Key learning aids to help you master the textbook material and prepare you for a successful career.

CHAPTER PREVIEW

The Chapter Preview summarizes the major issues discussed in the chapter, and provides students with a visual outline of the key topics.

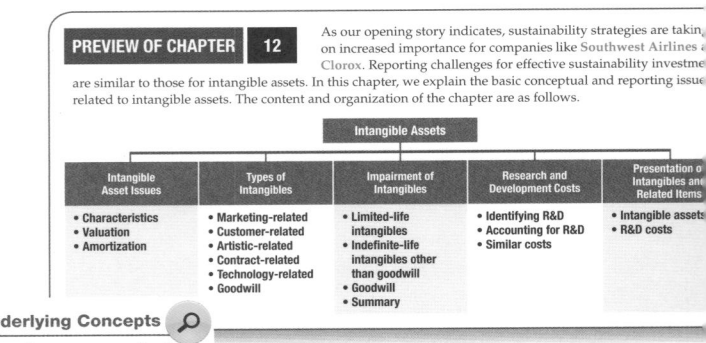

UNDERLYING CONCEPTS

The Underlying Concepts highlight and explain major conceptual topics in the chapter.

Underlying Concepts

The controversy surrounding the accounting for R&D expenditures reflects a debate about whether such expenditures meet the definition of an asset. If so, then an "expense all R&D costs" policy results in overstated expenses and understated assets.

WHAT DO THE NUMBERS MEAN?

The "What do the numbers mean?" boxes further students' understanding of key concepts with practical, real-world examples.

What do the numbers mean? *DEFINITELY INDEFINITE*

The importance of intangible asset classification as either limited-life or indefinite-life is illustrated in the experience of Outdoor Channel Holdings. Here's what happened. Outdoor Channel recorded an intangible asset related to the value of an important distributor relationship, purchased from another company. At that time, it classified the relationship as indefinite-life. Thus, in the first two years of the asset's life, Outdoor Channel recorded no amortization expense on this asset. In the third year, investors were surprised to find that Outdoor Channel changed the classification of the distributor relationship

to limited-life, with an expected life of 21.33 years (a fairly definite useful life) and, shortly thereafter, wrote off the intangible completely.

Apparently, the company was overly optimistic about the expected future cash flows arising from the distributor relationship. As a result of that optimism, income in the second year was overstated by $9.5 million, or 14 percent, and the impairment recorded in the third year amounted to 7 percent of assets. From indefinite-life to limited-life to worthless in two short years—investors were surely hurt by Outdoor aggressive intangible asset classification.

Source: Jack Ciesielski, *The AAO Weblog, www.accountingobserver.com/blog/* (January 12, 2007).

INTERNATIONAL PERSPECTIVE

International Perspectives provide students with specific examples of how global companies (and other countries) implement key accounting regulations. They also provide examples of how and where IFRS differs from GAAP.

International Perspective

IFRS requires the capitalization of appropriate development expenditures. This conflicts with GAAP.

EVOLVING ISSUE

The Evolving Issue feature introduces and discusses a current topic in the accounting industry in which the profession may be encountering controversy or nearing resolution. The feature shows how the key standard-setting organizations make decisions to adjust to the changing global business environment.

Evolving Issue *RECOGNITION OF R&D AND INTERNALLY GENER*

The requirement that companies expense immediately all R&D costs (as well as start-up costs) incurred internally is a practical solution. It ensures consistency in practice and uniformity among companies. But the practice of immediately writing off expenditures made in the expectation of benefiting future periods is conceptually incorrect.

Proponents of immediate expensing contend that from an income statement standpoint, long-run application of this standard frequently makes little difference. They argue that because of the ongoing nature of most companies' R&D activities, the amount of R&D cost charged to expense each accounting period is about the same, whether there is immediate expensing or capitalization and subsequent amortization.

Others criticize this practice. They believe that the balance

showed a significant relat... subsequent benefits in th... earnings, and shareholder v... Another study found that... earnings usefulness for co... from capitalizing to exp... decline appears to persist...

The current accountin... generated intangible ass... trade-offs made among r... and cost-benefit consider... completed some limited-... for intangible assets, and... joint project on the acco...

DEMONSTRATION PROBLEM

The Demonstration Problem provides a model for how to solve end-of-chapter material.

DEMONSTRATION PROBLEM

Sky Co., organized in 2014, provided you with the following information.

1. Purchased a license for $20,000 on July 1, 2014. The license gives Sky exclusive rights to sell its services in the tri-state region and will expire on July 1, 2022.
2. Purchased a patent on January 2, 2015, for $40,000. It is estimated to have a 5-year life.
3. Costs incurred to develop an exclusive Internet connection process as of June 1, 2015, were $45,000. The process has an indefinite life.
4. On April 1, 2015, Sky Co. purchased a small circuit board manufacturer for $350,000. Goodwill recorded in the transaction was $90,000.
5. On July 1, 2015, legal fees for successful defense of the patent purchased on January 2, 2015, were $11,400.
6. Research and development costs incurred as of September 1, 2015, were $75,000.

Instructions

(a) Prepare the journal entries to record all the entries related to the patent during 2015.
(b) At December 31, 2015, an impairment test is performed on the license purchased in 2014. It is estimated that the net cash flows to be received from the license will be $13,000, and its fair value is $7,000. Compute the amount of impairment, if any, to be recorded on December 31, 2015.
(c) What is the amount to be reported for intangible assets on the balance sheet at December 31, 2014? At December 31, 2015?

FASB CODIFICATION

The FASB Codification refers students to the relevant FASB literature for the key concepts presented in each chapter.

FASB CODIFICATION

FASB Codification References

[1] FASB ASC 350-10-05. [Predecessor literature: "Goodwill and Other Intangible Assets," *Statement of Financial Accounting Standards No. 142* (Norwalk, Conn.: FASB, 2001).]

[2] FASB ASC 350-30-35. [Predecessor literature: "Goodwill and Other Intangible Assets," *Statement of Financial Accounting Standards No. 142* (Norwalk, Conn.: FASB, 2001), par. 11.]

[3] FASB ASC 805-10. [Predecessor literature: "Business Combinations," *Statement of Financial Accounting Standards No. 141R* (Norwalk, Conn.: FASB, 2007).]

[4] FASB ASC 350-30-35. [Predecessor literature: "Goodwill and Other Intangible Assets," *Statement of Financial Accounting Standards No. 142* (Norwalk, Conn.: FASB, 2001), par. B55.]

[5] FASB ASC 805-10-20. [Predecessor literature: "Business Combinations," *Statement of Financial Accounting Standards No. 141R* (Norwalk, Conn.: FASB, 2007).]

USING YOUR JUDGMENT

The Using Your Judgment section provides students with real-world homework problems covering topics such as financial reporting, financial statement analysis, and professional research.

USING YOUR JUDGMENT

FINANCIAL REPORTING

Financial Reporting Problem

P&G The Procter & Gamble Company (P&G)

The financial statements of P&G are presented in Appendix 5B. The company's complete annual report, including the notes to the financial statements, can be accessed at the book's companion website, **www.wiley.com/college/kieso**.

Instructions

Refer to P&G's financial statements and the accompanying notes to answer the following questions.

(a) Does P&G report any intangible assets, especially goodwill, in its 2011 financial statements and accompanying notes?
(b) How much research and development (R&D) cost was expensed by P&G in 2010 and 2011? What percentage of sales revenue and net income did P&G spend on R&D in 2010 and 2011?

PROBLEMS SET B

In addition to the B Set of Exercises, we now provide an additional set of problems for each chapter, based on the problems in the textbook. The B Set of Problems are available in *WileyPLUS* and on the book's companion website, at **www.wiley.com/college/kieso**.

PROBLEMS SET B

See the book's companion website, at **www.wiley.com/college/kieso**, for an additional set of problems.

IFRS INSIGHTS

IFRS Insights offer students a detailed discussion as well as assessment material of international accounting standards at the end of each chapter.

IFRS INSIGHTS

There are some significant differences between IFRS and GAAP in the accounting for both intangible assets and impairments. IFRS related to intangible assets is presented in *IAS 38* ("Intangible Assets"). IFRS related to impairments is found in *IAS 36* ("Impairment of Assets").

kieso
weygandt
warfield
team for success

2014 FASB Update
Chapter 18
Revenue Recognition

INTERMEDIATE
FIFTEENTH EDITION
ACCOUNTING

WILEY

Donald E. Kieso PhD, CPA
Northern Illinois University
DeKalb, Illinois

Jerry J. Weygandt PhD, CPA
University of Wisconsin—Madison
Madison, Wisconsin

Terry D. Warfield, PhD
University of Wisconsin—Madison
Madison, Wisconsin

WILEY

Dedicated to
*our wives, **Donna, Enid, and Mary**,*
for their love,
support, and encouragement

Vice President & Executive Publisher	George Hoffman
Associate Publisher	Christopher DeJohn
Senior Acquisitions Editor	Michael McDonald
Content Editor	Brian Kamins
Senior Development Editor	Terry Ann Tatro
Development Editor	Margaret Thompson
Editorial Operations Manager	Yana Mermel
Senior Content Manager	Dorothy Sinclair
Senior Production Editor	Valerie Vargas
Associate Director of Marketing	Amy Scholz
Marketing Manager	Jesse Cruz
Senior Product Designer	Allie K. Morris
Product Designer	Greg Chaput
Senior Designer	Maureen Eide
Designer	Kristine Carney
Production Management Services	Ingrao Associates
Creative Director	Harry Nolan
Senior Photo Editor	Mary Ann Price
Senior Editorial Assistant	Jackie MacKenzie
Cover Photo	JB Broccard/Getty Images, Inc.
Chapter Opener Photo	JB Broccard/Getty Images, Inc.
Cover Credit	JB Broccard/Getty Images, Inc.

This book was set in Palatino LT Std by Aptara®, Inc. and printed and bound by Courier Kendallville. The cover was printed by Courier Kendallville.

This book is printed on acid-free paper. ∞

To order books or for customer service, please call 1-800-CALL WILEY (225-5945).

Material from the Uniform CPA Examinations and Unofficial Answers, copyright © 1965, 1966, 1967, 1968, 1969, 1970, 1971, 1972, 1973, 1974, 1975, 1976, 1977, 1978, 1979, 1980, 1981, 1982, 1983, 1984, 1985, 1986, 1987, 1988, 1990, 1991, 1992, and 1993 by the American Institute of Certified Public Accountants, Inc., is adapted with permission.

This book contains quotations from *Accounting Research Bulletins, Accounting Principles Board Opinions, Accounting Principles Board Statements, Accounting Interpretations,* and *Accounting Terminology Bulletins,* copyright © 1953, 1956, 1966, 1968, 1969, 1970, 1971, 1972, 1973, 1974, 1975, 1976, 1977, 1978, 1979, 1980, 1981, 1982 by the American Institute of Certified Public Accountants, Inc., 1211 Avenue of the Americas, New York, NY 10036.

This book contains citations from various FASB pronouncements. Copyright © by Financial Accounting Standards Board, 401 Merritt 7, P.O. Box 5116, Norwalk, CT 06856 U.S.A. Reprinted with permission. Copies of complete documents are available from Financial Accounting Standards Board.

Material from the Certificate in Management Accounting Examinations, copyright © 1975, 1976, 1977, 1978, 1979, 1980, 1981, 1982, 1983, 1984, 1985, 1986, 1987, 1988, 1989, 1990, 1991, 1992, and 1993 by the Institute of Certified Management Accountants, 10 Paragon Drive, Montvale, NJ 07645, is adapted with permission.

Material from the Certified Internal Auditor Examinations, copyright © May 1984, November 1984, May 1986 by The Institute of Internal Auditors, 249 Maitland Ave., Altemonte Springs, FL 32701, is adapted with permission.

The financial statements and accompanying notes reprinted from the 2011 Annual Report of Procter & Gamble Company are courtesy of P&G, copyright © 2011, all rights reserved.

ISBN-13   978-1-118-98531-1
BRV ISBN-13   978-1-118-93878-2

Printed in the United States of America

10 9 8 7 6 5 4 3 2 1

Brief Contents

1 Financial Accounting and Accounting Standards 2

2 Conceptual Framework for Financial Reporting 42

3 The Accounting Information System 82

4 Income Statement and Related Information 158

5 Balance Sheet and Statement of Cash Flows 212

6 Accounting and the Time Value of Money 286

7 Cash and Receivables 344

8 Valuation of Inventories: A Cost-Basis Approach 414

9 Inventories: Additional Valuation Issues 472

10 Acquisition and Disposition of Property, Plant, and Equipment 536

11 Depreciation, Impairments, and Depletion 588

12 Intangible Assets 648

13 Current Liabilities and Contingencies 700

14 Long-Term Liabilities 762

15 Stockholders' Equity 820

16 Dilutive Securities and Earnings per Share 882

17 Investments 950

18 Revenue Recognition 1040

19 Accounting for Income Taxes 1116

20 Accounting for Pensions and Postretirement Benefits 1182

21 Accounting for Leases 1268

22 Accounting Changes and Error Analysis 1342

23 Statement of Cash Flows 1410

24 Full Disclosure in Financial Reporting 1486

Author Commitment

Don Kieso

Donald E. Kieso, PhD, CPA, received his bachelor's degree from Aurora University and his doctorate in accounting from the University of Illinois. He has served as chairman of the Department of Accountancy and is currently the KPMG Emeritus Professor of Accountancy at Northern Illinois University. He has public accounting experience with Price Waterhouse & Co. (San Francisco and Chicago) and Arthur Andersen & Co. (Chicago) and research experience with the Research Division of the American Institute of Certified Public Accountants (New York). He has done post-doctorate work as a Visiting Scholar at the University of California at Berkeley and is a recipient of NIU's Teaching Excellence Award and four Golden Apple Teaching Awards. Professor Kieso is the author of other accounting and business books and is a member of the American Accounting Association, the American Institute of Certified Public Accountants, and the Illinois CPA Society. He has served as a member of the Board of Directors of the Illinois CPA Society, then AACSB's Accounting Accreditation Committees, the State of Illinois Comptroller's Commission, as Secretary-Treasurer of the Federation of Schools of Accountancy, and as Secretary-Treasurer of the American Accounting Association. Professor Kieso is currently serving on the Board of Trustees and Executive Committee of Aurora University, as a member of the Board of Directors of Kishwaukee Community Hospital, and as Treasurer and Director of Valley West Community Hospital. From 1989 to 1993, he served as a charter member of the National Accounting Education Change Commission. He is the recipient of the Outstanding Accounting Educator Award from the Illinois CPA Society, the FSA's Joseph A. Silvoso Award of Merit, the NIU Foundation's Humanitarian Award for Service to Higher Education, a Distinguished Service Award from the Illinois CPA Society, and in 2003 an honorary doctorate from Aurora University.

Jerry Weygandt

Jerry J. Weygandt, PhD, CPA, is Arthur Andersen Alumni Emeritus Professor of Accounting at the University of Wisconsin—Madison. He holds a Ph.D. in accounting from the University of Illinois. Articles by Professor Weygandt have appeared in the *Accounting Review, Journal of Accounting Research, Accounting Horizons, Journal of Accountancy,* and other academic and professional journals. These articles have examined such financial reporting issues as accounting for price-level adjustments, pensions, convertible securities, stock option contracts, and interim reports. Professor Weygandt is author of other accounting and financial reporting books and is a member of the American Accounting Association, the American Institute of Certified Public Accountants, and the Wisconsin Society of Certified Public Accountants. He has served on numerous committees of the American Accounting Association and as a member of the editorial board of the Accounting Review; he also has served as President and Secretary-Treasurer of the American Accounting Association. In addition, he has been actively involved with the American Institute of Certified Public Accountants and has been a member of the Accounting Standards Executive Committee (AcSEC) of that organization. He has served on the FASB task force that examined the reporting issues related to accounting for income taxes and served as a trustee of the Financial Accounting Foundation. Professor Weygandt has received the Chancellor's Award for Excellence in Teaching and the Beta Gamma Sigma Dean's Teaching Award. He is on the board of directors of M & I Bank of Southern Wisconsin. He is the recipient of the Wisconsin Institute of CPA's Outstanding Educator's Award and the Lifetime Achievement Award. In 2001, he received the American Accounting Association's Outstanding Educator Award.

Terry Warfield

Terry D. Warfield, PhD, is the Pricewater-houseCoopers Professor in Accounting at the University of Wisconsin—Madison. He received a B.S. and M.B.A. from Indiana University and a Ph.D. in accounting from the University of Iowa. Professor Warfield's area of expertise is financial reporting, and prior to his academic career, he worked for five years in the banking industry. He served as the Academic Accounting Fellow in the Office of the Chief Accountant at the U.S. Securities and Exchange Commission in Washington, D.C. from 1995–1996. Professor Warfield's primary research interests concern financial accounting standards and disclosure policies. He has published scholarly articles in *The Accounting Review, Journal of Accounting and Economics, Research in Accounting Regulation,* and *Accounting Horizons,* and he has served on the editorial boards of *The Accounting Review, Accounting Horizons,* and *Issues in Accounting Education.* He has served as president of the Financial Accounting and Reporting Section, the Financial Accounting Standards Committee of the American Accounting Association (Chair 1995–1996), and on the AAA-FASB Research Conference Committee. He also served on the Financial Accounting Standards Advisory Council of the Financial Accounting Standards Board. Professor Warfield has received teaching awards at both the University of Iowa and the University of Wisconsin, and he was named to the Teaching Academy at the University of Wisconsin in 1995. Professor Warfield has developed and published several case studies based on his research for use in accounting classes. These cases have been selected for the AICPA Professor-Practitioner Case Development Program and have been published in *Issues in Accounting Education.*

From the Authors

Accounting continues to be one of the most employable, sought-after majors, according to entry-level job site **CollegeGrad.com**. One reason for this interest is found in the statement by former Secretary of the Treasury and Economic Advisor to the President, Lawrence Summers. He noted that the single-most important innovation shaping our capital markets was the idea of generally accepted accounting principles (GAAP). We agree with Mr. Summers. Relevant and reliable financial information is a necessity for viable capital markets. Without it, our markets would be chaotic, and our standard of living would decrease.

This textbook is the market leader in providing the tools needed to understand what GAAP is and how it is applied in practice. Mastery of this material will be invaluable to you in whatever field you select.

Through many editions, this textbook has continued to reflect the constant changes taking place in the GAAP environment. This edition continues this tradition, which has become even more significant as the financial reporting environment is exploding with major change. Here are three areas of major importance that are now incorporated extensively into this edition of the textbook.

Convergence of U.S. GAAP and IFRS

As mentioned above, the most important innovation shaping our capital markets was the idea of U.S. GAAP. It might be said that it would be even better if we had one common set of accounting rules for the whole world, which will make it easier for international investors to compare the financial results of companies from different countries. That is happening quickly as U.S. GAAP and international accounting standards are converging. The convergence process has resulted in a number of common standards between U.S. GAAP and **International Financial Reporting Standards (IFRS)**. And you have the chance to be on the ground floor as we develop for you the similarities and differences in the two systems that ultimately will be one.

> "If this textbook helps you appreciate the challenges, worth, and limitations of financial reporting, if it encourages you to evaluate critically and understand financial accounting concepts and practice, and if it prepares you for advanced study, professional examinations, and the successful and ethical pursuit of your career in accounting or business in a global economy, then we will have attained our objectives."

A Fair Value Movement

The FASB believes that fair value information is more relevant to users than historical cost. As a result, there is more information that is being reported on this basis, and even more will occur in the future. The financial press is full of articles discussing how financial institutions must fair value their assets, which has led to massive losses during the recent credit crisis. In addition, additional insight into the reliability related to fair values is being addressed and disclosed to help investors make important capital allocation decisions. We devote a considerable amount of material that discusses and illustrates fair value concepts in this edition.

A New Way of Looking at Generally Accepted Accounting Principles (GAAP)

Learning GAAP used to be a daunting task, as it is comprised of many standards that vary in form, completeness, and structure. Fortunately, the profession has developed the Financial Accounting Standards Board Codification (often referred to as the Codification). This Codification provides in one place all the GAAP related to a given topic. This textbook is the first to incorporate this Codification—it will make learning GAAP easier and more interesting!

Intermediate Accounting is the market-leading textbook in providing the tools needed to understand what GAAP is and how it is applied in practice. With this Fifteenth Edition, we strive to continue to provide the material needed to understand this subject area. The textbook is comprehensive and up-to-date. We also include proven pedagogical tools, designed to help you learn more effectively and to answer the changing needs of this course. Look inside the front cover for a detailed description of all of the learning tools of the textbook.

We are excited about *Intermediate Accounting*, Fifteenth Edition. We believe it meets an important objective of providing useful information to educators and students interested in learning about both GAAP and IFRS. Suggestions and comments from users of this textbook will be appreciated. Please feel free to e-mail any one of us at *AccountingAuthors@yahoo.com*.

Donald E. Kieso
DeKalb, Illinois

Jerry J. Weygandt
Madison, Wisconsin

Terry D. Warfield
Madison, Wisconsin

What's New?

The Fifteenth Edition expands our emphasis on student learning and improves upon a teaching and learning package that instructors and students have rated the highest in customer satisfaction. Based on extensive reviews, focus groups, and interactions with other intermediate accounting instructors and students, we have developed a number of new pedagogical features and content changes, designed both to help students learn more effectively and to answer the changing needs of the course.

Evolving Issues

As we continue to strive to reflect the constant changes in the accounting environment, we have added a new feature to the Fifteenth Edition, **Evolving Issues**, which highlight and discuss areas in which the profession may be encountering controversy or nearing resolution. Our hope is that these high-interest boxes will increase student engagement, as well as serve as classroom discussion points. For another source of high-interest material, see the **What Do the Numbers Mean?** boxes, most of which are new to this edition.

Demonstration Problems

We understand that students often struggle to apply accounting concepts to realistic business situations. As a result, we include a new **Demonstration Problem** before the end-of-chapter problem material, to serve as a model to help students with their homework assignments.

Updated IFRS Insights Content

We have updated the end-of-chapter section, **IFRS Insights**, throughout the textbook. In addition, in the *Relevant Facts* section, we now present *Similarities* as well as *Differences* between GAAP and IFRS to increase student understanding.

Major Content Revisions

In response to the changing environment, we have significantly revised several chapters.

Chapter 2 Conceptual Framework for Financial Reporting
- New footnote material on the FASB's additional guidance related to the use of fair value in financial statements.
- Updated discussion plus added an illustration on the five steps of revenue recognition.
- Revised Constraints section, as now only cost constraint is included in the conceptual framework.

Chapter 4 Income Statement and Related Information
- Revised Format of the Income Statement section, adding discussion on the intermediate components of the income statement and presenting the multiple-step before the single-step format to reflect current practice.
- Revised Reporting Irregular Items section, to broaden focus on irregular and unusual items. Updated discussion throughout as well as added new material on noncontrolling interest.
- Updated Comprehensive Income discussion, to reflect the most recent accounting standards.
- New illustration showing and explaining the revised income statement sections.

Chapter 18 Revenue Recognition
- We anticipate a new FASB ruling on the revenue recognition principle. As a result, please see the book's companion website, at **www.wiley.com/college/kieso**, for the latest information as well as the availability of an updated, replacement chapter.

Chapter 23 Statement of Cash Flows
- Reorganized chapter, to present the indirect method through preparation of the statement of cash flows first, followed by the discussion of the direct method as well as the advantages and disadvantages of both methods.
- New Evolving Issue, "Direct versus Indirect Controversy," on the arguments in favor of each method.

See the next two pages for a complete list of content revisions by chapter.

Content Changes by Chapter

Chapter 1 Financial Accounting and Accounting Standards
- New opening story, about how the U.S. can improve its financial reporting system to provide reliable accounting information.
- Updated Types of Pronouncements section and increased coverage of the EITF.
- New WDNM box on how different countries' cultures impede international convergence efforts.
- Updated International Accounting Convergence discussion in *IFRS Insights* section.
- New **Evolving Issue**, on the use of fair value accounting.

Chapter 2 Conceptual Framework for Financial Reporting
- Updated WDNM box on earnings with recent information about **Facebook**'s reporting of its first earnings after going public.
- New footnote on the liquidation basis of accounting.
- New footnote material on the FASB's additional guidance related to use of fair value in financial statements.
- Updated discussion plus added an illustration on the five steps of revenue recognition.
- Revised Constraints section, as now only cost constraint is included in the conceptual framework.

Chapter 3 The Accounting Information System
- Revised discussion/terminology used to reflect anticipated new wording of revenue recognition principle.
- Updated material on economic crime in opening story.
- Updated graphics to increase student engagement.
- New WDNM box on companies' need to update their accounting information systems yet unwillingness to interrupt their operations to do so.

Chapter 4 Income Statement and Related Information
- Revised opening story, to discuss **Groupon**'s recent pro forma reporting.
- Revised Format of the Income Statement section, adding discussion on the intermediate components of the income statement and presenting the multiple-step before single-step format to reflect current practice.
- Revised Reporting Irregular Items section, to broaden focus on irregular and unusual items. Updated discussion throughout as well as added discussion on noncontrolling interest.
- Updated Comprehensive Income discussion, to reflect most recent accounting standards.
- New Underlying Concepts marginal note, about how the income statement provides information that is central to the objective of financial reporting.
- Revised the WDNM box on managing earnings to discuss a recent study that reinforces concerns about earnings management.
- New illustration showing and explaining the revised income statement sections.

- New WDNM box on the importance of the top line, in addition to the bottom line, in the income statement when analyzing companies.
- New **Evolving Issue**, on income reporting.

Chapter 5 Balance Sheet and Statement of Cash Flows
- Updated WDNM box on the airline industry, to include recent merger activity.
- Replaced several examples of real-company financial statements.
- Added noncontrolling interest line item to the balance sheet, to reflect recent FASB pronouncement.
- Moved most of **P&G**'s annual report from Appendix 5B to book's companion website.
- New **Evolving Issue**, on balance sheet reporting.

Chapter 6 Accounting and the Time Value of Money
- New opening story, about developing fair value estimates and applying fair value guidance to specific examples.
- New WDNM box on how starting a savings account earlier can significantly affect the value of a retirement fund.
- Revised WDNM box on Fed's ability to adjust interest rates by adding discussion on Fed's more recent use of quantitative easing.

Chapter 7 Cash and Receivables
- New opening story, about banks' boosting earnings by releasing loan loss reserves.
- New WDNM boxes, on tax incentives for companies to move their cash overseas, and recent trends of companies to delay payment of bills.
- New discussion on repurchase agreements (see footnote 14).
- New **Evolving Issue**, on how existing GAAP results in allowances for loan loss that tend to be at their lowest level when they are needed most, the beginning of a downward-trending economic cycle.

Chapter 8 Valuation of Inventories: A Cost-Basis Approach
- New opening story, about why some companies are switching from LIFO to FIFO.

Chapter 9 Inventories: Additional Valuation Issues
- New opening story, about why investors need comparable information about inventory when evaluating retailers' financial statements.

Chapter 10 Acquisition and Disposition of Property, Plant, and Equipment
- New opening story, about importance of capital expenditures and how they can affect a company's income.

Chapter 11 Depreciation, Impairments, and Depletion
- New **Evolving Issue**, on whether to account for exploration costs in the oil and gas industry using full-cost or successful-efforts.

Chapter 12 Intangible Assets
- New opening story, on increasing amount of sustainability information provided by companies.
- New Underlying Concepts marginal note about surrounding controversy for R&D accounting.
- Added more real-world examples to Contract-Related Intangible Assets section.
- Completely rewritten WDNM box, discussing the patent battles between e-tailers and cell phone companies.
- New discussion (footnotes) on qualitative assessment to determine impairment of indefinite-life intangibles.
- Revised WDNM box on impairment risk, to discuss more recent case of **Bank of America**.
- New **Evolving Issue**, on the recognition of R&D and internally generated intangibles.
- Moved Appendix 12A, Accounting for Computer Software Costs, to book's companion website.

Chapter 13 Current Liabilities and Contingencies
- New **Evolving Issue**, on how to account for greenhouse gases.

Chapter 14 Long-Term Liabilities
- New opening story, about the impact of long-term debt on governments and companies.
- New **Evolving Issue**, on how the FASB believes that using the fair value option for liabilities makes sense, as the valuation of a liability is related to a company's credit standing.

Chapter 15 Stockholders' Equity
- Updated opening story, on the global IPO market.
- New WDNM boxes, on Delaware as a tax haven for companies, whether buybacks signal good or bad news about companies, and an analysis of recent company dividend payouts.
- Revised WDNM box to include more recent information about companies going public with two or more classes of stock.
- New information and illustration on recent company buybacks.

Chapter 16 Dilutive Securities and Earnings per Share
- Revised opening story, updating information about companies' use of options and restricted stock.
- Updated material to include recent convergence material on accounting for financial instruments with characteristics of both debt and equity.
- New **Evolving Issue**, on accounting for convertible debt.
- New illustration on company equity grants.
- New footnote on rationale for why companies are moving away from options to restricted stock, and revised footnote about how EPS effects of noncontrolling interest should be presented.
- Completely revised WDNM box, about the effect of companies that expense stock options on their stock prices.

Chapter 17 Investments
- Revised opening story, to include recent FASB position on how banking industry values loans.
- New footnotes on FASB's current exploration for a new impairment model for financial instruments as well as additional disclosures required for items reclassified out of accumulated other comprehensive income.
- New **Evolving Issues**, on fair value controversy as well as proposed new classification and measurement model for financial assets.

- New material on FASB required disclosures for financial instruments, with special emphasis on Level 3 measurements.

Chapter 18 Revenue Recognition
- Updated WDNM boxes, to reflect new disclosure requirements for gift-card issuers and to stress importance of companies reporting sales on a net basis.

Chapter 19 Accounting for Income Taxes
- Updated footnotes on determining the true cost of taxes and deferred tax assets (**Sony**'s experience in post-quake Japan).
- New **Evolving Issue**, on uncertain tax positions.
- New WDNM box, about creative tax accounting at **Apple**, **Google**, and **GE**.

Chapter 20 Accounting for Pensions and Postretirement Benefits
- Updated opening story on pension plan choices.
- Updated statistics on size of pension plan assets globally.
- Updated chart on defined benefit/defined contribution plan mix.
- New **Evolving Issue**, on companies' voluntary choice to abandon corridor amortization.
- Updated WDNM box on funded status of pension plans.
- New WDNM box on guarantees for the PBGC.
- New IFRS Insight section reflecting major amendments to IFRS for pensions (*IAS 19*).

Chapter 21 Accounting for Leases
- Updated opening story on aircraft leasing data and added information about **Rite-Aid**'s off-balance-sheet obligations.
- New **Evolving Issue**, on proposal to address off-balance-sheet reporting of leases.

Chapter 22 Accounting Changes and Error Analysis
- Updated opening story, of recent accounting changes mandated by the FASB and subsequent company restatements.
- Revised WDNM box, on need to protect company statements from negative effects of fraud.

Chapter 23 Statement of Cash Flows
- Reorganized chapter, to present the indirect method through preparation of the statement of cash flows first, followed by the discussion of the direct method as well as advantages and disadvantages of both methods.
- New WDNM box, on how cash flow management can affect the quality of accounting information.
- Reformatted "Direct versus Indirect Controversy" as new **Evolving Issue**, to highlight the arguments in favor of each method.
- Updated WDNM box to show how banks' use of investment classifications can affect operating cash flows.

Chapter 24 Full Disclosure in Financial Reporting
- New discussion in Differential Disclosure section about costs and benefits of a "one size fits all" reporting package.
- New **Evolving Issues**, on ensuring the quantity and quality of financial disclosure, and interim reporting rules.
- New footnote on FASB going concern project.
- New WDNM box, on the difference between British and U.S. forecasting.

Teaching and Learning Supplementary Material

For Instructors

Active-Teaching Aids

Instructors can take advantage of the resources and support available in *WileyPLUS* and the Wiley Faculty Network, as well as a number of helpful assets (such as the Instructor's Manual, Test Bank, PowerPoint presentations, and Solutions Manual) at our book's companion site, **www.wiley.com/college/kieso**..

In addition, instructors will find that we have made a number of additions and enhancements to the Fifteenth Edition instructor and student resources.

Test Bank/Computerized Test Bank. We have made several key enhancements to the Test Bank, both in print and in *WileyPLUS*. These include:

- Newly authored Test Bank questions to cover recent topical additions/expansions (e.g., IFRS, revenue recognition, and fair value).
- New Critical Thinking Questions added to Exercises.
- Removal of outdated questions.

WileyPLUS now includes numerous questions from the Test Bank, offering simple multiple-choice and more complex exercises and problems. Many of these exercises/problems will be algorithmic.

Instructor's Manual, Vols. 1 and 2. Included in each chapter are lecture outlines with teaching tips, chapter reviews, illustrations, and review quizzes.

Solutions Manual, Vols. 1 and 2. Each volume contains detailed solutions to all Brief Exercises, Exercises, and Problems in the textbook, as well as suggested answers to the Concepts for Analysis and *Using Your Judgment* questions and cases.

Narrated PowerPoints. Brief chapter-based videos walk the students through the core concepts in each chapter, as outlined in the PowerPoint Slides.

For Students

Active-Learning Aids

The book's companion site for students, **www.wiley.com/ college/kieso**, is home to a number of helpful learning aids, including a B Set of Exercises, B Set of Problems, Self-Study Tests and Additional Self-Tests, Excel templates, annual reports, and a complete glossary of key terms.

B Set of Problems. In addition to the **B Set of Exercises**, we now provide an additional set of problems for each chapter, based on the problems in the textbook. The B Sets of Exercises and Problems are available in *WileyPLUS* and at the book's companion site.

Student Videos. Three new types of videos will be available in *WileyPLUS*:

- Mini lecture videos from Terry Warfield on select difficult topics in intermediate accounting.
- Exercise solution walkthrough videos where a student can see how an exercise similar to one in the textbook is solved.
- Accounting skills videos that demonstrate the basic concepts and skills needed for students to understand how to solve a multitude of intermediate accounting problems.

Student Study Guide, Vols. 1 and 2. Each chapter of the Study Guide contains a chapter review, chapter outline, and a glossary of key terms. Demonstration problems, multiple-choice, true/false, matching, and other exercises are included. Available for purchase at the book's companion site.

Problem-Solving Survival Guide, Vols. 1 and 2. This study guide contains exercises and problems that help students develop their intermediate accounting problem-solving skills. Explanations assist in the approach, set-up, and completion of accounting problems. Tips alert students to common pitfalls and misconceptions. Available for purchase at the book's companion site.

Rockford Corporation: An Accounting Practice Set. This practice set helps students review the accounting cycle and the preparation of financial statements. Available for purchase at the book's companion site. The **computerized Rockford practice set** is a general ledger software version of the printed practice set, also available in *WileyPLUS*.

Gateway to the Profession (accessed at www.wiley.com/college/kieso)

Expanding beyond technical accounting knowledge, the **Gateway to the Profession** materials emphasize certain skills necessary to become a successful accountant or financial manager. The following materials will help students develop needed professional skills:

- Financial Statement Analysis Primer
- Database of Real Companies
- Writing Handbook
- Working in Teams
- Ethics in Accounting

We also include chapter-level resources that help students process and understand key course concepts:

- Interactive Tutorials
- Expanded Discussions
- Spreadsheet Tools
- Additional Internet Links

WileyPLUS

WileyPLUS is a research-based, online environment for effective teaching and learning.

The market-leading homework experience in *WileyPLUS* offers:

A Blank Sheet of Paper Effect

The *WileyPLUS* homework experience, which includes type-ahead for account title entry, imitates a blank sheet of paper format so that students use recall memory when doing homework and will do better in class, on exams, and in their professions.

A Professional Worksheet Style

The professional, worksheet-style problem layouts help students master accounting skills while doing homework that directly applies to the classroom and the real world.

The Opportunity to Catch Mistakes Earlier

Multi-part problems further help students focus by providing feedback at the part-level. Students can catch their mistakes earlier and access content-specific resources at the point of learning.

More Assessment Options

All brief exercises, exercises, and problems from the textbook are now available for assignment in *WileyPLUS* in static or algorithmic format.

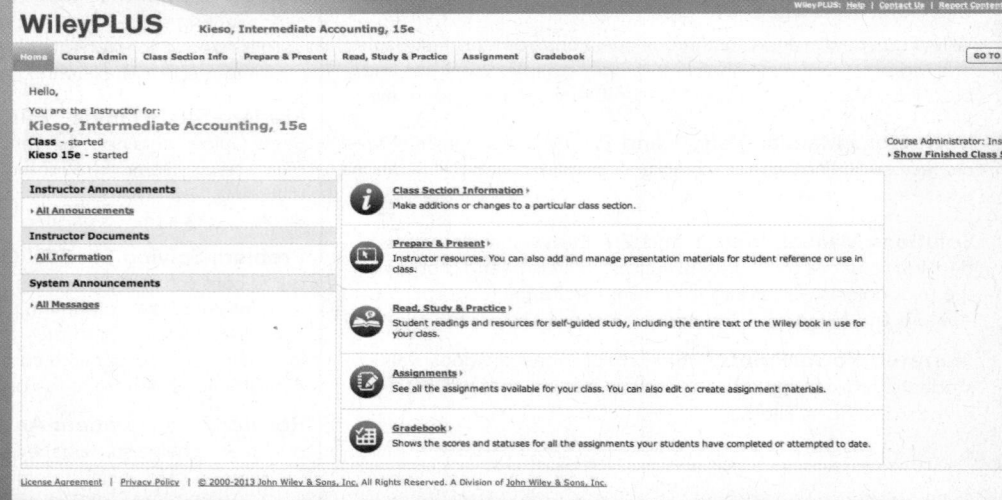

WileyPLUS includes a full ebook, interactive tutorials, assessment capabilities, and Blackboard integration.

Quantum®

Accelerate Learning and Improve Test Scores!

Quantum helps students master the core accounting topics and skills needed to be successful in their accounting course.

Personal Step-by-Step Feedback and Immediate Answers to Student Questions

Quantum uses powerful artificial intelligence technology to interpret and explain why individual student answers are right or wrong with personal step-by-step feedback.

Rather than wait until the next day to ask their instructor, students can now ask questions any time and get the real-time help needed to understand and master the material.

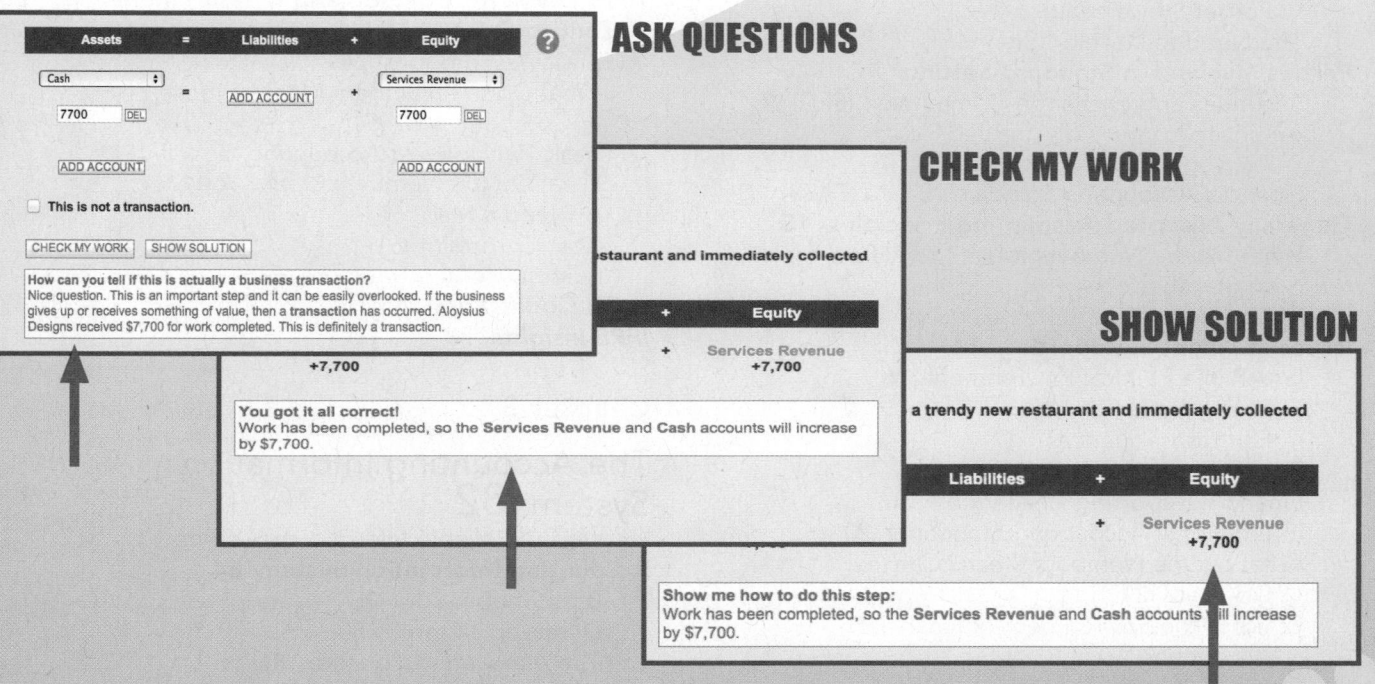

Target Areas Where Students Need Most Help

Students also receive real-time **"How Am I Doing?"** progress reports showing concept mastery and specific skills requiring more practice.

Quantum provides the individualized feedback that is proven to increase test scores at least a full letter grade with less study time.

Contents

Chapter 1

Financial Accounting and Accounting Standards 2
We Can Do Better

Financial Statements and Financial Reporting 4
   Accounting and Capital Allocation 4
   What Do the Numbers Mean? It's the Accounting 5
   Objective of Financial Reporting 5
   What Do the Numbers Mean? Don't Forget Stewardship 6
   The Need to Develop Standards 7

Parties Involved in Standard-Setting 7
   Securities and Exchange Commission (SEC) 7
   American Institute of Certified Public Accountants (AICPA) 9
   Financial Accounting Standards Board (FASB) 10

Generally Accepted Accounting Principles 13
   What Do the Numbers Mean? You Have to Step Back 14
   FASB Codification 14

Issues in Financial Reporting 16
   GAAP in a Political Environment 16
   Evolving Issue Fair Value, Fair Consequences? 17
   The Expectations Gap 17
   Financial Reporting Challenges 18
   International Accounting Standards 20
   What Do the Numbers Mean? Can You Do That? 21
   Ethics in the Environment of Financial Accounting 21
   Conclusion 21

FASB Codification 23
IFRS Insights 31

Chapter 2

Conceptual Framework for Financial Reporting 40
What Is It?

Conceptual Framework 42
   Need for a Conceptual Framework 42
   What Do the Numbers Mean? What's Your Principle? 43
   Development of a Conceptual Framework 43
   Overview of the Conceptual Framework 44

First Level: Basic Objective 45
Second Level: Fundamental Concepts 45
   Qualitative Characteristics of Accounting Information 45
   What Do the Numbers Mean? Living in a Material World 48
   What Do the Numbers Mean? Show Me the Earnings! 50
   Basic Elements 52

Third Level: Recognition and Measurement Concepts 53
   Basic Assumptions 54
   What Do the Numbers Mean? Whose Company Is It? 54
   Basic Principles of Accounting 56
   What Do the Numbers Mean? You May Need a Map 61
   Cost Constraint 61
   Summary of the Structure 63

FASB Codification 65
IFRS Insights 78

Chapter 3

The Accounting Information System 82
Needed: A Reliable Information System

Accounting Information System 84
   Basic Terminology 84
   Debits and Credits 85
   The Accounting Equation 86
   Financial Statements and Ownership Structure 88

The Accounting Cycle 89
   Identifying and Recording Transactions and Other Events 89
   Journalizing 91
   Posting 92
   Trial Balance 96
   Adjusting Entries 96
   What Do the Numbers Mean? Am I Covered? 107
   Adjusted Trial Balance 108
   Preparing Financial Statements 108

What Do the Numbers Mean?
24/7 Accounting 110
Closing 110
Post-Closing Trial Balance 113
Reversing Entries—An Optional Step 113
The Accounting Cycle Summarized 114
What Do the Numbers Mean? Hey, It's
Complicated 114
**Financial Statements for a Merchandising
Company 114**
Income Statement 114
Statement of Retained Earnings 115
Balance Sheet 115
What Do the Numbers Mean? Statements,
Please 117
Closing Entries 117
APPENDIX 3A **Cash-Basis Accounting versus
Accrual-Basis Accounting 118**
Conversion from Cash Basis to Accrual Basis 120
Service Revenue Computation 121
Operating Expense Computation 122
Theoretical Weaknesses of the Cash Basis 123
APPENDIX 3B **Using Reversing Entries 124**
Illustration of Reversing Entries—Accruals 124
Illustration of Reversing Entries—Deferrals 125
Summary of Reversing Entries 126
APPENDIX 3C **Using a Worksheet: The Accounting
Cycle Revisited 127**
Worksheet Columns 127
Trial Balance Columns 127
Adjustments Columns 127
Adjustments Entered on the Worksheet 127
Adjusted Trial Balance 129
Income Statement and Balance
Sheet Columns 129
**Preparing Financial Statements
from a Worksheet 130**
IFRS Insights 153

Chapter 4

**Income Statement and Related
Information 158**
Financial Statements Are Changing
Income Statement 160
Usefulness of the Income Statement 160
Limitations of the Income Statement 160
Quality of Earnings 161
What Do the Numbers Mean? Four: The
Loneliest Number 162
Format of the Income Statement 162
Elements of the Income Statement 162
Intermediate Components of the
Income Statement 164
What Do the Numbers Mean? Top Line or
Bottom Line? 166

Condensed Income Statements 166
Single-Step Income Statements 167
Reporting Various Income Items 168
What Do the Numbers Mean? Are One-Time
Charges Bugging You? 169
Unusual Gains and Losses 169
Discontinued Operations 170
Extraordinary Items 173
What Do the Numbers Mean? Extraordinary
Times 175
Noncontrolling Interest 176
Summary of Various Income Items 176
Earnings per Share 177
What Do the Numbers Mean? Different
Income Concepts 179
Other Reporting Issues 179
Accounting Changes and Errors 179
Retained Earnings Statement 181
Comprehensive Income 182
Evolving Issue Income Reporting 185
FASB Codification 188
IFRS Insights 205

Chapter 5

**Balance Sheet and Statement
of Cash Flows 212**
Hey, It Doesn't Balance!
Balance Sheet 214
Usefulness of the Balance Sheet 214
Limitations of the Balance Sheet 215
What Do the Numbers Mean? Grounded 215
Classification in the Balance Sheet 215
What Do the Numbers Mean? "Show Me
the Assets!" 223
What Do the Numbers Mean? Warning Signals 226
Balance Sheet Format 226
Statement of Cash Flows 228
What Do the Numbers Mean? Watch That
Cash Flow 228
Purpose of the Statement of Cash Flows 228
Content and Format of the Statement
of Cash Flows 229
Overview of the Preparation of the
Statement of Cash Flows 230
Usefulness of the Statement of Cash Flows 232
What Do the Numbers Mean? "There Ought
to Be a Law" 235
Additional Information 236
Supplemental Disclosures 236
What Do the Numbers Mean? What About
Your Commitments? 238
Techniques of Disclosure 239
Evolving Issue Balance Sheet Reporting:
Gross or Net? 243
APPENDIX 5A **Ratio Analysis—A Reference 245**
Using Ratios to Analyze Performance 245

APPENDIX 5B **Specimen Financial Statements:**
  The Procter & Gamble Company 246
FASB Codification 255
IFRS Insights 277

Chapter 6

Accounting and the Time Value of Money 286
How Do I Measure That?
Basic Time Value Concepts 288
  Applications of Time Value Concepts 288
  The Nature of Interest 289
  Simple Interest 290
  Compound Interest 290
  What Do the Numbers Mean? A Pretty
    Good Start 291
  Fundamental Variables 294
Single-Sum Problems 294
  Future Value of a Single Sum 295
  Present Value of a Single Sum 296
  Solving for Other Unknowns in
    Single-Sum Problems 298
Annuities 299
  Future Value of an Ordinary Annuity 300
  What Do the Numbers Mean? Don't Wait
    to Make That Contribution! 302
  Future Value of an Annuity Due 303
  Examples of Future Value of Annuity
    Problems 304
  Present Value of an Ordinary Annuity 306
  What Do the Numbers Mean? Up in Smoke 308
  Present Value of an Annuity Due 308
  Examples of Present Value of Annuity
    Problems 309
More Complex Situations 311
  Deferred Annuities 311
  Valuation of Long-Term Bonds 313
  Effective-Interest Method of Amortization
    of Bond Discount or Premium 314
Present Value Measurement 315
  Choosing an Appropriate Interest Rate 316
  What Do the Numbers Mean? How Low Can
    They Go? 316
  Example of Expected Cash Flow 316
FASB Codification 320

Chapter 7

Cash and Receivables 344
Please Release Me?
Cash 346
  What Is Cash? 346
  Reporting Cash 346
  Summary of Cash-Related Items 348
  What Do the Numbers Mean? Luck of
    the Irish 349

Accounts Receivable 349
  Recognition of Accounts Receivable 351
  Valuation of Accounts Receivable 352
  What Do the Numbers Mean?
    I'm Still Waiting 358
Notes Receivable 359
  Recognition of Notes Receivable 359
  Valuation of Notes Receivable 363
  What Do the Numbers Mean? Economic
    Consequences and Write-Offs 364
Special Issues 364
  Fair Value Option 365
  Disposition of Accounts and Notes
    Receivable 365
  What Do the Numbers Mean? Return
    to Lender 371
  Presentation and Analysis 372
  Evolving Issue A Cure for "Too Little,
    Too Late"? 374
APPENDIX 7A **Cash Controls 376**
Using Bank Accounts 376
The Imprest Petty Cash System 377
Physical Protection of Cash Balances 378
Reconciliation of Bank Balances 378
APPENDIX 7B **Impairments of Receivables 381**
Impairment Measurement and Reporting 382
  Impairment Loss Example 382
  Recording Impairment Losses 383
  What Do the Numbers Mean? Lost in
    Translation 383
FASB Codification 385
IFRS Insights 408

Chapter 8

Valuation of Inventories: A Cost-Basis Approach 414
To Switch or Not to Switch
Inventory Issues 416
  Classification 416
  Inventory Cost Flow 417
  Inventory Control 419
  What Do the Numbers Mean? Staying Lean 420
  Basic Issues in Inventory Valuation 420
Physical Goods Included in Inventory 421
  Goods in Transit 421
  Consigned Goods 422
  Special Sales Agreements 422
  What Do the Numbers Mean?
    No Parking! 423
  Effect of Inventory Errors 423
Costs Included in Inventory 425
  Product Costs 426
  Period Costs 426
  Treatment of Purchase Discounts 426
  What Do the Numbers Mean? You May
    Need a Map 427

Which Cost Flow Assumption to Adopt? 428
Specific Identification 428
Average-Cost 429
First-In, First-Out (FIFO) 430
Last-In, First-Out (LIFO) 431
Special Issues Related to LIFO 432
LIFO Reserve 432
What Do the Numbers Mean? Comparing
Apples to Apples 433
LIFO Liquidation 434
Dollar-Value LIFO 435
What Do the Numbers Mean?
Quite a Difference 440
Comparison of LIFO Approaches 440
Major Advantages of LIFO 441
Major Disadvantages of LIFO 442
Basis for Selection of Inventory Method 443
Evolving Issue Repeat LIFO! 445
Inventory Valuation Methods—Summary
Analysis 445
FASB Codification 449

Chapter 9

Inventories: Additional Valuation Issues 472
Not What It Seems to Be

Lower-of-Cost-or-Market 474
Ceiling and Floor 475
How Lower-of-Cost-or-Market Works 476
Methods of Applying Lower-of-Cost-or-
Market 477
Recording "Market" Instead of Cost 478
Use of an Allowance 479
Use of an Allowance—Multiple Periods 480
What Do the Numbers Mean?
"Put It in Reverse" 480
Evaluation of the Lower-of-Cost-or-Market
Rule 481
Valuation Bases 481
Valuation at Net Realizable Value 481
Valuation Using Relative Sales Value 482
Purchase Commitments—A Special Problem 483
**The Gross Profit Method of Estimating
Inventory 485**
Computation of Gross Profit Percentage 486
Evaluation of Gross Profit Method 488
What Do the Numbers Mean? The Squeeze 488
Retail Inventory Method 488
Retail-Method Concepts 489
Retail Inventory Method with Markups and
Markdowns—Conventional Method 490
Special Items Relating to Retail Method 493
Evaluation of Retail Inventory Method 493
Presentation and Analysis 494
Presentation of Inventories 494
Analysis of Inventories 495

APPENDIX 9A **LIFO Retail Methods 497**
Stable Prices—LIFO Retail Method 497
**Fluctuating Prices—Dollar-Value LIFO
Retail Method 498**
**Subsequent Adjustments Under Dollar-Value
LIFO Retail 500**
Changing from Conventional Retail to LIFO 501
FASB Codification 504
IFRS Insights 525

Chapter 10

Acquisition and Disposition of Property, Plant, and Equipment 536
Watch Your Spending

Property, Plant, and Equipment 538
Acquisition of Property, Plant,
and Equipment 538
Cost of Land 539
Cost of Buildings 539
Cost of Equipment 540
Self-Constructed Assets 540
Interest Costs During Construction 541
What Do the Numbers Mean? What's in
Your Interest? 546
Observations 547
Valuation of Property, Plant, and Equipment 547
Cash Discounts 547
Deferred-Payment Contracts 547
Lump-Sum Purchases 548
Issuance of Stock 549
Exchanges of Nonmonetary Assets 550
What Do the Numbers Mean?
About Those Swaps 555
Accounting for Contributions 555
Other Asset Valuation Methods 556
Costs Subsequent to Acquisition 556
What Do the Numbers Mean? Disconnected 557
Additions 558
Improvements and Replacements 558
Rearrangement and Reinstallation 559
Repairs 559
Summary of Costs Subsequent to
Acquisition 560
**Disposition of Property, Plant,
and Equipment 560**
Sale of Plant Assets 560
Involuntary Conversion 561
Miscellaneous Problems 561
FASB Codification 564

Chapter 11

Depreciation, Impairments, and Depletion 588
Here Come the Write-Offs

Depreciation—A Method of Cost Allocation 590
  Factors Involved in the Depreciation Process 590
  What Do the Numbers Mean? Alphabet Dupe 592
  Methods of Depreciation 592
  Special Depreciation Methods 595
  What Do the Numbers Mean? Decelerating Depreciation 597
  Special Depreciation Issues 598
  What Do the Numbers Mean? Depreciation Choices 601

Impairments 601
  Recognizing Impairments 601
  Measuring Impairments 602
  Restoration of Impairment Loss 603
  Impairment of Assets to Be Disposed Of 603

Depletion 604
  Establishing a Depletion Base 605
  Write-Off of Resource Cost 606
  Estimating Recoverable Reserves 607
  What Do the Numbers Mean? Reserve Surprise 607
  Liquidating Dividends 607
  Continuing Controversy 608
  Evolving Issue Full-Cost or Successful-Efforts? 609

Presentation and Analysis 609
  Presentation of Property, Plant, Equipment, and Natural Resources 609
  Analysis of Property, Plant, and Equipment 611
  APPENDIX 11A **Income Tax Depreciation 614**
Modified Accelerated Cost Recovery System 614
  Tax Lives (Recovery Periods) 614
  Tax Depreciation Methods 615
  Example of MACRS 615
Optional Straight-Line Method 616
Tax versus Book Depreciation 617
FASB Codification 618
IFRS Insights 637

Chapter 12

Intangible Assets 648
Is This Sustainable?
Intangible Asset Issues 650
  Characteristics 650
  Valuation 650
  Amortization of Intangibles 651
  What Do the Numbers Mean? Definitely Indefinite 653
Types of Intangible Assets 653
  Marketing-Related Intangible Assets 653
  What Do the Numbers Mean? Keep Your Hands Off My Intangible! 654

Customer-Related Intangible Assets 654
Artistic-Related Intangible Assets 655
Contract-Related Intangible Assets 655
Technology-Related Intangible Assets 656
What Do the Numbers Mean? Patent Battles 657
What Do the Numbers Mean? The Value of a Secret Formula 658
Goodwill 658

Impairment of Intangible Assets 662
  Impairment of Limited-Life Intangibles 662
  Impairment of Indefinite-Life Intangibles Other Than Goodwill 662
  Impairment of Goodwill 663
  Impairment Summary 664
  What Do the Numbers Mean? Impairment Risk 665

Research and Development Costs 665
  Identifying R&D Activities 666
  Accounting for R&D Activities 667
  Costs Similar to R&D Costs 667
  What Do the Numbers Mean? Branded 670

Presentation of Intangibles and Related Items 670
  Presentation of Intangible Assets 670
  Presentation of Research and Development Costs 672
  Evolving Issue Recognition of R&D and Internally Generated Intangibles 673
FASB Codification 676
IFRS Insights 693

Chapter 13

Current Liabilities and Contingencies 700
Now You See It, Now You Don't
Current Liabilities 702
  Accounts Payable 703
  Notes Payable 703
  Current Maturities of Long-Term Debt 705
  Short-Term Obligations Expected to Be Refinanced 705
  What Do the Numbers Mean? What About That Short-Term Debt? 707
  Dividends Payable 707
  Customer Advances and Deposits 707
  Unearned Revenues 708
  What Do the Numbers Mean? Microsoft's Liabilities—Good or Bad? 708
  Sales Taxes Payable 709
  Income Taxes Payable 709
  Employee-Related Liabilities 710
Contingencies 715
  Gain Contingencies 715
  Loss Contingencies 716
  What Do the Numbers Mean? Frequent Flyers 722

What Do the Numbers Mean? More
    Disclosure, Please 726
Presentation and Analysis 726
    Presentation of Current Liabilities 726
    Presentation of Contingencies 728
    Analysis of Current Liabilities 729
    Evolving Issue Greenhouse Gases: Let's Be
      Standard-Setters 730
FASB Codification 733
IFRS Insights 753

Chapter 14

Long-Term Liabilities 762
Going Long
Bonds Payable 764
    Issuing Bonds 764
    Types of Bonds 764
    What Do the Numbers Mean?
      All About Bonds 765
    Valuation of Bonds Payable—Discount
      and Premium 766
    What Do the Numbers Mean?
      How's My Rating? 768
    Bonds Issued at Par on Interest Date 768
    Bonds Issued at Discount or Premium on
      Interest Date 768
    Bonds Issued Between Interest Dates 770
    Effective-Interest Method 770
    Costs of Issuing Bonds 774
    Extinguishment of Debt 775
    What Do the Numbers Mean? Your Debt Is
      Killing My Equity 776
Long-Term Notes Payable 776
    Notes Issued at Face Value 777
    Notes Not Issued at Face Value 777
    Special Notes Payable Situations 779
    Mortgage Notes Payable 782
    Fair Value Option 782
Reporting and Analyzing Liabilities 783
    Off-Balance-Sheet Financing 783
    What Do the Numbers Mean?
      Obligated 785
    Presentation and Analysis of
      Long-Term Debt 786
    Evolving Issue Fair Value of Liabilities:
      Pick a Number, Any Number 788
APPENDIX 14A **Troubled-Debt**
  Restructurings 790
Settlement of Debt 791
    Transfer of Assets 791
    Granting of Equity Interest 791
Modification of Terms 792
    Example 1—No Gain for Debtor 792
    Example 2—Gain for Debtor 795
Concluding Remarks 796

FASB Codification 798
IFRS Insights 815

Chapter 15

Stockholders' Equity 820
It's a Global Market
The Corporate Form of Organization 822
    State Corporate Law 822
    What Do the Numbers Mean?
      1209 North Orange Street 822
    Capital Stock or Share System 823
    Variety of Ownership Interests 824
Corporate Capital 824
    Issuance of Stock 825
    What Do the Numbers Mean? The Case of the
      Disappearing Receivable 829
    Reacquisition of Shares 829
    What Do the Numbers Mean? Buybacks—Good
      or Bad? 830
Preferred Stock 834
    Features of Preferred Stock 834
    What Do the Numbers Mean?
      A Class (B) Act 836
    Accounting for and Reporting
      Preferred Stock 836
Dividend Policy 837
    Financial Condition and Dividend
      Distributions 837
    Types of Dividends 838
    Stock Dividends and Stock Splits 841
    What Do the Numbers Mean?
      Splitsville 844
    What Do the Numbers Mean? Dividends Up,
      Dividends Down 846
    Disclosure of Restrictions on Retained
      Earnings 846
Presentation and Analysis of Stockholders'
  Equity 847
    Presentation 847
    Analysis 849
APPENDIX 15A **Dividend Preferences and Book**
  Value per Share 852
Dividend Preferences 852
Book Value per Share 853
FASB Codification 856
IFRS Insights 874

Chapter 16

**Dilutive Securities and Earnings
per Share 882**
Kicking the Habit
Dilutive Securities 884
    Debt and Equity 884
    Accounting for Convertible Debt 884

Convertible Preferred Stock 886
What Do the Numbers Mean? How Low Can
  You Go? 887
Stock Warrants 887
Evolving Issue Is That All Debt? 890
Accounting for Stock Compensation 893
Stock-Option Plans 893
Restricted Stock 894
Employee Stock-Purchase Plans 896
Disclosure of Compensation Plans 897
Debate over Stock-Option Accounting 897
What Do the Numbers Mean? A Little Honesty
  Goes a Long Way 899
Computing Earnings per Share 899
Earnings per Share—Simple Capital
  Structure 900
Earnings per Share—Complex Capital
  Structure 904
What Do the Numbers Mean? Pro Forma
  EPS Confusion 911
APPENDIX 16A **Accounting for Stock-Appreciation
  Rights 913**
SARS—Share-Based Equity Awards 914
SARS—Share-Based Liability Awards 914
Stock-Appreciation Rights Example 915
APPENDIX 16B **Comprehensive Earnings
  per Share Example 916**
Diluted Earnings per Share 918
FASB Codification 923
IFRS Insights 941

Chapter 17

Investments 950
What to Do?

Investments in Debt Securities 952
Debt Investment Classifications 952
Held-to-Maturity Securities 953
Available-for-Sale Securities 955
What Do the Numbers Mean? What Is
  Fair Value? 959
Trading Securities 959
Investments in Equity Securities 960
Holdings of Less Than 20% 961
What Do the Numbers Mean? More Disclosure,
  Please 964
Holdings Between 20% and 50% 964
Holdings of More Than 50% 966
What Do the Numbers Mean? Who's in
  Control Here? 967
Additional Measurement Issues 967
Fair Value Option 967
Evolving Issue Fair Value Controversy 968
Impairment of Value 969
Reclassifications and Transfers 970
Reclassification Adjustments 970
Transfers Between Categories 974

Summary of Reporting Treatment of
  Securities 975
Evolving Issue Classification and Measurement—
  The Long Road 975
APPENDIX 17A **Accounting for Derivative
  Instruments 977**
Defining Derivatives 977
Who Uses Derivatives, and Why? 978
Producers and Consumers 978
Speculators and Arbitrageurs 979
Basic Principles in Accounting for Derivatives 980
Example of Derivative Financial Instrument—
  Speculation 980
Differences Between Traditional and Derivative
  Financial Instruments 983
Derivatives Used for Hedging 983
What Do the Numbers Mean?
  Risky Business 984
Fair Value Hedge 984
Cash Flow Hedge 987
Other Reporting Issues 989
Embedded Derivatives 989
Qualifying Hedge Criteria 989
Summary of Derivatives Accounting 990
Comprehensive Hedge Accounting Example 991
Fair Value Hedge 992
Financial Statement Presentation of an Interest
  Rate Swap 994
Controversy and Concluding Remarks 995
APPENDIX 17B **Variable-Interest Entities 996**
What About GAAP? 997
Consolidation of Variable-Interest Entities 997
Some Examples 998
What Is Happening in Practice? 999
APPENDIX 17C **Fair Value Disclosures 999**
**Disclosure of Fair Value Information: Financial
  Instruments 1000**
**Disclosure of Fair Values: Impaired
  Assets or Liabilities 1003**
Conclusion 1003
FASB Codification 1005
IFRS Insights 1026

Chapter 18

Revenue Recognition 1040
It's Back

Overview of Revenue Recognition 1042
Guidelines for Revenue Recognition 1043
Departures from the Sale Basis 1044
What Do the Numbers Mean? Liability or
  Revenue? 1045
**Revenue Recognition at Point of
  Sale (Delivery) 1045**
Sales with Discounts 1046
Sales with Right of Return 1047
Sales with Buybacks 1049

Bill and Hold Sales 1050
Principal-Agent Relationships 1050
What Do the Numbers Mean? Grossed Out 1051
Trade Loading and Channel Stuffing 1053
What Do the Numbers Mean?
  No Take-Backs 1053
Multiple-Deliverable Arrangements 1054
Summary 1056
Revenue Recognition before Delivery 1057
Percentage-of-Completion Method 1058
Completed-Contract Method 1063
Long-Term Contract Losses 1064
What Do the Numbers Mean?
  Less Conservative 1067
Disclosures in Financial Statements 1068
Completion-of-Production Basis 1068
Revenue Recognition after Delivery 1068
Installment-Sales Method 1068
Cost-Recovery Method 1077
Deposit Method 1078
Summary and Concluding Remarks 1079
APPENDIX 18A **Revenue Recognition**
  for Franchises 1081
Initial Franchise Fees 1082
Example of Entries for Initial Franchise
  Fee 1082
Continuing Franchise Fees 1083
Bargain Purchases 1083
Options to Purchase 1084
Franchisor's Cost 1084
Disclosures of Franchisors 1084
FASB Codification 1086
IFRS Insights 1109

Chapter 19

Accounting for Income Taxes 1116
How Much Is Enough?
Fundamentals of Accounting for
  Income Taxes 1118
Future Taxable Amounts and Deferred Taxes 1119
What Do the Numbers Mean?
  "Real Liabilities" 1122
Future Deductible Amounts and Deferred
  Taxes 1123
What Do the Numbers Mean? "Real Assets" 1125
Deferred Tax Asset—Valuation Allowance 1125
Income Statement Presentation 1126
Specific Differences 1127
Tax Rate Considerations 1130
What Do the Numbers Mean? Global
  Tax Rates 1131
Accounting for Net Operating Losses 1132
Loss Carryback 1132
Loss Carryforward 1132
Loss Carryback Example 1133
Loss Carryforward Example 1134

What Do the Numbers Mean? NOLs: Good
  News or Bad? 1138
Financial Statement Presentation 1138
Balance Sheet 1138
What Do the Numbers Mean? Imagination
  at Work 1140
Income Statement 1141
Evolving Issue Uncertain Tax Positions 1143
Review of the Asset-Liability Method 1144
APPENDIX 19A **Comprehensive Example of**
  Interperiod Tax Allocation 1147
First Year—2013 1147
Taxable Income and Income Taxes
  Payable—2013 1148
Computing Deferred Income Taxes—
  End of 2013 1148
Deferred Tax Expense (Benefit) and the Journal
  Entry to Record Income Taxes—2013 1149
Financial Statement Presentation—2013 1150
Second Year—2014 1151
Taxable Income and Income Taxes
  Payable—2014 1152
Computing Deferred Income Taxes—End
  of 2014 1152
Deferred Tax Expense (Benefit) and the Journal
  Entry to Record Income Taxes—2014 1153
Financial Statement Presentation—2014 1153
FASB Codification 1156
IFRS Insights 1175

Chapter 20

Accounting for Pensions and Postretirement Benefits 1182
Where Have All the Pensions Gone?
Nature of Pension Plans 1184
Defined Contribution Plan 1185
Defined Benefit Plan 1185
What Do the Numbers Mean? Which Plan
  Is Right for You? 1186
The Role of Actuaries in Pension Accounting 1187
Accounting for Pensions 1187
Alternative Measures of the Liability 1187
Recognition of the Net Funded Status of the
  Pension Plan 1189
Components of Pension Expense 1189
Using a Pension Worksheet 1192
2014 Entries and Worksheet 1192
Amortization of Prior Service Cost (PSC) 1194
2015 Entries and Worksheet 1195
Gain or Loss 1197
What Do the Numbers Mean? Pension Costs
  Ups and Downs 1198
Corridor Amortization 1199
Evolving Issue Bye Bye Corridor 1202
2016 Entries and Worksheet 1202
What Do the Numbers Mean? Roller Coaster 1204

Reporting Pension Plans in Financial Statements 1204
Within the Financial Statements 1205
Within the Notes to the Financial Statements 1207
Example of Pension Note Disclosure 1208
2017 Entries and Worksheet—A Comprehensive Example 1210
Special Issues 1211
What Do the Numbers Mean? Who Guarantees the Guarantor? 1213
Concluding Observations 1215
APPENDIX 20A **Accounting for Postretirement Benefits 1217**
Accounting Guidance 1217
Differences Between Pension Benefits and Healthcare Benefits 1218
What Do the Numbers Mean? OPEBs—How Big Are They? 1219
Postretirement Benefits Accounting Provisions 1219
Obligations Under Postretirement Benefits 1220
Postretirement Expense 1220
Illustrative Accounting Entries 1221
2014 Entries and Worksheet 1221
Recognition of Gains and Losses 1223
2015 Entries and Worksheet 1223
Amortization of Net Gain or Loss in 2016 1224
Disclosures in Notes to the Financial Statements 1225
Actuarial Assumptions and Conceptual Issues 1225
What Do the Numbers Mean? Want Some Bad News? 1227
FASB Codification 1229
IFRS Insights 1250

Chapter 21

Accounting for Leases 1268
More Companies Ask, "Why Buy?"
The Leasing Environment 1270
Who Are the Players? 1270
Advantages of Leasing 1272
What Do the Numbers Mean? Off-Balance-Sheet Financing 1273
Conceptual Nature of a Lease 1273
Accounting by the Lessee 1274
Capitalization Criteria 1275
Asset and Liability Accounted for Differently 1278
Capital Lease Method (Lessee) 1278
Operating Method (Lessee) 1281
What Do the Numbers Mean? Restatements on the Menu 1281
Comparison of Capital Lease with Operating Lease 1282
Evolving Issue Are You Liable? 1283
Accounting by the Lessor 1284
Economics of Leasing 1284
Classification of Leases by the Lessor 1285

Direct-Financing Method (Lessor) 1286
Operating Method (Lessor) 1289
Special Lease Accounting Problems 1289
Residual Values 1290
Sales-Type Leases (Lessor) 1296
What Do the Numbers Mean? Xerox Takes on the SEC 1298
Bargain-Purchase Option (Lessee) 1298
Initial Direct Costs (Lessor) 1298
Current versus Noncurrent 1299
Disclosing Lease Data 1300
Unresolved Lease Accounting Problems 1302
Evolving Issue Lease Accounting—If It Quacks Like a Duck 1303
APPENDIX 21A **Sale-Leasebacks 1306**
Determining Asset Use 1307
Lessee 1307
Lessor 1308
Sale-Leaseback Example 1308
FASB Codification 1313
IFRS Insights 1331

Chapter 22

Accounting Changes and Error Analysis 1342
In the Dark
Accounting Changes 1344
Changes in Accounting Principle 1344
What Do the Numbers Mean? Quite a Change 1346
Retrospective Accounting Change Approach 1346
What Do the Numbers Mean? Change Management 1348
Direct and Indirect Effects of Changes 1355
Impracticability 1356
Changes in Accounting Estimates 1357
Prospective Reporting 1357
Disclosures 1358
Changes in Reporting Entity 1359
Accounting Errors 1359
Example of Error Correction 1361
Summary of Accounting Changes and Correction of Errors 1363
What Do the Numbers Mean? Can I Get My Money Back? 1364
Motivations for Change of Accounting Method 1365
Error Analysis 1366
Balance Sheet Errors 1366
Income Statement Errors 1367
Balance Sheet and Income Statement Errors 1367
Comprehensive Example: Numerous Errors 1370
What Do the Numbers Mean? Guard the Financial Statements! 1372

Preparation of Financial Statements with
Error Corrections 1373
APPENDIX 22A **Changing from or to the
Equity Method 1377**
Change from the Equity Method 1377
Dividends in Excess of Earnings 1377
Change to the Equity Method 1378
FASB Codification 1381
IFRS Insights 1404

Chapter 23

Statement of Cash Flows 1410
Show Me the Money!
Preparation of the Statement of Cash Flows 1412
Usefulness of the Statement of Cash Flows 1412
Classification of Cash Flows 1413
What Do the Numbers Mean? How's My
Cash Flow? 1414
Format of the Statement of Cash Flows 1415
Steps in Preparation 1415
Illustrations—Tax Consultants Inc. 1416
Step 1: Determine the Change in Cash 1417
Step 2: Determine Net Cash Flow from
Operating Activities 1417
What Do the Numbers Mean? Earnings and Cash
Flow Management? 1419
Step 3: Determine Net Cash Flows from Investing
and Financing Activities 1419
Statement of Cash Flows—2013 1419
Illustration—2014 1420
Illustration—2015 1423
Sources of Information for the Statement
of Cash Flows 1426
Net Cash Flow from Operating Activities—
Direct Method 1428
Evolving Issue Direct versus Indirect 1433
Special Problems in Statement Preparation 1434
Adjustments to Net Income 1434
Accounts Receivable (Net) 1438
What Do the Numbers Mean? Not What
It Seems 1439
Other Working Capital Changes 1440
Net Losses 1440
Significant Noncash Transactions 1441
What Do the Numbers Mean? Cash
Flow Tool 1442
Use of a Worksheet 1443
Preparation of the Worksheet 1444
Analysis of Transactions 1444
Preparation of Final Statement 1451
FASB Codification 1454
IFRS Insights 1480

Chapter 24

Full Disclosure in Financial
Reporting 1486
High-Quality Financial Reporting—Always in Fashion
Full Disclosure Principle 1488
Increase in Reporting Requirements 1489
Differential Disclosure 1489
Evolving Issue Disclosure—Quantity
and Quality 1490
Notes to the Financial Statements 1491
Accounting Policies 1491
Common Notes 1491
What Do the Numbers Mean? Footnote
Secrets 1493
Disclosure Issues 1493
Disclosure of Special Transactions or Events 1493
Post-Balance-Sheet Events
(Subsequent Events) 1495
Reporting for Diversified (Conglomerate)
Companies 1497
Interim Reports 1501
Evolving Issue It's Faster but Is It Better? 1507
Auditor's and Management's Reports 1508
Auditor's Report 1508
What Do the Numbers Mean? Heart of
the Matter 1511
Management's Reports 1511
Current Reporting Issues 1513
Reporting on Financial Forecasts
and Projections 1513
What Do the Numbers Mean? Global
Forecasts 1515
Internet Financial Reporting 1516
What Do the Numbers Mean? New Formats,
New Disclosure 1517
Fraudulent Financial Reporting 1517
What Do the Numbers Mean? Disclosure
Overload 1519
Criteria for Making Accounting and Reporting
Choices 1520
APPENDIX 24A **Basic Financial Statement
Analysis 1522**
Perspective on Financial Statement Analysis 1522
Ratio Analysis 1523
Limitations of Ratio Analysis 1524
Comparative Analysis 1526
Percentage (Common-Size) Analysis 1527
FASB Codification 1530
IFRS Insights 1548

Index I-1

Acknowledgments

Intermediate Accounting has benefited greatly from the input of focus group participants, manuscript reviewers, those who have sent comments by letter or e-mail, ancillary authors, and proofers. We greatly appreciate the constructive suggestions and innovative ideas of reviewers and the creativity and accuracy of the ancillary authors and checkers.

Prior Edition Reviewers

We greatly appreciate the over 250 reviewers who have assisted with the prior editions of Intermediate Accounting. *Please visit the book's companion website, at **www.wiley.com/college/kieso**, for a full listing of these instructors who have been invaluable in the development and continued improvement of our textbook.*

Fifteenth Edition

Wendy Bailey, *Northeastern University;* Samuel Bass, *Missouri State University;* Susan Bennett, *Wake Technical Community College;* Elise A. Boyas, *University of Pittsburgh;* Jeff Brothers, *Regis University;* John Brozovsky, *Virginia Polytechnic Institute and State University;* Helen Brubeck, *San Jose State University;* Janie Casello Bouges, *University of Massachusetts—Lowell;* Tim Cangeleri, *St. Joseph's College;* Kimberly D. Charland, *Kansas State University;* Elizabeth Conner, *University of Colorado—Denver;* Ming Lu Chun, *Santa Monica College;* Natalie Churyk, *Northern Illinois University;* Eugene Comiskey, *Georgia Institute of Technology;* Tim Coville, *St. John's University;* Illia Dichev, *Emory University;* Bob Eskew, *Purdue University;* Tony Greig, *University of Wisconsin—Madison;* Lynne Hendrix, *Hope College;* Travis Holt, *University of Tennessee;* Allen Hunt, *Southern Illinois University;* John Jiang, *Michigan State University;* Mary Jo Jones, *Eastern University;* Lisa Koonce, *University of Texas—Austin;* Barbara Kren, *Marquette University;* Gaurav Kumar, *University of Arkansas—Little Rock;* Zining Li, *Southern Methodist University;* Ellen Lippman, *University of Portland;* Daphne Main, *Loyola University—New Orleans.*

S.A. Marino, *Westchester Community College;* Ariel Markelevich, *Suffolk University;* Linda McDaniel, *University of Kentucky;* K. Bryan Menk, *Virginia State University;* Gerald Miller, *The College of New Jersey;* Kathleen Moffitt, *Texas State University—San Marcos;* Kanalis Ockree, *Washburn University;* Felicia Olagbemi, *Colorado State University;* Mitch Oler, *Virginia Polytechnic Institute and State University;* Keith Patterson, *Brigham Young University—Idaho;* Charles Pendola, *St. Joseph's College;* Pete Poznanski, *Cleveland State University;* Jay Price, *Utah State University;* Terence Reilly, *Albright University;* Ken Reichelt, *Louisiana State University;* Ada Rodriguez, *Lehman College, CUNY;* Jack Rude, *Bloomsburg University;* Michael Ruff, *Bentley University;* August Saibeni, *Cosumnes River College;* Alexander J. Sannella, *Rutgers University;* Richard Schneible, *University of Albany SUNY;* Stephen Stubben, *University of North Carolina—Chapel Hill;* Stefanie Tate, *University of Massachusetts—Lowell;* Dan Teed, *Troy University;* Robin Thomas, *North Carolina State University;* Thomas Tyson, *St. John Fisher College;* Dan Wangerin, *Michigan State University;* Donna Whitten, *Purdue University North Central;* Kenneth Winter, *University of Wisconsin—Madison;* David Wright, *University of Michigan;* Jim Zapapas, *Regis University;* Lin Zheng, *Mercer University.*

Special thanks to Kurt Pany, Arizona State University, for his input on auditor disclosure issues, and to Stephen A. Zeff, Rice University, for his comments on international accounting.

In addition, we thank the following colleagues who contributed to several of the unique features of this edition.

Gateway to the Profession and Codification Cases

Katie Adler, *Deloitte LLP, Chicago;* Jack Cathey, *University of North Carolina—Charlotte;* Michelle Ephraim, *Worcester Polytechnic Institute;* Erik Frederickson, *Madison, Wisconsin;* Danielle Griffin, *KPMG, Chicago;* Jason Hart, *Deloitte LLP, Milwaukee;* Frank Heflin, *Florida State University;* Mike Katte, *SC Johnson, Racine, WI;* Kelly Krieg, *E & Y, Milwaukee;* Jeremy Kunicki, *Walgreens;* Courtney Meier, *Deloitte LLP, Milwaukee;* Andrew Prewitt, *KPMG, Chicago;* Jeff Seymour, *KPMG, Minneapolis;* Matt Sullivan, *Deloitte LLP, Milwaukee;* Matt Tutaj, *Deloitte LLP, Chicago;* Jen Vaughn, *PricewaterhouseCoopers, Chicago;* Erin Viel, *PricewaterhouseCoopers, Milwaukee.*

Ancillary Authors, Contributors, Proofers, and Accuracy Checkers

LuAnn Bean, *Florida Institute of Technology;* Mary Ann Benson; John C. Borke, *University of Wisconsin—Platteville;* Jack Cathey, *University of North Carolina—Charlotte;* Jim Emig, *Villanova University;* Larry Falcetto, *Emporia State University;* Coby Harmon, *University of California, Santa Barbara;* Marilyn F. Hunt, Douglas W. Kieso, *Aurora University;* Mark Kohlbeck, *Florida Atlantic University;* Steven Lifland, *High Point University;* Ming Lu, *Santa Monica College;* Maureen Mascha, *Marquette University;* Barbara Muller, *Arizona State University;* Jill Misuraca, *University of Tampa;* Yvonne Phang, *Borough of Manhattan Community College;* John Plouffe, *California State Polytechnic University—Pomona;* Mark Riley, *Northern Illinois University;* Lynn Stallworth, *Appalachian State University;* Diane Tanner, *University of North Florida;* Sheila Viel, *University of Wisconsin—Milwaukee;* Dick D. Wasson, *Southwestern College;* Melanie Yon, *San Diego University.*

Advisory Board

We gratefully acknowledge the following members of the Intermediate Accounting *Advisory Board for their advice and assistance with this edition.*

Steve Balsam, *Temple University;* Jack Cathey, *University of North Carolina—Charlotte;* Uday Chandra, *State University of New York at Albany;* Ruben Davila, *University of Southern California;* Doug deVidal, *University of Texas—Austin;* Sunita Goel, *Siena College;* Jeffrey Hales, *Georgia Institute of Technology;* Celina Jozsi,

University of South Florida; Jocelyn Kauffunger, *University of Pittsburgh*; Adam Koch, *University of Virginia*; Roger Martin, *University of Virginia*; Mark Riley, *Northern Illinois University*; Karen Turner, *University of Northern Colorado*.

Practicing Accountants and Business Executives

From the fields of corporate and public accounting, we owe thanks to the following practitioners for their technical advice and for consenting to interviews.

Mike Crooch, *FASB (retired)*; Tracy Golden, *Deloitte LLP*; John Gribble, *PricewaterhouseCoopers (retired)*; Darien Griffin, *S.C. Johnson & Son*; Michael Lehman, *Sun Microsystems, Inc.*; Tom Linsmeier, *FASB*; Michele Lippert, *Evoke.com*; Sue McGrath, *Vision Capital Management*; David Miniken, *Sweeney Conrad*; Robert Sack, *University of Virginia*; Clare Schulte, *Deloitte LLP*; Willie Sutton, *Mutual Community Savings Bank, Durham, NC*; Lynn Turner, *former SEC Chief Accountant*; Rachel Woods, *PricewaterhouseCoopers*; Arthur Wyatt, *Arthur Andersen & Co., and the University of Illinois—Urbana*.

Finally, we appreciate the exemplary support and professional commitment given us by the development, marketing, production, and editorial staffs of John Wiley & Sons, including the following: George Hoffman, Susan Elbe, Chris DeJohn, Michael McDonald, Amy Scholz, Jesse Cruz, Valerie Vargas, Brian Kamins, Jackie MacKenzie, Allie Morris, Greg Chaput, Harry Nolan, Maureen Eide, and Kristine Carney. Thanks, too, to Suzanne Ingrao for her production work, to Denise Showers and the staff at Aptara®, Inc. for their work on the textbook, Cyndy Taylor, and to Matt Gauthier and the staff at Integra Publishing Services for their work on the solutions manual.

We also appreciate the cooperation of the American Institute of Certified Public Accountants and the Financial Accounting Standards Board in permitting us to quote from their pronouncements. We thank The Procter & Gamble Company for permitting us to use its 2011 annual report for our specimen financial statements. We also acknowledge permission from the American Institute of Certified Public Accountants, the Institute of Management Accountants, and the Institute of Internal Auditors to adapt and use material from the Uniform CPA Examinations, the CMA Examinations, and the CIA Examinations, respectively.

Suggestions and comments from users of this book will be appreciated. Please feel free to e-mail any one of us at *AccountingAuthors@yahoo.com*.

Donald E. Kieso
Somonauk, Illinois

Jerry J. Weygandt
Madison, Wisconsin

Terry D. Warfield
Madison, Wisconsin

1 Financial Accounting and Accounting Standards

LEARNING OBJECTIVES

After studying this chapter, you should be able to:

1 Identify the major financial statements and other means of financial reporting.

2 Explain how accounting assists in the efficient use of scarce resources.

3 Identify the objective of financial reporting.

4 Explain the need for accounting standards.

5 Identify the major policy-setting bodies and their role in the standard-setting process.

6 Explain the meaning of generally accepted accounting principles (GAAP) and the role of the Codification for GAAP.

7 Describe the impact of user groups on the rule-making process.

8 Describe some of the challenges facing financial reporting.

9 Understand issues related to ethics and financial accounting.

We Can Do Better

A recent report says it best: "Accounting information is central to the functioning of international capital markets and to managing small businesses, conducting effective government, understanding business processes, and . . . how economic decisions are made. . . . Across the globe, a common characteristic of economies that flourish is the presence of reliable accounting information."

Many in the United States take pride in our system of financial reporting as being the most robust and transparent in the world. But most would also comment that we can do better, particularly in light of the many accounting scandals that have occurred at companies like **AIG**, **WorldCom**, and **Lehman Brothers**, and the financial crisis of 2008.

To better understand where we are today, the Center for Audit Quality conducts a yearly survey that measures investor confidence in such categories as U.S. capital markets, audited financial information, and U.S. publicly traded companies. Here are the results:

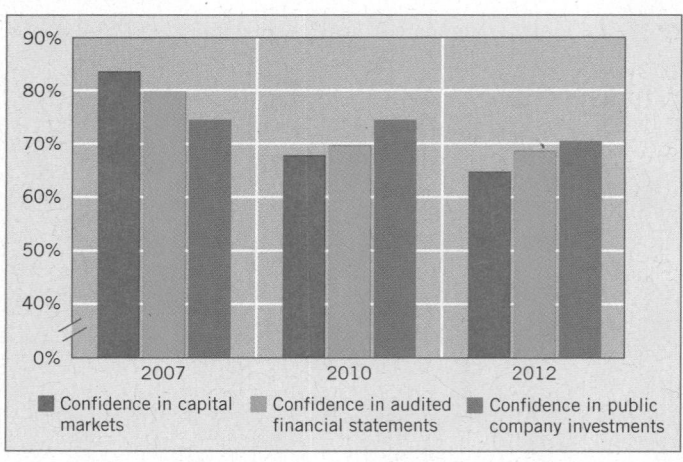

■ Confidence in capital markets ■ Confidence in audited financial statements ■ Confidence in public company investments

The results indicate that the 2008 financial crisis took a bite out of investor confidence. While investor confidence in U.S. markets, auditors, and public companies has stabilized, the question is how can we improve? Here are some possibilities on how we can enhance the existing system of financial reporting.

1. Today, equity securities are broadly held, with approximately half of American households investing in stocks. This presents a challenge—investors have expressed concerns that **one-size-fits-all financial reports do not meet the needs of the spectrum of investors** who rely on those reports. While many individual investors are more interested in summarized, plain-English reports, market analysts and other investment professionals may desire information at a far more detailed level than is currently provided. Technology may help customize the information that the different types of investors desire.

2. Companies also express concerns with the complexity of the financial reporting system. Companies assert that **when preparing financial reports, it is difficult to ensure compliance with the voluminous and complex requirements contained in U.S. GAAP and SEC reporting rules**. This is a particularly heavy burden on smaller, non-public companies, which may have fewer resources to comply with the wide range of rules.

3. We also need to consider the broader array of information that investors need to make informed decisions. As some have noted, the percentage of a company's market value that can be attributed to accounting book value has declined significantly from the days of a bricks-and-mortar economy. **Thus, we may want to consider a more comprehensive business reporting model, including both financial and nonfinancial key performance indicators.**

4. Finally, we must also consider **how to deliver all of this information in a timelier manner**. In a world where messages can be sent across the world in a blink of an eye, it is ironic that the analysis of financial information is still subject to many manual processes, resulting in delays, increased costs, and errors.

Thus, improving financial reporting involves more than simply trimming or reworking the existing accounting literature. In some cases, major change is already underway. For example:

- The FASB and IASB are working on a convergence project, which will contribute to less-complex, more-understandable standards in the important areas of revenue recognition, leasing, and financial instruments.
- Standard-setters are exploring expanded reporting of key performance indicators, including reports on sustainability and a disclosure framework project to improve the effectiveness of disclosures to clearly communicate the information that is most important to users of financial statements. This project, combined with the introduction of a private-company reporting framework, could go a long way to address one-size-fits-all challenges.
- The SEC now requires the delivery of financial reports using eXtensible Business Reporting Language (XBRL). Reporting through XBRL allows timelier reporting via the Internet and allows statement users to transform accounting reports to meet their specific needs.

Each of these projects will hopefully support improvements in the quality of financial reporting and increase confidence in U.S. capital markets.

Sources: Adapted from The Pathways Commission, "Charting a National Strategy for the Next Generation of Accountants" (AAA, AICPA, July 2012); Conrad W. Hewitt, "Opening Remarks Before the Initial Meeting of the SEC Advisory Committee on Improvements to Financial Reporting," U.S. Securities and Exchange Commission, Washington, D.C. (August 2, 2007); and Center for Audit Quality, *Main Street Investor Survey* (September 2012). See *www.fasb.org* for updates on FASB/IASB convergence, disclosure, and private company decision-making projects.

CONCEPTUAL FOCUS

> See the **Underlying Concepts** on pages 6 and 7.
> Read the **Evolving Issue** on page 17 for a discussion of the use of fair value accounting.

INTERNATIONAL FOCUS

> See the **International Perspectives** on pages 8, 9, 10, 17, and 20.
> Read the **IFRS Insights** on pages 31–39 for a discussion of:
  —International standard-setting organizations
  —Hierarchy of IFRS
  —International accounting convergence

| PREVIEW OF CHAPTER | 1 |

As our opening story indicates, the U.S. system of financial reporting has long been the most robust and transparent in the world. However, to ensure that it continues to provide the most relevant and reliable financial information to users, a number of financial reporting issues must be resolved. These issues include such matters as adopting global standards, increasing fair value reporting, and meeting multiple user needs. This chapter explains the environment of financial reporting and the many factors affecting it, as follows.

Financial Accounting and Accounting Standards

Financial Statements and Financial Reporting	Parties Involved in Standard-Setting	Generally Accepted Accounting Principles	Issues in Financial Reporting
• Accounting and capital allocation • Objective • Need to develop standards	• Securities and Exchange Commission • American Institute of CPAs • Financial Accounting Standards Board	• FASB Codification	• Political environment • Expectations gap • Financial reporting challenges • International accounting standards • Ethics

FINANCIAL STATEMENTS AND FINANCIAL REPORTING

LEARNING OBJECTIVE ❶
Identify the major financial statements and other means of financial reporting.

The essential characteristics of accounting are (1) the identification, measurement, and communication of financial information about (2) economic entities to (3) interested parties. Financial accounting is the process that culminates in the preparation of financial reports on the enterprise for use by both internal and external parties. Users of these financial reports include investors, creditors, managers, unions, and government agencies. In contrast, **managerial accounting** is the process of identifying, measuring, analyzing, and communicating financial information needed by management to plan, control, and evaluate a company's operations.

Financial statements are the principal means through which a company communicates its financial information to those outside it. These statements provide a company's history quantified in money terms. The financial statements most frequently provided are (1) the balance sheet, (2) the income statement, (3) the statement of cash flows, and (4) the statement of owners' or stockholders' equity. Note disclosures are an integral part of each financial statement.

Some financial information is better provided, or can be provided only, by means of financial reporting other than formal financial statements. Examples include the president's letter or supplementary schedules in the corporate annual report, prospectuses, reports filed with government agencies, news releases, management's forecasts, and social or environmental impact statements. Companies may need to provide such information because of authoritative pronouncement, regulatory rule, or custom. Or they may supply it because management wishes to disclose it voluntarily.

In this textbook, we focus on the development of two types of financial information: (1) the basic financial statements and (2) related disclosures.

Accounting and Capital Allocation

LEARNING OBJECTIVE ❷
Explain how accounting assists in the efficient use of scarce resources.

Resources are limited. As a result, people try to conserve them and ensure that they are used effectively. Efficient use of resources often determines whether a business thrives. This fact places a substantial burden on the accounting profession.

Accountants must measure performance accurately and fairly on a timely basis, so that the right managers and companies are able to attract investment capital. For example, relevant and reliable financial information allows investors and creditors to compare the income and assets employed by such companies as IBM, McDonald's, Microsoft, and Ford. Because these users can assess the relative return and risks associated with investment opportunities, they channel resources more effectively. Illustration 1-1 shows how this process of capital allocation works.

ILLUSTRATION 1-1
Capital Allocation
Process

Financial Reporting	**Users (present and potential)**	**Capital Allocation**
The financial information a company provides to help users with capital allocation decisions about the company.	Investors and creditors use financial reports to make their capital allocation decisions.	The process of determining how and at what cost money is allocated among competing interests.

An effective process of capital allocation is critical to a healthy economy. It promotes productivity, encourages innovation, and provides an efficient and liquid market for buying and selling securities and obtaining and granting credit. Unreliable and irrelevant information leads to poor capital allocation, which adversely affects the securities markets.

What do the numbers mean? IT'S THE ACCOUNTING

"It's the accounting." That's what many investors seem to be saying these days. Even the slightest hint of any accounting irregularity at a company leads to a subsequent pounding of the company's stock price. For example, the *Wall Street Journal* has run the following headlines related to accounting and its effects on the economy.

- Stocks take a beating as accounting woes spread beyond Enron.
- Quarterly reports from IBM and Goldman Sachs sent stocks tumbling.
- VeriFone finds accounting issues; stock price cut in half.

- Bank of America admits hiding debt.
- Facebook, Zynga, Groupon: IPO drops due to accounting, not valuation.

It now has become clear that investors must trust the accounting numbers, or they will abandon the market and put their resources elsewhere. With investor uncertainty, the cost of capital increases for companies who need additional resources. In short, relevant and reliable financial information is necessary for markets to be efficient.

Objective of Financial Reporting

What is the objective **(or purpose)** of financial reporting? The objective of general-purpose financial reporting is to **provide financial information about the reporting entity that is useful to present and potential equity investors, lenders, and other creditors in** decisions about providing resources to the entity. Those decisions involve buying, selling, or holding equity and debt instruments, and providing or settling loans and other forms of credit. Information that is decision-useful to capital providers (investors) may also be helpful to other users of financial reporting who are not investors. Let's examine each of the elements of this objective.[1]

3 LEARNING OBJECTIVE
Identify the objective of financial reporting.

General-Purpose Financial Statements

General-purpose financial statements provide financial reporting information to a wide variety of users. For example, when The Hershey Company issues its financial statements, these statements help shareholders, creditors, suppliers, employees, and regulators to better understand its financial position and related performance. Hershey's users need this type of information to make effective decisions. To be cost-effective in providing this information, general-purpose financial statements are most appropriate. In other words, general-purpose financial statements provide at the **least cost the most useful information possible**.

Equity Investors and Creditors

The objective of financial reporting **identifies investors and creditors as the primary users for general-purpose financial statements**. Identifying investors and creditors as the primary users provides an important focus of general-purpose financial reporting. For example, when Hershey issues its financial statements, its primary focus is on investors and creditors because they have the most critical and immediate need for information in financial reports. Investors and creditors need this financial information to assess

---

[1]Chapter 1, "The Objective of General Purpose Financial Reporting," and Chapter 3, "Qualitative Characteristics of Useful Financial Information," *Statement of Financial Accounting Concepts No. 8* (Norwalk, Conn.: FASB, September 2010), par. OB2.

Underlying Concepts

While the objective of financial reporting is focused on investors and creditors, financial statements may still meet the needs of others.

Hershey's ability to generate net cash inflow and to understand management's ability to protect and enhance the assets of the company, which will be used to generate future net cash inflows. As a result, the primary user groups are not management, regulators, or some other non-investor group.

Entity Perspective

As part of the objective of general-purpose financial reporting, an **entity perspective** is adopted. Companies are viewed as separate and distinct from their owners (present shareholders) using this perspective. The assets of Hershey are viewed as assets of the company and not of a specific creditor or shareholder. Rather, these investors have claims on Hershey's assets in the form of liability or equity claims. The entity perspective is consistent with the present business environment where most companies engaged in financial reporting have substance distinct from their investors (both shareholders and creditors). Thus, a perspective that financial reporting should be focused only on the needs of shareholders—often referred to as the **proprietary perspective**—is not considered appropriate.

What do the numbers mean? DON'T FORGET STEWARDSHIP

In addition to providing decision-useful information about future cash flows, management also is accountable to investors for the custody and safekeeping of the company's economic resources and for their efficient and profitable use. For example, the management of **The Hershey Company** has the responsibility for protecting its economic resources from unfavorable effects of economic factors, such as price changes, and technological and social changes. Because Hershey's performance in discharging its responsibilities (referred to as its **stewardship** responsibilities) usually affects its ability to generate net cash inflows, financial reporting may also provide decision-useful information to assess management performance in this role.

Source: Chapter 1, "The Objective of General Purpose Financial Reporting," and Chapter 3, "Qualitative Characteristics of Useful Financial Information," *Statement of Financial Accounting Concepts No. 8* (Norwalk, Conn.: FASB, September 2010), paras. OB4–OB10.

Decision-Usefulness

Investors are interested in financial reporting because it provides information that is useful for making decisions (referred to as the **decision-usefulness** approach). As indicated earlier, when making these decisions, investors are interested in assessing (1) the company's ability to generate net cash inflows and (2) management's ability to protect and enhance the capital providers' investments. Financial reporting should therefore help investors assess the amounts, timing, and uncertainty of prospective cash inflows from dividends or interest, and the proceeds from the sale, redemption, or maturity of securities or loans. In order for investors to make these assessments, the economic resources of an enterprise, the claims to those resources, and the changes in them must be understood. Financial statements and related explanations should be a primary source for determining this information.

The emphasis on "assessing cash flow prospects" does not mean that the cash basis is preferred over the accrual basis of accounting. Information based on accrual accounting better indicates a company's present and continuing ability to generate favorable cash flows than does information limited to the financial effects of cash receipts and payments.

Recall from your first accounting course the objective of **accrual-basis accounting:** It ensures that a company records events that change its financial statements in the periods in which the events occur, rather than only in the periods in which it receives or pays cash. Using the accrual basis to determine net income means that a company recognizes revenues when it provides the goods or services rather than when it receives cash. Similarly, it recognizes expenses when it incurs them rather than when it pays them. Under accrual accounting, a company generally recognizes revenues when it makes sales. The company can then relate the revenues to the economic environment of the period in which they occurred. Over the long run, trends in revenues and expenses are generally more meaningful than trends in cash receipts and disbursements.[2]

The Need to Develop Standards

The main controversy in setting accounting standards is, "Whose rules should we play by, and what should they be?" The answer is not immediately clear. Users of financial accounting statements have both coinciding and conflicting needs for information of various types. To meet these needs, and to satisfy the stewardship reporting responsibility of management, companies prepare a single set of **general-purpose financial statements**. Users expect these statements to present fairly, clearly, and completely the company's financial operations.

The accounting profession has attempted to develop a set of standards that are generally accepted and universally practiced. Otherwise, each company would have to develop its own standards. Further, readers of financial statements would have to familiarize themselves with every company's peculiar accounting and reporting practices. It would be almost impossible to prepare statements that could be compared.

This common set of standards and procedures is called **generally accepted accounting principles (GAAP)**. The term "generally accepted" means either that an authoritative accounting rule-making body has established a principle of reporting in a given area or that over time a given practice has been accepted as appropriate because of its universal application.[3] Although principles and practices continue to provoke both debate and criticism, most members of the financial community recognize them as the standards that over time have proven to be most useful. We present a more extensive discussion of what constitutes GAAP later in this chapter.

4 LEARNING OBJECTIVE
Explain the need for accounting standards.

Underlying Concepts
Preparing financial statements prepared according to accepted accounting standards contributes to the comparability of accounting information.

PARTIES INVOLVED IN STANDARD-SETTING

Three organizations are instrumental in the development of financial accounting standards (GAAP) in the United States:

1. Securities and Exchange Commission (SEC)
2. American Institute of Certified Public Accountants (AICPA)
3. Financial Accounting Standards Board (FASB)

5 LEARNING OBJECTIVE
Identify the major policy-setting bodies and their role in the standard-setting process.

Securities and Exchange Commission (SEC)

External financial reporting and auditing developed in tandem with the growth of the industrial economy and its capital markets. However, when the stock market crashed in

---

[2]As used here, cash flow means "cash generated and used in operations." The term *cash flows* also frequently means cash obtained by borrowing and used to repay borrowing, cash used for investments in resources and obtained from the disposal of investments, and cash contributed by or distributed to owners.

[3]The terms *principles* and *standards* are used interchangeably in practice and throughout this textbook.

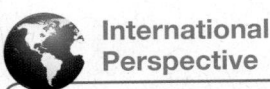

1929 and the nation's economy plunged into the Great Depression, there were calls for increased government regulation of business, especially financial institutions and the stock market.

As a result of these events, the federal government established the **Securities and Exchange Commission (SEC)** to help develop and standardize financial information presented to stockholders. The SEC is a federal agency. It administers the Securities Exchange Act of 1934 and several other acts. Most companies that issue securities to the public or are listed on a stock exchange are required to file audited financial statements with the SEC. In addition, the SEC has broad powers to prescribe, in whatever detail it desires, the accounting practices and standards to be employed by companies that fall within its jurisdiction. The SEC currently exercises oversight over 12,000 companies that are listed on the major exchanges (e.g., the New York Stock Exchange and the Nasdaq).

Public/Private Partnership

At the time the SEC was created, no group—public or private—issued accounting standards. The SEC encouraged the creation of a private standard-setting body because it believed that the private sector had the appropriate resources and talent to achieve this daunting task. As a result, accounting standards have developed in the private sector either through the American Institute of Certified Public Accountants (AICPA) or the Financial Accounting Standards Board (FASB).

The SEC has affirmed its support for the FASB by indicating that financial statements conforming to standards set by the FASB are presumed to have substantial authoritative support. In short, the **SEC requires registrants to adhere to GAAP**. In addition, the SEC indicated in its reports to Congress that "it continues to believe that the initiative for establishing and improving accounting standards should remain in the private sector, subject to Commission oversight."

SEC Oversight

The SEC's partnership with the private sector works well. The SEC acts with remarkable restraint in the area of developing accounting standards. Generally, **the SEC relies on the FASB to develop accounting standards**.

The SEC's involvement in the development of accounting standards varies. In some cases, the SEC rejects a standard proposed by the private sector. In other cases, the SEC prods the private sector into taking quicker action on certain reporting problems, such as accounting for investments in debt and equity securities and the reporting of derivative instruments. In still other situations, the SEC communicates problems to the FASB, responds to FASB exposure drafts, and provides the FASB with counsel and advice upon request.

The SEC's mandate is to establish accounting principles. The private sector, therefore, must listen carefully to the views of the SEC. In some sense, the private sector is the formulator and the implementor of the standards.[4] However, when the private sector fails to address accounting problems as quickly as the SEC would like, the partnership between the SEC and the private sector can be strained. This occurred in the deliberations on the

[4]One writer described the relationship of the FASB and SEC and the development of financial reporting standards using the analogy of a pearl. The pearl (a financial reporting standard) "is formed by the reaction of certain oysters (FASB) to an irritant (the SEC)—usually a grain of sand—that becomes embedded inside the shell. The oyster coats this grain with layers of nacre, and ultimately a pearl is formed. The pearl is a joint result of the irritant (SEC) and oyster (FASB); without both, it cannot be created." John C. Burton, "Government Regulation of Accounting and Information," *Journal of Accountancy* (June 1982).

accounting for business combinations and intangible assets. It is also highlighted by concerns over the accounting for off-balance-sheet special-purpose entities, highlighted in the failure of Enron and, more recently, the subprime crises that led to the failure of IndyMac Bank.

Enforcement

As we indicated earlier, companies listed on a stock exchange must submit their financial statements to the SEC. If the SEC believes that an accounting or disclosure irregularity exists regarding the form or content of the financial statements, it sends a deficiency letter to the company. Companies usually resolve these deficiency letters quickly. If disagreement continues, the SEC may issue a "stop order," which prevents the registrant from issuing or trading securities on the exchanges. The Department of Justice may also file criminal charges for violations of certain laws. The SEC process, private sector initiatives, and civil and criminal litigation help to ensure the integrity of financial reporting for public companies.

International Perspective

The U.S. legal system is based on English common law, whereby the government generally allows professionals to make the rules. The private sector, therefore, develops these rules (standards). Conversely, some countries have followed codified law, which leads to government-run accounting systems.

American Institute of Certified Public Accountants (AICPA)

The American Institute of Certified Public Accountants (AICPA), which is the national professional organization of practicing Certified Public Accountants (CPAs), has been an important contributor to the development of GAAP. Various committees and boards established since the founding of the AICPA have contributed to this effort.

Committee on Accounting Procedure

At the urging of the SEC, the AICPA appointed the Committee on Accounting Procedure in 1939. The Committee on Accounting Procedure (CAP) composed of practicing CPAs, issued 51 Accounting Research Bulletins during the years 1939 to 1959. These bulletins dealt with a variety of accounting problems. But this problem-by-problem approach failed to provide the needed structured body of accounting principles. In response, in 1959 the AICPA created the Accounting Principles Board.

Accounting Principles Board

The major purposes of the Accounting Principles Board (APB) were to (1) advance the written expression of accounting principles, (2) determine appropriate practices, and (3) narrow the areas of difference and inconsistency in practice. To achieve these objectives, the APB's mission was twofold: to develop an overall conceptual framework to assist in the resolution of problems as they become evident and to substantively research individual issues before the AICPA issued pronouncements. The Board's 18 to 21 members, selected primarily from public accounting, also included representatives from industry and academia. The Board's official pronouncements, called APB Opinions, were intended to be based mainly on research studies and be supported by reason and analysis. Between its inception in 1959 and its dissolution in 1973, the APB issued 31 opinions.

Unfortunately, the APB came under fire early, charged with lack of productivity and failing to act promptly to correct alleged accounting abuses. Later, the APB tackled numerous thorny accounting issues, only to meet a buzz saw of opposition from industry and CPA firms. It also ran into occasional governmental interference. In 1971, the accounting profession's leaders, anxious to avoid governmental rule-making, appointed a Study Group on Establishment of Accounting Principles. Commonly known as the Wheat Committee for its chair Francis Wheat, this group examined the organization and operation of the APB and determined the necessary changes to attain better results. The Study Group submitted its recommendations to the AICPA Council in the spring of 1972, which led to the replacement of the APB with the Financial Accounting Standards Board (FASB) in 1973.

Changing Role of the AICPA

When the FASB replaced the Accounting Principles Board, the AICPA established the **Accounting Standards Executive Committee (AcSEC)** as the committee authorized to speak for the AICPA in the area of financial accounting and reporting. It does so through various written communications:

Audit and Accounting Guides summarize the accounting practices of specific industries and provide specific guidance on matters not addressed by the FASB. Examples are accounting for casinos, airlines, colleges and universities, banks, insurance companies, and many others.

Statements of Position (SOPs) provide guidance on financial reporting topics until the FASB sets standards on the issue in question. SOPs may update, revise, and clarify audit and accounting guides or provide free-standing guidance.

Practice Bulletins indicate the AcSEC's views on narrow financial reporting issues not considered by the FASB.

The role of the AICPA in standard-setting has diminished. The FASB and the AICPA agree that the AICPA and AcSEC no longer will issue authoritative accounting guidance for public companies. Furthermore, while the AICPA has been the leader in developing auditing standards through its Auditing Standards Board, the Sarbanes-Oxley Act of 2002 requires the Public Company Accounting Oversight Board to oversee the development of auditing standards. The AICPA continues to develop and grade the CPA examination, which is administered in all 50 states.

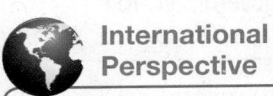

International Perspective

The CPA exam is administered internationally at testing sites in Bahrain, Kuwait, Japan, Lebanon, United Arab Emirates (UAE), and Brazil. The CPA exam now has some coverage of IFRS knowledge as part of the financial reporting section of the exam (see *www.aicpa.org/cpa-exam*).

Financial Accounting Standards Board (FASB)

The Wheat Committee's recommendations resulted in the creation of a new standard-setting structure composed of three organizations—the Financial Accounting Foundation (FAF), the Financial Accounting Standards Board (FASB), and the Financial Accounting Standards Advisory Council (FASAC). The **Financial Accounting Foundation** selects the members of the FASB and the Advisory Council, funds their activities, and generally oversees the FASB's activities.

The major operating organization in this three-part structure is the Financial Accounting Standards Board (FASB). Its mission is to establish and improve standards of financial accounting and reporting for the guidance and education of the public, which includes issuers, auditors, and users of financial information. The expectations of success and support for the new FASB relied on several significant differences between it and its predecessor, the APB:

1. *Smaller membership.* The FASB consists of seven members, replacing the relatively large 18-member APB.

2. *Full-time, remunerated membership.* FASB members are well-paid, full-time members appointed for renewable 5-year terms. The APB members volunteered their part-time work.

3. *Greater autonomy.* The APB was a senior committee of the AICPA. The FASB is not part of any single professional organization. It is appointed by and answerable only to the Financial Accounting Foundation.

4. *Increased independence.* APB members retained their private positions with firms, companies, or institutions. FASB members must sever all such ties.

5. *Broader representation.* All APB members were required to be CPAs and members of the AICPA. Currently, it is not necessary to be a CPA to be a member of the FASB.

In addition to research help from its own staff, the FASB relies on the expertise of various task force groups formed for various projects and on the **Financial Accounting Standards Advisory Council (FASAC)**. The FASAC consults with the FASB on major policy and technical issues and also helps select task force members. Illustration 1-2 shows the current organizational structure for the development of financial reporting standards.[5]

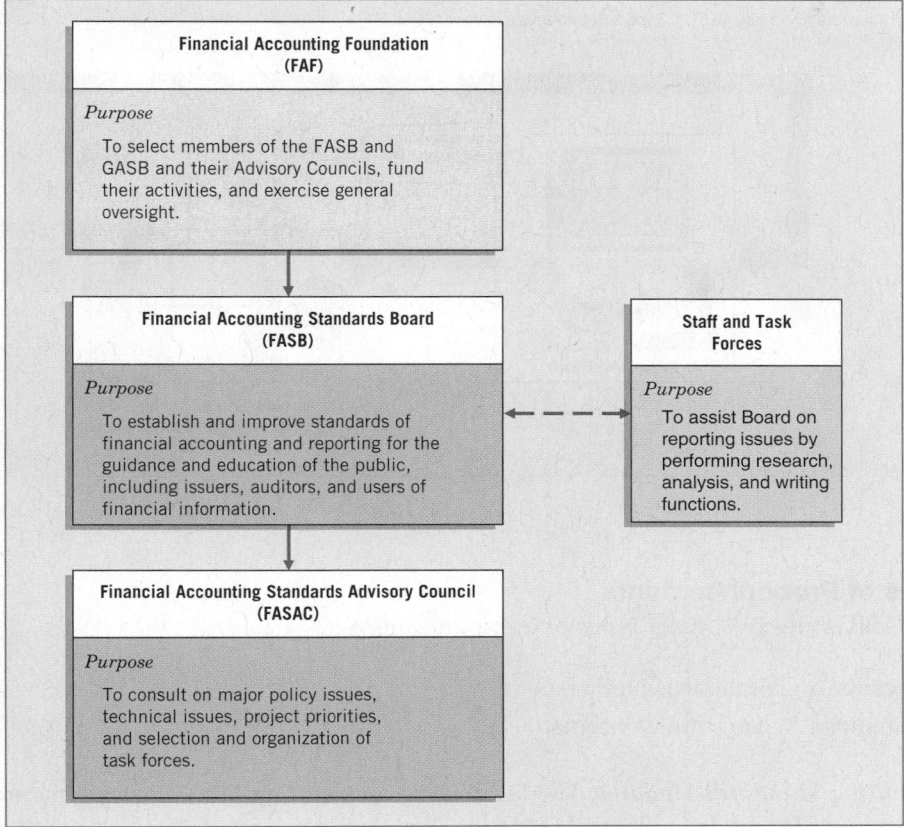

ILLUSTRATION 1-2
Organizational Structure for Setting Accounting Standards

Due Process

In establishing financial accounting standards, the FASB relies on two basic premises. (1) The FASB should be responsive to the needs and viewpoints of the entire economic community, not just the public accounting profession. (2) It should operate in full view of the public through a "due process" system that gives interested persons ample opportunity to make their views known. To ensure the achievement of these goals, the FASB follows specific steps to develop a typical FASB pronouncement, as Illustration 1-3 (page 12) shows.

The passage of new FASB guidance in the form of an Accounting Standards Update requires the support of four of the seven Board members. FASB pronouncements are considered GAAP and thereby binding in practice. All ARBs and APB Opinions implemented by 1973 (when the FASB formed) continue to be effective until amended or superseded by FASB pronouncements. In recognition of possible misconceptions of the term "principles," the FASB uses the term **financial accounting standards** in its pronouncements.

[5]Other advisory groups, such as the Investors Technical Advisory Committee (ITAC), the Not-for-Profit Advisor Committee (NAC), the Valuation Resource Group (VRG), and the recently established Private Company Financial Reporting Committee (PCFRC), share their views and experience with the Board on matters related to projects on the Board's agenda, from the perspective of various constituencies and/or in areas of specific expertise.

ILLUSTRATION 1-3
The Due Process System
of the FASB

Types of Pronouncements

The FASB issues two major types of pronouncements:

1. Accounting Standards Updates.
2. Financial Accounting Concepts.

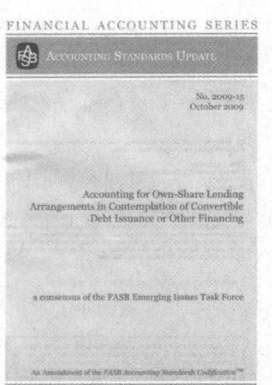

Accounting Standards Updates. The FASB issues accounting pronouncements through **Accounting Standards Updates** (Updates). These Updates amend the Accounting Standards Codification, which represents the source of authoritative accounting standards, other than standards issued by the SEC. Each Update explains how the Codification has been amended and also includes information to help the reader understand the changes and when those changes will be effective. Common forms of amendments are accounting standards issued that address a broad area of accounting practice (such as the accounting for leases) or interpretations that modify or extend existing standards. Prior standard-setters such as the APB also issued interpretations of APB Opinions.

A second type of Update is a consensus of the **Emerging Issues Task Force (EITF)**, created in 1984 by the FASB. The EITF is comprised of representatives from CPA firms and financial statement preparers. Observers from the SEC and AICPA also attend EITF meetings. The purpose of the task force is to reach a consensus on how to account for new and unusual financial transactions that may potentially create differing financial reporting practices. Examples include accounting for pension plan terminations, revenue from barter transactions by Internet companies, and excessive amounts paid to takeover specialists. The EITF also provided timely guidance for the accounting for loans and investments in the wake of the credit crisis.

The EITF helps the FASB in many ways. The EITF identifies controversial accounting problems as they arise. The EITF determines whether it can quickly resolve them or whether to involve the FASB in solving them. In essence, it becomes a "problem filter" for the FASB. Thus, the FASB will hopefully work on more pervasive long-term problems, while the EITF deals with short-term emerging issues.

We cannot overestimate the importance of the EITF. In one year, for example, the task force examined 61 emerging financial reporting issues and arrived at a consensus on approximately 75 percent of them. The FASB reviews and approves all EITF consensuses. And the SEC indicated that it will view consensus solutions as preferred accounting. Further, it requires persuasive justification for departing from them.

Financial Accounting Concepts. As part of a long-range effort to move away from the problem-by-problem approach, the FASB in November 1978 issued the first in a series of **Statements of Financial Accounting Concepts** as part of its conceptual framework project. (The Concepts Statement can be accessed at *http://www.fasb.org/.*) The series sets forth fundamental objectives and concepts that the Board uses in developing future standards of financial accounting and reporting. The Board intends to form a cohesive set of interrelated concepts—a conceptual framework—that will serve as tools for solving existing and emerging problems in a consistent manner. Unlike a Statement of Financial Accounting Standards, **a Statement of Financial Accounting Concepts does not establish GAAP**. Concepts statements, however, pass through the same due process system (preliminary views, public hearing, exposure draft, etc.) as do standards statements.

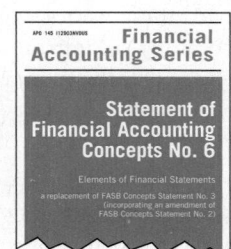

GENERALLY ACCEPTED ACCOUNTING PRINCIPLES

Generally accepted accounting principles (GAAP) have substantial authoritative support. The AICPA's Code of Professional Conduct requires that members prepare financial statements in accordance with GAAP. Specifically, Rule 203 of this Code prohibits a member from expressing an unqualified opinion on financial statements that contain a material departure from generally accepted accounting principles.

6 LEARNING OBJECTIVE

Explain the meaning of generally accepted accounting principles (GAAP) and the role of the Codification for GAAP.

What is GAAP? The major sources of GAAP come from the organizations discussed earlier in this chapter. It is composed of a mixture of over 2,000 documents that have been developed over the last 70 years or so. It includes APB Opinions, FASB Standards, and AICPA Research Bulletins. In addition, the FASB has issued **interpretations** and **FASB Staff Positions** that modified or extended existing standards. The APB also issued interpretations of APB Opinions. Both types of interpretations are considered authoritative for purposes of determining GAAP. Since replacing the APB, the FASB has issued over 160 standards, 48 interpretations, and nearly 100 staff positions. Illustration 1-4 highlights the many different types of documents that comprise GAAP.

ILLUSTRATION 1-4
GAAP Documents

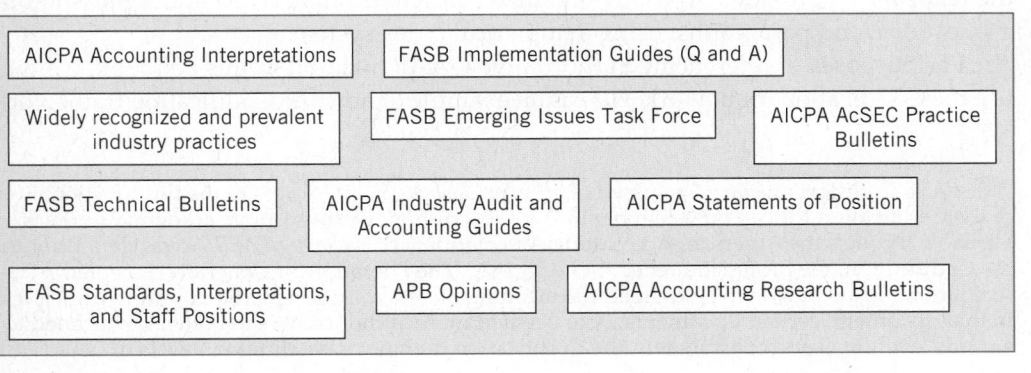

Should the accounting profession have principles-based standards or rules-based standards? Critics of the profession today say that over the past three decades, standard-setters have moved away from broad accounting principles aimed at ensuring that companies' financial statements are fairly presented.

Instead, these critics say, standard-setters have moved toward drafting voluminous rules that, if technically followed in "check-box" fashion, may shield auditors and companies from legal liability. That has resulted in companies creating complex capital structures that comply with GAAP but hide billions of dollars of debt and other obligations. To add fuel to the fire, the chief accountant of the enforcement division of the SEC noted, "One can violate SEC laws and still comply with GAAP."

In short, what he is saying is that it is not enough just to check the boxes. This point was reinforced by the Chief Accountant of the SEC, who remarked that judgments should result in "accounting that reflects the substance of the transaction, as well as being in accordance with the literature." That is, you have to exercise judgment in applying GAAP to achieve high-quality reporting.

Sources: Adapted from S. Liesman, "SEC Accounting Cop's Warning: Playing by the Rules May Not Head Off Fraud Issues," *Wall Street Journal* (February 12, 2002), p. C7. See also "Study Pursuant to Section 108(d) of the Sarbanes-Oxley Act of 2002 on the Adoption by the United States Financial Reporting System of a Principles-Based Accounting System," *SEC* (July 25, 2003); and E. Orenstein, "Accounting as Art vs. Science, and the Role of Professional Judgment," *Accounting Matters*, FEI Financial Reporting Blog (November, 2009).

FASB Codification

Historically, the documents that comprised GAAP varied in format, completeness, and structure. In some cases, these documents were inconsistent and difficult to interpret. As a result, financial statement preparers sometimes were not sure whether they had the right GAAP. Determining what was authoritative and what was not became difficult.

In response to these concerns, the FASB developed the **Financial Accounting Standards Board Accounting Standards Codification** (or more simply, "the Codification"). The FASB's primary goal in developing the Codification is to provide in one place all the authoritative literature related to a particular topic. This will simplify user access to all authoritative U.S. generally accepted accounting principles. The Codification changes the way GAAP is documented, presented, and updated. It explains what GAAP is and eliminates nonessential information such as redundant document summaries, basis for conclusions sections, and historical content. In short, the Codification integrates and synthesizes existing GAAP; it does not create new GAAP. It creates one level of GAAP, which is considered authoritative. All other accounting literature is considered non-authoritative.[6]

To provide easy access to this Codification, the FASB also developed the **Financial Accounting Standards Board Codification Research System (CRS)**. CRS is an online, real-time database that provides easy access to the Codification. The Codification and the related CRS provide a topically organized structure, subdivided into topic, subtopics, sections, and paragraphs, using a numerical index system.

For purposes of referencing authoritative GAAP material in this textbook, we will use the Codification framework. Here is an example of how the Codification framework

[6]The FASB Codification can be accessed at *http://asc.fasb.org/home*. Access to the full functionality of the Codification Research System requires a subscription. Reduced-price academic access is available through the American Accounting Association (see *aaahq.org/FASB/Access.cfm*). Prior to the Codification, the profession relied on *FASB 162*, "The Hierarchy of Generally Accepted Accounting Principles," which defined the meaning of generally accepted accounting principles. In that document, certain documents were deemed more authoritative than others, which led to various levels of GAAP. Fortunately, the Codification does not have different levels of GAAP.

is cited, using Receivables as the example. The purpose of the search shown below is to determine GAAP for accounting for loans and trade receivables not held for sale subsequent to initial measurement.

Topic	Go to FASB ASC 310 to access the Receivables topic.
Subtopics	Go to FASB ASC 310-10 to access the Overall Subtopic of the Topic 310.
Sections	Go to FASB ASC 310-10-35 to access the Subsequent Measurement Section of the Subtopic 310-10.
Paragraph	Go to FASB ASC 310-10-35-47 to access the Loans and Trade Receivables not Held for Sale paragraph of Section 310-10-35.

Illustration 1-5 shows the Codification framework graphically.

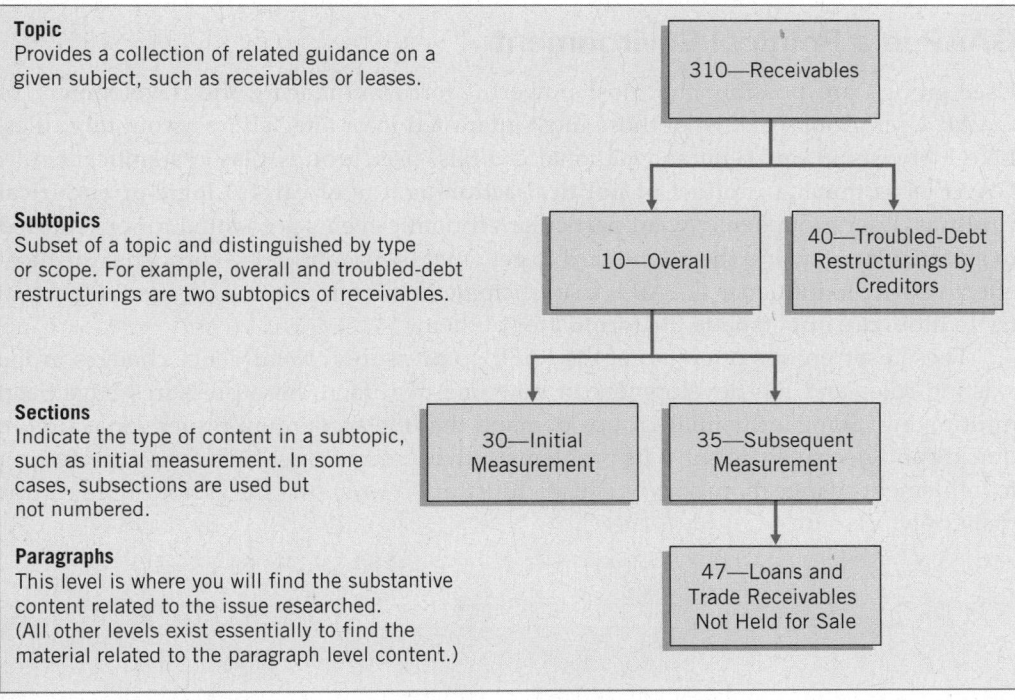

ILLUSTRATION 1-5
FASB Codification Framework

What happens if the Codification does not cover a certain type of transaction or event? In that case, other accounting literature should be considered, such as FASB Concept Statements, international financial reporting standards, and other professional literature. This will happen only rarely.

The expectations for the Codification are high. It is hoped that the Codification will enable users to better understand what GAAP is. As a result, the time to research accounting issues and the risk of noncompliance with GAAP will be reduced, sometimes substantially. In addition, the Web-based format will make updating easier, which will help users stay current with GAAP.[7]

[7]To increase the usefulness of the Codification for public companies, relevant authoritative content issued by the SEC is included in the Codification. In the case of SEC content, an "S" precedes the section number.

See the FASB Codification section at the end of each chapter for Codification references and exercises.

For individuals (like you) attempting to learn GAAP, the Codification will be invaluable. It streamlines and simplifies how to determine what GAAP is, which will lead to better financial accounting and reporting. We provide references to the Codification throughout this textbook, using a numbering system. For example, a bracket with a number, such as **[1]**, indicates that the citation to the FASB Codification can be found in the FASB Codification section at the end of the chapter (immediately before the assignment materials).

ISSUES IN FINANCIAL REPORTING

LEARNING OBJECTIVE 7
Describe the impact of user groups on the rule-making process.

Since the implementation of GAAP may affect many interests, much discussion occurs about who should develop GAAP and to whom it should apply. We discuss some of the major issues below.

GAAP in a Political Environment

User groups are possibly the most powerful force influencing the development of GAAP. User groups consist of those most interested in or affected by accounting rules. Like lobbyists in our state and national capitals, user groups play a significant role. **GAAP is as much a product of political action as it is of careful logic or empirical findings.** User groups may want particular economic events accounted for or reported in a particular way, and they fight hard to get what they want. They know that the most effective way to influence GAAP is to participate in the formulation of these rules or to try to influence or persuade the formulator of them.

These user groups often target the FASB, to pressure it to influence changes in the existing rules and the development of new ones.[8] In fact, these pressures have been multiplying. Some influential groups demand that the accounting profession act more quickly and decisively to solve its problems. Other groups resist such action, preferring to implement change more slowly, if at all. Illustration 1-6 shows the various user groups that apply pressure.

ILLUSTRATION 1-6
User Groups that Influence the Formulation of Accounting Standards

[8]FASB board members acknowledged that they undertook many of the Board's projects, such as "Accounting for Contingencies," "Accounting for Pensions," "Statement of Cash Flows," and "Accounting for Derivatives," due to political pressure.

Should there be politics in establishing GAAP for financial accounting and reporting? Why not? We have politics at home; at school; at the fraternity, sorority, and dormitory; at the office; and at church, temple, and mosque. Politics is everywhere. GAAP is part of the real world, and it cannot escape politics and political pressures.

That is not to say that politics in establishing GAAP is a negative force. Considering the **economic consequences**[9] of many accounting rules, special interest groups should vocalize their reactions to proposed rules. What the Board should *not* do is issue pronouncements that are primarily politically motivated. While paying attention to its constituencies, the Board should base GAAP on sound research and a conceptual framework that has its foundation in economic reality.

Evolving Issue   FAIR VALUE, FAIR CONSEQUENCES?

No recent accounting issue better illustrates the economic consequences of accounting than the current debate over the use of fair value accounting for financial assets. Both the FASB and the International Accounting Standards Board (IASB) have standards requiring the use of fair value accounting for financial assets, such as investments and other financial instruments. Fair value provides the most relevant and reliable information for investors about these assets and liabilities. However, in the wake of the recent credit crisis, some countries, their central banks, and bank regulators want to suspend fair value accounting, based on concerns that use of fair value accounting, which calls for recording significant losses on poorly performing loans and investments, could scare investors and depositors and lead to a "run on the bank."

For example, in 2009, Congress ordered the FASB to change its accounting rules so as to reduce the losses banks reported, as the values of their securities had crumbled. These changes were generally supported by banks. But these changes produced a strong reaction from some investors, with one investor group complaining that the changes would "effectively gut the transparent application of fair value measurement." The group also says suspending fair value accounting would delay the recovery of the banking system.

Such political pressure on accounting standard-setters is not confined to the United States. For example, French President Nicolas Sarkozy urged his European Union counterparts to back changes to accounting rules and give banks and insurers some breathing space amid the market turmoil. And more recently, international finance ministers are urging the FASB and IASB to accelerate their work on accounting standards, including the fair value guidance for financial instruments. It is unclear whether these political pressures will have an effect on fair value accounting, but there is no question that the issue has stirred significant worldwide political debate. In short, the numbers have consequences.

Sources: Adapted from Ben Hall and Nikki Tait, "Sarkozy Seeks EU Accounting Change," *The Financial Times Limited* (September 30, 2008); Floyd Norris, "Banks Are Set to Receive More Leeway on Asset Values," *The New York Times* (March 31, 2009); and E. Orenstein, "G20 Finance Ministers Urge FASB, IASB Converge Key Standards by Mid-2013 at the Latest," FEI Financial Reporting Blog (April 2012).

The Expectations Gap

The **Sarbanes-Oxley Act** was passed in response to a string of accounting scandals at companies like **Enron**, **Cendant**, **Sunbeam**, **Rite-Aid**, **Xerox**, and **WorldCom**. This law increased the resources for the SEC to combat fraud and curb poor reporting practices.[10] And the SEC has increased its policing efforts, approving new auditor independence rules and materiality guidelines

 International Perspective

Foreign accounting firms that provide an audit report for a U.S.-listed company are subject to the authority of the accounting oversight board (mandated by the Sarbanes-Oxley Act).

---

[9]*Economic consequences* means the impact of accounting reports on the wealth positions of issuers and users of financial information, and the decision-making behavior resulting from that impact. The resulting behavior of these individuals and groups could have detrimental financial effects on the providers of the financial information. See Stephen A. Zeff, "The Rise of 'Economic Consequences'," *Journal of Accountancy* (December 1978), pp. 56–63. We extend appreciation to Professor Zeff for his insights on this chapter.

[10]*Sarbanes-Oxley Act of 2002*, H. R. Rep. No. 107-610 (2002).

for financial reporting. In addition, the Sarbanes-Oxley Act introduces sweeping changes to the institutional structure of the accounting profession. The following are some of the key provisions of the legislation.

- Establishes an oversight board, the **Public Company Accounting Oversight Board (PCAOB)**, for accounting practices. The PCAOB has oversight and enforcement authority and establishes auditing, quality control, and independence standards and rules.

- Implements stronger independence rules for auditors. Audit partners, for example, are required to rotate every five years, and auditors are prohibited from offering certain types of consulting services to corporate clients.

- Requires CEOs and CFOs to personally certify that financial statements and disclosures are accurate and complete, and requires CEOs and CFOs to forfeit bonuses and profits when there is an accounting restatement.

- Requires audit committees to be comprised of independent members and members with financial expertise.

- Requires codes of ethics for senior financial officers.

In addition, Section 404 of the Sarbanes-Oxley Act requires public companies to attest to the effectiveness of their internal controls over financial reporting. **Internal controls** are a system of checks and balances designed to prevent and detect fraud and errors. Most companies have these systems in place, but many have never completely documented them. Companies are finding that it is a costly process but perhaps badly needed.

While there continues to be debate about the benefits and costs of Sarbanes-Oxley (especially for smaller companies), studies at the time of the act's implementation provide compelling evidence that there was much room for improvement. For example, one study documented 424 companies with deficiencies in internal control.[11] Many problems involved closing the books, revenue recognition deficiencies, reconciling accounts, or dealing with inventory. **SunTrust Bank**, for example, fired three officers after discovering errors in how the company calculates its allowance for bad debts. And **Visteon**, a car parts supplier, said it found problems recording and managing receivables from its largest customer, **Ford Motor**.

Will these changes be enough? The **expectations gap**—what the public thinks accountants *should* do and what accountants think they *can* do—is difficult to close. Due to the number of fraudulent reporting cases, some question whether the profession is doing enough. Although the profession can argue rightfully that accounting cannot be responsible for every financial catastrophe, it must continue to strive to meet the needs of society. However, efforts to meet these needs will become more costly to society. The development of a highly transparent, clear, and reliable system will require considerable resources.

Financial Reporting Challenges

LEARNING OBJECTIVE
Describe some of the challenges facing financial reporting.

While our reporting model has worked well in capturing and organizing financial information in a useful and reliable fashion, much still needs to be done. For example, if we move to the year 2025 and look back at financial reporting today, we might read the following.

- *Nonfinancial measurements.* Financial reports failed to provide some key performance measures widely used by management, such as customer satisfaction indexes,

---

[11]Leah Townsend, "Internal Control Deficiency Disclosures—Interim Alert," *Yellow Card—Interim Trend Alert* (April 12, 2005), Glass, Lewis & Co., LLC.

backlog information, reject rates on goods purchased, as well as the results of companies' sustainability efforts.

- *Forward-looking information.* Financial reports failed to provide forward-looking information needed by present and potential investors and creditors. One individual noted that financial statements in 2014 should have started with the phrase, "Once upon a time," to signify their use of historical cost and accumulation of past events.

- *Soft assets.* Financial reports focused on hard assets (inventory, plant assets) but failed to provide much information about a company's soft assets (intangibles). The best assets are often intangible. Consider Microsoft's know-how and market dominance, Wal-Mart's expertise in supply chain management, and Procter & Gamble's brand image.

- *Timeliness.* Companies only prepared financial statements quarterly and provided audited financials annually. Little to no real-time financial statement information was available.

- *Understandability.* Investors and market regulators were raising concerns about the complexity and lack of understandability of financial reports.

We believe each of these challenges must be met for the accounting profession to provide the type of information needed for an efficient capital allocation process. We are confident that changes will occur, based on these positive signs:

- Already, some companies voluntarily disclose information deemed relevant to investors. Often such information is nonfinancial. For example, banking companies now disclose data on loan growth, credit quality, fee income, operating efficiency, capital management, and management strategy. Increasingly, companies are preparing reports on their sustainability efforts by reporting such information as water use and conservation, carbon impacts, and labor practices. In some cases, "integrated reports" are provided, which incorporate sustainability reports into the traditional annual report, leading some to call for standards for sustainability reporting.

- Initially, companies used the Internet to provide limited financial data. Now, most companies publish their annual reports in several formats on the Web. The most innovative companies offer sections of their annual reports in a format that the user can readily manipulate, such as in an electronic spreadsheet format. Companies also format their financial reports using eXtensible Business Reporting Language (XBRL), which permits quicker and lower-cost access to companies' financial information.

- More accounting standards now require the recording or disclosing of fair value information. For example, companies either record investments in stocks and bonds, debt obligations, and derivatives at fair value, or companies show information related to fair values in the notes to the financial statements. The FASB and the IASB have a converged standard on fair value measures, which should enhance the usefulness of fair value measures in financial statements.

- The FASB is now working on projects that address disclosure effectiveness and a reporting framework for non-public companies. The projects could go a long way toward addressing complexity and understandability of the information in financial statements, allowing for more-effective, less-complex, and flexible reporting to meet the needs of investors.

Changes in these directions will enhance the relevance of financial reporting and provide useful information to financial statement readers.

International Accounting Standards

Former Secretary of the Treasury, Lawrence Summers, has indicated that the single most important innovation shaping the capital markets was the idea of generally accepted accounting principles. He went on to say that we need something similar internationally.

We believe that the Secretary is right. Relevant and reliable financial information is a necessity for viable capital markets. Unfortunately, companies outside the United States often prepare financial statements using standards different from U.S. GAAP (or simply GAAP). As a result, international companies such as Coca-Cola, Microsoft, and IBM have to develop financial information in different ways. Beyond the additional costs these companies incur, users of the financial statements often must understand at least two sets of accounting standards. (Understanding one set is hard enough!) It is not surprising, therefore, that there is a growing demand for one set of high-quality international standards.

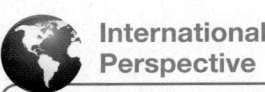

International Perspective

IFRS includes the standards, referred to as International Financial Reporting Standards (IFRS), developed by the IASB. The predecessor to the IASB issued International Accounting Standards (IAS).

Presently, there are two sets of rules accepted for international use—GAAP and International Financial Reporting Standards (IFRS), issued by the London-based International Accounting Standards Board (IASB). U.S. companies that list overseas are still permitted to use GAAP, and foreign companies listed on U.S. exchanges are permitted to use IFRS. As you will learn, there are many similarities between GAAP and IFRS.

Already over 115 countries use IFRS, and the European Union now requires all listed companies in Europe (over 7,000 companies) to use it. The SEC laid out a roadmap by which all U.S. companies might be required to use IFRS by 2015. Most parties recognize that global markets will best be served if only one set of accounting standards is used. For example, the FASB and the IASB formalized their commitment to the convergence of GAAP and IFRS by issuing a memorandum of understanding (often referred to as the Norwalk agreement). The two Boards agreed to use their best efforts to:

- Make their existing financial reporting standards fully compatible as soon as practicable, and
- Coordinate their future work programs to ensure that once achieved, compatibility is maintained.

International Perspective

The adoption of IFRS by U.S. companies would make it easier to compare U.S. and foreign companies, as well as for U.S. companies to raise capital in foreign markets.

As a result of this agreement, the two Boards identified a number of short-term and long-term projects that would lead to convergence. For example, one short-term project was for the FASB to issue a rule that permits a fair value option for financial instruments. This rule was issued in 2007, and now the FASB and the IASB follow the same accounting in this area. Conversely, the IASB completed a project related to borrowing costs, which makes IFRS consistent with GAAP. Long-term convergence projects relate to such issues as revenue recognition, the conceptual framework, and leases.

Because convergence is such an important issue, we provide a discussion of international accounting standards at the end of each chapter called **IFRS Insights**. This feature will help you understand the changes that are taking place in the financial reporting area as we move to one set of international standards. In addition, throughout the textbook, we provide *International Perspectives* in the margins to help you understand the international reporting environment.

One of the more difficult issues related to convergence and international accounting standards is that countries have different cultures and customs. For example, the former chair of the IASB explained it this way regarding Europe:

> "In the U.K. everything is permitted unless it is prohibited. In Germany, it is the other way around; everything is prohibited unless it is permitted. In the Netherlands,

everything is prohibited even if it is permitted. And in France, everything is permitted even if it is prohibited. Add in countries like Japan, the United States and China, it becomes very difficult to meet the needs of each of these countries."

With this diversity of thinking around the world, it understandable why accounting convergence has been so elusive.

Source: Sir D. Tweedie, "Remarks at the Robert P. Maxon Lectureship," George Washington University (April 7, 2010).

Ethics in the Environment of Financial Accounting

Robert Sack, a noted commentator on the subject of accounting ethics, observed, "Based on my experience, new graduates tend to be idealistic . . . thank goodness for that! Still it is very dangerous to think that your armor is all in place and say to yourself, 'I would have never given in to that.' The pressures don't explode on us; they build, and we often don't recognize them until they have us."

9 LEARNING OBJECTIVE
Understand issues related to ethics and financial accounting.

These observations are particularly appropriate for anyone entering the business world. In accounting, as in other areas of business, we frequently encounter ethical dilemmas. Some of these dilemmas are simple and easy to resolve. However, many are not, requiring difficult choices among allowable alternatives.

Companies that concentrate on "maximizing the bottom line," "facing the challenges of competition," and "stressing short-term results" place accountants in an environment of conflict and pressure. Basic questions such as, "Is this way of communicating financial information good or bad?" "Is it right or wrong?" and "What should I do in the circumstance?" cannot always be answered by simply adhering to GAAP or following the rules of the profession. Technical competence is not enough when encountering ethical decisions.

Doing the right thing is not always easy or obvious. The pressures "to bend the rules," "to play the game," or "to just ignore it" can be considerable. For example, "Will my decision affect my job performance negatively?" "Will my superiors be upset?" and "Will my colleagues be unhappy with me?" are often questions business people face in making a tough ethical decision. The decision is more difficult because there is no comprehensive ethical system to provide guidelines.

**Gateway to
the Profession**

*Expanded Discussion
of Ethical Issues in
Financial Reporting*

Time, job, client, personal, and peer pressures can complicate the process of ethical sensitivity and selection among alternatives. Throughout this textbook, **we present ethical considerations to help sensitize you** to the type of situations you may encounter in the performance of your professional responsibility.

Conclusion

Bob Herz, former FASB chairman, believes that there are three fundamental considerations the FASB must keep in mind in its rule-making activities: (1) improvement in financial reporting, (2) simplification of the accounting literature and the rule-making process, and (3) international convergence. These are notable objectives, and the Board is making good progress on all three dimensions. Issues such as off-balance-sheet financing, measurement of fair values, enhanced criteria for revenue recognition, and stock option accounting are examples of where the Board has exerted leadership. Improvements in financial reporting should follow.

Also, the Board is making it easier to understand what GAAP is. GAAP has been contained in a number of different documents. The lack of a single source makes it difficult to access and understand generally accepted principles. As discussed earlier, the Codification now organizes existing GAAP by accounting topic regardless of its source (FASB Statements, APB Opinions, and so on). The codified standards are then considered to be GAAP and to be authoritative. All other literature will be considered nonauthoritative.

Finally, international convergence is underway. Some projects already are completed and differences eliminated. Many more are on the drawing board. It appears to be only a matter of time until we will have one set of global accounting standards that will be established by the IASB. The profession has many challenges, but it has responded in a timely, comprehensive, and effective manner.

You will want to read the IFRS INSIGHTS on pages 31–39 for discussion of IFRS and the international reporting environment.

KEY TERMS

Accounting Principles Board (APB), 9

Accounting Research Bulletins, 9

Accounting Standards Updates, 12

accrual-basis accounting, 6

American Institute of Certified Public Accountants (AICPA), 9

APB Opinions, 9

Auditing Standards Board, 10

Committee on Accounting Procedure (CAP), 9

decision-usefulness, 6

Emerging Issues Task Force (EITF), 12

entity perspective, 6

expectations gap, 18

FASB Staff Positions, 13

financial accounting, 4

Financial Accounting Standards Board (FASB), 10

Financial Accounting Standards Board Accounting Standards Codification (Codification), 14

Financial Accounting Standards Board Codification Research System (CRS), 14

financial reporting, 4

financial statements, 4

SUMMARY OF LEARNING OBJECTIVES

1 **Identify the major financial statements and other means of financial reporting.** Companies most frequently provide (1) the balance sheet, (2) the income statement, (3) the statement of cash flows, and (4) the statement of owners' or stockholders' equity. Financial reporting other than financial statements may take various forms. Examples include the president's letter and supplementary schedules in the corporate annual report, prospectuses, reports filed with government agencies, news releases, management's forecasts, and descriptions of a company's social or environmental impact.

2 **Explain how accounting assists in the efficient use of scarce resources.** Accounting provides reliable, relevant, and timely information to managers, investors, and creditors to allow resource allocation to the most efficient enterprises. Accounting also provides measurements of efficiency (profitability) and financial soundness.

3 **Identify the objective of financial reporting.** The objective of general-purpose financial reporting is to provide financial information about the reporting entity that is useful to present and potential equity investors, lenders, and other creditors in decisions about providing resources to the entity through equity investments and loans or other forms of credit. Information that is decision-useful to investors may also be helpful to other users of financial reporting who are not investors.

4 **Explain the need for accounting standards.** The accounting profession has attempted to develop a set of standards that is generally accepted and universally practiced. Without this set of standards, each company would have to develop its own standards. Readers of financial statements would have to familiarize themselves with every company's peculiar accounting and reporting practices. As a result, it would be almost impossible to prepare statements that could be compared.

5 **Identify the major policy-setting bodies and their role in the standard-setting process.** The *Securities and Exchange Commission (SEC)* is a federal agency that has the broad powers to prescribe, in whatever detail it desires, the accounting standards to be employed by companies that fall within its jurisdiction. The *American Institute of Certified Public Accountants (AICPA)* issued standards through its Committee on Accounting Procedure and Accounting Principles Board. The *Financial Accounting Standards Board (FASB)* establishes and improves standards of financial accounting and reporting for the guidance and education of the public.

6 **Explain the meaning of generally accepted accounting principles (GAAP) and the role of the Codification for GAAP.** Generally accepted accounting principles (GAAP) are those principles that have substantial authoritative support, such as FASB standards, interpretations, and Staff Positions, APB Opinions and interpretations, AICPA Accounting Research Bulletins, and other authoritative pronouncements. All these documents and others are now classified in one document referred to as the Codification. The purpose of the Codification is to simplify user access to all authoritative U.S. GAAP. The Codification changes the way GAAP is documented, presented, and updated.

7 **Describe the impact of user groups on the rule-making process.** User groups may want particular economic events accounted for or reported in a particular way, and they fight hard to get what they want. They especially target the FASB to influence changes in existing GAAP and in the development of new rules. Because of the accelerated rate of change and the increased complexity of our economy, these pressures have been multiplying. GAAP is as much a product of political action as it is of careful logic or empirical findings. The IASB is working with the FASB toward international convergence of GAAP.

8 **Describe some of the challenges facing financial reporting.** Financial reports fail to provide (1) some key performance measures widely used by management, (2) forward-looking information needed by investors and creditors, (3) sufficient information on a company's soft assets (intangibles), (4) real-time financial information, and (5) easy-to-comprehend information.

9 **Understand issues related to ethics and financial accounting.** Financial accountants are called on for moral discernment and ethical decision-making. Decisions sometimes are difficult because a public consensus has not emerged to formulate a comprehensive ethical system that provides guidelines in making ethical judgments.

generally accepted accounting principles (GAAP), 7

general-purpose financial statements, 5

International Accounting Standards Board (IASB), 20

International Financial Reporting Standards (IFRS), 20

interpretations, 13

objective of financial reporting, 5

Public Company Accounting Oversight Board (PCAOB), 18

Sarbanes-Oxley Act, 17

Securities and Exchange Commission (SEC), 8

Statements of Financial Accounting Concepts, 13

Wheat Committee, 9

FASB CODIFICATION

Exercises

Academic access to the FASB Codification is available through university subscriptions, obtained from the American Accounting Association (at *http://aaahq.org/FASB/Access.cfm*), for an annual fee of $150. This subscription covers an unlimited number of students within a single institution. Once this access has been obtained by your school, you should log in (at *http://aaahq.org/ascLogin.cfm*) to prepare responses to the following exercises.

CE1-1 Describe the main elements of the link labeled "Help, FAQ, Learning Guide, and About the Codification."

CE1-2 Describe the procedures for providing feedback.

CE1-3 Briefly describe the purpose and content of the "What's New" link.

An additional accounting research case can be found in the Using Your Judgment section, on page 30.

Be sure to check the book's companion website for a Review and Analysis Exercise, with solution.

 Brief Exercises, Exercises, Problems, and many more learning and assessment tools and resources are available for practice in WileyPLUS.

QUESTIONS

1. Differentiate broadly between financial accounting and managerial accounting.
2. Differentiate between "financial statements" and "financial reporting."
3. How does accounting help the capital allocation process?
4. What is the objective of financial reporting?
5. Briefly explain the meaning of decision-usefulness in the context of financial reporting.
6. Of what value is a common set of standards in financial accounting and reporting?
7. What is the likely limitation of "general-purpose financial statements"?
8. In what way is the Securities and Exchange Commission concerned about and supportive of accounting principles and standards?
9. What was the Committee on Accounting Procedure, and what were its accomplishments and failings?
10. For what purposes did the AICPA in 1959 create the Accounting Principles Board?
11. Distinguish among Accounting Research Bulletins, Opinions of the Accounting Principles Board, and Statements of the Financial Accounting Standards Board.
12. If you had to explain or define "generally accepted accounting principles or standards," what essential characteristics would you include in your explanation?
13. In what ways was it felt that the pronouncements issued by the Financial Accounting Standards Board would carry greater weight than the opinions issued by the Accounting Principles Board?
14. How are FASB preliminary views and FASB exposure drafts related to FASB "statements"?
15. Distinguish between FASB Accounting Standards Updates and FASB Statements of Financial Accounting Concepts.
16. What is Rule 203 of the Code of Professional Conduct?
17. The chairman of the FASB at one time noted that "the flow of standards can only be slowed if (1) producers focus less on quarterly earnings per share and tax benefits and more on quality products, and (2) accountants and lawyers rely less on rules and law and more on professional judgment and conduct." Explain his comment.
18. What is the purpose of FASB Staff Positions?
19. Explain the role of the Emerging Issues Task Force in establishing generally accepted accounting principles.
20. What is the difference between the Codification and the Codification Research System?
21. What are the primary advantages of having a Codification of generally accepted accounting principles?
22. What are the sources of pressure that change and influence the development of GAAP?
23. Some individuals have indicated that the FASB must be cognizant of the economic consequences of its pronouncements. What is meant by "economic consequences"? What dangers exist if politics play too much of a role in the development of GAAP?
24. If you were given complete authority in the matter, how would you propose that GAAP should be developed and enforced?
25. One writer recently noted that 99.4 percent of all companies prepare statements that are in accordance with GAAP. Why then is there such concern about fraudulent financial reporting?
26. What is the "expectations gap"? What is the profession doing to try to close this gap?
27. The Sarbanes-Oxley Act was enacted to combat fraud and curb poor reporting practices. What are some key provisions of this legislation?
28. What are some of the major challenges facing the accounting profession?
29. How are financial accountants challenged in their work to make ethical decisions? Is technical mastery of GAAP not sufficient to the practice of financial accounting?

CONCEPTS FOR ANALYSIS

CA1-1 (FASB and Standard-Setting) Presented below are four statements which you are to identify as true or false. If false, explain why the statement is false.

1. GAAP is the term used to indicate the whole body of FASB authoritative literature.
2. Any company claiming compliance with GAAP must comply with most standards and interpretations but does not have to follow the disclosure requirements.
3. The primary governmental body that has influence over the FASB is the SEC.
4. The FASB has a government mandate and therefore does not have to follow due process in issuing a standard.

CA1-2 (GAAP and Standard-Setting) Presented below are four statements which you are to identify as true or false. If false, explain why the statement is false.

1. The objective of financial statements emphasizes a stewardship approach for reporting financial information.
2. The purpose of the objective of financial reporting is to prepare a balance sheet, an income statement, a statement of cash flows, and a statement of owners' or stockholders' equity.
3. Because they are generally shorter, FASB interpretations are subject to less due process, compared to FASB standards.
4. The objective of financial reporting uses an entity rather than a proprietary approach in determining what information to report.

CA1-3 (Financial Reporting and Accounting Standards) Answer the following multiple-choice questions.

1. GAAP stands for:
   (a) governmental auditing and accounting practices.
   (b) generally accepted attest principles.
   (c) government audit and attest policies.
   (d) generally accepted accounting principles.
2. Accounting standard-setters use the following process in establishing accounting standards:
   (a) Research, exposure draft, discussion paper, standard.
   (b) Discussion paper, research, exposure draft, standard.
   (c) Research, preliminary views, discussion paper, standard.
   (d) Research, discussion paper, exposure draft, standard.
3. GAAP is comprised of:
   (a) FASB standards, interpretations, and concepts statements.
   (b) FASB financial standards.
   (c) FASB standards, interpretations, EITF consensuses, and accounting rules issued by FASB predecessor organizations.
   (d) any accounting guidance included in the FASB Codification.
4. The authoritative status of the conceptual framework is as follows.
   (a) It is used when there is no standard or interpretation related to the reporting issues under consideration.
   (b) It is not as authoritative as a standard but takes precedence over any interpretation related to the reporting issue.
   (c) It takes precedence over all other authoritative literature.
   (d) It has no authoritative status.
5. The objective of financial reporting places most emphasis on:
   (a) reporting to capital providers.
   (b) reporting on stewardship.
   (c) providing specific guidance related to specific needs.
   (d) providing information to individuals who are experts in the field.
6. General-purpose financial statements are prepared primarily for:
   (a) internal users.
   (b) external users.
   (c) auditors.
   (d) government regulators.
7. Economic consequences of accounting standard-setting means:
   (a) standard-setters must give first priority to ensuring that companies do not suffer any adverse effect as a result of a new standard.
   (b) standard-setters must ensure that no new costs are incurred when a new standard is issued.
   (c) the objective of financial reporting should be politically motivated to ensure acceptance by the general public.
   (d) accounting standards can have detrimental impacts on the wealth levels of the providers of financial information.
8. The expectations gap is:
   (a) what financial information management provides and what users want.
   (b) what the public thinks accountants should do and what accountants think they can do.
   (c) what the governmental agencies want from standard-setting and what the standard-setters provide.
   (d) what the users of financial statements want from the government and what is provided.

CA1-4 (Financial Accounting) Omar Morena has recently completed his first year of studying accounting. His instructor for next semester has indicated that the primary focus will be the area of financial accounting.

Instructions
  (a) Differentiate between financial accounting and managerial accounting.
  (b) One part of financial accounting involves the preparation of financial statements. What are the financial statements most frequently provided?
  (c) What is the difference between financial statements and financial reporting?

CA1-5 (Objective of Financial Reporting) Karen Sepan, a recent graduate of the local state university, is presently employed by a large manufacturing company. She has been asked by Jose Martinez, controller, to prepare the company's response to a current Preliminary Views published by the Financial Accounting Standards Board (FASB). Sepan knows that the FASB has a conceptual framework, and she believes that these concept statements could be used to support the company's response to the Preliminary Views. She has prepared a rough draft of the response citing the objective of financial reporting.

Instructions
  (a) Identify the objective of financial reporting.
  (b) Describe the level of sophistication expected of the users of financial information by the objective of financial reporting.

CA1-6 (Accounting Numbers and the Environment) Hardly a day goes by without an article appearing on the crises affecting many of our financial institutions in the United States. It is estimated that the savings and loan (S&L) debacle of the 1980s, for example, ended up costing $500 billion ($2,000 for every man, woman, and child in the United States). Some argue that if the S&Ls had been required to report their investments at fair value instead of cost, large losses would have been reported earlier, which would have signaled regulators to close those S&Ls and, therefore, minimize the losses to U.S. taxpayers.

Instructions
Explain how reported accounting numbers might affect an individual's perceptions and actions. Cite two examples.

CA1-7 (Need for GAAP) Some argue that having various organizations establish accounting principles is wasteful and inefficient. Rather than mandating accounting rules, each company could voluntarily disclose the type of information it considered important. In addition, if an investor wants additional information, the investor could contact the company and pay to receive the additional information desired.

Instructions
Comment on the appropriateness of this viewpoint.

CA1-8 (AICPA's Role in Rule-Making) One of the major groups that has been involved in the standard-setting process is the American Institute of Certified Public Accountants. Initially, it was the primary organization that established accounting principles in the United States. Subsequently, it relinquished its power to the FASB.

Instructions
  (a) Identify the two committees of the AICPA that established accounting principles prior to the establishment of the FASB.
  (b) Speculate as to why these two organizations failed. In your answer, identify steps the FASB has taken to avoid failure.
  (c) What is the present role of the AICPA in the rule-making environment?

CA1-9 (FASB Role in Rule-Making) A press release announcing the appointment of the trustees of the new Financial Accounting Foundation stated that the Financial Accounting Standards Board (to be appointed by the trustees) ". . . will become the established authority for setting accounting principles under which corporations report to the shareholders and others" (AICPA news release July 20, 1972).

Instructions
  (a) Identify the sponsoring organization of the FASB and the process by which the FASB arrives at a decision and issues an accounting standard.
  (b) Indicate the major types of pronouncements issued by the FASB and the purposes of each of these pronouncements.

CA1-10 (Politicization of GAAP) Some accountants have said that politicization in the development and acceptance of generally accepted accounting principles (i.e., rule-making) is taking place. Some use the term "politicization" in a narrow sense to mean the influence by governmental agencies, particularly the Securities and Exchange Commission, on the development of generally accepted accounting principles. Others use it more broadly to mean the compromise that results when the bodies responsible for developing generally accepted accounting principles are pressured by interest groups (SEC, American Accounting Association, businesses through their various organizations, Institute of Management Accountants, financial analysts, bankers, lawyers, and so on).

Instructions

(a) The Committee on Accounting Procedure of the AICPA was established in the mid- to late 1930s and functioned until 1959, at which time the Accounting Principles Board came into existence. In 1973, the Financial Accounting Standards Board was formed and the APB went out of existence. Do the reasons these groups were formed, their methods of operation while in existence, and the reasons for the demise of the first two indicate an increasing politicization (as the term is used in the broad sense) of accounting standard-setting? Explain your answer by indicating how the CAP, the APB, and the FASB operated or operate. Cite specific developments that tend to support your answer.

(b) What arguments can be raised to support the "politicization" of accounting rule-making?

(c) What arguments can be raised against the "politicization" of accounting rule-making?

(CMA adapted)

CA1-11 (Models for Setting GAAP) Presented below are three models for setting GAAP.

1. The purely political approach, where national legislative action decrees GAAP.
2. The private, professional approach, where GAAP is set and enforced by private professional actions only.
3. The public/private mixed approach, where GAAP is basically set by private-sector bodies that behave as though they were public agencies and whose standards to a great extent are enforced through governmental agencies.

Instructions

(a) Which of these three models best describes standard-setting in the United States? Comment on your answer.

(b) Why do companies, financial analysts, labor unions, industry trade associations, and others take such an active interest in standard-setting?

(c) Cite an example of a group other than the FASB that attempts to establish accounting standards. Speculate as to why another group might wish to set its own standards.

 CA1-12 (GAAP Terminology) Wayne Rogers, an administrator at a major university, recently said, "I've got some CDs in my IRA, which I set up to beat the IRS." As elsewhere, in the world of accounting and finance, it often helps to be fluent in abbreviations and acronyms.

Instructions

Presented below is a list of common accounting acronyms. Identify the term for which each acronym stands, and provide a brief definition of each term.

(a) AICPA	(e) FAF	(i) CPA
(b) CAP	(f) FASAC	(j) FASB
(c) ARB	(g) SOP	(k) SEC
(d) APB	(h) GAAP	(l) IASB

 CA1-13 (Rule-Making Issues) When the FASB issues new pronouncements, the implementation date is usually 12 months from date of issuance, with early implementation encouraged. Karen Weller, controller, discusses with her financial vice president the need for early implementation of a rule that would result in a fairer presentation of the company's financial condition and earnings. When the financial vice president determines that early implementation of the rule will adversely affect the reported net income for the year, he discourages Weller from implementing the rule until it is required.

Instructions

Answer the following questions.

(a) What, if any, is the ethical issue involved in this case?

(b) Is the financial vice president acting improperly or immorally?

(c) What does Weller have to gain by advocacy of early implementation?

(d) Which stakeholders might be affected by the decision against early implementation?

(CMA adapted)

CA1-14 (Securities and Exchange Commission) The U.S. Securities and Exchange Commission (SEC) was created in 1934 and consists of five commissioners and a large professional staff. The SEC professional staff is organized into five divisions and several principal offices. The primary objective of the SEC is to support fair securities markets. The SEC also strives to foster enlightened stockholder participation in corporate decisions of publicly traded companies. The SEC has a significant presence in financial markets, the development of accounting practices, and corporation-shareholder relations, and has the power to exert influence on entities whose actions lie within the scope of its authority.

Instructions

(a) Explain from where the Securities and Exchange Commission receives its authority.

(b) Describe the official role of the Securities and Exchange Commission in the development of financial accounting theory and practices.

(c) Discuss the interrelationship between the Securities and Exchange Commission and the Financial Accounting Standards Board with respect to the development and establishment of financial accounting theory and practices.

(CMA adapted)

 CA1-15 (Financial Reporting Pressures) Presented below is abbreviated testimony from Troy Normand in the WorldCom case. He was a manager in the corporate reporting department and is one of five individuals who pleaded guilty. He is testifying in hopes of receiving no prison time when he is ultimately sentenced.

Q. Mr. Normand, if you could just describe for the jury how the meeting started and what was said during the meeting?

A. I can't recall exactly who initiated the discussion, but right away Scott Sullivan acknowledged that he was aware we had problems with the entries, David Myers had informed him, and we were considering resigning.

He said that he respected our concerns but that we weren't being asked to do anything that he believed was wrong. He mentioned that he acknowledged that the company had lost focus quite a bit due to the preparations for the Sprint merger, and that he was putting plans in place and projects in place to try to determine where the problems were, why the costs were so high.

He did say he believed that the initial statements that we produced, that the line costs in those statements could not have been as high as they were, that he believed something was wrong and there was no way that the costs were that high.

I informed him that I didn't believe the entry we were being asked to do was right, that I was scared, and I didn't want to put myself in a position of going to jail for him or the company. He responded that he didn't believe anything was wrong, nobody was going to be going to jail, but that if it later was found to be wrong, that he would be the person going to jail, not me.

He asked that I stay, don't jump off the plane, let him land it softly, that's basically how he put it. And he mentioned that he had a discussion with Bernie Ebbers, asking Bernie to reduce projections going forward and that Bernie had refused.

Q. Mr. Normand, you said that Mr. Sullivan said something about don't jump out of the plane. What did you understand him to mean when he said that?

A. Not to quit.

Q. During this meeting, did Mr. Sullivan say anything about whether you would be asked to make entries like this in the future?

A. Yes, he made a comment that from that point going forward we wouldn't be asked to record any entries, high-level late adjustments, that the numbers would be the numbers.

Q. What did you understand that to be mean, the numbers would be the numbers?

A. That after the preliminary statements were issued, with the exception of any normal transaction, valid transaction, we wouldn't be asked to be recording any more late entries.

Q. I believe you testified that Mr. Sullivan said something about the line cost numbers not being accurate. Did he ask you to conduct any analysis to determine whether the line cost numbers were accurate?

A. No, he did not.

Q. Did anyone ever ask you to do that?

A. No.

Q. Did you ever conduct any such analysis?

A. No, I didn't.

Q. During this meeting, did Mr. Sullivan ever provide any accounting justification for the entry you were asked to make?

A. No, he did not.

Q. Did anything else happen during the meeting?

A. I don't recall anything else.

Q. How did you feel after this meeting?

A. Not much better actually. I left his office not convinced in any way that what we were asked to do was right. However, I did question myself to some degree after talking with him wondering whether I was making something more out of what was really there.

Instructions

Answer the following questions.

(a) What appears to be the ethical issue involved in this case?

(b) Is Troy Normand acting improperly or immorally?

(c) What would you do if you were Troy Normand?

(d) Who are the major stakeholders in this case?

CA1-16 (Economic Consequences) Presented below are comments made in the financial press.

Instructions

Prepare responses to the requirements in each item.

(a) Rep. John Dingell, at one time the ranking Democrat on the House Commerce Committee, threw his support behind the FASB's controversial derivatives accounting standard and encouraged the FASB to adopt the rule promptly. Indicate why a member of Congress might feel obligated to comment on this proposed FASB standard.

(b) In a strongly worded letter to Senator Lauch Faircloth (R-NC) and House Banking Committee Chairman Jim Leach (R-IA), the American Institute of Certified Public Accountants (AICPA) cautioned against government intervention in the accounting standard-setting process, warning that it had the potential of jeopardizing U.S. capital markets. Explain how government intervention could possibly affect capital markets adversely.

CA1-17 (GAAP and Economic Consequences) The following letter was sent to the SEC and the FASB by leaders of the business community.

Dear Sirs:

The FASB has been struggling with accounting for derivatives and hedging for many years. The FASB has now developed, over the last few weeks, a new approach that it proposes to adopt as a final standard. We understand that the Board intends to adopt this new approach as a final standard without exposing it for public comment and debate, despite the evident complexity of the new approach, the speed with which it has been developed and the significant changes to the exposure draft since it was released more than one year ago. Instead, the Board plans to allow only a brief review by selected parties, limited to issues of operationality and clarity, and would exclude questions as to the merits of the proposed approach.

As the FASB itself has said throughout this process, its mission does not permit it to consider matters that go beyond accounting and reporting considerations. Accordingly, the FASB may not have adequately considered the wide range of concerns that have been expressed about the derivatives and hedging proposal, including concerns related to the potential impact on the capital markets, the weakening of companies' ability to manage risk, and the adverse control implications of implementing costly and complex new rules imposed at the same time as other major initiatives, including the Year 2000 issues and a single European currency. We believe that these crucial issues must be considered, if not by the FASB, then by the Securities and Exchange Commission, other regulatory agencies, or Congress.

We believe it is essential that the FASB solicit all comments in order to identify and address all material issues that may exist before issuing a final standard. We understand the desire to bring this process to a prompt conclusion, but the underlying issues are so important to this nation's businesses, the customers they serve and the economy as a whole that expediency cannot be the dominant consideration. As a result, we urge the FASB to expose its new proposal for public comment, following the established due process procedures that are essential to acceptance of its standards, and providing sufficient time to affected parties to understand and assess the new approach.

We also urge the SEC to study the comments received in order to assess the impact that these proposed rules may have on the capital markets, on companies' risk management practices, and on management and financial controls. These vital public policy matters deserve consideration as part of the Commission's oversight responsibilities.

We believe that these steps are essential if the FASB is to produce the best possible accounting standard while minimizing adverse economic effects and maintaining the competitiveness of U.S. businesses in the international marketplace.

Very truly yours,

(This letter was signed by the chairs of 22 of the largest U.S. companies.)

Instructions

Answer the following questions.

(a) Explain the "due process" procedures followed by the FASB in developing a financial reporting standard.

(b) What is meant by the term "economic consequences" in accounting standard-setting?

   (c) What economic consequences arguments are used in this letter?
   (d) What do you believe is the main point of the letter?
   (e) Why do you believe a copy of this letter was sent by the business community to influential members of the U.S. Congress?

USING YOUR JUDGMENT

FINANCIAL REPORTING

Financial Reporting Problem

Beverly Crusher, a new staff accountant, is confused because of the complexities involving accounting standard-setting. Specifically, she is confused by the number of bodies issuing financial reporting standards of one kind or another and the level of authoritative support that can be attached to these reporting standards. Beverly decides that she must review the environment in which accounting standards are set, if she is to increase her understanding of the accounting profession.

   Beverly recalls that during her accounting education there was a chapter or two regarding the environment of financial accounting and the development of GAAP. However, she remembers that her instructor placed little emphasis on these chapters.

Instructions
(a) Help Beverly by identifying key organizations involved in accounting rule-making.
(b) Beverly asks for guidance regarding authoritative support. Please assist her by explaining what is meant by authoritative support.
(c) Give Beverly a historical overview of how rule-making has evolved so that she will not feel that she is the only one to be confused.
(d) What authority for compliance with GAAP has existed throughout the history of rule-making?

BRIDGE TO THE PROFESSION

Professional Research

As a newly enrolled accounting major, you are anxious to better understand accounting institutions and sources of accounting literature. As a first step, you decide to explore the FASB Conceptual Framework.

Instructions
Go to the FASB website, *http://www.fasb.org*, to access the FASB Concepts Statements. When you have accessed the documents, you can use the search tool in your Internet browser to respond to the following items. (Provide paragraph citations.)
(a) What is the objective of financial reporting?
(b) What other means are there of communicating information, besides financial statements?
(c) Indicate some of the users and the information they are most directly concerned with in economic decision-making.

Additional Professional Resources

See the book's companion website, at **www.wiley.com/college/kieso**, for professional simulations as well as other study resources.

Most agree that there is a need for one set of international accounting standards. Here is why:

10 LEARNING OBJECTIVE

Compare the procedures related to financial accounting and accounting standards under GAAP and IFRS.

- *Multinational corporations.* Today's companies view the entire world as their market. For example, Coca-Cola, Intel, and McDonald's generate more than 50 percent of their sales outside the United States, and many foreign companies, such as Toyota, Nestlé, and Sony, find their largest market to be the United States.
- *Mergers and acquisitions.* The mergers between Fiat/Chrysler and Vodafone/Mannesmann suggest that we will see even more such business combinations in the future.
- *Information technology.* As communication barriers continue to topple through advances in technology, companies and individuals in different countries and markets are becoming more comfortable buying and selling goods and services from one another.
- *Financial markets.* Financial markets are of international significance today. Whether it is currency, equity securities (stocks), bonds, or derivatives, there are active markets throughout the world trading these types of instruments.

RELEVANT FACTS

- International standards are referred to as *International Financial Reporting Standards (IFRS)*, developed by the International Accounting Standards Board (IASB). Recent events in the global capital markets have underscored the importance of financial disclosure and transparency not only in the United States but in markets around the world. As a result, many are examining which accounting and financial disclosure rules should be followed.
- U.S standards, referred to as generally accepted accounting principles (GAAP), are developed by the Financial Accounting Standards Board (FASB). The fact that there are differences between what is in this textbook (which is based on U.S. standards) and IFRS should not be surprising because the FASB and IASB have responded to different user needs. In some countries, the primary users of financial statements are private investors; in others, the primary users are tax authorities or central government planners. It appears that the United States and the international standard-setting environment are primarily driven by meeting the needs of investors and creditors.
- The internal control standards applicable to Sarbanes-Oxley (SOX) apply only to large public companies listed on U.S. exchanges. There is a continuing debate as to whether non-U.S. companies should have to comply with this extra layer of regulation. Debate about international companies (non-U.S.) adopting SOX-type standards centers on whether the benefits exceed the costs. The concern is that the higher costs of SOX compliance are making the U.S. securities markets less competitive.
- The textbook mentions a number of ethics violations, such as at WorldCom, AIG, and Lehman Brothers. These problems have also occurred internationally, for example, at Satyam Computer Services (India), Parmalat (Italy), and Royal Ahold (the Netherlands).
- IFRS tends to be simpler in its accounting and disclosure requirements; some people say more "principles-based." GAAP is more detailed; some people say more "rules-based." This difference in approach has resulted in a debate about the merits of "principles-based" versus "rules-based" standards.

- The SEC allows foreign companies that trade shares in U.S. markets to file their IFRS financial statements without reconciliation to GAAP.

ABOUT THE NUMBERS

World markets are becoming increasingly intertwined. International consumers drive Japanese cars, wear Italian shoes and Scottish woolens, drink Brazilian coffee and Indian tea, eat Swiss chocolate bars, sit on Danish furniture, watch U.S. movies, and use Arabian oil. The tremendous variety and volume of both exported and imported goods indicates the extensive involvement in international trade—for many companies, the world is their market. To provide some indication of the extent of globalization of economic activity, Illustration IFRS1-1 provides a listing of the top 20 global companies in terms of sales.

ILLUSTRATION IFRS1-1
Global Companies

Rank ($ millions)	Company	Country	Revenues	Rank ($ millions)	Company	Country	Revenues
1	Wal-Mart Stores	U.S.	421,849	11	Total	France	186,055
2	Royal Dutch Shell	Netherlands	378,152	12	ConocoPhillips	U.S.	184,966
3	ExxonMobil	U.S.	354,674	13	Volkswagen	Germany	168,041
4	BP	U.K.	308,928	14	AXA	France	162,236
5	Sinopec Group	China	273,422	15	Fannie Mae	U.S.	153,825
6	China National Petroleum	China	240,192	16	General Electric	U.S.	151,628
				17	ING Group	Netherlands	147,052
7	State Grid	China	226,294	18	Glencore International	Switzerland	144,978
8	Toyota Motor	Japan	221,760				
9	Japan Post Holdings	Japan	203,958	19	Berkshire Hathaway	U.S.	136,185
10	Chevron	U.S.	196,337	20	General Motors	U.S.	135,592

Source: http://money.cnn.com/magazines/fortune/global500/2011/.

As capital markets are increasingly integrated, companies have greater flexibility in deciding where to raise capital. In the absence of market integration, there can be company-specific factors that make it cheaper to raise capital and list/trade securities in one location versus another. With the integration of capital markets, the automatic linkage between the location of the company and location of the capital market is loosening. As a result, companies have expanded choices of where to raise capital, either equity or debt. The move toward adoption of International Financial Reporting Standards has and will continue to facilitate this movement.

International Standard-Setting Organizations

For many years, many nations have relied on their own standard-setting organizations. For example, Canada has the Accounting Standards Board, Japan has the Accounting Standards Board of Japan, Germany has the German Accounting Standards Committee, and the United States has the Financial Accounting Standards Board (FASB). The standards issued by these organizations are sometimes principles-based, rules-based, tax-oriented, or business-based. In other words, they often differ in concept and objective. Starting in 2000, two major standard-setting bodies have emerged as the primary standard-setting bodies in the world. One organization is based in London, United Kingdom, and is called the **International Accounting Standards Board (IASB)**. The IASB issues **International Financial Reporting Standards (IFRS)**, which are used on most foreign exchanges. These standards may also be used by foreign companies listing on U.S. securities exchanges. As indicated earlier, IFRS is presently used in over 115 countries and is rapidly gaining acceptance in other countries as well.

It is generally believed that IFRS has the best potential to provide a common platform on which companies can report and investors can compare financial information. As a result, our discussion focuses on IFRS and the organization involved in developing these standards—the International Accounting Standards Board (IASB). (A detailed discussion of the U.S. system is provided in the chapter.) The two organizations that have a role in international standard-setting are the **International Organization of Securities Commissions (IOSCO)** and the IASB.

International Organization of Securities Commissions (IOSCO)

The International Organization of Securities Commissions (IOSCO) does not set accounting standards. Instead, this organization is dedicated to ensuring that the global markets can operate in an efficient and effective basis. The member agencies (such as from France, Germany, New Zealand, and the U.S. SEC) have resolved to:

- Cooperate to promote high standards of regulation in order to maintain just, efficient, and sound markets.
- Exchange information on their respective experiences in order to promote the development of domestic markets.
- Unite their efforts to establish standards and an effective surveillance of international securities transactions.
- Provide mutual assistance to promote the integrity of the markets by a rigorous application of the standards and by effective enforcement against offenses.

A landmark year for IOSCO was 2005 when it endorsed the IOSCO Memorandum of Understanding (MOU) to facilitate cross-border cooperation, reduce global systemic risk, protect investors, and ensure fair and efficient securities markets. (For more information, go to *http://www.iosco.org/*.)

International Accounting Standards Board (IASB)

The standard-setting structure internationally is composed of four organizations—the International Accounting Standards Committee Foundation, the International Accounting Standards Board (IASB), a Standards Advisory Council, and an International Financial Reporting Interpretations Committee (IFRIC). The trustees of the **International Accounting Standards Committee Foundation (IASCF)** select the members of the IASB and the Standards Advisory Council, fund their activities, and generally oversee the IASB's activities. The IASB is the major operating unit in this four-part structure. Its mission is to develop, in the public interest, a single set of high-quality and understandable IFRS for general-purpose financial statements.

In addition to research help from its own staff, the IASB relies on the expertise of various task force groups formed for various projects and on the **Standards Advisory Council (SAC)**. The SAC consults with the IASB on major policy and technical issues and also helps select task force members. IFRIC develops implementation guidance for consideration by the IASB. Illustration IFRS1-2 (page 34) shows the current organizational structure for the setting of international standards.

As indicated, the standard-setting structure internationally is very similar to the standard-setting structure in the United States (see Illustration 1-2 on page 11). One notable difference is the size of the Board—the IASB has 14 members, while the FASB has just seven members. The larger IASB reflects the need for broader geographic representation in the international setting.

ILLUSTRATION IFRS1-2
International Standard-Setting Structure

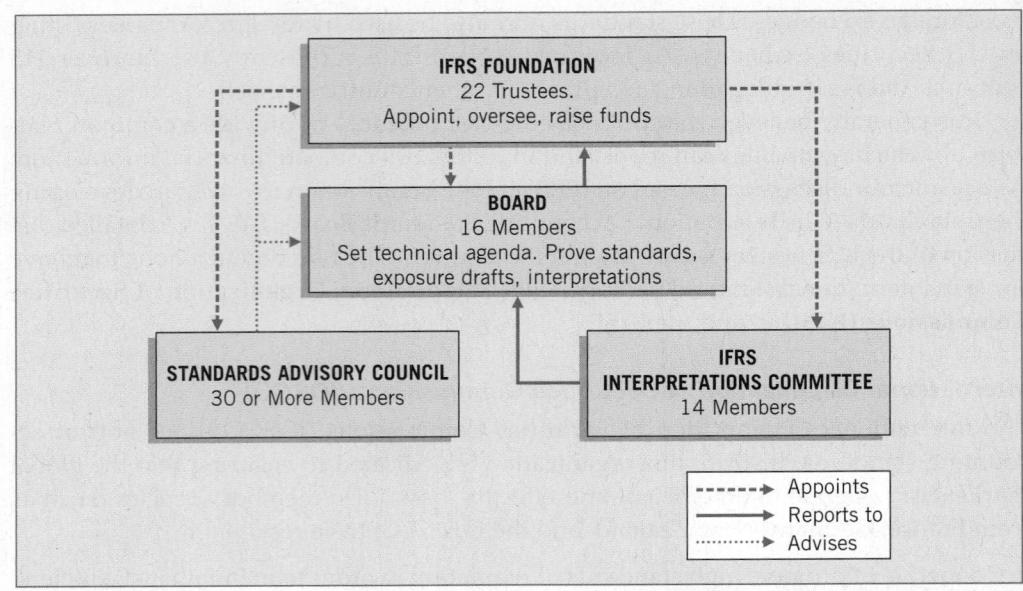

Types of Pronouncements

The IASB issues three major types of pronouncements:

1. International Financial Reporting Standards.

2. Framework for Financial Reporting.

3. International Financial Reporting Interpretations.

International Financial Reporting Standards. Financial accounting standards issued by the IASB are referred to as International Financial Reporting Standards (IFRS). The IASB has issued 13 of these standards to date, covering such subjects as business combinations and share-based payments. Prior to the IASB (formed in 2001), standard-setting on the international level was done by the International Accounting Standards Committee, which issued International Accounting Standards (IAS). The committee issued 41 IASs, many of which have been amended or superseded by the IASB. Those still remaining are considered under the umbrella of IFRS.

Framework for Financial Reporting. As part of a long-range effort to move away from the problem-by-problem approach, the International Accounting Standards Committee (predecessor to the IASB) issued a document entitled "Framework for the Preparation and Presentation of Financial Statements" (also referred to simply as the Framework). This Framework sets forth fundamental objectives and concepts that the Board uses in developing future standards of financial reporting. The intent of the document is to form a cohesive set of interrelated concepts—a conceptual framework—that will serve as tools for solving existing and emerging problems in a consistent manner. For example, the objective of general-purpose financial reporting discussed earlier is part of this Framework. The Framework and any changes to it pass through the same due process (discussion paper, public hearing, exposure draft, etc.) as an IFRS. However, this Framework is not an IFRS and hence does not define standards for any particular measurement or disclosure issue. Nothing in this Framework overrides any specific international accounting standard.

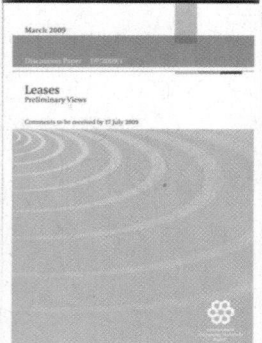

International Financial Reporting Interpretations. Interpretations issued by the **International Financial Reporting Interpretations Committee (IFRIC)** are also considered authoritative and must be followed. These interpretations cover (1) newly identified financial reporting issues not specifically dealt with in IFRS, and (2) issues where unsatisfactory or conflicting interpretations have developed, or seem likely to develop, in the absence of authoritative guidance. The IFRIC has issued over 15 of these interpretations to date. In keeping with the IASB's own approach to setting standards, the IFRIC applies a principles-based approach in providing interpretative guidance. To this end, the IFRIC looks first to the Framework for the Preparation and Presentation of Financial Statements as the foundation for formulating a consensus. It then looks to the principles articulated in the applicable standard, if any, to develop its interpretative guidance and to determine that the proposed guidance does not conflict with provisions in IFRS.

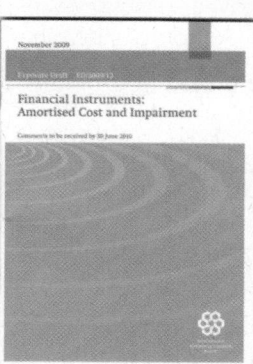

IFRIC helps the IASB in many ways. For example, emerging issues often attract public attention. If not resolved quickly, they can lead to financial crises and scandal. They can also undercut public confidence in current reporting practices. Similar to the EITF in the United States, IFRIC can address controversial accounting problems as they arise. It determines whether it can resolve them or whether to involve the IASB in solving them. In essence, it becomes a "problem filter" for the IASB. Thus, the IASB will hopefully work on more pervasive long-term problems, while the IFRIC deals with short-term emerging issues.

Hierarchy of IFRS

Because it is a private organization, the IASB has no regulatory mandate and therefore no enforcement mechanism. Similar to the U.S. setting, in which the Securities and Exchange Commission enforces the use of FASB standards for public companies, the IASB relies on other regulators to enforce the use of its standards. For example, effective January 1, 2005, the European Union required publicly traded member country companies to use IFRS.

Certain changes have been implemented with respect to use of IFRS in the United States. For example, under American Institute of Certified Public Accountants (AICPA) rules, a member of the AICPA can only report on financial statements prepared in accordance with standards promulgated by standard-setting bodies designated by the AICPA Council. In May 2008, the AICPA Council voted to designate the IASB in London as an international accounting standard-setter for purposes of establishing international financial accounting and reporting principles, and to make related amendments to its rules to provide AICPA members with the option to use IFRS.

Any company indicating that it is preparing its financial statements in conformity with IFRS must use all of the standards and interpretations. The following **hierarchy** is used to determine what recognition, valuation, and disclosure requirements should be used. Companies first look to:

1. International Financial Reporting Standards;

2. International Accounting Standards; and

3. Interpretations originated by the International Financial Reporting Interpretations Committee (IFRIC) or the former Standing Interpretations Committee (SIC).

In the absence of a standard or an interpretation, the following sources in descending order are used: (1) the requirements and guidance in standards and interpretations dealing with similar and related issues; (2) the Framework for financial reporting; and (3) most recent pronouncements of other standard-setting bodies that use a similar conceptual framework to develop accounting standards, other accounting literature, and accepted industry practices, to the extent they do not conflict with the above. The overriding requirement of IFRS is that the financial statements provide a fair presentation (often referred to as a "true and fair view"). Fair representation is assumed to occur if a company follows the guidelines established in IFRS.

International Accounting Convergence

The SEC recognizes that the establishment of a single, widely accepted set of high-quality accounting standards benefits both global capital markets and U.S. investors. U.S. investors will make better-informed investment decisions if they obtain high-quality financial information from U.S. companies that are more comparable to the presently available information from non-U.S. companies operating in the same industry or line of business. Thus, the SEC appears committed to move to IFRS, assuming that certain conditions are met. These conditions are spelled out in a document, referred to as the "**Roadmap**" and in a policy statement issued by the SEC in early 2010.[12]

The FASB and the IASB have been working diligently to (1) make their existing financial reporting standards fully compatible as soon as is practicable, and (2) coordinate their future work programs to ensure that once achieved, compatibility is maintained. This process is referred to as *convergence*, and the Boards have made significant progress in developing high-quality converged standards. However, much work needs to be done. The Boards have identified the issuance of converged standards on financial instruments (investments), revenue, and leases as a key milestone in the convergence process.

SEC Staff Paper on Incorporation of IFRS. The SEC has monitored the convergence process through a staff Work Plan, which considers specific areas and factors relevant to a commission determination as to whether, when, and how the current financial reporting system for U.S. companies should be transitioned to a system incorporating IFRS. Execution of the Work Plan (which addresses such areas as independence of standard- setting, investor understanding of IFRS, and auditor readiness), combined with the completion of the convergence projects of the FASB and the IASB according to their current work plan, will position the SEC to make a decision on required use of IFRS by U.S. issuers.

In July 2012, the SEC staff issued its final report related to the Work Plan elements.[13] The main thrust of the report is that we will have to wait and see for a commission decision on required use of IFRS in the United States. Although the Staff Report did not set out to answer the fundamental question of whether transitioning to IFRS is in the best interests of the U.S. securities markets generally and U.S. investors specifically, it appears that it is unlikely companies would be required to change to IFRS in the near future. Rather, there would be a transition period in which this would be accomplished. With respect to this transition, the SEC staff has suggested gradual incorporation of IFRS into the U.S. financial reporting system.[14]

The approach to incorporation is an "endorsement approach." Rather than adopting IFRS at a point in time (sometimes referred to as a "big bang"), the endorsement approach specifies that the FASB and IASB continue their convergence efforts (over a 5–7-year transition period) to align GAAP and IFRS. As a result, these converged standards (which are also IFRS) will be incorporated into GAAP.

At the end of this period, a U.S. company that is compliant with GAAP would also be compliant with IFRS. Following the transition period, there would be an ongoing endorsement period of IFRS by the FASB to determine if newly issued IFRS will become part of GAAP. Illustration IFRS1-3 shows the timeline for the international accounting convergence process.

[12] "Roadmap for the Potential Use of Financial Statements Prepared in Accordance with International Financial Reporting Standards by U.S. Issuers," *SEC Release No. 33-8982* (November 14, 2008), and "Statement in Support of Convergence and Global Accounting Standards," *SEC Release Nos. 33-9109; 34-61578* (February 24, 2010).

[13] "Work Plan for the Consideration of Incorporating International Financial Reporting Standards into the Financial Reporting System for U.S. Issuers: Final Staff Report SEC" (July 13, 2012), *http://www.sec.gov/spotlight/globalaccountingstandards/ifrs-work-plan-final-report.pdf*.

[14] SEC Staff Paper, "Work Plan for the Consideration of Incorporating International Financial Reporting Standards into the Financial Reporting System for U.S. Issuers: Exploring a Possible Method of Incorporation" (May 26, 2011), available at *www.sec.gov*.

ILLUSTRATION IFRS1-3
International Accounting Convergence Timeline

Transition Period. In the transition period, the FASB and SEC will execute a transition plan for evaluating IFRS for incorporation into GAAP. The transition plan groups IFRS into one of three categories, as summarized in Illustration IFRS1-4.

Category	Transition Plan
1. IFRS subject to current active convergence projects.	The FASB and IASB target completion of active projects (e.g., financial instruments, revenue recognition, and leases) in 2013.
2. IFRS included on the IASB's current standard-setting agenda.	The FASB evaluates other standards that the IASB is likely to issue in the near term to determine potential differences from GAAP. The FASB will review the individual standards to determine how best to incorporate the standards into GAAP.
3. All other existing IFRS not subject to current standard-setting and areas not addressed by IFRS.	The FASB assesses the IFRS not subject to current standard-setting plans for potential incorporation into GAAP. Prospective application of new requirements will be permitted whenever possible after giving consideration to comparability, reliability, cost and benefit, and other relevant factors.

ILLUSTRATION IFRS1-4
Transition Period Elements

As indicated, in the transition period, the FASB will continue to work with the IASB in a convergence process to develop converged standards and to evaluate other existing IFRS for incorporation in GAAP.

Ongoing Endorsement Period. After the transition period, the FASB will continue to have an active role in international standard-setting. This role would differ considerably from the FASB's current standard-setting role and responsibilities. Most significantly, the FASB would participate along with other constituents in the IASB's process for developing IFRS rather than serving as the principal body responsible for developing new accounting standards or modifying existing standards in GAAP.

However, in the ongoing endorsement process, the FASB retains the authority to modify or add to the requirements of newly issued IFRS. Under the endorsement approach, the SEC maintains its oversight of the FASB as the designated U.S. standard-setter. As a result, the SEC staff could issue guidance similar to its process for issuing staff accounting bulletins, although the staff expects that these occurrences would be rare.

Summary. Incorporation of IFRS through the endorsement approach works toward the goal of a single set of high-quality, globally accepted accounting standards, while doing so in a practical manner and in a way that minimizes both the cost and effort needed to incorporate IFRS into the U.S. financial reporting system. The gradual implementation of IFRS reduces adoption costs. Importantly, this IFRS incorporation approach retains GAAP as the basis of financial reporting for U.S. issuers. This avoids the complexities and costs associated with changing the many references to GAAP in U.S. laws and contracts. Based on the endorsement approach, which has been generally well-received by the financial reporting community in the United States, any U.S. incorporation of IFRS in GAAP will occur over several years.

ON THE HORIZON

Financial statements prepared according to IFRS have become an important standard around the world for communicating financial information to investors and creditors. The SEC and the FASB are working with their international counterparts to achieve the goal of a single set of high-quality financial reporting standards for use around the world. While there are still many bumps in the road to the establishment of one set of worldwide standards, we are optimistic that this goal can be achieved, which will be of value to all.

IFRS SELF-TEST QUESTIONS

1. IFRS stands for:
   (a) International Federation of Reporting Services.
   (b) Independent Financial Reporting Standards.
   (c) International Financial Reporting Standards.
   (d) Integrated Financial Reporting Services.
2. The major key players on the international side are the:
   (a) IASB and FASB.   (c) SEC and FASB.
   (b) IOSCO and the SEC.   (d) IASB and IOSCO.
3. IFRS is comprised of:
   (a) International Financial Reporting Standards and FASB Financial Reporting Standards.
   (b) International Financial Reporting Standards, International Accounting Standards, and International Accounting Interpretations.
   (c) International Accounting Standards and International Accounting Interpretations.
   (d) FASB Financial Reporting Standards and International Accounting Standards.
4. The authoritative status of the Framework for the Preparation and Presentation of Financial Statements is as follows:
   (a) It is used when there is no standard or interpretation related to the reporting issues under consideration.
   (b) It is not as authoritative as a standard but takes precedence over any interpretation related to the reporting issue.
   (c) It takes precedence over all other authoritative literature.
   (d) It has no authoritative status.
5. Which of the following statements is **true**?
   (a) The IASB has the same number of members as the FASB.
   (b) The IASB structure has both advisory and interpretation functions, but no trustees.
   (c) The IASB has been in existence longer than the FASB.
   (d) The IASB structure is quite similar to the FASB's, except the IASB has a larger number of board members.

IFRS CONCEPTS AND APPLICATION

IFRS1-1 Who are the two key international players in the development of international accounting standards? Explain their role.

IFRS1-2 What might explain the fact that different accounting standard-setters have developed accounting standards that are sometimes quite different in nature?

IFRS1-3 What is the benefit of a single set of high-quality accounting standards?

IFRS1-4 Briefly describe FASB/IASB convergence process and the principles that guide their convergence efforts.

Financial Reporting Case

IFRS1-5 The following comments were made at an Annual Conference of the Financial Executives Institute (FEI).

There is an irreversible movement toward the harmonization of financial reporting throughout the world. The international capital markets require an end to:

1. The confusion caused by international companies announcing different results depending on the set of accounting standards applied.
2. Companies in some countries obtaining unfair commercial advantages from the use of particular national accounting standards.
3. The complications in negotiating commercial arrangements for international joint ventures caused by different accounting requirements.
4. The inefficiency of international companies having to understand and use a myriad of different accounting standards depending on the countries in which they operate and the countries in which they raise capital and debt. Executive talent is wasted on keeping up to date with numerous sets of accounting standards and the never-ending changes to them.
5. The inefficiency of investment managers, bankers, and financial analysts as they seek to compare financial reporting drawn up in accordance with different sets of accounting standards.

Instructions

(a) What is the International Accounting Standards Board?
(b) What stakeholders might benefit from the use of International Accounting Standards?
(c) What do you believe are some of the major obstacles to convergence?

Professional Research

IFRS1-6 As a newly enrolled accounting major, you are anxious to better understand accounting institutions and sources of accounting literature. As a first step, you decide to explore the IASB's Framework for the Preparation and Presentation of Financial Statements.

Instructions

Access the IASB Framework at the IASB website (*http://eifrs.iasb.org/*). (Click on the IFRS tab and then register for free eIFRS access if necessary.) When you have accessed the documents, you can use the search tool in your Internet browser to respond to the following items. (Provide paragraph citations.)

(a) What is the objective of financial reporting?
(b) What other means are there of communicating information, besides financial statements?
(c) Indicate some of the users and the information they are most directly concerned with in economic decision-making.

International Financial Reporting Problem
Marks and Spencer plc

IFRS1-7 The financial statements of Marks and Spencer plc (M&S) are available at the book's companion website or can be accessed at *http://annualreport.marksandspencer.com/_assets/downloads/Marks-and-Spencer-Annual-report-and-financial-statements-2012.pdf.*

Instructions

Refer to M&S's financial statements and the accompanying notes to answer the following questions.

(a) What is the company's main line of business?
(b) In what countries does the company operate?
(c) What is the address of the company's corporate headquarters?
(d) What is the company's reporting currency?

ANSWERS TO IFRS SELF-TEST QUESTIONS

1. c **2.** d **3.** b **4.** a **5.** d

> **Remember to check the book's companion website to find additional resources for this chapter.**

Conceptual Framework for Financial Reporting

After studying this chapter, you should be able to:

1 Describe the usefulness of a conceptual framework.

2 Describe the FASB's efforts to construct a conceptual framework.

3 Understand the objective of financial reporting.

4 Identify the qualitative characteristics of accounting information.

5 Define the basic elements of financial statements.

6 Describe the basic assumptions of accounting.

7 Explain the application of the basic principles of accounting.

8 Describe the impact that the cost constraint has on reporting accounting information.

What Is It?

Everyone agrees that accounting needs a framework—a conceptual framework, so to speak—that will help guide the development of standards. To understand the importance of developing this framework, let's see how you would respond in the following two situations.

Situation 1: "Taking a Long Shot . . . "

To supplement donations collected from its general community solicitation, Tri-Cities United Charities holds an annual lottery sweepstakes. In this year's sweepstakes, United Charities is offering a grand prize of $1,000,000 to a single winning ticket holder. A total of 10,000 tickets have been printed, and United Charities plans to sell all the tickets at a price of $150 each.

Since its inception, the sweepstakes has attracted area-wide interest, and United Charities has always been able to meet its sales target. However, in the unlikely event that it might fail to sell a sufficient number of tickets to cover the grand prize, United Charities has reserved the right to cancel the sweepstakes and to refund the price of the tickets to holders.

In recent years, a fairly active secondary market for tickets has developed. This year, buying–selling prices have varied between $75 and $95 before stabilizing at about $90.

When the tickets first went on sale this year, multimillionaire Phil N. Tropic, well-known in Tri-Cities civic circles as a generous but sometimes eccentric donor, bought one of the tickets from United Charities, paying $150 cash.

How would you answer the following questions?

1. Should Phil N. Tropic recognize his lottery ticket as an asset in his financial statements?

2. Assuming that Phil N. Tropic recognizes the lottery ticket as an asset, at what amount should it be reported? Some possible answers are $150, $100, and $90.

Situation 2: The $20 Million Question

The Hard Rock Mining Company has just completed the first year of operations at its new strip mine, the Lonesome Doe. Hard Rock spent $10 million for the land and $20 million in preparing the site for mining operations. The mine is expected to operate for 20 years. Hard Rock is subject to environmental statutes requiring it to restore the Lonesome Doe mine site on completion of mining operations.

Based on its experience and industry data, as well as current technology, Hard Rock forecasts that restoration will cost about $10 million when it is undertaken. Of those costs, about $4 million is for restoring the topsoil that was removed in preparing the site for mining operations (prior to opening the mine). The rest is directly proportional to the depth of the mine, which in turn is directly proportional to the amount of ore extracted.

CONCEPTUAL FOCUS

This chapter summarizes conceptual elements that will be referred to throughout subsequent chapters.

INTERNATIONAL FOCUS

> See the **International Perspectives** on pages 43, 44, 54, and 55.
> Read the **IFRS Insights** on pages 78–81 for a discussion of:
> —Financial statement elements
> —Conceptual framework Work Plan

How would you answer the following questions?

1. Should Hard Rock recognize a liability for site restoration in conjunction with the opening of the Lonesome Doe Mine? If so, what is the amount of that liability?

2. After Hard Rock has operated the Lonesome Doe Mine for 5 years, new technology is introduced that reduces Hard Rock's estimated future restoration costs to $7 million, $3 million of which relates to restoring the topsoil. How should Hard Rock account for this change in its estimated future liability?

The answer to the questions on the two situations depends on how assets and liabilities are defined and how they should be valued. Hopefully, this chapter will provide you with a framework to resolve questions like these.

Sources: Adapted from Todd Johnson and Kim Petrone, *The FASB Cases on Recognition and Measurement*, Second Edition (New York: John Wiley and Sons, Inc., 1996).

PREVIEW OF CHAPTER 2

As our opening story indicates, users of financial statements can face difficult questions about the recognition and measurement of financial items. To help develop the type of financial information that can be used to answer these questions, financial accounting and reporting relies on a conceptual framework. In this chapter, we discuss the basic concepts underlying the conceptual framework as follows.

Conceptual Framework for Financial Reporting

Conceptual Framework	First Level: Basic Objective	Second Level: Fundamental Concepts	Third Level: Recognition and Measurement Concepts
• Need • Development • Overview		• Qualitative characteristics • Basic elements	• Basic assumptions • Basic principles • Cost constraint • Summary of the structure

CONCEPTUAL FRAMEWORK

A **conceptual framework** establishes the concepts that underlie financial reporting. A conceptual framework is a coherent system of concepts that flow from an objective. The objective identifies the purpose of financial reporting. The other concepts provide guidance on (1) identifying the boundaries of financial reporting; (2) selecting the transactions, other events, and circumstances to be represented; (3) how they should be recognized and measured; and (4) how they should be summarized and reported.[1]

Need for a Conceptual Framework

Why do we need a conceptual framework? First, to be useful, rule-making should build on and relate to an established body of concepts. A soundly developed conceptual framework thus enables the FASB to issue **more useful and consistent pronouncements over time; a coherent set of standards should result**. Indeed, without the guidance provided by a soundly developed framework, standard-setting ends up being based on individual concepts developed by each member of the standard-setting body. The following observation by a former standard-setter highlights the problem.

> "As our professional careers unfold, each of us develops a technical conceptual framework. Some individual frameworks are sharply defined and firmly held; others are vague and weakly held; still others are vague and firmly held. . . . At one time or another, most of us have felt the discomfort of listening to somebody buttress a preconceived conclusion by building a convoluted chain of shaky reasoning. Indeed, perhaps on occasion we have voiced such thinking ourselves. . . . My experience . . . taught me many lessons. A major one was that most of us have a natural tendency and an incredible talent for processing new facts in such a way that our prior conclusions remain intact.[2]

In other words, standard-setting that is based on personal conceptual frameworks will lead to different conclusions about identical or similar issues than it did previously. As a result, standards will not be consistent with one another, and past decisions may not be indicative of future ones. Furthermore, the framework should increase financial statement users' understanding of and confidence in financial reporting. It should enhance comparability among companies' financial statements.

Second, as a result of a soundly developed conceptual framework, the profession should be able to more quickly solve new and emerging **practical problems by referring to an existing framework of basic theory**. For example, Sunshine Mining sold two issues of bonds. It can redeem them either with $1,000 in cash or with 50 ounces of silver, whichever is worth more at maturity. Both bond issues have a stated interest rate of 8.5 percent. At what amounts should Sunshine or the buyers of the bonds record them? What is the amount of the premium or discount on the bonds? And how should Sunshine amortize this amount, if the bond redemption payments are to be made in silver (the future value of which is unknown at the date of issuance)? Consider that

---

[1] "Chapter 1, The Objective of General Purpose Financial Reporting" and "Chapter 3, Qualitative Characteristics of Useful Financial Information," *Statement of Financial Accounting Concepts No. 8* (Norwalk, Conn.: FASB, September 2010). Recall from our discussion in Chapter 1 that while the conceptual framework and any changes to it pass through the same due process (discussion paper, public hearing, exposure draft, etc.) as do the other FASB pronouncements, the framework is not authoritative. That is, the framework does not define standards for any particular measurement or disclosure issue, and nothing in the framework overrides any specific FASB pronouncement that is included in the Codification.

[2] C. Horngren, "Uses and Limitations of a Conceptual Framework," *Journal of Accountancy* (April 1981), p. 90.

Sunshine cannot know, at the date of issuance, the value of future silver bond redemption payments.

It is difficult, if not impossible, for the FASB to prescribe the proper accounting treatment quickly for situations like this or like those represented in our opening story. Practicing accountants, however, must resolve such problems on a daily basis. How? Through good judgment and with the help of a universally accepted conceptual framework, practitioners can quickly focus on an acceptable treatment.

What do the numbers mean? WHAT'S YOUR PRINCIPLE?

The need for a conceptual framework is highlighted by accounting scandals such as those at Enron and Lehman Brothers. To restore public confidence in the financial reporting process, many have argued that regulators should move toward principles-based rules. They believe that companies exploited the detailed provisions in rules-based pronouncements to manage accounting reports, rather than report the economic substance of transactions. For example, many of the off–balance-sheet arrangements of Enron avoided transparent reporting by barely achieving 3 percent outside equity ownership, a requirement in an obscure accounting rule interpretation. Enron's financial engineers were able to structure transactions to achieve a desired accounting treatment, even if that accounting treatment did not reflect the transaction's true nature. Under principles-based rules, hopefully top management's financial reporting focus will shift from demonstrating compliance with rules to demonstrating that a company has attained the objective of financial reporting.

Development of a Conceptual Framework

Over the years, numerous organizations developed and published their own conceptual frameworks, but no single framework was universally accepted and relied on in practice. In 1976, the FASB began to develop a conceptual framework that would be a basis for setting accounting rules and for resolving financial reporting controversies. The FASB has since issued seven Statements of Financial Accounting Concepts that relate to financial reporting for business enterprises.[3] They are as follows.

2 LEARNING OBJECTIVE
Describe the FASB's efforts to construct a conceptual framework.

1. *SFAC No. 1*, "Objectives of Financial Reporting by Business Enterprises," presents the goals and purposes of accounting (superseded by *SFAC No. 8*, Chapter 1).
2. *SFAC No. 2*, "Qualitative Characteristics of Accounting Information," examines the characteristics that make accounting information useful (superseded by *SFAC No. 8*, Chapter 3).
3. *SFAC No. 3*, "Elements of Financial Statements of Business Enterprises," provides definitions of items in financial statements, such as assets, liabilities, revenues, and expenses (superseded by *SFAC No. 6*).
4. *SFAC No. 5*, "Recognition and Measurement in Financial Statements of Business Enterprises," sets forth fundamental recognition and measurement criteria and guidance on what information should be formally incorporated into financial statements and when.
5. *SFAC No. 6*, "Elements of Financial Statements," replaces *SFAC No. 3* and expands its scope to include not-for-profit organizations.

International Perspective

The IASB has also issued a conceptual framework. The FASB and the IASB have agreed on a joint project to develop a common and improved conceptual framework. The project is being conducted in phases. Phase A on objectives and qualitative characteristics was issued in 2010.

---

[3]The FASB also issued a Statement of Financial Accounting Concepts that relates to nonbusiness organizations: "Objectives of Financial Reporting by Nonbusiness Organizations," *Statement of Financial Accounting Concepts No. 4* (December 1980).

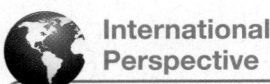
International Perspective

SFAC No. 8 is the product of a joint conceptual framework project of the FASB and IASB.

6. *SFAC No. 7*, "Using Cash Flow Information and Present Value in Accounting Measurements," provides a framework for using expected future cash flows and present values as a basis for measurement.

7. *SFAC No. 8*, Chapter 1, "The Objective of General Purpose Financial Reporting," and Chapter 3, "Qualitative Characteristics of Useful Financial Information," replaces *SFAC No. 1* and *No. 2*.

Overview of the Conceptual Framework

Illustration 2-1 provides an overview of the FASB's conceptual framework.[4]

ILLUSTRATION 2-1
Framework for Financial Reporting

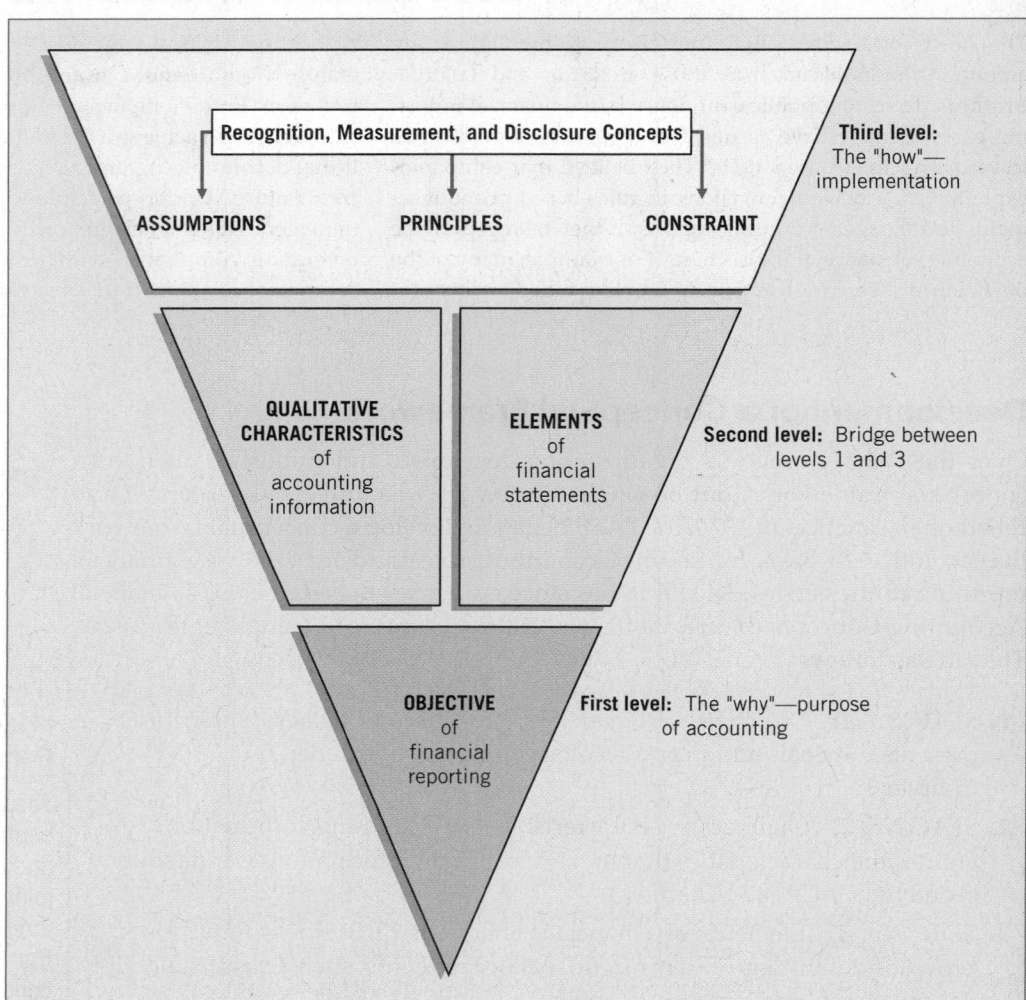

The first level identifies the **objective of financial reporting**—that is, the purpose of financial reporting. The second level provides the **qualitative characteristics** that make accounting information useful and the **elements of financial statements** (assets, liabilities, and so on). The third level identifies the **recognition, measurement, and disclosure concepts** used in establishing and applying accounting standards and the specific concepts to implement the objective. These concepts include assumptions, principles, and a cost constraint that describe the present reporting environment. We examine these three levels of the conceptual framework next.

[4]Adapted from William C. Norby, *The Financial Analysts Journal* (March–April 1982), p. 22.

FIRST LEVEL: BASIC OBJECTIVE

The objective of financial reporting is the foundation of the conceptual framework. Other aspects of the framework—qualitative characteristics, elements of financial statements, recognition, measurement, and disclosure—flow logically from the objective. Those aspects of the framework help to ensure that financial reporting achieves its objective.

The objective of general-purpose financial reporting is to provide financial information about the reporting entity that is **useful to present and potential equity investors, lenders, and other creditors in making decisions about providing resources to the entity**. Those decisions involve buying, selling, or holding equity and debt instruments, and providing or settling loans and other forms of credit. Information that is **decision-useful** to capital providers may also be useful to other users of financial reporting, who are not capital providers.[5]

As indicated in Chapter 1, to provide information to decision-makers, companies prepare general-purpose financial statements. General-purpose financial reporting helps users who lack the ability to demand all the financial information they need from an entity and therefore must rely, at least partly, on the information provided in financial reports. However, an implicit assumption is that users need reasonable knowledge of business and financial accounting matters to understand the information contained in financial statements. This point is important. It means that financial statement preparers assume a level of competence on the part of users. This assumption impacts the way and the extent to which companies report information.

SECOND LEVEL: FUNDAMENTAL CONCEPTS

The objective (first level) focuses on the purpose of financial reporting. Later, we will discuss the ways in which this purpose is implemented (third level). What, then, is the purpose of the second level? The second level provides conceptual building blocks that explain the qualitative characteristics of accounting information and define the elements of financial statements.[6] That is, the second level forms a bridge between the **why** of accounting (the objective) and the **how** of accounting (recognition, measurement, and financial statement presentation).

Qualitative Characteristics of Accounting Information

Should companies like Walt Disney or Kellogg's provide information in their financial statements on how much it costs them to acquire their assets (historical cost basis) or how much the assets are currently worth (fair value basis)? Should PepsiCo combine and show as one company the four main segments of its business, or should it report PepsiCo Beverages, Frito Lay, Quaker Foods, and PepsiCo International as four separate segments?

How does a company choose an acceptable accounting method, the amount and types of information to disclose, and the format in which to present it? The answer: By determining **which alternative provides the most useful information for decision-making purposes (decision-usefulness)**. The FASB identified the **qualitative characteristics** of accounting information that distinguish better (more useful) information from

---

[5] "Chapter 1, The Objective of General Purpose Financial Reporting," *Statement of Financial Accounting Concepts No. 8* (Norwalk, Conn.: FASB, September 2010), par. OB2.

[6] "Chapter 3, Qualitative Characteristics of Useful Financial Information," *Statement of Financial Accounting Concepts No. 8* (Norwalk, Conn.: FASB, September 2010).

inferior (less useful) information for decision-making purposes. In addition, the FASB identified a cost constraint as part of the conceptual framework (discussed later in the chapter). As Illustration 2-2 shows, the characteristics may be viewed as a hierarchy.

ILLUSTRATION 2-2
Hierarchy of Accounting Qualities

As indicated by Illustration 2-2, qualitative characteristics are either fundamental or enhancing characteristics, depending on how they affect the decision-usefulness of information. Regardless of classification, each qualitative characteristic contributes to the decision-usefulness of financial reporting information. However, providing useful financial information is limited by a pervasive constraint on financial reporting—cost should not exceed the benefits of a reporting practice.

Fundamental Quality—Relevance

Relevance is one of the two fundamental qualities that make accounting information useful for decision-making. Relevance and related ingredients of this fundamental quality are shown below.

To have **relevance**, accounting information must be capable of making a difference in a decision. Information with no bearing on a decision is irrelevant. Financial information is capable of making a difference when it has predictive value, confirmatory value, or both.

Financial information has **predictive value** if it has value as an input to predictive processes used by investors to form their own expectations about the future. For example, if potential investors are interested in purchasing common shares in **UPS (United Parcel Service)**, they may analyze its current resources and claims to those resources, its dividend payments, and its past income performance to predict the amount, timing, and uncertainty of UPS's future cash flows.

Relevant information also helps users confirm or correct prior expectations; it has **confirmatory value**. For example, when UPS issues its year-end financial statements, it confirms or changes past (or present) expectations based on previous evaluations. It follows that predictive value and confirmatory value are interrelated. For example, information about the current level and structure of UPS's assets and liabilities helps users predict its ability to take advantage of opportunities and to react to adverse situations. The same information helps to confirm or correct users' past predictions about that ability.

Materiality is a company-specific aspect of relevance. Information is material if omitting it or misstating it could influence decisions that users make on the basis of the reported financial information. An individual company determines whether information is material because both the nature and/or magnitude of the item(s) to which the information relates must be considered in the context of an individual company's financial report. Information is *immaterial,* and therefore irrelevant, if it would have no impact on a decision-maker. In short, **it must make a difference** or a company need not disclose it.

Assessing materiality is one of the more challenging aspects of accounting because it requires evaluating both the **relative size and importance** of an item. However, it is difficult to provide firm guidelines in judging when a given item is or is not material. Materiality varies both with relative amount and with relative importance. For example, the two sets of numbers in Illustration 2-3 indicate relative size.

	Company A	Company B
Sales	$10,000,000	$100,000
Costs and expenses	9,000,000	90,000
Income from operations	$ 1,000,000	$ 10,000
Unusual gain	$ 20,000	$ 5,000

ILLUSTRATION 2-3
Materiality Comparison

During the period in question, the revenues and expenses, and therefore the net incomes of Company A and Company B, are proportional. Each reported an unusual gain. In looking at the abbreviated income figures for Company A, it appears insignificant whether the amount of the unusual gain is set out separately or merged with the regular operating income. The gain is only 2 percent of the operating income. If merged, it would not seriously distort the income figure. Company B has had an unusual gain of only $5,000. However, it is relatively much more significant than the larger gain realized by Company A. For Company B, an item of $5,000 amounts to 50 percent of its income from operations. Obviously, the inclusion of such an item in operating income would affect the amount of that income materially. Thus, we see the importance of the **relative size** of an item in determining its materiality.

Companies and their auditors generally adopt the rule of thumb that anything under 5 percent of net income is considered immaterial. However, much can depend on specific rules. For example, one market regulator indicates that a company may use this percentage for an initial assessment of materiality, but it must also consider other factors.[7] For example, companies can no longer fail to record items in order to meet

[7]"Materiality," *SEC Staff Accounting Bulletin No. 99* (Washington, D.C.: SEC, 1999). The auditing profession also adopted this same concept of materiality. See "Audit Risk and Materiality in Conducting an Audit," *Statement on Auditing Standards No. 47* (New York: AICPA, 1983), par. 6.

consensus analysts' earnings numbers, preserve a positive earnings trend, convert a loss to a profit or vice versa, increase management compensation, or hide an illegal transaction like a bribe. In other words, **companies must consider both quantitative and qualitative factors in determining whether an item is material**.

Thus, it is generally not feasible to specify uniform quantitative thresholds at which an item becomes material. Rather, materiality judgments should be made in the context of the nature and the amount of an item. Materiality factors into a great many internal accounting decisions, too. Examples of such judgments that companies must make include the amount of classification required in a subsidiary expense ledger, the degree of accuracy required in allocating expenses among the departments of a company, and the extent to which adjustments should be made for accrued and deferred items. Only by **the exercise of good judgment and professional expertise** can reasonable and appropriate answers be found with respect to materiality issues.

What do the numbers mean? *LIVING IN A MATERIAL WORLD*

The first line of defense for many companies caught "cooking the books" had been to argue that a questionable accounting item is immaterial. That defense did not work so well in the wake of accounting meltdowns at Enron and Global Crossing and the tougher rules on materiality issued by the SEC (*SAB 99*).

For example, the SEC alleged in a case against Sunbeam that the company's many immaterial adjustments added up to a material misstatement that misled investors about the company's financial position. More recently, the SEC called for a number of companies, such as Jack in the Box, McDonald's, and AIG, to restate prior financial statements for the effects of incorrect accounting. In some cases, the restatements did not meet traditional materiality thresholds. Don Nicholaisen, then SEC chief accountant, observed that whether the amount is material or not, some transactions appear to be "flat out intended to mislead investors." In essence he is saying that any wrong accounting for a transaction can represent important information to the users of financial statements.

Responding to new concerns about materiality, blue-chip companies such as IBM and General Electric are providing expanded disclosures of transactions that used to fall below the materiality radar. As a result, some good may yet come from the recent accounting failures.

Sources: Adapted from K. Brown and J. Weil, "A Lot More Information Is 'Material' After Enron," *Wall Street Journal Online* (February 22, 2002); S. D. Jones and R. Gibson, "Restaurants Serve Up Restatements," *Wall Street Journal* (January 26, 2005), p. C3; and R. McTauge, "Nicholaisen Says Restatement Needed When Deal Lacks Business Purpose," *Securities Regulation & Law Reporter* (May 9, 2005).

Fundamental Quality—Faithful Representation

Faithful representation is the second fundamental quality that makes accounting information useful for decision-making. Faithful representation and related ingredients of this fundamental quality are shown below.

Faithful representation means that the numbers and descriptions match what really existed or happened. Faithful representation is a necessity because most users have neither the time nor the expertise to evaluate the factual content of the information. For example, if **General Motors'** income statement reports sales of $60,510 million when it had sales of $40,510 million, then the statement fails to faithfully represent the proper sales amount. To be a faithful representation, information must be complete, neutral, and free of material error.

Completeness. **Completeness** means that all the information that is necessary for faithful representation is provided. An omission can cause information to be false or misleading and thus not be helpful to the users of financial reports. For example, when **Citigroup** fails to provide information needed to assess the value of its subprime loan receivables (toxic assets), the information is not complete and therefore not a faithful representation of their values.

Neutrality. **Neutrality** means that a company cannot select information to favor one set of interested parties over another. Unbiased information must be the overriding consideration. For example, in the notes to financial statements, tobacco companies such as **R.J. Reynolds** should not suppress information about the numerous lawsuits that have been filed because of tobacco-related health concerns—even though such disclosure is damaging to the company.

Neutrality in rule-making has come under increasing attack. Some argue that the FASB should not issue pronouncements that cause undesirable economic effects on an industry or company. We disagree. Accounting rules (and the standard-setting process) must be free from bias, or we will no longer have credible financial statements. Without credible financial statements, individuals will no longer use this information. An analogy demonstrates the point: Many individuals bet on boxing matches because such contests are assumed not to be fixed. But nobody bets on wrestling matches. Why? Because the public assumes that wrestling matches are rigged. If financial information is biased (rigged), the public will lose confidence and no longer use it.[8]

Free from Error. An information item that is **free from error** will be a more accurate (faithful) representation of a financial item. For example, if **JPMorgan Chase** misstates its loan losses, its financial statements are misleading and not a faithful representation of its financial results. However, faithful representation does not imply total freedom from error. This is because most financial reporting measures involve estimates of various types that incorporate management's judgment. For example, management

---

[8]Sometimes, in practice, it has been acceptable to invoke prudence or conservatism as a justification for an accounting treatment under conditions of uncertainty. **Prudence** or **conservatism** means when in doubt, choose the solution that will be least likely to overstate assets or income and/or understate liabilities or expenses. The framework indicates that prudence or conservatism generally is in conflict with the quality of neutrality. This is because being prudent or conservative likely leads to a bias in the reported financial position and financial performance. In fact, introducing biased understatement of assets (or overstatement of liabilities) in one period frequently leads to overstating financial performance in later periods—a result that cannot be described as prudent. This is inconsistent with neutrality, which encompasses freedom from bias. Accordingly, the framework does not include prudence or conservatism as desirable qualities of financial reporting information. See "Chapter 3, Qualitative Characteristics of Useful Financial Information," *Statement of Financial Accounting Concepts No. 8* (Norwalk, Conn.: FASB, September 2010), paras. BC3.27–BC3.29.

must estimate the amount of uncollectible accounts to determine bad debt expense. And determination of depreciation expense requires estimation of useful lives of plant and equipment, as well as the salvage value of the assets.

What do the numbers mean?   SHOW ME THE EARNINGS!

The emergence of new-economy businesses on the Internet has led to the development of new measures of performance. When Priceline.com splashed on the dot-com scene, it touted steady growth in a measure called "unique offers by users" to explain its heady stock price. To draw investors to its stock, Drugstore.com focused on the number of "unique customers" at its website. After all, new businesses call for new performance measures, right?

Not necessarily. In fact, these indicators failed to show any consistent relationship between profits and website visits. Eventually, as the graphs below show, the profits never materialized, stock prices fell, and the dot-com bubble burst.

Some have not learned a lesson from this experience. Facebook, one of the hottest IPOs of the recent social media craze, gave investors a big jolt when it reported its first earnings after going public. While its revenues from online advertisers were up 32 percent compared to the prior year's quarter, its marketing and sales expenses increased dramatically and the company failed to exceed analysts' expectations for its earnings. The result? The stock dropped to an all-time low.

The lesson for investors? Keep an eye on reliable financial measures of performance and be sure to count the expenses and net income, rather than focusing on only the top line.

Sources: Story and graphs adapted from Gretchen Morgenson, "How Did They Value Stocks? Count the Absurd Ways," *New York Times* (March 18, 2001), section 3, p. 1; and B. Stone, "Facebook Bellyflops Into Its First Earnings Report," *www.businessweek.com* (July 26, 2012).

Enhancing Qualities

Enhancing qualitative characteristics are complementary to the fundamental qualitative characteristics. These characteristics distinguish more-useful information from less-useful information. Enhancing characteristics, shown below, are comparability, verifiability, timeliness, and understandability.

Comparability. Information that is measured and reported in a similar manner for different companies is considered comparable. Comparability enables users to identify the real similarities and differences in economic events between companies. For example, historically the accounting for pensions in Japan differed from that in the United States. In Japan, companies generally recorded little or no charge to income for these costs. U.S. companies recorded pension cost as incurred. As a result, it is difficult to compare and evaluate the financial results of Toyota or Honda to General Motors or Ford. Investors can only make valid evaluations if comparable information is available.

Another type of comparability, consistency, is present when a company applies the same accounting treatment to similar events, from period to period. Through such application, the company shows consistent use of accounting standards. The idea of consistency does not mean, however, that companies cannot switch from one accounting method to another. A company can change methods, but it must first demonstrate that the newly adopted method is preferable to the old. If approved, the company must then disclose the nature and effect of the accounting change, as well as the justification for it, in the financial statements for the period in which it made the change.[9] When a change in accounting principles occurs, the auditor generally refers to it in an explanatory paragraph of the audit report. This paragraph identifies the nature of the change and refers the reader to the note in the financial statements that discusses the change in detail.[10]

Verifiability. Verifiability occurs when independent measurers, using the same methods, obtain similar results. Verifiability occurs in the following situations.

1. Two independent auditors count PepsiCo's inventory and arrive at the same physical quantity amount for inventory. Verification of an amount for an asset therefore can occur by simply counting the inventory (referred to as *direct verification*).
2. Two independent auditors compute PepsiCo's inventory value at the end of the year using the FIFO method of inventory valuation. Verification may occur by checking the inputs (quantity and costs) and recalculating the outputs (ending inventory value) using the same accounting convention or methodology (referred to as *indirect verification*).

Timeliness. Timeliness means having information available to decision-makers before it loses its capacity to influence decisions. Having relevant information available sooner

Surveys indicate that users highly value consistency. They note that a change tends to destroy the comparability of data before and after the change. Some companies assist users to understand the pre- and post-change data. Generally, however, users say they lose the ability to analyze over time. GAAP guidelines (discussed in Chapter 22) on accounting changes are designed to improve the comparability of the data before and after the change.

These provisions are specified in "Reports on Audited Financial Statements," *Statement on Auditing Standards No. 58* (New York: AICPA, April 1988), par. 34.

can enhance its capacity to influence decisions. A lack of timeliness, on the other hand, can rob information of its usefulness. For example, if **Dell** waited to report its interim results until nine months after the period, the information would be much less useful for decision-making purposes.

Understandability. Decision-makers vary widely in the types of decisions they make, how they make decisions, the information they already possess or can obtain from other sources, and their ability to process the information. For information to be useful, there must be a connection (linkage) between these users and the decisions they make. This link, **understandability**, is the quality of information that lets reasonably informed users see its significance. Understandability is enhanced when information is classified, characterized, and presented clearly and concisely.

For example, assume that **Google** issues a three-months' report that shows interim earnings have declined significantly. This interim report provides relevant and faithfully represented information for decision-making purposes. Some users, upon reading the report, decide to sell their shares. Other users, however, do not understand the report's content and significance. They are surprised when Google declares a smaller year-end dividend and the share price declines. Thus, although Google presented highly relevant information that was a faithful representation, it was useless to those who did not understand it.

Thus, users of financial reports are assumed to have a reasonable knowledge of business and economic activities. In making decisions, users also should review and analyze the information with reasonable diligence. Information that is relevant and faithfully represented should not be excluded from financial reports solely because it is too complex or difficult for some users to understand without assistance.[11]

Basic Elements

LEARNING OBJECTIVE **5**
Define the basic elements of financial statements.

An important aspect of developing any theoretical structure is the body of **basic elements** or definitions to be included in it. Accounting uses many terms with distinctive and specific meanings. These terms constitute the language of business or the jargon of accounting.

One such term is **asset**. Is it merely something we own? Or is an asset something we have the right to use, as in the case of leased equipment? Or is it anything of value used by a company to generate revenues—in which case, should we also consider the managers of a company as an asset?

As this example and the lottery ticket example in the opening story illustrate, it therefore seems necessary to develop basic definitions for the elements of financial statements. *SFAC No. 6* defines the 10 interrelated elements that most directly relate to measuring the performance and financial status of a business enterprise. We list them on the next page for review and information purposes; you need not memorize these definitions at this point. We will explain and examine each of these elements in more detail in subsequent chapters.

The FASB classifies the elements into two distinct groups. The first group of three elements—assets, liabilities, and equity—describes amounts of resources and claims to resources at a **moment in time**. The other seven elements describe transactions, events, and circumstances that affect a company during a **period of time**. The first class, affected by elements of the second class, provides at any time the cumulative result of all changes. This interaction is referred to as "articulation." That is, key figures in one financial statement correspond to balances in another.

---

[11]"Chapter 3, Qualitative Characteristics of Useful Financial Information," *Statement of Financial Accounting Concepts No. 8* (Norwalk, Conn.: FASB, September 2010), paras. QC30–QC31.

ELEMENTS OF FINANCIAL STATEMENTS

ASSETS. Probable future economic benefits obtained or controlled by a particular entity as a result of past transactions or events.

LIABILITIES. Probable future sacrifices of economic benefits arising from present obligations of a particular entity to transfer assets or provide services to other entities in the future as a result of past transactions or events.

EQUITY. Residual interest in the assets of an entity that remains after deducting its liabilities. In a business enterprise, the equity is the ownership interest.

INVESTMENTS BY OWNERS. Increases in net assets of a particular enterprise resulting from transfers to it from other entities of something of value to obtain or increase ownership interests (or equity) in it. Assets are most commonly received as investments by owners, but that which is received may also include services or satisfaction or conversion of liabilities of the enterprise.

DISTRIBUTIONS TO OWNERS. Decreases in net assets of a particular enterprise resulting from transferring assets, rendering services, or incurring liabilities by the enterprise to owners. Distributions to owners decrease ownership interests (or equity) in an enterprise.

COMPREHENSIVE INCOME. Change in equity (net assets) of an entity during a period from transactions and other events and circumstances from nonowner sources. It includes all changes in equity during a period except those resulting from investments by owners and distributions to owners.

REVENUES. Inflows or other enhancements of assets of an entity or settlement of its liabilities (or a combination of both) during a period from delivering or producing goods, rendering services, or other activities that constitute the entity's ongoing major or central operations.

EXPENSES. Outflows or other using up of assets or incurrences of liabilities (or a combination of both) during a period from delivering or producing goods, rendering services, or carrying out other activities that constitute the entity's ongoing major or central operations.

GAINS. Increases in equity (net assets) from peripheral or incidental transactions of an entity and from all other transactions and other events and circumstances affecting the entity during a period except those that result from revenues or investments by owners.

LOSSES. Decreases in equity (net assets) from peripheral or incidental transactions of an entity and from all other transactions and other events and circumstances affecting the entity during a period except those that result from expenses or distributions to owners.[12]

THIRD LEVEL: RECOGNITION AND MEASUREMENT CONCEPTS

The third level of the framework consists of concepts that implement the basic objective of level one. These concepts explain how companies should recognize, measure, and report financial elements and events. The FASB sets forth most of these in its *Statement of Financial Accounting Concepts No. 5*, "Recognition and Measurement in Financial Statements of Business Enterprises." According to *SFAC No. 5*, to be recognized, an item (event or transaction) must meet the definition of an "element of

6 LEARNING OBJECTIVE
Describe the basic assumptions of accounting.

"Elements of Financial Statements," *Statement of Financial Accounting Concepts No. 6* (Stamford, Conn.: FASB, December 1985), pp. ix and x.

financial statements" as defined in *SFAC No. 6* and must be measurable. Most aspects of current practice follow these recognition and measurement concepts.

The accounting profession continues to use the concepts in *SFAC No. 5* as operational guidelines. Here, we identify the concepts as basic assumptions, principles, and a cost constraint. Not everyone uses this classification system, so focus your attention more on **understanding the concepts** than on how we classify and organize them. These concepts serve as guidelines in responding to controversial financial reporting issues.

Basic Assumptions

Four basic assumptions underlie the financial accounting structure: (1) **economic entity**, (2) **going concern**, (3) **monetary unit**, and (4) **periodicity**. We'll look at each in turn.

International Perspective

Phase D of the conceptual framework convergence project addresses the reporting entity.

Economic Entity Assumption

The economic entity assumption **means that economic activity can be identified with a particular unit of accountability**. In other words, a company keeps its activity separate and distinct from its owners and any other business unit.[13] At the most basic level, the economic entity assumption dictates that Panera Bread Company record the company's financial activities separate from those of its owners and managers. Equally important, financial statement users need to be able to distinguish the activities and elements of different companies, such as General Motors, Ford, and Chrysler. If users could not distinguish the activities of different companies, how would they know which company financially outperformed the other?

The entity concept does not apply solely to the segregation of activities among competing companies, such as Home Depot and Lowe's. An individual, department, division, or an entire industry could be considered a separate entity if we choose to define it in this manner. Thus, **the entity concept does not necessarily refer to a legal entity.** A parent and its subsidiaries are separate **legal** entities, but merging their activities for accounting and reporting purposes does not violate the **economic entity** assumption.[14]

What do the numbers mean?   *WHOSE COMPANY IS IT?*

The importance of the entity assumption is illustrated by scandals involving W. R. Grace and, more recently, Adelphia. In both cases, senior company employees entered into transactions that blurred the line between the employee's financial interests and those of the company. At Adelphia, among many other self-dealings, the company guaranteed over $2 billion of loans to the founding family. W. R. Grace used company funds to pay for an apartment and chef for the company chairman. As a result of these transactions, these insiders benefitted at the expense of shareholders. Additionally, the financial statements failed to disclose the transactions. Such disclosure would have allowed shareholders to sort out the impact of the employee transactions on company results.

---

[13]Recently, the FASB has proposed to link the definition of an entity to its financial reporting objective. That is, a reporting entity is described as a circumscribed area of business activity of interest to present and potential equity investors, lenders, and other capital providers. See IASB/FASB, "The Reporting Entity," *Exposure Draft ED/2010/2: Conceptual Framework for Financial Reporting* (March 2010).

[14]The concept of the entity is changing. For example, defining the "outer edges" of companies is now harder. Public companies often consist of multiple public subsidiaries, each with joint ventures, licensing arrangements, and other affiliations. Increasingly, companies form and dissolve joint ventures or customer-supplier relationships in a matter of months or weeks. These "virtual companies" raise accounting issues about how to account for the entity. As discussed in footnote 13, the FASB (and IASB) is addressing these issues in the entity phase of its conceptual framework project.

Going Concern Assumption

Most accounting methods rely on the going concern assumption—**that the company will have a long life**. Despite numerous business failures, most companies have a fairly high continuance rate. As a rule, we expect companies to last long enough to fulfill their objectives and commitments.

This assumption has significant implications. The historical cost principle would be of limited usefulness if we assume eventual liquidation. Under a liquidation approach, for example, a company would better state asset values at net realizable value (sales price less costs of disposal) than at acquisition cost. **Depreciation and amortization policies are justifiable and appropriate only if we assume some permanence to the company.** If a company adopts the liquidation approach, the current/noncurrent classification of assets and liabilities loses much of its significance. Labeling anything a fixed or long-term asset would be difficult to justify. Indeed, listing liabilities on the basis of priority in liquidation would be more reasonable.

The going concern assumption applies in most business situations. **Only where liquidation appears imminent is the assumption inapplicable.** In these cases, a total revaluation of assets and liabilities can provide information that closely approximates the company's net realizable value. You will learn more about accounting problems related to a company in liquidation in advanced accounting courses.[15]

Monetary Unit Assumption

The monetary unit assumption means that money is the common denominator of economic activity and provides an appropriate basis for accounting measurement and analysis. That is, the monetary unit is the most effective means of expressing to interested parties changes in capital and exchanges of goods and services. **The monetary unit is relevant, simple, universally available, understandable, and useful.** Application of this assumption depends on the even more basic assumption that quantitative data are useful in communicating economic information and in making rational economic decisions.

In the United States, accounting ignores price-level changes (inflation and deflation) and assumes that the unit of measure—the dollar—remains reasonably stable. We therefore use the monetary unit assumption to justify adding 1984 dollars to 2014 dollars without any adjustment. The FASB in *SFAC No. 5* indicated that it expects the dollar, unadjusted for inflation or deflation, to continue to be used to measure items recognized in financial statements. Only if circumstances change dramatically (such as if the United States experiences high inflation similar to that in many South American countries) will the FASB again consider "inflation accounting."

 International Perspective

Due to their experiences with persistent inflation, several South American countries produce "constant-currency" financial reports. Typically, companies in these countries use a general price-level index to adjust for the effects of inflation.

Periodicity Assumption

To measure the results of a company's activity accurately, we would need to wait until it liquidates. Decision-makers, however, cannot wait that long for such information. Users need to know a company's performance and economic status on a timely basis so that

[15] In response to minimal guidance addressing when it is appropriate to apply, or how to apply, the liquidation basis of accounting, the FASB recently issued a *Proposed Accounting Standards Update*, "Presentation of Financial Statements (Topic 205)—The Liquidation Basis of Accounting" (July 2, 2012). In brief, companies would prepare financial statements using the liquidation basis of accounting when liquidation is imminent (when either a plan for liquidation has been approved or a plan for liquidation is being imposed by other forces, such as involuntary bankruptcy). If liquidation accounting is used, financial statements should reflect relevant information about a company's resources and obligations in liquidation by measuring and presenting assets and liabilities at the amount of cash or other consideration that the company expects to collect or pay in liquidation, along with disclosures about the plan for liquidation, the methods and significant assumptions used to measure assets and liabilities, the type and amount of costs and income accrued, and the expected duration of liquidation.

they can evaluate and compare firms, and take appropriate actions. Therefore, companies must report information periodically.

The **periodicity** (or **time period**) **assumption** implies that a company can divide its economic activities into artificial time periods. These time periods vary, but the most common are monthly, quarterly, and yearly.

The shorter the time period, the more difficult it is to determine the proper net income for the period. A month's results usually prove less verifiable than a quarter's results, and a quarter's results are likely to be less verifiable than a year's results. Investors desire and demand that a company quickly process and disseminate information. Yet the quicker a company releases the information, the more likely the information will include errors. **This phenomenon provides an interesting example of the trade-off between timeliness and accuracy (free from error) in preparing financial data.**

The problem of defining the time period becomes more serious as product cycles shorten and products become obsolete more quickly. Many believe that, given technology advances, companies need to provide more online, real-time financial information to ensure the availability of relevant information.

Basic Principles of Accounting

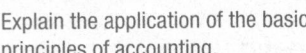

LEARNING OBJECTIVE 7
Explain the application of the basic principles of accounting.

We generally use four basic **principles of accounting** to record and report transactions: (1) measurement, (2) revenue recognition, (3) expense recognition, and (4) full disclosure. We look at each in turn.

Measurement Principle

We presently have a "mixed-attribute" system that permits the use of various measurement bases. The most commonly used measurements are based on historical cost and fair value. Here, we discuss each.

Historical Cost. GAAP requires that companies account for and report many assets and liabilities on the basis of acquisition price. This is often referred to as the **historical cost principle.** Historical cost has an important advantage over other valuations: **It is generally thought to be verifiable.**

To illustrate this advantage, consider the problems if companies select current selling price instead. Companies might have difficulty establishing a value for unsold items. Every member of the accounting department might value the assets differently. Further, how often would it be necessary to establish sales value? All companies close their accounts at least annually. But some compute their net income every month. Those companies would have to place a sales value on every asset each time they wished to determine income. Critics raise similar objections against current cost (replacement cost, present value of future cash flows) and any other basis of valuation **except historical cost.**

What about liabilities? Do companies account for them on a cost basis? Yes, they do. Companies issue liabilities, such as bonds, notes, and accounts payable, in exchange for assets (or services), for an agreed-upon price. **This price, established by the exchange transaction, is the "cost" of the liability.** A company uses this amount to record the liability in the accounts and report it in financial statements. Thus, many users prefer historical cost because it provides them with a **verifiable benchmark** for measuring historical trends.

Fair Value. **Fair value** is defined as "the price that would be received to sell an asset or paid to transfer a liability in an orderly transaction between market participants at the measurement date." Fair value is therefore a market-based measure. **[1]** Recently, GAAP

Gateway to the Profession

Expanded Discussion of Accounting and Changing Prices

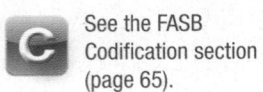

See the FASB Codification section (page 65).

has increasingly called for use of fair value measurements in the financial statements. This is often referred to as the **fair value principle**. Fair value information may be more useful than historical cost for certain types of assets and liabilities and in certain industries. For example, companies report many financial instruments, including derivatives, at fair value. Certain industries, such as brokerage houses and mutual funds, prepare their basic financial statements on a fair value basis.

At initial acquisition, historical cost equals fair value. In subsequent periods, as market and economic conditions change, historical cost and fair value often diverge. Thus, fair value measures or estimates often provide more relevant information about the expected future cash flows related to the asset or liability. For example, when long-lived assets decline in value, a fair value measure determines any impairment loss. The FASB believes that fair value information is more relevant to users than historical cost. Fair value measurement, it is argued, provides better insight into the value of a company's assets and liabilities (its financial position) and a better basis for assessing future cash flow prospects.

Recently the Board has taken the additional step of giving companies the option to use fair value (referred to as the **fair value option**) as the basis for measurement of financial assets and financial liabilities. **[2]** The Board considers fair value more relevant than historical cost because it reflects the current cash equivalent value of financial instruments. As a result companies now have the option to record fair value in their accounts for most financial instruments, including such items as receivables, investments, and debt securities.

Use of fair value in financial reporting is increasing. However, measurement based on fair value introduces increased subjectivity into accounting reports when fair value information is not readily available. To increase consistency and comparability in fair value measures, the FASB established a fair value hierarchy that provides insight into the priority of valuation techniques to use to determine fair value. As shown in Illustration 2-4, the fair value hierarchy is divided into three broad levels.

ILLUSTRATION 2-4
Fair Value Hierarchy

As Illustration 2-4 indicates, Level 1 is the least subjective because it is based on quoted prices, like a closing stock price in the *Wall Street Journal*. Level 2 is more subjective and would rely on evaluating similar assets or liabilities in active markets. At the most subjective level, Level 3, much judgment is needed, based on the best information available, to arrive at a relevant and representationally faithful fair value measurement.[16]

[16]For major groups of assets and liabilities, companies must disclose (1) the fair value measurement and (2) the fair value hierarchy level of the measurements as a whole, classified by Level 1, 2, or 3. Given the judgment involved, it follows that the more a company depends on Level 3 to determine fair values, the more information about the valuation process the company will need to disclose. Thus, additional disclosures are required for Level 3 measurements; we discuss these disclosures in more detail in subsequent chapters.

Recently, the FASB issued additional guidance related to issues surrounding the use of fair value in financial statements (Accounting Standards Update 2011–04, *Amendments to Achieve Common Fair Value Measurement and Disclosure Requirements in U.S. GAAP and IFRS*). A major benefit of the guidance is to provide a better definitional structure of what is meant by fair value and an improved understanding of how fair value should be measured.

It is easy to arrive at fair values when markets are liquid with many traders, but fair value answers are not readily available in other situations. For example, how do you value the mortgage assets of a subprime lender such as New Century given that the market for these securities has essentially disappeared? A great deal of expertise and sound judgment will be needed to arrive at appropriate answers. GAAP also provides guidance on estimating fair values when market-related data is not available. In general, these valuation issues relate to Level 3 fair value measurements. These measurements may be developed using expected cash flow and present value techniques, as described in *Statement of Financial Accounting Concepts No. 7*, "Using Cash Flow Information and Present Value in Accounting," discussed in Chapter 6.

As indicated above, we presently have a "mixed-attribute" system that permits the use of historical cost and fair value. Although the historical cost principle continues to be an important basis for valuation, recording and reporting of fair value information is increasing. The recent measurement and disclosure guidance should increase consistency and comparability when fair value measurements are used in the financial statements and related notes.

Revenue Recognition Principle

When a company agrees to perform a service or sell a product to a customer, it has a **performance obligation**. When the company satisfies this performance obligation, it recognizes revenue. The revenue recognition principle therefore requires that companies recognize revenue in the accounting period in which the performance obligation is satisfied. To illustrate, assume that Klinke Cleaners cleans clothing on June 30 but customers do not claim and pay for their clothes until the first week of July. Klinke should record revenue in June when it performed the service (satisfied the performance obligation) rather than in July when it received the cash. At June 30, Klinke would report a receivable on its balance sheet and revenue in its income statement for the service performed.

To illustrate the revenue recognition principle in more detail, assume that Boeing Corporation signs a contract to sell airplanes to Delta Air Lines for $100 million. To determine when to recognize revenue, Boeing uses the five steps shown in Illustration 2-5.

Many revenue transactions pose few problems because the transaction is initiated and completed at the same time. However, when to recognize revenue in other certain situations is often more difficult. The risk of errors and misstatements is significant. Chapter 18 discusses revenue recognition issues in more detail.[17]

Expense Recognition Principle

As indicated in the discussion of financial statement elements, expenses are defined as outflows or other "using up" of assets or incurring of liabilities (or a combination of both) during a period as a result of delivering or producing goods and/or performing services. It follows then that recognition of expenses is related to net changes in assets and earning revenues. In practice, the approach for recognizing expenses is, "Let the expense follow the revenues." This approach is the expense recognition principle.

To illustrate, companies recognize expenses not when they pay wages or make a product, but when the work (service) or the product actually contributes to revenue. Thus, companies tie expense recognition to revenue recognition. That is, by matching **efforts (expenses) with accomplishment (revenues), the expense recognition principle**

---

[17]The framework illustrated here is based on that proposed by the FASB and IASB in their joint project on revenue. See "Revenue from Contracts with Customers," *Proposed Accounting Standards Update (Revised)* (Norwalk, Conn.: FASB, November 14, 2011, and January 4, 2012). The Boards hope to issue a converged standard in early 2013. Application of this new framework to many revenue arrangements results in similar revenue recognition outcomes compared to the current framework (based on earned and realized criteria). However, a new, more general model was needed to respond to the growth of revenue arrangements for which the prior model did not address.

s implemented in accordance with the definition of expense (outflows or other using up of assets or incurring of liabilities).[18]

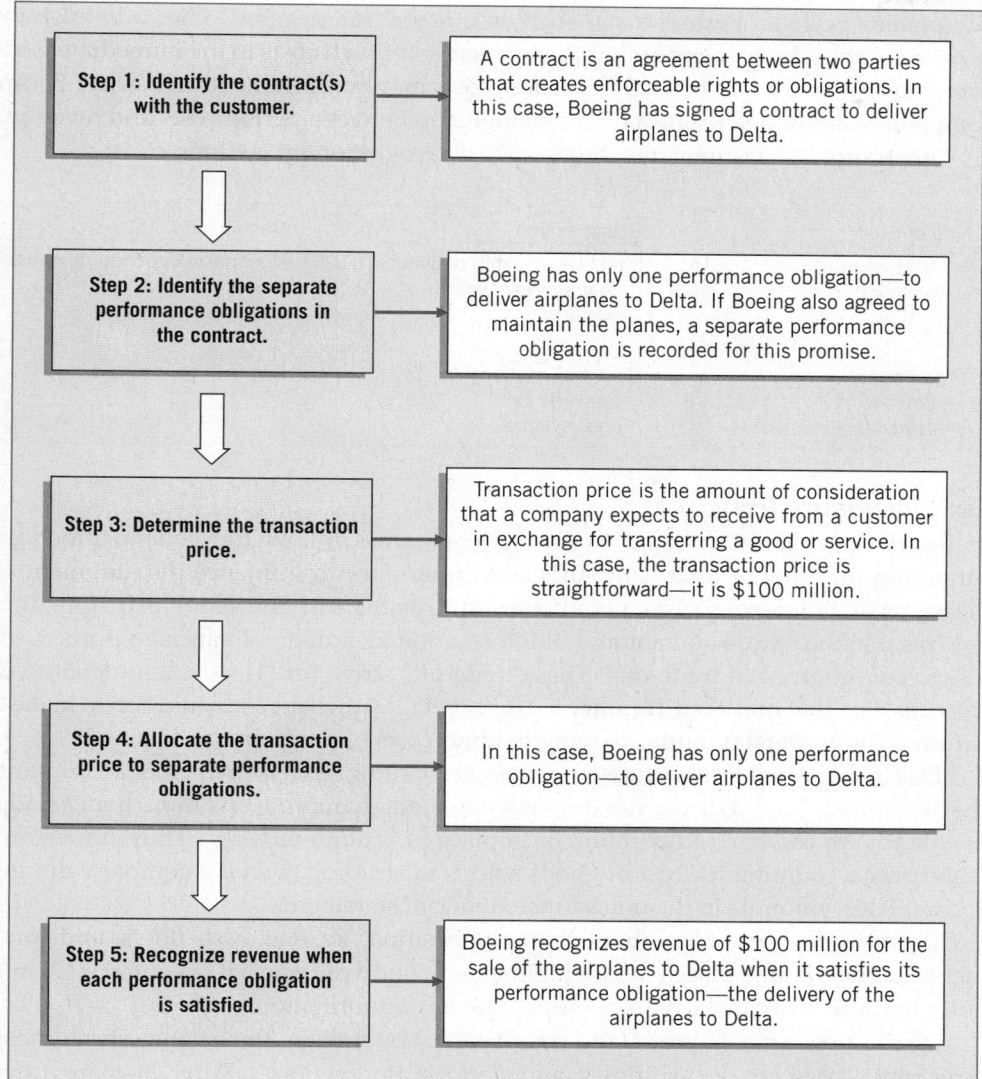

ILLUSTRATION 2-5
The Five Steps of
Revenue Recognition

Step 1: Identify the contract(s) with the customer.

A contract is an agreement between two parties that creates enforceable rights or obligations. In this case, Boeing has signed a contract to deliver airplanes to Delta.

Step 2: Identify the separate performance obligations in the contract.

Boeing has only one performance obligation—to deliver airplanes to Delta. If Boeing also agreed to maintain the planes, a separate performance obligation is recorded for this promise.

Step 3: Determine the transaction price.

Transaction price is the amount of consideration that a company expects to receive from a customer in exchange for transferring a good or service. In this case, the transaction price is straightforward—it is $100 million.

Step 4: Allocate the transaction price to separate performance obligations.

In this case, Boeing has only one performance obligation—to deliver airplanes to Delta.

Step 5: Recognize revenue when each performance obligation is satisfied.

Boeing recognizes revenue of $100 million for the sale of the airplanes to Delta when it satisfies its performance obligation—the delivery of the airplanes to Delta.

Some costs, however, are difficult to associate with revenue. As a result, some other approach must be developed. Often, companies use a "rational and systematic" allocation policy that will approximate the expense recognition principle. This type of expense recognition involves assumptions about the benefits that a company receives as well as the cost associated with those benefits. For example, a company like **Intel** or **Motorola** allocates the cost of a long-lived asset over all of the accounting periods during which it uses the asset because the asset contributes to the generation of revenue throughout its useful life.

Companies charge some costs to the current period as expenses (or losses) simply because they cannot determine a connection with revenue. Examples of these types of costs are officers' salaries and other administrative expenses.

This approach is commonly referred to as the **matching principle**. However, there is much debate about the conceptual validity of the matching principle. A major concern is that matching permits companies to defer certain costs and treat them as assets on the balance sheet. In fact, these costs may not have future benefits. If abused, this principle permits the balance sheet to become a "dumping ground" for unmatched costs.

Costs are generally classified into two groups: **product costs** and **period costs**. Product costs, such as material, labor, and overhead, attach to the product. Companies carry these costs into future periods if they recognize the revenue from the product in subsequent periods. Period costs, such as officers' salaries and other administrative expenses, attach to the period. Companies charge off such costs in the immediate period, even though benefits associated with these costs may occur in the future. Why? Because companies cannot determine a direct relationship between period costs and revenue.

Illustration 2-6 summarizes these expense recognition procedures.

ILLUSTRATION 2-6
Expense Recognition

Type of Cost	Relationship	Recognition
Product costs: • Material • Labor • Overhead	Direct relationship between cost and revenue.	Recognize in period of revenue (matching).
Period costs: • Salaries • Administrative costs	No direct relationship between cost and revenue.	Expense as incurred.

Full Disclosure Principle

In deciding what information to report, companies follow the general practice of providing information that is of sufficient importance to influence the judgment and decisions of an informed user. Often referred to as the full disclosure principle, it recognizes that the nature and amount of information included in financial reports reflect a series of judgmental trade-offs. These trade-offs strive for (1) sufficient detail to disclose matters that **make a difference** to users, yet (2) sufficient condensation to make the **information understandable**, keeping in mind costs of preparing and using it.

Disclosure is not a substitute for proper accounting. As a former chief accountant of the SEC noted, "Good disclosure does not cure bad accounting any more than an adjective or adverb can be used without, or in place of, a noun or verb." Thus, for example, cash-basis accounting for cost of goods sold is misleading even if a company discloses accrual-basis amounts in the notes to the financial statements.

Users find information about financial position, income, cash flows, and investments in one of three places: (1) within the main body of financial statements, (2) in the notes to those statements, or (3) as supplementary information.

As discussed in Chapter 1, the financial statements are the balance sheet, income statement, statement of cash flows, and statement of owners' equity. They are a structured means of communicating financial information. To be recognized in the main body of financial statements, **an item should meet the definition of a basic element, be measurable with sufficient certainty, and be relevant and reliable.**[19]

The notes to financial statements generally amplify or explain the items presented in the main body of the statements. If the main body of the financial statements gives an incomplete picture of the performance and position of the company, the notes should provide the additional information needed. Information in the notes does not have to be quantifiable, nor does it need to qualify as an element. Notes can be partially or totally narrative. Examples of notes include descriptions of the accounting policies and methods used in measuring the elements reported in the statements, explanations of uncertainties and contingencies, and statistics and details too voluminous for inclusion in the statements. The notes can be essential to understanding the company's performance and position.

Supplementary information may include details or amounts that present a different perspective from that adopted in the financial statements. It may be quantifiable information that is high in relevance but low in faithful representation. For example, or

---

[19]*SFAC No. 5*, par. 63.

and gas companies typically provide information on proven reserves as well as the related discounted cash flows.

Supplementary information may also include management's explanation of the financial information and its discussion of the significance of that information. For example, many business combinations have produced financing arrangements that demand new accounting and reporting practices and principles. In each of these situations, the same problem must be faced: making sure the company presents enough information to ensure that the **reasonably prudent investor** will not be misled.

We discuss the content, arrangement, and display of financial statements, along with other facets of full disclosure, in Chapters 4, 5, and 24.[20]

What do the numbers mean?   YOU MAY NEED A MAP

Beyond touting nonfinancial measures to investors (see the "What Do the Numbers Mean?" box on page 50), many companies increasingly promote the performance of their companies through the reporting of various "pro forma" earnings measures. A recent survey of newswire reports found 36 instances of the reporting of pro forma measures in just a three-day period.

Pro forma measures are standard measures (such as earnings) that companies adjust, usually for one-time or nonrecurring items. For example, companies usually adjust earnings for the effects of an extraordinary item. Such adjustments make the numbers more comparable to numbers reported in periods without the unusual item.

However, rather than increasing comparability, it appears that some companies use pro forma reporting to accentuate the positive in their results. Examples include Yahoo! and Cisco, which define pro forma income after adding back payroll tax expense. Level 8 Systems transformed an operating loss into a pro forma profit by adding back expenses for depreciation and amortization of intangible assets.

Lynn Turner, former chief accountant at the SEC, calls such earnings measures EBS—"Everything but Bad Stuff." To provide investors a more complete picture of company profitability, not the story preferred by management, the SEC issued Regulation G (REG G). REG G requires companies to reconcile non-GAAP financial measures to GAAP, thereby giving investors a roadmap to analyze adjustments companies make to their GAAP numbers to arrive at pro forma results.

Sources: Adapted from Gretchen Morgenson, "How Did They Value Stocks? Count the Absurd Ways," *New York Times* (March 18, 2001), section 3, p. 1; and Gretchen Morgenson, "Expert Advice: Focus on Profit," *New York Times* (March 18, 2001), section 3, p. 14. See also SEC Regulation G, "Conditions for Use of Non-GAAP Financial Measures," Release No. 33–8176 (March 28, 2003).

Cost Constraint

In providing information with the qualitative characteristics that make it useful, companies must consider an overriding factor that limits (constrains) the reporting. This is referred to as the cost constraint (the cost-benefit relationship). That is, companies must weigh the costs of providing the information against the benefits that can be derived from using it. Rule-making bodies and governmental agencies use cost-benefit analysis before making final their informational requirements. In order to justify requiring a particular measurement or disclosure, the benefits perceived to be derived from it must exceed the costs perceived to be associated with it.

A corporate executive made the following remark to the FASB about a proposed rule: "In all my years in the financial arena, I have never seen such an absolutely ridiculous proposal. . . . To dignify these 'actuarial' estimates by recording them as assets and liabilities would be virtually unthinkable except for the fact that the FASB has done equally stupid things in the past. . . . For God's sake, use common sense just this once."[21] Although extreme, this remark indicates the frustration expressed by members of the business community about rule-making, and whether the benefits of a given pronouncement exceed the costs.

8 LEARNING OBJECTIVE

Describe the impact that the cost constraint has on reporting accounting information.

[20]Recently, the FASB started a project on disclosure effectiveness to better communicate the information that is most important to users of financial statements. The Board hopes that a sharper focus on important information will result in a reduced volume of notes to the financial statements.

[21]"Decision-Usefulness: The Overriding Objective," *FASB Viewpoints* (October 19, 1983), p. 4.

The difficulty in cost-benefit analysis is that the costs and especially the benefits are not always evident or measurable. The costs are of several kinds: costs of collecting and processing, of disseminating, of auditing, of potential litigation, of disclosure to competitors, and of analysis and interpretation. Benefits to preparers may include greater management control and access to capital at a lower cost. Users may receive better information for allocation of resources, tax assessment, and rate regulation. As noted earlier, benefits are generally more difficult to quantify than are costs.

The implementation of the provisions of the Sarbanes-Oxley Act illustrates the challenges in assessing costs and benefits of standards. One study estimated the increased costs of complying with the new internal-control standards related to the financial reporting process to be an average of $7.8 million per company. However, the study concluded that "quantifying the benefits of improved more reliable financial reporting is not fully possible."[22]

Despite the difficulty in assessing the costs and benefits of its rules, the FASB attempts to determine that each proposed pronouncement will fill a significant need and that the costs imposed to meet the rule are justified in relation to overall benefits of

ILLUSTRATION 2-7
Conceptual Framework for Financial Reporting

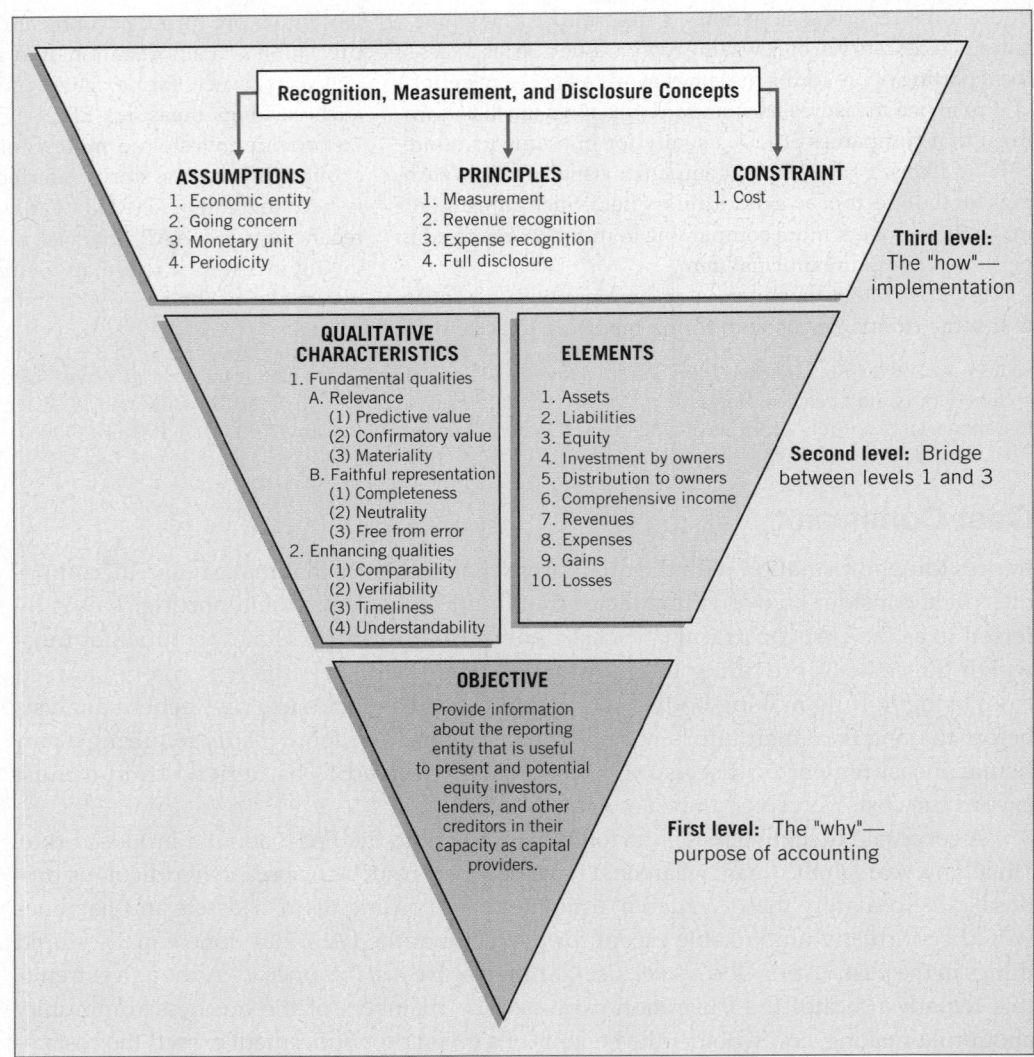

the resulting information. In addition, the Board seeks input on costs and benefits as part of its due process.[23]

Summary of the Structure

Illustration 2-7 (page 62) presents the conceptual framework discussed in this chapter. It is similar to Illustration 2-1 except that it provides additional information for each level. We cannot overemphasize the usefulness of this conceptual framework in helping to understand many of the problem areas that we examine in later chapters.

You will want to read the **IFRS INSIGHTS** on pages 78–81 for discussion of how IFRS relates to the conceptual framework.

SUMMARY OF LEARNING OBJECTIVES

1 **Describe the usefulness of a conceptual framework.** The accounting profession needs a conceptual framework to (1) build on and relate to an established body of concepts and objectives, (2) provide a framework for solving new and emerging practical problems, (3) increase financial statement users' understanding of and confidence in financial reporting, and (4) enhance comparability among companies' financial statements.

2 **Describe the FASB's efforts to construct a conceptual framework.** The FASB issued seven Statements of Financial Accounting Concepts that relate to financial reporting for business enterprises. These concept statements provide the basis for the conceptual framework. They include objectives, qualitative characteristics, and elements. In addition, measurement and recognition concepts are developed. The FASB and the IASB are now working on a joint project to develop an improved common conceptual framework that provides a sound foundation for developing future accounting standards.

3 **Understand the objective of financial reporting.** The objective of general-purpose financial reporting is to provide financial information about the reporting entity that is **useful to present and potential equity investors, lenders, and other creditors** in making decisions about providing resources to the entity. Those decisions involve buying, selling, or holding equity and debt instruments, and providing or settling loans and other forms of credit. Information that is decision-useful to capital providers may also be helpful to other users of financial reporting who are not capital providers.

4 **Identify the qualitative characteristics of accounting information.** The overriding criterion by which accounting choices can be judged is decision-usefulness—that is, providing information that is most useful for decision-making. Relevance and faithful representation are the two fundamental qualities that make information decision-useful. Relevant information makes a difference in a decision by having predictive or confirmatory value and is material. Faithful representation is characterized by completeness, neutrality, and being free from error. Enhancing qualities of useful information are (1) comparability, (2) verifiability, (3) timeliness, and (4) understandability.

5 **Define the basic elements of financial statements.** The basic elements of financial statements are (1) assets, (2) liabilities, (3) equity, (4) investments by owners, (5) distributions to owners, (6) comprehensive income, (7) revenues, (8) expenses, (9) gains, and (10) losses. We define these 10 elements on page 53.

6 **Describe the basic assumptions of accounting.** Four basic assumptions underlying financial accounting are as follows. (1) *Economic entity:* The activity of a company can be kept separate and distinct from its owners and any other business unit.

KEY TERMS

assumption, *54*
comparability, *51*
completeness, *49*
conceptual framework, *42*
confirmatory value, *47*
conservatism, *49(n)*
consistency, *51*
cost constraint (cost-benefit relationship), *61*
economic entity assumption, *54*
elements, basic, *52*
expense recognition principle, *58*
fair value, *56*
fair value option, *57*
fair value principle, *57*
faithful representation, *49*
financial statements, *60*
free from error, *49*
full disclosure principle, *60*
general-purpose financial reporting, *45*
going concern assumption, *55*
historical cost principle, *56*
matching principle, *59(n)*
materiality, *47*
monetary unit assumption, *55*
neutrality, *49*
notes to financial statements, *60*
objective of financial reporting, *45*
period costs, *59*

---

[23]For example, as part of its project on "Share-Based Payment" **[3]**, the Board conducted a field study and surveyed commercial software providers to collect information on the costs of measuring the fair values of share-based compensation arrangements.

periodicity (time period)
     assumption, *56*

predictive value, *47*

principles of
     accounting, *56*

product costs, *59*

prudence, *49(n)*

qualitative
     characteristics, *45*

relevance, *46*

revenue recognition
     principle, *58*

supplementary
     information, *60*

timeliness, *51*

understandability, *52*

verifiability, *51*

(2) *Going concern:* The company will have a long life. (3) *Monetary unit:* Money is the common denominator by which economic activity is conducted, and the monetary unit provides an appropriate basis for measurement and analysis. (4) *Periodicity:* The economic activities of a company can be divided into artificial time periods.

7 **Explain the application of the basic principles of accounting.** (1) *Measurement principle:* GAAP permits the use of historical cost, fair value, and other valuation bases. Although the historical cost principle (measurement based on acquisition price) continues to be an important basis for valuation, recording and reporting of fair value information is increasing. (2) *Revenue recognition principle:* A company recognizes revenue when it satisfies a performance obligation. (3) *Expense recognition principle:* As a general rule, companies recognize expenses when the service or the product actually makes its contribution to revenue (commonly referred to as *matching*). (4) *Full disclosure principle:* Companies generally provide information that is of sufficient importance to influence the judgment and decisions of an informed user.

8 **Describe the impact that the cost constraint has on reporting accounting information.** The cost of providing the information must be weighed against the benefits that can be derived from using the information.

DEMONSTRATION PROBLEM

Jeremy Meadow Corporation has hired you to review its accounting records prior to the closing of the revenue and expense accounts as of December 31, the end of the current fiscal year. The following information comes to your attention.

1. During the current year, Jeremy Meadow Corporation changed its policy in regard to expensing purchases of small tools. In the past, it had expensed these purchases because they amounted to less than 2% of net income. Now, the president has decided that the company should follow a policy of capitalization and subsequent depreciation. It is expected that purchases of small tools will not fluctuate greatly from year to year.

2. The company constructed a warehouse at a cost of $1,000,000. It had been depreciating the asset on a straight-line basis over 10 years. In the current year, the controller doubled depreciation expense because the replacement cost of the warehouse had increased significantly.

3. When the balance sheet was prepared, the preparer omitted detailed information as to the amount of cash on deposit in each of several banks. Only the total amount of cash under a caption "Cash in banks" was presented.

4. On July 15 of the current year, Jeremy Meadow Corporation purchased an undeveloped tract of land at a cost of $320,000. The company spent $80,000 in subdividing the land and getting it ready for sale. An appraisal of the property at the end of the year indicated that the land was now worth $500,000. Although none of the lots were sold, the company recognized revenue of $180,000, less related expenses of $80,000, for a net income on the project of $100,000.

5. For a number of years, the company used the FIFO method for inventory valuation purposes. During the current year, the president noted that all the other companies in the industry had switched to the LIFO method. The company decided not to switch to LIFO because net income would decrease $830,000.

Instructions
State whether or not you agree with the decisions made by Jeremy Meadow Corporation. Support your answers with reference, whenever possible, to the generally accepted principles, assumptions, and cost constraint applicable in the circumstances.

Solution

1. From the facts, it is difficult to determine whether to agree or disagree. Consistency, of course, is violated in this situation although its violation may not be material. Furthermore, the change of accounting policies regarding the treatment of small tools cannot be judged good or bad but would depend on the circumstances. In this case, it seems that the result will be approximately the same

whether the corporation capitalizes and expenses, or simply expenses each period, since the purchases are fairly uniform. Perhaps from a cost standpoint (expediency), it might be best to continue the present policy rather than become involved in detailed depreciation schedules, assuming that purchases remain fairly uniform. On the other hand, the president may believe there is a significant unrecorded asset that should be shown on the balance sheet. If such is the case, capitalization and subsequent depreciation would be more appropriate.

2. Disagree. At the present time, accountants do not recognize price level or current value adjustments in the accounts. Hence, it is misleading to deviate from the historical cost principle because conjecture or opinion can take place. Also, depreciation is not so much a matter of valuation as it is a means of cost allocation. Assets are not depreciated on the basis of a decline in their fair value. Rather, they are depreciated on the basis of a systematic charge of expired cost against revenues.

3. Agree. The full disclosure principle recognizes that reasonable condensation and summarization of the details of a corporation's operations and financial position are essential to readability and comprehension. Thus, in determining what is full disclosure, the accountant must decide whether omission will mislead readers of the financial statements. Generally, companies present only the total amount of cash on a balance sheet unless some special circumstance is involved (such as a possible restriction on the use of the cash). In most cases, however, the company's presentation would be considered appropriate and in accordance with the full disclosure principle.

4. Disagree. The historical cost principle indicates that companies account for assets and liabilities on the basis of cost. If sales value were selected, for example, it would be extremely difficult to establish an appraisal value for the given item without selling it. Note, too, that the revenue recognition principle provides guidance on when revenue should be recognized. Revenue should be recognized when the performance obligation is satisfied. In this case, the revenue was not recognized because the critical event, "sale of the land," had not occurred.

5. From the facts, it is difficult to determine whether to agree or disagree with the president. The president's approach is not a violation of any principle. Consistency requires that accounting entities give accountable events the same accounting treatment from period to period for a given business enterprise. It says nothing concerning consistency of accounting principles among business enterprises. From a comparability viewpoint, it might be useful to report the information on a LIFO basis. But, as indicated above, there is no requirement to do so.

FASB CODIFICATION

FASB Codification References

[1] FASB ASC 820-10. [Predecessor literature: "Fair Value Measurement," *Statement of Financial Accounting Standards No. 157* (Norwalk, Conn.: FASB, September 2006).]

[2] FASB ASC 825-10-25. [Predecessor literature: "The Fair Value Option for Financial Assets and Liabilities," *Statement of Financial Accounting Standards No. 159* (Norwalk, Conn.: FASB, 2007).]

[3] FASB ASC 718-10. [Predecessor literature: "Share-Based Payment," *Financial Accounting Standards No. 123(R)* (Norwalk, Conn.: FASB, 2004).]

Exercises

If your school has a subscription to the FASB Codification, go to *http://aaahq.org/ascLogin.cfm* to log in and prepare responses to the following. Provide Codification references for your responses.

CE2-1 Access the glossary ("Master Glossary") at the FASB Codification website to answer the following.

    (a) What is the definition of fair value?
    (b) What is the definition of revenue?
    (c) What is the definition of comprehensive income?

CE2-2 Briefly describe how the organization of the FASB Codification corresponds to the elements of financial statements.

An additional accounting research case can be found in the Using Your Judgment section, on page 77.

Be sure to check the book's companion website for a Review and Analysis Exercise, with solution.

WileyPLUS Brief Exercises, Exercises, Problems, and many more learning and assessment tools and resources are available for practice in WileyPLUS.

QUESTIONS

1. What is a conceptual framework? Why is a conceptual framework necessary in financial accounting?

2. What is the primary objective of financial reporting?

3. What is meant by the term "qualitative characteristics of accounting information"?

4. Briefly describe the two fundamental qualities of useful accounting information.

5. How is materiality (or immateriality) related to the proper presentation of financial statements? What factors and mea-sures should be considered in assessing the material-ity of a misstatement in the presentation of a financial statement?

6. What are the enhancing qualities of the qualitative charac-teristics? What is the role of enhancing qualities in the conceptual framework?

7. According to the FASB conceptual framework, the objec-tive of financial reporting for business enterprises is based on the needs of the users of financial statements. Explain the level of sophistication that the Board assumes about the users of financial statements.

8. What is the distinction between comparability and consistency?

9. Why is it necessary to develop a definitional framework for the basic elements of accounting?

10. Expenses, losses, and distributions to owners are all de-creases in net assets. What are the distinctions among them?

11. Revenues, gains, and investments by owners are all in-creases in net assets. What are the distinctions among them?

12. What are the four basic assumptions that underlie the financial accounting structure?

13. The life of a business is divided into specific time periods, usually a year, to measure results of operations for each such time period and to portray financial conditions at the end of each period.

    (a) This practice is based on the accounting assumption that the life of the business consists of a series of time periods and that it is possible to measure accurately the results of operations for each period. Comment on the validity and necessity of this assumption.

    (b) What has been the effect of this practice on account-ing? What is its relation to the accrual system? What

influence has it had on accounting entries and methodology?

14. What is the basic accounting problem created by the mon-etary unit assumption when there is significant inflation? What appears to be the FASB position on a stable mone-tary unit?

15. The chairman of the board of directors of the company for which you are chief accountant has told you that he has little use for accounting figures based on historical cost. He believes that replacement values are of far more significance to the board of directors than "out-of-date costs." Present some arguments to convince him that ac-counting data should still be based on historical cost.

16. What is the definition of fair value?

17. What is the fair value option? Explain how use of the fair value option reflects application of the fair value principle.

18. Briefly describe the fair value hierarchy.

19. Explain the revenue recognition principle.

20. What is a performance obligation, and how is it used to determine when revenue should be recognized?

21. What are the five steps used to determine the proper time to recognize revenue?

22. Selane Eatery operates a catering service specializing in business luncheons for large corporations. Selane requires customers to place their orders 2 weeks in advance of the scheduled events. Selane bills its customers on the tenth day of the month following the date of service and re-quires that payment be made within 30 days of the billing date. Conceptually, when should Selane recognize reve-nue related to its catering service?

23. Mogilny Company paid $135,000 for a machine. The Accumulated Depreciation—Equipment account has a bal-ance of $46,500 at the present time. The company could sell the machine today for $150,000. The company president believes that the company has a "right to this gain." What does the president mean by this statement? Do you agree?

24. Three expense recognition methods (associating cause and effect, systematic and rational allocation, and immediate recognition) were discussed in the text under the expense rec-ognition principle. Indicate the basic nature of each of these expense recognition methods and give two examples of each.

25. *Statement of Financial Accounting Concepts No. 5* identifies four characteristics that an item must have before it is recognized in the financial statements. What are these four characteristics?

26. Briefly describe the types of information concerning financial position, income, and cash flows that might be provided (a) within the main body of the financial statements, (b) in the notes to the financial statements, or (c) as supplementary information.

27. In January 2015, Janeway Inc. doubled the amount of its outstanding stock by selling on the market an additional 10,000 shares to finance an expansion of the business. You propose that this information be shown by a footnote on the balance sheet as of December 31, 2014. The president objects, claiming that this sale took place after December 31, 2014, and therefore should not be shown. Explain your position.

28. Describe the major constraint inherent in the presentation of accounting information.

29. What are some of the costs of providing accounting information? What are some of the benefits of accounting information? Describe the cost-benefit factors that should

be considered when new accounting standards are being proposed.

30. The treasurer of Landowska Co. has heard that conservatism is a doctrine that is followed in accounting and, therefore, proposes that several policies be followed that are conservative in nature. State your opinion with respect to each of the policies listed.

(a) The company gives a 2-year warranty to its customers on all products sold. The estimated warranty costs incurred from this year's sales should be entered as an expense this year instead of an expense in the period in the future when the warranty is made good.

(b) When sales are made on account, there is always uncertainty about whether the accounts are collectible. Therefore, the treasurer recommends recording the sale when the cash is received from the customers.

(c) A personal liability lawsuit is pending against the company. The treasurer believes there is an even chance that the company will lose the suit and have to pay damages of $200,000 to $300,000. The treasurer recommends that a loss be recorded and a liability created in the amount of $300,000.

BRIEF EXERCISES

4 BE2-1 Match the qualitative characteristics below with the following statements.

1. Relevance
2. Faithful representation
3. Predictive value
4. Confirmatory value
5. Comparability
6. Completeness
7. Neutrality
8. Timeliness

(a) Quality of information that permits users to identify similarities in and differences between two sets of economic phenomena.
(b) Having information available to users before it loses its capacity to influence decisions.
(c) Information about an economic phenomenon that has value as an input to the processes used by capital providers to form their own expectations about the future.
(d) Information that is capable of making a difference in the decisions of users in their capacity as capital providers.
(e) Absence of bias intended to attain a predetermined result or to induce a particular behavior.

4 BE2-2 Match the qualitative characteristics below with the following statements.

1. Timeliness
2. Completeness
3. Free from error
4. Understandability
5. Faithful representation
6. Relevance
7. Neutrality
8. Confirmatory value

(a) Quality of information that assures users that information represents the economic phenomena that it purports to represent.
(b) Information about an economic phenomenon that corrects past or present expectations based on previous evaluations.
(c) The extent to which information is accurate in representing the economic substance of a transaction.
(d) Includes all the information that is necessary for a faithful representation of the economic phenomena that it purports to represent.
(e) Quality of information that allows users to comprehend its meaning.

4 **BE2-3** Discuss whether the changes described in each of the cases below require recognition in the CPA's audit report as to consistency. (Assume that the amounts are material.)

    (a) The company changed its inventory method to FIFO from weighted-average, which had been used in prior years.

    (b) The company disposed of one of the two subsidiaries that had been included in its consolidated statements for prior years.

    (c) The estimated remaining useful life of plant property was reduced because of obsolescence.

4 **BE2-4** Identify which qualitative characteristic of accounting information is best described in each item below. (Do not use relevance and faithful representation.)

    (a) The annual reports of Best Buy Co. are audited by certified public accountants.

    (b) Black & Decker and Cannondale Corporation both use the FIFO cost flow assumption.

    (c) Starbucks Corporation has used straight-line depreciation since it began operations.

    (d) Motorola issues its quarterly reports immediately after each quarter ends.

4 **BE2-5** Presented below are three different transactions related to materiality. Explain whether you would classify these transactions as material.

    (a) Blair Co. has reported a positive trend in earnings over the last 3 years. In the current year, it reduces its bad debt allowance to ensure another positive earnings year. The impact of this adjustment is equal to 3% of net income.

    (b) Hindi Co. has an extraordinary gain of $3.1 million on the sale of plant assets and a $3.3 million loss on the sale of investments. It decides to net the gain and loss because the net effect is considered immaterial. Hindi Co.'s income for the current year was $10 million.

    (c) Damon Co. expenses all capital equipment under $25,000 on the basis that it is immaterial. The company has followed this practice for a number of years.

5 **BE2-6** For each item below, indicate to which category of elements of financial statements it belongs.

    (a) Retained earnings   **(e)** Depreciation   **(h)** Dividends

    (b) Sales   **(f)** Loss on sale of equipment   **(i)** Gain on sale of investment

    (c) Additional paid-in capital   **(g)** Interest payable   **(j)** Issuance of common stock

    (d) Inventory

6 **BE2-7** Identify which basic assumption of accounting is best described in each item below.

    (a) The economic activities of FedEx Corporation are divided into 12-month periods for the purpose of issuing annual reports.

    (b) Solectron Corporation, Inc. does not adjust amounts in its financial statements for the effects of inflation.

    (c) Walgreen Co. reports current and noncurrent classifications in its balance sheet.

    (d) The economic activities of General Electric and its subsidiaries are merged for accounting and reporting purposes.

7 **BE2-8** Identify which basic principle of accounting is best described in each item below.

    (a) Norfolk Southern Corporation reports revenue in its income statement when the performance obligation is satisfied instead of when the cash is collected.

    (b) Yahoo! recognizes depreciation expense for a machine over the 2-year period during which that machine helps the company earn revenue.

    (c) Oracle Corporation reports information about pending lawsuits in the notes to its financial statements.

    (d) Eastman Kodak Company reports land on its balance sheet at the amount paid to acquire it, even though the estimated fair value is greater.

7 **BE2-9** Vande Velde Company made three investments during 2014. (1) It purchased 1,000 shares of Sastre Company, a start-up company. Vande Velde made the investment based on valuation estimates from an internally developed model. (2) It purchased 2,000 shares of GE stock, which trades on the NYSE. (3) It invested $10,000 in local development authority bonds. Although these bonds do not trade on an active market, their value closely tracks movements in U.S. Treasury bonds. Where will Vande Velde report these investments in the fair value hierarchy?

6 **BE2-10** If the going concern assumption is not made in accounting, discuss the differences in the amounts shown in the financial statements for the following items.

    (a) Land.

    (b) Unamortized bond premium.

    (c) Depreciation expense on equipment.

    (d) Inventory.

    (e) Prepaid insurance.

6 7 8 BE2-11 What accounting assumption, principle, or constraint would Target Corporation use in each of the situations below?

   (a) Target was involved in litigation over the last year. This litigation is disclosed in the financial statements.
   (b) Target allocates the cost of its depreciable assets over the life it expects to receive revenue from these assets.
   (c) Target records the purchase of a new Dell PC at its cash equivalent price.

5 BE2-12 Explain how you would decide whether to record each of the following expenditures as an asset or an expense. Assume all items are material.

   (a) Legal fees paid in connection with the purchase of land are $1,500.
   (b) Eduardo, Inc. paves the driveway leading to the office building at a cost of $21,000.
   (c) A meat market purchases a meat-grinding machine at a cost of $3,500.
   (d) On June 30, Monroe and Meno, medical doctors, pay 6 months' office rent to cover the month of July and the next 5 months.
   (e) Smith's Hardware Company pays $9,000 in wages to laborers for construction on a building to be used in the business.
   (f) Alvarez's Florists pays wages of $2,100 for the month an employee who serves as driver of their delivery truck.

EXERCISES

1 3 E2-1 (Usefulness, Objective of Financial Reporting) Indicate whether the following statements about the conceptual framework are true or false. If false, provide a brief explanation supporting your position.

   (a) Accounting rule-making that relies on a body of concepts will result in useful and consistent pronouncements.
   (b) General-purpose financial reports are most useful to company insiders in making strategic business decisions.
   (c) Accounting standards based on individual conceptual frameworks generally will result in consistent and comparable accounting reports.
   (d) Capital providers are the only users who benefit from general-purpose financial reporting.
   (e) Accounting reports should be developed so that users without knowledge of economics and business can become informed about the financial results of a company.
   (f) The objective of financial reporting is the foundation from which the other aspects of the framework logically result.

1 3 4 E2-2 (Usefulness, Objective of Financial Reporting, Qualitative Characteristics) Indicate whether the following statements about the conceptual framework are true or false. If false, provide a brief explanation supporting your position.

   (a) The fundamental qualitative characteristics that make accounting information useful are relevance and verifiability.
   (b) Relevant information only has predictive value, confirmatory value, or both.
   (c) Information that is a faithful representation is characterized as having predictive or confirmatory value.
   (d) Comparability pertains only to the reporting of information in a similar manner for different companies.
   (e) Verifiability is solely an enhancing characteristic for faithful representation.
   (f) In preparing financial reports, it is assumed that users of the reports have reasonable knowledge of business and economic activities.

4 8 E2-3 (Qualitative Characteristics) *SFAC No. 8* identifies the qualitative characteristics that make accounting information useful. Presented below are a number of questions related to these qualitative characteristics and underlying constraint.

   (a) What is the quality of information that enables users to confirm or correct prior expectations?
   (b) Identify the pervasive constraint developed in the conceptual framework.
   (c) The chairman of the SEC at one time noted, "If it becomes accepted or expected that accounting principles are determined or modified in order to secure purposes other than economic measurement, we assume a grave risk that confidence in the credibility of our financial information system

will be undermined." Which qualitative characteristic of accounting information should ensure that such a situation will not occur? (Do not use faithful representation.)

(d) Muruyama Corp. switches from FIFO to average-cost to FIFO over a 2-year period. Which qualitative characteristic of accounting information is not followed?

(e) Assume that the profession permits the savings and loan industry to defer losses on investments it sells because immediate recognition of the loss may have adverse economic consequences on the industry. Which qualitative characteristic of accounting information is not followed? (Do not use relevance or faithful representation.)

(f) What are the two fundamental qualities that make accounting information useful for decision-making?

(g) Watteau Inc. does not issue its first-quarter report until after the second quarter's results are reported. Which qualitative characteristic of accounting is not followed? (Do not use relevance.)

(h) Predictive value is an ingredient of which of the two fundamental qualities that make accounting information useful for decision-making purposes?

(i) Duggan, Inc. is the only company in its industry to depreciate its plant assets on a straight-line basis. Which qualitative characteristic of accounting information may not be followed?

(j) Roddick Company has attempted to determine the replacement cost of its inventory. Three different appraisers arrive at substantially different amounts for this value. The president, nevertheless, decides to report the middle value for external reporting purposes. Which qualitative characteristic of information is lacking in these data? (Do not use relevance or faithful representation.)

4 E2-4 (Qualitative Characteristics) The qualitative characteristics that make accounting information useful for decision-making purposes are as follows.

Relevance	Neutrality	Verifiability
Faithful representation	Completeness	Understandability
Predictive value	Timeliness	Comparability
Confirmatory value	Materiality	Free from error

Instructions

Identify the appropriate qualitative characteristic(s) to be used given the information provided below.

(a) Qualitative characteristic being employed when companies in the same industry are using the same accounting principles.

(b) Quality of information that confirms users' earlier expectations.

(c) Imperative for providing comparisons of a company from period to period.

(d) Ignores the economic consequences of a standard or rule.

(e) Requires a high degree of consensus among individuals on a given measurement.

(f) Predictive value is an ingredient of this fundamental quality of information.

(g) Four qualitative characteristics that are related to both relevance and faithful representation.

(h) An item is not recorded because its effect on income would not change a decision.

(i) Neutrality is an ingredient of this fundamental quality of accounting information.

(j) Two fundamental qualities that make accounting information useful for decision-making purposes.

(k) Issuance of interim reports is an example of what enhancing quality of relevance?

5 E2-5 (Elements of Financial Statements) Ten interrelated elements that are most directly related to measuring the performance and financial status of an enterprise are provided below.

Assets	Distributions to owners	Expenses
Liabilities	Comprehensive income	Gains
Equity	Revenues	Losses
Investments by owners		

Instructions

Identify the element or elements associated with the 12 items below.

(a) Arises from peripheral or incidental transactions.

(b) Obligation to transfer resources arising from a past transaction.

(c) Increases ownership interest.

(d) Declares and pays cash dividends to owners.

(e) Increases in net assets in a period from nonowner sources.

(f) Items characterized by service potential or future economic benefit.

(g) Equals increase in assets less liabilities during the year, after adding distributions to owners and subtracting investments by owners.

(h) Arises from income statement activities that constitute the entity's ongoing major or central operations.

(i) Residual interest in the assets of the enterprise after deducting its liabilities.

(j) Increases assets during a period through sale of product.
(k) Decreases assets during the period by purchasing the company's own stock.
(l) Includes all changes in equity during the period, except those resulting from investments by owners and distributions to owners.

6 7 8 E2-6 (Assumptions, Principles, and Constraint) Presented below are the assumptions, principles, and constraint used in this chapter.

1. Economic entity assumption	5. Measurement principle (historical cost)	7. Expense recognition principle
2. Going concern assumption		8. Full disclosure principle
3. Monetary unit assumption	6. Measurement principle (fair value)	9. Cost constraint
4. Periodicity assumption		10. Revenue recognition principle

Instructions
Identify by number the accounting assumption, principle, or constraint that describes each situation below. Do not use a number more than once.

(a) Allocates expenses to revenues in the proper period.
(b) Indicates that fair value changes subsequent to purchase are not recorded in the accounts. (Do not use revenue recognition principle.)
(c) Ensures that all relevant financial information is reported.
(d) Rationale why plant assets are not reported at liquidation value. (Do not use historical cost principle.)
(e) Indicates that personal and business record keeping should be separately maintained.
(f) Separates financial information into time periods for reporting purposes.
(g) Assumes that the dollar is the "measuring stick" used to report on financial performance.

6 7 8 E2-7 (Assumptions, Principles, and Constraint) Presented below are a number of operational guidelines and practices that have developed over time.

Instructions
Select the assumption, principle, or constraint that most appropriately justifies these procedures and practices. (Do not use qualitative characteristics.)

(a) Fair value changes are not recognized in the accounting records.
(b) Financial information is presented so that investors will not be misled.
(c) Intangible assets are capitalized and amortized over periods benefited.
(d) Repair tools are expensed when purchased.
(e) Agricultural companies use fair value for purposes of valuing crops.
(f) Each enterprise is kept as a unit distinct from its owner or owners.
(g) All significant post-balance-sheet events are reported.
(h) Revenue is recorded at point of sale.
(i) All important aspects of bond indentures are presented in financial statements.
(j) Rationale for accrual accounting.
(k) The use of consolidated statements is justified.
(l) Reporting must be done at defined time intervals.
(m) An allowance for doubtful accounts is established.
(n) Goodwill is recorded only at time of purchase.
(o) A company charges its sales commission costs to expense.

7 E2-8 (Full Disclosure Principle) Presented below are a number of facts related to Weller, Inc. Assume that no mention of these facts was made in the financial statements and the related notes.

Instructions
Assume that you are the auditor of Weller, Inc. and that you have been asked to explain the appropriate accounting and related disclosure necessary for each of these items.

(a) The company decided that, for the sake of conciseness, only net income should be reported on the income statement. Details as to revenues, cost of goods sold, and expenses were omitted.
(b) Equipment purchases of $170,000 were partly financed during the year through the issuance of a $110,000 notes payable. The company offset the equipment against the notes payable and reported plant assets at $60,000.
(c) Weller has reported its ending inventory at $2,100,000 in the financial statements. No other information related to inventories is presented in the financial statements and related notes.
(d) The company changed its method of valuing inventories from weighted-average to FIFO. No mention of this change was made in the financial statements.

7 E2-9 (Accounting Principles—Comprehensive) Presented below are a number of business transactions that occurred during the current year for Gonzales, Inc.

Instructions

In each of the situations, discuss the appropriateness of the journal entries in terms of generally accepted accounting principles.

(a) The president of Gonzales, Inc. used his expense account to purchase a new Suburban solely for personal use. The following journal entry was made.

Miscellaneous Expense	29,000	
Cash		29,000

(b) Merchandise inventory that cost $620,000 is reported on the balance sheet at $690,000, the expected selling price less estimated selling costs. The following entry was made to record this increase in value.

Inventory	70,000	
Sales Revenue		70,000

(c) The company is being sued for $500,000 by a customer who claims damages for personal injury apparently caused by a defective product. Company attorneys feel extremely confident that the company will have no liability for damages resulting from the situation. Nevertheless, the company decides to make the following entry.

Loss from Lawsuit	500,000	
Liability for Lawsuit		500,000

(d) Because the general level of prices increased during the current year, Gonzales, Inc. determined that there was a $16,000 understatement of depreciation expense on its equipment and decided to record it in its accounts. The following entry was made.

Depreciation Expense	16,000	
Accumulated Depreciation—Equipment		16,000

(e) Gonzales, Inc. has been concerned about whether intangible assets could generate cash in case of liquidation. As a consequence, goodwill arising from a purchase transaction during the current year and recorded at $800,000 was written off as follows.

Retained Earnings	800,000	
Goodwill		800,000

(f) Because of a "fire sale," equipment obviously worth $200,000 was acquired at a cost of $155,000. The following entry was made.

Equipment	200,000	
Cash		155,000
Sales Revenue		45,000

7 E2-10 (Accounting Principles—Comprehensive) Presented below is information related to Cramer, Inc.

Instructions

Comment on the appropriateness of the accounting procedures followed by Cramer, Inc.

(a) Depreciation expense on the building for the year was $60,000. Because the building was increasing in value during the year, the controller decided to charge the depreciation expense to retained earnings instead of to net income. The following entry is recorded.

Retained Earnings	60,000	
Accumulated Depreciation—Buildings		60,000

(b) Materials were purchased on January 1, 2014, for $120,000 and this amount was entered in the Materials account. On December 31, 2014, the materials would have cost $141,000, so the following entry is made.

Inventory	21,000	
Gain on Inventories		21,000

(c) During the year, the company purchased equipment through the issuance of common stock. The stock had a par value of $135,000 and a fair value of $450,000. The fair value of the equipment was not easily determinable. The company recorded this transaction as follows.

Equipment	135,000	
Common Stock		135,000

(d) During the year, the company sold certain equipment for $285,000, recognizing a gain of $69,000. Because the controller believed that new equipment would be needed in the near future, she decided to defer the gain and amortize it over the life of any new equipment purchased.

(e) An order for $61,500 has been received from a customer for products on hand. This order was shipped on January 9, 2015. The company made the following entry in 2014.

Accounts Receivable	61,500	
Sales Revenue		61,500

EXERCISES SET B

See the book's companion website, at **www.wiley.com/college/kieso**, for an additional set of exercises.

CONCEPTS FOR ANALYSIS

CA2-1 (Conceptual Framework—General) Wayne Cooper has some questions regarding the theoretical framework in which GAAP is set. He knows that the FASB and other predecessor organizations have attempted to develop a conceptual framework for accounting theory formulation. Yet, Wayne's supervisors have indicated that these theoretical frameworks have little value in the practical sense (i.e., in the real world). Wayne did notice that accounting rules seem to be established after the fact rather than before. He thought this indicated a lack of theory structure but never really questioned the process at school because he was too busy doing the homework.

Wayne feels that some of his anxiety about accounting theory and accounting semantics could be alleviated by identifying the basic concepts and definitions accepted by the profession and considering them in light of his current work. By doing this, he hopes to develop an appropriate connection between theory and practice.

Instructions
(a) Help Wayne recognize the purpose of and benefit of a conceptual framework.
(b) Identify any Statements of Financial Accounting Concepts issued by the FASB that may be helpful to Wayne in developing his theoretical background.

CA2-2 (Conceptual Framework—General) The Financial Accounting Standards Board (FASB) has developed a conceptual framework for financial accounting and reporting. The FASB has issued eight Statements of Financial Accounting Concepts. These statements are intended to set forth the objective and fundamentals that will be the basis for developing financial accounting and reporting standards. The objective identifies the goals and purposes of financial reporting. The fundamentals are the underlying concepts of financial accounting that guide the selection of transactions, events, and circumstances to be accounted for; their recognition and measurement; and the means of summarizing and communicating them to interested parties.

The purpose of the statement on qualitative characteristics is to examine the characteristics that make accounting information useful. These characteristics or qualities of information are the ingredients that make information useful and the qualities to be sought when accounting choices are made.

Instructions
(a) Identify and discuss the benefits that can be expected to be derived from the FASB's conceptual framework study.
(b) What is the most important quality for accounting information as identified in the conceptual framework? Explain why it is the most important.
(c) *Statement of Financial Accounting Concepts No. 8* describes a number of key characteristics or qualities for accounting information. Briefly discuss the importance of any three of these qualities for financial reporting purposes.

(CMA adapted)

CA2-3 (Objective of Financial Reporting) Homer Winslow and Jane Alexander are discussing various aspects of the FASB's concepts statement on the objective of financial reporting. Homer indicates that this pronouncement provides little, if any, guidance to the practicing professional in resolving accounting controversies. He believes that the statement provides such broad guidelines that it would be impossible to apply the objective to present-day reporting problems. Jane concedes this point but indicates that the objective is still needed to provide a starting point for the FASB in helping to improve financial reporting.

Instructions

(a) Indicate the basic objective established in the conceptual framework.

(b) What do you think is the meaning of Jane's statement that the FASB needs a starting point to resolve accounting controversies?

 CA2-4 (Qualitative Characteristics) Accounting information provides useful information about business transactions and events. Those who provide and use financial reports must often select and evaluate accounting alternatives. The FASB statement on qualitative characteristics of accounting information examines the characteristics of accounting information that make it useful for decision-making. It also points out that various limitations inherent in the measurement and reporting process may necessitate trade-offs or sacrifices among the characteristics of useful information.

Instructions

(a) Describe briefly the following characteristics of useful accounting information.

(1) Relevance.   (4) Comparability.

(2) Faithful representation.   (5) Consistency.

(3) Understandability.

(b) For each of the following pairs of information characteristics, give an example of a situation in which one of the characteristics may be sacrificed in return for a gain in the other.

(1) Relevance and faithful representation.   (3) Comparability and consistency.

(2) Relevance and consistency.   (4) Relevance and understandability.

(c) What criterion should be used to evaluate trade-offs between information characteristics?

CA2-5 (Revenue Recognition Principle) After the presentation of your report on the examination of the financial statements to the board of directors of Piper Publishing Company, one of the new directors expresses surprise that the income statement assumes that an equal proportion of the revenue is recognized with the publication of every issue of the company's magazine. She feels that the "crucial event" in the process of earning revenue in the magazine business is the cash sale of the subscription. She says that she does not understand why most of the revenue cannot be "recognized" in the period of the cash sale.

Instructions

Discuss the propriety of timing the recognition of revenue in Piper Publishing Company's accounts with:

(a) The cash sale of the magazine subscription.

(b) The publication of the magazine every month.

(c) Both events, by recognizing a portion of the revenue with the cash sale of the magazine subscription and a portion of the revenue with the publication of the magazine every month.

CA2-6 (Expense Recognition Principle) An accountant must be familiar with the concepts involved in determining earnings of a business entity. The amount of earnings reported for a business entity is dependent on the proper recognition, in general, of revenues and expenses for a given time period. In some situations, costs are recognized as expenses at the time of product sale. In other situations, guidelines have been developed for recognizing costs as expenses or losses by other criteria.

Instructions

(a) Explain the rationale for recognizing costs as expenses at the time of product sale.

(b) What is the rationale underlying the appropriateness of treating costs as expenses of a period instead of assigning the costs to an asset? Explain.

(c) In what general circumstances would it be appropriate to treat a cost as an asset instead of as an expense? Explain.

(d) Some expenses are assigned to specific accounting periods on the basis of systematic and rational allocation of asset cost. Explain the underlying rationale for recognizing expenses on the basis of systematic and rational allocation of asset cost.

(e) Identify the conditions under which it would be appropriate to treat a cost as a loss.

(AICPA adapted)

CA2-7 (Expense Recognition Principle) Accountants try to prepare income statements that are as accurate as possible. A basic requirement in preparing accurate income statements is to record costs and revenues properly. Proper recognition of costs and revenues requires that costs resulting from typical business operations be recognized in the period in which they expired.

Instructions

(a) List three criteria that can be used to determine whether such costs should appear as charges in the income statement for the current period.

(b) As generally presented in financial statements, the following items or procedures have been criticized as improperly recognizing costs. Briefly discuss each item from the viewpoint of matching costs with revenues and suggest corrective or alternative means of presenting the financial information.

    (1) Receiving and handling costs.

    (2) Cash discounts on purchases.

CA2-8 (Expense Recognition Principle) Daniel Barenboim sells and erects shell houses, that is, frame structures that are completely finished on the outside but are unfinished on the inside except for flooring, partition studding, and ceiling joists. Shell houses are sold chiefly to customers who are handy with tools and who have time to do the interior wiring, plumbing, wall completion and finishing, and other work necessary to make the shell houses livable dwellings.

Barenboim buys shell houses from a manufacturer in unassembled packages consisting of all lumber, roofing, doors, windows, and similar materials necessary to complete a shell house. Upon commencing operations in a new area, Barenboim buys or leases land as a site for its local warehouse, field office, and display houses. Sample display houses are erected at a total cost of $30,000 to $44,000 including the cost of the unassembled packages. The chief element of cost of the display houses is the unassembled packages, inasmuch as erection is a short, low-cost operation. Old sample models are torn down or altered into new models every 3 to 7 years. Sample display houses have little salvage value because dismantling and moving costs amount to nearly as much as the cost of an unassembled package.

Instructions

    (a) A choice must be made between (1) expensing the costs of sample display houses in the periods in which the expenditure is made and (2) spreading the costs over more than one period. Discuss the advantages of each method.

    (b) Would it be preferable to amortize the cost of display houses on the basis of (1) the passage of time or (2) the number of shell houses sold? Explain.

(AICPA adapted)

CA2-9 (Qualitative Characteristics) Recently, your uncle, Carlos Beltran, who knows that you always have your eye out for a profitable investment, has discussed the possibility of your purchasing some corporate bonds. He suggests that you may wish to get in on the "ground floor" of this deal. The bonds being issued by Neville Corp. are 10-year debentures which promise a 40% rate of return. Neville manufactures novelty/party items.

You have told Neville that, unless you can take a look at its financial statements, you would not feel comfortable about such an investment. Believing that this is the chance of a lifetime, Uncle Carlos has procured a copy of Neville's most recent, unaudited financial statements which are a year old. These statements were prepared by Mrs. Andy Neville. You peruse these statements, and they are quite impressive. The balance sheet showed a debt-to-equity ratio of 0.10 and, for the year shown, the company reported net income of $2,424,240.

The financial statements are not shown in comparison with amounts from other years. In addition, no significant note disclosures about inventory valuation, depreciation methods, loan agreements, etc. are available.

Instructions

Write a letter to Uncle Carlos explaining why it would be unwise to base an investment decision on the financial statements that he has provided to you. Be sure to explain why these financial statements are neither relevant nor representationally faithful.

CA2-10 (Expense Recognition Principle) Anderson Nuclear Power Plant will be "mothballed" at the end of its useful life (approximately 20 years) at great expense. The expense recognition principle requires that expenses be matched to revenue. Accountants Ana Alicia and Ed Bradley argue whether it is better to allocate the expense of mothballing over the next 20 years or ignore it until mothballing occurs.

Instructions

Answer the following questions.

    (a) What stakeholders should be considered?

    (b) What ethical issue, if any, underlies the dispute?

    (c) What alternatives should be considered?

    (d) Assess the consequences of the alternatives.

    (e) What decision would you recommend?

CA2-11 (Cost Constraint) The AICPA Special Committee on Financial Reporting proposed the following constraints related to financial reporting.

    1. Business reporting should exclude information outside of management's expertise or for which management is not the best source, such as information about competitors.

2. Management should not be required to report information that would significantly harm the company's competitive position.
3. Management should not be required to provide forecasted financial statements. Rather, management should provide information that helps users forecast for themselves the company's financial future.
4. Other than for financial statements, management need report only the information it knows. That is, management should be under no obligation to gather information it does not have, or does not need, to manage the business.
5. Companies should present certain elements of business reporting only if users and management agree they should be reported—a concept of flexible reporting.
6. Companies should not have to report forward-looking information unless there are effective deterrents to unwarranted litigation that discourages companies from doing so.

Instructions
For each item, briefly discuss how the proposed constraint addresses concerns about the costs and benefits of financial reporting.

USING YOUR JUDGMENT

FINANCIAL REPORTING

Financial Reporting Problem

P&G **The Procter & Gamble Company (P&G)**
The financial statements of P&G are presented in Appendix 5B. The company's complete annual report, including the notes to the financial statements, can be accessed at the book's companion website, **www.wiley.com/college/kieso**.

Instructions
Refer to P&G's financial statements and the accompanying notes to answer the following questions.
(a) Using the notes to the consolidated financial statements, determine P&G's revenue recognition policies. Discuss the impact of trade promotions on P&G's financial statements.
(b) Give two examples of where historical cost information is reported in P&G's financial statements and related notes. Give two examples of the use of fair value information reported in either the financial statements or related notes.
(c) How can we determine that the accounting principles used by P&G are prepared on a basis consistent with those of last year?
(d) What is P&G's accounting policy related to advertising? What accounting principle does P&G follow regarding accounting for advertising? Where are advertising expenses reported in the financial statements?

Comparative Analysis Case
The Coca-Cola Company and PepsiCo, Inc.

Instructions
Go to the book's companion website, and use information found there to answer the following questions related to The Coca-Cola Company and PepsiCo, Inc.
(a) What are the primary lines of business of these two companies as shown in their notes to the financial statements?
(b) Which company has the dominant position in beverage sales?
(c) How are inventories for these two companies valued? What cost allocation method is used to report inventory? How does their accounting for inventories affect comparability between the two companies?
(d) Which company changed its accounting policies, which then affected the consistency of the financial results from the previous year? What were these changes?

Financial Statement Analysis Case
Wal-Mart Stores, Inc.

Wal-Mart Stores, Inc. provided the following disclosure in a recent annual report.

> *New accounting pronouncement (partial)* . . . the Securities and Exchange Commission issued Staff Accounting Bulletin No. 101—"Revenue Recognition in Financial Statements" (*SAB 101*). This SAB deals with various revenue recognition issues, several of which are common within the retail industry. As a result of the issuance of this SAB . . . the Company is currently evaluating the effects of the SAB on its method of recognizing revenues related to layaway sales and will make any accounting method changes necessary during the first quarter of [next year].

In response to *SAB 101*, Wal-Mart changed its revenue recognition policy for layaway transactions, in which Wal-Mart sets aside merchandise for customers who make partial payment. Before the change, Wal-Mart recognized all revenue on the sale at the time of the layaway. After the change, Wal-Mart does not recognize revenue until customers satisfy all payment obligations and take possession of the merchandise.

Instructions

(a) Discuss the expected effect on income (1) in the year that Wal-Mart makes the changes in its revenue recognition policy, and (2) in the years following the change.

(b) Evaluate the extent to which Wal-Mart's previous revenue policy was consistent with the revenue recognition principle.

(c) If all retailers had used a revenue recognition policy similar to Wal-Mart's before the change, are there any concerns with respect to the qualitative characteristic of comparability? Explain.

Accounting, Analysis, and Principles

William Murray achieved one of his life-long dreams by opening his own business, The Caddie Shack Driving Range, on May 1, 2014. He invested $20,000 of his own savings in the business. He paid $6,000 cash to have a small building constructed to house the operations and spent $800 on golf clubs, golf balls, and yardage signs. Murray leased 4 acres of land at a cost of $1,000 per month. (He paid the first month's rent in cash.) During the first month, advertising costs totaled $750, of which $150 was unpaid at the end of the month. Murray paid his three nephews $400 for retrieving golf balls. He deposited in the company's bank account all revenues from customers ($4,700). On May 15, Murray withdrew $800 in cash for personal use. On May 31, the company received a utility bill for $100 but did not immediately pay it. On May 31, the balance in the company bank account was $15,100.

Murray is feeling pretty good about results for the first month, but his estimate of profitability ranges from a loss of $4,900 to a profit of $1,650.

Accounting

Prepare a balance sheet at May 31, 2014. Murray appropriately records any depreciation expense on a quarterly basis. How could Murray have determined that the business operated at a profit of $1,650? How could Murray conclude that the business operated at a loss of $4,900?

Analysis

Assume Murray has asked you to become a partner in his business. Under the partnership agreement, after paying him $10,000, you would share equally in all future profits. Which of the two income measures above would be more useful in deciding whether to become a partner? Explain.

Principles

What is income according to GAAP? What concepts do the differences in the three income measures for The Caddie Shack Driving Range illustrate?

BRIDGE TO THE PROFESSION

Professional Research

Your aunt recently received the annual report for a company in which she has invested. The report notes that the statements have been prepared in accordance with "generally accepted accounting principles." She has also heard that certain terms have special meanings in accounting relative to everyday use. She would like you to explain the meaning of terms she has come across related to accounting.

Instructions

Go to *http://www.fasb.org* and access the FASB Concepts Statements and respond to the following items. (Provide paragraph citations.) When you have accessed the documents, you can use the search tool in your Internet browser.

(a) How is "materiality" defined in the conceptual framework?

(b) The concepts statements provide several examples in which specific quantitative materiality guidelines are provided to firms. Identity at least two of these examples. Do you think the materiality guidelines should be quantified? Why or why not?

(c) The concepts statements discuss the concept of "articulation" between financial statement elements. Briefly summarize the meaning of this term and how it relates to an entity's financial statements.

Additional Professional Resources

See the book's companion website, at **www.wiley.com/college/kieso**, for professional simulations as well as other study resources.

IFRS > INSIGHTS

LEARNING OBJECTIVE 9

Compare the conceptual frameworks underlying GAAP and IFRS.

The IASB and the FASB are working on a joint project to develop a common conceptual framework. This framework is based on the existing conceptual frameworks underlying GAAP and IFRS. The objective of this joint project is to develop a conceptual framework that leads to standards that are principles-based and internally consistent and that leads to the most useful financial reporting.

RELEVANT FACTS

Following are the key similarities and differences between GAAP and IFRS related to the conceptual framework.

Similarities

- In 2010, the IASB and FASB completed the first phase of a jointly created conceptual framework. In this first phase, they agreed on the objective of financial reporting and a common set of desired qualitative characteristics. These were presented in the Chapter 2 discussion. Note that prior to this converged phase, the IASB Framework gave more emphasis to the objective of providing information on management's performance (stewardship).

- The existing conceptual frameworks underlying GAAP and IFRS are very similar. That is, they are organized in a similar manner (objective, elements, qualitative characteristics, etc.). There is no real need to change many aspects of the existing frameworks other than to converge different ways of discussing essentially the same concepts.

- The converged framework should be a single document, unlike the two conceptual frameworks that presently exist. It is unlikely that the basic structure related to the concepts will change.

- Both the IASB and FASB have similar measurement principles, based on historical cost and fair value. In 2011, the Boards issued a converged standard fair value measurement so that the definition of fair value, measurement techniques, and disclosures are the same between GAAP and IFRS when fair value is used in financial statements.

Differences

- Although both GAAP and IFRS are increasing the use of fair value to report assets, at this point IFRS has adopted it more broadly. As examples, under IFRS, companies can apply fair value to property, plant, and equipment; natural resources; and in some cases, intangible assets.

- GAAP has a concept statement to guide estimation of fair values when market-related data is not available (*Statement of Financial Accounting Concepts No. 7*, "Using Cash Flow Information and Present Value in Accounting"). The IASB has not issued a similar concept statement; it has issued a fair value standard *(IFRS 13)* that is converged with GAAP.

- The monetary unit assumption is part of each framework. However, the unit of measure will vary depending on the currency used in the country in which the company is incorporated (e.g., Chinese yuan, Japanese yen, and British pound). IFRS makes an explicit assumption that financial statements are prepared on an accrual basis.

- The economic entity assumption is also part of each framework, although some cultural differences result in differences in its application. For example, in Japan many companies have formed alliances that are so strong that they act similar to related corporate divisions although they are not actually part of the same company.

ABOUT THE NUMBERS

Financial Statement Elements

While the conceptual framework that underlies IFRS is very similar to that used to develop GAAP, the elements identified and their definitions under IFRS are different. The IASB elements and their definitions are as follows.

Assets. A resource controlled by the entity as a result of past events and from which future economic benefits are expected to flow to the entity.

Liabilities. A present obligation of the entity arising from past events, the settlement of which is expected to result in an outflow from the entity of resources embodying economic benefits. Liabilities may be legally enforceable via a contract or law, but need not be, i.e., they can arise due to normal business practice or customs.

Equity. A residual interest in the assets of the entity after deducting all its liabilities.

Income. Increases in economic benefits that result in increases in equity (other than those related to contributions from shareholders). Income includes both revenues (resulting from ordinary activities) and gains.

Expenses. Decreases in economic benefits that result in decreases in equity (other than those related to distributions to shareholders). Expenses includes losses that are not the result of ordinary activities.

Conceptual Framework Work Plan

The work on the conceptual framework is being done in phases. As discussed, Phase A related to objectives and qualitative characteristics has been issued in 2010. Work on the remaining core phases—(1) a chapter on the reporting entity (Phase D), (2) a chapter related to measurement (Phase C), and (3) elements and recognition (Phase B)—are currently on hold as the focus is on completing key convergence projects on revenue, financial instruments, and leases.

ON THE HORIZON

The IASB and the FASB face a difficult task in attempting to update, modify, and complete a converged conceptual framework. There are many difficult issues. For example: How do we trade off characteristics such as highly relevant information that is difficult to verify? How do we define control when we are developing a definition of an asset? Is a liability the future sacrifice itself or the obligation to make the sacrifice? Should a single measurement method, such as historical cost or fair value, be used, or does it depend on whether it is an asset or liability that is being measured? We are optimistic that the new document will be a significant improvement over its predecessors and will lead to principles-based standards that help users of the financial statements make better decisions.

IFRS SELF-TEST QUESTIONS

1. Which of the following statements about the IASB and FASB conceptual frameworks is **not** correct?
   (a) The IASB conceptual framework does not identify the element *comprehensive income*.
   (b) The existing IASB and FASB conceptual frameworks are organized in similar ways.
   (c) The FASB and IASB agree that the objective of financial reporting is to provide useful information to investors and creditors.
   (d) IFRS does not allow use of fair value as a measurement basis.
2. Which of the following statements is **false**?
   (a) The monetary unit assumption is used under IFRS.
   (b) Under IFRS, companies may use fair value for property, plant, and equipment.
   (c) The FASB and IASB are working on a joint conceptual framework project.
   (d) Under IFRS, there are the same number of financial statement elements as in GAAP.
3. Companies that use IFRS:
   (a) must report all their assets on the statement of financial position (balance sheet) at fair value.
   (b) may report property, plant, and equipment and natural resources at fair value.
   (c) may refer to a concept statement on estimating fair values when market data are not available.
   (d) may only use historical cost as the measurement basis in financial reporting.
4. The issues that the FASB and IASB must address in developing a common conceptual framework include all of the following **except**:
   (a) should the characteristic of relevance be traded-off in favor of information that is verifiable?
   (b) should a single measurement method such as historical cost be used?
   (c) should the common framework lead to standards that are principles-based or rules-based?
   (d) should the role of financial reporting focus on internal decision-making as well as providing information to assist users in decision-making?
5. With respect to the converged FASB/IASB conceptual framework:
   (a) work is being conducted on the framework as a whole, and it will not be issued until all parts are completed.
   (b) work on the framework has a higher priority than projects on revenue and leases.
   (c) work is being conducted on the framework in phases, and completed parts will be issued as completed.
   (d) the framework will not address measurement issues.

IFRS CONCEPTS AND APPLICATION

IFRS2-1 What two assumptions are central to the IASB conceptual framework?

IFRS2-2 Do the IASB and FASB conceptual frameworks differ in terms of the role of financial reporting? Explain.

IFRS2-3 What are some of the differences in elements in the IASB and FASB conceptual frameworks?

IFRS2-4 What are some of the challenges to the FASB and IASB in developing a converged conceptual framework?

Financial Reporting Case

IFRS2-5 As discussed in Chapter 1, the International Accounting Standards Board (IASB) develops accounting standards for many international companies. The IASB also has developed a conceptual framework to help guide the setting of accounting standards. While the FASB and IASB have issued converged concepts statements on the objective and qualitative characteristics, other parts of their frameworks differ.

Instructions

Briefly discuss the similarities and differences between the FASB and IASB conceptual frameworks as related to elements and their definitions.

Professional Research

IFRS2-6 Your aunt recently received the annual report for a company in which she has invested. The report notes that the statements have been prepared in accordance with IFRS. She has also heard that certain terms have special meanings in accounting relative to everyday use. She would like you to explain the meaning of terms she has come across related to accounting.

Instructions

Access the IASB Framework at the IASB website (*http://eifrs.iasb.org/*). (Click on the IFRS tab and then register for free eIFRS access if necessary.) When you have accessed the documents, you can use the search tool in your Internet browser to prepare responses to the following items. (Provide paragraph citations.)

- **(a)** How is "materiality" defined in the framework?
- **(b)** Briefly discuss how materiality relates to (1) the relevance of financial information, and (2) completeness.
- **(c)** Your aunt observes that under IFRS, the financial statements are prepared on the accrual basis. According to the framework, what does "accrual basis" mean?

International Financial Reporting Problem
Marks and Spencer plc

IFRS2-7 The financial statements of Marks and Spencer plc (M&S) are available at the book's companion website or can be accessed at *http://annualreport.marksandspencer.com/_assets/downloads/Marks-and-Spencer-Annual-report-and-financial-statements-2012.pdf*.

Instructions

Refer to M&S's financial statements and the accompanying notes to answer the following questions.

- **(a)** Using the notes to the consolidated financial statements, determine M&S's revenue recognition policies.
- **(b)** Give two examples of where historical cost information is reported in M&S's financial statements and related notes. Give two examples of the use of fair value information reported in either the financial statements or related notes.
- **(c)** How can we determine that the accounting principles used by M&S are prepared on a basis consistent with those of last year?
- **(d)** What is M&S's accounting policy related to refunds and loyalty schemes? Why does M&S include the accounting for refunds and loyalty schemes in its critical accounting estimates and judgments?

ANSWERS TO IFRS SELF-TEST QUESTIONS

1. d **2.** d **3.** b **4.** d **5.** c

> **Remember to check the book's companion website to find additional resources for this chapter.**

3 The Accounting Information System

Needed: A Reliable Information System

Maintaining a set of accounting records is not optional. Regulators require that businesses prepare and retain a set of records and documents that can be audited. The U.S. Foreign Corrupt Practices Act, for example, requires public companies to "make and keep books, records, and accounts, which, in reasonable detail, accurately and fairly reflect the transactions and dispositions of the assets." But beyond these two reasons, a company that fails to keep an accurate record of its business transactions may lose revenue and is more likely to operate inefficiently.

One reason accurate records are not provided is because of economic crime or corruption. It is clear that economic crime remains a persistent and difficult problem for many companies. For example, it was recently estimated that 53 percent of U.S. companies experienced significant economic crime. And its global counterparts are not far behind, with a reported rate of 43 percent. While global rates appear lower, U.S. companies often have more stringent internal controls and are more likely to find and report crime. Presented to the right is a chart that indicates the types of economic crime experienced in a recent period.

The top four economic crimes are asset misappropriation, accounting fraud, bribery and corruption, and cybercrime. Cybercrime is a new phenomenon as new types of fraud are emerging in this area. Smartphones and tablet devices, social media, and cloud computing all offer companies interesting business opportunities but can also lead to risks related to the disclosure of sensitive and confidential data.

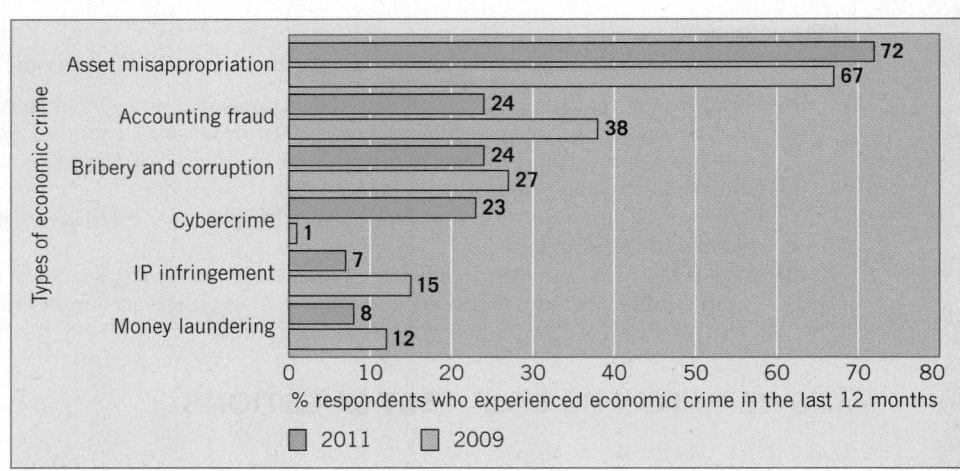

In some of these cases, such as money laundering or infringement of intellectual property, a sound system of internal controls focused on financial accounting and reporting may not work. Nonetheless, many believe that effective internal control sends a message that a company is serious about finding not only economic crime but also errors or misstatements. As a result, many companies are taking a proactive look as to how they can better prevent both economic crime as well as basic errors in their systems. The chart on the next page indicates the percentage of companies that identified certain factors influencing their decision to implement controls to deter economic crime.

Reasons for Internal Controls	U.S.	Global
Sarbanes-Oxley Act	99%	84%
U.S. Patriot Act	85	29
Advice from external consultants	63	50
FCPA/OECD Anti-Bribery Convention	38	23
Public discussion/media	38	33
Federal sentencing guidelines	38	29
Incidents of economic crime	31	34
Local legislation	24	51
Bad experience and/or advice from law enforcement	17	36

CONCEPTUAL FOCUS

> See the **Underlying Concepts** on page 90.

INTERNATIONAL FOCUS

> Read the **IFRS Insights** on pages 153–157 for a discussion of:
—Accounting system internal controls
—First-time adoption of IFRS

What happens when companies fail to keep an accurate record of their business transactions? Consider **Adecco**, the largest international employment services company, which confirmed existence of weakness in its internal controls systems and Adecco staffing operations in certain countries. Manipulation involved such matters as reconciliation of payroll bank accounts, accounts receivable, and documentation in revenue recognition. These irregularities forced an indefinite delay in reporting the company's income figures, which led to significant decline in share price. Or consider **Nortel Networks Corp.**, which overstated and understated its reserve accounts to manage its earnings. This eventually led to the liquidation of the company.

Even the use of computers is no assurance of accuracy and efficiency. "The conversion to a new system called MasterNet fouled up data processing records to the extent that **Bank of America** was frequently unable to produce or deliver customer statements on a timely basis," said an executive at one of the country's largest banks.

Although these situations may occur only rarely in large organizations, they illustrate the point: Companies must properly maintain accounts and detailed records or face unnecessary costs.

Sources: Adapted from "Economic Crime: People, Culture, and Controls," *The Fourth Biennial Global Economic Crime Survey* (Pricewaterhouse-Coopers, 2007); and "Cybercrime: Protecting Against the Growing Threat," *Global Economic Crime Survey* (PricewaterhouseCoopers, 2012).

PREVIEW OF CHAPTER **3**

As the opening story indicates, a reliable information system is a necessity for all companies. The purpose of this chapter is to explain and illustrate the features of an accounting information system. The content and organization of this chapter are as follows.

The Accounting Information System

Accounting Information System	The Accounting Cycle	Financial Statements for Merchandisers
• Basic terminology • Debits and credits • Accounting equation • Financial statements and ownership structure	• Identifying and recording • Journalizing • Posting • Trial balance • Adjusting entries • Adjusted trial balance • Preparing financial statements • Closing • Post-closing trial balance • Reversing entries	• Income statement • Statement of retained earnings • Balance sheet • Closing entries

ACCOUNTING INFORMATION SYSTEM

LEARNING OBJECTIVE **1**

Understand basic accounting terminology.

An **accounting information system** collects and processes transaction data and then disseminates the financial information to interested parties. Accounting information systems vary widely from one business to another. Various factors shape these systems: the nature of the business and the transactions in which it engages, the size of the firm, the volume of data to be handled, and the informational demands that management and others require.

As we discussed in Chapters 1 and 2, in response to the requirements of the Sarbanes-Oxley Act, companies are placing a renewed focus on their accounting systems to ensure relevant and reliable information is reported in financial statements.[1] A good accounting information system helps management answer such questions as:

- How much and what kind of debt is outstanding?
- Were our sales higher this period than last?
- What assets do we have?
- What were our cash inflows and outflows?
- Did we make a profit last period?
- Are any of our product lines or divisions operating at a loss?
- Can we safely increase our dividends to stockholders?
- Is our rate of return on net assets increasing?

Management can answer many other questions with the data provided by an efficient accounting system. A well-devised accounting information system benefits every type of company.

Basic Terminology

Financial accounting rests on a set of concepts (discussed in Chapters 1 and 2) for identifying, recording, classifying, and interpreting transactions and other events relating to enterprises. You therefore need to understand the **basic terminology employed in collecting accounting data**.

BASIC TERMINOLOGY

EVENT. A happening of consequence. An event generally is the source or cause of changes in assets, liabilities, and equity. Events may be external or internal.

TRANSACTION. An **external event** involving a transfer or exchange between two or more entities.

ACCOUNT. A systematic arrangement that shows the effect of transactions and other events on a specific element (asset, liability, and so on). Companies keep a separate account

---

[1]A recent survey indicated nearly one in three companies view the benefits of Sarbanes-Oxley (SOX) to outweigh its costs. Approximately half of the companies believe the costs exceed the benefits of SOX to some degree. Management view their companies generally as benefiting from SOX but overall have a slightly negative view toward the legislation. In a large percentage of companies, the internal control over financial reporting has improved since SOX became a requirement. See "Where U.S.-Listed Companies Stand: Reviewing Cost, Time, Effort and Processes," *2012 Sarbanes-Oxley Compliance Survey* (Protiviti Company, May 2012).

for each asset, liability, revenue, and expense, and for capital (owners' equity). Because the format of an account often resembles the letter T, it is sometimes referred to as a **T-account**. (See Illustration 3-3, page 87.)

REAL AND NOMINAL ACCOUNTS. **Real** (permanent) **accounts** are asset, liability, and equity accounts; they appear on the balance sheet. **Nominal** (temporary) **accounts** are revenue, expense, and dividend accounts; except for dividends, they appear on the income statement. Companies periodically close nominal accounts; they do not close real accounts.

LEDGER. The book (or computer printouts) containing the accounts. A **general ledger** is a collection of all the asset, liability, owners' equity, revenue, and expense accounts. A **subsidiary ledger** contains the details related to a given general ledger account.

JOURNAL. The "book of original entry" where the company initially records transactions and selected other events. Various amounts are transferred from the book of original entry, the journal, to the ledger. Entering transaction data in the journal is known as **journalizing**.

POSTING. The process of transferring the essential facts and figures from the book of original entry to the ledger accounts.

TRIAL BALANCE. The list of all open accounts in the ledger and their balances. The trial balance taken immediately after all adjustments have been posted is called an **adjusted trial balance**. A trial balance taken immediately after closing entries have been posted is called a **post-closing** (or **after-closing**) **trial balance**. Companies may prepare a trial balance at any time.

ADJUSTING ENTRIES. Entries made at the end of an accounting period to bring all accounts up to date on an accrual basis, so that the company can prepare correct financial statements.

FINANCIAL STATEMENTS. Statements that reflect the collection, tabulation, and final summarization of the accounting data. Four statements are involved. (1) The **balance sheet** shows the financial condition of the enterprise at the end of a period. (2) The **income statement** measures the results of operations during the period. (3) The **statement of cash flows** reports the cash provided and used by operating, investing, and financing activities during the period. (4) The **statement of retained earnings** reconciles the balance of the retained earnings account from the beginning to the end of the period.

CLOSING ENTRIES. The formal process by which the enterprise reduces all nominal accounts to zero and determines and transfers the net income or net loss to an owners' equity account. Also known as "closing the ledger," "closing the books," or merely "closing."

Debits and Credits

The terms **debit** (Dr.) and **credit** (Cr.) mean left and right, respectively. These terms do not mean increase or decrease, but instead describe *where* a company makes entries in the recording process. That is, when a company enters an amount on the left side of an account, it **debits** the account. When it makes an entry on the right side, it **credits** the account. When comparing the totals of the two sides, an account shows a **debit balance** if the total of the debit amounts exceeds the credits. An account shows a **credit balance** if the credit amounts exceed the debits.

The positioning of debits on the left and credits on the right is simply an accounting custom. We could function just as well if we reversed the sides. However, the United

2 LEARNING OBJECTIVE

Explain double-entry rules.

States adopted the custom, now the rule, of having debits on the left side of an account and credits on the right side, similar to the custom of driving on the right-hand side of the road. This rule applies to all accounts.

The equality of debits and credits provides the basis for the double-entry system of recording transactions (sometimes referred to as double-entry bookkeeping). Under the universally used **double-entry accounting** system, a company records the dual (two-sided) effect of each transaction in appropriate accounts. This system provides a logical method for recording transactions. It also offers a means of proving the accuracy of the recorded amounts. If a company records every transaction with equal debits and credits, then the sum of all the debits to the accounts must equal the sum of all the credits.

Illustration 3-1 presents the basic guidelines for an accounting system. Increases to all asset and expense accounts occur on the left (or debit side) and decreases on the right (or credit side). Conversely, increases to all liability and revenue accounts occur on the right (or credit side) and decreases on the left (or debit side). A company increases stockholders' equity accounts, such as Common Stock and Retained Earnings, on the credit side, but increases Dividends on the debit side.

ILLUSTRATION 3-1
Double-Entry (Debit and Credit) Accounting System

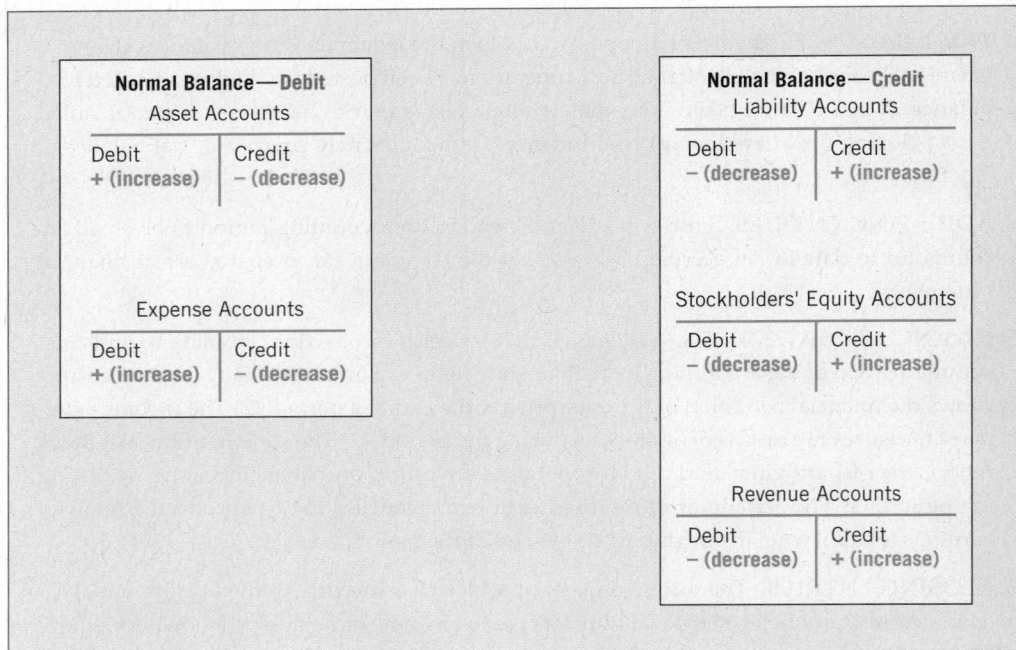

The Accounting Equation

In a double-entry system, for every debit there must be a credit, and vice versa. This leads us, then, to the basic equation in accounting (Illustration 3-2).

ILLUSTRATION 3-2
The Basic Accounting Equation

Illustration 3-3 expands this equation to show the accounts that make up stockholders' equity. The figure also shows the debit/credit rules and effects on each type of account. Study this diagram carefully. It will help you understand the fundamentals of the double-entry system. Like the basic equation, the expanded equation must also balance (total debits equal total credits).

ILLUSTRATION 3-3
Expanded Equation and Debit/Credit Rules and Effects

Every time a transaction occurs, the elements of the accounting equation change. However, the basic equality remains. To illustrate, consider the following eight different transactions for Perez Inc.

1. Owners invest $40,000 in exchange for common stock.

2. Disburse $600 cash for secretarial wages.

3. Purchase office equipment priced at $5,200, giving a 10 percent promissory note in exchange.

4. Receive $4,000 cash for services performed.

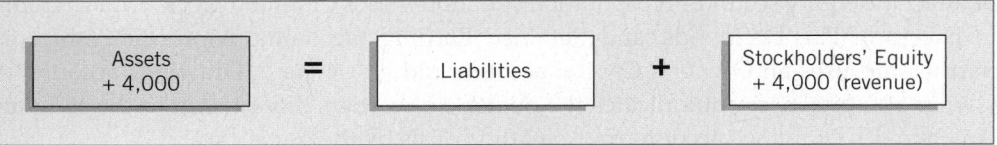

5. Pay off a short-term liability of $7,000.

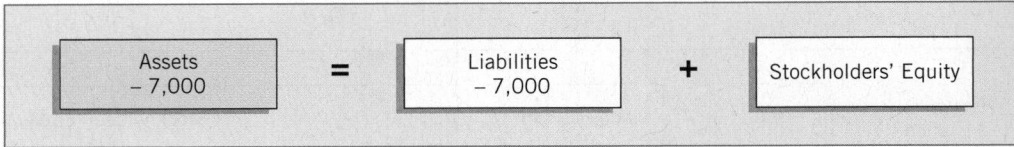

6. Declare a cash dividend of $5,000.

7. Convert a long-term liability of $80,000 into common stock.

8. Pay cash of $16,000 for a delivery van.

Financial Statements and Ownership Structure

The stockholders' equity section of the balance sheet reports common stock and retained earnings. The income statement reports revenues and expenses. The statement of retained earnings reports dividends. Because a company transfers dividends, revenues, and expenses to retained earnings at the end of the period, a change in any one of these three items affects stockholders' equity. Illustration 3-4 shows the stockholders' equity relationships.

The company's ownership structure dictates the types of accounts that are part of, or affect the equity section. A corporation commonly uses Common Stock, Paid-in Capital in Excess of Par, Dividends, and Retained Earnings accounts. A proprietorship or a partnership uses an Owner's Capital account and an Owner's Drawings account. An Owner's Capital account indicates the owner's or owners' investment in the company. An Owner's Drawings account tracks withdrawals by the owner(s).

ILLUSTRATION 3-4
Financial Statements and
Ownership Structure

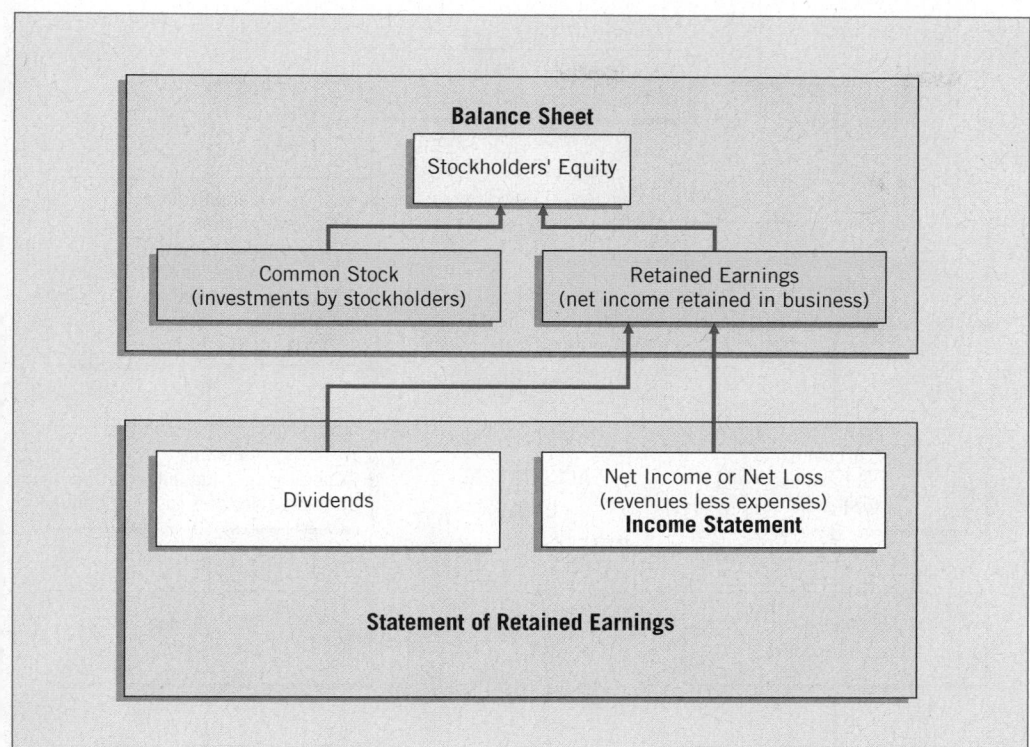

Illustration 3-5 summarizes and relates the transactions affecting owners' equity to the nominal (temporary) and real (permanent) classifications and to the types of business ownership.

ILLUSTRATION 3-5
Effects of Transactions on
Owners' Equity Accounts

		Ownership Structure			
		Proprietorships and Partnerships		Corporations	
Transactions Affecting Owners' Equity	Impact on Owners' Equity	Nominal (Temporary) Accounts	Real (Permanent) Accounts	Nominal (Temporary) Accounts	Real (Permanent) Accounts
Investment by owner(s)	Increase		Capital		Common Stock and related accounts
Revenues recognized	Increase	Revenue		Revenue	
Expenses incurred	Decrease	Expense }	Capital	Expense }	Retained
Withdrawal by owner(s)	Decrease	Drawing		Dividends	Earnings

THE ACCOUNTING CYCLE

Illustration 3-6 (on page 90) shows the steps in the **accounting cycle**. A company normally uses these accounting procedures to record transactions and prepare financial statements.

3 LEARNING OBJECTIVE
Identify steps in the accounting cycle.

Identifying and Recording Transactions and Other Events

The first step in the accounting cycle is analysis of transactions and selected other events. The first problem is to determine what to record. Although GAAP provides guidelines, no simple rules exist that state which events a company should record. Although

ILLUSTRATION 3-6
The Accounting Cycle

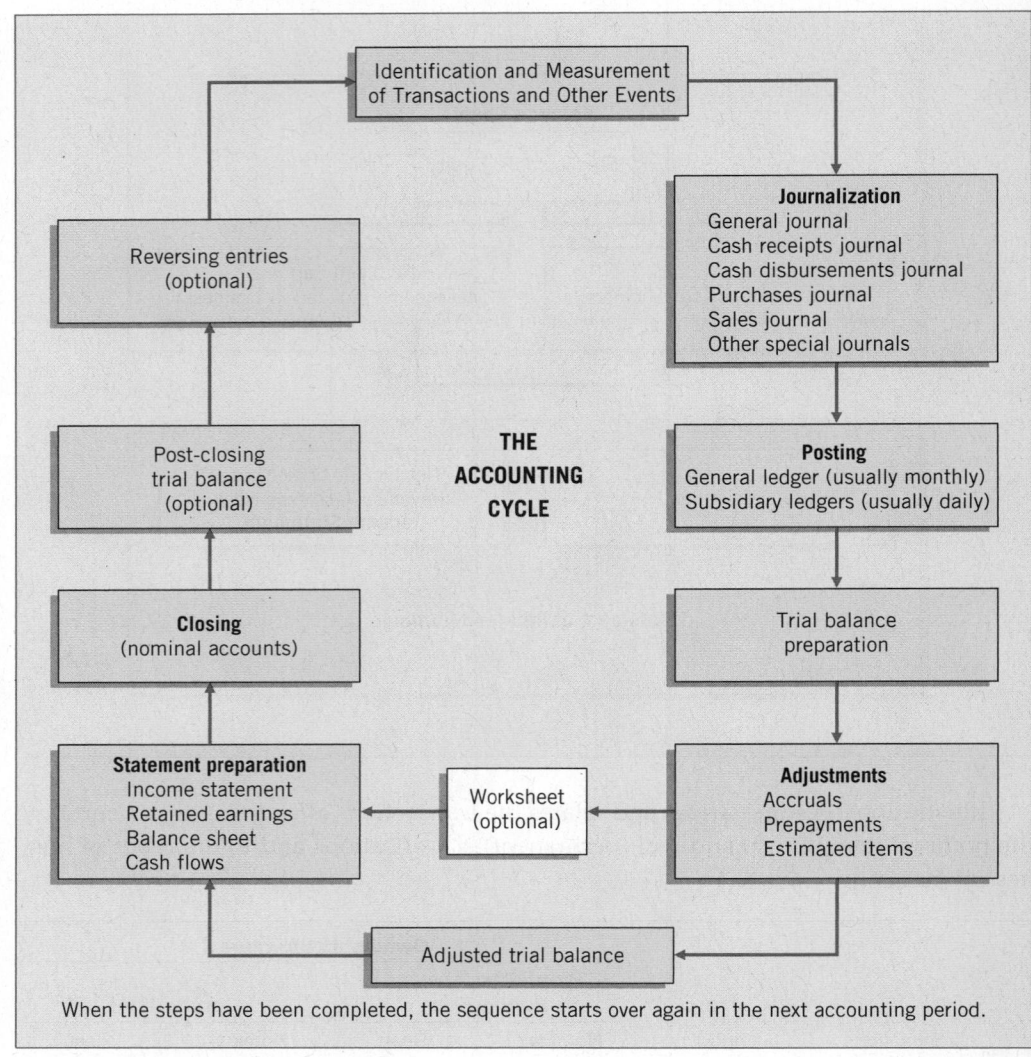

THE ACCOUNTING CYCLE

- Identification and Measurement of Transactions and Other Events
- **Journalization**
  General journal
  Cash receipts journal
  Cash disbursements journal
  Purchases journal
  Sales journal
  Other special journals
- **Posting**
  General ledger (usually monthly)
  Subsidiary ledgers (usually daily)
- Trial balance preparation
- **Adjustments**
  Accruals
  Prepayments
  Estimated items
- Worksheet (optional)
- **Statement preparation**
  Income statement
  Retained earnings
  Balance sheet
  Cash flows
- **Closing** (nominal accounts)
- Post-closing trial balance (optional)
- Reversing entries (optional)
- Adjusted trial balance

When the steps have been completed, the sequence starts over again in the next accounting period.

changes in a company's personnel or managerial policies may be important, the company should not record these items in the accounts. On the other hand, a company should record all cash sales or purchases—no matter how small.

The concepts we presented in Chapter 2 determine what to recognize in the accounts. An item should be recognized in the financial statements if it is an element, is measurable, and is relevant and representationally faithful. Consider human resources. **R. G. Barry & Co.** at one time reported as supplemental data total assets of $14,055,926, including $986,094 for "Net investments in human resources." **AT&T** and **ExxonMobil** also experimented with human resource accounting. Should we value employees for balance sheet and income statement purposes? Certainly skilled employees are an important asset (highly relevant), but the problems of determining their value and measuring it reliably have not yet been solved. Consequently, human resources are not recorded. Perhaps when measurement techniques become more sophisticated and accepted, such information will be presented, if only in supplemental form.

The FASB uses the phrase "transactions and other events and circumstances that affect a business enterprise" to describe the sources or causes of changes in an entity's assets, liabilities, and equity.[2] Events are of two types. (1) **External**

Underlying Concepts

Assets are probable economic benefits controlled by a particular entity as a result of a past transaction or event. Do human resources of a company meet this definition?

[2]"Elements of Financial Statements of Business Enterprises," *Statement of Financial Accounting Concepts No. 6* (Stamford, Conn.: FASB, 1985), pp. 259–260.

events involve interaction between an entity and its environment, such as a transaction with another entity, a change in the price of a good or service that an entity buys or sells, a flood or earthquake, or an improvement in technology by a competitor. (2) **Internal events** occur within an entity, such as using buildings and machinery in operations, or transferring or consuming raw materials in production processes.

Many events have both external and internal elements. For example, hiring an employee, which involves an exchange of salary for labor, is an external event. Using the services of labor is part of production, an internal event. Further, an entity may initiate and control events, such as the purchase of merchandise or use of a machine. Or, events may be beyond its control, such as an interest rate change, theft, or a tax hike.

Transactions are types of external events. They may be an exchange between two entities where each receives and sacrifices value, such as purchases and sales of goods or services. Or, transactions may be transfers in one direction only. For example, an entity may incur a liability without directly receiving value in exchange, such as charitable contributions. Other examples include investments by owners, distributions to owners, payment of taxes, gifts, casualty losses, and thefts.

In short, a company records as many events as possible that affect its financial position. As discussed earlier in the case of human resources, it omits some events because of tradition and others because of complicated measurement problems. Recently, however, the accounting profession shows more receptiveness to accepting the challenge of measuring and reporting events previously viewed as too complex and immeasurable.

Journalizing

A company records in **accounts** those transactions and events that affect its assets, liabilities, and equities. The **general ledger** contains all the asset, liability, and stockholders' equity accounts. An account (see Illustration 3-3, on page 87) shows the effect of transactions on particular asset, liability, equity, revenue, and expense accounts.

4 LEARNING OBJECTIVE
Record transactions in journals, post to ledger accounts, and prepare a trial balance.

In practice, companies do not record transactions and selected other events originally in the ledger. A transaction affects two or more accounts, each of which is on a different page in the ledger. Therefore, in order to have a complete record of each transaction or other event in one place, a company uses a **journal** (also called "the book of original entry"). In its simplest form, a **general journal** chronologically lists transactions and other events, expressed in terms of debits and credits to accounts.

Illustration 3-7 shows the technique of journalizing, using the first two transactions for Softbyte, Inc. These transactions were:

September 1   Stockholders invested $15,000 cash in the corporation in exchange for shares of stock.
                 Purchased computer equipment for $7,000 cash.

The J1 indicates these two entries are on the first page of the general journal.

GENERAL JOURNAL				J1
Date	Account Titles and Explanation	Ref.	Debit	Credit
2014 Sept. 1	Cash		15,000	
	Common Stock			15,000
	(Issued shares of stock for cash)			
1	Equipment		7,000	
	Cash			7,000
	(Purchased equipment for cash)			

ILLUSTRATION 3-7
Technique of Journalizing

Each **general journal entry** consists of four parts: (1) the accounts and amounts to be debited (Dr.), (2) the accounts and amounts to be credited (Cr.), (3) a date, and (4) an explanation. A company enters debits first, followed by the credits (slightly indented). The explanation begins below the name of the last account to be credited and may take one or more lines. A company completes the "Ref." column at the time it posts the accounts.

In some cases, a company uses **special journals** in addition to the general journal. Special journals summarize transactions possessing a common characteristic (e.g., cash receipts, sales, purchases, cash payments). As a result, using them reduces bookkeeping time.

Gateway to the Profession

Expanded Discussion of Special Journals

Posting

Transferring journal entries to the ledger accounts is called **posting**. Posting involves the following steps.

1. In the **ledger**, in the appropriate columns of the account(s) debited, enter the date, journal page, and debit amount shown in the journal.

2. In the reference column of the **journal**, write the account number to which the debit amount was posted.

3. In the **ledger**, in the appropriate columns of the account(s) credited, enter the date, journal page, and credit amount shown in the journal.

4. In the reference column of the **journal**, write the account number to which the credit amount was posted.

Illustration 3-8 diagrams these four steps, using the first journal entry of Softbyte, Inc. The illustration shows the general ledger accounts in **standard account form**. Some companies call this form the **three-column form of account** because it has three money

ILLUSTRATION 3-8
Posting a Journal Entry

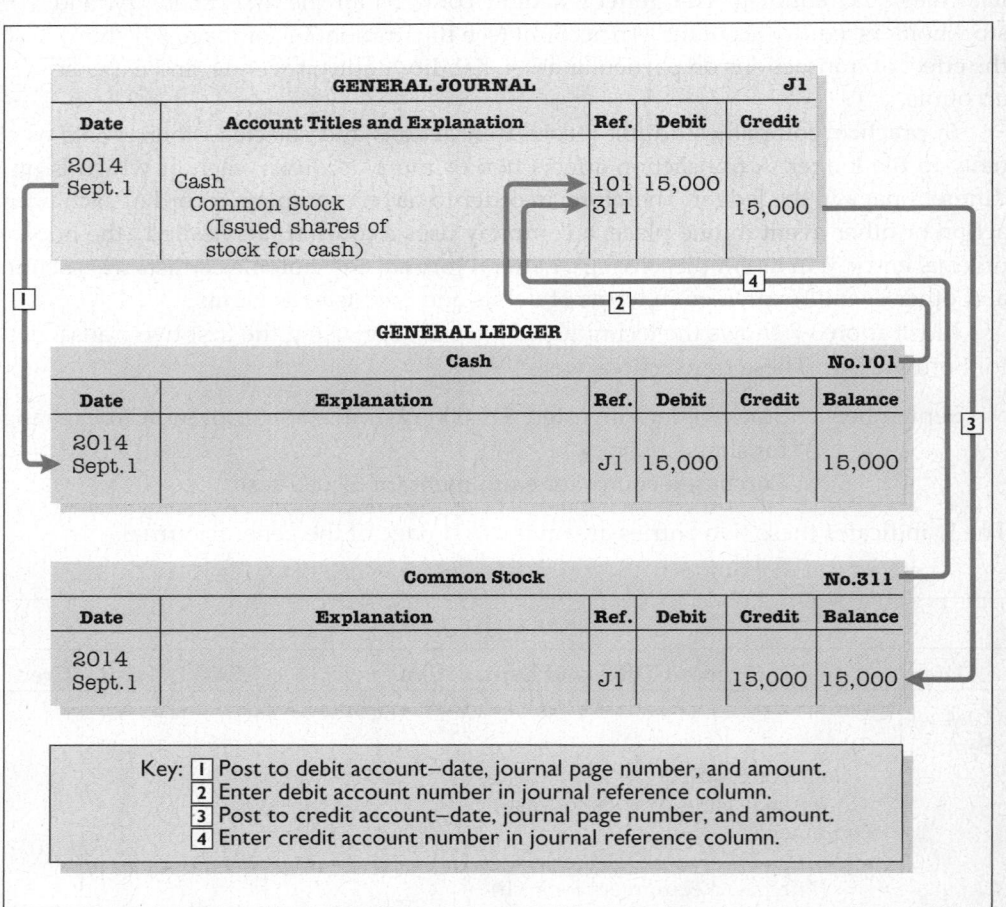

columns—debit, credit, and balance. The balance in the account is determined after each transaction. The explanation space and reference columns provide special information about the transaction. The boxed numbers indicate the sequence of the steps.

The numbers in the "Ref." column of the general journal refer to the ledger accounts to which a company posts the respective items. For example, the "101" placed in the column to the right of "Cash" indicates that the company posted this $15,000 item to Account No. 101 in the ledger.

The posting of the general journal is completed when a company records all of the posting reference numbers opposite the account titles in the journal. Thus, the number in the posting reference column serves two purposes. (1) It indicates the ledger account number of the account involved. (2) It indicates the completion of posting for the particular item. Each company selects its own numbering system for its ledger accounts. Many begin numbering with asset accounts and then follow with liabilities, owners' equity, revenue, and expense accounts, in that order.

The ledger accounts in Illustration 3-8 show the accounts after completion of the posting process. The reference J1 (General Journal, page 1) indicates the source of the data transferred to the ledger account.

An Expanded Example

To show an expanded example of the basic steps in the recording process, we use the October transactions of Pioneer Advertising Agency Inc. Pioneer's accounting period is a month. Illustrations 3-9 through 3-18 show the journal entry and posting of each transaction. For simplicity, we use a T-account form instead of the standard account form. Study the transaction analyses carefully.

The purpose of transaction analysis is (1) to identify the type of account involved, and (2) to determine whether a debit or a credit is required. You should always perform this type of analysis before preparing a journal entry. Doing so will help you understand the journal entries discussed in this chapter as well as more complex journal entries in later chapters. Keep in mind that every journal entry affects one or more of the following items: assets, liabilities, stockholders' equity, revenues, or expenses.

1. October 1: Stockholders invest $100,000 cash in an advertising venture to be known as Pioneer Advertising Agency Inc.

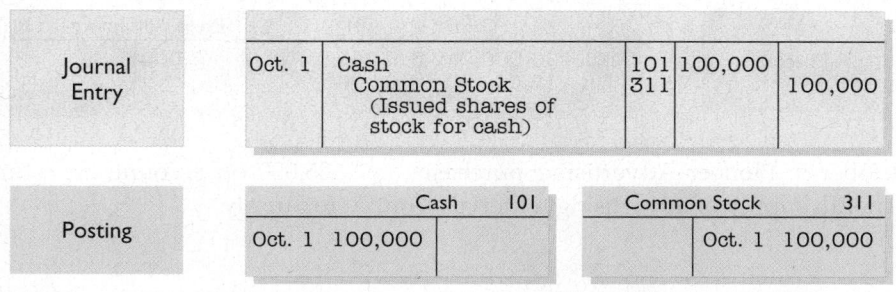

ILLUSTRATION 3-9
Investment of Cash by Stockholders

2. October 1: Pioneer Advertising purchases office equipment costing $50,000 by signing a 3-month, 12%, $50,000 note payable.

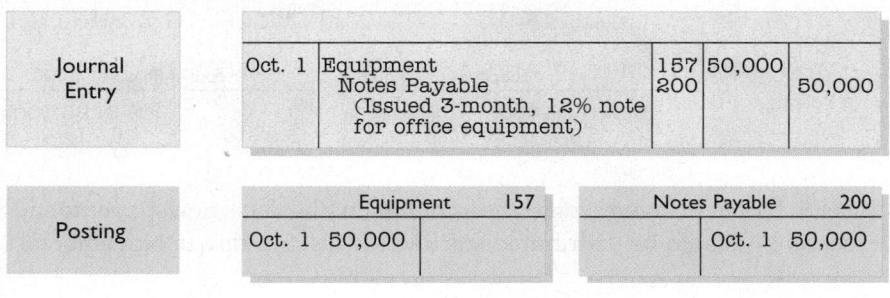

ILLUSTRATION 3-10
Purchase of Office Equipment

3. October 2: Pioneer Advertising receives a $12,000 cash advance from R. Knox, a client, for advertising services that are expected to be completed by December 31.

ILLUSTRATION 3-11
Receipt of Cash for
Future Service

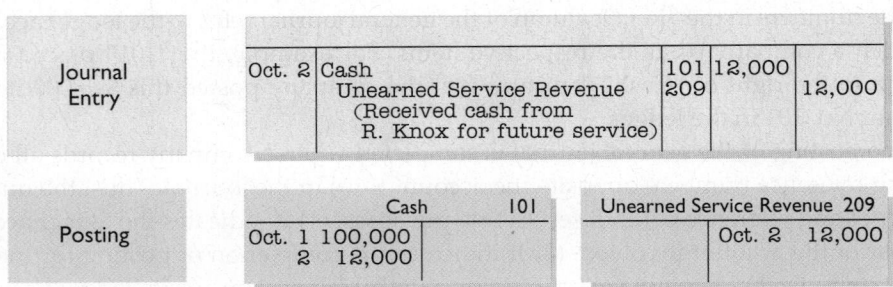

4. October 3: Pioneer Advertising pays $9,000 office rent, in cash, for October.

ILLUSTRATION 3-12
Payment of Monthly
Rent

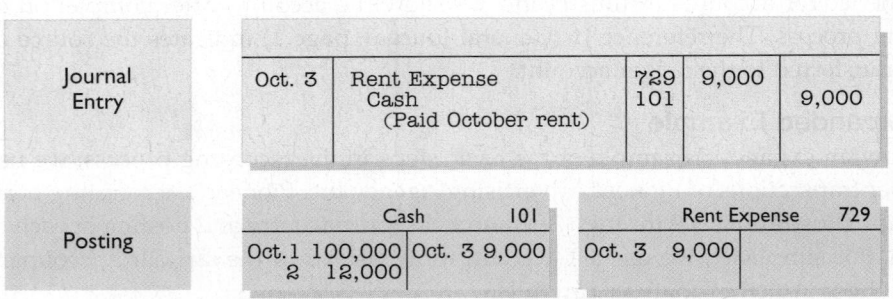

5. October 4: Pioneer Advertising pays $6,000 for a one-year insurance policy that will expire next year on September 30.

ILLUSTRATION 3-13
Payment for Insurance

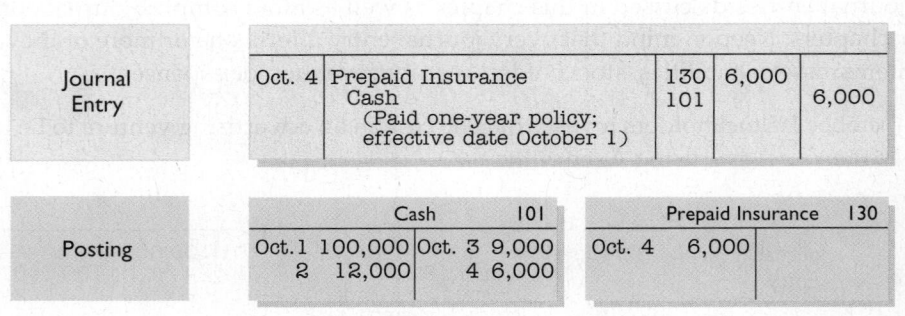

6. October 5: Pioneer Advertising purchases, for $25,000 on account, an estimated 3-month supply of advertising materials from Aero Supply.

ILLUSTRATION 3-14
Purchase of Supplies on
Account

7. October 9: Pioneer Advertising signs a contract with a local newspaper for advertising inserts (flyers) to be distributed starting the last Sunday in November. Pioneer will start work on the content of the flyers in November. Payment of $7,000 is due following delivery of the Sunday papers containing the flyers.

Journal Entry	A business transaction has not occurred. There is only an agreement between Pioneer Advertising and the newspaper for the services to be performed in November. Therefore, no journal entry is necessary in October.

ILLUSTRATION 3-15
Signing a Contract

8. October 20: Pioneer Advertising's board of directors declares and pays a $5,000 cash dividend to stockholders.

ILLUSTRATION 3-16
Declaration and Payment of Dividend by Corporation

Journal Entry	Oct. 20	Dividends	332	5,000	
		Cash	101		5,000
		(Declared and paid a cash dividend)			

Posting

Cash	101		
Oct.1	100,000	Oct. 3	9,000
2	12,000	4	6,000
		20	5,000

Dividends	332		
Oct. 20	5,000		

9. October 26: Pioneer Advertising pays employee salaries and wages in cash. Employees are paid once a month, every four weeks. The total payroll is $10,000 per week, or $2,000 per day. In October, the pay period began on Monday, October 1. As a result, the pay period ended on Friday, October 26, with salaries and wages of $40,000 being paid.

ILLUSTRATION 3-17
Payment of Salaries and Wages

Journal Entry	Oct. 26	Salaries and Wages Expense	726	40,000	
		Cash	101		40,000
		(Paid salaries to date)			

Posting

Cash	101		
Oct.1	100,000	Oct.3	9,000
2	12,000	4	6,000
		20	5,000
		26	40,000

Salaries and Wages Expense	726	
Oct.26	40,000	

10. October 31: Pioneer Advertising receives $28,000 in cash and bills Copa Company $72,000 for advertising services of $100,000 performed in October.

ILLUSTRATION 3-18
Recognize Revenue for Services Performed

Journal Entry	Oct. 31	Cash	101	28,000	
		Accounts Receivable	112	72,000	
		Service Revenue	400		100,000
		(Recognize revenue for services performed)			

Posting

Cash	101		
Oct.1	100,000	Oct.3	9,000
2	12,000	4	6,000
31	28,000	20	5,000
		26	40,000

Accounts Receivable	112	
Oct. 31	72,000	

Service Revenue	400	
	Oct. 31	100,000

Trial Balance

A **trial balance** is a list of accounts and their balances at a given time. A company usually prepares a trial balance at the end of an accounting period. The trial balance lists the accounts in the order in which they appear in the ledger, with debit balances listed in the left column and credit balances in the right column. The totals of the two columns must agree.

The trial balance proves the mathematical equality of debits and credits after posting. Under the double-entry system, this equality occurs when the sum of the debit account balances equals the sum of the credit account balances. A trial balance also uncovers errors in journalizing and posting. In addition, it is useful in the preparation of financial statements. The procedures for preparing a trial balance consist of:

1. List the account titles and their balances in the appropriate debit or credit column.
2. Total the debit and credit columns.
3. Prove the equality of the two columns.

Illustration 3-19 presents the trial balance prepared from the ledger of Pioneer Advertising Agency Inc. Note that the total debits ($287,000) equal the total credits ($287,000). A trial balance also often shows account numbers to the left of the account titles.

ILLUSTRATION 3-19
Trial Balance
(Unadjusted)

PIONEER ADVERTISING AGENCY INC.
TRIAL BALANCE
OCTOBER 31, 2014

	Debit	Credit
Cash	$ 80,000	
Accounts Receivable	72,000	
Supplies	25,000	
Prepaid Insurance	6,000	
Equipment	50,000	
Notes Payable		$ 50,000
Accounts Payable		25,000
Unearned Service Revenue		12,000
Common Stock		100,000
Dividends	5,000	
Service Revenue		100,000
Salaries and Wages Expense	40,000	
Rent Expense	9,000	
	$287,000	$287,000

A trial balance does not prove that a company recorded all transactions or that the ledger is correct. Numerous errors may exist even though the trial balance columns agree. For example, the trial balance may balance even when a company (1) fails to journalize a transaction, (2) omits posting a correct journal entry, (3) posts a journal entry twice, (4) uses incorrect accounts in journalizing or posting, or (5) makes offsetting errors in recording the amount of a transaction. In other words, as long as a company posts equal debits and credits, even to the wrong account or in the wrong amount, the total debits will equal the total credits.

LEARNING OBJECTIVE 5
Explain the reasons for preparing adjusting entries and identify major types of adjusting entries.

Adjusting Entries

In order for revenues to be recorded in the period in which services are performed and for expenses to be recognized in the period in which they are incurred, companies make **adjusting entries**. In short, adjustments ensure that a company like McDonald's follows the revenue recognition and expense recognition principles.

The use of adjusting entries makes it possible to report on the balance sheet the appropriate assets, liabilities, and owners' equity at the statement date. Adjusting entries also make it possible to report on the income statement the proper revenues and expenses for the period. However, the trial balance—the first pulling together of the transaction data—may not contain up-to-date and complete data. This occurs for the following reasons.

1. Some events are not recorded daily because it is not efficient to do so. Examples are the use of supplies and the earning of wages by employees.

2. Some costs are not recorded during the accounting period because these costs expire with the passage of time rather than as a result of recurring daily transactions. Examples of such costs are building and equipment depreciation and rent and insurance.

3. Some items may be unrecorded. An example is a utility service bill that will not be received until the next accounting period.

Adjusting entries are required every time a company, such as Coca-Cola, prepares financial statements. At that time, Coca-Cola must analyze each account in the trial balance to determine whether it is complete and up-to-date for financial statement purposes. The analysis requires a thorough understanding of Coca-Cola's operations and the interrelationship of accounts. Because of this involved process, usually a skilled accountant prepares the adjusting entries. In gathering the adjustment data, Coca-Cola may need to make inventory counts of supplies and repair parts. Further, it may prepare supporting schedules of insurance policies, rental agreements, and other contractual commitments. Companies often prepare adjustments after the balance sheet date. However, they date the entries as of the balance sheet date.

Types of Adjusting Entries

Adjusting entries are classified as either deferrals or accruals. Each of these classes has two subcategories, as Illustration 3-20 shows.

Deferrals:

1. **Prepaid expenses:** Expenses paid in cash before they are used or consumed.
2. **Unearned revenues:** Cash received before services are performed.

Accruals:

1. **Accrued revenues:** Revenues for services performed but not yet received in cash or recorded.
2. **Accrued expenses:** Expenses incurred but not yet paid in cash or recorded.

ILLUSTRATION 3-20
Categories of Adjusting Entries

We review specific examples and explanations of each type of adjustment in subsequent sections. We base each example on the October 31 trial balance of Pioneer Advertising Agency Inc. (Illustration 3-19). We assume that Pioneer uses an accounting period of one month. Thus, Pioneer will make monthly adjusting entries, dated October 31.

Adjusting Entries for Deferrals

To defer means to postpone or delay. **Deferrals** are expenses or revenues that are recognized at a date later than the point when cash was originally exchanged. The two types of deferrals are prepaid expenses and unearned revenues.

If a company does not make an adjustment for these deferrals, the asset and liability are overstated, and the related expense and revenue are understated. For example, in Pioneer's trial balance (Illustration 3-19), the balance in the asset Supplies shows only supplies purchased. This balance is overstated; the related expense account, Supplies Expense, is understated because the cost of supplies used has not been recognized. Thus, the adjusting entry for deferrals will decrease a balance sheet account and increase an income statement account. Illustration 3-21 shows the effects of adjusting entries for deferrals.

ILLUSTRATION 3-21
Adjusting Entries for
Deferrals

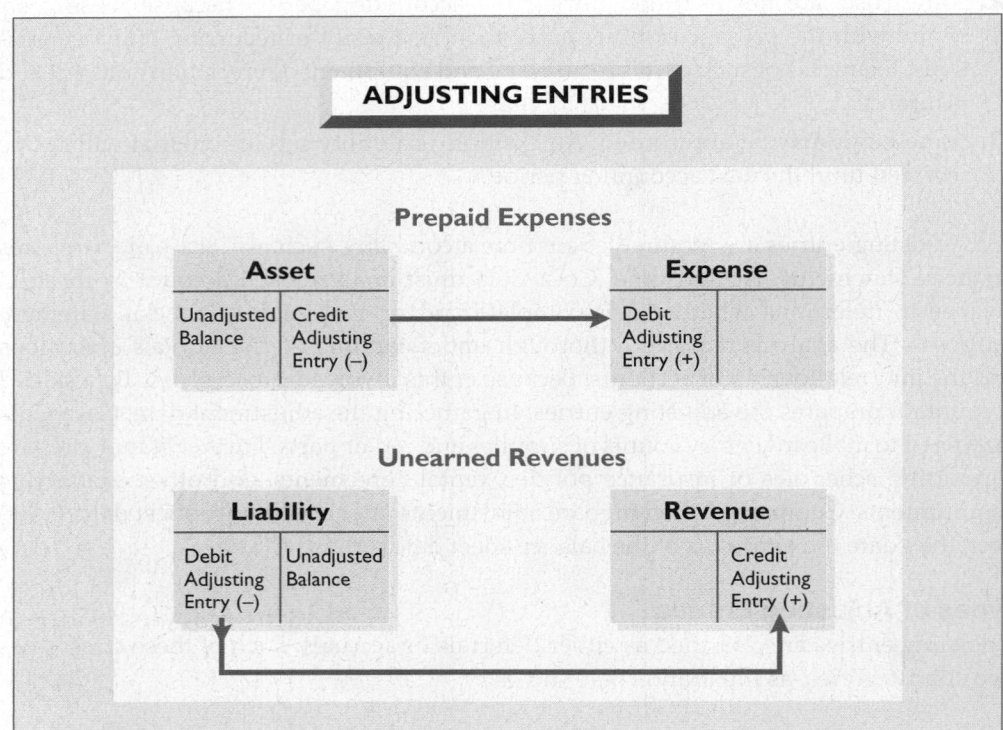

Prepaid Expenses. Assets paid for and recorded before a company uses them are called **prepaid expenses**. When expenses are prepaid, a company debits an asset account to show the service or benefit it will receive in the future. Examples of common prepayments are insurance, supplies, advertising, and rent. In addition, companies make prepayments when they purchase buildings and equipment.

Prepaid expenses are costs that expire either with the passage of time (e.g., rent and insurance) or through use and consumption (e.g., supplies). The expiration of these costs does not require daily entries, an unnecessary and impractical task. Accordingly, a company like **Walgreens** usually postpones the recognition of such cost expirations until it prepares financial statements. At each statement date, Walgreens makes adjusting entries to record the expenses that apply to the current accounting period and to show the remaining amounts in the asset accounts.

As shown above, prior to adjustment, assets are overstated and expenses are understated. **Thus, an adjusting entry for prepaid expenses results in a debit to an expense account and a credit to an asset account.**

Supplies. A business may use several different types of supplies. For example, a CPA firm will use office supplies such as stationery, envelopes, and accounting paper. An advertising firm will stock advertising supplies such as graph paper, video film, and poster paper. Supplies are generally debited to an asset account when they are acquired. Recognition of supplies used is generally deferred until the adjustment process. At that time, a physical inventory (count) of supplies is taken. The difference between the balance in the Supplies (asset) account and the cost of supplies on hand represents the supplies used (an expense) for the period.

For example, Pioneer Advertising purchased advertising supplies costing $25,000 on October 5. Pioneer therefore debited the asset Supplies. This account shows a balance of $25,000 in the October 31 trial balance (see Illustration 3-19 on page 96). An inventory count at the close of business on October 31 reveals that $10,000 of supplies are still on hand. Thus, the cost of supplies used is $15,000 ($25,000 − $10,000). The analysis and adjustment for advertising supplies is summarized in Illustration 3-22.

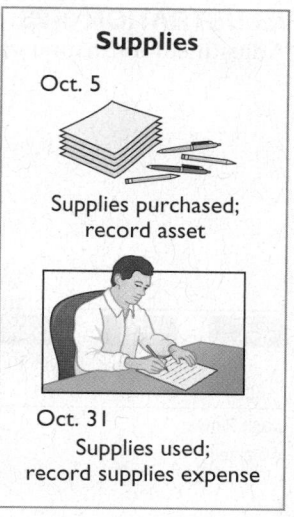

Supplies

Oct. 5

Supplies purchased;
record asset

Oct. 31
Supplies used;
record supplies expense

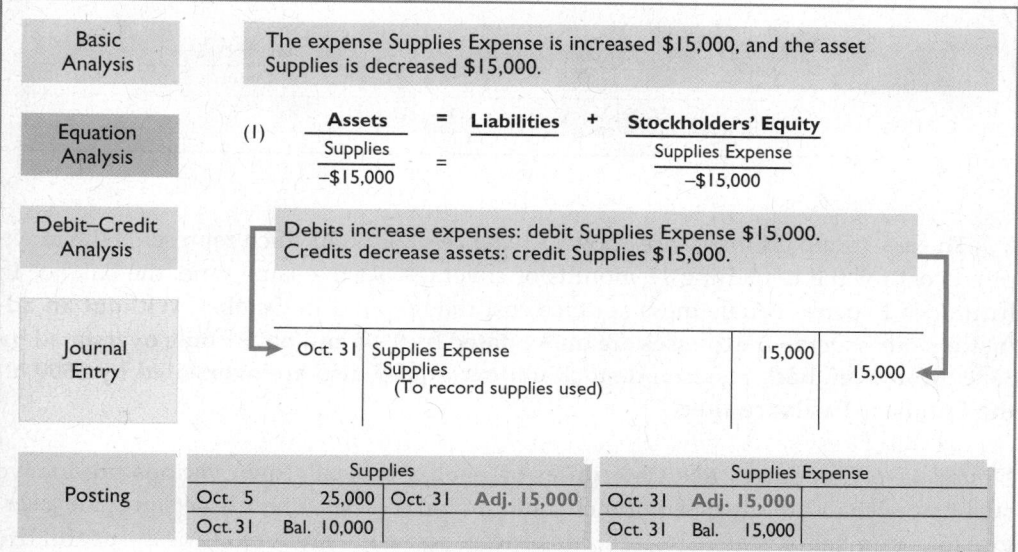

Basic Analysis	The expense Supplies Expense is increased $15,000, and the asset Supplies is decreased $15,000.		

Equation Analysis

(1)

Assets	**=**	**Liabilities**	**+**	**Stockholders' Equity**
Supplies				Supplies Expense
−$15,000	=			−$15,000

Debit–Credit Analysis

Debits increase expenses: debit Supplies Expense $15,000.
Credits decrease assets: credit Supplies $15,000.

Journal Entry

Oct. 31	Supplies Expense	15,000	
	Supplies		15,000
	(To record supplies used)		

Posting

Supplies				Supplies Expense		
Oct. 5	25,000	Oct. 31	Adj. 15,000	Oct. 31	Adj. 15,000	
Oct. 31	Bal. 10,000			Oct. 31	Bal. 15,000	

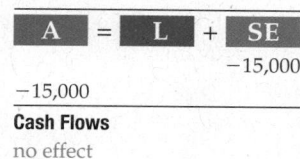

A	=	L	+	SE

−15,000

−15,000

Cash Flows
no effect

ILLUSTRATION 3-22
Adjustment for Supplies

After adjustment, the asset account Supplies shows a balance of $10,000, which equals the cost of supplies on hand at the statement date. In addition, Supplies Expense shows a balance of $15,000, which equals the cost of supplies used in October. **Without an adjusting entry, October expenses are understated and net income overstated by $15,000. Moreover, both assets and stockholders' equity are overstated by $15,000 on the October 31 balance sheet.**

Insurance. Most companies maintain fire and theft insurance on merchandise and equipment, personal liability insurance for accidents suffered by customers, and automobile insurance on company cars and trucks. The extent of protection against loss determines the cost of the insurance (the amount of the premium to be paid). The insurance policy specifies the term and coverage. The minimum term usually covers one year, but three- to five-year terms are available and may offer lower annual premiums. A company usually debits insurance premiums to the asset account Prepaid Insurance when paid. At the financial statement date, it then debits Insurance Expense and credits Prepaid Insurance for the cost that expired during the period.

For example, on October 4, Pioneer Advertising paid $6,000 for a one-year fire insurance policy. Coverage began on October 1. Pioneer debited the cost of the premium to Prepaid Insurance at that time. This account still shows a balance of $6,000 in the October 31 trial balance. The analysis and adjustment for insurance is summarized in Illustration 3-23 (page 100).

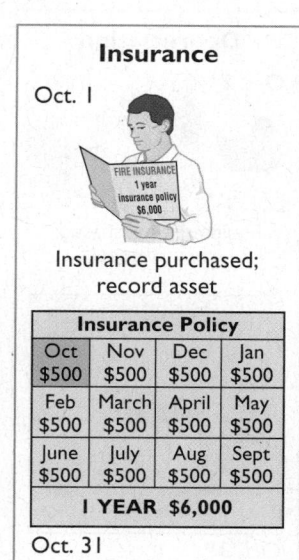

Insurance

Oct. 1

Insurance purchased;
record asset

Insurance Policy			
Oct $500	Nov $500	Dec $500	Jan $500
Feb $500	March $500	April $500	May $500
June $500	July $500	Aug $500	Sept $500
1 YEAR $6,000			

Oct. 31
Insurance expired;
record insurance expense.

ILLUSTRATION 3-23
Adjustment for Insurance

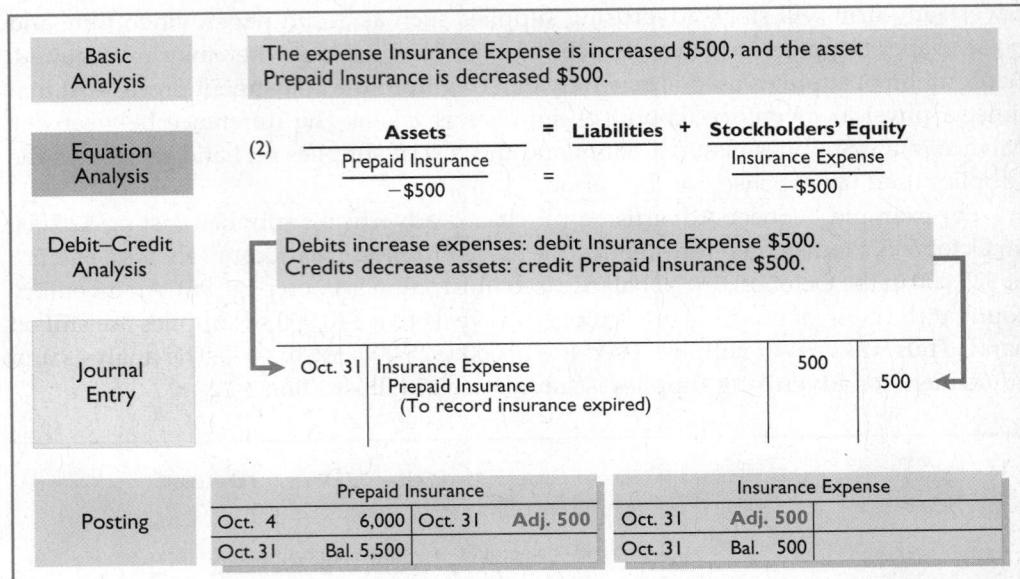

Basic Analysis	The expense Insurance Expense is increased $500, and the asset Prepaid Insurance is decreased $500.

Equation Analysis	(2)	Assets = Liabilities + Stockholders' Equity

Prepaid Insurance = Insurance Expense
−$500 = −$500

Debit–Credit Analysis: Debits increase expenses: debit Insurance Expense $500. Credits decrease assets: credit Prepaid Insurance $500.

Journal Entry:

Oct. 31	Insurance Expense	500	
	Prepaid Insurance		500
	(To record insurance expired)		

Posting:

Prepaid Insurance			
Oct. 4	6,000	Oct. 31	Adj. 500
Oct. 31	Bal. 5,500		

Insurance Expense		
Oct. 31	Adj. 500	
Oct. 31	Bal. 500	

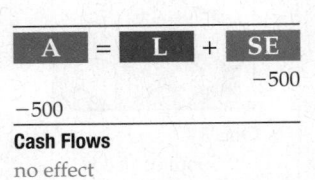

A	=	L	+	SE
				−500

−500

Cash Flows

no effect

The asset Prepaid Insurance shows a balance of $5,500, which represents the unexpired cost for the remaining 11 months of coverage. At the same time, the balance in Insurance Expense equals the insurance cost that expired in October. **Without an adjusting entry, October expenses are understated by $500 and net income overstated by $500. Moreover, both assets and stockholders' equity also are overstated by $500 on the October 31 balance sheet.**

Depreciation. Companies like Caterpillar or Boeing typically own various productive facilities, such as buildings, equipment, and motor vehicles. These assets provide a service for a number of years. The term of service is commonly referred to as the **useful life** of the asset. Because Caterpillar, for example, expects an asset such as a building to provide service for many years, Caterpillar records the building as an asset, rather than an expense, in the year the building is acquired. Caterpillar records such assets at cost, as required by the historical cost principle.

To follow the expense recognition principle, Caterpillar reports a portion of the cost of a long-lived asset as an expense during each period of the asset's useful life. Depreciation is the process of allocating the cost of an asset to expense over its useful life in a rational and systematic manner.

Need for depreciation adjustment. Generally accepted accounting principles (GAAP) view the acquisition of productive facilities as a long-term prepayment for services. The need for making periodic adjusting entries for depreciation is, therefore, the same as we described for other prepaid expenses. That is, a company recognizes the expired cost (expense) during the period and reports the unexpired cost (asset) at the end of the period. The primary causes of depreciation of a productive facility are actual use, deterioration due to the elements, and obsolescence. For example, at the time Caterpillar acquires an asset, the effects of these factors cannot be known with certainty. Therefore, Caterpillar must estimate them. **Thus, depreciation is an estimate rather than a factual measurement of the expired cost.**

To estimate depreciation expense, Caterpillar often divides the cost of the asset by its useful life. For example, if Caterpillar purchases equipment for $10,000 and expects its useful life to be 10 years, Caterpillar records annual depreciation of $1,000.

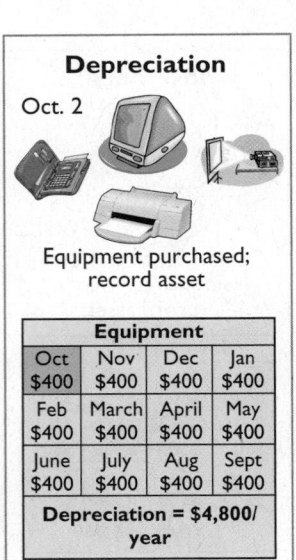

Depreciation

Oct. 2

Equipment purchased; record asset

Equipment			
Oct $400	Nov $400	Dec $400	Jan $400
Feb $400	March $400	April $400	May $400
June $400	July $400	Aug $400	Sept $400
Depreciation = $4,800/ year			

Oct. 31

Depreciation recognized; record depreciation expense

In the case of Pioneer Advertising, it estimates depreciation on its office equipment to be $4,800 a year (cost $50,000 less salvage value $2,000 divided by useful life of 10 years), or $400 per month. The analysis and adjustment for depreciation is summarized in Illustration 3-24.

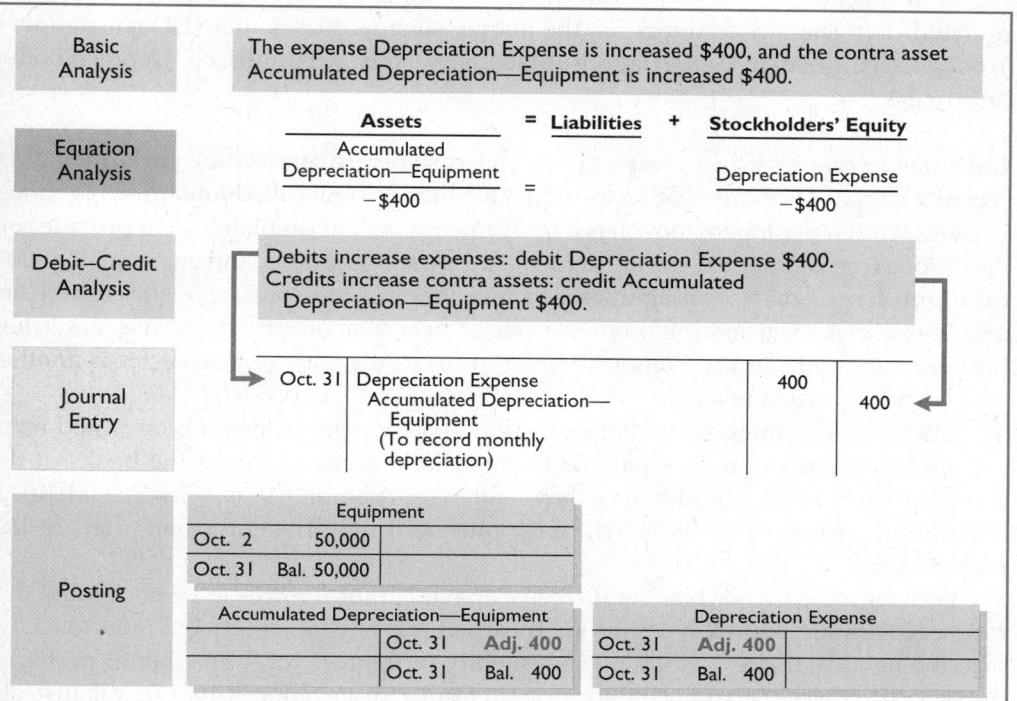

ILLUSTRATION 3-24
Adjustment for Depreciation

The balance in the Accumulated Depreciation—Equipment account will increase $400 each month. Therefore, after recording and posting the adjusting entry at November 30, the balance will be $800.

Statement presentation. Accumulated Depreciation—Equipment is a contra asset account. A **contra asset account** offsets an asset account on the balance sheet. This means that the Accumulated Depreciation—Equipment account offsets the Equipment account on the balance sheet. Its normal balance is a credit. Pioneer uses this account instead of crediting Equipment in order to disclose both the original cost of the equipment and the total expired cost to date. In the balance sheet, Pioneer deducts Accumulated Depreciation—Equipment from the related asset account as follows.

Equipment	$50,000	
Less: Accumulated depreciation—equipment	400	$49,600

ILLUSTRATION 3-25
Balance Sheet Presentation of Accumulated Depreciation

The **book value** of any depreciable asset is the difference between its cost and its related accumulated depreciation. In Illustration 3-25, the book value of the equipment at the balance sheet date is $49,600. Note that the asset's book value generally differs from its fair value. The reason: **Depreciation is an allocation concept, not a valuation concept.** That is, depreciation **allocates an asset's cost to the periods in which it is used. Depreciation does not attempt to report the actual change in the value of the asset.**

Depreciation expense identifies that portion of the asset's cost that expired during the period (in this case, October). **Without this adjusting entry, total assets, total stockholders' equity, and net income are overstated, and depreciation expense is understated.**

A company records depreciation expense for each piece of equipment, such as trucks or machinery, and for all buildings. A company also establishes related accumulated depreciation accounts for the above, such as Accumulated Depreciation—Trucks, Accumulated Depreciation—Machinery, and Accumulated Depreciation—Buildings.

Unearned Revenues

Oct. 2

Cash is received in advance;
liability is recorded

Oct. 31
Some service has been
performed; some revenue
is recorded

Unearned Revenues. When companies receive cash before services are performed, they record a liability by increasing (crediting) a liability account called unearned revenues. In other words, a company now has a performance obligation (liability) to provide service to one its customers. Items like rent, magazine subscriptions, and customer deposits for future service may result in unearned revenues. Airlines, such as Delta, American, and Southwest, treat receipts from the sale of tickets as unearned revenue until they provide the flight service. Tuition received prior to the start of a semester is another example of unearned revenue.

Unearned revenues are the opposite of prepaid expenses. Indeed, unearned revenue on the books of one company is likely to be a prepayment on the books of the company that made the advance payment. For example, if we assume identical accounting periods, a landlord will have unearned rent revenue when a tenant has prepaid rent.

When a company such as Intel receives payment for services to be performed in a future accounting period, it credits an unearned revenue (a liability) account to recognize the liability that exists. Intel subsequently recognizes revenue when it performs the service. However, making daily entries to record this revenue is impractical. Instead, Intel delays recognition of revenue until the adjustment process. Then, Intel makes an adjusting entry to record the revenue for services performed during the period and to show the liability that remains at the end of the accounting period. In the typical case, liabilities are overstated and revenues are understated prior to adjustment. **Thus, the adjusting entry for unearned revenues results in a debit (decrease) to a liability account and a credit (increase) to a revenue account.**

For example, Pioneer Advertising received $12,000 on October 2 from R. Knox for advertising services expected to be completed by December 31. Pioneer credited the payment to Unearned Service Revenue. This liability account shows a balance of $12,000 in the October 31 trial balance. Based on an evaluation of the service Pioneer performed for Knox during October, the company determines that it should recognize $4,000 of revenue in October. The liability (Unearned Service Revenue) is therefore decreased and stockholders' equity (Service Revenue) is increased, as shown in Illustration 3-26.

The liability Unearned Service Revenue now shows a balance of $8,000. This amount represents the remaining advertising services expected to be performed in the future. At the same time, Service Revenue shows total revenue recognized in October of $104,000. **Without this adjustment, revenues and net income are understated by $4,000 in the income statement. Moreover, liabilities will be overstated and stockholders' equity will be understated by $4,000 on the October 31 balance sheet.**

Adjusting Entries for Accruals

The second category of adjusting entries is accruals. Companies make adjusting entries for accruals to record revenues for services performed and expenses incurred in the current accounting period. Without an accrual adjustment, the revenue account (and the

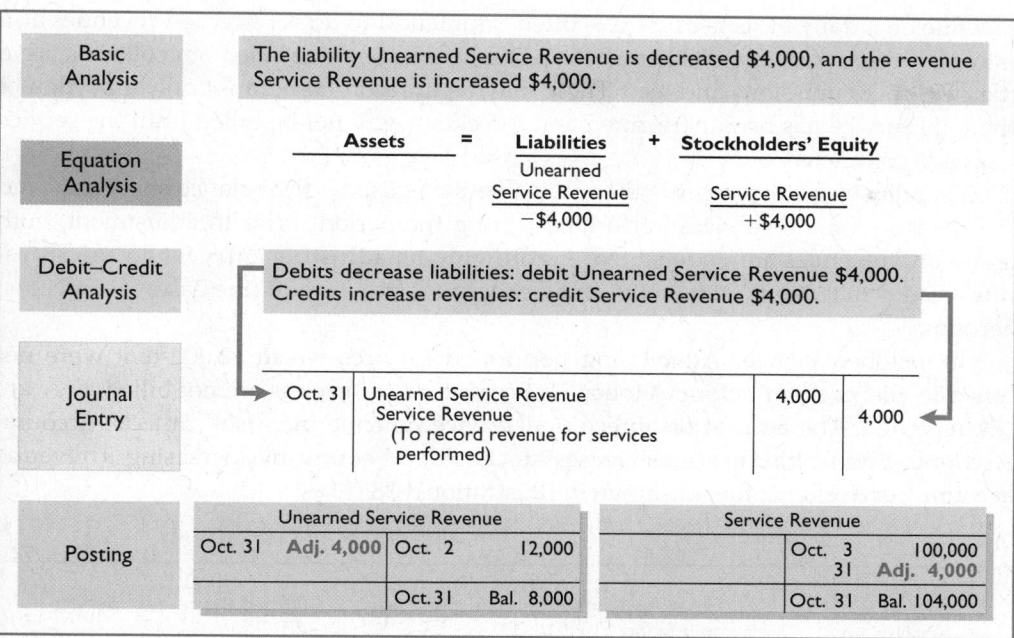

ILLUSTRATION 3-26
Adjustment for
Unearned Service
Revenue

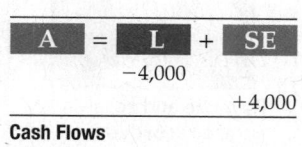

related asset account) or the expense account (and the related liability account) are understated. Thus, the adjusting entry for accruals **will increase both a balance sheet and an income statement account**. Illustration 3-27 shows adjusting entries for accruals.

ILLUSTRATION 3-27
Adjusting Entries for
Accruals

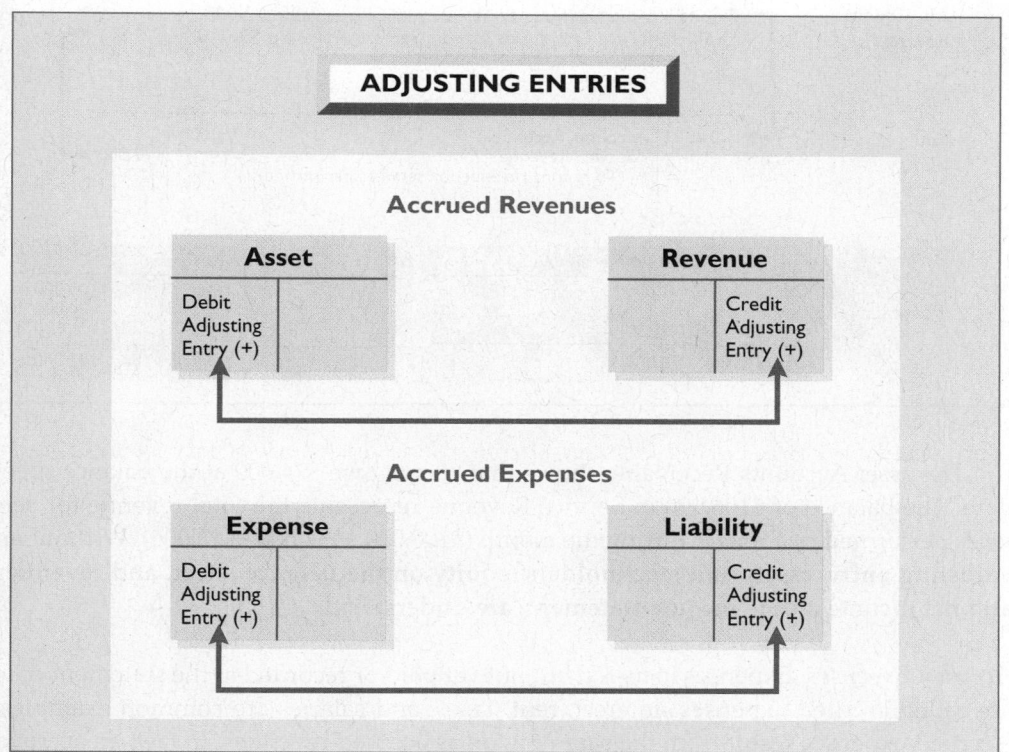

Accrued Revenues. Revenues for services performed but not yet recorded at the statement date are **accrued revenues**. Accrued revenues may accumulate (accrue) with the passing of time, as in the case of interest revenue. These are unrecorded because the earning of interest does not involve daily transactions. Companies do not record interest revenue on a daily basis because it is often impractical to do so. Accrued revenues also may result from services that have been performed but not yet billed nor collected, as in the case of commissions and fees. These may be unrecorded because only a portion of the total service has been performed and the clients will not be billed until the service has been completed.

An adjusting entry records the receivable that exists at the balance sheet date and the revenue for the services performed during the period. Prior to adjustment, both assets and revenues are understated. Accordingly, **an adjusting entry** for accrued revenues results in a debit (increase) to an asset account and a credit (increase) to a revenue account.

In October, Pioneer Advertising performed services worth $2,000 that were not billed to clients on or before October 31. Because these services are not billed, they are not recorded. The accrual of unrecorded service revenue increases an asset account, Accounts Receivable. It also increases stockholders' equity by increasing a revenue account, Service Revenue, as shown in Illustration 3-28.

Accrued Revenues

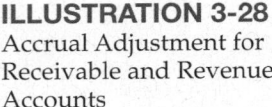

Revenue and receivable are recorded for unbilled services

ILLUSTRATION 3-28
Accrual Adjustment for Receivable and Revenue Accounts

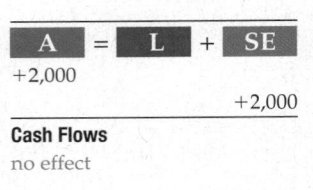

A	=	L	+	SE
+2,000				
				+2,000

Cash Flows
no effect

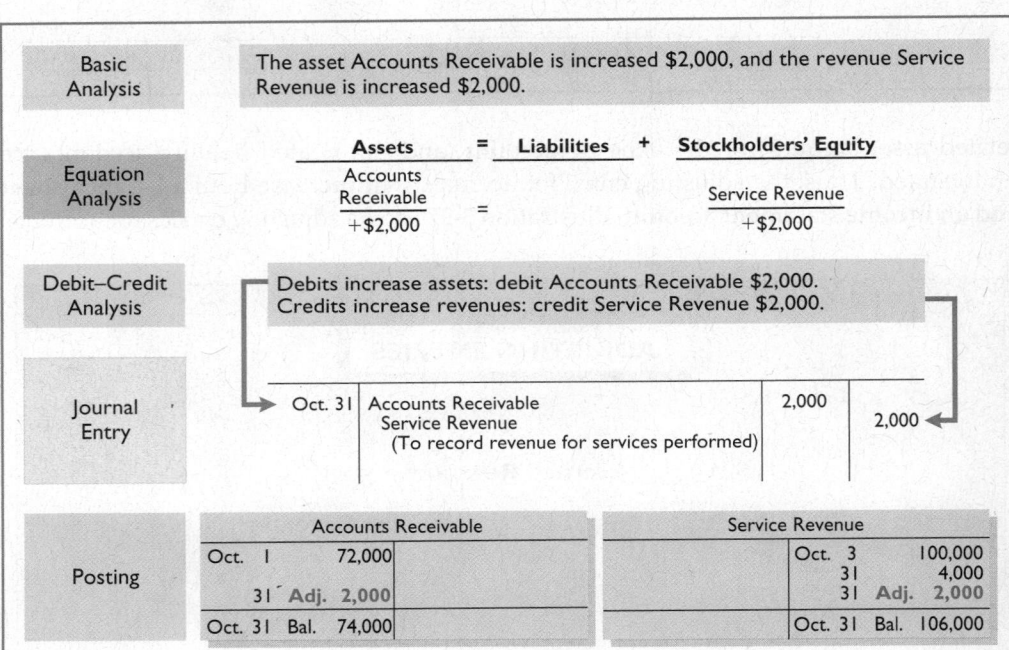

The asset Accounts Receivable shows that clients owe $74,000 at the balance sheet date. The balance of $106,000 in Service Revenue represents the total revenue for services performed by Pioneer during the month ($100,000 + $4,000 + $2,000). **Without an adjusting entry, assets and stockholders' equity on the balance sheet, and revenues and net income on the income statement, are understated.**

Accrued Expenses. Expenses incurred but not yet paid or recorded at the statement date are called **accrued expenses**. Interest, rent, taxes, and salaries are common examples. Accrued expenses result from the same causes as accrued revenues. In fact, an accrued expense on the books of one company is an accrued revenue to another company. For example, the $2,000 accrual of service revenue by Pioneer is an accrued expense to the client that received the service.

Adjustments for accrued expenses record the obligations that exist at the balance sheet date and recognize the expenses that apply to the current accounting period. Prior to adjustment, both liabilities and expenses are understated. Therefore, the adjusting entry for accrued expenses results in a debit (increase) to an expense account and a credit (increase) to a liability account.

Accrued interest. Pioneer Advertising signed a three-month note payable in the amount of $50,000 on October 1. The note requires interest at an annual rate of 12 percent. Three factors determine the amount of the interest accumulation: (1) the face value of the note; (2) the interest rate, which is always expressed as an annual rate; and (3) the length of time the note is outstanding. For Pioneer, the total interest due on the $50,000 note at its maturity date three months' in the future is $1,500 ($50,000 × 12% × 3/12), or $500 for one month. Illustration 3-29 shows the formula for computing interest and its application to Pioneer. Note that the formula expresses the time period as a fraction of a year.

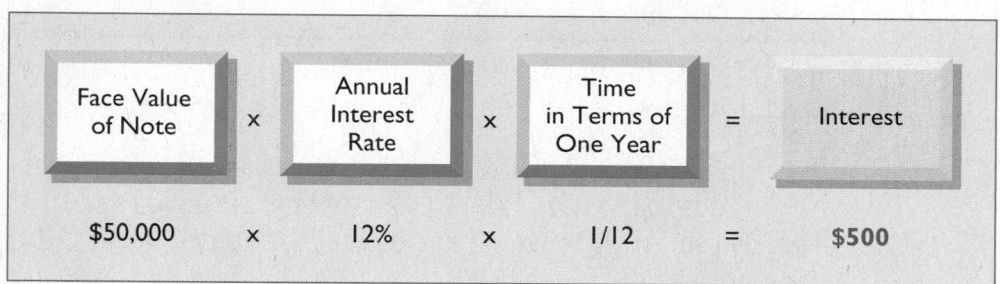

ILLUSTRATION 3-29
Formula for Computing Interest

As Illustration 3-30 shows, the accrual of interest at October 31 increases a liability account, Interest Payable. It also decreases stockholders' equity by increasing an expense account, Interest Expense.

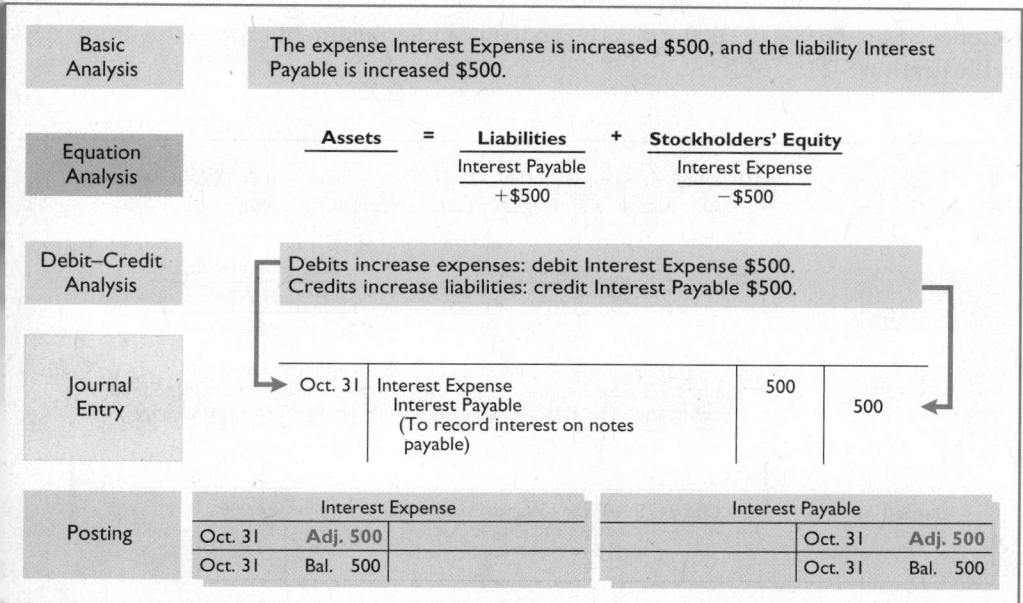

ILLUSTRATION 3-30
Adjustment for Interest

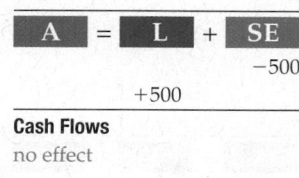

Interest Expense shows the interest charges for the month of October. Interest Payable shows the amount of interest owed at the statement date. Pioneer will not pay this amount until the note comes due at the end of three months. Why does Pioneer use the

Interest Payable account instead of crediting Notes Payable? By recording interest payable separately, Pioneer discloses the two different types of obligations—interest and principal—in the accounts and statements. **Without this adjusting entry, liabilities and interest expense are understated, and both net income and stockholders' equity are overstated.**

Accrued salaries and wages. Companies pay for some types of expenses, such as employee salaries and wages, after the services have been performed. For example, Pioneer Advertising last paid salaries and wages on October 26. It will not pay salaries and wages again until November 23. However, as shown in the calendar below, three working days remain in October (October 29–31).

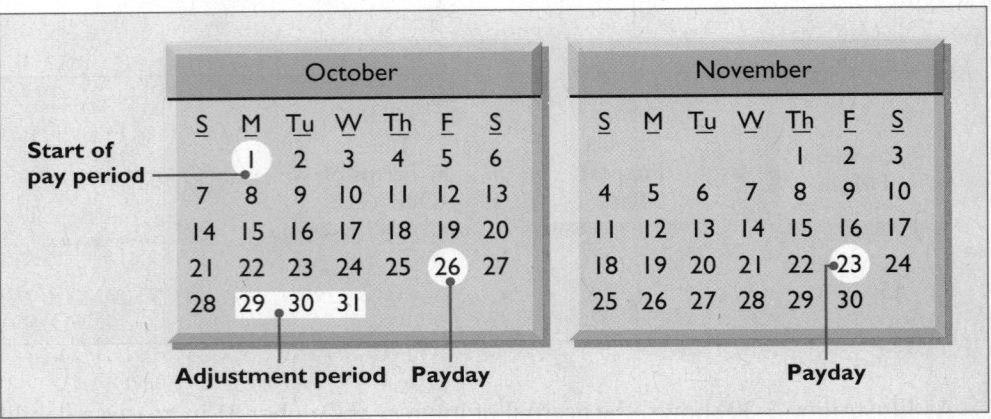

At October 31, the salaries and wages for these days represent an accrued expense and a related liability to Pioneer. The employees receive total salaries and wages of $10,000 for a five-day work week, or $2,000 per day. Thus, accrued salaries and wages at October 31 are $6,000 ($2,000 × 3). The analysis and adjustment process is summarized in Illustration 3-31.

ILLUSTRATION 3-31
Adjustment for Salaries and Wages Expense

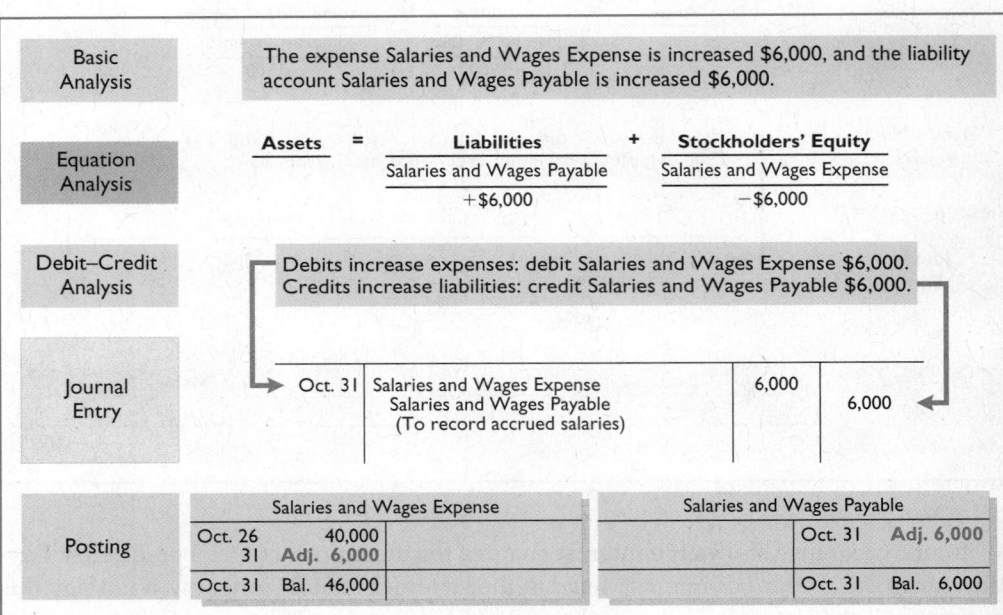

After this adjustment, the balance in Salaries and Wages Expense of $46,000 (23 days × $2,000) is the actual salaries and wages expense for October. The balance in Salaries and Wages Payable of $6,000 is the amount of the liability for salaries and wages owed as of October 31. **Without the $6,000 adjustment for salaries, both Pioneer's expenses and liabilities are understated by $6,000.**

Pioneer pays salaries and wages every four weeks. Consequently, the next payday is November 23, when it will again pay total salaries and wages of $40,000. The payment consists of $6,000 of salaries and wages payable at October 31 plus $34,000 of salaries and wages expense for November (17 working days as shown in the November calendar × $2,000). Therefore, Pioneer makes the following entry on November 23.

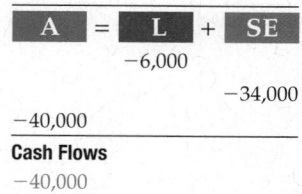

	Nov. 23		
Salaries and Wages Payable		6,000	
Salaries and Wages Expense		34,000	
Cash			40,000
(To record November 23 payroll)			

A = L + SE
−6,000
−34,000
−40,000

Cash Flows
−40,000

This entry eliminates the liability for Salaries and Wages Payable that Pioneer recorded in the October 31 adjusting entry. This entry also records the proper amount of Salaries and Wages Expense for the period between November 1 and November 23.

What do the numbers mean?   AM I COVERED?

Rather than purchasing insurance to cover casualty losses and other obligations, some companies "self-insure." That is, a company decides to pay for any possible claims, as they arise, out of its own resources. The company also purchases an insurance policy to cover losses that exceed certain amounts.

For example, **Almost Family, Inc.**, a healthcare services company, has a self-insured employee health-benefit program.

However, Almost Family ran into accounting problems when it failed to record an accrual of the liability for benefits not covered by its back-up insurance policy. This led to restatement of Almost Family's fiscal results for the accrual of the benefit expense.

Bad debts. Proper recognition of revenues and expenses dictates recording bad debts as an expense of the period in which a company recognizes revenue for services performed instead of the period in which the company writes off the accounts or notes. The proper valuation of the receivable balance also requires recognition of uncollectible receivables. Proper recognition and valuation require an adjusting entry.

At the end of each period, a company such as **General Mills** estimates the amount of receivables that will later prove to be uncollectible. General Mills bases the estimate on various factors: the amount of bad debts it experienced in past years, general economic conditions, how long the receivables are past due, and other factors that indicate the extent of uncollectibility. To illustrate, assume that, based on past experience, Pioneer Advertising reasonably estimates a bad debt expense for the month of $1,600. The analysis and adjustment process for bad debts is summarized in Illustration 3-32 (page 108).

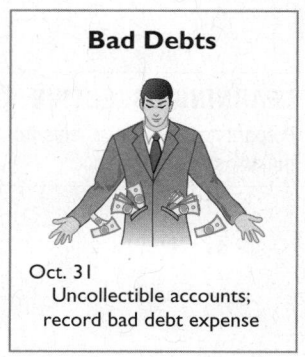

Bad Debts

Oct. 31
Uncollectible accounts;
record bad debt expense

ILLUSTRATION 3-32
Adjustment for Bad Debt
Expense

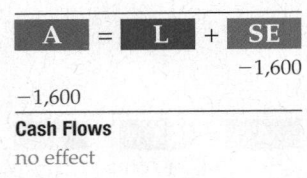

Cash Flows
no effect

A company often expresses bad debts as a percentage of the revenue on account for the period. Or, a company may compute bad debts by adjusting Allowance for Doubtful Accounts to a certain percentage of the trade accounts receivable and trade notes receivable at the end of the period.

Adjusted Trial Balance

After journalizing and posting all adjusting entries, Pioneer Advertising prepares another trial balance from its ledger accounts (shown in Illustration 3-33 on page 109). This trial balance is called an **adjusted trial balance**. The purpose of an adjusted trial balance is to **prove the equality** of the total debit balances and the total credit balances in the ledger after all adjustments. Because the accounts contain all data needed for financial statements, the adjusted trial balance is the **primary basis for the preparation of financial statements**.

Preparing Financial Statements

LEARNING OBJECTIVE 6
Prepare financial statements from
the adjusted trial balance.

As indicated above, **Pioneer Advertising can prepare financial statements directly from the adjusted trial balance.** Illustrations 3-34 (page 109) and 3-35 (page 110) show the interrelationships of data in the adjusted trial balance and the financial statements.

As Illustration 3-34 shows, Pioneer prepares the income statement from the revenue and expense accounts. Next, it derives the retained earnings statement from the retained earnings and dividends accounts and the net income (or net loss) shown in the income statement.

ILLUSTRATION 3-33
Adjusted Trial Balance

PIONEER ADVERTISING AGENCY INC.
ADJUSTED TRIAL BALANCE
OCTOBER 31, 2014

	Debit	Credit
Cash	$ 80,000	
Accounts Receivable	74,000	
Allowance for Doubtful Accounts		$ 1,600
Supplies	10,000	
Prepaid Insurance	5,500	
Equipment	50,000	
Accumulated Depreciation—Equipment		400
Notes Payable		50,000
Accounts Payable		25,000
Interest Payable		500
Unearned Service Revenue		8,000
Salaries and Wages Payable		6,000
Common Stock		100,000
Dividends	5,000	
Service Revenue		106,000
Salaries and Wages Expense	46,000	
Supplies Expense	15,000	
Rent Expense	9,000	
Insurance Expense	500	
Interest Expense	500	
Depreciation Expense	400	
Bad Debt Expense	1,600	
	$297,500	$297,500

ILLUSTRATION 3-34
Preparation of the
Income Statement and
Retained Earnings
Statement from the
Adjusted Trial Balance

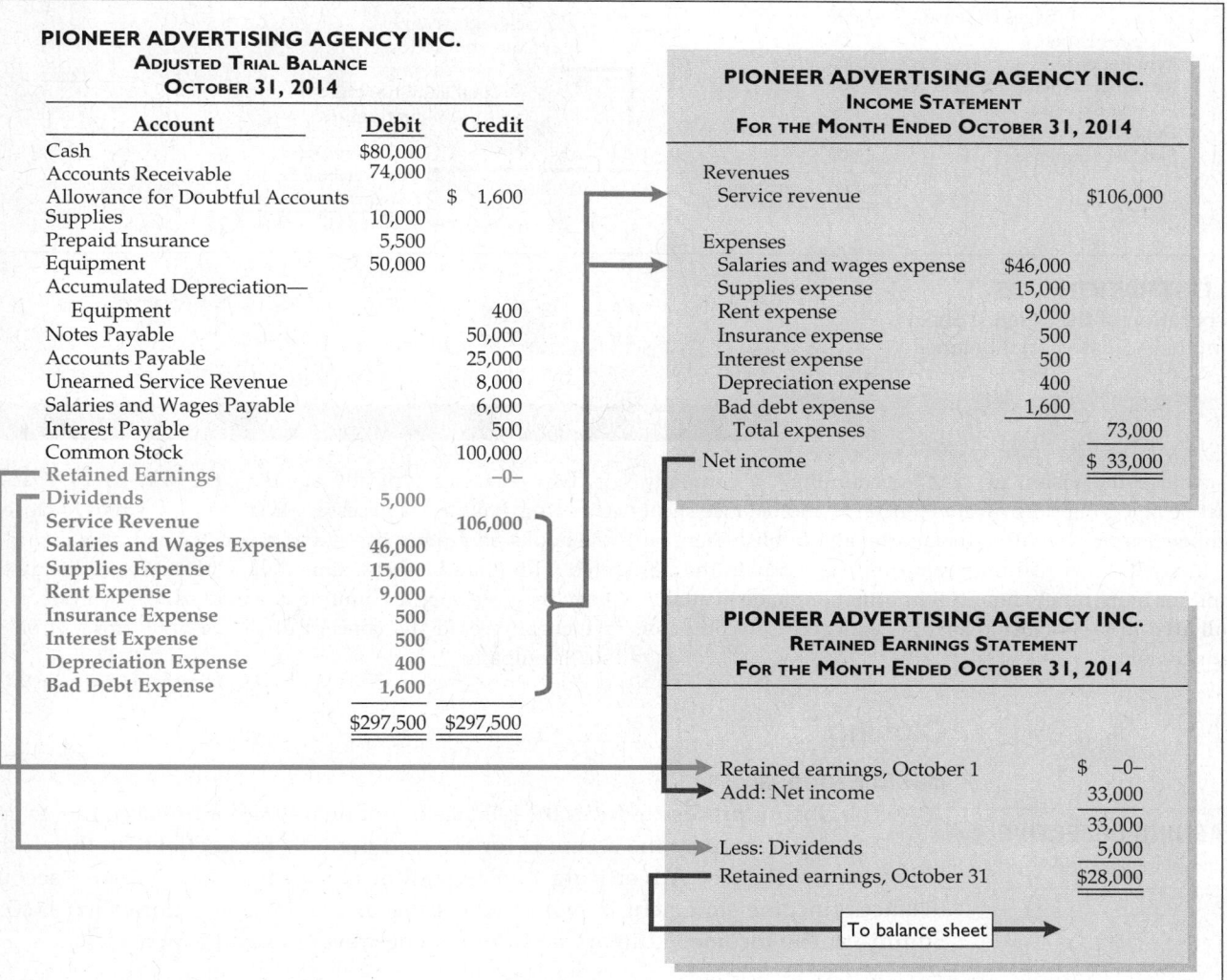

As Illustration 3-35 shows, Pioneer then prepares the balance sheet from the asset and liability accounts, the common stock account, and the ending retained earnings balance as reported in the retained earnings statement.

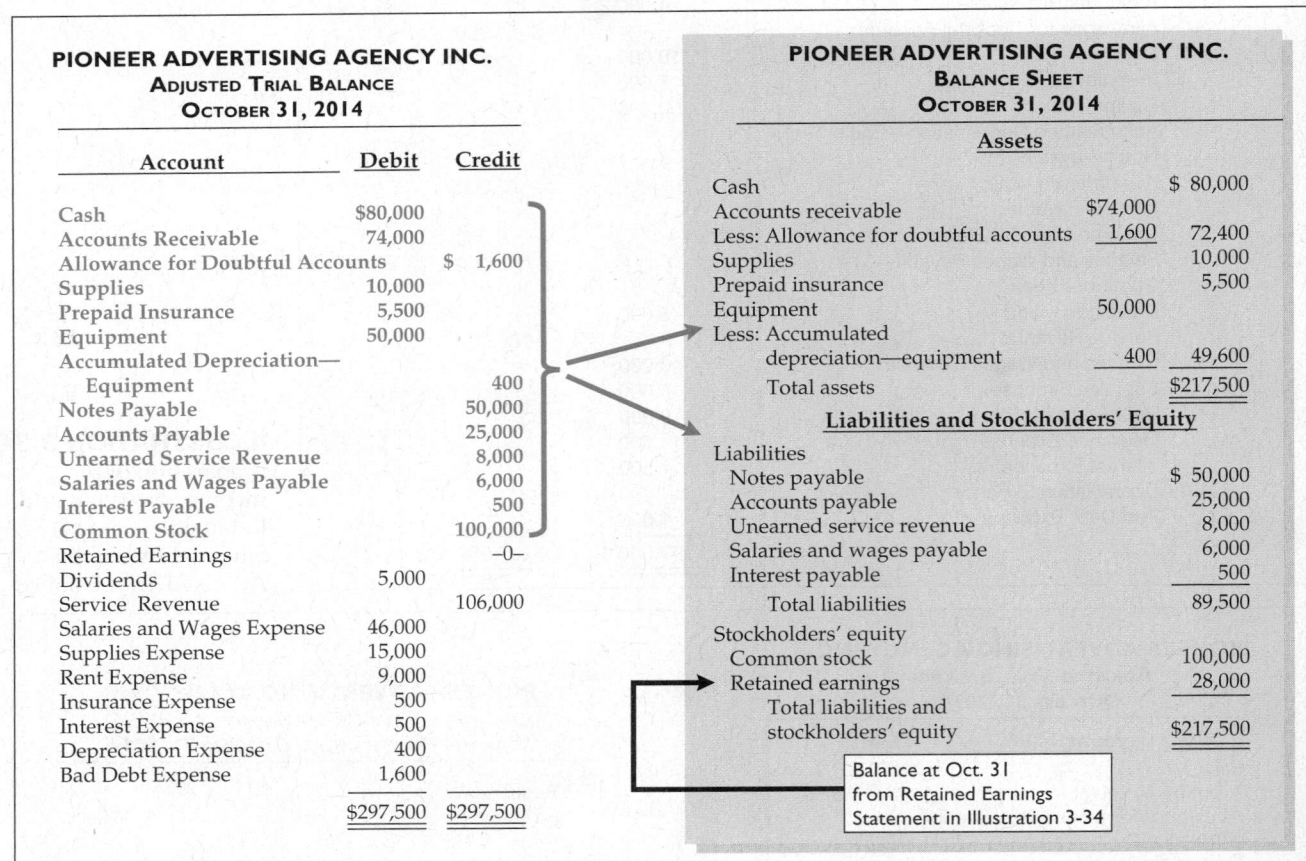

ILLUSTRATION 3-35
Preparation of the Balance Sheet
from the Adjusted Trial Balance

To achieve the vision of "24/7 accounting," a company must be able to update revenue, income, and balance sheet numbers every day within the quarter and publish them on the Internet. Such real-time reporting responds to the demand for more timely financial information made available to all investors—not just to analysts with access to company management.

Two obstacles typically stand in the way of 24/7 accounting: having the necessary accounting systems to close the books on a daily basis, and reliability concerns associated with unaudited real-time data. Only a few companies have the necessary accounting capabilities. Cisco Systems, which pioneered the concept of the 24-hour close, is one such company.

Closing

Basic Process

LEARNING OBJECTIVE 7
Prepare closing entries.

The closing process reduces the balance of nominal (temporary) accounts to zero in order to prepare the accounts for the next period's transactions. In the closing process, Pioneer Advertising transfers all of the revenue and expense account balances (income statement items) to a clearing or suspense account called Income Summary. The Income Summary account matches revenues and expenses.

Pioneer uses this clearing account only at the end of each accounting period. The account represents the net income or net loss for the period. It then transfers this amount (the net income or net loss) to an owners' equity account. (For a corporation, the owners' equity account is retained earnings; for proprietorships and partnerships, it is a capital account.) Companies post all such **closing entries** to the appropriate general ledger accounts.

Closing Entries

In practice, companies generally prepare closing entries only at the end of a company's annual accounting period. However, to illustrate the journalizing and posting of closing entries, we will assume that Pioneer Advertising closes its books monthly. Illustration 3-36 shows the closing entries at October 31.

ILLUSTRATION 3-36
Closing Entries Journalized

GENERAL JOURNAL				J3
Date	Account Titles and Explanation		Debit	Credit
	Closing Entries			
	(1)			
Oct. 31	Service Revenue		106,000	
	Income Summary			106,000
	(To close revenue account)			
	(2)			
31	Income Summary		73,000	
	Supplies Expense			15,000
	Depreciation Expense			400
	Insurance Expense			500
	Salaries and Wages Expense			46,000
	Rent Expense			9,000
	Interest Expense			500
	Bad Debt Expense			1,600
	(To close expense accounts)			
	(3)			
31	Income Summary		33,000	
	Retained Earnings			33,000
	(To close net income to retained earnings)			
	(4)			
31	Retained Earnings		5,000	
	Dividends			5,000
	(To close dividends to retained earnings)			

A couple of cautions about preparing closing entries. (1) Avoid unintentionally doubling the revenue and expense balances rather than zeroing them. (2) Do not close Dividends through the Income Summary account. **Dividends are not expenses, and they are not a factor in determining net income.**

Posting Closing Entries

Illustration 3-37 (page 112) shows the posting of closing entries and the underlining (ruling) of accounts. All temporary accounts have zero balances after posting the closing entries. In addition, note that the balance in Retained Earnings represents the accumulated undistributed earnings of Pioneer at the end of the accounting period. Pioneer reports this

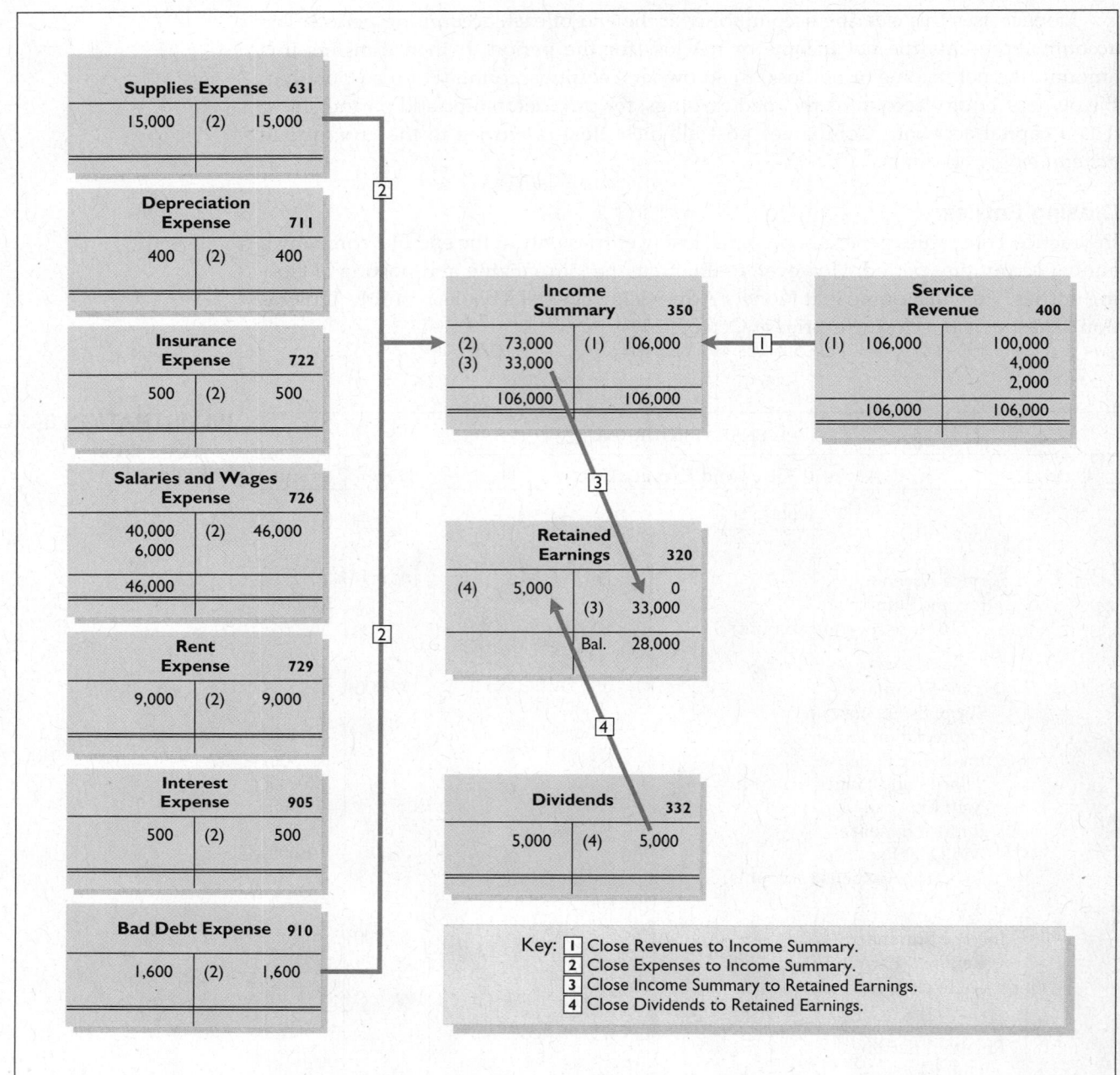

ILLUSTRATION 3-37
Posting of Closing Entries

amount in the balance sheet as the ending amount reported on the retained earnings statement. As noted above, **Pioneer uses the Income Summary account only in closing.** It does not journalize and post entries to this account during the year.

As part of the closing process, Pioneer totals, balances, and double-underlines the **temporary accounts**—revenues, expenses, and dividends—as shown in T-account form in Illustration 3-37. It does not close the **permanent accounts**—assets, liabilities, and stockholders' equity (Common Stock and Retained Earnings). Instead, Pioneer draws a single underline beneath the current period entries for the permanent accounts. The account balance is then entered below the single underline and is carried forward to the next period (see, for example, Retained Earnings).

After the closing process, each income statement account and the dividend account are balanced out to zero and are ready for use in the next accounting period.

Post-Closing Trial Balance

Recall that a trial balance is prepared after entering the regular transactions of the period, and that a second trial balance (the adjusted trial balance) occurs after posting the adjusting entries. A company may take a third trial balance after posting the closing entries. The trial balance after closing is called the post-closing trial balance. The purpose of the post-closing trial balance is **to prove the equality of the permanent account balances that the company carries forward into the next accounting period**. Since all temporary accounts will have zero balances, **the post-closing trial balance will contain only permanent (real)—balance sheet—accounts**.

Illustration 3-38 shows the post-closing trial balance of Pioneer Advertising Agency Inc.

ILLUSTRATION 3-38
Post-Closing Trial Balance

PIONEER ADVERTISING AGENCY INC. POST-CLOSING TRIAL BALANCE OCTOBER 31, 2014		
Account	Debit	Credit
Cash	$ 80,000	
Accounts Receivable	74,000	
Allowance for Doubtful Accounts		$ 1,600
Supplies	10,000	
Prepaid Insurance	5,500	
Equipment	50,000	
Accumulated Depreciation—Equipment		400
Notes Payable		50,000
Accounts Payable		25,000
Unearned Service Revenue		8,000
Salaries and Wages Payable		6,000
Interest Payable		500
Common Stock		100,000
Retained Earnings		28,000
	$219,500	$219,500

A post-closing trial balance provides evidence that the company has properly journalized and posted the closing entries. It also shows that the accounting equation is in balance at the end of the accounting period. However, like the other trial balances, it does not prove that Pioneer has recorded all transactions or that the ledger is correct. For example, the post-closing trial balance will balance if a transaction is not journalized and posted, or if a transaction is journalized and posted twice.

Reversing Entries—An Optional Step

Some accountants prefer to reverse the effects of certain adjusting entries by making a reversing entry at the beginning of the next accounting period. A reversing entry is the exact opposite of the adjusting entry made in the previous period. **Use of reversing entries is an optional bookkeeping procedure; it is not a required step in the accounting cycle.** Accordingly, we have chosen to cover this topic in Appendix 3B at the end of the chapter.

The Accounting Cycle Summarized

A summary of the steps in the accounting cycle shows a logical sequence of the accounting procedures used during a fiscal period:

1. Enter the transactions of the period in appropriate journals.

2. Post from the journals to the ledger (or ledgers).

3. Take an unadjusted trial balance (trial balance).

4. Prepare adjusting journal entries and post to the ledger(s).

5. Take a trial balance after adjusting (adjusted trial balance).

6. Prepare the financial statements from the second trial balance.

7. Prepare closing journal entries and post to the ledger(s).

8. Take a post-closing trial balance (**optional**).

9. Prepare reversing entries (**optional**) and post to the ledger(s).

A company normally completes all of these steps in every fiscal period.

What do the numbers mean?   HEY, IT'S COMPLICATED

The economic volatility of the past few years has left companies hungering for more timely and uniform financial information to help them react quickly to fast-changing conditions. As one expert noted, companies were extremely focused on trying to reduce costs and plan for the future better, but a lot of them discovered that they didn't have the information they needed and they didn't have the ability to get that information. The unsteady recession environment also made it risky for companies to interrupt their operations to get new systems up to speed.

So what to do? Try to piecemeal upgrades each year or start a major overhaul of their internal systems? Best Buy, for example, has standardized as many of its systems as possible and has been steadily upgrading them over the past decade. Acquisitions can wreak havoc on reporting systems. Best Buy is choosy about when to standardize for companies it acquires, but it sometimes has to implement new systems after international deals.

In other situations, a major overhaul is needed. For example, it is common for companies with a steady stream of acquisitions to have 50 to 70 general ledger systems. In those cases, a company cannot react well unless its systems are made compatible. So is it the big bang (major overhaul) or the piecemeal approach? It seems to depend. One thing is certain—good accounting systems are a necessity. Without one, the risk of failure is high.

Source: Emily Chasan, "The Financial-Data Dilemma," *Wall Street Journal* (July 24, 2012), p. B4.

FINANCIAL STATEMENTS FOR A MERCHANDISING COMPANY

LEARNING OBJECTIVE 8
Prepare financial statements for a merchandising company.

Pioneer Advertising Agency Inc. is a service company. In this section, we show a detailed set of financial statements for a merchandising company, Uptown Cabinet Corp. The financial statements (see pages 115–116) are prepared from the adjusted trial balance.

Income Statement

The income statement for Uptown, shown in Illustration 3-39, is self-explanatory. The income statement classifies amounts into such categories as gross profit on sales, income from operations, income before taxes, and net income. Although earnings per share information is required to be shown on the face of the income statement for a corporation, we omit this item here as it will be discussed more fully later in the textbook. *For homework problems, do not present earnings per share information unless required to do so.*

UPTOWN CABINET CORP.
INCOME STATEMENT
FOR THE YEAR ENDED DECEMBER 31, 2014

Net sales			$400,000
Cost of goods sold			316,000
Gross profit on sales			84,000
Selling expenses			
Salaries and wages expense (sales)		$20,000	
Advertising expense		10,200	
Total selling expenses		30,200	
Administrative expenses			
Salaries and wages expense (general)	$19,000		
Depreciation expense—equipment	6,700		
Property tax expense	5,300		
Rent expense	4,300		
Bad debt expense	1,000		
Telephone and Internet expense	600		
Insurance expense	360		
Total administrative expenses		37,260	
Total selling and administrative expenses			67,460
Income from operations			16,540
Other revenues and gains			
Interest revenue			800
			17,340
Other expenses and losses			
Interest expense			1,700
Income before income taxes			15,640
Income tax			3,440
Net income			$ 12,200

ILLUSTRATION 3-39
Income Statement for a
Merchandising Company

Statement of Retained Earnings

A corporation may retain the net income earned in the business, or it may distribute it
to stockholders by payment of dividends. In Illustration 3-40, Uptown added the net
income earned during the year to the balance of retained earnings on January 1, thereby
increasing the balance of retained earnings. Deducting dividends of $2,000 results in the
ending retained earnings balance of $26,400 on December 31.

UPTOWN CABINET CORP.
STATEMENT OF RETAINED EARNINGS
FOR THE YEAR ENDED DECEMBER 31, 2014

Retained earnings, January 1	$16,200
Add: Net income	12,200
	28,400
Less: Dividends	2,000
Retained earnings, December 31	$26,400

ILLUSTRATION 3-40
Statement of Retained
Earnings for a
Merchandising Company

Balance Sheet

The balance sheet for Uptown, shown in Illustration 3-41 (page 116), is a classified balance
sheet. Interest receivable, inventory, prepaid insurance, and prepaid rent are included as
current assets. Uptown considers these assets current because they will be converted into

cash or used by the business within a relatively short period of time. Uptown deducts the amount of Allowance for Doubtful Accounts from the total of accounts, notes, and interest receivable because it estimates that only $54,800 of $57,800 will be collected in cash.

ILLUSTRATION 3-41
Balance Sheet for a
Merchandising Company

UPTOWN CABINET CORP.
BALANCE SHEET
AS OF DECEMBER 31, 2014

Assets

Current assets			
Cash			$ 1,200
Notes receivable	$16,000		
Accounts receivable	41,000		
Interest receivable	800	$57,800	
Less: Allowance for doubtful accounts		3,000	54,800
Inventory			40,000
Prepaid insurance			540
Prepaid rent			500
Total current assets			97,040
Property, plant, and equipment			
Equipment		67,000	
Less: Accumulated depreciation—equipment		18,700	
Total property, plant, and equipment			48,300
Total assets			$145,340

Liabilities and Stockholders' Equity

Current liabilities			
Notes payable			$ 20,000
Accounts payable			13,500
Property taxes payable			2,000
Income taxes payable			3,440
Total current liabilities			38,940
Long-term liabilities			
Bonds payable, due June 30, 2022			30,000
Total liabilities			68,940
Stockholders' equity			
Common stock, $5.00 par value, issued and outstanding, 10,000 shares		$50,000	
Retained earnings		26,400	
Total stockholders' equity			76,400
Total liabilities and stockholders' equity			$145,340

In the property, plant, and equipment section, Uptown deducts the Accumulated Depreciation—Equipment from the cost of the equipment. The difference represents the book or carrying value of the equipment.

The balance sheet shows property taxes payable as a current liability because it is an obligation that is payable within a year. The balance sheet also shows other short-term liabilities such as accounts payable.

The bonds payable, due in 2022, are long-term liabilities. As a result, the balance sheet shows the account in a separate section. (The company paid interest on the bonds on December 31.)

Because Uptown is a corporation, the capital section of the balance sheet, called the stockholders' equity section in the illustration, differs somewhat from the capital section for a proprietorship. Total stockholders' equity consists of the common stock, which is the original investment by stockholders, and the earnings retained in the business. *For homework purposes, unless instructed otherwise, prepare an unclassified balance sheet.*

The use of a worksheet at the end of each month or quarter enables a company to prepare interim financial statements even though it closes the books only at the end of each year. For example, assume that Google closes its books on December 31, but it wants monthly financial statements. To do this, at the end of January, Google prepares an adjusted trial balance (using a worksheet as illustrated in Appendix 3C) to supply the information needed for statements for January.

At the end of February, it uses a worksheet again. Note that because Google did not close the accounts at the end of January, the income statement taken from the adjusted trial balance on February 28 will present the net income for two months. If Google wants an income statement for only the month of February, the company obtains it by subtracting the items in the January income statement from the corresponding items in the income statement for the two months of January and February.

If Google executes such a process daily, it can realize "24/7 accounting" (see the "What Do the Numbers Mean?" box on page 110).

Closing Entries

Uptown makes closing entries in its general journal as shown below.

DECEMBER 31, 2014		
Interest Revenue	800	
Sales Revenue	400,000	
Income Summary		400,800
(To close revenues to Income Summary)		
Income Summary	388,600	
Cost of Goods Sold		316,000
Salaries and Wages Expense (sales)		20,000
Advertising Expense		10,200
Salaries and Wages Expense (general)		19,000
Depreciation Expense		6,700
Rent Expense		4,300
Property Tax Expense		5,300
Bad Debt Expense		1,000
Telephone and Internet Expense		600
Insurance Expense		360
Interest Expense		1,700
Income Tax Expense		3,440
(To close expenses to Income Summary)		
Income Summary	12,200	
Retained Earnings		12,200
(To close Income Summary to Retained Earnings)		
Retained Earnings	2,000	
Dividends		2,000
(To close Dividends to Retained Earnings)		

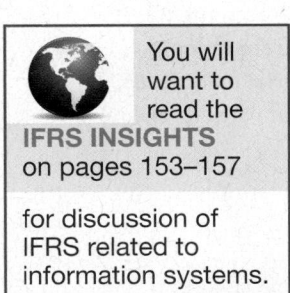

You will want to read the **IFRS INSIGHTS** on pages 153–157 for discussion of IFRS related to information systems.

SUMMARY OF LEARNING OBJECTIVES

1 Understand basic accounting terminology. Understanding the following eleven terms helps in understanding key accounting concepts: (1) Event. (2) Transaction. (3) Account. (4) Real and nominal accounts. (5) Ledger. (6) Journal. (7) Posting. (8) Trial balance. (9) Adjusting entries. (10) Financial statements. (11) Closing entries.

2 Explain double-entry rules. The left side of any account is the debit side; the right side is the credit side. All asset and expense accounts are increased on the left or

KEY TERMS

account, *84*
accounting cycle, *89*
accounting information
   system, *84*
accrued expenses, *104*
accrued revenues, *103*
adjusted trial
   balance, *85, 108*
adjusting entry, *85, 96*

balance sheet, *85*

book value, *101*

closing entries, *85, 111*

closing process, *110*

contra asset account, *101*

credit, *85*

debit, *85*

depreciation, *100*

double-entry
   accounting, *86*

event, *84*

financial statements, *85*

general journal, *91*

general ledger, *85, 91*

income statement, *85*

journal, *85*

journalizing, *85*

ledger, *85*

nominal accounts, *85*

post-closing trial
   balance, *85, 113*

posting, *85, 92*

prepaid expenses, *98*

real accounts, *85*

reversing entries, *113*

special journals, *92*

statement of cash
   flows, *85*

statement of retained
   earnings, *85*

subsidiary ledger, *85*

T-account, *85*

transaction, *84*

trial balance, *85, 96*

unearned revenues, *102*

debit side and decreased on the right or credit side. Conversely, all liability and revenue accounts are increased on the right or credit side and decreased on the left or debit side. Stockholders' equity accounts, Common Stock and Retained Earnings, are increased on the credit side. Dividends is increased on the debit side.

3 **Identify steps in the accounting cycle.** The basic steps in the accounting cycle are (1) identifying and measuring transactions and other events; (2) journalizing; (3) posting; (4) preparing an unadjusted trial balance; (5) making adjusting entries; (6) preparing an adjusted trial balance; (7) preparing financial statements; and (8) closing.

4 **Record transactions in journals, post to ledger accounts, and prepare a trial balance.** The simplest journal form chronologically lists transactions and events expressed in terms of debits and credits to particular accounts. The items entered in a general journal must be transferred (posted) to the general ledger. Companies should prepare an unadjusted trial balance at the end of a given period after they have recorded the entries in the journal and posted them to the ledger.

5 **Explain the reasons for preparing adjusting entries and identify major types of adjusting entries.** Adjustments achieve a proper recognition of revenues and expenses, so as to determine net income for the current period and to achieve an accurate statement of end-of-the-period balances in assets, liabilities, and owners' equity accounts. The major types of adjusting entries are deferrals (prepaid expenses and unearned revenues) and accruals (accrued revenues and accrued expenses).

6 **Prepare financial statements from the adjusted trial balance.** Companies can prepare financial statements directly from the adjusted trial balance. The income statement is prepared from the revenue and expense accounts. The statement of retained earnings is prepared from the retained earnings account, dividends, and net income (or net loss). The balance sheet is prepared from the asset, liability, and equity accounts.

7 **Prepare closing entries.** In the closing process, the company transfers all of the revenue and expense account balances (income statement items) to a clearing account called Income Summary, which is used only at the end of the fiscal year. Revenues and expenses are matched in the Income Summary account. The net result of this matching represents the net income or net loss for the period. That amount is then transferred to an owners' equity account (Retained Earnings for a corporation and capital accounts for proprietorships and partnerships).

8 **Prepare financial statements for a merchandising company.** The financial statements for a merchandiser differ from those for a service company, as a merchandiser must account for gross profit on sales. The accounting cycle, however, is performed the same.

APPENDIX 3A   **CASH-BASIS ACCOUNTING VERSUS ACCRUAL-BASIS ACCOUNTING**

LEARNING OBJECTIVE 9

Differentiate the cash basis of accounting from the accrual basis of accounting.

Most companies use **accrual-basis accounting**: They recognize revenue when the performance obligation is satisfied and expenses in the period incurred, without regard to the time of receipt or payment of cash.

Some small companies and the average individual taxpayer, however, use a strict or modified cash-basis approach. Under the **strict cash basis**, companies record revenue only when they receive cash. They record expenses only when they disperse cash. Determining income on the cash basis rests upon collecting revenue and paying expenses. The cash basis ignores two principles: the revenue recognition principle and the expense recognition principle. Consequently, cash-basis financial statements are not in conformity with GAAP.

An illustration will help clarify the differences between accrual-basis and cash-basis accounting. Assume that Quality Contractor signs an agreement to construct a garage for $22,000. In January, Quality begins construction, incurs costs of $18,000 on credit, and by the end of January delivers a finished garage to the buyer. In February, Quality collects $22,000 cash from the customer. In March, Quality pays the $18,000 due the creditors. Illustrations 3A-1 and 3A-2 show the net incomes for each month under cash-basis accounting and accrual-basis accounting.

QUALITY CONTRACTOR INCOME STATEMENT—CASH BASIS FOR THE MONTH OF				
	January	February	March	Total
Cash receipts	$–0–	$22,000	$ –0–	$22,000
Cash payments	–0–	–0–	18,000	18,000
Net income (loss)	$–0–	$22,000	$(18,000)	$ 4,000

ILLUSTRATION 3A-1
Income Statement—Cash Basis

QUALITY CONTRACTOR INCOME STATEMENT—ACCRUAL BASIS FOR THE MONTH OF				
	January	February	March	Total
Revenues	$22,000	$–0–	$–0–	$22,000
Expenses	18,000	–0–	–0–	18,000
Net income (loss)	$ 4,000	$–0–	$–0–	$ 4,000

ILLUSTRATION 3A-2
Income Statement—Accrual Basis

For the three months combined, total net income is the same under both cash-basis accounting and accrual-basis accounting. The difference is in the **timing** of revenues and expenses. The basis of accounting also affects the balance sheet. Illustrations 3A-3 and 3A-4 (page 120) show Quality Contractor's balance sheets at each month-end under the cash basis and the accrual basis.

QUALITY CONTRACTOR BALANCE SHEET—CASH BASIS AS OF			
	January 31	February 28	March 31
Assets			
Cash	$–0–	$22,000	$4,000
Total assets	$–0–	$22,000	$4,000
Liabilities and Owners' Equity			
Owners' equity	$–0–	$22,000	$4,000
Total liabilities and owners' equity	$–0–	$22,000	$4,000

ILLUSTRATION 3A-3
Balance Sheets—Cash Basis

ILLUSTRATION 3A-4
Balance Sheets—Accrual
Basis

QUALITY CONTRACTOR			
BALANCE SHEET—ACCRUAL BASIS			
AS OF			
	January 31	February 28	March 31
Assets			
Cash	$ –0–	$22,000	$4,000
Accounts receivable	22,000	–0–	–0–
Total assets	$22,000	$22,000	$4,000
Liabilities and Owners' Equity			
Accounts payable	$18,000	$18,000	$ –0–
Owners' equity	4,000	4,000	4,000
Total liabilities and owners' equity	$22,000	$22,000	$4,000

Analysis of Quality's income statements and balance sheets shows the ways in which cash-basis accounting is inconsistent with basic accounting theory:

1. The cash basis understates revenues and assets from the construction and delivery of the garage in January. It ignores the $22,000 of accounts receivable, representing a near-term future cash inflow.
2. The cash basis understates expenses incurred with the construction of the garage and the liability outstanding at the end of January. It ignores the $18,000 of accounts payable, representing a near-term future cash outflow.
3. The cash basis understates owners' equity in January by not recognizing the revenues and the asset until February. It also overstates owners' equity in February by not recognizing the expenses and the liability until March.

In short, cash-basis accounting violates the accrual concept underlying financial reporting.

The **modified cash basis** is a mixture of the cash basis and the accrual basis. It is based on the strict cash basis but with modifications that have substantial support, such as capitalizing and depreciating plant assets or recording inventory. This method is often followed by professional services firms (doctors, lawyers, accountants, and consultants) and by retail, real estate, and agricultural operations.[3]

CONVERSION FROM CASH BASIS TO ACCRUAL BASIS

Not infrequently, companies want to convert a cash basis or a modified cash basis set of financial statements to the accrual basis for presentation to investors and creditors. To illustrate this conversion, assume that Dr. Diane Windsor, like many small business owners, keeps her accounting records on a cash basis. In the year 2014, Dr. Windsor

---

[3]Companies in the following situations might use a cash or modified cash basis.

(1) A company that is primarily interested in cash flows (for example, a group of physicians that distributes cash-basis earnings for salaries and bonuses).

(2) A company that has a limited number of financial statement users (small, closely held company with little or no debt).

(3) A company that has operations that are relatively straightforward (small amounts of inventory, long-term assets, or long-term debt).

received $300,000 from her patients and paid $170,000 for operating expenses, resulting in an excess of cash receipts over disbursements of $130,000 ($300,000 − $170,000). At January 1 and December 31, 2014, she has accounts receivable, unearned service revenue, accrued liabilities, and prepaid expenses as shown in Illustration 3A-5.

	January 1, 2014	December 31, 2014
Accounts receivable	$12,000	$9,000
Unearned service revenue	–0–	4,000
Accrued liabilities	2,000	5,500
Prepaid expenses	1,800	2,700

ILLUSTRATION 3A-5
Financial Information Related to Dr. Diane Windsor

Service Revenue Computation

To convert the amount of cash received from patients to service revenue on an accrual basis, we must consider changes in accounts receivable and unearned service revenue during the year. Accounts receivable at the beginning of the year represents revenues recognized last year that are collected this year. Ending accounts receivable indicates revenues recognized this year that are not yet collected. Therefore, to compute revenue on an accrual basis, we subtract beginning accounts receivable and add ending accounts receivable, as the formula in Illustration 3A-6 shows.

ILLUSTRATION 3A-6
Conversion of Cash Receipts to Revenue— Accounts Receivable

Similarly, beginning unearned service revenue represents cash received last year for revenues recognized this year. Ending unearned service revenue results from collections this year that will be recognized as revenue next year. Therefore, to compute revenue on an accrual basis, we add beginning unearned service revenue and subtract ending unearned service revenue, as the formula in Illustration 3A-7 shows.

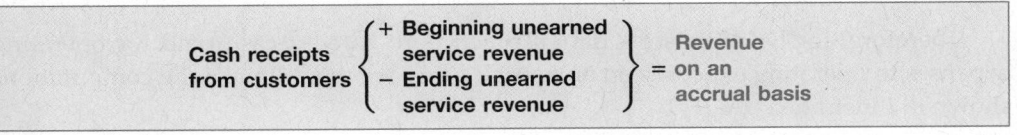

ILLUSTRATION 3A-7
Conversion of Cash Receipts to Revenue— Unearned Service Revenue

Therefore, for Dr. Windsor's dental practice, to convert cash collected from customers to service revenue on an accrual basis, we would make the computations shown in Illustration 3A-8.

Cash receipts from customers		$300,000
− Beginning accounts receivable	$(12,000)	
+ Ending accounts receivable	9,000	
+ Beginning unearned service revenue	–0–	
− Ending unearned service revenue	(4,000)	(7,000)
Service revenue (accrual)		$293,000

ILLUSTRATION 3A-8
Conversion of Cash Receipts to Service Revenue

Operating Expense Computation

To convert cash paid for operating expenses during the year to operating expenses on an accrual basis, we must consider changes in prepaid expenses and accrued liabilities. First, we need to recognize as this year's expenses the amount of beginning prepaid expenses. (The cash payment for these occurred last year.) Therefore, to arrive at operating expense on an accrual basis, we add the beginning prepaid expenses balance to cash paid for operating expenses.

Conversely, ending prepaid expenses result from cash payments made this year for expenses to be reported next year. (Under the accrual basis, Dr. Windsor would have deferred recognizing these payments as expenses until a future period.) To convert these cash payments to operating expenses on an accrual basis, we deduct ending prepaid expenses from cash paid for expenses, as the formula in Illustration 3A-9 shows.

ILLUSTRATION 3A-9
Conversion of Cash Payments to Expenses—Prepaid Expenses

Cash paid for operating expenses { + Beginning prepaid expenses − Ending prepaid expenses } = Expenses on an accrual basis

Similarly, beginning accrued liabilities result from expenses recognized last year that require cash payments this year. Ending accrued liabilities relate to expenses recognized this year that have not been paid. To arrive at expenses on an accrual basis, we deduct beginning accrued liabilities and add ending accrued liabilities to cash paid for expenses, as the formula in Illustration 3A-10 shows.

ILLUSTRATION 3A-10
Conversion of Cash Payments to Expenses—Accrued Liabilities

Cash paid for operating expenses { − Beginning accrued liabilities + Ending accrued liabilities } = Expenses on an accrual basis

Therefore, for Dr. Windsor's dental practice, to convert cash paid for operating expenses to operating expenses on an accrual basis, we would make the computations shown in Illustration 3A-11.

ILLUSTRATION 3A-11
Conversion of Cash Paid to Operating Expenses

Cash paid for operating expenses		$170,000
+ Beginning prepaid expense	$ 1,800	
− Ending prepaid expense	(2,700)	
− Beginning accrued liabilities	(2,000)	
+ Ending accrued liabilities	5,500	2,600
Operating expenses (accrual)		$172,600

This entire conversion can be completed in worksheet form, as shown in Illustration 3A-12.

	Home Insert Page Layout Formulas Data Review View				
	P18 *fx*				
	A	B	C	D	E
1					
2	**DIANE WINDSOR, D.D.S.**				
3	Conversion of Income Statement Data from Cash Basis to Accrual Basis				
4	For the Year 2014				
5		Cash			Accrual
6		Basis	Adjustments		Basis
7	Account Titles		Add	Deduct	
8	Collections from customers	$300,000			
9	– Accounts receivable, Jan. 1			$12,000	
10	+ Accounts receivable, Dec. 31		$9,000		
11	+ Unearned service revenue, Jan. 1		—	—	
12	– Unearned service revenue, Dec. 31			4,000	
13	Service revenue				$293,000
14	Disbursement for expenses	170,000			
15	+ Prepaid expenses, Jan. 1		1,800		
16	– Prepaid expenses, Dec. 31			2,700	
17	– Accrued liabilities, Jan. 1			2,000	
18	+ Accrued liabilities, Dec. 31		5,500		
19	Operating expenses				172,600
20	Excess of cash collections over disbursements—cash basis	$130,000			
21	Net income—accrual basis				$120,400
22					

Using this approach, we adjust collections and disbursements on a cash basis to revenue and expense on an accrual basis, to arrive at accrual net income. In any conversion from the cash basis to the accrual basis, depreciation or amortization is an additional expense in arriving at net income on an accrual basis.

THEORETICAL WEAKNESSES OF THE CASH BASIS

The cash basis reports exactly when cash is received and when cash is disbursed. To many people, that information represents something concrete. Isn't cash what it is all about? Does it make sense to invent something, design it, produce it, market and sell it, if you aren't going to get cash for it in the end? Many frequently say, "Cash is the real bottom line," and also, "Cash is the oil that lubricates the economy." If so, then what is the merit of accrual accounting?

Today's economy is considerably more lubricated by credit than by cash. The accrual basis, not the cash basis, recognizes all aspects of the credit phenomenon. Investors, creditors, and other decision-makers seek timely information about a company's *future* cash flows. Accrual-basis accounting provides this information by reporting the cash inflows and outflows associated with earnings activities as soon as these companies can estimate these cash flows with an acceptable degree of certainty. Receivables and payables are forecasters of future cash inflows and outflows. In other words, accrual-basis accounting aids in predicting future cash flows by reporting transactions and other events with cash consequences at the time the transactions and events occur, rather than when the cash is received and paid.

KEY TERMS

accrual-basis
  accounting, *118*
modified cash basis, *120*
strict cash basis, *118*

SUMMARY OF LEARNING OBJECTIVE FOR APPENDIX 3A

9 **Differentiate the cash basis of accounting from the accrual basis of accounting.** The cash basis of accounting records revenues when cash is received and expenses when cash is paid. The accrual basis recognizes revenue when the performance obligation is satisfied and expenses in the period incurred, without regard to the time of the receipt or payment of cash. Accrual-basis accounting is theoretically preferable because it provides information about future cash inflows and outflows associated with earnings activities as soon as companies can estimate these cash flows with an acceptable degree of certainty. Cash-basis accounting is not in conformity with GAAP.

APPENDIX 3B **USING REVERSING ENTRIES**

LEARNING OBJECTIVE 10
Identify adjusting entries that may be reversed.

Use of reversing entries simplifies the recording of transactions in the next accounting period. The use of reversing entries, however, does not change the amounts reported in the financial statements for the previous period.

ILLUSTRATION OF REVERSING ENTRIES—ACCRUALS

A company most often uses reversing entries to reverse two types of adjusting entries: accrued revenues and accrued expenses. To illustrate the optional use of reversing entries for accrued expenses, we use the following transaction and adjustment data.

1. October 24 (initial salaries and wages entry): Paid $4,000 of salaries and wages incurred between October 10 and October 24.

2. October 31 (adjusting entry): Incurred salaries and wages between October 25 and October 31 of $1,200, to be paid in the November 8 payroll.

3. November 8 (subsequent salaries and wages entry): Paid salaries and wages of $2,500. Of this amount, $1,200 applied to accrued salaries and wages payable at October 31 and $1,300 to salaries and wages payable for November 1 through November 8.

Illustration 3B-1 shows the comparative entries.

The comparative entries show that the first three entries are the same whether or not the company uses reversing entries. The last two entries differ. The November 1 reversing entry eliminates the $1,200 balance in Salaries and Wages Payable, created by the October 31 adjusting entry. The reversing entry also creates a $1,200 credit balance in the Salaries and Wages Expense account. As you know, it is unusual for an expense account to have a credit balance. However, the balance is correct in this instance. Why? Because the company will debit the entire amount of the first salaries and wages payment in the new accounting period to Salaries and Wages Expense. This debit eliminates the credit balance. The resulting debit balance in the expense account will equal the salaries and wages expense incurred in the new accounting period ($1,300 in this example).

REVERSING ENTRIES NOT USED				REVERSING ENTRIES USED		
Initial Salary Entry						
Oct. 24	Salaries and Wages Expense	4,000		Oct. 24	Salaries and Wages Expense	4,000
	Cash		4,000		Cash		4,000
Adjusting Entry						
Oct. 31	Salaries and Wages Expense	1,200		Oct. 31	Salaries and Wages Expense	1,200
	Salaries and Wages Payable		1,200		Salaries and Wages Payable		1,200
Closing Entry						
Oct. 31	Income Summary	5,200		Oct. 31	Income Summary	5,200
	Salaries and Wages Expense		5,200		Salaries and Wages Expense		5,200
Reversing Entry						
Nov. 1	No entry is made.			Nov. 1	Salaries and Wages Payable	1,200
					Salaries and Wages Expense		1,200
Subsequent Salary Entry						
Nov. 8	Salaries and Wages Payable	1,200		Nov. 8	Salaries and Wages Expense	2,500
	Salaries and Wages Expense	1,300			Cash		2,500
	Cash		2,500			

ILLUSTRATION 3B-1
Comparison of Entries for Accruals, with and without Reversing Entries

When a company makes reversing entries, it debits all cash payments of expenses to the related expense account. This means that on November 8 (and every payday), the company debits Salaries and Wages Expense for the amount paid without regard to the existence of any accrued salaries and wages payable. Repeating the same entry simplifies the recording process in an accounting system.

ILLUSTRATION OF REVERSING ENTRIES—DEFERRALS

Up to this point, we assumed the recording of all deferrals as prepaid expense or unearned revenue. In some cases, though, a company records deferrals directly in expense or revenue accounts. When this occurs, a company may also reverse deferrals.

To illustrate the use of reversing entries for prepaid expenses, we use the following transaction and adjustment data.

1. December 10 (initial entry): Purchased $20,000 of office supplies with cash.
2. December 31 (adjusting entry): Determined that $5,000 of office supplies are on hand.

Illustration 3B-2 (page 126) shows the comparative entries.

After the adjusting entry on December 31 (regardless of whether using reversing entries), the asset account Supplies shows a balance of $5,000, and Supplies Expense shows a balance of $15,000. If the company initially debits Supplies Expense when it purchases the supplies, it then makes a reversing entry to return to the expense account the cost of unconsumed supplies. The company then continues to debit Supplies Expense for additional purchases of supplies during the next period.

Deferrals are generally entered in real accounts (assets and liabilities), thus making reversing entries unnecessary. This approach is used because it is advantageous for items that a company needs to apportion over several periods (e.g., supplies and parts inventories). However, for other items that do not follow this regular pattern and that may or may not involve two or more periods, a company ordinarily enters them initially

REVERSING ENTRIES NOT USED				REVERSING ENTRIES USED		
Initial Purchase of Supplies Entry						
Dec. 10	Supplies	20,000		Dec. 10	Supplies Expense	20,000
	Cash		20,000		Cash	20,000
Adjusting Entry						
Dec. 31	Supplies Expense	15,000		Dec. 31	Supplies	5,000
	Supplies		15,000		Supplies Expense	5,000
Closing Entry						
Dec. 31	Income Summary	15,000		Dec. 31	Income Summary	15,000
	Supplies Expense		15,000		Supplies Expense	15,000
Reversing Entry						
Jan. 1	No entry			Jan. 1	Supplies Expense	5,000
					Supplies	5,000

ILLUSTRATION 3B-2
Comparison of Entries for Deferrals, with and without Reversing Entries

in revenue or expense accounts. The revenue and expense accounts may not require adjusting, and the company thus systematically closes them to Income Summary.

Using the nominal accounts adds consistency to the accounting system. It also makes the recording more efficient, particularly when a large number of such transactions occur during the year. For example, the bookkeeper knows to expense invoice items (except for capital asset acquisitions). He or she need not worry whether an item will result in a prepaid expense at the end of the period because the company will make adjustments at the end of the period.

SUMMARY OF REVERSING ENTRIES

We summarize guidelines for reversing entries as follows.

1. All accruals should be reversed.
2. All deferrals for which a company debited or credited the original cash transaction to an expense or revenue account should be reversed.
3. Adjusting entries for depreciation and bad debts are not reversed.

Recognize that reversing entries do not have to be used. Therefore, some accountants avoid them entirely.

SUMMARY OF LEARNING OBJECTIVE FOR APPENDIX 3B

10 **Identify adjusting entries that may be reversed.** Reversing entries are most often used to reverse two types of adjusting entries: accrued revenues and accrued expenses. Deferrals may also be reversed if the initial entry to record the transaction is made to an expense or revenue account.

APPENDIX 3C	USING A WORKSHEET: THE ACCOUNTING CYCLE REVISITED

n this appendix, we provide an additional illustration of the end-of-period steps n the accounting cycle and illustrate the use of a worksheet in this process. Using a worksheet often facilitates the end-of-period (monthly, quarterly, or annually) ccounting and reporting process. Use of a worksheet helps a company prepare the inancial statements on a more timely basis. How? With a worksheet, a company need not wait until it journalizes and posts the adjusting and closing entries.

11 LEARNING OBJECTIVE
Prepare a 10-column worksheet.

A company prepares a worksheet either on columnar paper or within a computer spreadsheet. In either form, a company uses the worksheet to adjust account balances and to prepare financial statements.

The worksheet does not replace the financial statements. Instead, it is an informal device for accumulating and sorting information needed for the financial statements. Completing the worksheet provides considerable assurance that a company properly handled all of the details related to the end-of-period accounting and statement preparation. The 10-column worksheet in Illustration 3C-1 (on page 128) provides columns for the first trial balance, adjustments, adjusted trial balance, income statement, and balance sheet.

WORKSHEET COLUMNS

Trial Balance Columns

Uptown Cabinet Corp., shown in Illustration 3C-1 (page 128), obtains data for the trial balance from its ledger balances at December 31. The amount for Inventory, $40,000, is the year-end inventory amount, which results from the application of a perpetual inventory system.

Adjustments Columns

After Uptown enters all adjustment data on the worksheet, it establishes the equality of the adjustment columns. It then extends the balances in all accounts to the adjusted trial balance columns.

ADJUSTMENTS ENTERED ON THE WORKSHEET

Items (a) through (g) below serve as the basis for the adjusting entries made in the worksheet for Uptown shown in Illustration 3C-1.

a) Depreciation of equipment at the rate of 10 percent per year based on original cost of $67,000.
b) Estimated bad debts of one-quarter of 1 percent of sales ($400,000).
c) Insurance expired during the year $360.
d) Interest accrued on notes receivable as of December 31, $800.
e) The Rent Expense account contains $500 rent paid in advance, which is applicable to next year.
f) Property taxes accrued December 31, $2,000.
g) Income taxes payable estimated $3,440.

Uptown Cabinet Corp.xls

Home | Insert | Page Layout | Formulas | Data | Review | View

P18 | fx

UPTOWN CABINET CORP.
Ten-Column Worksheet
For the Year Ended December 31, 2014

Account Titles	Trial Balance Dr.	Cr.	Adjustments Dr.	Cr.	Adjusted Trial Balance Dr.	Cr.	Income Statement Dr.	Cr.	Balance Sheet Dr.	Cr.
Cash	1,200				1,200				1,200	
Notes receivable	16,000				16,000				16,000	
Accounts receivable	41,000				41,000				41,000	
Allowance for doubtful accounts		2,000		(b) 1,000		3,000				3,000
Inventory	40,000				40,000				40,000	
Prepaid insurance	900			(c) 360	540				540	
Equipment	67,000				67,000				67,000	
Accumulated depreciation—equipment		12,000		(a) 6,700		18,700				18,700
Notes payable		20,000				20,000				20,000
Accounts payable		13,500				13,500				13,500
Bonds payable		30,000				30,000				30,000
Common stock		50,000				50,000				50,000
Retained earnings, Jan. 1, 2014		16,200				16,200				16,200
Dividends	2,000				2,000				2,000	
Sales revenue		400,000				400,000		400,000		
Cost of goods sold	316,000				316,000		316,000			
Salaries and wages expense (sales)	20,000				20,000		20,000			
Advertising expense	10,200				10,200		10,200			
Salaries and wages expense (general)	19,000				19,000		19,000			
Telephone and Internet expense	600				600		600			
Rent expense	4,800			(e) 500	4,300		4,300			
Property tax expense	3,300		(f) 2,000		5,300		5,300			
Interest expense	1,700				1,700		1,700			
Totals	543,700	543,700								
Depreciation expense			(a) 6,700		6,700		6,700			
Bad debt expense			(b) 1,000		1,000		1,000			
Insurance expense			(c) 360		360		360			
Interest receivable			(d) 800		800				800	
Interest revenue				(d) 800		800		800		
Prepaid rent			(e) 500		500				500	
Property taxes payable				(f) 2,000		2,000				2,000
Income tax expense			(g) 3,440		3,440		3,440			
Income tax payable				(g) 3,440		3,440				3,440
Totals			14,800	14,800	557,640	557,640	388,600	400,800		
Net income							12,200			12,200
Totals							400,800	400,800	169,040	169,040

ILLUSTRATION 3C-1
Use of a Worksheet

The adjusting entries shown on the December 31, 2014, worksheet are as follows.

(a)

Depreciation Expense	6,700	
Accumulated Depreciation—Equipment		6,700

(b)

Bad Debt Expense	1,000	
Allowance for Doubtful Accounts		1,000

(c)

Insurance Expense	360	
Prepaid Insurance		360

(d)

Interest Receivable	800	
Interest Revenue		800

(e)

Prepaid Rent	500	
Rent Expense		500

(f)

Property Tax Expense	2,000	
Property Taxes Payable		2,000

(g)

Income Tax Expense	3,440	
Income Taxes Payable		3,440

Uptown Cabinet transfers the adjusting entries to the Adjustments columns of the worksheet, often designating each by letter. The trial balance lists any new accounts resulting from the adjusting entries, as illustrated on the worksheet. (For example, see the accounts listed in rows 32 through 40 in Illustration 3C-1.) Uptown then totals and balances the Adjustments columns.

Adjusted Trial Balance

The adjusted trial balance shows the balance of all accounts after adjustment at the end of the accounting period. For example, Uptown adds the $2,000 shown opposite the Allowance for Doubtful Accounts in the Trial Balance Cr. column to the $1,000 in the Adjustments Cr. column. The company then extends the $3,000 total to the Adjusted Trial Balance Cr. column. Similarly, Uptown reduces the $900 debit opposite Prepaid Insurance by the $360 credit in the Adjustments column. The result, $540, is shown in the Adjusted Trial Balance Dr. column.

Income Statement and Balance Sheet Columns

Uptown extends all the debit items in the Adjusted Trial Balance columns into the Income Statement or Balance Sheet columns to the right. It similarly extends all the credit items.

The next step is to total the Income Statement columns. Uptown needs the amount of net income or loss for the period to balance the debit and credit columns. The net income of $12,200 is shown in the Income Statement Dr. column because revenues exceeded expenses by that amount.

Uptown then balances the Income Statement columns. The company also enters the net income of $12,200 in the Balance Sheet Cr. column as an increase in retained earnings.

PREPARING FINANCIAL STATEMENTS FROM A WORKSHEET

The worksheet provides the information needed for preparation of the financial statements without reference to the ledger or other records. In addition, the worksheet sorts that data into appropriate columns, which facilitates the preparation of the statements. The financial statements of Uptown Cabinet are shown in Chapter 3 (pages 115–116).

SUMMARY OF LEARNING OBJECTIVE FOR APPENDIX 3C

11 **Prepare a 10-column worksheet.** The 10-column worksheet provides columns for the first trial balance, adjustments, adjusted trial balance, income statement, and balance sheet. The worksheet does not replace the financial statements. Instead, it is an informal device for accumulating and sorting information needed for the financial statements.

DEMONSTRATION PROBLEM

Nalezny Advertising Agency was founded by Casey Hayward in January 2005. Presented below are both the adjusted and unadjusted trial balances as of December 31, 2014.

NALEZNY ADVERTISING AGENCY
TRIAL BALANCE
DECEMBER 31, 2014

	Unadjusted		Adjusted	
	Dr.	Cr.	Dr.	Cr.
Cash	$ 11,000		$ 11,000	
Accounts Receivable	20,000		21,500	
Supplies	8,400		5,000	
Equipment	60,000		60,000	
Accumulated Depreciation—Equipment		$ 28,000		$ 35,000
Accounts Payable		5,000		5,000
Unearned Advertising Revenue		7,000		5,600
Salaries and Wages Payable		–0–		1,300
Common Stock		10,000		10,000
Retained Earnings		4,800		4,800
Advertising Revenue		58,600		61,500
Salaries and Wages Expense	10,000		11,300	
Depreciation Expense			7,000	
Supplies Expense			3,400	
Rent Expense	4,000		4,000	
	$113,400	$113,400	$123,200	$123,200

Instructions

(a) Journalize the annual adjusting entries that were made.

(b) Prepare an income statement for the year ending December 31, 2014, and a balance sheet at December 31.

(c) Describe the remaining steps in the accounting cycle to be completed by Nalezny for 2014.

Solution

(a)

Dec. 31	Accounts Receivable	1,500	
	Advertising Revenue		1,500
31	Unearned Advertising Revenue	1,400	
	Advertising Revenue		1,400
31	Supplies Expense	3,400	
	Supplies		3,400
31	Depreciation Expense	7,000	
	Accumulated Depreciation—Equipment		7,000
31	Salaries and Wages Expense	1,300	
	Salaries and Wages Payable		1,300

(b)

NALEZNY ADVERTISING AGENCY
INCOME STATEMENT
FOR THE YEAR ENDED DECEMBER 31, 2014

Revenues		
Advertising revenue		$61,500
Expenses		
Salaries and wages expense	$11,300	
Depreciation expense	7,000	
Rent expense	4,000	
Supplies expense	3,400	
Total expenses		25,700
Net income		$35,800

NALEZNY ADVERTISING AGENCY
BALANCE SHEET
DECEMBER 31, 2014

Assets

Cash		$11,000
Accounts receivable		21,500
Supplies		5,000
Equipment	$60,000	
Less: Accumulated depreciation—equipment	35,000	25,000
Total assets		$62,500

Liabilities and Stockholders' Equity

Liabilities		
Accounts payable		$ 5,000
Unearned advertising revenue		5,600
Salaries and wage payable		1,300
Total liabilities		11,900
Stockholders' equity		
Common stock	$10,000	
Retained earnings	40,600*	50,600
Total liabilities and stockholders' equity		$62,500

*Retained earnings, Jan. 1, 2014	$ 4,800
Add: Net income	35,800
Retained earnings, Dec. 31, 2014	$40,600

(c) Following preparation of financial statements (part (b)), Nalezny would prepare closing entries to reduce the temporary accounts to zero. Some companies prepare a post-closing trial balance and reversing entries.

WileyPLUS Brief Exercises, Exercises, Problems, and many more learning and assessment tools and resources are available for practice in WileyPLUS.

Note: All asterisked Questions, Exercises, and Problems relate to material in the appendices to the chapter.

QUESTIONS

1. Give an example of a transaction that results in:
   (a) A decrease in an asset and a decrease in a liability.
   (b) A decrease in one asset and an increase in another asset.
   (c) A decrease in one liability and an increase in another liability.

2. Do the following events represent business transactions? Explain your answer in each case.
   (a) A computer is purchased on account.
   (b) A customer returns merchandise and is given credit on account.
   (c) A prospective employee is interviewed.
   (d) The owner of the business withdraws cash from the business for personal use.
   (e) Merchandise is ordered for delivery next month.

3. Name the accounts debited and credited for each of the following transactions.
   (a) Billing a customer for work done.
   (b) Receipt of cash from customer on account.
   (c) Purchase of office supplies on account.
   (d) Purchase of 15 gallons of gasoline for the delivery truck.

4. Why are revenue and expense accounts called temporary or nominal accounts?

5. Andrea Pafko, a fellow student, contends that the double-entry system means that each transaction must be recorded twice. Is Andrea correct? Explain.

6. Is it necessary that a trial balance be taken periodically? What purpose does it serve?

7. Indicate whether each of the following items is a real or nominal account and whether it appears in the balance sheet or the income statement.

(a) Prepaid Rent.
(b) Salaries and Wages Payable.
(c) Inventory.
(d) Accumulated Depreciation—Equipment.
(e) Equipment.
(f) Service Revenue.
(g) Salaries and Wages Expense.
(h) Supplies.

8. Employees are paid every Saturday for the preceding work week. If a balance sheet is prepared on Wednesday, December 31, what does the amount of wages earned during the first three days of the week (12/29, 12/30, 12/31) represent? Explain.

9. (a) How are the components of revenues and expenses different for a merchandising company? (b) Explain the income measurement process of a merchandising company.

10. What differences are there between the trial balance before closing and the trial balance after closing with respect to the following accounts?
    (a) Accounts Payable.
    (b) Expense accounts.
    (c) Revenue accounts.
    (d) Retained Earnings account.
    (e) Cash.

11. What are adjusting entries and why are they necessary?

12. What are closing entries and why are they necessary?

13. Jay Hawk, maintenance supervisor for Boston Insurance Co., has purchased a riding lawnmower and accessories to be used in maintaining the grounds around corporate headquarters. He has sent the following information to the accounting department.

Cost of mower and accessories	$4,000	Date purchased	7/1/14
Estimated useful life	5 yrs	Monthly salary of groundskeeper	$1,100
Salvage value	$0	Estimated annual fuel cost	$150

Compute the amount of depreciation expense (related to the mower and accessories) that should be reported on Boston's December 31, 2014, income statement. Assume straight-line depreciation.

14. Midwest Enterprises made the following entry on December 31, 2014.

Interest Expense	10,000	
Interest Payable		10,000
(To record interest expense due on loan from Anaheim National Bank)		

What entry would Anaheim National Bank make regarding its outstanding loan to Midwest Enterprises? Explain why this must be the case.

*15. Distinguish between cash-basis accounting and accrual-basis accounting. Why is accrual-basis accounting acceptable for most businesses and the cash-basis unacceptable in the preparation of an income statement and a balance sheet?

*16. When salaries and wages expense for the year is computed, why are beginning accrued salaries and wages subtracted from, and ending accrued salaries and wages added to, salaries and wages paid during the year?

*17. List two types of transactions that would receive different accounting treatment using (a) strict cash-basis accounting, and (b) a modified cash basis.

*18. What are reversing entries, and why are they used?

*19. "A worksheet is a permanent accounting record, and its use is required in the accounting cycle." Do you agree? Explain.

BRIEF EXERCISES

4 **BE3-1** Transactions for Mehta Company for the month of May are presented below. Prepare journal entries for each of these transactions. (You may omit explanations.)

May	1	B.D. Mehta invests $4,000 cash in exchange for common stock in a small welding corporation.
	3	Buys equipment on account for $1,100.
	13	Pays $400 to landlord for May rent.
	21	Bills Noble Corp. $500 for welding work done.

4 **BE3-2** Agazzi Repair Shop had the following transactions during the first month of business as a proprietorship. Journalize the transactions. (Omit explanations.)

Aug.	2	Invested $12,000 cash and $2,500 of equipment in the business.
	7	Purchased supplies on account for $500. (Debit asset account.)
	12	Performed services for clients, for which $1,300 was collected in cash and $670 was billed to the clients.
	15	Paid August rent $600.
	19	Counted supplies and determined that only $270 of the supplies purchased on August 7 are still on hand.

4 **5** **BE3-3** On July 1, 2014, Crowe Co. pays $15,000 to Zubin Insurance Co. for a 3-year insurance policy. Both companies have fiscal years ending December 31. For Crowe Co., journalize the entry on July 1 and the adjusting entry on December 31.

4 **5** **BE3-4** Using the data in BE3-3, journalize the entry on July 1 and the adjusting entry on December 31 for Zubin Insurance Co. Zubin uses the accounts Unearned Service Revenue and Service Revenue.

4 **5** **BE3-5** Assume that on February 1, Procter & Gamble (P&G) paid $720,000 in advance for 2 years' insurance coverage. Prepare P&G's February 1 journal entry and the annual adjusting entry on June 30.

4 **5** **BE3-6** LaBouche Corporation owns a warehouse. On November 1, it rented storage space to a lessee (tenant) for 3 months for a total cash payment of $2,400 received in advance. Prepare LaBouche's November 1 journal entry and the December 31 annual adjusting entry.

4 **5** **BE3-7** Dresser Company's weekly payroll, paid on Fridays, totals $8,000. Employees work a 5-day week. Prepare Dresser's adjusting entry on Wednesday, December 31, and the journal entry to record the $8,000 cash payment on Friday, January 2.

5 **BE3-8** Included in Gonzalez Company's December 31 trial balance is a note receivable of $12,000. The note is a 4-month, 10% note dated October 1. Prepare Gonzalez's December 31 adjusting entry to record $300 of accrued interest, and the February 1 journal entry to record receipt of $12,400 from the borrower.

5 BE3-9 Prepare the following adjusting entries at August 31 for Walgreens.

(a) Interest on notes payable of $300 is accrued.
(b) Services performed but unbilled total $1,400.
(c) Salaries and wages earned by employees of $700 have not been recorded.
(d) Bad debt expense for year is $900.

Use the following account titles: Service Revenue, Accounts Receivable, Interest Expense, Interest Payable, Salaries and Wages Expense, Salaries and Wages Payable, Allowance for Doubtful Accounts, and Bad Debt Expense.

5 BE3-10 At the end of its first year of operations, the trial balance of Alonzo Company shows Equipment $30,000 and zero balances in Accumulated Depreciation—Equipment and Depreciation Expense. Depreciation for the year is estimated to be $2,000. Prepare the adjusting entry for depreciation at December 31, and indicate the balance sheet presentation for the equipment at December 31.

7 BE3-11 Side Kicks has year-end account balances of Sales Revenue $808,900; Interest Revenue $13,500; Cost of Goods Sold $556,200; Administrative Expenses $189,000; Income Tax Expense $35,100; and Dividends $18,900. Prepare the year-end closing entries.

9 *BE3-12 Kelly Company had cash receipts from customers in 2014 of $142,000. Cash payments for operating expenses were $97,000. Kelly has determined that at January 1, accounts receivable was $13,000, and prepaid expenses were $17,500. At December 31, accounts receivable was $18,600, and prepaid expenses were $23,200. Compute (a) service revenue and (b) operating expenses.

10 *BE3-13 Assume that Best Buy made a December 31 adjusting entry to debit Salaries and Wages Expense and credit Salaries and Wages Payable for $4,200 for one of its departments. On January 2, Best Buy paid the weekly payroll of $7,000. Prepare Best Buy's (a) January 1 reversing entry; (b) January 2 entry (assuming the reversing entry was prepared); and (c) January 2 entry (assuming the reversing entry was not prepared).

EXERCISES

4 E3-1 (Transaction Analysis—Service Company) Beverly Crusher is a licensed CPA. During the first month of operations of her business (a sole proprietorship), the following events and transactions occurred.

April	2	Invested $32,000 cash and equipment valued at $14,000 in the business.
	2	Hired a secretary-receptionist at a salary of $290 per week payable monthly.
	3	Purchased supplies on account $700. (Debit an asset account.)
	7	Paid office rent of $600 for the month.
	11	Completed a tax assignment and billed client $1,100 for services rendered. (Use Service Revenue account.)
	12	Received $3,200 advance on a management consulting engagement.
	17	Received cash of $2,300 for services completed for Ferengi Co.
	21	Paid insurance expense $110.
	30	Paid secretary-receptionist $1,160 for the month.
	30	A count of supplies indicated that $120 of supplies had been used.
	30	Purchased a new computer for $6,100 with personal funds. (The computer will be used exclusively for business purposes.)

Instructions
Journalize the transactions in the general journal. (Omit explanations.)

4 E3-2 (Corrected Trial Balance) The trial balance of Wanda Landowska Company (shown on the next page) does not balance. Your review of the ledger reveals the following. (a) Each account had a normal balance. (b) The debit footings in Prepaid Insurance, Accounts Payable, and Property Tax Expense were each understated $100. (c) A transposition error was made in Accounts Receivable and Service Revenue; the correct balances for Accounts Receivable and Service Revenue are $2,750 and $6,690, respectively. (d) A debit posting to Advertising Expense of $300 was omitted. (e) A $1,500 cash drawing by the owner was debited to Owner's Capital and credited to Cash.

WANDA LANDOWSKA COMPANY
TRIAL BALANCE
APRIL 30, 2014

	Debit	Credit
Cash	$ 4,800	
Accounts Receivable	2,570	
Prepaid Insurance	700	
Equipment		$ 8,000
Accounts Payable		4,500
Property Taxes Payable	560	
Owner's Capital		11,200
Service Revenue	6,960	
Salaries and Wages Expense	4,200	
Advertising Expense	1,100	
Property Tax Expense		800
	$20,890	$24,500

Instructions

Prepare a correct trial balance.

4 **E3-3 (Corrected Trial Balance)** The trial balance of Blues Traveler Corporation does not balance.

BLUES TRAVELER CORPORATION
TRIAL BALANCE
APRIL 30, 2014

	Debit	Credit
Cash	$ 5,912	
Accounts Receivable	5,240	
Supplies	2,967	
Equipment	6,100	
Accounts Payable		$ 7,044
Common Stock		8,000
Retained Earnings		2,000
Service Revenue		5,200
Office Expense	4,320	
	$24,539	$22,244

An examination of the ledger shows these errors.

1. Cash received from a customer on account was recorded (both debit and credit) as $1,380 instead of $1,830.
2. The purchase on account of a computer costing $3,200 was recorded as a debit to Office Expense and a credit to Accounts Payable.
3. Services were performed on account for a client, $2,250, for which Accounts Receivable was debited $2,250 and Service Revenue was credited $225.
4. A payment of $95 for telephone charges was entered as a debit to Office Expense and a debit to Cash.
5. The Service Revenue account was totaled at $5,200 instead of $5,280.

Instructions

From this information prepare a corrected trial balance.

4 **E3-4 (Corrected Trial Balance)** The trial balance of Watteau Co. (shown on the next page) does not balance.

WATTEAU CO.
TRIAL BALANCE
JUNE 30, 2014

	Debit	Credit
Cash		$ 2,870
Accounts Receivable	$ 3,231	
Supplies	800	
Equipment	3,800	
Accounts Payable		2,666
Unearned Service Revenue	1,200	
Common Stock		6,000
Retained Earnings		3,000
Service Revenue		2,380
Salaries and Wages Expense	3,400	
Office Expense	940	
	$13,371	$16,916

Each of the listed accounts should have a normal balance per the general ledger. An examination of the ledger and journal reveals the following errors.

1. Cash received from a customer on account was debited for $570, and Accounts Receivable was credited for the same amount. The actual collection was for $750.
2. The purchase of a computer printer on account for $500 was recorded as a debit to Supplies for $500 and a credit to Accounts Payable for $500.
3. Services were performed on account for a client for $890. Accounts Receivable was debited for $890 and Service Revenue was credited for $89.
4. A payment of $65 for telephone charges was recorded as a debit to Office Expense for $65 and a debit to Cash for $65.
5. When the Unearned Service Revenue account was reviewed, it was found that service revenue amounting to $325 was performed prior to June 30 (related to Unearned Service Revenue).
6. A debit posting to Salaries and Wages Expense of $670 was omitted.
7. A payment on account for $206 was credited to Cash for $206 and credited to Accounts Payable for $260.
8. A dividend of $575 was debited to Salaries and Wages Expense for $575 and credited to Cash for $575.

Instructions
Prepare a correct trial balance. (*Note:* It may be necessary to add one or more accounts to the trial balance.)

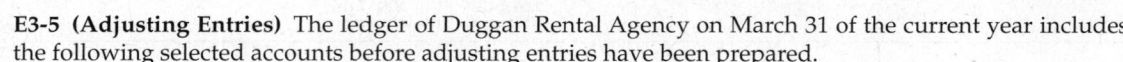

5 **E3-5 (Adjusting Entries)** The ledger of Duggan Rental Agency on March 31 of the current year includes the following selected accounts before adjusting entries have been prepared.

	Debit	Credit
Prepaid Insurance	$ 3,600	
Supplies	2,800	
Equipment	25,000	
Accumulated Depreciation—Equipment		$ 8,400
Notes Payable		20,000
Unearned Rent Revenue		9,300
Rent Revenue		60,000
Interest Expense	–0–	
Salaries and Wages Expense	14,000	

An analysis of the accounts shows the following.

1. The equipment depreciates $250 per month.
2. One-third of the unearned rent was recognized as revenue during the quarter.
3. Interest of $500 is accrued on the notes payable.
4. Supplies on hand total $850.
5. Insurance expires at the rate of $300 per month.

Instructions .

Prepare the adjusting entries at March 31, assuming that adjusting entries are made quarterly. Additional accounts are Depreciation Expense, Insurance Expense, Interest Payable, and Supplies Expense. (Omit explanations.)

5 **E3-6 (Adjusting Entries)** Karen Weller, D.D.S., opened a dental practice on January 1, 2014. During the first month of operations, the following transactions occurred.

1. Performed services for patients who had dental plan insurance. At January 31, $750 of such services was performed but not yet billed to the insurance companies.
2. Utility expenses incurred but not paid prior to January 31 totaled $520.
3. Purchased dental equipment on January 1 for $80,000, paying $20,000 in cash and signing a $60,000, 3-year note payable. The equipment depreciates $400 per month. Interest is $500 per month.
4. Purchased a one-year malpractice insurance policy on January 1 for $12,000.
5. Purchased $1,600 of dental supplies. On January 31, determined that $500 of supplies were on hand.

Instructions

Prepare the adjusting entries on January 31. (Omit explanations.) Account titles are Accumulated Depreciation—Equipment, Depreciation Expense, Service Revenue, Accounts Receivable, Insurance Expense, Interest Expense, Interest Payable, Prepaid Insurance, Supplies, Supplies Expense, Utilities Expense, and Accounts Payable.

5 **E3-7 (Analyze Adjusted Data)** A partial adjusted trial balance of Piper Company at January 31, 2014, shows the following.

PIPER COMPANY **ADJUSTED TRIAL BALANCE** **JANUARY 31, 2014**		
	Debit	Credit
Supplies	$ 700	
Prepaid Insurance	2,400	
Salaries and Wages Payable		$ 800
Unearned Service Revenue		750
Supplies Expense	950	
Insurance Expense	400	
Salaries and Wages Expense	1,800	
Service Revenue		2,000

Instructions

Answer the following questions, assuming the year begins January 1.

(a) If the amount in Supplies Expense is the January 31 adjusting entry, and $850 of supplies was purchased in January, what was the balance in Supplies on January 1?
(b) If the amount in Insurance Expense is the January 31 adjusting entry, and the original insurance premium was for one year, what was the total premium and when was the policy purchased?
(c) If $2,500 of salaries was paid in January, what was the balance in Salaries and Wages Payable at December 31, 2013?
(d) If $1,600 was received in January for services performed in January, what was the balance in Unearned Service Revenue at December 31, 2013?

5 **E3-8 (Adjusting Entries)** Andy Roddick is the new owner of Ace Computer Services. At the end of August 2014, his first month of ownership, Roddick is trying to prepare monthly financial statements. Below is some information related to unrecorded expenses that the business incurred during August.

1. At August 31, Roddick owed his employees $1,900 in wages that will be paid on September 1.
2. At the end of the month, he had not yet received the month's utility bill. Based on past experience, he estimated the bill would be approximately $600.
3. On August 1, Roddick borrowed $30,000 from a local bank on a 15-year mortgage. The annual interest rate is 8%.
4. A telephone bill in the amount of $117 covering August charges is unpaid at August 31.

Instructions

Prepare the adjusting journal entries as of August 31, 2014, suggested by the information above.

5 **E3-9** **(Adjusting Entries)** Selected accounts of Urdu Company are shown below.

Supplies				Accounts Receivable		
Beg. Bal.	800	10/31	470	10/17	2,400	
				10/31	1,650	

Salaries and Wages Expense			Salaries and Wages Payable		
10/15	800			10/31	600
10/31	600				

Unearned Service Revenue				Supplies Expense	
10/31	400	10/20	650	10/31	470

Service Revenue		
	10/17	2,400
	10/31	1,650
	10/31	400

Instructions

From an analysis of the T-accounts, reconstruct (a) the October transaction entries, and (b) the adjusting journal entries that were made on October 31, 2014. Prepare explanations for each journal entry.

5 **E3-10** **(Adjusting Entries)** Greco Resort opened for business on June 1 with eight air-conditioned units. Its trial balance on August 31 is as follows.

GRECO RESORT TRIAL BALANCE AUGUST 31, 2014		
	Debit	Credit
Cash	$ 19,600	
Prepaid Insurance	4,500	
Supplies	2,600	
Land	20,000	
Buildings	120,000	
Equipment	16,000	
Accounts Payable		$ 4,500
Unearned Rent Revenue		4,600
Mortgage Payable		60,000
Common Stock		91,000
Retained Earnings		9,000
Dividends	5,000	
Rent Revenue		76,200
Salaries and Wages Expense	44,800	
Utilities Expenses	9,200	
Maintenance and Repairs Expense	3,600	
	$245,300	$245,300

Other data:

1. The balance in prepaid insurance is a one-year premium paid on June 1, 2014.
2. An inventory count on August 31 shows $450 of supplies on hand.
3. Annual depreciation rates are buildings (4%) and equipment (10%). Salvage value is estimated to be 10% of cost.
4. Unearned Rent Revenue of $3,800 was earned prior to August 31.
5. Salaries of $375 were unpaid at August 31.
6. Rentals of $800 were due from tenants at August 31.
7. The mortgage interest rate is 8% per year.

Instructions

(a) Journalize the adjusting entries on August 31 for the 3-month period June 1–August 31. (Omit explanations.)

(b) Prepare an adjusted trial balance on August 31.

6 **E3-11 (Prepare Financial Statements)** The adjusted trial balance of Anderson Cooper Co. as of December 31, 2014, contains the following.

ANDERSON COOPER CO.
ADJUSTED TRIAL BALANCE
DECEMBER 31, 2014

Account Titles	Dr.	Cr.
Cash	$19,472	
Accounts Receivable	6,920	
Prepaid Rent	2,280	
Equipment	18,050	
Accumulated Depreciation—Equipment		$ 4,895
Notes Payable		5,700
Accounts Payable		5,472
Common Stock		20,000
Retained Earnings		11,310
Dividends	3,000	
Service Revenue		11,590
Salaries and Wages Expense	6,840	
Rent Expense	2,260	
Depreciation Expense	145	
Interest Expense	83	
Interest Payable		83
	$59,050	$59,050

Instructions

(a) Prepare an income statement.

(b) Prepare a statement of retained earnings.

(c) Prepare a classified balance sheet.

6 **E3-12 (Prepare Financial Statements)** Santo Design Agency was founded by Thomas Grant in January 2008. Presented below is the adjusted trial balance as of December 31, 2014.

SANTO DESIGN AGENCY
ADJUSTED TRIAL BALANCE
DECEMBER 31, 2014

	Dr.	Cr.
Cash	$ 11,000	
Accounts Receivable	21,500	
Supplies	5,000	
Prepaid Insurance	2,500	
Equipment	60,000	
Accumulated Depreciation—Equipment		$ 35,000
Accounts Payable		5,000
Interest Payable		150
Notes Payable		5,000
Unearned Service Revenue		5,600
Salaries and Wages Payable		1,300
Common Stock		10,000
Retained Earnings		3,500
Service Revenue		61,500
Salaries and Wages Expense	11,300	
Insurance Expense	850	
Interest Expense	500	
Depreciation Expense	7,000	
Supplies Expense	3,400	
Rent Expense	4,000	
	$127,050	$127,050

Instructions

(a) Prepare an income statement and a statement of retained earnings for the year ending December 31, 2014, and an unclassified balance sheet at December 31.

(b) Answer the following questions.

  (1) If the note has been outstanding 6 months, what is the annual interest rate on that note?

  (2) If the company paid $17,500 in salaries in 2014, what was the balance in Salaries and Wages Payable on December 31, 2013?

7 8 E3-13 (Closing Entries) The adjusted trial balance of Lopez Company shows the following data pertaining to sales at the end of its fiscal year, October 31, 2014: Sales Revenue $800,000, Delivery Expense $12,000, Sales Returns and Allowances $24,000, and Sales Discounts $15,000.

Instructions

(a) Prepare the revenues section of the income statement.

(b) Prepare separate closing entries for (1) sales and (2) the contra accounts to sales.

7 8 E3-14 (Closing Entries) Presented below is information related to Gonzales Corporation for the month of January 2014.

Cost of goods sold	$208,000	Salaries and wages expense	$ 61,000
Delivery expense	7,000	Sales discounts	8,000
Insurance expense	12,000	Sales returns and allowances	13,000
Rent expense	20,000	Sales revenue	350,000

Instructions

Prepare the necessary closing entries.

8 E3-15 (Missing Amounts) Presented below is financial information for two different companies.

	Alatorre Company	Eduardo Company
Sales revenue	$90,000	(d)
Sales returns and allowances	(a)	$ 5,000
Net sales	81,000	95,000
Cost of goods sold	56,000	(e)
Gross profit	(b)	38,000
Operating expenses	15,000	23,000
Net income	(c)	15,000

Instructions

Compute the missing amounts.

7 E3-16 (Closing Entries for a Corporation) Presented below are selected account balances for Homer Winslow Co. as of December 31, 2014.

Inventory 12/31/14	$ 60,000	Cost of Goods Sold	$225,700
Common Stock	75,000	Selling Expenses	16,000
Retained Earnings	45,000	Administrative Expenses	38,000
Dividends	18,000	Income Tax Expense	30,000
Sales Returns and Allowances	12,000		
Sales Discounts	15,000		
Sales Revenue	410,000		

Instructions

Prepare closing entries for Homer Winslow Co. on December 31, 2014. (Omit explanations.)

4 E3-17 (Transactions of a Corporation, Including Investment and Dividend) Scratch Miniature Golf and Driving Range Inc. was opened on March 1 by Scott Verplank. The following selected events and transactions occurred during March.

Mar. 1 Invested $50,000 cash in the business in exchange for common stock.

  3 Purchased Michelle Wie's Golf Land for $38,000 cash. The price consists of land $10,000, building $22,000, and equipment $6,000. (Make one compound entry.)

  5 Advertised the opening of the driving range and miniature golf course, paying advertising expenses of $1,600.

  6 Paid cash $1,480 for a one-year insurance policy.

  10 Purchased golf equipment for $2,500 from Singh Company, payable in 30 days.

Mar. 18	Received golf fees of $1,200 in cash.
25	Declared and paid a $500 cash dividend.
30	Paid wages of $900.
30	Paid Singh Company in full.
31	Received $750 of fees in cash.

Scratch uses the following accounts: Cash, Prepaid Insurance, Land, Buildings, Equipment, Accounts Payable, Common Stock, Dividends, Service Revenue, Advertising Expense, and Salaries and Wages Expense.

Instructions
Journalize the March transactions. (Provide explanations for the journal entries.)

9 *E3-18 (Cash to Accrual Basis)** Jill Accardo, M.D., maintains the accounting records of Accardo Clinic on a cash basis. During 2014, Dr. Accardo collected $142,600 from her patients and paid $55,470 in expenses. At January 1, 2014, and December 31, 2014, she had accounts receivable, unearned service revenue, accrued expenses, and prepaid expenses as follows. (All long-lived assets are rented.)

	January 1, 2014	December 31, 2014
Accounts receivable	$9,250	$15,927
Unearned service revenue	2,840	4,111
Accrued expenses	3,435	2,108
Prepaid expenses	1,917	3,232

Instructions
Prepare a schedule that converts Dr. Accardo's "excess of cash collected over cash disbursed" for the year 2014 to net income on an accrual basis for the year 2014.

9 *E3-19 (Cash and Accrual Basis)** Wayne Rogers Corp. maintains its financial records on the cash basis of accounting. Interested in securing a long-term loan from its regular bank, Wayne Rogers Corp. requests you as its independent CPA to convert its cash-basis income statement data to the accrual basis. You are provided with the following summarized data covering 2013, 2014, and 2015.

	2013	2014	2015
Cash receipts from sales:			
On 2013 sales	$295,000	$160,000	$ 30,000
On 2014 sales	–0–	355,000	90,000
On 2015 sales			408,000
Cash payments for expenses:			
On 2013 expenses	185,000	67,000	25,000
On 2014 expenses	40,000[a]	160,000	55,000
On 2015 expenses		45,000[b]	218,000

[a]Prepayments of 2014 expenses.
[b]Prepayments of 2015 expenses.

Instructions
(a) Using the data above, prepare abbreviated income statements for the years 2013 and 2014 on the cash basis.
(b) Using the data above, prepare abbreviated income statements for the years 2013 and 2014 on the accrual basis.

5 10 *E3-20 (Adjusting and Reversing Entries)** When the accounts of Daniel Barenboim Inc. are examined, the adjusting data listed below are uncovered on December 31, the end of an annual fiscal period.

1. The prepaid insurance account shows a debit of $5,280, representing the cost of a 2-year fire insurance policy dated August 1 of the current year.
2. On November 1, Rent Revenue was credited for $1,800, representing revenue from a subrental for a 3-month period beginning on that date.
3. Purchase of advertising materials for $800 during the year was recorded in the Advertising Expense account. On December 31, advertising materials of $290 are on hand.
4. Interest of $770 has accrued on notes payable.

Instructions
Prepare the following in general journal form.

(a) The adjusting entry for each item.
(b) The reversing entry for each item where appropriate.

11 *E3-21 (Worksheet) Presented below are selected accounts for Alvarez Company as reported in the worksheet at the end of May 2014.

		Alvarez Company.xls					
Home Insert Page Layout Formulas Data Review View							
P18 fx							
A	B	C	D	E	F	G	
		ALVAREZ CO.					
		Worksheet					
		For The Month Ended May 31, 2014					
	Adjusted Trial Balance		Income Statement		Balance Sheet		
Account Titles	Dr.	Cr.	Dr.	Cr.	Dr.	Cr.	
Cash	9,000						
Inventory	80,000						
Sales Revenue		450,000					
Sales Returns and Allowances	10,000						
Sales Discounts	5,000						
Cost of Goods Sold	250,000						

Instructions

Complete the worksheet by extending amounts reported in the adjusted trial balance to the appropriate columns in the worksheet. Do not total individual columns.

11 *E3-22 (Worksheet and Balance Sheet Presentation) The adjusted trial balance for Ed Bradley Co. is presented in the following worksheet for the month ended April 30, 2014.

		Ed Bradley Co.xls					
Home Insert Page Layout Formulas Data Review View							
P18 fx							
A	B	C	D	E	F	G	
		ED BRADLEY CO.					
		Worksheet (PARTIAL)					
		For The Month Ended April 30, 2014					
	Adjusted Trial Balance		Income Statement		Balance Sheet		
Account Titles	Dr.	Cr.	Dr.	Cr.	Dr.	Cr.	
Cash	$18,972						
Accounts Receivable	6,920						
Prepaid Rent	2,280						
Equipment	18,050						
Accumulated Depreciation—Equipment		$4,895					
Notes Payable		5,700					
Accounts Payable		4,472					
Common Stock		34,960					
Retained Earnings—April 1, 2014		1,000					
Dividends	6,650						
Service Revenue		12,590					
Salaries and Wages Expense	6,840						
Rent Expense	3,760						
Depreciation Expense	145						
Interest Expense	83						
Interest Payable		83					

Instructions

Complete the worksheet and prepare a classified balance sheet.

11 *E3-23 (Partial Worksheet Preparation)* Jurassic Park Co. prepares monthly financial statements from a worksheet. Selected portions of the January worksheet showed the following data.

	Jurassic Park Co.xls						
Home Insert Page Layout Formulas Data Review View							
P18	fx						
	A	B	C	D	E	F	G
1							
2	**JURASSIC PARK CO.**						
3	Worksheet (PARTIAL)						
4	For The Month Ended Jan. 31, 2014						
5						Adjusted	
6		Trial Balance		Adjustments		Trial Balance	
7	Account Titles	Dr.	Cr.	Dr.	Cr.	Dr.	Cr.
8	Supplies	3,256			(a) 1,500	1,756	
9	Accumulated Depreciation—Equipment		6,682		(b) 257		6,939
10	Interest Payable		100		(c) 50		150
11	Supplies Expense			(a) 1,500		1,500	
12	Depreciation Expense			(b) 257		257	
13	Interest Expense			(c) 50		50	

During February, no events occurred that affected these accounts. But at the end of February, the following information was available.

(a) Supplies on hand $715
(b) Monthly depreciation $257
(c) Accrued interest $ 50

Instructions
Reproduce the data that would appear in the February worksheet, and indicate the amounts that would be shown in the January income statement.

EXERCISES SET B

See the book's companion website, at **www.wiley.com/college/kieso**, for an additional set of exercises.

PROBLEMS

4 6 7 **P3-1 (Transactions, Financial Statements—Service Company)** Listed below are the transactions of Yasunari Kawabata, D.D.S., for the month of September.

Sept.   1   Kawabata begins practice as a dentist and invests $20,000 cash.
       2   Purchases dental equipment on account from Green Jacket Co. for $17,280.
       4   Pays rent for office space, $680 for the month.
       4   Employs a receptionist, Michael Bradley.
       5   Purchases dental supplies for cash, $942.
       8   Receives cash of $1,690 from patients for services performed.
      10   Pays miscellaneous office expenses, $430.
      14   Bills patients $5,820 for services performed.
      18   Pays Green Jacket Co. on account, $3,600.
      19   Withdraws $3,000 cash from the business for personal use.
      20   Receives $980 from patients on account.
      25   Bills patients $2,110 for services performed.
      30   Pays the following expenses in cash: Salaries and wages $1,800; miscellaneous office expenses $85.
      30   Dental supplies used during September, $330.

Instructions

(a) Enter the transactions shown above in appropriate general ledger accounts (use T-accounts). Use the following ledger accounts: Cash, Accounts Receivable, Supplies, Equipment, Accumulated Depreciation—Equipment, Accounts Payable, Owner's Capital, Service Revenue, Rent Expense, Office Expense, Salaries and Wages Expense, Supplies Expense, Depreciation Expense, and Income Summary. Allow 10 lines for the Cash and Income Summary accounts, and 5 lines for each of the other accounts needed. Record depreciation using a 5-year life on the equipment, the straight-line method, and no salvage value. Do not use a drawing account.

(b) Prepare a trial balance.

(c) Prepare an income statement, a statement of owner's equity, and an unclassified balance sheet.

(d) Close the ledger.

(e) Prepare a post-closing trial balance.

5 6 P3-2 (Adjusting Entries and Financial Statements) Mason Advertising Agency was founded in January 2010. Presented below are adjusted and unadjusted trial balances as of December 31, 2014.

	MASON ADVERTISING AGENCY TRIAL BALANCE DECEMBER 31, 2014			
	Unadjusted		Adjusted	
	Dr.	Cr.	Dr.	Cr.
Cash	$ 11,000		$ 11,000	
Accounts Receivable	20,000		23,500	
Supplies	8,400		3,000	
Prepaid Insurance	3,350		2,500	
Equipment	60,000		60,000	
Accumulated Depreciation—Equipment		$ 28,000		$ 33,000
Accounts Payable		5,000		5,000
Interest Payable		–0–		150
Notes Payable		5,000		5,000
Unearned Service Revenue		7,000		5,600
Salaries and Wages Payable		–0–		1,300
Common Stock		10,000		10,000
Retained Earnings		3,500		3,500
Service Revenue		58,600		63,500
Salaries and Wages Expense	10,000		11,300	
Insurance Expense			850	
Interest Expense	350		500	
Depreciation Expense			5,000	
Supplies Expense			5,400	
Rent Expense	4,000		4,000	
	$117,100	$117,100	$127,050	$127,050

Instructions

(a) Journalize the annual adjusting entries that were made. (Omit explanations.)

(b) Prepare an income statement and a statement of retained earnings for the year ending December 31, 2014, and an unclassified balance sheet at December 31.

(c) Answer the following questions.
   (1) If the note has been outstanding 3 months, what is the annual interest rate on that note?
   (2) If the company paid $12,500 in salaries and wages in 2014, what was the balance in Salaries and Wages Payable on December 31, 2013?

5 P3-3 (Adjusting Entries) A review of the ledger of Baylor Company at December 31, 2014, produces the following data pertaining to the preparation of annual adjusting entries.

1. Salaries and Wages Payable $0. There are eight employees. Salaries and wages are paid every Friday for the current week. Five employees receive $700 each per week, and three employees earn $600 each per week. December 31 is a Tuesday. Employees do not work weekends. All employees worked the last 2 days of December.

2. Unearned Rent Revenue $429,000. The company began subleasing office space in its new building on November 1. Each tenant is required to make a $5,000 security deposit that is not refundable until occupancy is terminated. At December 31, the company had the following rental contracts that are paid in full for the entire term of the lease.

Date	Term (in months)	Monthly Rent	Number of Leases
Nov. 1	6	$6,000	5
Dec. 1	6	$8,500	4

3. Prepaid Advertising $13,200. This balance consists of payments on two advertising contracts. The contracts provide for monthly advertising in two trade magazines. The terms of the contracts are as shown below.

Contract	Date	Amount	Number of Magazine Issues
A650	May 1	$6,000	12
B974	Oct. 1	7,200	24

The first advertisement runs in the month in which the contract is signed.

4. Notes Payable $60,000. This balance consists of a note for one year at an annual interest rate of 12%, dated June 1.

Instructions

Prepare the adjusting entries at December 31, 2014. (Show all computations).

P3-4 (Financial Statements, Adjusting and Closing Entries) The trial balance of Bellemy Fashion Center contained the following accounts at November 30, the end of the company's fiscal year.

BELLEMY FASHION CENTER
TRIAL BALANCE
NOVEMBER 30, 2014

	Debit	Credit
Cash	$ 28,700	
Accounts Receivable	33,700	
Inventory	45,000	
Supplies	5,500	
Equipment	133,000	
Accumulated Depreciation—Equipment		$ 24,000
Notes Payable		51,000
Accounts Payable		48,500
Common Stock		90,000
Retained Earnings		8,000
Sales Revenue		757,200
Sales Returns and Allowances	4,200	
Cost of Goods Sold	495,400	
Salaries and Wages Expense	140,000	
Advertising Expense	26,400	
Utilities Expenses	14,000	
Maintenance and Repairs Expense	12,100	
Delivery Expense	16,700	
Rent Expense	24,000	
	$978,700	$978,700

Adjustment data:

1. Supplies on hand totaled $1,500.
2. Depreciation is $15,000 on the equipment.
3. Interest of $11,000 is accrued on notes payable at November 30.

Other data:

1. Salaries expense is 70% selling and 30% administrative.
2. Rent expense and utilities expenses are 80% selling and 20% administrative.
3. $30,000 of notes payable are due for payment next year.
4. Maintenance and repairs expense is 100% administrative.

Instructions

(a) Journalize the adjusting entries.
(b) Prepare an adjusted trial balance.
(c) Prepare a multiple-step income statement and retained earnings statement for the year and a classified balance sheet as of November 30, 2014.
(d) Journalize the closing entries.
(e) Prepare a post-closing trial balance.

5 **P3-5 (Adjusting Entries)** The accounts listed below appeared in the December 31 trial balance of the Savard Theater.

	Debit	Credit
Equipment	$192,000	
Accumulated Depreciation—Equipment		$ 60,000
Notes Payable		90,000
Admissions Revenue		380,000
Advertising Expense	13,680	
Salaries and Wages Expense	57,600	
Interest Expense	1,400	

Instructions

(a) From the account balances listed above and the information given below, prepare the annual adjusting entries necessary on December 31. (Omit explanations.)
  (1) The equipment has an estimated life of 16 years and a salvage value of $24,000 at the end of that time. (Use straight-line method.)
  (2) The note payable is a 90-day note given to the bank October 20 and bearing interest at 8%. (Use 360 days for denominator.)
  (3) In December, 2,000 coupon admission books were sold at $30 each. They could be used for admission any time after January 1.
  (4) Advertising expense paid in advance and included in Advertising Expense $1,100.
  (5) Salaries and wages accrued but unpaid $4,700.
(b) What amounts should be shown for each of the following on the income statement for the year?
  (1) Interest expense.   (3) Advertising expense.
  (2) Admissions revenue.   (4) Salaries and wages expense.

5 **6** **P3-6 (Adjusting Entries and Financial Statements)** The following are the trial balance and the other information related to Yorkis Perez, a consulting engineer.

YORKIS PEREZ, CONSULTING ENGINEER
TRIAL BALANCE
DECEMBER 31, 2014

	Debit	Credit
Cash	$ 29,500	
Accounts Receivable	49,600	
Allowance for Doubtful Accounts		$ 750
Inventory	1,960	
Prepaid Insurance	1,100	
Equipment	25,000	
Accumulated Depreciation—Equipment		6,250
Notes Payable		7,200
Owner's Capital		35,010
Service Revenue		100,000
Rent Expense	9,750	
Salaries and Wages Expense	30,500	
Utilities Expenses	1,080	
Office Expense	720	
	$149,210	$149,210

1. Fees received in advance from clients $6,000.
2. Services performed for clients that were not recorded by December 31, $4,900.
3. Bad debt expense for the year is $1,430.
4. Insurance expired during the year $480.
5. Equipment is being depreciated at 10% per year.
6. Yorkis Perez gave the bank a 90-day, 10% note for $7,200 on December 1, 2014.
7. Rent of the building is $750 per month. The rent for 2014 has been paid, as has that for January 2015.
8. Office salaries and wages earned but unpaid December 31, 2014, $2,510.

Instructions

(a) From the trial balance and other information given, prepare annual adjusting entries as of December 31, 2014. (Omit explanations.)

(b) Prepare an income statement for 2014, a statement of owner's equity, and a classified balance sheet. Yorkis Perez withdrew $17,000 cash for personal use during the year.

5 6 P3-7 (Adjusting Entries and Financial Statements) Rolling Hills Golf Inc. was organized on July 1, 2014. Quarterly financial statements are prepared. The unadjusted trial balance and adjusted trial balance on September 30 are shown here.

<table>
<tr><td colspan="5" align="center">ROLLING HILLS GOLF INC.
TRIAL BALANCE
SEPTEMBER 30, 2014</td></tr>
<tr><td></td><td colspan="2" align="center">Unadjusted</td><td colspan="2" align="center">Adjusted</td></tr>
<tr><td></td><td align="center">Dr.</td><td align="center">Cr.</td><td align="center">Dr.</td><td align="center">Cr.</td></tr>
<tr><td>Cash</td><td>$ 6,700</td><td></td><td>$ 6,700</td><td></td></tr>
<tr><td>Accounts Receivable</td><td>400</td><td></td><td>1,000</td><td></td></tr>
<tr><td>Prepaid Rent</td><td>1,800</td><td></td><td>900</td><td></td></tr>
<tr><td>Supplies</td><td>1,200</td><td></td><td>180</td><td></td></tr>
<tr><td>Equipment</td><td>15,000</td><td></td><td>15,000</td><td></td></tr>
<tr><td>Accumulated Depreciation—Equipment</td><td></td><td></td><td></td><td>$ 350</td></tr>
<tr><td>Notes Payable</td><td></td><td>$ 5,000</td><td></td><td>5,000</td></tr>
<tr><td>Accounts Payable</td><td></td><td>1,070</td><td></td><td>1,070</td></tr>
<tr><td>Salaries and Wages Payable</td><td></td><td></td><td></td><td>600</td></tr>
<tr><td>Interest Payable</td><td></td><td></td><td></td><td>50</td></tr>
<tr><td>Unearned Rent Revenue</td><td></td><td>1,000</td><td></td><td>800</td></tr>
<tr><td>Common Stock</td><td></td><td>14,000</td><td></td><td>14,000</td></tr>
<tr><td>Retained Earnings</td><td></td><td>0</td><td></td><td>0</td></tr>
<tr><td>Dividends</td><td>600</td><td></td><td>600</td><td></td></tr>
<tr><td>Service Revenue</td><td></td><td>14,100</td><td></td><td>14,700</td></tr>
<tr><td>Rent Revenue</td><td></td><td>700</td><td></td><td>900</td></tr>
<tr><td>Salaries and Wages Expense</td><td>8,800</td><td></td><td>9,400</td><td></td></tr>
<tr><td>Rent Expense</td><td>900</td><td></td><td>1,800</td><td></td></tr>
<tr><td>Depreciation Expense</td><td></td><td></td><td>350</td><td></td></tr>
<tr><td>Supplies Expense</td><td></td><td></td><td>1,020</td><td></td></tr>
<tr><td>Utilities Expenses</td><td>470</td><td></td><td>470</td><td></td></tr>
<tr><td>Interest Expense</td><td></td><td></td><td>50</td><td></td></tr>
<tr><td></td><td>$35,870</td><td>$35,870</td><td>$37,470</td><td>$37,470</td></tr>
</table>

Instructions

(a) Journalize the adjusting entries that were made.

(b) Prepare an income statement and a retained earnings statement for the 3 months ending September 30 and a classified balance sheet at September 30.

(c) Identify which accounts should be closed on September 30.

(d) If the note bears interest at 12%, how many months has it been outstanding?

5 6 P3-8 (Adjusting Entries and Financial Statements) Vedula Advertising Agency was founded by Murali Vedula in January 2009. Presented on the next page are both the adjusted and unadjusted trial balances as of December 31, 2014.

VEDULA ADVERTISING AGENCY
TRIAL BALANCE
DECEMBER 31, 2014

	Unadjusted		Adjusted	
	Dr.	Cr.	Dr.	Cr.
Cash	$ 11,000		$ 11,000	
Accounts Receivable	16,000		19,500	
Supplies	9,400		6,500	
Prepaid Insurance	3,350		1,790	
Equipment	60,000		60,000	
Accumulated Depreciation—Equipment		$ 25,000		$ 30,000
Notes Payable		8,000		8,000
Accounts Payable		2,000		2,000
Interest Payable		0		560
Unearned Service Revenue		5,000		3,100
Salaries and Wages Payable		0		820
Common Stock		20,000		20,000
Retained Earnings		5,500		5,500
Dividends	10,000		10,000	
Service Revenue		57,600		63,000
Salaries and Wages Expense	9,000		9,820	
Insurance Expense			1,560	
Interest Expense			560	
Depreciation Expense			5,000	
Supplies Expense			2,900	
Rent Expense	4,350		4,350	
	$123,100	$123,100	$132,980	$132,980

Instructions

(a) Journalize the annual adjusting entries that were made.

(b) Prepare an income statement and a retained earnings statement for the year ended December 31, and a classified balance sheet at December 31.

(c) Identify which accounts should be closed on December 31.

(d) If the note has been outstanding 10 months, what is the annual interest rate on that note?

(e) If the company paid $10,500 in salaries and wages in 2014, what was the balance in Salaries and Wages Payable on December 31, 2013?

4 5 **6 7** **P3-9 (Adjusting and Closing)** Presented below is the trial balance of the Crestwood Golf Club, Inc. as of December 31. The books are closed annually on December 31.

CRESTWOOD GOLF CLUB, INC.
TRIAL BALANCE
DECEMBER 31

	Debit	Credit
Cash	$ 15,000	
Accounts Receivable	13,000	
Allowance for Doubtful Accounts		$ 1,100
Prepaid Insurance	9,000	
Land	350,000	
Buildings	120,000	
Accumulated Depreciation—Buildings		38,400
Equipment	150,000	
Accumulated Depreciation—Equipment		70,000
Common Stock		400,000
Retained Earnings		82,000
Dues Revenue		200,000
Green Fees Revenue		5,900
Rent Revenue		17,600
Utilities Expenses	54,000	
Salaries and Wages Expense	80,000	
Maintenance and Repairs Expense	24,000	
	$815,000	$815,000

Instructions

(a) Enter the balances in ledger accounts. Allow five lines for each account.
(b) From the trial balance and the information given below, prepare annual adjusting entries and post to the ledger accounts. (Omit explanations.)
  (1) The buildings have an estimated life of 30 years with no salvage value (straight-line method).
  (2) The equipment is depreciated at 10% per year.
  (3) Insurance expired during the year $3,500.
  (4) The rent revenue represents the amount received for 11 months for dining facilities. The December rent has not yet been received.
  (5) It is estimated that 12% of the accounts receivable will be uncollectible.
  (6) Salaries and wages earned but not paid by December 31, $3,600.
  (7) Dues received in advance from members $8,900.
(c) Prepare an adjusted trial balance.
(d) Prepare closing entries and post.

P3-10 (Adjusting and Closing) Presented below is the December 31 trial balance of New York Boutique.

NEW YORK BOUTIQUE TRIAL BALANCE DECEMBER 31		
	Debit	Credit
Cash	$ 18,500	
Accounts Receivable	32,000	
Allowance for Doubtful Accounts		$ 700
Inventory, December 31	80,000	
Prepaid Insurance	5,100	
Equipment	84,000	
Accumulated Depreciation—Equipment		35,000
Notes Payable		28,000
Common Stock		80,600
Retained Earnings		10,000
Sales Revenue		600,000
Cost of Goods Sold	408,000	
Salaries and Wages Expense (sales)	50,000	
Advertising Expense	6,700	
Salaries and Wages Expense (administrative)	65,000	
Supplies Expense	5,000	
	$754,300	$754,300

Instructions

(a) Construct T-accounts and enter the balances shown.
(b) Prepare adjusting journal entries for the following and post to the T-accounts. (Omit explanations.) Open additional T-accounts as necessary. (The books are closed yearly on December 31.)
  (1) Bad debt expense is estimated to be $1,400.
  (2) Equipment is depreciated based on a 7-year life (no salvage value).
  (3) Insurance expired during the year $2,550.
  (4) Interest accrued on notes payable $3,360.
  (5) Sales salaries and wages earned but not paid $2,400.
  (6) Advertising paid in advance $700.
  (7) Office supplies on hand $1,500, charged to Supplies Expense when purchased.
(c) Prepare closing entries and post to the accounts.

*P3-11 (Cash and Accrual Basis) On January 1, 2014, Norma Smith and Grant Wood formed a computer sales and service company in Soapsville, Arkansas, by investing $90,000 cash. The new company, Arkansas Sales and Service, has the following transactions during January.

1. Pays $6,000 in advance for 3 months' rent of office, showroom, and repair space.
2. Purchases 40 personal computers at a cost of $1,500 each, 6 graphics computers at a cost of $2,500 each, and 25 printers at a cost of $300 each, paying cash upon delivery.

3. Sales, repair, and office employees earn $12,600 in salaries and wages during January, of which $3,000 was still payable at the end of January.

4. Sells 30 personal computers at $2,550 each, 4 graphics computers for $3,600 each, and 15 printers for $500 each; $75,000 is received in cash in January, and $23,400 is sold on a deferred payment basis.

5. Other operating expenses of $8,400 are incurred and paid for during January; $2,000 of incurred expenses are payable at January 31.

Instructions

(a) Using the transaction data above, prepare (1) a cash-basis income statement and (2) an accrual-basis income statement for the month of January.

(b) Using the transaction data above, prepare (1) a cash-basis balance sheet and (2) an accrual-basis balance sheet as of January 31, 2014.

(c) Identify the items in the cash-basis financial statements that make cash-basis accounting inconsistent with the theory underlying the elements of financial statements.

5 **6** **7** **11** *P3-12 (Worksheet, Balance Sheet, Adjusting and Closing Entries)** Cooke Company has a fiscal year ending on September 30. Selected data from the September 30 worksheet are presented below.

Cooke Co.xls

Home   Insert   Page Layout   Formulas   Data   Review   View

P18   fx

	A	B	C	D	E
1					
2		**COOKE COMPANY**			
3		Worksheet			
4		For The Month Ended September 30, 2014			
5		Trial Balance		Adjusted Trial Balance	
6	Account Titles	Dr.	Cr.	Dr.	Cr.
7	Cash	37,400		37,400	
8	Supplies	18,600		4,200	
9	Prepaid Insurance	31,900		3,900	
10	Land	80,000		80,000	
11	Equipment	120,000		120,000	
12	Accumulated Depreciation—Equipment		36,200		42,000
13	Accounts Payable		14,600		14,600
14	Unearned Service Revenue		2,700		700
15	Mortgage Payable		50,000		50,000
16	Common Stock		107,700		107,700
17	Retained Earnings, Sept. 1, 2014		2,000		2,000
18	Dividends	14,000		14,000	
19	Service Revenue		278,500		280,500
20	Salaries and Wages Expense	109,000		109,000	
21	Maintenance and Repairs Expense	30,500		30,500	
22	Advertising Expense	9,400		9,400	
23	Utilities Expenses	16,900		16,900	
24	Property Tax Expense	18,000		21,000	
25	Interest Expense	6,000		12,000	
26	Totals	491,700	491,700		
27	Insurance Expense			28,000	
28	Supplies Expense			14,400	
29	Interest Payable				6,000
30	Depreciation Expense			5,800	
31	Property Taxes Payable				3,000
32	Totals			506,500	506,500

Instructions

(a) Prepare a complete worksheet.

(b) Prepare a classified balance sheet. (*Note:* $10,000 of the mortgage payable is due for payment in the next fiscal year.)

(c) Journalize the adjusting entries using the worksheet as a basis.

(d) Journalize the closing entries using the worksheet as a basis.

(e) Prepare a post-closing trial balance.

PROBLEMS SET B

See the book's companion website, at **www.wiley.com/college/kieso**, for an additional set of problems.

USING YOUR JUDGMENT

FINANCIAL REPORTING

Financial Reporting Problem

P&G

The Procter & Gamble Company (P&G)

The financial statements of **P&G** are presented in Appendix 5B. The company's complete annual report, including the notes to the financial statements, can be accessed at the book's companion website, **www. wiley.com/college/kieso**.

Instructions

Refer to these financial statements and the accompanying notes to answer the following questions.

(a) What were P&G's total assets at June 30, 2011? At June 30, 2010?

(b) How much cash (and cash equivalents) did P&G have on June 30, 2011?

(c) What were P&G's research and development costs in 2010? In 2011?

(d) What were P&G's revenues in 2010? In 2011?

(e) Using P&G's financial statements and related notes, identify items that may result in adjusting entries for deferrals and accruals.

(f) What were the amounts of P&G's depreciation and amortization expense in 2009, 2010, and 2011?

Comparative Analysis Case

The Coca-Cola Company and PepsiCo, Inc.

Instructions

Go to the book's companion website and use information found there to answer the following questions related to The Coca-Cola Company and PepsiCo, Inc.

(a) Which company had the greater percentage increase in total assets from 2010 to 2011?

(b) Using the Selected Financial Data section of these two companies, determine their 5-year average growth rates related to net sales and income from continuing operations.

(c) Which company had more depreciation and amortization expense for 2011? Provide a rationale as to why there is a difference in these amounts between the two companies.

Financial Statement Analysis Case

Kellogg Company

Kellogg Company has its headquarters in Battle Creek, Michigan. The company manufactures and sells ready-to-eat breakfast cereals and convenience foods including cookies, toaster pastries, and cereal bars.

Selected data from Kellogg Company's 2011 annual report follows (dollar amounts in millions).

	2011	2010	2009
Sales	$13,198.00	$12,397.00	$12,575.00
Gross profit %	41.28	42.66	42.87
Operating profit	1,976.00	1,990.00	2,001.00
Net cash flow less capital expenditures	1,001.00	534.00	1,266.00
Net earnings	1,231.00	1,247.00	1,212.00

In its annual reports, Kellogg Company has indicated that it plans to achieve sustainability of its operating results with operating principles that emphasize profit-rich, sustainable sales growth, as well as cash flow and return on invested capital. Kellogg believes its steady earnings growth, strong cash flow, and continued investment during a multi-year period demonstrates the strength and flexibility of its business model.

Instructions

(a) Compute the percentage change in sales, operating profit, net cash flow less capital expenditures, and net earnings from year to year for the years presented.

(b) Evaluate Kellogg's performance. Which trend seems most favorable? Which trend seems least favorable? What are the implications of these trends for Kellogg's sustainable performance objectives? Explain.

Accounting, Analysis, and Principles

The Amato Theater is nearing the end of the year and is preparing for a meeting with its bankers to discuss the renewal of a loan. The accounts listed below appeared in the December 31, 2014, trial balance.

	Debit	Credit
Prepaid Advertising	$ 6,000	
Equipment	192,000	
Accumulated Depreciation—Equipment		$ 60,000
Notes Payable		90,000
Unearned Service Revenue		17,500
Ticket Revenue		360,000
Advertising Expense	18,680	
Salaries and Wages Expense	67,600	
Interest Expense	1,400	

Additional information is available as follows.

1. The equipment has an estimated useful life of 16 years and a salvage value of $40,000 at the end of that time. Amato uses the straight-line method for depreciation.

2. The note payable is a one-year note given to the bank January 31 and bearing interest at 10%. Interest is calculated on a monthly basis.

3. Late in December 2014, the theater sold 350 coupon ticket books at $50 each. One hundred fifty of these ticket books can be used only for admission any time after January 1, 2015. The cash received was recorded as Unearned Service Revenue.

4. Advertising paid in advance was $6,000 and was debited to Prepaid Advertising. The company has used $2,500 of the advertising as of December 31, 2014.

5. Salaries and wages accrued but unpaid at December 31, 2014, were $3,500.

Accounting

Prepare any adjusting journal entries necessary for the year ended December 31, 2014.

Analysis

Determine Amato's income before and after recording the adjusting entries. Use your analysis to explain why Amato's bankers should be willing to wait for Amato to complete its year-end adjustment process before making a decision on the loan renewal.

Principles

Although Amato's bankers are willing to wait for the adjustment process to be completed before they receive financial information, they would like to receive financial reports more frequently than annually or even quarterly. What trade-offs, in terms of relevance and faithful representation, are inherent in preparing financial statements for shorter accounting time periods?

BRIDGE TO THE PROFESSION

Professional Research

Recording transactions in the accounting system requires knowledge of the important characteristics of the elements of financial statements, such as assets and liabilities. In addition, accountants must understand the inherent uncertainty in accounting measures and distinctions between related accounting concepts that are important in evaluating the effects of transactions on the financial statements.

Instructions

Go to *http://aaahq.org/asclogin.cfm* to log in and provide explanations for the following items. (Provide paragraph citations.) When you have accessed the documents, you can use the search tool in your Internet browser.

(a) The three essential characteristics of assets.

(b) The three essential characteristics of liabilities.

(c) Uncertainty and its effect on financial statements.

(d) The difference between realization and recognition.

Additional Professional Resources

See the book's companion website, at **www.wiley.com/college/kieso**, for professional simulations as well as other study resources.

FRS ▸ INSIGHTS

As indicated in this chapter, companies must have an effective accounting system. In the wake of accounting scandals at U.S. companies like **Sunbeam**, **Rite-Aid**, **Xerox**, and **WorldCom**, U.S. lawmakers demanded higher assurance on the quality of accounting reports. Since the passage of the Sarbanes-Oxley Act of 2002 (SOX), companies that trade on U.S. exchanges are required to place renewed focus on their accounting systems to ensure accurate reporting.

12 LEARNING OBJECTIVE

Compare the accounting information systems under GAAP and IFRS.

RELEVANT FACTS

Following are the key similarities and differences between GAAP and IFRS related to accounting information systems.

Similarities

International companies use the same set of procedures and records to keep track of transaction data. Thus, the material in Chapter 3 dealing with the account, general rules of debit and credit, and steps in the recording process—the journal, ledger, and chart of accounts—is the same under both GAAP and IFRS.

Transaction analysis is the same under GAAP and IFRS but, as you will see in later chapters, different standards sometimes impact how transactions are recorded.

Both the FASB and IASB go beyond the basic definitions provided in this textbook for the key elements of financial statements, that is, assets, liabilities, equity, revenues, and expenses.

A trial balance under IFRS follows the same format as shown in the textbook. As shown in the textbook, dollar signs are typically used only in the trial balance and the financial statements. The same practice is followed under IFRS, using the currency of the country in which the reporting company is headquartered.

Differences

- Rules for accounting for specific events sometimes differ across countries. For example, European companies rely less on historical cost and more on fair value than U.S. companies. Despite the differences, the double-entry accounting system is the basis of accounting systems worldwide.

- Internal controls are a system of checks and balances designed to prevent and detect fraud and errors. While most public U.S. companies have these systems in place, many non-U.S. companies have never completely documented them nor had an independent auditor attest to their effectiveness. Both of these actions are required under SOX. These enhanced internal control standards apply only to large public companies listed on U.S. exchanges.

ABOUT THE NUMBERS

Accounting System Internal Controls

There is continuing debate over whether foreign issuers should have to comply with the extra layer of regulation related to internal controls attestation.[4] Companies find that internal control review is a costly process but needed. One study estimates the cost of compliance for U.S. companies at over $35 billion, with audit fees doubling in the first year of compliance. At the same time, examination of internal controls indicates lingering problems in the way companies operate. One study of first compliance with the internal control testing provisions documented material weaknesses for about 13 percent of companies reporting in 2004 and 2005.

Debate about requiring foreign companies to comply with SOX centers on whether the higher costs of a good information system are making the U.S. securities markets less competitive. Presented below are statistics for initial public offerings (IPOs) in the years since the passage of SOX.

Share of IPO Proceeds: U.S., Europe, and China (U.S. $, billions)

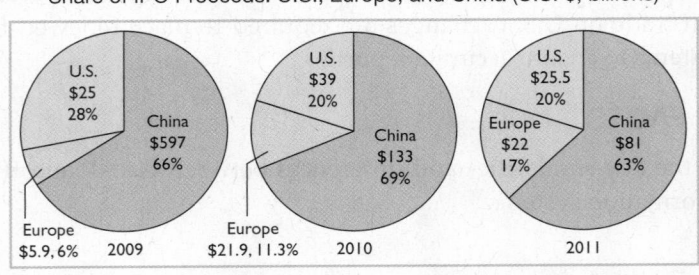

	2009 IPOs	2010 IPOs	2011 IPOs
U.S.	69	168	134
Europe	126	380	430
China	208	502	432

Source: PricewaterhouseCoopers, U.S. IPO Watch: 2011 Analysis and Trends.

Note the U.S. share of IPOs has steadily declined. Some critics of the SOX provision attribute the decline to the increased cost of complying with the internal control rules. Others, looking at these same trends, are not so sure about SOX being the cause of the relative decline of U.S. IPOs. These commentators argue that growth in non-U.S. markets is a natural consequence of general globalization of capital flows.

---

[4]See Greg Ip, Kara Scannel, and Deborah Solomon, "Trade Winds in Call to Deregulate Business: A Global Twist," *Wall Street Journal* (January 25, 2007), p. A1.

First-Time Adoption of IFRS

As discussed in Chapter 1, IFRS is growing in acceptance around the world. For example, recent statistics indicate 40 percent of the Global Fortune 500 companies use IFRS. And the chair of the IASB predicts that IFRS adoption will grow from its current level of over 115 countries to nearly 150 countries in the near future.

When countries accept IFRS for use as accepted accounting policies, companies need guidance to ensure that their first IFRS financial statements contain high-quality information. Specifically, *IFRS 1* requires that information in a company's first IFRS statements (1) be transparent, (2) provide a suitable starting point, and (3) have a cost that does not exceed the benefits. As a result, many companies will be going through a substantial conversion process to switch from their reporting standards to IFRS.

The overriding principle in converting to IFRS is full retrospective application of IFRS. Retrospective application—recasting prior financial statements on the basis of IFRS—provides financial statement users with comparable information. As indicated, the objective of the conversion process is to present a set of IFRS statements as if the company always reported using IFRS. To achieve this objective, a company follows these steps:

1. Identify the timing of its first IFRS statements.
2. Prepare an opening balance sheet at the date of transition to IFRS.
3. Select accounting principles that comply with IFRS, and apply these principles retrospectively.
4. Make extensive disclosures to explain the transition to IFRS.

Once a company decides to convert to IFRS, it must decide on the transition date and the reporting date. The transition date is the beginning of the earliest period for which full comparative IFRS information is presented. The reporting date is the closing balance sheet date for the first IFRS financial statements.

To illustrate, assume that FirstChoice Company plans to provide its first IFRS statements for the year ended December 31, 2016. FirstChoice decides to present comparative information for one year only. Therefore, its date of transition to IFRS is January 1, 2015, and its reporting date is December 31, 2016. The timeline for first-time adoption is presented in the following graphic.

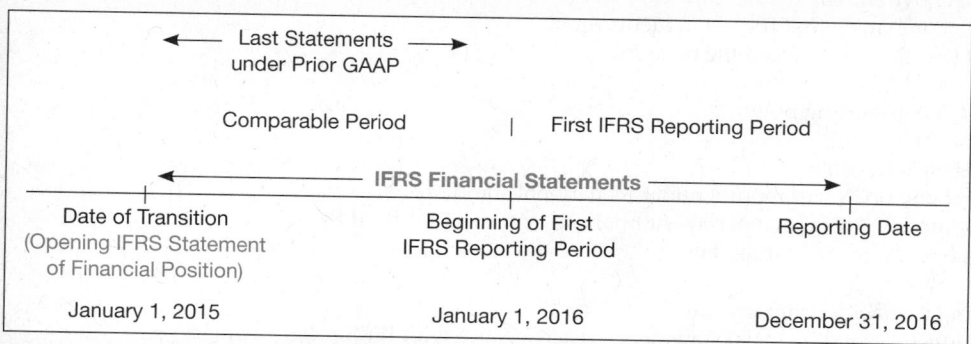

The graphic shows the following.

1. The opening IFRS statement of financial position for FirstChoice on January 1, 2015, serves as the starting point (date of transition) for the company's accounting under IFRS.
2. The first full IFRS statements are shown for FirstChoice for December 31, 2016. In other words, a minimum of two years of IFRS statements must be presented before

a conversion to IFRS occurs. As a result, FirstChoice must prepare at least one year of comparative financial statements for 2016 using IFRS.

3. FirstChoice presents financial statements in accordance with GAAP annually to December 31, 2015.

Following this conversion process, FirstChoice provides users of the financial statements with comparable IFRS statements for 2015 and 2016. Upon first-time adoption of IFRS, a company must present at least one year of comparative information under IFRS.

ON THE HORIZON

The basic recording process shown in this textbook is followed by companies around the globe. It is unlikely to change in the future. The definitional structure of assets, liabilities, equity, revenues, and expenses may change over time as the IASB and FASB evaluate their overall conceptual framework for establishing accounting standards. In addition, high-quality international accounting requires both high-quality accounting standards and high-quality auditing. Similar to the convergence of GAAP and IFRS, there is a movement to improve international auditing standards. The International Auditing and Assurance Standards Board (IAASB) functions as an independent standard-setting body. It works to establish high-quality auditing and assurance and quality-control standards throughout the world. Whether the IAASB adopts internal control provisions similar to those in SOX remains to be seen. You can follow developments in the international audit arena at *http://www.ifac.org/iaasb/*.

IFRS SELF-TEST QUESTIONS

1. Which statement is **correct** regarding IFRS?
   (a) IFRS reverses the rules of debits and credits, that is, debits are on the right and credits are on the left.
   (b) IFRS uses the same process for recording transactions as GAAP.
   (c) The chart of accounts under IFRS is different because revenues follow assets.
   (d) None of the above statements are correct.
2. Information in a company's first IFRS statements must:
   (a) have a cost that does not exceed the benefits.
   (b) be transparent.
   (c) provide a suitable starting point.
   (d) All the above.
3. The transition date is the date:
   (a) when a company no longer reports under its national standards.
   (b) when the company issues its most recent financial statement under IFRS.
   (c) three years prior to the reporting date.
   (d) None of the above.
4. When converting to IFRS, a company must:
   (a) recast previously issued financial statements in accordance with IFRS.
   (b) use GAAP in the reporting period but subsequently use IFRS.
   (c) prepare at least three years of comparative statements.
   (d) use GAAP in the transition year but IFRS in the reporting year.
5. The purpose of presenting comparative information in the transition to IFRS is:
   (a) to ensure that the information is a faithful representation.
   (b) in accordance with the Sarbanes-Oxley Act.
   (c) to provide users of the financial statements with information on GAAP in one period and IFRS in the other period.
   (d) to provide users of the financial statements with information on IFRS for at least two periods.

IFRS CONCEPTS AND APPLICATION

IFRS3-1 How is the date of transition and the date of reporting determined in first-time adoption of IFRS?

IFRS3-2 What are the characteristics of high-quality information in a company's first IFRS financial statements?

IFRS3-3 What are the steps to be completed in preparing the opening IFRS statement of financial position?

IFRS3-4 Becker Ltd. is planning to adopt IFRS and prepare its first IFRS financial statements at December 31, 2015. What is the date of Becker's opening balance sheet, assuming one year of comparative information? What periods will be covered in Becker's first IFRS financial statements?

Professional Research

IFRS3-5 Recording transactions in the accounting system requires knowledge of the important characteristics of the elements of financial statements, such as assets and liabilities. In addition, accountants must understand the inherent uncertainty in accounting measures and distinctions between related accounting concepts that are important in evaluating the effects of transactions on the financial statements.

Instructions

Access the IASB Framework at the IASB website (*http://eifrs.iasb.org/*). (Click on the IFRS tab and then register for free eIFRS access if necessary.) When you have accessed the documents, you can use the search tool in your Internet browser to respond to the following items. (Provide paragraph citations.)

(a) Provide the definition of an asset and discuss how the economic benefits embodied in an asset might flow to a company.
(b) Provide the definition of a liability and discuss how a company might satisfy a liability.
(c) What is "accrual basis"? How do adjusting entries illustrate application of the accrual basis?

International Financial Reporting Problem
Marks and Spencer plc

IFRS3-6 The financial statements of **Marks and Spencer plc (M&S)** are available at the book's companion website or can be accessed at *http://annualreport.marksandspencer.com/_assets/downloads/Marks-and-Spencer-Annual-report-and-financial-statements-2012.pdf*.

Instructions

Refer to M&S's financial statements and the accompanying notes to answer the following questions.

(a) What were M&S's total assets at 31 March 2012? At 2 April 2011?
(b) How much cash (and cash equivalents) did M&S have on 31 March 2012?
(c) What were M&S's selling and marketing expenses in 2012? In 2011?
(d) What were M&S's revenues in 2012? In 2011?
(e) Using M&S's financial statements and related notes, identify items that may result in adjusting entries for prepayments and accruals.
(f) What were the amounts of M&S's depreciation and amortization expense in 2011 and 2012?

ANSWERS TO IFRS SELF-TEST QUESTIONS

1. b **2.** d **3.** d **4.** a **5.** d

Remember to check the book's companion website to find additional resources for this chapter.

Income Statement and Related Information

LEARNING OBJECTIVES

After studying this chapter, you should be able to:

1 Understand the uses and limitations of an income statement.

2 Describe the content and format of the income statement.

3 Prepare an income statement.

4 Explain how to report various income items.

5 Identify where to report earnings per share information.

6 Understand the reporting of accounting changes and errors.

7 Prepare a retained earnings statement.

8 Explain how to report other comprehensive income.

Financial Statements Are Changing

The 2011 annual report of **Groupon** presents the following additional information in its financial statements regarding a calculation of its consolidated segment operating (loss) income (CSOI).

The following is a reconciliation of CSOI to the most comparable U.S. GAAP measure, "Loss from operations," for the years ended December 31, 2010 and 2011.

	Year Ended December 31,	
	2010	2011
(in thousands)		
Loss from operations	$(420,344)	$(233,386)
Adjustments:		
Stock-based compensation	36,168	93,590
Acquisition-related costs	203,183	(4,537)
Total adjustments	239,351	89,053
CSOI	$(180,993)	$(144,333)

Management of Groupon explained that CSOI is the consolidated operating (loss) income, after adjustment for acquisition-related costs and stock-based compensation expense. They explained, "We consider CSOI to be an important measure for management to evaluate the performance of our business as it excludes certain non-cash expenses. We believe it is important to view CSOI as a complement to our entire consolidated statements of operations. When evaluating our performance, you should consider CSOI as a complement to other financial performance measures, including various cash flow metrics, net loss and our other U.S. GAAP results."

Why do companies report these adjusted income numbers (sometimes referred to as pro forma measures)? One major reason is that companies believe some items on the income statement are not representative of operating results. Here is another example, using **Amazon.com**. At one time, Amazon reported in a separate schedule adjustments to net income for items such as share-based compensation, amortization of goodwill and intangibles, impairment charges, and equity in losses of its subsidiaries. All these adjustments make the adjusted income measure higher than reported income. Amazon defends its pro forma reporting, saying it gives better insight into the fundamental operations of the business. However, while management asserts pro forma is useful to investors, others raise concerns.

Skeptics of pro forma reporting often note that these adjustments generally lead to higher adjusted net income and, as a result, often report *earnings before bad stuff (EBS)*. In Groupon's case, the add-backs more than halved its operating loss in 2010 and resulted in an improving trend in operating performance over the two-year period. And pro forma puffery is not an isolated phenomenon. In a recent four-quarter earnings cycle, nearly 50 percent of S&P 500 companies also reported an income measure that they adjusted for certain items. Analysis of pro forma to GAAP numbers indicate that about 30 percent of the S&P 500 companies report pro forma income in excess of operating income. In general, pro forma profits were 18 percent higher than operating earnings. Another concern with pro forma is that it is difficult to compare these adjusted numbers because companies have different views as to what is fundamental to their business.

In many ways, the pro forma reporting practices by companies like Groupon and Amazon represent implied criticisms of certain financial reporting standards, including how the information is presented on the income statement. In response, the SEC issued Regulation G, which requires companies to reconcile non-GAAP financial measures to GAAP. This regulation provides investors with a roadmap to analyze adjustments that companies make to their GAAP numbers to arrive at pro forma results. Regulation G helps investors compare one company's pro forma measures with results reported by another company.

The FASB (and IASB) are working on a joint project on financial statement presentation to address users' concerns about these practices. Users believe too many alternatives exist for classifying and reporting income statement information. They note that information is often highly aggregated and inconsistently presented. As a result, it is difficult to assess the financial performance of the company and compare its results with other companies. This trend toward more transparent income reporting is encouraging, but managers still like pro forma reporting, as indicated by a recent survey in response to the FASB financial statement presentation project. Over 55 percent polled indicated they would continue to practice pro forma reporting, even with a revised income statement format.

CONCEPTUAL FOCUS

> See the **Underlying Concepts** on pages 161 and 179.
> Read the **Evolving Issue** on page 185 for a discussion of income reporting.

INTERNATIONAL FOCUS

> See the **International Perspectives** on pages 169, 174, and 183.
> Read the **IFRS Insights** on pages 205–211 for a discussion of:
  —Income reporting
  —Expense classifications

Sources: A. Stuart, "A New Vision for Accounting: Robert Herz and FASB Are Preparing a Radical New Format for Financial Statements," *CFO Magazine* (February 2008), pp. 49–53; SEC Regulation G, *"Conditions for Use of Non-GAAP Financial Measures,"* Release No. 33-8176 (March 28, 2003) and *Compliance & Disclosure Interpretations: Non-GAAP Financial Measures* (January 15, 2010), available at *www.sec.gov/divisions/corpfin/guidance/nongaapinterp.htm*; and R. Cyran, A. Currie, and R. Cox, "Fuzzy Accounting Enriches Groupon," *The New York Times* (June 12, 2011).

PREVIEW OF CHAPTER	4

As indicated in the opening story, companies are attempting to provide income statement information they believe is useful for decision-making. Investors need complete and comparable information on income and its components to assess company profitability correctly. In this chapter, we examine the many different types of revenues, expenses, gains, and losses that affect the income statement and related information, as follows.

Income Statement and Related Information

Income Statement	Format of the Income Statement	Reporting Various Income Items	Other Reporting Issues
• Usefulness • Limitations • Quality of earnings	• Elements • Intermediate components • Condensed income statements • Single-step income statements	• Unusual gains and losses • Discontinued operations • Extraordinary items • Noncontrolling interest • Earnings per share	• Accounting changes and errors • Retained earnings statement • Comprehensive income

INCOME STATEMENT

LEARNING OBJECTIVE 1
Understand the uses and limitations of
an income statement.

The **income statement** is the report that measures the success of company operations for a given period of time. (It is also often called the statement of income or statement of earnings.[1]) The business and investment community uses the income statement to determine profitability, investment value, and creditworthiness. It provides investors and creditors with information that helps them predict the **amounts, timing, and uncertainty of future cash flows**.

Usefulness of the Income Statement

Which company did better
last year?

The income statement helps users of financial statements predict future cash flows in a number of ways. For example, investors and creditors use the income statement information to:

1. *Evaluate the past performance of the company.* Examining revenues and expenses indicates how the company performed and allows comparison of its performance to its competitors. For example, analysts use the income data provided by Ford to compare its performance to that of Toyota.

2. *Provide a basis for predicting future performance.* Information about past performance helps to determine important trends that, if continued, provide information about future performance. For example, General Electric at one time reported consistent increases in revenues. Obviously, past success does not necessarily translate into future success. However, analysts can better predict future revenues, and hence earnings and cash flows, if a reasonable correlation exists between past and future performance.

3. *Help assess the risk or uncertainty of achieving future cash flows.* Information on the various components of income—revenues, expenses, gains, and losses—highlights the relationships among them. It also helps to assess the risk of not achieving a particular level of cash flows in the future. For example, investors and creditors often segregate IBM's operating performance from other nonrecurring sources of income because IBM primarily generates revenues and cash through its operations. Thus, results from continuing operations usually have greater significance for predicting future performance than do results from nonrecurring activities and events.

In summary, information in the income statement—revenues, expenses, gains, and losses—helps users evaluate past performance. It also provides insights into the likelihood of achieving a particular level of cash flows in the future.

Limitations of the Income Statement

You left something out!

Because net income is an estimate and reflects a number of assumptions, income statement users need to be aware of certain limitations associated with its information. Some of these limitations include:

1. *Companies omit items from the income statement that they cannot measure reliably.* Current practice prohibits recognition of certain items from the determination of income even though the effects of these items can arguably affect the company's

---

[1]We will use the term *income statement* except in situations where a company reports other comprehensive income (discussed later in the chapter). In that case, we will use the term statement of comprehensive income.

performance. For example, a company may not record unrealized gains and losses on certain investment securities in income when there is uncertainty that it will ever realize the changes in value. In addition, more and more companies, like **Cisco Systems** and **Microsoft**, experience increases in value due to brand recognition, customer service, and product quality. A common framework for identifying and reporting these types of values is still lacking.

2. *Income numbers are affected by the accounting methods employed.* One company may depreciate its plant assets on an accelerated basis; another chooses straight-line depreciation. Assuming all other factors are equal, the first company will report lower income. In effect, we are comparing apples to oranges.

3. *Income measurement involves judgment.* For example, one company in good faith may estimate the useful life of an asset to be 20 years while another company uses a 15-year estimate for the same type of asset. Similarly, some companies may make optimistic estimates of future warranty costs and bad debt write-offs, which result in lower expense and higher income.

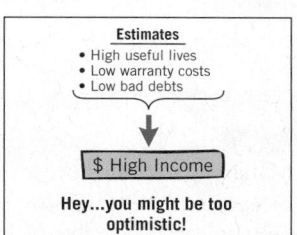

In summary, several limitations of the income statement reduce the usefulness of its information for predicting the amounts, timing, and uncertainty of future cash flows.

Quality of Earnings

So far, our discussion has highlighted the importance of information in the income statement for investment and credit decisions, including the evaluation of the company and its managers.[2] Companies try to meet or beat Wall Street expectations so that the market price of their stock and the value of management's stock options increase. As a result, companies have incentives to manage income to meet earnings targets or to make earnings look less risky.

The SEC has expressed concern that the motivations to meet earnings targets may override good business practices. This erodes the quality of earnings and the quality of financial reporting. As indicated by one SEC chairperson, "Managing may be giving way to manipulation; integrity may be losing out to illusion."[3] As a result, the SEC has taken decisive action to prevent the practice of earnings management.

What is **earnings management**? It is often defined as the planned timing of revenues, expenses, gains, and losses to smooth out bumps in earnings. In most cases, companies use earnings management to increase income in the current year at the expense of income in future years. For example, they prematurely recognize sales in order to boost earnings. As one commentator noted, "it's like popping a cork in [opening] a bottle of wine before it is ready."

Companies also use earnings management to decrease current earnings in order to increase income in the future. The classic case is the use of "cookie jar" reserves. Companies establish these reserves by using unrealistic assumptions to estimate liabilities for such items as loan losses, restructuring charges, and warranty returns. The companies then reduce these reserves in the future to increase reported income in the future.

> **Underlying Concepts**
>
> The income statement provides important information to help assess the amounts, timing, and uncertainty of future cash flows—the central element of the objective of financial reporting.

[2]In support of the usefulness of income information, accounting researchers have documented an association between companies' market prices and reported incomes. See W. H. Beaver, "Perspectives on Recent Capital Markets Research," *The Accounting Review* (April 2002), pp. 453–474.

[3]A. Levitt, "The Numbers Game," Remarks to NYU Center for Law and Business, September 28, 1998 (Securities and Exchange Commission, 1998).

Such earnings management negatively affects the **quality of earnings** if it distorts the information in a way that is less useful for predicting future earnings and cash flows. Markets rely on trust. The bond between shareholders and the company must remain strong. Investors or others losing faith in the numbers reported in the financial statements will damage U.S. capital markets. As we mentioned in the opening story, we need heightened scrutiny of income measurement and reporting to ensure the quality of earnings and investors' confidence in the income statement.

What do the numbers mean? FOUR: THE LONELIEST NUMBER

Managing earnings up or down adversely affects the quality of earnings. Why do companies engage in such practices? Some recent research concludes that many companies tweak quarterly earnings to meet investor expectations. How do they do it? Research findings indicate that companies tend to nudge their earnings numbers up by a 10th of a cent or two. That lets them round results up to the highest cent, as illustrated in the following chart.

Source: Joseph Grundfest and Nadya Malenko, Stanford University.

What the research shows is that the number "4" appeared less often in the 10th's place than any other digit and signifi-

cantly less often than would be expected by chance. This effect is called "quadrophobia." For the typical company in the study, an increase of $31,000 in quarterly net income would boost earnings per share by a 10th of a cent. A more recent analysis of quarterly results for more than 2,600 companies found that rounding up remains more common than rounding down.

Another recent study reinforces the concerns about earnings management. Based on a survey of 169 public-company chief financial officers (and with in-depth interviews of 12), the study concludes that high-quality earnings are sustainable when backed by actual cash flows and "avoiding unreliable long-term estimates." However, about 20 percent of firms manage earnings to misrepresent their economic performance. And when they do manage earnings, it could move EPS by an average of 10 percent.

Is such earnings management a problem for investors? It is if they cannot determine the impact on earnings quality. Indeed, the surveyed CFOs "believe that it is difficult for outside observers to unravel earnings management, especially when such earnings are managed using subtle unobservable choices or real actions." What's an investor to do? The survey authors say the CFOs "advocate paying close attention to the key managers running the firm, the lack of correlation between earnings and cash flows, significant deviations between firm and peer experience, and unusual behavior in accruals."

Sources: S. Thurm, "For Some Firms, a Case of 'Quadrophobia'," *Wall Street Journal* (February 14, 2010); and H. Greenberg, "CFOs Concede Earnings Are 'Managed'," *www.cnbc.com* (July 19, 2012). (The study referred to is by I. Dichev, J. Graham, C. Harvey, and S. Rajgopal, "Earnings Quality: Evidence from the Field," Emory University Working Paper (July 2012).

FORMAT OF THE INCOME STATEMENT

Elements of the Income Statement

LEARNING OBJECTIVE 2

Describe the content and format of the income statement.

Net income results from revenue, expense, gain, and loss transactions. The income statement summarizes these transactions. This method of income measurement, the **transaction approach**, focuses on the income-related activities that have occurred during the period.[4] The statement can further classify income by customer, product line, or function, or by operating and nonoperating, continuing and discontinued, and regular and irregular categories.[5] The following lists more formal definitions of income-related items, referred to as the major elements of the income statement.

ELEMENTS OF FINANCIAL STATEMENTS

REVENUES. Inflows or other enhancements of assets of an entity or settlements of its liabilities during a period from delivering or producing goods, rendering services, or other activities that constitute the entity's ongoing major or central operations.

EXPENSES. Outflows or other using-up of assets or incurrences of liabilities during a period from delivering or producing goods, rendering services, or carrying out other activities that constitute the entity's ongoing major or central operations.

GAINS. Increases in equity (net assets) from peripheral or incidental transactions of an entity except those that result from revenues or investments by owners.

LOSSES. Decreases in equity (net assets) from peripheral or incidental transactions of an entity except those that result from expenses or distributions to owners.[6]

Revenues take many forms, such as sales, fees, interest, dividends, and rents. Expenses also take many forms, such as cost of goods sold, depreciation, interest, rent, salaries and wages, and taxes. Gains and losses also are of many types, resulting from the sale of investments or plant assets, settlement of liabilities, and write-offs of assets due to impairments or casualty.

The distinction between revenues and gains, and between expenses and losses, depend to a great extent on the typical activities of the company. For example, when **McDonald's** sells a hamburger, it records the selling price as revenue. However, when McDonald's sells land, it records any excess of the selling price over the book value as a gain. This difference in treatment results because the sale of the hamburger is part of McDonald's regular operations. The sale of land is not.

We cannot overemphasize the importance of reporting these elements. Most decision-makers find the *parts* of a financial statement to be more useful than the whole. As we indicated earlier, investors and creditors are interested in predicting the amounts, timing, and uncertainty of future income and cash flows. Having income statement elements shown in some detail and in comparison with prior years' data allows decision-makers to better assess future income and cash flows.

---

[4]The most common alternative to the transaction approach is the **capital maintenance approach** to income measurement. Under this approach, a company determines income for the period based on the change in equity, after adjusting for capital contributions (e.g., investments by owners) or distributions (e.g., dividends). The main drawback associated with the capital maintenance approach is that the components of income are not evident in its measurement. The Internal Revenue Service uses the capital maintenance approach to identify unreported income and refers to this approach as the "net worth check."

[5]The term "irregular" encompasses transactions and other events that are derived from developments outside the normal operations of the business.

[6]"Elements of Financial Statements," *Statement of Financial Accounting Concepts No. 6* (Stamford, Conn.: FASB, 1985), paras. 78–89.

Intermediate Components of the Income Statement

LEARNING OBJECTIVE **3**

Prepare an income statement.

It is common for companies to present some or all of the following sections and totals within the income statement as shown in Illustration 4-1. This format is often referred to as the **multiple-step income statement.**

ILLUSTRATION 4-1
Income Statement
Sections

1. **OPERATING SECTION.** A report of the revenues and expenses of the company's principal operations.
   (a) **Sales or Revenue Section.** A subsection presenting sales, discounts, allowances, returns, and other related information. Its purpose is to arrive at the net amount of sales revenue.
   (b) **Cost of Goods Sold Section.** A subsection that shows the cost of goods that were sold to produce the sales.
   (c) **Selling Expenses.** A subsection that lists expenses resulting from the company's efforts to make sales.
   (d) **Administrative or General Expenses.** A subsection reporting expenses of general administration.[7]

2. **NONOPERATING SECTION.** A report of revenues and expenses resulting from secondary or auxiliary activities of the company. In addition, special gains and losses that are infrequent or unusual, but not both, are normally reported in this section. Generally these items break down into two main subsections:
   (a) **Other Revenues and Gains.** A list of the revenues recognized or gains incurred, generally net of related expenses, from nonoperating transactions.
   (b) **Other Expenses and Losses.** A list of the expenses or losses incurred, generally net of any related incomes, from nonoperating transactions.

3. **INCOME TAX.** A section reporting federal and state taxes levied on income from continuing operations.

4. **DISCONTINUED OPERATIONS.** Material gains or losses resulting from the disposition of a component of the business.

5. **EXTRAORDINARY ITEMS.** Unusual and infrequent material gains and losses.

6. **NONCONTROLLING INTEREST.** Allocation of income to noncontrolling shareholders.

7. **EARNINGS PER SHARE.**

As indicated, companies report all revenues, gains, expenses, and losses on the income statement. This statement separates operating transactions from nonoperating transactions, and matches costs and expenses with related revenues. It highlights certain intermediate components of income that analysts use to compute ratios for assessing the performance of the company. Companies present nonoperating revenues, gains, expenses, and losses in a separate section, before income taxes and income from operations. Companies report irregular items, such as discontinued operations of a component of a business and extraordinary items, as separate elements in the income statement. Segregating income with different characteristics and providing intermediate income figures helps readers evaluate earnings information in assessing the amounts, timing, and uncertainty of future cash flows.

[7]Although the content of the operating section is always the same, the organization of the material can differ. The breakdown above uses a **natural expense classification**. Manufacturing concerns and merchandising companies in the wholesale trade commonly use this. Another classification of operating expenses, recommended for retail stores, uses a **functional expense classification** of administrative, occupancy, publicity, buying, and selling expenses.

Illustration 4-2 presents an income statement for Cabrera Company. Cabrera's income statement includes all of the major items shown in Illustration 4-1, except for discontinued operations, extraordinary items, and noncontrolling interest. In arriving at net income, the statement presents the following subtotals and totals: gross profit, income from operations, income before income tax, and net income.[8]

ILLUSTRATION 4-2
Multiple-Step Income Statement

CABRERA COMPANY			
INCOME STATEMENT			
FOR THE YEAR ENDED DECEMBER 31, 2014			
Sales			
Sales revenue			$3,053,081
Less: Sales discounts		$ 24,241	
Sales returns and allowances		56,427	80,668
Net sales			2,972,413
Cost of goods sold			1,982,541
Gross profit			989,872
Operating Expenses			
Selling expenses			
Sales salaries and commissions	$202,644		
Sales office salaries	59,200		
Travel and entertainment	48,940		
Advertising expense	38,315		
Delivery expense	41,209		
Shipping supplies and expense	24,712		
Postage and stationery	16,788		
Telephone and Internet expense	12,215		
Depreciation of sales equipment	9,005	453,028	
Administrative expenses			
Officers' salaries	186,000		
Office salaries	61,200		
Legal and professional services	23,721		
Utilities expense	23,275		
Insurance expense	17,029		
Depreciation of building	18,059		
Depreciation of office equipment	16,000		
Stationery, supplies, and postage	2,875		
Miscellaneous office expenses	2,612	350,771	803,799
Income from operations			186,073
Other Revenues and Gains			
Dividend revenue		98,500	
Rent revenue		72,910	171,410
			357,483
Other Expenses and Losses			
Interest on bonds and notes			126,060
Income before income tax			231,423
Income tax			66,934
Net income for the year			$ 164,489
Earnings per common share			$1.74

The disclosure of net sales is useful because Cabrera reports regular revenues as a separate item. It discloses irregular or incidental revenues elsewhere in the income statement. As a result, analysts can more easily understand and assess trends in revenue from continuing operations.

Similarly, the reporting of gross profit provides a useful number for evaluating performance and predicting future earnings. Statement readers may study the trend in gross

[8]Companies must include *earnings per share* or *net loss per share* on the face of the income statement.

profits to determine how successfully a company uses its resources. They also may use that information to understand how competitive pressure affected profit margins.

Finally, disclosing income from operations highlights the difference between regular and irregular or incidental activities. This disclosure helps users recognize that incidental or irregular activities are unlikely to continue at the same level. Furthermore, disclosure of operating earnings may assist in comparing different companies and assessing operating efficiencies.

What do the numbers mean? TOP LINE OR BOTTOM LINE?

The importance of the components of income, as well as the bottom line, is illustrated in the recent case of Chipotle. Its stock had climbed fourfold in five years and for good reason. The company had been reporting surprisingly high bottom-line income and investors were clamoring to buy. However, in a recent month, that pattern was broken—that is, Chipotle posted solid earnings, but investors sold. The reason? Analysts attribute the sell-off to Chipotle missing its target for *revenues*. The stock fell 21 percent, from $404 to $317, in a day. And Chipotle was not alone. Six in 10 large companies reported results in that same quarter that missed revenue targets. In response to the bad revenue news, Priceline.com fell $117 to $562 after reporting revenue that was lower than analysts had expected. The story has been the same for dozens of companies across industries, from Coach, a luxury goods retailer, to Boston Scientific, which sells medical devices, to glass-container maker Owens-Illinois.

The recent focus on the top line, revenue, arises because market expectations for revenues do not seem to jive with the companies' optimistic profit picture. For example, revenues are expected to drop by about 2 percent in 2013 for companies in the S&P 500. And while companies might report a surprise in earnings, analysts will be focusing on revenues. Companies have been able to cut costs to compensate—laying off workers, squeezing remaining staff, and using technology to run more efficiently—but there's a limit to how much you can squeeze your workers and use technology to produce more. U.S. companies are just about as lean as any time in history.

As one analyst noted (in this economic environment), "you won't be able to grow earnings much faster than revenue. . . . Analysts will have to revise down their earnings." So watch the top line, as well as the bottom line.

Source: Associated Press, "Why Some Stocks Are Sinking Despite Big Profits," *The New York Times* (August 12, 2012).

Condensed Income Statements

In some cases, a single income statement cannot possibly present all the desired expense detail. To solve this problem, a company includes only the totals of expense groups in the statement of income. It then also prepares supplementary schedules to support the totals. This format may thus reduce the income statement itself to a few lines on a single sheet. For this reason, readers who wish to study all the reported data on operations must give their attention to the supporting schedules. For example, consider the income statement shown in Illustration 4-3 for Cabrera Company. This statement is a condensed version of the more detailed multiple-step statement presented in Illustration 4-2 (page 165). It is more representative of the type found in practice. Illustration 4-4 then shows an example of a supporting schedule, cross-referenced as Note D and detailing the selling expenses.

How much detail should a company include in the income statement? On the one hand, a company wants to present a simple, summarized statement so that readers can readily discover important factors. On the other hand, it wants to disclose the results of all activities and to provide more than just a skeleton report. As we showed in Illustrations 4-3 and 4-4, the income statement always includes certain basic elements, but companies can present them in various formats.

ILLUSTRATION 4-3
Condensed Income
Statement

CABRERA COMPANY		
INCOME STATEMENT		
FOR THE YEAR ENDED DECEMBER 31, 2014		
Net sales		$2,972,413
Cost of goods sold		1,982,541
Gross profit		989,872
Selling expenses (see Note D)	$453,028	
Administrative expenses	350,771	803,799
Income from operations		186,073
Other revenues and gains		171,410
		357,483
Other expenses and losses		126,060
Income before income tax		231,423
Income tax		66,934
Net income for the year		$ 164,489
Earnings per share		$1.74

ILLUSTRATION 4-4
Sample Supporting
Schedule

Note D: Selling expenses	
Sales salaries and commissions	$202,644
Sales office salaries	59,200
Travel and entertainment	48,940
Advertising expense	38,315
Delivery expense	41,209
Shipping supplies and expense	24,712
Postage and stationery	16,788
Telephone and Internet expense	12,215
Depreciation of sales equipment	9,005
Total selling expenses	$453,028

Single-Step Income Statements

In reporting revenues, gains, expenses, and losses, some companies often use a format known as the **single-step income statement** instead of a multiple-step income statement. The single-step statement consists of just two groupings: revenues and expenses. Expenses are deducted from revenues to arrive at net income or loss, hence the expression "single-step." Frequently, companies report income tax separately as the last item before net income to indicate its relationship to income before income tax. Illustration 4-5 (page 168) shows the single-step income statement of Cabrera Company.

Companies that use the single-step income statement in financial reporting typically do so because of its simplicity. That is, **the primary advantage of the single-step format lies in its simple presentation and the absence of any implication that one type of revenue or expense item has priority over another**. This format thus eliminates potential classification problems.[9]

[9]*Accounting Trends and Techniques* (New York: AICPA) recently reported that of the 500 companies surveyed, 411 employed the multiple-step form, and 89 employed the single-step income statement format. This is a reversal from 1983, when 314 used the single-step form and 286 used the multiple-step form.

ILLUSTRATION 4-5
Single-Step Income
Statement

CABRERA COMPANY		
INCOME STATEMENT		
FOR THE YEAR ENDED DECEMBER 31, 2014		
Revenues		
Net sales	$2,972,413	
Dividend revenue	98,500	
Rent revenue	72,910	
Total revenues		3,143,823
Expenses		
Cost of goods sold	1,982,541	
Selling expenses	453,028	
Administrative expenses	350,771	
Interest expense	126,060	
Income tax expense	66,934	
Total expenses		2,979,334
Net income		$ 164,489
Earnings per common share		$1.74

REPORTING VARIOUS INCOME ITEMS

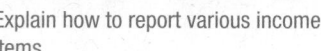

LEARNING OBJECTIVE **4**

Explain how to report various income items.

GAAP allows flexibility in the presentation of the components of income. How-ever, the FASB developed specific guidelines in two important areas: what to include in income and how to report certain unusual or irregular items.

What should be reported in net income and where it should be reported is con-troversial. For example, should companies report a gain or loss on sale of an investment as part of net income or report it directly in retained earnings? Should a company report a loss on discontinued operations differently than interest expense? What we therefore need is consistent and comparable income reporting practices. Developing a framework for reporting income components is important to ensure useful information.

Furthermore, as our opening story discusses, we need consistent and comparable income reporting practices to avoid "promotional" information reported by companies.[10] Some users advocate a **current operating performance approach** to income reporting. These analysts argue that the most useful income measure reflects only regular and re-curring revenue and expense elements. Some irregular items do not reflect a company's future earning power.

In contrast, others warn that a focus on operating income potentially misses impor-tant information about a company's performance. Any gain or loss experienced by the company, whether directly or indirectly related to operations, contributes to its long-run profitability. As one analyst notes, "write-offs matter. . . . They speak to the volatility of (past) earnings."[11] As a result, analysts can use some nonoperating items to assess the riskiness of future earnings. Furthermore, determining which items are operating and which are irregular or unusual requires judgment. This might lead to differences in the treatment of irregular items and to possible manipulation of income measures.

[10]The FASB and the IASB are working on a joint project on financial statement presentation, which is studying how to best report income as well as information presented in the balance sheet and the statement of cash flows. See *http://www.fasb.org/project/financial_statement_presentation.shtml*.

[11]D. McDermott, "Latest Profit Data Stir Old Debate Between Net and Operating Income," *Wall Street Journal* (May 3, 1999). A recent survey of 500 large public companies (*Accounting Trends and Techniques—2012* (New York: AICPA)) documented that 106 of the 500 survey companies reported a write-down of assets (see also Illustration 4-6 on page 169). This highlights the importance of good reporting for these irregular items.

So, what to do? The accounting profession has **adopted a** modified all-inclusive concept. In this approach, companies record most items, including unusual or irregular ones, as part of net income.[12] In addition, companies are required to highlight these items in the financial statements so that users can better determine the long-run earning power of the company. These income items fall into four general categories, which we discuss in the following sections:

1. Unusual gains and losses.
2. Discontinued operations.
3. Extraordinary items.
4. Noncontrolling interest.

International Perspective

In many countries, the "modified all-inclusive" income statement approach does not parallel that of the United States. For example, companies in these countries take some gains and losses directly to owners' equity accounts instead of reporting them on the income statement.

Unusual Gains and Losses

The following items may need separate disclosure in the income statement to help users predict the amounts, timing, and uncertainty of future cash flows.

* Losses on the write-down or write-off of receivables; inventories; property, plant, and equipment; deferred research and development costs; or other intangible assets.
* Gains or losses from exchange or translation of foreign currencies, including those relating to major devaluations and revaluations.
* Restructuring charges.
* Other gains or losses from sale or abandonment of property, plant, or equipment used in the business.
* Effects of a strike, including those against competitors and major suppliers.
* Adjustment of accruals on long-term contracts. **[1]**

See the FASB Codification section (page 188).

Illustration 4-6 identifies the most common types of unusual gains and losses reported in a survey of 500 large companies. Note that more than 40 percent of the surveyed firms reported restructuring charges, and nearly 60 percent of the companies reported write-downs or gains or losses on asset sales.

ILLUSTRATION 4-6
Number of Unusual Items Reported in a Recent Year by 500 Large Companies

Companies sometimes show these unusual gains and losses with their normal recurring revenues and expenses. For example, **PepsiCo, Inc.** presented an unusual charge in its income statement, as Illustration 4-7 (page 170) shows.

[12]The FASB issued a statement of concepts that offers some guidance on this topic: "Recognition and Measurement in Financial Statements of Business Enterprises," *Statement of Financial Accounting Concepts No. 5* (Stamford, Conn.: FASB, 1984).

ILLUSTRATION 4-7
Income Statement
Presentation of Unusual
Charges

PepsiCo, Inc.
(in millions)

Net sales	$20,917
Costs and expenses, net	
Cost of sales	8,525
Selling, general, and administrative expenses	9,241
Amortization of intangible assets	199
Unusual items (Note 2)	290
Operating income	$ 2,662

Note 2 (Restructuring Charge)	
Dispose and write down assets	$183
Improve productivity	94
Strengthen the international bottler structure	13
Net loss	$290

The net charge to strengthen the international bottler structure includes proceeds of $87 million associated with a settlement related to a previous Venezuelan bottler agreement, which were partially offset by related costs.

Restructuring charges, like the one PepsiCo reported in Note 2 above, are common in recent years (see also Illustration 4-6 on page 169). A **restructuring charge** relates to a major reorganization of company affairs, such as costs associated with employee lay-offs, plant closing costs, write-offs of assets, and so on. A company should not report a restructuring charge as an extraordinary item because these write-offs are part of a company's ordinary and typical activities.

Companies tend to **report unusual items in a separate section just above "Income from operations before income taxes,"** especially when there are multiple unusual items. For example, when General Electric experienced multiple unusual items in one year, it reported them in a separate "Unusual items" section of the income statement below "Income before unusual items and income taxes." *When preparing a multiple-step income statement for homework purposes, you should report unusual gains and losses in the "Other revenues and gains" or "Other expenses and losses" section unless you are instructed to prepare a separate unusual items section.*[13]

Discontinued Operations

A **discontinued operation** occurs when two things happen: (1) a company eliminates the results of operations of a component of the business, and (2) there is no significant involvement in that component after the disposal transaction. **[2]**

To illustrate a **component**, S. C. Johnson manufactures and sells consumer products. It has several product groups, each with different product lines and brands. For S. C. Johnson, a product group is the lowest level at which it can clearly distinguish the operations and cash flows from the rest of the company's operations. Therefore, each product group is a component of the company. If a component were disposed of, S. C. Johnson would classify it as a discontinued operation.

[13]Many companies report "one-time items." However, some companies take restructuring charges practically every year. Citicorp (now Citigroup) took restructuring charges six years in a row; Eastman Kodak Co. did so five out of six years. Research indicates that the market discounts the earnings of companies that report a series of "nonrecurring" items. Such evidence supports the contention that these elements reduce the quality of earnings. See J. Elliott and D. Hanna, "Repeated Accounting Write-Offs and the Information Content of Earnings," *Journal of Accounting Research* (Supplement, 1996).

Here is another example. Assume that Softso Inc. has experienced losses with certain brands in its beauty-care products group. As a result, Softso decides to sell that part of its business. It will discontinue any continuing involvement in the product group after the sale. In this case, Softso eliminates the operations and the cash flows of the product group from its ongoing operations and reports it as a discontinued operation.

On the other hand, assume Softso decides to remain in the beauty-care business but will discontinue the brands that experienced losses. Because Softso cannot differentiate the cash flows from the brands from the cash flows of the product group as a whole, it cannot consider the brands a component. Softso does not classify any gain or loss on the sale of the brands as a discontinued operation.

Companies report as discontinued operations (in a separate income statement category) the gain or loss from **disposal of a component of a business**. In addition, companies report the **results of operations of a component that has been or will be disposed of** separately from continuing operations. Companies show the effects of discontinued operations net of tax as a separate category, after continuing operations. **[3]**

To illustrate, Multiplex Products, Inc., a highly diversified company, decides to discontinue its electronics division. During the current year, the electronics division lost $300,000 (net of tax). Multiplex sold the division at the end of the year at a loss of $500,000 (net of tax). Illustration 4-8 shows the reporting of discontinued operations for Multiplex.

Income from continuing operations		$20,000,000
Discontinued operations		
Loss from operation of discontinued electronics		
division (net of tax)	$300,000	
Loss from disposal of electronics division (net of tax)	500,000	(800,000)
Net income		$19,200,000

ILLUSTRATION 4-8
Income Statement Presentation of Discontinued Operations

Companies use the phrase **"Income from continuing operations"** only when gains or losses on discontinued operations occur.[14]

A company that reports a discontinued operation must report per share amounts for discontinued operations either on the face of the income statement or in the notes to the financial statements. To illustrate, consider the income statement for Poquito Industries Inc., shown in Illustration 4-9 (page 172). Poquito had 100,000 shares outstanding for the entire year. Notice the order in which Poquito shows the data, with per share information at the bottom. The Poquito income statement, as Illustration 4-9 shows, is highly condensed. Poquito would need to describe items such as "Other expenses and losses" and "Discontinued operations" fully and appropriately in the statement or related notes.

Intraperiod Tax Allocation

As indicated in Illustration 4-8, companies report discontinued operations on the income statement net of tax. The allocation of tax to this item is called intraperiod tax allocation, that is, allocation within a period. It relates the income tax expense (sometimes referred to as the income tax provision) of the fiscal period to the specific items that give rise to the amount of the income tax provision.

Intraperiod tax allocation helps financial statement users better understand the impact of income taxes on the various components of net income. For example, readers

[14]In practice, a company will generally report only one line on the income statement, such as "Loss on discontinued operations," and then in the notes explain the two components of the loss that total $800,000. *For homework purposes, report both amounts on the face of the income statement, net of tax, if both amounts are provided.*

ILLUSTRATION 4-9
Income Statement

POQUITO INDUSTRIES INC.
INCOME STATEMENT
FOR THE YEAR ENDED DECEMBER 31, 2014

Sales revenue		$1,420,000
Cost of goods sold		600,000
Gross profit		820,000
Selling and administrative expenses		320,000
Other revenues and gains		
Interest revenue	$ 10,000	
Other expenses and losses		
Loss on disposal of part of Textile Division	(5,000)	
Loss on sale of investments	(30,000)	(25,000)
Income from operations		475,000
Interest expense		15,000
Income before income tax		460,000
Income tax		184,000
Income from continuing operations		276,000
Discontinued operations		
Income from operations of Pizza Division, less		
applicable income tax of $24,800	54,000	
Loss on disposal of Pizza Division, less		
applicable income tax of $41,000	(90,000)	(36,000)
Net income		$240,000
Per share		
Income from continuing operations		$2.76
Income from operations of discontinued division, net of tax		0.54
Loss on disposal of discontinued operation, net of tax		(0.90)
Net income		$2.40

of financial statements will understand how much income tax expense relates to "Income from continuing operations" and how much to discontinued operations. This approach helps users to better predict the amount, timing, and uncertainty of future cash flows. In addition, intraperiod tax allocation discourages statement readers from using pretax measures of performance when evaluating financial results, and thereby recognizes that income tax expense is a real cost.

Companies use intraperiod tax allocation on the income statement for the following items: (1) income from continuing operations, (2) discontinued operations, and (3) extraordinary items (discussed below). The general concept is **"let the tax follow the income."**

To compute the income tax expense attributable to "Income from continuing operations," a company computes the income tax expense related to both the revenue and expense transactions as well as other income and expense used in determining this income subtotal. (In this computation, the company does not consider the tax consequences of items excluded from the determination of "Income from continuing operations.") Companies then associate a separate tax effect (e.g., for discontinued operations). Here, we look in more detail at the calculation of intraperiod tax allocation for a discontinued gain or discontinued loss.

Discontinued Operations (Gain)

In applying the concept of intraperiod tax allocation, assume that Schindler Co. has income before income tax of $250,000. It has a gain of $100,000 from a discontinued operation. Assuming a 30 percent income tax rate, Schindler presents the following information on the income statement.

Income before income tax		$250,000
Income tax		75,000
Income from continuing operations		175,000
Gain on discontinued operations	$100,000	
Less: Applicable income tax	30,000	70,000
Net income		$245,000

ILLUSTRATION 4-10
Intraperiod Tax Allocation, Discontinued Operations Gain

Schindler determines the income tax of $75,000 ($250,000 × 30%) attributable to "Income before income tax" from revenue and expense transactions related to this income. Schindler omits the tax consequences of items excluded from the determination of "Income before income tax." The company shows a separate tax effect of $30,000 related to the "Gain on discontinued operations."

Discontinued Operations (Loss)

To illustrate the reporting of a loss from discontinued operations, assume that Schindler Co. has income before income tax of $250,000. It also has a loss from discontinued operations of $100,000. Assuming a 30 percent tax rate, Schindler presents the income tax on the income statement as shown in Illustration 4-11. In this case, the loss provides a positive tax benefit of $30,000. Schindler, therefore, subtracts it from the $100,000 loss.

Income before income tax		$250,000
Income tax		75,000
Income from continuing operations		175,000
Loss from discontinued operations	$100,000	
Less: Applicable income tax reduction	30,000	70,000
Net income		$105,000

ILLUSTRATION 4-11
Intraperiod Tax Allocation, Discontinued Operations Loss

Companies may also report the tax effect of a discontinued item by means of a note disclosure, as illustrated below.

Income before income tax		$250,000
Income tax		75,000
Income from continuing operations		175,000
Loss on discontinued operations, less applicable		
income tax reduction (Note 1)		70,000
Net income		$105,000

Note 1: During the year, the Company suffered a loss on discontinuing operations of $70,000, net of applicable income tax reduction of $30,000.

ILLUSTRATION 4-12
Note Disclosure of Intraperiod Tax Allocation

Extraordinary Items

Extraordinary items are nonrecurring **material** items that differ significantly from a company's typical business activities. The criteria for extraordinary items are as follows.

Extraordinary items are events and transactions that are distinguished by their unusual nature **and** by the infrequency of their occurrence. Classifying an event or transaction as an extraordinary item requires meeting **both** of the following criteria:

(a) *Unusual nature.* The underlying event or transaction should possess a high degree of abnormality and be of a type clearly unrelated to, or only incidentally related to, the ordinary and typical activities of the company, taking into account the environment in which it operates.

(b) *Infrequency of occurrence.* The underlying event or transaction should be of a type that the company does not reasonably expect to recur in the foreseeable future, taking into account the environment in which the company operates. **[4]**

Only rarely does an event or transaction clearly meet the criteria for an extraordinary item.[15] For example, a company classifies gains or losses as extraordinary if they **resulted directly from a major casualty** (such as an earthquake), an **expropriation**, or a **prohibition under a newly enacted law or regulation**. Such circumstances clearly meet the criteria of unusual and infrequent. For example, Weyerhaeuser Company (forest and lumber) incurred an extraordinary item (an approximate $36 million loss) as a result of volcanic activity at Mount St. Helens. The eruption destroyed standing timber, logs, buildings, equipment, and transportation systems covering 68,000 acres.

In determining whether an item is extraordinary, **a company must consider the environment in which it operates**. The environment includes such factors as industry characteristics, geographic location, and the nature and extent of governmental regulations. Thus, the FASB accords extraordinary item treatment to the loss from hail damages to a tobacco grower's crops if hailstorm damage in its locality is rare. On the other hand, frost damage to a citrus grower's crop in Florida does not qualify as extraordinary because frost damage normally occurs there every three or four years.

Similarly, when a company sells the only significant security investment it has ever owned, the gain or loss meets the criteria of an extraordinary item. Another company, however, that has a portfolio of securities acquired for investment purposes would not report such a sale as an extraordinary item. Sale of such securities is part of its ordinary and typical activities.

In addition, considerable judgment must be exercised in determining whether to report an item as extraordinary. For example, the government condemned the forestlands of some paper companies to preserve state or national parks or forests. Is such an event extraordinary, or is it part of a paper company's normal operations? Such determination is not easy. Much depends on the frequency of previous condemnations, the expectation of future condemnations, materiality, and the like.[16]

Extraordinary Gains

To illustrate the reporting of an extraordinary gain, assume that Logan Co. has income before income tax and extraordinary item of $250,000. It has an extraordinary gain of $100,000 from a condemnation settlement received on one its properties. Assuming a 30 percent income tax rate, Logan presents the following information on the income statement.

ILLUSTRATION 4-13
Extraordinary Gain

Income before income tax and extraordinary item		$250,000
Income tax		75,000
Income before extraordinary item		175,000
Extraordinary gain—condemnation settlement	$100,000	
Less: Applicable income tax	30,000	70,000
Net income		$245,000

---

[15]*Accounting Trends and Techniques—2012* (New York: AICPA) indicates that just 1 of the 500 companies surveyed reported an extraordinary item.

[16]Because assessing the materiality of individual items requires judgment, determining what is extraordinary is difficult. However, in making materiality judgments, companies should consider extraordinary items individually and not in the aggregate. **[5]**

Logan determines the income tax of $75,000 ($250,000 × 30%) attributable to "Income before income tax and extraordinary item" from revenue and expense transactions related to this income. Logan omits the tax consequences of items excluded from the determination of "Income before income tax and extraordinary item." The company shows a separate tax effect of $30,000 related to the "Extraordinary gain—condemnation settlement."

Extraordinary Losses

To illustrate the reporting of an extraordinary loss, assume that Logan Co. has income before income tax and extraordinary item of $250,000. It suffers an extraordinary loss from a major casualty of $100,000. Assuming a 30 percent tax rate, Logan presents the income tax on the income statement as shown in Illustration 4-14. In this case, the loss provides a positive tax benefit of $30,000. Logan, therefore, subtracts it from the $100,000 loss.

Income before income tax and extraordinary item		$250,000
Income tax		75,000
Income before extraordinary item		175,000
Extraordinary item—casualty loss	$100,000	
Less: Applicable income tax reduction	30,000	70,000
Net income		$105,000

ILLUSTRATION 4-14
Intraperiod Tax Allocation, Extraordinary Loss

Companies may also report the tax effect of an extraordinary item by means of a note disclosure, as illustrated below.

Income before income tax and extraordinary item	$250,000
Income tax	75,000
Income before extraordinary item	175,000
Extraordinary item—casualty loss, less applicable income tax reduction (Note 1)	70,000
Net income	$105,000

Note 1: During the year, the Company suffered a major casualty loss of $70,000, net of applicable income tax reduction of $30,000.

ILLUSTRATION 4-15
Note Disclosure of Intraperiod Tax Allocation

A presentation showing both discontinued operations and extraordinary items is shown in Illustration 4-19 (page 178).[17]

What do the numbers mean? *EXTRAORDINARY TIMES*

No event better illustrates the difficulties of determining whether a transaction meets the definition of extraordinary than the financial impacts of the terrorist attack on the World Trade Center on September 11, 2001.

To many, this event, which resulted in the tragic loss of lives, jobs, and in some cases entire businesses, clearly meets the criteria for unusual and infrequent. For example, in the wake of the terrorist attack that destroyed the World Trade Center and turned much of lower Manhattan including Wall Street into a war zone, airlines, insurance companies, and other businesses recorded major losses due to property damage, business disruption, and suspension of airline travel and of securities trading.

But, to the surprise of many, the FASB did not permit extraordinary item reporting for losses arising from the terrorist attacks. The reason? After much deliberation, the

---

[17]As indicated earlier, discontinued operations and extraordinary items are shown net of tax, while unusual gains and losses are not reported net of tax. The Board specifically **prohibited a net-of-tax treatment for these latter items**, to ensure that users of financial statements can easily differentiate extraordinary items—reported net of tax—from material items that are unusual or infrequent, but not both.

Emerging Issues Task Force (EITF) of the FASB decided that measurement of the possible loss was too difficult.

Take the airline industry as an example. What portion of the airlines' losses after September 11 was related to the terrorist attack, and what portion was due to the ongoing recession? Also, the FASB did not want companies to use the attack as a reason for reporting as extraordinary some losses that had little direct relationship to the attack. Indeed, energy company AES and shoe retailer Footstar, which both were experiencing profit pressure before 9/11, put some of the blame for their poor performance on the attack. The FASB came to a similar conclusion—no extraordinary treatment—for the effects of the recent huricanes Katrina and Sandy.

Sources: Julie Creswell, "Bad News Bearers Shift the Blame," *Fortune* (October 15, 2001), p. 44; and CFO Journal, "Companies Must Walk Fine Line in Accounting for Sandy," *Wall Street Journal* (November 13, 2012).

Noncontrolling Interest

A company like The Coca-Cola Company owns substantial interests in other companies. Coca-Cola generally consolidates the financial results of these companies into its own financial statements. In these cases, Coca-Cola is referred to as the parent, and the other companies are referred to as subsidiaries. Noncontrolling interest is then the portion of equity (net assets) interest in a subsidiary not attributable to the parent company.

To illustrate, assume that Coca-Cola acquires 70 percent of the outstanding stock of Koch Company. Because Coca-Cola owns more than 50 percent of Koch, it consolidates Koch's financial results with its own. Consolidated net income is then allocated to the controlling (Coca-Cola) and noncontrolling shareholders' percentage of ownership in Koch. In other words, under this arrangement, the ownership of Koch is divided into two classes: (1) the majority interest represented by stockholders who own the controlling interest and (2) the noncontrolling interest (sometimes referred to as the minority interest) represented by stockholders who are not part of the controlling group. When Coca-Cola prepares a consolidated income statement, GAAP requires that net income be allocated to the controlling and noncontrolling interest. This allocation is reported at the bottom of the income statement, after net income.

An example of how Coca-Cola reports its noncontrolling interest is shown in Illustration 4-16.

ILLUSTRATION 4-16
Presentation of
Noncontrolling Interest

The Coca-Cola Company	
Consolidated net income	$8,634
Less: Net income attributable to noncontrolling interests	62
Net income attributable to shareowners of The Coca-Cola Company	$8,572

The noncontrolling interest amounts are not an expense or dividend, but are allocations of net income (loss) to the noncontrolling interest. **[6]**

Summary of Various Income Items

Because of the numerous intermediate income figures created by the reporting of irregular items, readers must carefully evaluate earnings information reported by the financial press. Illustration 4-17 summarizes the basic concepts that we previously discussed. Although simplified, the chart provides a useful framework for determining the treatment of special items affecting the income statement.

Type of Situation	Criteria	Examples	Placement on Income Statement
Unusual gains or losses, not considered extraordinary	Material; character typical of the customary business activities; unusual or infrequent but not both.	Write-downs of receivables, inventories; adjustments of accrued contract prices; gains or losses from fluctuations of foreign exchange; gains or losses from sales of assets used in business.	Show in separate section above income before extraordinary items. Often reported in "Other revenues and gains" or "Other expenses and losses" section. **(Not shown net of tax.)**
Discontinued operations	Disposal of a component of a business for which the company can clearly distinguish operations and cash flows from the rest of the company's operations.	Sale by diversified company of major division that represents only activities in electronics industry. Food distributor that sells wholesale to supermarket chains and through fast-food restaurants decides to discontinue the division that sells to one of two classes of customers.	Show in separate section after continuing operations but before extraordinary items. **(Shown net of tax.)**
Extraordinary items	Material, and both unusual and infrequent (nonrecurring).	Gains or losses resulting from casualties, an expropriation, or a prohibition under a new law.	Show in separate section entitled "Extraordinary items." **(Shown net of tax.)**
Noncontrolling interest	Allocation of net income or loss divided between two classes: (1) the majority interest represented by the shareholders who own the controlling interest, and (2) the noncontrolling interest (often referred to as the *minority interest*).	Net profit (loss) attributable to noncontrolling shareholders.	Report as a separate item below net income or loss as an allocation of the net income or loss **(not as an item of income or expense).**

ILLUSTRATION 4-17
Summary of Various Items in the Income Statement

Earnings per Share

5 LEARNING OBJECTIVE
Identify where to report earnings per share information.

A company customarily sums up the results of its operations in one important figure: net income. However, the financial world has widely accepted an even more distilled and compact figure as the most significant business indicator—**earnings per share (EPS)**.

The computation of earnings per share is usually straightforward. **Earnings per share is net income minus preferred dividends (income available to common stockholders), divided by the weighted average of common shares outstanding.**[18]

To illustrate, assume that Lancer, Inc. reports net income of $350,000. It declares and pays preferred dividends of $50,000 for the year. The weighted-average number of common shares outstanding during the year is 100,000 shares. Lancer computes earnings per share of $3, as shown in Illustration 4-18.

$$\frac{\text{Net Income} - \text{Preferred Dividends}}{\text{Weighted Average of Common Shares Outstanding}} = \text{Earnings per Share}$$

$$\frac{\$350,000 - \$50,000}{100,000} = \$3$$

ILLUSTRATION 4-18
Equation Illustrating Computation of Earnings per Share

Note that EPS measures the number of dollars earned by each share of common stock. It does not represent the dollar amount paid to stockholders in the form of dividends.

Prospectuses, proxy material, and annual reports to stockholders commonly use the "net income per share" or "earnings per share" ratio. The financial press, statistical

[18]In calculating earnings per share, companies deduct preferred dividends from net income if the dividends are declared or if they are cumulative though not declared. Only the net income attributable to the controlling interest should be used in computing earnings per share.

services like Standard & Poor's, and Wall Street securities analysts also highlight EPS. Because of its importance, **companies must disclose earnings per share on the face of the income statement**. A company that reports a discontinued operation or an extraordinary item must report per share amounts for these line items either on the face of the income statement or in the notes to the financial statements. **[7]**

To illustrate, consider the income statement for Poquito Industries Inc. shown in Illustration 4-19. Notice the order in which Poquito shows the data, with per share information at the bottom. Assume that the company had 100,000 shares outstanding for the entire year. The Poquito income statement, as Illustration 4-19 shows, is highly condensed. Poquito would need to describe items such as "Loss on disposal of part of Textile Division," "Discontinued operations," and "Extraordinary item" fully and appropriately in the statement or related notes.

ILLUSTRATION 4-19
Income Statement

POQUITO INDUSTRIES INC. INCOME STATEMENT FOR THE YEAR ENDED DECEMBER 31, 2014		
Sales revenue		$1,420,000
Cost of goods sold		600,000
Gross profit		820,000
Selling and administrative expenses		320,000
Income from operations		500,000
Other revenues and gains		
Interest revenue		10,000
Other expenses and losses		
Loss on disposal of part of Textile Division	$ 5,000	
Loss on sale of investments	45,000	50,000
Income from continuing operations before income tax		460,000
Income tax		184,000
Income from continuing operations		276,000
Discontinued operations		
Income from operations of Pizza Division, less applicable income tax of $24,800	54,000	
Loss on disposal of Pizza Division, less applicable income tax of $41,000	90,000	36,000
Income before extraordinary item		240,000
Extraordinary item—loss from earthquake, less applicable income tax of $23,000		45,000
Net income		$ 195,000
Per share of common stock		
Income from continuing operations		$2.76
Income from operations of discontinued division, net of tax		0.54
Loss on disposal of discontinued operation, net of tax		0.90
Income before extraordinary item		2.40
Extraordinary loss, net of tax		0.45
Net income		$1.95

Many corporations have simple capital structures that include only common stock. For these companies, a presentation such as "Earnings per common share" is appropriate on the income statement. In many instances, however, companies' earnings per share are subject to dilution (reduction) in the future because existing contingencies permit the issuance of additional common shares. **[8]**[19]

[19]The earnings per share effects of noncontrolling interest should also be presented. In addition, the amounts of income from continuing operations and discontinued operations (if present) attributable to the controlling interest should be disclosed. We discuss the computational problems involved in accounting for these dilutive securities in earnings per share computations in Chapter 16.

What do the numbers mean? DIFFERENT INCOME CONCEPTS

As mentioned in the opening story, the FASB and the IASB are collaborating on a joint project related to presentation of financial statements. In 2008, these two groups issued an exposure draft that presented examples of what these new financial statements might look like. The Boards also conducted field tests on two groups: preparers and users. Preparers were asked to recast their financial statements and then comment on the results. Users examined the recast statements and commented on their usefulness.

One part of the field test asked analysts to indicate which primary performance metric they use or create from a company's income statement. They were provided with the following options: (a) Net income; (b) Pretax income; (c) Income before interest and taxes (EBIT); (d) Income before interest, taxes, depreciation, and amortization (EBITDA); (e) Operating income; (f) Comprehensive income; and (g) Other. The adjacent chart highlights their responses.

As indicated, Operating income (31%) and EBITDA (27%) were identified as the two primary performance metrics that

respondents use or create from a company's income statement. A majority of the respondents identified a primary performance metric that uses net income as its foundation (pretax income would be in this group). Clearly, users and preparers look at more than just the bottom-line income number, which supports the common practice of providing subtotals within the income statement.

Source: "FASB-IASB Report on Analyst Field Test Results," Financial Statement Presentation Informational Board Meeting (September 21, 2009).

OTHER REPORTING ISSUES

In this section, we discuss reporting issues related to (1) accounting changes and errors, (2) retained earnings statement, and (3) comprehensive income.

6 LEARNING OBJECTIVE

Understand the reporting of accounting changes and errors.

Accounting Changes and Errors

Changes in accounting principle, change in estimates, and corrections of errors require unique reporting provisions.

Changes in Accounting Principle

Changes in accounting occur frequently in practice because important events or conditions may be in dispute or uncertain at the statement date. One type of accounting change results when a company adopts a different accounting principle. **Changes in accounting principle** include a change in the method of inventory pricing from FIFO to average-cost, or a change in accounting for construction contracts from the percentage-of-completion to the completed-contract method. [9][20]

A company recognizes a change in accounting principle by making a **retrospective adjustment** to the financial statements. Such an adjustment recasts the prior years' statements on a basis consistent with the newly adopted principle. The company records the cumulative effect of the change for prior periods as an adjustment to beginning retained earnings of the earliest year presented.

To illustrate, Gaubert Inc. decided in March 2014 to change from FIFO to weighted-average inventory pricing. Gaubert's income before income tax, using the new weighted-average method in 2014, is $30,000. Illustration 4-20 (page 180) presents the pretax income data for 2012 and 2013 for this example.

Underlying Concepts

Companies can change principles, but they must demonstrate that the newly adopted principle is preferable to the old one. Such changes result in lost consistency from period to period.

---

[20]In Chapter 22, we examine in greater detail the problems related to accounting changes, and changes in estimates and errors.

ILLUSTRATION 4-20
Calculation of a Change
in Accounting Principle

Year	FIFO	Weighted-Average Method	Excess of FIFO over Weighted-Average Method
2012	$40,000	$35,000	$5,000
2013	30,000	27,000	3,000
Total			$8,000

Illustration 4-21 shows the information Gaubert presented in its comparative income statements, based on a 30 percent tax rate.

ILLUSTRATION 4-21
Income Statement
Presentation of a Change
in Accounting Principle

	2014	2013	2012
Income before income tax	$30,000	$27,000	$35,000
Income tax	9,000	8,100	10,500
Net income	$21,000	$18,900	$24,500

Thus, under the retrospective approach, the company recasts the prior years' income numbers under the newly adopted method. This approach therefore preserves comparability across years.

Changes in Accounting Estimates

Changes in accounting estimates are inherent in the accounting process. For example, companies estimate useful lives and salvage values of depreciable assets, uncollectible receivables, inventory obsolescence, and the number of periods expected to benefit from a particular expenditure. Not infrequently, due to time, circumstances, or new information, even estimates originally made in good faith must be changed. A company accounts for such changes in estimates in the period of change if they affect only that period, or in the period of change and future periods if the change affects both.

To illustrate a change in estimate that affects only the period of change, assume that DuPage Materials Corp. consistently estimated its bad debt expense at 1 percent of credit sales. In 2014, however, DuPage determines that it must revise upward the estimate of bad debts for the current year's credit sales to 2 percent, or double the prior years' percentage. The 2 percent rate is necessary to reduce accounts receivable to net realizable value. Using 2 percent results in a bad debt charge of $240,000, or double the amount using the 1 percent estimate for prior years. DuPage records the bad debt expense and related allowance at December 31, 2014, as follows.

Bad Debt Expense	240,000	
Allowance for Doubtful Accounts		240,000

DuPage includes the entire change in estimate in 2014 income because the change does not affect future periods. **Companies do not handle changes in estimate retrospectively.** That is, such changes are not carried back to adjust prior years. **Changes in estimate are not considered errors.**

Corrections of Errors

Errors occur as a result of mathematical mistakes, mistakes in the application of accounting principles, or oversight or misuse of facts that existed at the time financial statements were prepared. In recent years, many companies have corrected for errors in their financial statements. The errors involved such items as improper reporting of revenue, accounting for stock options, allowances for receivables, inventories, and other provisions.

Companies correct errors by making proper entries in the accounts and reporting the corrections in the financial statements. Corrections of errors are treated as **prior period adjustments**, similar to changes in accounting principles. Companies record a correction of an error in the year in which it is discovered. They report the error in the financial statements as an adjustment to the beginning balance of retained earnings. If a company prepares comparative financial statements, it should restate the prior statements for the effects of the error.

To illustrate, in 2015, Hillsboro Co. determined that it incorrectly overstated its accounts receivable and sales revenue by $100,000 in 2014. In 2015, Hillsboro makes the following entry to correct for this error (ignore income taxes).

Retained Earnings	100,000	
Accounts Receivable		100,000

Beginning retained earnings is debited in 2015 because sales revenue, and therefore net income, was overstated in 2014 (hence, Retained Earnings was overstated). Accounts Receivable is credited to reduce this overstated balance to the correct amount.

Summary

The impact of changes in accounting principle and error corrections are debited or credited directly to retained earnings for the amounts related to prior periods. Illustration 4-22 summarizes the basic concepts related to these two items, as well as the accounting and reporting for changes in estimates. Although simplified, the chart provides a useful framework for determining the treatment of special items affecting the income statement.

ILLUSTRATION 4-22
Summary of Accounting Changes and Errors

Type of Situation	Criteria	Examples	Placement on Income Statement
Changes in accounting principle	Change from one generally accepted accounting principle to another.	Change in the basis of inventory pricing from FIFO to average-cost.	Recast prior years' income statement on the same basis as the newly adopted principle. **(Shown net of tax.)**
Changes in estimates	Normal, recurring corrections and adjustments.	Changes in the realizability of receivables and inventories; changes in estimated lives of equipment, intangible assets; changes in estimated liability for warranty costs, income taxes, and salary payments.	Show change only in the affected accounts in current and future periods. **(Not shown net of tax.)**
Corrections of errors	Mistake, misuse of facts.	Error in reporting income and expenses.	Treat as prior period adjustment; restate prior years' income statements to correct for error. **(Shown net of tax.)**

Retained Earnings Statement

Net income increases retained earnings. A net loss decreases retained earnings. Both cash and stock dividends decrease retained earnings. Changes in accounting principles (generally) and prior period adjustments may increase or decrease retained earnings. Companies charge or credit these adjustments (net of tax) to the opening balance of retained earnings. This excludes the adjustments from the determination of net income for the current period.

Companies may show retained earnings information in different ways. For example, some companies prepare a separate retained earnings statement, as Illustration 4-23 (page 182) shows.

7 LEARNING OBJECTIVE
Prepare a retained earnings statement.

ILLUSTRATION 4-23
Retained Earnings
Statement

STRICKER INC.		
RETAINED EARNINGS STATEMENT		
FOR THE YEAR ENDED DECEMBER 31, 2014		
Retained earnings, January 1, as reported		$1,050,000
Correction for understatement of net income in prior period (inventory error)		50,000
Retained earnings, January 1, as adjusted		1,100,000
Add: Net income		360,000
		1,460,000
Less: Cash dividends	$100,000	
Stock dividends	200,000	300,000
Retained earnings, December 31		$1,160,000

The reconciliation of the beginning to the ending balance in retained earnings provides information about why net assets increased or decreased during the year.[21] The association of dividend distributions with net income for the period indicates what management is doing with earnings: It may be "plowing back" into the business part or all of the earnings, distributing all current income, or distributing current income plus the accumulated earnings of prior years.

Restrictions of Retained Earnings

Companies often restrict retained earnings to comply with contractual requirements, board of directors' policy, or current necessity. Generally, companies disclose in the notes to the financial statements the amounts of restricted retained earnings. In some cases, companies transfer the amount of retained earnings restricted to an account titled **Appropriated Retained Earnings**. The retained earnings section may therefore report two separate amounts—(1) retained earnings free (unrestricted) and (2) retained earnings appropriated (restricted). The total of these two amounts equals the total retained earnings.

Comprehensive Income

LEARNING OBJECTIVE 8

Explain how to report other comprehensive income.

Companies generally include in income all revenues, expenses, gains, and losses recognized during the period. These items are classified within the income statement so that financial statement readers can better understand the significance of various components of net income. Changes in accounting principles and corrections of errors are excluded from the calculation of net income because their effects relate to prior periods.

In recent years, there is increased use of fair values for measuring assets and liabilities. Furthermore, possible reporting of gains and losses related to changes in fair value have placed a strain on income reporting. Because fair values are continually changing, some argue that recognizing these gains and losses in net income is misleading. The FASB agrees and has identified a limited number of transactions that should be recorded in other comprehensive income, which affects accumulated other comprehensive income reported in stockholders' equity. One example is unrealized gains and losses on available-for-sale securities.[22] These gains and losses are excluded from net income, thereby

[21]*Accounting Trends and Techniques—2012* (New York: AICPA) indicates that most companies (490 of 500 surveyed) present changes in retained earnings either within the statement of stockholders' equity (486 firms) or in a separate statement of retained earnings (4 firms). Only 1 of the 500 companies prepares a combined statement of income and retained earnings.

[22]We further discuss available-for-sale securities in Chapter 17. Additional examples of other comprehensive items are translation gains and losses on foreign currency, unrealized gains and losses on certain hedging transactions, and adjustments related to pensions. Corrections of errors and changes in accounting principles are not considered other comprehensive income items.

educing volatility in net income due to fluctuations in fair value. At the same time, disclosure of the potential gain or loss is provided.

Companies include these items that bypass the income statement in a measure called comprehensive income. **Comprehensive income** includes all changes in equity during a period *except* those resulting from investments by owners and distributions to owners. Comprehensive income, therefore, includes the following: all revenues and gains, expenses and losses reported in net income, and all gains and losses that bypass net income but affect stockholders' equity. These items—non-owner changes in equity that bypass the income statement—are referred to as **other comprehensive income**.

International Perspective

> GAAP and IFRS are now converged with respect to comprehensive income reporting.

Companies must display the components of other comprehensive income in one of two ways: (1) a single continuous statement (**one statement approach**) or (2) two separate, but consecutive statements of net income and other comprehensive income (**two statement approach**). The one statement approach is often referred to as the statement of comprehensive income. The two statement approach uses the traditional term income statement for the first statement and the comprehensive income statement for the second statement. **[10]**

Under either approach, companies display each component of net income and each component of other comprehensive income. In addition, net income and comprehensive income are reported. Companies are not required to report earnings per share information related to comprehensive income.[23]

We illustrate these two alternatives in the next two sections. In each case, assume that V. Gill Inc. reports the following information for 2014: sales revenue $800,000; cost of goods sold $600,000; operating expenses $90,000; and an unrealized holding gain on available-for-sale securities of $30,000, net of tax.

One Statement Approach

In this approach, the traditional net income is a subtotal, with total comprehensive income shown as a final total. The combined statement has the advantage of not requiring the creation of a new financial statement. However, burying net income as a subtotal on the statement is a disadvantage. Illustration 4-24 shows the one statement format for V. Gill.

V. GILL INC. STATEMENT OF COMPREHENSIVE INCOME FOR THE YEAR ENDED DECEMBER 31, 2014	
Sales revenue	$800,000
Cost of goods sold	600,000
Gross profit	200,000
Operating expenses	90,000
Net income	110,000
Other comprehensive income	
Unrealized holding gain, net of tax	30,000
Comprehensive income	$140,000

ILLUSTRATION 4-24
One Statement Format:
Comprehensive Income

[23]A company must display the components of other comprehensive income either (1) net of related tax effects, or (2) before related tax effects, with one amount shown for the aggregate amount of tax related to the total amount of other comprehensive income. Both alternatives must show each component of other comprehensive income, net of related taxes either in the face of the statement or in the notes. *Accounting Trends and Techniques—2012* indicates that 89 of 90 surveyed companies reporting tax effects provided it in the notes.

Two Statement Approach

Illustration 4-25 shows the two statement format for V. Gill. Reporting comprehensive income in a separate statement indicates that the gains and losses identified as other comprehensive income have the same status as traditional gains and losses.

ILLUSTRATION 4-25

Two Statement Format: Comprehensive Income

V. GILL INC.
INCOME STATEMENT
FOR THE YEAR ENDED DECEMBER 31, 2014

Sales revenue	$800,000
Cost of goods sold	600,000
Gross profit	200,000
Operating expenses	90,000
Net income	$110,000

V. GILL INC.
COMPREHENSIVE INCOME STATEMENT
FOR THE YEAR ENDED DECEMBER 31, 2014

Net income	$110,000
Other comprehensive income	
Unrealized holding gain, net of tax	30,000
Comprehensive income	$140,000

Statement of Stockholders' Equity

In addition to a comprehensive income statement, companies also present a **statement of stockholders' equity** (often referred to as statement of changes in stockholders' equity). This statement reports the changes in each stockholders' equity account and in total stockholders' equity during the year. Companies often prepare **in columnar form** the statement of stockholders' equity. In this format, they use columns for each account and for total stockholders' equity. Stockholders' equity is generally comprised of contributed capital (common and preferred stock and additional paid-in capital), retained earnings, and the accumulated balances in other comprehensive income. The statement reports the change in each stockholders' equity account and in total stockholders' equity for the period. The following items are disclosed in this statement.

1. Contributions (issuances of shares) and distributions (dividends) to owners.

2. Reconciliation of the carrying amount of each component of stockholders' equity from the beginning to the end of the period.

To illustrate, assume the same information for V. Gill (on page 183). The company has the following stockholders' equity account balances at the beginning of 2014: Common Stock $300,000, Retained Earnings $50,000, and Accumulated Other Comprehensive Income $60,000. No changes in the Common Stock account occurred during the year. Illustration 4-26 shows a statement of stockholders' equity for V. Gill.

V. GILL INC. STATEMENT OF STOCKHOLDERS' EQUITY FOR THE YEAR ENDED DECEMBER 31, 2014				
	Total	Retained Earnings	Accumulated Other Comprehensive Income	Common Stock
Beginning balance	$410,000	$ 50,000	$60,000	$300,000
Net income	110,000	110,000		
Other comprehensive income				
Unrealized holding gain, net of tax	30,000		30,000	
Ending balance	$550,000	$160,000	$90,000	$300,000

ILLUSTRATION 4-26
Presentation of
Comprehensive Income
in Stockholders' Equity
Statement

Balance Sheet Presentation

Regardless of the display format used, V. Gill reports **accumulated other comprehensive income** of $90,000 in the stockholders' equity section of the balance sheet as follows.

V. GILL INC. BALANCE SHEET AS OF DECEMBER 31, 2014 (STOCKHOLDERS' EQUITY SECTION)	
Stockholders' equity	
Common stock	$300,000
Retained earnings	160,000
Accumulated other comprehensive income	90,000
Total stockholders' equity	$550,000

ILLUSTRATION 4-27
Presentation of
Accumulated Other
Comprehensive Income
in the Balance Sheet

 You will
want to
read the
IFRS INSIGHTS
on pages 205–211

for discussion of
IFRS related to the
income statement.

By providing information on the components of comprehensive income, as well as accumulated other comprehensive income, the company communicates information about all changes in net assets. With this information, users will better understand the quality of the company's earnings.

Evolving Issue   INCOME REPORTING

As indicated in the chapter, information reported in the income statement is important to meeting the objective of financial reporting. However, there is debate over income reporting practices, be it the controversy over pro forma reporting or whether to report comprehensive income in a one statement or a two statement format. In response to these debates and to differences between income reporting under U.S. GAAP and IFRS, standard-setters are working on a project to improve the usefulness of the income statement.

Work to date has resulted in two core principles for financial statement presentation (for the income statement, balance sheet, and the statement of cash flows) based on the objective of financial reporting:

1. **Disaggregate information so that it is useful in predicting an entity's future cash flows.** Disaggregation means separating resources by the activity in which they are used and by their economic characteristics.

2. **Portray a cohesive financial picture of a company's activities.** A cohesive financial picture means that the relationship between items across financial statements is clear and that a company's financial statements complement each other as much as possible.

Cohesiveness will be addressed by using the same classifications across the balance sheet, income statement, and statement of cash flows. The proposed model classifies activities as business or financing, although some have suggested that each statement be segregated into operating, investing, and financing activities.

The statement presentation project is currently inactive on the Boards' joint agenda (see *www.fasb.org* and click on Inactive Joint FASB/IASB Projects under the Projects tab), but it is expected to restart once the projects on financial instruments, revenue recognition, and leases are completed.

KEY TERMS

accumulated other comprehensive income, *185*

Appropriated Retained Earnings, *182*

capital maintenance approach, *163(n)*

changes in accounting estimates, *180*

changes in accounting principle, *179*

comprehensive income, *183*

current operating performance approach, *168*

discontinued operation, *170*

earnings management, *161*

earnings per share, *177*

extraordinary items, *173*

income statement, *160*

intraperiod tax allocation, *171*

modified all-inclusive concept, *169*

multiple-step income statement, *164*

noncontrolling (minority) interest, *176*

other comprehensive income, *183*

prior period adjustments, *181*

quality of earnings, *162*

single-step income statement, *167*

statement of comprehensive income, *160(n)*

statement of stockholders' equity, *184*

transaction approach, *162*

SUMMARY OF LEARNING OBJECTIVES

1 Understand the uses and limitations of an income statement. The income statement provides investors and creditors with information that helps them predict the amounts, timing, and uncertainty of future cash flows. Also, the income statement helps users determine the risk (level of uncertainty) of not achieving particular cash flows. The limitations of an income statement are as follows. (1) The statement does not include many items that contribute to general growth and well-being of a company. (2) Income numbers are often affected by the accounting methods used. (3) Income measures are subject to estimates.

The transaction approach focuses on the activities that occurred during a given period. Instead of presenting only a net change in net assets, it discloses the components of the change. The transaction approach to income measurement requires the use of revenue, expense, loss, and gain accounts.

2 Describe the content and format of the income statement. The major elements of the income statement are as follows. (1) *Revenues:* Inflows or other enhancements of assets of an entity or settlements of its liabilities during a period from delivering or producing goods, rendering services, or other activities that constitute the entity's ongoing major or central operations. (2) *Expenses:* Outflows or other using-up of assets or incurrences of liabilities during a period from delivering or producing goods, rendering services, or carrying out other activities that constitute the entity's ongoing major or central operations. (3) *Gains:* Increases in equity (net assets) from peripheral or incidental transactions of an entity except those that result from revenues or investments by owners. (4) *Losses:* Decreases in equity (net assets) from peripheral or incidental transactions of an entity except those that result from expenses or distributions to owners.

3 Prepare an income statement. In a single-step income statement, just two groupings exist: revenues and expenses. Expenses are deducted from revenues to arrive at net income or loss—a single subtraction. Frequently, companies report income tax separately as the last item before net income.

A multiple-step income statement shows two further classifications: (1) a separation of operating results from those obtained through the subordinate or nonoperating activities of the company, and (2) a classification of expenses by functions, such as merchandising or manufacturing, selling, and administration.

4 Explain how to report various income items. Companies generally include irregular gains or losses or nonrecurring items in the income statement as follows. (1) Other items of a material amount that are of an unusual or nonrecurring nature and are not considered extraordinary are separately disclosed as a component of continuing operations. (2) Discontinued operations of a component of a business are classified as a separate item, after continuing operations. (3) The unusual, material, nonrecurring items that are significantly different from the customary business activities are shown in a separate section for extraordinary items, below discontinued operations. If a company holds a noncontrolling interest in a subsidiary company, it must present an allocation of net income or loss that is attributable to the noncontrolling interest.

5 **Identify where to report earnings per share information.** Because of the inherent dangers of focusing attention solely on earnings per share, the profession concluded that companies must disclose earnings per share on the face of the income statement. A company that reports a discontinued operation or an extraordinary item must report per share amounts for these line items either on the face of the income statement or in the notes to the financial statements.

6 **Understand the reporting of accounting changes and errors.** Changes in accounting principle and corrections of errors are adjusted through retained earnings. Changes in estimates are a normal part of the accounting process. The effects of these changes are handled prospectively, with the effects recorded in income in the period of change and in future periods without adjustment to retained earnings.

7 **Prepare a retained earnings statement.** The retained earnings statement should disclose net income (loss), dividends, adjustments due to changes in accounting principles, error corrections, and restrictions of retained earnings.

8 **Explain how to report other comprehensive income.** Companies report the components of other comprehensive income in one of two ways: (1) a single statement of comprehensive income (one statement format) or (2) in a second statement (two statement format).

DEMONSTRATION PROBLEM

Presented below are 11 income statement items from Braun Company for the year ended December 31, 2014.

Sales revenue	$2,700,000
Cost of goods sold	1,150,000
Interest revenue	15,000
Loss from abandonment of plant assets	45,000
Gain from extinguishment of debt	28,000
Unrealized holding loss on an available-for-sale investment, net of tax	12,000
Selling expenses	290,000
Administrative expenses	190,000
Effect of change in estimated useful lives of fixed assets	35,000
Loss from earthquake (unusual and infrequent)	30,000
Gain on disposal of a component of Braun's business	50,000

Instructions
(a) Using the information above, prepare a condensed multiple-step income statement. Assume a tax rate of 30% and 100,000 shares of common stock outstanding during 2014.
(b) Compute comprehensive income for Braun in 2014.

Solution

(a)

BRAUN COMPANY
INCOME STATEMENT
FOR THE YEAR ENDED DECEMBER 31, 2014

Sales revenue		$2,700,000
Cost of goods sold		1,150,000
Gross profit		1,550,000
Selling expenses	$290,000	
Administrative expenses	190,000	480,000
Income from operations		1,070,000
Other revenues and gains		
Interest revenue	15,000	
Gain on debt extinguishment	28,000	43,000

Other expenses and losses		
Loss from plant abandonment		(45,000)
Income before income taxes		1,068,000
Income taxes (30%)		320,400
Income from continuing operations		747,600
Discontinued operations		
Gain from disposal of component of business	50,000	
Less: Applicable income tax	15,000	35,000
Income before extraordinary items		782,600
Extraordinary items		
Loss from earthquake	30,000	
Less: Applicable income tax	9,000	(21,000)
Net income		$ 761,600
Per share of common stock		
Income from continuing operations		$ 7.48
Discontinued operations		0.35
Income before extraordinary item		7.83
Extraordinary item, net of tax		(0.21)
Net income		$ 7.61

(b) Net income	$761,600	
Unrealized holding loss on available-for-sale investment, net of tax	12,000	
Comprehensive income	$749,600	

C FASB CODIFICATION

FASB Codification References

[1] FASB ASC 225-20-45-4. [Predecessor literature: "Reporting the Results of Operations," *Opinions of the Accounting Principles Board No. 30* (New York: AICPA, 1973), par. 23, as amended by "Accounting for the Impairment or Disposal of Long-lived Assets," *Statement of Financial Accounting Standards No. 144* (Norwalk, Conn.: FASB, 2001).]

[2] FASB ASC 224-20-45-2. [Predecessor literature: "Reporting the Results of Operations," *Opinions of the Accounting Principles Board No. 30* (New York: AICPA, 1973), par. 20.]

[3] FASB ASC 205-20-45. [Predecessor literature: "Accounting for the Impairment or Disposal of Long-lived Assets," *Statement of Financial Accounting Standards No. 144* (Norwalk, Conn.: FASB, 2001), par. 4.]

[4] FASB ASC 225-20-45-2. [Predecessor literature: "Reporting the Results of Operations," *Opinions of the Accounting Principles Board No. 30* (New York: AICPA, 1973), par. 20.]

[5] FASB ASC 225-20-45-3. [Predecessor literature: "Reporting the Results of Operations," *Opinions of the Accounting Principles Board No. 30* (New York: AICPA, 1973), par. 24, as amended by "Accounting for the Impairment or Disposal of Long-lived Assets," *Statement of Financial Accounting Standards No. 144* (Norwalk, Conn.: FASB, 2001).]

[6] FASB ASC 810-10-45. [Predecessor literature: "Consolidated Financial Statements," *Accounting Research Bulletin No. 51* (August 1959).]

[7] FASB ASC 260. [Predecessor literature: "Earnings Per Share," *Statement of Financial Accounting Standards No. 128* (Norwalk, Conn.: FASB, 1996).]

[8] FASB ASC 260-10-10-2. [Predecessor literature: "Earnings Per Share," *Statement of Financial Accounting Standards No. 128* (Norwalk, Conn.: FASB, 1996), par. 11.]

[9] FASB ASC 250. [Predecessor literature: "Accounting Changes and Error Corrections," *Statement of Financial Accounting Standards No. 154* (Norwalk, Conn.: FASB, 2005).]

[10] FASB ASC 220. [Predecessor literature: "Reporting Comprehensive Income," *Statement of Financial Accounting Standards No. 130* (Norwalk, Conn.: FASB, 1997).]

Exercises

If your school has a subscription to the FASB Codification, go to *http://aahq.org/asclogin.cfm* to log in and prepare responses to the following. Provide Codification references for your responses.

CE4-1 Access the glossary ("Master Glossary") to answer the following.
  (a) What is a change in accounting estimate?
  (b) How is a change in accounting principle distinguished from a "change in accounting estimate effected by a change in accounting principle"?
  (c) What is the formal definition of comprehensive income?

CE4-2 What distinguishes an item that is "unusual in nature" from an item that is considered "extraordinary"?

CE4-3 Enyart Company experienced a catastrophic loss in the second quarter of the year. The loss meets the criteria for extraordinary item reporting, but Enyart's controller is unsure whether this item should be reported as extraordinary in the second quarter interim report. Advise the controller.

CE4-4 What guidance does the SEC provide for public companies with respect to the reporting of the "effect of preferred stock dividends and accretion of carrying amount of preferred stock on earnings per share"?

An additional Codification case can be found in the Using Your Judgment section, on page 205.

Be sure to check the book's companion website for a Review and Analysis Exercise, with solution.

WileyPLUS   **Brief Exercises, Exercises, Problems, and many more learning and assessment tools and resources are available for practice in WileyPLUS.**

QUESTIONS

1. What kinds of questions about future cash flows do investors and creditors attempt to answer with information in the income statement?

2. How can information based on past transactions be used to predict future cash flows?

3. Identify at least two situations in which important changes in value are not reported in the income statement.

4. Identify at least two situations in which application of different accounting methods or accounting estimates results in difficulties in comparing companies.

5. Explain the transaction approach to measuring income. Why is the transaction approach to income measurement preferable to other ways of measuring income?

6. What is earnings management?

7. How can earnings management affect the quality of earnings?

8. Why should caution be exercised in the use of the net income figure derived in an income statement? What are the objectives of generally accepted accounting principles in their application to the income statement?

9. A *Wall Street Journal* article noted that **Apple** reported higher income than its competitors by using a more aggressive policy for recognizing revenue on future upgrades to its products. Some contend that Apple's quality of earnings is low. What does the term "quality of earnings" mean?

10. What is the major distinction (a) between revenues and gains and (b) between expenses and losses?

11. What are the advantages and disadvantages of the single-step income statement?

12. What is the basis for distinguishing between operating and nonoperating items?

13. Distinguish between the modified all-inclusive income statement and the current operating performance income statement. According to present generally accepted accounting principles, which is recommended? Explain.

14. How should correction of errors be reported in the financial statements?

15. Discuss the appropriate treatment in the financial statements of each of the following.

  (a) An amount of $113,000 realized in excess of the cash surrender value of an insurance policy on the life of one of the founders of the company who died during the year.

  (b) A profit-sharing bonus to employees computed as a percentage of net income.

  (c) Additional depreciation on factory machinery because of an error in computing depreciation for the previous year.

  (d) Rent received from subletting a portion of the office space.

(e) A patent infringement suit, brought 2 years ago against the company by another company, was settled this year by a cash payment of $725,000.

(f) A reduction in the Allowance for Doubtful Accounts balance because the account appears to be considerably in excess of the probable loss from uncollectible receivables.

16. Indicate where the following items would ordinarily appear on the financial statements of Boleyn, Inc. for the year 2014.

(a) The service life of certain equipment was changed from 8 to 5 years. If a 5-year life had been used previously, additional depreciation of $425,000 would have been charged.

(b) In 2014, a flood destroyed a warehouse that had a book value of $1,600,000. Floods are rare in this locality.

(c) In 2014, the company wrote off $1,000,000 of inventory that was considered obsolete.

(d) An income tax refund related to the 2011 tax year was received.

(e) In 2011, a supply warehouse with an expected useful life of 7 years was erroneously expensed.

(f) Boleyn, Inc. changed from weighted-average to FIFO inventory pricing.

17. Indicate the section of a multiple-step income statement in which each of the following is shown.

(a) Loss on inventory write-down.

(b) Loss from strike.

(c) Bad debt expense.

(d) Loss on disposal of a component of the business.

(e) Gain on sale of machinery.

(f) Interest revenue.

(g) Depreciation expense.

(h) Material write-offs of notes receivable.

18. Perlman Land Development, Inc. purchased land for $70,000 and spent $30,000 developing it. It then sold the land for $160,000. Sheehan Manufacturing purchased land for a future plant site for $100,000. Due to a change in plans, Sheehan later sold the land for $160,000. Should these two companies report the land sales, both at gains of $60,000, in a similar manner?

19. You run into Greg Norman at a party and begin discussing financial statements. Greg says, "I prefer the single-step income statement because the multiple-step format generally overstates income." How should you respond to Greg?

20. Santo Corporation has eight expense accounts in its general ledger which could be classified as selling expenses. Should Santo report these eight expenses separately in its income statement or simply report one total amount for selling expenses?

21. Cooper Investments reported an unusual gain from th[e] sale of certain assets in its 2014 income statement. Ho[w] does intraperiod tax allocation affect the reporting of thi[s] unusual gain?

22. Discuss the appropriate treatment in the income state[ment] for the following items:

(a) Loss on discontinued operations.

(b) Noncontrolling interest allocation.

(c) Earnings per share.

(d) Gain on sale of equipment.

23. Lebron Co. owns most but not all of the shares of it[s] subsidiary Bryant Inc. Lebron reported net income o[f] $124,700. The amount to be attributed to the noncontro[l-]ling interest in Bryant is $30,000. Indicate how Lebron wi[ll] report the noncontrolling interest in its income statemen[t.]

24. What effect does intraperiod tax allocation have o[n] reported net income?

25. Neumann Company computed earnings per share a[s] follows.

$$\frac{\text{Net income}}{\text{Common shares outstanding at year-end}}$$

Neumann has a simple capital structure. What possibl[e] errors might the company have made in the computation[?] Explain.

26. Qualls Corporation reported 2014 earnings per shar[e] of $7.21. In 2015, Qualls reported earnings per share a[s] follows.

On income before extraordinary item	$6.40
On extraordinary item	1.88
On net income	$8.28

Is the increase in earnings per share from $7.21 to $8.28 [a] favorable trend?

27. What is meant by "tax allocation within a period"? Wha[t] is the justification for such practice?

28. When does tax allocation within a period become neces[-]sary? How should this allocation be handled?

29. During 2014, Liselotte Company earned income of $1,500,00[0] before income taxes and realized a gain of $450,000 on [a] government-forced condemnation sale of a division plan[t] facility. The income is subject to income taxation at the rat[e] of 34%. The gain on the sale of the plant is taxed at 30%[.] Proper accounting suggests that the unusual gain b[e] reported as an extraordinary item. Illustrate an appropriat[e] presentation of these items in the income statement.

30. On January 30, 2013, a suit was filed against Frazie[r] Corporation under the Environmental Protection Act. O[n] August 6, 2014, Frazier Corporation agreed to settle th[e] action and pay $920,000 in damages to certain curren[t] and former employees. How should this settlement b[e] reported in the 2014 financial statements? Discuss.

31. Linus Paper Company decided to close two small pulp mills in Conway, New Hampshire, and Corvallis, Oregon. Would these closings be reported in a separate section entitled "Discontinued operations after income from continuing operations"? Discuss.

32. What major types of items are reported in the retained earnings statement?

33. Generally accepted accounting principles usually require the use of accrual accounting to "fairly present" income. If the cash receipts and disbursements method of accounting will "clearly reflect" taxable income, why does this method not usually also "fairly present" income?

34. State some of the more serious problems encountered in seeking to achieve the ideal measurement of periodic net income. Explain what accountants do as a practical alternative.

35. What is meant by the terms *elements* and *items* as they relate to the income statement? Why might items have to be disclosed in the income statement?

36. What are the two ways that other comprehensive income may be displayed (reported)?

37. How should the disposal of a component of a business be disclosed in the income statement?

BRIEF EXERCISES

BE4-1 Starr Co. had sales revenue of $540,000 in 2014. Other items recorded during the year were:

Cost of goods sold	$330,000
Salaries and wages expense	120,000
Income tax expense	25,000
Increase in value of company reputation	15,000
Other operating expenses	10,000
Unrealized gain on value of patents	20,000

Prepare a single-step income statement for Starr for 2014. Starr has 100,000 shares of stock outstanding.

BE4-2 Brisky Corporation had net sales of $2,400,000 and interest revenue of $31,000 during 2014. Expenses for 2014 were cost of goods sold $1,450,000; administrative expenses $212,000; selling expenses $280,000; and interest expense $45,000. Brisky's tax rate is 30%. The corporation had 100,000 shares of common stock authorized and 70,000 shares issued and outstanding during 2014. Prepare a single-step income statement for the year ended December 31, 2014.

BE4-3 Using the information provided in BE4-2, prepare a condensed multiple-step income statement for Brisky Corporation.

BE4-4 Finley Corporation had income from continuing operations of $10,600,000 in 2014. During 2014, it disposed of its restaurant division at an after-tax loss of $189,000. Prior to disposal, the division operated at a loss of $315,000 (net of tax) in 2014. Finley had 10,000,000 shares of common stock outstanding during 2014. Prepare a partial income statement for Finley beginning with income from continuing operations.

BE4-5 Stacy Corporation had income before income taxes for 2014 of $6,300,000. In addition, it suffered an unusual and infrequent pretax loss of $770,000 from a volcano eruption. The corporation's tax rate is 30%. Prepare a partial income statement for Stacy beginning with income before income taxes. The corporation had 5,000,000 shares of common stock outstanding during 2014.

BE4-6 During 2014, Williamson Company changed from FIFO to weighted-average inventory pricing. Pretax income in 2013 and 2012 (Williamson's first year of operations) under FIFO was $160,000 and $180,000, respectively. Pretax income using weighted-average pricing in the prior years would have been $145,000 in 2013 and $170,000 in 2012. In 2014, Williamson Company reported pretax income (using weighted-average pricing) of $180,000. Show comparative income statements for Williamson Company, beginning with "Income before income tax," as presented on the 2014 income statement. (The tax rate in all years is 30%.)

BE4-7 Vandross Company has recorded bad debt expense in the past at a rate of 1½% of net sales. In 2014, Vandross decides to increase its estimate to 2%. If the new rate had been used in prior years, cumulative bad debt expense would have been $380,000 instead of $285,000. In 2014, bad debt expense will be $120,000 instead of $90,000. If Vandross's tax rate is 30%, what amount should it report as the cumulative effect of changing the estimated bad debt rate?

BE4-8 In 2014, Hollis Corporation reported net income of $1,000,000. It declared and paid preferred stock dividends of $250,000. During 2014, Hollis had a weighted average of 190,000 common shares outstanding. Compute Hollis's 2014 earnings per share.

7 **BE4-9** Portman Corporation has retained earnings of $675,000 at January 1, 2014. Net income during 2014 was $1,400,000, and cash dividends declared and paid during 2014 totaled $75,000. Prepare a retained earnings statement for the year ended December 31, 2014.

6 **7** **BE4-10** Using the information from BE4-9, prepare a retained earnings statement for the year ended December 31, 2014. Assume an error was discovered: land costing $80,000 (net of tax) was charged to maintenance and repairs expense in 2011.

8 **BE4-11** On January 1, 2014, Richards Inc. had cash and common stock of $60,000. At that date, the company had no other asset, liability, or equity balances. On January 2, 2014, it purchased for cash $20,000 of equity securities that it classified as available-for-sale. It received cash dividends of $3,000 during the year on these securities. In addition, it has an unrealized holding gain on these securities of $4,000 net of tax. Determine the following amounts for 2014: (a) net income, (b) comprehensive income, (c) other comprehensive income, and (d) accumulated other comprehensive income (end of 2014).

EXERCISES

2 **E4-1 (Computation of Net Income)** Presented below are changes in all the account balances of Fritz Reiner Furniture Co. during the current year, except for retained earnings.

	Increase (Decrease)		Increase (Decrease)
Cash	$ 79,000	Accounts Payable	$ (51,000)
Accounts Receivable (net)	45,000	Bonds Payable	82,000
Inventory	127,000	Common Stock	125,000
Investments	(47,000)	Paid-In Capital in Excess of Par—Common Stock	13,000

Instructions

Compute the net income for the current year, assuming that there were no entries in the Retained Earnings account except for net income and a dividend declaration of $19,000 which was paid in the current year.

2 **4** **E4-2 (Compute Income Measures)** Presented below is information related to Viel Company at December 31, 2014, the end of its first year of operations.

Sales revenue	$310,000
Cost of goods sold	140,000
Selling and administrative expenses	50,000
Gain on sale of plant assets	30,000
Unrealized gain on available-for-sale investments	10,000
Interest expense	6,000
Loss on discontinued operations	12,000
Allocation to noncontrolling interest	40,000
Dividends declared and paid	5,000

Instructions

Compute the following: (a) income from operations, (b) net income, (c) net income attributable to Viel Company's controlling shareholders, (d) comprehensive income, and (e) retained earnings balance at December 31, 2014.

2 **4** **E4-3 (Income Statement Items)** Presented below are certain account balances of Paczki Products Co.

Rent revenue	$ 6,500	Sales discounts	$ 7,800
Interest expense	12,700	Selling expenses	99,400
Beginning retained earnings	114,400	Sales revenue	390,000
Ending retained earnings	134,000	Income tax expense	31,000
Dividend revenue	71,000	Cost of goods sold	184,400
Sales returns and allowances	12,400	Administrative expenses	82,500
Allocation to noncontrolling interest	17,000		

Instructions

From the foregoing, compute the following: (a) total net revenue, (b) net income, (c) dividends declared, and (d) income attributable to controlling stockholders.

2 **3** **E4-4 (Single-Step Income Statement)** The financial records of LeRoi Jones Inc. were destroyed by fire at the end of 2014. Fortunately, the controller had kept certain statistical data related to the income statement as follows.

1. The beginning merchandise inventory was $92,000 and decreased 20% during the current year.
2. Sales discounts amount to $17,000.
3. 20,000 shares of common stock were outstanding for the entire year.
4. Interest expense was $20,000.
5. The income tax rate is 30%.
6. Cost of goods sold amounts to $500,000.
7. Administrative expenses are 20% of cost of goods sold but only 8% of gross sales.
8. Four-fifths of the operating expenses relate to sales activities.

Instructions

From the foregoing information prepare an income statement for the year 2014 in single-step form.

 E4-5 (Multiple-Step and Single-Step) Two accountants for the firm of Elwes and Wright are arguing about the merits of presenting an income statement in a multiple-step versus a single-step format. The discussion involves the following 2014 information related to P. Bride Company ($000 omitted).

Administrative expense	
Officers' salaries	$ 4,900
Depreciation of office furniture and equipment	3,960
Cost of goods sold	60,570
Rent revenue	17,230
Selling expense	
Delivery expense	2,690
Sales commissions	7,980
Depreciation of sales equipment	6,480
Sales revenue	96,500
Income tax	9,070
Interest expense	1,860

Instructions

(a) Prepare an income statement for the year 2014 using the multiple-step form. Common shares outstanding for 2014 total 40,550 (000 omitted).
(b) Prepare an income statement for the year 2014 using the single-step form.
(c) Which one do you prefer? Discuss.

 E4-6 (Multiple-Step and Extraordinary Items) The following balances were taken from the books of Maria Conchita Alonzo Corp. on December 31, 2014.

Interest revenue	$ 86,000	Accumulated depreciation—equipment	$ 40,000
Cash	51,000	Accumulated depreciation—buildings	28,000
Sales revenue	1,380,000	Notes receivable	155,000
Accounts receivable	150,000	Selling expenses	194,000
Prepaid insurance	20,000	Accounts payable	170,000
Sales returns and allowances	150,000	Bonds payable	100,000
Allowance for doubtful accounts	7,000	Administrative and general expenses	97,000
Sales discounts	45,000	Accrued liabilities	32,000
Land	100,000	Interest expense	60,000
Equipment	200,000	Notes payable	100,000
Buildings	140,000	Loss from earthquake damage	
Cost of goods sold	621,000	(extraordinary item)	150,000
		Common stock	500,000
		Retained earnings	21,000

Assume the total effective tax rate on all items is 34%.

Instructions

Prepare a multiple-step income statement; 100,000 shares of common stock were outstanding during the year.

 E4-7 (Multiple-Step and Single-Step) The accountant of Latifa Shoe Co. has compiled the following information from the company's records as a basis for an income statement for the year ended December 31, 2014.

Rent revenue	$ 29,000
Interest expense	18,000
Market appreciation on land above cost	31,000
Salaries and wages expense (selling)	114,800
Supplies (selling)	17,600
Income tax	37,400
Salaries and wages expense (administrative)	135,900

Other administrative expenses	$ 51,700
Cost of goods sold	496,000
Net sales	980,000
Depreciation on plant assets (70% selling, 30% administrative)	65,000
Cash dividends declared	16,000

There were 20,000 shares of common stock outstanding during the year.

Instructions
(a) Prepare a multiple-step income statement.
(b) Prepare a single-step income statement.
(c) Which format do you prefer? Discuss.

3 4 5 **E4-8 (Income Statement, EPS)** Presented below are selected ledger accounts of Tucker Corporation as of December 31, 2014.

Cash	$ 50,000
Administrative expenses	100,000
Selling expenses	80,000
Net sales	540,000
Cost of goods sold	210,000
Cash dividends declared (2014)	20,000
Cash dividends paid (2014)	15,000
Discontinued operations (loss before income taxes)	40,000
Depreciation expense, not recorded in 2013	30,000
Retained earnings, December 31, 2013	90,000
Effective tax rate 30%	

Instructions
(a) Compute net income for 2014.
(b) Prepare a partial income statement beginning with income from continuing operations before income tax, and including appropriate earnings per share information. Assume 10,000 shares of common stock were outstanding during 2014.

3 4 5 7 **E4-9 (Multiple-Step Statement with Retained Earnings)** Presented below is information related to Ivan Calderon Corp. for the year 2014.

Net sales	$1,300,000	Write-off of inventory due to obsolescence	$ 80,000
Cost of goods sold	780,000	Depreciation expense omitted by accident in 2013	55,000
Selling expenses	65,000	Casualty loss (extraordinary item) before taxes	50,000
Administrative expenses	48,000	Cash dividends declared	45,000
Dividend revenue	20,000	Retained earnings at December 31, 2013	980,000
Interest revenue	7,000	Effective tax rate of 34% on all items	

Instructions
(a) Prepare a multiple-step income statement for 2014. Assume that 60,000 shares of common stock are outstanding.
(b) Prepare a separate retained earnings statement for 2014.

5 **E4-10 (Earnings per Share)** The stockholders' equity section of Tkachuk Corporation appears below as of December 31, 2014.

8% preferred stock, $50 par value, authorized		
100,000 shares, outstanding 90,000 shares		$ 4,500,000
Common stock, $1.00 par, authorized and issued 10 million shares		10,000,000
Additional paid-in capital		20,500,000
Retained earnings	$134,000,000	
Net income	33,000,000	167,000,000
		$202,000,000

Net income for 2014 reflects a total effective tax rate of 34%. Included in the net income figure is a loss of $18,000,000 (before tax) as a result of a major casualty, which should be classified as an extraordinary item. Preferred stock dividends of $360,000 were declared and paid in 2014. Dividends of $1,000,000 were declared and paid to common stockholders in 2014.

Instructions
Compute earnings per share data as it should appear on the income statement of Tkachuk Corporation.

3 4 5 7 **E4-11 (Condensed Income Statement—Periodic Inventory Method)** The following are selected ledger accounts of Spock Corporation at December 31, 2014.

Cash	$ 185,000	Salaries and wages expense (sales)	$284,000
Inventory	535,000	Salaries and wages expense (office)	346,000
Sales revenue	4,275,000	Purchase returns	15,000
Unearned sales revenue	117,000	Sales returns and allowances	79,000
Purchases	2,786,000	Freight-in	72,000
Sales discounts	34,000	Accounts receivable	142,500
Purchase discounts	27,000	Sales commissions	83,000
Selling expenses	69,000	Telephone and Internet expense (sales)	17,000
Accounting and legal services	33,000	Utilities expense (office)	32,000
Insurance expense (office)	24,000	Miscellaneous office expenses	8,000
Advertising expense	54,000	Rent revenue	240,000
Delivery expense	93,000	Extraordinary loss (before tax)	70,000
Depreciation expense (office equipment)	48,000	Interest expense	176,000
Depreciation expense (sales equipment)	36,000	Common stock ($10 par)	900,000

Spock's effective tax rate on all items is 34%. A physical inventory indicates that the ending inventory is $686,000.

Instructions

Prepare a condensed 2014 income statement for Spock Corporation.

7 **E4-12 (Retained Earnings Statement)** Eddie Zambrano Corporation began operations on January 1, 2011. During its first 3 years of operations, Zambrano reported net income and declared dividends as follows.

	Net Income	Dividends Declared
2011	$ 40,000	$ –0–
2012	125,000	50,000
2013	160,000	50,000

The following information relates to 2014.

Income before income tax	$240,000
Prior period adjustment: understatement of 2012 depreciation expense (before taxes)	$ 25,000
Cumulative decrease in income from change in inventory methods (before taxes)	$ 35,000
Dividends declared (of this amount, $25,000 will be paid on Jan. 15, 2015)	$100,000
Effective tax rate	40%

Instructions

(a) Prepare a 2014 retained earnings statement for Eddie Zambrano Corporation.

(b) Assume Eddie Zambrano Corp. restricted retained earnings in the amount of $70,000 on December 31, 2014. After this action, what would Zambrano report as total retained earnings in its December 31, 2014, balance sheet?

5 **E4-13 (Earnings per Share)** At December 31, 2013, Shiga Naoya Corporation had the following stock outstanding.

10% cumulative preferred stock, $100 par, 107,500 shares	$10,750,000
Common stock, $5 par, 4,000,000 shares	20,000,000

During 2014, Shiga Naoya did not issue any additional common stock. The following also occurred during 2014.

Income from continuing operations before taxes	$23,650,000
Discontinued operations (loss before taxes)	$ 3,225,000
Preferred dividends declared	$ 1,075,000
Common dividends declared	$ 2,200,000
Effective tax rate	35%

Instructions

Compute earnings per share data as it should appear in the 2014 income statement of Shiga Naoya Corporation. (Round to two decimal places.)

4 **E4-14 (Change in Accounting Principle)** Tim Mattke Company began operations in 2012 and for simplicity reasons, adopted weighted-average pricing for inventory. In 2014, in accordance with other companies in its industry, Mattke changed its inventory pricing to FIFO. The pretax income data is reported below.

Year	Weighted-Average	FIFO
2012	$370,000	$395,000
2013	390,000	430,000
2014	410,000	450,000

Instructions

(a) What is Mattke's net income in 2014? Assume a 35% tax rate in all years.
(b) Compute the cumulative effect of the change in accounting principle from weighted-average to FIFO inventory pricing.
(c) Show comparative income statements for Tim Mattke Company, beginning with income before income tax, as presented on the 2014 income statement.

3 8 E4-15 (Comprehensive Income) Roxanne Carter Corporation reported the following for 2014: net sales $1,200,000; cost of goods sold $750,000; selling and administrative expenses $320,000; and an unrealized holding gain on available-for-sale securities $18,000.

Instructions

Prepare a statement of comprehensive income, using (a) the one statement format, and (b) the two statement format. (Ignore income taxes and earnings per share.)

7 8 E4-16 (Comprehensive Income) C. Reither Co. reports the following information for 2014: sales revenue $700,000; cost of goods sold $500,000; operating expenses $80,000; and an unrealized holding loss on available-for-sale securities for 2014 of $60,000. It declared and paid a cash dividend of $10,000 in 2014.

C. Reither Co. has January 1, 2014, balances in common stock $350,000; accumulated other comprehensive income $80,000; and retained earnings $90,000. It issued no stock during 2014.

Instructions

Prepare a statement of stockholders' equity.

3 4 5 7 8 E4-17 (Various Reporting Formats) The following information was taken from the records of Roland Carlson Inc. for the year 2014. Income tax applicable to income from continuing operations $187,000; income tax applicable to loss on discontinued operations $25,500; income tax applicable to extraordinary gain $32,300; income tax applicable to extraordinary loss $20,400; and unrealized holding gain on available-for-sale securities $15,000.

Extraordinary gain	$ 95,000	Cash dividends declared	$ 150,000
Loss on discontinued operations	75,000	Retained earnings January 1, 2014	600,000
Administrative expenses	240,000	Cost of goods sold	850,000
Rent revenue	40,000	Selling expenses	300,000
Extraordinary loss	60,000	Sales revenue	1,900,000

Shares outstanding during 2014 were 100,000.

Instructions

(a) Prepare a single-step income statement.
(b) Prepare a comprehensive income statement for 2014, using the two statement format.
(c) Prepare a retained earnings statement for 2014.

EXERCISES SET B

See the book's companion website, at **www.wiley.com/college/kieso**, for an additional set of exercises.

PROBLEMS

3 4 5 7 P4-1 (Multiple-Step Income, Retained Earnings) The following information is related to Dickinson Company for 2014.

Retained earnings balance, January 1, 2014	$ 980,000
Sales revenue	25,000,000
Cost of goods sold	16,000,000
Interest revenue	70,000
Selling and administrative expenses	4,700,000
Write-off of goodwill	820,000
Income taxes for 2014	1,244,000
Gain on the sale of investments (normal recurring)	110,000
Loss due to flood damage—extraordinary item (net of tax)	390,000
Loss on the disposition of the wholesale division (net of tax)	440,000
Loss on operations of the wholesale division (net of tax)	90,000

Dividends declared on common stock		$250,000
Dividends declared on preferred stock		80,000

Dickinson Company decided to discontinue its entire wholesale operations and to retain its manufacturing operations. On September 15, Dickinson sold the wholesale operations to Rogers Company. During 2014, there were 500,000 shares of common stock outstanding all year.

Instructions

Prepare a multiple-step income statement and a retained earnings statement.

P4-2 (Single-Step Income, Retained Earnings, Periodic Inventory) Presented below is the trial balance of Thompson Corporation at December 31, 2014.

THOMPSON CORPORATION
TRIAL BALANCE
DECEMBER 31, 2014

	Debit	Credit
Purchase Discounts		$ 10,000
Cash	$ 189,700	
Accounts Receivable	105,000	
Rent Revenue		18,000
Retained Earnings		160,000
Salaries and Wages Payable		18,000
Sales Revenue		1,100,000
Notes Receivable	110,000	
Accounts Payable		49,000
Accumulated Depreciation—Equipment		28,000
Sales Discounts	14,500	
Sales Returns and Allowances	17,500	
Notes Payable		70,000
Selling Expenses	232,000	
Administrative Expenses	99,000	
Common Stock		300,000
Income Tax Expense	53,900	
Cash Dividends	45,000	
Allowance for Doubtful Accounts		5,000
Supplies	14,000	
Freight-In	20,000	
Land	70,000	
Equipment	140,000	
Bonds Payable		100,000
Gain on Sale of Land		30,000
Accumulated Depreciation—Buildings		19,600
Inventory	89,000	
Buildings	98,000	
Purchases	610,000	
Totals	$1,907,600	$1,907,600

A physical count of inventory on December 31 resulted in an inventory amount of $64,000; thus, cost of goods sold for 2014 is $645,000.

Instructions

Prepare a single-step income statement and a retained earnings statement. Assume that the only changes in retained earnings during the current year were from net income and dividends. Thirty thousand shares of common stock were outstanding the entire year.

P4-3 (Irregular Items) Maher Inc. reported income from continuing operations before taxes during 2014 of $790,000. Additional transactions occurring in 2014 but not considered in the $790,000 are as follows.

1. The corporation experienced an uninsured flood loss (extraordinary) in the amount of $90,000 during the year. The tax rate on this item is 46%.
2. At the beginning of 2012, the corporation purchased a machine for $54,000 (salvage value of $9,000) that had a useful life of 6 years. The bookkeeper used straight-line depreciation for 2012, 2013, and 2014 but failed to deduct the salvage value in computing the depreciation base.
3. Sale of securities held as a part of its portfolio resulted in a loss of $57,000 (pretax).

4. When its president died, the corporation realized $150,000 from an insurance policy. The cash surrender value of this policy had been carried on the books as an investment in the amount of $46,000 (the gain is nontaxable).
5. The corporation disposed of its recreational division at a loss of $115,000 before taxes. Assume that this transaction meets the criteria for discontinued operations.
6. The corporation decided to change its method of inventory pricing from average-cost to the FIFO method. The effect of this change on prior years is to increase 2012 income by $60,000 and decrease 2013 income by $20,000 before taxes. The FIFO method has been used for 2014. The tax rate on these items is 40%.

Instructions

Prepare an income statement for the year 2014 starting with income from continuing operations before taxes. Compute earnings per share as it should be shown on the face of the income statement. Common shares outstanding for the year are 120,000 shares. (Assume a tax rate of 30% on all items, unless indicated otherwise.)

3 4 5 6 7 **P4-4 (Multiple- and Single-Step Income, Retained Earnings)** The following account balances were included in the trial balance of Twain Corporation at June 30, 2014.

Sales revenue	$1,578,500	Depreciation expense (office	
Sales discounts	31,150	furniture and equipment)	$ 7,250
Cost of goods sold	896,770	Property tax expense	7,320
Salaries and wages expense (sales)	56,260	Bad debt expense (selling)	4,850
Sales commissions	97,600	Maintenance and repairs	
Travel expense (salespersons)	28,930	expense (administration)	9,130
Delivery expense	21,400	Office expense	6,000
Entertainment expense	14,820	Sales returns and allowances	62,300
Telephone and Internet expense (sales)	9,030	Dividends received	38,000
Depreciation expense (sales equipment)	4,980	Interest expense	18,000
Maintenance and repairs expense (sales)	6,200	Income tax expense	102,000
Miscellaneous selling expenses	4,715	Depreciation understatement	
Office supplies used	3,450	due to error—2011 (net of tax)	17,700
Telephone and Internet expense		Dividends declared on	
(administration)	2,820	preferred stock	9,000
		Dividends declared on common	
		stock	37,000

The Retained Earnings account had a balance of $337,000 at July 1, 2013. There are 80,000 shares of common stock outstanding.

Instructions

(a) Using the multiple-step form, prepare an income statement and a retained earnings statement for the year ended June 30, 2014.
(b) Using the single-step form, prepare an income statement and a retained earnings statement for the year ended June 30, 2014.

3 4 5 6 7 **P4-5 (Irregular Items)** Presented below is a combined single-step income and retained earnings statement for Nerwin Company for 2014.

		(000 omitted)
Net sales revenue		$640,000
Costs and expenses		
Cost of goods sold	$500,000	
Selling, general, and administrative expenses	66,000	
Other, net	17,000	583,000
Income before income tax		57,000
Income tax		19,400
Net income		37,600
Retained earnings at beginning of period, as previously reported	141,000	
Adjustment required for correction of error	(7,000)	
Retained earnings at beginning of period, as restated		134,000
Dividends on common stock		(12,200)
Retained earnings at end of period		$159,400

Additional facts are as follows.

1. "Selling, general, and administrative expenses" for 2014 included a charge of $8,500,000 that was usual but infrequently occurring.

2. "Other, net" for 2014 included an extraordinary item (charge) of $6,000,000. If the extraordinary item (charge) had not occurred, income taxes for 2014 would have been $21,400,000 instead of $19,400,000.
3. "Adjustment required for correction of an error" was a result of a change in estimate (useful life of certain assets reduced to 8 years and a catch-up adjustment made).
4. Nerwin Company disclosed earnings per common share for net income in the notes to the financial statements.

Instructions

Determine from these additional facts whether the presentation of the facts in the Nerwin Company income and retained earnings statement is appropriate. If the presentation is not appropriate, describe the appropriate presentation and discuss its theoretical rationale. (Do not prepare a revised statement.)

 P4-6 (Retained Earnings Statement, Prior Period Adjustment) Below is the Retained Earnings account for the year 2014 for Acadian Corp.

Retained earnings, January 1, 2014		$257,600
Add:		
Gain on sale of investments (net of tax)	$41,200	
Net income	84,500	
Refund on litigation with government, related to the year 2011 (net of tax)	21,600	
Recognition of income earned in 2013, but omitted from income statement in that year (net of tax)	25,400	172,700
		430,300
Deduct:		
Loss on discontinued operations (net of tax)	35,000	
Write-off of goodwill (net of tax)	60,000	
Cumulative effect on income of prior years in changing from LIFO to FIFO inventory valuation in 2014 (net of tax)	23,200	
Cash dividends declared	32,000	150,200
Retained earnings, December 31, 2014		$280,100

Instructions

(a) Prepare a corrected retained earnings statement. Acadian Corp. normally sells investments of the type mentioned above. FIFO inventory was used in 2014 to compute net income.
(b) State where the items that do not appear in the corrected retained earnings statement should be shown.

 P4-7 (Income Statement, Irregular Items) Wade Corp. has 150,000 shares of common stock outstanding. In 2014, the company reports income from continuing operations before income tax of $1,210,000. Additional transactions not considered in the $1,210,000 are as follows.

1. In 2014, Wade Corp. sold equipment for $40,000. The machine had originally cost $80,000 and had accumulated depreciation of $30,000. The gain or loss is considered ordinary.
2. The company discontinued operations of one of its subsidiaries during the current year at a loss of $190,000 before taxes. Assume that this transaction meets the criteria for discontinued operations. The loss from operations of the discontinued subsidiary was $90,000 before taxes; the loss from disposal of the subsidiary was $100,000 before taxes.
3. An internal audit discovered that amortization of intangible assets was understated by $35,000 (net of tax) in a prior period. The amount was charged against retained earnings.
4. The company had a gain of $125,000 on the condemnation of much of its property. The gain is taxed at a total effective rate of 40%. Assume that the transaction meets the requirements of an extraordinary item.

Instructions

Analyze the above information and prepare an income statement for the year 2014, starting with income from continuing operations before income tax. Compute earnings per share as it should be shown on the face of the income statement. (Assume a total effective tax rate of 38% on all items, unless otherwise indicated.)

PROBLEMS SET B

See the book's companion website, at **www.wiley.com/college/kieso**, for an additional set of problems.

CONCEPTS FOR ANALYSIS

CA4-1 (Identification of Income Statement Deficiencies) O'Malley Corporation was incorporated and began business on January 1, 2014. It has been successful and now requires a bank loan for additional working capital to finance expansion. The bank has requested an audited income statement for the year 2014. The accountant for O'Malley Corporation provides you with the following income statement which O'Malley plans to submit to the bank.

O'MALLEY CORPORATION		
INCOME STATEMENT		
Sales revenue		$850,000
Dividends		32,300
Gain on recovery of insurance proceeds from		
earthquake loss (extraordinary)		38,500
		920,800
Less:		
Selling expenses	$101,100	
Cost of goods sold	510,000	
Advertising expense	13,700	
Loss on obsolescence of inventories	34,000	
Loss on discontinued operations	48,600	
Administrative expense	73,400	780,800
Income before income tax		140,000
Income tax		56,000
Net income		$ 84,000

Instructions
Indicate the deficiencies in the income statement presented above. Assume that the corporation desires a single-step income statement.

CA4-2 (Earnings Management) Bobek Inc. has recently reported steadily increasing income. The company reported income of $20,000 in 2011, $25,000 in 2012, and $30,000 in 2013. A number of market analysts have recommended that investors buy the stock because they expect the steady growth in income to continue. Bobek is approaching the end of its fiscal year in 2014, and it again appears to be a good year. However, it has not yet recorded warranty expense.

Based on prior experience, this year's warranty expense should be around $5,000, but some managers have approached the controller to suggest a larger, more conservative warranty expense should be recorded this year. Income before warranty expense is $43,000. Specifically, by recording a $7,000 warranty accrual this year, Bobek could report an increase in income for this year and still be in a position to cover its warranty costs in future years.

Instructions
(a) What is earnings management?
(b) Assume income before warranty expense is $43,000 for both 2014 and 2015 and that total warranty expense over the 2-year period is $10,000. What is the effect of the proposed accounting in 2014? In 2015?
(c) What is the appropriate accounting in this situation?

CA4-3 (Earnings Management) Charlie Brown, controller for Kelly Corporation, is preparing the company's income statement at year-end. He notes that the company lost a considerable sum on the sale of some equipment it had decided to replace. Since the company has sold equipment routinely in the past, Brown knows the losses cannot be reported as extraordinary. He also does not want to highlight it as a material loss since he feels that will reflect poorly on him and the company. He reasons that if the company had recorded more depreciation during the assets' lives, the losses would not be so great. Since depreciation is included among the company's operating expenses, he wants to report the losses along with the company's expenses, where he hopes it will not be noticed.

Instructions
(a) What are the ethical issues involved?
(b) What should Brown do?

CA4-4 (Income Reporting Items) Simpson Corp. is an entertainment firm that derives approximately 30% of its income from the Casino Knights Division, which manages gambling facilities. As auditor for Simpson Corp., you have recently overheard the following discussion between the controller and financial vice president.

VICE PRESIDENT: If we sell the Casino Knights Division, it seems ridiculous to segregate the results of the sale in the income statement. Separate categories tend to be absurd and confusing to the stockholders. I believe that we should simply report the gain on the sale as other income or expense without detail.

CONTROLLER: Professional pronouncements would require that we report this information separately in the income statement. If a sale of this type is considered unusual and infrequent, it must be reported as an extraordinary item.

VICE PRESIDENT: What about the walkout we had last month when employees were upset about their commission income? Would this situation not also be an extraordinary item?

CONTROLLER: I am not sure whether this item would be reported as extraordinary or not.

VICE PRESIDENT: Oh well, it doesn't make any difference because the net effect of all these items is immaterial, so no disclosure is necessary.

Instructions

(a) On the basis of the foregoing discussion, answer the following questions. Who is correct about handling the sale? What would be the correct income statement presentation for the sale of the Casino Knights Division?

(b) How should the walkout by the employees be reported?

(c) What do you think about the vice president's observation on materiality?

(d) What are the earnings per share implications of these topics?

CA4-5 (Identification of Income Statement Weaknesses) The following financial statement was prepared by employees of Walters Corporation.

WALTERS CORPORATION
INCOME STATEMENT
YEAR ENDED DECEMBER 31, 2014

Revenues		
Gross sales, including sales taxes	$1,044,300	
Less: Returns, allowances, and cash discounts	56,200	
Net sales	988,100	
Dividends, interest, and purchase discounts	30,250	
Recoveries of accounts written off in prior years	13,850	
Total revenues		1,032,200
Costs and expenses		
Cost of goods sold, including sales taxes	465,900	
Salaries and related payroll expenses	60,500	
Rent	19,100	
Delivery expense and freight-in	3,400	
Bad debt expense	27,800	
Total costs and expenses		576,700
Income before extraordinary items		455,500
Extraordinary items		
Loss on discontinued styles (Note 1)	71,500	
Loss on sale of marketable securities (Note 2)	39,050	
Loss on sale of warehouse (Note 3)	86,350	
Total extraordinary items		196,900
Net income		$ 258,600
Net income per share of common stock		$2.30

Note 1: New styles and rapidly changing consumer preferences resulted in a $71,500 loss on the disposal of discontinued styles and related accessories.

Note 2: The corporation sold an investment in marketable securities at a loss of $39,050. The corporation normally sells securities of this nature.

Note 3: The corporation sold one of its warehouses at an $86,350 loss.

Instructions

Identify and discuss the weaknesses in classification and disclosure in the single-step income statement above. You should explain why these treatments are weaknesses and what the proper presentation of the items would be in accordance with GAAP.

CA4-6 (Classification of Income Statement Items) As audit partner for Grupo and Rijo, you are in charge of reviewing the classification of unusual items that have occurred during the current year. The following material items have come to your attention.

1. A merchandising company incorrectly overstated its ending inventory 2 years ago. Inventory for all other periods is correctly computed.
2. An automobile dealer sells for $137,000 an extremely rare 1930 S type Invicta which it purchased for $21,000 10 years ago. The Invicta is the only such display item the dealer owns.
3. A drilling company during the current year extended the estimated useful life of certain drilling equipment from 9 to 15 years. As a result, depreciation for the current year was materially lowered.
4. A retail outlet changed its computation for bad debt expense from 1% to ½ of 1% of sales because of changes in its customer clientele.
5. A mining concern sells a foreign subsidiary engaged in uranium mining, although it (the seller) continues to engage in uranium mining in other countries.
6. A steel company changes from the average-cost method to the FIFO method for inventory costing purposes.
7. A construction company, at great expense, prepared a major proposal for a government loan. The loan is not approved.
8. A water pump manufacturer has had large losses resulting from a strike by its employees early in the year.
9. Depreciation for a prior period was incorrectly understated by $950,000. The error was discovered in the current year.
10. A large sheep rancher suffered a major loss because the state required that all sheep in the state be killed to halt the spread of a rare disease. Such a situation has not occurred in the state for 20 years.
11. A food distributor that sells wholesale to supermarket chains and to fast-food restaurants (two distinguishable classes of customers) decides to discontinue the division that sells to one of the two classes of customers.

Instructions

From the foregoing information, indicate in what section of the income statement or retained earnings statement these items should be classified. Provide a brief rationale for your position.

CA4-7 (Comprehensive Income) Willie Nelson, Jr., controller for Jenkins Corporation, is preparing the company's financial statements at year-end. Currently, he is focusing on the income statement and determining the format for reporting comprehensive income. During the year, the company earned net income of $400,000 and had unrealized gains on available-for-sale securities of $15,000. In the previous year, net income was $410,000, and the company had no unrealized gains or losses.

Instructions

(a) Show how income and comprehensive income will be reported on a comparative basis for the current and prior years, using the two statement format.
(b) Show how income and comprehensive income will be reported on a comparative basis for the current and prior years, using the one statement format.
(c) Which format should Nelson recommend?

USING YOUR JUDGMENT

FINANCIAL REPORTING

Financial Reporting Problem

_P&G_ The Procter & Gamble Company (P&G)

The financial statements of P&G are presented in Appendix 5B. The company's complete annual report, including the notes to the financial statements, can be accessed at the book's companion website, **www.wiley.com/college/kieso**.

Instructions

Refer to P&G's financial statements and the accompanying notes to answer the following questions.

(a) What type of income statement format does P&G use? Indicate why this format might be used to present income statement information.

(b) What are P&G's primary revenue sources?

(c) Compute P&G's gross profit for each of the years 2009–2011. Explain why gross profit decreased in 2011.

(d) Why does P&G make a distinction between operating and nonoperating revenue?

(e) What financial ratios did P&G choose to report in its "Financial Summary" section covering the years 2001–2011?

Comparative Analysis Case

The Coca-Cola Company and PepsiCo, Inc.

Instructions

Go to the book's companion website and use information found there to answer the following questions related to The Coca-Cola Company and PepsiCo, Inc.

(a) What type of income format(s) is used by these two companies? Identify any differences in income statement format between these two companies.

(b) What are the gross profits, operating profits, and net incomes for these two companies over the 3-year period 2009–2011? Which company has had better financial results over this period of time?

(c) Identify the irregular items reported by these two companies in their income statements over the 3-year period 2009–2011. Do these irregular items appear to be significant?

Financial Statement Analysis Cases

Case 1 Bankruptcy Prediction

The Z-score bankruptcy prediction model uses balance sheet and income information to arrive at a Z-Score, which can be used to predict financial distress:

$$Z = \frac{\text{Working capital}}{\text{Total assets}} \times 1.2 + \frac{\text{Retained earnings}}{\text{Total assets}} \times 1.4 + \frac{\text{EBIT}}{\text{Total assets}} \times 3.3 + \frac{\text{Sales}}{\text{Total assets}} \times .99 + \frac{\text{MV equity}}{\text{Total liabilities}} \times 0.6$$

EBIT is earnings before interest and taxes. MV equity is the market value of common equity, which can be determined by multiplying stock price by shares outstanding.

Following extensive testing, it has been shown that companies with Z-scores above 3.0 are unlikely to fail; those with Z-scores below 1.81 are very likely to fail. While the original model was developed for publicly held manufacturing companies, the model has been modified to apply to companies in various industries, emerging companies, and companies not traded in public markets.

Instructions

(a) Use information in the financial statements of a company like Walgreens or Deere & Co. to compute the Z-score for the past 2 years.

(b) Interpret your result. Where does the company fall in the financial distress range?

(c) The Z-score uses EBIT as one of its elements. Why do you think this income measure is used?

Case 2 Dresser Industries

Dresser Industries provides products and services to oil and natural gas exploration, production, transmission, and processing companies. The following is taken from a recent income statement. (Dollar amounts are in millions.)

Sales revenue	$2,697.0
Service revenue	1,933.9
Share of earnings of unconsolidated affiliates	92.4
Total revenues	4,723.3
Cost of sales	1,722.7
Cost of services	1,799.9
Total costs of sales and services	3,522.6

Gross earnings	$1,200.7
Selling, engineering, administrative and general expenses	(919.8)
Special charges	(70.0)
Other income (deductions)	
Interest expense	(47.4)
Interest earned	19.1
Other, net	4.8
Earnings before income taxes and other items below	187.4
Income taxes	(79.4)
Noncontrolling interest	(10.3)
Earnings from continuing operations	97.7
Discontinued operations	(35.3)
Earnings before extraordinary items	62.4
Extraordinary items	(6.3)
Net earnings	$ 56.1

Instructions

Assume that 177,636,000 shares of stock were issued and outstanding. Prepare the per share portion of the income statement. Remember to begin with "Earnings from continuing operations."

Case 3 P/E Ratios

One of the more closely watched ratios by investors is the price/earnings (P/E) ratio. By dividing price per share by earnings per share, analysts get insight into the value the market attaches to a company's earnings. More specifically, a high P/E ratio (in comparison to companies in the same industry) may suggest the stock is overpriced. Also, there is some evidence that companies with low P/E ratios are underpriced and tend to outperform the market. However, the ratio can be misleading.

P/E ratios are sometimes misleading because the E (earnings) is subject to a number of assumptions and estimates that could result in overstated earnings and a lower P/E. Some analysts conduct "revenue analysis" to evaluate the quality of an earnings number. Revenues are less subject to management estimates and all earnings must begin with revenues. These analysts also compute the price-to-sales ratio (PSR = price per share ÷ sales per share) to assess whether a company is performing well compared to similar companies. If a company has a price-to-sales ratio significantly higher than its competitors, investors may be betting on a stock that has yet to prove itself. [*Source:* Janice Revell, "Beyond P/E," *Fortune* (May 28, 2001), p. 174.]

Instructions

(a) Identify some of the estimates or assumptions that could result in overstated earnings.

(b) Compute the P/E ratio and the PSR for Tootsie Roll and Hershey for 2011.

(c) Use these data to compare the quality of each company's earnings.

Accounting, Analysis, and Principles

Counting Crows Inc. provided the following information for the year 2014.

Retained earnings, January 1, 2014	$ 600,000
Administrative expenses	240,000
Selling expenses	300,000
Sales revenue	1,900,000
Cash dividends declared	80,000
Cost of goods sold	850,000
Extraordinary gain	95,000
Loss on discontinued operations	75,000
Rent revenue	40,000
Unrealized holding gain on available-for-sale securities	17,000
Income tax applicable to continuing operations	187,000
Income tax benefit applicable to loss on discontinued operations	25,500
Income tax applicable to extraordinary gain	32,300
Income tax applicable to unrealized holding gain on available-for-sale securities	2,000

Accounting

Prepare (a) a single-step income statement for 2014, (b) a retained earnings statement for 2014, and (c) a statement of comprehensive income using the two statement format. Shares outstanding during 2014 were 100,000.

Analysis

Explain how a multiple-step income statement format can provide useful information to a financial statement user.

Principles

In a recent meeting with its auditor, Counting Crows' management argued that the company should be able to prepare a pro forma income statement with some one-time administrative expenses reported similar to extraordinary items and discontinued operations. Is such reporting consistent with the qualitative characteristics of accounting information as discussed in the conceptual framework? Explain.

BRIDGE TO THE PROFESSION

 ## Professional Research: FASB Codification

Your client took accounting a number of years ago and was unaware of comprehensive income reporting. He is not convinced that any accounting standards exist for comprehensive income.

Instructions

Go to *http://aahq.org/asclogin.cfm* to log in and prepare responses to the following. Provide Codification references for your responses.

(a) What authoritative literature addresses comprehensive income? When was it issued?

(b) Provide the definition of comprehensive income.

(c) Define classifications within net income and give examples.

(d) Define classifications within other comprehensive income and give examples.

(e) What are reclassification adjustments?

Additional Professional Resources

See the book's companion website, at **www.wiley.com/college/kieso**, for professional simulations as well as other study resources.

IFRS ⟩ INSIGHTS

As in GAAP, the income statement is a required statement for IFRS. In addition, the content and presentation of an IFRS income statement is similar to the one used for GAAP. *IAS 1*, "Presentation of Financial Statements," provides general guidelines for the reporting of income statement information. Subsequently, a number of international standards have been issued that provide additional guidance to issues related to income statement presentation.

9 LEARNING OBJECTIVE

Compare the accounting procedures for income reporting under GAAP and IFRS.

RELEVANT FACTS

Following are the key similarities and differences between GAAP and IFRS related to the income statement.

Similarities

- Both GAAP and IFRS require companies to indicate the amount of net income attributable to noncontrolling interest.

- Both GAAP and IFRS follow the same presentation guidelines for discontinued operations, but IFRS defines a discontinued operation more narrowly. Both standard-setters have indicated a willingness to develop a similar definition to be used in the joint project on financial statement presentation.
- Both GAAP and IFRS have items that are recognized in equity as part of comprehensive income but do not affect net income. Both GAAP and IFRS allow a one statement or two statement approach to preparing the statement of comprehensive income.

Differences

- Presentation of the income statement under GAAP follows either a single-step or multiple-step format. IFRS does not mention a single-step or multiple-step approach. In addition, under GAAP, companies must report an item as extraordinary if it is unusual in nature and infrequent in occurrence. Extraordinary items are prohibited under IFRS.
- Under IFRS, companies must classify expenses by either nature or function. GAAP does not have that requirement, but the SEC requires a functional presentation.
- IFRS identifies certain minimum items that should be presented on the income statement. GAAP has no minimum information requirements. However, the SEC rules have more rigorous presentation requirements.
- IFRS does not define key measures like income from operations. SEC regulations define many key measures and provide requirements and limitations on companies reporting non-GAAP/IFRS information.
- Under IFRS, revaluation of property, plant, and equipment, and intangible assets is permitted and is reported as other comprehensive income. The effect of this difference is that application of IFRS results in more transactions affecting equity but not net income.

ABOUT THE NUMBERS
Income Reporting

Illustration IFRS4-1 provides a summary of the primary income items under IFRS. As indicated in the table, similar to GAAP, companies report all revenues, gains, expenses, and losses on the income statement and, at the end of the period, close them to Income Summary. They provide useful subtotals on the income statement, such as gross profit, income from operations, income before income tax, and net income. Companies classify discontinued operations of a component of a business as a separate item in the income statement, after "Income from continuing operations." Companies present other income and expense in a separate section, before income from operations. Providing intermediate income figures helps readers evaluate earnings information in assessing the amounts, timing, and uncertainty of future cash flows.

Expense Classifications

Companies are required to present an analysis of expenses classified either by their nature (such as cost of materials used, direct labor incurred, delivery expense, advertising expense, employee benefits, depreciation expense, and amortization expense) or their function (such as cost of goods sold, selling expenses, and administrative expenses).

Type of Situation	Criteria	Examples	Placement on Income Statement
Sales or service revenues	Revenue arising from the ordinary activities of the company	Sales revenue, service revenue	Sales or revenue section
Cost of goods sold	Expense arising from the cost of inventory sold or services provided	In a merchandising company, cost of goods sold; in a service company, cost of services	Deduct from sales (to arrive at gross profit) or service revenue
Selling and administrative expenses	Expenses arising from the ordinary activities of the company	Sales salaries, delivery expense, rent, depreciation, utilities	Deduct from gross profit; if the function-of-expense approach is used, depreciation and amortization expense and labor costs must be disclosed
Other income and expense	Gains and losses and other ancillary revenues and expenses	Gain on sale of long-lived assets, impairment loss on intangible assets, investment revenue, dividend and interest revenue, casualty losses	Report as part of income from operations
Financing costs	Separates cost of financing from operating costs	Interest expense	Report in separate section between income from operations and income before income tax
Income tax	Levies imposed by governmental bodies on the basis of income	Taxes computed on income before income tax	Report in separate section between income before income tax and net income
Discontinued operations	A component of a company that has either been disposed of or is classified as held-for-sale	A sale by diversified company of a major division representing its only activities in the electronics industry. Food distributor that sells wholesale to supermarkets decides to discontinue the division in a major geographic area	Report gains or losses on discontinued operations net of tax in a separate section between income from continuing operations and net income
Non-controlling interest	Allocation of net income of loss divided between two classes: (1) the majority interest represented by the shareholders who own the controlling interest, and (2) the non-controlling interest (often referred to as the minority interest)	Net profit (loss) attributable to non-controlling shareholders	Report as a separate item below net income or loss as an allocation of the net income or loss (not as an item of income or expense)

ILLUSTRATION IFRS4-1
Summary of Income Items under IFRS

An advantage of the **nature-of-expense method** is that it is simple to apply because allocations of expense to different functions are not necessary. For manufacturing companies that must allocate costs to the product produced, using a nature-of-expense approach permits companies to report expenses without making arbitrary allocations.

The **function-of-expense method**, however, is often viewed as more relevant because this method identifies the major cost drivers of the company and therefore helps users assess whether these amounts are appropriate for the revenue generated. As indicated, a disadvantage of this method is that the allocation of costs to the varying functions may be arbitrary and therefore the expense classification becomes misleading.

To illustrate these two methods, assume that the accounting firm of Telaris Co. performs audit, tax, and consulting services. It has the following revenues and expenses.

Service revenues	$400,000
Cost of services	
Staff salaries (related to various services performed)	145,000
Supplies expense (related to various services performed)	10,000
Selling expenses	
Advertising costs	20,000
Entertainment expense	3,000
Administrative expenses	
Utilities expense	5,000
Depreciation on building	12,000

If Telaris Co. uses the nature-of-expense approach, its income statement presents each expense item but does not classify the expenses into various subtotals, as follows.

TELARIS CO.
INCOME STATEMENT
FOR THE MONTH OF JANUARY 2014

Service revenues	$400,000
Staff salaries	145,000
Supplies expense	10,000
Advertising costs	20,000
Utilities expense	5,000
Depreciation on building	12,000
Entertainment expense	3,000
Net income	$205,000

If Telaris uses the function-of-expense approach, its income statement is as follows.

TELARIS CO.
INCOME STATEMENT
FOR THE MONTH OF JANUARY 2014

Service revenues	$400,000
Cost of services	155,000
Selling expenses	23,000
Administrative expenses	17,000
Net income	$205,000

The function-of-expense method is generally used in practice although many companies believe both approaches have merit. These companies use the function-of-expense approach on the income statement but provide detail of the expenses (as in the nature-of-expense approach) in the notes to the financial statements. The IASB-FASB discussion paper on financial statement presentation also recommends the dual approach.

ON THE HORIZON

The IASB and FASB are working on a project that would rework the structure of financial statements. One stage of this project will address the issue of how to classify various items in the income statement. A main goal of this new approach is to provide information that better represents how businesses are run. The FASB and IASB have issued a proposal to require comprehensive income be reported in a combined statement of comprehensive income. This approach draws attention away from just one number—net income.

IFRS SELF-TEST QUESTIONS

1. Which of the following is **not** reported in an income statement under IFRS?
   (a) Discontinued operations.
   (b) Extraordinary items.
   (c) Cost of goods sold.
   (d) Income tax.

2. Which of the following statements is **correct** regarding income reporting under IFRS?
   (a) IFRS does not permit revaluation of property, plant, and equipment, and intangible assets.
   (b) IFRS provides the same options for reporting comprehensive income as GAAP.
   (c) Companies must classify expenses by nature.
   (d) IFRS provides a definition for all items presented in the income statement.

3. Which statement is **correct** regarding IFRS?
   (a) An advantage of the nature-of-expense method is that it is simple to apply because allocations of expense to different functions are not necessary.
   (b) The function-of-expense approach never requires arbitrary allocations.
   (c) An advantage of the function-of-expense method is that allocation of costs to the varying functions is rarely arbitrary.
   (d) IFRS requires use of the nature-of-expense approach.

4. The non-controlling interest section of the income statement is:
   (a) required under GAAP but not under IFRS.
   (b) required under IFRS but not under GAAP.
   (c) required under IFRS and GAAP.
   (d) not reported under GAAP or IFRS.

5. Which of the following is **not** an acceptable way of displaying the components of other comprehensive income under IFRS?
   (a) Within the statement of retained earnings.
   (b) Second income statement.
   (c) Combined statement of comprehensive income.
   (d) All of these choices are acceptable.

IFRS CONCEPTS AND APPLICATION

IFRS4-1 Explain the difference between the "nature-of-expense" and "function-of-expense" classifications.

IFRS4-2 Discuss the appropriate treatment in the income statement for the following items:

(a) Loss on discontinued operations.
(b) Non-controlling interest allocation.

IFRS4-3 Bradshaw Company experienced a loss that was deemed to be both unusual in nature and infrequent in occurrence. How should Bradshaw report this item in accordance with IFRS?

IFRS4-4 Presented below is information related to Viel Company at December 31, 2014, the end of its first year of operations.

Sales revenue	$310,000
Cost of goods sold	140,000
Selling and administrative expenses	50,000
Gain on sale of plant assets	30,000
Unrealized gain on non-trading equity securities	10,000
Interest expense	6,000
Loss on discontinued operations	12,000
Allocation to non-controlling interest	40,000
Dividends declared and paid	5,000

Instructions

Compute the following: (a) income from operations, (b) net income, (c) net income attributable to Viel Company controlling shareholders, (d) comprehensive income, and (e) retained earnings balance at December 31, 2014. (Ignore income taxes.)

IFRS4-5 Below is the income statement for a British company, Avon Rubber plc. Avon prepares its financial statements in accordance with IFRS.

Avon Rubber plc
Consolidated Income Statement for the Year Ended 30 September

	2011	2010
Continuing operations		
Revenue	107,600	117,574
Cost of sales	(77,892)	(89,256)
Gross profit	29,708	28,318
Distribution costs	(4,832)	(4,527)
Administrative expenses	(13,740)	(14,536)
Other operating income	—	—
Operating profit/(loss) from continuing operations	11,136	9,255
Operating profit/(loss) is analysed as:		
Before depreciation, amortization and exceptional items	15,723	13,577
Depreciation and amortization	(4,587)	(4,322)
Operating profit/(loss) before exceptional items	11,136	9,255
Exceptional operating items		
Finance income	5	16
Finance costs	(486)	(985)
Other finance income	(443)	(1,152)
Profit/(loss) before taxation	991	(12,391)
Taxation	(3,094)	(2,808)
Profit/(loss) for the year from continuing operations	(2,103)	(15,199)
Discontinued operations		
Profit/(loss) for the year from discontinued operations	—	—
Loss for the year	—	—
Earnings/(loss) per share		
Basic	25.2p	15.2p
Diluted	23.3p	14.4p
Earnings/(loss) per share from continuing operations		
Basic	25.2p	15.2p
Diluted	23.3p	14.4p

Instructions

(a) Review the Avon Rubber income statement and identify at least three differences between the IFRS income statement and an income statement of a U.S. company as presented in the chapter.

(b) Identify any irregular items reported by Avon Rubber. Is the reporting of these irregular items in Avon's income statement similar to reporting of these items in U.S. companies' income statements? Explain.

Professional Research

IFRS4-6 Your client took accounting a number of years ago and was unaware of comprehensive income reporting. He is not convinced that any accounting standards exist for comprehensive income.

Instructions

Access the IFRS authoritative literature at the IASB website (*http://www.iasb.org/*). (Click on the IFRS tab and then register for free eIFRS access if necessary.) When you have accessed the documents, you can use the search tool in your Internet browser to respond to the following questions. (Provide paragraph citations.)

(a) What IFRS addresses reporting in the statement of comprehensive income? When was it issued?
(b) Provide the definition of total comprehensive income.
(c) Explain the rationale for presenting additional line items, headings, and subtotals in the statement of comprehensive income.
(d) What items of income or expense may be presented either in the statement of comprehensive income or in the notes?

International Financial Reporting Problem
Marks and Spencer plc

IFRS4-7 The financial statements of **Marks and Spencer plc (M&S)** are available at the book's companion website or can be accessed at *http://annualreport.marksandspencer.com/_assets/downloads/Marks-and-Spencer-Annual-report-and-financial-statements-2012.pdf.*

Instructions

Refer to M&S's financial statements and the accompanying notes to answer the following questions.

(a) What type of income statement format does M&S use? Indicate why this format might be used to present income statement information.
(b) What are M&S's primary revenue sources?
(c) Compute M&S's gross profit for each of the years 2011 and 2012. Explain why gross profit increased in 2012.
(d) Why does M&S make a distinction between operating and non-operating profit?
(e) Does M&S report any non-GAAP measures? Explain.

ANSWERS TO IFRS SELF-TEST QUESTIONS

1. b **2.** b **3.** a **4.** c **5.** a

Remember to check the book's companion website to find additional resources for this chapter.

After studying this chapter, you should be able to:

1 Explain the uses and limitations of a balance sheet.

2 Identify the major classifications of the balance sheet.

3 Prepare a classified balance sheet using the report and account formats.

4 Indicate the purpose of the statement of cash flows.

5 Identify the content of the statement of cash flows.

6 Prepare a basic statement of cash flows.

7 Understand the usefulness of the statement of cash flows.

8 Determine which balance sheet information requires supplemental disclosure.

9 Describe the major disclosure techniques for the balance sheet.

Hey, It Doesn't Balance!

A good accounting student knows by now that Total Assets = Total Liabilities + Total Equity. From this equation, we can also determine net assets, which are determined as follows: Total Assets − Total Liabilities = Net Assets. O.K., this is simple so far. But let's look at the recent discussion paper by the FASB/IASB on how the statement of financial position (the balance sheet) should be structured.

The statement of financial position is divided into five major parts, with many assets and liabilities netted against one another. Here is the general framework for the new statement of financial position:

BUSINESS
    Operating assets and liabilities
    Investing assets and liabilities
FINANCING
    Financing assets
    Financing liabilities
INCOME TAXES
DISCONTINUED OPERATIONS
EQUITY

The statement does look a bit different than the traditional balance sheet. Let's put some numbers to the statement and see how it works. (See the example on the facing page.)

Well, it does balance—in that net assets equal equity—but isn't it important to know total assets and total liabilities? As some have observed, the statement of financial position will not balance the way we expect it to. That is, assets won't equal liabilities and equity. This is because the assets and liabilities are grouped into the business, financing, discontinued operations, and income taxes categories. This new model raises a number of questions, such as:

- Does separating "business activities from financing activities" provide information that is more decision-useful?
- Does information on income taxes and discontinued operations merit separate categories?

The FASB and IASB are working to get answers to these and other questions about this proposed model. One thing is for sure—adoption of the new financial statements will be a dramatic change but hopefully one for the better.

STATEMENT OF FINANCIAL POSITION		
BUSINESS		
Operating		
Inventories	$ 400,000	
Receivables	200,000	
Total short-term assets		$ 600,000
Property (net)	500,000	
Intangible assets	50,000	
Total long-term assets		550,000
Accounts payable	30,000	
Wages payable	40,000	
Total short-term liabilities		(70,000)
Lease liability	10,000	
Other long-term debt	35,000	
Total long-term liabilities		(45,000)
Net operating assets		**1,035,000**
Investing		
Trading securities	45,000	
Other securities	5,000	
Total investing assets		50,000
TOTAL NET BUSINESS ASSETS		**1,085,000**
FINANCING		
Financing assets		
Cash	30,000	
Total financing assets		30,000
Financing liabilities		
Short- and long-term borrowing	130,000	
Total financing liabilities		(130,000)
NET FINANCING LIABILITIES		**(100,000)**
DISCONTINUED OPERATIONS		
Assets held for sale		420,000
INCOME TAXES		
Deferred income taxes		70,000
NET ASSETS		**$1,475,000**
EQUITY		
Share capital—ordinary	$1,000,000	
Retained earnings	475,000	
TOTAL EQUITY		**$1,475,000**

CONCEPTUAL FOCUS

> See the **Underlying Concepts** on pages 227, 228, 237, 240, and 241.
> Read the **Evolving Issue** on page 243 for a discussion of balance sheet reporting.

INTERNATIONAL FOCUS

> See the **International Perspectives** on pages 231 and 242.
> Read the **IFRS Insights** on pages 277–284 for a discussion of:
> —Classification in the statement of financial position
> —Equity
> —Revaluation equity
> —Fair presentation

Sources: Marie Leone and Tim Reason, "How Extreme Is the Makeover?" *CFO Magazine* (March 1, 2009); and *Preliminary Views on Financial Statement Presentation*, FASB/IASB Discussion Paper (October 2008).

PREVIEW OF CHAPTER	**5**

As the opening story indicates, the FASB and IASB are working to improve the presentation of financial information on the balance sheet, as well as other financial statements. In this chapter, we examine the many different types of assets, liabilities, and equity items that affect the balance sheet and the statement of cash flows. The content and organization of the chapter are as follows.

Balance Sheet and Statement of Cash Flows

Balance Sheet	Statement of Cash Flows	Additional Information
• Usefulness • Limitations • Classification • Format	• Purpose • Content and format • Preparation overview • Usefulness	• Supplemental disclosures • Techniques of disclosure

BALANCE SHEET

LEARNING OBJECTIVE **1**
Explain the uses and limitations of a balance sheet.

The **balance sheet**, sometimes referred to as the **statement of financial position**, reports the assets, liabilities, and stockholders' equity of a business enterprise at a specific date. This financial statement provides information about the nature and amounts of investments in enterprise resources, obligations to creditors, and the owners' equity in net resources. It therefore helps in predicting the amounts, timing, and uncertainty of future cash flows.

Usefulness of the Balance Sheet

By providing information on assets, liabilities, and stockholders' equity, the balance sheet provides a basis for computing rates of return and evaluating the capital structure of the enterprise. Analysts also use information in the balance sheet to assess a company's risk[1] and future cash flows. In this regard, analysts use the balance sheet to assess a company's liquidity, solvency, and financial flexibility.

Liquidity describes "the amount of time that is expected to elapse until an asset is realized or otherwise converted into cash or until a liability has to be paid."[2] Creditors are interested in short-term liquidity ratios, such as the ratio of cash (or near cash) to short-term liabilities. These ratios indicate whether a company, like **Amazon.com**, will have the resources to pay its current and maturing obligations. Similarly, stockholders assess liquidity to evaluate the possibility of future cash dividends or the buyback of shares. In general, the greater Amazon's liquidity, the lower its risk of failure.

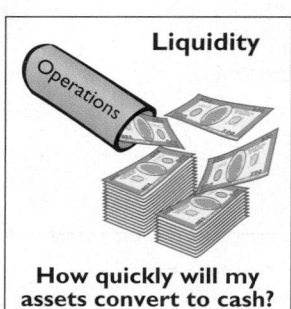

Liquidity

Operations

How quickly will my assets convert to cash?

Solvency refers to the ability of a company to pay its debts as they mature. For example, when a company carries a high level of long-term debt relative to assets, it has lower solvency than a similar company with a low level of long-term debt. Companies with higher debt are relatively more risky because they will need more of their assets to meet their fixed obligations (interest and principal payments).

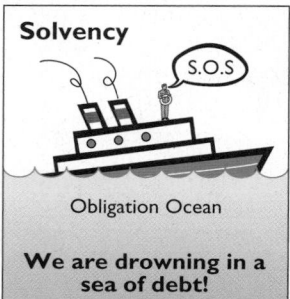

Solvency

S.O.S

Obligation Ocean

We are drowning in a sea of debt!

Liquidity and solvency affect a company's **financial flexibility**, which measures the "ability of an enterprise to take effective actions to alter the amounts and timing of cash flows so it can respond to unexpected needs and opportunities."[3] For example, a company may become so loaded with debt—so financially inflexible—that it has little or no sources of cash to finance expansion or to pay off maturing debt. A company with a high degree of financial flexibility is better able to survive bad times, to recover from unexpected setbacks, and to take advantage of profitable and unexpected investment opportunities. Generally, the greater an enterprise's financial flexibility, the lower its risk of failure.

Limitations of the Balance Sheet

Some of the major limitations of the balance sheet are:

Hmm... I wonder if they will pay me back?

1. Most assets and liabilities are reported at **historical cost**. As a result, the information provided in the balance sheet is often criticized for not reporting a more relevant fair value. For example, **Georgia-Pacific** owns timber and other assets that may appreciate in value after purchase. Yet, Georgia-Pacific reports any increase only if and when it sells the assets.

[1]Risk conveys the unpredictability of future events, transactions, circumstances, and results of the company.

[2]"Reporting Income, Cash Flows, and Financial Position of Business Enterprises," *Proposed Statement of Financial Accounting Concepts* (Stamford, Conn.: FASB, 1981), par. 29.

[3]"Reporting Income, Cash Flows, and Financial Position of Business Enterprises," *Proposed Statement of Financial Accounting Concepts* (Stamford, Conn.: FASB, 1981), par. 25.

2. Companies use **judgments and estimates** to determine many of the items reported in the balance sheet. For example, in its balance sheet, Dell estimates the amount of receivables that it will collect, the useful life of its warehouses, and the number of computers that will be returned under warranty.

3. The balance sheet necessarily **omits many items that are of financial value** but that a company cannot record objectively. For example, the knowledge and skill of Intel employees in developing new computer chips are arguably the company's most significant assets. However, because Intel cannot reliably measure the value of its employees and other intangible assets (such as customer base, research superiority, and reputation), it does not recognize these items in the balance sheet. Similarly, many liabilities are reported in an "off-balance-sheet" manner, if at all.

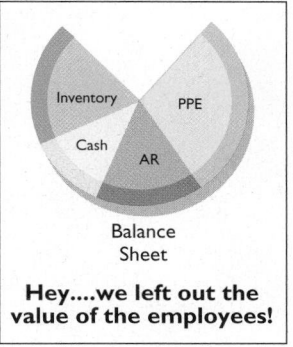

Balance Sheet

Hey....we left out the value of the employees!

The bankruptcy of Enron, the seventh-largest U.S. company at the time, highlights the omission of important items in the balance sheet. In Enron's case, it failed to disclose certain off-balance-sheet financing obligations in its main financial statements.[4]

What do the numbers mean?   GROUNDED

The terrorist attacks of September 11, 2001, showed how vulnerable the major airlines are to falling demand for their services. Since that infamous date, major airlines have reduced capacity and slashed jobs to avoid bankruptcy. United Airlines, Northwest Airlines, US Airways, and several smaller competitors filed for bankruptcy in the wake of 9/11.

Delta Airlines made the following statements in its annual report issued shortly after 9/11:

"If we are unsuccessful in further reducing our operating costs . . . we will need to restructure our costs under Chapter 11 of the U.S. Bankruptcy Code. . . . We have substantial liquidity needs and there is no assurance that

we will be able to obtain the necessary financing to meet those needs on acceptable terms, if at all."

These financial flexibility challenges have continued, exacerbated by ever-increasing fuel prices, labor costs, and the economic downturn in response to the financial crisis. Not surprisingly, several of the major airlines (Delta and Northwest, Continental and United, and Airtran and Southwest) merged recently as a way to build some competitive synergies and to bolster their financial flexibility. Others (American Airlines and US Airways) are exploring mergers.

Source: R. Seaney, "Airline Mergers: Good for Travelers?" *http://abcnews.go.com/Travel/airline-merger-mania-cost/story?id=16227892* (April 27, 2012).

Classification in the Balance Sheet

Balance sheet accounts are **classified**. That is, balance sheets group together similar items to arrive at significant subtotals. Furthermore, the material is arranged so that important relationships are shown.

The FASB has often noted that the parts and subsections of financial statements can be more informative than the whole. Therefore, the FASB discourages the reporting of summary accounts alone (total assets, net assets, total liabilities, etc.). Instead, companies should report and classify individual items in sufficient detail to permit users to assess the amounts, timing, and uncertainty of future cash flows. Such

2 LEARNING OBJECTIVE

Identify the major classifications of the balance sheet.

---

[4]We discuss several of these omitted items (such as leases and other off-balance-sheet arrangements) in later chapters. See Wayne Upton, Jr., *Special Report: Business and Financial Reporting, Challenges from the New Economy* (Norwalk, Conn.: FASB, 2001); and U.S. Securities and Exchange Commission, "Disclosure in Management's Discussion and Analysis about Off-Balance Sheet Arrangements and Aggregate Contractual Obligations," *http://www.sec.gov/rules/final/33-8182.htm* (May 2003).

classification also makes it easier for users to evaluate the company's liquidity, financial flexibility, profitability, and risk.

To classify items in financial statements, companies group those items with similar characteristics and separate items with different characteristics.[5] For example, companies should report separately:

1. Assets that differ in their **type or expected function** in the company's central operations or other activities. For example, **IBM** reports merchandise inventories separately from property, plant, and equipment.

2. Assets and liabilities with **different implications for the company's financial flexibility**. For example, a company that uses assets in its operations, like **Walgreens**, should report those assets separately from assets held for investment and assets subject to restrictions, such as leased equipment.

3. Assets and liabilities with **different general liquidity characteristics**. For example, **Boeing Company** reports cash separately from inventories.

The three general classes of items included in the balance sheet are assets, liabilities, and equity. We defined them in Chapter 2 as follows.

ELEMENTS OF THE BALANCE SHEET

1. **ASSETS.** Probable future economic benefits obtained or controlled by a particular entity as a result of past transactions or events.

2. **LIABILITIES.** Probable future sacrifices of economic benefits arising from present obligations of a particular entity to transfer assets or provide services to other entities in the future as a result of past transactions or events.

3. **EQUITY.** Residual interest in the assets of an entity that remains after deducting its liabilities. In a business enterprise, the equity is the ownership interest.[6]

Companies then further divide these items into several subclassifications. Illustration 5-1 indicates the general format of balance sheet presentation.

ILLUSTRATION 5-1
Balance Sheet
Classifications

Assets	Liabilities and Owners' Equity
Current assets	Current liabilities
Long-term investments	Long-term debt
Property, plant, and equipment	Owners' (stockholders') equity
Intangible assets	
Other assets	

A company may classify the balance sheet in some other manner, but in practice you usually see little departure from these major subdivisions. A proprietorship or partnership does present the classifications within the owners' equity section a little differently, as we will show later in the chapter.

---

[5]"Reporting Income, Cash Flows, and Financial Positions of Business Enterprises," *Proposed Statement of Financial Accounting Concepts* (Stamford, Conn.: FASB, 1981), par. 51.

[6]"Elements of Financial Statements of Business Enterprises," *Statement of Financial Accounting Concepts No. 6* (Stamford, Conn.: FASB, 1985), paras. 25, 35, and 49.

Current Assets

Current assets are cash and other assets a company expects to convert into cash, sell, or consume either in one year or in the operating cycle, whichever is longer. The operating cycle is the average time between when a company acquires materials and supplies and when it receives cash for sales of the product (for which it acquired the materials and supplies). The cycle operates from cash through inventory, production, receivables, and back to cash. When several operating cycles occur within one year (which is generally the case for service companies), a company uses the one-year period. If the operating cycle is more than one year, a company uses the longer period.

Current assets are presented in the balance sheet in order of liquidity. The five major items found in the current assets section, and their bases of valuation, are shown in Illustration 5-2.

Item	Basis of Valuation
Cash and cash equivalents	Fair value
Short-term investments	Generally, fair value
Receivables	Estimated amount collectible
Inventories	Lower-of-cost-or-market
Prepaid expenses	Cost

ILLUSTRATION 5-2
Current Assets and Basis of Valuation

A company does not report these five items as current assets if it does not expect to realize them in one year or in the operating cycle, whichever is longer. For example, a company excludes from the current assets section cash restricted for purposes other than payment of current obligations or for use in current operations. **Generally, if a company expects to convert an asset into cash or to use it to pay a current liability within a year or the operating cycle, whichever is longer, it classifies the asset as current.**

This rule, however, is subject to interpretation. A company classifies an investment in common stock as either a current asset or a noncurrent asset depending on management's intent. When it has small holdings of common stocks or bonds that it will hold long-term, it should not classify them as current.

Although a current asset is well defined, certain theoretical problems also develop. For example, how is including prepaid expenses in the current assets section justified? The rationale is that if a company did not pay these items in advance, it would instead need to use other current assets during the operating cycle. If we follow this logic to its ultimate conclusion, however, any asset previously purchased saves the use of current assets during the operating cycle and would be considered current.

Another problem occurs in the current-asset definition when a company consumes plant assets during the operating cycle. Conceptually, it seems that a company should place in the current assets section an amount equal to the current depreciation charge on the plant assets, because it will consume them in the next operating cycle. However, this conceptual problem is ignored. This example illustrates that the formal distinction made between some current and noncurrent assets is somewhat arbitrary.

Cash. Cash is generally considered to consist of currency and demand deposits (monies available on demand at a financial institution). **Cash equivalents** are short-term highly liquid investments that will mature within three months or less. Most companies use the caption "Cash and cash equivalents," and they indicate that this amount approximates fair value.

A company must disclose any restrictions or commitments related to the availability of cash. As an example, see the excerpt from the annual report of **Alterra Healthcare Corp.** in Illustration 5-3 (page 218).

ILLUSTRATION 5-3
Balance Sheet
Presentation of
Restricted Cash

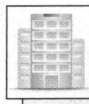

Alterra Healthcare Corp.

Current assets

Cash	$18,728,000
Restricted cash and investments (Note 7)	7,191,000

Note 7: Restricted Cash and Investments. Restricted cash and investments consist of certificates of deposit restricted as collateral for lease arrangements and debt service with interest rates ranging from 4.0% to 5.5%.

Alterra Healthcare restricted cash to meet an obligation due currently. Therefore, Alterra included this restricted cash under current assets.

If a company restricts cash for purposes other than current obligations, it excludes the cash from current assets. Illustration 5-4 shows an example of this, from the annual report of Owens Corning, Inc.

ILLUSTRATION 5-4
Balance Sheet
Presentation of Current
and Noncurrent
Restricted Cash

Owens Corning, Inc.
(in millions)

Current assets	
Cash and cash equivalents	$ 70
Restricted securities—Fibreboard—current portion (Note 23)	900
Other assets	
Restricted securities—Fibreboard (Note 23)	938

Note 23 (in part). The Insurance Settlement funds are held in and invested by the Fibreboard Settlement Trust (the "Trust") and are available to satisfy Fibreboard's pending and future asbestos related liabilities. . . . The assets of the Trust are comprised of cash and marketable securities (collectively, the "Trust Assets") and are reflected on Owens Corning's consolidated balance sheet as restricted assets. These assets are reflected as current assets or other assets, with each category denoted "Restricted securities—Fibreboard."

Short-Term Investments. Companies group investments in debt and equity securities into three separate portfolios for valuation and reporting purposes:

Held-to-maturity: Debt securities that a company has the positive intent and ability to hold to maturity.

Trading: Debt and equity securities bought and held primarily for sale in the near term to generate income on short-term price differences.

Available-for-sale: Debt and equity securities not classified as held-to-maturity or trading securities.

A company should report trading securities (whether debt or equity) as current assets. It classifies individual held-to-maturity and available-for-sale securities as current or noncurrent depending on the circumstances. It should report held-to-maturity securities at amortized cost. All trading and available-for-sale securities are reported at fair value. [1][7]

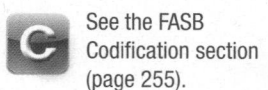

See the FASB
Codification section
(page 255).

[7]Under the fair value option, companies may elect to use fair value as the measurement basis for selected financial assets and liabilities. For these companies, some of their financial assets (and liabilities) may be recorded at historical cost, while others are recorded at fair value. [2]

For example, Illustration 5-5 is an excerpt from the annual report of Intuit Inc. with respect to its available-for-sale investments.

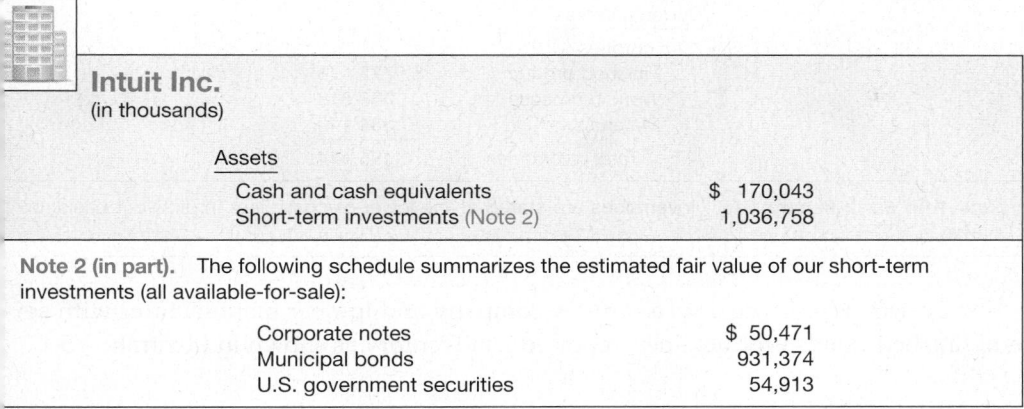

Intuit Inc.		
(in thousands)		
Assets		
Cash and cash equivalents	$ 170,043	
Short-term investments (Note 2)	1,036,758	
Note 2 (in part). The following schedule summarizes the estimated fair value of our short-term investments (all available-for-sale):		
Corporate notes	$ 50,471	
Municipal bonds	931,374	
U.S. government securities	54,913	

ILLUSTRATION 5-5
Balance Sheet
Presentation of
Investments in Securities

Receivables. A company should clearly identify any anticipated loss due to uncollectibles, the amount and nature of any nontrade receivables, and any receivables used as collateral. Major categories of receivables should be shown in the balance sheet or the related notes. For receivables arising from unusual transactions (such as sale of property, or a loan to affiliates or employees), companies should separately classify these as long-term, unless collection is expected within one year. Stanley Black & Decker reported its receivables as shown in Illustration 5-6.

Stanley Black & Decker		
(in millions)		
Current assets		
Cash and cash equivalents	$ 906.9	
Accounts and notes receivable, net	1,553.2	
Inventories, net	1,438.6	
Prepaid expenses	209.0	
Other current assets	215.0	
Total current assets	4,322.7	
Note B (in part): Accounts and Notes Receivable		
Trade accounts receivable	$1,484.0	
Trade notes receivable	100.3	
Other accounts receivables	32.8	
Gross accounts and notes receivable	1,617.1	
Allowance for doubtful accounts	(63.9)	
Accounts and notes receivable, net	$1,553.2	

ILLUSTRATION 5-6
Balance Sheet
Presentation of
Receivables

Inventories. To present inventories properly, a company discloses the basis of valuation (e.g., lower-of-cost-or-market) and the cost flow assumption used (e.g., FIFO or LIFO). A manufacturing concern (like Abbott Laboratories, shown in Illustration 5-7 on page 220) also indicates the stage of completion of the inventories.

ILLUSTRATION 5-7
Balance Sheet
Presentation of
Inventories, Showing
Stage of Completion

Abbott Laboratories
(in thousands)

Current assets

Inventories

Finished products	$ 772,478
Work in process	338,818
Materials	384,148
Total inventories	1,495,444

Note 1 (in part): Inventories. Inventories are stated at the lower-of-cost- (first-in, first-out basis) or-market.

Weyerhaeuser Company, a forestry company and lumber manufacturer with several finished-goods product lines, reported its inventory as shown in Illustration 5-8.

ILLUSTRATION 5-8
Balance Sheet
Presentation of
Inventories, Showing
Product Lines

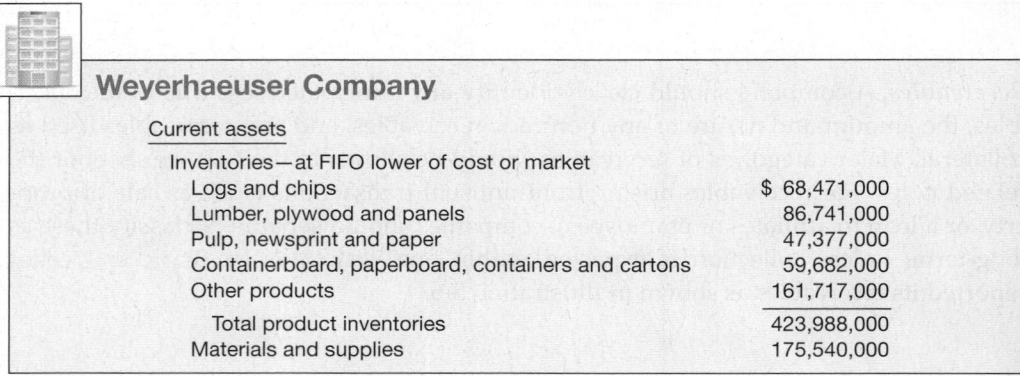

Weyerhaeuser Company

Current assets

Inventories—at FIFO lower of cost or market

Logs and chips	$ 68,471,000
Lumber, plywood and panels	86,741,000
Pulp, newsprint and paper	47,377,000
Containerboard, paperboard, containers and cartons	59,682,000
Other products	161,717,000
Total product inventories	423,988,000
Materials and supplies	175,540,000

Prepaid Expenses. A company includes prepaid expenses in current assets if it will receive benefits (usually services) within one year or the operating cycle, whichever is longer. As we discussed earlier, these items are current assets because if they had not already been paid, they would require the use of cash during the next year or the operating cycle. A company reports prepaid expenses at the amount of the unexpired or unconsumed cost.

A common example is the prepayment for an insurance policy. A company classifies it as a prepaid expense because the payment precedes the receipt of the benefit of coverage. Other common prepaid expenses include prepaid rent, advertising, taxes, and office or operating supplies. Hasbro, Inc., for example, listed its prepaid expenses in current assets as shown in Illustration 5-9.

ILLUSTRATION 5-9
Balance Sheet
Presentation of Prepaid
Expenses

Hasbro, Inc.
(in thousands)

Current assets

Cash and cash equivalents	$ 715,400
Accounts receivable, less allowances of $27,700	556,287
Inventories	203,337
Prepaid expenses and other current assets	243,291
Total current assets	$1,718,315

Noncurrent Assets

Noncurrent assets are those not meeting the definition of current assets. They include a variety of items, as we discuss in the following sections.

Long-Term Investments. **Long-term investments,** often referred to simply as investments, normally consist of one of four types:

1. Investments in securities, such as bonds, common stock, or long-term notes.
2. Investments in tangible fixed assets not currently used in operations, such as land held for speculation.
3. Investments set aside in special funds, such as a sinking fund, pension fund, or plant expansion fund. This includes the cash surrender value of life insurance.
4. Investments in nonconsolidated subsidiaries or affiliated companies.

Companies expect to hold long-term investments for many years. They usually present them on the balance sheet just below "Current assets," in a separate section called "Investments." Realize that many securities classified as long-term investments are, in fact, readily marketable. But a company does not include them as current assets unless it **intends to convert them to cash in the short-term**—that is, within a year or in the operating cycle, whichever is longer. As indicated earlier, securities classified as available-for-sale are reported at fair value, and held-to-maturity securities are reported at amortized cost.

Motorola, Inc. reported its investments section, located between "Property, plant, and equipment" and "Other assets," as shown in Illustration 5-10.

Motorola, Inc.
(in millions)

Investments	
Equity investments	$ 872
Other investments	2,567
Fair value adjustment to available-for-sale securities	2,487
Total	$5,926

ILLUSTRATION 5-10
Balance Sheet Presentation of Long-Term Investments

Property, Plant, and Equipment. **Property, plant, and equipment** are tangible long-lived assets used in the regular operations of the business. These assets consist of physical property such as land, buildings, machinery, furniture, tools, and wasting resources (timberland, minerals). With the exception of land, a company either depreciates (e.g., buildings) or depletes (e.g., timberlands or oil reserves) these assets.

Mattel, Inc. presented its property, plant, and equipment in its balance sheet as shown in Illustration 5-11 (page 222).

A company discloses the basis it uses to value property, plant, and equipment; any liens against the properties; and accumulated depreciation—usually in the notes to the financial statements.

ILLUSTRATION 5-11
Balance Sheet
Presentation of Property,
Plant, and Equipment

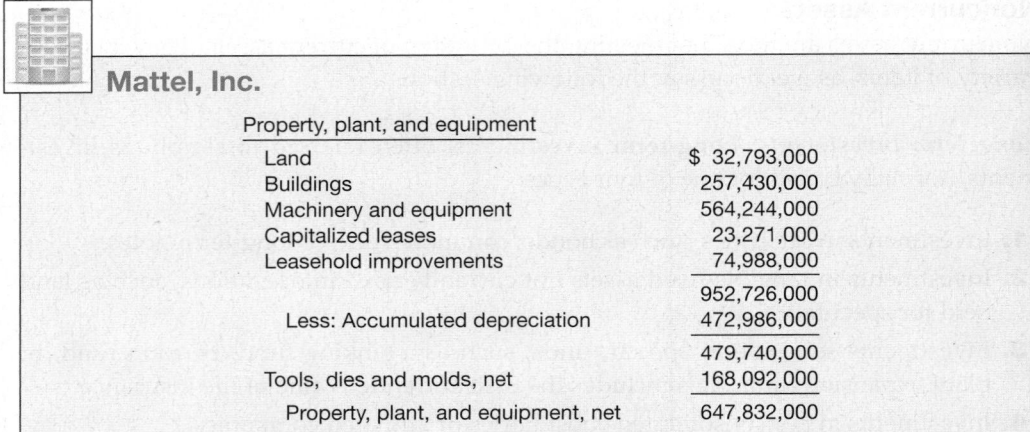

Mattel, Inc.

Property, plant, and equipment	
Land	$ 32,793,000
Buildings	257,430,000
Machinery and equipment	564,244,000
Capitalized leases	23,271,000
Leasehold improvements	74,988,000
	952,726,000
Less: Accumulated depreciation	472,986,000
	479,740,000
Tools, dies and molds, net	168,092,000
Property, plant, and equipment, net	647,832,000

Intangible Assets. Intangible assets lack physical substance and are not financial instruments (see page 238 for the definition of a financial instrument). They include patents, copyrights, franchises, goodwill, trademarks, trade names, and customer lists. A company writes off (amortizes) limited-life intangible assets over their useful lives. It periodically assesses indefinite-life intangibles (such as goodwill) for impairment. Intangibles can represent significant economic resources, yet financial analysts often ignore them, because valuation is difficult.

PepsiCo, Inc. reported intangible assets in its balance sheet as shown in Illustration 5-12.

ILLUSTRATION 5-12
Balance Sheet
Presentation of
Intangible Assets

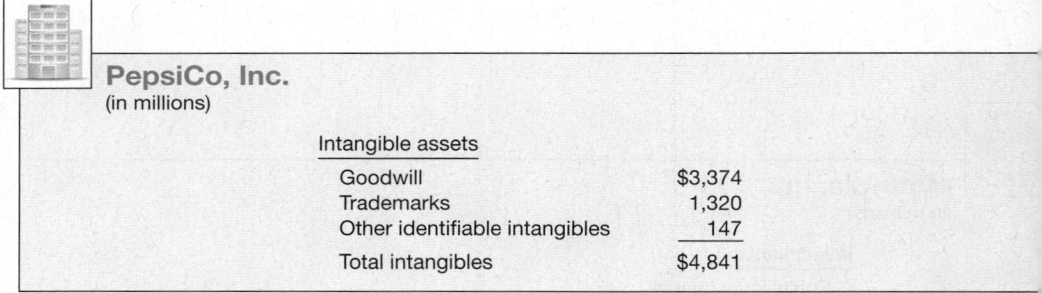

PepsiCo, Inc.
(in millions)

Intangible assets	
Goodwill	$3,374
Trademarks	1,320
Other identifiable intangibles	147
Total intangibles	$4,841

Other Assets. The items included in the section "Other assets" vary widely in practice. Some include items such as long-term prepaid expenses, prepaid pension cost, and non-current receivables. Other items that might be included are assets in special funds, deferred income taxes, property held for sale, and restricted cash or securities. A company should limit this section to include only unusual items sufficiently different from assets included in specific categories.

Liabilities
Similar to assets, companies classify liabilities as current or long-term.

Current Liabilities. Current liabilities are the obligations that a company reasonably expects to liquidate either through the use of current assets or the creation of other current liabilities. This concept includes:

1. Payables resulting from the acquisition of goods and services: accounts payable, wages payable, taxes payable, and so on.

2. Collections received in advance for the delivery of goods or performance of services, such as unearned rent revenue or unearned subscriptions revenue.

3. Other liabilities whose liquidation will take place within the operating cycle, such as the portion of long-term bonds to be paid in the current period or short-term obligations arising from the purchase of equipment.

At times, a liability that is payable within the next year is not included in the current liabilities section. This occurs either when the company expects to refinance the debt through another long-term issue [3] or to retire the debt out of noncurrent assets. This approach is used because liquidation does not result from the use of current assets or the creation of other current liabilities.

Companies do not report current liabilities in any consistent order. In general, though, companies most commonly list notes payable, accounts payable, or short-term debt as the first item. Income taxes payable, current maturities of long-term debt, or other current liabilities are commonly listed last. For example, see Halliburton Company's current liabilities section in Illustration 5-13.

Halliburton Company
(in millions)

Current liabilities	
Short-term notes payable	$1,570
Accounts payable	782
Accrued employee compensation and benefits	267
Unearned revenues	386
Income taxes payable	113
Accrued special charges	6
Current maturities of long-term debt	8
Other current liabilities	694
Total current liabilities	3,826

ILLUSTRATION 5-13
Balance Sheet Presentation of Current Liabilities

Current liabilities include such items as trade and nontrade notes and accounts payable, advances received from customers, and current maturities of long-term debt. If the amounts are material, companies classify income taxes and other accrued items separately. A company should fully describe in the notes any information about a secured liability—for example, stock held as collateral on notes payable—to identify the assets providing the security.

The excess of total current assets over total current liabilities is referred to as **working capital** (or sometimes **net working capital**). Working capital represents the net amount of a company's relatively liquid resources. That is, it is the liquidity buffer available to meet the financial demands of the operating cycle.

Companies seldom disclose on the balance sheet an amount for working capital. But bankers and other creditors compute it as an indicator of the short-run liquidity of a company. To determine the actual liquidity and availability of working capital to meet current obligations, however, requires analysis of the composition of the current assets and their nearness to cash.

Before the dot-com bubble burst, concerns about liquidity and solvency led creditors of many dot-com companies to demand more assurances that these companies could pay their bills when due. A key indicator for creditors is the amount of working capital. For example, when a report predicted that Amazon.com's working capital would turn negative, the company's vendors began to explore steps that would ensure that Amazon would pay them.

Some vendors demanded that their dot-com customers sign notes stating that the goods shipped to them would serve as collateral for the transaction. Other vendors began shipping goods on consignment—an arrangement whereby the vendor retains ownership of the goods until a third party buys and pays for them.

Another recent bubble in the real estate market created a working capital and liquidity crisis for no less a revered financial institution than Bear Stearns. What happened? Bear Stearns was one of the biggest investors in mortgage-backed securities. But when the housing market cooled off and the value of the collateral backing Bear Stearns's mortgage securities dropped dramatically, the market began to question Bear Stearns's ability to meet its obligations. The result: The Federal Reserve stepped in to avert a collapse of the company, backing a bailout plan that guaranteed *$30 billion* of Bear Stearns's investments. This paved the way for a buy-out by JPMorgan Chase at $2 per share (later amended to $10 a share)—quite a bargain since Bear Stearns had been trading above $80 a share just a month earlier.

Source: Robin Sidel, Greg Ip, Michael M. Phillips, and Kate Kelly, "The Week That Shook Wall Street: Inside the Demise of Bear Stearns," *Wall Street Journal* (March 18, 2008), p. A1.

Long-Term Liabilities. Long-term liabilities are obligations that a company does not reasonably expect to liquidate within the normal operating cycle. Instead, it expects to pay them at some date beyond that time. The most common examples are bonds payable, notes payable, some deferred income tax amounts, lease obligations, and pension obligations. **Companies classify long-term liabilities that mature within the current operating cycle as current liabilities if payment of the obligation requires the use of current assets.**

Generally, long-term liabilities are of three types:

1. Obligations arising from specific financing situations, such as the issuance of bonds, long-term lease obligations, and long-term notes payable.
2. Obligations arising from the ordinary operations of the company, such as pension obligations and deferred income tax liabilities.
3. Obligations that depend on the occurrence or non-occurrence of one or more future events to confirm the amount payable, the payee, or the date payable, such as service or product warranties and other contingencies.

Companies generally provide a great deal of supplementary disclosure for long-term liabilities because most long-term debt is subject to various covenants and restrictions for the protection of lenders.[8]

It is desirable to report any premium or discount separately as an addition to or subtraction from the bonds payable. Companies frequently describe the terms of all long-term liability agreements (including maturity date or dates, rates of interest, nature of obligation, and any security pledged to support the debt) in notes to the financial statements. Illustration 5-14 provides an example of this, taken from an excerpt from The Great Atlantic & Pacific Tea Company's financials.

[8]Companies usually explain the pertinent rights and privileges of the various securities (both debt and equity) outstanding in the notes to the financial statements. Examples of information that companies should disclose are dividend and liquidation preferences, participation rights, call prices and dates, conversion or exercise prices or rates and pertinent dates, sinking fund requirements, unusual voting rights, and significant terms of contracts to issue additional shares. **[4]**

The Great Atlantic & Pacific Tea Company, Inc.

Total current liabilities	$978,109,000
Long-term debt (See note)	254,312,000
Obligations under capital leases	252,618,000
Deferred income taxes	57,167,000
Other non-current liabilities	127,321,000

Note: Indebtedness. Debt consists of:	
9.5% senior notes, due in annual installments of $10,000,000	$ 40,000,000
Mortgages and other notes due through 2011 (average interest rate of 9.9%)	107,604,000
Bank borrowings at 9.7%	67,225,000
Commercial paper at 9.4%	100,102,000
	314,931,000
Less: Current portion	(60,619,000)
Total long-term debt	$254,312,000

ILLUSTRATION 5-14
Balance Sheet Presentation of Long-Term Debt

Owners' Equity

The **owners' equity** (**stockholders' equity**) section is one of the most difficult sections to prepare and understand. This is due to the complexity of capital stock agreements and the various restrictions on stockholders' equity imposed by state corporation laws, liability agreements, and boards of directors. Companies usually divide the section into six parts:

STOCKHOLDERS' EQUITY SECTION

1. **CAPITAL STOCK.** The par or stated value of the shares issued.
2. **ADDITIONAL PAID-IN CAPITAL.** The excess of amounts paid in over the par or stated value.
3. **RETAINED EARNINGS.** The corporation's undistributed earnings.
4. **ACCUMULATED OTHER COMPREHENSIVE INCOME.** The aggregate amount of the other comprehensive income items.
5. **TREASURY STOCK.** Generally, the amount of ordinary shares repurchased.
6. **NONCONTROLLING INTEREST (MINORITY INTEREST).** A portion of the equity of subsidiaries not wholly owned by the reporting company.

For capital stock, companies must disclose the par value and the authorized, issued, and outstanding share amounts. A company usually presents the additional paid-in capital in one amount although subtotals are informative if the sources of additional capital are varied and material. The retained earnings amount may be divided between the **unappropriated** (the amount that is usually available for dividend distribution) and **restricted** (e.g., by bond indentures or other loan agreements) amounts. In addition, companies show any capital stock reacquired (treasury stock) as a reduction of stockholders' equity. Accumulated other comprehensive income includes such items as unrealized gains and losses on available-for-sale investments and unrealized gains and losses on certain derivative transactions. Noncontrolling interest (discussed in Chapter 4 and sometimes referred to as *minority interest*) is also shown as a separate item (where applicable) as a part of equity.

Illustration 5-15 (page 226) presents an example of the stockholders' equity section from **Las Vegas Sands Corporation**.

The ownership or stockholders' equity accounts in a corporation differ considerably from those in a partnership or proprietorship. Partners show separately their permanent

ILLUSTRATION 5-15
Balance Sheet
Presentation of
Stockholders' Equity

Las Vegas Sands Corporation

Equity

Preferred stock, $0.001 par value, 50,000,000 shares authorized, 3,614,923 shares issued and outstanding	$ 207,356
Common stock, $0.001 par value, 1,000,000,000 shares authorized, 707,507,982 shares issued and outstanding	708
Capital in excess of par value	5,444,705
Accumulated other comprehensive income	129,519
Retained earnings	880,703
Total Las Vegas Sands Corp. stockholders' equity	6,662,991
Noncontrolling interests	1,268,197
Total equity	$7,931,188

capital accounts and the balance in their temporary accounts (drawing accounts). Proprietorships ordinarily use a single capital account that handles all of the owner's equity transactions.

What do the numbers mean? *WARNING SIGNALS*

Analysts use balance sheet information in models designed to predict financial distress. Researcher E. I. Altman pioneered a bankruptcy-prediction model that derives a "Z-score" by combining balance sheet and income measures in the following equation.

$$Z = \frac{\text{Working capital}}{\text{Total assets}} \times 1.2 + \frac{\text{Retained earnings}}{\text{Total assets}} \times 1.4$$
$$+ \frac{\text{EBIT}}{\text{Total assets}} \times 3.3 + \frac{\text{Sales}}{\text{Total assets}} \times 0.99 + \frac{\text{MV equity}}{\text{Total liabilities}} \times 0.6$$

Following extensive testing, Altman found that companies with Z-scores above 3.0 are unlikely to fail. Those with Z-scores below 1.81 are very likely to fail.

Altman developed the original model for publicly held manufacturing companies. He and others have modified the model to apply to companies in various industries, emerging companies, and companies not traded in public markets.

At one time, the use of Z-scores was virtually unheard of among practicing accountants. Today, auditors, management consultants, and courts of law use this measure to help evaluate the overall financial position and trends of a firm. In addition, banks use Z-scores for loan evaluation. While a low score does not guarantee bankruptcy, the model has been proven accurate in many situations.

Source: Adapted from E. I. Altman and E. Hotchkiss, *Corporate Financial Distress and Bankruptcy,* Third Edition (New York: John Wiley and Sons, 2005).

Balance Sheet Format

LEARNING OBJECTIVE **3**

Prepare a classified balance sheet using the report and account formats.

One common arrangement that companies use in presenting a classified balance sheet is the **account form**. It lists assets, by sections, on the left side, and liabilities and stockholders' equity, by sections, on the right side. The main disadvantage is the need for a sufficiently wide space in which to present the items side by side. Often, the account form requires two facing pages.

To avoid this disadvantage, the **report form** lists the sections one above the other, on the same page. See, for example, Illustration 5-16, which lists assets, followed by liabilities and stockholders' equity directly below, on the same page.[9]

[9]*Accounting Trends and Techniques* (New York: AICPA) recently indicates that all of the 500 companies surveyed use either the "report form" (484) or the "account form" (16), sometimes collectively referred to as the "customary form."

SCIENTIFIC PRODUCTS, INC.
BALANCE SHEET
DECEMBER 31, 2014

ILLUSTRATION 5-16
Classified Report Form
Balance Sheet

Underlying Concepts

The presentation of balance sheet information meets the objective of financial reporting—to provide information about entity resources, claims to resources, and changes in them.

Assets

Current assets

Cash		$ 42,485
Investments (available-for-sale)		28,250
Accounts receivable	$165,824	
Less: Allowance for doubtful accounts	1,850	163,974
Notes receivable		23,000
Inventories—at average-cost		489,713
Supplies on hand		9,780
Prepaid expenses		16,252
Total current assets		$ 773,454

Long-term investments

Equity investments		87,500

Property, plant, and equipment

Land—at cost		125,000
Buildings—at cost	975,800	
Less: Accumulated depreciation	341,200	634,600
Total property, plant, and equipment		759,600

Intangible assets

Goodwill		100,000
Total assets		$1,720,554

Liabilities and Stockholders' Equity

Current liabilities

Notes payable to banks		$ 50,000
Accounts payable		197,532
Accrued interest on notes payable		500
Income taxes payable		62,520
Accrued salaries, wages, and other liabilities		9,500
Deposits received from customers		420
Total current liabilities		$ 320,472

Long-term debt

Twenty-year 12% debentures, due January 1, 2022		500,000
Total liabilities		820,472

Stockholders' equity

Paid in on capital stock		
Preferred, 7%, cumulative		
Authorized, issued, and outstanding,		
30,000 shares of $10 par value	$300,000	
Common—		
Authorized, 500,000 shares of		
$1 par value; issued and		
outstanding, 400,000 shares	400,000	
Additional paid-in capital	37,500	$737,500
Retained earnings		153,182
Accumulated other comprehensive income		8,650
Less: Treasury stock		12,750
Equity attributable to Scientific Products, Inc.		886,582
Equity attributable to noncontrolling interest		13,500
Total stockholders' equity		900,082
Total liabilities and stockholders' equity		$1,720,554

Infrequently, companies use other balance sheet formats. For example, companies sometimes deduct current liabilities from current assets to arrive at working capital. Or, they deduct all liabilities from all assets.

STATEMENT OF CASH FLOWS

LEARNING OBJECTIVE 4

Indicate the purpose of the statement of cash flows.

Chapter 2 indicated that an important element of the objective of financial reporting is "assessing the amounts, timing, and uncertainty of cash flows." The three financial statements we have looked at so far—the income statement, the statement of stockholders' equity, and the balance sheet—each present some information about the cash flows of an enterprise during a period. But they do so to a limited extent. For instance, the income statement provides information about resources provided by operations but not exactly cash. The statement of stockholders' equity shows the amount of cash used to pay dividends or purchase treasury stock. Comparative balance sheets might show what assets the company has acquired or disposed of, and what liabilities it has incurred or liquidated.

🔍 **Underlying Concepts**

The statement of cash flows meets the objective of financial reporting—to help assess the amounts, timing, and uncertainty of future cash flows.

Useful as they are, none of these statements presents a detailed summary of all the cash inflows and outflows, or the sources and uses of cash during the period. To fill this need, the FASB requires the statement of cash flows (also called the **cash flow statement**). **[5]**

What do the numbers mean? WATCH THAT CASH FLOW

Investors usually focus on net income measured on an accrual basis. However, information on cash flows can be important for assessing a company's liquidity, financial flexibility, and overall financial performance. The graph below shows **W. T. Grant**'s financial performance over 7 years.

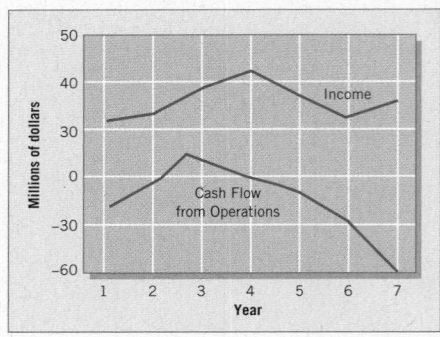

Although W. T. Grant showed consistent profits and even some periods of earnings growth, its cash flow began to "go south" starting in about year 3. The company filed for bankruptcy shortly after year 7. Financial statement readers who studied the company's cash flows would have found early warnings of its problems. The Grant experience is a classic case, illustrating the importance of cash flows as an early-warning signal of financial problems.

A more recent retailer case is **Target**. Although Target has shown good profits, some are concerned that a bit too much of its sales have been made on credit rather than cash. Why is this a problem? Like W. T. Grant, the earnings of profitable lenders can get battered in future periods if they have to start adding large amounts to their bad-loan reserve to catch up with credit losses. And if losses ramp up on Target-branded credit cards, Target may get hit in this way.

Source: Peter Eavis, "Is Target Corp.'s Credit Too Generous?" *Wall Street Journal* (March 11, 2008), p. C1.

Purpose of the Statement of Cash Flows

The primary purpose of a statement of cash flows is to provide relevant information about the cash receipts and cash payments of an enterprise during a period. To achieve this purpose, the statement of cash flows reports the following: (1) the cash effects of operations during a period, (2) investing transactions, (3) financing transactions, and (4) the net increase or decrease in cash during the period.[10]

---

[10]The FASB recommends the basis as "cash and cash equivalents." **Cash equivalents** are liquid investments that mature within three months or less.

Reporting the sources, uses, and net increase or decrease in cash helps investors, creditors, and others know what is happening to a company's most liquid resource. Because most individuals maintain a checkbook and prepare a tax return on a cash basis, they can comprehend the information reported in the statement of cash flows.

The statement of cash flows provides answers to the following simple but important questions:

1. Where did the cash come from during the period?
2. What was the cash used for during the period?
3. What was the change in the cash balance during the period?

Content and Format of the Statement of Cash Flows

Companies classify cash receipts and cash payments during a period into three different activities in the statement of cash flows—operating, investing, and financing activities, defined as follows.

5 LEARNING OBJECTIVE
Identify the content of the statement of cash flows.

1. **Operating activities** involve the cash effects of transactions that enter into the determination of net income.
2. **Investing activities** include making and collecting loans and acquiring and disposing of investments (both debt and equity) and property, plant, and equipment.
3. **Financing activities** involve liability and owners' equity items. They include (a) obtaining resources from owners and providing them with a return on their investment, and (b) borrowing money from creditors and repaying the amounts borrowed.

Illustration 5-17 shows the basic format of the statement of cash flows.

STATEMENT OF CASH FLOWS	
Cash flows from operating activities	$XXX
Cash flows from investing activities	XXX
Cash flows from financing activities	XXX
Net increase (decrease) in cash	XXX
Cash at beginning of year	XXX
Cash at end of year	$XXX

ILLUSTRATION 5-17
Basic Format of Cash Flow Statement

Illustration 5-18 (page 230) graphs the inflows and outflows of cash classified by activity.

The statement's value is that it helps users evaluate liquidity, solvency, and financial flexibility. As stated earlier, **liquidity** refers to the "nearness to cash" of assets and liabilities. **Solvency** is the firm's ability to pay its debts as they mature. **Financial flexibility** is a company's ability to respond and adapt to financial adversity and unexpected needs and opportunities.

We have devoted Chapter 23 entirely to the detailed preparation and content of the statement of cash flows. The intervening chapters will cover several elements and complex topics that affect the content of a typical statement of cash flows. The presentation in this chapter is introductory—a reminder of the existence of the statement of cash flows and its usefulness.

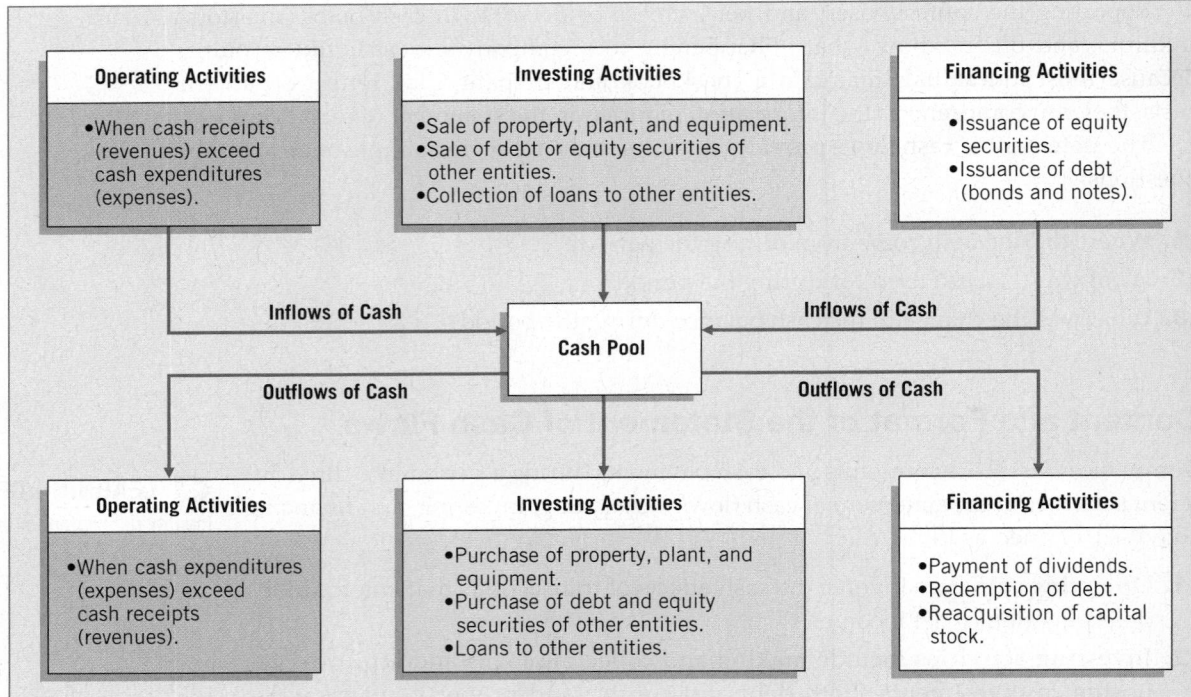

ILLUSTRATION 5-18
Cash Inflows and
Outflows

Overview of the Preparation of the Statement of Cash Flows

Sources of Information

LEARNING OBJECTIVE **6**
Prepare a basic statement of cash flows.

Companies obtain the information to prepare the statement of cash flows from several sources: (1) comparative balance sheets, (2) the current income statement, and (3) selected transaction data.

The following simple example demonstrates how companies use these sources in preparing a statement of cash flows.

On January 1, 2014, in its first year of operations, Telemarketing Inc. issued 50,000 shares of $1 par value common stock for $50,000 cash. The company rented its office space, furniture, and telecommunications equipment and performed marketing services throughout the first year. In June 2014, the company purchased land for $15,000. Illustration 5-19 shows the company's comparative balance sheets at the beginning and end of 2014.

ILLUSTRATION 5-19
Comparative Balance
Sheets

TELEMARKETING INC. BALANCE SHEETS			
	Dec. 31, 2014	Jan. 1, 2014	Increase/Decrease
Assets			
Cash	$31,000	$–0–	$31,000 Increase
Accounts receivable	41,000	–0–	41,000 Increase
Land	15,000	–0–	15,000 Increase
Total	$87,000	$–0–	
Liabilities and Stockholders' Equity			
Accounts payable	$12,000	$–0–	12,000 Increase
Common stock	50,000	–0–	50,000 Increase
Retained earnings	25,000	–0–	25,000 Increase
Total	$87,000	$–0–	

llustration 5-20 presents the income statement and additional information.

TELEMARKETING INC.	
INCOME STATEMENT	
FOR THE YEAR ENDED DECEMBER 31, 2014	
Revenues	$172,000
Operating expenses	120,000
Income before income tax	52,000
Income tax	13,000
Net income	$ 39,000

Additional information:
Dividends of $14,000 were paid during the year.

ILLUSTRATION 5-20
Income Statement Data

Preparing the Statement of Cash Flows

Preparing the statement of cash flows from these sources involves four steps:

1. Determine the net cash provided by (or used in) operating activities.
2. Determine the net cash provided by (or used in) investing and financing activities.
3. Determine the change (increase or decrease) in cash during the period.
4. Reconcile the change in cash with the beginning and the ending cash balances.

Net cash provided by operating activities is the excess of cash receipts over cash payments from operating activities. Companies determine this amount by converting net income on an accrual basis to a cash basis. To do so, they add to or deduct from net income those items in the income statement that do not affect cash. This procedure requires that a company analyze not only the current year's income statement but also the comparative balance sheets and selected transaction data.

Analysis of Telemarketing's comparative balance sheets reveals two items that will affect the computation of net cash provided by operating activities:

1. The increase in accounts receivable reflects a noncash increase of $41,000 in revenues.
2. The increase in accounts payable reflects a noncash increase of $12,000 in expenses.

Therefore, to arrive at net cash provided by operating activities, Telemarketing Inc. deducts from net income the increase in accounts receivable ($41,000), and it adds back to net income the increase in accounts payable ($12,000). As a result of these adjustments, the company determines net cash provided by operating activities to be $10,000, computed as shown in Illustration 5-21.

Net income		$39,000
Adjustments to reconcile net income		
to net cash provided by operating activities:		
Increase in accounts receivable	$(41,000)	
Increase in accounts payable	12,000	(29,000)
Net cash provided by operating activities		$10,000

ILLUSTRATION 5-21
Computation of Net
Cash Provided by
Operating Activities

Next, the company determines its investing and financing activities. Telemarketing Inc.'s only **investing activity** was the land purchase. It had two **financing activities**. (1) Common stock increased $50,000 from the issuance of 50,000 shares for cash. (2) The company paid $14,000 cash in dividends. Knowing the amounts provided/used by operating, investing, and financing activities, the company determines the **net increase in cash**. Illustration 5-22 (page 232) presents Telemarketing Inc.'s statement of cash flows for 2014.

International Perspective

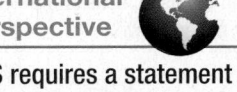

IFRS requires a statement of cash flows. Both IFRS and GAAP specify that the cash flows must be classified as operating, investing, or financing.

ILLUSTRATION 5-22
Statement of Cash Flows

TELEMARKETING INC. STATEMENT OF CASH FLOWS FOR THE YEAR ENDED DECEMBER 31, 2014		
Cash flows from operating activities		
Net income		$39,000
Adjustments to reconcile net income to net cash provided by operating activities:		
Increase in accounts receivable	$(41,000)	
Increase in accounts payable	12,000	(29,000)
Net cash provided by operating activities		10,000
Cash flows from investing activities		
Purchase of land	(15,000)	
Net cash used by investing activities		(15,000)
Cash flows from financing activities		
Issuance of common stock	50,000	
Payment of cash dividends	(14,000)	
Net cash provided by financing activities		36,000
Net increase in cash		31,000
Cash at beginning of year		–0–
Cash at end of year		$31,000

The increase in cash of $31,000 reported in the statement of cash flows **agrees with** the increase of $31,000 in cash calculated from the comparative balance sheets.

Significant Noncash Activities

Not all of a company's significant activities involve cash. Examples of significant noncash activities are:

1. Issuance of common stock to purchase assets.

2. Conversion of bonds into common stock.

3. Issuance of debt to purchase assets.

4. Exchanges of long-lived assets.

Significant financing and investing activities that do not affect cash are not reported in the body of the statement of cash flows. Rather, these activities are reported in either a separate schedule at the bottom of the statement of cash flows or in separate notes to the financial statements. Such reporting of these noncash activities satisfies the full disclosure principle.

Illustration 5-23 shows an example of a comprehensive statement of cash flows. Note that the company purchased equipment through the issuance of $50,000 of bonds, which is a significant noncash transaction. *In solving homework assignments, you should present significant noncash activities in a separate schedule at the bottom of the statement of cash flows.*

Usefulness of the Statement of Cash Flows

LEARNING OBJECTIVE 7
Understand the usefulness of the statement of cash flows.

"Happiness is a positive cash flow" is certainly true. Although net income provides a long-term measure of a company's success or failure, cash is its lifeblood. Without cash, a company will not survive. For small and newly developing companies, cash flow is the single most important element for survival. Even medium and large companies must control cash flow.

Creditors examine the cash flow statement carefully because they are concerned about being paid. They begin their examination by finding net cash provided by operating activities. A high amount indicates that a company is able to generate sufficient cash from

ILLUSTRATION 5-23
Comprehensive
Statement of Cash Flows

NESTOR COMPANY
STATEMENT OF CASH FLOWS
FOR THE YEAR ENDED DECEMBER 31, 2014

Cash flows from operating activities		
Net income		$320,750
Adjustments to reconcile net income to net cash provided by operating activities:		
Depreciation expense	$ 88,400	
Amortization of intangibles	16,300	
Gain on sale of plant assets	(8,700)	
Increase in accounts receivable (net)	(11,000)	
Decrease in inventory	15,500	
Decrease in accounts payable	(9,500)	91,000
Net cash provided by operating activities		411,750
Cash flows from investing activities		
Sale of plant assets	90,500	
Purchase of equipment	(182,500)	
Purchase of land	(70,000)	
Net cash used by investing activities		(162,000)
Cash flows from financing activities		
Payment of cash dividend	(19,800)	
Issuance of common stock	100,000	
Redemption of bonds	(50,000)	
Net cash provided by financing activities		30,200
Net increase in cash		279,950
Cash at beginning of year		135,000
Cash at end of year		$414,950
Noncash investing and financing activities		
Purchase of equipment through issuance of $50,000 of bonds		

operations to pay its bills without further borrowing. Conversely, a low or negative amount of net cash provided by operating activities indicates that a company may have to borrow or issue equity securities to acquire sufficient cash to pay its bills. Consequently, creditors look for answers to the following questions in the company's cash flow statements.

1. How successful is the company in generating net cash provided by operating activities?
2. What are the trends in net cash flow provided by operating activities over time?
3. What are the major reasons for the positive or negative net cash provided by operating activities?

You should recognize that companies can fail even though they report net income. The difference between net income and net cash provided by operating activities can be substantial. Companies such as W. T. Grant Company and Prime Motor Inn, for example, reported high net income numbers but negative net cash provided by operating activities. Eventually, both companies filed for bankruptcy.

In addition, substantial increases in receivables and/or inventory can explain the difference between positive net income and negative net cash provided by operating activities. For example, in its first year of operations, Hu Inc. reported a net income of $80,000. Its net cash provided by operating activities, however, was a negative $95,000, as shown in Illustration 5-24 (page 234).

Hu could easily experience a "cash crunch" because it has its cash tied up in receivables and inventory. If Hu encounters problems in collecting receivables, or if inventory moves slowly or becomes obsolete, its creditors may have difficulty collecting on their loans.

ILLUSTRATION 5-24
Negative Net Cash
Provided by Operating
Activities

HU INC.		
NET CASH FLOW FROM OPERATING ACTIVITIES		
Cash flows from operating activities		
Net income		$ 80,000
Adjustments to reconcile net income to net cash provided by		
operating activities:		
Increase in receivables	$ (75,000)	
Increase in inventories	(100,000)	(175,000)
Net cash provided by operating activities		$(95,000)

Financial Liquidity

Readers of financial statements often assess liquidity by using the **current cash debt coverage**. It indicates whether the company can pay off its current liabilities from its operations in a given year. Illustration 5-25 shows the formula for this ratio.

ILLUSTRATION 5-25
Formula for Current
Cash Debt Coverage

$$\frac{\text{Net Cash Provided by Operating Activities}}{\text{Average Current Liabilities}} = \text{Current Cash Debt Coverage}$$

The higher the current cash debt coverage, the less likely a company will have liquidity problems. For example, a ratio near 1:1 is good. It indicates that the company can meet all of its current obligations from internally generated cash flow.

Financial Flexibility

The **cash debt coverage** provides information on financial flexibility. It indicates a company's ability to repay its liabilities from net cash provided by operating activities, without having to liquidate the assets employed in its operations. Illustration 5-26 shows the formula for this ratio. Notice its similarity to the current cash debt coverage. However, because it uses average total liabilities in place of average current liabilities, it takes a somewhat longer-range view.

ILLUSTRATION 5-26
Formula for Cash Debt
Coverage

$$\frac{\text{Net Cash Provided by Operating Activities}}{\text{Average Total Liabilities}} = \text{Cash Debt Coverage}$$

The higher this ratio, the less likely the company will experience difficulty in meeting its obligations as they come due. It signals whether the company can pay its debts and survive if external sources of funds become limited or too expensive.

Free Cash Flow

A more sophisticated way to examine a company's financial flexibility is to develop a free cash flow analysis. **Free cash flow** is the amount of discretionary cash flow a company has. It can use this cash flow to purchase additional investments, retire its debt, purchase treasury stock, or simply add to its liquidity. Financial statement users calculate free cash flow as shown in Illustration 5-27.

ILLUSTRATION 5-27
Formula for Free Cash
Flow

$$\text{Net Cash Provided by Operating Activities} - \text{Capital Expenditures} - \text{Dividends} = \text{Free Cash Flow}$$

In a free cash flow analysis, we first deduct capital spending, to indicate it is the least discretionary expenditure a company generally makes. (Without continued efforts to maintain and expand facilities, it is unlikely that a company can continue to maintain its competitive position.) We then deduct dividends. Although a company *can* cut its dividend, it usually will do so only in **a financial emergency**. The amount resulting after these deductions is the company's free cash flow. Obviously, the greater the amount of free cash flow, the greater the company's financial flexibility.

Questions that a free cash flow analysis answers are:

1. Is the company able to pay its dividends without resorting to external financing?

2. If business operations decline, will the company be able to maintain its needed capital investment?

3. What is the amount of discretionary cash flow that can be used for additional investment, retirement of debt, purchase of treasury stock, or addition to liquidity?

Illustration 5-28 is a free cash flow analysis using the cash flow statement for Nestor Company (shown in Illustration 5-23 on page 233).

NESTOR COMPANY	
FREE CASH FLOW ANALYSIS	
Net cash provided by operating activities	$411,750
Less: Capital expenditures	252,500
Dividends	19,800
Free cash flow	$139,450

ILLUSTRATION 5-28
Free Cash Flow
Computation

This computation shows that Nestor has a positive, and substantial, net cash provided by operating activities of $411,750. Nestor's statement of cash flows reports that the company purchased equipment of $182,500 and land of $70,000 for total capital spending of $252,500. Nestor has more than sufficient cash flow to meet its dividend payment and therefore has satisfactory financial flexibility.

As you can see from looking back at Illustration 5-23 (page 233), Nestor used its free cash flow to redeem bonds and add to its liquidity. If it finds additional investments that are profitable, it can increase its spending without putting its dividend or basic capital spending in jeopardy. Companies that have strong financial flexibility can take advantage of profitable investments even in tough times. In addition, strong financial flexibility frees companies from worry about survival in poor economic times. In fact, those with strong financial flexibility often fare better in a poor economy because they can take advantage of opportunities that other companies cannot.

What do the numbers mean?   *"THERE OUGHT TO BE A LAW"*

As one manager noted, "There ought to be a law that before you can buy a stock, you must be able to read a balance sheet." We agree, and the same can be said for a statement of cash flows.

Krispy Kreme Doughnuts provides an example of how stunning earnings growth can hide real problems. Not long ago, the doughnut maker was a glamour stock with a 50 percent earnings per share growth rate and a price-earnings ratio around 70. Seven months later, its stock price had dropped 72 percent. What happened? Stockholders alleged that Krispy Kreme may have been inflating its revenues and not taking enough bad debt expense (which inflated both assets and income). In addition, Krispy Kreme's operating cash flow was negative. Most financially sound companies generate positive cash flow.

On the next page are additional examples of how one rating agency rated the earnings quality of some companies, using some key balance sheet and statement of cash flow measurements.

Earnings-Quality Winners	Company	Earnings-Quality Indicators	Earnings-Quality Losers	Company	Earnings-Quality Indicators
	Avon Products	Strong cash flow		Ford Motor	High debt and underfunded pension plan
	Capital One Financial	Conservatively capitalized		Kroger	High goodwill and debt
	Ecolab	Good management of working capital		Ryder System	Negative free cash flow
	Timberland	Minimal off-balance-sheet commitments		Teco Energy	Selling assets to meet liquidity needs

Another rating organization uses a metric to adjust for shortcomings in amounts reported in the balance sheet. Just as improving balance sheet and cash flow information is a leading indicator of improved earnings, a deteriorating balance sheet and statement of cash flows warn of earnings declines (and falling stock prices). This was the case at **Avon**; its strong cash flow rating subsequently declined, such that its free cash flow was just 76 percent of net income. This raised red flags about the results on foreign investments by Avon.

Sources: Adapted from Gretchen Morgenson, "How Did They Value Stocks? Count the Absurd Ways," *New York Times on the Web* (March 18, 2001); K. Badanhausen, J. Gage, C. Hall, and M. Ozanian, "Beyond Balance Sheet: Earnings Quality," *Forbes.com* (January 28, 2005); and H. Karp, "Avon's Investments Fall Short," *Wall Street Journal* (December 8, 2011).

ADDITIONAL INFORMATION

LEARNING OBJECTIVE 8

Determine which balance sheet information requires supplemental disclosure.

In both Chapter 4 and this chapter, we have discussed the primary financial statements that all companies prepare in accordance with GAAP. However, the primary financial statements cannot provide the complete picture related to the financial position and financial performance of the company. Additional descriptive information in supplemental disclosures and certain techniques of disclosure expand on and amplify the items presented in the main body of the statements.

Supplemental Disclosures

The balance sheet is not complete if a company simply lists the assets, liabilities, and owners' equity accounts. It still needs to provide important supplemental information. This may be information not presented elsewhere in the statement, or it may elaborate on items in the balance sheet. The four types of information that are usually supplemental to account titles and amounts presented in the balance sheet are as follows.

SUPPLEMENTAL BALANCE SHEET INFORMATION

1. **CONTINGENCIES.** Material events that have an uncertain outcome.
2. **ACCOUNTING POLICIES.** Explanations of the valuation methods used or the basic assumptions made concerning inventory valuations, depreciation methods, investments in subsidiaries, etc.
3. **CONTRACTUAL SITUATIONS.** Explanations of certain restrictions or covenants attached to specific assets or, more likely, to liabilities.
4. **FAIR VALUES.** Disclosures of fair values, particularly for financial instruments.

Contingencies

A **contingency** is an existing situation involving uncertainty as to possible gain (gain contingency) or loss (loss contingency) that will ultimately be resolved when one or more future events occur or fail to occur. In short, contingencies are material events with an uncertain future. Examples of gain contingencies are tax operating-loss carryforwards or company litigation against another party. Typical loss contingencies relate to litigation, environmental issues, possible tax assessments, or government investigations. We examine the accounting and reporting requirements involving contingencies more fully in Chapter 13.

Accounting Policies

GAAP recommends disclosure for all significant accounting principles and methods that involve selection from among alternatives or those that are peculiar to a given industry. **[6]** For instance, companies can compute inventories under several cost flow assumptions (e.g., LIFO and FIFO), depreciate plant and equipment under several accepted methods (e.g., double-declining-balance and straight-line), and carry investments at different valuations (e.g., cost, equity, and fair value). Sophisticated users of financial statements know of these possibilities and examine the statements closely to determine the methods used.

Companies must also disclose information about the nature of their operations, the use of estimates in preparing financial statements, certain significant estimates, and vulnerabilities due to certain concentrations. **[7]** Illustration 5-29 shows an example of such a disclosure.

Chesapeake Corporation

Risks and Uncertainties. Chesapeake operates in three business segments which offer a diversity of products over a broad geographic base. The Company is not dependent on any single customer, group of customers, market, geographic area or supplier of materials, labor or services. Financial statements include, where necessary, amounts based on the judgments and estimates of management. These estimates include allowances for bad debts, accruals for landfill closing costs, environmental remediation costs, loss contingencies for litigation, self-insured medical and workers' compensation insurance and determinations of discount and other rate assumptions for pensions and postretirement benefit expenses.

ILLUSTRATION 5-29
Balance Sheet Disclosure of Significant Risks and Uncertainties

Disclosure of significant accounting principles and methods and of risks and uncertainties is particularly useful if given in a separate **Summary of Significant Accounting Policies** preceding the notes to the financial statements or as the initial note.

Contractual Situations

Companies should disclose contractual situations, if significant, in the notes to the financial statements. For example, they must clearly state the essential provisions of lease contracts, pension obligations, and stock option plans in the notes. Analysts want to know not only the amount of the liabilities but also how the different contractual provisions affect the company at present and in the future.

Companies must disclose the following commitments if the amounts are material: commitments related to obligations to maintain working capital, to limit the payment of dividends, to restrict the use of assets, and to require the maintenance of certain financial ratios. Management must exercise considerable judgment to determine whether omission of such information is misleading. The rule in this situation is, "When in doubt, disclose." It is better to disclose a little too much information than not enough.

Many of the recent accounting scandals related to the nondisclosure of significant contractual obligations. In response, the SEC has mandated that companies disclose contractual obligations in a tabular summary in the management discussion and analysis section of the company's annual report.

Presented below, as an example, is a disclosure from The Procter & Gamble Company.

Contractual Commitments, as of June 30, 2011 (in millions of dollars)

	Total	Less Than 1 Year	1–3 Years	3–5 Years	After 5 Years
Recorded Liabilities					
Total debt	$31,494	$ 9,933	$ 5,959	$5,095	$10,507
Capital leases	407	46	89	75	197
Uncertain tax positions (1)	77	77	—	—	—
Other					
Interest payments relating to long-term debt	9,897	1,002	1,744	1,313	5,838
Operating leases (2)	1,499	264	416	314	505
Minimum pension funding (3)	1,070	391	679	—	—
Purchase obligations (4)	3,012	1,351	1,130	258	273
Total contractual commitments	$47,456	$13,064	$10,017	$7,055	$17,320

(1)As of June 30, 2011, the Company's Consolidated Balance Sheet reflects a liability for uncertain tax positions of $2.4 billion, including $555 million of interest and penalties. Due to the high degree of uncertainty regarding the timing of future cash outflows of liabilities for uncertain tax positions beyond one year, a reasonable estimate of the period of cash settlement beyond twelve months from the balance sheet date of June 30, 2011 cannot be made.
(2)Operating lease obligations are shown net of guaranteed sublease income.
(3)Represents future pension payments to comply with local funding requirements. The projected payments beyond fiscal year 2014 are not currently determinable.
(4)Primarily reflects future contractual payments under various take-or-pay arrangements entered into as part of the normal course of business.

Fair Values

As we have discussed, fair value information may be more useful than historical cost for certain types of assets and liabilities. This is particularly so in the case of financial instruments. **Financial instruments** are defined as cash, an ownership interest, or a contractual right to receive or obligation to deliver cash or another financial instrument. Such contractual rights to receive cash or other financial instruments are assets. Contractual obligations to pay are liabilities. Cash, investments, accounts receivable, and payables are examples of financial instruments.

Given the expanded use of fair value measurements, as discussed in Chapter 2, GAAP also has expanded disclosures about fair value measurements. [8] To increase consistency and comparability in the use of fair value measures, companies follow a fair value hierarchy that provides insight into how to determine fair value. The hierarchy has three levels. **Level 1** measures (the least subjective) are based on observable inputs, such as market prices for identical assets or liabilities. **Level 2** measures (more subjective) are based on market-based inputs other than those included in Level 1, such as those based on market prices for similar assets or liabilities. **Level 3** measures (most subjective) are based on unobservable inputs, such as a company's own data or assumptions.[11]

For major groups of assets and liabilities, companies must make the following fair value disclosures: (1) the fair value measurement and (2) the fair value hierarchy level of the measurements as a whole, classified by Level 1, 2, or 3. Illustration 5-30 provides a disclosure for Devon Energy for its assets and liabilities measured at fair value.

[11]Level 3 fair value measurements may be developed using expected cash flow and present value techniques, as described in "Using Cash Flow Information and Present Value in Accounting," *Statement of Financial Accounting Concepts No. 7*, as discussed in Chapter 6.

Devon Energy Corporation

Note 7: Fair Value Measurements (in part). Certain of Devon's assets and liabilities are reported at fair value in the accompanying balance sheets. The following table provides fair value measurement information for such assets and liabilities.

	Total Fair Value	Quoted Prices in Active Markets (Level 1)	Significant Other Observable Inputs (Level 2)	Significant Unobservable Inputs (Level 3)
		(In millions)		
Assets:				
Short-term investments	$ 341	$ 341	$ —	$ —
Investment in Chevron common stock	1,327	1,327	—	—
Financial instruments	8	—	8	—
Liabilities:				
Financial instruments	497	—	497	—
Asset retirement obligation (ARO)	1,300	—	—	1,300

Fair Value Measurements Using:

GAAP establishes a fair value hierarchy that prioritizes the inputs to valuation techniques used to measure fair value. As presented in the table above, this hierarchy consists of three broad levels. Level 1 inputs on the hierarchy consist of unadjusted quoted prices in active markets for identical assets and liabilities and have the highest priority. Level 3 inputs have the lowest priority. Devon uses appropriate valuation techniques based on the available inputs to measure the fair values of its assets and liabilities. When available, Devon measures fair value using Level 1 inputs because they generally provide the most reliable evidence of fair value.

ILLUSTRATION 5-30
Disclosure of Fair Values

In addition, companies must provide significant additional disclosure related to Level 3 measurements. The disclosures related to Level 3 are substantial and must identify what assumptions the company used to generate the fair value numbers and any related income effects. Companies will want to use Level 1 and 2 measurements as much as possible. In most cases, these valuations should be very reliable, as the fair value measurements are based on market information. In contrast, a company that uses Level 3 measurements extensively must be carefully evaluated to understand the impact these valuations have on the financial statements.

Techniques of Disclosure

Companies should disclose as completely as possible the effect of various contingencies on financial condition, the methods of valuing assets and liabilities, and the company's contracts and agreements. To disclose this pertinent information, companies may use parenthetical explanations, notes, cross-reference and contra items, and supporting schedules.

9 LEARNING OBJECTIVE
Describe the major disclosure techniques for the balance sheet.

Parenthetical Explanations
Companies often provide additional information by parenthetical explanations following the item. For example, Illustration 5-31 shows a parenthetical explanation of the

Ford Motor Company

Stockholders' Equity (in millions)
Common stock, par value $0.01 per share (1,837 million shares issued) $18

ILLUSTRATION 5-31
Parenthetical Disclosure of Shares Issued—Ford Motor Company

Underlying Concepts

The user-specific quality of *understandability* requires accountants to be careful in describing transactions and events.

number of shares issued by Ford Motor Company on the balance sheet under "Stockholders' equity."

This additional pertinent balance sheet information adds clarity and completeness. It has an advantage over a note because it brings the additional information into the **body of the statement** where readers will less likely overlook it. Companies, however, should avoid lengthy parenthetical explanations, which might be distracting.

Notes

Companies use notes if they cannot conveniently show additional explanations as parenthetical explanations. Illustration 5-32 shows how International Paper Company reported its inventory costing methods in its accompanying notes.

ILLUSTRATION 5-32
Note Disclosure

International Paper Company

Note 11

Inventories by major category were (millions):

Raw materials	$ 371
Finished pulp, paper and packaging products	1,796
Finished lumber and panel products	184
Operating supplies	351
Other	16
Total inventories	$2,718

The last-in, first-out inventory method is used to value most of International Paper's U.S. inventories. Approximately 70% of total raw materials and finished products inventories were valued using this method. If the first-in, first-out method had been used, it would have increased total inventories balances by approximately $170 million.

Companies commonly use notes to disclose the following: the existence and amount of any preferred stock dividends in arrears, the terms of or obligations imposed by purchase commitments, special financial arrangements and instruments, depreciation policies, any changes in the application of accounting principles, and the existence of contingencies.

Notes therefore must present all essential facts as completely and succinctly as possible. Careless wording may mislead rather than aid readers. Notes should add to the total information made available in the financial statements, not raise unanswered questions or contradict other portions of the statements. The note disclosures in Illustration 5-33 show the presentation of such information.

ILLUSTRATION 5-33
More Note Disclosures

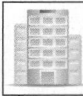

Alberto-Culver Company

Note 3: Long-Term Debt. Various borrowing arrangements impose restrictions on such items as total debt, working capital, dividend payments, treasury stock purchases and interest expense. The company was in compliance with these arrangements and $68 million of consolidated retained earnings was not restricted as to the payment of dividends and purchases of treasury stock.

ILLUSTRATION 5-33
(Continued)

Apple Inc.

Note 7: Commitments and Contingencies.

Other Commitments

As of September 24, 2011, the Company had outstanding off-balance sheet commitments for outsourced manufacturing and component purchases of $13.9 billion. Additionally, other outstanding obligations were $2.4 billion as of September 24, 2011, and were comprised mainly of commitments under long term supply agreements to make additional inventory component prepayments and to acquire capital equipment, commitments to acquire product tooling and manufacturing process equipment, and commitments related to advertising, research and development, Internet and telecommunications services and other obligations.

Underlying Concepts

The FASB recently issued an invitation to comment on disclosure effectiveness, in order to get input on how disclosures in the footnotes can be made more useful.

Willamette Industries, Inc.

Note 4: Property, Plant, and Equipment (partial): The company changed its accounting estimates relating to depreciation. The estimated service lives for most machinery and equipment were extended five years. The change was based upon a study performed by the company's engineering department, comparisons to typical industry practices, and the effect of the company's extensive capital investments which have resulted in a mix of assets with longer productive lives due to technological advances. As a result of the change, net income was increased $51,900, or $0.46 per diluted share.

Cross-Reference and Contra Items

Companies "cross-reference" a direct relationship between an asset and a liability on the balance sheet. For example, as shown in Illustration 5-34, on December 31, 2014, a company might show the following entries—one listed among the current assets, and the other listed among the current liabilities.

ILLUSTRATION 5-34
Cross-Referencing and Contra Items

Current Assets (in part)	
Cash on deposit with sinking fund trustee for redemption of bonds payable—see Current liabilities	$800,000

Current Liabilities (in part)	
Bonds payable to be redeemed in 2015—see Current assets	$2,300,000

This cross-reference points out that the company will redeem $2,300,000 of bonds payable currently, for which it has only set aside $800,000. Therefore, it needs additional cash from unrestricted cash, from sales of investments, from profits, or from some other source. Alternatively, the company can show the same information parenthetically.

Another common procedure is to establish contra or adjunct accounts. A **contra account** on a balance sheet reduces either an asset, liability, or owners' equity account. Examples include Accumulated Depreciation and Discount on Bonds Payable. Contra accounts provide some flexibility in presenting the financial information. With the use of the Accumulated Depreciation account, for example, a reader of the statement can see the original cost of the asset as well as the depreciation to date.

An **adjunct account**, on the other hand, increases either an asset, liability, or owners equity account. An example is Premium on Bonds Payable, which, when added to the Bonds Payable account, describes the total bond liability of the company.

Supporting Schedules

Often a company needs a separate schedule to present more detailed information about certain assets or liabilities, as shown in Illustration 5-35.

ILLUSTRATION 5-35
Disclosure through Use of Supporting Schedules

| Property, plant, and equipment | | | | |
| Land, buildings, equipment, and other fixed assets—net (see Schedule 3) | | | $643,300 | |

SCHEDULE 3
LAND, BUILDINGS, EQUIPMENT, AND OTHER FIXED ASSETS

	Total	Land	Buildings	Equip.	Other Fixed Assets
Balance January 1, 2014	$740,000	$46,000	$358,000	$260,000	$76,000
Additions in 2014	161,200		120,000	38,000	3,200
	901,200	46,000	478,000	298,000	79,200
Assets retired or sold in 2014	31,700			27,000	4,700
Balance December 31, 2014	869,500	46,000	478,000	271,000	74,500
Depreciation taken to January 1, 2014	196,000		102,000	78,000	16,000
Depreciation taken in 2014	56,000		28,000	24,000	4,000
	252,000		130,000	102,000	20,000
Depreciation on assets retired in 2014	25,800			22,000	3,800
Depreciation accumulated December 31, 2014	226,200		130,000	80,000	16,200
Book value of assets	$643,300	$46,000	$348,000	$191,000	$58,300

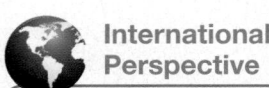

International Perspective

Internationally, accounting terminology is a problem. Confusion arises even between nations that share a language. For example, U.S. investors normally think of "stock" as "equity" or "ownership." To the British, "stocks" means inventory. In the United States, "fixed assets" generally refers to "property, plant, and equipment." In Britain, the category includes more items.

Terminology

The account titles in the general ledger do not necessarily represent the best terminology for balance sheet purposes. Companies often use brief account titles and include technical terms that only accountants understand. But many persons unacquainted with accounting terminology examine balance sheets. Thus, balance sheets should contain descriptions that readers will generally understand and clearly interpret.

For example, companies have used the term "reserve" in differing ways: to describe amounts deducted from assets (contra accounts such as accumulated depreciation and allowance for doubtful accounts), as a part of the title of contingent or estimated liabilities, and to describe an appropriation of retained earnings. Because of the different meanings attached to this term, misinterpretation often resulted from its use. Therefore, the profession has recommended that companies use the word **reserve** only to describe an appropriation of retained earnings. The use of the term in this narrower sense—to describe appropriated retained earnings—has resulted in a better understanding of its significance when it appears in a balance sheet. However, the term "appropriated" appears more logical, and we encourage its use.

For years, the profession has recommended that the use of the word **surplus** be discontinued in balance sheet presentations of stockholders' equity. The use of the terms *capital surplus, paid-in surplus,* and *earned surplus* is confusing. Although condemned by the profession, these terms appear all too frequently in current financial statements.

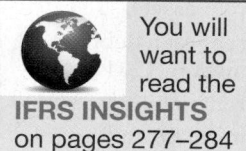

You will want to read the **IFRS INSIGHTS** on pages 277–284 for discussion of IFRS related to the balance sheet and statement of cash flows.

Evolving Issue — BALANCE SHEET REPORTING: GROSS OR NET?

In addition to the issue of financial statement presentation discussed in the opening story, a second area of controversy for balance sheet reporting is the issue of offsetting (or netting) of assets and liabilities. It is generally accepted that offsetting of recognized assets and recognized liabilities detracts from the ability of users both to understand the transactions and conditions that have occurred and to assess the company's future cash flows. In other words, providing information on assets, liabilities, and stockholders' equity helps users to compute rates of return and evaluate capital structure. However, netting assets and liabilities limits a user's ability to assess the future economic benefits and obligations. That is, offsetting hides the existence of assets and liabilities, making it difficult to evaluate liquidity, solvency, and financial flexibility. As a result, GAAP does not permit the reporting of summary accounts alone (e.g., total assets, net assets, and total liabilities).

Recently, the IASB and FASB have worked to develop common criteria for offsetting on the balance sheet. Current offsetting rules under IFRS are more restrictive than GAAP. The rules proposed would allow offsetting only in rare circumstances (e.g., when right of offset is legally enforceable).

Implementation of these new rules in the United States would result in a dramatic "grossing up" of balance sheets (particularly for financial institutions). For example, one study estimated that the new rules would gross up U.S. banks' balance sheets by $900 billion (or an average of 68%, ranging from a 31.4% increase for Citigroup to 104.7% for Morgan Stanley).* Not surprisingly, the FASB received significant push-back from some of its constituents (particularly financial institutions) to the proposed rules.

As a result, to date the Boards have not been able to agree on a converged standard, thereby stalling this project. However, the Boards have issued converged disclosure requirements. The disclosure rules require companies to disclose both gross information and net information about instruments and transactions that are eligible for offset in the balance sheet. While the Boards have not been able to develop a converged set of criteria for offsetting, the information provided under the new converged disclosure rules should enable users of a company's financial statements to evaluate the effects of netting arrangements on its financial position. In doing so, the new rules support the full disclosure principle.

*See Y. N'Diaye, "S&P: Accounting Rule Could Boost Bank Balance Sheets by Average 68%," *https://mninews.deutsche-boerse.com* (September 22, 2011).

SUMMARY OF LEARNING OBJECTIVES

1 Explain the uses and limitations of a balance sheet. The balance sheet provides information about the nature and amounts of investments in a company's resources, obligations to creditors, and owners' equity. The balance sheet contributes to financial reporting by providing a basis for (1) computing rates of return, (2) evaluating the capital structure of the enterprise, and (3) assessing the liquidity, solvency, and financial flexibility of the enterprise.

KEY TERMS

account form, *226*
adjunct account, *242*
available-for-sale investments, *218*
balance sheet, *214*
cash debt coverage, *234*
contingency, *237*
contra account, *241*

current assets, 217

current cash debt
  coverage, 234

current liabilities, 222

financial flexibility, 214

financial instruments, 238

financing activities, 229

free cash flow, 234

held-to-maturity
  investments, 218

intangible assets, 222

investing activities, 229

liquidity, 214

long-term
  investments, 221

long-term liabilities, 224

operating activities, 229

owners' (stockholders')
  equity, 225

property, plant, and
  equipment, 221

report form, 226

reserve, 242

solvency, 214

statement of cash
  flows, 228

trading investments, 218

working capital, 223

Three limitations of a balance sheet are as follows. (1) The balance sheet does not reflect fair value because accountants use a historical cost basis in valuing and reporting most assets and liabilities. (2) Companies must use judgments and estimates to determine certain amounts, such as the collectibility of receivables and the useful life of long-term tangible and intangible assets. (3) The balance sheet omits many items that are of financial value to the business but cannot be recorded objectively, such as human resources, customer base, and reputation.

2 Identify the major classifications of the balance sheet. The general elements of the balance sheet are assets, liabilities, and equity. The major classifications of assets are current assets; long-term investments; property, plant, and equipment; intangible assets; and other assets. The major classifications of liabilities are current and long-term liabilities. The balance sheet of a corporation generally classifies owners' equity as capital stock, additional paid-in capital, and retained earnings.

3 Prepare a classified balance sheet using the report and account formats. The report form lists liabilities and stockholders' equity directly below assets on the same page. The account form lists assets, by sections, on the left side, and liabilities and stockholders' equity, by sections, on the right side.

4 Indicate the purpose of the statement of cash flows. The primary purpose of a statement of cash flows is to provide relevant information about a company's cash receipts and cash payments during a period. Reporting the sources, uses, and net change in cash enables financial statement readers to know what is happening to a company's most liquid resource.

5 Identify the content of the statement of cash flows. In the statement of cash flows, companies classify the period's cash receipts and cash payments into three different activities. (1) *Operating activities:* Involve the cash effects of transactions that enter into the determination of net income. (2) *Investing activities:* Include making and collecting loans, and acquiring and disposing of investments (both debt and equity) and of property, plant, and equipment. (3) *Financing activities:* Involve liability and owners' equity items. Financing activities include (a) obtaining capital from owners and providing them with a return on their investment, and (b) borrowing money from creditors and repaying the amounts borrowed.

6 Prepare a basic statement of cash flows. The information to prepare the statement of cash flows usually comes from comparative balance sheets, the current income statement, and selected transaction data. Companies follow four steps to prepare the statement of cash flows from these sources. (1) Determine the net cash provided by (or used in) operating activities. (2) Determine the net cash provided by (or used in) investing and financing activities. (3) Determine the change (increase or decrease) in cash during the period. (4) Reconcile the change in cash with the beginning and ending cash balances.

7 Understand the usefulness of the statement of cash flows. Creditors examine the statement of cash flows carefully because they are concerned about being paid. The net cash flow provided by operating activities in relation to the company's liabilities is helpful in making this assessment. Two ratios used in this regard are the current cash debt ratio and the cash debt ratio. In addition, the amount of free cash flow provides creditors and stockholders with a picture of the company's financial flexibility.

8 Determine which balance sheet information requires supplemental disclosure. Four types of information normally are supplemental to account titles and amounts presented in the balance sheet. (1) *Contingencies:* Material events that have an uncertain outcome. (2) *Accounting policies:* Explanations of the valuation methods used or the basic assumptions made concerning inventory valuation, depreciation methods, investments in subsidiaries, etc. (3) *Contractual situations:* Explanations of certain restrictions or covenants attached to specific assets or, more likely, to liabilities. (4) *Fair values:* Disclosures related to fair values, particularly related to financial instruments.

9 **Describe the major disclosure techniques for the balance sheet.** Companies use four methods to disclose pertinent information in the balance sheet. (1) *Parenthetical explanations:* Parenthetical information provides additional information or description following the item. (2) *Notes:* A company uses notes if it cannot conveniently show additional explanations or descriptions as parenthetical explanations. (3) *Cross-reference and contra items:* Companies "cross-reference" a direct relationship between an asset and a liability on the balance sheet. (4) *Supporting schedules:* Often a company uses a separate schedule to present more detailed information than just the single summary item shown in the balance sheet.

APPENDIX 5A	RATIO ANALYSIS—A REFERENCE

USING RATIOS TO ANALYZE PERFORMANCE

Analysts and other interested parties can gather qualitative information from financial statements by examining relationships between items on the statements and identifying trends in these relationships. A useful starting point in developing this information is ratio analysis.

10 **LEARNING OBJECTIVE**
Identify the major types of financial ratios and what they measure.

A **ratio** expresses the mathematical relationship between one quantity and another. **Ratio analysis** expresses the relationship among pieces of selected financial statement data, in a **percentage**, a **rate**, or a simple **proportion**.

To illustrate, IBM Corporation recently had current assets of $46,970 million and current liabilities of $39,798 million. We find the ratio between these two amounts by dividing current assets by current liabilities. The alternative means of expression are:

Percentage: Current assets are 118% of current liabilities.
Rate: Current assets are 1.18 times as great as current liabilities.
Proportion: The relationship of current assets to current liabilities is 1.18:1.

To analyze financial statements, we classify ratios into four types, as follows.

MAJOR TYPES OF RATIOS

LIQUIDITY RATIOS. Measures of the company's short-term ability to pay its maturing obligations.

ACTIVITY RATIOS. Measures of how effectively the company uses its assets.

PROFITABILITY RATIOS. Measures of the degree of success or failure of a given company or division for a given period of time.

COVERAGE RATIOS. Measures of the degree of protection for long-term creditors and investors.

**Gateway to
the Profession**

*Expanded Discussion
of Financial
Statement Analysis*

In Chapter 5, we discussed three measures related to the statement of cash flows (current cash debt coverage, cash debt coverage, and free cash flow). Throughout the remainder of the textbook, we provide ratios to help you understand and interpret the information presented in financial statements. Illustration 5A-1 presents the ratios that we will use throughout the textbook. You should find this chart helpful as you examine these ratios in more detail in the following chapters. An appendix to Chapter 24 further discusses financial statement analysis.

ILLUSTRATION 5A-1
A Summary of Financial Ratios

Ratio	Formula	Purpose or Use
I. Liquidity		
1. Current ratio	$\dfrac{\text{Current assets}}{\text{Current liabilities}}$	Measures short-term debt-paying ability
2. Quick or acid-test ratio	$\dfrac{\text{Cash, short-term investments, and net receivables}}{\text{Current liabilities}}$	Measures immediate short-term liquidity
3. Current cash debt coverage	$\dfrac{\text{Net cash provided by operating activities}}{\text{Average current liabilities}}$	Measures a company's ability to pay off its current liabilities in a given year from its operations
II. Activity		
4. Accounts receivable turnover	$\dfrac{\text{Net sales}}{\text{Average trade receivables (net)}}$	Measures liquidity of receivables
5. Inventory turnover	$\dfrac{\text{Cost of goods sold}}{\text{Average inventory}}$	Measures liquidity of inventory
6. Asset turnover	$\dfrac{\text{Net sales}}{\text{Average total assets}}$	Measures how efficiently assets are used to generate sales
III. Profitability		
7. Profit margin on sales	$\dfrac{\text{Net income}}{\text{Net sales}}$	Measures net income generated by each dollar of sales
8. Return on assets	$\dfrac{\text{Net income}}{\text{Average total assets}}$	Measures overall profitability of assets
9. Return on common stock equity	$\dfrac{\text{Net income minus preferred dividends}}{\text{Average common stockholders' equity}}$	Measures profitability of owners' investment
10. Earnings per share	$\dfrac{\text{Net income minus preferred dividends}}{\text{Weighted-average number of shares outstanding}}$	Measures net income earned on each share of common stock
11. Price-earnings ratio	$\dfrac{\text{Market price of stock}}{\text{Earnings per share}}$	Measures the ratio of the market price per share to earnings per share
12. Payout ratio	$\dfrac{\text{Cash dividends}}{\text{Net income}}$	Measures percentage of earnings distributed in the form of cash dividends
IV. Coverage		
13. Debt to assets	$\dfrac{\text{Total liabilities}}{\text{Total assets}}$	Measures the percentage of total assets provided by creditors
14. Times interest earned	$\dfrac{\text{Income before income taxes and interest expense}}{\text{Interest expense}}$	Measures ability to meet interest payments as they come due
15. Cash debt coverage	$\dfrac{\text{Net cash provided by operating activities}}{\text{Average total liabilities}}$	Measures a company's ability to repay its total liabilities in a given year from its operations
16. Book value per share	$\dfrac{\text{Common stockholders' equity}}{\text{Outstanding shares}}$	Measures the amount each share would receive if the company were liquidated at the amounts reported on the balance sheet
17. Free cash flow	Net cash provided by operating activities − Capital expenditures − Dividends	Measures the amount of discretionary cash flow

SUMMARY OF LEARNING OBJECTIVE FOR APPENDIX 5A

KEY TERMS

activity ratios, *245*
coverage ratios, *245*
liquidity ratios, *245*
profitability ratios, *245*
ratio analysis, *245*

10 **Identify the major types of financial ratios and what they measure.**
Ratios express the mathematical relationship between one quantity and another, expressed as a percentage, a rate, or a proportion. *Liquidity* ratios measure the short-term ability to pay maturing obligations. *Activity* ratios measure the effectiveness of asset usage. *Profitability* ratios measure the success or failure of an enterprise. *Coverage* ratios measure the degree of protection for long-term creditors and investors.

APPENDIX 5B SPECIMEN FINANCIAL STATEMENTS: THE PROCTER & GAMBLE COMPANY

The Procter & Gamble Company (P&G) manufactures and markets a range of consumer products in various countries throughout the world. The company markets over 300 branded products in more than 160 countries. It manages its business in six product segments: Fabric and Home Care, Baby and Family Care, Beauty Care, Health Care, Snacks, and Pet Care and Grooming.

The content and organization of corporate annual reports have become fairly standardized. Excluding the public relations part of the report (pictures, products, etc.), the following are the traditional financial portions of the annual report:

- Letter to the Stockholders
- Financial Highlights
- Management's Discussion and Analysis
- Management Certification of Financial Statements
- Management's Report on Internal Control
- Auditor's Reports
- Financial Statements
- Notes to the Financial Statements
- Supplementary Financial Information (e.g., 10-year financial summary)

The following pages contain excerpts from the president's letter and the financial statements from P&G's 2011 annual report. **The complete P&G annual report can be accessed at the book's companion website, www.wiley.com/college/kieso.** You will see examples of the standard annual report elements by examining the P&G annual report.

We do not expect that you will comprehend P&G's financial statements and the accompanying notes in their entirety at your first reading. But we expect that by the time you complete the material in this textbook, your level of understanding and interpretive ability will have grown enormously.

At this point, we recommend that you go online and take 20 to 30 minutes to scan the annual report, especially the financial statements and notes. Your goal should be to familiarize yourself with the contents and accounting elements. Throughout the following 19 chapters, when you are asked to refer to specific parts of P&G's financial statements, do so! Then, when you have completed reading this textbook, we challenge you to reread P&G's financials to see how much greater and more sophisticated your understanding of them has become.

Letter to Shareholders

Dear Shareholders,

Last year, I described P&G's Purpose-inspired Growth Strategy, which is to touch and improve more consumers' lives in more parts of the world more completely. I told you that we intend to deliver total shareholder return that consistently ranks P&G among the top third of our peers—the best performing consumer products companies in the world. To do this, we must deliver the Company's long-term annual growth goals, which are to:

- **Grow organic sales 1% to 2% faster than market growth in the categories and countries where we compete.**
- **Deliver core earnings per share (core EPS) growth of high single to low double digits.**
- **Generate free cash flow productivity of 90% or greater.**

We made meaningful progress toward these long-term goals for fiscal 2011, despite significant external challenges.

- **Organic sales grew 4%. Organic volume grew 5%.**
- **Core earnings per share grew 8%.**
- **Free cash flow productivity was 84% of net earnings.**

We increased our quarterly dividend by 9%, making this the 121st consecutive year that P&G has paid a dividend and the 55th consecutive year that the dividend has increased.

Over the past 55 years, P&G's dividend has increased at an annual compound average rate of approximately 9.5%. In total, we paid approximately $5.8 billion in dividends in fiscal 2011. We also returned $7.0 billion to shareholders through the repurchase of P&G stock. Based on our current market capitalization, dividends and share repurchase, we provided shareholders with an effective cash yield of nearly 7%, with additional potential for capital appreciation.

This is good performance in a very demanding business and economic environment. It is not yet great performance. I am confident, however, that we will continue to grow our business on the strength of our Purpose-inspired Growth Strategy:

- **We are executing the strategy as planned, with unrelenting focus on innovation.**
- **We are increasing productivity, which frees up resources to invest in innovation.**
- **We continue to strengthen our portfolio of businesses.**
- **We are tackling growth challenges head on.**
- **We have solid, executable plans in place to capture the enormous growth potential that our strategy creates.**

Further, P&G people are inspired and are performing heroically to improve lives, to grow our business, and to create value for our shareholders.

Robert A. McDonald
Chairman of the Board, President and
Chief Executive Officer

Financials

Net Sales ($ billions)

Year	
11	$82.6
10	$78.9
09	$76.7
08	$79.3
07	$72.4

Operating Cash Flow ($ billions)

Year	
11	$13.2
10	$16.1
09	$14.9
08	$15.0
07	$13.4

Diluted Net Earnings (per common share)

Year	
11	$3.93
10	$4.11
09	$4.26
08	$3.64
07	$3.04

Financial Highlights (Unaudited)

Amounts in millions, except per share amounts	2011	2010	2009	2008	2007
Net Sales	$82,559	$78,938	$76,694	$79,257	$72,441
Operating Income	15,818	16,021	15,374	15,979	14,485
Net Earnings	11,797	12,736	13,436	12,075	10,340
Net Earnings Margin from Continuing Operations	14.3%	13.9%	13.9%	14.2%	13.3%
Diluted Net Earnings per Common Share from Continuing Operations	$ 3.93	$ 3.53	$ 3.39	$ 3.40	$ 2.84
Diluted Net Earnings per Common Share	3.93	4.11	4.26	3.64	3.04
Dividends per Common Share	1.97	1.80	1.64	1.45	1.28

Consolidated Statements of Earnings

Amounts in millions except per share amounts; Years ended June 30	2011	2010	2009
NET SALES	$82,559	$78,938	$76,694
Cost of products sold	40,768	37,919	38,690
Selling, general and administrative expense	25,973	24,998	22,630
OPERATING INCOME	15,818	16,021	15,374
Interest expense	831	946	1,358
Other non-operating income/(expense), net	202	(28)	397
EARNINGS FROM CONTINUING OPERATIONS BEFORE INCOME TAXES	15,189	15,047	14,413
Income taxes on continuing operations	3,392	4,101	3,733
NET EARNINGS FROM CONTINUING OPERATIONS	11,797	10,946	10,680
NET EARNINGS FROM DISCONTINUED OPERATIONS	—	1,790	2,756
NET EARNINGS	$11,797	$12,736	$13,436
BASIC NET EARNINGS PER COMMON SHARE:			
Earnings from continuing operations	$ 4.12	$ 3.70	$ 3.55
Earnings from discontinued operations	—	0.62	0.94
BASIC NET EARNINGS PER COMMON SHARE	4.12	4.32	4.49
DILUTED NET EARNINGS PER COMMON SHARE:			
Earnings from continuing operations	3.93	3.53	3.39
Earnings from discontinued operations	—	0.58	0.87
DILUTED NET EARNINGS PER COMMON SHARE	3.93	4.11	4.26
DIVIDENDS PER COMMON SHARE	$ 1.97	$ 1.80	$ 1.64

Consolidated Balance Sheets

Amounts in millions; June 30

Assets	2011	2010
CURRENT ASSETS		
Cash and cash equivalents	$ 2,768	$ 2,879
Accounts receivable	6,275	5,335
INVENTORIES		
Materials and supplies	2,153	1,692
Work in process	717	604
Finished goods	4,509	4,088
Total inventories	7,379	6,384
Deferred income taxes	1,140	990
Prepaid expenses and other current assets	4,408	3,194
TOTAL CURRENT ASSETS	21,970	18,782
PROPERTY, PLANT AND EQUIPMENT		
Buildings	7,753	6,868
Machinery and equipment	32,820	29,294
Land	934	850
Total property, plant and equipment	41,507	37,012
Accumulated depreciation	(20,214)	(17,768)
NET PROPERTY, PLANT AND EQUIPMENT	21,293	19,244
GOODWILL AND OTHER INTANGIBLE ASSETS		
Goodwill	57,562	54,012
Trademarks and other intangible assets, net	32,620	31,636
NET GOODWILL AND OTHER INTANGIBLE ASSETS	90,182	85,648
OTHER NONCURRENT ASSETS	4,909	4,498
TOTAL ASSETS	$138,354	$128,172

Liabilities and Shareholders' Equity	2011	2010
CURRENT LIABILITIES		
Accounts payable	$ 8,022	$ 7,251
Accrued and other liabilities	9,290	8,559
Debt due within one year	9,981	8,472
TOTAL CURRENT LIABILITIES	27,293	24,282
LONG-TERM DEBT	22,033	21,360
DEFERRED INCOME TAXES	11,070	10,902
OTHER NONCURRENT LIABILITIES	9,957	10,189
TOTAL LIABILITIES	70,353	66,733
SHAREHOLDERS' EQUITY		
Convertible Class A preferred stock, stated value $1 per share (600 shares authorized)	1,234	1,277
Non-Voting Class B preferred stock, stated value $1 per share (200 shares authorized)	—	—
Common stock, stated value $1 per share (10,000 shares authorized; shares issued: 2011—4,007.9, 2010—4,007.6)	4,008	4,008
Additional paid-in capital	62,405	61,697
Reserve for ESOP debt retirement	(1,357)	(1,350)
Accumulated other comprehensive income/(loss)	(2,054)	(7,822)
Treasury stock, at cost (shares held: 2011—1,242.2, 2010—1,164.1)	(67,278)	(61,309)
Retained earnings	70,682	64,614
Noncontrolling interest	361	324
TOTAL SHAREHOLDERS' EQUITY	68,001	61,439
TOTAL LIABILITIES AND SHAREHOLDERS' EQUITY	$138,354	$128,172

Consolidated Statements of Shareholders' Equity

Dollars in millions/Shares in thousands	Common Shares Outstanding	Common Stock	Preferred Stock	Additional Paid-In Capital	Reserve for ESOP Debt Retirement	Accumulated Other Comprehensive Income/(loss)	Non-controlling Interest	Treasury Stock	Retained Earnings	Total
BALANCE JUNE 30, 2008	3,032,717	$4,002	$1,366	$60,307	$(1,325)	$ 3,746	$290	$(47,588)	$48,986	$69,784
Net earnings									13,436	13,436
Other comprehensive income:										
Financial statement translation						(6,151)				(6,151)
Hedges and investment securities, net of $452 tax						748				748
Defined benefit retirement plans, net of $879 tax						(1,701)				(1,701)
Total comprehensive income										$ 6,332
Cumulative impact for adoption of new accounting guidance[1]									(84)	(84)
Dividends to shareholders:										
Common									(4,852)	(4,852)
Preferred, net of tax benefits									(192)	(192)
Treasury purchases	(98,862)							(6,370)		(6,370)
Employee plan issuances	16,841	5		804				428		1,237
Preferred stock conversions	4,992		(42)	7				35		—
Shares tendered for Folgers coffee subsidiary	(38,653)							(2,466)		(2,466)
ESOP debt impacts					(15)				15	—
Noncontrolling interest							(7)			(7)
BALANCE JUNE 30, 2009	2,917,035	4,007	1,324	61,118	(1,340)	(3,358)	283	(55,961)	57,309	63,382
Net earnings									12,736	12,736
Other comprehensive income:										
Financial statement translation						(4,194)				(4,194)
Hedges and investment securities, net of $520 tax						867				867
Defined benefit retirement plans, net of $465 tax						(1,137)				(1,137)
Total comprehensive income										$ 8,272
Dividends to shareholders:										
Common									(5,239)	(5,239)
Preferred, net of tax benefits									(219)	(219)
Treasury purchases	(96,759)							(6,004)		(6,004)
Employee plan issuances	17,616	1		574				616		1,191
Preferred stock conversions	5,579		(47)	7				40		—
ESOP debt impacts					(10)				27	17
Noncontrolling interest				(2)			41			39
BALANCE JUNE 30, 2010	2,843,471	4,008	1,277	61,697	(1,350)	(7,822)	324	(61,309)	64,614	61,439
Net earnings									11,797	11,797
Other comprehensive income:										
Financial statement translation						6,493				6,493
Hedges and investment securities, net of $711 tax						(1,178)				(1,178)
Defined benefit retirement plans, net of $302 tax						453				453
Total comprehensive income										$17,565
Dividends to shareholders:										
Common									(5,534)	(5,534)
Preferred, net of tax benefits									(233)	(233)
Treasury purchases	(112,729)							(7,039)		(7,039)
Employee plan issuances	29,729	—		702				1,033		1,735
Preferred stock conversions	5,266		(43)	6				37		—
ESOP debt impacts					(7)				38	31
Noncontrolling interest				—			37			37
BALANCE JUNE 30, 2011	2,765,737	$4,008	$1,234	$62,405	$(1,357)	$(2,054)	$361	$(67,278)	$70,682	$68,001

(1) Cumulative impact of adopting new accounting guidance relates to split-dollar life insurance arrangements.

Consolidated Statements of Cash Flows

Amounts in millions; Years ended June 30	2011	2010	2009
CASH AND CASH EQUIVALENTS, BEGINNING OF YEAR	$ 2,879	$ 4,781	$ 3,313
OPERATING ACTIVITIES			
Net earnings	11,797	12,736	13,436
Depreciation and amortization	2,838	3,108	3,082
Share-based compensation expense	414	453	516
Deferred income taxes	128	36	596
Gain on sale of businesses	(203)	(2,670)	(2,377)
Change in accounts receivable	(426)	(14)	415
Change in inventories	(501)	86	721
Change in accounts payable, accrued and other liabilities	358	2,446	(742)
Change in other operating assets and liabilities	(1,190)	(305)	(758)
Other	16	196	30
TOTAL OPERATING ACTIVITIES	13,231	16,072	14,919
INVESTING ACTIVITIES			
Capital expenditures	(3,306)	(3,067)	(3,238)
Proceeds from asset sales	225	3,068	1,087
Acquisitions, net of cash acquired	(474)	(425)	(368)
Change in investments	73	(173)	166
TOTAL INVESTING ACTIVITIES	(3,482)	(597)	(2,353)
FINANCING ACTIVITIES			
Dividends to shareholders	(5,767)	(5,458)	(5,044)
Change in short-term debt	151	(1,798)	(2,420)
Additions to long-term debt	1,536	3,830	4,926
Reductions of long-term debt	(206)	(8,546)	(2,587)
Treasury stock purchases	(7,039)	(6,004)	(6,370)
Impact of stock options and other	1,302	721	681
TOTAL FINANCING ACTIVITIES	(10,023)	(17,255)	(10,814)
EFFECT OF EXCHANGE RATE CHANGES ON CASH AND CASH EQUIVALENTS	163	(122)	(284)
CHANGE IN CASH AND CASH EQUIVALENTS	(111)	(1,902)	1,468
CASH AND CASH EQUIVALENTS, END OF YEAR	$ 2,768	$ 2,879	$ 4,781
SUPPLEMENTAL DISCLOSURE			
Cash payments for:			
Interest	$ 806	$ 1,184	$ 1,226
Income taxes	2,992	4,175	3,248
Assets acquired through non-cash capital leases	13	20	8
Divestiture of coffee business in exchange for shares of P&G stock	—	—	2,466

DEMONSTRATION PROBLEMS

Demonstration Problem 1: Assume that Sanchez Company has the following accounts at the end of the current year.

1. Common Stock.
2. Discount on Bonds Payable.
3. Treasury Stock (at cost).
4. Notes Payable (short-term).
5. Raw Materials.
6. Preferred Stock Investments (long-term).
7. Unearned Rent Revenue.
8. Work in Process.
9. Copyrights.
10. Buildings.
11. Notes Receivable (short-term).
12. Cash.
13. Salaries and Wages Payable.
14. Accumulated Depreciation—Buildings.
15. Accumulated Other Comprehensive Income.
16. Cash Restricted for Plant Expansion.
16. Land Held for Future Plant Site.
17. Noncontrolling Interest.
18. Allowance for Doubtful Accounts—Accounts Receivable.
19. Retained Earnings.
20. Paid-in Capital in Excess of Par—Common Stock.
21. Unearned Subscriptions Revenue.
22. Receivables—Officers (due in one year).
23. Finished Goods.
24. Accounts Receivable.
25. Bonds Payable (due in 4 years).

Instructions

Prepare a classified balance sheet in good form. (No monetary amounts are necessary.)

Solution to Demonstration Problem 1

SANCHEZ COMPANY
BALANCE SHEET
DECEMBER 31, 20XX

Assets

Current assets

Cash (less cash restricted for plant expansion)		$XXX
Accounts receivable	$XXX	
Less: Allowance for doubtful accounts	XXX	XXX
Notes receivable		XXX
Receivables—officers		XXX
Inventory		
Finished goods	XXX	
Work in process	XXX	
Raw materials	XXX	XXX
Total current assets		$XXX

Long-term investments

Preferred stock investments	XXX	
Land held for future plant site	XXX	
Cash restricted for plant expansion	XXX	
Total long-term investments		XXX

Property, plant, and equipment

Buildings	XXX	
Less: Accumulated depreciation—buildings	XXX	XXX

Intangible assets

Copyrights		XXX
Total assets		$XXX

Liabilities and Stockholders' Equity

Current liabilities

Salaries and wages payable	$XXX	
Notes payable (short-term)	XXX	
Unearned subscriptions revenue	XXX	
Unearned rent revenue	XXX	
Total current liabilities		$XXX

Long-term debt

Bonds payable (due in four years)	XXX	
Discount on bonds payable	(XXX)	XXX
Total liabilities		XXX

Stockholders' equity

Capital stock:		
Common stock	$XXX	
Additional paid-in capital:		
Paid in capital in excess of par—common stock	XXX	
Total paid-in capital		XXX
Retained earnings		XXX
Accumulated other comprehensive income		XXX
Treasury stock (at cost)		(XXX)
Total equity attributable to Sanchez shareholders		XXX
Equity attributable to noncontrolling interest		XXX
Total liabilities and stockholders' equity		$XXX

Demonstration Problem 2: Cassy Corporation's balance sheet at the end of 2013 included the following items.

Current assets	$282,000		Current liabilities	$180,000
Land	36,000		Bonds payable	120,000
Buildings	144,000		Common stock	216,000
Equipment	108,000		Retained earnings	52,800
Accumulated depreciation—buildings	(36,000)		Total	$568,800
Accumulated depreciation—equipment	(13,200)			
Patents	48,000			
Total	$568,800			

The following information is available for 2014.

1. Treasury stock was purchased at a cost of $13,200.
2. Cash dividends of $36,000 were declared and paid.
3. A long-term investment in stock was purchased for $19,200.
4. Current assets other than cash increased by $34,800. Current liabilities increased by $15,600.
5. Depreciation expense was $4,800 on the building and $10,800 on equipment.
6. Net income was $66,000.
7. Bonds payable of $60,000 were issued.
8. An addition to the building was completed at a cost of $32,400.
9. Patent amortization was $3,000.
10. Equipment (cost $24,000 and accumulated depreciation $9,600) was sold for $12,000.

Instructions

(a) Prepare a balance sheet at December 31, 2014.
(b) Prepare a statement of cash flows for 2014.

Solution to Demonstration Problem 2

(a)

CASSY CORPORATION
BALANCE SHEET
DECEMBER 31, 2014

Assets

Current assets ($282,000 + $34,800 + $39,000)			$355,800
Long-term investments			19,200
Property, plant, and equipment			
Land		$ 36,000	
Buildings ($144,000 + $32,400)	$176,400		
Less: Accumulated depreciation—buildings			
($36,000 + $4,800)	40,800	135,600	
Equipment ($108,000 − $24,000)	84,000		
Less: Accumulated depreciation—equipment			
($13,200 − $9,600 + $10,800)	14,400	69,600	
Total			241,200
Intangible assets—patents			
($48,000 − $3,000)			45,000
Total assets			$661,200

Liabilities and Stockholders' Equity

Current liabilities ($180,000 + $15,600)		$195,600
Long-term liabilities		
Bonds payable ($120,000 + $60,000)		180,000
Total liabilities		375,600

Stockholders' equity		
Common stock	$216,000	
Retained earnings ($52,800 + $66,000 − $36,000)	82,800	
Total	298,800	
Less: Cost of treasury stock	(13,200)	
Total stockholders' equity		285,600
Total liabilities and stockholders' equity		$661,200

Notes: The amount determined for current assets is computed last and is a "plug" figure. That is, total liabilities and stockholders' equity is computed because information is available to determine this amount. Because the total assets amount is the same as the total liabilities and stockholders' equity amount, the amount of total assets is determined. Information is available to compute all the asset amounts except current assets. Therefore, current assets can be determined by deducting the total of all the other asset balances from the total asset balance (i.e., $661,200 − $45,000 − $241,200 − $19,200).

(b)

CASSY CORPORATION
STATEMENT OF CASH FLOWS
FOR THE YEAR ENDED DECEMBER 31, 2014

Cash flows from operating activities		
Net income		$66,000
Adjustments to reconcile net income to net cash provided by operating activities:		
Loss on sale of equipment	$ 2,400	
Depreciation expense	15,600	
Patent amortization	3,000	
Increase in current liabilities	15,600	
Increase in current assets (other than cash)	(34,800)	1,800
Net cash provided by operating activities		67,800
Cash flows from investing activities		
Sale of equipment	12,000	
Addition to building	(32,400)	
Investment in stock	(19,200)	
Net cash used by investing activities		(39,600)
Cash flows from financing activities		
Issuance of bonds	60,000	
Payment of dividends	(36,000)	
Purchase of treasury stock	(13,200)	
Net cash provided by financing activities		10,800
Net increase in cash		$39,000

FASB CODIFICATION

FASB Codification References

[1] FASB ASC 320-10-35-1. [Predecessor literature: "Accounting for Certain Investments in Debt and Equity Securities," *Statement of Financial Accounting Standards No. 115* (Norwalk, Conn.: FASB, 1993).]

[2] FASB ASC 825-10-25-1. [Predecessor literature: "The Fair Value Option for Financial Assets and Liabilities, Including an Amendment of FASB Statement No. 115," *Statement of Financial Accounting Standards No. 159* (Norwalk, Conn.: FASB, February 2007).]

[3] FASB ASC 470-10-05-6. [Predecessor literature: "Classification of Short-term Obligations Expected to Be Refinanced," *Statement of Financial Accounting Standards No. 6* (Stamford, Conn.: FASB, 1975).]

[4] FASB ASC 505-10-50. [Predecessor literature: "Disclosure of Information about Capital Structure," *Statement of Financial Accounting Standards No. 129* (Norwalk: FASB, 1997), par. 4).]

[5] FASB ASC 230-10-05. [Predecessor literature: "Statement of Cash Flows," *Statement of Financial Accounting Standards No. 95* (Stamford, Conn.: FASB, 1987).]

[6] FASB ASC 235-10-05. [Predecessor literature: "Disclosure of Accounting Policies," *Opinions of the Accounting Principles Board No. 22* (New York: AICPA, 1972).]

[7] FASB ASC 275-10-05. [Predecessor literature: "Disclosure of Certain Significant Risks and Uncertainties," *Statement of Position 94-6* (New York: AICPA, 1994).]

[8] FASB ASC 820-10-15. [Predecessor literature: "Fair Value Measurement," *Statement of Financial Accounting Standards No. 157* (Norwalk, Conn.: FASB, September 2006).]

Exercises

If your school has a subscription to the FASB Codification, go to *http://aaahq.org/asclogin.cfm* to log in and prepare responses to the following. Provide Codification references for your responses.

CE5-1 Access the Codification glossary ("Master Glossary") to answer the following.

    (a) What is the definition provided for current assets?
    (b) What is the definition of an intangible asset? In what section of the Codification are intangible assets addressed?
    (c) What are cash equivalents?
    (d) What are financing activities?

CE5-2 What guidance does the Codification provide on the classification of current liabilities?

CE5-3 What guidance does the Codification provide concerning the format of accounting disclosures?

CE5-4 What are the objectives related to the statement of cash flows?

An additional Codification case can be found in the Using Your Judgment section, on page 277.

Be sure to check the book's companion website for a Review and Analysis Exercise, with solution.

WileyPLUS

Brief Exercises, Exercises, Problems, and many more learning and assessment tools and resources are available for practice in WileyPLUS.

QUESTIONS

1. How does information from the balance sheet help users of the financial statements?

2. What is meant by solvency? What information in the balance sheet can be used to assess a company's solvency?

3. A recent financial magazine indicated that the airline industry has poor financial flexibility. What is meant by financial flexibility, and why is it important?

4. Discuss at least two situations in which estimates could affect the usefulness of information in the balance sheet.

5. Perez Company reported an increase in inventories in the past year. Discuss the effect of this change on the current ratio (current assets ÷ current liabilities). What does this tell a statement user about Perez Company's liquidity?

6. What is meant by liquidity? Rank the following assets from one to five in order of liquidity.

    (a) Goodwill.

    (b) Inventory.

    (c) Buildings.

    (d) Short-term investments.

    (e) Accounts receivable.

7. What are the major limitations of the balance sheet as a source of information?

8. Discuss at least two items that are important to the value of companies like **Intel** or **IBM** but that are not recorded in their balance sheets. What are some reasons why these items are not recorded in the balance sheet?

9. How does separating current assets from property, plant, and equipment in the balance sheet help analysts?

10. In its December 31, 2014, balance sheet Oakley Corporation reported as an asset, "Net notes and accounts receivable, $7,100,000." What other disclosures are necessary?

11. Should available-for-sale securities always be reported as a current asset? Explain.

12. What is the relationship between current assets and current liabilities?

13. The New York Knicks, Inc. sold 10,000 season tickets at $2,000 each. By December 31, 2014, 16 of the 40 home games had been played. What amount should be reported as a current liability at December 31, 2014?

14. What is working capital? How does working capital relate to the operating cycle?

15. In what section of the balance sheet should the following items appear, and what balance sheet terminology would you use?

(a) Treasury stock (recorded at cost).

(b) Checking account at bank.

(c) Land (held as an investment).

(d) Sinking fund.

(e) Unamortized premium on bonds payable.

(f) Copyrights.

(g) Pension fund assets.

(h) Premium on capital stock.

(i) Long-term investments (pledged against bank loans payable).

16. Where should the following items be shown on the balance sheet, if shown at all?

(a) Allowance for doubtful accounts.

(b) Merchandise held on consignment.

(c) Advances received on sales contract.

(d) Cash surrender value of life insurance.

(e) Land.

(f) Merchandise out on consignment.

(g) Franchises.

(h) Accumulated depreciation of equipment.

(i) Materials in transit—purchased f.o.b. destination.

17. State the generally accepted accounting principle applicable to balance sheet valuation of each of the following assets.

(a) Trade accounts receivable.

(b) Land.

(c) Inventories.

(d) Trading securities (common stock of other companies).

(e) Prepaid expenses.

18. Refer to the definition of assets on page 216. Discuss how a leased building might qualify as an asset of the lessee (tenant) under this definition.

19. Kathleen Battle says, "Retained earnings should be reported as an asset, since it is earnings which are reinvested in the business." How would you respond to Battle?

20. The creditors of Chester Company agree to accept promissory notes for the amount of its indebtedness with a proviso that two-thirds of the annual profits must be applied to their liquidation. How should these notes be reported on the balance sheet of the issuing company? Give a reason for your answer.

21. What is the purpose of a statement of cash flows? How does it differ from a balance sheet and an income statement?

22. The net income for the year for Genesis, Inc. is $750,000, but the statement of cash flows reports that the net cash provided by operating activities is $640,000. What might account for the difference?

23. Net income for the year for Carrie, Inc. was $750,000, but the statement of cash flows reports that net cash provided by operating activities was $860,000. What might account for the difference?

24. Differentiate between operating activities, investing activities, and financing activities.

25. Each of the following items must be considered in preparing a statement of cash flows. Indicate where each item is to be reported in the statement, if at all. Assume that net income is reported as $90,000.

(a) Accounts receivable increased from $34,000 to $39,000 from the beginning to the end of the year.

(b) During the year, 10,000 shares of preferred stock with a par value of $100 per share were issued at $115 per share.

(c) Depreciation expense amounted to $14,000, and bond premium amortization amounted to $5,000.

(d) Land increased from $10,000 to $30,000.

26. Sergey Co. has net cash provided by operating activities of $1,200,000. Its average current liabilities for the period are $1,000,000, and its average total liabilities are $1,500,000. Comment on the company's liquidity and financial flexibility, given this information.

27. Net income for the year for Tanizaki, Inc. was $750,000, but the statement of cash flows reports that net cash provided by operating activities was $860,000. Tanizaki also reported capital expenditures of $75,000 and paid dividends in the amount of $30,000. Compute Tanizaki's free cash flow.

28. What is the purpose of a free cash flow analysis?

29. What are some of the techniques of disclosure for the balance sheet?

30. What is a "Summary of Significant Accounting Policies"?

31. What types of contractual obligations must be disclosed in great detail in the notes to the balance sheet? Why do you think these detailed provisions should be disclosed?

32. What is the profession's recommendation in regard to the use of the term "surplus"? Explain.

BRIEF EXERCISES

3 **BE5-1** Harding Corporation has the following accounts included in its December 31, 2014, trial balance: Accounts Receivable $110,000; Inventory $290,000; Allowance for Doubtful Accounts $8,000; Patents $72,000; Prepaid Insurance $9,500; Accounts Payable $77,000; Cash $30,000. Prepare the current assets section of the balance sheet, listing the accounts in proper sequence.

3 **BE5-2** Koch Corporation's adjusted trial balance contained the following asset accounts at December 31, 2014: Cash $7,000; Land $40,000; Patents $12,500; Accounts Receivable $90,000; Prepaid Insurance $5,200; Inventory $30,000; Allowance for Doubtful Accounts $4,000; Equity Investments (trading) $11,000. Prepare the current assets section of the balance sheet, listing the accounts in proper sequence.

3 **BE5-3** Included in Outkast Company's December 31, 2014, trial balance are the following accounts: Prepaid Rent $5,200; Debt Investments (trading) $56,000; Unearned Fees $17,000; Land (held for investment) $39,000; Notes Receivable (long-term) $42,000. Prepare the long-term investments section of the balance sheet.

3 **BE5-4** Lowell Company's December 31, 2014, trial balance includes the following accounts: Inventory $120,000; Buildings $207,000; Accumulated Depreciation—Equipment $19,000; Equipment $190,000; Land (held for investment) $46,000; Accumulated Depreciation—Buildings $45,000; Land $71,000; Timberland $70,000. Prepare the property, plant, and equipment section of the balance sheet.

3 **BE5-5** Crane Corporation has the following accounts included in its December 31, 2014, trial balance: Equity Investments (trading) $21,000; Goodwill $150,000; Prepaid Insurance $12,000; Patents $220,000; Franchises $130,000. Prepare the intangible assets section of the balance sheet.

3 **BE5-6** Patrick Corporation's adjusted trial balance contained the following asset accounts at December 31, 2014: Prepaid Rent $12,000; Goodwill $50,000; Franchise Fees Receivable $2,000; Franchises $47,000; Patents $33,000; Trademarks $10,000. Prepare the intangible assets section of the balance sheet.

3 **BE5-7** Thomas Corporation's adjusted trial balance contained the following liability accounts at December 31, 2014: Bonds Payable (due in 3 years) $100,000; Accounts Payable $72,000; Notes Payable (due in 90 days) $22,500; Salaries and Wages Payable $4,000; Income Taxes Payable $7,000. Prepare the current liabilities section of the balance sheet.

3 **BE5-8** Included in Adams Company's December 31, 2014, trial balance are the following accounts: Accounts Payable $220,000; Pension Liability $375,000; Discount on Bonds Payable $29,000; Unearned Rent Revenue $41,000; Bonds Payable $400,000; Salaries and Wages Payable $27,000; Interest Payable $12,000; Income Taxes Payable $29,000. Prepare the current liabilities section of the balance sheet.

3 **BE5-9** Use the information presented in BE5-8 for Adams Company to prepare the long-term liabilities section of the balance sheet.

3 **BE5-10** Hawthorn Corporation's adjusted trial balance contained the following accounts at December 31, 2014: Retained Earnings $120,000; Common Stock $750,000; Bonds Payable $100,000; Paid-in Capital in Excess of Par—Common Stock $200,000; Goodwill $55,000; Accumulated Other Comprehensive Loss $150,000; Noncontrolling Interest $35,000. Prepare the stockholders' equity section of the balance sheet.

3 **BE5-11** Stowe Company's December 31, 2014, trial balance includes the following accounts: Investment in Common Stock $70,000; Retained Earnings $114,000; Trademarks $31,000; Preferred Stock $152,000; Common Stock $55,000; Deferred Income Taxes $88,000; Paid-in Capital in Excess of Par—Common Stock $174,000; Noncontrolling Interest $63,000. Prepare the stockholders' equity section of the balance sheet.

6 **BE5-12** Keyser Beverage Company reported the following items in the most recent year.

Net income	$40,000
Dividends paid	5,000
Increase in accounts receivable	10,000
Increase in accounts payable	7,000
Purchase of equipment (capital expenditure)	8,000
Depreciation expense	4,000
Issue of notes payable	20,000

Compute net cash provided by operating activities, the net change in cash during the year, and free cash flow.

6 **BE5-13** Ames Company reported 2014 net income of $151,000. During 2014, accounts receivable increased by $13,000 and accounts payable increased by $9,500. Depreciation expense was $44,000. Prepare the cash flows from operating activities section of the statement of cash flows.

6 **BE5-14** Martinez Corporation engaged in the following cash transactions during 2014.

Sale of land and building	$191,000
Purchase of treasury stock	40,000
Purchase of land	37,000
Payment of cash dividend	95,000
Purchase of equipment	53,000
Issuance of common stock	147,000
Retirement of bonds	100,000

Compute the net cash provided (used) by investing activities.

6 **BE5-15** Use the information presented in BE5-14 for Martinez Corporation to compute the net cash used (provided) by financing activities.

7 **BE5-16** Using the information in BE5-14, determine Martinez's free cash flow, assuming that it reported net cash provided by operating activities of $400,000.

EXERCISES

2 3 **E5-1 (Balance Sheet Classifications)** Presented below are a number of balance sheet accounts of Deep Blue Something, Inc.

(a) Investment in Preferred Stock.
(b) Treasury Stock.
(c) Common Stock.
(d) Dividends Payable.
(e) Accumulated Depreciation—Equipment.
(f) Construction in Process.
(g) Petty Cash.

(h) Interest Payable.
(i) Deficit.
(j) Equity Investments (trading).
(k) Income Taxes Payable.
(l) Unearned Subscriptions Revenue.
(m) Work in Process.
(n) Salaries and Wages Payable.

Instructions
For each of the accounts above, indicate the proper balance sheet classification. In the case of borderline items, indicate the additional information that would be required to determine the proper classification.

2 3 **E5-2 (Classification of Balance Sheet Accounts)** Presented below are the captions of Faulk Company's balance sheet.

(a) Current assets.
(b) Investments.
(c) Property, plant, and equipment.
(d) Intangible assets.
(e) Other assets.

(f) Current liabilities.
(g) Noncurrent liabilities.
(h) Capital stock.
(i) Additional paid-in capital.
(j) Retained earnings.

Instructions
Indicate by letter where each of the following items would be classified.

1. Preferred stock.
2. Goodwill.
3. Salaries and wages payable.
4. Accounts payable.
5. Buildings.
6. Equity investments (trading).
7. Current maturity of long-term debt.
8. Premium on bonds payable.
9. Allowance for doubtful accounts.
10. Accounts receivable.

11. Cash surrender value of life insurance.
12. Notes payable (due next year).
13. Supplies.
14. Common stock.
15. Land.
16. Bond sinking fund.
17. Inventory.
18. Prepaid insurance.
19. Bonds payable.
20. Income taxes payable.

2 3 **E5-3 (Classification of Balance Sheet Accounts)** Assume that Fielder Enterprises uses the following headings on its balance sheet.

(a) Current assets.
(b) Investments.
(c) Property, plant, and equipment.
(d) Intangible assets.
(e) Other assets.

(f) Current liabilities.
(g) Long-term liabilities.
(h) Capital stock.
(i) Paid-in capital in excess of par.
(j) Retained earnings.

Instructions

Indicate by letter how each of the following usually should be classified. If an item should appear in a note to the financial statements, use the letter "N" to indicate this fact. If an item need not be reported at all on the balance sheet, use the letter "X."

1. Prepaid insurance.
2. Stock owned in affiliated companies.
3. Unearned service revenue.
4. Advances to suppliers.
5. Unearned rent revenue.
6. Preferred stock.
7. Additional paid-in capital on preferred stock.
8. Copyrights.
9. Petty cash fund.
10. Sales taxes payable.
11. Accrued interest on notes receivable.

12. Twenty-year issue of bonds payable that will mature within the next year. (No sinking fund exists, and refunding is not planned.)
13. Machinery retired from use and held for sale.
14. Fully depreciated machine still in use.
15. Accrued interest on bonds payable.
16. Salaries that company budget shows will be paid to employees within the next year.
17. Discount on bonds payable. (Assume related to bonds payable in item 12.)
18. Accumulated depreciation—buildings.
19. Noncontrolling interest.

2 3 **E5-4 (Preparation of a Classified Balance Sheet)** Assume that Denis Savard Inc. has the following accounts at the end of the current year.

1. Common Stock.
2. Discount on Bonds Payable.
3. Treasury Stock (at cost).
4. Notes Payable (short-term).
5. Raw Materials.
6. Preferred Stock Investments (long-term).
7. Unearned Rent Revenue.
8. Work in Process.
9. Copyrights.
10. Buildings.
11. Notes Receivable (short-term).
12. Cash.
13. Salaries and Wages Payable.

14. Accumulated Depreciation—Buildings.
15. Restricted Cash for Plant Expansion.
16. Land Held for Future Plant Site.
17. Allowance for Doubtful Accounts.
18. Retained Earnings.
19. Paid-in Capital in Excess of Par—Common Stock.
20. Unearned Subscriptions Revenue.
21. Receivables—Officers (due in one year).
22. Inventory (finished goods).
23. Accounts Receivable.
24. Bonds Payable (due in 4 years).
25. Noncontrolling Interest.

Instructions

Prepare a classified balance sheet in good form. (No monetary amounts are necessary.)

3 **E5-5 (Preparation of a Corrected Balance Sheet)** Uhura Company has decided to expand its operations. The bookkeeper recently completed the balance sheet presented below in order to obtain additional funds for expansion.

UHURA COMPANY
BALANCE SHEET
FOR THE YEAR ENDED 2014

Current assets	
Cash	$230,000
Accounts receivable (net)	340,000
Inventory (lower-of-average-cost-or-market)	401,000
Equity investments (trading)—at cost (fair value $120,000)	140,000
Property, plant, and equipment	
Buildings (net)	570,000
Equipment (net)	160,000
Land held for future use	175,000

Intangible assets	
Goodwill	80,000
Cash surrender value of life insurance	90,000
Prepaid expenses	12,000
Current liabilities	
Accounts payable	135,000
Notes payable (due next year)	125,000
Pension obligation	82,000
Rent payable	49,000
Premium on bonds payable	53,000
Long-term liabilities	
Bonds payable	500,000
Stockholders' equity	
Common stock, $1.00 par, authorized	
400,000 shares, issued 290,000	290,000
Additional paid-in capital	160,000
Retained earnings	?

Instructions

Prepare a revised balance sheet given the available information. Assume that the accumulated depreciation balance for the buildings is $160,000 and for the equipment, $105,000. The allowance for doubtful accounts has a balance of $17,000. The pension obligation is considered a long-term liability.

2 3 **E5-6 (Corrections of a Balance Sheet)** The bookkeeper for Geronimo Company has prepared the following balance sheet as of July 31, 2014.

GERONIMO COMPANY
BALANCE SHEET
AS OF JULY 31, 2014

Cash	$ 69,000	Notes and accounts payable	$ 44,000
Accounts receivable (net)	40,500	Long-term liabilities	75,000
Inventory	60,000	Stockholders' equity	155,500
Equipment (net)	84,000		$274,500
Patents	21,000		
	$274,500		

The following additional information is provided.

1. Cash includes $1,200 in a petty cash fund and $15,000 in a bond sinking fund.
2. The net accounts receivable balance is comprised of the following two items: (a) accounts receivable $44,000 and (b) allowance for doubtful accounts $3,500.
3. Inventory costing $5,300 was shipped out on consignment on July 31, 2014. The ending inventory balance does not include the consigned goods. Receivables in the amount of $5,300 were recognized on these consigned goods.
4. Equipment had a cost of $112,000 and an accumulated depreciation balance of $28,000.
5. Income taxes payable of $6,000 were accrued on July 31. Geronimo Company, however, had set up a cash fund to meet this obligation. This cash fund was not included in the cash balance but was offset against the income taxes payable amount.

Instructions

Prepare a corrected classified balance sheet as of July 31, 2014, from the available information, adjusting the account balances using the additional information.

3 **E5-7 (Current Assets Section of the Balance Sheet)** Presented below are selected accounts of Yasunari Kawabata Company at December 31, 2014.

Inventory (finished goods)	$ 52,000	Cost of Goods Sold	$2,100,000
Unearned Service Revenue	90,000	Notes Receivable	40,000
Equipment	253,000	Accounts Receivable	161,000
Inventory (work in process)	34,000	Inventory (raw materials)	207,000
Cash	37,000	Supplies Expense	60,000
Equity Investments (short-term)	31,000	Allowance for Doubtful Accounts	12,000
Customer Advances	36,000	Licenses	18,000
Restricted Cash for Plant Expansion	50,000	Additional Paid-in Capital	88,000
		Treasury Stock	22,000

The following additional information is available.

1. Inventories are valued at lower-of-cost-or-market using LIFO.
2. Equipment is recorded at cost. Accumulated depreciation, computed on a straight-line basis, is $50,600.
3. The short-term investments have a fair value of $29,000. (Assume they are trading securities.)
4. The notes receivable are due April 30, 2016, with interest receivable every April 30. The notes bear interest at 6%. (*Hint:* Accrued interest due on December 31, 2014.)
5. The allowance for doubtful accounts applies to the accounts receivable. Accounts receivable of $50,000 are pledged as collateral on a bank loan.
6. Licenses are recorded net of accumulated amortization of $14,000.
7. Treasury stock is recorded at cost.

Instructions

Prepare the current assets section of Yasunari Kawabata Company's December 31, 2014, balance sheet, with appropriate disclosures.

2 ▶ **E5-8 (Current vs. Long-term Liabilities)** Frederic Chopin Corporation is preparing its December 31, 2014, balance sheet. The following items may be reported as either a current or long-term liability.

1. On December 15, 2014, Chopin declared a cash dividend of $2.50 per share to stockholders of record on December 31. The dividend is payable on January 15, 2015. Chopin has issued 1,000,000 shares of common stock, of which 50,000 shares are held in treasury.
2. At December 31, bonds payable of $100,000,000 are outstanding. The bonds pay 12% interest every September 30 and mature in installments of $25,000,000 every September 30, beginning September 30, 2015.
3. At December 31, 2013, customer advances were $12,000,000. During 2014, Chopin collected $30,000,000 of customer advances; advances of $25,000,000 should be recognized in income.

Instructions

For each item above, indicate the dollar amounts to be reported as a current liability and as a long-term liability, if any.

2 3 **E5-9 (Current Assets and Current Liabilities)** The current assets and current liabilities sections of the balance sheet of Allessandro Scarlatti Company appear as follows.

ALLESSANDRO SCARLATTI COMPANY
BALANCE SHEET (PARTIAL)
DECEMBER 31, 2014

Cash		$ 40,000	Accounts payable	$ 61,000
Accounts receivable	$89,000		Notes payable	67,000
Less: Allowance for				$128,000
doubtful accounts	7,000	82,000		
Inventory		171,000		
Prepaid expenses		9,000		
		$302,000		

The following errors in the corporation's accounting have been discovered:

1. January 2015 cash disbursements entered as of December 2014 included payments of accounts payable in the amount of $39,000, on which a cash discount of 2% was taken.
2. The inventory included $27,000 of merchandise that had been received at December 31 but for which no purchase invoices had been received or entered. Of this amount, $12,000 had been received on consignment; the remainder was purchased f.o.b. destination, terms 2/10, n/30.
3. Sales for the first four days in January 2015 in the amount of $30,000 were entered in the sales journal as of December 31, 2014. Of these, $21,500 were sales on account and the remainder were cash sales.

4. Cash, not including cash sales, collected in January 2015 and entered as of December 31, 2014, totaled $35,324. Of this amount, $23,324 was received on account after cash discounts of 2% had been deducted; the remainder represented the proceeds of a bank loan.

Instructions

(a) Restate the current assets and current liabilities sections of the balance sheet in accordance with good accounting practice. (Assume that both accounts receivable and accounts payable are recorded gross.)

(b) State the net effect of your adjustments on Allessandro Scarlatti Company's retained earnings balance.

2 3 **E5-10 (Current Liabilities)** Norma Smith is the controller of Baylor Corporation and is responsible for the preparation of the year-end financial statements. The following transactions occurred during the year.

(a) On December 20, 2014, a former employee filed a legal action against Baylor for $100,000 for wrongful dismissal. Management believes the action to be frivolous and without merit. The likelihood of payment to the employee is remote.

(b) Bonuses to key employees based on net income for 2014 are estimated to be $150,000.

(c) On December 1, 2014, the company borrowed $600,000 at 8% per year. Interest is paid quarterly.

(d) Credit sales for the year amounted to $10,000,000. Baylor's expense provision for doubtful accounts is estimated to be 3% of credit sales.

(e) On December 15, 2014, the company declared a $2.00 per share dividend on the 40,000 shares of common stock outstanding, to be paid on January 5, 2015.

(f) During the year, customer advances of $160,000 were received; $50,000 of this amount was earned by December 31, 2014.

Instructions

For each item above, indicate the dollar amount to be reported as a current liability. If a liability is not reported, explain why.

3 **E5-11 (Balance Sheet Preparation)** Presented below is the adjusted trial balance of Kelly Corporation at December 31, 2014.

	Debit	Credit
Cash	$?	
Supplies	1,200	
Prepaid Insurance	1,000	
Equipment	48,000	
Accumulated Depreciation—Equipment		$ 4,000
Trademarks	950	
Accounts Payable		10,000
Salaries and Wages Payable		500
Unearned Service Revenue		2,000
Bonds Payable (due 2021)		9,000
Common Stock		10,000
Retained Earnings		25,000
Service Revenue		10,000
Salaries and Wages Expense	9,000	
Insurance Expense	1,400	
Rent Expense	1,200	
Interest Expense	900	
Total	$?	$?

Additional information:

1. Net loss for the year was $2,500.

2. No dividends were declared during 2014.

Instructions

Prepare a classified balance sheet as of December 31, 2014.

3 **E5-12 (Preparation of a Balance Sheet)** Presented below is the trial balance of Scott Butler Corporation at December 31, 2014.

	Debit	Credit
Cash	$ 197,000	
Sales Revenue		$ 8,100,000
Debt Investments (trading) (at cost, $145,000)	153,000	
Cost of Goods Sold	4,800,000	
Debt Investments (long-term)	299,000	
Equity Investments (long-term)	277,000	
Notes Payable (short-term)		90,000
Accounts Payable		455,000
Selling Expenses	2,000,000	
Investment Revenue		63,000
Land	260,000	
Buildings	1,040,000	
Dividends Payable		136,000
Accrued Liabilities		96,000
Accounts Receivable	435,000	
Accumulated Depreciation—Buildings		152,000
Allowance for Doubtful Accounts		25,000
Administrative Expenses	900,000	
Interest Expense	211,000	
Inventory	597,000	
Gain (extraordinary)		80,000
Notes Payable (long-term)		900,000
Equipment	600,000	
Bonds Payable		1,000,000
Accumulated Depreciation—Equipment		60,000
Franchises	160,000	
Common Stock ($5 par)		1,000,000
Treasury Stock	191,000	
Patents	195,000	
Retained Earnings		78,000
Paid-in Capital in Excess of Par		80,000
Totals	$12,315,000	$12,315,000

Instructions

Prepare a balance sheet at December 31, 2014, for Scott Butler Corporation. (Ignore income taxes.)

5 **E5-13 (Statement of Cash Flows—Classifications)** The major classifications of activities reported in the statement of cash flows are operating, investing, and financing. Classify each of the transactions listed below as:

1. Operating activity—add to net income.
2. Operating activity—deduct from net income.
3. Investing activity.
4. Financing activity.
5. Reported as significant noncash activity.

The transactions are as follows.

(a) Issuance of common stock.
(b) Purchase of land and building.
(c) Redemption of bonds.
(d) Sale of equipment.
(e) Depreciation of machinery.
(f) Amortization of patent.
(g) Issuance of bonds for plant assets.

(h) Payment of cash dividends.
(i) Exchange of furniture for office equipment.
(j) Purchase of treasury stock.
(k) Loss on sale of equipment.
(l) Increase in accounts receivable during the year.
(m) Decrease in accounts payable during the year.

6 **E5-14 (Preparation of a Statement of Cash Flows)** The comparative balance sheets of Constantine Cavamanlis Inc. at the beginning and the end of the year 2014 are as follows.

CONSTANTINE CAVAMANLIS INC.
BALANCE SHEETS

Assets	Dec. 31, 2014	Jan. 1, 2014	Inc./Dec.
Cash	$ 45,000	$ 13,000	$32,000 Inc.
Accounts receivable	91,000	88,000	3,000 Inc.
Equipment	39,000	22,000	17,000 Inc.
Less: Accumulated depreciation—equipment	17,000	11,000	6,000 Inc.
Total	$158,000	$112,000	
Liabilities and Stockholders' Equity			
Accounts payable	$ 20,000	$ 15,000	5,000 Inc.
Common stock	100,000	80,000	20,000 Inc.
Retained earnings	38,000	17,000	21,000 Inc.
Total	$158,000	$112,000	

Net income of $44,000 was reported, and dividends of $23,000 were paid in 2014. New equipment was purchased and none was sold.

Instructions

Prepare a statement of cash flows for the year 2014.

6 7 E5-15 (Preparation of a Statement of Cash Flows) Presented below is a condensed version of the comparative balance sheets for Zubin Mehta Corporation for the last two years at December 31.

	2014	2013
Cash	$177,000	$ 78,000
Accounts receivable	180,000	185,000
Investments	52,000	74,000
Equipment	298,000	240,000
Accumulated depreciation—equipment	(106,000)	(89,000)
Current liabilities	134,000	151,000
Common stock	160,000	160,000
Retained earnings	307,000	177,000

Additional information:

Investments were sold at a loss (not extraordinary) of $10,000; no equipment was sold; cash dividends paid were $30,000; and net income was $160,000.

Instructions

(a) Prepare a statement of cash flows for 2014 for Zubin Mehta Corporation.

(b) Determine Zubin Mehta Corporation's free cash flow.

6 7 E5-16 (Preparation of a Statement of Cash Flows) A comparative balance sheet for Shabbona Corporation is presented below.

	December 31	
Assets	2014	2013
Cash	$ 73,000	$ 22,000
Accounts receivable	82,000	66,000
Inventory	180,000	189,000
Land	71,000	110,000
Equipment	260,000	200,000
Accumulated depreciation—equipment	(69,000)	(42,000)
Total	$597,000	$545,000
Liabilities and Stockholders' Equity		
Accounts payable	$ 34,000	$ 47,000
Bonds payable	150,000	200,000
Common stock ($1 par)	214,000	164,000
Retained earnings	199,000	134,000
Total	$597,000	$545,000

Additional information:

1. Net income for 2014 was $125,000. No gains or losses were recorded in 2014.
2. Cash dividends of $60,000 were declared and paid.
3. Bonds payable amounting to $50,000 were retired through issuance of common stock.

Instructions
(a) Prepare a statement of cash flows for 2014 for Shabbona Corporation.
(b) Determine Shabbona Corporation's current cash debt coverage, cash debt coverage, and free cash flow. Comment on its liquidity and financial flexibility.

3 6 E5-17 (Preparation of a Statement of Cash Flows and a Balance Sheet) Grant Wood Corporation's balance sheet at the end of 2013 included the following items.

Current assets	$235,000	Current liabilities	$150,000
Land	30,000	Bonds payable	100,000
Buildings	120,000	Common stock	180,000
Equipment	90,000	Retained earnings	44,000
Accum. depr.—buildings	(30,000)	Total	$474,000
Accum. depr.—equipment	(11,000)		
Patents	40,000		
Total	$474,000		

The following information is available for 2014.

1. Net income was $55,000.
2. Equipment (cost $20,000 and accumulated depreciation $8,000) was sold for $10,000.
3. Depreciation expense was $4,000 on the building and $9,000 on equipment.
4. Patent amortization was $2,500.
5. Current assets other than cash increased by $29,000. Current liabilities increased by $13,000.
6. An addition to the building was completed at a cost of $27,000.
7. A long-term investment in stock was purchased for $16,000.
8. Bonds payable of $50,000 were issued.
9. Cash dividends of $30,000 were declared and paid.
10. Treasury stock was purchased at a cost of $11,000.

Instructions
(Show only totals for current assets and current liabilities.)
(a) Prepare a statement of cash flows for 2014.
(b) Prepare a balance sheet at December 31, 2014.

6 7 E5-18 (Preparation of a Statement of Cash Flows, Analysis) The comparative balance sheets of Madrasah Corporation at the beginning and end of the year 2014 appear below.

MADRASAH CORPORATION			
BALANCE SHEETS			
Assets	Dec. 31, 2014	Jan. 1, 2014	Inc./Dec.
Cash	$ 20,000	$ 13,000	$ 7,000 Inc.
Accounts receivable	106,000	88,000	18,000 Inc.
Equipment	39,000	22,000	17,000 Inc.
Less: Accumulated depreciation—equipment	17,000	11,000	6,000 Inc.
Total	$148,000	$112,000	
Liabilities and Stockholders' Equity			
Accounts payable	$ 20,000	$ 15,000	5,000 Inc.
Common stock	100,000	80,000	20,000 Inc.
Retained earnings	28,000	17,000	11,000 Inc.
Total	$148,000	$112,000	

Net income of $44,000 was reported, and dividends of $33,000 were paid in 2014. New equipment was purchased and none was sold.

Instructions
(a) Prepare a statement of cash flows for the year 2014.

(b) Compute the current ratio (current assets ÷ current liabilities) as of January 1, 2014, and December 31, 2014, and compute free cash flow for the year 2014.

(c) In light of the analysis in (b), comment on Madrasah's liquidity and financial flexibility.

EXERCISES SET B

See the book's companion website, at **www.wiley.com/college/kieso**, for an additional set of exercises.

PROBLEMS

3 **P5-1** **(Preparation of a Classified Balance Sheet, Periodic Inventory)** Presented below is a list of accounts in alphabetical order.

Accounts Receivable	Inventory—Ending
Accumulated Depreciation—Buildings	Land
Accumulated Depreciation—Equipment	Land for Future Plant Site
Accumulated Other Comprehensive Income	Loss from Flood
Advances to Employees	Noncontrolling Interest
Advertising Expense	Notes Payable (due next year)
Allowance for Doubtful Accounts	Paid-in Capital in Excess of Par—Preferred Stock
Bond Sinking Fund	Patents
Bonds Payable	Payroll Taxes Payable
Buildings	Pension Liability
Cash (in bank)	Petty Cash
Cash (on hand)	Preferred Stock
Cash Surrender Value of Life Insurance	Premium on Bonds Payable
Commission Expense	Prepaid Rent
Common Stock	Purchase Returns and Allowances
Copyrights	Purchases
Debt Investments (trading)	Retained Earnings
Dividends Payable	Salaries and Wages Expense (sales)
Equipment	Salaries and Wages Payable
Freight-In	Sales Discounts
Gain on Disposal of Equipment	Sales Revenue
Interest Receivable	Treasury Stock (at cost)
Inventory—Beginning	Unearned Subscriptions Revenue

Instructions
Prepare a classified balance sheet in good form. (No monetary amounts are to be shown.)

3 **P5-2** **(Balance Sheet Preparation)** Presented below are a number of balance sheet items for Montoya, Inc., for the current year, 2014.

Goodwill	$ 125,000	Accumulated depreciation—equipment	$ 292,000
Payroll taxes payable	177,591	Inventory	239,800
Bonds payable	300,000	Rent payable (short-term)	45,000
Discount on bonds payable	15,000	Income taxes payable	98,362
Cash	360,000	Rent payable (long-term)	480,000
Land	480,000	Common stock, $1 par value	200,000
Notes receivable	445,700	Preferred stock, $10 par value	150,000
Notes payable (to banks)	265,000	Prepaid expenses	87,920
Accounts payable	490,000	Equipment	1,470,000
Retained earnings	?	Equity investments (trading)	121,000
Income taxes receivable	97,630	Accumulated depreciation—buildings	270,200
Notes payable (long-term)	1,600,000	Buildings	1,640,000

Instructions
Prepare a classified balance sheet in good form. Common stock authorized was 400,000 shares, and preferred stock authorized was 20,000 shares. Assume that notes receivable and notes payable are short-term, unless stated otherwise. Cost and fair value of equity investments (trading) are the same.

3 **P5-3** **(Balance Sheet Adjustment and Preparation)** The adjusted trial balance of Eastwood Company and other related information for the year 2014 are presented as follows.

EASTWOOD COMPANY
ADJUSTED TRIAL BALANCE
DECEMBER 31, 2014

	Debit	Credit
Cash	$ 41,000	
Accounts Receivable	163,500	
Allowance for Doubtful Accounts		$ 8,700
Prepaid Insurance	5,900	
Inventory	208,500	
Equity Investments (long-term)	339,000	
Land	85,000	
Construction in Process (building)	124,000	
Patents	36,000	
Equipment	400,000	
Accumulated Depreciation—Equipment		240,000
Discount on Bonds Payable	20,000	
Accounts Payable		148,000
Accrued Liabilities		49,200
Notes Payable		94,000
Bonds Payable		200,000
Common Stock		500,000
Paid-in Capital in Excess of Par—Common Stock		45,000
Retained Earnings		138,000
	$1,422,900	$1,422,900

Additional information:

1. The LIFO method of inventory value is used.
2. The cost and fair value of the long-term investments that consist of stocks and bonds is the same.
3. The amount of the Construction in Progress account represents the costs expended to date on a building in the process of construction. (The company rents factory space at the present time.) The land on which the building is being constructed cost $85,000, as shown in the trial balance.
4. The patents were purchased by the company at a cost of $40,000 and are being amortized on a straight-line basis.
5. Of the discount on bonds payable, $2,000 will be amortized in 2015.
6. The notes payable represent bank loans that are secured by long-term investments carried at $120,000. These bank loans are due in 2015.
7. The bonds payable bear interest at 8% payable every December 31, and are due January 1, 2025.
8. 600,000 shares of common stock of a par value of $1 were authorized, of which 500,000 shares were issued and outstanding.

Instructions
Prepare a balance sheet as of December 31, 2014, so that all important information is fully disclosed.

3 **P5-4 (Preparation of a Corrected Balance Sheet)** The balance sheet of Kishwaukee Corporation as of December 31, 2014, is as follows.

KISHWAUKEE CORPORATION
BALANCE SHEET
DECEMBER 31, 2014

Assets	
Goodwill (Note 2)	$ 120,000
Buildings (Note 1)	1,640,000
Inventory	312,100
Land	950,000
Accounts receivable	170,000
Treasury stock (50,000 shares)	87,000
Cash on hand	175,900
Assets allocated to trustee for plant expansion	
Cash in bank	70,000
Debt investments (held-to-maturity)	138,000
	$3,663,000

Equities

Notes payable (Note 3)	$ 600,000
Common stock, authorized and issued, 1,000,000 shares, no par	1,150,000
Retained earnings	803,000
Noncontrolling interest	55,000
Appreciation capital (Note 1)	570,000
Income tax payable	75,000
Reserve for depreciation recorded to date on the building	410,000
	$3,663,000

Note 1: Buildings are stated at cost, except for one building that was recorded at appraised value. The excess of appraisal value over cost was $570,000. Depreciation has been recorded based on cost.

Note 2: Goodwill in the amount of $120,000 was recognized because the company believed that book value was not an accurate representation of the fair value of the company. The gain of $120,000 was credited to Retained Earnings.

Note 3: Notes payable are long-term except for the current installment due of $100,000.

Instructions

Prepare a corrected classified balance sheet in good form. The notes above are for information only.

 P5-5 (Balance Sheet Adjustment and Preparation) Presented below is the balance sheet of Sargent Corporation for the current year, 2014.

SARGENT CORPORATION
BALANCE SHEET
DECEMBER 31, 2014

Current assets	$ 485,000	Current liabilities	$ 380,000
Investments	640,000	Long-term liabilities	1,000,000
Property, plant, and equipment	1,720,000	Stockholders' equity	1,770,000
Intangible assets	305,000		$3,150,000
	$3,150,000		

The following information is presented.

1. The current assets section includes cash $150,000, accounts receivable $170,000 less $10,000 for allowance for doubtful accounts, inventories $180,000, and unearned rent revenue $5,000. Inventoy is stated on the lower-of-FIFO-cost-or-market.
2. The investments section includes the cash surrender value of a life insurance contract $40,000; investments in common stock, short-term (trading) $80,000 and long-term (available-for-sale) $270,000; and bond sinking fund $250,000. The cost and fair value of investments in common stock are the same.
3. Property, plant, and equipment includes buildings $1,040,000 less accumulated depreciation $360,000; equipment $450,000 less accumulated depreciation $180,000; land $500,000; and land held for future use $270,000.
4. Intangible assets include a franchise $165,000; goodwill $100,000; and discount on bonds payable $40,000.
5. Current liabilities include accounts payable $140,000; notes payable—short-term $80,000 and long-term $120,000; and income taxes payable $40,000.
6. Long-term liabilities are composed solely of 7% bonds payable due 2022.
7. Stockholders' equity has preferred stock, no par value, authorized 200,000 shares, issued 70,000 shares for $450,000; and common stock, $1.00 par value, authorized 400,000 shares, issued 100,000 shares at an average price of $10. In addition, the corporation has retained earnings of $320,000.

Instructions

Prepare a balance sheet in good form, adjusting the amounts in each balance sheet classification as affected by the information given above.

3 6 7 P5-6 (Preparation of a Statement of Cash Flows and a Balance Sheet) Lansbury Inc. had the following balance sheet at December 31, 2013.

LANSBURY INC.
BALANCE SHEET
DECEMBER 31, 2013

Cash	$ 20,000	Accounts payable	$ 30,000
Accounts receivable	21,200	Notes payable (long-term)	41,000
Investments	32,000	Common stock	100,000
Plant assets (net)	81,000	Retained earnings	23,200
Land	40,000		$194,200
	$194,200		

During 2014, the following occurred.

1. Lansbury Inc. sold part of its investment portfolio for $15,000. This transaction resulted in a gain of $3,400 for the firm. The company classifies its investments as available-for-sale.
2. A tract of land was purchased for $18,000 cash.
3. Long-term notes payable in the amount of $16,000 were retired before maturity by paying $16,000 cash.
4. An additional $20,000 in common stock was issued at par.
5. Dividends of $8,200 were declared and paid to stockholders.
6. Net income for 2014 was $32,000 after allowing for depreciation of $11,000.
7. Land was purchased through the issuance of $30,000 in bonds.
8. At December 31, 2014, Cash was $32,000, Accounts Receivable was $41,600, and Accounts Payable remained at $30,000.

Instructions

(a) Prepare a statement of cash flows for 2014.
(b) Prepare an unclassified balance sheet as it would appear at December 31, 2014.
(c) How might the statement of cash flows help the user of the financial statements? Compute two cash flow ratios.

1 3 6 7 P5-7 (Preparation of a Statement of Cash Flows and Balance Sheet) Aero Inc. had the following balance sheet at December 31, 2013.

AERO INC.
BALANCE SHEET
DECEMBER 31, 2013

Cash	$ 20,000	Accounts payable	$ 30,000
Accounts receivable	21,200	Bonds payable	41,000
Investments	32,000	Common stock	100,000
Plant assets (net)	81,000	Retained earnings	23,200
Land	40,000		$194,200
	$194,200		

During 2014, the following occurred.

1. Aero liquidated its available-for-sale investment portfolio at a loss of $5,000.
2. A tract of land was purchased for $38,000.
3. An additional $30,000 in common stock was issued at par.
4. Dividends totaling $10,000 were declared and paid to stockholders.
5. Net income for 2014 was $35,000, including $12,000 in depreciation expense.
6. Land was purchased through the issuance of $30,000 in additional bonds.
7. At December 31, 2014, Cash was $70,200, Accounts Receivable was $42,000, and Accounts Payable was $40,000.

Instructions

(a) Prepare a statement of cash flows for the year 2014 for Aero.
(b) Prepare the unclassified balance sheet as it would appear at December 31, 2014.
(c) Compute Aero's free cash flow and current cash debt coverage for 2014.
(d) Use the analysis of Aero to illustrate how information in the balance sheet and statement of cash flows helps the user of the financial statements.

PROBLEMS SET B

See the book's companion website, at **www.wiley.com/college/kieso**, for an additional set of problems.

CONCEPTS FOR ANALYSIS

CA5-1 (Reporting the Financial Effects of Varied Transactions) In an examination of Arenes Corporation as of December 31, 2014, you have learned that the following situations exist. No entries have been made in the accounting records for these items.

1. The corporation erected its present factory building in 1999. Depreciation was calculated by the straight-line method, using an estimated life of 35 years. Early in 2014, the board of directors conducted a careful survey and estimated that the factory building had a remaining useful life of 25 years as of January 1, 2014.
2. An additional assessment of 2013 income taxes was levied and paid in 2014.
3. When calculating the accrual for officers' salaries at December 31, 2014, it was discovered that the accrual for officers' salaries for December 31, 2013, had been overstated.
4. On December 15, 2014, Arenes Corporation declared a cash dividend on its common stock outstanding, payable February 1, 2015, to the common stockholders of record December 31, 2014.

Instructions
Describe fully how each of the items above should be reported in the financial statements of Arenes Corporation for the year 2014.

CA5-2 (Identifying Balance Sheet Deficiencies) The assets of Fonzarelli Corporation are presented below (000s omitted).

FONZARELLI CORPORATION
BALANCE SHEET (PARTIAL)
DECEMBER 31, 2014

Assets

Current assets		
Cash		$ 100,000
Unclaimed payroll checks		27,500
Debt investments (trading) (fair value $30,000) at cost		37,000
Accounts receivable (less bad debt reserve)		75,000
Inventory—at lower-of-cost- (determined by the next-in, first-out method) or-market		240,000
Total current assets		479,500
Tangible assets		
Land (less accumulated depreciation)		80,000
Buildings and equipment	$800,000	
Less: Accumulated depreciation	250,000	550,000
Net tangible assets		630,000
Long-term investments		
Stocks and bonds		100,000
Treasury stock		70,000
Total long-term investments		170,000
Other assets		
Discount on bonds payable		19,400
Sinking fund		975,000
Total other assets		994,400
Total assets		$2,273,900

Instructions

Indicate the deficiencies, if any, in the foregoing presentation of Fonzarelli Corporation's assets.

CA5-3 (Critique of Balance Sheet Format and Content) Presented below is the balance sheet of Sameed Brothers Corporation (000s omitted).

SAMEED BROTHERS CORPORATION
BALANCE SHEET
DECEMBER 31, 2014

<u>Assets</u>

Current assets		
Cash	$26,000	
Marketable securities	18,000	
Accounts receivable	25,000	
Inventory	20,000	
Supplies	4,000	
Stock investment in subsidiary company	20,000	$113,000
Investments		
Treasury stock		25,000
Property, plant, and equipment		
Buildings and land	91,000	
Less: Reserve for depreciation	31,000	60,000
Other assets		
Cash surrender value of life insurance		19,000
Total assets		$217,000

<u>Liabilities and Stockholders' Equity</u>

Current liabilities		
Accounts payable	$22,000	
Reserve for income taxes	15,000	
Customers' accounts with credit balances	1	$ 37,001
Deferred credits		
Unamortized premium on bonds payable		2,000
Long-term liabilities		
Bonds payable		60,000
Total liabilities		99,001
Common stock		
Common stock, par $5	85,000	
Earned surplus	24,999	
Cash dividends declared	8,000	117,999
Total liabilities and stockholders' equity		$217,000

Instructions

Evaluate the balance sheet presented. State briefly the proper treatment of any item criticized.

CA5-4 (Presentation of Property, Plant, and Equipment) Carol Keene, corporate comptroller for Dumaine Industries, is trying to decide how to present "Property, plant, and equipment" in the balance sheet. She realizes that the statement of cash flows will show that the company made a significant investment in purchasing new equipment this year, but overall she knows the company's plant assets are rather old. She feels that she can disclose one figure titled "Property, plant, and equipment, net of depreciation," and the result will be a low figure. However, it will not disclose the age of the assets. If she chooses to show the cost less accumulated depreciation, the age of the assets will be apparent. She proposes the following.

Property, plant, and equipment, net of depreciation	$10,000,000
rather than	
Property, plant, and equipment	$50,000,000
Less: Accumulated depreciation	40,000,000
Net book value	$10,000,000

Instructions

Answer the following questions.

(a) What are the ethical issues involved?

(b) What should Keene do?

CA5-5 (Cash Flow Analysis) The partner in charge of the Kappeler Corporation audit comes by your desk and leaves a letter he has started to the CEO and a copy of the cash flow statement for the year ended December 31, 2014. Because he must leave on an emergency, he asks you to finish the letter by explaining: (1) the disparity between net income and cash flow, (2) the importance of operating cash flow, (3) the renewable source(s) of cash flow, and (4) possible suggestions to improve the cash position.

KAPPELER CORPORATION
STATEMENT OF CASH FLOWS
FOR THE YEAR ENDED DECEMBER 31, 2014

Cash flows from operating activities		
Net income		$ 100,000
Adjustments to reconcile net income to net cash provided by		
operating activities:		
Depreciation expense	$ 10,000	
Amortization expense	1,000	
Loss on sale of fixed assets	5,000	
Increase in accounts receivable (net)	(40,000)	
Increase in inventory	(35,000)	
Decrease in accounts payable	(41,000)	(100,000)
Net cash provided by operating activities		–0–
Cash flows from investing activities		
Sale of plant assets	25,000	
Purchase of equipment	(100,000)	
Purchase of land	(200,000)	
Net cash used by investing activities		(275,000)
Cash flows from financing activities		
Payment of dividends	(10,000)	
Redemption of bonds	(100,000)	
Net cash used by financing activities		(110,000)
Net decrease in cash		(385,000)
Cash balance, January 1, 2014		400,000
Cash balance, December 31, 2014		$ 15,000

Date

President Kappeler, CEO
Kappeler Corporation
125 Wall Street
Middleton, Kansas 67458

Dear Mr. Kappeler:

I have good news and bad news about the financial statements for the year ended December 31, 2014. The good news is that net income of $100,000 is close to what we predicted in the strategic plan last year, indicating strong performance this year. The bad news is that the cash balance is seriously low. Enclosed is the Statement of Cash Flows, which best illustrates how both of these situations occurred simultaneously . . .

Instructions

Complete the letter to the CEO, including the four components requested by your boss.

USING YOUR JUDGMENT

FINANCIAL REPORTING

Financial Reporting Problem

P&G **The Procter & Gamble Company (P&G)**

The financial statements of P&G are presented in Appendix 5B. The company's complete annual report, including the notes to the financial statments, can be accessed at the book's companion website, **www.wiley.com/college/kieso**.

Instructions

Refer to P&G's financial statements and the related information in the annual report to answer the following questions.

(a) What alternative formats could P&G have adopted for its balance sheet? Which format did it adopt?

(b) Identify the various techniques of disclosure P&G might have used to disclose additional pertinent financial information. Which technique does it use in its financials?

(c) In what classifications are P&G's investments reported? What valuation basis does P&G use to report its investments? How much working capital did P&G have on June 30, 2011? On June 30, 2010?

(d) What were P&G's cash flows from its operating, investing, and financing activities for 2011? What were its trends in net cash provided by operating activities over the period 2009 to 2011? Explain why the change in accounts payable and in accrued and other liabilities is added to net income to arrive at net cash provided by operating activities.

(e) Compute P&G's (1) current cash debt coverage, (2) cash debt coverage, and (3) free cash flow for 2011. What do these ratios indicate about P&G's financial condition?

Comparative Analysis Case

The Coca-Cola Company and PepsiCo, Inc.

Instructions

Go to the book's companion website and use information found there to answer the following questions related to The Coca-Cola Company and PepsiCo, Inc.

(a) What format(s) did these companies use to present their balance sheets?

(b) How much working capital did each of these companies have at the end of 2011? Speculate as to their rationale for the amount of working capital they maintain.

(c) What is the most significant difference in the asset structure of the two companies? What causes this difference?

(d) What are the companies' annual and 5-year (2007–2011) growth rates in total assets and long-term debt?

(e) What were these two companies' trends in net cash provided by operating activities over the period 2007–2011?

(f) Compute both companies' (1) current cash debt coverage, (2) cash debt coverage, and (3) free cash flow. What do these ratios indicate about the financial condition of the two companies?

Financial Statement Analysis Cases

Case 1: Uniroyal Technology Corporation

Uniroyal Technology Corporation (UTC), with corporate offices in Sarasota, Florida, is organized into three operating segments. The high-performance plastics segment is responsible for research, development, and manufacture of a wide variety of products, including orthopedic braces, graffiti-resistant seats for buses and airplanes, and a static-resistant plastic used in the central processing units of microcomputers. The coated fabrics segment manufactures products such as automobile seating, door and instrument panels, and specialty items such as waterproof seats for personal watercraft and stain-resistant, easy-cleaning upholstery fabrics. The foams and adhesives segment develops and manufactures products used in commercial roofing applications.

The following items relate to operations in a recent year.

1. Serious pressure was placed on profitability by sharply increasing raw material prices. Some raw materials increased in price 50% during the past year. Cost containment programs were instituted and

product prices were increased whenever possible, which resulted in profit margins actually improving over the course of the year.

2. The company entered into a revolving credit agreement, under which UTC may borrow the lesser of $15,000,000 or 80% of eligible accounts receivable. At the end of the year, approximately $4,000,000 was outstanding under this agreement. The company plans to use this line of credit in the upcoming year to finance operations and expansion.

Instructions

(a) Should investors be informed of raw materials price increases, such as described in item 1? Does the fact that the company successfully met the challenge of higher prices affect the answer? Explain.

(b) How should the information in item 2 be presented in the financial statements of UTC?

Case 2: Sherwin-Williams Company

Sherwin-Williams, based in Cleveland, Ohio, manufactures a wide variety of paint and other coatings, which are marketed through its specialty stores and in other retail outlets. The company also manufactures paint for automobiles. The Automotive Division has had financial difficulty. During a recent year, five branch locations of the Automotive Division were closed, and new management was put in place for the branches remaining.

The following titles were shown on Sherwin-Williams's balance sheet for that year.

Accounts payable	Machinery and equipment
Accounts receivable, less allowance	Other accruals
Accrued taxes	Other capital
Buildings	Other current assets
Cash and cash equivalents	Other long-term liabilities
Common stock	Postretirement obligations other than pensions
Employee compensation payable	Retained earnings
Finished goods inventories	Short-term investments
Intangibles and other assets	Taxes payable
Land	Work in process and raw materials inventories
Long-term debt	

Instructions

(a) Organize the accounts in the general order in which they would have been presented in a classified balance sheet.

(b) When several of the branch locations of the Automotive Division were closed, what balance sheet accounts were most likely affected? Did the balance in those accounts decrease or increase?

Case 3: Deere & Company

Presented below is the SEC-mandated disclosure of contractual obligations provided by Deere & Company in a recent annual report. Deere & Company reported current assets of $27,208 and total current liabilities of $15,922 at year-end. All dollars are in millions.

Aggregate Contractual Obligations

The payment schedule for the company's contractual obligations at year-end in millions of dollars is as follows:

	Total	Less than 1 year	2&3 years	4&5 years	More than 5 years
Debt					
Equipment operations	$ 2,061	$ 130	$ 321		$1,610
Financial services	19,598	8,515	7,025	$3,003	1,055
Total	21,659	8,645	7,346	3,003	2,665
Interest on debt	3,857	941	1,102	557	1,257
Purchase obligations	3,212	3,172	26	9	5
Operating leases	358	100	120	58	80
Capital leases	29	3	6	4	16
Total	$29,115	$12,861	$8,600	$3,631	$4,023

Instructions

(a) Compute Deere & Company's working capital and current ratio (current assets ÷ current liabilities) with and without the contractual obligations reported in the schedule.

(b) Briefly discuss how the information provided in the contractual obligation disclosure would be useful in evaluating Deere & Company for loans (1) due in one year and (2) due in five years.

Case 4: Amazon.com

The incredible growth of Amazon.com has put fear into the hearts of traditional retailers. Amazon's stock price has soared to amazing levels. However, it is often pointed out in the financial press that it took the company several years to report its first profit. The following financial information is taken from a recent annual report.

($ in millions)	Current Year	Prior Year
Current assets	$ 3,373	$2,929
Total assets	4,363	3,696
Current liabilities	2,532	1,899
Total liabilities	3,932	3,450
Cash provided by operations	702	733
Capital expenditures	216	204
Dividends paid	0	0
Net income(loss)	190	359
Sales	10,711	8,490

Instructions

(a) Calculate free cash flow for Amazon for the current and prior years, and discuss its ability to finance expansion from internally generated cash. Thus far Amazon has avoided purchasing large warehouses. Instead, it has used those of others. It is possible, however, that in order to increase customer satisfaction the company may have to build its own warehouses. If this happens, how might your impression of its ability to finance expansion change?

(b) Discuss any potential implications of the change in Amazon's cash provided by operations from the prior year to the current year.

Accounting, Analysis, and Principles

Early in January 2015, Hopkins Company is preparing for a meeting with its bankers to discuss a loan request. Its bookkeeper provided the following accounts and balances at December 31, 2014.

	Debit	Credit
Cash	$ 75,000	
Accounts Receivable (net)	38,500	
Inventory	65,300	
Equipment (net)	84,000	
Patents	15,000	
Notes and Accounts Payable		$ 52,000
Notes Payable (due 2016)		75,000
Common Stock		100,000
Retained Earnings		50,800
	$277,800	$277,800

Except for the following items, Hopkins has recorded all adjustments in its accounts.

1. Cash includes $500 petty cash and $15,000 in a bond sinking fund.
2. Net accounts receivable is comprised of $52,000 in accounts receivable and $13,500 in allowance for doubtful accounts.
3. Equipment had a cost of $112,000 and accumulated depreciation of $28,000.
4. On January 8, 2015, one of Hopkins' customers declared bankruptcy. At December 31, 2014, this customer owed Hopkins $9,000.

Accounting

Prepare a corrected December 31, 2014, balance sheet for Hopkins Company.

Analysis

Hopkins' bank is considering granting an additional loan in the amount of $45,000, which will be due December 31, 2015. How can the information in the balance sheet provide useful information to the bank about Hopkins' ability to repay the loan?

Principles

In the upcoming meeting with the bank, Hopkins plans to provide additional information about the fair value of its equipment and some internally generated intangible assets related to its customer lists. This information indicates that Hopkins has significant unrealized gains on these assets, which are not reflected on the balance sheet. What objections is the bank likely to raise about the usefulness of this information in evaluating Hopkins for the loan renewal?

BRIDGE TO THE PROFESSION

 ## Professional Research: FASB Codification

In light of the full disclosure principle, investors and creditors need to know the balances for assets, liabilities, and equity as well as the accounting policies adopted by management to measure the items reported in the balance sheet.

Instructions

If your school has a subscription to the FASB Codification, go to *http://aaahq.org/asclogin.cfm* to log in and prepare responses to the following. Provide Codification references for your responses.

(a) Identify the literature that addresses the disclosure of accounting policies.

(b) How are accounting policies defined in the literature?

(c) What are the three scenarios that would result in detailed disclosure of the accounting methods used?

(d) What are some examples of common disclosures that are required under this statement?

Additional Professional Resources

See the book's companion website, at **www.wiley.com/college/kieso**, for professional simulations as well as other study resources.

FRS > INSIGHTS

...s in GAAP, the balance sheet and the statement of cash flows are required statements for IFRS. In addition, the content and presentation of an IFRS statement of ...nancial position (balance sheet) and cash flow statement are similar to those used ...or GAAP. In general, the disclosure requirements related to the balance sheet and ...he statement of cash flows are much more extensive and detailed in the United ...tates. *IAS 1*, "Presentation of Financial Statements," provides the overall IFRS require-...ents for balance sheet information. *IAS 7*, "Cash Flow Statements," provides the over-...ll IFRS requirements for cash flow information. IFRS insights on the statement of cash ...ows are presented in Chapter 23.

11 LEARNING OBJECTIVE

Compare the accounting procedures related to the balance sheet under GAAP and IFRS.

RELEVANT FACTS

Following are the key similarities and differences between GAAP and IFRS related to the balance sheet.

Similarities

- Both IFRS and GAAP allow the use of title "balance sheet" or "statement of financial position." IFRS recommends but does not require the use of the title "statement of financial position" rather than balance sheet.
- Both IFRS and GAAP require disclosures about (1) accounting policies followed, (2) judgments that management has made in the process of applying the entity's accounting policies, and (3) the key assumptions and estimation uncertainty that could result in a material adjustment to the carrying amounts of assets and liabilities within the next financial year. Comparative prior period information must be presented and financial statements must be prepared annually.
- IFRS and GAAP require presentation of non-controlling interests in the equity section of the balance sheet.

Differences

- IFRS requires a classified statement of financial position except in very limited situations. IFRS follows the same guidelines as this textbook for distinguishing between current and non-current assets and liabilities. However, under GAAP, public companies must follow SEC regulations, which require specific line items. In addition, specific GAAP mandates certain forms of reporting for this information.
- Under IFRS, current assets are usually listed in the reverse order of liquidity. For example, under GAAP cash is listed first, but under IFRS it is listed last.
- IFRS has many differences in terminology that you will notice in this textbook. For example, in the sample statement of financial position illustrated on page 279 notice in the equity section common stock is called share capital—ordinary.
- Use of the term "reserve" is discouraged in GAAP, but there is no such prohibition in IFRS.

ABOUT THE NUMBERS

Classification in the Statement of Financial Position

Statement of financial position accounts are **classified**. That is, a statement of financial position groups together similar items to arrive at significant subtotals. Furthermore, the material is arranged so that important relationships are shown. The IASB indicate that the parts and subsections of financial statements are more informative than the whole. Therefore, the IASB discourages the reporting of summary accounts alone (total assets, net assets, total liabilities, etc.).

Instead, companies should report and classify individual items in sufficient detail to permit users to assess the amounts, timing, and uncertainty of future cash flows. Such classification also makes it easier for users to evaluate the company's liquidity and financial flexibility, profitability, and risk. Companies then further divide these items into several subclassifications. A representative statement of financial position presentation is shown on the next page.

SCIENTIFIC PRODUCTS, INC.
STATEMENT OF FINANCIAL POSITION
DECEMBER 31, 2014

Assets

Non-current assets

Long-term investments

Investments in held-for-collection securities	$ 82,000	
Land held for future development	5,500	$ 87,500

Property, plant, and equipment

Land		125,000
Buildings	$975,800	
Less: Accumulated depreciation	341,200	634,600
Total property, plant, and equipment		759,600

Intangible assets

Capitalized development costs		6,000
Goodwill		66,000
Other identifiable intangible assets		28,000	100,000
Total non-current assets			947,100

Current assets

Inventories		489,713
Prepaid expenses		16,252
Accounts receivable	165,824	
Less: Allowance for doubtful accounts	1,850	163,974
Short-term investments		51,030
Cash and cash equivalents		52,485
Total current assets			773,454
Total assets			$1,720,554

Equity and Liabilities

Equity

Share capital—preference	$300,000	
Share capital—ordinary	400,000	
Share premium—preference	10,000	
Share premium—ordinary	27,500	
Retained earnings	153,182	
Accumulated other comprehensive income	8,650	
Less: Treasury shares	12,750	
Equity attributable to Scientific Products, Inc.	$886,582	
Equity attributable to non-controlling interest	13,500	
Total equity		$ 900,082

Non-current liabilities

Bond liabilities due January 31, 2022	425,000	
Provisions related to pensions	75,000	
Total non-current liabilities	500,000	

Current liabilities

Notes payable	80,000	
Accounts payable	197,532	
Interest payable	20,500	
Salary and wages payable	5,560	
Provisions related to warranties	12,500	
Deposits received from customers	4,380	
Total current liabilities	320,472	
Total liabilities		820,472
Total equity and liabilities		$1,720,554

The statement presented is in "report form" format. Some companies use other statement of financial position formats. For example, companies sometimes deduct current liabilities from current assets to arrive at working capital. Or, they deduct all liabilities from all assets. Some companies report the subtotal *net assets*, which equals total assets minus total liabilities.

Equity

The **equity** (also referred to as **shareholders' equity**) section is one of the most difficult sections to prepare and understand. This is due to the complexity of ordinary and preference share agreements and the various restrictions on equity imposed by corporation laws, liability agreements, and boards of directors. Companies usually divide the section into six parts

---

EQUITY SECTION

1. **SHARE CAPITAL.** The par or stated value of shares issued. It includes ordinary shares (sometimes referred to as *common shares*) and preference shares (sometimes referred to as *preferred shares*).

2. **SHARE PREMIUM.** The excess of amounts paid-in over the par or stated value.

3. **RETAINED EARNINGS.** The corporation's undistributed earnings.

4. **ACCUMULATED OTHER COMPREHENSIVE INCOME.** The aggregate amount of the other comprehensive income items.

5. **TREASURY SHARES.** Generally, the amount of ordinary shares repurchased.

6. **NON-CONTROLLING INTEREST (MINORITY INTEREST).** A portion of the equity of subsidiaries not owned by the reporting company.

For ordinary shares, companies must disclose the par value and the authorized, issued, and outstanding share amounts. The same holds true for preference shares. A company usually presents the share premium (for both ordinary and preference shares) in one amount, although subtotals are informative if the sources of additional capital are varied and material. The retained earnings amount may be divided between the **unappropriated** (the amount that is usually available for dividend distribution) and **restricted** (e.g., by bond indentures or other loan agreements) amounts. In addition, companies show any shares reacquired (treasury shares) as a reduction of equity.

Accumulated other comprehensive income (sometimes referred to as *reserves* or *other reserves*) includes such items as unrealized gains and losses on non-trading equity investments and unrealized gains and losses on certain derivative transactions Non-controlling interest, sometimes referred to as minority interest, is also shown as a separate item (where applicable) as a part of equity.

Delhaize Group presented its equity section as follows.

Delhaize Group
(000,000)

Share capital	€ 50
Share premium	2,725
Treasury shares	(56)
Retained earnings	2,678
Other reserves	(1,254)
Shareholders' equity	4,143
Minority interests	52
Total equity	€ 4,195

Many companies reporting under IFRS often use the term "reserve" as an all-inclusive catch-all for items such as retained earnings, share premium, and accumulated other comprehensive income.

Revaluation Equity

GAAP and IFRS differ in the IFRS provision for balance sheet revaluations of property, plant, and equipment. Under the *revaluation model*, revaluations are recorded and reported as part of equity. To illustrate, Richardson Company uses IFRS and has property and equipment on an historical cost basis of $2,000,000. At the end of the year, Richardson appraises its property and equipment and determines it had a revaluation increase of $243,000.

Richardson records this revaluation under IFRS with an increase to property and equipment as well as a valuation reserve in equity. A note to the financial statements explains the change in the revaluation equity account from one period to the next, as shown below for Richardson Company, assuming a beginning balance of $11,345,000.

Note 30. Reserves (in part) (,000)	2014
Properties Revaluation Reserve	
Balance at beginning of year	$11,345
Increase (decrease) on revaluation of plant and equipment	243
Impairment losses	—
Reversals of impairment losses	—
Balance at end of year	$11,588

Fair Presentation

Companies must present fairly the financial position, financial performance, and cash flows of the company. Fair presentation means the faithful representation of transactions and events using the definitions and recognition criteria in the IASB conceptual framework. It is presumed that the use of IFRS with appropriate disclosure results in financial statements that are fairly presented. In other words, inappropriate use of accounting policies cannot be overcome by explanatory notes to the financial statements. In some rare cases, as indicated in Chapter 2, companies can use a "true and fair" override. This situation develops, for example, when the IFRS for a given company appears to conflict with the objective of financial reporting. This situation might occur when a regulatory body indicates that a specific IFRS may be misleading. As indicated earlier, a true and fair override is highly unlikely in today's reporting environment.

One recent and highly publicized exception is the case of Société Générale (SocGen), a French bank. The bank used the true and fair rule to justify reporting losses that occurred in 2008 in the prior year. Although allowed under the true and fair rule, such reporting was questioned because it permitted the bank to "take a bath," that is, record as many losses as possible in 2007, which was already a bad year for the bank. As a result, SocGen's 2008 reports looked better. [See F. Norris, "SocGen Changes Its Numbers," *The New York Times* (May 13, 2008).]

ON THE HORIZON

The FASB and the IASB are working on a project to converge their standards related to financial statement presentation. A key feature of the proposed framework is that each of the statements will be organized, in the same format, to separate an entity's financing activities from its operating and investing activities and, further, to separate financing activities into transactions with owners and creditors. Thus, the same classifications used in the statement of financial position would also be used in the statement of comprehensive income and the statement of cash flows. The project has three phases. You can follow the joint financial presentation project at the following link: *http://www.fasb.org/project/financial_statement_ presentation.shtml.*

IFRS SELF-TEST QUESTIONS

1. Which of the following statements about IFRS and GAAP accounting and reporting requirements for the balance sheet is **not** correct?
   (a) Both IFRS and GAAP distinguish between current and non-current assets and liabilities.
   (b) The presentation formats required by IFRS and GAAP for the balance sheet are similar.
   (c) Both IFRS and GAAP require that comparative information be reported.
   (d) One difference between the reporting requirements under IFRS and those of the GAAP balance sheet is that an IFRS balance sheet may list long-term assets first.

2. Current assets under IFRS are listed generally:
   (a) by importance.
   (b) in the reverse order of their expected conversion to cash.
   (c) by longevity.
   (d) alphabetically.

3. Companies that use IFRS:
   (a) may report all their assets on the statement of financial position at fair value.
   (b) are not allowed to net assets (assets − liabilities) on their statement of financial positions.
   (c) may report non-current assets before current assets on the statement of financial position.
   (d) do not have any guidelines as to what should be reported on the statement of financial position.

4. Franco Company uses IFRS and owns property, plant, and equipment with a historical cost of $5,000,000. At December 31, 2013, the company reported a valuation reserve of $690,000. At December 31, 2014, the property, plant, and equipment was appraised at $5,325,000. The valuation reserve will show what balance at December 31, 2014?
   (a) $365,000.
   (b) $325,000.
   (c) $690,000.
   (d) $0.

5. A company has purchased a tract of land and expects to build a production plant on the land in approximately 5 years. During the 5 years before construction, the land will be idle. Under IFRS, the land should be reported as:
   (a) land expense.
   (b) property, plant, and equipment.
   (c) an intangible asset.
   (d) a long-term investment.

IFRS CONCEPTS AND APPLICATION

IFRS5-1 Where can authoritative IFRS guidance be found related to the statement of financial position (balance sheet) and the statement of cash flows?

IFRS5-2 Briefly describe some of the similarities and differences between GAAP and IFRS with respect to statement of financial position (balance sheet) reporting.

IFRS5-3 Briefly describe the convergence efforts related to financial statement presentation.

IFRS5-4 Rainmaker Company prepares its financial statements in accordance with IFRS. In 2014, Rainmaker recorded the following revaluation adjustments related to its buildings and land: The company's building increased in value by $200,000; its land declined by $35,000. How will these revaluation adjustments affect Rainmaker's balance sheet? Will the reporting differ under GAAP? Explain.

International Reporting Case

IFRS5-5 Presented below is the balance sheet for Tomkins plc, a British company.

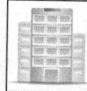

Tomkins plc
Consolidated Balance Sheet
(amounts in £ millions)

Non-current assets	
Goodwill	436.0
Other intangible assets	78.0
Property, plant and equipment	1,122.8
Investments in associates	20.6
Trade and other receivables	81.1
Deferred tax assets	82.9
Post-employment benefit surpluses	1.3
	1,822.7
Current assets	
Inventories	590.8
Trade and other receivables	753.0
Income tax recoverable	49.0
Available-for-sale investments	1.2
Cash and cash equivalents	445.0
	1,839.0
Assets held for sale	11.9
Total assets	3,673.6
Current liabilities	
Bank overdrafts	4.8
Bank and other loans	11.2
Obligations under finance leases	1.0
Trade and other payables	677.6
Income tax liabilities	15.2
Provisions	100.3
	810.1
Non-current liabilities	
Bank and other loans	687.3
Obligations under finance leases	3.6
Trade and other payables	27.1
Post-employment benefit obligations	343.5
Deferred tax liabilities	25.3
Income tax liabilities	79.5
Provisions	19.2
	1,185.5
Total liabilities	1,995.6
Net assets	1,678.0
Capital and reserves	
Ordinary share capital	79.6
Share premium account	799.2
Own shares	(8.2)
Capital redemption reserve	921.8
Currency translation reserve	(93.0)
Available-for-sale reserve	(0.9)
Accumulated deficit	(161.9)
Shareholders' equity	1,536.6
Minority interests	141.4
Total equity	1,678.0

Instructions

(a) Identify at least three differences in balance sheet reporting between British and U.S. firms, as shown in Tomkins' balance sheet.

(b) Review Tomkins' balance sheet and identify how the format of this financial statement provides useful information, as illustrated in the chapter.

Professional Research

IFRS5-6 In light of the full disclosure principle, investors and creditors need to know the balances for assets, liabilities, and equity, as well as the accounting policies adopted by management to measure the items reported in the statement of financial position.

Instructions

Access the IFRS authoritative literature at the IASB website (*http://eifrs.iasb.org/*). (If necessary, click on the IFRS tab and then register for eIFRS free access.) When you have accessed the documents, you can use the search tool in your Internet browser to respond to the following questions. (Provide paragraph citations.)

(a) Identify the literature that addresses the disclosure of accounting policies.

(b) How are accounting policies defined in the literature?

(c) What are the guidelines concerning consistency in applying accounting policies?

(d) What are some examples of common disclosures that are required under this statement?

International Financial Reporting Problem
Marks and Spencer plc

IFRS5-7 The financial statements of **Marks and Spencer plc (M&S)** are available at the book's companion website or can be accessed at *http://annualreport.marksandspencer.com/_assets/downloads/Marks-and-Spencer-Annual-report-and-financial-statements-2012.pdf*.

Instructions

Refer to M&S's financial statements and the accompanying notes to answer the following questions.

(a) What alternative formats could M&S have adopted for its statement of financial position? Which format did it adopt?

(b) Identify the various techniques of disclosure M&S might have used to disclose additional pertinent financial information. Which technique does it use in its financials?

(c) In what classifications are M&S's investments reported? What valuation basis does M&S use to report its investments? How much working capital did M&S have on 31 March 2012? On 2 April 2011?

(d) What were M&S's cash flows from its operating, investing, and financing activities for 2012? What were its trends in net cash provided by operating activities over the period 2011 to 2012? Explain why the change in accounts payable and in accrued and other liabilities is added to net income to arrive at net cash provided by operating activities.

(e) Compute M&S's (1) current cash debt coverage, (2) cash debt coverage, and (3) free cash flow for 2012. What do these ratios indicate about M&S's financial conditions?

ANSWERS TO IFRS SELF-TEST QUESTIONS

1. b **2.** b **3.** c **4.** b **5.** d

Remember to check the book's companion website to find additional resources for this chapter.

6 Accounting and the Time Value of Money

How Do I Measure That?

A significant part of accounting is measurement. And as we discussed in Chapter 2, we have a mixed-attribute measurement model. That is, many items are measured based on historical cost (e.g., property, plant, and equipment, inventory), but increasingly accounting measurements are based on fair value (e.g., financial instruments, impairments). Determining fair value of an item is fairly straightforward when market prices are available (Level 1 in the fair value hierarchy). However, when a market price is not available, accountants must rely on valuation models to develop a fair value estimate (Level 3 of the fair value hierarchy).

Developing fair value estimates based on a valuation model generally involves discounted cash flow techniques, which has three primary elements: (1) estimating the amounts and timing of future cash flows, (2) developing probability estimates for those cash flows, and (3) determining the appropriate discount rate to apply to the expected cash flows to arrive at a fair value estimate. Seems pretty straightforward, right? Actually, this can be a challenging process when applied to a variety of complex assets and liabilities for which GAAP requires a fair value estimate.

Many companies, particularly financial institutions, faced this challenge during the financial crisis when securities markets seized up to the point that valid market prices for investments and loans were not readily available. Major banks, such as **HSBC Holdings**, **Wells Fargo**, and **Bank of America**, confronted this issue with respect to their mortgage-backed securities and interest rate swaps used to hedge interest rate risk. **Kohl's Department Stores** dealt with a similar situation for its investment in auction rates securities (ARS). The fair value of ARS is generally determined at quarterly auctions. However, these auctions failed during the financial crisis, and Kohl's and other ARS investors were forced to use a valuation model rather than market prices to determine fair value.

The FASB provides fair value estimation guidance (FASB ASC 820), but the Board also performs ongoing assessment of whether and to what extent additional valuation guidance is needed. In this regard, the Board established the **Valuation Resource Group (VRG)**. The VRG is comprised of accounting and valuation professionals, preparers and users of financial statements, regulators, and other industry representatives. The VRG provides the Board and the FASB staff with multiple viewpoints on application issues relating to fair value for financial reporting purposes. Here is a sampling of the issues discussed by the VRG:

- Measurement of contingent consideration in a business combination.
- Incorporating multi-period excess earnings in valuing intangible assets.
- Effects of premiums and discounts in fair value measurements.

- Determining the carrying amount of a reporting unit when performing the goodwill impairment test.
- Measurement uncertainty analysis disclosures.

As indicated, the list of topics is revealing as to the variety and complexity of the issues that must be addressed in implementing the fair value measurement principle. Discussion of these items by the VRG helped the FASB develop appropriate approaches for applying fair value guidance to specific examples. For example, with respect to the contingent consideration topic, the VRG noted that taxes must be considered when developing future cash flow estimates and that, in some cases, these tax effects are different for assets and liabilities.

The VRG has and will provide good counsel to the FASB with respect to applying the fair value measurement principle. After studying this chapter, you should have a better understanding of time value of money principles and discounted cash flow techniques as they are applied in accounting measurements.

Sources: Ernst and Young, "Valuation Resource Group: Highlights of November 2010 Meeting," *Hot Topic—Update on Major Accounting and Auditing Activities, No. 2010-59* (5 November 2010).

PREVIEW OF CHAPTER 6

As we indicated in the opening story, as a financial expert in today's accounting environment, you will be expected to make present and future value measurements and to understand their implications. The purpose of this chapter is to present the tools and techniques that will help you measure the present value of future cash inflows and outflows. The content and organization of the chapter are as follows.

Accounting and the Time Value of Money

Basic Time Value Concepts	Single-Sum Problems	Annuities	More Complex Situations	Present Value Measurement
• Applications • The nature of interest • Simple interest • Compound interest • Fundamental variables	• Future value of a single sum • Present value of a single sum • Solving for other unknowns	• Future value of ordinary annuity • Future value of annuity due • Examples of FV of annuity • Present value of ordinary annuity • Present value of annuity due • Examples of PV of annuity	• Deferred annuities • Valuation of long-term bonds • Effective-interest method of bond discount/premium amortization	• Choosing an appropriate interest rate • Example of expected cash flow

BASIC TIME VALUE CONCEPTS

LEARNING OBJECTIVE ❶

Identify accounting topics where the time value of money is relevant.

In accounting (and finance), the phrase **time value of money** indicates a relationship between time and money—that a dollar received today is worth more than a dollar promised at some time in the future. Why? Because of the opportunity to invest today's dollar and receive interest on the investment. Yet, when deciding among investment or borrowing alternatives, it is essential to be able to compare today's dollar and tomorrow's dollar on the same footing—to compare "apples to apples." Investors do that by using the concept of **present value**, which has many applications in accounting.

Applications of Time Value Concepts

Financial reporting uses different measurements in different situations—historical cost for equipment, net realizable value for inventories, fair value for investments. As we discussed in Chapters 2 and 5, the FASB increasingly is requiring the use of fair values in the measurement of assets and liabilities. According to the FASB's recent guidance on fair value measurements, the most useful fair value measures are based on market prices in active markets. Within the fair value hierarchy these are referred to as Level 1. Recall that Level 1 fair value measures are the least subjective because they are based on quoted prices, such as a closing stock price in the *Wall Street Journal*.

However, for many assets and liabilities, market-based fair value information is not readily available. In these cases, fair value can be estimated based on the expected future cash flows related to the asset or liability. Such fair value estimates are generally considered Level 3 (most subjective) in the fair value hierarchy because they are based on unobservable inputs, such as a company's own data or assumptions related to the expected future cash flows associated with the asset or liability. As discussed in the fair value guidance, present value techniques are used to convert expected cash flows into present values, which represent an estimate of fair value. **[1]**

⊙ See the FASB Codification section (page 320).

Because of the increased use of present values in this and other contexts, it is important to understand present value techniques.[1] We list some of the applications of present value-based measurements to accounting topics below; we discuss many of these in the following chapters.

> ### PRESENT VALUE-BASED ACCOUNTING MEASUREMENTS
>
> 1. **NOTES.** Valuing noncurrent receivables and payables that carry no stated interest rate or a lower than market interest rate.
> 2. **LEASES.** Valuing assets and obligations to be capitalized under long-term leases and measuring the amount of the lease payments and annual leasehold amortization.
> 3. **PENSIONS AND OTHER POSTRETIREMENT BENEFITS.** Measuring service cost components of employers' postretirement benefits expense and postretirement benefits obligation.
> 4. **LONG-TERM ASSETS.** Evaluating alternative long-term investments by discounting future cash flows. Determining the value of assets acquired under deferred payment contracts. Measuring impairments of assets.

[1]GAAP addresses present value as a measurements basis for a broad array of transactions, such as accounts and loans receivable **[2]**, leases **[3]**, postretirement benefits **[4]**, asset impairments **[5]**, and stock-based compensation **[6]**.

5. STOCK-BASED COMPENSATION. Determining the fair value of employee services in compensatory stock-option plans.

6. BUSINESS COMBINATIONS. Determining the value of receivables, payables, liabilities, accruals, and commitments acquired or assumed in a "purchase."

7. DISCLOSURES. Measuring the value of future cash flows from oil and gas reserves for disclosure in supplementary information.

8. ENVIRONMENTAL LIABILITIES. Determining the fair value of future obligations for asset retirements.

In addition to accounting and business applications, compound interest, annuity, and present value concepts apply to personal finance and investment decisions. In purchasing a home or car, planning for retirement, and evaluating alternative investments, you will need to understand time value of money concepts.

The Nature of Interest

Interest is payment for the use of money. It is the excess cash received or repaid over and above the amount lent or borrowed (**principal**). For example, Corner Bank lends Hillfarm Company $10,000 with the understanding that it will repay $11,500. The excess over $10,000, or $1,500, represents interest expense for Hillfarm and interest revenue for Corner Bank.

The lender generally states the amount of interest as a rate over a specific period of time. For example, if Hillfarm borrowed $10,000 for one year before repaying $11,500, the rate of interest is 15 percent per year ($1,500 ÷ $10,000). The custom of expressing interest as a percentage rate is an established business practice.[2] In fact, business managers make investing and borrowing decisions on the basis of the rate of interest involved, rather than on the actual dollar amount of interest to be received or paid.

How is the interest rate determined? One important factor is the level of credit risk (risk of nonpayment) involved. Other factors being equal, the higher the credit risk, the higher the interest rate. Low-risk borrowers like **Microsoft** or **Intel** can probably obtain a loan at or slightly below the going market rate of interest. However, a bank would probably charge the neighborhood delicatessen several percentage points above the market rate, if granting the loan at all.

The amount of interest involved in any financing transaction is a function of three variables:

VARIABLES IN INTEREST COMPUTATION

1. PRINCIPAL. The amount borrowed or invested.

2. INTEREST RATE. A percentage of the outstanding principal.

3. TIME. The number of years or fractional portion of a year that the principal is outstanding.

Thus, the following three relationships apply:

- The larger the principal amount, the larger the dollar amount of interest.
- The higher the interest rate, the larger the dollar amount of interest.
- The longer the time period, the larger the dollar amount of interest.

Federal law requires the disclosure of interest rates on an annual basis in all contracts. That is, instead of stating the rate as "1% per month," contracts must state the rate as "12% per year" if it is simple interest or "12.68% per year" if it is compounded monthly.

Simple Interest

LEARNING OBJECTIVE **2**
Distinguish between simple and compound interest.

Companies compute **simple interest** on the amount of the principal only. It is the return on (or growth of) the principal for one time period. The following equation expresses simple interest.[3]

$$\text{Interest} = p \times i \times n$$

where

p = principal .
i = rate of interest for a single period
n = number of periods

To illustrate, Barstow Electric Inc. borrows $10,000 for 3 years with a simple interest rate of 8% per year. It computes the total interest it will pay as follows.

$$
\begin{aligned}
\text{Interest} &= p \times i \times n \\
&= \$10,000 \times .08 \times 3 \\
&= \$2,400
\end{aligned}
$$

If Barstow borrows $10,000 for 3 months at 8%, the interest is $200, computed as follows.

$$
\begin{aligned}
\text{Interest} &= \$10,000 \times .08 \times 3/12 \\
&= \$200
\end{aligned}
$$

Compound Interest

LEARNING OBJECTIVE **3**
Use appropriate compound interest tables.

John Maynard Keynes, the legendary English economist, supposedly called it magic. Mayer Rothschild, the founder of the famous European banking firm, proclaimed it the eighth wonder of the world. Today, people continue to extol its wonder and its power. The object of their affection? Compound interest.

We compute **compound interest** on principal **and** on any interest earned that has not been paid or withdrawn. It is the return on (or growth of) the principal for two or more time periods. Compounding computes interest not only on the principal but also on the interest earned to date on that principal, assuming the interest is left on deposit.

To illustrate the difference between simple and compound interest, assume that Vasquez Company deposits $10,000 in the Last National Bank, where it will earn simple interest of 9% per year. It deposits another $10,000 in the First State Bank, where it will earn compound interest of 9% per year compounded annually. In both cases, Vasquez will not withdraw any interest until 3 years from the date of deposit. Illustration 6-1 shows the computation of interest Vasquez will receive, as well as its accumulated year-end balance.

ILLUSTRATION 6-1
Simple vs. Compound Interest

Last National Bank				*First State Bank*		
Simple Interest Calculation	Simple Interest	Accumulated Year-End Balance		Compound Interest Calculation	Compound Interest	Accumulated Year-End Balance
Year 1 $10,000.00 × 9%	$ 900.00	$10,900.00		Year 1 $10,000.00 × 9%	$ 900.00	$10,900.00
Year 2 $10,000.00 × 9%	900.00	$11,800.00		Year 2 $10,900.00 × 9%	981.00	$11,881.00
Year 3 $10,000.00 × 9%	900.00	$12,700.00		Year 3 $11,881.00 × 9%	1,069.29	$12,950.29
	$2,700.00		→ $250.29 ←		$2,950.29	
			Difference			

---

[3]Business mathematics and business finance textbooks traditionally state simple interest as I (interest) = P (principal) $\times$ R (rate) $\times$ T (time).

Note in Illustration 6-1 that simple interest uses the initial principal of $10,000 to compute the interest in all 3 years. **Compound interest uses the accumulated balance (principal plus interest to date) at each year-end to compute interest in the succeeding year.** This explains the larger balance in the compound interest account.

Obviously, any rational investor would choose compound interest, if available, over simple interest. In the example above, compounding provides $250.29 of additional interest revenue. For practical purposes, compounding assumes that unpaid interest earned becomes a part of the principal. Furthermore, the accumulated balance at the end of each year becomes the new principal sum on which interest is earned during the next year.

Compound interest is the typical interest computation applied in business situations. This occurs particularly in our economy, where companies use and finance large amounts of long-lived assets over long periods of time. Financial managers view and evaluate their investment opportunities in terms of a series of periodic returns, each of which they can reinvest to yield additional returns. Simple interest usually applies only to short-term investments and debts that involve a time span of one year or less.

What do the numbers mean? *A PRETTY GOOD START*

The continuing debate on Social Security reform provides a great context to illustrate the power of compounding. One proposed idea is for the government to give $1,000 to every citizen at birth. This gift would be deposited in an account that would earn interest tax-free until the citizen retires. Assuming the account earns a modest 5% annual return until retirement at age 65, the $1,000 would grow to $23,839. With monthly compounding, the $1,000 deposited at birth would grow to $25,617.

Why start so early? If the government waited until age 18 to deposit the money, it would grow to only $9,906 with annual compounding. That is, reducing the time invested by a third results in more than a 50% reduction in retirement money. This example illustrates the importance of starting early when the power of compounding is involved.

Compound Interest Tables (see pages 334–343)

We present five different types of compound interest tables at the end of this chapter. These tables should help you study this chapter as well as solve other problems involving interest.

INTEREST TABLES AND THEIR CONTENTS

1. FUTURE VALUE OF 1 *TABLE.* Contains the amounts to which 1 will accumulate if deposited now at a specified rate and left for a specified number of periods (Table 6-1).

2. PRESENT VALUE OF 1 *TABLE.* Contains the amounts that must be deposited now at a specified rate of interest to equal 1 at the end of a specified number of periods (Table 6-2).

3. FUTURE VALUE OF AN ORDINARY ANNUITY OF 1 *TABLE.* Contains the amounts to which periodic rents of 1 will accumulate if the payments (rents) are invested at the **end** of each period at a specified rate of interest for a specified number of periods (Table 6-3).

4. PRESENT VALUE OF AN ORDINARY ANNUITY OF 1 *TABLE.* Contains the amounts that must be deposited now at a specified rate of interest to permit withdrawals of 1 at the **end** of regular periodic intervals for the specified number of periods (Table 6-4).

5. PRESENT VALUE OF AN ANNUITY DUE OF 1 *TABLE.* Contains the amounts that must be deposited now at a specified rate of interest to permit withdrawals of 1 at the **beginning** of regular periodic intervals for the specified number of periods (Table 6-5).

Illustration 6-2 lists the general format and content of these tables. It shows how much principal plus interest a dollar accumulates to at the end of each of five periods, at three different rates of compound interest.

ILLUSTRATION 6-2
Excerpt from Table 6-1

FUTURE VALUE OF 1 AT COMPOUND INTEREST (EXCERPT FROM TABLE 6-1, PAGE 334)			
Period	9%	10%	11%
1	1.09000	1.10000	1.11000
2	1.18810	1.21000	1.23210
3	1.29503	1.33100	1.36763
4	1.41158	1.46410	1.51807
5	1.53862	1.61051	1.68506

The compound tables rely on basic formulas. For example, the formula to determine the future value factor (*FVF*) for 1 is:

$$FVF_{n,i} = (1 + i)^n$$

where

$FVF_{n,i}$ = future value factor for n periods at i interest

n = number of periods

i = rate of interest for a single period

Gateway to the Profession

Financial Calculator and Spreadsheet Tools

Financial calculators include preprogrammed $FVF_{n,i}$ and other time value of money formulas.

To illustrate the use of interest tables to calculate compound amounts, assume an interest rate of 9%. Illustration 6-3 shows the future value to which 1 accumulates (the future value factor).

ILLUSTRATION 6-3
Accumulation of Compound Amounts

Period	Beginning-of-Period Amount	Multiplier × (1 + i)	End-of-Period = Amount*	Formula (1 + i)ⁿ
1	1.00000	1.09	1.09000	$(1.09)^1$
2	1.09000	1.09	1.18810	$(1.09)^2$
3	1.18810	1.09	1.29503	$(1.09)^3$

*Note that these amounts appear in Table 6-1 in the 9% column.

Throughout our discussion of compound interest tables, note the intentional use of the term **periods** instead of **years**. Interest is generally expressed in terms of an annual rate. However, many business circumstances dictate a compounding period of less than one year. In such circumstances, a company must convert the annual interest rate to correspond to the length of the period. To convert the "annual interest rate" into the "compounding period interest rate," a company **divides the annual rate by the number of compounding periods per year**.

In addition, companies determine the number of periods by **multiplying the number of years involved by the number of compounding periods per year**. To illustrate, assume an investment of $1 for 6 years at 8% annual interest compounded **quarterly**. Using Table 6-1, page 334, read the factor that appears in the 2% column on the 24th row—6 years × 4 compounding periods per year, namely 1.60844, or approximately $1.61. Thus, all compound interest tables use the term **periods**, not **years**, to express th quantity of n. Illustration 6-4 shows how to determine (1) the interest rate per compounding period and (2) the number of compounding periods in four situations of differing compounding frequency.[4]

12% Annual Interest Rate over 5 Years Compounded	Interest Rate per Compounding Period	Number of Compounding Periods
Annually (1)	.12 ÷ 1 = .12	5 years × 1 compounding per year = 5 periods
Semiannually (2)	.12 ÷ 2 = .06	5 years × 2 compoundings per year = 10 periods
Quarterly (4)	.12 ÷ 4 = .03	5 years × 4 compoundings per year = 20 periods
Monthly (12)	.12 ÷ 12 = .01	5 years × 12 compoundings per year = 60 periods

ILLUSTRATION 6-4
Frequency of Compounding

How often interest is compounded can substantially affect the rate of return. For example, a 9% annual interest compounded **daily** provides a 9.42% yield, or a difference of 0.42%. The 9.42% is the **effective yield**.[5] The annual interest rate (9%) is the **stated**, **nominal**, or **face rate**. When the compounding frequency is greater than once a year, the effective-interest rate will always exceed the stated rate.

Illustration 6-5 shows how compounding for five different time periods affects the effective yield and the amount earned by an investment of $10,000 for one year.

Interest Rate	Compounding Periods				
	Annually	Semiannually	Quarterly	Monthly	Daily
8%	8.00% $800	8.16% $816	8.24% $824	8.30% $830	8.33% $833
9%	9.00% $900	9.20% $920	9.31% $931	9.38% $938	9.42% $942
10%	10.00% $1,000	10.25% $1,025	10.38% $1,038	10.47% $1,047	10.52% $1,052

ILLUSTRATION 6-5
Comparison of Different Compounding Periods

[4]Because interest is theoretically earned (accruing) every second of every day, it is possible to calculate interest that is **compounded continuously**. Using the natural, or Napierian, system of logarithms facilitates computations involving continuous compounding. As a practical matter, however, most business transactions assume interest to be compounded no more frequently than daily.

[5]The formula for calculating the **effective rate**, in situations where the compounding frequency (n) is greater than once a year, is as follows.

$$\text{Effective rate} = (1 + i)^n - 1$$

To illustrate, if the stated annual rate is 8% compounded quarterly (or 2% per quarter), the effective annual rate is:

$$
\begin{aligned}
\text{Effective rate} &= (1 + .02)^4 - 1 \\
&= (1.02)^4 - 1 \\
&= 1.0824 - 1 \\
&= .0824 \\
&= 8.24\%
\end{aligned}
$$

Fundamental Variables

The following four variables are fundamental to all compound interest problems.

FUNDAMENTAL VARIABLES

1. **RATE OF INTEREST.** This rate, unless otherwise stated, is an annual rate that must be adjusted to reflect the length of the compounding period if less than a year.
2. **NUMBER OF TIME PERIODS.** This is the number of compounding periods. (A period may be equal to or less than a year.)
3. **FUTURE VALUE.** The value at a future date of a given sum or sums invested assuming compound interest.
4. **PRESENT VALUE.** The value now (present time) of a future sum or sums discounted assuming compound interest.

Illustration 6-6 depicts the relationship of these four fundamental variables in a **time diagram**.

ILLUSTRATION 6-6
Basic Time Diagram

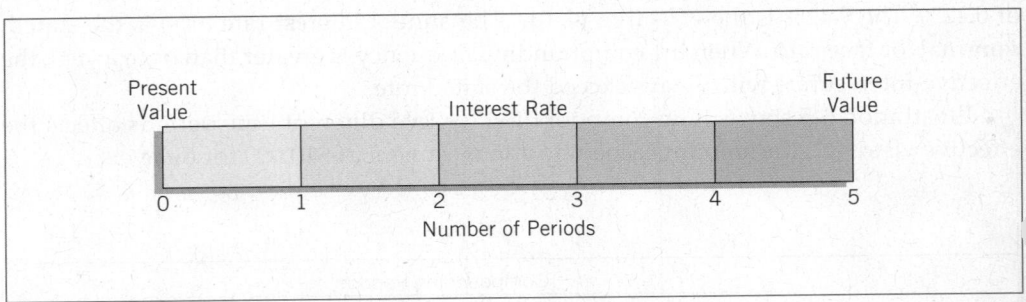

In some cases, all four of these variables are known. However, at least one variable is unknown in many business situations. To better understand and solve the problems in this chapter, we encourage you to sketch compound interest problems in the form of the preceding time diagram.

SINGLE-SUM PROBLEMS

Many business and investment decisions involve a single amount of money that either exists now or will in the future. Single-sum problems are generally classified into one of the following two categories.

1. Computing the **unknown future value** of a known single sum of money that is invested now for a certain number of periods at a certain interest rate.
2. Computing the **unknown present value** of a known single sum of money in the future that is discounted for a certain number of periods at a certain interest rate.

When analyzing the information provided, determine first whether the problem involves a future value or a present value. Then apply the following general rules, depending on the situation:

- **If solving for a future value,** *accumulate* all cash flows to a future point. In this instance, interest increases the amounts or values over time so that the future value exceeds the present value.

- **If solving for a present value**, *discount* all cash flows from the future to the present. In this case, **discounting** reduces the amounts or values, so that the present value is less than the future amount.

Preparation of time diagrams aids in identifying the unknown as an item in the future or the present. Sometimes the problem involves neither a future value nor a present value. Instead, the unknown is the interest or discount rate, or the number of compounding or discounting periods.

Future Value of a Single Sum

To determine the **future value** of a single sum, multiply the future value factor by its present value (principal), as follows.

$$FV = PV \, (FVF_{n,i})$$

where

FV = future value

PV = present value (principal or single sum)

$FVF_{n,i}$ = future value factor for n periods at i interest

To illustrate, Bruegger Co. wants to determine the future value of $50,000 invested for 5 years compounded annually at an interest rate of 11%. Illustration 6-7 shows this investment situation in time-diagram form.

ILLUSTRATION 6-7
Future Value Time
Diagram ($n = 5, i = 11\%$)

Using the future value formula, Bruegger solves this investment problem as follows.

$$\text{Future value} = PV \, (FVF_{n,i})$$
$$= \$50,000 \, (FVF_{5,11\%})$$
$$= \$50,000 \, (1 + .11)^5$$
$$= \$50,000 \, (1.68506)$$
$$= \$84,253$$

To determine the future value factor of 1.68506 in the formula above, Bruegger uses a financial calculator or reads the appropriate table, in this case Table 6-1 (11% column and the 5-period row).

Companies can apply this time diagram and formula approach to routine business situations. To illustrate, assume that **Commonwealth Edison Company** deposited $250 million in an escrow account with **Northern Trust Company** at the beginning of 2014 as a commitment toward a power plant to be completed December 31, 2017. How much will the company have on deposit at the end of 4 years if interest is 10%, compounded semiannually?

With a known present value of $250 million, a total of 8 compounding periods (4 × 2), and an interest rate of 5% per compounding period (.10 ÷ 2), the company can time-diagram this problem and determine the future value as shown in Illustration 6-8.

ILLUSTRATION 6-8
Future Value Time
Diagram ($n = 8$, $i = 5\%$)

$$\text{Future value} = \$250,000,000 \ (FVF_{8,5\%})$$
$$= \$250,000,000 \ (1 + .05)^8$$
$$= \$250,000,000 \ (1.47746)$$
$$= \$369,365,000$$

Using a future value factor found in Table 6-1 (5% column, 8-period row), we find that the deposit of $250 million will accumulate to $369,365,000 by December 31, 2017.

Present Value of a Single Sum

The Bruegger example on page 295 showed that $50,000 invested at an annually compounded interest rate of 11% will equal $84,253 at the end of 5 years. It follows, then, that $84,253, 5 years in the future, is worth $50,000 now. That is, $50,000 is the present value of $84,253. The **present value** is the amount needed to invest now, to produce a known future value.

The present value is always a smaller amount than the known future value, due to earned and accumulated interest. In determining the future value, a company moves forward in time using a process of **accumulation**. In determining present value, it moves backward in time using a process of **discounting**.

As indicated earlier, a "present value of 1 table" appears at the end of this chapter as Table 6-2. Illustration 6-9 demonstrates the nature of such a table. It shows the present value of 1 for five different periods at three different rates of interest.

ILLUSTRATION 6-9
Excerpt from Table 6-2

PRESENT VALUE OF 1 AT COMPOUND INTEREST			
(EXCERPT FROM TABLE 6-2, PAGE 337)			
Period	9%	10%	11%
1	0.91743	0.90909	0.90090
2	0.84168	0.82645	0.81162
3	0.77218	0.75132	0.73119
4	0.70843	0.68301	0.65873
5	0.64993	0.62092	0.59345

The following formula is used to determine the present value of 1 (present value factor):

$$PVF_{n,i} = \frac{1}{(1 + i)^n}$$

where

$PVF_{n,i}$ = present value factor for n periods at i interest

To illustrate, assuming an interest rate of 9%, the present value of 1 discounted for three different periods is as shown in Illustration 6-10.

Discount Periods	1	÷	$(1 + i)^n$	=	Present Value*	Formula $1/(1 + i)^n$
1	1.00000		1.09		.91743	$1/(1.09)^1$
2	1.00000		$(1.09)^2$		.84168	$1/(1.09)^2$
3	1.00000		$(1.09)^3$		.77218	$1/(1.09)^3$

*Note that these amounts appear in Table 6-2 in the 9% column.

ILLUSTRATION 6-10
Present Value of $1 Discounted at 9% for Three Periods

The present value of any single sum (future value), then, is as follows.

$$PV = FV (PVF_{n,i})$$

where

PV = present value

FV = future value

$PVF_{n,i}$ = present value factor for n periods at i interest

To illustrate, what is the present value of $84,253 to be received or paid in 5 years discounted at 11% compounded annually? Illustration 6-11 shows this problem as a time diagram.

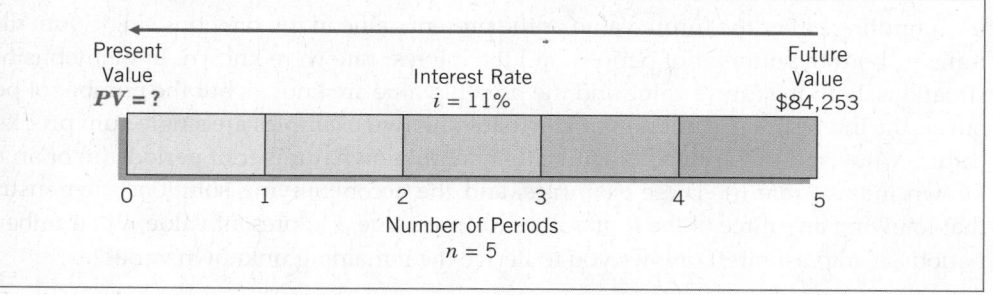

Present Value
$PV = ?$

Interest Rate
$i = 11\%$

Future Value
$84,253

Number of Periods
$n = 5$

ILLUSTRATION 6-11
Present Value Time Diagram ($n = 5, i = 11\%$)

Using the formula, we solve this problem as follows.

$$\text{Present value} = FV (PVF_{n,i})$$
$$= \$84{,}253 \ (PVF_{5,11\%})$$
$$= \$84{,}253 \left(\frac{1}{(1 + .11)^5} \right)$$
$$= \$84{,}253 \ (.59345)$$
$$= \$50{,}000 \ (\text{rounded by } \$.06)$$

To determine the present value factor of 0.59345, use a financial calculator or read the present value of a single sum in Table 6-2 (11% column, 5-period row).

The time diagram and formula approach can be applied in a variety of situations. For example, assume that your rich uncle decides to give you $2,000 for a trip to Europe when you graduate from college 3 years from now. He proposes to finance the trip by investing a sum of money now at 8% compound interest that will provide you with $2,000 upon your graduation. The only conditions are that you graduate and that you tell him how much to invest now.

To impress your uncle, you set up the time diagram in Illustration 6-12 and solve this problem as follows.

ILLUSTRATION 6-12
Present Value Time
Diagram ($n = 3$, $i = 8\%$)

$$\text{Present value} = 2,000 \ (PVF_{3,8\%})$$

$$= \$2,000 \left(\frac{1}{(1 + .08)^3} \right)$$

$$= \$2,000 \ (.79383)$$

$$= \$1,587.66$$

Advise your uncle to invest $1,587.66 now to provide you with $2,000 upon graduation. To satisfy your uncle's other condition, you must pass this course (and many more).

Solving for Other Unknowns in Single-Sum Problems

In computing either the future value or the present value in the previous single-sum illustrations, both the number of periods and the interest rate were known. In many business situations, both the future value and the present value are known, but the number of periods or the interest rate is unknown. The following two examples are single-sum problems (future value and present value) with either an unknown number of periods (n) or an unknown interest rate (i). These examples, and the accompanying solutions, demonstrate that knowing any three of the four values (future value, FV; present value, PV; number of periods, n; interest rate, i) allows you to derive the remaining unknown variable.

Example—Computation of the Number of Periods

The Village of Somonauk wants to accumulate $70,000 for the construction of a veterans monument in the town square. At the beginning of the current year, the Village deposited $47,811 in a memorial fund that earns 10% interest compounded annually. How many years will it take to accumulate $70,000 in the memorial fund?

In this illustration, the Village knows both the present value ($47,811) and the future value ($70,000), along with the interest rate of 10%. Illustration 6-13 depicts this investment problem as a time diagram.

ILLUSTRATION 6-13
Time Diagram to Solve
for Unknown Number of
Periods

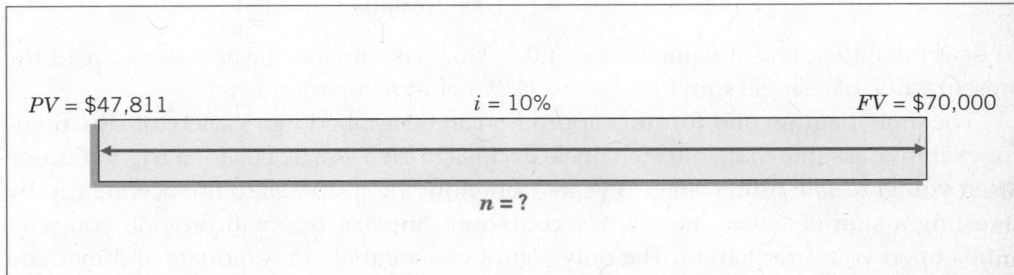

Knowing both the present value and the future value allows the Village to solve for the unknown number of periods. It may use either the future value or the present value formulas, as shown in Illustration 6-14.

Future Value Approach	Present Value Approach
$FV = PV (FVF_{n,10\%})$	$PV = FV (PVF_{n,10\%})$
$\$70,000 = \$47,811 (FVF_{n,10\%})$	$\$47,811 = \$70,000 (PVF_{n,10\%})$
$FVF_{n,10\%} = \dfrac{\$70,000}{\$47,811} = 1.46410$	$PVF_{n,10\%} = \dfrac{\$47,811}{\$70,000} = .68301$

ILLUSTRATION 6-14
Solving for Unknown Number of Periods

Using the future value factor of 1.46410, refer to Table 6-1 and read down the 10% column to find that factor in the 4-period row. Thus, it will take 4 years for the $47,811 to accumulate to $70,000 if invested at 10% interest compounded annually. Or, using the present value factor of 0.68301, refer to Table 6-2 and read down the 10% column to find that factor in the 4-period row.

Example—Computation of the Interest Rate

Advanced Design, Inc. needs $1,409,870 for basic research 5 years from now. The company currently has $800,000 to invest for that purpose. At what rate of interest must it invest the $800,000 to fund basic research projects of $1,409,870, 5 years from now?

The time diagram in Illustration 6-15 depicts this investment situation.

ILLUSTRATION 6-15
Time Diagram to Solve for Unknown Interest Rate

Advanced Design may determine the unknown interest rate from either the future value approach or the present value approach, as Illustration 6-16 shows.

Future Value Approach	Present Value Approach
$FV = PV (FVF_{5,i})$	$PV = FV (PVF_{5,i})$
$\$1,409,870 = \$800,000 (FVF_{5,i})$	$\$800,000 = \$1,409,870 (PVF_{5,i})$
$FVF_{5,i} = \dfrac{\$1,409,870}{\$800,000} = 1.76234$	$PVF_{5,i} = \dfrac{\$800,000}{\$1,409,870} = .56743$

ILLUSTRATION 6-16
Solving for Unknown Interest Rate

Using the future value factor of 1.76234, refer to Table 6-1 and read across the 5-period row to find that factor in the 12% column. Thus, the company must invest the $800,000 at 12% to accumulate to $1,409,870 in 5 years. Or, using the present value factor of .56743 and Table 6-2, again find that factor at the juncture of the 5-period row and the 12% column.

ANNUITIES

The preceding discussion involved only the accumulation or discounting of a single principal sum. However, many situations arise in which a series of dollar amounts are paid or received periodically, such as installment loans or sales; regular, partially recovered invested funds; or a series of realized cost savings.

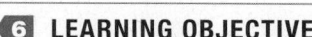

6 LEARNING OBJECTIVE
Solve future value of ordinary and annuity due problems.

For example, a life insurance contract involves a series of equal payments made at equal intervals of time. Such a process of periodic payment represents the accumulation of a sum of money through an annuity. An **annuity**, by definition, requires the following: (1) periodic payments or receipts (called **rents**) of the same amount, (2) the same-length interval between such rents, and (3) compounding of **interest** once each interval. The **future value of an annuity** is the sum of all the rents plus the accumulated compound interest on them.

Note that the rents may occur at either the beginning or the end of the periods. If the rents occur at the end of each period, an annuity is classified as an **ordinary annuity**. If the rents occur at the beginning of each period, an annuity is classified as an **annuity due**.

Future Value of an Ordinary Annuity

One approach to determining the future value of an annuity computes the value to which **each** of the rents in the series will accumulate, and then totals their individual future values.

For example, assume that $1 is deposited at the **end** of each of 5 years (an ordinary annuity) and earns 12% interest compounded annually. Illustration 6-17 shows the computation of the future value, using the "future value of 1" table (Table 6-1) for each of the five $1 rents.

ILLUSTRATION 6-17
Solving for the Future Value of an Ordinary Annuity

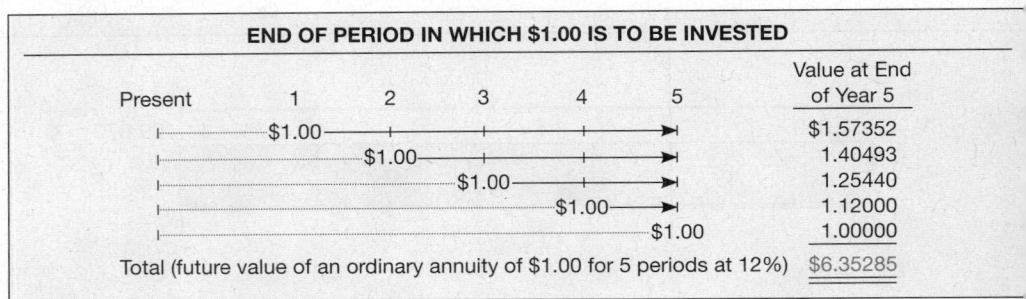

	END OF PERIOD IN WHICH $1.00 IS TO BE INVESTED					
Present	1	2	3	4	5	Value at End of Year 5
	$1.00					$1.57352
		$1.00				1.40493
			$1.00			1.25440
				$1.00		1.12000
					$1.00	1.00000
Total (future value of an ordinary annuity of $1.00 for 5 periods at 12%)						$6.35285

Because an ordinary annuity consists of rents deposited at the end of the period, those rents earn no interest during the period. For example, the third rent earns interest for only two periods (periods four and five). It earns no interest for the third period since it is not deposited until the end of the third period. When computing the future value of an ordinary annuity, the number of compounding periods will always be **one less than the number of rents**.

The foregoing procedure for computing the future value of an ordinary annuity always produces the correct answer. However, it can become cumbersome if the number of rents is large. A formula provides a more efficient way of expressing the future value of an ordinary annuity of 1. This formula sums the individual rents plus the compound interest, as follows.

$$FVF\text{-}OA_{n,i} = \frac{(1 + i)^n - 1}{i}$$

where

$$FVF\text{-}OA_{n,i} = \text{future value factor of an ordinary annuity}$$
$$i = \text{rate of interest per period}$$
$$n = \text{number of compounding periods}$$

For example, $FVF\text{-}OA_{5,12\%}$ refers to the value to which an ordinary annuity of 1 will accumulate in 5 periods at 12% interest.

Using the formula above has resulted in the development of tables, similar to those used for the "future value of 1" and the "present value of 1" for both an ordinary annuity and an annuity due. Illustration 6-18 provides an excerpt from the "future value of an ordinary annuity of 1" table.

FUTURE VALUE OF AN ORDINARY ANNUITY OF 1 (EXCERPT FROM TABLE 6-3, PAGE 339)			
Period	10%	11%	12%
1	1.00000	1.00000	1.00000
2	2.10000	2.11000	2.12000
3	3.31000	3.34210	3.37440
4	4.64100	4.70973	4.77933
5	6.10510	6.22780	6.35285*

*Note that this annuity table factor is the same as the sum of the future values of 1 factors shown in Illustration 6-17.

ILLUSTRATION 6-18
Excerpt from Table 6-3

Interpreting the table, if $1 is invested at the end of each year for 4 years at 11% interest compounded annually, the value of the annuity at the end of the fourth year is $4.71 (4.70973 × $1.00). Now, multiply the factor from the appropriate line and column of the table by the dollar amount of **one rent** involved in an ordinary annuity. The result: the accumulated sum of the rents and the compound interest to the date of the last rent.

The following formula computes the future value of an ordinary annuity.

$$\text{Future value of an ordinary annuity} = R\ (FVF\text{-}OA_{n,i})$$

where

$$R = \text{periodic rent}$$
$$FVF\text{-}OA_{n,i} = \text{future value of an ordinary annuity}$$
$$\text{factor for } n \text{ periods at } i \text{ interest}$$

To illustrate, what is the future value of five $5,000 deposits made at the end of each of the next 5 years, earning interest of 12%? Illustration 6-19 depicts this problem as a time diagram.

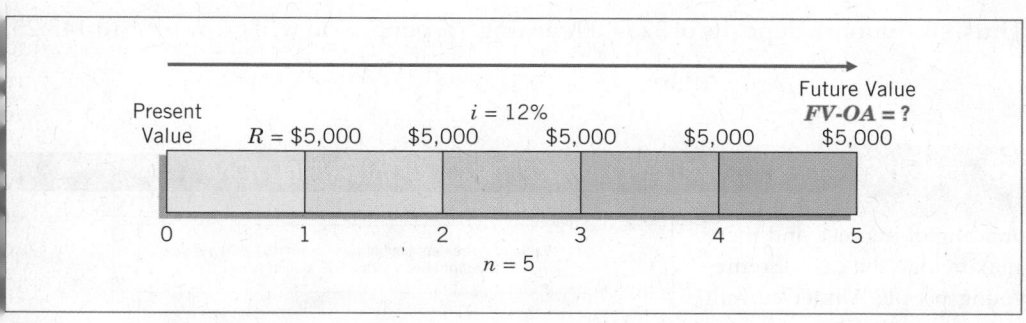

ILLUSTRATION 6-19
Time Diagram for Future Value of Ordinary Annuity ($n = 5$, $i = 12\%$)

Use of the formula solves this investment problem as follows.

$$\text{Future value of an ordinary annuity} = R\ (FVF\text{-}OA_{n,i})$$
$$= 5,000\ (FVF\text{-}OA_{5,12\%})$$
$$= \$5,000 \left(\frac{(1 + .12)^5 - 1}{.12} \right)$$
$$= \$5,000\ (6.35285)$$
$$= \$31,764.25$$

To determine the future value of an ordinary annuity factor of 6.35285 in the formula on page 301, use a financial calculator or read the appropriate table, in this case, Table 6-3 (12% column and the 5-period row).

To illustrate these computations in a business situation, assume that Hightown Electronics deposits $75,000 at the end of each 6-month period for the next 3 years, to accumulate enough money to meet debts that mature in 3 years. What is the future value that the company will have on deposit at the end of 3 years if the annual interest rate is 10%? The time diagram in Illustration 6-20 depicts this situation.

ILLUSTRATION 6-20
Time Diagram for Future Value of Ordinary Annuity ($n = 6$, $i = 5\%$)

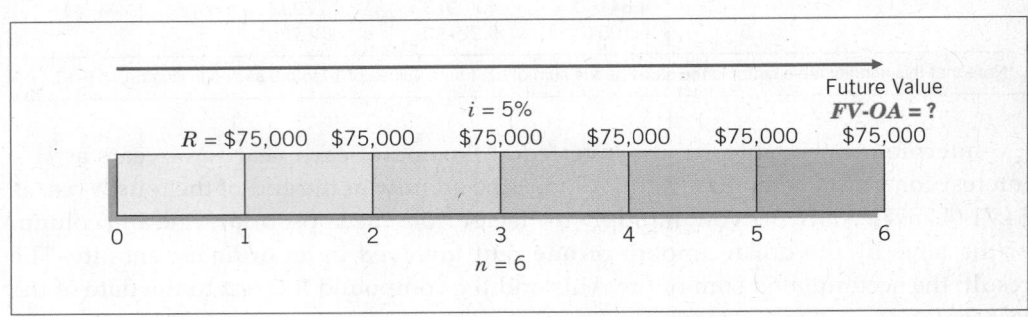

The formula solution for the Hightown Electronics situation is as follows.

$$\text{Future value of an ordinary annuity} = R\ (FVF\text{-}OA_{n,i})$$
$$= \$75,000\ (FVF\text{-}OA_{6,5\%})$$
$$= \$75,000 \left(\frac{(1 + .05)^6 - 1}{.05} \right)$$
$$= \$75,000\ (6.80191)$$
$$= \$510,143.25$$

Thus, six 6-month deposits of $75,000 earning 5% per period will grow to $510,143.25.

What do the numbers mean?   DON'T WAIT TO MAKE THAT CONTRIBUTION!

There is great power in compounding of interest, and there is no better illustration of this maxim than the case of retirement savings, especially for young people. Under current tax rules for individual retirement accounts (IRAs), you can contribute up to $5,000 in an investment fund, which will grow tax-free until you reach retirement age. What's more, you get a tax deduction for the amount contributed in the current year. Financial planners encourage young people to take advantage of the tax benefits of IRAs. By starting early, you can use the power of compounding to grow a pretty good nest egg. As shown in the adjacent chart, starting earlier can have a big impact on the value of your retirement fund.

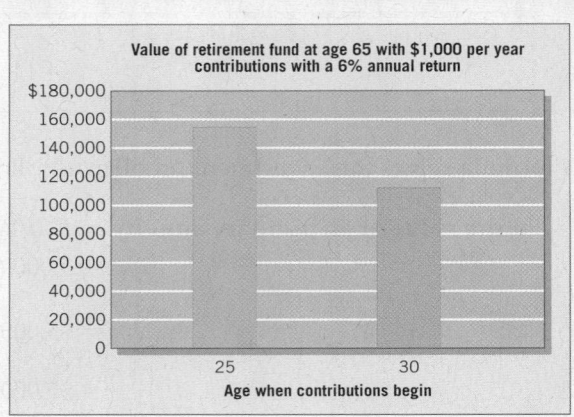

As shown, by setting aside $1,000 each year, beginning when you are 25 and assuming a rate of return of 6%, your retirement account at age 65 will have a tidy balance of $154,762 ($1,000 × 154.76197 (*FVF-OA*$_{40,6\%}$)). That's the power of compounding. Not too bad you say, but hey, there are a lot of things you might want to spend that $1,000 on (clothes, a trip to Vegas or Europe, new golf clubs). However, if you delay starting those contributions until age 30, your retirement fund will grow only to a value of $111,435 ($1,000 × 111.43478 (*FVF-OA*$_{35,6\%}$)). That is quite a haircut—about 28%. That is, by delaying or missing contributions, you miss out on the power of compounding and put a dent in your projected nest egg.

Source: Adapted from T. Rowe Price, "A Roadmap to Financial Security for Young Adults," *Invest with Confidence* (*troweprice.com*).

Future Value of an Annuity Due

The preceding analysis of an ordinary annuity assumed that the periodic rents occur at the **end** of each period. Recall that an **annuity due** assumes periodic rents occur at the **beginning** of each period. This means an annuity due will accumulate interest during the first period (in contrast to an ordinary annuity rent, which will not). In other words, the two types of annuities differ in the number of interest accumulation periods involved even though the same number of rents occur.

If rents occur at the end of a period (ordinary annuity), in determining the **future value of an annuity** there will be one less interest period than if the rents occur at the beginning of the period (annuity due). Illustration 6-21 shows this distinction.

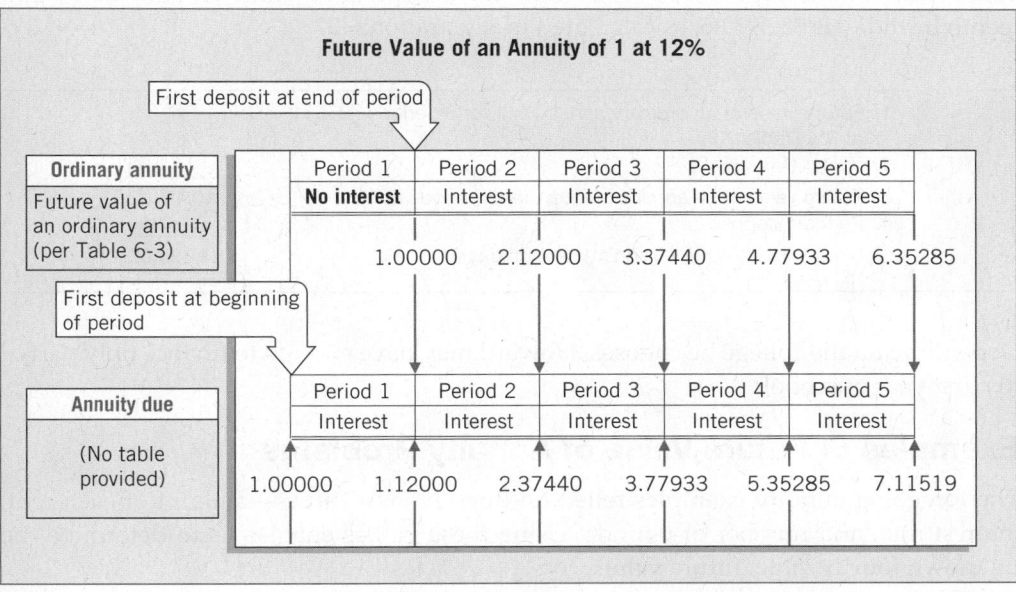

ILLUSTRATION 6-21
Comparison of the Future Value of an Ordinary Annuity with an Annuity Due

In this example, the cash flows from the annuity due come exactly one period earlier than for an ordinary annuity. As a result, the future value of the annuity due factor is exactly 12% higher than the ordinary annuity factor. For example, the value of an ordinary annuity factor at the end of period one at 12% is 1.00000, whereas for an annuity due it is 1.12000.

To find the future value of an annuity due factor, multiply the future value of an ordinary annuity factor by 1 plus the interest rate. For example, to determine the future value of an annuity due interest factor for 5 periods at 12% compound interest, simply multiply the future value of an ordinary annuity interest factor for 5 periods (6.35285), by one plus the interest rate (1 + .12), to arrive at 7.11519 (6.35285 × 1.12).

To illustrate the use of the ordinary annuity tables in converting to an annuity due, assume that Sue Lotadough plans to deposit $800 a year on each birthday of her son Howard. She makes the first deposit on his tenth birthday, at 6% interest compounded annually. Sue wants to know the amount she will have accumulated for college expenses by her son's eighteenth birthday.

If the first deposit occurs on Howard's tenth birthday, Sue will make a total of 8 deposits over the life of the annuity (assume no deposit on the eighteenth birthday), as shown in Illustration 6-22. Because all the deposits are made at the beginning of the periods, they represent an annuity due.

ILLUSTRATION 6-22
Annuity Due Time
Diagram

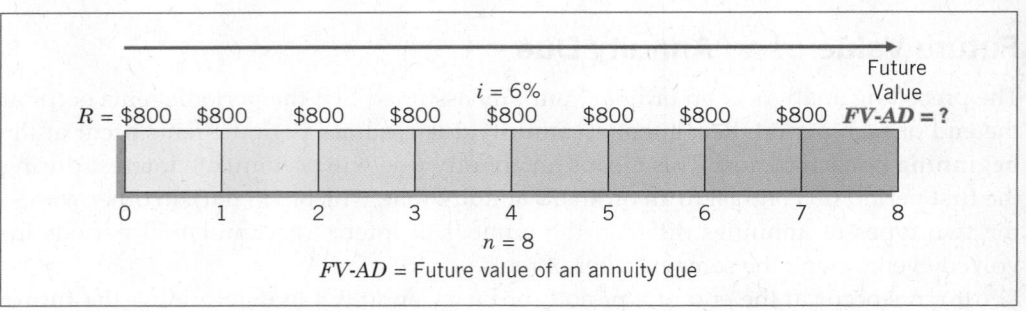

Referring to the "future value of an ordinary annuity of 1" table for 8 periods at 6%, Sue finds a factor of 9.89747. She then multiplies this factor by (1 + .06) to arrive at the future value of an annuity due factor. As a result, the accumulated value on Howard's eighteenth birthday is $8,393.06, as calculated in Illustration 6-23.

ILLUSTRATION 6-23
Computation of
Accumulated Value of
Annuity Due

1. Future value of an ordinary annuity of 1 for 8 periods at 6% (Table 6-3)		9.89747
2. Factor (1 + .06)	×	1.06
3. Future value of an annuity due of 1 for 8 periods at 6%		10.49132
4. Periodic deposit (rent)	×	$800
5. Accumulated value on son's 18th birthday		$8,393.06

Depending on the college he chooses, Howard may have enough to finance only part of his first year of school.

Examples of Future Value of Annuity Problems

The foregoing annuity examples relied on three known values—amount of each rent, interest rate, and number of periods. Using these values enables us to determine the unknown fourth value, future value.

The first two future value problems we present illustrate the computations of (1) the amount of the rents and (2) the number of rents. The third problem illustrates the computation of the future value of an annuity due.

Computation of Rent

Assume that you plan to accumulate $14,000 for a down payment on a condominium apartment 5 years from now. For the next 5 years, you earn an annual return of 8% compounded semiannually. How much should you deposit at the end of each 6-month period?

The $14,000 is the future value of 10 (5 × 2) semiannual end-of-period payments of an unknown amount, at an interest rate of 4% (8% ÷ 2). Illustration 6-24 depicts this problem as a time diagram.

Using the formula for the future value of an ordinary annuity, you determine the amount of each rent as follows.

$$\text{Future value of an ordinary annuity} = R\ (FVF\text{-}OA_{n,i})$$
$$\$14{,}000 = R\ (FVF\text{-}OA_{10,4\%})$$
$$\$14{,}000 = R\ (12.00611)$$
$$R = \$1{,}166.07$$

Thus, you must make 10 semiannual deposits of $1,166.07 each in order to accumulate $14,000 for your down payment.

Computation of the Number of Periodic Rents

Suppose that a company's goal is to accumulate $117,332 by making periodic deposits of $20,000 at the end of each year, which will earn 8% compounded annually while accumulating. How many deposits must it make?

The $117,332 represents the future value of $n(?)$ $20,000 deposits, at an 8% annual rate of interest. Illustration 6-25 depicts this problem in a time diagram.

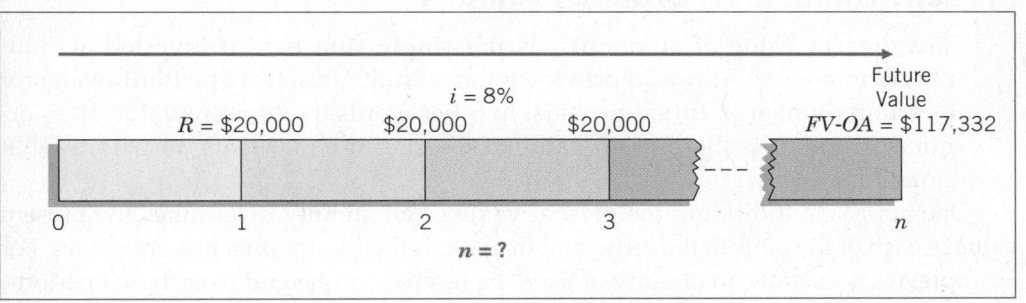

Using the future value of an ordinary annuity formula, the company obtains the following factor.

$$\text{Future value of an ordinary annuity} = R\ (FVF\text{-}OA_{n,i})$$
$$\$117{,}332 = \$20{,}000\ (FVF\text{-}OA_{n,8\%})$$
$$FVF\text{-}OA_{n,8\%} = \frac{\$117{,}332}{\$20{,}000} = 5.86660$$

Use Table 6-3 and read down the 8% column to find 5.86660 in the 5-period row. Thus, the company must make five deposits of $20,000 each.

Computation of the Future Value

To create his retirement fund, Walter Goodwrench, a mechanic, now works weekends. Mr. Goodwrench deposits $2,500 today in a savings account that earns 9% interest.

He plans to deposit $2,500 every year for a total of 30 years. How much cash will Mr. Goodwrench accumulate in his retirement savings account, when he retires in 30 years? Illustration 6-26 depicts this problem in a time diagram.

ILLUSTRATION 6-26
Future Value Annuity
Due Time Diagram
($n = 30$, $i = 9$%)

Using the "future value of an ordinary annuity of 1" table, Mr. Goodwrench computes the solution as shown in Illustration 6-27.

ILLUSTRATION 6-27
Computation of
Accumulated Value of
an Annuity Due

1. Future value of an ordinary annuity of 1 for 30 periods at 9%	136.30754
2. Factor (1 + .09)	× 1.09
3. Future value of an annuity due of 1 for 30 periods at 9%	148.57522
4. Periodic rent	× $2,500
5. Accumulated value at end of 30 years	$371,438

Present Value of an Ordinary Annuity

LEARNING OBJECTIVE **7**
Solve present value of ordinary and
annuity due problems.

The present value of an annuity is **the single sum** that, if invested at compound interest now, would provide for an annuity (a series of withdrawals) for a certain number of future periods. In other words, the present value of an ordinary annuity is the present value of a series of equal rents, to withdraw at equal intervals.

One approach to finding the present value of an annuity determines the present value of each of the rents in the series and then totals their individual present values. For example, we may view an annuity of $1, to be received at the **end** of each of 5 periods, as separate amounts. We then compute each present value using the table of present values (see Table 6-2 on pages 336–337), assuming an interest rate of 12%. Illustration 6-28 shows this approach.

ILLUSTRATION 6-28
Solving for the Present
Value of an Ordinary
Annuity

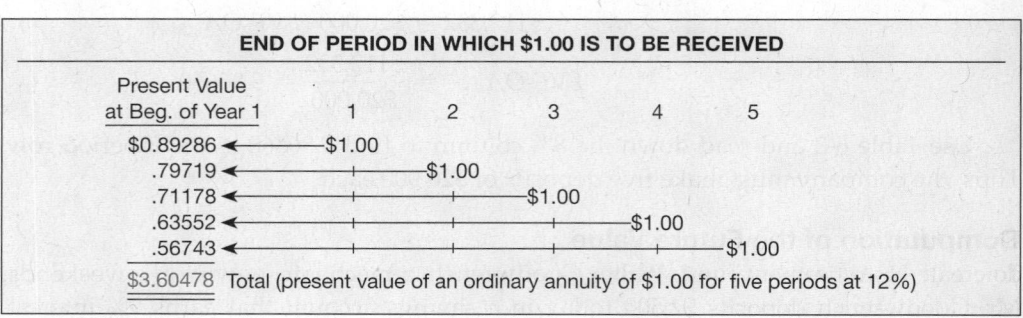

This computation tells us that if we invest the single sum of $3.61 today at 12% interest for 5 periods, we will be able to withdraw $1 at the end of each period for 5 periods. We can summarize this cumbersome procedure by the following formula.

$$PVF\text{-}OA_{n,i} = \frac{1 - \dfrac{1}{(1 + i)^n}}{i}$$

The expression $PVF\text{-}OA_{n,i}$ refers to the present value of an ordinary annuity of 1 factor for n periods at i interest. Ordinary annuity tables base present values on this formula. Illustration 6-29 shows an excerpt from such a table.

ILLUSTRATION 6-29
Excerpt from Table 6-4

PRESENT VALUE OF AN ORDINARY ANNUITY OF 1 (EXCERPT FROM TABLE 6-4, PAGE 341)			
Period	10%	11%	12%
1	0.90909	0.90090	0.89286
2	1.73554	1.71252	1.69005
3	2.48685	2.44371	2.40183
4	3.16986	3.10245	3.03735
5	3.79079	3.69590	3.60478*

*Note that this annuity table factor is equal to the sum of the present value of 1 factors shown in Illustration 6-28.

The general formula for the present value of any ordinary annuity is as follows.

Present value of an ordinary annuity = $R\ (PVF\text{-}OA_{n,i})$

where

R = periodic rent (ordinary annuity)

$PVF\text{-}OA_{n,i}$ = present value of an ordinary annuity of 1 for n periods at i interest

To illustrate with an example, what is the present value of rental receipts of $6,000 each, to be received at the end of each of the next 5 years when discounted at 12%? This problem may be time-diagrammed and solved as shown in Illustration 6-30.

ILLUSTRATION 6-30
Present Value of
Ordinary Annuity Time
Diagram

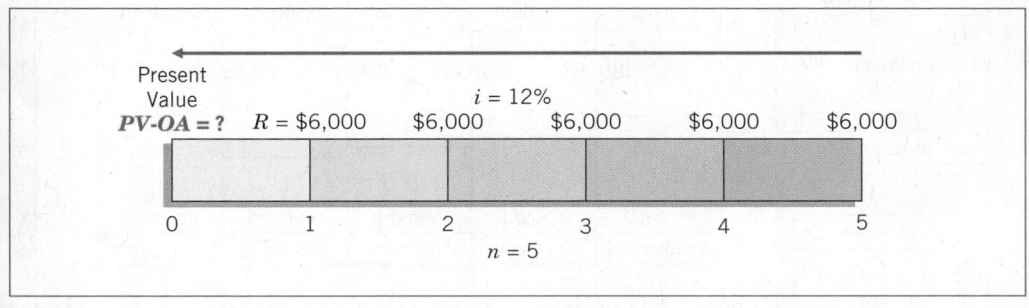

The formula for this calculation is as shown below.

Present value of an ordinary annuity = $R\ (PVF\text{-}OA_{n,i})$

$$= \$6,000\ (PVF\text{-}OA_{5,12\%})$$

$$= \$6,000\ (3.60478)$$

$$= \$21,628.68$$

The present value of the 5 ordinary annuity rental receipts of $6,000 each is $21,628.68. To determine the present value of the ordinary annuity factor 3.60478, use a financial calculator or read the appropriate table, in this case Table 6-4 (12% column and 5-period row).

What do the numbers mean?   UP IN SMOKE

Time value of money concepts also can be relevant to public policy debates. For example, several states had to determine how to receive the payments from tobacco companies as settlement for a national lawsuit against the companies for the healthcare costs of smoking.

The State of Wisconsin was due to collect 25 years of payments totaling $5.6 billion. The state could wait to collect the payments, or it could sell the payments to an investment bank (a process called *securitization*). If it were to sell the payments, it would receive a lump-sum payment today of $1.26 billion. Is this a good deal for the state? Assuming a discount rate of 8% and that the payments will be received in equal amounts (e.g., an annuity), the present value of the tobacco payment is:

$5.6 billion ÷ 25 = $224 million

$224 million × 10.67478* = $2.39 billion

PV-OA (i = 8%, n = 25)

Why would some in the state be willing to take just $1.26 billion today for an annuity whose present value is almost twice that amount? One reason is that Wisconsin was facing a hole in its budget that could be plugged in part by the lump-sum payment. Also, some believed that the risk of not getting paid by the tobacco companies in the future makes it prudent to get the money earlier.

If this latter reason has merit, then the present value computation above should have been based on a higher interest rate. Assuming a discount rate of 15%, the present value of the annuity is $1.448 billion ($5.6 billion ÷ 25 = $224 million; $224 million × 6.46415), which is much closer to the lump-sum payment offered to the State of Wisconsin.

Present Value of an Annuity Due

In our discussion of the present value of an ordinary annuity, we discounted the final rent based on the number of rent periods. In determining the present value of an annuity due, there is always one fewer discount period. Illustration 6-31 shows this distinction.

ILLUSTRATION 6-31
Comparison of Present Value of an Ordinary Annuity with an Annuity Due

Because each cash flow comes exactly one period sooner in the present value of the annuity due, the present value of the cash flows is exactly 12% higher than the present value of an ordinary annuity. Thus, **to find the present value of an annuity due factor, multiply the present value of an ordinary annuity factor by 1 plus the interest rate** (that is, 1 + i).

To determine the present value of an annuity due interest factor for 5 periods at 12% interest, take the present value of an ordinary annuity for 5 periods at 12% interest (3.60478) and multiply it by 1.12 to arrive at the present value of an annuity due, 4.03735 (3.60478 × 1.12). We provide present value of annuity due factors in Table 6-5.

To illustrate, Space Odyssey, Inc., rents a communications satellite for 4 years with annual rental payments of $4.8 million to be made at the beginning of each year. If the relevant annual interest rate is 11%, what is the present value of the rental obligations? Illustration 6-32 shows the company's time diagram for this problem.

ILLUSTRATION 6-32
Present Value of Annuity Due Time Diagram ($n = 4$, $i = 11\%$)

Illustration 6-33 shows the computations to solve this problem.

1. Present value of an ordinary annuity of 1 for 4 periods at 11% (Table 6-4)	3.10245
2. Factor (1 + .11)	× 1.11
3. Present value of an annuity due of 1 for 4 periods at 11%	3.44372
4. Periodic deposit (rent)	× $4,800,000
5. Present value of payments	$16,529,856

ILLUSTRATION 6-33
Computation of Present Value of an Annuity Due

Using Table 6-5 also locates the desired factor 3.44371 and computes the present value of the lease payments to be $16,529,808. (The difference in computations is due to rounding.)

Examples of Present Value of Annuity Problems

In the following three examples, we demonstrate the computation of (1) the present value, (2) the interest rate, and (3) the amount of each rent.

Computation of the Present Value of an Ordinary Annuity

You have just won a lottery totaling $4,000,000. You learn that you will receive a check in the amount of $200,000 at the end of each of the next 20 years. What amount have you really won? That is, what is the present value of the $200,000 checks you will receive over the next 20 years? Illustration 6-34 (page 310) shows a time diagram of this enviable situation (assuming an appropriate interest rate of 10%).

You calculate the present value as follows.

$$\text{Present value of an ordinary annuity} = R\ (PVF\text{-}OA_{n,i})$$
$$= \$200{,}000\ (PVF\text{-}OA_{20,10\%})$$
$$= \$200{,}000\ (8.51356)$$
$$= \$1{,}702{,}712$$

ILLUSTRATION 6-34
Time Diagram to Solve
for Present Value of
Lottery Payments

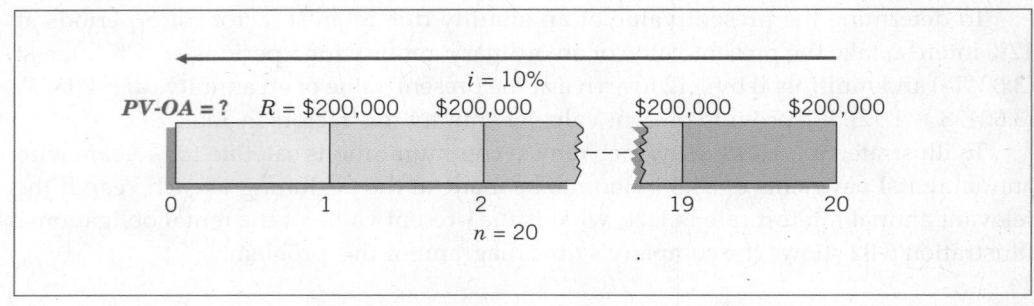

As a result, if the state deposits $1,702,712 now and earns 10% interest, it can withdraw $200,000 a year for 20 years to pay you the $4,000,000.

Computation of the Interest Rate

Many shoppers use credit cards to make purchases. When you receive the statement for payment, you may pay the total amount due or you may pay the balance in a certain number of payments. For example, assume you receive a statement from **MasterCard** with a balance due of $528.77. You may pay it off in 12 equal monthly payments of $50 each, with the first payment due one month from now. What rate of interest would you be paying?

The $528.77 represents the present value of the 12 payments of $50 each at an unknown rate of interest. The time diagram in Illustration 6-35 depicts this situation.

ILLUSTRATION 6-35
Time Diagram to Solve
for Effective-Interest Rate
on Loan

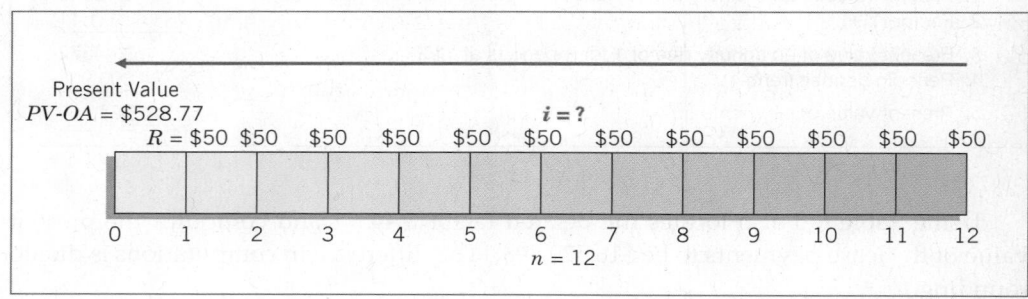

You calculate the rate as follows.

$$\text{Present value of an ordinary annuity} = R\,(PVF\text{-}OA_{n,i})$$
$$\$528.77 = \$50\,(PVF\text{-}OA_{12,i})$$
$$(PVFOA_{12,i}) = \frac{\$528.77}{\$50} = 10.57540$$

Referring to Table 6-4 and reading across the 12-period row, you find 10.57534 in the 2% column. Since 2% is a monthly rate, the nominal annual rate of interest is 24% (12 × 2%). The effective annual rate is 26.82423% $[(1 + .02)^{12} - 1]$. Obviously, you are better off paying the entire bill now if possible.

Computation of a Periodic Rent

Norm and Jackie Remmers have saved $36,000 to finance their daughter Dawna's college education. They deposited the money in the Bloomington Savings and Loan Association, where it earns 4% interest compounded semiannually. What equal amounts can their daughter withdraw at the end of every 6 months during her 4 college years, without exhausting the fund? Illustration 6-36 shows a time diagram of this situation.

ILLUSTRATION 6-36
Time Diagram for
Ordinary Annuity for a
College Fund

Determining the answer by simply dividing $36,000 by 8 withdrawals is wrong. Why? Because that ignores the interest earned on the money remaining on deposit. Dawna must consider that interest is compounded semiannually at 2% (4% ÷ 2) for 8 periods (4 years × 2). Thus, using the same present value of an ordinary annuity formula, she determines the amount of each withdrawal that she can make as follows.

$$\text{Present value of an ordinary annuity} = R \, (PVF\text{-}OA_{n,i})$$
$$\$36,\!000 = R \, (PVF\text{-}OA_{8,2\%})$$
$$\$36,\!000 = R \, (7.32548)$$
$$R = \$4,\!914.35$$

MORE COMPLEX SITUATIONS

Solving time value problems often requires using more than one table. For example, a business problem may need computations of both present value of a single sum and present value of an annuity. Two such common situations are:

8 LEARNING OBJECTIVE
Solve present value problems related to deferred annuities and bonds.

1. Deferred annuities.
2. Bond problems.

Deferred Annuities

A **deferred annuity** is an annuity in which the rents begin after a specified number of periods. A deferred annuity does not begin to produce rents until two or more periods have expired. For example, "an **ordinary annuity** of six annual rents deferred 4 years" means that no rents will occur during the first 4 years and that the first of the six rents will occur at the end of the fifth year. "An **annuity due** of six annual rents deferred 4 years" means that no rents will occur during the first 4 years and that the first of six rents will occur at the beginning of the fifth year.

Future Value of a Deferred Annuity
Computing the future value of a deferred annuity is relatively straightforward. Because there is no accumulation or investment on which interest may accrue, the future value of a deferred annuity is the same as the future value of an annuity not deferred. That is, computing the future value simply ignores the deferred period.

To illustrate, assume that Sutton Corporation plans to purchase a land site in 6 years for the construction of its new corporate headquarters. Because of cash flow problems, Sutton budgets deposits of $80,000 on which it expects to earn 5% annually, only at the end of the fourth, fifth, and sixth periods. What future value will Sutton have accumulated at the end of the sixth year? Illustration 6-37 (page 312) shows a time diagram of this situation.

ILLUSTRATION 6-37
Time Diagram for Future
Value of Deferred
Annuity

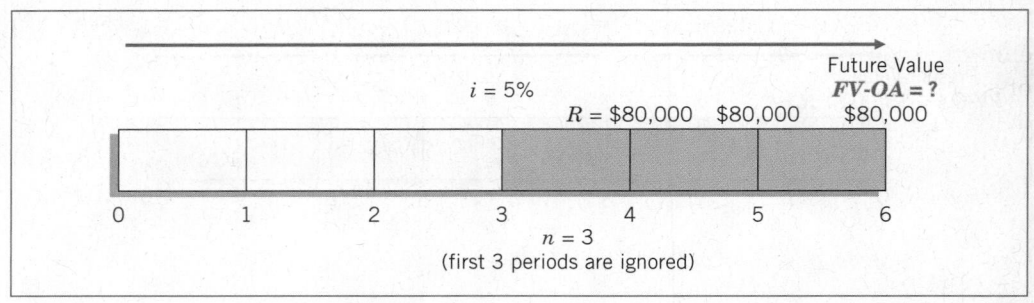

Sutton determines the value accumulated by using the standard formula for the future value of an ordinary annuity:

$$\text{Future value of an ordinary annuity} = R\ (FVF\text{-}OA_{n,i})$$
$$= \$80,000\ (FVF\text{-}OA_{3,5\%})$$
$$= \$80,000\ (3.15250)$$
$$= \$252,200$$

Present Value of a Deferred Annuity

Computing the present value of a deferred annuity must recognize the interest that accrues on the original investment during the deferral period.

To compute the present value of a deferred annuity, we compute the present value of an ordinary annuity of 1 as if the rents had occurred for the entire period. We then subtract the present value of rents that were not received during the deferral period. We are left with the present value of the rents actually received subsequent to the deferral period.

To illustrate, Bob Bender has developed and copyrighted tutorial software for students in advanced accounting. He agrees to sell the copyright to Campus Micro Systems for 6 annual payments of $5,000 each. The payments will begin 5 years from today. Given an annual interest rate of 8%, what is the present value of the 6 payments?

This situation is an ordinary annuity of 6 payments deferred 4 periods. The time diagram in Illustration 6-38 depicts this sales agreement.

ILLUSTRATION 6-38
Time Diagram for
Present Value of Deferred
Annuity

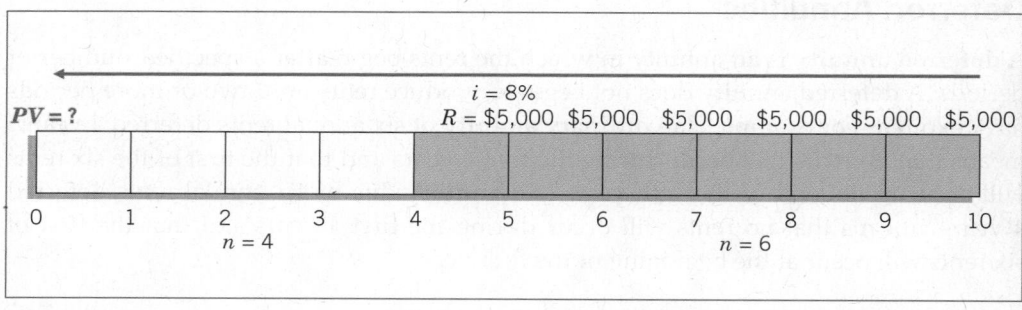

Two options are available to solve this problem. The first is to use only Table 6-4, as shown in Illustration 6-39.

ILLUSTRATION 6-39
Computation of the
Present Value of a
Deferred Annuity

1. Each periodic rent		$5,000
2. Present value of an ordinary annuity of 1 for total periods (10) [number of rents (6) plus number of deferred periods (4)] at 8%	6.71008	
3. Less: Present value of an ordinary annuity of 1 for the number of deferred periods (4) at 8%	3.31213	
4. Difference		× 3.39795
5. Present value of 6 rents of $5,000 deferred 4 periods		$16,989.75

The subtraction of the present value of an annuity of 1 for the deferred periods eliminates the nonexistent rents during the deferral period. It converts the present value of an ordinary annuity of $1.00 for 10 periods to the present value of 6 rents of $1.00, deferred 4 periods.

Alternatively, Bender can use both Table 6-2 and Table 6-4 to compute the present value of the 6 rents. He can first discount the annuity 6 periods. However, because the annuity is deferred 4 periods, he must treat the present value of the annuity as a future amount to be discounted another 4 periods. The time diagram in Illustration 6-40 depicts this two-step process.

ILLUSTRATION 6-40
Time Diagram for Present Value of Deferred Annuity (2-Step Process)

Calculation using formulas would be done in two steps, as follows.

Step 1: Present value of
an ordinary annuity $= R\ (PVF\text{-}OA_{n,i})$

$= \$5,000\ (PVF\text{-}OA_{6,8\%})$

$= \$5,000\ (4.62288)$
(Table 6-4, Present value of an ordinary annuity)

$= \$23,114.40$

Step 2: Present value of
a single sum $= FV\ (PVF_{n,i})$

$= \$23,114.40\ (PVF_{4,8\%})$

$= \$23,114.40\ (.73503)$
(Table 6-2, Present value of a single sum)

$= \$16,989.78$

The present value of $16,989.78 computed above is the same as in Illustration 6-39 although computed differently. (The $0.03 difference is due to rounding.)

Valuation of Long-Term Bonds

A long-term bond produces two cash flows: (1) periodic interest payments during the life of the bond, and (2) the principal (face value) paid at maturity. At the date of issue, bond buyers determine the present value of these two cash flows using the market rate of interest.

The periodic interest payments represent an annuity. The principal represents a single-sum problem. The current market value of the bonds is the combined present values of the interest annuity and the principal amount.

To illustrate, Alltech Corporation on January 1, 2014, issues $100,000 of 9% bonds due in 5 years with interest payable annually at year-end. The current market rate of interest for bonds of similar risk is 11%. What will the buyers pay for this bond issue?

The time diagram in Illustration 6-41 depicts both cash flows.

ILLUSTRATION 6-41
Time Diagram to Solve
for Bond Valuation

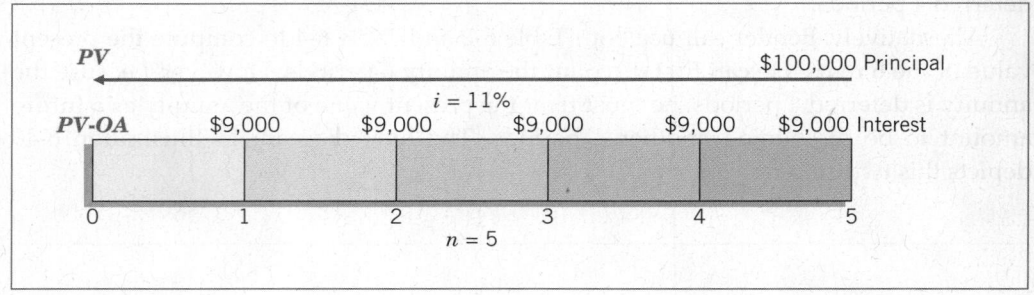

Alltech computes the present value of the two cash flows by discounting at 11% as follows.

ILLUSTRATION 6-42
Computation of the
Present Value of an
Interest-Bearing Bond

1. Present value of the principal: FV $(PVF_{5,11\%})$ = \$100,000 (.59345)	\$59,345.00
2. Present value of the interest payments: R $(PVF\text{-}OA_{5,11\%})$ = \$9,000 (3.69590)	33,263.10
3. Combined present value (market price)—carrying value of bonds	\$92,608.10

By paying \$92,608.10 at date of issue, the buyers of the bonds will realize an effective yield of 11% over the 5-year term of the bonds. This is true because Alltech discounted the cash flows at 11%.

Effective-Interest Method of Amortization of Bond Discount or Premium

In the previous example (Illustration 6-42), Alltech Corporation issued bonds at a discount, computed as follows.

ILLUSTRATION 6-43
Computation of Bond
Discount

Maturity value (face amount) of bonds		\$100,000.00
Present value of the principal	\$59,345.00	
Present value of the interest	33,263.10	
Proceeds (present value and cash received)		(92,608.10)
Discount on bonds issued		\$ 7,391.90

Alltech amortizes (writes off to interest expense) the amount of this discount over the life of the bond issue.

The preferred procedure for amortization of a discount or premium is the **effective-interest method**. Under the effective-interest method:

**Gateway to
the Profession**

*Use of Spreadsheets to
Calculate Bond Amortization*

1. The company issuing the bond first computes bond interest expense by multiplying the carrying value of the bonds at the beginning of the period by the effective-interest rate.

2. The company then determines the bond discount or premium amortization by comparing the bond interest expense with the interest to be paid.

Illustration 6-44 depicts the computation of bond amortization.

ILLUSTRATION 6-44
Amortization
Computation

The effective-interest method produces a periodic interest expense equal to a **constant percentage of the carrying value of the bonds**. Since the percentage used is the effective rate of interest incurred by the borrower at the time of issuance, the effective-interest method results in matching expenses with revenues.

We can use the data from the Alltech Corporation example to illustrate the effective-interest method of amortization. Alltech issued $100,000 face value of bonds at a discount of $7,391.90, resulting in a carrying value of $92,608.10. Illustration 6-45 shows the effective-interest amortization schedule for Alltech's bonds.

ILLUSTRATION 6-45
Effective-Interest
Amortization Schedule

SCHEDULE OF BOND DISCOUNT AMORTIZATION
5-YEAR, 9% BONDS SOLD TO YIELD 11%

Date	Cash Interest Paid	Interest Expense	Bond Discount Amortization	Carrying Value of Bonds
1/1/12				$ 92,608.10
12/31/12	$ 9,000[a]	$10,186.89[b]	$1,186.89[c]	93,794.99[d]
12/31/13	9,000	10,317.45	1,317.45	95,112.44
12/31/14	9,000	10,462.37	1,462.37	96,574.81
12/31/15	9,000	10,623.23	1,623.23	98,198.04
12/31/16	9,000	10,801.96[e]	1,801.96	100,000.00
	$45,000	$52,391.90	$7,391.90	

[a]$100,000 × .09 = $9,000
[b]$92,608.10 × .11 = $10,186.89
[c]$10,186.89 − $9,000 = $1,186.89
[d]$92,608.10 + $1,186.89 = $93,794.99
[e]$0.18 difference due to rounding.

We use the amortization schedule illustrated above for note and bond transactions in Chapters 7 and 14.

PRESENT VALUE MEASUREMENT

In the past, most accounting calculations of present value relied on the most likely cash flow amount. *Concepts Statement No. 7* introduces an **expected cash flow approach.**[6] It uses a range of cash flows and incorporates the probabilities of those cash flows to provide a more relevant measurement of present value.

9 LEARNING OBJECTIVE
Apply expected cash flows to present value measurement.

To illustrate the expected cash flow model, assume that there is a 30% probability that future cash flows will be $100, a 50% probability that they will be $200, and a 20% probability that they will be $300. In this case, the expected cash flow would be $190 [($100 × 0.3) + ($200 × 0.5) + ($300 × 0.2)]. Traditional present value approaches would use the most likely estimate ($200). However, that estimate fails to consider the different probabilities of the possible cash flows.

---

[6]"Using Cash Flow Information and Present Value in Accounting Measurements," *Statement of Financial Accounting Concepts No. 7* (Norwalk, Conn.: FASB, 2000).

Choosing an Appropriate Interest Rate

After determining expected cash flows, a company must then use the proper interest rate to discount the cash flows. The interest rate used for this purpose has three components:

THREE COMPONENTS OF INTEREST

1. **PURE RATE OF INTEREST (2%–4%).** This would be the amount a lender would charge if there were no possibilities of default and no expectation of inflation.

2. **EXPECTED INFLATION RATE OF INTEREST (0%–?).** Lenders recognize that in an inflationary economy, they are being paid back with less valuable dollars. As a result, they increase their interest rate to compensate for this loss in purchasing power. When inflationary expectations are high, interest rates are high.

3. **CREDIT RISK RATE OF INTEREST (0%–5%).** The government has little or no credit risk (i.e., risk of nonpayment) when it issues bonds. A business enterprise, however, depending upon its financial stability, profitability, etc., can have a low or a high credit risk.

The FASB takes the position that after computing the expected cash flows, a company should discount those cash flows by the **risk-free rate of return**. That rate is defined as **the pure rate of return plus the expected inflation rate**. The Board notes that the expected cash flow framework adjusts for credit risk because it incorporates the probability of receipt or payment into the computation of expected cash flows. Therefore, the rate used to discount the expected cash flows should consider only the pure rate of interest and the inflation rate.

What do the numbers mean? HOW LOW CAN THEY GO?

Management of the level of interest rates is an important policy tool of the Federal Reserve Bank and its chair, Ben Bernanke. Through a number of policy options, the Fed has the ability to move interest rates up or down, and these rate changes can affect the wealth of all market participants. For example, if the Fed wants to raise rates (because the overall economy is getting overheated), it can raise the *discount rate,* which is the rate banks pay to borrow money from the Fed. This rate increase will factor into the rates banks and other creditors use to lend money. As a result, companies will think twice about borrowing money to expand their businesses. The result will be a slowing economy. A rate cut does just the opposite. It makes borrowing cheaper, and it can help the economy expand as more companies borrow to expand their operations.

Keeping rates low had been the Fed's policy in the early 2000s. The low rates did help keep the economy humming.

But these same low rates may have also resulted in too much real estate lending and the growth of a real estate bubble, as the price of housing was fueled by cheaper low-interest mortgage loans. But, as the old saying goes, "What goes up, must come down." That is what real estate prices did, triggering massive loan write-offs, a seizing up of credit markets, and a slowing economy.

So just when a rate cut might help the economy, the Fed's rate-cutting toolbox is empty. As a result, the Fed began to explore other options, such as repurchasing long-term government bonds—referred to as "quantitative easing." These repurchases put money into the market, increase the demand for long-term bonds, and reduce long-term interest rates. The Fed has conducted three rounds of quantitative easing in an attempt to spur the economy out of its persistent funk.

Source: Adam Shell, "Five Investments to Consider if the Fed Uncorks QE3," *USA TODAY* (September 1, 2012).

Example of Expected Cash Flow

To illustrate, assume that Al's Appliance Outlet offers a 2-year warranty on all products sold. In 2014, Al's Appliance sold $250,000 of a particular type of clothes dryer. Al's Appliance entered into an agreement with Ralph's Repair to provide all warranty service on the dryers sold in 2014. To determine the warranty expense to record in 2014 and the amount of warranty liability to record on the December 31, 2014, balance sheet, Al's Appliance must measure the fair value of the agreement. Since there is not a ready market for these warranty contracts, Al's Appliance uses expected cash flow techniques to value the warranty obligation.

Based on prior warranty experience, Al's Appliance estimates the expected cash outflows associated with the dryers sold in 2014, as shown in Illustration 6-46.

	Cash Flow Estimate	×	Probability Assessment	=	Expected Cash Flow
2014	$3,800		20%		$ 760
	6,300		50%		3,150
	7,500		30%		2,250
	Total				$6,160
2015	$5,400		30%		$1,620
	7,200		50%		3,600
	8,400		20%		1,680
	Total				$6,900

ILLUSTRATION 6-46
Expected Cash Outflows—Warranties

Applying expected cash flow concepts to these data, Al's Appliance estimates warranty cash outflows of $6,160 in 2014 and $6,900 in 2015.

Illustration 6-47 shows the present value of these cash flows, assuming a risk-free rate of 5% and cash flows occurring at the end of the year.

Year	Expected Cash Flow	×	PV Factor, i = 5%	=	Present Value
2014	$6,160		0.95238		$ 5,866.66
2015	6,900		0.90703		6,258.51
	Total				$12,125.17

ILLUSTRATION 6-47
Present Value of Cash Flows

SUMMARY OF LEARNING OBJECTIVES

1 Identify accounting topics where the time value of money is relevant. Some of the applications of present value–based measurements to accounting topics are (1) notes, (2) leases, (3) pensions and other postretirement benefits, (4) long-term assets, (5) sinking funds, (6) business combinations, (7) disclosures, and (8) installment contracts.

2 Distinguish between simple and compound interest. See items 1 and 2 in the Fundamental Concepts on page 318.

3 Use appropriate compound interest tables. In order to identify which of the five compound interest tables to use, determine whether you are solving for (1) the future value of a single sum, (2) the present value of a single sum, (3) the future value of a series of sums (an annuity), or (4) the present value of a series of sums (an annuity). In addition, when a series of sums (an annuity) is involved, identify whether these sums are received or paid (1) at the beginning of each period (annuity due) or (2) at the end of each period (ordinary annuity).

4 Identify variables fundamental to solving interest problems. The following four variables are fundamental to all compound interest problems. (1) *Rate of interest:*

KEY TERMS

annuity, *300*
annuity due, *300*
compound interest, *290*
deferred annuity, *311*
discounting, *295*
effective yield, *293*
effective-interest method, *314*
expected cash flow approach, *315*
face rate, *293*
future value, *294*
future value of an annuity, *300*
interest, *289*
nominal rate, *293*
ordinary annuity, *300*
present value, *294*

principal, *289*
risk-free rate of return, *316*
simple interest, *290*
stated rate, *293*
time value of money, *288*

unless otherwise stated, an annual rate, adjusted to reflect the length of the compounding period if less than a year. (2) *Number of time periods:* the number of compounding periods (a period may be equal to or less than a year). (3) *Future value:* the value at a future date of a given sum or sums invested assuming compound interest. (4) *Present value:* the value now (present time) of a future sum or sums discounted assuming compound interest.

5 ▸ **Solve future and present value of 1 problems.** See items 5(a) and 6(a) in the Fundamental Concepts below.

6 ▸ **Solve future value of ordinary and annuity due problems.** See item 5(b) in the Fundamental Concepts below.

7 ▸ **Solve present value of ordinary and annuity due problems.** See item 6(b) in the Fundamental Concepts on page 319.

8 ▸ **Solve present value problems related to deferred annuities and bonds.** Deferred annuities are annuities in which rents begin after a specified number of periods. The future value of a deferred annuity is computed the same as the future value of an annuity not deferred. To find the present value of a deferred annuity, compute the present value of an ordinary annuity of 1 as if the rents had occurred for the entire period, and then subtract the present value of rents not received during the deferral period. The current market price of bonds combines the present values of the interest annuity and the principal amount.

9 ▸ **Apply expected cash flows to present value measurement.** The expected cash flow approach uses a range of cash flows and the probabilities of those cash flows to provide the most likely estimate of expected cash flows. The proper interest rate used to discount the cash flows is the risk-free rate of return.

FUNDAMENTAL CONCEPTS

1. **SIMPLE INTEREST.** Interest on principal only, regardless of interest that may have accrued in the past.

2. **COMPOUND INTEREST.** Interest accrues on the unpaid interest of past periods as well as on the principal.

3. **RATE OF INTEREST.** Interest is usually expressed as an annual rate, but when the compounding period is shorter than one year, the interest rate for the shorter period must be determined.

4. **ANNUITY.** A series of payments or receipts (called rents) that occur at equal intervals of time. Types of annuities:
   (a) **Ordinary Annuity.** Each rent is payable (receivable) at the end of the period.
   (b) **Annuity Due.** Each rent is payable (receivable) at the beginning of the period.

5. **FUTURE VALUE.** Value at a later date of a single sum that is invested at compound interest.
   (a) **Future Value of 1** (or value of a single sum). The future value of $1 (or a single given sum), *FV*, at the end of *n* periods at *i* compound interest rate (Table 6-1).
   (b) **Future Value of an Annuity.** The future value of a series of rents invested at compound interest. In other words, the accumulated total that results from a series of equal deposits at regular intervals invested at compound interest. Both deposits and interest increase the accumulation.

(1) **Future Value of an Ordinary Annuity.** The future value on the date of the last rent (Table 6-3).

(2) **Future Value of an Annuity Due.** The future value one period after the date of the last rent. When an annuity due table is not available, use Table 6-3 with the following formula.

$$\text{Value of annuity due of 1 for } n \text{ rents} = \text{(Value of ordinary annuity for } n \text{ rents)} \times (1 + \text{interest rate})$$

6. **PRESENT VALUE.** The value at an earlier date (usually now) of a given future sum discounted at compound interest.

(a) **Present Value of 1** (or present value of a single sum). The present value (worth) of $1 (or a given sum), due n periods hence, discounted at i compound interest (Table 6-2).

(b) **Present Value of an Annuity.** The present value (worth) of a series of rents discounted at compound interest. In other words, it is the sum when invested at compound interest that will permit a series of equal withdrawals at regular intervals.

(1) **Present Value of an Ordinary Annuity.** The value now of $1 to be received or paid at the end of each period (rents) for n periods, discounted at i compound interest (Table 6-4).

(2) **Present Value of an Annuity Due.** The value now of $1 to be received or paid at the beginning of each period (rents) for n periods, discounted at i compound interest (Table 6-5). To use Table 6-4 for an annuity due, apply this formula.

$$\text{Present value of annuity due of 1 for } n \text{ rents} = \text{(Present value of an ordinary annuity of } n \text{ rents)} \times (1 + \text{interest rate})$$

DEMONSTRATION PROBLEM

Messier Company is a manufacturer of cycling equipment. It is facing several decisions involving time value of money considerations.

Instructions

Provide the requested information for (a)–(d) below. (Round all answers to the nearest dollar.)

(a) Messier recently signed a lease for a new office building for a lease period of 10 years. Under the lease agreement, a security deposit of $12,000 is made, with the deposit to be returned at the expiration of the lease, with interest compounded at 10% per year. What amount will the company receive at the time the lease expires?

(b) Recently, the vice president of operations of the company has requested construction of a new plant to meet the increasing demand for the company's bikes. After a careful evaluation of the request, the board of directors has decided to raise funds for the new plant by issuing $3,000,000 of 11% term corporate bonds on March 1, 2014, due on March 1, 2029, with interest payable each March 1 and September 1. At the time of issuance, the market interest rate for similar financial instruments is 10%. Determine the selling price of the bonds.

(c) The company, having issued the bonds in part (b), is committed to make annual sinking fund deposits of $90,000. The deposits are made on the last day of each year and yield a return of 10%. Will the fund at the end of 15 years be sufficient to retire the bonds? If not, what will the deficiency be?

(d) Messier has 50 employees. Recently, after a long negotiation with the local labor union, the company decided to initiate a pension plan as a part of its employee compensation plan. The plan will start on January 1, 2014. Each employee covered by the plan is entitled to a pension payment each year after retirement. As required by accounting standards, the controller of the company needs to report the pension obligation (liability). The following estimates have been collected.

Average length of time to retirement	15 years
Expected life duration after retirement	10 years
Total pension payment expected each year after retirement for all employees	$800,000 per year

On the basis of the information above, determine the present value of the pension liability. Assume payment made at the end of the year and the interest rate to be used is 8%.

Solution

(a) Future value of $12,000 at 10% for 10 years

($12,000 × 2.59374) = $ 31,125

(b) Formula for the interest payments:

$PV\text{-}OA = R\ (PVF\text{-}OA_{n,i})$
$PV\text{-}OA = \$165,000\ (PVF\text{-}OA_{30,5\%})$
$PV\text{-}OA = \$165,000\ (15.37245)$
$PV\text{-}OA = \$2,536,454$

Formula for the principal:

$PV = FV\ (PVF_{n,i})$
$PV = \$3,000,000\ (PVF_{30,5\%})$
$PV = \$3,000,000\ (0.23138)$
$PV = \$694,140$

The selling price of the bonds = $2,536,454 + $694,140 = $3,230,594.

(c) Future value of an ordinary annuity of $90,000
at 10% for 15 years ($90,000 × 31.77248) $2,859,523

Deficiency ($3,000,000 − $2,859,523) $ 140,477

(d) Compute the value of the deferred annuity and then discount
that amount to the present.

(i) Present value of the expected annual pension payments at the end of the tenth year:

$PV\text{-}OA = R\ (PVF\text{-}OA_{n,i})$
$PV\text{-}OA = \$800,000\ (PVF\text{-}OA_{10,8\%})$
$PV\text{-}OA = \$800,000\ (6.71008)$
$PV\text{-}OA = \$5,368,064$

(ii) Present value of the expected annual pension payments at the beginning of the current year:

$PV = FV\ (PVF_{n,i})$
$PV = \$5,368,064\ (PVF_{15,8\%})$
$PV = \$5,368,064\ (0.31524)$
$PV = \$1,692,228$

The company's pension obligation (liability) is $1,692,228.

FASB CODIFICATION

FASB Codification References

[1] FASB ASC 820-10. [Predecessor literature: "Fair Value Measurement," *Statement of Financial Accounting Standards No. 157* (Norwalk, Conn.: FASB, September 2006).]

[2] FASB ASC 310-10. [Predecessor literature: "Accounting by Creditors for Impairment of a Loan," *FASB Statement No. 114* (Norwalk, Conn.: FASB, May 1993).]

[3] FASB ASC 840-30-30. [Predecessor literature: "Accounting for Leases," *FASB Statement No. 13* as amended and interpreted through May 1980 (Stamford, Conn.: FASB, 1980).]

[4] FASB ASC 715-30-35. [Predecessor literature: "Employers' Accounting for Pension Plans," *Statement of Financial Accounting Standards No. 87* (Stamford, Conn.: FASB, 1985).]

[5] FASB ASC 360-10-35. [Predecessor literature: "Accounting for the Impairment or Disposal of Long-Lived Assets," *Statement of Financial Accounting Standards No. 144* (Norwalk, Conn.: FASB, 2001).]

[6] FASB ASC 718-10-10. [Predecessor literature: "Accounting for Stock-Based Compensation," *Statement of Financial Accounting Standards No. 123* (Norwalk, Conn: FASB, 1995); and "Share-Based Payment," *Statement of Financial Accounting Standard No. 123(R)* (Norwalk, Conn: FASB, 2004).]

Exercises

If your school has a subscription to the FASB Codification, go to *http://aaahq.org/asclogin.cfm* to log in and prepare responses to the following. Provide Codification references for your responses.

CE6-1 Access the glossary ("Master Glossary") to answer the following.
(a) What is the definition of present value?
(b) Briefly describe the term "discount rate adjustment technique."
(c) Identify the other codification references to present value.

CE6-2 In addition to the list of topics identified in footnote 1 on page 288, identify three areas in which present value is used as a measurement basis. Briefly describe one topic related to:
(a) Assets.   **(b)** Liabilities.   **(c)** Revenues or expenses.

CE6-3 What is interest cost? Briefly describe imputation of interest.

An additional Codification case can be found in the Using Your Judgment section, on page 333.

Be sure to check the book's companion website for a Review and Analysis Exercise, with solution.

WileyPLUS Brief Exercises, Exercises, Problems, and many more learning and assessment tools and resources are available for practice in WileyPLUS.

QUESTIONS

1. What is the time value of money? Why should accountants have an understanding of compound interest, annuities, and present value concepts?

2. Identify three situations in which accounting measures are based on present values. Do these present value applications involve single sums or annuities, or both single sums and annuities? Explain.

3. What is the nature of interest? Distinguish between "simple interest" and "compound interest."

4. What are the components of an interest rate? Why is it important for accountants to understand these components?

5. The following are a number of values taken from compound interest tables involving the same number of periods and the same rate of interest. Indicate what each of these four values represents.

(a) 6.71008.   **(c)** .46319.
(b) 2.15892.   **(d)** 14.48656.

6. Jose Oliva is considering two investment options for a $1,500 gift he received for graduation. Both investments have 8% annual interest rates. One offers quarterly compounding; the other compounds on a semiannual basis. Which investment should he choose? Why?

7. Regina Henry deposited $20,000 in a money market certificate that provides interest of 10% compounded quarterly if the amount is maintained for 3 years. How much will Regina Henry have at the end of 3 years?

8. Will Smith will receive $80,000 on December 31, 2019 (5 years from now), from a trust fund established by his father. Assuming the appropriate interest rate for discounting is 12% (compounded semiannually), what is the present value of this amount today?

9. What are the primary characteristics of an annuity? Differentiate between an "ordinary annuity" and an "annuity due."

10. Kehoe, Inc. owes $40,000 to Ritter Company. How much would Kehoe have to pay each year if the debt is retired through four equal payments (made at the end of the year), given an interest rate on the debt of 12%? (Round to two decimal places.)

11. The Kellys are planning for a retirement home. They estimate they will need $200,000 4 years from now to purchase this home. Assuming an interest rate of 10%, what amount must be deposited at the end of each of the 4 years to fund the home price? (Round to two decimal places.)

12. Assume the same situation as in Question 11, except that the four equal amounts are deposited at the beginning of the period rather than at the end. In this case, what amount must be deposited at the beginning of each period? (Round to two decimals.)

13. Explain how the future value of an ordinary annuity interest table is converted to the future value of an annuity due interest table.

14. Explain how the present value of an ordinary annuity interest table is converted to the present value of an annuity due interest table.

15. In a book named *Treasure,* the reader has to figure out where a 2.2 pound, 24 kt gold horse has been buried. If the horse is found, a prize of $25,000 a year for 20 years is provided. The actual cost to the publisher to purchase an annuity to pay for the prize is $245,000. What interest rate (to the nearest percent) was used to determine the amount of the annuity? (Assume end-of-year payments.)

16. Alexander Enterprises leases property to Hamilton, Inc. Because Hamilton, Inc. is experiencing financial difficulty, Alexander agrees to receive five rents of $20,000 at the end of each year, with the rents deferred 3 years. What is the present value of the five rents discounted at 12%?

17. Answer the following questions.

    (a) On May 1, 2014, Goldberg Company sold some machinery to Newlin Company on an installment contract basis. The contract required five equal annual payments, with the first payment due on May 1, 2014. What present value concept is appropriate for this situation?

    (b) On June 1, 2014, Seymour Inc. purchased a new machine that it does not have to pay for until May 1, 2016. The total payment on May 1, 2016, will include both principal and interest. Assuming interest at a 12% rate, the cost of the machine would be the total payment multiplied by what time value of money concept?

    (c) Costner Inc. wishes to know how much money it will have available in 5 years if five equal amounts of $35,000 are invested, with the first amount invested immediately. What interest table is appropriate for this situation?

    (d) Megan Hoffman invests in a "jumbo" $200,000, 3-year certificate of deposit at First Wisconsin Bank. What table would be used to determine the amount accumulated at the end of 3 years?

18. Recently, Glenda Estes was interested in purchasing a Honda Acura. The salesperson indicated that the price of the car was either $27,600 cash or $6,900 at the end of each of 5 years. Compute the effective-interest rate to the nearest percent that Glenda would pay if she chooses to make the five annual payments.

19. Recently, property/casualty insurance companies have been criticized because they reserve for the total loss as much as 5 years before it may happen. The IRS has joined the debate because it says the full reserve is unfair from a taxation viewpoint. What do you believe is the IRS position?

BRIEF EXERCISES

(Unless instructed otherwise, round answers to the nearest dollar.)

BE6-1 Chris Spear invested $15,000 today in a fund that earns 8% compounded annually. To what amount will the investment grow in 3 years? To what amount would the investment grow in 3 years if the fund earns 8% annual interest compounded semiannually?

BE6-2 Tony Bautista needs $25,000 in 4 years. What amount must he invest today if his investment earns 12% compounded annually? What amount must he invest if his investment earns 12% annual interest compounded quarterly?

BE6-3 Candice Willis will invest $30,000 today. She needs $150,000 in 21 years. What annual interest rate must she earn?

BE6-4 Bo Newman will invest $10,000 today in a fund that earns 5% annual interest. How many years will it take for the fund to grow to $17,100?

6 **BE6-5** Sally Medavoy will invest $8,000 a year for 20 years in a fund that will earn 12% annual interest. If the first payment into the fund occurs today, what amount will be in the fund in 20 years? If the first payment occurs at year-end, what amount will be in the fund in 20 years?

6 **BE6-6** Steve Madison needs $250,000 in 10 years. How much must he invest at the end of each year, at 11% interest, to meet his needs?

5 **BE6-7** John Fillmore's lifelong dream is to own his own fishing boat to use in his retirement. John has recently come into an inheritance of $400,000. He estimates that the boat he wants will cost $300,000 when he retires in 5 years. How much of his inheritance must he invest at an annual rate of 12% (compounded annually) to buy the boat at retirement?

5 **BE6-8** Refer to the data in BE6-7. Assuming quarterly compounding of amounts invested at 12%, how much of John Fillmore's inheritance must be invested to have enough at retirement to buy the boat?

6 **BE6-9** Morgan Freeman is investing $16,380 at the end of each year in a fund that earns 10% interest. In how many years will the fund be at $100,000?

7 **BE6-10** Henry Quincy wants to withdraw $30,000 each year for 10 years from a fund that earns 8% interest. How much must he invest today if the first withdrawal is at year-end? How much must he invest today if the first withdrawal takes place immediately?

7 **BE6-11** Leon Tyler's VISA balance is $793.15. He may pay it off in 12 equal end-of-month payments of $75 each. What interest rate is Leon paying?

7 **BE6-12** Maria Alvarez is investing $300,000 in a fund that earns 8% interest compounded annually. What equal amounts can Maria withdraw at the end of each of the next 20 years?

6 **BE6-13** Adams Inc. will deposit $30,000 in a 12% fund at the end of each year for 8 years beginning December 31, 2014. What amount will be in the fund immediately after the last deposit?

7 **BE6-14** Amy Monroe wants to create a fund today that will enable her to withdraw $25,000 per year for 8 years, with the first withdrawal to take place 5 years from today. If the fund earns 8% interest, how much must Amy invest today?

8 **BE6-15** Clancey Inc. issues $2,000,000 of 7% bonds due in 10 years with interest payable at year-end. The current market rate of interest for bonds of similar risk is 8%. What amount will Clancey receive when it issues the bonds?

7 **BE6-16** Zach Taylor is settling a $20,000 loan due today by making 6 equal annual payments of $4,727.53. Determine the interest rate on this loan, if the payments begin one year after the loan is signed.

7 **BE6-17** Consider the loan in BE6-16. What payments must Zach Taylor make to settle the loan at the same interest rate but with the 6 payments beginning on the day the loan is signed?

EXERCISES

(Unless instructed otherwise, round answers to the nearest dollar. Interest rates are per annum unless otherwise indicated.)

3 **E6-1 (Using Interest Tables)** For each of the following cases, indicate (a) to what rate columns, and (b) to what number of periods you would refer in looking up the interest factor.

1. In a future value of 1 table

Annual Rate	Number of Years Invested	Compounded
a. 9%	9	Annually
b. 12%	5	Quarterly
c. 10%	15	Semiannually

2. In a present value of an annuity of 1 table

Annual Rate	Number of Years Involved	Number of Rents Involved	Frequency of Rents
a. 9%	25	25	Annually
b. 10%	15	30	Semiannually
c. 12%	7	28	Quarterly

2 5 E6-2 (Simple and Compound Interest Computations) Alan Jackson invests $20,000 at 8% annual interest, leaving the money invested without withdrawing any of the interest for 8 years. At the end of the 8 years, Alan withdraws the accumulated amount of money.

Instructions

(a) Compute the amount Alan would withdraw assuming the investment earns simple interest.

(b) Compute the amount Alan would withdraw assuming the investment earns interest compounded annually.

(c) Compute the amount Alan would withdraw assuming the investment earns interest compounded semiannually.

5 6 7 E6-3 (Computation of Future Values and Present Values) Using the appropriate interest table, answer each of the following questions. (Each case is independent of the others.)

(a) What is the future value of $7,000 at the end of 5 periods at 8% compounded interest?

(b) What is the present value of $7,000 due 8 periods hence, discounted at 11%?

(c) What is the future value of 15 periodic payments of $7,000 each made at the end of each period and compounded at 10%?

(d) What is the present value of $7,000 to be received at the end of each of 20 periods, discounted at 5% compound interest?

6 7 E6-4 (Computation of Future Values and Present Values) Using the appropriate interest table, answer the following questions. (Each case is independent of the others).

(a) What is the future value of 20 periodic payments of $4,000 each made at the beginning of each period and compounded at 8%?

(b) What is the present value of $2,500 to be received at the beginning of each of 30 periods, discounted at 10% compound interest?

(c) What is the future value of 15 deposits of $2,000 each made at the beginning of each period and compounded at 10%? (Future value as of the end of the fifteenth period.)

(d) What is the present value of six receipts of $1,000 each received at the beginning of each period, discounted at 9% compounded interest?

7 E6-5 (Computation of Present Value) Using the appropriate interest table, compute the present values of the following periodic amounts due at the end of the designated periods.

(a) $30,000 receivable at the end of each period for 8 periods compounded at 12%.

(b) $30,000 payments to be made at the end of each period for 16 periods at 9%.

(c) $30,000 payable at the end of the seventh, eighth, ninth, and tenth periods at 12%.

5 6 7 E6-6 (Future Value and Present Value Problems) Presented below are three unrelated situations.

(a) Dwayne Wade Company recently signed a lease for a new office building, for a lease period of 10 years. Under the lease agreement, a security deposit of $12,000 is made, with the deposit to be returned at the expiration of the lease, with interest compounded at 10% per year. What amount will the company receive at the time the lease expires?

(b) Serena Williams Corporation, having recently issued a $20 million, 15-year bond issue, is committed to make annual sinking fund deposits of $600,000. The deposits are made on the last day of each year and yield a return of 10%. Will the fund at the end of 15 years be sufficient to retire the bonds? If not, what will the deficiency be?

(c) Under the terms of his salary agreement, president Rex Walters has an option of receiving either an immediate bonus of $40,000, or a deferred bonus of $70,000 payable in 10 years. Ignoring tax considerations and assuming a relevant interest rate of 8%, which form of settlement should Walters accept?

8 E6-7 (Computation of Bond Prices) What would you pay for a $50,000 debenture bond that matures in 15 years and pays $5,000 a year in interest if you wanted to earn a yield of:

(a) 8%?   (b) 10%?   (c) 12%?

8 E6-8 (Computations for a Retirement Fund) Clarence Weatherspoon, a super salesman contemplating retirement on his fifty-fifth birthday, decides to create a fund on an 8% basis that will enable him to withdraw $20,000 per year on June 30, beginning in 2018 and continuing through 2021. To develop this fund, Clarence intends to make equal contributions on June 30 of each of the years 2014–2017.

Instructions

(a) How much must the balance of the fund equal on June 30, 2017, in order for Clarence Weatherspoon to satisfy his objective?

(b) What are each of Clarence's contributions to the fund?

5 **E6-9 (Unknown Rate)** LEW Company purchased a machine at a price of $100,000 by signing a note payable, which requires a single payment of $123,210 in 2 years. Assuming annual compounding of interest, what rate of interest is being paid on the loan?

5 **E6-10 (Unknown Periods and Unknown Interest Rate)** Consider the following independent situations.

  (a) Mike Finley wishes to become a millionaire. His money market fund has a balance of $92,296 and has a guaranteed interest rate of 10%. How many years must Mike leave that balance in the fund in order to get his desired $1,000,000?

  (b) Assume that Sally Williams desires to accumulate $1 million in 15 years using her money market fund balance of $182,696. At what interest rate must Sally's investment compound annually?

7 **E6-11 (Evaluation of Purchase Options)** Sosa Excavating Inc. is purchasing a bulldozer. The equipment has a price of $100,000. The manufacturer has offered a payment plan that would allow Sosa to make 10 equal annual payments of $16,274.53, with the first payment due one year after the purchase.

Instructions

  (a) How much total interest will Sosa pay on this payment plan?

  (b) Sosa could borrow $100,000 from its bank to finance the purchase at an annual rate of 9%. Should Sosa borrow from the bank or use the manufacturer's payment plan to pay for the equipment?

7 **E6-12 (Analysis of Alternatives)** The Black Knights Inc., a manufacturer of low-sugar, low-sodium, low-cholesterol TV dinners, would like to increase its market share in the Sunbelt. In order to do so, Black Knights has decided to locate a new factory in the Panama City area. Black Knights will either buy or lease a site depending upon which is more advantageous. The site location committee has narrowed down the available sites to the following three buildings.

  Building A: Purchase for a cash price of $600,000, useful life 25 years.

  Building B: Lease for 25 years with annual lease payments of $69,000 being made at the beginning of the year.

  Building C: Purchase for $650,000 cash. This building is larger than needed; however, the excess space can be sublet for 25 years at a net annual rental of $7,000. Rental payments will be received at the end of each year. The Black Knights Inc. has no aversion to being a landlord.

Instructions

In which building would you recommend that The Black Knights Inc. locate, assuming a 12% cost of funds?

8 **E6-13 (Computation of Bond Liability)** George Hincapie Inc. manufactures cycling equipment. Recently, the vice president of operations of the company has requested construction of a new plant to meet the increasing demand for the company's bikes. After a careful evaluation of the request, the board of directors has decided to raise funds for the new plant by issuing $2,000,000 of 11% term corporate bonds on March 1, 2014, due on March 1, 2029, with interest payable each March 1 and September 1. At the time of issuance, the market interest rate for similar financial instruments is 10%.

Instructions

As the controller of the company, determine the selling price of the bonds.

8 **E6-14 (Computation of Pension Liability)** Nerwin, Inc. is a furniture manufacturing company with 50 employees. Recently, after a long negotiation with the local labor union, the company decided to initiate a pension plan as a part of its compensation plan. The plan will start on January 1, 2014. Each employee covered by the plan is entitled to a pension payment each year after retirement. As required by accounting standards, the controller of the company needs to report the pension obligation (liability). On the basis of a discussion with the supervisor of the Personnel Department and an actuary from an insurance company, the controller develops the following information related to the pension plan.

Average length of time to retirement	15 years
Expected life duration after retirement	10 years
Total pension payment expected each year after retirement for all employees. Payment made at the end of the year.	$700,000 per year

The interest rate to be used is 8%.

Instructions

On the basis of the information above, determine the present value of the pension obligation (liability).

5 **6** **E6-15 (Investment Decision)** Andrew Bogut just received a signing bonus of $1,000,000. His plan is to invest this payment in a fund that will earn 8%, compounded annually.

Instructions

(a) If Bogut plans to establish the AB Foundation once the fund grows to $1,999,000, how many years until he can establish the foundation?

(b) Instead of investing the entire $1,000,000, Bogut invests $300,000 today and plans to make 9 equal annual investments into the fund beginning one year from today. What amount should the payments be if Bogut plans to establish the $1,999,000 foundation at the end of 9 years?

6 **E6-16 (Retirement of Debt)** Jesper Parnevik borrowed $70,000 on March 1, 2012. This amount plus accrued interest at 12% compounded semiannually is to be repaid March 1, 2022. To retire this debt, Jesper plans to contribute to a debt retirement fund five equal amounts starting on March 1, 2017, and for the next 4 years. The fund is expected to earn 10% per annum.

Instructions

How much must be contributed each year by Jesper Parnevik to provide a fund sufficient to retire the debt on March 1, 2022?

7 **E6-17 (Computation of Amount of Rentals)** Your client, Keith Moreland Leasing Company, is preparing a contract to lease a machine to Souvenirs Corporation for a period of 25 years. Moreland has an investment cost of $365,755 in the machine, which has a useful life of 25 years and no salvage value at the end of that time. Your client is interested in earning an 11% return on its investment and has agreed to accept 25 equal rental payments at the end of each of the next 25 years.

Instructions

You are requested to provide Moreland with the amount of each of the 25 rental payments that will yield an 11% return on investment.

7 **E6-18 (Least Costly Payoff)** Assume that Sonic Foundry Corporation has a contractual debt outstanding. Sonic has available two means of settlement. It can either make immediate payment of $2,600,000, or it can make annual payments of $300,000 for 15 years, each payment due on the last day of the year.

Instructions

Which method of payment do you recommend, assuming an expected effective interest rate of 8% during the future period?

7 **E6-19 (Least Costly Payoff)** Assuming the same facts as those in E6-18 except that the payments must begin now and be made on the first day of each of the 15 years, what payment method would you recommend?

9 **E6-20 (Expected Cash Flows)** For each of the following, determine the expected cash flows.

	Cash Flow Estimate	Probability Assessment
(a)	$ 4,800	20%
	6,300	50%
	7,500	30%
(b)	$ 5,400	30%
	7,200	50%
	8,400	20%
(c)	$(1,000)	10%
	3,000	80%
	5,000	10%

9 **E6-21 (Expected Cash Flows and Present Value)** Keith Bowie is trying to determine the amount to set aside so that he will have enough money on hand in 2 years to overhaul the engine on his vintage used car. While there is some uncertainty about the cost of engine overhauls in 2 years, by conducting some research online, Keith has developed the following estimates.

Engine Overhaul Estimated Cash Outflow	Probability Assessment
$200	10%
450	30%
600	50%
750	10%

Instructions

How much should Keith Bowie deposit today in an account earning 6%, compounded annually, so that he will have enough money on hand in 2 years to pay for the overhaul?

9 **E6-22 (Fair Value Estimate)** Killroy Company owns a trade name that was purchased in an acquisition of McClellan Company. The trade name has a book value of $3,500,000, but according to GAAP, it is assessed for impairment on an annual basis. To perform this impairment test, Killroy must estimate the fair value of the trade name. (You will learn more about intangible asset impairments in Chapter 12.) It has developed the following cash flow estimates related to the trade name based on internal information. Each cash flow estimate reflects Killroy's estimate of annual cash flows over the next 8 years. The trade name is assumed to have no salvage value after the 8 years. (Assume the cash flows occur at the end of each year.)

Cash Flow Estimate	Probability Assessment
$380,000	20%
630,000	50%
750,000	30%

Instructions

(a) What is the estimated fair value of the trade name? Killroy determines that the appropriate discount rate for this estimation is 8%.

(b) Is the estimate developed for part (a) a Level 1 or Level 3 fair value estimate? Explain.

EXERCISES SET B

See the book's companion website, at **www.wiley.com/college/kieso**, for an additional set of exercises.

PROBLEMS

(Unless instructed otherwise, round answers to the nearest dollar. Interest rates are per annum unless otherwise indicated.)

5 **7** **P6-1 (Various Time Value Situations)** Answer each of these unrelated questions.

(a) On January 1, 2014, Fishbone Corporation sold a building that cost $250,000 and that had accumulated depreciation of $100,000 on the date of sale. Fishbone received as consideration a $240,000 non-interest-bearing note due on January 1, 2017. There was no established exchange price for the building, and the note had no ready market. The prevailing rate of interest for a note of this type on January 1, 2014, was 9%. At what amount should the gain from the sale of the building be reported?

(b) On January 1, 2014, Fishbone Corporation purchased 300 of the $1,000 face value, 9%, 10-year bonds of Walters Inc. The bonds mature on January 1, 2024, and pay interest annually beginning January 1, 2015. Fishbone purchased the bonds to yield 11%. How much did Fishbone pay for the bonds?

(c) Fishbone Corporation bought a new machine and agreed to pay for it in equal annual installments of $4,000 at the end of each of the next 10 years. Assuming that a prevailing interest rate of 8% applies to this contract, how much should Fishbone record as the cost of the machine?

(d) Fishbone Corporation purchased a special tractor on December 31, 2014. The purchase agreement stipulated that Fishbone should pay $20,000 at the time of purchase and $5,000 at the end of each of the next 8 years. The tractor should be recorded on December 31, 2014, at what amount, assuming an appropriate interest rate of 12%?

(e) Fishbone Corporation wants to withdraw $120,000 (including principal) from an investment fund at the end of each year for 9 years. What should be the required initial investment at the beginning of the first year if the fund earns 11%?

5 **6** **P6-2 (Various Time Value Situations)** Using the appropriate interest table, provide the solution to each of
7 the following four questions by computing the unknowns.

(a) What is the amount of the payments that Ned Winslow must make at the end of each of 8 years to accumulate a fund of $90,000 by the end of the eighth year, if the fund earns 8% interest, compounded annually?

(b) Robert Hitchcock is 40 years old today and he wishes to accumulate $500,000 by his sixty-fifth birthday so he can retire to his summer place on Lake Hopatcong. He wishes to accumulate this amount by making equal deposits on his fortieth through his sixty-fourth birthdays. What annual deposit must Robert make if the fund will earn 12% interest compounded annually?

(c) Diane Ross has $20,000 to invest today at 9% to pay a debt of $47,347. How many years will it take her to accumulate enough to liquidate the debt?

(d) Cindy Houston has a $27,600 debt that she wishes to repay 4 years from today; she has $19,553 that she intends to invest for the 4 years. What rate of interest will she need to earn annually in order to accumulate enough to pay the debt?

5 7 P6-3 (Analysis of Alternatives) Assume that Wal-Mart Stores, Inc. has decided to surface and maintain for 10 years a vacant lot next to one of its stores to serve as a parking lot for customers. Management is considering the following bids involving two different qualities of surfacing for a parking area of 12,000 square yards.

Bid A: A surface that costs $5.75 per square yard to install. This surface will have to be replaced at the end of 5 years. The annual maintenance cost on this surface is estimated at 25 cents per square yard for each year except the last year of its service. The replacement surface will be similar to the initial surface.

Bid B: A surface that costs $10.50 per square yard to install. This surface has a probable useful life of 10 years and will require annual maintenance in each year except the last year, at an estimated cost of 9 cents per square yard.

Instructions

Prepare computations showing which bid should be accepted by Wal-Mart. You may assume that the cost of capital is 9%, that the annual maintenance expenditures are incurred at the end of each year, and that prices are not expected to change during the next 10 years.

7 P6-4 (Evaluating Payment Alternatives) Howie Long has just learned he has won a $500,000 prize in the lottery. The lottery has given him two options for receiving the payments. (1) If Howie takes all the money today, the state and federal governments will deduct taxes at a rate of 46% immediately. (2) Alternatively, the lottery offers Howie a payout of 20 equal payments of $36,000 with the first payment occurring when Howie turns in the winning ticket. Howie will be taxed on each of these payments at a rate of 25%.

Instructions

Assuming Howie can earn an 8% rate of return (compounded annually) on any money invested during this period, which pay-out option should he choose?

5 7 P6-5 (Analysis of Alternatives) Julia Baker died, leaving to her husband Brent an insurance policy contract that provides that the beneficiary (Brent) can choose any one of the following four options.

(a) $55,000 immediate cash.

(b) $4,000 every 3 months payable at the end of each quarter for 5 years.

(c) $18,000 immediate cash and $1,800 every 3 months for 10 years, payable at the beginning of each 3-month period.

(d) $4,000 every 3 months for 3 years and $1,500 each quarter for the following 25 quarters, all payments payable at the end of each quarter.

Instructions

If money is worth 2½% per quarter, compounded quarterly, which option would you recommend that Brent exercise?

8 P6-6 (Purchase Price of a Business) During the past year, Stacy McGill planted a new vineyard on 150 acres of land that she leases for $30,000 a year. She has asked you, as her accountant, to assist her in determining the value of her vineyard operation.

The vineyard will bear no grapes for the first 5 years (1–5). In the next 5 years (6–10), Stacy estimates that the vines will bear grapes that can be sold for $60,000 each year. For the next 20 years (11–30), she expects the harvest will provide annual revenues of $110,000. But during the last 10 years (31–40) of the vineyard's life, she estimates that revenues will decline to $80,000 per year.

During the first 5 years, the annual cost of pruning, fertilizing, and caring for the vineyard is estimated at $9,000; during the years of production, 6–40, these costs will rise to $12,000 per year. The relevant market rate of interest for the entire period is 12%. Assume that all receipts and payments are made at the end of each year.

Instructions

Dick Button has offered to buy Stacy's vineyard business by assuming the 40-year lease. On the basis of the current value of the business, what is the minimum price Stacy should accept?

5 6 7 **P6-7 (Time Value Concepts Applied to Solve Business Problems)** Answer the following questions related to Dubois Inc.

(a) Dubois Inc. has $600,000 to invest. The company is trying to decide between two alternative uses of the funds. One alternative provides $80,000 at the end of each year for 12 years, and the other is to receive a single lump-sum payment of $1,900,000 at the end of the 12 years. Which alternative should Dubois select? Assume the interest rate is constant over the entire investment.

(b) Dubois Inc. has completed the purchase of new Dell computers. The fair value of the equipment is $824,150. The purchase agreement specifies an immediate down payment of $200,000 and semiannual payments of $76,952 beginning at the end of 6 months for 5 years. What is the interest rate, to the nearest percent, used in discounting this purchase transaction?

(c) Dubois Inc. loans money to John Kruk Corporation in the amount of $800,000. Dubois accepts an 8% note due in 7 years with interest payable semiannually. After 2 years (and receipt of interest for 2 years), Dubois needs money and therefore sells the note to Chicago National Bank, which demands interest on the note of 10% compounded semiannually. What is the amount Dubois will receive on the sale of the note?

(d) Dubois Inc. wishes to accumulate $1,300,000 by December 31, 2024, to retire bonds outstanding. The company deposits $200,000 on December 31, 2014, which will earn interest at 10% compounded quarterly, to help in the retirement of this debt. In addition, the company wants to know how much should be deposited at the end of each quarter for 10 years to ensure that $1,300,000 is available at the end of 2024. (The quarterly deposits will also earn at a rate of 10%, compounded quarterly.) (Round to even dollars.)

7 **P6-8 (Analysis of Alternatives)** Ellison Inc., a manufacturer of steel school lockers, plans to purchase a new punch press for use in its manufacturing process. After contacting the appropriate vendors, the purchasing department received differing terms and options from each vendor. The Engineering Department has determined that each vendor's punch press is substantially identical and each has a useful life of 20 years. In addition, Engineering has estimated that required year-end maintenance costs will be $1,000 per year for the first 5 years, $2,000 per year for the next 10 years, and $3,000 per year for the last 5 years. Following is each vendor's sale package.

> **Vendor A:** $55,000 cash at time of delivery and 10 year-end payments of $18,000 each. Vendor A offers all its customers the right to purchase at the time of sale a separate 20-year maintenance service contract, under which Vendor A will perform all year-end maintenance at a one-time initial cost of $10,000.

> **Vendor B:** Forty semiannual payments of $9,500 each, with the first installment due upon delivery. Vendor B will perform all year-end maintenance for the next 20 years at no extra charge.

> **Vendor C:** Full cash price of $150,000 will be due upon delivery.

Instructions

Assuming that both Vendors A and B will be able to perform the required year-end maintenance, that Ellison's cost of funds is 10%, and the machine will be purchased on January 1, from which vendor should the press be purchased?

5 7 **P6-9 (Analysis of Business Problems)** James Kirk is a financial executive with McDowell Enterprises. Although James Kirk has not had any formal training in finance or accounting, he has a "good sense" for numbers and has helped the company grow from a very small company ($500,000 sales) to a large operation ($45 million in sales). With the business growing steadily, however, the company needs to make a number of difficult financial decisions in which James Kirk feels a little "over his head." He therefore has decided to hire a new employee with "numbers" expertise to help him. As a basis for determining whom to employ, he has decided to ask each prospective employee to prepare answers to questions relating to the following situations he has encountered recently. Here are the questions.

(a) In 2013, McDowell Enterprises negotiated and closed a long-term lease contract for newly constructed truck terminals and freight storage facilities. The buildings were constructed on land owned by the company. On January 1, 2014, McDowell took possession of the leased property. The 20-year lease is effective for the period January 1, 2014, through December 31, 2033. Advance rental payments of $800,000 are payable to the lessor (owner of facilities) on January 1 of each of the first 10 years of the lease term. Advance payments of $400,000 are due on January 1 for each of the last 10 years of the lease term. McDowell has an option to purchase all the leased facilities for $1 on December 31, 2033. At the time the lease was negotiated, the fair value of the truck terminals and freight storage facilities was approximately $7,200,000. If the company had borrowed the money to purchase the facilities, it would have had to pay 10% interest. Should the company have purchased rather than leased the facilities?

(b) Last year the company exchanged a piece of land for a non-interest-bearing note. The note is to be paid at the rate of $15,000 per year for 9 years, beginning one year from the date of disposal of the land. An appropriate rate of interest for the note was 11%. At the time the land was originally purchased, it cost $90,000. What is the fair value of the note?

(c) The company has always followed the policy to take any cash discounts on goods purchased. Recently, the company purchased a large amount of raw materials at a price of $800,000 with terms 1/10, n/30 on which it took the discount. McDowell has recently estimated its cost of funds at 10%. Should McDowell continue this policy of always taking the cash discount?

5 7 P6-10 (Analysis of Lease vs. Purchase) Dunn Inc. owns and operates a number of hardware stores in the New England region. Recently, the company has decided to locate another store in a rapidly growing area of Maryland. The company is trying to decide whether to purchase or lease the building and related facilities.

Purchase: The company can purchase the site, construct the building, and purchase all store fixtures. The cost would be $1,850,000. An immediate down payment of $400,000 is required, and the remaining $1,450,000 would be paid off over 5 years at $350,000 per year (including interest payments made at end of year). The property is expected to have a useful life of 12 years, and then it will be sold for $500,000. As the owner of the property, the company will have the following out-of-pocket expenses each period.

Property taxes (to be paid at the end of each year)	$40,000
Insurance (to be paid at the beginning of each year)	27,000
Other (primarily maintenance which occurs at the end of each year)	16,000
	$83,000

Lease: First National Bank has agreed to purchase the site, construct the building, and install the appropriate fixtures for Dunn Inc. if Dunn will lease the completed facility for 12 years. The annual costs for the lease would be $270,000. Dunn would have no responsibility related to the facility over the 12 years. The terms of the lease are that Dunn would be required to make 12 annual payments (the first payment to be made at the time the store opens and then each following year). In addition, a deposit of $100,000 is required when the store is opened. This deposit will be returned at the end of the twelfth year, assuming no unusual damage to the building structure or fixtures.

Instructions

Which of the two approaches should Dunn Inc. follow? (Currently, the cost of funds for Dunn Inc. is 10%.)

8 P6-11 (Pension Funding) You have been hired as a benefit consultant by Jean Honore, the owner of Attic Angels. She wants to establish a retirement plan for herself and her three employees. Jean has provided the following information. The retirement plan is to be based upon annual salary for the last year before retirement and is to provide 50% of Jean's last-year annual salary and 40% of the last-year annual salary for each employee. The plan will make annual payments at the beginning of each year for 20 years from the date of retirement. Jean wishes to fund the plan by making 15 annual deposits beginning January 1, 2014. Invested funds will earn 12% compounded annually. Information about plan participants as of January 1, 2014, is as follows.

Jean Honore, owner: Current annual salary of $48,000; estimated retirement date January 1, 2039.

Colin Davis, flower arranger: Current annual salary of $36,000; estimated retirement date January 1, 2044.

Anita Baker, sales clerk: Current annual salary of $18,000; estimated retirement date January 1, 2034.

Gavin Bryars, part-time bookkeeper: Current annual salary of $15,000; estimated retirement date January 1, 2029.

In the past, Jean has given herself and each employee a year-end salary increase of 4%. Jean plans to continue this policy in the future.

Instructions

(a) Based upon the above information, what will be the annual retirement benefit for each plan participant? (Round to the nearest dollar.) (*Hint:* Jean will receive raises for 24 years.)

(b) What amount must be on deposit at the end of 15 years to ensure that all benefits will be paid? (Round to the nearest dollar.)

(c) What is the amount of each annual deposit Jean must make to the retirement plan?

8 P6-12 (Pension Funding) Craig Brokaw, newly appointed controller of STL, is considering ways to reduce his company's expenditures on annual pension costs. One way to do this is to switch STL's pension fund assets from First Security to NET Life. STL is a very well-respected computer manufacturer that recently has experienced a sharp decline in its financial performance for the first time in its 25-year history. Despite financial problems, STL still is committed to providing its employees with good pension and postretirement health benefits.

Under its present plan with First Security, STL is obligated to pay $43 million to meet the expected value of future pension benefits that are payable to employees as an annuity upon their retirement from the company. On the other hand, NET Life requires STL to pay only $35 million for identical future pension benefits. First Security is one of the oldest and most reputable insurance companies in North America. NET Life has a much weaker reputation in the insurance industry. In pondering the significant difference in annual pension costs, Brokaw asks himself, "Is this too good to be true?"

Instructions

Answer the following questions.

(a) Why might NET Life's pension cost requirement be $8 million less than First Security's requirement for the same future value?

(b) What ethical issues should Craig Brokaw consider before switching STL's pension fund assets?

(c) Who are the stakeholders that could be affected by Brokaw's decision?

7 9 **P6-13 (Expected Cash Flows and Present Value)** Danny's Lawn Equipment sells high-quality lawn mowers and offers a 3-year warranty on all new lawn mowers sold. In 2014, Danny sold $300,000 of new specialty mowers for golf greens for which Danny's service department does not have the equipment to do the service. Danny has entered into an agreement with Mower Mavens to provide all warranty service on the special mowers sold in 2014. Danny wishes to measure the fair value of the agreement to determine the warranty liability for sales made in 2014. The controller for Danny's Lawn Equipment estimates the following expected warranty cash outflows associated with the mowers sold in 2014.

Year	Cash Flow Estimate	Probability Assessment
2015	$2,500	20%
	4,000	60%
	5,000	20%
2016	$3,000	30%
	5,000	50%
	6,000	20%
2017	$4,000	30%
	6,000	40%
	7,000	30%

Instructions

Using expected cash flow and present value techniques, determine the value of the warranty liability for the 2014 sales. Use an annual discount rate of 5%. Assume all cash flows occur at the end of the year.

7 9 **P6-14 (Expected Cash Flows and Present Value)** At the end of 2014, Sawyer Company is conducting an impairment test and needs to develop a fair value estimate for machinery used in its manufacturing operations. Given the nature of Sawyer's production process, the equipment is for special use. (No secondhand market values are available.) The equipment will be obsolete in 2 years, and Sawyer's accountants have developed the following cash flow information for the equipment.

Year	Net Cash Flow Estimate	Probability Assessment
2015	$6,000	40%
	9,000	60%
2016	$ (500)	20%
	2,000	60%
	4,000	20%
	Scrap value	
2016	$ 500	50%
	900	50%

Instructions

Using expected cash flow and present value techniques, determine the fair value of the machinery at the end of 2014. Use a 6% discount rate. Assume all cash flows occur at the end of the year.

8 9 **P6-15 (Fair Value Estimate)** Murphy Mining Company recently purchased a quartz mine that it intends to work for the next 10 years. According to state environmental laws, Murphy must restore the mine site to its original natural prairie state after it ceases mining operations at the site. To properly account for the mine, Murphy must estimate the fair value of this asset retirement obligation. This amount will be recorded as a liability and added to the value of the mine on Murphy's books. (You will learn more about these asset retirement obligations in Chapters 10 and 13.)

There is no active market for retirement obligations such as these, but Murphy has developed the following cash flow estimates based on its prior experience in mining-site restoration. It will take 3 years to restore the mine site when mining operations cease in 10 years. Each estimated cash outflow reflects an annual payment at the end of each year of the 3-year restoration period.

Restoration Estimated Cash Outflow	Probability Assessment
$15,000	10%
22,000	30%
25,000	50%
30,000	10%

Instructions

(a) What is the estimated fair value of Murphy's asset retirement obligation? Murphy determines that the appropriate discount rate for this estimation is 5%. Round calculations to the nearest dollar.

(b) Is the estimate developed for part (a) a Level 1 or Level 3 fair value estimate? Explain.

PROBLEMS SET B

See the book's companion website, at **www.wiley.com/college/kieso**, for an additional set of problems.

USING YOUR JUDGMENT

FINANCIAL REPORTING

P&G **Financial Reporting Problem**

The Procter & Gamble Company (P&G)

The financial statements of P&G are presented in Appendix 5B. The company's complete annual report, including the notes to the financial statements, can be accessed at the book's companion website, **www.wiley.com/college/kieso**.

Instructions

(a) Examining each item in P&G's balance sheet, identify those items that require present value, discounting, or interest computations in establishing the amount reported. (The accompanying notes are an additional source for this information.)

(b) (1) What interest rates are disclosed by P&G as being used to compute interest and present values? (2) Why are there so many different interest rates applied to P&G's financial statement elements (assets, liabilities, revenues, and expenses)?

Financial Statement Analysis Case

Consolidated Natural Gas Company

Consolidated Natural Gas Company (CNG), with corporate headquarters in Pittsburgh, Pennsylvania, is one of the largest producers, transporters, distributors, and marketers of natural gas in North America.

Periodically, the company experiences a decrease in the value of its gas- and oil-producing properties, and a special charge to income was recorded in order to reduce the carrying value of those assets.

Assume the following information. In 2013, CNG estimated the cash inflows from its oil- and gas-producing properties to be $375,000 per year. During 2014, the write-downs described above caused the estimate to be decreased to $275,000 per year. Production costs (cash outflows) associated with all these properties were estimated to be $125,000 per year in 2013, but this amount was revised to $155,000 per year in 2014.

Instructions

(Assume that all cash flows occur at the end of the year.)

(a) Calculate the present value of net cash flows for 2013–2015 (three years), using the 2013 estimates and a 10% discount factor.

(b) Calculate the present value of net cash flows for 2014–2016 (three years), using the 2014 estimates and a 10% discount factor.

(c) Compare the results using the two estimates. Is information on future cash flows from oil- and gas-producing properties useful, considering that the estimates must be revised each year? Explain.

Accounting, Analysis, and Principles

Johnson Co. accepts a note receivable from a customer in exchange for some damaged inventory. The note requires the customer make semiannual installments of $50,000 each for 10 years. The first installment begins six months from the date the customer took delivery of the damaged inventory. Johnson's management estimates that the fair value of the damaged inventory is $679,517.

Accounting

(a) What interest rate is Johnson implicitly charging the customer? Express the rate as an annual rate but assume semiannual compounding.

(b) At what dollar amount do you think Johnson should record the note receivable on the day the customer takes delivery of the damaged inventory?

Analysis

Assume the note receivable for damaged inventory makes up a significant portion of Johnson's assets. If interest rates increase, what happens to the fair value of the receivable? Briefly explain why.

Principles

The Financial Accounting Standards Board recently issued an accounting standard that allows companies to report assets such as notes receivable at fair value. Discuss how fair value versus historical cost potentially involves a trade-off of one desired quality of accounting information against another.

BRIDGE TO THE PROFESSION

Professional Research

At a recent meeting of the accounting staff in your company, the controller raised the issue of using present value techniques to conduct impairment tests for some of the company's fixed assets. Some of the more senior members of the staff admitted having little knowledge of present value concepts in this context, but they had heard about a FASB Concepts Statement that may be relevant. As the junior staff in the department, you have been asked to conduct some research of the authoritative literature on this topic and report back at the staff meeting next week.

Instructions

If your school has a subscription to the FASB Codification, go to *http://aaahq.org/asclogin.cfm* to log in and access the FASB Statements of Financial Accounting Concepts. When you have accessed the documents, you can use the search tool in your Internet browser to respond to the following items. (Provide paragraph citations.)

(a) Identify the recent concept statement that addresses present value measurement in accounting.

(b) What are some of the contexts in which present value concepts are applied in accounting measurement?

(c) Provide definitions for the following terms:
  (1) Best estimate.
  (2) Estimated cash flow (contrasted to expected cash flow).
  (3) Fresh-start measurement.
  (4) Interest methods of allocation.

Additional Professional Resources

See the book's companion website, at **www.wiley.com/college/kieso**, for professional simulations as well as other study resources.

Remember to check the book's companion website to find additional resources for this chapter.

TABLE 6-1   FUTURE VALUE OF 1 (FUTURE VALUE OF A SINGLE SUM)

$$FVF_{n,i} = (1 + i)^n$$

(n) Periods	2%	2½%	3%	4%	5%	6%
1	1.02000	1.02500	1.03000	1.04000	1.05000	1.06000
2	1.04040	1.05063	1.06090	1.08160	1.10250	1.12360
3	1.06121	1.07689	1.09273	1.12486	1.15763	1.19102
4	1.08243	1.10381	1.12551	1.16986	1.21551	1.26248
5	1.10408	1.13141	1.15927	1.21665	1.27628	1.33823
6	1.12616	1.15969	1.19405	1.26532	1.34010	1.41852
7	1.14869	1.18869	1.22987	1.31593	1.40710	1.50363
8	1.17166	1.21840	1.26677	1.36857	1.47746	1.59385
9	1.19509	1.24886	1.30477	1.42331	1.55133	1.68948
10	1.21899	1.28008	1.34392	1.48024	1.62889	1.79085
11	1.24337	1.31209	1.38423	1.53945	1.71034	1.89830
12	1.26824	1.34489	1.42576	1.60103	1.79586	2.01220
13	1.29361	1.37851	1.46853	1.66507	1.88565	2.13293
14	1.31948	1.41297	1.51259	1.73168	1.97993	2.26090
15	1.34587	1.44830	1.55797	1.80094	2.07893	2.39656
16	1.37279	1.48451	1.60471	1.87298	2.18287	2.54035
17	1.40024	1.52162	1.65285	1.94790	2.29202	2.69277
18	1.42825	1.55966	1.70243	2.02582	2.40662	2.85434
19	1.45681	1.59865	1.75351	2.10685	2.52695	3.02560
20	1.48595	1.63862	1.80611	2.19112	2.65330	3.20714
21	1.51567	1.67958	1.86029	2.27877	2.78596	3.39956
22	1.54598	1.72157	1.91610	2.36992	2.92526	3.60354
23	1.57690	1.76461	1.97359	2.46472	3.07152	3.81975
24	1.60844	1.80873	2.03279	2.56330	3.22510	4.04893
25	1.64061	1.85394	2.09378	2.66584	3.38635	4.29187
26	1.67342	1.90029	2.15659	2.77247	3.55567	4.54938
27	1.70689	1.94780	2.22129	2.88337	3.73346	4.82235
28	1.74102	1.99650	2.28793	2.99870	3.92013	5.11169
29	1.77584	2.04641	2.35657	3.11865	4.11614	5.41839
30	1.81136	2.09757	2.42726	3.24340	4.32194	5.74349
31	1.84759	2.15001	2.50008	3.37313	4.53804	6.08810
32	1.88454	2.20376	2.57508	3.50806	4.76494	6.45339
33	1.92223	2.25885	2.65234	3.64838	5.00319	6.84059
34	1.96068	2.31532	2.73191	3.79432	5.25335	7.25103
35	1.99989	2.37321	2.81386	3.94609	5.51602	7.68609
36	2.03989	2.43254	2.89828	4.10393	5.79182	8.14725
37	2.08069	2.49335	2.98523	4.26809	6.08141	8.63609
38	2.12230	2.55568	3.07478	4.43881	6.38548	9.15425
39	2.16474	2.61957	3.16703	4.61637	6.70475	9.70351
40	2.20804	2.68506	3.26204	4.80102	7.03999	10.28572

TABLE 6-1   FUTURE VALUE OF 1

8%	9%	10%	11%	12%	15%	(n) Periods
1.08000	1.09000	1.10000	1.11000	1.12000	1.15000	1
1.16640	1.18810	1.21000	1.23210	1.25440	1.32250	2
1.25971	1.29503	1.33100	1.36763	1.40493	1.52088	3
1.36049	1.41158	1.46410	1.51807	1.57352	1.74901	4
1.46933	1.53862	1.61051	1.68506	1.76234	2.01136	5
1.58687	1.67710	1.77156	1.87041	1.97382	2.31306	6
1.71382	1.82804	1.94872	2.07616	2.21068	2.66002	7
1.85093	1.99256	2.14359	2.30454	2.47596	3.05902	8
1.99900	2.17189	2.35795	2.55803	2.77308	3.51788	9
2.15892	2.36736	2.59374	2.83942	3.10585	4.04556	10
2.33164	2.58043	2.85312	3.15176	3.47855	4.65239	11
2.51817	2.81267	3.13843	3.49845	3.89598	5.35025	12
2.71962	3.06581	3.45227	3.88328	4.36349	6.15279	13
2.93719	3.34173	3.79750	4.31044	4.88711	7.07571	14
3.17217	3.64248	4.17725	4.78459	5.47357	8.13706	15
3.42594	3.97031	4.59497	5.31089	6.13039	9.35762	16
3.70002	4.32763	5.05447	5.89509	6.86604	10.76126	17
3.99602	4.71712	5.55992	6.54355	7.68997	12.37545	18
4.31570	5.14166	6.11591	7.26334	8.61276	14.23177	19
4.66096	5.60441	6.72750	8.06231	9.64629	16.36654	20
5.03383	6.10881	7.40025	8.94917	10.80385	18.82152	21
5.43654	6.65860	8.14028	9.93357	12.10031	21.64475	22
5.87146	7.25787	8.95430	11.02627	13.55235	24.89146	23
6.34118	7.91108	9.84973	12.23916	15.17863	28.62518	24
6.84847	8.62308	10.83471	13.58546	17.00000	32.91895	25
7.39635	9.39916	11.91818	15.07986	19.04007	37.85680	26
7.98806	10.24508	13.10999	16.73865	21.32488	43.53532	27
8.62711	11.16714	14.42099	18.57990	23.88387	50.06561	28
9.31727	12.17218	15.86309	20.62369	26.74993	57.57545	29
10.06266	13.26768	17.44940	22.89230	29.95992	66.21177	30
10.86767	14.46177	19.19434	25.41045	33.55511	76.14354	31
11.73708	15.76333	21.11378	28.20560	37.58173	87.56507	32
12.67605	17.18203	23.22515	31.30821	42.09153	100.69983	33
13.69013	18.72841	25.54767	34.75212	47.14252	115.80480	34
14.78534	20.41397	28.10244	38.57485	52.79962	133.17552	35
15.96817	22.25123	30.91268	42.81808	59.13557	153.15185	36
17.24563	24.25384	34.00395	47.52807	66.23184	176.12463	37
18.62528	26.43668	37.40434	52.75616	74.17966	202.54332	38
20.11530	28.81598	41.14479	58.55934	83.08122	232.92482	39
21.72452	31.40942	45.25926	65.00087	93.05097	267.86355	40

TABLE 6-2 PRESENT VALUE OF 1 (PRESENT VALUE OF A SINGLE SUM)

$$PVF_{n,i} = \frac{1}{(1+i)^n} = (1+i)^{-n}$$

(n) Periods	2%	2½%	3%	4%	5%	6%
1	.98039	.97561	.97087	.96154	.95238	.94340
2	.96117	.95181	.94260	.92456	.90703	.89000
3	.94232	.92860	.91514	.88900	.86384	.83962
4	.92385	.90595	.88849	.85480	.82270	.79209
5	.90573	.88385	.86261	.82193	.78353	.74726
6	.88797	.86230	.83748	.79031	.74622	.70496
7	.87056	.84127	.81309	.75992	.71068	.66506
8	.85349	.82075	.78941	.73069	.67684	.62741
9	.83676	.80073	.76642	.70259	.64461	.59190
10	.82035	.78120	.74409	.67556	.61391	.55839
11	.80426	.76214	.72242	.64958	.58468	.52679
12	.78849	.74356	.70138	.62460	.55684	.49697
13	.77303	.72542	.68095	.60057	.53032	.46884
14	.75788	.70773	.66112	.57748	.50507	.44230
15	.74301	.69047	.64186	.55526	.48102	.41727
16	.72845	.67362	.62317	.53391	.45811	.39365
17	.71416	.65720	.60502	.51337	.43630	.37136
18	.70016	.64117	.58739	.49363	.41552	.35034
19	.68643	.62553	.57029	.47464	.39573	.33051
20	.67297	.61027	.55368	.45639	.37689	.31180
21	.65978	.59539	.53755	.43883	.35894	.29416
22	.64684	.58086	.52189	.42196	.34185	.27751
23	.63416	.56670	.50669	.40573	.32557	.26180
24	.62172	.55288	.49193	.39012	.31007	.24698
25	.60953	.53939	.47761	.37512	.29530	.23300
26	.59758	.52623	.46369	.36069	.28124	.21981
27	.58586	.51340	.45019	.34682	.26785	.20737
28	.57437	.50088	.43708	.33348	.25509	.19563
29	.56311	.48866	.42435	.32065	.24295	.18456
30	.55207	.47674	.41199	.30832	.23138	.17411
31	.54125	.46511	.39999	.29646	.22036	.16425
32	.53063	.45377	.38834	.28506	.20987	.15496
33	.52023	.44270	.37703	.27409	.19987	.14619
34	.51003	.43191	.36604	.26355	.19035	.13791
35	.50003	.42137	.35538	.25342	.18129	.13011
36	.49022	.41109	.34503	.24367	.17266	.12274
37	.48061	.40107	.33498	.23430	.16444	.11579
38	.47119	.39128	.32523	.22529	.15661	.10924
39	.46195	.38174	.31575	.21662	.14915	.10306
40	.45289	.37243	.30656	.20829	.14205	.09722

TABLE 6-2   PRESENT VALUE OF 1

8%	9%	10%	11%	12%	15%	(n) Periods
.92593	.91743	.90909	.90090	.89286	.86957	1
.85734	.84168	.82645	.81162	.79719	.75614	2
.79383	.77218	.75132	.73119	.71178	.65752	3
.73503	.70843	.68301	.65873	.63552	.57175	4
.68058	.64993	.62092	.59345	.56743	.49718	5
.63017	.59627	.56447	.53464	.50663	.43233	6
.58349	.54703	.51316	.48166	.45235	.37594	7
.54027	.50187	.46651	.43393	.40388	.32690	8
.50025	.46043	.42410	.39092	.36061	.28426	9
.46319	.42241	.38554	.35218	.32197	.24719	10
.42888	.38753	.35049	.31728	.28748	.21494	11
.39711	.35554	.31863	.28584	.25668	.18691	12
.36770	.32618	.28966	.25751	.22917	.16253	13
.34046	.29925	.26333	.23199	.20462	.14133	14
.31524	.27454	.23939	.20900	.18270	.12289	15
.29189	.25187	.21763	.18829	.16312	.10687	16
.27027	.23107	.19785	.16963	.14564	.09293	17
.25025	.21199	.17986	.15282	.13004	.08081	18
.23171	.19449	.16351	.13768	.11611	.07027	19
.21455	.17843	.14864	.12403	.10367	.06110	20
.19866	.16370	.13513	.11174	.09256	.05313	21
.18394	.15018	.12285	.10067	.08264	.04620	22
.17032	.13778	.11168	.09069	.07379	.04017	23
.15770	.12641	.10153	.08170	.06588	.03493	24
.14602	.11597	.09230	.07361	.05882	.03038	25
.13520	.10639	.08391	.06631	.05252	.02642	26
.12519	.09761	.07628	.05974	.04689	.02297	27
.11591	.08955	.06934	.05382	.04187	.01997	28
.10733	.08216	.06304	.04849	.03738	.01737	29
.09938	.07537	.05731	.04368	.03338	.01510	30
.09202	.06915	.05210	.03935	.02980	.01313	31
.08520	.06344	.04736	.03545	.02661	.01142	32
.07889	.05820	.04306	.03194	.02376	.00993	33
.07305	.05340	.03914	.02878	.02121	.00864	34
.06763	.04899	.03558	.02592	.01894	.00751	35
.06262	.04494	.03235	.02335	.01691	.00653	36
.05799	.04123	.02941	.02104	.01510	.00568	37
.05369	.03783	.02674	.01896	.01348	.00494	38
.04971	.03470	.02430	.01708	.01204	.00429	39
.04603	.03184	.02210	.01538	.01075	.00373	40

TABLE 6-3   FUTURE VALUE OF AN ORDINARY ANNUITY OF 1

$$FVF\text{-}OA_{n,i} = \frac{(1+i)^n - 1}{i}$$

(n) Periods	2%	2½%	3%	4%	5%	6%
1	1.00000	1.00000	1.00000	1.00000	1.00000	1.00000
2	2.02000	2.02500	2.03000	2.04000	2.05000	2.06000
3	3.06040	3.07563	3.09090	3.12160	3.15250	3.18360
4	4.12161	4.15252	4.18363	4.24646	4.31013	4.37462
5	5.20404	5.25633	5.30914	5.41632	5.52563	5.63709
6	6.30812	6.38774	6.46841	6.63298	6.80191	6.97532
7	7.43428	7.54743	7.66246	7.89829	8.14201	8.39384
8	8.58297	8.73612	8.89234	9.21423	9.54911	9.89747
9	9.75463	9.95452	10.15911	10.58280	11.02656	11.49132
10	10.94972	11.20338	11.46338	12.00611	12.57789	13.18079
11	12.16872	12.48347	12.80780	13.48635	14.20679	14.97164
12	13.41209	13.79555	14.19203	15.02581	15.91713	16.86994
13	14.68033	15.14044	15.61779	16.62684	17.71298	18.88214
14	15.97394	16.51895	17.08632	18.29191	19.59863	21.01507
15	17.29342	17.93193	18.59891	20.02359	21.57856	23.27597
16	18.63929	19.38022	20.15688	21.82453	23.65749	25.67253
17	20.01207	20.86473	21.76159	23.69751	25.84037	28.21288
18	21.41231	22.38635	23.41444	25.64541	28.13238	30.90565
19	22.84056	23.94601	25.11687	27.67123	30.53900	33.75999
20	24.29737	25.54466	26.87037	29.77808	33.06595	36.78559
21	25.78332	27.18327	28.67649	31.96920	35.71925	39.99273
22	27.29898	28.86286	30.53678	34.24797	38.50521	43.39229
23	28.84496	30.58443	32.45288	36.61789	41.43048	46.99583
24	30.42186	32.34904	34.42647	39.08260	44.50200	50.81558
25	32.03030	34.15776	36.45926	41.64591	47.72710	54.86451
26	33.67091	36.01171	38.55304	44.31174	51.11345	59.15638
27	35.34432	37.91200	40.70963	47.08421	54.66913	63.70577
28	37.05121	39.85980	42.93092	49.96758	58.40258	68.52811
29	38.79223	41.85630	45.21885	52.96629	62.32271	73.63980
30	40.56808	43.90270	47.57542	56.08494	66.43885	79.05819
31	42.37944	46.00027	50.00268	59.32834	70.76079	84.80168
32	44.22703	48.15028	52.50276	62.70147	75.29883	90.88978
33	46.11157	50.35403	55.07784	66.20953	80.06377	97.34316
34	48.03380	52.61289	57.73018	69.85791	85.06696	104.18376
35	49.99448	54.92821	60.46208	73.65222	90.32031	111.43478
36	51.99437	57.30141	63.27594	77.59831	95.83632	119.12087
37	54.03425	59.73395	66.17422	81.70225	101.62814	127.26812
38	56.11494	62.22730	69.15945	85.97034	107.70955	135.90421
39	58.23724	64.78298	72.23423	90.40915	114.09502	145.05846
40	60.40198	67.40255	75.40126	95.02552	120.79977	154.76197

TABLE 6-3 FUTURE VALUE OF AN ORDINARY ANNUITY OF 1

8%	9%	10%	11%	12%	15%	(n) Periods
1.00000	1.00000	1.00000	1.00000	1.00000	1.00000	1
2.08000	2.09000	2.10000	2.11000	2.12000	2.15000	2
3.24640	3.27810	3.31000	3.34210	3.37440	3.47250	3
4.50611	4.57313	4.64100	4.70973	4.77933	4.99338	4
5.86660	5.98471	6.10510	6.22780	6.35285	6.74238	5
7.33592	7.52334	7.71561	7.91286	8.11519	8.75374	6
8.92280	9.20044	9.48717	9.78327	10.08901	11.06680	7
10.63663	11.02847	11.43589	11.85943	12.29969	13.72682	8
12.48756	13.02104	13.57948	14.16397	14.77566	16.78584	9
14.48656	15.19293	15.93743	16.72201	17.54874	20.30372	10
16.64549	17.56029	18.53117	19.56143	20.65458	24.34928	11
18.97713	20.14072	21.38428	22.71319	24.13313	29.00167	12
21.49530	22.95339	24.52271	26.21164	28.02911	34.35192	13
24.21492	26.01919	27.97498	30.09492	32.39260	40.50471	14
27.15211	29.36092	31.77248	34.40536	37.27972	47.58041	15
30.32428	33.00340	35.94973	39.18995	42.75328	55.71747	16
33.75023	36.97371	40.54470	44.50084	48.88367	65.07509	17
37.45024	41.30134	45.59917	50.39593	55.74972	75.83636	18
41.44626	46.01846	51.15909	56.93949	63.43968	88.21181	19
45.76196	51.16012	57.27500	64.20283	72.05244	102.44358	20
50.42292	56.76453	64.00250	72.26514	81.69874	118.81012	21
55.45676	62.87334	71.40275	81.21431	92.50258	137.63164	22
60.89330	69.53194	79.54302	91.14788	104.60289	159.27638	23
66.76476	76.78981	88.49733	102.17415	118.15524	184.16784	24
73.10594	84.70090	98.34706	114.41331	133.33387	212.79302	25
79.95442	93.32398	109.18177	127.99877	150.33393	245.71197	26
87.35077	102.72314	121.09994	143.07864	169.37401	283.56877	27
95.33883	112.96822	134.20994	159.81729	190.69889	327.10408	28
03.96594	124.13536	148.63093	178.39719	214.58275	377.16969	29
13.28321	136.30754	164.49402	199.02088	241.33268	434.74515	30
23.34587	149.57522	181.94343	221.91317	271.29261	500.95692	31
34.21354	164.03699	201.13777	247.32362	304.84772	577.10046	32
45.95062	179.80032	222.25154	275.52922	342.42945	644.66553	33
58.62667	196.98234	245.47670	306.83744	384.52098	765.36535	34
72.31680	215.71076	271.02437	341.58955	431.66350	881.17016	35
87.10215	236.12472	299.12681	380.16441	484.46312	1014.34568	36
03.07032	258.37595	330.03949	422.98249	543.59869	1167.49753	37
20.31595	282.62978	364.04343	470.51056	609.83053	1343.62216	38
38.94122	309.06646	401.44778	523.26673	684.01020	1546.16549	39
59.05652	337.88245	442.59256	581.82607	767.09142	1779.09031	40

TABLE 6-4   PRESENT VALUE OF AN ORDINARY ANNUITY OF 1

$$PVF\text{-}OA_{n,i} = \frac{1 - \frac{1}{(1 + i)^n}}{i}$$

(n) Periods	2%	2½%	3%	4%	5%	6%
1	.98039	.97561	.97087	.96154	.95238	.94340
2	1.94156	1.92742	1.91347	1.88609	1.85941	1.83339
3	2.88388	2.85602	2.82861	2.77509	2.72325	2.67301
4	3.80773	3.76197	3.71710	3.62990	3.54595	3.46511
5	4.71346	4.64583	4.57971	4.45182	4.32948	4.21236
6	5.60143	5.50813	5.41719	5.24214	5.07569	4.91732
7	6.47199	6.34939	6.23028	6.00205	5.78637	5.58238
8	7.32548	7.17014	7.01969	6.73274	6.46321	6.20979
9	8.16224	7.97087	7.78611	7.43533	7.10782	6.80169
10	8.98259	8.75206	8.53020	8.11090	7.72173	7.36009
11	9.78685	9.51421	9.25262	8.76048	8.30641	7.88687
12	10.57534	10.25776	9.95400	9.38507	8.86325	8.38384
13	11.34837	10.98319	10.63496	9.98565	9.39357	8.85268
14	12.10625	11.69091	11.29607	10.56312	9.89864	9.29498
15	12.84926	12.38138	11.93794	11.11839	10.37966	9.71225
16	13.57771	13.05500	12.56110	11.65230	10.83777	10.10590
17	14.29187	13.71220	13.16612	12.16567	11.27407	10.47726
18	14.99203	14.35336	13.75351	12.65930	11.68959	10.82760
19	15.67846	14.97889	14.32380	13.13394	12.08532	11.15812
20	16.35143	15.58916	14.87747	13.59033	12.46221	11.46992
21	17.01121	16.18455	15.41502	14.02916	12.82115	11.76408
22	17.65805	16.76541	15.93692	14.45112	13.16300	12.04158
23	18.29220	17.33211	16.44361	14.85684	13.48857	12.30338
24	18.91393	17.88499	16.93554	15.24696	13.79864	12.55036
25	19.52346	18.42438	17.41315	15.62208	14.09394	12.78336
26	20.12104	18.95061	17.87684	15.98277	14.37519	13.00317
27	20.70690	19.46401	18.32703	16.32959	14.64303	13.21053
28	21.28127	19.96489	18.76411	16.66306	14.89813	13.40616
29	21.84438	20.45355	19.18845	16.98371	15.14107	13.59072
30	22.39646	20.93029	19.60044	17.29203	15.37245	13.76483
31	22.93770	21.39541	20.00043	17.58849	15.59281	13.92909
32	23.46833	21.84918	20.38877	17.87355	15.80268	14.08404
33	23.98856	22.29188	20.76579	18.14765	16.00255	14.23023
34	24.49859	22.72379	21.13184	18.41120	16.19290	14.36814
35	24.99862	23.14516	21.48722	18.66461	16.37419	14.49825
36	25.48884	23.55625	21.83225	18.90828	16.54685	14.62099
37	25.96945	23.95732	22.16724	19.14258	16.71129	14.73678
38	26.44064	24.34860	22.49246	19.36786	16.86789	14.84602
39	26.90259	24.73034	22.80822	19.58448	17.01704	14.94907
40	27.35548	25.10278	23.11477	19.79277	17.15909	15.04630

TABLE 6-4   PRESENT VALUE OF AN ORDINARY ANNUITY OF 1

8%	9%	10%	11%	12%	15%	(n) Periods
.92593	.91743	.90909	.90090	.89286	.86957	1
1.78326	1.75911	1.73554	1.71252	1.69005	1.62571	2
2.57710	2.53130	2.48685	2.44371	2.40183	2.28323	3
3.31213	3.23972	3.16986	3.10245	3.03735	2.85498	4
3.99271	3.88965	3.79079	3.69590	3.60478	3.35216	5
4.62288	4.48592	4.35526	4.23054	4.11141	3.78448	6
5.20637	5.03295	4.86842	4.71220	4.56376	4.16042	7
5.74664	5.53482	5.33493	5.14612	4.96764	4.48732	8
6.24689	5.99525	5.75902	5.53705	5.32825	4.77158	9
6.71008	6.41766	6.14457	5.88923	5.65022	5.01877	10
7.13896	6.80519	6.49506	6.20652	5.93770	5.23371	11
7.53608	7.16073	6.81369	6.49236	6.19437	5.42062	12
7.90378	7.48690	7.10336	6.74987	6.42355	5.58315	13
8.24424	7.78615	7.36669	6.98187	6.62817	5.72448	14
8.55948	8.06069	7.60608	7.19087	6.81086	5.84737	15
8.85137	8.31256	7.82371	7.37916	6.97399	5.95424	16
9.12164	8.54363	8.02155	7.54879	7.11963	6.04716	17
9.37189	8.75563	8.20141	7.70162	7.24967	6.12797	18
9.60360	8.95012	8.36492	7.83929	7.36578	6.19823	19
9.81815	9.12855	8.51356	7.96333	7.46944	6.25933	20
10.01680	9.29224	8.64869	8.07507	7.56200	6.31246	21
10.20074	9.44243	8.77154	8.17574	7.64465	6.35866	22
10.37106	9.58021	8.88322	8.26643	7.71843	6.39884	23
10.52876	9.70661	8.98474	8.34814	7.78432	6.43377	24
10.67478	9.82258	9.07704	8.42174	7.84314	6.46415	25
10.80998	9.92897	9.16095	8.48806	7.89566	6.49056	26
10.93516	10.02658	9.23722	8.54780	7.94255	6.51353	27
11.05108	10.11613	9.30657	8.60162	7.98442	6.53351	28
11.15841	10.19828	9.36961	8.65011	8.02181	6.55088	29
11.25778	10.27365	9.42691	8.69379	8.05518	6.56598	30
11.34980	10.34280	9.47901	8.73315	8.08499	6.57911	31
11.43500	10.40624	9.52638	8.76860	8.11159	6.59053	32
11.51389	10.46444	9.56943	8.80054	8.13535	6.60046	33
11.58693	10.51784	9.60858	8.82932	8.15656	6.60910	34
11.65457	10.56682	9.64416	8.85524	8.17550	6.61661	35
11.71719	10.61176	9.67651	8.87859	8.19241	6.62314	36
11.77518	10.65299	9.70592	8.89963	8.20751	6.62882	37
11.82887	10.69082	9.73265	8.91859	8.22099	6.63375	38
11.87858	10.72552	9.75697	8.93567	8.23303	6.63805	39
11.92461	10.75736	9.77905	8.95105	8.24378	6.64178	40

TABLE 6-5 PRESENT VALUE OF AN ANNUITY DUE OF 1

$$PVF\text{-}AD_{n,i} = 1 + \frac{1 - \dfrac{1}{(1+i)^{n-1}}}{i}$$

(n) Periods	2%	2½%	3%	4%	5%	6%
1	1.00000	1.00000	1.00000	1.00000	1.00000	1.00000
2	1.98039	1.97561	1.97087	1.96154	1.95238	1.94340
3	2.94156	2.92742	2.91347	2.88609	2.85941	2.83339
4	3.88388	3.85602	3.82861	3.77509	3.72325	3.67301
5	4.80773	4.76197	4.71710	4.62990	4.54595	4.46511
6	5.71346	5.64583	5.57971	5.45182	5.32948	5.21236
7	6.60143	6.50813	6.41719	6.24214	6.07569	5.91732
8	7.47199	7.34939	7.23028	7.00205	6.78637	6.58238
9	8.32548	8.17014	8.01969	7.73274	7.46321	7.20979
10	9.16224	8.97087	8.78611	8.43533	8.10782	7.80169
11	9.98259	9.75206	9.53020	9.11090	8.72173	8.36009
12	10.78685	10.51421	10.25262	9.76048	9.30641	8.88687
13	11.57534	11.25776	10.95400	10.38507	9.86325	9.38384
14	12.34837	11.98319	11.63496	10.98565	10.39357	9.85268
15	13.10625	12.69091	12.29607	11.56312	10.89864	10.29498
16	13.84926	13.38138	12.93794	12.11839	11.37966	10.71225
17	14.57771	14.05500	13.56110	12.65230	11.83777	11.10590
18	15.29187	14.71220	14.16612	13.16567	12.27407	11.47726
19	15.99203	15.35336	14.75351	13.65930	12.68959	11.82760
20	16.67846	15.97889	15.32380	14.13394	13.08532	12.15812
21	17.35143	16.58916	15.87747	14.59033	13.46221	12.46992
22	18.01121	17.18455	16.41502	15.02916	13.82115	12.76408
23	18.65805	17.76541	16.93692	15.45112	14.16300	13.04158
24	19.29220	18.33211	17.44361	15.85684	14.48857	13.30338
25	19.91393	18.88499	17.93554	16.24696	14.79864	13.55036
26	20.52346	19.42438	18.41315	16.62208	15.09394	13.78336
27	21.12104	19.95061	18.87684	16.98277	15.37519	14.00317
28	21.70690	20.46401	19.32703	17.32959	15.64303	14.21053
29	22.28127	20.96489	19.76411	17.66306	15.89813	14.40616
30	22.84438	21.45355	20.18845	17.98371	16.14107	14.59072
31	23.39646	21.93029	20.60044	18.29203	16.37245	14.76483
32	23.93770	22.39541	21.00043	18.58849	16.59281	14.92909
33	24.46833	22.84918	21.38877	18.87355	16.80268	15.08404
34	24.98856	23.29188	21.76579	19.14765	17.00255	15.23023
35	25.49859	23.72379	22.13184	19.41120	17.19290	15.36814
36	25.99862	24.14516	22.48722	19.66461	17.37419	15.49825
37	26.48884	24.55625	22.83225	19.90828	17.54685	15.62099
38	26.96945	24.95732	23.16724	20.14258	17.71129	15.73678
39	27.44064	25.34860	23.49246	20.36786	17.86789	15.84602
40	27.90259	25.73034	23.80822	20.58448	18.01704	15.94907

TABLE 6-5   PRESENT VALUE OF AN ANNUITY DUE OF 1

8%	9%	10%	11%	12%	15%	(n) Periods
1.00000	1.00000	1.00000	1.00000	1.00000	1.00000	1
1.92593	1.91743	1.90909	1.90090	1.89286	1.86957	2
2.78326	2.75911	2.73554	2.71252	2.69005	2.62571	3
3.57710	3.53130	3.48685	3.44371	3.40183	3.28323	4
4.31213	4.23972	4.16986	4.10245	4.03735	3.85498	5
4.99271	4.88965	4.79079	4.69590	4.60478	4.35216	6
5.62288	5.48592	5.35526	5.23054	5.11141	4.78448	7
6.20637	6.03295	5.86842	5.71220	5.56376	5.16042	8
6.74664	6.53482	6.33493	6.14612	5.96764	5.48732	9
7.24689	6.99525	6.75902	6.53705	6.32825	5.77158	10
7.71008	7.41766	7.14457	6.88923	6.65022	6.01877	11
8.13896	7.80519	7.49506	7.20652	6.93770	6.23371	12
8.53608	8.16073	7.81369	7.49236	7.19437	6.42062	13
8.90378	8.48690	8.10336	7.74987	7.42355	6.58315	14
9.24424	8.78615	8.36669	7.98187	7.62817	6.72448	15
9.55948	9.06069	8.60608	8.19087	7.81086	6.84737	16
9.85137	9.31256	8.82371	8.37916	7.97399	6.95424	17
10.12164	9.54363	9.02155	8.54879	8.11963	7.04716	18
10.37189	9.75563	9.20141	8.70162	8.24967	7.12797	19
10.60360	9.95012	9.36492	8.83929	8.36578	7.19823	20
10.81815	10.12855	9.51356	8.96333	8.46944	7.25933	21
11.01680	10.29224	9.64869	9.07507	8.56200	7.31246	22
11.20074	10.44243	9.77154	9.17574	8.64465	7.35866	23
11.37106.	10.58021	9.88322	9.26643	8.71843	7.39884	24
11.52876	10.70661	9.98474	9.34814	8.78432	7.43377	25
11.67478	10.82258	10.07704	9.42174	8.84314	7.46415	26
11.80998	10.92897	10.16095	9.48806	8.89566	7.49056	27
11.93518	11.02658	10.23722	9.54780	8.94255	7.51353	28
12.05108	11.11613	10.30657	9.60162	8.98442	7.53351	29
12.15841	11.19828	10.36961	9.65011	9.02181	7.55088	30
12.25778	11.27365	10.42691	9.69379	9.05518	7.56598	31
12.34980	11.34280	10.47901	9.73315	9.08499	7.57911	32
12.43500	11.40624	10.52638	9.76860	9.11159	7.59053	33
12.51389	11.46444	10.56943	9.80054	9.13535	7.60046	34
12.58693	11.51784	10.60858	9.82932	9.15656	7.60910	35
12.65457	11.56682	10.64416	9.85524	9.17550	7.61661	36
12.71719	11.61176	10.67651	9.87859	9.19241	7.62314	37
12.77518	11.65299	10.70592	9.89963	9.20751	7.62882	38
12.82887	11.69082	10.73265	9.91859	9.22099	7.63375	39
12.87858	11.72552	10.75697	9.93567	9.23303	7.63805	40

Please Release Me?

In recent quarters, several U.S. banks have reported increases in net income compared to the same quarter in the previous year. How did the market greet this news? With a resounding "blah." For example, **Wells Fargo**'s report led to a share price decline of 8.4 percent, and **Citigroup** saw a 1.7 percent drop in its share price when it announced earnings. What gives?

It seems that the source of earnings increase matters to the market. And in the case of banks, a significant portion of recent earnings increases are the result of decreases in the banks' bad debt expense, not increased revenues on loans and investments. These decreases happen when the banks' reserves that have accumulated in the allowance for loan losses are judged to be too high. How big is the effect? As shown in the chart below, in a recent quarter, of the $14.3 billion in earnings reported by the top 10 U.S. banks, $3.5 billion came from releasing loan loss reserves. For Citi, without the reserve release, it would have reported a loss.

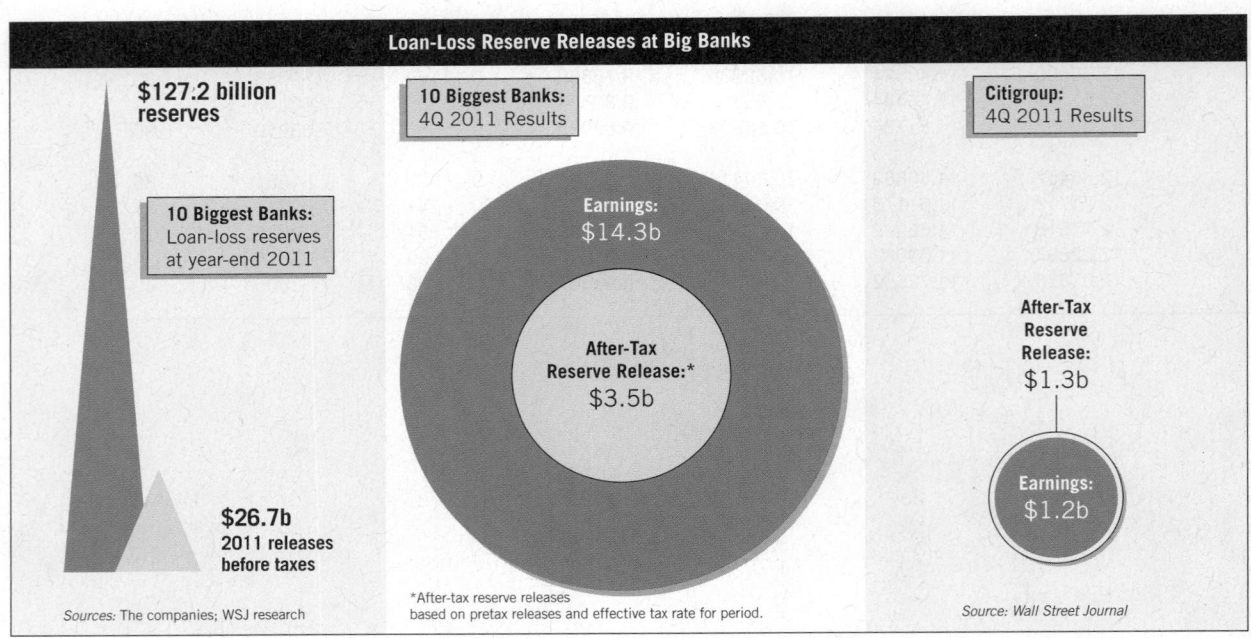

Loan-Loss Reserve Releases at Big Banks

$127.2 billion reserves

10 Biggest Banks: Loan-loss reserves at year-end 2011

$26.7b 2011 releases before taxes

10 Biggest Banks: 4Q 2011 Results

Earnings: $14.3b

After-Tax Reserve Release:* $3.5b

Citigroup: 4Q 2011 Results

After-Tax Reserve Release: $1.3b

Earnings: $1.2b

*After-tax reserve releases based on pretax releases and effective tax rate for period.

Sources: The companies; WSJ research

Source: Wall Street Journal

As shown in the left side of the chart, the 10 largest banks had $127.2 billion in the allowance for loan losses at the end of 2011, and $26.7 billion was drawn down (released) in that same year.

So is this a problem? Supposedly, reserves should be released when there is a decline in the likelihood that loans will not be paid. However, some market-watchers doubt that banks can afford to keep up the pace of reserve releases. Lowering reserves could increase pressure on profits that are being hit by slow economic growth, low interest rates, and tighter rules. According to one analyst, "The releases are masking some horrible operating performance. . . . The bottom line is your earnings power is decreasing."

CONCEPTUAL FOCUS

> See the **Underlying Concepts** on pages 352, 356, and 373.
> Read the **Evolving Issue** on page 374 for a discussion of accounting for loan losses.

INTERNATIONAL FOCUS

> See the **International Perspectives** on pages 365, 370, and 372.
> Read the **IFRS Insights** on pages 408–412 for a discussion of:
—Impairment evaluation
—Recovery of impairment losses

To be fair, analysts often criticize banks when they increase the allowance for loan losses during profitable periods. In some cases, the banks are accused of managing earnings. That is, in good times they increase loan loss reserves, which reduces (or smoothes) earnings. Then in bad times, the reserves can be released, thereby increasing earnings. The SEC has reprimanded some banks for this alleged earnings management—in not only the tough times, but the good times as well.

Sources: S. Kapner, "Citi Shines, but Investors Shrug," *Wall Street Journal* (October 18, 2011), p. C1; and M. Rapoport, "Banks Depleting Earnings Backstop: Days Numbered for Using Reserves to Increase Profit," *Wall Street Journal* (February 8, 2012), p. C1.

PREVIEW OF CHAPTER 7

As our opening story indicates, measurement and remeasurement of the allowance for doubtful accounts has important implications for accurate reporting of net accounts receivable, operating profits, net income, and assets. In this chapter, we discuss cash and receivables—two assets that are important to banks such as **Citigroup** and nonbank companies such as **Wal-Mart Stores, Inc.** The content and organization of the chapter are as follows.

Cash and Receivables

Cash	Accounts Receivable	Notes Receivable	Special Issues
• What is cash? • Reporting cash • Summary of cash-related items	• Recognition of accounts receivable • Valuation of accounts receivable	• Recognition of notes receivable • Valuation of notes receivable	• Fair value option • Disposition of accounts and notes receivable • Presentation and analysis

CASH

What Is Cash?

LEARNING OBJECTIVE
Identify items considered cash.

Cash, the most liquid of assets, is the standard medium of exchange and the basis for measuring and accounting for all other items. Companies generally classify cash as a current asset. Cash consists of coin, currency, and available funds on deposit at the bank. Negotiable instruments such as money orders, certified checks, cashier's checks, personal checks, and bank drafts are also viewed as cash. What about savings accounts? Banks do have the legal right to demand notice before withdrawal. But, because banks rarely demand prior notice, savings accounts nevertheless are considered cash.

Some negotiable instruments provide small investors with an opportunity to earn interest. These items, more appropriately classified as temporary investments than as cash, include money market funds, money market savings certificates, certificates of deposit (CDs), and similar types of deposits and "short-term paper."[1] These securities usually contain restrictions or penalties on their conversion to cash. Money market funds that provide checking account privileges, however, are usually classified as cash.

Certain items present classification problems: Companies treat **postdated checks and I.O.U.s** as receivables. They also treat **travel advances** as receivables if collected from employees or deducted from their salaries. Otherwise, companies classify the travel advance as a prepaid expense. **Postage stamps on hand** are classified as part of office supplies inventory or as a prepaid expense. Because **petty cash funds and change funds are used** to meet current operating expenses and liquidate current liabilities, companies include these funds in current assets as cash.

Reporting Cash

LEARNING OBJECTIVE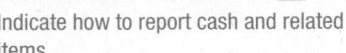
Indicate how to report cash and related items.

Although the reporting of cash is relatively straightforward, a number of issues merit special attention. These issues relate to the reporting of:

1. Cash equivalents.
2. Restricted cash.
3. Bank overdrafts.

Cash Equivalents

A current classification that has become popular is "Cash and cash equivalents."[2] **Cash equivalents** are short-term, highly liquid investments that are both (a) readily convertible to known amounts of cash, and (b) so near their maturity that they present insignificant risk of changes in value because of changes in interest rates. Generally, only investments with original maturities of three months or less qualify under these definitions. Examples of cash

---

[1]A variety of "short-term paper" is available for investment. For example, **certificates of deposit** (CDs) represent formal evidence of indebtedness, issued by a bank, subject to withdrawal under the specific terms of the instrument. Issued in various denominations, they have maturities anywhere from 7 days to 10 years and generally pay interest at the short-term interest rate in effect at the date of issuance.

In **money-market funds**, a variation of the mutual fund, the mix of Treasury bills and commercial paper making up the fund's portfolio determines the yield. Most money-market funds require an initial minimum investment of $1,000; many allow withdrawal by check or wire transfer.

Treasury bills are U.S. government obligations generally issued with 4-, 13-, and 26-week maturities; they are sold at weekly government auctions in denominations of $1,000 up to a maximum purchase of $5 million.

Commercial paper is a short-term note issued by corporations with good credit ratings. Often issued in $5,000 and $10,000 denominations, these notes generally yield a higher rate than Treasury bills.

[2]*Accounting Trends and Techniques* recently indicated that approximately 2 percent of the companies surveyed use the caption "Cash," 89 percent use "Cash and cash equivalents," and 2 percent use a caption such as "Cash and marketable securities" or similar terminology.

equivalents are Treasury bills, commercial paper, and money market funds. Some companies combine cash with temporary investments on the balance sheet. In these cases, they describe the amount of the temporary investments either parenthetically or in the notes.

Most individuals think of cash equivalents as cash. Unfortunately, that is not always the case. Companies like Kohl's and ADC Telecommunications have found out the hard way and are taking sizable write-downs on cash equivalents. Their losses resulted because they purchased auction-rate notes that declined in value. These notes carry interest rates that usually reset weekly and often have long-maturity dates (as long as 30 years). Companies argued that such notes should be classified as cash equivalents because they can be routinely traded at auction on a daily basis. (In short, they are liquid and risk-free.) Auditors agreed and permitted cash-equivalent treatment even though maturities extended well beyond three months. But when the credit crunch hit, the auctions stopped, and the value of these securities dropped because no market existed. In retrospect, the cash-equivalent classification was misleading.

It now appears likely that the FASB will eliminate the cash-equivalent classification from financial statement presentations altogether. Companies will now report only cash. If an asset is not cash and is short-term in nature, it should be reported as a temporary investment. An interesting moral to this story is that when times are good, some careless accounting may work. But in bad times, it quickly becomes apparent that sloppy accounting can lead to misleading and harmful effects for users of the financial statements.

Restricted Cash

Petty cash, payroll, and dividend funds are examples of cash set aside for a particular purpose. In most situations, these fund balances are not material. Therefore, companies do not segregate them from cash in the financial statements. When material in amount, companies segregate restricted cash from "regular" cash for reporting purposes. Companies classify restricted cash either in the current assets or in the long-term assets section, depending on the date of availability or disbursement. Classification in the current section is appropriate if using the cash for payment of existing or maturing obligations (within a year or the operating cycle, whichever is longer). On the other hand, companies show the restricted cash in the long-term section of the balance sheet if holding the cash for a longer period of time. Among other potential restrictions, companies need to determine whether any of the cash in accounts outside the United States is restricted by regulations against exportation of currency.

Cash classified in the long-term section is frequently set aside for plant expansion, retirement of long-term debt, or, in the case of International Thoroughbred Breeders, for entry fee deposits.

International Thoroughbred Breeders

Restricted cash and investments (See Note)	$3,730,000

Note: Restricted Cash. At year-end, the Company had approximately $3,730,000, which was classified as restricted cash and investments. These funds are primarily cash received from horsemen for nomination and entry fees to be applied to upcoming racing meets, purse winnings held in trust for horsemen, and amounts held for unclaimed ticketholder winnings.

ILLUSTRATION 7-1
Disclosure of Restricted Cash

Banks and other lending institutions often require customers to maintain minimum cash balances in checking or savings accounts. The SEC defines these minimum balances, called compensating balances, as "that portion of any demand deposit (or any time deposit or certificate of deposit) maintained by a corporation which constitutes support for existing borrowing arrangements of the corporation with a lending institution. Such arrangements would include both outstanding borrowings and the assurance of future credit availability." [1]

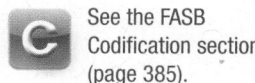

See the FASB Codification section (page 385).

To avoid misleading investors about the amount of cash available to meet recurring obligations, the SEC recommends that companies state separately **legally restricted deposits** held as compensating balances against **short-term** borrowing arrangements among the "Cash and cash equivalent items" in current assets. Companies should classify separately restricted deposits held as compensating balances against **long-term** borrowing arrangements as noncurrent assets in either the investments or other assets sections, using a caption such as "Cash on deposit maintained as compensating balance." In cases where compensating balance arrangements exist without agreements that restrict the use of cash amounts shown on the balance sheet, companies should describe the arrangements and the amounts involved in the notes.

Bank Overdrafts

Bank overdrafts occur when a company writes a check for more than the amount in its cash account. Companies should report bank overdrafts in the current liabilities section, adding them to the amount reported as accounts payable. If material, companies should disclose these items separately, either on the face of the balance sheet or in the related notes.[3]

Bank overdrafts are generally not offset against the cash account. A major exception is when available cash is present in another account in the same bank on which the overdraft occurred. Offsetting in this case is required.

Summary of Cash-Related Items

Cash and cash equivalents include the medium of exchange and most negotiable instruments. If the item cannot be quickly converted to coin or currency, a company separately classifies it as an investment, receivable, or prepaid expense. Companies segregate and classify cash that is unavailable for payment of currently maturing liabilities in the long-term assets section. Illustration 7-2 summarizes the classification of cash-related items.

ILLUSTRATION 7-2
Classification of Cash-Related Items

Classification of Cash, Cash Equivalents, and Noncash Items		
Item	Classification	Comment
Cash	Cash	If unrestricted, report as cash. If restricted, identify and classify as current and noncurrent assets.
Petty cash and change funds	Cash	Report as cash.
Short-term paper	Cash equivalents	Investments with maturity of less than 3 months, often combined with cash.
Short-term paper	Temporary investments	Investments with maturity of 3 to 12 months.
Postdated checks and I.O.U.s	Receivables	Assumed to be collectible.
Travel advances	Receivables	Assumed to be collected from employees or deducted from their salaries.
Postage on hand (as stamps or in postage meters)	Prepaid expenses	May also be classified as office supplies inventory.
Bank overdrafts	Current liability	If right of offset exists, reduce cash.
Compensating balances	Cash separately classified as a deposit maintained as compensating balance	Classify as current or noncurrent in the balance sheet. Disclose separately in notes details of the arrangement.

[3]Bank overdrafts usually occur because of a simple oversight by the company writing the check. Banks often expect companies to have overdrafts from time to time and therefore negotiate a fee as payment for this possible occurrence. However, at one time, E. F. Hutton (a large brokerage firm) began intentionally overdrawing its accounts by astronomical amounts—on some days exceeding $1 billion—thus obtaining interest-free loans that it could invest. Because the amounts were so large and fees were not negotiated in advance, E. F. Hutton came under criminal investigation for its actions.

Recently, Apple executives explained what they are planning to do with their $98 billion in cash (pay a $2.65 dividend and buy back some of their shares). However, what they were really talking about was not the full $98 billion but the $34 billion the company has here in the United States. The other $64 billion is sitting in overseas subsidiaries and may never find its way back to the United States. The reason: U.S. tax laws allow companies to defer taxes on their profits from international operations until they bring the cash back into the country.

So what do many companies do? Either the cash just sits there in foreign bank accounts or is reinvested in factories and acquisitions overseas. After all, why should a company send its cash back to the United States when it can reinvest this cash overseas without any tax payments? As a result, companies now have the incentive to move as much of their earnings overseas to low-tax jurisdictions such as a country like Ireland. As one expert noted, it cannot be the luck of the Irish that explains the extraordinary and systematic profitability of Irish subsidiaries of U.S. companies.

So when investors analyze an annual report and find a company reporting a large cash balance, they may believe that this cash is available for increased dividends or for acquisitions in the United States. But that is not necessarily so—much of the cash may be overseas and may never return.

Unfortunately, the problem is getting bigger, not smaller. Untaxed foreign earnings are now growing at a much faster rate than earnings generated in the United States. For example, in a recent five-year period, the accumulated untaxed foreign earnings have reached over $1 trillion and are growing at a rate of 22 percent as compared to 5 percent for domestic earnings. A majority of these earnings are concentrated in three sectors—health care, technology, and industrials. Presented below is a chart that shows total accumulated untaxed foreign earnings, untaxed foreign earnings for the current year and its relationship to net income, and cash flow provided by operations for the top five companies in the S&P 500. Note that the top 40 companies in the S&P 500 have 73 percent of the total untaxed foreign earnings in the index.

Company	Accumulated Untaxed Foreign Earnings (UFE)*	Untaxed Foreign Earnings in Current Year*	Untaxed Foreign Earnings as a % of Net Income	Untaxed Foreign Earnings as a % of Operating Cash Flow
Microsoft	$ 44,800	$15,300	66%	57%
Pfizer	63,000	14,800	169	73
ExxonMobil	47,000	12,000	28	22
Apple	23,400	11,100	43	30
General Electric	102,000	8,000	56	24

*In $ millions.

What this all tells us is that the U.S. taxpayer is presently holding the bag because many of these companies may never be taxed as the cash from these earnings will not be invested in the Unites States. At a minimum, investors need more information about foreign earnings, the amount of cash in foreign deposits, and cash generated from foreign operations where untaxed foreign earnings were reported. Capital markets are well served when good information is provided. You would think that cash is cash and the amount is certain, but unfortunately some cash is better than other cash.

Source: J. Ciesielski, "Growing, Glowing Earnings: S&P 500's 2011 Untaxed Income," *The Analyst's Accounting Observer* (March 26, 2012).

ACCOUNTS RECEIVABLE

Receivables are claims held against customers and others for money, goods, or services. For financial statement purposes, companies classify receivables as either **current** (short-term) or **noncurrent** (long-term). Companies expect to collect **current receivables** within a year or during the current operating cycle, whichever is longer. They classify all other receivables as **noncurrent**. Receivables are further classified in the balance sheet as either trade or nontrade receivables.

3 LEARNING OBJECTIVE
Define receivables and identify the different types of receivables.

Customers often owe a company amounts for goods bought or services rendered. A company may subclassify these **trade receivables**, usually the most significant item it possesses, into accounts receivable and notes receivable. **Accounts receivable** are oral promises of the purchaser to pay for goods and services sold. They represent "open accounts" resulting from short-term extensions of credit. A company normally collects them within 30 to 60 days. **Notes receivable** are written promises to pay a certain sum of money on a specified future date. They may arise from sales, financing, or other transactions. Notes may be short-term or long-term.

Nontrade receivables arise from a variety of transactions. Some examples of nontrade receivables are:

1. Advances to officers and employees.
2. Advances to subsidiaries.
3. Deposits paid to cover potential damages or losses.
4. Deposits paid as a guarantee of performance or payment.
5. Dividends and interest receivable.
6. Claims against:
   (a) Insurance companies for casualties sustained.
   (b) Defendants under suit.
   (c) Governmental bodies for tax refunds.
   (d) Common carriers for damaged or lost goods.
   (e) Creditors for returned, damaged, or lost goods.
   (f) Customers for returnable items (crates, containers, etc.).

Because of the peculiar nature of nontrade receivables, companies generally report them as separate items in the balance sheet. Illustration 7-3 shows the reporting of trade and nontrade receivables in the balance sheets of **Molson Coors Brewing Company** and **Seaboard Corporation**.

Molson Coors Brewing Company (in thousands)	
Current assets	
Cash and cash equivalents	$ 377,023
Accounts and notes receivable	
Trade, less allowance for doubtful accounts of $8,827	758,526
Current notes receivable and other receivables, less allowance for doubtful accounts of $3,181	112,626
Inventories	369,521
Maintenance and operating supplies, less allowance for obsolete supplies of $10,556	34,782
Other current assets, less allowance for advertising supplies of $948	124,336
Total current assets	$1,776,814

Seaboard Corporation (in thousands)		
Current assets		
Cash and cash equivalents		$ 47,346
Short-term investments		286,660
Receivables		
Trade	$251,005	
Due from foreign affiliates	90,019	
Other	26,349	
		367,373
Allowance for doubtful accounts		(8,060)
Net receivables		359,313
Inventories		392,946
Deferred income taxes		19,558
Other current assets		77,710
Total current assets		$1,183,533

ILLUSTRATION 7-3
Receivables Balance Sheet Presentations

The basic issues in accounting for accounts and notes receivable are the same: **recognition**, **valuation**, and **disposition**. We discuss these basic issues for accounts and notes receivable next.

Recognition of Accounts Receivable

In most receivables transactions, the amount to be recognized is the exchange price between the two parties. **The exchange price is the amount due from the debtor** (a customer or a borrower). Some type of business document, often an invoice, serves as evidence of the exchange price. Two factors may complicate the measurement of the exchange price: (1) the availability of discounts (trade and cash discounts), and (2) the length of time between the sale and the due date of payments (the interest element).

Trade Discounts

Prices may be subject to a trade or quantity discount. Companies use such **trade discounts** to avoid frequent changes in catalogs, to alter prices for different quantities purchased, or to hide the true invoice price from competitors.

Trade discounts are commonly quoted in percentages. For example, say your cell phone has a list price of $90, and the manufacturer sells it to **Best Buy** for list less a 30 percent trade discount. The manufacturer then records the receivable at $63 per phone. The manufacturer, per normal practice, simply deducts the trade discount from the list price and bills the customer net.

As another example, **Maxwell House** at one time sold a 10-ounce jar of its instant coffee listing at $5.85 to supermarkets for $5.05, a trade discount of approximately 14 percent. The supermarkets in turn sold the instant coffee for $5.20 per jar. Maxwell House records the receivable and related sales revenue at $5.05 per jar, not $5.85.

Cash Discounts (Sales Discounts)

Companies offer **cash discounts (sales discounts)** to induce prompt payment. Cash discounts generally presented in terms such as 2/10, n/30 (2 percent if paid within 10 days, gross amount due in 30 days), or 2/10, E.O.M., net 30, E.O.M. (2 percent if paid any time before the tenth day of the following month, with full payment due by the thirtieth of the following month).

Companies usually take sales discounts unless their cash is severely limited. Why? A company that receives a 1 percent reduction in the sales price for payment within 10 days, total payment due within 30 days, effectively earns 18.25 percent [$.01 \div (20/365)$], or at least avoids that rate of interest cost.

Companies usually record sales and related sales discount transactions by entering the receivable and sale at the gross amount. Under this method, companies recognize sales discounts only when they receive payment within the discount period. The income statement shows sales discounts as a deduction from sales to arrive at net sales.

Some contend that sales discounts not taken reflect penalties added to an established price to encourage prompt payment. That is, the seller offers sales on account at a slightly higher price than if selling for cash. The cash discount offered offsets the increase. Thus, customers who pay within the discount period actually purchase at the cash price. Those who pay after expiration of the discount period pay a penalty for the delay—an amount in excess of the cash price. Per this reasoning, some companies record sales and receivables net. They subsequently debit any discounts not taken to Accounts Receivable and credit to Sales Discounts Forfeited. The entries in Illustration 7-4 (page 352) show the difference between the gross and net methods.

If using the gross method, a company reports sales discounts as a deduction from sales in the income statement. Proper expense recognition dictates that the company also reasonably estimates the expected discounts to be taken and charges that amount

ILLUSTRATION 7-4
Entries under Gross and
Net Methods of
Recording Cash (Sales)
Discounts

Gross Method			Net Method		
Sales of $10,000, terms 2/10, n/30					
Accounts Receivable	10,000		Accounts Receivable	9,800	
Sales Revenue		10,000	Sales Revenue		9,800
Payment on $4,000 of sales received within discount period					
Cash	3,920		Cash	3,920	
Sales Discounts	80		Accounts Receivable		3,920
Accounts Receivable		4,000			
Payment on $6,000 of sales received after discount period					
Cash	6,000		Accounts Receivable	120	
Accounts Receivable		6,000	Sales Discounts Forfeited		120
			Cash	6,000	
			Accounts Receivable		6,000

against sales. If using the net method, a company considers Sales Discounts Forfeited as an "Other revenue" item.[4]

Theoretically, the recognition of Sales Discounts Forfeited is correct. The receivable is stated closer to its realizable value, and the net sales figure measures the revenue recognized from the sale. As a practical matter, however, companies seldom use the net method because it requires additional analysis and bookkeeping. For example, the net method requires adjusting entries to record sales discounts forfeited on accounts receivable that have passed the discount period.

Nonrecognition of Interest Element

Ideally, a company should measure receivables in terms of their present value, that is, the discounted value of the cash to be received in the future. When expected cash receipts require a waiting period, the receivable face amount is not worth the amount that the company ultimately receives.

To illustrate, assume that **Best Buy** makes a sale on account for $1,000 with payment due in four months. The applicable annual rate of interest is 12 percent, and payment is made at the end of four months. The present value of that receivable is not $1,000 but $961.54 ($1,000 × .96154). In other words, the $1,000 Best Buy receives four months from now is not the same as the $1,000 received today.

Theoretically, any revenue after the period of sale is interest revenue. In practice, companies ignore interest revenue related to accounts receivable because the amount of the discount is not usually material in relation to the net income for the period. The profession specifically excludes from present value considerations "receivables arising from transactions with customers in the normal course of business which are due in customary trade terms not exceeding approximately one year." [2]

> **Underlying Concepts**
>
> Materiality means it must make a difference to a decision-maker. The FASB believes that present value concepts can be ignored for short-term receivables.

Valuation of Accounts Receivable

LEARNING OBJECTIVE 5
Explain accounting issues related to valuation of accounts receivable.

Reporting of receivables involves (1) classification and (2) valuation on the balance sheet. Classification involves determining the length of time each receivable will be outstanding. Companies classify receivables intended to be collected within a

---

[4]To the extent that discounts not taken reflect a short-term financing, some argue that companies could use an interest revenue account to record these amounts.

year or the operating cycle, whichever is longer, as current. All other receivables are classified as long-term.

Companies value and report short-term receivables at net realizable value—**the net amount they expect to receive in cash.** Determining net realizable value requires estimating both uncollectible receivables and any returns or allowances to be granted.

Uncollectible Accounts Receivable

As one revered accountant aptly noted, the credit manager's idea of heaven probably would be a place where everyone (eventually) paid his or her debts.[5] Unfortunately, this situation often does not occur. For example, a customer may not be able to pay because of a decline in its sales revenue due to a downturn in the economy. Similarly, individuals may be laid off from their jobs or faced with unexpected hospital bills. Companies record credit losses as debits to Bad Debt Expense (or Uncollectible Accounts Expense). Such losses are a normal and necessary risk of doing business on a credit basis.

Two methods are used in accounting for uncollectible accounts: (1) the direct write-off method and (2) the allowance method. The following sections explain these methods.

Direct Write-Off Method for Uncollectible Accounts

Under the direct write-off method, when a company determines a particular account to be uncollectible, it charges the loss to Bad Debt Expense. Assume, for example, that on December 10 Cruz Co. writes off as uncollectible Yusado's $8,000 balance. The entry is:

December 10

Bad Debt Expense	8,000	
Accounts Receivable (Yusado)		8,000
(To record write-off of Yusado account)		

Under this method, Bad Debt Expense will show only **actual losses** from uncollectibles. The company will report accounts receivable at its gross amount.

Supporters of the **direct write-off-method** (which is often used for tax purposes) contend that it records facts, not estimates. It assumes that a good account receivable resulted from each sale, and that later events revealed certain accounts to be uncollectible and worthless. From a practical standpoint, this method is simple and convenient to apply. But the direct write-off method is theoretically deficient. It usually fails to record expenses in the same period as associated revenues. Nor does it result in receivables being stated at net realizable value on the balance sheet. **As a result, using the direct write-off method is not considered appropriate, except when the amount uncollectible is immaterial.**

Allowance Method for Uncollectible Accounts

The allowance method of accounting for bad debts involves estimating uncollectible accounts at the end of each period. This ensures that companies state receivables on the balance sheet at their net realizable value. Net realizable value is the net amount the company expects to receive in cash. The FASB considers the collectibility of receivables a loss contingency. Thus, the allowance method is appropriate in situations where it is probable that an asset has been impaired and that the amount of the loss can be reasonably estimated. **[3]**

Although estimates are involved, companies can predict the percentage of uncollectible receivables from past experiences, present market conditions, and an analysis of the outstanding balances. Many companies set their credit policies to provide for a certain percentage of uncollectible accounts. (In fact, many feel that failure to reach that

---

[5]William J. Vatter, *Managerial Accounting* (Englewood Cliffs, N.J.: Prentice-Hall, 1950), p. 60.

percentage means that they are losing sales due to overly restrictive credit policies.) Thus, the FASB requires the allowance method for financial reporting purposes when bad debts are material in amount. This method has three essential features:

1. Companies **estimate** uncollectible accounts receivable. They match this estimated expense **against revenues** in the same accounting period in which they record the revenues.
2. Companies debit estimated uncollectibles to Bad Debt Expense and credit them to Allowance for Doubtful Accounts (a contra asset account) through an adjusting entry at the end of each period.
3. When companies write off a specific account, they debit actual uncollectibles to Allowance for Doubtful Accounts and credit that amount to Accounts Receivable.

Recording Estimated Uncollectibles. To illustrate the allowance method, assume that Brown Furniture has credit sales of $1,800,000 in 2014. Of this amount, $150,000 remains uncollected at December 31. The credit manager estimates that $10,000 of these sales will be uncollectible. The adjusting entry to record the estimated uncollectibles is:

December 31, 2014

Bad Debt Expense	10,000	
Allowance for Doubtful Accounts		10,000
(To record estimate of uncollectible accounts)		

Brown reports Bad Debt Expense in the income statement as an operating expense. Thus, the estimated uncollectibles are matched with sales in 2014. Brown records the expense in the same year it made the sales.

As Illustration 7-5 shows, the company deducts the allowance account from accounts receivable in the current assets section of the balance sheet.

ILLUSTRATION 7-5
Presentation of
Allowance for Doubtful
Accounts

BROWN FURNITURE		
BALANCE SHEET (PARTIAL)		
Current assets		
Cash		$ 15,000
Accounts receivable	$150,000	
Less: Allowance for doubtful accounts	10,000	140,000
Inventory		300,000
Prepaid insurance		25,000
Total current assets		$480,000

Allowance for Doubtful Accounts shows the estimated amount of claims on customers that the company expects will become uncollectible in the future.[6] Companies use a contra account instead of a direct credit to Accounts Receivable because they do not know which customers will not pay. The credit balance in the allowance account will absorb the specific write-offs when they occur. The amount of $140,000 in Illustration 7-5 represents the **net realizable value** of the accounts receivable at the statement date. **Companies do not close Allowance for Doubtful Accounts at the end of the fiscal year.**

---

[6]The account description employed for the allowance account is usually Allowance for Doubtful Accounts or simply Allowance. *Accounting Trends and Techniques* recently indicated that approximately 83 percent of the companies surveyed used "allowance" in their description.

Recording the Write-Off of an Uncollectible Account. When companies have exhausted all means of collecting a past-due account and collection appears impossible, the company should write off the account. In the credit card industry, for example, it is standard practice to write off accounts that are 210 days past due.

To illustrate a receivables write-off, assume that the financial vice president of Brown Furniture authorizes a write-off of the $1,000 balance owed by Randall Co. on March 1, 2015. The entry to record the write-off is:

	March 1, 2015		
Allowance for Doubtful Accounts		1,000	
Accounts Receivable (Randall Co.)			1,000
(Write-off of Randall Co. account)			

Bad Debt Expense does not increase when the write-off occurs. **Under the allowance method, companies debit every bad debt write-off to the allowance account rather than to Bad Debt Expense.** A debit to Bad Debt Expense would be incorrect because the company has already recognized the expense when it made the adjusting entry for estimated bad debts. Instead, the entry to record the write-off of an uncollectible account reduces both Accounts Receivable and Allowance for Doubtful Accounts.

Recovery of an Uncollectible Account. Occasionally, a company collects from a customer after it has written off the account as uncollectible. The company makes two entries to record the recovery of a bad debt: (1) It reverses the entry made in writing off the account. This reinstates the customer's account. (2) It journalizes the collection in the usual manner.

To illustrate, assume that on July 1, 2015, Randall Co. pays the $1,000 amount that Brown had written off on March 1. These are the entries:

	July 1, 2015		
Accounts Receivable (Randall Co.)		1,000	
Allowance for Doubtful Accounts			1,000
(To reverse write-off of account)			
Cash		1,000	
Accounts Receivable (Randall Co.)			1,000
(Collection of account)			

Note that the recovery of a bad debt, like the write-off of a bad debt, affects **only balance sheet accounts**. The net effect of the two entries above is a debit to Cash and a credit to Allowance for Doubtful Accounts for $1,000.[7]

Bases Used for Allowance Method. To simplify the preceding explanation, we assumed we knew the amount of the expected uncollectibles. In "real life," companies must estimate that amount when they use the allowance method. Two bases are used to determine this amount: **(1) percentage of sales** and **(2) percentage of receivables**. Both bases are generally accepted. The choice is a management decision. It depends on the relative emphasis that management wishes to give to expenses and revenues on the one hand or to net realizable value of the accounts receivable on the other. The choice is whether to emphasize income statement or balance sheet relationships. Illustration 7-6 (page 356) compares the two bases.

---

[7]If using the direct write-off approach, the company debits the amount collected to Cash and credits a revenue account entitled Uncollectible Amounts Recovered, with proper notation in the customer's account.

ILLUSTRATION 7-6
Comparison of Bases for
Estimating Uncollectibles

Underlying Concepts

The percentage-of-sales method illustrates the expense recognition principle, which relates expenses to revenues recognized.

The percentage-of-sales basis results in a better matching of expenses with revenues—an income statement viewpoint. The percentage-of-receivables basis produces the better estimate of net realizable value—a balance sheet viewpoint. Under both bases, the company must determine its past experience with bad debt losses.

Percentage-of-sales (income statement) approach. In the **percentage-of-sales approach**, management estimates what percentage of credit sales will be uncollectible. This percentage is based on past experience and anticipated credit policy.

The company applies this percentage to either total credit sales or net credit sales of the current year. To illustrate, assume that Gonzalez Company elects to use the percentage-of-sales basis. It concludes that 1 percent of net credit sales will become uncollectible. If net credit sales for 2014 are $800,000, the estimated bad debts expense is $8,000 (1% × $800,000). The adjusting entry is:

December 31, 2014

Bad Debt Expense	8,000	
Allowance for Doubtful Accounts		8,000

After the adjusting entry is posted, assuming the allowance account already has a credit balance of $1,723, the accounts of Gonzalez Company will show the following:

ILLUSTRATION 7-7
Bad Debt Accounts
after Posting

Bad Debt Expense			Allowance for Doubtful Accounts		
Dec. 31 Adj.	8,000			Jan. 1 Bal.	1,723
				Dec. 31 Adj.	8,000
				Dec. 31 Bal.	9,723

The amount of bad debt expense and the related credit to the allowance account are unaffected by any balance currently existing in the allowance account. Because the bad debt expense estimate is related to a nominal account (Sales Revenue), any balance in the allowance is ignored. Therefore, the percentage-of-sales method achieves a proper matching of cost and revenues. This method is frequently referred to as the **income statement approach**.

Percentage-of-receivables (balance sheet) approach. Using past experience, a company can estimate the percentage of its outstanding receivables that will become uncollectible, without identifying specific accounts. This procedure provides a reasonably accurate estimate of the receivables' realizable value. But, it does not fit the concept of matching cost and revenues. Rather, it simply reports receivables in the balance sheet at net realizable value. Hence, it is referred to as the **percentage-of-receivables** (or balance sheet) **approach**.

Companies may apply this method using one **composite rate** that reflects an estimate of the uncollectible receivables. Or, companies may set up an **aging schedule** of accounts receivable, which applies a different percentage based on past experience to the various age categories. An aging schedule also identifies which accounts require special attention by indicating the extent to which certain accounts are past due. The schedule of Wilson & Co. in Illustration 7-8 is an example.

ILLUSTRATION 7-8
Accounts Receivable Aging Schedule

WILSON & CO.
AGING SCHEDULE

Name of Customer	Balance Dec. 31	Under 60 days	60–90 days	91–120 days	Over 120 days
Western Stainless Steel Corp.	$ 98,000	$ 80,000	$18,000		
Brockway Steel Company	320,000	320,000			
Freeport Sheet & Tube Co.	55,000				$55,000
Allegheny Iron Works	74,000	60,000		$14,000	
	$547,000	$460,000	$18,000	$14,000	$55,000

Summary

Age	Amount	Percentage Estimated to Be Uncollectible	Required Balance in Allowance
Under 60 days old	$460,000	4%	$18,400
60–90 days old	18,000	15%	2,700
91–120 days old	14,000	20%	2,800
Over 120 days	55,000	25%	13,750
Year-end balance of allowance for doubtful accounts			$37,650

Wilson reports bad debt expense of $37,650 for this year, assuming that no balance existed in the allowance account.

To change the illustration slightly, **assume that the allowance account had a credit balance of $800 before adjustment**. In this case, Wilson adds $36,850 ($37,650 − $800) to the allowance account and makes the following entry.

| Bad Debt Expense | 36,850 | |
| Allowance for Doubtful Accounts | | 36,850 |

Wilson therefore states the balance in the allowance account at $37,650. **If the Allowance for Doubtful Accounts balance before adjustment had a debit balance of $200**, then Wilson records bad debt expense of $37,850 ($37,650 desired balance + $200 debit balance). In the percentage-of-receivables method, Wilson cannot ignore the balance in the allowance account because the percentage is related to a real account (Accounts Receivable).

Companies usually do not prepare an aging schedule to determine bad debt expense. Rather, they prepare it as a control device to determine the composition of receivables and to identify delinquent accounts. Companies base the estimated loss percentage developed for each category on previous loss experience and the advice of credit department personnel.

Whether using a composite rate or an aging schedule, the primary objective of the percentage of outstanding receivables method for financial statement purposes is to report receivables in the balance sheet at net realizable value. However, it is deficient in that it may not match the bad debt expense to the period in which the sale takes place.

The allowance for doubtful accounts as a percentage of receivables will vary, depending on the industry and the economic climate. Companies such as **Eastman Kodak**, **General Electric**, and **Monsanto** have recorded allowances ranging from $3 to $6 per $100 of accounts receivable. Other large companies, such as **CPC International** ($1.48), **Texaco** ($1.23), and **USX Corp.** ($0.78), have had bad debt allowances of less than $1.50 per $100. At the other extreme are hospitals that allow for $15 to $20 per $100 of accounts receivable.

Regardless of the method chosen—percentage-of-sales or -receivables—determining the expense associated with uncollectible accounts requires a large degree of judgment. Recent concern exists that, similar to **Citigroup** in our opening story, some banks use this judgment to manage earnings. By overestimating the amounts of uncollectible loans in a good earnings year, the bank can "save for a rainy day" in a future period. In future (less-profitable) periods, banks can reduce the overly conservative allowance for loan loss account to increase earnings.[8]

What do the numbers mean? *I'M STILL WAITING*

Small companies are in a bind. Many of their suppliers are demanding payment earlier, and their customers (represented by their accounts receivable) are taking longer to pay. That means companies with the least clout get squeezed the hardest. As one company executive noted, "The slowdown of currency, of money, the exchange, puts us in a very precarious position."

The average time small companies took to collect accounts receivable increased to 27 days in 2010 from about 23 days in the previous four-year period. Many small companies are seeing their payments from larger customers stretch from 30 days to 60 and even 90 days after an invoice is issued. **Wal-Mart Stores, Inc.**, for example, took 29.5 days to pay its bills in the first quarter of 2010, up from 27 days a year earlier. **Apple** took 52 days, up from 43 days a year earlier. As one individual stated, "If you are working with one of these large companies, as your only customer, they have the power. They can go to somebody else, but you can't go anywhere."

The chart on the right indicates that, overall, companies are increasing their payment times past the due date regardless of their size. For example, in the first quarter of 2012, companies paid their bills an average of 7.6 days past due, a 14.1 percent increase from the same period the previous period. The very small companies and the large companies generally have delayed payment the most.

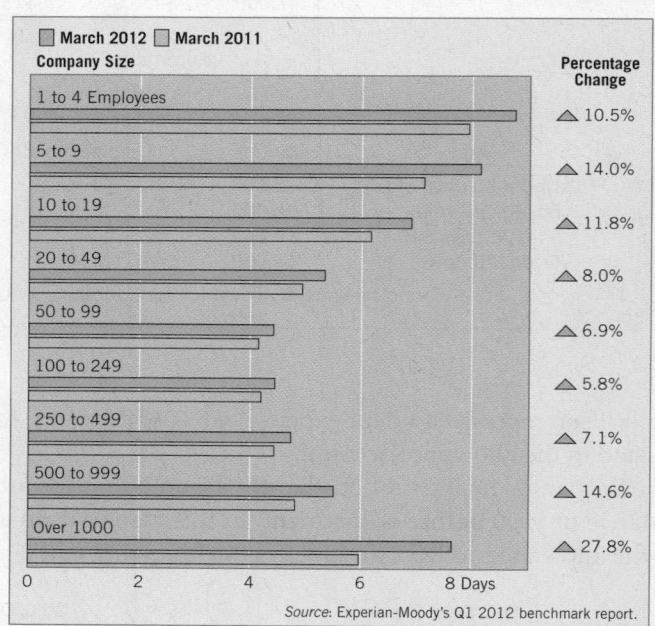

Source: Experian-Moody's Q1 2012 benchmark report.

The recession is taking its toll. As companies get squeezed between late payments and tighter credit terms, nonpayments often result. As a result, much judgment must be exercised in determining the proper percentage to record for bad debts.

Sources: Anonymous, "A Cash-Flow Crisis Is the Recession's Legacy," *Bloomberg Businessweek* (March 28–April 3, 2011), pp. 59–60; and A. Loten, "Small Firms' Big Customers Are Slow to Pay," *Wall Street Journal* (June 7, 2012), p. B7.

---

[8] The SEC brought action against **Suntrust Banks**, requiring a reversal of $100 million of bad debt expense. This reversal increased after-tax profit by $61 million. Recall from our earnings management discussion in Chapter 4 that increasing or decreasing income through management manipulation can reduce the quality of financial reports.

NOTES RECEIVABLE

A note receivable is supported by a formal **promissory note**, a written promise to pay a certain sum of money at a specific future date. Such a note is a negotiable instrument that a **maker** signs in favor of a designated **payee** who may legally and readily sell or otherwise transfer the note to others. Although all notes contain an interest element because of the time value of money, companies classify them as interest-bearing or non-interest-bearing. **Interest-bearing notes** have a stated rate of interest. Zero-interest-bearing notes (non-interest-bearing) include interest as part of their face amount. Notes receivable are considered fairly liquid, even if long-term, because companies may easily convert them to cash (although they might pay a fee to do so).

6 **LEARNING OBJECTIVE**
Explain accounting issues related to recognition and valuation of notes receivable.

Companies frequently accept notes receivable from customers who need to extend the payment period of an outstanding receivable. Or they require notes from high-risk or new customers. In addition, companies often use notes in loans to employees and subsidiaries, and in the sales of property, plant, and equipment. In some industries (e.g., the pleasure and sport boat industry), notes support all credit sales. The majority of notes, however, originate from lending transactions. The basic issues in accounting for notes receivable are the same as those for accounts receivable: **recognition**, **valuation**, **and disposition**.

Recognition of Notes Receivable

Companies generally record short-term notes at face value (less allowances) because the interest implicit in the maturity value is immaterial. A general rule is that notes treated as cash equivalents (maturities of three months or less and easily converted to cash) are not subject to premium or discount amortization.

However, companies should record and report long-term notes receivable at the **present value of the cash they expect to collect**. When the interest stated on an interest-bearing note equals the effective (market) rate of interest, the note sells at face value.[9] When the stated rate differs from the market rate, the cash exchanged (present value) differs from the face value of the note. Companies then record this difference, either a discount or a premium, and amortize it over the life of a note to approximate the effective (market) interest rate. This illustrates one of the many situations in which time value of money concepts are applied to accounting measurement.

Note Issued at Face Value

To illustrate the discounting of a note issued at face value, assume that Bigelow Corp. lends Scandinavian Imports $10,000 in exchange for a $10,000, three-year note bearing interest at 10 percent annually. The market rate of interest for a note of similar risk is also 10 percent. We show the time diagram depicting both cash flows in Illustration 7-9 (page 360).

---

[9]The **stated interest rate**, also referred to as the face rate or the coupon rate, is the rate contracted as part of the note. The **effective-interest rate**, also referred to as the market rate or the effective yield, is the rate used in the market to determine the value of the note—that is, the discount rate used to determine present value.

ILLUSTRATION 7-9
Time Diagram for Note
Issued at Face Value

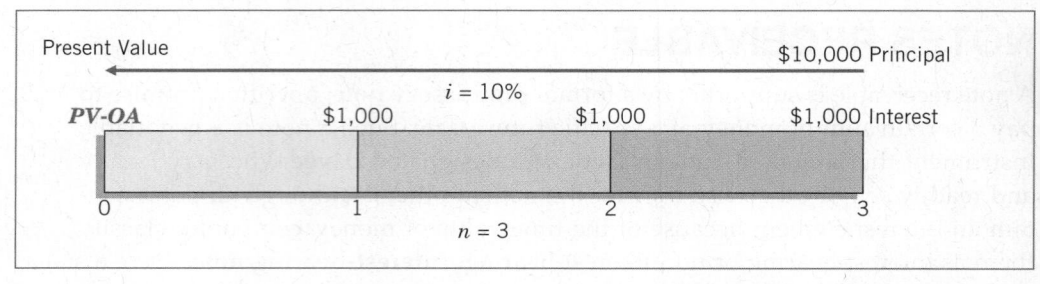

Bigelow computes the present value or exchange price of the note as follows.

ILLUSTRATION 7-10
Present Value of Note—
Stated and Market Rates
the Same

Face value of the note		$10,000
Present value of the principal:		
$10,000 ($PVF_{3,10\%}$) = $10,000 × .75132	$7,513	
Present value of the interest:		
$1,000 ($PVF\text{-}OA_{3,10\%}$) = $1,000 × 2.48685	2,487	
Present value of the note		10,000
Difference		$ –0–

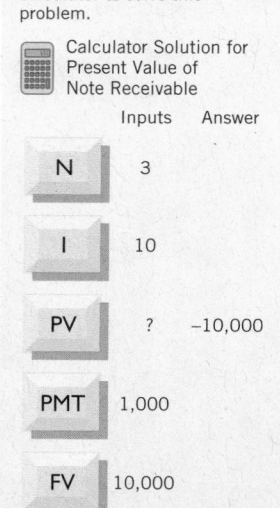

You can use a financial
calculator to solve this
problem.

Calculator Solution for
Present Value of
Note Receivable

	Inputs	Answer
N	3	
I	10	
PV	?	–10,000
PMT	1,000	
FV	10,000	

In this case, the present value of the note equals its face value because the effective and stated rates of interest are also the same. Bigelow records the receipt of the note as follows.

Notes Receivable	10,000	
Cash		10,000

Bigelow recognizes the interest earned each year as follows.

Cash	1,000	
Interest Revenue		1,000

Note Not Issued at Face Value

Zero-Interest-Bearing Notes. If a company receives a zero-interest-bearing note, its present value is the cash paid to the issuer. Because the company knows both the future amount and the present value of the note, it can compute the interest rate. This rate is often referred to as the **implicit interest rate**. Companies record the difference between the future (face) amount and the present value (cash paid) as a discount and amortize it to interest revenue over the life of the note.

To illustrate, Jeremiah Company receives a three-year, $10,000 zero-interest-bearing note, the present value of which is $7,721.80. The implicit rate that equates the total cash to be received ($10,000 at maturity) to the present value of the future cash flows ($7,721.80) is 9 percent (the present value of 1 for three periods at 9 percent is .77218). We show the time diagram depicting the one cash flow in Illustration 7-11.

ILLUSTRATION 7-11
Time Diagram for Zero-Interest-Bearing Note

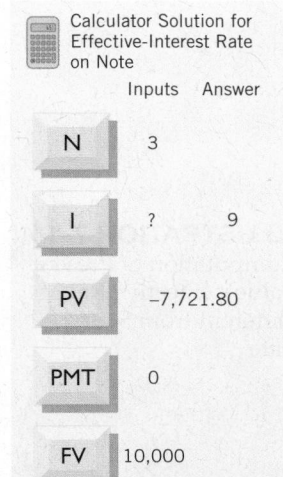

Jeremiah records the transaction as follows.

Notes Receivable	10,000.00	
Discount on Notes Receivable ($10,000 − $7,721.80)		2,278.20
Cash		7,721.80

Discount on Notes Receivable is a valuation account. Companies report it on the balance sheet as a contra asset account to notes receivable. They then amortize the discount, and recognize interest revenue annually using the **effective-interest method**. Illustration 7-12 shows the three-year discount amortization and interest revenue schedule.

ILLUSTRATION 7-12
Discount Amortization Schedule—Effective-Interest Method

	Cash Received	Interest Revenue	Discount Amortized	Carrying Amount of Note
	SCHEDULE OF NOTE DISCOUNT AMORTIZATION EFFECTIVE-INTEREST METHOD 0% NOTE DISCOUNTED AT 9%			
Date of issue				$ 7,721.80
End of year 1	$ –0–	$ 694.96[a]	$ 694.96[b]	8,416.76[c]
End of year 2	–0–	757.51	757.51	9,174.27
End of year 3	–0–	825.73[d]	825.73	10,000.00
	$ –0–	$2,278.20	$2,278.20	

[a]$7,721.80 × .09 = $694.96
[b]$694.96 − 0 = $694.96
[c]$7,721.80 + $694.96 = $8,416.76
[d]5¢ adjustment to compensate for rounding

Jeremiah records interest revenue at the end of the first year using the effective-interest method as follows.

Discount on Notes Receivable	694.96	
Interest Revenue ($7,721.80 × 9%)		694.96

The amount of the discount, $2,278.20 in this case, represents the interest revenue Jeremiah will receive from the note over the three years.

Interest-Bearing Notes. Often the stated rate and the effective rate differ. The zero-interest-bearing note is one example.

To illustrate a more common situation, assume that Morgan Corp. makes a loan to Marie Co. and receives in exchange a three-year, $10,000 note bearing interest at 10 percent annually. The market rate of interest for a note of similar risk is 12 percent. We show the time diagram depicting both cash flows in Illustration 7-13 (page 362).

ILLUSTRATION 7-13
Time Diagram for
Interest-Bearing Note

Morgan computes the present value of the two cash flows as follows.

ILLUSTRATION 7-14
Computation of Present
Value—Effective Rate
Different from Stated
Rate

Face value of the note		$10,000
Present value of the principal:		
$10,000 (*PVF*$_{3,12\%}$) = $10,000 × .71178	$7,118	
Present value of the interest:		
$1,000 (*PVF-OA*$_{3,12\%}$) = $1,000 × 2.40183	2,402	
Present value of the note		9,520
Difference (Discount)		$ 480

In this case, because the effective rate of interest (12 percent) exceeds the stated rate (10 percent), the present value of the note is less than the face value. That is, Morgan exchanged the note at a **discount**. Morgan records the receipt of the note at a discount as follows.

Notes Receivable	10,000	
Discount on Notes Receivable		480
Cash		9,520

Morgan then amortizes the discount and recognizes interest revenue annually using the **effective-interest method**. Illustration 7-15 shows the three-year discount amortization and interest revenue schedule.

ILLUSTRATION 7-15
Discount Amortization
Schedule—Effective-
Interest Method

SCHEDULE OF NOTE DISCOUNT AMORTIZATION
EFFECTIVE-INTEREST METHOD
10% NOTE DISCOUNTED AT 12%

	Cash Received	Interest Revenue	Discount Amortized	Carrying Amount of Note
Date of issue				$ 9,520
End of year 1	$1,000[a]	$1,142[b]	$142[c]	9,662[d]
End of year 2	1,000	1,159	159	9,821
End of year 3	1,000	1,179	179	10,000
	$3,000	$3,480	$480	

[a]$10,000 × 10% = $1,000   [c]$1,142 − $1,000 = $142
[b]$9,520 × 12% = $1,142   [d]$9,520 + $142 = $9,662

On the date of issue, the note has a present value of $9,520. Its unamortized discount—additional interest revenue spread over the three-year life of the note—is $480.

At the end of year 1, Morgan receives $1,000 in cash. But its interest revenue is $1,142 ($9,520 × 12%). The difference between $1,000 and $1,142 is the amortized discount, $142. Morgan records receipt of the annual interest and amortization of the discount for the first year as follows (amounts per amortization schedule).

Cash	1,000	
Discount on Notes Receivable	142	
Interest Revenue		1,142

The carrying amount of the note is now $9,662 ($9,520 + $142). Morgan repeats this process until the end of year 3.

When the present value exceeds the face value, the note is exchanged at a premium. Companies record the premium on a note receivable as a debit and amortize it using the effective-interest method over the life of the note as annual reductions in the amount of interest revenue recognized.

Notes Received for Property, Goods, or Services. When a **note is received in exchange for property, goods, or services** in a bargained transaction entered into at arm's length, the stated interest rate is presumed to be fair unless:

1. No interest rate is stated, or
2. The stated interest rate is unreasonable, or
3. The face amount of the note is materially different from the current cash sales price for the same or similar items or from the current fair value of the debt instrument. **[4]**

In these circumstances, the company measures the present value of the note by the fair value of the property, goods, or services or by an amount that reasonably approximates the fair value of the note.

Calculator Solution for
Effective-Interest
Rate on Note

To illustrate, Oasis Development Co. sold a corner lot to Rusty Pelican as a restaurant site. Oasis accepted in exchange a five-year note having a maturity value of $35,247 and no stated interest rate. The land originally cost Oasis $14,000. At the date of sale, the land had a fair value of $20,000. Given the criterion above, Oasis uses the fair value of the land, $20,000, as the present value of the note. Oasis therefore records the sale as:

Notes Receivable	35,247	
Discount on Notes Receivable ($35,247 − $20,000)		15,247
Land		14,000
Gain on Disposal of Land ($20,000 − $14,000)		6,000

Oasis amortizes the discount to interest revenue over the five-year life of the note using the effective-interest method.

Choice of Interest Rate

In note transactions, other factors involved in the exchange, such as the fair value of the property, goods, or services, determine the effective or real interest rate. But, if a company cannot determine that fair value and if the note has no ready market, determining the present value of the note is more difficult. To estimate the present value of a note under such circumstances, the company must approximate an applicable interest rate that may differ from the stated interest rate. This process of interest-rate approximation is called **imputation**. The resulting interest rate is called an *imputed interest rate*.

The prevailing rates for similar instruments, from issuers with similar credit ratings, affect the choice of a rate. Restrictive covenants, collateral, payment schedule, and the existing prime interest rate also impact the choice. A company determines the imputed interest rate when it receives the note. It ignores any subsequent changes in prevailing interest rates.

Valuation of Notes Receivable

Like accounts receivable, companies record and report short-term notes receivable at their net realizable value—that is, at their face amount less all necessary allowances. The primary notes receivable allowance account is Allowance for Doubtful Accounts. The computations and estimations involved in valuing short-term notes receivable and in recording bad debt expense and the related allowance **exactly parallel that for trade accounts receivable**. Companies estimate the amount of uncollectibles by using either a percentage-of-sales revenue or an analysis of the receivables.

Long-term notes receivable involve additional estimation problems. For example, the value of a note receivable can change significantly over time from its original cost. That is, with the passage of time, historical numbers become less and less relevant. As discussed earlier (in Chapters 2, 5, and 6), the FASB requires that for financial instruments such as receivables, companies disclose not only their cost but also their fair value in the notes to the financial statements.

Impairments. A note receivable may become impaired. A note receivable is considered **impaired** when it is probable that the creditor will be unable to collect all amounts due (both principal and interest) according to the contractual terms of the receivable. In this case, a loss is recorded for the amount of the impairment. Appendix 7B further discusses impairments of receivables.

What do the numbers mean? ECONOMIC CONSEQUENCES AND WRITE-OFFS

The massive write-downs that financial firms are posting have begun to spur a backlash among some investors and executives, who are blaming accounting rules for exaggerating the losses and are seeking new, more forgiving ways to value investments.

The rules—which last made headlines back in the Enron era—require companies to value many of the securities they hold at whatever price prevails in the market, no matter how sharply those prices swing.

Some analysts and executives argue this triggers a domino effect. The market falls, forcing banks to take write-offs, pushing the market lower, causing more write-offs. Companies like AIG and Citicorp argue that their write-downs may never actually result in a true charge to the company. It's a sore point because companies feel they are being forced to take big financial hits on holdings that they have no intention of actually selling at current prices.

Companies believe they are strong enough to simply keep the holdings in their portfolios until the crisis passes. Forcing companies to value securities based on what they would fetch if sold today "is an attempt to apply liquidation accounting to a going concern," says one analyst. Bob Herz, former FASB chairperson, acknowledges the difficulty but notes, "you tell me what a better answer is. . . . Is just pretending that things aren't decreasing in value a better answer? Should you just let everybody say they think it's going to recover?"

Others who favor the use of market values say that for all its imperfections, market value also imposes discipline on companies. "It forces you to realistically confront what's happening to you much quicker, so it plays a useful purpose," said Sen. Jack Reed (D., R.I.), a member of the Senate banking committee.

Japan stands out as an example of how ignoring problems can lead to years-long stagnation. "Look at Japan, where they ignored write-downs at all their financial institutions when loans went bad," said Jeff Mahoney, general counsel at the Council for Institutional Investors.

In addition, companies don't always have the luxury of waiting out a storm until assets recover the long-term value that executives believe exists. A classic example relates to many European banks that hold loans to countries like Greece, Spain, Ireland, and Portugal. Although these loans are clearly toxic (values overstated), some banks still contend that they should not be written down (partly because they can be held to maturity). However, this contention is suspect, and impairment losses are rising. For example, Bankia Group, Spain's third largest bank, recently restated its 2011 results to show a €3.3 billion ($4.2 billion) loss rather than the previously reported €40.9 billion profit.

Sources: Adapted from David Reilly, "Wave of Write-Offs Rattles Market: Accounting Rules Blasted as Dow Falls; A $600 Billion Toll?" *Wall Street Journal* (March 1, 2008), p. Al; and J. Weil, "The E4 Smiled While Spain's Banks Cooked the Books," *Bloomberg* (June 14, 2012).

SPECIAL ISSUES

Three additional special issues for accounting and reporting of receivables relate to the following.

1. Fair value option.

2. Disposition of receivables.

3. Presentation and disclosure.

Fair Value Option

Recently, the FASB has given companies the option to use fair value as the basis of measurement in the financial statements. [5] The Board believes that fair value measurement for financial instruments provides more relevant and understandable information than historical cost. It considers fair value to be more relevant because it reflects the current cash equivalent value of financial instruments. As a result, companies now have the option to record fair value in their accounts for most financial instruments, including receivables.

7 LEARNING OBJECTIVE
Explain the fair value option.

International Perspective

IFRS also has the fair value option.

If companies choose the **fair value option**, the receivables are recorded at fair value, with unrealized holding gains or losses reported as part of net income. An **unrealized holding gain or loss** is the net change in the fair value of the receivable from one period to another, exclusive of interest revenue. As a result, the company reports the receivable at fair value each reporting date. In addition, it reports the change in value as part of net income.

Companies may elect to use the fair value option at the time the financial instrument is originally recognized or when some event triggers a new basis of accounting (such as when a business acquisition occurs). If a company elects the fair value option for a financial instrument, it must continue to use fair value measurement for that instrument until the company no longer owns this instrument. If the company does not elect the fair value option for a given financial instrument at the date of recognition, it may not use this option on that specific instrument in subsequent periods.

Recording Fair Value Option

Assume that Escobar Company has notes receivable that have a fair value of $810,000 and a carrying amount of $620,000. Escobar decides on December 31, 2014, to use the fair value option for these receivables. This is the first valuation of these recently acquired receivables. Having elected to use the fair value option, Escobar must value these receivables **at fair value in all subsequent periods in which it holds these receivables**. Similarly, if Escobar elects *not* to use the fair value option, it must use its carrying amount for all future periods.

When using the fair value option, Escobar reports the receivables at fair value, with any unrealized holding gains and losses reported as part of net income. The **unrealized holding gain** is the difference between the fair value and the carrying amount at December 31, 2014, which for Escobar is $190,000 ($810,000 − $620,000). At December 31, 2014, Escobar makes an adjusting entry to record the increase in value of notes receivable and to record the unrealized holding gain, as follows.

December 31, 2014

Notes Receivable	190,000	
Unrealized Holding Gain or Loss—Income		190,000

Escobar adds the difference between fair value and the cost of the notes receivable to arrive at the fair value reported on the balance sheet. In subsequent periods, the company will report **any change in fair value** as an unrealized holding gain or loss. For example, if at December 31, 2015, the fair value of the notes receivable is $800,000, Escobar would recognize an unrealized holding loss of $10,000 ($810,000 − $800,000) and reduce the Notes Receivable account.

Disposition of Accounts and Notes Receivable

In the normal course of events, companies collect accounts and notes receivable when due and then remove them from the books. However, the growing size and significance of credit sales and receivables has led to changes in this "normal

8 LEARNING OBJECTIVE
Explain accounting issues related to disposition of accounts and notes receivable.

course of events." **In order to accelerate the receipt of cash from receivables, the owner may transfer accounts or notes receivables to another company for cash.**

There are various reasons for this early transfer. First, for competitive reasons, providing sales financing for customers is virtually mandatory in many industries. In the sale of durable goods, such as automobiles, trucks, industrial and farm equipment, computers, and appliances, most sales are on an installment contract basis. Many major companies in these industries have created wholly owned subsidiaries specializing in receivables financing. For example, Ford has Ford Motor Credit, and John Deere has John Deere Credit.

Second, the **holder** may sell receivables because money is tight and access to normal credit is unavailable or too expensive. Also, a firm may sell its receivables, instead of borrowing, to avoid violating existing lending agreements.

Finally, billing and collection of receivables are often time-consuming and costly. Credit card companies such as MasterCard, Visa, American Express, Diners Club, Discover, and others take over the collection process and provide merchants with immediate cash.

Conversely, some **purchasers** of receivables buy them to obtain the legal protection of ownership rights afforded a purchaser of assets versus the lesser rights afforded a secured creditor. In addition, banks and other lending institutions may need to purchase receivables because of legal lending limits. That is, they cannot make any additional loans but they can buy receivables and charge a fee for this service.

The transfer of receivables to a third party for cash happens in one of two ways:

1. Secured borrowing.
2. Sales of receivables.

Secured Borrowing

A company often uses receivables as collateral in a borrowing transaction. In fact, a creditor often requires that the debtor designate (assign) or pledge[10] receivables as security for the loan. If the loan is not paid when due, the creditor can convert the collateral to cash—that is, collect the receivables.

To illustrate, on March 1, 2014, Howat Mills, Inc. provides (assigns) $700,000 of its accounts receivable to Citizens Bank as collateral for a $500,000 note. Howat Mills continues to collect the accounts receivable; the account debtors are not notified of the arrangement. Citizens Bank assesses a finance charge of 1 percent of the accounts receivable and interest on the note of 12 percent. Howat Mills makes monthly payments to the bank for all cash it collects on the receivables. Illustration 7-16 shows the entries for the secured borrowing for Howat Mills and Citizens Bank.

In addition to recording the collection of receivables, Howat Mills must recognize all discounts, returns and allowances, and bad debts. Each month Howat Mills uses the proceeds from the collection of the accounts receivable to retire the note obligation. In addition, it pays interest on the note.[11]

Sales of Receivables

Sales of receivables have increased substantially in recent years. A common type is a sale to a factor. **Factors** are finance companies or banks that buy receivables from businesses

[10]If a company transfers the receivables for custodial purposes, the custodial arrangement is often referred to as a **pledge**.

[11]What happens if Citizens Bank collected the transferred accounts receivable rather than Howat Mills? Citizens Bank would simply remit the cash proceeds to Howat Mills, and Howat Mills would make the same entries shown in Illustration 7-16. As a result, Howat Mills reports these "collaterized" receivables as an asset on the balance sheet.

Howat Mills, Inc.			Citizens Bank		
Transfer of accounts receivable and issuance of note on March 1, 2014					
Cash	493,000		Notes Receivable	500,000	
Interest Expense	7,000*		Interest Revenue		7,000*
Notes Payable		500,000	Cash		493,000
*(1% × $700,000)					
Collection in March of $440,000 of accounts less cash discounts of $6,000 plus receipt of $14,000 sales returns					
Cash	434,000				
Sales Discounts	6,000				
Sales Returns and Allowances	14,000		(No entry)		
Accounts Receivable					
($440,000 + $14,000 = $454,000)		454,000			
Remitted March collections plus accrued interest to the bank on April 1, 2014					
Interest Expense	5,000*		Cash	439,000	
Notes Payable	434,000		Interest Revenue		5,000*
Cash		439,000	Notes Receivable		434,000
*($500,000 × .12 × 1/12)					
Collection in April of the balance of accounts less $2,000 written off as uncollectible					
Cash	244,000				
Allowance for Doubtful Accounts	2,000		(No entry)		
Accounts Receivable		246,000*			
*($700,000 − $454,000)					
Remitted the balance due of $66,000 ($500,000 − $434,000) on the note plus interest on May 1, 2014					
Interest Expense	660*		Cash	66,660	
Notes Payable	66,000		Interest Revenue		660*
Cash		66,660	Notes Receivable		66,000
*($66,000 × .12 × 1/12)					

ILLUSTRATION 7-16
Entries for Transfer of Receivables—Secured Borrowing

for a fee and then collect the remittances directly from the customers. **Factoring receivables** is traditionally associated with the textile, apparel, footwear, furniture, and home furnishing industries.[12] Illustration 7-17 shows a typical factoring arrangement.

ILLUSTRATION 7-17
Basic Procedures in Factoring

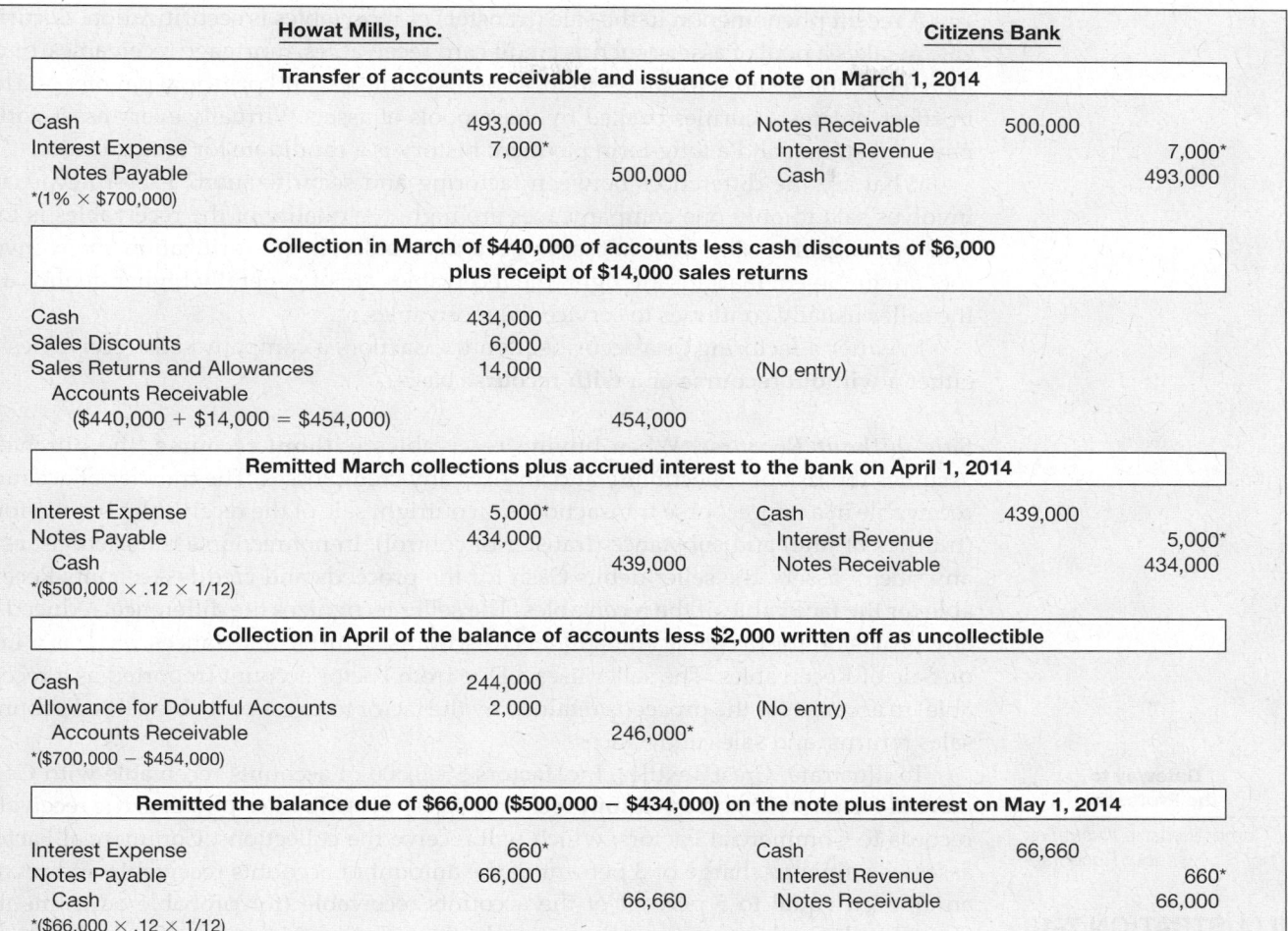

[12]Credit cards like **MasterCard** and **Visa** are a type of factoring arrangement. Typically, the purchaser of the receivable charges a ¾–1½ percent commission of the receivables purchased (the commission is 4–5 percent for credit card factoring).

A recent phenomenon in the sale (transfer) of receivables is securitization. **Securitization** takes a pool of assets, such as credit card receivables, mortgage receivables, or car loan receivables, and sells shares in these pools of interest and principal payments. This, in effect, creates securities backed by these pools of assets. Virtually every asset with a payment stream and a long-term payment history is a candidate for securitization.

What are the differences between factoring and securitization? Factoring usually involves sale to only one company, fees are high, the quality of the receivables is low, and the seller afterward does not service the receivables. In a securitization, many investors are involved, margins are tight, the receivables are of generally higher quality, and the seller usually continues to service the receivables.

In either a factoring or a securitization transaction, a company sells receivables on either a **without recourse** or a **with recourse** basis.[13]

Sale without Recourse. When buying receivables **without recourse**, the purchaser assumes the risk of collectibility and absorbs any credit losses. The transfer of accounts receivable in a nonrecourse transaction is an outright sale of the receivables both in form (transfer of title) and substance (transfer of control). In nonrecourse transactions, as in any sale of assets, the seller debits Cash for the proceeds and credits Accounts Receivable for the face value of the receivables. The seller recognizes the difference, reduced by any provision for probable adjustments (discounts, returns, allowances, etc.), as a Loss on Sale of Receivables. The seller uses a Due from Factor account (reported as a receivable) to account for the proceeds retained by the factor to cover probable sales discounts, sales returns, and sales allowances.

To illustrate, Crest Textiles, Inc. factors $500,000 of accounts receivable with Commercial Factors, Inc., on a **without recourse** basis. Crest Textiles transfers the receivable records to Commercial Factors, which will receive the collections. Commercial Factors assesses a finance charge of 3 percent of the amount of accounts receivable and retains an amount equal to 5 percent of the accounts receivable (for probable adjustments). Crest Textiles and Commercial Factors make the following journal entries for the receivables transferred without recourse.

Gateway to the Profession

Comprehensive Illustration of Sale without Recourse

ILLUSTRATION 7-18
Entries for Sale of Receivables without Recourse

Crest Textiles, Inc.			Commercial Factors, Inc.		
Cash	460,000		Accounts (Notes) Receivable	500,000	
Due from Factor	25,000*		Due to Customer (Crest Textiles)		25,000
Loss on Sale of Receivables	15,000**		Interest Revenue		15,000
Accounts (Notes) Receivable		500,000	Cash		460,000
*(5% × $500,000) **(3% × $500,000)					

In recognition of the sale of receivables, Crest Textiles records a loss of $15,000. The factor's net income will be the difference between the financing revenue of $15,000 and the amount of any uncollectible receivables.

Sale with Recourse. For receivables sold **with recourse**, the seller guarantees payment to the purchaser in the event the debtor fails to pay. To record this type of transaction, the seller uses a **financial components approach** because the seller has a continuing involvement with the receivable. Values are now assigned to such components as the

---

[13]**Recourse** is the right of a transferee of receivables to receive payment from the transferor of those receivables for (1) failure of the debtors to pay when due, (2) the effects of prepayments, or (3) adjustments resulting from defects in the eligibility of the transferred receivables. **[6]**

recourse provision, servicing rights, and agreement to reacquire. In this approach, each party to the sale only recognizes the assets and liabilities that it controls after the sale.

To illustrate, assume the same information as in Illustration 7-18 for Crest Textiles and for Commercial Factors, except that Crest Textiles sold the receivables on a with recourse basis. Crest Textiles determines that this recourse liability has a fair value of $6,000. To determine the loss on the sale of the receivables, Crest Textiles computes the net proceeds from the sale as follows.

ILLUSTRATION 7-19
Net Proceeds
Computation

Cash received	$460,000	
Due from factor	25,000	$485,000
Less: Recourse liability		6,000
Net proceeds		$479,000

Net proceeds are cash or other assets received in a sale less any liabilities incurred. Crest Textiles then computes the loss as follows.

ILLUSTRATION 7-20
Loss on Sale
Computation

Carrying (book) value	$500,000
Net proceeds	479,000
Loss on sale of receivables	$ 21,000

Illustration 7-21 shows the journal entries for both Crest Textiles and Commercial Factors for the receivables sold with recourse.

ILLUSTRATION 7-21
Entries for Sale of
Receivables with
Recourse

Crest Textiles, Inc.			Commercial Factors, Inc.		
Cash	460,000		Accounts Receivable	500,000	
Due from Factor	25,000		Due to Customer		
Loss on Sale of			(Crest Textiles)		25,000
Receivables	21,000		Interest Revenue		15,000
Accounts (Notes)			Cash		460,000
Receivable		500,000			
Recourse Liability		6,000			

In this case, Crest Textiles recognizes a loss of $21,000. In addition, it records a liability of $6,000 to indicate the probable payment to Commercial Factors for uncollectible receivables. If Commercial Factors collects all the receivables, Crest Textiles eliminates its recourse liability and increases income. Commercial Factors' net income is the interest revenue of $15,000. It will have no bad debts related to these receivables.

Secured Borrowing versus Sale
The FASB concluded that a sale occurs only if the seller surrenders control of the receivables to the buyer. The following three conditions must be met before a company can record a sale:

1. The transferred asset has been isolated from the transferor (put beyond reach of the transferor and its creditors).

**Gateway to
the Profession**

*Tutorial on the Disposition
of Receivables*

2. The transferees have obtained the right to pledge or exchange either the transferred assets or beneficial interests in the transferred assets.

3. The transferor does not maintain effective control over the transferred assets through an agreement to repurchase or redeem them before their maturity.

If the three conditions are met, a sale occurs. Otherwise, the transferor should record the transfer as a secured borrowing. If sale accounting is appropriate, a company must still consider assets obtained and liabilities incurred in the transaction. Illustration 7-22 shows the rules of accounting for transfers of receivables.

ILLUSTRATION 7-22
Accounting for Transfers
of Receivables

**International
Perspective**

With recent changes in U.S. GAAP, the accounting guidance for transfers is substantially converged.

As indicated, if there is continuing involvement in a sale transaction, a company must record the assets obtained and liabilities incurred.[14]

[14]In response to the financial crisis, which was partly caused by securitizations gone bad (see the "What Do the Numbers Mean?" box on page 371), the FASB issued new rules to tighten up the conditions when a transfer of receivables is recorded as a sale. The changes in the rules apply primarily to transfers that involve participating interests (which is the case for many securitizations). In order for a transfer with participating interests to be accounted for as a sale, all participating investors must have a pro rata share ownership interest in the transferred assets. That is, all parties to the transfer must receive benefits or be exposed to risks of the transferred assets in proportion to their ownership share. If these criteria are not met (e.g., some investors get paid first or others absorb more losses than others on the transferred receivables), then the transfer is accounted for as a secured borrowing. **[7]** As a result of these new rules, sale treatment for transfers of receivables will be significantly reduced.

In response to the use of **repurchase agreements** by some financial institutions during the financial crisis (e.g., **Lehman Brothers'** Repo 105) to "window-dress" their balance sheets and show lower leverage, the FASB also recently issued new guidance on transfers of assets in repurchase agreements. **[8]** The new rules tighten the requirements for meeting the control criterion, which raises the bar for companies to be able to assert sale accounting in a repurchase agreement.

It used to be that lenders of mortgages and other types of debt securities carried them on their books as a loan receivable. But thanks to Wall Street, many lenders learned how to package these loans together and sell (securitize) them, and record a gain on the sale. In fact, virtually every asset with a payment stream and a long-term payment history is a candidate for securitization. And, for a while, everyone was happy to be part of the mortgage securitization game. The graphic below illustrates the way the process worked.

Borrower	**Lender**	**Investment Bank**	**Investors**
Works with a lender to get a home-purchase loan or a refinancing.	Often sells loan to investment bank or special-purpose entity.	Packages the loans into a mortgage-backed security deal, often known as a securitization. Sells the securitization, sorted by risk, to investors. Lower-rated slices take the first defaults when mortgages go bad but offer higher returns.	Choose what to buy based on their appetites for risk and reward.
What they get			
Financing needed to purchase a home or cash from refinancing.	Takes upfront fees for making the loan.	Collects fees for packaging the loans into bond deal.	Earn interest on the securities and absorb any gain or loss in price.
If the loan goes bad			
House can be repossessed.	Can be forced to take back loan if there's an early default or documentation is questionable.	May push back loan to lender, or be forced to eat any loss.	May have legal recourse against the bank if they can show the quality of the loan or loan documentation was misrepresented.

As indicated, once the mortgage loan is signed by the borrower, the lender sells the loans to an investment bank or a trust (special-purpose entity), reports a gain, and generally earns fees for servicing the debt. The trust, with the help of the investment bank, raises the money to buy these loans by selling some type of interest-bearing security to the investing public. These investors are happy because they earn a return that they believe is excellent, given the risk they take.

There were two big problems with these arrangements. First, as indicated in our discussion in the text, the lender has to make sure it does not keep control. Otherwise, it cannot sell the receivable *and* receive gain-on-sale treatment. Unfortunately, the accounting rules were loose enough that lenders were able to argue that they do not have control in most cases. Second, lenders realized that lending to subprime borrowers could be very profitable. They focused on these customers because the bank earns a fee for origination of the loan, sells the loans for a gain, and earns servicing revenue— a triple bump to the bottom line. However, when the housing market collapsed, the subprime borrowers could not repay their loans, and the credit markets collapsed. The result was a credit crisis.

So, who loses? Investors, primarily. But many investors are not ready to let lenders off the hook. They argue that in many of these sales, the lender must take back loans that defaulted or contained mistakes or fraud (bogus appraisals, inflated borrower incomes, and other misrepresentations). For example, Countrywide Financial Corp., the largest mortgage lender in the United States, indicated that its liability for such claims increased by nearly $600 million from March 31, 2007, to March 31, 2008.

The moral of the story is that accounting matters. Lenders have strong incentives to want to report upfront gains on sales of loans. But, in most cases, these gains should never have been booked. In response, the FASB has issued new rules to tighten up "gain-on-sale" accounting for securitizations with participating interests (see footnote 14 on page 370). With these new rules, lenders will have to keep the loan on its balance sheet. Under these conditions, lenders would be much less likely to lend so much money to individuals with poor credit ratings.

Source: M. Hudson, "How Wall Street Stoked the Mortgage Meltdown," *Wall Street Journal* (June 27, 2007), p. A10.

Presentation and Analysis

Presentation of Receivables

The general rules in classifying receivables are:

1. Segregate the different types of receivables that a company possesses, if material.
2. Appropriately offset the valuation accounts against the proper receivable accounts.
3. Determine that receivables classified in the current assets section will be converted into cash within the year or the operating cycle, whichever is longer.
4. Disclose any loss contingencies that exist on the receivables.
5. Disclose any receivables designated or pledged as collateral.
6. Disclose the nature of credit risk inherent in the receivables, how that risk is analyzed and assessed in arriving at the allowance for credit losses, and the changes and reasons for those changes in the allowance for credit losses.

With respect to additional disclosures, companies are required to disaggregate based on type of receivable. In response to demands for additional information about credit risk, the FASB recently issued rules for companies to provide the following disclosures about its receivables on a disaggregated basis: (1) a roll-forward schedule of the allowance for doubtful accounts from the beginning of the reporting period to the end of the reporting period, (2) the nonaccrual status of receivables by class of receivables, and (3) impaired receivables by type of receivable. In addition, companies should disclose credit quality indicators and the aging of past due receivables. **[9]**

Companies must disclose concentrations of credit risk for all financial instruments (including receivables). Concentrations of credit risk exist when receivables have common characteristics that may affect their collection. These common characteristics might be companies in the same industry or same region of the country. For example, Quantum Corporation reported that sales of its disk drives to its top five customers (including Hewlett-Packard) represented nearly 40 percent of its revenues in a recent year. Financial statements users want to know if a substantial amount of receivables from such sales are to customers facing uncertain economic conditions.

International Perspective

Holding receivables that it will receive in a foreign currency represents risk that the exchange rate may move against the company. This results in a decrease in the amount collected in terms of U.S. dollars. Companies engaged in cross-border transactions often "hedge" these receivables by buying contracts to exchange currencies at specified amounts at future dates.

No numerical guidelines are provided as to what is meant by a "concentration of credit risk."[15]

The assets sections of Colton Corporation's balance sheet in Illustration 7-23 show many of the disclosures required for receivables.

Analysis of Receivables

Accounts Receivable Turnover. Analysts frequently compute financial ratios to evaluate the liquidity of a company's accounts receivable. To assess the liquidity of the receivables, they use the accounts receivable turnover ratio. This ratio measures the number of times, on average, a company collects receivables during the period. The ratio is computed by dividing net sales by average (net) receivables outstanding during the year. Theoretically, the numerator should include only net credit sales, but this information is frequently unavailable. However, if the relative amounts of credit and cash sales remain fairly constant, the trend indicated by the ratio will still be valid. Barring significant seasonal

---

[15]Three items should be disclosed with an identified concentration: (1) information on the characteristic that determines the concentration, (2) the amount of loss that could occur upon nonperformance, and (3) information on any collateral related to the receivable. **[10]**

ILLUSTRATION 7-23
Disclosure of Receivables

COLTON CORPORATION
BALANCE SHEET (PARTIAL)
AS OF DECEMBER 31, 2014

Current assets		
Cash and cash equivalents		$ 1,870,250
Accounts and notes receivable (Note 2)	$10,509,673	
Less: Allowance for doubtful accounts	500,226	
	10,009,447	
Advances to subsidiaries due 9/30/14	2,090,000	
Federal income taxes refundable	146,704	
Dividends and interest receivable	75,500	
Other receivables and claims (including debit		
balances in accounts payable)	174,620	12,496,271
Total current assets		$14,366,521
Noncurrent receivables		
Notes receivable from officers and key employees		376,090
Claims receivable (litigation settlement to be collected		
over four years)		585,000

Segregate different types of receivables

Note 2: Accounts and Notes Receivable. All noncurrent receivables are due within five years from the balance sheet date. Trade receivables that are less than three months past due are not considered impaired. At December 31, the aging analysis of receivables is as follows.

Amounts ($000)	Total	Neither Past Due or Impaired	<30 days	30–60 days	60–90 days	90–120 days	>120 days
					Past Due but Not Impaired		
2014	10,510	5,115	2,791	1,582	570	360	92

Disclose aging of receivables

As at December 31, 2014, trade receivables at initial value of $109 were impaired and fully provided for. The following table summarises movements in the provision for impairment of receivables.

	Total $000
At January 1, 2014	98
Expense for the year	26
Written off	(9)
Recoveries	(6)
At December 31, 2014	109

Presentation of impaired receivables

Certain subsidiaries transferred receivable balances amounting to $1,014 to a bank in exchange for cash during the year ended December 31, 2014. The transaction has been accounted for as a secured borrowing. In case of default under the loan agreement, the borrower has the right to receive the cash flows from the receivables transferred. Without default, the subsidiaries will collect the receivables and assign new receivables as collateral.

Disclose collateral arrangements

factors, average receivables outstanding can be computed from the beginning and ending balances of net trade receivables.

To illustrate, **Best Buy** reported 2011 net sales of $50,705 million, its beginning and ending accounts receivable balances were $2,288 million and $2,348 million, respectively. Illustration 7-24 shows the computation of its accounts receivable turnover.

Underlying Concepts

Providing information that will help users assess a company's current liquidity and prospective cash flows is a primary objective of accounting.

$$\frac{\text{Net Sales}}{\text{Average Trade Receivables (net)}} = \text{Accounts Receivable Turnover}$$

$$\frac{\$50,705}{(\$2,288 + \$2,348)/2} = 21.9 \text{ times, or every 16.7 days } (365 \div 21.9)$$

ILLUSTRATION 7-24
Computation of Accounts Receivable Turnover

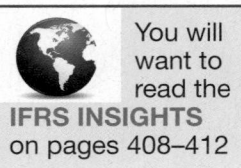

You will want to read the **IFRS INSIGHTS** on pages 408–412

for discussion of IFRS related to cash and receivables.

This information[16] shows how successful the company is in collecting its outstanding receivables. If possible, an aging schedule should also be prepared to help determine how long receivables have been outstanding. A satisfactory accounts receivable turnover may have resulted because certain receivables were collected quickly though others have been outstanding for a relatively long period. An aging schedule would reveal such patterns.

Often the accounts receivable turnover is transformed to **days to collect accounts receivable or days outstanding**—an average collection period. In this case, 21.9 is divided into 365 days, resulting in 16.7 days. Companies frequently use the average collection period to assess the effectiveness of a company's credit and collection policies. The general rule is that the average collection period should not greatly exceed the credit term period. That is, if customers are given a 60-day period for payment, then the average collection period should not be too much in excess of 60 days.

🔍 Evolving Issue   A CURE FOR "TOO LITTLE, TOO LATE"?

A significant accounting weakness revealed during the financial crisis relates to the accounting for loan losses (or allowance for doubtful accounts). The concern is that the existing GAAP (and IFRS) results in allowances for loan loss that tend to be at their lowest level when they are needed the most—at the beginning of a downward-trending economic cycle (the "too little, too late" concern). Therefore, the FASB and IASB have been working to develop a standard that ensures that the allowance for loan loss balance better reflects all estimated credit losses.

The Boards agree that a company should recognize an impairment in net income when it does not expect to collect all contractual amounts due on a loan. Furthermore, the Boards indicate that it is inappropriate to defer an impairment loss over the life of a loan. In other words, if a company does not expect to collect all amounts due, a loss exists and should be recognized immediately. The Boards are exploring two different approaches to an improved impairment model.

The first approach, referred to as the three-bucket approach, would classify loans and other financial assets into three buckets, which reflect assets of increasing severity of impairment. In this model, financial assets start out in Bucket 1 with reserves equal to 12 months of expected losses. Then, assets move to Bucket 2 or 3, and reserves increase to reflect expected losses over the life of those assets

if the credit quality deteriorates and if there is an expectation that substantially all of the contractual cash flows will not be recovered.

In response to criticisms that the three-bucket model is overly complex, the FASB is exploring a second model—referred to as the "Current Expected Credit Loss" (CECL) model. Unlike the three-bucket approach, the CECL model uses a single-measurement objective—current estimate of lifetime expected credit losses—in contrast to the three-bucket model's requirement to distinguish between "12 months of expected credit losses" (Bucket 1) and "lifetime expected credit losses" (Buckets 2 and 3).

Under the CECL model, the impairment estimate reflects management's estimate of the contractual cash flows that the company does not expect to collect. Thus, the balance sheet will reflect the current estimate of expected credit losses at the reporting date, while the income statement will indicate the effects of credit deterioration or improvement that has taken place during the period.

While these proposed models represent a significant change from current practice, they have gained support because the loan loss allowance captures expected losses in response to deterioration in credit quality. In addition, in contrast to current GAAP, which is based on an "incurred loss" model, estimated loan losses are recognized earlier.

Source: K. Tysiac, "FASB Takes New Path in Contentious Financial Instruments Project," *Journal of Accountancy* (August 31, 2012).

---

[16]Several figures other than 365 could be used. A common alternative is 360 days because it is divisible by 30 (days) and 12 (months). *Use 365 days in any homework computations.*

SUMMARY OF LEARNING OBJECTIVES

1 Identify items considered cash. To be reported as "cash," an asset must be readily available for the payment of current obligations and free from contractual restrictions that limit its use in satisfying debts. Cash consists of coin, currency, and available funds on deposit at the bank. Negotiable instruments such as money orders, certified checks, cashier's checks, personal checks, and bank drafts are also viewed as cash. Savings accounts are usually classified as cash.

2 Indicate how to report cash and related items. Companies report cash as a current asset in the balance sheet. The reporting of other related items are as follows. (1) *Restricted cash:* The SEC recommends that companies state separately legally restricted deposits held as compensating balances against short-term borrowing among the "Cash and cash equivalent items" in current assets. Restricted deposits held against long-term borrowing arrangements should be separately classified as noncurrent assets in either the investments or other assets sections. (2) *Bank overdrafts:* Companies should report overdrafts in the current liabilities section and usually add them to the amount reported as accounts payable. If material, these items should be separately disclosed either on the face of the balance sheet or in the related notes. (3) *Cash equivalents:* Companies often report this item together with cash as "Cash and cash equivalents."

3 Define receivables and identify the different types of receivables. Receivables are claims held against customers and others for money, goods, or services. The receivables are classified into three types: (1) current or noncurrent, (2) trade or nontrade, and (3) accounts receivable or notes receivable.

4 Explain accounting issues related to recognition of accounts receivable. Two issues that may complicate the measurement of accounts receivable are (1) the availability of discounts (trade and cash discounts), and (2) the length of time between the sale and the payment due dates (the interest element).

Ideally, companies should measure receivables in terms of their present value—that is, the discounted value of the cash to be received in the future. The profession specifically excludes from the present value considerations receivables arising from normal business transactions that are due in customary trade terms within approximately one year.

5 Explain accounting issues related to valuation of accounts receivable. Companies value and report short-term receivables at net realizable value—the net amount expected to be received in cash, which is not necessarily the amount legally receivable. Determining net realizable value requires estimating uncollectible receivables.

6 Explain accounting issues related to recognition and valuation of notes receivable. Companies record short-term notes at face value and long-term notes receivable at the present value of the cash they expect to collect. When the interest stated on an interest-bearing note equals the effective (market) rate of interest, the note sells at face value. When the stated rate differs from the effective rate, a company records either a discount or premium. Like accounts receivable, companies record and report short-term notes receivable at their net realizable value. The same is also true of long-term receivables.

7 Explain the fair value option. Companies have the option to record receivables at fair value. Once the fair value option is chosen, the receivable is reported on the balance sheet at fair value, with the change in fair value recorded in income.

8 Explain accounting issues related to disposition of accounts and notes receivable. To accelerate the receipt of cash from receivables, the owner may transfer the receivables to another company for cash in one of two ways. (1) *Secured borrowing:*

KEY TERMS

accounts receivable, *350*
accounts receivable turnover, *372*
aging schedule, *357*
allowance method, *353*
bank overdrafts, *348*
cash, *346*
cash discounts, *351*
cash equivalents, *346*
compensating balances, *347*
direct write-off method, *353*
factoring receivables, *367*
fair value option, *365*
financial components approach, *368*
imputed interest rate, *363*
net realizable value, *353*
nontrade receivables, *350*
notes receivable, *350*
percentage-of-receivables approach, *357*
percentage-of-sales approach, *356*
promissory note, *359*
receivables, *349*
restricted cash, *347*
sales discounts, *351*
securitization, *368*
trade discounts, *351*
trade receivables, *349*
unrealized holding gain or loss, *365*
without recourse, *368*
with recourse, *368*
zero-interest-bearing notes, *359*

A creditor often requires that the debtor designate or pledge receivables as security for the loan. (2) *Sales (factoring) of receivables:* Factors are finance companies or banks that buy receivables from businesses and then collect the remittances directly from the customers. In many cases, transferors may have some continuing involvement with the receivable sold. Companies use a financial components approach to record this type of transaction.

9 **Describe how to report and analyze receivables.** Companies should report receivables with appropriate offset of valuation accounts against receivables, classify receivables as current or noncurrent, identify pledged or designated receivables, and disclose the credit risk inherent in the receivables. Analysts assess receivables based on turnover and the days outstanding.

APPENDIX 7A   CASH CONTROLS

LEARNING OBJECTIVE **10**
Explain common techniques employed to control cash.

Cash is the asset most susceptible to improper diversion and use. Management faces two problems in accounting for cash transactions: (1) to establish proper controls to prevent any unauthorized transactions by officers or employees, and (2) to provide information necessary to properly manage cash on hand and cash transactions. Yet even with sophisticated control devices, errors can and do happen. For example, the *Wall Street Journal* ran a story entitled "A $7.8 Million Error Has a Happy Ending for a Horrified Bank." The story described how **Manufacturers Hanover Trust Co.** mistakenly overpaid about $7.8 million in cash dividends to its stockholders. (As implied in the headline, most stockholders returned the monies.)

To safeguard cash and to ensure the accuracy of the accounting records for cash, companies need effective **internal control** over cash. Provisions of the Sarbanes-Oxley Act call for enhanced efforts to increase the quality of internal control (for cash and other assets). Such efforts are expected to result in improved financial reporting. In this appendix, we discuss some of the basic control issues related to cash.

USING BANK ACCOUNTS

To obtain desired control objectives, a company can vary the number and location of banks and the types of bank accounts. For large companies operating in multiple locations, the location of bank accounts can be important. Establishing collection accounts in strategic locations can accelerate the flow of cash into the company by shortening the time between a customer's mailing of a payment and the company's use of the cash. Multiple collection centers generally reduce the size of a company's **collection float**. This is the difference between the amount on deposit according to the company's records and the amount of collected cash according to the bank record.

Large, multilocation companies frequently use **lockbox accounts** to collect in cities with heavy customer billing. The company rents a local post office box and authorizes a local bank to pick up the remittances mailed to that box number. The bank empties the box at least once a day and immediately credits the company's account for collections. The greatest advantage of a lockbox is that it accelerates the availability of collected cash. Generally, in a lockbox arrangement the bank microfilms the checks for record purposes and provides the company with a deposit slip, a list of collections, and any customer correspondence. Thus, a lockbox system improves the control over cash and accelerates collection of

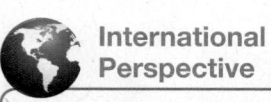
International Perspective

Multinational corporations often have cash accounts in more than one currency. For financial statement purposes, these corporations typically translate these currencies into U.S. dollars, using the exchange rate in effect at the balance sheet date.

cash. If the income generated from accelerating the receipt of funds exceeds the cost of the lockbox system, then it is a worthwhile undertaking.

The **general checking account** is the principal bank account in most companies and frequently the only bank account in small businesses. A company deposits in and disburses cash from this account. A company cycles all transactions through it. For example, a company deposits from and disburses to all other bank accounts through the general checking account.

Companies use **imprest bank accounts** to make a specific amount of cash available for a limited purpose. The account acts as a clearing account for a large volume of checks or for a specific type of check. To clear a specific and intended amount through the imprest account, a company transfers that amount from the general checking account or other source. Companies often use imprest bank accounts for disbursing payroll checks, dividends, commissions, bonuses, confidential expenses (e.g., officers' salaries), and travel expenses.

THE IMPREST PETTY CASH SYSTEM

Almost every company finds it necessary to pay small amounts for miscellaneous expenses such as taxi fares, minor office supplies, and employees' lunches. Disbursements by check for such items is often impractical, yet some control over them is important. A simple method of obtaining reasonable control, while adhering to the rule of disbursement by check, is the imprest system for petty cash disbursements. This is how the system works:

1. The company designates a petty cash custodian, and gives the custodian a small amount of currency from which to make payments. It records transfer of funds to petty cash as:

Petty Cash	300	
Cash		300

2. The petty cash custodian obtains signed receipts from each individual to whom he or she pays cash, attaching evidence of the disbursement to the petty cash receipt. Petty cash transactions are not recorded until the fund is reimbursed; someone other than the petty cash custodian records those entries.

3. When the supply of cash runs low, the custodian presents to the controller or accounts payable cashier a request for reimbursement supported by the petty cash receipts and other disbursement evidence. The custodian receives a company check to replenish the fund. At this point, the company records transactions based on petty cash receipts.

Supplies Expense	42	
Postage Expense	53	
Miscellaneous Expense	76	
Cash Over and Short	2	
Cash		173

4. If the company decides that the amount of cash in the petty cash fund is excessive, it lowers the fund balance as follows.

Cash	50	
Petty Cash		50

Subsequent to establishment, a company makes entries to the Petty Cash account only to increase or decrease the size of the fund.

A company uses a **Cash Over and Short** account when the petty cash fund fails to prove out. That is, an error occurs such as incorrect change, overpayment of expense, or lost receipt. If cash proves out **short** (i.e., the sum of the receipts and cash in the fund is less than the imprest amount), the company debits the shortage to the Cash Over and

Short account. If cash proves out **over**, it credits the overage to Cash Over and Short. The company closes Cash Over and Short only at the end of the year. It generally shows Cash Over and Short on the income statement as an "Other expense or revenue."

There are usually expense items in the fund except immediately after reimbursement. Therefore, to maintain accurate financial statements, a company must reimburse the funds at the end of each accounting period and also when nearly depleted.

Under the imprest system, the petty cash custodian is responsible at all times for the amount of the fund on hand either as cash or in the form of signed receipts. These receipts provide the evidence required by the disbursing officer to issue a reimbursement check. Further, a company follows two additional procedures to obtain more complete control over the petty cash fund:

1. A superior of the petty cash custodian makes surprise counts of the fund from time to time to determine that a satisfactory accounting of the fund has occurred.
2. The company cancels or mutilates petty cash receipts after they have been submitted for reimbursement, so that they cannot be used to secure a second reimbursement.

PHYSICAL PROTECTION OF CASH BALANCES

Not only must a company safeguard cash receipts and cash disbursements through internal control measures, but it must also protect the cash on hand and in banks. Because receipts become cash on hand and disbursements are made from cash in banks, adequate control of receipts and disbursements is part of the protection of cash balances, along with certain other procedures.

Physical protection of cash is so elementary a necessity that it requires little discussion. A company should make every effort to minimize the cash on hand in the office. It should only have on hand a petty cash fund, the current day's receipts, and perhaps funds for making change. Insofar as possible, it should keep these funds in a vault, safe, or locked cash drawer. The company should transmit intact each day's receipts to the bank as soon as practicable. Accurately stating the amount of available cash both in internal management reports and in external financial statements is also extremely important.

Every company has a record of cash received, disbursed, and the balance. Because of the many cash transactions, however, errors or omissions may occur in keeping this record. Therefore, a company must periodically prove the balance shown in the general ledger. It can count cash actually present in the office—petty cash, change funds, and undeposited receipts—for comparison with the company records. For cash on deposit, a company prepares a bank reconciliation—a reconciliation of the company's record and the bank's record of the company's cash.

RECONCILIATION OF BANK BALANCES

At the end of each calendar month the bank supplies each customer with a **bank statement** (a copy of the bank's account with the customer) together with the customer's checks that the bank paid during the month.[17] If neither the bank nor the customer made any errors, if all deposits made and all checks drawn by the customer reached the bank

---

[17]As we mentioned in Chapter 7, paper checks continue to be used as a means of payment. However, ready availability of desktop publishing software and hardware has created new opportunities for check fraud in the form of duplicate, altered, and forged checks. At the same time, new fraud-fighting technologies, such as ultraviolet imaging, high-capacity barcodes, and biometrics, are being developed. These technologies convert paper documents into electronically processed document files, thereby reducing the risk of fraud.

within the same month, and if no unusual transactions occurred that affected either the company's or the bank's record of cash, the balance of cash reported by the bank to the customer equals that shown in the customer's own records. This condition seldom occurs due to one or more of the reconciling items presented below. Hence, a company expects differences between its record of cash and the bank's record. Therefore, it must reconcile the two to determine the nature of the differences between the two amounts.

RECONCILING ITEMS

1. **DEPOSITS IN TRANSIT.** End-of-month deposits of cash recorded on the depositor's books in one month are received and recorded by the bank in the following month.
2. **OUTSTANDING CHECKS.** Checks written by the depositor are recorded when written but may not be recorded by (may not "clear") the bank until the next month.
3. **BANK CHARGES.** Charges recorded by the bank against the depositor's balance for such items as bank services, printing checks, **not-sufficient-funds (NSF) checks**, and safe-deposit box rentals. The depositor may not be aware of these charges until the receipt of the bank statement.
4. **BANK CREDITS.** Collections or deposits by the bank for the benefit of the depositor that may be unknown to the depositor until receipt of the bank statement. Examples are note collection for the depositor and interest earned on interest-bearing checking accounts.
5. **BANK OR DEPOSITOR ERRORS.** Errors on either the part of the bank or the part of the depositor cause the bank balance to disagree with the depositor's book balance.

A **bank reconciliation** is a schedule explaining any differences between the bank's and the company's records of cash. If the difference results only from transactions not yet recorded by the bank, the company's record of cash is considered correct. But, if some part of the difference arises from other items, either the bank or the company must adjust its records.

A company may prepare two forms of a bank reconciliation. One form reconciles from the bank statement balance to the book balance or vice versa. The other form reconciles both the bank balance and the book balance to a correct cash balance. Most companies use this latter form. Illustration 7A-1 shows a sample of that form and its common reconciling items.

Balance per bank statement (end of period)		$$$
Add: Deposits in transit	$$	
Undeposited receipts (cash on hand)	$$	
Bank errors that understate the bank statement balance	$$	$$
		$$$
Deduct: Outstanding checks	$$	
Bank errors that overstate the bank statement balance	$$	$$
Correct cash balance		$$$
Balance per depositor's books		$$$
Add: Bank credits and collections not yet recorded in the books	$$	
Book errors that understate the book balance	$$	$$
		$$$
Deduct: Bank charges not yet recorded in the books	$$	
Book errors that overstate the book balance	$$	$$
Correct cash balance		$$$

ILLUSTRATION 7A-1
Bank Reconciliation Form and Content

This form of reconciliation consists of two sections: (1) "Balance per bank statement" and (2) "Balance per depositor's books." Both sections end with the same "Correct cash balance." The correct cash balance is the amount to which the books must be adjusted and is the amount reported on the balance sheet. **Companies prepare adjusting journal entries for all the addition and deduction items appearing in the "Balance per depositor's books" section.** Companies should immediately call to the bank's attention any errors attributable to it.

To illustrate, Nugget Mining Company's books show a cash balance at the Denver National Bank on November 30, 2014, of $20,502. The bank statement covering the month of November shows an ending balance of $22,190. An examination of Nugget's accounting records and November bank statement identified the following reconciling items.

1. A deposit of $3,680 that Nugget mailed November 30 does not appear on the bank statement.
2. Checks written in November but not charged to the November bank statement are:

Check #7327	$ 150
#7348	4,820
#7349	31

3. Nugget has not yet recorded the $600 of interest collected by the bank November 20 on Sequoia Co. bonds held by the bank for Nugget.
4. Bank service charges of $18 are not yet recorded on Nugget's books.
5. The bank returned one of Nugget's customer's checks for $220 with the bank statement, marked "NSF." The bank treated this bad check as a disbursement.
6. Nugget discovered that it incorrectly recorded check #7322, written in November for $131 in payment of an account payable, as $311.
7. A check for Nugent Oil Co. in the amount of $175 that the bank incorrectly charged to Nugget accompanied the statement.

Nugget reconciled the bank and book balances to the correct cash balance of $21,044 as shown in Illustration 7A-2.

ILLUSTRATION 7A-2
Sample Bank
Reconciliation

NUGGET MINING COMPANY
BANK RECONCILIATION
DENVER NATIONAL BANK, NOVEMBER 30, 2014

Balance per bank statement (end of period)			$22,190
Add: Deposit in transit	(1)	$3,680	
Bank error—incorrect check charged to account by bank	(7)	175	3,855
			26,045
Deduct: Outstanding checks	(2)		5,001
Correct cash balance			$21,044
Balance per books			$20,502
Add: Interest collected by the bank	(3)	$ 600	
Error in recording check #7322	(6)	180	780
			21,282
Deduct: Bank service charges	(4)	18	
NSF check returned	(5)	220	238
Correct cash balance			$21,044

The journal entries required to adjust and correct Nugget's books in early December 2014 are taken from the items in the "Balance per books" section and are as follows.

Cash	600	
Interest Revenue		600
(To record interest on Sequoia Co. bonds, collected by bank)		
Cash	180	
Accounts Payable		180
(To correct error in recording amount of check #7322)		
Office Expense (bank charges)	18	
Cash		18
(To record bank service charges for November)		
Accounts Receivable	220	
Cash		220
(To record customer's check returned NSF)		

After posting the entries, Nugget's cash account will have a balance of $21,044. Nugget should return the Nugent Oil Co. check to Denver National Bank, informing the bank of the error.

Gateway to the Profession

Expanded Discussion of a Four-Column Bank Reconciliation

SUMMARY OF LEARNING OBJECTIVE FOR APPENDIX 7A

KEY TERMS

bank reconciliation, *379*
imprest system for petty cash, *377*
not-sufficient-funds (NSF) checks, *379*

10 **Explain common techniques employed to control cash.** The common techniques employed to control cash are as follows. (1) *Using bank accounts:* A company can vary the number and location of banks and the types of accounts to obtain desired control objectives. (2) *The imprest petty cash system:* It may be impractical to require small amounts of various expenses be paid by check, yet some control over them is important. (3) *Physical protection of cash balances:* Adequate control of receipts and disbursements is a part of the protection of cash balances. Every effort should be made to minimize the cash on hand in the office. (4) *Reconciliation of bank balances:* Cash on deposit is not available for count and is proved by preparing a bank reconciliation.

APPENDIX 7B   **IMPAIRMENTS OF RECEIVABLES**

Companies continually evaluate their receivables to determine their ultimate collectibility. As discussed in the chapter, the FASB considers the collectibility of receivables a *loss contingency*. Thus, the allowance method is appropriate in situations where it is probable that an asset has been impaired and the amount of the loss can be reasonably estimated. Generally, companies start with historical loss rates and modify these rates for changes in economic conditions that could affect a borrower's ability to repay the loan. The discussion in the chapter assumed use of this approach to determine the amount of bad debts to be recorded for a period.

However, for long-term receivables such as loans that are identified as impaired, companies perform an additional impairment evaluation.[18] GAAP has specific rules for

11 LEARNING OBJECTIVE
Describe the accounting for a loan impairment.

---

[18]A loan is defined as "a contractual right to receive money on demand or on fixed and determinable dates that is recognized as an asset in the creditor's statement of financial position." For example, accounts receivable with terms exceeding one year are considered loans. **[11]**

measurement and reporting of these impairments. These rules relate to determining the value of these loans and how much loss to recognize if the holder of the loans plans to keep them in hope that the market will recover. More complex rules arise when these loans are sold as part of the securitization process, especially when the original terms of the notes are modified.[19]

IMPAIRMENT MEASUREMENT AND REPORTING

A company considers a loan receivable impaired when it is probable, based on current information and events, that it will not collect all amounts due (both principal and interest). If a loan is determined to be individually impaired, the company should measure the loss due to the **impairment**. This impairment loss is calculated as the difference between the investment in the loan (generally the principal plus accrued interest) and the expected future cash flows discounted at the loan's historical effective-interest rate.[20] When using the historical effective loan rate, the value of the investment will change only if some of the legally contracted cash flows are reduced. A company recognizes a loss in this case because the expected future cash flows are now lower. The company ignores interest rate changes caused by current economic events that affect the fair value of the loan. In estimating future cash flows, the creditor should use reasonable and supportable assumptions and projections. **[13]**

Impairment Loss Example

At December 31, 2013, Ogden Bank recorded an investment of $100,000 in a loan to Carl King. The loan has an historical effective-interest rate of 10 percent, the principal is due in full at maturity in three years, and interest is due annually. Unfortunately, King is experiencing financial difficulty and thinks he will have a difficult time making full payment. The loan officer performs a review of the loan's expected future cash flows and utilizes the present value method for measuring the required impairment loss. Illustration 7B-1 shows the cash flow schedule prepared by the loan officer.

ILLUSTRATION 7B-1
Impaired Loan Cash Flows

Dec. 31	Contractual Cash Flow	Expected Cash Flow	Loss of Cash Flow
2014	$ 10,000	$ 5,000	$ 5,000
2015	10,000	5,000	5,000
2016	$110,000	105,000	5,000
Total cash flows	$130,000	$115,000	$15,000

As indicated, this loan is impaired. The expected cash flows of $115,000 are less than the contractual cash flows, including principal and interest, of $130,000. The amount of the impairment to be recorded equals the difference between the recorded investment of $100,000 and the present value of the expected cash flows, as shown in Illustration 7B-2.

[19]Note that the impairment test shown in this appendix only applies to specific loans. However, if the loans are bundled into a security (e.g., the mortgage-backed securities), the impairment test is different. Impairments of securities are measured based on fair value. We discuss this accounting in Chapter 17.

[20]The creditor may also, for the sake of expediency, use the market price of the loan (if such a price is available) or the fair value of the collateral if it is a collateralized loan. **[12]** Recognize that if the value of the investment is based on the historical rate, generally the resultant value will not be equal to the fair value of the loan in subsequent periods. We consider this accounting inconsistent with fair value principles as applied to other financial instruments.

Recorded investment		$100,000
Less: Present value of $100,000 due in 3 years at 10%		
(Table 6-2); *FV* (*PVF*$_{3,10\%}$); ($100,000 × .75132)	$75,132	
Present value of $5,000 interest payable annually		
for 3 years at 10% R (*PVF-OA*$_{3,10\%}$); ($5,000 × 2.48685)	12,434	87,566
Loss on impairment		$ 12,434

ILLUSTRATION 7B-2
Computation of
Impairment Loss

The loss due to the impairment is $12,434. Why isn't it $15,000 ($130,000 − $115,000)? Because Ogden Bank must measure the loss at a present-value amount, not at an undiscounted amount, when it records the loss.

Recording Impairment Losses

Ogden Bank (the creditor) recognizes an impairment loss of $12,434 by debiting Bad Debt Expense for the expected loss. At the same time, it reduces the overall value of the receivable by crediting Allowance for Doubtful Accounts. The journal entry to record the loss is therefore as follows.[21]

Bad Debt Expense	12,434	
Allowance for Doubtful Accounts		12,434

What entry does Carl King (the debtor) make? The debtor makes no entry because he still legally owes $100,000.

In some cases, debtors like King negotiate a modification in the terms of the loan agreement. In such cases, the accounting entries from Ogden Bank are the same as the situation in which the loan officer must estimate the future cash flows—except that the calculation for the amount of the loss becomes more reliable (because the revised expected cash flow amounts are contractually specified in the loan agreement).[22] The entries related to the debtor in this case often change; they are discussed in Appendix 14A.

What do the numbers mean? *LOST IN TRANSLATION*

Floyd Norris, noted financial writer for the *New York Times*, recently wrote in his blog that he attended a conference to discuss the financial crisis in subprime lending. He highlighted, and provided "translations" of, some of the statements he heard at that conference:

- "There is a problem of misaligned incentives."

   Translation: Many parties in the lending process were complicit in not performing due diligence on loans because there were lots of fees to be had if the loans were made, good loans or bad.

- "It is pretty clear that there was a failure in some key assumptions that were supporting our analytics and our models."

   Translation: The rating agencies that evaluated the risk level of these securities made many miscalculations. Some structured finance products that were given superior ratings are no longer worth much.

- "The plumbing of the U.S. economy has been deeply damaged. It is a long window of vulnerability."

   Translation: The U.S. has caused a financial crisis as a result of poor lending practices, and many financial institutions are fighting to survive.

- "I'm glad that this time we did not cause it."

   Translation: Other countries realized they had caused financial crises in the past but were not to blame for the current U.S. financial situation.

[21]In the event of a loan write-off, the company charges the loss against the allowance. In subsequent periods, if revising estimated expected cash flows based on new information, the company adjusts the allowance account and bad debt expense account (either increased or decreased depending on whether conditions improved or worsened) in the same fashion as the original impairment. We use the terms "loss" and "bad debt expense" interchangeably throughout this discussion. Companies should charge losses related to receivables transactions to Bad Debt Expense or the related Allowance for Doubtful Accounts because they use these accounts to recognize changes in values affecting receivables.

[22]Many alternatives are permitted to recognize income by Ogden Bank in subsequent periods. **[14]**

- "What you see is what you get. If you don't see it, it will get you."

  Translation: A large number of financial institutions have to take losses on assets that are not reported on their

balance sheets. Their continuing interest in some of the loans that they supposedly sold is now coming back to them and they will have to report losses.

Source: Floyd Norris blog, *http://www.norris.blogs.nytimes.com/* (accessed June 2008).

KEY TERM

impairment, *382*

SUMMARY OF LEARNING OBJECTIVE FOR APPENDIX 7B

11 **Describe the accounting for a loan impairment.** A creditor bases an impairment loan loss on the difference between the present value of the future cash flows (using the historical effective-interest rate) and the carrying amount of the note.

DEMONSTRATION PROBLEM

The trial balance before adjustment for Slamar Company shows the following balances.

	Debit	Credit
Net sales	$860,000	
Accounts receivable	338,000	
Allowance for doubtful accounts		$4,240

Consider the following independent situations:

1. To obtain additional cash, Slamar factors without recourse $50,000 of accounts receivable with Pierce Finance. The finance charge is 11% of the amount factored.
2. To obtain a 1-year loan of $75,000, Slamar assigns $80,000 of specific receivable accounts to Milo Financial. The finance charge is 9% of the loan; the cash is received and the accounts turned over to Milo Financial.
3. The company wants to maintain Allowance for Doubtful Accounts at 6% of gross accounts receivable.
4. The company wishes to increase the allowance account by 2% of net sales.

Instructions

(a) Using the data above, give the journal entries required to record situations 1–4.
(b) Discuss how analysis based on the current ratio and the accounts receivable turnover would be affected if Slamar had transferred the receivables in situation 1 using a secured borrowing.

Solution

(a)

1.	Cash		44,500	
	Loss on Sale of Receivables ($50,000 × 11%)		5,500	
	Accounts Receivable			50,000
2.	Cash		68,250	
	Interest Expense ($75,000 × 9%)		6,750	
	Notes Payable			75,000

3.	Bad Debt Expense	24,520	
	Allowance for Doubtful Accounts [($338,000 × 6%) + $4,240]		24,520
4.	Bad Debt Expense	17,200	
	Allowance for Doubtful Accounts ($860,000 × 2%)		17,200

(b) With a secured borrowing, the receivables would stay on Slamar's books, and Slamar would record a note payable. This would reduce the current ratio and accounts receivable turnover.

FASB CODIFICATION

FASB Codification References

[1] FASB ASC 210-10-S99-1. [Predecessor literature: "Amendments to Regulations S-X and Related Interpretations and Guidelines Regarding the Disclosure of Compensating Balances and Short-Term Borrowing Arrangements," *Accounting Series Release No. 148*, Securities and Exchange Commission (November 13, 1973).]

[2] FASB ASC 835-30-15-3. [Predecessor literature: "Interest on Receivables and Payables," *Opinions of the Accounting Principles Board No. 21* (New York: AICPA, 1971), par. 3(a).]

[3] FASB ASC 310-10-35-8. [Predecessor literature: "Accounting for Contingencies," *Statement of Financial Accounting Standards No. 5* (Stamford, Conn.: FASB, 1975), par. 8.]

[4] FASB ASC 835-30-05. [Predecessor literature: "Interest on Receivables and Payables," *Opinions of the Accounting Principles Board No. 21* (New York: AICPA, 1971), par. 3(a).]

[5] FASB ASC 825-10-25. [Predecessor literature: "The Fair Value Option for Financial Assets and Liabilities—Including an Amendment to FASB No. 115," *Statement of Financial Accounting Standards No. 159* (Norwalk, Conn.: FASB, 2007).]

[6] FASB ASC 860-40 and FASB ASC 860-10-5-15. [Predecessor literature: "Accounting for Transfers and Servicing of Financial Assets and Extinguishments of Liabilities," *Statement of Financial Accounting Standards No. 140* (Stamford, Conn.: FASB, 2000), p. 155.]

[7] FASB ASC 860-10-40. [Predecessor literature: None.]

[8] FASB ASC 860. [Predecessor literature: "Transfers and Servicing," *Accounting Standards Update 2011–03* (April 2011).]

[9] FASB ASC 310-10-50. [Predecessor literature: None.]

[10] FASB ASC 825-10-50-20 through 22. [Predecessor literature: "Disclosures about Fair Value of Financial Instruments," *Statement of Financial Accounting Standards No. 107* (Norwalk, Conn.: FASB, 1991), par. 15.]

[11] FASB ASC 310-10-35-22. [Predecessor literature: "Accounting by Creditors for Impairment of a Loan," *FASB Statement No. 114* (Norwalk, Conn.: FASB, May 1993).]

[12] FASB ASC 310-10-35-22. [Predecessor literature: "Accounting by Creditors for Impairment of a Loan," *FASB Statement No. 114* (Norwalk, Conn.: FASB, May 1993), par. 13.]

[13] FASB ASC 310-10-35-26. [Predecessor literature: "Accounting by Creditors for Impairment of a Loan," *FASB Statement No. 114* (Norwalk, Conn.: FASB, May 1993), par. 15.]

[14] FASB ASC 310-10-35-40. [Predecessor literature: "Accounting by Creditors for Impairment of a Loan—Income Recognition and Disclosures," *FASB Statement No. 118* (Norwalk, Conn.: FASB, October 1994).]

Exercises

If your school has a subscription to the FASB Codification, go to *http://aaahq.org/asclogin.cfm* to log in and prepare responses to the following. Provide Codification references for your responses.

CE7-1 Access the glossary ("Master Glossary") to answer the following.

(a) What is the definition of cash?
(b) What is the definition of securitization?
(c) What are the three contexts that give rise to recourse?

CE7-2 Carrie Underwood believes that by establishing a loss contingency for uncollectible receivables, a company provides financial protection against the loss. What does the authoritative literature say about this belief?

CE7-3 In addition to securitizations, what are the other types of transfers of financial assets identified in the Codification?

CE7-4 The controller for Nesheim Construction Company believes that it is appropriate to offset a note payable to Oregon Bank against an account receivable from Oregon Bank related to remodeling services provided to the bank. What is the authoritative guidance concerning the criteria to be met to allow such offsetting?

An additional Codification case can be found in the Using Your Judgment section, on page 407.

Be sure to check the book's companion website for a Review and Analysis Exercise, with solution.

WileyPLUS
Brief Exercises, Exercises, Problems, and many more learning and assessment tools and resources are available for practice in WileyPLUS.

Note: All asterisked Questions, Exercises, and Problems relate to material in the appendices to the chapter.

QUESTIONS

1. What may be included under the heading of "cash"?

2. In what accounts should the following items be classified?
   (a) Coins and currency.
   (b) U.S. Treasury (government) bonds.
   (c) Certificate of deposit.
   (d) Cash in a bank that is in receivership.
   (e) NSF check (returned with bank statement).
   (f) Deposit in foreign bank (exchangeability limited).
   (g) Postdated checks.
   (h) Cash to be used for retirement of long-term bonds.
   (i) Deposits in transit.
   (j) 100 shares of Dell stock (intention is to sell in one year or less).
   (k) Savings and checking accounts.
   (l) Petty cash.
   (m) Stamps.
   (n) Travel advances.

3. Define a "compensating balance." How should a compensating balance be reported?

4. Springsteen Inc. reported in a recent annual report "Restricted cash for debt redemption." What section of the balance sheet would report this item?

5. What are the reasons that a company gives trade discounts? Why are trade discounts not recorded in the accounts like cash discounts?

6. What are two methods of recording accounts receivable transactions when a cash discount situation is involved? Which is more theoretically correct? Which is used in practice more of the time? Why?

7. What are the basic problems that occur in the valuation of accounts receivable?

8. What is the theoretical justification of the allowance method as contrasted with the direct write-off method of accounting for bad debts?

9. Indicate how well the percentage-of-sales method and the aging method accomplish the objectives of the allowance method of accounting for bad debts.

10. Of what merit is the contention that the allowance method lacks the objectivity of the direct write-off method? Discuss in terms of accounting's measurement function.

11. Explain how the accounting for bad debts can be used for earnings management.

12. Because of calamitous earthquake losses, Bernstein Company, one of your client's oldest and largest customers, suddenly and unexpectedly became bankrupt. Approximately 30% of your client's total sales have been made to Bernstein Company during each of the past several years. The amount due from Bernstein Company—none of which is collectible—equals 22% of total accounts receivable, an amount that is considerably in excess of what was determined to be an adequate provision for doubtful accounts at the close of the preceding year. How would your client record the write-off of the Bernstein Company

receivable if it is using the allowance method of accounting for bad debts? Justify your suggested treatment.

13. What is the normal procedure for handling the collection of accounts receivable previously written off using the direct write-off method? The allowance method?

14. On January 1, 2014, Lombard Co. sells property for which it had paid $690,000 to Sargent Company, receiving in return Sargent's zero-interest-bearing note for $1,000,000 payable in 5 years. What entry would Lombard make to record the sale, assuming that Lombard frequently sells similar items of property for a cash sales price of $640,000?

15. What is "imputed interest"? In what situations is it necessary to impute an interest rate for notes receivable? What are the considerations in imputing an appropriate interest rate?

16. What is the fair value option? Where do companies that elect the fair value option report unrealized holding gains and losses?

17. Indicate three reasons why a company might sell its receivables to another company.

18. When is the financial components approach to recording the transfers of receivables used? When should a transfer of receivables be recorded as a sale?

19. Moon Hardware is planning to factor some of its receivables. The cash received will be used to pay for inventory purchases. The factor has indicated that it will require "recourse" on the sold receivables. Explain to the controller of Moon Hardware what "recourse" is and how the recourse will be reflected in Moon's financial statements after the sale of the receivables.

20. Horizon Outfitters Company includes in its trial balance for December 31 an item for Accounts Receivable $789,000. This balance consists of the following items:

Due from regular customers	$523,000
Refund receivable on prior year's income taxes (an established claim)	15,500
Travel advance to employees	22,000
Loan to wholly owned subsidiary	45,500
Advances to creditors for goods ordered	61,000
Accounts receivable assigned as security for loans payable	75,000
Notes receivable past due plus interest on these notes	47,000
Total	$789,000

Illustrate how these items should be shown in the balance sheet as of December 31.

21. What is the accounts receivable turnover, and what type of information does it provide?

22. You are evaluating Woodlawn Racetrack for a potential loan. An examination of the notes to the financial statements indicates restricted cash at year-end amounts to $100,000. Explain how you would use this information in evaluating Woodlawn's liquidity.

*23. Distinguish among the following: (1) a general checking account, (2) an imprest bank account, and (3) a lockbox account.

*24. What are the general rules for measuring and recognizing gain or loss by both the debtor and the creditor in an impairment?

*25. What is meant by impairment of a loan? Under what circumstances should a creditor recognize an impaired loan?

BRIEF EXERCISES

1 **BE7-1** Kraft Enterprises owns the following assets at December 31, 2014.

Cash in bank—savings account	68,000	Checking account balance	17,000
Cash on hand	9,300	Postdated checks	750
Cash refund due from IRS	31,400	Certificates of deposit (180-day)	90,000

What amount should be reported as cash?

4 **BE7-2** Restin Co. uses the gross method to record sales made on credit. On June 1, 2014, it made sales of $50,000 with terms 3/15, n/45. On June 12, 2014, Restin received full payment for the June 1 sale. Prepare the required journal entries for Restin Co.

4 **BE7-3** Use the information from BE7-2, assuming Restin Co. uses the net method to account for cash discounts. Prepare the required journal entries for Restin Co.

5 **BE7-4** Wilton, Inc. had net sales in 2014 of $1,400,000. At December 31, 2014, before adjusting entries, the balances in selected accounts were: Accounts Receivable $250,000 debit, and Allowance for Doubtful Accounts $2,400 credit. If Wilton estimates that 2% of its net sales will prove to be uncollectible, prepare the December 31, 2014, journal entry to record bad debt expense.

5 **BE7-5** Use the information presented in BE7-4 for Wilton, Inc.

(a) Instead of estimating the uncollectibles at 2% of net sales, assume that 10% of accounts receivable will prove to be uncollectible. Prepare the entry to record bad debt expense.

(b) Instead of estimating uncollectibles at 2% of net sales, assume Wilton prepares an aging schedule that estimates total uncollectible accounts at $24,600. Prepare the entry to record bad debt expense.

6 **BE7-6** Milner Family Importers sold goods to Tung Decorators for $30,000 on November 1, 2014, accepting Tung's $30,000, 6-month, 6% note. Prepare Milner's November 1 entry, December 31 annual adjusting entry, and May 1 entry for the collection of the note and interest.

6 **BE7-7** Dold Acrobats lent $16,529 to Donaldson, Inc., accepting Donaldson's 2-year, $20,000, zero-interest-bearing note. The implied interest rate is 10%. Prepare Dold's journal entries for the initial transaction, recognition of interest each year, and the collection of $20,000 at maturity.

8 **BE7-8** On October 1, 2014, Chung, Inc. assigns $1,000,000 of its accounts receivable to Seneca National Bank as collateral for a $750,000 note. The bank assesses a finance charge of 2% of the receivables assigned and interest on the note of 9%. Prepare the October 1 journal entries for both Chung and Seneca.

8 **BE7-9** Wood Incorporated factored $150,000 of accounts receivable with Engram Factors Inc. on a without-recourse basis. Engram assesses a 2% finance charge of the amount of accounts receivable and retains an amount equal to 6% of accounts receivable for possible adjustments. Prepare the journal entry for Wood Incorporated and Engram Factors to record the factoring of the accounts receivable to Engram.

8 **BE7-10** Use the information in BE7-9 for Wood. Assume that the receivables are sold with recourse. Prepare the journal entry for Wood to record the sale, assuming that the recourse liability has a fair value of $7,500.

8 **BE7-11** Arness Woodcrafters sells $250,000 of receivables to Commercial Factors, Inc. on a with recourse basis. Commercial assesses a finance charge of 5% and retains an amount equal to 4% of accounts receivable. Arness estimates the fair value of the recourse liability to be $8,000. Prepare the journal entry for Arness to record the sale.

8 **BE7-12** Use the information presented in BE7-11 for Arness Woodcrafters but assume that the recourse liability has a fair value of $4,000, instead of $8,000. Prepare the journal entry and discuss the effects of this change in the value of the recourse liability on Arness's financial statements.

9 **BE7-13** Recent financial statements of General Mills, Inc. report net sales of $12,442,000,000. Accounts receivable are $912,000,000 at the beginning of the year and $953,000,000 at the end of the year. Compute General Mills' accounts receivable turnover. Compute General Mills' average collection period for accounts receivable in days.

10 *BE7-14** Finman Company designated Jill Holland as petty cash custodian and established a petty cash fund of $200. The fund is reimbursed when the cash in the fund is at $15. Petty cash receipts indicate funds were disbursed for office supplies $94 and miscellaneous expense $87. Prepare journal entries for the establishment of the fund and the reimbursement.

10 *BE7-15** Horton Corporation is preparing a bank reconciliation and has identified the following potential reconciling items. For each item, indicate if it is (1) added to balance per bank statement, (2) deducted from balance per bank statement, (3) added to balance per books, or (4) deducted from balance per books.

(a) Deposit in transit $5,500.
(b) Bank service charges $25.
(c) Interest credited to Horton's account $31.

(d) Outstanding checks $7,422.
(e) NSF check returned $377.

10 *BE7-16** Use the information presented in BE7-15 for Horton Corporation. Prepare any entries necessary to make Horton's accounting records correct and complete.

11 *BE7-17** Assume that Toni Braxton Company has recently fallen into financial difficulties. By reviewing all available evidence on December 31, 2014, one of Toni Braxton's creditors, the National American Bank, determined that Toni Braxton would pay back only 65% of the principal at maturity. As a result, the bank decided that the loan was impaired. If the loss is estimated to be $225,000, what entry(ies) should National American Bank make to record this loss?

EXERCISES

1 **E7-1 (Determining Cash Balance)** The controller for Clint Eastwood Co. is attempting to determine the amount of cash to be reported on its December 31, 2014, balance sheet. The following information is provided.

1. Commercial savings account of $600,000 and a commercial checking account balance of $900,000 are held at First National Bank of Yojimbo.

2. Money market fund account held at Volonte Co. (a mutual fund organization) permits Eastwood to write checks on this balance, $5,000,000.
3. Travel advances of $180,000 for executive travel for the first quarter of next year (employee to reimburse through salary reduction).
4. A separate cash fund in the amount of $1,500,000 is restricted for the retirement of long-term debt.
5. Petty cash fund of $1,000.
6. An I.O.U. from Marianne Koch, a company customer, in the amount of $190,000.
7. A bank overdraft of $110,000 has occurred at one of the banks the company uses to deposit its cash receipts. At the present time, the company has no deposits at this bank.
8. The company has two certificates of deposit, each totaling $500,000. These CDs have a maturity of 120 days.
9. Eastwood has received a check that is dated January 12, 2015, in the amount of $125,000.
10. Eastwood has agreed to maintain a cash balance of $500,000 at all times at First National Bank of Yojimbo to ensure future credit availability.
11. Eastwood has purchased $2,100,000 of commercial paper of Sergio Leone Co. which is due in 60 days.
12. Currency and coin on hand amounted to $7,700.

Instructions

(a) Compute the amount of cash to be reported on Eastwood Co.'s balance sheet at December 31, 2014.
(b) Indicate the proper reporting for items that are not reported as cash on the December 31, 2014, balance sheet.

E7-2 (Determining Cash Balance) Presented below are a number of independent situations.

Instructions

For each individual situation, determine the amount that should be reported as cash. If the item(s) is not reported as cash, explain the rationale.

1. Checking account balance $925,000; certificate of deposit $1,400,000; cash advance to subsidiary of $980,000; utility deposit paid to gas company $180.
2. Checking account balance $600,000; an overdraft in special checking account at same bank as normal checking account of $17,000; cash held in a bond sinking fund $200,000; petty cash fund $300; coins and currency on hand $1,350.
3. Checking account balance $590,000; postdated check from customer $11,000; cash restricted due to maintaining compensating balance requirement of $100,000; certified check from customer $9,800; postage stamps on hand $620.
4. Checking account balance at bank $37,000; money market balance at mutual fund (has checking privileges) $48,000; NSF check received from customer $800.
5. Checking account balance $700,000; cash restricted for future plant expansion $500,000; short-term Treasury bills $180,000; cash advance received from customer $900 (not included in checking account balance); cash advance of $7,000 to company executive, payable on demand; refundable deposit of $26,000 paid to federal government to guarantee performance on construction contract.

E7-3 (Financial Statement Presentation of Receivables) Jim Carrie Company shows a balance of $181,140 in the Accounts Receivable account on December 31, 2013. The balance consists of the following.

Installment accounts due in 2014	$23,000
Installment accounts due after 2014	34,000
Overpayments to vendors	2,640
Due from regular customers, of which $40,000 represents	
accounts pledged as security for a bank loan	79,000
Advances to employees	1,500
Advance to subsidiary company (due in 2015)	81,000

Instructions

Illustrate how the information above should be shown on the balance sheet of Jim Carrie Company on December 31, 2013.

E7-4 (Determining Ending Accounts Receivable) Your accounts receivable clerk, Mitra Adams, to whom you pay a salary of $1,500 per month, has just purchased a new Acura. You decided to test the accuracy of the accounts receivable balance of $82,000 as shown in the ledger.

The following information is available for your *first year* in business.

(1) Collections from customers	$198,000
(2) Merchandise purchased	320,000
(3) Ending merchandise inventory	90,000
(4) Goods are marked to sell at 40% above cost	

Instructions

Compute an estimate of the ending balance of accounts receivable from customers that should appear in the ledger and any apparent shortages. Assume that all sales are made on account.

4 ▶ **E7-5 (Recording Sales Gross and Net)** On June 3, Arnold Company sold to Chester Company merchandise having a sale price of $3,000 with terms of 2/10, n/60, f.o.b. shipping point. An invoice totaling $90, terms n/30, was received by Chester on June 8 from John Booth Transport Service for the freight cost. On June 12, the company received a check for the balance due from Chester Company.

Instructions

(a) Prepare journal entries on the Arnold Company books to record all the events noted above under each of the following bases.

(1) Sales and receivables are entered at gross selling price.

(2) Sales and receivables are entered at net of cash discounts.

(b) Prepare the journal entry under basis 2, assuming that Chester Company did not remit payment until July 29.

4 ▶ **E7-6 (Recording Sales Transactions)** Presented below is information from Perez Computers Incorporated.

July	1	Sold $20,000 of computers to Robertson Company with terms 3/15, n/60. Perez uses the gross method to record cash discounts.
	10	Perez received payment from Robertson for the full amount owed from the July transactions.
	17	Sold $200,000 in computers and peripherals to The Clark Store with terms of 2/10, n/30.
	30	The Clark Store paid Perez for its purchase of July 17.

Instructions

Prepare the necessary journal entries for Perez Computers.

5 ▶ **E7-7 (Recording Bad Debts)** Duncan Company reports the following financial information before adjustments.

	Dr.	Cr.
Accounts Receivable	$100,000	
Allowance for Doubtful Accounts		$ 2,000
Sales Revenue (all on credit)		900,000
Sales Returns and Allowances	50,000	

Instructions

Prepare the journal entry to record Bad Debt Expense assuming Duncan Company estimates bad debts at (a) 1% of net sales and (b) 5% of accounts receivable.

5 ▶ **E7-8 (Recording Bad Debts)** At the end of 2014, Aramis Company has accounts receivable of $800,000 and an allowance for doubtful accounts of $40,000. On January 16, 2015, Aramis Company determined that its receivable from Ramirez Company of $6,000 will not be collected, and management authorized its write-off.

Instructions

(a) Prepare the journal entry for Aramis Company to write off the Ramirez receivable.

(b) What is the net realizable value of Aramis Company's accounts receivable before the write-off of the Ramirez receivable?

(c) What is the net realizable value of Aramis Company's accounts receivable after the write-off of the Ramirez receivable?

5 ▶ **E7-9 (Computing Bad Debts and Preparing Journal Entries)** The trial balance before adjustment of Reba McIntyre Inc. shows the following balances.

	Dr.	Cr.
Accounts Receivable	$90,000	
Allowance for Doubtful Accounts	1,750	
Sales Revenue (all on credit)		$680,000

Instructions

Give the entry for estimated bad debts assuming that the allowance is to provide for doubtful accounts on the basis of (a) 4% of gross accounts receivable and (b) 1% of net sales.

5 ▶ **E7-10 (Bad-Debt Reporting)** The chief accountant for Dickinson Corporation provides you with the following list of accounts receivable written off in the current year.

Date	Customer	Amount
March 31	E. L. Masters Company	$7,800
June 30	Stephen Crane Associates	6,700
September 30	Amy Lowell's Dress Shop	7,000
December 31	R. Frost, Inc.	9,830

Dickinson Corporation follows the policy of debiting Bad Debt Expense as accounts are written off. The chief accountant maintains that this procedure is appropriate for financial statement purposes because the Internal Revenue Service will not accept other methods for recognizing bad debts.

All of Dickinson Corporation's sales are on a 30-day credit basis. Sales for the current year total $2,200,000, and research has determined that bad debt losses approximate 2% of sales.

Instructions

(a) Do you agree or disagree with Dickinson's policy concerning recognition of bad debt expense? Why or why not?

(b) By what amount would net income differ if bad debt expense was computed using the percentage-of-sales approach?

E7-11 (Bad Debts—Aging) Danica Patrick, Inc. includes the following account among its trade receivables.

	Hopkins Co.				
1/1	Balance forward	700	1/28	Cash (#1710)	1,100
1/20	Invoice #1710	1,100	4/2	Cash (#2116)	1,350
3/14	Invoice #2116	1,350	4/10	Cash (1/1 Balance)	155
4/12	Invoice #2412	1,710	4/30	Cash (#2412)	1,000
9/5	Invoice #3614	490	9/20	Cash (#3614 and	
10/17	Invoice #4912	860		part of #2412)	790
11/18	Invoice #5681	2,000	10/31	Cash (#4912)	860
12/20	Invoice #6347	800	12/1	Cash (#5681)	1,250
			12/29	Cash (#6347)	800

Instructions

Age the balance and specify any items that apparently require particular attention at year-end.

E7-12 (Journalizing Various Receivable Transactions) Presented below is information related to James Garfield Corp.

July 1 James Garfield Corp. sold to Warren Harding Co. merchandise having a sales price of $8,000 with terms 2/10, net/60. Garfield records its sales and receivables net.

5 Accounts receivable of $9,000 (gross) are factored with Andrew Jackson Credit Corp. without recourse at a financing charge of 9%. Cash is received for the proceeds; collections are handled by the finance company. (These accounts were all past the discount period.)

9 Specific accounts receivable of $9,000 (gross) are pledged to Alf Landon Credit Corp. as security for a loan of $6,000 at a finance charge of 6% of the amount of the loan. The finance company will make the collections. (All the accounts receivable are past the discount period.)

Dec. 29 Warren Harding Co. notifies Garfield that it is bankrupt and will pay only 10% of its account. Give the entry to write off the uncollectible balance using the allowance method. (*Note*: First record the increase in the receivable on July 11 when the discount period passed.)

Instructions

Prepare all necessary entries in general journal form for Garfield Corp.

E7-13 (Assigning Accounts Receivable) On April 1, 2014, Rasheed Company assigns $400,000 of its accounts receivable to the Third National Bank as collateral for a $200,000 loan due July 1, 2014. The assignment agreement calls for Rasheed Company to continue to collect the receivables. Third National Bank assesses a finance charge of 2% of the accounts receivable, and interest on the loan is 10% (a realistic rate of interest for a note of this type).

Instructions

(a) Prepare the April 1, 2014, journal entry for Rasheed Company.

(b) Prepare the journal entry for Rasheed's collection of $350,000 of the accounts receivable during the period from April 1, 2014, through June 30, 2014.

(c) On July 1, 2014, Rasheed paid Third National all that was due from the loan it secured on April 1, 2014. Prepare the journal entry to record this payment.

5 8 **E7-14 (Journalizing Various Receivable Transactions)** The trial balance before adjustment for Phil Collins Company shows the following balances.

	Dr.	Cr.
Accounts Receivable	$82,000	
Allowance for Doubtful Accounts	2,120	
Sales Revenue		$430,000

Instructions

Using the data above, give the journal entries required to record each of the following cases. (Each situation is independent.)

1. To obtain additional cash, Collins factors without recourse $25,000 of accounts receivable with Stills Finance. The finance charge is 10% of the amount factored.
2. To obtain a 1-year loan of $55,000, Collins assigns $65,000 of specific receivable accounts to Crosby Financial. The finance charge is 8% of the loan; the cash is received and the accounts turned over to Crosby Financial.
3. The company wants to maintain the Allowance for Doubtful Accounts at 5% of gross accounts receivable.
4. The company wishes to increase the allowance account by 1½% of net sales.

8 **E7-15 (Transfer of Receivables with Recourse)** Ames Quartet Inc. factors receivables with a carrying amount of $200,000 to Joffrey Company for $160,000 on a with recourse basis.

Instructions

The recourse provision has a fair value of $1,000. This transaction should be recorded as a sale. Prepare the appropriate journal entry to record this transaction on the books of Ames Quartet Inc.

8 **E7-16 (Transfer of Receivables with Recourse)** Beyoncé Corporation factors $175,000 of accounts receivable with Kathleen Battle Financing, Inc. on a with recourse basis. Kathleen Battle Financing will collect the receivables. The receivables records are transferred to Kathleen Battle Financing on August 15, 2014. Kathleen Battle Financing assesses a finance charge of 2% of the amount of accounts receivable and also reserves an amount equal to 4% of accounts receivable to cover probable adjustments.

Instructions

(a) What conditions must be met for a transfer of receivables with recourse to be accounted for as a sale?
(b) Assume the conditions from part (a) are met. Prepare the journal entry on August 15, 2014, for Beyoncé to record the sale of receivables, assuming the recourse obligation has a fair value of $2,000.

8 **E7-17 (Transfer of Receivables without Recourse)** JFK Corp. factors $300,000 of accounts receivable with LBJ Finance Corporation on a without recourse basis on July 1, 2014. The receivables records are transferred to LBJ Finance, which will receive the collections. LBJ Finance assesses a finance charge of 1½% of the amount of accounts receivable and retains an amount equal to 4% of accounts receivable to cover sales discounts, returns, and allowances. The transaction is to be recorded as a sale.

Instructions

(a) Prepare the journal entry on July 1, 2014, for JFK Corp. to record the sale of receivables without recourse.
(b) Prepare the journal entry on July 1, 2014, for LBJ Finance Corporation to record the purchase of receivables without recourse.

6 **E7-18 (Note Transactions at Unrealistic Interest Rates)** On July 1, 2014, Agincourt Inc. made two sales.

1. It sold land having a fair value of $700,000 in exchange for a 4-year zero-interest-bearing promissory note in the face amount of $1,101,460. The land is carried on Agincourt's books at a cost of $590,000.
2. It rendered services in exchange for a 3%, 8-year promissory note having a face value of $400,000 (interest payable annually).

Agincourt Inc. recently had to pay 8% interest for money that it borrowed from British National Bank. The customers in these two transactions have credit ratings that require them to borrow money at 12% interest.

Instructions

Record the two journal entries that should be recorded by Agincourt Inc. for the sales transactions above that took place on July 1, 2014.

6 7 **E7-19 (Notes Receivable with Unrealistic Interest Rate)** On December 31, 2012, Ed Abbey Co. performed environmental consulting services for Hayduke Co. Hayduke was short of cash, and Abbey Co. agreed to accept a $200,000 zero-interest-bearing note due December 31, 2014, as payment in full. Hayduke is somewhat of a credit risk and typically borrows funds at a rate of 10%. Abbey is much more creditworthy and has various lines of credit at 6%.

Instructions

(a) Prepare the journal entry to record the transaction of December 31, 2012, for the Ed Abbey Co.

(b) Assuming Ed Abbey Co.'s fiscal year-end is December 31, prepare the journal entry for December 31, 2013.

(c) Assuming Ed Abbey Co.'s fiscal year-end is December 31, prepare the journal entry for December 31, 2014.

9 **E7-20 (Analysis of Receivables)** Presented below is information for Jones Company.

1. Beginning-of-the-year Accounts Receivable balance was $15,000.
2. Net sales (all on account) for the year were $100,000. Jones does not offer cash discounts.
3. Collections on accounts receivable during the year were $70,000.

Instructions

(a) Prepare (summary) journal entries to record the items noted above.

(b) Compute Jones's accounts receivable turnover for the year. The company does not believe it will have any bad debts.

(c) Use the turnover ratio computed in (b) to analyze Jones's liquidity. The turnover ratio last year was 6.0.

8 **E7-21 (Transfer of Receivables)** Use the information for Jones Company as presented in E7-20. Jones is planning to factor some accounts receivable at the end of the year. Accounts totaling $25,000 will be transferred to Credit Factors, Inc. with recourse. Credit Factors will retain 5% of the balances for probable adjustments and assesses a finance charge of 4%. The fair value of the recourse obligation is $1,200.

Instructions

(a) Prepare the journal entry to record the sale of the receivables.

(b) Compute Jones's accounts receivable turnover for the year, assuming the receivables are sold, and discuss how factoring of receivables affects the turnover ratio.

10 ***E7-22 (Petty Cash)** Carolyn Keene, Inc. decided to establish a petty cash fund to help ensure internal control over its small cash expenditures. The following information is available for the month of April.

1. On April 1, it established a petty cash fund in the amount of $200.
2. A summary of the petty cash expenditures made by the petty cash custodian as of April 10 is as follows.

Delivery charges paid on merchandise purchased	$60.00
Supplies purchased and used	25.00
Postage expense	33.00
I.O.U. from employees	17.00
Miscellaneous expense	36.00

The petty cash fund was replenished on April 10. The balance in the fund was $27.

3. The petty cash fund balance was increased $100 to $300 on April 20.

Instructions

Prepare the journal entries to record transactions related to petty cash for the month of April.

10 ***E7-23 (Petty Cash)** The petty cash fund of Fonzarelli's Auto Repair Service, a sole proprietorship, contains the following.

1. Coins and currency		$ 15.20
2. Postage stamps		2.90
3. An I.O.U. from Richie Cunningham, an employee, for cash advance		40.00
4. Check payable to Fonzarelli's Auto Repair from Pottsie Weber, an employee, marked NSF		34.00
5. Vouchers for the following:		
Stamps	$ 20.00	
Two Rose Bowl tickets for Nick Fonzarelli	170.00	
Printer cartridge	14.35	204.35
		$296.45

The general ledger account Petty Cash has a balance of $300.

Instructions

Prepare the journal entry to record the reimbursement of the petty cash fund.

10 *E7-24 (**Bank Reconciliation and Adjusting Entries**) Angela Lansbury Company deposits all receipts and makes all payments by check. The following information is available from the cash records.

June 30 Bank Reconciliation

Balance per bank	$ 7,000
Add: Deposits in transit	1,540
Deduct: Outstanding checks	(2,000)
Balance per books	$ 6,540

Month of July Results

	Per Bank	Per Books
Balance July 31	$8,650	$9,250
July deposits	5,000	5,810
July checks	4,000	3,100
July note collected (not included in July deposits)	1,000	—
July bank service charge	15	—
July NSF check from a customer, returned by the bank (recorded by bank as a charge)	335	—

Instructions

(a) Prepare a bank reconciliation going from balance per bank and balance per book to correct cash balance.

(b) Prepare the general journal entry or entries to correct the Cash account.

10 *E7-25 (**Bank Reconciliation and Adjusting Entries**) Logan Bruno Company has just received the August 31, 2014, bank statement, which is summarized below.

County National Bank	Disbursements	Receipts	Balance
Balance, August 1			$ 9,369
Deposits during August		$32,200	41,569
Note collected for depositor, including $40 interest		1,040	42,609
Checks cleared during August	$34,500		8,109
Bank service charges	20		8,089
Balance, August 31			8,089

The general ledger Cash account contained the following entries for the month of August.

Cash

Balance, August 1	10,050	Disbursements in August	34,903
Receipts during August	35,000		

Deposits in transit at August 31 are $3,800, and checks outstanding at August 31 total $1,050. Cash on hand at August 31 is $310. The bookkeeper improperly entered one check in the books at $146.50 which was written for $164.50 for supplies (expense); it cleared the bank during the month of August.

Instructions

(a) Prepare a bank reconciliation dated August 31, 2014, proceeding to a correct balance.

(b) Prepare any entries necessary to make the books correct and complete.

(c) What amount of cash should be reported in the August 31 balance sheet?

11 *E7-26 (**Impairments**) On December 31, 2014, Iva Majoli Company borrowed $62,092 from Paris Bank, signing a 5-year, $100,000 zero-interest-bearing note. The note was issued to yield 10% interest. Unfortunately, during 2016, Majoli began to experience financial difficulty. As a result, at December 31, 2016, Paris Bank determined that it was probable that it would receive back only $75,000 at maturity. The market rate of interest on loans of this nature is now 11%.

Instructions

(a) Prepare the entry to record the issuance of the loan by Paris Bank on December 31, 2014.

(b) Prepare the entry, if any, to record the impairment of the loan on December 31, 2016, by Paris Bank.

11 *E7-27 (Impairments)* On December 31, 2014, Conchita Martinez Company signed a $1,000,000 note to Sauk City Bank. The market interest rate at that time was 12%. The stated interest rate on the note was 10%, payable annually. The note matures in 5 years. Unfortunately, because of lower sales, Conchita Martinez's financial situation worsened. On December 31, 2016, Sauk City Bank determined that it was probable that the company would pay back only $600,000 of the principal at maturity. However, it was considered likely that interest would continue to be paid, based on the $1,000,000 loan.

Instructions

(a) Determine the amount of cash Conchita Martinez received from the loan on December 31, 2014.
(b) Prepare a note amortization schedule for Sauk City Bank up to December 31, 2016.
(c) Determine the loss on impairment that Sauk City Bank should recognize on December 31, 2016.

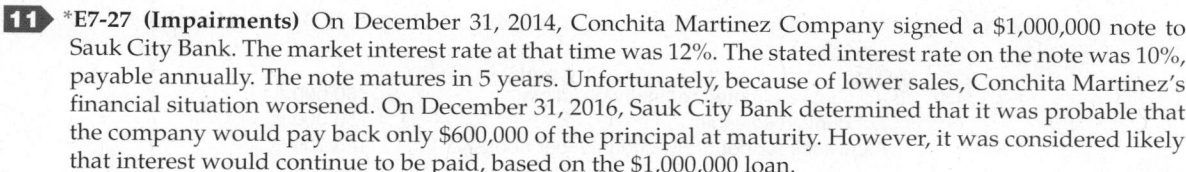

EXERCISES SET B

See the book's companion website, at **www.wiley.com/college/kieso**, for an additional set of exercises.

PROBLEMS

2 **P7-1 (Determine Proper Cash Balance)** Francis Equipment Co. closes its books regularly on December 31, but at the end of 2014 it held its cash book open so that a more favorable balance sheet could be prepared for credit purposes. Cash receipts and disbursements for the first 10 days of January were recorded as December transactions. The information is given below.

1. January cash receipts recorded in the December cash book totaled $45,640, of which $28,000 represents cash sales, and $17,640 represents collections on account for which cash discounts of $360 were given.
2. January cash disbursements recorded in the December check register liquidated accounts payable of $22,450 on which discounts of $250 were taken.
3. The ledger has not been closed for 2014.
4. The amount shown as inventory was determined by physical count on December 31, 2014.

The company uses the periodic method of inventory.

Instructions

(a) Prepare any entries you consider necessary to correct Francis's accounts at December 31.
(b) To what extent was Francis Equipment Co. able to show a more favorable balance sheet at December 31 by holding its cash book open? (Compute working capital and the current ratio.) Assume that the balance sheet that was prepared by the company showed the following amounts:

	Dr.	Cr.
Cash	$39,000	
Accounts receivable	42,000	
Inventory	67,000	
Accounts payable		$45,000
Other current liabilities		14,200

5 **P7-2 (Bad-Debt Reporting)** The following are a series of unrelated situations.

1. Halen Company's unadjusted trial balance at December 31, 2014, included the following accounts.

	Debit	Credit
Allowance for doubtful accounts	$4,000	
Net sales		$1,200,000

Halen Company estimates its bad debt expense to be 1½% of net sales. Determine its bad debt expense for 2014.

2. An analysis and aging of Stuart Corp. accounts receivable at December 31, 2014, disclosed the following.

Amounts estimated to be uncollectible	$ 180,000
Accounts receivable	1,750,000
Allowance for doubtful accounts (per books)	125,000

What is the net realizable value of Stuart's receivables at December 31, 2014?

3. Shore Co. provides for doubtful accounts based on 3% of credit sales. The following data are available for 2014.

Credit sales during 2014	$2,400,000
Allowance for doubtful accounts 1/1/14	17,000
Collection of accounts written off in prior years	
(customer credit was reestablished)	8,000
Customer accounts written off as uncollectible during 2014	30,000

What is the balance in Allowance for Doubtful Accounts at December 31, 2014?

4. At the end of its first year of operations, December 31, 2014, Darden Inc. reported the following information.

Accounts receivable, net of allowance for doubtful accounts	$950,000
Customer accounts written off as uncollectible during 2014	24,000
Bad debt expense for 2014	84,000

What should be the balance in accounts receivable at December 31, 2014, before subtracting the allowance for doubtful accounts?

5. The following accounts were taken from Bullock Inc.'s trial balance at December 31, 2014.

	Debit	Credit
Net credit sales		$750,000
Allowance for doubtful accounts	$ 14,000	
Accounts receivable	310,000	

If doubtful accounts are 3% of accounts receivable, determine the bad debt expense to be reported for 2014.

Instructions

Answer the questions relating to each of the five independent situations as requested.

5 **P7-3 (Bad-Debt Reporting—Aging)** Manilow Corporation operates in an industry that has a high rate of bad debts. Before any year-end adjustments, the balance in Manilow's Accounts Receivable account was $555,000 and Allowance for Doubtful Accounts had a credit balance of $40,000. The year-end balance reported in the balance sheet for Allowance for Doubtful Accounts will be based on the aging schedule shown below.

Days Account Outstanding	Amount	Probability of Collection
Less than 16 days	$300,000	.98
Between 16 and 30 days	100,000	.90
Between 31 and 45 days	80,000	.85
Between 46 and 60 days	40,000	.80
Between 61 and 75 days	20,000	.55
Over 75 days	15,000	.00

Instructions

(a) What is the appropriate balance for Allowance for Doubtful Accounts at year-end?

(b) Show how accounts receivable would be presented on the balance sheet.

(c) What is the dollar effect of the year-end bad debt adjustment on the before-tax income?

(CMA adapted)

5 **P7-4 (Bad-Debt Reporting)** From inception of operations to December 31, 2014, Fortner Corporation provided for uncollectible accounts receivable under the allowance method. Provisions were made monthly at 2% of credit sales, bad debts written off were charged to the allowance account; recoveries of bad debts previously written off were credited to the allowance account, and no year-end adjustments to the allowance account were made. Fortner's usual credit terms are net 30 days.

The balance in Allowance for Doubtful Accounts was $130,000 at January 1, 2014. During 2014, credit sales totaled $9,000,000, interim provisions for doubtful accounts were made at 2% of credit sales, $90,000 of bad debts were written off, and recoveries of accounts previously written off amounted to $15,000. Fortner installed a computer system in November 2014, and an aging of accounts receivable was prepared for the first time as of December 31, 2014. A summary of the aging is as follows.

Classification by Month of Sale	Balance in Each Category	Estimated % Uncollectible
November–December 2014	$1,080,000	2%
July–October	650,000	10%
January–June	420,000	25%
Prior to 1/1/14	150,000	80%
	$2,300,000	

Based on the review of collectibility of the account balances in the "prior to 1/1/14" aging category, additional receivables totaling $60,000 were written off as of December 31, 2014. The 80% uncollectible estimate applies to the remaining $90,000 in the category. Effective with the year ended December 31, 2014, Fortner adopted a different method for estimating the allowance for doubtful accounts at the amount indicated by the year-end aging analysis of accounts receivable.

Instructions

(a) Prepare a schedule analyzing the changes in Allowance for Doubtful Accounts for the year ended December 31, 2014. Show supporting computations in good form. (*Hint:* In computing the 12/31/14 allowance, subtract the $60,000 write-off.)

(b) Prepare the journal entry for the year-end adjustment to Allowance for Doubtful Accounts balance as of December 31, 2014.

(AICPA adapted)

5 **P7-5 (Bad-Debt Reporting)** Presented below is information related to the Accounts Receivable accounts of Gulistan Inc. during the current year 2014.

1. An aging schedule of the accounts receivable as of December 31, 2014, is as follows.

Age	Net Debit Balance	% to Be Applied after Correction Is Made
Under 60 days	$172,342	1%
60–90 days	136,490	3%
91–120 days	39,924*	6%
Over 120 days	23,644	$3,700 definitely uncollectible; estimated remainder uncollectible is 25%
	$372,400	

*The $3,240 write-off of receivables is related to the 91-to-120 day category.

2. The Accounts Receivable control account has a debit balance of $372,400 on December 31, 2014.
3. Two entries were made in the Bad Debt Expense account during the year: (1) a debit on December 31 for the amount credited to Allowance for Doubtful Accounts, and (2) a credit for $3,240 on November 3, 2014, and a debit to Allowance for Doubtful Accounts because of a bankruptcy.
4. Allowance for Doubtful Accounts is as follows for 2014.

	Allowance for Doubtful Accounts				
Nov. 3	Uncollectible accounts written off	3,240	Jan. 1	Beginning balance	8,750
			Dec. 31	5% of $372,400	18,620

5. A credit balance exists in Accounts Receivable (60–90 days) of $4,840, which represents an advance on a sales contract.

Instructions

Assuming that the books have not been closed for 2014, make the necessary correcting entries.

3 4 5 **P7-6 (Journalize Various Accounts Receivable Transactions)** The balance sheet of Starsky Company at December 31, 2013, includes the following.

Notes receivable	$ 36,000	
Accounts receivable	182,100	
Less: Allowance for doubtful accounts	17,300	$200,800

Transactions in 2014 include the following.

1. Accounts receivable of $138,000 were collected including accounts of $60,000 on which 2% sales discounts were allowed.
2. $5,300 was received in payment of an account which was written off the books as worthless in 2013.
3. Customer accounts of $17,500 were written off during the year.
4. At year-end, Allowance for Doubtful Accounts was estimated to need a balance of $20,000. This estimate is based on an analysis of aged accounts receivable.

Instructions

Prepare all journal entries necessary to reflect the transactions above.

8 ▶ P7-7 (Assigned Accounts Receivable—Journal Entries) Salen Company finances some of its current operations by assigning accounts receivable to a finance company. On July 1, 2014, it assigned, under guarantee, specific accounts amounting to $150,000. The finance company advanced to Salen 80% of the accounts assigned (20% of the total to be withheld until the finance company has made its full recovery), less a finance charge of ½% of the total accounts assigned.

On July 31, Salen Company received a statement that the finance company had collected $80,000 of these accounts and had made an additional charge of ½% of the total accounts outstanding as of July 31. This charge is to be deducted at the time of the first remittance due Salen Company from the finance company. (*Hint:* Make entries at this time.) On August 31, 2014, Salen Company received a second statement from the finance company, together with a check for the amount due. The statement indicated that the finance company had collected an additional $50,000 and had made a further charge of ½% of the balance outstanding as of August 31.

Instructions

Make all entries on the books of Salen Company that are involved in the transactions above.

(AICPA adapted)

6 ▶ P7-8 (Notes Receivable with Realistic Interest Rate) On October 1, 2014, Arden Farm Equipment Company sold a pecan-harvesting machine to Valco Brothers Farm, Inc. In lieu of a cash payment Valco Brothers Farm gave Arden a 2-year, $120,000, 8% note (a realistic rate of interest for a note of this type). The note required interest to be paid annually on October 1. Arden's financial statements are prepared on a calendar-year basis.

Instructions

Assuming Valco Brothers Farm fulfills all the terms of the note, prepare the necessary journal entries for Arden Farm Equipment Company for the entire term of the note.

6 ▶ P7-9 (Notes Receivable Journal Entries) On December 31, 2014, Oakbrook Inc. rendered services to Beghun Corporation at an agreed price of $102,049, accepting $40,000 down and agreeing to accept the balance in four equal installments of $20,000 receivable each December 31. An assumed interest rate of 11% is imputed.

Instructions

Prepare the entries that would be recorded by Oakbrook Inc. for the sale and for the receipts and interest on the following dates. (Assume that the effective-interest method is used for amortization purposes.)

(a) December 31, 2014. (c) December 31, 2016. (e) December 31, 2018.
(b) December 31, 2015. (d) December 31, 2017.

6 ▶ P7-10 (Comprehensive Receivables Problem) Braddock Inc. had the following long-term receivable account balances at December 31, 2013.

Note receivable from sale of division	$1,500,000
Note receivable from officer	400,000

Transactions during 2014 and other information relating to Braddock's long-term receivables were as follows.

1. The $1,500,000 note receivable is dated May 1, 2013, bears interest at 9%, and represents the balance of the consideration received from the sale of Braddock's electronics division to New York Company. Principal payments of $500,000 plus appropriate interest are due on May 1, 2014, 2015, and 2016. The first principal and interest payment was made on May 1, 2014. Collection of the note installments is reasonably assured.
2. The $400,000 note receivable is dated December 31, 2013, bears interest at 8%, and is due on December 31, 2016. The note is due from Sean May, president of Braddock Inc. and is collateralized by 10,000 shares of Braddock's common stock. Interest is payable annually on December 31, and all interest payments were paid on their due dates through December 31, 2014. The quoted market price of Braddock's common stock was $45 per share on December 31, 2014.

3. On April 1, 2014, Braddock sold a patent to Pennsylvania Company in exchange for a $100,000 zero-interest-bearing note due on April 1, 2016. There was no established exchange price for the patent, and the note had no ready market. The prevailing rate of interest for a note of this type at April 1, 2014, was 12%. The present value of $1 for two periods at 12% is 0.797 (use this factor). The patent had a carrying value of $40,000 at January 1, 2014, and the amortization for the year ended December 31, 2014, would have been $8,000. The collection of the note receivable from Pennsylvania is reasonably assured.

4. On July 1, 2014, Braddock sold a parcel of land to Splinter Company for $200,000 under an installment sale contract. Splinter made a $60,000 cash down payment on July 1, 2014, and signed a 4-year 11% note for the $140,000 balance. The equal annual payments of principal and interest on the note will be $45,125 payable on July 1, 2015, through July 1, 2018. The land could have been sold at an established cash price of $200,000. The cost of the land to Braddock was $150,000. Circumstances are such that the collection of the installments on the note is reasonably assured.

Instructions

(a) Prepare the long-term receivables section of Braddock's balance sheet at December 31, 2014.

(b) Prepare a schedule showing the current portion of the long-term receivables and accrued interest receivable that would appear in Braddock's balance sheet at December 31, 2014.

(c) Prepare a schedule showing interest revenue from the long-term receivables that would appear on Braddock's income statement for the year ended December 31, 2014.

8 9 P7-11 (Income Effects of Receivables Transactions) Sandburg Company requires additional cash for its business. Sandburg has decided to use its accounts receivable to raise the additional cash and has asked you to determine the income statement effects of the following contemplated transactions.

1. On July 1, 2014, Sandburg assigned $400,000 of accounts receivable to Keller Finance Company. Sandburg received an advance from Keller of 80% of the assigned accounts receivable less a commission of 3% on the advance. Prior to December 31, 2014, Sandburg collected $220,000 on the assigned accounts receivable, and remitted $232,720 to Keller, $12,720 of which represented interest on the advance from Keller.

2. On December 1, 2014, Sandburg sold $300,000 of net accounts receivable to Wunsch Company for $270,000. The receivables were sold outright on a without recourse basis.

3. On December 31, 2014, an advance of $120,000 was received from First Bank by pledging $160,000 of Sandburg's accounts receivable. Sandburg's first payment to First Bank is due on January 30, 2015.

Instructions

Prepare a schedule showing the income statement effects for the year ended December 31, 2014, as a result of the above facts.

10 *P7-12 (Petty Cash, Bank Reconciliation) Bill Jovi is reviewing the cash accounting for Nottleman, Inc., a local mailing service. Jovi's review will focus on the petty cash account and the bank reconciliation for the month ended May 31, 2014. He has collected the following information from Nottleman's bookkeeper for this task.

Petty Cash

1. The petty cash fund was established on May 10, 2014, in the amount of $250.
2. Expenditures from the fund by the custodian as of May 31, 2014, were evidenced by approved receipts for the following.

Postage expense	$33.00
Mailing labels and other supplies	65.00
I.O.U. from employees	30.00
Shipping charges (to customer)	57.45
Newspaper advertising	22.80
Miscellaneous expense	15.35

On May 31, 2014, the petty cash fund was replenished and increased to $300; currency and coin in the fund at that time totaled $26.40.

Bank Reconciliation

THIRD NATIONAL BANK BANK STATEMENT			
	Disbursements	Receipts	Balance
Balance, May 1, 2014			$8,769
Deposits		$28,000	
Note payment direct from customer (interest of $30)		930	
Checks cleared during May	$31,150		
Bank service charges	27		
Balance, May 31, 2014			6,522

Nottleman's Cash Account

Balance, May 1, 2014	$ 8,850
Deposits during May 2014	31,000
Checks written during May 2014	(31,835)

Deposits in transit are determined to be $3,000, and checks outstanding at May 31 total $850. Cash on hand (besides petty cash) at May 31, 2014, is $246.

Instructions

(a) Prepare the journal entries to record the transactions related to the petty cash fund for May.

(b) Prepare a bank reconciliation dated May 31, 2014, proceeding to a correct cash balance, and prepare the journal entries necessary to make the books correct and complete.

(c) What amount of cash should be reported in the May 31, 2014, balance sheet?

10 *P7-13 **(Bank Reconciliation and Adjusting Entries)** The cash account of Aguilar Co. showed a ledger balance of $3,969.85 on June 30, 2014. The bank statement as of that date showed a balance of $4,150. Upon comparing the statement with the cash records, the following facts were determined.

1. There were bank service charges for June of $25.
2. A bank memo stated that Bao Dai's note for $1,200 and interest of $36 had been collected on June 29, and the bank had made a charge of $5.50 on the collection. (No entry had been made on Aguilar's books when Bao Dai's note was sent to the bank for collection.)
3. Receipts for June 30 for $3,390 were not deposited until July 2.
4. Checks outstanding on June 30 totaled $2,136.05.
5. The bank had charged the Aguilar Co.'s account for a customer's uncollectible check amounting to $253.20 on June 29.
6. A customer's check for $90 had been entered as $60 in the cash receipts journal by Aguilar on June 15.
7. Check no. 742 in the amount of $491 had been entered in the cash journal as $419, and check no. 747 in the amount of $58.20 had been entered as $582. Both checks had been issued to pay for purchases of equipment.

Instructions

(a) Prepare a bank reconciliation dated June 30, 2014, proceeding to a correct cash balance.

(b) Prepare any entries necessary to make the books correct and complete.

10 *P7-14 **(Bank Reconciliation and Adjusting Entries)** Presented below is information related to Haselhof Inc.

Balance per books at October 31, $41,847.85; receipts $173,523.91; disbursements $164,893.54. Balance per bank statement November 30, $56,274.20.

The following checks were outstanding at November 30.

1224	$1,635.29
1230	2,468.30
1232	2,125.15
1233	482.17

Included with the November bank statement and not recorded by the company were a bank debit memo for $27.40 covering bank charges for the month, a debit memo for $372.13 for a customer's check returned and marked NSF, and a credit memo for $1,400 representing bond interest collected by the bank in the name of Haselhof Inc. Cash on hand at November 30 recorded and awaiting deposit amounted to $1,915.40.

Instructions

(a) Prepare a bank reconciliation (to the correct balance) at November 30, for Haselhof Inc. from the information above.

(b) Prepare any journal entries required to adjust the cash account at November 30.

11 *P7-15 **(Loan Impairment Entries)** On January 1, 2014, Botosan Company issued a $1,200,000, 5-year, zero-interest-bearing note to National Organization Bank. The note was issued to yield 8% annual interest. Unfortunately, during 2015 Botosan fell into financial trouble due to increased competition. After reviewing all available evidence on December 31, 2015, National Organization Bank decided that the loan was impaired. Botosan will probably pay back only $800,000 of the principal at maturity.

Instructions

(a) Prepare journal entries for both Botosan Company and National Organization Bank to record the issuance of the note on January 1, 2014. (Round to the nearest $10.)

(b) Assuming that both Botosan Company and National Organization Bank use the effective-interest method to amortize the discount, prepare the amortization schedule for the note.

(c) Under what circumstances can National Organization Bank consider Botosan's note to be impaired?

(d) Compute the loss National Organization Bank will suffer from Botosan's financial distress on December 31, 2015. What journal entries should be made to record this loss?

PROBLEMS SET B

See the book's companion website, at **www.wiley.com/college/kieso**, for an additional set of problems.

CONCEPTS FOR ANALYSIS

CA7-1 (Bad-Debt Accounting) Simms Company has significant amounts of trade accounts receivable. Simms uses the allowance method to estimate bad debts instead of the direct write-off method. During the year, some specific accounts were written off as uncollectible, and some that were previously written off as uncollectible were collected.

Instructions
(a) What are the deficiencies of the direct write-off method?
(b) What are the two basic allowance methods used to estimate bad debts, and what is the theoretical justification for each?
(c) How should Simms account for the collection of the specific accounts previously written off as uncollectible?

CA7-2 (Various Receivable Accounting Issues) Kimmel Company uses the net method of accounting for sales discounts. Kimmel also offers trade discounts to various groups of buyers.

On August 1, 2014, Kimmel sold some accounts receivable on a without recourse basis. Kimmel incurred a finance charge.

Kimmel also has some notes receivable bearing an appropriate rate of interest. The principal and total interest are due at maturity. The notes were received on October 1, 2014, and mature on September 30, 2016. Kimmel's operating cycle is less than one year.

Instructions
(a) **(1)** Using the net method, how should Kimmel account for the sales discounts at the date of sale? What is the rationale for the amount recorded as sales under the net method?
(2) Using the net method, what is the effect on Kimmel's sales revenues and net income when customers do not take the sales discounts?
(b) What is the effect of trade discounts on sales revenues and accounts receivable? Why?
(c) How should Kimmel account for the accounts receivable factored on August 1, 2014? Why?
(d) How should Kimmel account for the note receivable and the related interest on December 31, 2014? Why?

CA7-3 (Bad-Debt Reporting Issues) Clark Pierce conducts a wholesale merchandising business that sells approximately 5,000 items per month with a total monthly average sales value of $250,000. Its annual bad debt rate has been approximately 1½% of sales. In recent discussions with his bookkeeper, Mr. Pierce has become confused by all the alternatives apparently available in handling the Allowance for Doubtful Accounts balance. The following information has been presented to Pierce.

1. An allowance can be set up (a) on the basis of a percentage of sales or (b) on the basis of a valuation of all past due or otherwise questionable accounts receivable. Those considered uncollectible can be charged to such allowance at the close of the accounting period, or specific items can be charged off directly against (1) Gross Sales or to (2) Bad Debt Expense in the year in which they are determined to be uncollectible.
2. Collection agency and legal fees, and so on, incurred in connection with the attempted recovery of bad debts can be charged to (a) Bad Debt Expense, (b) Allowance for Doubtful Accounts, (c) Legal Expense, or (d) Administrative Expense.
3. Debts previously written off in whole or in part but currently recovered can be credited to (a) Other Revenue, (b) Bad Debt Expense, or (c) Allowance for Doubtful Accounts.

Instructions

Which of the foregoing methods would you recommend to Mr. Pierce in regard to (1) allowances and charge-offs, (2) collection expenses, and (3) recoveries? State briefly and clearly the reasons supporting your recommendations.

CA7-4 (Basic Note and Accounts Receivable Transactions)

Part 1: On July 1, 2014, Wallace Company, a calendar-year company, sold special-order merchandise on credit and received in return an interest-bearing note receivable from the customer. Wallace Company will receive interest at the prevailing rate for a note of this type. Both the principal and interest are due in one lump sum on June 30, 2015.

Instructions

When should Wallace Company report interest revenue from the note receivable? Discuss the rationale for your answer.

Part 2: On December 31, 2014, Wallace Company had significant amounts of accounts receivable as a result of credit sales to its customers. Wallace uses the allowance method based on credit sales to estimate bad debts. Past experience indicates that 2% of credit sales normally will not be collected. This pattern is expected to continue.

Instructions

(a) Discuss the rationale for using the allowance method based on credit sales to estimate bad debts. Contrast this method with the allowance method based on the balance in the trade receivables accounts.

(b) How should Wallace Company report the allowance for doubtful accounts on its balance sheet at December 31, 2014? Also, describe the alternatives, if any, for presentation of bad debt expense in Wallace Company's 2014 income statement.

(AICPA adapted)

CA7-5 (Sale of Notes Receivable) Corrs Wholesalers Co. sells industrial equipment for a standard 3-year note receivable. Revenue is recognized at time of sale. Each note is secured by a lien on the equipment and has a face amount equal to the equipment's list price. Each note's stated interest rate is below the customer's market rate at date of sale. All notes are to be collected in three equal annual installments beginning one year after sale. Some of the notes are subsequently sold to a bank with recourse, some are subsequently sold without recourse, and some are retained by Corrs. At year end, Corrs evaluates all outstanding notes receivable and provides for estimated losses arising from defaults.

Instructions

(a) What is the appropriate valuation basis for Corrs's notes receivable at the date it sells equipment?

(b) How should Corrs account for the sale, without recourse, of a February 1, 2014, note receivable sold on May 1, 2014? Why is it appropriate to account for it in this way?

(c) At December 31, 2014, how should Corrs measure and account for the impact of estimated losses resulting from notes receivable that it

(1) Retained and did **not** sell?

(2) Sold to bank with recourse?

(AICPA adapted)

CA7-6 (Zero-Interest-Bearing Note Receivable) On September 30, 2013, Rolen Machinery Co. sold a machine and accepted the customer's zero-interest-bearing note. Rolen normally makes sales on a cash basis. Since the machine was unique, its sales price was not determinable using Rolen's normal pricing practices.

After receiving the first of two equal annual installments on September 30, 2014, Rolen immediately sold the note with recourse. On October 9, 2015, Rolen received notice that the note was dishonored, and it paid all amounts due. At all times prior to default, the note was reasonably expected to be paid in full.

Instructions

(a) (1) How should Rolen determine the sales price of the machine?

(2) How should Rolen report the effects of the zero-interest-bearing note on its income statement for the year ended December 31, 2013? Why is this accounting presentation appropriate?

(b) What are the effects of the sale of the note receivable with recourse on Rolen's income statement for the year ended December 31, 2014, and its balance sheet at December 31, 2014?

(c) How should Rolen account for the effects of the note being dishonored?

CA7-7 (Reporting of Notes Receivable, Interest, and Sale of Receivables) On July 1, 2014, Moresan Company sold special-order merchandise on credit and received in return an interest-bearing note receivable from the customer. Moresan will receive interest at the prevailing rate for a note of this type. Both the principal and interest are due in one lump sum on June 30, 2015.

On September 1, 2014, Moresan sold special-order merchandise on credit and received in return a zero-interest-bearing note receivable from the customer. The prevailing rate of interest for a note of this type is determinable. The note receivable is due in one lump sum on August 31, 2016.

Moresan also has significant amounts of trade accounts receivable as a result of credit sales to its customers. On October 1, 2014, some trade accounts receivable were assigned to Indigo Finance Company on a non-notification (Moresan handles collections) basis for an advance of 75% of their amount at an interest charge of 8% on the balance outstanding.

On November 1, 2014, other trade accounts receivable were sold on a without recourse basis. The factor withheld 5% of the trade accounts receivable factored as protection against sales returns and allowances and charged a finance charge of 3%.

Instructions

(a) How should Moresan determine the interest revenue for 2014 on the:
   (1) Interest-bearing note receivable? Why?
   (2) Zero-interest-bearing note receivable? Why?

(b) How should Moresan report the interest-bearing note receivable and the zero-interest-bearing note receivable on its balance sheet at December 31, 2014?

(c) How should Moresan account for subsequent collections on the trade accounts receivable assigned on October 1, 2014, and the payments to Indigo Finance? Why?

(d) How should Moresan account for the trade accounts receivable factored on November 1, 2014? Why?

(AICPA adapted)

CA7-8 (Accounting for Zero-Interest-Bearing Note) Soon after beginning the year-end audit work on March 10 at Engone Company, the auditor has the following conversation with the controller.

CONTROLLER: The year ended March 31st should be our most profitable in history and, as a consequence, the board of directors has just awarded the officers generous bonuses.

AUDITOR: I thought profits were down this year in the industry, according to your latest interim report.

CONTROLLER: Well, they were down, but 10 days ago we closed a deal that will give us a substantial increase for the year.

AUDITOR: Oh, what was it?

CONTROLLER: Well, you remember a few years ago our former president bought stock in Henderson Enterprises because he had those grandiose ideas about becoming a conglomerate. For 6 years we have not been able to sell this stock, which cost us $3,000,000 and has not paid a nickel in dividends. Thursday we sold this stock to Bimini Inc. for $4,000,000. So, we will have a gain of $700,000 ($1,000,000 pretax) which will increase our net income for the year to $4,000,000, compared with last year's $3,800,000. As far as I know, we'll be the only company in the industry to register an increase in net income this year. That should help the market value of the stock!

AUDITOR: Do you expect to receive the $4,000,000 in cash by March 31st, your fiscal year-end?

CONTROLLER: No. Although Bimini Inc. is an excellent company, they are a little tight for cash because of their rapid growth. Consequently, they are going to give us a $4,000,000 zero-interest-bearing note with payments of $400,000 per year for the next 10 years. The first payment is due on March 31 of next year.

AUDITOR: Why is the note zero-interest-bearing?

CONTROLLER: Because that's what everybody agreed to. Since we don't have any interest-bearing debt, the funds invested in the note do not cost us anything and besides, we were not getting any dividends on the Henderson Enterprises stock.

Instructions

Do you agree with the way the controller has accounted for the transaction? If not, how should the transaction be accounted for?

CA7-9 (Receivables Management) As the manager of the accounts receivable department for Beavis Leather Goods, Ltd., you recently noticed that Kelly Collins, your accounts receivable clerk who is paid $1,200 per month, has been wearing unusually tasteful and expensive clothing. (This is Beavis's first year in business.) This morning, Collins drove up to work in a brand new Lexus.

Naturally suspicious by nature, you decide to test the accuracy of the accounts receivable balance of $192,000 as shown in the ledger. The following information is available for your first year (precisely 9 months ended September 30, 2014) in business.

(1) Collections from customers	$188,000
(2) Merchandise purchased	360,000
(3) Ending merchandise inventory	90,000
(4) Goods are marked to sell at 40% above cost.	

Instructions

Assuming all sales were made on account, compute the ending accounts receivable balance that should appear in the ledger, noting any apparent shortage. Then, draft a memo dated October 3, 2014, to Mark Price, the branch manager, explaining the facts in this situation. Remember that this problem is serious, and you do not want to make hasty accusations.

CA7-10 (Bad-Debt Reporting) Marvin Company is a subsidiary of Hughes Corp. The controller believes that the yearly allowance for doubtful accounts for Marvin should be 2% of net credit sales. Given the recession and the high interest rate environment, the president, nervous that the parent company might expect the subsidiary to sustain its 10% growth rate, suggests that the controller increase the allowance for doubtful accounts to 3% yearly. The president thinks that the lower net income, which reflects a 6% growth rate, will be a more sustainable rate for Marvin Company.

Instructions

(a) In a recessionary environment with tight credit and high interest rates:
   (1) Identify steps Marvin Company might consider to improve the accounts receivable situation.
   (2) Then evaluate each step identified in terms of the risks and costs involved.
(b) Should the controller be concerned with Marvin Company's growth rate in estimating the allowance? Explain your answer.
(c) Does the president's request pose an ethical dilemma for the controller? Give your reasons.

USING YOUR JUDGMENT

FINANCIAL REPORTING

Financial Reporting Problem

P&G The Procter & Gamble Company (P&G)

The financial statements of P&G are presented in Appendix 5B. The company's complete annual report, including the notes to the financial statements, can be accessed at the book's companion website, **www.wiley.com/college/kieso**.

Instructions

Refer to P&G's financial statements and the accompanying notes to answer the following questions.

(a) What criteria does P&G use to classify "Cash and cash equivalents" as reported in its balance sheet?
(b) As of June 30, 2011, what balances did P&G have in cash and cash equivalents? What were the major uses of cash during the year?
(c) P&G reports no allowance for doubtful accounts, suggesting that bad debt expense is not material for this company. Is it reasonable that a company like P&G would not have material bad debt expense? Explain.

Comparative Analysis Case

The Coca-Cola Company and PepsiCo, Inc.

Instructions

Go to the book's companion website and use the information found there to answer the following questions related to The Coca-Cola Company and PepsiCo, Inc.

(a) What were the cash and cash equivalents reported by Coca-Cola and PepsiCo at the end of 2011? What does each company classify as cash equivalents?

(b) What were the accounts receivable (net) for Coca-Cola and PepsiCo at the end of 2011? Which company reports the greater allowance for doubtful accounts (amount and percentage of gross receivable) at the end of 2011?

(c) Assuming that all "net operating revenues" (Coca-Cola) and all "net sales" (PepsiCo) were net *credit* sales, compute the accounts receivable turnover for 2011 for Coca-Cola and PepsiCo; also compute the days outstanding for receivables. What is your evaluation of the difference?

Financial Statement Analysis Cases

Case 1 Occidental Petroleum Corporation

Occidental Petroleum Corporation reported the following information in a recent annual report.

Occidental Petroleum Corporation
Consolidated Balance Sheets
(in millions)

Assets at December 31,	Current year	Prior year
Current assets		
Cash and cash equivalents	$ 683	$ 146
Trade receivables, net of allowances	804	608
Receivables from joint ventures, partnerships, and other	330	321
Inventories	510	491
Prepaid expenses and other	147	307
Total current assets	2,474	1,873
Long-term receivables, net	264	275

Notes to Consolidated Financial Statements

Cash and Cash Equivalents. Cash equivalents consist of highly liquid investments. Cash equivalents totaled approximately $661 million and $116 million at current and prior year-ends, respectively.

Trade Receivables. Occidental has agreement to sell, under a revolving sale program, an undivided percentage ownership interest in a designated pool of non-interest-bearing receivables. Under this program, Occidental serves as the collection agent with respect to the receivables sold. An interest in new receivables is sold as collections are made from customers. The balance sold at current year-end was $360 million.

Instructions

(a) What items other than coin and currency may be included in "cash"?

(b) What items may be included in "cash equivalents"?

(c) What are compensating balance arrangements, and how should they be reported in financial statements?

(d) What are the possible differences between cash equivalents and short-term (temporary) investments?

(e) Assuming that the sale agreement meets the criteria for sale accounting, cash proceeds were $345 million, the carrying value of the receivables sold was $360 million, and the fair value of the recourse liability was $15 million, what was the effect on income from the sale of receivables?

(f) Briefly discuss the impact of the transaction in (e) on Occidental's liquidity.

Case 2 Microsoft Corporation

Microsoft is the leading developer of software in the world. To continue to be successful Microsoft must generate new products, which requires significant amounts of cash. The following is the current asset and current liability information from Microsoft's current balance sheets (in millions). Following the Microsoft data is the current asset and current liability information from Oracle's current balance sheets (in millions). Oracle is another major software developer.

Microsoft Corporation

Balance Sheets (partial)
As of June 30
(in millions)

Current assets	2011	2010
Cash and equivalents	$ 9,610	$ 5,505
Short-term investments	43,162	31,283
Accounts receivable	14,987	13,014
Other	7,159	5,874
Total current assets	$74,918	$55,676
Total current liabilities	$28,774	$26,147

Oracle

Balance Sheets (partial)
As of May 31
(in millions)

Current assets	2011	2010
Cash and equivalents	$16,163	$ 9,914
Short-term investments	12,685	8,555
Receivables	6,628	5,585
Other current assets	3,698	2,950
Total current assets	$39,174	$27,004
Current liabilities	$14,192	$14,691

Part 1 (Cash and Cash Equivalents)

Instructions

(a) What is the definition of a cash equivalent? Give some examples of cash equivalents. How do cash equivalents differ from other types of short-term investments?

(b) Calculate (1) the current ratio and (2) working capital for each company for 2011 and discuss your results.

(c) Is it possible to have too many liquid assets?

Part 2 (Accounts Receivable)

Microsoft provided the following disclosure related to its accounts receivable.

Allowance for Doubtful Accounts. The allowance for doubtful accounts reflects our best estimate of probable losses inherent in the accounts receivable balance. We determine the allowance based on known troubled accounts, historical experience, and other currently available evidence. Activity in the allowance for doubtful accounts is as follows:

(in millions)

Year Ended June 30	Balance at beginning of period	Charged to costs and expenses	Write-offs	Balance at end of period
2009	$153	$360	$(62)	$451
2010	451	45	(121)	375
2011	375	14	(56)	333

Instructions

(a) Compute Microsoft's accounts receivable turnover for 2011 and discuss your results. Microsoft had sales revenue of $69,943 million in 2011.

(b) Reconstruct the summary journal entries for 2011 based on the information in the disclosure.

(c) Briefly discuss how the accounting for bad debts affects the analysis in Part 2 (a).

Accounting, Analysis, and Principles

The Flatiron Pub provides catering services to local businesses. The following information was available for The Flatiron Pub for the years ended December 31, 2013 and 2014.

	December 31, 2013	December 31, 2014
Cash	$ 2,000	$ 1,685
Accounts receivable	46,000	?
Allowance for doubtful accounts	550	?
Other current assets	8,500	7,925
Current liabilities	37,000	44,600
Total credit sales	205,000	255,000
Collections on accounts receivable	190,000	228,000

Flatiron management is preparing for a meeting with its bank concerning renewal of a loan and has collected the following information related to the above balances.

1. The cash reported at December 31, 2014, reflects the following items: petty cash $1,575 and postage stamps $110. The other current assets balance at December 31, 2014, includes the checking account balance of $4,000.

2. On November 30, 2014, Flatiron agreed to accept a 6-month, $5,000 note bearing 12% interest, payable at maturity, from a major client in settlement of a $5,000 bill. The above balances do not reflect this transaction.

3. Flatiron factored some accounts receivable at the end of 2014. It transferred accounts totaling $10,000 to Final Factor, Inc. with recourse. Final Factor will receive the collections from Flatiron's customers and will retain 2% of the balances. Final Factor assesses Flatiron a finance charge of 3% on this transfer. The fair value of the recourse liability is $400. However, management has determined that the amount due from the factor and the fair value of the resource obligation have not been recorded, and neither are included in the balances above.

4. Flatiron charged off uncollectible accounts with balances of $1,600. On the basis of the latest available information, the 2014 provision for bad debts is estimated to be 2.5% of accounts receivable.

Accounting

(a) Based on the above transactions, determine the balance for (1) Accounts Receivable and (2) Allowance for Doubtful Accounts at December 31, 2014.

(b) Prepare the current assets section of The Flatiron Pub's balance sheet at December 31, 2014.

Analysis

(a) Compute Flatiron's current ratio and accounts receivable turnover for December 31, 2014. Use these measures to analyze Flatiron's liquidity. The accounts receivable turnover in 2013 was 4.37.

(b) Discuss how the analysis you did above of Flatiron's liquidity would be affected if Flatiron had transferred the receivables in a secured borrowing transaction.

Principles

What is the conceptual basis for recording bad debt expense based on the percentage-of-receivables approach at December 31, 2014?

BRIDGE TO THE PROFESSION

Professional Research: FASB Codification

As the new staff person in your company's treasury department, you have been asked to conduct research related to a proposed transfer of receivables. Your supervisor wants the authoritative sources for the following items that are discussed in the securitization agreement.

Instructions

If your school has a subscription to the FASB Codification, go to *http://aaahq.org/asclogin.cfm* to log in and prepare responses to the following. Provide Codification references for your responses.

(a) Identify relevant Codification section that addresses transfers of receivables.

(b) What are the objectives for reporting transfers of receivables?

(c) Provide definitions for the following:

   (1) Transfer.

   (2) Recourse.

   (3) Collateral.

(d) Provide other examples (besides recourse and collateral) that qualify as continuing involvement.

Additional Professional Resources

See the book's companion website, at **www.wiley.com/college/kieso**, for professional simulations as well as other study resources.

IFRS INSIGHTS

LEARNING OBJECTIVE 12

Compare the accounting procedures for cash and receivables under GAAP and IFRS.

The basic accounting and reporting issues related to recognition and measurement of receivables, such as the use of allowance accounts, how to record discounts, use of the allowance method to account for bad debts, and factoring, are similar for both IFRS and GAAP. *IAS 1* ("Presentation of Financial Statements") is the only standard that discusses issues specifically related to cash. *IFRS 7* ("Financial Instruments: Disclosure") and *IAS 39* ("Financial Instruments: Recognition and Measurement") are the two international standards that address issues related to financial instruments and more specifically receivables.

RELEVANT FACTS

Following are the key similarities and differences between GAAP and IFRS related to cash and receivables.

Similarities

- The accounting and reporting related to cash is essentially the same under both IFRS and GAAP. In addition, the definition used for cash equivalents is the same.

- Like GAAP, cash and receivables are generally reported in the current assets section of the statement of financial position under IFRS.

- Similar to GAAP, IFRS requires that loans and receivables be accounted for at amortized cost, adjusted for allowances for doubtful accounts. IFRS sometimes refers to these allowances as *provisions*. The entry to record the allowance would be as follows.

Bad Debt Expense	xxxxxx	
Provision for Doubtful Accounts		xxxxxx

Differences

- Under IFRS, companies may report cash and receivables as the last items in current assets under IFRS. Under GAAP, these items are reported in order of liquidity.

- While IFRS implies that receivables with different characteristics should be reported separately, there is no standard that mandates this segregation. GAAP has explicit guidance in the area.

- The fair value option is similar under GAAP and IFRS but not identical. The international standard related to the fair value option is subject to certain qualifying criteria not in the U.S. standard. In addition, there is some difference in the financial instruments covered.

- Under IFRS, bank overdrafts are generally reported as cash. Under GAAP, such balances are reported as liabilities.

- IFRS and GAAP differ in the criteria used to account for transfers of receivables. IFRS is a combination of an approach focused on risks and rewards and loss of control. GAAP uses loss of control as the primary criterion. In addition, IFRS generally permits partial transfers; GAAP does not.

ABOUT THE NUMBERS

Impairment Evaluation Process

IFRS provides detailed guidelines to assess whether receivables should be considered uncollectible (often referred to as *impaired*). GAAP does not identify a specific approach. Under IFRS, companies assess their receivables for impairment each reporting period and start the impairment assessment by considering whether objective evidence indicates that one or more loss events have occurred. Examples of possible loss events are:

- Significant financial problems of the customer.
- Payment defaults.
- Renegotiation of terms of the receivable due to financial difficulty of the customer.
- Measurable decrease in estimated future cash flows from a group of receivables since initial recognition, although the decrease cannot yet be identified with individual assets in the group.

A receivable is considered impaired when a loss event indicates a negative impact on the estimated future cash flows to be received from the customer (*IAS 39*, paragraphs 58–70). The IASB requires that the impairment assessment should be performed as follows.

1. Receivables that are individually significant are considered for impairment separately; if impaired, the company recognizes it. Receivables that are not individually significant may also be assessed individually, but it is not necessary to do so.

2. Any receivable individually assessed that is not considered impaired is included with a group of assets with similar credit-risk characteristics and collectively assessed for impairment.

3. Any receivables **not individually assessed are collectively assessed** for impairment.

To illustrate, assume that Hector Company has the following receivables classified into individually significant and all other receivables.

Individually significant receivables		
Yaan Company	$ 40,000	
Randon Inc.	100,000	
Fernando Co.	60,000	
Blanchard Ltd.	50,000	$250,000
All other receivables		500,000
Total		$750,000

Hector determines that Yaan's receivable is impaired by $15,000, and Blanchard's receivable is totally impaired. Both Randon's and Fernando's receivables are not considered impaired. Hector also determines a composite rate of 2% is appropriate to measure impairment on all other receivables. The total impairment is computed as follows.

Accounts Receivable Impairments		
Individually assessed receivables		
Yaan Company		$15,000
Blanchard Ltd.		50,000
Collectively assessed receivables	$500,000	
Add: Randon Inc.	100,000	
Fernando Co.	60,000	
Total collectively assessed receivables	$660,000	
Collectively assessed impairments ($660,000 × 2%)		13,200
Total impairment		$78,200

Hector therefore has an impairment related to its receivables of $78,200. The most controversial part of this computation is that Hector must include in the collective assessment the receivables from Randon and Fernando that were individually assessed and not considered impaired. The rationale for including Randon and Fernando in the collective assessment is that companies often do not have all the information at hand to make an informed decision for individual assessment.

Recovery of Impairment Loss

The accounting for loan impairments is similar between GAAP and IFRS. Subsequent to recording an impairment, events or economic conditions may change such that the extent of the impairment loss decreases (e.g., due to an impairment in the debtor's credit rating). Under IFRS, some or all of the previously recognized impairment loss shall be reversed either directly, with a debit to Accounts Receivable, or by debiting the allowance account and crediting Bad Debt Expense. Such reversals of impairment losses are not allowed under GAAP.

To illustrate, recall the Ogden Bank impairment example of page 382. In that situation, Ogden Bank (the creditor) recognized an impairment loss of $12,434 by debiting Bad Debt Expense for the expected loss. At the same time, it reduced the overall value of the receivable by crediting Allowance for Doubtful Accounts. Ogden made the following entry to record the loss.

Bad Debt Expense	12,434	
Allowance for Doubtful Accounts		12,434

Now, assume that in the year following the impairment recorded by Ogden, Carl King (the borrower) has worked his way out of financial difficulty. Ogden now expects to receive all payments on the loan according to the original loan terms. Based on this new information, the present value of the expected payments is $100,000. Thus, Ogden makes the following entry to reverse the previously recorded impairment.

Allowance for Doubtful Accounts	12,434	
Bad Debt Expense		12,434

Note that the reversal of impairment losses shall not result in carrying amount of the receivable that exceeds the amortized cost that would have been reported had the impairment not been recognized. Under GAAP, reversal of an impairment is not permitted. Rather, the balance of the loan after the impairment becomes the new basis for the loan.

ON THE HORIZON

The question of recording fair values for financial instruments will continue to be an important issue to resolve as the Boards work toward convergence. Both the IASB and the FASB have indicated that they believe that financial statements would be more transparent and understandable if companies recorded and reported all financial instruments at fair value. That said, in *IFRS 9*, which was issued in 2009, the IASB created a split model, where some financial instruments are recorded at fair value but other financial assets, such as loans and receivables, can be accounted for at amortized cost if certain criteria are met. Critics say that this can result in two companies with identical securities accounting for those securities in different ways. A proposal by the FASB would require that nearly all financial instruments, including loans and receivables, be accounted for at fair value. It has been suggested that *IFRS 9* will likely be changed or replaced as the FASB and IASB continue to deliberate the best treatment for financial instruments. In fact, one member of the IASB said that companies should ignore *IFRS 9* and continue to report under the old standard, because in his opinion, it is extremely likely that it would be changed before the mandatory adoption date of this standard in 2015.

IFRS SELF-TEST QUESTIONS

1. Under IFRS, cash and cash equivalents are reported:
   (a) the same as GAAP.
   (b) as separate items.
   (c) similar to GAAP, except for the reporting of bank overdrafts.
   (d) always as the first items in the current assets section.

2. Under IFRS, receivables are to be reported on the balance sheet at:
   (a) amortized cost.
   (b) amortized cost adjusted for estimated loss provisions.
   (c) historical cost.
   (d) replacement cost.

3. Which of the following statements is **false**?
   (a) Receivables include equity securities purchased by the company.
   (b) Receivables include credit card receivables.
   (c) Receivables include amounts owed by employees as result of company loans to employees.
   (d) Receivables include amounts resulting from transactions with customers.

4. Under IFRS:
   (a) the entry to record estimated uncollected accounts is the same as GAAP.
   (b) loans and receivables should only be tested for impairment as a group.
   (c) it is always acceptable to use the direct write-off method.
   (d) all financial instruments are recorded at fair value.

5. Which of the following statements is **true**?
   (a) The fair value option requires that some types of financial instruments be recorded at fair value.
   (b) The fair value option requires that all noncurrent financial instruments be recorded at amortized cost.
   (c) The fair value option allows, but does not require, that some types of financial instruments be recorded at fair value.
   (d) The FASB and IASB would like to reduce the reliance on fair value accounting for financial instruments in the future.

IFRS CONCEPTS AND APPLICATION

IFRS7-1 Briefly describe the impairment evaluation process and assessment of receivables on an individual or collective basis.

IFRS7-2 What are some steps taken by both the FASB and IASB to move to fair value measurement for financial instruments? In what ways have some of the approaches differed?

IFRS7-3 On December 31, 2014, Firth Company borrowed $62,092 from Paris Bank, signing a 5-year, $100,000 zero-interest-rate note. The note was issued to yield 10% interest. Unfortunately, during 2016, Firth began to experience financial difficulty. As a result, at December 31, 2016, Paris Bank determined that it was probable that it would collect only $75,000 at maturity. The market rate of interest on loans of this nature is now 11%.

Instructions

(a) Prepare the entry (if any) to record the impairment of the loan on December 31, 2016, by Paris Bank.
(b) Prepare the entry on March 31, 2017, if Paris learns that Firth will be able to repay the loan under the original terms.

Professional Research

IFRS7-4 As the new staff person in your company's treasury department, you have been asked to conduct research related to a proposed transfer of receivables. Your supervisor wants the authoritative sources for the following items that are discussed in the receivables transfer agreement.

Instructions

Access the IFRS authoritative literature at the IASB website (*http://eifrs.iasb.org/*). (Click on the IFRS tab and then register for free eIFRS access if necessary.) When you have accessed the documents, you can use the search tool in your Internet browser to prepare responses to the following items. **(a)** Identify relevant IFRSs that address transfers of receivables. **(b)** What are the objectives for reporting transfers of receivables? **(c)** Provide the definition for "Amortized cost."

International Financial Reporting Problem
Marks and Spencer plc

IFRS7-5 The financial statements of **Marks and Spencer plc (M&S)** are available at the book's companion website or can be accessed at *http://annualreport.marksandspencer.com/_assets/downloads/Marks-and-Spencer-Annual-report-and-financial-statements-2012.pdf*.

Instructions
Refer to M&S's financial statements and the accompanying notes to answer the following questions.

(a) What criteria does M&S use to classify "Cash and cash equivalents" as reported in its statement of financial position?
(b) As of 31 March 2012, what balances did M&S have in cash and cash equivalents? What were the major uses of cash during the year?
(c) What amounts related to trade receivables does M&S report? Does M&S have any past due but not impaired receivables?

ANSWERS TO IFRS SELF-TEST QUESTIONS

1. c **2.** b **3.** a **4.** a **5.** c

Remember to check the book's companion website to find additional resources for this chapter.

Valuation of Inventories: A Cost-Basis Approach

To Switch or Not to Switch

Many companies use the last-in, first-out (LIFO) cost flow assumption in the accounting for inventories. LIFO has a lot going for it in terms of tax savings and providing an income number that better reflects the gross profit associated with inventories with different historical costs. However, in the wake of international convergence discussions (LIFO is not permitted under IFRS) and tax policy debates (LIFO is one of a number of "tax loopholes" that if closed could help address our budget and deficit challenges), more companies are seriously considering the switch from LIFO to first-in, first-out (FIFO) or average-cost inventory methods. For example, of the 449 large public companies surveyed by the AICPA in 2012, just 163 indicated LIFO use (a 25% decline relative to 2001). Here are some of the reasons to support the switch from LIFO.

- While many believe that LIFO provides a more useful income measure, other methods, such as FIFO and average-cost, better reflect the current value of inventory on the balance sheet.

- Many companies discontinued LIFO use to support uniformity of inventory valuation across operations. That is, companies were using LIFO in their U.S. operations but FIFO and/or average-cost in international units. The switch from LIFO simplifies the external reporting for these multinational companies.

- There is also a "bandwagon" effect—when some companies make the switch, their peers likely follow suit to enhance comparability for financial statement users.

- The recent periods of low inflation have resulted in less significant tax benefits associated with LIFO use. That is, in times of rising costs, by expensing the most recently purchased items, cost of goods sold is higher (compared to FIFO or average-cost) and taxable income is lower. A number of companies do not believe the smaller tax benefits of LIFO offset the costs. For example, **Kraft Foods** switched from LIFO to average-cost in 2009, noting that in the recent stable price environment, its cost of goods sold was $95 million *higher* under average-cost.

CONCEPTUAL FOCUS

> See the **Underlying Concepts** on pages 422, 425, and 427.
> Read the **Evolving Issue** on page 445 for a discussion of LIFO.

INTERNATIONAL FOCUS

> See the **International Perspectives** on pages 421, 426, 429, 431, and 444.
> **IFRS Insights** related to inventory are presented in Chapter 9 on pages 525–534.

• Finally, the companies most resistant to make the switch from LIFO are those with large inventory balances. That is, the higher the inventory balance, the higher the additional tax payment will be upon the switch to FIFO. However, a growing number of companies have implemented just-in-time (JIT) or other lean manufacturing techniques, under which much lower inventories are kept on hand. In the extreme, JIT leads to zero inventory and no LIFO effect relative to other methods. For example, **JCPenney** recently switched from LIFO to FIFO in the same period that it rolled out its "Door-to-Floor" lean inventory strategy. As a result, the accounting effect of the change to FIFO was immaterial.

The merits of LIFO use (about which you will learn more in this chapter) are many. However, these benefits appear to be waning. We expect more companies to weigh a voluntary switch away from LIFO in the future.

Source: Adapted from L. Hughes, J. Livingstone, and D. Upton, "Switching from LIFO: Strategies for Change," *The CPA Journal* (April 2011), pp. 26–29.

PREVIEW OF CHAPTER **8**

As our opening story indicates, the accounting choice related to inventory is affected by operating strategies, tax consequences, and is important for providing information that is useful for predicting financial performance. In this chapter, we discuss the basic issues related to accounting and reporting for inventory. The content and organization of the chapter are as follows.

Valuation of Inventories: A Cost-Basis Approach

Inventory Issues	Physical Goods Included in Inventory	Costs Included in Inventory	Cost Flow Assumptions	LIFO: Special Issues	Basis for Selection
• Classification • Cost flow • Control • Basic inventory valuation	• Goods in transit • Consigned goods • Special sales agreements • Effect of inventory errors	• Product costs • Period costs • Purchase discounts	• Specific identification • Average-cost • FIFO • LIFO	• LIFO reserve • LIFO liquidation • Dollar-value LIFO • Comparison of LIFO approaches • Advantages of LIFO • Disadvantages of LIFO	• Summary of inventory valuation methods

INVENTORY ISSUES
Classification

Inventories are asset items that a company holds for sale in the ordinary course of business, or goods that it will use or consume in the production of goods to be sold. The description and measurement of inventory require careful attention. The investment in inventories is frequently the largest current asset of merchandising (retail) and manufacturing businesses.

A **merchandising concern**, such as Wal-Mart Stores, Inc., usually purchases its merchandise in a form ready for sale. It reports the cost assigned to unsold units left on hand as **merchandise inventory**. Only one inventory account, Inventory, appears in the financial statements.

Manufacturing concerns, on the other hand, produce goods to sell to merchandising firms. Many of the largest U.S. businesses are manufacturers, such as Boeing, IBM, ExxonMobil, Procter & Gamble, Ford, and Motorola. Although the products they produce may differ, manufacturers normally have three inventory accounts—Raw Materials, Work in Process, and Finished Goods.

A company reports the cost assigned to goods and materials on hand but not yet placed into production as **raw materials inventory**. Raw materials include the wood to make a baseball bat or the steel to make a car. These materials can be traced directly to the end product.

At any point in a continuous production process, some units are only partially processed. The cost of the raw material for these unfinished units, plus the direct labor cost applied specifically to this material and a ratable share of manufacturing overhead costs, constitute the **work in process inventory**.

Companies report the costs identified with the completed but unsold units on hand at the end of the fiscal period as **finished goods inventory**. Illustration 8-1 contrasts the financial statement presentation of inventories of Wal-Mart Stores, Inc. (a merchandising company) with those of Sherwin-Williams Company (a manufacturing company.) The remainder of the balance sheet is essentially similar for the two types of companies.

ILLUSTRATION 8-1
Comparison of Presentation of Current Assets for Merchandising and Manufacturing Companies

Merchandising Company
Wal-Mart Stores, Inc.

Balance Sheet
January 31, 2012

Current assets (in millions)	
Cash and cash equivalents	$ 6,550
Receivables, net	5,937
Inventories	40,714
Prepaid expenses and other	1,774
Total current assets	$54,975

Manufacturing Company
Sherwin-Williams Company

Balance Sheet
December 31, 2011

Current assets (in thousands)		
Cash and cash equivalents		$ 32,696
Accounts receivable, less allowance		989,873
Inventories:		
Finished goods	$730,727	
Work in process and raw materials	196,082	926,809
Deferred income taxes		149,207
Other current assets		163,008
Total current assets		$ 2,261,593

A manufacturing company like Sherwin-Williams also might include a Manufacturing or Factory **Supplies Inventory** account. In it, Sherwin-Williams would include such items as machine oils, nails, cleaning material, and the like—supplies that are used in production but are not the primary materials being processed.

Illustration 8-2 shows the differences in the flow of costs through a merchandising company and a manufacturing company.

ILLUSTRATION 8-2
Flow of Costs through Manufacturing and Merchandising Companies

Inventory Cost Flow

Companies that sell or produce goods report inventory and cost of goods sold at the end of each accounting period. The flow of costs for a company is as follows. Beginning inventory plus the cost of goods purchased is the cost of goods available for sale. As goods are sold, they are assigned to cost of goods sold. Those goods that are not sold by the end of the accounting period represent ending inventory. Illustration 8-3 describes these relationships.

2 LEARNING OBJECTIVE
Distinguish between perpetual and periodic inventory systems.

ILLUSTRATION 8-3
Inventory Cost Flow

Companies use one of two types of systems for maintaining accurate inventory records for these costs—the perpetual system or the periodic system.

Perpetual System

A **perpetual inventory system** continuously tracks changes in the Inventory account. That is, a company records all purchases and sales (issues) of goods directly in the Inventory account **as they occur**. The accounting features of a perpetual inventory system are as follows.

1. Purchases of merchandise for resale or raw materials for production are debited to Inventory rather than to Purchases.

2. Freight-in is debited to Inventory, not Purchases. Purchase returns and allowances and purchase discounts are credited to Inventory rather than to separate accounts.

3. Cost of goods sold is recorded at the time of each sale by debiting Cost of Goods Sold and crediting Inventory.

4. A subsidiary ledger of individual inventory records is maintained as a control measure. The subsidiary records show the quantity and cost of each type of inventory on hand.

The perpetual inventory system provides a continuous record of the balances in both the Inventory account and the Cost of Goods Sold account.

Periodic System

Under a **periodic inventory system**, a company determines the quantity of inventory on hand only periodically, as the name implies. It records all acquisitions of inventory during the accounting period by debiting the Purchases account. A company then adds the total in the Purchases account at the end of the accounting period to the cost of the inventory on hand at the beginning of the period. This sum determines the total cost of the goods available for sale during the period.

To compute the cost of goods sold, the company then subtracts the ending inventory from the cost of goods available for sale. Note that under a periodic inventory system, the cost of goods sold is a residual amount that depends on a physical count of ending inventory. This process is referred to as "taking a physical inventory." Companies that use the periodic system take a physical inventory at least once a year.

Comparing Perpetual and Periodic Systems

To illustrate the difference between a perpetual and a periodic system, assume that Fesmire Company had the following transactions during the current year.

Beginning inventory	100 units at $6 = $ 600
Purchases	900 units at $6 = $5,400
Sales	600 units at $12 = $7,200
Ending inventory	400 units at $6 = $2,400

Fesmire records these transactions during the current year as shown in Illustration 8-4.

When a company uses a perpetual inventory system and a difference exists between the perpetual inventory balance and the physical inventory count, it needs a separate entry to adjust the perpetual inventory account. To illustrate, assume that at the end of the reporting period, the perpetual inventory account reported an inventory balance of $4,000. However, a physical count indicates inventory of $3,800 is actually on hand. The entry to record the necessary write-down is as follows.

Inventory Over and Short	200	
Inventory		200

Perpetual inventory overages and shortages generally represent a misstatement of cost of goods sold. The difference results from normal and expected shrinkage, breakage,

Perpetual Inventory System		Periodic Inventory System	
Beginning inventory, 100 units at $6			
The Inventory account shows the inventory on hand at $600.		The Inventory account shows the inventory on hand at $600.	
Purchase 900 units at $6			
Inventory	5,400	Purchases	5,400
Accounts Payable	5,400	Accounts Payable	5,400
Sale of 600 units at $12			
Accounts Receivable	7,200	Accounts Receivable	7,200
Sales Revenue	7,200	Sales Revenue	7,200
Cost of Goods Sold	3,600	(No entry)	
(600 at $6)			
Inventory	3,600		
End-of-period entries for inventory accounts, 400 units at $6			
No entry necessary.		Inventory (ending, by count)	2,400
The Inventory account shows the ending		Cost of Goods Sold	3,600
balance of $2,400 ($600 + $5,400 − $3,600).		Purchases	5,400
		Inventory (beginning)	600

ILLUSTRATION 8-4
Comparative Entries—
Perpetual vs. Periodic

shoplifting, incorrect recordkeeping, and the like. Inventory Over and Short therefore adjusts Cost of Goods Sold. In practice, companies sometimes report Inventory Over and Short in the "Other revenues and gains" or "Other expenses and losses" section of the income statement.

Note that a company using the periodic inventory system does not report the account Inventory Over and Short. The reason: The periodic method does not have accounting records against which to compare the physical count. As a result, a company buries inventory overages and shortages in cost of goods sold.

Inventory Control

For various reasons, management is vitally interested in inventory planning and control. Whether a company manufactures or merchandises goods, it needs an accurate accounting system with up-to-date records. It may lose sales and customers if it does not stock products in the desired style, quality, and quantity. Further, companies must monitor inventory levels carefully to limit the financing costs of carrying large amounts of inventory.

In a perfect world, companies would like a continuous record of both their inventory levels and their cost of goods sold. The popularity and affordability of accounting software makes the perpetual system cost-effective for many kinds of businesses. Companies like Target, Best Buy, and Sears Holdings now incorporate the recording of sales with optical scanners at the cash register into perpetual inventory systems.

However, many companies cannot afford a complete perpetual system. But, most of these companies need current information regarding their inventory levels, to protect against stock-outs or overpurchasing, and to aid in preparation of monthly or quarterly financial data. As a result, these companies use a **modified perpetual inventory system**. This system provides detailed inventory records of increases and decreases in quantities only—not dollar amounts. It is merely a memorandum device outside the double-entry system, which helps in determining the level of inventory at any point in time.

Whether a company maintains a complete perpetual inventory in quantities and dollars or a modified perpetual inventory system, it probably takes a physical inventory once a year. No matter what type of inventory records companies use, they all face the danger of loss and error. Waste, breakage, theft, improper entry, failure to prepare or record requisitions, and other similar possibilities may cause the inventory records to differ from the actual inventory on hand. Thus, **all companies** need periodic verification of the inventory records by actual count, weight, or measurement, with the counts compared with the detailed inventory records. As indicated earlier, a company corrects the records to agree with the quantities actually on hand.

Insofar as possible, companies should take the physical inventory near the end of their fiscal year, to properly report inventory quantities in their annual accounting reports. Because this is not always possible, however, physical inventories taken within two or three months of the year's end are satisfactory if a company maintains detailed inventory records with a fair degree of accuracy.[1]

What do the numbers mean? *STAYING LEAN*

Wal-Mart Stores, Inc. uses its buying power in the supply chain to purchase an increasing proportion of its goods directly from manufacturers and on a combined basis across geographic borders. Wal-Mart estimates that it saves 5–15% across its supply chain by implementing direct purchasing on a combined basis for the 15 countries in which it operates. Thus, Wal-Mart has a good handle on what products it needs to stock, and it gets the best prices when it purchases.

Wal-Mart also provides a classic example of the use of tight inventory controls. Department managers use a scanner that when placed over the bar code corresponding to a particular item, will tell them how many of the items the store sold yesterday, last week, and over the same period last year. It will tell them how many of those items are in stock, how many are on the way, and how many the neighboring Walmart stores are carrying (in case one store runs out). Wal-Mart's inventory management practices have helped it become one of the top-ranked companies on the Fortune 500 in terms of sales.

Source: J. Birchall, "Walmart Aims to Cut Supply Chain Cost," *Financial Times* (January 4, 2010).

Basic Issues in Inventory Valuation

Goods sold (or used) during an accounting period seldom correspond exactly to the goods bought (or produced) during that period. As a result, inventories either increase or decrease during the period. Companies must then allocate the cost of all the goods available for sale (or use) between the goods that were sold or used and those that are still on hand. The **cost of goods available for sale or use** is the *sum* of (1) the cost of the goods on hand at the beginning of the period, and (2) the cost of the goods acquired or produced during the period. The **cost of goods sold** is the *difference* between (1) the cost of goods available for sale during the period, and (2) the cost of goods on hand at the end of the period. Illustration 8-5 shows these calculations.

ILLUSTRATION 8-5
Computation of Cost of Goods Sold

Beginning inventory, Jan. 1	$100,000
Cost of goods acquired or produced during the year	800,000
Total cost of goods available for sale	900,000
Ending inventory, Dec. 31	(200,000)
Cost of goods sold during the year	$700,000

---

[1]Some companies have developed methods of determining inventories, including statistical sampling, that are sufficiently reliable to make unnecessary an annual physical count of each item of inventory.

Valuing inventories can be complex. It requires determining the following.

1. The physical goods to include in inventory (who owns the goods?—goods in transit, consigned goods, special sales agreements).

2. The costs to include in inventory (product vs. period costs).

3. The cost flow assumption to adopt (specific identification, average-cost, FIFO, LIFO, retail, etc.)

We explore these basic issues in the next three sections.

International Perspective

Who owns the goods, as well as the costs to include in inventory, are essentially accounted for the same under IFRS and GAAP.

PHYSICAL GOODS INCLUDED IN INVENTORY

Technically, a company should record purchases when it obtains legal title to the goods. In practice, however, a company records acquisitions when it receives the goods. Why? Because it is difficult to determine the exact time of legal passage of title for every purchase. In addition, no material error likely results from such a practice if consistently applied. Illustration 8-6 indicates the general guidelines companies use in evaluating whether the seller or buyer reports an item as inventory. Exceptions to the general guidelines can arise for goods in transit and consigned goods.

3 LEARNING OBJECTIVE

Determine the goods included in inventory and the effects of inventory errors on the financial statements.

ILLUSTRATION 8-6
Guidelines for
Determining Ownership

Goods in Transit

Sometimes purchased merchandise remains in transit—not yet received—at the end of a fiscal period. The accounting for these shipped goods depends on who owns them. For example, a company like Walgreens determines ownership by applying the "passage of title" rule. If a supplier ships goods to Walgreens **f.o.b. shipping point**, title passes to Walgreens when the supplier delivers the goods to the common carrier, who acts as an agent for Walgreens. (The abbreviation f.o.b. stands for free on board.) If the supplier ships the goods **f.o.b. destination**, title passes to Walgreens only when it receives the goods from the common carrier. "Shipping point" and "destination" are often designated by a particular location, for example, f.o.b. Denver.

When Walgreens obtains legal title to goods, it must record them as purchases in that fiscal period, assuming a periodic inventory system. Thus, goods shipped to Walgreens f.o.b. shipping point, but in transit at the end of the period, belong to Walgreens. It should show the purchase in its records because legal title to these goods passed to

Walgreens upon shipment of the goods. To disregard such purchases results in understating inventories and accounts payable in the balance sheet, and understating purchases and ending inventories in the income statement.

Consigned Goods

Companies market certain products through a **consignment** shipment. Under this arrangement, a company like Williams' Art Gallery (the consignor) ships various art merchandise to Sotheby's Holdings (the consignee), who acts as Williams' agent in selling the consigned goods. Sotheby's agrees to accept the goods without any liability, except to exercise due care and reasonable protection from loss or damage, until it sells the goods to a third party. When Sotheby's sells the goods, it remits the revenue, less a selling commission and expenses incurred in accomplishing the sale, to Williams.

Goods out on consignment remain the property of the consignor (Williams in the example above). Williams thus includes the goods in its inventory at purchase price or production cost. Occasionally, and only for a significant amount, the consignor shows the inventory out on consignment as a separate item. Sometimes a consignor reports the inventory on consignment in the notes to the financial statements. For example, Eagle Clothes, Inc. reported the following related to consigned goods: "Inventories consist of finished goods shipped on consignment to customers of the Company's subsidiary April-Marcus, Inc."

The consignee makes no entry to the inventory account for goods received. Remember, these goods remain the property of the consignor until sold. In fact, the consignee should be extremely careful *not* to include any of the goods consigned as a part of inventory.

Special Sales Agreements

As we indicated earlier, transfer of legal title is the general guideline used to determine whether a company should include an item in inventory. Unfortunately, transfer of legal title and the underlying substance of the transaction often do not match. For example, legal title may have passed to the purchaser, but the seller of the goods retains the risks of ownership. Conversely, transfer of legal title may not occur, but the economic substance of the transaction is such that the seller no longer retains the risks of ownership.

Two special sales situations are illustrated here to indicate the types of problems companies encounter in practice:

1. Sales with buyback agreement.
2. Sales with high rates of return.

Sales with Buyback Agreement

Sometimes an enterprise finances its inventory without reporting either the liability or the inventory on its balance sheet. This approach, often referred to as a **product financing arrangement**, usually involves a "sale" with either an implicit or explicit "buyback" agreement.

To illustrate, Hill Enterprises transfers ("sells") inventory to Chase, Inc. and simultaneously agrees to repurchase this merchandise at a specified price over a specified period of time. Chase then uses the inventory as collateral and borrows against it. Chase uses the loan proceeds to pay Hill, which repurchases the inventory in the future. Chase employs the proceeds from repayment to meet its loan obligation.

The essence of this transaction is that Hill Enterprises is financing its inventory—and retaining risk of ownership—even though it transferred to Chase technical legal title to the merchandise. By structuring a transaction in

Underlying Concepts

Recognizing revenue at the time the inventory is "parked" violates the revenue recognition principle. That is, a performance obligation is met when the risks and rewards of ownership are transferred to the buyer.

this manner, Hill avoids personal property taxes in certain states. Other advantages of this transaction for Hill are the removal of the current liability from its balance sheet and the ability to manipulate income. For Chase, the purchase of the goods may solve a LIFO liquidation problem (discussed later), or Chase may enter into a similar reciprocal agreement at a later date.

These arrangements are often described in practice as "**parking transactions**." In this situation, Hill simply parks the inventory on Chase's balance sheet for a short period of time. Generally, when a repurchase agreement exists, Hill should report the inventory and related liability on its books. **[1]** The reason? Hill has retained the risks and rewards of ownership.

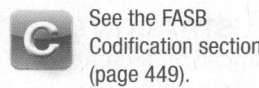

See the FASB Codification section (page 449).

Sales with High Rates of Return

In industries such as publishing, music, toys, and sporting goods, formal or informal agreements often exist that permit purchasers to return inventory for a full or partial refund.

To illustrate, Quality Publishing Company sells textbooks to Campus Bookstores with an agreement that Campus may return for full credit any books not sold. Historically, Campus Bookstores returned approximately 25 percent of the textbooks from Quality Publishing. How should Quality Publishing report its sales transactions?

One alternative is to record the sale at the full amount and establish an estimated sales returns and allowances account until the return period has expired. A second possibility is to not record any sales until circumstances indicate the amount of inventory the buyer will return. The key question is: Under what circumstances should Quality Publishing consider the inventory sold? The answer is that **when Quality Publishing can reasonably estimate the amount of returns**, it should consider the goods sold but establish a return liability for the amount of the estimated returns. Conversely, if returns are unpredictable, Quality Publishing should not consider the goods sold and it should not remove the goods from its inventory. **[2]**

What do the numbers mean?   NO PARKING!

In one of the more elaborate accounting frauds, employees at Kurzweil Applied Intelligence Inc. booked millions of dollars in phony inventory sales during a two-year period that straddled two audits and an initial public stock offering. They dummied up phony shipping documents and logbooks to support bogus sales transactions. Then they shipped high-tech equipment, not to customers, but to a public warehouse for "temporary" storage, where some of it sat for 17 months. (Kurzweil still had ownership.)

To foil auditors' attempts to verify the existence of the inventory, Kurzweil employees moved the goods from warehouse to warehouse. To cover the fraudulently recorded sales transactions as auditors closed in, the employees brought back the still-hidden goods, under the pretense that the goods were returned by customers. When auditors uncovered the fraud, the bottom dropped out of Kurzweil's stock.

Similar inventory shenanigans occurred at Delphi, which used side-deals with third parties to get inventory off its books and to record sales. The overstatement in income eventually led to a bankruptcy filing for Delphi.

More recently and with an international twist, concerns about inventory shenanigans are surfacing in China. Following years of torrid growth, the global economic slowdown has resulted in a huge buildup of unsold goods that is cluttering shop floors, clogging car dealerships, and filling factory warehouses. The large inventory overhang is raising alarms about phantom profits and suspect economic data coming out of China.

Sources: Adapted from "Anatomy of a Fraud," *BusinessWeek* (September 16, 1996), pp. 90–94; J. McCracken, "Delphi Executives Named in Suit over Inventory Practices," *Wall Street Journal* (May 5, 2005), p. A3; and K. Bradsher, "China Confronts Mounting Piles of Unsold Goods," *New York Times* (August 23, 2012).

Effect of Inventory Errors

Items incorrectly included or excluded in determining cost of goods sold through inventory misstatements will result in errors in the financial statements. Let's look at two cases, assuming a periodic inventory system.

Ending Inventory Misstated

What would happen if **IBM** correctly records its beginning inventory and purchases, but fails to include some items in ending inventory? In this situation, we would have the following effects on the financial statements at the end of the period.

ILLUSTRATION 8-7
Financial Statement
Effects of Misstated
Ending Inventory

Balance Sheet		Income Statement	
Inventory	Understated	Cost of goods sold	Overstated
Retained earnings	Understated		
Working capital	Understated	Net income	Understated
Current ratio	Understated		

If ending inventory is understated, working capital (current assets less current liabilities) and the current ratio (current assets divided by current liabilities) are understated. If cost of goods sold is overstated, then net income is understated.

To illustrate the effect on net income over a two-year period (2013–2014), assume that Jay Weiseman Corp. understates its ending inventory by $10,000 in 2013; all other items are correctly stated. The effect of this error is to decrease net income in 2013 and to increase net income in 2014. The error is counterbalanced (offset) in 2014 because beginning inventory is understated and net income is overstated. As Illustration 8-8 shows, the income statement misstates the net income figures for both 2013 and 2014 although the *total* for the two years is correct.

ILLUSTRATION 8-8
Effect of Ending
Inventory Error on Two
Periods

JAY WEISEMAN CORP.
(All Figures Assumed)

	Incorrect Recording		Correct Recording	
	2013	2014	2013	2014
Revenues	$100,000	$100,000	$100,000	$100,000
Cost of goods sold				
Beginning inventory	25,000	20,000	25,000	30,000
Purchased or produced	45,000	60,000	45,000	60,000
Goods available for sale	70,000	80,000	70,000	90,000
Less: Ending inventory	20,000*	40,000	30,000	40,000
Cost of goods sold	50,000	40,000	40,000	50,000
Gross profit	50,000	60,000	60,000	50,000
Administrative and selling expenses	40,000	40,000	40,000	40,000
Net income	$ 10,000	$ 20,000	$ 20,000	$ 10,000

Total income
for two years = $30,000

Total income
for two years = $30,000

*Ending inventory understated by $10,000 in 2013.

If Weiseman *overstates* ending inventory in 2013, the reverse effect occurs. Inventory, working capital, current ratio, and net income are overstated, and cost of goods sold is understated. The effect of the error on net income will be counterbalanced in 2014, but the income statement misstates both years' net income figures.

Purchases and Inventory Misstated

Suppose that Bishop Company does not record as a purchase certain goods that it owns and does not count them in ending inventory. The effect on the financial statements (assuming this is a purchase on account) is as follows.

ILLUSTRATION 8-9
Financial Statement
Effects of Misstated
Purchases and Inventory

Balance Sheet		Income Statement	
Inventory	Understated	Purchases	Understated
Retained earnings	No effect	Cost of goods sold	No effect
Accounts payable	Understated	Net income	No effect
Working capital	No effect	Inventory (ending)	Understated
Current ratio	Overstated		

Omission of goods from purchases and inventory results in an understatement of inventory and accounts payable in the balance sheet. It also results in an understatement of purchases and ending inventory in the income statement. However, the omission of such goods does not affect net income for the period. Why not? Because Bishop understates both purchases and ending inventory by the same amount—the error is thereby offset in cost of goods sold. Total working capital is unchanged, but the current ratio is overstated because of the omission of equal amounts from inventory and accounts payable.

To illustrate the effect on the current ratio, assume that Bishop *understated* accounts payable and ending inventory by $40,000. Illustration 8-10 shows the understated and correct data.

ILLUSTRATION 8-10
Effects of Purchases and
Ending Inventory Errors

Purchases and Ending Inventory Understated		Purchases and Ending Inventory Correct	
Current assets	$120,000	Current assets	$160,000
Current liabilities	$ 40,000	Current liabilities	$ 80,000
Current ratio	3 to 1	Current ratio	2 to 1

The understated data indicate a current ratio of 3 to 1, whereas the correct ratio is 2 to 1. Thus, understatement of accounts payable and ending inventory can lead to a "window-dressing" of the current ratio. That is, Bishop can make the current ratio appear better than it is.

If Bishop *overstates* both purchases (on account) and ending inventory, then the effects on the balance sheet are exactly the reverse. The financial statements overstate inventory and accounts payable, and understate the current ratio. The overstatement does not affect cost of goods sold and net income because the errors offset one another. Similarly, working capital is not affected.

Underlying Concepts

When inventory is misstated, its presentation is not representationally faithful.

We cannot overemphasize the importance of proper inventory measurement in presenting accurate financial statements. For example, Leslie Fay, a women's apparel maker, had accounting irregularities that wiped out one year's net income and caused a restatement of the prior year's earnings. One reason: It inflated inventory and deflated cost of goods sold. Anixter Bros. Inc. had to restate its income by $1.7 million because an accountant in the antenna manufacturing division overstated the ending inventory, thereby reducing its cost of sales. Similarly, AM International allegedly recorded as sold products that were only being rented. As a result, inaccurate inventory and sales figures inappropriately added $7.9 million to pretax income.

COSTS INCLUDED IN INVENTORY

4 LEARNING OBJECTIVE
Understand the items to include as inventory cost.

One of the most important problems in dealing with inventories concerns the dollar amount at which to carry the inventory in the accounts. **Companies generally account for the acquisition of inventories, like other assets, on a cost basis.**

Product Costs

Product costs are those costs that "attach" to the inventory. As a result, a company records product costs in the inventory account. These costs are directly connected with bringing the goods to the buyer's place of business and converting such goods to a salable condition. Such charges include freight charges on goods purchased, other direct costs of acquisition, and labor and other production costs incurred in processing the goods up to the time of sale.

It seems proper also to allocate to inventories a share of any buying costs or expenses of a purchasing department, storage costs, and other costs incurred in storing or handling the goods before their sale. However, because of the practical difficulties involved in allocating such costs and expenses, companies usually exclude these items in valuing inventories.

A manufacturing company's costs include direct materials, direct labor, and manufacturing overhead costs. Manufacturing overhead costs include indirect materials, indirect labor, and various costs, such as depreciation, taxes, insurance, and heat and electricity.

Period Costs

Period costs are those costs that are indirectly related to the acquisition or production of goods. Period costs such as selling expenses and, under ordinary circumstances, general and administrative expenses are therefore not included as part of inventory cost.

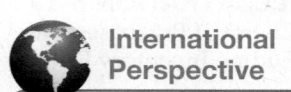

International Perspective

GAAP has more detailed rules related to the accounting for inventories, compared to IFRS.

Yet, conceptually, these expenses are as much a cost of the product as the initial purchase price and related freight charges attached to the product. Why then do companies exclude these costs from inventoriable items? Because companies generally consider selling expenses as more directly related to the cost of goods sold than to the unsold inventory. In addition, period costs, especially administrative expenses, are so unrelated or indirectly related to the immediate production process that any allocation is purely arbitrary.[2]

Interest is another period cost. Companies usually expense **interest costs** associated with getting inventories ready for sale. Supporters of this approach argue that interest costs are really a **cost of financing**. Others contend that interest costs incurred to finance activities associated with readying inventories for sale are as much a **cost of the asset** as materials, labor, and overhead. Therefore, they reason, companies should capitalize interest costs.

The FASB ruled that companies should capitalize interest costs related to assets constructed for internal use or assets produced as discrete projects (such as ships or real estate projects) for sale or lease [4].[3] The FASB emphasized that these discrete projects should take considerable time, entail substantial expenditures, and be likely to involve significant amounts of interest cost. A company should not capitalize interest costs for inventories that it routinely manufactures or otherwise produces in large quantities on a repetitive basis. In this case, the informational benefit does not justify the cost.

Treatment of Purchase Discounts

The use of a **Purchase Discounts** account in a periodic inventory system indicates that the company is reporting its purchases and accounts payable at the gross amount. If a

---

[2]Companies should not record abnormal freight, handling costs, and amounts of wasted materials (spoilage) as inventory costs. If the costs associated with the actual level of spoilage or product defects are greater than the costs associated with normal spoilage or defects, the company should charge the excess as an expense in the current period. **[3]**

[3]The reporting rules related to interest cost capitalization have their greatest impact in accounting for long-term assets. We therefore discuss them in Chapter 10.

company uses this **gross method**, it reports purchase discounts as a deduction from purchases on the income statement.

Another approach is to record the purchases and accounts payable at an amount **net of the cash discounts**. In this approach, the company records failure to take a purchase discount within the discount period in a Purchase Discounts Lost account. If a company uses this **net method**, it considers purchase discounts lost as a financial expense and reports it in the "Other expenses and losses" section of the income statement. This treatment is considered better for two reasons. (1) It provides a correct reporting of the cost of the asset and related liability. (2) It can measure management inefficiency by holding management responsible for discounts not taken.

To illustrate the difference between the gross and net methods, assume the following transactions.

ILLUSTRATION 8-11
Entries under Gross and Net Methods

Gross Method		Net Method	
Purchase cost $10,000, terms 2/10, net 30			
Purchases	10,000	Purchases	9,800
Accounts Payable	10,000	Accounts Payable	9,800
Invoices of $4,000 are paid within discount period			
Accounts Payable	4,000	Accounts Payable	3,920
Purchase Discounts	80	Cash	3,920
Cash	3,920		
Invoices of $6,000 are paid after discount period			
Accounts Payable	6,000	Accounts Payable	5,880
Cash	6,000	Purchase Discounts Lost	120
		Cash	6,000

Many believe that the somewhat more complicated net method is not justified by the resulting benefits. This could account for the widespread use of the less logical but simpler gross method. In addition, some contend that management is reluctant to report in the financial statements the amount of purchase discounts lost.

Underlying Concepts 🔍

Not using the net method because of resultant difficulties is an example of the application of the cost constraint.

What do the numbers mean? YOU MAY NEED A MAP

Does it really matter *where* a company reports certain costs in its income statement as long as it includes them all as expenses in computing income?

For e-tailers, such as **Amazon.com** or **Drugstore.com**, *where* they report certain selling costs does appear to be important. Contrary to well-established retailer practices, these companies insist on reporting some selling costs—fulfillment costs related to inventory shipping and warehousing—as part of administrative expenses, instead of as cost of goods sold. This practice is allowable within GAAP, *if* applied consistently and adequately disclosed. Although the practice doesn't affect the bottom line, it does make the e-tailers' gross margins look better. For example, at one time Amazon

reported $265 million of these costs in one quarter. Some experts thought Amazon should include those charges in costs of goods sold, which would substantially lower its gross profit, as shown below (in millions).

	E-tailer Reporting	Traditional Reporting
Sales	$2,795	$2,795
Cost of goods sold	2,132	2,397
Gross profit	$ 663	$ 398
Gross margin %	24%	14%

Similarly, if **Drugstore.com** and **eToys.com** made similar adjustments, their gross margins would go from positive to negative.

Thus, if you want to be able to compare the operating results of e-tailers to other traditional retailers, it might be a good idea to have a good accounting map in order to navigate their income statements and how they report certain selling costs.

Source: Adapted from P. Elstrom, "The End of Fuzzy Math?" *BusinessWeek, e.Biz—Net Worth* (December 11, 2000). According to GAAP **[5]**, companies must disclose the accounting policy for classifying these selling costs in income.

WHICH COST FLOW ASSUMPTION TO ADOPT?

LEARNING OBJECTIVE **5**

Describe and compare the cost flow assumptions used to account for inventories.

During any given fiscal period, companies typically purchase merchandise at several different prices. If a company prices inventories at cost and it made numerous purchases at different unit costs, which cost price should it use? Conceptually, a specific identification of the given items sold and unsold seems optimal. But this measure often proves both expensive and impossible to achieve. Consequently, companies use one of several systematic inventory cost flow assumptions.

Indeed, the actual physical flow of goods and the cost flow assumption often greatly differ. **There is no requirement that the cost flow assumption adopted be consistent with the physical movement of goods.** A company's major objective in selecting a method should be to choose the one that, under the circumstances, most clearly reflects periodic income. **[6]**

To illustrate, assume that Call-Mart Inc. had the following transactions in its first month of operations.

Date	Purchases	Sold or Issued	Balance
March 2	2,000 @ $4.00		2,000 units
March 15	6,000 @ $4.40		8,000 units
March 19		4,000 units	4,000 units
March 30	2,000 @ $4.75		6,000 units

From this information, Call-Mart computes the ending inventory of 6,000 units and the cost of goods available for sale (beginning inventory + purchases) of $43,900 [(2,000 at $4.00) + (6,000 at $4.40) + (2,000 at $4.75)]. The question is, which price or prices should it assign to the 6,000 units of ending inventory? The answer depends on which cost flow assumption it uses.

Specific Identification

Specific identification calls for identifying each item sold and each item in inventory. A company includes in cost of goods sold the costs of the specific items sold. It includes in inventory the costs of the specific items on hand. This method may be used only in instances where it is practical to separate physically the different purchases made. As a result, most companies only use this method when handling a relatively small number of costly, easily distinguishable items. In the retail trade, this includes some types of jewelry, fur coats, automobiles, and some furniture. In manufacturing, it includes special orders and many products manufactured under a job cost system.

To illustrate, assume that Call-Mart Inc.'s 6,000 units of inventory consists of 1,000 units from the March 2 purchase, 3,000 from the March 15 purchase, and 2,000 from the March 30 purchase. Illustration 8-12 shows how Call-Mart computes the ending inventory and cost of goods sold.

Date	No. of Units	Unit Cost	Total Cost
March 2	1,000	$4.00	$ 4,000
March 15	3,000	4.40	13,200
March 30	2,000	4.75	9,500
Ending inventory	6,000		$26,700

Cost of goods available for sale (computed in previous section)	$43,900
Deduct: Ending inventory	26,700
Cost of goods sold	$17,200

ILLUSTRATION 8-12
Specific Identification Method

This method appears ideal. Specific identification matches actual costs against actual revenue. Thus, a company reports ending inventory at actual cost. In other words, **under specific identification the cost flow matches the physical flow of the goods**. On closer observation, however, this method has certain deficiencies.

Some argue that specific identification allows a company to manipulate net income. For example, assume that a wholesaler purchases identical plywood early in the year at three different prices. When it sells the plywood, the wholesaler can select either the lowest or the highest price to charge to expense. It simply selects the plywood from a specific lot for delivery to the customer. A business manager, therefore, can manipulate net income by delivering to the customer the higher- or lower-priced item, depending on whether the company seeks lower or higher reported earnings for the period.

Another problem relates to the arbitrary allocation of costs that sometimes occurs with specific inventory items. For example, a company often faces difficulty in relating shipping charges, storage costs, and discounts directly to a given inventory item. This results in allocating these costs somewhat arbitrarily, leading to a "breakdown" in the precision of the specific identification method.[4]

International Perspective

IFRS indicates specific identification is the preferred inventory method, unless it is impracticable to use.

Average-Cost

As the name implies, the **average-cost method** prices items in the inventory on the basis of the average cost of all similar goods available during the period. To illustrate use of the periodic inventory method (amount of inventory computed at the end of the period), Call-Mart computes the ending inventory and cost of goods sold using a **weighted-average method** as follows.

Date of Invoice	No. Units	Unit Cost	Total Cost
March 2	2,000	$4.00	$ 8,000
March 15	6,000	4.40	26,400
March 30	2,000	4.75	9,500
Total goods available	10,000		$43,900

Weighted-average cost per unit $\dfrac{\$43,900}{10,000} = \$4.39$

Inventory in units   6,000 units
Ending inventory   6,000 × $4.39 = $26,340

Cost of goods available for sale	$43,900
Deduct: Ending inventory	26,340
Cost of goods sold	$17,560

ILLUSTRATION 8-13
Weighted-Average Method—Periodic Inventory

[4]The motion picture industry provides a good illustration of the cost allocation problem. Often actors receive a percentage of net income for a given movie or television program. Some actors, however, have alleged that their programs have been extremely profitable to the motion picture studios but they have received little in the way of profit-sharing. Actors contend that the studios allocate additional costs to successful projects to avoid sharing profits.

In computing the average cost per unit, Call-Mart includes the beginning inventory, if any, both in the total units available and in the total cost of goods available.

Companies use the **moving-average method** with perpetual inventory records. Illustration 8-14 shows the application of the average-cost method for perpetual records.

ILLUSTRATION 8-14
Moving-Average
Method—Perpetual
Inventory

Date	Purchased		Sold or Issued		Balance	
March 2	(2,000 @ $4.00)	$ 8,000			(2,000 @ $4.00)	$ 8,000
March 15	(6,000 @ 4.40)	26,400			(8,000 @ 4.30)	34,400
March 19			(4,000 @ $4.30)			
				$17,200	(4,000 @ 4.30)	17,200
March 30	(2,000 @ 4.75)	9,500			(6,000 @ 4.45)	26,700

In this method, Call-Mart computes a **new average unit cost** each time it makes a purchase. For example, on March 15, after purchasing 6,000 units for $26,400, Call-Mart has 8,000 units costing $34,400 ($8,000 plus $26,400) on hand. The average unit cost is $34,400 divided by 8,000, or $4.30. Call-Mart uses this unit cost in costing withdrawals until it makes another purchase. At that point, Call-Mart computes a new average unit cost. Accordingly, the company shows the cost of the 4,000 units withdrawn on March 19 at $4.30, for a total cost of goods sold of $17,200. On March 30, following the purchase of 2,000 units for $9,500, Call-Mart determines a new unit cost of $4.45, for an ending inventory of $26,700.

Companies often use average-cost methods for practical rather than conceptual reasons. These methods are both simple to apply and objective. They are not as subject to income manipulation as some of the other inventory pricing methods. In addition, proponents of the average-cost methods reason that measuring a specific physical flow of inventory is often impossible. Therefore, it is better to cost items on an average-price basis. This argument is particularly persuasive when dealing with similar inventory items.

First-In, First-Out (FIFO)

The **FIFO (first-in, first-out) method** assumes that a company uses goods in the order in which it purchases them. In other words, the FIFO method assumes that **the first goods purchased are the first used** (in a manufacturing concern) **or the first sold** (in a merchandising concern). The inventory remaining must therefore represent the most recent purchases.

To illustrate, assume that Call-Mart uses the periodic inventory system. It determines its cost of the ending inventory by taking the cost of the most recent purchase and working back until it accounts for all units in the inventory. Call-Mart determines its ending inventory and cost of goods sold as shown in Illustration 8-15.

ILLUSTRATION 8-15
FIFO Method—Periodic
Inventory

Date	No. Units	Unit Cost	Total Cost
March 30	2,000	$4.75	$ 9,500
March 15	4,000	4.40	17,600
Ending inventory	6,000		$27,100

Cost of goods available for sale	$43,900	
Deduct: Ending inventory	27,100	
Cost of goods sold	$16,800	

If Call-Mart instead uses a perpetual inventory system in quantities and dollars, it attaches a cost figure to each withdrawal. Then the cost of the 4,000 units removed on March 19 consists of the cost of the items purchased on March 2 and March 15. Illustration 8-16 shows the inventory on a FIFO basis perpetual system for Call-Mart.

Date	Purchased		Sold or Issued		Balance	
March 2	(2,000 @ $4.00)	$ 8,000			2,000 @ $4.00	$ 8,000
March 15	(6,000 @ 4.40)	26,400			2,000 @ 4.00 }	34,400
					6,000 @ 4.40 }	
March 19			2,000 @ $4.00 }		4,000 @ 4.40	17,600
			2,000 @ 4.40 }			
			($16,800)			
March 30	(2,000 @ 4.75)	9,500			4,000 @ 4.40 }	27,100
					2,000 @ 4.75 }	

ILLUSTRATION 8-16
FIFO Method—Perpetual Inventory

Here, the ending inventory is $27,100, and the cost of goods sold is $16,800 [(2,000 @ $4.00) + (2,000 @ $4.40)].

Notice that in these two FIFO examples, the cost of goods sold ($16,800) and ending inventory ($27,100) are the same. **In all cases where FIFO is used, the inventory and cost of goods sold would be the same at the end of the month whether a perpetual or periodic system is used.** Why? Because the same costs will always be first in and, therefore, first out. This is true whether a company computes cost of goods sold as it sells goods throughout the accounting period (the perpetual system) or as a residual at the end of the accounting period (the periodic system).

One objective of FIFO is to approximate the physical flow of goods. When the physical flow of goods is actually first-in, first-out, the FIFO method closely approximates specific identification. At the same time, it prevents manipulation of income. With FIFO, a company cannot pick a certain cost item to charge to expense.

Another advantage of the FIFO method is that the ending inventory is close to current cost. Because the first goods in are the first goods out, the ending inventory amount consists of the most recent purchases. This is particularly true with rapid inventory turnover. This approach generally approximates replacement cost on the balance sheet when price changes have not occurred since the most recent purchases.

However, the FIFO method fails to match current costs against current revenues on the income statement. A company charges the oldest costs against the more current revenue, possibly distorting gross profit and net income.

Last-In, First-Out (LIFO)

The **LIFO (last-in, first-out) method** matches the cost of the last goods purchased against revenue. If Call-Mart Inc. uses a periodic inventory system, it assumes that **the cost of the total quantity sold or issued during the month comes from the most recent purchases**. Call-Mart prices the ending inventory by using the total units as a basis of computation and disregards the exact dates of sales or issuances. For example, Call-Mart would assume that the cost of the 4,000 units withdrawn absorbed the 2,000 units purchased on March 30 and 2,000 of the 6,000 units purchased on March 15. Illustration 8-17 (page 432) shows how Call-Mart computes the inventory and related cost of goods sold, using the periodic inventory method.

If Call-Mart keeps a perpetual inventory record in quantities and dollars, use of the LIFO method results in **different ending inventory and cost of goods sold amounts**

International Perspective

IFRS does not permit LIFO.

ILLUSTRATION 8-17
LIFO Method—Periodic
Inventory

Date of Invoice	No. Units	Unit Cost	Total Cost
March 2	2,000	$4.00	$ 8,000
March 15	4,000	4.40	17,600
Ending inventory	6,000		$25,600

Goods available for sale		$43,900
Deduct: Ending inventory		25,600
Cost of goods sold		$18,300

than the amounts calculated under the periodic method. Illustration 8-18 shows these differences under the perpetual method.

ILLUSTRATION 8-18
LIFO Method—Perpetual
Inventory

Date	Purchased		Sold or Issued	Balance	
March 2	(2,000 @ $4.00)	$ 8,000		2,000 @ $4.00	$ 8,000
March 15	(6,000 @ 4.40)	26,400		2,000 @ 4.00 ⎱ 6,000 @ 4.40 ⎰	34,400
March 19			(4,000 @ $4.40) $17,600	2,000 @ 4.00 ⎱ 2,000 @ 4.40 ⎰	16,800
March 30	(2,000 @ 4.75)	9,500		2,000 @ 4.00 ⎱ 2,000 @ 4.40 ⎰ 2,000 @ 4.75 ⎰	26,300

The month-end periodic inventory computation presented in Illustration 8-17 (inventory $25,600 and cost of goods sold $18,300) shows a different amount from the perpetual inventory computation (inventory $26,300 and cost of goods sold $17,600). The periodic system matches the total withdrawals for the month with the total purchases for the month in applying the last-in, first-out method. In contrast, the perpetual system matches each withdrawal with the immediately preceding purchases. In effect, the periodic computation assumed that Call-Mart included the cost of the goods that it purchased on March 30 in the sale or issue on March 19.

**Gateway to
the Profession**

*Tutorial on Inventory
Methods*

SPECIAL ISSUES RELATED TO LIFO
LIFO Reserve

LEARNING OBJECTIVE **6**
Explain the significance and use of a LIFO reserve.

Many companies use LIFO for tax and external reporting purposes. However, they maintain a FIFO, average-cost, or standard cost system for internal reporting purposes. There are several reasons to do so. (1) Companies often base their pricing decisions on a FIFO, average, or standard cost assumption, rather than on a LIFO basis. (2) Recordkeeping on some other basis is easier because the LIFO assumption usually does not approximate the physical flow of the product. (3) Profit-sharing and other bonus arrangements often depend on a non-LIFO inventory assumption. (4) The use of a pure LIFO system is troublesome for interim periods, which require estimates of year-end quantities and prices.

The difference between the inventory method used for internal reporting purposes and LIFO is the Allowance to Reduce Inventory to LIFO account or the **LIFO reserve**. The change in the allowance balance from one period to the next is the **LIFO effect**. The LIFO effect is the adjustment that companies must make to the accounting records in a given year.

To illustrate, assume that Acme Boot Company uses the FIFO method for internal reporting purposes and LIFO for external reporting purposes. At January 1, 2014, the Allowance to Reduce Inventory to LIFO balance is $20,000. At December 31, 2014, the balance should be $50,000. As a result, Acme Boot realizes a LIFO effect of $30,000 and makes the following entry at year-end.

Cost of Goods Sold	30,000	
Allowance to Reduce Inventory to LIFO		30,000

Acme Boot deducts Allowance to Reduce Inventory to LIFO from inventory to ensure that it states the inventory on a LIFO basis at year-end.

Companies should disclose either the LIFO reserve or the replacement cost of the inventory, as shown in Illustration 8-19. **[7]**

American Maize-Products Company

Inventories (Note 3)	$80,320,000

Note 3: Inventories. At December 31, $31,516,000 of inventories were valued using the LIFO method. This amount is less than the corresponding replacement value by $3,765,000.

ILLUSTRATION 8-19
Note Disclosures of LIFO Reserve

Brown Shoe Company, Inc.
(in thousands)

	Current Year	Previous Year
Inventories, (Note 1)	$365,989	$362,274

Note 1 (partial): Inventories. Inventories are valued at the lower of cost or market determined principally by the last-in, first-out (LIFO) method. If the first-in, first-out (FIFO) cost method had been used, inventories would have been $11,709 higher in the current year and $13,424 higher in the previous year.

What do the numbers mean?   COMPARING APPLES TO APPLES

Investors commonly use the current ratio to evaluate a company's liquidity. They compute the current ratio as current assets divided by current liabilities. A higher current ratio indicates that a company is better able to meet its current obligations when they come due. However, it is not meaningful to compare the current ratio for a company using LIFO to one for a company using FIFO. It would be like comparing apples to oranges since the two companies measure inventory (and cost of goods sold) differently.

To make the current ratio comparable on an apples-to-apples basis, analysts use the LIFO reserve. The following adjustments should do the trick:

> Inventory Adjustment: LIFO inventory + LIFO reserve = FIFO inventory

(For cost of goods sold, deduct the *change* in the LIFO reserve from LIFO cost of goods sold to yield the comparable FIFO amount.)

For Brown Shoe, Inc. (see Illustration 8-19), with current assets of $487.8 million and current liabilities of $217.8 million, the current ratio using LIFO is $487.8 ÷ $217.8 = 2.2. After adjusting for the LIFO effect, Brown Shoe's current ratio under FIFO would be ($487.8 + $11.7) ÷ $217.8 = 2.3.

Thus, without the LIFO adjustment, the Brown Shoe current ratio is understated.

LIFO Liquidation

Up to this point, we have emphasized a **specific-goods approach** to costing LIFO inventories (also called **traditional LIFO** or **unit LIFO**). This approach is often unrealistic for two reasons:

1. When a company has many different inventory items, the accounting cost of tracking each inventory item is expensive.
2. Erosion of the LIFO inventory can easily occur. Referred to as **LIFO liquidation**, this often distorts net income and leads to substantial tax payments.

To understand the LIFO liquidation problem, assume that Basler Co. has 30,000 pounds of steel in its inventory on December 31, 2014, with cost determined on a specific-goods LIFO approach.

	Ending Inventory (2014)		
	Pounds	Unit Cost	LIFO Cost
2011	8,000	$ 4	$ 32,000
2012	10,000	6	60,000
2013	7,000	9	63,000
2014	5,000	10	50,000
	30,000		$205,000

As indicated, the ending 2014 inventory for Basler comprises costs from past periods. These costs are called **layers** (increases from period to period). The first layer is identified as the base layer. Illustration 8-20 shows the layers for Basler.

ILLUSTRATION 8-20
Layers of LIFO Inventory

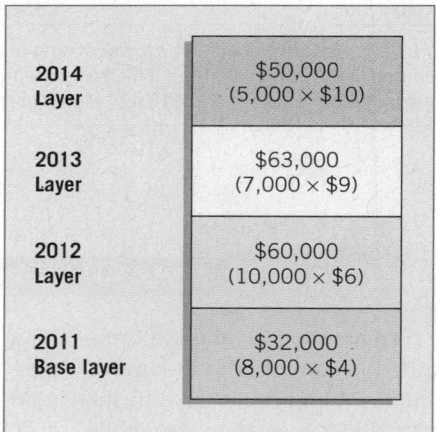

Note the increased price of steel over the four-year period. In 2015, due to metal shortages, Basler had to liquidate much of its inventory (a LIFO liquidation). At the end of 2015, only 6,000 pounds of steel remained in inventory. Because the company uses LIFO, Basler liquidates the most recent layer, 2014, first, followed by the 2013 layer, and so on. The result: Basler matches costs from preceding periods against sales revenues reported in current dollars. As Illustration 8-21 shows, this leads to a distortion in net income and increased taxable income in the current period. Unfortunately, **LIFO liquidations can occur frequently when using a specific-goods LIFO approach.**

ILLUSTRATION 8-21
LIFO Liquidation

To alleviate the LIFO liquidation problems and to simplify the accounting, companies can combine goods into pools. A **pool** groups items of a similar nature. Thus, instead of only identical units, a company combines, and counts as a group, a number of similar units or products. This method, the specific-goods pooled LIFO approach, usually results in fewer LIFO liquidations. Why? Because the reduction of one quantity in the pool may be offset by an increase in another.

The specific-goods pooled LIFO approach eliminates some of the disadvantages of the specific-goods (traditional) accounting for LIFO inventories. This pooled approach, using quantities as its measurement basis, however, creates other problems.

First, most companies continually change the mix of their products, materials, and production methods. As a result, in employing a pooled approach using quantities, companies must continually redefine the pools. This can be time-consuming and costly. Second, even when practical, the approach often results in an erosion ("LIFO liquidation") of the layers, thereby losing much of the LIFO costing benefit. Erosion of the layers occurs when a specific good or material in the pool is replaced with another good or material. The new item may not be similar enough to be treated as part of the old pool. Therefore, a company may need to recognize any inflationary profit deferred on the old goods as it replaces them.

Dollar-Value LIFO

The dollar-value LIFO method overcomes the problems of redefining pools and eroding layers. **The dollar-value LIFO method determines and measures any increases and decreases in a pool in terms of total dollar value, not the physical quantity of the goods in the inventory pool.**

Such an approach has two important advantages over the specific-goods pooled approach. First, companies may include a broader range of goods in a dollar-value LIFO pool. Second, a dollar-value LIFO pool permits replacement of goods that are similar items, similar in use, or interchangeable. (In contrast, a specific-goods LIFO pool only allows replacement of items that are substantially identical.)

8 LEARNING OBJECTIVE

Explain the dollar-value LIFO method.

Gateway to the Profession

Tutorial on Dollar-Value LIFO

Thus, dollar-value LIFO techniques help protect LIFO layers from erosion. Because of this advantage, companies frequently use the dollar-value LIFO method in practice.[5] Companies use the more traditional LIFO approaches only when dealing with few goods and expecting little change in product mix.

Under the dollar-value LIFO method, one pool may contain the entire inventory. However, companies generally use several pools.[6] In general, the more goods included in a pool, the more likely that increases in the quantities of some goods will offset decreases in other goods in the same pool. Thus, companies avoid liquidation of the LIFO layers. It follows that having fewer pools means less cost and less chance of a reduction of a LIFO layer.[7]

Dollar-Value LIFO Example

To illustrate how the dollar-value LIFO method works, assume that Enrico Company first adopts dollar-value LIFO on December 31, 2013 (base period). The inventory at current prices on that date was $20,000. The inventory on December 31, 2014, at current prices is $26,400.

Can we conclude that Enrico's inventory quantities increased 32 percent during the year ($26,400 ÷ $20,000 = 132%)? First, we need to ask: What is the value of the ending inventory in terms of beginning-of-the-year prices? Assuming that prices have increased 20 percent during the year, the ending inventory at beginning-of-the-year prices amounts to $22,000 ($26,400 ÷ 120%). Therefore, the inventory quantity has increased only 10 percent, or from $20,000 to $22,000 in terms of beginning-of-the-year prices.

The next step is to price this real-dollar quantity increase. This real-dollar quantity increase of $2,000 valued at year-end prices is $2,400 (120% × $2,000). This increment (layer) of $2,400, when added to the beginning inventory of $20,000, totals $22,400 for the December 31, 2014, inventory, as shown below.

First layer—(beginning inventory) in terms of 100	$20,000
Second layer—(2014 increase) in terms of 120	2,400
Dollar-value LIFO inventory, December 31, 2014	$22,400

Note that a layer forms only when the ending inventory at base-year prices exceeds the beginning inventory at base-year prices. And only when a new layer forms must Enrico compute a new index.

---

[5] A study by James M. Reeve and Keith G. Stanga disclosed that the vast majority of respondent companies applying LIFO use the dollar-value method or the dollar-value retail method to apply LIFO. Only a small minority of companies use the specific-goods (unit LIFO) approach or the specific-goods pooling approach. See J.M. Reeve and K.G. Stanga, "The LIFO Pooling Decision," *Accounting Horizons* (June 1987), p. 27.

[6] The Reeve and Stanga study (*ibid.*) reports that most companies have only a few pools—the median is six for retailers and three for nonretailers. But the distributions are highly skewed; some companies have 100 or more pools. Retailers that use LIFO have significantly more pools than nonretailers. About a third of the nonretailers (mostly manufacturers) use a single pool for their entire LIFO inventory.

[7] A later study shows that when quantities are increasing, multiple pools over a period of time may produce (under rather general conditions) significantly higher cost of goods sold deductions than a single-pool approach. When a stock-out occurs, a single-pool approach may lessen the layer liquidation for that year, but it may not erase the cumulative cost of goods sold advantage accruing to the use of multiple pools built up over the preceding years. See William R. Coon and Randall B. Hayes, "The Dollar Value LIFO Pooling Decision: The Conventional Wisdom Is Too General," *Accounting Horizons* (December 1989), pp. 57–70.

Comprehensive Dollar-Value LIFO Example

To illustrate the use of the dollar-value LIFO method in a more complex situation, assume that Bismark Company develops the following information.

December 31		Inventory at End-of-Year Prices	÷	Price Index (percentage)	=	End-of-Year Inventory at Base-Year Prices
(Base year)	2011	$200,000		100		$200,000
	2012	299,000		115		260,000
	2013	300,000		120		250,000
	2014	351,000		130		270,000

At December 31, 2011, Bismark computes the ending inventory under dollar-value LIFO as $200,000, as Illustration 8-22 shows.

Ending Inventory at Base-Year Prices	Layer at Base-Year Prices		Price Index (percentage)		Ending Inventory at LIFO Cost
$200,000	$200,000	×	100	=	$200,000

ILLUSTRATION 8-22
Computation of 2011 Inventory at LIFO Cost

At December 31, 2012, a comparison of the ending inventory at base-year prices ($260,000) with the beginning inventory at base-year prices ($200,000) indicates that the quantity of goods (in base-year prices) increased $60,000 ($260,000 − $200,000). Bismark prices this increment (layer) at the 2012 index of 115 percent to arrive at a new layer of $69,000. Ending inventory for 2012 is $269,000, composed of the beginning inventory of $200,000 and the new layer of $69,000. Illustration 8-23 shows the computations.

Ending Inventory at Base-Year Prices	Layers at Base-Year Prices			Price Index (percentage)		Ending Inventory at LIFO Cost
$260,000	2011	$200,000	×	100	=	$200,000
	2012	60,000	×	115	=	69,000
		$260,000				$269,000

ILLUSTRATION 8-23
Computation of 2012 Inventory at LIFO Cost

At December 31, 2013, a comparison of the ending inventory at base-year prices ($250,000) with the beginning inventory at base-year prices ($260,000) indicates a decrease in the quantity of goods of $10,000 ($250,000 − $260,000). If the ending inventory at base-year prices is less than the beginning inventory at base-year prices, **a company must subtract the decrease from the most recently added layer. When a decrease occurs, the company "peels off" previous layers at the prices in existence when it added the layers.** In Bismark's situation, this means that it removes $10,000 in base-year prices from the 2012 layer of $60,000 at base-year prices. It values the balance of $50,000 ($60,000 − $10,000) at base-year prices at the 2012 price index of 115 percent. As a result, it now values this 2012 layer at $57,500 ($50,000 × 115%). Therefore, Bismark computes the ending inventory at $257,500, consisting of the beginning inventory of $200,000 and the second layer of $57,500. Illustration 8-24 (page 438) shows the computations for 2013.

ILLUSTRATION 8-24
Computation of 2013
Inventory at LIFO Cost

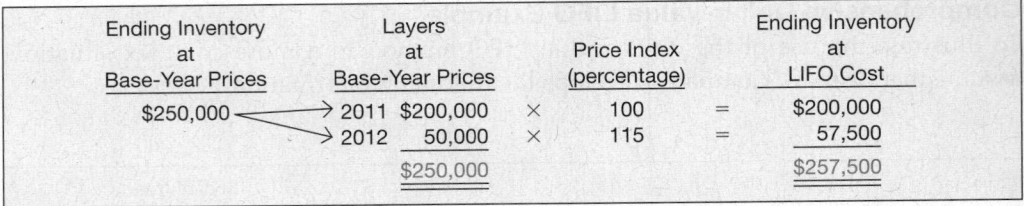

Note that if Bismark eliminates a layer or base (or portion thereof), it cannot rebuild it in future periods. That is, the layer is gone forever.

At December 31, 2014, a comparison of the ending inventory at base-year prices ($270,000) with the beginning inventory at base-year prices ($250,000) indicates an increase in the quantity of goods (in base-year prices) of $20,000 ($270,000 − $250,000). After converting the $20,000 increase, using the 2014 price index, the ending inventory is $283,500, composed of the beginning layer of $200,000, a 2012 layer of $57,500, and a 2014 layer of $26,000 ($20,000 × 130%). Illustration 8-25 shows this computation.

ILLUSTRATION 8-25
Computation of 2014
Inventory at LIFO Cost

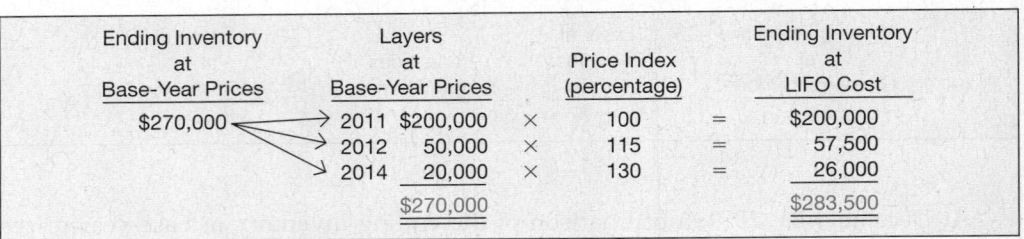

The ending inventory at base-year prices must always equal the total of the layers at base-year prices. Checking that this situation exists will help to ensure correct dollar-value computations.

Selecting a Price Index

Obviously, price changes are critical in dollar-value LIFO. How do companies determine the price indexes? Many companies use the general price-level index that the federal government prepares and publishes each month. The most popular general external price-level index is the **Consumer Price Index for Urban Consumers** (CPI-U).[8] Companies also use more-specific external price indexes. For instance, various organizations compute and publish daily indexes for most commodities (gold, silver, other metals, corn, wheat, and other farm products). Many trade associations prepare indexes for specific product lines or industries. Any of these indexes may be used for dollar-value LIFO purposes.

When a relevant specific external price index is not readily available, a company may compute its own specific internal price index. The desired approach is to price ending inventory at the most current cost. Therefore, a company that chose to compute its own specific internal price index would ordinarily determine current cost by referring to the actual cost of the goods it most recently had purchased. The price index provides a measure of the change in price or cost levels between the base year and the current year. The company then computes the index for each year after the base year. The general formula for computing the index is as follows.

---

[8]Indexes may be **general** (composed of several commodities, goods, or services) or **specific** (for one commodity, good, or service). Additionally, they may be **external** (computed by an outside party, such as the government, commodity exchange, or trade association) or **internal** (computed by the enterprise for its own product or service).

$$\frac{\text{Ending Inventory for the Period at Current Cost}}{\text{Ending Inventory for the Period at Base-Year Cost}} = \text{Price Index for Current Year}$$

ILLUSTRATION 8-26
Formula for Computing
a Price Index

This approach is generally referred to as the **double-extension method**. As its name implies, the value of the units in inventory is extended at *both* base-year prices and current-year prices.

To illustrate this computation, assume that Toledo Company's base-year inventory (January 1, 2014) consisted of the following.

Items	Quantity	Cost per Unit	Total Cost
A	1,000	$ 6	$ 6,000
B	2,000	20	40,000
January 1, 2014, inventory at base-year costs			$46,000

Examination of the ending inventory indicates that the company holds 3,000 units of Item A and 6,000 units of Item B on December 31, 2014. The most recent actual purchases related to these items were as follows.

Items	Purchase Date	Quantity Purchased	Cost per Unit
A	December 1, 2014	4,000	$ 7
B	December 15, 2014	5,000	25
B	November 16, 2014	1,000	22

Toledo double-extends the inventory as shown in Illustration 8-27.

Items	Units	12/31/14 Inventory at Base-Year Costs — Base-Year Cost per Unit	Total	Units	12/31/14 Inventory at Current-Year Costs — Current-Year Cost per Unit	Total
A	3,000	$ 6	$ 18,000	3,000	$ 7	$ 21,000
B	6,000	20	120,000	5,000	25	125,000
B				1,000	22	22,000
			$138,000			$168,000

ILLUSTRATION 8-27
Double-Extension
Method of Determining
a Price Index

After the inventories are double-extended, Toledo uses the formula in Illustration 8-26 to develop the index for the current year (2014), as follows.

$$\frac{\text{Ending Inventory for the Period at Current Cost}}{\text{Ending Inventory for the Period at Base-Year Cost}} = \frac{\$168,000}{\$138,000} = 121.74\%$$

ILLUSTRATION 8-28
Computation of 2014
Index

Toledo then applies this index (121.74%) to the layer added in 2014. Note in this Illustration that Toledo used the most recent actual purchases to determine current cost. Alternatively, it could have used other approaches such as FIFO and average-cost. Whichever flow assumption is adopted, a company must use it consistently from one period to another.

Use of the double-extension method is time-consuming and difficult where substantial technological change has occurred or where many items are involved. That is, as time passes, the company must determine a new base-year cost for new products, and must keep a base-year cost for each inventory item.[9]

What do the numbers mean? QUITE A DIFFERENCE

As indicated, significant differences can arise in inventory measured according to current cost and dollar-value LIFO. Let's look at an additional summary example.

Truman Company uses the dollar-value LIFO method of computing its inventory. Inventory for the last three years is as shown below.

Year Ended December 31	Inventory at Current-Year Cost	Price Index
2012	$60,000	100
2013	84,000	105
2014	87,000	116

The values of the 2012, 2013, and 2014 inventories using the dollar-value LIFO method are presented in the table below.

As indicated, consistent with LIFO costing in times of rising prices, the dollar-value LIFO inventory amount is less than inventory stated at end-of-year prices. The company did not add layers at the 2014 prices. This is because the increase in inventory at end-of-year (current) prices was primarily due to higher prices. Also, establishing the LIFO layers based on price-adjusted dollars relative to base-year layers reduces the likelihood of a LIFO liquidation.

Year	Inventory at End-of-Year Prices	Inventory at Base-Year Prices	Layers at Base-Year Prices	×	Price-Index Layers at LIFO Cost	Dollar-Value LIFO Inventory
2012	$60,000	$60,000 ÷ 100 = $60,000	2012 $60,000	×	100 = $60,000	$60,000
2013	84,000	$84,000 ÷ 105 = $80,000	2012 $60,000	×	100 = $60,000	
			2013 20,000	×	105 = $21,000	$81,000
2014	87,000	$87,000 ÷ 116 = $75,000	2012 $60,000	×	100 = $60,000	
			2013 15,000	×	105 = $15,750	$75,750

Comparison of LIFO Approaches

We present three different approaches to computing LIFO inventories in this chapter—specific-goods LIFO, specific-goods pooled LIFO, and dollar-value LIFO. As we indicated earlier, the use of the specific-goods LIFO is unrealistic. Most companies have numerous goods in inventory at the end of a period. Costing (pricing) them on a unit basis is extremely expensive and time-consuming.

The specific-goods pooled LIFO approach reduces recordkeeping and clerical costs. In addition, it is more difficult to erode the layers because the reduction of one quantity in the pool may be offset by an increase in another. Nonetheless, the pooled approach using quantities as its measurement basis can lead to untimely LIFO liquidations.

As a result, **most companies using a LIFO system employ dollar-value LIFO**. Although the approach appears complex, the logic and the computations are actually quite simple, after determining an appropriate index.

[9]To simplify the analysis, companies may use another approach, initially sanctioned by the Internal Revenue Service for tax purposes. Under this method, a company obtains an index from an outside source or by double-extending only a sample portion of the inventory. For example, the IRS allows all companies to use as their inflation rate for a LIFO pool 80 percent of the inflation rate reported by the appropriate consumer or producer price indexes prepared by the Bureau of Labor Statistics (BLS). Once the company obtains the index, it divides the ending inventory at current cost by the index to find the base-year cost. Using generally available external indexes greatly simplifies LIFO computations, and frees companies from having to compute internal indexes.

However, problems do exist with the dollar-value LIFO method. The selection of the items to be put in a pool can be subjective.[10] Such a determination, however, is extremely important because manipulation of the items in a pool without conceptual justification can affect reported net income. For example, the SEC noted that some companies have set up pools that are easy to liquidate. As a result, to increase income, a company simply decreases inventory, thereby matching low-cost inventory items to current revenues.

To curb this practice, the SEC has taken a much harder line on the number of pools that companies may establish. In a well-publicized case, **Stauffer Chemical Company** increased the number of LIFO pools from 8 to 280, boosting its net income by $16,515,000 or approximately 13 percent. Stauffer justified the change in its annual report on the basis of "achieving a better matching of cost and revenue." The SEC required Stauffer to reduce the number of its inventory pools, contending that some pools were inappropriate and alleging income manipulation.

Major Advantages of LIFO

One obvious advantage of LIFO approaches is that the LIFO cost flow often approximates the physical flow of the goods in and out of inventory. For instance, in a coal pile, the last coal in is the first coal out because it is on the top of the pile. The coal remover is not going to take the coal from the bottom of the pile! The coal taken first is the coal placed on the pile last.

> **9 LEARNING OBJECTIVE**
> Identify the major advantages and disadvantages of LIFO.

However, this is one of only a few situations where the actual physical flow corresponds to LIFO. Therefore, most adherents of LIFO use other arguments for its widespread use, as follows.

Matching

LIFO matches the more recent costs against current revenues to provide a better measure of current earnings. During periods of inflation, many challenge the quality of non-LIFO earnings, noting that failing to match current costs against current revenues **creates transitory or "paper" profits ("inventory profits")**. Inventory profits occur when the inventory costs matched against sales are less than the inventory replacement cost. This results in understating the cost of goods sold and overstating profit. Using LIFO (rather than a method such as FIFO) matches current costs against revenues, thereby reducing inventory profits.

Tax Benefits/Improved Cash Flow

LIFO's popularity mainly stems from its tax benefits. As long as the price level increases and inventory quantities do not decrease, a deferral of income tax occurs. Why? Because a company matches the items it most recently purchased (at the higher price level) against revenues. For example, when **Fuqua Industries** switched to LIFO, it realized a tax savings of about $4 million. Even if the price level decreases later, the company still temporarily deferred its income taxes. Thus, use of LIFO in such situations improves a company's cash flow.[11]

---

[10]It is suggested that companies analyze how inventory purchases are affected by price changes, how goods are stocked, how goods are used, and if future liquidations are likely. See William R. Cron and Randall Hayes, *ibid.*, p. 57.

[11]In periods of rising prices, the use of fewer pools will translate into greater income tax benefits through the use of LIFO. The use of fewer pools allows companies to offset inventory reductions on some items and inventory increases in others. In contrast, the use of more pools increases the likelihood of liquidating old, low-cost inventory layers and incurring negative tax consequences. See Reeve and Stanga, *ibid.*, pp. 28–29.

The tax law requires that if a company uses LIFO for tax purposes, it must also use LIFO for financial accounting purposes[12] (although neither tax law nor GAAP requires a company to pool its inventories in the same manner for book and tax purposes). This requirement is often referred to as the **LIFO conformity rule**. Other inventory valuation methods do not have this requirement.

Future Earnings Hedge

With LIFO, future price declines will not substantially affect a company's future reported earnings. The reason: Since the company records the most recent inventory as sold first, there is not much ending inventory at high prices vulnerable to a price decline. Thus LIFO eliminates or substantially minimizes write-downs to market as a result of price decreases. In contrast, inventory costed under FIFO is more vulnerable to price declines, which can reduce net income substantially.

Major Disadvantages of LIFO

Despite its advantages, LIFO has the following drawbacks.

Reduced Earnings

Many corporate managers view the lower profits reported under the LIFO method in inflationary times as a distinct disadvantage. They would rather have higher reported profits than lower taxes. Some fear that investors may misunderstand an accounting change to LIFO, and that the lower profits may cause the price of the company's stock to fall.

Inventory Understated

LIFO may have a distorting effect on a company's balance sheet. The inventory valuation is normally outdated because the oldest costs remain in inventory. This understatement makes the working capital position of the company appear worse than it really is. A good example is Caterpillar, which uses LIFO costing for most of its inventory, valued at $14.5 billion at year-end 2011. Under FIFO costing, Caterpillar's inventories have a value of $16.7 billion—approximately 5 percent higher than the LIFO amount.

The magnitude and direction of this variation between the carrying amount of inventory and its current price depend on the degree and direction of the price changes and the amount of inventory turnover. The combined effect of rising product prices and avoidance of inventory liquidations increases the difference between the inventory carrying value at LIFO and current prices of that inventory. This magnifies the balance sheet distortion attributed to the use of LIFO.

Physical Flow

LIFO does not approximate the physical flow of the items except in specific situations (such as the coal pile discussed earlier). Originally, companies could use LIFO only in certain circumstances. This situation has changed over the years. Now, physical flow characteristics no longer determine whether a company may employ LIFO.

Involuntary Liquidation/Poor Buying Habits

If a company eliminates the base or layers of old costs, it may match old, irrelevant costs against current revenues. A distortion in reported income for a given period may result, as well as detrimental income tax consequences. For example, Caterpillar recently experienced a LIFO liquidation, resulting in an increased tax bill of $60 million.[13]

---

[12]Management often selects an accounting procedure because a lower tax results from its use, instead of an accounting method that is conceptually more appealing. Throughout this textbook, we identify accounting procedures that provide income tax benefits to the user.

[13]Companies should disclose the effects on income of LIFO inventory liquidations in the notes to the financial statements. **[8]**

Because of the liquidation problem, LIFO may cause poor buying habits. A company may simply purchase more goods and match these goods against revenue to avoid charging the old costs to expense. Furthermore, recall that with LIFO, a company may attempt to manipulate its net income at the end of the year simply by altering its pattern of purchases.[14]

One survey uncovered the following reasons why companies reject LIFO.[15]

Reasons to Reject LIFO	Number	% of Total*
No expected tax benefits		
No required tax payment	34	16%
Declining prices	31	15
Rapid inventory turnover	30	14
Immaterial inventory	26	12
Miscellaneous tax related	38	17
	159	74%
Regulatory or other restrictions	26	12%
Excessive cost		
High administrative costs	29	14%
LIFO liquidation–related costs	12	6
	41	20%
Other adverse consequences		
Lower reported earnings	18	8%
Bad accounting	7	3
	25	11%

*Percentage totals more than 100% as some companies offered more than one explanation.

ILLUSTRATION 8-29
Why Do Companies Reject LIFO? Summary of Responses

BASIS FOR SELECTION OF INVENTORY METHOD

How does a company choose among the various inventory methods? Although no absolute rules can be stated, preferability for LIFO usually occurs in either of the following circumstances: (1) if selling prices and revenues have been increasing faster than costs, thereby distorting income, and (2) in situations where LIFO has been traditional, such as department stores and industries where a fairly constant "base stock" is present (such as refining, chemicals, and glass).[16]

Conversely, LIFO is probably inappropriate in the following circumstances: (1) where prices tend to lag behind costs; (2) in situations where specific identification is traditional, such as in the sale of automobiles, farm equipment, art, and antique jewelry; or (3) where unit costs tend to decrease as production increases, thereby nullifying the tax benefit that LIFO might provide.[17]

10 **LEARNING OBJECTIVE**
Understand why companies select given inventory methods.

[14]For example, General Tire and Rubber accelerated raw material purchases at the end of the year to minimize the book profit from a liquidation of LIFO inventories and to minimize income taxes for the year.

[15]Michael H. Granof and Daniel Short, "Why Do Companies Reject LIFO?" *Journal of Accounting, Auditing, and Finance* (Summer 1984), pp. 323–333 and Table 1, p. 327.

[16]*Accounting Trends and Techniques—2012* reports that of 669 inventory method disclosures, 163 used LIFO, 312 used FIFO, 133 used average-cost, and 56 used other methods. As discussed in the opening story, because of steady or falling raw materials costs and costs savings from electronic data interchange and just-in-time technologies in recent years, many businesses using LIFO no longer experience substantial tax benefits. Even some companies for which LIFO is creating a benefit are finding that the administrative costs associated with LIFO are higher than the LIFO benefit obtained. As a result, some companies are moving to FIFO or average-cost.

[17]See Barry E. Cushing and Marc J. LeClere, "Evidence on the Determinants of Inventory Accounting Policy Choice," *The Accounting Review* (April 1992), pp. 355–366 and Table 4, p. 363, for a list of factors hypothesized to affect FIFO–LIFO choices.

Tax consequences are another consideration. Switching from FIFO to LIFO usually results in an immediate tax benefit. However, switching from LIFO to FIFO can result in a substantial tax burden. For example, when Chrysler changed from LIFO to FIFO, it became responsible for an additional $53 million in taxes that the company had deferred over 14 years of LIFO inventory valuation. Why, then, would Chrysler, and other companies, change to FIFO? The major reason was the profit crunch of that era. Although Chrysler showed a loss of $7.6 million after the switch, the loss would have been $20 million *more* if the company had not changed its inventory valuation from LIFO to FIFO.

It is questionable whether companies should switch from LIFO to FIFO for the sole purpose of increasing reported earnings. Intuitively, we would assume that companies with higher reported earnings would have a higher share valuation (common stock price). However, some studies have indicated that the users of financial data exhibit a much higher sophistication than might be expected. Share prices are the same and, in some cases, even higher under LIFO in spite of lower reported earnings.[18]

The concern about reduced income resulting from adoption of LIFO has even less substance now because the IRS has also relaxed the LIFO conformity rule which requires a company employing LIFO for tax purposes to use it for book purposes as well. The IRS has also relaxed restrictions against providing non-LIFO income numbers as supplementary information. As a result, companies now provide supplemental non-LIFO disclosures. While not intended to override the basic LIFO method adopted for financial reporting, these disclosures may be useful in comparing operating income and working capital with companies not on LIFO.

For example, Sherwin-Williams Company, a LIFO user, presented the information in its annual report as shown in Illustration 8-30.

ILLUSTRATION 8-30
Supplemental Non-LIFO
Disclosure

Sherwin-Williams Company

Inventories were stated at the lower of cost or market with cost determined principally on the last-in, first-out (LIFO) method. The following presents the effect on inventories, net income and net income per common share had the Company used the first-in, first-out (FIFO) inventory valuation method adjusted for income taxes at the statutory rate and assuming no other adjustments.

	2011	2010
Percentage of total inventories on LIFO	77%	76%
Excess of FIFO over LIFO	$378,986	$277,164
(Decrease) increase in net income due to LIFO	(62,636)	(16,394)
(Decrease) increase in net income per common share due to LIFO	(.59)	(.15)

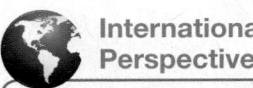

International Perspective

Many U.S. companies that have international operations use LIFO for U.S. purposes but use FIFO for their foreign subsidiaries.

Relaxation of the LIFO conformity rule has led some companies to select LIFO as their inventory valuation method because they will be able to disclose FIFO income numbers in the financial reports if they so desire.[19]

Companies often combine inventory methods. For example, John Deere uses LIFO for most of its inventories, and prices the remainder using FIFO. The Hershey Company follows the same practice. One reason for these practices is

---

[18]See, for example, Shyam Sunder, "Relationship Between Accounting Changes and Stock Prices: Problems of Measurement and Some Empirical Evidence," *Empirical Research in Accounting: Selected Studies, 1973* (Chicago: University of Chicago), pp. 1–40. But see Robert Moren Brown, "Short-Range Market Reaction to Changes to LIFO Accounting Using Preliminary Earnings Announcement Dates," *The Journal of Accounting Research* (Spring 1980), which found that companies that do change to LIFO suffer a short-run decline in the price of their stock.

[19]Note that a company can use one variation of LIFO for financial reporting purposes and another for tax without violating the LIFO conformity rule. Such a relaxation has caused many problems because the general approach to accounting for LIFO has been "whatever is good for tax is good for financial reporting."

that certain product lines can be highly susceptible to deflation instead of inflation. In addition, if the level of inventory is unstable, unwanted involuntary liquidations may result in certain product lines if using LIFO. Finally, for high inventory turnover in certain product lines, a company cannot justify LIFO's additional recordkeeping and expense. In such cases, a company often uses average-cost because it is easy to compute.[20]

Although a company may use a variety of inventory methods to assist in accurate computation of net income, once it selects a pricing method, it must apply it consistently thereafter. If conditions indicate that the inventory pricing method in use is unsuitable, the company must seriously consider all other possibilities before selecting another method. It should clearly explain any change and disclose its effect in the financial statements.

Evolving Issue   *REPEAL LIFO!*

In some situations, use of LIFO can result in significant tax savings for companies. For example, Sherwin-Williams Company estimates its tax bill would increase by $16 million if it were to change from LIFO to FIFO. The option to use LIFO to reduce taxes has become a political issue because of the growing federal deficit. Some are proposing elimination of LIFO (and other tax law changes) to help reduce the federal deficit. Why pick on LIFO? Well, one recent budget estimate indicates that repeal of LIFO would help plug the budget deficit with over $61 billion in additional tax collections. In addition, since IFRS does not permit LIFO, its repeal will contribute to international accounting convergence.

Source: R. Bloom and W. Cenker, "The Death of LIFO?" *Journal of Accountancy* (January 2009), pp. 44–49.

Inventory Valuation Methods—Summary Analysis

The preceding sections of this chapter described a number of inventory valuation methods. Here we present a brief summary of the three major inventory methods to show the effects these valuation methods have on the financial statements. This comparison assumes periodic inventory procedures and the following selected data.

Selected Data		
Beginning cash balance		$ 7,000
Beginning retained earnings		$10,000
Beginning inventory:	4,000 units @ $3	$12,000
Purchases:	6,000 units @ $4	$24,000
Sales:	5,000 units @ $12	$60,000
Operating expenses		$10,000
Income tax rate		40%

Illustration 8-31 (page 446) shows the comparative results on net income of the use of average-cost, FIFO, and LIFO. Notice that gross profit and net income are lowest under LIFO, highest under FIFO, and somewhere in the middle under average-cost.

[20]For an interesting discussion of the reasons for and against the use of FIFO and average-cost, see Michael H. Granof and Daniel G. Short, "For Some Companies, FIFO Accounting Makes Sense," *Wall Street Journal* (August 30, 1982); and the subsequent rebuttal by Gary C. Biddle, "Taking Stock of Inventory Accounting Choices," *Wall Street Journal* (September 15, 1982).

ILLUSTRATION 8-31
Comparative Results of
Average-Cost, FIFO, and
LIFO Methods

	Average-Cost	FIFO	LIFO
Sales	$60,000	$60,000	$60,000
Cost of goods sold	18,000[a]	16,000[b]	20,000[c]
Gross profit	42,000	44,000	40,000
Operating expenses	10,000	10,000	10,000
Income before taxes	32,000	34,000	30,000
Income taxes (40%)	12,800	13,600	12,000
Net income	$19,200	$20,400	$18,000

[a]4,000 @ $3 = $12,000
6,000 @ $4 = 24,000
$36,000

$36,000 ÷ 10,000 = $3.60
$3.60 × 5,000 = $18,000

[b]4,000 @ $3 = $12,000
1,000 @ $4 = 4,000
$16,000

[c]5,000 @ $4 = $20,000

Illustration 8-32 shows the final balances of selected items at the end of the period.

ILLUSTRATION 8-32
Balances of Selected
Items under Alternative
Inventory Valuation
Methods

	Inventory	Gross Profit	Taxes	Net Income	Retained Earnings	Cash
Average-Cost	$18,000 (5,000 × $3.60)	$42,000	$12,800	$19,200	$29,200 ($10,000 + $19,200)	$20,200[a]
FIFO	$20,000 (5,000 × $4)	$44,000	$13,600	$20,400	$30,400 ($10,000 + $20,400)	$19,400[a]
LIFO	$16,000 (4,000 × $3) (1,000 × $4)	$40,000	$12,000	$18,000	$28,000 ($10,000 + $18,000)	$21,000[a]

[a]Cash at year-end	=	Beg. Balance	+	Sales	−	Purchases	−	Operating expenses	−	Taxes
Average-cost—$20,200	=	$7,000	+	$60,000	−	$24,000	−	$10,000	−	$12,800
FIFO—$19,400	=	$7,000	+	$60,000	−	$24,000	−	$10,000	−	$13,600
LIFO—$21,000	=	$7,000	+	$60,000	−	$24,000	−	$10,000	−	$12,000

LIFO results in the highest cash balance at year-end (because taxes are lower). This example assumes that prices are rising. The opposite result occurs if prices are declining.

KEY TERMS

average-cost method, *429*

consigned goods, *422*

cost flow
    assumptions, *428*

dollar-value LIFO, *435*

double-extension
    method, *439*

finished goods
    inventory, *416*

first-in, first-out (FIFO)
    method, *430*

f.o.b. destination, *421*

f.o.b. shipping point, *421*

gross method, *427*

inventories, *416*

last-in, first-out (LIFO)
    method, *431*

SUMMARY OF LEARNING OBJECTIVES

1 Identify major classifications of inventory. Only one inventory account, Inventory, appears in the financial statements of a merchandising concern. A manufacturer normally has three inventory accounts: Raw Materials, Work in Process, and Finished Goods. Companies report the cost assigned to goods and materials on hand but not yet placed into production as raw materials inventory. They report the cost of the raw materials on which production has been started but not completed, plus the direct labor cost applied specifically to this material and a ratable share of manufacturing overhead costs, as work in process inventory. Finally, they report the costs identified with the completed but unsold units on hand at the end of the fiscal period as finished goods inventory.

2 Distinguish between perpetual and periodic inventory systems. A perpetual inventory system maintains a continuous record of inventory changes in the Inventory account. That is, a company records all purchases and sales (issues) of goods directly in the Inventory account as they occur. Under a periodic inventory system, companies determine the quantity of inventory on hand only periodically. A company debits a Purchases account, but the Inventory account remains the same. It determines cost of goods sold at the end of the period by subtracting ending inventory from cost of goods available for sale. A company ascertains ending inventory by physical count.

3 **Determine the goods included in inventory and the effects of inventory errors on the financial statements.** Companies record purchases of inventory when they obtain legal title to the goods (generally when they receive the goods). Shipping terms must be evaluated to determine when legal title passes, and careful consideration must be made for cost of goods sold on consignment and sales with buy-back agreements and high rates of return. *If the company misstates ending inventory:* (1) In the balance sheet, the inventory and retained earnings will be misstated, which will lead to miscalculation of the working capital and current ratio, and (2) in the income statement, the cost of goods sold and net income will be misstated. *If the company misstates purchases (and related accounts payable) and inventory:* (1) In the balance sheet, the inventory and accounts payable will be misstated, which will lead to miscalculation of the current ratio, and (2) in the income statement, purchases and ending inventory will be misstated.

4 **Understand the items to include as inventory cost.** Product costs are those costs that attach to the inventory and are recorded in the Inventory account. Such charges include freight charges on goods purchased, other direct costs of acquisition, and labor and other production costs incurred in processing the goods up to the time of sale. Period costs are those costs that are indirectly related to the acquisition or production of goods. These changes, such as selling expense and general and administrative expenses, are therefore not included as part of inventory cost.

5 **Describe and compare the cost flow assumptions used to account for inventories.** (1) *Average-cost* prices items in the inventory on the basis of the average cost of all similar goods available during the period. (2) *First-in, first-out (FIFO)* assumes that a company uses goods in the order in which it purchases them. The inventory remaining must therefore represent the most recent purchases. (3) *Last-in, first-out (LIFO)* matches the cost of the last goods purchased against revenue.

6 **Explain the significance and use of a LIFO reserve.** The difference between the inventory method used for internal reporting purposes and LIFO is referred to as Allowance to Reduce Inventory to LIFO, or the LIFO reserve. The change in LIFO reserve is referred to as the LIFO effect. Companies should disclose either the LIFO reserve or the replacement cost of the inventory in the financial statements.

7 **Understand the effect of LIFO liquidations.** LIFO liquidations match costs from preceding periods against sales revenues reported in current dollars. This distorts net income and results in increased taxable income in the current period. LIFO liquidations can occur frequently when using a specific-goods LIFO approach.

8 **Explain the dollar-value LIFO method.** For the dollar-value LIFO method, companies determine and measure increases and decreases in a pool in terms of total dollar value, not the physical quantity of the goods in the inventory pool.

9 **Identify the major advantages and disadvantages of LIFO.** The major advantages of LIFO are the following. (1) It matches recent costs against current revenues to provide a better measure of current earnings. (2) As long as the price level increases and inventory quantities do not decrease, a deferral of income tax occurs in LIFO. (3) Because of the deferral of income tax, cash flow improves. Major disadvantages are (1) reduced earnings, (2) understated inventory, (3) does not approximate physical flow of the items except in peculiar situations, and (4) involuntary liquidation issues.

10 **Understand why companies select given inventory methods.** Companies ordinarily prefer LIFO in the following circumstances: (1) if selling prices and revenues have been increasing faster than costs and (2) if a company has a fairly constant "base stock." Conversely, LIFO would probably not be appropriate in the following circumstances: (1) if sale prices tend to lag behind costs, (2) if specific identification is traditional, and (3) when unit costs tend to decrease as production increases, thereby nullifying the tax benefit that LIFO might provide.

LIFO effect, *432*

LIFO liquidation, *434*

LIFO reserve, *432*

merchandise
inventory, *416*

modified perpetual
inventory system, *419*

moving-average
method, *430*

net method, *427*

net of the cash
discounts, *427*

period costs, *426*

periodic inventory
system, *418*

perpetual inventory
system, *418*

product costs, *426*

Purchase Discounts, *426*

raw materials
inventory, *416*

specific-goods pooled
LIFO approach, *435*

specific identification, *428*

weighted-average
method, *429*

work in process
inventory, *416*

DEMONSTRATION PROBLEM

Clinton Company makes specialty cases for smart phones and other handheld devices. The company has experienced strong growth, and you are especially interested in how well Clinton is managing its inventory balances. You have collected the following information for the current year.

Inventory at the beginning of year	$ 1,555 million
Inventory at the end of year, before any adjustments	$ 1,267 million
Total cost of goods sold, before any adjustments	$17,844 million

The company values inventory at lower-of-cost (using LIFO cost flow assumption)-or-market.

Instructions

Prepare a schedule (a computer worksheet would serve well) showing the impact of the following items on Clinton's inventory turnover.

(a) Shipping contracts changed 2 months ago from f.o.b. shipping point to f.o.b. destination. At the end of the year, $5 million of products are en route to China (and will not arrive until after financial statements are released). Current inventory balances do not reflect this change in policy.

(b) During the year, Clinton recorded sales and costs of goods sold on $2 million of units shipped to various wholesalers on consignment. At year-end, none of these units have been sold by wholesalers.

(c) To be more consistent with industry inventory valuation practices, Clinton changed from LIFO to FIFO for its inventory of iPad cases. This inventory is currently carried at $724 million. Data for this item of inventory for the year are as follows.

Month	Units Purchased	Inventory Sold	Price per Unit	Units Balance
January 1	100		$3.10	100
April 15	150		3.20	250
October 25		130		120
November 10	250		3.50	370
December 20		150		220

(d) Explain to Clinton management the advantages of adopting the LIFO cost flow assumption. Are there any drawbacks? Explain.

Solution

(a)–(c)

	A	B	C	D	E	F
		Unadjusted Balance	Adjustment (a)	Adjustment (b)	Adjustment (c)	Adjusted Balance
3	Beginning inventory	$ 1,555.00	–	–	–	$ 1,555.00
4	Ending inventory	1,267.00	$ 5.00	$ 2.00	$ 46.00	1,320.00
5	Average inventory	1,411.00	–	–	–	1,437.50
6	Cost of goods sold	17,844.00	$(5.00)	$(2.00)	$(46.00)	17,791.00
7	Inventory turnover	12.65	–	–	–	12.38
8						
9	Explanation		Goods officially change hands at the point of destination.	Clinton should include the goods on consignment to other sellers.	Ending inventory under FIFO would be $770 (220 @ $3.50), which is $46 ($770 - $724) lower than LIFO.	

(d) The major advantages of the LIFO inventory method include better matching of costs with revenues, deferral of income taxes, improved cash flow, and minimization of the impact of future price declines on future earnings. Better matching arises in the use of LIFO because the most recent costs are matched with current revenues. In times of rising prices, this matching will result in lower taxable income, which in turn will reduce current taxes. The deferral of taxes under LIFO contributes to a higher cash flow. As illustrated in the analysis above, the switch to FIFO resulted in a higher ending inventory, which leads to a lower cost of goods sold and higher income. Thus, Clinton's reported income will be higher but so will its taxes. Note that under LIFO, future taxes may be higher when lower cost items of inventory are sold in future periods and matched with higher sales prices.

FASB CODIFICATION

FASB Codification References

[1] FASB ASC 470-40-05. [Predecessor literature: "Accounting for Product Financing Arrangements," *Statement of Financial Accounting Standards No. 49* (Stamford, Conn.: FASB, 1981).]

[2] FASB ASC 605-15-15. [Predecessor literature: "Revenue Recognition When Right of Return Exists," *Statement of Financial Accounting Standards No. 48* (Stamford, Conn.: FASB, 1981).]

[3] FASB ASC 330-10-30-7. [Predecessor literature: "Inventory Costs: An Amendment of ARB No. 43, Chapter 4," *Statement of Financial Accounting Standards No. 151* (Norwalk, Conn.: FASB 2004).]

[4] FASB ASC 835-20-05. [Predecessor literature: "Capitalization of Interest Cost," *Statement of Financial Accounting Standards No. 34* (Stamford, Conn.: FASB, 1979).]

[5] FASB ASC 645-45-05. [Predecessor literature: "Accounting for Shipping and Handling Fees and Costs," *EITF No. 00–10* (2000).]

[6] FASB ASC 330-10-30. [Predecessor literature: "Restatement and Revision of Accounting Research Bulletins," *Accounting Research Bulletin No. 43* (New York: AICPA, 1953), Ch. 4, Statement 4.]

[7] FASB ASC 330-10-S99-1. [Predecessor literature: "AICPA Task Force on LIFO Inventory Problems, *Issues Paper* (New York: AICPA, November 30, 1984), pp. 2–24.]

[8] FASB ASC 330-10-S99-3. [Predecessor literature: "AICPA Task Force on LIFO Inventory Problems, *Issues Paper* (New York: AICPA, November 30, 1984), pp. 36–37.]

Exercises

If your school has a subscription to the FASB Codification, go to *http://aaahq.org/asclogin.cfm* to log in and prepare responses to the following. Provide Codification references for your responses.

CE8-1 Access the glossary ("Master Glossary") to answer the following.
    (a) What is the definition provided for inventory?
    (b) What is a customer?
    (c) Under what conditions is a distributor considered a customer?
    (d) What is a product financing arrangement? What inventory measurement issues are raised through these arrangements?

CE8-2 Due to rising fuel costs, your client, Overstock.com, is considering adding a charge for shipping and handling costs on products sold through its website. What is the authoritative guidance for reporting these costs?

CE8-3 What guidance does the Codification provide concerning reporting inventories above cost?

CE8-4 What is the nature of the SEC guidance concerning the reporting of LIFO liquidations?

An additional Codification case can be found in the Using Your Judgment section, on page 471.

Be sure to check the book's companion website for a Review and Analysis Exercise, with solution.

WileyPLUS   Brief Exercises, Exercises, Problems, and many more learning and assessment tools and resources are available for practice in WileyPLUS.

QUESTIONS

1. In what ways are the inventory accounts of a retailing company different from those of a manufacturing company?

2. Why should inventories be included in (a) a statement of financial position and (b) the computation of net income?

3. What is the difference between a perpetual inventory and a physical inventory? If a company maintains a perpetual inventory, should its physical inventory at any date be equal to the amount indicated by the perpetual inventory records? Why?

4. Mishima, Inc. indicated in a recent annual report that approximately $19 million of merchandise was received on consignment. Should Mishima, Inc. report this amount on its balance sheet? Explain.

5. What is a product financing arrangement? How should product financing arrangements be reported in the financial statements?

6. Where, if at all, should the following items be classified on a balance sheet?
   (a) Goods out on approval to customers.
   (b) Goods in transit that were recently purchased f.o.b. destination.
   (c) Land held by a realty firm for sale.
   (d) Raw materials.
   (e) Goods received on consignment.
   (f) Manufacturing supplies.

7. At the balance sheet date, Clarkson Company held title to goods in transit amounting to $214,000. This amount was omitted from the purchases figure for the year and also from the ending inventory. What is the effect of this omission on the net income for the year as calculated when the books are closed? What is the effect on the company's financial position as shown in its balance sheet? Is materiality a factor in determining whether an adjustment for this item should be made?

8. Define "cost" as applied to the valuation of inventories.

9. Distinguish between product costs and period costs as they relate to inventory.

10. Ford Motor Co. is considering alternate methods of accounting for the cash discounts it takes when paying suppliers promptly. One method suggested was to report these discounts as financial income when payments are made. Comment on the propriety of this approach.

11. Zonker Inc. purchases 500 units of an item at an invoice cost of $30,000. What is the cost per unit? If the goods are shipped f.o.b. shipping point and the freight bill was $1,500, what is the cost per unit if Zonker Inc. pays the freight charges? If these items were bought on 2/10, n/30 terms and the invoice and the freight bill were paid within the 10-day period, what would be the cost per unit?

12. Specific identification is sometimes said to be the ideal method of assigning cost to inventory and to cost of goods sold. Briefly indicate the arguments for and against this method of inventory valuation.

13. FIFO, average-cost, and LIFO methods are often used instead of specific identification for inventory valuation purposes. Compare these methods with the specific identification method, discussing the theoretical propriety of each method in the determination of income and asset valuation.

14. How might a company obtain a price index in order to apply dollar-value LIFO?

15. Describe the LIFO double-extension method. Using the following information, compute the index at December 31, 2014, applying the double-extension method to a LIFO pool consisting of 25,500 units of product A and 10,350 units of product B. The base-year cost of product A is $10.20 and of product B is $37.00. The price at December 31, 2014, for product A is $21.00 and for product B is $45.60. (Round to two decimal places.)

16. As compared with the FIFO method of costing inventories, does the LIFO method result in a larger or smaller net income in a period of rising prices? What is the comparative effect on net income in a period of falling prices?

17. What is the dollar-value method of LIFO inventory valuation? What advantage does the dollar-value method have over the specific goods approach of LIFO inventory valuation? Why will the traditional LIFO inventory costing method and the dollar-value LIFO inventory costing method produce different inventory valuations if the composition of the inventory base changes?

18. Explain the following terms.
   (a) LIFO layer.
   (b) LIFO reserve.
   (c) LIFO effect.

19. On December 31, 2013, the inventory of Powhattan Company amounts to $800,000. During 2014, the company decides to use the dollar-value LIFO method of costing inventories. On December 31, 2014, the inventory is $1,053,000 at December 31, 2014, prices. Using the December 31, 2013, price level of 100 and the December 31, 2014, price level of 108, compute the inventory value at December 31, 2014, under the dollar-value LIFO method.

20. In an article that appeared in the *Wall Street Journal*, the phrases "phantom (paper) profits" and "high LIFO profits" through involuntary liquidation were used. Explain these phrases.

BRIEF EXERCISES

1 ▶ **BE8-1** Included in the December 31 trial balance of Rivera Company are the following assets.

Cash	$ 190,000	Work in process	$200,000
Equipment (net)	1,100,000	Accounts receivable (net)	400,000
Prepaid insurance	41,000	Patents	110,000
Raw materials	335,000	Finished goods	170,000

Prepare the current assets section of the December 31 balance sheet.

2 ▶ **BE8-2** Matlock Company uses a perpetual inventory system. Its beginning inventory consists of 50 units that cost $34 each. During June, the company purchased 150 units at $34 each, returned 6 units for credit, and sold 125 units at $50 each. Journalize the June transactions.

4 ▶ **BE8-3** Stallman Company took a physical inventory on December 31 and determined that goods costing $200,000 were on hand. Not included in the physical count were $25,000 of goods purchased from Pelzer Corporation, f.o.b. shipping point, and $22,000 of goods sold to Alvarez Company for $30,000, f.o.b. destination. Both the Pelzer purchase and the Alvarez sale were in transit at year-end. What amount should Stallman report as its December 31 inventory?

3 ▶ **BE8-4** Bienvenu Enterprises reported cost of goods sold for 2014 of $1,400,000 and retained earnings of $5,200,000 at December 31, 2014. Bienvenu later discovered that its ending inventories at December 31, 2013 and 2014, were overstated by $110,000 and $35,000, respectively. Determine the corrected amounts for 2014 cost of goods sold and December 31, 2014, retained earnings.

5 ▶ **BE8-5** Amsterdam Company uses a periodic inventory system. For April, when the company sold 600 units, the following information is available.

	Units	Unit Cost	Total Cost
April 1 inventory	250	$10	$ 2,500
April 15 purchase	400	12	4,800
April 23 purchase	350	13	4,550
	1,000		$11,850

Compute the April 30 inventory and the April cost of goods sold using the average-cost method.

5 ▶ **BE8-6** Data for Amsterdam Company are presented in BE8-5. Compute the April 30 inventory and the April cost of goods sold using the FIFO method.

5 ▶ **BE8-7** Data for Amsterdam Company are presented in BE8-5. Compute the April 30 inventory and the April cost of goods sold using the LIFO method.

8 ▶ **BE8-8** Midori Company had ending inventory at end-of-year prices of $100,000 at December 31, 2013; $119,900 at December 31, 2014; and $134,560 at December 31, 2015. The year-end price indexes were 100 at 12/31/13, 110 at 12/31/14, and 116 at 12/31/15. Compute the ending inventory for Midori Company for 2013 through 2015 using the dollar-value LIFO method.

8 ▶ **BE8-9** Arna, Inc. uses the dollar-value LIFO method of computing its inventory. Data for the past 3 years follow.

Year Ended December 31	Inventory at Current-Year Cost	Price Index
2013	$19,750	100
2014	22,140	108
2015	25,935	114

Instructions

Compute the value of the 2014 and 2015 inventories using the dollar-value LIFO method.

EXERCISES

4 **E8-1 (Inventoriable Costs)** Presented below is a list of items that may or may not be reported as inventory in a company's December 31 balance sheet.

1. Goods out on consignment at another company's store.
2. Goods sold on an installment basis (bad debts can be reasonably estimated).
3. Goods purchased f.o.b. shipping point that are in transit at December 31.
4. Goods purchased f.o.b. destination that are in transit at December 31.
5. Goods sold to another company, for which our company has signed an agreement to repurchase at a set price that covers all costs related to the inventory.
6. Goods sold where large returns are predictable.
7. Goods sold f.o.b. shipping point that are in transit at December 31.
8. Freight charges on goods purchased.
9. Interest costs incurred for inventories that are routinely manufactured.
10. Costs incurred to advertise goods held for resale.
11. Materials on hand not yet placed into production by a manufacturing firm.
12. Office supplies.
13. Raw materials on which a manufacturing firm has started production but which are not completely processed.
14. Factory supplies.
15. Goods held on consignment from another company.
16. Costs identified with units completed by a manufacturing firm but not yet sold.
17. Goods sold f.o.b. destination that are in transit at December 31.
18. Short-term investments in stocks and bonds that will be resold in the near future.

Instructions
Indicate which of these items would typically be reported as inventory in the financial statements. If an item should **not** be reported as inventory, indicate how it should be reported in the financial statements.

4 **E8-2 (Inventoriable Costs)** In your audit of Jose Oliva Company, you find that a physical inventory on December 31, 2014, showed merchandise with a cost of $441,000 was on hand at that date. You also discover the following items were all excluded from the $441,000.

1. Merchandise of $61,000 which is held by Oliva on consignment. The consignor is the Max Suzuki Company.
2. Merchandise costing $38,000 which was shipped by Oliva f.o.b. destination to a customer on December 31, 2014. The customer was expected to receive the merchandise on January 6, 2015.
3. Merchandise costing $46,000 which was shipped by Oliva f.o.b. shipping point to a customer on December 29, 2014. The customer was scheduled to receive the merchandise on January 2, 2015.
4. Merchandise costing $83,000 shipped by a vendor f.o.b. destination on December 30, 2014, and received by Oliva on January 4, 2015.
5. Merchandise costing $51,000 shipped by a vendor f.o.b. shipping point on December 31, 2014, and received by Oliva on January 5, 2015.

Instructions
Based on the above information, calculate the amount that should appear on Oliva's balance sheet at December 31, 2014, for inventory.

4 **E8-3 (Inventoriable Costs)** Assume that in an annual audit of Harlowe Inc. at December 31, 2014, you find the following transactions near the closing date.

1. A special machine, fabricated to order for a customer, was finished and specifically segregated in the back part of the shipping room on December 31, 2014. The customer was billed on that date and the machine excluded from inventory although it was shipped on January 4, 2015.
2. Merchandise costing $2,800 was received on January 3, 2015, and the related purchase invoice recorded January 5. The invoice showed the shipment was made on December 29, 2014, f.o.b. destination.
3. A packing case containing a product costing $3,400 was standing in the shipping room when the physical inventory was taken. It was not included in the inventory because it was marked "Hold for shipping instructions." Your investigation revealed that the customer's order was dated December 18, 2014, but that the case was shipped and the customer billed on January 10, 2015. The product was a stock item of your client.

4. Merchandise received on January 6, 2015, costing $680 was entered in the purchase journal on January 7, 2015. The invoice showed shipment was made f.o.b. supplier's warehouse on December 31, 2014. Because it was not on hand at December 31, it was not included in inventory.
5. Merchandise costing $720 was received on December 28, 2014, and the invoice was not recorded. You located it in the hands of the purchasing agent; it was marked "on consignment."

Instructions

Assuming that each of the amounts is material, state whether the merchandise should be included in the client's inventory, and give your reason for your decision on each item.

2 4 **E8-4 (Inventoriable Costs—Perpetual)** Colin Davis Machine Company maintains a general ledger account for each class of inventory, debiting such accounts for increases during the period and crediting them for decreases. The transactions below relate to the Raw Materials inventory account, which is debited for materials purchased and credited for materials requisitioned for use.

1. An invoice for $8,100, terms f.o.b. destination, was received and entered January 2, 2014. The receiving report shows that the materials were received December 28, 2013.
2. Materials costing $28,000, shipped f.o.b. destination, were not entered by December 31, 2013, "because they were in a railroad car on the company's siding on that date and had not been unloaded."
3. Materials costing $7,300 were returned to the supplier on December 29, 2013, and were shipped f.o.b. shipping point. The return was entered on that date, even though the materials are not expected to reach the supplier's place of business until January 6, 2014.
4. An invoice for $7,500, terms f.o.b. shipping point, was received and entered December 30, 2013. The receiving report shows that the materials were received January 4, 2014, and the bill of lading shows that they were shipped January 2, 2014.
5. Materials costing $19,800 were received December 30, 2013, but no entry was made for them because "they were ordered with a specified delivery of no earlier than January 10, 2014."

Instructions

Prepare correcting general journal entries required at December 31, 2013, assuming that the books have not been closed.

3 4 **E8-5 (Inventoriable Costs—Error Adjustments)** Craig Company asks you to review its December 31, 2014, inventory values and prepare the necessary adjustments to the books. The following information is given to you.

1. Craig uses the periodic method of recording inventory. A physical count reveals $234,890 of inventory on hand at December 31, 2014.
2. Not included in the physical count of inventory is $13,420 of merchandise purchased on December 15 from Browser. This merchandise was shipped f.o.b. shipping point on December 29 and arrived in January. The invoice arrived and was recorded on December 31.
3. Included in inventory is merchandise sold to Champy on December 30, f.o.b. destination. This merchandise was shipped after it was counted. The invoice was prepared and recorded as a sale on account for $12,800 on December 31. The merchandise cost $7,350, and Champy received it on January 3.
4. Included in inventory was merchandise received from Dudley on December 31 with an invoice price of $15,630. The merchandise was shipped f.o.b. destination. The invoice, which has not yet arrived, has not been recorded.
5. Not included in inventory is $8,540 of merchandise purchased from Glowser Industries. This merchandise was received on December 31 after the inventory had been counted. The invoice was received and recorded on December 30.
6. Included in inventory was $10,438 of inventory held by Craig on consignment from Jackel Industries.
7. Included in inventory is merchandise sold to Kemp f.o.b. shipping point. This merchandise was shipped after it was counted. The invoice was prepared and recorded as a sale for $18,900 on December 31. The cost of this merchandise was $10,520, and Kemp received the merchandise on January 5.
8. Excluded from inventory was a carton labeled "Please accept for credit." This carton contains merchandise costing $1,500 which had been sold to a customer for $2,600. No entry had been made to the books to reflect the return, but none of the returned merchandise seemed damaged.

Instructions

(a) Determine the proper inventory balance for Craig Company at December 31, 2014.
(b) Prepare any correcting entries to adjust inventory to its proper amount at December 31, 2014. Assume the books have not been closed.

4 **E8-6 (Determining Merchandise Amounts—Periodic)** Two or more items are omitted in each of the following tabulations of income statement data. Fill in the amounts that are missing.

	2013	2014	2015
Sales revenue	$290,000	$?	$410,000
Sales returns and allowances	11,000	13,000	?
Net sales	?	347,000	?
Beginning inventory	20,000	32,000	?
Ending inventory	?	?	?
Purchases	?	260,000	298,000
Purchase returns and allowances	5,000	8,000	10,000
Freight-in	8,000	9,000	12,000
Cost of goods sold	233,000	?	293,000
Gross profit on sales	46,000	91,000	97,000

4 **E8-7 (Purchases Recorded Net)** Presented below are transactions related to Tom Brokaw, Inc.

May 10 Purchased goods billed at $15,000 subject to cash discount terms of 2/10, n/60.
　　11 Purchased goods billed at $13,200 subject to terms of 1/15, n/30.
　　19 Paid invoice of May 10.
　　24 Purchased goods billed at $11,500 subject to cash discount terms of 2/10, n/30.

Instructions

(a) Prepare general journal entries for the transactions above under the assumption that purchases are to be recorded at net amounts after cash discounts and that discounts lost are to be treated as financial expense.

(b) Assuming no purchase or payment transactions other than those given above, prepare the adjusting entry required on May 31 if financial statements are to be prepared as of that date.

4 **E8-8 (Purchases Recorded, Gross Method)** Cruise Industries purchased $10,800 of merchandise on February 1, 2014, subject to a trade discount of 10% and with credit terms of 3/15, n/60. It returned $2,500 (gross price before trade or cash discount) on February 4. The invoice was paid on February 13.

Instructions

(a) Assuming that Cruise uses the perpetual method for recording merchandise transactions, record the purchase, return, and payment using the gross method.

(b) Assuming that Cruise uses the periodic method for recording merchandise transactions, record the purchase, return, and payment using the gross method.

(c) At what amount would the purchase on February 1 be recorded if the net method were used?

2 **E8-9 (Periodic versus Perpetual Entries)** Fong Sai-Yuk Company sells one product. Presented below is information for January for Fong Sai-Yuk Company.

Jan. 1 Inventory　　100 units at $5 each
　　 4 Sale　　　　 80 units at $8 each
　　11 Purchase　　150 units at $6 each
　　13 Sale　　　　 120 units at $8.75 each
　　20 Purchase　　160 units at $7 each
　　27 Sale　　　　 100 units at $9 each

Fong Sai-Yuk uses the FIFO cost flow assumption. All purchases and sales are on account.

Instructions

(a) Assume Fong Sai-Yuk uses a periodic system. Prepare all necessary journal entries, including the end-of-month closing entry to record cost of goods sold. A physical count indicates that the ending inventory for January is 110 units.

(b) Compute gross profit using the periodic system.

(c) Assume Fong Sai-Yuk uses a perpetual system. Prepare all necessary journal entries.

(d) Compute gross profit using the perpetual system.

3 **E8-10 (Inventory Errors—Periodic)** Ann M. Martin Company makes the following errors during the current year. (Evaluate each case independently and assume ending inventory in the following year is correctly stated.)

1. Ending inventory is overstated, but purchases and related accounts payable are recorded correctly.
2. Both ending inventory and purchases and related accounts payable are understated. (Assume this purchase was recorded and paid for in the following year.)
3. Ending inventory is correct, but a purchase on account was not recorded. (Assume this purchase was recorded and paid for in the following year.)

Instructions
Indicate the effect of each of these errors on working capital, current ratio (assume that the current ratio is greater than 1), retained earnings, and net income for the current year and the subsequent year.

3 **E8-11 (Inventory Errors)** At December 31, 2013, Stacy McGill Corporation reported current assets of $370,000 and current liabilities of $200,000. The following items may have been recorded incorrectly.

1. Goods purchased costing $22,000 were shipped f.o.b. shipping point by a supplier on December 28. McGill received and recorded the invoice on December 29, 2013, but the goods were not included in McGill's physical count of inventory because they were not received until January 4, 2014.
2. Goods purchased costing $15,000 were shipped f.o.b. destination by a supplier on December 26. McGill received and recorded the invoice on December 31, but the goods were not included in McGill's 2013 physical count of inventory because they were not received until January 2, 2014.
3. Goods held on consignment from Claudia Kishi Company were included in McGill's December 31, 2013, physical count of inventory at $13,000.
4. Freight-in of $3,000 was debited to advertising expense on December 28, 2013.

Instructions
(a) Compute the current ratio based on McGill's balance sheet.
(b) Recompute the current ratio after corrections are made.
(c) By what amount will income (before taxes) be adjusted up or down as a result of the corrections?

3 **E8-12 (Inventory Errors)** The net income per books of Linda Patrick Company was determined without knowledge of the errors indicated.

Year	Net Income per Books	Error in Ending Inventory	
2009	$50,000	Overstated	$ 3,000
2010	52,000	Overstated	9,000
2011	54,000	Understated	11,000
2012	56,000	No error	
2013	58,000	Understated	2,000
2014	60,000	Overstated	8,000

Instructions
Prepare a worksheet to show the adjusted net income figure for each of the 6 years after taking into account the inventory errors.

2 **5** **E8-13 (FIFO and LIFO—Periodic and Perpetual)** Inventory information for Part 311 of Monique Aaron Corp. discloses the following information for the month of June.

June 1	Balance	300 units @ $10	June 10	Sold	200 units @ $24
11	Purchased	800 units @ $12	15	Sold	500 units @ $25
20	Purchased	500 units @ $13	27	Sold	300 units @ $27

Instructions
(a) Assuming that the periodic inventory method is used, compute the cost of goods sold and ending inventory under (1) LIFO and (2) FIFO.
(b) Assuming that the perpetual inventory method is used and costs are computed at the time of each withdrawal, what is the value of the ending inventory at LIFO?
(c) Assuming that the perpetual inventory method is used and costs are computed at the time of each withdrawal, what is the gross profit if the inventory is valued at FIFO?
(d) Why is it stated that LIFO usually produces a lower gross profit than FIFO?

5 **E8-14 (FIFO, LIFO and Average-Cost Determination)** John Adams Company's record of transactions for the month of April was as follows.

Purchases			Sales		
April 1 (balance on hand)	600 @ $ 6.00		April 3	500 @ $10.00	
4	1,500 @ 6.08		9	1,400 @ 10.00	
8	800 @ 6.40		11	600 @ 11.00	
13	1,200 @ 6.50		23	1,200 @ 11.00	
21	700 @ 6.60		27	900 @ 12.00	
29	500 @ 6.79			4,600	
	5,300				

Instructions

(a) Assuming that periodic inventory records are kept in units only, compute the inventory at April 30 using (1) LIFO and (2) average-cost.

(b) Assuming that perpetual inventory records are kept in dollars, determine the inventory using (1) FIFO and (2) LIFO.

(c) Compute cost of goods sold assuming periodic inventory procedures and inventory priced at FIFO.

(d) In an inflationary period, which inventory method—FIFO, LIFO, average-cost—will show the highest net income?

5 **E8-15 (FIFO, LIFO, Average-Cost Inventory)** Shania Twain Company was formed on December 1, 2013. The following information is available from Twain's inventory records for Product BAP.

	Units	Unit Cost
January 1, 2014 (beginning inventory)	600	$ 8.00
Purchases:		
January 5, 2014	1,200	9.00
January 25, 2014	1,300	10.00
February 16, 2014	800	11.00
March 26, 2014	600	12.00

A physical inventory on March 31, 2014, shows 1,600 units on hand.

Instructions

Prepare schedules to compute the ending inventory at March 31, 2014, under each of the following inventory methods.

(a) FIFO.   (b) LIFO.   (c) Weighted-average (round unit costs to two decimal places).

5 **E8-16 (Compute FIFO, LIFO, Average-Cost—Periodic)** Presented below is information related to Blowfish radios for the Hootie Company for the month of July.

Date	Transaction	Units In	Unit Cost	Total	Units Sold	Selling Price	Total
July 1	Balance	100	$4.10	$ 410			
6	Purchase	800	4.20	3,360			
7	Sale				300	$7.00	$ 2,100
10	Sale				300	7.30	2,190
12	Purchase	400	4.50	1,800			
15	Sale				200	7.40	1,480
18	Purchase	300	4.60	1,380			
22	Sale				400	7.40	2,960
25	Purchase	500	4.58	2,290			
30	Sale				200	7.50	1,500
	Totals	2,100		$9,240	1,400		$10,230

Instructions

(a) Assuming that the periodic inventory method is used, compute the inventory cost at July 31 under each of the following cost flow assumptions.

(1) FIFO.

(2) LIFO.

(3) Weighted-average.

(b) Answer the following questions.

(1) Which of the methods used above will yield the lowest figure for gross profit for the income statement? Explain why.

(2) Which of the methods used above will yield the lowest figure for ending inventory for the balance sheet? Explain why.

2 **5** **E8-17 (FIFO and LIFO—Periodic and Perpetual)** The following is a record of Pervis Ellison Company's transactions for Boston Teapots for the month of May 2014.

May 1	Balance 400 units @ $20	May 10	Sale 300 units @ $38
12	Purchase 600 units @ $25	20	Sale 540 units @ $38
28	Purchase 400 units @ $30		

Instructions

(a) Assuming that perpetual inventories are **not** maintained and that a physical count at the end of the month shows 560 units on hand, what is the cost of the ending inventory using (1) FIFO and (2) LIFO?

(b) Assuming that perpetual records are maintained and they tie into the general ledger, calculate the ending inventory using (1) FIFO and (2) LIFO.

5 E8-18 (FIFO and LIFO; Income Statement Presentation) The board of directors of Ichiro Corporation is considering whether or not it should instruct the accounting department to shift from a first-in, first-out (FIFO) basis of pricing inventories to a last-in, first-out (LIFO) basis. The following information is available.

Sales	21,000 units @ $50
Inventory, January 1	6,000 units @ 20
Purchases	6,000 units @ 22
	10,000 units @ 25
	7,000 units @ 30
Inventory, December 31	8,000 units @ ?
Operating expenses	$200,000

Instructions

Prepare a condensed income statement for the year on both bases for comparative purposes.

5 E8-19 (FIFO and LIFO Effects) You are the vice president of finance of Sandy Alomar Corporation, a retail company that prepared two different schedules of gross margin for the first quarter ended March 31, 2014. These schedules appear below.

	Sales ($5 per unit)	Cost of Goods Sold	Gross Margin
Schedule 1	$150,000	$124,900	$25,100
Schedule 2	150,000	129,400	20,600

The computation of cost of goods sold in each schedule is based on the following data.

	Units	Cost per Unit	Total Cost
Beginning inventory, January 1	10,000	$4.00	$40,000
Purchase, January 10	8,000	4.20	33,600
Purchase, January 30	6,000	4.25	25,500
Purchase, February 11	9,000	4.30	38,700
Purchase, March 17	11,000	4.40	48,400

Jane Torville, the president of the corporation, cannot understand how two different gross margins can be computed from the same set of data. As the vice president of finance, you have explained to Ms. Torville that the two schedules are based on different assumptions concerning the flow of inventory costs, i.e., FIFO and LIFO. Schedules 1 and 2 were not necessarily prepared in this sequence of cost flow assumptions.

Instructions

Prepare two separate schedules computing cost of goods sold and supporting schedules showing the composition of the ending inventory under both cost flow assumptions.

5 E8-20 (FIFO and LIFO—Periodic) Johnny Football Shop began operations on January 2, 2014. The following stock record card for footballs was taken from the records at the end of the year.

Date	Voucher	Terms	Units Received	Unit Invoice Cost	Gross Invoice Amount
1/15	10624	Net 30	50	$20	$1,000
3/15	11437	1/5, net 30	65	16	1,040
6/20	21332	1/10, net 30	90	15	1,350
9/12	27644	1/10, net 30	84	12	1,008
11/24	31269	1/10, net 30	76	11	836
	Totals		365		$5,234

A physical inventory on December 31, 2014, reveals that 100 footballs were in stock. The bookkeeper informs you that all the discounts were taken. Assume that Johnny Football Shop uses the invoice price less discount for recording purchases.

Instructions

(a) Compute the December 31, 2014, inventory using the FIFO method.

(b) Compute the 2014 cost of goods sold using the LIFO method.

(c) What method would you recommend to the owner to minimize income taxes in 2014, using the inventory information for footballs as a guide?

6 E8-21 (LIFO Effect) The following example was provided to encourage the use of the LIFO method. In a nutshell, LIFO subtracts inflation from inventory costs, deducts it from taxable income, and records it in a LIFO reserve account on the books. The LIFO benefit grows as inflation widens the gap between current-year and past-year (minus inflation) inventory costs. This gap is:

	With LIFO	Without LIFO
Revenues	$3,200,000	$3,200,000
Cost of goods sold	2,800,000	2,800,000
Operating expenses	150,000	150,000
Operating income	250,000	250,000
LIFO adjustment	40,000	0
Taxable income	$ 210,000	$ 250,000
Income taxes @ 36%	$ 75,600	$ 90,000
Cash flow	$ 174,400	$ 160,000
Extra cash	$ 14,400	0
Increased cash flow	9%	0%

Instructions

(a) Explain what is meant by the LIFO reserve account.

(b) How does LIFO subtract inflation from inventory costs?

(c) Explain how the cash flow of $174,400 in this example was computed. Explain why this amount may not be correct.

(d) Why does a company that uses LIFO have extra cash? Explain whether this situation will always exist.

5 8 E8-22 (Alternative Inventory Methods—Comprehensive) Tori Amos Corporation began operations on December 1, 2013. The only inventory transaction in 2013 was the purchase of inventory on December 10, 2013, at a cost of $20 per unit. None of this inventory was sold in 2013. Relevant information is as follows.

Ending inventory units		
December 31, 2013		100
December 31, 2014, by purchase date		
December 2, 2014	100	
July 20, 2014	50	150

During the year, the following purchases and sales were made.

Purchases		Sales	
March 15	300 units at $24	April 10	200
July 20	300 units at 25	August 20	300
September 4	200 units at 28	November 18	150
December 2	100 units at 30	December 12	200

The company uses the periodic inventory method.

Instructions

(a) Determine ending inventory under (1) specific identification, (2) FIFO, (3) LIFO, and (4) average-cost.

(b) Determine ending inventory using dollar-value LIFO. Assume that the December 2, 2014, purchase cost is the current cost of inventory. (*Hint:* The beginning inventory is the base layer priced at $20 per unit.)

8 E8-23 (Dollar-Value LIFO) Oasis Company has used the dollar-value LIFO method for inventory cost determination for many years. The following data were extracted from Oasis' records.

Date	Price Index	Ending Inventory at Base Prices	Ending Inventory at Dollar-Value LIFO
December 31, 2014	105	$92,000	$92,600
December 31, 2015	?	97,000	98,350

Instructions

Calculate the index used for 2015 that yielded the above results.

8 **E8-24 (Dollar-Value LIFO)** The dollar-value LIFO method was adopted by Enya Corp. on January 1, 2014. Its inventory on that date was $160,000. On December 31, 2014, the inventory at prices existing on that date amounted to $140,000. The price level at January 1, 2014, was 100, and the price level at December 31, 2014, was 112.

Instructions
(a) Compute the amount of the inventory at December 31, 2014, under the dollar-value LIFO method.
(b) On December 31, 2015, the inventory at prices existing on that date was $172,500, and the price level was 115. Compute the inventory on that date under the dollar-value LIFO method.

8 **E8-25 (Dollar-Value LIFO)** Presented below is information related to Dino Radja Company.

Date	Ending Inventory (End-of-Year Prices)	Price Index
December 31, 2011	$ 80,000	100
December 31, 2012	115,500	105
December 31, 2013	108,000	120
December 31, 2014	122,200	130
December 31, 2015	154,000	140
December 31, 2016	176,900	145

Instructions
Compute the ending inventory for Dino Radja Company for 2011 through 2016 using the dollar-value LIFO method.

8 **E8-26 (Dollar-Value LIFO)** The following information relates to the Jimmy Johnson Company.

Date	Ending Inventory (End-of-Year Prices)	Price Index
December 31, 2010	$ 70,000	100
December 31, 2011	90,300	105
December 31, 2012	95,120	116
December 31, 2013	105,600	120
December 31, 2014	100,000	125

Instructions
Use the dollar-value LIFO method to compute the ending inventory for Johnson Company for 2010 through 2014.

EXERCISES SET B

See the book's companion website, at **www.wiley.com/college/kieso**, for an additional set of exercises.

PROBLEMS

4 **5** **P8-1 (Various Inventory Issues)** The following independent situations relate to inventory accounting.
8

1. Kim Co. purchased goods with a list price of $175,000, subject to trade discounts of 20% and 10%, with no cash discounts allowable. How much should Kim Co. record as the cost of these goods?
2. Keillor Company's inventory of $1,100,000 at December 31, 2014, was based on a physical count of goods priced at cost and before any year-end adjustments relating to the following items.
   (a) Goods shipped from a vendor f.o.b. shipping point on December 24, 2014, at an invoice cost of $69,000 to Keillor Company were received on January 4, 2015.
   (b) The physical count included $29,000 of goods billed to Sakic Corp. f.o.b. shipping point on December 31, 2014. The carrier picked up these goods on January 3, 2015.
   What amount should Keillor report as inventory on its balance sheet?
3. Zimmerman Corp. had 1,500 units of part M.O. on hand May 1, 2014, costing $21 each. Purchases of part M.O. during May were as follows.

	Units	Unit Cost
May 9	2,000	$22.00
17	3,500	23.00
26	1,000	24.00

A physical count on May 31, 2014, shows 2,000 units of part M.O. on hand. Using the FIFO method, what is the cost of part M.O. inventory at May 31, 2014? Using the LIFO method, what is the inventory cost? Using the average-cost method, what is the inventory cost?

4. Ashbrook Company adopted the dollar-value LIFO method on January 1, 2014 (using internal price indexes and multiple pools). The following data are available for inventory pool A for the 2 years following adoption of LIFO.

Inventory	At Base-Year Cost	At Current-Year Cost
1/1/14	$200,000	$200,000
12/31/14	240,000	264,000
12/31/15	256,000	286,720

Computing an internal price index and using the dollar-value LIFO method, at what amount should the inventory be reported at December 31, 2015?

5. Donovan Inc., a retail store chain, had the following information in its general ledger for the year 2015.

Merchandise purchased for resale	$909,400
Interest on notes payable to vendors	8,700
Purchase returns	16,500
Freight-in	22,000
Freight-out (delivery expense)	17,100
Cash discounts on purchases	6,800

What is Donovan's inventoriable cost for 2015?

Instructions

Answer each of the preceding questions about inventories, and explain your answers.

3 4 P8-2 (Inventory Adjustments) Dimitri Company, a manufacturer of small tools, provided the following information from its accounting records for the year ended December 31, 2014.

Inventory at December 31, 2014 (based on physical count of goods in Dimitri's plant, at cost, on December 31, 2014)	$1,520,000
Accounts payable at December 31, 2014	1,200,000
Net sales (sales less sales returns)	8,150,000

Additional information is as follows.

1. Included in the physical count were tools billed to a customer f.o.b. shipping point on December 31, 2014. These tools had a cost of $31,000 and were billed at $40,000. The shipment was on Dimitri's loading dock waiting to be picked up by the common carrier.

2. Goods were in transit from a vendor to Dimitri on December 31, 2014. The invoice cost was $76,000, and the goods were shipped f.o.b. shipping point on December 29, 2014.

3. Work in process inventory costing $30,000 was sent to an outside processor for plating on December 30, 2014.

4. Tools returned by customers and held pending inspection in the returned goods area on December 31, 2014, were not included in the physical count. On January 8, 2015, the tools costing $32,000 were inspected and returned to inventory. Credit memos totaling $47,000 were issued to the customers on the same date.

5. Tools shipped to a customer f.o.b. destination on December 26, 2014, were in transit at December 31, 2014, and had a cost of $26,000. Upon notification of receipt by the customer on January 2, 2015, Dimitri issued a sales invoice for $42,000.

6. Goods, with an invoice cost of $27,000, received from a vendor at 5:00 p.m. on December 31, 2014, were recorded on a receiving report dated January 2, 2015. The goods were not included in the physical count, but the invoice was included in accounts payable at December 31, 2014.

7. Goods received from a vendor on December 26, 2014, were included in the physical count. However, the related $56,000 vendor invoice was not included in accounts payable at December 31, 2014, because the accounts payable copy of the receiving report was lost.

8. On January 3, 2015, a monthly freight bill in the amount of $8,000 was received. The bill specifically related to merchandise purchased in December 2014, one-half of which was still in the inventory at December 31, 2014. The freight charges were not included in either the inventory or in accounts payable at December 31, 2014.

Instructions

Using the format shown below, prepare a schedule of adjustments as of December 31, 2014, to the initial amounts per Dimitri's accounting records. Show separately the effect, if any, of each of the eight transactions on the December 31, 2014, amounts. If the transactions would have no effect on the initial amount shown, enter NONE.

	Inventory	Accounts Payable	Net Sales
Initial amounts	$1,520,000	$1,200,000	$8,150,000
Adjustments—increase (decrease)			
1			
2			
3			
4			
5			
6			
7			
8			
Total adjustments			
Adjusted amounts	$	$	$

(AICPA adapted)

4 **P8-3 (Purchases Recorded Gross and Net)** Some of the transactions of Torres Company during August are listed below. Torres uses the periodic inventory method.

August 10 Purchased merchandise on account, $12,000, terms 2/10, n/30.
13 Returned part of the purchase of August 10, $1,200, and received credit on account.
15 Purchased merchandise on account, $16,000, terms 1/10, n/60.
25 Purchased merchandise on account, $20,000, terms 2/10, n/30.
28 Paid invoice of August 15 in full.

Instructions

(a) Assuming that purchases are recorded at gross amounts and that discounts are to be recorded when taken:
(1) Prepare general journal entries to record the transactions.
(2) Describe how the various items would be shown in the financial statements.
(b) Assuming that purchases are recorded at net amounts and that discounts lost are treated as financial expenses:
(1) Prepare general journal entries to enter the transactions.
(2) Prepare the adjusting entry necessary on August 31 if financial statements are to be prepared at that time.
(3) Describe how the various items would be shown in the financial statements.
(c) Which of the two methods do you prefer and why?

2 5 **P8-4 (Compute FIFO, LIFO, and Average-Cost)** Hull Company's record of transactions concerning part X for the month of April was as follows.

Purchases		Sales	
April 1 (balance on hand)	100 @ $5.00	April 5	300
4	400 @ 5.10	12	200
11	300 @ 5.30	27	800
18	200 @ 5.35	28	150
26	600 @ 5.60		
30	200 @ 5.80		

Instructions

(a) Compute the inventory at April 30 on each of the following bases. Assume that perpetual inventory records are kept in units only. Carry unit costs to the nearest cent.
(1) First-in, first-out (FIFO).
(2) Last-in, first-out (LIFO).
(3) Average-cost.
(b) If the perpetual inventory record is kept in dollars, and costs are computed at the time of each withdrawal, what amount would be shown as ending inventory in (1), (2), and (3) above? (Carry average unit costs to four decimal places.)

2 5 P8-5 (Compute FIFO, LIFO, and Average-Cost) Some of the information found on a detail inventory card for Slatkin Inc. for the first month of operations is as follows.

	Received		Issued,	Balance,
Date	No. of Units	Unit Cost	No. of Units	No. of Units
January 2	1,200	$3.00		1,200
7			700	500
10	600	3.20		1,100
13			500	600
18	1,000	3.30	300	1,300
20			1,100	200
23	1,300	3.40		1,500
26			800	700
28	1,600	3.50		2,300
31			1,300	1,000

Instructions

(a) From these data compute the ending inventory on each of the following bases. Assume that perpetual inventory records are kept in units only. (Carry unit costs to the nearest cent and ending inventory to the nearest dollar.)

(1) First-in, first-out (FIFO).

(2) Last-in, first-out (LIFO).

(3) Average-cost.

(b) If the perpetual inventory record is kept in dollars, and costs are computed at the time of each withdrawal, would the amounts shown as ending inventory in (1), (2), and (3) above be the same? Explain and compute. (Round average unit costs to four decimal places.)

 2 5 P8-6 (Compute FIFO, LIFO, Average-Cost—Periodic and Perpetual) Ehlo Company is a multiproduct firm. Presented below is information concerning one of its products, the Hawkeye.

Date	Transaction	Quantity	Price/Cost
1/1	Beginning inventory	1,000	$12
2/4	Purchase	2,000	18
2/20	Sale	2,500	30
4/2	Purchase	3,000	23
11/4	Sale	2,200	33

Instructions

Compute cost of goods sold, assuming Ehlo uses:

(a) Periodic system, FIFO cost flow.

(b) Perpetual system, FIFO cost flow.

(c) Periodic system, LIFO cost flow.

(d) Perpetual system, LIFO cost flow.

(e) Periodic system, weighted-average cost flow.

(f) Perpetual system, moving-average cost flow.

 5 P8-7 (Financial Statement Effects of FIFO and LIFO) The management of Tritt Company has asked its accounting department to describe the effect upon the company's financial position and its income statements of accounting for inventories on the LIFO rather than the FIFO basis during 2014 and 2015. The accounting department is to assume that the change to LIFO would have been effective on January 1, 2014, and that the initial LIFO base would have been the inventory value on December 31, 2013. Presented below are the company's financial statements and other data for the years 2014 and 2015 when the FIFO method was employed.

	Financial Position as of		
	12/31/13	12/31/14	12/31/15
Cash	$ 90,000	$130,000	$154,000
Accounts receivable	80,000	100,000	120,000
Inventory	120,000	140,000	176,000
Other assets	160,000	170,000	200,000
Total assets	$450,000	$540,000	$650,000
Accounts payable	$ 40,000	$ 60,000	$ 80,000
Other liabilities	70,000	80,000	110,000
Common stock	200,000	200,000	200,000
Retained earnings	140,000	200,000	260,000
Total liabilities and equity	$450,000	$540,000	$650,000

	Income for Years Ended	
	12/31/14	12/31/15
Sales revenue	$900,000	$1,350,000
Less: Cost of goods sold	505,000	756,000
Other expenses	205,000	304,000
	710,000	1,060,000
Income before income taxes	190,000	290,000
Income taxes (40%)	76,000	116,000
Net income	$114,000	$ 174,000

Other data:

1. Inventory on hand at December 31, 2013, consisted of 40,000 units valued at $3.00 each.
2. Sales (all units sold at the same price in a given year):

   2014—150,000 units @ $6.00 each   2015—180,000 units @ $7.50 each

3. Purchases (all units purchased at the same price in given year):

   2014—150,000 units @ $3.50 each   2015—180,000 units @ $4.40 each

4. Income taxes at the effective rate of 40% are paid on December 31 each year.

Instructions
Name the account(s) presented in the financial statements that would have different amounts for 2015 if LIFO rather than FIFO had been used, and state the new amount for each account that is named. Show computations.

(CMA adapted)

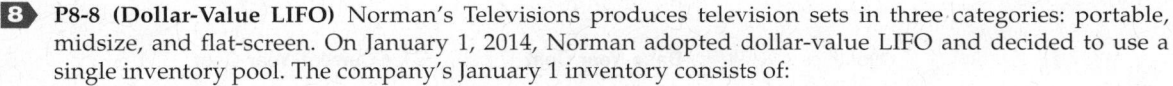 **P8-8 (Dollar-Value LIFO)** Norman's Televisions produces television sets in three categories: portable, midsize, and flat-screen. On January 1, 2014, Norman adopted dollar-value LIFO and decided to use a single inventory pool. The company's January 1 inventory consists of:

Category	Quantity	Cost per Unit	Total Cost
Portable	6,000	$100	$ 600,000
Midsize	8,000	250	2,000,000
Flat-screen	3,000	400	1,200,000
	17,000		$3,800,000

During 2014, the company had the following purchases and sales.

Category	Quantity Purchased	Cost per Unit	Quantity Sold	Selling Price per Unit
Portable	15,000	$110	14,000	$150
Midsize	20,000	300	24,000	405
Flat-screen	10,000	500	6,000	600
	45,000		44,000	

Instructions
(Round to four decimals.)

(a) Compute ending inventory, cost of goods sold, and gross profit.
(b) Assume the company uses three inventory pools instead of one. Repeat instruction (a).

 P8-9 (Internal Indexes—Dollar-Value LIFO) On January 1, 2014, Bonanza Wholesalers Inc. adopted the dollar-value LIFO inventory method for income tax and external financial reporting purposes. However, Bonanza continued to use the FIFO inventory method for internal accounting and management purposes. In applying the LIFO method, Bonanza uses internal conversion price indexes and the multiple pools approach under which substantially identical inventory items are grouped into LIFO inventory pools. The following data were available for inventory pool no. 1, which comprises products A and B, for the 2 years following the adoption of LIFO.

		FIFO Basis per Records	
	Units	Unit Cost	Total Cost
Inventory, 1/1/14			
Product A	10,000	$30	$300,000
Product B	9,000	25	225,000
			$525,000
Inventory, 12/31/14			
Product A	17,000	36	$612,000
Product B	9,000	26	234,000
			$846,000
Inventory, 12/31/15			
Product A	13,000	40	$520,000
Product B	10,000	32	320,000
			$840,000

Instructions

(a) Prepare a schedule to compute the internal conversion price indexes for 2014 and 2015. Round indexes to two decimal places.

(b) Prepare a schedule to compute the inventory amounts at December 31, 2014 and 2015, using the dollar-value LIFO inventory method.

(AICPA adapted)

8 ▶ P8-10 (Internal Indexes—Dollar-Value LIFO) Presented below is information related to Kaisson Corporation for the last 3 years.

Item	Quantities in Ending Inventories	Base-Year Cost Unit Cost	Base-Year Cost Amount	Current-Year Cost Unit Cost	Current-Year Cost Amount
December 31, 2013					
A	9,000	$2.00	$18,000	$2.20	$19,800
B	6,000	3.00	18,000	3.55	21,300
C	4,000	5.00	20,000	5.40	21,600
Totals			$56,000		$62,700
December 31, 2014					
A	9,000	$2.00	$18,000	$2.60	$23,400
B	6,800	3.00	20,400	3.75	25,500
C	6,000	5.00	30,000	6.40	38,400
Totals			$68,400		$87,300
December 31, 2015					
A	8,000	$2.00	$16,000	$2.70	$21,600
B	8,000	3.00	24,000	4.00	32,000
C	6,000	5.00	30,000	6.20	37,200
Totals			$70,000		$90,800

Instructions

Compute the ending inventories under the dollar-value LIFO method for 2013, 2014, and 2015. The base period is January 1, 2013, and the beginning inventory cost at that date was $45,000. Compute indexes to two decimal places.

8 ▶ P8-11 (Dollar-Value LIFO) Richardson Company cans a variety of vegetable-type soups. Recently, the company decided to value its inventories using dollar-value LIFO pools. The clerk who accounts for inventories does not understand how to value the inventory pools using this new method, so, as a private consultant, you have been asked to teach him how this new method works.

He has provided you with the following information about purchases made over a 6-year period.

Date	Ending Inventory (End-of-Year Prices)	Price Index
Dec. 31, 2010	$ 80,000	100
Dec. 31, 2011	111,300	105
Dec. 31, 2012	108,000	120
Dec. 31, 2013	128,700	130
Dec. 31, 2014	147,000	140
Dec. 31, 2015	174,000	145

You have already explained to him how this inventory method is maintained, but he would feel better about it if you were to leave him detailed instructions explaining how these calculations are done and why he needs to put all inventories at a base-year value.

Instructions

(a) Compute the ending inventory for Richardson Company for 2010 through 2015 using dollar-value LIFO.

(b) Using your computation schedules as your illustration, write a step-by-step set of instructions explaining how the calculations are done. Begin your explanation by briefly explaining the theory behind this inventory method, including the purpose of putting all amounts into base-year price levels.

PROBLEMS SET B

See the book's companion website, at **www.wiley.com/college/kieso**, for an additional set of problems.

CONCEPTS FOR ANALYSIS

CA8-1 (Inventoriable Costs) You are asked to travel to Milwaukee to observe and verify the inventory of the Milwaukee branch of one of your clients. You arrive on Thursday, December 30, and find that the inventory procedures have just been started. You spot a railway car on the sidetrack at the unloading door and ask the warehouse superintendent, Buck Rogers, how he plans to inventory the contents of the car. He responds, "We are not going to include the contents in the inventory."

Later in the day, you ask the bookkeeper for the invoice on the carload and the related freight bill. The invoice lists the various items, prices, and extensions of the goods in the car. You note that the carload was shipped December 24 from Albuquerque, f.o.b. Albuquerque, and that the total invoice price of the goods in the car was $35,300. The freight bill called for a payment of $1,500. Terms were net 30 days. The bookkeeper affirms the fact that this invoice is to be held for recording in January.

Instructions

(a) Does your client have a liability that should be recorded at December 31? Discuss.

(b) Prepare a journal entry(ies), if required, to reflect any accounting adjustment required. Assume a perpetual inventory system is used by your client.

(c) For what possible reason(s) might your client wish to postpone recording the transaction?

CA8-2 (Inventoriable Costs) Brian Erlacher, an inventory control specialist, is interested in better understanding the accounting for inventories. Although Brian understands the more sophisticated computer inventory control systems, he has little knowledge of how inventory cost is determined. In studying the records of Strider Enterprises, which sells normal brand-name goods from its own store and on consignment through Chavez Inc., he asks you to answer the following questions.

Instructions

(a) Should Strider Enterprises include in its inventory normal brand-name goods purchased from its suppliers but not yet received if the terms of purchase are f.o.b. shipping point (manufacturer's plant)? Why?

(b) Should Strider Enterprises include freight-in expenditures as an inventory cost? Why?

(c) If Strider Enterprises purchases its goods on terms 2/10, net 30, should the purchases be recorded gross or net? Why?

(d) What are products on consignment? How should they be reported in the financial statements?

(AICPA adapted)

CA8-3 (Inventoriable Costs) George Solti, the controller for Garrison Lumber Company, has recently hired you as assistant controller. He wishes to determine your expertise in the area of inventory accounting and therefore asks you to answer the following unrelated questions.

   (a) A company is involved in the wholesaling and retailing of automobile tires for foreign cars. Most of the inventory is imported, and it is valued on the company's records at the actual inventory cost plus freight-in. At year-end, the warehousing costs are prorated over cost of goods sold and ending inventory. Are warehousing costs considered a product cost or a period cost?

   (b) A certain portion of a company's "inventory" is composed of obsolete items. Should obsolete items that are not currently consumed in the production of "goods or services to be available for sale" be classified as part of inventory?

   (c) A company purchases airplanes for sale to others. However, until they are sold, the company charters and services the planes. What is the proper way to report these airplanes in the company's financial statements?

   (d) A company wants to buy coal deposits but does not want the financing for the purchase to be reported on its financial statements. The company therefore establishes a trust to acquire the coal deposits. The company agrees to buy the coal over a certain period of time at specified prices. The trust is able to finance the coal purchase and pay off the loan as it is paid by the company for the minerals. How should this transaction be reported?

CA8-4 (Accounting Treatment of Purchase Discounts) Shawnee Corp., a household appliances dealer, purchases its inventories from various suppliers. Shawnee has consistently stated its inventories at the lower-of-cost (FIFO)-or-market.

Instructions
Shawnee is considering alternate methods of accounting for the cash discounts it takes when paying its suppliers promptly. From a theoretical standpoint, discuss the acceptability of each of the following methods.

   (a) Financial income when payments are made.

   (b) Reduction of cost of goods sold for the period when payments are made.

   (c) Direct reduction of purchase cost.

(AICPA adapted)

CA8-5 (General Inventory Issues) In January 2014, Susquehanna Inc. requested and secured permission from the commissioner of the Internal Revenue Service to compute inventories under the last-in, first-out (LIFO) method and elected to determine inventory cost under the dollar-value LIFO method. Susquehanna Inc. satisfied the commissioner that cost could be accurately determined by use of an index number computed from a representative sample selected from the company's single inventory pool.

Instructions
   (a) Why should inventories be included in (1) a balance sheet and (2) the computation of net income?

   (b) The Internal Revenue Code allows some accountable events to be considered differently for income tax reporting purposes and financial accounting purposes, while other accountable events must be reported the same for both purposes. Discuss why it might be desirable to report some accountable events differently for financial accounting purposes than for income tax reporting purposes.

   (c) Discuss the ways and conditions under which the FIFO and LIFO inventory costing methods produce different inventory valuations. Do not discuss procedures for computing inventory cost.

(AICPA adapted)

CA8-6 (LIFO Inventory Advantages) Jane Yoakam, president of Estefan Co., recently read an article that claimed that at least 100 of the country's largest 500 companies were either adopting or considering adopting the last-in, first-out (LIFO) method for valuing inventories. The article stated that the firms were switching to LIFO to (1) neutralize the effect of inflation in their financial statements, (2) eliminate inventory profits, and (3) reduce income taxes. Ms. Yoakam wonders if the switch would benefit her company.

   Estefan currently uses the first-in, first-out (FIFO) method of inventory valuation in its periodic inventory system. The company has a high inventory turnover rate, and inventories represent a significant proportion of the assets.

   Ms. Yoakam has been told that the LIFO system is more costly to operate and will provide little benefit to companies with high turnover. She intends to use the inventory method that is best for the company in the long run rather than selecting a method just because it is the current fad.

Instructions

(a) Explain to Ms. Yoakam what "inventory profits" are and how the LIFO method of inventory valuation could reduce them.

(b) Explain to Ms. Yoakam the conditions that must exist for Estefan Co. to receive tax benefits from a switch to the LIFO method.

CA8-7 (Average-Cost, FIFO, and LIFO) Prepare a memorandum containing responses to the following items.

(a) Describe the cost flow assumptions used in average-cost, FIFO, and LIFO methods of inventory valuation.

(b) Distinguish between weighted-average-cost and moving-average-cost for inventory costing purposes.

(c) Identify the effects on both the balance sheet and the income statement of using the LIFO method instead of the FIFO method for inventory costing purposes over a substantial time period when purchase prices of inventoriable items are rising. State why these effects take place.

CA8-8 (LIFO Application and Advantages) Geddes Corporation is a medium-sized manufacturing company with two divisions and three subsidiaries, all located in the United States. The Metallic Division manufactures metal castings for the automotive industry, and the Plastic Division produces small plastic items for electrical products and other uses. The three subsidiaries manufacture various products for other industrial users.

Geddes Corporation plans to change from the lower of first-in, first-out (FIFO)-cost-or market method of inventory valuation to the last-in, first-out (LIFO) method of inventory valuation to obtain tax benefits. To make the method acceptable for tax purposes, the change also will be made for its annual financial statements.

Instructions

(a) Describe the establishment of and subsequent pricing procedures for each of the following LIFO inventory methods.

(1) LIFO applied to units of product when the periodic inventory system is used.

(2) Application of the dollar-value method to LIFO units of product.

(b) Discuss the specific advantages and disadvantages of using the dollar-value LIFO application as compared to specific goods LIFO (unit LIFO). (Ignore income tax considerations.)

(c) Discuss the general advantages and disadvantages claimed for LIFO methods.

CA8-9 (Dollar-Value LIFO Issues) Arruza Co. is considering switching from the specific-goods LIFO approach to the dollar-value LIFO approach. Because the financial personnel at Arruza know very little about dollar-value LIFO, they ask you to answer the following questions.

(a) What is a LIFO pool?

(b) Is it possible to use a LIFO pool concept and not use dollar-value LIFO? Explain.

(c) What is a LIFO liquidation?

(d) How are price indexes used in the dollar-value LIFO method?

(e) What are the advantages of dollar-value LIFO over specific-goods LIFO?

CA8-10 (FIFO and LIFO) Harrisburg Company is considering changing its inventory valuation method from FIFO to LIFO because of the potential tax savings. However, management wishes to consider all of the effects on the company, including its reported performance, before making the final decision.

The inventory account, currently valued on the FIFO basis, consists of 1,000,000 units at $8 per unit on January 1, 2014. There are 1,000,000 shares of common stock outstanding as of January 1, 2014, and the cash balance is $400,000.

The company has made the following forecasts for the period 2014–2016.

	2014	2015	2016
Unit sales (in millions of units)	1.1	1.0	1.3
Sales price per unit	$10	$12	$12
Unit purchases (in millions of units)	1.0	1.1	1.2
Purchase price per unit	$8	$9	$10
Annual depreciation (in thousands of dollars)	$300	$300	$300
Cash dividends per share	$0.15	$0.15	$0.15
Cash payments for additions to and replacement of plant and equipment (in thousands of dollars)	$350	$350	$350
Income tax rate	40%	40%	40%
Operating expenses (exclusive of depreciation) as a percent of sales	15%	15%	15%
Common shares outstanding (in millions)	1	1	1

Instructions

(a) Prepare a schedule that illustrates and compares the following data for Harrisburg Company under the FIFO and the LIFO inventory method for 2014–2016. Assume the company would begin LIFO at the beginning of 2014.

    (1) Year-end inventory balances.   **(3)** Earnings per share.

    (2) Annual net income after taxes.   **(4)** Cash balance.

    Assume all sales are collected in the year of sale and all purchases, operating expenses, and taxes are paid during the year incurred.

(b) Using the data above, your answer to (a), and any additional issues you believe need to be considered, prepare a report that recommends whether or not Harrisburg Company should change to the LIFO inventory method. Support your conclusions with appropriate arguments.

(CMA adapted)

CA8-11 (LIFO Choices) Wilkens Company uses the LIFO method for inventory costing. In an effort to lower net income, company president Mike Wilkens tells the plant accountant to take the unusual step of recommending to the purchasing department a large purchase of inventory at year-end. The price of the item to be purchased has nearly doubled during the year, and the item represents a major portion of inventory value.

Instructions

Answer the following questions.

(a) Identify the major stakeholders. If the plant accountant recommends the purchase, what are the consequences?

(b) If Wilkens Company were using the FIFO method of inventory costing, would Mike Wilkens give the same order? Why or why not?

USING YOUR JUDGMENT

FINANCIAL REPORTING

Financial Statement Analysis Cases

Case 1 T J International

T J International was founded in 1969 as Trus Joist International. The firm, a manufacturer of specialty building products, has its headquarters in Boise, Idaho. The company, through its partnership in the Trus Joist MacMillan joint venture, develops and manufactures engineered lumber. This product is a high-quality substitute for structural lumber and uses lower-grade wood and materials formerly considered waste. The company also is majority owner of the Outlook Window Partnership, which is a consortium of three wood and vinyl window manufacturers.

Following is T J International's adapted income statement and information concerning inventories from its annual report.

T J International	
Sales	$618,876,000
Cost of goods sold	475,476,000
Gross profit	143,400,000
Selling and administrative expenses	102,112,000
Income from operations	41,288,000
Other expense	24,712,000
Income before income tax	16,576,000
Income taxes	7,728,000
Net income	$ 8,848,000

Inventories. Inventories are valued at the lower of cost or market and include material, labor, and production overhead costs. Inventories consisted of the following:

	Current Year	Prior Year
Finished goods	$27,512,000	$23,830,000
Raw materials and work-in-progress	34,363,000	33,244,000
	61,875,000	57,074,000
Reduction to LIFO cost	(5,263,000)	(3,993,000)
	$56,612,000	$53,081,000

The last-in, first-out (LIFO) method is used for determining the cost of lumber, veneer, Microllam lumber, TJI joists, and open web joists. Approximately 35 percent of total inventories at the end of the current year were valued using the LIFO method. The first-in, first-out (FIFO) method is used to determine the cost of all other inventories.

Instructions

(a) How much would income before taxes have been if FIFO costing had been used to value all inventories?

(b) If the income tax rate is 46.6%, what would income tax have been if FIFO costing had been used to value all inventories? In your opinion, is this difference in net income between the two methods material? Explain.

(c) Does the use of a different costing system for different types of inventory mean that there is a different physical flow of goods among the different types of inventory? Explain.

Case 2 Noven Pharmaceuticals, Inc.

Noven Pharmaceuticals, Inc., headquartered in Miami, Florida, describes itself in a recent annual report as follows.

Noven Pharmaceuticals, Inc.

Noven is a place of ideas—a company where scientific excellence and state-of-the-art manufacturing combine to create new answers to human needs. Our transdermal delivery systems speed drugs painlessly and effortlessly into the bloodstream by means of a simple skin patch. This technology has proven applications in estrogen replacement, but at Noven we are developing a variety of systems incorporating bestselling drugs that fight everything from asthma, anxiety and dental pain to cancer, heart disease and neurological illness. Our research portfolio also includes new technologies, such as iontophoresis, in which drugs are delivered through the skin by means of electrical currents, as well as products that could satisfy broad consumer needs, such as our anti-microbial mouthrinse.

Noven also reported in its annual report that its activities to date have consisted of product development efforts, some of which have been independent and some of which have been completed in conjunction with **Rhone-Poulenc Rorer (RPR)** and **Ciba-Geigy**. The revenues so far have consisted of money received from licensing fees, "milestone" payments (payments made under licensing agreements when certain stages of the development of a certain product have been completed), and interest on its investments. The company expects that it will have significant revenue in the upcoming fiscal year from the launch of its first product, a transdermal estrogen delivery system.

The current assets portion of Noven's balance sheet follows.

Cash and cash equivalents	$12,070,272
Securities held to maturity	23,445,070
Inventory of supplies	1,264,553
Prepaid and other current assets	825,159
Total current assets	$37,605,054

Inventory of supplies is recorded at the lower-of-cost (first-in, first-out)-or-net realizable value and consists mainly of supplies for research and development.

Instructions

(a) What would you expect the physical flow of goods for a pharmaceutical manufacturer to be most like: FIFO, LIFO, or random (flow of goods does not follow a set pattern)? Explain.

(b) What are some of the factors that Noven should consider as it selects an inventory measurement method?

(c) Suppose that Noven had $49,000 in an inventory of transdermal estrogen delivery patches. These patches are from an initial production run and will be sold during the coming year. Why do you think that this amount is not shown in a separate inventory account? In which of the accounts shown is the inventory likely to be? At what point will the inventory be transferred to a separate inventory account?

Case 3   SUPERVALU

SUPERVALU reported the following data in its annual report.

	Feb. 27, 2010	Feb. 26, 2011	Feb. 25, 2012
Total revenues	$40,597	$37,534	$36,100
Cost of sales (using LIFO)	31,444	29,124	28,010
Year-end inventories using FIFO	2,606	2,552	2,492
Year-end inventories using LIFO	2,342	2,270	2,150

(a) Compute SUPERVALU's inventory turnovers for 2011 and 2012, using:

   (1) Cost of sales and LIFO inventory.

   (2) Cost of sales and FIFO inventory.

(b) Some firms calculate inventory turnover using sales rather than cost of goods sold in the numerator. Calculate SUPERVALU's 2011 and 2012 turnover, using:

   (1) Sales and LIFO inventory.

   (2) Sales and FIFO inventory.

(c) Describe the method that SUPERVALU's appears to use.

(d) State which method you would choose to evaluate SUPERVALU's performance. Justify your choice.

Accounting, Analysis, and Principles

Englehart Company sells two types of pumps. One is large and is for commercial use. The other is smaller and is used in residential swimming pools. The following inventory data is available for the month of March.

	Units	Price per Unit	Total
Residential Pumps			
Inventory at Feb. 28:	200	$ 400	$ 80,000
Purchases:			
March 10	500	$ 450	$225,000
March 20	400	$ 475	$190,000
March 30	300	$ 500	$150,000
Sales:			
March 15	500	$ 540	$270,000
March 25	400	$ 570	$228,000
Inventory at March 31:	500		
Commercial Pumps			
Inventory at Feb. 28:	600	$ 800	$480,000
Purchases:			
March 3	600	$ 900	$540,000
March 12	300	$ 950	$285,000
March 21	500	$1,000	$500,000
Sales:			
March 18	900	$1,080	$972,000
March 29	600	$1,140	$684,000
Inventory at March 31:	500		

Accounting

(a) Assuming Englehart uses a periodic inventory system, determine the cost of inventory on hand at March 31 and the cost of goods sold for March under first-in, first-out (FIFO).

(b) Assume Englehart uses dollar-value LIFO and one pool, consisting of the combination of residential and commercial pumps. Determine the cost of inventory on hand at March 31 and the cost of goods sold for March. Assume Englehart's initial adoption of LIFO is on March 1. Use the double-extension method to determine the appropriate price indices. (*Hint:* The price index for February 28/March 1 should be 1.00.) (Round the index to three decimal places.)

Analysis

(a) Assume you need to compute a current ratio for Englehart. Which inventory method (FIFO or dollar-value LIFO) do you think would give you a more meaningful current ratio?

(b) Some of Englehart's competitors use LIFO inventory costing and some use FIFO. How can an analyst compare the results of companies in an industry, when some use LIFO and others use FIFO?

Principles

Can companies change from one inventory accounting method to another? If a company changes to an inventory accounting method used by most of its competitors, what are the trade-offs in terms of the conceptual framework discussed in Chapter 2 of the textbook?

BRIDGE TO THE PROFESSION

Professional Research: FASB Codification

In conducting year-end inventory counts, your audit team is debating the impact of the client's right of return policy both on inventory valuation and revenue recognition. The assistant controller argues that there is no need to worry about the return policies since they have not changed in a while. The audit senior wants a more authoritative answer and has asked you to conduct some research of the authoritative literature before she presses the point with the client.

Instructions

If your school has a subscription to the FASB Codification, go to *http://aaahq.org/asclogin.cfm* to log in and prepare responses to the following. Provide Codification references for your responses.

(a) What is the authoritative guidance for revenue recognition when right of return exists?

(b) When is this guidance important for a company?

(c) Sales with high rates of return can ultimately cause inventory to be misstated. Why are returns allowed? Should different industries be able to make different types of return policies?

(d) In what situations would a reasonable estimate of returns be difficult to make?

Additional Professional Resources

See the book's companion website, at **www.wiley.com/college/kieso**, for professional simulations as well as other study resources.

Remember to check the book's companion website to find additional resources for this chapter.

Inventories: Additional Valuation Issues

Not What It Seems to Be

Investors need comparable information about inventory when evaluating a retailer's financial statements. To do so, investors need to determine what inventory method a retailer is using (FIFO, LIFO, average-cost, or a combination of methods) and then adjust the company to a common method. That is a good start. What investors often then do is compute relevant information about the company such as inventory turnover, number of days sales in inventory, gross profit rate, and liquidity measures such as the acid-test ratio. These calculations are critical. Inventory is a significant component of working capital and the gross profit resulting from sales of inventory is often viewed as the most important income component in measuring a retailer's progress. For example, consider the financial statements of **Best Buy** shown in the following table. Inventory comprises over 50 percent of current assets, and gross profit represents 24 percent of sales revenue.

BEST BUY ($ IN MILLIONS)			
Consolidated Balance Sheets		**Consolidated Statements of Earnings**	
Current Assets		Revenue	$50,705
Cash and cash equivalents	$ 1,199	Cost of goods sold	38,132
Receivables	2,288	Gross profit	$12,573
Merchandise inventories	5,731		
Other current assets	1,101	Net income (loss)	$ (1,231)
Total current assets	$10,319		

Therefore, analysis is based on these numbers. However, there often are still questions about the reliability of the information reported in the financial statements. That is, subjective estimates are involved because of the possible impairment of the inventory. For example, Best Buy provides disclosures related to inventory in its annual report, shown on the next page.

CONCEPTUAL FOCUS

> See the **Underlying Concepts** on pages 479, 480, and 484.

INTERNATIONAL FOCUS

> See the **International Perspectives** on pages 474, 475, and 482.
> Read the **IFRS Insights** on pages 525–534 for a discussion of:
  —Lower-of-cost-or-net realizable value (LCNRV)
  —Agricultural inventory

As indicated in the table below, subjective estimates concerning the measurement and valuation of inventory (related to markdowns and inventory losses) could have a significant impact on an investor's ability to compare inventory levels (and their impact on gross profit) at Best Buy relative to other retailers. Thus, inventory balances may not be what they seem, not only due to the cost flow assumptions (e.g., LIFO/FIFO) you learned about in Chapter 8 but also due to significant markdowns and losses that you will learn about in this chapter.

Critical Accounting Estimates in Preparation of the Financial Statements: Inventory	Judgments and Uncertainties
We value our inventory at the lower of cost or market through the establishment of markdown and inventory loss adjustments.	
Our inventory valuation reflects markdowns for the excess of the cost over the amount we expect to realize from the ultimate sale or other disposal of the inventory. Markdowns establish a new cost basis for our inventory. Subsequent changes in facts or circumstances do not result in the reversal of previously recorded markdowns or an increase in that newly established cost basis.	Our markdown adjustment contains uncertainties because the calculation requires management to make assumptions and to apply judgment regarding inventory aging, forecast consumer demand, the promotional environment and technological obsolescence.
Our inventory valuation also reflects adjustments for anticipated physical inventory losses (e.g., theft) that have occurred since the last physical inventory. Physical inventory counts are taken on a regular basis to ensure that the inventory reported in our consolidated financial statements is properly stated.	Our inventory loss adjustment contains uncertainties because the calculation requires management to make assumptions and to apply judgment regarding a number of factors, including historical results and current inventory loss trends.

PREVIEW OF CHAPTER 9

As our opening story indicates, information on inventories is important to investors. In this chapter, we discuss some of the valuation and estimation concepts that companies use to develop relevant inventory information. The content and organization of the chapter are as follows.

Inventories: Additional Valuation Issues

Lower-of-Cost-or-Market	Valuation Bases	Gross Profit Method	Retail Inventory Method	Presentation and Analysis
• Ceiling and floor • How LCM works • Application of LCM • "Market" • Use of allowance • Multiple periods • Evaluation of rule	• Net realizable value • Relative sales value • Purchase commitments	• Gross profit percentage • Evaluation of method	• Concepts • Conventional method • Special items • Evaluation of method	• Presentation • Analysis

LOWER-OF-COST-OR-MARKET

Inventories are recorded at their cost. However, if inventory declines in value below its original cost, a major departure from the historical cost principle occurs. Whatever the reason for a decline—obsolescence, price-level changes, or damaged goods—a company should write down the inventory to market to report this loss. **A company abandons the historical cost principle when the future utility (revenue-producing ability) of the asset drops below its original cost.** Companies therefore **report inventories at the lower-of-cost-or-market** at each reporting period.

Illustration 9-1 shows how **Target** and **Best Buy** reported this information.

ILLUSTRATION 9-1
Lower-of-Cost-or-Market
Disclosures

Target
(in millions)   As of January 28, 2012

Current Assets	
Inventory	$7,918

Notes to Consolidated Financial Statements (in part)

11. Inventory

Substantially all inventory and the related cost of sales are accounted for under the retail inventory accounting method (RIM) using the last-in, first-out (LIFO) method. Inventory is stated at the lower of LIFO cost or market. Cost includes purchase price as reduced by vendor income. Inventory is also reduced for estimated losses related to shrinkage and markdowns. The LIFO provision is calculated based on inventory levels, markup rates and internally measured retail price indices.

Best Buy
(in millions)   March 3, 2012

Current Assets	
Merchandise inventories	$5,731

Summary of Significant Accounting Policies (in part)

Merchandise inventories are recorded at the lower of cost using either the average cost or first-in-first-out method, or market.

International Perspective

IFRS defines *market* as net realizable value; GAAP defines *market* as replacement cost subject to certain constraints.

Recall that **cost** is the acquisition price of inventory computed using one of the historical cost-based methods—specific identification, average-cost, FIFO, or LIFO. The term **market** in the phrase "the lower-of-cost-or-market" (LCM) generally means the cost to replace the item by purchase or reproduction. For a retailer like **Nordstrom**, the term "market" refers to the market in which it purchases goods, not the market in which it sells them. For a manufacturer like **William Wrigley Jr.**, the term "market" refers to the cost to reproduce. Thus the rule really means that **companies value goods at cost or cost to replace, whichever is lower**.

For example, say **Target** purchased a **Timex** wristwatch for $30 for resale. Target can sell the wristwatch for $48.95 and replace it for $25. It should therefore value the wristwatch at $25 for inventory purposes under the lower-of-cost-or-market rule. Target can use the lower-of-cost-or-market rule of valuation after applying any of the cost flow methods discussed above to determine the inventory cost.

A departure from cost is justified because **a company should charge a loss of utility against revenues in the period in which the loss occurs**, not in the period of sale. Note also that the lower-of-cost-or-market method is **a conservative approach to inventory valuation**. That is, when doubt exists about the value of an asset, a company should use the lower value for the asset, which also reduces net income.

Ceiling and Floor

Why use replacement cost to represent market value? Because a decline in the replacement cost of an item usually reflects or predicts a decline in selling price. Using replacement cost allows a company to maintain a consistent rate of gross profit on sales (normal profit margin). Sometimes, however, a reduction in the replacement cost of an item fails to indicate a corresponding reduction in its utility. This requires using two additional valuation limitations to value ending inventory—net realizable value and net realizable value less a normal profit margin.

Net realizable value (NRV) is the estimated selling price in the ordinary course of business, less reasonably predictable costs of completion and disposal (often referred to as net selling price). A normal profit margin is subtracted from that amount to arrive at net realizable value less a normal profit margin.

To illustrate, assume that Jerry Mander Corp. has unfinished inventory with a sales value of $1,000, estimated cost of completion and disposal of $300, and a normal profit margin of 10 percent of sales. Jerry Mander determines the following net realizable value.

Inventory—sales value	$1,000
Less: Estimated cost of completion and disposal	300
Net realizable value	700
Less: Allowance for normal profit margin (10% of sales)	100
Net realizable value less a normal profit margin	$ 600

ILLUSTRATION 9-2
Computation of Net Realizable Value

The general lower-of-cost-or-market rule is: A company values inventory at the lower-of-cost-or-market, with market limited to an amount that is not more than net realizable value or less than net realizable value less a normal profit margin. [1]

The upper limit (ceiling) is the net realizable value of inventory. The lower limit (floor) is the net realizable value less a normal profit margin. What is the rationale for these two limitations? Establishing these limits for the value of the inventory prevents companies from over- or understating inventory.

The maximum limitation, **not to exceed the net realizable value (ceiling),** prevents overstatement of the value of obsolete, damaged, or shopworn inventories. That is, if the replacement cost of an item exceeds its net realizable value, a company should not report inventory at replacement cost. The company can receive only the selling price less cost of disposal. To report the inventory at replacement cost would result in an overstatement of inventory and understatement of the loss in the current period.

To illustrate, assume that Staples paid $1,000 for a color laser printer that it can now replace for $900. The printer's net realizable value is $700. At what amount should Staples report the laser printer in its financial statements? To report the replacement cost of $900 overstates the ending inventory and understates the loss for the period. Therefore, Staples should report the printer at $700.

The minimum limitation (floor) is **not to be less than net realizable value reduced by an allowance for an approximately normal profit margin.** The floor establishes a value below which a company should not price inventory, regardless of replacement cost. It makes no sense to price inventory below net realizable value less a normal margin. This minimum amount (floor) measures

 See the FASB Codification section (page 504).

International Perspective

IFRS does not use a ceiling or floor to determine market.

what the company can receive for the inventory and still earn a normal profit. Use of a floor deters understatement of inventory and overstatement of the loss in the current period.

Illustration 9-3 graphically presents the guidelines for valuing inventory at the lower-of-cost-or-market.

ILLUSTRATION 9-3
Inventory Valuation—
Lower-of-Cost-or-Market

How Lower-of-Cost-or-Market Works

The **designated market value** is the amount that a company compares to cost. It is **always the middle value of three amounts**: replacement cost, net realizable value, and net realizable value less a normal profit margin. To illustrate how to compute designated market value, assume the information relative to the inventory of Regner Foods, Inc., as shown in Illustration 9-4.

ILLUSTRATION 9-4
Computation of
Designated Market Value

Food	Replacement Cost	Net Realizable Value (Ceiling)	Net Realizable Value Less a Normal Profit Margin (Floor)	Designated Market Value
Spinach	$ 88,000	$120,000	$104,000	$104,000
Carrots	90,000	100,000	70,000	90,000
Cut beans	45,000	40,000	27,500	40,000
Peas	36,000	72,000	48,000	48,000
Mixed vegetables	105,000	92,000	80,000	92,000

Designated Market Value Decision:

Spinach	Net realizable value less a normal profit margin is selected because it is the middle value.
Carrots	Replacement cost is selected because it is the middle value.
Cut beans	Net realizable value is selected because it is the middle value.
Peas	Net realizable value less a normal profit margin is selected because it is the middle value.
Mixed vegetables	Net realizable value is selected because it is the middle value.

Regner Foods then compares designated market value to cost to determine the lower-of-cost-or-market. It determines the final inventory value as shown in Illustration 9-5.

ILLUSTRATION 9-5
Determining Final
Inventory Value

Food	Cost	Replacement Cost	Net Realizable Value (Ceiling)	Net Realizable Value Less a Normal Profit Margin (Floor)	Designated Market Value	Final Inventory Value
Spinach	$ 80,000	$ 88,000	$120,000	$104,000	$104,000	$ 80,000
Carrots	100,000	90,000	100,000	70,000	90,000	90,000
Cut beans	50,000	45,000	40,000	27,500	40,000	40,000
Peas	90,000	36,000	72,000	48,000	48,000	48,000
Mixed vegetables	95,000	105,000	92,000	80,000	92,000	92,000
						$350,000

Final Inventory Value:

Spinach	Cost ($80,000) is selected because it is lower than designated market value (net realizable value less a normal profit margin).
Carrots	Designated market value (replacement cost, $90,000) is selected because it is lower than cost.
Cut beans	Designated market value (net realizable value, $40,000) is selected because it is lower than cost.
Peas	Designated market value (net realizable value less a normal profit margin, $48,000) is selected because it is lower than cost.
Mixed vegetables	Designated market value (net realizable value, $92,000) is selected because it is lower than cost.

The application of the lower-of-cost-or-market rule incorporates only losses in value that occur in the normal course of business from such causes as style changes, shift in demand, or regular shop wear. A company reduces damaged or deteriorated goods to net realizable value. When material, it may carry such goods in separate inventory accounts.

Methods of Applying Lower-of-Cost-or-Market

In the Regner Foods illustration, we assumed that the company applied the lower-of-cost-or-market rule to each individual type of food. However, companies may apply the lower-of-cost-or-market rule either directly to each item, to each category, or to the total of the inventory. If a company follows a major category or total inventory approach in applying the lower-of-cost-or-market rule, increases in market prices tend to offset decreases in market prices. To illustrate, assume that Regner Foods separates its food products into two major categories, frozen and canned, as shown in Illustration 9-6.

ILLUSTRATION 9-6
Alternative Applications
of Lower-of-Cost-or-
Market

	Cost	Designated Market	Lower-of-Cost-or-Market by: Individual Items	Major Categories	Total Inventory
Frozen					
Spinach	$ 80,000	$104,000	$ 80,000		
Carrots	100,000	90,000	90,000		
Cut beans	50,000	40,000	40,000		
Total frozen	230,000	234,000		$230,000	
Canned					
Peas	90,000	48,000	48,000		
Mixed vegetables	95,000	92,000	92,000		
Total canned	185,000	140,000		140,000	
Total	$415,000	$374,000	$350,000	$370,000	$374,000

If Regner Foods applied the lower-of-cost-or-market rule to individual items, the amount of inventory is $350,000. If applying the rule to major categories, it jumps to

$370,000. If applying LCM to the total inventory, it totals $374,000. Why this difference? When a company uses a major categories or total inventory approach, market values higher than cost offset market values lower than cost. For Regner Foods, using the major categories approach partially offsets the high market value for spinach. Using the total inventory approach totally offsets the high market value for spinach.

Companies usually price inventory on an item-by-item basis. In fact, tax rules require that companies use an individual-item basis barring practical difficulties. In addition, the individual-item approach gives the most conservative valuation for balance sheet purposes.[1] Often, a company prices inventory on a total-inventory basis when it offers only one end product (comprised of many different raw materials). If it produces several end products, a company might use a category approach instead. The method selected should be the one that most clearly reflects income. **Whichever method a company selects, it should apply the method consistently from one period to another.**[2]

Recording "Market" Instead of Cost

One of two methods may be used to record the income effect of valuing inventory at market. One method, referred to as the **cost-of-goods-sold method**, debits cost of goods sold for the write-down of the inventory to market. As a result, the company does not report a loss in the income statement because the cost of goods sold already includes the amount of the loss. The second method, referred to as the **loss method**, debits a loss account for the write-down of the inventory to market. We use the following inventory data for Ricardo Company to illustrate entries under both methods.

Cost of goods sold (before adjustment to market)	$108,000
Ending inventory (cost)	82,000
Ending inventory (at market)	70,000

Illustration 9-7 shows the entries for both the cost-of-goods-sold and loss methods, assuming the use of a perpetual inventory system.

ILLUSTRATION 9-7
Accounting for the Reduction of Inventory to Market—Perpetual Inventory System

Cost-of-Goods-Sold Method		Loss Method	
To reduce inventory from cost to market			
Cost of Goods Sold 12,000		Loss Due to Decline of Inventory to Market 12,000	
Inventory	12,000	Inventory	12,000

The cost-of-goods-sold method buries the loss in the Cost of Goods Sold account. The loss method, by identifying the loss due to the write-down, shows the loss separate from Cost of Goods Sold in the income statement.

Illustration 9-8 contrasts the differing amounts reported in the income statement under the two approaches, using data from the Ricardo example.

---

[1]If a company uses dollar-value LIFO, determining the LIFO cost of an individual item may be more difficult. The company might decide that it is more appropriate to apply the lower-of-cost-or-market rule to the total amount of each pool. The AICPA Task Force on LIFO Inventory Problems concluded that the most reasonable approach to applying the lower-of-cost-or-market provisions to LIFO inventories is to base the determination on reasonable groupings of items. A pool constitutes a reasonable grouping.

[2]Inventory accounting for financial statement purposes can be different from income tax purposes. For example, companies cannot use the lower-of-cost-or-market rule with LIFO for tax purposes. However, companies may use the lower-of-cost-or-market and LIFO for financial accounting purposes.

Cost-of-Goods-Sold Method	
Sales revenue	$200,000
Cost of goods sold (after adjustment to market*)	120,000
Gross profit on sales	$ 80,000
*Cost of goods sold (before adjustment to market)	$108,000
Difference between inventory at cost and market ($82,000 − $70,000)	12,000
Cost of goods sold (after adjustment to market)	$120,000
Loss Method	
Sales revenue	$200,000
Cost of goods sold	108,000
Gross profit on sales	92,000
Loss due to decline of inventory to market	12,000
	$ 80,000

ILLUSTRATION 9-8
Income Statement Presentation—Cost-of-Goods-Sold and Loss Methods of Reducing Inventory to Market

GAAP does not specify a particular account to debit for the write-down. We believe the loss method presentation is preferable because it clearly discloses the loss resulting from a decline in inventory to market.

Use of an Allowance

Instead of crediting the Inventory account for market adjustments, companies generally use an allowance account, often referred to as Allowance to Reduce Inventory to Market. For example, using an allowance account under the loss method, Ricardo Company makes the following entry to record the inventory write-down to market.

Loss Due to Decline of Inventory to Market	12,000	
Allowance to Reduce Inventory to Market		12,000

Underlying Concepts

The income statement under the cost-of-goods-sold method presentation lacks *representational faithfulness*. The cost-of-goods-sold method does not indicate what it purports to represent. However, allowing this presentation illustrates the concept of materiality.

Use of the allowance account results in reporting both the cost and the market of the inventory. Ricardo reports inventory in the balance sheet as follows.

Inventory (at cost)	$ 82,000
Allowance to reduce inventory to market	(12,000)
Inventory (at market)	$ 70,000

ILLUSTRATION 9-9
Presentation of Inventory Using an Allowance Account

The use of the allowance under the cost-of-goods-sold or loss method permits the balance sheet to reflect inventory measured at $82,000, although the balance sheet shows a net amount of $70,000. It also keeps subsidiary inventory ledgers and records in correspondence with the control account without changing prices. *For homework purposes, use an allowance account to record market adjustments, unless instructed otherwise.*

With respect to accounting for the allowance in the subsequent period, if the company still has on hand the merchandise in question, it should retain the allowance account. If it does not keep that account, the company will overstate beginning inventory and cost of goods. However, **if the company has sold the goods**, then it should close the account. It then establishes a "new allowance account" for any decline in inventory value that takes place in the current year.[3]

---

[3]The AICPA Task Force on LIFO Inventory Problems concluded that for LIFO inventories, companies should close the allowance from the prior year and should base the allowance at the end of the year on a new lower-of-cost-or-market computation. **[2]**

Use of an Allowance—Multiple Periods

Underlying Concepts

The inconsistency in the presentation of inventory is an example of the trade-off between *relevance and faithful representation*. Market is more relevant than cost, and cost is more representationally faithful than market. Apparently, relevance takes precedence in a down market, and faithful representation is more important in an up market.

In general, accountants leave the allowance account on the books. They merely adjust the balance at the next year-end to agree with the discrepancy between cost and the lower-of-cost-or-market at that balance sheet date. Thus, if prices are falling, the company records an additional write-down. If prices are rising, the company records an increase in income, as shown in Illustration 9-10.

We can think of the net increase in income as the excess of the credit effect of closing the beginning allowance balance over the debit effect of setting up the current year-end allowance account. Recognizing the increases and decreases has the same effect on net income as closing the allowance balance to beginning inventory or to cost of goods sold.

ILLUSTRATION 9-10
Effect on Net Income of Reducing Inventory to Market

Date	Inventory at Cost	Inventory at Market	Amount Required in Valuation Account	Adjustment of Valuation Account Balance	Effect on Net Income
Dec. 31, 2013	$188,000	$176,000	$12,000	$12,000 inc.	Decrease
Dec. 31, 2014	194,000	187,000	7,000	5,000 dec.	Increase
Dec. 31, 2015	173,000	174,000	0	7,000 dec.	Increase
Dec. 31, 2016	182,000	180,000	2,000	2,000 inc.	Decrease

What do the numbers mean? "PUT IT IN REVERSE"

The lower-of-cost-or-market rule is designed to provide timely information about the decline in the value of inventory. When the value of inventory declines, income takes a hit in the period of the write-down.

What happens in the periods after the write-down? For some companies, gross margins and bottom lines get a boost when they sell inventory that had been written down in a previous period. For example, as the table below shows, Vishay Intertechnology, Transwitch, and Cisco Systems reported gains from selling inventory that had previously been written down. The table also evaluates how clearly these companies disclosed the effects of the reversal of inventory write-downs.

For Transwitch, the reversal of fortunes amounted to 23 percent of net income. The problem is that the $600,000 credit had little to do with the company's ongoing operations, and the company did not do a good job disclosing the effect of the reversal on current-year profitability.

Even when companies do disclose a reversal, it is sometimes hard to determine the impact on income. For example, Intel disclosed that it had sold inventory that had been written down in prior periods but did not specify how much reserved inventory was sold.

Transparency of financial reporting should be a top priority. With better disclosure of the reversals that boost profits in the current period, financial transparency would also get a boost.

Company	Gain from Reversal	Disclosure
Vishay Intertechnology	Not available	Poor—The semiconductor company did not mention the gain in its earnings announcement. Two weeks later in an SEC filing, Vishay disclosed the gain on the inventory that it had written down.
Transwitch	$600,000	Poor—The company did not mention the gain in its earnings announcement. Three weeks later in an SEC filing, the company disclosed the gain on the inventory that it had written down.
Cisco Systems	$525 million	Good—The networking giant detailed in its earnings release and in SEC filings the gains from selling inventory it had previously written off.

Source: S. E. Ante, "The Secret Behind Those Profit Jumps," *BusinessWeek Online* (December 8, 2003).

Evaluation of the Lower-of-Cost-or-Market Rule

The lower-of-cost-or-market rule suffers some conceptual deficiencies:

1. A company recognizes decreases in the value of the asset and the charge to expense in the period in which the loss in utility occurs—not in the period of sale. On the other hand, it recognizes increases in the value of the asset only at the point of sale. This inconsistent treatment can distort income data.

2. Application of the rule results in inconsistency because a company may value the inventory at cost in one year and at market in the next year.

3. Lower-of-cost-or-market values the inventory in the balance sheet conservatively, but its effect on the income statement may or may not be conservative. Net income for the year in which a company takes the loss is definitely lower. Net income of the subsequent period may be higher than normal if the expected reductions in sales price do not materialize.

4. Application of the lower-of-cost-or-market rule uses a "normal profit" in determining inventory values. Since companies estimate "normal profit" based on past experience (which they may not attain in the future), this subjective measure presents an opportunity for income manipulation.

Many financial statement users appreciate the lower-of-cost-or-market rule because they at least know that it prevents overstatement of inventory. In addition, recognizing all losses but anticipating no gains generally avoids overstating income.

VALUATION BASES

Valuation at Net Realizable Value

For the most part, companies record inventory at cost or at the lower-of-cost-or-market.[4] However, many believe that for purposes of applying the lower-of-cost-or-market rule, companies should define "market" as **net realizable value** (selling price less estimated costs to complete and sell) rather than as replacement cost. This argument is based on the fact that the amount that companies will collect from this inventory in the future is the net realizable value.[5]

Under limited circumstances, support exists for **recording inventory at net realizable value**, even if that amount is above cost. GAAP permits this exception to the

2 LEARNING OBJECTIVE
Explain when companies value inventories at net realizable value.

---

[4]Manufacturing companies frequently employ a **standardized cost system** that predetermines the unit costs for material, labor, and manufacturing overhead and that values raw materials, work in process, and finished goods inventories at their standard costs. For financial reporting purposes, it is acceptable to price inventories at standard costs if there is no significant difference between the actual costs and standard costs. If there is a significant difference, companies should adjust the inventory amounts to actual cost. In *Accounting Research and Terminology Bulletin, Final Edition,* the profession notes that **"standard costs are acceptable if adjusted at reasonable intervals to reflect current conditions."** Burlington Industries and Hewlett-Packard use standard costs for valuing at least a portion of their inventories.

[5]"The Accounting Basis of Inventories," *Accounting Research Study No. 13* (New York: AICPA, 1973) recommends that companies adopt net realizable value. We also should note that companies frequently fail to apply the rules of lower-of-cost-or-market in practice. For example, companies rarely compute and apply the lower limit—net realizable value less a normal markup—because it is a fairly subjective computation. In addition, companies often do not reduce inventory to market unless its disposition is expected to result in a loss. Furthermore, if the net realizable value of finished goods exceeds cost, companies usually assume that both work in process and raw materials do also. In practice, therefore, authoritative literature [3] is considered a guide, and accountants often exercise professional judgment in lieu of following the pronouncements literally.

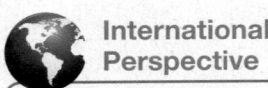

International Perspective

Similar to GAAP, certain agricultural products and mineral products can be reported at net realizable value using IFRS.

normal recognition rule under the following conditions: (1) when there is a controlled market with a quoted price applicable to all quantities, and (2) when no significant costs of disposal are involved. For example, mining companies ordinarily report inventories of certain minerals (rare metals, especially) at selling prices because there is often a controlled market without significant costs of disposal. Similar treatment is given agricultural products that are immediately marketable at quoted prices.

A third reason for allowing valuation at net realizable value is that sometimes it is too difficult to obtain the cost figures. Cost figures are not difficult to determine in, say, a manufacturing plant, where the company combines various raw materials and purchased parts to create a finished product. The manufacturer can use the cost basis to account for various items in inventory because it knows the cost of each individual component part. The situation is different in a meat-packing plant, however. The "raw material" consists of, say, cattle, each unit of which the company purchases as a whole and then divides into parts that are the products. Instead of one product out of many raw materials or parts, the meat-packing company makes many products from one "unit" of raw material. To allocate the cost of the animal "on the hoof" into the cost of, say, ribs, chuck, and shoulders, is a practical impossibility. It is much easier and more useful for the company to determine the market price of the various products and value them in the inventory at selling price less the various costs necessary to get them to market (costs such as shipping and handling). Hence, because of a peculiarity of the industry, meat-packing companies sometimes carry **inventories at sales price less distribution costs**.

Valuation Using Relative Sales Value

LEARNING OBJECTIVE ③

Explain when companies use the relative sales value method to value inventories.

A special problem arises when a company buys a group of varying units in a single **lump-sum purchase**, also called a **basket purchase**. To illustrate, assume that Woodland Developers purchases land for $1 million that it will subdivide into 400 lots. These lots are of different sizes and shapes but can be roughly sorted into three groups graded A, B, and C. As Woodland sells the lots, it apportions the purchase cost of $1 million among the lots sold and the lots remaining on hand.

You might wonder why Woodland would not simply divide the total cost of $1 million by 400 lots, to get a cost of $2,500 for each lot. This approach would not recognize that the lots vary in size, shape, and attractiveness. Therefore, to accurately value each unit, the common and most logical practice is to allocate the total among the various units on the basis of their **relative sales value**.

Illustration 9-11 shows the allocation of relative sales value for the Woodland Developers example.

ILLUSTRATION 9-11
Allocation of Costs, Using Relative Sales Value

Lots	Number of Lots	Sales Price per Lot	Total Sales Price	Relative Sales Price	Total Cost	Cost Allocated to Lots	Cost per Lot
A	100	$10,000	$1,000,000	100/250	$1,000,000	$ 400,000	$4,000
B	100	6,000	600,000	60/250	1,000,000	240,000	2,400
C	200	4,500	900,000	90/250	1,000,000	360,000	1,800
			$2,500,000			$1,000,000	

Woodland determines the cost of lots sold and the gross profit, using the amounts given in the "Cost per Lot" column, as follows.

Lots	Number of Lots Sold	Cost per Lot	Cost of Lots Sold	Sales	Gross Profit
A	77	$4,000	$308,000	$ 770,000	$ 462,000
B	80	2,400	192,000	480,000	288,000
C	100	1,800	180,000	450,000	270,000
			$680,000	$1,700,000	$1,020,000

ILLUSTRATION 9-12
Determination of Gross Profit, Using Relative Sales Value

The ending inventory is therefore $320,000 ($1,000,000 − $680,000).

Woodland also can compute this inventory amount another way. The ratio of cost to selling price for all the lots is $1 million divided by $2,500,000, or 40 percent. Accordingly, if the total sales price of lots sold is, say $1,700,000, then the cost of the lots sold is 40 percent of $1,700,000, or $680,000. The inventory of lots on hand is then $1 million less $680,000, or $320,000.

The petroleum industry widely uses the relative sales value method to value (at cost) the many products and by-products obtained from a barrel of crude oil.

Purchase Commitments—A Special Problem

In many lines of business, a company's survival and continued profitability depends on its having a sufficient stock of merchandise to meet customer demand. Consequently, it is quite common for a company to make **purchase commitments**, which are agreements to buy inventory weeks, months, or even years in advance. Generally, the seller retains title to the merchandise or materials covered in the purchase commitments. Indeed, the goods may exist only as natural resources as unplanted seed (in the case of agricultural commodities), or as work in process (in the case of a product).[6]

4 LEARNING OBJECTIVE
Discuss accounting issues related to purchase commitments.

Usually, it is not necessary for the buyer to make any entries to reflect commitments for purchases of goods that the seller has not shipped. Ordinary orders, for which the buyer and seller will determine prices at the time of shipment and **which are subject to cancellation**, do not represent either an asset or a liability to the buyer. Therefore, the buyer need not record such purchase commitments or report them in the financial statements.

What happens, though, if a buyer enters into a formal, noncancelable purchase contract? Even then, the buyer recognizes no asset or liability at the date of inception, **because the contract is "executory" in nature**: Neither party has fulfilled its part of the contract. However, if material, the buyer should disclose such contract details in a note to its financial statements. Illustration 9-13 shows an example of a purchase commitment disclosure.

Note 1: Contracts for the purchase of raw materials in 2014 have been executed in the amount of $600,000. The market price of such raw materials on December 31, 2013, is $640,000.

ILLUSTRATION 9-13
Disclosure of Purchase Commitment

In the disclosure in Illustration 9-13, the contract price was less than the market price at the balance sheet date. **If the contract price is greater than the market price and the buyer expects that losses will occur when the purchase is effected, the buyer**

One study noted that about 30 percent of public companies have purchase commitments outstanding, with an estimated value of $725 billion ("SEC Staff Report on Off-Balance Sheet Arrangements, Special Purpose Entities, and Related Issues," http://www.sec.gov/news/ studies/soxoffbalancerpt.pdf, June 2005). Purchase commitments are popular because the buyer can secure a supply of inventory at a known price. The seller also benefits in these arrangements by knowing how much to produce.

should recognize losses in the period during which such declines in market prices take place. [4][7]

As an example, at one time many Northwest forest-product companies such as **Boise Cascade, Georgia-Pacific,** and **Weyerhaeuser** signed long-term timber-cutting contracts with the **U.S. Forest Service.** These contracts required that the companies pay $310 per thousand board feet for timber-cutting rights. Unfortunately, the market price for timber-cutting rights in the latter part of the year dropped to $80 per thousand board feet. As a result, a number of these companies had long-term contracts that, if fulfilled, would result in substantial future losses.

To illustrate the accounting problem, assume that St. Regis Paper Co. signed timber-cutting contracts to be executed in 2015 at a price of $10,000,000. Assume further that the market price of the timber cutting rights on December 31, 2014, dropped to $7,000,000. St. Regis would make the following entry on December 31, 2014.

Unrealized Holding Gain or Loss—Income (Purchase Commitments)	3,000,000	
Estimated Liability on Purchase Commitments		3,000,000

St. Regis would report this unrealized holding loss in the income statement under "Other expenses and losses." And because the contract is to be executed within the next fiscal year, St. Regis would report the Estimated Liability on Purchase Commitments in the current liabilities section on the balance sheet. When St. Regis cuts the timber at a cost of $10 million, it would make the following entry.

Purchases (Inventory)	7,000,000	
Estimated Liability on Purchase Commitments	3,000,000	
Cash		10,000,000

The result of the purchase commitment was that St. Regis paid $10 million for a contract worth only $7 million. It recorded the loss in the previous period—when the price actually declined.

If St. Regis can partially or fully recover the contract price before it cuts the timber, it reduces the Estimated Liability on Purchase Commitments. In that case, it then reports in the period of the price increase a resulting gain for the amount of the partial or full recovery. For example, Congress permitted some of the forest-products companies to buy out of their contracts at reduced prices in order to avoid potential bankruptcies. To illustrate assume that Congress permitted St. Regis to reduce its contract price and therefore its commitment by $1,000,000. The entry to record this transaction is as follows.

Estimated Liability on Purchase Commitments	1,000,000	
Unrealized Holding Gain or Loss—Income (Purchase Commitments)		1,000,000

If the market price at the time St. Regis cuts the timber is more than $2,000,000 below the contract price, St. Regis will have to recognize an additional loss in the period of cutting and record the purchase at the lower-of-cost-or-market.

---

[7]There is a long-standing controversy on the accounting in this area. See, for example, Yuji Ijiri, *Recognition of Contractual Rights and Obligations, Research Report* (Stamford, Conn.: FASB, 1980), who argues that companies should capitalize firm purchase commitments. "Firm" means that it is unlikely that companies can avoid performance under the contract without a severe penalty.

Also, see Mahendra R. Gujarathi and Stanley F. Biggs, "Accounting for Purchase Commitments: Some Issues and Recommendations," *Accounting Horizons* (September 1988), pp. 75–78. They conclude, "Recording an asset and liability on the date of inception for the noncancelable purchase commitments is suggested as the first significant step towards alleviating the accounting problems associated with the issue. At year-end, the potential gains and losses should be treated as contingencies which provide a coherent structure for the reporting of such gains and losses."

Are purchasers at the mercy of market price declines? Not totally. Purchasers can protect themselves against the possibility of market price declines of goods under contract by hedging. In **hedging**, the purchaser in the purchase commitment simultaneously enters into a contract in which it agrees to sell in the future the same quantity of the same (or similar) goods at a fixed price. Thus the company holds a *buy position* in a purchase commitment and a *sell position* in a futures contract in the same commodity. The purpose of the hedge is to offset the price risk of the buy and sell positions. The company will be better off under one contract by approximately (maybe exactly) the same amount by which it is worse off under the other contract.

For example, St. Regis Paper Co. could have hedged its purchase commitment contract with a futures contract for timber rights of the same amount. In that case, its loss of $3,000,000 on the purchase commitment could have been offset by a $3,000,000 gain on the futures contract.[8]

As easy as this makes it sound, accounting for purchase commitments is still unsettled and controversial. Some argue that companies should report purchase commitments as assets and liabilities at the time they sign the contract. Others believe that the present recognition at the delivery date is more appropriate. *FASB Concepts Statement No. 6* states, "a purchase commitment involves both an item that might be recorded as an asset and an item that might be recorded as a liability. That is, it involves both a right to receive assets and an obligation to pay. . . . If both the right to receive assets and the obligation to pay were recorded at the time of the purchase commitment, the nature of the loss and the valuation account that records it when the price falls would be clearly seen." Although the discussion in *Concepts Statement No. 6* does not exclude the possibility of recording assets and liabilities for purchase commitments, it contains no conclusions or implications about whether companies should record them.[9]

THE GROSS PROFIT METHOD OF ESTIMATING INVENTORY

Companies take a physical inventory to verify the accuracy of the perpetual inventory records or, if no records exist, to arrive at an inventory amount. Sometimes, however, taking a physical inventory is impractical. In such cases, companies use substitute measures to approximate inventory on hand.

5 LEARNING OBJECTIVE
Determine ending inventory by applying the gross profit method.

One substitute method of verifying or determining the inventory amount is the **gross profit method** (also called the **gross margin method**). Auditors widely use this method in situations where they need only an estimate of the company's inventory (e.g., interim reports). Companies also use this method when fire or other catastrophe destroys either inventory or inventory records. The gross profit method relies on three assumptions:

1. The beginning inventory plus purchases equal total goods to be accounted for.
2. Goods not sold must be on hand.
3. The sales, reduced to cost, deducted from the sum of the opening inventory plus purchases, equal ending inventory.

To illustrate, assume that Cetus Corp. has a beginning inventory of $60,000 and purchases of $200,000, both at cost. Sales at selling price amount to $280,000. The gross profit on selling price is 30 percent.

---

[8] Appendix 17A provides a complete discussion of hedging and the use of derivatives such as futures.

[9] "Elements of Financial Statements," *Statement of Financial Accounting Concepts No. 6* (Stamford, Conn.: FASB, 1985), paras. 251–253.

Cetus applies the gross profit method as follows.

ILLUSTRATION 9-14
Application of Gross
Profit Method

Beginning inventory (at cost)		$ 60,000
Purchases (at cost)		200,000
Goods available (at cost)		260,000
Sales (at selling price)	$280,000	
Less: Gross profit (30% of $280,000)	84,000	
Sales (at cost)		196,000
Approximate inventory (at cost)		$ 64,000

The current period's records contain all the information Cetus needs to compute inventory at cost, except for the gross profit percentage. Cetus determines the gross profit percentage by reviewing company policies or prior period records. In some cases, companies must adjust this percentage if they consider prior periods unrepresentative of the current period.[10]

Computation of Gross Profit Percentage

In most situations, the gross profit percentage is stated as a percentage of selling price. The previous illustration, for example, used a 30 percent gross profit on sales. Gross profit on selling price is the common method for quoting the profit for several reasons. (1) Most companies state goods on a retail basis, not a cost basis. (2) A profit quoted on selling price is lower than one based on cost. This lower rate gives a favorable impression to the consumer. (3) The gross profit based on selling price can never exceed 100 percent.[11]

In Illustration 9-14, the gross profit was a given. But how did Cetus derive that figure? To see how to compute a gross profit percentage, assume that an article cost $15 and sells for $20, a gross profit of $5. As shown in the computations in Illustration 9-15, this markup is ¼ or 25 percent of retail, and ⅓ or, 33⅓ percent of cost.

ILLUSTRATION 9-15
Computation of Gross
Profit Percentage

$$\frac{\text{Markup}}{\text{Retail}} = \frac{\$5}{\$20} = 25\% \text{ at retail} \qquad \frac{\text{Markup}}{\text{Cost}} = \frac{\$5}{\$15} = 33\tfrac{1}{3}\% \text{ on cost}$$

Although companies normally compute the gross profit on the basis of selling price, you should understand the basic relationship between markup on cost and markup on

[10]An alternative method of estimating inventory using the gross profit percentage is considered by some to be less complicated than the traditional method. This alternative method uses the standard income statement format as follows. (Assume the same data as in the Cetus example above.)

Relationships			Solution	
Sales revenue		$280,000		$280,000
Cost of sales				
Beginning inventory	$ 60,000		$ 60,000	
Purchases	200,000		200,000	
Goods available for sale	260,000		260,000	
Ending inventory	(3) ?		(3) 64,000 Est.	
Cost of goods sold		(2) ?		(2)196,000 Est.
Gross profit on sales (30%)		(1) ?		(1) 84,000 Est.

Compute the unknowns as follows: first the gross profit amount, then cost of goods sold, and finally the ending inventory, as shown below.

   (1) $280,000 × 30% = $84,000 (gross profit on sales).
   (2) $280,000 − $84,000 = $196,000 (cost of goods sold).
   (3) $260,000 − $196,000 = $64,000 (ending inventory).

[11]The terms *gross margin percentage, rate of gross profit,* and *percentage markup* are synonymous, although companies more commonly use *markup* in reference to cost and *gross profit* in reference to sales.

selling price. For example, assume that a company marks up a given item by 25 percent. What, then, is the **gross profit on selling price**? To find the answer, assume that the item sells for $1. In this case, the following formula applies.

$$\textbf{Cost + Gross profit = Selling price}$$
$$C + .25C = SP$$
$$(1 + .25)C = SP$$
$$1.25C = \$1.00$$
$$C = \$0.80$$

The gross profit equals $0.20 ($1.00 − $0.80). The rate of gross profit on selling price is therefore 20 percent ($0.20/$1.00).

Conversely, assume that the gross profit on selling price is 20 percent. What is the **markup on cost**? To find the answer, again assume that the item sells for $1. Again, the same formula holds:

$$\textbf{Cost + Gross profit = Selling price}$$
$$C + .20SP = SP$$
$$C = (1 - .20)SP$$
$$C = .80SP$$
$$C = .80(\$1.00)$$
$$C = \$0.80$$

As in the previous example, the markup equals $0.20 ($1.00 − $0.80). The markup on cost is 25 percent ($0.20/$0.80).

Retailers use the following formulas to express these relationships:

1. Gross profit on selling price = $\dfrac{\text{Percentage markup on cost}}{100\% + \text{Percentage markup on cost}}$

2. Percentage markup on cost = $\dfrac{\text{Gross profit on selling price}}{100\% - \text{Gross profit on selling price}}$

ILLUSTRATION 9-16
Formulas Relating to
Gross Profit

To understand how to use these formulas, consider their application in the following calculations.

Gross Profit on Selling Price		Percentage Markup on Cost
Given: 20%	$\longrightarrow$ $\dfrac{.20}{1.00 - .20} = 25\%$	
Given: 25%	$\longrightarrow$ $\dfrac{.25}{1.00 - .25} = 33\frac{1}{3}\%$	
$\dfrac{.25}{1.00 + .25} = 20\%$ $\longleftarrow$		Given: 25%
$\dfrac{.50}{1.00 + .50} = 33\frac{1}{3}\%$ $\longleftarrow$		Given: 50%

ILLUSTRATION 9-17
Application of Gross
Profit Formulas

Because selling price exceeds cost and with the gross profit amount the same for both, **gross profit on selling price will always be less than the related percentage based on cost**. Note that companies do not multiply sales by a cost-based markup percentage. Instead, they must convert the gross profit percentage to a percentage based on selling price.

Evaluation of Gross Profit Method

What are the major disadvantages of the gross profit method? One disadvantage is that **it provides an estimate**. As a result, companies must take a physical inventory once a year to verify the inventory. Second, the gross profit method **uses past percentages** in determining the markup. Although the past often provides answers to the future, a current rate is more appropriate. Note that whenever significant fluctuations occur, companies should adjust the percentage as appropriate. Third, companies must be **careful in applying a blanket gross profit rate**. Frequently, a store or department handles merchandise with widely varying rates of gross profit. In these situations, the company may need to apply the gross profit method by subsections, lines of merchandise, or a similar basis that classifies merchandise according to their respective rates of gross profit. The gross profit method is normally unacceptable for financial reporting purposes because it provides only an estimate. GAAP requires a physical inventory as additional verification of the inventory indicated in the records. Nevertheless, GAAP permits the gross profit method to determine ending inventory for interim (generally quarterly) reporting purposes, provided a company discloses the use of this method. Note that the gross profit method will follow closely the inventory method used (FIFO, LIFO, average-cost) because it relies on historical records.

What do the numbers mean?   THE SQUEEZE

Managers and analysts closely follow gross profits. A small change in the gross profit rate can significantly affect the bottom line. At one time, Apple suffered a textbook case of shrinking gross profits. In response to pricing wars in the personal computer market, Apple had to quickly reduce the price of its signature Macintosh computers—reducing prices more quickly than it could reduce its costs. As a result, its gross profit rate fell from 44 percent to 40 percent in one year. Though the drop of 4 percent seems small, its impact on the bottom line caused Apple's stock price to drop from $57 per share to $27.50 per share in a two-month period (with a recent share price over $500, it would have been great to get into Apple stock at those lower prices!)

As another, more recent example, Nike—the largest global manufacturer of athletic footwear—in a recent quarter reported earnings that indicated falling gross profit, leading market analysts to adjust Nike's stock price downward. The cause—continuing downward pressure on its gross profit. On the positive side, an increase in the gross profit rate provides a positive signal to the market. For example, just a 1 percent boost in Dr. Pepper's gross profit rate cheered the market, indicating the company was able to avoid the squeeze of increased commodity costs by raising its prices.

Sources: Trefis, "Nike's Earnings Reiterate Gross Margin Pressure," *http://seekingalpha.com* (March 23, 2011); and D. Kardous, "Higher Pricing Helps Boost Dr. Pepper Snapple's Net," *Wall Street Journal Online* (June 5, 2008).

RETAIL INVENTORY METHOD

LEARNING OBJECTIVE 6

Determine ending inventory by applying the retail inventory method.

Accounting for inventory in a retail operation presents several challenges. Retailers with certain types of inventory may use the specific identification method to value their inventories. Such an approach makes sense when a retailer holds significant individual inventory units, such as automobiles, pianos, or fur coats. However, imagine attempting to use such an approach at Target, Home Depot, Sears Holdings, or Bloomingdale's—high-volume retailers that have many different types of merchandise. It would be extremely difficult to determine the cost of each sale, to enter cost codes on the tickets, to change the codes to reflect declines in value of the merchandise, to allocate costs such as transportation, and so on.

An alternative is to compile the inventories at retail prices. For most retailers, an observable pattern between cost and price exists. The retailer can then use a formula to convert retail prices to cost. This method is called the retail inventory method. **It requires** that the retailer keep a record of (1) the total cost and retail value of goods purchased, (2) the total cost and retail value of the goods available for sale, and (3) the sales for the period. Use of the retail inventory method is very common. For example, Safeway super-markets, Target, Wal-Mart, and Best Buy use the retail inventory method.

Here is how it works at a company like Best Buy. Beginning with the retail value of the goods available for sale, Best Buy deducts the sales revenue for the period. This cal-culation determines an estimated inventory (goods on hand) at retail. It next computes the cost-to-retail ratio for all goods. The formula for this computation is to divide the total goods available for sale at cost by the total goods available at retail price. Finally, to obtain ending inventory at cost, Best Buy applies the cost-to-retail ratio to the ending inventory valued at retail. Illustration 9-18 shows the retail inventory method calcula-tions for Best Buy (assumed data).

ILLUSTRATION 9-18
Retail Inventory Method

BEST BUY (current period)	Cost	Retail
Beginning inventory	$14,000	$ 20,000
Purchases	63,000	90,000
Goods available for sale	$77,000	110,000
Deduct: Sales revenue		85,000
Ending inventory, at retail		$ 25,000

Cost-to-retail ratio ($77,000 ÷ $110,000) = 70%
Ending inventory at cost (70% of $25,000) = $17,500

There are different versions of the retail inventory method. These include the **con-ventional** method (based on lower-of-average-cost-or-market), the **cost** method, the **LIFO retail** method, and the **dollar-value LIFO** retail method. Regardless of which ver-sion a company uses, the IRS, various retail associations, and the accounting profession all sanction use of the retail inventory method. One of its advantages is that a company like Best Buy can approximate the inventory balance **without a physical count**. How-ever, to avoid a potential overstatement of the inventory, Target makes periodic inven-tory counts. Such counts are especially important in retail operations where loss due to shoplifting or breakage is common.

The retail inventory method is particularly useful for any type of **interim report** because such reports usually need a fairly quick and reliable measure of the inventory. Also, similar to use of the gross profit method, insurance adjusters often use this method to **estimate losses** from fire, flood, or other type of casualty. This method also acts as a **control device** because a company will have to explain any deviations from a physical count at the end of the year. Finally, the retail method **expedites the physical inventory count** at the end of the year. The crew taking the physical inventory need record only the retail price of each item. The crew does not need to look up each item's invoice cost, thereby saving time and expense.

Retail-Method Concepts

The amounts shown in the "Retail" column of Illustration 9-18 above represent the orig-inal retail prices, assuming no price changes. In practice, though, retailers frequently mark up or mark down the prices they charge buyers.

For retailers, the term markup means an additional markup of the original retail price. (In another context, such as the gross profit discussion on pages 485–488, we often think of markup on the basis of cost.) Markup cancellations are decreases in prices of merchandise that the retailer had marked up above the original retail price.

In a competitive market, retailers often need to use **markdowns**, which are decreases in the original sales prices. Such cuts in sales prices may be necessary because of a decrease in the general level of prices, special sales, soiled or damaged goods, overstocking, and market competition. Markdowns are common in retailing these days. **Markdown cancellations** occur when the markdowns are later offset by increases in the prices of goods that the retailer had marked down—such as after a one-day sale, for example. Neither a markup cancellation nor a markdown cancellation can exceed the original markup or markdown.

To illustrate these concepts, assume that Designer Clothing Store recently purchased 100 dress shirts from Marroway, Inc. The cost for these shirts was $1,500, or $15 a shirt. Designer Clothing established the selling price on these shirts at $30 a shirt. The shirts were selling quickly in anticipation of Father's Day, so the manager added a markup of $5 per shirt. This markup made the price too high for customers, and sales slowed. The manager then reduced the price to $32. At this point we would say that the shirts at Designer Clothing have had a markup of $5 and a markup cancellation of $3.

Right after Father's Day, the manager marked down the remaining shirts to a sale price of $23. At this point, an additional markup cancellation of $2 has taken place, and a $7 markdown has occurred. If the manager later increases the price of the shirts to $24, a markdown cancellation of $1 would occur.

Retail Inventory Method with Markups and Markdowns—Conventional Method

Retailers use markup and markdown concepts in developing the proper inventory valuation at the end of the accounting period. To obtain the appropriate inventory figures, companies must give proper treatment to markups, markup cancellations, markdowns, and markdown cancellations.

To illustrate the different possibilities, consider the data for In-Fusion Inc., shown in Illustration 9-19. In-Fusion can calculate its ending inventory at cost under two assumptions, A and B. (We'll explain the reasons for the two later.)

Assumption A: Computes a cost ratio after markups (and markup cancellations) but before markdowns.

Assumption B: Computes a cost ratio after both markups and markdowns (and cancellations).

The computations for In-Fusion are:

Ending inventory at retail × Cost ratio = Value of ending inventory

Assumption A: $12,500 × 53.9% = $6,737.50

Assumption B: $12,500 × 54.7% = $6,837.50

The question becomes: Which assumption and which percentage should In-Fusion use to compute the ending inventory valuation? The answer depends on which retail inventory method In-Fusion chooses.

One approach uses only assumption A (a cost ratio using markups but not markdowns). It approximates the lower-of-average-cost-or-market. We will refer to this approach as the **conventional retail inventory method** or the **lower-of-cost-or-market approach**.

To understand why this method considers only the markups, not the markdowns, in the cost percentage, you must understand how a retail business operates. A markup normally indicates an increase in the market value of the item. On the other hand, a markdown means a decline in the utility of that item. Therefore, to approximate the lower-of-cost-or-market, we would consider markdowns a current loss and so would not

	Cost	Retail
Beginning inventory	$ 500	$ 1,000
Purchases (net)	20,000	35,000
Markups		3,000
Markup cancellations		1,000
Markdowns		2,500
Markdown cancellations		2,000
Sales (net)		25,000

ILLUSTRATION 9-19
Retail Inventory Method
with Markups and
Markdowns

IN-FUSION INC.

	Cost		Retail
Beginning inventory	$ 500		$ 1,000
Purchases (net)	20,000		35,000
Merchandise available for sale	20,500		36,000
Add: Markups		$3,000	
Less: Markup cancellations		1,000	
Net markups			2,000
	20,500		38,000

$$\text{(A)} \qquad \text{Cost-to-retail ratio} = \frac{\$20,500}{\$38,000} = 53.9\%$$

Deduct:			
Markdowns		2,500	
Markdown cancellations		(2,000)	
Net markdowns			500
	$20,500		37,500

$$\text{(B)} \qquad \text{Cost-to-retail ratio} = \frac{\$20,500}{\$37,500} = 54.7\%$$

Deduct: Sales (net)		25,000
Ending inventory at retail		$12,500

include them in calculating the cost-to-retail ratio. Omitting the markdowns would make the cost-to-retail ratio lower, which leads to an approximate lower-of-cost-or-market.

An example will make the distinction between the two methods clear. In-Fusion purchased two items for $5 apiece; the original sales price was $10 each. One item was subsequently written down to $2. Assuming no sales for the period, **if markdowns are considered** in the cost-to-retail ratio (assumption B—the **cost method**), we compute the ending inventory in the following way.

ILLUSTRATION 9-20
Retail Inventory Method
Including Markdowns—
Cost Method

Markdowns Included in Cost-to-Retail Ratio

	Cost	Retail
Purchases	$10	$20
Deduct: Markdowns		8
Ending inventory, at retail		$12

$$\text{Cost-to-retail ratio} = \frac{\$10}{\$12} = 83.3\%$$

$$\text{Ending inventory at cost } (\$12 \times .833) = \$10$$

This approach (the cost method) reflects an **average cost** of the two items of the commodity without considering the loss on the one item. It values ending inventory at $10.

If **markdowns are not considered** in the cost-to-retail ratio (assumption A—the **conventional retail method**), we compute the ending inventory as follows.

ILLUSTRATION 9-21
Retail Inventory Method
Excluding Markdowns—
Conventional Method
(LCM)

Markdowns Not Included in Cost-to-Retail Ratio		
	Cost	Retail
Purchases	$10	$20
Cost-to-retail ratio = $\dfrac{\$10}{\$20}$ = 50%		
Deduct: Markdowns		8
Ending inventory, at retail		$12
Ending inventory at cost ($12 × .50) = $6		

Under this approach (the conventional retail method, in which markdowns are **not considered**), ending inventory would be $6. The inventory valuation of $6 reflects two inventory items, one inventoried at $5 and the other at $1. It reflects the fact that In-Fusion reduced the sales price from $10 to $2, and reduced the cost from $5 to $1.[12]

To approximate the lower-of-cost-or-market, In-Fusion must establish the **cost-to-retail ratio**. It does this by dividing the cost of goods available for sale by the sum of the original retail price of these goods plus the net markups. This calculation excludes markdowns and markdown cancellations. Illustration 9-22 shows the basic format for the retail inventory method using the lower-of-cost-or-market approach along with the In-Fusion Inc. information.

ILLUSTRATION 9-22
Comprehensive
Conventional Retail
Inventory Method
Format

IN-FUSION INC.			
	Cost		Retail
Beginning inventory	$ 500		$ 1,000
Purchases (net)	20,000		35,000
Totals	20,500		36,000
Add: Net markups			
Markups		$3,000	
Markup cancellations		1,000	2,000
Totals	$20,500 ⟷		38,000
Deduct: Net markdowns			
Markdowns		2,500	
Markdown cancellations		2,000	500
Sales price of goods available			37,500
Deduct: Sales (net)			25,000
Ending inventory, at retail			$12,500

$$\text{Cost-to-retail ratio} = \frac{\text{Cost of goods available}}{\text{Original retail price of goods available, plus net markups}}$$

$$= \frac{\$20,500}{\$38,000} = \underline{53.9\%}$$

Ending inventory at lower-of-cost-or-market (53.9% × $12,500) = $6,737.50

[12]This figure is not really market (replacement cost), but it is net realizable value less the normal margin that is allowed. In other words, the sale price of the goods written down is $2, but subtracting a normal margin of 50 percent ($5 cost, $10 price), the figure becomes $1.

Because an averaging effect occurs, an exact lower-of-cost-or-market inventory valuation is ordinarily not obtained, but an adequate approximation can be achieved. In contrast, adding net markups **and** deducting net markdowns yields **approximate cost**.

Special Items Relating to Retail Method

The retail inventory method becomes more complicated when we consider such items as freight-in, purchase returns and allowances, and purchase discounts. In the retail method, we treat such items as follows.

- **Freight costs** are part of the purchase cost.
- **Purchase returns** are ordinarily considered as a reduction of the price at both cost and retail.
- **Purchase discounts and allowances** usually are considered as a reduction of the cost of purchases.

In short, the treatment for the items affecting the cost column of the retail inventory approach follows the computation for cost of goods available for sale.[13]

Note also that **sales returns and allowances** are considered as proper adjustments to gross sales. However, when sales are recorded gross, companies do not recognize **sales discounts**. To adjust for the sales discount account in such a situation would provide an ending inventory figure at retail that would be overvalued.

In addition, a number of special items require careful analysis:

- **Transfers-in** from another department are reported in the same way as purchases from an outside company.
- **Normal shortages** (breakage, damage, theft, shrinkage) should reduce the retail column because these goods are no longer available for sale. Such costs are reflected in the selling price because a certain amount of shortage is considered normal in a retail enterprise. As a result, companies do not consider this amount in computing the cost-to-retail percentage. Rather, to arrive at ending inventory at retail, they show normal shortages as a deduction similar to sales.
- **Abnormal shortages**, on the other hand, are deducted from both the cost and retail columns and reported as a special inventory amount or as a loss. To do otherwise distorts the cost-to-retail ratio and overstates ending inventory.
- **Employee discounts** (given to employees to encourage loyalty, better performance, and so on) are deducted from the retail column in the same way as sales. These discounts should not be considered in the cost-to-retail percentage because they do not reflect an overall change in the selling price.[14]

Illustration 9-23 (page 494) shows some of these concepts. The company, Extreme Sport Apparel, determines its inventory using the conventional retail inventory method.

Evaluation of Retail Inventory Method

Companies like Gap Inc., Home Depot, or your local department store use the retail inventory method of computing inventory for the following reasons: (1) to permit the computation of net income without a physical count of inventory, (2) as a control measure in determining inventory shortages, (3) in regulating quantities of merchandise on hand, and (4) for insurance information.

---

[13]When the purchase allowance is not reflected by a reduction in the selling price, no adjustment is made to the retail column.

[14]Note that if employee sales are recorded gross, no adjustment is necessary for employee discounts in the retail column.

ILLUSTRATION 9-23
Conventional Retail
Inventory Method—
Special Items Included

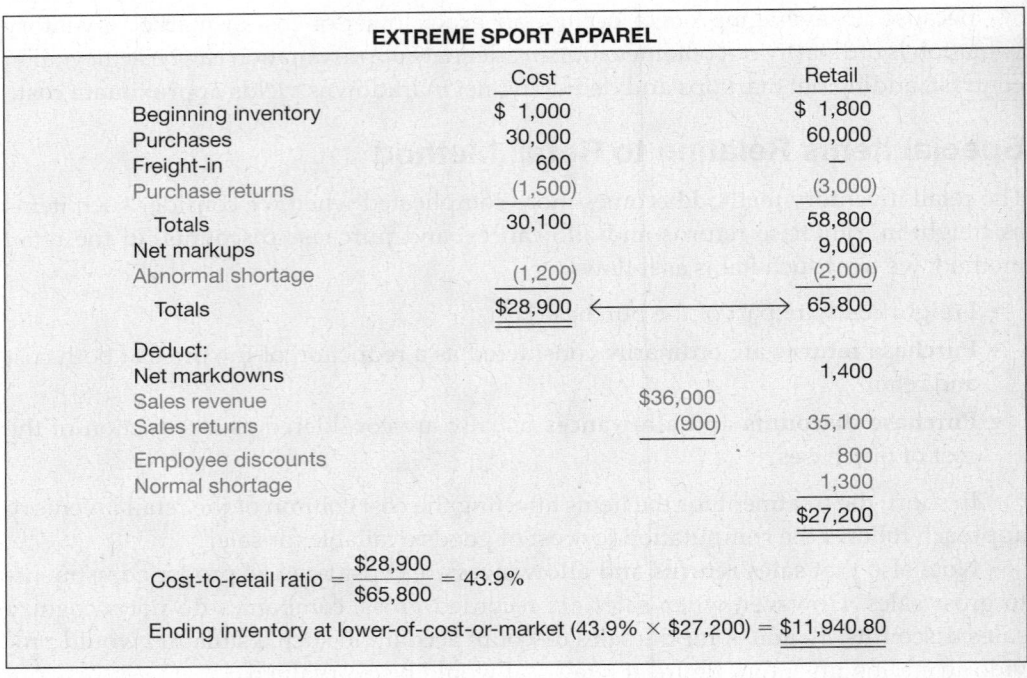

EXTREME SPORT APPAREL		
	Cost	Retail
Beginning inventory	$ 1,000	$ 1,800
Purchases	30,000	60,000
Freight-in	600	—
Purchase returns	(1,500)	(3,000)
Totals	30,100	58,800
Net markups		9,000
Abnormal shortage	(1,200)	(2,000)
Totals	$28,900 ⟵ ⟶	65,800
Deduct:		
Net markdowns		1,400
Sales revenue	$36,000	
Sales returns	(900)	35,100
Employee discounts		800
Normal shortage		1,300
		$27,200

$$\text{Cost-to-retail ratio} = \frac{\$28,900}{\$65,800} = 43.9\%$$

Ending inventory at lower-of-cost-or-market (43.9% × $27,200) = $11,940.80

One characteristic of the retail inventory method is that it **has an averaging effect on varying rates of gross profit**. This can be problematic when companies apply the method to an entire business, where rates of gross profit vary among departments. There is no allowance for possible distortion of results because of such differences. Companies refine the retail method under such conditions by computing inventory separately by departments or by classes of merchandise with similar gross profits. In addition, the reliability of this method assumes that the distribution of items in inventory is similar to the "mix" in the total goods available for sale.

PRESENTATION AND ANALYSIS
Presentation of Inventories

LEARNING OBJECTIVE 7
Explain how to report and analyze inventory.

Accounting standards require financial statement disclosure of the composition of the inventory, inventory financing arrangements, and the inventory costing methods employed. The standards also require the consistent application of costing methods from one period to another.

Manufacturers should report the inventory composition either in the balance sheet or in a separate schedule in the notes. The relative mix of raw materials, work in process, and finished goods helps in assessing liquidity and in computing the stage of inventory completion.

Significant or unusual financing arrangements relating to inventories may require note disclosure. Examples include transactions with related parties, product financing arrangements, firm purchase commitments, involuntary liquidation of LIFO inventories, and pledging of inventories as collateral. Companies should present inventories pledged as collateral for a loan in the current assets section rather than as an offset to the liability.

A company should also report the basis on which it states inventory amounts (lower-of-cost-or-market) and the method used in determining cost (LIFO, FIFO, average-cost, etc.). For example, the annual report of **Mumford of Wyoming** contains the following disclosures.

Mumford of Wyoming

Note A: Significant Accounting Policies

Live feeder cattle and feed—last-in, first-out (LIFO) cost, which is below approximate market	$854,800
Live range cattle—lower of principally identified cost or market	$1,240,500
Live sheep and supplies—lower of first-in, first-out (FIFO) cost or market	$674,000
Dressed meat and by-products—principally at market less allowances for distribution and selling expenses	$362,630

ILLUSTRATION 9-24
Disclosure of Inventory Methods

Illustration 9-24 shows that a company can use different pricing methods for different elements of its inventory. If Mumford changes the method of pricing any of its inventory elements, it must report a change in accounting principle. For example, if Mumford changes its method of accounting for live sheep from FIFO to average-cost, it should separately report this change, along with the effect on income, in the current and prior periods. Changes in accounting principle require an explanatory paragraph in the auditor's report describing the change in method.

Fortune Brands, Inc. reported its inventories in its annual report as follows (note the "trade practice" followed in classifying inventories among the current assets).

Fortune Brands, Inc.

Current assets

(in millions)	December 31
Inventories	
Maturing spirits	$1,243.0
Other raw materials, supplies and work in process	322.7
Finished products	450.9
Total inventories	$2,016.6

Significant Accounting Policies (in part)

Inventories   The first-in, first-out (FIFO) inventory method is our principal inventory method across all segments. In accordance with generally recognized trade practice, maturing spirits inventories are classified as current assets, although the majority of these inventories ordinarily will not be sold within one year, due to the duration of aging processes. Inventory provisions are recorded to reduce inventory to the lower of cost or market value for obsolete or slow moving inventory based on assumptions about future demand and marketability of products, the impact of new product introductions, inventory turns, product spoilage and specific identification of items, such as product discontinuance or engineering/material changes.

ILLUSTRATION 9-25
Disclosure of Trade Practice in Valuing Inventories

Analysis of Inventories

As our opening story illustrates, the amount of inventory that a company carries can have significant economic consequences. As a result, companies must manage inventories. But, inventory management is a double-edged sword. It requires constant attention. On the one hand, management wants to stock a great variety and quantity of items. Doing so will provide customers with the greatest selection. However, such an inventory policy may incur excessive carrying costs (e.g., investment, storage, insurance, taxes, obsolescence, and damage). On the other hand, low inventory levels lead to stockouts, lost sales, and disgruntled customers.

Using financial ratios helps companies to chart a middle course between these two dangers. Common ratios used in the management and evaluation of inventory levels are inventory turnover and a related measure, average days to sell inventory.

Inventory Turnover

The inventory turnover measures the number of times on average a company sells the inventory during the period. It measures the liquidity of the inventory. To compute inventory turnover, divide the cost of goods sold by the average inventory on hand during the period.

Barring seasonal factors, analysts compute average inventory from beginning and ending inventory balances. For example, in its 2011 annual report Kellogg Company reported a beginning inventory of $1,056 million, an ending inventory of $1,132 million, and cost of goods sold of $7,750 million for the year. Illustration 9-26 shows the inventory turnover formula and Kellogg Company's 2011 ratio computation below.

ILLUSTRATION 9-26
Inventory Turnover

$$\text{Inventory Turnover} = \frac{\text{Cost of Goods Sold}}{\text{Average Inventory}} = \frac{\$7,750}{(\$1,132 + \$1,056)/2} = 7.08 \text{ times}$$

You will want to read the
IFRS INSIGHTS
on pages 525–534

for discussion of IFRS related to inventories.

Average Days to Sell Inventory

A variant of the inventory turnover is the average days to sell inventory. This measure represents the average number of days' sales for which a company has inventory on hand. For example, the inventory turnover for Kellogg Company of 7.08 times divided into 365 is approximately 51.6 days.

There are typical levels of inventory in every industry. However, companies that keep their inventory at lower levels with higher turnovers than those of their competitors, and that still can satisfy customer needs, are the most successful.

KEY TERMS

average days to sell inventory, *496*

conventional retail inventory method, *490*

cost-of-goods-sold method, *478*

cost-to-retail ratio, *489*

designated market value, *476*

gross profit method, *485*

gross profit percentage, *486*

hedging, *485*

inventory turnover, *496*

loss method, *478*

lower limit (floor), *475*

lower-of-cost-or-market (LCM), *475*

lump-sum (basket) purchase, *482*

markdown, *490*

SUMMARY OF LEARNING OBJECTIVES

1 **Describe and apply the lower-of-cost-or-market rule.** If inventory declines in value below its original cost, for whatever reason, a company should write down the inventory to reflect this loss. The general rule is to abandon the historical cost principle when the future utility (revenue-producing ability) of the asset drops below its original cost.

2 **Explain when companies value inventories at net realizable value.** Companies value inventory at net realizable value when (1) there is a controlled market with a quoted price applicable to all quantities, (2) no significant costs of disposal are involved, and (3) the cost figures are too difficult to obtain.

3 **Explain when companies use the relative sales value method to value inventories.** When a company purchases a group of varying units at a single lump-sum price—a so-called basket purchase—the company may allocate the total purchase price to the individual items on the basis of relative sales value.

4 **Discuss accounting issues related to purchase commitments.** Accounting for purchase commitments is controversial. Some argue that companies should report purchase commitment contracts as assets and liabilities at the time the contract is signed. Others believe that recognition at the delivery date is most appropriate. The

FASB neither excludes nor recommends the recording of assets and liabilities for purchase commitments. However, companies record losses when market prices fall relative to the commitment price.

5 **Determine ending inventory by applying the gross profit method.** Companies follow these steps to determine ending inventory by the gross profit method. (1) Compute the gross profit percentage on selling price. (2) Compute gross profit by multiplying net sales by the gross profit percentage. (3) Compute cost of goods sold by subtracting gross profit from net sales. (4) Compute ending inventory by subtracting cost of goods sold from total goods available for sale.

6 **Determine ending inventory by applying the retail inventory method.** Companies follow these steps to determine ending inventory by the conventional retail method. (1) To estimate inventory at retail, deduct the sales for the period from the retail value of the goods available for sale. (2) To find the cost-to-retail ratio for all goods passing through a department or firm, divide the total goods available for sale at cost by the total goods available at retail. (3) Convert the inventory valued at retail to approximate cost by applying the cost-to-retail ratio.

7 **Explain how to report and analyze inventory.** Accounting standards require financial statement disclosure of (1) the composition of the inventory (in the balance sheet or a separate schedule in the notes), (2) significant or unusual inventory financing arrangements, and (3) inventory costing methods employed (which may differ for different elements of inventory). Accounting standards also require the consistent application of costing methods from one period to another. Common ratios used in the management and evaluation of inventory levels are inventory turnover and average days to sell inventory.

markdown cancellations, *490*

market (for LCM), *474*

markup, *489*

markup cancellations, *489*

net realizable value (NRV), *475*

net realizable value less a normal profit margin, *475*

purchase commitments, *483*

retail inventory method, *488*

upper limit (ceiling), *475*

APPENDIX **9A**	**LIFO RETAIL METHODS**

A number of retail establishments have changed from the more conventional treatment to a **LIFO retail method**. For example, the world's largest retailer, **Wal-Mart Stores, Inc.**, uses the LIFO retail method. The primary reason to do so is for the tax advantages associated with valuing inventories on a LIFO basis. In addition, adoption of LIFO results in a better matching of costs and revenues.

8 **LEARNING OBJECTIVE**
Determine ending inventory by applying the LIFO retail methods.

The use of LIFO retail is made under two assumptions: (1) stable prices and (2) fluctuating prices.

STABLE PRICES—LIFO RETAIL METHOD

It is much more complex to compute the final inventory balance using a LIFO flow than using the conventional retail method. Under the LIFO retail method, companies like Wal-Mart or Target consider **both markups and markdowns** in obtaining the proper cost-to-retail percentage. Furthermore, since the LIFO method is concerned only with the additional layer, or the amount that should be subtracted from the previous layer, the beginning inventory is excluded from the cost-to-retail percentage.

A major assumption of the LIFO retail method is that the markups and markdowns apply only to the goods purchased during the current period and not to the beginning inventory. This assumption is debatable and may explain why some companies do not adopt this method.

Illustration 9A-1 presents the major concepts involved in the LIFO retail method applied to the Hernandez Company. Note that, to simplify the accounting, we have assumed that the price level has remained unchanged.

ILLUSTRATION 9A-1
LIFO Retail Method—
Stable Prices

	Cost	Retail
Beginning inventory—2014	$ 27,000	$ 45,000
Net purchases during the period	346,500	480,000
Net markups		20,000
Net markdowns		(5,000)
Total (excluding beginning inventory)	346,500 ⟷ 495,000
Total (including beginning inventory)	$373,500	540,000
Net sales during the period		(484,000)
Ending inventory at retail		$ 56,000

Establishment of cost-to-retail percentage under
assumptions of LIFO retail ($346,500 ÷ $495,000) = 70%

Illustration 9A-2 indicates that the inventory is composed of two layers: the beginning inventory and the additional increase that occurred in the inventory this period (2014). When we start the next period (2015), the beginning inventory will be composed of those two layers. If an increase in inventory occurs again, an additional layer will be added.

ILLUSTRATION 9A-2
Ending Inventory at
LIFO Cost, 2014—Stable
Prices

Ending Inventory at Retail Prices—2014	Layers at Retail Prices		Cost-to-Retail (Percentage)		Ending Inventory at LIFO Cost
$56,000	2013	$45,000 ×	60%*	=	$27,000
	2014	11,000 ×	70	=	7,700
		$56,000			$34,700

$\dfrac{*\$27,000}{\$45,000}$ (prior year's cost-to-retail)

However, if the final inventory figure is below the beginning inventory, Hernandez must reduce the beginning inventory starting with the most recent layer. For example, assume that the ending inventory for 2015 at retail is $50,000. Illustration 9A-3 shows the computation of the ending inventory at cost. Notice that the 2014 layer is reduced from $11,000 to $5,000.

ILLUSTRATION 9A-3
Ending Inventory at
LIFO Cost, 2015—Stable
Prices

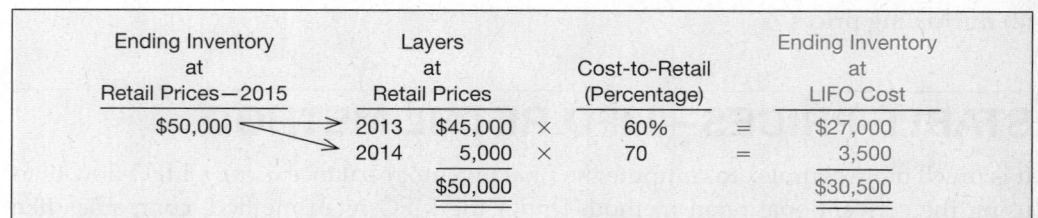

Ending Inventory at Retail Prices—2015	Layers at Retail Prices		Cost-to-Retail (Percentage)		Ending Inventory at LIFO Cost
$50,000	2013	$45,000 ×	60%	=	$27,000
	2014	5,000 ×	70	=	3,500
		$50,000			$30,500

FLUCTUATING PRICES—DOLLAR-VALUE LIFO RETAIL METHOD

The previous example simplified the LIFO retail method by ignoring changes in the selling price of the inventory. Let us now assume that a change in the price level of the inventories occurs (as is usual). If the price level does change, the company must

eliminate the price change so as to measure the real increase in inventory, not the dollar increase. This approach is referred to as the dollar-value LIFO retail method.

To illustrate, assume that the beginning inventory had a retail market value of $10,000 and the ending inventory had a retail market value of $15,000. Assume further that the price level has risen from 100 to 125. It is inappropriate to suggest that a real increase in inventory of $5,000 has occurred. Instead, the company must deflate the ending inventory at retail, as the computation in Illustration 9A-4 shows.

Ending inventory at retail (deflated) $15,000 ÷ 1.25*	$12,000	
Beginning inventory at retail	10,000	
Real increase in inventory at retail	$ 2,000	
Ending inventory at retail on LIFO basis:		
First layer	$10,000	
Second layer ($2,000 × 1.25)	2,500	$12,500

*1.25 = 125 ÷ 100

ILLUSTRATION 9A-4
Ending Inventory at Retail—Deflated and Restated

This approach is essentially the dollar-value LIFO method discussed in Chapter 8. In computing the LIFO inventory under a dollar-value LIFO approach, the company finds the dollar increase in inventory and deflates it to beginning-of-the-year prices. This indicates whether actual increases or decreases in quantity have occurred. If an increase in quantities occurs, the company prices this increase at the new index, in order to compute the value of the new layer. If a decrease in quantities happens, the company subtracts the increase from the most recent layers to the extent necessary.

The following computations, based on those in Illustration 9A-1 for Hernandez Company, illustrate the differences between the dollar-value LIFO retail method and the regular LIFO retail approach. Assume that the current 2014 price index is 112 (prior year = 100) and that the inventory ($56,000) has remained unchanged. In comparing Illustrations 9A-1 and 9A-5 (see below), note that the computations involved in finding the cost-to-retail percentage are exactly the same. However, the dollar-value method determines the increase that has occurred in the inventory in terms of base-year prices.

	Cost	Retail
Beginning inventory—2014	$ 27,000	$ 45,000
Net purchases during the period	346,500	480,000
Net markups		20,000
Net markdowns		(5,000)
Total (excluding beginning inventory)	346,500 ⟵⟶	495,000
Total (including beginning inventory)	$373,500	540,000
Net sales during the period at retail		(484,000)
Ending inventory at retail		$ 56,000
Establishment of cost-to-retail percentage under assumptions of LIFO retail ($346,500 ÷ $495,000) =		70%
A. Ending inventory at retail prices deflated to base-year prices ($56,000 ÷ 1.12)		$50,000
B. Beginning inventory (retail) at base-year prices		45,000
C. Inventory increase (retail) from beginning of period		$ 5,000

ILLUSTRATION 9A-5
Dollar-Value LIFO Retail Method—Fluctuating Prices

From this information, we compute the inventory amount at cost:

ILLUSTRATION 9A-6
Ending Inventory at LIFO Cost, 2014—Fluctuating Prices

Ending Inventory at Base-Year Retail Prices—2014	Layers at Base-Year Retail Prices		Price Index (percentage)		Cost-to-Retail (percentage)		Ending Inventory at LIFO Cost
$50,000	2013	$45,000 ×	100%	×	60%	=	$27,000
	2014	5,000 ×	112	×	70	=	3,920
		$50,000					$30,920

As Illustration 9A-6 shows, before the conversion to cost takes place, Hernandez must restate layers of a particular year to the prices in effect in the year when the layer was added.

Note the difference between the LIFO approach (stable prices) and the dollar-value LIFO method as indicated below.

ILLUSTRATION 9A-7
Comparison of Effect of Price Assumptions

	LIFO (stable prices)	LIFO (fluctuating prices)
Beginning inventory	$27,000	$27,000
Increment	7,700	3,920
Ending inventory	$34,700	$30,920

The difference of $3,780 ($34,700 − $30,920) results from an increase in the **price** of goods, not from an increase in the **quantity** of goods.

SUBSEQUENT ADJUSTMENTS UNDER DOLLAR-VALUE LIFO RETAIL

The dollar-value LIFO retail method follows the same procedures in subsequent periods as the traditional dollar-value method discussed in Chapter 8. That is, when a real increase in inventory occurs, Hernandez adds a new layer.

To illustrate, using the data from the previous example, assume that the retail value of the 2015 ending inventory at current prices is $64,800, the 2015 price index is 120 percent of base-year, and the cost-to-retail percentage is 75 percent. In base-year dollars, the ending inventory is therefore $54,000 ($64,800/120%). Illustration 9A-8 shows the computation of the ending inventory at LIFO cost.

ILLUSTRATION 9A-8
Ending Inventory at LIFO Cost, 2015—Fluctuating Prices

Ending Inventory at Base-Year Retail Prices—2015	Layers at Base-Year Retail Prices		Price Index (percentage)		Cost-to-Retail (percentage)		Ending Inventory at LIFO Cost
$54,000	2013	$45,000 ×	100%	×	60%	=	$27,000
	2014	5,000 ×	112	×	70	=	3,920
	2015	4,000 ×	120	×	75	=	3,600
		$54,000					$34,520

Conversely, when a real decrease in inventory develops, Hernandez "peels off" previous layers at prices in existence when the layers were added. To illustrate, assume that in 2015 the ending inventory in base-year prices is $48,000. The computation of the LIFO inventory is as follows.

Ending Inventory at Base-Year Retail Prices—2015	Layers at Base-Year Retail Prices		Price Index (percentage)		Cost-to-Retail (percentage)		Ending Inventory at LIFO Cost
$48,000	2013	$45,000 ×	100%	×	60%	=	$27,000
	2014	3,000 ×	112	×	70	=	2,352
		$48,000					$29,352

ILLUSTRATION 9A-9
Ending Inventory at LIFO Cost, 2015—Fluctuating Prices

The advantages and disadvantages of the lower-of-cost-or-market method (conventional retail) versus LIFO retail are the same for retail operations as for non-retail operations. As a practical matter, a company's selection of which retail inventory method to use often involves determining which method provides a lower taxable income. It might appear that retail LIFO will provide the lower taxable income in a period of rising prices. But this is not always the case. LIFO will provide an approximate current cost matching, but it states ending inventory at cost. The conventional retail method may have a large write-off because of the use of the lower-of-cost-or-market approach, which may offset the LIFO current cost matching.

CHANGING FROM CONVENTIONAL RETAIL TO LIFO

Because conventional retail is a lower-of-cost-or-market approach, the company must restate beginning inventory to a cost basis when changing from the conventional retail to the LIFO method.[15] The usual approach is to compute the cost basis from the purchases of the prior year, adjusted for both markups and markdowns.[16]

To illustrate, assume that Hakeman Clothing Store employs the conventional retail method but wishes to change to the LIFO retail method beginning in 2015. The amounts shown on the company's books are as follows.

	At Cost	At Retail
Inventory, January 1, 2014	$ 5,210	$ 15,000
Net purchases in 2014	47,250	100,000
Net markups in 2014		7,000
Net markdowns in 2014		2,000
Sales revenue in 2014		95,000

Illustration 9A-10 (page 502) shows computation of ending inventory under the **conventional retail method** for 2014.

[15]Changing from the conventional retail method to LIFO retail represents a change in accounting principle. We provide an expanded discussion of accounting principle changes in Chapter 22.

[16]A logical question to ask is, "Why are only the purchases from the prior period considered and not also the beginning inventory?" Apparently, the IRS believes that "the purchases-only approach" provides a more reasonable cost basis. The IRS position is debatable. However, for our purposes, it seems appropriate to use the purchases-only approach.

ILLUSTRATION 9A-10
Conventional Retail
Inventory Method

	Cost	Retail
Inventory January 1, 2014	$ 5,210	$ 15,000
Net purchases	47,250	100,000
Net additional markups		7,000
	$52,460	122,000
Net markdowns		(2,000)
Sales revenue		(95,000)
Ending inventory at retail		$ 25,000
Establishment of cost-to-retail percentage ($52,460 ÷ $122,000) =		43%
December 31, 2014, inventory at cost		
Inventory at retail		$ 25,000
Cost-to-retail ratio		× 43%
Inventory at cost under conventional retail		$ 10,750

Hakeman Clothing can then quickly approximate the ending inventory for 2014 under the **LIFO retail method,** as shown in Illustration 9A-11.

ILLUSTRATION 9A-11
Conversion to LIFO
Retail Inventory Method

December 31, 2014, Inventory at LIFO Cost

$$\text{Ending inventory} = \frac{\text{Retail}}{\$25,000} \times \frac{\text{Ratio}}{45\%^*} = \frac{\text{LIFO}}{\$11,250}$$

*The cost-to-retail ratio was computed as follows.

$$\frac{\text{Net purchases at cost}}{\substack{\text{Net purchases at retail plus}\\\text{markups less markdowns}}} = \frac{\$47,250}{\$100,000 + \$7,000 - \$2,000} = 45\%$$

The difference of $500 ($11,250 − $10,750) between the LIFO retail method and the conventional retail method in the ending inventory for 2014 is the amount by which the company must adjust beginning inventory for 2015. The entry to adjust the inventory to a cost basis is as follows.

Inventory	500	
Adjustment to Record Inventory at Cost		500

KEY TERMS

dollar-value LIFO retail method, *499*

LIFO retail method, *497*

SUMMARY OF LEARNING OBJECTIVE FOR APPENDIX 9A

8 **Determine ending inventory by applying the LIFO retail methods.** The application of LIFO retail is made under two assumptions: stable prices and fluctuating prices.

Procedures under stable prices: (a) Because the LIFO method is a cost method, both markups and markdowns must be considered in obtaining the proper cost-to-retail percentage. (b) Since the LIFO method is concerned only with the additional layer, or the amount that should be subtracted from the previous layer, the beginning inventory is excluded from the cost-to-retail percentage. (c) The markups and markdowns apply only to the goods purchased during the current period and not to the beginning inventory.

Procedures under fluctuating prices: The steps are the same as for stable prices except that in computing the LIFO inventory under a dollar-value LIFO approach, the dollar increase in inventory is found and deflated to beginning-of-the-year prices. Doing so will determine whether actual increases or decreases in quantity have occurred. If quantities increase, this increase is priced at the new index to compute the new layer. If quantities decrease, the decrease is subtracted from the most recent layers to the extent necessary.

DEMONSTRATION PROBLEM

Norwood Company makes miniature circuit boards that are components of wireless phones and personal organizers. The company has experienced strong growth, and you are especially interested in how well Norwood is managing its inventory balances. You have collected the following information for the current year.

Inventory at the beginning of year	$ 1,026,000
Inventory at the end of year, before any adjustments	1,007,000
Total cost of goods sold, before any adjustments	11,776,000

The company values inventory at lower-of-cost (using LIFO cost flow assumption)-or-market.

Instructions

(a) Compute Norwood's inventory turnover before any adjustment.

(b) Recompute the inventory turnover after adjusting Norwood's inventory information for the following items.

   1. During the year, Norwood recorded sales and costs of goods sold on $22,000 of units shipped to various wholesalers on consignment. At year-end, none of these units have been sold by wholesalers.

   2. Shipping contracts changed 2 months ago from f.o.b. shipping point to f.o.b. destination point. At the end of the year, $25,000 of products are en route to China and will not arrive until after financial statements are released. Current inventory balances do not reflect this change in policy.

   3. At the end of the year, Norwood determined that a certain section of inventory with an historical cost of $112,000 has a replacement cost of $100,800, net realizable value of $101,000 and net realizable value less a normal profit margin of $90,400. There is no need to make a lower-of-cost-or-market adjustment to other inventory.

Solution

(a) $$\frac{\$11,776,000}{(\$1,026,000 \times \$1,007,000)/2} = 11.6 \text{ times}$$

(b) Adjustments to ending inventory

Item	Adjustment to Ending Inventory	Explanation
1. Consigned goods	$22,000	Norwood should count the goods it has consigned in other stores.
2. Goods in transit	$25,000	Goods officially change hands at the point of destination. Norwood should still show these goods in inventory (not cost of goods sold), until they reach the destination.
3. Lower-of-cost-or-market	$(11,200)	($112,000 − $100,800). The correct valuation is $100,800 since the market designation of $100,800 is less than the original cost.

$$\text{Adjusted inventory turnover} = \frac{\$11,740,000^a}{(\$1,026,000 \times \$1,042,800^b)/2}$$
$$= 11.3 \text{ times}$$

[a]Cost of goods sold: $11,776,000 − $22,000 − $25,000 + $11,200 = $11,740,200
[b]Ending inventory: $1,007,000 + $22,000 + $25,000 − $11,200 = $1,042,800

FASB CODIFICATION

FASB Codification References

[1] FASB ASC 330-10-35. [Predecessor literature: "Restatement and Revision of Accounting Research Bulletins," *Accounting Research Bulletin No. 43* (New York: AICPA, 1953), Ch. 4, par. 8.]

[2] FASB ASC 330-10-S99-3. [Predecessor literature: "AICPA Task Force on LIFO Inventory Problems," *Issues Paper* (New York: AICPA, November 30, 1984), pp. 50–55.]

[3] FASB ASC 330-10-35. [Predecessor literature: "Restatement and Revision of Accounting Research Bulletins," *Accounting Research Bulletin No. 43* (New York: AICPA, 1953), Ch. 4.]

[4] FASB ASC 330-10-35-16 through 18. [Predecessor literature: "Restatement and Revision of Accounting Research Bulletins," *Accounting Research Bulletin No. 43* (New York: AICPA, 1953), Ch. 4, par. 16.]

Exercises

If your school has a subscription to the FASB Codification, go to *http://aaahq.org/asclogin.cfm* to log in and prepare responses to the following. Provide Codification references for your responses.

CE9-1 Access the glossary ("Master Glossary") to answer the following.

(a) What is the definition of inventory?
(b) What is the definition of market as it relates to inventory?
(c) What is the definition of net realizable value?

CE9-2 Based on increased competition for one of its key products, Tutaj Company is concerned that it will not be able to sell its products at a price that would cover its costs. Since the company is already having a bad year, the sales manager proposes writing down the inventory to the lowest level possible, so that all the bad news will be in the current year. Explain to the sales manager the rationale for lower-of-cost-or-market adjustments, according to GAAP.

CE9-3 What are the provisions for subsequent measurement of inventory in the context of a hedging transaction?

CE9-4 What is the nature of the SEC guidance concerning inventory disclosures?

An additional Codification case can be found in the Using Your Judgment section, on page 525.

Be sure to check the book's companion website for a Review and Analysis Exercise, with solution.

 Brief Exercises, Exercises, Problems, and many more learning and assessment tools and resources are available for practice in WileyPLUS.

Note: All asterisked Questions, Exercises, and Problems relate to material in the appendix to the chapter.

QUESTIONS

1. Where there is evidence that the utility of inventory goods, as part of their disposal in the ordinary course of business, will be less than cost, what is the proper accounting treatment?

2. Explain the rationale for the ceiling and floor in the lower-of-cost-or-market method of valuing inventories.

3. Why are inventories valued at the lower-of-cost-or-market? What are the arguments against the use of the LCM method of valuing inventories?

4. What approaches may be employed in applying the lower-of-cost-or-market procedure? Which approach is normally used and why?

5. In some instances, accounting principles require a departure from valuing inventories at cost alone. Determine the proper unit inventory price in the following cases.

	Cases				
	1	2	3	4	5
Cost	$15.90	$16.10	$15.90	$15.90	$15.90
Net realizable value	14.50	19.20	15.20	10.40	16.40
Net realizable value less normal profit	12.80	17.60	13.75	8.80	14.80
Market (replacement cost)	14.80	17.20	12.80	9.70	16.80

6. What method(s) might be used in the accounts to record a loss due to a price decline in the inventories? Discuss.

7. What factors might call for inventory valuation at sales prices (net realizable value or market price)?

8. Under what circumstances is relative sales value an appropriate basis for determining the price assigned to inventory?

9. At December 31, 2014, Ashley Co. has outstanding purchase commitments for 150,000 gallons, at $6.20 per gallon, of a raw material to be used in its manufacturing process. The company prices its raw material inventory at cost or market, whichever is lower. Assuming that the market price as of December 31, 2014, is $5.90, how would you treat this situation in the accounts?

10. What are the major uses of the gross profit method?

11. Distinguish between gross profit as a percentage of cost and gross profit as a percentage of sales price. Convert the following gross profit percentages based on cost to gross profit percentages based on sales price: 25% and $33\frac{1}{3}$%. Convert the following gross profit percentages based on sales price to gross profit percentages based on cost: $33\frac{1}{3}$% and 60%.

12. Adriana Co., with annual net sales of $5 million, maintains a markup of 25% based on cost. Adriana's expenses average 15% of net sales. What is Adriana's gross profit and net profit in dollars?

13. A fire destroys all of the merchandise of Assante Company on February 10, 2014. Presented below is information compiled up to the date of the fire.

Inventory, January 1, 2014	$ 400,000
Sales revenue to February 10, 2014	1,950,000
Purchases to February 10, 2014	1,140,000
Freight-in to February 10, 2014	60,000
Rate of gross profit on selling price	40%

What is the approximate inventory on February 10, 2014?

14. What conditions must exist for the retail inventory method to provide valid results?

15. The conventional retail inventory method yields results that are essentially the same as those yielded by the lower-of-cost-or-market method. Explain. Prepare an illustration of how the retail inventory method reduces inventory to market.

16. **(a)** Determine the ending inventory under the conventional retail method for the furniture department of Mayron Department Stores from the following data.

	Cost	Retail
Inventory, Jan. 1	$ 149,000	$ 283,500
Purchases	1,400,000	2,160,000
Freight-in	70,000	
Markups, net		92,000
Markdowns, net		48,000
Sales revenue		2,175,000

(b) If the results of a physical inventory indicated an inventory at retail of $295,000, what inferences would you draw?

17. **Deere and Company** reported inventory in its balance sheet as follows.

Inventories $1,999,100,000

What additional disclosures might be necessary to present the inventory fairly?

18. Of what significance is inventory turnover to a retail store?

*19. What modifications to the conventional retail method are necessary to approximate a LIFO retail flow?

BRIEF EXERCISES

1 2 BE9-1 Presented below is information related to Rembrandt Inc.'s inventory.

(per unit)	Skis	Boots	Parkas
Historical cost	$190.00	$106.00	$53.00
Selling price	212.00	145.00	73.75
Cost to distribute	19.00	8.00	2.50
Current replacement cost	203.00	105.00	51.00
Normal profit margin	32.00	29.00	21.25

Determine the following: (a) the two limits to market value (i.e., the ceiling and the floor) that should be used in the lower-of-cost-or-market computation for skis, (b) the cost amount that should be used in the lower-of-cost-or-market comparison of boots, and (c) the market amount that should be used to value parkas on the basis of the lower-of-cost-or-market.

1 2 BE9-2 Floyd Corporation has the following four items in its ending inventory.

Item	Cost	Replacement Cost	Net Realizable Value (NRV)	NRV Less Normal Profit Margin
Jokers	$2,000	$2,050	$2,100	$1,600
Penguins	5,000	5,100	4,950	4,100
Riddlers	4,400	4,550	4,625	3,700
Scarecrows	3,200	2,990	3,830	3,070

Determine the final lower-of-cost-or-market inventory value for each item.

1 2 BE9-3 Kumar Inc. uses a perpetual inventory system. At January 1, 2014, inventory was $214,000 at both cost and market value. At December 31, 2014, the inventory was $286,000 at cost and $265,000 at market value. Prepare the necessary December 31 entry under (a) the cost-of-goods-sold method and (b) the loss method.

3 BE9-4 Bell, Inc. buys 1,000 computer game CDs from a distributor who is discontinuing those games. The purchase price for the lot is $8,000. Bell will group the CDs into three price categories for resale, as indicated below.

Group	No. of CDs	Price per CD
1	100	$ 5
2	800	10
3	100	15

Determine the cost per CD for each group, using the relative sales value method.

4 BE9-5 Kemper Company signed a long-term noncancelable purchase commitment with a major supplier to purchase raw materials in 2015 at a cost of $1,000,000. At December 31, 2014, the raw materials to be purchased have a market value of $950,000. Prepare any necessary December 31, 2014, entry.

4 BE9-6 Use the information for Kemper Company from BE9-5. In 2015, Kemper paid $1,000,000 to obtain the raw materials which were worth $950,000. Prepare the entry to record the purchase.

5 BE9-7 Fosbre Corporation's April 30 inventory was destroyed by fire. January 1 inventory was $150,000, and purchases for January through April totaled $500,000. Sales revenue for the same period were $700,000. Fosbre's normal gross profit percentage is 35% on sales. Using the gross profit method, estimate Fosbre's April 30 inventory that was destroyed by fire.

6 BE9-8 Boyne Inc. had beginning inventory of $12,000 at cost and $20,000 at retail. Net purchases were $120,000 at cost and $170,000 at retail. Net markups were $10,000; net markdowns were $7,000; and sales revenue was $147,000. Compute ending inventory at cost using the conventional retail method.

7 BE9-9 In its 2012 annual report, Gap Inc. reported inventory of $1,615 million on January 25, 2012, and $1,620 million on January 29, 2011, cost of sales of $9,275 million for fiscal year 2012, and net sales of $14,549 million. Compute Gap's inventory turnover and the average days to sell inventory for the fiscal year 2012.

8 *BE9-10 Use the information for Boyne Inc. from BE9-8. Compute ending inventory at cost using the LIFO retail method.

8 *BE9-11 Use the information for Boyne Inc. from BE9-8, and assume the price level increased from 100 at the beginning of the year to 115 at year-end. Compute ending inventory at cost using the dollar-value LIFO retail method.

EXERCISES

1 2 **E9-1 (Lower-of-Cost-or-Market)** The inventory of 3T Company on December 31, 2014, consists of the following items.

Part No.	Quantity	Cost per Unit	Cost to Replace per Unit
110	600	$ 90	$100
111	1,000	60	52
112	500	80	76
113	200	170	180
120	400	205	208
121[a]	1,600	16	14
122	300	240	235

[a]Part No. 121 is obsolete and has a realizable value of $0.20 each as scrap.

Instructions

(a) Determine the inventory as of December 31, 2014, by the lower-of-cost-or-market method, applying this method directly to each item.

(b) Determine the inventory by the lower-of-cost-or-market method, applying the method to the total of the inventory.

1 2 **E9-2 (Lower-of-Cost-or-Market)** Smashing Pumpkins Company uses the lower-of-cost-or-market method, on an individual-item basis, in pricing its inventory items. The inventory at December 31, 2014, consists of products D, E, F, G, H, and I. Relevant per-unit data for these products appear below.

	Item D	Item E	Item F	Item G	Item H	Item I
Estimated selling price	$120	$110	$95	$90	$110	$90
Cost	75	80	80	80	50	36
Replacement cost	120	72	70	30	70	30
Estimated selling expense	30	30	30	25	30	30
Normal profit	20	20	20	20	20	20

Instructions

Using the lower-of-cost-or-market rule, determine the proper unit value for balance sheet reporting purposes at December 31, 2014, for each of the inventory items above.

1 2 **E9-3 (Lower-of-Cost-or-Market)** Michael Bolton Company follows the practice of pricing its inventory at the lower-of-cost-or-market, on an individual-item basis.

Item No.	Quantity	Cost per Unit	Cost to Replace	Estimated Selling Price	Cost of Completion and Disposal	Normal Profit
1320	1,200	$3.20	$3.00	$4.50	$0.35	$1.25
1333	900	2.70	2.30	3.50	0.50	0.50
1426	800	4.50	3.70	5.00	0.40	1.00
1437	1,000	3.60	3.10	3.20	0.25	0.90
1510	700	2.25	2.00	3.25	0.80	0.60
1522	500	3.00	2.70	3.80	0.40	0.50
1573	3,000	1.80	1.60	2.50	0.75	0.50
1626	1,000	4.70	5.20	6.00	0.50	1.00

Instructions

From the information above, determine the amount of Bolton Company inventory.

1 2 **E9-4 (Lower-of-Cost-or-Market—Journal Entries)** Corrs Company began operations in 2013 and determined its ending inventory at cost and at lower-of-cost-or-market at December 31, 2013, and December 31, 2014. This information is presented below.

	Cost	Lower-of-Cost-or-Market
12/31/13	$346,000	$327,000
12/31/14	410,000	395,000

Instructions

(a) Prepare the journal entries required at December 31, 2013, and December 31, 2014, assuming that the inventory is recorded at market, and a perpetual inventory system (direct method) is used.

(b) Prepare journal entries required at December 31, 2013, and December 31, 2014, assuming that the inventory is recorded at cost and an allowance account is adjusted at each year-end under a perpetual system.

(c) Which of the two methods above provides the higher net income in each year?

1 2 E9-5 (Lower-of-Cost-or-Market—Valuation Account) Presented below is information related to Candlebox Enterprises.

	Jan. 31	Feb. 28	Mar. 31	Apr. 30
Inventory at cost	$15,000	$15,100	$17,000	$13,000
Inventory at the lower-of-cost-or-market	14,500	12,600	15,600	12,300
Purchases for the month		20,000	24,000	26,500
Sales revenue for the month		29,000	35,000	40,000

Instructions

(a) From the information, prepare (as far as the data permit) monthly income statements in columnar form for February, March, and April. The inventory is to be shown in the statement at cost, the gain or loss due to market fluctuations is to be shown separately, and a valuation account is to be set up for the difference between cost and the lower of cost or market.

(b) Prepare the journal entry required to establish the valuation account at January 31 and entries to adjust it monthly thereafter.

1 2 E9-6 (Lower-of-Cost-or-Market—Error Effect) Winans Company uses the lower-of-cost-or-market method, on an individual-item basis, in pricing its inventory items. The inventory at December 31, 2013, included product X. Relevant per-unit data for product X appear below.

Estimated selling price	$45
Cost	40
Replacement cost	35
Estimated selling expense	14
Normal profit	9

There were 1,000 units of product X on hand at December 31, 2013. Product X was incorrectly valued at $35 per unit for reporting purposes. All 1,000 units were sold in 2014.

Instructions

Compute the effect of this error on net income for 2013 and the effect on net income for 2014, and indicate the direction of the misstatement for each year.

3 E9-7 (Relative Sales Value Method) Phil Collins Realty Corporation purchased a tract of unimproved land for $55,000. This land was improved and subdivided into building lots at an additional cost of $34,460. These building lots were all of the same size but owing to differences in location were offered for sale at different prices as follows.

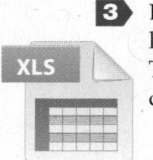

Group	No. of Lots	Price per Lot
1	9	$3,000
2	15	4,000
3	17	2,400

Operating expenses for the year allocated to this project total $18,200. Lots unsold at the year-end were as follows.

Group 1	5 lots
Group 2	7 lots
Group 3	2 lots

Instructions

At the end of the fiscal year Phil Collins Realty Corporation instructs you to arrive at the net income realized on this operation to date.

3 **E9-8 (Relative Sales Value Method)** During 2014, Pretenders Furniture Company purchases a carload of wicker chairs. The manufacturer sells the chairs to Pretenders for a lump sum of $59,850 because it is discontinuing manufacturing operations and wishes to dispose of its entire stock. Three types of chairs are included in the carload. The three types and the estimated selling price for each are listed below.

Type	No. of Chairs	Estimated Selling Price Each
Lounge chairs	400	$90
Armchairs	300	80
Straight chairs	700	50

During 2014, Pretenders sells 200 lounge chairs, 100 armchairs, and 120 straight chairs.

Instructions
What is the amount of gross profit realized during 2014? What is the amount of inventory of unsold straight chairs on December 31, 2014?

4 **E9-9 (Purchase Commitments)** Marvin Gaye Company has been having difficulty obtaining key raw materials for its manufacturing process. The company therefore signed a long-term noncancelable purchase commitment with its largest supplier of this raw material on November 30, 2014, at an agreed price of $400,000. At December 31, 2014, the raw material had declined in price to $365,000.

Instructions
What entry would you make on December 31, 2014, to recognize these facts?

4 **E9-10 (Purchase Commitments)** At December 31, 2014, Indigo Girls Company has outstanding noncancelable purchase commitments for 36,000 gallons, at $3.00 per gallon, of raw material to be used in its manufacturing process. The company prices its raw material inventory at cost or market, whichever is lower.

Instructions
(a) Assuming that the market price as of December 31, 2014, is $3.30, how would this matter be treated in the accounts and statements? Explain.
(b) Assuming that the market price as of December 31, 2014, is $2.70, instead of $3.30, how would you treat this situation in the accounts and statements?
(c) Give the entry in January 2015, when the 36,000-gallon shipment is received, assuming that the situation given in (b) above existed at December 31, 2014, and that the market price in January 2015 was $2.70 per gallon. Give an explanation of your treatment.

5 **E9-11 (Gross Profit Method)** Each of the following gross profit percentages is expressed in terms of cost.

1. 20%.   3. $33\frac{1}{3}$%.
2. 25%.   4. 50%.

Instructions
Indicate the gross profit percentage in terms of sales for each of the above.

5 **E9-12 (Gross Profit Method)** Mark Price Company uses the gross profit method to estimate inventory for monthly reporting purposes. Presented below is information for the month of May.

Inventory, May 1	$ 160,000
Purchases (gross)	640,000
Freight-in	30,000
Sales revenue	1,000,000
Sales returns	70,000
Purchase discounts	12,000

Instructions
(a) Compute the estimated inventory at May 31, assuming that the gross profit is 30% of sales.
(b) Compute the estimated inventory at May 31, assuming that the gross profit is 30% of cost.

5 **E9-13 (Gross Profit Method)** Tim Legler requires an estimate of the cost of goods lost by fire on March 9. Merchandise on hand on January 1 was $38,000. Purchases since January 1 were $72,000; freight-in, $3,400; purchase returns and allowances, $2,400. Sales are made at $33\frac{1}{3}$% above cost and totaled $100,000 to March 9. Goods costing $10,900 were left undamaged by the fire; remaining goods were destroyed.

Instructions
(a) Compute the cost of goods destroyed.
(b) Compute the cost of goods destroyed, assuming that the gross profit is $33\frac{1}{3}$% of sales.

5 E9-14 (Gross Profit Method) Rasheed Wallace Company lost most of its inventory in a fire in December just before the year-end physical inventory was taken. The corporation's books disclosed the following.

Beginning inventory	$170,000	Sales revenue	$650,000
Purchases for the year	390,000	Sales returns	24,000
Purchase returns	30,000	Rate of gross profit on net sales	40%

Merchandise with a selling price of $21,000 remained undamaged after the fire. Damaged merchandise with an original selling price of $15,000 had a net realizable value of $5,300.

Instructions

Compute the amount of the loss as a result of the fire, assuming that the corporation had no insurance coverage.

5 E9-15 (Gross Profit Method) You are called by Tim Duncan of Spurs Co. on July 16 and asked to prepare a claim for insurance as a result of a theft that took place the night before. You suggest that an inventory be taken immediately. The following data are available.

Inventory, July 1	$ 38,000
Purchases—goods placed in stock July 1–15	85,000
Sales revenue—goods delivered to customers (gross)	116,000
Sales returns—goods returned to stock	4,000

Your client reports that the goods on hand on July 16 cost $30,500, but you determine that this figure includes goods of $6,000 received on a consignment basis. Your past records show that sales are made at approximately 40% over cost. Duncan's insurance covers only goods owned.

Instructions

Compute the claim against the insurance company.

5 E9-16 (Gross Profit Method) Gheorghe Moresan Lumber Company handles three principal lines of merchandise with these varying rates of gross profit on cost.

Lumber	25%
Millwork	30%
Hardware and fittings	40%

On August 18, a fire destroyed the office, lumber shed, and a considerable portion of the lumber stacked in the yard. To file a report of loss for insurance purposes, the company must know what the inventories were immediately preceding the fire. No detail or perpetual inventory records of any kind were maintained. The only pertinent information you are able to obtain are the following facts from the general ledger, which was kept in a fireproof vault and thus escaped destruction.

	Lumber	Millwork	Hardware
Inventory, Jan. 1, 2014	$ 250,000	$ 90,000	$ 45,000
Purchases to Aug. 18, 2014	1,500,000	375,000	160,000
Sales revenue to Aug. 18, 2014	2,080,000	533,000	210,000

Instructions

Submit your estimate of the inventory amounts immediately preceding the fire.

5 E9-17 (Gross Profit Method) Presented below is information related to Aaron Rodgers Corporation for the current year.

Beginning inventory	$ 600,000	
Purchases	1,500,000	
Total goods available for sale		$2,100,000
Sales revenue		2,500,000

Instructions

Compute the ending inventory, assuming that **(a)** gross profit is 45% of sales; **(b)** gross profit is 60% of cost; **(c)** gross profit is 35% of sales; and **(d)** gross profit is 25% of cost.

6 **E9-18 (Retail Inventory Method)** Presented below is information related to Bobby Engram Company.

	Cost	Retail
Beginning inventory	$ 58,000	$100,000
Purchases (net)	122,000	200,000
Net markups		10,345
Net markdowns		26,135
Sales revenue		186,000

Instructions
  (a) Compute the ending inventory at retail.
  (b) Compute a cost-to-retail percentage (round to two decimals) under the following conditions.
      (1) Excluding both markups and markdowns.
      (2) Excluding markups but including markdowns.
      (3) Excluding markdowns but including markups.
      (4) Including both markdowns and markups.
  (c) Which of the methods in (b) above (1, 2, 3, or 4) does the following?
      (1) Provides the most conservative estimate of ending inventory.
      (2) Provides an approximation of lower-of-cost-or-market.
      (3) Is used in the conventional retail method.
  (d) Compute ending inventory at lower-of-cost-or-market (round to nearest dollar).
  (e) Compute cost of goods sold based on (d).
  (f) Compute gross margin based on (d).

6 **E9-19 (Retail Inventory Method)** Presented below is information related to Ricky Henderson Company.

	Cost	Retail
Beginning inventory	$ 200,000	$ 280,000
Purchases	1,375,000	2,140,000
Markups		95,000
Markup cancellations		15,000
Markdowns		35,000
Markdown cancellations		5,000
Sales revenue		2,200,000

Instructions
Compute the inventory by the conventional retail inventory method.

6 **E9-20 (Retail Inventory Method)** The records of Ellen's Boutique report the following data for the month of April.

Sales revenue	$99,000	Purchases (at cost)	$48,000
Sales returns	2,000	Purchases (at sales price)	88,000
Markups	10,000	Purchase returns (at cost)	2,000
Markup cancellations	1,500	Purchase returns (at sales price)	3,000
Markdowns	9,300	Beginning inventory (at cost)	30,000
Markdown cancellations	2,800	Beginning inventory (at sales price)	46,500
Freight on purchases	2,400		

Instructions
Compute the ending inventory by the conventional retail inventory method.

7 **E9-21 (Analysis of Inventories)** The financial statements of ConAgra Foods, Inc.'s 2012 annual report disclose the following information.

(in millions)	May 27, 2012	May 29, 2011	May 30, 2010
Inventories	$1,870	$1,803	$1,598

	Fiscal Year	
	2012	2011
Net sales	$13,263	$12,303
Cost of goods sold	10,436	9,390
Net income	474	818

Instructions
Compute ConAgra's **(a)** inventory turnover and **(b)** the average days to sell inventory for 2012 and 2011.

8 *E9-22 (Retail Inventory Method—Conventional and LIFO)** Helen Keller Company began operations on January 1, 2013, adopting the conventional retail inventory system. None of the company's merchandise was marked down in 2013 and, because there was no beginning inventory, its ending inventory for 2013 of $38,100 would have been the same under either the conventional retail system or the LIFO retail system.

On December 31, 2014, the store management considers adopting the LIFO retail system and desires to know how the December 31, 2014, inventory would appear under both systems. All pertinent data regarding purchases, sales, markups, and markdowns are shown below. There has been no change in the price level.

	Cost	Retail
Inventory, Jan. 1, 2014	$ 38,100	$ 60,000
Markdowns (net)		13,000
Markups (net)		22,000
Purchases (net)	130,900	178,000
Sales (net)		167,000

Instructions
Determine the cost of the 2014 ending inventory under both **(a)** the conventional retail method and **(b)** the LIFO retail method.

8 *E9-23 (Retail Inventory Method—Conventional and LIFO)** Leonard Bernstein Company began operations late in 2013 and adopted the conventional retail inventory method. Because there was no beginning inventory for 2013 and no markdowns during 2013, the ending inventory for 2013 was $14,000 under both the conventional retail method and the LIFO retail method. At the end of 2014, management wants to compare the results of applying the conventional and LIFO retail methods. There was no change in the price level during 2014. The following data are available for computations.

	Cost	Retail
Inventory, January 1, 2014	$14,000	$20,000
Sales revenue		80,000
Net markups		9,000
Net markdowns		1,600
Purchases	58,800	81,000
Freight-in	7,500	
Estimated theft		2,000

Instructions
Compute the cost of the 2014 ending inventory under both **(a)** the conventional retail method and **(b)** the LIFO retail method.

8 *E9-24 (Dollar-Value LIFO Retail)** You assemble the following information for Seneca Department Store, which computes its inventory under the dollar-value LIFO method.

	Cost	Retail
Inventory on January 1, 2014	$216,000	$300,000
Purchases	364,800	480,000
Increase in price level for year		9%

Instructions
Compute the cost of the inventory on December 31, 2014, assuming that the inventory at retail is **(a)** $294,300 and **(b)** $365,150.

8 *E9-25 (Dollar-Value LIFO Retail)** Presented below is information related to Langston Hughes Corporation.

	Price Index	LIFO Cost	Retail
Inventory on December 31, 2014, when dollar-value LIFO is adopted	100	$36,000	$ 74,500
Inventory, December 31, 2015	110	?	100,100

Instructions

Compute the ending inventory under the dollar-value LIFO method at December 31, 2015. The cost-to-retail ratio for 2015 was 60%.

8 *E9-26 (Conventional Retail and Dollar-Value LIFO Retail)** Amiras Corporation began operations on January 1, 2014, with a beginning inventory of $30,100 at cost and $50,000 at retail. The following information relates to 2014.

	Retail
Net purchases ($108,500 at cost)	$150,000
Net markups	10,000
Net markdowns	5,000
Sales revenue	126,900

Instructions

(a) Assume Amiras decided to adopt the conventional retail method. Compute the ending inventory to be reported in the balance sheet.

(b) Assume instead that Amiras decides to adopt the dollar-value LIFO retail method. The appropriate price indexes are 100 at January 1 and 110 at December 31. Compute the ending inventory to be reported in the balance sheet.

(c) On the basis of the information in part (b), compute cost of goods sold.

8 *E9-27 (Dollar-Value LIFO Retail)** Connie Chung Corporation adopted the dollar-value LIFO retail inventory method on January 1, 2013. At that time the inventory had a cost of $54,000 and a retail price of $100,000. The following information is available.

	Year-End Inventory at Retail	Current Year Cost—Retail %	Year-End Price Index
2013	$118,720	57%	106
2014	138,750	60%	111
2015	125,350	61%	115
2016	162,500	58%	125

The price index at January 1, 2013, is 100.

Instructions

Compute the ending inventory at December 31 of the years 2013–2016. (Round to the nearest dollar.)

8 *E9-28 (Change to LIFO Retail)** John Olerud Ltd., a local retailing concern in the Bronx, New York, has decided to change from the conventional retail inventory method to the LIFO retail method starting on January 1, 2015. The company recomputed its ending inventory for 2014 in accordance with the procedures necessary to switch to LIFO retail. The inventory computed was $212,600.

Instructions

Assuming that John Olerud Ltd.'s ending inventory for 2014 under the conventional retail inventory method was $205,000, prepare the appropriate journal entry on January 1, 2015.

EXERCISES SET B

See the book's companion website, at **www.wiley.com/college/kieso**, for an additional set of exercises.

PROBLEMS

1 **2** **P9-1 (Lower-of-Cost-or-Market)** Remmers Company manufactures desks. Most of the company's desks are standard models and are sold on the basis of catalog prices. At December 31, 2014, the following finished desks appear in the company's inventory.

Finished Desks	A	B	C	D
2014 catalog selling price	$450	$480	$900	$1,050
FIFO cost per inventory list 12/31/14	470	450	830	960
Estimated current cost to manufacture (at December 31, 2014, and early 2015)	460	430	610	1,000
Sales commissions and estimated other costs of disposal	50	60	80	130
2015 catalog selling price	500	540	900	1,200

The 2014 catalog was in effect through November 2014, and the 2015 catalog is effective as of December 1, 2014. All catalog prices are net of the usual discounts. Generally, the company attempts to obtain a 20% gross profit on selling price and has usually been successful in doing so.

Instructions

At what amount should each of the four desks appear in the company's December 31, 2014, inventory, assuming that the company has adopted a lower-of-FIFO-cost-or-market approach for valuation of inventories on an individual-item basis?

P9-2 (Lower-of-Cost-or-Market) Garcia Home Improvement Company installs replacement siding, windows, and louvered glass doors for single-family homes and condominium complexes in northern New Jersey and southern New York. The company is in the process of preparing its annual financial statements for the fiscal year ended May 31, 2014, and Jim Alcide, controller for Garcia, has gathered the following data concerning inventory.

At May 31, 2014, the balance in Garcia's Raw Materials Inventory account was $408,000, and Allowance to Reduce Inventory to Market had a credit balance of $27,500. Alcide summarized the relevant inventory cost and market data at May 31, 2014, in the schedule below.

Alcide assigned Patricia Devereaux, an intern from a local college, the task of calculating the amount that should appear on Garcia's May 31, 2014, financial statements for inventory under the lower-of-cost-or-market rule as applied to each item in inventory. Devereaux expressed concern over departing from the historical cost principle.

	Cost	Replacement Cost	Sales Price	Net Realizable Value	Normal Profit
Aluminum siding	$ 70,000	$ 62,500	$ 64,000	$ 56,000	$ 5,100
Cedar shake siding	86,000	79,400	94,000	84,800	7,400
Louvered glass doors	112,000	124,000	186,400	168,300	18,500
Thermal windows	140,000	126,000	154,800	140,000	15,400
Total	$408,000	$391,900	$499,200	$449,100	$46,400

Instructions

(a) (1) Determine the proper balance in Allowance to Reduce Inventory to Market at May 31, 2014.

(2) For the fiscal year ended May 31, 2014, determine the amount of the gain or loss that would be recorded due to the change in Allowance to Reduce Inventory to Market.

(b) Explain the rationale for the use of the lower-of-cost-or-market rule as it applies to inventories.

(CMA adapted)

P9-3 (Entries for Lower-of-Cost-or-Market—Cost-of-Goods-Sold and Loss) Malone Company determined its ending inventory at cost and at lower-of-cost-or-market at December 31, 2013, December 31, 2014, and December 31, 2015, as shown below.

	Cost	Lower-of-Cost-or-Market
12/31/13	$650,000	$650,000
12/31/14	780,000	712,000
12/31/15	905,000	830,000

Instructions

(a) Prepare the journal entries required at December 31, 2014, and at December 31, 2015, assuming that the cost-of-goods-sold method of adjusting to lower-of-cost-or-market is used.

(b) Prepare the journal entries required at December 31, 2014, and at December 31, 2015, assuming that the loss method of adjusting to lower-of-cost-or-market is used.

5 **P9-4 (Gross Profit Method)** Eastman Company lost most of its inventory in a fire in December just before the year-end physical inventory was taken. Corporate records disclose the following.

Inventory (beginning)	$ 80,000	Sales revenue	$415,000
Purchases	290,000	Sales returns	21,000
Purchase returns	28,000	Gross profit % based on	
		net selling price	35%

Merchandise with a selling price of $30,000 remained undamaged after the fire, and damaged merchandise has a net realizable value of $8,150. The company does not carry fire insurance on its inventory.

Instructions

Prepare a formal labeled schedule computing the fire loss incurred. (Do not use the retail inventory method.)

5 **P9-5 (Gross Profit Method)** On April 15, 2015, fire damaged the office and warehouse of Stanislaw Corporation. The only accounting record saved was the general ledger, from which the trial balance below was prepared.

STANISLAW CORPORATION		
TRIAL BALANCE		
MARCH 31, 2015		
Cash	$ 20,000	
Accounts receivable	40,000	
Inventory, December 31, 2014	75,000	
Land	35,000	
Buildings	110,000	
Accumulated depreciation		$ 41,300
Equipment	3,600	
Accounts payable		23,700
Other accrued expenses		10,200
Common stock		100,000
Retained earnings		52,000
Sales revenue		135,000
Purchases	52,000	
Miscellaneous expense	26,600	
	$362,200	$362,200

The following data and information have been gathered.

1. The fiscal year of the corporation ends on December 31.
2. An examination of the April bank statement and canceled checks revealed that checks written during the period April 1–15 totaled $13,000: $5,700 paid to accounts payable as of March 31, $3,400 for April merchandise shipments, and $3,900 paid for other expenses. Deposits during the same period amounted to $12,950, which consisted of receipts on account from customers with the exception of a $950 refund from a vendor for merchandise returned in April.
3. Correspondence with suppliers revealed unrecorded obligations at April 15 of $15,600 for April merchandise shipments, including $2,300 for shipments in transit (f.o.b. shipping point) on that date.
4. Customers acknowledged indebtedness of $46,000 at April 15, 2015. It was also estimated that customers owed another $8,000 that will never be acknowledged or recovered. Of the acknowledged indebtedness, $600 will probably be uncollectible.
5. The companies insuring the inventory agreed that the corporation's fire-loss claim should be based on the assumption that the overall gross profit rate for the past 2 years was in effect during the current year. The corporation's audited financial statements disclosed this information:

	Year Ended December 31	
	2014	2013
Net sales	$530,000	$390,000
Net purchases	280,000	235,000
Beginning inventory	50,000	66,000
Ending inventory	75,000	50,000

    6. Inventory with a cost of $7,000 was salvaged and sold for $3,500. The balance of the inventory was a total loss.

Instructions

Prepare a schedule computing the amount of inventory fire loss. The supporting schedule of the computation of the gross profit should be in good form.

(AICPA adapted)

P9-6 (Retail Inventory Method) The records for the Clothing Department of Sharapova's Discount Store are summarized below for the month of January.

> Inventory, January 1: at retail $25,000; at cost $17,000
> Purchases in January: at retail $137,000; at cost $82,500
> Freight-in: $7,000
> Purchase returns: at retail $3,000; at cost $2,300
> Transfers in from suburban branch: at retail $13,000; at cost $9,200
> Net markups: $8,000
> Net markdowns: $4,000
> Inventory losses due to normal breakage, etc.: at retail $400
> Sales revenue at retail: $95,000
> Sales returns: $2,400

Instructions

    (a) Compute the inventory for this department as of January 31, at retail prices.

    (b) Compute the ending inventory using lower-of-average-cost-or-market.

P9-7 (Retail Inventory Method) Presented below is information related to Waveland Inc.

	Cost	Retail
Inventory, 12/31/14	$250,000	$ 390,000
Purchases	914,500	1,460,000
Purchase returns	60,000	80,000
Purchase discounts	18,000	—
Gross sales revenue (after employee discounts)	—	1,410,000
Sales returns	—	97,500
Markups	—	120,000
Markup cancellations	—	40,000
Markdowns	—	45,000
Markdown cancellations	—	20,000
Freight-in	42,000	—
Employee discounts granted	—	8,000
Loss from breakage (normal)	—	4,500

Instructions

Assuming that Waveland Inc. uses the conventional retail inventory method, compute the cost of its ending inventory at December 31, 2015.

P9-8 (Retail Inventory Method) Fuque Inc. uses the retail inventory method to estimate ending inventory for its monthly financial statements. The following data pertain to a single department for the month of October 2015.

Inventory, October 1, 2015	
At cost	$ 52,000
At retail	78,000
Purchases (exclusive of freight and returns)	
At cost	272,000
At retail	423,000
Freight-in	16,600
Purchase returns	
At cost	5,600
At retail	8,000
Markups	9,000
Markup cancellations	2,000
Markdowns (net)	3,600
Normal spoilage and breakage	10,000
Sales revenue	390,000

Instructions

    (a) Using the conventional retail method, prepare a schedule computing estimated lower-of-cost-or-market inventory for October 31, 2015.

    (b) A department store using the conventional retail inventory method estimates the cost of its ending inventory as $60,000. An accurate physical count reveals only $47,000 of inventory at lower-of-cost-or-market. List the factors that may have caused the difference between the computed inventory and the physical count.

 P9-9 (Statement and Note Disclosure, LCM, and Purchase Commitment) Maddox Specialty Company, a division of Lost World Inc., manufactures three models of gear shift components for bicycles that are sold to bicycle manufacturers, retailers, and catalog outlets. Since beginning operations in 1990, Maddox has used normal absorption costing and has assumed a first-in, first-out cost flow in its perpetual inventory system. The balances of the inventory accounts at the end of Maddox's fiscal year, November 30, 2014, are shown below. The inventories are stated at cost before any year-end adjustments.

Finished goods	$647,000
Work in process	112,500
Raw materials	264,000
Factory supplies	69,000

The following information relates to Maddox's inventory and operations.

1. The finished goods inventory consists of the items analyzed below.

	Cost	Market
Down tube shifter		
Standard model	$ 67,500	$ 67,000
Click adjustment model	94,500	89,000
Deluxe model	108,000	110,000
Total down tube shifters	270,000	266,000
Bar end shifter		
Standard model	83,000	90,050
Click adjustment model	99,000	97,550
Total bar end shifters	182,000	187,600
Head tube shifter		
Standard model	78,000	77,650
Click adjustment model	117,000	119,300
Total head tube shifters	195,000	196,950
Total finished goods	$647,000	$650,550

2. One-half of the head tube shifter finished goods inventory is held by catalog outlets on consignment.
3. Three-quarters of the bar end shifter finished goods inventory has been pledged as collateral for a bank loan.
4. One-half of the raw materials balance represents derailleurs acquired at a contracted price 20% above the current market price. The market value of the rest of the raw materials is $127,400.
5. The total market value of the work in process inventory is $108,700.
6. Included in the cost of factory supplies are obsolete items with an historical cost of $4,200. The market value of the remaining factory supplies is $65,900.
7. Maddox applies the lower-of-cost-or-market method to each of the three types of shifters in finished goods inventory. For each of the other three inventory accounts, Maddox applies the lower-of-cost-or-market method to the total of each inventory account.
8. Consider all amounts presented above to be material in relation to Maddox's financial statements taken as a whole.

Instructions

    (a) Prepare the inventory section of Maddox's balance sheet as of November 30, 2014, including any required note(s).

    (b) Without prejudice to your answer to (a), assume that the market value of Maddox's inventories is less than cost. Explain how this decline would be presented in Maddox's income statement for the fiscal year ended November 30, 2014.

(c) Assume that Maddox has a firm purchase commitment for the same type of derailleur included in the raw materials inventory as of November 30, 2014, and that the purchase commitment is at a contracted price 15% greater than the current market price. These derailleurs are to be delivered to Maddox after November 30, 2014. Discuss the impact, if any, that this purchase commitment would have on Maddox's financial statements prepared for the fiscal year ended November 30, 2014.

(CMA adapted)

 P9-10 (Lower-of-Cost-or-Market) Fiedler Co. follows the practice of valuing its inventory at the lower-of-cost-or-market. The following information is available from the company's inventory records as of December 31, 2014.

Item	Quantity	Unit Cost	Replacement Cost/Unit	Estimated Selling Price/Unit	Completion & Disposal Cost/Unit	Normal Profit Margin/Unit
A	1,100	$7.50	$8.40	$10.50	$1.50	$1.80
B	800	8.20	7.90	9.40	0.90	1.20
C	1,000	5.60	5.40	7.20	1.15	0.60
D	1,000	3.80	4.20	6.30	0.80	1.50
E	1,400	6.40	6.30	6.70	0.70	1.00

Instructions

Greg Forda is an accounting clerk in the accounting department of Fiedler Co., and he cannot understand why the market value keeps changing from replacement cost to net realizable value to something that he cannot even figure out. Greg is very confused, and he is the one who records inventory purchases and calculates ending inventory. You are the manager of the department and an accountant.

(a) Calculate the lower-of-cost-or-market using the "individual item" approach.
(b) Show the journal entry he will need to make in order to write down the ending inventory from cost to market.
(c) Then write a memo to Greg explaining what designated market value is as well as how it is computed. Use your calculations to aid in your explanation.

8 *P9-11 (Conventional and Dollar-Value LIFO Retail)** As of January 1, 2014, Aristotle Inc. installed the retail method of accounting for its merchandise inventory.

To prepare the store's financial statements at June 30, 2014, you obtain the following data.

	Cost	Selling Price
Inventory, January 1	$ 30,000	$ 43,000
Markdowns		10,500
Markups		9,200
Markdown cancellations		6,500
Markup cancellations		3,200
Purchases	104,800	155,000
Sales revenue		154,000
Purchase returns	2,800	4,000
Sales returns and allowances		8,000

Instructions

(a) Prepare a schedule to compute Aristotle's June 30, 2014, inventory under the conventional retail method of accounting for inventories.
(b) Without prejudice to your solution to part (a), assume that you computed the June 30, 2014, inventory to be $59,400 at retail and the ratio of cost to retail to be 70%. The general price level has increased from 100 at January 1, 2014, to 108 at June 30, 2014. Prepare a schedule to compute the June 30, 2014, inventory at the June 30 price level under the dollar-value LIFO retail method.

(AICPA adapted)

 8 *P9-12 (Retail, LIFO Retail, and Inventory Shortage)** Late in 2011, Joan Seceda and four other investors took the chain of Becker Department Stores private, and the company has just completed its third year of operations under the ownership of the investment group. Andrea Selig, controller of Becker Department Stores, is in the process of preparing the year-end financial statements. Based on the preliminary financial statements, Seceda has expressed concern over inventory shortages, and she has asked Selig to determine whether an abnormal amount of theft and breakage has occurred. The accounting records of Becker Department Stores contain the following amounts on November 30, 2014, the end of the fiscal year.

	Cost	Retail
Beginning inventory	$ 68,000	$100,000
Purchases	255,000	400,000
Net markups		50,000
Net markdowns		110,000
Sales revenue		320,000

According to the November 30, 2014, physical inventory, the actual inventory at retail is $115,000.

Instructions
(a) Describe the circumstances under which the retail inventory method would be applied and the advantages of using the retail inventory method.
(b) Assuming that prices have been stable, calculate the value, at cost, of Becker Department Stores' ending inventory using the last-in, first-out (LIFO) retail method. Be sure to furnish supporting calculations.
(c) Estimate the amount of shortage, at retail, that has occurred at Becker Department Stores during the year ended November 30, 2014.
(d) Complications in the retail method can be caused by such items as (1) freight-in costs, (2) purchase returns and allowances, (3) sales returns and allowances, and (4) employee discounts. Explain how each of these four special items is handled in the retail inventory method.

(CMA adapted)

8 *P9-13 (Change to LIFO Retail)** Diderot Stores Inc., which uses the conventional retail inventory method, wishes to change to the LIFO retail method beginning with the accounting year ending December 31, 2014. Amounts as shown below appear on the store's books before adjustment.

	Cost	Retail
Inventory, January 1, 2014	$ 15,800	$ 24,000
Purchases in 2014	116,200	184,000
Markups in 2014		12,000
Markdowns in 2014		5,500
Sales revenue in 2014		175,000

You are to assume that all markups and markdowns apply to 2014 purchases, and that it is appropriate to treat the entire inventory as a single department.

Instructions
Compute the inventory at December 31, 2014, under the following methods.
(a) The conventional retail method.
(b) The last-in, first-out retail method, effecting the change in method as of January 1, 2014. Assume that the cost-to-retail percentage for 2013 was recomputed correctly in accordance with procedures necessary to change to LIFO. This ratio was 59%.

(AICPA adapted)

8 *P9-14 (Change to LIFO Retail; Dollar-Value LIFO Retail)** Davenport Department Store converted from the conventional retail method to the LIFO retail method on January 1, 2014, and is now considering converting to the dollar-value LIFO inventory method. During your examination of the financial statements for the year ended December 31, 2015, management requested that you furnish a summary showing certain computations of inventory cost for the past 3 years.
Here is the available information.

1. The inventory at January 1, 2013, had a retail value of $56,000 and cost of $29,800 based on the conventional retail method.
2. Transactions during 2013 were as follows.

	Cost	Retail
Purchases	$311,000	$554,000
Purchase returns	5,200	10,000
Purchase discounts	6,000	
Gross sales revenue (after employee discounts)		551,000
Sales returns		9,000
Employee discounts		3,000
Freight-in	17,600	
Net markups		20,000
Net markdowns		12,000

3. The retail value of the December 31, 2014, inventory was $75,600, the cost ratio for 2014 under the LIFO retail method was 61%, and the regional price index was 105% of the January 1, 2014, price level.

4. The retail value of the December 31, 2015, inventory was $62,640, the cost ratio for 2015 under the LIFO retail method was 60%, and the regional price index was 108% of the January 1, 2014, price level.

Instructions

(a) Prepare a schedule showing the computation of the cost of inventory on hand at December 31, 2013, based on the conventional retail method.

(b) Prepare a schedule showing the recomputation of the inventory to be reported on December 31, 2013, in accordance with procedures necessary to convert from the conventional retail method to the LIFO retail method beginning January 1, 2014. Assume that the retail value of the December 31, 2013, inventory was $60,000.

(c) Without prejudice to your solution to part (b), assume that you computed the December 31, 2013, inventory (retail value $60,000) under the LIFO retail method at a cost of $33,300. Prepare a schedule showing the computations of the cost of the store's 2014 and 2015 year-end inventories under the dollar-value LIFO method.

(AICPA adapted)

PROBLEMS SET B

See the book's companion website, at **www.wiley.com/college/kieso**, for an additional set of problems.

CONCEPTS FOR ANALYSIS

CA9-1 (Lower-of-Cost-or-Market) You have been asked by the financial vice president to develop a short presentation on the lower-of-cost-or-market method for inventory purposes. The financial VP needs to explain this method to the president because it appears that a portion of the company's inventory has declined in value.

Instructions

The financial VP asks you to answer the following questions.

(a) What is the purpose of the lower-of-cost-or-market method?

(b) What is meant by "market"? (*Hint:* Discuss the ceiling and floor constraints.)

(c) Do you apply the lower-of-cost-or-market method to each individual item, to a category, or to the total of the inventory? Explain.

(d) What are the potential disadvantages of the lower-of-cost-or-market method?

CA9-2 (Lower-of-Cost-or-Market) The market value of Lake Corporation's inventory has declined below its cost. Sheryl Conan, the controller, wants to use the loss method to write down inventory because it more clearly discloses the decline in market value and does not distort the cost of goods sold. Her supervisor, financial vice president Dick Wright, prefers the cost-of-goods-sold method to write down inventory because it does not call attention to the decline in market value.

Instructions

Answer the following questions.

(a) What, if any, is the ethical issue involved?

(b) Is any stakeholder harmed if Dick Wright's preference is used?

(c) What should Sheryl Conan do?

CA9-3 (Lower-of-Cost-or-Market) Ogala Corporation purchased a significant amount of raw materials inventory for a new product that it is manufacturing.

Ogala uses the lower-of-cost-or-market rule for these raw materials. The replacement cost of the raw materials is above the net realizable value, and both are below the original cost.

Ogala uses the average-cost inventory method for these raw materials. In the last 2 years, each purchase has been at a lower price than the previous purchase, and the ending inventory quantity for each period has been higher than the beginning inventory quantity for that period.

Instructions

(a) (1) At which amount should Ogala's raw materials inventory be reported on the balance sheet? Why?

(2) In general, why is the lower-of-cost-or-market rule used to report inventory?

(b) What would have been the effect on ending inventory and cost of goods sold had Ogala used the LIFO inventory method instead of the average-cost inventory method for the raw materials? Why?

 CA9-4 (Retail Inventory Method) Saurez Company, your client, manufactures paint. The company's president, Maria Saurez, has decided to open a retail store to sell Saurez paint as well as wallpaper and other supplies that would be purchased from other suppliers. She has asked you for information about the conventional retail method of pricing inventories at the retail store.

Instructions

Prepare a report to the president explaining the retail method of pricing inventories. Your report should include the following points.

(a) Description and accounting features of the method.
(b) The conditions that may distort the results under the method.
(c) A comparison of the advantages of using the retail method with those of using cost methods of inventory pricing.
(d) The accounting theory underlying the treatment of net markdowns and net markups under the method.

(AICPA adapted)

CA9-5 (Cost Determination, LCM, Retail Method) Olson Corporation, a retailer and wholesaler of national brand-name household lighting fixtures, purchases its inventories from various suppliers.

Instructions

(a) (1) What criteria should be used to determine which of Olson's costs are inventoriable?
(2) Are Olson's administrative costs inventoriable? Defend your answer.
(b) (1) Olson uses the lower-of-cost-or-market rule for its wholesale inventories. What are the theoretical arguments for that rule?
(2) The replacement cost of the inventories is below the net realizable value less a normal profit margin, which, in turn, is below the original cost. What amount should be used to value the inventories? Why?
(c) Olson calculates the estimated cost of its ending inventories held for sale at retail using the conventional retail inventory method. How would Olson treat the beginning inventories and net markdowns in calculating the cost ratio used to determine its ending inventories? Why?

(AICPA adapted)

CA9-6 (Purchase Commitments) Prophet Company signed a long-term purchase contract to buy timber from the U.S. Forest Service at $300 per thousand board feet. Under these terms, Prophet must cut and pay $6,000,000 for this timber during the next year. Currently, the market value is $250 per thousand board feet. At this rate, the market price is $5,000,000. Jerry Herman, the controller, wants to recognize the loss in value on the year-end financial statements, but the financial vice president, Billie Hands, argues that the loss is temporary and should be ignored. Herman notes that market value has remained near $250 for many months, and he sees no sign of significant change.

Instructions

(a) What are the ethical issues, if any?
(b) Is any particular stakeholder harmed by the financial vice president's decision?
(c) What should the controller do?

USING YOUR JUDGMENT

FINANCIAL REPORTING

Financial Reporting Problem

P&G **The Procter & Gamble Company (P&G)**

The financial statements of P&G are presented in Appendix 5B. The company's complete annual report, including the notes to the financial statements, can be accessed at the book's companion website, **www.wiley.com/college/kieso**.

Instructions

Refer to P&G's financial statements and the accompanying notes to answer the following questions.

(a) How does P&G value its inventories? Which inventory costing method does P&G use as a basis for reporting its inventories?

(b) How does P&G report its inventories in the balance sheet? In the notes to its financial statements, what three descriptions are used to classify its inventories?

(c) What costs does P&G include in Inventory and Cost of Products Sold?

(d) What was P&G's inventory turnover in 2011? What is its gross profit percentage? Evaluate P&G's inventory turnover and its gross profit percentage.

Comparative Analysis Case

The Coca-Cola Company and PepsiCo, Inc.

Instructions

Go to the book's companion website and use information found there to answer the following questions related to The Coca-Cola Company and PepsiCo, Inc.

(a) What is the amount of inventory reported by Coca-Cola at December 31, 2011, and by PepsiCo at December 31, 2011? What percent of total assets is invested in inventory by each company?

(b) What inventory costing methods are used by Coca-Cola and PepsiCo? How does each company value its inventories?

(c) In the notes, what classifications (description) are used by Coca-Cola and PepsiCo to categorize their inventories?

(d) Compute and compare the inventory turnovers and days to sell inventory for Coca-Cola and PepsiCo for 2011. Indicate why there might be a significant difference between the two companies.

Financial Statement Analysis Cases

Case 1   Robots, Inc.

Robots, Inc. reported the following information regarding 2013–2014 inventory.

Robots, Inc.		
	2014	2013
Current assets		
Cash	$ 153,010	$ 538,489
Accounts receivable, net of allowance for doubtful accounts		
of $46,000 in 2014 and $160,000 in 2013	1,627,980	2,596,291
Inventories (Note 2)	1,340,494	1,734,873
Other current assets	123,388	90,592
Assets of discontinued operations	—	32,815
Total current assets	3,244,872	4,993,060

Notes to Consolidated Financial Statements

Note 1 (in part): Nature of Business and Significant Accounting Policies

Inventories—Inventories are stated at the lower-of-cost-or-market. Cost is determined by the last-in, first-out (LIFO) method by the parent company and by the first-in, first-out (FIFO) method by its subsidiaries.

Note 2: Inventories

Inventories consist of the following.

	2014	2013
Raw materials	$1,264,646	$2,321,178
Work in process	240,988	171,222
Finished goods and display units	129,406	711,252
Total inventories	1,635,040	3,203,652
Less: Amount classified as long-term	294,546	1,468,779
Current portion	$1,340,494	$1,734,873

Inventories are stated at the lower of cost determined by the LIFO method or market for Robots, Inc. Inventories for the two wholly-owned subsidiaries, Robot Command, Inc. (U.S.) and Robot Limited (U.K.), are stated on the FIFO method which amounted to $566,000 at October 31, 2013. No inventory is stated on the FIFO method at October 31, 2014. Included in inventory stated at FIFO cost was $32,815 at October 31, 2013, of Robot Command inventory classified as an asset from discontinued operations (see Note 14). If the FIFO method had been used for the entire consolidated group, inventories after an adjustment to the lower-of-cost-or-market would have been approximately $2,000,000 and $3,800,000 at October 31, 2014 and 2013, respectively.

Inventory has been written down to estimated net realizable value, and results of operations for 2014, 2013, and 2012 include a corresponding charge of approximately $868,000, $960,000, and $273,000, respectively, which represents the excess of LIFO cost over market.

Inventory of $294,546 and $1,468,779 at October 31, 2014 and 2013, respectively, shown on the balance sheet as a noncurrent asset represents that portion of the inventory that is not expected to be sold currently.

Reduction in inventory quantities during the years ended October 31, 2014, 2013, and 2012 resulted in liquidation of LIFO inventory quantities carried at a lower cost prevailing in prior years as compared with the cost of fiscal 2011 purchases. The effect of these reductions was to decrease the net loss by approximately $24,000, $157,000, and $90,000 at October 31, 2014, 2013, and 2012, respectively.

Instructions

(a) Why might Robots, Inc., use two different methods for valuing inventory?

(b) Comment on why Robots, Inc., might disclose how its LIFO inventories would be valued under FIFO.

(c) Why does the LIFO liquidation reduce operating costs?

(d) Comment on whether Robots, Inc. would report more or less income if it had been on a FIFO basis for all its inventory.

Case 2 Barrick Gold Corporation

Barrick Gold Corporation, with headquarters in Toronto, Canada, is the world's most profitable and largest gold mining company outside South Africa. Part of the key to Barrick's success has been due to its ability to maintain cash flow while improving production and increasing its reserves of gold-containing property. In the most recent year, Barrick achieved record growth in cash flow, production, and reserves.

The company maintains an aggressive policy of developing previously identified target areas that have the possibility of a large amount of gold ore, and that have not been previously developed. Barrick limits the riskiness of this development by choosing only properties that are located in politically stable regions, and by the company's use of internally generated funds, rather than debt, to finance growth.

Barrick's inventories are as follows.

Barrick Gold Corporation	
Inventories (in millions, US dollars)	
Current	
Gold in process	$133
Mine operating supplies	82
	$215
Non-current (included in Other assets)	
Ore in stockpiles	$65

Instructions

(a) Why do you think that there are no finished goods inventories? Why do you think the raw material, ore in stockpiles, is considered to be a non-current asset?

(b) Consider that Barrick has no finished goods inventories. What journal entries are made to record a sale?

(c) Suppose that gold bullion that cost $1.8 million to produce was sold for $2.4 million. The journal entry was made to record the sale, but no entry was made to remove the gold from the gold in process inventory. How would this error affect the following?

Balance Sheet		Income Statement	
Inventory	?	Cost of goods sold	?
Retained earnings	?	Net income	?
Accounts payable	?		
Working capital	?		
Current ratio	?		

Accounting, Analysis, and Principles

Englehart Company sells two types of pumps. One is large and is for commercial use. The other is smaller and is used in residential swimming pools. The following inventory data is available for the month of March.

	Units	Price per Unit	Total
Residential Pumps			
Inventory at Feb. 28:	200	$ 400	$ 80,000
Purchases:			
March 10	500	$ 450	$225,000
March 20	400	$ 475	$190,000
March 30	300	$ 500	$150,000
Sales:			
March 15	500	$ 540	$270,000
March 25	400	$ 570	$228,000
Inventory at March 31:	500		
Commercial Pumps			
Inventory at Feb. 28:	600	$ 800	$480,000
Purchases:			
March 3	600	$ 900	$540,000
March 12	300	$ 950	$285,000
March 21	500	$1,000	$500,000
Sales:			
March 18	900	$1,080	$972,000
March 29	600	$1,140	$684,000
Inventory at March 31:	500		

In addition to the above information, due to a downturn in the economy that has hit Englehart's commercial customers especially hard, Englehart expects commercial pump prices from March 31 onward to be considerably different (and lower) than at the beginning of and during March. Englehart has developed the following additional information.

	Commercial Pumps	Residential Pumps
Expected selling price (per unit, net of costs to sell)	$1,050	$580
Replacement cost	$ 900	$550

The normal profit margin is 16.67% of cost. Englehart uses the FIFO accounting method.

Accounting

(a) Determine the dollar amount that Englehart should report on its March 31 balance sheet for inventory. Assume Englehart applies lower-of-cost-or-market at the individual product level.

(b) Repeat part (a) but assume Englehart applies lower-of-cost-or-market at the major category level. Englehart places both commercial and residential pumps into the same (and only) category.

Analysis

Which of the two approaches above (individual product level or major categories) for applying LCM do you think gives the financial statement reader better information?

Principles

Assume that during April, the replacement cost of commercial pumps rebounds to $1,050 (assume this will be designated market value).

(a) Briefly describe how Englehart will report in its April financial statements the inventory remaining from March 31.

(b) Briefly describe the conceptual trade-offs inherent in the accounting in part (a).

BRIDGE TO THE PROFESSION

 ## Professional Research: FASB Codification

Jones Co. is in a technology-intensive industry. Recently, one of its competitors introduced a new product with technology that might render obsolete some of Jones's inventory. The accounting staff wants to follow the appropriate authoritative literature in determining the accounting for this significant market event.

Instructions

If your school has a subscription to the FASB Codification, go to *http://aaahq.org/asclogin.cfm* to log in and prepare responses to the following. Provide Codification references for your responses.

(a) Identify the primary authoritative guidance for the accounting for inventories. What is the predecessor literature?

(b) List three types of goods that are classified as inventory. What characteristic will automatically exclude an item from being classified as inventory?

(c) Define "market" as used in the phrase "lower-of-cost-or-market."

(d) Explain when it is acceptable to state inventory above cost and which industries allow this practice.

Additional Professional Resources

See the book's companion website, at **www.wiley.com/college/kieso**, for professional simulations as well as other study resources.

 IFRS INSIGHTS

The major IFRS requirements related to accounting and reporting for inventories are found in *IAS 2* ("Inventories"), *IAS 18* ("Revenue"), and *IAS 41* ("Agriculture"). In most cases, IFRS and GAAP are the same. The major differences are that IFRS prohibits the use of the LIFO cost flow assumption and records market in the lower-of-cost-or-market differently.

9 LEARNING OBJECTIVE

Compare the accounting procedures related to valuation of inventories under GAAP and IFRS.

RELEVANT FACTS

Following are the key similarities and differences between GAAP and IFRS related to inventories.

Similarities

- IFRS and GAAP account for inventory acquisitions at historical cost and evaluate inventory for lower-of-cost-or-market subsequent to acquisition.
- Who owns the goods—goods in transit, consigned goods, special sales agreements—as well as the costs to include in inventory are essentially accounted for the same under IFRS and GAAP.

Differences

- The requirements for accounting for and reporting inventories are more principles-based under IFRS. That is, GAAP provides more detailed guidelines in inventory accounting.
- A major difference between IFRS and GAAP relates to the LIFO cost flow assumption. GAAP permits the use of LIFO for inventory valuation. IFRS prohibits its use. FIFO and average-cost are the only two acceptable cost flow assumptions permitted under IFRS. Both sets of standards permit specific identification where appropriate.
- In the lower-of-cost-or-market test for inventory valuation, IFRS defines market as net realizable value. GAAP, on the other hand, defines market as replacement cost subject to the constraints of net realizable value (the ceiling) and net realizable value less a normal markup (the floor). IFRS does not use a ceiling or a floor to determine market.
- Under GAAP, if inventory is written down under the lower-of-cost-or-market valuation, the new basis is now considered its cost. As a result, the inventory may not be written back up to its original cost in a subsequent period. Under IFRS, the write-down may be reversed in a subsequent period up to the amount of the previous write-down. Both the write-down and any subsequent reversal should be reported on the income statement. IFRS accounting for lower-of-cost-or-market is discussed more fully in the *About the Numbers* section below.
- IFRS requires both biological assets and agricultural produce at the point of harvest to be reported at net realizable value. GAAP does not require companies to account for all biological assets in the same way. Furthermore, these assets generally are not reported at net realizable value. Disclosure requirements also differ between the two sets of standards. IFRS accounting for agriculture and biological assets is discussed more fully in the *About the Numbers* section.

ABOUT THE NUMBERS

Lower-of-Cost-or-Net Realizable Value (LCNRV)

Inventories are recorded at their cost. However, if inventory declines in value below its original cost, a major departure from the historical cost principle occurs. Whatever the reason for a decline—obsolescence, price-level changes, or damaged goods—a company should write down the inventory to net realizable value to report this loss. **A company abandons the historical cost principle when the future utility (revenue-producing ability) of the asset drops below its original cost.**

Net Realizable Value

Recall that **cost** is the acquisition price of inventory computed using one of the historical cost-based methods—specific identification, average-cost, or FIFO. The term **net realizable value (NRV)** refers to the net amount that a company expects to realize from the sale of inventory. Specifically, net realizable value is the estimated selling price in the normal course of business less estimated costs to complete and estimated costs to make a sale.

To illustrate, assume that Mander Corp. has unfinished inventory with a cost of $950, a sales value of $1,000, estimated cost of completion of $50, and estimated selling costs of $200. Mander's net realizable value is computed as follows.

Inventory value—unfinished		$1,000
Less: Estimated cost of completion	$ 50	
Estimated cost to sell	200	250
Net realizable value		$ 750

Mander reports inventory on its statement of financial position (balance sheet) at $750. In its income statement, Mander reports a Loss on Inventory Write-Down of $200 ($950−$750).

A departure from cost is justified because inventories should not be reported at amounts higher than their expected realization from sale or use. In addition, a company like Mander should charge the loss of utility against revenues in the period in which the loss occurs, not in the period of sale. Companies therefore report their inventories at the **lower-of-cost-or-net realizable value (LCNRV)** at each reporting date.

Illustration of LCNRV

As indicated, a company values inventory at LCNRV. A company estimates net realizable value based on the most reliable evidence of the inventories' realizable amounts (expected selling price, expected costs to completion, and expected costs to sell). To illustrate, Regner Foods computes its inventory at LCNRV, as shown in Illustration IFRS9-1.

Food	Cost	Net Realizable Value	Final Inventory Value
Spinach	$ 80,000	$120,000	$ 80,000
Carrots	100,000	110,000	100,000
Cut beans	50,000	40,000	40,000
Peas	90,000	72,000	72,000
Mixed vegetables	95,000	92,000	92,000
			$384,000

Final Inventory Value:	
Spinach	Cost ($80,000) is selected because it is lower than net realizable value.
Carrots	Cost ($100,000) is selected because it is lower than net realizable value.
Cut beans	Net realizable value ($40,000) is selected because it is lower than cost.
Peas	Net realizable value ($72,000) is selected because it is lower than cost.
Mixed vegetables	Net realizable value ($92,000) is selected because it is lower than cost.

ILLUSTRATION IFRS9-1
LCNRV Data

As indicated, the final inventory value of $384,000 equals the sum of the LCNRV for each of the inventory items. That is, Regner Foods applies the LCNRV rule to each individual type of food. Similar to GAAP, under IFRS, companies may apply the LCNRV rule to a group of similar or related items, or to the total of the inventory. If a company follows a group-of-similar-or-related-items or total-inventory approach in determining LCNRV, increases in market prices tend to offset decreases in market prices. In most situations, companies price inventory on an item-by-item basis. In fact, tax rules in some countries require that companies use an individual-item basis, barring practical difficulties.

In addition, the individual-item approach gives the lowest valuation for statement of financial position purposes. In some cases, a company prices inventory on a total-inventory basis when it offers only one end product (comprised of many different raw materials). If it produces several end products, a company might use a similar-or-related approach instead. **Whichever method a company selects, it should apply the method consistently from one period to another.**

Recording Net Realizable Value Instead of Cost

Similar to GAAP, one of two methods may be used to record the income effect of valuing inventory at net realizable value. One method, referred to as the **cost-of-goods-sold method**, debits cost of goods sold for the write-down of the inventory to net realizable value. As a result, the company does not report a loss in the income statement because the cost of goods sold already includes the amount of the loss. The second method, referred to as the **loss method**, debits a loss account for the write-down of the inventory to net realizable value. We use the following inventory data for Ricardo Company to illustrate entries under both methods.

Cost of goods sold (before adjustment to net realizable value)	$108,000
Ending inventory (cost)	82,000
Ending inventory (at net realizable value)	70,000

Illustration IFRS9-2 shows the entries for both the cost-of-goods-sold and loss methods, assuming the use of a perpetual inventory system.

ILLUSTRATION IFRS9-2
LCNRV Entries

Cost-of-Goods-Sold Method		Loss Method	
To reduce inventory from cost to net realizable value			
Cost of Goods Sold	12,000	Loss Due to Decline	
Inventory	12,000	of Inventory to Net	
		Realizable Value	12,000
		Inventory	12,000

The cost-of-goods-sold method buries the loss in the Cost of Goods Sold account. The loss method, by identifying the loss due to the write-down, shows the loss separate from Cost of Goods Sold in the income statement. Illustration IFRS9-3 contrasts the differing amounts reported in the income statement under the two approaches, using data from the Ricardo example.

Cost-of-Goods-Sold Method	
Sales revenue	$200,000
Cost of goods sold (after adjustment to net realizable value*)	120,000
Gross profit on sales	$ 80,000
*Cost of goods sold (before adjustment to net realizable value)	$108,000
Difference between inventory at cost and net realizable value ($82,000 − $70,000)	12,000
Cost of goods sold (after adjustment to net realizable value)	$120,000
Loss Method	
Sales revenue	$200,000
Cost of goods sold	108,000
Gross profit on sales	92,000
Loss due to decline of inventory to net realizable value	12,000
	$ 80,000

IFRS does not specify a particular account to debit for the write-down. We believe the loss method presentation is preferable because it clearly discloses the loss resulting from a decline in inventory net realizable values.

Use of an Allowance

Instead of crediting the Inventory account for net realizable value adjustments, companies generally use an allowance account, often referred to as Allowance to Reduce Inventory to Net Realizable Value. For example, using an allowance account under the loss method, Ricardo Company makes the following entry to record the inventory write-down to net realizable value.

Loss Due to Decline of Inventory to Net Realizable Value	12,000	
Allowance to Reduce Inventory to Net Realizable Value		12,000

Use of the allowance account results in reporting both the cost and the net realizable value of the inventory. Ricardo reports inventory in the statement of financial position as follows.

Inventory (at cost)	$82,000
Allowance to reduce inventory to net realizable value	(12,000)
Inventory (at net realizable value)	$70,000

The use of the allowance under the cost-of-goods-sold or loss method permits both the income statement and the statement of financial position to reflect inventory measured at $82,000, although the statement of financial position shows a net amount of $70,000. It also keeps subsidiary inventory ledgers and records in correspondence with the control account without changing prices. *For homework purposes, use an allowance account to record net realizable value adjustments, unless instructed otherwise.*

Recovery of Inventory Loss

In periods following the write-down, economic conditions may change such that the net realizable value of inventories previously written down may be *greater* than cost or there is clear evidence of an increase in the net realizable value. In this situation, the amount of the write-down is reversed, with the reversal limited to the amount of the original write-down.

Continuing the Ricardo example, assume that in the subsequent period, market conditions change, such that the net realizable value increases to $74,000 (an increase of $4,000). As a result, only $8,000 is needed in the allowance. Ricardo makes the following entry, using the loss method.

Allowance to Reduce Inventory to Net Realizable Value	4,000	
Recovery of Inventory Loss ($74,000 − $70,000)		4,000

Valuation Bases

For the most part, companies record inventory at LCNRV. However, there are some situations in which companies depart from the LCNRV rule. Such treatment may be justified in situations when cost is difficult to determine, the items are readily marketable at quoted market prices, and units of product are interchangeable. In this section, we discuss agricultural assets (including biological assets and agricultural produce), for which net realizable value is the general rule for valuing inventory.

Agricultural Inventory

Under IFRS, net realizable value measurement is used for inventory when the inventory is related to agricultural activity. In general, agricultural activity results in two types of agricultural assets: (1) biological assets or (2) agricultural produce at the point of harvest.

A **biological asset** (classified as a non-current asset) is a living animal or plant, such as sheep, cows, fruit trees, or cotton plants. **Agricultural produce** is the harvested product of a biological asset, such as wool from a sheep, milk from a dairy cow, picked fruit from a fruit tree, or cotton from a cotton plant.

Biological assets are measured on initial recognition and at the end of each reporting period at fair value less costs to sell (net realizable value). Companies record a gain or loss due to changes in the net realizable value of biological assets in income when it arises. For example, a gain may arise on initial recognition of a biological asset, such as when a calf is born. A gain or loss may arise on initial recognition of agricultural produce as a result of harvesting. Losses may arise on initial recognition for agricultural assets because costs to sell are deducted in determining fair value less costs to sell.

Agricultural produce (which are harvested from biological assets) are measured at fair value less costs to sell (net realizable value) at the point of harvest. Once harvested, the net realizable value of the agricultural produce becomes its cost, and this asset is accounted for similar to other inventories held for sale in the normal course of business. Measurement at fair value or selling price less point-of-sale costs corresponds to the net realizable value measure in the LCNRV test (selling price less estimated costs to complete and sell) since at harvest, the agricultural product is complete and is ready for sale.

Illustration of Agricultural Accounting at Net Realizable Value

To illustrate the accounting at net realizable value for agricultural assets, assume that Bancroft Dairy produces milk for sale to local cheese-makers. Bancroft began operations on January 1, 2014, by purchasing 420 milking cows for $460,000. Bancroft provides the following information related to the milking cows.

Milking cows		
Carrying value, January 1, 2014*		$460,000
Change in fair value due to growth and price changes	$35,000	
Decrease in fair value due to harvest	(1,200)	
Change in carrying value		33,800
Carrying value, January 31, 2014		$493,800
Milk harvested during January**		$ 36,000

*The carrying value is measured at fair value less costs to sell (net realizable value). The fair value of milking cows is determined based on market prices of livestock of similar age, breed, and genetic merit.
**Milk is initially measured at its fair value less costs to sell (net realizable value) at the time of milking. The fair value of milk is determined based on market prices in the local area.

As indicated, the carrying value of the milking cows increased during the month. Part of the change is due to changes in market prices (less costs to sell) for milking cows. The change in market price may also be affected by growth—the increase in value as the cows mature and develop increased milking capacity. At the same time, as mature cows are milked, their milking capacity declines (fair value decrease due to harvest). For example, changes in fair value arising from growth and harvesting from mature cows can be estimated based on changes in market prices of different age cows in the herd.

Bancroft makes the following entry to record the change in carrying value of the milking cows.

Biological Asset—Milking Cows ($493,800 − $460,000)	33,800	
Unrealized Holding Gain or Loss—Income		33,800

As a result of this entry, Bancroft's statement of financial position reports Biological Asset—Milking Cows as a non-current asset at fair value less costs to sell (net realizable value). In addition, the unrealized gains and losses are reported as other income and expense on the income statement. In subsequent periods at each reporting date, Bancroft continues to report Biological Asset—Milking Cows at net realizable value and records any related unrealized gains or losses in income. Because there is a ready market for the biological assets (milking cows), valuation at net realizable value provides more relevant information about these assets.

In addition to recording the change in the biological asset, Bancroft makes the following summary entry to record the milk harvested for the month of January.

Milk Inventory	36,000	
Unrealized Holding Gain or Loss—Income		36,000

The milk inventory is recorded at net realizable value at the time it is harvested, and Unrealized Holding Gain or Loss—Income is recognized in income. As with the biological assets, net realizable value is considered the most relevant for purposes of valuation at harvest. What happens to the milk inventory that Bancroft recorded upon harvesting the milk from the cows? Assuming the milk harvested in January was sold to a local cheese-maker for $38,500, Bancroft records the sale as follows.

Cash	38,500	
Cost of Goods Sold	36,000	
Milk Inventory		36,000
Sales Revenue		38,500

Thus, once harvested, the net realizable value of the harvested milk becomes its cost, and the milk is accounted for similar to other inventories held for sale in the normal course of business.

A final note: Some animals or plants may not be considered biological assets but would be classified and accounted for as other types of assets (not at net realizable value). For example, a pet shop may hold an inventory of dogs purchased from breeders that it then sells. Because the pet shop is not breeding the dogs, these dogs are not considered biological assets. As a result, the dogs are accounted for as inventory held for sale (at LCNRV).

ON THE HORIZON

One issue that will be difficult to resolve relates to the use of the LIFO cost flow assumption. As indicated, IFRS specifically prohibits its use. Conversely, the LIFO cost flow assumption is widely used in the United States because of its favorable tax advantages. In addition, many argue that LIFO from a financial reporting point of view provides a better matching of current costs against revenue and therefore enables companies to compute a more realistic income.

IFRS SELF-TEST QUESTIONS

1. All of the following are key similarities between GAAP and IFRS with respect to accounting for inventories **except**:
   (a) costs to include in inventories are similar.
   (b) LIFO cost flow assumption where appropriate is used by both sets of standards.
   (c) fair value valuation of inventories is prohibited by both sets of standards.
   (d) guidelines on ownership of goods are similar.

2. All of the following are key differences between GAAP and IFRS with respect to accounting for inventories **except** the:
   (a) definition of the lower-of-cost-or-market test for inventory valuation differs between GAAP and IFRS.
   (b) average-cost method is prohibited under IFRS.
   (c) inventory basis determination for write-downs differs between GAAP and IFRS.
   (d) guidelines are more principles-based under IFRS than they are under GAAP.

3. Starfish Company (a company using GAAP and the LIFO inventory method) is considering changing to IFRS and the FIFO inventory method. How would a comparison of these methods affect Starfish's financials?
   (a) During a period of inflation, working capital would decrease when IFRS and the FIFO inventory method are used as compared to GAAP and LIFO.
   (b) During a period of inflation, the taxes will decrease when IFRS and the FIFO inventory method are used as compared to GAAP and LIFO.
   (c) During a period of inflation, net income would be greater if IFRS and the FIFO inventory method are used as compared to GAAP and LIFO.
   (d) During a period of inflation, the current ratio would decrease when IFRS and the FIFO inventory method are used as compared to GAAP and LIFO.

4. Assume that Darcy Industries had the following inventory values.

Inventory cost (on December 31, 2014)	$1,500
Inventory market (on December 31, 2014)	$1,350
Inventory net realizable value (on December 31, 2014)	$1,320

   Under IFRS, what is the inventory carrying value on December 31, 2014?
   (a) $1,500.
   (b) $1,570.
   (c) $1,560.
   (d) $1,320.

5. Under IFRS, agricultural activity results in which of the following types of assets?
      I. Agricultural produce
      II. Biological assets
   (a) I only.
   (b) II only.
   (c) I and II.
   (d) Neither I nor II.

IFRS CONCEPTS AND APPLICATION

IFRS9-1 Briefly describe some of the similarities and differences between GAAP and IFRS with respect to the accounting for inventories.

IFRS9-2 LaTour Inc. is based in France and prepares its financial statements in accordance with IFRS. In 2014, it reported cost of goods sold of $578 million and average inventory of $154 million. Briefly discuss how analysis of LaTour's inventory turnover (and comparisons to a company using GAAP) might be affected by differences in inventory accounting between IFRS and GAAP.

IFRS9-3 Reed Pentak, a finance major, has been following globalization and made the following observation concerning accounting convergence: "I do not see many obstacles concerning development of a single accounting standard for inventories." Prepare a response to Reed to explain the main obstacle to achieving convergence in the area of inventory accounting.

IFRS9-4 Briefly describe the valuation of (a) biological assets and (b) agricultural produce.

IFRS9-5 In some instances, accounting principles require a departure from valuing inventories at cost alone. Determine the proper unit inventory price in the following cases.

	Cases				
	1	2	3	4	5
Cost	$15.90	$16.10	$15.90	$15.90	$15.90
Sales price	14.80	19.20	15.20	10.40	17.80
Estimated cost to complete	1.50	1.90	1.65	.80	1.00
Estimated cost to sell	.50	.70	.55	.40	.60

IFRS9-6 Riegel Company uses the LCNRV method, on an individual-item basis, in pricing its inventory items. The inventory at December 31, 2014, consists of products D, E, F, G, H, and I. Relevant per unit data for these products appear below.

	Item D	Item E	Item F	Item G	Item H	Item I
Estimated selling price	$120	$110	$95	$90	$110	$90
Cost	75	80	80	80	50	36
Cost to complete	30	30	25	35	30	30
Selling costs	10	18	10	20	10	20

Using the LCNRV rule, determine the proper unit value for statement of financial position reporting purposes at December 31, 2014, for each of the inventory items above.

IFRS9-7 Dover Company began operations in 2014 and determined its ending inventory at cost and at LCNRV at December 31, 2014, and December 31, 2015. This information is presented below.

	Cost	Net Realizable Value
12/31/14	$346,000	$322,000
12/31/15	410,000	390,000

(a) Prepare the journal entries required at December 31, 2014, and December 31, 2015, assuming that the inventory is recorded at LCNRV and a perpetual inventory system using the cost-of-goods-sold method is used.

(b) Prepare journal entries required at December 31, 2014, and December 31, 2015, assuming that the inventory is recorded at cost and a perpetual system using the loss method is used.

(c) Which of the two methods above provides the higher net income in each year?

IFRS9-8 Keyser's Fleece Inc. holds a drove of sheep. Keyser shears the sheep on a semiannual basis and then sells the harvested wool into the specialty knitting market. Keyser has the following information related to the shearing sheep at January 1, 2014, and during the first six months of 2014.

	Shearing Sheep
Carrying value (equal to net realizable value), January 1, 2014	$74,000
Change in fair value due to growth and price changes	4,700
Change in fair value due to harvest	(575)
Wool harvested during the first 6 months (at NRV)	9,000

Prepare the journal entry(ies) for Keyser's biological asset (shearing sheep) for the first six months of 2014.

IFRS9-9 Refer to the data in IFRS9-8 for Keyser's Fleece Inc. Prepare the journal entries for (a) the wool harvested in the first six months of 2014, and (b) the wool harvested that is sold for $10,500 in July 2014.

Professional Research

IFRS9-10 Jones Co. is in a technology-intensive industry. Recently, one of its competitors introduced a new product with technology that might render obsolete some of Jones's inventory. The accounting staff wants to follow the appropriate authoritative literature in determining the accounting for this significant market event.

Instructions

Access the IFRS authoritative literature at the IASB website (*http://eifrs.iasb.org/*). (Click on the IFRS tab and then register for free eIFRS access if necessary.) When you have accessed the documents, you can use the search tool in your Internet browser to respond to the following questions. (Provide paragraph citations.)

  (a) Identify the authoritative literature addressing inventory pricing.
  (b) List three types of goods that are classified as inventory. What characteristic will automatically exclude an item from being classified as inventory?
  (c) Define "net realizable value" as used in the phrase "lower-of-cost-or-net realizable value."
  (d) Explain when it is acceptable to state inventory above cost and which industries allow this practice.

International Financial Reporting Problem
Marks and Spencer plc

IFRS9-11 The financial statements of Marks and Spencer plc (M&S) are available at the book's companion website or can be accessed at *http://annualreport.marksandspencer.com/_assets/downloads/ Marks-and-Spencer-Annual-report-and-financial-statements-2012.pdf*.

Instructions

Refer to M&S's financial statements and the accompanying notes to answer the following questions.

  (a) How does M&S value its inventories? Which inventory costing method does M&S use as a basis for reporting its inventories?
  (b) How does M&S report its inventories in the statement of financial position? In the notes to its financial statements, what three descriptions are used to classify its inventories?
  (c) What costs does M&S include in Inventory and Cost of Sales?
  (d) What was M&S's inventory turnover in 2012? What is its gross profit percentage? Evaluate M&S's inventory turnover and its gross profit percentage.

ANSWERS TO IFRS SELF-TEST QUESTIONS

1. b **2.** b **3.** c **4.** d **5.** c

LEARNING OBJECTIVES

After studying this chapter, you should be able to:

1 Describe property, plant, and equipment.

2 Identify the costs to include in initial valuation of property, plant, and equipment.

3 Describe the accounting problems associated with self-constructed assets.

4 Describe the accounting problems associated with interest capitalization.

5 Understand accounting issues related to acquiring and valuing plant assets.

6 Describe the accounting treatment for costs subsequent to acquisition.

7 Describe the accounting treatment for the disposal of property, plant, and equipment.

Watch Your Spending

Investments in long-lived assets, such as property, plant, and equipment, are important elements in many companies' balance sheets. As Table 1 shows, capital expenditures on structures and equipment (whether new or used) are starting to grow again after the effects of the 2008 financial crisis.

Table 1: Total Capital Expenditures by Type for All U.S. Businesses, 2001 to 2010

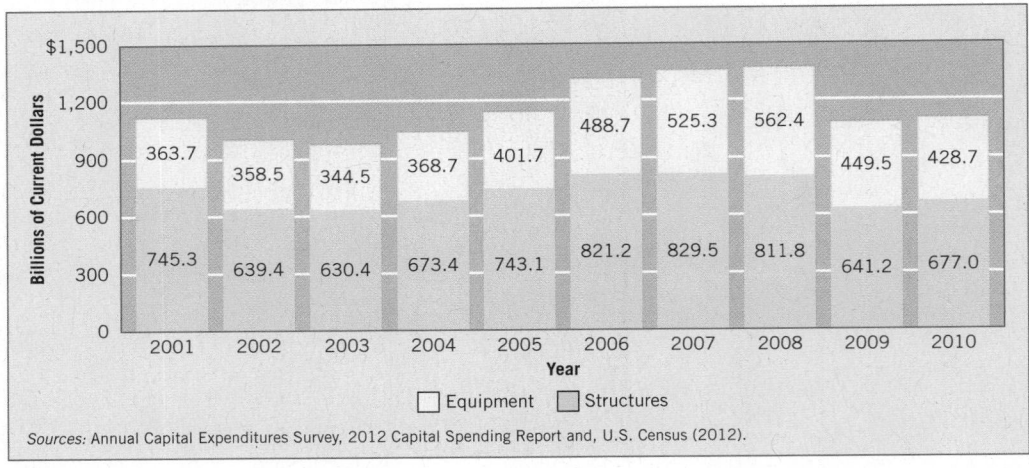

Sources: Annual Capital Expenditures Survey, 2012 Capital Spending Report and, U.S. Census (2012).

Unfortunately, Table 1 also shows that capital expenditures' growth is overall stagnant in the last 10 years. However, better times may be ahead. To illustrate, the food and beverage industry increased its capital expenditures by 20 percent in 2011 and is estimated to increase them again by 4 percent in 2012. Table 2 identifies the five companies in this industry with the largest capital expenditures in 2011 and 2012.

Table 2: Capital Spending ($ in millions)

Company	2012 Budget	% Change from 2011	2011 Actual	2011 Budget	% Change from 2010 Actual	2010 Actual
Anheuser-Busch InBev	$3,200	2%	$3,256	$2,800	31%	$2,350
Coca-Cola	3,100M	6	2,920	3,100	40	2,215
PepsiCo	3,000	9	3,300	3,700	14	3,253
Kraft Foods	2,000	13	1,771	1,800	9	1,661
Tyson	825	28	643	700	27	550

Capital expenditures are significant for many companies. For example, at **Jet Blue Airways**, plant assets are 69 percent of its total assets. For **Wal-Mart Stores, Inc.**, it's 53 percent. Conversely, **Microsoft**'s percentage is just 3 percent. Amounts for companies' capital expenditures are reported on a company's balance sheet and directly affect such items as total assets, depreciation expense, cash flows, and net income. Companies that overspend in this area find that income is reduced as depreciation increases without corresponding increases in revenues. As a result, these companies often lose financial flexibility. That is, they find themselves in a cash bind as their cash flows from operations can no longer meet their obligations.

A good example is **Baker Hughes, Inc.** (an oilfield-services company), which in the first half of 2012 reported cash flow from operations of $24 million but capital expenditures of $1,442 million. Although the company is presently stable, the unfavorable relationship of cash flow from operations to capital expenditures is a cause for concern.

Companies can also affect income by reducing capital expenditures. For example, **Cintas** (a uniform rental business) cut back on capital expenditures in recent years. In response, depreciation expense declined to $152 million in 2010 relative to $158 million in the prior year. That lifted its earnings per share by seven cents. Similarly, **Norfolk Southern** added eight cents per share to its bottom line through lower depreciation charges.

Thus, not only do companies have to be careful in planning the proper amount of capital expenditures, but users must understand the impact of these expenditures on measures of financial performance. As illustrated by the examples above, the level of capital expenditures, depreciation expense, cash flow from operations, and net income all play a role in assessing a company's ability to generate future cash flows.

Sources: Adapted from L. Strauss, "Depreciation: An Appreciation," *Barrons Online* (April 30, 2011); and D. Phelps, "Top 100 Capital Spending Report: Greek Yogurt Plants Are Stacking Up," *www.FoodProcessing.com* (April 9, 2012).

CONCEPTUAL FOCUS

> See the **Underlying Concepts** on pages 538, 542, and 557.

INTERNATIONAL FOCUS

> See the **International Perspectives** on pages 538, 542, 546, 550, and 555.
> **IFRS Insights** related to property, plant, and equipment are presented in Chapter 11.

PREVIEW OF CHAPTER | **10**

As we indicate in the opening story, a company like **Jet Blue Airways** has a substantial investment in property, plant, and equipment. Conversely, other companies, such as **Microsoft**, have a minor investment in these types of assets. In this chapter, we discuss the proper accounting for the acquisition, use, and disposition of property, plant, and equipment. The content and organization of the chapter are as follows.

Acquisition and Disposition of Property, Plant, and Equipment

Acquisition	Valuation	Costs Subsequent to Acquisition	Disposition
• Acquisition costs: land, buildings, equipment • Self-constructed assets • Interest costs • Observations	• Cash discounts • Deferred contracts • Lump-sum purchases • Stock issuance • Nonmonetary exchanges • Contributions • Other valuation methods	• Additions • Improvements and replacements • Rearrangement and reinstallation • Repairs • Summary	• Sale • Involuntary conversion • Miscellaneous problems

PROPERTY, PLANT, AND EQUIPMENT

Companies like Boeing, Target, and Starbucks use assets of a durable nature. Such assets are called **property, plant, and equipment**. Other terms commonly used are **plant assets** and **fixed assets**. We use these terms interchangeably. Property, plant, and equipment include land, building structures (offices, factories, warehouses), and equipment (machinery, furniture, tools). The major characteristics of property, plant, and equipment are as follows.

1. *They are acquired for use in operations and not for resale.* Only assets used in normal business operations are classified as property, plant, and equipment. For example, an idle building is more appropriately classified separately as an investment. Land developers or subdividers classify land as inventory.

2. *They are long-term in nature and usually depreciated.* Property, plant, and equipment yield services over a number of years. Companies allocate the cost of the investment in these assets to future periods through periodic depreciation charges. The exception is land, which is depreciated only if a material decrease in value occurs, such as a loss in fertility of agricultural land because of poor crop rotation, drought, or soil erosion.

3. *They possess physical substance.* Property, plant, and equipment are tangible assets characterized by physical existence or substance. This differentiates them from intangible assets, such as patents or goodwill. Unlike raw material, however, property, plant, and equipment do not physically become part of a product held for resale.

 Underlying Concepts

Fair value is relevant to inventory but less so for property, plant, and equipment which, consistent with the going-concern assumption, are held for use in the business, not for sale like inventory.

Acquisition of Property, Plant, and Equipment

Most companies use historical cost as the basis for valuing property, plant, and equipment. **Historical cost** measures the cash or cash equivalent price of obtaining the asset and bringing it to the location and condition necessary for its intended use. For example, companies like Kellogg Co. consider the purchase price, freight costs, sales taxes, and installation costs of a productive asset as part of the asset's cost. It then allocates these costs to future periods through depreciation. Further, Kellogg **adds to the asset's original cost** any related costs incurred **after the asset's acquisition**, such as additions, improvements, or replacements, **if they provide future service potential**. Otherwise, Kellogg expenses these costs immediately.[1]

Subsequent to acquisition, companies should not write up property, plant, and equipment to reflect fair value when it is above cost. The main reasons for this position are as follows.

International Perspective

Under international accounting standards, historical cost is the benchmark (preferred) treatment for property, plant, and equipment. However, companies may also use revalued amounts. When using revaluation, companies must revalue the class of assets regularly.

1. Historical cost involves actual, not hypothetical, transactions and so is the most reliable.

2. Companies should not anticipate gains and losses but should recognize gains and losses only when the asset is sold.

Even those who favor fair value measurement for inventory and financial instruments often take the position that property, plant, and equipment should not be revalued. The major concern is the difficulty of developing a reliable fair value for these types

---

[1]Additional costs to be included in the cost of property, plant, and equipment are those related to asset retirement obligations (AROs). These costs, such as those related to decommissioning nuclear facilities or reclamation or restoration of a mining facility, reflect a legal requirement to retire the asset at the end of its useful life. The expected costs are recorded in the asset cost and depreciated over the useful life (see Chapter 13).

of assets. For example, how does one value a General Motors automobile manufacturing plant or a nuclear power plant owned by Consolidated Edison?

However, if the fair value of the property, plant, and equipment is less than its carrying amount, the asset may be written down. These situations occur when the asset is impaired (discussed in Chapter 11) and in situations where the asset is being held for sale. A long-lived asset classified as held for sale should be measured at the lower of its carrying amount or fair value less costs to sell. In that case, a reasonable valuation for the asset can be obtained, based on the sales price. A long-lived asset is not depreciated if it is classified as held for sale. This is because such assets are not being used to generate revenues. **[1]**

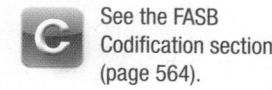

See the FASB Codification section (page 564).

Cost of Land

All expenditures made to acquire land and ready it for use are considered part of the land cost. Thus, when Wal-Mart Stores, Inc. or Home Depot purchases land on which to build a new store, its land costs typically include (1) the purchase price; (2) closing costs, such as title to the land, attorney's fees, and recording fees; (3) costs incurred in getting the land in condition for its intended use, such as grading, filling, draining, and clearing; (4) assumption of any liens, mortgages, or encumbrances on the property; and (5) any additional land improvements that have an indefinite life.

Gateway to the Profession

Expanded Discussion of Alternative Valuation Methods

For example, when Home Depot purchases land for the purpose of constructing a building, it considers all costs incurred up to the excavation for the new building as land costs. **Removal of old buildings—clearing, grading, and filling—is a land cost because this activity is necessary to get the land in condition for its intended purpose.** Home Depot treats any proceeds from getting the land ready for its intended use, such as salvage receipts on the demolition of an old building or the sale of cleared timber, as **reductions in the price of the land**.

In some cases, when Home Depot purchases land, it may assume certain obligations on the land such as back taxes or liens. In such situations, the cost of the land is the cash paid for it, plus the encumbrances. In other words, if the purchase price of the land is $50,000 cash but Home Depot assumes accrued property taxes of $5,000 and liens of $10,000, its land cost is $65,000.

Home Depot also might incur **special assessments** for local improvements, such as pavements, street lights, sewers, and drainage systems. It should charge these costs to the Land account because they are relatively permanent in nature. That is, after installation, they are maintained by the local government. In addition, Home Depot should charge any permanent improvements it makes, such as landscaping, to the Land account. It records separately any **improvements with limited lives**, such as private driveways, walks, fences, and parking lots, as Land Improvements. These costs are depreciated over their estimated lives.

Generally, land is part of property, plant, and equipment. However, if the major purpose of acquiring and holding land is speculative, a company more appropriately classifies the land as an **investment**. If a real estate concern holds the land for resale, it should classify the land as **inventory**.

In cases where land is held as an investment, what accounting treatment should be given for taxes, insurance, and other direct costs incurred while holding the land? Many believe these costs should be capitalized. The reason: They are not generating revenue from the investment at this time. Companies generally use this approach except when the asset is currently producing revenue (such as rental property).

Cost of Buildings

The cost of buildings should include all expenditures related directly to their acquisition or construction. These costs include (1) materials, labor, and overhead costs incurred during construction, and (2) professional fees and building permits. Generally, companies contract others to construct their buildings. Companies consider all costs incurred, from excavation to completion, as part of the building costs.

But how should companies account for an old building that is on the site of a newly proposed building? Is the cost of removal of the old building a cost of the land or a cost of the new building? Recall that **if a company purchases land with an old building on it, then the cost of demolition less its salvage value is a cost of getting the land ready for its intended use and relates to the land rather than to the new building**. In other words, all costs of getting an asset ready for its intended use are costs of that asset.

Cost of Equipment

The term "equipment" in accounting includes delivery equipment, office equipment, machinery, furniture and fixtures, furnishings, factory equipment, and similar fixed assets. The cost of such assets includes the purchase price, freight and handling charges incurred, insurance on the equipment while in transit, cost of special foundations if required, assembling and installation costs, and costs of conducting trial runs. Costs thus include all expenditures incurred in acquiring the equipment and preparing it for use.

Self-Constructed Assets

LEARNING OBJECTIVE 3
Describe the accounting problems associated with self-constructed assets.

Occasionally, companies construct their own assets. Determining the cost of such machinery and other fixed assets can be a problem. Without a purchase price or contract price, the company must allocate costs and expenses to arrive at the cost of the **self-constructed asset**. Materials and direct labor used in construction pose no problem. A company can trace these costs directly to work and material orders related to the fixed assets constructed.

However, the assignment of indirect costs of manufacturing creates special problems. These indirect costs, called **overhead** or burden, include power, heat, light, insurance, property taxes on factory buildings and equipment, factory supervisory labor, depreciation of fixed assets, and supplies.

Companies can handle indirect costs in one of two ways:

1. *Assign no fixed overhead to the cost of the constructed asset.* The major argument for this treatment is that indirect overhead is generally fixed in nature. It does not increase as a result of a company constructing its own plant or equipment. This approach assumes that the company will have the same costs regardless of whether it constructs the asset or not. Therefore, to charge a portion of the overhead costs to the equipment will normally reduce current expenses and consequently overstate income of the current period. However, the company would assign to the cost of the constructed asset variable overhead costs that increase as a result of the construction.

2. *Assign a portion of all overhead to the construction process.* This approach, called a **full-costing approach**, follows the belief that costs should attach to all products and assets manufactured or constructed. Under this approach, a company assigns a portion of all overhead to the construction process, as it would to normal production. Advocates say that failure to allocate overhead costs understates the initial cost of the asset and results in an inaccurate future allocation.

Companies should assign to the asset **a pro rata portion** of the fixed overhead to determine its cost. Companies use this treatment extensively because many believe that it results in a better recognition of these costs in periods benefited.

If the allocated overhead results in recording construction costs in excess of the costs that an outside independent producer would charge, the company should record the excess overhead as a period loss rather than capitalize it. This avoids capitalizing the asset at more than its probable fair value.[2]

Interest Costs During Construction

The proper accounting for interest costs has been a long-standing controversy. Three approaches have been suggested to account for the interest incurred in financing the construction of property, plant, and equipment:

4 LEARNING OBJECTIVE

Describe the accounting problems associated with interest capitalization.

1. *Capitalize no interest charges during construction.* Under this approach, interest is considered a cost of financing and not a cost of construction. Some contend that if a company had used stock (equity) financing rather than debt, it would not incur this cost. The major argument against this approach is that the use of cash, whatever its source, has an associated implicit interest cost, which should not be ignored.

2. *Charge construction with all costs of funds employed, whether identifiable or not.* This method maintains that the cost of construction should include the cost of financing, whether by cash, debt, or stock. Its advocates say that all costs necessary to get an asset ready for its intended use, including interest, are part of the asset's cost. Interest, whether actual or imputed, is a cost, just as are labor and materials. A major criticism of this approach is that imputing the cost of equity capital (stock) is subjective and outside the framework of an historical cost system.

3. *Capitalize only the actual interest costs incurred during construction.* This approach agrees in part with the logic of the second approach—that interest is just as much a cost as are labor and materials. But this approach capitalizes only interest costs incurred through debt financing. (That is, it does not try to determine the cost of equity financing.) Under this approach, a company that uses debt financing will have an asset of higher cost than a company that uses stock financing. Some consider this approach unsatisfactory because they believe the cost of an asset should be the same whether it is financed with cash, debt, or equity.

Illustration 10-1 shows how a company might add interest costs (if any) to the cost of the asset under the three capitalization approaches.

ILLUSTRATION 10-1
Capitalization of Interest Costs

---

[2]A committee of the AICPA argues against allocation of overhead. Instead, it supports capitalization of only direct costs (costs directly related to the specific activities involved in the construction process). AcSEC was concerned that the allocation of overhead costs may lead to overly aggressive allocations and therefore misstatements of income. In addition, not reporting these costs as period costs during the construction period may affect comparisons of period costs and resulting net income from one period to the next. See Accounting Standards Executive Committee, "Accounting for Certain Costs and Activities Related to Property, Plant, and Equipment," Exposure Draft (New York: AICPA, June 29, 2001).

GAAP requires the third approach—capitalizing actual interest (with modification). This method follows the concept that the **historical cost of acquiring an asset includes all costs (including interest) incurred to bring the asset to the condition and location necessary for its intended use.** The rationale for this approach is that during construction, the asset is not generating revenues. Therefore, a company should defer (capitalize) interest costs. **[2]** Once construction is complete, the asset is ready for its intended use and a company can earn revenues. At this point, the company should report interest as an expense and match it to these revenues. It follows that the company should expense any interest cost incurred in purchasing an asset that is ready for its intended use.

To implement this general approach, companies consider three items:

1. Qualifying assets.
2. Capitalization period.
3. Amount to capitalize.

Underlying Concepts

The objective of capitalizing interest is to obtain a measure of acquisition cost that reflects a company's total investment in the asset and to charge that cost to future periods benefited.

Qualifying Assets

To qualify for interest capitalization, assets must require a period of time to get them ready for their intended use. A company capitalizes interest costs starting with the first expenditure related to the asset. Capitalization continues until the company substantially readies the asset for its intended use.

Assets that qualify for interest cost capitalization include assets under construction for a company's own use (including buildings, plants, and large machinery) and assets intended for sale or lease that are constructed or otherwise produced as discrete projects (e.g., ships or real estate developments).

Examples of assets that do not qualify for interest capitalization are (1) assets that are in use or ready for their intended use, and (2) assets that the company does not use in its earnings activities and that are not undergoing the activities necessary to get them ready for use. Examples of this second type include land remaining undeveloped and assets not used because of obsolescence, excess capacity, or need for repair.

International Perspective

Recently, IFRS changed to require companies to capitalize borrowing costs related to qualifying assets. These changes were made as part of the IASB's and FASB's convergence project.

Capitalization Period

The **capitalization period** is the period of time during which a company must capitalize interest. It begins with the presence of three conditions:

1. Expenditures for the asset have been made.
2. Activities that are necessary to get the asset ready for its intended use are in progress.
3. Interest cost is being incurred.

Interest capitalization **continues as long as these three conditions are present.** The capitalization period ends when the asset is substantially complete and ready for its intended use.

Amount to Capitalize

The amount of interest to capitalize is limited to the lower of actual interest cost incurred during the period or avoidable interest. **Avoidable interest** is the amount of interest cost during the period that a company could theoretically avoid if it had not made expenditures for the asset. If the actual interest cost for the period is $90,000 and the avoidable interest is $80,000, the company capitalizes only $80,000. Or, if the actual interest cost is $80,000 and the avoidable interest is $90,000, it still capitalizes only $80,000. In no situation should interest cost include a cost of capital charge for stockholders' equity. Furthermore, GAAP requires interest capitalization for a qualifying asset only if its effect, compared with the effect of expensing interest, is material. **[3]**

To apply the avoidable interest concept, a company determines the potential amount of interest that it may capitalize during an accounting period by multiplying the interest rate(s) by the **weighted-average accumulated expenditures** for qualifying assets during the period.

Weighted-Average Accumulated Expenditures. In computing the weighted-average accumulated expenditures, a company weights the construction expenditures by the amount of time (fraction of a year or accounting period) that it can incur interest cost on the expenditure.

To illustrate, assume a 17-month bridge construction project with current-year payments to the contractor of $240,000 on March 1, $480,000 on July 1, and $360,000 on November 1. The company computes the weighted-average accumulated expenditures for the year ended December 31 as follows.

Date	Expenditures Amount	×	Capitalization Period*	=	Weighted-Average Accumulated Expenditures
March 1	$ 240,000		10/12		$200,000
July 1	480,000		6/12		240,000
November 1	360,000		2/12		60,000
	$1,080,000				$500,000

*Months between date of expenditure and date interest capitalization stops or end of year, whichever comes first (in this case December 31).

ILLUSTRATION 10-2
Computation of Weighted-Average Accumulated Expenditures

To compute the weighted-average accumulated expenditures, a company weights the expenditures by the amount of time that it can incur interest cost on each one. For the March 1 expenditure, the company associates 10 months' interest cost with the expenditure. For the expenditure on July 1, it incurs only 6 months' interest costs. For the expenditure made on November 1, the company incurs only 2 months of interest cost.

Interest Rates. Companies follow the below principles in selecting the appropriate interest rates to be applied to the weighted-average accumulated expenditures:

1. For the portion of weighted-average accumulated expenditures that is less than or equal to any amounts borrowed specifically to finance construction of the assets, **use the interest rate incurred on the specific borrowings**.

2. For the portion of weighted-average accumulated expenditures that is greater than any debt incurred specifically to finance construction of the assets, **use a weighted average of interest rates incurred on all other outstanding debt during the period.**[3]

[3]The interest rate to be used may rely exclusively on an average rate of all the borrowings, if desired. For our purposes, we use the specific borrowing rate followed by the average interest rate because we believe it to be more conceptually consistent. Either method can be used; GAAP does not provide explicit guidance on this measurement. For a discussion of this issue and others related to interest capitalization, see Kathryn M. Means and Paul M. Kazenski, "SFAS 34: Recipe for Diversity," *Accounting Horizons* (September 1988); and Wendy A. Duffy, "A Graphical Analysis of Interest Capitalization," *Journal of Accounting Education* (Fall 1990).

Illustration 10-3 shows the computation of a weighted-average interest rate for debt greater than the amount incurred specifically to finance construction of the assets.

ILLUSTRATION 10-3
Computation of
Weighted-Average
Interest Rate

	Principal	Interest
12%, 2-year note	$ 600,000	$ 72,000
9%, 10-year bonds	2,000,000	180,000
7.5%, 20-year bonds	5,000,000	375,000
	$7,600,000	$627,000

$$\text{Weighted-average interest rate} = \frac{\text{Total interest}}{\text{Total principal}} = \frac{\$627,000}{\$7,600,000} = 8.25\%$$

Comprehensive Example of Interest Capitalization

To illustrate the issues related to interest capitalization, assume that on November 1, 2013, Shalla Company contracted Pfeifer Construction Co. to construct a building for $1,400,000 on land costing $100,000 (purchased from the contractor and included in the first payment). Shalla made the following payments to the construction company during 2014.

January 1	March 1	May 1	December 31	Total
$210,000	$300,000	$540,000	$450,000	$1,500,000

Pfeifer Construction completed the building, ready for occupancy, on December 31, 2014. Shalla had the following debt outstanding at December 31, 2014.

Specific Construction Debt

1. 15%, 3-year note to finance purchase of land and construction of the building, dated December 31, 2013, with interest payable annually on December 31 — $750,000

Other Debt

2. 10%, 5-year note payable, dated December 31, 2010, with interest payable annually on December 31 — $550,000
3. 12%, 10-year bonds issued December 31, 2009, with interest payable annually on December 31 — $600,000

Shalla computed the weighted-average accumulated expenditures during 2014 as shown in Illustration 10-4.

ILLUSTRATION 10-4
Computation of
Weighted-Average
Accumulated
Expenditures

Expenditures		Current-Year Capitalization	Weighted-Average
Date	Amount ×	Period =	Accumulated Expenditures
January 1	$ 210,000	12/12	$210,000
March 1	300,000	10/12	250,000
May 1	540,000	8/12	360,000
December 31	450,000	0	0
	$1,500,000		$820,000

Note that the expenditure made on December 31, the last day of the year, does not have any interest cost.

Shalla computes the avoidable interest as shown in Illustration 10-5.

ILLUSTRATION 10-5
Computation of
Avoidable Interest

Weighted-Average Accumulated Expenditures	×	Interest Rate	=	Avoidable Interest
$750,000		.15 (construction note)		$112,500
70,000[a]		.1104 (weighted average of		7,728
$820,000		other debt)[b]		$120,228

[a]The amount by which the weighted-average accumulated expenditures exceeds the specific construction loan.

[b]Weighted-average interest rate computation:

	Principal	Interest
10%, 5-year note	$ 550,000	$ 55,000
12%, 10-year bonds	600,000	72,000
	$1,150,000	$127,000

$$\text{Weighted-average interest rate} = \frac{\text{Total interest}}{\text{Total principal}} = \frac{\$127,000}{\$1,150,000} = 11.04\%$$

The company determines the actual interest cost, which represents the maximum amount of interest that it may capitalize during 2014, as shown in Illustration 10-6.

ILLUSTRATION 10-6
Computation of Actual
Interest Cost

Construction note	$750,000 × .15 = $112,500
5-year note	$550,000 × .10 = 55,000
10-year bonds	$600,000 × .12 = 72,000
Actual interest	$239,500

The interest cost that Shalla capitalizes is the lesser of $120,228 (avoidable interest) and $239,500 (actual interest), or $120,228.

Shalla records the following journal entries during 2014:

January 1

Land	100,000	
Buildings (or Construction in Process)	110,000	
Cash		210,000

Gateway to the Profession

Tutorial on Interest Capitalization

March 1

Buildings	300,000	
Cash		300,000

May 1

Buildings	540,000	
Cash		540,000

December 31

Buildings	450,000	
Cash		450,000
Buildings (Capitalized Interest)	120,228	
Interest Expense ($239,500 − $120,228)	119,272	
Cash ($112,500 + $55,000 + $72,000)		239,500

Shalla should write off capitalized interest cost as part of depreciation over the useful life of the assets involved and not over the term of the debt. It should disclose the total interest cost incurred during the period, with the portion charged to expense and the portion capitalized indicated.

At December 31, 2014, Shalla discloses the amount of interest capitalized either as part of the nonoperating section of the income statement or in the notes accompanying the financial statements. We illustrate both forms of disclosure, in Illustrations 10-7 and 10-8.[4]

ILLUSTRATION 10-7
Capitalized Interest
Reported in the Income
Statement

Income from operations		XXXX
Other expenses and losses:		
Interest expense	$239,500	
Less: Capitalized interest	120,228	119,272
Income before income taxes		XXXX
Income taxes		XXX
Net income		XXXX

ILLUSTRATION 10-8
Capitalized Interest
Disclosed in a Note

Note 1: Accounting Policies. *Capitalized Interest.* During 2014, total interest cost was $239,500, of which $120,228 was capitalized and $119,272 was charged to expense.

What do the numbers mean? WHAT'S IN YOUR INTEREST?

The requirement to capitalize interest can significantly impact financial statements. For example, when earnings of building manufacturer Jim Walter's Corporation dropped from $1.51 to $1.17 per share, the company offset 11 cents per share of the decline by capitalizing the interest on coal mining projects and several plants under construction.

How do statement users determine the impact of interest capitalization on a company's bottom line? They examine the notes to the financial statements. Companies with material interest capitalization must disclose the amounts of capitalized interest relative to total interest costs. For example,

Anadarko Petroleum Corporation capitalized nearly 30 percent of its total interest costs in a recent year and provided the following footnote related to capitalized interest.

Financial Footnotes
Total interest costs incurred during the year were $82,415,000. Of this amount, the Company capitalized $24,716,000. Capitalized interest is included as part of the cost of oil and gas properties. The capitalization rates are based on the Company's weighted-average cost of borrowings used to finance the expenditures.

Special Issues Related to Interest Capitalization

Two issues related to interest capitalization merit special attention:

1. Expenditures for land.

2. Interest revenue.

Expenditures for Land. When a company purchases land with the intention of developing it for a particular use, interest costs associated with those expenditures qualify for interest capitalization. If it purchases land as a site for a structure (such as a plant site), **interest costs capitalized during the period of construction are part of the cost of the plant, not the land**. Conversely, if the company develops land for lot sales, it includes any capitalized interest cost as part of the acquisition cost of the developed land. However, it should **not** capitalize interest costs involved in purchasing land held **for speculation** because the asset is ready for its intended use.

International Perspective

IFRS requires that interest revenue earned on specific borrowings should offset interest costs capitalized. The rationale is that the interest revenue earned is directly related to the interest cost incurred on the specific borrowing.

Interest Revenue. Companies frequently borrow money to finance construction of assets. They temporarily invest the excess borrowed funds in interest-bearing securities until they need the funds to pay for construction. During the early stages of construction, interest revenue earned may exceed the interest cost incurred on the borrowed funds.

---

[4]In subsequent years of a multi-year project, Shalla would follow the same procedures as presented for year 1. That is, interest to be capitalized each year is determined, based on weighted-average expenditures in that year multiplied by the appropriate interest rate, and then compared to actual interest. Total interest for the year is then allocated to interest expense and capitalized interest.

Should companies offset interest revenue against interest cost when determining the amount of interest to capitalize as part of the construction cost of assets? In general, **companies should not net or offset interest revenue against interest cost**. Temporary or short-term investment decisions are not related to the interest incurred as part of the acquisition cost of assets. Therefore, companies should capitalize the interest incurred on qualifying assets whether or not they temporarily invest excess funds in short-term securities. Some criticize this approach because a company can defer the interest cost but report the interest revenue in the current period.

Observations

The interest capitalization requirement is still debated. From a conceptual viewpoint, many believe that, for the reasons mentioned earlier, companies should either capitalize **no interest cost** or **all interest costs**, actual or imputed.

VALUATION OF PROPERTY, PLANT, AND EQUIPMENT

Like other assets, **companies should record property, plant, and equipment at the fair value of what they give up or at the fair value of the asset received, whichever is more clearly evident**. However, the process of asset acquisition sometimes obscures fair value. For example, if a company buys land and buildings together for one price, how does it determine separate values for the land and buildings? We examine these types of accounting problems in the following sections.

> **5 LEARNING OBJECTIVE**
> Understand accounting issues related to acquiring and valuing plant assets.

Cash Discounts

When a company purchases plant assets subject to cash discounts for prompt payment, how should it report the discount? If it takes the discount, the company should consider the discount as a reduction in the purchase price of the asset. But should the company reduce the asset cost even if it does not take the discount?

Two points of view exist on this question. One approach considers the discount—whether taken or not—as a reduction in the cost of the asset. The rationale for this approach is that the real cost of the asset is the cash or cash equivalent price of the asset. In addition, some argue that the terms of cash discounts are so attractive that failure to take them indicates management error or inefficiency.

Proponents of the other approach argue that failure to take the discount should not always be considered a loss. The terms may be unfavorable, or it might not be prudent for the company to take the discount. At present, companies use both methods though most prefer the former method.

Deferred-Payment Contracts

Companies frequently purchase plant assets on long-term credit contracts, using notes, mortgages, bonds, or equipment obligations. **To properly reflect cost, companies account for assets purchased on long-term credit contracts at the present value of the consideration exchanged between the contracting parties at the date of the transaction.**

For example, Greathouse Company purchases an asset today in exchange for a $10,000 zero-interest-bearing note payable four years from now. The company would not record the asset at $10,000. Instead, the present value of the $10,000 note establishes the exchange price of the transaction (the purchase price of the asset). Assuming an appropriate interest rate of 9 percent at which to discount this single payment of $10,000 due four years from now, Greathouse records this asset at $7,084.30 ($10,000 × .70843). [See Table 6-2 (page 337) for the present value of a single sum, $PV = \$10,000\ (PVF_{4,9\%})$.]

When no interest rate is stated or if the specified rate is unreasonable, the company imputes an appropriate interest rate. The objective is to approximate the interest rate that the buyer and seller would negotiate at arm's length in a similar borrowing transaction. In imputing an interest rate, companies consider such factors as the borrower's credit rating, the amount and maturity date of the note, and prevailing interest rates. **The company uses the cash exchange price of the asset acquired (if determinable) as the basis for recording the asset and measuring the interest element.**

To illustrate, Sutter Company purchases a specially built robot spray painter for its production line. The company issues a $100,000, five-year, zero-interest-bearing note to Wrigley Robotics, Inc. for the new equipment. The prevailing market rate of interest for obligations of this nature is 10 percent. Sutter is to pay off the note in five $20,000 installments, made at the end of each year. Sutter cannot readily determine the fair value of this specially built robot. Therefore, Sutter approximates the robot's value by establishing the fair value (present value) of the note. Entries for the date of purchase and dates of payments, plus computation of the present value of the note, are as follows.

Date of Purchase

Equipment	75,816*	
Discount on Notes Payable	24,184	
Notes Payable		100,000

*Present value of note $= \$20,000\ (PVF\text{-}OA_{5,10\%})$
$= \$20,000\ (3.79079)$; Table 6-4
$= \$75,816$

End of First Year

Interest Expense	7,582	
Notes Payable	20,000	
Cash		20,000
Discount on Notes Payable		7,582

Interest expense in the first year under the effective-interest approach is $7,582 [($100,000 − $24,184) × 10%]. The entry at the end of the second year to record interest and principal payment is as follows.

End of Second Year

Interest Expense	6,340	
Notes Payable	20,000	
Cash		20,000
Discount on Notes Payable		6,340

Interest expense in the second year under the effective-interest approach is $6,340 [($100,000 − $24,184) − ($20,000 − $7,582)] × 10%.

If Sutter did not impute an interest rate for deferred-payment contracts, it would record the asset at an amount greater than its fair value and overstate depreciation expense. In addition, Sutter would understate interest expense in the income statement for all periods involved.

Lump-Sum Purchases

A special problem of valuing fixed assets arises when a company purchases a group of plant assets at a single **lump-sum price**. When this common situation occurs, the company allocates the total cost among the various assets on the basis of their relative fair values. The assumption is that costs will vary in direct proportion to fair value. This is the same principle that companies apply to allocate a lump-sum cost among different inventory items.

To determine fair value, a company should use valuation techniques that are appropriate in the circumstances. In some cases, a single valuation technique will be appropriate. In other cases, multiple valuation approaches might have to be used.[5]

To illustrate, Norduct Homes, Inc. decides to purchase several assets of a small heating concern, Comfort Heating, for $80,000. Comfort Heating is in the process of liquidation. Its assets sold are:

	Book Value	Fair Value
Inventory	$30,000	$ 25,000
Land	20,000	25,000
Building	35,000	50,000
	$85,000	$100,000

Norduct Homes allocates the $80,000 purchase price on the basis of the relative fair values (assuming specific identification of costs is impracticable) in the following manner.

Inventory $\dfrac{\$25,000}{\$100,000} \times \$80,000 = \$20,000$

Land $\dfrac{\$25,000}{\$100,000} \times \$80,000 = \$20,000$

Building $\dfrac{\$50,000}{\$100,000} \times \$80,000 = \$40,000$

ILLUSTRATION 10-9
Allocation of Purchase Price—Relative Fair Value Basis

Issuance of Stock

When companies acquire property by issuing securities, such as common stock, the par or stated value of such stock fails to properly measure the property cost. If trading of the stock is active, **the market price of the stock issued is a fair indication of the cost of the property acquired. The stock is a good measure of the current cash equivalent price.**

For example, Upgrade Living Co. decides to purchase some adjacent land for expansion of its carpeting and cabinet operation. In lieu of paying cash for the land, the company issues to Deedland Company 5,000 shares of common stock (par value $10) that have a fair value of $12 per share. Upgrade Living Co. records the following entry.

Land (5,000 × $12)	60,000	
Common Stock		50,000
Paid-In Capital in Excess of Par—Common Stock		10,000

If the company cannot determine the market price of the common stock exchanged, it establishes the fair value of the property. It then uses the value of the property as the basis for recording the asset and issuance of the common stock.

---

[5]The valuation approaches that should be used are the market, income, or cost approach, or a combination of these approaches. The *market approach* uses observable prices and other relevant information generated by market transactions involving comparable assets. The *income approach* uses valuation techniques to convert future amounts (for example, cash flows or earnings) to a single present value amount (discounted). The *cost approach* is based on the amount that currently would be required to replace the service capacity of an asset (often referred to as current replacement cost). In determining the fair value, the company should assume the highest and best use of the asset. **[4]**

Exchanges of Nonmonetary Assets

The proper accounting for exchanges of nonmonetary assets, such as property, plant, and equipment, is controversial.[6] Some argue that companies should account for these types of exchanges based on the fair value of the asset given up or the fair value of the asset received, with a gain or loss recognized. Others believe that they should account for exchanges based on the recorded amount (book value) of the asset given up, with no gain or loss recognized. Still others favor an approach that recognizes losses in all cases but defers gains in special situations.

Ordinarily, companies account for the exchange of nonmonetary assets on the basis of **the fair value of the asset given up or the fair value of the asset received, whichever is clearly more evident. [5]** Thus, companies **should recognize immediately** any gains or losses on the exchange. The rationale for immediate recognition is that most transactions have **commercial substance**, and therefore gains and losses should be recognized.

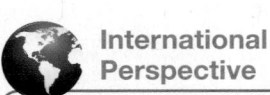

International Perspective

The FASB changed its accounting for exchanges to converge with IFRS. Previously, the FASB used a "similar in nature" criterion for exchanged assets to determine whether gains should be recognized. With use of the commercial substance test, GAAP and IFRS are now very similar.

Meaning of Commercial Substance

As indicated above, fair value is the basis for measuring an asset acquired in a nonmonetary exchange if the transaction has commercial substance. An exchange has commercial substance if the future cash flows change as a result of the transaction. That is, if the two parties' economic positions change, the transaction has commercial substance.

For example, Andrew Co. exchanges some of its equipment for land held by Roddick Inc. It is likely that the timing and amount of the cash flows arising for the land will differ significantly from the cash flows arising from the equipment. As a result, both Andrew Co. and Roddick Inc. are in different economic positions. Therefore, the exchange has commercial substance, and the companies recognize a gain or loss on the exchange.

What if companies exchange similar assets, such as one truck for another truck? Even in an exchange of similar assets, a change in the economic position of the company can result. For example, let's say the useful life of the truck received is significantly longer than that of the truck given up. The cash flows for the trucks can differ significantly. As a result, the transaction has commercial substance, and the company should use fair value as a basis for measuring the asset received in the exchange.

However, it is possible to exchange similar assets but not have a significant difference in cash flows. That is, the company is in the same economic position as before the exchange. In that case, the company recognizes a loss but generally defers a gain.

As we will see in the following examples, use of fair value generally results in recognizing a gain or loss at the time of the exchange. Consequently, companies must determine if the transaction has commercial substance. To make this determination, they must carefully evaluate the cash flow characteristics of the assets exchanged.[7]

Illustration 10-10 summarizes asset exchange situations and the related accounting.

---

[6]Nonmonetary assets are items whose price in terms of the monetary unit may change over time. Monetary assets—cash and short- or long-term accounts and notes receivable—are fixed in terms of units of currency by contract or otherwise.

[7]The determination of the commercial substance of a transaction requires significant judgment. In determining whether future cash flows change, it is necessary to do one of two things. (1) Determine whether the risk, timing, and amount of cash flows arising for the asset received differ from the cash flows associated with the outbound asset. Or, (2) evaluate whether cash flows are affected with the exchange versus without the exchange. Also note that if companies cannot determine fair values of the assets exchanged, then they should use recorded book values in accounting for the exchange.

Type of Exchange	Accounting Guidance
Exchange has commercial substance.	Recognize gains and losses immediately.
Exchange lacks commercial substance—no cash received.	Defer gains; recognize losses immediately.
Exchange lacks commercial substance—cash received.	Recognize partial gain; recognize losses immediately.*

*If cash is 25% or more of the fair value of the exchange, recognize entire gain because earnings process is complete.

ILLUSTRATION 10-10
Accounting for Exchanges

As Illustration 10-10 indicates, companies immediately recognize losses they incur on all exchanges. The accounting for gains depends on whether the exchange has commercial substance. If the exchange has commercial substance, the company recognizes the gain immediately. However, the profession modifies the rule for immediate recognition of a gain when an exchange lacks commercial substance: **If the company receives no cash in such an exchange, it defers recognition of a gain. If the company receives cash in such an exchange, it recognizes part of the gain immediately.**

To illustrate the accounting for these different types of transactions, we examine various loss and gain exchange situations.

Exchanges—Loss Situation

When a company exchanges nonmonetary assets and a loss results, the company recognizes the loss immediately. The rationale: Companies should not value assets at more than their cash equivalent price. If the loss were deferred, assets would be overstated. Therefore, companies recognize a loss immediately whether the exchange has commercial substance or not.

For example, Information Processing, Inc. trades its used machine for a new model at Jerrod Business Solutions Inc. The exchange has commercial substance. The used machine has a book value of $8,000 (original cost $12,000 less $4,000 accumulated depreciation) and a fair value of $6,000. The new model lists for $16,000. Jerrod gives Information Processing a trade-in allowance of $9,000 for the used machine. Information Processing computes the cost of the new asset as follows.

List price of new machine	$16,000
Less: Trade-in allowance for used machine	9,000
Cash payment due	7,000
Fair value of used machine	6,000
Cost of new machine	$13,000

ILLUSTRATION 10-11
Computation of Cost of New Machine

Information Processing records this transaction as follows.

Equipment	13,000	
Accumulated Depreciation—Equipment	4,000	
Loss on Disposal of Equipment	2,000	
Equipment		12,000
Cash		7,000

We verify the loss on the disposal of the used machine as follows.

Fair value of used machine	$6,000
Less: Book value of used machine	8,000
Loss on disposal of used machine	$2,000

ILLUSTRATION 10-12
Computation of Loss on Disposal of Used Machine

Why did Information Processing not use the trade-in allowance or the book value of the old asset as a basis for the new equipment? The company did not use the trade-in allowance because it included a price concession (similar to a price discount). Few individuals pay list price for a new car. Dealers such as Jerrod often inflate trade-in allowances on the used car so that actual selling prices fall below list prices. To record the car at list price would state it at an amount in excess of its cash equivalent price because of the new car's inflated list price. Similarly, use of book value in this situation would overstate the value of the new machine by $2,000.[8]

Exchanges—Gain Situation

Has Commercial Substance. Now let's consider the situation in which a nonmonetary exchange has commercial substance and a gain is realized. In such a case, a company usually records the cost of a nonmonetary asset acquired in exchange for another nonmonetary asset at the **fair value of the asset given up** and immediately recognizes a gain. The company should use the **fair value of the asset received** only if it is more clearly evident than the fair value of the asset given up.

To illustrate, Interstate Transportation Company exchanged a number of used trucks plus cash for a semi-truck. The used trucks have a combined book value of $42,000 (cost $64,000 less $22,000 accumulated depreciation). Interstate's purchasing agent, experienced in the secondhand market, indicates that the used trucks have a fair value of $49,000. In addition to the trucks, Interstate must pay $11,000 cash for the semi-truck. Interstate computes the cost of the semi-truck as follows.

ILLUSTRATION 10-13
Computation of
Semi-Truck Cost

Fair value of trucks exchanged	$49,000
Cash paid	11,000
Cost of semi-truck	$60,000

Interstate records the exchange transaction as follows.

Trucks (semi)	60,000	
Accumulated Depreciation—Trucks	22,000	
Trucks (used)		64,000
Gain on Disposal of Trucks		7,000
Cash		11,000

The gain is the difference between the fair value of the used trucks and their book value. We verify the computation as follows.

ILLUSTRATION 10-14
Computation of Gain on
Disposal of Used Trucks

Fair value of used trucks		$49,000
Cost of used trucks	$64,000	
Less: Accumulated depreciation	22,000	
Book value of used trucks		(42,000)
Gain on disposal of used trucks		$ 7,000

In this case, Interstate is in a different economic position, and therefore the transaction has commercial substance. Thus, it **recognizes a gain**.

Lacks Commercial Substance—No Cash Received. We now assume that the Interstate Transportation Company exchange lacks commercial substance. That is, the economic

---

[8]Recognize that for Jerrod (the dealer), the asset given up in the exchange is considered inventory. As a result, Jerrod records a sale and related cost of goods sold. The used machine received by Jerrod is recorded at fair value.

position of Interstate did not change significantly as a result of this exchange. In this case, Interstate defers the gain of $7,000 and reduces the basis of the semi-truck. Illustration 10-15 shows two different but acceptable computations to illustrate this reduction.

Fair value of semi-truck	$60,000		Book value of used trucks	$42,000
Less: Gain deferred	7,000	OR	Plus: Cash paid	11,000
Basis of semi-truck	$53,000		Basis of semi-truck	$53,000

ILLUSTRATION 10-15
Basis of Semi-Truck—Fair Value vs. Book Value

Interstate records this transaction as follows.

Trucks (semi)	53,000	
Accumulated Depreciation—Trucks	22,000	
Trucks (used)		64,000
Cash		11,000

If the exchange lacks commercial substance, the company recognizes the gain (reflected in the basis of the semi-truck) through lower depreciation expense or when it later sells the semi-truck, not at the time of the exchange.

Lacks Commercial Substance—Some Cash Received. When a company receives cash (sometimes referred to as "boot") in an exchange that lacks commercial substance, it must immediately recognize a portion of the gain.[9] Illustration 10-16 shows the general formula for gain recognition when an exchange includes some cash.

$$\frac{\text{Cash Received (Boot)}}{\text{Cash Received (Boot)} + \text{Fair Value of Other Assets Received}} \times \text{Total Gain} = \frac{\text{Recognized}}{\text{Gain}}$$

ILLUSTRATION 10-16
Formula for Gain Recognition, Some Cash Received

To illustrate, assume that Queenan Corporation traded in used machinery with a book value of $60,000 (cost $110,000 less accumulated depreciation $50,000) and a fair value of $100,000. It receives in exchange a machine with a fair value of $90,000 plus cash of $10,000. Illustration 10-17 shows calculation of the total gain on the exchange.

Fair value of machine given up	$100,000
Less: Book value of machine given up	60,000
Total gain	$ 40,000

ILLUSTRATION 10-17
Computation of Total Gain

Generally, when a transaction lacks commercial substance, a company defers any gain. But because Queenan received $10,000 in cash, it recognizes a partial gain. The portion of the gain a company recognizes is the ratio of monetary assets (cash in this case) to the total consideration received. Queenan computes the partial gain as follows.

$$\frac{\$10,000}{\$10,000 + \$90,000} \times \$40,000 = \$4,000$$

ILLUSTRATION 10-18
Computation of Gain Based on Ratio of Cash Received to Total Consideration Received

[9]When the monetary consideration is significant, i.e., **25 percent or more** of the fair value of the exchange, both parties consider the transaction a **monetary exchange**. Such "monetary" exchanges rely on the fair values to measure the gains or losses that are recognized in their entirety. **[6]**

Because Queenan recognizes only a gain of $4,000 on this transaction, it defers the remaining $36,000 ($40,000 − $4,000) and reduces the basis (recorded cost) of the new machine. Illustration 10-19 shows the computation of the basis.

ILLUSTRATION 10-19
Computation of Basis

Fair value of new machine	$90,000		Book value of old machine	$60,000
Less: Gain deferred	36,000	OR	Less: Portion of book value presumed sold	6,000*
Basis of new machine	$54,000		Basis of new machine	$54,000

$$*\frac{\$10,000}{\$100,000} \times \$60,000 = \$6,000$$

Queenan records the transaction with the following entry.

Cash	10,000	
Machinery (new)	54,000	
Accumulated Depreciation—Machinery	50,000	
Machinery (old)		110,000
Gain on Disposal of Machinery		4,000

The rationale for the treatment of a partial gain is as follows. Before a nonmonetary exchange that includes some cash, a company has an unrecognized gain, which is the difference between the book value and the fair value of the old asset. When the exchange occurs, a portion of the fair value is converted to a more liquid asset. The ratio of this liquid asset to the total consideration received is the portion of the total gain that the company realizes. Thus, the company recognizes and records that amount.

Illustration 10-20 presents in summary form the accounting requirements for recognizing gains and losses on exchanges of nonmonetary assets.[10]

ILLUSTRATION 10-20
Summary of Gain and Loss Recognition on Exchanges of Nonmonetary Assets

1. Compute the total gain or loss on the transaction. This amount is equal to the difference between the fair value of the asset given up and the book value of the asset given up.
2. If a loss is computed in step 1, always recognize the entire loss.
3. If a gain is computed in step 1,
    (a) and the exchange has commercial substance, recognize the entire gain.
    (b) and the exchange lacks commercial substance,
        (1) and no cash is involved, no gain is recognized.
        (2) and some cash is given, no gain is recognized.
        (3) and some cash is received, the following portion of the gain is recognized:

$$\frac{\text{Cash Received (Boot)}}{\text{Cash Received (Boot)} + \text{Fair Value of Other Assets Received}} \times \text{Total Gain}^*$$

*If the amount of cash exchanged is 25% or more, both parties recognize entire gain or loss.

Companies disclose in their financial statements nonmonetary exchanges during a period. Such disclosure indicates the nature of the transaction(s), the method of accounting for the assets exchanged, and gains or losses recognized on the exchanges. **[7]**

[10]Adapted from an article by Robert Capettini and Thomas E. King, "Exchanges of Nonmonetary Assets: Some Changes," *The Accounting Review* (January 1976).

In a press release, Roy Olofson, former vice president of finance for Global Crossing, accused company executives of improperly describing the company's revenue to the public. He said the company had improperly recorded long-term sales immediately rather than over the term of the contract, had improperly booked as cash transactions swaps of capacity with other carriers, and had fired him when he blew the whistle.

The accounting for the swaps involves exchanges of similar network capacity. Companies have said they engage in such deals because swapping is quicker and less costly than building segments of their own networks, or because such pacts provide redundancies to make their own networks more reliable. In one expert's view, an exchange of similar network capacity is the equivalent of trading a blue truck for a red truck—it shouldn't boost a company's revenue.

But Global Crossing and Qwest, among others, counted as revenue the money received from the other company in the swap. (In general, in transactions involving leased capacity, the companies booked the revenue over the life of the contract.) Some of these companies then treated their own purchases as capital expenditures, which were not run through the income statement. Instead, the spending led to the addition of assets on the balance sheet (and an inflated bottom line).

The SEC questioned some of these capacity exchanges, because it appeared they were a device to pad revenue. This reaction was not surprising, since revenue growth was a key factor in the valuation of companies such as Global Crossing and Qwest during the craze for tech stocks in the late 1990s and 2000.

Source: Adapted from Henny Sender, "Telecoms Draw Focus for Moves in Accounting," *Wall Street Journal* (March 26, 2002), p. C7.

Accounting for Contributions

Companies sometimes receive or make contributions (donations or gifts). Such contributions, nonreciprocal transfers, transfer assets in one direction. A contribution is often some type of asset (such as cash, securities, land, buildings, or use of facilities), but it also could be the forgiveness of a debt.

When companies acquire assets as donations, a strict cost concept dictates that the valuation of the asset should be zero. However, a departure from the historical cost principle seems justified; the only costs incurred (legal fees and other relatively minor expenditures) are not a reasonable basis of accounting for the assets acquired. To record nothing is to ignore the economic realities of an increase in wealth and assets. Therefore, companies use the **fair value of the asset** to establish its value on the books.

What then is the proper accounting for the credit in this transaction? Some believe the credit should be made to Donated Capital (an additional paid-in capital account). This approach views the increase in assets from a donation as contributed capital, rather than as earned revenue.

International Perspective

IFRS provides detailed guidance on how to account for contributions and government grants.

Others argue that companies should report donations as revenues from contributions. Their reasoning is that only the owners of a business contribute capital. At issue in this approach is whether the company should report revenue immediately or over the period that the asset is employed. For example, to attract new industry a city may offer land, but the receiving enterprise may incur additional costs in the future (e.g., transportation or higher state income taxes) because the location is not the most desirable. As a consequence, some argue that the company should defer the revenue and recognize it as the costs are incurred.

The FASB's position is that **in general, companies should recognize contributions received as revenues in the period received. [8]**[11] Companies measure contributions at the fair value of the assets received. **[9]** To illustrate, Max Wayer Meat Packing, Inc. has

---

[11]GAAP is silent on how to account for the transfers of assets from governmental units to business enterprises. However, we believe that the basic requirements should hold also for these types of contributions. Therefore, companies should record all assets at fair value and all credits as revenue.

recently accepted a donation of land with a fair value of $150,000 from the Memphis Industrial Development Corp. In return, Max Wayer Meat Packing promises to build a packing plant in Memphis. Max Wayer's entry is:

Land	150,000	
Contribution Revenue		150,000

When a company contributes a nonmonetary asset, it should record the amount of the donation as an expense at the fair value of the donated asset. If a difference exists between the fair value of the asset and its book value, the company should recognize a gain or loss. To illustrate, Kline Industries donates land to the city of Los Angeles for a city park. The land cost $80,000 and has a fair value of $110,000. Kline Industries records this donation as follows.

Contribution Expense	110,000	
Land		80,000
Gain on Disposal of Land		30,000

In some cases, companies promise to give (pledge) some type of asset in the future. Should companies record this promise immediately or when they give the assets? If the promise is **unconditional** (depends only on the passage of time or on demand by the recipient for performance), the company should report the contribution expense and related payable immediately. If the promise is **conditional**, the company recognizes expense in the period benefited by the contribution, generally when it transfers the asset.

Other Asset Valuation Methods

The exception to the historical cost principle for assets acquired through donation is based on fair value. Another exception is the prudent cost concept. This concept states that if for some reason a company ignorantly paid too much for an asset originally, it is theoretically preferable to charge a loss immediately.

For example, assume that a company constructs an asset at a cost much greater than its present economic usefulness. It would be appropriate to charge these excess costs as a loss to the current period, rather than capitalize them as part of the cost of the asset. In practice, the need to use the prudent cost approach seldom develops. Companies typically either use good reasoning in paying a given price or fail to recognize that they have overpaid.

What happens, on the other hand, if a company makes a bargain purchase or internally constructs a piece of equipment at a cost savings? Such savings should not result in immediate recognition of a gain under any circumstances.

COSTS SUBSEQUENT TO ACQUISITION

LEARNING OBJECTIVE 6

Describe the accounting treatment for costs subsequent to acquisition.

After installing plant assets and readying them for use, a company incurs additional costs that range from ordinary repairs to significant additions. The major problem is allocating these costs to the proper time periods. **In general, costs incurred to achieve greater future benefits should be capitalized, whereas expenditures that simply maintain a given level of services should be expensed.** In order to capitalize costs, one of three conditions must be present:

1. The useful life of the asset must be increased.
2. The quantity of units produced from the asset must be increased.
3. The quality of the units produced must be enhanced.

For example, a company like Boeing should expense expenditures that do not increase an asset's future benefits. That is, it expenses immediately ordinary repairs that maintain the existing condition of the asset or restore it to normal operating efficiency.

Companies expense most expenditures below an established arbitrary minimum amount, say, $100 or $500. Although conceptually this treatment may be incorrect, expediency demands it. Otherwise, companies would set up depreciation schedules for an item such as a wastepaper basket.

The distinction between a **capital expenditure (asset)** and a **revenue expenditure (expense)** is not always clear-cut. Yet, in most cases, **consistent application of a capital/expense policy** is more important than attempting to provide general theoretical guidelines for each transaction. Generally, companies incur four major types of expenditures relative to existing assets.

Underlying Concepts 🔍

Expensing long-lived wastepaper baskets is an application of the materiality concept.

MAJOR TYPES OF EXPENDITURES

ADDITIONS. Increase or extension of existing assets.

IMPROVEMENTS AND REPLACEMENTS. Substitution of an improved asset for an existing one.

REARRANGEMENT AND REINSTALLATION. Movement of assets from one location to another.

REPAIRS. Expenditures that maintain assets in condition for operation.

What do the numbers mean?   DISCONNECTED

It all started with a check of the books by an internal auditor for WorldCom Inc. The telecom giant's newly installed chief executive had asked for a financial review, and the auditor was spot-checking records of capital expenditures. She found the company was using an unorthodox technique to account for one of its biggest expenses: charges paid to local telephone networks to complete long-distance calls.

Instead of recording these charges as operating expenses, WorldCom recorded a significant portion as capital expenditures. The maneuver was worth hundreds of millions of dollars to WorldCom's bottom line. It effectively turned a loss for all of 2001 and the first quarter of 2002 into a profit. The graph below compares WorldCom's accounting to that under GAAP. Soon after this discovery, WorldCom filed for bankruptcy.

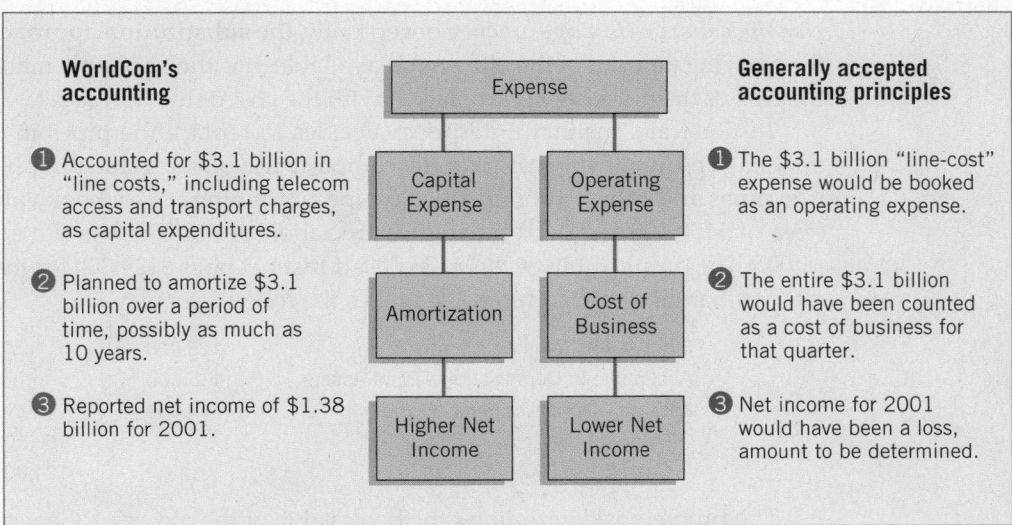

Source: Adapted from Jared Sandberg, Deborah Solomon, and Rebecca Blumenstein, "Inside WorldCom's Unearthing of a Vast Accounting Scandal," *Wall Street Journal* (June 27, 2002), p. A1.

Additions

Additions should present no major accounting problems. By definition, **companies capitalize any addition to plant assets because a new asset is created**. For example, the addition of a wing to a hospital, or of an air conditioning system to an office, increases the service potential of that facility. Companies should capitalize such expenditures and match them against the revenues that will result in future periods.

One problem that arises in this area is the accounting for any changes related to the existing structure as a result of the addition. Is the cost incurred to tear down an old wall, to make room for the addition, a cost of the addition or an expense or loss of the period? The answer is that it depends on the original intent. If the company had anticipated building an addition later, then this cost of removal is a proper cost of the addition. But if the company had not anticipated this development, it should properly report the removal as a loss in the current period on the basis of inefficient planning. Normally, the company retains the carrying amount of the old wall in the accounts, although theoretically the company should remove it.

Improvements and Replacements

Companies substitute one asset for another through **improvements** and **replacements**. What is the difference between an improvement and a replacement? An **improvement** (**betterment**) is the substitution of a **better asset** for the one currently used (say, a concrete floor for a wooden floor). A **replacement**, on the other hand, is the substitution of a **similar asset** (a wooden floor for a wooden floor).

Many times improvements and replacements result from a general policy to modernize or rehabilitate an older building or piece of equipment. The problem is differentiating these types of expenditures from normal repairs. Does the expenditure increase the **future service potential** of the asset? Or does it merely **maintain the existing level** of service? Frequently, the answer is not clear-cut. Good judgment is required to correctly classify these expenditures.

If the expenditure increases the future service potential of the asset, a company should capitalize it. The accounting is therefore handled in one of three ways, depending on the circumstances:

1. *Use the substitution approach.* Conceptually, the **substitution approach** is correct if the carrying amount of the old asset is available. It is then a simple matter to remove the cost of the old asset and replace it with the cost of the new asset.

   To illustrate, Instinct Enterprises decides to replace the pipes in its plumbing system. A plumber suggests that the company use plastic tubing in place of the cast iron pipes and copper tubing. The old pipe and tubing have a book value of $15,000 (cost of $150,000 less accumulated depreciation of $135,000), and a scrap value of $1,000. The plastic tubing costs $125,000. If Instinct pays $124,000 for the new tubing after exchanging the old tubing, it makes the following entry:

Plant Assets (plumbing system)	125,000	
Accumulated Depreciation—Plant Assets	135,000	
Loss on Disposal of Plant Assets	14,000	
Plant Assets		150,000
Cash ($125,000 − $1,000)		124,000

   The problem is determining the book value of the old asset. Generally, the components of a given asset depreciate at different rates. However, generally no separate accounting is made. For example, the tires, motor, and body of a truck depreciate at different rates, but most companies use one rate for the entire truck. Companies can set separate depreciation rates, but it is often impractical. If a company cannot determine the carrying amount of the old asset, it adopts one of two other approaches.

2. *Capitalize the new cost.* Another approach capitalizes the improvement and keeps the carrying amount of the old asset on the books. The justification for this approach is that the item is sufficiently depreciated to reduce its carrying amount almost to zero. Although this assumption may not always be true, the differences are often insignificant. Companies usually handle improvements in this manner.

3. *Charge to accumulated depreciation.* In cases when a company does not improve the quantity or quality of the asset itself but instead extends its useful life, the company debits the expenditure to Accumulated Depreciation rather than to an asset account. The theory behind this approach is that the replacement extends the useful life of the asset and thereby recaptures some or all of the past depreciation. The net carrying amount of the asset is the same whether debiting the asset or accumulated depreciation.

Rearrangement and Reinstallation

Companies incur **rearrangement and reinstallation costs** to benefit future periods. An example is the rearrangement and reinstallation of machines to facilitate future production.

If a company like **The Coca-Cola Company** can determine or estimate the original installation cost and the accumulated depreciation to date, it handles the rearrangement and reinstallation cost as a replacement. If not, which is generally the case, Coca-Cola should capitalize the new costs (if material in amount) as an asset to be amortized over future periods expected to benefit. If these costs are immaterial, if they cannot be separated from other operating expenses, or if their future benefit is questionable, the company should immediately expense them.

Repairs

A company makes **ordinary repairs** to maintain plant assets in operating condition. It charges ordinary repairs to an expense account in the period incurred, on the basis that **it is the primary period benefited**. Maintenance charges that occur regularly include replacing minor parts, lubricating and adjusting equipment, repainting, and cleaning. A company treats these as ordinary operating expenses.

It is often difficult to distinguish a repair from an improvement or replacement. The major consideration is whether the expenditure benefits more than one year or one operating cycle, whichever is longer. If a **major repair** (such as an overhaul) occurs, several periods will benefit. A company should handle the cost as an addition, improvement, or replacement.[12]

An interesting question is whether a company can accrue planned maintenance overhaul costs *before* the actual costs are incurred. For example, assume that **Southwest Airlines** schedules major overhauls of its planes every three years. Should Southwest be permitted to accrue these costs and related liability over the three-year period? Some argue that this accrue-in-advance approach better matches expenses to revenues and reports Southwest's obligation for these costs. However, reporting a liability is inappropriate. To whom does Southwest owe? In other words, Southwest has no obligation to an outside party until it has to pay for the overhaul costs, and therefore it has no liability. As a result, companies are not permitted to accrue in advance for planned major overhaul costs either for interim or annual periods. **[10]**

---

[12]A committee of the AICPA has proposed (see footnote 2) that companies expense as incurred costs involved for planned major expenditures unless they represent an *additional* component or the *replacement* of an existing component.

Summary of Costs Subsequent to Acquisition

Illustration 10-21 summarizes the accounting treatment for various costs incurred subsequent to the acquisition of capitalized assets.

ILLUSTRATION 10-21
Summary of Costs
Subsequent to
Acquisition of Property,
Plant, and Equipment

Type of Expenditure	Normal Accounting Treatment
Additions	Capitalize cost of addition to asset account.
Improvements and replacements	(a) **Carrying value known:** Remove cost of and accumulated depreciation on old asset, recognizing any gain or loss. Capitalize cost of improvement/ replacement. (b) **Carrying value unknown:** 1. If the asset's useful life is extended, debit accumulated depreciation for cost of improvement/replacement. 2. If the quantity or quality of the asset's productivity is increased, capitalize cost of improvement/replacement to asset account.
Rearrangement and reinstallation	(a) If original installation cost is **known**, account for cost of rearrangement/ reinstallation as a replacement (carrying value known). (b) If original installation cost is **unknown** and rearrangement/reinstallation cost is **material** in amount and benefits future periods, capitalize as an asset. (c) If original installation cost is **unknown** and rearrangement/reinstallation cost is **not material or future benefit is questionable**, expense the cost when incurred.
Repairs	(a) **Ordinary:** Expense cost of repairs when incurred. (b) **Major:** As appropriate, treat as an addition, improvement, or replacement.

DISPOSITION OF PROPERTY, PLANT, AND EQUIPMENT

LEARNING OBJECTIVE 7

Describe the accounting treatment for the disposal of property, plant, and equipment.

A company, like Intel, may retire plant assets voluntarily or dispose of them by sale, exchange, involuntary conversion, or abandonment. Regardless of the type of disposal, depreciation must be taken up to the date of disposition. Then, Intel should remove all accounts related to the retired asset. Generally, the book value of the specific plant asset does not equal its disposal value. As a result, a gain or loss develops. The reason: Depreciation is an estimate of cost allocation and not a process of valuation. **The gain or loss is really a correction of net income** for the years during which Intel used the fixed asset.

Intel should show gains or losses on the disposal of plant assets in the income statement along with other items from customary business activities. However, if it sold, abandoned, spun off, or otherwise disposed of the "operations of a component of a business," then it should report the results separately in the discontinued operations section of the income statement (as discussed in Chapter 4). That is, Intel should report any gain or loss from disposal of a business component with the related results of discontinued operations.

Sale of Plant Assets

Companies record depreciation for the period of time between the date of the last depreciation entry and the date of sale. To illustrate, assume that Barret Company recorded depreciation on a machine costing $18,000 for 9 years at the rate of $1,200 per year. If it sells the machine in the middle of the tenth year for $7,000, Barret records depreciation to the date of sale as:

Depreciation Expense ($1,200 × $\frac{1}{2}$)	600	
Accumulated Depreciation—Machinery		600

The entry for the sale of the asset then is:

Cash	7,000	
Accumulated Depreciation—Machinery	11,400	
[($1,200 × 9) + $600]		
Machinery		18,000
Gain on Disposal of Machinery		400

The book value of the machinery at the time of the sale is $6,600 ($18,000 − $11,400). Because the machinery sold for $7,000, the amount of the gain on the sale is $400.

Involuntary Conversion

Sometimes an asset's service is terminated through some type of **involuntary conversion** such as fire, flood, theft, or condemnation. Companies report the difference between the amount recovered (e.g., from a condemnation award or insurance recovery), if any, and the asset's book value as a gain or loss. They treat these gains or losses like any other type of disposition. In some cases, these gains or losses may be reported as extraordinary items in the income statement **if the conditions of the disposition are unusual and infrequent in nature**.

To illustrate, Camel Transport Corp. had to sell a plant located on company property that stood directly in the path of an interstate highway. For a number of years, the state had sought to purchase the land on which the plant stood, but the company resisted. The state ultimately exercised its right of eminent domain, which the courts upheld. In settlement, Camel received $500,000, which substantially exceeded the $200,000 book value of the plant and land (cost of $400,000 less accumulated depreciation of $200,000). Camel made the following entry.

Cash	500,000	
Accumulated Depreciation—Plant Assets	200,000	
Plant Assets		400,000
Gain on Disposal of Plant Assets		300,000

If the conditions surrounding the condemnation are judged to be unusual and infrequent, Camel's gain of $300,000 is reported as an extraordinary item.

Some object to the recognition of a gain or loss in certain *involuntary* conversions. For example, the federal government often condemns forests for national parks. The paper companies that owned these forests must report a gain or loss on the condemnation. However, companies such as **Georgia-Pacific** contend that no gain or loss should be reported because they must replace the condemned forest land immediately and so are in the same economic position as they were before. The issue is whether condemnation and subsequent purchase should be viewed as one or two transactions. GAAP requires "that a gain or loss be recognized when a nonmonetary asset is involuntarily converted to monetary assets even though an enterprise reinvests or is obligated to reinvest the monetary assets in replacement nonmonetary assets." **[11]**

Miscellaneous Problems

If a company scraps or abandons an asset without any cash recovery, it recognizes a loss equal to the asset's book value. If scrap value exists, the gain or loss that occurs is the difference between the asset's scrap value and its book value. If an asset still can be used even though it is fully depreciated, it may be kept on the books at historical cost less depreciation.

Companies must disclose in notes to the financial statements the amount of fully depreciated assets in service. For example, **Petroleum Equipment Tools Inc.** in its annual report disclosed, "The amount of fully depreciated assets included in property, plant, and equipment at December 31 amounted to approximately $98,900,000."

KEY TERMS

additions, *558*

avoidable interest, *542*

capital expenditure, *557*

capitalization period, *542*

commercial
 substance, *550*

fixed assets, *538*

historical cost, *538*

improvements
 (betterments), *558*

involuntary
 conversion, *561*

lump-sum price, *548*

major repairs, *559*

nonmonetary assets, *550*

nonreciprocal
 transfers, *555*

ordinary repairs, *559*

plant assets, *538*

property, plant, and
 equipment, *538*

prudent cost, *556*

rearrangement and
 reinstallation costs, *559*

replacements, *558*

revenue expenditure, *557*

self-constructed asset, *540*

weighted-average
 accumulated
 expenditures, *543*

SUMMARY OF LEARNING OBJECTIVES

1 Describe property, plant, and equipment. The major characteristics of property, plant, and equipment are as follows. (1) They are acquired for use in operations and not for resale. (2) They are long-term in nature and usually subject to depreciation. (3) They possess physical substance.

2 Identify the costs to include in initial valuation of property, plant, and equipment. The costs included in initial valuation of property, plant, and equipment are as follows.

Cost of land: Includes all expenditures made to acquire land and to ready it for use. Land costs typically include (1) the purchase price; (2) closing costs, such as title to the land, attorney's fees, and recording fees; (3) costs incurred in getting the land in condition for its intended use, such as grading, filling, draining, and clearing; (4) assumption of any liens, mortgages, or encumbrances on the property; and (5) any additional land improvements that have an indefinite life.

Cost of buildings: Includes all expenditures related directly to their acquisition or construction. These costs include (1) materials, labor, and overhead costs incurred during construction, and (2) professional fees and building permits.

Cost of equipment: Includes the purchase price, freight and handling charges incurred, insurance on the equipment while in transit, cost of special foundations if required, assembling and installation costs, and costs of conducting trial runs.

3 Describe the accounting problems associated with self-constructed assets. Indirect costs of manufacturing create special problems because companies cannot easily trace these costs directly to work and material orders related to the constructed assets. Companies might handle these costs in one of two ways. (1) Assign no fixed overhead to the cost of the constructed asset, or (2) assign a portion of all overhead to the construction process. Companies use the second method extensively.

4 Describe the accounting problems associated with interest capitalization. Only actual interest (with modifications) should be capitalized. The rationale for this approach is that during construction, the asset is not generating revenue and therefore companies should defer (capitalize) interest cost. Once construction is completed, the asset is ready for its intended use and revenues can be recognized. Any interest cost incurred in purchasing an asset that is ready for its intended use should be expensed.

5 Understand accounting issues related to acquiring and valuing plant assets. The following issues relate to acquiring and valuing plant assets. (1) *Cash discounts:* Whether taken or not, they are generally considered a reduction in the cost of the asset; the real cost of the asset is the cash or cash equivalent price of the asset. (2) *Deferred-payment contracts:* Companies account for assets purchased on long-term credit contracts at the present value of the consideration exchanged between the contracting parties. (3) *Lump-sum purchase:* Allocate the total cost among the various assets on the basis of their relative fair values. (4) *Issuance of stock:* If the stock is actively traded, the market price of the stock issued is a fair indication of the cost of the property acquired. If the market price of the common stock exchanged is not determinable, establish the fair value of the property and use it as the basis for recording the asset and issuance of the common stock. (5) *Exchanges of nonmonetary assets*: The accounting for exchanges of nonmonetary assets depends on whether the exchange has commercial substance. See Illustrations 10-10 (page 551) and 10-20 (page 554) for summaries of how to account for exchanges. (6) *Contributions:* Record at the fair value of the asset received, and credit revenue for the same amount.

6 **Describe the accounting treatment for costs subsequent to acquisition.** Illustration 10-21 (page 560) summarizes how to account for costs subsequent to acquisition.

7 **Describe the accounting treatment for the disposal of property, plant, and equipment.** Regardless of the time of disposal, companies take depreciation up to the date of disposition and then remove all accounts related to the retired asset. Gains or losses on the retirement of plant assets are shown in the income statement along with other items that arise from customary business activities. Gains or losses on involuntary conversions, if unusual and infrequent, may be reported as extraordinary items.

DEMONSTRATION PROBLEM

Columbia Company, which manufactures machine tools, had the following transactions related to plant assets in 2014.

Asset A: On June 2, 2014, Columbia purchased a stamping machine at a retail price of $12,000. Columbia paid 6% sales tax on this purchase. Columbia paid a contractor $2,800 for a specially wired platform for the machine, to ensure noninterrupted power to the machine. Columbia estimates the machine will have a 4-year useful life, with a salvage value of $2,000 at the end of 4 years. The machine was put into use on July 1, 2014.

Asset B: On January 1, 2014, Columbia, Inc. signed a fixed-price contract for construction of a warehouse facility at a cost of $1,000,000. It was estimated that the project will be completed by December 31, 2014. On March 1, 2014, to finance the construction cost, Columbia borrowed $1,000,000 payable April 1, 2015, plus interest at the rate of 10%. During 2014, Columbia made deposit and progress payments totaling $750,000 under the contract; the weighted-average amount of accumulated expenditures was $400,000 for the year. The excess-borrowed funds were invested in short-term securities, from which Columbia realized investment revenue of $13,000. The warehouse was completed on December 1, 2014, at which time Columbia made the final payment to the contractor. Columbia estimates the warehouse will have a 25-year useful life, with a salvage value of $20,000.

Columbia uses straight-line depreciation and employs the "half-year" convention in accounting for partial-year depreciation. Columbia's fiscal year ends on December 31.

Instructions

(a) At what amount should Columbia record the acquisition cost of the machine?
(b) What amount of capitalized interest should Columbia include in the cost of the warehouse?
(c) On July 1, 2016, Columbia decides to outsource its stamping operation to Medek, Inc. As part of this plan, Columbia sells the machine (and the platform) to Medek, Inc. for $7,000. What is the impact of this disposal on Columbia's 2016 income before taxes?

Solution

(a) Historical cost is measured by the cash or cash equivalent price of obtaining the asset and bringing it to the location and condition for its intended use. For Columbia, this is:

Price	$12,000
Tax ($12,000 × .06)	720
Platform	2,800
Total	$15,520

(b) $40,000 ($400,000 × .10)—Weighted-Average Accumulated Expenditures × Interest Rate = Avoidable Interest

Since Columbia has outstanding debt incurred specifically for the construction project, in an amount greater than the weighted-average accumulated expenditures of $400,000, the interest rate of 10% is used for capitalization purposes. Capitalization stops upon completion of the project at December 31, 2014. Therefore, the avoidable interest is $40,000, which is less than the actual interest. The investment revenue of $13,000 is irrelevant to the question addressed in this problem because such interest earned on the unexpended portion of the loan is not to be offset against the amount eligible for capitalization.

(c) The income effect is a gain or loss, determined by comparing the book value of the asset to the disposal value:

Cost	$15,520
Less: Accumulated depreciation	
($1,690 + $3,380 + $1,690)	6,760*
Book value of machine and platform	8,760
Less: Cash received for machine and platform	7,000
Loss before income taxes	$ 1,760

*Depreciable base: $15,520 − $2,000 = $13,520. Depreciation expense: $13,520 ÷ 4 = $3,380 per year.

2014: ½ year ($3,380 × .50)		$1,690
2015: full year		3,380
2016: ½ year		1,690
Total		$6,760

FASB CODIFICATION

FASB Codification References

[1] FASB ASC 360-10-35-43. [Predecessor literature: "Accounting for the Impairment or Disposal of Long-lived Assets," *Statement of Financial Accounting Standards No. 144* (Norwalk, Conn.: FASB, 2001), par. 34.]

[2] FASB ASC 835-20-05. [Predecessor literature: "Capitalization of Interest Cost," *Statement of Financial Accounting Standards No. 34* (Stamford, Conn.: FASB, 1979).]

[3] FASB ASC 835-20-15-4. [Predecessor literature: "Determining Materiality for Capitalization of Interest Cost," *Statement of Financial Accounting Standards No. 42* (Stamford, Conn.: FASB, 1980), par. 10.]

[4] FASB ASC 820-10-35. [Predecessor literature: "(Predecessor literature: "Fair Value Measurement," *Statement of Financial Accounting Standards No. 157* (Norwalk, Conn.: FASB, September 2006), paras. 13–18.]

[5] FASB ASC 845-10-30. [Predecessor literature: "Accounting for Nonmonetary Transactions," *Opinions of the Accounting Principles Board No. 29* (New York: AICPA, 1973), par. 18, and "Exchanges of Nonmonetary Assets, an Amendment of *APB Opinion No. 29*," *Statement of Financial Accounting Standards No. 153* (Norwalk, Conn.: FASB, 2004).]

[6] FASB ASC 845-10-25-6. [Predecessor literature: "Interpretations of *APB Opinion No. 29*," EITF Abstracts No. 01-02 (Norwalk, Conn.: FASB, 2002).]

[7] FASB ASC 845-10-50-1. [Predecessor literature: "Accounting for Nonmonetary Transactions," *Opinions of the Accounting Principles Board No. 29* (New York: AICPA, 1973), par. 28, and "Exchanges of Nonmonetary Assets, an Amendment of *APB Opinion No. 29*," *Statement of Financial Accounting Standards No. 153* (Norwalk, Conn.: FASB, 2004).]

[8] FASB ASC 958-605-25-2. [Predecessor literature: "Accounting for Contributions Received and Contributions Made," *Statement of Financial Accounting Standards No. 116* (Norwalk, Conn.: FASB, 1993).]

[9] FASB ASC 845-10-30. [Predecessor literature: "Accounting for Nonmonetary Transactions," *Opinions of the Accounting Principles Board No. 29* (New York: AICPA, 1973), par. 18, and "Exchanges of Nonmonetary Assets, an Amendment of *APB Opinion No. 29*," *Statement of Financial Accounting Standards No. 153* (Norwalk, Conn.: FASB, 2004).]

[10] FASB ASC 360-10-25-5. [Predecessor literature: "Accounting for Planned Major Maintenance Activities," FASB Staff Position AUG-AIR-1 (Norwalk, Conn.: FASB, September 2006), par. 5.]

[11] FASB ASC 605-40-25-2. [Predecessor literature: "Accounting for Involuntary Conversions of Nonmonetary Assets to Monetary Assets," *FASB Interpretation No. 30* (Stamford, Conn.: FASB, 1979), summary paragraph.]

Exercises

If your school has a subscription to the FASB Codification, go to *http://aaahq.org/asclogin.cfm* to log in and prepare responses to the following. Provide Codification references for your responses.

CE10-1 Access the glossary ("Master Glossary") to answer the following.

(a) What does it mean to "capitalize" an item?

(b) What is the definition of a nonmonetary asset?

(c) What is a nonreciprocal transfer?

(d) What is the definition of "contribution"?

CE10-2 Herb Scholl, the owner of Scholl's Company, wonders whether interest costs associated with developing land can ever be capitalized. What does the Codification say on this matter?

CE10-3 What guidance does the Codification provide on the accrual of costs associated with planned major maintenance activities?

CE10-4 Briefly describe how the purchases and sales of inventory with the same counterparty are similar to the accounting for other nonmonetary exchanges.

An additional Codification case can be found in the Using Your Judgment section, on page 586.

Be sure to check the book's companion website for a Review and Analysis Exercise, with solution.

WileyPLUS Brief Exercises, Exercises, Problems, and many more learning and assessment tools and resources are available for practice in WileyPLUS.

QUESTIONS

1. What are the major characteristics of plant assets?

2. Mickelson Inc. owns land that it purchased on January 1, 2000, for $450,000. At December 31, 2014, its current value is $770,000 as determined by appraisal. At what amount should Mickelson report this asset on its December 31, 2014, balance sheet? Explain.

3. Name the items, in addition to the amount paid to the former owner or contractor, that may properly be included as part of the acquisition cost of the following plant assets.

(a) Land.

(b) Machinery and equipment.

(c) Buildings.

4. Indicate where the following items would be shown on a balance sheet.

(a) A lien that was attached to the land when purchased.

(b) Landscaping costs.

(c) Attorney's fees and recording fees related to purchasing land.

(d) Variable overhead related to construction of machinery.

(e) A parking lot servicing employees in the building.

(f) Cost of temporary building for workers during construction of building.

(g) Interest expense on bonds payable incurred during construction of a building.

(h) Assessments for sidewalks that are maintained by the city.

(i) The cost of demolishing an old building that was on the land when purchased.

5. Two positions have normally been taken with respect to the recording of fixed manufacturing overhead as an element of the cost of plant assets constructed by a company for its own use:

(a) It should be excluded completely.

(b) It should be included at the same rate as is charged to normal operations.

What are the circumstances or rationale that support or deny the application of these methods?

6. The Buildings account of Postera Inc. includes the following items that were used in determining the basis for depreciating the cost of a building.

(a) Organization and promotion expenses.

(b) Architect's fees.

(c) Interest and taxes during construction.

(d) Interest revenue on investments held to fund construction of a building.

Do you agree with these charges? If not, how would you deal with each of the items above in the corporation's books and in its annual financial statements?

7. Burke Company has purchased two tracts of land. One tract will be the site of its new manufacturing plant, while the other is being purchased with the hope that it will be sold in the next year at a profit. How should these two tracts of land be reported in the balance sheet?

8. One financial accounting issue encountered when a company constructs its own plant is whether the interest cost on funds borrowed to finance construction should be capitalized and then amortized over the life of the assets constructed. What is the justification for capitalizing such interest?

9. Provide examples of assets that do not qualify for interest capitalization.

10. What interest rates should be used in determining the amount of interest to be capitalized? How should the amount of interest to be capitalized be determined?

11. How should the amount of interest capitalized be disclosed in the notes to the financial statements? How should interest revenue from temporarily invested excess funds borrowed to finance the construction of assets be accounted for?

12. Discuss the basic accounting problem that arises in handling each of the following situations.

  (a) Assets purchased by issuance of common stock.

  (b) Acquisition of plant assets by gift or donation.

  (c) Purchase of a plant asset subject to a cash discount.

  (d) Assets purchased on a long-term credit basis.

  (e) A group of assets acquired for a lump sum.

  (f) An asset traded in or exchanged for another asset.

13. Magilke Industries acquired equipment this year to be used in its operations. The equipment was delivered by the suppliers, installed by Magilke, and placed into operation. Some of it was purchased for cash with discounts available for prompt payment. Some of it was purchased under long-term payment plans for which the interest charges approximated prevailing rates. What costs should Magilke capitalize for the new equipment purchased this year? Explain.

14. Schwartzkopf Co. purchased for $2,200,000 property that included both land and a building to be used in operations. The seller's book value was $300,000 for the land and $900,000 for the building. By appraisal, the fair value was estimated to be $500,000 for the land and $2,000,000 for the building. At what amount should Schwartzkopf report the land and the building at the end of the year?

15. Pueblo Co. acquires machinery by paying $10,000 cash and signing a $5,000, 2-year, zero-interest-bearing note payable. The note has a present value of $4,208, and Pueblo purchased a similar machine last month for $13,500. At what cost should the new equipment be recorded?

16. Stan Ott is evaluating two recent transactions involving exchanges of equipment. In one case, the exchange has commercial substance. In the second situation, the exchange lacks commercial substance. Explain to Stan the differences in accounting for these two situations.

17. Crowe Company purchased a heavy-duty truck on July 1, 2011, for $30,000. It was estimated that it would have a useful life of 10 years and then would have a trade-in value of $6,000. The company uses the straight-line method. It was traded on August 1, 2015, for a similar truck costing $42,000; $16,000 was allowed as trade-in value (also fair value) on the old truck and $26,000 was paid in cash. A comparison of expected cash flows for the trucks indicates the exchange lacks commercial substance. What is the entry to record the trade-in?

18. Once equipment has been installed and placed in operation, subsequent expenditures relating to this equipment are frequently thought of as repairs or general maintenance and, hence, chargeable to operations in the period in which the expenditure is made. Actually, determination of whether such an expenditure should be charged to operations or capitalized involves a much more careful analysis of the character of the expenditure. What are the factors that should be considered in making such a decision? Discuss fully.

19. What accounting treatment is normally given to the following items in accounting for plant assets?

  (a) Additions.

  (b) Major repairs.

  (c) Improvements and replacements.

20. New machinery, which replaced a number of employees, was installed and put in operation in the last month of the fiscal year. The employees had been dismissed after payment of an extra month's wages, and this amount was added to the cost of the machinery. Discuss the propriety of the charge. If it was improper, describe the proper treatment.

21. To what extent do you consider the following items to be proper costs of the fixed asset? Give reasons for your opinions.

  (a) Overhead of a business that builds its own equipment.

  (b) Cash discounts on purchases of equipment.

  (c) Interest paid during construction of a building.

  (d) Cost of a safety device installed on a machine.

  (e) Freight on equipment returned before installation, for replacement by other equipment of greater capacity.

  (f) Cost of moving machinery to a new location.

  (g) Cost of plywood partitions erected as part of the remodeling of the office.

  (h) Replastering of a section of the building.

  (i) Cost of a new motor for one of the trucks.

22. Neville Enterprises has a number of fully depreciated assets that are still being used in the main operations of the business. Because the assets are fully depreciated, the president of the company decides not to show them on the balance sheet or disclose this information in the notes. Evaluate this procedure.

23. What are the general rules for how gains or losses on retirement of plant assets should be reported in income?

BRIEF EXERCISES

2 **BE10-1** Previn Brothers Inc. purchased land at a price of $27,000. Closing costs were $1,400. An old building was removed at a cost of $10,200. What amount should be recorded as the cost of the land?

4 **BE10-2** Hanson Company is constructing a building. Construction began on February 1 and was completed on December 31. Expenditures were $1,800,000 on March 1, $1,200,000 on June 1, and $3,000,000 on December 31. Compute Hanson's weighted-average accumulated expenditures for interest capitalization purposes.

4 **BE10-3** Hanson Company (see BE10-2) borrowed $1,000,000 on March 1 on a 5-year, 12% note to help finance construction of the building. In addition, the company had outstanding all year a 10%, 5-year, $2,000,000 note payable and an 11%, 4-year, $3,500,000 note payable. Compute the weighted-average interest rate used for interest capitalization purposes.

4 **BE10-4** Use the information for Hanson Company from BE10-2 and BE10-3. Compute avoidable interest for Hanson Company.

5 **BE10-5** Garcia Corporation purchased a truck by issuing an $80,000, 4-year, zero-interest-bearing note to Equinox Inc. The market rate of interest for obligations of this nature is 10%. Prepare the journal entry to record the purchase of this truck.

5 **BE10-6** Mohave Inc. purchased land, building, and equipment from Laguna Corporation for a cash payment of $315,000. The estimated fair values of the assets are land $60,000, building $220,000, and equipment $80,000. At what amounts should each of the three assets be recorded?

5 **BE10-7** Fielder Company obtained land by issuing 2,000 shares of its $10 par value common stock. The land was recently appraised at $85,000. The common stock is actively traded at $40 per share. Prepare the journal entry to record the acquisition of the land.

5 **BE10-8** Navajo Corporation traded a used truck (cost $20,000, accumulated depreciation $18,000) for a small computer worth $3,300. Navajo also paid $500 in the transaction. Prepare the journal entry to record the exchange. (The exchange has commercial substance.)

5 **BE10-9** Use the information for Navajo Corporation from BE10-8. Prepare the journal entry to record the exchange, assuming the exchange lacks commercial substance.

5 **BE10-10** Mehta Company traded a used welding machine (cost $9,000, accumulated depreciation $3,000) for office equipment with an estimated fair value of $5,000. Mehta also paid $3,000 cash in the transaction. Prepare the journal entry to record the exchange. (The exchange has commercial substance.)

5 **BE10-11** Cheng Company traded a used truck for a new truck. The used truck cost $30,000 and has accumulated depreciation of $27,000. The new truck is worth $37,000. Cheng also made a cash payment of $36,000. Prepare Cheng's entry to record the exchange. (The exchange lacks commercial substance.)

5 **BE10-12** Slaton Corporation traded a used truck for a new truck. The used truck cost $20,000 and has accumulated depreciation of $17,000. The new truck is worth $35,000. Slaton also made a cash payment of $33,000. Prepare Slaton's entry to record the exchange. (The exchange has commercial substance.)

6 **BE10-13** Indicate which of the following costs should be expensed when incurred.

    (a) $13,000 paid to rearrange and reinstall machinery.
    (b) $200,000 paid for addition to building.
    (c) $200 paid for tune-up and oil change on delivery truck.
    (d) $7,000 paid to replace a wooden floor with a concrete floor.
    (e) $2,000 paid for a major overhaul on a truck, which extends the useful life.

7 **BE10-14** Ottawa Corporation owns machinery that cost $20,000 when purchased on July 1, 2011. Depreciation has been recorded at a rate of $2,400 per year, resulting in a balance in accumulated depreciation of $8,400 at December 31, 2014. The machinery is sold on September 1, 2015, for $10,500. Prepare journal entries to (a) update depreciation for 2015 and (b) record the sale.

7 **BE10-15** Use the information presented for Ottawa Corporation in BE10-14, but assume the machinery is sold for $5,200 instead of $10,500. Prepare journal entries to (a) update depreciation for 2015 and (b) record the sale.

EXERCISES

2 **E10-1 (Acquisition Costs of Realty)** The following expenditures and receipts are related to land, land improvements, and buildings acquired for use in a business enterprise. The receipts are enclosed in parentheses.

(a)	Money borrowed to pay building contractor (signed a note)	$(275,000)
(b)	Payment for construction from note proceeds	275,000
(c)	Cost of land fill and clearing	8,000
(d)	Delinquent real estate taxes on property assumed by purchaser	7,000
(e)	Premium on 6-month insurance policy during construction	6,000
(f)	Refund of 1-month insurance premium because construction completed early	(1,000)
(g)	Architect's fee on building	22,000
(h)	Cost of real estate purchased as a plant site (land $200,000 and building $50,000)	250,000
(i)	Commission fee paid to real estate agency	9,000
(j)	Installation of fences around property	4,000
(k)	Cost of razing and removing building	11,000
(l)	Proceeds from salvage of demolished building	(5,000)
(m)	Interest paid during construction on money borrowed for construction	13,000
(n)	Cost of parking lots and driveways	19,000
(o)	Cost of trees and shrubbery planted (permanent in nature)	14,000
(p)	Excavation costs for new building	3,000

Instructions
Identify each item by letter and list the items in columnar form, using the headings shown below. All receipt amounts should be reported in parentheses. For any amounts entered in the Other Accounts column, also indicate the account title.

Item	Land	Land Improvements	Buildings	Other Accounts

2 **E10-2 (Acquisition Costs of Realty)** Martin Buber Co. purchased land as a factory site for $400,000. The process of tearing down two old buildings on the site and constructing the factory required 6 months.

The company paid $42,000 to raze the old buildings and sold salvaged lumber and brick for $6,300. Legal fees of $1,850 were paid for title investigation and drawing the purchase contract. Martin Buber paid $2,200 to an engineering firm for a land survey, and $68,000 for drawing the factory plans. The land survey had to be made before definitive plans could be drawn. Title insurance on the property cost $1,500, and a liability insurance premium paid during construction was $900. The contractor's charge for construction was $2,740,000. The company paid the contractor in two installments: $1,200,000 at the end of 3 months and $1,540,000 upon completion. Interest costs of $170,000 were incurred to finance the construction.

Instructions
Determine the cost of the land and the cost of the building as they should be recorded on the books of Martin Buber Co. Assume that the land survey was for the building.

2 **E10-3 (Acquisition Costs of Trucks)** Kelly Clarkson Corporation operates a retail computer store. To improve delivery services to customers, the company purchases four new trucks on April 1, 2014. The terms of acquisition for each truck are described below.

1. Truck #1 has a list price of $15,000 and is acquired for a cash payment of $13,900.
2. Truck #2 has a list price of $16,000 and is acquired for a down payment of $2,000 cash and a zero-interest-bearing note with a face amount of $14,000. The note is due April 1, 2015. Clarkson would normally have to pay interest at a rate of 10% for such a borrowing, and the dealership has an incremental borrowing rate of 8%.
3. Truck #3 has a list price of $16,000. It is acquired in exchange for a computer system that Clarkson carries in inventory. The computer system cost $12,000 and is normally sold by Clarkson for $15,200. Clarkson uses a perpetual inventory system.
4. Truck #4 has a list price of $14,000. It is acquired in exchange for 1,000 shares of common stock in Clarkson Corporation. The stock has a par value per share of $10 and a market price of $13 per share.

Instructions
Prepare the appropriate journal entries for the above transactions for Clarkson Corporation.

2 3 **E10-4 (Purchase and Self-Constructed Cost of Assets)** Worf Co. both purchases and constructs various equipment it uses in its operations. The following items for two different types of equipment were recorded in random order during the calendar year 2014.

Purchase

Cash paid for equipment, including sales tax of $5,000	$105,000
Freight and insurance cost while in transit	2,000
Cost of moving equipment into place at factory	3,100
Wage cost for technicians to test equipment	4,000
Insurance premium paid during first year of operation on this equipment	1,500
Special plumbing fixtures required for new equipment	8,000
Repair cost incurred in first year of operations related to this equipment	1,300

Construction

Material and purchased parts (gross cost $200,000; failed to take 2% cash discount)	$200,000
Imputed interest on funds used during construction (stock financing)	14,000
Labor costs	190,000
Allocated overhead costs (fixed—$20,000; variable—$30,000)	50,000
Profit on self-construction	30,000
Cost of installing equipment	4,400

Instructions

Compute the total cost for each of these two pieces of equipment. If an item is not capitalized as a cost of the equipment, indicate how it should be reported.

2 3 4 **E10-5 (Treatment of Various Costs)** Ben Sisko Supply Company, a newly formed corporation, incurred the following expenditures related to Land, to Buildings, and to Machinery and Equipment.

Abstract company's fee for title search		$ 520
Architect's fees		3,170
Cash paid for land and dilapidated building thereon		87,000
Removal of old building	$20,000	
Less: Salvage	5,500	14,500
Interest on short-term loans during construction		7,400
Excavation before construction for basement		19,000
Machinery purchased (subject to 2% cash discount, which was not taken)		55,000
Freight on machinery purchased		1,340
Storage charges on machinery, necessitated by noncompletion of building when machinery was delivered		2,180
New building constructed (building construction took 6 months from date of purchase of land and old building)		485,000
Assessment by city for drainage project		1,600
Hauling charges for delivery of machinery from storage to new building		620
Installation of machinery		2,000
Trees, shrubs, and other landscaping after completion of building (permanent in nature)		5,400

Instructions

Determine the amounts that should be debited to Land, to Buildings, and to Machinery and Equipment. Assume the benefits of capitalizing interest during construction exceed the cost of implementation. Indicate how any costs not debited to these accounts should be recorded.

3 4 **E10-6 (Correction of Improper Cost Entries)** Plant acquisitions for selected companies are as follows.

1. Belanna Industries Inc. acquired land, buildings, and equipment from a bankrupt company, Torres Co., for a lump-sum price of $700,000. At the time of purchase, Torres's assets had the following book and appraisal values.

	Book Values	Appraisal Values
Land	$200,000	$150,000
Buildings	250,000	350,000
Equipment	300,000	300,000

To be conservative, the company decided to take the lower of the two values for each asset acquired. The following entry was made.

Land	150,000	
Buildings	250,000	
Equipment	300,000	
Cash		700,000

2. Harry Enterprises purchased store equipment by making a $2,000 cash down payment and signing a 1-year, $23,000, 10% note payable. The purchase was recorded as follows.

Equipment	27,300	
Cash		2,000
Notes Payable		23,000
Interest Payable		2,300

3. Kim Company purchased office equipment for $20,000, terms 2/10, n/30. Because the company intended to take the discount, it made no entry until it paid for the acquisition. The entry was:

Equipment	20,000	
Cash		19,600
Purchase Discounts		400

4. Kaisson Inc. recently received at zero cost land from the Village of Cardassia as an inducement to locate its business in the Village. The appraised value of the land is $27,000. The company made no entry to record the land because it had no cost basis.

5. Zimmerman Company built a warehouse for $600,000. It could have purchased the building for $740,000. The controller made the following entry.

Buildings	740,000	
Cash		600,000
Profit on Construction		140,000

Instructions
Prepare the entry that should have been made at the date of each acquisition.

4 **E10-7 (Capitalization of Interest)** Harrisburg Furniture Company started construction of a combination office and warehouse building for its own use at an estimated cost of $5,000,000 on January 1, 2014. Harrisburg expected to complete the building by December 31, 2014. Harrisburg has the following debt obligations outstanding during the construction period.

Construction loan—12% interest, payable semiannually, issued	
December 31, 2013	$2,000,000
Short-term loan—10% interest, payable monthly, and principal payable	
at maturity on May 30, 2015	1,400,000
Long-term loan—11% interest, payable on January 1 of each	
year. Principal payable on January 1, 2018	1,000,000

Instructions
(Carry all computations to two decimal places.)

(a) Assume that Harrisburg completed the office and warehouse building on December 31, 2014, as planned at a total cost of $5,200,000, and the weighted-average amount of accumulated expenditures was $3,600,000. Compute the avoidable interest on this project.

(b) Compute the depreciation expense for the year ended December 31, 2015. Harrisburg elected to depreciate the building on a straight-line basis and determined that the asset has a useful life of 30 years and a salvage value of $300,000.

4 **E10-8 (Capitalization of Interest)** On December 31, 2013, Main Inc. borrowed $3,000,000 at 12% payable annually to finance the construction of a new building. In 2014, the company made the following expenditures related to this building: March 1, $360,000; June 1, $600,000; July 1, $1,500,000; December 1, $1,500,000. The building was completed in February 2015. Additional information is provided as follows.

1. Other debt outstanding
10-year, 13% bond, December 31, 2007, interest payable annually	$4,000,000
6-year, 10% note, dated December 31, 2011, interest payable annually	$1,600,000
2. March 1, 2014, expenditure included land costs of $150,000
3. Interest revenue earned in 2014 $49,000

Instructions
(a) Determine the amount of interest to be capitalized in 2014 in relation to the construction of the building.

(b) Prepare the journal entry to record the capitalization of interest and the recognition of interest expense, if any, at December 31, 2014.

4 **E10-9 (Capitalization of Interest)** On July 31, 2014, Amsterdam Company engaged Minsk Tooling Company to construct a special-purpose piece of factory machinery. Construction was begun immediately and was completed on November 1, 2014. To help finance construction, on July 31 Amsterdam issued a $300,000, 3-year, 12% note payable at Netherlands National Bank, on which interest is payable each July 31. $200,000 of the proceeds of the note was paid to Minsk on July 31. The remainder of the proceeds was temporarily invested in short-term marketable securities (trading securities) at 10% until November 1. On November 1, Amsterdam made a final $100,000 payment to Minsk. Other than the note to Netherlands, Amsterdam's only outstanding liability at December 31, 2014, is a $30,000, 8%, 6-year note payable, dated January 1, 2011, on which interest is payable each December 31.

Instructions

    (a) Calculate the interest revenue, weighted-average accumulated expenditures, avoidable interest, and total interest cost to be capitalized during 2014. (Round all computations to the nearest dollar.)

    (b) Prepare the journal entries needed on the books of Amsterdam Company at each of the following dates.

        (1) July 31, 2014.

        (2) November 1, 2014.

        (3) December 31, 2014.

4 **E10-10 (Capitalization of Interest)** The following three situations involve the capitalization of interest.

Situation I: On January 1, 2014, Oksana Baiul, Inc. signed a fixed-price contract to have Builder Associates construct a major plant facility at a cost of $4,000,000. It was estimated that it would take 3 years to complete the project. Also on January 1, 2014, to finance the construction cost, Oksana Baiul borrowed $4,000,000 payable in 10 annual installments of $400,000, plus interest at the rate of 10%. During 2014, Oksana Baiul made deposit and progress payments totaling $1,500,000 under the contract; the weighted-average amount of accumulated expenditures was $800,000 for the year. The excess borrowed funds were invested in short-term securities, from which Oksana Baiul realized investment income of $250,000.

Instructions

What amount should Oksana Baiul report as capitalized interest at December 31, 2014?

Situation II: During 2014, Midori Ito Corporation constructed and manufactured certain assets and incurred the following interest costs in connection with those activities.

	Interest Costs Incurred
Warehouse constructed for Ito's own use	$30,000
Special-order machine for sale to unrelated customer, produced according to customer's specifications	9,000
Inventories routinely manufactured, produced on a repetitive basis	8,000

All of these assets required an extended period of time for completion.

Instructions

Assuming the effect of interest capitalization is material, what is the total amount of interest costs to be capitalized?

Situation III: Peggy Fleming, Inc. has a fiscal year ending April 30. On May 1, 2014, Peggy Fleming borrowed $10,000,000 at 11% to finance construction of its own building. Repayments of the loan are to commence the month following completion of the building. During the year ended April 30, 2015, expenditures for the partially completed structure totaled $7,000,000. These expenditures were incurred evenly throughout the year. Interest earned on the unexpended portion of the loan amounted to $650,000 for the year.

Instructions

How much should be shown as capitalized interest on Peggy Fleming's financial statements at April 30, 2015?
(CPA adapted)

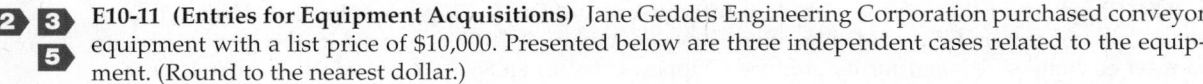 **E10-11 (Entries for Equipment Acquisitions)** Jane Geddes Engineering Corporation purchased conveyor equipment with a list price of $10,000. Presented below are three independent cases related to the equipment. (Round to the nearest dollar.)

    (a) Geddes paid cash for the equipment 8 days after the purchase. The vendor's credit terms are 2/10, n/30. Assume that equipment purchases are initially recorded gross.

    (b) Geddes traded in equipment with a book value of $2,000 (initial cost $8,000), and paid $9,500 in cash one month after the purchase. The old equipment could have been sold for $400 at the date of trade. (The exchange has commercial substance.)

    (c) Geddes gave the vendor a $10,800 zero-interest-bearing note for the equipment on the date of purchase. The note was due in one year and was paid on time. Assume that the effective-interest rate in the market was 9%.

Instructions

Prepare the general journal entries required to record the acquisition and payment in each of the independent cases above.

E10-12 (Entries for Asset Acquisition, Including Self-Construction) Below are transactions related to Duffner Company.

(a) The City of Pebble Beach gives the company 5 acres of land as a plant site. The fair value of this land is determined to be $81,000.

(b) 13,000 shares of common stock with a par value of $50 per share are issued in exchange for land and buildings. The property has been appraised at a fair value of $810,000, of which $180,000 has been allocated to land and $630,000 to buildings. The stock of Duffner Company is not listed on any exchange, but a block of 100 shares was sold by a stockholder 12 months ago at $65 per share, and a block of 200 shares was sold by another stockholder 18 months ago at $58 per share.

(c) No entry has been made to remove from the accounts for Materials, Direct Labor, and Overhead the amounts properly chargeable to plant asset accounts for machinery constructed during the year. The following information is given relative to costs of the machinery constructed.

Materials used	$12,500
Factory supplies used	900
Direct labor incurred	15,000
Additional overhead (over regular) caused by construction of machinery, excluding factory supplies used	2,700
Fixed overhead rate applied to regular manufacturing operations	60% of direct labor cost
Cost of similar machinery if it had been purchased from outside suppliers	44,000

Instructions

Prepare journal entries on the books of Duffner Company to record these transactions.

E10-13 (Entries for Acquisition of Assets) Presented below is information related to Zonker Company.

1. On July 6, Zonker Company acquired the plant assets of Doonesbury Company, which had discontinued operations. The appraised value of the property is:

Land	$ 400,000
Buildings	1,200,000
Equipment	800,000
Total	$2,400,000

Zonker Company gave 12,500 shares of its $100 par value common stock in exchange. The stock had a market price of $168 per share on the date of the purchase of the property.

2. Zonker Company expended the following amounts in cash between July 6 and December 15, the date when it first occupied the building.

Repairs to building	$105,000
Construction of bases for equipment to be installed later	135,000
Driveways and parking lots	122,000
Remodeling of office space in building, including new partitions and walls	161,000
Special assessment by city on land	18,000

3. On December 20, the company paid cash for equipment, $260,000, subject to a 2% cash discount, and freight on equipment of $10,500.

Instructions

Prepare entries on the books of Zonker Company for these transactions.

E10-14 (Purchase of Equipment with Zero-Interest-Bearing Debt) Chippewas Inc. has decided to purchase equipment from Central Michigan Industries on January 2, 2014, to expand its production capacity to meet customers' demand for its product. Chippewas issues an $800,000, 5-year, zero-interest-bearing note to Central Michigan for the new equipment when the prevailing market rate of interest for obligations of this nature is 12%. The company will pay off the note in five $160,000 installments due at the end of each year over the life of the note.

Instructions

(Round to nearest dollar in all computations.)

(a) Prepare the journal entry(ies) at the date of purchase.

(b) Prepare the journal entry(ies) at the end of the first year to record the payment and interest, assuming that the company employs the effective-interest method.

(c) Prepare the journal entry(ies) at the end of the second year to record the payment and interest.

(d) Assuming that the equipment had a 10-year life and no salvage value, prepare the journal entry necessary to record depreciation in the first year. (Straight-line depreciation is employed.)

E10-15 (Purchase of Computer with Zero-Interest-Bearing Debt) Cardinals Corporation purchased a computer on December 31, 2013, for $105,000, paying $30,000 down and agreeing to pay the balance in five equal installments of $15,000 payable each December 31 beginning in 2014. An assumed interest rate of 10% is implicit in the purchase price.

Instructions
(Round to two decimal places.)

(a) Prepare the journal entry(ies) at the date of purchase.

(b) Prepare the journal entry(ies) at December 31, 2014, to record the payment and interest (effective-interest method employed).

(c) Prepare the journal entry(ies) at December 31, 2015, to record the payment and interest (effective-interest method employed).

E10-16 (Asset Acquisition) Hayes Industries purchased the following assets and constructed a building as well. All this was done during the current year.

Assets 1 and 2: These assets were purchased as a lump sum for $100,000 cash. The following information was gathered.

Description	Initial Cost on Seller's Books	Depreciation to Date on Seller's Books	Book Value on Seller's Books	Appraised Value
Machinery	$100,000	$50,000	$50,000	$90,000
Equipment	60,000	10,000	50,000	30,000

Asset 3: This machine was acquired by making a $10,000 down payment and issuing a $30,000, 2-year, zero-interest-bearing note. The note is to be paid off in two $15,000 installments made at the end of the first and second years. It was estimated that the asset could have been purchased outright for $35,900.

Asset 4: This machinery was acquired by trading in used machinery. (The exchange lacks commercial substance.) Facts concerning the trade-in are as follows.

Cost of machinery traded	$100,000
Accumulated depreciation to date of sale	40,000
Fair value of machinery traded	80,000
Cash received	10,000
Fair value of machinery acquired	70,000

Asset 5: Equipment was acquired by issuing 100 shares of $8 par value common stock. The stock had a market price of $11 per share.

Construction of Building: A building was constructed on land purchased last year at a cost of $150,000. Construction began on February 1 and was completed on November 1. The payments to the contractor were as follows.

Date	Payment
2/1	$120,000
6/1	360,000
9/1	480,000
11/1	100,000

To finance construction of the building, a $600,000, 12% construction loan was taken out on February 1. The loan was repaid on November 1. The firm had $200,000 of other outstanding debt during the year at a borrowing rate of 8%.

Instructions
Record the acquisition of each of these assets.

E10-17 (Nonmonetary Exchange) Busytown Corporation, which manufactures shoes, hired a recent college graduate to work in its accounting department. On the first day of work, the accountant was assigned to total a batch of invoices with the use of an adding machine. Before long, the accountant, who had never before seen such a machine, managed to break the machine. Busytown Corporation gave the machine plus $340 to Dick Tracy Business Machine Company (dealer) in exchange for a new machine. Assume the following information about the machines.

	Busytown Corp. (Old Machine)	Dick Tracy Co. (New Machine)
Machine cost	$290	$270
Accumulated depreciation	140	–0–
Fair value	85	425

Instructions

For each company, prepare the necessary journal entry to record the exchange. (The exchange has commercial substance.)

5 **E10-18 (Nonmonetary Exchange)** Cannondale Company purchased an electric wax melter on April 30, 2014, by trading in its old gas model and paying the balance in cash. The following data relate to the purchase.

List price of new melter	$15,800
Cash paid	10,000
Cost of old melter (5-year life, $700 salvage value)	11,200
Accumulated depreciation—old melter (straight-line)	6,300
Secondhand fair value of old melter	5,200

Instructions

Prepare the journal entry(ies) necessary to record this exchange, assuming that the exchange **(a)** has commercial substance, and **(b)** lacks commercial substance. Cannondale's fiscal year ends on December 31, and depreciation has been recorded through December 31, 2013.

5 **E10-19 (Nonmonetary Exchange)** Carlos Arruza Company exchanged equipment used in its manufacturing operations plus $3,000 in cash for similar equipment used in the operations of Tony LoBianco Company. The following information pertains to the exchange.

	Carlos Arruza Co.	Tony LoBianco Co.
Equipment (cost)	$28,000	$28,000
Accumulated depreciation	19,000	10,000
Fair value of equipment	12,500	15,500
Cash given up	3,000	

Instructions

(a) Prepare the journal entries to record the exchange on the books of both companies. Assume that the exchange lacks commercial substance.

(b) Prepare the journal entries to record the exchange on the books of both companies. Assume that the exchange has commercial substance.

5 **E10-20 (Nonmonetary Exchange)** Dana Ashbrook Inc. has negotiated the purchase of a new piece of automatic equipment at a price of $8,000 plus trade-in, f.o.b. factory. Dana Ashbrook Inc. paid $8,000 cash and traded in used equipment. The used equipment had originally cost $62,000; it had a book value of $42,000 and a secondhand fair value of $47,800, as indicated by recent transactions involving similar equipment. Freight and installation charges for the new equipment required a cash payment of $1,100.

Instructions

(a) Prepare the general journal entry to record this transaction, assuming that the exchange has commercial substance.

(b) Assuming the same facts as in (a) except that fair value information for the assets exchanged is not determinable, prepare the general journal entry to record this transaction.

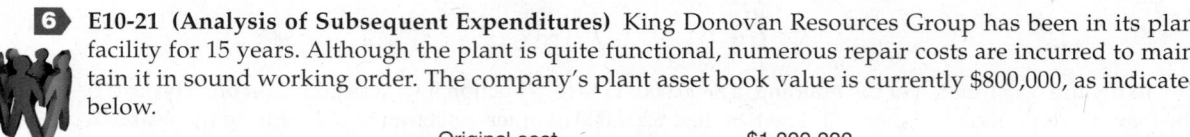

6 **E10-21 (Analysis of Subsequent Expenditures)** King Donovan Resources Group has been in its plant facility for 15 years. Although the plant is quite functional, numerous repair costs are incurred to maintain it in sound working order. The company's plant asset book value is currently $800,000, as indicated below.

Original cost	$1,200,000
Accumulated depreciation	400,000
Book value	$ 800,000

During the current year, the following expenditures were made to the plant facility.

(a) Because of increased demands for its product, the company increased its plant capacity by building a new addition at a cost of $270,000.

(b) The entire plant was repainted at a cost of $23,000.

(c) The roof was an asbestos cement slate. For safety purposes, it was removed and replaced with a wood shingle roof at a cost of $61,000. Book value of the old roof was $41,000.

(d) The electrical system was completely updated at a cost of $22,000. The cost of the old electrical system was not known. It is estimated that the useful life of the building will not change as a result of this updating.

(e) A series of major repairs were made at a cost of $47,000, because parts of the wood structure were rotting. The cost of the old wood structure was not known. These extensive repairs are estimated to increase the useful life of the building.

Instructions

Indicate how each of these transactions would be recorded in the accounting records.

6 **E10-22 (Analysis of Subsequent Expenditures)** The following transactions occurred during 2014. Assume that depreciation of 10% per year is charged on all machinery and 5% per year on buildings, on a straight-line basis, with no estimated salvage value. Depreciation is charged for a full year on all fixed assets acquired during the year, and no depreciation is charged on fixed assets disposed of during the year.

Jan. 30   A building that cost $132,000 in 1997 is torn down to make room for a new building. The wrecking contractor was paid $5,100 and was permitted to keep all materials salvaged.

Mar. 10   Machinery that was purchased in 2007 for $16,000 is sold for $2,900 cash, f.o.b. purchaser's plant. Freight of $300 is paid on the sale of this machinery.

Mar. 20   A gear breaks on a machine that cost $9,000 in 2009. The gear is replaced at a cost of $2,000. The replacement does not extend the useful life of the machine but does make the machine more efficient.

May 18   A special base installed for a machine in 2008 when the machine was purchased has to be replaced at a cost of $5,500 because of defective workmanship on the original base. The cost of the machinery was $14,200 in 2008. The cost of the base was $3,500, and this amount was charged to the Machinery account in 2008.

June 23   One of the buildings is repainted at a cost of $6,900. It had not been painted since it was constructed in 2010.

Instructions

(Round to the nearest dollar.)

Prepare general journal entries for the transactions.

6 **E10-23 (Analysis of Subsequent Expenditures)** Plant assets often require expenditures subsequent to acquisition. It is important that they be accounted for properly. Any errors will affect both the balance sheets and income statements for a number of years.

Instructions

For each of the following items, indicate whether the expenditure should be capitalized (C) or expensed (E) in the period incurred.

(a) _____ Improvement.
(b) _____ Replacement of a minor broken part on a machine.
(c) _____ Expenditure that increases the useful life of an existing asset.
(d) _____ Expenditure that increases the efficiency and effectiveness of a productive asset but does not increase its salvage value.
(e) _____ Expenditure that increases the efficiency and effectiveness of a productive asset and increases the asset's salvage value.
(f) _____ Expenditure that increases the quality of the output of the productive asset.
(g) _____ Improvement to a machine that increased its fair market value and its production capacity by 30% without extending the machine's useful life.
(h) _____ Ordinary repairs.

7 **E10-24 (Entries for Disposition of Assets)** On December 31, 2014, Travis Tritt Inc. has a machine with a book value of $940,000. The original cost and related accumulated depreciation at this date are as follows.

Machine	$1,300,000
Less: Accumulated depreciation	360,000
Book value	$ 940,000

Depreciation is computed at $60,000 per year on a straight-line basis.

Instructions

Presented below is a set of independent situations. For each independent situation, indicate the journal entry to be made to record the transaction. Make sure that depreciation entries are made to update the book value of the machine prior to its disposal.

(a) A fire completely destroys the machine on August 31, 2015. An insurance settlement of $430,000 was received for this casualty. Assume the settlement was received immediately.

(b) On April 1, 2015, Tritt sold the machine for $1,040,000 to Dwight Yoakam Company.

(c) On July 31, 2015, the company donated this machine to the Mountain King City Council. The fair value of the machine at the time of the donation was estimated to be $1,100,000.

7 **E10-25 (Disposition of Assets)** On April 1, 2014, Gloria Estefan Company received a condemnation award of $430,000 cash as compensation for the forced sale of the company's land and building, which stood in the path of a new state highway. The land and building cost $60,000 and $280,000, respectively, when they were acquired. At April 1, 2014, the accumulated depreciation relating to the building amounted to $160,000. On August 1, 2014, Estafan purchased a piece of replacement property for cash. The new land cost $90,000, and the new building cost $400,000.

Instructions
Prepare the journal entries to record the transactions on April 1 and August 1, 2014.

EXERCISES SET B

See the book's companion website, at **www.wiley.com/college/kieso**, for an additional set of exercises.

PROBLEMS

2 **P10-1 (Classification of Acquisition and Other Asset Costs)** At December 31, 2013, certain accounts included in the property, plant, and equipment section of Reagan Company's balance sheet had the following balances.

Land	$230,000
Buildings	890,000
Leasehold improvements	660,000
Equipment	875,000

During 2014, the following transactions occurred.

1. Land site number 621 was acquired for $850,000. In addition, to acquire the land Reagan paid a $51,000 commission to a real estate agent. Costs of $35,000 were incurred to clear the land. During the course of clearing the land, timber and gravel were recovered and sold for $13,000.

2. A second tract of land (site number 622) with a building was acquired for $420,000. The closing statement indicated that the land value was $300,000 and the building value was $120,000. Shortly after acquisition, the building was demolished at a cost of $41,000. A new building was constructed for $330,000 plus the following costs.

Excavation fees	$38,000
Architectural design fees	11,000
Building permit fee	2,500
Imputed interest on funds used	
during construction (stock financing)	8,500

The building was completed and occupied on September 30, 2014.

3. A third tract of land (site number 623) was acquired for $650,000 and was put on the market for resale.

4. During December 2014, costs of $89,000 were incurred to improve leased office space. The related lease will terminate on December 31, 2016, and is not expected to be renewed. (*Hint:* Leasehold improvements should be handled in the same manner as land improvements.)

5. A group of new machines was purchased under a royalty agreement that provides for payment of royalties based on units of production for the machines. The invoice price of the machines was $87,000, freight costs were $3,300, installation costs were $2,400, and royalty payments for 2014 were $17,500.

Instructions
(a) Prepare a detailed analysis of the changes in each of the following balance sheet accounts for 2014.

Land	Leasehold Improvements
Buildings	Equipment

Disregard the related accumulated depreciation accounts.

(b) List the items in the situation that were not used to determine the answer to (a) above, and indicate where, or if, these items should be included in Reagan's financial statements.

(AICPA adapted)

2 7 P10-2 (Classification of Acquisition Costs) Selected accounts included in the property, plant, and equipment section of Lobo Corporation's balance sheet at December 31, 2013, had the following balances.

Land	$ 300,000
Land improvements	140,000
Buildings	1,100,000
Equipment	960,000

During 2014, the following transactions occurred.

1. A tract of land was acquired for $150,000 as a potential future building site.
2. A plant facility consisting of land and building was acquired from Mendota Company in exchange for 20,000 shares of Lobo's common stock. On the acquisition date, Lobo's stock had a closing market price of $37 per share on a national stock exchange. The plant facility was carried on Mendota's books at $110,000 for land and $320,000 for the building at the exchange date. Current appraised values for the land and building, respectively, are $230,000 and $690,000.
3. Items of machinery and equipment were purchased at a total cost of $400,000. Additional costs were incurred as follows.

Freight and unloading	$13,000
Sales taxes	20,000
Installation	26,000

4. Expenditures totaling $95,000 were made for new parking lots, streets, and sidewalks at the corporation's various plant locations. These expenditures had an estimated useful life of 15 years.
5. A machine costing $80,000 on January 1, 2006, was scrapped on June 30, 2014. Double-declining-balance depreciation has been recorded on the basis of a 10-year life.
6. A machine was sold for $20,000 on July 1, 2014. Original cost of the machine was $44,000 on January 1, 2011, and it was depreciated on the straight-line basis over an estimated useful life of 7 years and a salvage value of $2,000.

Instructions
(Round to the nearest dollar.)

(a) Prepare a detailed analysis of the changes in each of the following balance sheet accounts for 2014.

Land   Buildings
Land Improvements   Equipment

(*Hint:* Disregard the related accumulated depreciation accounts.)

(b) List the items in the fact situation that were not used to determine the answer to (a), showing the pertinent amounts and supporting computations in good form for each item. In addition, indicate where, or if, these items should be included in Lobo's financial statements.

(AICPA adapted)

2 3 5 P10-3 (Classification of Land and Building Costs) Spitfire Company was incorporated on January 2, 2015, but was unable to begin manufacturing activities until July 1, 2015, because new factory facilities were not completed until that date.

The Land and Buildings account reported the following items during 2015.

January 31	Land and buildings	$160,000
February 28	Cost of removal of building	9,800
May 1	Partial payment of new construction	60,000
May 1	Legal fees paid	3,770
June 1	Second payment on new construction	40,000
June 1	Insurance premium	2,280
June 1	Special tax assessment	4,000
June 30	General expenses	36,300
July 1	Final payment on new construction	30,000
December 31	Asset write-up	53,800
		399,950
December 31	Depreciation—2015 at 1%	(4,000)
December 31, 2015	Account balance	$395,950

The following additional information is to be considered.

1. To acquire land and building, the company paid $80,000 cash and 800 shares of its 8% cumulative preferred stock, par value $100 per share. Fair value of the stock is $117 per share.
2. Cost of removal of old buildings amounted to $9,800, and the demolition company retained all materials of the building.
3. Legal fees covered the following.

Cost of organization	$ 610
Examination of title covering purchase of land	1,300
Legal work in connection with construction contract	1,860
	$3,770

4. Insurance premium covered the building for a 2-year term beginning May 1, 2015.
5. The special tax assessment covered street improvements that are permanent in nature.
6. General expenses covered the following for the period from January 2, 2015, to June 30, 2015.

President's salary	$32,100
Plant superintendent's salary—supervision of new building	4,200
	$36,300

7. Because of a general increase in construction costs after entering into the building contract, the board of directors increased the value of the building $53,800, believing that such an increase was justified to reflect the current market at the time the building was completed. Retained earnings was credited for this amount.
8. Estimated life of building—50 years.
   Depreciation for 2015—1% of asset value (1% of $400,000, or $4,000).

Instructions

(a) Prepare entries to reflect correct land, buildings, and depreciation accounts at December 31, 2015.
(b) Show the proper presentation of land, buildings, and depreciation on the balance sheet at December 31, 2015.

(AICPA adapted)

P10-4 (Dispositions, Including Condemnation, Demolition, and Trade-In) Presented below is a schedule of property dispositions for Hollerith Co.

					Schedule of Property Dispositions
	Cost	Accumulated Depreciation	Cash Proceeds	Fair Value	Nature of Disposition
Land	$40,000	—	$31,000	$31,000	Condemnation
Building	15,000	—	3,600	—	Demolition
Warehouse	70,000	$16,000	74,000	74,000	Destruction by fire
Machine	8,000	2,800	900	7,200	Trade-in
Furniture	10,000	7,850	—	3,100	Contribution
Automobile	9,000	3,460	2,960	2,960	Sale

The following additional information is available.

Land: On February 15, a condemnation award was received as consideration for unimproved land held primarily as an investment, and on March 31, another parcel of unimproved land to be held as an investment was purchased at a cost of $35,000.

Building: On April 2, land and building were purchased at a total cost of $75,000, of which 20% was allocated to the building on the corporate books. The real estate was acquired with the intention of demolishing the building, and this was accomplished during the month of November. Cash proceeds received in November represent the net proceeds from demolition of the building.

Warehouse: On June 30, the warehouse was destroyed by fire. The warehouse was purchased January 2, 2011, and had depreciated $16,000. On December 27, the insurance proceeds and other funds were used to purchase a replacement warehouse at a cost of $90,000.

Machine: On December 26, the machine was exchanged for another machine having a fair value of $6,300 and cash of $900 was received. (The exchange lacks commercial substance.)

Furniture: On August 15, furniture was contributed to a qualified charitable organization. No other contributions were made or pledged during the year.

Automobile: On November 3, the automobile was sold to Jared Winger, a stockholder.

Instructions

Indicate how these items would be reported on the income statement of Hollerith Co.

(AICPA adapted)

2 4 P10-5 (Classification of Costs and Interest Capitalization) On January 1, 2014, Blair Corporation purchased for $500,000 a tract of land (site number 101) with a building. Blair paid a real estate broker's commission of $36,000, legal fees of $6,000, and title guarantee insurance of $18,000. The closing statement indicated that the land value was $500,000 and the building value was $100,000. Shortly after acquisition, the building was razed at a cost of $54,000.

Blair entered into a $3,000,000 fixed-price contract with Slatkin Builders, Inc. on March 1, 2014, for the construction of an office building on land site number 101. The building was completed and occupied on September 30, 2015. Additional construction costs were incurred as follows.

Plans, specifications, and blueprints	$21,000
Architects' fees for design and supervision	82,000

The building is estimated to have a 40-year life from date of completion and will be depreciated using the 150% declining-balance method.

To finance construction costs, Blair borrowed $3,000,000 on March 1, 2014. The loan is payable in 10 annual installments of $300,000 starting on March 1, 2015, plus interest at the rate of 10%. Blair's weighted-average amounts of accumulated building construction expenditures were as follows.

For the period March 1 to December 31, 2014	$1,300,000
For the period January 1 to September 30, 2015	1,900,000

Instructions

(a) Prepare a schedule that discloses the individual costs making up the balance in the land account in respect of land site number 101 as of September 30, 2015.

(b) Prepare a schedule that discloses the individual costs that should be capitalized in the office building account as of September 30, 2015. Show supporting computations in good form.

(AICPA adapted)

2 4 P10-6 (Interest During Construction) Grieg Landscaping began construction of a new plant on December 1, 2014. On this date, the company purchased a parcel of land for $139,000 in cash. In addition, it paid $2,000 in surveying costs and $4,000 for a title insurance policy. An old dwelling on the premises was demolished at a cost of $3,000, with $1,000 being received from the sale of materials.

Architectural plans were also formalized on December 1, 2014, when the architect was paid $30,000. The necessary building permits costing $3,000 were obtained from the city and paid for on December 1 as well. The excavation work began during the first week in December with payments made to the contractor as follows.

Date of Payment	Amount of Payment
March 1	$240,000
May 1	330,000
July 1	60,000

The building was completed on July 1, 2015.

To finance construction of this plant, Grieg borrowed $600,000 from the bank on December 1, 2014. Grieg had no other borrowings. The $600,000 was a 10-year loan bearing interest at 8%.

Instructions

Compute the balance in each of the following accounts at December 31, 2014, and December 31, 2015. (Round amounts to the nearest dollar.)

(a) Land.

(b) Buildings.

(c) Interest Expense.

4 P10-7 (Capitalization of Interest) Laserwords Inc. is a book distributor that had been operating in its original facility since 1987. The increase in certification programs and continuing education requirements in several professions has contributed to an annual growth rate of 15% for Laserwords since 2009. Laserwords' original facility became obsolete by early 2014 because of the increased sales volume and the fact that Laserwords now carries CDs in addition to books.

On June 1, 2014, Laserwords contracted with Black Construction to have a new building constructed for $4,000,000 on land owned by Laserwords. The payments made by Laserwords to Black Construction are shown in the schedule below.

Date	Amount
July 30, 2014	$ 900,000
January 30, 2015	1,500,000
May 30, 2015	1,600,000
Total payments	$4,000,000

Construction was completed and the building was ready for occupancy on May 27, 2015. Laserwords had no new borrowings directly associated with the new building but had the following debt outstanding at May 31, 2015, the end of its fiscal year.

10%, 5-year note payable of $2,000,000, dated April 1, 2011, with interest payable annually on April 1.
12%, 10-year bond issue of $3,000,000 sold at par on June 30, 2007, with interest payable annually on June 30.

The new building qualifies for interest capitalization. The effect of capitalizing the interest on the new building, compared with the effect of expensing the interest, is material.

Instructions
(a) Compute the weighted-average accumulated expenditures on Laserwords' new building during the capitalization period.
(b) Compute the avoidable interest on Laserwords' new building. (Round to one decimal place.)
(c) Some interest cost of Laserwords Inc. is capitalized for the year ended May 31, 2015.
  (1) Identify the items relating to interest costs that must be disclosed in Laserwords' financial statements.
  (2) Compute the amount of each of the items that must be disclosed.

(CMA adapted)

P10-8 (Nonmonetary Exchanges) Holyfield Corporation wishes to exchange a machine used in its operations. Holyfield has received the following offers from other companies in the industry.

1. Dorsett Company offered to exchange a similar machine plus $23,000. (The exchange has commercial substance for both parties.)
2. Winston Company offered to exchange a similar machine. (The exchange lacks commercial substance for both parties.)
3. Liston Company offered to exchange a similar machine, but wanted $3,000 in addition to Holyfield's machine. (The exchange has commercial substance for both parties.)

In addition, Holyfield contacted Greeley Corporation, a dealer in machines. To obtain a new machine, Holyfield must pay $93,000 in addition to trading in its old machine.

	Holyfield	Dorsett	Winston	Liston	Greeley
Machine cost	$160,000	$120,000	$152,000	$160,000	$130,000
Accumulated depreciation	60,000	45,000	71,000	75,000	–0–
Fair value	92,000	69,000	92,000	95,000	185,000

Instructions
For each of the four independent situations, prepare the journal entries to record the exchange on the books of each company.

P10-9 (Nonmonetary Exchanges) On August 1, Hyde, Inc. exchanged productive assets with Wiggins, Inc. Hyde's asset is referred to below as "Asset A," and Wiggins' is referred to as "Asset B." The following facts pertain to these assets.

	Asset A	Asset B
Original cost	$96,000	$110,000
Accumulated depreciation (to date of exchange)	40,000	47,000
Fair value at date of exchange	60,000	75,000
Cash paid by Hyde, Inc.	15,000	
Cash received by Wiggins, Inc.		15,000

Instructions

(a) Assuming that the exchange of Assets A and B has commercial substance, record the exchange for both Hyde, Inc. and Wiggins, Inc. in accordance with generally accepted accounting principles.

(b) Assuming that the exchange of Assets A and B lacks commercial substance, record the exchange for both Hyde, Inc. and Wiggins, Inc. in accordance with generally accepted accounting principles.

5 P10-10 (Nonmonetary Exchanges) During the current year, Marshall Construction trades an old crane that has a book value of $90,000 (original cost $140,000 less accumulated depreciation $50,000) for a new crane from Brigham Manufacturing Co. The new crane cost Brigham $165,000 to manufacture and is classified as inventory. The following information is also available.

	Marshall Const.	Brigham Mfg. Co.
Fair value of old crane	$ 82,000	
Fair value of new crane		$200,000
Cash paid	118,000	
Cash received		118,000

Instructions

(a) Assuming that this exchange is considered to have commercial substance, prepare the journal entries on the books of (1) Marshall Construction and (2) Brigham Manufacturing.

(b) Assuming that this exchange lacks commercial substance for Marshall, prepare the journal entries on the books of Marshall Construction.

(c) Assuming the same facts as those in (a), except that the fair value of the old crane is $98,000 and the cash paid is $102,000, prepare the journal entries on the books of (1) Marshall Construction and (2) Brigham Manufacturing.

(d) Assuming the same facts as those in (b), except that the fair value of the old crane is $97,000 and the cash paid $103,000, prepare the journal entries on the books of (1) Marshall Construction and (2) Brigham Manufacturing.

2 5 P10-11 (Purchases by Deferred Payment, Lump-Sum, and Nonmonetary Exchanges) Klamath Company, a manufacturer of ballet shoes, is experiencing a period of sustained growth. In an effort to expand its production capacity to meet the increased demand for its product, the company recently made several acquisitions of plant and equipment. Rob Joffrey, newly hired in the position of fixed-asset accountant, requested that Danny Nolte, Klamath's controller, review the following transactions.

Transaction 1: On June 1, 2014, Klamath Company purchased equipment from Wyandot Corporation. Klamath issued a $28,000, 4-year, zero-interest-bearing note to Wyandot for the new equipment. Klamath will pay off the note in four equal installments due at the end of each of the next 4 years. At the date of the transaction, the prevailing market rate of interest for obligations of this nature was 10%. Freight costs of $425 and installation costs of $500 were incurred in completing this transaction. The appropriate factors for the time value of money at a 10% rate of interest are given below.

Future value of $1 for 4 periods	1.46
Future value of an ordinary annuity for 4 periods	4.64
Present value of $1 for 4 periods	0.68
Present value of an ordinary annuity for 4 periods	3.17

Transaction 2: On December 1, 2014, Klamath Company purchased several assets of Yakima Shoes Inc., a small shoe manufacturer whose owner was retiring. The purchase amounted to $220,000 and included the assets listed below. Klamath Company engaged the services of Tennyson Appraisal Inc., an independent appraiser, to determine the fair values of the assets which are also presented below.

	Yakima Book Value	Fair Value
Inventory	$ 60,000	$ 50,000
Land	40,000	80,000
Buildings	70,000	120,000
	$170,000	$250,000

During its fiscal year ended May 31, 2015, Klamath incurred $8,000 for interest expense in connection with the financing of these assets.

Transaction 3: On March 1, 2015, Klamath Company exchanged a number of used trucks plus cash for vacant land adjacent to its plant site. (The exchange has commercial substance.) Klamath intends to use the land for a parking lot. The trucks had a combined book value of $35,000, as Klamath had recorded $20,000 of accumulated depreciation against these assets. Klamath's purchasing agent, who has had previous dealings in the secondhand market, indicated that the trucks had a fair value of $46,000 at the time of the transaction. In addition to the trucks, Klamath Company paid $19,000 cash for the land.

Instructions

(a) Plant assets such as land, buildings, and equipment receive special accounting treatment. Describe the major characteristics of these assets that differentiate them from other types of assets.

(b) For each of the three transactions described above, determine the value at which Klamath Company should record the acquired assets. Support your calculations with an explanation of the underlying rationale.

(c) The books of Klamath Company show the following additional transactions for the fiscal year ended May 31, 2015.

(1) Acquisition of a building for speculative purposes.

(2) Purchase of a 2-year insurance policy covering plant equipment.

(3) Purchase of the rights for the exclusive use of a process used in the manufacture of ballet shoes.

For each of these transactions, indicate whether the asset should be classified as a plant asset. If it is a plant asset, explain why it is. If it is not a plant asset, explain why not, and identify the proper classification.

(CMA adapted)

PROBLEMS SET B

See the book's companion website, at **www.wiley.com/college/kieso**, for an additional set of problems.

CONCEPTS FOR ANALYSIS

CA10-1 (Acquisition, Improvements, and Sale of Realty) Tonkawa Company purchased land for use as its corporate headquarters. A small factory that was on the land when it was purchased was torn down before construction of the office building began. Furthermore, a substantial amount of rock blasting and removal had to be done to the site before construction of the building foundation began. Because the office building was set back on the land far from the public road, Tonkawa Company had the contractor construct a paved road that led from the public road to the parking lot of the office building.

Three years after the office building was occupied, Tonkawa Company added four stories to the office building. The four stories had an estimated useful life of 5 years more than the remaining estimated useful life of the original office building.

Ten years later, the land and building were sold at an amount more than their net book value, and Tonkawa Company had a new office building constructed in another state for use as its new corporate headquarters.

Instructions

(a) Which of the expenditures above should be capitalized? How should each be depreciated or amortized? Discuss the rationale for your answers.

(b) How would the sale of the land and building be accounted for? Include in your answer an explanation of how to determine the net book value at the date of sale. Discuss the rationale for your answer.

CA10-2 (Accounting for Self-Constructed Assets) Troopers Medical Labs, Inc., began operations 5 years ago producing stetrics, a new type of instrument it hoped to sell to doctors, dentists, and hospitals. The demand for stetrics far exceeded initial expectations, and the company was unable to produce enough stetrics to meet demand.

The company was manufacturing its product on equipment that it built at the start of its operations. To meet demand, more efficient equipment was needed. The company decided to design and build the equipment, because the equipment currently available on the market was unsuitable for producing stetrics.

In 2014, a section of the plant was devoted to development of the new equipment and a special staff was hired. Within 6 months, a machine developed at a cost of $714,000 increased production dramatically and reduced labor costs substantially. Elated by the success of the new machine, the company built three more machines of the same type at a cost of $441,000 each.

Instructions

(a) In general, what costs should be capitalized for self-constructed equipment?

(b) Discuss the propriety of including in the capitalized cost of self-constructed assets:

 (1) The increase in overhead caused by the self-construction of fixed assets.

 (2) A proportionate share of overhead on the same basis as that applied to goods manufactured for sale.

(c) Discuss the proper accounting treatment of the $273,000 ($714,000 − $441,000) by which the cost of the first machine exceeded the cost of the subsequent machines. This additional cost should not be considered research and development costs.

CA10-3 (Capitalization of Interest) Vania Magazine Company started construction of a warehouse building for its own use at an estimated cost of $5,000,000 on January 1, 2013, and completed the building on December 31, 2013. During the construction period, Vania has the following debt obligations outstanding.

Construction loan—12% interest, payable semiannually, issued December 31, 2012	$2,000,000
Short-term loan—10% interest, payable monthly, and principal payable at maturity, on May 30, 2014	1,400,000
Long-term loan—11% interest, payable on January 1 of each year; principal payable on January 1, 2016	1,000,000

Total cost amounted to $5,200,000, and the weighted average of accumulated expenditures was $3,500,000.

Jane Esplanade, the president of the company, has been shown the costs associated with this construction project and capitalized on the balance sheet. She is bothered by the "avoidable interest" included in the cost. She argues that, first, all the interest is unavoidable—no one lends money without expecting to be compensated for it. Second, why can't the company use all the interest on all the loans when computing this avoidable interest? Finally, why can't her company capitalize all the annual interest that accrued over the period of construction?

Instructions

(Round the weighted-average interest rate to two decimal places.)

You are the manager of accounting for the company. In a memo, explain what avoidable interest is, how you computed it (being especially careful to explain why you used the interest rates that you did), and why the company cannot capitalize all its interest for the year. Attach a schedule supporting any computations that you use.

CA10-4 (Nonmonetary Exchanges) You have two clients that are considering trading machinery with each other. Although the machines are different from each other, you believe that an assessment of expected cash flows on the exchanged assets will indicate the exchange lacks commercial substance. Your clients would prefer that the exchange be deemed to have commercial substance, to allow them to record gains. Here are the facts:

	Client A	Client B
Original cost	$100,000	$150,000
Accumulated depreciation	40,000	80,000
Fair value	80,000	100,000
Cash received (paid)	(20,000)	20,000

Instructions

(a) Record the trade-in on Client A's books assuming the exchange has commercial substance.

(b) Record the trade-in on Client A's books assuming the exchange lacks commercial substance.

(c) Write a memo to the controller of Company A indicating and explaining the dollar impact on current and future statements of treating the exchange as having, versus lacking, commercial substance.

(d) Record the entry on Client B's books assuming the exchange has commercial substance.

(e) Record the entry on Client B's books assuming the exchange lacks commercial substance.

(f) Write a memo to the controller of Company B indicating and explaining the dollar impact on current and future statements of treating the exchange as having, versus lacking, commercial substance.

CA10-5 (Costs of Acquisition) The invoice price of a machine is $50,000. Various other costs relating to the acquisition and installation of the machine including transportation, electrical wiring, special base, and so on amount to $7,500. The machine has an estimated life of 10 years, with no salvage value at the end of that period.

The owner of the business suggests that the incidental costs of $7,500 be charged to expense immediately for the following reasons.

1. If the machine should be sold, these costs cannot be recovered in the sales price.

2. The inclusion of the $7,500 in the machinery account on the books will not necessarily result in a closer approximation of the market price of this asset over the years, because of the possibility of changing demand and supply levels.

3. Charging the $7,500 to expense immediately will reduce federal income taxes.

Instructions

Discuss each of the points raised by the owner of the business.

(AICPA adapted)

CA10-6 (Cost of Land vs. Building—Ethics) Tones Company purchased a warehouse in a downtown district where land values are rapidly increasing. Gerald Carter, controller, and Wilma Ankara, financial vice president, are trying to allocate the cost of the purchase between the land and the building. Noting that depreciation can be taken only on the building, Carter favors placing a very high proportion of the cost on the warehouse itself, thus reducing taxable income and income taxes. Ankara, his supervisor, argues that the allocation should recognize the increasing value of the land, regardless of the depreciation potential of the warehouse. Besides, she says, net income is negatively impacted by additional depreciation and will cause the company's stock price to go down.

Instructions

Answer the following questions.

(a) What stakeholder interests are in conflict?

(b) What ethical issues does Carter face?

(c) How should these costs be allocated?

USING YOUR JUDGMENT

FINANCIAL REPORTING

Financial Statement Analysis Case

Johnson & Johnson

Johnson & Johnson, the world's leading and most diversified health-care corporation, serves its customers through specialized worldwide franchises. Each of its franchises consists of a number of companies throughout the world that focus on a particular health-care market, such as surgical sutures, consumer pharmaceuticals, or contact lenses. Information related to its property, plant, and equipment in its 2011 annual report is shown in the notes to the financial statements below.

---

1. Property, Plant and Equipment and Depreciation

Property, plant and equipment are stated at cost. The Company utilizes the straight-line method of depreciation over the estimated useful lives of the assets:

Building and building equipment	20–40 years
Land and leasehold improvements	10–20 years
Machinery and equipment	2–13 years

4. Property, Plant and Equipment

At the end of 2011 and 2010, property, plant and equipment at cost and accumulated depreciation were:

(dollars in millions)	2011	2010
Land and land improvements	$ 754	$ 738
Buildings and building equipment	9,389	9,079
Machinery and equipment	19,182	18,032
Construction in progress	2,504	2,577
	31,829	30,426
Less accumulated depreciation	17,090	15,873
	$14,739	$14,553

The Company capitalizes interest expense as part of the cost of construction of facilities and equipment. Interest expense capitalized in 2011, 2010 and 2009 was $84 million, $73 million and $101 million, respectively.

Depreciation expense, including the amortization of capitalized interest in 2011, 2010 and 2009 was $2.3 billion, $2.2 billion and $2.1 billion, respectively.

Johnson & Johnson's provided the following selected information in its 2011 cash flow statement.

Johnson & Johnson
2011 Annual Report

Consolidated Financial Statements (excerpts)

Net cash flows from operating activities	$14,298
Cash flows from investing activities	
Additions to property, plant and equipment	(2,893)
Proceeds from the disposal of assets	1,342
Acquisitions, net of cash acquired	(2,797)
Purchases of investments	(29,882)
Sales of investments	30,396
Other (primarily intangibles)	(778)
Net cash used by investing activities	(4,612)
Cash flows from financing activities	
Dividends to shareholders	(6,156)
Repurchase of common stock	(2,525)
Proceeds from short-term debt	9,729
Retirement of short-term debt	(11,200)
Proceeds from long-term debt	4,470
Retirement of long-term debt	(16)
Proceeds from the exercise of stock options/excess tax benefits	1,246
Net cash used by financing activities	(4,452)
Effect of exchange rate changes on cash and cash equivalents	(47)
Increase in cash and cash equivalents	5,187
Cash and cash equivalents, beginning of year (Note 1)	19,355
Cash and cash equivalents, end of year (Note 1)	$24,542
Supplemental cash flow data	
Cash paid during the year for:	
Interest	$ 576
Income taxes	2,970

Instructions

(a) What was the cost of buildings and building equipment at the end of 2011?

(b) Does Johnson & Johnson use a conservative or liberal method to depreciate its property, plant, and equipment?

(c) What was the actual interest expense paid by the company in 2011?

(d) What is Johnson & Johnson's free cash flow? From the information provided, comment on Johnson & Johnson's financial flexibility.

Accounting, Analysis, and Principles

Durler Company purchased equipment on January 2, 2010, for $112,000. The equipment had an estimated useful life of 5 years with an estimated salvage value of $12,000. Durler uses straight-line depreciation on all assets. On January 2, 2014, Durler exchanged this equipment plus $12,000 in cash for newer equipment. The old equipment has a fair value of $50,000.

Accounting

Prepare the journal entry to record the exchange on the books of Durler Company. Assume that the exchange has commercial substance.

Analysis

How will this exchange affect comparisons of the return on asset ratio for Durler in the year of the exchange compared to prior years?

Principles

How does the concept of commercial substance affect the accounting and analysis of this exchange?

BRIDGE TO THE PROFESSION

 ## Professional Research: FASB Codification

Your client is in the planning phase for a major plant expansion, which will involve the construction of a new warehouse. The assistant controller does not believe that interest cost can be included in the cost of the warehouse, because it is a financing expense. Others on the planning team believe that some interest cost can be included in the cost of the warehouse, but no one could identify the specific authoritative guidance for this issue. Your supervisor asks you to research this issue.

Instructions

If your school has a subscription to the FASB Codification, go to *http://aaahq.org/asclogin.cfm* to log in and prepare responses to the following. Provide Codification references for your responses.

(a) Is it permissible to capitalize interest into the cost of assets? Provide authoritative support for your answer.

(b) What are the objectives for capitalizing interest?

(c) Discuss which assets qualify for interest capitalization.

(d) Is there a limit to the amount of interest that may be capitalized in a period?

(e) If interest capitalization is allowed, what disclosures are required?

Additional Professional Resources

See the book's companion website, at **www.wiley.com/college/kieso**, for professional simulations as well as other study resources.

Remember to check the book's companion website to find additional resources for this chapter.

11 Depreciation, Impairments, and Depletion

Here Come the Write-Offs

The credit crisis starting in late 2008 affected many financial and nonfinancial institutions. Many of the statistics related to this crisis are sobering, as noted below.

- In October 2008, the FTSE 100 in the United Kingdom suffered its biggest one-day fall since October 1987. The index closed at its lowest level since October 2004.
- The Dow Jones Industrial Average fell below the 8,000 level for the first time since 2003.
- Germany's benchmark DAX tumbled after the collapse of the proposed rescue plan for **Hypo Real Estate**.
- Tightening credit and less disposable income led to Japanese electronic groups losing value. The Nikkei fell to its lowest point since February 2004.
- The Hong Kong Hang Seng dropped in line with the rest of Asia, closing below 17,000 points for the first time in two years in October 2008 and below 11,000 by November of that year.
- Governments spent billions of dollars bailing out financial institutions.

Although some financial rebound has occurred since October 2008, it is clear that most economies of the world are now in a slower growth pattern. This slowdown raises many questions related to the proper accounting for many long-term assets, such as property, plant, and equipment; intangible assets; and many types of financial assets. One of the most difficult issues relates to the possibility of higher impairment charges related to these assets and the related disclosures that may be needed. The following is an example of a recent impairment charge taken by **Fujitsu Limited**.

Impairment Losses (in part)

Due to the worsening of the global business environment, Fujitsu recognized consolidated impairment losses of 58.9 billion yen in relation to property, plant, and equipment of businesses with decreased profitability. The main losses are as follows:

(1) Property, Plant, and Equipment of LSI Business
Impairment losses related to the property, plant, and equipment of the LSI business of Fujitsu Microelectronics Limited totaled 49.9 billion yen. In January, Fujitsu Microelectronics announced business reforms in response to a sharp downturn in customer demand that began last autumn.

(2) Property, Plant, and Equipment of Optical Transmission Systems and Other Businesses
Consolidated impairment losses of 8.9 billion yen were recognized in relation to the property, plant, and equipment of the optical transmission systems business, the electronic components business and other businesses due to their decreased profitability.

(3) Property, Plant, and Equipment of HDD Business (included in business restructuring expenses)
Impairment losses of 16.2 billion yen have been recognized in relation to the property, plant, and equipment of the reorganized HDD business. These losses are included in business restructuring expenses. The impairment loss includes 5.3 billion yen recognized in the third quarter for the discontinuation of the HDD head business.

Impairment losses for property, plant, and equipment for many companies in the next few years will be substantial. Here are some of the questions that will need to be addressed regarding possible impairments.

1. How often should a company test for impairment?

2. What are key impairment indicators?

3. What disclosures are necessary for impairments?

4. How do companies match their cash flows to the asset that is potentially impaired?

Assessing whether a company has impaired assets is difficult. For example, in addition to the technical accounting issues, the environment can change quickly. Reduced spending by consumers, lack of confidence in global economic decisions, and higher volatility in both stock and commodity markets are factors to consider. Nevertheless, for investors and creditors to have assurance that the amounts reported on the balance sheet for property, plant, and equipment are relevant and representationally faithful, appropriate impairment charges must be reported on a timely basis.

Source: A portion of this discussion is taken from "Top 10 Tips for Impairment Testing," PricewaterhouseCoopers (December 2008).

CONCEPTUAL FOCUS

> See the **Underlying Concepts** on pages 592, 593, 594, and 601.
> Read the **Evolving Issue** on page 609 for a discussion of using the full-cost versus successful-efforts method for accounting for exploration costs.

INTERNATIONAL FOCUS

> See the **International Perspectives** on pages 597, 602, 603, and 609.
> Read the **IFRS Insights** on pages 637–646 for a discussion of:
— Component depreciation
— Impairments
— Revaluations

PREVIEW OF CHAPTER | **11**

As noted in the opening story, both U.S. and foreign companies are affected by impairment rules. These rules recognize that when economic conditions deteriorate, companies may need to write off an asset's cost to indicate the decline in its usefulness. The purpose of this chapter is to examine the depreciation process and the methods of writing off the cost of property, plant, and equipment and natural resources. The content and organization of the chapter are as follows.

Depreciation, Impairments, and Depletion

Depreciation	Impairments	Depletion	Presentation and Analysis
• Factors involved	• Recognizing impairments	• Establishing a base	• Presentation
• Methods of depreciation	• Measuring impairments	• Write-off of resource cost	• Analysis
• Special methods	• Restoration of loss	• Estimating reserves	
• Special issues	• Assets to be disposed of	• Liquidating dividends	
		• Continuing controversy	

DEPRECIATION—A METHOD OF COST ALLOCATION

Most individuals at one time or another purchase and trade in an automobile. The automobile dealer and the buyer typically discuss what the trade-in value of the old car is. Also, they may talk about what the trade-in value of the new car will be in several years. In both cases, a decline in value is considered to be an example of depreciation.

To accountants, however, depreciation is not a matter of valuation. Rather, **depreciation is a means of cost allocation.** Depreciation **is the accounting process of allocating the cost of tangible assets to expense in a systematic and rational manner to those periods expected to benefit from the use of the asset.** For example, a company like Goodyear (one of the world's largest tire manufacturers) does not depreciate assets on the basis of a decline in their fair value. Instead, it depreciates through systematic charges to expense.

This approach is employed because the value of the asset may fluctuate between the time the asset is purchased and the time it is sold or junked. Attempts to measure these interim value changes have not been well received because values are difficult to measure objectively. Therefore, Goodyear charges the asset's cost to depreciation expense over its estimated life. It makes no attempt to value the asset at fair value between acquisition and disposition. Companies use the cost allocation approach because it recognizes the expense in the periods expected to benefit and because fluctuations in fair value are uncertain and difficult to measure.

When companies write off the cost of long-lived assets over a number of periods, they typically use the term **depreciation.** They use the term depletion to describe the reduction in the cost of natural resources (such as timber, gravel, oil, and coal) over a period of time. The expiration of intangible assets, such as patents or copyrights, is called amortization.

Factors Involved in the Depreciation Process

Before establishing a pattern of charges to revenue, a company must answer three basic questions:

1. What depreciable base is to be used for the asset?
2. What is the asset's useful life?
3. What method of cost apportionment is best for this asset?

The answers to these questions involve combining several estimates into one single figure. Note the calculations assume perfect knowledge of the future, which is never attainable.

Depreciable Base for the Asset

The base established for depreciation is a function of two factors: the original cost, and salvage or disposal value. We discussed historical cost in Chapter 10. **Salvage value** is the estimated amount that a company will receive when it sells the asset or removes it from service. It is the amount to which a company writes down or depreciates the asset during its useful life. If an asset has a cost of $10,000 and a salvage value of $1,000, its depreciation base is $9,000.

ILLUSTRATION 11-1
Computation of
Depreciation Base

Original cost	$10,000
Less: Salvage value	1,000
Depreciation base	$ 9,000

From a practical standpoint, companies often assign a zero salvage value. Some long-lived assets, however, have substantial salvage values.

Estimation of Service Lives

The service life of an asset often differs from its physical life. A piece of machinery may be physically capable of producing a given product for many years beyond its service life. But a company may not use the equipment for all that time because the cost of producing the product in later years may be too high. For example, the old Slater cotton mill in Pawtucket, Rhode Island, is preserved in remarkable physical condition as an historic landmark in U.S. industrial development, although its service life was terminated many years ago.[1]

Companies retire assets for two reasons: **physical factors** (such as casualty or expiration of physical life) and **economic factors** (obsolescence). Physical factors are the wear and tear, decay, and casualties that make it difficult for the asset to perform indefinitely. These physical factors set the outside limit for the service life of an asset.

We can classify the economic or functional factors into three categories:

1. **Inadequacy** results when an asset ceases to be useful to a company because the demands of the firm have changed. An example would be the need for a larger building to handle increased production. Although the old building may still be sound, it may have become inadequate for the company's purpose.

2. **Supersession** is the replacement of one asset with another more efficient and economical asset. Examples would be the replacement of the mainframe computer with a PC network, or the replacement of the Boeing 767 with the Boeing 787.

3. **Obsolescence** is the catchall for situations not involving inadequacy and supersession.

Because the distinction between these categories appears artificial, it is probably best to consider economic factors collectively instead of trying to make distinctions that are not clear-cut.

To illustrate the concepts of physical and economic factors, consider a new nuclear power plant. Which is more important in determining the useful life of a nuclear power plant—physical factors or economic factors? The limiting factors seem to be (1) ecological considerations, (2) competition from other power sources, and (3) safety concerns. Physical life does not appear to be the primary factor affecting useful life. Although the plant's physical life may be far from over, the plant may become obsolete in 10 years.

For a house, physical factors undoubtedly are more important than the economic or functional factors relative to useful life. Whenever the physical nature of the asset primarily determines useful life, maintenance plays an extremely vital role. The better the maintenance, the longer the life of the asset.[2]

In most cases, a company estimates the useful life of an asset based on its past experience with the same or similar assets. Others use sophisticated statistical methods to establish a useful life for accounting purposes. And in some cases, companies select arbitrary service lives. In a highly industrial economy such as that of the United States, where research and innovation are so prominent, technological factors have as much effect, if not more, on service lives of tangible plant assets as physical factors do.

---

[1]Taken from J. D. Coughlan and W. K. Strand, *Depreciation Accounting, Taxes and Business Decisions* (New York: The Ronald Press, 1969), pp. 10–12.

[2]The airline industry also illustrates the type of problem involved in estimation. In the past, aircraft were assumed not to wear out—they just became obsolete. However, some jets have been in service as long as 20 years, and maintenance of these aircraft has become increasingly expensive. As a result, some airlines now replace aircraft not because of obsolescence but because of physical deterioration.

What do the numbers mean? ALPHABET DUPE

Some companies try to imply that depreciation is not a cost. For example, in their press releases they will often make a bigger deal over earnings before interest, taxes, depreciation, and amortization (often referred to as EBITDA) than net income under GAAP. They like it because it "dresses up" their earnings numbers. Some on Wall Street buy this hype because they don't like the allocations that are required to determine net income. Some banks, without batting an eyelash, even let companies base their loan covenants on EBITDA.

For example, look at Premier Parks, which operates the Six Flags chain of amusement parks. Premier touts its EBITDA performance. But that number masks a big part of how the company operates—and how it spends its money. Premier argues that analysts should ignore depreciation for big-ticket items like roller coasters because the rides have a long life. Critics, however, say that the amusement industry has to spend as much as 50 percent of its EBITDA just to keep its rides and attractions current. Those expenses are not optional—let the rides get a little rusty, and ticket sales start to tail off. That means analysts really should view depreciation associated with the costs of maintaining the rides (or buying new ones) as an everyday expense. It also means investors in those companies should have strong stomachs.

What's the risk of trusting a fad accounting measure? Just look at one year's bankruptcy numbers. Of the 147 companies tracked by Moody's that defaulted on their debt, most borrowed money based on EBITDA performance. The bankers in those deals probably wish they had looked at a few other factors. On the other hand, nonfinancial companies in the S&P 500 generated a substantial EBITDA margin of 20.9 percent in 2011. Some analysts are concerned that such a high number suggests that companies are reluctant to incur costs and want to stockpile cash. The lesson? Investors will do well to avoid focus on any single accounting measure.

Sources: Adapted from Herb Greenberg, "Alphabet Dupe: Why EBITDA Falls Short," *Fortune* (July 10, 2000), p. 240; and V. Monga, "Operating Efficiency Runs High at U.S. Firms," *Wall Street Journal* (February 28, 2012), p. B7.

Methods of Depreciation

LEARNING OBJECTIVE
Compare activity, straight-line, and decreasing-charge methods of depreciation.

The third factor involved in the depreciation process is the **method** of cost apportionment. The profession requires that the depreciation method employed be "systematic and rational." Companies may use a number of depreciation methods, as follows.

1. Activity method (units of use or production).
2. Straight-line method.
3. Decreasing-charge methods (accelerated):
   (a) Sum-of-the-years'-digits.
   (b) Declining-balance method.
4. Special depreciation methods:
   (a) Group and composite methods.
   (b) Hybrid or combination methods.[3]

 Underlying Concepts

Depreciation attempts to recognize the cost of an asset to the periods that benefit from the use of that asset.

To illustrate these depreciation methods, assume that Stanley Coal Mines recently purchased an additional crane for digging purposes. Illustration 11-2 contains the pertinent data concerning this purchase.

ILLUSTRATION 11-2
Data Used to Illustrate
Depreciation Methods

Cost of crane	$500,000
Estimated useful life	5 years
Estimated salvage value	$ 50,000
Productive life in hours	30,000 hours

[3]*Accounting Trends and Techniques—2012* reports that of its 500 surveyed companies, for reporting purposes, 490 used straight-line, 9 used declining-balance, 2 used sum-of-the-years'-digits, 9 used an accelerated method (not specified), 12 used units-of-production, and 17 used group/composite.

Activity Method

The **activity method** (also called the **variable-charge** or **units-of-production approach**) assumes that depreciation is **a function of use or productivity, instead of the passage of time**. A company considers the life of the asset in terms of either the **output** it provides (units it produces) or an **input** measure such as the number of hours it works. Conceptually, the proper cost association relies on output instead of hours used, but often the output is not easily measurable. In such cases, an input measure such as machine hours is a more appropriate method of measuring the dollar amount of depreciation charges for a given accounting period.

The crane poses no particular depreciation problem. Stanley can measure the usage (hours) relatively easily. If Stanley uses the crane for 4,000 hours the first year, the depreciation charge is:

$$\frac{\textbf{(Cost less salvage value)} \times \textbf{Hours this year}}{\textbf{Total estimated hours}} = \textbf{Depreciation charge}$$

$$\frac{(\$500{,}000 - \$50{,}000) \times 4{,}000}{30{,}000} = \$60{,}000$$

ILLUSTRATION 11-3
Depreciation Calculation, Activity Method—Crane Example

The major limitation of this method is that it is inappropriate in situations in which depreciation is a function of time instead of activity. For example, a building steadily deteriorates due to the elements (time) regardless of its use. In addition, where economic or functional factors affect an asset, independent of its use, the activity method loses much of its significance. For example, if a company is expanding rapidly, a particular building may soon become obsolete for its intended purposes. In both cases, activity is irrelevant. Another problem in using an activity method is the difficulty of estimating units of output or service hours received.

In cases where loss of services results from activity or productivity, the activity method does the best to record expenses in the same period as associated revenues. Companies that desire low depreciation during periods of low productivity, and high depreciation during high productivity, either adopt or switch to an activity method. In this way, a plant running at 40 percent of capacity generates 60 percent lower depreciation charges. **Inland Steel**, for example, switched to units-of-production depreciation at one time and reduced its losses by $43 million, or $1.20 per share.

Straight-Line Method

The **straight-line method** considers depreciation as a **function of time rather than a function of usage**. Companies widely use this method because of its simplicity. The straight-line procedure is often the most conceptually appropriate, too. When creeping obsolescence is the primary reason for a limited service life, the decline in usefulness may be constant from period to period. Stanley computes the depreciation charge for the crane as follows.

Underlying Concepts

If benefits flow on a "straight-line" basis, then justification exists for recording the cost of the asset on a straight-line basis with these benefits.

$$\frac{\textbf{Cost less salvage value}}{\textbf{Estimated service life}} = \textbf{Depreciation charge}$$

$$\frac{\$500{,}000 - \$50{,}000}{5} = \$90{,}000$$

ILLUSTRATION 11-4
Depreciation Calculation, Straight-Line Method—Crane Example

The major objection to the straight-line method is that it rests on two tenuous assumptions. (1) The asset's economic usefulness is the same each year, and (2) the maintenance and repair expense is essentially the same each period.

One additional problem that occurs in using straight-line—as well as some others—is that distortions in the rate of return analysis (income/assets) develop.

Illustration 11-5 indicates how the rate of return increases, given constant revenue flows, because the asset's book value decreases.

ILLUSTRATION 11-5
Depreciation and Rate of Return Analysis—Crane Example

Year	Depreciation Expense	Undepreciated Asset Balance (book value)	Income (after depreciation expense)	Rate of Return (Income ÷ Assets)
0		$500,000		
1	$90,000	410,000	$100,000	24.4%
2	90,000	320,000	100,000	31.2%
3	90,000	230,000	100,000	43.5%
4	90,000	140,000	100,000	71.4%
5	90,000	50,000	100,000	200.0%

Decreasing-Charge Methods

The **decreasing-charge methods** provide for a higher depreciation cost in the earlier years and lower charges in later periods. Because these methods allow for higher early-year charges than in the straight-line method, they are often called **accelerated depreciation methods**.

What is the main justification for this approach? The rationale is that companies should charge more depreciation in earlier years because the asset is most productive in its earlier years. Furthermore, the accelerated methods provide a constant cost because the depreciation charge is lower in the later periods, at the time when the repair and maintenance costs are often higher. Generally, companies use one of two decreasing-charge methods: the sum-of-the-years'-digits method or the declining-balance method.

Sum-of-the-Years'-Digits. The **sum-of-the-years'-digits method** results in a decreasing depreciation charge based on a decreasing fraction of depreciable cost (original cost less salvage value). Each fraction uses the sum of the years as a denominator $(5 + 4 + 3 + 2 + 1 = 15)$. The numerator is the number of years of estimated life remaining as of the beginning of the year. In this method, the numerator decreases year by year, and the denominator remains constant $(5/15, 4/15, 3/15, 2/15, \text{and } 1/15)$. At the end of the asset's useful life, the balance remaining should equal the salvage value. Illustration 11-6 shows this method of computation.[4]

ILLUSTRATION 11-6
Sum-of-the-Years'-Digits Depreciation Schedule— Crane Example

Year	Depreciation Base	Remaining Life in Years	Depreciation Fraction	Depreciation Expense	Book Value, End of Year
1	$450,000	5	5/15	$150,000	$350,000
2	450,000	4	4/15	120,000	230,000
3	450,000	3	3/15	90,000	140,000
4	450,000	2	2/15	60,000	80,000
5	450,000	1	1/15	30,000	50,000[a]
		15	15/15	$450,000	

[a]Salvage value.

[4]What happens if the estimated service life of the asset is, let us say, 51 years? How would we calculate the sum-of-the-years'-digits? Fortunately mathematicians have developed the following formula that permits easy computation:

$$\frac{n(n + 1)}{2} = \frac{51(51 + 1)}{2} = 1{,}326$$

Declining-Balance Method. The declining-balance method utilizes a depreciation rate (expressed as a percentage) that is some multiple of the straight-line method. For example, the double-declining rate for a 10-year asset is 20 percent (double the straight-line rate, which is 1/10 or 10 percent). Companies apply the constant rate to the declining book value each year.

Unlike other methods, the declining-balance method **does not deduct the salvage value** in computing the depreciation base. The declining-balance rate is multiplied by the book value of the asset at the beginning of each period. Since the depreciation charge reduces the book value of the asset each period, applying the constant-declining-balance rate to a successively lower book value results in lower depreciation charges each year. This process continues until the book value of the asset equals its estimated salvage value. At that time, the company discontinues depreciation.

Companies use various multiples in practice. For example, the double-declining-balance method depreciates assets at twice (200 percent) the straight-line rate. Illustration 11-7 shows Stanley's depreciation charges if using the double-declining approach.

Year	Book Value of Asset First of Year	Rate on Declining Balance[a]	Depreciation Expense	Balance Accumulated Depreciation	Book Value, End of Year
1	$500,000	40%	$200,000	$200,000	$300,000
2	300,000	40%	120,000	320,000	180,000
3	180,000	40%	72,000	392,000	108,000
4	108,000	40%	43,200	435,200	64,800
5	64,800	40%	14,800[b]	450,000	50,000

[a]Based on twice the straight-line rate of 20% ($90,000/$450,000 = 20%; 20% × 2 = 40%).
[b]Limited to $14,800 because book value should not be less than salvage value.

ILLUSTRATION 11-7
Double-Declining
Depreciation Schedule—
Crane Example

Companies often switch from the declining-balance method to the straight-line method near the end of the asset's useful life to ensure that they depreciate the asset only to its salvage value.[5]

Special Depreciation Methods

Sometimes companies adopt special depreciation methods. Reasons for doing so might be that a company's assets have unique characteristics, or the nature of the industry. Two of these special methods are:

4 LEARNING OBJECTIVE
Explain special depreciation methods.

1. Group and composite methods.
2. Hybrid or combination methods.

Group and Composite Methods

Companies often depreciate multiple-asset accounts using one rate. For example, AT&T might depreciate telephone poles, microwave systems, or switchboards by groups.

Two methods of depreciating multiple-asset accounts exist: the group method and the composite method. The choice of method depends on the nature of the assets involved. Companies frequently use the group method when the assets are similar in nature and

[5]A pure form of the declining-balance method (sometimes appropriately called the "fixed percentage of book value method") has also been suggested as a possibility. This approach finds a rate that depreciates the asset exactly to salvage value at the end of its expected useful life. The formula for determination of this rate is as follows.

$$\text{Depreciation rate} = 1 - \sqrt[n]{\frac{\text{Salvage value}}{\text{Acquisition cost}}}$$

The life in years is n. After computing the depreciation rate, a company applies it on the declining book value of the asset from period to period, which means that depreciation expense will be successively lower. This method is not used extensively in practice due to cumbersome computations. Further, it is not permitted for tax purposes.

have approximately the same useful lives. They use the **composite approach** when the assets are dissimilar and have different lives. The group method more closely approximates a single-unit cost procedure because the dispersion from the average is not as great. The computation for group or composite methods is essentially the same: find an average and depreciate on that basis.

Companies determine the **composite depreciation rate** by dividing the depreciation per year by the total cost of the assets. To illustrate, Mooney Motors establishes the composite depreciation rate for its fleet of cars, trucks, and campers as shown in Illustration 11-8.

ILLUSTRATION 11-8
Depreciation Calculation, Composite Basis

Asset	Original Cost	Salvage Value	Depreciation Cost	Estimated Life (yrs.)	Depreciation per Year (straight-line)
Cars	$145,000	$25,000	$120,000	3	$40,000
Trucks	44,000	4,000	40,000	4	10,000
Campers	35,000	5,000	30,000	5	6,000
	$224,000	$34,000	$190,000		$56,000

$$\text{Composite depreciation rate} = \frac{\$56,000}{\$224,000} = 25\%$$

Composite life = 3.39 years ($190,000 ÷ $56,000)

If there are no changes in the asset account, Mooney will depreciate the group of assets to the residual or salvage value at the rate of $56,000 ($224,000 × 25%) a year. As a result, it will take Mooney 3.39 years to depreciate these assets. The length of time it takes a company to depreciate its assets on a composite basis is called the **composite life**.

We can highlight the differences between the group or composite method and the single-unit depreciation method by looking at asset retirements. If Mooney retires an asset before or after the average service life of the group is reached, it buries the resulting gain or loss in the Accumulated Depreciation account. This practice is justified because Mooney will retire some assets before the average service life and others after the average life. For this reason, the debit to Accumulated Depreciation is the difference between original cost and cash received. Mooney does not record a gain or loss on disposition.

To illustrate, suppose that Mooney Motors sold one of the campers with a cost of $5,000 for $2,600 at the end of the third year. The entry is:

Accumulated Depreciation—Plant Assets	2,400	
Cash	2,600	
Cars, Trucks, and Campers		5,000

If Mooney purchases a new type of asset (mopeds, for example), it must compute a new depreciation rate and apply this rate in subsequent periods.

Illustration 11-9 presents a typical financial statement disclosure of the group depreciation method for **Ampco-Pittsburgh Corporation**.

ILLUSTRATION 11-9
Disclosure of Group Depreciation Method

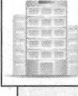

Ampco-Pittsburgh Corporation

Depreciation rates are based on estimated useful lives of the asset groups. Gains or losses on normal retirements or replacements of depreciable assets, subject to composite depreciation methods, are not recognized; the difference between the cost of the assets retired or replaced and the related salvage value is charged or credited to the accumulated depreciation.

The group or composite method simplifies the bookkeeping process and tends to average out errors caused by over- or underdepreciation. As a result, gains or losses on disposals of assets do not distort periodic income.

On the other hand, the unit method (depreciation of single assets) has several advantages over the group or composite methods. (1) It simplifies the computation mathematically. (2) It identifies gains and losses on disposal. (3) It isolates depreciation on idle equipment. (4) It represents the best estimate of the depreciation of each asset, not the result of averaging the cost over a longer period of time. As a consequence, companies generally use the unit method.[6] *Unless stated otherwise, you should use the unit method in homework problems.*

Hybrid or Combination Methods

In addition to the depreciation methods already discussed, companies are free to develop their own special or tailor-made depreciation methods. GAAP requires only that the method result in the allocation of an asset's cost over the asset's life in a **systematic and rational manner**.

For example, the steel industry widely uses a hybrid depreciation method, called the **production variable method**, that is a combination straight-line/activity approach. The following note from **WHX Corporation**'s annual report explains one variation of this method.

WHX Corporation

The Company utilizes the modified units of production method of depreciation which recognizes that the depreciation of steelmaking machinery is related to the physical wear of the equipment as well as a time factor. The modified units of production method provides for straight-line depreciation charges modified (adjusted) by the level of raw steel production. In the prior year, depreciation under the modified units of production method was $21.6 million or 40% less than straight-line depreciation, and in the current year it was $1.1 million or 2% more than straight-line depreciation.

Gateway to the Profession

Expanded Discussion— Special Depreciation Methods

ILLUSTRATION 11-10
Disclosure of Hybrid Depreciation Method

What do the numbers mean? DECELERATING DEPRECIATION

Which depreciation method should management select? Many believe that the method that best matches revenues with expenses should be used. For example, if revenues generated by the asset are constant over its useful life, select straight-line depreciation. On the other hand, if revenues are higher (or lower) at the beginning of the asset's life, then use a decreasing (or increasing) method. Thus, if a company can reliably estimate revenues from the asset, selecting a depreciation method that best matches costs with those revenues would seem to provide the most useful information to investors and creditors for assessing the future cash flows from the asset.

Managers in the real estate industry face a different challenge when considering depreciation choices. Real estate managers object to traditional depreciation methods because in their view, real estate often does not decline in value. In addition, because real estate is highly debt-financed, most real estate concerns report losses in earlier years of operations when the sum of depreciation and interest exceeds the revenue from the real estate project. As a result, real estate companies, like **Kimco Realty**, argue for some form of **increasing-charge** method of depreciation (lower depreciation at the beginning and higher depreciation at the end). With such a method, companies would report higher total assets and net income in the earlier years of the project.[7]

---

[6]A committee of the AICPA has indicated in an exposure draft that companies should use the unit approach whenever feasible. In fact, it indicates that an even better way to depreciate property, plant, and equipment is to use *component depreciation*. Under component depreciation, a company should depreciate over its expected useful life any part or portion of property, plant, and equipment that can be separately identified as an asset. For example, a company could separate the various components of a building (e.g., roof, heating and cooling system, elevator, leasehold improvements) and depreciate each component over its useful life.

[7]In this regard, real estate investment trusts (REITs) often report (in addition to net income) an earnings measure, funds from operations (FFO), that adjusts income for depreciation expense and other noncash expenses. This method is not GAAP. There is mixed empirical evidence about whether FFO or GAAP income is more useful to real estate investment trust investors. See, for example, Richard Gore and David Stott, "Toward a More Informative Measure of Operating Performance in the REIT Industry: Net Income vs. FFO," *Accounting Horizons* (December 1998); and Linda Vincent, "The Information Content of FFO for REITs," *Journal of Accounting and Economics* (January 1999).

International Perspective

IFRS requires use of component depreciation.

Special Depreciation Issues

We still need to discuss several special issues related to depreciation:

1. How should companies compute depreciation for partial periods?
2. Does depreciation provide for the replacement of assets?
3. How should companies handle revisions in depreciation rates?

Depreciation and Partial Periods

Companies seldom purchase plant assets on the first day of a fiscal period or dispose of them on the last day of a fiscal period. A practical question is: How much depreciation should a company charge for the partial periods involved?

In computing depreciation expense for partial periods, companies must determine the depreciation expense for the full year and then prorate this depreciation expense between the two periods involved. This process should continue throughout the useful life of the asset.

Assume, for example, that Steeltex Company purchases an automated drill machine with a five-year life for $45,000 (no salvage value) on June 10, 2013. The company's fiscal year ends December 31. Steeltex therefore charges depreciation for only $6\frac{2}{3}$ months during that year. The total depreciation for a full year (assuming straight-line depreciation) is $9,000 ($45,000/5). The depreciation for the first, partial year is therefore:

$$\frac{6\frac{2}{3}}{12} \times \$9,000 = \$5,000$$

The partial-period calculation is relatively simple when Steeltex uses straight-line depreciation. But how is partial-period depreciation handled when it uses an accelerated method such as sum-of-the-years'-digits or double-declining-balance? As an illustration, assume that Steeltex purchased another machine for $10,000 on July 1, 2013, with an estimated useful life of five years and no salvage value. Illustration 11-11 shows the depreciation figures for 2013, 2014, and 2015.

ILLUSTRATION 11-11
Calculation of Partial-Period Depreciation, Two Accelerated Methods

	Sum-of-the-Years'-Digits	Double-Declining-Balance
1st full year	(5/15 × $10,000) = $3,333.33	(40% × $10,000) = $4,000
2nd full year	(4/15 × 10,000) = 2,666.67	(40% × 6,000) = 2,400
3rd full year	(3/15 × 10,000) = 2,000.00	(40% × 3,600) = 1,440

Depreciation from July 1, 2013, to December 31, 2013

| 6/12 × $3,333.33 = $1,666.67 | 6/12 × $4,000 = $2,000 |

Depreciation for 2014

6/12 × $3,333.33 = $1,666.67	6/12 × $4,000 = $2,000
6/12 × 2,666.67 = 1,333.33	6/12 × 2,400 = 1,200
$3,000.00	$3,200

or ($10,000 − $2,000) × 40% = $3,200

Depreciation for 2015

6/12 × $2,666.67 = $1,333.33	6/12 × $2,400 = $1,200
6/12 × 2,000.00 = 1,000.00	6/12 × 1,440 = 720
$2,333.33	$1,920

or ($10,000 − $5,200) × 40% = $1,920

Sometimes a company like Steeltex modifies the process of allocating costs to a partial period to handle acquisitions and disposals of plant assets more simply. One variation is to take no depreciation in the year of acquisition and a full year's depreciation in the year of disposal. Other variations charge one-half year's depreciation both in the year of acquisition and in the year of disposal (referred to as the **half-year convention**), or charge a full year in the year of acquisition and none in the year of disposal.

In fact, Steeltex may adopt any one of these fractional-year policies in allocating cost to the first and last years of an asset's life so long as it applies the method consistently. However, **unless otherwise stipulated, companies normally compute depreciation on the basis of the nearest full month**.

Illustration 11-12 shows depreciation allocated under five different fractional-year policies using the straight-line method on the $45,000 automated drill machine purchased by Steeltex Company on June 10, 2013, discussed earlier.

Machine Cost = $45,000	Depreciation Allocated per Period Over 5-Year Life*					
Fractional-Year Policy	2013	2014	2015	2016	2017	2018
1. Nearest fraction of a year.	$5,000[a]	$9,000	$9,000	$9,000	$9,000	$4,000[b]
2. Nearest full month.	5,250[c]	9,000	9,000	9,000	9,000	3,750[d]
3. Half year in period of acquisition and disposal.	4,500	9,000	9,000	9,000	9,000	4,500
4. Full year in period of acquisition, none in period of disposal.	9,000	9,000	9,000	9,000	9,000	–0–
5. None in period of acquisition, full year in period of disposal.	–0–	9,000	9,000	9,000	9,000	9,000

[a]6.667/12 ($9,000)   [b]5.333/12 ($9,000)   [c]7/12 ($9,000)   [d]5/12 ($9,000)
*Rounded to nearest dollar.

ILLUSTRATION 11-12
Fractional-Year
Depreciation Policies

Depreciation and Replacement of Property, Plant, and Equipment

A common misconception about depreciation is that it provides funds for the replacement of fixed assets. Depreciation is like other expenses in that it reduces net income. It differs, though, in that **it does not involve a current cash outflow**.

To illustrate why depreciation does not provide funds for replacement of plant assets, assume that a business starts operating with plant assets of $500,000 that have a useful life of five years. The company's balance sheet at the beginning of the period is:

Plant assets $500,000	Stockholders' equity $500,000	

If we assume that the company earns no revenue over the five years, the income statements are:

	Year 1	Year 2	Year 3	Year 4	Year 5
Revenue	$ –0–	$ –0–	$ –0–	$ –0–	$ –0–
Depreciation	(100,000)	(100,000)	(100,000)	(100,000)	(100,000)
Loss	$(100,000)	$(100,000)	$(100,000)	$(100,000)	$(100,000)

Total depreciation of the plant assets over the five years is $500,000. The balance sheet at the end of the five years therefore is:

Plant assets –0–	Stockholders' equity –0–	

This extreme example illustrates that depreciation **in no way** provides funds for the replacement of assets. **The funds for the replacement of the assets come from the revenues** (generated through use of the asset). Without the revenues, no income materializes and no cash inflow results.

Revision of Depreciation Rates

When purchasing a plant asset, companies carefully determine depreciation rates based on past experience with similar assets and other pertinent information. The provisions for depreciation are only estimates, however. Companies may need to revise them during the life of the asset. Unexpected physical deterioration or unforeseen obsolescence may decrease the estimated useful life of the asset. Improved maintenance procedures, revision of operating procedures, or similar developments may prolong the life of the asset beyond the expected period.[8]

For example, assume that **International Paper Co.** purchased machinery with an original cost of $90,000. It estimates a 20-year life with no salvage value. However, during year 6, International Paper estimates that it will use the machine for an additional 25 years. Its total life, therefore, will be 30 years instead of 20. Depreciation has been recorded at the rate of 1/20 of $90,000, or $4,500 per year by the straight-line method. On the basis of a 30-year life, International Paper should have recorded depreciation as 1/30 of $90,000, or $3,000 per year. It has therefore overstated depreciation, and understated net income, by $1,500 for each of the past five years, or a total amount of $7,500. Illustration 11-13 shows this computation.

ILLUSTRATION 11-13
Computation of
Accumulated Difference
Due to Revisions

	Per Year	For 5 Years
Depreciation charged per books (1/20 × $90,000)	$4,500	$22,500
Depreciation based on a 30-year life (1/30 × $90,000)	(3,000)	(15,000)
Excess depreciation charged	$1,500	$ 7,500

International Paper should report this change in estimate in the current and prospective periods (prospectively): It should not make any changes in previously reported results. And it does not adjust opening balances nor attempt to "catch up" for prior periods. The reason? Changes in estimates are a continual and inherent part of any estimation process. Continual restatement of prior periods would occur for revisions of estimates unless handled prospectively. Therefore, no entry is made at the time the change in estimate occurs. Charges for depreciation in subsequent periods (assuming use of the straight-line method) are determined by **dividing the remaining book value less any salvage value by the remaining estimated life**.

ILLUSTRATION 11-14
Computing Depreciation
after Revision of
Estimated Life

Machinery	$90,000
Less: Accumulated depreciation	22,500
Book value of machinery at end of 5th year	$67,500

Depreciation (future periods) = $67,500 book value ÷ 25 years remaining life = $2,700

The entry to record depreciation for each of the remaining 25 years is:

Depreciation Expense	2,700	
Accumulated Depreciation—Machinery		2,700

[8]As an example of a change in operating procedures, **General Motors (GM)** used to write off its tools—such as dies and equipment used to manufacture car bodies—over the life of the body type. Through this procedure, it expensed tools twice as fast as **Ford** and three times as fast as **Chrysler**. However, it slowed the depreciation process on these tools and lengthened the lives on its plant and equipment. These revisions reduced depreciation and amortization charges by approximately $1.23 billion, or $2.55 per share, in the year of the change. In Chapter 22, we provide a more complete discussion of changes in estimates.

The amount of depreciation expense recorded depends on both the depreciation method used and estimates of service lives and salvage values of the assets. Differences in these choices and estimates can significantly impact a company's reported results and can make it difficult to compare the depreciation numbers of different companies.

For example, when Willamette Industries extended the estimated service lives of its machinery and equipment by five years, it increased income by nearly $54 million (see Note 4 to the right).

An analyst determines the impact of these management choices and judgments on the amount of depreciation expense by examining the notes to financial statements. For example, Willamette Industries provided the following note to its financial statements.

Note 4: Property, Plant, and Equipment (partial)	
	Range of Useful Lives
Land	—
Buildings	15–35
Machinery & equipment	5–25
Furniture & fixtures	3–15

During the year, the estimated service lives for most machinery and equipment were extended five years. The change was based upon a study performed by the company's engineering department, comparisons to typical industry practices, and the effect of the company's extensive capital investments which have resulted in a mix of assets with longer productive lives due to technological advances. As a result of the change, net income was increased by $54,000,000.

IMPAIRMENTS

The general accounting standard of **lower-of-cost-or-market for inventories does not apply to property, plant, and equipment**. Even when property, plant, and equipment has suffered partial obsolescence, accountants have been reluctant to reduce the asset's carrying amount. Why? Because, unlike inventories, it is difficult to arrive at a fair value for property, plant, and equipment that is not subjective and arbitrary.

For example, Falconbridge Ltd. Nickel Mines had to decide whether to write off all or a part of its property, plant, and equipment in a nickel-mining operation in the Dominican Republic. The project had been incurring losses because nickel prices were low and operating costs were high. Only if nickel prices increased by approximately 33 percent would the project be reasonably profitable. Whether a write-off was appropriate depended on the future price of nickel. Even if the company decided to write off the asset, how much should be written off?

Recognizing Impairments

As discussed in the opening story, the credit crisis starting in late 2008 has affected many financial and nonfinancial institutions. As a result of the global slump, many companies are considering write-offs of some of their long-lived assets. These write-offs are referred to as impairments.

Various events and changes in circumstances might lead to an impairment. Examples are:

• A significant decrease in the fair value of an asset.

• A significant change in the extent or manner in which an asset is used.

• A significant adverse change in legal factors or in the business climate that affects the value of an asset.

5 LEARNING OBJECTIVE

Explain the accounting issues related to asset impairment.

Underlying Concepts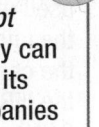

The *going concern concept* assumes that the company can recover the investment in its assets. Under GAAP, companies do not report the fair value of long-lived assets because a going concern does not plan to sell such assets. However, if the assumption of being able to recover the cost of the investment is not valid, then a company should report a reduction in value.

- An accumulation of costs significantly in excess of the amount originally expected to acquire or construct an asset.
- A projection or forecast that demonstrates continuing losses associated with an asset.

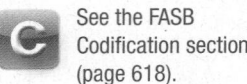

See the FASB
Codification section
(page 618).

These events or changes in circumstances indicate that the company may not be able to recover the carrying amount of the asset. In that case, a **recoverability test** is used to determine whether an impairment has occurred. **[1]**

To apply the first step of the recoverability test, a company like **UPS** estimates the future net cash flows expected from the **use of that asset and its eventual disposition**. If the sum of the expected future net cash flows (undiscounted) is **less than the carrying amount** of the asset, UPS considers the asset impaired. Conversely, if the sum of the expected future net cash flows (undiscounted) is **equal to or greater than the carrying amount** of the asset, no impairment has occurred.

The recoverability test therefore screens for asset impairment. For example, if the expected future net cash flows from an asset are $400,000 and its carrying amount is $350,000, no impairment has occurred. However, if the expected future net cash flows are $300,000, an impairment has occurred. The rationale for the recoverability test relies on a basic presumption: A balance sheet should report long-lived assets at no more than the carrying amounts that are recoverable.

Measuring Impairments

If the recoverability test indicates an impairment, UPS computes a loss. The **impairment loss** is the amount by which the carrying amount of the asset **exceeds its fair value**. How does UPS determine the fair value of an asset? It is measured based on the market price if an active market for the asset exists. If no active market exists, UPS uses the **present value of expected future net cash flows to determine fair value**.

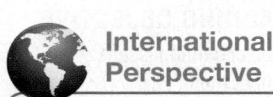

**International
Perspective**

IFRS also uses a fair value test to measure the impairment loss. However, IFRS does not use the first-stage recoverability test used under GAAP—comparing the undiscounted cash flows to the carrying amount. As a result, the IFRS test is more strict than GAAP.

To summarize, the process of determining an impairment loss is as follows.

1. Review events or changes in circumstances for possible impairment.
2. If the review indicates a possible impairment, apply the recoverability test. If the sum of the expected future net cash flows from the long-lived asset is less than the carrying amount of the asset, an impairment has occurred.
3. Assuming an impairment, the impairment loss is the amount by which the carrying amount of the asset exceeds the fair value of the asset. The fair value is the market price of the asset or the present value of expected future net cash flows.

Impairment—Example 1

M. Alou Inc. has equipment that, due to changes in its use, it reviews for possible impairment. The equipment's carrying amount is $600,000 ($800,000 cost less $200,000 accumulated depreciation). Alou determines the expected future net cash flows (undiscounted) from the use of the equipment and its eventual disposal to be $650,000.

The recoverability test indicates that the $650,000 of expected future net cash flows from the equipment's use exceed the carrying amount of $600,000. As a result, no impairment occurred. (Recall that the undiscounted future net cash flows must be less than the carrying amount for Alou to deem an asset to be impaired and to measure the impairment loss.) Therefore, M. Alou Inc. does not recognize an impairment loss in this case.

Impairment—Example 2

Assume the same facts as in Example 1, except that the expected future net cash flows from Alou's equipment are $580,000 (instead of $650,000). The recoverability test indicates that the expected future net cash flows of $580,000 from the use of the asset are less than its carrying amount of $600,000. Therefore, an impairment has occurred.

The difference between the carrying amount of Alou's asset and its fair value is the impairment loss. Assuming this asset has a fair value of $525,000, Illustration 11-15 shows the loss computation.

Carrying amount of the equipment	$600,000
Fair value of equipment	(525,000)
Loss on impairment	$ 75,000

ILLUSTRATION 11-15
Computation of
Impairment Loss

M. Alou records the impairment loss as follows.

Loss on Impairment	75,000	
Accumulated Depreciation—Equipment		75,000

M. Alou Inc. reports the impairment loss as part of income from continuing operations, in the "Other expenses and losses" section. Generally, Alou **should not report this loss as an extraordinary item**. Costs associated with an impairment loss are the same costs that would flow through operations and that it would report as part of continuing operations. Alou will continue to use these assets in operations. Therefore, it should not report the loss below "Income from continuing operations."

A company that recognizes an impairment loss should disclose the asset(s) impaired, the events leading to the impairment, the amount of the loss, and how it determined fair value (disclosing the interest rate used, if appropriate).

Restoration of Impairment Loss

After recording an impairment loss, the reduced carrying amount of an asset held for use becomes its new cost basis. A company does not change the new cost basis except for depreciation or amortization in future periods or for additional impairments.

To illustrate, assume that Damon Company at December 31, 2013, has equipment with a carrying amount of $500,000. Damon determines this asset is impaired and writes it down to its fair value of $400,000. At the end of 2014, Damon determines that the fair value of the asset is $480,000. The carrying amount of the equipment should not change in 2014 except for the depreciation taken in 2014. Damon **may not restore an impairment loss for an asset held for use**. The rationale for not writing the asset up in value is that the new cost basis puts the impaired asset on an equal basis with other assets that are unimpaired.

International Perspective

IFRS permits write-ups for subsequent recoveries of impairment, back up to the original amount before the impairment. GAAP prohibits those write-ups, except for assets to be disposed of.

Impairment of Assets to Be Disposed Of

What happens if a company intends to dispose of the impaired asset, instead of holding it for use? At one time, Kroger recorded an impairment loss of $54 million on property, plant, and equipment it no longer needed due to store closures. In this case, Kroger reports the impaired asset at the lower-of-cost-or-net realizable value (fair value less costs to sell). Because Kroger intends to dispose of the assets in a short period of time, it uses net realizable value in order to provide a better measure of the net cash flows that it will receive from these assets.

Kroger does not depreciate or amortize assets held for disposal during the period it holds them. The rationale is that depreciation is inconsistent with the notion of assets to be disposed of and with the use of the lower-of-cost-or-net realizable value. In other words, **assets held for disposal are like inventory; companies should report them at the lower-of-cost-or-net realizable value**.

Because Kroger will recover assets held for disposal through sale rather than through operations, it continually revalues them. Each period, the assets are reported at the lower-of-cost-or-net realizable value. Thus, **Kroger can write up or down an asset held for disposal in future periods, as long as the carrying value after the write-up never exceeds the carrying amount of the asset before the impairment**. Companies should report losses or gains related to these impaired assets as part of **income from continuing operations**.

Illustration 11-16 summarizes the key concepts in accounting for impairments.

ILLUSTRATION 11-16
Graphic of Accounting
for Impairments

DEPLETION

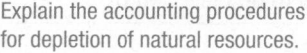

LEARNING OBJECTIVE **6**

Explain the accounting procedures
for depletion of natural resources.

Natural resources, often called wasting assets, include petroleum, minerals, and timber. They have two main features: (1) the complete removal (consumption) of the asset, and (2) replacement of the asset only by an act of nature. Unlike plant and equipment, natural resources are consumed physically over the period of use and do not maintain their physical characteristics. Still, the accounting problems associated with natural resources are similar to those encountered with fixed assets. The questions to be answered are:

1. How do companies establish the cost basis for write-off?

2. What pattern of allocation should companies employ?

Recall that the accounting profession uses the term **depletion** for the process of allocating the cost of natural resources.

Establishing a Depletion Base

How do we determine the depletion base for natural resources? For example, a company like ExxonMobil makes sizable expenditures to find natural resources. And for every successful discovery, there are many failures. Furthermore, the company encounters long delays between the time it incurs costs and the time it obtains the benefits from the extracted resources. As a result, a company in the extractive industries, like ExxonMobil, frequently adopts a conservative policy in accounting for the expenditures related to finding and extracting natural resources.

Computation of the depletion base involves four factors: (1) acquisition cost of the deposit, (2) exploration costs, (3) development costs, and (4) restoration costs.

Acquisition Costs

Acquisition cost is the price ExxonMobil pays to obtain the property right to search and find an undiscovered natural resource. It also can be the price paid for an already-discovered resource. A third type of acquisition cost can be lease payments for property containing a productive natural resource. Included in these acquisition costs are royalty payments to the owner of the property.

Generally, the acquisition cost of natural resources is recorded in an account titled Undeveloped Property. ExxonMobil later assigns that cost to the natural resource if exploration efforts are successful. If the efforts are unsuccessful, it writes off the acquisition cost as a loss.

Exploration Costs

As soon as a company has the right to use the property, it often incurs exploration costs needed to find the resource. When exploration costs are substantial, some companies capitalize them into the depletion base. In the oil and gas industry, where the costs of finding the resource are significant and the risks of finding the resource are very uncertain, most large companies expense these costs. Smaller oil and gas companies often capitalize these exploration costs. We examine the unique issues related to the oil and gas industry on pages 608–609 (see "Continuing Controversy").

Development Costs

Companies divide development costs into two parts: (1) tangible equipment costs and (2) intangible development costs. Tangible equipment costs include all of the transportation and other heavy equipment needed to extract the resource and get it ready for market. Because companies can move the heavy equipment from one extracting site to another, companies do not normally include **tangible equipment costs in the depletion base**. Instead, they use separate depreciation charges to allocate the costs of such equipment. However, some tangible assets (e.g., a drilling rig foundation) cannot be moved. Companies depreciate these assets over their useful life or the life of the resource, whichever is shorter.

Intangible development costs, on the other hand, are such items as drilling costs, tunnels, shafts, and wells. These costs have no tangible characteristics but are needed for the production of the natural resource. **Intangible development costs are considered part of the depletion base.**

Restoration Costs

Companies sometimes incur substantial costs to restore property to its natural state after extraction has occurred. These are restoration costs. Companies consider **restoration costs part of the depletion base**. The amount included in the depletion base is the fair value of the obligation to restore the property after extraction. A more complete discussion of the accounting for restoration costs and related liabilities (sometimes referred to as asset retirement obligations) is provided in Chapter 13. Similar to other long-lived assets, companies deduct from the depletion base any salvage value to be received on the property.

Write-Off of Resource Cost

Once the company establishes the depletion base, the next problem is determining how to allocate the cost of the natural resource to accounting periods.

Normally, companies compute depletion (often referred to as cost depletion) on a **units-of-production method** (an activity approach). Thus, depletion is a function of the number of units extracted during the period. In this approach, the total cost of the natural resource less salvage value is divided by the number of units estimated to be in the resource deposit, to obtain a **cost per unit of product**. To compute depletion, the cost per unit is then multiplied by the number of units extracted.

For example, MaClede Co. acquired the right to use 1,000 acres of land in Alaska to mine for gold. The lease cost is $50,000, and the related exploration costs on the property are $100,000. Intangible development costs incurred in opening the mine are $850,000. Total costs related to the mine before the first ounce of gold is extracted are, therefore, $1,000,000. MaClede estimates that the mine will provide approximately 100,000 ounces of gold. Illustration 11-17 shows computation of the depletion cost per unit (depletion rate).

ILLUSTRATION 11-17
Computation of
Depletion Rate

$$\frac{\text{Total cost} - \text{Salvage value}}{\text{Total estimated units available}} = \text{Depletion cost per unit}$$

$$\frac{\$1,000,000}{100,000} = \$10 \text{ per ounce}$$

If MaClede extracts 25,000 ounces in the first year, then the depletion for the year is $250,000 (25,000 ounces × $10). It records the depletion as follows.

Inventory (gold)	250,000	
Gold Mine		250,000

MaClede debits Inventory for the total depletion for the year and credits Gold Mine to reduce the carrying value of the natural resource. MaClede credits Inventory when it sells the inventory and debits Cost of Goods Sold. The amount not sold remains in inventory and is reported in the current assets section of the balance sheet.[9]

Sometimes companies use an Accumulated Depletion account. In that case, MaClede's balance sheet would present the cost of the natural resource and the amount of accumulated depletion entered to date as follows.

ILLUSTRATION 11-18
Balance Sheet
Presentation of Natural
Resource

Gold mine (at cost)	$1,000,000	
Less: Accumulated depletion	250,000	$750,000

For purposes of homework, credit depletion to the asset account.

[9] The tax law has long provided a deduction against revenue from oil, gas, and most minerals for the greater of cost or percentage depletion. The percentage (statutory) depletion allows some companies a write-off ranging from 5 percent to 22 percent (depending on the natural resource) of gross revenue received. As a result of this tax benefit, the amount of depletion may exceed the cost assigned to a given natural resource. An asset's carrying amount may be zero, but the company may take a depletion deduction if it has gross revenue. The significance of the percentage depletion allowance is now greatly reduced since Congress repealed it for most oil and gas companies.

MaClede may also depreciate on a units-of-production basis the tangible equipment used in extracting the gold. This approach is appropriate if it can directly assign the estimated lives of the equipment to one given resource deposit. If MaClede uses the equipment on more than one job, other cost allocation methods such as straight-line or accelerated depreciation methods would be more appropriate.

Estimating Recoverable Reserves

Sometimes companies need to change the estimate of recoverable reserves. They do so either because they have new information or because more sophisticated production processes are available. Natural resources such as oil and gas deposits and some rare metals have recently provided the greatest challenges. Estimates of these reserves are in large measure merely "knowledgeable guesses."

This problem is the **same as accounting for changes in estimates for the useful lives of plant and equipment**. The procedure is to **revise the depletion rate on a prospective basis**: A company divides the remaining cost by the new estimate of the recoverable reserves. This approach has much merit because the required estimates are so uncertain.

What do the numbers mean? *RESERVE SURPRISE*

Cuts in the estimates of oil and natural gas reserves at **Royal Dutch Shell**, **El Paso Corporation**, and other energy companies at one time highlighted the importance of reserve disclosures. Investors appeared to believe that these disclosures provide useful information for assessing the future cash flows from a company's oil and gas reserves. For example, when Shell's estimates turned out to be overly optimistic (to the tune of 3.9 billion barrels or 20 percent of reserves), Shell's stock price fell.

The experience at Shell and other companies has led the SEC to look at how companies are estimating their "proved" reserves. *Proved reserves* are quantities of oil and gas that can be shown "with reasonable certainty to be recoverable in future years. . . ." The phrase "reasonable certainty" is crucial to this guidance, but differences in interpretation of what is reasonably certain can result in a wide range of estimates.

In one case, for example, **ExxonMobil**'s estimate was 29 percent higher than an estimate the SEC developed. Exxon-Mobil was more optimistic about the effects of new technology that enables the industry to retrieve more of the oil and gas it finds. Thus, to ensure the continued usefulness of reserve information disclosures, the SEC continues to work on a measurement methodology that keeps up with technology changes in the oil and gas industry.

Sources: S. Labaton and J. Gerth, "At Shell, New Accounting and Rosier Outlook," *New York Times* (*nytimes.com*) (March 12, 2004); and J. Ball, C. Cummins, and B. Bahree, "Big Oil Differs with SEC on Methods to Calculate the Industry's Reserves," *Wall Street Journal* (February 24, 2005), p. C1.

Liquidating Dividends

A company often owns as its only major asset a property from which it intends to extract natural resources. If the company does not expect to purchase additional properties, it may gradually distribute to stockholders their capital investments by paying **liquidating dividends**, which are dividends greater than the amount of accumulated net income.

The major accounting problem is to distinguish between dividends that are a return of capital and those that are not. Because the dividend is a return of the investor's original contribution, the company issuing a liquidating dividend should debit Paid-in Capital in Excess of Par for that portion related to the original investment, instead of debiting Retained Earnings.

To illustrate, at year-end, Callahan Mining had a retained earnings balance of $1,650,000, accumulated depletion on mineral properties of $2,100,000, and paid-in capital in excess of par of $5,435,493. Callahan's board declared a dividend of $3 per share on the 1,000,000 shares outstanding. It records the $3,000,000 cash dividend as follows.

Retained Earnings	1,650,000	
Paid-in Capital in Excess of Par—Common Stock	1,350,000	
Cash		3,000,000

Callahan must inform stockholders that the $3 dividend per share represents a $1.65 ($1,650,000 ÷ 1,000,000 shares) per share return on investment and a $1.35 ($1,350,000 ÷ 1,000,000 shares) per share liquidating dividend.

Continuing Controversy

A major controversy relates to the accounting for exploration costs in the oil and gas industry. Conceptually, the question is whether unsuccessful ventures are a cost of those that are successful. Those who hold the **full-cost concept** argue that the cost of drilling a dry hole is a cost needed to find the commercially profitable wells. Others believe that companies should capitalize only the costs of successful projects. This is the **successful-efforts concept**. Its proponents believe that the only relevant measure for a project is the cost directly related to that project, and that companies should report any remaining costs as period charges. In addition, they argue that an unsuccessful company will end up capitalizing many costs that will make it, over a short period of time, show no less income than does one that is successful.[10]

The FASB has attempted to narrow the available alternatives, with little success. Here is a brief history of the debate.

1. *1977—The FASB required oil and gas companies to follow successful-efforts accounting.* Small oil and gas producers, voicing strong opposition, lobbied extensively in Congress. Governmental agencies assessed the implications of this standard from a public interest perspective and reacted contrary to the FASB's position.[11]

2. *1978—In response to criticisms of the FASB's actions, the SEC reexamined the issue and found both the successful-efforts and full-cost approaches inadequate. Neither method, said the SEC, reflects the economic substance of oil and gas exploration.* As a substitute, the SEC argued in favor of a yet-to-be developed method, **reserve recognition accounting (RRA)**, which it believed would provide more useful information. Under RRA, as soon as a company discovers oil, it reports the value of the oil on the balance sheet and in the income statement. Thus, RRA is a fair value approach, in contrast to full-costing and successful-efforts, which are historical cost approaches. The use of RRA would make a substantial difference in the balance sheets and income statements of oil companies. For example, **Atlantic Richfield Co.** at one time reported net producing property of $2.6 billion. Under RRA, the same properties would be valued at $11.8 billion.

3. *1979–1981—As a result of the SEC's actions, the FASB issued another standard that suspended the requirement that companies follow successful-efforts accounting.*

---

[10]Large international oil companies such as **ExxonMobil** use the successful-efforts approach. Most of the smaller, exploration-oriented companies use the full-cost approach. The differences in net income figures under the two methods can be staggering. Analysts estimated that the difference between full-cost and successful-efforts for **ChevronTexaco** would be $500 million over a 10-year period (income lower under successful-efforts).

[11]The Department of Energy indicated that companies using the full-cost method at that time would reduce their exploration activities because of the unfavorable earnings impact associated with successful-efforts accounting. The Justice Department asked the SEC to postpone adoption of one uniform method of accounting in the oil and gas industry until the SEC could determine whether the information reported to investors would be enhanced and competition constrained by adoption of the successful-efforts method.

Therefore, full-costing was again permissible. In attempting to implement RRA, however, the SEC encountered practical problems in estimating **(1) the amount of the reserves**, **(2) the future production costs**, **(3) the periods of expected disposal**, **(4) the discount rate**, **and (5) the selling price**. Companies needed an estimate for each of these to arrive at an accurate valuation of existing reserves. Estimating the future selling price, appropriate discount rate, and future extraction and delivery costs of reserves that are years away from realization can be a formidable task.

4. *1981—The SEC abandoned RRA in the primary financial statements of oil and gas producers.* The SEC decided that RRA did not possess the required degree of reliability for use as a primary method of financial reporting. However, it continued to stress the need for some form of fair-value-based disclosure for oil and gas reserves. As a result, the profession now requires fair value disclosures for those natural resources.

Currently, companies can use either the full-cost approach or the successful-efforts approach. It does seem ironic that Congress directed the FASB to develop one method of accounting for the oil and gas industry, and when the FASB did so, the government chose not to accept it. Subsequently, the SEC attempted to develop a new approach, failed, and then urged the FASB to develop the disclosure requirements in this area. After all these changes, the two alternatives still exist.[12]

International Perspective

IFRS also permits companies to use either full-cost or successful-efforts approaches.

Evolving Issue | *FULL-COST OR SUCCESSFUL-EFFORTS?*

The controversy in the oil and gas industry provides a number of lessons. First, it demonstrates the strong influence that the federal government has in financial reporting matters. Second, the concern for economic consequences places pressure on the FASB to weigh the economic effects of any required standard. Third, the experience with RRA highlights the problems that accompany any proposed change from an historical cost to a fair value approach. Fourth, this controversy illustrates the difficulty of establishing standards when affected groups have differing viewpoints.

Indeed, failure to consider the economic consequences of accounting principles is a frequent criticism of the profession. However, the neutrality concept requires that the statements be free from bias. Freedom from bias requires that the statements reflect economic reality, even if undesirable effects occur. Finally, the debate over oil and gas accounting reinforces the need for a conceptual framework with carefully developed guidelines for recognition, measurement, and reporting, so that interested parties can more easily resolve issues of this nature in the future.

PRESENTATION AND ANALYSIS
Presentation of Property, Plant, Equipment, and Natural Resources

A company should disclose the basis of valuation—usually historical cost—for property, plant, equipment, and natural resources along with pledges, liens, and other commitments related to these assets. It should not offset any liability secured by property, plant, equipment, and natural resources against these assets. Instead, this obligation should be reported in the liabilities section. The company should

7 LEARNING OBJECTIVE

Explain how to report and analyze property, plant, equipment, and natural resources.

---

[12]One requirement of the full-cost approach is that companies can capitalize costs only up to a ceiling, which is the present value of company reserves. Companies must expense costs above that ceiling. When the price of oil fell in the mid-1980s, so did the present value of companies' reserves, which forced expensing of costs beyond the ceiling. Companies lobbied for leniency, but the SEC decided that the write-offs had to be taken. **Mesa Limited Partnerships** restated its $31 million profit to a $169 million loss, and **Pacific Lighting** restated its $44.5 million profit to a $70.5 million loss.

segregate property, plant, and equipment not currently employed as producing assets in the business (such as idle facilities or land held as an investment) from assets used in operations.

When depreciating assets, a company credits a valuation account such as Accumulated Depreciation—Equipment. Using an accumulated depreciation account permits the user of the financial statements to see the original cost of the asset and the amount of depreciation that the company charged to expense in past years.

When depleting natural resources, some companies use an accumulated depletion account. Many, however, simply credit the natural resource account directly. The rationale for this approach is that the natural resources are physically consumed, making direct reduction of the cost of the natural resources appropriate.

Because of the significant impact on the financial statements of the depreciation method(s) used, companies should disclose the following.

1. Depreciation expense for the period.

2. Balances of major classes of depreciable assets, by nature and function.

3. Accumulated depreciation, either by major classes of depreciable assets or in total.

4. A general description of the method or methods used in computing depreciation with respect to major classes of depreciable assets. **[2]**[13]

Special disclosure requirements relate to the oil and gas industry. Companies engaged in these activities must disclose the following in their financial statements: (1) the basic method of accounting for those costs incurred in oil and gas producing activities (e.g., full-cost versus successful-efforts), and (2) how the company disposes of costs relating to extractive activities (e.g., dispensing immediately versus depreciation and depletion). **[3]**[14]

The 2011 annual report of International Paper Company in Illustration 11-19 shows an acceptable disclosure. It uses condensed balance sheet data supplemented with details and policies in notes to the financial statements.

ILLUSTRATION 11-19
Disclosures for Property,
Plant, Equipment, and
Natural Resources

International Paper Company

Consolidated Balance Sheet (partial)

In millions at December 31	2011	2010
Assets		
Total current assets	$10,456	$ 8,028
Plants, properties and equipment, net	11,817	12,002
Forestlands	660	747
Investments	632	1,092
Goodwill	2,346	2,308
Deferred charges and other assets	1,082	1,191
Total assets	$26,993	$25,368

[13]Some believe that companies should disclose the average useful life of the assets or the range of years of asset life to help users understand the age and life of property, plant, and equipment.

[14]Public companies, in addition to these two required disclosures, must include as supplementary information numerous schedules reporting reserve quantities; capitalized costs; acquisition, exploration, and development activities; and a standardized measure of discounted future net cash flows related to proved oil and gas reserve quantities. Given the importance of these disclosures, the SEC has issued rules for disclosures to help investors better understand the nature of oil and gas company operations. These rules provide updated guidance on (1) estimates of quantities of proved reserves, (2) estimates of future net revenues, and (3) disclosure of reserve information. See "Modernization of Oil and Gas Reporting," SEC Financial Reporting Release No. 78 (Release No. 33-8995) (December 31, 2008).

ILLUSTRATION 11-19
(*continued*)

Note 1 (partial)

Plants, Properties and Equipment.   Plants, properties and equipment are stated at cost, less accumulated depreciation. Expenditures for betterments are capitalized, whereas normal repairs and maintenance are expensed as incurred. The units-of-production method of depreciation is used for major pulp and paper mills, and the straight-line method is used for other plants and equipment. Annual straight-line depreciation rates are, for buildings—2 1/2% to 8 1/2%, and for machinery and equipment—5% to 33%.

Forestlands.   At December 31, 2011, International Paper and its subsidiaries owned or managed approximately 325,000 acres of forestlands in Brazil, and through licenses and forest management agreements, had harvesting rights on government-owned forestlands in Russia. Costs attributable to timber are charged against income as trees are cut. The rate charged is determined annually based on the relationship of incurred costs to estimated current merchantable volume.

Note 7 (partial)

Plants, properties and equipment by major classification were:

In millions at December 31	2011	2010
Pulp, paper and packaging facilities		
Mills	$22,494	$22,935
Packaging plants	6,358	6,534
Other plants, properties and equipment	1,556	1,524
Gross cost	30,408	30,993
Less: Accumulated depreciation	18,591	18,991
Plants, properties and equipment, net	$11,817	$12,002

In millions	2011	2010	2009
Depreciation expense	$1,263	$1,396	$1,416

Analysis of Property, Plant, and Equipment

Analysts evaluate assets relative to activity (turnover) and profitability.

Asset Turnover

How efficiently a company uses its assets to generate sales is measured by the **asset turnover**. This ratio divides net sales by average total assets for the period. The resulting number is the dollars of sales produced by each dollar invested in assets. To illustrate, we use the following data from the Johnson & Johnson 2011 annual report. Illustration 11-20 shows computation of the asset turnover.

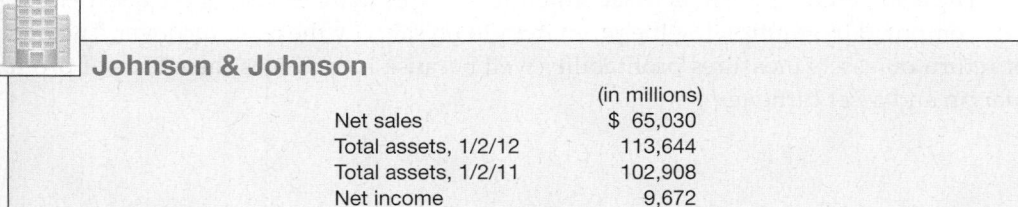

Johnson & Johnson

	(in millions)
Net sales	$ 65,030
Total assets, 1/2/12	113,644
Total assets, 1/2/11	102,908
Net income	9,672

$$\text{Asset turnover} = \frac{\text{Net sales}}{\text{Average total assets}}$$

$$= \frac{\$65,030}{(\$113,644 + \$102,908)/2}$$

$$= .60$$

ILLUSTRATION 11-20
Asset Turnover

The asset turnover shows that Johnson & Johnson generated sales of $0.60 per dollar of assets in the year ended January 2, 2012.

  Asset turnovers vary considerably among industries. For example, a large utility like Ameren has a ratio of 0.32 times. A large grocery chain like Kroger has a ratio of 2.73 times. Thus, in comparing performance among companies based on the asset turnover ratio, you need to consider the ratio within the context of the industry in which a company operates.

Profit Margin on Sales

Another measure for analyzing the use of property, plant, and equipment is the **profit margin on sales** (return on sales). Calculated as net income divided by net sales, this profitability ratio does not, by itself, answer the question of how profitably a company uses its assets. But by relating the profit margin on sales to the asset turnover during a period of time, we can ascertain how profitably the company used assets during that period of time in a measure of the return on assets. Using the Johnson & Johnson data shown on page 611, we compute the profit margin on sales and the return on assets as follows.

ILLUSTRATION 11-21
Profit Margin on Sales

$$\text{Profit margin on sales} = \frac{\text{Net income}}{\text{Net sales}}$$
$$= \frac{\$9{,}672}{\$65{,}030}$$
$$= 14.87\%$$

$$\text{Return on assets} = \text{Profit margin on sales} \times \text{Asset turnover}$$
$$= 14.87\% \times .6006$$
$$= 8.93\%$$

Return on Assets

The **return on assets (ROA)** is computed directly by dividing net income by average total assets. Using Johnson & Johnson's data, we compute the ratio as follows.

ILLUSTRATION 11-22
Return on Assets

$$\text{Return on assets} = \frac{\text{Net income}}{\text{Average total assets}}$$
$$= \frac{\$9{,}672}{(\$113{,}644 + \$102{,}908)/2}$$
$$= 8.93\%$$

The 8.93 percent return on assets computed in this manner equals the 8.93 percent rate computed by multiplying the profit margin on sales by the asset turnover. The rate of return on assets measures profitability well because it combines the effects of profit margin and asset turnover.

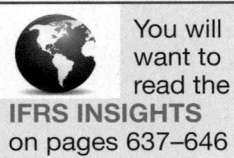

You will want to read the **IFRS INSIGHTS** on pages 637–646

for discussion of IFRS related to property, plant, and equipment.

KEY TERMS

accelerated depreciation methods, *594*

activity method, *593*

amortization, *590*

asset turnover, *611*

composite approach, *596*

composite depreciation rate, *596*

cost depletion, *606*

SUMMARY OF LEARNING OBJECTIVES

1 **Explain the concept of depreciation.** Depreciation allocates the cost of tangible assets to expense in a systematic and rational manner to those periods expected to benefit from the use of the asset.

2 **Identify the factors involved in the depreciation process.** Three factors involved in the depreciation process are (1) determining the depreciation base for the asset, (2) estimating service lives, and (3) selecting a method of cost apportionment (depreciation).

3 **Compare activity, straight-line, and decreasing-charge methods of depreciation.** (1) *Activity method:* Assumes that depreciation is a function of use or productivity instead of the passage of time. The life of the asset is considered in terms of either the output it provides, or an input measure such as the number of hours it works. (2) *Straight-line method:* Considers depreciation a function of time instead of a function of usage. The straight-line procedure is often the most conceptually appropriate when the decline in usefulness is constant from period to period. (3) *Decreasing-charge methods:* Provide for a higher depreciation cost in the earlier years and lower charges in later periods. The main justification for this approach is that the asset is the most productive in its early years.

4 **Explain special depreciation methods.** Two special depreciation methods are as follows. (1) *Group and composite methods:* The group method is frequently used when the assets are fairly similar in nature and have approximately the same useful lives. The composite method may be used when the assets are dissimilar and have different lives. (2) *Hybrid or combination methods:* These methods may combine straight-line/activity approaches.

5 **Explain the accounting issues related to asset impairment.** The process to determine an impairment loss is as follows. (1) Review events and changes in circumstances for possible impairment. (2) If events or changes suggest impairment, determine if the sum of the expected future net cash flows from the long-lived asset is less than the carrying amount of the asset. If less, measure the impairment loss. (3) The impairment loss is the amount by which the carrying amount of the asset exceeds the fair value of the asset.

After a company records an impairment loss, the reduced carrying amount of the long-lived asset is its new cost basis. Impairment losses may not be restored for assets held for use. If the company expects to dispose of the asset, it should report the impaired asset at the lower-of-cost-or-net realizable value. It is not depreciated. It can be continuously revalued, as long as the write-up is never to an amount greater than the carrying amount before impairment.

6 **Explain the accounting procedures for depletion of natural resources.** To account for depletion of natural resources, companies (1) establish the depletion base and (2) write off resource cost. Four factors are part of establishing the depletion base: (a) acquisition costs, (b) exploration costs, (c) development costs, and (d) restoration costs. To write off resource cost, companies normally compute depletion on the units-of-production method. Thus, depletion is a function of the number of units withdrawn during the period. To obtain a cost per unit of product, the total cost of the natural resource less salvage value is divided by the number of units estimated to be in the resource deposit, to obtain a cost per unit of product. To compute depletion, this cost per unit is multiplied by the number of units withdrawn.

7 **Explain how to report and analyze property, plant, equipment, and natural resources.** The basis of valuation for property, plant, and equipment and for natural resources should be disclosed along with pledges, liens, and other commitments related to these assets. Companies should not offset any liability secured by property, plant, and equipment or by natural resources against these assets, but should report it in the liabilities section. When depreciating assets, credit a valuation account normally called Accumulated Depreciation. When depleting assets, use an accumulated depletion account, or credit the depletion directly to the natural resource account. Companies engaged in significant oil and gas producing activities must provide additional disclosures about these activities. Analysis may be performed to evaluate the asset turnover, profit margin on sales, and return on assets.

declining-balance method, 595

decreasing-charge methods, 594

depletion, 590, 604

depreciation, 590

depreciation base, 590

development costs, 605

double-declining-balance method, 595

exploration costs, 605

full-cost concept, 608

group method, 595

impairment, 601

inadequacy, 591

liquidating dividends, 607

natural resources, 604

obsolescence, 591

percentage depletion, 606(n)

profit margin on sales, 612

recoverability test, 602

reserve recognition accounting (RRA), 608

restoration costs, 605

return on assets (ROA), 612

salvage value, 590

straight-line method, 593

successful-efforts concept, 608

sum-of-the-years'-digits method, 594

supersession, 591

| APPENDIX **11A** | **INCOME TAX DEPRECIATION** |

LEARNING OBJECTIVE **8**
Describe income tax methods
of depreciation.

For the most part, a financial accounting course does not address issues related to the computation of income taxes. However, because the concepts of tax depreciation are similar to those of book depreciation and because tax depreciation methods are sometimes adopted for book purposes, we present an overview of this subject.

Congress passed the Accelerated Cost Recovery System (ACRS) as part of the Economic Recovery Tax Act of 1981. The goal was to stimulate capital investment through faster write-offs and to bring more uniformity to the write-off period. For assets purchased in the years 1981 through 1986, companies use ACRS and its preestablished "cost recovery periods" for various classes of assets.

In the Tax Reform Act of 1986 Congress enacted a **Modified Accelerated Cost Recovery System**, known as **MACRS**. It applies to depreciable assets placed in service in 1987 and later. The following discussion is based on these MACRS rules. Realize that tax depreciation rules are subject to change annually.[15]

MODIFIED ACCELERATED COST RECOVERY SYSTEM

The computation of depreciation under MACRS differs from the computation under GAAP in three respects: (1) a mandated tax life, which is generally shorter than the economic life; (2) cost recovery on an accelerated basis; and (3) an assigned salvage value of zero.

Tax Lives (Recovery Periods)

Each item of depreciable property belongs to a property class. The recovery period (depreciable tax life) of an asset depends on its property class. Illustration 11A-1 presents the MACRS property classes.

ILLUSTRATION 11A-1
MACRS Property Classes

3-year property	Includes small tools, horses, and assets used in research and development activities
5-year property	Includes automobiles, trucks, computers and peripheral equipment, and office machines
7-year property	Includes office furniture and fixtures, agriculture equipment, oil exploration and development equipment, railroad track, manufacturing equipment, and any property not designated by law as being in any other class
10-year property	Includes railroad tank cars, mobile homes, boilers, and certain public utility property
15-year property	Includes roads, shrubbery, and certain low-income housing
20-year property	Includes waste-water treatment plants and sewer systems
27.5-year property	Includes residential rental property
39-year property	Includes nonresidential real property

[15]For example, in an effort to jump-start the economy following the September 11, 2001, terrorist attacks, Congress passed the Job Creation and Worker Assistance Act of 2002 (the Act). The Act allows a 30 percent first-year bonus depreciation for assets placed into service after September 11, 2001, but before September 11, 2004. A follow-up provision enacted in 2003 extended the tax savings to assets placed in service before January 1, 2005. And in 2010, Congress extended bonus depreciation for smaller companies. These laws encourage companies to invest in fixed assets because they can front-load depreciation expense, which lowers taxable income and amount of taxes companies pay in the early years of an asset's life. Although the Act may be a good thing for the economy, it can distort cash flow measures—making them look artificially strong when the allowances are in place but reversing once the bonus depreciation expires. See D. Zion and B. Carcache, "Bonus Depreciation Boomerang," *Credit Suisse First Boston Equity Research* (February 19, 2004).

Tax Depreciation Methods

Companies compute depreciation expense using the tax basis—usually the cost—of the asset. The depreciation method depends on the MACRS property class, as shown below.

MACRS Property Class	Depreciation Method
3-, 5-, 7-, and 10-year property	Double-declining-balance
15- and 20-year property	150% declining-balance
27.5- and 39-year property	Straight-line

ILLUSTRATION 11A-2
Depreciation Method for Various MACRS Property Classes

Depreciation computations for income tax purposes are based on the **half-year convention**. That is, a half year of depreciation is allowable in the year of acquisition and in the year of disposition.[16] A company depreciates an asset to a zero value so that there is no salvage value at the end of its MACRS life.

Use of IRS-published tables, shown in Illustration 11A-3, simplifies application of these depreciation methods.

MACRS Depreciation Rates by Class of Property

Recovery Year	3-year (200% DB)	5-year (200% DB)	7-year (200% DB)	10-year (200% DB)	15-year (150% DB)	20-year (150% DB)
1	33.33	20.00	14.29	10.00	5.00	3.750
2	44.45	32.00	24.49	18.00	9.50	7.219
3	14.81*	19.20	17.49	14.40	8.55	6.677
4	7.41	11.52*	12.49	11.52	7.70	6.177
5		11.52	8.93*	9.22	6.93	5.713
6		5.76	8.92	7.37	6.23	5.285
7			8.93	6.55*	5.90*	4.888
8			4.46	6.55	5.90	4.522
9				6.56	5.91	4.462*
10				6.55	5.90	4.461
11				3.28	5.91	4.462
12					5.90	4.461
13					5.91	4.462
14					5.90	4.461
15					5.91	4.462
16					2.95	4.461
17						4.462
18						4.461
19						4.462
20						4.461
21						2.231

*Switchover to straight-line depreciation.

ILLUSTRATION 11A-3
IRS Table of MACRS Depreciation Rates, by Property Class

Example of MACRS

To illustrate depreciation computations under both MACRS and GAAP straight-line accounting, assume the following facts for a computer and peripheral equipment purchased by Denise Rode Company on January 1, 2013.

---

[16]The tax law requires mid-quarter and mid-month conventions for MACRS purposes in certain circumstances.

Acquisition Date	January 1, 2013
Cost	$100,000
Estimated useful life	7 years
Estimated salvage value	$16,000
MACRS class life	5 years
MACRS method	200% declining-balance
GAAP method	Straight-line
Disposal proceeds—January 2, 2020	$11,000

Using the rates from the MACRS depreciation rate schedule for a 5-year class of property, Rode computes depreciation as follows for tax purposes.

ILLUSTRATION 11A-4
Computation of MACRS Depreciation

MACRS Depreciation

2013	$100,000 × .20 =	$ 20,000
2014	$100,000 × .32 =	32,000
2015	$100,000 × .192 =	19,200
2016	$100,000 × .1152 =	11,520
2017	$100,000 × .1152 =	11,520
2018	$100,000 × .0576 =	5,760
	Total depreciation	$100,000

Rode computes the depreciation under GAAP straight-line method, with $16,000 of estimated salvage value and an estimated useful life of 7 years, as shown in Illustration 11A-5.

ILLUSTRATION 11A-5
Computation of GAAP Depreciation

GAAP Depreciation

($100,000 − $16,000) ÷ 7 = $12,000 annual depreciation

× 7 years

1/1/13–1/2/20 $84,000 total depreciation

The MACRS depreciation recovers the total cost of the asset on an accelerated basis. But, a taxable gain of $11,000 results from the sale of the asset at January 2, 2020. Therefore, the net effect on taxable income for the years 2013 through 2020 is $89,000 ($100,000 depreciation − $11,000 gain).

Under GAAP, the company recognizes a loss on disposal of $5,000 ($16,000 book value − $11,000 disposal proceeds). The net effect on income before income taxes for the years 2013 through 2020 is $89,000 ($84,000 depreciation + $5,000 loss), the same as the net effect of MACRS on taxable income.

Even though the net effects are equal in amount, the deferral of income tax payments under MACRS from early in the life of the asset to later in life is desirable. The different amounts of depreciation for income tax reporting and financial GAAP reporting in each year are a matter of timing and result in temporary differences, which require **interperiod tax allocation**. (See Chapter 19 for an extended treatment of this topic.)

OPTIONAL STRAIGHT-LINE METHOD

An alternate MACRS method exists for determining depreciation deductions. Based on the straight-line method, it is referred to as the **optional** (elective) **straight-line method**. This method applies to the six classes of property described earlier. The alternate

MACRS applies the straight-line method to the MACRS recovery periods. It ignores salvage value.

Under the optional straight-line method, in the first year in which the property is put in service, the company deducts half of the amount of depreciation that would be permitted for a full year (half-year convention). *Use the half-year convention for homework problems.*

TAX VERSUS BOOK DEPRECIATION

GAAP requires that companies allocate the cost of depreciable assets to expense over the expected useful life of the asset in a systematic and rational manner. Some argue that from a cost-benefit perspective it would be better for companies to adopt the MACRS approach in order to eliminate the necessity of maintaining two different sets of records.

However, the tax laws and financial reporting have different objectives. The purpose of taxation is to raise revenue from constituents in an equitable manner. The purpose of financial reporting is to reflect the economic substance of a transaction as closely as possible and to help predict the amounts, timing, and uncertainty of future cash flows. Because these objectives differ, the adoption of one method for both tax and book purposes in all cases is not in accordance with GAAP.

KEY TERM

Modified Accelerated
  Cost Recovery System
  (MACRS), *614*

```
SUMMARY OF LEARNING OBJECTIVE
       FOR APPENDIX 11A
```

8 **Describe income tax methods of depreciation.** Congress enacted a Modified Accelerated Cost Recovery System (MACRS) in the Tax Reform Act of 1986. It applies to depreciable assets placed in service in 1987 and later. The computation of depreciation under MACRS differs from the computation under GAAP in three respects: (1) a mandated tax life, which is generally shorter than the economic life; (2) cost recovery on an accelerated basis; and (3) an assigned salvage value of zero.

DEMONSTRATION PROBLEM

Norwel Company manufactures miniature circuit boards used in smartphones. On June 5, 2014, Norwel purchased a circuit board stamping machine at a retail price of $24,000. Norwel paid 5% sales tax on this purchase and hired a contractor to build a specially wired platform for the machine for $1,800, to meet OSHA safety requirements. Norwel estimates the machine will have a 5-year useful life, with a salvage value of $2,000 at the end of 5 years. Norwel uses straight-line depreciation and employs the "half-year" convention in accounting for partial-year depreciation. Norwel's fiscal year ends on December 31.

Instructions
  (a) At what amount should Norwel record the acquisition cost of the machine?
  (b) How much depreciation expense should Norwel record in 2014 and in 2015?
  (c) At what amount will the machine be reported in Norwel's balance sheet at December 31, 2015?
  (d) During 2016, Norwel's circuit board business is experiencing significant competition from companies with more advanced low-heat circuit boards. As a result, at June 30, 2016, Norwel conducts an impairment evaluation of the stamping machine purchased in 2014. Norwel determines that undiscounted future cash flows for the machine are estimated to be $15,200 and the fair value of the machine, based on prices in the re-sale market, to be $13,400. Prepare the journal entry to record an impairment, if any, on the stamping machine.

Solution

(a) Historical cost is measured by the cash or cash equivalent price of obtaining the asset and bringing it to the location and condition for its intended use. For Norwel, this is:

Price	$24,000
Tax ($24,000 × .05)	1,200
Platform	1,800
Total	$27,000

(b) Depreciable base: $27,000 − $2,000 = $25,000

Depreciation expense: $25,000 ÷ 5 = $5,000 per year

> 2014: 1/2 year = $5,000 × .50 = $2,500
> 2015: full year = $5,000

(c) The amount reported on the balance sheet is the cost of the asset less accumulated depreciation:

Machinery	$27,000
Less: Accumulated depreciation	7,500
Book value	$19,500

(d) Norwel first conducts the recoverability test, comparing the book value of the machine to the undiscounted future cash flows. This indicates the future cash flows ($15,200) are less than the book value ($17,000*).

*Cost	$27,000
Less: Accumulated depreciation	
($2,500 + $5,000 + $2,500)	10,000
Book value of machine and platform	$17,000

Thus, Norwel will record an impairment, based on comparison of the fair value of the machine and platform to the book value. The entry is as follows.

Loss on Impairment ($17,000 − $13,400)	3,600	
Accumulated Depreciation—Machinery		3,600

FASB CODIFICATION

FASB Codification References

[1] FASB ASC 360-10-05. [Predecessor literature: "Accounting for the Impairment or Disposal of Long-lived Assets," *Statement of Financial Accounting Standards No. 144* (Norwalk, Conn.: 2001).]

[2] FASB ASC 360-10-50-1. [Predecessor literature: "Omnibus Opinion—1967," *Opinions of the Accounting Principles Board No. 12* (New York: AICPA, 1967), par. 5.]

[3] FASB ASC 932-235-50-1. [Predecessor literature: "Disclosures about Oil and Gas Producing Activities," *Statement of Financial Accounting Standards Board No. 69* (Stamford, Conn.: FASB, 1982).]

Exercises

If your school has a subscription to the FASB Codification, go to *http://aaahq.org/asclogin.cfm* to log in and prepare responses to the following. Provide Codification references for your responses.

CE11-1 Access the glossary ("Master Glossary") to answer the following.

    (a) What is the definition of amortization?
    (b) What is the definition of impairment?
    (c) What is the definition of recoverable amount?
    (d) What are activities, as they relate to the construction of an asset?

CE11-2 Your client, Barriques Inc., is contemplating a restructuring of its operations, including the possibility of spinning off some of its assets to the original owners. However, management is unsure of the accounting for any impairment on the assets. What does the authoritative literature say about these types of impairments?

CE11-3 Your great-uncle, who is a CPA, is impressed that you are majoring in accounting. But, he believes that depreciation is something that companies do based on past practice, not on the basis of any authoritative guidance. Provide the authoritative literature to support the practice of fixed-asset depreciation.

CE11-4 What is the nature of SEC guidance concerning property, plant, and equipment disclosures?

An additional Codification case can be found in the Using Your Judgment section, on page 637.

Be sure to check the book's companion website for a Review and Analysis Exercise, with solution.

WileyPLUS

Brief Exercises, Exercises, Problems, and many more learning and assessment tools and resources are available for practice in WileyPLUS.

Note: All asterisked Questions, Exercises, and Problems relate to material in the appendix to the chapter.

QUESTIONS

1. Distinguish among depreciation, depletion, and amortization.

2. Identify the factors that are relevant in determining the annual depreciation charge, and explain whether these factors are determined objectively or whether they are based on judgment.

3. Some believe that accounting depreciation measures the decline in the value of fixed assets. Do you agree? Explain.

4. Explain how estimation of service lives can result in unrealistically high carrying values for fixed assets.

5. The plant manager of a manufacturing firm suggested in a conference of the company's executives that accountants should speed up depreciation on the machinery in the finishing department because improvements were rapidly making those machines obsolete, and a depreciation fund big enough to cover their replacement is needed. Discuss the accounting concept of depreciation and the effect on a business concern of the depreciation recorded for plant assets, paying particular attention to the issues raised by the plant manager.

6. For what reasons are plant assets retired? Define inadequacy, supersession, and obsolescence.

7. What basic questions must be answered before the amount of the depreciation charge can be computed?

8. Workman Company purchased a machine on January 2, 2014, for $800,000. The machine has an estimated useful life of 5 years and a salvage value of $100,000. Depreciation was computed by the 150% declining-balance method. What is the amount of accumulated depreciation at the end of December 31, 2015?

9. Silverman Company purchased machinery for $162,000 on January 1, 2014. It is estimated that the machinery will have a useful life of 20 years, salvage value of $15,000, production of 84,000 units, and working hours of 42,000. During 2014, the company uses the machinery for 14,300 hours, and the machinery produces 20,000 units. Compute depreciation under the straight-line, units-of-output, working hours, sum-of-the-years'-digits, and double-declining-balance methods.

10. What are the major factors considered in determining what depreciation method to use?

11. Under what conditions is it appropriate for a business to use the composite method of depreciation for its plant assets? What are the advantages and disadvantages of this method?

12. If Remmers, Inc. uses the composite method and its composite rate is 7.5% per year, what entry should it make when plant assets that originally cost $50,000 and have been used for 10 years are sold for $14,000?

13. A building that was purchased on December 31, 2000, for $2,500,000 was originally estimated to have a life of 50 years with no salvage value at the end of that time. Depreciation has been recorded through 2014. During 2015, an examination of the building by an engineering firm discloses that its estimated useful life is 15 years after 2014. What should be the amount of depreciation for 2015?

14. Charlie Parker, president of Spinners Company, has recently noted that depreciation increases cash provided by operations and therefore depreciation is a good source of funds. Do you agree? Discuss.

15. Andrea Torbert purchased a computer for $8,000 on July 1, 2014. She intends to depreciate it over 4 years using the double-declining-balance method. Salvage value is $1,000. Compute depreciation for 2015.

16. Walkin Inc. is considering the write-down of its long-term plant because of a lack of profitability. Explain to the management of Walkin how to determine whether a write-down is permitted.

17. Last year, Wyeth Company recorded an impairment on an asset held for use. Recent appraisals indicate that the asset has increased in value. Should Wyeth record this recovery in value?

18. Toro Co. has equipment with a carrying amount of $700,000. The expected future net cash flows from the equipment are $705,000, and its fair value is $590,000. The equipment is expected to be used in operations in the future. What amount (if any) should Toro report as an impairment to its equipment?

19. Explain how gains or losses on impaired assets should be reported in income.

20. It has been suggested that plant and equipment could be replaced more quickly if depreciation rates for income tax and accounting purposes were substantially increased. As a result, business operations would receive the benefit of more modern and more efficient plant facilities. Discuss the merits of this proposition.

21. Neither depreciation on replacement cost nor depreciation adjusted for changes in the purchasing power of the dollar has been recognized as generally accepted accounting principles for inclusion in the primary financial statements. Briefly present the accounting treatment that might be used to assist in the maintenance of the ability of a company to replace its productive capacity.

22. List (a) the similarities and (b) the differences in the accounting treatments of depreciation and cost depletion.

23. Describe cost depletion and percentage depletion. Why is the percentage depletion method permitted?

24. In what way may the use of percentage depletion violate sound accounting theory?

25. In the extractive industries, businesses may pay dividends in excess of net income. What is the maximum permissible? How can this practice be justified?

26. The following statement appeared in a financial magazine: "RRA—or Rah-Rah, as it's sometimes dubbed—has kicked up quite a storm. Oil companies, for example, are convinced that the approach is misleading. Major accounting firms agree." What is RRA? Why might oil companies believe that this approach is misleading?

27. Shumway Oil uses successful-efforts accounting and also provides full-cost results as well. Under full-cost, Shumway Oil would have reported retained earnings of $42 million and net income of $4 million. Under successful-efforts, retained earnings were $29 million, and net income was $3 million. Explain the difference between full-costing and successful-efforts accounting.

28. Target in 2012 reported net income of $2.9 billion, net sales of $69.8 billion, and average total assets of $45.2 billion. What is Target's asset turnover? What is Target's return on assets?

***29.** What is a modified accelerated cost recovery system (MACRS)? Speculate as to why this system is now required for tax purposes.

BRIEF EXERCISES

2 3 **BE11-1** Fernandez Corporation purchased a truck at the beginning of 2014 for $50,000. The truck is estimated to have a salvage value of $2,000 and a useful life of 160,000 miles. It was driven 23,000 miles in 2014 and 31,000 miles in 2015. Compute depreciation expense for 2014 and 2015.

2 3 **BE11-2** Lockard Company purchased machinery on January 1, 2014, for $80,000. The machinery is estimated to have a salvage value of $8,000 after a useful life of 8 years. (a) Compute 2014 depreciation expense using the straight-line method. (b) Compute 2014 depreciation expense using the straight-line method assuming the machinery was purchased on September 1, 2014.

2 3 **BE11-3** Use the information for Lockard Company given in BE11-2. (a) Compute 2014 depreciation expense using the sum-of-the-years'-digits method. (b) Compute 2014 depreciation expense using the sum-of-the-years'-digits method, assuming the machinery was purchased on April 1, 2014.

2 **3** **BE11-4** Use the information for Lockard Company given in BE11-2. (a) Compute 2014 depreciation expense using the double-declining-balance method. (b) Compute 2014 depreciation expense using the double-declining-balance method, assuming the machinery was purchased on October 1, 2014.

2 **3** **BE11-5** Cominsky Company purchased a machine on July 1, 2015, for $28,000. Cominsky paid $200 in title fees and county property tax of $125 on the machine. In addition, Cominsky paid $500 shipping charges for delivery, and $475 was paid to a local contractor to build and wire a platform for the machine on the plant floor. The machine has an estimated useful life of 6 years with a salvage value of $3,000. Determine the depreciation base of Cominsky's new machine. Cominsky uses straight-line depreciation.

4 **BE11-6** Dickinson Inc. owns the following assets.

Asset	Cost	Salvage	Estimated Useful Life
A	$70,000	$7,000	10 years
B	50,000	5,000	5 years
C	82,000	4,000	12 years

Compute the composite depreciation rate and the composite life of Dickinson's assets.

4 **BE11-7** Holt Company purchased a computer for $8,000 on January 1, 2013. Straight-line depreciation is used, based on a 5-year life and a $1,000 salvage value. In 2015, the estimates are revised. Holt now feels the computer will be used until December 31, 2016, when it can be sold for $500. Compute the 2015 depreciation.

5 **BE11-8** Jurassic Company owns equipment that cost $900,000 and has accumulated depreciation of $380,000. The expected future net cash flows from the use of the asset are expected to be $500,000. The fair value of the equipment is $400,000. Prepare the journal entry, if any, to record the impairment loss.

6 **BE11-9** Everly Corporation acquires a coal mine at a cost of $400,000. Intangible development costs total $100,000. After extraction has occurred, Everly must restore the property (estimated fair value of the obligation is $80,000), after which it can be sold for $160,000. Everly estimates that 4,000 tons of coal can be extracted. If 700 tons are extracted the first year, prepare the journal entry to record depletion.

7 **BE11-10** In its 2011 annual report, Campbell Soup Company reports beginning-of-the-year total assets of $6,276 million, end-of-the-year total assets of $6,862 million, total sales of $7,719 million, and net income of $805 million. (a) Compute Campbell's asset turnover. (b) Compute Campbell's profit margin on sales. (c) Compute Campbell's return on assets using (1) asset turnover and profit margin and (2) net income.

8 *****BE11-11** Francis Corporation purchased an asset at a cost of $50,000 on March 1, 2014. The asset has a useful life of 8 years and a salvage value of $4,000. For tax purposes, the MACRS class life is 5 years. Compute tax depreciation for each year 2014–2019.

EXERCISES

2 **3** **E11-1 (Depreciation Computations—SL, SYD, DDB)** Deluxe Ezra Company purchases equipment on January 1, Year 1, at a cost of $469,000. The asset is expected to have a service life of 12 years and a salvage value of $40,000.

Instructions

(a) Compute the amount of depreciation for each of Years 1 through 3 using the straight-line depreciation method.

(b) Compute the amount of depreciation for each of Years 1 through 3 using the sum-of-the-years'-digits method.

(c) Compute the amount of depreciation for each of Years 1 through 3 using the double-declining-balance method. (In performing your calculations, round constant percentage to the nearest one-hundredth of a point and round answers to the nearest dollar.)

2 **3** **E11-2 (Depreciation—Conceptual Understanding)** Rembrandt Company acquired a plant asset at the beginning of Year 1. The asset has an estimated service life of 5 years. An employee has prepared depreciation schedules for this asset using three different methods to compare the results of using one method with the results of using other methods. You are to assume that the following schedules have been correctly prepared for this asset using (1) the straight-line method, (2) the sum-of-the-years'-digits method, and (3) the double-declining-balance method.

Year	Straight-Line	Sum-of-the-Years'-Digits	Double-Declining-Balance
1	$ 9,000	$15,000	$20,000
2	9,000	12,000	12,000
3	9,000	9,000	7,200
4	9,000	6,000	4,320
5	9,000	3,000	1,480
Total	$45,000	$45,000	$45,000

Instructions

Answer the following questions.

(a) What is the cost of the asset being depreciated?
(b) What amount, if any, was used in the depreciation calculations for the salvage value for this asset?
(c) Which method will produce the highest charge to income in Year 1?
(d) Which method will produce the highest charge to income in Year 4?
(e) Which method will produce the highest book value for the asset at the end of Year 3?
(f) If the asset is sold at the end of Year 3, which method would yield the highest gain (or lowest loss) on disposal of the asset?

E11-3 (Depreciation Computations—SYD, DDB—Partial Periods) Judds Company purchased a new plant asset on April 1, 2014, at a cost of $711,000. It was estimated to have a service life of 20 years and a salvage value of $60,000. Judds' accounting period is the calendar year.

Instructions

(a) Compute the depreciation for this asset for 2014 and 2015 using the sum-of-the-years'-digits method.
(b) Compute the depreciation for this asset for 2014 and 2015 using the double-declining-balance method.

E11-4 (Depreciation Computations—Five Methods) Jon Seceda Furnace Corp. purchased machinery for $315,000 on May 1, 2014. It is estimated that it will have a useful life of 10 years, salvage value of $15,000, production of 240,000 units, and working hours of 25,000. During 2015, Seceda Corp. uses the machinery for 2,650 hours, and the machinery produces 25,500 units.

Instructions

From the information given, compute the depreciation charge for 2015 under each of the following methods. (Round to the nearest dollar.)

(a) Straight-line.   (d) Sum-of-the-years'-digits.
(b) Units-of-output.   (e) Declining-balance (use 20% as the annual rate).
(c) Working hours.

E11-5 (Depreciation Computations—Four Methods) Robert Parish Corporation purchased a new machine for its assembly process on August 1, 2014. The cost of this machine was $117,900. The company estimated that the machine would have a salvage value of $12,900 at the end of its service life. Its life is estimated at 5 years, and its working hours are estimated at 21,000 hours. Year-end is December 31.

Instructions

Compute the depreciation expense under the following methods. Each of the following should be considered unrelated.

(a) Straight-line depreciation for 2014.
(b) Activity method for 2014, assuming that machine usage was 800 hours.
(c) Sum-of-the-years'-digits for 2015.
(d) Double-declining-balance for 2015.

E11-6 (Depreciation Computations—Five Methods, Partial Periods) Muggsy Bogues Company purchased equipment for $212,000 on October 1, 2014. It is estimated that the equipment will have a useful life of 8 years and a salvage value of $12,000. Estimated production is 40,000 units and estimated working hours are 20,000. During 2014, Bogues uses the equipment for 525 hours and the equipment produces 1,000 units.

Instructions

Compute depreciation expense under each of the following methods. Bogues is on a calendar-year basis ending December 31.

(a) Straight-line method for 2014.
(b) Activity method (units of output) for 2014.

(c) Activity method (working hours) for 2014.
(d) Sum-of-the-years'-digits method for 2016.
(e) Double-declining-balance method for 2015.

2 3 E11-7 (Different Methods of Depreciation) Jackel Industries presents you with the following information.

Description	Date Purchased	Cost	Salvage Value	Life in Years	Depreciation Method	Accumulated Depreciation to 12/31/15	Depreciation for 2016
Machine A	2/12/14	$142,500	$16,000	10	(a)	$33,350	(b)
Machine B	8/15/13	(c)	21,000	5	SL	29,000	(d)
Machine C	7/21/12	75,400	23,500	8	DDB	(e)	(f)
Machine D	10/12/(g)	219,000	69,000	5	SYD	70,000	(h)

Instructions
Complete the table for the year ended December 31, 2016. The company depreciates all assets using the half-year convention.

2 3 E11-8 (Depreciation Computation—Replacement, Nonmonetary Exchange) George Zidek Corporation bought a machine on June 1, 2012, for $31,000, f.o.b. the place of manufacture. Freight to the point where it was set up was $200, and $500 was expended to install it. The machine's useful life was estimated at 10 years, with a salvage value of $2,500. On June 1, 2013, an essential part of the machine is replaced, at a cost of $1,980, with one designed to reduce the cost of operating the machine. The cost of the old part and related depreciation cannot be determined with any accuracy.

On June 1, 2016, the company buys a new machine of greater capacity for $35,000, delivered, trading in the old machine which has a fair value and trade-in allowance of $20,000. To prepare the old machine for removal from the plant cost $75, and expenditures to install the new one were $1,500. It is estimated that the new machine has a useful life of 10 years, with a salvage value of $4,000 at the end of that time. (The exchange has commercial substance.)

Instructions
Assuming that depreciation is to be computed on the straight-line basis, compute the annual depreciation on the new equipment that should be provided for the fiscal year beginning June 1, 2016. (Round to the nearest dollar.)

4 E11-9 (Composite Depreciation) Presented below is information related to LeBron James Manufacturing Corporation.

Asset	Cost	Estimated Salvage	Estimated Life (in years)
A	$40,500	$5,500	10
B	33,600	4,800	9
C	36,000	3,600	9
D	19,000	1,500	7
E	23,500	2,500	6

Instructions
(a) Compute the rate of depreciation per year to be applied to the plant assets under the composite method.
(b) Prepare the adjusting entry necessary at the end of the year to record depreciation for the year.
(c) Prepare the entry to record the sale of asset D for cash of $4,800. It was used for 6 years, and depreciation was entered under the composite method.

2 3 E11-10 (Depreciation Computations, SYD) Five Satins Company purchased a piece of equipment at the beginning of 2011. The equipment cost $430,000. It has an estimated service life of 8 years and an expected salvage value of $70,000. The sum-of-the-years'-digits method of depreciation is being used. Someone has already correctly prepared a depreciation schedule for this asset. This schedule shows that $60,000 will be depreciated for a particular calendar year.

Instructions
Show calculations to determine for what particular year the depreciation amount for this asset will be $60,000.

2 3 4 E11-11 (Depreciation—Change in Estimate) Machinery purchased for $60,000 by Tom Brady Co. in 2010 was originally estimated to have a life of 8 years with a salvage value of $4,000 at the end of that time. Depreciation has been entered for 5 years on this basis. In 2015, it is determined that the total estimated life should be 10 years with a salvage value of $4,500 at the end of that time. Assume straight-line depreciation.

Instructions
(a) Prepare the entry to correct the prior years' depreciation, if necessary.
(b) Prepare the entry to record depreciation for 2015.

E11-12 (Depreciation Computation—Addition, Change in Estimate) In 1987, Herman Moore Company completed the construction of a building at a cost of $2,000,000 and first occupied it in January 1988. It was estimated that the building will have a useful life of 40 years and a salvage value of $60,000 at the end of that time.

Early in 1998, an addition to the building was constructed at a cost of $500,000. At that time, it was estimated that the remaining life of the building would be, as originally estimated, an additional 30 years, and that the addition would have a life of 30 years and a salvage value of $20,000.

In 2016, it is determined that the probable life of the building and addition will extend to the end of 2047, or 20 years beyond the original estimate.

Instructions
(a) Using the straight-line method, compute the annual depreciation that would have been charged from 1988 through 1997.
(b) Compute the annual depreciation that would have been charged from 1998 through 2015.
(c) Prepare the entry, if necessary, to adjust the account balances because of the revision of the estimated life in 2016.
(d) Compute the annual depreciation to be charged, beginning with 2016.

E11-13 (Depreciation—Replacement, Change in Estimate) Greg Maddox Company constructed a building at a cost of $2,200,000 and occupied it beginning in January 1995. It was estimated at that time that its life would be 40 years, with no salvage value.

In January 2015, a new roof was installed at a cost of $300,000, and it was estimated then that the building would have a useful life of 25 years from that date. The cost of the old roof was $160,000.

Instructions
(a) What amount of depreciation should have been charged annually from the years 1995 to 2014? (Assume straight-line depreciation.)
(b) What entry should be made in 2015 to record the replacement of the roof?
(c) Prepare the entry in January 2015 to record the revision in the estimated life of the building, if necessary.
(d) What amount of depreciation should be charged for the year 2015?

E11-14 (Error Analysis and Depreciation, SL and SYD) Mike Devereaux Company shows the following entries in its Equipment account for 2015. All amounts are based on historical cost.

		Equipment				
2015				2015		
Jan. 1	Balance	134,750		June 30	Cost of equipment sold	
Aug. 10	Purchases	32,000			(purchased prior	
12	Freight on equipment				to 2015)	23,000
	purchased	700				
25	Installation costs	2,700				
Nov. 10	Repairs	500				

Instructions
(a) Prepare any correcting entries necessary.
(b) Assuming that depreciation is to be charged for a full year on the ending balance in the asset account, compute the proper depreciation charge for 2015 under each of the methods listed below. Assume an estimated life of 10 years, with no salvage value. The machinery included in the January 1, 2015, balance was purchased in 2013.
(1) Straight-line. (2) Sum-of-the-years'-digits.

E11-15 (Depreciation for Fractional Periods) On March 10, 2016, Lost World Company sells equipment that it purchased for $192,000 on August 20, 2009. It was originally estimated that the equipment would have a life of 12 years and a salvage value of $16,800 at the end of that time, and depreciation has been computed on that basis. The company uses the straight-line method of depreciation.

Instructions
(a) Compute the depreciation charge on this equipment for 2009, for 2016, and the total charge for the period from 2010 to 2015, inclusive, under each of the six following assumptions with respect to partial periods.

(1) Depreciation is computed for the exact period of time during which the asset is owned. (Use 365 days for base.)

(2) Depreciation is computed for the full year on the January 1 balance in the asset account.

(3) Depreciation is computed for the full year on the December 31 balance in the asset account.

(4) Depreciation for one-half year is charged on plant assets acquired or disposed of during the year.

(5) Depreciation is computed on additions from the beginning of the month following acquisition and on disposals to the beginning of the month following disposal.

(6) Depreciation is computed for a full period on all assets in use for over one-half year, and no depreciation is charged on assets in use for less than one-half year. (Use 365 days for base.)

(b) Briefly evaluate the methods above, considering them from the point of view of basic accounting theory as well as simplicity of application.

E11-16 (Impairment) Presented below is information related to equipment owned by Suarez Company at December 31, 2014.

Cost	$9,000,000
Accumulated depreciation to date	1,000,000
Expected future net cash flows	7,000,000
Fair value	4,800,000

Assume that Suarez will continue to use this asset in the future. As of December 31, 2014, the equipment has a remaining useful life of 4 years.

Instructions

(a) Prepare the journal entry (if any) to record the impairment of the asset at December 31, 2014.

(b) Prepare the journal entry to record depreciation expense for 2015.

(c) The fair value of the equipment at December 31, 2015, is $5,100,000. Prepare the journal entry (if any) necessary to record this increase in fair value.

E11-17 (Impairment) Assume the same information as E11-16, except that Suarez intends to dispose of the equipment in the coming year. It is expected that the cost of disposal will be $20,000.

Instructions

(a) Prepare the journal entry (if any) to record the impairment of the asset at December 31, 2014.

(b) Prepare the journal entry (if any) to record depreciation expense for 2015.

(c) The asset was not sold by December 31, 2015. The fair value of the equipment on that date is $5,300,000. Prepare the journal entry (if any) necessary to record this increase in fair value. It is expected that the cost of disposal is still $20,000.

E11-18 (Impairment) The management of Petro Garcia Inc. was discussing whether certain equipment should be written off as a charge to current operations because of obsolescence. This equipment has a cost of $900,000 with depreciation to date of $400,000 as of December 31, 2014. On December 31, 2014, management projected its future net cash flows from this equipment to be $300,000 and its fair value to be $230,000. The company intends to use this equipment in the future.

Instructions

(a) Prepare the journal entry (if any) to record the impairment at December 31, 2014.

(b) Where should the gain or loss (if any) on the write-down be reported in the income statement?

(c) At December 31, 2015, the equipment's fair value increased to $260,000. Prepare the journal entry (if any) to record this increase in fair value.

(d) What accounting issues did management face in accounting for this impairment?

E11-19 (Depletion Computations—Timber) Stanislaw Timber Company owns 9,000 acres of timberland purchased in 2003 at a cost of $1,400 per acre. At the time of purchase, the land without the timber was valued at $400 per acre. In 2004, Stanislaw built fire lanes and roads, with a life of 30 years, at a cost of $84,000. Every year, Stanislaw sprays to prevent disease at a cost of $3,000 per year and spends $7,000 to maintain the fire lanes and roads. During 2005, Stanislaw selectively logged and sold 700,000 board feet of timber, of the estimated 3,500,000 board feet. In 2006, Stanislaw planted new seedlings to replace the trees cut at a cost of $100,000.

Instructions

(a) Determine the depreciation expense and the cost of timber sold related to depletion for 2005.

(b) Stanislaw has not logged since 2005. If Stanislaw logged and sold 900,000 board feet of timber in 2016, when the timber cruise (appraiser) estimated 5,000,000 board feet, determine the cost of timber sold related to depletion for 2016.

6 **E11-20 (Depletion Computations—Oil)** Diderot Drilling Company has leased property on which oil has been discovered. Wells on this property produced 18,000 barrels of oil during the past year that sold at an average sales price of $55 per barrel. Total oil resources of this property are estimated to be 250,000 barrels.

The lease provided for an outright payment of $500,000 to the lessor (owner) before drilling could be commenced and an annual rental of $31,500. A premium of 5% of the sales price of every barrel of oil removed is to be paid annually to the lessor. In addition, Diderot (lessee) is to clean up all the waste and debris from drilling and to bear the costs of reconditioning the land for farming when the wells are abandoned. The estimated fair value, at the time of the lease, of this clean-up and reconditioning is $30,000.

Instructions
From the provisions of the lease agreement, you are to compute the cost per barrel for the past year, exclusive of operating costs, to Diderot Drilling Company.

6 **E11-21 (Depletion Computations—Timber)** Forda Lumber Company owns a 7,000-acre tract of timber purchased in 2000 at a cost of $1,300 per acre. At the time of purchase, the land was estimated to have a value of $300 per acre without the timber. Forda Lumber Company has not logged this tract since it was purchased. In 2014, Forda had the timber cruised. The cruise (appraiser) estimated that each acre contained 8,000 board feet of timber. In 2014, Forda built 10 miles of roads at a cost of $7,840 per mile. After the roads were completed, Forda logged and sold 3,500 trees containing 850,000 board feet.

Instructions
(a) Determine the cost of timber sold related to depletion for 2014.
(b) If Forda depreciates the logging roads on the basis of timber cut, determine the depreciation expense for 2014.
(c) If Forda plants five seedlings at a cost of $4 per seedling for each tree cut, how should Forda treat the reforestation?

6 **E11-22 (Depletion Computations—Mining)** Alcide Mining Company purchased land on February 1, 2014, at a cost of $1,190,000. It estimated that a total of 60,000 tons of mineral was available for mining. After it has removed all the natural resources, the company will be required to restore the property to its previous state because of strict environmental protection laws. It estimates the fair value of this restoration obligation at $90,000. It believes it will be able to sell the property afterwards for $100,000. It incurred developmental costs of $200,000 before it was able to do any mining. In 2014, resources removed totaled 30,000 tons. The company sold 22,000 tons.

Instructions
Compute the following information for 2014.

(a) Per unit material cost.
(b) Total material cost of December 31, 2014, inventory.
(c) Total material cost in cost of goods sold at December 31, 2014.

6 **E11-23 (Depletion Computations—Minerals)** At the beginning of 2014, Aristotle Company acquired a mine for $970,000. Of this amount, $100,000 was ascribed to the land value and the remaining portion to the minerals in the mine. Surveys conducted by geologists have indicated that approximately 12,000,000 units of the ore appear to be in the mine. Aristotle incurred $170,000 of development costs associated with this mine prior to any extraction of minerals. It also determined that the fair value of its obligation to prepare the land for an alternative use when all of the mineral has been removed was $40,000. During 2014, 2,500,000 units of ore were extracted and 2,100,000 of these units were sold.

Instructions
Compute the following.

(a) The total amount of depletion for 2014.
(b) The amount that is charged as an expense for 2014 for the cost of the minerals sold during 2014.

7 **E11-24 (Ratio Analysis)** The 2011 Annual Report of Tootsie Roll Industries contains the following information.

(in millions)	December 31, 2011	December 31, 2010
Total assets	$857.9	$858.0
Total liabilities	191.9	190.6
Net sales	528.4	517.1
Net income	43.9	53.0

Instructions

Compute the following ratios for Tootsie Roll for 2011.

- **(a)** Asset turnover.
- **(b)** Return on assets.
- **(c)** Profit margin on sales.
- **(d)** How can the asset turnover be used to compute the return on assets?

8 *E11-25 (Book vs. Tax (MACRS) Depreciation)** Futabatei Enterprises purchased a delivery truck on January 1, 2014, at a cost of $27,000. The truck has a useful life of 7 years with an estimated salvage value of $6,000. The straight-line method is used for book purposes. For tax purposes, the truck, having an MACRS class life of 7 years, is classified as 5-year property; the optional MACRS tax rate tables are used to compute depreciation. In addition, assume that for 2014 and 2015 the company has revenues of $200,000 and operating expenses (excluding depreciation) of $130,000.

Instructions

- **(a)** Prepare income statements for 2014 and 2015. (The final amount reported on the income statement should be income before income taxes.)
- **(b)** Compute taxable income for 2014 and 2015.
- **(c)** Determine the total depreciation to be taken over the useful life of the delivery truck for both book and tax purposes.
- **(d)** Explain why depreciation for book and tax purposes will generally be different over the useful life of a depreciable asset.

8 *E11-26 (Book vs. Tax (MACRS) Depreciation)** Shimei Inc. purchased computer equipment on March 1, 2014, for $31,000. The computer equipment has a useful life of 10 years and a salvage value of $1,000. For tax purposes, the MACRS class life is 5 years.

Instructions

- **(a)** Assuming that the company uses the straight-line method for book and tax purposes, what is the depreciation expense reported in (1) the financial statements for 2014 and (2) the tax return for 2014?
- **(b)** Assuming that the company uses the double-declining-balance method for both book and tax purposes, what is the depreciation expense reported in (1) the financial statements for 2014 and (2) the tax return for 2014?
- **(c)** Why is depreciation for tax purposes different from depreciation for book purposes even if the company uses the same depreciation method to compute them both?

EXERCISES SET B

See the book's companion website, at **www.wiley.com/college/kieso**, for an additional set of exercises.

PROBLEMS

2 3 **P11-1 (Depreciation for Partial Period—SL, SYD, and DDB)** Alladin Company purchased Machine #201 on May 1, 2014. The following information relating to Machine #201 was gathered at the end of May.

Price	$85,000
Credit terms	2/10, n/30
Freight-in	$ 800
Preparation and installation costs	$ 3,800
Labor costs during regular production operations	$10,500

It is expected that the machine could be used for 10 years, after which the salvage value would be zero. Alladin intends to use the machine for only 8 years, however, after which it expects to be able to sell it for $1,500. The invoice for Machine #201 was paid May 5, 2014. Alladin uses the calendar year as the basis for the preparation of financial statements.

Instructions

(a) Compute the depreciation expense for the years indicated using the following methods. (Round to the nearest dollar.)

    (1) Straight-line method for 2014.

    (2) Sum-of-the-years'-digits method for 2015.

    (3) Double-declining-balance method for 2014.

(b) Suppose Kate Crow, the president of Alladin, tells you that because the company is a new organization, she expects it will be several years before production and sales reach optimum levels. She asks you to recommend a depreciation method that will allocate less of the company's depreciation expense to the early years and more to later years of the assets' lives. What method would you recommend?

2 3 **P11-2 (Depreciation for Partial Periods—SL, Act., SYD, and Declining-Balance)** The cost of equipment purchased by Charleston, Inc., on June 1, 2014, is $89,000. It is estimated that the machine will have a $5,000 salvage value at the end of its service life. Its service life is estimated at 7 years, its total working hours are estimated at 42,000, and its total production is estimated at 525,000 units. During 2014, the machine was operated 6,000 hours and produced 55,000 units. During 2015, the machine was operated 5,500 hours and produced 48,000 units.

Instructions

Compute depreciation expense on the machine for the year ending December 31, 2014, and the year ending December 31, 2015, using the following methods.

    (a) Straight-line.   (d) Sum-of-the-years'-digits.

    (b) Units-of-output.   (e) Declining-balance (twice the straight-line rate).

    (c) Working hours.

2 3 **P11-3 (Depreciation—SYD, Act., SL, and DDB)** The following data relate to the Machinery account of Eshkol, Inc. at December 31, 2014.

	Machinery			
	A	B	C	D
Original cost	$46,000	$51,000	$80,000	$80,000
Year purchased	2009	2010	2011	2013
Useful life	10 years	15,000 hours	15 years	10 years
Salvage value	$ 3,100	$ 3,000	$ 5,000	$ 5,000
Depreciation method	Sum-of-the-years'-digits	Activity	Straight-line	Double-declining-balance
Accum. depr. through 2014*	$31,200	$35,200	$15,000	$16,000

*In the year an asset is purchased, Eshkol, Inc. does not record any depreciation expense on the asset. In the year an asset is retired or traded in, Eshkol, Inc. takes a full year's depreciation on the asset.

The following transactions occurred during 2015.

(a) On May 5, Machine A was sold for $13,000 cash. The company's bookkeeper recorded this retirement in the following manner in the cash receipts journal.

Cash	13,000	
Machinery (Machine A)		13,000

(b) On December 31, it was determined that Machine B had been used 2,100 hours during 2015.

(c) On December 31, before computing depreciation expense on Machine C, the management of Eshkol, Inc. decided the useful life remaining from January 1, 2015, was 10 years.

(d) On December 31, it was discovered that a machine purchased in 2014 had been expensed completely in that year. This machine cost $28,000 and has a useful life of 10 years and no salvage value. Management has decided to use the double-declining-balance method for this machine, which can be referred to as "Machine E."

Instructions

Prepare the necessary correcting entries for the year 2015. Record the appropriate depreciation expense on the above-mentioned machines.

2 3 **P11-4 (Depreciation and Error Analysis)** A depreciation schedule for semi-trucks of Ichiro Manufacturing Company was requested by your auditor soon after December 31, 2015, showing the additions, retirements, depreciation, and other data affecting the income of the company in the 4-year period 2012 to 2015, inclusive. The following data were ascertained.

Balance of Trucks account, Jan. 1, 2012	
Truck No. 1 purchased Jan. 1, 2009, cost	$18,000
Truck No. 2 purchased July 1, 2009, cost	22,000
Truck No. 3 purchased Jan. 1, 2011, cost	30,000
Truck No. 4 purchased July 1, 2011, cost	24,000
Balance, Jan. 1, 2012	$94,000

The Accumulated Depreciation—Trucks account previously adjusted to January 1, 2012, and entered in the ledger, had a balance on that date of $30,200 (depreciation on the four trucks from the respective dates of purchase, based on a 5-year life, no salvage value). No charges had been made against the account before January 1, 2012.

Transactions between January 1, 2012, and December 31, 2015, which were recorded in the ledger, are as follows.

July 1, 2012 Truck No. 3 was traded for a larger one (No. 5), the agreed purchase price of which was $40,000. Ichiro Mfg. Co. paid the automobile dealer $22,000 cash on the transaction. The entry was a debit to Trucks and a credit to Cash, $22,000. The transaction has commercial substance.

Jan. 1, 2013 Truck No. 1 was sold for $3,500 cash; entry debited Cash and credited Trucks, $3,500.

July 1, 2014 A new truck (No. 6) was acquired for $42,000 cash and was charged at that amount to the Trucks account. (Assume truck No. 2 was not retired.)

July 1, 2014 Truck No. 4 was damaged in a wreck to such an extent that it was sold as junk for $700 cash. Ichiro Mfg. Co. received $2,500 from the insurance company. The entry made by the bookkeeper was a debit to Cash, $3,200, and credits to Miscellaneous Income, $700, and Trucks, $2,500.

Entries for depreciation had been made at the close of each year as follows: 2012, $21,000; 2013, $22,500; 2014, $25,050; and 2015, $30,400.

Instructions

(a) For each of the 4 years, compute separately the increase or decrease in net income arising from the company's errors in determining or entering depreciation or in recording transactions affecting trucks, ignoring income tax considerations.

(b) Prepare one compound journal entry as of December 31, 2015, for adjustment of the Trucks account to reflect the correct balances as revealed by your schedule, assuming that the books have not been closed for 2015.

3 6 P11-5 (Depletion and Depreciation—Mining) Khamsah Mining Company has purchased a tract of mineral land for $900,000. It is estimated that this tract will yield 120,000 tons of ore with sufficient mineral content to make mining and processing profitable. It is further estimated that 6,000 tons of ore will be mined the first and last year and 12,000 tons every year in between. (Assume 11 years of mining operations.) The land will have a salvage value of $30,000.

The company builds necessary structures and sheds on the site at a cost of $36,000. It is estimated that these structures can serve 15 years but, because they must be dismantled if they are to be moved, they have no salvage value. The company does not intend to use the buildings elsewhere. Mining machinery installed at the mine was purchased secondhand at a cost of $60,000. This machinery cost the former owner $150,000 and was 50% depreciated when purchased. Khamsah Mining estimates that about half of this machinery will still be useful when the present mineral resources have been exhausted, but that dismantling and removal costs will just about offset its value at that time. The company does not intend to use the machinery elsewhere. The remaining machinery will last until about one-half the present estimated mineral ore has been removed and will then be worthless. Cost is to be allocated equally between these two classes of machinery.

Instructions

(a) As chief accountant for the company, you are to prepare a schedule showing estimated depletion and depreciation costs for each year of the expected life of the mine.

(b) Also compute the depreciation and depletion for the first year assuming actual production of 5,000 tons. Nothing occurred during the year to cause the company engineers to change their estimates of either the mineral resources or the life of the structures and equipment.

6 P11-6 (Depletion, Timber, and Extraordinary Loss) Conan O'Brien Logging and Lumber Company owns 3,000 acres of timberland on the north side of Mount Leno, which was purchased in 2002 at a cost of $550 per acre. In 2014, O'Brien began selectively logging this timber tract. In May 2014, Mount Leno erupted, burying the timberland of O'Brien under a foot of ash. All of the timber on the O'Brien tract was downed. In addition, the logging roads, built at a cost of $150,000, were destroyed, as well as the logging equipment, with a net book value of $300,000.

At the time of the eruption, O'Brien had logged 20% of the estimated 500,000 board feet of timber. Prior to the eruption, O'Brien estimated the land to have a value of $200 per acre after the timber was harvested. O'Brien includes the logging roads in the depletion base.

O'Brien estimates it will take 3 years to salvage the downed timber at a cost of $700,000. The timber can be sold for pulp wood at an estimated price of $3 per board foot. The value of the land is unknown, but must be considered nominal due to future uncertainties.

Instructions

(a) Determine the depletion cost per board foot for the timber harvested prior to the eruption of Mount Leno.

(b) Prepare the journal entry to record the depletion prior to the eruption.

(c) If this tract represents approximately half of the timber holdings of O'Brien, determine the amount of the extraordinary loss due to the eruption of Mount Leno for the year ended December 31, 2014.

 P11-7 (Natural Resources—Timber) Bronson Paper Products purchased 10,000 acres of forested timberland in March 2014. The company paid $1,700 per acre for this land, which was above the $800 per acre most farmers were paying for cleared land. During April, May, June, and July 2014, Bronson cut enough timber to build roads using moveable equipment purchased on April 1, 2014. The cost of the roads was $250,000, and the cost of the equipment was $225,000; this equipment was expected to have a $9,000 salvage value and would be used for the next 15 years. Bronson selected the straight-line method of depreciation for the moveable equipment. Bronson began actively harvesting timber in August and by December had harvested and sold 540,000 board feet of timber of the estimated 6,750,000 board feet available for cutting.

In March 2015, Bronson planted new seedlings in the area harvested during the winter. Cost of planting these seedlings was $120,000. In addition, Bronson spent $8,000 in road maintenance and $6,000 for pest spraying during calendar-year 2015. The road maintenance and spraying are annual costs. During 2015, Bronson harvested and sold 774,000 board feet of timber of the estimated 6,450,000 board feet available for cutting.

In March 2016, Bronson again planted new seedlings at a cost of $150,000, and also spent $15,000 on road maintenance and pest spraying. During 2016, the company harvested and sold 650,000 board feet of timber of the estimated 6,500,000 board feet available for cutting.

Instructions

Compute the amount of depreciation and depletion expense for each of the 3 years (2014, 2015, and 2016). Assume that the roads are usable only for logging and therefore are included in the depletion base.

 P11-8 (Comprehensive Fixed-Asset Problem) Darby Sporting Goods Inc. has been experiencing growth in the demand for its products over the last several years. The last two Olympic Games greatly increased the popularity of basketball around the world. As a result, a European sports retailing consortium entered into an agreement with Darby's Roundball Division to purchase basketballs and other accessories on an increasing basis over the next 5 years.

To be able to meet the quantity commitments of this agreement, Darby had to obtain additional manufacturing capacity. A real estate firm located an available factory in close proximity to Darby's Roundball manufacturing facility, and Darby agreed to purchase the factory and used machinery from Encino Athletic Equipment Company on October 1, 2013. Renovations were necessary to convert the factory for Darby's manufacturing use.

The terms of the agreement required Darby to pay Encino $50,000 when renovations started on January 1, 2014, with the balance to be paid as renovations were completed. The overall purchase price for the factory and machinery was $400,000. The building renovations were contracted to Malone Construction at $100,000. The payments made, as renovations progressed during 2014, are shown below. The factory was placed in service on January 1, 2015.

	1/1	4/1	10/1	12/31
Encino	$50,000	$90,000	$110,000	$150,000
Malone		30,000	30,000	40,000

On January 1, 2014, Darby secured a $500,000 line-of-credit with a 12% interest rate to finance the purchase cost of the factory and machinery, and the renovation costs. Darby drew down on the line-of-credit to meet the payment schedule shown above; this was Darby's only outstanding loan during 2014.

Bob Sprague, Darby's controller, will capitalize the maximum allowable interest costs for this project. Darby's policy regarding purchases of this nature is to use the appraisal value of the land for book purposes and prorate the balance of the purchase price over the remaining items. The building had originally cost Encino $300,000 and had a net book value of $50,000, while the machinery originally cost $125,000 and had a net book value of $40,000 on the date of sale. The land was recorded on Encino's books at $40,000. An appraisal, conducted by independent appraisers at the time of acquisition, valued the land at $290,000, the building at $105,000, and the machinery at $45,000.

Angie Justice, chief engineer, estimated that the renovated plant would be used for 15 years, with an estimated salvage value of $30,000. Justice estimated that the productive machinery would have a remaining useful life of 5 years and a salvage value of $3,000. Darby's depreciation policy specifies the 200% declining-balance method for machinery and the 150% declining-balance method for the plant. One-half year's depreciation is taken in the year the plant is placed in service, and one-half year is allowed when the property is disposed of or retired. Darby uses a 360-day year for calculating interest costs.

Instructions

(a) Determine the amounts to be recorded on the books of Darby Sporting Goods Inc. as of December 31, 2014, for each of the following properties acquired from Encino Athletic Equipment Company.

    (1) Land.   **(2)** Buildings.   **(3)** Machinery.

(b) Calculate Darby Sporting Goods Inc.'s 2015 depreciation expense, for book purposes, for each of the properties acquired from Encino Athletic Equipment Company.

(c) Discuss the arguments for and against the capitalization of interest costs.

(CMA adapted)

P11-9 (Impairment) Roland Company uses special strapping equipment in its packaging business. The equipment was purchased in January 2013 for $10,000,000 and had an estimated useful life of 8 years with no salvage value. At December 31, 2014, new technology was introduced that would accelerate the obsolescence of Roland's equipment. Roland's controller estimates that expected future net cash flows on the equipment will be $6,300,000 and that the fair value of the equipment is $5,600,000. Roland intends to continue using the equipment, but it is estimated that the remaining useful life is 4 years. Roland uses straight-line depreciation.

Instructions

(a) Prepare the journal entry (if any) to record the impairment at December 31, 2014.

(b) Prepare any journal entries for the equipment at December 31, 2015. The fair value of the equipment at December 31, 2015, is estimated to be $5,900,000.

(c) Repeat the requirements for (a) and (b), assuming that Roland intends to dispose of the equipment and that it has not been disposed of as of December 31, 2015.

 P11-10 (Comprehensive Depreciation Computations) Kohlbeck Corporation, a manufacturer of steel products, began operations on October 1, 2013. The accounting department of Kohlbeck has started the fixed-asset and depreciation schedule presented on page 632. You have been asked to assist in completing this schedule. In addition to ascertaining that the data already on the schedule are correct, you have obtained the following information from the company's records and personnel.

1. Depreciation is computed from the first of the month of acquisition to the first of the month of disposition.
2. Land A and Building A were acquired from a predecessor corporation. Kohlbeck paid $800,000 for the land and building together. At the time of acquisition, the land had an appraised value of $90,000, and the building had an appraised value of $810,000.
3. Land B was acquired on October 2, 2013, in exchange for 2,500 newly issued shares of Kohlbeck's common stock. At the date of acquisition, the stock had a par value of $5 per share and a fair value of $30 per share. During October 2013, Kohlbeck paid $16,000 to demolish an existing building on this land so it could construct a new building.
4. Construction of Building B on the newly acquired land began on October 1, 2014. By September 30, 2015, Kohlbeck had paid $320,000 of the estimated total construction costs of $450,000. It is estimated that the building will be completed and occupied by July 2016.
5. Certain equipment was donated to the corporation by a local university. An independent appraisal of the equipment when donated placed the fair value at $40,000 and the salvage value at $3,000.
6. Machinery A's total cost of $182,900 includes installation expense of $600 and normal repairs and maintenance of $14,900. Salvage value is estimated at $6,000. Machinery A was sold on February 1, 2015.
7. On October 1, 2014, Machinery B was acquired with a down payment of $5,740 and the remaining payments to be made in 11 annual installments of $6,000 each beginning October 1, 2014. The prevailing interest rate was 8%. The following data were abstracted from present value tables (rounded).

Present value of $1.00 at 8%		Present value of an ordinary annuity of $1.00 at 8%	
10 years	.463	10 years	6.710
11 years	.429	11 years	7.139
15 years	.315	15 years	8.559

KOHLBECK CORPORATION
Fixed-Asset and Depreciation Schedule
For Fiscal Years Ended September 30, 2014, and September 30, 2015

Assets	Acquisition Date	Cost	Salvage	Depreciation Method	Estimated Life in Years	Depreciation Expense Year Ended September 30	
						2014	2015
Land A	October 1, 2013	$ (1)	N/A*	N/A	N/A	N/A	N/A
Building A	October 1, 2013	(2)	$40,000	Straight-line	(3)	$13,600	(4)
Land B	October 2, 2013	(5)	N/A	N/A	N/A	N/A	N/A
Building B	Under Construction	$320,000 to date	—	Straight-line	30	—	(6)
Donated Equipment	October 2, 2013	(7)	3,000	150% declining-balance	10	(8)	(9)
Machinery A	October 2, 2013	(10)	6,000	Sum-of-the-years'-digits	8	(11)	(12)
Machinery B	October 1, 2014	(13)	—	Straight-line	20	—	(14)

*N/A—Not applicable

Instructions

For each numbered item on the schedule above, supply the correct amount. (Round each answer to the nearest dollar.)

2 3 P11-11 (Depreciation for Partial Periods—SL, Act., SYD, and DDB) On January 1, 2012, a machine was purchased for $90,000. The machine has an estimated salvage value of $6,000 and an estimated useful life of 5 years. The machine can operate for 100,000 hours before it needs to be replaced. The company closed its books on December 31 and operates the machine as follows: 2012, 20,000 hours; 2013, 25,000 hours; 2014, 15,000 hours; 2015, 30,000 hours; and 2016, 10,000 hours.

Instructions

(a) Compute the annual depreciation charges over the machine's life assuming a December 31 year-end for each of the following depreciation methods.

   (1) Straight-line method.   (3) Sum-of-the-years'-digits method.
   (2) Activity method.   (4) Double-declining-balance method.

(b) Assume a fiscal year-end of September 30. Compute the annual depreciation charges over the asset's life applying each of the following methods.

   (1) Straight-line method.   (3) Double-declining-balance method.
   (2) Sum-of-the-years'-digits method.

2 3 8 *P11-12 (Depreciation—SL, DDB, SYD, Act., and MACRS)** On January 1, 2013, Locke Company, a small machine-tool manufacturer, acquired for $1,260,000 a piece of new industrial equipment. The new equipment had a useful life of 5 years, and the salvage value was estimated to be $60,000. Locke estimates that the new equipment can produce 12,000 machine tools in its first year. It estimates that production will decline by 1,000 units per year over the remaining useful life of the equipment.

The following depreciation methods may be used: (1) straight-line, (2) double-declining-balance, (3) sum-of-the-years'-digits, and (4) units-of-output. For tax purposes, the class life is 7 years. Use the MACRS tables for computing depreciation.

Instructions

(a) Which depreciation method would maximize net income for financial statement reporting for the 3-year period ending December 31, 2015? Prepare a schedule showing the amount of accumulated depreciation at December 31, 2015, under the method selected. Ignore present value, income tax, and deferred income tax considerations.

(b) Which depreciation method (MACRS or optional straight-line) would minimize net income for income tax reporting for the 3-year period ending December 31, 2015? Determine the amount of accumulated depreciation at December 31, 2015. Ignore present value considerations.

(AICPA adapted)

PROBLEMS SET B

See the book's companion website, at **www.wiley.com/college/kieso**, for an additional set of problems.

CONCEPTS FOR ANALYSIS

CA11-1 (Depreciation Basic Concepts) Burnitz Manufacturing Company was organized on January 1, 2014. During 2014, it has used in its reports to management the straight-line method of depreciating its plant assets.

On November 8, you are having a conference with Burnitz's officers to discuss the depreciation method to be used for income tax and stockholder reporting. James Bryant, president of Burnitz, has suggested the use of a new method, which he feels is more suitable than the straight-line method for the needs of the company during the period of rapid expansion of production and capacity that he foresees. Following is an example in which the proposed method is applied to a fixed asset with an original cost of $248,000, an estimated useful life of 5 years, and a salvage value of approximately $8,000.

Year	Years of Life Used	Fraction Rate	Depreciation Expense	Accumulated Depreciation at End of Year	Book Value at End of Year
1	1	1/15	$16,000	$ 16,000	$232,000
2	2	2/15	32,000	48,000	200,000
3	3	3/15	48,000	96,000	152,000
4	4	4/15	64,000	160,000	88,000
5	5	5/15	80,000	240,000	8,000

The president favors the new method because he has heard that:

1. It will increase the funds recovered during the years near the end of the assets' useful lives when maintenance and replacement disbursements are high.
2. It will result in increased write-offs in later years and thereby will reduce taxes.

Instructions
(a) What is the purpose of accounting for depreciation?
(b) Is the president's proposal within the scope of generally accepted accounting principles? In making your decision, discuss the circumstances, if any, under which use of the method would be reasonable and those, if any, under which it would not be reasonable.
(c) The president wants your advice on the following issues.
   (1) Do depreciation charges recover or create funds? Explain.
   (2) Assume that the Internal Revenue Service accepts the proposed depreciation method in this case. If the proposed method were used for stockholder and tax reporting purposes, how would it affect the availability of cash flows generated by operations?

CA11-2 (Unit, Group, and Composite Depreciation) The certified public accountant is frequently called upon by management for advice regarding methods of computing depreciation. Of comparable importance, although it arises less frequently, is the question of whether the depreciation method should be based on consideration of the assets as units, as a group, or as having a composite life.

Instructions
(a) Briefly describe the depreciation methods based on treating assets as (1) units and (2) a group or as having a composite life.
(b) Present the arguments for and against the use of each of the two methods.
(c) Describe how retirements are recorded under each of the two methods.

(AICPA adapted)

CA11-3 (Depreciation—Strike, Units-of-Production, Obsolescence) Presented on page 634 are three different and unrelated situations involving depreciation accounting. Answer the question(s) at the end of each situation.

Situation I: Recently, Broderick Company experienced a strike that affected a number of its operating plants. The controller of this company indicated that it was not appropriate to report depreciation expense during this period because the equipment did not depreciate and an improper matching of costs and revenues would result. She based her position on the following points.

1. It is inappropriate to charge the period with costs for which there are no related revenues arising from production.
2. The basic factor of depreciation in this instance is wear and tear. Because equipment was idle, no wear and tear occurred.

Instructions
Comment on the appropriateness of the controller's comments.

Situation II: Etheridge Company manufactures electrical appliances, most of which are used in homes. Company engineers have designed a new type of blender which, through the use of a few attachments, will perform more functions than any blender currently on the market. Demand for the new blender can be projected with reasonable probability. In order to make the blenders, Etheridge needs a specialized machine that is not available from outside sources. It has been decided to make such a machine in Etheridge's own plant.

Instructions
(a) Discuss the effect of projected demand in units for the new blenders (which may be steady, decreasing, or increasing) on the determination of a depreciation method for the machine.
(b) What other matters should be considered in determining the depreciation method? (Ignore income tax considerations.)

Situation III: Haley Paper Company operates a 300-ton-per-day kraft pulp mill and four sawmills in Wisconsin. The company is in the process of expanding its pulp mill facilities to a capacity of 1,000 tons per day and plans to replace three of its older, less efficient sawmills with an expanded facility. One of the mills to be replaced did not operate for most of 2014 (current year), and there are no plans to reopen it before the new sawmill facility becomes operational.

In reviewing the depreciation rates and in discussing the salvage values of the sawmills that were to be replaced, it was noted that if present depreciation rates were not adjusted, substantial amounts of plant costs on these three mills would not be depreciated by the time the new mill came on stream.

Instructions
What is the proper accounting for the four sawmills at the end of 2014?

 CA11-4 (Depreciation Concepts) As a cost accountant for San Francisco Cannery, you have been approached by Phil Perriman, canning room supervisor, about the 2014 costs charged to his department. In particular, he is concerned about the line item "depreciation." Perriman is very proud of the excellent condition of his canning room equipment. He has always been vigilant about keeping all equipment serviced and well oiled. He is sure that the huge charge to depreciation is a mistake; it does not at all reflect the cost of minimal wear and tear that the machines have experienced over the last year. He believes that the charge should be considerably lower.

The machines being depreciated are six automatic canning machines. All were put into use on January 1, 2014. Each cost $625,000, having a salvage value of $55,000 and a useful life of 12 years. San Francisco depreciates this and similar assets using double-declining-balance depreciation. Perriman has also pointed out that if you used straight-line depreciation, the charge to his department would not be so great.

Instructions
Write a memo to Phil Perriman to clear up his misunderstanding of the term "depreciation." Also, calculate year-1 depreciation on all machines using both methods. Explain the theoretical justification for double-declining-balance and why, in the long run, the aggregate charge to depreciation will be the same under both methods.

CA11-5 (Depreciation Choice—Ethics) Jerry Prior, Beeler Corporation's controller, is concerned that net income may be lower this year. He is afraid upper-level management might recommend cost reductions by laying off accounting staff, including him.

Prior knows that depreciation is a major expense for Beeler. The company currently uses the double-declining-balance method for both financial reporting and tax purposes, and he's thinking of selling equipment that, given its age, is primarily used when there are periodic spikes in demand. The equipment has a carrying value of $2,000,000 and a fair value of $2,180,000. The gain on the sale would be reported in the income statement. He doesn't want to highlight this method of increasing income. He thinks, "Why don't I increase the estimated useful lives and the salvage values? That will decrease depreciation expense and require less extensive disclosure, since the changes are accounted for prospectively. I may be able to save my job and those of my staff."

Instructions
Answer the following questions.

(a) Who are the stakeholders in this situation?
(b) What are the ethical issues involved?
(c) What should Prior do?

USING YOUR JUDGMENT

FINANCIAL REPORTING

Financial Reporting Problem

P&G **The Procter & Gamble Company (P&G)**

The financial statements of P&G are presented in Appendix 5B. The company's complete annual report, including the notes to the financial statements, can be accessed at the book's companion website, **www. wiley.com/college/kieso**.

Instructions
Refer to P&G's financial statements and the accompanying notes to answer the following questions.

(a) What descriptions are used by P&G in its balance sheet to classify its property, plant, and equipment?
(b) What method or methods of depreciation does P&G use to depreciate its property, plant, and equipment?
(c) Over what estimated useful lives does P&G depreciate its property, plant, and equipment?
(d) What amounts for depreciation and amortization expense did P&G charge to its income statement in 2011, 2010, and 2009?
(e) What were the capital expenditures for property, plant, and equipment made by P&G in 2011, 2010, and 2009?

Comparative Analysis Case

The Coca-Cola Company and PepsiCo., Inc.

Instructions
Go to the book's companion website and use information found there to answer the following questions related to The Coca-Cola Company and PepsiCo, Inc.

(a) What amount is reported in the balance sheets as property, plant, and equipment (net) of Coca-Cola at December 31, 2011, and of PepsiCo at December 31, 2011? What percentage of total assets is invested in property, plant, and equipment by each company?
(b) What depreciation methods are used by Coca-Cola and PepsiCo for property, plant, and equipment? How much depreciation was reported by Coca-Cola and PepsiCo in 2011? In 2010?
(c) Compute and compare the following ratios for Coca-Cola and PepsiCo for 2011.
   (1) Asset turnover.
   (2) Profit margin on sales.
   (3) Return on assets.
(d) What amount was spent in 2011 for capital expenditures by Coca-Cola and PepsiCo? What amount of interest was capitalized in 2011?

Financial Statement Analysis Case

McDonald's Corporation

McDonald's is the largest and best-known global food-service retailer, with more than 32,000 restaurants in 118 countries. On any day, McDonald's serves approximately 1 percent of the world's population. Presented on the next page is information related to McDonald's property and equipment.

McDonald's Corporation
Summary of Significant Accounting Policies Section

Property and Equipment. Property and equipment are stated at cost, with depreciation and amortization provided using the straight-line method over the following estimated useful lives: buildings—up to 40 years; leasehold improvements—the lesser of useful lives of assets or lease terms, which generally include option periods; and equipment—three to 12 years.

[In the notes to the financial statements:]

Property and Equipment
Net property and equipment consisted of:

	December 31	
(In millions)	2011	2010
Land	$ 5,328.3	$ 5,200.5
Buildings and improvements on owned land	13,079.9	12,399.4
Buildings and improvements on leased land	12,021.8	11,732.0
Equipment, signs and seating	4,757.2	4,608.5
Other	550.4	542.0
	35,737.6	34,482.4
Accumulated depreciation and amortization	(12,903.1)	(12,421.8)
Net property and equipment	$22,834.5	$22,060.6

Depreciation and amortization expense was (in millions): 2011—$1,329.6; 2010—$1,200.4; 2009—$1,160.8.

[In its 6-year summary, McDonald's provides the following information.]

Cash Provided by Operations

(dollars in millions)	2011	2010	2009
Cash provided by operations	$7,150	$6,342	$5,751
Capital expenditures	$2,730	$2,135	$1,952

Instructions

(a) What method of depreciation does McDonald's use?

(b) Does depreciation and amortization expense cause cash flow from operations to increase? Explain.

(c) What does the schedule of cash flow measures indicate?

Accounting, Analysis, and Principles

Electroboy Enterprises, Inc. operates several stores throughout the western United States. As part of an operational and financial reporting review in a response to a downturn in its markets, the company's management has decided to perform an impairment test on five stores (combined). The five stores' sales have declined due to aging facilities and competition from a rival that opened new stores in the same markets. Management has developed the following information concerning the five stores as of the end of fiscal 2013.

Original cost	$36 million
Accumulated depreciation	$10 million
Estimated remaining useful life	4 years
Estimated expected future annual cash flows (not discounted)	$4.0 million per year
Appropriate discount rate	5 percent

Accounting

(a) Determine the amount of impairment loss, if any, that Electroboy should report for fiscal 2013 and the book value at which Electroboy should report the five stores on its fiscal year-end 2013 balance sheet. Assume that the cash flows occur at the end of each year.

(b) Repeat part (a), but instead assume that (1) the estimated remaining useful life is 10 years, (2) the estimated annual cash flows are $2,720,000 per year, and (3) the appropriate discount rate is 6 percent.

Analysis

Assume that you are a financial analyst and you participate in a conference call with Electroboy management in early 2014 (before Electroboy closes the books on fiscal 2013). During the conference call, you learn that management is considering selling the five stores, but the sale won't likely be completed until the second quarter of fiscal 2014. Briefly discuss what implications this would have for Electroboy's 2013 financial statements. Assume the same facts as in part (b) above.

Principles

Electroboy management would like to know the accounting for the impaired asset in periods subsequent to the impairment. Can the assets be written back up? Briefly discuss the conceptual arguments for this accounting.

BRIDGE TO THE PROFESSION

Professional Research: FASB Codification

Matt Holmes recently joined Klax Company as a staff accountant in the controller's office. Klax Company provides warehousing services for companies in several midwestern cities.

The location in Dubuque, Iowa, has not been performing well due to increased competition and the loss of several customers that have recently gone out of business. Matt's department manager suspects that the plant and equipment may be impaired and wonders whether those assets should be written down. Given the company's prior success, this issue has never arisen in the past, and Matt has been asked to conduct some research on this issue.

Instructions

If your school has a subscription to the FASB Codification, go to *http://aaahq.org/asclogin.cfm* to log in and prepare responses to the following. Provide Codification references for your responses.

(a) What is the authoritative guidance for asset impairments? Briefly discuss the scope of the standard (i.e., explain the types of transactions to which the standard applies).

(b) Give several examples of events that would cause an asset to be tested for impairment. Does it appear that Klax should perform an impairment test? Explain.

(c) What is the best evidence of fair value? Describe alternate methods of estimating fair value.

Additional Professional Resources

See the book's companion website, at **www.wiley.com/college/kieso**, for professional simulations as well as other study resources.

IFRS INSIGHTS

GAAP adheres to many of the same principles of IFRS in the accounting for property, plant, and equipment. Major differences relate to use of component depreciation, impairments, and revaluations.

9 LEARNING OBJECTIVE
Compare the accounting for property, plant, and equipment under GAAP and IFRS.

RELEVANT FACTS

Following are the key similarities and differences between GAAP and IFRS related to property, plant, and equipment.

Similarities

• The definition of property, plant, and equipment is essentially the same under GAAP and IFRS.

- Under both GAAP and IFRS, changes in depreciation method and changes in useful life are treated in the current and future periods. Prior periods are not affected.
- The accounting for plant asset disposals is the same under GAAP and IFRS.
- The accounting for the initial costs to acquire natural resources is similar under GAAP and IFRS.
- Under both GAAP and IFRS, interest costs incurred during construction must be capitalized. Recently, IFRS converged to GAAP.
- The accounting for exchanges of non-monetary assets is essentially the same between IFRS and GAAP. GAAP requires that gains on exchanges of non-monetary assets be recognized if the exchange has commercial substance. This is the same framework used in IFRS.
- GAAP and IFRS both view depreciation as allocation of cost over an asset's life. GAAP permits the same depreciation methods (straight-line, diminishing-balance, units-of-production) as IFRS.

Differences

- IFRS requires component depreciation. Under GAAP, component depreciation is permitted but is rarely used.
- Under IFRS, companies can use either the historical cost model or the revaluation model. GAAP does not permit revaluations of property, plant, and equipment or mineral resources.
- In testing for impairments of long-lived assets, GAAP uses a different model than IFRS to test for impairments (details of the IFRS impairment test is presented in the *About the Numbers* discussion). As long as future undiscounted cash flows exceed the carrying amount of the asset, no impairment is recorded. The IFRS impairment test is stricter. However, unlike GAAP, reversals of impairment losses are permitted.

ABOUT THE NUMBERS

Component Depreciation

Under IFRS, companies are required to use **component depreciation**. IFRS requires that each part of an item of property, plant, and equipment that is significant to the total cost of the asset must be depreciated separately. Companies therefore have to exercise judgment to determine the proper allocations to the components. As an example, when a company like Nokia purchases a building, it must determine how the various building components (e.g., the foundation, structure, roof, heating and cooling system, and elevators) should be segregated and depreciated.

To illustrate the accounting for component depreciation, assume that EuroAsia Airlines purchases an airplane for $100,000,000 on January 1, 2014. The airplane has a useful life of 20 years and a residual value of $0. EuroAsia uses the straight-line method of depreciation for all its airplanes. EuroAsia identifies the following components, amounts, and useful lives, as shown in Illustration IFRS11-1.

ILLUSTRATION IFRS11-1
Airplane Components

Components	Component Amount	Component Useful Life
Airframe	$60,000,000	20 years
Engine components	32,000,000	8 years
Other components	8,000,000	5 years

Illustration IFRS11-2 shows the computation of depreciation expense for EuroAsia for 2014.

Components	Component Amount	÷	Useful Life	=	Component Depreciation
Airframe	$ 60,000,000		20		$3,000,000
Engine components	32,000,000		8		4,000,000
Other components	8,000,000		5		1,600,000
Total	$100,000,000				$8,600,000

ILLUSTRATION IFRS11-2
Computation of Component Depreciation

As indicated, EuroAsia records depreciation expense of $8,600,000 in 2014 as follows.

Depreciation Expense	8,600,000	
Accumulated Depreciation—Airplane		8,600,000

On the statement of financial position at the end of 2014, EuroAsia reports the airplane as a single amount. The presentation is shown in Illustration IFRS11-3.

Non-current assets	
Airplane	$100,000,000
Less: Accumulated depreciation—airplane	8,600,000
	$ 91,400,000

ILLUSTRATION IFRS11-3
Presentation of Carrying Amount of Airplane

In many situations, a company may not have a good understanding of the cost of the individual components purchased. In that case, the cost of individual components should be estimated based on reference to current market prices (if available), discussion with experts in valuation, or use of other reasonable approaches.

Recognizing Impairments

As discussed in the textbook, the credit crisis starting in late 2008 has affected many financial and non-financial institutions. As a result of this global slump, many companies are considering write-offs of some of their long-lived assets. These write-offs are referred to as **impairments**. The accounting for impairments is different under GAAP and IFRS.

A long-lived tangible asset is impaired when a company is not able to recover the asset's carrying amount either through using it or by selling it. To determine whether an asset is impaired, **on an annual basis, companies review the asset for indicators of impairments**—that is, a decline in the asset's cash-generating ability through use or sale. This review should consider internal sources (e.g., adverse changes in performance) and external sources (e.g., adverse changes in the business or regulatory environment) of information. **If impairment indicators are present, then an impairment test must be conducted.** This test compares the asset's recoverable amount with its carrying amount. If the carrying amount is higher than the recoverable amount, the difference is an impairment loss. If the recoverable amount is greater than the carrying amount, no impairment is recorded.

Recoverable amount is defined as the higher of fair value less costs to sell or value-in-use. **Fair value less costs to sell** means what the asset could be sold for after deducting costs of disposal. **Value-in-use** is the present value of cash flows expected from the future use and eventual sale of the asset at the end of its useful life. Illustration IFRS11-4 (page 640) highlights the nature of the impairment test.

**ILLUSTRATION
IFRS11-4**
Impairment Test

If either the fair value less costs to sell or value-in-use is higher than the carrying amount, there is no impairment. If both the fair value less costs to sell and value-in-use are lower than the carrying amount, a loss on impairment occurs.

Example: No Impairment

Assume that Cruz Company performs an impairment test for its equipment. The carrying amount of Cruz's equipment is $200,000, its fair value less costs to sell is $180,000, and its value-in-use is $205,000. In this case, the value-in-use of Cruz's equipment is higher than its carrying amount of $200,000. As a result, there is no impairment. (If a company can more readily determine value-in-use (or fair value less costs to sell) and it determines that no impairment is needed, it is not required to compute the other measure.)

Example: Impairment

Assume the same information for Cruz Company above except that the value-in-use of Cruz's equipment is $175,000 rather than $205,000. Cruz measures the impairment loss as the difference between the carrying amount of $200,000 and the higher of fair value less costs to sell ($180,000) or value-in-use ($175,000). Cruz therefore uses the fair value less cost of disposal to record an impairment loss of $20,000 ($200,000 − $180,000). Cruz makes the following entry to record the impairment loss.

Loss on Impairment	20,000	
Accumulated Depreciation—Equipment		20,000

Loss on Impairment is reported in the income statement in the "Other income and expense" section. The company then either credits Equipment or Accumulated Depreciation—Equipment to reduce the carrying amount of the equipment for the impairment. *For purposes of homework, credit accumulated depreciation when recording an impairment for a depreciable asset.*

Reversal of Impairment Loss

After recording the impairment loss, the recoverable amount becomes the basis of the impaired asset. What happens if a review in a future year indicates that the asset is no longer impaired because the recoverable amount of the asset is higher than the carrying amount? In that case, the impairment loss may be reversed.

To illustrate, assume that Tan Company purchases equipment on January 1, 2014, for $300,000, with a useful life of three years, and no residual value. Its depreciation and related carrying amount over the three years is as follows.

Year	Depreciation Expense	Carrying Amount
2014	$100,000 ($300,000/3)	$200,000
2015	$100,000 ($300,000/3)	$100,000
2016	$100,000 ($300,000/3)	0

At December 31, 2014, Tan determines it has an impairment loss of $20,000 and therefore makes the following entry.

Loss on Impairment	20,000	
Accumulated Depreciation—Equipment		20,000

Tan's depreciation expense and related carrying amount after the impairment is as indicated in Illustration IFRS11-5.

Year	Depreciation Expense	Carrying Amount
2015	$90,000 ($180,000/2)	$90,000
2016	$90,000 ($180,000/2)	0

ILLUSTRATION IFRS11-5
Carrying Value of Impaired Asset

At the end of 2015, Tan determines that the recoverable amount of the equipment is $96,000, which is greater than its carrying amount of $90,000. In this case, Tan reverses the previously recognized impairment loss with the following entry.

Accumulated Depreciation—Equipment	6,000	
Recovery of Loss from Impairment		6,000

The recovery of the impairment loss is reported in the "Other income and expense" section of the income statement. The carrying amount of Tan's equipment is now $96,000 ($90,000 + $6,000) at December 31, 2015. The general rule related to reversals of impairments is as follows. The amount of the recovery of the loss is limited to the carrying amount that would result if the impairment had not occurred. For example, the carrying amount of Tan's equipment at the end of 2015 would be $100,000, assuming no impairment. The $6,000 recovery is therefore permitted because Tan's carrying amount on the equipment is now only $96,000.

However, any recovery above $10,000 is not permitted. The reason is that any recovery above $10,000 results in Tan carrying the asset at a value above its historical cost.

Revaluations

Up to this point, we have assumed that companies use the historical cost principle to value long-lived tangible assets after acquisition. However, under IFRS companies have a choice. They may value these assets at cost or at fair value.

Recognizing Revaluations

Network Rail (a company in Great Britain) is an example of a company that elected to use fair values to account for its railroad network. Its use of fair value led to an increase of £4,289 million to its long-lived tangible assets. When companies choose to fair value their long-lived tangible assets subsequent to acquisition, they account for the change in the fair value by adjusting the appropriate asset account and establishing an unrealized gain on the revalued long-lived tangible asset. This unrealized gain is often referred to as **revaluation surplus**.

Revaluation—Land. To illustrate revaluation of land, assume that Siemens Group purchased land for $1,000,000 on January 5, 2014. The company elects to use revaluation accounting for the land in subsequent periods. At December 31, 2014, the land's fair value is $1,200,000. The entry to record the land at fair value is as follows.

Land	200,000	
Unrealized Gain on Revaluation (land)		200,000

The land is reported on the statement of financial position at $1,200,000, and Unrealized Gain on Revaluation (land) increases other comprehensive income in the statement of comprehensive income. In addition, if this is the only revaluation adjustment to date, the statement of financial position reports accumulated other comprehensive income of $200,000.

Revaluation—Depreciable Assets. To illustrate the accounting for revaluations of depreciable assets, assume that Lenovo Group purchases equipment for $500,000 on January 2, 2014. The equipment has a useful life of five years, is depreciated using the straight-line method of depreciation, and its residual value is zero. Lenovo chooses to revalue its equipment to fair value over the life of the equipment. Lenovo records depreciation expense of $100,000 ($500,000 ÷ 5) at December 31, 2014, as follows.

December 31, 2014

Depreciation Expense	100,000	
Accumulated Depreciation—Equipment		100,000
(To record depreciation expense in 2014)		

After this entry, Lenovo's equipment has a carrying amount of $400,000 ($500,000 − $100,000). Lenovo receives an independent appraisal for the fair value of equipment at December 31, 2014, which is $460,000. To report the equipment at fair value, Lenovo does the following.

1. Reduces the Accumulated Depreciation—Equipment account to zero.
2. Reduces the Equipment account by $40,000—it then is reported at its fair value of $460,000.
3. Records Unrealized Gain on Revaluation (equipment) for the difference between the fair value and carrying amount of the equipment, or $60,000 ($460,000 − $400,000).

The entry to record this revaluation at December 31, 2014, is as follows.

December 31, 2014

Accumulated Depreciation—Equipment	100,000	
Equipment		40,000
Unrealized Gain on Revaluation (equipment)		60,000
(To adjust the equipment to fair value and		
record revaluation increase)		

The equipment is now reported at its fair value of $460,000 ($500,000 − $40,000). As an alternative to the one shown here, companies restate on a proportionate basis the cost and accumulated depreciation of the asset, such that the carrying amount of the asset after revaluation equals its revalued amount.

The increase in the fair value of $60,000 is reported on the statement of comprehensive income as other comprehensive income. In addition, the ending balance is reported in accumulated other comprehensive income on the statement of financial position in the equity section. Illustration IFRS11-6 shows the presentation of revaluation elements.

ILLUSTRATION IFRS11-6
Financial Statement Presentation—Revaluations

On the statement of comprehensive income:	
Depreciation expense	$100,000
Other comprehensive income	
Unrealized gain on revaluation (equipment)	$ 60,000
On the statement of financial position:	
Non-current assets	
Equipment ($500,000 − $40,000)	$460,000
Accumulated depreciation—equipment ($100,000 − $100,000)	–0–
Carrying amount	$460,000
Equity	
Accumulated other comprehensive income	$ 60,000

As indicated, at December 31, 2014, the carrying amount of the equipment is now $460,000. Lenovo reports depreciation expense of $100,000 in the income statement and Unrealized Gain on Revaluation (equipment) of $60,000 in "Other comprehensive income." Assuming no change in the useful life of the equipment, depreciation in 2015 is $115,000 ($460,000 ÷ 4).

In summary, a revaluation increase generally goes to equity. A revaluation decrease is reported as an expense (as an impairment loss), unless it offsets previously recorded revaluation increases. If the revaluation increase offsets a revaluation decrease that went to expense, then the increase is reported in income. **Under no circumstances can the Accumulated Other Comprehensive Income account related to revaluations have a negative balance.**

ON THE HORIZON

With respect to revaluations, as part of the conceptual framework project, the Boards will examine the measurement bases used in accounting. It is too early to say whether a converged conceptual framework will recommend fair value measurement (and revaluation accounting) for property, plant, and equipment. However, this is likely to be one of the more contentious issues, given the long-standing use of historical cost as a measurement basis in GAAP.

IFRS SELF-TEST QUESTIONS

1. Mandall Company constructed a warehouse for $280,000 on January 2, 2014. Mandall estimates that the warehouse has a useful life of 20 years and no residual value. Construction records indicate that $40,000 of the cost of the warehouse relates to its heating, ventilation, and air conditioning (HVAC) system, which has an estimated useful life of only 10 years. What is the first year of depreciation expense using straight-line component depreciation under IFRS?
   (a) $28,000.   (c) $16,000.
   (b) $14,000.   (d) $4,000.

2. Francisco Corporation is constructing a new building at a total initial cost of $10,000,000. The building is expected to have a useful life of 50 years with no residual value. The building's finished surfaces (e.g., roof cover and floor cover) are 5% of this cost and have a useful life of 20 years. Building services systems (e.g., electric, heating, and plumbing) are 20% of the cost and have a useful life of 25 years. The depreciation in the first year using component depreciation, assuming straight-line depreciation with no residual value, is:
   (a) $200,000.   (c) $255,000.
   (b) $215,000.   (d) None of the above.

3. Which of the following statements is **correct**?
   (a) Both IFRS and GAAP permit revaluation of property, plant, and equipment.
   (b) IFRS permits revaluation of property, plant, and equipment but not GAAP.
   (c) Both IFRS and GAAP do not permit revaluation of property, plant, and equipment.
   (d) GAAP permits revaluation of property, plant, and equipment but not IFRS.

4. Hilo Company has land that cost $350,000 but now has a fair value of $500,000. Hilo Company decides to use the revaluation method specified in IFRS to account for the land. Which of the following statements is **correct**?
   (a) Hilo Company must continue to report the land at $350,000.
   (b) Hilo Company would report a net income increase of $150,000 due to an increase in the value of the land.
   (c) Hilo Company would debit Revaluation Surplus for $150,000.
   (d) Hilo Company would credit Revaluation Surplus by $150,000.

5. Under IFRS, value-in-use is defined as:
   (a) net realizable value.
   (b) fair value.
   (c) future cash flows discounted to present value.
   (d) total future undiscounted cash flows.

IFRS CONCEPTS AND APPLICATION

IFRS11-1 Walkin Inc. is considering the write-down of its long-term plant because of a lack of profitability. Explain to the management of Walkin how to determine whether a write-down is permitted.

IFRS11-2 Last year, Wyeth Company recorded an impairment on an asset held for use. Recent appraisals indicate that the asset has increased in value. Should Wyeth record this recovery in value?

IFRS11-3 Toro Co. has equipment with a carrying amount of $700,000. The value-in-use of the equipment is $705,000, and its fair value less costs of disposal is $590,000. The equipment is expected to be used in operations in the future. What amount (if any) should Toro report as an impairment to its equipment?

IFRS11-4 Explain how gains or losses on impaired assets should be reported in income.

IFRS11-5 Tanaka Company has land that cost $15,000,000. Its fair value on December 31, 2014, is $20,000,000. Tanaka chooses the revaluation model to report its land. Explain how the land and its related valuation should be reported.

IFRS11-6 Why might a company choose not to use revaluation accounting?

IFRS11-7 Ortiz purchased a piece of equipment that cost $202,000 on January 1, 2014. The equipment has the following components.

Component	Cost	Residual Value	Estimated Useful Life
A	$70,000	$7,000	10 years
B	50,000	5,000	5 years
C	82,000	4,000	12 years

Compute the depreciation expense for this equipment at December 31, 2014.

IFRS11-8 Tan Chin Company purchases a building for $11,300,000 on January 2, 2014. An engineer's report shows that of the total purchase price, $11,000,000 should be allocated to the building (with a 40-year life), $150,000 to 15-year property, and $150,000 to 5-year property. No residual (salvage) value should be considered. Compute depreciation expense for 2014 using component depreciation.

IFRS11-9 Brazil Group purchases a vehicle at a cost of $50,000 on January 2, 2014. Individual components of the vehicle and useful lives are as follows.

	Cost	Useful Lives
Tires	$ 6,000	2 years
Transmission	10,000	5 years
Trucks	34,000	10 years

Instructions

(Assume no residual (salvage) value.)

(a) Compute depreciation expense for 2014, assuming Brazil depreciates the vehicle as a single unit.
(b) Compute depreciation expense for 2014, assuming Brazil uses component depreciation.
(c) Why might a company want to use component depreciation to depreciate its assets?

IFRS11-10 Jurassic Company owns machinery that cost $900,000 and has accumulated depreciation of $380,000. The present value of expected future net cash flows from the use of the asset are expected to be $500,000. The fair value less cost of disposal of the equipment is $400,000. Prepare the journal entry, if any, to record the impairment loss.

IFRS11-11 Presented below is information related to equipment owned by Pujols Company at December 31, 2014.

Cost (residual value $0)	$9,000,000
Accumulated depreciation to date	1,000,000
Value-in-use	5,500,000
Fair value less cost of disposal	4,400,000

Assume that Pujols will continue to use this asset in the future. As of December 31, 2014, the equipment has a remaining useful life of 8 years. Pujols uses straight-line depreciation.

Instructions

(a) Prepare the journal entry (if any) to record the impairment of the asset at December 31, 2014.

(b) Prepare the journal entry to record depreciation expense for 2015.

(c) The recoverable amount of the equipment at December 31, 2015, is $6,050,000. Prepare the journal entry (if any) necessary to record this increase.

IFRS11-12 Assume the same information as in IFRS11-11, except that Pujols intends to dispose of the equipment in the coming year.

Instructions

(a) Prepare the journal entry (if any) to record the impairment of the asset at December 31, 2014.

(b) Prepare the journal entry (if any) to record depreciation expense for 2015.

(c) The asset was not sold by December 31, 2015. The fair value of the equipment on that date is $5,100,000. Prepare the journal entry (if any) necessary to record this increase. It is expected that the cost of disposal is $20,000.

IFRS11-13 Falcetto Company acquired equipment on January 1, 2013, for $12,000. Falcetto elects to value this class of equipment using revaluation accounting. This equipment is being depreciated on a straight-line basis over its 6-year useful life. There is no residual value at the end of the 6-year period. The appraised value of the equipment approximates the carrying amount at December 31, 2013 and 2015. On December 31, 2014, the fair value of the equipment is determined to be $7,000.

Instructions

(a) Prepare the journal entries for 2013 related to the equipment.

(b) Prepare the journal entries for 2014 related to the equipment.

(c) Determine the amount of depreciation expense that Falcetto will record on the equipment in 2015.

International Reporting Case

IFRS11-14 Companies following international accounting standards are permitted to revalue fixed assets above the assets' historical costs. Such revaluations are allowed under various countries' standards and the standards issued by the IASB. Liberty International, a real estate company headquartered in the United Kingdom (U.K.), follows U.K. standards. In a recent year, Liberty disclosed the following information on revaluations of its tangible fixed assets. The revaluation reserve measures the amount by which tangible fixed assets are recorded above historical cost and is reported in Liberty's stockholders' equity.

Liberty International

Completed Investment Properties

Completed investment properties are professionally valued on a market value basis by external valuers at the balance sheet date. Surpluses and deficits arising during the year are reflected in the revalution reserve.

Liberty reported the following additional data. Amounts for Kimco Realty (which follows GAAP) in the same year are provided for comparison.

	Liberty (pounds sterling, in thousands)	Kimco (dollars, in millions)
Total revenues	£ 741	$ 517
Average total assets	5,577	4,696
Net income	125	297

Instructions

(a) Compute the following ratios for Liberty and Kimco.

    (1) Return on assets.

    (2) Profit margin on sales.

    (3) Asset turnover.

    How do these companies compare on these performance measures?

(b) Liberty reports a revaluation surplus of £1,952. Assume that £1,550 of this amount arose from an increase in the net replacement value of investment properties during the year. Prepare the journal entry to record this increase.

(c) Under U.K. (and IASB) standards, are Liberty's assets and equity overstated? If so, why? When comparing Liberty to U.S. companies, like Kimco, what adjustments would you need to make in order to have valid comparisons of ratios such as those computed in (a) above?

Professional Research

IFRS11-15 Matt Holmes recently joined Klax Company as a staff accountant in the controller's office. Klax Company provides warehousing services for companies in several European cities. The location in Koblenz, Germany, has not been performing well due to increased competition and the loss of several customers that have recently gone out of business. Matt's department manager suspects that the plant and equipment may be impaired and wonders whether those assets should be written down. Given the company's prior success, this issue has never arisen in the past, and Matt has been asked to conduct some research on this issue.

Instructions

Access the IFRS authoritative literature at the IASB website (*http://eifrs.iasb.org/*). (Click on the IFRS tab and then register for free eIFRS access if necessary.) When you have accessed the documents, you can use the search tool in your Internet browser to respond to the following questions. (Provide paragraph citations.)

(a) What is the authoritative guidance for asset impairments? Briefly discuss the scope of the standard (i.e., explain the types of transactions to which the standard applies).
(b) Give several examples of events that would cause an asset to be tested for impairment. Does it appear that Klax should perform an impairment test? Explain.
(c) What is the best evidence of fair value? Describe alternate methods of estimating fair value.

International Financial Reporting Problem
Marks and Spencer plc

IFRS11-16 The financial statements of **Marks and Spencer plc (M&S)** are available at the book's companion website or can be accessed at *http://annualreport.marksandspencer.com/_assets/downloads/Marks-and-Spencer-Annual-report-and-financial-statements-2012.pdf*.

Instructions

Refer to M&S's financial statements and the accompanying notes to answer the following questions.

(a) What descriptions are used by M&S in its statement of financial position to classify its property, plant, and equipment?
(b) What method or methods of depreciation does M&S use to depreciate its property, plant, and equipment?
(c) Over what estimated useful lives does M&S depreciate its property, plant, and equipment?
(d) What amounts for depreciation and amortization expense did M&S charge to its income statement in 2012 and 2011?
(e) What were the capital expenditures for property, plant, and equipment made by M&S in 2012 and 2011?

ANSWERS TO IFRS SELF-TEST QUESTIONS

1. c **2.** c **3.** b **4.** d **5.** c

Remember to check the book's companion website to find additional resources for this chapter.

12 Intangible Assets

Is This Sustainable?

Companies are increasing their focus on sustainability issues. Companies like **Southwest Airlines**, **Clorox**, and **Northrop Grumman** are executing strategic initiatives including fuel-spill control, use of recycled materials, and water conservation. Why the growing importance of responsible management of resource use? One reason is that market participants are now more interested in investing in companies that are pursuing sustainability strategies.

For example, as indicated in the following graph, sustainable investing by professional portfolio managers in the United States has increased from below $500 billion in the mid-1990s to over $2.5 trillion (or 12.5% of the total under management) in 2010.

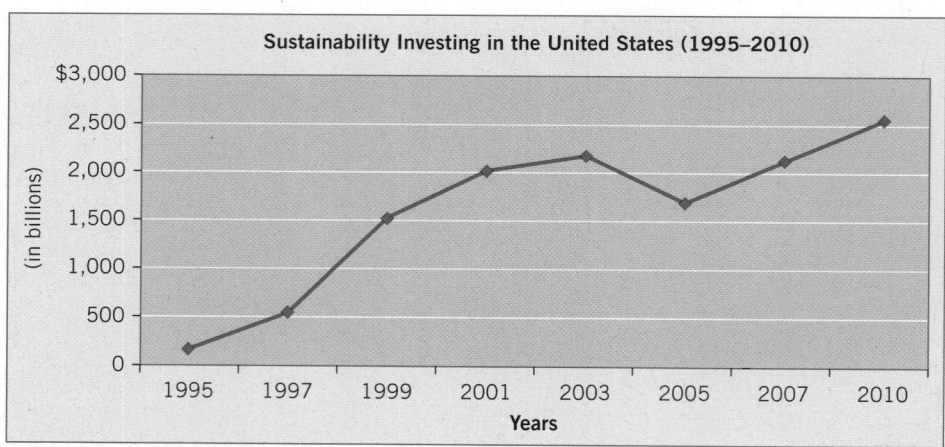

Source: Social Investment Forum.

In light of investor focus on sustainability, it is not surprising that companies are increasing the amount of information reported to the market about their sustainability efforts. However, rather than adding a line item in the income statement or balance sheet, companies instead provide more useful information about the future cash flow consequences of sustainability strategies, which are intangible and usually "nonfinancial" in nature.

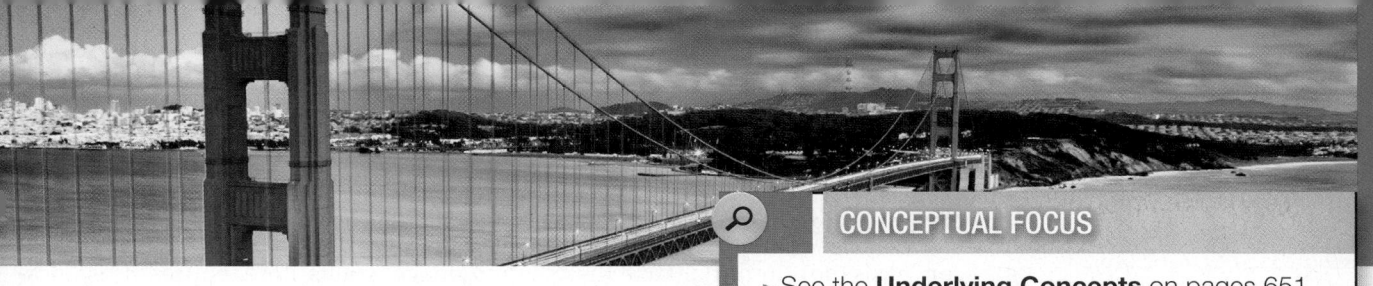

Consider, for example, the disclosure of information about greenhouse gases. In 2010, the Securities and Exchange Commission clarified the circumstances in which public companies should disclose information related to climate change, as well as the impact on financial performance of their efforts to manage the consequences of greenhouse gas emissions. So here's the paradox: If nonfinancial data, such as greenhouse gas emissions per dollar of revenue, is included in a financial report for investors, how can it still be called nonfinancial?

As with the reporting of research and development expenditures and other intangible assets—many of which do not show up on a balance sheet or income statement—companies are now exploring ways to combine the nonfinancial information with mandated disclosures in what is called an **integrated report**. In such a report, a company might disclose data on any of dozens of metrics beyond conventional balance sheet accounting, whether they are "integrated" or released separately. Practitioners collectively refer sustainability reporting as **ESG** for the three major categories of data—environmental, social, and corporate governance.

While 228 U.S. companies issued a sustainability report in 2011, there was significant variation in the content and format. Only a handful, like those prepared by **Clorox**, **Northrop Grumman**, **SAS**, **Genentech**, and **Polymer Group Inc.**, integrated a sustainability report with the financial statements. As with accounting reports prepared under GAAP, perhaps sustainability reporting is in need of standards?

Sources: S. Lopresti and P. Lilak, "Do Investors Care About Sustainability?" *PwC* (March 2012); and E. Rostin, "Non-Financial Data Are Material: The Sustainability Paradox," *www.bloombergnews.com* (April 13, 2012).

CONCEPTUAL FOCUS

> See the **Underlying Concepts** on pages 651, 659, and 662.
> Read the **Evolving Issue** on page 673 for a discussion of recognition of R&D and internally generated intangibles.

INTERNATIONAL FOCUS

> See the **International Perspectives** on pages 652 and 666.
> Read the **IFRS Insights** on pages 693–699 for a discussion of:
> —Development costs
> —Impairments of intangibles

PREVIEW OF CHAPTER 12

As our opening story indicates, sustainability strategies are taking on increased importance for companies like Southwest Airlines and Clorox. Reporting challenges for effective sustainability investments are similar to those for intangible assets. In this chapter, we explain the basic conceptual and reporting issues related to intangible assets. The content and organization of the chapter are as follows.

Intangible Assets

Intangible Asset Issues	Types of Intangibles	Impairment of Intangibles	Research and Development Costs	Presentation of Intangibles and Related Items
• Characteristics • Valuation • Amortization	• Marketing-related • Customer-related • Artistic-related • Contract-related • Technology-related • Goodwill	• Limited-life intangibles • Indefinite-life intangibles other than goodwill • Goodwill • Summary	• Identifying R&D • Accounting for R&D • Similar costs	• Intangible assets • R&D costs

INTANGIBLE ASSET ISSUES
Characteristics

LEARNING OBJECTIVE ❶
Describe the characteristics of
intangible assets.

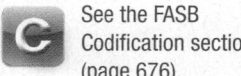

See the FASB
Codification section
(page 676).

Gap Inc.'s most important asset is its brand image, not its store fixtures. The Coca-Cola Company's success comes from its secret formula for making Coca-Cola, not its plant facilities. America Online's subscriber base, not its Internet connection equipment, provides its most important asset. The U.S. economy is dominated by information and service providers. For these companies, their major assets are often intangible in nature.

What exactly are intangible assets? **Intangible assets** have two main characteristics. **[1]**

1. *They lack physical existence.* Tangible assets such as property, plant, and equipment have physical form. Intangible assets, in contrast, derive their value from the rights and privileges granted to the company using them.
2. *They are not financial instruments.* Assets such as bank deposits, accounts receivable, and long-term investments in bonds and stocks also lack physical substance. However, financial instruments derive their value from the right (claim) to receive cash or cash equivalents in the future. Financial instruments are not classified as intangibles.

In most cases, intangible assets provide benefits over a period of years. Therefore, companies normally classify them as long-term assets.

Following a discussion of the general valuation and accounting provisions for intangible assets, we present a more extensive discussion of the types of intangible assets and their accounting.

Valuation
Purchased Intangibles

LEARNING OBJECTIVE ❷
Identify the costs to include in the
initial valuation of intangible assets.

Companies **record at cost** intangibles purchased from another party. Cost includes all acquisition costs plus expenditures to make the intangible asset ready for its intended use. Typical costs include purchase price, legal fees, and other incidental expenses.

Sometimes companies acquire intangibles in exchange for stock or other assets. In such cases, **the cost of the intangible is the fair value of the consideration given or the fair value of the intangible received, whichever is more clearly evident**. What if a company buys several intangibles, or a combination of intangibles and tangibles? In such a "basket purchase," the company should allocate the cost on the basis of fair values. Essentially, the accounting treatment for purchased intangibles closely parallels that for purchased tangible assets.[1]

Internally Created Intangibles

Sometimes a company may incur substantial research and development (R&D) costs to create an intangible. For example, Google expensed the R&D costs incurred to develop its valuable search engine. Costs incurred internally to create intangibles are generally expensed.

---

[1]The accounting in this section relates to the acquisition of a single asset or group of assets. The accounting for intangible assets acquired in a **business combination** (transaction in which the purchaser obtains control of one or more businesses) is discussed later in this chapter.

How do companies justify this approach? Some argue that the costs incurred internally to create intangibles bear no relationship to their real value. Therefore, they reason, expensing these costs is appropriate. Others note that it is difficult to associate internal costs with a specific intangible. Still others contend that due to the underlying subjectivity related to intangibles, companies should follow a conservative approach—that is, expense as incurred. As a result, **companies capitalize only direct costs** incurred in developing the intangible, such as legal costs, and expense the rest.

Underlying Concepts

The controversy surrounding the accounting for R&D expenditures reflects a debate about whether such expenditures meet the definition of an asset. If so, then an "expense all R&D costs" policy results in overstated expenses and understated assets.

Amortization of Intangibles

The allocation of the cost of intangible assets in a systematic way is called amortization. Intangibles have either a limited (finite) useful life or an indefinite useful life. For example, a company like Walt Disney Company has both types of intangibles. Disney **amortizes** its **limited-life** intangible assets (e.g., copyrights on its movies and licenses related to its branded products). It **does not amortize indefinite-life** intangible assets (e.g., the Disney trade name or its Internet domain name).

3 LEARNING OBJECTIVE

Explain the procedure for amortizing intangible assets.

Limited-Life Intangibles

Companies amortize their limited-life intangibles by systematic charges to expense over their useful life. The useful life should reflect the periods over which these assets will contribute to cash flows. Disney, for example, considers these factors in determining useful life:

1. The expected use of the asset by the company.

2. The expected useful life of another asset or a group of assets to which the useful life of the intangible asset may relate (such as lease rights to a studio lot).

3. Any legal, regulatory, or contractual provisions that may limit the useful life.

4. Any provisions (legal, regulatory, or contractual) that enable renewal or extension of the asset's legal or contractual life without substantial cost. This factor assumes that there is evidence to support renewal or extension. Disney also must be able to accomplish renewal or extension without material modifications of the existing terms and conditions.

5. The effects of obsolescence, demand, competition, and other economic factors. Examples include the stability of the industry, known technological advances, legislative action that results in an uncertain or changing regulatory environment, and expected changes in distribution channels.

6. The level of maintenance expenditure required to obtain the expected future cash flows from the asset. For example, a material level of required maintenance in relation to the carrying amount of the asset may suggest a very limited useful life. **[2]**

The amount of amortization expense for a limited-life intangible asset should reflect the pattern in which the company consumes or uses up the asset, if the company can reliably determine that pattern. For example, assume that Second Wave, Inc. purchases a license to provide a specified quantity of a gene product called Mega. Second Wave should amortize the cost of the license following the pattern of use of Mega. If Second Wave's license calls for it to provide 30 percent of the total the first year, 20 percent the second year, and 10 percent per year until the license expires, it would amortize the license cost using that pattern. If it cannot determine the pattern of production or consumption, Second Wave should use the straight-line method of amortization. (*For homework problems, assume the use of the straight-line method unless stated otherwise.*) **When Second Wave amortizes these licenses, it should show the charges as expenses. It should credit either the appropriate asset accounts or separate accumulated amortization accounts.**

The amount of an intangible asset to be amortized should be its cost less residual value. The residual value is assumed to be zero unless at the end of its useful life the intangible asset has value to another company. For example, if Hardy Co. commits to purchasing an intangible asset from U2D Co. at the end of the asset's useful life, U2D Co. should reduce the cost of its intangible asset by the residual value. Similarly, U2D Co. should consider fair values, if reliably determined, for residual values.

What happens if the life of a limited-life intangible asset changes? In that case, the remaining carrying amount should be amortized over the revised remaining useful life. Companies should, on a regular basis, evaluate the limited-life intangibles for **impairment**. Similar to the accounting for property, plant, and equipment, an impairment loss should be recognized if the carrying amount of the intangible is not recoverable and its carrying amount exceeds its fair value. (We will cover impairment of intangibles in more detail later in the chapter.)

Indefinite-Life Intangibles

If no factors (legal, regulatory, contractual, competitive, or other) limit the useful life of an intangible asset, a company considers its useful life indefinite. An **indefinite life** means that there is no foreseeable limit on the period of time over which the intangible asset is expected to provide cash flows. A company **does not amortize** an intangible asset with an indefinite life. To illustrate, assume that Double Clik Inc. acquired a trademark that it uses to distinguish a leading consumer product. It renews the trademark every 10 years. All evidence indicates that this trademarked product will generate cash flows for an indefinite period of time. In this case, the trademark has an indefinite life; Double Clik does not record any amortization.

International Perspective

IFRS requires capitalization of some development costs.

Companies should test indefinite-life intangibles for **impairment** at least annually. As we will discuss in more detail later in the chapter, the **impairment test** for indefinite-life intangibles differs from the one for limited-life intangibles. Only the fair value test is performed for indefinite-life intangibles; there is no recoverability test for these intangibles. The reason? Indefinite-life intangible assets might never fail the undiscounted cash flows recoverability test because cash flows could extend indefinitely into the future.

Illustration 12-1 summarizes the accounting treatment for intangible assets.

ILLUSTRATION 12-1
Accounting Treatment for Intangibles

Type of Intangible	Manner Acquired		Amortization	Impairment Test
	Purchased	Internally Created		
Limited-life intangibles	Capitalize	Expense*	Over useful life	Recoverability test and then fair value test
Indefinite-life intangibles	Capitalize	Expense*	Do not amortize	Fair value test only

*Except for direct costs, such as legal costs.

The importance of intangible asset classification as either limited-life or indefinite-life is illustrated in the experience of Outdoor Channel Holdings. Here's what happened. Outdoor Channel recorded an intangible asset related to the value of an important distributor relationship, purchased from another company. At that time, it classified the relationship as indefinite-life. Thus, in the first two years of the asset's life, Outdoor Channel recorded no amortization expense on this asset. In the third year, investors were surprised to find that Outdoor Channel changed the classification of the distributor relationship to limited-life, with an expected life of 21.33 years (a fairly definite useful life) and, shortly thereafter, wrote off this intangible completely.

Apparently, the company was overly optimistic about the expected future cash flows arising from the distributor relationship. As a result of that optimism, income in the second year was overstated by $9.5 million, or 14 percent, and the impairment recorded in the third year amounted to 7 percent of assets. From indefinite-life to limited-life to worthless in two short years—investors were surely hurt by Outdoor's aggressive intangible asset classification.

Source: Jack Ciesielski, *The AAO Weblog, www.accountingobserver.com/blog/* (January 12, 2007).

TYPES OF INTANGIBLE ASSETS

As indicated, the accounting for intangible assets depends on whether the intangible has a limited or an indefinite life. There are many different types of intangibles, often classified into the following six major categories. **[3]**

4 **LEARNING OBJECTIVE**
Describe the types of intangible assets.

1. Marketing-related intangible assets.

2. Customer-related intangible assets.

3. Artistic-related intangible assets.

4. Contract-related intangible assets.

5. Technology-related intangible assets.

6. Goodwill.

Marketing-Related Intangible Assets

Companies primarily use **marketing-related intangible assets** in the marketing or promotion of products or services. Examples are trademarks or trade names, newspaper mastheads, Internet domain names, and noncompetition agreements.

A trademark or trade name is a word, phrase, or symbol that distinguishes or identifies a particular company or product. Trade names like Kleenex, Pepsi-Cola, Buick, Excedrin, Wheaties, and Sunkist create immediate product identification in our minds, thereby enhancing marketability. Under common law, the right to use a trademark or trade name, whether registered or not, rests exclusively with the original user as long as the original user continues to use it. Registration with the U.S. Patent and Trademark Office provides legal protection for an **indefinite number of renewals for periods of 10 years each**. Therefore, a company that uses an established trademark or trade name may properly consider it to have an indefinite life and does not amortize its cost.

If a company buys a trademark or trade name, it capitalizes the cost at the purchase price. If a company develops a trademark or trade name, it capitalizes costs related to securing it, such as attorney fees, registration fees, design costs, consulting fees, and successful legal defense costs. However, it excludes research and development costs. When the total cost of a trademark or trade name is insignificant, a company simply expenses it.

The value of a marketing-related intangible can be substantial. Consider Internet **domain names**. The name Drugs.com at one time sold for $800,000. The bidding for the name Loans.com approached $500,000. An expansion of domain names will allow industries to use terms like .cars or even Internet slang like lol. This expansion has led to a new wave of domain name activity. For a fee of $185,000, companies can register their own domain names. Applications received include company names (such as Microsoft, which would have the name .microsoft) and for city-based domains (such as .nyc and .berlin).

Company names also identify qualities and characteristics that companies work hard and spend much to develop. In a recent year, an estimated 1,230 companies took on new names in an attempt to forge new identities and paid over $250 million to corporate-identity consultants. Among these were Primerica (formerly American Can), Navistar (formerly International Harvester), and Nissan (formerly Datsun).

What do the numbers mean? KEEP YOUR HANDS OFF MY INTANGIBLE!

Companies go to great extremes to protect their valuable intangible assets. Consider how the creators of the highly successful game *Trivial Pursuit* protected their creation. First, they copyrighted the 6,000 questions that are at the heart of the game. Then they shielded the *Trivial Pursuit* name by applying for a registered trademark. As a third mode of protection, they obtained a design patent on the playing board's design as a unique graphic creation.

Another example is the iPhone trade name. Cisco Systems sued Apple for using the iPhone trade name when Apple introduced its hot new phone in 2007. Not so fast, said Cisco, which had held the iPhone trade name since 2000 and was using it on its own Voice over Internet Protocol (VoIP) products. The two companies came to an agreement for joint use of the name. It was not disclosed what Apple paid for this arrangement, but it is not surprising why Apple would want to settle—to avoid a costly delay to the launch of its highly anticipated iPhone.

Source: Nick Wingfield, "Apple, Cisco Reach Accord Over iPhone," *Wall Street Journal Online* (February 22, 2007).

Customer-Related Intangible Assets

Customer-related intangible assets result from interactions with outside parties. Examples include customer lists, order or production backlogs, and both contractual and noncontractual customer relationships.

To illustrate, assume that Green Market Inc. acquires the customer list of a large newspaper for $6,000,000 on January 1, 2014. This customer database includes names, contact information, order history, and demographic information. Green Market expects to benefit from the information evenly over a three-year period. In this case, the customer list is a limited-life intangible that Green Market should amortize on a straight-line basis.

Green Market records the purchase of the customer list and the amortization of the customer list at the end of each year as follows.

January 1, 2014

Customer List	6,000,000	
Cash		6,000,000
(To record purchase of customer list)		

December 31, 2014, 2015, 2016

Amortization Expense	2,000,000	
Customer List (or Accumulated Customer List Amortization)		2,000,000
(To record amortization expense)		

The preceding example assumed no residual value for the customer list. But what if Green Market determines that it can sell the list for $60,000 to another company at the end of three years? In that case, Green Market should subtract this residual value from the cost in order to determine the amortization expense for each year. Amortization expense would be $1,980,000, as shown in Illustration 12-2.

Cost	$6,000,000
Less: Residual value	60,000
Amortization base	$5,940,000
Amortization expense per period: $1,980,000 ($5,940,000 ÷ 3)	

ILLUSTRATION 12-2
Calculation of Amortization Expense with Residual Value

Companies should assume a zero residual value unless the asset's useful life is less than the economic life and reliable evidence is available concerning the residual value. **[4]**

Artistic-Related Intangible Assets

Artistic-related intangible assets involve ownership rights to plays, literary works, musical works, pictures, photographs, and video and audiovisual material. Copyrights protect these ownership rights.

A **copyright** is a federally granted right that all authors, painters, musicians, sculptors, and other artists have in their creations and expressions. A copyright is granted for the **life of the creator plus 70 years**. It gives the owner or heirs the exclusive right to reproduce and sell an artistic or published work. Copyrights are not renewable.

Copyrights can be valuable. In the late 1990s, **Walt Disney Company** faced the loss of its copyright on Mickey Mouse, which could have affected sales of billions of dollars of Mickey-related goods and services (including theme parks). This copyright was so important that Disney and many other big entertainment companies fought all the way to the Supreme Court—and won an extension of copyright lives from 50 to 70 years.

As another example, **Really Useful Group** owns copyrights on the musicals of Andrew Lloyd Webber—*Cats, Phantom of the Opera, Jesus Christ Superstar*, and others. The company has little in the way of tangible assets, yet analysts value it at over $300 million.

Companies capitalize the costs of acquiring and defending a copyright. They amortize any capitalized costs over the useful life of the copyright if less than its legal life (life of the creator plus 70 years). For example, Really Useful Group should allocate the costs of its copyrights to the years in which it expects to receive the benefits. The difficulty of determining the number of years over which it will receive benefits typically encourages a company like Really Useful Group to write off these costs over a fairly short period of time. Companies must expense the research and development costs that lead to a copyright as those costs are incurred.

Contract-Related Intangible Assets

Contract-related intangible assets represent the value of rights that arise from contractual arrangements. Examples are franchise and licensing agreements, construction permits, broadcast rights, and service or supply contracts.

A **franchise** is a contractual arrangement under which the franchisor grants the franchisee the right to sell certain products or services, to use certain trademarks or trade names, or to perform certain functions, usually within a designated geographical area. When you purchase a Prius from a **Toyota** dealer, fill up your tank at the corner **Shell** station, eat lunch at **Subway**, or make reservations at a **Marriott** hotel, you are dealing with franchises.

The franchisor, having developed a unique concept or product, protects its concept or product through a patent, copyright, or trademark or trade name. The franchisee acquires the right to exploit the franchisor's idea or product by signing a franchise agreement.

Another type of franchise, granted by a governmental body, permits the business to use public property in performing its services. Examples are the use of city streets for a bus line or taxi service; the use of public land for telephone, electric, and cable television lines; and the use of airwaves for radio or TV broadcasting. Such operating rights are referred to as licenses or permits. For example, Fox, CBS, and NBC recently agreed to pay $27.9 billion for the right to broadcast NFL football games over an eight-year period.

Franchises and licenses may be for a definite period of time, for an indefinite period of time, or perpetual. The company securing the franchise or license carries an intangible asset account (entitled Franchises or Licenses) on its books, only when it can identify costs with the acquisition of the operating right. (Such costs might be legal fees or an advance lump-sum payment, for example.) **A company should amortize the cost of a franchise (or license) with a limited life as an operating expense over the life of the franchise.** It should not amortize a franchise with an indefinite life nor a perpetual franchise; the company should instead carry such franchises at cost.

Annual payments made under a franchise agreement should be entered as operating expenses in the period in which they are incurred. These payments do not represent an asset since they do not relate to *future rights* to use the property.

Technology-Related Intangible Assets

Technology-related intangible assets relate to innovations or technological advances. Examples are patented technology and trade secrets granted by the U.S. Patent and Trademark Office.

A patent gives the holder exclusive right to use, manufacture, and sell a product or process **for a period of 20 years** without interference or infringement by others. Companies such as Merck, Polaroid, and Xerox were founded on patents and built on the exclusive rights thus granted.[2] The two principal kinds of patents are **product patents**, which cover actual physical products, and **process patents**, which govern the process of making products.

If a company like Qualcomm purchases a patent from an inventor, the purchase price represents its cost. Qualcomm can capitalize other costs incurred in connection with securing a patent, as well as attorneys' fees and other unrecovered costs of a successful legal suit to protect the patent, as part of the patent cost. However, it **must expense as incurred** any research and development costs related to the **development** of the product, process, or idea that it subsequently patents. (We discuss accounting for research and development costs in more detail on pages 665–667.)

Companies should amortize the cost of a patent over its legal life or its useful life (the period in which benefits are received), **whichever is shorter**. If Qualcomm owns a patent from the date it is granted and expects the patent to be useful during its entire legal life, the company should amortize it over 20 years. If it appears that the patent will be useful for a shorter period of time, say for five years, it should amortize its cost over five years.

---

[2]Consider the opposite result. Sir Alexander Fleming, who discovered penicillin, decided not to use a patent to protect his discovery. He hoped that foregoing a patent would help companies produce the medication more quickly. Companies, however, refused to develop it because they did not have the patent shield and, therefore, were afraid to make the investment.

Changing demand, new inventions superseding old ones, inadequacy, and other factors often limit the useful life of a patent to less than the legal life. For example, the useful life of pharmaceutical patents is frequently less than the legal life because of the testing and approval period that follows their issuance. A typical drug patent has several years knocked off its 20-year legal life. Why? Because a drug-maker spends one to four years on animal tests, four to six years on human tests, and two to three years for the Food and Drug Administration to review the tests. All this time occurs *after* issuing the patent but *before* the product goes on pharmacists' shelves.

What do the numbers mean? PATENT BATTLES

From online retailing to cell phone features, global competition is bringing to the boiling point battles over patents. For example, to protect its patented "one-click" shopping technology that saves your shipping and credit card information when you shop online, Amazon.com filed a complaint against Barnesandnoble.com, its rival in the e-tailing wars.

The smartphone industry is another patent battleground. For example, Nokia filed patent lawsuits against Apple (and Apple countersued) over cell phone features such as swiping gestures on touch screens and the "app store" for downloading software. Apple also targeted HTC for infringing on Apple's patented feature that allows screens to detect more than one finger touch at a time. This facilitates the popular zoom-in and zoom-out capability. HTC, in turn, sued Apple for infringing on patented technology that helps extend battery life.

Sources: Adapted from L. Rohde, "Amazon, Barnes and Noble Settle Patent Dispute," *CNN.com* (March 8, 2002); and J. Mintz, "Smart Phone Makers in Legal Fights over Patents," *Wisconsin State Journal* (December 19, 2010), p. F4.

As mentioned earlier, companies capitalize the costs of defending copyrights. The accounting treatment for a patent defense is similar. **A company charges all unrecovered legal fees and other costs incurred in successfully defending a patent suit to Patents,** an asset account. Such costs should be amortized along with acquisition cost over the remaining useful life of the patent.

Amortization expense should reflect the pattern, if reliably determined, in which a company uses up the patent.[3] A company may credit amortization of patents directly to the Patents account or to an Accumulated Patent Amortization account. To illustrate, assume that Harcott Co. incurs $180,000 in legal costs on January 1, 2014, to successfully defend a patent. The patent's useful life after defense is 12 years, amortized on a straight-line basis. Harcott records the legal fees and the amortization at the end of 2014 as follows.

January 1, 2014

Patents	180,000	
Cash		180,000
(To record legal fees related to patent)		

December 31, 2014

Amortization Expense ($180,000 ÷ 12)	15,000	
Patents (or Accumulated Patent Amortization)		15,000
(To record amortization of patent)		

We've indicated that a patent's useful life should not extend beyond its legal life of 20 years. However, companies often make small modifications or additions that lead to a new patent. For example, Astra Zeneca plc filed for additional patents on minor modifications to its heartburn drug Prilosec. The effect may be to extend the life of the old

[3]Companies may compute amortization on a units-of-production basis in a manner similar to that described for depreciation on property, plant, and equipment.

patent. If the new patent provides essentially the same benefits, Astra Zeneca can apply the unamortized costs of the old patent to the new patent.[4]

Alternatively, if a patent becomes impaired because demand drops for the product, the asset should be written down or written off immediately to expense.

What do the numbers mean? THE VALUE OF A SECRET FORMULA

After several espionage cases were uncovered, the secrets contained within the Los Alamos nuclear lab seemed easier to check out than a library book. But The Coca-Cola Company has managed to keep the recipe for the world's best-selling soft drink under wraps for more than 100 years. The company offers almost no information about its lifeblood, and the only written copy of the formula resides in a bank vault in Atlanta. This handwritten sheet is available to no one except by vote of Coca-Cola's board of directors.

Can't science offer some clues? Coke purportedly contains 17 to 18 ingredients. That includes the usual caramel color and corn syrup, as well as a blend of oils known as 7X (rumored to be a mix of orange, lemon, cinnamon, and others). Distilling natural products like these is complicated since they are made of thousands of compounds. One ingredient you will not find, by the way, is cocaine. Although the original formula did contain trace amounts, today's Coke doesn't. When was it removed? That too is a secret.

Some experts indicate that the power of the Coca-Cola formula and related brand image account for almost $72 billion, or roughly 6 percent, of Coke's $1,128 billion stock value.

Sources: Adapted from Reed Tucker, "How Has Coke's Formula Stayed a Secret?" *Fortune* (July 24, 2000), p. 42; and "Best Global Brands 2011," *www.interbrand.com* (accessed July 5, 2012).

Goodwill

LEARNING OBJECTIVE 5

Explain the accounting issues for recording goodwill.

Although companies may capitalize certain costs incurred in developing specifically identifiable assets such as patents and copyrights, the amounts capitalized are generally insignificant. But companies do record material amounts of intangible assets when purchasing them, particularly in situations involving a business combination (the purchase of another business).

To illustrate, assume that Portofino Company decides to purchase Aquinas Company. In this situation, Portofino measures the assets acquired and the liabilities assumed at fair value. In measuring these assets and liabilities, Portofino must identify all the assets and liabilities of Aquinas. As a result, Portofino may recognize some assets or liabilities not previously recognized by Aquinas. For example, Portofino may recognize intangible assets such as a brand name, patent, or customer list that were not recorded by Aquinas. In this case, Aquinas may not have recognized these assets because they were developed internally and charged to expense.

In many business combinations, the purchasing company records goodwill. Goodwill is measured as the excess of the cost of the purchase over the fair value of the identifiable net assets (assets less liabilities) purchased. For example, if Portofino paid $2,000,000 to purchase Aquinas's identifiable net assets (with a fair value of $1,500,000), Portofino records goodwill of $500,000. Goodwill is therefore measured as a residual rather than measured directly. That is why goodwill is sometimes referred to as a **plug**, a **gap filler**, or a **master valuation account**.[5]

---

[4]Another classic example is Eli Lilly's drug Prozac (prescribed to treat depression). In 1998, this product accounted for 43 percent of Eli Lilly's sales. The patent on Prozac expired in 2001, and the company was unable to extend its protection with a second-use patent for the use of Prozac to treat appetite disorders. Sales of the product slipped substantially as generic equivalents entered the market.

[5]GAAP **[5]** provides detailed guidance regarding the recognition of identifiable intangible assets in a business combination. With this guidance, companies should recognize more identifiable intangible assets, and less goodwill, in the financial statements as a result of business combinations.

Conceptually, goodwill represents the future economic benefits arising from the other assets acquired in a business combination that are not individually identified and separately recognized. It is often called "the most intangible of the intangible assets" because it is identified only with the business as a whole. The only way to sell goodwill is to sell the business.

Recording Goodwill

Internally Created Goodwill. **Goodwill generated internally should not be capitalized in the accounts.** The reason? Measuring the components of goodwill is simply too complex, and associating any costs with future benefits is too difficult. The future benefits of goodwill may have no relationship to the costs incurred in the development of that goodwill. To add to the mystery, goodwill may even exist in the absence of specific costs to develop it. Finally, because no objective transaction with outside parties takes place, a great deal of subjectivity—even misrepresentation—may occur.

Purchased Goodwill. As indicated earlier, **goodwill is recorded only when an entire business is purchased**. To record goodwill, a company compares the fair value of the net tangible and identifiable intangible assets with the purchase price of the acquired business. The difference is considered goodwill. **Goodwill is the residual—the excess of cost over fair value of the identifiable net assets acquired.**

To illustrate, Multi-Diversified, Inc. decides that it needs a parts division to supplement its existing tractor distributorship. The president of Multi-Diversified is interested in buying Tractorling Company, a small concern in Chicago. Illustration 12-3 presents the balance sheet of Tractorling Company.

> **Underlying Concepts** 🔍
>
> Capitalizing goodwill only when it is purchased in an arm's-length transaction, and not capitalizing any goodwill generated internally, is another example of faithful representation winning out over relevance.

ILLUSTRATION 12-3
Tractorling Co. Balance Sheet

TRACTORLING CO. BALANCE SHEET AS OF DECEMBER 31, 2014			
Assets		**Liabilities and Equity**	
Cash	$ 25,000	Current liabilities	$ 55,000
Accounts receivable	35,000	Capital stock	100,000
Inventory	42,000	Retained earnings	100,000
Property, plant, and equipment, net	153,000		
Total assets	$255,000	Total liabilities and equity	$255,000

After considerable negotiation, Tractorling Company decides to accept Multi-Diversified's offer of $400,000. What, then, is the value of the goodwill, if any?

The answer is not obvious. Tractorling's historical cost-based balance sheet does not disclose the fair values of its identifiable assets. Suppose, though, that as the negotiations progress, Multi-Diversified investigates Tractorling's underlying assets to determine their fair values. Such an investigation may be accomplished either through a purchase audit undertaken by Multi-Diversified or by an independent appraisal from some other source. The investigation determines the valuations shown in Illustration 12-4 (page 660).

Normally, differences between current fair value and book value are more common among long-term assets than among current assets. Cash obviously poses no problems as to value. Receivables normally are fairly close to current valuation although they may at times need certain adjustments due to inadequate bad debt provisions. Liabilities usually are stated at book value. However, if interest rates have changed since the company incurred the liabilities, a different valuation (such as present value based on

Gateway to the Profession

Expanded Discussion— Valuing Goodwill

ILLUSTRATION 12-4
Fair Value of Tractorling's
Net Assets

Fair Values	
Cash	$ 25,000
Accounts receivable	35,000
Inventory	122,000
Property, plant, and equipment, net	205,000
Patents	18,000
Liabilities	(55,000)
Fair value of net assets	$350,000

expected cash flows) is appropriate. Careful analysis must be made to determine that no unrecorded liabilities are present.

The $80,000 difference in Tractorling's inventories ($122,000 − $42,000) could result from a number of factors. The most likely is that the company uses LIFO. Recall that during periods of inflation, LIFO better matches expenses against revenues. However, it also creates a balance sheet distortion. Ending inventory consists of older layers costed at lower valuations.

In many cases, the values of long-term assets such as property, plant, and equipment, and intangibles may have increased substantially over the years. This difference could be due to inaccurate estimates of useful lives, continual expensing of small expenditures (say, less than $300), inaccurate estimates of residual values, and the discovery of some unrecorded assets. (For example, in Tractorling's case, analysis determines Patents have a fair value of $18,000.) Or, fair values may have substantially increased.

Since the investigation now determines the fair value of net assets to be $350,000, why would Multi-Diversified pay $400,000? Undoubtedly, Tractorling points to its established reputation, good credit rating, top management team, well-trained employees, and so on. These factors make the value of the business greater than $350,000. Multi-Diversified places a premium on the future earning power of these attributes as well as on the basic asset structure of the company today.

Multi-Diversified labels the difference between the purchase price of $400,000 and the fair value of net assets of $350,000 as goodwill. Goodwill is viewed as one or a group of unidentifiable values (intangible assets), the cost of which "is measured by the difference between the cost of the group of assets or enterprise acquired and the sum of the assigned costs of individual tangible and identifiable intangible assets acquired less liabilities assumed."[6] This procedure for valuation is called a **master valuation approach**. It assumes goodwill covers all the values that cannot be specifically identified with any identifiable tangible or intangible asset. Illustration 12-5 shows this approach.

ILLUSTRATION 12-5
Determination of
Goodwill—Master
Valuation Approach

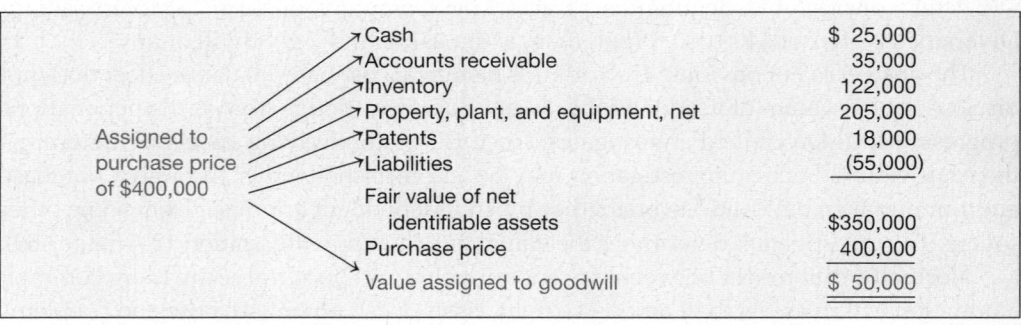

	Cash	$ 25,000
	Accounts receivable	35,000
	Inventory	122,000
Assigned to	Property, plant, and equipment, net	205,000
purchase price	Patents	18,000
of $400,000	Liabilities	(55,000)
	Fair value of net identifiable assets	$350,000
	Purchase price	400,000
	Value assigned to goodwill	$ 50,000

[6]The FASB expressed concern about measuring goodwill as a residual but noted that there is no real measurement alternative since goodwill is not separable from the company as a whole. **[6]**

Multi-Diversified records this transaction as follows.

Cash	25,000	
Accounts Receivable	35,000	
Inventory	122,000	
Property, Plant, and Equipment	205,000	
Patents	18,000	
Goodwill	50,000	
Liabilities		55,000
Cash		400,000

Companies often identify goodwill on the balance sheet as the **excess of cost over the fair value** of the net assets acquired.

Goodwill Write-Off

Companies that recognize goodwill in a business combination **consider it to have an indefinite life and therefore should not amortize it**. Although goodwill may decrease in value over time, predicting the actual life of goodwill and an appropriate pattern of amortization is extremely difficult. In addition, investors find the amortization charge of little use in evaluating financial performance.

Furthermore, the investment community wants to know the amount invested in goodwill, which often is the largest intangible asset on a company's balance sheet. Therefore, **companies adjust its carrying value only when goodwill is impaired**. This approach significantly impacts the income statements of some companies.

Some believe that goodwill's value eventually disappears. Therefore, they argue, companies should charge goodwill to expense over the periods affected, to better match expense with revenues. Others note that the accounting treatment for purchased goodwill and goodwill created internally should be consistent. They point out that companies immediately expense goodwill created internally and should follow the same treatment for purchased goodwill. Though these arguments may have some merit, nonamortization of goodwill combined with an adequate impairment test should provide the most useful financial information to the investment community. We discuss the accounting for goodwill impairments later in the chapter.

Bargain Purchase

In a few cases, the purchaser in a business combination pays *less than* the fair value of the identifiable net assets. Such a situation is referred to as a **bargain purchase**. A bargain purchase results from a market imperfection. That is, the seller would have been better off to sell the assets individually than in total. However, situations do occur (e.g., a forced liquidation or distressed sale due to the death of a company founder) in which the purchase price is less than the value of the net identifiable assets. **This excess amount is recorded as a gain by the purchaser.**

The FASB notes that an economic gain is inherent in a bargain purchase. The purchaser is better off by the amount by which the fair value of what is acquired exceeds the amount paid. Some expressed concern that some companies may attempt inappropriate gain recognition by making an intentional error in measurement of the assets or liabilities. As a result, the FASB requires companies to disclose the nature of this gain transaction. Such disclosure will help users to better evaluate the quality of the earnings reported.[7]

---

[7]This gain is not reported as an extraordinary item, **[7]** which is consistent with convergence in international accounting standards. IFRS does not permit extraordinary item reporting.

IMPAIRMENT OF INTANGIBLE ASSETS

LEARNING OBJECTIVE 6

Explain the accounting issues related to intangible-asset impairments.

In some cases, the carrying amount of a long-lived asset (property, plant, and equipment, or intangible assets) is not recoverable. Therefore, a company needs to record a write-off. As discussed in Chapter 11, this write-off is referred to as an **impairment**.

Impairment of Limited-Life Intangibles

The rules that apply to **impairments of property, plant, and equipment also apply to limited-life intangibles**. As discussed in Chapter 11, a company should review property, plant, and equipment for impairment at certain points—whenever events or changes in circumstances indicate that the carrying amount of the asset may not be recoverable. In performing this **recoverability test**, the company estimates the future cash flows expected from use of the asset and its eventual disposal. If the sum of the expected future net cash flows (undiscounted) is less than the carrying amount of the asset, the company would measure and recognize an impairment loss. **[8]**

The company then uses the **fair value test**. This test measures the impairment loss by comparing the asset's fair value with its carrying amount. The impairment loss is the carrying amount of the asset less the fair value of the impaired asset. As with other impairments, the loss on the limited-life intangible is reported as part of income from continuing operations. The entry generally appears in the "Other expenses and losses" section.

To illustrate, assume that Lerch, Inc. has a patent on how to extract oil from shale rock. Unfortunately, several recent non-shale oil discoveries adversely affected the demand for shale-oil technology. Thus, the patent has provided little income to date. As a result, Lerch performs a recoverability test. It finds that the expected future net cash flows from this patent are $35 million. Lerch's patent has a carrying amount of $60 million. Because the expected future net cash flows of $35 million are less than the carrying amount of $60 million, Lerch must determine an impairment loss.

Discounting the expected future net cash flows at its market rate of interest, Lerch determines the fair value of its patent to be $20 million. Illustration 12-6 shows the impairment loss computation (based on fair value).

ILLUSTRATION 12-6
Computation of Loss on Impairment of Patent

Carrying amount of patent	$60,000,000
Less: Fair value (based on present value computation)	20,000,000
Loss on impairment	$40,000,000

Lerch records this loss as follows.

Loss on Impairment	40,000,000	
Patents		40,000,000

Underlying Concepts

The basic attributes of intangibles, their uncertainty as to future benefits, and their uniqueness have discouraged valuation in excess of cost.

After recognizing the impairment, the reduced carrying amount of the patents is its new cost basis. Lerch should amortize the patent's new cost over its remaining useful life or legal life, whichever is shorter. Even if shale-oil prices increase in subsequent periods and the value of the patent increases, Lerch **may not recognize restoration of the previously recognized impairment loss**.

Impairment of Indefinite-Life Intangibles Other Than Goodwill

Companies should test indefinite-life intangibles other than goodwill for impairment at least annually. The impairment test for an indefinite-life asset other than goodwill is a **fair value test**. This test compares the fair value of the intangible asset with the asset's carrying amount. If the fair value is less than the carrying amount, the company recognizes an impairment. Companies use this one-step test because many indefinite-life assets easily meet the recoverability test (because cash flows may extend many years into the future). **Thus, companies do not use the recoverability test.**

To illustrate, assume that Arcon Radio purchased a broadcast license for $2,000,000. The license is renewable every 10 years if the company provides appropriate service and does not violate Federal Communications Commission (FCC) rules. Arcon Radio has renewed the license with the FCC twice, at a minimal cost. Because it expects cash flows to last indefinitely, Arcon reports the license as an indefinite-life intangible asset. Recently, the FCC decided to auction significantly more of these licenses. As a result, Arcon Radio expects reduced cash flows for the remaining two years of its existing license. It performs an impairment test and determines that the fair value of the intangible asset is $1,500,000. Arcon therefore reports an impairment loss of $500,000, computed as follows.

Carrying amount of broadcast license	$2,000,000
Less: Fair value of broadcast license	1,500,000
Loss on impairment	$ 500,000

ILLUSTRATION 12-7
Computation of Loss on Impairment of Broadcast License

Arcon Radio now reports the license at $1,500,000, its fair value. Even if the value of the license increases in the remaining two years, Arcon may not restore the previously recognized impairment loss.

Companies have the option to perform a qualitative assessment to determine whether it is more likely than not (i.e., a likelihood of more than 50 percent) that an indefinite-life intangible asset is impaired. **[9]** If the qualitative assessment indicates that the fair value of the reporting unit is more likely than not to be greater than the carrying value (i.e., the asset is not impaired), **the company need not continue with the fair value test**. As a result, use of the qualitative assessment option should reduce both the cost and complexity of performing the impairment test.[8]

Impairment of Goodwill

Goodwill must be tested for impairment at least annually. **The impairment rule for goodwill is a two-step process.** First, a company compares the fair value of the reporting unit to its carrying amount, including goodwill. If the fair value of the reporting unit exceeds the carrying amount, goodwill is not impaired. The company does not have to do anything else. Similar to other indefinite-life intangibles, companies may instead perform an optional qualitative assessment to determine whether it is more likely than not that goodwill is impaired. If the qualitative assessment indicates that the fair value of the reporting unit is more likely than not to be greater than the carrying value, the company need not continue with the two-step impairment test.[9]

To illustrate, assume that Kohlbuy Corporation has three divisions. It purchased one division, Pritt Products, four years ago for $2 million. Unfortunately, Pritt experienced operating losses over the last three quarters. Kohlbuy management is now reviewing the

[8] Examples of events and circumstances to be evaluated include but are not limited to (1) deterioration in general economic conditions; (2) an increased competitive environment, a decline in market-dependent multiples or metrics, a change in the market for a company's products or services, or a regulatory or political development; (3) cost factors such as increases in raw materials, labor, or other costs that have a negative effect on earnings; and (4) overall financial performance such as negative or declining cash flows or a decline in actual or planned revenue or earnings.

[9] The qualitative assessment examines similar factors as those used in the optional qualitative test for other indefinite-life intangibles but are based on events and circumstances related to the reporting unit. **[10]**

division for purposes of recognizing an impairment. Illustration 12-8 lists the Pritt Division's net assets, including the associated goodwill of $900,000 from the purchase.

ILLUSTRATION 12-8
Net Assets of Pritt Division, Including Goodwill

Cash	$ 200,000
Accounts receivable	300,000
Inventory	700,000
Property, plant, and equipment (net)	800,000
Goodwill	900,000
Accounts and notes payable	(500,000)
Net assets	$2,400,000

Kohlbuy determines that the fair value of Pritt Division is $2,800,000. **Because the fair value of the division exceeds the carrying amount of the net assets, Kohlbuy does not recognize any impairment.**

However, if the fair value of Pritt Division were less than the carrying amount of the net assets, then Kohlbuy would perform a second step to determine possible impairment. In the second step, Kohlbuy determines the fair value of the goodwill (implied value of goodwill) and compares it to its carrying amount. To illustrate, assume that the fair value of the Pritt Division is $1,900,000 instead of $2,800,000. Illustration 12-9 computes the implied value of the goodwill in this case.[10]

ILLUSTRATION 12-9
Determination of Implied Value of Goodwill

Fair value of Pritt Division	$1,900,000
Less: Net identifiable assets (excluding goodwill) ($2,400,000 − $900,000)	1,500,000
Implied value of goodwill	$ 400,000

Kohlbuy then compares the implied value of the goodwill to the recorded goodwill to measure the impairment, as shown in Illustration 12-10.

ILLUSTRATION 12-10
Measurement of Goodwill Impairment

Carrying amount of goodwill	$900,000
Less: Implied value of goodwill	400,000
Loss on impairment	$500,000

Impairment Summary

Illustration 12-11 summarizes the impairment tests for various intangible assets.

ILLUSTRATION 12-11
Summary of Intangible Asset Impairment Tests

Type of Intangible Asset	Impairment Test
Limited life	Recoverability test, then fair value test
Indefinite life other than goodwill	Fair value test*
Goodwill	Fair value test on reporting unit, then fair value test on implied goodwill*
	*An optional qualitative assessment may be performed to determine whether the fair value test needs to be performed.

[10] Illustration 12-9 assumes that the carrying amount equals the fair value of net identifiable assets (excluding goodwill). If different, companies use the fair value of the net identifiable assets (excluding goodwill) to determine the implied goodwill.

As shown in the chart below, goodwill impairments spiked in 2008 and 2009, coinciding with the stock market downturn in the wake of the financial crisis.

A spike in impairments when the market declines is understandable because declines in stock price are indicators that the fair values of acquired assets have declined below the carrying value. And while there is a declining trend in impairments in 2009 and 2010, notable goodwill impairments are being reported. For example, Microsoft posted a goodwill impairment charge of $6.3 billion in 2012. Some are expecting more goodwill impairments for other companies with book values well above market value of equity ($1.8 trillion for about 10 percent of companies in the S&P 500 at the end of 2001). As one analyst noted, "Anybody looking at a decline in market price could see the company was placing a much higher value on its assets than the market thought they were worth."

Investors need to keep watch. Such asset write-downs—for brand names, franchise rights, and other intangible assets (including goodwill)—are important because they tell investors that management have concluded their companies' future cash flows will not achieve previous estimates.

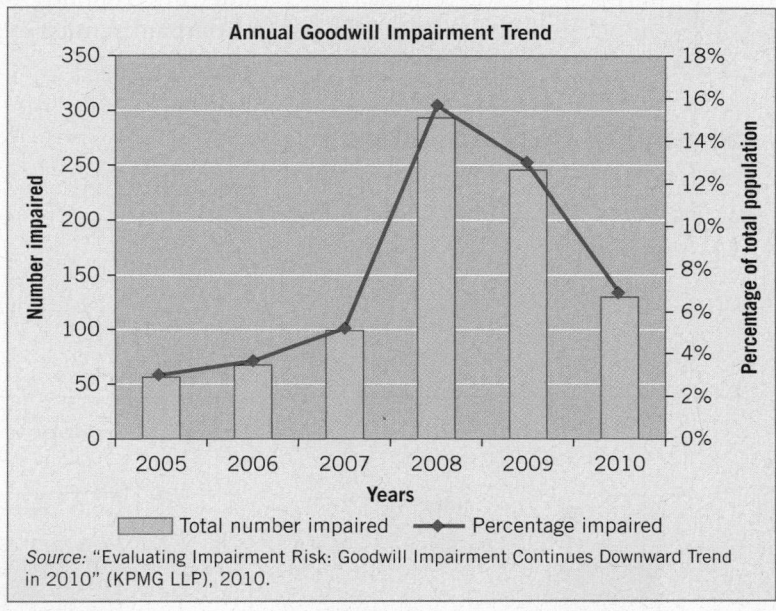

Source: "Evaluating Impairment Risk: Goodwill Impairment Continues Downward Trend in 2010" (KPMG LLP), 2010.

Sources: M. Murphy, "The Big Number," *Wall Street Journal* (November 16, 2011), p. B5; and S. Thurm, "Buyers Beware: The Goodwill Games," *Wall Street Journal* (August 13, 2012).

RESEARCH AND DEVELOPMENT COSTS

Research and development (R&D) costs are not in themselves intangible assets. However, we present the accounting for R&D costs here because R&D activities frequently result in the development of patents or copyrights (such as a new product, process, idea, formula, composition, or literary work) that may provide future value.

7 LEARNING OBJECTIVE
Identify the conceptual issues related to research and development costs.

Many companies spend considerable sums on research and development. Illustration 12-12 (page 666) shows the outlays for R&D made by selected global companies.

Two difficulties arise in accounting for R&D expenditures: (1) identifying the costs associated with particular activities, projects, or achievements, and (2) determining the

ILLUSTRATION 12-12
R&D Outlays, as a
Percentage of Sales

Company	Sales (millions)	R&D/Sales
Canon	$3,557,433	8.65%
Daimler	€106,540	3.92%
GlaxoSmithKline	£27,387	14.64%
Johnson & Johnson	$65,030	11.61%
Nokia	€38,659	14.52%
Roche	CHF42,531	19.58%
Procter & Gamble	$82,559	2.42%
Samsung	₩ 165,002	6.05%

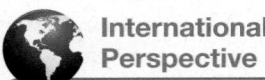

International Perspective

IFRS requires the capitalization of appropriate development expenditures. This conflicts with GAAP.

magnitude of the future benefits and length of time over which such benefits may be realized. Because of these latter uncertainties, the FASB has simplified the accounting practice in this area. **Companies must expense all research and development costs when incurred. [11]**

Identifying R&D Activities

Illustration 12-13 shows the definitions for **research activities** and **development activities**. These definitions differentiate research and development costs from other similar costs. **[12]**

ILLUSTRATION 12-13
Research Activities
versus Development
Activities

Research Activities	Development Activities
Planned search or critical investigation aimed at discovery of new knowledge.	Translation of research findings or other knowledge into a plan or design for a new product or process or for a significant improvement to an existing product or process whether intended for sale or use.
Examples	**Examples**
Laboratory research aimed at discovery of new knowledge; searching for applications of new research findings.	Conceptual formulation and design of possible product or process alternatives; construction of prototypes and operation of pilot plants.

R&D activities do not include routine or periodic alterations to existing products, production lines, manufacturing processes, and other ongoing operations, even though these alterations may represent improvements. For example, routine ongoing efforts to refine, enrich, or improve the qualities of an existing product are not considered R&D activities.

Accounting for R&D Activities

8 LEARNING OBJECTIVE

Describe the accounting for research and development and similar costs.

The costs associated with R&D activities and the accounting treatments accorded them are as follows.

1. *Materials, equipment, and facilities.* Expense the entire costs, **unless the items have alternative future uses** (in other R&D projects or otherwise). If there are alternative future uses, carry the items as inventory and allocate as consumed, or capitalize and depreciate as used.

2. *Personnel.* Expense as incurred salaries, wages, and other related costs of personnel engaged in R&D.

3. *Purchased intangibles.* Recognize and measure at fair value. After initial recognition, account for in accordance with their nature (as either limited-life or indefinite-life intangibles).[11]

4. *Contract services.* Expense the costs of services performed by others in connection with the R&D as incurred.

5. *Indirect costs.* Include a reasonable allocation of indirect costs in R&D costs, except for general and administrative cost, which must be clearly related in order to be included in R&D. **[14]**

Consistent with item 1 above, if a company owns a research facility that conducts R&D activities and that has alternative future uses (in other R&D projects or otherwise), it should capitalize the facility as an operational asset. The company accounts for depreciation and other costs related to such research facilities as R&D expenses.[12]

To illustrate, assume that Next Century Incorporated develops, produces, and markets laser machines for medical, industrial, and defense uses.[13] Illustration 12-14 (on the next page) lists the types of expenditures related to its laser-machine activities, along with the recommended accounting treatment.

Costs Similar to R&D Costs

Many costs have characteristics similar to research and development costs. Examples are:

1. Start-up costs for a new operation.
2. Initial operating losses.
3. Advertising costs.
4. Computer software costs.

---

[11]If R&D-related intangibles (often referred to as **in-process R&D**) are also acquired in a business combination, they are also recognized and measured at fair value. After initial recognition, these intangible assets are accounted for in accordance with their nature (as either limited-life or indefinite-life intangibles). **[13]**

[12]Companies in **the extractive industries** can use the following accounting treatment for the unique costs of research, exploration, and development activities and for those costs that are similar to but not classified as R&D costs: (1) expense as incurred, (2) capitalize and either depreciate or amortize over an appropriate period of time, or (3) accumulate as part of inventoriable costs. Choice of the appropriate accounting treatment for such costs is based on the degree of certainty of future benefits and the principle of matching revenues and expenses.

[13]Sometimes companies conduct R&D activities for other companies under a contractual arrangement. In this case, the contract usually specifies that the company performing the R&D work be reimbursed for all direct costs and certain specific indirect costs, plus a profit element. Because reimbursement is expected, the company doing the R&D work records the R&D costs as a receivable. The company for whom the work has been performed reports these costs as R&D and expenses them as incurred. For a more complete discussion of how an enterprise should account for funding of its R&D by others, see **[15]**.

NEXT CENTURY INCORPORATED

Type of Expenditure	Accounting Treatment	Rationale
1. Construction of long-range research facility for use in current and future projects (three-story, 400,000-square-foot building).	Capitalize and depreciate as R&D expense.	Has alternative future use.
2. Acquisition of R&D equipment for use on current project only.	Expense immediately as R&D.	Research cost.
3. Acquisition of machinery for use on current and future R&D projects.	Capitalize and depreciate as R&D expense.	Has alternative future use.
4. Purchase of materials for use on current and future R&D projects.	Inventory and allocate to R&D projects; expense as consumed.	Has alternative future use.
5. Salaries of research staff designing new laser bone scanner.	Expense immediately as R&D.	Research cost.
6. Research costs incurred under contract with New Horizon, Inc., and billable monthly.	Record as a receivable.	Not R&D cost (reimbursable expense).
7. Material, labor, and overhead costs of prototype laser scanner.	Expense immediately as R&D.	Development cost.
8. Costs of testing prototype and design modifications.	Expense immediately as R&D.	Development cost.
9. Legal fees to obtain patent on new laser scanner.	Capitalize as patent and amortize to overhead as part of cost of goods manufactured.	Direct cost of patent.
10. Executive salaries.	Expense as operating expense.	Not R&D cost (general and administrative expense).
11. Cost of marketing research to promote new laser scanner.	Expense as operating expense.	Not R&D cost (selling expense).
12. Engineering costs incurred to advance the laser scanner to full production stage.	Expense immediately as R&D.	Development cost.
13. Costs of successfully defending patent on laser scanner.	Capitalize as patent and amortize to overhead as part of cost of goods manufactured.	Direct cost of patent.
14. Commissions to sales staff marketing new laser scanner.	Expense as operating expense.	Not R&D cost (selling expense).

ILLUSTRATION 12-14
Sample R&D
Expenditures and Their
Accounting Treatment

For the most part, these costs are expensed as incurred, similar to the accounting for R&D costs. We briefly explain these costs in the following sections.

Start-Up Costs

Start-up costs are incurred for one-time activities to start a new operation. Examples include opening a new plant, introducing a new product or service, or conducting business in a new territory. Start-up costs include organizational costs, such as legal and state fees incurred to organize a new business entity.

The accounting for start-up costs is straightforward: **Expense start-up costs as incurred.** The profession recognizes that companies incur start-up costs with the expectation of future revenues or increased efficiencies. However, to determine the amount and timing of future benefits is so difficult that a conservative approach—expensing these costs as incurred—is required. **[16]**

To illustrate examples of start-up costs, assume that U.S.-based Hilo Beverage Company decides to construct a new plant in Brazil. This represents Hilo's first entry into the Brazilian market. Hilo plans to introduce the company's major U.S. brands into Brazil on a locally produced basis. The following costs might be involved:

1. Travel-related costs; costs related to employee salaries; and costs related to feasibility studies, accounting, tax, and government affairs.

2. Training of local employees related to product, maintenance, computer systems, finance, and operations.

3. Recruiting, organizing, and training related to establishing a distribution network.

Hilo Beverage should expense all these start-up costs as incurred.

Start-up activities commonly occur at the same time as activities involving the acquisition of assets. For example, as it is incurring start-up costs for the new plant, Hilo probably is also buying or building property, plant, equipment, and inventory. Hilo should not immediately expense the costs of these tangible assets. Instead, it should report them on the balance sheet using appropriate GAAP reporting guidelines.

Initial Operating Losses

Some contend that companies should be allowed to capitalize initial operating losses incurred in the start-up of a business. They argue that such operating losses are an unavoidable cost of starting a business.

For example, assume that Hilo lost money in its first year of operations and wishes to capitalize this loss. Hilo's CEO argues that as the company becomes profitable, it will offset these losses in future periods. What do you think? We believe that this approach is unsound since losses have no future service potential and therefore cannot be considered an asset.

GAAP requires that operating losses during the early years **should not be capitalized**. In short, **the accounting and reporting standards should be no different for an enterprise trying to establish a new business than they are for other enterprises. [17]**[14]

Advertising Costs

Over the years, **PepsiCo** has hired various pop stars, such as Elton John and Beyoncé, to advertise its products. How should it report such advertising costs related to its star spokespeople? Pepsi could expense the costs in various ways:

1. When the pop stars have completed their singing assignments.

2. The first time the advertising runs.

3. Over the estimated useful life of the advertising.

4. In an appropriate fashion to each of the three periods identified above.

5. Over the period revenues are expected to result.

For the most part, Pepsi must expense advertising costs as incurred or the first time the advertising takes place. Whichever of these two approaches is followed, the results are essentially the same. On the other hand, companies record as assets any tangible assets used in advertising, such as billboards or blimps. The rationale is that such assets do have alternative future uses. Again the profession has taken a conservative approach to recording advertising costs because defining and measuring the future benefits can be so difficult. **[18]**[15]

Computer Software Costs

A special problem arises in distinguishing R&D costs from selling and administrative activities. The FASB's intent was that companies exclude from the definition of R&D activities the acquisition, development, or improvement of a product or process **for use in their selling or administrative activities**. For example, the costs of software incurred by an airline

Gateway to the Profession

Expanded Discussion—Software Development Costs

---

[14]A company is considered to be in the developing stages when it is directing its efforts toward establishing a new business and either the company has not started the principal operations or it has earned no significant revenue.

[15]There are some exceptions for immediate expensing of advertising costs when they relate to direct-response advertising, but that subject is beyond the scope of this book.

in improving its computerized reservation system or the costs incurred in developing a company's management information system **are not** research and development costs.

For many companies, developing a strong brand image is as important as developing the products they sell. Now more than ever, companies see the power of a strong brand, enhanced by significant and effective advertising investments.

As the following chart indicates, the value of brand investments is substantial. Coca-Cola heads the list with an estimated brand value of about $72 billion.

The World's 10 Most Valuable Brands (in billions)	
1 Coca-Cola	$71.9
2 IBM	69.9
3 Microsoft	59.0
4 Google	55.3
5 GE	42.8
6 McDonald's	35.6
7 Intel	35.2
8 Apple	33.5
9 Disney	29.0
10 HP	28.9

Source: 2011 data, from Interbrand Corp.

Occasionally you may find the value of a brand included in a company's financial statements under goodwill. But generally you will not find the estimated values of brands recorded in companies' balance sheets. The reason? The subjectivity that goes into estimating a brand's value. In some cases, analysts base an estimate of brand value on opinion polls or on some multiple of ad spending. For example, in estimating the brand values shown to the left, Interbrand Corp. estimates the percentage of the overall future revenues the brand will generate and then discounts the net cash flows, to arrive at a present value.

Some analysts believe that information on brand values is relevant. Others voice valid concerns about the reliability of brand value estimates due to subjectivity in the estimates for revenues, costs, and the risk component of the discount rate. For example, another brand valuation firm, Millward Brown, ranks Apple as number one with an estimated brand value of $183 billion (or about one-third of Apple's market value). These data support the highly subjective nature of brand valuation estimates.

Sources: "Best Global Brands 2011," *www.interbrand.com* (accessed July 5, 2012); and S. Vranica and J. Hansegard, "Ikea Discloses an $11 Billion Secret," *Wall Street Journal* (August 9, 2012).

PRESENTATION OF INTANGIBLES AND RELATED ITEMS
Presentation of Intangible Assets

LEARNING OBJECTIVE 9

Indicate the presentation of intangible assets and related items.

The reporting of intangible assets is similar to the reporting of property, plant, and equipment. However, contra accounts are not normally shown for intangibles on the balance sheet. As Illustration 12-15 shows, on the balance sheet companies should report as a separate item all intangible assets other than goodwill. If goodwill is present, companies should report it separately. The FASB concluded that since goodwill and other intangible assets differ significantly from other types of assets, such disclosure benefits users of the balance sheet.

On the income statement, companies should present amortization expense and impairment losses for intangible assets other than goodwill separately and as part of continuing operations. Again, see Illustration 12-15. Goodwill impairment losses should also be presented as a separate line item in the continuing operations section, unless the goodwill impairment is associated with a discontinued operation.

The notes to the financial statements should include information about acquired intangible assets, including the aggregate amortization expense for each of the succeeding five years. If separate accumulated amortization accounts are not used, accumulated amortization should be disclosed in the notes. The notes should include information about changes in the carrying amount of goodwill during the period.

ILLUSTRATION 12-15
Intangible Asset
Disclosures

HARBAUGH COMPANY

Balance Sheet (partial)
(in thousands)

Intangible assets (Note C)	$3,840
Goodwill (Note D)	2,575

Income Statement (partial)
(in thousands)

as part of Continuing operations

Amortization expense	$380
Impairment losses (goodwill)	46

Notes to the Financial Statements

Note C: Acquired Intangible Assets

	As of December 31, 2014	
	Gross Carrying Amount	Accumulated Amortization
Amortized intangible assets		
Trademark	$2,000	$(100)
Customer list	500	(310)
Other	60	(10)
Total	$2,560	$(420)
Unamortized intangible assets		
Licenses	$1,300	
Trademark	400	
Total	$1,700	

Types of intangibles and carrying values

Aggregate Amortization Expense

For year ended 12/31/14	$380

Estimated Amortization Expense

For year ended 12/31/15	$200
For year ended 12/31/16	90
For year ended 12/31/17	70
For year ended 12/31/18	60
For year ended 12/31/19	50

Current and future expense

Note D: Goodwill
The changes in the carrying amount of goodwill for the year ended December 31, 2014, are as follows.

($000s)	Technology Segment	Communications Segment	Total
Balance as of January 1, 2014	$1,413	$904	$2,317
Goodwill acquired during year	189	115	304
Impairment losses	—	(46)	(46)
Balance as of December 31, 2014	$1,602	$973	$2,575

Goodwill by segment and carrying values

The Communications segment is tested for impairment in the third quarter, after the annual forecasting process. Due to an increase in competition in the Texas and Louisiana cable industry, operating profits and cash flows were lower than expected in the fourth quarter of 2013 and the first and second quarters of 2014. Based on that trend, the earnings forecast for the next 5 years was revised. In September 2014, a goodwill impairment loss of $46 was recognized in the Communications reporting unit. The fair value of that reporting unit was estimated using the expected present value of future cash flows.

Impairment methodology

Presentation of Research and Development Costs

Companies should disclose in the financial statements (generally in the notes) the total R&D costs charged to expense each period for which they present an income statement. Merck & Co., Inc., a global research pharmaceutical company, reported both internal and acquired research and development in its recent income statement, as shown in Illustration 12-16.

ILLUSTRATION 12-16
Income Statement
Disclosure of R&D Costs

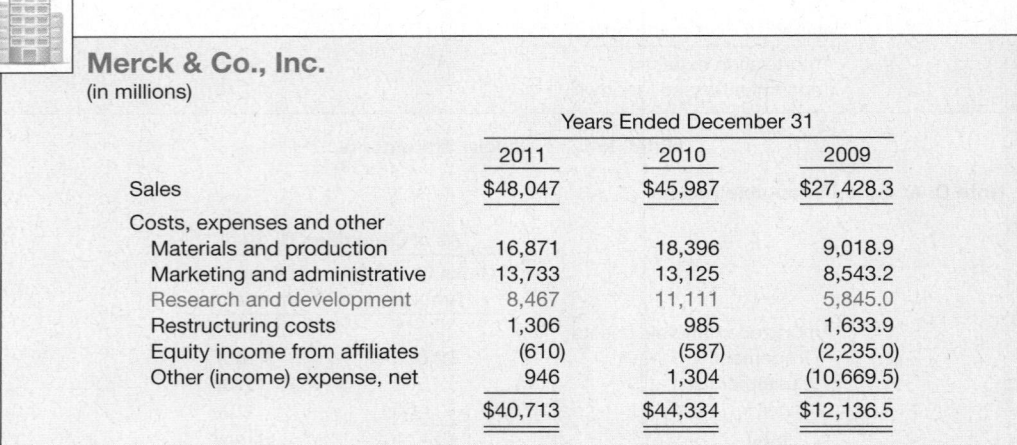

Merck & Co., Inc.
(in millions)

	Years Ended December 31		
	2011	2010	2009
Sales	$48,047	$45,987	$27,428.3
Costs, expenses and other			
Materials and production	16,871	18,396	9,018.9
Marketing and administrative	13,733	13,125	8,543.2
Research and development	8,467	11,111	5,845.0
Restructuring costs	1,306	985	1,633.9
Equity income from affiliates	(610)	(587)	(2,235.0)
Other (income) expense, net	946	1,304	(10,669.5)
	$40,713	$44,334	$12,136.5

In addition, Merck provides a discussion about R&D expenditures in its annual report, as shown in Illustration 12-17.

ILLUSTRATION 12-17
Merck's R&D Disclosure

Merck & Co., Inc.

Research and development in the pharmaceutical industry is inherently a long-term process. The following data show the trend of the Company's research and development spending. For the period 1998 to 2011, the compounded annual growth rate in research and development was approximately 21%.

You will want to read the
IFRS INSIGHTS
on pages 693–699

for discussion of IFRS related to intangible assets.

Evolving Issue *RECOGNITION OF R&D AND INTERNALLY GENERATED INTANGIBLES*

The requirement that companies expense immediately all R&D costs (as well as start-up costs) incurred internally is a practical solution. It ensures consistency in practice and uniformity among companies. But the practice of immediately writing off expenditures made in the expectation of benefiting future periods is conceptually incorrect.

Proponents of immediate expensing contend that from an income statement standpoint, long-run application of this standard frequently makes little difference. They argue that because of the ongoing nature of most companies' R&D activities, the amount of R&D cost charged to expense each accounting period is about the same, whether there is immediate expensing or capitalization and subsequent amortization.

Others criticize this practice. They believe that the balance sheet should report an intangible asset related to expenditures that have future benefit. To preclude capitalization of all R&D expenditures removes from the balance sheet what may be a company's most valuable asset.

Indeed, research findings indicate that capitalizing R&D costs may be helpful to investors. For example, one study showed a significant relationship between R&D outlays and subsequent benefits in the form of increased productivity, earnings, and shareholder value for R&D-intensive companies. Another study found that there was a significant decline in earnings usefulness for companies that were forced to switch from capitalizing to expensing R&D costs, and that the decline appears to persist over time.

The current accounting for R&D and other internally generated intangible assets represents one of the many trade-offs made among relevance, faithful representation, and cost-benefit considerations. The FASB and IASB have completed some limited-scope projects on the accounting for intangible assets, and the Boards have contemplated a joint project on the accounting for identifiable intangible assets (i.e., excluding goodwill). Such a project would address concerns that the current accounting requirements lead to inconsistent treatments for some types of intangible assets depending on how they arise. (See *http://www.ifrs.org/Current+Projects/IASB+Projects/Intangible+Assets/Intangible+Assets.htm*.)

Sources for research studies: Baruch Lev and Theodore Sougiannis, "The Capitalization, Amortization, and Value-Relevance of R&D," *Journal of Accounting and Economics* (February 1996); and Martha L. Loudder and Bruce K. Behn, "Alternative Income Determination Rules and Earnings Usefulness: The Case of R&D Costs," *Contemporary Accounting Research* (Fall 1995).

SUMMARY OF LEARNING OBJECTIVES

KEY TERMS

amortization, *651*

bargain purchase, *661*

business combination, *650(n)*

copyright, *655*

development activities, *666*

fair value test, *662*

franchise, *655*

goodwill, *658*

impairment, *662*

indefinite-life intangibles, *651*

intangible assets, *650*

license (permit), *656*

limited-life intangibles, *651*

master valuation approach, *660*

organizational costs, *668*

1 **Describe the characteristics of intangible assets.** Intangible assets have two main characteristics: (1) They lack physical existence, and (2) they are not financial instruments. In most cases, intangible assets provide services over a period of years and so are normally classified as long-term assets.

2 **Identify the costs to include in the initial valuation of intangible assets.** Intangibles are recorded at cost. Cost includes all acquisition costs and expenditures needed to make the intangible asset ready for its intended use. If intangibles are acquired in exchange for stock or other assets, the cost of the intangible is the fair value of the consideration given or the fair value of the intangible received, whichever is more clearly evident. When a company makes a "basket purchase" of several intangibles or a combination of intangibles and tangibles, it should allocate the cost on the basis of fair values.

3 **Explain the procedure for amortizing intangible assets.** Intangibles have either a limited useful life or an indefinite useful life. Companies amortize limited-life intangibles. They do not amortize indefinite-life intangibles. Limited-life intangibles should be amortized by systematic charges to expense over their useful life. The useful life should reflect the period over which these assets will contribute to cash flows. The patent, *656*

recoverability test, *662*

research activities, *666*

research and development (R&D) costs, *665*

start-up costs, *668*

trademark, trade name, *653*

amount to report for amortization expense should reflect the pattern in which a company consumes or uses up the asset, if it can reliably determine that pattern. Otherwise, use a straight-line approach.

4 **Describe the types of intangible assets.** Major types of intangibles are (1) *marketing-related intangibles*, used in the marketing or promotion of products or services; (2) *customer-related intangibles*, resulting from interactions with outside parties; (3) *artistic-related intangibles*, giving ownership rights to such items as plays and literary works; (4) *contract-related intangibles*, representing the value of rights that arise from contractual arrangements; (5) *technology-related intangibles*, relating to innovations or technological advances; and (6) *goodwill*, arising from business combinations.

5 **Explain the accounting issues for recording goodwill.** Unlike receivables, inventories, and patents that a company can sell or exchange individually in the marketplace, goodwill can be identified only with the company as a whole. Goodwill is a "going concern" valuation and is recorded only when an entire business is purchased. A company should not capitalize goodwill generated internally. The future benefits of goodwill may have no relationship to the costs incurred in the development of that goodwill. Goodwill may exist even in the absence of specific costs to develop it.

To record goodwill, a company compares the fair value of the net tangible and identifiable intangible assets with the purchase price of the acquired business. The difference is considered goodwill. Goodwill is the residual. Goodwill is often identified on the balance sheet as the excess of cost over the fair value of the net assets acquired.

6 **Explain the accounting issues related to intangible-asset impairments.** Impairment occurs when the carrying amount of the intangible asset is not recoverable. Companies use a recoverability test and a fair value test to determine impairments for limited-life intangibles. They use only a fair value test for indefinite-life intangibles. Goodwill impairments require a two-step process. First, test the fair value of the reporting unit, then do the fair value test on implied goodwill.

7 **Identify the conceptual issues related to research and development costs.** R&D costs are not in themselves intangible assets, but R&D activities frequently result in the development of something a company patents or copyrights. The difficulties in accounting for R&D expenditures are (1) identifying the costs associated with particular activities, projects, or achievements, and (2) determining the magnitude of the future benefits and length of time over which a company may realize such benefits. Because of these latter uncertainties, companies are required to expense all research and development costs when incurred.

8 **Describe the accounting for research and development and similar costs.** Illustration 12-14 (page 668) shows typical costs associated with R&D activities and the accounting treatment accorded them. Many costs have characteristics similar to R&D costs. Examples are start-up costs, initial operating losses, and advertising costs. For the most part, these costs are expensed as incurred, similar to the accounting for R&D costs.

9 **Indicate the presentation of intangible assets and related items.** On the balance sheet, companies should report all intangible assets other than goodwill as a separate item. Contra accounts are not normally shown. If goodwill is present, it too should be reported as a separate item. On the income statement, companies should report amortization expense and impairment losses in continuing operations. The notes to the financial statements have additional detailed information. Financial statements must disclose the total R&D costs charged to expense each period for which an income statement is presented.

DEMONSTRATION PROBLEM

Sky Co., organized in 2014, provided you with the following information.

1. Purchased a license for $20,000 on July 1, 2014. The license gives Sky exclusive rights to sell its services in the tri-state region and will expire on July 1, 2022.
2. Purchased a patent on January 2, 2015, for $40,000. It is estimated to have a 5-year life.
3. Costs incurred to develop an exclusive Internet connection process as of June 1, 2015, were $45,000. The process has an indefinite life.
4. On April 1, 2015, Sky Co. purchased a small circuit board manufacturer for $350,000. Goodwill recorded in the transaction was $90,000.
5. On July 1, 2015, legal fees for successful defense of the patent purchased on January 2, 2015, were $11,400.
6. Research and development costs incurred as of September 1, 2015, were $75,000.

Instructions

(a) Prepare the journal entries to record all the entries related to the patent during 2015.
(b) At December 31, 2015, an impairment test is performed on the license purchased in 2014. It is estimated that the net cash flows to be received from the license will be $13,000, and its fair value is $7,000. Compute the amount of impairment, if any, to be recorded on December 31, 2015.
(c) What is the amount to be reported for intangible assets on the balance sheet at December 31, 2014? At December 31, 2015?

Solution

(a)

January 2, 2015		
Patents	40,000	
Cash		40,000

July 1, 2015		
Patents	11,400	
Cash		11,400

December 31, 2015		
Patent Amortization Expense	9,267	
Patents		9,267

Computation of patent expense:

$40,000 × 12/60 =	$8,000
$11,400 × 6/54 =	1,267
Total	$9,267

(b) Computation of impairment loss:

Cost	$20,000
Less: Accumulated amortization ($20,000 × 18/96)	3,750
Book value	$16,250

Book value of $16,250 is greater than net cash flows of $13,000. Therefore, the license is impaired. The impairment loss is computed as follows.

Book value	$16,250
Fair value	7,000
Loss on impairment	$ 9,250

(c) Intangible assets as of December 31, 2014:

License	$18,750*
*Cost	$20,000
Less: Accumulated amortization ($20,000 × 6/96)	1,250
Total	$18,750

Intangible assets as of December 31, 2015:

License	$ 7,000
Patents ($40,000 + $11,400 − $9,267)	$42,133
Goodwill	$90,000

All the costs to develop the Internet connection process and the research and development costs are expensed as incurred.

FASB CODIFICATION

FASB Codification References

[1] FASB ASC 350-10-05. [Predecessor literature: "Goodwill and Other Intangible Assets," *Statement of Financial Accounting Standards No. 142* (Norwalk, Conn.: FASB, 2001).]

[2] FASB ASC 350-30-35. [Predecessor literature: "Goodwill and Other Intangible Assets," *Statement of Financial Accounting Standards No. 142* (Norwalk, Conn.: FASB, 2001), par. 11.]

[3] FASB ASC 805-10. [Predecessor literature: "Business Combinations," *Statement of Financial Accounting Standards No. 141R* (Norwalk, Conn.: FASB, 2007).]

[4] FASB ASC 350-30-35. [Predecessor literature: "Goodwill and Other Intangible Assets," *Statement of Financial Accounting Standards No. 142* (Norwalk, Conn.: FASB, 2001), par. B55.]

[5] FASB ASC 805-10-20. [Predecessor literature: "Business Combinations," *Statement of Financial Accounting Standards No. 141R* (Norwalk, Conn.: FASB, 2007).]

[6] FASB ASC 805-10-30. [Predecessor literature: "Business Combinations," *Statement of Financial Accounting Standards No. 141R* (Norwalk, Conn.: FASB, 2007).]

[7] FASB ASC 805-10-30. [Predecessor literature: "Business Combinations," *Statement of Financial Accounting Standards No. 141R* (Norwalk, Conn.: FASB, 2007).]

[8] FASB ASC 360-10-05. [Predecessor literature: "Accounting for the Impairment or Disposal of Long-lived Assets," *Statement of Financial Accounting Standards No. 144* (Norwalk, Conn.: 2001).]

[9] FASB ASC 350-30-35-17A-19. [Predecessor literature: "Goodwill and Other Intangible Assets," *Statement of Financial Accounting Standards No. 142* (Norwalk, Conn.: FASB, 2001).]

[10] FASB ASC 350-20-35. [Predecessor literature: "Goodwill and Other Intangible Assets," *Statement of Financial Accounting Standards No. 142* (Norwalk, Conn.: FASB, 2001).]

[11] FASB ASC 735-10-25-1. [Predecessor literature: "Accounting for Research and Development Costs," *Statement of Financial Accounting Standards No. 2* (Stamford, Conn.: FASB, 1974), par. 12.]

[12] FASB ASC Master Glossary. [Predecessor literature: "Accounting for Research and Development Costs," *Statement of Financial Accounting Standards No. 2* (Stamford, Conn.: FASB, 1974), par. 8.]

[13] FASB ASC 805-10. [Predecessor literature: "Business Combinations," *Statement of Financial Accounting Standards No. 141–Revised* (Norwalk, Conn.: FASB, 2007), par. E11.]

[14] FASB ASC 730-10-25-2. [Predecessor literature: "Accounting for Research and Development Costs," *Statement of Financial Accounting Standards No. 2* (Stamford, Conn.: FASB, 1974), par. 11.]

[15] FASB ASC 730-20-05. [Predecessor literature: "Research and Development Arrangements," *Statement of Financial Accounting Standards No. 68* (Stamford, Conn.: FASB, 1982).]

[16] FASB ASC 720-15-25. [Predecessor literature: "Reporting on the Costs of Start-up Activities," *Statement of Position 98-5* (New York: AICPA, 1998).]

[17] FASB ASC 915-205-45-1. [Predecessor literature: "Accounting and Reporting by Development Stage Enterprises," *Statement of Financial Accounting Standards No. 7* (Stamford, Conn.: FASB, 1975), par. 10.]

[18] FASB ASC 720-35-05-3. [Predecessor literature: "Reporting on Advertising Costs," *Statement of Position 93-7* (New York: AICPA, 1993).]

Exercises

If your school has a subscription to the FASB Codification, go to *http://aaahq.org/asclogin.cfm* to log in and prepare responses to the following. Provide Codification references for your responses.

CE12-1 Access the Codification glossary ("Master Glossary") to answer the following.

   (a) What is the definition provided for an intangible asset?
   (b) What is the definition of goodwill?
   (c) What is the definition of research and development (R&D)?
   (d) What is a development stage entity?

CE12-2 Your friend Harry does not understand the concept of an indefinite-life intangible asset. He wonders, "Does this mean the life is infinite?" What does the authoritative literature say about indefinite-life intangible assets?

CE12-3 What guidance does the Codification provide concerning the disclosure of research and development (R&D) costs?

CE12-4 What is the nature of the authoritative guidance for advertising costs for entertainment companies?

An additional Codification case can be found in the Using Your Judgment section, on page 692.

Be sure to check the book's companion website for a Review and Analysis Exercise, with solution.

WileyPLUS   Brief Exercises, Exercises, Problems, and many more learning and assessment tools and resources are available for practice in WileyPLUS.

QUESTIONS

1. What are the two main characteristics of intangible assets?

2. If intangibles are acquired for stock, how is the cost of the intangible determined?

3. Intangibles have either a limited useful life or an indefinite useful life. How should these two different types of intangibles be amortized?

4. Why does the accounting profession make a distinction between internally created intangibles and purchased intangibles?

5. In 2014, Ghostbusters Corp. spent $420,000 for "goodwill" visits by sales personnel to key customers. The purpose of these visits was to build a solid, friendly relationship for the future and to gain insight into the problems and needs of the companies served. How should this expenditure be reported?

6. What are factors to be considered in estimating the useful life of an intangible asset?

7. What should be the pattern of amortization for a limited-life intangible?

8. Columbia Sportswear Company acquired a trademark that is helpful in distinguishing one of its new products. The trademark is renewable every 10 years at minimal cost. All evidence indicates that this trademarked product will generate cash flows for an indefinite period of time. How should this trademark be amortized?

9. McNabb Company spent $190,000 developing a new process, $45,000 in legal fees to obtain a patent, and $91,000 to market the process that was patented, all in the year 2014. How should these costs be accounted for in 2014?

10. Izzy Inc. purchased a patent for $350,000 which has an estimated useful life of 10 years. Its pattern of use or consumption cannot be reliably determined. Prepare the entry to record the amortization of the patent in its first year of use.

11. Explain the difference between artistic-related intangible assets and contract-related intangible assets.

12. What is goodwill? What is a bargain purchase?

13. Under what circumstances is it appropriate to record goodwill in the accounts? How should goodwill, properly recorded on the books, be written off in order to conform with generally accepted accounting principles?

14. In examining financial statements, financial analysts often write off goodwill immediately. Comment on this procedure.

15. Braxton Inc. is considering the write-off of a limited-life intangible because of its lack of profitability. Explain to the management of Braxton how to determine whether a write-off is permitted.

16. Last year, Zeno Company recorded an impairment on an intangible asset held for use. Recent appraisals indicate that the asset has increased in value. Should Zeno record this recovery in value?

17. Explain how losses on impaired intangible assets should be reported in income.

18. Simon Company determines that its goodwill is impaired. It finds that its implied goodwill is $360,000 and its recorded goodwill is $400,000. The fair value of its identifiable assets is $1,450,000. What is the amount of goodwill impaired?

19. What is the nature of research and development costs?

20. Research and development activities may include (a) personnel costs, (b) materials and equipment costs, and (c) indirect costs. What is the recommended accounting treatment for these three types of R&D costs?

21. Which of the following activities should be expensed currently as R&D costs?

(a) Testing in search for or evaluation of product or process alternatives.

(b) Engineering follow-through in an early phase of commercial production.

(c) Legal work in connection with patent applications or litigation, and the sale or licensing of patents.

22. Indicate the proper accounting for the following items.

(a) Organization costs.   (c) Operating losses.

(b) Advertising costs.

23. In 2013, Austin Powers Corporation developed a new product that will be marketed in 2014. In connection with the development of this product, the following costs were incurred in 2013: research and development costs $400,000; materials and supplies consumed $60,000; and compensation paid to research consultants $125,000. It is anticipated that these costs will be recovered in 2016. What is the amount of research and development costs that Austin Powers should record in 2013 as a charge to expense?

24. Recently, a group of university students decided to incorporate for the purposes of selling a process to recycle the waste product from manufacturing cheese. Some of the initial costs involved were legal fees and office expenses incurred in starting the business, state incorporation fees, and stamp taxes. One student wishes to charge these costs against revenue in the current period. Another wishes to defer these costs and amortize them in the future. Which student is correct?

25. An intangible asset with an estimated useful life of 30 years was acquired on January 1, 2004, for $540,000. On January 1, 2014, a review was made of intangible assets and their expected service lives, and it was determined that this asset had an estimated useful life of 30 more years from the date of the review. What is the amount of amortization for this intangible in 2014?

BRIEF EXERCISES

2 3 **BE12-1** Celine Dion Corporation purchases a patent from Salmon Company on January 1, 2014, for $54,000. The patent has a remaining legal life of 16 years. Celine Dion feels the patent will be useful for 10 years. Prepare Celine Dion's journal entries to record the purchase of the patent and 2014 amortization.

2 3 **BE12-2** Use the information provided in BE12-1. Assume that at January 1, 2016, the carrying amount of the patent on Celine Dion's books is $43,200. In January, Celine Dion spends $24,000 successfully defending a patent suit. Celine Dion still feels the patent will be useful until the end of 2023. Prepare the journal entries to record the $24,000 expenditure and 2016 amortization.

2 3 **BE12-3** Larry Byrd, Inc., spent $68,000 in attorney fees while developing the trade name of its new product, the Mean Bean Machine. Prepare the journal entries to record the $68,000 expenditure and the first year's amortization, using an 8-year life.

2 3 **BE12-4** Gershwin Corporation obtained a franchise from Sonic Hedgehog Inc. for a cash payment of $120,000 on April 1, 2014. The franchise grants Gershwin the right to sell certain products and services for a period of 8 years. Prepare Gershwin's April 1 journal entry and December 31 adjusting entry.

5 **BE12-5** On September 1, 2014, Winans Corporation acquired Aumont Enterprises for a cash payment of $700,000. At the time of purchase, Aumont's balance sheet showed assets of $620,000, liabilities of $200,000, and owners' equity of $420,000. The fair value of Aumont's assets is estimated to be $800,000. Compute the amount of goodwill acquired by Winans.

6 **BE12-6** Kenoly Corporation owns a patent that has a carrying amount of $300,000. Kenoly expects future net cash flows from this patent to total $210,000. The fair value of the patent is $110,000. Prepare Kenoly's journal entry, if necessary, to record the loss on impairment.

6 **BE12-7** Waters Corporation purchased Johnson Company 3 years ago and at that time recorded goodwill of $400,000. The Johnson Division's net assets, including the goodwill, have a carrying amount of $800,000. The fair value of the division is estimated to be $1,000,000. Prepare Waters' journal entry, if necessary, to record impairment of the goodwill.

6 **BE12-8** Use the information provided in BE12-7. Assume that the fair value of the division is estimated to be $750,000 and the implied goodwill is $350,000. Prepare Waters' journal entry, if necessary, to record impairment of the goodwill.

8 **BE12-9** Capriati Corporation commenced operations in early 2014. The corporation incurred $60,000 of costs such as fees to underwriters, legal fees, state fees, and promotional expenditures during its formation. Prepare journal entries to record the $60,000 expenditure and 2014 amortization, if any.

8 **BE12-10** Treasure Land Corporation incurred the following costs in 2014.

Cost of laboratory research aimed at discovery of new knowledge	$120,000
Cost of testing in search for product alternatives	100,000
Cost of engineering activity required to advance the design of a product to the manufacturing stage	210,000
	$430,000

Prepare the necessary 2014 journal entry or entries for Treasure Land.

8 **BE12-11** Indicate whether the following items are capitalized or expensed in the current year.

(a) Purchase cost of a patent from a competitor.   (c) Organizational costs.
(b) Research and development costs.   (d) Costs incurred internally to create goodwill.

3 9 **BE12-12** Nieland Industries had one patent recorded on its books as of January 1, 2014. This patent had a book value of $288,000 and a remaining useful life of 8 years. During 2014, Nieland incurred research and development costs of $96,000 and brought a patent infringement suit against a competitor. On December 1, 2014, Nieland received the good news that its patent was valid and that its competitor could not use the process Nieland had patented. The company incurred $85,000 to defend this patent. At what amount should patent(s) be reported on the December 31, 2014, balance sheet, assuming monthly amortization of patents?

3 9 **BE12-13** Sinise Industries acquired two copyrights during 2014. One copyright related to a textbook that was developed internally at a cost of $9,900. This textbook is estimated to have a useful life of 3 years from September 1, 2014, the date it was published. The second copyright (a history research textbook) was purchased from University Press on December 1, 2014, for $24,000. This textbook has an indefinite useful life. How should these two copyrights be reported on Sinise's balance sheet as of December 31, 2014?

EXERCISES

1 4 **E12-1 (Classification Issues—Intangibles)** Presented below is a list of items that could be included in the intangible assets section of the balance sheet.

1. Investment in a subsidiary company.
2. Timberland.
3. Cost of engineering activity required to advance the design of a product to the manufacturing stage.

4. Lease prepayment (6 months' rent paid in advance).
5. Cost of equipment obtained.
6. Cost of searching for applications of new research findings.
7. Costs incurred in the formation of a corporation.
8. Operating losses incurred in the start-up of a business.
9. Training costs incurred in start-up of new operation.
10. Purchase cost of a franchise.
11. Goodwill generated internally.
12. Cost of testing in search for product alternatives.
13. Goodwill acquired in the purchase of a business.
14. Cost of developing a patent.
15. Cost of purchasing a patent from an inventor.
16. Legal costs incurred in securing a patent.
17. Unrecovered costs of a successful legal suit to protect the patent.
18. Cost of conceptual formulation of possible product alternatives.
19. Cost of purchasing a copyright.
20. Research and development costs.
21. Long-term receivables.
22. Cost of developing a trademark.
23. Cost of purchasing a trademark.

Instructions
(a) Indicate which items on the list above would generally be reported as intangible assets in the balance sheet.
(b) Indicate how, if at all, the items not reportable as intangible assets would be reported in the financial statements.

1 4 E12-2 (Classification Issues—Intangibles) Presented below is selected information related to Martin Burke Inc. at year-end. All these accounts have debit balances.

Cable television franchises	Film contract rights
Music copyrights	Customer lists
Research and development costs	Prepaid expenses
Goodwill	Covenants not to compete
Cash	Brand names
Discount on notes payable	Notes receivable
Accounts receivable	Investments in affiliated companies
Property, plant, and equipment	Organization costs
Internet domain name	Land

Instructions
Identify which items should be classified as an intangible asset. For those items not classified as an intangible asset, indicate where they would be reported in the financial statements.

1 4 E12-3 (Classification Issues—Intangible Assets) Joni Hyde Inc. has the following amounts reported in its general ledger at the end of the current year.

Organization costs	$24,000
Trademarks	15,000
Discount on bonds payable	35,000
Deposits with advertising agency for ads to promote goodwill of company	10,000
Excess of cost over fair value of net identifiable assets of acquired subsidiary	75,000
Cost of equipment acquired for research and development projects; the equipment has an alternative future use	90,000
Costs of developing a secret formula for a product that is expected to be marketed for at least 20 years	80,000

Instructions
(a) On the basis of the information above, compute the total amount to be reported by Hyde for intangible assets on its balance sheet at year-end.
(b) If an item is not to be included in intangible assets, explain its proper treatment for reporting purposes.

3 **8** **E12-4 (Intangible Amortization)** Presented below is selected information for Alatorre Company.

1. Alatorre purchased a patent from Vania Co. for $1,000,000 on January 1, 2012. The patent is being amortized over its remaining legal life of 10 years, expiring on January 1, 2022. During 2014, Alatorre determined that the economic benefits of the patent would not last longer than 6 years from the date of acquisition. What amount should be reported in the balance sheet for the patent, net of accumulated amortization, at December 31, 2014?

2. Alatorre bought a franchise from Alexander Co. on January 1, 2013, for $400,000. The carrying amount of the franchise on Alexander's books on January 1, 2013, was $500,000. The franchise agreement had an estimated useful life of 30 years. Because Alatorre must enter a competitive bidding at the end of 2015, it is unlikely that the franchise will be retained beyond 2022. What amount should be amortized for the year ended December 31, 2014?

3. On January 1, 2014, Alatorre incurred organization costs of $275,000. What amount of organization expense should be reported in 2014?

4. Alatorre purchased the license for distribution of a popular consumer product on January 1, 2014, for $150,000. It is expected that this product will generate cash flows for an indefinite period of time. The license has an initial term of 5 years but by paying a nominal fee, Alatorre can renew the license indefinitely for successive 5-year terms. What amount should be amortized for the year ended December 31, 2014?

Instructions
Answer the questions asked about each of the factual situations.

2 **3** **E12-5 (Correct Intangible Assets Account)** As the recently appointed auditor for William J. Bryan Corpo-
7 ration, you have been asked to examine selected accounts before the 6-month financial statements of June 30, 2014, are prepared. The controller for William J. Bryan Corporation mentions that only one account is kept for intangible assets. The account is shown below.

Intangible Assets

		Debit	Credit	Balance
Jan. 4	Research and development costs	940,000		940,000
Jan. 5	Legal costs to obtain patent	75,000		1,015,000
Jan. 31	Payment of 7 months' rent on property leased by Bryan	91,000		1,106,000
Feb. 11	Premium on common stock		250,000	856,000
March 31	Unamortized bond discount on bonds due March 31, 2034	84,000		940,000
April 30	Promotional expenses related to start-up of business	207,000		1,147,000
June 30	Operating losses for first 6 months	241,000		1,388,000

Instructions
Prepare the entry or entries necessary to correct this account. Assume that the patent has a useful life of 10 years.

3 **8** **E12-6 (Recording and Amortization of Intangibles)** Rolanda Marshall Company, organized in 2013, has set up a single account for all intangible assets. The following summary discloses the debit entries that have been recorded during 2014.

1/2/14	Purchased patent (8-year life)	$ 350,000
4/1/14	Purchase goodwill (indefinite life)	360,000
7/1/14	Purchased franchise with 10-year life; expiration date 7/1/24	450,000
8/1/14	Payment of copyright (5-year life)	156,000
9/1/14	Research and development costs	215,000
		$1,531,000

Instructions
Prepare the necessary entries to clear the Intangible Assets account and to set up separate accounts for distinct types of intangibles. Make the entries as of December 31, 2014, recording any necessary amortization and reflecting all balances accurately as of that date. (Use straight-line amortization.)

2 3 **E12-7 (Accounting for Trade Name)** In early January 2013, Outkast Corporation applied for a trade name, incurring legal costs of $16,000. In January 2014, Outkast incurred $7,800 of legal fees in a successful defense of its trade name.

Instructions
- **(a)** Compute 2013 amortization, 12/31/13 book value, 2014 amortization, and 12/31/14 book value if the company amortizes the trade name over 10 years.
- **(b)** Compute the 2014 amortization and the 12/31/14 book value, assuming that at the beginning of 2014, Outkast determines that the trade name will provide no future benefits beyond December 31, 2017.
- **(c)** Ignoring the response for part (b), compute the 2015 amortization and the 12/31/15 book value, assuming that at the beginning of 2015, based on new market research, Outkast determines that the fair value of the trade name is $15,000. Estimated total future cash flows from the trade name is $16,000 on January 3, 2015.

8 **E12-8 (Accounting for Organization Costs)** Horace Greeley Corporation was organized in 2013 and began operations at the beginning of 2014. The company is involved in interior design consulting services. The following costs were incurred prior to the start of operations.

Attorney's fees in connection with organization of the company	$15,000
Purchase of drafting and design equipment	10,000
Costs of meetings of incorporators to discuss organizational activities	7,000
State filing fees to incorporate	1,000
	$33,000

Instructions
- **(a)** Compute the total amount of organization costs incurred by Greeley.
- **(b)** Prepare the journal entry to record organization costs for 2014.

2 3 **E12-9 (Accounting for Patents, Franchises, and R&D)** Jimmy Carter Company has provided information
7 on intangible assets as follows.

A patent was purchased from Gerald Ford Company for $2,000,000 on January 1, 2013. Carter estimated the remaining useful life of the patent to be 10 years. The patent was carried in Ford's accounting records at a net book value of $2,000,000 when Ford sold it to Carter.

During 2014, a franchise was purchased from Ronald Reagan Company for $480,000. In addition, 5% of revenue from the franchise must be paid to Reagan. Revenue from the franchise for 2014 was $2,500,000. Carter estimates the useful life of the franchise to be 10 years and takes a full year's amortization in the year of purchase.

Carter incurred research and development costs in 2014 as follows.

Materials and equipment	$142,000
Personnel	189,000
Indirect costs	102,000
	$433,000

Carter estimates that these costs will be recouped by December 31, 2017. The materials and equipment purchased have no alternative uses.

On January 1, 2014, because of recent events in the field, Carter estimates that the remaining life of the patent purchased on January 1, 2013, is only 5 years from January 1, 2014.

Instructions
- **(a)** Prepare a schedule showing the intangibles section of Carter's balance sheet at December 31, 2014. Show supporting computations in good form.
- **(b)** Prepare a schedule showing the income statement effect (related to expenses) for the year ended December 31, 2014, as a result of the facts above. Show supporting computations in good form.

(AICPA adapted)

2 3 **E12-10 (Accounting for Patents)** During 2010, George Winston Corporation spent $170,000 in research and development costs. As a result, a new product called the New Age Piano was patented. The patent was obtained on October 1, 2010, and had a legal life of 20 years and a useful life of 10 years. Legal costs of $18,000 related to the patent were incurred as of October 1, 2010.

Instructions

(a) Prepare all journal entries required in 2010 and 2011 as a result of the transactions above.

(b) On June 1, 2012, Winston spent $9,480 to successfully prosecute a patent infringement suit. As a result, the estimate of useful life was extended to 12 years from June 1, 2012. Prepare all journal entries required in 2012 and 2013.

(c) In 2014, Winston determined that a competitor's product would make the New Age Piano obsolete and the patent worthless by December 31, 2015. Prepare all journal entries required in 2014 and 2015.

E12-11 (Accounting for Patents) Tones Industries has the following patents on its December 31, 2013, balance sheet.

Patent Item	Initial Cost	Date Acquired	Useful Life at Date Acquired
Patent A	$30,600	3/1/10	17 years
Patent B	$15,000	7/1/11	10 years
Patent C	$14,400	9/1/12	4 years

The following events occurred during the year ended December 31, 2014.

1. Research and development costs of $245,700 were incurred during the year.
2. Patent D was purchased on July 1 for $36,480. This patent has a useful life of 9½ years.
3. As a result of reduced demands for certain products protected by Patent B, a possible impairment of Patent B's value may have occurred at December 31, 2014. The controller for Tones estimates the expected future cash flows from Patent B will be as follows.

Year	Expected Future Cash Flows
2015	$2,000
2016	2,000
2017	2,000

The proper discount rate to be used for these flows is 8%. (Assume that the cash flows occur at the end of the year.)

Instructions

(a) Compute the total carrying amount of Tones' patents on its December 31, 2013, balance sheet.

(b) Compute the total carrying amount of Tones' patents on its December 31, 2014, balance sheet.

E12-12 (Accounting for Goodwill) Fred Moss, owner of Moss Interiors, is negotiating for the purchase of Zweifel Galleries. The balance sheet of Zweifel is given in an abbreviated form below.

ZWEIFEL GALLERIES
BALANCE SHEET
AS OF DECEMBER 31, 2014

Assets		Liabilities and Stockholders' Equity		
Cash	$100,000	Accounts payable		$ 50,000
Land	70,000	Notes payable (long-term)		300,000
Buildings (net)	200,000	Total liabilities		350,000
Equipment (net)	175,000	Common stock	$200,000	
Copyrights (net)	30,000	Retained earnings	25,000	225,000
Total assets	$575,000	Total liabilities and stockholders' equity		$575,000

Moss and Zweifel agree that:

1. Land is undervalued by $30,000.
2. Equipment is overvalued by $5,000.

Zweifel agrees to sell the gallery to Moss for $350,000.

Instructions

Prepare the entry to record the purchase of Zweifel Galleries on Moss's books.

3 5 **E12-13 (Accounting for Goodwill)** On July 1, 2014, Brigham Corporation purchased Young Company by paying $250,000 cash and issuing a $100,000 note payable to Steve Young. At July 1, 2014, the balance sheet of Young Company was as follows.

Cash	$ 50,000	Accounts payable	$200,000
Accounts receivable	90,000	Stockholders' equity	235,000
Inventory	100,000		$435,000
Land	40,000		
Buildings (net)	75,000		
Equipment (net)	70,000		
Trademarks	10,000		
	$435,000		

The recorded amounts all approximate current values except for land (fair value of $60,000), inventory (fair value of $125,000), and trademarks (fair value of $15,000).

Instructions

(a) Prepare the July 1 entry for Brigham Corporation to record the purchase.

(b) Prepare the December 31 entry for Brigham Corporation to record amortization of intangibles. The trademark has an estimated useful life of 4 years with a residual value of $3,000.

6 **E12-14 (Copyright Impairment)** Presented below is information related to copyrights owned by Walter de la Mare Company at December 31, 2014.

Cost	$8,600,000
Carrying amount	4,300,000
Expected future net cash flows	4,000,000
Fair value	3,200,000

Assume that Walter de la Mare Company will continue to use this copyright in the future. As of December 31, 2014, the copyright is estimated to have a remaining useful life of 10 years.

Instructions

(a) Prepare the journal entry (if any) to record the impairment of the asset at December 31, 2014. The company does not use accumulated amortization accounts.

(b) Prepare the journal entry to record amortization expense for 2015 related to the copyrights.

(c) The fair value of the copyright at December 31, 2015, is $3,400,000. Prepare the journal entry (if any) necessary to record the increase in fair value.

5 6 **E12-15 (Goodwill Impairment)** Presented below is net asset information related to the Carlos Division of Santana, Inc.

CARLOS DIVISION
NET ASSETS
AS OF DECEMBER 31, 2014
(IN MILLIONS)

Cash	$ 50
Accounts receivable	200
Property, plant, and equipment (net)	2,600
Goodwill	200
Less: Notes payable	(2,700)
Net assets	$ 350

The purpose of the Carlos Division is to develop a nuclear-powered aircraft. If successful, traveling delays associated with refueling could be substantially reduced. Many other benefits would also occur. To date, management has not had much success and is deciding whether a write-down at this time is appropriate. Management estimated its future net cash flows from the project to be $400 million. Management has also received an offer to purchase the division for $335 million. All identifiable assets' and liabilities' book and fair value amounts are the same.

Instructions

(a) Prepare the journal entry (if any) to record the impairment at December 31, 2014.

(b) At December 31, 2015, it is estimated that the division's fair value increased to $345 million. Prepare the journal entry (if any) to record this increase in fair value.

8 **E12-16 (Accounting for R&D Costs)** Leontyne Price Company from time to time embarks on a research program when a special project seems to offer possibilities. In 2013, the company expends $325,000 on a research project, but by the end of 2013 it is impossible to determine whether any benefit will be derived from it.

Instructions

(a) What account should be charged for the $325,000, and how should it be shown in the financial statements?

(b) The project is completed in 2014, and a successful patent is obtained. The R&D costs to complete the project are $110,000. The administrative and legal expenses incurred in obtaining patent number 472-1001-84 in 2014 total $16,000. The patent has an expected useful life of 5 years. Record these costs in journal entry form. Also, record patent amortization (full year) in 2014.

(c) In 2015, the company successfully defends the patent in extended litigation at a cost of $47,200, thereby extending the patent life to December 31, 2022. What is the proper way to account for this cost? Also, record patent amortization (full year) in 2015.

(d) Additional engineering and consulting costs incurred in 2015 required to advance the design of a product to the manufacturing stage total $60,000. These costs enhance the design of the product considerably. Discuss the proper accounting treatment for this cost.

8 **E12-17 (Accounting for R&D Costs)** Thomas More Company incurred the following costs during the current year in connection with its research and development activities.

Cost of equipment acquired that will have alternative uses in future R&D projects over the next 5 years (uses straight-line depreciation)	$280,000
Materials consumed in R&D projects	59,000
Consulting fees paid to outsiders for R&D projects	100,000
Personnel costs of persons involved in R&D projects	128,000
Indirect costs reasonably allocable to R&D projects	50,000
Materials purchased for future R&D projects	34,000

Instructions
Compute the amount to be reported as research and development expense by More on its current year income statement. Assume equipment is purchased at the beginning of the year.

EXERCISES SET B

See the book's companion website, at **www.wiley.com/college/kieso**, for an additional set of exercises.

PROBLEMS

2 **3** **P12-1 (Correct Intangible Assets Account)** Reichenbach Co., organized in 2013, has set up a single account for all intangible assets. The following summary discloses the debit entries that have been recorded during 2014 and 2015.

Intangible Assets

7/1/14	8-year franchise; expiration date 6/30/22	$ 48,000
10/1/14	Advance payment on laboratory space (2-year lease)	24,000
12/31/14	Net loss for 2013 including state incorporation fee, $1,000, and related legal fees of organizing, $5,000 (all fees incurred in 2013)	16,000
1/2/15	Patent purchased (10-year life)	84,000
3/1/15	Cost of developing a secret formula (indefinite life)	75,000
4/1/15	Goodwill purchased (indefinite life)	278,400
6/1/15	Legal fee for successful defense of patent purchased above	12,650
9/1/15	Research and development costs	160,000

Instructions
Prepare the necessary entries to clear the Intangible Assets account and to set up separate accounts for distinct types of intangibles. Make the entries as of December 31, 2015, recording any necessary amortization and reflecting all balances accurately as of that date. (Ignore income tax effects.)

2 **3** **P12-2 (Accounting for Patents)** Fields Laboratories holds a valuable patent (No. 758-6002-1A) on a precipitator that prevents certain types of air pollution. Fields does not manufacture or sell the products and processes it develops. Instead, it conducts research and develops products and processes which it patents, and then assigns the patents to manufacturers on a royalty basis. Occasionally it sells a patent. The history of Fields patent number 758-6002-1A is as follows.

Date	Activity	Cost
2005–2006	Research conducted to develop precipitator	$384,000
Jan. 2007	Design and construction of a prototype	87,600
March 2007	Testing of models	42,000
Jan. 2008	Fees paid engineers and lawyers to prepare patent application; patent granted June 30, 2008	59,500
Nov. 2009	Engineering activity necessary to advance the design of the precipitator to the manufacturing stage	81,500
Dec. 2010	Legal fees paid to successfully defend precipitator patent	42,000
April 2011	Research aimed at modifying the design of the patented precipitator	43,000
July 2015	Legal fees paid in unsuccessful patent infringement suit against a competitor	34,000

Fields assumed a useful life of 17 years when it received the initial precipitator patent. On January 1, 2013, it revised its useful life estimate downward to 5 remaining years. Amortization is computed for a full year if the cost is incurred prior to July 1, and no amortization for the year if the cost is incurred after June 30. The company's year ends December 31.

Instructions
Compute the carrying value of patent No. 758-6002-1A on each of the following dates:

   (a) December 31, 2008.
   (b) December 31, 2012.
   (c) December 31, 2015.

2 **3** **P12-3 (Accounting for Franchise, Patents, and Trademark)** Information concerning Sandro Corporation's intangible assets is as follows.

   1. On January 1, 2014, Sandro signed an agreement to operate as a franchisee of Hsian Copy Service, Inc. for an initial franchise fee of $75,000. Of this amount, $15,000 was paid when the agreement was signed, and the balance is payable in 4 annual payments of $15,000 each, beginning January 1, 2015. The agreement provides that the down payment is not refundable and no future services are required of the franchisor. The present value at January 1, 2014, of the 4 annual payments discounted at 14% (the implicit rate for a loan of this type) is $43,700. The agreement also provides that 5% of the revenue from the franchise must be paid to the franchisor annually. Sandro's revenue from the franchise for 2014 was $900,000. Sandro estimates the useful life of the franchise to be 10 years. (*Hint:* You may want to refer to Chapter 18 to determine the proper accounting treatment for the franchise fee and payments.)
   2. Sandro incurred $65,000 of experimental and development costs in its laboratory to develop a patent that was granted on January 2, 2014. Legal fees and other costs associated with registration of the patent totaled $17,600. Sandro estimates that the useful life of the patent will be 8 years.
   3. A trademark was purchased from Shanghai Company for $36,000 on July 1, 2011. Expenditures for successful litigation in defense of the trademark totaling $10,200 were paid on July 1, 2014. Sandro estimates that the useful life of the trademark will be 20 years from the date of acquisition.

Instructions
   (a) Prepare a schedule showing the intangible assets section of Sandro's balance sheet at December 31, 2014. Show supporting computations in good form.
   (b) Prepare a schedule showing all expenses resulting from the transactions that would appear on Sandro's income statement for the year ended December 31, 2014. Show supporting computations in good form.

(AICPA adapted)

8 **9** **P12-4 (Accounting for R&D Costs)** During 2012, Robin Wright Tool Company purchased a building site for its proposed research and development laboratory at a cost of $60,000. Construction of the building was started in 2012. The building was completed on December 31, 2013, at a cost of $320,000 and was placed in service on January 2, 2014. The estimated useful life of the building for depreciation purposes was 20 years. The straight-line method of depreciation was to be employed, and there was no estimated residual value.

Management estimates that about 50% of the projects of the research and development group will result in long-term benefits (i.e., at least 10 years) to the corporation. The remaining projects either benefit the current period or are abandoned before completion. A summary of the number of projects and the direct costs incurred in conjunction with the research and development activities for 2014 appears below.

	Number of Projects	Salaries and Employee Benefits	Other Expenses (excluding Building Depreciation Charges)
Completed projects with long-term benefits	15	$ 90,000	$50,000
Abandoned projects or projects that benefit the current period	10	65,000	15,000
Projects in process—results indeterminate	5	40,000	12,000
Total	30	$195,000	$77,000

Upon recommendation of the research and development group, Robin Wright Tool Company acquired a patent for manufacturing rights at a cost of $88,000. The patent was acquired on April 1, 2013, and has an economic life of 10 years.

Instructions

If generally accepted accounting principles were followed, how would the items above relating to research and development activities be reported on the following financial statements?

(a) The company's income statement for 2014.

(b) The company's balance sheet as of December 31, 2014.

Be sure to give account titles and amounts, and briefly justify your presentation.

(CMA adapted)

 P12-5 (Goodwill, Impairment) On July 31, 2014, Mexico Company paid $3,000,000 to acquire all of the common stock of Conchita Incorporated, which became a division of Mexico. Conchita reported the following balance sheet at the time of the acquisition.

Current assets	$ 800,000	Current liabilities	$ 600,000
Noncurrent assets	2,700,000	Long-term liabilities	500,000
Total assets	$3,500,000	Stockholders' equity	2,400,000
		Total liabilities and stockholders' equity	$3,500,000

It was determined at the date of the purchase that the fair value of the identifiable net assets of Conchita was $2,750,000. Over the next 6 months of operations, the newly purchased division experienced operating losses. In addition, it now appears that it will generate substantial losses for the foreseeable future. At December 31, 2014, Conchita reports the following balance sheet information.

Current assets	$ 450,000
Noncurrent assets (including goodwill recognized in purchase)	2,400,000
Current liabilities	(700,000)
Long-term liabilities	(500,000)
Net assets	$1,650,000

It is determined that the fair value of the Conchita Division is $1,850,000. The recorded amount for Conchita's net assets (excluding goodwill) is the same as fair value, except for property, plant, and equipment, which has a fair value $150,000 above the carrying value.

Instructions

(a) Compute the amount of goodwill recognized, if any, on July 31, 2014.

(b) Determine the impairment loss, if any, to be recorded on December 31, 2014.

(c) Assume that fair value of the Conchita Division is $1,600,000 instead of $1,850,000. Determine the impairment loss, if any, to be recorded on December 31, 2014.

(d) Prepare the journal entry to record the impairment loss, if any, and indicate where the loss would be reported in the income statement.

P12-6 (Comprehensive Intangible Assets) Montana Matt's Golf Inc. was formed on July 1, 2013, when Matt Magilke purchased the Old Master Golf Company. Old Master provides video golf instruction at kiosks in shopping malls. Magilke plans to integrate the instructional business into his golf equipment and accessory stores. Magilke paid $770,000 cash for Old Master. At the time, Old Master's balance sheet reported assets of $650,000 and liabilities of $200,000 (thus owners' equity was $450,000). The fair value of Old Master's assets is estimated to be $800,000. Included in the assets is the Old Master trade name with a fair value of $10,000 and a copyright on some instructional books with a fair value of $24,000. The trade name has a remaining life of 5 years and can be renewed at nominal cost indefinitely. The copyright has a remaining life of 40 years.

Instructions

(a) Prepare the intangible assets section of Montana Matt's Golf Inc. at December 31, 2013. How much amortization expense is included in Montana Matt's income for the year ended December 31, 2013? Show all supporting computations.

(b) Prepare the journal entry to record amortization expense for 2014. Prepare the intangible assets section of Montana Matt's Golf Inc. at December 31, 2014. (No impairments are required to be recorded in 2014.)

(c) At the end of 2015, Magilke is evaluating the results of the instructional business. Due to fierce competition from online and television (e.g., the Golf Channel), the Old Master reporting unit has been losing money. Its book value is now $500,000. The fair value of the Old Master reporting unit is $420,000. The implied value of goodwill is $90,000. Magilke has collected the following information related to the company's intangible assets.

Intangible Asset	Expected Cash Flows (undiscounted)	Fair Values
Trade names	$ 9,000	$ 3,000
Copyrights	30,000	25,000

Prepare the journal entries required, if any, to record impairments on Montana Matt's intangible assets. (Assume that any amortization for 2015 has been recorded.) Show supporting computations.

PROBLEMS SET B

See the book's companion website, at **www.wiley.com/college/kieso**, for an additional set of problems.

CONCEPTS FOR ANALYSIS

CA12-1 (Accounting for Pre-Opening Costs) After securing lease commitments from several major stores, Auer Shopping Center, Inc. was organized and built a shopping center in a growing suburb.

The shopping center would have opened on schedule on January 1, 2014, if it had not been struck by a severe tornado in December. Instead, it opened for business on October 1, 2014. All of the additional construction costs that were incurred as a result of the tornado were covered by insurance.

In July 2013, in anticipation of the scheduled January opening, a permanent staff had been hired to promote the shopping center, obtain tenants for the uncommitted space, and manage the property.

A summary of some of the costs incurred in 2013 and the first nine months of 2014 follows.

	2013	January 1, 2014 through September 30, 2014
Interest on mortgage bonds	$720,000	$540,000
Cost of obtaining tenants	300,000	360,000
Promotional advertising	540,000	557,000

The promotional advertising campaign was designed to familiarize shoppers with the center. Had it been known in time that the center would not open until October 2014, the 2013 expenditure for promotional advertising would not have been made. The advertising had to be repeated in 2014.

All of the tenants who had leased space in the shopping center at the time of the tornado accepted the October occupancy date on condition that the monthly rental charges for the first 9 months of 2014 be canceled.

Instructions

Explain how each of the costs for 2013 and the first 9 months of 2014 should be treated in the accounts of the shopping center corporation. Give the reasons for each treatment.

(AICPA adapted)

CA12-2 (Accounting for Patents) On June 30, 2014, your client, Ferry Company, was granted two patents covering plastic cartons that it had been producing and marketing profitably for the past 3 years. One patent covers the manufacturing process, and the other covers the related products.

Ferry executives tell you that these patents represent the most significant breakthrough in the industry in the past 30 years. The products have been marketed under the registered trademarks Evertight, Duratainer, and Sealrite. Licenses under the patents have already been granted by your client to other manufacturers in the United States and abroad, and are producing substantial royalties.

On July 1, Ferry commenced patent infringement actions against several companies whose names you recognize as those of substantial and prominent competitors. Ferry's management is optimistic that these suits will result in a permanent injunction against the manufacture and sale of the infringing products as well as collection of damages for loss of profits caused by the alleged infringement.

The financial vice president has suggested that the patents be recorded at the discounted value of expected net royalty receipts.

Instructions
- **(a)** What is the meaning of "discounted value of expected net receipts"? Explain.
- **(b)** How would such a value be calculated for net royalty receipts?
- **(c)** What basis of valuation for Ferry's patents would be generally accepted in accounting? Give supporting reasons for this basis.
- **(d)** Assuming no practical problems of implementation, and ignoring generally accepted accounting principles, what is the preferable basis of valuation for patents? Explain.
- **(e)** What would be the preferable theoretical basis of amortization? Explain.
- **(f)** What recognition, if any, should be made of the infringement litigation in the financial statements for the year ending September 30, 2014? Discuss.

(AICPA adapted)

CA12-3 (Accounting for Research and Development Costs) Cuevas Co. is in the process of developing a revolutionary new product. A new division of the company was formed to develop, manufacture, and market this new product. As of year-end (December 31, 2014), the new product has not been manufactured for resale. However, a prototype unit was built and is in operation.

Throughout 2014, the new division incurred certain costs. These costs include design and engineering studies, prototype manufacturing costs, administrative expenses (including salaries of administrative personnel), and market research costs. In addition, approximately $900,000 in equipment (with an estimated useful life of 10 years) was purchased for use in developing and manufacturing the new product. Approximately $315,000 of this equipment was built specifically for the design development of the new product. The remaining $585,000 of equipment was used to manufacture the pre-production prototype and will be used to manufacture the new product once it is in commercial production.

Instructions
- **(a)** How are "research" and "development" defined in the authoritative literature (GAAP)?
- **(b)** Briefly indicate the practical and conceptual reasons for the conclusion reached by the Financial Accounting Standards Board on accounting and reporting practices for research and development costs.
- **(c)** In accordance with GAAP, how should the various costs of Cuevas described above be recorded on the financial statements for the year ended December 31, 2014?

(AICPA adapted)

CA12-4 (Accounting for Research and Development Costs) Czeslaw Corporation's research and development department has an idea for a project it believes will culminate in a new product that would be very profitable for the company. Because the project will be very expensive, the department requests approval from the company's controller, Jeff Reid.

Reid recognizes that corporate profits have been down lately and is hesitant to approve a project that will incur significant expenses that cannot be capitalized due to the requirements of the authoritative literature. He knows that if they hire an outside firm that does the work and obtains a patent for the process, Czeslaw Corporation can purchase the patent from the outside firm and record the expenditure as an asset. Reid knows that the company's own R&D department is first-rate, and he is confident they can do the work well.

Instructions
Answer the following questions.
- **(a)** Who are the stakeholders in this situation?
- **(b)** What are the ethical issues involved?
- **(c)** What should Reid do?

USING YOUR JUDGMENT

FINANCIAL REPORTING

Financial Reporting Problem

P&G **The Procter & Gamble Company (P&G)**

The financial statements of P&G are presented in Appendix 5B. The company's complete annual report, including the notes to the financial statements, can be accessed at the book's companion website, **www.wiley.com/college/kieso**.

Instructions

Refer to P&G's financial statements and the accompanying notes to answer the following questions.

(a) Does P&G report any intangible assets, especially goodwill, in its 2011 financial statements and accompanying notes?

(b) How much research and development (R&D) cost was expensed by P&G in 2010 and 2011? What percentage of sales revenue and net income did P&G spend on R&D in 2010 and 2011?

Comparative Analysis Case

The Coca-Cola Company and PepsiCo, Inc.

Instructions

Go to the book's companion website and use information found there to answer the following questions related to **The** Coca-Cola Company and PepsiCo, Inc.

(a) (1) What amounts for intangible assets were reported in their respective balance sheets by Coca-Cola and PepsiCo?

(2) What percentage of total assets is each of these reported amounts?

(3) What was the change in the amount of intangibles from 2010 to 2011 for Coca-Cola and PepsiCo?

(b) (1) On what basis and over what periods of time did Coca-Cola and PepsiCo amortize their intangible assets?

(2) What were the amounts of accumulated amortization reported by Coca-Cola and PepsiCo at the end of 2011 and 2010?

(3) What was the composition of the identifiable and unidentifiable intangible assets reported by Coca-Cola and PepsiCo at the end of 2011?

Financial Statement Analysis Cases

Case 1: Merck and Johnson & Johnson

Merck & Co., Inc. and Johnson & Johnson are two leading producers of health-care products. Each has considerable assets, and each expends considerable funds each year toward the development of new products. The development of a new health-care product is often very expensive, and risky. New products frequently must undergo considerable testing before approval for distribution to the public. For example, it took Johnson & Johnson 4 years and $200 million to develop its 1-DAY ACUVUE contact lenses. Below are some basic data compiled from the financial statements of these two companies.

(all dollars in millions)	Johnson & Johnson	Merck
Total assets	$53,317	$42,573
Total revenue	47,348	22,939
Net income	8,509	5,813
Research and development expense	5,203	4,010
Intangible assets	11,842	2,765

Instructions

(a) What kinds of intangible assets might a health-care products company have? Does the composition of these intangibles matter to investors—that is, would it be perceived differently if all of Merck's intangibles were goodwill than if all of its intangibles were patents?

(b) Suppose the president of Merck has come to you for advice. He has noted that by eliminating research and development expenditures the company could have reported $4 billion more in net income. He is frustrated because much of the research never results in a product, or the products take years to develop. He says shareholders are eager for higher returns, so he is considering eliminating research and development expenditures for at least a couple of years. What would you advise?

(c) The notes to Merck's financial statements note that Merck has goodwill of $1.1 billion. Where does recorded goodwill come from? Is it necessarily a good thing to have a lot of goodwill on a company's books?

Case 2: Analysis of Goodwill

As a new intern for the local branch office of a national brokerage firm, you are excited to get an assignment that allows you to use your accounting expertise. Your supervisor provides you the spreadsheet below, which contains data for the most recent quarter for three companies that the firm has been recommending to its clients as "buys." Each of the companies' returns on assets has outperformed their industry cohorts in the past. But, given recent challenges in their markets, there is concern that the companies may experience operating challenges and lower earnings. (All numbers in millions, except return on assets.)

Company	Fair Value of Company	Book Value (Net Assets)	Carrying Value of Goodwill	Return on Assets
Sprint Nextel	$36,361	$51,271	$30,718	3.5%
Washington Mutual	11,742	23,941	9,062	2.4%
E* Trade Financial	1,639	4,104	2,035	5.6%

Instructions

(a) The fair value for each of these companies is lower than the corresponding book value. What implications does this have for each company's future prospects?

(b) To date, none of these companies has recorded goodwill impairments. Your supervisor suspects that they will need to record impairments in the near future, but he is unsure about the goodwill impairment rules. Is it likely that these companies will recognize impairments? Explain.

(c) Estimate the amount of goodwill impairment for each company and prepare the journal entry to record the impairment. For each company, you may assume that the book value less the carrying value of the goodwill approximates the fair value of the companies' net assets.

(d) Discuss the effects of your entries in part (c) on your evaluation of these companies based on the return on assets ratio.

Accounting, Analysis, and Principles

On January 2, 2014, Raconteur Corp. reported the following intangible assets: (1) copyright with a carrying value of $15,000, and (2) a trade name with a carrying value of $8,500. The trade name has a remaining life of 5 years and can be renewed at nominal cost indefinitely. The copyright has a remaining life of 10 years.

At December 31, 2014, Raconteur assessed the intangible assets for possible impairment and developed the following information.

	Estimated Undiscounted Expected Future Cash Flows	Estimated Fair Value
Copyright	$20,000	$16,000
Trade name	10,000	5,000

Accounting

Prepare any journal entries required for Raconteur's intangible assets at December 31, 2014.

Analysis

Many stock analysts indicate a preference for less-volatile operating income measures. Such measures make it easier to predict future income and cash flows, using reported income measures. How does the accounting for impairments of intangible assets affect the volatility of operating income?

Principles

Many accounting issues involve a trade-off between the primary characteristics of relevant and representationally faithful information. How does the accounting for intangible asset impairments reflect this trade-off?

BRIDGE TO THE PROFESSION

 ## Professional Research: FASB Codification

King Company is contemplating the purchase of a smaller company, which is a distributor of King's products. Top management of King is convinced that the acquisition will result in significant synergies in its selling and distribution functions. The financial management group (of which you are a part) has been asked to prepare some analysis of the effects of the acquisition on the combined company's financial statements. This is the first acquisition for King, and some of the senior staff insist that based on their recollection of goodwill accounting, any goodwill recorded on the acquisition will result in a "drag" on future earnings for goodwill amortization. Other younger members on the staff argue that goodwill accounting has changed. Your supervisor asks you to research this issue.

Instructions

If your school has a subscription to the FASB Codification, go to *http://aaahq.org/asclogin.cfm* to log in and prepare responses to the following. Provide Codification references for your responses.

(a) Identify the accounting literature that addresses goodwill and other intangible assets.

(b) Define goodwill.

(c) Is goodwill subject to amortization? Explain.

(d) When goodwill is recognized by a subsidiary, should it be tested for impairment at the consolidated level or the subsidiary level? Discuss.

Additional Professional Resources

See the book's companion website, at **www.wiley.com/college/kieso**, for professional simulations as well as other study resources.

IFRS > INSIGHTS

There are some significant differences between IFRS and GAAP in the accounting for both intangible assets and impairments. IFRS related to intangible assets is presented in *IAS 38* ("Intangible Assets"). IFRS related to impairments is found in *IAS 36* ("Impairment of Assets").

10 **LEARNING OBJECTIVE**
Compare the accounting for intangible assets under GAAP and IFRS.

RELEVANT FACTS

Following are the key similarities and differences between GAAP and IFRS related to intangible assets.

Similarities

- Like GAAP, under IFRS intangible assets (1) lack physical substance and (2) are not financial instruments. In addition, under IFRS an intangible asset is identifiable. To be identifiable, an intangible asset must either be separable from the company (can be sold or transferred) or it arises from a contractual or legal right from which economic benefits will flow to the company. Fair value is used as the measurement basis for intangible assets under IFRS, if it is more clearly evident.

- With issuance of a recent converged statement on business combinations (*IFRS 3* and *SFAS No. 141—Revised*), IFRS and GAAP are very similar for intangibles acquired in a business combination. That is, companies recognize an intangible asset separately from goodwill if the intangible represents contractual or legal rights or is capable of being separated or divided and sold, transferred, licensed, rented, or exchanged. In addition, under both GAAP and IFRS, companies recognize acquired in-process research and development (IPR&D) as a separate intangible asset if it meets the definition of an intangible asset and its fair value can be measured reliably.

- As in GAAP, under IFRS the costs associated with research and development are segregated into the two components. Costs in the research phase are always expensed under both IFRS and GAAP.

Differences

- IFRS permits revaluation on limited-life intangible assets. Revaluations are not permitted for goodwill and other indefinite-life intangible assets.

- IFRS permits some capitalization of internally generated intangible assets (e.g., brand value) if it is probable there will be a future benefit and the amount can be reliably measured. GAAP requires expensing of all costs associated with internally generated intangibles.

- IFRS requires an impairment test at each reporting date for long-lived assets and intangibles, and records an impairment if the asset's carrying amount exceeds its recoverable amount. The recoverable amount is the higher of the asset's fair value less costs to sell and its value-in-use. **Value-in-use** is the future cash flows to be derived from the particular assets, discounted to present value. Under GAAP, impairment loss is measured as the excess of the carrying amount over the asset's fair value.

- IFRS allows reversal of impairment losses when there has been a change in economic conditions or in the expected use of limited-life intangibles. Under GAAP, impairment losses cannot be reversed for assets to be held and used; the impairment loss results in a new cost basis for the asset. IFRS and GAAP are similar in the accounting for impairments of assets held for disposal.

- Under IFRS, costs in the development phase of a research and development project are capitalized once technological feasibility (referred to as **economic viability**) is achieved.

ABOUT THE NUMBERS
Development Costs

Businesses frequently incur costs on a variety of intangible resources, such as scientific or technological knowledge, market research, intellectual property, and brand names. These costs are commonly referred to as research and development (R&D) costs. Intangible assets that might arise from these expenditures include patents, computer software, copyrights, and trademarks. For example, Nokia incurred R&D costs to develop its cell phones, resulting in patents related to its technology. In determining the accounting for these costs, Nokia must determine whether its R&D project is at a sufficiently advanced stage to be considered economically viable. To perform this assessment, Nokia evaluates costs incurred during the research phase and the development phase. Illustration IFRS12-1 indicates the two stages of research and development activities, along with the accounting treatment for costs incurred during these phases.

ILLUSTRATION IFRS12-1
Research and Development Stages

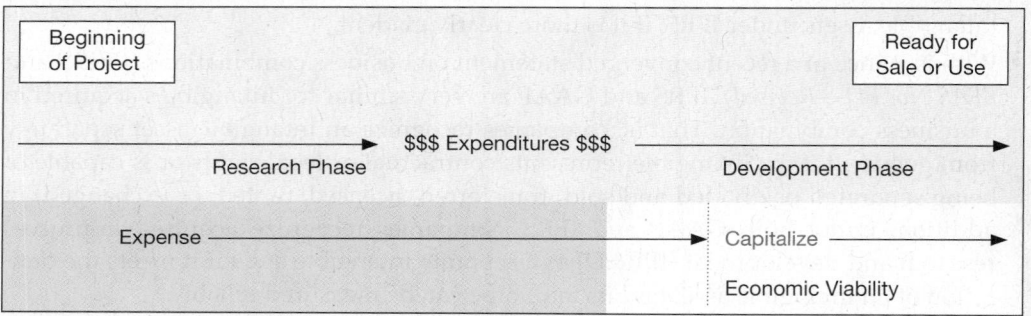

As indicated, all costs incurred in the research phase are expensed as incurred. Once a project moves to the development phase, certain development costs are capitalized. Specifically, development costs are capitalized when certain criteria are met, indicating that an economically viable intangible asset will result from the R&D project. In essence, economic viability indicates that the project is far enough along in the process such that the economic benefits of the R&D project will flow to the company. Therefore, development costs incurred from that point forward meet the recognition criteria and should be recorded as an intangible asset.

In summary, companies expense all research phase costs and some development phase costs. Certain development costs are capitalized once economic viability criteria are met.

Impairment of Intangible Assets

An intangible asset is **impaired** when a company is not able to recover the asset's carrying amount either through using it or by selling it. As discussed in Chapter 11, to determine whether a long-lived asset (property, plant, and equipment, or intangible asset) is impaired, a review is made of the asset's cash-generating ability through use or sale. If the carrying amount is higher than the recoverable amount, the difference is an impairment loss. If the recoverable amount is greater than the carrying amount, no impairment is recorded. The specific procedures for recording impairments depend on the type of intangible asset—limited-life or indefinite-life (including goodwill).

Impairment of Limited-Life Intangibles

The rules that apply to **impairments of property, plant, and equipment also apply to limited-life intangibles**. At each statement of financial position date, a company should review limited-life intangibles for impairment. Information indicating that an impairment test should be performed might be internal (e.g., physical damage or adverse changes in performance) or external (e.g., adverse changes in the business or regulatory environment, or technological or competitive developments). If there is an indication that an intangible asset is impaired, the company performs an impairment test: compare the carrying value of the intangible asset to the recoverable amount.

Recall that **recoverable amount** is defined as the higher of fair value less costs to sell or value-in-use. Fair value less costs to sell means what the asset could be sold for after deducting costs of disposal. Value-in-use is the present value of cash flows expected from the future use and eventual sale of the asset at the end of its useful life. The **impairment loss** is the carrying amount of the asset less the recoverable amount of the impaired asset. As with other impairments, the loss is reported in profit or loss.

Companies generally report the loss in the "Other income and expense" section. To illustrate, assume that Lerch, Inc. has a patent on how to extract oil from shale rock, with a carrying value of $5,000,000 at the end of 2014. Unfortunately, several recent non-shale-oil discoveries adversely affected the demand for shale-oil technology, indicating that the patent is impaired. Lerch determines the recoverable amount for the patent, based on value-in-use (because there is no active market for the patent). Lerch estimates the patent's value-in-use at $2,000,000, based on the discounted expected future net cash flows at its market rate of interest. Illustration IFRS12-2 shows the impairment loss computation (based on value-in-use).

Carrying value of patent	$5,000,000
Recoverable amount (based on value-in-use)	(2,000,000)
Loss on impairment	$3,000,000

ILLUSTRATION IFRS12-2
Computation of Loss on Impairment of Patent

Lerch records this loss as follows.

Loss on Impairment	3,000,000	
Patents		3,000,000

After recognizing the impairment, the recoverable amount of $2,000,000 is the new cost basis of the patent. Lerch should amortize the patent's recoverable amount (new carrying amount) over its remaining useful life or legal life, whichever is shorter.

Reversal of Impairment Loss

What happens if a review in a future year indicates that an intangible asset is no longer impaired because the recoverable amount of the asset is higher than the carrying amount? In that case, the impairment loss may be reversed. To illustrate, continuing the Lerch patent example, assume that the remaining life of the patent is five years with zero residual value. Recall the carrying value of the patent after impairment is $2,000,000 ($5,000,000 − $3,000,000). Thus, Lerch's amortization is $400,000 ($2,000,000 ÷ 5) over the remaining five years of the patent's life. The amortization expense and related carrying amount after the impairment is shown in Illustration IFRS12-3.

Early in 2016, based on improving conditions in the market for shale-oil technology, Lerch remeasures the recoverable amount of the patent to be $1,750,000. In this case, Lerch reverses a portion of the recognized impairment loss with the following entry.

Patents ($1,750,000 − $1,600,000)	150,000	
Recovery of Loss on Impairment		150,000

ILLUSTRATION IFRS12-3
Post-Impairment Carrying Value of Patent

Year	Amortization Expense	Carrying Amount	
2015	$400,000	$1,600,000	($2,000,000 − $400,000)
2016	400,000	1,200,000	($1,600,000 − $400,000)
2017	400,000	800,000	($1,200,000 − $400,000)
2018	400,000	400,000	($800,000 − $400,000)
2019	400,000	0	($400,000 − $400,000)

The recovery of the impairment loss is reported in the "Other income and expense" section of the income statement. The carrying amount of the patent is now $1,750,000 ($1,600,000 + $150,000). Assuming the remaining life of the patent is four years, Lerch records $437,500 ($1,750,000 ÷ 4) amortization expense in 2016.

Impairment of Indefinite-Life Intangibles Other Than Goodwill

Companies test indefinite-life intangibles (including goodwill) for impairment annually. To illustrate, assume that Arcon Radio purchased a broadcast license for $2,000,000. The license is renewable every 10 years if the company provides appropriate service and does not violate Government Communications Commission (GCC) rules. Arcon Radio has renewed the license with the GCC twice, at a minimal cost. Because it expects cash flows to last indefinitely, Arcon reports the license as an indefinite-life intangible asset. Recently, the GCC decided to issue significantly more of these licenses, which will reduce the value of Arcon's license. Based on recent auctions of similar licenses, Arcon Radio estimates the fair value less costs to sell (the recoverable amount) of its license to be $1,500,000. Arcon therefore reports an impairment loss of $500,000, computed as follows.

ILLUSTRATION IFRS12-4
Computation of Loss on Impairment of Broadcast License

Carrying value of broadcast license	$ 2,000,000
Recoverable amount (based on fair value less costs to sell)	(1,500,000)
Loss on impairment	$ 500,000

Impairment of Goodwill

The timing of the impairment test for goodwill is the same as that for other indefinite-life intangibles. That is, companies must test goodwill at least annually. However, because goodwill generates cash flows only in combination with other assets, the impairment test is conducted based on the cash-generating unit to which the goodwill is assigned. Recall from our discussion in Chapter 11 that companies identify a **cash-generating unit** based on the smallest identifiable group of assets that generate cash flows independently of the cash flows from other assets. Under IFRS, when a company records goodwill in a business combination, it must assign the goodwill to the cash-generating unit that is expected to benefit from the synergies and other benefits arising from the business combination.

To illustrate, assume that Kohlbuy Corporation has three divisions. It purchased one division, Pritt Products, four years ago for $2 million. Unfortunately, Pritt experienced operating losses over the last three quarters. Kohlbuy management is now reviewing the division (the cash-generating unit), for purposes of its annual impairment testing. Illustration IFRS12-5 lists the Pritt Division's net assets, including the associated goodwill of $900,000 from the purchase.

ILLUSTRATION IFRS12-5
Net Assets of Pritt Division, Including Goodwill

Property, plant, and equipment (net)	$ 800,000
Goodwill	900,000
Inventory	700,000
Receivables	300,000
Cash	200,000
Accounts and notes payable	(500,000)
Net assets	$2,400,000

Kohlbuy determines the recoverable amount for the Pritt Division to be $2,800,000, based on a value-in-use estimate. **Because the recoverable amount of the division exceeds the carrying amount of the net assets, Kohlbuy does not recognize any impairment.** However, if the recoverable amount for the Pritt Division were less than the carrying amount of the net assets, then Kohlbuy must record an impairment. To illustrate, assume that the recoverable amount for the Pritt Division is $1,900,000 instead of $2,800,000. Illustration IFRS12-6 computes the amount of the impairment loss to be recorded.

Recoverable amount of Pritt Division	$ 1,900,000	
Net identifiable assets	(2,400,000)	
Loss on impairment	$ 500,000	

ILLUSTRATION IFRS12-6
Determination of Impairment for the Pritt Division

Kohlbuy makes the following entry to record the impairment.

Loss on Impairment	500,000	
Goodwill		500,000

Following this entry, the carrying value of the goodwill is $400,000 ($900,000 − $500,000). If conditions change in subsequent periods, such that the recoverable amount of the Pritt Division's assets other than goodwill exceeds their carrying value, Kohlbuy may reverse an impairment loss on the Pritt Division assets other than goodwill. **Goodwill impairment loss reversals are not permitted.**

ON THE HORIZON

The IASB and FASB have identified a project, in a very preliminary stage, which would consider expanded recognition of internally generated intangible assets. As indicated, IFRS permits more recognition of intangibles compared to GAAP. Thus, it will be challenging to develop converged standards for intangible assets, given the long-standing prohibition on capitalizing internally generated intangible assets and research and development in GAAP. Learn more about the timeline for the intangible asset project at the IASB website *http://www.iasb.org/current_Projects/IASB_Projects/IASB_Work_Plan.htm.*

IFRS SELF-TEST QUESTIONS

1. All of the following are key similarities between GAAP and IFRS with respect to accounting for intangible assets **except**:
    (a) for accounting purposes, costs associated with research and development activities are segregated into the two components.
    (b) the accounting for intangibles acquired in a business combination.
    (c) recovery of impairments on intangibles other than goodwill.
    (d) the accounting for impairments of assets held for disposal.
2. Research and development costs are:
    (a) expensed under GAAP.
    (b) expensed under IFRS.
    (c) expensed under both GAAP and IFRS.
    (d) None of the above.
3. Which of the following statements is **correct**?
    (a) Both IFRS and GAAP permit revaluation of property, plant, and equipment, and intangible assets (except for goodwill).
    (b) GAAP permits capitalization of development costs.
    (c) IFRS requires capitalization of research and development costs once economic viability is met.
    (d) IFRS requires capitalization of development costs once economic viability is met.

4. A loss on impairment of an intangible asset under IFRS is the asset's:
    (a) carrying amount less the expected future net cash flows.
    (b) carrying amount less its recoverable amount.
    (c) recoverable amount less the expected future net cash flows.
    (d) book value less its fair value.
5. Recovery of impairment is recognized under IFRS for all the following **except**:
    (a) patent held for sale.   (c) trademark.
    (b) patent held for use.   (d) goodwill.

IFRS CONCEPTS AND APPLICATION

IFRS12-1 Where can authoritative IFRS guidance related to intangible assets be found?

IFRS12-2 Briefly describe some of the similarities and differences between GAAP and IFRS with respect to the accounting for intangible assets.

IFRS12-3 Briefly discuss the convergence efforts that are underway in the area of intangible assets.

IFRS12-4 Treasure Land Corporation incurred the following costs in 2014.

Cost of laboratory research aimed at discovery of new knowledge	$120,000
Cost of testing in search for product alternatives	100,000
Cost of engineering activity required to advance the design of a product to the manufacturing stage	210,000
Prototype testing subsequent to meeting economic viability	75,000
	$505,000

Prepare the necessary 2014 journal entry(ies) for Treasure Land.

IFRS12-5 Indicate whether the following items are capitalized or expensed in the current year.

(a) Purchase cost of a patent from a competitor.
(b) Research costs.
(c) Development costs (after achieving economic viability).
(d) Organizational costs.
(e) Costs incurred internally to create goodwill.

IFRS12-6 Kenoly Corporation owns a patent that has a carrying amount of $300,000. Kenoly expects future net cash flows from this patent to total $210,000 over its remaining life of 10 years. The recoverable amount of the patent is $110,000. Prepare Kenoly's journal entry, if necessary, to record the loss on impairment.

IFRS12-7 Use the information in IFRS12-6. Assume that at the end of the year following the impairment (after recording amortization expense), the estimated recoverable amount for the patent is $130,000. Prepare Kenoly's journal entry, if needed.

IFRS12-8 Waters Corporation purchased Johnson Company 3 years ago and at that time recorded goodwill of $400,000. The Johnson Division's net assets, including the goodwill, have a carrying amount of $800,000. The recoverable amount of the division is estimated to be $1,000,000. Prepare Waters' journal entry, if necessary, to record impairment of the goodwill.

IFRS12-9 Use the information provided in IFRS12-8. Assume that the recoverable amount of the division is estimated to be $750,000. Prepare Waters' journal entry, if necessary, to record impairment of the goodwill.

IFRS12-10 Margaret Avery Company from time to time embarks on a research program when a special project seems to offer possibilities. In 2012, the company expends $325,000 on a research project, but by the end of 2012, it is impossible to determine whether any benefit will be derived from it.

(a) What account should be charged for the $325,000, and how should it be shown in the financial statements?
(b) The project is completed in 2013, and a successful patent is obtained. The R&D costs to complete the project are $130,000 ($36,000 of these costs were incurred after achieving economic viability). The

administrative and legal expenses incurred in obtaining patent number 472-1001-84 in 2013 total $24,000. The patent has an expected useful life of 5 years. Record these costs in journal entry form. Also, record patent amortization (full year) in 2013.

(c) In 2014, the company successfully defends the patent in extended litigation at a cost of $47,200, thereby extending the patent life to December 31, 2021. What is the proper way to account for this cost? Also, record patent amortization (full year) in 2014.

(d) Additional engineering and consulting costs incurred in 2014 required to advance the design of a new version of the product to the manufacturing stage total $60,000. These costs enhance the design of the product considerably, but it is highly uncertain if there will be a market for the new version of the product. Discuss the proper accounting treatment for this cost.

Professional Research

IFRS12-11 King Company is contemplating the purchase of a smaller company, which is a distributor of King's products. Top management of King is convinced that the acquisition will result in significant synergies in its selling and distribution functions. The financial management group (of which you are a part) has been asked to analyze the effects of the acquisition on the combined company's financial statements. This is the first acquisition for King, and some of the senior staff insist that based on their recollection of goodwill accounting, any goodwill recorded on the acquisition will result in a "drag" on future earnings for goodwill amortization. Other younger members on the staff argue that goodwill accounting has changed. Your supervisor asks you to research this issue.

Instructions

Access the IFRS authoritative literature at the IASB website (*http://eifrs.iasb.org/*). (Click on the IFRS tab and then register for free eIFRS access if necessary.) When you have accessed the documents, you can use the search tool in your Internet browser to respond to the following questions. (Provide paragraph citations.)

(a) Identify the accounting literature that addresses goodwill and other intangible assets.
(b) Define goodwill.
(c) Is goodwill subject to amortization? Explain.
(d) When goodwill is recognized by a subsidiary, should it be tested for impairment at the consolidated level or the subsidiary level? Discuss.

International Financial Reporting Problem
Marks and Spencer plc

IFRS12-12 The financial statements of **Marks and Spencer plc (M&S)** are available at the book's companion website or can be accessed at *http://corporate.marksandspencer.com/documents/publications/2012/Annual_Report_2012*.

Instructions

Refer to M&S's financial statements and the accompanying notes to answer the following questions.

(a) Does M&S report any intangible assets and goodwill in its financial statements and accompanying notes? Briefly explain.
(b) How much selling and marketing expenses does M&S report in 2011 and 2012? Briefly discuss the significance of these expenses to M&S's operating results.

ANSWERS TO IFRS SELF-TEST QUESTIONS

1. c **2.** a **3.** d **4.** b **5.** d

Remember to check the book's companion website to find additional resources for this chapter.

13 Current Liabilities and Contingencies

After studying this chapter, you should be able to:

1 Describe the nature, type, and valuation of current liabilities.

2 Explain the classification issues of short-term debt expected to be refinanced.

3 Identify types of employee-related liabilities.

4 Identify the criteria used to account for and disclose gain and loss contingencies.

5 Explain the accounting for different types of loss contingencies.

6 Indicate how to present and analyze liabilities and contingencies.

Now You See It, Now You Don't

A look at the liabilities side of the balance sheet of the company **Beru AG Corporation**, dated March 31, 2003, shows how international standards have changed regarding the reporting of financial information. Here is how one liability was shown on this date:

Anticipated losses arising from pending transactions	3,285,000 euros

Do you believe a liability should be reported for such transactions? *Anticipated losses* means the losses have not yet occurred. *Pending transactions* means that the condition that might cause the loss has also not occurred. So where is the liability? To whom does the company owe something? Where is the obligation?

German accounting rules in 2003 were permissive. They allowed companies to report liabilities for possible future events. In essence, the establishment of this general-purpose "liability" provides a buffer for Beru if losses do materialize. If you take a more skeptical view, you might say the accounting rules let Beru smooth its income by charging expenses in good years and reducing expenses in bad years.

The story has a happy ending: European companies switched to International Financial Reporting Standards (IFRS) in 2005. Under IFRS, liabilities like "Anticipated losses arising from pending transactions" disappear. So when we look at Beru's 2005 financial statements, we find a note stating that the company has reported as liabilities only obligations arising from past transactions that can be reasonably estimated.

Standard-setters continue to work on the financial reporting of certain "contingent" liabilities, such as those related to pending lawsuits and other possible losses for which a company might be liable. As you will learn in this chapter, standard-setters have provided much more transparency in reporting liability-type transactions. However, much still needs to be done. For example, the IASB is considering major changes in how to recognize and measure contingent liabilities. The task will not be easy. Consider a simple illustration involving a company that sells hamburgers:

- The hamburgers are sold in a jurisdiction where the law states that the seller must pay $100,000 to each customer that purchases a contaminated hamburger;
- At the end of the reporting period, the company has sold one hamburger; and
- Past experience indicates there is a one in a million chance that a hamburger sold by the entity is contaminated. No other information is available.

Does the company have a liability? What is the conceptual justification, if any, to record a liability or for that matter, not to record a liability? And if you conclude that the sale of the hamburger results in a liability, how do you measure it? Another way to ask the question is whether the hamburger issue is a recognition issue or a measurement issue. This example illustrates some of the difficult questions that the IASB faces in this area.

The FASB recently proposed expanded disclosure about the nature of contingencies, more quantitative and qualitative background on contingencies, and, maybe most welcome of all, required tabular presentation of the changes in contingencies, including explanation of the changes. Note that these disclosures are similar to those required in IFRS. What's not to like about these enhanced disclosures? Well quite a bit,

CONCEPTUAL FOCUS

> See the **Underlying Concepts** on pages 702, 707, 712, 721, and 725.
> Read the **Evolving Issue** on page 730 for a discussion of how to account for greenhouse gases.

INTERNATIONAL FOCUS

> See the **International Perspectives** on pages 706, 727, and 729.
> Read the **IFRS Insights** on pages 753–761 for a discussion of:
  —Refinancing criteria
  —Provisions
  —Contingencies

according to early responses by some companies and the legal profession. These parties are concerned that the information in these enhanced disclosures could be used against them in a lawsuit, and they are voicing strong opposition to the proposed rules. We do not know the end of this liability story. However, the controversy over the proposed rules illustrates the challenges of developing accounting rules for liabilities that meet the needs of investors while avoiding harm to the companies reporting the information.

PREVIEW OF CHAPTER   13

As our opening story indicates, the convergence of GAAP and IFRS should lead to improved reporting of liabilities. In this chapter, we explain the basic issues related to accounting and reporting for current and contingent liabilities. The content and organization of the chapter are as follows.

Current Liabilities and Contingencies

Current Liabilities	Contingencies	Presentation and Analysis
• Accounts payable • Notes payable • Current maturities of long-term debt • Short-term obligations • Dividends payable • Customer advances and deposits, unearned revenues • Taxes payable • Employee-related liabilities	• Gain contingencies • Loss contingencies	• Presentation of current liabilities • Presentation of contingencies • Analysis of current liabilities

CURRENT LIABILITIES

The question, "What is a liability?" is not easy to answer. For example, is preferred stock a liability or an ownership claim? The first reaction is to say that preferred stock is in fact an ownership claim, and companies should report it as part of stockholders' equity. In fact, preferred stock has many elements of debt as well.[1] The issuer (and in some cases the holder) often has the right to call the stock within a specific period of time—making it similar to a repayment of principal. The dividend on the preferred stock is in many cases almost guaranteed (the cumulative provision)—making it look like interest. As a result, preferred stock is but one of many financial instruments that are difficult to classify.[2]

Underlying Concepts

To determine the appropriate classification of specific financial instruments, companies need proper definitions of assets, liabilities, and equities. They often use the conceptual framework definitions as the basis for resolving controversial classification issues.

To help resolve some of these controversies, the FASB, as part of its conceptual framework, defined liabilities as **"probable future sacrifices of economic benefits arising from present obligations of a particular entity to transfer assets or provide services to other entities in the future as a result of past transactions or events."**[3] In other words, a liability has three essential characteristics:

1. It is a present obligation that entails settlement by probable future transfer or use of cash, goods, or services.

2. It is an unavoidable obligation.

3. The transaction or other event creating the obligation has already occurred.

Because liabilities involve future disbursements of assets or services, one of their most important features is the date on which they are payable. A company must satisfy currently maturing obligations in the ordinary course of business to continue operating. Liabilities with a more distant due date do not, as a rule, represent a claim on the company's current resources. They are therefore in a slightly different category. This feature gives rise to the basic division of liabilities into (1) current liabilities and (2) long-term debt.

Recall that current assets are cash or other assets that companies reasonably expect to convert into cash, sell, or consume in operations within a single operating cycle or within a year (if completing more than one cycle each year). Current liabilities are **"obligations whose liquidation is reasonably expected to require use of existing resources properly classified as current assets, or the creation of other current liabilities."** [2] This definition has gained wide acceptance because it recognizes operating cycles of varying lengths in different industries. This definition also considers the important relationship between current assets and current liabilities. [3]

The operating cycle is the period of time elapsing between the acquisition of goods and services involved in the manufacturing process and the final cash realization resulting from sales and subsequent collections. Industries that manufacture products requiring an aging process, and certain capital-intensive industries, have an operating cycle of considerably more than one year. On the other hand, most retail and service establishments have several operating cycles within a year.

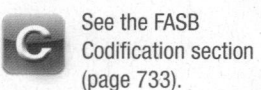

See the FASB Codification section (page 733).

---

[1]This illustration is not just a theoretical exercise. In practice, a number of preferred stock issues have all the characteristics of a debt instrument, except that they are called and legally classified as preferred stock. In some cases, the IRS has even permitted companies to treat the dividend payments as interest expense for tax purposes.

[2]The FASB has issued a standard to address the accounting for some of these securities [1] and is working with the IASB on a broader project to address the accounting for securities with debt and equity features.

[3]"Elements of Financial Statements of Business Enterprises," *Statement of Financial Accounting Concepts No. 6* (Stamford, Conn.: FASB, 1980).

Here are some typical current liabilities:

1. Accounts payable.
2. Notes payable.
3. Current maturities of long-term debt.
4. Short-term obligations expected to be refinanced.
5. Dividends payable.
6. Customer advances and deposits.
7. Unearned revenues.
8. Sales taxes payable.
9. Income taxes payable.
10. Employee-related liabilities.

Accounts Payable

Accounts payable, or **trade accounts payable,** are balances owed to others for goods, supplies, or services purchased on open account. Accounts payable arise because of the time lag between the receipt of services or acquisition of title to assets and the payment for them. The terms of the sale (e.g., 2/10, n/30 or 1/10, E.O.M.) usually state this period of extended credit, commonly 30 to 60 days.

Most companies record liabilities for purchases of goods upon receipt of the goods. If title has passed to the purchaser before receipt of the goods, the company should record the transaction at the time of title passage. A company must pay special attention to transactions occurring near the end of one accounting period and at the beginning of the next. It needs to ascertain that the record of goods received (the inventory) agrees with the liability (accounts payable), and that it records both in the proper period.

Measuring the amount of an account payable poses no particular difficulty. The invoice received from the creditor specifies the due date and the exact outlay in money that is necessary to settle the account. The only calculation that may be necessary concerns the amount of cash discount. See Chapter 8 for illustrations of entries related to accounts payable and purchase discounts.

Notes Payable

Notes payable are written promises to pay a certain sum of money on a specified future date. They may arise from purchases, financing, or other transactions. Some industries require notes (often referred to as **trade notes payable**) as part of the sales/purchases transaction in lieu of the normal extension of open account credit. Notes payable to banks or loan companies generally arise from cash loans. Companies classify notes as short-term or long-term, depending on the payment due date. Notes may also be interest-bearing or zero-interest-bearing.

Interest-Bearing Note Issued

Assume that Castle National Bank agrees to lend $100,000 on March 1, 2014, to Landscape Co. if Landscape signs a $100,000, 6 percent, four-month note. Landscape records the cash received on March 1 as follows.

	March 1	
Cash	100,000	
Notes Payable		100,000
(To record issuance of 6%, 4-month note to Castle National Bank)		

If Landscape prepares financial statements semiannually, it makes the adjusting entry (shown at the top of page 704) to recognize interest expense and interest payable of $2,000 ($100,000 $\times$ 6% $\times$ 4/12) at June 30.

June 30

Interest Expense	2,000	
Interest Payable		2,000
(To accrue interest for 4 months on Castle National Bank note)		

If Landscape prepares financial statements monthly, its adjusting entry at the end of each month is $500 ($100,000 × 6% × 1/12).

At maturity (July 1), Landscape must pay the face value of the note ($100,000) plus $2,000 interest ($100,000 × 6% × 4/12). Landscape records payment of the note and accrued interest as follows.

July 1

Notes Payable	100,000	
Interest Payable	2,000	
Cash		102,000
(To record payment of Castle National Bank interest-bearing note and accrued interest at maturity)		

Zero-Interest-Bearing Note Issued

A company may issue a zero-interest-bearing note instead of an interest-bearing note. A zero-interest-bearing note does not explicitly state an interest rate on the face of the note. **Interest is still charged**, however. At maturity, the borrower must pay back an amount greater than the cash received at the issuance date. In other words, the borrower receives in cash the present value of the note. The present value equals the face value of the note at maturity minus the interest or discount charged by the lender for the term of the note. In essence, the bank takes its fee "up front" rather than on the date the note matures.

To illustrate, assume that Landscape issues a $102,000, four-month, zero-interest-bearing note to Castle National Bank. The present value of the note is $100,000.[4] Landscape records this transaction as follows.

March 1

Cash	100,000	
Discount on Notes Payable	2,000	
Notes Payable		102,000
(To record issuance of 4-month, zero-interest-bearing note to Castle National Bank)		

Landscape credits the Notes Payable account for the face value of the note, which is $2,000 more than the actual cash received. It debits the difference between the cash received and the face value of the note to Discount on Notes Payable. **Discount on Notes Payable is a contra account to Notes Payable, and therefore is subtracted from Notes Payable on the balance sheet.** Illustration 13-1 shows the balance sheet presentation on March 1.

ILLUSTRATION 13-1
Balance Sheet
Presentation of Discount

Current liabilities		
Notes payable	$102,000	
Less: Discount on notes payable	2,000	$100,000

The amount of the discount, $2,000 in this case, represents the cost of borrowing $100,000 for 4 months. Accordingly, Landscape charges the discount to interest expense over the life of the note. That is, the Discount on Notes Payable balance **represents interest expense chargeable to future periods**. Thus, Landscape should not debit

[4]The bank discount rate used in this example to find the present value is 5.96 percent.

Interest Expense for $2,000 at the time of obtaining the loan. We discuss additional accounting issues related to notes payable in Chapter 14.

Current Maturities of Long-Term Debt

PepsiCo reports as part of its current liabilities the portion of bonds, mortgage notes, and other long-term indebtedness that matures within the next fiscal year. It categorizes this amount as current maturities of long-term debt. Companies, like PepsiCo, exclude long-term debts maturing currently as current liabilities if they are to be:

1. Retired by assets accumulated for this purpose that properly have not been shown as current assets,

2. Refinanced, or retired from the proceeds of a new debt issue, or

3. Converted into capital stock.

In these situations, the use of current assets or the creation of other current liabilities does not occur. Therefore, classification as a current liability is inappropriate. A company should disclose the plan for liquidation of such a debt either parenthetically or by a note to the financial statements. When only a part of a long-term debt is to be paid within the next 12 months, as in the case of serial bonds that it retires through a series of annual installments, **the company reports the maturing portion of long-term debt as a current liability**, and the remaining portion as a long-term debt.

However, a company should classify as current any liability that is **due on demand** (callable by the creditor) or will be due on demand within a year (or operating cycle, if longer). Liabilities often become callable by the creditor when there is a violation of the debt agreement. For example, most debt agreements specify a given level of equity to debt be maintained, or specify that working capital be of a minimum amount. If the company violates an agreement, it must classify the debt as current because it is a reasonable expectation that existing working capital will be used to satisfy the debt. Only if a company can show that it is **probable** that it will cure (satisfy) the violation within the grace period specified in the agreements can it classify the debt as noncurrent. **[4]**

Short-Term Obligations Expected to Be Refinanced

Short-term obligations are debts scheduled to mature within one year after the date of a company's balance sheet or within its operating cycle, whichever is longer. Some short-term obligations are expected to be refinanced on a long-term basis. These short-term obligations will not require the use of working capital during the next year (or operating cycle).[5]

2 LEARNING OBJECTIVE

Explain the classification issues of short-term debt expected to be refinanced.

At one time, the accounting profession generally supported the exclusion of short-term obligations from current liabilities if they were "expected to be refinanced." But the profession provided no specific guidelines, so companies determined whether a short-term obligation was "expected to be refinanced" based solely on management's **intent** to refinance on a long-term basis. Classification was not clear-cut. For example, a company might obtain a five-year bank loan but handle the actual financing with 90-day notes, which it must keep turning over (renewing). In this case, is the loan a long-term debt or a current liability? Another example was the Penn Central Railroad before it went bankrupt. The railroad was deep into short-term debt but classified it as long-term debt. Why? Because the railroad believed it had commitments from lenders to keep

---

[5]*Refinancing a short-term obligation on a long-term basis* means either replacing it with a long-term obligation or equity securities, or renewing, extending, or replacing it with short-term obligations for an uninterrupted period extending beyond one year (or the operating cycle, if longer) from the date of the enterprise's balance sheet.

refinancing the short-term debt. When those commitments suddenly disappeared, it was "good-bye Pennsy." As the Greek philosopher Epictetus once said, "Some things in this world are not and yet appear to be."

Refinancing Criteria

To resolve these classification problems, the accounting profession has developed criteria for determining the circumstances under which short-term obligations may be properly excluded from current liabilities. A company is required to exclude a short-term obligation from current liabilities if **both** of the following conditions are met:

1. It must **intend to refinance** the obligation on a long-term basis.
2. It must **demonstrate an ability** to consummate the refinancing. [5]

Intention to refinance on a long-term basis means that the company intends to refinance the short-term obligation so that it will not require the use of working capital during the ensuing fiscal year (or operating cycle, if longer).

The company demonstrates the **ability** to consummate the refinancing by:

(a) **Actually refinancing** the short-term obligation by issuing a long-term obligation or equity securities after the date of the balance sheet but before it is issued; or

(b) Entering into a **financing agreement** that clearly permits the company to refinance the debt on a long-term basis on terms that are readily determinable.

If an actual refinancing occurs, the portion of the short-term obligation to be excluded from current liabilities may not exceed the proceeds from the new obligation or equity securities used to retire the short-term obligation. For example, Montavon Winery had $3,000,000 of short-term debt. Subsequent to the balance sheet date, but before issuing the balance sheet, the company issued 100,000 shares of common stock, intending to use the proceeds to liquidate the short-term debt at its maturity. If Montavon's net proceeds from the sale of the 100,000 shares total $2,000,000, it can exclude from current liabilities only $2,000,000 of the short-term debt.

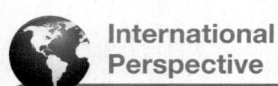
International Perspective

IFRS requires that the current portion of long-term debt be classified as current unless an agreement to refinance on a long-term basis is completed before the date of the financial statements.

An additional question is whether a company should exclude from current liabilities a short-term obligation if it is paid off after the balance sheet date and replaced by long-term debt before the balance sheet is issued. To illustrate, Marquardt Company pays off short-term debt of $40,000 on January 17, 2015, and issues long-term debt of $100,000 on February 3, 2015. Marquardt's financial statements, dated December 31, 2014, are to be issued March 1, 2015. Should Marquardt exclude the $40,000 short-term debt from current liabilities? No—here's why: Repayment of the short-term obligation required the use of **existing** current assets **before** the company obtained funds through long-term financing. Therefore, Marquardt must include the short-term obligations in current liabilities at the balance sheet date (as shown in Illustration 13-2).

ILLUSTRATION 13-2
Short-Term Debt Paid Off after Balance Sheet Date and Later Replaced by Long-Term Debt

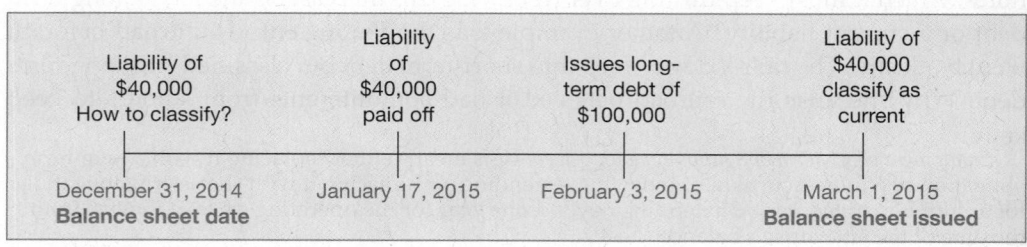

What do the numbers mean? WHAT ABOUT THAT SHORT-TERM DEBT?

The evaluation of credit quality involves more than simply assessing a company's ability to repay loans. Credit analysts also evaluate debt management strategies. Analysts and investors will reward what they view as prudent management decisions with lower debt service costs and a higher stock price. The wrong decisions can bring higher debt costs and lower stock prices.

General Electric Capital Corp., a subsidiary of General Electric, experienced the negative effects of market scrutiny of its debt management policies. Analysts complained that GE had been slow to refinance its mountains of short-term debt. GE had issued these current obligations, with maturities of 270 days or less, when interest rates were low. However, in light of expectations that the Fed would raise interest rates,

analysts began to worry about the higher interest costs GE would pay when it refinanced these loans. Some analysts recommended that it was time to reduce dependence on short-term credit. The reasoning goes that a shift to more dependable long-term debt, thereby locking in slightly higher rates for the long-term, is the better way to go.

Thus, scrutiny of GE debt strategies led to analysts' concerns about GE's earnings prospects. Investors took the analysis to heart, and GE experienced a two-day 6 percent drop in its stock price. Recently, GE and other companies, such as UPS, have responded to these criticisms and have been increasing issuance of long-term debt to lock-in continuing low interest rates.

Sources: Adapted from Steven Vames, "Credit Quality, Stock Investing Seem to Go Hand in Hand," *Wall Street Journal* (April 1, 2002), p. R4; and V. Monga, "Companies Feast on Cheap Money Market for 30-Year Bonds, Priced at Stark Lows, Brings Out GE, UPS and Other Once-Shy Issuers," *Wall Street Journal* (October 8, 2012).

Dividends Payable

A cash dividend payable is an amount owed by a corporation to its stockholders as a result of board of directors' authorization. At the date of declaration, the corporation assumes a liability that places the stockholders in the position of creditors in the amount of dividends declared. Because companies always pay cash dividends within one year of declaration (generally within three months), they classify them as current liabilities.

On the other hand, companies do not recognize accumulated but undeclared dividends on cumulative preferred stock as a liability. Why? Because preferred dividends in arrears are not an obligation until the board of directors authorizes the payment. Nevertheless, companies should disclose the amount of cumulative dividends unpaid in a note, or show it parenthetically in the capital stock section.

Dividends payable in the form of additional shares of stock are not recognized as a liability. Such **stock dividends** (as we discuss in Chapter 15) do not require future outlays of assets or services. Companies generally report such undistributed stock dividends in the stockholders' equity section because they represent retained earnings in the process of transfer to paid-in capital.

Underlying Concepts

Preferred dividends in arrears do represent a probable future economic sacrifice, but the expected sacrifice does not result from a past transaction or past event. The sacrifice will result from a future event (declaration by the board of directors). Note disclosure improves the predictive value of the financial statements.

Customer Advances and Deposits

Current liabilities may include returnable cash deposits received from customers and employees. Companies may receive deposits from customers to guarantee performance of a contract or service or as guarantees to cover payment of expected future obligations. For example, a company like Alltel Corp. often requires a deposit on equipment that customers use to connect to the Internet or to access its other services. Alltel also may receive deposits from customers as guarantees for possible damage to property. Additionally, some companies require their employees to make deposits for the return of keys or other company property.

The classification of these items as current or noncurrent liabilities depends on the time between the date of the deposit and the termination of the relationship that required the deposit.

Unearned Revenues

A magazine publisher, such as Golf Digest, receives payment when a customer subscribes to its magazines. An airline company, such as American Airlines, sells tickets for future flights. And software companies, like Microsoft, issue coupons that allow customers to upgrade to the next version of their software. How do these companies account for **unearned revenues** that they receive before delivering goods or rendering services?

1. When a company receives an advance payment, it debits Cash, and credits a current liability account identifying the source of the unearned revenue.
2. When a company recognizes revenue, it debits the unearned revenue account, and credits a revenue account.

To illustrate, assume that Allstate University sells 10,000 season football tickets at $50 each for its five-game home schedule. Allstate University records the sales of season tickets as follows.

August 6

Cash	500,000	
Unearned Sales Revenue		500,000
(To record sale of 10,000 season tickets)		

As each game is completed, Allstate University makes the following entry.

September 7

Unearned Sales Revenue	100,000	
Sales Revenue		100,000
(To record football ticket revenue)		

The account Unearned Sales Revenue represents unearned revenue. Allstate University reports it as a current liability in the balance sheet as the school has a performance obligation. As the school recognizes revenue, it reclassifies the amount from Unearned Sales Revenue to Sales Revenue. Unearned revenue is material for some companies. In the airline industry, for example, tickets sold for future flights represent almost 50 percent of total current liabilities.

Illustration 13-3 shows specific unearned revenue and revenue accounts used in elected types of businesses.

ILLUSTRATION 13-3
Unearned Revenue and
Revenue Accounts

Type of Business	Account Title	
	Unearned Revenue	Revenue
Airline	Unearned Ticket Revenue	Passenger Revenue
Magazine publisher	Unearned Subscription Revenue	Subscription Revenue
Hotel	Unearned Rent Revenue	Rent Revenue
Auto dealer	Unearned Warranty Revenue	Warranty Revenue
Retailers	Unearned Gift Card Revenue	Sales Revenue

The balance sheet reports obligations for any commitments that are redeemable in goods and services. The income statement reports revenues related to performance obligations satisfied during the period.

What do the numbers mean? MICROSOFT'S LIABILITIES—GOOD OR BAD?

Users of financial statements generally examine current liabilities to assess a company's liquidity and overall financial flexibility. Companies must pay many current liabilities, such as accounts payable, wages payable, and taxes payable, sooner rather than later. A substantial increase in these liabilities should raise a red flag about a company's financial position.

This is not the case for all current liabilities. For example, **Microsoft** has a current liability entitled "Short-term unearned revenue" of $18,653 million in 2012 that has increased year after year. Unearned revenue is a liability that arises from sales of Microsoft products such as *Internet Explorer* and *Windows*. Microsoft also has provided coupons for upgrades to its programs to bolster sales of its XBox consoles. At the time of a sale, customers pay not only for the current version of the software but also for future upgrades. Microsoft recognizes sales revenue from the current version of the software and records as a liability (unearned revenue) the value of future upgrades to the software that it "owes" to customers.

Market analysts read such an increase in unearned revenue as a positive signal about Microsoft's sales and profitability. When Microsoft's sales are growing, its unearned revenue account increases. Thus, an *increase* in a liability is good news about Microsoft sales. At the same time, a decline in unearned revenue is bad news. As one analyst noted, a slowdown or reversal of the growth in Microsoft's unearned revenues indicates slowing sales, which is bad news for investors. Thus, increases in current liabilities can sometimes be viewed as good signs instead of bad.

Sources: Adapted from David Bank, "Some Fans Cool to Microsoft, Citing Drop in Old Indicator," *Wall Street Journal* (October 28, 1999); and Bloomberg News, "Microsoft Profit Hit by Deferred Sales; Forecast Raised," *The Globe and Mail* (January 26, 2007), p. B8.

Sales Taxes Payable

Retailers like **Wal-Mart**, **Best Buy**, and **Gap Inc.** must collect sales taxes from customers on transfers of tangible personal property and on certain services and then must remit these taxes to the proper governmental authority. Gap, for example, sets up a liability to provide for taxes collected from customers but not yet remitted to the tax authority. The Sales Taxes Payable account should reflect the liability for sales taxes due various governments.

The entry below illustrates use of the Sales Taxes Payable account on a sale of $3,000 when a 4 percent sales tax is in effect.

Cash	3,120	
Sales Revenue		3,000
Sales Taxes Payable		120

Sometimes the sales tax collections credited to the liability account are not equal to the liability as computed by the governmental formula. In such a case, Gap makes an adjustment of the liability account by recognizing a gain or a loss on sales tax collections.

Many companies do not segregate the sales tax and the amount of the sale at the time of sale. Instead, the company credits both amounts in total in the Sales Revenue account. Then, to reflect correctly the actual amount of sales and the liability for sales taxes, the company would debit the Sales Revenue account for the amount of the sales taxes due the government on these sales, and would credit the Sales Taxes Payable account for the same amount.

To illustrate, assume that the Sales Revenue account balance of $150,000 includes sales taxes of 4 percent. Thus, the amount recorded in the Sales Revenue account is comprised of the sales amount plus sales tax of 4 percent of the sales amount. Sales therefore are $144,230.77 ($150,000 ÷ 1.04) and the sales tax liability is $5,769.23 ($144,230.77 × 0.04; or $150,000 − $144,230.77). The following entry would record the amount due the taxing unit.

Sales Revenue	5,769.23	
Sales Taxes Payable		5,769.23

Income Taxes Payable

Any federal or state income tax varies in proportion to the amount of annual income. Using the best information and advice available, a business must prepare an income tax return and compute the income taxes payable resulting from the operations of the

**Gateway to
the Profession**

*Expanded Discussion
of Property Taxes
Payable*

current period. Corporations should classify as a current liability the taxes payable on net income, as computed per the tax return.[6] Unlike a corporation, proprietorships and partnerships are not taxable entities. Because the individual proprietor and the members of a partnership are subject to personal income taxes on their share of the business's taxable income, income tax liabilities do not appear on the financial statements of proprietorships and partnerships.

Most corporations must make periodic tax payments throughout the year in an authorized bank depository or a Federal Reserve Bank. These payments are based upon estimates of the total annual tax liability. As the estimated total tax liability changes, the periodic contributions also change. If in a later year the taxing authority assesses an additional tax on the income of an earlier year, the company should credit Income Taxes Payable and charge the related debit to current operations.

Differences between taxable income under the tax laws and accounting income under generally accepted accounting principles sometimes occur. Because of these differences, the amount of income taxes payable to the government in any given year may differ substantially from income tax expense as reported on the financial statements. Chapter 19 is devoted solely to income tax matters and presents an extensive discussion of this complex topic.

Employee-Related Liabilities

LEARNING OBJECTIVE **3**
Identify types of employee-related liabilities.

Companies also report as a current liability amounts owed to employees for salaries or wages at the end of an accounting period. In addition, they often also report as current liabilities the following items related to employee compensation.

1. Payroll deductions.
2. Compensated absences.
3. Bonuses.

Payroll Deductions

The most common types of payroll deductions are taxes, insurance premiums, employee savings, and union dues. **To the extent that a company has not remitted the amounts deducted to the proper authority at the end of the accounting period, it should recognize them as current liabilities.**

Social Security Taxes. Since January 1, 1937, Social Security legislation has provided federal Old Age, Survivor, and Disability Insurance (OASDI) benefits for certain individuals and their families. Funds for these payments come from taxes levied on both the employer and the employee. Employers collect the employee's share of this tax by deducting it from the employee's gross pay, and remit it to the government along with their share. The government taxes both the employer and the employee at the same rate, currently 6.2 percent based on the employee's gross pay up to a $113,700 annual limit. The OASDI tax is usually referred to as FICA (the Federal Insurance Contribution Act).

In 1965, Congress passed the first federal health insurance program for the aged—popularly known as **Medicare**. This two-part program alleviates the high cost of medical care for those over age 65. A separate Hospital Insurance tax, paid by both the employee and the employer at the rate of 1.45 percent on the employee's total compensation,

---

[6]Corporate taxes are based on a progressive tax rate structure. Companies with taxable income of $50,000 or less are taxed at a 15 percent rate. Higher levels of income are taxed at much higher rates.

finances the Basic Plan, which provides hospital and other institutional services.[7] The Voluntary Plan covers the major part of doctors' bills and other medical and health services. Monthly payments from all who enroll, plus matching funds from the federal government, finance this plan.

The combination of the OASDI tax (FICA) and the federal Hospital Insurance Tax is commonly referred to as the Social Security tax. The combined rate for these taxes, 7.65 percent on an employee's wages to $113,700 and 1.45 percent in excess of $113,700, changes intermittently by acts of Congress. **Companies should report the amount of unremitted employee and employer Social Security tax on gross wages paid as a current liability.**

Unemployment Taxes. Another payroll tax levied by the federal government in co-operation with state governments provides a system of unemployment insurance. All employers who meet the following criteria are subject to the Federal Unemployment Tax Act (FUTA): (1) those who paid wages of $1,500 or more during any calendar quarter in the year or preceding year, or (2) those who employed at least one individual on at least one day in each of 20 weeks during the current or preceding calendar year.

Only employers pay the unemployment tax. The rate of this tax is 6.2 percent on the first $7,000 of compensation paid to each employee during the calendar year. The employer receives a tax credit not to exceed 5.4 percent for contributions paid to a state plan for unemployment compensation. Thus, if an employer is subject to a state unemployment tax of 5.4 percent or more, it pays only 0.8 percent tax to the federal government.

State unemployment compensation laws differ both from the federal law and among various states. Therefore, employers must refer to the unemployment tax laws in each state in which they pay wages and salaries. The normal state tax may range from 3 percent to 7 percent or higher. However, all states provide for some form of **merit rating**, which reduces the state contribution rate. Employers who display by their benefit and contribution experience that they provide steady employment may receive this reduction—if the size of the state fund is adequate. In order not to penalize an employer who has earned a reduction in the state contribution rate, federal law allows a credit of 5.4 percent, even when the effective state contribution rate is less than 5.4 percent.

To illustrate, Appliance Repair Co. has a taxable payroll of $100,000. It is subject to a federal rate of 6.2 percent and a state contribution rate of 5.7 percent. However, its stable employment experience reduces the company's state rate to 1 percent. Appliance Repair computes its federal and state unemployment taxes as shown in Illustration 13-4.

State unemployment tax payment (1% × $100,000)	$1,000
Federal unemployment tax [(6.2% − 5.4%) × $100,000]	800
Total federal and state unemployment tax	$1,800

ILLUSTRATION 13-4
Computation of Unemployment Taxes

Companies pay federal unemployment tax quarterly, and file a tax form annually. Companies also generally pay state contributions quarterly as well. Because both the federal and the state unemployment taxes accrue on earned compensation, companies should record the amount of accrued but unpaid employer contributions **as an operating expense and as a current liability when preparing financial statements at year-end.**

Income Tax Withholding. Federal and some state income tax laws require employers to withhold from each employee's pay the applicable income tax due on those wages. The

---

[7]As a result of the new health-care law, the Affordable Care Act, the actual rate for Medicare is higher for married couples, generally with incomes in excess of $250,000.

employer computes the amount of income tax to withhold according to a government-prescribed formula or withholding tax table. That amount depends on the length of the pay period and each employee's taxable wages, marital status, and claimed dependents. If the income tax withheld plus the employee and the employer Social Security taxes exceeds specified amounts per month, the employer must make remittances to the government during the month. Illustration 13-5 summarizes payroll deductions and liabilities.

ILLUSTRATION 13-5
Summary of Payroll
Liabilities

Item	Who Pays	
Income tax withholding		
FICA taxes—employee share	Employee	Employer reports these
Union dues		amounts as liabilities
FICA taxes—employer share		until remitted.
Federal unemployment	Employer	
State unemployment		

Payroll Deductions Example. Assume a weekly payroll of $10,000 entirely subject to FICA and Medicare (7.65%), federal (0.8%) and state (4%) unemployment taxes, with income tax withholding of $1,320 and union dues of $88 deducted. The company records the salaries and wages paid and the **employee payroll deductions** as follows.

Salaries and Wages Expense	10,000	
Withholding Taxes Payable		1,320
FICA Taxes Payable		765
Union Dues Payable		88
Cash		7,827

It records the **employer payroll taxes** as follows.

Payroll Tax Expense	1,245	
FICA Taxes Payable		765
FUTA Taxes Payable		80
SUTA Taxes Payable		400

The employer must remit to the government its share of FICA tax along with the amount of FICA tax deducted from each employee's gross compensation. It records all unremitted employer FICA taxes as payroll tax expense and payroll tax payable.[8]

Compensated Absences

Underlying Concepts

When these four conditions exist, all elements in the definition of a liability exist. In addition, the expense recognition principle requires that the company report the expense for the services in the period consumed.

Compensated absences are paid absences from employment—such as vacation, illness, and holidays.[9] Companies should accrue a liability for the cost of compensation for future absences if **all of the following conditions** exist. **[6]**

(a) The employer's obligation relating to employees' rights to receive compensation for future absences is attributable to employees' services **already rendered**.

(b) The obligation relates to the rights that **vest or accumulate**.

(c) Payment of the compensation is **probable**.

(d) The amount can be **reasonably estimated**. **[7]**

[8]A manufacturing company allocates all of the payroll costs (wages, payroll taxes, and fringe benefits) to appropriate cost accounts such as Direct Labor, Indirect Labor, Sales Salaries, Administrative Salaries, and the like. This abbreviated and somewhat simplified discussion of payroll costs and deductions is not indicative of the volume of records and clerical work that may be involved in maintaining a sound and accurate payroll system.

[9]In addition, companies provide **postemployment benefits** to past or inactive employees **after employment but prior to retirement**. Examples include salary continuation, supplemental unemployment benefits, severance pay, job training, and continuation of health and life insurance coverage.

Illustration 13-6 shows an example of an accrual for compensated absences, in an excerpt from the balance sheet of **Clarcor Inc.**

Clarcor Inc.

Current liabilities	
Accounts payable	$ 6,308
Accrued salaries, wages and commissions	2,278
Compensated absences	2,271
Accrued pension liabilities	1,023
Other accrued liabilities	4,572
	$16,452

ILLUSTRATION 13-6
Balance Sheet Presentation of Accrual for Compensated Absences

If an employer meets conditions (a), (b), and (c) but does not accrue a liability because of a failure to meet condition (d), it should disclose that fact. Illustration 13-7 shows an example of such a disclosure, in a note from the financial statements of **Gotham Utility Company.**

Gotham Utility Company

Employees of the Company are entitled to paid vacation, personal, and sick days off, depending on job status, length of service, and other factors. Due to numerous differing union contracts and other agreements with nonunion employees, it is impractical to estimate the amount of compensation for future absences, and, accordingly, no liability has been reported in the accompanying financial statements. The Company's policy is to recognize the cost of compensated absences when actually paid to employees; compensated absence payments to employees totaled $2,786,000.

ILLUSTRATION 13-7
Disclosure of Policy for Compensated Absences

The following considerations are relevant to the accounting for compensated absences.

Vested rights exist when an employer has an obligation to make payment to an employee even after terminating his or her employment. Thus, vested rights are not contingent on an employee's future service. **Accumulated rights** are those that employees can carry forward to future periods if not used in the period in which earned. For example, assume that you earn four days of vacation pay as of December 31, the end of your employer's fiscal year. Company policy is that you will be paid for this vacation time even if you terminate employment. In this situation, your four days of vacation pay are vested, and your employer must accrue the amount.

Now assume that your vacation days are not vested but that you can carry the four days over into later periods. Although the rights are not vested, they are accumulated rights for which the employer must make an accrual. However, the amount of the accrual is adjusted to allow for estimated forfeitures due to turnover.

A modification of the general rules relates to the issue of **sick pay**. If sick pay benefits vest, a company must accrue them. If sick pay benefits accumulate but do not vest, a company may choose whether to accrue them. Why this distinction? Companies may administer compensation designated as sick pay in one of two ways. In some companies, employees receive sick pay only if illness causes their absence. Therefore, these companies may or may not accrue a liability because its payment depends on future employee illness. Other companies allow employees to accumulate unused sick pay and take compensated time off from work even when not ill. For this type of sick pay, a company must accrue a liability because the company will pay it, regardless of whether employees become ill.

Companies should recognize the expense and related liability for compensated absences in the year earned by employees. For example, if new employees receive rights to two weeks' paid vacation at the beginning of their second year of employment, a company considers the vacation pay to be earned during the first year of employment.

What rate should a company use to accrue the compensated absence cost—the current rate or an estimated future rate? GAAP is silent on this subject. Therefore, companies will likely use the current rather than future rate. The future rate is less certain and raises time value of money issues. To illustrate, assume that Amutron Inc. began operations on January 1, 2014. The company employs 10 individuals and pays each $480 per week. Employees earned 20 unused vacation weeks in 2014. In 2015, the employees used the vacation weeks, but now they each earn $540 per week. Amutron accrues the accumulated vacation pay on December 31, 2014, as follows.

Salaries and Wages Expense	9,600	
Salaries and Wages Payable ($480 × 20)		9,600

At December 31, 2014, the company reports on its balance sheet a liability of $9,600. In 2015, it records the payment of vacation pay as follows.

Salaries and Wages Payable	9,600	
Salaries and Wages Expense	1,200	
Cash ($540 × 20)		10,800

In 2015, the use of the vacation weeks extinguishes the liability. Note that Amutron records the difference between the amount of cash paid and the reduction in the liability account as an adjustment to Salaries and Wages Expense in the period when paid. This difference arises because it accrues the liability account at the rates of pay in effect during the period when employees **earned** the compensated time. The cash paid, however, depends on the rates in effect during the period when employees **used** the compensated time. If Amutron used the future rates of pay to compute the accrual in 2014, then the cash paid in 2015 would equal the liability.[10]

**Gateway to
the Profession**

*Expanded Discussion
of Bonus
Computations*

Bonus Agreements

Many companies give a **bonus** to certain or all employees in addition to their regular salaries or wages. Frequently the bonus amount depends on the company's yearly profit. For example, employees at **Ford Motor Company** share in the success of the company's operations on the basis of a complicated formula using net income as its primary basis for computation. A company may consider **bonus payments to employees** as additional wages and should include them as a deduction in determining the net income for the year.

To illustrate the entries for an employee bonus, assume that Palmer Inc. shows income for the year 2014 of $100,000. It will pay out bonuses of $10,700 in January 2015. Palmer makes an adjusting entry dated December 31, 2014, to record the bonuses as follows.

Salaries and Wages Expense	10,700	
Salaries and Wages Payable		10,700

In January 2015, when Palmer pays the bonus, it makes this journal entry:

Salaries and Wages Payable	10,700	
Cash		10,700

---

[10]Some companies also have obligations for benefits paid to employees after they retire. The accounting and reporting standards for postretirement benefit payments are complex. These standards relate to two different types of **postretirement benefits**: (1) pensions, and (2) postretirement health-care and life insurance benefits. We discuss these issues extensively in Chapter 20.

Palmer should show the expense account in the income statement as an operating expense. **The liability, Salaries and Wages Payable, is usually payable within a short period of time. Companies should include it as a current liability in the balance sheet.** Similar to bonus agreements are contractual agreements for **conditional expenses**. Examples would be agreements covering rents or royalty payments conditional on the amount of revenues recognized or the quantity of product produced or extracted. Conditional expenses based on revenues or units produced are usually less difficult to compute than bonus arrangements.

For example, assume that a lease calls for a fixed rent payment of $500 per month and 1 percent of all sales over $300,000 per year. The company's annual rent obligation would amount to $6,000 plus $0.01 of each dollar of revenue over $300,000. Or, a royalty agreement may give to a patent owner $1 for every ton of product resulting from the patented process, or give to a mineral rights owner $0.50 on every barrel of oil extracted. As the company produces or extracts each additional unit of product, it creates an additional obligation, usually a current liability.

CONTINGENCIES

Companies often are involved in situations where uncertainty exists about whether an obligation to transfer cash or other assets has arisen and/or the amount that will be required to settle the obligation. For example:

- **Merck** may be a defendant in a lawsuit, and any payment is contingent upon the outcome of a settlement or an administrative or court proceeding.
- **Ford Motor Company** provides a warranty for a car it sells, and any payments are contingent on the number of cars that qualify for benefits under the warranty.
- **Briggs & Stratton** acts as a guarantor on a loan for another entity, and any payment is contingent on whether the other entity defaults.

Broadly, these situations are called contingencies. A **contingency** is "an existing condition, situation, or set of circumstances involving uncertainty as to possible gain **(gain contingency)** or loss **(loss contingency)** to an enterprise that will ultimately be resolved when one or more future events occur or fail to occur." **[8]**[11]

Gain Contingencies

Gain contingencies are claims or rights to receive assets (or have a liability reduced) whose existence is uncertain but which may become valid eventually. The typical gain contingencies are:

1. Possible receipts of monies from gifts, donations, asset sales, and so on.
2. Possible refunds from the government in tax disputes.
3. Pending court cases with a probable favorable outcome.
4. Tax loss carryforwards (discussed in Chapter 19).

Companies follow a conservative policy in this area; they do not record gain contingencies. A company discloses gain contingencies in the notes only when a high probability exists for realizing them. As a result, it is unusual to find information about

[11]According to *Accounting Trends and Techniques—2012,* the most common gain contingencies are related to operating loss carryforwards and other tax credits and to tax credit carryforwards.

contingent gains in the financial statements and the accompanying notes. Illustration 13-8 presents an example of a gain contingency disclosure.

ILLUSTRATION 13-8
Disclosure of Gain
Contingency

BMC Industries, Inc.

Note 13: Legal Matters. In the first quarter, a U.S. District Court in Miami, Florida, awarded the Company a $5.1 million judgment against Barth Industries (Barth) of Cleveland, Ohio and its parent, Nesco Holdings, Inc. (Nesco). The judgment relates to an agreement under which Barth and Nesco were to help automate the plastic lens production plant in Fort Lauderdale, Florida. The Company has not recorded any income relating to this judgment because Barth and Nesco have filed an appeal.

Loss Contingencies

LEARNING OBJECTIVE 5
Explain the accounting for different types of loss contingencies.

Loss contingencies involve possible losses. A liability incurred as a result of a loss contingency is by definition a contingent liability. **Contingent liabilities** depend on the occurrence of one or more future events to confirm either the amount payable, the payee, the date payable, or its existence. That is, these factors depend on a contingency.

International Perspective

IFRS uses the term *provisions* to refer to estimated liabilities.

Likelihood of Loss

When a loss contingency exists, the likelihood that the future event or events will confirm the incurrence of a liability can range from probable to remote. The FASB uses the terms **probable, reasonably possible,** and **remote** to identify three areas within that range and assigns the following meanings.

Probable. The future event or events are likely to occur.

Reasonably possible. The chance of the future event or events occurring is more than remote but less than likely.

Remote. The chance of the future event or events occurring is slight.

Companies should accrue an estimated loss from a loss contingency by a charge to expense and a liability recorded only if **both** of the following conditions are met.[12]

1. Information available prior to the issuance of the financial statements indicates that it is **probable that a liability has been incurred** at the date of the financial statements.

2. The amount of the loss can be **reasonably estimated**.

To record a liability, a company does not need to know the exact payee nor the exact date payable. **What a company must know is whether it is probable that it incurred a liability.**

To meet the second criterion, a company needs to be able to reasonably determine an amount for the liability. To determine a reasonable estimate of the liability, a company may use its own experience, experience of other companies in the industry, engineering or research studies, legal advice, or educated guesses by qualified personnel. Illustration 13-9 shows disclosure of an accrual recorded for a loss contingency, from the annual report of **Quaker State Oil Refining Company**.

---

[12]We discuss loss contingencies that result in the incurrence of a liability in this chapter. We discuss loss contingencies that result in the impairment of an asset (e.g., collectibility of receivables or threat of expropriation of assets) in other sections of this textbook.

ILLUSTRATION 13-9
Disclosure of Accrual for
Loss Contingency

Quaker State Oil Refining Company

Note 5: Contingencies. During the period from November 13 to December 23, a change in an additive component purchased from one of its suppliers caused certain oil refined and shipped to fail to meet the Company's low-temperature performance requirements. The Company has recalled this product and has arranged for reimbursement to its customers and the ultimate consumers of all costs associated with the product. Estimated cost of the recall program, net of estimated third party reimbursement, in the amount of $3,500,000 has been charged to current operations.

Use of the terms probable, reasonably possible, and remote to classify contingencies involves judgment and subjectivity. Illustration 13-10 lists examples of loss contingencies and the general accounting treatment accorded them.

ILLUSTRATION 13-10
Accounting Treatment of
Loss Contingencies

Usually Accrued

Loss Related to:

1. Collectibility of receivables
2. Obligations related to product warranties and product defects
3. Premiums offered to customers

Not Accrued

Loss Related to:

4. Risk of loss or damage of enterprise property by fire, explosion, or other hazards
5. General or unspecified business risks
6. Risk of loss from catastrophes assumed by property and casualty insurance companies, including reinsurance companies

May Be Accrued*

Loss Related to:

7. Threat of expropriation of assets
8. Pending or threatened litigation
9. Actual or possible claims and assessments**
10. Guarantees of indebtedness of others
11. Obligations of commercial banks under "standby letters of credit"
12. Agreements to repurchase receivables (or the related property) that have been sold

*Should be accrued when both criteria—probable and reasonably estimable—are met.
**Estimated amounts of losses incurred prior to the balance sheet date but settled subsequently should be accrued as of the balance sheet date.

Practicing accountants express concern over the diversity that now exists in the interpretation of "probable," "reasonably possible," and "remote." Current practice relies heavily on the exact language used in responses received from lawyers (such language is necessarily biased and protective rather than predictive). As a result, accruals and disclosures of contingencies vary considerably in practice. Some of the more common loss contingencies are:[13]

1. Litigation, claims, and assessments.
2. Guarantee and warranty costs.
3. Premiums and coupons.
4. Environmental liabilities.

[13]*Accounting Trends and Techniques—2012* indicates that 500 companies report loss contingencies for the following: litigation, 355; environmental, 195; possible tax assessments, 124; insurance, 154; governmental investigation, 101; and others, 71.

As discussed in the opening story, companies do not record or report in the notes to the financial statements general risk contingencies inherent in business operations (e.g., the possibility of war, strike, uninsurable catastrophes, or a business recession).

Litigation, Claims, and Assessments

Companies must consider the following factors, among others, in determining whether to record a liability with respect to **pending or threatened** litigation and actual or possible **claims** and **assessments**.

1. The **time period** in which the underlying cause of action occurred.
2. The **probability** of an unfavorable outcome.
3. The ability to make a **reasonable estimate** of the amount of loss.

To report a loss and a liability in the financial statements, **the cause for litigation must have occurred on or before the date of the financial statements**. It does not matter that the company became aware of the existence or possibility of the lawsuit or claims after the date of the financial statements but before issuing them. To evaluate the probability of an unfavorable outcome, a company considers the following: the nature of the litigation, the progress of the case, the opinion of legal counsel, its own and others' experience in similar cases, and any management response to the lawsuit.

Companies can seldom predict the outcome of pending litigation, however, with any assurance. And, even if evidence available at the balance sheet date does not favor the company, it is hardly reasonable to expect the company to publish in its financial statements a dollar estimate of the probable negative outcome. Such specific disclosures might weaken the company's position in the dispute and encourage the plaintiff to intensify its efforts. A typical example of the wording of such a disclosure is the note to the financial statements of **Apple Inc.**, relating to its litigation concerning repetitive stress injuries, as shown in Illustration 13-11.

ILLUSTRATION 13-11
Disclosure of Litigation

Apple Inc.

"Repetitive Stress Injury" Litigation. The Company is named in numerous lawsuits (fewer than 100) alleging that the plaintiff incurred so-called "repetitive stress injury" to the upper extremities as a result of using keyboards and/or mouse input devices sold by the Company. In a trial of one of these cases (*Dorsey v. Apple*) in the United States District Court for the Eastern District of New York, the jury rendered a verdict in favor of the Company, and final judgment in favor of the Company has been entered. The other cases are in various stages of pretrial activity. These suits are similar to those filed against other major suppliers of personal computers. Ultimate resolution of the litigation against the Company may depend on progress in resolving this type of litigation in the industry overall.

With respect to **unfiled suits** and **unasserted claims and assessments**, a company must determine (1) the degree of **probability** that a suit may be filed or a claim or assessment may be asserted, and (2) the **probability** of an unfavorable outcome. For example, assume that the Federal Trade Commission investigates the Nawtee Company for restraint of trade, and institutes enforcement proceedings. Private claims of triple damages for redress often follow such proceedings. In this case, Nawtee must determine the probability of the claims being asserted **and** the probability of triple damages being awarded. If both are probable, if the loss is reasonably estimable, and if the cause for action is dated on or before the date of the financial statements, then Nawtee should accrue the liability.[14]

Guarantee and Warranty Costs

A warranty **(product guarantee)** is a promise made by a seller to a buyer to make good on a deficiency of quantity, quality, or performance in a product. Manufacturers commonly use it as a sales promotion technique. Automakers, for instance, "hyped" their sales by extending their new-car warranty to seven years or 100,000 miles. For a specified period of time following the date of sale to the consumer, the manufacturer may promise to bear all or part of the cost of replacing defective parts, to perform any necessary repairs or servicing without charge, to refund the purchase price, or even to "double your money back."

Warranties and guarantees entail future costs. These additional costs, sometimes called "after costs" or "post-sale costs," frequently are significant. Although the future cost is indefinite as to amount, due date, and even customer, a liability is probable in most cases. Companies should recognize this liability in the accounts if they can reasonably estimate it. The estimated amount of the liability includes all the costs that the company will incur after sale and delivery and that are incident to the correction of defects or deficiencies required under the warranty provisions. Warranty costs are a classic example of a loss contingency.

Companies use two basic methods of accounting for warranty costs: (1) the cash-basis method and (2) the accrual method.

Cash Basis. Under the **cash-basis method**, companies expense warranty costs as incurred. In other words, a **seller or manufacturer charges warranty costs to the period in which it complies with the warranty**. The company does not record a liability for future costs arising from warranties, nor does it charge the period of sale. Companies frequently justify use of this method, the only one recognized for income tax purposes, on the basis of expediency when warranty costs are immaterial or when the warranty period is relatively short. A company uses the cash-basis method when it does not accrue a warranty liability in the year of sale either because:

1. It is not probable that a liability has been incurred, or

2. It cannot reasonably estimate the amount of the liability.

Accrual Basis. If it is probable that customers will make warranty claims and a company can reasonably estimate the costs involved, the company must use the accrual method. Under the **accrual method**, companies charge warranty costs to operating expense **in the year of sale**. The accrual method is the generally accepted method. Companies should use it whenever the warranty is an integral and inseparable part of the sale and is viewed as a loss contingency. We refer to this approach as the expense warranty approach.

Example of expense warranty approach. To illustrate the expense warranty method, assume that Denson Machinery Company begins production on a new machine in July 2014,

---

[14]Companies need not disclose contingencies involving an unasserted claim or assessment when no claimant has come forward unless (1) it is considered probable that a claim will be asserted, and (2) there is a reasonable possibility that the outcome will be unfavorable. The FASB recently had a project to develop disclosures that are sufficient to enable users of financial statements to assess the likelihood, timing, and amount of future cash flows associated with loss contingencies. As indicated in the opening story, this project and its proposed recommendations were extremely controversial. Although the SEC continues to focus on these disclosures, the FASB has now removed the project from its active agenda (see *http://www.cooley.com/66716*).

and sells 100 units at $5,000 each by its year-end, December 31, 2014. Each machine is under warranty for one year. Denson estimates, based on past experience with a similar machine, that the warranty cost will average $200 per unit. Further, as a result of parts replacements and services rendered in compliance with machinery warranties, it incurs $4,000 in warranty costs in 2014 and $16,000 in 2015.

1. Sale of 100 machines at $5,000 each, July through December 2014:

Cash or Accounts Receivable	500,000	
Sales Revenue		500,000
(To record sales revenue)		

2. Recognition of warranty expense, July through December 2014:

Warranty Expense	4,000	
Cash, Inventory, Accrued Payroll		4,000
(Warranty costs incurred)		
Warranty Expense	16,000	
Warranty Liability		16,000
(To accrue estimated warranty costs)		

The December 31, 2014, balance sheet reports "Warranty liability" as a current liability of $16,000, and the income statement for 2014 reports "Warranty expense" of $20,000.

3. Recognition of warranty costs incurred in 2015 (on 2014 machinery sales):

Warranty Liability	16,000	
Cash, Inventory, Accrued Payroll		16,000
(Warranty costs incurred)		

If Denson Machinery applies the cash-basis method, it reports $4,000 as warranty expense in 2014 and $16,000 as warranty expense in 2015. It records all of the sale price as revenue in 2014. In many instances, application of the cash-basis method fails to record the warranty costs relating to the products sold during a given period with the revenues derived from such products. As such, **it violates the expense recognition principle**. However, where ongoing warranty policies exist year after year, the differences between the cash and the expense warranty bases probably would not be so great.

Sales warranty approach. A warranty is sometimes **sold separately from the product**. For example, when you purchase a television set or Blu-ray player, you are entitled to the manufacturer's warranty. You also will undoubtedly be offered an extended warranty on the product at an additional cost.[15]

In this case, the seller should recognize separately the sale of the television or Blu-ray player, with the manufacturer's warranty and the sale of the extended warranty. **[9]** This approach is referred to as the sales warranty approach. **Companies defer revenue on the sale of the extended warranty** and generally recognize it on a straight-line basis over the life of the contract. The seller of the warranty defers revenue because it has an obligation to perform services over the life of the contract. The seller should only defer and amortize costs that vary with, and are directly related to, the sale of the contracts (mainly commissions). It expenses those costs, such as employees' salaries, advertising, and general and administrative expenses, that it would have incurred even if it did not sell a contract.

To illustrate, assume you purchase a new automobile from Hanlin Auto for $20,000. In addition to the regular warranty on the auto (the manufacturer will pay for all repairs

---

[15]A company separately prices a contract if the customer has the option to purchase the services provided under the contract for an expressly stated amount separate from the price of the product. An extended warranty or product maintenance contract usually meets these conditions.

for the first 36,000 miles or three years, whichever comes first), you purchase at a cost of $600 an extended warranty that protects you for an additional three years or 36,000 miles. Hanlin Auto records the sale of the automobile (with the regular warranty) and the sale of the extended warranty on January 2, 2014, as follows.

Cash	20,600	
Sales Revenue		20,000
Unearned Warranty Revenue		600

It recognizes revenue at the end of the fourth year (using straight-line amortization) as follows.

Unearned Warranty Revenue	200	
Warranty Revenue		200

Because the extended warranty contract only starts after the regular warranty expires, Hanlin Auto defers revenue recognition until the fourth year. If it incurs the costs of performing services under the extended warranty contract on other than a straight-line basis (as historical evidence might indicate), Hanlin Auto should recognize revenue over the contract period as it performs services under the contract. **[10]**[16]

Premiums and Coupons

Numerous companies offer premiums (either on a limited or continuing basis) to customers in return for boxtops, certificates, coupons, labels, or wrappers. The premium may be silverware, dishes, a small appliance, a toy, or free transportation. Also, **printed coupons** that can be redeemed for a cash discount on items purchased are extremely popular. A more recent marketing innovation is the **cash rebate**, which the buyer can obtain by returning the store receipt, a rebate coupon, and Universal Product Code (UPC label) or "bar code" to the manufacturer.[17]

Companies offer premiums, coupon offers, and rebates to stimulate sales. Thus companies should charge the **costs of premiums and coupons to expense in the period of the sale** that benefits from the plan. The period that benefits is not necessarily the period in which the company offered the premium. At the end of the accounting period, many premium offers may be outstanding and must be redeemed when presented in subsequent periods. In order to reflect the existing current liability and to match costs with revenues, the company estimates the number of outstanding premium offers that customers will present for redemption. The company then charges the cost of premium offers to Premium Expense. It credits the outstanding performance obligation to an account titled Premium Liability.

The following example illustrates the accounting treatment for a premium offer. Fluffy Cakemix Company offered its customers a large, nonbreakable mixing bowl in exchange for 25 cents and 10 boxtops. The mixing bowl costs Fluffy Cakemix Company 75 cents, and the company estimates that customers will redeem 60 percent of the boxtops. The premium offer began in June 2014 and resulted in the transactions journalized

Underlying Concepts 🔍

Warranties and coupons are loss contingencies that satisfy the conditions necessary for a liability. Regarding the income statement, the *expense recognition principle* requires that companies report the related expense in the period in which the sale occurs.

---

[16]The FASB requires additional disclosure requirements for warranties. A company must disclose its accounting policy and the method used to determine its warranty liability, and must present a tabular reconciliation of the changes in the product warranty liability. **[11]**

[17]Nearly 40 percent of cash rebates never get redeemed, and some customers complain about how difficult the rebate process is. See B. Grow, "The Great Rebate Runaround," *BusinessWeek* (December 5, 2005), pp. 34–37. Approximately 4 percent of coupons are redeemed. Redeemed coupons eventually make their way to the corporate headquarters of the stores that accept them. From there they are shipped to clearinghouses operated by A. C. Nielsen Company (of TV-rating fame) that count them and report back to the manufacturers who, in turn, reimburse the stores.

below. Fluffy Cakemix Company records purchase of 20,000 mixing bowls at 75 cents as follows.

Inventory of Premiums	15,000	
Cash		15,000

The entry to record sales of 300,000 boxes of cake mix at 80 cents would be:

Cash	240,000	
Sales Revenue		240,000

Fluffy records the actual redemption of 60,000 boxtops, the receipt of 25 cents per 10 boxtops, and the delivery of the mixing bowls as follows.

Cash [(60,000 ÷ 10) × $0.25]	1,500	
Premium Expense	3,000	
Inventory of Premiums		4,500
Computation: (60,000 ÷ 10) × $0.75 = $4,500		

Finally, Fluffy makes an end-of-period adjusting entry for estimated liability for outstanding premium offers (boxtops) as follows.

Premium Expense	6,000	
Premium Liability		6,000

Computation:

Total boxtops sold in 2014	300,000
Total estimated redemptions (60%)	180,000
Boxtops redeemed in 2014	60,000
Estimated future redemptions	120,000
Cost of estimated claims outstanding (120,000 ÷ 10) × ($0.75 − $0.25) = $6,000	

The December 31, 2014, balance sheet of Fluffy Cakemix Company reports an "Inventory of premiums" of $10,500 for the premium mixing bowls as a current asset and "Premium liability" of $6,000 as a current liability. The 2014 income statement reports a $9,000 "Premium expense" among the selling expenses.

What do the numbers mean? FREQUENT FLYERS

Numerous companies offer premiums to customers in the form of a promise of future goods or services as an incentive for purchases today. Premium plans that have widespread adoption are the frequent-flyer programs used by all major airlines. On the basis of mileage accumulated, frequent-flyer members receive discounted or free airline tickets. Airline customers can earn miles toward free travel by making long-distance phone calls, staying in hotels, and charging gasoline and groceries on a credit card. Those free tickets represent an enormous potential liability because people using them may displace paying passengers.

When airlines first started offering frequent-flyer bonuses, everyone assumed that they could accommodate the free-ticket holders with otherwise-empty seats. That made the additional cost of the program so minimal that airlines didn't accrue it or report the small liability. But, as more and more paying passengers have been crowded off flights by frequent-flyer awardees, the loss of revenues has grown enormously. For example, Delta Air Lines reported liabilities of over $4.5 billion for frequent-flyer tickets.

Environmental Liabilities

Estimates to clean up existing toxic waste sites total upward of $752 billion over a 30-year period. In addition, cost estimates of cleaning up our air and preventing future deterioration of the environment run even higher. These costs are likely to only grow, considering "Superfund legislation." This federal legislation provides the Environmental

Protection Agency (EPA) with the power to clean up waste sites and charge the clean-up costs to parties the EPA deems responsible for contaminating the site. These potentially responsible parties can have a significant liability.

In many industries, the construction and operation of long-lived assets involves obligations for the retirement of those assets. When a mining company opens up a strip mine, it may also commit to restore the land once it completes mining. Similarly, when an oil company erects an offshore drilling platform, it may be legally obligated to dismantle and remove the platform at the end of its useful life.

Accounting Recognition of Asset Retirement Obligations. A company must recognize an **asset retirement obligation (ARO)** when it has an existing legal obligation associated with the retirement of a long-lived asset and when it can reasonably estimate the amount of the liability. Companies should record the ARO at fair value. **[12]**

Obligating events. Examples of existing legal obligations, which require recognition of a liability include, but are not limited to:

- Decommissioning nuclear facilities;
- Dismantling, restoring, and reclamation of oil and gas properties;
- Certain closure, reclamation, and removal costs of mining facilities; and
- Closure and post-closure costs of landfills.

In order to capture the benefits of these long-lived assets, **the company is generally legally obligated for the costs associated with retirement of the asset, whether the company hires another party to perform the retirement activities or performs the activities with its own workforce and equipment.** AROs give rise to various recognition patterns. For example, the obligation may arise at the outset of the asset's use (e.g., erection of an oil-rig), or it may build over time (e.g., a landfill that expands over time).

Measurement. A company initially measures an ARO at fair value, which is defined as the amount that the company would pay in an active market to settle the ARO. While active markets do not exist for many AROs, companies should estimate fair value based on the best information available. Such information could include market prices of similar liabilities, if available. Alternatively, companies may use present value techniques to estimate fair value.

Recognition and allocation. To record an ARO in the financial statements, a company includes the cost associated with the ARO in the carrying amount of the related long-lived asset, and records a liability for the same amount. It records an asset retirement cost as part of the related asset because these costs are directly related to operating the asset and are necessary to prepare the asset for its intended use. Therefore, the specific asset (e.g., mine, drilling platform, nuclear power plant) should be increased because the future economic benefit comes from the use of this productive asset. **Companies should not record the capitalized asset retirement costs in a separate account because there is no future economic benefit that can be associated with these costs alone.**

In subsequent periods, companies allocate the cost of the ARO to expense over the period of the related asset's useful life. Companies may use the straight-line method for this allocation, as well as other systematic and rational allocations.

Example of ARO accounting provisions. To illustrate the accounting for AROs, assume that on January 1, 2014, Wildcat Oil Company erected an oil platform in the Gulf of

Mexico. Wildcat is legally required to dismantle and remove the platform at the end of its useful life, estimated to be five years. Wildcat estimates that dismantling and removal will cost $1,000,000. Based on a 10 percent discount rate, the fair value of the asset retirement obligation is estimated to be $620,920 ($1,000,000 × .62092). Wildcat records this ARO as follows.

January 1, 2014

Drilling Platform	620,920	
Asset Retirement Obligation		620,920

During the life of the asset, Wildcat allocates the asset retirement cost to expense. Using the straight-line method, Wildcat makes the following entries to record this expense.

December 31, 2014, 2015, 2016, 2017, 2018

Depreciation Expense ($620,920 ÷ 5)	124,184	
Accumulated Depreciation—Plant Assets		124,184

In addition, Wildcat must accrue interest expense each period. Wildcat records interest expense and the related increase in the asset retirement obligation on December 31, 2014, as follows.

December 31, 2014

Interest Expense ($620,920 × 10%)	62,092	
Asset Retirement Obligation		62,092

On January 10, 2019, Wildcat contracts with Rig Reclaimers, Inc. to dismantle the platform at a contract price of $995,000. Wildcat makes the following journal entry to record settlement of the ARO.

January 10, 2019

Asset Retirement Obligation	1,000,000	
Gain on Settlement of ARO		5,000
Cash		995,000

Companies provide extensive disclosure regarding environmental liabilities. In addition, some believe that companies should record more of these liabilities. The SEC recommends that companies not delay recognition of a liability due to significant uncertainty. The SEC argues that if the liability is within a range, and no amount within the range is the best estimate, then management should recognize the minimum amount of the range. That treatment is in accordance with GAAP. The SEC also believes that companies should report environmental liabilities in the balance sheet independent of recoveries from third parties. Thus, companies may not net possible insurance recoveries against liabilities but must show them separately. Because there is much litigation regarding recovery of insurance proceeds, these "assets" appear to be gain contingencies. Therefore, companies should not report these on the balance sheet.[18]

---

[18]As we indicated earlier, the FASB requires that, when some amount within the range appears at the time to be a better estimate than any other amount within the range, a company accrues that amount. When no amount within the range is a better estimate than any other amount, the company accrues the dollar amount at the low end of the range and discloses the dollar amount at the high end of the range. Unfortunately, in many cases, zero may arguably be the low point of the range, resulting in no liability being recognized. **[13], [14]**

Self-Insurance

As discussed earlier, contingencies are not recorded for general risks (e.g., losses that might arise due to poor expected economic conditions). Similarly, companies do not record contingencies for more specific future risks such as allowances for repairs. The reason: These items do meet the definition of a liability because they do not arise from a past transaction but instead relate to future events.

Some companies take out insurance policies against the potential losses from fire, flood, storm, and accident. Other companies do not. The reasons: Some risks are not insurable, the insurance rates are prohibitive (e.g., earthquakes and riots), or they make a business decision to self-insure. Self-insurance is another item that is not recognized as a contingency.

Despite its name, **self-insurance** is **not insurance but risk assumption**. Any company that assumes its own risks puts itself in the position of incurring expenses or losses as they happen. There is little theoretical justification for the establishment of a liability based on a hypothetical charge to insurance expense. This is "as if" accounting. The conditions for accrual stated in GAAP are not satisfied prior to the occurrence of the event. Until that time there is no diminution in the value of the property. And unlike an insurance company, which has contractual obligations to reimburse policyholders for losses, a company can have no such obligation to itself and, hence, no liability either before or after the occurrence of damage. **[15]**[19]

The note shown in Illustration 13-12 from the annual report of **Molson Coors Brewing Company** is typical of the self-insurance disclosure.

Molson Coors Brewing Company

Notes to Financial Statements (in part)

Note 21: Insurance. We are self-insured for certain insurable risks consisting primarily of employee health insurance programs, as well as workers' compensation, general liability, automobile liability, and property insurance deductibles or retentions . . . we fully insured future risks for long-term disability, and, in most states, workers' compensation, but maintained a self-insured position for workers' compensation for certain self-insured states and for claims incurred prior to the inception of the insurance coverage in Colorado in 1997.

ILLUSTRATION 13-12
Disclosure of Self-Insurance

Exposure to **risks of loss resulting from uninsured past injury to others**, however, is an existing condition involving uncertainty about the amount and timing of losses that may develop. In such a case, a contingency exists. A company with a fleet of vehicles for example, would have to accrue uninsured losses resulting from injury to others or damage to the property of others that took place prior to the date of the financial statements (if the experience of the company or other information enables it to make a reasonable estimate of the liability). However, it should not establish a liability for **expected future injury** to others or damage to the property of others, even if it can reasonably estimate the amount of losses.

[19]A commentary in *Forbes* (June 15, 1974, p. 42) stated its position on this matter quite succinctly: "The simple and unquestionable fact of life is this: Business is cyclical and full of unexpected surprises. Is it the role of accounting to disguise this unpleasant fact and create a fairyland of smoothly rising earnings? Or, should accounting reflect reality, warts and all—floods, expropriations and all manner of rude shocks?"

On November 19, 2001, Enron filed its third-quarter financial statements and reported on its balance sheet debt of approximately $13 billion. Yet on the same day, at a meeting to discuss its liquidity crisis, Enron informed its bankers that its debt was approximately $38 billion. Company officers described the difference of *$25 billion* as being either off-balance-sheet or on the balance sheet other than debt.

As a result of the Enron bankruptcy and other financial reporting scandals, Congress passed the Sarbanes-Oxley Act of 2002. One of its provisions mandates that the Securities and Exchange Commission conduct a study to determine the extent of off-balance-sheet transactions occurring in U.S. businesses.

Table 1 below indicates the extent of disclosure and recognition of contingent liabilities. The study classified contingent liabilities into three categories: (1) litigation contingent liabilities, (2) environmental liabilities, and (3) guarantees. The statistics provided relate to reports filed by 10,100 companies listed on the U.S. stock exchanges in 2005.

Table 1		
Type of Contingency	Companies Disclosing	Companies Recording
Litigation contingent liabilities	46.3%	5.1%
Environmental contingent liabilities	10.2%	5.1%
Guarantees	35.4%	10.2%

As Table 1 indicates, approximately 46 percent of companies disclosed litigation contingent liabilities, but only 5.1 percent recorded any liability related to these contingencies. On the other hand, 35 percent of the companies disclosed guarantees but a third of these companies (10.2 percent) recorded a liability for these contingencies.

Table 2 below shows the dollar amounts of the contingent liabilities companies disclosed and recorded.

Table 2		
Type of Contingency	Companies Disclosing ($ millions)	Companies Recording ($ millions)
Litigation contingent liabilities	$52,354	$11,814
Environmental contingent liabilities	$23,414	$18,723
Guarantees	$46,535,399	$123,949

Table 2 indicates that companies disclosed litigation contingent liabilities of approximately $52 billion, but recorded only $11.8 billion as liabilities. Incredibly, companies disclosed more than *$46 trillion* of guarantees, a small fraction of which (just $124 billion) they recorded as liabilities.

The results of this study suggest that the FASB must continue to address the issue of contingencies to ensure that companies provide relevant and representationally faithful information for these types of financial events.

Source: "Report and Recommendations Pursuant to Section 401(c) of the Sarbanes-Oxley Act of 2002 on Arrangements with Off-Balance Sheet Implications, Special Purpose Entities, and Transparency of Filings by Issuers," United States Securities and Exchange Commission, Office of Chief Accountant, Office of Economic Analyses, Division of Corporation Finance (June 2005).

PRESENTATION AND ANALYSIS
Presentation of Current Liabilities

LEARNING OBJECTIVE [6]

Indicate how to present and analyze liabilities and contingencies.

In practice, current liabilities are usually recorded and reported in financial statements at their full maturity value. Because of the short time periods involved, frequently less than one year, the difference between the present value of a current liability and the maturity value is usually not large. The profession accepts as immaterial any slight overstatement of liabilities that results from carrying current liabilities at maturity value. **[16]**[20]

[20]GAAP specifically exempts from present value measurements those payables arising from transactions with suppliers in the normal course of business that do not exceed approximately one year.

The current liabilities accounts are commonly presented as the first classification in the liabilities and stockholders' equity section of the balance sheet. Within the current liabilities section, companies may list the accounts in order of maturity, in descending order of amount, or in order of liquidation preference. Illustration 13-13 presents an excerpt of **Best Buy Co.**'s financial statements that is representative of the reports of large corporations.

ILLUSTRATION 13-13
Balance Sheet
Presentation of Current
Liabilities

Best Buy Co.
(dollars in thousands)

	March 3, 2012	February 26, 2011
Current assets		
Cash and cash equivalents	$ 1,199	$ 1,103
Short-term investments	—	22
Receivables	2,288	2,348
Merchandise inventories	5,731	5,897
Other current assets	1,079	1,103
Total current assets	$10,297	$10,473
Current liabilities		
Accounts payable	$ 5,364	$ 4,894
Unredeemed gift card liabilities	456	474
Accrued compensation and related expenses	539	570
Accrued liabilities	1,685	1,471
Accrued income taxes	288	256
Short-term debt	480	557
Current portion of long-term debt	43	441
Total current liabilities	$ 8,855	$ 8,663

Detail and supplemental information concerning current liabilities should be sufficient to meet the requirement of full disclosure. Companies should clearly identify secured liabilities, as well as indicate the related assets pledged as collateral. If the due date of any liability can be extended, a company should disclose the details. Companies should not offset current liabilities against assets that it will apply to their liquidation. Finally, current maturities of long-term debt are classified as current liabilities.

International Perspective

Companies reporting under IFRS often report noncurrent liabilities before current liabilities.

A major exception exists when a company will pay a currently maturing obligation from assets classified as long-term. For example, if a company will retire a bond payable using a bond sinking fund that is classified as a long-term asset, it should report the bonds payable in the long-term liabilities section. Presentation of this debt in the current liabilities section would distort the working capital position of the company.

If a company excludes a short-term obligation from current liabilities because of refinancing, it should include the following in the note to the financial statements:

1. A general description of the financing agreement.

2. The terms of any new obligation incurred or to be incurred.

3. The terms of any equity security issued or to be issued.

When a company expects to refinance on a long-term basis by issuing equity securities, it is not appropriate to include the short-term obligation in stockholders' equity. At the date of the balance sheet, the obligation is a liability and not stockholders' equity. Illustration 13-14 (on page 728) shows the disclosure requirements for an actual refinancing situation.

ILLUSTRATION 13-14
Actual Refinancing of
Short-Term Debt

	December 31, 2014
Current liabilities	
Accounts payable	$ 3,600,000
Accrued payables	2,500,000
Income taxes payable	1,100,000
Current portion of long-term debt	1,000,000
Total current liabilities	$ 8,200,000
Long-term debt	
Notes payable refinanced in January 2015 (Note 1)	$ 2,000,000
11% bonds due serially through 2025	15,000,000
Total long-term debt	$17,000,000

Note 1: On January 19, 2015, the Company issued 50,000 shares of common stock and received proceeds totaling $2,385,000, of which $2,000,000 was used to liquidate notes payable that matured on February 1, 2015. Accordingly, such notes payable have been classified as long-term debt at December 31, 2014.

Presentation of Contingencies

A company records a loss contingency and a liability if the loss is both probable and estimable. But, if the loss is **either probable or estimable but not both**, and if there is at least a **reasonable possibility** that a company may have incurred a liability, it must disclose the following in the notes.

1. The nature of the contingency.
2. An estimate of the possible loss or range of loss or a statement that an estimate cannot be made.

Illustration 13-15 presents an extensive litigation disclosure note from the financial statements of **Raymark Corporation**. The note indicates that Raymark charged actual losses to operations and that a further liability may exist, but that the company cannot currently estimate this liability.

ILLUSTRATION 13-15
Disclosure of Loss
Contingency through
Litigation

Raymark Corporation

Note I: Litigation. Raymark is a defendant or co-defendant in a substantial number of lawsuits alleging wrongful injury and/or death from exposure to asbestos fibers in the air. The following table summarizes the activity in these lawsuits:

Claims	
Pending at beginning of year	8,719
Received during year	4,494
Settled or otherwise disposed of	(1,445)
Pending at end of year	11,768
Average indemnification cost	$3,364
Average cost per case, including defense costs	$6,499
Trial activity	
Verdicts for the Company	23
Total trials	36

The following table presents the cost of defending asbestos litigation, together with related insurance and workers' compensation expenses.

Included in operating profit	$ 1,872,000
Nonoperating expense	9,077,000
Total	$10,949,000

The Company is seeking to reasonably determine its liability. However, it is not possible to predict which theory of insurance will apply, the number of lawsuits still to be filed, the cost of settling and defending the existing and unfiled cases, or the ultimate impact of these lawsuits on the Company's consolidated financial statements.

Companies should disclose certain other contingent liabilities, even though the possibility of loss may be remote, as follows.

1. Guarantees of indebtedness of others.

2. Obligations of commercial banks under "stand-by letters of credit."

3. Guarantees to repurchase receivables (or any related property) that have been sold or assigned.

International Perspective

GAAP provides more guidance on the content of disclosures about contingencies than does IFRS.

Disclosure should include the nature and amount of the guarantee and, if estimable, the amount that the company can recover from outside parties.[21] **Cities Service Company** disclosed its guarantees of others' indebtedness in the following note.

Cities Service Company

Note 10: Contingent Liabilities. The Company and certain subsidiaries have guaranteed debt obligations of approximately $62 million of companies in which substantial stock investments are held. Also, under long-term agreements with certain pipeline companies in which stock interests are held, the Company and its subsidiaries have agreed to provide minimum revenue for product shipments. The Company has guaranteed mortgage debt ($80 million) incurred by a 50 percent owned tanker affiliate for construction of tankers which are under long-term charter contracts to the Company and others. It is not anticipated that any loss will result from any of the above described agreements.

ILLUSTRATION 13-16
Disclosure of Guarantees of Indebtedness

Analysis of Current Liabilities

The distinction between current liabilities and long-term debt is important. It provides information about the liquidity of the company. Liquidity regarding a liability is the expected time to elapse before its payment. In other words, a liability soon to be paid is a current liability. A liquid company is better able to withstand a financial downturn. Also, it has a better chance of taking advantage of investment opportunities that develop.

Analysts use certain basic ratios such as net cash flow provided by operating activities to current liabilities, and the turnover ratios for receivables and inventory, to assess liquidity. Two other ratios used to examine liquidity are the current ratio and the acid-test ratio.

Current Ratio

The **current ratio** is the ratio of total current assets to total current liabilities. Illustration 13-17 shows its formula.

$$\text{Current ratio} = \frac{\text{Current assets}}{\text{Current liabilities}}$$

ILLUSTRATION 13-17
Formula for Current Ratio

The ratio is frequently expressed as a coverage of so many times. Sometimes it is called the **working capital ratio** because working capital is the excess of current assets over current liabilities.

---

[21]As discussed earlier (footnote 16), the FASB has issued additional disclosure and recognition requirements for guarantees. The interpretation responds to confusion about the reporting of guarantees used in certain transactions. The new rules expand existing disclosure requirements for most guarantees, including loan guarantees such as standby letters of credit. It also will result in companies recognizing more liabilities at fair value for the obligations assumed under a guarantee. **[17]**

A satisfactory current ratio does not disclose that a portion of the current assets may be tied up in slow-moving inventories. With inventories, especially raw materials and work in process, there is a question of how long it will take to transform them into the finished product and what ultimately will be realized in the sale of the merchandise. Eliminating the inventories, along with any prepaid expenses, from the amount of current assets might provide better information for short-term creditors. Therefore, some analysts use the acid-test ratio in place of the current ratio.

Acid-Test Ratio

Many analysts favor an **acid-test** or **quick ratio** that relates total current liabilities to cash, marketable securities, and receivables. Illustration 13-18 shows the formula for this ratio. As you can see, the acid-test ratio does not include inventories.

ILLUSTRATION 13-18
Formula for Acid-Test Ratio

$$\text{Acid-test ratio} = \frac{\text{Cash} + \text{Short-term investments} + \text{Net receivables}}{\text{Current liabilities}}$$

To illustrate the computation of these two ratios, we use the information for **Best Buy Co.** in Illustration 13-13 (on page 727). Illustration 13-19 shows the computation of the current and acid-test ratios for Best Buy.

ILLUSTRATION 13-19
Computation of Current and Acid-Test Ratios for Best Buy Co.

$$\text{Current ratio} = \frac{\text{Current assets}}{\text{Current liabilities}} = \frac{\$10,297}{\$8,855} = 1.16 \text{ times}$$

$$\text{Acid-test ratio} = \frac{\text{Cash} + \text{Short-term investments} + \text{Net receivables}}{\text{Current liabilities}} = \frac{\$3,487}{\$8,855} = 0.39 \text{ times}$$

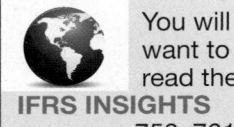

You will want to read the **IFRS INSIGHTS** on pages 753–761 for discussion of IFRS related to current liabilities and contingencies.

From this information, it appears that Best Buy's current position is adequate. However, the acid-test ratio is well below 1. A comparison to another retailer, **RadioShack**, whose current ratio is 2.73 and whose acid-test ratio is 1.44, indicates that Best Buy is less liquid and carrying more inventory than its industry counterparts.

🔍 **Evolving Issue**   *GREENHOUSE GASES: LET'S BE STANDARD-SETTERS*

Ok, here is your chance to determine what to do about a very fundamental issue—how to account for greenhouse gases (GHG), often referred to as carbon emissions. Many governments are trying a market-based system, in which companies pay for an excessive amount of carbon emissions put into the atmosphere. In this market-based system, companies are granted carbon allowance permits. Each permit allows them to discharge, as an example, one metric ton of carbon dioxide (CO_2). In some cases, companies may receive a number of these permits free—in other situations, they must pay for them. Other approaches require companies only to pay when they exceed a certain amount. The question is, how to account for these permits and related liabilities? For example, what happens when the permits issued by the government are free? Should an asset and revenue be reported? And if an

asset is recorded, should the debit be to an intangible asset or inventory? Also, should the company recognize a liability related to its pollution? And how do we account for companies that have to purchase permits because they have exceeded their allowance?

Two views seem to have emerged. The first is referred to as the **net liability approach**. In this approach, a company does not recognize an asset or liability. A company only recognizes a liability once GHG exceed the permits granted. To illustrate, Holton Refinery receives permits on January 1, 2014, representing the right to emit 10,000 tons of GHG for the year 2014. Other data:

- The market price of each permit at date of issuance is $10 per ton.

- During the year, Holton emits 12,000 tons.
- The market price for a permit is now $16 per ton at December 31, 2014.

Under the net liability approach, Holton records only a liability of $32,000 for the additional amount that it must pay for the 2,000 permits it must purchase at $16 per ton.

Another approach is referred to as the **government grant approach**. In this approach, permits granted by the government are recorded at their fair value based on the initial price of $10 per ton. The asset recorded is an intangible asset. At the same time, an Unearned Revenue account is credited, which is subsequently recognized in income over the 2014 year. During 2014, a liability and a related emission expense of $132,000 is recognized (10,000 tons × $10 + 2,000 tons × $16). The chart below compares the results of each approach on the financial statements.

Net Liability Approach		Government Grant Approach
Income Statement		
Revenues	$ 0	$100,000
Emission expenses	32,000	132,000
Net loss	$32,000	$ 32,000
Balance Sheet		
Assets	$ 0	$100,000
Liabilities	32,000	132,000

So what do you think—net liability or government grant approach? As indicated, companies presently can report this information either way, plus some other variants which were not mentioned here. Please feel free to contact the FASB regarding your views.

SUMMARY OF LEARNING OBJECTIVES

1 **Describe the nature, type, and valuation of current liabilities.** Current liabilities are obligations whose liquidation a company reasonably expects to require the use of current assets or the creation of other current liabilities. Theoretically, liabilities should be measured by the present value of the future outlay of cash required to liquidate them. In practice, companies usually record and report current liabilities at their full maturity value.

There are several types of current liabilities, such as (1) accounts payable, (2) notes payable, (3) current maturities of long-term debt, (4) dividends payable, (5) customer advances and deposits, (6) unearned revenues, (7) taxes payable, and (8) employee-related liabilities.

2 **Explain the classification issues of short-term debt expected to be refinanced.** A short-term obligation is excluded from current liabilities if both of the following conditions are met. (1) The company must intend to refinance the obligation on a long-term basis, *and* (2) it must demonstrate an ability to consummate the refinancing.

3 **Identify types of employee-related liabilities.** The employee-related liabilities are (1) payroll deductions, (2) compensated absences, and (3) bonus agreements.

4 **Identify the criteria used to account for and disclose gain and loss contingencies.** Gain contingencies are not recorded. Instead, they are disclosed in the notes only when the probabilities are high that a gain contingency will occur. A company should accrue an estimated loss from a loss contingency by charging expense and recording a liability only if *both* of the following conditions are met. (1) Information available prior to the issuance of the financial statements indicates that it is probable

KEY TERMS

accumulated rights, *713*

acid-test (quick) ratio, *730*

asset retirement obligation, *723*

bonus, *714*

cash dividend payable, *707*

compensated absences, *712*

contingency, *715*

contingent liabilities, *716*

current liabilities, *702*

current maturities of long-term debt, *705*

current ratio, *729*

expense warranty approach, *719*

FICA, *710*

FUTA, *711*

gain contingencies, *715*

liabilities, *702*

litigation, claims, and assessments, *718*

loss contingencies, *716*

notes payable (trade notes payable), *703*

OASDI, *710*

operating cycle, *702*

preferred dividends in arrears, *707*

premium, *721*

probable (contingency), *716*

reasonably possible (contingency), *716*

remote (contingency), *716*

returnable cash deposits, *707*

sales warranty approach, *720*

self-insurance, *725*

short-term obligations expected to be refinanced, *705*

Social Security tax, *711*

trade accounts payable, *703*

trade notes payable, *703*

unearned revenues, *708*

vested rights, *713*

warranty, *719*

working capital ratio, *729*

that a liability has been incurred at the date of the financial statements, and (2) the amount of the loss can be reasonably estimated.

5 **Explain the accounting for different types of loss contingencies.** The following factors must be considered in determining whether to record a liability with respect to pending or threatened litigation and actual or possible claims and assessments: (1) the time period in which the underlying cause for action occurred, (2) the probability of an unfavorable outcome, and (3) the ability to reasonably estimate the amount of loss.

If it is probable that customers will make claims under warranties relating to goods or services that have been sold and it can reasonably estimate the costs involved, the company uses the accrual method. It charges warranty costs under the accrual basis to operating expense in the year of sale.

Premiums, coupon offers, and rebates are made to stimulate sales. Companies should charge their costs to expense in the period of the sale that benefits from the premium plan.

A company must recognize asset retirement obligations when it has an existing legal obligation related to the retirement of a long-lived asset and it can reasonably estimate the amount.

6 **Indicate how to present and analyze liabilities and contingencies.** The current liability accounts are usually presented as the first classification in the liabilities and stockholders' equity section of the balance sheet. Within the current liabilities section, companies may list the accounts in order of maturity, in descending order of amount, or in order of liquidation preference. Detail and supplemental information concerning current liabilities should be sufficient to meet the requirement of full disclosure. If the loss is either probable or estimable but not both, and if there is at least a reasonable possibility that a company may have incurred a liability, it should disclose in the notes both the nature of the contingency and an estimate of the possible loss. Two ratios used to analyze liquidity are the current and acid-test ratios.

DEMONSTRATION PROBLEM

Listed below are selected transactions of Baileys' Department Store for the current year ending December 31.

1. On December 5, the store received $500 from the Jackson Players as a deposit to be returned after certain furniture to be used in stage production was returned on January 15.
2. During December, cash sales totaled $798,000, which includes the 5% sales tax that must be remitted to the state by the fifteenth day of the following month.
3. On December 10, the store purchased for cash three delivery trucks for $120,000. The trucks were purchased in a state that applies a 5% sales tax.
4. The store determined it will cost $100,000 to restore the area (considered a land improvement) surrounding one of its store parking lots, when the store is closed in 2 years. Baileys' estimates the fair value of the obligation at December 31 is $84,000.
5. As a result of uninsured accidents during the year, personal injury suits for $350,000 and $60,000 have been filed against the company. It is the judgment of Baileys' legal counsel that an unfavorable outcome is unlikely in the $60,000 case but that an unfavorable verdict approximating $250,000 (reliably estimated) will probably result in the $350,000 case.
6. Baileys' Midwest store division consisting of 12 stores in "Tornado Alley" is uninsurable because of the special risk of injury to customers, employees, and losses due to severe weather and subpar construction standards in older malls. The year 2014 is considered one of the safest (luckiest) in the division's history because no loss due to injury or casualty was suffered. Having suffered an average of three casualties a year during the rest of the past decade (ranging from $60,000 to $700,000), management is certain that next year the company will probably not be so fortunate.

Instructions

(a) Prepare all the journal entries necessary to record the transactions noted above as they occurred and any adjusting journal entries relative to the transactions that would be required to present fair financial statements at December 31. Date each entry. For simplicity, assume that adjusting entries are recorded only once a year on December 31.

(b) For items 5 and 6, indicate what should be reported relative to each situation in the financial statements and accompanying notes. Explain why.

Solution

(a)

1. Dec. 5	Cash		500	
	Due to Customer			500
2. Dec. 1–31	Cash		798,000	
	Sales Revenue ($798,000 ÷ 1.05)			760,000
	Sales Taxes Payable ($760,000 × .05)			38,000
3. Dec. 10	Trucks ($120,000 × 1.05)		126,000	
	Cash			126,000
4. Dec. 31	Land Improvements		84,000	
	Asset Retirement Obligation			84,000
5.	Lawsuit Loss		250,000	
	Lawsuit Liability			250,000

6. No entry required.

(b) 5. A loss and a liability have been recorded in the first case because (i) information is available prior to the issuance of the financial statements that indicates it is probable that a liability had been incurred at the date of the financial statements and (ii) the amount is reasonably estimable. That is, the occurrence of the uninsured accidents during the year plus the outstanding injury suits and the attorney's estimate of probable loss required recognition of a loss contingency.

6. Even though Baileys' Midwest store division is uninsurable due to high risk and has sustained repeated losses in the past, as of the balance sheet date no assets have been impaired or liabilities incurred, nor is an amount reasonably estimable. Therefore, this situation does not satisfy the criteria for recognition of a loss contingency. Also, unless a casualty has occurred or there is some other evidence to indicate impairment of an asset prior to the issuance of the financial statements, there is no disclosure required relative to a loss contingency. Disclosure is required when one or both of the criteria for a loss contingency are not satisfied and there is a reasonable possibility that a liability may have been incurred or an asset impaired, or it is probable that a claim will be asserted and there is a reasonable possibility of an unfavorable outcome.

FASB CODIFICATION

FASB Codification References

[1] FASB ASC 480-10-05. [Predecessor literature: "Accounting for Certain Financial Instruments with Characteristics of Both Liabilities and Equity," *Statement of Financial Accounting Standards No. 150* (Norwalk, Conn.: FASB, 2003).]

[2] FASB ASC 210-10-45-6. [Predecessor literature: Committee on Accounting Procedure, American Institute of Certified Public Accountants, "Accounting Research and Terminology Bulletins," Final Edition (New York: AICPA, 1961), p. 21.]

[3] FASB ASC 470-10-05-7. [Predecessor literature: "Classification of Short-term Obligations Expected to Be Refinanced," *Statement of Financial Accounting Standards No. 6* (Stamford, Conn.: FASB, 1975), par. 2.]

[4] FASB ASC 470-10-45-11. [Predecessor literature: "Classification of Obligations That Are Callable by the Creditor," *Statement of Financial Accounting Standards No. 78* (Stamford, Conn.: FASB, 1983).]

[5] FASB ASC 470-10-45-14. [Predecessor literature: "Classification of Short-term Obligations Expected to Be Refinanced," *Statement of Financial Accounting Standards No. 6* (Stamford, Conn.: FASB, 1975), paras. 10 and 11.]

[6] FASB ASC 710-10-25-1. [Predecessor literature: "Accounting for Compensated Absences," *Statement of Financial Accounting Standards No. 43* (Stamford, Conn.: FASB, 1980), par. 6.]

[7] FASB ASC 712-10-05. [Predecessor literature: "Employers' Accounting for Postemployment Benefits," *Statement of Financial Accounting Standards No. 112* (Norwalk, Conn.: FASB, November 1992), par. 18.]

[8] FASB ASC 450-10-05-4. [Predecessor literature: "Accounting for Contingencies," *Statement of Financial Accounting Standards No. 5* (Stamford, Conn.: FASB, 1975), par. 1.]

[9] FASB ASC 605-20-25. [Predecessor literature: "Accounting for Separately Extended Warranty and Product Maintenance Contracts," *FASB Technical Bulletin No. 90-1* (Stamford, Conn.: FASB, 1990).]

[10] FASB ASC 605-20-25-3. [Predecessor literature: "Accounting for Separately Extended Warranty and Product Maintenance Contracts," *FASB Technical Bulletin No. 90-1* (Stamford, Conn.: FASB, 1990).]

[11] FASB ASC 460-10-50-8. [Predecessor literature: "Guarantor's Accounting and Disclosure Requirements for Guarantees, Including Indirect Guarantees of Indebtedness of Others," *FASB Interpretation No. 45* (Norwalk, Conn.: FASB, 2002).]

[12] FASB ASC 410-20-05. [Predecessor literature: "Accounting for Asset Retirement Obligations," *Statement of Financial Accounting Standards No. 143* (Norwalk, Conn.: FASB, 2001).]

[13] FASB ASC 450-20-30-1. [Predecessor literature: "Reasonable Estimation of the Amount of a Loss," *FASB Interpretation No. 14* (Stamford, Conn.: FASB, 1976), par. 3.]

[14] FASB ASC 450-10-05. [Predecessor literature: "Accounting for Contingencies," *FASB Statement No. 5* (Stamford, Conn.: FASB, 1975).]

[15] FASB ASC 450-20-55-5. [Predecessor literature: "Accounting for Contingencies," *FASB Statement No. 5* (Stamford, Conn.: FASB, 1975), par. 28.]

[16] FASB ASC 835-30-15-3. [Predecessor literature: "Interest on Receivables and Payables," *Opinions of the Accounting Principles Board No. 21* (New York: AICPA, 1971), par. 3.]

[17] FASB ASC 460-10-50-8. [Predecessor literature: "Guarantor's Accounting and Disclosure Requirements for Guarantees, Including Indirect Guarantees of Indebtedness of Others," *FASB Interpretation No. 45* (Norwalk, Conn.: FASB, 2002).]

Exercises

If your school has a subscription to the FASB Codification, go to *http://aaahq.org/asclogin.cfm* to log in and prepare responses to the following. Provide Codification references for your responses.

CE13-1 Access the glossary ("Master Glossary") to answer the following.

    (a) What is an asset retirement obligation?
    (b) What is the definition of "current liabilities"?
    (c) What does it mean if something is "reasonably possible"?
    (d) What is a warranty?

CE13-2 What must an entity disclose about its asset retirement obligations?

CE13-3 What are three examples of estimates that are used in accounting that are not contingencies? Can you explain why they are not considered contingencies?

CE13-4 Under what conditions must an employer accrue a liability for employees' compensation for future absences?

An additional Codification case can be found in the Using Your Judgment section, on page 753.

Be sure to check the book's companion website for a Review and Analysis Exercise, with solution.

WileyPLUS Brief Exercises, Exercises, Problems, and many more learning and assessment tools and resources are available for practice in WileyPLUS.

QUESTIONS

1. Distinguish between a current liability and a long-term debt.

2. Assume that your friend Will Morris, who is a music major, asks you to define and discuss the nature of a liability. Assist him by preparing a definition of a liability and by explaining to him what you believe are the elements or factors inherent in the concept of a liability.

3. Why is the liabilities section of the balance sheet of primary significance to bankers?

4. How are current liabilities related by definition to current assets? How are current liabilities related to a company's operating cycle?

5. Leon Wight, a newly hired loan analyst, is examining the current liabilities of a corporate loan applicant. He observes that unearned revenues have declined in the current year compared to the prior year. Is this a positive indicator about the client's liquidity? Explain.

6. How is present value related to the concept of a liability?

7. What is the nature of a "discount" on notes payable?

8. How should a debt callable by the creditor be reported in the debtor's financial statements?

9. Under what conditions should a short-term obligation be excluded from current liabilities?

10. What evidence is necessary to demonstrate the ability to consummate the refinancing of short-term debt?

11. Discuss the accounting treatment or disclosure that should be accorded a declared but unpaid cash dividend, an accumulated but undeclared dividend on cumulative preferred stock, and a stock dividend distributable.

12. How does unearned revenue arise? Why can it be classified properly as a current liability? Give several examples of business activities that result in unearned revenues.

13. What are compensated absences?

14. Under what conditions must an employer accrue a liability for the cost of compensated absences?

15. Under what conditions is an employer required to accrue a liability for sick pay? Under what conditions is an employer permitted but not required to accrue a liability for sick pay?

16. Faith Battle operates a health food store, and she has been the only employee. Her business is growing, and she is considering hiring some additional staff to help her in the store. Explain to her the various payroll deductions that she will have to account for, including their potential impact on her financial statements, if she hires additional staff.

17. Define (a) a contingency and (b) a contingent liability.

18. Under what conditions should a contingent liability be recorded?

19. Distinguish between a determinable current liability and a contingent liability. Give two examples of each type.

20. How are the terms "probable," "reasonably possible," and "remote" related to contingent liabilities?

21. Contrast the cash-basis method and the accrual method of accounting for warranty costs.

22. Grant Company has had a record-breaking year in terms of growth in sales and profitability. However, market research indicates that it will experience operating losses in two of its major businesses next year. The controller has proposed that the company record a provision for these future losses this year, since it can afford to take the charge and still show good results. Advise the controller on the appropriateness of this charge.

23. How does the expense warranty approach differ from the sales warranty approach?

24. Southeast Airlines Inc. awards members of its Flightline program a second ticket at half price, valid for 2 years anywhere on its flight system, when a full-price ticket is purchased. How would you account for the full-fare and half-fare tickets?

25. Pacific Airlines Co. awards members of its Frequent Fliers Club one free round-trip ticket, anywhere on its flight system, for every 50,000 miles flown on its planes. How would you account for the free ticket award?

26. When must a company recognize an asset retirement obligation?

27. Should a liability be recorded for risk of loss due to lack of insurance coverage? Discuss.

28. What factors must be considered in determining whether or not to record a liability for pending litigation? For threatened litigation?

29. Within the current liabilities section, how do you believe the accounts should be listed? Defend your position.

30. How does the acid-test ratio differ from the current ratio? How are they similar?

31. When should liabilities for each of the following items be recorded on the books of an ordinary business corporation?

    (a) Acquisition of goods by purchase on credit.

    (b) Officers' salaries.

    (c) Special bonus to employees.

    (d) Dividends.

    (e) Purchase commitments.

BRIEF EXERCISES

1 **BE13-1** Roley Corporation uses a periodic inventory system and the gross method of accounting for purchase discounts. On July 1, Roley purchased $60,000 of inventory, terms 2/10, n/30, FOB shipping point. Roley paid freight costs of $1,200. On July 3, Roley returned damaged goods and received credit of $6,000. On July 10, Roley paid for the goods. Prepare all necessary journal entries for Roley.

BE13-2 Upland Company borrowed $40,000 on November 1, 2014, by signing a $40,000, 9%, 3-month note. Prepare Upland's November 1, 2014, entry; the December 31, 2014, annual adjusting entry; and the February 1, 2015, entry.

BE13-3 Takemoto Corporation borrowed $60,000 on November 1, 2014, by signing a $61,350, 3-month, zero-interest-bearing note. Prepare Takemoto's November 1, 2014, entry; the December 31, 2014, annual adjusting entry; and the February 1, 2015, entry.

BE13-4 At December 31, 2014, Burr Corporation owes $500,000 on a note payable due February 15, 2015. (a) If Burr refinances the obligation by issuing a long-term note on February 14 and using the proceeds to pay off the note due February 15, how much of the $500,000 should be reported as a current liability at December 31, 2014? (b) If Burr pays off the note on February 15, 2015, and then borrows $1,000,000 on a long-term basis on March 1, how much of the $500,000 should be reported as a current liability at December 31, 2014, the end of the fiscal year?

BE13-5 Sport Pro Magazine sold 12,000 annual subscriptions on August 1, 2014, for $18 each. Prepare Sport Pro's August 1, 2014, journal entry and the December 31, 2014, annual adjusting entry, assuming the magazines are published and delivered monthly.

BE13-6 Dillons Corporation made credit sales of $30,000 which are subject to 6% sales tax. The corporation also made cash sales which totaled $20,670 including the 6% sales tax. (a) Prepare the entry to record Dillons' credit sales. (b) Prepare the entry to record Dillons' cash sales.

BE13-7 Lexington Corporation's weekly payroll of $24,000 included FICA taxes withheld of $1,836, federal taxes withheld of $2,990, state taxes withheld of $920, and insurance premiums withheld of $250. Prepare the journal entry to record Lexington's payroll.

BE13-8 Kasten Inc. provides paid vacations to its employees. At December 31, 2014, 30 employees have each earned 2 weeks of vacation time. The employees' average salary is $500 per week. Prepare Kasten's December 31, 2014, adjusting entry.

BE13-9 Mayaguez Corporation provides its officers with bonuses based on net income. For 2014, the bonuses total $350,000 and are paid on February 15, 2015. Prepare Mayaguez's December 31, 2014, adjusting entry and the February 15, 2015, entry.

BE13-10 Scorcese Inc. is involved in a lawsuit at December 31, 2014. (a) Prepare the December 31 entry assuming it is probable that Scorcese will be liable for $900,000 as a result of this suit. (b) Prepare the December 31 entry, if any, assuming it is *not* probable that Scorcese will be liable for any payment as a result of this suit.

BE13-11 Buchanan Company recently was sued by a competitor for patent infringement. Attorneys have determined that it is probable that Buchanan will lose the case and that a reasonable estimate of damages to be paid by Buchanan is $300,000. In light of this case, Buchanan is considering establishing a $100,000 self-insurance allowance. What entry(ies), if any, should Buchanan record to recognize this loss contingency?

BE13-12 Calaf's Drillers erects and places into service an off-shore oil platform on January 1, 2015, at a cost of $10,000,000. Calaf is legally required to dismantle and remove the platform at the end of its useful life in 10 years. Calaf estimates it will cost $1,000,000 to dismantle and remove the platform at the end of its useful life in 10 years. (The fair value at January 1, 2015, of the dismantle and removal costs is $450,000.) Prepare the entry to record the asset retirement obligation.

BE13-13 Streep Factory provides a 2-year warranty with one of its products which was first sold in 2014. In that year, Streep spent $70,000 servicing warranty claims. At year-end, Streep estimates that an additional $400,000 will be spent in the future to service warranty claims related to 2014 sales. Prepare Streep's journal entry to record the $70,000 expenditure and the December 31 adjusting entry, assuming the expenditures are inventory costs.

BE13-14 Leppard Corporation sells DVD players. The corporation also offers its customers a 2-year warranty contract. During 2014, Leppard sold 20,000 warranty contracts at $99 each. The corporation spent $180,000 servicing warranties during 2014, and it estimates that an additional $900,000 will be spent in the future to service the warranties. Prepare Leppard's journal entries for (a) the sale of contracts, (b) the cost of servicing the warranties, and (c) the recognition of warranty revenue. Assume the service costs are inventory costs.

BE13-15 Wynn Company offers a set of building blocks to customers who send in 3 UPC codes from Wynn cereal, along with 50¢. The block sets cost Wynn $1.10 each to purchase and 60¢ each to mail to customers. During 2014, Wynn sold 1,200,000 boxes of cereal. The company expects 30% of the UPC codes to be sent in. During 2014, 120,000 UPC codes were redeemed. Prepare Wynn's December 31, 2014, adjusting entry.

EXERCISES

1 ▶ **E13-1 (Balance Sheet Classification of Various Liabilities)** How would each of the following items be reported on the balance sheet?

(a) Accrued vacation pay.
(b) Estimated taxes payable.
(c) Service warranties on appliance sales.
(d) Bank overdraft.
(e) Employee payroll deductions unremitted.
(f) Unpaid bonus to officers.
(g) Deposit received from customer to guarantee performance of a contract.
(h) Sales taxes payable.
(i) Gift certificates sold to customers but not yet redeemed.

(j) Premium offers outstanding.
(k) Discount on notes payable.
(l) Personal injury claim pending.
(m) Current maturities of long-term debts to be paid from current assets.
(n) Cash dividends declared but unpaid.
(o) Dividends in arrears on preferred stock.
(p) Loans from officers.

1 ▶ **E13-2 (Accounts and Notes Payable)** The following are selected 2014 transactions of Sean Astin Corporation.

Sept. 1 Purchased inventory from Encino Company on account for $50,000. Astin records purchases gross and uses a periodic inventory system.
Oct. 1 Issued a $50,000, 12-month, 8% note to Encino in payment of account.
Oct. 1 Borrowed $50,000 from the Shore Bank by signing a 12-month, zero-interest-bearing $54,000 note.

Instructions
(a) Prepare journal entries for the selected transactions above.
(b) Prepare adjusting entries at December 31.
(c) Compute the total net liability to be reported on the December 31 balance sheet for:
  (1) The interest-bearing note.
  (2) The zero-interest-bearing note.

2 ▶ **E13-3 (Refinancing of Short-Term Debt)** On December 31, 2014, Hattie McDaniel Company had $1,200,000 of short-term debt in the form of notes payable due February 2, 2015. On January 21, 2015, the company issued 25,000 shares of its common stock for $38 per share, receiving $950,000 proceeds after brokerage fees and other costs of issuance. On February 2, 2015, the proceeds from the stock sale, supplemented by an additional $250,000 cash, are used to liquidate the $1,200,000 debt. The December 31, 2014, balance sheet is issued on February 23, 2015.

Instructions
Show how the $1,200,000 of short-term debt should be presented on the December 31, 2014, balance sheet, including note disclosure.

2 ▶ **E13-4 (Refinancing of Short-Term Debt)** On December 31, 2014, Kate Holmes Company has $7,000,000 of short-term debt in the form of notes payable to Gotham State Bank due in 2015. On January 28, 2015, Holmes enters into a refinancing agreement with Gotham that will permit it to borrow up to 60% of the gross amount of its accounts receivable. Receivables are expected to range between a low of $6,000,000 in May to a high of $8,000,000 in October during the year 2015. The interest cost of the maturing short-term debt is 15%, and the new agreement calls for a fluctuating interest at 1% above the prime rate on notes due in 2019. Holmes's December 31, 2014, balance sheet is issued on February 15, 2015.

Instructions
Prepare a partial balance sheet for Holmes at December 31, 2014, showing how its $7,000,000 of short-term debt should be presented, including footnote disclosure.

3 ▶ **E13-5 (Compensated Absences)** Matt Broderick Company began operations on January 2, 2013. It employs 9 individuals who work 8-hour days and are paid hourly. Each employee earns 10 paid vacation days and 6 paid sick days annually. Vacation days may be taken after January 15 of the year following the year in which they are earned. Sick days may be taken as soon as they are earned; unused sick days accumulate. Additional information is as follows.

Actual Hourly Wage Rate		Vacation Days Used by Each Employee		Sick Days Used by Each Employee	
2013	2014	2013	2014	2013	2014
$10	$11	0	9	4	5

Matt Broderick Company has chosen to accrue the cost of compensated absences at rates of pay in effect during the period when earned and to accrue sick pay when earned.

Instructions

(a) Prepare journal entries to record transactions related to compensated absences during 2013 and 2014.

(b) Compute the amounts of any liability for compensated absences that should be reported on the balance sheet at December 31, 2013 and 2014.

E13-6 (Compensated Absences) Assume the facts in E13-5 except that Matt Broderick Company has chosen not to accrue paid sick leave until used, and has chosen to accrue vacation time at expected future rates of pay without discounting. The company used the following projected rates to accrue vacation time.

Year in Which Vacation Time Was Earned	Projected Future Pay Rates Used to Accrue Vacation Pay
2013	$10.75
2014	11.60

Instructions

(a) Prepare journal entries to record transactions related to compensated absences during 2013 and 2014.

(b) Compute the amounts of any liability for compensated absences that should be reported on the balance sheet at December 31, 2013, and 2014.

E13-7 (Adjusting Entry for Sales Tax) During the month of June, Rowling Boutique had cash sales of $233,200 and credit sales of $153,700, both of which include the 6% sales tax that must be remitted to the state by July 15.

Instructions

Prepare the adjusting entry that should be recorded to fairly present the June 30 financial statements.

E13-8 (Payroll Tax Entries) The payroll of YellowCard Company for September 2013 is as follows.

Total payroll was $480,000, of which $110,000 is exempt from Social Security tax because it represented amounts paid in excess of $113,700 to certain employees. The amount paid to employees in excess of $7,000 was $400,000. Income taxes in the amount of $80,000 were withheld, as was $9,000 in union dues. The state unemployment tax is 3.5%, but YellowCard Company is allowed a credit of 2.3% by the state for its unemployment experience. Also, assume that the current FICA tax is 7.65% on an employee's wages to $113,700 and 1.45% in excess of $113,700. No employee for YellowCard makes more than $125,000. The federal unemployment tax rate is 0.8% after state credit.

Instructions

Prepare the necessary journal entries if the wages and salaries paid and the employer payroll taxes are recorded separately.

E13-9 (Payroll Tax Entries) Green Day Hardware Company's payroll for November 2014 is summarized below.

			Amount Subject to Payroll Taxes	
			Unemployment Tax	
Payroll	Wages Due	FICA	Federal	State
Factory	$120,000	$120,000	$40,000	$40,000
Sales	32,000	32,000	4,000	4,000
Administrative	36,000	36,000	—	—
Total	$188,000	$188,000	$44,000	$44,000

At this point in the year, some employees have already received wages in excess of those to which payroll taxes apply. Assume that the state unemployment tax is 2.5%. The FICA rate is 7.65% on an employee's wages to $113,700 and 1.45% in excess of $113,700. Of the $188,000 wages subject to FICA tax, $20,000 of the sales wages is in excess of $113,700. Federal unemployment tax rate is 0.8% after credits. Income tax withheld amounts to $16,000 for factory, $7,000 for sales, and $6,000 for administrative.

Instructions

(a) Prepare a schedule showing the employer's total cost of wages for November by function. (Round all computations to nearest dollar.)

(b) Prepare the journal entries to record the factory, sales, and administrative payrolls including the employer's payroll taxes.

E13-10 (Warranties) Soundgarden Company sold 200 color laser copiers in 2014 for $4,000 apiece, together with a one-year warranty. Maintenance on each copier during the warranty period averages $330.

Instructions

(a) Prepare entries to record the sale of the copiers and the related warranty costs, assuming that the accrual method is used. Actual warranty costs incurred in 2014 were $17,000.

(b) On the basis of the data above, prepare the appropriate entries, assuming that the cash-basis method is used.

5 E13-11 (Warranties) Sheryl Crow Equipment Company sold 500 Rollomatics during 2014 at $6,000 each. During 2014, Crow spent $20,000 servicing the 2-year warranties that accompany the Rollomatic. All applicable transactions are on a cash basis.

Instructions

(a) Prepare 2014 entries for Crow using the expense warranty approach. Assume that Crow estimates the total cost of servicing the warranties will be $120,000 for 2 years.

(b) Prepare 2014 entries for Crow assuming that the warranties are not an integral part of the sale. Assume that of the sales total, $150,000 relates to sales of warranty contracts. Crow estimates the total cost of servicing the warranties will be $120,000 for 2 years. Estimate revenues to be recognized on the basis of costs incurred and estimated costs.

5 E13-12 (Premium Entries) No Doubt Company includes 1 coupon in each box of soap powder that it packs, and 10 coupons are redeemable for a premium (a kitchen utensil). In 2014, No Doubt Company purchased 8,800 premiums at 80 cents each and sold 110,000 boxes of soap powder at $3.30 per box; 44,000 coupons were presented for redemption in 2014. It is estimated that 60% of the coupons will eventually be presented for redemption.

Instructions

Prepare all the entries that would be made relative to sales of soap powder and to the premium plan in 2014.

4 5 E13-13 (Contingencies) Presented below are three independent situations. Answer the question at the end of each situation.

1. During 2014, Salt-n-Pepa Inc. became involved in a tax dispute with the IRS. Salt-n-Pepa's attorneys have indicated that they believe it is probable that Salt-n-Pepa will lose this dispute. They also believe that Salt-n-Pepa will have to pay the IRS between $900,000 and $1,400,000. After the 2014 financial statements were issued, the case was settled with the IRS for $1,200,000. What amount, if any, should be reported as a liability for this contingency as of December 31, 2014?

2. On October 1, 2014, Alan Jackson Chemical was identified as a potentially responsible party by the Environmental Protection Agency. Jackson's management along with its counsel have concluded that it is probable that Jackson will be responsible for damages, and a reasonable estimate of these damages is $5,000,000. Jackson's insurance policy of $9,000,000 has a deductible clause of $500,000. How should Alan Jackson Chemical report this information in its financial statements at December 31, 2014?

3. Melissa Etheridge Inc. had a manufacturing plant in Sudan, which was destroyed in the civil war. It is not certain who will compensate Etheridge for this destruction, but Etheridge has been assured by governmental officials that it will receive a definite amount for this plant. The amount of the compensation will be less than the fair value of the plant, but more than its book value. How should the contingency be reported in the financial statements of Etheridge Inc.?

5 E13-14 (Asset Retirement Obligation) Oil Products Company purchases an oil tanker depot on January 1, 2014, at a cost of $600,000. Oil Products expects to operate the depot for 10 years, at which time it is legally required to dismantle the depot and remove the underground storage tanks. It is estimated that it will cost $75,000 to dismantle the depot and remove the tanks at the end of the depot's useful life.

Instructions

(a) Prepare the journal entries to record the depot and the asset retirement obligation for the depot on January 1, 2014. Based on an effective-interest rate of 6%, the present value of the asset retirement obligation on January 1, 2014, is $41,879.

(b) Prepare any journal entries required for the depot and the asset retirement obligation at December 31, 2014. Oil Products uses straight-line depreciation; the estimated salvage value for the depot is zero.

(c) On December 31, 2023, Oil Products pays a demolition firm to dismantle the depot and remove the tanks at a price of $80,000. Prepare the journal entry for the settlement of the asset retirement obligation.

5 E13-15 (Premiums) Presented below and on page 740 are three independent situations.

1. Hairston Stamp Company records stamp service revenue and provides for the cost of redemptions in the year stamps are sold to licensees. Hairston's past experience indicates that only 80% of the

stamps sold to licensees will be redeemed. Hairston's liability for stamp redemptions was $13,000,000 at December 31, 2013. Additional information for 2014 is as follows.

Stamp service revenue from stamps sold to licensees	$9,500,000
Cost of redemptions (stamps sold prior to 1/1/14)	6,000,000

If all the stamps sold in 2014 were presented for redemption in 2015, the redemption cost would be $5,200,000. What amount should Hairston report as a liability for stamp redemptions at December 31, 2014?

2. In packages of its products, Burnitz Inc. includes coupons that may be presented at retail stores to obtain discounts on other Burnitz products. Retailers are reimbursed for the face amount of coupons redeemed plus 10% of that amount for handling costs. Burnitz honors requests for coupon redemption by retailers up to 3 months after the consumer expiration date. Burnitz estimates that 60% of all coupons issued will ultimately be redeemed. Information relating to coupons issued by Burnitz during 2014 is as follows.

Consumer expiration date	12/31/14
Total face amount of coupons issued	$800,000
Total payments to retailers as of 12/31/14	330,000

What amount should Burnitz report as a liability for unredeemed coupons at December 31, 2014?

3. Roland Company sold 700,000 boxes of pie mix under a new sales promotional program. Each box contains one coupon, which submitted with $4.00, entitles the customer to a baking pan. Roland pays $6.00 per pan and $0.50 for handling and shipping. Roland estimates that 70% of the coupons will be redeemed, even though only 250,000 coupons had been processed during 2014. What amount should Roland report as a liability for unredeemed coupons at December 31, 2014?

(AICPA adapted)

6 **E13-16 (Financial Statement Impact of Liability Transactions)** Presented below is a list of possible transactions.

1. Purchased inventory for $80,000 on account (assume perpetual system is used).
2. Issued an $80,000 note payable in payment on account (see item 1 above).
3. Recorded accrued interest on the note from item 2 above.
4. Borrowed $100,000 from the bank by signing a 6-month, $112,000, zero-interest-bearing note.
5. Recognized 4 months' interest expense on the note from item 4 above.
6. Recorded cash sales of $75,260, which includes 6% sales tax.
7. Recorded wage expense of $35,000. The cash paid was $25,000; the difference was due to various amounts withheld.
8. Recorded employer's payroll taxes.
9. Accrued accumulated vacation pay.
10. Recorded an asset retirement obligation.
11. Recorded bonuses due to employees.
12. Recorded a contingent loss on a lawsuit that the company will probably lose.
13. Accrued warranty expense (assume expense warranty approach).
14. Paid warranty costs that were accrued in item 13 above.
15. Recorded sales of product and related warranties (assume sales warranty approach).
16. Paid warranty costs under contracts from item 15 above.
17. Recognized warranty revenue (see item 15 above).
18. Recorded estimated liability for premium claims outstanding.

Instructions
Set up a table using the format shown below and analyze the effect of the 18 transactions on the financial statement categories indicated.

#	Assets	Liabilities	Owners' Equity	Net Income
1				

Use the following code:

I: Increase   D: Decrease   NE: No net effect

6 **E13-17 (Ratio Computations and Discussion)** Sprague Company has been operating for several years, and on December 31, 2014, presented the following balance sheet.

SPRAGUE COMPANY
BALANCE SHEET
DECEMBER 31, 2014

Cash	$ 40,000	Accounts payable	$ 80,000
Receivables	75,000	Mortgage payable	140,000
Inventory	95,000	Common stock ($1 par)	150,000
Plant assets (net)	220,000	Retained earnings	60,000
	$430,000		$430,000

The net income for 2014 was $25,000. Assume that total assets are the same in 2013 and 2014.

Instructions

Compute each of the following ratios. For each of the four, indicate the manner in which it is computed and its significance as a tool in the analysis of the financial soundness of the company.

(a) Current ratio.   (c) Debt to assets.
(b) Acid-test ratio.   (d) Return on assets.

6 **E13-18 (Ratio Computations and Analysis)** Prior Company's condensed financial statements provide the following information.

PRIOR COMPANY
BALANCE SHEET

	Dec. 31, 2014	Dec. 31, 2013
Cash	$ 52,000	$ 60,000
Accounts receivable (net)	198,000	80,000
Short-term investments	80,000	40,000
Inventory	440,000	360,000
Prepaid expenses	3,000	7,000
Total current assets	$ 773,000	$ 547,000
Property, plant, and equipment (net)	857,000	853,000
Total assets	$1,630,000	$1,400,000
Current liabilities	240,000	160,000
Bonds payable	400,000	400,000
Common stockholders' equity	990,000	840,000
Total liabilities and stockholders' equity	$1,630,000	$1,400,000

INCOME STATEMENT
FOR THE YEAR ENDED 2014

Sales revenue	$1,640,000
Cost of goods sold	(800,000)
Gross profit	840,000
Selling and administrative expenses	(440,000)
Interest expense	(40,000)
Net income	$ 360,000

Instructions

(a) Determine the following for 2014.
  (1) Current ratio at December 31.
  (2) Acid-test ratio at December 31.
  (3) Accounts receivable turnover.
  (4) Inventory turnover.
  (5) Return on assets.
  (6) Profit margin on sales.
(b) Prepare a brief evaluation of the financial condition of Prior Company and of the adequacy of its profits.

6 **E13-19 (Ratio Computations and Effect of Transactions)** Presented below is information related to Carver Inc.

CARVER INC.
BALANCE SHEET
DECEMBER 31, 2014

Cash		$ 45,000	Notes payable (short-term)	$ 50,000
Receivables	$110,000		Accounts payable	32,000
Less: Allowance	15,000	95,000	Accrued liabilities	5,000
Inventory		170,000	Common stock (par $5)	260,000
Prepaid insurance		8,000	Retained earnings	141,000
Land		20,000		
Equipment (net)		150,000		
		$488,000		$488,000

CARVER INC.
INCOME STATEMENT
FOR THE YEAR ENDED DECEMBER 31, 2014

Sales revenue		$1,400,000
Cost of goods sold		
Inventory, Jan. 1, 2014	$200,000	
Purchases	790,000	
Cost of goods available for sale	990,000	
Inventory, Dec. 31, 2014	(170,000)	
Cost of goods sold		820,000
Gross profit on sales		580,000
Operating expenses		170,000
Net income		$ 410,000

Instructions

(a) Compute the following ratios or relationships of Carver Inc. Assume that the ending account balances are representative unless the information provided indicates differently.
  (1) Current ratio.
  (2) Inventory turnover.
  (3) Accounts receivable turnover.
  (4) Earnings per share.
  (5) Profit margin on sales.
  (6) Return on assets on December 31, 2014.

(b) Indicate for each of the following transactions whether the transaction would improve, weaken, or have no effect on the current ratio of Carver Inc. at December 31, 2014.
  (1) Write off an uncollectible account receivable, $2,200.
  (2) Purchase additional capital stock for cash.
  (3) Pay $40,000 on notes payable (short-term).
  (4) Collect $23,000 on accounts receivable.
  (5) Buy equipment on account.
  (6) Give an existing creditor a short-term note in settlement of account.

EXERCISES SET B

See the book's companion website, at **www.wiley.com/college/kieso**, for an additional set of exercises.

PROBLEMS

P13-1 (Current Liability Entries and Adjustments) Described below are certain transactions of Edwardson Corporation. The company uses the periodic inventory system.

1. On February 2, the corporation purchased goods from Martin Company for $70,000 subject to cash discount terms of 2/10, n/30. Purchases and accounts payable are recorded by the corporation at net amounts after cash discounts. The invoice was paid on February 26.
2. On April 1, the corporation bought a truck for $50,000 from General Motors Company, paying $4,000 in cash and signing a one-year, 12% note for the balance of the purchase price.
3. On May 1, the corporation borrowed $83,000 from Chicago National Bank by signing a $92,000 zero-interest-bearing note due one year from May 1.
4. On August 1, the board of directors declared a $300,000 cash dividend that was payable on September 10 to stockholders of record on August 31.

Instructions

(a) Make all the journal entries necessary to record the transactions above using appropriate dates.
(b) Edwardson Corporation's year-end is December 31. Assuming that no adjusting entries relative to the transactions above have been recorded, prepare any adjusting journal entries concerning interest that are necessary to present fair financial statements at December 31. Assume straight-line amortization of discounts.

P13-2 (Liability Entries and Adjustments) Listed below are selected transactions of Schultz Department Store for the current year ending December 31.

1. On December 5, the store received $500 from the Selig Players as a deposit to be returned after certain furniture to be used in stage production was returned on January 15.
2. During December, cash sales totaled $798,000, which includes the 5% sales tax that must be remitted to the state by the fifteenth day of the following month.
3. On December 10, the store purchased for cash three delivery trucks for $120,000. The trucks were purchased in a state that applies a 5% sales tax.
4. The store determined it will cost $100,000 to restore the area (considered a land improvement) surrounding one of its store parking lots, when the store is closed in 2 years. Schultz estimates the fair value of the obligation at December 31 is $84,000.

Instructions

Prepare all the journal entries necessary to record the transactions noted above as they occurred and any adjusting journal entries relative to the transactions that would be required to present fair financial statements at December 31. Date each entry. For simplicity, assume that adjusting entries are recorded only once a year on December 31.

P13-3 (Payroll Tax Entries) Cedarville Company pays its office employee payroll weekly. Below is a partial list of employees and their payroll data for August. Because August is their vacation period, vacation pay is also listed.

Employee	Earnings to July 31	Weekly Pay	Vacation Pay to Be Received in August
Mark Hamill	$4,200	$200	—
Karen Robbins	3,500	150	$300
Brent Kirk	2,700	110	220
Alec Guinness	7,400	250	—
Ken Sprouse	8,000	330	660

Assume that the federal income tax withheld is 10% of wages. Union dues withheld are 2% of wages. Vacations are taken the second and third weeks of August by Robbins, Kirk, and Sprouse. The state unemployment tax rate is 2.5% and the federal is 0.8%, both on a $7,000 maximum. The FICA rate is 7.65% on employee and employer on a maximum of $113,700 per employee. In addition, a 1.45% rate is charged both employer and employee for an employee's wages in excess of $113,700.

Instructions

Make the journal entries necessary for each of the four August payrolls. The entries for the payroll and for the company's liability are made separately. Also make the entry to record the monthly payment of accrued payroll liabilities.

3 ▶ **P13-4 (Payroll Tax Entries)** Below is a payroll sheet for Otis Import Company for the month of September 2014. The company is allowed a 1% unemployment compensation rate by the state; the federal unemployment tax rate is 0.8% and the maximum for both is $7,000. Assume a 10% federal income tax rate for all employees and a 7.65% FICA tax on employee and employer on a maximum of $113,700. In addition, 1.45% is charged both employer and employee for an employee's wages in excess of $113,700 per employee.

Name	Earnings to Aug. 31	September Earnings	Income Tax Withholding	FICA	Unemployment Tax State	Federal
B.D. Williams	$ 6,800	$ 800				
D. Raye	6,500	700				
K. Baker	7,600	1,100				
F. Lopez	13,600	1,900				
A. Daniels	107,000	13,000				
B. Kingston	112,000	16,000				

Instructions

(a) Complete the payroll sheet and make the necessary entry to record the payment of the payroll.

(b) Make the entry to record the payroll tax expenses of Otis Import Company.

(c) Make the entry to record the payment of the payroll liabilities created. Assume that the company pays all payroll liabilities at the end of each month.

5 ▶ **P13-5 (Warranties, Accrual, and Cash Basis)** Brooks Corporation sells computers under a 2-year warranty contract that requires the corporation to replace defective parts and to provide the necessary repair labor. During 2014, the corporation sells for cash 400 computers at a unit price of $2,500. On the basis of past experience, the 2-year warranty costs are estimated to be $155 for parts and $185 for labor per unit. (For simplicity, assume that all sales occurred on December 31, 2014.) The warranty is not sold separately from the computer.

Instructions

(a) Record any necessary journal entries in 2014, applying the cash-basis method.

(b) Record any necessary journal entries in 2014, applying the expense warranty accrual method.

(c) What liability relative to these transactions would appear on the December 31, 2014, balance sheet and how would it be classified if the cash-basis method is applied?

(d) What liability relative to these transactions would appear on the December 31, 2014, balance sheet and how would it be classified if the expense warranty accrual method is applied?

In 2015, the actual warranty costs to Brooks Corporation were $21,400 for parts and $39,900 for labor.

(e) Record any necessary journal entries in 2015, applying the cash-basis method.

(f) Record any necessary journal entries in 2015, applying the expense warranty accrual method.

5 ▶ **P13-6 (Extended Warranties)** Dos Passos Company sells televisions at an average price of $900 and also offers to each customer a separate 3-year warranty contract for $90 that requires the company to perform periodic services and to replace defective parts. During 2014, the company sold 300 televisions and 270 warranty contracts for cash. It estimates the 3-year warranty costs as $20 for parts and $40 for labor, and accounts for warranties separately. Assume sales occurred on December 31, 2014, and straight-line recognition of warranty revenues occurs.

Instructions

(a) Record any necessary journal entries in 2014.

(b) What liability relative to these transactions would appear on the December 31, 2014, balance sheet and how would it be classified?

In 2015, Dos Passos Company incurred actual costs relative to 2014 television warranty sales of $2,000 for parts and $4,000 for labor.

(c) Record any necessary journal entries in 2015 relative to 2014 television warranties.

(d) What amounts relative to the 2014 television warranties would appear on the December 31, 2015, balance sheet and how would they be classified?

4 **5** ▶ **P13-7 (Warranties, Accrual, and Cash Basis)** Alvarado Company sells a machine for $7,400 with a 12-month warranty agreement that requires the company to replace all defective parts and to provide the repair labor at no cost to the customers. With sales being made evenly throughout the year, the company sells 600 machines in 2014 (warranty expense is incurred half in 2014 and half in 2015). As a result of product testing, the company estimates that the warranty cost is $390 per machine ($170 parts and $220 labor).

Instructions

Assuming that actual warranty costs are incurred exactly as estimated, what journal entries would be made relative to the following facts?

(a) Under application of the expense warranty accrual method for:
  (1) Sale of machinery in 2014.
  (2) Warranty costs incurred in 2014.
  (3) Warranty expense charged against 2014 revenues.
  (4) Warranty costs incurred in 2015.

(b) Under application of the cash-basis method for:
  (1) Sale of machinery in 2014.
  (2) Warranty costs incurred in 2014.
  (3) Warranty expense charged against 2014 revenues.
  (4) Warranty costs incurred in 2015.

(c) What amount, if any, is disclosed in the balance sheet as a liability for future warranty costs as of December 31, 2014, under each method?

(d) Which method best reflects the income in 2014 and 2015 of Alvarado Company? Why?

5 **P13-8 (Premium Entries)** To stimulate the sales of its Alladin breakfast cereal, Loptien Company places 1 coupon in each box. Five coupons are redeemable for a premium consisting of a children's hand puppet. In 2015, the company purchases 40,000 puppets at $1.50 each and sells 480,000 boxes of Alladin at $3.75 a box. From its experience with other similar premium offers, the company estimates that 40% of the coupons issued will be mailed back for redemption. During 2015, 115,000 coupons are presented for redemption.

Instructions

Prepare the journal entries that should be recorded in 2015 relative to the premium plan.

5 **6** **P13-9 (Premium Entries and Financial Statement Presentation)** Sycamore Candy Company offers an MP3 download (seven-single medley) as a premium for every five candy bar wrappers presented by customers together with $2.50. The candy bars are sold by the company to distributors for 30 cents each. The purchase price of each download code to the company is $2.25. In addition, it costs 50 cents to distribute each code. The results of the premium plan for the years 2014 and 2015 are as follows. (All purchases and sales are for cash.)

	2014	2015
MP3 codes purchased	250,000	330,000
Candy bars sold	2,895,400	2,743,600
Wrappers redeemed	1,200,000	1,500,000
2014 wrappers expected to be redeemed in 2015	290,000	
2015 wrappers expected to be redeemed in 2016		350,000

Instructions

(a) Prepare the journal entries that should be made in 2014 and 2015 to record the transactions related to the premium plan of the Sycamore Candy Company.

(b) Indicate the account names, amounts, and classifications of the items related to the premium plan that would appear on the balance sheet and the income statement at the end of 2014 and 2015.

4 **5** **P13-10 (Loss Contingencies: Entries and Essay)** On November 24, 2014, 26 passengers on Windsor Airlines Flight No. 901 were injured upon landing when the plane skidded off the runway. Personal injury suits for damages totaling $9,000,000 were filed on January 11, 2015, against the airline by 18 injured passengers. The airline carries no insurance. Legal counsel has studied each suit and advised Windsor that it can reasonably expect to pay 60% of the damages claimed. The financial statements for the year ended December 31, 2014, were issued February 27, 2015.

Instructions

(a) Prepare any disclosures and journal entries required by the airline in preparation of the December 31, 2014, financial statements.

(b) Ignoring the November 24, 2014, accident, what liability due to the risk of loss from lack of insurance coverage should Windsor Airlines record or disclose? During the past decade, the company has experienced at least one accident per year and incurred average damages of $3,200,000. Discuss fully.

4 **5** **P13-11 (Loss Contingencies: Entries and Essays)** Polska Corporation, in preparation of its December 31, 2014, financial statements, is attempting to determine the proper accounting treatment for each of the following situations.

1. As a result of uninsured accidents during the year, personal injury suits for $350,000 and $60,000 have been filed against the company. It is the judgment of Polska's legal counsel that an unfavorable outcome is unlikely in the $60,000 case but that an unfavorable verdict approximating $250,000 will probably result in the $350,000 case.

2. Polska Corporation owns a subsidiary in a foreign country that has a book value of $5,725,000 and an estimated fair value of $9,500,000. The foreign government has communicated to Polska its intention to expropriate the assets and business of all foreign investors. On the basis of settlements other firms have received from this same country, Polska expects to receive 40% of the fair value of its properties as final settlement.

3. Polska's chemical product division consisting of five plants is uninsurable because of the special risk of injury to employees and losses due to fire and explosion. The year 2014 is considered one of the safest (luckiest) in the division's history because no loss due to injury or casualty was suffered. Having suffered an average of three casualties a year during the rest of the past decade (ranging from $60,000 to $700,000), management is certain that next year the company will probably not be so fortunate.

Instructions

(a) Prepare the journal entries that should be recorded as of December 31, 2014, to recognize each of the situations above.

(b) Indicate what should be reported relative to each situation in the financial statements and accompanying notes. Explain why.

5 **P13-12 (Warranties and Premiums)** Garison Music Emporium carries a wide variety of musical instruments, sound reproduction equipment, recorded music, and sheet music. Garison uses two sales promotion techniques—warranties and premiums—to attract customers.

Musical instruments and sound equipment are sold with a one-year warranty for replacement of parts and labor. The estimated warranty cost, based on past experience, is 2% of sales.

The premium is offered on the recorded and sheet music. Customers receive a coupon for each dollar spent on recorded music or sheet music. Customers may exchange 200 coupons and $20 for a digital MP3 player. Garison pays $32 for each player and estimates that 60% of the coupons given to customers will be redeemed.

Garison's total sales for 2014 were $7,200,000—$5,700,000 from musical instruments and sound reproduction equipment and $1,500,000 from recorded music and sheet music. Replacement parts and labor for warranty work totaled $164,000 during 2014. A total of 6,500 players used in the premium program were purchased during the year and there were 1,200,000 coupons redeemed in 2014.

The accrual method is used by Garison to account for the warranty and premium costs for financial reporting purposes. The balances in the accounts related to warranties and premiums on January 1, 2014, were as shown below.

Inventory of Premiums	$ 37,600
Premium Liability	44,800
Warranty Liability	136,000

Instructions

Garison Music Emporium is preparing its financial statements for the year ended December 31, 2014. Determine the amounts that will be shown on the 2014 financial statements for the following.

(a) Warranty Expense.
(b) Warranty Liability.
(c) Premium Expense.

(d) Inventory of Premiums.
(e) Premium Liability.

(CMA adapted)

 4 5 **P13-13 (Liability Errors)** You are the independent auditor engaged to audit Millay Corporation's December 31, 2014, financial statements. Millay manufactures household appliances. During the course of your audit, you discovered the following contingent liabilities.

1. Millay began production of a new dishwasher in June 2014 and, by December 31, 2014, sold 120,000 to various retailers for $500 each. Each dishwasher is under a one-year warranty. The company estimates that its warranty expense per dishwasher will amount to $25. At year-end, the company had already paid out $1,000,000 in warranty expenses. Millay's income statement shows warranty expenses of $1,000,000 for 2014. Millay accounts for warranty costs on the accrual basis.

2. In response to your attorney's letter, Morgan Sondgeroth, Esq., has informed you that Millay has been cited for dumping toxic waste into the Kishwaukee River. Clean-up costs and fines amount to $2,750,000. Although the case is still being contested, Sondgeroth is certain that Millay will most probably have to pay the fine and clean-up costs. No disclosure of this situation was found in the financial statements.

3. Millay is the defendant in a patent infringement lawsuit by Megan Drabek over Millay's use of a hydraulic compressor in several of its products. Sondgeroth claims that, if the suit goes against Millay, the loss may be as much as $5,000,000. However, Sondgeroth believes the loss of this suit to be only reasonably possible. Again, no mention of this suit is made in the financial statements.

As presented, these contingencies are not reported in accordance with GAAP, which may create problems in issuing a favorable audit report. You feel the need to note these problems in the work papers.

Instructions

Heading each page with the name of the company, balance sheet date, and a brief description of the problem, write a brief narrative for each of the above issues in the form of **a memorandum** to be incorporated in the audit work papers. Explain what led to the discovery of each problem, what the problem really is, and what you advised your client to do (along with any appropriate journal entries) in order to bring these contingencies in accordance with GAAP.

P13-14 (Warranty and Coupon Computation) Schmitt Company must make computations and adjusting entries for the following independent situations at December 31, 2015.

1. Its line of amplifiers carries a 3-year warranty against defects. On the basis of past experience the estimated warranty costs related to dollar sales are first year after sale—2% of sales revenue; second year after sale—3% of sales revenue; and third year after sale—5% of sales revenue. Sales and actual warranty expenditures for the first 3 years of business were:

	Sales Revenue	Warranty Expenditures
2013	$ 800,000	$ 6,500
2014	1,100,000	17,200
2015	1,200,000	62,000

Instructions

Compute the amount that Schmitt Company should report as a liability in its December 31, 2015, balance sheet. Assume that all sales are made evenly throughout each year with warranty expenses also evenly spaced relative to the rates above.

2. With some of its products, Schmitt Company includes coupons that are redeemable in merchandise. The coupons have no expiration date and, in the company's experience, 40% of them are redeemed. The liability for unredeemed coupons at December 31, 2014, was $9,000. During 2015, coupons worth $30,000 were issued, and merchandise worth $8,000 was distributed in exchange for coupons redeemed.

Instructions

Compute the amount of the liability that should appear on the December 31, 2015, balance sheet.

(AICPA adapted)

PROBLEMS SET B

See the book's companion website, at **www.wiley.com/college/kieso**, for an additional set of problems.

CONCEPTS FOR ANALYSIS

CA13-1 (Nature of Liabilities) Presented below is the current liabilities section of Micro Corporation.

	($000)	
	2015	2014
Current liabilities		
Notes payable	$ 68,713	$ 7,700
Accounts payable	179,496	101,379
Compensation to employees	60,312	31,649
Accrued liabilities	158,198	77,621
Income taxes payable	10,486	26,491
Current maturities of long-term debt	16,592	6,649
Total current liabilities	$493,797	$251,489

Instructions
Answer the following questions.

(a) What are the essential characteristics that make an item a liability?
(b) How does one distinguish between a current liability and a long-term liability?
(c) What are accrued liabilities? Give three examples of accrued liabilities that Micro might have.
(d) What is the theoretically correct way to value liabilities? How are current liabilities usually valued?
(e) Why are notes payable reported first in the current liabilities section?
(f) What might be the items that comprise Micro's liability for "Compensation to employees"?

CA13-2 (Current versus Noncurrent Classification) Rodriguez Corporation includes the following items in its liabilities at December 31, 2014.

1. Notes payable, $25,000,000, due June 30, 2015.
2. Deposits from customers on equipment ordered by them from Rodriguez, $6,250,000.
3. Salaries and wages payable, $3,750,000, due January 14, 2015.

Instructions
Indicate in what circumstances, if any, each of the three liabilities above would be excluded from current liabilities.

CA13-3 (Refinancing of Short-Term Debt) Dumars Corporation reports in the current liability section of its balance sheet at December 31, 2014 (its year-end), short-term obligations of $15,000,000, which includes the current portion of 12% long-term debt in the amount of $10,000,000 (matures in March 2015). Management has stated its intention to refinance the 12% debt whereby no portion of it will mature during 2015. The date of issuance of the financial statements is March 25, 2015.

Instructions
(a) Is management's intent enough to support long-term classification of the obligation in this situation?
(b) Assume that Dumars Corporation issues $13,000,000 of 10-year debentures to the public in January 2015 and that management intends to use the proceeds to liquidate the $10,000,000 debt maturing in March 2015. Furthermore, assume that the debt maturing in March 2015 is paid from these proceeds prior to the issuance of the financial statements. Will this have any impact on the balance sheet classification at December 31, 2014? Explain your answer.
(c) Assume that Dumars Corporation issues common stock to the public in January and that management intends to entirely liquidate the $10,000,000 debt maturing in March 2015 with the proceeds of this equity securities issue. In light of these events, should the $10,000,000 debt maturing in March 2015 be included in current liabilities at December 31, 2014?
(d) Assume that Dumars Corporation, on February 15, 2015, entered into a financing agreement with a commercial bank that permits Dumars Corporation to borrow at any time through 2016 up to $15,000,000 at the bank's prime rate of interest. Borrowings under the financing agreement mature three years after the date of the loan. The agreement is not cancelable except for violation of a provision with which compliance is objectively determinable. No violation of any provision exists at the date of issuance of the financial statements. Assume further that the current portion of long-term debt does not mature until August 2015. In addition, management intends to refinance the $10,000,000 obligation under the terms of the financial agreement with the bank, which is expected to be financially capable of honoring the agreement.
  (1) Given these facts, should the $10,000,000 be classified as current on the balance sheet at December 31, 2014?
  (2) Is disclosure of the refinancing method required?

CA13-4 (Loss Contingencies) On February 1, 2015, one of the huge storage tanks of Viking Manufacturing Company exploded. Windows in houses and other buildings within a one-mile radius of the explosion were severely damaged, and a number of people were injured. As of February 15, 2015 (when the December 31, 2014, financial statements were completed and sent to the publisher for printing and public distribution), no suits had been filed or claims asserted against the company as a consequence of the explosion. The company fully anticipates that suits will be filed and claims asserted for injuries and damages. Because the casualty was uninsured and the company considered at fault, Viking Manufacturing will have to cover the damages from its own resources.

Instructions
Discuss fully the accounting treatment and disclosures that should be accorded the casualty and related contingent losses in the financial statements dated December 31, 2014.

CA13-5 (Loss Contingency) Presented below is a note disclosure for Matsui Corporation.

> **Litigation and Environmental:** The Company has been notified, or is a named or a potentially responsible party in a number of governmental (federal, state and local) and private actions associated with environmental matters, such as those relating to hazardous wastes, including certain sites which are on the United States EPA National Priorities List ("Superfund"). These actions seek clean-up costs, penalties and/or damages for personal injury or to property or natural resources.
>
> In 2014, the Company recorded a pre-tax charge of $56,229,000, included in the "Other expense (income)—net" caption of the Company's consolidated income statements, as an additional provision for environmental matters. These expenditures are expected to take place over the next several years and are indicative of the Company's commitment to improve and maintain the environment in which it operates. At December 31, 2014, environmental accruals amounted to $69,931,000, of which $61,535,000 are considered noncurrent and are included in the "Deferred credits and other liabilities" caption of the Company's consolidated balance sheets.
>
> While it is impossible at this time to determine with certainty the ultimate outcome of environmental matters, it is management's opinion, based in part on the advice of independent counsel (after taking into account accruals and insurance coverage applicable to such actions) that when the costs are finally determined they will not have a material adverse effect on the financial position of the Company.

Instructions

Answer the following questions.

   (a) What conditions must exist before a loss contingency can be recorded in the accounts?

   (b) Suppose that Matsui Corporation could not reasonably estimate the amount of the loss, although it could establish with a high degree of probability the minimum and maximum loss possible. How should this information be reported in the financial statements?

   (c) If the amount of the loss is uncertain, how would the loss contingency be reported in the financial statements?

CA13-6 (Warranties and Loss Contingencies) The following two independent situations involve loss contingencies.

Part 1: Benson Company sells two products, Grey and Yellow. Each carries a one-year warranty.

   1. Product Grey—Product warranty costs, based on past experience, will normally be 1% of sales.

   2. Product Yellow—Product warranty costs cannot be reasonably estimated because this is a new product line. However, the chief engineer believes that product warranty costs are likely to be incurred.

Instructions

How should Benson report the estimated product warranty costs for each of the two types of merchandise above? Discuss the rationale for your answer. Do not discuss disclosures that should be made in Benson's financial statements or notes.

Part 2: Constantine Company is being sued for $4,000,000 for an injury caused to a child as a result of alleged negligence while the child was visiting the Constantine Company plant in March 2014. The suit was filed in July 2014. Constantine's lawyer states that it is probable that Constantine will lose the suit and be found liable for a judgment costing anywhere from $400,000 to $2,000,000. However, the lawyer states that the most probable judgment is $1,000,000.

Instructions

How should Constantine report the suit in its 2014 financial statements? Discuss the rationale for your answer. Include in your answer disclosures, if any, that should be made in Constantine's financial statements or notes.

(AICPA adapted)

 CA13-7 (Warranties) The Dotson Company, owner of Bleacher Mall, charges Rich Clothing Store a rental fee of $600 per month plus 5% of yearly profits over $500,000. Matt Rich, the owner of the store, directs his accountant, Ron Hamilton, to increase the estimate of bad debt expense and warranty costs in order to keep profits at $475,000.

Instructions

Answer the following questions.

   (a) Should Hamilton follow his boss's directive?

   (b) Who is harmed if the estimates are increased?

   (c) Is Matt Rich's directive ethical?

USING YOUR JUDGMENT

FINANCIAL REPORTING

Financial Reporting Problem

P&G **The Procter & Gamble Company (P&G)**

The financial statements of P&G are presented in Appendix 5B. The company's complete annual report, including the notes to the financial statements, can be accessed at the book's companion website, **www.wiley.com/college/kieso**.

Instructions

Refer to these financial statements and the accompanying notes to answer the following questions.

(a) What was P&G's 2011 short-term debt and related weighted-average interest rate on this debt?

(b) What was P&G's 2011 working capital, acid-test ratio, and current ratio? Comment on P&G's liquidity.

(c) What types of commitments and contingencies has P&G's reported in its financial statements? What is management's reaction to these contingencies?

Comparative Analysis Case

The Coca-Cola Company and PepsiCo, Inc.

Instructions

Go to the book's companion website and use information found there to answer the following questions related to The Coca-Cola Company and PepsiCo, Inc.

(a) How much working capital do each of these companies have at the end of 2011?

(b) Compute each company's (a) current cash debt coverage, (b) cash debt coverage, (c) current ratio, (d) acid-test ratio, (e) accounts receivable turnover, and (f) inventory turnover for 2011. Comment on each company's overall liquidity.

(c) In PepsiCo's financial statements, it reports in the long-term debt section "short-term borrowings, reclassified." How can short-term borrowings be classified as long-term debt?

(d) What types of loss or gain contingencies do these two companies have at the end of 2011?

Financial Statement Analysis Cases

Case 1   Northland Cranberries

Despite being a publicly traded company only since 1987, Northland Cranberries of Wisconsin Rapids, Wisconsin, is one of the world's largest cranberry growers. During its short life as a publicly traded corporation, it has engaged in an aggressive growth strategy. As a consequence, the company has taken on significant amounts of both short-term and long-term debt. The following information is taken from recent annual reports of the company.

Northland Cranberries

	Current Year	Prior Year
Current assets	$ 6,745,759	$ 5,598,054
Total assets	107,744,751	83,074,339
Current liabilities	10,168,685	4,484,687
Total liabilities	73,118,204	49,948,787
Shareholders' equity	34,626,547	33,125,552
Net sales	21,783,966	18,051,355
Cost of goods sold	13,057,275	8,751,220
Interest expense	3,654,006	2,393,792
Income tax expense	1,051,000	1,917,000
Net income	1,581,707	2,942,954

Instructions

(a) Evaluate the company's liquidity by calculating and analyzing working capital and the current ratio.

(b) The discussion of the company's liquidity, shown below, was provided by the company in the Management Discussion and Analysis section of the company's annual report. Comment on whether you agree with management's statements, and what might be done to remedy the situation.

The lower comparative current ratio in the current year was due to $3 million of short-term borrowing then outstanding which was incurred to fund the Yellow River Marsh acquisitions last year. As a result of the extreme seasonality of its business, the company does not believe that its current ratio or its underlying stated working capital at the current, fiscal year-end is a meaningful indication of the Company's liquidity. As of March 31 of each fiscal year, the Company has historically carried no significant amounts of inventories and by such date all of the Company's accounts receivable from its crop sold for processing under the supply agreements have been paid in cash, with the resulting cash received from such payments used to reduce indebtedness. The Company utilizes its revolving bank credit facility, together with cash generated from operations, to fund its working capital requirements throughout its growing season.

Case 2   Mohican Company

Presented below is the current liabilities section and related note of Mohican Company.

| | (dollars in thousands) | |
	Current Year	Prior Year
Current liabilities		
Current portion of long-term debt	$ 15,000	$ 10,000
Short-term debt	2,668	405
Accounts payable	29,495	42,427
Accrued warranty	16,843	16,741
Accrued marketing programs	17,512	16,585
Other accrued liabilities	35,653	33,290
Accrued and deferred income taxes	16,206	17,348
Total current liabilities	$133,377	$136,796

Notes to Consolidated Financial Statements

Note 1 (in part): Summary of Significant Accounting Policies and Related Data
Accrued Warranty   The company provides an accrual for future warranty costs based upon the relationship of prior years' sales to actual warranty costs.

Instructions

Answer the following questions.

(a) What is the difference between the cash basis and the accrual basis of accounting for warranty costs?

(b) Under what circumstance, if any, would it be appropriate for Mohican Company to recognize deferred revenue on warranty contracts?

(c) If Mohican Company recognized deferred revenue on warranty contracts, how would it recognize this revenue in subsequent periods?

Case 3   BOP Clothing Co.

As discussed in the chapter, an important consideration in evaluating current liabilities is a company's operating cycle. The operating cycle is the average time required to go from cash to cash in generating revenue. To determine the length of the operating cycle, analysts use two measures: the average days to sell inventory (*inventory days*) and the average days to collect receivables (*receivable days*). The inventory-days computation measures the average number of days it takes to move an item from raw materials or purchase to final sale (from the day it comes in the company's door to the point it is converted to cash or an account receivable). The receivable-days computation measures the average number of days it takes to collect an account.

Most businesses must then determine how to finance the period of time when the liquid assets are tied up in inventory and accounts receivable. To determine how much to finance, companies first determine accounts payable days—how long it takes to pay creditors. Accounts payable days measures the number of days it takes to pay a supplier invoice. Consider the following operating cycle worksheet for BOP Clothing Co.

	2013	2014
Cash	$ 45,000	$ 30,000
Accounts receivable	250,000	325,000
Inventory	830,000	800,000
Accounts payable	720,000	775,000
Purchases	1,100,000	1,425,000
Cost of goods sold	1,145,000	1,455,000
Sales	1,750,000	1,950,000
Operating Cycle		
Inventory days[1]	264.6	200.7
Receivable days[2]	52.1	60.8
Operating cycle	316.7	261.5
Less: Accounts payable days[3]	238.9	198.5
Days to be financed	77.8	63.0
Working capital	$ 405,000	$ 380,000
Current ratio	1.56	1.49
Acid-test ratio	0.41	0.46

[1]Inventory days = (Inventory × 365) ÷ Cost of goods sold
[2]Receivable days = (Accounts receivable × 365) ÷ Sales
[3]Accounts payable days = (Accounts payable × 365) ÷ Purchases

Purchases = Cost of goods sold + Ending inventory − Beginning inventory.
The ratios above assume that other current assets and liabilities are negligible.

These data indicate that BOP has reduced its overall operating cycle (to 261.5 days) as well as the number of days to be financed with sources of funds other than accounts payable (from 78 to 63 days). Most businesses cannot finance the operating cycle with accounts payable financing alone, so working capital financing, usually short-term interest-bearing loans, is needed to cover the shortfall. In this case, BOP would need to borrow less money to finance its operating cycle in 2014 than in 2013.

Instructions

(a) Use the BOP analysis to briefly discuss how the operating cycle data relate to the amount of working capital and the current and acid-test ratios.

(b) Select two other real companies that are in the same industry and complete the operating cycle worksheet, along with the working capital and ratio analysis. Briefly summarize and interpret the results. To simplify the analysis, you may use ending balances to compute turnover ratios.

[Adapted from Operating Cycle Worksheet at *www.entrepreneur.com*]

Accounting, Analysis, and Principles

(*Note:* For any part of this problem requiring an interest or discount rate, use 10%.)

YellowCard Company manufactures accessories for iPods. It had the following selected transactions during 2014.

1. YellowCard provides a 2-year warranty on its docking stations, which it began selling in 2014. During 2014, YellowCard spent $6,000 servicing warranty claims. At year-end, YellowCard estimates that an additional $45,000 will be spent in the future to service warranties related to 2014 sales.

2. YellowCard has a $200,000 loan outstanding from First Trust Corp. The loan is set to mature on February 28, 2015. For several years, First Trust has agreed to extend the loan, as long as YellowCard makes all its quarterly interest payments (interest is due on the last days of each February, May, August, and November) and maintains an acid-test ratio (also called "quick ratio") of at least 1.25. First Trust has provided YellowCard a "commitment letter" indicating that First Trust will extend the loan another 12 months, providing YellowCard makes the interest payment due on March 31.

3. During 2013, YellowCard constructed a small manufacturing facility specifically to manufacture one particular accessory. YellowCard paid the construction contractor $5,000,000 cash (which was the total contract price) and placed the facility into service on January 1, 2014. Because of technological change, YellowCard anticipates that the manufacturing facility will be useful for no more than 10 years. The local government where the facility is located required that, at the end of the 10-year period, Yellow-Card remediate the facility so that it can be used as a community center. YellowCard estimates the cost of remediation to be $500,000.

Accounting

Prepare all 2014 journal entries relating to (a) YellowCard's warranties, (b) YellowCard's loan from First Trust Corp., and (c) the new manufacturing facility YellowCard opened on January 1, 2014.

Analysis

Describe how the transactions above affect ratios that might be used to assess YellowCard's liquidity. How important is the commitment letter that YellowCard has from First Trust Corp. to these ratios?

Principles

YellowCard is contemplating offering an extended warranty. If customers pay an additional $50 at the time of product purchase, YellowCard would extend the warranty an additional two years. Would the extended warranty meet the definition of a liability under current generally accepted accounting principles? Briefly explain.

BRIDGE TO THE PROFESSION

Professional Research: FASB Codification

Pleasant Co. manufactures specialty bike accessories. The company is known for product quality, and it has offered one of the best warranties in the industry on its higher-priced products—a lifetime guarantee, performing all the warranty work in its own shops. The warranty on these products is included in the sales price.

Due to the recent introduction and growth in sales of some products targeted to the low-price market, Pleasant is considering partnering with another company to do the warranty work on this line of products, if customers purchase a service contract at the time of original product purchase. Pleasant has called you to advise the company on the accounting for this new warranty arrangement.

Instructions

If your school has a subscription to the FASB Codification, go to *http://aaahq.org/asclogin.cfm* to log in and prepare responses to the following. Provide Codification references for your responses.

(a) Identify the accounting literature that addresses the accounting for the type of separately priced warranty that Pleasant is considering.

(b) When are warranty contracts considered separately priced?

(c) What are incremental direct acquisition costs and how should they be treated?

Additional Professional Resources

See the book's companion website, at **www.wiley.com/college/kieso**, for professional simulations as well as other study resources.

IFRS > INSIGHTS

IFRS and GAAP have similar definitions for liabilities. IFRS related to reporting and recognition of liabilities is found in *IAS 1* ("Presentation of Financial Statements") and *IAS 37* ("Provisions, Contingent Liabilities, and Contingent Assets").

7 LEARNING OBJECTIVE

Compare the accounting procedures for current liabilities and contingencies under GAAP and IFRS.

RELEVANT FACTS

Following are the key similarities and differences between GAAP and IFRS related to current liabilities and contingencies.

Similarities

- Similar to U.S. practice, IFRS requires that companies present current and non-current liabilities on the face of the statement of financial position (balance sheet), with current liabilities generally presented in order of liquidity. However, many companies using IFRS present non-current liabilities before current liabilities on the statement of financial position.

- The basic definition of a liability under GAAP and IFRS is very similar. In a more technical way, liabilities are defined by the IASB as a present obligation of the entity arising from past events, the settlement of which is expected to result in an outflow from the entity of resources embodying economic benefits. Liabilities may be legally enforceable via a contract or law but need not be. That is, they can arise due to normal business practices or customs.

- IFRS requires that companies classify liabilities as current or non-current on the face of the statement of financial position (balance sheet), except in industries where a presentation based on liquidity would be considered to provide more useful information (such as financial institutions).

Differences

- Under IFRS, the measurement of a provision related to a contingency is based on the best estimate of the expenditure required to settle the obligation. If a range of estimates is predicted and no amount in the range is more likely than any other amount in the range, the "midpoint" of the range is used to measure the liability. In GAAP, the minimum amount in a range is used.

- Both IFRS and GAAP prohibit the recognition of liabilities for future losses. However, IFRS permits recognition of a restructuring liability, once a company has committed to a restructuring plan. GAAP has additional criteria (i.e., related to communicating the plan to employees) before a restructuring liability can be established.

- IFRS and GAAP are similar in the treatment of asset retirement obligations (AROs). However, the recognition criteria for an ARO are more stringent under GAAP: The ARO is not recognized unless there is a present legal obligation and the fair value of the obligation can be reasonably estimated.

- Under IFRS, short-term obligations expected to be refinanced can be classified as non-current if the refinancing is completed by the financial statement date. GAAP uses the date the financial statements are issued.

- IFRS uses the term *provisions* to refer to estimated liabilities. Under IFRS, contingencies are not recorded but are often disclosed. The accounting for provisions under IFRS and estimated liabilities under GAAP are very similar.

- GAAP uses the term *contingency* in a different way than IFRS. Contingent liabilities are not recognized in the financial statements under IFRS, whereas under GAAP, a contingent liability is sometimes recognized.

ABOUT THE NUMBERS

Refinancing Criteria

The IASB has developed criteria for determining the circumstances under which short-term obligations may be properly excluded from current liabilities. Specifically, a company can exclude a short-term obligation from current liabilities if both of the following conditions are met:

1. It must intend to refinance the obligation on a long-term basis; and
2. It must have an unconditional right to defer settlement of the liability for at least 12 months after the reporting date.

Intention to refinance on a long-term basis means that the company intends to refinance the short-term obligation so that it will not require the use of working capital during the ensuing fiscal year (or operating cycle, if longer). Entering into a financing arrangement that clearly permits the company to refinance the debt on a long-term basis on terms that are readily determinable before the next reporting date is one way to satisfy the second condition. In addition, the fact that a company has the right to refinance at any time and intends to do so permits the company to classify the liability as non-current.

To illustrate, assume that Haddad Company provides the following information related to its note payable.

- Issued note payable of $3,000,000 on November 30, 2013, due on February 28, 2014. Haddad's reporting date is December 31, 2013.
- Haddad intends to extend the maturity date of the loan (refinance the loan) to June 30, 2015.
- Its December 31, 2013, financial statements are authorized for issue on March 15, 2014.
- The necessary paperwork to refinance the loan is completed on January 15, 2014. Haddad did not have an unconditional right to defer settlement of the obligation at December 31, 2013.

A graphical representation of the refinancing events is provided in Illustration IFRS13-1.

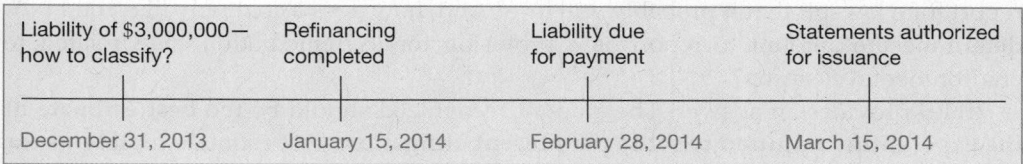

ILLUSTRATION IFRS13-1
Refinancing Events

In this case, Haddad must classify its note payable as a current liability because the refinancing was not completed by December 31, 2013, the financial reporting date. Only if the refinancing was completed before December 31, 2013, can Haddad classify the note obligation as non-current. The rationale: Refinancing a liability after the statement of financial position date does not affect the liquidity or solvency at the date of the statement of financial position, the reporting of which should reflect contractual agreements in force on that date.

What happens if Haddad has both the intention and the discretion (within the loan agreement) to refinance or roll over its $3,000,000 note payable to June 30, 2015? In this case, Haddad should classify the note payable as non-current because it has the ability to defer the payment to June 30, 2015.

Provisions

As indicated in the *Relevant Facts* section, a **provision** is a liability of uncertain timing or amount (sometimes referred to as an *estimated liability*). Provisions are very common and may be reported either as current or non-current depending on the date of expected payment. Common types of provisions are obligations related to litigation, warrantees or product guarantees, business restructurings, and environmental damage.

The difference between a provision and other liabilities (such as accounts or notes payable, salaries payable, and dividends payable) is that **a provision has greater uncertainty about the timing or amount of the future expenditure required to settle the obligation**. For example, when Siemens AG reports an accounts payable, there is an invoice or formal agreement as to the existence and the amount of the liability. Similarly, when Siemens accrues interest payable, the timing and the amount are known.[22]

[22]The distinction is important because provisions are subject to disclosure requirements that do not apply to other types of payables.

Recognition of a Provision

Companies accrue an expense and related liability for a provision only if the following three conditions are met:

1. A company has a present obligation (legal or constructive) as a result of a past event;

2. It is probable that an outflow of resources embodying economic benefits will be required to settle the obligation; and.

3. A reliable estimate can be made of the amount of the obligation.

If any of these three conditions are not met, no provision is recognized.

In applying the first condition, the past event (often referred to as the *past obligatory event*) must have occurred. In applying the second condition, the term **probable** is defined as "more likely than not to occur." This phrase is interpreted to mean the probability of occurrence is greater than 50 percent. If the probability is 50 percent or less, the provision is not recognized.

Measurement of Provisions

How does a company like Toyota, for example, determine the amount to report for its warranty cost on its automobiles? How does a company like Carrefour determine its liability for customer refunds? Or, how does Novartis determine the amount to report for a lawsuit that it probably will lose? And, how does a company like Total S.A. determine the amount to report as a provision for its remediation costs related to environmental clean-up?

IFRS provides an answer: The amount recognized should be the **best estimate of the expenditure required to settle the present obligation**. Best estimate represents the amount that a company would pay to settle the obligation at the statement of financial position date.

Measurement Examples. In determining the best estimate, the management of a company must use judgment, based on past or similar transactions, discussions with experts, and any other pertinent information. Here is how this judgment might be used in three different types of situations to arrive at best estimate:

- *Toyota warranties.* Toyota sells many cars and must make an estimate of the number of warranty repairs and related costs it will incur. Because it is dealing with a large population of automobiles, it is often best to weight all possible outcomes by associated probabilities. For example, it might determine that 80 percent of its cars will not have any warranty cost, 12 percent will have substantial costs, and 8 percent will have a much smaller cost. In this case, by weighting all the possible outcomes by their associated probabilities, Toyota **arrives at an expected value** for its warranty liability.

- *Carrefour refunds.* Carrefour sells many items at varying selling prices. Refunds to customers for products sold may be viewed as a continuous range of refunds, with each point in the range having the same probability of occurrence. In this case, the **midpoint in the range** can be used as the basis for measuring the amount of the refunds.

- *Novartis lawsuit.* Large companies like Novartis are involved in numerous litigation issues related to their products. Where a single obligation such as a lawsuit is being measured, **the most likely outcome** of the lawsuit may be the best estimate of the liability.

Common Types of Provisions

Here are some common areas for which provisions may be recognized in the financial statements:

1. Lawsuits
2. Warranties
3. Premiums
4. Environmental
5. Onerous contracts
6. Restructuring

IFRS accounting guidance is similar to GAAP for these items. Although companies generally report only one current and one non-current amount for provisions in the statement of financial position, IFRS also requires extensive disclosure related to provisions in the notes to the financial statements. Companies do not record or report in the notes to the financial statements general risk contingencies inherent in business operations (e.g., the possibility of war, strike, uninsurable catastrophes, or a business recession).

Onerous Contract Provisions

Sometimes, companies have what are referred to as **onerous contracts**. These contracts are ones in which "the unavoidable costs of meeting the obligations exceed the economic benefits expected to be received." An example of an onerous contract is a loss recognized on unfavorable non-cancelable purchase commitments related to inventory items.

To illustrate another situation, assume that Sumart Sports operates profitably in a factory that it has leased and on which it pays monthly rentals. Sumart decides to relocate its operations to another facility. However, the lease on the old facility continues for the next three years. Unfortunately, Sumart cannot cancel the lease nor will it be able to sublet the factory to another party. The expected costs to satisfy this onerous contract are $200,000. In this case, Sumart makes the following entry.

Loss on Lease Contract	200,000	
Lease Contract Liability		200,000

The expected costs should reflect the least net cost of exiting from the contract, which is the lower of (1) the cost of fulfilling the contract, or (2) the compensation or penalties arising from failure to fulfill the contract.

Contingencies

In a general sense, all provisions are contingent because they are uncertain in timing or amount. However, IFRS uses the term "contingent" for liabilities and assets that are not recognized in the financial statements.

Contingent Liabilities

Contingent liabilities are not recognized in the financial statements because they are (1) a possible obligation (not yet confirmed as a present obligation), (2) a present obligation for which it is not probable that payment will be made, or (3) a present obligation for which a reliable estimate of the obligation cannot be made. Examples of contingent liabilities are:

• A lawsuit in which it is only possible that the company might lose.
• A guarantee related to collectability of a receivable.

Illustration IFRS13-2 presents the general guidelines for the accounting and reporting of contingent liabilities.

Outcome	Probability*	Accounting Treatment
Virtually certain	At least 90%	Report as liability (provision).
Probable (more likely than not)	51–89% probable	Report as liability (provision).
Possible but not probable	5–50%	Disclosure required.
Remote	Less than 5%	No disclosure required.

*In practice, the percentages for virtually certain and remote may deviate from those presented here.

ILLUSTRATION IFRS13-2
Contingent Liability Guidelines

Unless the possibility of any outflow in settlement is remote, companies should disclose the contingent liability at the end of the reporting period, providing a brief description of the nature of the contingent liability and, where practicable:

1. An estimate of its financial effect;

2. An indication of the uncertainties relating to the amount or timing of any outflow; and

3. The possibility of any reimbursement.

Contingent Assets

A **contingent asset** is a possible asset that arises from past events and whose existence will be confirmed by the occurrence or non-occurrence of uncertain future events not wholly within the control of the company. Typical contingent assets are:

1. Possible receipts of monies from gifts, donations, bonuses.

2. Possible refunds from the government in tax disputes.

3. Pending court cases with a probable favorable outcome.

Contingent assets are not recognized on the statement of financial position. If realization of the contingent asset is virtually certain, it is no longer considered a contingent asset and is recognized as an asset. **Virtually certain** is generally interpreted to be at least a probability of 90 percent or more.

The general rules related to contingent assets are presented in Illustration IFRS13-3.

ILLUSTRATION IFRS13-3
Contingent Asset Guidelines

Outcome	Probability*	Accounting Treatment
Virtually certain	At least 90% probable	Report as asset (no longer contingent).
Probable (more likely than not)	51–90% probable	Disclose.
Possible but not probable	5–50%	No disclosure required.
Remote	Less than 5%	No disclosure required.

*In practice, the percentages for virtually certain and remote may deviate from those presented here.

Contingent assets are disclosed when an inflow of economic benefits is considered more likely than not to occur (greater than 50 percent). However, it is important that disclosures for contingent assets avoid giving misleading indications of the likelihood of income arising. As a result, it is not surprising that the thresholds for allowing recognition of contingent assets are more stringent relative to those for liabilities.

What might be an example of a contingent asset that becomes an asset to be recorded? To illustrate, assume that Marcus Realty leases a property to **Marks and Spencer plc (M&S)**. The contract is non-cancelable for five years. On December 1, 2013, before the end of the contract, M&S withdraws from the contract and is required to pay £245,000 as a penalty. At the time M&S cancels the contract, a receivable and related income should be reported by Marcus. The disclosure includes the nature and, where practicable, the estimated financial effects of the asset.

IFRS SELF-TEST QUESTIONS

1. The presentation of current and non-current liabilities in the statement of financial position (balance sheet):

(a) is shown only on GAAP financial statements.

(b) is shown on both a GAAP and an IFRS statement of financial position.

(c) is always shown with current liabilities reported first in an IFRS statement of financial position.

(d) includes contingent liabilities under IFRS.

2. In accounting for short-term debt expected to be refinanced to long-term debt:

(a) GAAP uses the authorization date to determine classification of short-term debt to be refinanced.

(b) IFRS uses the authorization date to determine classification of short-term debt to be refinanced.

(c) IFRS uses the financial statement date to determine classification of short-term debt to be refinanced.

(d) GAAP uses the date of issue, but only for secured debt, to determine classification of short-term debt to be refinanced.

3. Under IFRS, a provision is the same as:

(a) a contingent liability. **(c)** a contingent gain.

(b) an estimated liability. **(d)** None of the above.

4. A typical provision is:

(a) bonds payable. **(c)** a warranty liability.

(b) cash. **(d)** accounts payable.

5. In determining the amount of a provision, a company using IFRS should generally measure:

(a) using the midpoint of the range between the lowest possible loss and the highest possible loss.

(b) using the minimum amount of the loss in the range.

(c) using the best estimate of the amount of the loss expected to occur.

(d) using the maximum amount of the loss in the range.

IFRS CONCEPTS AND APPLICATION

IFRS13-1 Under what conditions should a short-term obligation be excluded from current liabilities?

IFRS13-2 What evidence is necessary to demonstrate the ability to defer settlement of short-term debt?

IFRS13-3 Define a provision, and give three examples of a provision.

IFRS13-4 Under what conditions should a provision be recorded?

IFRS13-5 Distinguish between a current liability, such as accounts payable, and a provision.

IFRS13-6 What is an onerous contract? Give two examples of an onerous contract.

IFRS13-7 On December 31, 2014, Alexander Company had $1,200,000 of short-term debt in the form of notes payable due February 2, 2015. On January 21, 2015, the company issued 25,000 ordinary shares for $36 per share, receiving $900,000 proceeds after brokerage fees and other costs of issuance. On February 2, 2015, the proceeds from the share sale, supplemented by an additional $300,000 cash, are used to liquidate the $1,200,000 debt. The December 31, 2014, statement of financial position is authorized for issue on February 23, 2015.

Instructions

Show how the $1,200,000 of short-term debt should be presented on the December 31, 2014, statement of financial position.

IFRS13-8 Presented below are two different situations related to Mckee Corporation's debt obligations. Mckee's next financial reporting date is December 31, 2014. The financial statements are authorized for issuance on March 1, 2015.

1. Mckee has a long-term obligation of $400,000, which is maturing over 4 years in the amount of $100,000 per year. The obligation is dated November 1, 2014, and the first maturity date is November 1, 2015.

2. Mckee has a short-term obligation due February 15, 2015. Its lender agrees to extend the maturity date of this loan to February 15, 2017. The agreement for extension is signed on January 15, 2015.

Instructions

Indicate how each of these debt obligations is reported on Mckee's statement of financial position on December 31, 2014.

IFRS13-9 The following situations relate to Bolivia Company.

1. Bolivia provides a warranty with all its products it sells. It estimates that it will sell 1,000,000 units of its product for the year ended December 31, 2014, and that its total revenue for the product will be $100,000,000. It also estimates that 60% of the product will have no defects, 30% will have major defects, and 10% will have minor defects. The cost of a minor defect is estimated to be $5 for each product sold, and the cost for a major defect cost is $15. The company also estimates that the minimum amount of warranty expense will be $2,000,000 and the maximum will be $10,000,000.

2. Bolivia is involved in a tax dispute with the tax authorities. The most likely outcome of this dispute is that Bolivia will lose and have to pay $400,000. The minimum it will lose is $20,000 and the maximum is $2,500,000.

Instructions

Prepare the journal entry to record provisions, if any, for Bolivia at December 31, 2014.

IFRS13-10 Kobayashi Corporation reports in the current liability section of its statement of financial position at December 31, 2014 (its year-end), short-term obligations of $15,000,000, which includes the current portion of 12% long-term debt in the amount of $10,000,000 (matures in March 2015). Management has stated its intention to refinance the 12% debt whereby no portion of it will mature during 2015. The date of issuance of the financial statements is March 25, 2015.

Instructions

(a) Is management's intent enough to support long-term classification of the obligation in this situation?

(b) Assume that Kobayashi Corporation issues $13,000,000 of 10-year debentures to the public in January 2015 and that management intends to use the proceeds to liquidate the $10,000,000 debt maturing in March 2015. Furthermore, assume that the debt maturing in March 2015 is paid from these proceeds prior to the authorization to issue the financial statements. Will this have any impact on the statement of financial position classification at December 31, 2014? Explain your answer.

(c) Assume that Kobayashi Corporation issues ordinary shares to the public in January and that management intends to entirely liquidate the $10,000,000 debt maturing in March 2015 with the proceeds of this equity securities issue. In light of these events, should the $10,000,000 debt maturing in March 2015 be included in current liabilities at December 31, 2014?

Professional Research

IFRS13-11 Hincapie Co. manufactures specialty bike accessories. The company is most well known for its product quality, and it has offered one of the best warranties in the industry on its higher-priced products—a lifetime guarantee. The warranty on these products is included in the sales price. Hincapie has a contract with a service company, which performs all warranty work on Hincapie products. Under the contract, Hincapie guarantees the service company at least $200,000 of warranty work for each year of the 3-year contract.

The recent economic recession has been hard on Hincapie's business, and sales for its higher-end products have been especially adversely impacted. As a result, Hincapie is planning to restructure its high-quality lines by moving manufacturing for those products into one of its other factories, shutting down assembly lines, and terminating workers. In order to keep some workers on-board, Hincapie plans to bring all warranty work in-house. It can terminate the current warranty contract by making a one-time termination payment of $75,000.

The restructuring plans have been discussed by management during November 2013; they plan to get approval from the board of directors at the December board meeting and execute the restructuring in early 2014. Given the company's past success, the accounting for restructuring activities has never come up. Hincapie would like you to do some research on how it should account for this restructuring according to IFRS.

Instructions

Access the IFRS authoritative literature at the IASB website (*http://eifrs.iasb.org/*). (Click on the IFRS tab and then register for free eIFRS access if necessary.) When you have accessed the documents, you can use the search tool in your Internet browser to respond to the following questions. (Provide paragraph citations.)

(a) Identify the accounting literature that addresses the accounting for the various costs that will be incurred in the restructuring.

(b) Advise Hincapie on the restructuring costs. When should Hincapie recognize liabilities arising from the restructuring? What costs can be included? What costs are excluded?

(c) Does Hincapie have a liability related to the service contract? Explain. If Hincapie has a liability, at what amount should it be recorded?

International Financial Reporting Problem
Marks and Spencer plc

IFRS13-12 The financial statements of **Marks and Spencer plc (M&S)** are available at the book's companion website or can be accessed at *http://annualreport.marksandspencer.com/_assets/downloads/ Marks-and-Spencer-Annual-report-and-financial-statements-2012.pdf*.

Instructions
Refer to M&S's financial statements and the accompanying notes to answer the following questions.

(a) What was M&S's 2012 short-term debt and related weighted-average interest rate on this debt?

(b) What was M&S's 2012 working capital, acid-test ratio, and current ratio? Comment on M&S's liquidity.

(c) What types of commitments and contingencies has M&S reported in its financial statements?

ANSWERS TO IFRS SELF-TEST QUESTIONS

1. b **2.** c **3.** b **4.** c **5.** c

Remember to check the book's companion website to find additional resources for this chapter.

14 Long-Term Liabilities

Going Long

The clock is ticking. Every second, it seems, someone in the world takes on more debt. The idea of a debt clock for an individual nation is familiar to anyone who has been to Times Square in New York, where the American public shortfall is revealed. The global debt clock shown below (accessed in October 2012) indicates the global figure for almost all government debts in dollar terms.

Current Global Public Debt

$ 049, 041, 235, 945, 311

Does it matter? After all, world governments owe the money to their own citizens, not to the Martians. But the rising total is important for two reasons. First, when government debt rises faster than economic output (as it has been doing in recent years), this implies more state interference in the economy and higher taxes in the future. Second, debt must be rolled over at regular intervals. This creates a recurring popularity test for individual governments, much like reality-TV contestants facing a public phone vote every week. Fail that vote, as various euro-zone governments have done, and the country (and its neighbors) can be plunged into crisis.

In addition to government debt, companies are issuing corporate debt at a record pace. Why this trend? For one thing, low interest rates and rising inflows into fixed-income funds have triggered record bond issuances as banks cut back lending. In addition, for some high-rated companies, it can be riskier to borrow from a bank than the bond markets. The reason: High-rated companies tend to rely on short-term commercial paper, backed up by undrawn loans, to fund working capital but are left stranded when these markets freeze up. Some are now financing themselves with longer-term bonds instead.

In fact, nonfinancial companies are issuing 30-year bonds at a record pace, as they look to increase long-term borrowings, lock in low interest rates, and take advantage of investor demand. The charts on the next page show the substantial increase in bonds issues as interest rates have fallen.

Companies, like **Phillip Morris**, **Medtronic**, **Plains All American Pipeline**, and **Simon Property Group**, have all sold 30-year bonds recently. Increases in the issuance of these bonds suggest confidence in the economy as investors appear comfortable holding such long-term investments. In addition, companies have a strong appetite for issuing these bonds

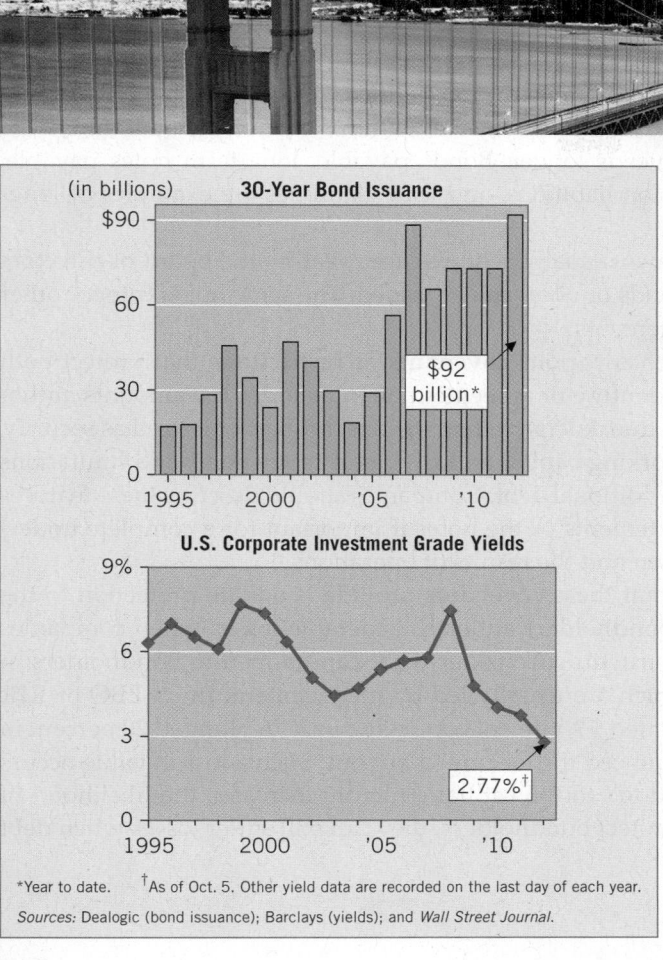

30-Year Bond Issuance
(in billions)

$90

60

30

$92 billion*

0

1995   2000   '05   '10

U.S. Corporate Investment Grade Yields

9%

6

3

2.77%†

0

1995   2000   '05   '10

*Year to date.   †As of Oct. 5. Other yield data are recorded on the last day of each year.
Sources: Dealogic (bond issuance); Barclays (yields); and *Wall Street Journal*.

CONCEPTUAL FOCUS

> See the **Underlying Concepts** on page 774.
> Read the **Evolving Issue** on page 788 for a discussion of recognizing debt using the fair value option.

INTERNATIONAL FOCUS

> See the **International Perspectives** on pages 770, 775, and 785.
> Read the **IFRS Insights** on pages 815–819 for a discussion of:
  —Effective-interest method
  —Extinguishments with modifications of terms

because they provide a substantial cash infusion at a relatively low interest rate. Hopefully, it will work out for both the investor and the company in the long run.

Sources: A. Sakoui and N. Bullock, "Companies Choose Bonds for Cheap Funds," *Financial Times* (October 12, 2009); *http://www.economist.com/content/global_debt_clock*; and V. Monga, "Companies Feast on Cheap Money Market for 30-Year Bonds, Priced at Stark Lows, Brings Out GE, UPS and Other Once-Shy Issuers," *Wall Street Journal* (October 8, 2012).

PREVIEW OF CHAPTER   14

As our opening story indicates, companies may rely on different forms of long-term borrowing, depending on market conditions and the features of various noncurrent liabilities. In this chapter, we explain the accounting issues related to long-term liabilities. The content and organization of the chapter are as follows.

Long-Term Liabilities

Bonds Payable	Valuation of Bonds Payable	Long-Term Notes Payable	Reporting and Analyzing Liabilities
• Issuing bonds • Types of bonds	• Issued at par • Issued at discount or premium • Issued between interest dates • Effective-interest method • Costs of issuing • Extinguishment	• Notes issued at face value • Notes not issued at face value • Special situations • Mortgage notes payable • Fair value option	• Off-balance-sheet financing • Presentation and analysis

BONDS PAYABLE

LEARNING OBJECTIVE 1

Describe the formal procedures associated with issuing long-term debt.

Long-term debt consists of probable future sacrifices of economic benefits arising from present obligations that are not payable within a year or the operating cycle of the company, whichever is longer. Bonds payable, long-term notes payable, mortgages payable, pension liabilities, and lease liabilities are examples of long-term liabilities.

A corporation, per its bylaws, usually requires approval by the board of directors and the stockholders before bonds or notes can be issued. The same holds true for other types of long-term debt arrangements.

Generally, long-term debt has various **covenants** or **restrictions** that protect both lenders and borrowers. The indenture or agreement often includes the amounts authorized to be issued, interest rate, due date(s), call provisions, property pledged as security, sinking fund requirements, working capital and dividend restrictions, and limitations concerning the assumption of additional debt. Companies should describe these features in the body of the financial statements or the notes if important for a complete understanding of the financial position and the results of operations.

Although it would seem that these covenants provide adequate protection to the long-term debtholder, many bondholders suffer considerable losses when companies add more debt to the capital structure. Consider what can happen to bondholders in leveraged buyouts (LBOs), which are usually led by management. In an LBO of **RJR Nabisco**, for example, solidly rated 9⅜ percent bonds due in 2016 plunged 20 percent in value when management announced the leveraged buyout. Such a loss in value occurs because the additional debt added to the capital structure increases the likelihood of default. Although covenants protect bondholders, they can still suffer losses when debt levels get too high.

Issuing Bonds

A bond arises from a contract known as a **bond indenture**. A bond represents a promise to pay (1) a sum of money at a designated maturity date, plus (2) periodic interest at a specified rate on the maturity amount (face value). Individual bonds are evidenced by a paper certificate and typically have a $1,000 face value. Companies usually make bond interest payments semiannually, although the interest rate is generally expressed as an annual rate. The main purpose of bonds is to borrow for the long term when the amount of capital needed is too large for one lender to supply. By issuing bonds in $100, $1,000, or $10,000 denominations, a company can divide a large amount of long-term indebtedness into many small investing units, thus enabling more than one lender to participate in the loan.

A company may sell an entire bond issue to an investment bank, which acts as a selling agent in the process of marketing the bonds. In such arrangements, investment banks may either underwrite the entire issue by guaranteeing a certain sum to the company, thus taking the risk of selling the bonds for whatever price they can get (firm underwriting). Or they may sell the bond issue for a commission on the proceeds of the sale (best-efforts underwriting). Alternatively, the issuing company may sell the bonds directly to a large institution, financial or otherwise, without the aid of an underwriter (private placement).

Types of Bonds

LEARNING OBJECTIVE 2

Identify various types of bond issues.

Presented on the next page, we define some of the more common types of bonds found in practice.

TYPES OF BONDS

SECURED AND UNSECURED BONDS. **Secured bonds** are backed by a pledge of some sort of collateral. Mortgage bonds are secured by a claim on real estate. Collateral trust bonds are secured by stocks and bonds of other corporations. Bonds not backed by collateral are **unsecured**. A **debenture bond** is unsecured. A "junk bond" is unsecured and also very risky, and therefore pays a high interest rate. Companies often use these bonds to finance leveraged buyouts.

TERM, SERIAL BONDS, AND CALLABLE BONDS. Bond issues that mature on a single date are called **term bonds**. Issues that mature in installments are called **serial bonds**. Serially maturing bonds are frequently used by school or sanitary districts, municipalities, or other local taxing bodies that receive money through a special levy. **Callable bonds** give the issuer the right to call and redeem the bonds prior to maturity.

CONVERTIBLE, COMMODITY-BACKED, AND DEEP-DISCOUNT BONDS. If bonds are convertible into other securities of the corporation for a specified time after issuance, they are **convertible bonds**.

Two types of bonds have been developed in an attempt to attract capital in a tight money market—commodity-backed bonds and deep-discount bonds. **Commodity-backed bonds** (also called **asset-linked bonds**) are redeemable in measures of a commodity, such as barrels of oil, tons of coal, or ounces of rare metal. To illustrate, **Sunshine Mining**, a silver-mining company, sold two issues of bonds redeemable with either $1,000 in cash or 50 ounces of silver, whichever is greater at maturity, and that have a stated interest rate of 8½ percent. The accounting problem is one of projecting the maturity value, especially since silver has fluctuated between $4 and $40 an ounce since issuance.

JCPenney Company sold the first publicly marketed long-term debt securities in the United States that do not bear interest. These **deep-discount bonds**, also referred to as **zero-interest debenture bonds**, are sold at a discount that provides the buyer's total interest payoff at maturity.

REGISTERED AND BEARER (COUPON) BONDS. Bonds issued in the name of the owner are **registered bonds** and require surrender of the certificate and issuance of a new certificate to complete a sale. A **bearer** or **coupon bond**, however, is not recorded in the name of the owner and may be transferred from one owner to another by mere delivery.

INCOME AND REVENUE BONDS. **Income bonds** pay no interest unless the issuing company is profitable. **Revenue bonds**, so called because the interest on them is paid from specified revenue sources, are most frequently issued by airports, school districts, counties, toll-road authorities, and governmental bodies.

What do the numbers mean? ALL ABOUT BONDS

How do investors monitor their bond investments? One way is to review the bond listings found in the newspaper or online. Corporate bond listings show the coupon (interest) rate, maturity date, and last price. However, because corporate bonds are more actively held by large institutional investors, the listings also indicate the current yield and the volume traded. Corporate bond listings would look like those below.

Issuer	Maturity	Amount ($ millions)	Price	Coupon	Yield
Wal-Mart Stores, Inc.	08/15/2037	3,000	145.4	6.50	3.69
General Electric	12/06/2017	4,000	118.2	5.25	1.58

The companies issuing the bonds are listed in the first column, in this case, Wal-Mart Stores, Inc. and General Electric. Immediately after the names is a column with the maturity date, followed by the amount and price of the bonds. As indicated, Wal-Mart pays a coupon rate of 6.5 percent and yields 3.69 percent. General Electric pays a coupon rate of 5.25 percent and yields 1.58 percent. The lower yield for General Electric arises because the time to maturity is much shorter than Wal-Mart's.

Also, interest rates and the bond's term to maturity have a real effect on bond prices. For example, an increase in interest rates will lead to a decline in bond values. Similarly, a decrease in interest rates will lead to a rise in bond values. The data reported in the table to the right, based on three different bond funds, demonstrate these relationships between interest rate changes and bond values.

Bond Price Changes in Response to Interest Rate Changes	1% Interest Rate Increase	1% Interest Rate Decrease
Short-term fund (2–5 years)	−2.5%	+2.5%
Intermediate-term fund (5 years)	−5%	+5%
Long-term fund (10 years)	−10%	+10%

Data source: The Vanguard Group.

Another factor that affects bond prices is the call feature, which decreases the value of the bond. Investors must be rewarded for the risk that the issuer will call the bond if interest rates decline, which would force the investor to reinvest at lower rates.

VALUATION OF BONDS PAYABLE—DISCOUNT AND PREMIUM

LEARNING OBJECTIVE 3

Describe the accounting valuation for bonds at date of issuance.

The issuance and marketing of bonds to the public does not happen overnight. It usually takes weeks or even months. First, the issuing company must arrange for underwriters that will help market and sell the bonds. Then, it must obtain the Securities and Exchange Commission's approval of the bond issue, undergo audits, and issue a prospectus (a document which describes the features of the bond and related financial information). Finally, the company must generally have the bond certificates printed. Frequently, the issuing company establishes the terms of a bond indenture well in advance of the sale of the bonds. Between the time the company sets these terms and the time it issues the bonds, the market conditions and the financial position of the issuing corporation may change significantly. Such changes affect the marketability of the bonds and thus their selling price.

The selling price of a bond issue is set by the supply and demand of buyers and sellers, relative risk, market conditions, and the state of the economy. The investment community values a bond at the **present value of its expected future cash flows**, which consist of (1) interest and (2) principal. The rate used to compute the present value of these cash flows is the interest rate that provides an acceptable return on an investment commensurate with the issuer's risk characteristics.

The interest rate written in the terms of the bond indenture (and often printed on the bond certificate) is known as the stated, coupon, or nominal rate. The issuer of the bonds sets this rate. The stated rate is expressed as a percentage of the face value of the bonds (also called the par value, principal amount, or maturity value).

If the rate employed by the investment community (buyers) differs from the stated rate, the present value of the bonds computed by the buyers (and the current purchase price) will differ from the face value of the bonds. The difference between the face value and the present value of the bonds determines the actual price that buyers pay for the bonds. This difference is either a discount or premium.[1]

---

[1]It is generally the case that the stated rate of interest on bonds is set in rather precise decimals (such as 6.875%). Companies usually attempt to align the stated rate as closely as possible with the market or effective rate at the time of issue.

- If the bonds sell for less than face value, they sell at a discount.
- If the bonds sell for more than face value, they sell at a premium.

The rate of interest actually earned by the bondholders is called the effective yield or market rate. If bonds sell at a discount, the effective yield exceeds the stated rate. Conversely, if bonds sell at a premium, the effective yield is lower than the stated rate. Several variables affect the bond's price while it is outstanding, most notably the market rate of interest. There is an inverse relationship between the market interest rate and the price of the bond.

Here we consider an example to illustrate the computation of the **present value of a bond issue**. Assume that ServiceMaster issues $100,000 in bonds, due in five years with 9 percent interest payable annually at year-end. At the time of issue, the market rate for such bonds is 11 percent. The time diagram in Illustration 14-1 depicts both the interest and the principal cash flows.

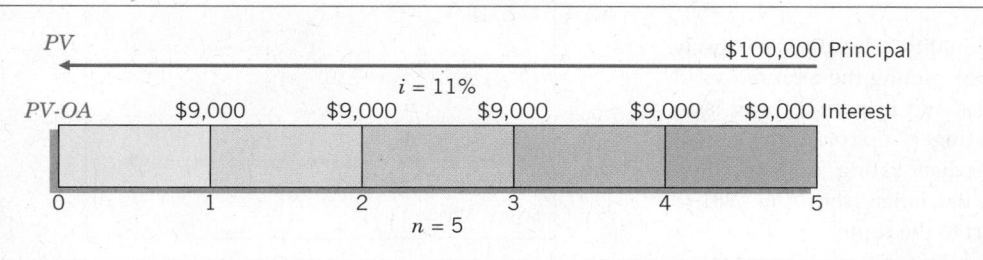

ILLUSTRATION 14-1
Time Diagram for Bond
Cash Flows

The actual principal and interest cash flows are discounted at an 11 percent rate for five periods, as shown in Illustration 14-2.

Present value of the principal:	
$100,000 × .59345 (Table 6-2)	$59,345.00
Present value of the interest payments:	
$9,000 × 3.69590 (Table 6-4)	33,263.10
Present value (selling price) of the bonds	$92,608.10

ILLUSTRATION 14-2
Present Value
Computation of Bond
Selling at a Discount

By paying $92,608.10 at the date of issue, investors earn an effective rate or yield of 11 percent over the five-year term of the bonds. These bonds would sell at a discount of $7,391.90 ($100,000 − $92,608.10). The price at which the bonds sell is typically stated as a **percentage** of the face or par value of the bonds. For example, the ServiceMaster bonds sold for 92.6 (92.6% of par). If ServiceMaster had received $102,000, then the bonds sold for 102 (102% of par).

When bonds sell at less than face value, it means that investors demand a rate of interest **higher** than the stated rate. Usually this occurs because the investors can earn a greater rate on alternative investments of equal risk. They cannot change the stated rate, so they refuse to pay face value for the bonds. Thus, by changing the amount invested, they alter the effective rate of return. The investors receive interest at the stated rate computed on the face value, but they actually earn at **an effective rate that exceeds the stated rate because they paid less than face value for the bonds**. (Later in the chapter, in Illustrations 14-6 and 14-7 (pages 772–773), we show an illustration for a bond that sells at a premium.)

What do the numbers mean? HOW'S MY RATING?

Two major publication companies, Moody's Investors Service and Standard & Poor's Corporation, issue quality ratings on every public debt issue. The following table summarizes the ratings issued by Standard & Poor's, along with historical default rates on bonds with different ratings.

Original rating	AAA	AA	A	BBB	BB	B	CCC
Default rate	0.52%	1.31	2.32	6.64	19.52	35.76	54.38

Data source: Standard & Poor's Corp.

As expected, bonds receiving the highest quality rating of AAA have the lowest historical default rates. Bonds rated below BBB, which are considered below investment grade ("junk bonds"), experience default rates ranging from 20 to 50 percent.

Debt ratings reflect credit quality. The market closely monitors these ratings when determining the required yield and pricing of bonds at issuance and in periods after issuance, especially if a bond's rating is upgraded or downgraded. Unfortunately, the median rating of companies assessed by Standard & Poor's has fallen from A in 1981 to BBB today, as shown in the chart to the right.

The BBB rating is the lowest possible "investment grade" or, to put it another way, is just one notch above "junk" bond status. It should be noted that investors who seek triple-A debt are running out of options. Standard & Poor's recently gave its top rating to just four U.S. industrial companies: Automatic Data Processing, ExxonMobil, Johnson & Johnson, and Microsoft.

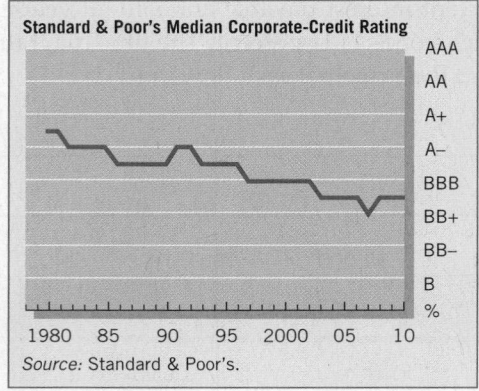

Source: Standard & Poor's.

Sources: A. Borrus, M. McNamee, and H. Timmons, "The Credit Raters: How They Work and How They Might Work Better," *BusinessWeek* (April 8, 2002), pp. 38–40; Standard and Poor's, *Global Fixed Income Research*, "Fallen Angel Activity" (February 6, 2007); and "Betting the Balance Sheet," *The Economist* (June 24, 2010).

Bonds Issued at Par on Interest Date

When a company issues bonds on an interest payment date at par (face value), it accrues no interest. No premium or discount exists. The company simply records the cash proceeds and the face value of the bonds. To illustrate, if Buchanan Company issues at par 10-year term bonds with a par value of $800,000, dated January 1, 2014, and bearing interest at an annual rate of 10 percent payable semiannually on January 1 and July 1, it records the following entry.

Cash	800,000	
Bonds Payable		800,000

Buchanan records the first semiannual interest payment of $40,000 ($800,000 × .10 × 1/2) on July 1, 2014, as follows.

Interest Expense	40,000	
Cash		40,000

It records accrued interest expense at December 31, 2014 (year-end), as follows.

Interest Expense	40,000	
Interest Payable		40,000

LEARNING OBJECTIVE 4

Apply the methods of bond discount and premium amortization.

Bonds Issued at Discount or Premium on Interest Date

If Buchanan Company issues the $800,000 of bonds on January 1, 2014, at 97 (meaning 97% of par), it records the issuance as shown on the top of the next page.

Cash ($800,000 × .97)	776,000	
Discount on Bonds Payable	24,000	
Bonds Payable		800,000

Recall from our earlier discussion that because of its relation to interest, **companies amortize the discount and charge it to interest expense over the period of time that the bonds are outstanding**.

The straight-line method amortizes a constant amount each interest period (in this case 20 interest periods).[2] For example, using the bond discount of $24,000, Buchanan amortizes $1,200 to interest expense each period for 20 periods ($24,000 ÷ 20).

Buchanan records the first semiannual interest payment of $40,000 ($800,000 × 10% × ½) and the bond discount on July 1, 2014, as follows.

Interest Expense	41,200	
Discount on Bonds Payable		1,200
Cash		40,000

At December 31, 2014, Buchanan makes the following adjusting entry.

Interest Expense	41,200	
Discount on Bonds Payable		1,200
Interest Payable		40,000

At the end of the first year, 2014, the balance in the Discount on Bonds Payable account is $21,600 ($24,000 − $1,200 − $1,200). Over the term of the bonds, the balance in Discount on Bonds Payable will decrease by the same amount until it has zero balance at the maturity date of the bonds.

If instead of issuing the bonds on January 1, 2014, Buchanan dates and sells the bonds on October 1, 2014, and if the fiscal year of the corporation ends on December 31, the discount amortized during 2014 would be only 3/12 of 1/10 of $24,000, or $600. Buchanan must also record three months of accrued interest on December 31.

Premium on Bonds Payable is accounted for in a manner similar to that for Discount on Bonds Payable. If Buchanan dates and sells 10-year bonds with a par value of $800,000 on January 1, 2014, at 103, it records the issuance as follows.

Cash ($800,000 × 1.03)	824,000	
Premium on Bonds Payable		24,000
Bonds Payable		800,000

With the bond premium of $24,000, Buchanan amortizes $1,200 to interest expense each period for 20 periods ($24,000 ÷ 20).

Buchanan records the first semiannual interest payment of $40,000 ($800,000 × 10% × ½) and the bond premium on July 1, 2014, as follows.

Interest Expense	38,800	
Premium on Bonds Payable	1,200	
Cash		40,000

At December 31, 2014, Buchanan makes the following adjusting entry.

Interest Expense	38,800	
Premium on Bonds Payable	1,200	
Interest Payable		40,000

Amortization of a discount increases interest expense. Amortization of a premium decreases interest expense. Later in the chapter, we discuss amortization of a discount or premium under the effective-interest method.

---

[2]The effective-interest method is preferred for amortization of discount or premium. To keep these initial illustrations simple, we have chosen to use the straight-line method.

The issuer may call some bonds at a stated price after a certain date. This call feature gives the issuing corporation the opportunity to reduce its bonded indebtedness or take advantage of lower interest rates. **Whether callable or not, a company must amortize any premium or discount over the bond's life to maturity because early redemption (call of the bond) is not a certainty.**

Bonds Issued Between Interest Dates

Companies usually make bond interest payments semiannually, on dates specified in the bond indenture. When companies issue bonds on other than the interest payment dates, **buyers of the bonds will pay the seller the interest accrued from the last interest payment date to the date of issue.** The purchasers of the bonds, in effect, pay the bond issuer in advance for that portion of the full six-months' interest payment to which they are not entitled because they have not held the bonds for that period. **Then, on the next semiannual interest payment date, purchasers will receive the full six-months' interest payment.**

To illustrate, assume that on March 1, 2014, Taft Corporation issues 10-year bonds, dated January 1, 2014, with a par value of $800,000. These bonds have an annual interest rate of 6 percent, payable semiannually on January 1 and July 1. Because Taft issues the bonds between interest dates, it records the bond issuance at **par plus accrued interest** as follows.

Cash	808,000	
Bonds Payable		800,000
Interest Expense ($800,000 × .06 × 2/12)		8,000
(Interest Payable might be credited instead)		

The purchaser advances two months' interest. On July 1, 2014, four months after the date of purchase, Taft pays the purchaser six months' interest. Taft makes the following entry on July 1, 2014.

Interest Expense	24,000	
Cash		24,000

The Interest Expense account now contains a debit balance of $16,000, which represents the proper amount of interest expense—four months at 6 percent on $800,000.

The illustration above was simplified by having the January 1, 2014, bonds issued on March 1, 2014, **at par**. If, however, Taft issued the 6 percent bonds at 102, its March 1 entry would be:

Cash [($800,000 × 1.02) + ($800,000 × .06 × 2/12)]	824,000	
Bonds Payable		800,000
Premium on Bonds Payable ($800,000 × .02)		16,000
Interest Expense		8,000

Taft would amortize the premium **from the date of sale** (March 1, 2014), not from the date of the bonds (January 1, 2014).

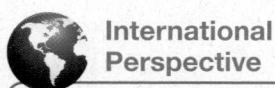
International Perspective

IFRS requires the use of the effective-interest method. GAAP permits the use of the straight-line method if not materially different than the effective-interest method.

Effective-Interest Method

The preferred procedure for amortization of a discount or premium is the effective-interest method (also called **present value amortization**). Under the effective-interest method, companies:

1. Compute bond interest expense first by multiplying the carrying value (book value) of the bonds at the beginning of the period by the effective-interest rate.[3]

---

[3]The carrying value is the face amount minus any unamortized discount or plus any unamortized premium. The term *carrying value* is synonymous with *book value*.

2. Determine the bond discount or premium amortization next by comparing the bond interest expense with the interest (cash) to be paid.

Illustration 14-3 depicts graphically the computation of the amortization.

The effective-interest method produces a periodic interest expense equal to **a constant percentage of the carrying value of the bonds**. Since the percentage is the effective rate of interest incurred by the borrower at the time of issuance, the effective-interest method matches expenses with revenues better than the straight-line method.

Both the effective-interest and straight-line methods result in the **same total amount of interest expense over the term of the bonds**. However, when the annual amounts are materially different, generally accepted accounting principles require use of the effective-interest method. **[1]**

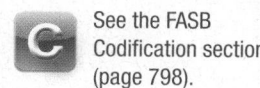

See the FASB
Codification section
(page 798).

Bonds Issued at a Discount

To illustrate amortization of a discount under the effective-interest method, Evermaster Corporation issued $100,000 of 8 percent term bonds on January 1, 2014, due on January 1, 2019, with interest payable each July 1 and January 1. Because the investors required an effective-interest rate of 10 percent, they paid $92,278 for the $100,000 of bonds, creating a $7,722 discount. Evermaster computes the $7,722 discount as follows.[4]

Maturity value of bonds payable		$100,000
Present value of $100,000 due in 5 years at 10%, interest payable		
semiannually (Table 6-2); $FV(PVF_{10,5\%})$; ($100,000 × .61391)	$61,391	
Present value of $4,000 interest payable semiannually for 5 years at		
10% annually (Table 6-4); $R(PVF\text{-}OA_{10,5\%})$; ($4,000 × 7.72173)	30,887	
Less: Proceeds from sale of bonds		92,278
Discount on bonds payable		$ 7,722

ILLUSTRATION 14-4
Computation of Discount
on Bonds Payable

The five-year amortization schedule appears in Illustration 14-5 (page 772).

Evermaster records the issuance of its bonds at a discount on January 1, 2014, as follows.

Cash	92,278	
Discount on Bonds Payable	7,722	
Bonds Payable		100,000

It records the first interest payment on July 1, 2014, and amortization of the discount as follows.

Interest Expense	4,614	
Discount on Bonds Payable		614
Cash		4,000

[4]Because companies pay interest semiannually, the interest rate used is 5% (10% × 6/12). The number of periods is 10 (5 years × 2).

ILLUSTRATION 14-5
Bond Discount
Amortization Schedule

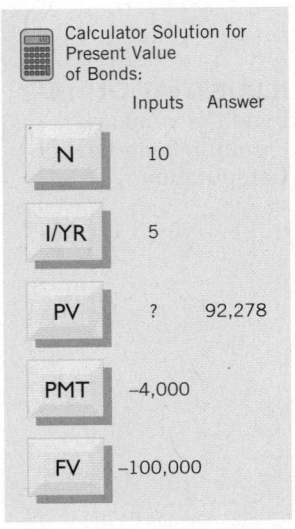

Calculator Solution for
Present Value
of Bonds:

	Inputs	Answer
N	10	
I/YR	5	
PV	?	92,278
PMT	–4,000	
FV	–100,000	

SCHEDULE OF BOND DISCOUNT AMORTIZATION
EFFECTIVE-INTEREST METHOD—SEMIANNUAL INTEREST PAYMENTS
5-YEAR, 8% BONDS SOLD TO YIELD 10%

Date	Cash Paid	Interest Expense	Discount Amortized	Carrying Amount of Bonds
1/1/14				$ 92,278
7/1/14	$ 4,000ᵃ	$ 4,614ᵇ	$ 614ᶜ	92,892ᵈ
1/1/15	4,000	4,645	645	93,537
7/1/15	4,000	4,677	677	94,214
1/1/16	4,000	4,711	711	94,925
7/1/16	4,000	4,746	746	95,671
1/1/17	4,000	4,783	783	96,454
7/1/17	4,000	4,823	823	97,277
1/1/18	4,000	4,864	864	98,141
7/1/18	4,000	4,907	907	99,048
1/1/19	4,000	4,952	952	100,000
	$40,000	$47,722	$7,722	

ᵃ$4,000 = $100,000 × .08 × 6/12
ᵇ$4,614 = $92,278 × .10 × 6/12
ᶜ$614 = $4,614 − $4,000
ᵈ$92,892 = $92,278 + $614

Evermaster records the interest expense accrued at December 31, 2014 (year-end), and amortization of the discount as follows.

Interest Expense	4,645	
Interest Payable		4,000
Discount on Bonds Payable		645

Bonds Issued at a Premium

Now assume that for the bond issue by Evermaster Corporation (page 771), investors are willing to accept an effective-interest rate of 6 percent. In that case, they would pay $108,530 or a premium of $8,530, computed as follows.

ILLUSTRATION 14-6
Computation of Premium
on Bonds Payable

Maturity value of bonds payable		$100,000
Present value of $100,000 due in 5 years at 6%, interest payable semiannually (Table 6-2); FV(PVF₁₀,₃%); ($100,000 × .74409)	$74,409	
Present value of $4,000 interest payable semiannually for 5 years at 6% annually (Table 6-4); R(PVF-OA₁₀,₃%); ($4,000 × 8.53020)	34,121	
Less: Proceeds from sale of bonds		108,530
Premium on bonds payable		$ 8,530

The five-year amortization schedule appears in Illustration 14-7.

Evermaster records the issuance of its bonds at a premium on January 1, 2014, as follows.

Cash	108,530	
Premium on Bonds Payable		8,530
Bonds Payable		100,000

Evermaster records the first interest payment on July 1, 2014, and amortization of the premium as follows.

Interest Expense	3,256	
Premium on Bonds Payable	744	
Cash		4,000

		SCHEDULE OF BOND PREMIUM AMORTIZATION		
	EFFECTIVE-INTEREST METHOD—SEMIANNUAL INTEREST PAYMENTS			
		5-YEAR, 8% BONDS SOLD TO YIELD 6%		
Date	Cash Paid	Interest Expense	Premium Amortized	Carrying Amount of Bonds
1/1/14				$108,530
7/1/14	$ 4,000ᵃ	$ 3,256ᵇ	$ 744ᶜ	107,786ᵈ
1/1/15	4,000	3,234	766	107,020
7/1/15	4,000	3,211	789	106,231
1/1/16	4,000	3,187	813	105,418
7/1/16	4,000	3,162	838	104,580
1/1/17	4,000	3,137	863	103,717
7/1/17	4,000	3,112	888	102,829
1/1/18	4,000	3,085	915	101,914
7/1/18	4,000	3,057	943	100,971
1/1/19	4,000	3,029	971	100,000
	$40,000	$31,470	$8,530	

ᵃ$4,000 = $100,000 × .08 × 6/12   ᶜ$744 = $4,000 − $3,256
ᵇ$3,256 = $108,530 × .06 × 6/12   ᵈ$107,786 = $108,530 − $744

ILLUSTRATION 14-7
Bond Premium
Amortization Schedule

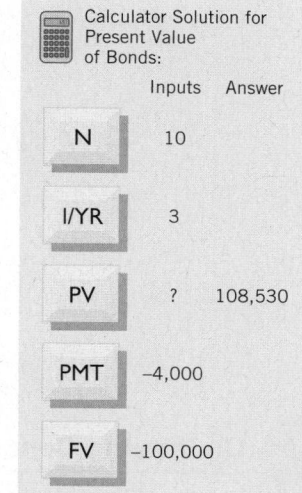

Calculator Solution for
Present Value
of Bonds:

	Inputs	Answer
N	10	
I/YR	3	
PV	?	108,530
PMT	−4,000	
FV	−100,000	

Evermaster should amortize the discount or premium as an adjustment to interest expense over the life of the bond in such a way as to result in a **constant rate of interest** when applied to the carrying amount of debt outstanding at the beginning of any given period.

Accruing Interest

In our previous examples, the interest payment dates and the date the financial statements were issued were essentially the same. For example, when Evermaster sold bonds at a premium, the two interest payment dates coincided with the financial reporting dates. However, what happens if Evermaster wishes to report financial statements at the end of February 2014? In this case, the company **prorates** the premium by the appropriate number of months, to arrive at the proper interest expense, as follows.

Interest accrual ($4,000 × ⅔)	$1,333.33
Premium amortized ($744 × ⅔)	(248.00)
Interest expense (Jan.–Feb.)	$1,085.33

ILLUSTRATION 14-8
Computation of Interest
Expense

Evermaster records this accrual as follows.

Interest Expense	1,085.33	
Premium on Bonds Payable	248.00	
Interest Payable		1,333.33

If the company prepares financial statements six months later, it follows the same procedure. That is, the premium amortized would be as follows.

Premium amortized (March–June) ($744 × ⅔)	$496.00
Premium amortized (July–August) ($766 × ⅓)	255.33
Premium amortized (March–August)	$751.33

ILLUSTRATION 14-9
Computation of
Premium Amortization

The interest-accrual computation is much simpler if the company uses the straight-line method. For example, the total premium is $8,530, which Evermaster allocates evenly over the five-year period. Thus, premium amortization per month is $142.17 ($8,530 ÷ 60 months).

Classification of Discount and Premium

Discount on bonds payable is **not an asset**. It does not provide any future economic benefit. In return for the use of borrowed funds, a company must pay interest. A bond discount means that the company borrowed less than the face or maturity value of the bond. It therefore faces an actual (effective) interest rate higher than the stated (nominal) rate. Conceptually, discount on bonds payable is a liability valuation account. That is, it reduces the face or maturity amount of the related liability.[5] This account is referred to as a **contra account**.

Similarly, premium on bonds payable has no existence apart from the related debt. The lower interest cost results because the proceeds of borrowing exceed the face or maturity amount of the debt. Conceptually, premium on bonds payable is a *liability* valuation account. It adds to the face or maturity amount of the related liability.[6] This account is referred to as an **adjunct account**. As a result, **companies report bond discounts and bond premiums as a direct deduction from or addition to the face amount of the bond**.

Costs of Issuing Bonds

Underlying Concepts

Because bond issue costs do not meet the definition of an asset, some argue they should be expensed at issuance.

The issuance of bonds involves engraving and printing costs, legal and accounting fees, commissions, promotion costs, and other similar charges. Companies are required to charge these costs to an asset account (usually long-term), often referred to as Unamortized Bond Issue Costs. Companies then allocate Unamortized Bond Issue Costs to expense over the life of the debt, in a manner similar to that used for discount on bonds. **[2]**

We disagree with this approach. Unamortized bond issue cost in our view is an expense (or a reduction of the related liability).

Apparently the FASB also disagrees with the current GAAP treatment and notes in *Concepts Statement No. 6* that debt issue cost is not considered an asset because it provides no future economic benefit. The cost of issuing bonds, in effect, reduces the proceeds of the bonds issued and increases the effective-interest rate. Companies may thus account for it the same as the unamortized discount.

There is an obvious difference between GAAP and *Concepts Statement No. 6*'s view of debt issue costs. However, until an issued standard supersedes existing GAAP, **unamortized bond issue costs are treated as a deferred charge and amortized over the life of the debt**.

To illustrate the accounting for costs of issuing bonds, assume that Microchip Corporation sold $20,000,000 of 10-year debenture bonds for $20,795,000 on January 1, 2014 (also the date of the bonds). Costs of issuing the bonds were $245,000. Microchip records the issuance of the bonds and amortization of the bond issue costs as follows.

January 1, 2014

Cash	20,550,000	
Unamortized Bond Issue Costs	245,000	
Premium on Bonds Payable		795,000
Bonds Payable		20,000,000
(To record issuance of bonds)		

December 31, 2014

Bond Issue Expense	24,500	
Unamortized Bond Issue Costs		24,500
(To amortize one year of bond issue costs—straight-line method)		

---

[5]"Elements of Financial Statements of Business Enterprises," *Statement of Financial Accounting Concepts No. 6* (Stamford, Conn.: FASB, 1980).

[6]*Ibid.*, par. 238.

Microchip continues to amortize the bond issue costs in the same way over the life of the bonds. Although the effective-interest method is preferred, in practice companies may use the straight-line method to amortize bond issue costs because it is easier and the results are not materially different.

International Perspective

IFRS requires that issue costs reduce the carrying amount of the bond, which increases the effective-interest rate.

Extinguishment of Debt

5 LEARNING OBJECTIVE
Describe the accounting for the extinguishment of debt.

How do companies record the payment of debt—often referred to as **extinguishment of debt**? If a company holds the bonds (or any other form of debt security) to maturity, the answer is straightforward: The company does not compute any gains or losses. It will have fully amortized any premium or discount and any issue costs at the date the bonds mature. As a result, the carrying amount will equal the maturity (face) value of the bond. As the maturity or face value will also equal the bond's fair value at that time, no gain or loss exists.

In some cases, a company extinguishes debt before its maturity date.[7] The amount paid on extinguishment or redemption before maturity, including any call premium and expense of reacquisition, is called the **reacquisition price**. On any specified date, the **net carrying amount** of the bonds is the amount payable at maturity, adjusted for unamortized premium or discount, and cost of issuance. Any excess of the net carrying amount over the reacquisition price is a **gain from extinguishment**. The excess of the reacquisition price over the net carrying amount is a **loss from extinguishment**. At the time of reacquisition, **the unamortized premium or discount, and any costs of issue applicable to the bonds, must be amortized up to the reacquisition date**.

To illustrate, assume that on January 1, 2007, General Bell Corp. issued at 97 bonds with a par value of $800,000, due in 20 years. It incurred bond issue costs totaling $16,000. Eight years after the issue date, General Bell calls the entire issue at 101 and cancels it.[8] At that time, the unamortized discount balance is $14,400, and the unamortized issue cost balance is $9,600. Illustration 14-10 indicates how General Bell computes the loss on redemption (extinguishment).

Reacquisition price ($800,000 × 1.01)		$808,000
Net carrying amount of bonds redeemed:		
Face value	$800,000	
Unamortized discount ($24,000* × 12/20)	(14,400)	
Unamortized issue costs ($16,000 × 12/20)		
(both amortized using straight-line basis)	(9,600)	(776,000)
Loss on redemption		$ 32,000

*[$800,000 × (1 − .97)]

ILLUSTRATION 14-10
Computation of Loss on Redemption of Bonds

[7]Some companies have attempted to extinguish debt through an in-substance defeasance. **In-substance defeasance** is an arrangement whereby a company provides for the future repayment of a long-term debt issue by placing purchased securities in an irrevocable trust. The company pledges the principal and interest of the securities in the trust to pay off the principal and interest of its own debt securities as they mature. However, it is not legally released from its primary obligation for the debt that is still outstanding. In some cases, debtholders are not even aware of the transaction and continue to look to the company for repayment. This practice is not considered an extinguishment of debt, and therefore the company does not record a gain or loss.

[8]The issuer of callable bonds must generally exercise the call on an interest date. Therefore, the amortization of any discount or premium will be up to date, and there will be no accrued interest. However, early extinguishments through purchases of bonds in the open market are more likely to be on other than an interest date. If the purchase is not made on an interest date, the discount or premium must be amortized, and the interest payable must be accrued from the last interest date to the date of purchase.

General Bell records the reacquisition and cancellation of the bonds as follows.

Bonds Payable	800,000	
Loss on Redemption of Bonds	32,000	
Discount on Bonds Payable		14,400
Unamortized Bond Issue Costs		9,600
Cash		808,000

Note that it is often advantageous for the issuer to acquire the **entire** outstanding bond issue and replace it with a new bond issue bearing a lower rate of interest. The replacement of an existing issuance with a new one is called **refunding**. Whether the early redemption or other extinguishment of outstanding bonds is a nonrefunding or a refunding situation, a company should recognize the difference (gain or loss) between the reacquisition price and the net carrying amount of the redeemed bonds in income of the period of redemption.[9]

What do the numbers mean? YOUR DEBT IS KILLING MY EQUITY

Traditionally, investors in the equity and bond markets operate in their own separate worlds. However, in recent volatile markets, even quiet murmurs in the bond market have been amplified into movements (usually negative) in share prices. At one extreme, these gyrations heralded the demise of a company well before the investors could sniff out the problem.

The swift decline of Enron in late 2001 provided the ultimate lesson: A company with no credit is no company at all. As one analyst remarked, "You can no longer have an opinion on a company's shares without having an appreciation for its credit rating." Indeed, other energy companies also felt the effect of Enron's troubles as lenders tightened or closed down the credit supply and raised interest rates on already-high levels of debt. The result? Stock prices took a hit.

Other industries are not immune from the negative shareholder effects of credit problems. For example, analysts at TheStreet.com compiled a list of companies with a focus on debt levels. Companies like Copel CIA (an energy distribution company) were rewarded with improved stock ratings, based on their manageable debt levels. In contrast, other companies with high debt levels and low ability to cover interest costs were not viewed very favorably. Among them is Goodyear Tire and Rubber, which reported debt six times greater than its equity.

Goodyear is a classic example of how swift and crippling a heavy debt-load can be. Not too long ago, Goodyear had a good credit rating and was paying a good dividend. But, with mounting operating losses, Goodyear's debt became a huge burden, its debt rating fell to junk status, the company cut its dividend, and its stock price dropped 80 percent. Only recently has Goodyear been able to dig out of its debt ditch. This was yet another example of stock prices taking a hit due to concerns about credit quality. Thus, even if your investment tastes are in equity, keep an eye on the liabilities.

Sources: Adapted from Steven Vames, "Credit Quality, Stock Investing Seem to Go Hand in Hand," *Wall Street Journal* (April 1, 2002), p. R4; Herb Greenberg, "The Hidden Dangers of Debt," *Fortune* (July 21, 2003), p. 153; and Christine Richard, "Holders of Corporate Bonds Seek Protection from Risk," *Wall Street Journal* (December 17–18, 2005), p. B4.

LONG-TERM NOTES PAYABLE

LEARNING OBJECTIVE

Explain the accounting for long-term notes payable.

The difference between current notes payable and **long-term notes payable** is the maturity date. As discussed in Chapter 13, short-term notes payable are those that companies expect to pay within a year or the operating cycle, whichever is longer. Long-term notes are similar in substance to bonds in that both have fixed maturity dates and carry either a stated or implicit interest rate. However, notes do not trade as readily as bonds in the organized public securities markets. Noncorporate and small corporate enterprises issue notes as their long-term instruments. Larger corporations issue both long-term notes and bonds.

[9]At one time, companies were required to report gains and losses on extinguishment of debt as extraordinary items. In response to increasing debt extinguishments as part of normal risk management, the FASB concluded that such gains or losses are neither unusual nor infrequent. As a result, the FASB eliminated the requirement for extraordinary item treatment for extinguishment of debt. **[3]**

Accounting for notes and bonds is quite similar. **Like a bond, a note is valued at the present value of its future interest and principal cash flows. The company amortizes any discount or premium over the life of the note**, just as it would the discount or premium on a bond.[10] Companies compute the present value of an **interest-bearing note**, record its issuance, and amortize any discount or premium and accrual of interest in the same way that they do for bonds (as shown on pages 768–773 of this chapter).

As you might expect, accounting for long-term notes payable parallels accounting for long-term notes receivable as was presented in Chapter 7.

Notes Issued at Face Value

In Chapter 7, we discussed the recognition of a $10,000, three-year note Scandinavian Imports issued at face value to Bigelow Corp. In this transaction, the stated rate and the effective rate were both 10 percent. The time diagram and present value computation on page 360 of Chapter 7 (see Illustration 7-9) for Bigelow Corp. are the same for the issuer of the note, Scandinavian Imports, in recognizing a note payable. Because the present value of the note and its face value are the same, $10,000, Scandinavian recognizes no premium or discount. It records the issuance of the note as follows.

Cash	10,000	
Notes Payable		10,000

Scandinavian Imports recognizes the interest incurred each year as follows.

Interest Expense	1,000	
Cash		1,000

Notes Not Issued at Face Value

Zero-Interest-Bearing Notes

If a company issues a zero-interest-bearing (non-interest-bearing) note[11] solely for cash, it measures the note's present value by the cash received. The implicit interest rate is the **rate that equates the cash received with the amounts to be paid in the future**. The issuing company records the difference between the face amount and the present value (cash received) as **a discount and amortizes that amount to interest expense over the life of the note**.

An example of such a transaction is Beneficial Corporation's offering of $150 million of zero-coupon notes (deep-discount bonds) having an eight-year life. With a face value of $1,000 each, these notes sold for $327—a deep discount of $673 each. The present value of each note is the cash proceeds of $327. We can calculate the interest rate by determining the rate that equates the amount the investor currently pays with the amount to be received in the future. Thus, Beneficial amortizes the discount over the eight-year life of the notes using an effective-interest rate of 15 percent.[12]

Calculator Solution for Effective Interest on Note:

	Inputs	Answer
N	8	
I/YR	?	15
PV	−327	
PMT	0	
FV	1,000	

---

[10]All payables that represent commitments to pay money at a determinable future date are subject to present value measurement techniques, except for the following specifically excluded types:
  1. Normal accounts payable due within one year.
  2. Security deposits, retainages, advances, or progress payments.
  3. Transactions between parent and subsidiary.
  4. Obligations payable at some indeterminable future date. **[4]**

[11]Although we use the term "note" throughout this discussion, the basic principles and methodology apply equally to other long-term debt instruments.

[12]$327 = $1,000(PVF_{8,i})$

$$PVF_{8,i} = \frac{\$327}{\$1,000} = .327$$

  .327 = 15% (in Table 6-2 locate .32690).

To illustrate the entries and the amortization schedule for a long-term note payable, assume that Turtle Cove Company issued the three-year, $10,000, zero-interest-bearing note to Jeremiah Company illustrated on page 361 of Chapter 7 (notes receivable). The implicit rate that equated the total cash to be paid ($10,000 at maturity) to the present value of the future cash flows ($7,721.80 cash proceeds at date of issuance) was 9 percent. (The present value of $1 for 3 periods at 9% is $0.77218.) Illustration 14-11 shows the time diagram for the single cash flow.

ILLUSTRATION 14-11
Time Diagram for Zero-Interest-Bearing Note

Turtle Cove records issuance of the note as follows.

Cash	7,721.80	
Discount on Notes Payable	2,278.20	
Notes Payable		10,000.00

Turtle Cove amortizes the discount and recognizes interest expense annually using the **effective-interest method**. Illustration 14-12 shows the three-year discount amortization and interest expense schedule. (This schedule is similar to the note receivable schedule of Jeremiah Company in Illustration 7-12.)

ILLUSTRATION 14-12
Schedule of Note Discount Amortization

SCHEDULE OF NOTE DISCOUNT AMORTIZATION				
EFFECTIVE-INTEREST METHOD				
0% NOTE DISCOUNTED AT 9%				
	Cash Paid	Interest Expense	Discount Amortized	Carrying Amount of Note
Date of issue				$ 7,721.80
End of year 1	$-0-	$ 694.96[a]	$ 694.96[b]	8,416.76[c]
End of year 2	-0-	757.51	757.51	9,174.27
End of year 3	-0-	825.73[d]	825.73	10,000.00
	$-0-	$2,278.20	$2,278.20	

[a]$7,721.80 × .09 = $694.96   [c]$7,721.80 + $694.96 = $8,416.76
[b]$694.96 − 0 = $694.96   [d]5¢ adjustment to compensate for rounding.

Turtle Cove records interest expense at the end of the first year using the effective-interest method as follows.

Interest Expense ($7,721.80 × 9%)	694.96	
Discount on Notes Payable		694.96

The total amount of the discount, $2,278.20 in this case, represents the expense that Turtle Cove Company will incur on the note over the three years.

Interest-Bearing Notes

The zero-interest-bearing note above is an example of the extreme difference between the stated rate and the effective rate. In many cases, the difference between these rates is not so great.

Consider the example from Chapter 7 where Marie Co. issued for cash a $10,000, three-year note bearing interest at 10 percent to Morgan Corp. The market rate of interest for a note of similar risk is 12 percent. Illustration 7-13 (page 362) shows the time diagram depicting the cash flows and the computation of the present value of this note. In this case, because the effective rate of interest (12%) is greater than the stated rate (10%), the present value of the note is less than the face value. That is, the note is exchanged at a **discount**. Marie Co. records the issuance of the note as follows.

Cash	9,520	
Discount on Notes Payable	480	
Notes Payable		10,000

Marie Co. then amortizes the discount and recognizes interest expense annually using the **effective-interest method**. Illustration 14-13 shows the three-year discount amortization and interest expense schedule.

<table>
<tr><td colspan="5" align="center">SCHEDULE OF NOTE DISCOUNT AMORTIZATION
EFFECTIVE-INTEREST METHOD
10% NOTE DISCOUNTED AT 12%</td></tr>
<tr><td></td><td>Cash
Paid</td><td>Interest
Expense</td><td>Discount
Amortized</td><td>Carrying
Amount
of Note</td></tr>
<tr><td>Date of issue</td><td></td><td></td><td></td><td>$ 9,520</td></tr>
<tr><td>End of year 1</td><td>$1,000[a]</td><td>$1,142[b]</td><td>$142[c]</td><td>9,662[d]</td></tr>
<tr><td>End of year 2</td><td>1,000</td><td>1,159</td><td>159</td><td>9,821</td></tr>
<tr><td>End of year 3</td><td>1,000</td><td>1,179</td><td>179</td><td>10,000</td></tr>
<tr><td></td><td>$3,000</td><td>$3,480</td><td>$480</td><td></td></tr>
<tr><td colspan="5">[a]$10,000 × 10% = $1,000   [c]$1,142 − $1,000 = $142
[b]$9,520 × 12% = $1,142   [d]$9,520 + $142 = $9,662</td></tr>
</table>

ILLUSTRATION 14-13
Schedule of Note Discount Amortization

Marie Co. records payment of the annual interest and amortization of the discount for the first year as follows (amounts per amortization schedule).

Interest Expense	1,142	
Discount on Notes Payable		142
Cash		1,000

When the present value exceeds the face value, Marie Co. exchanges the note at a premium. It does so by recording the premium as a credit and amortizing it using the effective-interest method over the life of the note as annual reductions in the amount of interest expense recognized.

Special Notes Payable Situations

Notes Issued for Property, Goods, or Services

Sometimes, companies may receive property, goods, or services in exchange for a note payable. When exchanging the debt instrument for property, goods, or services in a bargained transaction entered into at arm's length, the stated interest rate is presumed to be fair unless:

1. No interest rate is stated, or

2. The stated interest rate is unreasonable, or

3. The stated face amount of the debt instrument is materially different from the current cash sales price for the same or similar items or from the current fair value of the debt instrument.

In these circumstances, the company measures the present value of the debt instrument by the fair value of the property, goods, or services or by an amount that reasonably approximates the fair value of the note. **[5]** If there is **no stated rate of interest, the amount of interest is the difference between the face amount of the note and the fair value of the property**.

For example, assume that Scenic Development Company sells land having a cash sale price of $200,000 to Health Spa, Inc. In exchange for the land, Health Spa gives a five-year, $293,866, zero-interest-bearing note. The $200,000 cash sale price represents the present value of the $293,866 note discounted at 8 percent for five years. Should both parties record the transaction on the sale date at the face amount of the note, which is $293,866? No—if they did, Health Spa's Land account and Scenic's sales would be overstated by $93,866 (the interest for five years at an effective rate of 8%). Similarly, interest revenue to Scenic and interest expense to Health Spa for the five-year period would be understated by $93,866.

Because the difference between the cash sale price of $200,000 and the $293,866 face amount of the note represents interest at an effective rate of 8 percent, the companies' transaction is recorded at the exchange date as shown in Illustration 14-14.

ILLUSTRATION 14-14
Entries for Noncash Note Transactions

Health Spa, Inc. (Buyer)			Scenic Development Company (Seller)		
Land	200,000		Notes Receivable	293,866	
Discount on Notes Payable	93,866		Discount on Notes Rec.		93,866
Notes Payable		293,866	Sales Revenue		200,000

During the five-year life of the note, Health Spa amortizes annually a portion of the discount of $93,866 as a charge to interest expense. Scenic Development records interest revenue totaling $93,866 over the five-year period by also amortizing the discount. The effective-interest method is required, unless the results obtained from using another method are not materially different from those that result from the effective-interest method.

Choice of Interest Rate

In note transactions, the effective or market interest rate is either evident or determinable by other factors involved in the exchange, such as the fair value of what is given or received. But, if a company cannot determine the fair value of the property, goods, services, or other rights, and if the note has no ready market, the problem of determining the present value of the note is more difficult. To estimate the present value of a note under such circumstances, a company must approximate an applicable interest rate that may differ from the stated interest rate. This process of interest-rate approximation is called imputation, and the resulting interest rate is called an imputed interest rate.

The prevailing rates for similar instruments of issuers with similar credit ratings affect the choice of a rate. Other factors such as restrictive covenants, collateral, payment schedule, and the existing prime interest rate also play a part. Companies determine the imputed interest rate when they issue a note; any subsequent changes in prevailing interest rates are ignored.

To illustrate, assume that on December 31, 2014, Wunderlich Company issued a promissory note to Brown Interiors Company for architectural services. The note has a face value of $550,000, a due date of December 31, 2019, and bears a stated interest rate of 2 percent, payable at the end of each year. Interest paid each period is therefore $11,000 ($550,000 × 2%). Wunderlich cannot readily determine the fair value of the architectural services, nor is the note readily marketable. On the basis of Wunderlich's credit rating, the absence of collateral, the prime interest rate at that date, and the prevailing interest on Wunderlich's other outstanding debt, the company imputes an 8 percent interest rate as appropriate in this circumstance. Illustration 14-15 shows the time diagram depicting both cash flows.

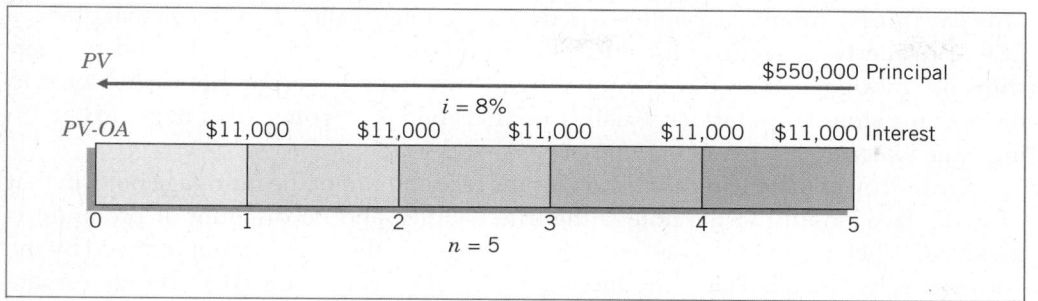

ILLUSTRATION 14-15
Time Diagram for
Interest-Bearing Note

The present value of the note and the imputed fair value of the architectural services are determined as follows.

Face value of the note		$550,000
Present value of $550,000 due in 5 years at 8% interest payable annually (Table 6-2); $FV(PVF_{5,8\%})$; ($550,000 × .68058)	$374,319	
Present value of $11,000 interest payable annually for 5 years at 8%; $R(PVF\text{-}OA_{5,8\%})$; ($11,000 × 3.99271)	43,920	
Present value of the note		(418,239)
Discount on notes payable		$131,761

ILLUSTRATION 14-16
Computation of Imputed
Fair Value and Note
Discount

Wunderlich records issuance of the note in payment for the architectural services as follows.

December 31, 2014

Buildings (or Construction in Process)	418,239	
Discount on Notes Payable	131,761	
Notes Payable		550,000

The five-year amortization schedule appears below.

SCHEDULE OF NOTE DISCOUNT AMORTIZATION
EFFECTIVE-INTEREST METHOD
2% NOTE DISCOUNTED AT 8% (IMPUTED)

Date	Cash Paid (2%)	Interest Expense (8%)	Discount Amortized	Carrying Amount of Note
12/31/14				$418,239
12/31/15	$11,000[a]	$ 33,459[b]	$ 22,459[c]	440,698[d]
12/31/16	11,000	35,256	24,256	464,954
12/31/17	11,000	37,196	26,196	491,150
12/31/18	11,000	39,292	28,292	519,442
12/31/19	11,000	41,558[e]	30,558	550,000
	$55,000	$186,761	$131,761	

[a]$550,000 × 2% = $11,000
[b]$418,239 × 8% = $33,459
[c]$33,459 − $11,000 = $22,459
[d]$418,239 + $22,459 = $440,698
[e]$3 adjustment to compensate for rounding.

ILLUSTRATION 14-17
Schedule of Discount
Amortization Using
Imputed Interest Rate

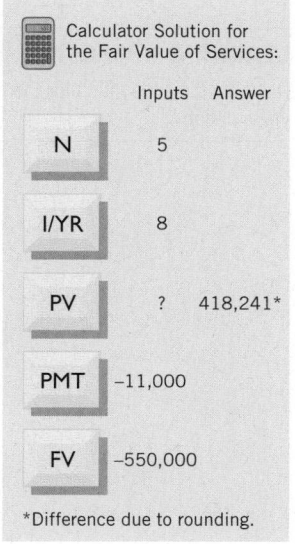

Calculator Solution for
the Fair Value of Services:

	Inputs	Answer
N	5	
I/YR	8	
PV	?	418,241*
PMT	−11,000	
FV	−550,000	

*Difference due to rounding.

Wunderlich records payment of the first year's interest and amortization of the discount as follows.

December 31, 2015

Interest Expense	33,459	
Discount on Notes Payable		22,459
Cash		11,000

Mortgage Notes Payable

The most common form of long-term notes payable is a mortgage note payable. A **mortgage note payable** is a promissory note secured by a document called a mortgage that pledges title to property as security for the loan. Individuals, proprietorships, and partnerships use mortgage notes payable more frequently than do corporations. (As noted in the opening story, corporations usually find that bond issues offer advantages in obtaining large loans.)

The borrower usually receives cash for the face amount of the mortgage note. In that case, the face amount of the note is the true liability, and no discount or premium is involved. When the lender assesses "points," however, the total amount received by the borrower is less than the face amount of the note.[13] Points raise the effective-interest rate above the rate specified in the note. A **point** is 1 percent of the face of the note.

For example, assume that Harrick Co. borrows $1,000,000, signing a 20-year mortgage note with a stated interest rate of 10.75 percent as part of the financing for a new plant. If Associated Savings demands 4 points to close the financing, Harrick will receive 4 percent less than $1,000,000—or $960,000—but it will be obligated to repay the entire $1,000,000 at the rate of $10,150 per month. Because Harrick received only $960,000, and must repay $1,000,000, its effective-interest rate is increased to approximately 11.3 percent on the money actually borrowed.

On the balance sheet, Harrick should report the mortgage note payable as a liability using a title such as "Mortgage Payable" or "Notes Payable—Secured," with a brief disclosure of the property pledged in notes to the financial statements.

Mortgages may be payable in full at maturity or in installments over the life of the loan. If payable at maturity, Harrick classifies its mortgage payable as a long-term liability on the balance sheet until such time as the approaching maturity date warrants showing it as a current liability. If it is payable in installments, Harrick shows the current installments due as current liabilities, with the remainder as a long-term liability.

Lenders have partially replaced the traditional **fixed-rate mortgage** with alternative mortgage arrangements. Most lenders offer **variable-rate mortgages** (also called *floating-rate* or *adjustable-rate* mortgages) featuring interest rates tied to changes in the fluctuating market rate. Generally, the variable-rate lenders adjust the interest rate at either one- or three-year intervals, pegging the adjustments to changes in the prime rate or the U.S. Treasury bond rate.

Fair Value Option

LEARNING OBJECTIVE
Describe the accounting for the fair value option.

As indicated earlier, noncurrent liabilities, such as bonds and notes payable, are generally measured at amortized cost (face value of the payable, adjusted for any payments and amortization of any premium or discount). However, companies have the option to record fair value in their accounts for most financial assets and liabilities, including bonds and notes payable. [6] As discussed in Chapter 7 (page 365), the FASB believes that fair value measurement for financial instruments, including financial liabilities, provides more relevant and understandable information than amortized cost. It considers fair value to be more relevant because it reflects the current cash equivalent value of financial instruments.

Fair Value Measurement

If companies choose the **fair value option**, noncurrent liabilities, such as bonds and notes payable, are recorded at fair value, with unrealized holding gains or losses reported as part of net income. An **unrealized holding gain or loss** is the net change in the

---

[13]Points, in mortgage financing, are analogous to the original issue discount of bonds.

fair value of the liability from one period to another, exclusive of interest expense recognized but not recorded. As a result, the company reports the liability at fair value each reporting date. In addition, it reports the change in value as part of net income.

To illustrate, Edmonds Company has issued $500,000 of 6 percent bonds at face value on May 1, 2014. Edmonds chooses the fair value option for these bonds. At December 31, 2014, the value of the bonds is now $480,000 because interest rates in the market have increased to 8 percent. The value of the debt securities falls because the bond is paying less than market rate for similar securities. Under the fair value option, Edmonds makes the following entry.

Bonds Payable	20,000	
Unrealized Holding Gain or Loss—Income		20,000

As the journal entry indicates, the value of the bonds declined. This decline leads to a reduction in the bond liability and a resulting unrealized holding gain, which is reported as part of net income. The value of Edmonds' debt declined because interest rates increased. It should be emphasized that Edmonds must continue to value the bonds payable at fair value in all subsequent periods.

Fair Value Controversy

With the Edmonds bonds, we assumed that the decline in value of the bonds was due to an interest rate increase. In other situations, the decline may occur because the bonds become more likely to default. That is, **if the creditworthiness of Edmonds Company declines, the value of its debt also declines**. If its creditworthiness declines, its bond investors are receiving a lower rate relative to investors with similar-risk investments. If Edmonds is using the fair value option, changes in the fair value of the bonds payable for a decline in creditworthiness are included as part of income. Some question how Edmonds can record a gain when its creditworthiness is becoming worse. As one writer noted, "It seems counterintuitive." However, the FASB notes that the debtholders' loss is the shareholders' gain. That is, the shareholders' claims on the assets of the company increase when the value of the debtholders' claims declines. In addition, the worsening credit position may indicate that the assets of the company are declining in value as well. Thus, the company may be reporting losses on the asset side, which will be offsetting gains on the liability side.[14]

REPORTING AND ANALYZING LIABILITIES

Reporting liabilities and long-term debt is one of the most controversial areas in financial reporting. Because long-term debt has a significant impact on the cash flows of the company, reporting requirements must be substantive and informative. One problem is that the definition of a liability established in *Concepts Statement No. 6* and the recognition criteria established in *Concepts Statement No. 5* are sufficiently imprecise that some continue to argue that certain obligations need not be reported as debt.

8 LEARNING OBJECTIVE
Explain the reporting of off-balance-sheet financing arrangements.

Off-Balance-Sheet Financing

What do Krispy Kreme, Cisco, Enron, and Adelphia Communications have in common? They all have been accused of using off-balance-sheet financing to minimize the reporting of debt on their balance sheets. Off-balance-sheet financing is an attempt to borrow monies in such a way to prevent recording the obligations. It has become an issue of

---

[14]This issue is discussed further in the "Evolving Issue" box on page 788.

extreme importance. Many allege that Enron, in one of the largest corporate failures on record, hid a considerable amount of its debt off the balance sheet. As a result, any company that uses off-balance-sheet financing today risks investors dumping the company's stock. Consequently, the company's share price will suffer. Nevertheless, a considerable amount of off-balance-sheet financing continues to exist. As one writer noted, "The basic drives of humans are few: to get enough food, to find shelter, and to keep debt off the balance sheet."

Different Forms

Off-balance-sheet financing can take many different forms:

1. *Non-consolidated subsidiary.* Under GAAP, a parent company does not have to consolidate a subsidiary company that is less than 50 percent owned. In such cases, the parent therefore does not report the assets and liabilities of the subsidiary. All the parent reports on its balance sheet is the investment in the subsidiary. As a result, users of the financial statements may not understand that the subsidiary has considerable debt for which the parent may ultimately be liable if the subsidiary runs into financial difficulty.

2. *Special-purpose entity (SPE).* A company creates a special-purpose entity (SPE) to perform a special project. To illustrate, assume that Clarke Company decides to build a new factory. However, management does not want to report the plant or the borrowing used to fund the construction on its balance sheet. It therefore creates an SPE, the purpose of which is to build the plant. (This arrangement is called a **project financing arrangement**.) The SPE finances and builds the plant. In return, Clarke guarantees that it or some outside party will purchase all the products produced by the plant. (Some refer to this as a **take-or-pay contract**.) As a result, Clarke might not report the asset or liability on its books. The accounting rules in this area are complex. We discuss the accounting for SPEs in Appendix 17B.

3. *Operating leases.* Another way that companies keep debt off the balance sheet is by leasing. Instead of owning the assets, companies lease them. Again, by meeting certain conditions, the company has to report only rent expense each period and to provide note disclosure of the transaction. Note that SPEs often use leases to accomplish off-balance-sheet treatment. We discuss accounting for lease transactions extensively in Chapter 21.

Rationale

Why do companies engage in off-balance-sheet financing? A major reason is that many believe that **removing debt enhances the quality of the balance sheet** and permits credit to be obtained more readily and at less cost.

Second, loan covenants often limit the amount of debt a company may have. As a result, the company uses off-balance-sheet financing because **these types of commitments might not be considered in computing the debt limitation**.

Third, some argue that the asset side of the balance sheet is severely understated. For example, companies that use LIFO costing for inventories and depreciate assets on an accelerated basis will often have carrying amounts for inventories and property, plant, and equipment that are much lower than their fair values. As an offset to these lower values, some believe that part of the debt does not have to be reported. In other words, **if companies report assets at fair values**, less pressure would undoubtedly exist for off-balance-sheet financing arrangements.

Whether the arguments above have merit is debatable. The general idea of "out of sight, out of mind" may not be true in accounting. Many users of financial statements indicate that they factor these off-balance-sheet financing arrangements into their computations when assessing debt-to-equity relationships. Similarly, many loan covenants also attempt to account for these complex arrangements. Nevertheless, many companies still believe that benefits will accrue if they omit certain obligations from the balance sheet.

As a response to off-balance-sheet financing arrangements, the FASB has increased disclosure (note) requirements. This response is consistent with an "efficient markets" philosophy: The important question is not whether the presentation is off-balance-sheet or not, but whether the items are disclosed at all. In addition, the SEC, in response to the Sarbanes-Oxley Act of 2002, now requires companies to provide related information in their management discussion and analysis sections. Specifically, companies must disclose (1) all contractual obligations in a tabular format and (2) contingent liabilities and commitments in either a textual or tabular format.[15]

We believe that recording more obligations on the balance sheet will enhance financial reporting. Given the problems with companies such as Enron, Dynegy, Williams Company, Chesapeake Energy, and Calpine, and the Sarbanes-Oxley requirements, we expect that less off-balance-sheet financing will occur in the future.

International Perspective

There is no comparable institution to the SEC in international securities markets. As a result, many international companies (those not registered with the SEC) are not required to provide disclosures such as those related to contractual obligations.

What do the numbers mean? OBLIGATED

The off-balance-sheet world is slowly but surely becoming more on-balance-sheet. New interpretations on guarantees (discussed in Chapter 13) and variable-interest entities (discussed in Appendix 17B) are doing their part to increase the amount of debt reported on corporate balance sheets.

In addition, the SEC has rules that require companies to disclose off-balance-sheet arrangements and contractual obligations that currently have, or are reasonably likely to have, a material future effect on the companies' financial condition. Companies now must include a tabular disclosure (following a prescribed format) in the management discussion and analysis section of the annual report. Presented below is Best Buy Co.'s tabular disclosure of its contractual obligations.

Best Buy Co.
Contractual Obligations

The following table presents information regarding our contractual obligations by fiscal year ($ in millions):

Contractual Obligations	Total	Less than 1 year	1–3 years	3–5 years	More than 5 years
Short-term debt obligations	$ 480	$ 480	—	—	—
Long-term debt obligations	1,498	—	$ 500	$ 349	$ 649
Capital lease obligations	81	18	35	11	17
Financing lease obligations	149	22	47	40	40
Interest payments	500	101	142	105	152
Operating lease obligations	7,517	1,216	2,217	1,732	2,352
Purchase obligations	3,548	1,771	1,499	278	—
	$13,773	$3,608	$4,440	$2,515	$3,210
Other					
Unrecognized tax benefits	$ 387	—	—	—	—
Deferred compensation	62	—	—	—	—

Note: For additional information refer to Note 8, Debt; Note 11, Leases; Note 13, Income Taxes and Note 15, Contingencies and Commitments, in the Notes to Consolidated Financial Statements, included in Item 8, Financial Statements and Supplementary Data, of this Annual Report on Form 10-K.

Enron's abuse of off-balance-sheet financing to hide debt was shocking and inappropriate. One silver lining in the Enron debacle, however, is that the standard-setting bodies in the accounting profession are now providing increased guidance on companies' reporting of contractual obligations. We believe the new SEC rule, which requires companies to report their obligations over a period of time, will be extremely useful to the investment community.

[15]It is unlikely that the FASB will be able to stop all types of off-balance-sheet transactions. Financial engineering is the "Holy Grail" of Wall Street. Developing new financial instruments and arrangements to sell and market to customers is not only profitable but also adds to the prestige of the investment firms that create them. Thus, new financial products will continue to appear that will test the ability of the FASB to develop appropriate accounting standards for them.

Presentation and Analysis of Long-Term Debt

Presentation of Long-Term Debt

LEARNING OBJECTIVE **9**

Indicate how to present and analyze long-term debt.

Companies that have large amounts and numerous issues of long-term debt frequently report only one amount in the balance sheet, supported with comments and schedules in the accompanying notes. Long-term debt that **matures within one year** should be reported as a current liability, unless using noncurrent assets to accomplish redemption. If the company plans to refinance debt, convert it into stock, or retire it from a bond retirement fund, it should continue to report the debt as noncurrent. However, the company should disclose the method it will use in its liquidation. **[7]**, **[8]**

Note disclosures generally indicate the nature of the liabilities, maturity dates, interest rates, call provisions, conversion privileges, restrictions imposed by the creditors, and assets designated or pledged as security. Companies should show any assets pledged as security for the debt in the assets section of the balance sheet. The fair value of the long-term debt should also be disclosed if it is practical to estimate fair value. Finally, companies must disclose future payments for sinking fund requirements and maturity amounts of long-term debt during each of the next five years. These disclosures aid financial statement users in evaluating the amounts and timing of future cash flows. Illustration 14-18 shows an example of the type of information provided for Target Corporation. Note that if the company has any off-balance-sheet financing, it must provide extensive note disclosure. **[9]**

ILLUSTRATION 14-18
Long-Term Debt
Disclosure

Target Corporation
(dollars in millions)

	January 28, 2012	January 29, 2011
Total current assets	$16,449	$17,213
Current liabilities		
Accounts payable	$ 6,857	$ 6,625
Accrued and other current liabilities	3,644	3,326
Unsecured debt and other borrowings	3,036	119
Nonrecourse debt collateralized by credit card receivables	750	—
Total current liabilities	14,287	10,070
Total noncurrent liabilities	16,522	18,148

19. Notes Payable and Long-Term Debt (in part)

At January 28, 2012, the carrying value and maturities of our debt portfolio were as follows:

Debt Maturities	January 28, 2012	
(millions)	Rate (a)	Balance
Due fiscal 2012–2016	2.8%	$ 6,281
Due fiscal 2017–2021	4.8	4,604
Due fiscal 2022–2026	8.7	64
Due fiscal 2027–2031	6.8	680
Due fiscal 2032–2036	6.3	551
Due fiscal 2037	6.8	3,500
Total notes and debentures	4.6	15,680
Swap valuation adjustments		114
Capital lease obligations		1,689
Less:		
Amounts due within one year		(3,786)
Long-term debt		$13,697

ILLUSTRATION 14-18
(*continued*)

(a) Reflects the weighted-average stated interest rate as of year-end.

Required principal payments on notes and debentures over the next five years are as follows:

Required Principal Payments (millions)	2012	2013	2014	2015	2016
Unsecured	$3,001	$501	$1,001	$27	$751
Nonrecourse	750	250	—	—	—
Total required principal payments	$3,751	$751	$1,001	$27	$751

Analysis of Long-Term Debt

Long-term creditors and stockholders are interested in a company's long-run solvency, particularly its ability to pay interest as it comes due and to repay the face value of the debt at maturity. Debt to assets and times interest earned are two ratios that provide information about debt-paying ability and long-run solvency.

Debt to Assets. The **debt to assets ratio** measures the percentage of the total assets provided by creditors. To compute it, divide total debt (both current and long-term liabilities) by total assets, as Illustration 14-19 shows.

$$\text{Debt to assets} = \frac{\text{Total liabilities}}{\text{Total assets}}$$

ILLUSTRATION 14-19
Computation of Debt to Assets Ratio

The higher the percentage of total liabilities to total assets, the greater the risk that the company may be unable to meet its maturing obligations.

Times Interest Earned. The **times interest earned** ratio indicates the company's ability to meet interest payments as they come due. As shown in Illustration 14-20, it is computed by dividing income before interest expense and income taxes by interest expense.

$$\text{Times interest earned} = \frac{\text{Income before income taxes and interest expense}}{\text{Interest expense}}$$

ILLUSTRATION 14-20
Computation of Times Interest Earned

To illustrate these ratios, we use data from **Target**'s 2011 annual report. Target has total liabilities of $30,809 million, total assets of $46,630 million, interest expense of $869 million, income taxes of $1,527 million, and net income of $2,929 million. We compute Target's debt to assets and times interest earned ratios as shown in Illustration 14-21.

Even though Target has a relatively high debt to assets percentage of 66.1 percent, its interest coverage of 6.12 times indicates it can easily meet its interest payments as they come due.

You will want to read the **IFRS INSIGHTS** on pages 815–819 for discussion of IFRS related to long-term liabilities.

$$\text{Debt to assets} = \frac{\$30,809}{\$46,630} = 66.1\%$$

$$\text{Times interest earned} = \frac{(\$2,929 + \$869 + \$1,527)}{\$869} = 6.12 \text{ times}$$

ILLUSTRATION 14-21
Computation of Long-Term Debt Ratios for Target

Evolving Issue *FAIR VALUE OF LIABILITIES: PICK A NUMBER, ANY NUMBER*

In 2011, Citigroup's third-quarter earnings rose 68 percent from a year earlier, partly due to an accounting adjustment. The accounting adjustment was a $1.9 billion gain related to a change in the valuation of its debt obligations. A similar situation resulted in the third quarter of 2011 for JPMorgan. Its results were enhanced by decreasing the value of its debt, also by $1.9 billion. How does a company recognize a gain on its debt when it has not sold it?

Here is how it works. Say a company records a $100 million liability for bonds it issues. Subsequently, the bond's credit rating drops from AA to BB. As a result, the price of the bond trading in the market drops to $90 million. As we discussed earlier, if the fair value option is used to value debt, the company makes the following entry.

Bonds Payable	10,000,000	
Unrealized Holding Gain		
or Loss—Income		10,000,000

Presto! The company's net income increases even though its credit rating drops. This result seems counterintuitive—how does a company that is actually doing worse have its income increase?

The FASB has struggled with this issue for years. It defends the present position by indicating that the valuation of a liability is related to its credit standing. Therefore, if a company's credit standing drops, the liability value drops as well. And if the value of a company's liability is less, the company is better off and should record a gain. It should be noted that it can work the other way as well. That is, if a company's credit standing increases, the value of the liability increases and therefore the company records a loss.

Another major argument in favor of the present approach is that by forcing companies to highlight their credit weakness, it raises a question about the asset side of the balance sheet. In other words, if you see a credit weakness, you should ask, "Where is the impaired asset?" If a company's credit is bad, it may mean there are losses on the asset side that are not being recognized or disclosed.

The FASB (and IASB) are debating this issue in the financial instruments project. Some have suggested that the gain or loss be part of other comprehensive income. Others disagree and believe it should be part of net income. Still others believe that changes in the value of the liability should not be reported in income until the liability is extinguished. As one expert noted, "At its worse, bank accounting can seem like the mirrors in a fun house. Reality is reflected, but the distortions can be very large."

Sources: Floyd Norris, "Distortions in Baffling Financial Statements," *The New York Times* (November 10, 2011); and Marie Leone, "The Fair Value Deadbeat Debate Returns," *CFO.com* (June 25, 2009).

KEY TERMS

bearer (coupon) bonds, *765*

bond discount, *767*

bond indenture, *764*

bond premium, *767*

callable bonds, *765*

carrying value, *770*

commodity-backed
  bonds, *765*

convertible bonds, *765*

debenture bonds, *765*

debt to assets ratio, *787*

deep-discount (zero-
  interest debenture)
  bonds, *765*

discount, *767*

effective-interest
  method, *770*

effective yield, or market
  rate, *767*

extinguishment of
  debt, *775*

face, par, principal, or
  maturity value, *766*

SUMMARY OF LEARNING OBJECTIVES

1 **Describe the formal procedures associated with issuing long-term debt.** Incurring long-term debt is often a formal procedure. The bylaws of corporations usually require approval by the board of directors and the stockholders before corporations can issue bonds or can make other long-term debt arrangements. Generally, long-term debt has various covenants or restrictions. The covenants and other terms of the agreement between the borrower and the lender are stated in the bond indenture or note agreement.

2 **Identify various types of bond issues.** Various types of bond issues are (1) secured and unsecured bonds; (2) term, serial, and callable bonds; (3) convertible, commodity-backed, and deep-discount bonds; (4) registered and bearer (coupon) bonds; and (5) income and revenue bonds. The variety in the types of bonds results from attempts to attract capital from different investors and risk-takers and to satisfy the cash flow needs of the issuers.

3 **Describe the accounting valuation for bonds at date of issuance.** The investment community values a bond at the present value of its future cash flows, which consist of interest and principal. The rate used to compute the present value of these cash flows is the interest rate that provides an acceptable return on an investment commensurate with the issuer's risk characteristics. The interest rate written in the terms of the bond indenture and ordinarily appearing on the bond certificate is the stated, coupon, or nominal rate. The issuer of the bonds sets the rate and expresses it as a percentage of the face value (also called the par value, principal amount, or maturity value) of the bonds. If the rate employed by the buyers differs from the stated rate, the present value of the bonds computed by the buyers will differ from the face value of the bonds. The difference between the face value and the present value of the bonds is either a discount or premium.

4 Apply the methods of bond discount and premium amortization. The discount (premium) is amortized and charged (credited) to interest expense over the life of the bonds. Amortization of a discount increases bond interest expense, and amortization of a premium decreases bond interest expense. The profession's preferred procedure for amortization of a discount or premium is the effective-interest method. Under the effective-interest method, (1) bond interest expense is computed by multiplying the carrying value of the bonds at the beginning of the period by the effective-interest rate; then, (2) the bond discount or premium amortization is determined by comparing the bond interest expense with the interest to be paid.

5 Describe the accounting for the extinguishment of debt. At the time of extinguishment (reacquisition, redemption, or refunding) of long-term debt, the unamortized premium or discount and any costs of issue applicable to the debt must be amortized up to the reacquisition date. The reacquisition price is the amount paid on extinguishment or redemption before maturity, including any call premium and expense of reacquisition. On any specified date, the net carrying amount of the debt is the amount payable at maturity, adjusted for unamortized premium or discount and issue costs. Any excess of the net carrying amount over the reacquisition price is a gain from extinguishment. The excess of the reacquisition price over the net carrying amount is a loss from extinguishment. Gains and losses on extinguishments are recognized currently in income.

6 Explain the accounting for long-term notes payable. Accounting procedures for notes and bonds are similar. Like a bond, a note is valued at the present value of its expected future interest and principal cash flows, with any discount or premium being similarly amortized over the life of the note. Whenever the face amount of the note does not reasonably represent the present value of the consideration in the exchange, a company must evaluate the entire arrangement in order to properly record the exchange and the subsequent interest.

7 Describe the accounting for the fair value option. Companies have the option to record fair value in their accounts for most financial assets and liabilities, including noncurrent liabilities. Fair value measurement for financial instruments, including financial liabilities, provides more relevant and understandable information than amortized cost. If companies choose the fair value option, noncurrent liabilities, such as bonds and notes payable, are recorded at fair value, with unrealized holding gains or losses reported as part of net income. An unrealized holding gain or loss is the net change in the fair value of the liability from one period to another, exclusive of interest expense recognized but not recorded.

8 Explain the reporting of off-balance-sheet financing arrangements. Off-balance-sheet financing is an attempt to borrow funds in such a way to prevent recording obligations. Examples of off-balance-sheet arrangements are (1) non-consolidated subsidiaries, (2) special-purpose entities, and (3) operating leases.

9 Indicate how to present and analyze long-term debt. Companies that have large amounts and numerous issues of long-term debt frequently report only one amount in the balance sheet and support this with comments and schedules in the accompanying notes. Any assets pledged as security for the debt should be shown in the assets section of the balance sheet. Long-term debt that matures within one year should be reported as a current liability, unless redemption is to be accomplished with other than current assets. If a company plans to refinance the debt, convert it into stock, or retire it from a bond retirement fund, it should continue to report it as noncurrent, accompanied

fair value option, *782*
imputation, *780*
imputed interest rate, *780*
income bonds, *765*
long-term debt, *764*
long-term notes payable, *776*
mortgage notes payable, *782*
off-balance-sheet financing, *783*
premium, *767*
refunding, *776*
registered bonds, *765*
revenue bonds, *765*
secured bonds, *765*
serial bonds, *765*
special-purpose entity (SPE), *784*
stated, coupon, or nominal rate, *766*
straight-line method, *769*
term bonds, *765*
times interest earned, *787*
zero-interest debenture bonds, *765*

with a note explaining the method it will use in the debt's liquidation. Disclosure is required of future payments for sinking fund requirements and maturity amounts of long-term debt during each of the next five years. Debt to assets and times interest earned are two ratios that provide information about debt-paying ability and long-run solvency.

| APPENDIX **14A** | **TROUBLED-DEBT RESTRUCTURINGS** |

LEARNING OBJECTIVE ❿
Describe the accounting for a debt restructuring.

Practically every day, the *Wall Street Journal* runs a story about some company in financial difficulty. In most troubled-debt situations, the creditor usually first recognizes a loss on impairment. Subsequently, the creditor either modifies the terms of the loan or the debtor settles the loan on terms unfavorable to the creditor. In unusual cases, the creditor forces the debtor into bankruptcy in order to ensure the highest possible collection on the loan. Illustration 14A-1 shows this continuum.

ILLUSTRATION 14A-1
Usual Progression in Troubled-Debt Situations

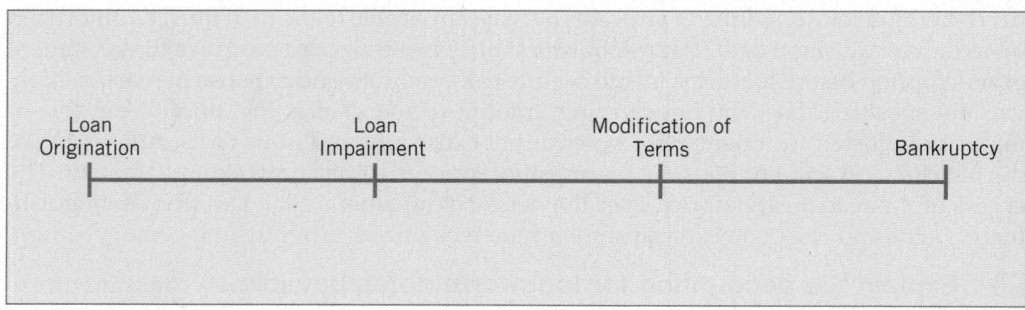

To illustrate, consider the case of **Huffy Corp.**, a name that adorned the first bicycle of many American children. Before its bankruptcy, Huffy's creditors likely recognized a loss on impairment. Subsequently, the creditors either modified the terms of the loan or settled it on terms unfavorable to the creditor. Finally, the creditors forced Huffy into bankruptcy, and the suppliers received a 30 percent equity stake in Huffy. These terms helped ensure the highest possible collection on the Huffy loan.

We discussed the accounting for loan impairments in Appendix 7B. The purpose of this appendix is to explain how creditors and debtors report information in financial statements related to troubled-debt restructurings.

🌐 **International Perspective**

IFRS generally assumes that all restructurings be accounted for as extinguishments of debt.

A **troubled-debt restructuring** occurs when a creditor "for economic or legal reasons related to the debtor's financial difficulties grants a concession to the debtor that it would not otherwise consider." **[10]** Thus, a troubled-debt restructuring does not apply to modifications of a debt obligation that reflect general economic conditions leading to a reduced interest rate. Nor does it apply to the refunding of an old debt with new debt having an effective-interest rate approximately equal to that of similar debt issued by nontroubled debtors. A troubled-debt restructuring involves one of two basic types of transactions:[16]

1. Settlement of debt at less than its carrying amount.

2. Continuation of debt with a modification of terms.

[16] Recently, the FASB issued Accounting Standards Update 2011-02, Receivables (Topic 310): *A Creditor's Determination of Whether a Restructuring Is a Troubled Debt Restructuring,* to help determine when a troubled-debt restructuring (TDR) occurs. The new rule provides additional guidance for determining whether a TDR has occurred by clarifying when the creditor has granted a concession and whether the debtor is experiencing financial difficulty. As a result of this rule, creditors will likely determine that more restructurings are troubled-debt restructurings, which will lead to more losses on receivables being reported.

SETTLEMENT OF DEBT

In addition to using cash, settling a debt obligation can involve either a transfer of noncash assets (real estate, receivables, or other assets) or the issuance of the debtor's stock. In these situations, **the creditor should account for the noncash assets or equity interest received at their fair value**.

The debtor must determine the excess of the carrying amount of the payable over the fair value of the assets or equity transferred (gain). Likewise, the creditor must determine the excess of the receivable over the fair value of those same assets or equity interests transferred (loss). The debtor recognizes a gain equal to the amount of the excess. The creditor normally charges the excess (loss) against Allowance for Doubtful Accounts. In addition, the debtor recognizes a gain or loss on disposition of assets to the extent that the fair value of those assets differs from their carrying amount (book value).

Transfer of Assets

Assume that American City Bank loaned $20,000,000 to Union Mortgage Company. Union Mortgage, in turn, invested these monies in residential apartment buildings. However, because of low occupancy rates, it cannot meet its loan obligations. American City Bank agrees to accept from Union Mortgage real estate with a fair value of $16,000,000 in full settlement of the $20,000,000 loan obligation. The real estate has a carrying value of $21,000,000 on the books of Union Mortgage. American City Bank (creditor) records this transaction as follows.

Land	16,000,000	
Allowance for Doubtful Accounts	4,000,000	
Notes Receivable (from Union Mortgage)		20,000,000

The bank records the real estate at fair value. Further, it makes a charge to Allowance for Doubtful Accounts to reflect the bad debt write-off.

Union Mortgage (debtor) records this transaction as follows.

Notes Payable (to American City Bank)	20,000,000	
Loss on Disposal of Land	5,000,000	
Land		21,000,000
Gain on Restructuring of Debt		4,000,000

Union Mortgage has a loss on the disposition of real estate in the amount of $5,000,000 (the difference between the $21,000,000 book value and the $16,000,000 fair value). It should show this as an ordinary loss on the income statement. In addition, it has a gain on restructuring of debt of $4,000,000 (the difference between the $20,000,000 carrying amount of the note payable and the $16,000,000 fair value of the real estate).

Granting of Equity Interest

Assume that American City Bank agrees to accept from Union Mortgage 320,000 shares of common stock ($10 par) that has a fair value of $16,000,000, in full settlement of the $20,000,000 loan obligation. American City Bank (creditor) records this transaction as follows.

Equity Investments	16,000,000	
Allowance for Doubtful Accounts	4,000,000	
Notes Receivable (from Union Mortgage)		20,000,000

It records the stock as an investment at the fair value at the date of restructure.

Union Mortgage (debtor) records this transaction as follows.

Notes Payable (to American City Bank)	20,000,000	
Common Stock		3,200,000
Paid-in Capital in Excess of Par—Common Stock		12,800,000
Gain on Restructuring of Debt		4,000,000

It records the stock issued in the normal manner. It records the difference between the par value and the fair value of the stock as additional paid-in capital.

MODIFICATION OF TERMS

In some cases, a debtor's serious short-run cash flow problems will lead it to request one or a combination of the following modifications:

1. Reduction of the stated interest rate.

2. Extension of the maturity date of the face amount of the debt.

3. Reduction of the face amount of the debt.

4. Reduction or deferral of any accrued interest.

The creditor's loss is based on expected cash flows discounted at the historical effective rate of the loan. **[11]** The debtor calculates its gain based on **undiscounted amounts**. As a consequence, **the gain recorded by the debtor will not equal the loss recorded by the creditor under many circumstances.**[17]

Two examples demonstrate the accounting for a troubled-debt restructuring by debtors and creditors:

1. The debtor does not record a gain.

2. The debtor does record a gain.

In both instances the creditor has a loss.

Example 1—No Gain for Debtor

This example demonstrates a restructuring in which the debtor records no gain.[18] On December 31, 2013, Morgan National Bank enters into a debt restructuring agreement with Resorts Development Company, which is experiencing financial difficulties. The bank restructures a $10,500,000 loan receivable issued at par (interest paid to date) by:

1. Reducing the principal obligation from $10,500,000 to $9,000,000;

2. Extending the maturity date from December 31, 2013, to December 31, 2017; and

3. Reducing the interest rate from 12% to 8%.

[17]In response to concerns expressed about this nonsymmetric treatment, the FASB stated that it did not address debtor accounting because expansion of the scope of the statement would delay its issuance. By basing the debtor calculation on undiscounted amounts, the amount of gain (if any) recognized by the debtor is reduced at the time the modification of terms occurs. If fair value were used, the gain recognized would be greater. The result of this approach is to spread the unrecognized gain over the life of the new agreement. We believe that this accounting is inappropriate and hopefully will change as more fair value measurements are introduced into the financial statements.

[18]Note that the examples given for restructuring assume the creditor made no previous entries for impairment. In actuality, it is likely that the creditor would have already made an entry when the loan initially became impaired. Restructuring would, therefore, simply require an adjustment of the initial estimated bad debt by the creditor. Recall, however, that the debtor makes no entry upon impairment.

Debtor Calculations

The total future cash flow, after restructuring of $11,880,000 ($9,000,000 of principal plus $2,880,000 of interest payments[19]), exceeds the total pre-restructuring carrying amount of the debt of $10,500,000. Consequently, **the debtor records no gain nor makes any adjustment** to the carrying amount of the payable. As a result, Resorts Development (debtor) makes no entry at the date of restructuring.

The debtor must compute a new effective-interest rate in order to record interest expense in future periods. The new effective-interest rate equates the present value of the future cash flows specified by the new terms with the pre-restructuring carrying amount of the debt. In this case, Resorts Development computes the new rate by relating the pre-restructure carrying amount ($10,500,000) to the total future cash flow ($11,880,000). The rate necessary to discount the total future cash flow ($11,880,000), to a present value equal to the remaining balance ($10,500,000), is 3.46613 percent.[20]

On the basis of the effective rate of 3.46613 percent, the debtor prepares the schedule shown in Illustration 14A-2.

ILLUSTRATION 14A-2
Schedule Showing Reduction of Carrying Amount of Note

RESORTS DEVELOPMENT CO. (DEBTOR)				
Date	Cash Paid (8%)	Interest Expense (3.46613%)	Reduction of Carrying Amount	Carrying Amount of Note
12/31/13				$10,500,000
12/31/14	$ 720,000[a]	$ 363,944[b]	$ 356,056[c]	10,143,944
12/31/15	720,000	351,602	368,398	9,775,546
12/31/16	720,000	338,833	381,167	9,394,379
12/31/17	720,000	325,621	394,379	9,000,000
	$2,880,000	$1,380,000	$1,500,000	

[a]$720,000 = $9,000,000 × .08
[b]$363,944 = $10,500,000 × 3.46613%
[c]$356,056 = $720,000 − $363,944

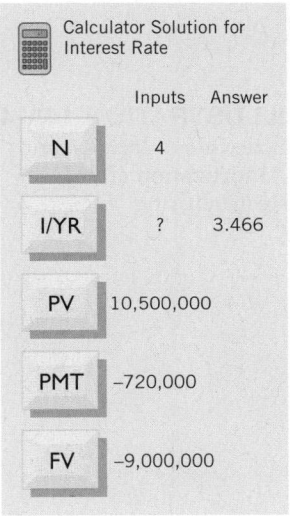

Calculator Solution for Interest Rate

	Inputs	Answer
N	4	
I/YR	?	3.466
PV	10,500,000	
PMT	−720,000	
FV	−9,000,000	

Thus, on December 31, 2014 (date of first interest payment after restructure), the debtor makes the following entry.

December 31, 2014

Notes Payable	356,056	
Interest Expense	363,944	
Cash		720,000

The debtor makes a similar entry (except for different amounts for debits to Notes Payable and Interest Expense) each year until maturity. At maturity, Resorts Development makes the following entry.

December 31, 2017

Notes Payable	9,000,000	
Cash		9,000,000

---

[19]Total interest payments are $9,000,000 × .08 × 4 years = $2,880,000.

[20]An accurate interest rate i can be found by using the formulas given at the tops of Tables 6-2 and 6-4 to set up the following equation.

$$\$10,500,000 = \underbrace{\frac{1}{(1+i)^4}}_{\text{(from Table 6-2)}} \times \$9,000,000 + \underbrace{\frac{1 - \dfrac{1}{(1+i)^4}}{i}}_{\text{(from Table 6-4)}} \times \$720,000$$

Solving algebraically for i, we find that $i = 3.46613\%$.

Creditor Calculations

Morgan National Bank (creditor) must calculate its loss based on the expected future cash flows discounted at the historical effective rate of the loan. It calculates this loss as shown in Illustration 14A-3.

ILLUSTRATION 14A-3
Computation of Loss to Creditor on Restructuring

Pre-restructure carrying amount		$10,500,000
Present value of restructured cash flows:		
Present value of $9,000,000 due in 4 years		
at 12%, interest payable annually (Table 6-2);		
$FV(PVF_{4,12\%})$; ($9,000,000 × .63552)	$5,719,680	
Present value of $720,000 interest payable annually for		
4 years at 12% (Table 6-4); $R(PVF\text{-}OA_{4,12\%})$;		
($720,000 × 3.03735)	2,186,892	
Present value of restructured cash flows		(7,906,572)
Loss on restructuring		$ 2,593,428

As a result, Morgan National Bank records bad debt expense as follows (assuming no establishment of an allowance balance from recognition of an impairment).

Bad Debt Expense	2,593,428	
Allowance for Doubtful Accounts		2,593,428

In subsequent periods, Morgan National Bank reports interest revenue based on the historical effective rate. Illustration 14A-4 provides the following interest and amortization information.

ILLUSTRATION 14A-4
Schedule of Interest and Amortization after Debt Restructuring

MORGAN NATIONAL BANK (CREDITOR)				
Date	Cash Received (8%)	Interest Revenue (12%)	Increase of Carrying Amount	Carrying Amount of Note
12/31/13				$7,906,572
12/31/14	$ 720,000[a]	$ 948,789[b]	$ 228,789[c]	8,135,361
12/31/15	720,000	976,243	256,243	8,391,604
12/31/16	720,000	1,006,992	286,992	8,678,596
12/31/17	720,000	1,041,404[d]	321,404[d]	9,000,000
Total	$2,880,000	$3,973,428	$1,093,428	

[a]$720,000 = $9,000,000 × .08
[b]$948,789 = $7,906,572 × .12
[c]$228,789 = $948,789 − $720,000
[d]$28 adjustment to compensate for rounding.

On December 31, 2014, Morgan National Bank makes the following entry.

December 31, 2014

Cash	720,000	
Allowance for Doubtful Accounts	228,789	
Interest Revenue		948,789

Morgan National Bank makes a similar entry (except for different amounts debited to Allowance for Doubtful Accounts and credited to Interest Revenue) each year until maturity. At maturity, the company makes the following entry.

December 31, 2017

Cash	9,000,000	
Allowance for Doubtful Accounts	1,500,000	
Notes Receivable		10,500,000

Example 2—Gain for Debtor

If the pre-restructure carrying amount exceeds the total future cash flows as a result of a modification of the terms, the debtor records a gain. To illustrate, assume the facts in the previous example except that Morgan National Bank reduces the principal to $7,000,000 (and extends the maturity date to December 31, 2017, and reduces the interest from 12% to 8%). The total future cash flow is now $9,240,000 ($7,000,000 of principal plus $2,240,000 of interest[21]), which is $1,260,000 ($10,500,000 − $9,240,000) less than the pre-restructure carrying amount of $10,500,000.

Under these circumstances, Resorts Development (debtor) reduces the carrying amount of its payable $1,260,000 and records a gain of $1,260,000. On the other hand, Morgan National Bank (creditor) debits its Bad Debt Expense for $4,350,444. Illustration 14A-5 shows this computation.

Pre-restructure carrying amount		$10,500,000
Present value of restructured cash flows:		
Present value of $7,000,000 due in 4 years at 12%, interest payable annually (Table 6-2); $FV(PVF_{4,12\%})$;		
($7,000,000 × .63552)	$4,448,640	
Present value of $560,000 interest payable annually for 4 years at 12% (Table 6-4); $R(PVF\text{-}OA_{4,12\%})$;		
($560,000 × 3.03735)	1,700,916	(6,149,556)
Creditor's loss on restructuring		$ 4,350,444

ILLUSTRATION 14A-5
Computation of Loss to Creditor on Restructuring

Illustration 14A-6 shows the entries to record the gain and loss on the debtor's and creditor's books at the date of restructure, December 31, 2013.

December 31, 2013 (date of restructure)				
Resorts Development Co. (Debtor)		**Morgan National Bank (Creditor)**		
Notes Payable	1,260,000	Bad Debt Expense	4,350,444	
Gain on Restructuring of Debt	1,260,000	Allowance for Doubtful Accounts		4,350,444

ILLUSTRATION 14A-6
Debtor and Creditor Entries to Record Gain and Loss on Note

For Resorts Development (debtor), because the new carrying value of the note ($10,500,000 − $1,260,000 = $9,240,000) equals the sum of the undiscounted cash flows ($9,240,000), the imputed interest rate is 0 percent. Consequently, all of the future cash flows reduce the principal balance, and the company recognizes no interest expense.

Morgan National reports the interest revenue in the same fashion as the previous example—that is, using the historical effective-interest rate applied toward the newly discounted value of the note. Illustration 14A-7 (on page 796) shows interest computations.

---

[21]Total interest payments are $7,000,000 × .08 × 4 years = $2,240,000.

ILLUSTRATION 14A-7
Schedule of Interest and
Amortization after Debt
Restructuring

MORGAN NATIONAL BANK (CREDITOR)				
Date	Cash Received (8%)	Interest Revenue (12%)	Increase in Carrying Amount	Carrying Amount of Note
12/31/13				$6,149,556
12/31/14	$ 560,000[a]	$ 737,947[b]	$177,947[c]	6,327,503
12/31/15	560,000	759,300	199,300	6,526,803
12/31/16	560,000	783,216	223,216	6,750,019
12/31/17	560,000	809,981[d]	249,981[d]	7,000,000
Total	$2,240,000	$3,090,444	$850,444	

[a]$560,000 = $7,000,000 × .08
[b]$737,947 = $6,149,556 × .12
[c]$177,947 = $737,947 − $560,000
[d]$21 adjustment to compensate for rounding.

The journal entries in Illustration 14A-8 demonstrate the accounting by debtor and creditor for periodic interest payments and final principal payment.

Resorts Development Co. (Debtor)		Morgan National Bank (Creditor)	
December 31, 2014 (date of first interest payment following restructure)			
Notes Payable 560,000		Cash 560,000	
Cash 560,000		Allowance for Doubtful Accounts 177,947	
		Interest Revenue 737,947	
December 31, 2015, 2016, and 2017 (dates of 2nd, 3rd, and last interest payments)			
(Debit and credit same accounts as 12/31/14 using applicable amounts from appropriate amortization schedules.)			
December 31, 2017 (date of principal payment)			
Notes Payable 7,000,000		Cash 7,000,000	
Cash 7,000,000		Allowance for Doubtful Accounts 3,500,000	
		Notes Receivable 10,500,000	

ILLUSTRATION 14A-8
Debtor and Creditor
Entries to Record
Periodic Interest and
Final Principal Payments

CONCLUDING REMARKS

The accounting for troubled debt is complex because the accounting standards allow for use of different measurement standards to determine the loss or gain reported. In addition, the assets and liabilities reported are sometimes not stated at historical cost or fair value, but at amounts adjusted for certain events but not others. This cumbersome accounting demonstrates the need for adoption of a comprehensive fair-value model for financial instruments that is consistent with finance concepts for pricing these financial instruments.

KEY TERM

troubled-debt
  restructuring, 790

SUMMARY OF LEARNING OBJECTIVE FOR APPENDIX 14A

10 **Describe the accounting for a debt restructuring.** There are two types of debt settlements: (1) transfer of noncash assets, and (2) granting of equity interest. Creditors and debtors record losses and gains on settlements based on fair values. For accounting purposes, there are also two types of restructurings with continuation of debt with modified terms: (1) the carrying amount of debt is less than the future cash flows, and (2) the carrying amount of debt exceeds the total future cash flows. Creditors record losses on these restructurings based on the expected future cash flows discounted at the historical effective-interest rate. The debtor determines its gain based on undiscounted cash flows.

DEMONSTRATION PROBLEM

Consider the following independent situations:

(a) On March 1, 2014, Heide Co. issued at 103 plus accrued interest $3,000,000, 9% bonds. The bonds are dated January 1, 2010, and pay interest semiannually on July 1 and January 1. In addition, Heide Co. incurred $27,000 of bond issuance costs. Compute the net amount of cash received by Heide Co. as a result of the issuance of these bonds.

(b) On January 1, 2014, Reymont Co. issued 9% bonds with a face value of $500,000 for $469,280 to yield 10%. The bonds are dated January 1, 2014, and pay interest annually. What amount is reported as bond discount on the issue date? Prepare the journal entry to record interest expense on December 31, 2014.

(c) Czeslaw Building Co. has a number of long-term bonds outstanding at December 31, 2014. These long-term bonds have the following sinking fund requirements and maturities for the next 6 years.

	Sinking Fund	Maturities
2015	$300,000	$100,000
2016	100,000	250,000
2017	100,000	100,000
2018	200,000	—
2019	200,000	150,000
2020	200,000	100,000

Indicate how this information should be reported in the financial statements at December 31, 2014.

Instructions
Prepare responses for each item above.

Solution

(a) Heide Co.

Selling price of the bonds ($3,000,000 × 103%)	$3,090,000
Accrued interest from January 1 to February 28, 2014 ($3,000,000 × 9% × 2/12)	45,000
Total cash received from issuance of the bonds	3,135,000
Less: Bond issuance costs	27,000
Net amount of cash received	$3,108,000

(b) Reymont Co.

Face value of bonds	$500,000
Issue price	(469,280)
Bond discount on issue late	$ 30,720

December 31, 2014

Interest Expense ($469,280 × 10%)	46,928	
Discount on Bonds Payable ($46,928 − $45,000)		1,928
Interest Payable ($500,000 × 9%)		45,000

(c) Czeslaw Building Co.

Maturities and sinking fund requirements on long-term debt for the next five year are as follows.

2015	$400,000	2018	$200,000
2016	350,000	2019	350,000
2017	200,000		

FASB CODIFICATION

FASB Codification References

[1] FASB ASC 835-30-55-2. [Predecessor literature: "Interest on Receivables and Payables," *Opinions of the Accounting Principles Board No. 21* (New York: AICPA, 1971), par. 16.]

[2] FASB ASC 835-30-35-2. [Predecessor literature: "Interest on Receivables and Payables," *Opinions of the Accounting Principles Board No. 21* (New York: AICPA, 1971), par. 15.]

[3] FASB ASC 470-50-45. [Predecessor literature: "Rescission of *FASB Statements No. 4, 44,* and *64* and Technical Corrections," *Statement of Accounting Standards No. 145* (Norwalk, Conn.: FASB, 2002).]

[4] FASB ASC 835-30-15-3. [Predecessor literature: "Interest on Receivables and Payables," *Opinions of the Accounting Principles Board No. 21* (New York: AICPA, 1971).]

[5] FASB ASC 835-30-05-2. [Predecessor literature: "Interest on Receivables and Payables," *Opinions of the Accounting Principles Board No. 21* (New York: AICPA, 1971), par. 12.]

[6] FASB ASC 825-10-25. [Predecessor literature: "The Fair Value Option for Financial Assets and Liabilities—Including an Amendment to FASB No. 115," *Statement of Financial Accounting Standards No. 159* (Norwalk, Conn.: FASB, 2007).]

[7] FASB ASC 470-10-50-4. [Predecessor literature: "Balance Sheet Classification of Short-Term Obligations Expected to Be Refinanced," *FASB Statement of Financial Accounting Standards No. 6* (Stamford, Conn.: FASB, 1975), par. 15.]

[8] FASB ASC 505-10-50-3. [Predecessor literature: "Disclosure of Information about Capital Structure," *FASB Statement of Financial Accounting Standards No. 129* (Norwalk, Conn.: 1997), par. 4.]

[9] FASB ASC 470-10-50-1. [Predecessor literature: "Disclosure of Long-Term Obligations," *FASB Statement of Financial Accounting Standards No. 47* (Stamford, Conn.: 1981), par. 10.]

[10] FASB ASC 310-40-15-2. [Predecessor literature: "Accounting by Debtors and Creditors for Troubled Debt Restructurings," *FASB Statement No. 15* (Norwalk, Conn.: FASB, June, 1977), par. 1.]

[11] FASB ASC 310-10-35. [Predecessor literature: "Accounting by Creditors for Impairment of a Loan," *FASB Statement No. 114* (Norwalk, Conn.: FASB, May 1993), par. 42.]

Exercises

If your school has a subscription to the FASB Codification, go to *http://aaahq.org/ascLogin.cfm* to log in and prepare responses to the following. Provide Codification references for your responses.

CE14-1 Access the glossary (Master Glossary) to answer the following.

    (a) What does the term "callable obligation" mean?
    (b) What is an imputed interest rate?
    (c) What is a long-term obligation?
    (d) What is the definition of "effective-interest rate"?

CE14-2 What guidance does the Codification provide on the disclosure of long-term obligations?

CE14-3 Describe how a company would classify debt that includes covenants. What conditions must exist in order to depart from the normal rule?

CE14-4 A company proposes to include in its SEC registration statement a balance sheet showing its subordinate debt as a portion of stockholders' equity. Will the SEC allow this? Why or why not?

An additional Codification case can be found in the Using Your Judgment section, on page 814.

Be sure to check the book's companion website for a Review and Analysis Exercise, with solution.

WileyPLUS   Brief Exercises, Exercises, Problems, and many more learning and assessment tools and resources are available for practice in WileyPLUS.

Note: All asterisked Questions, Exercises, and Problems relate to material in the appendix to the chapter.

(Unless instructed otherwise, round all answers to the nearest dollar.)

QUESTIONS

1. (a) From what sources might a corporation obtain funds through long-term debt? (b) What is a bond indenture? What does it contain? (c) What is a mortgage?

2. Potlatch Corporation has issued various types of bonds such as term bonds, income bonds, and debentures. Differentiate between term bonds, mortgage bonds, debenture bonds, income bonds, callable bonds, registered bonds, bearer or coupon bonds, convertible bonds, commodity-backed bonds, and deep discount bonds.

3. Distinguish between the following interest rates for bonds payable:

  (a) Yield rate.   **(d)** Market rate.

  (b) Nominal rate.   **(e)** Effective rate.

  (c) Stated rate.

4. Distinguish between the following values relative to bonds payable:

  (a) Maturity value.   **(c)** Market (fair) value.

  (b) Face value.   **(d)** Par value.

5. Under what conditions of bond issuance does a discount on bonds payable arise? Under what conditions of bond issuance does a premium on bonds payable arise?

6. How should discount on bonds payable be reported on the financial statements? Premium on bonds payable?

7. What are the two methods of amortizing discount and premium on bonds payable? Explain each.

8. Zopf Company sells its bonds at a premium and applies the effective-interest method in amortizing the premium. Will the annual interest expense increase or decrease over the life of the bonds? Explain.

9. Briggs and Stratton reported unamortized debt issue costs of $5.1 million. How should the costs of issuing these bonds be accounted for and classified in the financial statements?

10. Will the amortization of Discount on Bonds Payable increase or decrease Bond Interest Expense? Explain.

11. What is the "call" feature of a bond issue? How does the call feature affect the amortization of bond premium or discount?

12. Why would a company wish to reduce its bond indebtedness before its bonds reach maturity? Indicate how this can be done and the correct accounting treatment for such a transaction.

13. How are gains and losses from extinguishment of a debt classified in the income statement? What disclosures are required of such transactions?

14. What is done to record properly a transaction involving the issuance of a non-interest-bearing long-term note in exchange for property?

15. How is the present value of a non-interest-bearing note computed?

16. When is the stated interest rate of a debt instrument presumed to be fair?

17. What are the considerations in imputing an appropriate interest rate?

18. Differentiate between a fixed-rate mortgage and a variable-rate mortgage.

19. What is the fair value option? Briefly describe the controversy of applying the fair value option to financial liabilities.

20. Pierre Company has a 12% note payable with a carrying value of $20,000. Pierre applies the fair value option to this note. Given an increase in market interest rates, the fair value of the note is $22,600. Prepare the entry to record the fair value option for this note.

21. What disclosures are required relative to long-term debt and sinking fund requirements?

22. What is off-balance-sheet financing? Why might a company be interested in using off-balance-sheet financing?

23. What are some forms of off-balance-sheet financing?

24. Explain how a non-consolidated subsidiary can be a form of off-balance-sheet financing.

*25. What are the types of situations that result in troubled debt?

*26. What are the general rules for measuring gain or loss by both creditor and debtor in a troubled-debt restructuring involving a settlement?

*27. **(a)** In a troubled-debt situation, why might the creditor grant concessions to the debtor?

  (b) What type of concessions might a creditor grant the debtor in a troubled-debt situation?

*28. What are the general rules for measuring and recognizing gain or loss by both the debtor and the creditor in a troubled-debt restructuring involving a modification of terms?

*29. What is meant by "accounting symmetry" between the entries recorded by the debtor and creditor in a troubled-debt restructuring involving a modification of terms? In what ways is the accounting for troubled-debt restructurings non-symmetrical?

*30. Under what circumstances would a transaction be recorded as a troubled-debt restructuring by only one of the two parties to the transaction?

BRIEF EXERCISES

3 **BE14-1** Whiteside Corporation issues $500,000 of 9% bonds, due in 10 years, with interest payable semiannually. At the time of issue, the market rate for such bonds is 10%. Compute the issue price of the bonds.

3 **4** **BE14-2** The Colson Company issued $300,000 of 10% bonds on January 1, 2014. The bonds are due January 1, 2020, with interest payable each July 1 and January 1. The bonds are issued at face value. Prepare Colson's journal entries for (a) the January issuance, (b) the July 1 interest payment, and (c) the December 31 adjusting entry.

3 **4** **BE14-3** Assume the bonds in BE14-2 were issued at 98. Prepare the journal entries for (a) January 1, (b) July 1, and (c) December 31. Assume The Colson Company records straight-line amortization semiannually.

3 **4** **BE14-4** Assume the bonds in BE14-2 were issued at 103. Prepare the journal entries for (a) January 1, (b) July 1, and (c) December 31. Assume The Colson Company records straight-line amortization semiannually.

3 **4** **BE14-5** Devers Corporation issued $400,000 of 6% bonds on May 1, 2014. The bonds were dated January 1, 2014, and mature January 1, 2017, with interest payable July 1 and January 1. The bonds were issued at face value plus accrued interest. Prepare Devers's journal entries for (a) the May 1 issuance, (b) the July 1 interest payment, and (c) the December 31 adjusting entry.

3 **4** **BE14-6** On January 1, 2014, JWS Corporation issued $600,000 of 7% bonds, due in 10 years. The bonds were issued for $559,224, and pay interest each July 1 and January 1. JWS uses the effective-interest method. Prepare the company's journal entries for (a) the January 1 issuance, (b) the July 1 interest payment, and (c) the December 31 adjusting entry. Assume an effective-interest rate of 8%.

3 **4** **BE14-7** Assume the bonds in BE14-6 were issued for $644,636 and the effective-interest rate is 6%. Prepare the company's journal entries for (a) the January 1 issuance, (b) the July 1 interest payment, and (c) the December 31 adjusting entry.

3 **4** **BE14-8** Teton Corporation issued $600,000 of 7% bonds on November 1, 2014, for $644,636. The bonds were dated November 1, 2014, and mature in 10 years, with interest payable each May 1 and November 1. Teton uses the effective-interest method with an effective rate of 6%. Prepare Teton's December 31, 2014, adjusting entry.

9 **BE14-9** At December 31, 2014, Hyasaki Corporation has the following account balances:

Bonds payable, due January 1, 2023	$2,000,000
Discount on bonds payable	88,000
Interest payable	80,000

Show how the above accounts should be presented on the December 31, 2014, balance sheet, including the proper classifications.

4 **BE14-10** Wasserman Corporation issued 10-year bonds on January 1, 2014. Costs associated with the bond issuance were $160,000. Wasserman uses the straight-line method to amortize bond issue costs. Prepare the December 31, 2014, entry to record 2014 bond issue cost amortization.

5 **BE14-11** On January 1, 2014, Henderson Corporation redeemed $500,000 of bonds at 99. At the time of redemption, the unamortized premium was $15,000 and unamortized bond issue costs were $5,250. Prepare the corporation's journal entry to record the reacquisition of the bonds.

6 **BE14-12** Coldwell, Inc. issued a $100,000, 4-year, 10% note at face value to Flint Hills Bank on January 1, 2014, and received $100,000 cash. The note requires annual interest payments each December 31. Prepare Coldwell's journal entries to record (a) the issuance of the note and (b) the December 31 interest payment.

6 **BE14-13** Samson Corporation issued a 4-year, $75,000, zero-interest-bearing note to Brown Company on January 1, 2014, and received cash of $47,664. The implicit interest rate is 12%. Prepare Samson's journal entries for (a) the January 1 issuance and (b) the December 31 recognition of interest.

6 **BE14-14** McCormick Corporation issued a 4-year, $40,000, 5% note to Greenbush Company on January 1, 2014, and received a computer that normally sells for $31,495. The note requires annual interest payments each December 31. The market rate of interest for a note of similar risk is 12%. Prepare McCormick's journal entries for (a) the January 1 issuance and (b) the December 31 interest.

6 **BE14-15** Shlee Corporation issued a 4-year, $60,000, zero-interest-bearing note to Garcia Company on January 1, 2014, and received cash of $60,000. In addition, Shlee agreed to sell merchandise to Garcia at an amount less than regular selling price over the 4-year period. The market rate of interest for similar notes is 12%. Prepare Shlee Corporation's January 1 journal entry.

7 **BE14-16** Shonen Knife Corporation has elected to use the fair value option for one of its notes payable. The note was issued at an effective rate of 11% and has a carrying value of $16,000. At year-end, Shonen Knife's borrowing rate has declined; the fair value of the note payable is now $17,500. (a) Determine the unrealized holding gain or loss on the note. (b) Prepare the entry to record any unrealized holding gain or loss.

EXERCISES

2 **E14-1 (Classification of Liabilities)** Presented below are various account balances of K.D. Lang Inc.

(a) Unamortized premium on bonds payable, of which $3,000 will be amortized during the next year.
(b) Bank loans payable of a winery, due March 10, 2018. (The product requires aging for 5 years before sale.)
(c) Serial bonds payable, $1,000,000, of which $200,000 are due each July 31.
(d) Amounts withheld from employees' wages for income taxes.
(e) Notes payable due January 15, 2017.
(f) Credit balances in customers' accounts arising from returns and allowances after collection in full of account.
(g) Bonds payable of $2,000,000 maturing June 30, 2016.
(h) Overdraft of $1,000 in a bank account. (No other balances are carried at this bank.)
(i) Deposits made by customers who have ordered goods.

Instructions
Indicate whether each of the items above should be classified on December 31, 2014, as a current liability, a long-term liability, or under some other classification. Consider each one independently from all others; that is, do not assume that all of them relate to one particular business. If the classification of some of the items is doubtful, explain why in each case.

2 **E14-2 (Classification)** The following items are found in the financial statements.

(a) Discount on bonds payable.
(b) Interest expense (credit balance).
(c) Unamortized bond issue costs.
(d) Gain on repurchase of debt.
(e) Mortgage payable (payable in equal amounts over next 3 years).
(f) Debenture bonds payable (maturing in 5 years).
(g) Notes payable (due in 4 years).
(h) Premium on bonds payable.
(i) Treasury bonds.
(j) Bonds payable (due in 3 years).

Instructions
Indicate how each of these items should be classified in the financial statements.

3 **4** **E14-3 (Entries for Bond Transactions)** Presented below are two independent situations.

1. On January 1, 2014, Simon Company issued $200,000 of 9%, 10-year bonds at par. Interest is payable quarterly on April 1, July 1, October 1, and January 1.
2. On June 1, 2014, Garfunkel Company issued $100,000 of 12%, 10-year bonds dated January 1 at par plus accrued interest. Interest is payable semiannually on July 1 and January 1.

Instructions
For each of these two independent situations, prepare journal entries to record the following.

(a) The issuance of the bonds.
(b) The payment of interest on July 1.
(c) The accrual of interest on December 31.

3 **4** **E14-4 (Entries for Bond Transactions—Straight-Line)** Celine Dion Company issued $600,000 of 10%, 20-year bonds on January 1, 2014, at 102. Interest is payable semiannually on July 1 and January 1. Dion Company uses the straight-line method of amortization for bond premium or discount.

Instructions
Prepare the journal entries to record the following.

(a) The issuance of the bonds.

(b) The payment of interest and the related amortization on July 1, 2014.

(c) The accrual of interest and the related amortization on December 31, 2014.

 E14-5 (Entries for Bond Transactions—Effective-Interest) Assume the same information as in E14-4, except that Celine Dion Company uses the effective-interest method of amortization for bond premium or discount. Assume an effective yield of 9.7705%.

Instructions

Prepare the journal entries to record the following. (Round to the nearest dollar.)

(a) The issuance of the bonds.

(b) The payment of interest and related amortization on July 1, 2014.

(c) The accrual of interest and the related amortization on December 31, 2014.

E14-6 (Amortization Schedule—Straight-Line) Devon Harris Company sells 10% bonds having a maturity value of $2,000,000 for $1,855,816. The bonds are dated January 1, 2014, and mature January 1, 2019. Interest is payable annually on January 1.

Instructions

Set up a schedule of interest expense and discount amortization under the straight-line method. (Round answers to the nearest cent.)

E14-7 (Amortization Schedule—Effective-Interest) Assume the same information as E14-6.

Instructions

Set up a schedule of interest expense and discount amortization under the effective-interest method. (*Hint:* The effective-interest rate must be computed.)

 E14-8 (Determine Proper Amounts in Account Balances) Presented below are three independent situations.

(a) CeCe Winans Corporation incurred the following costs in connection with the issuance of bonds: (1) printing and engraving costs, $12,000; (2) legal fees, $49,000; and (3) commissions paid to underwriter, $60,000. What amount should be reported as Unamortized Bond Issue Costs, and where should this amount be reported on the balance sheet?

(b) George Gershwin Co. sold $2,000,000 of 10%, 10-year bonds at 104 on January 1, 2014. The bonds were dated January 1, 2014, and pay interest on July 1 and January 1. If Gershwin uses the straight-line method to amortize bond premium or discount, determine the amount of interest expense to be reported on July 1, 2014, and December 31, 2014.

(c) Ron Kenoly Inc. issued $600,000 of 9%, 10-year bonds on June 30, 2014, for $562,500. This price provided a yield of 10% on the bonds. Interest is payable semiannually on December 31 and June 30. If Kenoly uses the effective-interest method, determine the amount of interest expense to record if financial statements are issued on October 31, 2014.

 E14-9 (Entries and Questions for Bond Transactions) On June 30, 2014, Mischa Auer Company issued $4,000,000 face value of 13%, 20-year bonds at $4,300,920, a yield of 12%. Auer uses the effective-interest method to amortize bond premium or discount. The bonds pay semiannual interest on June 30 and December 31.

Instructions

(Round answers to the nearest cent.)

(a) Prepare the journal entries to record the following transactions.

   (1) The issuance of the bonds on June 30, 2014.

   (2) The payment of interest and the amortization of the premium on December 31, 2014.

   (3) The payment of interest and the amortization of the premium on June 30, 2015.

   (4) The payment of interest and the amortization of the premium on December 31, 2015.

(b) Show the proper balance sheet presentation for the liability for bonds payable on the December 31, 2015, balance sheet.

(c) Provide the answers to the following questions.

   (1) What amount of interest expense is reported for 2015?

   (2) Will the bond interest expense reported in 2015 be the same as, greater than, or less than the amount that would be reported if the straight-line method of amortization were used?

   (3) Determine the total cost of borrowing over the life of the bond.

   (4) Will the total bond interest expense for the life of the bond be greater than, the same as, or less than the total interest expense if the straight-line method of amortization were used?

E14-10 (Entries for Bond Transactions) On January 1, 2014, Aumont Company sold 12% bonds having a maturity value of $500,000 for $537,907.37, which provides the bondholders with a 10% yield. The bonds are dated January 1, 2014, and mature January 1, 2019, with interest payable December 31 of each year. Aumont Company allocates interest and unamortized discount or premium on the effective-interest basis.

Instructions

(Round answers to the nearest cent.)

(a) Prepare the journal entry at the date of the bond issuance.
(b) Prepare a schedule of interest expense and bond amortization for 2014–2016.
(c) Prepare the journal entry to record the interest payment and the amortization for 2014.
(d) Prepare the journal entry to record the interest payment and the amortization for 2016.

3 **E14-11 (Information Related to Various Bond Issues)** Karen Austin Inc. has issued three types of debt on January 1, 2014, the start of the company's fiscal year.

(a) $10 million, 10-year, 15% unsecured bonds, interest payable quarterly. Bonds were priced to yield 12%.
(b) $25 million par of 10-year, zero-coupon bonds at a price to yield 12% per year.
(c) $20 million, 10-year, 10% mortgage bonds, interest payable annually to yield 12%.

Instructions

Prepare a schedule that identifies the following items for each bond: (1) maturity value, (2) number of interest periods over life of bond, (3) stated rate per each interest period, (4) effective-interest rate per each interest period, (5) payment amount per period, and (6) present value of bonds at date of issue.

3 **4** **E14-12 (Entry for Redemption of Bond; Bond Issue Costs)** On January 2, 2009, Banno Corporation issued **5** $1,500,000 of 10% bonds at 97 due December 31, 2018. Legal and other costs of $24,000 were incurred in connection with the issue. Interest on the bonds is payable annually each December 31. The $24,000 issue costs are being deferred and amortized on a straight-line basis over the 10-year term of the bonds. The discount on the bonds is also being amortized on a straight-line basis over the 10 years. (Straight-line is not materially different in effect from the preferable "interest method.")

The bonds are callable at 101 (i.e., at 101% of face amount), and on January 2, 2014, Banno called $900,000 face amount of the bonds and redeemed them.

Instructions

Ignoring income taxes, compute the amount of loss, if any, to be recognized by Banno as a result of retiring the $900,000 of bonds in 2014 and prepare the journal entry to record the redemption.

(AICPA adapted)

3 **4** **E14-13 (Entries for Redemption and Issuance of Bonds)** Matt Perry, Inc. had outstanding $6,000,000 of **5** 11% bonds (interest payable July 31 and January 31) due in 10 years. On July 1, it issued $9,000,000 of 10%, 15-year bonds (interest payable July 1 and January 1) at 98. A portion of the proceeds was used to call the 11% bonds at 102 on August 1. Unamortized bond discount and issue cost applicable to the 11% bonds were $120,000 and $30,000, respectively.

Instructions

Prepare the journal entries necessary to record issue of the new bonds and the refunding of the bonds.

3 **4** **E14-14 (Entries for Redemption and Issuance of Bonds)** On June 30, 2006, County Company issued 12% **5** bonds with a par value of $800,000 due in 20 years. They were issued at 98 and were callable at 104 at any date after June 30, 2014. Because of lower interest rates and a significant change in the company's credit rating, it was decided to call the entire issue on June 30, 2015, and to issue new bonds. New 10% bonds were sold in the amount of $1,000,000 at 102; they mature in 20 years. County Company uses straight-line amortization. Interest payment dates are December 31 and June 30.

Instructions

(a) Prepare journal entries to record the redemption of the old issue and the sale of the new issue on June 30, 2015.
(b) Prepare the entry required on December 31, 2015, to record the payment of the first 6 months' interest and the amortization of premium on the bonds.

3 **4** **E14-15 (Entries for Redemption and Issuance of Bonds)** Linda Day George Company had bonds out- **5** standing with a maturity value of $300,000. On April 30, 2014, when these bonds had an unamortized discount of $10,000, they were called in at 104. To pay for these bonds, George had issued other bonds a month earlier bearing a lower interest rate. The newly issued bonds had a life of 10 years. The new bonds were issued at 103 (face value $300,000). Issue costs related to the new bonds were $3,000.

Instructions

Ignoring interest, compute the gain or loss and record this refunding transaction.

(AICPA adapted)

6 **E14-16 (Entries for Zero-Interest-Bearing Notes)** On January 1, 2014, Ellen Greene Company makes the two following acquisitions.

1. Purchases land having a fair value of $200,000 by issuing a 5-year, zero-interest-bearing promissory note in the face amount of $337,012.
2. Purchases equipment by issuing a 6%, 8-year promissory note having a maturity value of $250,000 (interest payable annually).

The company has to pay 11% interest for funds from its bank.

Instructions
(Round answers to the nearest cent.)

(a) Record the two journal entries that should be recorded by Ellen Greene Company for the two purchases on January 1, 2014.
(b) Record the interest at the end of the first year on both notes using the effective-interest method.

6 **E14-17 (Imputation of Interest)** Presented below are two independent situations.

(a) On January 1, 2014, Robin Wright Inc. purchased land that had an assessed value of $350,000 at the time of purchase. A $550,000, zero-interest-bearing note due January 1, 2017, was given in exchange. There was no established exchange price for the land, nor a ready fair value for the note. The interest rate charged on a note of this type is 12%. Determine at what amount the land should be recorded at January 1, 2014, and the interest expense to be reported in 2014 related to this transaction.
(b) On January 1, 2014, Field Furniture Co. borrowed $5,000,000 (face value) from Gary Sinise Co., a major customer, through a zero-interest-bearing note due in 4 years. Because the note was zero-interest-bearing, Field Furniture agreed to sell furniture to this customer at lower than market price. A 10% rate of interest is normally charged on this type of loan. Prepare the journal entry to record this transaction and determine the amount of interest expense to report for 2014.

6 **E14-18 (Imputation of Interest with Right)** On January 1, 2014, Margaret Avery Co. borrowed and received $400,000 from a major customer evidenced by a zero-interest-bearing note due in 3 years. As consideration for the zero-interest-bearing feature, Avery agrees to supply the customer's inventory needs for the loan period at lower than the market price. The appropriate rate at which to impute interest is 8%.

Instructions

(a) Prepare the journal entry to record the initial transaction on January 1, 2014. (Round all computations to the nearest dollar.)
(b) Prepare the journal entry to record any adjusting entries needed at December 31, 2014. Assume that the sales of Avery's product to this customer occur evenly over the 3-year period.

7 **E14-19 (Fair Value Option)** Fallen Company commonly issues long-term notes payable to its various lenders. Fallen has had a pretty good credit rating such that its effective borrowing rate is quite low (less than 8% on an annual basis). Fallen has elected to use the fair value option for the long-term notes issued to Barclay's Bank and has the following data related to the carrying and fair value for these notes.

	Carrying Value	Fair Value
December 31, 2014	$54,000	$54,000
December 31, 2015	44,000	42,500
December 31, 2016	36,000	38,000

Instructions

(a) Prepare the journal entry at December 31 (Fallen's year-end) for 2014, 2015, and 2016, to record the fair value option for these notes.
(b) At what amount will the note be reported on Fallen's 2015 balance sheet?
(c) What is the effect of recording the fair value option on these notes on Fallen's 2016 income?
(d) Assuming that general market interest rates have been stable over the period, does the fair value data for the notes indicate that Fallen's creditworthiness has improved or declined in 2016? Explain.

9 **E14-20 (Long-Term Debt Disclosure)** At December 31, 2014, Redmond Company has outstanding three long-term debt issues. The first is a $2,000,000 note payable which matures June 30, 2017. The second is a $6,000,000 bond issue which matures September 30, 2018. The third is a $12,500,000 sinking fund debenture with annual sinking fund payments of $2,500,000 in each of the years 2016 through 2020.

Instructions
Prepare the required note disclosure for the long-term debt at December 31, 2014.

10 ***E14-21 (Settlement of Debt)*** Strickland Company owes $200,000 plus $18,000 of accrued interest to Moran State Bank. The debt is a 10-year, 10% note. During 2014, Strickland's business deteriorated due to a faltering regional economy. On December 31, 2014, Moran State Bank agrees to accept an old machine and cancel the entire debt. The machine has a cost of $390,000, accumulated depreciation of $221,000, and a fair value of $180,000.

Instructions

(a) Prepare journal entries for Strickland Company and Moran State Bank to record this debt settlement.

(b) How should Strickland report the gain or loss on the disposition of machine and on restructuring of debt in its 2014 income statement?

(c) Assume that, instead of transferring the machine, Strickland decides to grant 15,000 shares of its common stock ($10 par) which has a fair value of $180,000 in full settlement of the loan obligation. If Moran State Bank treats Strickland's stock as a trading investment, prepare the entries to record the transaction for both parties.

10 ***E14-22 (Term Modification without Gain—Debtor's Entries)*** On December 31, 2014, the American Bank enters into a debt restructuring agreement with Barkley Company, which is now experiencing financial trouble. The bank agrees to restructure a 12%, issued at par, $3,000,000 note receivable by the following modifications:

1. Reducing the principal obligation from $3,000,000 to $2,400,000.
2. Extending the maturity date from December 31, 2014, to January 1, 2018.
3. Reducing the interest rate from 12% to 10%.

Barkley pays interest at the end of each year. On January 1, 2018, Barkley Company pays $2,400,000 in cash to Firstar Bank.

Instructions

(a) Will the gain recorded by Barkley be equal to the loss recorded by American Bank under the debt restructuring?

(b) Can Barkley Company record a gain under the term modification mentioned above? Explain.

(c) Assuming that the interest rate Barkley should use to compute interest expense in future periods is 1.4276%, prepare the interest payment schedule of the note for Barkley Company after the debt restructuring.

(d) Prepare the interest payment entry for Barkley Company on December 31, 2016.

(e) What entry should Barkley make on January 1, 2018?

10 ***E14-23 (Term Modification without Gain—Creditor's Entries)*** Using the same information as in E14-22, answer the following questions related to American Bank (creditor).

Instructions

(a) What interest rate should American Bank use to calculate the loss on the debt restructuring?

(b) Compute the loss that American Bank will suffer from the debt restructuring. Prepare the journal entry to record the loss.

(c) Prepare the interest receipt schedule for American Bank after the debt restructuring.

(d) Prepare the interest receipt entry for American Bank on December 31, 2016.

(e) What entry should American Bank make on January 1, 2018?

10 ***E14-24 (Term Modification with Gain—Debtor's Entries)*** Use the same information as in E14-22 above except that American Bank reduced the principal to $1,900,000 rather than $2,400,000. On January 1, 2018, Barkley pays $1,900,000 in cash to American Bank for the principal.

Instructions

(a) Can Barkley Company record a gain under this term modification? If yes, compute the gain for Barkley Company.

(b) Prepare the journal entries to record the gain on Barkley's books.

(c) What interest rate should Barkley use to compute its interest expense in future periods? Will your answer be the same as in E14-22 above? Why or why not?

(d) Prepare the interest payment schedule of the note for Barkley Company after the debt restructuring.

(e) Prepare the interest payment entries for Barkley Company on December 31, of 2015, 2016, and 2017.

(f) What entry should Barkley make on January 1, 2018?

10 ***E14-25 (Term Modification with Gain—Creditor's Entries)*** Using the same information as in E14-22 and E14-24, answer the following questions related to American Bank (creditor).

Instructions

(a) Compute the loss American Bank will suffer under this new term modification. Prepare the journal entry to record the loss on American's books.

(b) Prepare the interest receipt schedule for American Bank after the debt restructuring.

(c) Prepare the interest receipt entry for American Bank on December 31, 2015, 2016, and 2017.

(d) What entry should American Bank make on January 1, 2018?

10 *E14-26 **(Debtor/Creditor Entries for Settlement of Troubled Debt)** Gottlieb Co. owes $199,800 to Ceballos Inc. The debt is a 10-year, 11% note. Because Gottlieb Co. is in financial trouble, Ceballos Inc. agrees to accept some property and cancel the entire debt. The property has a book value of $90,000 and a fair value of $140,000.

Instructions

(a) Prepare the journal entry on Gottlieb's books for debt restructure.

(b) Prepare the journal entry on Ceballos's books for debt restructure.

10 *E14-27 **(Debtor/Creditor Entries for Modification of Troubled Debt)** Vargo Corp. owes $270,000 to First Trust. The debt is a 10-year, 12% note due December 31, 2014. Because Vargo Corp. is in financial trouble, First Trust agrees to extend the maturity date to December 31, 2016, reduce the principal to $220,000, and reduce the interest rate to 5%, payable annually on December 31.

Instructions

(a) Prepare the journal entries on Vargo's books on December 31, 2014, 2015, 2016.

(b) Prepare the journal entries on First Trust's books on December 31, 2014, 2015, 2016.

EXERCISES SET B

See the book's companion website, at **www.wiley.com/college/kieso**, for an additional set of exercises.

PROBLEMS

 P14-1 (Analysis of Amortization Schedule and Interest Entries) The following amortization and interest schedule reflects the issuance of 10-year bonds by Capulet Corporation on January 1, 2008, and the subsequent interest payments and charges. The company's year-end is December 31, and financial statements are prepared once yearly.

		Amortization Schedule		
Year	Cash	Interest	Amount Unamortized	Carrying Value
1/1/2008			$5,651	$ 94,349
2008	$11,000	$11,322	5,329	94,671
2009	11,000	11,361	4,968	95,032
2010	11,000	11,404	4,564	95,436
2011	11,000	11,452	4,112	95,888
2012	11,000	11,507	3,605	96,395
2013	11,000	11,567	3,038	96,962
2014	11,000	11,635	2,403	97,597
2015	11,000	11,712	1,691	98,309
2016	11,000	11,797	894	99,106
2017	11,000	11,894		100,000

Instructions

(a) Indicate whether the bonds were issued at a premium or a discount and how you can determine this fact from the schedule.

(b) Indicate whether the amortization schedule is based on the straight-line method or the effective-interest method, and how you can determine which method is used.

(c) Determine the stated interest rate and the effective-interest rate.

(d) On the basis of the schedule above, prepare the journal entry to record the issuance of the bonds on January 1, 2008.

(e) On the basis of the schedule above, prepare the journal entry or entries to reflect the bond transactions and accruals for 2008. (Interest is paid January 1.)

(f) On the basis of the schedule above, prepare the journal entry or entries to reflect the bond transactions and accruals for 2015. Capulet Corporation does not use reversing entries.

P14-2 (Issuance and Redemption of Bonds) Venezuela Co. is building a new hockey arena at a cost of $2,500,000. It received a downpayment of $500,000 from local businesses to support the project, and now needs to borrow $2,000,000 to complete the project. It therefore decides to issue $2,000,000 of 10.5%, 10-year bonds. These bonds were issued on January 1, 2013, and pay interest annually on each January 1. The bonds yield 10%. Venezuela paid $50,000 in bond issue costs related to the bond sale.

Instructions

(a) Prepare the journal entry to record the issuance of the bonds and the related bond issue costs incurred on January 1, 2013.

(b) Prepare a bond amortization schedule up to and including January 1, 2017, using the effective-interest method.

(c) Assume that on July 1, 2016, Venezuela Co. redeems half of the bonds at a cost of $1,065,000 plus accrued interest. Prepare the journal entry to record this redemption.

P14-3 (Negative Amortization) Good-Deal Inc. developed a new sales gimmick to help sell its inventory of new automobiles. Because many new car buyers need financing, Good-Deal offered a low downpayment and low car payments for the first year after purchase. It believes that this promotion will bring in some new buyers.

On January 1, 2014, a customer purchased a new $33,000 automobile, making a downpayment of $1,000. The customer signed a note indicating that the annual rate of interest would be 8% and that quarterly payments would be made over 3 years. For the first year, Good-Deal required a $400 quarterly payment to be made on April 1, July 1, October 1, and January 1, 2015. After this one-year period, the customer was required to make regular quarterly payments that would pay off the loan as of January 1, 2017.

Instructions

(a) Prepare a note amortization schedule for the first year.

(b) Indicate the amount the customer owes on the contract at the end of the first year.

(c) Compute the amount of the new quarterly payments.

(d) Prepare a note amortization schedule for these new payments for the next 2 years.

(e) What do you think of the new sales promotion used by Good-Deal?

P14-4 (Issuance and Redemption of Bonds; Income Statement Presentation) Holiday Company issued its 9%, 25-year mortgage bonds in the principal amount of $3,000,000 on January 2, 2000, at a discount of $150,000, which it proceeded to amortize by charges to expense over the life of the issue on a straight-line basis. The indenture securing the issue provided that the bonds could be called for redemption in total but not in part at any time before maturity at 104% of the principal amount, but it did not provide for any sinking fund.

On December 18, 2014, the company issued its 11%, 20-year debenture bonds in the principal amount of $4,000,000 at 102, and the proceeds were used to redeem the 9%, 25-year mortgage bonds on January 2, 2015. The indenture securing the new issue did not provide for any sinking fund or for redemption before maturity.

Instructions

(a) Prepare journal entries to record the issuance of the 11% bonds and the redemption of the 9% bonds.

(b) Indicate the income statement treatment of the gain or loss from redemption and the note disclosure required.

P14-5 (Comprehensive Bond Problem) In each of the following independent cases the company closes its books on December 31.

1. Sanford Co. sells $500,000 of 10% bonds on March 1, 2014. The bonds pay interest on September 1 and March 1. The due date of the bonds is September 1, 2017. The bonds yield 12%. Give entries through December 31, 2015.

2. Titania Co. sells $400,000 of 12% bonds on June 1, 2014. The bonds pay interest on December 1 and June 1. The due date of the bonds is June 1, 2018. The bonds yield 10%. On October 1, 2015, Titania buys back $120,000 worth of bonds for $126,000 (includes accrued interest). Give entries through December 1, 2016.

Instructions

For the two cases prepare all of the relevant journal entries from the time of sale until the date indicated. Use the effective-interest method for discount and premium amortization (construct amortization tables where applicable). Amortize premium or discount on interest dates and at year-end. (Assume that no reversing entries were made.)

3 4 5 P14-6 (Issuance of Bonds between Interest Dates, Straight-Line, Redemption) Presented below are selected transactions on the books of Simonson Corporation.

May 1, 2014	Bonds payable with a par value of $900,000, which are dated January 1, 2014, are sold at 106 plus accrued interest. They are coupon bonds, bear interest at 12% (payable annually at January 1), and mature January 1, 2024. (Use interest expense account for accrued interest.)
Dec. 31	Adjusting entries are made to record the accrued interest on the bonds, and the amortization of the proper amount of premium. (Use straight-line amortization.)
Jan. 1, 2015	Interest on the bonds is paid.
April 1	Bonds with par value of $360,000 are called at 102 plus accrued interest, and redeemed. (Bond premium is to be amortized only at the end of each year.)
Dec. 31	Adjusting entries are made to record the accrued interest on the bonds, and the proper amount of premium amortized.

Instructions

(Round to two decimal places.)

Prepare journal entries for the transactions above.

3 4 5 P14-7 (Entries for Life Cycle of Bonds) On April 1, 2014, Seminole Company sold 15,000 of its 11%, 15-year, $1,000 face value bonds at 97. Interest payment dates are April 1 and October 1, and the company uses the straight-line method of bond discount amortization. On March 1, 2015, Seminole took advantage of favorable prices of its stock to extinguish 6,000 of the bonds by issuing 200,000 shares of its $10 par value common stock. At this time, the accrued interest was paid in cash. The company's stock was selling for $31 per share on March 1, 2015.

Instructions

Prepare the journal entries needed on the books of Seminole Company to record the following.

(a) April 1, 2014: issuance of the bonds.
(b) October 1, 2014: payment of semiannual interest.
(c) December 31, 2014: accrual of interest expense.
(d) March 1, 2015: extinguishment of 6,000 bonds. (No reversing entries made.)

6 P14-8 (Entries for Zero-Interest-Bearing Note) On December 31, 2014, Faital Company acquired a computer from Plato Corporation by issuing a $600,000 zero-interest-bearing note, payable in full on December 31, 2018. Faital Company's credit rating permits it to borrow funds from its several lines of credit at 10%. The computer is expected to have a 5-year life and a $70,000 salvage value.

Instructions

(Round answers to the nearest cent.)

(a) Prepare the journal entry for the purchase on December 31, 2014.
(b) Prepare any necessary adjusting entries relative to depreciation (use straight-line) and amortization (use effective-interest method) on December 31, 2015.
(c) Prepare any necessary adjusting entries relative to depreciation and amortization on December 31, 2016.

6 P14-9 (Entries for Zero-Interest-Bearing Note; Payable in Installments) Sabonis Cosmetics Co. purchased machinery on December 31, 2013, paying $50,000 down and agreeing to pay the balance in four equal installments of $40,000 payable each December 31. An assumed interest of 8% is implicit in the purchase price.

Instructions

Prepare the journal entries that would be recorded for the purchase and for the payments and interest on the following dates. (Round answers to the nearest cent.)

(a) December 31, 2013.   (d) December 31, 2016.
(b) December 31, 2014.   (e) December 31, 2017.
(c) December 31, 2015.

3 4 5 9 P14-10 (Comprehensive Problem: Issuance, Classification, Reporting) Presented on the next page are four independent situations.

(a) On March 1, 2015, Wilke Co. issued at 103 plus accrued interest $4,000,000, 9% bonds. The bonds are dated January 1, 2015, and pay interest semiannually on July 1 and January 1. In addition, Wilke Co. incurred $27,000 of bond issuance costs. Compute the net amount of cash received by Wilke Co. as a result of the issuance of these bonds.

(b) On January 1, 2014, Langley Co. issued 9% bonds with a face value of $700,000 for $656,992 to yield 10%. The bonds are dated January 1, 2014, and pay interest annually. What amount is reported for interest expense in 2014 related to these bonds, assuming that Langley used the effective-interest method for amortizing bond premium and discount?

(c) Tweedie Building Co. has a number of long-term bonds outstanding at December 31, 2014. These long-term bonds have the following sinking fund requirements and maturities for the next 6 years.

	Sinking Fund	Maturities
2015	$300,000	$100,000
2016	100,000	250,000
2017	100,000	100,000
2018	200,000	—
2019	200,000	150,000
2020	200,000	100,000

Indicate how this information should be reported in the financial statements at December 31, 2014.

(d) In the long-term debt structure of Beckford Inc., the following three bonds were reported: mortgage bonds payable $10,000,000; collateral trust bonds $5,000,000; bonds maturing in installments, secured by plant equipment $4,000,000. Determine the total amount, if any, of debenture bonds outstanding.

P14-11 (Effective-Interest Method) Samantha Cordelia, an intermediate accounting student, is having difficulty amortizing bond premiums and discounts using the effective-interest method. Furthermore, she cannot understand why GAAP requires that this method be used instead of the straight-line method. She has come to you with the following problem, looking for help.

On June 30, 2014, Hobart Company issued $2,000,000 face value of 11%, 20-year bonds at $2,171,600, a yield of 10%. Hobart Company uses the effective-interest method to amortize bond premiums or discounts. The bonds pay semiannual interest on June 30 and December 31. Prepare an amortization schedule for four periods.

Instructions
Using the data above for illustrative purposes, write a short memo (1–1.5 pages double-spaced) to Samantha, explaining what the effective-interest method is, why it is preferable, and how it is computed. (Do not forget to include an amortization schedule, referring to it whenever necessary.)

*P14-12 (Debtor/Creditor Entries for Continuation of Troubled Debt) Daniel Perkins is the sole shareholder of Perkins Inc., which is currently under protection of the U.S. bankruptcy court. As a "debtor in possession," he has negotiated the following revised loan agreement with United Bank. Perkins Inc.'s $600,000, 12%, 10-year note was refinanced with a $600,000, 5%, 10-year note.

Instructions
(a) What is the accounting nature of this transaction?
(b) Prepare the journal entry to record this refinancing:
   (1) On the books of Perkins Inc.
   (2) On the books of United Bank.
(c) Discuss whether generally accepted accounting principles provide the proper information useful to managers and investors in this situation.

*P14-13 (Restructure of Note under Different Circumstances) Halvor Corporation is having financial difficulty and therefore has asked Frontenac National Bank to restructure its $5 million note outstanding. The present note has 3 years remaining and pays a current rate of interest of 10%. The present market rate for a loan of this nature is 12%. The note was issued at its face value.

Instructions
Presented below and on the next page are four independent situations. Prepare the journal entry that Halvor and Frontenac National Bank would make for each of these restructurings.

(a) Frontenac National Bank agrees to take an equity interest in Halvor by accepting common stock valued at $3,700,000 in exchange for relinquishing its claim on this note. The common stock has a par value of $1,700,000.
(b) Frontenac National Bank agrees to accept land in exchange for relinquishing its claim on this note. The land has a book value of $3,250,000 and a fair value of $4,000,000.
(c) Frontenac National Bank agrees to modify the terms of the note, indicating that Halvor does not have to pay any interest on the note over the 3-year period.

(d) Frontenac National Bank agrees to reduce the principal balance due to $4,166,667 and require interest only in the second and third year at a rate of 10%.

10 *P14-14 (Debtor/Creditor Entries for Continuation of Troubled Debt with New Effective Interest) Crocker Corp. owes D. Yaeger Corp. a 10-year, 10% note in the amount of $330,000 plus $33,000 of accrued interest. The note is due today, December 31, 2014. Because Crocker Corp. is in financial trouble, D. Yaeger Corp. agrees to forgive the accrued interest, $30,000 of the principal, and to extend the maturity date to December 31, 2017. Interest at 10% of revised principal will continue to be due on 12/31 each year.

Assume the following present value factors for 3 periods.

	2¼%	2⅜%	2½%	2⅝%	2¾%	3%
Single sum	.93543	.93201	.92859	.92521	.92184	.91514
Ordinary annuity of 1	2.86989	2.86295	2.85602	2.84913	2.84226	2.82861

Instructions
(a) Compute the new effective-interest rate for Crocker Corp. following restructure. (*Hint:* Find the interest rate that establishes approximately $363,000 as the present value of the total future cash flows.)
(b) Prepare a schedule of debt reduction and interest expense for the years 2014 through 2017.
(c) Compute the gain or loss for D. Yaeger Corp. and prepare a schedule of receivable reduction and interest revenue for the years 2014 through 2017.
(d) Prepare all the necessary journal entries on the books of Crocker Corp. for the years 2014, 2015, and 2016.
(e) Prepare all the necessary journal entries on the books of D. Yaeger Corp. for the years 2014, 2015, and 2016.

PROBLEMS SET B

See the book's companion website, at **www.wiley.com/college/kieso**, for an additional set of problems.

CONCEPTS FOR ANALYSIS

CA14-1 (Bond Theory: Balance Sheet Presentations, Interest Rate, Premium) On January 1, 2014, Nichols Company issued for $1,085,800 its 20-year, 11% bonds that have a maturity value of $1,000,000 and pay interest semiannually on January 1 and July 1. Bond issue costs were not material in amount. Below are three presentations of the long-term liability section of the balance sheet that might be used for these bonds at the issue date.

1. Bonds payable (maturing January 1, 2034)	$1,000,000
Unamortized premium on bonds payable	85,800
Total bond liability	$1,085,800
2. Bonds payable—principal (face value $1,000,000 maturing January 1, 2034)	$ 142,050[a]
Bonds payable—interest (semiannual payment $55,000)	943,750[b]
Total bond liability	$1,085,800
3. Bonds payable—principal (maturing January 1, 2034)	$1,000,000
Bonds payable—interest ($55,000 per period for 40 periods)	2,200,000
Total bond liability	$3,200,000

[a]The present value of $1,000,000 due at the end of 40 (6-month) periods at the yield rate of 5% per period.
[b]The present value of $55,000 per period for 40 (6-month) periods at the yield rate of 5% per period.

Instructions
(a) Discuss the conceptual merit(s) of each of the date-of-issue balance sheet presentations shown above for these bonds.
(b) Explain why investors would pay $1,085,800 for bonds that have a maturity value of only $1,000,000.

(c) Assuming that a discount rate is needed to compute the carrying value of the obligations arising from a bond issue at any date during the life of the bonds, discuss the conceptual merit(s) of using for this purpose:

    (1) The coupon or nominal rate.

    (2) The effective or yield rate at date of issue.

(d) If the obligations arising from these bonds are to be carried at their present value computed by means of the current market rate of interest, how would the bond valuation at dates subsequent to the date of issue be affected by an increase or a decrease in the market rate of interest?

(AICPA adapted)

CA14-2 (Bond Theory: Price, Presentation, and Redemption) On March 1, 2014, Sealy Company sold its 5-year, $1,000 face value, 9% bonds dated March 1, 2014, at an effective annual interest rate (yield) of 11%. Interest is payable semiannually, and the first interest payment date is September 1, 2014. Sealy uses the effective-interest method of amortization. Bond issue costs were incurred in preparing and selling the bond issue. The bonds can be called by Sealy at 101 at any time on or after March 1, 2015.

Instructions

    (a) (1) How would the selling price of the bond be determined?

        (2) Specify how all items related to the bonds would be presented in a balance sheet prepared immediately after the bond issue was sold.

    (b) What items related to the bond issue would be included in Sealy's 2014 income statement, and how would each be determined?

    (c) Would the amount of bond discount amortization using the effective-interest method of amortization be lower in the second or third year of the life of the bond issue? Why?

    (d) Assuming that the bonds were called in and redeemed on March 1, 2015, how should Sealy report the redemption of the bonds on the 2015 income statement?

(AICPA adapted)

CA14-3 (Bond Theory: Amortization and Gain or Loss Recognition)

Part I: The appropriate method of amortizing a premium or discount on issuance of bonds is the effective-interest method.

Instructions

    (a) What is the effective-interest method of amortization and how is it different from and similar to the straight-line method of amortization?

    (b) How is amortization computed using the effective-interest method, and why and how do amounts obtained using the effective-interest method differ from amounts computed under the straight-line method?

Part II: Gains or losses from the early extinguishment of debt that is refunded can theoretically be accounted for in three ways:

    1. Amortized over remaining life of old debt.

    2. Amortized over the life of the new debt issue.

    3. Recognized in the period of extinguishment.

Instructions

    (a) Develop supporting arguments for each of the three theoretical methods of accounting for gains and losses from the early extinguishment of debt.

    (b) Which of the methods above is generally accepted and how should the appropriate amount of gain or loss be shown in a company's financial statements?

(AICPA adapted)

CA14-4 (Off-Balance-Sheet Financing) Matt Ryan Corporation is interested in building its own soda can manufacturing plant adjacent to its existing plant in Partyville, Kansas. The objective would be to ensure a steady supply of cans at a stable price and to minimize transportation costs. However, the company has been experiencing some financial problems and has been reluctant to borrow any additional cash to fund the project. The company is not concerned with the cash flow problems of making payments, but rather with the impact of adding additional long-term debt to its balance sheet.

    The president of Ryan, Andy Newlin, approached the president of the Aluminum Can Company (ACC), its major supplier, to see if some agreement could be reached. ACC was anxious to work out an arrangement, since it seemed inevitable that Ryan would begin its own can production. The Aluminum Can Company could not afford to lose the account.

    After some discussion, a two-part plan was worked out. First, ACC was to construct the plant on Ryan's land adjacent to the existing plant. Second, Ryan would sign a 20-year purchase agreement. Under the purchase agreement, Ryan would express its intention to buy all of its cans from ACC, paying a unit price which at normal capacity would cover labor and material, an operating management fee, and the debt service requirements on the plant. The expected unit price, if transportation costs are taken into consideration, is lower than current market. If Ryan did not take enough production in any one year and if the excess cans could not be sold at a high enough price on the open market, Ryan agrees to make up any cash shortfall so that ACC could make the payments on its debt. The bank will be willing to make a 20-year loan for the plant, taking the plant and the purchase agreement as collateral. At the end of 20 years, the plant is to become the property of Ryan.

Instructions

    (a) What are project financing arrangements using special-purpose entities?

    (b) What are take-or-pay contracts?

    (c) Should Ryan record the plant as an asset together with the related obligation?

    (d) If not, should Ryan record an asset relating to the future commitment?

    (e) What is meant by off-balance-sheet financing?

CA14-5 (Bond Issue) Donald Lennon is the president, founder, and majority owner of Wichita Medical Corporation, an emerging medical technology products company. Wichita is in dire need of additional capital to keep operating and to bring several promising products to final development, testing, and production. Donald, as owner of 51% of the outstanding stock, manages the company's operations. He places heavy emphasis on research and development and long-term growth. The other principal stockholder is Nina Friendly who, as a nonemployee investor, owns 40% of the stock. Nina would like to deemphasize the R & D functions and emphasize the marketing function to maximize short-run sales and profits from existing products. She believes this strategy would raise the market price of Wichita's stock.

All of Donald's personal capital and borrowing power is tied up in his 51% stock ownership. He knows that any offering of additional shares of stock will dilute his controlling interest because he won't be able to participate in such an issuance. But, Nina has money and would likely buy enough shares to gain control of Wichita. She then would dictate the company's future direction, even if it meant replacing Donald as president and CEO.

The company already has considerable debt. Raising additional debt will be costly, will adversely affect Wichita's credit rating, and will increase the company's reported losses due to the growth in interest expense. Nina and the other minority stockholders express opposition to the assumption of additional debt, fearing the company will be pushed to the brink of bankruptcy. Wanting to maintain his control and to preserve the direction of "his" company, Donald is doing everything to avoid a stock issuance and is contemplating a large issuance of bonds, even if it means the bonds are issued with a high effective-interest rate.

Instructions

    (a) Who are the stakeholders in this situation?

    (b) What are the ethical issues in this case?

    (c) What would you do if you were Donald?

USING YOUR JUDGMENT

FINANCIAL REPORTING

Financial Reporting Problem

The Procter & Gamble Company (P&G)

The financial statements of **P&G** are presented in Appendix 5B. The company's complete annual report, including the notes to the financial statements, can be accessed at the book's companion website, **www.wiley.com/college/kieso**.

Instructions

Refer to P&G's 2011 financial statements and the accompanying notes to answer the following questions.

(a) What cash outflow obligations related to the repayment of long-term debt does P&G have over the next 5 years?

(b) P&G indicates that it believes that it has the ability to meet business requirements in the foreseeable future. Prepare an assessment of its liquidity, solvency, and financial flexibility using ratio analysis.

Comparative Analysis Case

The Coca-Cola Company and PepsiCo, Inc.

Instructions

Go to the book's companion website and use information found there to answer the following questions related to The Coca-Cola Company and PepsiCo, Inc.

(a) Compute the debt to assets and the times interest earned ratios for these two companies. Comment on the quality of these two ratios for both Coca-Cola and PepsiCo.

(b) What is the difference between the fair value and the historical cost (carrying amount) of each company's debt at year-end 2011? Why might a difference exist in these two amounts?

(c) Both companies have debt issued in foreign countries. Speculate as to why these companies may use foreign debt to finance their operations. What risks are involved in this strategy, and how might they adjust for this risk?

Financial Statement Analysis Case

Commonwealth Edison Co.

The following article appeared in the *Wall Street Journal*.

> **Bond Markets**
>
> *Giant Commonwealth Edison Issue Hits Resale Market With $70 Million Left Over*
>
> NEW YORK—Commonwealth Edison Co.'s slow-selling new 9¼% bonds were tossed onto the resale market at a reduced price with about $70 million still available from the $200 million offered Thursday, dealers said.
>
> The Chicago utility's bonds, rated double-A by Moody's and double-A-minus by Standard & Poor's, originally had been priced at 99.803, to yield 9.3% in 5 years. They were marked down yesterday the equivalent of about $5.50 for each $1,000 face amount, to about 99.25, where their yield jumped to 9.45%.

Instructions

(a) How will the development above affect the accounting for Commonwealth Edison's bond issue?

(b) Provide several possible explanations for the markdown and the slow sale of Commonwealth Edison's bonds.

Accounting, Analysis, and Principles

The following information is taken from the 2014 annual report of Bugant, Inc. Bugant's fiscal year ends December 31 of each year. Bugant's December 31, 2014, balance sheet is as follows.

Bugant, Inc.
Balance Sheet
December 31, 2014

Assets	
Cash	$ 450
Inventory	1,800
Total current assets	2,250
Plant and equipment	2,000
Accumulated depreciation	(160)
Total assets	$4,090
Liabilities	
Bonds payable (net of discount)	$1,426
Stockholders' equity	
Common stock	1,500
Retained earnings	1,164
Total liabilities and stockholders' equity	$4,090

Note X: Long Term Debt:
On January 1, 2015, Bugant issued bonds with face value of $1,500 and a coupon rate equal to 10%. The bonds were issued to yield 12% and mature on January 1, 2020.

Additional information concerning 2015 is as follows.

1. Sales were $3,500, all for cash.
2. Purchases were $2,000, all paid in cash.
3. Salaries were $700, all paid in cash.
4. Property, plant, and equipment was originally purchased for $2,000 and is depreciated straight-line over a 25-year life with no salvage value.
5. Ending inventory was $1,900.
6. Cash dividends of $100 were declared and paid by Bugant.
7. Ignore taxes.
8. The market rate of interest on bonds of similar risk was 12% during all of 2015.
9. Interest on the bonds is paid semiannually each June 30 and December 31.

Accounting
Prepare a balance sheet for Bugant, Inc. at December 31, 2015, and an income statement for the year ending December 31, 2015. Assume semiannual compounding of the bond interest.

Analysis
Use common ratios for analysis of long-term debt to assess Bugant's long-run solvency. Has Bugant's solvency changed much from 2014 to 2015? Bugant's net income in 2014 was $550 and interest expense was $169.

Principles
Recently, the FASB and the IASB allowed companies the option of recognizing in their financial statements the fair values of their long-term debt. That is, companies have the option to change the balance sheet value of their long-term debt to the debt's fair value and report the change in balance sheet value as a gain or loss in income. In terms of the qualitative characteristics of accounting information (Chapter 2), briefly describe the potential trade-off(s) involved in reporting long-term debt at its fair value.

BRIDGE TO THE PROFESSION

 ## Professional Research: FASB Codification

Wie Company has been operating for just 2 years, producing specialty golf equipment for women golfers. To date, the company has been able to finance its successful operations with investments from its principal owner, Michelle Wie, and cash flows from operations. However, current expansion plans will require some borrowing to expand the company's production line.

As part of the expansion plan, Wie will acquire some used equipment by signing a zero-interest-bearing note. The note has a maturity value of $50,000 and matures in 5 years. A reliable fair value measure for the equipment is not available, given the age and specialty nature of the equipment. As a result, Wie's accounting staff is unable to determine an established exchange price for recording the equipment (nor the interest rate to be used to record interest expense on the long-term note). They have asked you to conduct some accounting research on this topic.

Instructions
If your school has a subscription to the FASB Codification, go to *http://aaahq.org/ascLogin.cfm* to log in and prepare responses to the following. Provide Codification references for your responses.

(a) Identify the authoritative literature that provides guidance on the zero-interest-bearing note. Use some of the examples to explain how the standard applies in this setting.

(b) How is present value determined when an established exchange price is not determinable and a note has no ready market? What is the resulting interest rate often called?

(c) Where should a discount or premium appear in the financial statements? What about issue costs?

Additional Professional Resources
See the book's companion website, at **www.wiley.com/college/kieso**, for professional simulations as well as other study resources.

As indicated in Chapter 13, IFRS and GAAP have similar definitions of liabilities.

RELEVANT FACTS

11 LEARNING OBJECTIVE

Compare the accounting procedures for long-term liabilities under GAAP and IFRS.

Following are the key similarities and differences between GAAP and IFRS related to long-term liabilities.

Similarities

- As indicated in our earlier discussions, GAAP and IFRS have similar liability definitions, and liabilities are classified as current and non-current.
- Much of the accounting for bonds and long-term notes is the same for GAAP and IFRS.

Differences

- Under GAAP, companies are permitted to use the straight-line method of amortization for bond discount or premium, provided that the amount recorded is not materially different than that resulting from effective-interest amortization. However, the effective-interest method is preferred and is generally used. Under IFRS, companies must use the effective-interest method.
- Under IFRS, companies do not use premium or discount accounts but instead show the bond at its net amount. For example, if a $100,000 bond was issued at 97, under IFRS a company would record:

Cash	97,000	
Bonds Payable		97,000

- Under GAAP, bond issue costs are recorded as an asset. Under IFRS, bond issue costs are netted against the carrying amount of the bonds.
- GAAP uses the term *troubled-debt restructurings* and has developed specific guidelines related to that category of loans. IFRS generally assumes that all restructurings will be accounted for as extinguishments of debt.
- IFRS requires a liability and related expense or cost be recognized when a contract is onerous. Under GAAP, losses on onerous contracts are generally not recognized under GAAP unless addressed by industry or transaction-specific requirements.

ABOUT THE NUMBERS
Effective-Interest Method

As discussed earlier, by paying more or less at issuance, investors earn a rate different than the coupon rate on the bond. Recall that the issuing company pays the contractual interest rate over the term of the bonds but also must pay the face value at maturity. If the bond is issued at a discount, the amount paid at maturity is more than the issue amount. If issued at a premium, the company pays less at maturity relative to the issue price.

The company records this adjustment to the cost as **bond interest expense** over the life of the bonds through a process called **amortization. Amortization of a discount increases bond interest expense. Amortization of a premium decreases bond interest expense.**

Under IFRS, the required procedure for amortization of a discount or premium is the **effective-interest method** (also called **present value amortization**). Under the effective-interest method, companies:

1. Compute bond interest expense first by multiplying the **carrying value** (book value) of the bonds at the beginning of the period by the effective-interest rate.

2. Determine the bond discount or premium amortization next by comparing the bond interest expense with the interest (cash) to be paid.

Illustration IFRS14-1 depicts graphically the computation of the amortization.

ILLUSTRATION IFRS14-1
Bond Discount and Premium Amortization Computation

The effective-interest method produces a periodic interest expense equal to **a constant percentage of the carrying value of the bonds**. The issuance of bonds involves engraving and printing costs, legal and accounting fees, commissions, promotion costs, and other similar charges. These costs should be recorded as a reduction to the issue amount of the bond payable and then amortized into expense over the life of the bond, through an adjustment to the effective-interest rate. For example, if the face value of the bond is $100,000 and issue costs are $1,000, then the bond payable (net of the bond issue costs) is recorded at $99,000. Thus, the effective-interest rate will be higher, based on the reduced carrying value.

Bonds Issued at a Discount

To illustrate amortization of a discount under the effective-interest method, Evermaster Corporation issued $100,000 of 8 percent term bonds on January 1, 2014, due on January 1, 2019, with interest payable each July 1 and January 1. Because the investors required an effective-interest rate of 10 percent, they paid $92,278 for the $100,000 of bonds, creating a $7,722 discount. Evermaster computes the $7,722 discount as follows.

ILLUSTRATION IFRS14-2
Computation of Discount on Bonds Payable

Maturity value of bonds payable		$100,000
Present value of $100,000 due in 5 years at 10%, interest payable semiannually (Table 6-2); $FV(PVF_{10,5\%})$; ($100,000 \times .61391$)	$61,391	
Present value of $4,000 interest payable semiannually for 5 years at 10% annually (Table 6-4); $R(PVF\text{-}OA_{10,5\%})$; ($4,000 \times 7.72173$)	30,887	
Proceeds from sale of bonds		(92,278)
Discount on bonds payable		$ 7,722

The five-year amortization schedule appears in Illustration IFRS14-3.

Evermaster records the issuance of its bonds at a discount on January 1, 2014, as follows.

Cash	92,278	
Bonds Payable		92,278

It records the first interest payment on July 1, 2014, and amortization of the discount as follows.

Interest Expense	4,614	
Bonds Payable		614
Cash		4,000

SCHEDULE OF BOND DISCOUNT AMORTIZATION				
EFFECTIVE-INTEREST METHOD—SEMIANNUAL INTEREST PAYMENTS				
5-YEAR, 8% BONDS SOLD TO YIELD 10%				
Date	Cash Paid	Interest Expense	Discount Amortized	Carrying Amount of Bonds
1/1/14				$ 92,278
7/1/14	$ 4,000[a]	$ 4,614[b]	$ 614[c]	92,892[d]
1/1/15	4,000	4,645	645	93,537
7/1/15	4,000	4,677	677	94,214
1/1/16	4,000	4,711	711	94,925
7/1/16	4,000	4,746	746	95,671
1/1/17	4,000	4,783	783	96,454
7/1/17	4,000	4,823	823	97,277
1/1/18	4,000	4,864	864	98,141
7/1/18	4,000	4,907	907	99,048
1/1/19	4,000	4,952	952	100,000
	$40,000	$47,722	$7,722	

[a]$4,000 = $100,000 × .08 × 6/12
[b]$4,614 = $92,278 × .10 × 6/12
[c]$614 = $4,614 − $4,000
[d]$92,892 = $92,278 + $614

ILLUSTRATION IFRS14-3
Bond Discount Amortization Schedule

Evermaster records the interest expense accrued at December 31, 2014 (year-end), and amortization of the discount as follows.

Interest Expense	4,645	
Interest Payable		4,000
Bonds Payable		645

Extinguishment with Modification of Terms

Practically every day, the *Wall Street Journal* or the *Financial Times* runs a story about some company in financial difficulty. Notable recent examples are Nakheel, Parmalat, and General Motors. In many of these situations, the creditor may grant a borrower concessions with respect to settlement. The creditor offers these concessions to ensure the highest possible collection on the loan. For example, a creditor may offer one or a combination of the following modifications:

1. Reduction of the stated interest rate.

2. Extension of the maturity date of the face amount of the debt.

3. Reduction of the face amount of the debt.

4. Reduction or deferral of any accrued interest.

As with other extinguishments, when a creditor grants favorable concessions on the terms of a loan, the debtor has an economic gain. Thus, the accounting for debt modifications is similar to that for other extinguishments. That is, the original obligation is extinguished, the new payable is recorded at fair value, and a gain is recognized for the difference in the fair value of the new obligation and the carrying value of the old obligation. Thus, under IFRS, debt modifications are similar to troubled-debt restructurings in GAAP. In general, IFRS treats debt modifications as debt extinguishments.

An exception to the general rule is when the modification of terms is not substantial. A substantial modification is defined as one in which the discounted cash flows under the terms of the new debt (using the historical effective-interest rate) differ by at least 10 percent of the carrying value of the original debt. If a modification is not substantial, the difference (gain) is deferred and amortized over the remaining life of the debt at the historical effective-interest rate. In the case of a non-substantial modification, in essence, the new loan is a continuation of the old loan. Therefore, the debtor should record interest at the historical effective-interest rate.

ON THE HORIZON

The FASB and IASB are currently involved in two projects, each of which has implications for the accounting for liabilities. One project is investigating approaches to differentiate between debt and equity instruments. The other project, the elements phase of the conceptual framework project, will evaluate the definitions of the fundamental building blocks of accounting. The results of these projects could change the classification of many debt and equity securities.

IFRS SELF-TEST QUESTIONS

1. Under IFRS, bond issuance costs, including the printing costs and legal fees associated with the issuance, should be:
   (a) expensed in the period when the debt is issued.
   (b) recorded as a reduction in the carrying value of bonds payable.
   (c) accumulated in a deferred charge account and amortized over the life of the bonds.
   (d) reported as an expense in the period the bonds mature or are redeemed.
2. Which of the following is stated correctly?
   (a) Current liabilities follow non-current liabilities on the statement of financial position under GAAP but non-current liabilities follow current liabilities under IFRS.
   (b) IFRS does not treat debt modifications as extinguishments of debt.
   (c) Bond issuance costs are recorded as a reduction of the carrying value of the debt under GAAP but are recorded as an asset and amortized to expense over the term of the debt under IFRS.
   (d) Under GAAP, bonds payable is recorded at the face amount and any premium or discount is recorded in a separate account. Under IFRS, bonds payable is recorded at the carrying value so no separate premium or discount accounts are used.
3. All of the following are differences between IFRS and GAAP in accounting for liabilities **except:**
   (a) When a bond is issued at a discount, GAAP records the discount in a separate contra liability account. IFRS records the bond net of the discount.
   (b) Under IFRS, bond issuance costs reduce the carrying value of the debt. Under GAAP, these costs are recorded as an asset and amortized to expense over the terms of the bond.
   (c) GAAP, but not IFRS, uses the term "troubled-debt restructurings."
   (d) GAAP, but not IFRS, uses the term "provisions" for contingent liabilities which are accrued.
4. On January 1, Patterson Inc. issued $5,000,000, 9% bonds for $4,695,000. The market rate of interest for these bonds is 10%. Interest is payable annually on December 31. Patterson uses the effective-interest method of amortizing bond discount. At the end of the first year, Patterson should report bonds payable of:
   (a) $4,725,500.   (c) $258,050.
   (b) $4,714,500.   (d) $4,745,000.
5. On January 1, Martinez Inc. issued $3,000,000, 11% bonds for $3,195,000. The market rate of interest for these bonds is 10%. Interest is payable annually on December 31. Martinez uses the effective-interest method of amortizing bond premium. At the end of the first year, Martinez should report bonds payable of:
   (a) $3,185,130.   (c) $3,173,550.
   (b) $3,184,500.   (d) $3,165,000.

IFRS CONCEPTS AND APPLICATION

IFRS14-1 What is the required method of amortizing discount and premium on bonds payable? Explain the procedures.

IFRS14-2 What are the general rules for measuring and recognizing gain or loss by a debt extinguishment with modification?

IFRS14-3 On January 1, 2014, JWS Corporation issued $600,000 of 7% bonds, due in 10 years. The bonds were issued for $559,224, and pay interest each July 1 and January 1. Prepare the company's journal entries for (a) the January 1 issuance, (b) the July 1 interest payment, and (c) the December 31 adjusting entry. Assume an effective-interest rate of 8%.

IFRS14-4 Assume the bonds in IFRS14-3 were issued for $644,636 and the effective-interest rate is 6%. Prepare the company's journal entries for (a) the January 1 issuance, (b) the July 1 interest payment, and (c) the December 31 adjusting entry. (Round to the nearest dollar.)

IFRS14-5 Foreman Company issued $800,000 of 10%, 20-year bonds on January 1, 2014, at 119.792 to yield 8%. Interest is payable semiannually on July 1 and January 1. Prepare the journal entries to record (a) the issuance of the bonds, (b) the payment of interest and the related amortization on July 1, 2014, and (c) the accrual of interest and the related amortization on December 31, 2014. (Round to the nearest dollar.)

IFRS14-6 Assume the same information as in IFRS14-5, except that the bonds were issued at 84.95 to yield 12%. Prepare the journal entries to record (a) the issuance of the bonds, (b) the payment of interest and related amortization on July 1, 2014, and (c) the accrual of interest and the related amortization on December 31, 2014. (Round to the nearest dollar.)

Professional Research

IFRS14-7 Wie Company has been operating for just 2 years, producing specialty golf equipment for women golfers. To date, the company has been able to finance its successful operations with investments from its principal owner, Michelle Wie, and cash flows from operations. However, current expansion plans will require some borrowing to expand the company's production line.

As part of the expansion plan, Wie is contemplating a borrowing on a note payable or issuance of bonds. In the past, the company has had little need for external borrowing so the management team has a number of questions concerning the accounting for these new non-current liabilities. They have asked you to conduct some research on this topic.

Instructions

Access the IFRS authoritative literature at the IASB website (*http://eifrs.iasb.org/*). (Click on the IFRS tab and then register for free eIFRS access if necessary.) When you have accessed the documents, you can use the search tool in your Internet browser to respond to the following questions. (Provide paragraph citations.)

(a) With respect to a decision of issuing notes or bonds, management is aware of certain costs (e.g., printing, marketing, selling) associated with a bond issue. How will these costs affect Wie's reported earnings in the year of issue and while the bonds are outstanding?

(b) If all goes well with the plant expansion, the financial performance of Wie Company could dramatically improve. As a result, Wie's market rate of interest (which is currently around 12%) could decline. This raises the possibility of retiring or exchanging the debt, in order to get a lower borrowing rate. How would such a debt extinguishment be accounted for?

International Financial Reporting Problem
Marks and Spencer plc

IFRS14-8 The financial statements of Marks and Spencer plc (M&S) are available at the book's companion website or can be accessed at *http://annualreport.marksandspencer.com/_assets/downloads/Marks-and-Spencer-Annual-report-and-financial-statements-2012.pdf*.

Instructions

Refer to M&S's financial statements and the accompanying notes to answer the following questions.

(a) What cash outflow obligations related to the repayment of long-term debt does M&S have over the next 5 years?

(b) M&S indicates that it believes that it has the ability to meet business requirements in the foreseeable future. Prepare an assessment of its liquidity, solvency, and financial flexibility using ratio analysis.

ANSWERS TO IFRS SELF-TEST QUESTIONS

1. b **2.** d **3.** d **4.** b **5.** b

> Remember to check the book's companion website to find additional resources for this chapter.

15 Stockholders' Equity

After studying this chapter, you should be able to:

1 Discuss the characteristics of the corporate form of organization.

2 Identify the key components of stockholders' equity.

3 Explain the accounting procedures for issuing shares of stock.

4 Describe the accounting for treasury stock.

5 Explain the accounting for and reporting of preferred stock.

6 Describe the policies used in distributing dividends.

7 Identify the various forms of dividend distributions.

8 Explain the accounting for small and large stock dividends, and for stock splits.

9 Indicate how to present and analyze stockholders' equity.

It's a Global Market

As mentioned in prior chapters, we are moving rapidly toward one set of global financial reporting standards and one "common language" for financial information. This change will probably lead to more consolidation of our capital markets. To understand how quickly the global financial world is changing, let's examine a few trends occurring on stock exchanges around the world.

In 2007, the New York Stock Exchange (NYSE) merged with Paris-based Euronext, creating the world's first transatlantic stock exchange. **NYSE Euronext** is the world's largest exchange group, now with 8,000 listed issuers representing over 40 percent of global equity trading in 2010. Similarly, NASDAQ, the world's largest electronic stock market, merged with OMX, the Nordic stock market operator. This electronic exchange operates in 29 countries, on six continents, and has over 4,000 listed issuers, with a market value of approximately $5.5 trillion. (Further exchange consolidation may be in the offing, with **IntercontinentalExchange** and international exchanges in Asia exploring mergers with NYSE Euronext.)

Another reason behind the movement to international financial reporting standards can be found in recent initial public offerings (IPOs). The emerging markets are driving the global IPO market. As shown in the following table, Greater China is at the top in IPO volume, with Poland, Korea, and India also in the top 10.

2011 Global IPOs by Domicile Country—Top 10 by Number of Deals		
Country	**Number of Deals**	**% of Global Total**
Greater China*	388	31.70%
Poland	137	11.20
United States	108	8.80
Australia	98	8.00
South Korea	69	5.60
Canada	64	5.20
India	40	3.30
Japan	37	3.00
United Kingdom	28	2.30
Indonesia	26	2.10
Rest of world** (52 countries)	230	18.80
Total	1,225	100.00%

Source: Based on the listed company domicile.
*Includes Mainland China, Hong Kong, and Taiwan.
**Includes countries with 1% or less of IPO activity by number of deals or capital raised.

Finally, globalization has also been an enormous boon for some of the biggest names in corporate America, along with investors who own the stocks in those companies. As shown in the following table, these 10 large U.S. companies—often called "multinationals" for good reason—have increasingly followed globalization of markets.

Company	Total Revenues	% of Revenues Overseas
Intel	$ 44	85
Dow	54	67
McDonald's	24	66
IBM	100	64
General Electric	149	54
Ford	129	51
Nike	21	50
Wal-Mart	420	45
ExxonMobil	342	45
Amazon.com	34	45

As indicated, **Intel** has 85 percent of its sales overseas, **McDonald's** in a recent year sold more hamburgers overseas than in the United States, and **Ford Motor Company**'s sales would be much less except for success in the European market. Overall, about 40 percent of profit for firms listed in the S&P 500 stock index are now coming in from overseas sales. Foreign exposure allows U.S.-based companies to capitalize on rapid growth in emerging markets like China, India, and Latin America, and earn much stronger profits than if they were totally dependent on the struggling U.S. economy. As one analyst noted, "[Returns for companies] . . . in the S&P 500 continue to outgrow the U.S. economy. Earnings power is decoupled from U.S. GDP."

Sources: Ernst and Young, *Growth During Economic Uncertainty: Global IPO Trends Report* (2012); *www. euronext.com;* and R. Newman, "Why U.S. Companies Aren't So American Anymore," *http://money.usnews.com* (June 30, 2011).

PREVIEW OF CHAPTER **15**

As our opening story indicates, the growth of global equity capital markets indicates that investors around the world need useful information. In this chapter, we explain the accounting issues related to the stockholders' equity of a corporation. The content and organization of the chapter are as follows.

Stockholders' Equity

The Corporate Form	Corporate Capital	Preferred Stock	Dividend Policy	Presentation and Analysis
• State corporate law • Capital stock or share system • Variety of ownership interests	• Issuance of stock • Reacquisition of shares	• Features • Accounting for and reporting preferred stock	• Financial condition and dividend distributions • Types of dividends • Stock dividends and stock splits • Disclosure of restrictions	• Presentation • Analysis

THE CORPORATE FORM OF ORGANIZATION

LEARNING OBJECTIVE 1

Discuss the characteristics of the corporate form of organization.

Of the three **primary forms of business organization**—the proprietorship, the partnership, and the corporation—the corporate form dominates. The corporation is by far the leader in terms of the aggregate amount of resources controlled, goods and services produced, and people employed. All of the "Fortune 500" largest industrial firms are corporations. Although the corporate form has a number of advantages (as well as disadvantages) over the other two forms, its principal advantage is its facility for attracting and accumulating large amounts of capital.

The special characteristics of the corporate form that affect accounting include:

1. Influence of state corporate law.
2. Use of the capital stock or share system.
3. Development of a variety of ownership interests.

State Corporate Law

Anyone who wishes to establish a corporation must submit **articles of incorporation** to the state in which incorporation is desired. After fulfilling requirements, the state issues a corporation charter, thereby recognizing the company as a legal entity subject to state law. Regardless of the number of states in which a corporation has operating divisions, it is incorporated in only one state.

It is to the company's advantage to incorporate in a state whose laws favor the corporate form of business organization. For example, consider that nearly half of all public corporations in the United States are incorporated in Delaware. Why Delaware? The state has a favorable tax and regulatory environment, resulting in Delaware being home to more corporations—public and private—than people.[1]

Each state has its own business incorporation act. The accounting for stockholders' equity follows the provisions of these acts. In many cases, states have adopted the principles contained in the Model Business Corporate Act prepared by the American Bar Association. State laws are complex and vary both in their provisions and in their definitions of certain terms. Some laws fail to define technical terms. As a result, terms often mean one thing in one state and another thing in a different state. These problems may be further compounded because legal authorities often interpret the effects and restrictions of the laws differently.

What do the numbers mean? 1209 NORTH ORANGE STREET

Nothing about 1209 North Orange Street hints at the secrets inside. It's a humdrum office building, a low-slung affair with a faded awning and a view of a parking garage. Hardly worth a second glance, if even a first one. But behind its doors is one of the most remarkable corporate collections in the world: 1209 North Orange, you see, is the legal address of no fewer than 285,000 separate businesses.

Its occupants, on paper, include giants like American Airlines, Apple, Bank of America, Berkshire Hathaway, Cargill, Coca-Cola, Ford, General Electric, Google, JPMorgan Chase, and Wal-Mart. These companies do business across the nation and around the world. Here at 1209 North Orange, they simply have a dropbox.

What brings these marquee names to 1209 North Orange, and to other Delaware addresses, also attracts less-upstanding corporate citizens. For instance, 1209 North Orange was, until recently, a business address of Timothy S. Durham, known as "the Midwest Madoff." On June 20, Durham was found guilty of bilking 5,000 mostly middle-class and elderly investors out of $207 million. It was also an address of Stanko Subotic, a Serbian businessman and convicted smuggler—just one of many Eastern Europeans drawn to the state.

Big corporations, small-time businesses, rogues, scoundrels, and worse—all have turned up at Delaware addresses in hopes of minimizing taxes, skirting regulations, plying friendly courts, or, when needed, covering their tracks.

[1]L. Wayne, "How Delaware Thrives as a Corporate Tax Haven," *The New York Times* (June 30, 2012).

Federal authorities worry that, in addition to the legitimate businesses flocking here, drug-traffickers, embezzlers, and money-launderers are increasingly heading to Delaware, too. It's easy to set up shell companies here, no questions asked.

Of course, business—the legal kind—has been the mainstay of Delaware since 1792, when the state established its Court of Chancery to handle business affairs. By the early 20th century, the state was writing friendly corporate and tax laws to lure companies from New York, New Jersey, and elsewhere. Today, Delaware regularly tops lists of domestic and foreign tax havens because it allows companies to lower their taxes in another state—for instance, the state in which they actually do business or have their headquarters—by shifting royalties and similar revenues to holding companies in Delaware, where they are not taxed. In tax circles, the arrangement is known as "the Delaware loophole." Over the last decade, the Delaware loophole has enabled corporations to reduce the taxes paid to other states by an estimated $9.5 billion.

Source: L. Wayne, "How Delaware Thrives as a Corporate Tax Haven," *The New York Times* (June 30, 2012).

Capital Stock or Share System

Stockholders' equity in a corporation generally consists of a large number of units or shares. Within a given class of stock, each share exactly equals every other share. The number of shares possessed determines each owner's interest. If a company has one class of stock divided into 1,000 shares, a person who owns 500 shares controls one-half of the ownership interest. One holding 10 shares has a one-hundredth interest.

Each share of stock has certain rights and privileges. Only by special contract can a company restrict these rights and privileges at the time it issues the shares. Owners must examine the articles of incorporation, stock certificates, and the provisions of the state law to ascertain such restrictions on or variations from the standard rights and privileges. In the absence of restrictive provisions, each share carries the following rights:

1. To share proportionately in profits and losses.

2. To share proportionately in management (the right to vote for directors).

3. To share proportionately in corporate assets upon liquidation.

4. To share proportionately in any new issues of stock of the same class—called the **preemptive right**.[2]

International Perspective

> In the United States, stockholders are treated equally as far as access to financial information. That is not always the case in other countries. For example, in Mexico, foreign investors as well as minority investors often have difficulty obtaining financial data. These restrictions are rooted in the habits of companies that, for many years, were tightly controlled by a few stockholders and managers.

The first three rights are self-explanatory. The last right is used to protect each stockholder's proportional interest in the company. **The preemptive right protects an existing stockholder from involuntary dilution of ownership interest.** Without this right, stockholders might find their interest reduced by the issuance of additional stock without their knowledge and at prices unfavorable to them. However, many corporations have eliminated the preemptive right. Why? Because this right makes it inconvenient for corporations to issue large amounts of additional stock, as they frequently do in acquiring other companies.

The share system easily allows one individual to transfer an interest in a company to another investor. For example, individuals owning shares in Google **may sell them to others at any time and at any price without obtaining the consent of the company or other stockholders**. Each share is personal property of the owner, who may dispose of it at will. Google simply maintains a list or subsidiary ledger of stockholders as a guide to dividend payments, issuance of stock rights, voting proxies, and the like. Because owners freely and frequently transfer shares, Google must revise the subsidiary

---

[2]This privilege is referred to as a **stock right** or **warrant**. The warrants issued in these situations are of short duration, unlike the warrants issued with other securities.

ledger of stockholders periodically, generally in advance of every dividend payment or stockholders' meeting.

In addition, the major stock exchanges require ownership controls that the typical corporation finds uneconomic to provide. Thus, corporations often use **registrars and transfer agents** who specialize in providing services for recording and transferring stock. The Uniform Stock Transfer Act and the Uniform Commercial Code govern the negotiability of stock certificates.

Variety of Ownership Interests

In every corporation, one class of stock must represent the basic ownership interest. That class is called common stock. **Common stock** is the residual corporate interest that bears the ultimate risks of loss and receives the benefits of success. Common stockholders are not guaranteed dividends or assets upon dissolution. But common stockholders generally control the management of the corporation and tend to profit most if the company is successful. In the event that a corporation has only one authorized issue of capital stock, that issue is by definition common stock, whether so designated in the charter or not.

International Perspective

The U.S. and British systems of corporate governance and finance depend to a large extent on equity financing and the widely dispersed ownership of shares traded in highly liquid markets. The German and Japanese systems have relied more on debt financing, interlocking stock ownership, and banker/director and worker/shareholder rights.

In an effort to broaden investor appeal, corporations may offer two or more classes of stock, each with different rights or privileges. As indicated in the preceding section, each share of stock of a given issue has the same four inherent rights as other shares of the same issue. By special stock contracts between the corporation and its stockholders, however, the stockholder may sacrifice certain of these rights in return for other special rights or privileges. Thus, special classes of stock, usually called **preferred stock**, are created. In return for any special preference, the preferred stockholder always sacrifices some of the inherent rights of common stock ownership.

A common type of preference is to give the preferred stockholders a prior claim on earnings. The corporation thus assures them a dividend, usually at a stated rate, before it distributes any amount to the common stockholders. In return for this preference, the preferred stockholders may sacrifice their right to a voice in management or their right to share in profits beyond the stated rate.

CORPORATE CAPITAL

LEARNING OBJECTIVE
Identify the key components of stockholders' equity.

Owners' equity in a corporation is defined as stockholders' equity, shareholders' equity, or corporate capital. The following three categories normally appear as part of stockholders' equity:

1. Capital stock.
2. Additional paid-in capital.
3. Retained earnings.

The first two categories, capital stock and additional paid-in capital, constitute contributed (paid-in) capital. **Retained earnings** represents the earned capital of the company. **Contributed (paid-in) capital** is the total amount paid in on capital stock—the amount provided by stockholders to the corporation for use in the business. Contributed capital includes items such as the par value of all outstanding stock and premiums less discounts on issuance. **Earned capital** is the capital that develops from profitable operations. It consists of all undistributed income that remains invested in the company.

Stockholders' equity is the difference between the assets and the liabilities of the company. That is, the owners' or stockholders' interest in a company like **The Walt Disney Company** is a **residual interest.**[3] **Stockholders' (owners') equity** represents the cumulative net contributions by stockholders plus retained earnings. As a residual interest, stockholders' equity has no existence apart from the assets and liabilities of Disney—stockholders' equity equals net assets. Stockholders' equity is not a claim to specific assets but a claim against a portion of the total assets. Its amount is not specified or fixed; it depends on Disney's profitability. Stockholders' equity grows if the company is profitable. It shrinks, or may disappear entirely, if Disney loses money.

Issuance of Stock

In issuing stock, companies follow these procedures. First, the state must authorize the stock, generally in a certificate of incorporation or charter. Next, the corporation offers shares for sale, entering into contracts to sell stock. Then, after receiving amounts for the stock, the corporation issues shares. The corporation generally makes no entry in the general ledger accounts when it receives its stock authorization from the state of incorporation.

3 LEARNING OBJECTIVE
Explain the accounting procedures for issuing shares of stock.

We discuss the accounting problems involved in the issuance of stock under the following topics.

1. Accounting for par value stock.
2. Accounting for no-par stock.
3. Accounting for stock issued in combination with other securities (lump-sum sales).
4. Accounting for stock issued in noncash transactions.
5. Accounting for costs of issuing stock.

Par Value Stock

The par value of a stock has no relationship to its fair value. At present, the par value associated with most capital stock issuances is very low. For example, **PepsiCo**'s par value is $1\frac{2}{3}$¢, **Kellogg**'s is $0.25, and **Hershey**'s is $1. Such values contrast dramatically with the situation in the early 1900s, when practically all stock issued had a par value of $100. Low par values help companies avoid the contingent liability associated with stock sold below par.[4]

To show the required information for issuance of par value stock, corporations maintain accounts for each class of stock as follows.

1. *Preferred Stock or Common Stock.* Together, these two stock accounts reflect the par value of the corporation's issued shares. The company credits these accounts when it originally issues the shares. It makes no additional entries in these accounts unless it issues additional shares or retires them.

2. *Paid-in Capital in Excess of Par (also called *Additional Paid-in Capital*).* The **Paid-in Capital in Excess of Par** account indicates any excess over par value paid in by stockholders in return for the shares issued to them. Once paid in, the excess over par becomes a part of the corporation's additional paid-in capital. The individual stockholder has no greater claim on the excess paid in than all other holders of the same class of shares.

[3]"Elements of Financial Statements," *Statement of Financial Accounting Concepts No. 6* (Stamford, Conn.: FASB, 1985), par. 60.

[4]Companies rarely, if ever, issue stock at a value below par value. If issuing stock below par, the company records the discount as a debit to Additional Paid-in Capital. In addition, the corporation may call on the original purchaser or the current holder of the shares issued below par to pay in the amount of the discount to prevent creditors from sustaining a loss upon liquidation of the corporation.

No-Par Stock

Many states permit the issuance of capital stock without par value, called **no-par stock**. The reasons for issuance of no-par stock are twofold. First, issuance of no-par stock **avoids the contingent liability** (see footnote 4) that might occur if the corporation issued par value stock at a discount. Second, some confusion exists over the relationship (or rather the absence of a relationship) between the par value and fair value. If shares have no-par value, **the questionable treatment of using par value as a basis for fair value never arises**. This is particularly advantageous whenever issuing stock for property items such as intangible or tangible fixed assets.

A major disadvantage of no-par stock is that some states levy a high tax on these issues. In addition, in some states the total issue price for no-par stock may be considered legal capital, which could reduce the flexibility in paying dividends.

Corporations sell no-par shares, like par value shares, for whatever price they will bring. However, unlike par value shares, corporations issue them without a premium or a discount. The exact amount received represents the credit to common or preferred stock. For example, Video Electronics Corporation is organized with authorized common stock of 10,000 shares without par value. Video Electronics makes only a memorandum entry for the authorization, inasmuch as no amount is involved. If Video Electronics then issues 500 shares for cash at $10 per share, it makes the following entry.

Cash	5,000	
Common Stock (no-par value)		5,000

If it issues another 500 shares for $11 per share, Video Electronics makes this entry:

Cash	5,500	
Common Stock (no-par value)		5,500

True no-par stock should be carried in the accounts at issue price without any additional paid-in capital or discount reported. But some states require that no-par stock have a stated value. The stated value is a minimum value below which a company cannot issue it. Thus, instead of being no-par stock, such stated-value stock becomes, in effect, stock with a very low par value. It thus is open to all the criticism and abuses that first encouraged the development of no-par stock.[5]

If no-par stock has a stated value of $5 per share but sells for $11, all such amounts in excess of $5 are recorded as additional paid-in capital, which in many states is fully or partially available for dividends. Thus, no-par value stock with a low stated value permits a new corporation to commence its operations with additional paid-in capital that may exceed its stated capital. For example, if a company issued 1,000 of the shares with a $5 stated value at $15 per share for cash, it makes the following entry.

Cash	15,000	
Common Stock		5,000
Paid-in Capital in Excess of Stated Value—Common Stock		10,000

Most corporations account for no-par stock with a stated value as if it were par value stock with par equal to the stated value.

Stock Issued with Other Securities (Lump-Sum Sales)

Generally, corporations sell classes of stock separately from one another. The reason to do so is to track the proceeds relative to each class, as well as relative to each lot. Occasionally, a corporation issues two or more classes of securities for a single payment

---

[5]*Accounting Trends and Techniques—2012* indicates that its 500 surveyed companies reported 461 issues of outstanding common stock, 453 par value issues, and 40 no-par issues; 3 of the no-par issues were shown at their stated (assigned) values.

or lump sum (e.g., in the acquisition of another company). The accounting problem in such lump-sum sales is how to allocate the proceeds among the several classes of securities. Companies use one of two methods of allocation: (1) the proportional method and (2) the incremental method.

Proportional Method. If the fair value or other sound basis for determining relative value is available for each class of security, **the company allocates the lump sum received among the classes of securities on a proportional basis**. For instance, assume a company issues 1,000 shares of $10 stated value common stock having a market price of $20 a share, and 1,000 shares of $10 par value preferred stock having a market price of $12 a share, for a lump sum of $30,000. Illustration 15-1 shows how the company allocates the $30,000 to the two classes of stock.

Fair value of common (1,000 × $20) =	$20,000
Fair value of preferred (1,000 × $12) =	12,000
Aggregate fair value	$32,000
Allocated to common: $\dfrac{\$20,000}{\$32,000} \times \$30,000 = \$18,750$	
Allocated to preferred: $\dfrac{\$12,000}{\$32,000} \times \$30,000 = \$11,250$	
Total allocation	$30,000

ILLUSTRATION 15-1
Allocation in Lump-Sum Securities Issuance— Proportional Method

Incremental Method. In instances where a company cannot determine the fair value of all classes of securities, it may use the incremental method. It uses the fair value of the securities as a basis for those classes that it knows, and allocates the remainder of the lump sum to the class for which it does not know the fair value. For instance, if a company issues 1,000 shares of $10 stated value common stock having a fair value of $20, and 1,000 shares of $10 par value preferred stock having no established fair value, for a lump sum of $30,000, it allocates the $30,000 to the two classes as shown in Illustration 15-2.

Lump-sum receipt	$30,000
Allocated to common (1,000 × $20)	(20,000)
Balance allocated to preferred	$10,000

ILLUSTRATION 15-2
Allocation in Lump-Sum Securities Issuance— Incremental Method

If a company cannot determine fair value for any of the classes of stock involved in a lump-sum exchange, it may need to use other approaches. It may rely on an expert's appraisal. Or, if the company knows that one or more of the classes of securities issued will have a determinable fair value in the near future, it may use a best estimate basis with the intent to adjust later, upon establishment of the future fair value.

Stock Issued in Noncash Transactions

Accounting for the issuance of shares of stock for property or services involves an issue of valuation. **The general rule is: Companies should record stock issued for services or property other than cash at either the fair value of the stock issued or the fair value of the noncash consideration received, whichever is more clearly determinable.**

If a company can readily determine both, and the transaction results from an arm's-length exchange, there will probably be little difference in their fair values. In such cases, the basis for valuing the exchange should not matter.

If a company cannot readily determine either the fair value of the stock it issues or the property or services it receives, it should employ an appropriate valuation technique.

Depending on available data, the valuation may be based on market transactions involving comparable assets or the use of discounted expected future cash flows. Companies should avoid the use of the book, par, or stated values as a basis of valuation for these transactions.

A company may exchange unissued stock or treasury stock (issued shares that it has reacquired but not retired) for property or services. If it uses treasury shares, the cost of the treasury shares **should not** be considered the decisive factor in establishing the fair value of the property or services. Instead, it should use the fair value of the treasury stock, if known, to value the property or services. Otherwise, if it does not know the fair value of the treasury stock, it should use the fair value of the property or services received, if determinable.

The following series of transactions illustrates the procedure for recording the issuance of 10,000 shares of $10 par value common stock for a patent for Marlowe Company, in various circumstances.

1. Marlowe cannot readily determine the fair value of the patent, but it knows the fair value of the stock is $140,000.

Patents	140,000	
Common Stock (10,000 shares × $10 per share)		100,000
Paid-in Capital in Excess of Par—Common Stock		40,000

2. Marlowe cannot readily determine the fair value of the stock, but it determines the fair value of the patent is $150,000.

Patents	150,000	
Common Stock (10,000 shares × $10 per share)		100,000
Paid-in Capital in Excess of Par—Common Stock		50,000

3. Marlowe cannot readily determine the fair value of the stock nor the fair value of the patent. An independent consultant values the patent at $125,000 based on discounted expected cash flows.

Patents	125,000	
Common Stock (10,000 shares × $10 share)		100,000
Paid-in Capital in Excess of Par—Common Stock		25,000

In corporate law, the board of directors has the power to set the value of noncash transactions. However, boards sometimes abuse this power. The issuance of stock for property or services has resulted in cases of overstated corporate capital through intentional overvaluation of the property or services received. The overvaluation of the stockholders' equity resulting from inflated asset values creates **watered stock**. The corporation should eliminate the "water" by simply writing down the overvalued assets.

If, as a result of the issuance of stock for property or services, a corporation undervalues the recorded assets, it creates **secret reserves**. An understated corporate structure (secret reserve) may also result from other methods: excessive depreciation or amortization charges, expensing capital expenditures, excessive write-downs of inventories or receivables, or any other understatement of assets or overstatement of liabilities. An example of a liability overstatement is an excessive provision for estimated product warranties that ultimately results in an understatement of owners' equity, thereby creating a secret reserve.

Costs of Issuing Stock

When a company like Walgreens issues common stock, it should report direct costs incurred to sell stock, such as underwriting costs, accounting and legal fees, printing costs, and taxes, as a reduction of the amounts paid in. Walgreens therefore debits issue costs to Paid-in Capital in Excess of Par—Common Stock because they are unrelated to corporate operations. In effect, **issue costs are a cost of financing**. As such, issue costs should reduce the proceeds received from the sale of the stock.

Walgreens should expense management salaries and other indirect costs related to the stock issue because it is difficult to establish a relationship between these costs and the sale proceeds. In addition, Walgreens expenses recurring costs, primarily registrar and transfer agents' fees, as incurred.

What do the numbers mean?   THE CASE OF THE DISAPPEARING RECEIVABLE

Sometimes companies issue stock but may not receive cash in return. As a result, a company records a receivable.

Controversy existed regarding the presentation of this receivable on the balance sheet. Some argued that the company should report the receivable as an asset similar to other receivables. Others argued that the company should report the receivable as a deduction from stockholders' equity (similar to the treatment of treasury stock). The SEC settled this issue: It requires companies to use the contra equity approach because the risk of collection in this type of transaction is often very high.

This accounting issue surfaced in Enron's accounting. Starting in early 2000, Enron issued shares of its common stock to four "special-purpose entities" in exchange for

which it received a note receivable. Enron then increased its assets (by recording a receivable) and stockholders' equity, a move the company now calls an accounting error. As a result of this accounting treatment, Enron overstated assets and stockholders' equity by $172 million in its 2000 audited financial statements and by $828 million in its unaudited 2001 statements. This $1 billion overstatement was 8.5 percent of Enron's previously reported stockholders' equity at that time.

As Lynn Turner, former chief accountant of the SEC, noted, "It is a basic accounting principle that you don't record equity until you get cash, and a note doesn't count as cash." Situations like this led investors, creditors, and suppliers to lose faith in the credibility of Enron, which eventually caused its bankruptcy.

Source: Adapted from Jonathan Weil, "Basic Accounting Tripped Up Enron—Financial Statements Didn't Add Up—Auditors Overlook a Simple Rule," *Wall Street Journal* (November 11, 2001), p. C1.

Reacquisition of Shares

Companies often buy back their own shares. In fact, share buybacks now exceed dividends as a form of distribution to stockholders. For example, oil producer **ConocoPhillips**, healthcare–products giant **Johnson & Johnson**, and discount retailer **Wal-Mart Stores** have ambitious buyback plans. As shown in Illustration 15-3, companies in the S&P 500 are on track to buy back more than $429 billion of their own shares in 2012.[6]

4 LEARNING OBJECTIVE
Describe the accounting for treasury stock.

ILLUSTRATION 15-3
Share Buybacks in 2012

Corporations purchase their outstanding stock for several reasons:

1. *To provide tax-efficient distributions of excess cash to shareholders.* Capital gain rates on sales of stock to the company by the stockholders have been approximately half the ordinary tax rate for many investors. This advantage has been somewhat diminished by recent changes in the tax law related to dividends.

[6]T. Lauricella, "Post-Rally Risks in U.S. Stocks," *Wall Street Journal* (October 1, 2012), p. C11.

2. *To increase earnings per share and return on equity.* Reducing both shares outstanding and stockholders' equity often enhances certain performance ratios. However, strategies to hype performance measures might increase performance in the short-run, but these tactics add no real long-term value.

3. *To provide stock for employee stock compensation contracts or to meet potential merger needs.* Honeywell Inc. reported that it would use part of its purchase of one million common shares for employee stock option contracts. Other companies acquire shares to have them available for business acquisitions.

4. *To thwart takeover attempts or to reduce the number of stockholders.* By reducing the number of shares held by the public, existing owners and managements bar "outsiders" from gaining control or significant influence. When Ted Turner attempted to acquire CBS, CBS started a substantial buyback of its stock. Companies may also use stock purchases to eliminate dissident stockholders.

5. *To make a market in the stock.* As one company executive noted, "Our company is trying to establish a floor for the stock." Purchasing stock in the marketplace creates a demand. This may stabilize the stock price or, in fact, increase it.

Some publicly held corporations have chosen to "go private," that is, to eliminate public (outside) ownership entirely by purchasing all of their outstanding stock. Companies often accomplish such a procedure through a **leveraged buyout (LBO)**, in which the company borrows money to finance the stock repurchases.

> ### 🔍 Underlying Concepts
>
> As we indicated in Chapter 2, an asset should have probable future economic benefits. Treasury stock simply reduces common stock outstanding.

After reacquiring shares, a company may either retire them or hold them in the treasury for reissue. If not retired, such shares are referred to as **treasury stock (treasury shares)**. Technically, treasury stock is a corporation's own stock, reacquired after having been issued and fully paid.

Treasury stock is not an asset. When a company purchases treasury stock, a reduction occurs in both assets and stockholders' equity. It is inappropriate to imply that a corporation can own a part of itself. A corporation may sell treasury stock to obtain funds, but that does not make treasury stock a balance sheet asset. When a corporation buys back some of its own outstanding stock, it has not acquired an asset; it reduces net assets.

The possession of treasury stock does not give the corporation the right to vote, to exercise preemptive rights as a stockholder, to receive cash dividends, or to receive assets upon corporate liquidation. **Treasury stock is essentially the same as unissued capital stock.** No one advocates classifying unissued capital stock as an asset in the balance sheet.[7]

| *What do the numbers mean?* | BUYBACKS—GOOD OR BAD? |

As indicated in Illustration 15-3, companies have ramped up repurchases of their own stock. Notable buyback companies are ExxonMobil, which recently bought back $5 billion of its stock during that period, and ConocoPhillips, which repurchased $3.1 billion of its shares. The surge in repurchases came as the prices of shares in the S&P 500 dropped 3.3 percent, meaning that companies bought more shares during a period when the market was falling. That is a far cry from some previous surges in buybacks, such as the one in the fourth quarter of 2007, when companies repurchased a record

---

[7]The possible justification for classifying these shares as assets is that the company will use them to liquidate a specific liability that appears on the balance sheet. *Accounting Trends and Techniques—2012* reported that out of 500 companies surveyed, 341 disclosed treasury stock, but none classified it as an asset.

dollar amount of shares even as the stock market was peaking.

Is this good or bad news for investors? Maybe neither. While it might appear that companies are getting better at timing their purchases (when prices are falling), they also buy shares for reasons that go beyond giving a boost to shareholders—everything from mergers and acquisitions to eliminating the impact of equity compensation. And unlike dividend payments, buybacks haven't been shown to make investors better off in the long run. For example, from 2004, when companies first were required to disclose monthly share repurchases, through the end of 2011, 31 percent of S&P 500 companies have seen the value of those shares fall and just 36 percent have returned more than 7 percent. As one analyst notes, "It's important to look at what a company is paying relative to what its shares are worth. If they overpay, wealth is being transferred to the sellers."

The conventional wisdom is that companies which buy back shares believe their shares are undervalued. Thus, analysts view the buyback announcement as an important piece of inside information about future company prospects. On the other hand, buybacks can actually hurt businesses and

their shareholders over the long run. For example, drug-makers Merck, Pfizer, and Amgen spent heavily on stock repurchases, possibly at the expense of research and development. And whether the buyback is a good thing appears to depend a lot on why the company did the buyback and what the repurchased shares were used for.

One study found that companies often increased their buybacks when earnings growth slowed. This allowed the companies to prop up earnings per share (based on fewer shares outstanding). Furthermore, many buybacks do not actually result in a net reduction in shares outstanding. For example, companies such as Microsoft and Broadcom bought back shares to meet share demands for stock option exercises, resulting in higher net shares outstanding when they reissued the repurchased shares to the option holders upon exercise. In this case, the buyback actually indicated a further dilution in the share ownership in the buyback company.

This does not mean you should never trust a buyback signal. But if the buyback is intended to manage the company's earnings or if the buyback results in dilution, take a closer look.

Sources: Adapted from W. Lazonick, "The Buyback Boondoggle," *BusinessWeek* (August 24, 2009); and B. Levisohn, "Beware All Those Buybacks," *Wall Street Journal* (September 29–30, 2012), p. B9.

Purchase of Treasury Stock

Companies use two general methods of handling treasury stock in the accounts: the cost method and the par value method. Both methods are generally acceptable. The cost method enjoys more widespread use.[8]

Gateway to the Profession

Discussion of Using Par or Stated Value for Treasury Stock Transactions

- The **cost method** results in debiting the Treasury Stock account for the reacquisition cost and in reporting this account as a deduction from the total paid-in capital **and** retained earnings on the balance sheet.

- The **par (stated) value method** records all transactions in treasury shares at their par value and reports the treasury stock as a deduction from capital stock only.

No matter which method a company uses, most states consider the cost of the treasury shares acquired as a restriction on retained earnings.

Companies generally use the cost method to account for treasury stock. This method derives its name from the fact that a company maintains the Treasury Stock account at the cost of the shares purchased.[9] Under the cost method, the company debits the Treasury Stock account for the cost of the shares acquired. Upon reissuance of the shares, it credits the account for this same cost. The original price received for the stock does not affect the entries to record the acquisition and reissuance of the treasury stock.

To illustrate, assume that Pacific Company issued 100,000 shares of $1 par value common stock at a price of $10 per share. In addition, it has retained earnings of $300,000.

---

[8]*Accounting Trends and Techniques—2012* indicates that of its selected list of 500 companies, of the 341 companies with treasury stock, all carried common stock in treasury at cost. Only one company carried preferred stock in treasury.

[9]If making numerous acquisitions of blocks of treasury shares at different prices, a company may use inventory costing methods—such as specific identification, average-cost, or FIFO—to identify the cost at date of reissuance.

Illustration 15-4 shows the stockholders' equity section on December 31, 2013, before purchase of treasury stock.

ILLUSTRATION 15-4
Stockholders' Equity
with No Treasury Stock

Stockholders' equity		
Paid-in capital		
Common stock, $1 par value, 100,000 shares		
issued and outstanding		$ 100,000
Additional paid-in capital		900,000
Total paid-in capital		1,000,000
Retained earnings		300,000
Total stockholders' equity		$1,300,000

On January 20, 2014, Pacific acquires 10,000 shares of its stock at $11 per share. Pacific records the reacquisition as follows.

January 20, 2014

Treasury Stock	110,000	
Cash		110,000

Note that Pacific debited Treasury Stock for the cost of the shares purchased. The original paid-in capital account, Common Stock, is not affected because the number of issued shares does not change. The same is true for the Paid-in Capital in Excess of Par—Common Stock account. Pacific deducts treasury stock from total paid-in capital and retained earnings in the stockholders' equity section.

Illustration 15-5 shows the stockholders' equity section for Pacific after purchase of the treasury stock.

ILLUSTRATION 15-5
Stockholders' Equity
with Treasury Stock

Stockholders' equity		
Paid-in capital		
Common stock, $1 par value, 100,000 shares		
issued and 90,000 outstanding		$ 100,000
Additional paid-in capital		900,000
Total paid-in capital		1,000,000
Retained earnings		300,000
Total paid-in capital and retained earnings		1,300,000
Less: Cost of treasury stock (10,000 shares)		110,000
Total stockholders' equity		$1,190,000

Pacific subtracts the cost of the treasury stock from the total of common stock, additional paid-in capital, and retained earnings. It therefore reduces stockholders' equity. Many states require a corporation to restrict retained earnings for the cost of treasury stock purchased. The restriction keeps intact the corporation's legal capital that it temporarily holds as treasury stock. When the corporation sells the treasury stock, it lifts the restriction.

Pacific discloses both the number of shares issued (100,000) and the number in the treasury (10,000). The difference is the number of shares of stock outstanding (90,000). The term **outstanding stock** means the number of shares of issued stock that stockholders own.

Sale of Treasury Stock

Companies usually reissue or retire treasury stock. When selling treasury shares, the accounting for the sale depends on the price. If the selling price of the treasury stock equals its cost, the company records the sale of the shares by debiting Cash and crediting

Treasury Stock. In cases where the selling price of the treasury stock is not equal to cost, then accounting for treasury stock sold **above cost** differs from the accounting for treasury stock sold **below cost**. However, the sale of treasury stock either above or below cost increases both total assets and stockholders' equity.

Sale of Treasury Stock above Cost. When the selling price of shares of treasury stock exceeds its cost, a company credits the difference to Paid-in Capital from Treasury Stock. To illustrate, assume that Pacific acquired 10,000 shares of its treasury stock at $11 per share. It now sells 1,000 shares at $15 per share on March 10. Pacific records the entry as follows.

March 10, 2014

Cash	15,000	
Treasury Stock		11,000
Paid-in Capital from Treasury Stock		4,000

There are two reasons why Pacific does not credit $4,000 to Gain on Sale of Treasury Stock. (1) Gains on sales occur when selling **assets**; treasury stock is not an asset. (2) A gain or loss should not be recognized from stock transactions with its own stockholders. Thus, Pacific should not include paid-in capital arising from the sale of treasury stock in the measurement of net income. Instead, it lists paid-in capital from treasury stock separately on the balance sheet, as a part of paid-in capital.

Sale of Treasury Stock below Cost. When a corporation sells treasury stock below its cost, it usually debits the excess of the cost over selling price to Paid-in Capital from Treasury Stock. Thus, if Pacific sells an additional 1,000 shares of treasury stock on March 21 at $8 per share, it records the sale as follows.

March 21, 2014

Cash	8,000	
Paid-in Capital from Treasury Stock	3,000	
Treasury Stock		11,000

We can make several observations based on the two sale entries (sale above cost and sale below cost). (1) Pacific credits Treasury Stock at cost in each entry. (2) Pacific uses Paid-in Capital from Treasury Stock for the difference between the cost and the resale price of the shares. (3) Neither entry affects the original paid-in capital account, Common Stock.

After eliminating the credit balance in Paid-in Capital from Treasury Stock, the corporation debits any additional excess of cost over selling price to Retained Earnings. To illustrate, assume that Pacific sells an additional 1,000 shares at $8 per share on April 10. Illustration 15-6 shows the balance in the Paid-in Capital from Treasury Stock account (before the April 10 purchase).

Paid-in Capital from Treasury Stock			
Mar. 21	3,000	Mar. 10	4,000
		Balance	1,000

ILLUSTRATION 15-6
Treasury Stock Transactions in Paid-in Capital Account

In this case, Pacific debits $1,000 of the excess to Paid-in Capital from Treasury Stock. It debits the remainder to Retained Earnings. The entry is:

April 10, 2014

Cash	8,000	
Paid-in Capital from Treasury Stock	1,000	
Retained Earnings	2,000	
Treasury Stock		11,000

Retiring Treasury Stock

The board of directors may approve the retirement of treasury shares. This decision results in cancellation of the treasury stock and a reduction in the number of shares of issued stock. Retired treasury shares have the status of authorized and unissued shares. The accounting effects are similar to the sale of treasury stock except that corporations debit the **paid-in capital accounts applicable to the retired shares** instead of cash. For example, if a corporation originally sells the shares at par, it debits Common Stock for the par value per share. If it originally sells the shares at $3 above par value, it also debits Paid-in Capital in Excess of Par—Common Stock for $3 per share at retirement.

PREFERRED STOCK

LEARNING OBJECTIVE 5

Explain the accounting for and reporting of preferred stock.

As noted earlier, preferred stock is a special class of shares that possesses certain preferences or features not possessed by the common stock.[10] The following features are those most often associated with preferred stock issues.

1. Preference as to dividends.
2. Preference as to assets in the event of liquidation.
3. Convertible into common stock.
4. Callable at the option of the corporation.
5. Nonvoting.

The features that distinguish preferred from common stock may be of a more restrictive and negative nature than preferences. For example, the preferred stock may be nonvoting, noncumulative, and nonparticipating.

Companies usually issue preferred stock with a par value, expressing the dividend preference as a **percentage of the par value**. Thus, holders of 8 percent preferred stock with a $100 par value are entitled to an annual dividend of $8 per share. This stock is commonly referred to as 8 percent preferred stock. In the case of no-par preferred stock, a corporation expresses a dividend preference as a **specific dollar amount** per share, for example, $7 per share. This stock is commonly referred to as $7 preferred stock.

A preference as to dividends does not assure the payment of dividends. It merely assures that **the corporation must pay the stated dividend rate or amount applicable to the preferred stock before paying any dividends on the common stock**.

A company often issues preferred stock (instead of debt) because of a high debt-to-equity ratio. In other instances, it issues preferred stock through private placements with other corporations at a lower-than-market dividend rate because the acquiring corporation receives largely tax-free dividends (owing to the IRS's 70 percent or 80 percent dividends received deduction).

Features of Preferred Stock

A corporation may attach whatever preferences or restrictions, in whatever combination it desires, to a preferred stock issue, as long as it does not specifically violate its state incorporation law. Also, it may issue more than one class of preferred stock. We discuss the most common features attributed to preferred stock on the next page.

[10]*Accounting Trends and Techniques—2012* reports that of its 500 surveyed companies, 35 had preferred stock outstanding.

Cumulative Preferred Stock

Cumulative preferred stock requires that if a corporation fails to pay a dividend in any year, it must make it up in a later year before paying any dividends to common stockholders. If the directors fail to declare a dividend at the normal date for dividend action, the dividend is said to have been "passed." Any passed dividend on cumulative preferred stock constitutes a dividend in arrears. Because no liability exists until the board of directors declares a dividend, a corporation does not record a dividend in arrears as a liability but discloses it in a note to the financial statements. A corporation seldom issues noncumulative preferred stock because a passed dividend is lost forever to the preferred stockholder. As a result, this stock issue would be less marketable.

Participating Preferred Stock

Holders of participating preferred stock share ratably with the common stockholders in any profit distributions beyond the prescribed rate. That is, 5 percent preferred stock, if fully participating, will receive not only its 5 percent return, but also dividends at the same rates as those paid to common stockholders if paying amounts in excess of 5 percent of par or stated value to common stockholders. Note that participating preferred stock may be only partially participating. Although seldom used, examples of companies that have issued participating preferred stock are LTV Corporation, Southern California Edison, and Allied Products Corporation.

Convertible Preferred Stock

Convertible preferred stock allows stockholders, at their option, to exchange preferred shares for common stock at a predetermined ratio. The convertible preferred stockholder not only enjoys a preferred claim on dividends but also has the option of converting into a common stockholder with unlimited participation in earnings.

Callable Preferred Stock

Callable preferred stock permits the corporation at its option to call or redeem the outstanding preferred shares at specified future dates and at stipulated prices. Many preferred issues are callable. The corporation usually sets the call or redemption price slightly above the original issuance price and commonly states it in terms related to the par value. The callable feature permits the corporation to use the capital obtained through the issuance of such stock until the need has passed or it is no longer advantageous.

The existence of a call price or prices tends to set a ceiling on the market price of the preferred shares unless they are convertible into common stock. When a corporation redeems preferred stock, it must pay any dividends in arrears.

Redeemable Preferred Stock

Recently, more and more issuances of preferred stock have features that make the security more like debt (legal obligation to pay) than an equity instrument. For example, redeemable preferred stock has a mandatory redemption period or a redemption feature that the issuer cannot control.

Previously, public companies were not permitted to report these debt-like preferred stock issues in equity, but they were not required to report them as a liability either. There were concerns about classification of these debt-like securities, which may have been reported as equity or in the "mezzanine" section of balance sheets between debt and equity. There also was diversity in practice as to how dividends on these securities were reported. The FASB now requires debt-like securities, such as redeemable preferred stock, to be classified as liabilities and be measured and accounted for similar to liabilities. [1]

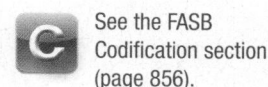

See the FASB Codification section (page 856).

What do the numbers mean? A CLASS (B) ACT

Some companies grant preferences to different shareholders by issuing different classes of common stock. Recent stock bids put the spotlight on dual-class stock structures. For example, ownership of Dow Jones & Co. was controlled by family members who owned Class B shares, which carry super voting powers. The same is true for the Ford family's control of Ford Motor Co. Class B shares are often criticized for protecting owners' interest at the expense of shareholder return. These shares often can determine if a takeover deal gets done, or not. Here are some notable companies with two-tiered shares.

Company	Votes Controlled by Class B Shareholders	Company	Votes Controlled by Class B Shareholders
Ford	40%	Estée Lauder	88%
New York Times	70%	Polo Ralph Lauren	88%
Meredith	71%	Martha Stewart Living	91%
Cablevision Systems	73%	1-800-Flowers	93%
Google	78%		

Data: Bloomberg Financial Markets, *BusinessWeek*, company documents.

For most retail investors, voting rights are not that important. Indeed, in 2011, 20 companies (including Zynga, Groupon, and LinkedIn) went public in the United States with two or more classes of stock. For family-controlled companies, issuing newer classes of lower or nonvoting stock effectively creates currency for acquisitions, increases liquidity, or puts a public value on the company without diluting the family's voting control. This was one of the main reasons Facebook gave when it created a dual-class share structure in 2009. In that IPO, Facebook founder Mark Zuckerberg owns only a quarter of the stock but still holds 57 percent of Facebook's voting rights. Thus, investors must carefully compare the apparent bargain prices for some classes of stock—they may end up as second-class citizens with no voting rights.

Sources: Adapted from Andy Serwer, "Dual-Listed Companies Aren't Fair or Balanced," *Fortune* (September 20, 2004), p. 83; Alex Halperin, "A Class (B) Act," *BusinessWeek* (May 28, 2007), p. 12; The Big Number, "20 Companies That Went Public in 2011 with Two or More Classes of Stock," *Wall Street Journal* (February 8, 2012), p. B5; and MoneyWatch, "Facebook's IPO by the Important Numbers," *www.cbsnews.com* (May 17, 2012).

Accounting for and Reporting Preferred Stock

The accounting for preferred stock at issuance is similar to that for common stock. A corporation allocates proceeds between the par value of the preferred stock and additional paid-in capital. To illustrate, assume that Bishop Co. issues 10,000 shares of $10 par value preferred stock for $12 cash per share. Bishop records the issuance as follows.

Cash	120,000	
Preferred Stock		100,000
Paid-in Capital in Excess of Par—Preferred Stock		20,000

Thus, Bishop maintains separate accounts for these different classes of shares.

In contrast to convertible bonds (recorded as a liability on the date of issue), corporations consider convertible preferred stock as a part of stockholders' equity. In addition, when exercising convertible preferred stock, there is no theoretical justification for recognition of a gain or loss. A company recognizes no gain or loss when dealing with stockholders in their capacity as business owners. Instead, the company **employs the book value method**: debit Preferred Stock, along with any related Paid-in Capital in Excess of Par—Preferred Stock, and credit Common Stock and Paid-in Capital in Excess of Par—Common Stock (if an excess exists).

Preferred stock generally has no maturity date. Therefore, no legal obligation exists to pay the preferred stockholder. As a result, companies classify preferred stock as part of stockholders' equity. Companies generally report preferred stock at par value as the first item in the stockholders' equity section. They report any excess over par value as part of additional paid-in capital. They also consider dividends on preferred stock as a distribution of income and not an expense. Companies must disclose the pertinent rights of the preferred stock outstanding. **[2]**

DIVIDEND POLICY

Dividend payouts can be important signals to the market. The practice of paying dividends declined sharply in the 1980s and 1990s as companies focused on growth and plowed profits back into the business. A resurgence in dividend payouts is due in large part to the dividend tax cut of 2003, which reduced the rate of tax on dividends to 15 percent (quite a bit lower than the ordinary income rate charged in the past). In addition, investors who were burned by accounting scandals in recent years began demanding higher payouts in the form of dividends. Why? A dividend check provides proof that at least some portion of a company's profits is genuine.[11] As one analyst noted, "Companies with the ability to grow dividends over time tend to be durable businesses with strong cash flow and relatively predictable earnings. . . . So you're more likely to get a return on your investment year in and year out."

6 **LEARNING OBJECTIVE**
Describe the policies used in distributing dividends.

Determining the proper amount of dividends to pay is a difficult financial management decision. Companies paying dividends are extremely reluctant to reduce or eliminate their dividend. They fear that the securities market might negatively view this action. As a consequence, dividend-paying companies will make every effort to continue to do so. In addition, the type of shareholder the company has (taxable or nontaxable, retail investor or institutional investor) plays a large role in determining dividend policy.

Very few companies pay dividends in amounts equal to their legally available retained earnings. The major reasons are as follows.

1. To maintain agreements (bond covenants) with specific creditors, to retain all or a portion of the earnings, in the form of assets, to build up additional protection against possible loss.

2. To meet state corporation requirements, that earnings equivalent to the cost of treasury shares purchased be restricted against dividend declarations.

3. To retain assets that would otherwise be paid out as dividends, to finance growth or expansion. This is sometimes called internal financing, reinvesting earnings, or "plowing" the profits back into the business.

4. To smooth out dividend payments from year to year by accumulating earnings in good years and using such accumulated earnings as a basis for dividends in bad years.

5. To build up a cushion or buffer against possible losses or errors in the calculation of profits.

The reasons above are self-explanatory except for the second. The laws of some states require that the corporation restrict its legal capital from distribution to stockholders, to protect against loss for creditors.[12] The applicable state law determines the legality of a dividend.

Financial Condition and Dividend Distributions

Effective management of a company requires attention to more than the legality of dividend distributions. Management must also consider economic conditions, most importantly, liquidity. Assume an extreme situation as shown in Illustration 15-7 (page 838).

---

[11]"Dividend Stocks: Yield, Growth, and Possible Tax Hikes," *T. Rowe Price Report* (Fall 2011). From 1926 to 2011, dividends have contributed 42% of the total return of the S&P 500 Index. See "Dividend Growth Stocks May Be Timely as the Economy Sputters," *T. Rowe Price Report* (Fall 2011).

[12]If the corporation buys its own outstanding stock, it reduces its legal capital and distributes assets to stockholders. If permitted, the corporation could, by purchasing treasury stock at any price desired, return to the stockholders their investments and leave creditors with little or no protection against loss.

ILLUSTRATION 15-7
Balance Sheet, Showing a
Lack of Liquidity

BALANCE SHEET			
Plant assets	$500,000	Capital stock	$400,000
	$500,000	Retained earnings	100,000
			$500,000

The depicted company has a retained earnings credit balance. Unless restricted, it can declare a dividend of $100,000. But because all its assets are plant assets used in operations, payment of a cash dividend of $100,000 would require the sale of plant assets or borrowing.

Even if a balance sheet shows current assets, as in Illustration 15-8, the question remains as to whether the company needs its cash for other purposes.

ILLUSTRATION 15-8
Balance Sheet, Showing
Cash but Minimal
Working Capital

BALANCE SHEET				
Cash	$100,000	Current liabilities		$ 60,000
Plant assets	460,000	Capital stock	$400,000	
	$560,000	Retained earnings	100,000	500,000
				$560,000

The existence of current liabilities strongly implies that the company needs some of the cash to meet current debts as they mature. In addition, day-to-day cash requirements for payrolls and other expenditures not included in current liabilities also require cash.

Thus, before declaring a dividend, management must consider **availability of funds to pay the dividend**. A company should not pay a dividend unless both the present and future financial position warrant the distribution.

The SEC encourages companies to disclose their dividend policy in their annual report, especially those that (1) have earnings but fail to pay dividends, or (2) do not expect to pay dividends in the foreseeable future. In addition, the SEC encourages companies that consistently pay dividends to indicate whether they intend to continue this practice in the future.

Types of Dividends

LEARNING OBJECTIVE 7
Identify the various forms of dividend
distributions.

Companies generally base dividend distributions either on accumulated profits (that is, retained earnings) or on some other capital item such as additional paid-in capital. Dividends are of the following types.

1. Cash dividends.

2. Property dividends.

3. Liquidating dividends.

Although commonly paid in cash, companies occasionally pay dividends in stock or some other asset.[13] **All dividends, except for stock dividends, reduce the total stockholders' equity in the corporation.** When declaring a stock dividend, the corporation does not pay out assets or incur a liability. It issues additional shares of stock to each stockholder and nothing more.

---

[13]*Accounting Trends and Techniques—2012* reported that of its 500 surveyed companies, 343 paid a cash dividend on common stock, 33 paid a cash dividend on preferred stock, 2 issued stock dividends, and 1 issued or paid dividends in kind. Some companies declare more than one type of dividend in a given year.

The natural expectation of any stockholder who receives a dividend is that the corporation has operated successfully. As a result, he or she is receiving a share of its profits. A company should disclose a liquidating dividend—that is, a dividend not based on retained earnings—to the stockholders so that they will not misunderstand its source.

Cash Dividends

The board of directors votes on the declaration of cash dividends. Upon approval of the resolution, the board declares a dividend. Before paying it, however, the company must prepare a current list of stockholders. For this reason, there is usually a time lag between declaration and payment. For example, the board of directors might approve a resolution at the January 10 (**date of declaration**) meeting and declare it payable February 5 (**date of payment**) to all stockholders of record January 25 (**date of record**).[14] In this example, the period from January 10 to January 25 gives time for the company to complete and register any transfers in process. The time from January 25 to February 5 provides an opportunity for the transfer agent or accounting department, depending on who does this work, to prepare a list of stockholders as of January 25 and to prepare and mail dividend checks.

A declared cash dividend is a liability. Because payment is generally required very soon, it is usually a current liability. Companies record the following entries to record the declaration and payment of a cash dividend. To illustrate, Roadway Freight Corp. on June 10 declared a cash dividend of 50 cents a share on 1.8 million shares payable July 16 to all stockholders of record June 24.

At date of declaration (June 10)

Retained Earnings (Cash Dividends Declared)	900,000	
Dividends Payable		900,000

At date of record (June 24)

No entry

At date of payment (July 16)

Dividends Payable	900,000	
Cash		900,000

To set up a ledger account that shows the amount of dividends declared during the year, Roadway Freight might debit Cash Dividends Declared instead of Retained Earnings at the time of declaration. It then closes this account to Retained Earnings at year-end.

A company may declare dividends either as a certain percent of par, such as a 6 percent dividend on preferred stock, or as an amount per share, such as 60 cents per share on no-par common stock. In the first case, the rate multiplied by the par value of outstanding shares equals the total dividend. In the second, the dividend equals the amount per share multiplied by the number of shares outstanding. **Companies do not declare or pay cash dividends on treasury stock.**

Dividend policies vary among corporations. Some companies, such as JP Morgan Chase, Clorox Co., and Tootsie Roll Industries, take pride in a long, unbroken string of quarterly dividend payments. They would lower or pass the dividend only if forced to do so by a sustained decline in earnings or a critical shortage of cash.

---

[14]Theoretically, the ex-dividend date is the day after the date of record. However, to allow time for transfer of the shares, the stock exchanges generally advance the ex-dividend date two to four days. Therefore, the party who owns the stock on the day prior to the expressed ex-dividend date receives the dividends. The party who buys the stock on and after the ex-dividend date does not receive the dividend. Between the declaration date and the ex-dividend date, the market price of the stock includes the dividend.

"Growth" companies, on the other hand, pay little or no cash dividends because their policy is to expand as rapidly as internal and external financing permit. For example, Questcor Pharmaceuticals Inc. has never paid cash dividends to its common stockholders. These investors hope that the price of their shares will appreciate in value. The investors will then realize a profit when they sell their shares. Many companies focus more on increasing share price, stock repurchase programs, and corporate earnings than on dividend payout.

Property Dividends

Dividends payable in assets of the corporation other than cash are called **property dividends** or **dividends in kind**. Property dividends may be merchandise, real estate, or investments, or whatever form the board of directors designates. Ranchers Exploration and Development Corp. reported one year that it would pay a fourth-quarter dividend in gold bars instead of cash. Because of the obvious difficulties of divisibility of units and delivery to stockholders, the usual property dividend is in the form of securities of other companies that the distributing corporation holds as an investment.

For example, after ruling that DuPont's 23 percent stock interest in General Motors (GM) violated antitrust laws, the Supreme Court ordered DuPont to divest itself of the GM stock within 10 years. The stock represented 63 million shares of GM's 281 million shares then outstanding. DuPont could not sell the shares in one block of 63 million. Further, it could not sell 6 million shares annually for the next 10 years without severely depressing the value of the GM stock. DuPont solved its problem by declaring a property dividend and distributing the GM shares as a dividend to its own stockholders.

When declaring a property dividend, the corporation should **restate at fair value the property it will distribute**, **recognizing any gain or loss** as the difference between the property's fair value and carrying value at date of declaration. The corporation may then record the declared dividend as a debit to Retained Earnings (or Property Dividends Declared) and a credit to Property Dividends Payable, at an amount equal to the fair value of the distributed property. Upon distribution of the dividend, the corporation debits Property Dividends Payable and credits the account containing the distributed asset (restated at fair value).

For example, Trendler, Inc. transferred to stockholders some of its equity investments costing $1,250,000 by declaring a property dividend on December 28, 2013, to be distributed on January 30, 2014, to stockholders of record on January 15, 2014. At the date of declaration, the securities have a fair value of $2,000,000. Trendler makes the following entries.

At date of declaration (December 28, 2013)		
Equity Investments	750,000	
Unrealized Holding Gain or Loss—Income		750,000
Retained Earnings (Property Dividends Declared)	2,000,000	
Property Dividends Payable		2,000,000

At date of distribution (January 30, 2014)		
Property Dividends Payable	2,000,000	
Equity Investments		2,000,000

Liquidating Dividends

Some corporations use paid-in capital as a basis for dividends. Without proper disclosure of this fact, stockholders may erroneously believe the corporation has been operating at a profit. To avoid this type of deception, intentional or unintentional, a clear statement of the source of every dividend should accompany the dividend check.

Dividends based on other than retained earnings are sometimes described as liqui-dating dividends. This term implies that such dividends are a return of the stockholder's investment rather than of profits. In other words, **any dividend not based on earnings reduces corporate paid-in capital and to that extent, it is a liquidating dividend.** Com-panies in the extractive industries may pay dividends equal to the total of accumulated income and depletion. The portion of these dividends in excess of accumulated income represents a return of part of the stockholder's investment.

For example, McChesney Mines Inc. issued a "dividend" to its common stockholders of $1,200,000. The cash dividend announcement noted that stockholders should consider $900,000 as income and the remainder a return of capital. McChesney Mines records the dividend as follows.

At date of declaration

Retained Earnings	900,000	
Paid-in Capital in Excess of Par—Common Stock	300,000	
Dividends Payable		1,200,000

At date of payment

Dividends Payable	1,200,000	
Cash		1,200,000

In some cases, management simply decides to cease business and declares a liqui-dating dividend. In these cases, liquidation may take place over a number of years to ensure an orderly and fair sale of assets. For example, when Overseas National Airways dissolved, it agreed to pay a liquidating dividend to its stockholders over a period of years equivalent to $8.60 per share. Each liquidating dividend payment in such cases reduces paid-in capital.

Stock Dividends and Stock Splits

Stock Dividends

If management wishes to "capitalize" part of the earnings (i.e., reclassify amounts from earned to contributed capital) and thus retain earnings in the business on a permanent basis, it may issue a stock dividend. In this case, **the company distrib-utes no assets.** Each stockholder maintains exactly the same proportionate interest in the corporation and the same total book value after the company issues the stock dividend. Of course, the book value per share is lower because each stock-holder holds more shares.

A stock dividend therefore is the issuance by a corporation of its own stock to its stockholders on a pro rata basis, without receiving any consideration. In record-ing a stock dividend, some believe that the company should transfer the **par value of the stock issued** as a dividend from retained earnings to capital stock. Others believe that it should transfer the **fair value of the stock issued**—its market value at the declaration date—from retained earnings to capital stock and additional paid-in capital.

The fair value position was adopted, at least in part, in order to influence the stock dividend policies of corporations. Evidently in 1941, both the New York Stock Exchange and many in the accounting profession regarded periodic stock dividends as objectionable. They believed that the term dividend when used with a distribution of additional stock was misleading because investors' net assets did not increase as a result of this "dividend." As a result, these groups decided to make it more difficult for corporations to sustain a series of such stock dividends out of their accumulated

8 LEARNING OBJECTIVE

Explain the accounting for small and large stock dividends, and for stock splits.

earnings, by requiring the use of fair value when it substantially exceeded book value.[15]

When the stock dividend is less than 20–25 percent of the common shares outstanding at the time of the dividend declaration, the company is therefore required to transfer the **fair value** of the stock issued from retained earnings. Stock dividends of less than 20–25 percent are often referred to as small (ordinary) stock dividends. This method of handling stock dividends is justified on the grounds that "many recipients of stock dividends look upon them as distributions of corporate earnings and usually in an amount equivalent to the fair value of the additional shares received." **[3]** We consider this argument unconvincing. It is generally agreed that stock dividends are not income to the recipients. Therefore, sound accounting should not recommend procedures simply because some recipients think they are income.[16]

To illustrate a small stock dividend, assume that Vine Corporation has outstanding 1,000 shares of $100 par value common stock and retained earnings of $50,000. If Vine declares a 10 percent stock dividend, it issues 100 additional shares to current stockholders. If the fair value of the stock at the time of the stock dividend is $130 per share, the entry is:

At date of declaration

Retained Earnings	13,000	
Common Stock Dividend Distributable		10,000
Paid-in Capital in Excess of Par—Common Stock		3,000

Note that the stock dividend does not affect any asset or liability. **The entry merely reflects a reclassification of stockholders' equity.** If Vine prepares a balance sheet between the dates of declaration and distribution, it should show the common stock dividend distributable in the stockholders' equity section as an addition to common stock (whereas it shows cash or property dividends payable as current liabilities).

When issuing the stock, the entry is:

At date of distribution

Common Stock Dividend Distributable	10,000	
Common Stock		10,000

No matter what the fair value is at the time of the stock dividend, each stockholder retains the same proportionate interest in the corporation.

Some state statutes specifically prohibit the issuance of stock dividends on treasury stock. In those states that permit treasury shares to participate in the distribution accompanying a stock dividend or stock split, the planned use of the treasury shares influences corporate practice. For example, if a corporation issues treasury shares in connection with employee stock options, the treasury shares may participate in the distribution because the corporation usually adjusts the number of shares under option for any stock dividends or splits. But no useful purpose is served by issuing additional shares to the treasury stock without a specific purpose, since they are essentially equivalent to authorized but unissued shares.

---

[15]This was perhaps the earliest instance of "economic consequences" affecting an accounting pronouncement. The Committee on Accounting Procedure described its action as required by "proper accounting and corporate policy." See Stephen A. Zeff, "The Rise of 'Economic Consequences,'" *The Journal of Accountancy* (December 1978), pp. 53–66.

[16]One study concluded that *small* stock dividends do not always produce significant amounts of extra value on the date after issuance (ex date) and that *large* stock dividends almost always fail to generate extra value on the ex-dividend date. Taylor W. Foster III and Don Vickrey, "The Information Content of Stock Dividend Announcements," *The Accounting Review,* Vol. LIII, No. 2 (April 1978), pp. 360–370.

To continue with our example of the effect of the small stock dividend, note in Illustration 15-9 that the stock dividend does not change the total stockholders' equity. Also, it does not change the proportion of the total shares outstanding held by each stockholder.

Before dividend	
Common stock, 1,000 shares at $100 par	$100,000
Retained earnings	50,000
Total stockholders' equity	$150,000
Stockholders' interests:	
A. 400 shares, 40% interest, book value	$ 60,000
B. 500 shares, 50% interest, book value	75,000
C. 100 shares, 10% interest, book value	15,000
	$150,000
After declaration but before distribution of 10% stock dividend	
If fair value ($130) is used as basis for entry:	
Common stock, 1,000 shares at $100 par	$100,000
Common stock distributable, 100 shares at $100 par	10,000
Paid-in capital in excess of par—common stock	3,000
Retained earnings ($50,000 − $13,000)	37,000
Total stockholders' equity	$150,000
After declaration and distribution of 10% stock dividend	
If fair value ($130) is used as basis for entry:	
Common stock, 1,100 shares at $100 par	$110,000
Paid-in capital in excess of par—common stock	3,000
Retained earnings ($50,000 − $13,000)	37,000
Total stockholders' equity	$150,000
Stockholders' interest:	
A. 440 shares, 40% interest, book value	$ 60,000
B. 550 shares, 50% interest, book value	75,000
C. 110 shares, 10% interest, book value	15,000
	$150,000

ILLUSTRATION 15-9
Effects of a Small (10%) Stock Dividend

Stock Splits

If a company has undistributed earnings over several years and accumulates a sizable balance in retained earnings, the market value of its outstanding shares likely increases. Stock issued at prices less than $50 a share can easily attain a market price in excess of $200 a share. The higher the market price of a stock, however, the less readily some investors can purchase it.

The managements of many corporations believe that better public relations depend on wider ownership of the corporation stock. They therefore target a market price sufficiently low to be within range of the majority of potential investors. To reduce the market price of shares, they use the common device of a **stock split**. For example, after its stock price increased by 25-fold, **Qualcomm Inc.** split its stock 4-for-1. Qualcomm's stock had risen above $500 per share, raising concerns that Qualcomm could not meet an analyst target of $1,000 per share. The split reduced the analysts' target to $250, which it could better meet with wider distribution of shares at lower trading prices.[17]

From an accounting standpoint, Qualcomm **records no entry for a stock split**. However, it enters a memorandum note to indicate the changed par value of the shares

---

[17]Another classic case is **Coca-Cola**. Coca-Cola recently split its stock for the 11th time. If it had not done all of these splits, one of Coke's original shares would be worth $10.3 *million*. See S. Jakab, "Coca-Cola's Currency Is Its Resilience," *Wall Street Journal* (July 16, 2012).

and the increased number of shares. Illustration 15-10 shows the lack of change in stockholders' equity for a 2-for-1 stock split on 1,000 shares of $100 par value stock with the par being halved upon issuance of the additional shares.

ILLUSTRATION 15-10
Effects of a Stock Split

Stockholders' Equity before 2-for-1 Split		Stockholders' Equity after 2-for-1 Split	
Common stock, 1,000 shares		Common stock, 2,000 shares	
at $100 par	$100,000	at $50 par	$100,000
Retained earnings	50,000	Retained earnings	50,000
	$150,000		$150,000

What do the numbers mean? SPLITSVILLE

Stock splits were all the rage in the booming stock market of the 1990s. Of major companies on the New York Stock Exchange, fewer than 80 companies split shares in 1990. By 1998, with stock prices soaring, over 200 companies split shares. Although the split does not increase a stockholder's proportionate ownership of the company, studies show that split shares usually outperform those that don't split, as well as the market as a whole, for several years after the split. In addition, the splits help the company keep the shares in more attractive price ranges.

What about when the market "turns south"? A number of companies who split their shares in the boom markets of the 1990s have since seen their share prices decline to a point considered too low. For example, Lucent traded at less than $5 a share following a 4-for-1 split. For some investors, these low-priced stocks are unattractive because some brokerage commissions rely on the number of shares traded, not the dollar amount. Others are concerned that low-priced shares are easier for would-be scamsters to manipulate. And if a company's per share price falls below $1 for 30 consecutive days, it is a violation of stock exchange listing requirements.

Some companies are considering reverse stock splits in which, say, 5 shares are consolidated into one. Thus, a stock previously trading at $5 per share would be part of an un-split share trading at $25. Unsplitting might thus avoid some of the negative consequences of a low trading price. The downside to this strategy is that analysts might view reverse splits as additional bad news about the direction of the stock price. For example, Webvan, a failed Internet grocer, did a 1-for-25 reverse split just before it entered bankruptcy. And struggling Tenet Healthcare executed a 1-for-4 reverse split in combination with a debt restructuring, in order to get its stock price into a more favorable trading range.

Sources: Adapted from David Henry, "Stocks: The Case for Unsplitting," *BusinessWeek Online* (April 1, 2002); and M. Murphy, "Tenet CFO Says Reverse Split Could Help Land New Business," *Wall Street Journal* (October 2, 2012).

Stock Split and Stock Dividend Differentiated

From a legal standpoint, a stock split differs from a stock dividend. How? A stock split increases the number of shares outstanding and decreases the par or stated value per share. **A stock dividend, although it increases the number of shares outstanding, does not decrease the par value; thus, it increases the total par value of outstanding shares.**

The reasons for issuing a stock dividend are numerous and varied. Stock dividends can be primarily a publicity gesture **because many consider stock dividends as dividends**. Another reason is that the corporation may simply wish to retain profits in the business by capitalizing a part of retained earnings. In such a situation, it makes a transfer on declaration of a stock dividend from earned capital to contributed capital.

A corporation may also use a stock dividend, like a stock split, to increase the marketability of the stock, although marketability is often a secondary consideration. If the stock dividend is large, it has the same effect on market price as a stock split. **Whenever corporations issue additional shares for the purpose of reducing the unit market price, then the distribution more closely resembles a stock split than a stock dividend. This effect usually results only if the number of shares issued is more than 20–25 percent of the number of shares previously outstanding. [4]** A stock dividend of more than 20–25 percent of the number of shares previously outstanding is called a large stock dividend.[18] Such a distribution should not be called a stock dividend but instead "a split-up effected in the form of a dividend" or "stock split."

Also, since a split-up effected in the form of a dividend does not alter the par value per share, companies generally are required to transfer the par value amount from retained earnings. In other words, companies transfer from retained earnings to capital stock **the par value of the stock issued**, as opposed to a transfer of the market price of the shares issued as in the case of a small stock dividend.[19] For example, Brown Group, Inc. at one time authorized a 2-for-1 split, effected in the form of a stock dividend. As a result of this authorization, it distributed approximately 10.5 million shares, and transferred more than $39 million representing the par value of the shares issued from Retained Earnings to the Common Stock account.

To illustrate a large stock dividend (stock split-up effected in the form of a dividend), Rockland Steel, Inc. declared a 30 percent stock dividend on November 20, payable December 29 to stockholders of record December 12. At the date of declaration, 1,000,000 shares, par value $10, are outstanding and with a fair value of $200 per share. The entries are:

At date of declaration (November 20)

Retained Earnings	3,000,000	
Common Stock Dividend Distributable		3,000,000

Computation: 1,000,000 shares   300,000 Additional shares
$\times$ 30% $\times$ $10 Par value
300,000 $3,000,000

At date of distribution (December 29)

Common Stock Dividend Distributable	3,000,000	
Common Stock		3,000,000

Illustration 15-11 summarizes and compares the effects in the balance sheet and related items of various types of dividends and stock splits.

ILLUSTRATION 15-11
Effects of Dividends and Stock Splits on Financial Statement Elements

Effect on:	Declaration of Cash Dividend	Payment of Cash Dividend	Declaration and Distribution of		
			Small Stock Dividend	Large Stock Dividend	Stock Split
Retained earnings	Decrease	–0–	Decrease[a]	Decrease[b]	–0–
Capital stock	–0–	–0–	Increase[b]	Increase[b]	–0–
Additional paid-in capital	–0–	–0–	Increase[c]	–0–	–0–
Total stockholders' equity	Decrease	–0–	–0–	–0–	–0–
Working capital	Decrease	–0–	–0–	–0–	–0–
Total assets	–0–	Decrease	–0–	–0–	–0–
Number of shares outstanding	–0–	–0–	Increase	Increase	Increase

[a]Market price of shares. [b]Par or stated value of shares. [c]Excess of market price over par.

[18]The SEC has added more precision to the 20–25 percent rule. Specifically, the SEC indicates that companies should consider distributions of 25 percent or more as a "split-up effected in the form of a dividend." Companies should account for distributions of less than 25 percent as a stock dividend. The SEC more precisely defined GAAP here. As a result, public companies follow the SEC rule.

[19]Often, a company records a split-up effected in the form of a dividend as a debit to Paid-in Capital instead of Retained Earnings to indicate that this transaction should affect only paid-in capital accounts. No reduction of retained earnings is required except as indicated by legal requirements. *For homework purposes, assume that the debit is to Retained Earnings.* See, for example, Taylor W. Foster III and Edmund Scribner, "Accounting for Stock Dividends and Stock Splits: Corrections to Textbook Coverage," *Issues in Accounting Education* (February 1998).

As the economy recovered from the financial crisis, a number of U.S. companies increased their dividend payout in a sign of growing confidence and rising cash balances. For example, early in 2011 a number of companies increased dividends, including **CVS/Caremark Corp.**, **Family Dollar Stores Inc.**, and **Schlumberger Ltd.** The number was up from the prior year amid concerns that dividend payouts would level off if the economy slows.

In such a slow growth environment, with interest rates persistently low and the tax treatment of dividends still favorable, an investment strategy focusing on stocks with the potential of *increasing* dividends may be particularly timely. Said one market watcher, "Investors too often overlook the importance of dividends, particularly the contribution to total return from reinvested dividends. . . . Dividends also can provide a good hedge against inflation in the form of a growing stream of income."

A look at the returns for "dividend growers" compared to "dividend cutters" in the following chart supports the advice to keep an eye on dividend growth.

Source: T. Rowe Price analysis based on Compustat data.

As indicated, from 1979 through the end of 2011, stocks in the Russell 1000 Index that were growing their dividends outperformed dividend-paying stocks, the index itself, non-dividend-paying stocks, and stocks that cut their dividends. During that time, an investment of $100 in dividend growers would have risen to $4,018 compared with $3,134 based on the index return. Dividend payers outperformed non-dividend payers during down and flat markets, and offered lower volatility of returns in all market environments.

Furthermore, the best performers are stocks with the combination of a relatively high yield—though not always

the very highest—and a high dividend growth rate. This is because high yields sometimes are a function of beaten-down stock prices due to poor corporate earnings prospects or other issues. Indeed, in such cases, dividend cuts could be in the offing. By contrast, stocks that have performed best historically have been those in which the company's true growth potential has been undervalued by investors. Thus, companies with growing dividends are signaling confidence about their future earnings and most likely to perform well throughout market cycles, which make them good candidates for long-term growth.

Source: "Dividend Growth Stocks May Be Timely as the Economy Sputters," *T. Rowe Price Report* (Fall 2011).

Disclosure of Restrictions on Retained Earnings

Many corporations restrict retained earnings or dividends, without any formal journal entries. Such restrictions are **best disclosed by note**. Parenthetical notations are sometimes used, but restrictions imposed by bond indentures and loan agreements commonly require an extended explanation. Notes provide a medium for more complete explanations and free the financial statements from abbreviated notations. The note disclosure should reveal the source of the restriction, pertinent provisions, and the amount of retained earnings subject to restriction, or the amount not restricted.

Restrictions may be based on the retention of a certain retained earnings balance, the ability to maintain certain working capital requirements, additional borrowing, and other considerations. The example from the annual report of **Alberto-Culver Company** in Illustration 15-12 shows a note disclosing potential restrictions on retained earnings and dividends.

Alberto-Culver Company
Note 3 (in part): The $200 million revolving credit facility, the term note, and the receivables agreement impose restrictions on such items as total debt, working capital, dividend payments, treasury stock purchases, and interest expense. At year-end, the company was in compliance with these arrangements, and $220 million of consolidated retained earnings was not restricted as to the payment of dividends.

ILLUSTRATION 15-12
Disclosure of Restrictions on Retained Earnings and Dividends

PRESENTATION AND ANALYSIS OF STOCKHOLDERS' EQUITY

Presentation

Balance Sheet

Illustration 15-13 shows a comprehensive stockholders' equity section from the balance sheet of Frost Company that includes most of the equity items we discussed in this chapter.

9 LEARNING OBJECTIVE
Indicate how to present and analyze stockholders' equity.

ILLUSTRATION 15-13
Comprehensive Stockholders' Equity Presentation

FROST COMPANY STOCKHOLDERS' EQUITY DECEMBER 31, 2014		
Capital stock		
Preferred stock, $100 par value, 7% cumulative, 100,000 shares authorized, 30,000 shares issued and outstanding		$ 3,000,000
Common stock, no-par, stated value $10 per share, 500,000 shares authorized, 400,000 shares issued		4,000,000
Common stock dividend distributable, 20,000 shares		200,000
Total capital stock		7,200,000
Additional paid-in capital[20]		
Excess over par—preferred	$150,000	
Excess over stated value—common	840,000	990,000
Total paid-in capital		8,190,000
Retained earnings		4,360,000
Total paid-in capital and retained earnings		12,550,000
Less: Cost of treasury stock (2,000 shares, common)		190,000
Accumulated other comprehensive loss[21]		360,000
Total stockholders' equity		$12,000,000

[20]*Accounting Trends and Techniques—2012* reports that of its 500 surveyed companies, 465 had additional paid-in capital.

[21]Companies may include a number of items in the "Accumulated other comprehensive income (loss)." *Accounting Trends and Techniques—2012* reports that of its 500 surveyed companies, 407 reported cumulative translation adjustments, 386 reported defined benefit postretirement plan adjustments (discussed in Chapter 20), 286 reported changes in the fair value of derivatives (discussed in Appendix 17A), and 218 reported unrealized losses/gains on certain investments (discussed in Chapter 17). A number of companies had more than one item.

Frost should disclose the pertinent rights and privileges of the various securities outstanding. For example, companies must disclose all of the following: dividend and liquidation preferences, participation rights, call prices and dates, conversion or exercise prices and pertinent dates, sinking fund requirements, unusual voting rights, and significant terms of contracts to issue additional shares. Liquidation preferences should be disclosed in the equity section of the balance sheet, rather than in the notes to the financial statements, to emphasize the possible effect of this restriction on future cash flows. [5]

Statement of Stockholders' Equity

The **statement of stockholders' equity** is frequently presented in the following basic format.

1. Balance at the beginning of the period.
2. Additions.
3. Deductions.
4. Balance at the end of the period.

Companies must disclose changes in the separate accounts comprising stockholders' equity, to make the financial statements sufficiently informative. Such changes may be disclosed in separate statements or in the basic financial statements or notes thereto.[22]

A **columnar format** for the presentation of changes in stockholders' equity items in published annual reports is gaining in popularity. An example is **ConAgra Foods**' statement of common stockholders' equity, shown in Illustration 15-14.

ConAgra Foods, Inc. and Subsidiaries

For the Fiscal Year Ended May 2012

(Dollars in millions except per share amounts)	Common Shares	Common Stock	Additional Paid-in Capital	Retained Earnings	Accumulated Other Comprehensive Income (Loss)	Treasury Stock	Noncontrolling Interests	Total Equity
Balance of May 29, 2011	567.9	$2,839.7	$899.1	$4,690.3	$ (91.2)	$(3,668.2)	$ 7.0	$4,676.7
Stock option and incentive plans			3.9	(1.3)		252.9		255.5
Currency translation adjustment, net of reclassification adjustment					(52.0)		(4.4)	(56.4)
Repurchase of common shares						(352.4)		(352.4)
Unrealized loss on securities					(0.1)			(0.1)
Derivative adjustment, net of reclassification adjustment					(89.1)			(89.1)
Acquisition of majority interest in ATFL							92.6	92.6
Activities of noncontrolling interests			(1.5)				1.3	(0.2)
Pension and postretirement healthcare benefits					(66.7)			(66.7)
Dividends declared on common stock; $0.95 per share				(391.8)				(391.8)
Net income attributable to ConAgra Foods, Inc.				467.9				467.9
Balance at May 27, 2012	567.9	$2,839.7	$901.5	$4,765.1	$(299.1)	$(3,767.7)	$96.5	$4,536.0

ILLUSTRATION 15-14
Columnar Format for Statement of Common Stockholders' Equity

[22]*Accounting Trends and Techniques—2012* reports that of the 500 companies surveyed, 486 presented statements of stockholders' equity, 4 presented separate statements of retained earnings only, 1 presented combined statements of income and retained earnings, and 9 presented changes in equity items in the notes only.

Analysis

Analysts use stockholders' equity ratios to evaluate a company's profitability and long-term solvency. We discuss and illustrate the following three ratios below.

1. Return on common stock equity.
2. Payout ratio.
3. Book value per share.

**Gateway to
the Profession**

Financial Analysis Primer

Return on Common Stock Equity

The return on common stock equity, often referred to as **return on equity (ROE)**, measures profitability from the common stockholders' viewpoint. This ratio shows how many dollars of net income the company earned for each dollar invested by the owners. Return on equity also helps investors judge the worthiness of a stock when the overall market is not doing well. For example, Best Buy shares dropped nearly 40 percent, along with the broader market in 2001–2002. But a review of its return on equity during this period and since shows a steady return of 20 to 22 percent while the overall market ROE declined from 16 percent to 8 percent. More importantly, Best Buy and other stocks, such as 3M and Procter & Gamble, recovered their lost market value, while other stocks with less robust ROEs stayed in the doldrums.

Return on equity equals net income less preferred dividends, divided by average common stockholders' equity. For example, assume that Gerber's Inc. had net income of $360,000, declared and paid preferred dividends of $54,000, and average common stockholders' equity of $2,550,000. Illustration 15-15 shows how to compute Gerber's ratio.

$$\text{Return on Common Stock Equity} = \frac{\text{Net Income} - \text{Preferred Dividends}}{\text{Average Common Stockholders' Equity}}$$

$$= \frac{\$360,000 - \$54,000}{\$2,550,000}$$

$$= 12\%$$

ILLUSTRATION 15-15
Computation of Return on Common Stock Equity

As shown in Illustration 15-15, when preferred stock is present, income available to common stockholders equals net income less preferred dividends. Similarly, the amount of common stock equity used in this ratio equals **total stockholders' equity less the par value of preferred stock**.

A company can improve its return on common stock equity through the prudent use of debt or preferred stock financing. Trading on the equity describes the practice of using borrowed money or issuing preferred stock in hopes of obtaining a higher rate of return on the money used. Shareholders win if return on the assets is higher than the cost of financing these assets. When this happens, the return on common stock equity will exceed the return on total assets. In short, the company is "trading on the equity at a gain." In this situation, the money obtained from bondholders or preferred stockholders earns enough to pay the interest or preferred dividends and leaves a profit for the common stockholders. On the other hand, if the cost of the financing is higher that the rate earned on the assets, the company is trading on equity at a loss and stockholders lose.

Payout Ratio

Another ratio of interest to investors, the payout ratio, is the ratio of cash dividends to net income. If preferred stock is outstanding, this ratio equals cash dividends paid to common stockholders, divided by net income available to common stockholders.

For example, assume that Troy Co. has cash dividends of $100,000 and net income of $500,000, and no preferred stock outstanding. Illustration 15-16 shows the payout ratio computation.

ILLUSTRATION 15-16
Computation of Payout Ratio

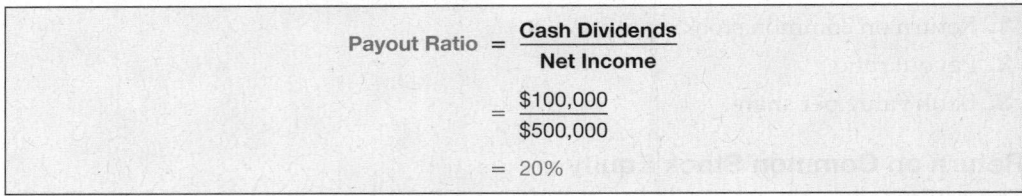

$$\text{Payout Ratio} = \frac{\text{Cash Dividends}}{\text{Net Income}}$$

$$= \frac{\$100,000}{\$500,000}$$

$$= 20\%$$

Recently, the payout ratio has plummeted. In 1982, more than half of earnings were converted to dividends. In the fourth quarter of 2011, just 36 percent of the earnings of the S&P 500 was distributed via dividends.[23]

Book Value per Share

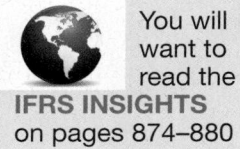

You will want to read the IFRS INSIGHTS on pages 874–880

for discussion of IFRS related to stockholders' equity.

A much-used basis for evaluating net worth is found in the book value or equity value per share of stock. Book value per share of stock is the amount each share would receive if the company were liquidated **on the basis of amounts reported on the balance sheet.** However, the figure loses much of its relevance if the valuations on the balance sheet fail to approximate fair value of the assets. Book value per share equals common stockholders' equity divided by outstanding common shares. Assume that Chen Corporation's common stockholders' equity is $1,000,000 and it has 100,000 shares of common stock outstanding. Illustration 15-17 shows its book value per share computation.

ILLUSTRATION 15-17
Computation of Book Value per Share

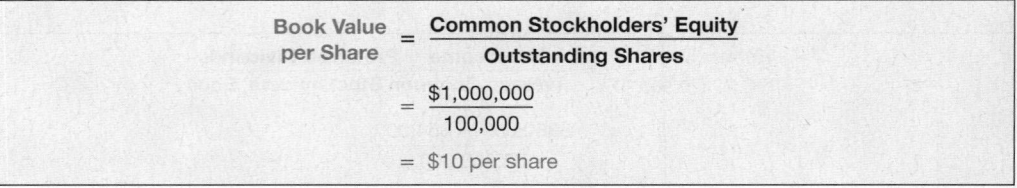

$$\frac{\text{Book Value}}{\text{per Share}} = \frac{\text{Common Stockholders' Equity}}{\text{Outstanding Shares}}$$

$$= \frac{\$1,000,000}{100,000}$$

$$= \$10 \text{ per share}$$

KEY TERMS

Additional Paid-in Capital, 825
book value per share, 850
callable preferred stock, 835
cash dividends, 839
common stock, 824
contributed (paid-in) capital, 824
convertible preferred stock, 835
cost method, 831
cumulative preferred stock, 835
dividend in arrears, 835
earned capital, 824
large stock dividend, 845
leveraged buyout (LBO), 830

SUMMARY OF LEARNING OBJECTIVES

1 **Discuss the characteristics of the corporate form of organization.** Among the specific characteristics of the corporate form that affect accounting are the (1) influence of state corporate law, (2) use of the capital stock or share system, and (3) development of a variety of ownership interests. In the absence of restrictive provisions, each share of stock carries the right to share proportionately in (1) profits and losses, (2) management (the right to vote for directors), (3) corporate assets upon liquidation, and (4) any new issues of stock of the same class (called the preemptive right).

2 **Identify the key components of stockholders' equity.** Stockholders' or owners' equity is classified into two categories: contributed capital and earned capital. Contributed capital (paid-in capital) describes the total amount paid in on capital stock. Put another way, it is the amount that stockholders invested in the corporation for use in the business. Contributed capital includes items such as the par value of all outstanding capital stock and premiums less any discounts on issuance. Earned capital is the

[23]R. Shaw, "S&P 500 Dividend Payout Ratio Still Giving Off Caution Signals," *http://seekingalpha.com* (January 16, 2012).

capital that develops if the business operates profitably; it consists of all undistributed income that remains invested in the company.

3 **Explain the accounting procedures for issuing shares of stock.** Accounts are kept for the following different types of stock. *Par value stock:* (a) preferred stock or common stock, (b) paid-in capital in excess of par or additional paid-in capital, and (c) discount on stock. *No-par stock:* common stock or common stock and additional paid-in capital, if stated value used. *Stock issued in combination with other securities (lump-sum sales):* The two methods of allocation available are (a) the proportional method and (b) the incremental method. *Stock issued in noncash transactions:* When issuing stock for services or property other than cash, the company should record the property or services at either the fair value of the stock issued, or the fair value of the noncash consideration received, whichever is more clearly determinable.

4 **Describe the accounting for treasury stock.** The cost method is generally used in accounting for treasury stock. This method derives its name from the fact that a company maintains the Treasury Stock account at the cost of the shares purchased. Under the cost method, a company debits the Treasury Stock account for the cost of the shares acquired and credits it for this same cost upon reissuance. The price received for the stock when originally issued does not affect the entries to record the acquisition and reissuance of the treasury stock.

5 **Explain the accounting for and reporting of preferred stock.** Preferred stock is a special class of shares that possesses certain preferences or features not possessed by the common stock. The features that are most often associated with preferred stock issues are (1) preference as to dividends, (2) preference as to assets in the event of liquidation, (3) convertible into common stock, (4) callable at the option of the corporation, and (5) nonvoting. At issuance, the accounting for preferred stock is similar to that for common stock. When convertible preferred stock is converted, a company uses the book value method. It debits Preferred Stock, along with any related Paid-in Capital in Excess of Par—Preferred Stock and credits Common Stock and Paid-in Capital in Excess of Par—Common Stock (if an excess exists).

6 **Describe the policies used in distributing dividends.** The state incorporation laws normally provide information concerning the legal restrictions related to the payment of dividends. Corporations rarely pay dividends in an amount equal to the legal limit. This is due, in part, to the fact that companies use assets represented by undistributed earnings to finance future operations of the business. If a company is considering declaring a dividend, it must ask two preliminary questions. (1) Is the condition of the corporation such that the dividend is **legally permissible**? (2) Is the condition of the corporation such that a dividend is **economically sound**?

7 **Identify the various forms of dividend distributions.** Dividends are of the following types: (1) cash dividends, (2) property dividends, (3) liquidating dividends (dividends based on other than retained earnings), and (4) stock dividends (the issuance by a corporation of its own stock to its stockholders on a pro rata basis, but without receiving consideration).

8 **Explain the accounting for small and large stock dividends, and for stock splits.** Generally accepted accounting principles require that the accounting for small stock dividends (less than 20–25 percent) rely on the fair value of the stock issued. When declaring a common stock dividend, a company debits Retained Earnings at the fair value of the stock it distributes. The entry includes a credit to Common Stock Dividend Distributable at par value times the number of shares, with any excess credited to Paid-in Capital in Excess of Par—Common Stock. If the number of shares issued exceeds 20–25 percent of the shares outstanding (large stock dividend), it debits Retained Earnings at par value and credits Common Stock Distributable—there is no additional paid-in capital.

A stock dividend is a capitalization of retained earnings that reduces retained earnings and increases certain contributed capital accounts. The par value per share and total

liquidating dividends, *839, 841*

lump-sum sales, *827*

no-par stock, *826*

Paid-in Capital in Excess of Par, *825*

par (stated) value method, *831*

participating preferred stock, *835*

payout ratio, *849*

preemptive right, *823*

preferred stock, *824, 834*

property dividends, *840*

redeemable preferred stock, *835*

residual interest, *825*

retained earnings, *824*

return on common stock equity, *849*

small (ordinary) stock dividends, *842*

stated value, *826*

statement of stockholders' equity, *848*

stock dividends, *841*

stock split, *843*

stockholders' (owners') equity, *825*

trading on the equity, *849*

treasury stock, *830*

Gateway to the Profession

Expanded Discussion of Quasi-Reorganization

stockholders' equity remain unchanged with a stock dividend, and all stockholders retain their same proportionate share of ownership. A stock split results in an increase or decrease in the number of shares outstanding, with a corresponding decrease or increase in the par or stated value per share. No accounting entry is required for a stock split.

9 **Indicate how to present and analyze stockholders' equity.** The stockholders' equity section of a balance sheet includes capital stock, additional paid-in capital, and retained earnings. A company might also present additional items such as treasury stock and accumulated other comprehensive income. Companies often provide a statement of stockholders' equity. Common ratios that use stockholders' equity amounts are return on common stock equity, payout ratio, and book value per share.

APPENDIX **15A**	DIVIDEND PREFERENCES AND BOOK VALUE PER SHARE

DIVIDEND PREFERENCES

LEARNING OBJECTIVE **10**

Explain the different types of preferred stock dividends and their effect on book value per share.

Illustrations 15A-1 to 15A-4 indicate the **effects** of various **dividend preferences** on dividend distributions to common and preferred stockholders. Assume that in 2014, Mason Company is to distribute $50,000 as cash dividends, its outstanding common stock has a par value of $400,000, and its 6 percent preferred stock has a par value of $100,000. Mason would distribute dividends to each class, employing the assumptions given, as follows.

1. If the preferred stock is noncumulative and nonparticipating:

ILLUSTRATION 15A-1
Dividend Distribution, Noncumulative and Nonparticipating Preferred

	Preferred	Common	Total
6% of $100,000	$6,000		$ 6,000
The remainder to common		$44,000	44,000
Totals	$6,000	$44,000	$50,000

2. If the preferred stock is cumulative and nonparticipating, and Mason Company did not pay dividends on the preferred stock in the preceding two years:

ILLUSTRATION 15A-2
Dividend Distribution, Cumulative and Nonparticipating Preferred, with Dividends in Arrears

	Preferred	Common	Total
Dividends in arrears, 6% of $100,000 for 2 years	$12,000		$12,000
Current year's dividend, 6% of $100,000	6,000		6,000
The remainder to common		$32,000	32,000
Totals	$18,000	$32,000	$50,000

3. If the preferred stock is noncumulative and is fully participating:[24]

---

[24]When preferred stock is participating, there may be different agreements as to how the participation feature is to be executed. However, in the absence of any specific agreement the following procedure is recommended:

   a. After the preferred stock is assigned its current year's dividend, the common stock will receive a "like" percentage of par value outstanding. In example (3) in Illustration 15A-3, this amounts to 6 percent of $400,000.

   b. In example (3), shown in Illustration 15A-3, the remainder of the declared dividend is $20,000. We divide this amount by total par value ($500,000) to find the rate of participation to be applied to each class of stock. In this case, the rate of participation is 4 percent ($20,000 ÷ $500,000), which we then multiply by the par value of each class of stock to determine the amount of participation.

	Preferred	Common	Total
Current year's dividend, 6%	$ 6,000	$24,000	$30,000
Participating dividend of 4%	4,000	16,000	20,000
Totals	$10,000	$40,000	$50,000

The participating dividend was determined as follows.
Current year's dividend:

Preferred, 6% of $100,000 = $ 6,000		
Common, 6% of $400,000 = 24,000	$ 30,000	
Amount available for participation ($50,000 − $30,000)	$ 20,000	
Par value of stock that is to participate ($100,000 + $400,000)	$500,000	
Rate of participation ($20,000 ÷ $500,000)	4%	
Participating dividend:		
Preferred, 4% of $100,000	$ 4,000	
Common, 4% of $400,000	16,000	
	$ 20,000	

ILLUSTRATION 15A-3
Dividend Distribution,
Noncumulative and
Fully Participating
Preferred

4. If the preferred stock is cumulative and is fully participating, and Mason Company did not pay dividends on the preferred stock in the preceding two years:

	Preferred	Common	Total
Dividends in arrears, 6% of $100,000 for 2 years	$12,000		$12,000
Current year's dividend, 6%	6,000	$24,000	30,000
Participating dividend, 1.6% ($8,000 ÷ $500,000)	1,600	6,400	8,000
Totals	$19,600	$30,400	$50,000

ILLUSTRATION 15A-4
Dividend Distribution,
Cumulative and Fully
Participating Preferred,
with Dividends in
Arrears

BOOK VALUE PER SHARE

Book value per share in its simplest form is computed as net assets divided by outstanding common shares at the end of the year. The computation of book value per share becomes more complicated if a company has preferred stock in its capital structure. For example, if preferred dividends are in arrears, if the preferred stock is participating, or if preferred stock has a redemption or liquidating value higher than its carrying amount, the company must allocate retained earnings between the preferred and common stockholders in computing book value.

To illustrate, assume that the following situation exists.

Stockholders' equity	Preferred	Common
Preferred stock, 5%	$300,000	
Common stock		$400,000
Excess of issue price over par of common stock		37,500
Retained earnings		162,582
Totals	$300,000	$600,082
Common shares outstanding		4,000
Book value per share		$150.02

ILLUSTRATION 15A-5
Computation of Book
Value per Share—No
Dividends in Arrears

The situation in Illustration 15A-5 assumes that no preferred dividends are in arrears and that the preferred is not participating. Now assume that the same facts exist except that the 5 percent preferred is cumulative, participating up to 8 percent, and that dividends for three years before the current year are in arrears. Illustration 15A-6 (page 854) shows how to compute the book value of the common stock, assuming that no action has yet been taken concerning dividends for the current year.

ILLUSTRATION 15A-6
Computation of Book Value per Share—with Dividends in Arrears

Stockholders' equity	Preferred	Common
Preferred stock, 5%	$300,000	
Common stock		$400,000
Excess of issue price over par of common stock		37,500
Retained earnings:		
Dividends in arrears (3 years at 5% a year)	45,000	
Current year requirement at 5%	15,000	20,000
Participating—additional 3%	9,000	12,000
Remainder to common		61,582
Totals	$369,000	$531,082
Shares outstanding		4,000
Book value per share		$132.77

In connection with the book value computation, the analyst must know how to handle the following items: the number of authorized and unissued shares; the number of treasury shares on hand; any commitments with respect to the issuance of unissued shares or the reissuance of treasury shares; and the relative rights and privileges of the various types of stock authorized. As an example, if the liquidating value of the preferred stock is higher than its carrying amount, the liquidating amount should be used in the book value computation.

SUMMARY OF LEARNING OBJECTIVE FOR APPENDIX 15A

10 **Explain the different types of preferred stock dividends and their effect on book value per share.** The dividend preferences of preferred stock affect the dividends paid to stockholders. Preferred stock can be (1) cumulative or noncumulative, and (2) fully participating, partially participating, or nonparticipating. If preferred dividends are in arrears, if the preferred stock is participating, or if preferred stock has a redemption or liquidation value higher than its carrying amount, allocate retained earnings between preferred and common stockholders in computing book value per share.

DEMONSTRATION PROBLEM

D'Ouville Company was formed on July 1, 2011. It was authorized to issue 500,000 shares of $10 par value common stock and 100,000 shares of 8%, $25 par value, cumulative and nonparticipating preferred stock. D'Ouville Company has a July 1–June 30 fiscal year. The following information relates to the stockholders' equity accounts of D'Ouville Company.

Common Stock: Prior to the 2013–2014 fiscal year, D'Ouville Company had 110,000 shares of outstanding common stock issued as follows.

1. 95,000 shares were issued for cash on July 1, 2011, at $31 per share.
2. On July 24, 2011, 5,000 shares were exchanged for a plot of land which cost the seller $70,000 in 2005 and had an estimated fair value of $220,000 on July 24, 2011.
3. 10,000 shares were issued on March 1, 2013, for $42 per share.

During the 2013–2014 fiscal year, the following transactions regarding common stock took place.

November 30, 2013   D'Ouville purchased 2,000 shares of its own stock on the open market at $39 per share. D'Ouville uses the cost method for treasury stock.

December 15, 2013	D'Ouville declared a 5% stock dividend for stockholders of record on January 15, 2014, to be issued on January 31, 2014. D'Ouville was having a liquidity problem and could not afford a cash dividend at the time. D'Ouville's common stock was selling at $52 per share on December 15, 2013.
June 20, 2014	D'Ouville sold 500 shares of its own common stock that it had purchased on November 30, 2013, for $21,000.

Preferred Stock: D'Ouville issued 100,000 shares of preferred stock at $44 per share on July 1, 2012.

Cash Dividends: D'Ouville has followed a schedule of declaring cash dividends in December and June, with payment being made to stockholders of record in the following month. The cash dividends which have been declared since inception of the company through June 30, 2014, are shown below.

Declaration Date	Common Stock	Preferred Stock
12/15/12	$0.30 per share	$0.50 per share
6/15/13	$0.30 per share	$0.50 per share
12/15/13	—	$0.50 per share

No cash dividends were declared during June 2014 due to the company's liquidity problems.

Retained Earnings: As of June 30, 2013, D'Ouville retained earnings account had a balance of $550,000. For the fiscal year ending June 30, 2014, D'Ouville reported net income of $120,000.

Instructions

Prepare the stockholders' equity section of the balance sheet, including appropriate notes, for D'Ouville Company as of June 30, 2014, as it should appear in its annual report to the shareholders.

Solution

D'OUVILLE COMPANY
STOCKHOLDERS' EQUITY
JUNE 30, 2014

Capital stock		
4% preferred stock, $25 par value, cumulative and nonparticipating, 100,000 shares authorized, 100,000 shares issued and outstanding—Note A		$2,500,000
Common stock, $10 par value, 500,000 shares authorized, 115,400 shares issued, with 1,500 shares held in the treasury		1,154,000
Additional paid-in capital		
On preferred stock	$1,900,000	
On common stock	2,711,800*	
On treasury stock	1,500	4,613,300
Total paid-in capital		8,267,300
Retained earnings		339,200**
Total paid-in capital and retained earnings		8,606,500
Less: Treasury stock, 1,500 shares at cost		58,500
Total stockholders' equity		$8,548,000

Note A: D'Ouville Company is in arrears on the preferred stock in the amount of $100,000.

*Premium on Common Stock:

Issue of 95,000 shares × ($31 − $10)	$1,995,000
Issue of 5,000 shares for plot of land ($220,000 − $50,000)	170,000
10,000 shares issued (3/1/13) [10,000 × ($42 − $10)]	320,000
5,400 shares as dividend [5,400 × ($52 − $10)]	226,800
	$2,711,800

**Retained Earnings:

Beginning balance	+	Income	−	Stock dividend	−	Preferred dividend	=	Ret. earnings, ending balance
$550,000	+ $120,000	−	$280,800	−	$50,000	=	$339,200

FASB CODIFICATION

FASB Codification References

[1] FASB ASC 480-10-05. [Predecessor literature: "Accounting for Certain Financial Instruments with Characteristics of Both Liabilities and Equity," *Statement of Financial Accounting Standards No. 150* (Norwalk Conn.: FASB, 2003).]

[2] FASB ASC 505-10-50-3. [Predecessor literature: "Disclosure of Information about Capital Structure," *Statement of Financial Accounting Standards No. 129* (Norwalk, Conn.: FASB, 1997).]

[3] FASB ASC 505-20-05-2. [Predecessor literature: American Institute of Certified Public Accountants, *Accounting Research and Terminology Bulletins, No. 43* (New York: AICPA, 1961), Ch. 7, par. 10.]

[4] FASB ASC 505-20-25-3. [Predecessor literature: American Institute of Certified Public Accountants, *Accounting Research and Terminology Bulletins, No. 43* (New York: AICPA, 1961), par. 13.]

[5] FASB ASC 505-10-50-3. [Predecessor literature: "Disclosure of Information about Capital Structure," *Statement of Financial Accounting Standards No. 129* (Norwalk, Conn.: FASB, February 1997), par. 4.]

Exercises

If your school has a subscription to the FASB Codification, go to *http://aaahq.org/ascLogin.cfm* to log in and prepare responses to the following. Provide Codification references for your responses.

CE15-1 Access the glossary ("Master Glossary") to answer the following.

    (a) What is a "convertible security"?
    (b) What is a "stock dividend"?
    (c) What is a "stock split"?
    (d) What are "participation rights"?

CE15-2 At what percentage point can the issuance of additional shares still qualify as a stock dividend, as opposed to a stock split?

CE15-3 A company plans to issue shares and wants to know the SEC's stance on the accounting treatment for the costs of issuing stock. Can these costs be deferred, or must they be expensed immediately?

CE15-4 If a company chooses to purchase its own shares and then either (1) retires the repurchased shares and issues additional shares, or (2) resells the repurchased shares, can a gain or loss be recognized by the company? Why or why not?

An additional Codification case can be found in the Using Your Judgment section, on page 873.

Be sure to check the book's companion website for a Review and Analysis Exercise, with solution.

WileyPLUS Brief Exercises, Exercises, Problems, and many more learning and assessment tools and resources are available for practice in WileyPLUS.

Note: All asterisked Questions, Exercises, and Problems relate to material in the appendix to the chapter.

QUESTIONS

1. In the absence of restrictive provisions, what are the basic rights of stockholders of a corporation?

2. Why is a preemptive right important?

3. Distinguish between common and preferred stock.

4. Why is the distinction between paid-in capital and retained earnings important?

5. Explain each of the following terms: authorized capital stock, unissued capital stock, issued capital stock, outstanding capital stock, and treasury stock.

6. What is meant by par value, and what is its significance to stockholders?

7. Describe the accounting for the issuance for cash of no-par value common stock at a price in excess of the stated value of the common stock.

8. Explain the difference between the proportional method and the incremental method of allocating the proceeds of lump-sum sales of capital stock.

9. What are the different bases for stock valuation when assets other than cash are received for issued shares of stock?

10. Explain how underwriting costs and accounting and legal fees associated with the issuance of stock should be recorded.

11. For what reasons might a corporation purchase its own stock?

12. Discuss the propriety of showing:

(a) Treasury stock as an asset.

(b) "Gain" or "loss" on sale of treasury stock as additions to or deductions from income.

(c) Dividends received on treasury stock as income.

13. What features or rights may alter the character of preferred stock?

14. Dagwood Inc. recently noted that its 4% preferred stock and 4% participating preferred stock, which are both cumulative, have priority as to dividends up to 4% of their par value. Its participating preferred stock participates equally with the common stock in any dividends in excess of 4%. What is meant by the term participating? Cumulative?

15. Where in the financial statements is preferred stock normally reported?

16. List possible sources of additional paid-in capital.

17. Satchel Inc. purchases 10,000 shares of its own previously issued $10 par common stock for $290,000. Assuming the shares are held in the treasury with intent to reissue, what effect does this transaction have on (a) net income, (b) total assets, (c) total paid-in capital, and (d) total stockholders' equity?

18. Indicate how each of the following accounts should be classified in the stockholders' equity section.

(a) Common Stock.

(b) Retained Earnings.

(c) Paid-in Capital in Excess of Par—Common Stock.

(d) Treasury Stock.

(e) Paid-in Capital from Treasury Stock.

(f) Paid-in Capital in Excess of Stated Value—Common Stock.

(g) Preferred Stock.

19. What factors influence the dividend policy of a company?

20. What are the principal considerations of a board of directors in making decisions involving dividend declarations? Discuss briefly.

21. Dividends are sometimes said to have been paid "out of retained earnings." What is the error, if any, in that statement?

22. Distinguish among: cash dividends, property dividends, liquidating dividends, and stock dividends.

23. Describe the accounting entry for a stock dividend, if any. Describe the accounting entry for a stock split, if any.

24. Stock splits and stock dividends may be used by a corporation to change the number of shares of its stock outstanding.

(a) What is meant by a stock split effected in the form of a dividend?

(b) From an accounting viewpoint, explain how the stock split effected in the form of a dividend differs from an ordinary stock dividend.

(c) How should a stock dividend that has been declared but not yet issued be classified in a balance sheet? Why?

25. The following comment appeared in the notes of Colorado Corporation's annual report: "Such distributions, representing proceeds from the sale of Sarazan, Inc., were paid in the form of partial liquidating dividends and were in lieu of a portion of the Company's ordinary cash dividends." How would a partial liquidating dividend be accounted for in the financial records?

26. This comment appeared in the annual report of MacCloud Inc.: "The Company could pay cash or property dividends on the Class A common stock without paying cash or property dividends on the Class B common stock. But if the Company pays any cash or property dividends on the Class B common stock, it would be required to pay at least the same dividend on the Class A common stock." How is a property dividend accounted for in the financial records?

27. For what reasons might a company restrict a portion of its retained earnings?

28. How are restrictions of retained earnings reported?

*****29.** McNabb Corp. had $100,000 of 7%, $20 par value preferred stock and 12,000 shares of $25 par value common stock outstanding throughout 2014.

(a) Assuming that total dividends declared in 2014 were $64,000, and that the preferred stock is not cumulative but is fully participating, common stockholders should receive 2014 dividends of what amount?

(b) Assuming that total dividends declared in 2014 were $64,000, and that the preferred stock is fully participating and cumulative with preferred dividends in arrears for 2013, preferred stockholders should receive 2014 dividends totaling what amount?

(c) Assuming that total dividends declared in 2014 were $30,000, that the preferred stock is cumulative, non-participating, and was issued on January 1, 2013, and that $5,000 of preferred dividends were declared and paid in 2013, the common stockholders should receive 2014 dividends totaling what amount?

3 **BE15-1** Buttercup Corporation issued 300 shares of $10 par value common stock for $4,500. Prepare Buttercup's journal entry.

3 **BE15-2** Swarten Corporation issued 600 shares of no-par common stock for $8,200. Prepare Swarten's journal entry if (a) the stock has no stated value, and (b) the stock has a stated value of $2 per share.

4 **9** **BE15-3** Wilco Corporation has the following account balances at December 31, 2014.

Common stock, $5 par value	$ 510,000
Treasury stock	90,000
Retained earnings	2,340,000
Paid-in capital in excess of par—common stock	1,320,000

Prepare Wilco's December 31, 2014, stockholders' equity section.

3 **BE15-4** Ravonette Corporation issued 300 shares of $10 par value common stock and 100 shares of $50 par value preferred stock for a lump sum of $13,500. The common stock has a market price of $20 per share, and the preferred stock has a market price of $90 per share. Prepare the journal entry to record the issuance.

3 **BE15-5** On February 1, 2014, Buffalo Corporation issued 3,000 shares of its $5 par value common stock for land worth $31,000. Prepare the February 1, 2014, journal entry.

3 **BE15-6** Moonwalker Corporation issued 2,000 shares of its $10 par value common stock for $60,000. Moonwalker also incurred $1,500 of costs associated with issuing the stock. Prepare Moonwalker's journal entry to record the issuance of the company's stock.

4 **BE15-7** Sprinkle Inc. has outstanding 10,000 shares of $10 par value common stock. On July 1, 2014, Sprinkle reacquired 100 shares at $87 per share. On September 1, Sprinkle reissued 60 shares at $90 per share. On November 1, Sprinkle reissued 40 shares at $83 per share. Prepare Sprinkle's journal entries to record these transactions using the cost method.

4 **BE15-8** Arantxa Corporation has outstanding 20,000 shares of $5 par value common stock. On August 1, 2014, Arantxa reacquired 200 shares at $80 per share. On November 1, Arantxa reissued the 200 shares at $70 per share. Arantxa had no previous treasury stock transactions. Prepare Arantxa's journal entries to record these transactions using the cost method.

5 **BE15-9** Hinges Corporation issued 500 shares of $100 par value preferred stock for $61,500. Prepare Hinges's journal entry.

6 **BE15-10** Woolford Inc. declared a cash dividend of $1.00 per share on its 2 million outstanding shares. The dividend was declared on August 1, payable on September 9 to all stockholders of record on August 15. Prepare all journal entries necessary on those three dates.

6 **7** **BE15-11** Cole Inc. owns shares of Marlin Corporation stock classified as an available-for-sale investment. At December 31, 2014, the available-for-sale securities were carried in Cole's accounting records at their cost of $875,000, which equals their fair value. On September 21, 2015, when the fair value of the securities was $1,200,000, Cole declared a property dividend whereby the Marlin securities are to be distributed on October 23, 2015 to stockholders of record on October 8, 2015. Prepare all journal entries necessary on those three dates.

6 **7** **BE15-12** Graves Mining Company declared, on April 20, a dividend of $500,000 payable on June 1. Of this amount, $125,000 is a return of capital. Prepare the April 20 and June 1 entries for Graves.

8 **BE15-13** Green Day Corporation has outstanding 400,000 shares of $10 par value common stock. The corporation declares a 5% stock dividend when the fair value of the stock is $65 per share. Prepare the journal entries for Green Day Corporation for both the date of declaration and the date of distribution.

8 **BE15-14** Use the information from BE15-13, but assume Green Day Corporation declared a 100% stock dividend rather than a 5% stock dividend. Prepare the journal entries for both the date of declaration and the date of distribution.

10 *****BE15-15** Nottebart Corporation has outstanding 10,000 shares of $100 par value, 6% preferred stock and 60,000 shares of $10 par value common stock. The preferred stock was issued in January 2014, and no dividends were declared in 2014 or 2015. In 2016, Nottebart declares a cash dividend of $300,000. How will the dividend be shared by common and preferred stockholders if the preferred is (a) noncumulative and (b) cumulative?

EXERCISES

3 **E15-1 (Recording the Issuances of Common Stock)** During its first year of operations, Collin Raye Corporation had the following transactions pertaining to its common stock.

Jan. 10	Issued 80,000 shares for cash at $6 per share.	
Mar. 1	Issued 5,000 shares to attorneys in payment of a bill for $35,000 for services rendered in helping the company to incorporate.	
July 1	Issued 30,000 shares for cash at $8 per share.	
Sept. 1	Issued 60,000 shares for cash at $10 per share.	

Instructions
  (a) Prepare the journal entries for these transactions, assuming that the common stock has a par value of $5 per share.
  (b) Prepare the journal entries for these transactions, assuming that the common stock is no-par with a stated value of $3 per share.

3 **E15-2 (Recording the Issuance of Common and Preferred Stock)** Kathleen Battle Corporation was organized on January 1, 2014. It is authorized to issue 10,000 shares of 8%, $100 par value preferred stock, and 500,000 shares of no-par common stock with a stated value of $1 per share. The following stock transactions were completed during the first year.

Jan. 10	Issued 80,000 shares of common stock for cash at $5 per share.
Mar. 1	Issued 5,000 shares of preferred stock for cash at $108 per share.
Apr. 1	Issued 24,000 shares of common stock for land. The asking price of the land was $90,000; the fair value of the land was $80,000.
May 1	Issued 80,000 shares of common stock for cash at $7 per share.
Aug. 1	Issued 10,000 shares of common stock to attorneys in payment of their bill of $50,000 for services rendered in helping the company organize.
Sept. 1	Issued 10,000 shares of common stock for cash at $9 per share.
Nov. 1	Issued 1,000 shares of preferred stock for cash at $112 per share.

Instructions
Prepare the journal entries to record the above transactions.

3 **E15-3 (Stock Issued for Land)** Twenty-five thousand shares reacquired by Elixir Corporation for $53 per share were exchanged for undeveloped land that has an appraised value of $1,700,000. At the time of the exchange, the common stock was trading at $62 per share on an organized exchange.

Instructions
  (a) Prepare the journal entry to record the acquisition of land assuming that the purchase of the stock was originally recorded using the cost method.
  (b) Briefly identify the possible alternatives (including those that are totally unacceptable) for quantifying the cost of the land and briefly support your choice.

3 **E15-4 (Lump-Sum Sale of Stock with Bonds)** Faith Evans Corporation is a regional company which is an SEC registrant. The corporation's securities are thinly traded on NASDAQ. Faith Evans Corp. has issued 10,000 units. Each unit consists of a $500 par, 12% subordinated debenture and 10 shares of $5 par common stock. The investment banker has retained 400 units as the underwriting fee. The other 9,600 units were sold to outside investors for cash at $880 per unit. Prior to this sale, the 2-week ask price of common stock was $40 per share. Twelve percent is a reasonable market yield for the debentures, and therefore the par value of the bonds is equal to the fair value.

Instructions
  (a) Prepare the journal entry to record Evans' transaction, under the following conditions.
    (1) Employing the incremental method.
    (2) Employing the proportional method, assuming the recent price quote on the common stock reflects fair value.
  (b) Briefly explain which method is, in your opinion, the better method.

3 **5** **E15-5 (Lump-Sum Sales of Stock with Preferred Stock)** Dave Matthew Inc. issues 500 shares of $10 par value common stock and 100 shares of $100 par value preferred stock for a lump sum of $100,000.

Instructions
  (a) Prepare the journal entry for the issuance when the market price of the common shares is $165 each and market price of the preferred is $230 each. (Round to nearest dollar.)

(b) Prepare the journal entry for the issuance when only the market price of the common stock is known and it is $170 per share.

3 4 E15-6 (Stock Issuances and Repurchase) Lindsey Hunter Corporation is authorized to issue 50,000 shares of $5 par value common stock. During 2014, Lindsey Hunter took part in the following selected transactions.

1. Issued 5,000 shares of stock at $45 per share, less costs related to the issuance of the stock totaling $7,000.
2. Issued 1,000 shares of stock for land appraised at $50,000. The stock was actively traded on a national stock exchange at approximately $46 per share on the date of issuance.
3. Purchased 500 shares of treasury stock at $43 per share. The treasury shares purchased were issued in 2010 at $40 per share.

Instructions
(a) Prepare the journal entry to record item 1.
(b) Prepare the journal entry to record item 2.
(c) Prepare the journal entry to record item 3 using the cost method.

4 E15-7 (Effect of Treasury Stock Transactions on Financials) Joe Dumars Company has outstanding 40,000 shares of $5 par common stock which had been issued at $30 per share. Joe Dumars then entered into the following transactions.

1. Purchased 5,000 treasury shares at $45 per share.
2. Resold 2,000 of the treasury shares at $49 per share.
3. Resold 500 of the treasury shares at $40 per share.

Instructions
Use the following code to indicate the effect each of the three transactions has on the financial statement categories listed in the table below, assuming Joe Dumars Company uses the cost method (I = Increase; D = Decrease; NE = No effect).

#	Assets	Liabilities	Stockholders' Equity	Paid-in Capital	Retained Earnings	Net Income
1						
2						
3						

3 E15-8 (Preferred Stock Entries and Dividends) Otis Thorpe Corporation has 10,000 shares of $100 par value, 8%, preferred stock and 50,000 shares of $10 par value common stock outstanding at December 31, 2014.

Instructions
Answer the questions in each of the following independent situations.
(a) If the preferred stock is cumulative and dividends were last paid on the preferred stock on December 31, 2011, what are the dividends in arrears that should be reported on the December 31, 2014, balance sheet? How should these dividends be reported?
(b) If the preferred stock is convertible into seven shares of $10 par value common stock and 4,000 shares are converted, what entry is required for the conversion assuming the preferred stock was issued at par value?
(c) If the preferred stock was issued at $107 per share, how should the preferred stock be reported in the stockholders' equity section?

3 4 E15-9 (Correcting Entries for Equity Transactions) Pistons Inc. recently hired a new accountant with extensive experience in accounting for partnerships. Because of the pressure of the new job, the accountant was unable to review what he had learned earlier about corporation accounting. During the first month, he made the following entries for the corporation's capital stock.

May 2	Cash	192,000	
	Capital Stock		192,000
	(Issued 12,000 shares of $5 par value common stock at $16 per share)		
10	Cash	600,000	
	Capital Stock		600,000
	(Issued 10,000 shares of $30 par value preferred stock at $60 per share)		

May 15	Capital Stock	15,000	
	Cash		15,000
	(Purchased 1,000 shares of common stock for the treasury at $15 per share)		
31	Cash	8,500	
	Capital Stock		5,000
	Gain on Sale of Stock		3,500
	(Sold 500 shares of treasury stock at $17 per share)		

Instructions

On the basis of the explanation for each entry, prepare the entries that should have been made for the capital stock transactions.

3 4 **E15-10 (Analysis of Equity Data and Equity Section Preparation)** For a recent 2-year period, the balance sheet of Santana Dotson Company showed the following stockholders' equity data at December 31 (in millions).

	2014	2013
Additional paid-in capital	$ 931	$ 817
Common stock	545	540
Retained earnings	7,167	5,226
Treasury stock	1,564	918
Total stockholders' equity	$7,079	$5,665
Common stock shares issued	218	216
Common stock shares authorized	500	500
Treasury stock shares	34	27

Instructions

(a) Answer the following questions.
  (1) What is the par value of the common stock?
  (2) What is the cost per share of treasury stock at December 31, 2014, and at December 31, 2013?
(b) Prepare the stockholders' equity section at December 31, 2014.

7 8 **E15-11 (Equity Items on the Balance Sheet)** The following are selected transactions that may affect stockholders' equity.

1. Recorded accrued interest earned on a note receivable.
2. Declared a cash dividend.
3. Declared and distributed a stock split.
4. Approved a retained earnings restriction.
5. Recorded the expiration of insurance coverage that was previously recorded as prepaid insurance.
6. Paid the cash dividend declared in item 2 above.
7. Recorded accrued interest expense on a note payable.
8. Declared a stock dividend.
9. Distributed the stock dividend declared in item 8.

Instructions

In the following table, indicate the effect each of the nine transactions has on the financial statement elements listed. Use the following code: I = Increase, D = Decrease, NE = No effect.

Item	Assets	Liabilities	Stockholders' Equity	Paid-in Capital	Retained Earnings	Net Income

7 **E15-12 (Cash Dividend and Liquidating Dividend)** Lotoya Davis Corporation has 10 million shares of common stock issued and outstanding. On June 1, the board of directors voted an 80 cents per share cash dividend to stockholders of record as of June 14, payable June 30.

Instructions
(a) Prepare the journal entry for each of the dates above assuming the dividend represents a distribution of earnings.
(b) How would the entry differ if the dividend were a liquidating dividend?

8 **E15-13 (Stock Split and Stock Dividend)** The common stock of Alexander Hamilton Inc. is currently selling at $120 per share. The directors wish to reduce the share price and increase share volume prior to a new issue. The per share par value is $10; book value is $70 per share. Nine million shares are issued and outstanding.

Instructions
Prepare the necessary journal entries assuming the following.
(a) The board votes a 2-for-1 stock split.
(b) The board votes a 100% stock dividend.
(c) Briefly discuss the accounting and securities market differences between these two methods of increasing the number of shares outstanding.

8 **E15-14 (Entries for Stock Dividends and Stock Splits)** The stockholders' equity accounts of G.K. Chesterton Company have the following balances on December 31, 2014.

Common stock, $10 par, 300,000 shares issued and outstanding	$3,000,000
Paid-in capital in excess of par—common stock	1,200,000
Retained earnings	5,600,000

Shares of G.K. Chesterton Company stock are currently selling on the Midwest Stock Exchange at $37.

Instructions
Prepare the appropriate journal entries for each of the following cases.
(a) A stock dividend of 5% is declared and issued.
(b) A stock dividend of 100% is declared and issued.
(c) A 2-for-1 stock split is declared and issued.

7 **8** **E15-15 (Dividend Entries)** The following data were taken from the balance sheet accounts of Masefield Corporation on December 31, 2013.

Current assets	$540,000
Debt investments	624,000
Common stock (par value $10)	500,000
Paid-in capital in excess of par	150,000
Retained earnings	840,000

Instructions
Prepare the required journal entries for the following unrelated items.
(a) A 5% stock dividend is declared and distributed at a time when the market price per share is $39.
(b) The par value of the common stock is reduced to $2 with a 5-for-1 stock split.
(c) A dividend is declared January 5, 2014, and paid January 25, 2014, in bonds held as an investment. The bonds have a book value of $100,000 and a fair value of $135,000.

6 **7** **8** **E15-16 (Computation of Retained Earnings)** The following information has been taken from the ledger accounts of Isaac Stern Corporation.

Total income since incorporation	$317,000
Total cash dividends paid	60,000
Total value of stock dividends distributed	30,000
Gains on treasury stock transactions	18,000
Unamortized discount on bonds payable	32,000

Instructions
Determine the current balance of retained earnings.

9 **E15-17 (Stockholders' Equity Section)** Bruno Corporation's post-closing trial balance at December 31, 2014, is shown on the next page.

BRUNO CORPORATION
POST-CLOSING TRIAL BALANCE
DECEMBER 31, 2014

	Dr.	Cr.
Accounts payable		$ 310,000
Accounts receivable	$ 480,000	
Accumulated depreciation—buildings		185,000
Additional paid-in capital in excess		
of par—common		1,300,000
From treasury stock		160,000
Allowance for doubtful accounts		30,000
Bonds payable		300,000
Buildings	1,450,000	
Cash	190,000	
Common stock ($1 par)		200,000
Dividends payable (preferred stock—cash)		4,000
Inventory	560,000	
Land	400,000	
Preferred stock ($50 par)		500,000
Prepaid expenses	40,000	
Retained earnings		301,000
Treasury stock (common at cost)	170,000	
Totals	$3,290,000	$3,290,000

At December 31, 2014, Bruno had the following number of common and preferred shares.

	Common	Preferred
Authorized	600,000	60,000
Issued	200,000	10,000
Outstanding	190,000	10,000

The dividends on preferred stock are $4 cumulative. In addition, the preferred stock has a preference in liquidation of $50 per share.

Instructions
Prepare the stockholders' equity section of Bruno's balance sheet at December 31, 2014.

(AICPA adapted)

  E15-18 (Dividends and Stockholders' Equity Section) Anne Cleves Company reported the following amounts in the stockholders' equity section of its December 31, 2013, balance sheet.

Preferred stock, 10%, $100 par (10,000 shares authorized, 2,000 shares issued)	$200,000
Common stock, $5 par (100,000 shares authorized, 20,000 shares issued)	100,000
Additional paid-in capital	125,000
Retained earnings	450,000
Total	$875,000

During 2014, Cleves took part in the following transactions concerning stockholders' equity.

1. Paid the annual 2013 $10 per share dividend on preferred stock and a $2 per share dividend on common stock. These dividends had been declared on December 31, 2013.
2. Purchased 1,700 shares of its own outstanding common stock for $40 per share. Cleves uses the cost method.
3. Reissued 700 treasury shares for land valued at $30,000.
4. Issued 500 shares of preferred stock at $105 per share.
5. Declared a 10% stock dividend on the outstanding common stock when the stock is selling for $45 per share.
6. Issued the stock dividend.
7. Declared the annual 2014 $10 per share dividend on preferred stock and the $2 per share dividend on common stock. These dividends are payable in 2015.

Instructions

(a) Prepare journal entries to record the transactions described above.

(b) Prepare the December 31, 2014, stockholders' equity section. Assume 2014 net income was $330,000.

9 ▸ E15-19 (Comparison of Alternative Forms of Financing) Shown below is the liabilities and stockholders' equity section of the balance sheet for Jana Kingston Company and Mary Ann Benson Company. Each has assets totaling $4,200,000.

Jana Kingston Co.		Mary Ann Benson Co.	
Current liabilities	$ 300,000	Current liabilities	$ 600,000
Long-term debt, 10%	1,200,000	Common stock ($20 par)	2,900,000
Common stock ($20 par)	2,000,000	Retained earnings (Cash	
Retained earnings (Cash		dividends, $328,000)	700,000
dividends, $220,000)	700,000		
	$4,200,000		$4,200,000

For the year, each company has earned the same income before interest and taxes.

	Jana Kingston Co.	Mary Ann Benson Co.
Income before interest and taxes	$1,200,000	$1,200,000
Interest expense	120,000	–0–
	1,080,000	1,200,000
Income taxes (45%)	486,000	540,000
Net income	$ 594,000	$ 660,000

At year end, the market price of Kingston's stock was $101 per share, and Benson's was $63.50.

Instructions

(a) Which company is more profitable in terms of return on total assets?

(b) Which company is more profitable in terms of return on common stock equity?

(c) Which company has the greater net income per share of stock? Neither company issued or reacquired shares during the year.

(d) From the point of view of net income, is it advantageous to the stockholders of Jana Kingston Co. to have the long-term debt outstanding? Why?

(e) What is the book value per share for each company?

9 ▸ E15-20 (Trading on the Equity Analysis) Presented below is information from the annual report of Emporia Plastics, Inc.

Operating income	$ 532,150
Bond interest expense	135,000
	397,150
Income taxes	183,432
Net income	$ 213,718
Bonds payable	$1,000,000
Common stock	875,000
Retained earnings	375,000

Instructions

(a) Compute the return on common stock equity and the rate of interest paid on bonds. (Assume balances for debt and equity accounts approximate averages for the year.)

(b) Is Emporia Plastics Inc. trading on the equity successfully? Explain.

10 ▸ *E15-21 (Preferred Dividends) The outstanding capital stock of Edna Millay Corporation consists of 2,000 shares of $100 par value, 8% preferred, and 5,000 shares of $50 par value common.

Instructions

Assuming that the company has retained earnings of $90,000, all of which is to be paid out in dividends, and that preferred dividends were not paid during the 2 years preceding the current year, state how much each class of stock should receive under each of the following conditions.

(a) The preferred stock is noncumulative and nonparticipating.

(b) The preferred stock is cumulative and nonparticipating.

(c) The preferred stock is cumulative and participating. (Round dividend rate percentages to four decimal places.)

10 *E15-22 **(Preferred Dividends)** Matt Schmidt Company's ledger shows the following balances on December 31, 2014.

7% Preferred stock—$10 par value, outstanding 20,000 shares	$ 200,000
Common stock—$100 par value, outstanding 30,000 shares	3,000,000
Retained earnings	630,000

Instructions

Assuming that the directors decide to declare total dividends in the amount of $366,000, determine how much each class of stock should receive under each of the conditions stated below. One year's dividends are in arrears on the preferred stock.

(a) The preferred stock is cumulative and fully participating.
(b) The preferred stock is noncumulative and nonparticipating.
(c) The preferred stock is noncumulative and is participating in distributions in excess of a 10% dividend rate on the common stock.

10 *E15-23 **(Preferred Stock Dividends)** Cajun Company has outstanding 2,500 shares of $100 par, 6% preferred stock and 15,000 shares of $10 par value common. The following schedule shows the amount of dividends paid out over the last 4 years.

Instructions

Allocate the dividends to each type of stock under assumptions (a) and (b). Express your answers in per-share amounts using the format shown below.

		Assumptions			
		(a) Preferred, noncumulative, and nonparticipating		**(b)** Preferred, cumulative, and fully participating	
Year	Paid-out	Preferred	Common	Preferred	Common
2012	$13,000				
2013	$26,000				
2014	$57,000				
2015	$76,000				

10 *E15-24 **(Computation of Book Value per Share)** Morgan Sondgeroth Inc. began operations in January 2012 and reported the following results for each of its 3 years of operations.

| 2012 | $260,000 net loss | 2013 | $40,000 net loss | 2014 | $800,000 net income |

At December 31, 2014, Morgan Sondgeroth Inc. capital accounts were as follows.

8% cumulative preferred stock, par value $100; authorized, issued, and outstanding 5,000 shares	$500,000
Common stock, par value $1.00; authorized 1,000,000 shares; issued and outstanding 750,000 shares	$750,000

Morgan Sondgeroth Inc. has never paid a cash or stock dividend. There has been no change in the capital accounts since Sondgeroth began operations. The state law permits dividends only from retained earnings.

Instructions

(a) Compute the book value of the common stock at December 31, 2014.
(b) Compute the book value of the common stock at December 31, 2014, assuming that the preferred stock has a liquidating value of $106 per share.

EXERCISES SET B

See the book's companion website, at **www.wiley.com/college/kieso**, for an additional set of exercises.

PROBLEMS

P15-1 (Equity Transactions and Statement Preparation) On January 5, 2014, Phelps Corporation received a charter granting the right to issue 5,000 shares of $100 par value, 8% cumulative and nonparticipating preferred stock, and 50,000 shares of $10 par value common stock. It then completed these transactions.

Jan. 11	Issued 20,000 shares of common stock at $16 per share.
Feb. 1	Issued to Sanchez Corp. 4,000 shares of preferred stock for the following assets: equipment with a fair value of $50,000; a factory building with a fair value of $160,000; and land with an appraised value of $270,000.
July 29	Purchased 1,800 shares of common stock at $17 per share. (Use cost method.)
Aug. 10	Sold the 1,800 treasury shares at $14 per share.
Dec. 31	Declared a $0.25 per share cash dividend on the common stock and declared the preferred dividend.
Dec. 31	Closed the Income Summary account. There was a $175,700 net income.

Instructions
(a) Record the journal entries for the transactions listed above.
(b) Prepare the stockholders' equity section of Phelps Corporation's balance sheet as of December 31, 2014.

P15-2 (Treasury Stock Transactions and Presentation) Clemson Company had the following stockholders' equity as of January 1, 2014.

Common stock, $5 par value, 20,000 shares issued	$100,000
Paid-in capital in excess of par—common stock	300,000
Retained earnings	320,000
Total stockholders' equity	$720,000

During 2014, the following transactions occurred.

Feb.	1	Clemson repurchased 2,000 shares of treasury stock at a price of $19 per share.
Mar.	1	800 shares of treasury stock repurchased above were reissued at $17 per share.
Mar.	18	500 shares of treasury stock repurchased above were reissued at $14 per share.
Apr.	22	600 shares of treasury stock repurchased above were reissued at $20 per share.

Instructions
(a) Prepare the journal entries to record the treasury stock transactions in 2014, assuming Clemson uses the cost method.
(b) Prepare the stockholders' equity section as of April 30, 2014. Net income for the first 4 months of 2014 was $130,000.

P15-3 (Equity Transactions and Statement Preparation) Hatch Company has two classes of capital stock outstanding: 8%, $20 par preferred and $5 par common. At December 31, 2014, the following accounts were included in stockholders' equity.

Preferred Stock, 150,000 shares	$ 3,000,000
Common Stock, 2,000,000 shares	10,000,000
Paid-in Capital in Excess of Par—Preferred Stock	200,000
Paid-in Capital in Excess of Par—Common Stock	27,000,000
Retained Earnings	4,500,000

The following transactions affected stockholders' equity during 2015.

Jan.	1	30,000 shares of preferred stock issued at $22 per share.
Feb.	1	50,000 shares of common stock issued at $20 per share.
June	1	2-for-1 stock split (par value reduced to $2.50).
July	1	30,000 shares of common treasury stock purchased at $10 per share. Hatch uses the cost method.
Sept.	15	10,000 shares of treasury stock reissued at $11 per share.
Dec.	31	The preferred dividend is declared, and a common dividend of 50¢ per share is declared.
Dec.	31	Net income is $2,100,000.

Instructions
Prepare the stockholders' equity section for Hatch Company at December 31, 2015. Show all supporting computations.

3 **5** **P15-4 (Stock Transactions—Lump Sum)** Seles Corporation's charter authorized issuance of 100,000 shares of $10 par value common stock and 50,000 shares of $50 preferred stock. The following transactions involving the issuance of shares of stock were completed. Each transaction is independent of the others.

1. Issued a $10,000, 9% bond payable at par and gave as a bonus one share of preferred stock, which at that time was selling for $106 a share.
2. Issued 500 shares of common stock for equipment. The equipment had been appraised at $7,100; the seller's book value was $6,200. The most recent market price of the common stock is $16 a share.
3. Issued 375 shares of common and 100 shares of preferred for a lump sum amounting to $10,800. The common had been selling at $14 and the preferred at $65.
4. Issued 200 shares of common and 50 shares of preferred for equipment. The common had a fair value of $16 per share; the equipment has a fair value of $6,500.

Instructions

Record the transactions listed above in journal entry form.

4 **P15-5 (Treasury Stock—Cost Method)** Before Gordon Corporation engages in the treasury stock transactions listed below, its general ledger reflects, among others, the following account balances (par value of its stock is $30 per share).

Paid-in Capital in Excess of Par—Common Stock	Common Stock	Retained Earnings
$99,000	$270,000	$80,000

Instructions

Record the treasury stock transactions (given below) under the cost method of handling treasury stock; use the FIFO method for purchase-sale purposes.

(a) Bought 380 shares of treasury stock at $40 per share.
(b) Bought 300 shares of treasury stock at $45 per share.
(c) Sold 350 shares of treasury stock at $42 per share.
(d) Sold 110 shares of treasury stock at $38 per share.

4 **7** **P15-6 (Treasury Stock—Cost Method—Equity Section Preparation)** Washington Company has the **9** following stockholders' equity accounts at December 31, 2014.

Common Stock ($100 par value, authorized 8,000 shares)	$480,000
Retained Earnings	294,000

Instructions

(a) Prepare entries in journal form to record the following transactions, which took place during 2015.
   (1) 280 shares of outstanding stock were purchased at $97 per share. (These are to be accounted for using the cost method.)
   (2) A $20 per share cash dividend was declared.
   (3) The dividend declared in (2) above was paid.
   (4) The treasury shares purchased in (1) above were resold at $102 per share.
   (5) 500 shares of outstanding stock were purchased at $105 per share.
   (6) 350 of the shares purchased in (5) above were resold at $96 per share.
(b) Prepare the stockholders' equity section of Washington Company's balance sheet after giving effect to these transactions, assuming that the net income for 2015 was $94,000. State law requires restriction of retained earnings for the amount of treasury stock.

4 **7** **P15-7 (Cash Dividend Entries)** The books of Conchita Corporation carried the following account balances as of December 31, 2014.

Cash	$ 195,000
Preferred Stock (6% cumulative, nonparticipating, $50 par)	300,000
Common Stock (no-par value, 300,000 shares issued)	1,500,000
Paid-in Capital in Excess of Par—Preferred Stock	150,000
Treasury Stock (common 2,800 shares at cost)	33,600
Retained Earnings	105,000

The company decided not to pay any dividends in 2014.

The board of directors, at their annual meeting on December 21, 2015, declared the following: "The current year dividends shall be 6% on the preferred and $.30 per share on the common. The dividends in arrears shall be paid by issuing 1,500 shares of treasury stock." At the date of declaration, the preferred is selling at $80 per share, and the common at $12 per share. Net income for 2015 is estimated at $77,000.

Instructions

(a) Prepare the journal entries required for the dividend declaration and payment, assuming that they occur simultaneously.

(b) Could Conchita Corporation give the preferred stockholders 2 years' dividends and common stockholders a 30 cents per share dividend, all in cash?

7 **8** **P15-8 (Dividends and Splits)** Myers Company provides you with the following condensed balance sheet information.

Assets		Liabilities and Stockholders' Equity		
Current assets	$ 40,000	Current and long-term liabilities		$100,000
Equity investments (trading)	60,000	Stockholders' equity		
Equipment (net)	250,000	Common stock ($5 par)	$ 20,000	
Intangibles	60,000	Paid-in capital in excess of par	110,000	
		Retained earnings	180,000	310,000
Total assets	$410,000			
		Total liabilities and stockholders' equity		$410,000

Instructions

For each transaction below, indicate the dollar impact (if any) on the following five items: (1) total assets, (2) common stock, (3) paid-in capital in excess of par, (4) retained earnings, and (5) stockholders' equity. (Each situation is independent.)

(a) Myers declares and pays a $0.50 per share cash dividend.

(b) Myers declares and issues a 10% stock dividend when the market price of the stock is $14 per share.

(c) Myers declares and issues a 30% stock dividend when the market price of the stock is $15 per share.

(d) Myers declares and distributes a property dividend. Myers gives one share of its equity investment (ABC stock) for every two shares of Myers Company stock held. Myers owns 10,000 shares of ABC. ABC is selling for $10 per share on the date the property dividend is declared.

(e) Myers declares a 2-for-1 stock split and issues new shares.

3 **4** **P15-9 (Stockholders' Equity Section of Balance Sheet)** The following is a summary of all relevant trans-
7 **9** actions of Vicario Corporation since it was organized in 2014.

In 2014, 15,000 shares were authorized and 7,000 shares of common stock ($50 par value) were issued at a price of $57. In 2015, 1,000 shares were issued as a stock dividend when the stock was selling for $60. Three hundred shares of common stock were bought in 2016 at a cost of $64 per share. These 300 shares are still in the company treasury.

In 2015, 10,000 preferred shares were authorized and the company issued 5,000 of them ($100 par value) at $113. Some of the preferred stock was reacquired by the company and later reissued for $4,700 more than it cost the company.

The corporation has earned a total of $610,000 in net income after income taxes and paid out a total of $312,600 in cash dividends since incorporation.

Instructions

Prepare the stockholders' equity section of the balance sheet in proper form for Vicario Corporation as of December 31, 2016. Account for treasury stock using the cost method.

8 **P15-10 (Stock Dividends and Stock Split)** Oregon Inc. $10 par common stock is selling for $110 per share. Four million shares are currently issued and outstanding. The board of directors wishes to stimulate interest in Oregon common stock before a forthcoming stock issue but does not wish to distribute capital at this time. The board also believes that too many adjustments to the stockholders' equity section, especially retained earnings, might discourage potential investors.

The board has considered three options for stimulating interest in the stock:

1. A 20% stock dividend.
2. A 100% stock dividend.
3. A 2-for-1 stock split.

Instructions

Acting as financial advisor to the board, you have been asked to report briefly on each option and, considering the board's wishes, make a recommendation. Discuss the effects of each of the foregoing options.

7 **8** **P15-11 (Stock and Cash Dividends)** Earnhart Corporation has outstanding 3,000,000 shares of common
9 stock of a par value of $10 each. The balance in its Retained Earnings account at January 1, 2014, was $24,000,000, and it then had Paid-in Capital in Excess of Par—Common Stock of $5,000,000. During 2014,

the company's net income was $4,700,000. A cash dividend of $0.60 a share was declared on May 5, 2014, and was paid June 30, 2014, and a 6% stock dividend was declared on November 30, 2014, and distributed to stockholders of record at the close of business on December 31, 2014. You have been asked to advise on the proper accounting treatment of the stock dividend.

The existing stock of the company is quoted on a national stock exchange. The market price of the stock has been as follows.

October 31, 2014	$31
November 30, 2014	$34
December 31, 2014	$38

Instructions

(a) Prepare the journal entry to record the declaration and payment of the cash dividend.

(b) Prepare the journal entry to record the declaration and distribution of the stock dividend.

(c) Prepare the stockholders' equity section (including schedules of retained earnings and additional paid-in capital) of the balance sheet of Earnhart Corporation for the year 2014 on the basis of the foregoing information. Draft a note to the financial statements setting forth the basis of the accounting for the stock dividend, and add separately appropriate comments or explanations regarding the basis chosen.

P15-12 (Analysis and Classification of Equity Transactions) Penn Company was formed on July 1, 2012. It was authorized to issue 300,000 shares of $10 par value common stock and 100,000 shares of 8% $25 par value, cumulative and nonparticipating preferred stock. Penn Company has a July 1–June 30 fiscal year.

The following information relates to the stockholders' equity accounts of Penn Company.

Common Stock

Prior to the 2014–2015 fiscal year, Penn Company had 110,000 shares of outstanding common stock issued as follows.

1. 85,000 shares were issued for cash on July 1, 2012, at $31 per share.
2. On July 24, 2012, 5,000 shares were exchanged for a plot of land which cost the seller $70,000 in 2006 and had an estimated fair value of $220,000 on July 24, 2012.
3. 20,000 shares were issued on March 1, 2013, for $42 per share.

During the 2014–2015 fiscal year, the following transactions regarding common stock took place.

November 30, 2014	Penn purchased 2,000 shares of its own stock on the open market at $39 per share. Penn uses the cost method for treasury stock.
December 15, 2014	Penn declared a 5% stock dividend for stockholders of record on January 15, 2015, to be issued on January 31, 2015. Penn was having a liquidity problem and could not afford a cash dividend at the time. Penn's common stock was selling at $52 per share on December 15, 2014.
June 20, 2015	Penn sold 500 shares of its own common stock that it had purchased on November 30, 2014, for $21,000.

Preferred Stock

Penn issued 40,000 shares of preferred stock at $44 per share on July 1, 2013.

Cash Dividends

Penn has followed a schedule of declaring cash dividends in December and June, with payment being made to stockholders of record in the following month. The cash dividends which have been declared since inception of the company through June 30, 2015, are shown below.

Declaration Date	Common Stock	Preferred Stock
12/15/13	$0.30 per share	$1.00 per share
6/15/14	$0.30 per share	$1.00 per share
12/15/14	—	$1.00 per share

No cash dividends were declared during June 2015 due to the company's liquidity problems.

Retained Earnings

As of June 30, 2014, Penn's retained earnings account had a balance of $690,000. For the fiscal year ending June 30, 2015, Penn reported net income of $40,000.

Instructions

Prepare the stockholders' equity section of the balance sheet, including appropriate notes, for Penn Company as of June 30, 2015, as it should appear in its annual report to the shareholders.

(CMA adapted)

PROBLEMS SET B

See the book's companion website, at **www.wiley.com/college/kieso**, for an additional set of problems.

CONCEPTS FOR ANALYSIS

CA15-1 (Preemptive Rights and Dilution of Ownership) Wallace Computer Company is a small, closely held corporation. Eighty percent of the stock is held by Derek Wallace, president. Of the remainder, 10% is held by members of his family and 10% by Kathy Baker, a former officer who is now retired. The balance sheet of the company at June 30, 2014, was substantially as shown below.

Assets		Liabilities and Stockholders' Equity	
Cash	$ 22,000	Current liabilities	$ 50,000
Other	450,000	Common stock	250,000
	$472,000	Retained earnings	172,000
			$472,000

Additional authorized common stock of $300,000 par value had never been issued. To strengthen the cash position of the company, Wallace issued common stock with a par value of $100,000 to himself at par for cash. At the next stockholders' meeting, Baker objected and claimed that her interests had been injured.

Instructions
(a) Which stockholder's right was ignored in the issue of shares to Derek Wallace?
(b) How may the damage to Baker's interests be repaired most simply?
(c) If Derek Wallace offered Baker a personal cash settlement and they agreed to employ you as an impartial arbitrator to determine the amount, what settlement would you propose? Present your calculations with sufficient explanation to satisfy both parties.

CA15-2 (Issuance of Stock for Land) Martin Corporation is planning to issue 3,000 shares of its own $10 par value common stock for two acres of land to be used as a building site.

Instructions
(a) What general rule should be applied to determine the amount at which the land should be recorded?
(b) Under what circumstances should this transaction be recorded at the fair value of the land?
(c) Under what circumstances should this transaction be recorded at the fair value of the stock issued?
(d) Assume Martin intentionally records this transaction at an amount greater than the fair value of the land and the stock. Discuss this situation.

CA15-3 (Conceptual Issues—Equity) Statements of Financial Accounting Concepts set forth financial accounting and reporting objectives and fundamentals that will be used by the Financial Accounting Standards Board in developing standards. *Concepts Statement No. 6* defines various elements of financial statements.

Instructions
Answer the following questions based on *SFAC No. 6.*

(a) Define and discuss the term "equity."
(b) What transactions or events change owners' equity?
(c) Define "investments by owners" and provide examples of this type of transaction. What financial statement element other than equity is typically affected by owner investments?
(d) Define "distributions to owners" and provide examples of this type of transaction. What financial statement element other than equity is typically affected by distributions?
(e) What are examples of changes within owners' equity that do not change the total amount of owners' equity?

CA15-4 (Stock Dividends and Splits) The directors of Merchant Corporation are considering the issuance of a stock dividend. They have asked you to discuss the proposed action by answering the following questions.

Instructions

(a) What is a stock dividend? How is a stock dividend distinguished from a stock split (1) from a legal standpoint, and (2) from an accounting standpoint?

(b) For what reasons does a corporation usually declare a stock dividend? A stock split?

(c) Discuss the amount, if any, of retained earnings to be capitalized in connection with a stock dividend.

(AICPA adapted)

CA15-5 (Stock Dividends) Kulikowski Inc., a client, is considering the authorization of a 10% common stock dividend to common stockholders. The financial vice president of Kulikowski wishes to discuss the accounting implications of such an authorization with you before the next meeting of the board of directors.

Instructions

(a) The first topic the vice president wishes to discuss is the nature of the stock dividend to the recipient. Discuss the case against considering the stock dividend as income to the recipient.

(b) The other topic for discussion is the propriety of issuing the stock dividend to all "stockholders of record" or to "stockholders of record exclusive of shares held in the name of the corporation as treasury stock." Discuss the case against issuing stock dividends on treasury shares.

(AICPA adapted)

CA15-6 (Stock Dividend, Cash Dividend, and Treasury Stock) Mask Company has 30,000 shares of $10 par value common stock authorized and 20,000 shares issued and outstanding. On August 15, 2014, Mask purchased 1,000 shares of treasury stock for $18 per share. Mask uses the cost method to account for treasury stock. On September 14, 2014, Mask sold 500 shares of the treasury stock for $20 per share.

In October 2014, Mask declared and distributed 1,950 shares as a stock dividend from unissued shares when the market price of the common stock was $21 per share.

On December 20, 2014, Mask declared a $1 per share cash dividend, payable on January 10, 2015, to shareholders of record on December 31, 2014.

Instructions

(a) How should Mask account for the purchase and sale of the treasury stock, and how should the treasury stock be presented in the balance sheet at December 31, 2014?

(b) How should Mask account for the stock dividend, and how would it affect the stockholders' equity at December 31, 2014? Why?

(c) How should Mask account for the cash dividend, and how would it affect the balance sheet at December 31, 2014? Why?

(AICPA adapted)

CA15-7 (Treasury Stock—Ethics) Lois Kenseth, president of Sycamore Corporation, is concerned about several large stockholders who have been very vocal lately in their criticisms of her leadership. She thinks they might mount a campaign to have her removed as the corporation's CEO. She decides that buying them out by purchasing their shares could eliminate them as opponents, and she is confident they would accept a "good" offer. Kenseth knows the corporation's cash position is decent, so it has the cash to complete the transaction. She also knows the purchase of these shares will increase earnings per share, which should make other investors quite happy. (Earnings per share is calculated by dividing net income available for the common shareholders by the weighted-average number of shares outstanding. Therefore, if the number of shares outstanding is decreased by purchasing treasury shares, earnings per share increases.)

Instructions

Answer the following questions.

(a) Who are the stakeholders in this situation?

(b) What are the ethical issues involved?

(c) Should Kenseth authorize the transaction?

<h2 style="text-align:center">USING YOUR JUDGMENT</h2>

FINANCIAL REPORTING

Financial Reporting Problem

P&G **The Procter & Gamble Company (P&G)**

The financial statements of **P&G** are presented in Appendix 5B. The company's complete annual report, including the notes to the financial statements, can be accessed at the book's companion website, **www. wiley.com/college/kieso**.

Instructions

Refer to P&G's financial statements and the accompanying notes to answer the following questions.

(a) What is the par or stated value of P&G's preferred stock?

(b) What is the par or stated value of P&G's common stock?

(c) What percentage of P&G's authorized common stock was issued at June 30, 2011?

(d) How many shares of common stock were outstanding at June 30, 2011, and June 30, 2010?

(e) What was the dollar amount effect of the cash dividends on P&G's stockholders' equity?

(f) What is P&G's return on common stock equity for 2011 and 2010?

(g) What is P&G's payout ratio for 2011 and 2010?

(h) What was the market price range (high/low) of P&G's common stock during the quarter ended June 30, 2011?

Comparative Analysis Case

The Coca-Cola Company and PepsiCo, Inc.

Instructions

Go to the book's companion website and use information found there to answer the following questions related to The Coca-Cola Company and PepsiCo, Inc.

(a) What is the par or stated value of Coca-Cola's and PepsiCo's common or capital stock?

(b) What percentage of authorized shares was issued by Coca-Cola at December 31, 2011, and by PepsiCo at December 31, 2011?

(c) How many shares are held as treasury stock by Coca-Cola at December 31, 2011, and by PepsiCo at December 31, 2011?

(d) How many Coca-Cola common shares are outstanding at December 31, 2011? How many PepsiCo shares of capital stock are outstanding at December 31, 2011?

(e) What amounts of cash dividends per share were declared by Coca-Cola and PepsiCo in 2011? What were the dollar amount effects of the cash dividends on each company's stockholders' equity?

(f) What are Coca-Cola's and PepsiCo's return on common/capital stock equity for 2011 and 2010? Which company gets the higher return on the equity of its shareholders?

(g) What are Coca-Cola's and PepsiCo's payout ratios for 2011?

(h) What was the market price range (high/low) for Coca-Cola's common stock and PepsiCo's capital stock during the fourth quarter of 2011? Which company's (Coca-Cola's or PepsiCo's) stock price increased more (%) during 2011?

Financial Statement Analysis Cases

Case 1 Kellogg Company

Kellogg Company is the world's leading producer of ready-to-eat cereal products. In recent years, the company has taken numerous steps aimed at improving its profitability and earnings per share. Presented below are some basic facts for Kellogg.

	2011	2010
Net sales	$13,198	$12,397
Net income	1,229	1,240
Total assets	11,901	11,847
Total liabilities	10,139	9,693
Common stock, $0.25 par value	105	105
Capital in excess of par value	522	495
Retained earnings	6,721	6,122
Treasury stock, at cost	3,130	2,650
Number of shares outstanding (in millions)	357	366

Instructions

(a) What are some of the reasons that management purchases its own stock?

(b) Explain how earnings per share might be affected by treasury stock transactions.

(c) Calculate the ratio of debt to assets for 2010 and 2011, and discuss the implications of the change.

Case 2   Wiebold, Incorporated

The following note related to stockholders' equity was reported in Wiebold, Inc.'s annual report.

On February 1, the Board of Directors declared a 3-for-2 stock split, distributed on February 22 to shareholders of record on February 10. Accordingly, all numbers of common shares, except unissued shares and treasury shares, and all per share data have been restated to reflect this stock split.

On the basis of amounts declared and paid, the annualized quarterly dividends per share were $0.80 in the current year and $0.75 in the prior year.

Instructions

(a) What is the significance of the date of record and the date of distribution?

(b) Why might Wiebold have declared a 3-for-2 for stock split?

(c) What impact does Wiebold's stock split have on (1) total stockholders' equity, (2) total par value, (3) outstanding shares, and (4) book value per share?

Accounting, Analysis, and Principles

On January 1, 2014, Agassi Corporation had the following stockholders' equity accounts.

Common Stock ($10 par value, 60,000 shares issued and outstanding)	$600,000
Paid-in Capital in Excess of Par—Common Stock	500,000
Retained Earnings	620,000

During 2014, the following transactions occurred.

Jan. 15	Declared and paid a $1.05 cash dividend per share to stockholders.
Apr. 15	Declared and paid a 10% stock dividend. The market price of the stock was $14 per share.
May 15	Reacquired 2,000 common shares at a market price of $15 per share.
Nov. 15	Reissued 1,000 shares held in treasury at a price of $18 per share.
Dec. 31	Determined that net income for the year was $370,000.

Accounting

Journalize the above transactions. (Include entries to close net income to Retained Earnings.) Determine the ending balances for Paid-in Capital, Retained Earnings, and Stockholders' Equity.

Analysis

Calculate the payout ratio and the return on common stock equity.

Principles

R. Federer is examining Agassi's financial statements and wonders whether the "gains" or "losses" on Agassi's treasury stock transactions should be included in income for the year. Briefly explain whether, and the conceptual reasons why, gains or losses on treasury stock transactions should be recorded in income.

BRIDGE TO THE PROFESSION

 ## Professional Research: FASB Codification

Recall from Chapter 13 that Hincapie Co. (a specialty bike-accessory manufacturer) is expecting growth in sales of some products targeted to the low-price market. Hincapie is contemplating a preferred stock issue to help finance this expansion in operations. The company is leaning toward participating preferred stock because ownership will not be diluted, but the investors will get an extra dividend if the company does well. The company management wants to be certain that its reporting of this transaction is transparent to its current shareholders and wants you to research the disclosure requirements related to its capital structure.

Instructions

If your school has a subscription to the FASB Codification, go to *http://aaahq.org/ascLogin.cfm* to log in and prepare responses to the following. Provide Codification references for your responses.

(a) Identify the authoritative literature that addresses disclosure of information about capital structure.

(b) Find definitions of the following:

   (1) Securities.

   (2) Participation rights.

   (3) Preferred stock.

(c) What information about securities must companies disclose? Discuss how Hincapie should report the proposed preferred stock issue.

Additional Professional Resources

See the book's companion website, at **www.wiley.com/college/kieso**, for professional simulations as well as other study resources.

 IFRS INSIGHTS

LEARNING OBJECTIVE 11
Compare the procedures for accounting for stockholders' equity under GAAP and IFRS.

The primary IFRS related to stockholders' equity are *IAS 1* ("Presentation of Financial Statements"), *IAS 32* ("Financial Instruments: Presentation"), and *IAS 39* ("Financial Instruments: Recognition and Measurement").

RELEVANT FACTS

Following are the key similarities and differences between GAAP and IFRS related to stockholders' equity.

Similarities

- The accounting for the issuance of shares and purchase of treasury stock are similar under both IFRS and GAAP.

- The accounting for declaration and payment of dividends and the accounting for stock splits are similar under both IFRS and GAAP.

Differences

- Major differences relate to terminology used, introduction of concepts such as revaluation surplus, and presentation of stockholders' equity information.

- Many countries have different investor groups than the United States. For example, in Germany, financial institutions like banks are not only the major creditors but often are the largest shareholders as well. In the United States and the United Kingdom, many companies rely on substantial investment from private investors.

- The accounting for treasury share retirements differs between IFRS and GAAP. Under GAAP, a company has three options: (1) charge the excess of the cost of treasury shares over par value to retained earnings, (2) allocate the difference between paid-in capital and retained earnings, or (3) charge the entire amount to paid-in capital. Under IFRS, the excess may have to be charged to paid-in capital, depending on the original transaction related to the issuance of the shares.

- The statement of changes in equity is usually referred to as the statement of stockholders' equity (or shareholders' equity) under GAAP.

- Both IFRS and GAAP use the term retained earnings. However, IFRS relies on the term "reserve" as a dumping ground for other types of equity transactions, such as other comprehensive income items as well as various types of unusual transactions related to convertible debt and share option contracts. GAAP relies on the account Accumulated Other Comprehensive Income (Loss). We also use this account in the discussion below, as it appears this account is gaining prominence within the IFRS literature.

- Under IFRS, it is common to report "revaluation surplus" related to increases or decreases in items such as property, plant, and equipment; mineral resources; and intangible assets. The term surplus is generally not used in GAAP. In addition, unrealized gains on the above items are not reported in the financial statements under GAAP.

ABOUT THE NUMBERS

Equity

Equity is the residual interest in the assets of the company after deducting all liabilities. Equity is often referred to as shareholders' equity, stockholders' equity, or corporate capital. Equity is often subclassified on the statement of financial position (balance sheet) into the following categories (as discussed in Chapter 5).

1. Share capital.

2. Share premium.

3. Retained earnings.

4. Accumulated other comprehensive income.

5. Treasury shares.

6. Non-controlling interest (minority interest).

Such classifications help financial statement users to better understand the legal or other restrictions related to the ability of the company to pay dividends or otherwise use its equity for certain defined purposes. Companies often make a distinction between contributed capital (paid-in capital) and earned capital. **Contributed capital (paid-in capital)** is the total amount paid in on capital shares—the amount provided by shareholders to the corporation for use in the business. Contributed capital includes items such as the par value of all outstanding shares and premiums less discounts on issuance. **Earned capital** is the capital that develops from profitable operations. It consists of all undistributed income that remains invested in the company. **Retained earnings** represents the earned capital of the company.

As indicated above, equity is a **residual interest** and therefore its value is derived from the amount of the corporations' assets and liabilities. Only in unusual cases will a company's equity equal the total fair value of its shares. For example, BMW recently had total equity of €20,265 million and a market capitalization of €21,160 million. BMW's equity represents the net contributions from shareholders (from both majority and minority shareholders) plus retained earnings and accumulated other comprehensive income. As a residual interest, its equity has no existence apart from the assets and liabilities of BMW—equity equals net assets. Equity is not a claim to specific assets but a claim against a portion of the total assets. Its amount is not specified or fixed; it depends on BMW's profitability. Equity grows if it is profitable. It shrinks, or may disappear entirely, if BMW loses money.

Issuance of Ordinary Shares

Under IFRS, the accounting for share issuances is similar to GAAP. The primary difference is the account titles. GAAP uses an account, Common Stock, for the par value of shares, while IFRS uses an account labeled Share Capital. What about no-par shares? In some countries, as in the United States, the total issue price for no-par shares may be considered legal capital, which could reduce the flexibility in paying dividends. Corporations sell no-par shares, like par value shares, for whatever price they will bring. However, unlike par value shares, corporations issue them without a premium or a discount. The exact amount received represents the credit to ordinary or preference shares.

For example, Video Electronics Corporation is organized with 10,000 ordinary shares authorized without par value. Video Electronics makes only a memorandum entry for the authorization, inasmuch as no amount is involved. If Video Electronics then issues 500 shares for cash at $10 per share, it makes the following entry.

Cash	5,000	
Share Capital—Ordinary		5,000

If it issues another 500 shares for $11 per share, Video Electronics makes this entry.

Cash	5,500	
Share Capital—Ordinary		5,500

True no-par shares should be carried in the accounts at issue price without any share premium reported. But some countries require that no-par shares have a **stated value**. The stated value is a minimum value below which a company cannot issue it. Thus, instead of being no-par shares, such stated-value shares become, in effect, shares with a very low par value. It thus is open to all the criticism and abuses that first encouraged the development of no-par shares.

If no-par shares have a stated value of $5 per share but sell for $11, all such amounts in excess of $5 are recorded as share premium, which in many jurisdictions is fully or partially available for dividends. Thus, no-par value shares, with a low stated value, permit a new corporation to commence its operations with share premium that may exceed its stated capital. For example, if a company issued 1,000 of the shares with a $5 stated value at $15 per share for cash, it makes the following entry.

Cash	15,000	
Share Capital—Ordinary		5,000
Share Premium—Ordinary		10,000

Most corporations account for no-par shares with a stated value as if they were par value shares with par equal to the stated value.

Accounting for and Reporting Preference Shares

The accounting for preference shares at issuance is similar to that for ordinary shares. A corporation allocates proceeds between the par value of the preference shares and share premium. To illustrate, assume that Bishop Co. issues 10,000 shares of $10 par value preference shares for $12 cash per share. Bishop records the issuance as follows.

Cash	120,000	
Share Capital—Preference		100,000
Share Premium—Preference		20,000

Thus, Bishop maintains separate accounts for these different classes of shares. Corporations consider convertible preference shares as a part of equity. In addition, when exercising convertible preference shares, there is no theoretical justification for recognition of a gain or loss. A company recognizes no gain or loss when dealing with shareholders in their capacity as business owners. Instead, the company **employs the book value method**: debit Share Capital—Preference, along with any related Share Premium—Preference; credit Share Capital—Ordinary and Share Premium—Ordinary (if an excess exists).

Preference shares generally have no maturity date. Therefore, no legal obligation exists to pay the preference shareholder. As a result, companies classify preference shares as part of equity. Companies generally report preference shares at par value as the first item in the equity section. They report any excess over par value as part of share premium. They also consider dividends on preference shares as a distribution of income and not an expense. Companies must disclose the pertinent rights of the preference shares outstanding.

Presentation of Equity

Statement of Financial Position

Illustration IFRS15-1 shows a comprehensive equity section from the statement of financial position of Frost Company that includes the equity items we discussed previously.

FROST COMPANY EQUITY DECEMBER 31, 2014		
Share capital—preference, $100 par value, 7% cumulative,		
100,000 shares authorized, 30,000 shares issued and outstanding	$3,000,000	
Share capital—ordinary, no-par, stated value $10 per share,		
500,000 shares authorized, 400,000 shares issued	4,000,000	
Ordinary share dividend distributable	200,000	$ 7,200,000
Share premium—preference	150,000	
Share premium—ordinary	840,000	990,000
Retained earnings		4,360,000
Treasury shares (2,000 ordinary shares)		(190,000)
Accumulated other comprehensive loss		(360,000)
Total equity		$12,000,000

ILLUSTRATION IFRS15-1
Comprehensive Equity Presentation

Frost should disclose the pertinent rights and privileges of the various securities outstanding. For example, companies must disclose all of the following: dividend and liquidation preferences, participation rights, call prices and dates, conversion or exercise prices and pertinent dates, sinking fund requirements, unusual voting rights, and significant terms of contracts to issue additional shares. Liquidation preferences should be disclosed in the equity section of the statement of financial position, rather than in the notes to the financial statements, to emphasize the possible effect of this restriction on future cash flows.

Presentation of Statement of Changes in Equity

Companies are also required to present a **statement of changes in equity**. The statement of changes in equity includes the following.

1. Total comprehensive income for the period, showing separately the total amounts attributable to owners of the parent and to non-controlling interests.

2. For each component of equity, the effects of retrospective application or retrospective restatement.

3. For each component of equity, a reconciliation between the carrying amount at the beginning and the end of the period, separately disclosing changes resulting from:
   (a) Profit or loss;
   (b) Each item of other comprehensive income; and
   (c) Transactions with owners in their capacity as owners, showing separately contributions by and distributions to owners and changes in ownership interests in subsidiaries that do not result in a loss of control.

A typical statement of changes in equity is shown in Illustration IFRS15-2.

ILLUSTRATION IFRS15-2
Statement of Changes in Equity

	Share Capital	Retained Earnings	Unrealized Holding Gain (Loss) on Non-Trading Equity Investments	Unrealized Holding Gain (Loss) on Property, Plant, and Equipment	Total
Balance—December 31, 2014	$600,000	$120,000	$22,000	$15,000	$ 757,000
Issue of Ordinary Shares	200,000				200,000
Total Comprehensive Income		70,000	11,000	8,000	89,000
Dividends		(20,000)			(20,000)
Balance—December 31, 2015	$800,000	$170,000	$33,000	$23,000	$1,026,000

In addition, companies are required to present, either in the statement of changes in equity or in the notes, the amount of dividends recognized as distributions to owners during the period and the related amount per share.

ON THE HORIZON

As indicated in earlier discussions, the IASB and the FASB are currently working on a project related to financial statement presentation. An important part of this study is to determine whether certain line items, subtotals, and totals should be clearly defined and required to be displayed in the financial statements. For example, it is likely that the statement of changes in equity and its presentation will be examined closely. In addition, the options of how to present other comprehensive income under GAAP will change in any converged standard.

IFRS SELF-TEST QUESTIONS

1. Which of the following does **not** represent a pair of GAAP/IFRS-comparable terms?
    (a) Additional paid-in capital/Share premium.
    (b) Treasury stock/Repurchase reserve.
    (c) Common stock/Share capital—ordinary.
    (d) Preferred stock/Preference shares.
2. Under IFRS, the amount of capital received in excess of par value would be credited to:
    (a) Retained Earnings.
    (b) Contributed Capital.
    (c) Share Premium.
    (d) Par value is not used under IFRS.
3. The term *reserves* is used under IFRS with reference to all of the following **except**:
    (a) gains and losses on revaluation of property, plant, and equipment.
    (b) capital received in excess of the par value of issued shares.
    (c) retained earnings.
    (d) fair value differences.
4. Which of the following is **false**?
    (a) Under GAAP, companies cannot record gains on transactions involving their own shares.
    (b) Under IFRS, companies cannot record gains on transactions involving their own shares.
    (c) Under IFRS, the statement of stockholders' equity is a required statement.
    (d) Under IFRS, a company records a revaluation surplus when it experiences an increase in the price of its common stock.
5. Under IFRS, a purchase by a company of its own shares results in:
    (a) an increase in treasury shares.
    (b) a decrease in assets.
    (c) a decrease in equity.
    (d) All of the above.

IFRS CONCEPTS AND APPLICATION

IFRS15-1 Where can authoritative IFRS guidance related to stockholders' equity be found?

IFRS15-2 Briefly describe some of the similarities and differences between GAAP and IFRS with respect to the accounting for stockholders' equity.

IFRS15-3 Briefly discuss the implications of the financial statement presentation project for the reporting of stockholders' equity.

IFRS15-4 Mary Tokar is comparing a GAAP-based company to a company that uses IFRS. Both companies report equity investments. The IFRS company reports unrealized losses on these investments under the heading "Reserves" in its equity section. However, Mary can find no similar heading in the GAAP-based company financial statements. Can Mary conclude that the GAAP-based company has no unrealized gains or losses on its non-trading equity investments? Explain.

IFRS15-5 Explain each of the following terms: authorized ordinary shares, unissued ordinary shares, issued ordinary shares, outstanding ordinary shares, and treasury shares.

IFRS15-6 Indicate how each of the following accounts should be classified in the equity section.

(a) Share Capital—Ordinary.
(b) Retained Earnings.
(c) Share Premium—Ordinary.
(d) Treasury Shares.
(e) Share Premium—Treasury.
(f) Share Capital—Preference.
(g) Accumulated Other Comprehensive Income.

IFRS15-7 Kaymer Corporation issued 300 shares of $10 par value ordinary shares for $4,500. Prepare Kaymer's journal entry.

IFRS15-8 Wilco Corporation has the following account balances at December 31, 2014.

Share capital—ordinary, $5 par value	$ 510,000
Treasury shares	90,000
Retained earnings	2,340,000
Share premium—ordinary	1,320,000

Instructions

Prepare Wilco's December 31, 2014, equity section.

IFRS15-9 Ravonette Corporation issued 300 shares of $10 par value ordinary shares and 100 shares of $50 par value preference shares for a lump sum of $13,500. The ordinary shares have a market price of $20 per share, and the preference shares have a market price of $90 per share.

Instructions

Prepare the journal entry to record the issuance.

IFRS15-10 Weisberg Corporation has 10,000 shares of $100 par value, 6%, preference shares and 50,000 ordinary shares of $10 par value outstanding at December 31, 2014.

Instructions

Answer the questions in each of the following independent situations.

(a) If the preference shares are cumulative and dividends were last paid on the preference shares on December 31, 2011, what are the dividends in arrears that should be reported on the December 31, 2014, statement of financial position? How should these dividends be reported?
(b) If the preference shares are convertible into seven shares of $10 par value ordinary shares and 3,000 shares are converted, what entry is required for the conversion, assuming the preference shares were issued at par value?
(c) If the preference shares were issued at $107 per share, how should the preference shares be reported in the equity section?

IFRS15-11 Teller Corporation's post-closing trial balance at December 31, 2014, was as follows.

TELLER CORPORATION
POST-CLOSING TRIAL BALANCE
DECEMBER 31, 2014

	Dr.	Cr.
Accounts payable		$ 310,000
Accounts receivable	$ 480,000	
Accumulated depreciation—building and equipment		185,000
Allowance for doubtful accounts		30,000
Bonds payable		700,000
Building and equipment	1,450,000	
Cash	190,000	
Dividends payable on preference shares—cash		4,000
Inventories	560,000	
Land	400,000	
Prepaid expenses	40,000	
Retained earnings		201,000
Share capital—ordinary ($1 par value)		200,000
Share capital—preference ($50 par value)		500,000
Share premium—ordinary		1,000,000
Share premium—treasury		160,000
Treasury shares—ordinary at cost	170,000	
Totals	$3,290,000	$3,290,000

At December 31, 2014, Teller had the following number of ordinary and preference shares.

	Ordinary	Preference
Authorized	600,000	60,000
Issued	200,000	10,000
Outstanding	190,000	10,000

The dividends on preference shares are $4 cumulative. In addition, the preference shares have a preference in liquidation of $50 per share.

Instructions

Prepare the equity section of Teller's statement of financial position at December 31, 2014.

Professional Research

IFRS15-12 Hincapie Co. (a specialty bike-accessory manufacturer) is expecting growth in sales of some products targeted to the low-price market. Hincapie is contemplating a preference share issue to help finance this expansion in operations. The company is leaning toward preference shares because ownership will not be diluted, but the investors will get an extra dividend if the company does well. The company management wants to be certain that its reporting of this transaction is transparent to its current shareholders and wants you to research the disclosure requirements related to its capital structure.

Instructions

Access the IFRS authoritative literature at the IASB website (*http://eifrs.iasb.org/*). (Click on the IFRS tab and then register for free eIFRS access if necessary.) When you have accessed the documents, you can use the search tool in your Internet browser to respond to the following questions. (Provide paragraph citations.)

(a) Identify the authoritative literature that addresses disclosure of information about capital structure.
(b) What information about share capital must companies disclose? Discuss how Hincapie should report the proposed preference share issue.

International Financial Reporting Problem
Marks and Spencer plc

IFRS15-13 The financial statements of **Marks and Spencer plc (M&S)** are available at the book's companion website or can be accessed at *http://annualreport.marksandspencer.com/_assets/downloads/Marks-and-Spencer-Annual-report-and-financial-statements-2012.pdf*.

Instructions

Refer to M&S's financial statements and the accompanying notes to answer the following questions.

(a) What is the par or stated value of M&S's preference shares?
(b) What is the par or stated value of M&S's ordinary shares?
(c) What percentage of M&S's authorized ordinary shares was issued at 31 March 2012?
(d) How many ordinary shares were outstanding at 31 March 2012, and 2 April 2011?
(e) What was the pound amount effect of the cash dividends on M&S's equity?
(f) What is M&S's return on ordinary share equity for 2012 and 2011?
(g) What is M&S's payout ratio for 2012 and 2011?

ANSWERS TO IFRS SELF-TEST QUESTIONS

1. b **2.** c **3.** b **4.** d **5.** d

Remember to check the book's companion website to find additional resources for this chapter.

LEARNING OBJECTIVES

After studying this chapter, you should be able to:

1 Describe the accounting for the issuance, conversion, and retirement of convertible securities.

2 Explain the accounting for convertible preferred stock.

3 Contrast the accounting for stock warrants and for stock warrants issued with other securities.

4 Describe the accounting for stock compensation plans.

5 Discuss the controversy involving stock compensation plans.

6 Compute earnings per share in a simple capital structure.

7 Compute earnings per share in a complex capital structure.

Kicking the Habit

Some habits die hard. Take stock options—called by some "the crack cocaine of incentives." Stock options are a form of compensation that gives key employees the choice to purchase shares at a given (usually lower-than-market) price. For many years, companies were hooked on these products. Why? The combination of a hot equity market and favorable accounting treatment made stock options the incentive of choice. They were compensation with no expense to the companies that granted them, and they were popular with key employees, so companies granted them with abandon. However, the accounting rules that took effect in 2005 required *expensing* the fair value of stock options. This new treatment has made it easier for companies to kick this habit.

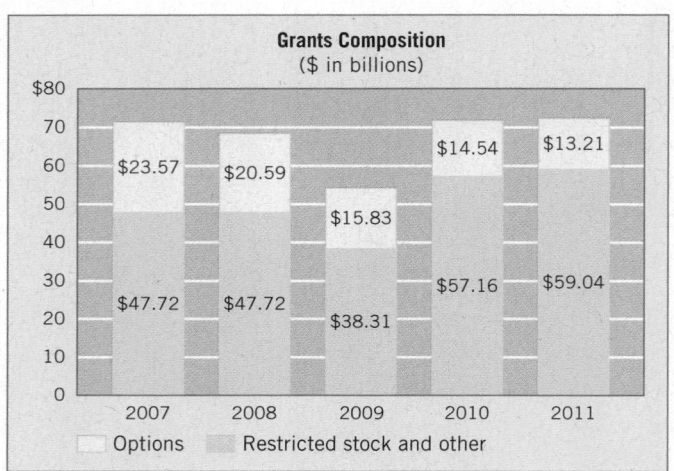

Grants Composition
($ in billions)

Year	Options	Restricted stock and other
2007	$23.57	$47.72
2008	$20.59	$47.72
2009	$15.83	$38.31
2010	$14.54	$57.16
2011	$13.21	$59.04

As shown in the chart above, a review of option use for the U.S. companies in the S&P 500 indicates a decline in the use of option-based compensation and an increase in restricted-stock plans. Fewer companies are granting stock options, following implementation of stock-option expensing. As a spokesperson at one company commented, "Once you begin expensing options, the attractiveness significantly drops."

CONCEPTUAL FOCUS

> See the **Underlying Concepts** on pages 890 and 897.
> Read the **Evolving Issue** on page 890 for a discussion of convertible debt.

INTERNATIONAL FOCUS

> See the **International Perspectives** on pages 885, 892, 896, 901, and 904.
> Read the **IFRS Insights** on pages 941–949 for a discussion of:
  —Accounting for convertible debt
  —Employee share-purchase plans

In the 1990s, executives with huge option stockpiles had an almost irresistible incentive to do whatever it took to increase the stock price and cash in their options. By reining in options, many companies are taking the first steps toward curbing both out-of-control executive pay and the era of corporate corruption that it spawned.

As indicated earlier, some of the ways that companies are curbing option grants include replacing options with restricted shares. Further analysis of these trends indicates that restricted-stock use is more than 10 times the magnitude of options grants in the financial industry. Even after excluding financial companies from the statistics, restricted shares are now the plan of choice. And in the information technology area (where in the past, share options were heavily favored), the fair value of restricted-share plans exceeds that for share options. In this industry, some companies are simply reducing option grants, without offering a replacement, while others, like **Microsoft** and **Yahoo!**, have switched to restricted-stock plans completely. Is this a good trend? Most believe it is; the requirement to expense stock-based compensation similar to other forms of compensation has changed the focus of compensation plans to rewarding talent and performance without breaking the bank. The positive impact on corporate behavior, while hard to measure, should benefit investors in years to come.

Sources: Adapted from: Louis Lavelle, "Kicking the Stock-Options Habit," *BusinessWeek Online* (February 16, 2005). Graph from J. Ciesielski, "S&P 500 Executive Pay: The Bread Keeps Rising," *The Analyst's Accounting Observer* (June 25, 2012).

| **PREVIEW OF CHAPTER** | **16** | As the opening story indicates, companies are rethinking the use of various forms of stock-based compensation. The purpose of this chapter is to discuss the proper accounting for stock-based |

compensation. In addition, the chapter examines issues related to other types of financial instruments, such as convertible securities, warrants, and contingent shares, including their effects on reporting earnings per share. The content and organization of the chapter are as follows.

Dilutive Securities and Earnings per Share

Dilutive Securities	**Accounting for Stock Compensation**	**Computing Earnings per Share**
• Debt and equity • Convertible debt • Convertible preferred stock • Stock warrants	• Stock-option plans • Restricted stock • Employee stock-purchase plans • Disclosure of compensation plans • Debate	• Simple capital structure • Complex capital structure

DILUTIVE SECURITIES

Debt and Equity

Many of the controversies related to the accounting for financial instruments such as stock options, convertible securities, and preferred stock relate to whether companies should report these instruments as a liability or as equity. For example, companies should classify nonredeemable common shares as equity because the issuer has no **obligation** to pay dividends or repurchase the stock. Declaration of dividends is at the issuer's discretion, as is the decision to repurchase the stock. Similarly, preferred stock that is not redeemable does not require the issuer to pay dividends or repurchase the stock. Thus, nonredeemable common or preferred stock lacks an important characteristic of a liability—an obligation to pay the holder of the common or preferred stock at some point in the future.

However the classification is not as clear-cut for other financial instruments. For example, in Chapter 15 we discussed the accounting for mandatorily redeemable preferred stock. Companies originally classified this security as part of equity. The SEC then prohibited equity classification, and most companies classified these securities between debt and equity on the balance sheet in a separate section often referred to as the "mezzanine section." The FASB now requires companies to report these types of securities as a liability.[1] **[1]**

In this chapter, we discuss securities that have characteristics of *both* debt and equity. For example, a convertible bond has both debt and equity characteristics. Should a company classify this security as debt, as equity, or as part debt and part equity? In addition, how should a company compute earnings per share if it has convertible bonds and other convertible securities in its capital structure? Convertible securities as well as options, warrants, and other securities are often called dilutive securities because upon exercise they may reduce (dilute) earnings per share.

Accounting for Convertible Debt

Convertible bonds can be changed into other corporate securities during some specified period of time after issuance. A convertible bond combines the benefits of a bond with the privilege of exchanging it for stock at the holder's option. Investors who purchase it desire the security of a bond holding (guaranteed interest and principal) plus the added option of conversion if the value of the stock appreciates significantly.

Corporations issue convertibles for two main reasons. One is to raise equity capital without giving up more ownership control than necessary. To illustrate, assume a company wants to raise $1 million; its common stock is selling at $45 a share. To raise the $1 million, the company would have to sell 22,222 shares (ignoring issue costs). By selling 1,000 bonds at $1,000 par, each convertible into 20 shares of common stock, the company could raise $1 million by committing only 20,000 shares of its common stock.

---

[1] The FASB (and IASB) have studied the accounting for financial instruments with characteristics of both debt and equity. At one time, the Boards proposed a definition of equity that is far more restrictive than current practice. Under the proposed "basic ownership approach," only common stock is classified as equity. All other instruments (e.g., preferred stock, options, and convertible debt) are classified as liabilities. Instruments classified as liabilities are measured at fair value, and changes are reported in income. Adoption of a narrow definition provides fewer opportunities to structure instruments and arrangements to achieve a desired accounting treatment. See "*Financial Instruments with Characteristics of Equity*" (November 30, 2007) at *http://www.fasb.org*. While the Boards have agreed on some provisions to improve and simplify the financial reporting requirements for financial instruments with characteristics of debt and equity, the project is currently inactive as the Boards have focused on other major convergence projects.

A second reason to issue convertibles is to obtain debt financing at cheaper rates. Many companies could issue debt only at high interest rates unless they attach a convertible covenant. The conversion privilege entices the investor to accept a lower interest rate than would normally be the case on a straight debt issue. For example, Amazon.com at one time issued convertible bonds that pay interest at an effective yield of 4.75 percent. This rate was much lower than Amazon would have had to pay by issuing straight debt. For this lower interest rate, the investor receives the right to buy Amazon's common stock at a fixed price until the bond's maturity.[2]

As indicated earlier, the accounting for convertible debt involves reporting issues at the time of (1) issuance, (2) conversion, and (3) retirement.

At Time of Issuance

The method for recording convertible bonds **at the date of issue follows the method used to record straight debt issues**. None of the proceeds are recorded as equity. Companies amortize to the maturity date any discount or premium that results from the issuance of convertible bonds. Why this treatment? Because it is difficult to predict when, if at all, conversion will occur. However, the accounting for convertible debt as a straight debt issue is controversial; we discuss it more fully later in the chapter.

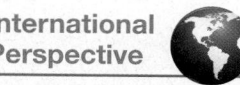

International Perspective

IFRS requires that the issuer of convertible debt record the liability and equity components separately.

At Time of Conversion

If converting bonds into other securities, a company uses the **book value method** to record the conversion. The book value method records the securities exchanged for the bond at the carrying amount (book value) of the bond.

To illustrate, assume that Hilton, Inc. has a $1,000 bond that is convertible into 10 shares of common stock (par value $10). At the time of conversion, the unamortized premium is $50. Hilton records the conversion of the bonds as follows.

Bonds Payable	1,000	
Premium on Bonds Payable	50	
Common Stock		100
Paid-in Capital in Excess of Par—Common Stock		950

Support for the book value approach is based on the argument that an agreement was established at the date of the issuance either to pay a stated amount of cash at maturity or to issue a stated number of shares of equity securities. Therefore, when the debtholder converts the debt to equity in accordance with the preexisting contract terms, the issuing company recognizes no gain or loss upon conversion.

Induced Conversions

Sometimes the issuer wishes to encourage prompt conversion of its convertible debt to equity securities in order to reduce interest costs or to improve its debt to equity ratio. Thus, the issuer may offer some form of additional consideration (such as cash or common stock), called a "sweetener," to **induce conversion**. The issuing company reports the sweetener as an expense of the current period. Its amount is the fair value of the additional securities or other consideration given.

---

[2]As with any investment, a buyer has to be careful. For example, Wherehouse Entertainment Inc., which had 6¼ percent convertibles outstanding, was taken private in a leveraged buyout. As a result, the convertible was suddenly as risky as a junk bond of a highly leveraged company with a coupon of only 6¼ percent. As one holder of the convertibles noted, "What's even worse is that the company will be so loaded down with debt that it probably won't have enough cash flow to make its interest payments. And the convertible debt we hold is subordinated to the rest of Wherehouse's debt." These types of situations make convertibles less attractive and lead to the introduction of takeover protection covenants in some convertible bond offerings. Or, sometimes convertibles are permitted to be called at par, and therefore the conversion premium may be lost.

Assume that Helloid, Inc. has outstanding $1,000,000 par value convertible debentures convertible into 100,000 shares of $1 par value common stock. Helloid wishes to reduce its annual interest cost. To do so, Helloid agrees to pay the holders of its convertible debentures an additional $80,000 if they will convert. Assuming conversion occurs, Helloid makes the following entry.

Debt Conversion Expense	80,000	
Bonds Payable	1,000,000	
Common Stock		100,000
Paid-in Capital in Excess of Par—Common Stock		900,000
Cash		80,000

Helloid records the additional $80,000 as **an expense of the current period** and not as a reduction of equity.

Some argue that the cost of a conversion inducement is a cost of obtaining equity capital. As a result, they contend, companies should recognize the cost of conversion as a cost of (a reduction of) the equity capital acquired, and not as an expense. However, the FASB indicated that when an issuer makes an additional payment to encourage conversion, the payment is for a service (bondholders converting at a given time) and should be reported as an expense. The issuing company does not report this expense as an extraordinary item. [2]

Retirement of Convertible Debt

As indicated earlier, the method for recording the **issuance** of convertible bonds follows that used in recording straight debt issues. Specifically this means that issuing companies should not attribute any portion of the proceeds to the conversion feature, nor should it credit a paid-in capital account.

Although some raise theoretical objections to this approach, to be consistent, companies need to recognize a gain or loss on **retiring convertible debt in the same way that they recognize a gain or loss on retiring nonconvertible debt**. For this reason, companies should report differences between the cash acquisition price of debt and its carrying amount **in current income as a gain or loss**.

Convertible Preferred Stock

LEARNING OBJECTIVE 2

Explain the accounting for convertible preferred stock.

Convertible preferred stock includes an option for the holder to convert preferred shares into a fixed number of common shares. The major difference between accounting for a convertible bond and convertible preferred stock at the date of issue is their classification. Convertible bonds are considered liabilities, whereas convertible preferreds (unless mandatory redemption exists) are considered part of stockholders' equity.

In addition, when stockholders exercise convertible preferred stock, there is no theoretical justification for recognizing a gain or loss. A company does not recognize a gain or loss when it deals with stockholders in their capacity as business owners. Therefore, companies do not recognize a gain or loss when stockholders exercise convertible preferred stock.

In accounting for the exercise of convertible preferred stock, a company uses the **book value method**. It debits Preferred Stock, along with any related Paid-in Capital in Excess of Par—Preferred Stock, and it credits Common Stock and Paid-in Capital in Excess of Par—Common Stock (if an excess exists). The treatment differs when the par value of the common stock issued **exceeds** the book value of the preferred stock. In that case, the company usually debits Retained Earnings for the difference.

To illustrate, assume Host Enterprises issued 1,000 shares of common stock (par value $2) upon conversion of 1,000 shares of preferred stock (par value $1) that was originally issued for a $200 premium. The entry would be:

Convertible Preferred Stock	1,000	
Paid-in Capital in Excess of Par—Preferred Stock	200	
Retained Earnings	800	
Common Stock		2,000

The rationale for the debit to Retained Earnings is that Host has offered the preferred stockholders an **additional return** to facilitate their conversion to common stock. In this example, Host charges the additional return to retained earnings. Many states, however, require that this charge simply reduce additional paid-in capital from other sources.

What do the numbers mean?   *HOW LOW CAN YOU GO?*

Financial engineers are always looking for the next innovation in security design to meet the needs of both issuers and investors. Consider the convertible bonds issued by **STMicroelectronics (STM)**. STM's 10-year bonds have a zero coupon and are convertible into STM common stock at an exercise price of $33.43. When issued, the bonds sold at an effective yield of −0.05 percent. That's right—a negative yield.

How could this happen? When STM issued the bonds, investors thought the options to convert were so valuable that they were willing to take zero interest payments and invest an amount *in excess of* the maturity value of the bonds.

In essence, the investors are paying interest to STM, and STM records interest revenue. Why would investors do this? If the stock price rises, as many thought it would for STM and many tech companies at this time, these bond investors could convert and get a big gain in the stock.

Investors did get some additional protection in the deal: They can redeem the $1,000 bonds after three years and receive $975 (and after five and seven years, for lower amounts), if it looks like the bonds will never convert. In the end, STM has issued bonds with a significant equity component. And because the entire bond issue is classified as debt, STM records negative interest expense.

Source: STM Financial Reports. See also Floyd Norris, "Legal but Absurd: They Borrow a Billion and Report a Profit," *The New York Times* (August 8, 2003), p. C1.

Stock Warrants

Warrants are certificates entitling the holder to acquire shares of stock at a certain price within a stated period. This option is similar to the conversion privilege in a convertible bond. Warrants, if exercised, become common stock and usually have a dilutive effect (reduce earnings per share) similar to that of the conversion of convertible securities. However, a substantial difference between convertible securities and stock warrants is that upon exercise of the warrants, the holder has to pay a certain amount of money to obtain the shares.

3 LEARNING OBJECTIVE

Contrast the accounting for stock warrants and for stock warrants issued with other securities.

The issuance of warrants or options to buy additional shares normally arises under three situations:

1. When issuing different types of securities, such as bonds or preferred stock, companies often include warrants **to make the security more attractive**—by providing an "equity kicker."

2. Upon the issuance of additional common stock, existing stockholders have a **preemptive right to purchase common stock** first. Companies may issue warrants to evidence that right.

3. Companies give warrants, often referred to as *stock options*, **to executives and employees** as a form of **compensation**.

The problems in accounting for stock warrants are complex and present many difficulties—some of which remain unresolved. The following sections address the accounting for stock warrants in the three situations listed above.

Stock Warrants Issued with Other Securities

Warrants issued with other securities are basically long-term options to buy common stock at a fixed price. Generally the life of warrants is five years, occasionally 10 years; very occasionally, a company may offer perpetual warrants.

A warrant works like this. **Tenneco, Inc.** offered a unit comprising one share of stock and one detachable warrant. As its name implies, the **detachable stock warrant** can be detached (separated) from the stock and traded as a separate security. The Tenneco warrant in this example is exercisable at $24.25 per share and good for five years. The unit (share of stock plus detachable warrant) sold for 22.75 ($22.75). Since the price of the common stock the day before the sale was 19.88 ($19.88), the difference suggests a price of 2.87 ($2.87) for the warrant.

The investor pays for the warrant in order to receive the right to buy the stock, at a fixed price of $24.25, sometime in the future. It would not be profitable at present for the purchaser to exercise the warrant and buy the stock, because the price of the stock was much below the exercise price.[3] But if, for example, the price of the stock rises to $30, the investor gains $2.88 ($30 − $24.25 − $2.87) on an investment of $2.87, a 100 percent increase! If the price never rises, the investor loses the full $2.87 per warrant.[4]

A company should allocate the proceeds from the sale of debt with detachable stock warrants **between the two securities**.[5] The profession takes the position that two separable instruments are involved, that is, (1) a bond and (2) a warrant giving the holder the right to purchase common stock at a certain price. Companies can trade detachable warrants separately from the debt. This allows the determination of a fair value. The two methods of allocation available are:

1. The proportional method.
2. The incremental method.

Proportional Method. At one time, **AT&T** issued bonds with detachable five-year warrants to buy one share of common stock (par value $5) at $25. At the time, a share of AT&T stock was selling for approximately $50. These warrants enabled AT&T to price its bond offering at par with an 8¾ percent yield (quite a bit lower than prevailing rates at that time). To account for the proceeds from this offering, AT&T would place a value on the two securities: (1) the value of the bonds without the warrants, and (2) the value of the warrants. The **proportional method** then allocates the proceeds using the proportion of the two amounts, based on fair values.

For example, assume that AT&T's bonds (par $1,000) sold for 99 without the warrants soon after their issue. The market price of the warrants at that time was $30. (Prior to sale the warrants will not have a fair value.) The allocation relies on an estimate of fair value, generally as established by an investment banker, or on the relative fair value of the bonds and the warrants soon after the company issues and trades them. The price paid for 10,000, $1,000 bonds with the warrants attached was par, or $10,000,000. Illustration 16-1 shows the proportional allocation of the bond proceeds between the bonds and warrants.

---

[3]Later in this discussion, we will show that the value of the warrant is normally determined on the basis of a relative fair value approach because of the difficulty of imputing a warrant value in any other manner.

[4]From the illustration, it is apparent that buying warrants can be an "all or nothing" proposition.

[5]A detachable warrant means that the warrant can sell separately from the bond. GAAP makes a distinction between detachable and nondetachable warrants because companies must sell nondetachable warrants with the security as a complete package. Thus, no allocation is permitted. **[3]**

Fair value of bonds (without warrants) ($10,000,000 × .99)		$ 9,900,000
Fair value of warrants (10,000 × $30)		300,000
Aggregate fair value		$10,200,000
Allocated to bonds:	$\dfrac{\$9,900,000}{\$10,200,000}$ × $10,000,000 =	$ 9,705,882
Allocated to warrants:	$\dfrac{\$300,000}{\$10,200,000}$ × $10,000,000 =	$ 294,118
Total allocation		$10,000,000

In this situation, the bonds sell at a discount. AT&T records the sale as follows.

Cash	9,705,882	
Discount on Bonds Payable	294,118	
Bonds Payable		10,000,000

In addition, AT&T sells warrants that it credits to paid-in capital. It makes the following entry.

Cash	294,118	
Paid-in Capital—Stock Warrants		294,118

AT&T may combine the entries if desired. Here, we show them separately, to indicate that the purchaser of the bond is buying not only a bond but also a possible future claim on common stock in the form of the stock warrant.

Assuming investors exercise all 10,000 warrants (one warrant per one share of stock), AT&T makes the following entry.

Cash (10,000 × $25)	250,000	
Paid-in Capital—Stock Warrants	294,118	
Common Stock (10,000 × $5)		50,000
Paid-in Capital in Excess of Par—Common Stock		494,118

What if investors fail to exercise the warrants? In that case, AT&T debits Paid-in Capital—Stock Warrants for $294,118 and credits Paid-in Capital—Expired Stock Warrants for a like amount. The additional paid-in capital reverts to the former stockholders.

Incremental Method. In instances where a company cannot determine the fair value of either the warrants or the bonds, it applies the **incremental method** used in lump-sum security purchases (as explained in Chapter 15, page 827). That is, the company uses the security for which it *can* determine the fair value. It allocates the remainder of the purchase price to the security for which it does not know the fair value.

For example, assume that the fair value of the AT&T warrants is $300,000, but the company cannot determine the fair value of the bonds without the warrants. Illustration 16-2 shows the amount allocated to the warrants and the stock in this case.

Lump-sum receipt	$10,000,000
Allocated to the warrants	(300,000)
Balance allocated to bonds	$ 9,700,000

Conceptual Questions. The question arises whether the allocation of value to the warrants is consistent with the handling of convertible debt, in which companies allocate no value to the conversion privilege. The FASB stated that the features of a convertible security are **inseparable** in the sense that choices are mutually exclusive. The holder either converts the bonds or redeems them for cash, but cannot do both. No basis, therefore, exists for recognizing the conversion value in the accounts.

Underlying Concepts

Reporting a convertible bond solely as debt is not representationally faithful. However, the cost constraint is used to justify the failure to allocate between debt and equity.

The Board, however, indicated that the issuance of bonds with **detachable warrants** involves *two* securities, one a debt security, which will remain outstanding until maturity, and the other a warrant to purchase common stock. At the time of issuance, separable instruments exist. The existence of two instruments therefore justifies separate treatment. **Nondetachable warrants**, however, **do not require an allocation of the proceeds between the bonds and the warrants**. Similar to the accounting for convertible bonds, companies record the entire proceeds from nondetachable warrants as debt.[6]

Evolving Issue   IS THAT ALL DEBT?

Many argue that the conversion feature of a convertible bond is not significantly different in nature from the call represented by a warrant. The question is whether, although the legal forms differ, sufficient similarities of substance exist to support the same accounting treatment. Some contend that inseparability *per se* is an insufficient basis for restricting allocation between identifiable components of a transaction.

Examples of allocation between assets of value in a single transaction *do* exist, such as allocation of values in basket purchases and separation of principal and interest in capitalizing long-term leases. Critics of the current accounting for convertibles say that to deny recognition of value to the conversion feature merely looks to the form of the instrument and does not deal with the substance of the transaction. In an exposure draft on this subject (project now inactive), the FASB indicates that companies should separate the debt and equity components of securities such as convertible debt or bonds issued with nondetachable warrants (see footnotes 1 and 6).

We agree with this position. In both situations (convertible debt and debt issued with warrants), the investor has made a payment to the company for an equity feature—the right to acquire an equity instrument in the future. The only real distinction between them is that the additional payment made when the equity instrument is formally acquired takes different forms. The warrant holder pays additional cash to the issuing company; the convertible debt holder pays for stock by forgoing the receipt of interest from conversion date until maturity date and by forgoing the receipt of the maturity value itself. Thus, the difference is one of method or form of payment only, rather than one of substance. However, until the profession officially reverses its stand with respect to accounting for convertible debt, companies will continue to report convertible debt and bonds issued with nondetachable warrants solely as debt.

Rights to Subscribe to Additional Shares

If the directors of a corporation decide to issue new shares of stock, the old stockholders generally have the right (**preemptive privilege**) to purchase newly issued shares in proportion to their holdings. This privilege, referred to as a stock right, saves existing stockholders from suffering a dilution of voting rights without their consent. Also, it may allow them to purchase stock somewhat below its fair value. Unlike the warrants issued with other securities, the warrants issued for stock rights are of short duration.

The certificate representing the stock right states the number of shares the holder of the right may purchase. Each share of stock owned ordinarily gives the owner one stock right. The certificate also states the price at which the new shares may be purchased. The

[6]GAAP requires that for convertible debt that can be settled in cash, companies should account for the liability and equity components separately. In deliberations of the debt/equity project (see footnote 1), the FASB has proposed that all convertible bonds be separated into liability and equity components. As indicated, this project is inactive at this time. **[4]** Academic research indicates that estimates of the debt and equity components of convertible bonds are subject to considerable measurement error. See Mary Barth, Wayne Landsman, and Richard Rendleman, Jr., "Option Pricing–Based Bond Value Estimates and a Fundamental Components Approach to Account for Corporate Debt," *The Accounting Review* (January 1998). This and other challenges explain in part the extended time needed to develop new standards in this area.

price is normally less than the current market price of such shares, which gives the rights a value in themselves. From the time they are issued until they expire, holders of stock rights may purchase and sell them like any other security.

Companies make only a memorandum entry when they issue rights to existing stockholders. This entry indicates the number of rights issued to existing stockholders in order to ensure that the company has additional unissued stock registered for issuance in case the rights are exercised. Companies make no formal entry at this time because they have not yet issued stock nor received cash.

If holders exercise the stock rights, a cash payment of some type usually is involved. If the company receives cash equal to the par value, it makes an entry crediting Common Stock at par value. If the company receives cash in excess of par value, it credits Paid-in Capital in Excess of Par—Common Stock. If it receives cash less than par value, a debit to Paid-in Capital in Excess of Par—Common Stock is appropriate.

Stock Compensation Plans

The third form of warrant arises in stock compensation plans to pay and motivate employees. This warrant is a stock option, which gives key employees the option to purchase common stock at a given price over an extended period of time.

A consensus of opinion is that effective compensation programs are ones that do the following: (1) base compensation on employee and company performance, (2) motivate employees to high levels of performance, (3) help retain executives and allow for recruitment of new talent, (4) maximize the employee's after-tax benefit and minimize the employer's after-tax cost, and (5) use performance criteria over which the employee has control. Straight cash-compensation plans (salary and perhaps a bonus), though important, are oriented to the short run. Many companies recognize that they need a longer-term compensation plan in addition to the cash component.

Long-term compensation plans attempt to develop company loyalty among key employees by giving them "a piece of the action"—that is, an equity interest. These plans, generally referred to as stock-based compensation plans, come in many forms. Essentially, they provide the employee with the opportunity to receive stock if the performance of the company (by whatever measure) is satisfactory. Typical performance measures focus on long-term improvements that are readily measurable and that benefit the company as a whole, such as increases in earnings per share, revenues, stock price, or market share.

As indicated in our opening story, companies are changing the way they use stock-based compensation. Illustration 16-3 indicates that option expense is a much smaller element of compensation relative to **restricted stock** at companies such as Ford and Wal-Mart.

Company	Fair Value of Option Grants	Fair Value of Restricted Stock Grants
Disney	$120.6	$515.1
Ford	37.3	124.4
Urban Outfitters	1.0	35.8
Wal-Mart Stores	19.6	550.9

ILLUSTRATION 16-3
2011 Company Equity Grants ($ in millions)

The major reasons for this change are two-fold. Critics often cited the indiscriminate use of stock options as a reason why company executives manipulated accounting numbers in an attempt to achieve higher share price. As a result, many responsible companies decided to cut back on the issuance of options, both to avoid such accounting manipulations and to head off investor doubts. In addition, GAAP now results in companies recording a higher expense when stock options are granted.

The data reported in Illustration 16-4 (page 892) reinforce the point that the fair value of stock grants is significant and increasing. The study documents that compensation increased 7.7 percent for S&P 500 executives in 2011, with equity grants being the biggest source of growth.

ILLUSTRATION 16-4
Compensation Elements

($ in millions)	2011	% Change from 2010
Salary	$ 1,781.3	0.2%
Bonus	648.8	−2.8
Fair value of equity grants	8389.1	13.8
Non-equity incentive compensation	2719.2	−2.9
Pension benefits	1309.2	11.9
All other	590.6	7.8
Total executive compensation	$15,438.2	7.7%

Illustration 16-4 shows that cash compensation is less than 20 percent of total compensation. The fair value of equity grants comprised approximately 54 percent of total compensation.

The Major Reporting Issue. Suppose that as an employee for Hurdle Inc., you receive options to purchase 10,000 shares of the firm's common stock as part of your compensation. The date you receive the options is referred to as the grant date. The options are good for 10 years. The market price and the exercise price for the stock are both $20 at the grant date. **What is the value of the compensation you just received?**

Some believe that what you have received has no value. They reason that because the difference between the market price and the exercise price is zero, no compensation results. Others argue these options do have value. If the stock price goes above $20 any time in the next 10 years and you exercise the options, you may earn substantial compensation. For example, if at the end of the fourth year, the market price of the stock is $30 and you exercise your options, you earn $100,000 [10,000 options × ($30 − $20)], ignoring income taxes.

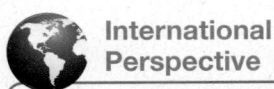

International Perspective

IFRS follows the same model as GAAP for recognizing share-based compensation.

The question for Hurdle is how to report the granting of these options. One approach measures compensation cost by the excess of the market price of the stock over its exercise price at the grant date. This approach is referred to as the intrinsic-value method. It measures what the holder would receive today if the option was immediately exercised. That intrinsic value **is the difference between the market price of the stock and the exercise price of the options at the grant date**. Using the intrinsic-value method, Hurdle would not recognize any compensation expense related to your options because at the grant date the market price equaled the exercise price. (In the preceding paragraph, those who answered that the options had no value were looking at the question from the intrinsic-value approach.)

The second way to look at the question of how to report the granting of these options bases the cost of employee stock options on the **fair value** of the stock options granted. Under this fair value method, companies use acceptable option-pricing models to value the options at the date of grant. These models take into account the many factors that determine an option's underlying value.[7]

GAAP requires that companies recognize compensation cost using the fair value method. **[5]** The FASB position is that companies should base the accounting for the cost of employee services on the fair value of compensation paid. This amount is presumed to be a measure of the value of the services received. We will discuss more about the politics of GAAP in this area later (see "Debate over Stock-Option Accounting," page 897). Let's first describe the procedures involved.

[7]These factors include the volatility of the underlying stock, the expected life of the options, the risk-free rate during the option life, and expected dividends during the option life.

ACCOUNTING FOR STOCK COMPENSATION
Stock-Option Plans

Stock-option plans involve two main accounting issues:

1. How to determine compensation expense.

2. Over what periods to allocate compensation expense.

Determining Expense

Under the fair value method, companies compute total compensation expense based on the fair value of the options expected to vest on the date they grant the options to the employee(s) (i.e., the **grant date**).[8] Public companies estimate fair value by using an option-pricing model, with some adjustments for the unique factors of employee stock options. No adjustments occur after the grant date in response to subsequent changes in the stock price—either up or down.

Allocating Compensation Expense

In general, a company recognizes compensation expense in the periods in which its employees perform the service—the service period. Unless otherwise specified, the service period is the vesting period—the time between the grant date and the vesting date. Thus, the company determines total compensation cost at the grant date and allocates it to the periods benefited by its employees' services.

Stock Compensation Example

An example will help show the accounting for a stock-option plan. Assume that on November 1, 2013, the stockholders of Chen Company approve a plan that grants the company's five executives options to purchase 2,000 shares each of the company's $1 par value common stock. The company grants the options on January 1, 2014. The executives may exercise the options at any time within the next 10 years. The option price per share is $60, and the market price of the stock at the date of grant is $70 per share.

Under the fair value method, the company computes total compensation expense by applying an acceptable fair value option-pricing model (such as the Black-Scholes option-pricing model). To keep this illustration simple, we assume that the fair value option-pricing model determines Chen's total compensation expense to be $220,000.

Basic Entries. Under the fair value method, a company recognizes the value of the options as an expense in the periods in which the employee performs services. In the case of Chen Company, assume that the expected period of benefit is two years, starting with the grant date. Chen would record the transactions related to this option contract as follows.

At date of grant (January 1, 2014)

No entry.

To record compensation expense for 2014 (December 31, 2014)

Compensation Expense	110,000	
Paid-in Capital—Stock Options ($220,000 ÷ 2)		110,000

To record compensation expense for 2015 (December 31, 2015)

Compensation Expense	110,000	
Paid-in Capital—Stock Options		110,000

---

[8]"To vest" means "to earn the rights to." An employee's award becomes vested at the date that the employee's right to receive or retain shares of stock or cash under the award is no longer contingent on remaining in the service of the employer.

As indicated, Chen allocates compensation expense evenly over the two-year service period.

Exercise. If Chen's executives exercise 2,000 of the 10,000 options (20 percent of the options) on June 1, 2017 (three years and five months after date of grant), the company records the following journal entry.

June 1, 2017

Cash (2,000 × $60)	120,000	
Paid-in Capital—Stock Options (20% × $220,000)	44,000	
Common Stock (2,000 × $1.00)		2,000
Paid-in Capital in Excess of Par—Common Stock		162,000

Expiration. If Chen's executives fail to exercise the remaining stock options before their expiration date, the company transfers the balance in the Paid-in Capital—Stock Options account to a more properly titled paid-in capital account, such as Paid-in Capital—Expired Stock Options. Chen records this transaction at the date of expiration as follows.

January 1, 2024 (expiration date)

Paid-in Capital—Stock Options	176,000	
Paid-in Capital—Expired Stock Options (80% × $220,000)		176,000

Adjustment. An unexercised stock option does not nullify the need to record the costs of services received from executives and attributable to the stock option plan. Under GAAP, a company therefore does not adjust compensation expense upon expiration of the options.

However, if an employee forfeits a stock option because **the employee fails to satisfy a service requirement** (e.g., leaves employment), the company should adjust the estimate of compensation expense recorded in the current period (as a change in estimate). A company records this change in estimate by debiting Paid-in Capital—Stock Options and crediting Compensation Expense for the amount of cumulative compensation expense recorded to date (thus decreasing compensation expense in the period of forfeiture).

Restricted Stock

As indicated earlier, many companies also use restricted stock (in some cases, replacing options altogether) to compensate employees. **Restricted-stock plans** transfer shares of stock to employees, subject to an agreement that the shares cannot be sold, transferred, or pledged until vesting occurs. Similar to stock options, these shares are subject to forfeiture if the conditions for vesting are not met.[9]

Major advantages of restricted-stock plans are:

1. *Restricted stock never becomes completely worthless.* In contrast, if the stock price does not exceed the exercise price for a stock option, the options are worthless. The restricted stock, however, still has value.
2. *Restricted stock generally results in less dilution to existing stockholders.* Restricted-stock awards are usually one-half to one-third the size of stock options. For example,

[9]Most companies base vesting on future service for a period of generally three to five years. Vesting may also be conditioned on some performance target such as revenue, net income, cash flows, or some combination of these three factors. The employee also collects dividends on the restricted stock, and these dividends generally must be repaid if forfeiture occurs.

if a company issues stock options on 1,000 shares, an equivalent restricted-stock offering might be 333 to 500 shares. The reason for the difference is that at the end of the vesting period, the restricted stock will have value, whereas the stock options may not. As a result, fewer shares are involved in restricted-stock plans, and therefore less dilution results if the stock price rises.

3. *Restricted stock better aligns the employee incentives with the companies' incentives.* The holder of restricted stock is essentially a stockholder and should be more interested in the long-term objectives of the company. In contrast, the recipients of stock options often have a short-run focus which leads to taking risks to hype the stock price for short-term gain to the detriment of the long-term.[10]

The accounting for restricted stock follows the same general principles as accounting for stock options at the date of grant. That is, the company determines the fair value of the restricted stock at the date of grant (usually the fair value of a share of stock) and then expenses that amount over the service period. Subsequent changes in the fair value of the stock are ignored for purposes of computing compensation expense.

Restricted Stock Example

Assume that on January 1, 2014, Ogden Company issues 1,000 shares of restricted stock to its CEO, Christie DeGeorge. Ogden's stock has a fair value of $20 per share on January 1, 2014. Additional information is as follows.

1. The service period related to the restricted stock is five years.
2. Vesting occurs if DeGeorge stays with the company for a five-year period.
3. The par value of the stock is $1 per share.

Ogden makes the following entry on the grant date (January 1, 2014).

Unearned Compensation	20,000	
Common Stock (1,000 × $1)		1,000
Paid-in Capital in Excess of Par—Common Stock (1,000 × $19)		19,000

The credits to Common Stock and Paid-in Capital in Excess of Par—Common Stock indicate that Ogden has issued shares of stock. The debit to Unearned Compensation (often referred to as Deferred Compensation Expense) identifies the total compensation expense the company will recognize over the five-year period. **Unearned Compensation represents the cost of services yet to be performed, which is not an asset.** Consequently, the company reports Unearned Compensation in stockholders' equity in the balance sheet, as a contra equity account (similar to the reporting of treasury stock at cost).

At December 31, 2014, Ogden records compensation expense of $4,000 (1,000 shares × $20 × 20%) as follows.

Compensation Expense	4,000	
Unearned Compensation		4,000

Ogden records compensation expense of $4,000 for each of the next four years (2015, 2016, 2017, and 2018).

---

[10]One important rationale for moving away from options to restricted stock is summarized by Bill Gates of **Microsoft**: "When you win [with options], you win the lottery. And when you don't win, you still want it. I can imagine an employee going home at night and considering two wildly different possibilities with his compensation program. Either he can buy six summer homes or no summer homes. Either he can send his kids to college 50 times, or no times. The variation is huge; much greater than most employees have an appetite for. And so as soon as they saw that options could go both ways, we proposed an economic equivalent. So what we do now is give shares, not options." See *http://www.mystockoptions.com/pdfs/Restricted%20Stock.pdf.*

What happens if DeGeorge leaves the company before the five years has elapsed? In this situation, DeGeorge forfeits her rights to the stock, and Ogden reverses the compensation expense already recorded.

For example, assume that DeGeorge leaves on February 3, 2016 (before any expense has been recorded during 2016). The entry to record this forfeiture is as follows.

Common Stock	1,000	
Paid-in Capital in Excess of Par—Common Stock	19,000	
Compensation Expense ($4,000 × 2)		8,000
Unearned Compensation		12,000

In this situation, Ogden reverses the compensation expense of $8,000 recorded through 2015. In addition, the company debits Common Stock and Paid-in Capital in Excess of Par—Common Stock, reflecting DeGeorge's forfeiture. It credits the balance of Unearned Compensation since none remains when DeGeorge leaves Ogden.

This accounting is similar to accounting for stock options when employees do not fulfill vesting requirements. Recall that once compensation expense is recorded for stock options, it is not reversed. The only exception is if the employee does not fulfill the vesting requirement, by leaving the company before vesting occurs.

In Ogden's restricted-stock plan, vesting never occurred because DeGeorge left the company before she met the service requirement. Because DeGeorge was never vested, she had to forfeit her shares. Therefore, the company must reverse compensation expense recorded to date.[11]

Employee Stock-Purchase Plans

Employee stock-purchase plans (ESPPs) generally permit all employees to purchase stock at a discounted price for a short period of time. The company often uses such plans to secure equity capital or to induce widespread ownership of its common stock among employees. These plans are considered compensatory unless they satisfy **all three** conditions presented below.

1. Substantially all full-time employees may participate on an equitable basis.
2. The discount from market is small. That is, the discount does not exceed the per share amount of costs avoided by not having to raise cash in a public offering. If the amount of the discount is 5 percent or less, no compensation needs to be recorded.
3. The plan offers no substantive option feature.

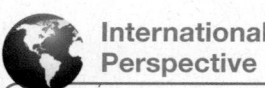 **International Perspective**

IFRS requires that any discount from the market price in employee stock-purchase plans be recorded as compensation expense.

For example, Masthead Company's stock-purchase plan allowed employees who met minimal employment qualifications to purchase its stock at a 5 percent reduction from market price for a short period of time. The reduction from market price is not considered compensatory. Why? Because the per share amount of the costs avoided by not having to raise the cash in a public offering equals 5 percent.

Companies that offer their employees a compensatory ESPP should record the compensation expense over the service life of the employees. It will be difficult for some companies to claim that their ESPPs are non-compensatory (and therefore not record compensation expense) unless they change their discount policy which in the past often was 15 percent. If they change their discount policy to 5 percent, participation in these plans will undoubtedly be lower. As a result, it is likely that some companies will end up dropping these plans.

---

[11]There are numerous variations on restricted-stock plans, including restricted-stock units (for which the shares are issued at the end of the vesting period) and restricted-stock plans with performance targets, such as EPS or stock price growth.

Disclosure of Compensation Plans

Companies must fully disclose the status of their compensation plans at the end of the periods presented. To meet these objectives, companies must make extensive disclosures. Specifically, a company with one or more share-based payment arrangements must disclose information that enables users of the financial statements to understand:

1. The nature and terms of such arrangements that existed during the period and the potential effects of those arrangements on shareholders.
2. The effect on the income statement of compensation cost arising from share-based payment arrangements.
3. The method of estimating the fair value of the goods or services received, or the fair value of the equity instruments granted (or offered to grant), during the period.
4. The cash flow effects resulting from share-based payment arrangements.

Illustration 16-5 (on page 898) presents the type of information disclosed for compensation plans.

Debate over Stock-Option Accounting

The FASB faced considerable opposition when it proposed the fair value method for accounting for stock options. This is not surprising, given that the fair value method results in greater compensation costs relative to the intrinsic-value model. One study documented that, on average, companies in the Standard & Poor's 500 stock index overstated earnings in a recent year by 10 percent through the use of the intrinsic-value method. (See the "What Do the Numbers Mean" box on page 899.) Nevertheless, some companies, such as **Coca-Cola**, **General Electric**, **Wachovia**, **Bank One**, and **The Washington Post**, decided to use the fair value method. As the CFO of Coca-Cola stated, "There is no doubt that stock options are compensation. If they weren't, none of us would want them."

Yet many in corporate America resisted the fair value method. Many small high-technology companies were especially vocal in their opposition, arguing that only through offering stock options can they attract top professional management. They contended that recognizing large amounts of compensation expense under these plans places them at a competitive disadvantage against larger companies that can withstand higher compensation charges. As one high-tech executive stated, "If your goal is to attack fat-cat executive compensation in multi-billion dollar firms, then please do so! But not at the expense of the people who are 'running lean and mean,' trying to build businesses and creating jobs in the process."

The stock-option saga is a classic example of the difficulty the FASB faces in issuing new accounting guidance. Many powerful interests aligned against the Board. Even some who initially appeared to support the Board's actions later reversed themselves. These efforts undermine the authority of the FASB, which in turn damages confidence in our financial reporting system.

Transparent financial reporting—including recognition of stock-based expense—should not be criticized because companies will report lower income. We may not like what the financial statements say, but we are always better off when the statements are representationally faithful to the underlying economic substance of transactions.

5 LEARNING OBJECTIVE

Discuss the controversy involving stock compensation plans.

Underlying Concepts 🔍

The stock-option controversy involves economic-consequence issues. The FASB believes companies should follow the neutrality concept. Others disagree, noting that factors other than accounting theory should be considered.

ILLUSTRATION 16-5
Stock-Option Plan
Disclosure

Description of plan

Valuation model
assumptions

Option plan activity
and balances

Option expense

Restricted-stock plan
details

Stock-Option Plan

The Company has a share-based compensation plan. The compensation cost that has been charged against income for the plan was $29.4 million, and $28.7 million for 2014 and 2013, respectively.

The Company's 2014 Employee Share-Option Plan (the Plan), which is shareholder-approved, permits the grant of share options and shares to its employees for up to 8 million shares of common stock. The Company believes that such awards better align the interests of its employees with those of its shareholders. Option awards are generally granted with an exercise price equal to the market price of the Company's stock at the date of grant; those option awards generally vest based on 5 years of continuous service and have 10-year contractual terms. Share awards generally vest over five years. Certain option and share awards provide for accelerated vesting if there is a change in control (as defined by the Plan).

The fair value of each option award is estimated on the date of grant using an option valuation model based on the assumptions noted in the following table.

	2014	2013
Expected volatility	25%–40%	24%–38%
Weighted-average volatility	33%	30%
Expected dividends	1.5%	1.5%
Expected term (in years)	5.3–7.8	5.5–8.0
Risk-free rate	6.3%–11.2%	6.0%–10.0%

A summary of option activity under the Plan as of December 31, 2014, and changes during the year then ended are presented below.

Options	Shares (000)	Weighted-Average Exercise Price	Weighted-Average Remaining Contractual Term	Aggregate Intrinsic Value ($000)
Outstanding at January 1, 2014	4,660	42		
Granted	950	60		
Exercised	(800)	36		
Forfeited or expired	(80)	59		
Outstanding at December 31, 2014	4,730	47	6.5	85,140
Exercisable at December 31, 2014	3,159	41	4.0	75,816

The weighted-average grant-date fair value of options granted during the years 2014 and 2013 was $19.57 and $17.46, respectively. The total intrinsic value of options exercised during the years ended December 31, 2014 and 2013, was $25.2 million, and $20.9 million, respectively.

As of December 31, 2014, there was $25.9 million of total unrecognized compensation cost related to nonvested share-based compensation arrangements granted under the Plan. That cost is expected to be recognized over a weighted-average period of 4.9 years. The total fair value of shares vested during the years ended December 31, 2014 and 2013, was $22.8 million and $21 million, respectively.

Restricted-Stock Awards

The Company also has a restricted-stock plan. The Plan is intended to retain and motivate the Company's Chief Executive Officer over the term of the award and to bring his total compensation package closer to median levels for Chief Executive Officers of comparable companies. The fair value of grants during the year was $1,889,000, or $35.68 per share, equivalent to 92% of the market price of a share of the Company's Common Stock on the date the award was granted.

Restricted-stock activity for the year ended 2014 is as follows.

	Shares	Price
Outstanding at December 31, 2013	57,990	—
Granted	149,000	$12.68
Vested	(19,330)	—
Forfeited	—	—
Outstanding at December 31, 2014	187,660	

By leaving stock-based compensation expense out of income, reported income is biased. Biased reporting not only raises concerns about the credibility of companies' reports, but also of financial reporting in general. Even good companies get tainted by the biased reporting of a few "bad apples." If we write standards to achieve some social, economic, or public policy goal, financial reporting loses its credibility.

As you have learned, GAAP requires companies to expense compensation paid in the form of stock options. However, before the change to require expensing, some companies voluntarily expensed options rather than simply disclosing the estimated costs in the notes to the financial statements. You might think investors would punish companies that decided to expense stock options. After all, most of corporate America has been battling for years to avoid having to expense them, worried that accounting for those perks would destroy

earnings. And indeed, Merrill Lynch estimated that if all S&P 500 companies were to expense options, reported profits would fall by as much as 10 percent.

Yet, this small band of big-name companies voluntarily made the switch to expensing, and investors for the most part showered them with love. As shown in the following table, with a few exceptions, the stock prices of the "expensers," from Cinergy to The Washington Post, outpaced the market after they announced the change.

Company	Estimated EPS		% Change Since Announcement
	Without Options	With Options Expensed	Company Stock Price
Cinergy	$ 2.80	$ 2.77	22.4%
The Washington Post	20.48	20.10	16.4
Computer Associates	−0.46	−0.62	11.1
Fannie Mae	6.15	6.02	6.7
Bank One	2.77	2.61	2.6
General Motors	5.84	5.45	2.6
Procter & Gamble	3.57	3.35	−2.3
Coca-Cola	1.79	1.70	−6.2
General Electric	1.65	1.61	−6.2
Amazon.com	0.04	−0.99	−11.4

Sources: Merrill Lynch; company reports.

The market's general positive reaction to the expensing of stock options provides a good case study supporting the value that investors place on transparent accounting and

reporting. It is puzzling why some companies continued to fight implementation of the expensing rule.

Source: David Stires, "A Little Honesty Goes a Long Way," *Fortune* (September 2, 2002), p. 186. Reprinted by permission. See also Troy Wolverton, "Foes of Expensing Welcome FASB Delay," *TheStreet.com* (October 15, 2004).

COMPUTING EARNINGS PER SHARE

As indicated earlier, stockholders and potential investors widely use earnings per share in evaluating the profitability of a company. As a result, much attention is given to earnings per share by the financial press. Earnings per share indicates the income earned by each share of common stock. Thus, **companies report earnings per share only for common stock**. For example, if Oscar Co. has net income of $300,000 and a weighted average of 100,000 shares of common stock outstanding for the year, earnings per share is $3 ($300,000 ÷ 100,000). Because of the importance of earnings per share information, most companies must report this information on the face of the income statement.[12] **[6]** The exception, due to cost-benefit considerations, is nonpublic companies.[13] Generally, companies report earnings per share information below

6 LEARNING OBJECTIVE
Compute earnings per share in a simple capital structure.

[12]For an article on the usefulness of reported EPS data and the application of the qualitative characteristics of accounting information to EPS data, see Lola W. Dudley, "A Critical Look at EPS," *Journal of Accountancy* (August 1985), pp. 102–111.

[13]A nonpublic enterprise is an enterprise (1) whose debt or equity securities are not traded in a public market on a foreign or domestic stock exchange or in the over-the-counter market (including securities quoted locally or regionally), or (2) that is not required to file financial statements with the SEC. An enterprise is not considered a nonpublic enterprise when its financial statements are issued in preparation for the sale of any class of securities in a public market.

net income in the income statement. Illustration 16-6 shows Oscar Co.'s income statement presentation of earnings per share.

ILLUSTRATION 16-6
Income Statement
Presentation of EPS

Net income	$300,000
Earnings per share	$3.00

When the income statement contains intermediate components of income (such as discontinued operations or extraordinary items), companies should disclose earnings per share for each component. The presentation in Illustration 16-7 is representative.

ILLUSTRATION 16-7
Income Statement
Presentation of EPS
Components

Earnings per share:	
Income from continuing operations	$4.00
Loss from discontinued operations, net of tax	0.60
Income before extraordinary item	3.40
Extraordinary gain, net of tax	1.00
Net income	$4.40

These disclosures enable the user of the financial statements to recognize the effects on EPS of income from continuing operations, as distinguished from income or loss from irregular items.[14]

Earnings per Share—Simple Capital Structure

A corporation's capital structure is **simple** if it consists only of common stock or includes no **potential common stock** that upon conversion or exercise could dilute earnings per common share. A capital structure is **complex** if it includes securities that could have a dilutive effect on earnings per common share.

The computation of earnings per share for a simple capital structure involves two items (other than net income)—(1) preferred stock dividends and (2) weighted-average number of shares outstanding.

Preferred Stock Dividends

As we indicated earlier, earnings per share relates to earnings per *common share*. When a company has both common and preferred stock outstanding, **it subtracts the current-year preferred stock dividend from net income to arrive at** income available to common stockholders. Illustration 16-8 shows the formula for computing earnings per share.

ILLUSTRATION 16-8
Formula for Computing
Earnings per Share

$$\text{Earnings per Share} = \frac{\text{Net Income} - \text{Preferred Dividends}}{\text{Weighted-Average Number of Shares Outstanding}}$$

In reporting earnings per share information, a company must calculate income available to common stockholders. To do so, the company subtracts dividends on preferred stock from each of the intermediate components of income (income from continuing operations and income before extraordinary items) and finally from net income. If a company declares dividends on preferred stock and a net loss occurs, **the**

---

[14]Companies should present, either on the face of the income statement or in the notes to the financial statements, per share amounts for discontinued operations and extraordinary items.

company adds the preferred dividend to the loss for purposes of computing the loss per share.

If the preferred stock is cumulative and the company has net income but declares no dividend in the current year, it subtracts **an amount equal to the dividend that it should have declared for the current year only**. If the stock is cumulative and the company reports a net loss, but declares no dividend in the current year, it **adds** an amount equal to the dividend to the net loss. The company should have included dividends in arrears for previous years in the previous years' computations.

International Perspective

The FASB and the IASB are working together on a project to improve EPS accounting by simplifying the computational guidance and thereby increasing the comparability of EPS data on an international basis.

Weighted-Average Number of Shares Outstanding

In all computations of earnings per share, the weighted-average number of shares outstanding during the period constitutes the basis for the per share amounts reported. Shares issued or purchased during the period affect the amount outstanding. Companies must **weight the shares by the fraction of the period they are outstanding**. The rationale for this approach is to find the equivalent number of whole shares outstanding for the year.

To illustrate, assume that Franks Inc. has changes in its common stock shares outstanding for the period as shown in Illustration 16-9.

Date	Share Changes	Shares Outstanding
January 1	Beginning balance	90,000
April 1	Issued 30,000 shares for cash	30,000
		120,000
July 1	Purchased 39,000 shares	(39,000)
		81,000
November 1	Issued 60,000 shares for cash	60,000
December 31	Ending balance	141,000

ILLUSTRATION 16-9
Shares Outstanding, Ending Balance— Franks Inc.

Franks computes the weighted-average number of shares outstanding as follows.

Dates Outstanding	(A) Shares Outstanding	(B) Fraction of Year	(C) Weighted Shares (A × B)
Jan. 1–Apr. 1	90,000	3/12	22,500
Apr. 1–July 1	120,000	3/12	30,000
July 1–Nov. 1	81,000	4/12	27,000
Nov. 1–Dec. 31	141,000	2/12	23,500
Weighted-average number of shares outstanding			103,000

ILLUSTRATION 16-10
Weighted-Average Number of Shares Outstanding

As Illustration 16-10 shows, 90,000 shares were outstanding for three months, which is equivalent to 22,500 whole shares for the entire year. Because Franks issued additional shares on April 1, it must weight these shares for the time outstanding. When the company purchased 39,000 shares on July 1, it reduced the shares outstanding. Therefore, from July 1 to November 1, only 81,000 shares were outstanding, which is equivalent to 27,000 shares. The issuance of 60,000 shares increases shares outstanding for the last two months of the year. Franks then makes a new computation to determine the proper weighted shares outstanding.

Stock Dividends and Stock Splits. When **stock dividends** or **stock splits** occur, companies need to restate the shares outstanding before the stock dividend or split, in order to compute the weighted-average number of shares. For example, assume that Vijay Corporation had 100,000 shares outstanding on January 1 and issued a 25 percent stock dividend on June 30. For purposes of computing a weighted-average for the current year, it assumes the additional 25,000 shares outstanding as a result of the stock dividend to be **outstanding since the beginning of the year**. Thus, the weighted-average for the year for Vijay is 125,000 shares.

Companies restate the issuance of a stock dividend or stock split, but not the issuance or repurchase of stock for cash. Why? Because stock splits and stock dividends do not increase or decrease the net assets of the company. The company merely issues additional shares of stock. Because of the added shares, it must restate the weighted-average shares. Restating allows valid comparisons of earnings per share between periods before and after the stock split or stock dividend. Conversely, the issuance or purchase of stock for cash **changes the amount of net assets**. As a result, the company either earns more or less in the future as a result of this change in net assets. Stated another way, **a stock dividend or split does not change the shareholders' total investment—** it only increases (unless it is a reverse stock split) the number of common shares representing this investment.

To illustrate how a stock dividend affects the computation of the weighted-average number of shares outstanding, assume that Sabrina Company has the following changes in its common stock shares during the year.

ILLUSTRATION 16-11
Shares Outstanding, Ending Balance—Sabrina Company

Date	Share Changes	Shares Outstanding
January 1	Beginning balance	100,000
March 1	Issued 20,000 shares for cash	20,000
		120,000
June 1	60,000 additional shares (50% stock dividend)	60,000
		180,000
November 1	Issued 30,000 shares for cash	30,000
December 31	Ending balance	210,000

Sabrina computes the weighted-average number of shares outstanding as follows.

ILLUSTRATION 16-12
Weighted-Average Number of Shares Outstanding—Stock Issue and Stock Dividend

Dates Outstanding	(A) Shares Outstanding	(B) Restatement	(C) Fraction of Year	(D) Weighted Shares (A × B × C)
Jan. 1–Mar. 1	100,000	1.50	2/12	25,000
Mar. 1–June 1	120,000	1.50	3/12	45,000
June 1–Nov. 1	180,000		5/12	75,000
Nov. 1–Dec. 31	210,000		2/12	35,000
Weighted-average number of shares outstanding				180,000

Sabrina must restate the shares outstanding prior to the stock dividend. The company adjusts the shares outstanding from January 1 to June 1 for the stock dividend, so that it now states these shares on the same basis as shares issued subsequent to the stock dividend. Sabrina does not restate shares issued after the stock dividend because they are on the new basis. The stock dividend simply restates existing shares. **The same type of treatment applies to a stock split.**

If a stock dividend or stock split occurs after the end of the year but before issuing the financial statements, a company must restate the weighted-average number of shares outstanding for the year (and any other years presented in comparative form). For example, assume that Hendricks Company computes its weighted-average number of shares as 100,000 for the year ended December 31, 2014. On January 15, 2015, before issuing the financial statements, the company splits its stock 3 for 1. In this case, the weighted-average number of shares used in computing earnings per share for 2014 is now 300,000 shares. If providing earnings per share information for 2013 as comparative information, Hendricks must also adjust it for the stock split.

Comprehensive Example

Let's study a comprehensive illustration for a simple capital structure. Darin Corporation has income before extraordinary item of $580,000 and an extraordinary gain, net of tax, of $240,000. In addition, it has declared preferred dividends of $1 per share on 100,000 shares of preferred stock outstanding. Darin also has the following changes in its common stock shares outstanding during 2014.

Dates	Share Changes	Shares Outstanding
January 1	Beginning balance	180,000
May 1	Purchased 30,000 treasury shares	(30,000)
		150,000
July 1	300,000 additional shares	
	(3-for-1 stock split)	300,000
		450,000
December 31	Issued 50,000 shares for cash	50,000
December 31	Ending balance	500,000

ILLUSTRATION 16-13
Shares Outstanding, Ending Balance— Darin Corp.

To compute the earnings per share information, Darin determines the weighted-average number of shares outstanding as follows.

Dates Outstanding	(A) Shares Outstanding	(B) Restatement	(C) Fraction of Year	(D) Weighted Shares (A × B × C)
Jan. 1–May 1	180,000	3	4/12	180,000
May 1–July 1	150,000	3	2/12	75,000
July 1–Dec. 31	450,000		6/12	225,000
Weighted-average number of shares outstanding				480,000

ILLUSTRATION 16-14
Weighted-Average Number of Shares Outstanding

In computing the weighted-average number of shares, the company ignores the shares sold on December 31, 2014, because they have not been outstanding during the year. Darin then divides the weighted-average number of shares into income before extraordinary item and net income to determine earnings per share. It subtracts its preferred dividends of $100,000 from income before extraordinary item ($580,000) to arrive at income before extraordinary item available to common stockholders of $480,000 ($580,000 − $100,000).

Deducting the preferred dividends from the income before extraordinary item also reduces net income without affecting the amount of the extraordinary item. The final amount is referred to as **income available to common stockholders**, as shown in Illustration 16-15.

ILLUSTRATION 16-15
Computation of Income Available to Common Stockholders

	(A) Income Information	(B) Weighted Shares	(C) Earnings per Share (A ÷ B)
Income before extraordinary item available to common stockholders	$480,000*	480,000	$1.00
Extraordinary gain (net of tax)	240,000	480,000	0.50
Income available to common stockholders	$720,000	480,000	$1.50

*$580,000 − $100,000

Darin must disclose the per share amount for the extraordinary item (net of tax) either on the face of the income statement or in the notes to the financial statements. Illustration 16-16 shows the income and per share information reported on the face of Darin's income statement.

ILLUSTRATION 16-16
Earnings per Share, with Extraordinary Item

Income before extraordinary item	$580,000
Extraordinary gain, net of tax	240,000
Net income	$820,000
Earnings per share:	
Income before extraordinary item	$1.00
Extraordinary item, net of tax	0.50
Net income	$1.50

Earnings per Share—Complex Capital Structure

LEARNING OBJECTIVE 7
Compute earnings per share in a complex capital structure.

The EPS discussion to this point applies to basic EPS for a simple capital structure. One problem with a **basic EPS** computation is that it fails to recognize the potential impact of a corporation's dilutive securities. As discussed at the beginning of the chapter, dilutive securities are securities that can be converted to common stock.[15] Upon conversion or exercise by the holder, the dilutive securities reduce (dilute) earnings per share. This adverse effect on EPS can be significant and, more importantly, *unexpected* unless financial statements call attention to their potential dilutive effect.

As indicated earlier, a complex capital structure exists when a corporation has convertible securities, options, warrants, or other rights that upon conversion or exercise could dilute earnings per share. When a company has a complex capital structure, **it generally reports both basic and diluted earnings per share**.

Computing diluted EPS is similar to computing basic EPS. The difference is that diluted EPS includes the effect of all potential dilutive common shares that were outstanding during the period. The formula in Illustration 16-17 shows the relationship between basic EPS and diluted EPS.

Some securities are antidilutive. Antidilutive securities are securities that upon conversion or exercise **increase** earnings per share (or reduce the loss per share). Companies with complex capital structures will not report diluted EPS if the securities in their capital structure are antidilutive. The purpose of presenting both basic and diluted EPS is to inform financial statement users of

International Perspective

The provisions in GAAP are substantially the same as those in *International Accounting Standard No. 33*, "Earnings per Share," issued by the IASB.

[15]Issuance of these types of securities is typical in mergers and compensation plans.

ILLUSTRATION 16-17
Relationship between
Basic and Diluted EPS

situations that will likely occur (basic EPS) and also to provide "worst case" dilutive situations (dilutive EPS). If the securities are antidilutive, the likelihood of conversion or exercise is considered remote. Thus, companies that have only antidilutive securities must report only the basic EPS number. We illustrated the computation of basic EPS in the prior section. In the following sections, we address the effects of convertible and other dilutive securities on EPS calculations.

Diluted EPS—Convertible Securities

At conversion, companies exchange convertible securities for common stock. Companies measure the dilutive effects of potential conversion on EPS using the **if-converted method**. This method for a convertible bond assumes (1) the conversion of the convertible securities at the beginning of the period (or at the time of issuance of the security, if issued during the period), and (2) the elimination of related interest, net of tax. Thus, the additional shares assumed issued increase the **denominator**—the weighted-average number of shares outstanding. The amount of interest expense, net of tax associated with those potential common shares, increases the **numerator**—net income.

Comprehensive Example—If-Converted Method. As an example, Mayfield Corporation has net income of $210,000 for the year and a weighted-average number of common shares outstanding during the period of 100,000 shares. The basic earnings per share is therefore $2.10 ($210,000 ÷ 100,000). The company has two convertible debenture bond issues outstanding. One is a 6 percent issue sold at 100 (total $1,000,000) in a prior year and convertible into 20,000 common shares. The other is a 10 percent issue sold at 100 (total $1,000,000) on April 1 of the current year and convertible into 32,000 common shares. The tax rate is 40 percent.

As Illustration 16-18 shows, to determine the numerator for diluted earnings per share, Mayfield adds back the interest on the if-converted securities, less the related tax effect. Because the if-converted method assumes conversion as of the beginning of the year, Mayfield assumes that it pays no interest on the convertibles during the year. The interest on the 6 percent convertibles is $60,000 for the year ($1,000,000 × 6%). The increased tax expense is $24,000 ($60,000 × 0.40). The interest added back net of taxes is $36,000 [$60,000 − $24,000, or simply $60,000 × (1 − 0.40)].

Net income for the year	$210,000
Add: Adjustment for interest (net of tax)	
6% debentures ($60,000 × [1 − .40])	36,000
10% debentures ($100,000 × 9/12 × [1 − .40])	45,000
Adjusted net income	$291,000

ILLUSTRATION 16-18
Computation of Adjusted
Net Income

Continuing with the information in Illustration 16-18, because Mayfield issues 10 percent convertibles subsequent to the beginning of the year, it weights the shares. In other words, it considers these shares to have been outstanding from April 1 to the end of the year. As a result, the interest adjustment to the numerator for these bonds reflects the interest for only nine months. Thus, the interest added back on the 10 percent convertible is $45,000 [$1,000,000 × 10% × 9/12 year × (1 − 0.4)]. The final item in Illustration 16-18 shows the adjusted net income. This amount becomes the numerator for Mayfield's computation of diluted earnings per share.

Mayfield then calculates the weighted-average number of shares outstanding, as shown in Illustration 16-19. This number of shares becomes the denominator for Mayfield's computation of diluted earnings per share.

ILLUSTRATION 16-19
Computation of
Weighted-Average
Number of Shares

Weighted-average number of shares outstanding	100,000
Add: Shares assumed to be issued:	
6% debentures (as of beginning of year)	20,000
10% debentures (as of date of issue, April 1; 9/12 × 32,000)	24,000
Weighted-average number of shares adjusted for dilutive securities	144,000

In its income statement, Mayfield reports basic and diluted earnings per share.[16] Illustration 16-20 shows this dual presentation.

ILLUSTRATION 16-20
Earnings per Share
Disclosure

Net income for the year	$210,000
Earnings per Share (Note X)	
Basic earnings per share ($210,000 ÷ 100,000)	$2.10
Diluted earnings per share ($291,000 ÷ 144,000)	$2.02

Other Factors. The example above assumed that Mayfield sold its bonds at the face amount. If it instead sold the bonds at a premium or discount, the company must adjust the interest expense each period to account for this occurrence. Therefore, the interest expense reported on the income statement is the amount of interest expense, net of tax, added back to net income. (It is not the interest paid in cash during the period.)

In addition, the conversion rate on a dilutive security may change during the period in which the security is outstanding. For the diluted EPS computation in such a situation, the **company uses the most dilutive conversion rate available**. For example, assume that a company issued a convertible bond on January 1, 2013, with a conversion rate of 10 common shares for each bond starting January 1, 2015. Beginning January 1, 2018, the conversion rate is 12 common shares for each bond, and beginning January 1, 2022, it is 15 common shares for each bond. In computing diluted EPS in 2013, the company uses the conversion rate of 15 shares to one bond.

A final issue relates to preferred stock. For example, assume that Mayfield's 6 percent convertible debentures were instead 6 percent convertible *preferred stock.* In that case, Mayfield considers the convertible preferred as potential common shares. Thus, it includes them in its diluted EPS calculations as shares outstanding. The company does not subtract preferred dividends from net income in computing the numerator. Why

---

[16]Conversion of bonds is dilutive because EPS with conversion ($2.02) is less than basic EPS ($2.10). See Appendix 16B for a comprehensive evaluation of antidilution with multiple securities.

not? Because for purposes of computing EPS, it assumes conversion of the convertible preferreds to outstanding common stock. The company uses net income as the numerator—it computes **no tax effect** because preferred dividends generally are not tax-deductible.

Diluted EPS—Options and Warrants

A company includes in diluted earnings per share stock options and warrants outstanding (whether or not presently exercisable), unless they are antidilutive. Companies use the **treasury-stock method** to include options and warrants and their equivalents in EPS computations.

The treasury-stock method assumes that the options or warrants are exercised at the beginning of the year (or date of issue if later), and that the company uses those proceeds to purchase common stock for the treasury. If the exercise price is lower than the market price of the stock, then the proceeds from exercise are insufficient to buy back all the shares. The company then adds the incremental shares remaining to the weighted-average number of shares outstanding for purposes of computing diluted earnings per share.

For example, if the exercise price of a warrant is $5 and the market price of the stock is $15, the treasury-stock method increases the shares outstanding. Exercise of the warrant results in one additional share outstanding, but the $5 received for the one share issued is insufficient to purchase one share in the market at $15. The company needs to exercise three warrants (and issue three additional shares) to produce enough money ($15) to acquire one share in the market. Thus, a net increase of two shares outstanding results.

To see this computation using larger numbers, assume 1,500 options outstanding at an exercise price of $30 for a common share and a common stock market price per share of $50. Through application of the treasury-stock method, the company would have 600 incremental shares outstanding, computed as shown in Illustration 16-21.[17]

Proceeds from exercise of 1,500 options (1,500 × $30)	$45,000
Shares issued upon exercise of options	1,500
Treasury shares purchasable with proceeds ($45,000 ÷ $50)	(900)
Incremental shares outstanding (potential common shares)	600

ILLUSTRATION 16-21
Computation of Incremental Shares

Thus, if the exercise price of the option or warrant is **lower** than the market price of the stock, dilution occurs. An exercise price of the option or warrant **higher** than the market price of the stock reduces common shares. In this case, the options or warrants are **antidilutive** because their assumed exercise leads to an increase in earnings per share.

For both options and warrants, exercise is assumed only if the average market price of the stock exceeds the exercise price during the reported period.[18] As a practical

---

[17]The incremental number of shares may be more simply computed:

$$\frac{\text{Market price} - \text{Option price}}{\text{Market price}} \times \text{Number of options} = \text{Number of shares}$$

$$\frac{\$50 - \$30}{\$50} \times 1{,}500 \text{ options} = 600 \text{ shares}$$

[18]Options and warrants have essentially the same assumptions and computational problems, although the warrants may allow or require the tendering of some other security, such as debt, in lieu of cash upon exercise. In such situations, the accounting becomes quite complex and is beyond the scope of this textbook.

matter, a simple average of the weekly or monthly prices is adequate, so long as the prices do not fluctuate significantly.

Comprehensive Example—Treasury-Stock Method. To illustrate application of the treasury-stock method, assume that Kubitz Industries, Inc. has net income for the period of $220,000. The average number of shares outstanding for the period was 100,000 shares. Hence, basic EPS—ignoring all dilutive securities—is $2.20. The average number of shares related to options outstanding (although not exercisable at this time), at an option price of $20 per share, is 5,000 shares. The average market price of the common stock during the year was $28. Illustration 16-22 shows the computation of EPS using the treasury-stock method.

ILLUSTRATION 16-22
Computation of Earnings per Share—Treasury-Stock Method

	Basic Earnings per Share	Diluted Earnings per Share
Average number of shares related to options outstanding		5,000
Option price per share		× $20
Proceeds upon exercise of options		$100,000
Average market price of common stock		$28
Treasury shares that could be repurchased with proceeds ($100,000 ÷ $28)		3,571
Excess of shares under option over the treasury shares that could be repurchased (5,000 − 3,571)—potential common incremental shares		1,429
Average number of common shares outstanding	100,000	100,000
Total average number of common shares outstanding and potential common shares	100,000 (A)	101,429 (C)
Net income for the year	$220,000 (B)	$220,000 (D)
Earnings per share	$2.20 (B ÷ A)	$2.17 (D ÷ C)

Contingent Issue Agreement

In business combinations, the acquirer may promise to issue additional shares—referred to as **contingent shares**—under certain conditions. Sometimes the company issues these contingent shares as a result of a **passage-of-time condition** or upon the attainment of a **certain earnings or market price level**. If this passage-of-time condition occurs during the current year, or if the company meets the earnings or market price **by the end of the year**, the company considers the contingent shares as outstanding for the computation of diluted earnings per share.[19]

For example, assume that Watts Corporation purchased Cardoza Company and agreed to give Cardoza's stockholders 20,000 additional shares in 2017 if Cardoza's net income in 2016 is $90,000. In 2015, Cardoza's net income is $100,000. Because Cardoza has already attained the 2016 stipulated earnings of $90,000, in computing diluted earnings per share for 2015, Watts would include the 20,000 contingent shares in the shares-outstanding computation.

Antidilution Revisited

In computing diluted EPS, a company must consider the aggregate of all dilutive securities. But first it must determine which potentially dilutive securities are in fact individually dilutive and which are antidilutive. **A company should exclude any**

[19]In addition to contingent issuances of stock, other situations that might lead to dilution are the issuance of participating securities and two-class common shares. The reporting of these types of securities in EPS computations is beyond the scope of this textbook.

security that is antidilutive, nor can the company use such a security to offset dilutive securities.

Recall that including antidilutive securities in earnings per share computations increases earnings per share (or reduces net loss per share). With options or warrants, whenever the exercise price exceeds the market price, the security is antidilutive. Convertible debt is antidilutive if the addition to income of the interest (net of tax) causes a greater percentage increase in income (numerator) than conversion of the bonds causes a percentage increase in common and potentially dilutive shares (denominator). In other words, convertible debt is antidilutive if conversion of the security causes common stock earnings to increase by a greater amount per additional common share than earnings per share was before the conversion.

To illustrate, assume that Martin Corporation has a 6 percent, $1,000,000 debt issue that is convertible into 10,000 common shares. Net income for the year is $210,000, the weighted-average number of common shares outstanding is 100,000 shares, and the tax rate is 40 percent. In this case, assumed conversion of the debt into common stock at the beginning of the year requires the following adjustments of net income and the weighted-average number of shares outstanding.

Net income for the year	$210,000	Average number of shares outstanding	100,000
Add: Adjustment for interest (net of tax) on 6% debentures		Add: Shares issued upon assumed conversion of debt	10,000
$60,000 × (1 − .40)	36,000	Average number of common and	
Adjusted net income	$246,000	potential common shares outstanding	110,000

Basic EPS = $210,000 ÷ 100,000 = $2.10
Diluted EPS = $246,000 ÷ 110,000 = $2.24 = **Antidilutive**

ILLUSTRATION 16-23
Test for Antidilution

As a shortcut, Martin can also identify the convertible debt as antidilutive by comparing the EPS resulting from conversion, $3.60 ($36,000 additional earnings ÷ 10,000 additional shares), with EPS before inclusion of the convertible debt, $2.10.

Companies should ignore antidilutive securities in all calculations and in computing diluted earnings per share. This approach is reasonable. The profession's intent was to inform the investor of the possible dilution that might occur in reported earnings per share and not to be concerned with securities that, if converted or exercised, would result in an increase in earnings per share. Appendix 16B to this chapter provides an extended example of how companies consider antidilution in a complex situation with multiple securities.

EPS Presentation and Disclosure

A company with a complex capital structure would present its EPS information as follows.

Earnings per common share	
Basic earnings per share	$3.30
Diluted earnings per share	$2.70

ILLUSTRATION 16-24
EPS Presentation—Complex Capital Structure

When the earnings of a period include irregular items, a company should show per share amounts (where applicable) for the following: income from continuing operations, income before extraordinary items, and net income. Companies that report a discontinued operation or an extraordinary item should present per share amounts **for those line items** either on the face of the income statement or in the notes to the financial statements. Illustration 16-25 (page 910) shows a presentation reporting extraordinary items.

ILLUSTRATION 16-25
EPS Presentation, with
Extraordinary Item

Basic earnings per share	
Income before extraordinary item	$3.80
Extraordinary item	(0.80)
Net income	$3.00
Diluted earnings per share	
Income before extraordinary item	$3.35
Extraordinary item	(0.65)
Net income	$2.70

A company must show earnings per share amounts for all periods presented. Also, the company should restate all prior period earnings per share amounts presented for stock dividends and stock splits. If it reports diluted EPS data for at least one period, the company should report such data for all periods presented, even if it is the same as basic EPS. When a company restates results of operations of a prior period as a result of an error or a change in accounting principle, it should also restate the earnings per share data shown for the prior periods. Complex capital structures and dual presentation of earnings per share require the following additional disclosures in note form.

1. Description of pertinent rights and privileges of the various securities outstanding.
2. A reconciliation of the numerators and denominators of the basic and diluted per share computations, including individual income and share amount effects of all securities that affect EPS.
3. The effect given preferred dividends in determining income available to common stockholders in computing basic EPS.
4. Securities that could potentially dilute basic EPS in the future that were excluded in the computation because they would be antidilutive.
5. Effect of conversions subsequent to year-end, but before issuing statements.

Illustration 16-26 presents the reconciliation and the related disclosure to meet the requirements of this standard.[20] **[7]**

ILLUSTRATION 16-26
Reconciliation for Basic
and Diluted EPS

	For the Year Ended 2014		
	Income (Numerator)	Shares (Denominator)	Per Share Amount
Income before extraordinary item	$7,500,000		
Less: Preferred stock dividends	45,000		
Basic EPS	7,455,000	3,991,666	$1.87
Warrants		30,768	
Convertible preferred stock	45,000	308,333	
4% convertible bonds (net of tax)	60,000	50,000	
Diluted EPS	$7,560,000	4,380,767	$1.73

Stock options to purchase 1,000,000 shares of common stock at $85 per share were outstanding during the second half of 2014 but were not included in the computation of diluted EPS because the options' exercise price was greater than the average market price of the common shares. The options were still outstanding at the end of year 2014 and expire on June 30, 2024.

[20]Note that GAAP has specific disclosure requirements regarding stock-based compensation plans and earnings per share disclosures as well. The earnings per share effects of noncontrolling interest (discussed in Chapter 4) should also be presented, with the amounts of income from continuing operations and discontinued operations (if present), attributable to the controlling interest disclosed. However, only the net income attributable to the controlling interest should be used in computing earnings per share.

What do the numbers mean? PRO FORMA EPS CONFUSION

Many companies are reporting pro forma EPS numbers along with GAAP-based EPS numbers in the financial information provided to investors. Pro forma earnings generally exceed GAAP earnings because the pro forma numbers exclude such items as restructuring charges, impairments of assets, R&D expenditures, and stock compensation expense. Here are some examples.

Company	GAAP EPS	Pro Forma EPS
Adaptec	$(0.62)	$ 0.05
Corning	(0.24)	0.09
General Motors	(0.41)	0.85
Honeywell International	(0.38)	0.44
International Paper	(0.57)	0.14
Qualcomm	(0.06)	0.20
Broadcom	(6.36)	(0.13)
Lucent Technologies	(2.16)	(0.27)

Source: Company press releases.

Another case of possibly misleading pro forma reporting is the case of social media darlings Facebook, Zynga, and Groupon. For example, social gaming company Zynga recently reported so much stock-compensation expense

($600 million) that it overwhelmed its operating profit; these expenses took operating profit negative to the tune of $406 million. The accounting? Zynga "window dressed" the expense by encouraging Wall Street analysts to use a non-GAAP pro forma accounting figure—"adjusted earnings before interest, taxes, depreciation and amortization"—that ignores the stock compensation. LinkedIn and Groupon also use non-GAAP metrics that exclude stock compensation. LinkedIn's $30 million stock-compensation expense roughly halved its operating profit, while Groupon's $94 million took operating profit $203 million into the red. Wall Street analysts tend to go along with the accounting hocus-pocus, as it allows them to justify higher valuations for stocks. Investors should remember, however, that employee equity awards are real costs.

As discussed in Chapter 4, SEC Regulation G requires companies to provide a clear reconciliation between pro forma and GAAP information. And this applies to EPS measures as well. This reconciliation is especially important, given the spike in pro forma reporting by companies adding back employee stock-option expense.

Sources: See M. Moran, A. J. Cohen, and K. Shaustyuk, "Stock Option Expensing: The Battle Has Been Won; Now Comes the Aftermath," *Portfolio Strategy/Accounting*, Goldman Sachs (March 17, 2005); and R. Winkler, "Stock and Awe at Facebook and Zynga," *Wall Street Journal* (February 16, 2012).

Summary of EPS Computation

As you can see, computation of earnings per share is a complex issue. It is a controversial area because many securities, although technically not common stock, have many of its basic characteristics. Indeed, some companies have issued these other securities rather than common stock in order to avoid an adverse dilutive effect on earnings per share. Illustrations 16-27 and 16-28 (page 912) display the elementary points of calculating earnings per share in a simple capital structure and in a complex capital structure.

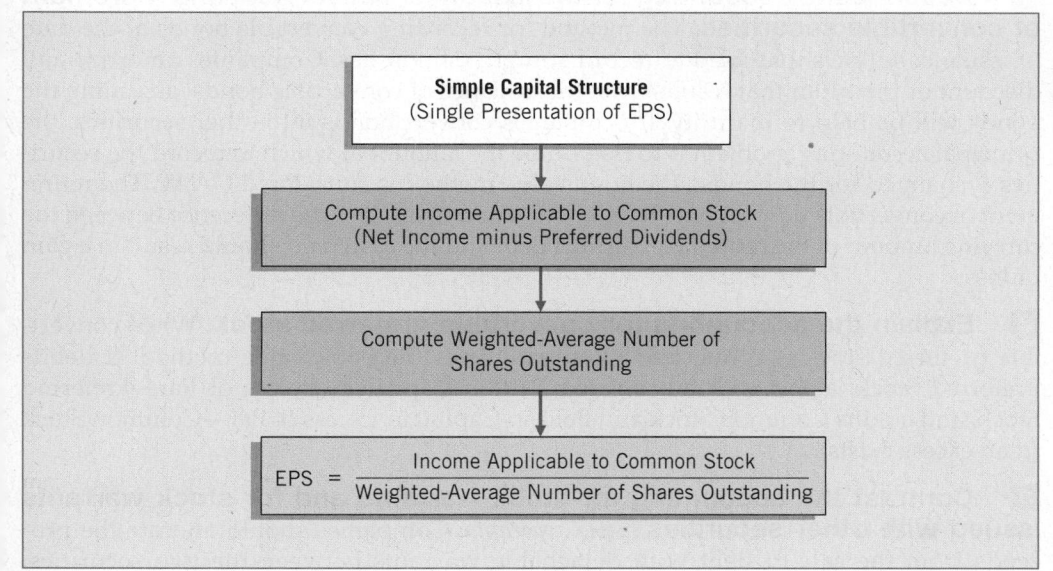

ILLUSTRATION 16-27
Calculating EPS, Simple Capital Structure

ILLUSTRATION 16-28
Calculating EPS,
Complex Capital
Structure

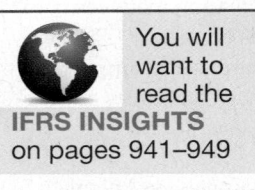

You will
want to
read the
IFRS INSIGHTS
on pages 941–949

for discussion of IFRS
related to dilutive
securities and
earnings per share.

KEY TERMS

antidilutive securities, *904*

basic EPS, *904*

complex capital
  structure, *900*

convertible bonds, *884*

convertible preferred
  stock, *886*

detachable stock
  warrants, *888*

diluted EPS, *904*

dilutive securities,
  884, 904

earnings per share, *899*

fair value method, *892*

grant date, *892*

if-converted method, *905*

income available
  to common
  stockholders, *900*

incremental method, *889*

induced conversion, *885*

SUMMARY OF LEARNING OBJECTIVES

1 **Describe the accounting for the issuance, conversion, and retirement of convertible securities.** The method for recording convertible bonds at the date of issuance follows that used to record straight debt issues. Companies amortize any discount or premium that results from the issuance of convertible bonds, assuming the bonds will be held to maturity. If companies convert bonds into other securities, the principal accounting problem is to determine the amount at which to record the securities exchanged for the bonds. The book value method is considered GAAP. The retirement of convertible debt is considered a debt retirement, and the difference between the carrying amount of the retired convertible debt and the cash paid should result in a gain or loss.

2 **Explain the accounting for convertible preferred stock.** When convertible preferred stock is converted, a company uses the book value method. It debits Preferred Stock, along with any related Paid-in Capital in Excess of Par—Preferred Stock, and credits Common Stock and Paid-in Capital in Excess of Par—Common Stock (if an excess exists).

3 **Contrast the accounting for stock warrants and for stock warrants issued with other securities.** *Stock warrants*: Companies should allocate the proceeds from the sale of debt with detachable warrants between the two securities.

Warrants that are detachable can be traded separately from the debt, and therefore companies can determine their fair value. Two methods of allocation are available: the proportional method and the incremental method. Nondetachable warrants do not require an allocation of the proceeds between the bonds and the warrants; companies record the entire proceeds as debt. *Stock rights*: No entry is required when a company issues rights to existing stockholders. The company needs only to make a memorandum entry to indicate the number of rights issued to existing stockholders and to ensure that the company has additional unissued stock registered for issuance in case the stockholders exercise the rights.

4 **Describe the accounting for stock compensation plans.** Companies must use the fair value approach to account for stock-based compensation. Under this approach, a company computes total compensation expense based on the fair value of the options that it expects to vest on the grant date. Companies recognize compensation expense in the periods in which the employee performs the services. Restricted-stock plans follow the same general accounting principles as those for stock options. Companies estimate total compensation cost at the grant date based on the fair value of the restricted stock; they expense that cost over the service period. If vesting does not occur, companies reverse the compensation expense.

5 **Discuss the controversy involving stock compensation plans.** When first proposed, there was considerable opposition to the recognition provisions contained in the fair value approach. The reason: that approach could result in substantial, previously unrecognized compensation expense. Corporate America, particularly the high-technology sector, vocally opposed the proposed standard. They believed that the standard would place them at a competitive disadvantage with larger companies that can withstand higher compensation charges. Offsetting such opposition is the need for greater transparency in financial reporting, on which our capital markets depend.

6 **Compute earnings per share in a simple capital structure.** When a company has both common and preferred stock outstanding, it subtracts the current-year preferred stock dividend from net income to arrive at income available to common stockholders. The formula for computing earnings per share is net income less preferred stock dividends, divided by the weighted-average number of shares outstanding.

7 **Compute earnings per share in a complex capital structure.** A complex capital structure requires a dual presentation of earnings per share, each with equal prominence on the face of the income statement. These two presentations are referred to as basic earnings per share and diluted earnings per share. Basic earnings per share relies on the number of weighted-average common shares outstanding (i.e., equivalent to EPS for a simple capital structure). Diluted earnings per share indicates the dilution of earnings per share that will occur if all potential issuances of common stock that would reduce earnings per share takes place. Companies with complex capital structures should exclude antidilutive securities when computing earnings per share.

intrinsic-value
method, *892*

proportional method, *888*

restricted-stock plans, *894*

service period, *893*

simple capital
structure, *900*

stock option, *891*

stock-based
compensation
plans, *891*

stock right, *890*

treasury-stock
method, *907*

warrants, *887*

weighted-average
number of shares
outstanding, *901*

APPENDIX **16A**	ACCOUNTING FOR STOCK-APPRECIATION RIGHTS

A major disadvantage of many stock-option plans is that an executive must pay income tax on the difference between the market price of the stock and the option price at the **date of exercise**. This feature of stock-option plans (those referred to as **nonqualified**) can be a financial hardship for an executive who wishes to keep the stock (rather than sell it immediately) because he or she would have to pay not

8 **LEARNING OBJECTIVE**
Explain the accounting for stock-appreciation rights plans.

only income tax but the option price as well. In another type of plan (an **incentive plan**), the executive pays no taxes at exercise but may need to borrow to finance the exercise price, which leads to related interest cost.

One solution to this problem was the creation of stock-appreciation rights (SARs). In this type of plan, the company gives an executive the right to receive compensation equal to the share appreciation. Share appreciation is the excess of the market price of the stock at the date of exercise over a pre-established price. The company may pay the share appreciation in cash, shares, or a combination of both.

The major advantage of SARs is that the executive often does not have to make a cash outlay at the date of exercise, but receives a payment for the share appreciation. Unlike shares acquired under a stock-option plan, the company does not issue the shares that constitute the basis for computing the appreciation in a SARs plan. Rather, the company simply awards the executive cash or stock having a fair value equivalent to the appreciation. The accounting for stock-appreciation rights depends on whether the company classifies the rights as equity or as a liability.

SARS—SHARE-BASED EQUITY AWARDS

Companies classify SARs as **equity awards** if at the date of exercise, the holder receives shares of stock from the company upon exercise. In essence, SARs are essentially equivalent to a stock option. The major difference relates to the form of payment. With the stock option, the holder pays the exercise price and then receives the stock. In an equity SAR, the holder receives shares in an amount equal to the **share-price appreciation** (the difference between the market price and the pre-established price). The accounting for SARs when they are equity awards follows the accounting used for stock options. At the date of grant, the company determines a fair value for the SAR and then allocates this amount to compensation expense over the service period of the employees.

SARS—SHARE-BASED LIABILITY AWARDS

Companies classify SARs as liability awards if at the date of exercise, the holder receives a cash payment. In this case the holder is not receiving additional shares of stock but a cash payment equal to the amount of share-price appreciation. The company's compensation expense therefore changes as the value of the liability changes.

A company uses the following approach to record share-based liability awards:

1. Measure the fair value of the award at the grant date and accrue compensation over the service period.

2. Remeasure the fair value each reporting period, until the award is settled. Adjust the compensation cost each period for changes in fair value prorated for the portion of the service period completed.

3. Once the service period is completed, determine compensation expense each subsequent period by reporting the full change in market price as an adjustment to compensation expense.

For liability awards, the company estimates the fair value of the SARs, using an option-pricing model. The company then allocates this total estimated compensation cost over the service period, recording expense (or a decrease in expense if fair value declines) in each period. At the end of each period, total compensation expense reported to date should equal the percentage of the total service period that has elapsed, multiplied by the total estimated compensation cost.

For example, assume that the service period is 40 percent complete and total estimated compensation is $100,000. The company reports cumulative compensation expense to date of $40,000 ($100,000 × .40).

The method of allocating compensation expense is called the **percentage approach**. In this method, in the first year of, say, a four-year plan, the company charges one-fourth of the estimated cost to date. In the second year, it charges off two-fourths, or 50 percent, of the estimated cost to date, less the amount already recognized in the first year. In the third year, it charges off three-fourths of the estimated cost to date, less the amount recognized previously. In the fourth year, it charges off the remaining compensation expense.

A special problem arises when the exercise date is later than the service period. In the previous example, if the stock-appreciation rights were not exercised at the end of four years, in the fifth year the company would have to account for the difference in the market price and the pre-established price. In this case, the company adjusts compensation expense whenever a change in the market price of the stock **occurs in subsequent reporting periods, until the rights expire or are exercised, whichever comes first**.

Increases or decreases in the fair value of the SAR between the date of grant and the exercise date, therefore, result in a change in the measure of compensation. Some periods will have credits to compensation expense if the fair value decreases from one period to the next. The credit to compensation expense, however, cannot exceed previously recognized compensation expense. In other words, **cumulative compensation expense cannot be negative**.

STOCK-APPRECIATION RIGHTS EXAMPLE

Assume that American Hotels, Inc. establishes a stock-appreciation rights plan on January 1, 2014. The plan entitles executives to receive cash at the date of exercise for the difference between the market price of the stock and the pre-established price of $10 on 10,000 SARs. The fair value of the SARs on December 31, 2014, is $3, and the service period runs for two years (2014–2015). Illustration 16A-1 indicates the amount of compensation expense to be recorded each period, assuming that the executives hold the SARs for three years, at which time they exercise the rights.

STOCK-APPRECIATION RIGHTS SCHEDULE OF COMPENSATION EXPENSE							
(1)	(2)	(3)	(4)	(5)			
Date	Fair Value	Cumulative Compensation Recognizable[a]	Percentage Accrued[b]	Cumulative Compensation Accrued to Date	Expense 2014	Expense 2015	Expense 2016
12/31/14	$3	$30,000	50%	$ 15,000	$15,000		
12/31/15	7	70,000	100%	55,000 70,000		$55,000	
12/31/16	5	50,000	100%	(20,000) $ 50,000			$(20,000)

[a]Cumulative compensation for unexercised SARs to be allocated to periods of service.
[b]The percentage accrued is based upon a two-year service period (2014–2015).

ILLUSTRATION 16A-1
Compensation Expense, Stock-Appreciation Rights

In 2014, American Hotels records compensation expense of $15,000 because 50 percent of the $30,000 total compensation cost estimated at December 31, 2014, is allocable to 2014. In 2015, the fair value increased to $7 per right ($70,000 total). The company recorded additional compensation expense of $55,000 ($70,000 minus $15,000).

The executives held the SARs through 2016, during which time the fair value declined to $5 (and the obligation to the executives equals $50,000). American Hotels recognizes the decrease by recording a $20,000 credit to compensation expense and a debit to Liability under Stock-Appreciation Plan. Note that after the service period ends, since the rights are still outstanding, the company adjusts the rights to market at December 31, 2016. Any such credit to compensation expense cannot exceed previous charges to expense attributable to that plan.

As the company records the compensation expense each period, the corresponding credit is to a liability account, because the company will pay the stock appreciation in cash. American Hotels records compensation expense in the first year as follows.

Compensation Expense	15,000	
Liability under Stock-Appreciation Plan		15,000

The company would credit the liability account for $55,000 again in 2015. In 2016, when it records negative compensation expense, American would debit the account for $20,000. The entry to record the negative compensation expense is as follows.

Liability under Stock-Appreciation Plan	20,000	
Compensation Expense		20,000

At December 31, 2016, the executives receive $50,000 (which equals the market price of the shares less the pre-established price). American would remove the liability with the following entry.

Liability under Stock-Appreciation Plan	50,000	
Cash		50,000

Compensation expense can increase or decrease substantially from one period to the next. The reason is that compensation expense is remeasured each year, which can lead to large swings in compensation expense.

KEY TERMS

percentage approach, *915*
share appreciation, *914*
stock-appreciation rights
   (SARs), *914*

SUMMARY OF LEARNING OBJECTIVE FOR APPENDIX 16A

8 **Explain the accounting for stock-appreciation rights plans.** The accounting for stock-appreciation rights depends on whether the rights are classified as equity- or liability-based. If equity-based, the accounting is similar to that used for stock options. If liability-based, companies remeasure compensation expense each period and allocate it over the service period using the percentage approach.

APPENDIX 16B   COMPREHENSIVE EARNINGS PER SHARE EXAMPLE

LEARNING OBJECTIVE 9
Compute earnings per share in a complex situation.

This appendix illustrates the method of computing dilution when many securities are involved. We present the following section of the balance sheet of Webster Corporation for analysis. Assumptions related to the capital structure follow the balance sheet.

WEBSTER CORPORATION
BALANCE SHEET (PARTIAL)
AT DECEMBER 31, 2014

Long-term debt	
Notes payable, 14%	$ 1,000,000
8% convertible bonds payable	2,500,000
10% convertible bonds payable	2,500,000
Total long-term debt	$ 6,000,000
Stockholders' equity	
10% cumulative, convertible preferred stock, par value $100;	
100,000 shares authorized, 25,000 shares issued and outstanding	$ 2,500,000
Common stock, par value $1, 5,000,000 shares authorized,	
500,000 shares issued and outstanding	500,000
Additional paid-in capital	2,000,000
Retained earnings	9,000,000
Total stockholders' equity	$14,000,000

ILLUSTRATION 16B-1
Balance Sheet for
Comprehensive
Illustration

Notes and Assumptions
December 31, 2014

1. Options were granted in July 2012 to purchase 50,000 shares of common stock at $20 per share. The average market price of Webster's common stock during 2014 was $30 per share. All options are still outstanding at the end of 2014.
2. Both the 8 percent and 10 percent convertible bonds were issued in 2013 at face value. Each convertible bond is convertible into 40 shares of common stock. (Each bond has a face value of $1,000.)
3. The 10 percent cumulative, convertible preferred stock was issued at the beginning of 2014 at par. Each share of preferred is convertible into four shares of common stock.
4. The average income tax rate is 40 percent.
5. The 500,000 shares of common stock were outstanding during the entire year.
6. Preferred dividends were not declared in 2014.
7. Net income was $1,750,000 in 2014.
8. No bonds or preferred stock were converted during 2014.

The computation of basic earnings per share for 2014 starts with the amount based upon the weighted-average number of shares outstanding, as shown in Illustration 16B-2.

Net income	$1,750,000
Less: 10% cumulative, convertible preferred stock dividend requirements	250,000
Income applicable to common stockholders	$1,500,000
Weighted-average number of shares outstanding	500,000
Earnings per common share ($1,500,000 ÷ 500,000)	$3.00

ILLUSTRATION 16B-2
Computation of Earnings
per Share—Simple
Capital Structure

Note the following points concerning this calculation.

1. When preferred stock is cumulative, the company subtracts the preferred dividend to arrive at income applicable to common stock, whether the dividend is declared or not.
2. The company must compute earnings per share of $3 as a starting point, because it is the per share amount that is subject to reduction due to the existence of convertible securities and options.

DILUTED EARNINGS PER SHARE

The steps for computing diluted earnings per share are:

1. Determine, for each dilutive security, the per share effect assuming exercise/conversion.

2. Rank the results from step 1 from smallest to largest earnings effect per share. That is, rank the results from most dilutive to least dilutive.

3. Beginning with the earnings per share based upon the weighted-average number of shares outstanding ($3), recalculate earnings per share by adding the smallest per share effects from step 2. If the results from this recalculation are less than $3, proceed to the next smallest per share effect and recalculate earnings per share. Continue this process so long as each recalculated earnings per share is smaller than the previous amount. The process will end either because there are no more securities to test or a particular security maintains or increases earnings per share (is antidilutive).

We'll now apply the three steps to Webster Corporation. (Note that net income and income available to common stockholders are not the same if preferred dividends are declared or cumulative.) Webster Corporation has four securities that could reduce EPS: options, 8 percent convertible bonds, 10 percent convertible bonds, and the convertible preferred stock.

The first step in the computation of diluted earnings per share is to determine a per share effect for each potentially dilutive security. Illustrations 16B-3 through 16B-6 illustrate these computations.

ILLUSTRATION 16B-3
Per Share Effect of Options (Treasury-Stock Method), Diluted Earnings per Share

Number of shares under option	50,000
Option price per share	× $20
Proceeds upon assumed exercise of options	$1,000,000
Average 2014 market price of common	$30
Treasury shares that could be acquired with proceeds ($1,000,000 ÷ $30)	33,333
Excess of shares under option over treasury shares that could be repurchased (50,000 − 33,333)	16,667
Per share effect:	
$\dfrac{\text{Incremental Numerator Effect}}{\text{Incremental Denominator Effect}} = \dfrac{\text{None}}{16,667 \text{ shares}} =$	$0

ILLUSTRATION 16B-4
Per Share Effect of 8% Bonds (If-Converted Method), Diluted Earnings per Share

Interest expense for year (8% × $2,500,000)	$200,000
Income tax reduction due to interest (40% × $200,000)	80,000
Interest expense avoided (net of tax)	$120,000
Number of common shares issued assuming conversion of bonds (2,500 bonds × 40 shares)	100,000
Per share effect:	
$\dfrac{\text{Incremental Numerator Effect}}{\text{Incremental Denominator Effect}} = \dfrac{\$120,000}{100,000 \text{ shares}} =$	$1.20

ILLUSTRATION 16B-5
Per Share Effect of 10% Bonds (If-Converted Method), Diluted Earnings per Share

Interest expense for year (10% × $2,500,000)	$250,000
Income tax reduction due to interest (40% × $250,000)	100,000
Interest expense avoided (net of tax)	$150,000
Number of common shares issued assuming conversion of bonds (2,500 bonds × 40 shares)	100,000
Per share effect:	
$\dfrac{\text{Incremental Numerator Effect}}{\text{Incremental Denominator Effect}} = \dfrac{\$150,000}{100,000 \text{ shares}} =$	$1.50

Dividend requirement on cumulative preferred (25,000 shares × $10)	$250,000	
Income tax effect (dividends not a tax deduction)	none	
Dividend requirement avoided	$250,000	
Number of common shares issued assuming conversion of preferred (4 × 25,000 shares)	100,000	
Per share effect:		
$\frac{\text{Incremental Numerator Effect}}{\text{Incremental Denominator Effect}} = \frac{\$250,000}{100,000 \text{ shares}} =$	$2.50	

ILLUSTRATION 16B-6
Per Share Effect of 10% Convertible Preferred (If-Converted Method), Diluted Earnings per Share

Illustration 16B-7 shows the ranking of all four potentially dilutive securities.

	Effect per Share
1. Options	$ 0
2. 8% convertible bonds	1.20
3. 10% convertible bonds	1.50
4. 10% convertible preferred	2.50

ILLUSTRATION 16B-7
Ranking of per Share Effects (Smallest to Largest), Diluted Earnings per Share

The next step is to determine earnings per share giving effect to the ranking in Illustration 16B-7. Starting with the earnings per share of $3 computed previously, add the incremental effects of the options to the original calculation, as follows.

Options	
Income applicable to common stockholders	$1,500,000
Add: Incremental numerator effect of options	none
Total	$1,500,000
Weighted-average number of shares outstanding	500,000
Add: Incremental denominator effect of options (Illustration 16B-3)	16,667
Total	516,667
Recomputed earnings per share ($1,500,000 ÷ 516,667 shares)	$2.90

ILLUSTRATION 16B-8
Recomputation of EPS Using Incremental Effect of Options

Since the recomputed earnings per share is reduced (from $3 to $2.90), the effect of the options is dilutive. Again, we could have anticipated this effect because the average market price ($30) exceeded the option price ($20).

Assuming that Webster converts the 8 percent bonds, recomputed earnings per share is as shown in Illustration 16B-9.

8% Convertible Bonds	
Numerator from previous calculation	$1,500,000
Add: Interest expense avoided (net of tax)	120,000
Total	$1,620,000
Denominator from previous calculation (shares)	516,667
Add: Number of common shares assumed issued upon conversion of bonds	100,000
Total	616,667
Recomputed earnings per share ($1,620,000 ÷ 616,667 shares)	$2.63

ILLUSTRATION 16B-9
Recomputation of EPS Using Incremental Effect of 8% Convertible Bonds

Since the recomputed earnings per share is reduced (from $2.90 to $2.63), the effect of the 8 percent bonds is dilutive.

Next, assuming Webster converts the 10 percent bonds, the company recomputes earnings per share as shown in Illustration 16B-10 (page 920).

ILLUSTRATION 16B-10
Recomputation of EPS Using Incremental Effect of 10% Convertible Bonds

10% Convertible Bonds	
Numerator from previous calculation	$1,620,000
Add: Interest expense avoided (net of tax)	150,000
Total	$1,770,000
Denominator from previous calculation (shares)	616,667
Add: Number of common shares assumed issued upon conversion of bonds	100,000
Total	716,667
Recomputed earnings per share ($1,770,000 ÷ 716,667 shares)	$2.47

Since the recomputed earnings per share is reduced (from $2.63 to $2.47), the effect of the 10 percent convertible bonds is dilutive.

The final step is the recomputation that includes the 10 percent preferred stock. This is shown in Illustration 16B-11.

ILLUSTRATION 16B-11
Recomputation of EPS Using Incremental Effect of 10% Convertible Preferred

10% Convertible Preferred	
Numerator from previous calculation	$1,770,000
Add: Dividend requirement avoided	250,000
Total	$2,020,000
Denominator from previous calculation (shares)	716,667
Add: Number of common shares assumed issued upon conversion of preferred	100,000
Total	816,667
Recomputed earnings per share ($2,020,000 ÷ 816,667 shares)	$2.47

Since the recomputed earnings per share is not reduced, the effect of the 10 percent convertible preferred is not dilutive. Diluted earnings per share is $2.47. The per share effects of the preferred are not used in the computation.

Finally, Illustration 16B-12 shows Webster Corporation's disclosure of earnings per share on its income statement.

ILLUSTRATION 16B-12
Income Statement Presentation, EPS

Net income	$1,750,000
Basic earnings per common share (Note X)	$3.00
Diluted earnings per common share	$2.47

A company uses income from continuing operations (adjusted for preferred dividends) to determine whether potential common stock is dilutive or antidilutive. Some refer to this measure as the **control number**. To illustrate, assume that Barton Company provides the following information.

ILLUSTRATION 16B-13
Barton Company Data

Income from continuing operations	$2,400,000
Loss from discontinued operations	3,600,000
Net loss	$1,200,000
Weighted-average number of shares outstanding	1,000,000
Potential common stock	200,000

Barton reports basic and dilutive earnings per share as follows.

ILLUSTRATION 16B-14
Basic and Diluted EPS

Basic earnings per share	
Income from continuing operations	$2.40
Loss from discontinued operations	3.60
Net loss	$1.20
Diluted earnings per share	
Income from continuing operations	$2.00
Loss from discontinued operations	3.00
Net loss	$1.00

As Illustration 16B-14 shows, basic earnings per share from continuing operations is higher than the diluted earnings per share from continuing operations. The reason: The diluted earnings per share from continuing operations includes an additional 200,000 shares of potential common stock in its denominator.[21]

Companies use income from continuing operations as the control number because many of them show income from continuing operations (or a similar line item above net income if it appears on the income statement) but report a final net loss due to a loss on discontinued operations. If a company uses final net loss as the control number, basic and diluted earnings per share would be the same because the potential common shares are antidilutive.[22]

**Gateway to
the Profession**

*EPS Illustration with Multiple
Dilutive Securities*

SUMMARY OF LEARNING OBJECTIVE FOR APPENDIX 16B

KEY TERM

control number, *920*

9 **Compute earnings per share in a complex situation.** For diluted EPS, make the following computations. (1) For each potentially dilutive security, determine the per share effect assuming exercise/conversion. (2) Rank the results from most dilutive to least dilutive. (3) Recalculate EPS starting with the most dilutive, and continue adding securities until EPS does not change or becomes larger.

DEMONSTRATION PROBLEM

On January 1, 2013, Scutaro Company issued 10-year, $200,000 face value, 6% bonds at par (payable annually on January 1). Each $1,000 bond is convertible into 30 shares of Garner $2 par value common stock. The company has had 10,000 shares of common stock (and no preferred stock) outstanding throughout its life. None of the bonds have been converted as of the end of 2014.

---

[21]A company that does not report a discontinued operation but reports an extraordinary item should use that line item (for example, income before extraordinary items) as the control number.

[22]If a company reports a loss from continuing operations, basic and diluted earnings per share will be the same because potential common stock will be antidilutive, even if the company reports final net income. The FASB believes that comparability of EPS information will be improved by using income from continuing operations as the control number.

Scutaro also has adopted a stock-option plan that granted options to key executives to purchase 4,000 shares of the company's common stock. The options were granted on January 2, 2013, and were exercisable 2 years after the date of grant if the grantee was still an employee of the company. The options expired 6 years from the date of grant. The option price was set at $4, and the fair value option-pricing model determines the total compensation expense to be $18,000. All of the options were exercised during the year 2015: 3,000 on January 3 when the market price was $6, and 1,000 on May 1 when the market price was $7 a share. (Ignore all tax effects.)

Instructions

(a) Prepare the journal entry Scutaro would have made on January 1, 2013, to record the issuance of the bonds.

(b) Prepare the journal entry to record interest expense and compensation expense in 2014.

(c) Scutaro's net income in 2014 was $30,000 and was $27,000 in 2013. Compute basic and diluted earnings per share for Scutaro for 2014 and 2013. Scutaro's average stock price was $4.40 in 2013 and $5 in 2014.

(d) Assume that 75 percent of the holders of Scutaro's convertible bonds convert their bonds to stock on June 30, 2015, when Scutaro's stock is trading at $8 per share. Scutaro pays $2 per bond to induce bondholders to convert. Prepare the journal entry to record the conversion.

Solution

(a) Under U.S. GAAP, proceeds from the issuance of convertible debt are recorded entirely as debt.

Cash	200,000	
Bonds Payable		200,000

(b)

December 31, 2014

Interest Expense	12,000	
Interest Payable		12,000
[To record interest expense for 2014 ($200,000 × 6%)]		
Compensation Expense	9,000	
Paid-in Capital—Stock Options		9,000
[To record compensation expense for 2014 (1/2 × $18,000)]		

(c)

Basic EPS	**2014**	**2013**
Net income (a)	$30,000	$27,000
Outstanding shares (b)	10,000	10,000
Basic EPS (a ÷ b)	$ 3.00	$ 2.70

Diluted EPS		
Net income	$30,000	$27,000
Add: Interest savings ($200,000 × 6%)	12,000	12,000
Adjusted net income (a)	$42,000	$39,000
Outstanding shares	10,000	10,000
Shares upon conversion (200 × 30)	6,000	6,000
Options (treasury-stock method)	800*	364*
Total shares for diluted EPS (b)	16,800	16,364
Diluted EPS (a ÷ b)	$ 2.50	$ 2.38

*Treasury-stock method:

	2014		**2013**	
Cash proceeds	($4 × 4,000)	$16,000		$16,000
Shares repurchased	($16,000 ÷ $5)	3,200	($16,000 ÷ $4.40)	3,636
Net shares issued	(4,000 − 3,200)	800	(4,000 − 3,636)	364

(d)	Bond Conversion Expense**		300	
	Bonds Payable		150,000	
	Common Stock*			9,000
	Paid-in-Capital in Excess of Par—Common Stock*			141,000
	Cash			300

*$200,000 × 75% = $150,000 of bonds converted
$150,000 ÷ $1,000 per bond = 150 bonds
150 bonds × 30 shares per bond = 4,500 new shares issued
4,500 shares × $2 par value = $9,000 increase in common stock account
$150,000 − $9,000 = $141,000 increase in paid-in capital account

**150 bonds X $2 per bond = $300 bond conversion expense

FASB CODIFICATION

FASB Codification References

[1] FASB ASC 480-10-25. [Predecessor literature: "Accounting for Certain Financial Instruments with Characteristics of Both Liabilities and Equity," *Statement of Financial Accounting Standards No. 150* (Norwalk, Conn.: FASB, 2003), par. 23.]

[2] FASB ASC 470-20-45. [Predecessor literature: "Induced Conversions of Convertible Debt," *Statement of Financial Accounting Standards No. 84* (Stamford, Conn.: FASB, 1985).]

[3] FASB ASC 470-20-25-1 to 2. [Predecessor literature: "Accounting for Convertible Debt and Debt Issued with Stock Purchase Warrants," *Opinions of the Accounting Principles Board No. 14* (New York, NY: AICPA, 1973).]

[4] FASB ASC 470-20-30. [Predecessor literature: "Accounting for Convertible Debt Instruments that May Be Settled in Cash Upon Conversion," *FASB Staff Position No. 14-1* (Norwalk, Conn: FASB, 2008).]

[5] FASB ASC 718-10-10. [Predecessor literature: "Accounting for Stock-Based Compensation," *Statement of Financial Accounting Standards No. 123* (Norwalk, Conn: FASB, 1995); and "Share-Based Payment," *Statement of Financial Accounting Standard No. 123(R)* (Norwalk, Conn: FASB, 2004).]

[6] FASB ASC 260-10-45-2. [Predecessor literature: "Earnings per Share," *Statement of Financial Accounting Standards No. 128* (Norwalk, Conn: FASB, 1997).]

[7] FASB ASC 260-10-50. [Predecessor literature: "Earnings per Share," *Statement of Financial Accounting Standards No. 128*, (Norwalk, Conn.: FASB, 1997.)]

Exercises

If your school has a subscription to the FASB Codification, go to *http://aaahq.org/ascLogin.cfm* to log in and prepare responses to the following. Provide Codification references for your responses.

CE16-1 Access the glossary ("Master Glossary") to answer the following.

(a) What is the definition of "basic earnings per share"?
(b) What is "dilution"?
(c) What is a "warrant"?
(d) What is a "grant date"?

CE16-2 For how many periods must a company present EPS data?

CE16-3 For each period that an income statement is presented, what must a company disclose about its EPS?

CE16-4 If a company's outstanding shares are increased through a stock dividend or a stock split, how would that alter the presentation of its EPS data?

An additional Codification case can be found in the Using Your Judgment section, on page 941.

Be sure to check the book's companion website for a Review and Analysis Exercise, with solution.

WileyPLUS | Brief Exercises, Exercises, Problems, and many more learning and assessment tools and resources are available for practice in WileyPLUS.

Note: All asterisked Questions, Exercises, and Problems relate to material in the appendices to the chapter.

QUESTIONS

1. What is meant by a dilutive security?

2. Briefly explain why corporations issue convertible securities.

3. Discuss the similarities and the differences between convertible debt and debt issued with stock warrants.

4. Bridgewater Corp. offered holders of its 1,000 convertible bonds a premium of $160 per bond to induce conversion into shares of its common stock. Upon conversion of all the bonds, Bridgewater Corp. recorded the $160,000 premium as a reduction of paid-in capital. Comment on Bridgewater's treatment of the $160,000 "sweetener."

5. Explain how the conversion feature of convertible debt has a value (a) to the issuer and (b) to the purchaser.

6. What are the arguments for giving separate accounting recognition to the conversion feature of debentures?

7. Four years after issue, debentures with a face value of $1,000,000 and book value of $960,000 are tendered for conversion into 80,000 shares of common stock immediately after an interest payment date. At that time, the market price of the debentures is 104, and the common stock is selling at $14 per share (par value $10). The company records the conversion as follows.

Bonds Payable	1,000,000	
Discount on Bonds Payable		40,000
Common Stock		800,000
Paid-in Capital in Excess of Par— Common Stock		160,000

Discuss the propriety of this accounting treatment.

8. On July 1, 2014, Roberts Corporation issued $3,000,000 of 9% bonds payable in 20 years. The bonds include detachable warrants giving the bondholder the right to purchase for $30 one share of $1 par value common stock at any time during the next 10 years. The bonds were sold for $3,000,000. The value of the warrants at the time of issuance was $100,000. Prepare the journal entry to record this transaction.

9. What are stock rights? How does the issuing company account for them?

10. Briefly explain the accounting requirements for stock compensation plans under GAAP.

11. Cordero Corporation has an employee stock-purchase plan which permits all full-time employees to purchase 10 shares of common stock on the third anniversary of their employment and an additional 15 shares on each subsequent anniversary date. The purchase price is set at the market price on the date purchased and no commission is charged. Discuss whether this plan would be considered compensatory.

12. What date or event does the profession believe should be used in determining the value of a stock option? What arguments support this position?

13. Over what period of time should compensation cost be allocated?

14. How is compensation expense computed using the fair value approach?

15. What are the advantages of using restricted stock to compensate employees?

16. At December 31, 2014, Reid Company had 600,000 shares of common stock issued and outstanding, 400,000 of which had been issued and outstanding throughout the year and 200,000 of which were issued on October 1, 2014. Net income for 2014 was $2,000,000, and dividends declared on preferred stock were $400,000. Compute Reid's earnings per common share. (Round to the nearest penny.)

17. What effect do stock dividends or stock splits have on the computation of the weighted-average number of shares outstanding?

18. Define the following terms.
    (a) Basic earnings per share.
    (b) Potentially dilutive security.
    (c) Diluted earnings per share.
    (d) Complex capital structure.
    (e) Potential common stock.

19. What are the computational guidelines for determining whether a convertible security is to be reported as part of diluted earnings per share?

20. Discuss why options and warrants may be considered potentially dilutive common shares for the computation of diluted earnings per share.

21. Explain how convertible securities are determined to be potentially dilutive common shares and how those convertible securities that are not considered to be potentially dilutive common shares enter into the determination of earnings per share data.

22. Explain the treasury-stock method as it applies to options and warrants in computing dilutive earnings per share data.

23. Earnings per share can affect market prices of common stock. Can market prices affect earnings per share? Explain.

24. What is meant by the term antidilution? Give an example.

25. What type of earnings per share presentation is required in a complex capital structure?

*26. How is antidilution determined when multiple securities are involved?

BRIEF EXERCISES

1 **BE16-1** Archer Inc. issued $4,000,000 par value, 7% convertible bonds at 99 for cash. If the bonds had not included the conversion feature, they would have sold for 95. Prepare the journal entry to record the issuance of the bonds.

1 **BE16-2** Petrenko Corporation has outstanding 2,000 $1,000 bonds, each convertible into 50 shares of $10 par value common stock. The bonds are converted on December 31, 2014, when the unamortized discount is $30,000 and the market price of the stock is $21 per share. Record the conversion using the book value approach.

2 **BE16-3** Pechstein Corporation issued 2,000 shares of $10 par value common stock upon conversion of 1,000 shares of $50 par value preferred stock. The preferred stock was originally issued at $60 per share. The common stock is trading at $26 per share at the time of conversion. Record the conversion of the preferred stock.

3 **BE16-4** Eisler Corporation issued 2,000 $1,000 bonds at 101. Each bond was issued with one detachable stock warrant. After issuance, the bonds were selling in the market at 98, and the warrants had a market price of $40. Use the proportional method to record the issuance of the bonds and warrants.

3 **BE16-5** McIntyre Corporation issued 2,000 $1,000 bonds at 101. Each bond was issued with one detachable stock warrant. After issuance, the bonds were selling separately at 98. The market price of the warrants without the bonds cannot be determined. Use the incremental method to record the issuance of the bonds and warrants.

4 **BE16-6** On January 1, 2014, Barwood Corporation granted 5,000 options to executives. Each option entitles the holder to purchase one share of Barwood's $5 par value common stock at $50 per share at any time during the next 5 years. The market price of the stock is $65 per share on the date of grant. The fair value of the options at the grant date is $150,000. The period of benefit is 2 years. Prepare Barwood's journal entries for January 1, 2014, and December 31, 2014 and 2015.

4 **BE16-7** Refer to the data for Barwood Corporation in BE16-6. Repeat the requirements assuming that instead of options, Barwood granted 2,000 shares of restricted stock.

4 **BE16-8** On January 1, 2014 (the date of grant), Lutz Corporation issues 2,000 shares of restricted stock to its executives. The fair value of these shares is $75,000, and their par value is $10,000. The stock is forfeited if the executives do not complete 3 years of employment with the company. Prepare the journal entry (if any) on January 1, 2014, and on December 31, 2014, assuming the service period is 3 years.

6 **BE16-9** Kalin Corporation had 2014 net income of $1,000,000. During 2014, Kalin paid a dividend of $2 per share on 100,000 shares of preferred stock. During 2014, Kalin had outstanding 250,000 shares of common stock. Compute Kalin's 2014 earnings per share.

6 **BE16-10** Douglas Corporation had 120,000 shares of stock outstanding on January 1, 2014. On May 1, 2014, Douglas issued 60,000 shares. On July 1, Douglas purchased 10,000 treasury shares, which were reissued on October 1. Compute Douglas's weighted-average number of shares outstanding for 2014.

6 **BE16-11** Tomba Corporation had 300,000 shares of common stock outstanding on January 1, 2014. On May 1, Tomba issued 30,000 shares. (a) Compute the weighted-average number of shares outstanding if the 30,000 shares were issued for cash. (b) Compute the weighted-average number of shares outstanding if the 30,000 shares were issued in a stock dividend.

7 **BE16-12** Rockland Corporation earned net income of $300,000 in 2014 and had 100,000 shares of common stock outstanding throughout the year. Also outstanding all year was $800,000 of 10% bonds, which are convertible into 16,000 shares of common. Rockland's tax rate is 40%. Compute Rockland's 2014 diluted earnings per share.

7 **BE16-13** DiCenta Corporation reported net income of $270,000 in 2014 and had 50,000 shares of common stock outstanding throughout the year. Also outstanding all year were 5,000 shares of cumulative preferred stock, each convertible into 2 shares of common. The preferred stock pays an annual dividend of $5 per share. DiCenta's tax rate is 40%. Compute DiCenta's 2014 diluted earnings per share.

7 **BE16-14** Bedard Corporation reported net income of $300,000 in 2014 and had 200,000 shares of common stock outstanding throughout the year. Also outstanding all year were 45,000 options to purchase common stock at $10 per share. The average market price of the stock during the year was $15. Compute diluted earnings per share.

6 **BE16-15** The 2014 income statement of Wasmeier Corporation showed net income of $480,000 and an extraordinary loss of $120,000. Wasmeier had 100,000 shares of common stock outstanding all year. Prepare Wasmeier's income statement presentation of earnings per share.

8 *BE16-16** Ferraro, Inc. established a stock-appreciation rights (SAR) program on January 1, 2014, which entitles executives to receive cash at the date of exercise for the difference between the market price of the stock and the pre-established price of $20 on 5,000 SARs. The required service period is 2 years. The fair value of the SARs are determined to be $4 on December 31, 2014, and $9 on December 31, 2015. Compute Ferraro's compensation expense for 2014 and 2015.

EXERCISES

1 **3** **E16-1 (Issuance and Conversion of Bonds)** For each of the unrelated transactions described below, present the entry(ies) required to record each transaction.

1. Grand Corp. issued $20,000,000 par value 10% convertible bonds at 99. If the bonds had not been convertible, the company's investment banker estimates they would have been sold at 95. Expenses of issuing the bonds were $70,000.
2. Hoosier Company issued $20,000,000 par value 10% bonds at 98. One detachable stock purchase warrant was issued with each $100 par value bond. At the time of issuance, the warrants were selling for $4.
3. Suppose **Sepracor, Inc.** called its convertible debt in 2014. Assume the following related to the transaction. The 11%, $10,000,000 par value bonds were converted into 1,000,000 shares of $1 par value common stock on July 1, 2014. On July 1, there was $55,000 of unamortized discount applicable to the bonds, and the company paid an additional $75,000 to the bondholders to induce conversion of all the bonds. The company records the conversion using the book value method.

1 **E16-2 (Conversion of Bonds)** Aubrey Inc. issued $4,000,000 of 10%, 10-year convertible bonds on June 1, 2014, at 98 plus accrued interest. The bonds were dated April 1, 2014, with interest payable April 1 and October 1. Bond discount is amortized semiannually on a straight-line basis.

On April 1, 2015, $1,500,000 of these bonds were converted into 30,000 shares of $20 par value common stock. Accrued interest was paid in cash at the time of conversion.

Instructions
(a) Prepare the entry to record the interest expense at October 1, 2014. Assume that accrued interest payable was credited when the bonds were issued. (Round to nearest dollar.)
(b) Prepare the entry(ies) to record the conversion on April 1, 2015. (Book value method is used.) Assume that the entry to record amortization of the bond discount and interest payment has been made.

1 **E16-3 (Conversion of Bonds)** Vargo Company has bonds payable outstanding in the amount of $500,000, and the Premium on Bonds Payable account has a balance of $7,500. Each $1,000 bond is convertible into 20 shares of preferred stock of par value of $50 per share. All bonds are converted into preferred stock.

Instructions
Assuming that the book value method was used, what entry would be made?

1 **E16-4 (Conversion of Bonds)** On January 1, 2013, when its $30 par value common stock was selling for $80 per share, Plato Corp. issued $10,000,000 of 8% convertible debentures due in 20 years. The conversion option allowed the holder of each $1,000 bond to convert the bond into five shares of the corporation's common stock. The debentures were issued for $10,800,000. The present value of the bond payments at the time of issuance was $8,500,000, and the corporation believes the difference between the present value and the amount paid is attributable to the conversion feature. On January 1, 2014, the corporation's $30 par value common stock was split 2 for 1, and the conversion rate for the bonds was adjusted accordingly. On January 1, 2015, when the corporation's $15 par value common stock was selling for $135 per share, holders of 30% of the convertible debentures exercised their conversion options. The corporation uses the straight-line method for amortizing any bond discounts or premiums.

Instructions
(a) Prepare in general journal form the entry to record the original issuance of the convertible debentures.

(b) Prepare in general journal form the entry to record the exercise of the conversion option, using the book value method. Show supporting computations in good form.

E16-5 (Conversion of Bonds) The December 31, 2014, balance sheet of Kepler Corp. is as follows.

10% callable, convertible bonds payable (semiannual interest dates April 30 and October 31; convertible into 6 shares of $25 par value common stock per $1,000 of bond principal; maturity date April 30, 2020)	$500,000	
Discount on bonds payable	10,240	$489,760

On March 5, 2015, Kepler Corp. called all of the bonds as of April 30 for the principal plus interest through April 30. By April 30, all bondholders had exercised their conversion to common stock as of the interest payment date. Consequently, on April 30, Kepler Corp. paid the semiannual interest and issued shares of common stock for the bonds. The discount is amortized on a straight-line basis. Kepler uses the book value method.

Instructions

Prepare the entry(ies) to record the interest expense and conversion on April 30, 2015. Reversing entries were made on January 1, 2015. (Round to the nearest dollar.)

E16-6 (Conversion of Bonds) On January 1, 2014, Gottlieb Corporation issued $4,000,000 of 10-year, 8% convertible debentures at 102. Interest is to be paid semiannually on June 30 and December 31. Each $1,000 debenture can be converted into eight shares of Gottlieb Corporation $100 par value common stock after December 31, 2015.

On January 1, 2016, $400,000 of debentures are converted into common stock, which is then selling at $110. An additional $400,000 of debentures are converted on March 31, 2016. The market price of the common stock is then $115. Accrued interest at March 31 will be paid on the next interest date.

Bond premium is amortized on a straight-line basis.

Instructions

Make the necessary journal entries for:

(a) December 31, 2015.	**(c)** March 31, 2016.
(b) January 1, 2016.	**(d)** June 30, 2016.

Record the conversions using the book value method.

E16-7 (Issuance of Bonds with Warrants) Illiad Inc. has decided to raise additional capital by issuing $170,000 face value of bonds with a coupon rate of 10%. In discussions with investment bankers, it was determined that to help the sale of the bonds, detachable stock warrants should be issued at the rate of one warrant for each $100 bond sold. The value of the bonds without the warrants is considered to be $136,000, and the value of the warrants in the market is $24,000. The bonds sold in the market at issuance for $152,000.

Instructions

(a) What entry should be made at the time of the issuance of the bonds and warrants?
(b) If the warrants were nondetachable, would the entries be different? Discuss.

E16-8 (Issuance of Bonds with Detachable Warrants) On September 1, 2014, Sands Company sold at 104 (plus accrued interest) 4,000 of its 9%, 10-year, $1,000 face value, nonconvertible bonds with detachable stock warrants. Each bond carried two detachable warrants. Each warrant was for one share of common stock at a specified option price of $15 per share. Shortly after issuance, the warrants were quoted on the market for $3 each. No fair value can be determined for the Sands Company bonds. Interest is payable on December 1 and June 1. Bond issue costs of $30,000 were incurred.

Instructions

Prepare in general journal format the entry to record the issuance of the bonds.

(AICPA adapted)

E16-9 (Issuance of Bonds with Stock Warrants) On May 1, 2014, Friendly Company issued 2,000 $1,000 bonds at 102. Each bond was issued with one detachable stock warrant. Shortly after issuance, the bonds were selling at 98, but the fair value of the warrants cannot be determined.

Instructions

(a) Prepare the entry to record the issuance of the bonds and warrants.
(b) Assume the same facts as part (a), except that the warrants had a fair value of $30. Prepare the entry to record the issuance of the bonds and warrants.

4 ▶ **E16-10 (Issuance and Exercise of Stock Options)** On November 1, 2014, Columbo Company adopted a stock-option plan that granted options to key executives to purchase 30,000 shares of the company's $10 par value common stock. The options were granted on January 2, 2015, and were exercisable 2 years after the date of grant if the grantee was still an employee of the company. The options expired 6 years from date of grant. The option price was set at $40, and the fair value option-pricing model determines the total compensation expense to be $450,000.

All of the options were exercised during the year 2017: 20,000 on January 3 when the market price was $67, and 10,000 on May 1 when the market price was $77 a share.

Instructions

Prepare journal entries relating to the stock option plan for the years 2015, 2016, and 2017. Assume that the employee performs services equally in 2015 and 2016.

4 ▶ **E16-11 (Issuance, Exercise, and Termination of Stock Options)** On January 1, 2015, Titania Inc. granted stock options to officers and key employees for the purchase of 20,000 shares of the company's $10 par common stock at $25 per share. The options were exercisable within a 5-year period beginning January 1, 2017, by grantees still in the employ of the company, and expiring December 31, 2021. The service period for this award is 2 years. Assume that the fair value option-pricing model determines total compensation expense to be $350,000.

On April 1, 2016, 2,000 options were terminated when the employees resigned from the company. The market price of the common stock was $35 per share on this date.

On March 31, 2017, 12,000 options were exercised when the market price of the common stock was $40 per share.

Instructions

Prepare journal entries to record issuance of the stock options, termination of the stock options, exercise of the stock options, and charges to compensation expense, for the years ended December 31, 2015, 2016, and 2017.

4 ▶ **E16-12 (Issuance, Exercise, and Termination of Stock Options)** On January 1, 2013, Nichols Corporation granted 10,000 options to key executives. Each option allows the executive to purchase one share of Nichols' $5 par value common stock at a price of $20 per share. The options were exercisable within a 2-year period beginning January 1, 2015, if the grantee is still employed by the company at the time of the exercise. On the grant date, Nichols' stock was trading at $25 per share, and a fair value option-pricing model determines total compensation to be $400,000.

On May 1, 2015, 8,000 options were exercised when the market price of Nichols' stock was $30 per share. The remaining options lapsed in 2017 because executives decided not to exercise their options.

Instructions

Prepare the necessary journal entries related to the stock option plan for the years 2013 through 2017.

4 ▶ **E16-13 (Accounting for Restricted Stock)** Derrick Company issues 4,000 shares of restricted stock to its CFO, Dane Yaping, on January 1, 2014. The stock has a fair value of $120,000 on this date. The service period related to this restricted stock is 4 years. Vesting occurs if Yaping stays with the company for 4 years. The par value of the stock is $5. At December 31, 2015, the fair value of the stock is $145,000.

Instructions

(a) Prepare the journal entries to record the restricted stock on January 1, 2014 (the date of grant), and December 31, 2015.

(b) On March 4, 2016, Yaping leaves the company. Prepare the journal entry (if any) to account for this forfeiture.

4 ▶ **E16-14 (Accounting for Restricted Stock)** Tweedie Company issues 10,000 shares of restricted stock to its CFO, Mary Tokar, on January 1, 2014. The stock has a fair value of $500,000 on this date. The service period related to this restricted stock is 5 years. Vesting occurs if Tokar stays with the company until December 31, 2018. The par value of the stock is $10. At December 31, 2014, the fair value of the stock is $450,000.

Instructions

(a) Prepare the journal entries to record the restricted stock on January 1, 2014 (the date of grant), and December 31, 2015.

(b) On July 25, 2018, Tokar leaves the company. Prepare the journal entry (if any) to account for this forfeiture.

6 **E16-15 (Weighted-Average Number of Shares)** Newton Inc. uses a calendar year for financial reporting. The company is authorized to issue 9,000,000 shares of $10 par common stock. At no time has Newton issued any potentially dilutive securities. Listed below is a summary of Newton's common stock activities.

1. Number of common shares issued and outstanding at December 31, 2012	2,000,000
2. Shares issued as a result of a 10% stock dividend on September 30, 2013	200,000
3. Shares issued for cash on March 31, 2014	2,000,000
Number of common shares issued and outstanding at December 31, 2014	4,200,000

4. A 2-for-1 stock split of Newton's common stock took place on March 31, 2015

Instructions

(a) Compute the weighted-average number of common shares used in computing earnings per common share for 2013 on the 2014 comparative income statement.

(b) Compute the weighted-average number of common shares used in computing earnings per common share for 2014 on the 2014 comparative income statement.

(c) Compute the weighted-average number of common shares to be used in computing earnings per common share for 2014 on the 2015 comparative income statement.

(d) Compute the weighted-average number of common shares to be used in computing earnings per common share for 2015 on the 2015 comparative income statement.

(CMA adapted)

6 **E16-16 (EPS: Simple Capital Structure)** On January 1, 2015, Wilke Corp. had 480,000 shares of common stock outstanding. During 2015, it had the following transactions that affected the common stock account.

February 1	Issued 120,000 shares
March 1	Issued a 10% stock dividend
May 1	Acquired 100,000 shares of treasury stock
June 1	Issued a 3-for-1 stock split
October 1	Reissued 60,000 shares of treasury stock

Instructions

(a) Determine the weighted-average number of shares outstanding as of December 31, 2015.

(b) Assume that Wilke Corp. earned net income of $3,456,000 during 2015. In addition, it had 100,000 shares of 9%, $100 par nonconvertible, noncumulative preferred stock outstanding for the entire year. Because of liquidity considerations, however, the company did not declare and pay a preferred dividend in 2015. Compute earnings per share for 2015, using the weighted-average number of shares determined in part (a).

(c) Assume the same facts as in part (b), except that the preferred stock was cumulative. Compute earnings per share for 2015.

(d) Assume the same facts as in part (b), except that net income included an extraordinary gain of $864,000 and a loss from discontinued operations of $432,000. Both items are net of applicable income taxes. Compute earnings per share for 2015.

6 **E16-17 (EPS: Simple Capital Structure)** Ace Company had 200,000 shares of common stock outstanding on December 31, 2015. During the year 2016, the company issued 8,000 shares on May 1 and retired 14,000 shares on October 31. For the year 2016, Ace Company reported net income of $249,690 after a casualty loss of $40,600 (net of tax).

Instructions

What earnings per share data should be reported at the bottom of its income statement, assuming that the casualty loss is extraordinary?

6 **E16-18 (EPS: Simple Capital Structure)** Flagstad Inc. presented the following data.

Net income	$2,500,000
Preferred stock: 50,000 shares outstanding,	
$100 par, 8% cumulative, not convertible	5,000,000
Common stock: Shares outstanding 1/1	750,000
Issued for cash, 5/1	300,000
Acquired treasury stock for cash, 8/1	150,000
2-for-1 stock split, 10/1	

Instructions

Compute earnings per share.

6 **E16-19 (EPS: Simple Capital Structure)** A portion of the combined statement of income and retained earnings of Seminole Inc. for the current year follows.

Income before extraordinary item	$15,000,000
Extraordinary loss, net of applicable income tax (Note 1)	1,340,000
Net income	13,660,000
Retained earnings at the beginning of the year	83,250,000
	96,910,000

Dividends declared:		
On preferred stock—$6.00 per share	$ 300,000	
On common stock—$1.75 per share	14,875,000	15,175,000
Retained earnings at the end of the year		$81,735,000

Note 1. During the year, Seminole Inc. suffered a major casualty loss of $1,340,000 after applicable income tax reduction of $1,200,000.

At the end of the current year, Seminole Inc. has outstanding 8,500,000 shares of $10 par common stock and 50,000 shares of 6% preferred. On April 1 of the current year, Seminole Inc. issued 1,000,000 shares of common stock for $32 per share to help finance the casualty.

Instructions
Compute the earnings per share on common stock for the current year as it should be reported to stock-holders.

6 **E16-20 (EPS: Simple Capital Structure)** On January 1, 2014, Lennon Industries had stock outstanding as follows.

6% Cumulative preferred stock, $100 par value, issued and outstanding 10,000 shares	$1,000,000
Common stock, $10 par value, issued and outstanding 200,000 shares	2,000,000

To acquire the net assets of three smaller companies, Lennon authorized the issuance of an additional 160,000 common shares. The acquisitions took place as shown below.

Date of Acquisition	Shares Issued
Company A April 1, 2014	50,000
Company B July 1, 2014	80,000
Company C October 1, 2014	30,000

On May 14, 2014, Lennon realized a $90,000 (before taxes) insurance gain on the expropriation of investments originally purchased in 2000.

On December 31, 2014, Lennon recorded net income of $300,000 before tax and exclusive of the gain.

Instructions
Assuming a 50% tax rate, compute the earnings per share data that should appear on the financial statements of Lennon Industries as of December 31, 2014. Assume that the expropriation is extraordinary.

6 **E16-21 (EPS: Simple Capital Structure)** At January 1, 2014, Langley Company's outstanding shares included the following.

> 280,000 shares of $50 par value, 7% cumulative preferred stock
> 900,000 shares of $1 par value common stock

Net income for 2014 was $2,530,000. No cash dividends were declared or paid during 2014. On February 15, 2015, however, all preferred dividends in arrears were paid, together with a 5% stock dividend on common shares. There were no dividends in arrears prior to 2014.

On April 1, 2014, 450,000 shares of common stock were sold for $10 per share, and on October 1, 2014, 110,000 shares of common stock were purchased for $20 per share and held as treasury stock.

Instructions
Compute earnings per share for 2014. Assume that financial statements for 2014 were issued in March 2015.

7 **E16-22 (EPS with Convertible Bonds, Various Situations)** In 2013, Chirac Enterprises issued, at par, 60 $1,000, 8% bonds, each convertible into 100 shares of common stock. Chirac had revenues of $17,500 and expenses other than interest and taxes of $8,400 for 2014. (Assume that the tax rate is 40%.) Throughout 2014, 2,000 shares of common stock were outstanding; none of the bonds was converted or redeemed.

Instructions

   (a) Compute diluted earnings per share for 2014.
   (b) Assume the same facts as those assumed for part (a), except that the 60 bonds were issued on September 1, 2014 (rather than in 2013), and none have been converted or redeemed.
   (c) Assume the same facts as assumed for part (a), except that 20 of the 60 bonds were actually converted on July 1, 2014.

7 **E16-23 (EPS with Convertible Bonds)** On June 1, 2012, Andre Company and Agassi Company merged to form Lancaster Inc. A total of 800,000 shares were issued to complete the merger. The new corporation reports on a calendar-year basis.

On April 1, 2014, the company issued an additional 400,000 shares of stock for cash. All 1,200,000 shares were outstanding on December 31, 2014.

Lancaster Inc. also issued $600,000 of 20-year, 8% convertible bonds at par on July 1, 2014. Each $1,000 bond converts to 40 shares of common at any interest date. None of the bonds have been converted to date.

Lancaster Inc. is preparing its annual report for the fiscal year ending December 31, 2014. The annual report will show earnings per share figures based upon a reported after-tax net income of $1,540,000. (The tax rate is 40%.)

Instructions

Determine the following for 2014.

   (a) The number of shares to be used for calculating:
      (1) Basic earnings per share.
      (2) Diluted earnings per share.
   (b) The earnings figures to be used for calculating:
      (1) Basic earnings per share.
      (2) Diluted earnings per share.

(CMA adapted)

7 **E16-24 (EPS with Convertible Bonds and Preferred Stock)** The Simon Corporation issued 10-year, $5,000,000 par, 7% callable convertible subordinated debentures on January 2, 2014. The bonds have a par value of $1,000, with interest payable annually. The current conversion ratio is 14:1, and in 2 years it will increase to 18:1. At the date of issue, the bonds were sold at 98. Bond discount is amortized on a straight-line basis. Simon's effective tax was 35%. Net income in 2014 was $9,500,000, and the company had 2,000,000 shares outstanding during the entire year.

Instructions

   (a) Prepare a schedule to compute both basic and diluted earnings per share.
   (b) Discuss how the schedule would differ if the security was convertible preferred stock.

7 **E16-25 (EPS with Convertible Bonds and Preferred Stock)** On January 1, 2014, Crocker Company issued 10-year, $2,000,000 face value, 6% bonds, at par. Each $1,000 bond is convertible into 15 shares of Crocker common stock. Crocker's net income in 2014 was $300,000, and its tax rate was 40%. The company had 100,000 shares of common stock outstanding throughout 2014. None of the bonds were converted in 2014.

Instructions

   (a) Compute diluted earnings per share for 2014.
   (b) Compute diluted earnings per share for 2014, assuming the same facts as above, except that $1,000,000 of 6% convertible preferred stock was issued instead of the bonds. Each $100 preferred share is convertible into 5 shares of Crocker common stock.

7 **E16-26 (EPS with Options, Various Situations)** Venzuela Company's net income for 2014 is $50,000. The only potentially dilutive securities outstanding were 1,000 options issued during 2013, each exercisable for one share at $6. None has been exercised, and 10,000 shares of common were outstanding during 2014. The average market price of Venzuela's stock during 2014 was $20.

Instructions

   (a) Compute diluted earnings per share. (Round to nearest cent.)
   (b) Assume the same facts as those assumed for part (a), except that the 1,000 options were issued on October 1, 2014 (rather than in 2013). The average market price during the last 3 months of 2014 was $20.

7 **E16-27 (EPS with Contingent Issuance Agreement)** Winsor Inc. recently purchased Holiday Corp., a large midwestern home painting corporation. One of the terms of the merger was that if Holiday's income for 2014 was $110,000 or more, 10,000 additional shares would be issued to Holiday's stockholders in 2015. Holiday's income for 2013 was $120,000.

Instructions
(a) Would the contingent shares have to be considered in Winsor's 2013 earnings per share computations?
(b) Assume the same facts, except that the 10,000 shares are contingent on Holiday's achieving a net income of $130,000 in 2014. Would the contingent shares have to be considered in Winsor's earnings per share computations for 2013?

7 **E16-28 (EPS with Warrants)** Howat Corporation earned $360,000 during a period when it had an average of 100,000 shares of common stock outstanding. The common stock sold at an average market price of $15 per share during the period. Also outstanding were 15,000 warrants that could be exercised to purchase one share of common stock for $10 for each warrant exercised.

Instructions
(a) Are the warrants dilutive?
(b) Compute basic earnings per share.
(c) Compute diluted earnings per share.

8 *E16-29 (Stock-Appreciation Rights)** On December 31, 2010, Beckford Company issues 150,000 stock-appreciation rights to its officers entitling them to receive cash for the difference between the market price of its stock and a pre-established price of $10. The fair value of the SARs is estimated to be $4 per SAR on December 31, 2011; $1 on December 31, 2012; $10 on December 31, 2013; and $9 on December 31, 2014. The service period is 4 years, and the exercise period is 7 years.

Instructions
(a) Prepare a schedule that shows the amount of compensation expense allocable to each year affected by the stock-appreciation rights plan.
(b) Prepare the entry at December 31, 2014, to record compensation expense, if any, in 2014.
(c) Prepare the entry on December 31, 2014, assuming that all 150,000 SARs are exercised.

8 *E16-30 (Stock-Appreciation Rights)** Capulet Company establishes a stock-appreciation rights program that entitles its new president Ben Davis to receive cash for the difference between the market price of the stock and a pre-established price of $30 (also market price) on December 31, 2010, on 30,000 SARs. The date of grant is December 31, 2010, and the required employment (service) period is 4 years. President Davis exercises all of the SARs in 2016. The fair value of the SARs is estimated to be $6 per SAR on December 31, 2011; $9 on December 31, 2012; $15 on December 31, 2013; $6 on December 31, 2014; and $18 on December 31, 2015.

Instructions
(a) Prepare a 5-year (2011–2015) schedule of compensation expense pertaining to the 30,000 SARs granted president Davis.
(b) Prepare the journal entry for compensation expense in 2011, 2014, and 2015 relative to the 30,000 SARs.

EXERCISES SET B

See the book's companion website, at **www.wiley.com/college/kieso**, for an additional set of exercises.

PROBLEMS

1 **3** **4** **P16-1 (Entries for Various Dilutive Securities)** The stockholders' equity section of Martino Inc. at the beginning of the current year appears below.

Common stock, $10 par value, authorized 1,000,000 shares, 300,000 shares issued and outstanding	$3,000,000
Paid-in capital in excess of par—common stock	600,000
Retained earnings	570,000

During the current year, the following transactions occurred.

1. The company issued to the stockholders 100,000 rights. Ten rights are needed to buy one share of stock at $32. The rights were void after 30 days. The market price of the stock at this time was $34 per share.

2. The company sold to the public a $200,000, 10% bond issue at 104. The company also issued with each $100 bond one detachable stock purchase warrant, which provided for the purchase of common stock at $30 per share. Shortly after issuance, similar bonds without warrants were selling at 96 and the warrants at $8.

3. All but 5,000 of the rights issued in (1) were exercised in 30 days.

4. At the end of the year, 80% of the warrants in (2) had been exercised, and the remaining were outstanding and in good standing.

5. During the current year, the company granted stock options for 10,000 shares of common stock to company executives. The company, using a fair value option-pricing model, determines that each option is worth $10. The option price is $30. The options were to expire at year-end and were considered compensation for the current year.

6. All but 1,000 shares related to the stock-option plan were exercised by year-end. The expiration resulted because one of the executives failed to fulfill an obligation related to the employment contract.

Instructions

(a) Prepare general journal entries for the current year to record the transactions listed above.

(b) Prepare the stockholders' equity section of the balance sheet at the end of the current year. Assume that retained earnings at the end of the current year is $750,000.

P16-2 (Entries for Conversion, Amortization, and Interest of Bonds) Volker Inc. issued $2,500,000 of convertible 10-year bonds on July 1, 2014. The bonds provide for 12% interest payable semiannually on January 1 and July 1. The discount in connection with the issue was $54,000, which is being amortized monthly on a straight-line basis.

The bonds are convertible after one year into 8 shares of Volker Inc.'s $100 par value common stock for each $1,000 of bonds.

On August 1, 2015, $250,000 of bonds were turned in for conversion into common stock. Interest has been accrued monthly and paid as due. At the time of conversion, any accrued interest on bonds being converted is paid in cash.

Instructions

Prepare the journal entries to record the conversion, amortization, and interest in connection with the bonds as of the following dates. (Round to the nearest dollar.)

(a) August 1, 2015. (Assume the book value method is used.)

(b) August 31, 2015.

(c) December 31, 2015, including closing entries for end-of-year.

(AICPA adapted)

P16-3 (Stock-Option Plan) Berg Company adopted a stock-option plan on November 30, 2013, that provided that 70,000 shares of $5 par value stock be designated as available for the granting of options to officers of the corporation at a price of $9 a share. The market price was $12 a share on November 30, 2014.

On January 2, 2014, options to purchase 28,000 shares were granted to president Tom Winter—15,000 for services to be rendered in 2014 and 13,000 for services to be rendered in 2015. Also on that date, options to purchase 14,000 shares were granted to vice president Michelle Bennett—7,000 for services to be rendered in 2014 and 7,000 for services to be rendered in 2015. The market price of the stock was $14 a share on January 2, 2014. The options were exercisable for a period of one year following the year in which the services were rendered. The fair value of the options on the grant date was $4 per option.

In 2015, neither the president nor the vice president exercised their options because the market price of the stock was below the exercise price. The market price of the stock was $8 a share on December 31, 2015, when the options for 2014 services lapsed.

On December 31, 2016, both president Winter and vice president Bennett exercised their options for 13,000 and 7,000 shares, respectively, when the market price was $16 a share.

Instructions

Prepare the necessary journal entries in 2013 when the stock-option plan was adopted, in 2014 when options were granted, in 2015 when options lapsed, and in 2016 when options were exercised.

P16-4 (Stock-Based Compensation) Assume that Amazon.com has a stock-option plan for top management. Each stock option represents the right to purchase a share of Amazon $1 par value common stock in the future at a price equal to the fair value of the stock at the date of the grant. Amazon has 5,000 stock options outstanding, which were granted at the beginning of 2014. The following data relate to the option grant.

Exercise price for options	$40
Market price at grant date (January 1, 2014)	$40
Fair value of options at grant date (January 1, 2014)	$6
Service period	5 years

Instructions

(a) Prepare the journal entry(ies) for the first year of the stock-option plan.

(b) Prepare the journal entry(ies) for the first year of the plan assuming that, rather than options, 700 shares of restricted stock were granted at the beginning of 2014.

(c) Now assume that the market price of Amazon stock on the grant date was $45 per share. Repeat the requirements for (a) and (b).

(d) Amazon would like to implement an employee stock-purchase plan for rank-and-file employees, but it would like to avoid recording expense related to this plan. Which of the following provisions must be in place for the plan to avoid recording compensation expense?

　(1) Substantially all employees may participate.

　(2) The discount from market is small (less than 5%).

　(3) The plan offers no substantive option feature.

　(4) There is no preferred stock outstanding.

 P16-5 (EPS with Complex Capital Structure) Amy Dyken, controller at Fitzgerald Pharmaceutical Industries, a public company, is currently preparing the calculation for basic and diluted earnings per share and the related disclosure for Fitzgerald's financial statements. Below is selected financial information for the fiscal year ended June 30, 2014.

FITZGERALD PHARMACEUTICAL INDUSTRIES
SELECTED BALANCE SHEET
INFORMATION
JUNE 30, 2014

Long-term debt	
Notes payable, 10%	$ 1,000,000
8% convertible bonds payable	5,000,000
10% bonds payable	6,000,000
Total long-term debt	$12,000,000
Shareholders' equity	
Preferred stock, 6% cumulative, $50 par value, 100,000 shares authorized, 25,000 shares issued and outstanding	$ 1,250,000
Common stock, $1 par, 10,000,000 shares authorized, 1,000,000 shares issued and outstanding	1,000,000
Additional paid-in capital	4,000,000
Retained earnings	6,000,000
Total shareholders' equity	$12,250,000

The following transactions have also occurred at Fitzgerald.

1. Options were granted on July 1, 2013, to purchase 200,000 shares at $15 per share. Although no options were exercised during fiscal year 2014, the average price per common share during fiscal year 2014 was $20 per share.

2. Each bond was issued at face value. The 8% convertible bonds will convert into common stock at 50 shares per $1,000 bond. The bonds are exercisable after 5 years and were issued in fiscal year 2013.

3. The preferred stock was issued in 2013.

4. There are no preferred dividends in arrears; however, preferred dividends were not declared in fiscal year 2014.

5. The 1,000,000 shares of common stock were outstanding for the entire 2014 fiscal year.

6. Net income for fiscal year 2014 was $1,500,000, and the average income tax rate is 40%.

Instructions

For the fiscal year ended June 30, 2014, calculate the following for Fitzgerald Pharmaceutical Industries.

(a) Basic earnings per share.
(b) Diluted earnings per share.

P16-6 (Basic EPS: Two-Year Presentation) Melton Corporation is preparing the comparative financial statements for the annual report to its shareholders for fiscal years ended May 31, 2014, and May 31, 2015. The income from operations for each year was $1,800,000 and $2,500,000, respectively. In both years, the company incurred a 10% interest expense on $2,400,000 of debt, an obligation that requires interest-only payments for 5 years. The company experienced a loss of $600,000 from a fire in its Scotsland facility in February 2015, which was determined to be an extraordinary loss. The company uses a 40% effective tax rate for income taxes.

The capital structure of Melton Corporation on June 1, 2013, consisted of 1 million shares of common stock outstanding and 20,000 shares of $50 par value, 6%, cumulative preferred stock. There were no preferred dividends in arrears, and the company had not issued any convertible securities, options, or warrants.

On October 1, 2013, Melton sold an additional 500,000 shares of the common stock at $20 per share. Melton distributed a 20% stock dividend on the common shares outstanding on January 1, 2014. On December 1, 2014, Melton was able to sell an additional 800,000 shares of the common stock at $22 per share. These were the only common stock transactions that occurred during the two fiscal years.

Instructions

(a) Identify whether the capital structure at Melton Corporation is a simple or complex capital structure, and explain why.
(b) Determine the weighted-average number of shares that Melton Corporation would use in calculating earnings per share for the fiscal year ended:
   (1) May 31, 2014.
   (2) May 31, 2015.
(c) Prepare, in good form, a comparative income statement, beginning with income from operations, for Melton Corporation for the fiscal years ended May 31, 2014, and May 31, 2015. This statement will be included in Melton's annual report and should display the appropriate earnings per share presentations.

(CMA adapted)

P16-7 (Computation of Basic and Diluted EPS) Charles Austin of the controller's office of Thompson Corporation was given the assignment of determining the basic and diluted earnings per share values for the year ending December 31, 2015. Austin has compiled the information listed below.

1. The company is authorized to issue 8,000,000 shares of $10 par value common stock. As of December 31, 2014, 2,000,000 shares had been issued and were outstanding.
2. The per share market prices of the common stock on selected dates were as follows.

	Price per Share
July 1, 2014	$20.00
January 1, 2015	21.00
April 1, 2015	25.00
July 1, 2015	11.00
August 1, 2015	10.50
November 1, 2015	9.00
December 31, 2015	10.00

3. A total of 700,000 shares of an authorized 1,200,000 shares of convertible preferred stock had been issued on July 1, 2014. The stock was issued at its par value of $25, and it has a cumulative dividend of $3 per share. The stock is convertible into common stock at the rate of one share of convertible preferred for one share of common. The rate of conversion is to be automatically adjusted for stock splits and stock dividends. Dividends are paid quarterly on September 30, December 31, March 31, and June 30.
4. Thompson Corporation is subject to a 40% income tax rate.
5. The after-tax net income for the year ended December 31, 2015, was $11,550,000.

The following specific activities took place during 2015.

1. January 1—A 5% common stock dividend was issued. The dividend had been declared on December 1, 2014, to all stockholders of record on December 29, 2014.

2. April 1—A total of 400,000 shares of the $3 convertible preferred stock was converted into common stock. The company issued new common stock and retired the preferred stock. This was the only conversion of the preferred stock during 2015.
3. July 1—A 2-for-1 split of the common stock became effective on this date. The board of directors had authorized the split on June 1.
4. August 1—A total of 300,000 shares of common stock were issued to acquire a factory building.
5. November 1—A total of 24,000 shares of common stock were purchased on the open market at $9 per share. These shares were to be held as treasury stock and were still in the treasury as of December 31, 2015.
6. Common stock cash dividends—Cash dividends to common stockholders were declared and paid as follows.

April 15—$0.30 per share

October 15—$0.20 per share

7. Preferred stock cash dividends—Cash dividends to preferred stockholders were declared and paid as scheduled.

Instructions

(a) Determine the number of shares used to compute basic earnings per share for the year ended December 31, 2015.
(b) Determine the number of shares used to compute diluted earnings per share for the year ended December 31, 2015.
(c) Compute the adjusted net income to be used as the numerator in the basic earnings per share calculation for the year ended December 31, 2015.

7 P16-8 (Computation of Basic and Diluted EPS) The information below pertains to Barkley Company for 2015.

Net income for the year	$1,200,000
7% convertible bonds issued at par ($1,000 per bond); each bond is convertible into 30 shares of common stock	2,000,000
6% convertible, cumulative preferred stock, $100 par value; each share is convertible into 3 shares of common stock	4,000,000
Common stock, $10 par value	6,000,000
Tax rate for 2015	40%
Average market price of common stock	$25 per share

There were no changes during 2015 in the number of common shares, preferred shares, or convertible bonds outstanding. There is no treasury stock. The company also has common stock options (granted in a prior year) to purchase 75,000 shares of common stock at $20 per share.

Instructions

(a) Compute basic earnings per share for 2015.
(b) Compute diluted earnings per share for 2015.

6 P16-9 (EPS with Stock Dividend and Extraordinary Items) Agassi Corporation is preparing the comparative financial statements to be included in the annual report to stockholders. Agassi employs a fiscal year ending May 31.

Income from operations before income taxes for Agassi was $1,400,000 and $660,000, respectively, for fiscal years ended May 31, 2015 and 2014. Agassi experienced an extraordinary loss of $400,000 because of an earthquake on March 3, 2015. A 40% combined income tax rate pertains to any and all of Agassi Corporation's profits, gains, and losses.

Agassi's capital structure consists of preferred stock and common stock. The company has not issued any convertible securities or warrants and there are no outstanding stock options.

Agassi issued 40,000 shares of $100 par value, 6% cumulative preferred stock in 2011. All of this stock is outstanding, and no preferred dividends are in arrears.

There were 1,000,000 shares of $1 par common stock outstanding on June 1, 2013. On September 1, 2013, Agassi sold an additional 400,000 shares of the common stock at $17 per share. Agassi distributed a 20% stock dividend on the common shares outstanding on December 1, 2014. These were the only common stock transactions during the past 2 fiscal years.

Instructions

(a) Determine the weighted-average number of common shares that would be used in computing earnings per share on the current comparative income statement for:
(1) The year ended May 31, 2014.
(2) The year ended May 31, 2015.

(b) Starting with income from operations before income taxes, prepare a comparative income statement for the years ended May 31, 2015 and 2014. The statement will be part of Agassi Corporation's annual report to stockholders and should include appropriate earnings per share presentation.

(c) The capital structure of a corporation is the result of its past financing decisions. Furthermore, the earnings per share data presented on a corporation's financial statements is dependent upon the capital structure.

    (1) Explain why Agassi Corporation is considered to have a simple capital structure.

    (2) Describe how earnings per share data would be presented for a corporation that has a complex capital structure.

(CMA adapted)

PROBLEMS SET B

See the book's companion website, at **www.wiley.com/college/kieso**, for an additional set of problems.

CONCEPTS FOR ANALYSIS

CA16-1 (Warrants Issued with Bonds and Convertible Bonds) Incurring long-term debt with an arrangement whereby lenders receive an option to buy common stock during all or a portion of the time the debt is outstanding is a frequent corporate financing practice. In some situations, the result is achieved through the issuance of convertible bonds; in others, the debt instruments and the warrants to buy stock are separate.

Instructions

    (a) (1) Describe the differences that exist in current accounting for original proceeds of the issuance of convertible bonds and of debt instruments with separate warrants to purchase common stock.

        (2) Discuss the underlying rationale for the differences described in (a)(1) above.

        (3) Summarize the arguments that have been presented in favor of accounting for convertible bonds in the same manner as accounting for debt with separate warrants.

    (b) At the start of the year, Huish Company issued $18,000,000 of 12% bonds along with detachable warrants to buy 1,200,000 shares of its $10 par value common stock at $18 per share. The bonds mature over the next 10 years, starting one year from date of issuance, with annual maturities of $1,800,000. At the time, Huish had 9,600,000 shares of common stock outstanding. The company received $20,040,000 for the bonds and the warrants. For Huish Company, 12% was a relatively low borrowing rate. If offered alone, at this time, the bonds would have sold in the market at a 22% discount. Prepare the journal entry (or entries) for the issuance of the bonds and warrants for the cash consideration received.

(AICPA adapted)

CA16-2 (Ethical Issues—Compensation Plan) The executive officers of Rouse Corporation have a performance-based compensation plan. The performance criteria of this plan is linked to growth in earnings per share. When annual EPS growth is 12%, the Rouse executives earn 100% of the shares; if growth is 16%, they earn 125%. If EPS growth is lower than 8%, the executives receive no additional compensation.

In 2014, Joan Devers, the controller of Rouse, reviews year-end estimates of bad debt expense and warranty expense. She calculates the EPS growth at 15%. Kurt Adkins, a member of the executive group, remarks over lunch one day that the estimate of bad debt expense might be decreased, increasing EPS growth to 16.1%. Devers is not sure she should do this because she believes that the current estimate of bad debts is sound. On the other hand, she recognizes that a great deal of subjectivity is involved in the computation.

Instructions

Answer the following questions.

    (a) What, if any, is the ethical dilemma for Devers?

    (b) Should Devers's knowledge of the compensation plan be a factor that influences her estimate?

    (c) How should Devers respond to Adkins's request?

CA16-3 (Stock Warrants—Various Types) For various reasons a corporation may issue warrants to purchase shares of its common stock at specified prices that, depending on the circumstances, may be less than, equal to, or greater than the current market price. For example, warrants may be issued:

1. To existing stockholders on a pro rata basis.
2. To certain key employees under an incentive stock-option plan.
3. To purchasers of the corporation's bonds.

Instructions
For each of the three examples of how stock warrants are used:

(a) Explain why they are used.
(b) Discuss the significance of the price (or prices) at which the warrants are issued (or granted) in relation to (1) the current market price of the company's stock, and (2) the length of time over which they can be exercised.
(c) Describe the information that should be disclosed in financial statements, or notes thereto, that are prepared when stock warrants are outstanding in the hands of the three groups listed above.

(AICPA adapted)

CA16-4 (Stock Compensation Plans) The following two items appeared on the Internet concerning the GAAP requirement to expense stock options.

WASHINGTON, D.C.—February 17, 2005 Congressman David Dreier (R–CA), Chairman of the House Rules Committee, and Congresswoman Anna Eshoo (D–CA) reintroduced legislation today that will preserve broad-based employee stock option plans and give investors critical information they need to understand how employee stock options impact the value of their shares.

"Last year, the U.S. House of Representatives overwhelmingly voted for legislation that would have ensured the continued ability of innovative companies to offer stock options to rank-and-file employees," Dreier stated. "Both the Financial Accounting Standards Board (FASB) and the Securities and Exchange Commission (SEC) continue to ignore our calls to address legitimate concerns about the impact of FASB's new standard on workers' ability to have an ownership stake in the New Economy, and its failure to address the real need of shareholders: accurate and meaningful information about a company's use of stock options."

"In December 2004, FASB issued a stock option expensing standard that will render a huge blow to the 21st century economy," Dreier said. "Their action and the SEC's apparent lack of concern for protecting shareholders, requires us to once again take a firm stand on the side of investors and economic growth. Giving investors the ability to understand how stock options impact the value of their shares is critical. And equally important is preserving the ability of companies to use this innovative tool to attract talented employees."

"Here We Go Again!" by Jack Ciesielski (2/21/2005, http://www.accountingobserver.com/blog/2005/02/here-we-go-again) On February 17, Congressman David Dreier (R–CA), and Congresswoman Anna Eshoo (D–CA), officially entered Silicon Valley's bid to gum up the launch of honest reporting of stock option compensation: They co-sponsored a bill to "preserve broad-based employee stock option plans and give investors critical information they need to understand how employee stock options impact the value of their shares." You know what "critical information" they mean: stuff like the stock compensation for the top five officers in a company, with a rigged value set as close to zero as possible. Investors *crave* this kind of information. Other ways the good Congresspersons want to "help" investors: The bill "also requires the SEC to study the effectiveness of those disclosures over three years, during which time, no new accounting standard related to the treatment of stock options could be recognized. Finally, the bill requires the Secretary of Commerce to conduct a study and report to Congress on the impact of broad-based employee stock option plans on expanding employee corporate ownership, skilled worker recruitment and retention, research and innovation, economic growth, and international competitiveness."

It's the old "four corners" basketball strategy: stall, stall, stall. In the meantime, hope for regime change at your opponent, the FASB.

Instructions
(a) What are the major recommendations of the stock-based compensation pronouncement?
(b) How do the provisions of GAAP in this area differ from the bill introduced by members of Congress (Dreier and Eshoo), which would require expensing for options issued to only the top five officers in a company? Which approach do you think would result in more useful information? (Focus on comparability.)

(c) The bill in Congress urges the FASB to develop a rule that preserves "the ability of companies to use this innovative tool to attract talented employees." Write a response to these Congress-people explaining the importance of neutrality in financial accounting and reporting.

CA16-5 (EPS: Preferred Dividends, Options, and Convertible Debt) "Earnings per share" (EPS) is the most featured, single financial statistic about modern corporations. Daily published quotations of stock prices have recently been expanded to include for many securities a "times earnings" figure that is based on EPS. Stock analysts often focus their discussions on the EPS of the corporations they study.

Instructions

(a) Explain how dividends or dividend requirements on any class of preferred stock that may be outstanding affect the computation of EPS.

(b) One of the technical procedures applicable in EPS computations is the "treasury-stock method." Briefly describe the circumstances under which it might be appropriate to apply the treasury-stock method.

(c) Convertible debentures are considered potentially dilutive common shares. Explain how convertible debentures are handled for purposes of EPS computations.

(AICPA adapted)

 CA16-6 (EPS, Antidilution) Brad Dolan, a stockholder of Rhode Corporation, has asked you, the firm's accountant, to explain why his stock warrants were not included in diluted EPS. In order to explain this situation, you must briefly explain what dilutive securities are, why they are included in the EPS calculation, and why some securities are antidilutive and thus not included in this calculation.

Rhode Corporation earned $228,000 during the period, when it had an average of 100,000 shares of common stock outstanding. The common stock sold at an average market price of $25 per share during the period. Also outstanding were 30,000 warrants that could be exercised to purchase one share of common stock at $30 per warrant.

Instructions

Write Mr. Dolan a 1–1.5-page letter explaining why the warrants are not included in the calculation.

USING YOUR JUDGMENT

FINANCIAL REPORTING

Financial Reporting Problem

P&G **The Procter & Gamble Company (P&G)**

The financial statements of **P&G** are presented in Appendix 5B. The company's complete annual report, including the notes to the financial statements, can be accessed at the book's companion website, **www.wiley.com/college/kieso**.

Instructions

Refer to P&G's financial statements and accompanying notes to answer the following questions.

(a) Under P&G's stock-based compensation plan, stock options are granted annually to key managers and directors.

(1) How many options were granted during 2011 under the plan?

(2) How many options were exercisable at June 30, 2011?

(3) How many options were exercised in 2011, and what was the average price of those exercised?

(4) How many years from the grant date do the options expire?

(5) To what accounts are the proceeds from these option exercises credited?

(6) What was the number of outstanding options at June 30, 2011, and at what average exercise price?

(b) What number of diluted weighted-average common shares outstanding was used by P&G in computing earnings per share for 2011, 2010, and 2009? What was P&G's diluted earnings per share in 2011, 2010, and 2009?

(c) What other stock-based compensation plans does P&G have?

Comparative Analysis Case

The Coca-Cola Company and PepsiCo, Inc.

Instructions

Go to the book's companion website and use information found there to answer the following questions related to The Coca-Cola Company and PepsiCo, Inc.

(a) What employee stock-option compensation plans are offered by Coca-Cola and PepsiCo?

(b) How many options are outstanding at year-end 2011 for both Coca-Cola and PepsiCo?

(c) How many options were granted by Coca-Cola and PepsiCo to officers and employees during 2011?

(d) How many options were exercised during 2011?

(e) What was the average exercise price for Coca-Cola and PepsiCo employees during 2011?

(f) What are the weighted-average number of shares used by Coca-Cola and PepsiCo in 2011, 2010, and 2009 to compute diluted earnings per share?

(g) What was the diluted net income per share for Coca-Cola and PepsiCo for 2011, 2010, and 2009?

Financial Statement Analysis Case

Ragatz, Inc.

Ragatz, Inc., a drug company, reported the following information. The company prepares its financial statements in accordance with GAAP.

	2014 (,000)
Current liabilities	$ 554,114
Convertible subordinated debt	648,020
Total liabilities	1,228,313
Stockholders' equity	176,413
Net income	58,333

Analysts attempting to compare Ragatz to drug companies that issue debt with detachable warrants may face a challenge due to differences in accounting for convertible debt.

Instructions

(a) Compute the following ratios for Ragatz, Inc. (Assume that year-end balances approximate annual averages.)

    (1) Return on assets.

    (2) Return on common stock equity.

    (3) Debt to assets ratio.

(b) Briefly discuss the operating performance and financial position of Ragatz. Industry averages for these ratios in 2014 were ROA 3.5%; return on equity 16%; and debt to assets 75%. Based on this analysis, would you make an investment in the company's 5% convertible bonds? Explain.

(c) Assume you want to compare Ragatz to an IFRS company like Merck (which issues nonconvertible debt with detachable warrants). Assuming that the fair value of the equity component of Ragatz's convertible bonds is $150,000, how would you adjust the analysis above to make valid comparisons between Ragatz and Merck?

Accounting, Analysis, and Principles

On January 1, 2013, Garner issued 10-year, $200,000 face value, 6% bonds at par. Each $1,000 bond is convertible into 30 shares of Garner $2 par value common stock. The company has had 10,000 shares of common stock (and no preferred stock) outstanding throughout its life. None of the bonds have been converted as of the end of 2014. (Ignore all tax effects.)

Accounting

(a) Prepare the journal entry Garner would have made on January 1, 2013, to record the issuance of the bonds.

(b) Garner's net income in 2014 was $30,000 and was $27,000 in 2013. Compute basic and diluted earnings per share for Garner for 2014 and 2013.

(c) Assume that 75% of the holders of Garner's convertible bonds convert their bonds to stock on June 30, 2015, when Garner's stock is trading at $32 per share. Garner pays $50 per bond to induce bondholders to convert. Prepare the journal entry to record the conversion.

Analysis

Show how Garner will report income and EPS for 2014 and 2013. Briefly discuss the importance of GAAP for EPS to analysts evaluating companies based on price-earnings ratios. Consider comparisons for a company over time, as well as comparisons between companies at a point in time.

Principles

In order to converge GAAP and IFRS, the FASB is considering whether the equity element of a convertible bond should be reported as equity. Describe how the journal entry you made in part (a) above would differ under IFRS. In terms of the accounting principles discussed in Chapter 2, what does IFRS for convertible debt accomplish that GAAP potentially sacrifices? What does GAAP for convertible debt accomplish that IFRS potentially sacrifices?

BRIDGE TO THE PROFESSION

 ## Professional Research: FASB Codification

Richardson Company is contemplating the establishment of a share-based compensation plan to provide long-run incentives for its top management. However, members of the compensation committee of the board of directors have voiced some concerns about adopting these plans, based on news accounts related to a recent accounting standard in this area. They would like you to conduct some research on this recent standard so they can be better informed about the accounting for these plans.

Instructions

If your school has a subscription to the FASB Codification, go to *http://aaahq.org/ascLogin.cfm* to log in and prepare responses to the following. Provide Codification references for your responses.

(a) Identify the authoritative literature that addresses the accounting for share-based payment compensation plans.

(b) Briefly discuss the objectives for the accounting for stock compensation. What is the role of fair value measurement?

(c) The Richardson Company board is also considering an employee share-purchase plan, but the Board does not want to record expense related to the plan. What criteria must be met to avoid recording expense on an employee stock-purchase plan?

Additional Professional Resources

See the book's companion website, at **www.wiley.com/college/kieso**, for professional simulations as well as other study resources.

IFRS > INSIGHTS

The primary IFRS related to financial instruments, including dilutive securities, is *IAS 39*, "Financial Instruments: Recognition and Measurement." The accounting for various forms of stock-based compensation under IFRS is found in *IFRS 2*, "Share-Based Payment." This standard was recently amended, resulting in significant convergence between IFRS and GAAP in this area. The IFRS addressing accounting and reporting for earnings per share computations is *IAS 33*, "Earnings per Share."

> **10** **LEARNING OBJECTIVE**
> Compare the accounting for dilutive securities and earnings per share under GAAP and IFRS.

RELEVANT FACTS

Following are the key similarities and differences between GAAP and IFRS related to dilutive securities and earnings per share.

Similarities

- IFRS and GAAP follow the same model for recognizing stock-based compensation: The fair value of shares and options awarded to employees is recognized over the period to which the employees' services relate.

- Although the calculation of basic and diluted earnings per share is similar between IFRS and GAAP, the Boards are working to resolve the few minor differences in EPS reporting. One proposal in the FASB project concerns contracts that can be settled in either cash or shares. IFRS requires that share settlement must be used, while GAAP gives companies a choice. The FASB project proposes adopting the IFRS approach, thus converging GAAP and IFRS in this regard.

Differences

- A significant difference between IFRS and GAAP is the accounting for securities with characteristics of debt and equity, such as convertible debt. Under GAAP, all of the proceeds of convertible debt are recorded as long-term debt. Under IFRS, convertible bonds are "bifurcated"—separated into the equity component (the value of the conversion option) of the bond issue and the debt component.

- Related to employee share-purchase plans, under IFRS, all employee share-purchase plans are deemed to be compensatory; that is, compensation expense is recorded for the amount of the discount. Under GAAP, these plans are often considered noncompensatory and therefore no compensation is recorded. Certain conditions must exist before a plan can be considered noncompensatory—the most important being that the discount generally cannot exceed 5 percent.

- Modification of a share option results in the recognition of any incremental fair value under both IFRS and GAAP. However, if the modification leads to a reduction, IFRS does not permit the reduction but GAAP does.

- Other EPS differences relate to (1) the treasury-stock method and how the proceeds from extinguishment of a liability should be accounted for, and (2) how to compute the weighted average of contingently issuable shares.

ABOUT THE NUMBERS

Accounting for Convertible Debt

Convertible debt is accounted for as a **compound instrument** because it contains both a liability and an equity component. IFRS requires that compound instruments be separated into their liability and equity components for purposes of accounting. Companies use the **"with-and-without" method** to value compound instruments. Illustration IFRS16-1 identifies the components used in the with-and-without method.

ILLUSTRATION IFRS16-1
Convertible Debt Components

| Fair value of convertible debt at date of issuance (with both debt and equity components) | − | Fair value of liability component at date of issuance, based on present value of cash flows | = | Equity component at date of issuance (without the debt component) |

As indicated, the equity component is the residual amount after subtracting the liability component. IFRS does not permit companies to assign a value to the equity amount first and then determine the liability component. To do so would be inconsistent with the definition of equity, which is considered a residual amount. To implement the with-and-without approach, companies do the following.

1. First, the company determines the total fair value of the convertible debt *with* both the liability and equity component. **This is straightforward, as this amount is the proceeds received upon issuance.**

2. The company then determines the liability component by computing the net present value of all contractual future cash flows discounted at the market rate of interest. This market rate is the rate the company would pay on similar nonconvertible debt.

3. In the final step, the company subtracts the liability component estimated in the second step from the fair value of the convertible debt (issue proceeds) to arrive at the equity component. That is, the equity component is the fair value of the convertible debt *without* the liability component.

Accounting at Time of Issuance

To illustrate the accounting for convertible debt, assume that Roche Group issues 2,000 convertible bonds at the beginning of 2013. The bonds have a four-year term with a stated rate of interest of 6 percent, and are issued at par with a face value of $1,000 per bond (the total proceeds received from issuance of the bonds are $2,000,000). Interest is payable annually at December 31. Each bond is convertible into 250 ordinary shares with a par value of $1. The market rate of interest on similar nonconvertible debt is 9 percent. The time diagram in Illustration IFRS16-2 depicts both the interest and principal cash flows.

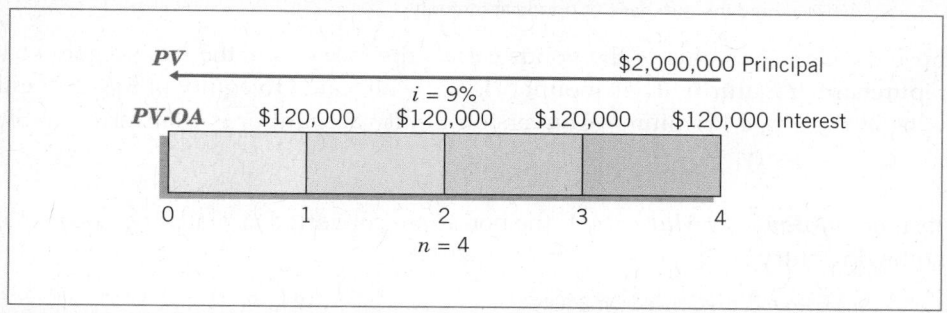

ILLUSTRATION IFRS16-2
Time Diagram for Convertible Bond

The liability component of the convertible debt is computed as shown in Illustration IFRS16-3.

Present value of principal: $2,000,000 × .70843 (Table 6-2; $n = 4$, $i = 9\%$)	$1,416,860
Present value of the interest payments: $120,000 × 3.23972 (Table 6-4; $n = 4$, $i = 9\%$)	388,766
Present value of the liability component	$1,805,626

ILLUSTRATION IFRS16-3
Fair Value of Liability Component of Convertible Bond

The equity component of Roche's convertible debt is then computed as shown in Illustration IFRS16-4.

Fair value of convertible debt at date of issuance	$2,000,000
Less: Fair value of liability component at date of issuance	1,805,626
Fair value of equity component at date of issuance	$ 194,374

ILLUSTRATION IFRS16-4
Equity Component of Convertible Bond

The journal entry to record this transaction is as follows.

Cash	2,000,000	
Bonds Payable		1,805,626
Share Premium—Conversion Equity		194,374

The liability component of Roche's convertible debt issue is recorded as Bonds Payable. As shown in Chapter 14, the amount of the discount relative to the face value of the bond is amortized at each reporting period so at maturity, the Bonds Payable account is reported at $2,000,000 (face value). The equity component of the convertible bond is recorded in the Share Premium—Conversion Equity account and is reported in the equity section of the statement of financial position. Because this amount is considered part of contributed capital, it does not change over the life of the convertible. **Transaction costs related to the liability and equity components are allocated in proportion to the proceeds received from the two components.** *For purposes of homework, use the Share Premium—Conversion Equity account to record the equity component.* **In practice, there may be considerable variation in the accounts used to record this component.**

Settlement of Convertible Bonds

We illustrate four settlement situations: (1) repurchase at maturity, (2) conversion at maturity, (3) conversion before maturity, and (4) repurchase before maturity.

Repurchase at Maturity. If the bonds are not converted at maturity, Roche makes the following entry to pay off the convertible debtholders.

Bonds Payable	2,000,000	
Cash		2,000,000
(To record the purchase of bonds at maturity)		

Because the carrying value of the bonds equals the face value, there is no gain or loss on repurchase at maturity. The amount originally allocated to equity of $194,374 either remains in the Share Premium—Conversion Equity account or is transferred to Share Premium—Ordinary.

Conversion of Bonds at Maturity. If the bonds are converted at maturity, Roche makes the following entry.

Share Premium—Conversion Equity	194,374	
Bonds Payable	2,000,000	
Share Capital—Ordinary		500,000
Share Premium—Ordinary		1,694,374
(To record the conversion of bonds at maturity)		

As indicated, Roche records a credit to Share Capital—Ordinary for $500,000 (2,000 bonds × 250 shares × $1 par) and the remainder to Share Premium—Ordinary for $1,694,374. There is no gain or loss on conversion at maturity. The original amount allocated to equity ($194,374) is transferred to the Share Premium—Ordinary account. As a result, Roche's equity has increased by a total of $2,194,374 through issuance and conversion of the convertible bonds. This accounting approach is often referred to as the **book value method** in that the carrying amount (book value) of the bond and related conversion equity determines the amount in the ordinary equity accounts.

Conversion of Bonds before Maturity. What happens if bonds are converted before maturity? To understand the accounting, we again use the Roche Group example. A schedule of bond amortization related to Roche's convertible bonds is shown in Illustration IFRS16-5.

SCHEDULE OF BOND AMORTIZATION
EFFECTIVE-INTEREST METHOD
6% BOND DISCOUNTED AT 9%

Date	Cash Paid	Interest Expense	Discount Amortized	Carrying Amount of Bonds
1/1/13				$1,805,626
12/31/13	$120,000	$162,506	$42,506	1,848,132
12/31/14	120,000	166,332	46,332	1,894,464
12/31/15	120,000	170,502	50,502	1,944,966
12/31/16	120,000	175,034*	55,034	2,000,000

*$13 difference due to rounding.

Assuming that Roche converts its bonds into ordinary shares on December 31, 2014, Roche debits the Bonds Payable account for its carrying value of $1,894,464 (see Illustration IFRS16-5). In addition, Roche credits Share Capital—Ordinary for $500,000 (2,000 × 250 × $1) and credits Share Premium—Ordinary for $1,588,838. The entry to record this conversion is as follows.

Share Premium—Conversion Equity	194,374	
Bonds Payable	1,894,464	
Share Capital—Ordinary		500,000
Share Premium—Ordinary		1,588,838
(To record the conversion of bonds before maturity)		

There is no gain or loss on conversion before maturity: The original amount allocated to equity ($194,374) is transferred to the Share Premium—Ordinary account.

Repurchase before Maturity. In some cases, companies decide to repurchase the convertible debt before maturity. The approach used for allocating the amount paid upon repurchase follows the approach used when the convertible bond was originally issued. That is, Roche determines the fair value of the liability component of the convertible bonds at December 31, 2014, and then subtracts this amount from the fair value of the convertible bond issue (including the equity component) to arrive at the value for the equity. After this allocation is completed:

1. The difference between the consideration allocated to the liability component and the carrying amount of the liability is recognized as a gain or loss, and

2. The amount of consideration relating to the equity component is recognized (as a reduction) in equity.

To illustrate, instead of converting the bonds on December 31, 2014, assume that Roche repurchases the convertible bonds from the bondholders. Pertinent information related to this conversion is as follows.

• Fair value of the convertible debt (including both liability and equity components), based on market prices at December 31, 2014, is $1,965,000.

• The fair value of the liability component is $1,904,900. This amount is based on computing the present value of a nonconvertible bond with a two-year term (which corresponds to the shortened time to maturity of the repurchased bonds).

We first determine the gain or loss on the liability component, as computed in Illustration IFRS16-6.

Present value of liability component at December 31, 2014 (given above)	$ 1,904,900
Carrying value of liability component at December 31, 2014 (per Illustration IFRS16-5)	(1,894,464)
Loss on repurchase	$ 10,436

Roche has a loss on this repurchase because the value of the debt extinguished is greater than its carrying amount. To determine any adjustment to equity, we compute the value of the equity as shown in Illustration IFRS16-7.

ILLUSTRATION IFRS16-7
Equity Adjustment on Repurchase of Convertible Bonds

Fair value of convertible debt at December 31, 2014 (**with equity component**)	$1,965,000
Less: Fair value of liability component at December 31, 2014 (similar 2-year nonconvertible debt)	1,904,900
Fair value of equity component at December 31, 2014 (**without debt component**)	$ 60,100

Roche makes the following compound journal entry to record the entire repurchase transaction.

Bonds Payable	1,894,464	
Share Premium—Conversion Equity	60,100	
Loss on Repurchase	10,436	
Cash		1,965,000
(To record the repurchase of convertible bonds)		

In summary, the repurchase results in a loss related to the liability component and a reduction in Share Premium—Conversion Equity. The remaining balance in Share Premium—Conversion Equity of $134,274 ($194,374 − $60,100) is often transferred to Share Premium—Ordinary upon the repurchase.

Employee Share-Purchase Plans

Employee share-purchase plans (ESPPs) generally permit all employees to purchase shares at a discounted price for a short period of time. The company often uses such plans to secure equity capital or to induce widespread ownership of its ordinary shares among employees. **These plans are considered compensatory and should be recorded as expense over the service period.**

To illustrate, assume that Masthead Company offers all its 1,000 employees the opportunity to participate in an employee share-purchase plan. Under the terms of the plan, the employees are entitled to purchase 100 ordinary shares (par value $1 per share) at a 20 percent discount. The purchase price must be paid immediately upon acceptance of the offer. In total, 800 employees accept the offer, and each employee purchases on average 80 shares. That is, the employees purchase a total of 64,000 shares. The weighted-average market price of the shares at the purchase date is $30 per share, and the weighted-average purchase price is $24 per share. The entry to record this transaction is as follows.

Cash (64,000 × $24)	1,536,000	
Compensation Expense [64,000 × ($30 − $24)]	384,000	
Share Capital—Ordinary (64,000 × $1)		64,000
Share Premium—Ordinary		1,856,000
(Issue shares in an employee share-purchase plan)		

The IASB indicates that there is no reason to treat broad-based employee share plans differently from other employee share plans. Some have argued that because these plans are used to raise capital, they should not be compensatory. However, IFRS requires recording expense for these arrangements. The Board notes that because these arrangements are available only to employees, it is sufficient to conclude that the benefits provided represent employee compensation.

ON THE HORIZON

The FASB has been working on a standard that will likely converge to IFRS in the accounting for convertible debt. Similar to the FASB, the IASB is examining the classification of hybrid securities; the IASB is seeking comment on a discussion document similar to the FASB Preliminary Views document, "*Financial Instruments with Characteristics of*

Equity." It is hoped that the Boards will develop a converged standard in this area. While GAAP and IFRS are similar as to the presentation of EPS, the Boards have been working together to resolve remaining differences related to earnings per share computations.

IFRS SELF-TEST QUESTIONS

1. All of the following are key similarities between GAAP and IFRS with respect to accounting for dilutive securities and EPS **except**:
    (a) the model for recognizing stock-based compensation.
    (b) the calculation of basic and diluted EPS.
    (c) the accounting for convertible debt.
    (d) the accounting for modifications of share options, when the value increases.
2. Which of the following statements is **correct**?
    (a) IFRS separates the proceeds of a convertible bond between debt and equity by determining the fair value of the debt component before the equity component.
    (b) Both IFRS and GAAP assume that when there is choice of settlement of an option for cash or shares, share settlement is assumed.
    (c) IFRS separates the proceeds of a convertible bond between debt and equity, based on relative fair values.
    (d) Both GAAP and IFRS separate the proceeds of convertible bonds between debt and equity.
3. Under IFRS, convertible bonds:
    (a) are separated into the bond component and the expense component.
    (b) are separated into debt and equity components.
    (c) are separated into their components based on relative fair values.
    (d) All of the above.
4. Mae Jong Corp. issues $1,000,000 of 10% bonds payable which may be converted into 10,000 shares of $2 par value ordinary shares. The market rate of interest on similar bonds is 12%. Interest is payable annually on December 31, and the bonds were issued for total proceeds of $1,000,000. In accounting for these bonds, Mae Jong Corp. will:
    (a) first assign a value to the equity component, then determine the liability component.
    (b) assign no value to the equity component since the conversion privilege is not separable from the bond.
    (c) first assign a value to the liability component based on the face amount of the bond.
    (d) use the "with-and-without" method to value the compound instrument.
5. Anazazi Co. offers all its 10,000 employees the opportunity to participate in an employee share-purchase plan. Under the terms of the plan, the employees are entitled to purchase 100 ordinary shares (par value $1 per share) at a 20% discount. The purchase price must be paid immediately upon acceptance of the offer. In total, 8,500 employees accept the offer, and each employee purchases on average 80 shares at $22 share (market price $27.50). Under IFRS, Anazazi Co. will record:
    (a) no compensation since the plan is used to raise capital, not compensate employees.
    (b) compensation expense of $5,500,000.
    (c) compensation expense of $18,700,000.
    (d) compensation expense of $3,740,000.

IFRS CONCEPTS AND APPLICATION

IFRS16-1 Where can authoritative IFRS be found related to dilutive securities, stock-based compensation, and earnings per share?

IFRS16-2 Briefly describe some of the similarities and differences between GAAP and IFRS with respect to the accounting for dilutive securities, stock-based compensation, and earnings per share.

IFRS16-3 Norman Co., a fast-growing golf equipment company, uses GAAP. It is considering the issuance of convertible bonds. The bonds mature in 10 years, have a face value of $400,000, and pay interest annually at a rate of 4%. The equity component of the bond issue has a fair value of $35,000. Greg Shark is curious as to the difference in accounting for these bonds if the company were to use IFRS. (a) Prepare the entry to record issuance of the bonds at par under GAAP. (b) Repeat the requirement for part (a), assuming application of IFRS to the bond issuance. (c) Which approach provides the better accounting? Explain.

IFRS16-4 Briefly discuss the convergence efforts that are under way by the IASB and FASB in the area of dilutive securities and earnings per share.

IFRS16-5 Explain how the conversion feature of convertible debt has a value (a) to the issuer and (b) to the purchaser.

IFRS16-6 What are the arguments for giving separate accounting recognition to the conversion feature of debentures?

IFRS16-7 Four years after issue, debentures with a face value of $1,000,000 and book value of $960,000 are tendered for conversion into 80,000 ordinary shares immediately after an interest payment date. At that time, the market price of the debentures is 104, and the ordinary shares are selling at $14 per share (par value $10). At date of issue, the company recorded Share Premium—Conversion Equity of $50,000. The company records the conversion as follows.

Bonds Payable	960,000	
Share Premium—Conversion Equity	50,000	
Share Capital—Ordinary		800,000
Share Premium—Ordinary		210,000

Discuss the propriety of this accounting treatment.

IFRS16-8 Cordero Corporation has an employee share-purchase plan which permits all full-time employees to purchase 10 ordinary shares on the third anniversary of their employment and an additional 15 shares on each subsequent anniversary date. The purchase price is set at the market price on the date purchased less a 10% discount. How is this discount accounted for by Cordero?

IFRS16-9 Archer Company issued $4,000,000 par value, 7% convertible bonds at 99 for cash. The net present value of the debt without the conversion feature is $3,800,000. Prepare the journal entry to record the issuance of the convertible bonds.

IFRS16-10 Petrenko Corporation has outstanding 2,000 $1,000 bonds, each convertible into 50 shares of $10 par value ordinary shares. The bonds are converted on December 31, 2014. The bonds payable has a carrying value of $1,950,000 and conversion equity of $20,000. Record the conversion using the book value method.

IFRS16-11 Angela Corporation issues 2,000 convertible bonds at January 1, 2013. The bonds have a 3-year life, and are issued at par with a face value of $1,000 per bond, giving total proceeds of $2,000,000. Interest is payable annually at 6%. Each bond is convertible into 250 ordinary shares (par value of $1). When the bonds are issued, the market rate of interest for similar debt without the conversion option is 8%.

Instructions

(a) Compute the liability and equity component of the convertible bond on January 1, 2013.
(b) Prepare the journal entry to record the issuance of the convertible bond on January 1, 2013.
(c) Prepare the journal entry to record the repurchase of the convertible bond for cash at January 1, 2016, its maturity date.

IFRS16-12 Assume the same information in IFRS16-11, except that Angela Corporation converts its convertible bonds on January 1, 2014.

Instructions

(a) Compute the carrying value of the bond payable on January 1, 2014.
(b) Prepare the journal entry to record the conversion on January 1, 2014.
(c) Assume that the bonds were repurchased on January 1, 2014, for $1,940,000 cash instead of being converted. The net present value of the liability component of the convertible bonds on January 1, 2014, is $1,900,000. Prepare the journal entry to record the repurchase on January 1, 2014.

IFRS16-13 Assume that Sarazan Company has a share-option plan for top management. Each share option represents the right to purchase a $1 par value ordinary share in the future at a price equal to the fair value of the shares at the date of the grant. Sarazan has 5,000 share options outstanding, which were granted at the beginning of 2014. The following data relate to the option grant.

Exercise price for options	$40
Market price at grant date (January 1, 2014)	$40
Fair value of options at grant date (January 1, 2014)	$6
Service period	5 years

Instructions

(a) Prepare the journal entry(ies) for the first year of the share-option plan.

(b) Prepare the journal entry(ies) for the first year of the plan assuming that, rather than options, 700 shares of restricted shares were granted at the beginning of 2014.

(c) Now assume that the market price of Sarazan shares on the grant date was $45 per share. Repeat the requirements for (a) and (b).

(d) Sarazan would like to implement an employee share-purchase plan for rank-and-file employees, but it would like to avoid recording expense related to this plan. Explain how employee share-purchase plans are recorded.

Professional Research

IFRS16-14 Richardson Company is contemplating the establishment of a share-based compensation plan to provide long-run incentives for its top management. However, members of the compensation committee of the board of directors have voiced some concerns about adopting these plans, based on news accounts related to a recent accounting standard in this area. They would like you to conduct some research on this recent standard so they can be better informed about the accounting for these plans.

Instructions

Access the IFRS authoritative literature at the IASB website (*http://eifrs.iasb.org/*). (Click on the IFRS tab and then register for free eIFRS access if necessary.) When you have accessed the documents, you can use the search tool in your Internet browser to respond to the following questions. (Provide paragraph citations.)

(a) Identify the authoritative literature that addresses the accounting for share-based payment compensation plans.

(b) Briefly discuss the objectives for the accounting for share-based compensation. What is the role of fair value measurement?

(c) The Richardson Company board is also considering an employee share-purchase plan, but the Board does not want to record expense related to the plan. What are the IFRS requirements for the accounting for an employee share-purchase plan?

International Financial Reporting Problem
Marks and Spencer plc

IFRS16-15 The financial statements of **Marks and Spencer plc (M&S)** are available at the book's companion website or can be accessed at *http://annualreport.marksandspencer.com/_assets/downloads/Marks-and-Spencer-Annual-report-and-financial-statements-2012.pdf*.

Instructions

Refer to M&S's financial statements and the accompanying notes to answer the following questions.

(a) Under M&S's share-based compensation plan, share options are granted annually to key managers and directors.
   (1) How many options were granted during 2012 under the plan?
   (2) How many options were exercisable at 31 March 2012?
   (3) How many options were exercised in 2012, and what was the average price of those exercised?
   (4) How many years from the grant date do the options expire?
   (5) To what accounts are the proceeds from these option exercises credited?
   (6) What was the number of outstanding options at 31 March 2012, and at what average exercise price?

(b) What number of diluted weighted-average shares outstanding was used by M&S in computing earnings per share for 2012 and 2011? What was M&S's diluted earnings per share in 2012 and 2011?

(c) What other share-based compensation plans does M&S have?

ANSWERS TO IFRS SELF-TEST QUESTIONS

1. c **2.** a **3.** b **4.** d **5.** d

> **Remember to check the book's companion website to find additional resources for this chapter.**

17 Investments

What to Do?

A few years ago, a bank reported an $87.3 million write-down on its mortgage-backed securities for the third quarter of 2008. However, the bank stated that it expected its actual losses to be only $44,000. The loss of $44,000 was equal to a modest loss on a condo foreclosure. The bank's regulator found "the accounting result absurd." And the bank regulator was right, as the bank, in the third quarter of 2009, raised its credit-loss estimate by **$263.1 million**, quite a difference from its original loss estimate of **$44,000**.

The discussion above highlights the challenge of valuing financial assets such as loans, derivatives, and other debt investments. The fundamental question that arose out of the example above and, more significantly, the recent financial crisis is: Should financial instruments be valued at amortized cost, fair value, or some other measure(s)? As one writer noted, the opinion that fair value accounting weakens financial and economic stability has persisted among many regulators and politicians. But some investors and others believe that fair value is the right answer because it is more transparent information. OK, so what to do?

Well, the FASB originally issued a proposal to account for just about all financial assets at fair value with gains and losses recorded in income (amortized cost would be disclosed for some financial assets). The FASB indicated this approach will provide the most relevant and transparent information about financial assets. In contrast, the IASB issued a new standard on financial assets (*IFRS 9*) that uses a mixed-attribute approach. Some of the financial assets are valued at amortized cost and others at fair value.

Interestingly, the European Union refused to consider adopting the requirements of *IFRS 9*, arguing that it contained **too much** fair value information. Nevertheless, the standard was issued and other countries that follow IFRS will have to implement the new standard in 2015. At the same time, as soon as the FASB issues its new standard, the IASB has indicated that it may revisit the valuation issue once again. Thus, the early reaction to *IFRS 9* indicates that, unfortunately, once again politics is raising its ugly head on an accounting issue. Some European regulators have suggested that the IASB's future funding may even depend on the IASB putting more limits on the use of fair value.

Now, let's go back to the FASB. Recently, the FASB dropped its plan to value loans at fair value and permits amortized cost accounting for these loans. This decision means banks will continue to value loans as they do today. This reversal is a big victory for the banking industry, which argued that the fair value approach would hurt lending and provide unnecessary volatility in their financial results. As a consequence, the FASB is moving much closer to the IASB's position. So after much discussion about what went wrong in the accounting for financial instruments during the financial crises, it looks like we are headed back to most of the same measurement rules that occurred before the financial collapse of 2008. We deem that unfortunate.

CONCEPTUAL FOCUS

> See the **Underlying Concepts** on pages 954, 955, and 957.
> Read the **Evolving Issues** on pages 968 and 975 for a discussion of the fair value controversy, and proposed classification and measurement model for financial instruments.

INTERNATIONAL FOCUS

> See the **International Perspectives** on pages 952, 953, 966, 968, 987, 989, and 995.
> Read the **IFRS Insights** on pages 1026–1039 for a discussion of:
> —Accounting for financial assets
> —Debt investments
> —Equity investments
> —Impairments

Sources: Adapted from Jonathan Weil, "Suing Wall Street Banks Never Looked So Shady," *http://www.bloomberg.com/* (February 28, 2010); and Rachel Sanderson and Jennifer Hughes, "Carried Forward," *Financial Times Online* (April 20, 2010).

PREVIEW OF CHAPTER	17

As indicated in the opening story, the accounting for financial assets is highly controversial. How to measure, recognize, and disclose this information is now being debated and discussed extensively. In this chapter, we address the accounting for debt and equity investments. Appendices to this chapter discuss the accounting for derivative instruments, variable-interest entities, and fair value disclosures. The content and organization of this chapter are as follows.

Investments

Investments in Debt Securities	Investments in Equity Securities	Additional Measurement Issues	Reclassifications and Transfers
• Debt investment classifications • Held-to-maturity securities • Available-for-sale securities • Trading securities	• Holdings of less than 20% • Holdings between 20% and 50% • Holdings of more than 50%	• Fair value option • Impairment of value	• Reclassification adjustments • Transfers between categories • Summary

INVESTMENTS IN DEBT SECURITIES

LEARNING OBJECTIVE 1

Identify the three categories of debt securities and describe the accounting and reporting treatment for each category.

Companies have different motivations for investing in securities issued by other companies.[1] **One motivation is to earn a high rate of return.** For example, companies like **Coca-Cola** and **PepsiCo** can receive interest revenue from a debt investment or dividend revenue from an equity investment. In addition, they can realize capital gains on both types of securities. **Another motivation for investing (in equity securities) is to secure certain operating or financing arrangements with another company.** For example, Coca-Cola and PepsiCo are able to exercise some control over bottler companies based on their significant (but not controlling) equity investments.

To provide useful information, companies account for investments based on the type of security (debt or equity) and their intent with respect to the investment. As indicated in Illustration 17-1, we organize our study of investments by type of security. Within this section, we explain the accounting for investments in debt. We address equity securities later in the chapter.

ILLUSTRATION 17-1
Summary of Investment Accounting Approaches

Type of Security	Management Intent	Valuation Approach
Debt	No plans to sell	Amortized cost
	Plan to sell	Fair value
Equity	Plan to sell	Fair value
	Exercise some control	Equity method

Debt securities represent a creditor relationship with another entity. Debt securities include U.S. government securities, municipal securities, corporate bonds, convertible debt, and commercial paper. Trade accounts receivable and loans receivable are not debt securities because they do not meet the definition of a security.

Debt Investment Classifications

Companies group investments in debt securities into three separate categories for accounting and reporting purposes:

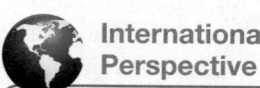

International Perspective

Under IFRS, debt investments are classified as either held-for-collection or trading.

- **Held-to-maturity:** Debt securities that the company has the positive intent and ability to hold to maturity.
- **Trading:** Debt securities bought and held primarily for sale in the near term to generate income on short-term price differences.
- **Available-for-sale:** Debt securities not classified as held-to-maturity or trading securities.

Illustration 17-2 identifies these categories, along with the accounting and reporting treatments required for each.

---

[1]A **security** is a share, participation, or other interest in property or in an enterprise of the issuer or an obligation of the issuer that has the following three characteristics. (1) It either is represented by an instrument issued in bearer or registered form or, if not represented by an instrument, is registered in books maintained to record transfers by or on behalf of the issuer. (2) It is commonly traded on securities exchanges or markets or, when represented by an instrument, is commonly recognized in any area in which it is issued or dealt in as a medium for investment. (3) It either is one of a class or series or by its terms is divisible into a class or series of shares, participations, interests, or obligations. **[1]**

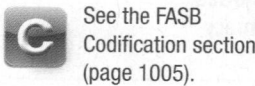

See the FASB Codification section (page 1005).

Category	Valuation	Unrealized Holding Gains or Losses	Other Income Effects
Held-to-maturity	Amortized cost	Not recognized	Interest when earned; gains and losses from sale.
Trading securities	Fair value	Recognized in net income	Interest when earned; gains and losses from sale.
Available-for-sale	Fair value	Recognized as other comprehensive income and as separate component of stockholders' equity	Interest when earned; gains and losses from sale.

ILLUSTRATION 17-2
Accounting for Debt
Securities by Category

International Perspective

> Under IFRS, held-for-collection debt investments are valued at amortized cost; all other investments are measured at fair value.

Amortized cost is the acquisition cost adjusted for the amortization of discount or premium, if appropriate. Fair value is the price that would be received to sell an asset or paid to transfer a liability in an orderly transaction between market participants at the measurement date. [2]

Held-to-Maturity Securities

Only debt securities can be classified as held-to-maturity. By definition, equity securities have no maturity date. A company like Starbucks should classify a debt security as **held-to-maturity** only if it has **both (1) the positive intent** and **(2) the ability to hold those securities to maturity**. It should not classify a debt security as held-to-maturity if it intends to hold the security for an indefinite period of time. Likewise, if Starbucks anticipates that a sale may be necessary due to changes in interest rates, foreign currency risk, liquidity needs, or other asset-liability management reasons, it should not classify the security as held-to-maturity.[2]

Companies account for held-to-maturity securities **at amortized cost**, not fair value. If management intends to hold certain investment securities to maturity and has no plans to sell them, fair values (selling prices) are not relevant for measuring and evaluating the cash flows associated with these securities. Finally, because companies do not adjust held-to-maturity securities to fair value, these securities do not increase the volatility of either reported earnings or reported capital as do trading securities and available-for-sale securities.

To illustrate the accounting for held-to-maturity debt securities, assume that Robinson Company purchased $100,000 of 8 percent bonds of Evermaster Corporation on January 1, 2013, at a discount, paying $92,278. The bonds mature January 1, 2018 and yield 10%. Interest is payable each July 1 and January 1. Robinson records the investment as follows.

2 LEARNING OBJECTIVE
Understand the procedures for discount and premium amortization on bond investments.

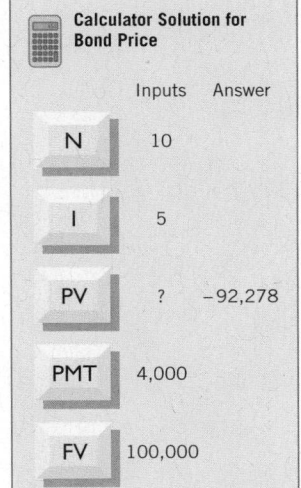

Calculator Solution for Bond Price

	Inputs	Answer
N	10	
I	5	
PV	?	–92,278
PMT	4,000	
FV	100,000	

January 1, 2013

Debt Investments	92,278	
Cash		92,278

[2]The FASB defines situations where, even though a company sells a security before maturity, it has constructively held the security to maturity, and thus does not violate the held-to-maturity requirement. These include selling a security close enough to maturity (such as three months) so that interest rate risk is no longer an important pricing factor.

However, companies must be extremely careful with debt securities held to maturity. If a company prematurely sells a debt security in this category, the sale may "taint" the entire held-to-maturity portfolio. That is, a management's statement regarding "intent" is no longer credible. Therefore, the company may have to reclassify the securities. This could lead to unfortunate consequences. An interesting by-product of this situation is that companies that wish to retire their debt securities early are finding it difficult to do so. The holder will not sell because the securities are classified as held-to-maturity.

Robinson uses a Debt Investments account to indicate the type of debt security purchased.[3]

As indicated in Chapter 14, companies must amortize premium or discount using the **effective-interest method** unless some other method—such as the straight-line method—yields a similar result. They apply the effective-interest method to bond investments in a way similar to that for bonds payable. To compute interest revenue, companies compute the effective-interest rate or yield at the time of investment and apply that rate to the beginning carrying amount (book value) for each interest period. The investment carrying amount is increased by the amortized discount or decreased by the amortized premium in each period.

Illustration 17-3 shows the effect of the discount amortization on the interest revenue that Robinson records each period for its investment in Evermaster bonds.

Underlying Concepts

The use of some simpler method that yields results similar to the effective-interest method is an application of the materiality concept.

ILLUSTRATION 17-3
Schedule of Interest
Revenue and Bond
Discount Amortization—
Effective-Interest Method

		8% Bonds Purchased to Yield 10%		
Date	Cash Received	Interest Revenue	Bond Discount Amortization	Carrying Amount of Bonds
1/1/13				$ 92,278
7/1/13	$ 4,000[a]	$ 4,614[b]	$ 614[c]	92,892[d]
1/1/14	4,000	4,645	645	93,537
7/1/14	4,000	4,677	677	94,214
1/1/15	4,000	4,711	711	94,925
7/1/15	4,000	4,746	746	95,671
1/1/16	4,000	4,783	783	96,454
7/1/16	4,000	4,823	823	97,277
1/1/17	4,000	4,864	864	98,141
7/1/17	4,000	4,907	907	99,048
1/1/18	4,000	4,952	952	100,000
	$40,000	$47,722	$7,722	

[a]$4,000 = $100,000 \times .08 \times {}^6/_{12}$
[b]$4,614 = $92,278 \times .10 \times {}^6/_{12}$
[c]$614 = $4,614 - $4,000$
[d]$92,892 = $92,278 + 614

Robinson records the receipt of the first semiannual interest payment on July 1, 2013 (using the data in Illustration 17-3), as follows.

July 1, 2013

Cash	4,000	
Debt Investments	614	
Interest Revenue		4,614

Because Robinson is on a calendar-year basis, it accrues interest and amortizes the discount at December 31, 2013, as follows.

December 31, 2013

Interest Receivable	4,000	
Debt Investments	645	
Interest Revenue		4,645

Again, Illustration 17-3 shows the interest and amortization amounts.

[3]Companies generally record investments acquired at par, at a discount, or at a premium in the accounts at cost, including brokerage and other fees but excluding the accrued interest. They generally do not record investments at maturity value. The use of a separate discount or premium account as a valuation account is acceptable procedure for investments, but in practice companies do not widely use it.

Robinson reports its investment in Evermaster bonds in its December 31, 2013, financial statements, as follows.

Balance Sheet	
Current assets	
Interest receivable	$ 4,000
Long-term investments	
Debt investments (held-to-maturity)	$93,537
Income Statement	
Other revenues and gains	
Interest revenue	$ 9,259

ILLUSTRATION 17-4
Reporting of Held-to-Maturity Securities

Sometimes, a company sells a held-to-maturity debt security so close to its maturity date that a change in the market interest rate would not significantly affect the security's fair value. Such a sale may be considered a sale at maturity and would not call into question the company's original intent to hold the investment to maturity. Let's assume, as an example, that Robinson Company sells its investment in Evermaster bonds on November 1, 2017, at $99^3/4$ plus accrued interest. The discount amortization from July 1, 2017, to November 1, 2017, is $635 ($4/6 \times 952). Robinson records this discount amortization as follows.

November 1, 2017

Debt Investments	635	
Interest Revenue		635

Illustration 17-5 shows the computation of the realized gain on the sale.

Selling price of bonds (exclusive of accrued interest)		$99,750
Less: Book value of bonds on November 1, 2017:		
Amortized cost, July 1, 2017	$99,048	
Add: Discount amortized for the period July 1, 2017, to November 1, 2017	635	99,683
Gain on sale of bonds		$ 67

ILLUSTRATION 17-5
Computation of Gain on Sale of Bonds

Robinson records the sale of the bonds as:

November 1, 2017

Cash	102,417	
Interest Revenue (4/6 × $4,000)		2,667
Debt Investments		99,683
Gain on Sale of Investments		67

The credit to Interest Revenue represents accrued interest for four months, for which the purchaser pays cash. The debit to Cash represents the selling price of the bonds plus accrued interest ($99,750 + $2,667$). The credit to Debt Investments represents the book value of the bonds on the date of sale. The credit to Gain on Sale of Investments represents the excess of the selling price over the book value of the bonds.

Available-for-Sale Securities

Companies like Amazon.com report **available-for-sale** securities at fair value. It records the unrealized gains and losses related to changes in the fair value of available-for-sale debt securities in an unrealized holding gain or loss account. Amazon adds (subtracts) this amount to other comprehensive income for the

Underlying Concepts 🔍

Recognizing unrealized gains and losses is an application of the concept of comprehensive income.

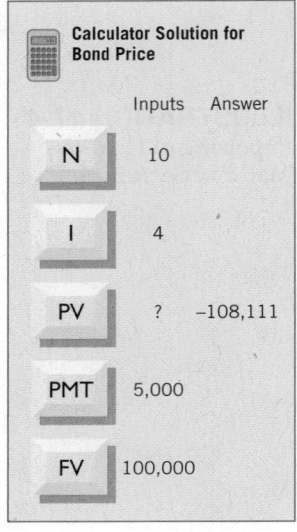

Calculator Solution for Bond Price

	Inputs	Answer
N	10	
I	4	
PV	?	−108,111
PMT	5,000	
FV	100,000	

period. Other comprehensive income is then added to (subtracted from) accumulated other comprehensive income, which is shown as a separate component of stockholders' equity until realized. Thus, **companies report available-for-sale securities at fair value on the balance sheet but do not report changes in fair value as part of net income until after selling the security**. This approach reduces the volatility of net income.

Example: Single Security

To illustrate the accounting for available-for-sale securities, assume that Graff Corporation purchases $100,000, 10 percent, five-year bonds on January 1, 2013, with interest payable on July 1 and January 1. The bonds sell for $108,111, which results in a bond premium of $8,111 and an effective-interest rate of 8 percent.

Graff records the purchase of the bonds as follows.

January 1, 2013

Debt Investments	108,111	
Cash		108,111

Illustration 17-6 discloses the effect of the premium amortization on the interest revenue Graff records each period using the effective-interest method.

ILLUSTRATION 17-6
Schedule of Interest Revenue and Bond Premium Amortization— Effective-Interest Method

		10% BONDS PURCHASED TO YIELD 8%		
Date	Cash Received	Interest Revenue	Bond Premium Amortization	Carrying Amount of Bonds
1/1/13				$108,111
7/1/13	$ 5,000[a]	$ 4,324[b]	$ 676[c]	107,435[d]
1/1/14	5,000	4,297	703	106,732
7/1/14	5,000	4,269	731	106,001
1/1/15	5,000	4,240	760	105,241
7/1/15	5,000	4,210	790	104,451
1/1/16	5,000	4,178	822	103,629
7/1/16	5,000	4,145	855	102,774
1/1/17	5,000	4,111	889	101,885
7/1/17	5,000	4,075	925	100,960
1/1/18	5,000	4,040	960	100,000
	$50,000	$41,889	$8,111	

[a]$5,000 = $100,000 × .10 × 6/12
[b]$4,324 = $108,111 × .08 × 6/12
[c]$676 = $5,000 − $4,324
[d]$107,435 = $108,111 − $676

The entry to record interest revenue on July 1, 2013, is as follows.

July 1, 2013

Cash	5,000	
Debt Investments		676
Interest Revenue		4,324

At December 31, 2013, Graff makes the following entry to recognize interest revenue.

December 31, 2013

Interest Receivable	5,000	
Debt Investments		703
Interest Revenue		4,297

As a result, Graff reports revenue for 2013 of $8,621 ($4,324 + $4,297).

To apply the fair value method to these debt investments, assume that at year-end the fair value of the bonds is $105,000 and that the carrying amount of the investments is $106,732. Comparing this fair value with the carrying amount (amortized cost) of the bonds at December 31, 2013, Graff recognizes an unrealized holding loss of $1,732 ($106,732 − $105,000). It reports this loss as other comprehensive income. Graff makes the following entry.

December 31, 2013

Unrealized Holding Gain or Loss—Equity	1,732	
Fair Value Adjustment (available-for-sale)		1,732

Graff uses a valuation account instead of crediting the Debt Investments account. The use of the **Fair Value Adjustment** (available-for-sale) account enables the company to maintain a record of its amortized cost. Because the adjustment account has a credit balance in this case, Graff subtracts it from the balance of the Debt Investments account to determine fair value. Graff reports this fair value amount on the balance sheet. At each reporting date, Graff reports the bonds at fair value with an adjustment to the Unrealized Holding Gain or Loss—Equity account.

Underlying Concepts 🔍

Companies report some debt securities at fair value not only because the information is relevant but also because it is representationally faithful.

Example: Portfolio of Securities

To illustrate the accounting for a portfolio of securities, assume that Webb Corporation has two debt securities classified as available-for-sale. Illustration 17-7 identifies the amortized cost, fair value, and the amount of the unrealized gain or loss.

ILLUSTRATION 17-7
Computation of Fair Value Adjustment— Available-for-Sale Securities (2014)

AVAILABLE-FOR-SALE DEBT SECURITY PORTFOLIO DECEMBER 31, 2014			
Investments	Amortized Cost	Fair Value	Unrealized Gain (Loss)
Watson Corporation 8% bonds	$ 93,537	$103,600	$ 10,063
Anacomp Corporation 10% bonds	200,000	180,400	(19,600)
Total of portfolio	$293,537	$284,000	(9,537)
Previous fair value adjustment balance			–0–
Fair value adjustment—Cr.			$ (9,537)

The fair value of Webb's available-for-sale portfolio totals $284,000. The gross unrealized gains are $10,063, and the gross unrealized losses are $19,600, resulting in a net unrealized loss of $9,537. That is, the fair value of available-for-sale securities is $9,537 lower than its amortized cost. Webb makes an adjusting entry to a valuation allowance to record the decrease in value and to record the loss as follows.

December 31, 2014

Unrealized Holding Gain or Loss—Equity	9,537	
Fair Value Adjustment (available-for-sale)		9,537

Webb reports the unrealized holding loss of $9,537 as other comprehensive income and a reduction of stockholders' equity. Recall that companies exclude from net income any unrealized holding gains and losses related to available-for-sale securities.

Sale of Available-for-Sale Securities

If a company sells bonds carried as investments in available-for-sale securities before the maturity date, it must make entries to remove from the Debt Investments account the amortized cost of bonds sold. To illustrate, assume that Webb Corporation sold the Watson bonds (from Illustration 17-7) on July 1, 2015, for $90,000, at which time it had an amortized cost of $94,214. Illustration 17-8 (on page 958) shows the computation of the realized loss.

ILLUSTRATION 17-8
Computation of Loss on
Sale of Bonds

Amortized cost (Watson bonds)	$94,214
Less: Selling price of bonds	90,000
Loss on sale of bonds	$ 4,214

Webb records the sale of the Watson bonds as follows.

July 1, 2015

Cash	90,000	
Loss on Sale of Investments	4,214	
Debt Investments		94,214

Webb reports this realized loss in the "Other expenses and losses" section of the income statement.[4] Assuming no other purchases and sales of bonds in 2015, Webb on December 31, 2015, prepares the information shown in Illustration 17-9.

ILLUSTRATION 17-9
Computation of Fair
Value Adjustment—
Available-for-Sale (2015)

AVAILABLE-FOR-SALE DEBT SECURITY PORTFOLIO DECEMBER 31, 2015			
Investments	Amortized Cost	Fair Value	Unrealized Gain (Loss)
Anacomp Corporation 10% bonds (total portfolio)	$200,000	$195,000	$(5,000)
Previous fair value adjustment balance—Cr.			(9,537)
Fair value adjustment—Dr.			$ 4,537

Webb has an unrealized holding loss of $5,000. However, the Fair Value Adjustment (available-for-sale) account already has a credit balance of $9,537. To reduce the adjustment account balance to $5,000, Webb debits it for $4,537, as follows.

December 31, 2015

Fair Value Adjustment (available-for-sale)	4,537	
Unrealized Holding Gain or Loss—Equity		4,537

Financial Statement Presentation

Webb's December 31, 2015, balance sheet and the 2015 income statement include the following items and amounts (the Anacomp bonds are long-term investments but are not intended to be held to maturity).

ILLUSTRATION 17-10
Reporting of Available-
for-Sale Securities

Balance Sheet	
Current assets	
Interest receivable	$ xxx
Investments	
Debt investments (available-for-sale)	$195,000
Stockholders' equity	
Accumulated other comprehensive loss	$ 5,000
Income Statement	
Other revenues and gains	
Interest revenue	$ xxx
Other expenses and losses	
Loss on sale of investments	$ 4,214

[4]On the date of sale, any unrealized gains or losses on the sold security is not adjusted in accumulated other comprehensive income. This adjustment occurs at year-end when the portfolio is evaluated for fair value adjustment.

Some favor including the unrealized holding gain or loss in net income rather than showing it as other comprehensive income.[5] However, some companies, particularly financial institutions, note that recognizing gains and losses on assets, but not liabilities, introduces substantial volatility in net income. They argue that hedges often exist between assets and liabilities so that gains in assets are offset by losses in liabilities, and vice versa. In short, to recognize gains and losses only on the asset side is unfair and not representative of the economic activities of the company.

This argument convinced the FASB. As a result, companies **do not include in net income** these unrealized gains and losses. **[3]** However, even this approach solves only some of the problems because **volatility of capital** still results. This is of concern to financial institutions because regulators restrict financial institutions' operations based on their level of capital. However, companies can still manage their net income by engaging in gains trading (i.e., selling the winners and holding the losers).

What do the numbers mean?   WHAT IS FAIR VALUE?

In the fall of 2000, Wall Street brokerage firm **Morgan Stanley** told investors that rumors of big losses in its bond portfolio were "greatly exaggerated." As it turns out, Morgan Stanley also was exaggerating.

As a result, the SEC accused Morgan Stanley of violating securities laws by overstating the value of certain bonds by $75 million. The SEC said the overvaluations stemmed more from wishful thinking than reality, which violated generally accepted accounting principles. "In effect, Morgan Stanley valued its positions at the price at which it thought a willing buyer and seller should enter into an exchange, rather than at a price at which a willing buyer and a willing seller would enter into a current exchange," the SEC wrote.

Especially egregious, stated one accounting expert, were the SEC's findings that Morgan Stanley in some instances used its own more optimistic assumptions as a substitute for external pricing sources. "What that is saying is: 'Fair value is what you want the value to be. Pick a number . . .' That's especially troublesome."

As indicated in the opening story, both the FASB and the IASB are assessing what is fair and what isn't when it comes to assigning valuations. Concerns over the issue caught fire after the collapses of **Enron Corp.** and other energy traders that abused the wide discretion given them under fair value accounting. Investors have expressed similar worries about some financial companies, which use internal—and subjectively designed—mathematical models to come up with valuations when market quotes aren't available. Similar concerns have been raised when companies revalue their debt obligations when they apply the fair value option.

Sources: Adapted from Susanne Craig and Jonathan Weil, "SEC Targets Morgan Stanley Values," *Wall Street Journal* (November 8, 2004), p. C3; Floyd Norris, "Distortions in Baffling Financial Statements," *The New York Times* (November 10, 2011); and Marie Leone, "The Fair Value Deadbeat Debate Returns," *CFO.com* (June 25, 2009).

Trading Securities

Companies hold **trading securities** with the intention of selling them in a short period of time. "Trading" in this context means frequent buying and selling. Companies thus use trading securities to generate profits from short-term differences in price. Companies generally hold these securities for less than three months, some for merely days or hours.

Companies report trading securities at fair value, with unrealized holding gains and losses reported as part of net income. Similar to held-to-maturity or available-for-sale investments, companies are required to amortize any discount or premium. A holding gain or loss is the net change in the fair value of a security from one period to another, exclusive of dividend or interest revenue recognized but not received. In short, the FASB says to adjust the trading securities to fair value, at each reporting date. In addition, companies report the change in value as part of net income, not other comprehensive income.

---

[5]In Chapter 4, we discussed the concept of, and reporting for, other comprehensive income.

To illustrate, assume that on December 31, 2014, Western Publishing Corporation determined its trading securities portfolio to be as shown in Illustration 17-11. (Assume that 2014 is the first year that Western Publishing held trading securities.) At the date of acquisition, Western Publishing recorded these trading securities at cost, including brokerage commissions and taxes, in the account entitled Debt Investments. This is the first valuation of this recently purchased portfolio.

ILLUSTRATION 17-11
Computation of Fair Value Adjustment—Trading Securities Portfolio (2014)

TRADING DEBT SECURITY PORTFOLIO DECEMBER 31, 2014			
Investments	Amortized Cost	Fair Value	Unrealized Gain (Loss)
Burlington Northern 6% bonds	$ 43,860	$ 51,500	$ 7,640
GM Corporation 7% bonds	184,230	175,200	(9,030)
Time Warner 8% bonds	86,360	91,500	5,140
Total of portfolio	$314,450	$318,200	3,750
Previous fair value adjustment balance			–0–
Fair value adjustment—Dr.			$ 3,750

The total cost of Western Publishing's trading portfolio is $314,450. The gross unrealized gains are $12,780 ($7,640 + $5,140), and the gross unrealized losses are $9,030, resulting in a net unrealized gain of $3,750. The fair value of trading securities is $3,750 greater than its cost.

At December 31, Western Publishing makes an adjusting entry to a valuation allowance, referred to as Fair Value Adjustment (trading), to record the increase in value and to record the unrealized holding gain.

December 31, 2014

Fair Value Adjustment (trading)	3,750	
Unrealized Holding Gain or Loss—Income		3,750

Because the Fair Value Adjustment account balance is a debit, Western Publishing adds it to the cost of the Debt Investments account to arrive at a fair value for the trading securities. Western Publishing reports this fair value amount on the balance sheet.

As with other debt investments, when a trading investment is sold, the Debt Investments account is reduced by the amount of the amortized cost of the bonds. Any realized gain or loss is recorded in the "Other expenses and losses" section of the income statement. The Fair Value Adjustment account is then adjusted at year-end for the unrealized gains or losses on the remaining securities in the trading investment portfolio.

When securities are actively traded, the FASB believes that the investments should be reported at fair value on the balance sheet. In addition, changes in fair value (unrealized gains and losses) should be reported in income. Such reporting on trading securities provides more relevant information to existing and prospective stockholders.

INVESTMENTS IN EQUITY SECURITIES

LEARNING OBJECTIVE 3

Identify the categories of equity securities and describe the accounting and reporting treatment for each category.

Equity securities represent ownership interests such as common, preferred, or other capital stock. They also include rights to acquire or dispose of ownership interests at an agreed-upon or determinable price, such as in warrants, rights, and call or put options. Companies do not treat convertible debt securities as equity securities. Nor do they treat as equity securities redeemable preferred stock (which must be redeemed for common stock). The cost of equity securities includes the purchase price of the security plus broker's commissions and other fees incidental to the purchase.

The degree to which one corporation (**investor**) acquires an interest in the common stock of another corporation (**investee**) generally determines the accounting treatment for the investment subsequent to acquisition. The classification of such investments depends on the percentage of the investee voting stock that is held by the investor:

1. Holdings of less than 20 percent (**fair value method**)—investor has passive interest.
2. Holdings between 20 percent and 50 percent (**equity method**)—investor has significant influence.
3. Holdings of more than 50 percent (**consolidated statements**)—investor has controlling interest.

Illustration 17-12 lists these levels of interest or influence and the corresponding valuation and reporting method that companies must apply to the investment.

Percentage of Ownership	0% ←→ 20% ←→ 50% ←→ 100%		
Level of Influence	Little or None	Significant	Control
Valuation Method	Fair Value Method	Equity Method	Consolidation

ILLUSTRATION 17-12
Levels of Influence Determine Accounting Methods

The accounting and reporting for equity securities therefore depend on the level of influence and the type of security involved, as shown in Illustration 17-13.

ILLUSTRATION 17-13
Accounting and Reporting for Equity Securities by Category

Category	Valuation	Unrealized Holding Gains or Losses	Other Income Effects
Holdings less than 20%			
1. Available-for-sale	Fair value	Recognized in "Other comprehensive income" and as separate component of stockholders' equity	Dividends declared; gains and losses from sale.
2. Trading	Fair value	Recognized in net income	Dividends declared; gains and losses from sale.
Holdings between 20% and 50%	Equity	Not recognized	Proportionate share of investee's net income.
Holdings more than 50%	Consolidation	Not recognized	Not applicable.

Holdings of Less Than 20%

When an investor has an interest of less than 20 percent, it is presumed that the investor has little or no influence over the investee. In such cases, if market prices are available subsequent to acquisition, the company values and reports the investment using the **fair value method**.[6] The fair value method requires that companies classify equity securities at acquisition as **available-for-sale securities** or **trading securities**. Because equity securities have no maturity date, companies cannot classify them as held-to-maturity.

[6]If an equity investment is not publicly traded, a company values the investment and reports it at cost in periods subsequent to acquisition. This approach is often referred to as the cost method. Companies recognize dividends when received. They value the portfolio and report it at acquisition cost. Companies only recognize gains or losses after selling the securities.

Available-for-Sale Securities

Upon acquisition, companies record available-for-sale securities at cost.[7] To illustrate, assume that on November 3, 2014, Republic Corporation purchased common stock of three companies, each investment representing less than a 20 percent interest.

	Cost
Northwest Industries, Inc.	$259,700
Campbell Soup Co.	317,500
St. Regis Pulp Co.	141,350
Total cost	$718,550

Republic records these investments as follows.

November 3, 2014

Equity Investments	718,550	
Cash		718,550

On December 6, 2014, Republic receives a cash dividend of $4,200 on its investment in the common stock of Campbell Soup Co. It records the cash dividend as follows.

December 6, 2014

Cash	4,200	
Dividend Revenue		4,200

All three of the investee companies reported net income for the year, but only Campbell Soup declared and paid a dividend to Republic. But, recall that when an investor owns less than 20 percent of the common stock of another corporation, it is presumed that the investor has relatively little influence on the investee. As a result, **net income of the investee is not a proper basis for recognizing income from the investment by the investor**. Why? Because the increased net assets resulting from profitable operations may be permanently retained for use in the investee's business. Therefore, **the investor recognizes net income only when the investee declares cash dividends**.

At December 31, 2014, Republic's available-for-sale equity security portfolio has the cost and fair value shown in Illustration 17-14.

ILLUSTRATION 17-14
Computation of Fair Value Adjustment—Available-for-Sale Equity Security Portfolio (2014)

AVAILABLE-FOR-SALE EQUITY SECURITY PORTFOLIO DECEMBER 31, 2014			
Investments	Cost	Fair Value	Unrealized Gain (Loss)
Northwest Industries, Inc.	$259,700	$275,000	$ 15,300
Campbell Soup Co.	317,500	304,000	(13,500)
St. Regis Pulp Co.	141,350	104,000	(37,350)
Total of portfolio	$718,550	$683,000	(35,550)
Previous fair value adjustment balance			–0–
Fair value adjustment—Cr.			$(35,550)

---

[7]Companies should record equity securities acquired in **exchange for noncash consideration** (property or services) at (1) the fair value of the consideration given, or (2) the fair value of the security received, whichever is more clearly determinable. Accounting for numerous purchases of securities requires the preservation of information regarding the cost of individual purchases, as well as the dates of purchases and sales. If specific identification is not possible, companies may use average-cost for multiple purchases of the same class of security. The **first-in, first-out method (FIFO)** of assigning costs to investments at the time of sale is also acceptable and normally employed.

For Republic's available-for-sale equity securities portfolio, the gross unrealized gains are $15,300, and the gross unrealized losses are $50,850 ($13,500 + $37,350), resulting in a net unrealized loss of $35,550. The fair value of the available-for-sale securities portfolio is below cost by $35,550.

As with available-for-sale **debt** securities, Republic records the net unrealized gains and losses related to changes in the fair value of available-for-sale **equity** securities in an Unrealized Holding Gain or Loss—Equity account. Republic reports this amount as a **part of other comprehensive income and as a component of other accumulated comprehensive income (reported in stockholders' equity) until realized**. In this case, Republic prepares an adjusting entry debiting the Unrealized Holding Gain or Loss—Equity account and crediting the Fair Value Adjustment account to record the decrease in fair value and to record the loss as follows.

December 31, 2014

Unrealized Holding Gain or Loss—Equity	35,550	
Fair Value Adjustment (available-for-sale)		35,550

On January 23, 2015, Republic sold all of its Northwest Industries, Inc. common stock receiving net proceeds of $287,220. Illustration 17-15 shows the computation of the realized gain on the sale.

Net proceeds from sale	$287,220
Cost of Northwest shares	259,700
Gain on sale of stock	$ 27,520

ILLUSTRATION 17-15
Computation of Gain on Sale of Stock

Republic records the sale as follows.

January 23, 2015

Cash	287,220	
Equity Investments		259,700
Gain on Sale of Investments		27,520

In addition, assume that on February 10, 2015, Republic purchased 20,000 shares of Continental Trucking at a market price of $12.75 per share plus brokerage commissions of $1,850 (total cost, $256,850).

Illustration 17-16 lists Republic's portfolio of available-for-sale securities, as of December 31, 2015.

ILLUSTRATION 17-16
Computation of Fair Value Adjustment— Available-for-Sale Equity Security Portfolio (2015)

AVAILABLE-FOR-SALE EQUITY SECURITY PORTFOLIO DECEMBER 31, 2015			
Investments	Cost	Fair Value	Unrealized Gain (Loss)
Continental Trucking	$256,850	$278,350	$ 21,500
Campbell Soup Co.	317,500	362,550	45,050
St. Regis Pulp Co.	141,350	139,050	(2,300)
Total of portfolio	$715,700	$779,950	64,250
Previous fair value adjustment balance—Cr.			(35,550)
Fair value adjustment—Dr.			$ 99,800

At December 31, 2015, the fair value of Republic's available-for-sale equity securities portfolio exceeds cost by $64,250 (unrealized gain). The Fair Value Adjustment account had a credit balance of $35,550 at December 31, 2015. To adjust its December 31, 2015, available-for-sale portfolio to fair value, the company debits the Fair Value Adjustment account for $99,800 ($35,550 + $64,250). Republic records this adjustment as follows.

December 31, 2015

Fair Value Adjustment (available-for-sale)	99,800	
Unrealized Holding Gain or Loss—Equity		99,800

Trading Securities

The accounting entries to record trading equity securities are the same as for available-for-sale equity securities, except for recording the unrealized holding gain or loss. For trading equity securities, companies **report the unrealized holding gain or loss as part of net income**. Thus, the account titled Unrealized Holding Gain or Loss—Income is used.

What do the numbers mean?   MORE DISCLOSURE, PLEASE

How to account for investment securities is a particularly sensitive area, given the large amounts of equity investments involved. And presently companies report investments in equity securities at cost, equity, fair value, and full consolidation, depending on the circumstances. As a recent SEC study noted, "there are so many different accounting treatments for investments that it raises the question of whether they are all needed."

Presented in the right-hand column is an estimate of the percentage of companies on the major exchanges that have investments in the equity of other entities.

As the table indicates, many companies have equity investments of some type. These investments can be substantial. For example, the total amount of equity-method investments appearing on company balance sheets is approximately

Investments in the Equity of Other Companies	
Categorized by Accounting Treatment	Percent of Companies
Presenting consolidated financial statements	91.1%
Reporting equity method investments	23.5
Reporting cost method investments*	17.4
Reporting available-for-sale investments	37.4
Reporting trading investments	6.2

*If the equity investments are not publicly traded, the company often accounts for the investment under the cost method. Changes in value are therefore not recognized unless there is impairment.

$403 billion, and the amount shown in the income statements in any one year for all companies is approximately $38 billion.

Source: "Report and Recommendations Pursuant to Section 401(c) of the Sarbanes-Oxley Act of 2002 on Arrangements with Off-Balance Sheet Implications, Special Purpose Entities, and Transparency of Filings by Issuers," United States Securities and Exchange Commission—Office of Chief Accountant, Office of Economic Analyses, Division of Corporation Finance (June 2005), pp. 36–39.

Holdings Between 20% and 50%

LEARNING OBJECTIVE 4

Explain the equity method of accounting and compare it to the fair value method for equity securities.

An investor corporation may hold an interest of less than 50 percent in an investee corporation and thus not possess legal control. However, an investment in voting stock of less than 50 percent can still give the investor the ability to exercise significant influence over the operating and financial policies of the investee company. **[4]** **Significant influence** may be indicated in several ways. Examples include representation on the board of directors, participation in policy-making processes, material intercompany transactions, interchange of managerial personnel, or technological dependency.

Another important consideration is the extent of ownership by an investor in relation to the concentration of other shareholdings. To achieve a reasonable degree of uniformity in application of the "significant influence" criterion, the profession concluded that an investment (direct or indirect) of 20 percent or more of the voting stock of an investee should lead to a presumption that in the absence of evidence to the contrary, an investor has the ability to exercise significant influence over an investee.[8]

[8]Cases in which an investment of 20 percent or more might not enable an investor to exercise significant influence include (1) the investee opposes the investor's acquisition of its stock, (2) the investor and investee sign an agreement under which the investor surrenders significant shareholder rights, (3) the investor's ownership share does not result in "significant influence" because majority ownership of the investee is concentrated among a small group of shareholders who operate the investee without regard to the views of the investor, and (4) the investor tries and fails to obtain representation on the investee's board of directors. **[5]**

In instances of "significant influence" (generally an investment of 20 percent or more), the investor must account for the investment using the **equity method**.

Equity Method

Under the equity method, the investor and the investee acknowledge a substantive economic relationship. The company originally records the investment at the cost of the shares acquired but subsequently adjusts the amount each period for changes in the investee's net assets. That is, **the investor's proportionate share of the earnings (losses) of the investee periodically increases (decreases) the investment's carrying amount. All cash dividends received by the investor from the investee also decrease the investment's carrying amount.** The equity method recognizes that investee's earnings increase investee's net assets, and that investee's losses and dividends decrease these net assets.

To illustrate the equity method and compare it with the fair value method, assume that Maxi Company purchases a 20 percent interest in Mini Company. To apply the fair value method in this example, assume that Maxi does not have the ability to exercise significant influence, and classifies the securities as available-for-sale. Where this example applies the equity method, assume that the 20 percent interest permits Maxi to exercise significant influence. Illustration 17-17 shows the entries.

ILLUSTRATION 17-17
Comparison of Fair Value Method and Equity Method

ENTRIES BY MAXI COMPANY			
Fair Value Method		Equity Method	
On January 2, 2014, Maxi Company acquired 48,000 shares (20% of Mini Company common stock) at a cost of $10 a share.			
Equity Investments	480,000	Equity Investments	480,000
Cash	480,000	Cash	480,000
For the year 2014, Mini Company reported net income of $200,000; Maxi Company's share is 20%, or $40,000.			
No entry		Equity Investments	40,000
		Investment Income	40,000
At December 31, 2014, the 48,000 shares of Mini Company have a fair value (market price) of $12 a share, or $576,000.			
Fair Value Adjustment		No entry	
(available-for-sale)	96,000		
Unrealized Holding Gain			
or Loss—Equity	96,000		
On January 28, 2015, Mini Company announced and paid a cash dividend of $100,000; Maxi Company received 20%, or $20,000.			
Cash	20,000	Cash	20,000
Dividend Revenue	20,000	Equity Investments	20,000
For the year 2015, Mini reported a net loss of $50,000; Maxi Company's share is 20%, or $10,000.			
No entry		Investment Loss	10,000
		Equity Investments	10,000
At December 31, 2015, the Mini Company 48,000 shares have a fair value (market price) of $11 a share, or $528,000.			
Unrealized Holding Gain			
or Loss—Equity	48,000	No entry	
Fair Value Adjustment			
(available-for-sale)	48,000		

Note that under the fair value method, Maxi reports as revenue only the cash dividends received from Mini. **The earning of net income by Mini (the investee) is not** considered a proper basis for recognition of income from the investment by Maxi (the investor). Why? Mini may permanently retain in the business any increased net assets resulting from its profitable operation. Therefore, Maxi only recognizes revenue when it receives dividends from Mini.

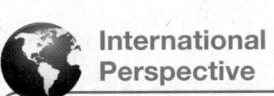

International Perspective

IFRS has similar accounting rules for significant influence equity investments.

Under the equity method, Maxi reports as revenue its share of the net income reported by Mini. Maxi records the cash dividends received from Mini as a decrease in the investment carrying value. As a result, Maxi records its share of the net income of Mini in the year when it is recognized. With significant influence, Maxi can ensure that Mini will pay dividends, if desired, on any net asset increases resulting from net income. To wait until receiving a dividend ignores the fact that Maxi is better off if the investee has earned income.

Using dividends as a basis for recognizing income poses an additional problem. For example, assume that the investee reports a net loss. However, the investor exerts influence to force a dividend payment from the investee. In this case, the investor reports income, even though the investee is experiencing a loss. **In other words, using dividends as a basis for recognizing income fails to report properly the economics of the situation.**

For some companies, equity accounting can be a real pain to the bottom line. For example, Amazon.com, the pioneer of Internet retailing, at one time struggled to turn a profit. Furthermore, some of Amazon's equity investments had resulted in Amazon's earnings performance going from bad to worse. At one time, Amazon disclosed equity stakes in such companies as Altera International, Basis Technology, Drugstore.com, and Eziba.com. These equity investees reported losses that made Amazon's already bad bottom line even worse, accounting for up to 22 percent of its reported loss in one year alone.

Investee Losses Exceed Carrying Amount. If an investor's share of the investee's losses exceeds the carrying amount of the investment, should the investor recognize additional losses? Ordinarily, the investor should discontinue applying the equity method and not recognize additional losses.

If the investor's potential loss is not limited to the amount of its original investment (by guarantee of the investee's obligations or other commitment to provide further financial support) or if imminent return to profitable operations by the investee appears to be assured, the investor should recognize additional losses. **[6]**

Holdings of More Than 50%

When one corporation acquires a voting interest of more than 50 percent in another corporation, it is said to have a controlling interest. In such a relationship, the investor corporation is referred to as the parent and the investee corporation as the subsidiary.

Companies present the investment in the common stock of the subsidiary as a long-term investment on the separate financial statements of the parent.

International Perspective

In contrast to U.S. firms, financial statements of non-U.S. companies often include both consolidated (group) statements and parent company financial statements.

When the parent treats the investment as a subsidiary, the parent generally prepares consolidated financial statements. Consolidated financial statements treat the parent and subsidiary corporations as a single economic entity. (Advanced accounting courses extensively discuss the subject of when and how to prepare consolidated financial statements.) Whether or not consolidated financial statements are prepared, the parent company generally accounts for the investment in the subsidiary **using the equity method** as explained in the previous section of this chapter.

Molson Coors Brewing Company owns 42 percent of the MillerCoors' brewing venture operating in the United States and Puerto Rico. As part of the agreement, Molson helps the MillerCoors unit produce and sell its products in the U.S. and Puerto Rican markets. Lenovo Group owns a significant percentage (45 percent) of the shares of Beijing Lenovo Parasaga Information Technology Co. (which develops and distributes computer software). Beijing Lenovo is important to Lenovo because it develops and sells the software that is used with Lenovo computers. In return, Beijing Lenovo depends on Lenovo to provide the products that make its software and services valuable, as well as perform significant customer and market support. Indeed, it can be said that to some extent Lenovo controls Beijing Lenovo, which would likely not exist without the support of Lenovo.

As you have learned, because a company like Lenovo owns less than 50 percent of the shares, it does not consolidate Beijing Lenovo but instead accounts for its investment using the *equity method*. Under the equity method, Lenovo reports a single income item for its profits from Beijing Lenovo and only the net amount of its investment in the statement of financial position. Equity method accounting gives Lenovo a pristine statement of financial position and income statement, by separating the assets and liabilities and the profit margins of the related companies from its laptop-computer businesses.

Some are critical of equity method accounting. They argue that some investees, like Beijing Lenovo, should be consolidated. The FASB has issued rules to consider other factors, in addition to voting interests, when determining whether an entity should be consolidated. We discuss these rules in Appendix 17B. The FASB has tightened up consolidation rules, so that companies will be more likely to consolidate more of their 20–50-percent-owned investments. Consolidation of entities, such as MillerCoors and Beijing Lenovo, is warranted if Molson and Lenovo effectively control their equity method investments.

ADDITIONAL MEASUREMENT ISSUES

Fair Value Option

As indicated in earlier chapters, companies have the option to report most financial instruments at fair value, with all gains and losses related to changes in fair value reported in the income statement. This option is applied on an instrument-by-instrument basis. The fair value option is generally available only at the time a company first purchases the financial asset or incurs a financial liability. If a company chooses to use the fair value option, it must measure this instrument at fair value until the company no longer has ownership.

> **5 LEARNING OBJECTIVE**
> Describe the accounting for the fair value option and for impairments of debt and equity investments.

For example, assume that Abbott Laboratories purchased debt securities in 2014 that it classified as held-to-maturity. Abbott does not choose to report this security using the fair value option. In 2015, Abbott buys another held-to-maturity debt security. Abbott decides to report this security using the fair value option. Once it chooses the fair value option for the security bought in 2015, the decision is irrevocable (may not be changed). In addition, Abbott does not have the option to value the held-to-maturity security purchased in 2014 at fair value in 2015 or in subsequent periods.

Many support the use of the fair value option as a step closer to total fair value reporting for financial instruments. They believe this treatment leads to an improvement in financial reporting. Others argue that the fair value option is confusing. A company can choose from period to period whether to use the fair value option for any new investment in a financial instrument. By permitting an instrument-by-instrument approach, companies are able to report some financial instruments at fair value but not others. To illustrate the accounting issues related to the fair value option, we discuss two different situations.

Available-for-Sale Securities

Available-for-sale securities are presently reported at fair value, with any unrealized gains and losses recorded as part of other comprehensive income. Assume that Hardy Company purchases stock in Fielder Company during 2014 that it classifies as available-for-sale. At December 31, 2014, the cost of this security is $100,000; its fair value at December 31, 2014, is $125,000. If Hardy chooses the fair value option to account for the Fielder Company stock, it makes the following entry at December 31, 2014.

Equity Investments	25,000	
Unrealized Holding Gain or Loss—Income		25,000

In this situation, Hardy uses an account titled Equity Investments to record the change in fair value at December 31. It does not use a Fair Value Adjustment account because the accounting for a fair value option is on an investment-by-investment basis rather than on a portfolio basis. Because Hardy selected the fair value option, the unrealized gain or loss is recorded as part of net income. Hardy must continue to use the fair value method to record this investment until it no longer has ownership of the security.

Equity Method Investments

Companies may also use the fair value option for investments that otherwise follow the equity method of accounting. To illustrate, assume that Durham Company holds a 28 percent stake in Suppan Inc. Durham purchased the investment in 2014 for $930,000. At December 31, 2014, the fair value of the investment is $900,000. Durham elects to report the investment in Suppan using the fair value option. The entry to record this investment is as follows.

Unrealized Holding Gain or Loss—Income	30,000	
Equity Investments		30,000

In contrast to equity method accounting, if the fair value option is chosen, Durham does not report its pro rata share of the income or loss from Suppan. In addition, any dividend payments are credited to Dividend Revenue and therefore do not reduce the Equity Investments account.

International Perspective

> IFRS does not allow the use of the fair value option for equity method investments. The FASB is considering a proposal to converge to IFRS in this area.

One major advantage of using the fair value option for this type of investment is that it addresses confusion about the equity method of accounting. In other words, what exactly does the one-line consolidation related to the equity method of accounting on the balance sheet tell investors? Many believe it does not provide information about liquidity or solvency, nor does it provide an indication of the worth of the company.

🔍 *Evolving Issue*   FAIR VALUE CONTROVERSY

The reporting of investment securities is controversial. Some believe that all securities should be reported at fair value. Others believe they all should be stated at amortized cost. Still others favor the present approach. Here are some of the major unresolved issues:

- *Measurement based on intent.* Companies classify debt securities as held-to-maturity, available-for-sale, or trading. As a result, companies can report three identical debt securities in three different ways in the financial

statements. Some argue such treatment is confusing. Furthermore, the held-to-maturity category relies on intent, a subjective evaluation. What is not subjective is the fair value of the debt instrument. In other words, the three classifications are subjective, resulting in arbitrary classifications.

- *Gains trading.* Companies can classify certain debt securities as held-to-maturity and therefore report them at amortized cost. Companies can classify other debt and equity securities as available-for-sale and report them at fair value, with the unrealized gain or loss reported as other comprehensive income. In either case, a company can become involved in "gains trading" (also referred to as "cherry picking," "snacking," or "sell the best and keep the rest"). In **gains trading**, companies sell their "winners," reporting the gains in income, and hold on to the losers.

- *Liabilities not fairly valued.* Many argue that if companies report investment securities at fair value, they also should report liabilities at fair value. Why? By recog-

nizing changes in value on only one side of the balance sheet (the asset side), a high degree of volatility can occur in the income and stockholders' equity amounts. Further, financial institutions are involved in asset and liability management (not just asset management). Viewing only one side may lead managers to make uneconomic decisions as a result of the accounting. The fair value option may address this concern to some extent. However, there is debate on the usefulness of fair value estimates for liabilities.

Impairment of Value

A company should evaluate every investment, at each reporting date, to determine if it has suffered impairment—a loss in value that is other than temporary. For example, if an investee experiences a bankruptcy or a significant liquidity crisis, the investor may suffer a permanent loss. **If the decline is judged to be other than temporary, a company writes down the cost basis of the individual security to a new cost basis.** The company accounts for the write-down as a realized loss. Therefore, it includes the amount in net income.

For debt securities, a company uses the impairment test to determine whether "it is probable that the investor will be unable to collect all amounts due according to the contractual terms."

For equity securities, the guideline is less precise. Any time realizable value is lower than the carrying amount of the investment, a company must consider an impairment. Factors involved include the length of time and the extent to which the fair value has been less than cost, the financial condition and near-term prospects of the issuer, and the intent and ability of the investor company to retain its investment to allow for any anticipated recovery in fair value.

To illustrate an impairment, assume that Strickler Company holds available-for-sale bond securities with a par value and amortized cost of $1 million. The fair value of these securities is $800,000. Strickler has previously reported an unrealized loss on these securities of $200,000 as part of other comprehensive income. In evaluating the securities, Strickler now determines that it probably will not collect all amounts due. In this case, it reports the unrealized loss of $200,000 as a loss on impairment of $200,000. Strickler includes this amount in income, with the bonds stated at their new cost basis. It records this impairment as follows.

Loss on Impairment	200,000	
Debt Investments		200,000

The new cost basis of the investment in debt securities is $800,000. Strickler includes subsequent increases and decreases in the fair value of impaired available-for-sale securities as other comprehensive income.[9]

Companies base impairment for debt and equity securities on a fair value test. This test differs slightly from the impairment test for loans that we discuss in Appendix 7B.

---

[9]In addition, any balance in the Unrealized Gain or Loss—Equity and Fair Value Adjustment accounts related to the impaired security would be eliminated. Companies may not amortize any discount related to the debt securities after recording the impairment. The new cost basis of impaired held-to-maturity securities does not change unless additional impairment occurs.

The FASB rejected the discounted cash flow alternative for securities because of the availability of market price information.[10]

An example of the criteria used by Caterpillar to assess impairment is provided in Illustration 17-18.

ILLUSTRATION 17-18
Disclosure of Impairment
Assessment Criteria

Caterpillar, Inc.
Notes to Financial Statements

Note 1.   Impairment of available-for-sale securities

Available-for-sale securities are reviewed monthly to identify market values below cost of 20% or more. If a decline for a debt security is in excess of 20% for six months, the investment is evaluated to determine if the decline is due to general declines in the marketplace or if the investment has been impaired and should be written down to market value. . . . After the six-month period, debt securities with declines from cost in excess of 20% are evaluated monthly for impairment. For equity securities, if a decline from cost of 20% or more continues for a 12-month period, an other than temporary impairment is recognized without continued analysis.

RECLASSIFICATIONS AND TRANSFERS
Reclassification Adjustments

LEARNING OBJECTIVE 6

Describe the reporting of reclassification adjustments and the accounting for transfers between categories.

As we indicated in Chapter 4, companies report changes in unrealized holding gains and losses related to available-for-sale securities as part of other comprehensive income. Companies may display the components of other comprehensive income in one of two ways: (1) in a combined statement of income and comprehensive income, or (2) in a separate statement of comprehensive income that begins with net income.

The reporting of changes in unrealized gains or losses in comprehensive income is straightforward unless a company sells securities during the year. In that case, double-counting results when the company reports realized gains or losses as part of net income but also shows the amounts as part of other comprehensive income in the current period or in previous periods.

To ensure that gains and losses are not counted twice when a sale occurs, a **reclassification adjustment** is necessary. To illustrate, assume that Open Company has the following two available-for-sale securities in its portfolio at the end of 2013 (its first year of operations).

ILLUSTRATION 17-19
Available-for-Sale
Security Portfolio (2013)

Investments	Cost	Fair Value	Unrealized Holding Gain (Loss)
Lehman Inc. common stock	$ 80,000	$105,000	$25,000
Woods Co. common stock	120,000	135,000	15,000
Total of portfolio	$200,000	$240,000	40,000
Previous fair value adjustment balance			–0–
Fair value adjustment—Dr.			$40,000

The entry to record the unrealized holding gain in 2013 is as follows.

Fair Value Adjustment (available-for-sale)	40,000	
Unrealized Holding Gain or Loss—Equity		40,000

---

[10]The FASB is currently exploring a new impairment model for financial instruments. The model focuses on the recognition of all expected losses which are "an estimate of contractual cash flows not expected to be collected." This differs from the current model, known as the incurred loss model, which requires evidence that a loss actually has occurred before the loss can be recorded.

If Open Company reports net income in 2013 of $350,000, it presents a statement of comprehensive income as follows.

ILLUSTRATION 17-20
Statement of
Comprehensive
Income (2013)

OPEN COMPANY STATEMENT OF COMPREHENSIVE INCOME FOR THE YEAR ENDED DECEMBER 31, 2013	
Net income	$350,000
Other comprehensive income	
Unrealized holding gain	40,000
Comprehensive income	$390,000

At December 31, 2013, Open Company reports on its balance sheet equity investments of $240,000 (cost $200,000 plus fair value adjustment of $40,000) and accumulated other comprehensive income in stockholders' equity of $40,000. The entry to transfer the unrealized holding gain—equity to accumulated other comprehensive income is as follows.

Unrealized Holding Gain or Loss—Equity	40,000	
Accumulated Other Comprehensive Income		40,000

In 2014, Open Company sells its Lehman Inc. common stock for $105,000 and realizes a gain on the sale of $25,000 ($105,000 − $80,000). The journal entry to record this transaction is as follows.

Cash	105,000	
Equity Investments		80,000
Gain on Sale of Investments		25,000

At the end of 2014, the fair value of the Woods Co. common stock increased an additional $20,000 ($155,000 − $135,000), to $155,000. Illustration 17-21 shows the computation of the change in the Fair Value Adjustment account (based on only the Woods Co. investment).

ILLUSTRATION 17-21
Available-for-Sale
Security Portfolio (2014)

Investments	Cost	Fair Value	Unrealized Holding Gain (Loss)
Woods Co. common stock	$120,000	$155,000	$35,000
Previous fair value adjustment balance—Dr.			(40,000)
Fair value adjustment—Cr.			$ (5,000)

The entry to record the unrealized holding gain in 2014 is as follows.

Unrealized Holding Gain or Loss—Equity	5,000	
Fair Value Adjustment (available-for-sale)		5,000

If we assume that Open Company reports net income of $720,000 in 2014, including the realized sale on the Lehman stock, its income statement is presented as shown in Illustration 17-22.

ILLUSTRATION 17-22
Statement of
Comprehensive
Income (2014)

OPEN COMPANY STATEMENT OF COMPREHENSIVE INCOME FOR THE YEAR ENDED DECEMBER 31, 2014	
Net income (includes $25,000 realized gain on Lehman shares)	$720,000
Other comprehensive income	
Unrealized holding loss	(5,000)
Comprehensive income	$715,000

At December 31, 2014, Open Company reports on its balance sheet equity investments of $155,000 (cost $120,000 plus a fair value adjustment of $35,000) and accumulated other comprehensive income in stockholders' equity of $35,000 ($40,000 − $5,000). The entry to transfer the unrealized holding loss—equity to accumulated other comprehensive income is as follows.

Accumulated Other Comprehensive Income	5,000	
Unrealized Holding Gain or Loss—Equity		5,000

In 2013, Open included the unrealized gain on the Lehman Co. common stock in comprehensive income. In 2014, Open sold the stock. It reported the realized gain ($25,000) in net income, which increased comprehensive income again. To avoid double-counting this gain, Open makes a reclassification adjustment to eliminate the realized gain from the computation of comprehensive income in 2014.

This reclassification adjustment may be made in the income statement, in accumulated other comprehensive income or in a note to the financial statements. The FASB prefers to show the reclassification amount in accumulated other comprehensive income in the notes to the financial statements.[11] For Open Company, this presentation is as shown in Illustration 17-23.

ILLUSTRATION 17-23
Note Disclosure of Reclassification Adjustments

OPEN COMPANY NOTES TO FINANCIAL STATEMENTS CHANGES IN ACCUMULATED OTHER COMPREHENSIVE INCOME		
Beginning balance, January 1, 2014		$40,000
Current-period other comprehensive income ($155,000 − $135,000)	$ 20,000	
Amount reclassified from accumulated other comprehensive income	(25,000)	
Unrealized holding loss		(5,000)
Ending balance, December 31, 2014		$35,000

Comprehensive Example

To provide a single-period example of the reporting of investment securities and related gain or loss on available-for-sale securities, assume that on January 1, 2014, Hinges Co. had cash and common stock of $50,000.[12] At that date, the company had no other asset, liability, or equity balance. On January 2, Hinges purchased for cash $50,000 of equity securities classified as available-for-sale. On June 30, Hinges sold part of the available-for-sale security portfolio, realizing a gain as shown in Illustration 17-24.

ILLUSTRATION 17-24
Computation of Realized Gain

Fair value of securities sold	$22,000
Less: Cost of securities sold	20,000
Realized gain	$ 2,000

---

[11]Recently, the FASB has proposed requiring companies to provide a tabular disclosure about items reclassified out of accumulated other comprehensive income. In general, for items reclassified to net income (e.g., gains or losses on available-for-sale securities), the disclosure includes the amount reclassified and identifies the line item affected on the income statement.

[12]We adapted this example from Dennis R. Beresford, L. Todd Johnson, and Cheri L. Reither, "Is a Second Income Statement Needed?" *Journal of Accountancy* (April 1996), p. 71.

Hinges did not purchase or sell any other securities during 2014. It received $3,000 in dividends during the year. At December 31, 2014, the remaining portfolio is as shown in Illustration 17-25.

Fair value of portfolio	$34,000
Less: Cost of portfolio	30,000
Unrealized gain	$ 4,000

ILLUSTRATION 17-25
Computation of
Unrealized Gain

Illustration 17-26 shows the company's income statement for 2014.

HINGES CO.
INCOME STATEMENT
FOR THE YEAR ENDED DECEMBER 31, 2014

Dividend revenue	$3,000
Realized gains on investment in securities	2,000
Net income	$5,000

ILLUSTRATION 17-26
Income Statement

The company reports its change in the unrealized holding gain in a statement of comprehensive income as follows.

HINGES CO.
STATEMENT OF COMPREHENSIVE INCOME
FOR THE YEAR ENDED DECEMBER 31, 2014

Net income (includes realized gain of $2,000)	$5,000
Other comprehensive income:	
Unrealized holding gain	4,000
Comprehensive income	$9,000

ILLUSTRATION 17-27
Statement of
Comprehensive Income

Its statement of stockholders' equity appears in Illustration 17-28.

HINGES CO.
STATEMENT OF STOCKHOLDERS' EQUITY
FOR THE YEAR ENDED DECEMBER 31, 2014

	Common Stock	Retained Earnings	Accumulated Other Comprehensive Income	Total
Beginning balance	$50,000	$ –0–	$–0–	$50,000
Add: Net income		5,000		5,000
Other comprehensive income			4,000*	4,000
Ending balance	$50,000	$5,000	$4,000	$59,000

*Total holding gains of $6,000 less reclassification adjustment of $2,000.

ILLUSTRATION 17-28
Statement of
Stockholders' Equity

The comparative balance sheet is shown below in Illustration 17-29.

ILLUSTRATION 17-29
Comparative Balance
Sheet

HINGES CO. COMPARATIVE BALANCE SHEET		
	1/1/14	12/31/14
Assets		
Cash	$50,000	$25,000
Equity investments (available-for-sale)		34,000
Total assets	$50,000	$59,000
Stockholders' equity		
Common stock	$50,000	$50,000
Retained earnings		5,000
Accumulated other comprehensive income		4,000
Total stockholders' equity	$50,000	$59,000

This example indicates how an unrealized gain or loss on available-for-sale securities affects all the financial statements. Note that a company must disclose the components that comprise accumulated other comprehensive income.

Transfers Between Categories

Companies account for transfers between any of the categories at fair value. Thus, if a company transfers available-for-sale securities to held-to-maturity investments, it records the new investments (held-to-maturity) at the date of transfer at **fair value** in the new category. Similarly, if it transfers held-to-maturity investments to available-for-sale investments, it records the new investments (available-for-sale) at **fair value**. This **fair value** rule assures that a company cannot omit recognition of fair value simply by transferring securities to the held-to-maturity category. Illustration 17-30 summarizes the accounting treatment for transfers.

ILLUSTRATION 17-30
Accounting for Transfers

Gateway to the Profession

Examples of the Entries for Recording Transfers Between Categories

Type of Transfer	Measurement Basis	Impact of Transfer on Stockholders' Equity*	Impact of Transfer on Net Income*
Transfer from trading to available-for-sale	Security transferred at fair value at the date of transfer, which is the new cost basis of the security.	The unrealized gain or loss at the date of transfer increases or decreases stockholders' equity.	The unrealized gain or loss at the date of transfer is recognized in income.
Transfer from available-for-sale to trading	Security transferred at fair value at the date of transfer, which is the new cost basis of the security.	The unrealized gain or loss at the date of transfer increases or decreases stockholders' equity.	The unrealized gain or loss at the date of transfer is recognized in income.
Transfer from held-to-maturity to available-for-sale**	Security transferred at fair value at the date of transfer.	The separate component of stockholders' equity is increased or decreased by the unrealized gain or loss at the date of transfer.	None
Transfer from available-for-sale to held-to-maturity	Security transferred at fair value at the date of transfer.	The unrealized gain or loss at the date of transfer carried as a separate component of stockholders' equity is amortized over the remaining life of the security.	None

*Assumes that adjusting entries to report changes in fair value for the current period are not yet recorded.
**According to GAAP, these types of transfers should be rare.

Summary of Reporting Treatment of Securities

Illustration 17-31 summarizes the major debt and equity securities and their reporting treatment.

Category*	Balance Sheet	Income Statement
Trading (debt and equity securities)	Investments shown at fair value. Current assets.	Interest and dividends are recognized as revenue. Unrealized holding gains and losses are included in net income.
Available-for-sale (debt and equity securities)	Investments shown at fair value. Current or long-term assets. Unrealized holding gains and losses are a separate component of stockholders' equity.	Interest and dividends are recognized as revenue. Unrealized holding gains and losses are **not** included in net income but in other comprehensive income.
Held-to-maturity (debt securities)	Investments shown at amortized cost. Current or long-term assets.	Interest is recognized as revenue.
Equity method and/or consolidation (equity securities)	Investments originally are carried at cost, are periodically adjusted by the investor's share of the investee's earnings or losses, and are decreased by all dividends received from the investee. Classified as long-term.	Revenue is recognized to the extent of the investee's earnings or losses reported subsequent to the date of investment.

*Companies have the option to report financial instruments at fair value with all gains and losses related to changes in fair value reported in the income statement. If a company chooses to use the fair value option for some of its financial instruments, these assets or liabilities should be reported separately from other financial instruments that use a different valuation basis. To accomplish separate reporting, a company may either (a) report separate line items for the fair value and non–fair value amounts or (b) report the total fair value and non–fair value amounts in one line and parenthetically report the fair value amount in that line also.[13]

ILLUSTRATION 17-31
Summary of Treatment of Major Debt and Equity Securities

Gateway to the Profession

Discussion of Special Issues Related to Investments

 You will want to read the IFRS INSIGHTS on pages 1026–1039 for discussion of IFRS related to the accounting for investments.

Evolving Issue   CLASSIFICATION AND MEASUREMENT—THE LONG ROAD

As discussed in the opening story, the FASB and IASB have been on divergent approaches to financial instrument classification and measurement. These differences have narrowed recently with the decision to permit a "Fair Value through Other Comprehensive Income" category for some debt instruments. The following table summarizes the agreed-upon approach in comparison to current GAAP.

Source: J.P. Morgan.

As indicated, under the new model, there will still be three "buckets" although the proportions of financial instruments within the new classifications will change. For example, the FV-NI category will likely be larger than the current trading category because publicly traded companies will likely be required to classify all equity securities (both marketable

[13]Not surprisingly, the disclosure requirements for investments and other financial assets and liabilities are extensive. We provide an expanded discussion with examples of these disclosure requirements in Appendix 17C.

and nonmarketable) in FV-NI. Currently, companies are able to classify some equities in the available-for-sale category if particular criteria are met. To the extent a company has traditionally classified a large portion of its equity securities in the available-for-sale category, more equity instruments accounted for in the FV-NI category could create more net income volatility than under current GAAP.

The FV-OCI category may be larger or smaller than a company's current available-for-sale category. On the one hand, equities will no longer be eligible for classification in this category, which will make it smaller. On the other hand, some instruments that are currently classified as held-to-

maturity will not be eligible for amortized cost classification and instead will end up being moved into the FV-OCI category.

For most companies, the amortized cost category generally will be smaller than the current held-to-maturity category because securities will no longer be eligible for classification in this category. Our expectation is that most of the instruments that will no longer meet the eligibility criteria for amortized cost accounting will likely move to the FV-OCI category.

The FASB is expected to issue a revised proposal in 2013. The IASB has specified that a revised *IFRS 9* will be effective for annual periods beginning on or after January 1, 2015.

Source: Adapted from D. Mott, "FASB and IASB Come Together on the Classification and Measurement of Debt Instruments," *Global Equity Research—Accounting Issues*, J.P. Morgan (25 May 2012).

KEY TERMS

amortized cost, *953*

available-for-sale securities, *952*

consolidated financial statements, *966*

controlling interest, *966*

debt securities, *952*

effective-interest method, *954*

equity method, *965*

equity securities, *960*

exchange for noncash consideration, *962(n)*

fair value, *953*

Fair Value Adjustment, *957*

fair value method, *961*

gains trading, *959*

held-to-maturity securities, *952*

holding gain or loss, *959*

impairment, *969*

investee, *961*

investor, *961*

parent, *966*

reclassification adjustment, *970*

security, *952(n)*

significant influence, *964*

subsidiary, *966*

trading securities, *952*

SUMMARY OF LEARNING OBJECTIVES

1 **Identify the three categories of debt securities and describe the accounting and reporting treatment for each category.** (1) Carry and report *held-to-maturity debt securities* at amortized cost. (2) Value *trading debt securities* for reporting purposes at fair value, with unrealized holding gains or losses included in net income. (3) Value *available-for-sale debt securities* for reporting purposes at fair value, with unrealized holding gains or losses reported as other comprehensive income and as a separate component of stockholders' equity.

2 **Understand the procedures for discount and premium amortization on bond investments.** Similar to bonds payable, companies should amortize discount or premium on bond investments using the effective-interest method. They apply the effective-interest rate or yield to the beginning carrying value of the investment for each interest period in order to compute interest revenue.

3 **Identify the categories of equity securities and describe the accounting and reporting treatment for each category.** The degree to which one corporation (investor) acquires an interest in the common stock of another corporation (investee) generally determines the accounting treatment for the investment. Long-term investments by one corporation in the common stock of another can be classified according to the percentage of the voting stock of the investee held by the investor.

4 **Explain the equity method of accounting and compare it to the fair value method for equity securities.** Under the equity method, the investor and the investee acknowledge a substantive economic relationship. The company originally records the investment at cost but subsequently adjusts the amount each period for changes in the net assets of the investee. That is, the investor's proportionate share of the earnings (losses) of the investee periodically increases (decreases) the investment's carrying amount. All dividends received by the investor from the investee decrease the investment's carrying amount. Under the fair value method, a company reports the equity investment at fair value each reporting period irrespective of the investee's earnings or dividends paid to it. A company applies the equity method to investment holdings between 20 percent and 50 percent of ownership. It applies the fair value method to holdings below 20 percent.

5 **Describe the accounting for the fair value option and for impairments of debt and equity investments.** Companies have the option to report most financial instruments at fair value, with all gains and losses related to changes in fair value reported in the income statement. This option is applied on an instrument-by-instrument basis. The fair value option is generally available only at the time a company first purchases the financial asset or incurs a financial liability. If a company chooses to use the fair value option, it must measure this instrument at fair value until the company no longer has ownership.

Impairments of debt and equity securities are losses in value that are determined to be other than temporary, are based on a fair value test, and are charged to income.

6 **Describe the reporting of reclassification adjustments and the accounting for transfers between categories.** A company needs a reclassification adjustment when it reports realized gains or losses as part of net income but also shows the amounts as part of other comprehensive income in the current or in previous periods. Companies should report unrealized holding gains or losses related to available-for-sale securities in other comprehensive income and the aggregate balance as accumulated comprehensive income on the balance sheet.

Transfers of securities between categories of investments should be accounted for at fair value, with unrealized holding gains or losses treated in accordance with the nature of the transfer.

APPENDIX 17A | **ACCOUNTING FOR DERIVATIVE INSTRUMENTS**

Until the early 1970s, most financial managers worked in a cozy, if unthrilling, world. Since then, constant change caused by volatile markets, new technology, and deregulation has increased the risks to businesses. In response, the financial community developed products to manage these risks.

7 LEARNING OBJECTIVE
Describe the uses of and accounting for derivatives.

These products—called **derivative financial instruments** or simply **derivatives**—are useful for managing risk. Companies use the fair values or cash flows of these instruments to offset the changes in fair values or cash flows of the at-risk assets. The development of powerful computing and communication technology has aided the growth in derivative use. This technology provides new ways to analyze information about markets as well as the power to process high volumes of payments.

DEFINING DERIVATIVES

In order to understand derivatives, consider the following examples.

Example 1—Forward Contract. Assume that a company like Dell believes that the price of Google's stock will increase substantially in the next 3 months. Unfortunately, it does not have the cash resources to purchase the stock today. Dell therefore enters into a contract with a broker for delivery of 10,000 shares of Google stock in 3 months at the price of $110 per share.

Dell has entered into a **forward contract**, a type of derivative. As a result of the contract, Dell **has received the right** to receive 10,000 shares of Google stock in 3 months. Further, it **has an obligation** to pay $110 per share at that time. What is the benefit of this derivative contract? Dell can buy Google stock today and take delivery in 3 months. If the price goes up, as it expects, Dell profits. If the price goes down, Dell loses.

Example 2—Option Contract. Now suppose that Dell needs 2 weeks to decide whether to purchase Google stock. It therefore enters into a different type of contract, one that gives it the right to purchase Google stock at its current price any time within the next 2 weeks. As part of the contract, the broker charges $3,000 for holding the contract open for 2 weeks at a set price.

Dell has now entered into an option contract, another type of derivative. As a result of this contract, **it has received the right but not the obligation** to purchase this stock. If the price of the Google stock increases in the next 2 weeks, Dell exercises its option. In this case, the cost of the stock is the price of the stock stated in the contract, plus the cost of the option contract. If the price does not increase, Dell does not exercise the contract but still incurs the cost for the option.

The forward contract and the option contract both involve a future delivery of stock. The value of the contract relies on the underlying asset—the Google stock. Thus, these financial instruments are known as derivatives because they **derive their value from** values of other assets (e.g., stocks, bonds, or commodities). Or, put another way, their value relates to a market-determined indicator (e.g., stock price, interest rates, or the Standard and Poor's 500 stock composite index).

In this appendix, we discuss the accounting for three different types of derivatives:

1. Financial forwards or financial futures.
2. Options.
3. Swaps.

WHO USES DERIVATIVES, AND WHY?

Whether to protect for changes in interest rates, the weather, stock prices, oil prices, or foreign currencies, derivative contracts help to smooth the fluctuations caused by various types of risks. A company that wants to ensure against certain types of business risks often uses derivative contracts to achieve this objective.[14]

Producers and Consumers

To illustrate, assume that Heartland Ag is a large producer of potatoes for the consumer market. The present price for potatoes is excellent. Unfortunately, Heartland needs two months to harvest its potatoes and deliver them to the market. Because Heartland expects the price of potatoes to drop in the coming months, it signs a forward contract. It agrees to sell its potatoes today at the current market price for delivery in 2 months.

Who would buy this contract? Suppose on the other side of the contract is **McDonald's Corporation**. McDonald's wants to have potatoes (for French fries) in 2 months and believes that prices will increase. McDonald's is therefore agreeable to accepting delivery in 2 months at current prices. It knows that it will need potatoes in 2 months and that it can make an acceptable profit at this price level.

In this situation, if the price of potatoes increases before delivery, Heartland loses and McDonald's wins. Conversely, if the price decreases, Heartland wins and McDonald's loses. However, the objective is not to gamble on the outcome. Regardless of which way the price moves, both Heartland and McDonald's have received a price at

[14]Derivatives are traded on many exchanges throughout the world. In addition, many derivative contracts (primarily interest rate swaps) are privately negotiated.

which they obtain an acceptable profit. In this case, although Heartland is a **producer** and McDonald's is a **consumer**, both companies are **hedgers**. They both **hedge their positions** to ensure an acceptable financial result.

Commodity prices are volatile. They depend on weather, crop production, and general economic conditions. For the producer and the consumer to plan effectively, it makes good sense to lock in specific future revenues or costs in order to run their businesses successfully.

Speculators and Arbitrageurs

In some cases, instead of McDonald's taking a position in the forward contract, a speculator may purchase the contract from Heartland. The speculator bets that the price of potatoes will rise, thereby increasing the value of the forward contract. The speculator, who may be in the market for only a few hours, will then sell the forward contract to another speculator or to a company like McDonald's.

Arbitrageurs also use derivatives. These market players attempt to exploit inefficiencies in markets. They seek to lock in profits by simultaneously entering into transactions in two or more markets. For example, an arbitrageur might trade in a futures contract. At the same time, the arbitrageur will also trade in the commodity underlying the futures contract, hoping to achieve small price gains on the difference between the two. Markets rely on speculators and arbitrageurs to keep the market liquid on a daily basis.

In these illustrations, we explained why Heartland (the producer) and McDonald's (the consumer) would become involved in a derivative contract. Consider other types of situations that companies face.

1. Airlines, like **Delta**, **Southwest**, and **United**, are affected by changes in the price of jet fuel.
2. Financial institutions, such as **Citigroup**, **Bankers Trust**, and **BMO Harris**, are involved in borrowing and lending funds that are affected by changes in interest rates.
3. Multinational corporations, like **Cisco Systems**, **Coca-Cola**, and **General Electric**, are subject to changes in foreign exchange rates.

In fact, most corporations are involved in some form of derivatives transactions. Companies give these reasons (in their annual reports) as to why they use derivatives:

1. **ExxonMobil** uses derivatives to hedge its exposure to fluctuations in interest rates, foreign currency exchange rates, and hydrocarbon prices.
2. **Caterpillar** uses derivatives to manage foreign currency exchange rates, interest rates, and commodity price exposure.
3. **Johnson & Johnson** uses derivatives to manage the impact of interest rate and foreign exchange rate changes on earnings and cash flows.

Many corporations use derivatives extensively and successfully. However, derivatives can be dangerous. All parties involved must understand the risks and rewards associated with these contracts.[15]

---

[15]There are some well-publicized examples of companies that have suffered considerable losses using derivatives. For example, companies such as **Fannie Mae** (U.S.), **Enron** (U.S.), **Showa Shell Sekiyu** (Japan), **Metallgesellschaft** (Germany), **Procter & Gamble** (U.S.), and **Air Products & Chemicals** (U.S.) incurred significant losses from investments in derivative instruments.

BASIC PRINCIPLES IN ACCOUNTING FOR DERIVATIVES

The FASB concluded that derivatives such as forwards and options are assets and liabilities. It also concluded that companies should report them in the balance sheet **at fair value**.[16] The Board believes that fair value will provide statement users the best information about derivatives. Relying on some other basis of valuation for derivatives, such as historical cost, does not make sense. Why? Because many derivatives have a historical cost of zero. Furthermore, the markets for derivatives, and the assets upon which derivatives' values rely, are well developed. As a result, the Board believes that companies can determine reliable fair value amounts for derivatives.[17]

On the income statement, a company should recognize any unrealized gain or loss in income, if it uses the derivative for speculation purposes. If using the derivative for hedging purposes, the accounting for any gain or loss depends on the type of hedge used. We discuss the accounting for hedged transactions later in the appendix.

In summary, companies follow these guidelines in accounting for derivatives.

1. Recognize derivatives in the financial statements as assets and liabilities.
2. Report derivatives at fair value.
3. Recognize gains and losses resulting from speculation in derivatives immediately in income.
4. Report gains and losses resulting from hedge transactions differently, depending on the type of hedge.

Example of Derivative Financial Instrument—Speculation

To illustrate the measurement and reporting of a derivative for speculative purposes, we examine a derivative whose value depends on the market price of Laredo Inc. common stock. A company can realize a gain from the increase in the value of the Laredo shares with the use of a derivative, such as a call option.[18] A **call option** gives the holder the right, but not the obligation, to buy shares at a preset price. This price is often referred to as the **strike price** or the **exercise price**.

---

[16]GAAP covers accounting and reporting for all derivative instruments, whether financial or not. In this appendix, we focus on derivative financial instruments because of their widespread use in practice. **[7]**

[17]As discussed in earlier chapters, fair value is defined as "the price that would be received to sell an asset or paid to transfer a liability in an orderly transaction between market participants at the measurement date." Fair value is therefore a market-based measure. The FASB has also developed a fair value hierarchy, which indicates the priority of valuation techniques to use to determine fair value. *Level 1* fair value measures are based on observable inputs that reflect quoted prices for identical assets or liabilities in active markets. *Level 2* measures are based on inputs other than quoted prices included in Level 1 but that can be corroborated with observable data. *Level 3* fair values are based on unobservable inputs (for example, a company's own data or assumptions). Thus, Level 1 is the most reliable because it is based on quoted prices, like a closing stock price in the *Wall Street Journal*. Level 2 is the next most reliable and would rely on evaluating similar assets or liabilities in active markets. For Level 3 (the least reliable), much judgment is needed, based on the best information available, to arrive at a relevant and reliable fair value measurement. **[8]**

[18]Investors can use a different type of option contract—a **put option**—to realize a gain if anticipating a decline in the Laredo stock value. A put option gives the holder the option to sell shares at a preset price. Thus, a put option **increases** in value when the underlying asset **decreases** in value.

For example, assume a company enters into a call option contract with Baird Investment Co., which gives it the option to purchase Laredo stock at $100 per share.[19] If the price of Laredo stock increases above $100, the company can exercise this option and purchase the shares for $100 per share. If Laredo's stock never increases above $100 per share, the call option is worthless.

Accounting Entries. To illustrate the accounting for a call option, assume that the company purchases a call option contract on January 2, 2014, when Laredo shares are trading at $100 per share. The contract gives it the option to purchase 1,000 shares (referred to as the **notional amount**) of Laredo stock at an option price of $100 per share. The option expires on April 30, 2014. The company purchases the call option for $400 and makes the following entry.

January 2, 2014

Call Option	400	
Cash		400

This payment is referred to as the **option premium**. It is generally much less than the cost of purchasing the shares directly. The option premium consists of two amounts: (1) intrinsic value and (2) time value. Illustration 17A-1 shows the formula to compute the option premium.

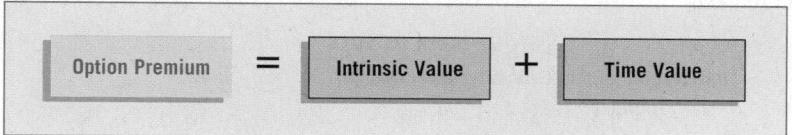

ILLUSTRATION 17A-1
Option Premium
Formula

Intrinsic value is the difference between the market price and the preset strike price at any point in time. It represents the amount realized by the option holder, if exercising the option immediately. On January 2, 2014, the intrinsic value is zero because the market price equals the preset strike price.

Time value refers to the option's value over and above its intrinsic value. Time value reflects the possibility that the option has a fair value greater than zero. How? Because there is some expectation that the price of Laredo shares will increase above the strike price during the option term. As indicated, the time value for the option is $400.[20]

The following additional data are available with respect to the call option.

Date	Market Price of Laredo Shares	Time Value of Call Option
March 31, 2014	$120 per share	$100
April 16, 2014	$115 per share	$ 60

As indicated, on March 31, 2014, the price of Laredo shares increases to $120 per share. The intrinsic value of the call option contract is now $20,000. That is, the company can exercise the call option and purchase 1,000 shares from Baird Investment for $100 per share. It can then sell the shares in the market for $120 per share. This gives the

[19]Baird Investment Co. is referred to as the **counterparty**. Counterparties frequently are investment bankers or other companies that hold inventories of financial instruments.

[20]This cost is estimated using option-pricing models, such as the Black-Scholes equation. The volatility of the underlying stock, the expected life of the option, the risk-free rate of interest, and expected dividends on the underlying stock during the option term affect the Black-Scholes fair value estimate.

company a gain of $20,000 ($120,000 − $100,000) on the option contract.[21] It records the increase in the intrinsic value of the option as follows.

March 31, 2014

Call Option	20,000	
Unrealized Holding Gain or Loss—Income		20,000

A market appraisal indicates that the time value of the option at March 31, 2014, is $100.[22] The company records this change in value of the option as follows.

March 31, 2014

Unrealized Holding Gain or Loss—Income	300	
Call Option ($400 − $100)		300

At March 31, 2014, the company reports the call option in its balance sheet at fair value of $20,100.[23] The unrealized holding gain increases net income for the period. The loss on the time value of the option decreases net income.

On April 16, 2014, the company settles the option before it expires. To properly record the settlement, it updates the value of the option for the decrease in the intrinsic value of $5,000 ([$20 − $15]) × 1,000) as follows.

April 16, 2014

Unrealized Holding Gain or Loss—Income	5,000	
Call Option		5,000

The decrease in the time value of the option of $40 ($100 − $60) is recorded as follows.

April 16, 2014

Unrealized Holding Gain or Loss—Income	40	
Call Option		40

Thus, at the time of the settlement, the call option's carrying value is as follows.

Call Option

January 2, 2014	400	March 31, 2014	300	
March 31, 2014	20,000	April 16, 2014	5,000	
		April 16, 2014	40	
Balance, April 16, 2014	15,060			

The company records the settlement of the option contract with Baird as follows.

April 16, 2014

Cash	15,000	
Loss on Settlement of Call Option	60	
Call Option		15,060

Illustration 17A-2 summarizes the effects of the call option contract on net income.

ILLUSTRATION 17A-2
Effect on Income—
Derivative Financial
Instrument

Date	Transaction	Income (Loss) Effect
March 31, 2014	Net increase in value of call option ($20,000 − $300)	$19,700
April 16, 2014	Decrease in value of call option ($5,000 + $40)	(5,040)
April 16, 2014	Settle call option	(60)
	Total net income	$14,600

[21]In practice, investors generally do not have to actually buy and sell the Laredo shares to settle the option and realize the gain. This is referred to as the **net settlement** feature of option contracts.

[22]The decline in value reflects both the decreased likelihood that the Laredo shares will continue to increase in value over the option period and the shorter time to maturity of the option contract.

[23]As indicated earlier, the total value of the option at any point in time equals the intrinsic value plus the time value.

The accounting summarized in Illustration 17A-2 is in accord with GAAP. That is, because the call option meets the definition of an asset, the company records it in the balance sheet on March 31, 2014. Furthermore, it reports the call option at fair value, with any gains or losses reported in income.

Differences Between Traditional and Derivative Financial Instruments

How does a traditional financial instrument differ from a derivative one? A derivative financial instrument has the following three basic characteristics. **[9]**

1. *The instrument has (1) one or more underlyings and (2) an identified payment provision.* An **underlying** is a specified interest rate, security price, commodity price, index of prices or rates, or other market-related variable. The interaction of the underlying, with the face amount or the number of units specified in the derivative contract (the notional amounts), determines payment. For example, the value of the call option increased in value when the value of the Laredo stock increased. In this case, the underlying is the stock price. To arrive at the payment provision, multiply the change in the stock price by the number of shares (notional amount).

2. *The instrument requires little or no investment at the inception of the contract.* To illustrate, the company paid a small premium to purchase the call option—an amount much less than if purchasing the Laredo shares as a direct investment.

3. *The instrument requires or permits net settlement.* As indicated in the call option example, the company could realize a profit on the call option without taking possession of the shares. This **net settlement** feature reduces the transaction costs associated with derivatives.

Illustration 17A-3 summarizes the differences between traditional and derivative financial instruments. Here, we use a trading security for the traditional financial instrument and a call option as an example of a derivative one.

Feature	Traditional Financial Instrument (Trading Security)	Derivative Financial Instrument (Call Option)
Payment provision	Stock price times the number of shares.	Change in stock price (underlying) times number of shares (notional amount).
Initial investment	Investor pays full cost.	Initial investment is much less than full cost.
Settlement	Deliver stock to receive cash.	Receive cash equivalent, based on changes in stock price times the number of shares.

ILLUSTRATION 17A-3
Features of Traditional and Derivative Financial Instruments

DERIVATIVES USED FOR HEDGING

Flexibility in use and the low-cost features of derivatives relative to traditional financial instruments explain the popularity of derivatives. An additional use for derivatives is in risk management. For example, companies such as Coca-Cola, ExxonMobil, and General Electric borrow and lend substantial amounts in credit markets. In doing so, they are exposed to significant **interest rate risk**. That is, they face substantial risk that the fair values or cash flows of interest-sensitive assets or liabilities will change if interest rates increase or decrease. These same companies also have significant international operations. As such, they are also exposed to **exchange rate risk**—the risk that changes in foreign currency exchange rates will negatively impact the profitability of their international businesses.

Companies can use derivatives to offset the negative impacts of changes in interest rates or foreign currency exchange rates. This use of derivatives is referred to as **hedging**. GAAP established accounting and reporting standards for derivative financial instruments used in hedging activities. The FASB allows special accounting for two types of hedges—fair value and cash flow hedges.[24]

What do the numbers mean? RISKY BUSINESS

As shown in the graph below, use of derivatives has grown substantially in the past 10 years. In fact, over *$450 trillion* (in notional amounts) in derivative contracts were in play at the end of 2010. The primary players in the market for derivatives are large companies and various financial institutions, which continue to find new uses for derivatives for speculation and risk management

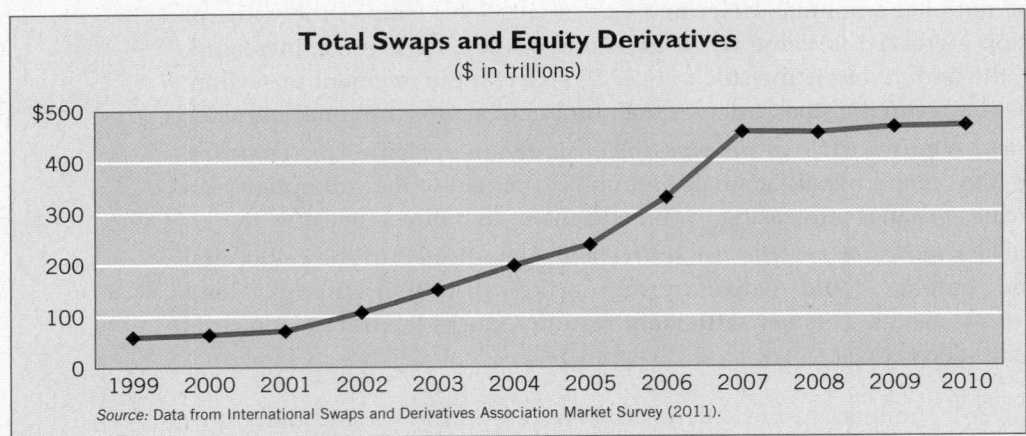

Total Swaps and Equity Derivatives
($ in trillions)

Source: Data from International Swaps and Derivatives Association Market Survey (2011).

Financial engineers continue to develop new uses for derivatives, many times through the use of increasingly complex webs of transactions, spanning a number of markets. As new uses for derivatives appear, the financial system as a whole can be dramatically affected. As a result, some market-watchers are concerned about the risk that a crisis in one company or sector could bring the entire financial system to its knees.

This was the case recently when credit default swaps were used to facilitate the sales of mortgage-backed securities (MBS). However, when the real estate market went south, the MBS defaulted, exposing large international financial institutions, like Barclays, AIG, and Bank of America, to massive losses. The losses were so widespread that government bailouts were required to prevent international securities markets from collapsing. In response, market regulators are proposing new rules to mitigate risks to broader markets from derivatives trading.

Source: P. Eavis, "Bill on Derivatives Overhaul Is Long Overdue," *Wall Street Journal* (April 14, 2010).

Fair Value Hedge

LEARNING OBJECTIVE 8
Explain how to account for a fair value hedge.

In a **fair value hedge**, a company uses a derivative to hedge (offset) the exposure to changes in the fair value of a recognized asset or liability or of an unrecognized commitment. In a perfectly hedged position, the gain or loss on the fair value of the derivative equals and offsets that of the hedged asset or liability.

[24]GAAP also addresses the accounting for certain foreign currency hedging transactions. In general, these transactions are special cases of the two hedges we discuss here. [10] Understanding of foreign currency hedging transactions requires knowledge related to consolidation of multinational entities, which is beyond the scope of this textbook.

Companies commonly use several types of fair value hedges. For example, companies use interest rate swaps to hedge the risk that changes in interest rates will impact the fair value of debt obligations. Or, they use put options to hedge the risk that an equity investment will decline in value.

To illustrate a fair value hedge, assume that on April 1, 2014, Hayward Co. purchases 100 shares of Sonoma stock at a market price of $100 per share. Hayward does not intend to actively trade this investment. It consequently classifies the Sonoma investment as available-for-sale. Hayward records this available-for-sale investment as follows.

April 1, 2014

Equity Investments	10,000	
Cash		10,000

Hayward records available-for-sale securities at fair value on the balance sheet. It reports unrealized gains and losses in equity as part of other comprehensive income.[25] Fortunately for Hayward, the value of the Sonoma shares increases to $125 per share during 2014. Hayward records the gain on this investment as follows.

December 31, 2014

Fair Value Adjustment (available-for-sale)	2,500	
Unrealized Holding Gain or Loss—Equity		2,500

Illustration 17A-4 indicates how Hayward reports the Sonoma investment in its balance sheet.

ILLUSTRATION 17A-4
Balance Sheet
Presentation of Available-for-Sale Securities

HAYWARD CO. BALANCE SHEET (PARTIAL) DECEMBER 31, 2014	
Assets	
Equity investments (available-for-sale)	$12,500
Stockholders' Equity	
Accumulated other comprehensive income	
Unrealized holding gain	$2,500

While Hayward benefits from an increase in the price of Sonoma shares, it is exposed to the risk that the price of the Sonoma stock will decline. To hedge this risk, Hayward locks in its gain on the Sonoma investment by purchasing a put option on 100 shares of Sonoma stock.

Hayward enters into the put option contract on January 2, 2015, and designates the option as a fair value hedge of the Sonoma investment. This put option (which expires in two years) gives Hayward the option to sell Sonoma shares at a price of $125. Since the exercise price equals the current market price, no entry is necessary at inception of the put option.[26]

January 2, 2015

No entry required. A memorandum indicates the signing of the put option contract and its designation as a fair value hedge for the Sonoma investment.

At December 31, 2015, the price of the Sonoma shares has declined to $120 per share. Hayward records the following entry for the Sonoma investment.

December 31, 2015

Unrealized Holding Gain or Loss—Income	500	
Fair Value Adjustment (available-for-sale)		500

[25]We discussed the distinction between trading and available-for-sale investments in the chapter.
[26]To simplify the example, we assume no premium is paid for the option.

Note that upon designation of the hedge, the accounting for the available-for-sale security changes from regular GAAP. That is, Hayward records the unrealized holding loss in income, not in equity. **If Hayward had not followed this accounting, a mismatch of gains and losses in the income statement would result.** Thus, special accounting for the hedged item (in this case, an available-for-sale security) is necessary in a fair value hedge.

The following journal entry records the increase in value of the put option on Sonoma shares.

December 31, 2015

Put Option	500	
Unrealized Holding Gain or Loss—Income		500

The decline in the price of Sonoma shares results in an increase in the fair value of the put option. That is, Hayward could realize a gain on the put option by purchasing 100 shares in the open market for $120 and then exercise the put option, selling the shares for $125. This results in a gain to Hayward of $500 (100 shares × [$125 − $120]).[27]

Illustration 17A-5 indicates how Hayward reports the amounts related to the Sonoma investment and the put option.

ILLUSTRATION 17A-5
Balance Sheet
Presentation of Fair Value
Hedge

HAYWARD CO.
BALANCE SHEET (PARTIAL)
DECEMBER 31, 2015

Assets	
Equity investments (available-for-sale)	$12,000
Put option	500

The increase in fair value on the option offsets or hedges the decline in value on Hayward's available-for-sale security. By using fair value accounting for both financial instruments, the financial statements reflect the underlying substance of Hayward's net exposure to the risks of holding Sonoma stock. By using fair value accounting for both these financial instruments, the balance sheet reports the amount that Hayward would receive on the investment and the put option contract if Hayward sold and settled them, respectively.

Illustration 17A-6 illustrates the reporting of the effects of the hedging transaction on income for the year ended December 31, 2015.

ILLUSTRATION 17A-6
Income Statement
Presentation of Fair Value
Hedge

HAYWARD CO.
INCOME STATEMENT (PARTIAL)
FOR THE YEAR ENDED DECEMBER 31, 2015

Other Income	
Unrealized holding gain—put option	$ 500
Unrealized holding loss—available-for-sale securities	(500)

The income statement indicates that the gain on the put option offsets the loss on the available-for-sale securities.[28] The reporting for these financial instruments, even when

---

[27]In practice, Hayward generally does not have to actually buy and sell the Sonoma shares to realize this gain. Rather, unless the counterparty wants to hold Hayward shares, Hayward can "close out" the contract by having the counterparty pay it $500 in cash. This is an example of the net settlement feature of derivatives.

[28]Note that the fair value changes in the option contract will not offset *increases* in the value of the Hayward investment. Should the price of Sonoma stock increase above $125 per share, Hayward would have no incentive to exercise the put option.

they reflect a hedging relationship, illustrates why the FASB argued that fair value accounting provides the most relevant information about financial instruments, including derivatives.

Cash Flow Hedge

Companies use **cash flow hedges** to hedge exposures to **cash flow risk**, which results from the variability in cash flows. The FASB allows special accounting for cash flow hedges. Generally, companies measure and report derivatives at fair value on the balance sheet. They report gains and losses directly in net income. However, companies account for derivatives used in cash flow hedges at fair value on the balance sheet, but they **record gains or losses in equity, as part of other comprehensive income**.

9 LEARNING OBJECTIVE

Explain how to account for a cash flow hedge.

To illustrate, assume that in September 2014, Allied Can Co. anticipates purchasing 1,000 metric tons of aluminum in January 2015. Concerned that prices for aluminum will increase in the next few months, Allied wants to hedge the risk that it might pay higher prices for inventory in January 2015. As a result, Allied enters into an aluminum futures contract.

International Perspective

Under IFRS, companies record unrealized holding gains or losses on cash flow hedges as adjustments to the value of the hedged item, not as "Other comprehensive income."

A **futures contract** gives the holder the right and the obligation to purchase an asset at a preset price for a specified period of time.[29] In this case, the aluminum futures contract gives Allied the right and the obligation to purchase 1,000 metric tons of aluminum for $1,550 per ton. This contract price is good until the contract expires in January 2015. The underlying for this derivative is the price of aluminum. If the price of aluminum rises above $1,550, the value of the futures contract to Allied increases. Why? Because Allied will be able to purchase the aluminum at the lower price of $1,550 per ton.[30]

Allied enters into the futures contract on September 1, 2014. Assume that the price to be paid today for inventory to be delivered in January—the **spot price**—equals the contract price. With the two prices equal, the futures contract has no value. Therefore, no entry is necessary.

September 2014

No entry required. A memorandum indicates the signing of the futures contract.

At December 31, 2014, the price for January delivery of aluminum increases to $1,575 per metric ton. Allied makes the following entry to record the increase in the value of the futures contract.

December 31, 2014

Futures Contract	25,000	
Unrealized Holding Gain or Loss—Equity		
([$1,575 − $1,550] × 1,000 tons)		25,000

Allied reports the futures contract in the balance sheet as a current asset. It reports the gain on the futures contract as part of other comprehensive income.

---

[29]A **futures contract** is a firm contractual agreement between a buyer and seller for a specified asset on a fixed date in the future which also trades on an exchange. The contract also has a standard specification so both parties know exactly what is being traded. A **forward** is similar but is not traded on an exchange and does not have standardized conditions.

[30]As with the earlier call option example, the actual aluminum does not have to be exchanged. Rather, the parties to the futures contract settle by paying the cash difference between the futures price and the price of aluminum on each settlement date.

Since Allied has not yet purchased and sold the inventory, this gain arises from an **anticipated transaction**. In this type of transaction, **a company accumulates in equity gains or losses on the futures contract as part of other comprehensive income until the period in which it sells the inventory, thereby affecting earnings**.

In January 2015, Allied purchases 1,000 metric tons of aluminum for $1,575 and makes the following entry.[31]

January 2015

Aluminum Inventory	1,575,000	
Cash ($1,575 × 1,000 tons)		1,575,000

At the same time, Allied makes final settlement on the futures contract. It records the following entry.

January 2015

Cash	25,000	
Futures Contract ($1,575,000 − $1,550,000)		25,000

Through use of the futures contract derivative, Allied fixes the cost of its inventory. The $25,000 futures contract settlement offsets the amount paid to purchase the inventory at the prevailing market price of $1,575,000. The result: net cash outflow of $1,550 per metric ton, as desired. As Illustration 17A-7 shows, Allied has therefore effectively hedged the cash flow for the purchase of inventory.

ILLUSTRATION 17A-7
Effect of Hedge on Cash Flows

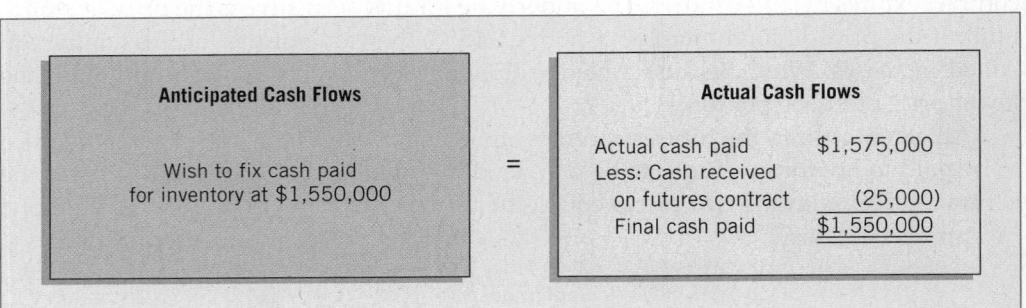

There are no income effects at this point. Allied accumulates in equity the gain on the futures contract as part of other comprehensive income until the period when it sells the inventory, affecting earnings through cost of goods sold.

For example, assume that Allied processes the aluminum into finished goods (cans). The total cost of the cans (including the aluminum purchases in January 2015) is $1,700,000. Allied sells the cans in July 2015 for $2,000,000, and records this sale as follows.

July 2015

Cash	2,000,000	
Sales Revenue		2,000,000
Cost of Goods Sold	1,700,000	
Inventory (cans)		1,700,000

Since the effect of the anticipated transaction has now affected earnings, Allied makes the following entry related to the hedging transaction.

---

[31]In practice, futures contracts are settled on a daily basis. For our purposes, we show only one settlement for the entire amount.

July 2015

Unrealized Holding Gain or Loss—Equity	25,000	
Cost of Goods Sold		25,000

The gain on the futures contract, which Allied reported as part of other comprehensive income, now reduces cost of goods sold. As a result, the cost of aluminum included in the overall cost of goods sold is $1,550,000. The futures contract has worked as planned. Allied has managed the cash paid for aluminum inventory and the amount of cost of goods sold.

OTHER REPORTING ISSUES

The preceding examples illustrate the basic reporting issues related to the accounting for derivatives. Next, we discuss the following additional issues:

10 **LEARNING OBJECTIVE**

Identify special reporting issues related to derivative financial instruments that cause unique accounting problems.

1. The accounting for embedded derivatives.
2. Qualifying hedge criteria.

Embedded Derivatives

As we indicated at the beginning of this appendix, rapid innovation in the development of complex financial instruments drove efforts toward unifying and improving the accounting standards for derivatives. In recent years, this innovation has led to the development of **hybrid securities**. These securities have characteristics of both debt and equity. They often combine traditional and derivative financial instruments.

For example, a convertible bond (discussed in Chapter 16) is a hybrid instrument. It consists of two parts: (1) a debt security, referred to as the **host security**, combined with (2) an option to convert the bond to shares of common stock, the **embedded derivative**.

To provide consistency in accounting for similar derivatives, a company must account for embedded derivatives similarly to other derivatives. Therefore, to account for an embedded derivative, a company **should separate it from the host security** and then account for it using the accounting for derivatives. This separation process is referred to as **bifurcation**.[32] Thus, a company investing in a convertible bond must separate the stock option component of the instrument. It then accounts for the derivative (the stock option) at fair value and the host instrument (the debt) according to GAAP, as if there were no embedded derivative.[33]

Qualifying Hedge Criteria

The FASB identified certain criteria that hedging transactions must meet before requiring the special accounting for hedges. The FASB designed these criteria to ensure the use of hedge accounting in a consistent manner across different hedge transactions. The general criteria relate to the following areas.

International Perspective

IFRS qualifying hedge criteria are similar to those used in GAAP.

1. *Documentation, risk management, and designation.* At inception of the hedge, there must be formal **documentation** of the hedging relationship, the company's **risk management** objective, and the strategy for undertaking the hedge. **Designation**

---

[32]A company can also designate such a derivative as a hedging instrument. The company would apply the hedge accounting provisions outlined earlier in the chapter.

[33]The issuer of the convertible bonds would not bifurcate the option component of the convertible bonds payable. GAAP explicitly precludes embedded derivative accounting for an embedded derivative that is indexed to a company's own common stock. If the conversion feature was tied to **another company's** stock, then the derivative would be bifurcated.

refers to identifying the hedging instrument, the hedged item or transaction, the nature of the risk being hedged, and how the hedging instrument will offset changes in the fair value or cash flows attributable to the hedged risk.

The FASB decided that documentation and designation are critical to the implementation of the special accounting for hedges. Without these requirements, companies might try to apply the hedge accounting provisions retroactively, only in response to negative changes in market conditions, to offset the negative impact of a transaction on the financial statements. Allowing special hedge accounting in such a setting could mask the speculative nature of the original transaction.

2. *Effectiveness of the hedging relationship.* At inception and on an ongoing basis, the hedging relationship should be highly effective in achieving offsetting changes in fair value or cash flows. Companies must assess effectiveness whenever preparing financial statements.

The general guideline for effectiveness is that the fair values or cash flows of the hedging instrument (the derivative) and the hedged item exhibit a high degree of correlation. In practice, high effectiveness is assumed when the correlation is close to one (e.g., within plus or minus .10). In our earlier hedging examples (put option and the futures contract on aluminum inventory), the fair values and cash flows are perfectly correlated. That is, when the cash payment for the inventory purchase increased, it offset, dollar for dollar, the cash received on the futures contract.

If the effectiveness criterion is not met, either at inception or because of changes following inception of the hedging relationship, the FASB no longer allows special hedge accounting. The company should then account for the derivative as a freestanding derivative.[34]

3. *Effect on reported earnings of changes in fair values or cash flows.* A change in the fair value of a hedged item or variation in the cash flow of a hedged forecasted transaction must have the potential to change the amount recognized in reported earnings.[35] There is no need for special hedge accounting if a company accounts for both the hedging instrument and the hedged item at fair value under existing GAAP. In this case, earnings will properly reflect the offsetting gains and losses.

For example, special accounting is not needed for a fair value hedge of a trading security, because a company accounts for both the investment and the derivative at fair value on the balance sheet with gains or losses reported in earnings. Thus, "special" hedge accounting is necessary only when there is a mismatch of the accounting effects for the hedging instrument and the hedged item under GAAP.[36]

Summary of Derivatives Accounting

Illustration 17A-8 summarizes the accounting provisions for derivatives and hedging transactions.

---

[34]That is, the accounting for the part of a derivative that is not effective in a hedge is at fair value, with gains and losses recorded in income.

[35]GAAP gives companies the option to measure most types of financial instruments—from equity investments to debt issued by the company—at fair value. Changes in fair value are recognized in net income each reporting period. Thus, GAAP provides companies with the opportunity to hedge their financial instruments without the complexity inherent in applying hedge accounting provisions. For example, if the fair value option is used, bifurcation of an embedded derivative is not required. **[11]**

[36]An important criterion specific to cash flow hedges is that the forecasted transaction in a cash flow hedge "is likely to occur." A company should support this probability (defined as significantly greater than the term "more likely than not") by observable facts such as frequency of similar past transactions and its financial and operational ability to carry out the transaction.

Derivative Use	Accounting for Derivative	Accounting for Hedged Item	Common Example
Speculation	At fair value with unrealized holding gains and losses recorded in income.	Not applicable.	Call or put option on an equity security.
Hedging			
Fair value	At fair value with holding gains and losses recorded in income.	At fair value with gains and losses recorded in income.	Put option to hedge an equity investment.
Cash flow	At fair value with unrealized holding gains and losses from the hedge recorded in other comprehensive income, and reclassified in income when the hedged transaction's cash flows affect earnings.	Use other generally accepted accounting principles for the hedged item.	Use of a futures contract to hedge a forecasted purchase of inventory.

As indicated, the general accounting for derivatives relies on fair values. GAAP also establishes special accounting guidance when companies use derivatives **for hedging purposes**. For example, when a company uses a put option to hedge price changes in an available-for-sale stock investment in a fair value hedge (see the Hayward example earlier), it records unrealized gains on the investment in earnings, which is not GAAP for available-for-sale securities without such a hedge. This special accounting is justified in order to accurately report the nature of the hedging relationship in the balance sheet (recording both the put option and the investment at fair value) and in the income statement (reporting offsetting gains and losses in the same period).

Special accounting also is used for cash flow hedges. Companies account for derivatives used in qualifying cash flow hedges at fair value on the balance sheet, but record unrealized holding gains or losses in other comprehensive income until selling or settling the hedged item. In a cash flow hedge, a company continues to record the hedged item at its historical cost.

Disclosure requirements for derivatives are complex. Recent pronouncements on fair value information and financial instruments provide a helpful disclosure framework for reporting derivative instruments. Appendix 17C illustrates many of these disclosures, except for discussion of hedging issues. In general, companies that have derivatives are required to disclose the objectives for holding or issuing those instruments (speculation or hedging), the hedging context (fair value or cash flow), and the strategies for achieving risk-management objectives.

COMPREHENSIVE HEDGE ACCOUNTING EXAMPLE

To provide a comprehensive example of hedge accounting, we examine the use of an interest rate swap. First, let's consider how swaps work and why companies use them.

Options and futures trade on organized securities exchanges. Because of this, options and futures have standardized terms. Although that standardization makes the trading easier, it limits the flexibility needed to tailor contracts to specific circumstances. In addition, most types of derivatives have relatively short time horizons, thereby excluding their use for reducing long-term risk exposure.

As a result, many corporations instead turn to the swap, a very popular type of derivative. A **swap** is a transaction between two parties in which the first party promises to make a payment to the second party. Similarly, the second party promises to make a simultaneous payment to the first party.

The most common type of swap is the **interest rate swap**. In this type, one party makes payments based on a fixed or floating rate, and the second party does just the opposite. In most cases, large money-center banks bring together the two parties. These banks handle the flow of payments between the parties, as shown in Illustration 17A-9.

ILLUSTRATION 17A-9
Swap Transaction

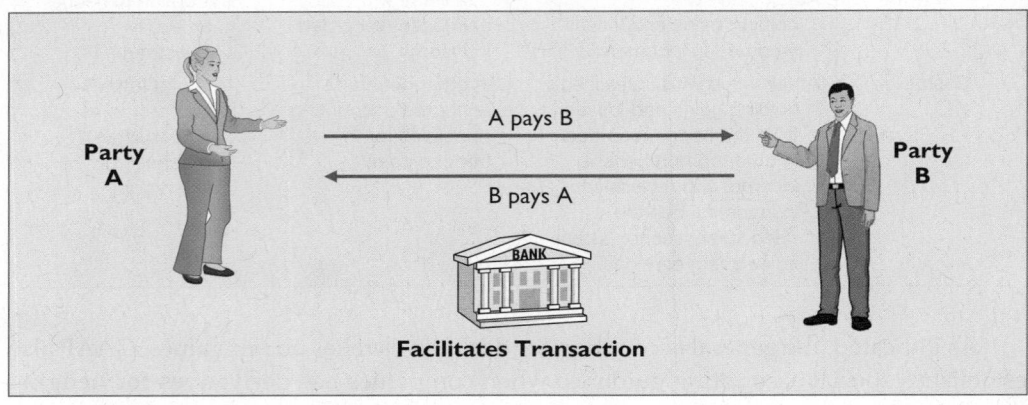

Fair Value Hedge

To illustrate the use of a swap in a fair value hedge, assume that Jones Company issues $1,000,000 of five-year, 8 percent bonds on January 2, 2014. Jones records this transaction as follows.

January 2, 2014		
Cash	1,000,000	
Bonds Payable		1,000,000

Jones offered a fixed interest rate to appeal to investors. But Jones is concerned that if market interest rates decline, the fair value of the liability will increase. The company will then suffer an economic loss.[37] To protect against the risk of loss, Jones hedges the risk of a decline in interest rates by entering into a five-year interest rate swap contract. Jones agrees to the following terms:

1. Jones will receive fixed payments at 8 percent (based on the $1,000,000 amount).
2. Jones will pay variable rates, based on the market rate in effect for the life of the swap contract. The variable rate at the inception of the contract is 6.8 percent.

As Illustration 17A-10 shows, this swap allows Jones to change the interest on the bonds payable from a fixed rate to a variable rate.

ILLUSTRATION 17A-10
Interest Rate Swap

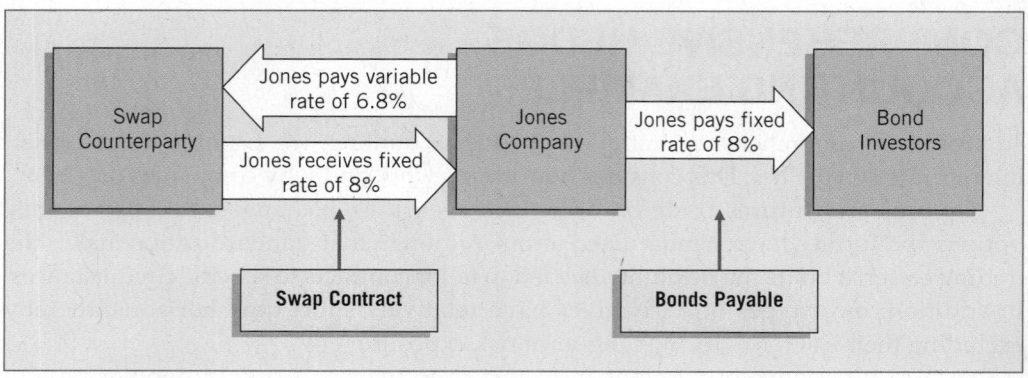

[37]This economic loss arises because Jones is locked into the 8 percent interest payments even if rates decline.

The settlement dates for the swap correspond to the interest payment dates on the debt (December 31). On each interest payment (settlement) date, Jones and the counterparty compute the difference between current market interest rates and the fixed rate of 8 percent, and determine the value of the swap.[38] If interest rates decline, the value of the swap contract to Jones increases (Jones has a gain), while at the same time Jones's fixed-rate debt obligation increases (Jones has an economic loss).

The swap is an effective risk-management tool in this setting. Its value relates to the same underlying (interest rates) that will affect the value of the fixed-rate bond payable. Thus, if the value of the swap goes up, it offsets the loss related to the debt obligation.

Assuming that Jones enters into the swap on January 2, 2014 (the same date as the issuance of the debt), the swap at this time has no value. Therefore, no entry is necessary.

January 2, 2014
No entry required. A memorandum indicates the signing of the swap contract.

At the end of 2014, Jones makes the interest payment on the bonds. It records this transaction as follows.

December 31, 2014

Interest Expense	80,000	
Cash (8% × $1,000,000)		80,000

At the end of 2014, market interest rates have declined substantially. Therefore, the value of the swap contract increases. Recall (see Illustration 17A-9) that in the swap, Jones receives a fixed rate of 8 percent, or $80,000 ($1,000,000 × 8%), and pays a variable rate (6.8%), or $68,000. Jones therefore receives $12,000 ($80,000 − $68,000) as a settlement payment on the swap contract on the first interest payment date. Jones records this transaction as follows.

December 31, 2014

Cash	12,000	
Interest Expense		12,000

In addition, a market appraisal indicates that the value of the interest rate swap has increased $40,000. Jones records this increase in value as follows.[39]

December 31, 2014

Swap Contract	40,000	
Unrealized Holding Gain or Loss—Income		40,000

Jones reports this swap contract in the balance sheet. It reports the gain on the hedging transaction in the income statement. Because interest rates have declined, the company records a loss and a related increase in its liability as follows.

December 31, 2014

Unrealized Holding Gain or Loss—Income	40,000	
Bonds Payable		40,000

Jones reports the loss on the hedging activity in net income. It adjusts bonds payable in the balance sheet to fair value (which deviates from normal accounting at amortized cost).

[38]The underlying for an interest rate swap is some index of market interest rates. The most commonly used index is the London Interbank Offer Rate, or LIBOR. In this example, we assume the LIBOR is 6.8 percent.

[39]Theoretically, this fair value change reflects the present value of expected future differences in variable and fixed interest rates.

Financial Statement Presentation of an Interest Rate Swap

Illustration 17A-11 indicates how Jones reports the asset and liability related to this hedging transaction on the balance sheet.

ILLUSTRATION 17A-11
Balance Sheet
Presentation of Fair
Value Hedge

JONES COMPANY BALANCE SHEET (PARTIAL) DECEMBER 31, 2014	
Current assets	
Swap contract	$40,000
Long-term liabilities	
Bonds payable	$1,040,000

The effect on Jones's balance sheet is the addition of the swap asset and an increase in the carrying value of the bonds payable. Illustration 17A-12 indicates how Jones reports the effects of this swap transaction in the income statement.

ILLUSTRATION 17A-12
Income Statement
Presentation of Fair
Value Hedge

JONES COMPANY INCOME STATEMENT (PARTIAL) FOR THE YEAR ENDED DECEMBER 31, 2014		
Interest expense ($80,000 − $12,000)		$68,000
Other income		
Unrealized holding gain—swap contract	$40,000	
Unrealized holding loss—bonds payable	(40,000)	
Net gain (loss)		$–0–

On the income statement, Jones reports interest expense of $68,000. Jones has effectively changed the debt's interest rate from fixed to variable. That is, by receiving a fixed rate and paying a variable rate on the swap, the company converts the fixed rate on the bond payable to variable. This results in an effective-interest rate of 6.8 percent in 2014.[40] Also, the gain on the swap offsets the loss related to the debt obligation. Therefore, the net gain or loss on the hedging activity is zero.

Illustration 17A-13 shows the overall impact of the swap transaction on the financial statements.

ILLUSTRATION 17A-13
Impact on Financial
Statements of Fair Value
Hedge

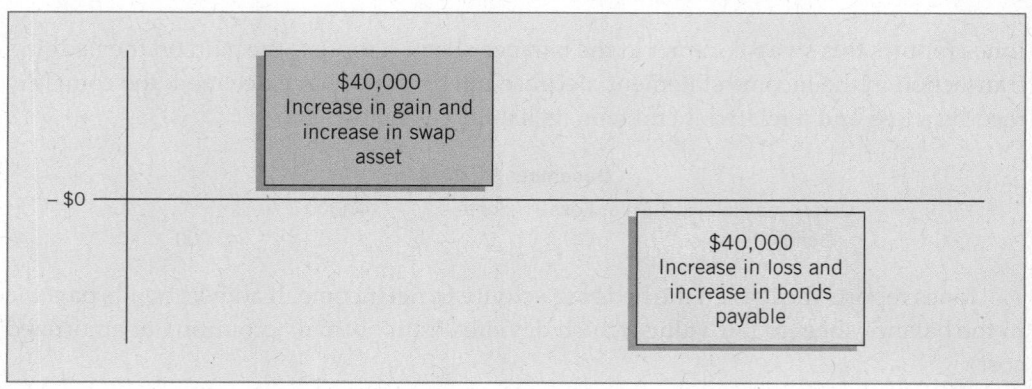

[40]Jones will apply similar accounting and measurement at future interest payment dates. Thus, if interest rates increase, Jones will continue to receive 8 percent on the swap (records a loss) but will also be locked into the fixed payments to the bondholders at an 8 percent rate (records a gain).

In summary, to account for fair value hedges (as illustrated in the Jones example) **record the derivative at its fair value in the balance sheet, and record any gains and losses in income**. Thus, the gain on the swap offsets or hedges the loss on the bond payable, due to the decline in interest rates.

By adjusting the hedged item (the bond payable in the Jones case) to fair value, with the gain or loss recorded in earnings, the accounting for the Jones bond payable deviates from amortized cost. This special accounting is justified in order to report accurately the nature of the hedging relationship between the swap and the bond payable in the balance sheet (both the swap and the debt obligation are recorded at fair value) and in the income statement (offsetting gains and losses are reported in the same period).[41]

International Perspective

International accounting for hedges (*IAS 39*) is similar to the provisions of GAAP.

CONTROVERSY AND CONCLUDING REMARKS

Companies need rules to properly measure and report derivatives in financial statements. However, some argue that reporting derivatives at fair value results in unrealized gains and losses that are difficult to interpret. Others raise concerns about the complexity and cost of implementing GAAP in this area.

However, we believe that the long-term benefits of using fair value and reporting derivatives at fair value will far outweigh any short-term implementation costs. As the volume and complexity of derivatives and hedging transactions continue to grow, so does the risk that investors and creditors will be exposed to unexpected losses arising from derivative transactions. Statement readers must have comprehensive information concerning many derivative financial instruments and the effects of hedging transactions using derivatives.

SUMMARY OF LEARNING OBJECTIVES FOR APPENDIX 17A

7 **Describe the uses of and accounting for derivatives.** Any company or individual that wants to ensure against different types of business risks may use derivative contracts to achieve this objective. In general, these transactions involve some type of hedge. Speculators also use derivatives, attempting to find an enhanced return. Speculators are very important to the derivatives market because they keep it liquid on a daily basis. Arbitrageurs attempt to exploit inefficiencies in various derivative contracts. A company primarily uses derivatives for purposes of hedging its exposure to fluctuations in interest rates, foreign currency exchange rates, and commodity prices.

Companies should recognize derivatives in the financial statements as assets and liabilities, and report them at fair value. Companies should recognize gains and losses resulting from speculation immediately in income. They report gains and losses resulting from hedge transactions in different ways, depending on the type of hedge.

KEY TERMS

anticipated transaction, *988*
arbitrageurs, *979*
bifurcation, *989*
call option, *980*
cash flow hedge, *987*
counterparty, *981(n)*
derivative financial instruments,
 derivatives, *977*
designation, *989*
documentation, *989*
embedded
 derivative, *989*
fair value hedge, *984*
forward contract, *977*
futures contract, *987*
hedging, *984*
highly effective, *990*
host security, *989*
hybrid security, *989*
interest rate swap, *992*
intrinsic value, *981*

---

[41]An interest rate swap can also be used in a cash flow hedge. A common setting is the cash flow risk inherent in having variable rate debt as part of a company's debt structure. In this situation, the variable debt issuer can hedge the cash flow risk by entering into a swap contract to receive variable rate cash flows but pay fixed rate. The cash received on the swap contract will offset the variable cash flows to be paid on the debt obligation.

net settlement, *982(n)*

notional amount, *981*

option contract, *978*

option premium, *981*

put option, *980(n)*

risk management, *989*

speculators, *979*

spot price, *987*

strike (exercise) price, *980*

swap, *991*

time value, *981*

underlying, *983*

Companies report derivative financial instruments in the balance sheet, and record them at fair value. Except for derivatives used in hedging, companies record realized and unrealized gains and losses on derivative financial instruments in income.

8 **Explain how to account for a fair value hedge.** A company records the derivative used in a qualifying fair value hedge at its fair value in the balance sheet, recording any gains and losses in income. In addition, the company also accounts for the item being hedged with the derivative at fair value. By adjusting the hedged item to fair value, with the gain or loss recorded in earnings, the accounting for the hedged item may deviate from GAAP in the absence of a hedge relationship. This special accounting is justified in order to report accurately the nature of the hedging relationship between the derivative hedging instruments and the hedged item. A company reports both in the balance sheet, reporting offsetting gains and losses in income in the same period.

9 **Explain how to account for a cash flow hedge.** Companies account for derivatives used in qualifying cash flow hedges at fair value on the balance sheet, but record gains or losses in equity as part of other comprehensive income. Companies accumulate these gains or losses, and reclassify them in income when the hedged transaction's cash flows affect earnings. Accounting is according to GAAP for the hedged item.

10 **Identify special reporting issues related to derivative financial instruments that cause unique accounting problems.** A company should separate a derivative that is embedded in a hybrid security from the host security, and account for it using the accounting for derivatives. This separation process is referred to as bifurcation. Special hedge accounting is allowed only for hedging relationships that meet certain criteria. The main criteria are as follows. (1) There is formal documentation of the hedging relationship, the company's risk-management objective, and the strategy for undertaking the hedge, and the company designates the derivative as either a cash flow or fair value hedge. (2) The company expects the hedging relationship to be highly effective in achieving offsetting changes in fair value or cash flows. (3) "Special" hedge accounting is necessary only when there is a mismatch of the accounting effects for the hedging instrument and the hedged item under GAAP.

APPENDIX 17B | **VARIABLE-INTEREST ENTITIES**

LEARNING OBJECTIVE 11
Describe the accounting for variable-interest entities.

The FASB has issued rules to address the concern that some companies are not reporting the risks and rewards of certain investments and other financial arrangements in their consolidated financial statements. **[12]** As one analyst noted, **Enron** showed the world the power of the idea that "if investors can't see it, they can't ask you about it—the 'it' being assets and liabilities."

What exactly did Enron do? First, it created a number of entities whose purpose was to hide debt, avoid taxes, and enrich certain management personnel to the detriment of the company and its stockholders. In effect, these entities, called **special-purpose entities (SPEs)**, appeared to be separate entities for which Enron had a limited economic interest. However, for many of these arrangements, Enron actually had a substantial economic interest. The risks and rewards of ownership were not shifted to the entities but remained with Enron. In short, Enron was obligated to repay investors in these SPEs when they were unsuccessful. Once Enron's problems were discovered, it soon became apparent that many other companies had similar problems.

WHAT ABOUT GAAP?

A reasonable question to ask with regard to SPEs is, "Why didn't GAAP prevent companies from hiding SPE debt and other risks, by forcing companies to include these obligations in their consolidated financial statements?" To understand why, we have to look at the basic rules of consolidation.

The GAAP rules indicate that consolidated financial statements are "usually necessary for a fair presentation when one of the companies in the group directly or indirectly has a controlling financial interest in other companies." They further note that "the usual condition for a controlling financial interest is ownership of a majority voting interest."[42] In other words, if a company like Intel owns more than 50 percent of the voting stock of another company, Intel consolidates that company. GAAP also indicates that controlling financial interest may be achieved through arrangements that do not involve voting interests. However, applying these guidelines in practice is difficult.

Whenever GAAP uses a clear line, like "greater than 50 percent," companies sometimes exploit the criterion. For example, some companies set up joint ventures in which each party owns exactly 50 percent. In that case, neither party consolidates. Or like Coca-Cola, a company may own less than 50 percent of the voting stock but maintain effective control through board of director relationships, supply relationships, or through some other type of financial arrangement.

So the FASB realized that changes had to be made to GAAP for consolidations, and it issued expanded consolidation guidelines. These guidelines define when a company should use factors other than voting interest to determine controlling financial interest. In this pronouncement, the FASB created a new risk-and-reward model to be used in situations where voting interests were unclear. The risk-and-reward model answers the basic questions of who stands to gain or lose the most from ownership in an SPE when ownership is uncertain.

In other words, we now have two models for consolidation:

1. **Voting-interest model**—If a company owns more than 50 percent of another company, then consolidate in most cases.
2. **Risk-and-reward model**—If a company is involved substantially in the economics of another company, then consolidate.

Operationally, the voting-interest model is easy to apply. It sets a "bright-line" ownership standard of more than 50 percent of the voting stock. However, if companies cannot determine control based on voting interest, they must use the risk-and-reward model.

CONSOLIDATION OF VARIABLE-INTEREST ENTITIES

To answer the question of who gains or loses when voting rights do not determine consolidation, the FASB developed the risk-and-reward model. In this model, the FASB introduced the notion of a variable-interest entity. A **variable-interest entity (VIE)** is an entity that has one of the following characteristics:

1. *Insufficient equity investment at risk.* Stockholders are assumed to have sufficient capital investment to support the entity's operations. If thinly capitalized, the entity is considered a VIE and is subject to the risk-and-reward model.

---

[42]"Consolidation of Certain Special Purpose Entities," Proposed Interpretation (Norwalk, Conn.: FASB, June 28, 2002).

2. *Stockholders lack decision-making rights.* In some cases, stockholders do not have the influence to control the company's destiny.

3. *Stockholders do not absorb the losses or receive the benefits of a normal stockholder.* In some entities, stockholders are shielded from losses related to their primary risks, or their returns are capped or must be shared with other parties.

Once the company determines that an entity is a variable-interest entity, it no longer can use the voting-interest model. The question that must then be asked is, "What party is exposed to the majority of the risks and rewards associated with the VIE?" This party is called the primary beneficiary and must consolidate the VIE. Illustration 17B-1 shows the decision model for the VIE consolidation model.[43]

ILLUSTRATION 17B-1
VIE Consolidation Model

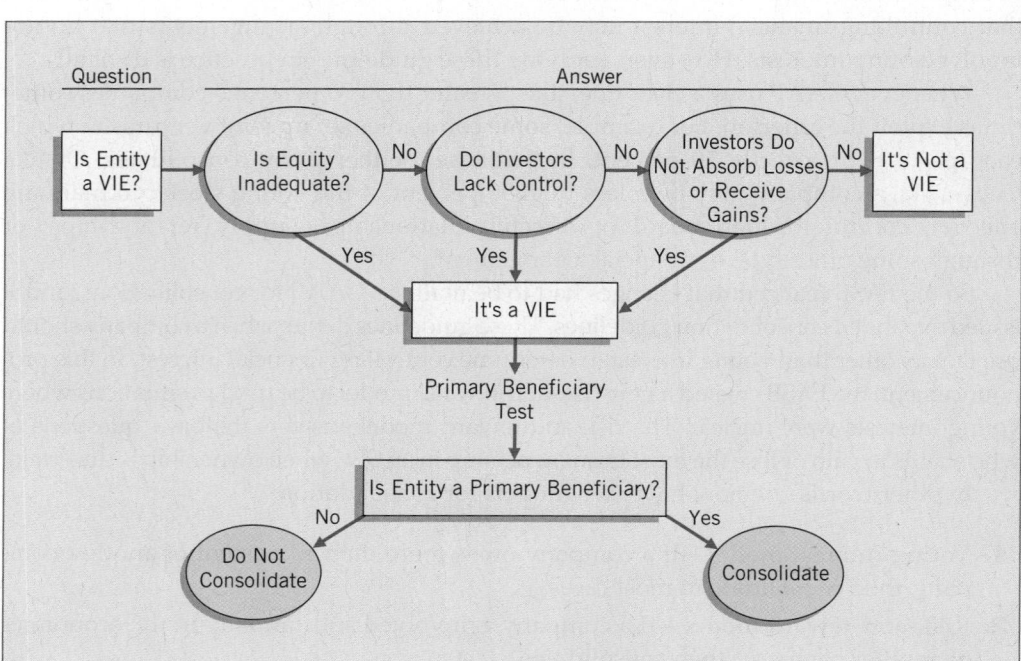

Some Examples

Let's look at a couple of examples to illustrate how this process works.

Example 1

Assume that Citigroup sells notes receivable to another entity called RAKO. RAKO's assets are financed in two ways: Lenders provide 90 percent, and investors provide the remaining 10 percent as an equity investment. If Citigroup does not guarantee the debt, Citigroup has low or nonexistent risk. Therefore, Citigroup would not consolidate the assets and liabilities of RAKO. On the other hand, if Citigroup guarantees RAKO's debt, then RAKO is a VIE, and Citigroup is the primary beneficiary. In that case, Citigroup must consolidate.

---

[43]In a recent amendment to the VIE consolidation rules, the FASB expanded the factors to be considered when deciding whether a VIE should be consolidated. The new guidelines require evaluation of qualitative factors related to the power to direct activities of the VIE and assessment of obligations to absorb losses or rights to receive benefits from the VIE. These qualitative factors must be considered in addition to the quantitative analysis of the expected losses of the entity to determine consolidation. **[13]** The IASB has recently issued new rules on consolidation that are similar to GAAP.

Example 2

San Diego Gas and Electric (SDGE) is required by law to buy power from small, local producers. In some cases, SDGE has contracts requiring it to purchase substantially all the power generated by these local companies over their lifetime. Because SDGE controls the outputs of the producers, they are VIEs. In this case, the risks and rewards related to ownership apply to SDGE. In other words, it is the primary beneficiary, and SDGE should include these producers in the consolidated financial statements.

Note that the primary beneficiary may have the risks and rewards of ownership through use of a variety of instruments and financial arrangements, such as equity investments, loans to the VIE, leases, derivatives, and guarantees. Potential VIEs include corporations, partnerships, limited liability companies, and majority-owned subsidiaries.

What Is Happening in Practice?

For most companies, the reporting related to VIEs will not materially affect their financial statements. As shown in Illustration 17B-2, one study of 509 companies with total market values over $500 million found that just 17 percent of the companies reviewed had a material impact when the VIE rules were first implemented.

Of the material VIEs disclosed in the study, the most common types (42 percent) were related to joint-venture equity investments, followed by off-balance-sheet lease arrangements (22 percent). In some cases, companies restructured transactions to avoid consolidation. For example, Pep Boys, Choice Point, Inc., and Anadarko all appear to have restructured their lease transactions to avoid consolidation. On the other hand, companies like eBay, Kimberly-Clark, and Williams-Sonoma Inc. had to consolidate their VIEs. With respect to the new guidelines for VIEs, companies began reporting under these rules in 2010. Some estimates have as much as $5 trillion of assets that could be brought on-balance-sheet under the new rules. As an example, JP Morgan reported in a recent annual report that up to $160 billion of credit card receivables and other mortgage-backed loans will have to be consolidated when it adopts the new rules.

In summary, companies are required to consolidate certain investments and other financing arrangements that previously were reported off-balance-sheet. As a result, financial statements should be more complete in reporting the risks and rewards of these transactions.

ILLUSTRATION 17B-2
Impact of Rule Involving Risk-and-Reward Model

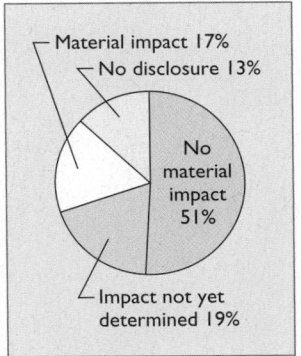

Source: Company Reports; *Glass, Lewis, & Co. Research Report* (November 6, 2003).

SUMMARY OF LEARNING OBJECTIVE FOR APPENDIX 17B

11 **Describe the accounting for variable-interest entities.** Special variable-interest accounting is used in situations where control cannot be determined based on voting rights. A company is required to consolidate a variable-interest entity if it is the primary beneficiary of the variable-interest entity.

KEY TERMS

risk-and-reward
  model, *997*

special-purpose entity
  (SPE), *996*

variable-interest entity
  (VIE), *997*

voting-interest
  model, *997*

APPENDIX 17C FAIR VALUE DISCLOSURES

As indicated in the chapter, the FASB believes that fair value information is relevant for making effective business decisions. However, others express concern about fair value measurements for two reasons: (1) the lack of reliability related to the fair value measurement in certain cases, and (2) the ability to manipulate fair value

12 LEARNING OBJECTIVE
Describe required fair value disclosures.

measurements to achieve financial results inconsistent with the underlying economics of the situation.

The Board recognizes these concerns and has attempted to develop a sound conceptual basis for measuring and reporting fair value information. In addition, it has placed emphasis on developing guidelines for reporting fair value information for financial instruments because many of these instruments have relatively active markets for which valuations can be reliably determined. The purpose of this appendix is to explain the disclosure requirements for financial instruments related to fair value information.

DISCLOSURE OF FAIR VALUE INFORMATION: FINANCIAL INSTRUMENTS

One requirement related to fair value disclosure is that both the cost and the fair value of all financial instruments be reported in the notes to the financial statements. **[14]** This enables readers of the financial statements to understand the fair value of the company's financial instruments and the potential gains and losses that might occur in the future as a result of these instruments.

The Board also decided that companies should disclose information that enables users to determine the extent of usage of fair value and the inputs used to implement fair value measurement. Two reasons for additional disclosure beyond the simple itemization of fair values are:

1. *Differing levels of reliability exist in the measurement of fair value information.* It therefore is important to understand the varying risks involved in measurement. It is difficult to incorporate these levels of uncertainty into the financial statements. Disclosure provides a framework for addressing the qualitative aspects related to risk and measurement.

2. *Changes in the fair value of financial instruments are reported differently in the financial statements, depending on the type of financial instrument involved and whether the fair value option is employed.* Note disclosure provides an opportunity to explain more precisely the impact that changes in the value of financial instruments have on financial results. In assessing the inputs, the Board recognizes that the reliability of the fair value measurement is of extreme importance. Many financial instruments are traded in active markets, and their valuation is not difficult. Other instruments are complex/illiquid, and their valuation is difficult.

To highlight these levels of reliability in valuation, the FASB established a fair value hierarchy. As discussed in Chapter 2 (page 57), this hierarchy identifies three broad levels—1, 2, and 3—related to the measurement of fair values. Level 1 is the most reliable measurement because fair value is based on quoted prices in active markets *for identical assets or liabilities.* Level 2 is less reliable; it is not based on quoted market prices for identical assets and liabilities but instead may be based on *similar assets or liabilities.* Level 3 is least reliable; it uses unobservable inputs that reflect the company's assumption as to the value of the financial instrument.

Illustration 17C-1 is an example of a fair value note disclosure for Sabathia Company. It includes both the fair value amounts and the reliability level. (A similar disclosure would be presented for liabilities.)

ILLUSTRATION 17C-1
Example of Fair Value
Hierarchy

		Fair Value Measurements at Reporting Data Using		
SABATHIA COMPANY				
NOTES TO THE FINANCIAL STATEMENTS				
($ in 000s)				
Description	Fair Value 12/31/14	Quoted Prices in Active Markets for Identical Assets (Level 1)	Significant Other Observable Inputs (Level 2)	Significant Unobservable Inputs (Level 3)
Trading securities	$115	$105	$10	
Available-for-sale securities	75	75		
Derivatives	60	25	15	$20
Venture capital investments	10			10
Total	$260	$205	$25	$30

For assets and liabilities measured at fair value and classified as Level 3, a reconciliation of Level 3 changes for the period is required. In addition, companies should report an analysis of how Level 3 changes in fair value affect total gains and losses and their impact on net income. Illustration 17C-2 is an example of this disclosure.

ILLUSTRATION 17C-2
Reconciliation of Level 3
Inputs

SABATHIA COMPANY
NOTES TO THE FINANCIAL STATEMENTS

($ in 000s)	Fair Value Measurements Using Significant Unobservable Inputs (Level 3)		
	Derivatives	Venture Capital Investments	Total
Beginning balance	$14	$11	$25
Total gains or losses (realized/unrealized)			
Included in earnings (or changes in net assets)	11	(3)	8
Included in other comprehensive income	4		4
Purchases, issuances, and settlements	(7)	2	(5)
Transfers in and/or out of Level 3	(2)		(2)
Ending balance	$20	$10	$30
The amount of total gains or losses for the period included in earnings (or changes in net assets) attributable to the change in unrealized gains or losses relating to assets still held at the reporting date	$7	$2	$9

Gains and losses (realized and unrealized) included in earnings (or changes in net assets) for the period (above) are reported in trading revenues and in other revenues as follows.

	Trading Revenues	Other Revenues
Total gains or losses included in earnings (or changes in net assets) for the period (as shown in the table above)	$11	$(3)
Change in unrealized gains or losses relating to assets still held at reporting date	$7	$2

Sabathia Company's disclosure provides to the user of the financial statements an understanding of the following:

1. The carrying amount and the fair value of the company's financial instruments segregated by level of reliability. Thus, the reader of the financial statements has a basis for judging what credence should be given to the fair value amounts.

2. For Level 3 financial instruments, a reconciliation of the balance from the beginning to the end of the period. This reconciliation enables the reader to understand the composition of the change. It is important because these calculations are most affected by subjective estimates and could be subject to manipulation.

3. The impact of changes in fair value on the net assets of the company from one period to the next.

For companies that choose to use the fair value option for some or all of their financial instruments **[15]**, they are permitted to incorporate the entire guidelines related to fair value measurement into one master schedule, or they can provide in a separate schedule information related solely to the fair value option.

Finally, companies must provide the following (with special emphasis on Level 3 measurements):

1. Quantitative information about significant unobservable inputs used for all Level 3 measurements.

2. A qualitative discussion about the sensitivity of recurring Level 3 measurements to changes in the unobservable inputs disclosed, including interrelationships between inputs.

3. A description of the company's valuation process.

4. Any transfers between Levels 1 and 2 of the fair value hierarchy.

5. Information about nonfinancial assets measured at fair value at amounts that differ from the assets' highest and best use.

6. The proper hierarchy classification for items that are not recognized on the balance sheet but are disclosed in the notes to the financial statements.

ILLUSTRATION 17C-3
Quantitative Information about Level 3 Fair Value Measurements

A typical disclosure related to Level 3 fair value measurements is presented in Illustration 17C-3.

($ in millions)	Fair Value at 12/31/2014	Valuation Technique(s)	Unobservable Input	Range (Weighted-Average)
Residential mortgage-backed securities	125	Discounted cash flow	Constant prepayment rate Probability of default Loss severity	3.5%–5.5% (4.5%) 5%–50% (10%) 40%–100% (60%)
Collateralized debt obligations	35	Consensus pricing	Offered quotes Comparability adjustments (%)	20–45 −10%–+15% (+5%)
Direct venture capital investments: Healthcare	53	Discounted cash flow	Weighted-average cost of capital Long-term revenue growth rate Long-term pretax operating margin Discount for lack of marketability[a] Control premium[a]	7%–16% (12.1%) 2%–5% (4.2%) 3%–20% (10.3%) 5%–20% (17%) 10%–30% (20%)
		Market-comparable companies	EBITDA multiple[b] Revenue multiple[b] Discount for lack of marketability[a] Control premium[a]	6.5–12 (9.5) 1.0–3.0 (2.0) 5%–20% (10%) 10%–20% (12%)
Credit contracts	38	Option model	Annualized volatility of credit[c] Counterparty credit risk[d] Own credit risk[d]	10%–20% 0.5–3.5% 0.3–2.0%

[a]Represents amounts used when the reporting entity has determined that market participants would take into account these premiums and discounts when pricing the investments.
[b]Represents amounts used when the reporting entity has determined that market participants would use such multiples when pricing the investments.
[c]Represents the range of the volatility curves used in the valuation analysis that the reporting entity has determined market participants would use when pricing the contracts.
[d]Represents the range of the credit default swap spread curves used in the valuation analysis that the reporting entity has determined market participants would use when pricing the contracts.

(*Note:* For liabilities, a similar table should be presented.)

DISCLOSURE OF FAIR VALUES: IMPAIRED ASSETS OR LIABILITIES

In addition to financial instruments, companies often have assets or liabilities that are remeasured on a nonrecurring basis due to impairment. In this case, the fair value hierarchy can highlight the reliability of the measurement, coupled with the related gain or loss for the period. Illustration 17C-4 highlights this disclosure for McClung Company.

ILLUSTRATION 17C-4
Disclosure of Fair Value, with Impairment

McCLUNG COMPANY				
NOTES TO THE FINANCIAL STATEMENTS				
($ in millions)		Fair Value Measurements Using		
Description	Year Ended 12/31/14	Quoted Prices in Active Markets for Identical Assets (Level 1)	Significant Other Observable Inputs (Level 2)	Significant Unobservable Inputs (Level 3)
Long-lived assets held and used	$75	—	$75	—
Goodwill	30	—	—	$30
Long-lived assets held for sale	26	—	26	—

Long-lived assets held and used with a carrying amount of $100 million were written down to their fair value of $75 million, resulting in an impairment charge of $25 million, which was included in earnings for the period.

Goodwill with a carrying amount of $65 million was written down to its implied fair value of $30 million, resulting in an impairment charge of $35 million, which was included in earnings for the period.

In accordance with the provisions of the Impairment or Disposal of Long-Lived Assets Subsections of FASB Codification Subtopic 360-10, long-lived assets held for sale with a carrying amount of $35 million were written down to their fair value of $26 million, less cost to sell of $6 million (or $20 million), resulting in a loss of $15 million, which was included in earnings for the period.

CONCLUSION

With recent joint FASB and IASB standard-setting efforts, we now have convergence with respect to fair value measurement, both in terms of the definition and measurement guidelines when fair value is the measurement approach in GAAP and IFRS. In addition, GAAP and IFRS have the same fair value disclosure requirements, as illustrated in this appendix. As the former chair of the IASB noted, this "marks the completion of a major convergence project and is a fundamentally important element of our joint response to the global crisis. The result is clearer and more consistent guidance on measuring fair value, where its use is already required."

SUMMARY OF LEARNING OBJECTIVE FOR APPENDIX 17C

12 **Describe required fair value disclosures.** The FASB has developed required fair value disclosures in response to concerns about the reliability of fair value measures. Disclosure elements include fair value amounts and reliability levels as well as impaired assets or liabilities.

DEMONSTRATION PROBLEM

Rogers Corporation carries an account in its general ledger called Investments, which contained the following debits for investment purchases and no credits.

Feb. 1, 2014	Jordy Company common stock, $100 par, 200 shares	$ 37,400
April 1	U.S. government bonds, 11%, due April 1, 2024, interest payable April 1 and October 1, 100 bonds at $1,000 each	100,000
July 1	Driver Company 12% bonds, par $50,000, dated March 1, 2010, purchased at par plus accrued interest, interest payable annually on March 1, due March 1, 2034	52,000

Instructions

(a) Prepare the entries necessary to classify the amounts into proper accounts, assuming that all the securities are classified as available-for-sale.

(b) Prepare the entry to record the accrued interest on December 31, 2014.

(c) The fair values of the securities on December 31, 2014, were:

Jordy Company common stock	$ 33,800 (1% of total shares)
U.S. government bonds	124,700
Driver Company bonds	58,600

What entry or entries, if any, would you recommend be made?

(d) The U.S. government bonds were sold on July 1, 2015, for $119,200 plus accrued interest. Give the proper entry.

(e) Now assume Rogers' investment in Jordy Company represents 30% of Jordy's shares. Prepare the 2014 entries for the investment in Jordy stock. In 2014, Jordy declared and paid dividends of $9,000 (on September 30) and reported net income of $30,000.

Solution

(a)

Equity Investments (available-for-sale)	37,400	
Debt Investments (available-for-sale)	150,000	
Interest Revenue ($50,000 × .12 × 4/12)	2,000	
Investments		189,400

(b)

December 31, 2014

Interest Receivable	7,750	
Interest Revenue		7,750

(c)

Available-for-Sale Portfolio
December 31, 2014

Securities	Cost	Fair Value	Unrealized Gain (Loss)
Jordy Company stock	$ 37,400	$ 33,800	$ (3,600)
U.S. government bonds	100,000	124,700	24,700
Driver Company bonds	50,000	58,600	8,600
Total	$187,400	$217,100	29,700
Previous fair value adjustment balance			0
Fair value adjustment—Dr.			$29,700

Fair Value Adjustment (available-for-sale)	29,700	
Unrealized Holding Gain or Loss—Equity		29,700

(d)

July 1, 2015

Cash ($119,200 + $2,750)	121,950	
Debt Investments (available-for-sale)		100,000
Interest Revenue ($100,000 × .11 × 3/12)		2,750
Gain on Sale of Investments		19,200

(e)

February 1, 2014

Equity Investments (Jordy Company)	37,400	
Cash		37,400

September 30, 2014

Cash	2,700	
Equity Investments (Jordy Company)		
(30% × $9,000)		2,700

December 31, 2014

Equity Investments (Jordy Company)	9,000	
Investment Income (30% × $30,000)		9,000

FASB CODIFICATION

FASB Codification References

[1] FASB ASC Glossary. [Predecessor literature: "Accounting for Certain Investments in Debt and Equity Securities," *Statement of Financial Accounting Standards No. 115* (Norwalk, Conn.: FASB, 1993), par. 137.]

[2] FASB ASC 820-10-20. [Predecessor literature: "Fair Value Measurement," *Statement of Financial Accounting Standards No. 157* (Norwalk, Conn.: FASB, September 2006).]

[3] FASB ASC 220. [Predecessor literature: "Reporting Comprehensive Income," *Statement of Financial Accounting Standards No. 130* (Norwalk, Conn.: FASB, 1997).]

[4] FASB ASC 323-10-15. [Predecessor literature: "The Equity Method of Accounting for Investments in Common Stock," *Opinions of the Accounting Principles Board No. 18* (New York: AICPA, 1971), par. 17.]

[5] FASB ASC 323-10-15-10. [Predecessor literature: "Criteria for Applying the Equity Method of Accounting for Investments in Common Stock," *Interpretations of the Financial Accounting Standards Board No. 35* (Stamford, Conn.: FASB, 1981).]

[6] FASB ASC 323-10-35. [Predecessor literature: "The Equity Method of Accounting for Investments in Common Stock," *Opinions of the Accounting Principles Board No. 18* (New York: AICPA, 1971), par. 19(i).]

[7] FASB ASC 815-10-05. [Predecessor literature: "Accounting for Derivative Instruments and Hedging Activities," *Statement of Financial Accounting Standards No. 133* (Stamford, Conn.: FASB, 1998).]

[8] FASB ASC 820-10. [Predecessor literature: "Fair Value Measurement," *Statement of Financial Accounting Standards No. 157* (Norwalk, Conn.: FASB, September 2006).]

[9] FASB ASC 815-10-05-4. [Predecessor literature: "Accounting for Derivative Instruments and Hedging Activities," *Statement of Financial Accounting Standards No. 133* (Stamford, Conn.: FASB, 1998), par. 249.]

[10] FASB ASC 815-10-05-4. [Predecessor literature: "Accounting for Derivative Instruments and Hedging Activities," *Statement of Financial Accounting Standards No. 133* (Stamford, Conn.: FASB, 1998).]

[11] FASB ASC 825-10-25-1. [Predecessor literature: "The Fair Value Option for Financial Assets and Liabilities, Including an Amendment of FASB Statement No. 115," *Statement of Financial Accounting Standards No. 159* (Norwalk, Conn.: FASB, February 2007).]

[12] FASB ASC 810-10-05. [Predecessor literature: "Consolidation of Variable Interest Entities (revised)—An Interpretation of ARB No. 51," *Financial Accounting Standards Interpretation No. 46(R)* (Norwalk, Conn.: FASB, December 2003).]

[13] FASB ASC 810-10-15. [Predecessor literature: "Consolidation of Variable Interest Entities (revised)—An Interpretation of ARB No. 51," *Financial Accounting Standards Interpretation No. 46(R)* (Norwalk, Conn.: FASB, December 2003).]

[14] FASB ASC 820-10. [Predecessor literature: "Fair Value Measurement," *Statement of Financial Accounting Standards No. 157* (Norwalk, Conn.: FASB, September 2006).]

[15] FASB ASC 825-10-25-1. (Predecessor literature: "The Fair Value Option for Financial Assets and Liabilities, Including an Amendment of FASB Statement No. 115," *Statement of Financial Accounting Standards No. 159* (Norwalk, Conn.: FASB, February 2007).]

Exercises

If your school has a subscription to the FASB Codification, go to *http://aaahq.org/ascLogin.cfm* to log in and prepare responses to the following. Provide Codification references for your responses.

CE17-1 Access the glossary ("Master Glossary") to answer the following.

(a) What are trading securities?
(b) What is the definition of "holding gain or loss"?
(c) What is a cash flow hedge?
(d) What is a fair value hedge?

CE17-2 What guidance does the SEC give for disclosures regarding accounting policies used for derivatives?

CE17-3 When would an investor discontinue applying the equity method in an investment? Are there any exceptions to this rule?

CE17-4 For balance sheet purposes, can the fair value of a derivative in a loss position be netted against the fair value of a derivative in a gain position?

An additional Codification case can be found in the Using Your Judgment section, on page 1026.

Be sure to check the book's companion website for a Review and Analysis Exercise, with solution.

WileyPLUS

Brief Exercises, Exercises, Problems, and many more learning and assessment tools and resources are available for practice in WileyPLUS.

Note: All asterisked Questions, Exercises, and Problems relate to material in the appendices to the chapter.

QUESTIONS

1. Distinguish between a debt security and an equity security.

2. What purpose does the variety in bond features (types and characteristics) serve?

3. What is the cost of a long-term investment in bonds?

4. Identify and explain the three types of classifications for investments in debt securities.

5. When should a debt security be classified as held-to-maturity?

6. Explain how trading securities are accounted for and reported.

7. At what amount should trading, available-for-sale, and held-to-maturity securities be reported on the balance sheet?

8. On July 1, 2014, Wheeler Company purchased $4,000,000 of Duggen Company's 8% bonds, due on July 1, 2021. The bonds, which pay interest semiannually on January 1 and July 1, were purchased for $3,500,000 to yield 10%. Determine the amount of interest revenue Wheeler should report on its income statement for the year ended December 31, 2014.

9. If the bonds in Question 8 are classified as available-for-sale and they have a fair value at December 31, 2014, of

$3,604,000, prepare the journal entry (if any) at December 31, 2014, to record this transaction.

10. Indicate how unrealized holding gains and losses should be reported for investments securities classified as trading, available-for-sale, and held-to-maturity.

11. (a) Assuming no Fair Value Adjustment (available-for-sale) account balance at the beginning of the year, prepare the adjusting entry at the end of the year if Laura Company's available-for-sale securities have a fair value $60,000 below cost. (b) Assume the same information as part (a), except that Laura Company has a debit balance in its Fair Value Adjustment account of $10,000 at the beginning of the year. Prepare the adjusting entry at year-end.

12. Identify and explain the different types of classifications for investments in equity securities.

13. Why are held-to-maturity investments applicable only to debt securities?

14. Hayes Company sold 10,000 shares of Kenyon Co. common stock for $27.50 per share, incurring $1,770 in brokerage commissions. These securities were classified as trading and originally cost $260,000. Prepare the entry to record the sale of these securities.

15. Distinguish between the accounting treatment for available-for-sale equity securities and trading equity securities.

16. What constitutes "significant influence" when an investor's financial interest is below the 50% level?

17. Explain how the investment account is affected by investee activities under the equity method.

18. Your classmate Kate believes that the equity method is applied with a strict application of the "20%" rule. Do you agree? Explain.

19. Hiram Co. uses the equity method to account for investments in common stock. What accounting should be made for dividends received from these investments subsequent to the date of investment?

20. Raleigh Corp. has an investment with a carrying value (equity method) on its books of $170,000 representing a 30% interest in Borg Company, which suffered a $620,000 loss this year. How should Raleigh Corp. handle its proportionate share of Borg's loss?

21. Where on the asset side of the balance sheet are trading securities, available-for-sale securities, and held-to-maturity securities reported? Explain.

22. Explain why reclassification adjustments are necessary.

23. Briefly discuss how a transfer of securities from the available-for-sale category to the trading category affects stockholders' equity and income.

24. When is a debt security considered impaired? Explain how to account for the impairment of an available-for-sale debt security.

25. What is the GAAP definition of fair value?

26. What is the fair value option?

27. Franklin Corp. has an investment that it has held for several years. When it purchased the investment, Franklin classified and accounted for it as available-for-sale. Can Franklin use the fair value option for this investment? Explain.

*28. What is meant by the term "underlying" as it relates to derivative financial instruments?

*29. What are the main distinctions between a traditional financial instrument and a derivative financial instrument?

*30. What is the purpose of a fair value hedge?

*31. In what situation will the unrealized holding gain or loss on an available-for-sale security be reported in income?

*32. Why might a company become involved in an interest rate swap contract to receive fixed interest payments and pay variable?

*33. What is the purpose of a cash flow hedge?

*34. Where are gains and losses related to cash flow hedges involving anticipated transactions reported?

*35. What are hybrid securities? Give an example of a hybrid security.

*36. Explain the difference between the voting-interest model and the risk-and-reward model used for consolidation.

*37. What is a variable-interest entity?

BRIEF EXERCISES

BE17-1 Garfield Company purchased, as a held-to-maturity investment, $80,000 of the 9%, 5-year bonds of Chester Corporation for $74,086, which provides an 11% return. Prepare Garfield's journal entries for (a) the purchase of the investment, and (b) the receipt of annual interest and discount amortization. Assume effective-interest amortization is used.

BE17-2 Use the information from BE17-1 but assume the bonds are purchased as an available-for-sale security. Prepare Garfield's journal entries for (a) the purchase of the investment, (b) the receipt of annual interest and discount amortization, and (c) the year-end fair value adjustment. (Assume a zero balance in the Fair Value Adjustment account.) The bonds have a year-end fair value of $75,500.

BE17-3 Carow Corporation purchased, as a held-to-maturity investment, $60,000 of the 8%, 5-year bonds of Harrison, Inc. for $65,118, which provides a 6% return. The bonds pay interest semiannually. Prepare Carow's journal entries for (a) the purchase of the investment, and (b) the receipt of semiannual interest and premium amortization. Assume effective-interest amortization is used.

BE17-4 Hendricks Corporation purchased trading investment bonds for $50,000 at par. At December 31, Hendricks received annual interest of $2,000, and the fair value of the bonds was $47,400. Prepare Hendricks' journal entries for (a) the purchase of the investment, (b) the interest received, and (c) the fair value adjustment. (Assume a zero balance in the Fair Value Adjustment account.)

BE17-5 Fairbanks Corporation purchased 400 shares of Sherman Inc. common stock as an available-for-sale investment for $13,200. During the year, Sherman paid a cash dividend of $3.25 per share. At year-end, Sherman stock was selling for $34.50 per share. Prepare Fairbanks' journal entries to record (a) the purchase of the investment, (b) the dividends received, and (c) the fair value adjustment. (Assume a zero balance in the Fair Value Adjustment account.)

3 **BE17-6** Use the information from BE17-5 but assume the stock was purchased as a trading security. Prepare Fairbanks' journal entries to record (a) the purchase of the investment, (b) the dividends received, and (c) the fair value adjustment.

4 **BE17-7** Zoop Corporation purchased for $300,000 a 30% interest in Murphy, Inc. This investment enables Zoop to exert significant influence over Murphy. During the year, Murphy earned net income of $180,000 and paid dividends of $60,000. Prepare Zoop's journal entries related to this investment.

3 **BE17-8** Cleveland Company has a stock portfolio valued at $4,000 (available-for-sale). Its cost was $3,300. If the Fair Value Adjustment account has a debit balance of $200, prepare the journal entry at year-end.

6 **BE17-9** The following information relates to Starbucks for the year ended October 2, 2011: net income 1,245.7 million; unrealized holding loss of $10.9 million related to available-for-sale securities during the year; accumulated other comprehensive income of $57.2 million on October 3, 2010. Assuming no other changes in accumulated other comprehensive income, determine (a) other comprehensive income for 2011, (b) comprehensive income for 2011, and (c) accumulated other comprehensive income at October 2, 2011.

5 **BE17-10** Hillsborough Co. has an available-for-sale investment in the bonds of Schuyler Corp. with a carrying (and fair) value of $70,000. Hillsborough determined that due to poor economic prospects for Schuyler, the bonds have decreased in value to $60,000. It is determined that this loss in value is other-than-temporary. Prepare the journal entry, if any, to record the reduction in value.

EXERCISES

1 **3** **E17-1 (Investment Classifications)** For the following investments identify whether they are:

1. Trading Securities
2. Available-for-Sale Securities
3. Held-to-Maturity Securities

Each case is independent of the other.

(a) A bond that will mature in 4 years was bought 1 month ago when the price dropped. As soon as the value increases, which is expected next month, it will be sold.

(b) 10% of the outstanding stock of Farm-Co was purchased. The company is planning on eventually getting a total of 30% of its outstanding stock.

(c) 10-year bonds were purchased this year. The bonds mature at the first of next year.

(d) Bonds that will mature in 5 years are purchased. The company would like to hold them until they mature, but money has been tight recently and they may need to be sold.

(e) Preferred stock was purchased for its constant dividend. The company is planning to hold the preferred stock for a long time.

(f) A bond that matures in 10 years was purchased. The company is investing money set aside for an expansion project planned 10 years from now.

2 **E17-2 (Entries for Held-to-Maturity Securities)** On January 1, 2013, Dagwood Company purchased at par 12% bonds having a maturity value of $300,000. They are dated January 1, 2013, and mature January 1, 2018, with interest receivable December 31 of each year. The bonds are classified in the held-to-maturity category.

Instructions

(a) Prepare the journal entry at the date of the bond purchase.

(b) Prepare the journal entry to record the interest received for 2013.

(c) Prepare the journal entry to record the interest received for 2014.

2 **E17-3 (Entries for Held-to-Maturity Securities)** On January 1, 2013, Hi and Lois Company purchased 12% bonds having a maturity value of $300,000 for $322,744.44. The bonds provide the bondholders with a 10% yield. They are dated January 1, 2013, and mature January 1, 2018, with interest receivable December 31 of each year. Hi and Lois Company uses the effective-interest method to allocate unamortized discount or premium. The bonds are classified in the held-to-maturity category.

Instructions

(a) Prepare the journal entry at the date of the bond purchase.

(b) Prepare a bond amortization schedule.

(c) Prepare the journal entry to record the interest received and the amortization for 2013.
(d) Prepare the journal entry to record the interest received and the amortization for 2014.

E17-4 (Entries for Available-for-Sale Securities) Assume the same information as in E17-3 except that the securities are classified as available-for-sale. The fair value of the bonds at December 31 of each year-end is as follows.

2013	$320,500	2016	$310,000
2014	$309,000	2017	$300,000
2015	$308,000		

Instructions
(a) Prepare the journal entry at the date of the bond purchase.
(b) Prepare the journal entries to record the interest received and recognition of fair value for 2013.
(c) Prepare the journal entry to record the recognition of fair value for 2014.

E17-5 (Effective-Interest versus Straight-Line Bond Amortization) On January 1, 2013, Phantom Company acquires $200,000 of Spiderman Products, Inc., 9% bonds at a price of $185,589. The interest is payable each December 31, and the bonds mature December 31, 2015. The investment will provide Phantom Company a 12% yield. The bonds are classified as held-to-maturity.

Instructions
(a) Prepare a 3-year schedule of interest revenue and bond discount amortization, applying the straight-line method.
(b) Prepare a 3-year schedule of interest revenue and bond discount amortization, applying the effective-interest method.
(c) Prepare the journal entry for the interest receipt of December 31, 2014, and the discount amortization under the straight-line method.
(d) Prepare the journal entry for the interest receipt of December 31, 2014, and the discount amortization under the effective-interest method.

E17-6 (Entries for Available-for-Sale and Trading Securities) The following information is available for Barkley Company at December 31, 2014, regarding its investments.

Securities	Cost	Fair Value
3,000 shares of Myers Corporation Common Stock	$40,000	$48,000
1,000 shares of Cole Incorporated Preferred Stock	25,000	22,000
	$65,000	$70,000

Instructions
(a) Prepare the adjusting entry (if any) for 2014, assuming the securities are classified as trading.
(b) Prepare the adjusting entry (if any) for 2014, assuming the securities are classified as available-for-sale.
(c) Discuss how the amounts reported in the financial statements are affected by the entries in (a) and (b).

E17-7 (Trading Securities Entries) On December 21, 2013, Bucky Katt Company provided you with the following information regarding its trading securities.

December 31, 2013

Investments (Trading)	Cost	Fair Value	Unrealized Gain (Loss)
Clemson Corp. stock	$20,000	$19,000	$(1,000)
Colorado Co. stock	10,000	9,000	(1,000)
Buffaloes Co. stock	20,000	20,600	600
Total of portfolio	$50,000	$48,600	(1,400)
Previous fair value adjustment balance			–0–
Fair value adjustment—Cr.			$(1,400)

During 2014, Colorado Company stock was sold for $9,400. The fair value of the stock on December 31, 2014, was Clemson Corp. stock—$19,100; Buffaloes Co. stock—$20,500.

Instructions

    (a) Prepare the adjusting journal entry needed on December 31, 2013.

    (b) Prepare the journal entry to record the sale of the Colorado Company stock during 2014.

    (c) Prepare the adjusting journal entry needed on December 31, 2014.

3 **E17-8 (Available-for-Sale Securities Entries and Reporting)** Satchel Corporation purchases equity securities costing $73,000 and classifies them as available-for-sale securities. At December 31, the fair value of the portfolio is $65,000.

Instructions

Prepare the adjusting entry to report the securities properly. Indicate the statement presentation of the accounts in your entry.

3 **E17-9 (Available-for-Sale Securities Entries and Financial Statement Presentation)** At December 31, 2013, the available-for-sale equity portfolio for Steffi Graf, Inc. is as follows.

Security	Cost	Fair Value	Unrealized Gain (Loss)
A	$17,500	$15,000	($2,500)
B	12,500	14,000	1,500
C	23,000	25,500	2,500
Total	$53,000	$54,500	1,500
Previous fair value adjustment balance—Dr.			400
Fair value adjustment—Dr.			$1,100

On January 20, 2014, Steffi Graf, Inc. sold security A for $15,100. The sale proceeds are net of brokerage fees.

Instructions

    (a) Prepare the adjusting entry at December 31, 2013, to report the portfolio at fair value.

    (b) Show the balance sheet presentation of the investment-related accounts at December 31, 2013. (Ignore notes presentation.)

    (c) Prepare the journal entry for the 2014 sale of security A.

6 **E17-10 (Comprehensive Income Disclosure)** Assume the same information as E17-9 and that Steffi Graf Inc. reports net income in 2013 of $120,000 and in 2014 of $140,000. Total holding gains (including any realized holding gain or loss) total $40,000.

Instructions

    (a) Prepare a statement of comprehensive income for 2013 starting with net income.

    (b) Prepare a statement of comprehensive income for 2014 starting with net income.

3 **E17-11 (Equity Securities Entries)** Arantxa Corporation made the following cash purchases of securities during 2014, which is the first year in which Arantxa invested in securities.

    1. On January 15, purchased 10,000 shares of Sanchez Company's common stock at $33.50 per share plus commission $1,980.

    2. On April 1, purchased 5,000 shares of Vicario Co.'s common stock at $52.00 per share plus commission $3,370.

    3. On September 10, purchased 7,000 shares of WTA Co.'s preferred stock at $26.50 per share plus commission $4,910.

On May 20, 2014, Arantxa sold 4,000 shares of Sanchez Company's common stock at a market price of $35 per share less brokerage commissions, taxes, and fees of $3,850. The year-end fair values per share were Sanchez $30, Vicario $55, and WTA $28. In addition, the chief accountant of Arantxa told you that Arantxa Corporation plans to hold these securities for the long term but may sell them in order to earn profits from appreciation in prices.

Instructions

    (a) Prepare the journal entries to record the above three security purchases.

    (b) Prepare the journal entry for the security sale on May 20.

    (c) Compute the unrealized gains or losses and prepare the adjusting entries for Arantxa on December 31, 2014.

3 **4** **E17-12 (Journal Entries for Fair Value and Equity Methods)** The following are two independent situations.

Situation 1: Conchita Cosmetics acquired 10% of the 200,000 shares of common stock of Martinez Fashion at a total cost of $13 per share on March 18, 2014. On June 30, Martinez declared and paid a $75,000 cash dividend. On December 31, Martinez reported net income of $122,000 for the year. At December 31, the market price of Martinez Fashion was $15 per share. The securities are classified as available-for-sale.

Situation 2: Monica, Inc. obtained significant influence over Seles Corporation by buying 30% of Seles's 30,000 outstanding shares of common stock at a total cost of $9 per share on January 1, 2014. On June 15, Seles declared and paid a cash dividend of $36,000. On December 31, Seles reported a net income of $85,000 for the year.

Instructions
Prepare all necessary journal entries in 2014 for both situations.

4 **E17-13 (Equity Method)** Parent Co. invested $1,000,000 in Sub Co. for 25% of its outstanding stock. Sub Co. pays out 40% of net income in dividends each year.

Instructions
Use the information in the following T-account for the investment in Sub to answer the following questions.

Investment in Sub Co.

1,000,000	
110,000	
	44,000

(a) How much was Parent Co.'s share of Sub Co.'s net income for the year?
(b) How much was Parent Co.'s share of Sub Co.'s dividends for the year?
(c) What was Sub Co.'s total net income for the year?
(d) What was Sub Co.'s total dividends for the year?

3 **E17-14 (Equity Investment—Trading)** Oregon Co. had purchased 200 shares of Washington Co. for $40 each this year and classified the investment as a trading security. Oregon Co. sold 100 shares of the stock for $45 each. At year-end, the price per share of the Washington Co. stock had dropped to $35.

Instructions
Prepare the journal entries for these transactions and any year-end adjustments.

3 **E17-15 (Equity Investments—Trading)** Kenseth Company has the following securities in its trading portfolio of securities on December 31, 2013.

Investments (Trading)	Cost	Fair Value
1,500 shares of Gordon, Inc., Common	$ 73,500	$ 69,000
5,000 shares of Wallace Corp., Common	180,000	175,000
400 shares of Martin, Inc., Preferred	60,000	61,600
	$313,500	$305,600

All of the securities were purchased in 2013.
In 2014, Kenseth completed the following securities transactions.

March 1 Sold the 1,500 shares of Gordon, Inc., Common, @ $45 less fees of $1,200
April 1   Bought 700 shares of Earnhart Corp., Common, @ $75 plus fees of $1,300

Kenseth Company's portfolio of trading securities appeared as follows on December 31, 2014.

Investments (Trading)	Cost	Fair Value
5,000 shares of Wallace Corp., Common	$180,000	$175,000
700 shares of Earnhart Corp., Common	53,800	50,400
400 shares of Martin, Inc., Preferred	60,000	58,000
	$293,800	$283,400

Instructions
Prepare the general journal entries for Kenseth Company for:

(a) The 2013 adjusting entry.
(b) The sale of the Gordon stock.
(c) The purchase of the Earnhart stock.
(d) The 2014 adjusting entry for the trading portfolio.

3 4 **E17-16 (Fair Value and Equity Method Compared)** Jaycie Phelps Inc. acquired 20% of the outstanding common stock of Theresa Kulikowski Inc. on December 31, 2013. The purchase price was $1,200,000 for 50,000 shares. Kulikowski Inc. declared and paid an $0.85 per share cash dividend on June 30 and on December 31, 2014. Kulikowski reported net income of $730,000 for 2014. The fair value of Kulikowski's stock was $27 per share at December 31, 2014.

Instructions
(a) Prepare the journal entries for Jaycie Phelps Inc. for 2013 and 2014, assuming that Phelps cannot exercise significant influence over Kulikowski. The securities should be classified as available-for-sale.
(b) Prepare the journal entries for Jaycie Phelps Inc. for 2013 and 2014, assuming that Phelps can exercise significant influence over Kulikowski.
(c) At what amount is the investment in securities reported on the balance sheet under each of these methods at December 31, 2014? What is the total net income reported in 2014 under each of these methods?

4 **E17-17 (Equity Method)** On January 1, 2014, Pennington Corporation purchased 30% of the common shares of Edwards Company for $180,000. During the year, Edwards earned net income of $80,000 and paid dividends of $20,000.

Instructions
Prepare the entries for Pennington to record the purchase and any additional entries related to this investment in Edwards Company in 2014.

5 **E17-18 (Impairment of Debt Securities)** Hagar Corporation has municipal bonds classified as available-for-sale at December 31, 2013. These bonds have a par value of $800,000, an amortized cost of $800,000, and a fair value of $720,000. The unrealized loss of $80,000 previously recognized as other comprehensive income and as a separate component of stockholders' equity is now determined to be other than temporary. That is, the company believes that impairment accounting is now appropriate for these bonds.

Instructions
(a) Prepare the journal entry to recognize the impairment. No entry is needed to adjust accumulated other comprehensive income.
(b) What is the new cost basis of the municipal bonds? Given that the maturity value of the bonds is $800,000, should Hagar Corporation amortize the difference between the carrying amount and the maturity value over the life of the bonds?
(c) At December 31, 2014, the fair value of the municipal bonds is $760,000. Prepare the entry (if any) to record this information.

3 5 **E17-19 (Fair Value Measurement)** Presented below is information related to the purchases of common stock by Lilly Company during 2014.

	Cost (at purchase date)	Fair Value (at December 31)
Investment in Arroyo Company stock	$100,000	$ 80,000
Investment in Lee Corporation stock	250,000	300,000
Investment in Woods Inc. stock	180,000	190,000
Total	$530,000	$570,000

Instructions
(Assume a zero balance for any Fair Value Adjustment account.)
(a) What entry would Lilly make at December 31, 2014, to record the investment in Arroyo Company stock if it chooses to report this security using the fair value option?
(b) What entry would Lilly make at December 31, 2014, to record the investment in Lee Corporation, assuming that Lilly wants to classify this security as available-for-sale? This security is the only available-for-sale security that Lilly presently owns.
(c) What entry would Lilly make at December 31, 2014, to record the investment in Woods Inc., assuming that Lilly wants to classify this investment as a trading security?

3 5 **E17-20 (Fair Value Measurement Issues)** Assume the same information as in E17-19 for Lilly Company. In addition, assume that the investment in the Woods Inc. stock was sold during 2015 for $195,000.

At December 31, 2015, the following information relates to its two remaining investments of common stock.

	Cost (at purchase date)	Fair Value (at December 31)
Investment in Arroyo Company stock	$100,000	$140,000
Investment in Lee Corporation stock	250,000	310,000
Total	$350,000	$450,000

Net income before any security gains and losses for 2015 was $905,000.

Instructions

(a) Compute the amount of net income or net loss that Lilly should report for 2015, taking into consideration Lilly's security transactions for 2015.

(b) Prepare the journal entry to record unrealized gain or loss related to the investment in Arroyo Company stock at December 31, 2015.

2 3 5 E17-21 (Fair Value Option) Presented below is selected information related to the financial instruments of Dawson Company at December 31, 2014. This is Dawson Company's first year of operations.

	Carrying Amount	Fair Value (at December 31)
Investment in debt securities (intent is to hold to maturity)	$ 40,000	$ 41,000
Investment in Chen Company stock	800,000	910,000
Bonds payable	220,000	195,000

Instructions

(a) Dawson elects to use the fair value option whenever possible. Assuming that Dawson's net income is $100,000 in 2014 before reporting any securities gains or losses, determine Dawson's net income for 2014.

(b) Record the journal entry, if any, necessary at December 31, 2014, to record the fair value option for the bonds payable.

7 *E17-22 (Derivative Transaction) On January 2, 2014, Jones Company purchases a call option for $300 on Merchant common stock. The call option gives Jones the option to buy 1,000 shares of Merchant at a strike price of $50 per share. The market price of a Merchant share is $50 on January 2, 2014 (the intrinsic value is therefore $0). On March 31, 2014, the market price for Merchant stock is $53 per share, and the time value of the option is $200.

Instructions

(a) Prepare the journal entry to record the purchase of the call option on January 2, 2014.

(b) Prepare the journal entry(ies) to recognize the change in the fair value of the call option as of March 31, 2014.

(c) What was the effect on net income of entering into the derivative transaction for the period January 2 to March 31, 2014?

8 *E17-23 (Fair Value Hedge) On January 2, 2014, MacCloud Co. issued a 4-year, $100,000 note at 6% fixed interest, interest payable semiannually. MacCloud now wants to change the note to a variable-rate note.

As a result, on January 2, 2014, MacCloud Co. enters into an interest rate swap where it agrees to receive 6% fixed and pay LIBOR of 5.7% for the first 6 months on $100,000. At each 6-month period, the variable rate will be reset. The variable rate is reset to 6.7% on June 30, 2014.

Instructions

(a) Compute the net interest expense to be reported for this note and related swap transaction as of June 30, 2014.

(b) Compute the net interest expense to be reported for this note and related swap transaction as of December 31, 2014.

9 *E17-24 (Cash Flow Hedge) On January 2, 2014, Parton Company issues a 5-year, $10,000,000 note at LIBOR, with interest paid annually. The variable rate is reset at the end of each year. The LIBOR rate for the first year is 5.8%.

Parton Company decides it prefers fixed-rate financing and wants to lock in a rate of 6%. As a result, Parton enters into an interest rate swap to pay 6% fixed and receive LIBOR based on $10 million. The variable rate is reset to 6.6% on January 2, 2015.

Instructions

(a) Compute the net interest expense to be reported for this note and related swap transactions as of December 31, 2014.

(b) Compute the net interest expense to be reported for this note and related swap transactions as of December 31, 2015.

8 *E17-25 (Fair Value Hedge)** Sarazan Company issues a 4-year, 7.5% fixed-rate interest only, nonprepayable $1,000,000 note payable on December 31, 2013. It decides to change the interest rate from a fixed rate to variable rate and enters into a swap agreement with M&S Corp. The swap agreement specifies that Sarazan will receive a fixed rate at 7.5% and pay variable with settlement dates that match the interest payments on the debt. Assume that interest rates have declined during 2014 and that Sarazan received $13,000 as an adjustment to interest expense for the settlement at December 31, 2014. The loss related to the debt (due to interest rate changes) was $48,000. The value of the swap contract increased $48,000.

Instructions

(a) Prepare the journal entry to record the payment of interest expense on December 31, 2014.

(b) Prepare the journal entry to record the receipt of the swap settlement on December 31, 2014.

(c) Prepare the journal entry to record the change in the fair value of the swap contract on December 31, 2014.

(d) Prepare the journal entry to record the change in the fair value of the debt on December 31, 2014.

7 *E17-26 (Call Option)** On August 15, 2013, Outkast Co. invested idle cash by purchasing a call option on Counting Crows Inc. common shares for $360. The notional value of the call option is 400 shares, and the option price is $40. The option expires on January 31, 2014. The following data are available with respect to the call option.

Date	Market Price of Counting Crows Shares	Time Value of Call Option
September 30, 2013	$48 per share	$180
December 31, 2013	$46 per share	65
January 15, 2014	$47 per share	30

Instructions

Prepare the journal entries for Outkast for the following dates.

(a) Investment in call option on Counting Crows shares on August 15, 2013.

(b) September 30, 2013—Outkast prepares financial statements.

(c) December 31, 2013—Outkast prepares financial statements.

(d) January 15, 2014—Outkast settles the call option on the Counting Crows shares.

9 *E17-27 (Cash Flow Hedge)** Hart Golf Co. uses titanium in the production of its specialty drivers. Hart anticipates that it will need to purchase 200 ounces of titanium in November 2014, for clubs that will be shipped in the spring and summer of 2015. However, if the price of titanium increases, this will increase the cost to produce the clubs, which will result in lower profit margins.

To hedge the risk of increased titanium prices, on May 1, 2014, Hart enters into a titanium futures contract and designates this futures contract as a cash flow hedge of the anticipated titanium purchase. The notional amount of the contract is 200 ounces, and the terms of the contract give Hart the option to purchase titanium at a price of $500 per ounce. The price will be good until the contract expires on November 30, 2014.

Assume the following data with respect to the price of the call options and the titanium inventory purchase.

Date	Spot Price for November Delivery
May 1, 2014	$500 per ounce
June 30, 2014	520 per ounce
September 30, 2014	525 per ounce

Instructions

Present the journal entries for the following dates/transactions.

(a) May 1, 2014—Inception of futures contract, no premium paid.

(b) June 30, 2014—Hart prepares financial statements.

(c) September 30, 2014—Hart prepares financial statements.

(d) October 5, 2014—Hart purchases 200 ounces of titanium at $525 per ounce and settles the futures contract.

(e) December 15, 2014—Hart sells clubs containing titanium purchased in October 2014 for $250,000. The cost of the finished goods inventory is $140,000.

(f) Indicate the amount(s) reported in the income statement related to the futures contract and the inventory transactions on December 31, 2014.

EXERCISES SET B

See the book's companion website, at **www.wiley.com/college/kieso**, for an additional set of exercises.

PROBLEMS

2 P17-1 (Debt Securities) Presented below is an amortization schedule related to Spangler Company's 5-year, $100,000 bond with a 7% interest rate and a 5% yield, purchased on December 31, 2012, for $108,660.

Date	Cash Received	Interest Revenue	Bond Premium Amortization	Carrying Amount of Bonds
12/31/12				$108,660
12/31/13	$7,000	$5,433	$1,567	107,093
12/31/14	7,000	5,354	1,646	105,447
12/31/15	7,000	5,272	1,728	103,719
12/31/16	7,000	5,186	1,814	101,905
12/31/17	7,000	5,095	1,905	100,000

The following schedule presents a comparison of the amortized cost and fair value of the bonds at year-end.

	12/31/13	12/31/14	12/31/15	12/31/16	12/31/17
Amortized cost	$107,093	$105,447	$103,719	$101,905	$100,000
Fair value	$106,500	$107,500	$105,650	$103,000	$100,000

Instructions

(a) Prepare the journal entry to record the purchase of these bonds on December 31, 2012, assuming the bonds are classified as held-to-maturity securities.

(b) Prepare the journal entry(ies) related to the held-to-maturity bonds for 2013.

(c) Prepare the journal entry(ies) related to the held-to-maturity bonds for 2015.

(d) Prepare the journal entry(ies) to record the purchase of these bonds, assuming they are classified as available-for-sale.

(e) Prepare the journal entry(ies) related to the available-for-sale bonds for 2013.

(f) Prepare the journal entry(ies) related to the available-for-sale bonds for 2015.

2 P17-2 (Available-for-Sale Debt Securities) On January 1, 2014, Novotna Company purchased $400,000, 8% bonds of Aguirre Co. for $369,114. The bonds were purchased to yield 10% interest. Interest is payable semiannually on July 1 and January 1. The bonds mature on January 1, 2019. Novotna Company uses the effective-interest method to amortize discount or premium. On January 1, 2016, Novotna Company sold the bonds for $370,726 after receiving interest to meet its liquidity needs.

Instructions

(a) Prepare the journal entry to record the purchase of bonds on January 1. Assume that the bonds are classified as available-for-sale.

(b) Prepare the amortization schedule for the bonds.

(c) Prepare the journal entries to record the semiannual interest on July 1, 2014, and December 31, 2014.

(d) If the fair value of Aguirre bonds is $372,726 on December 31, 2015, prepare the necessary adjusting entry. (Assume the fair value adjustment balance on January 1, 2015, is a debit of $3,375.)

(e) Prepare the journal entry to record the sale of the bonds on January 1, 2016.

2 3 **P17-3 (Available-for-Sale Investments)** Cardinal Paz Corp. carries an account in its general ledger called Investments, which contained debits for investment purchases, and no credits, with the following descriptions.

Feb. 1, 2014	Sharapova Company common stock, $100 par, 200 shares	$ 37,400
April 1	U.S. government bonds, 11%, due April 1, 2024, interest payable April 1 and October 1, 110 bonds of $1,000 par each	110,000
July 1	McGrath Company 12% bonds, par $50,000, dated March 1, 2014, purchased at 104 plus accrued interest, interest payable annually on March 1, due March 1, 2034	54,000

Instructions
(Round all computations to the nearest dollar.)

(a) Prepare entries necessary to classify the amounts into proper accounts, assuming that all the securities are classified as available-for-sale.
(b) Prepare the entry to record the accrued interest and the amortization of premium on December 31, 2014, using the straight-line method.
(c) The fair values of the investments on December 31, 2014, were:

Sharapova Company common stock	$ 31,800
U.S. government bonds	124,700
McGrath Company bonds	58,600

What entry or entries, if any, would you recommend be made?
(d) The U.S. government bonds were sold on July 1, 2015, for $119,200 plus accrued interest. Give the proper entry.

2 **P17-4 (Available-for-Sale Debt Investments)** Presented below is information taken from a bond investment amortization schedule with related fair values provided. These bonds are classified as available-for-sale.

	12/31/14	12/31/15	12/31/16
Amortized cost	$491,150	$519,442	$550,000
Fair value	$497,000	$509,000	$550,000

Instructions
(a) Indicate whether the bonds were purchased at a discount or at a premium.
(b) Prepare the adjusting entry to record the bonds at fair value at December 31, 2014. The Fair Value Adjustment account has a debit balance of $1,000 prior to adjustment.
(c) Prepare the adjusting entry to record the bonds at fair value at December 31, 2015.

3 **P17-5 (Equity Securities Entries and Disclosures)** Parnevik Company has the following securities in its investment portfolio on December 31, 2014 (all securities were purchased in 2014): (1) 3,000 shares of Anderson Co. common stock which cost $58,500, (2) 10,000 shares of Munter Ltd. common stock which cost $580,000, and (3) 6,000 shares of King Company preferred stock which cost $255,000. The Fair Value Adjustment account shows a credit of $10,100 at the end of 2014.

In 2015, Parnevik completed the following securities transactions.

1. On January 15, sold 3,000 shares of Anderson's common stock at $22 per share less fees of $2,150.
2. On April 17, purchased 1,000 shares of Castle's common stock at $33.50 per share plus fees of $1,980.

On December 31, 2015, the market prices per share of these securities were Munter $61, King $40, and Castle $29. In addition, the accounting supervisor of Parnevik told you that, even though all these securities have readily determinable fair values, Parnevik will not actively trade these securities because the top management intends to hold them for more than one year.

Instructions
(a) Prepare the entry for the security sale on January 15, 2015.
(b) Prepare the journal entry to record the security purchase on April 17, 2015.
(c) Compute the unrealized gains or losses and prepare the adjusting entry for Parnevik on December 31, 2015.
(d) How should the unrealized gains or losses be reported on Parnevik's balance sheet?

3 **P17-6 (Trading and Available-for-Sale Securities Entries)** McElroy Company has the following portfolio of investment securities at September 30, 2014, its last reporting date.

Trading Securities	Cost	Fair Value
Horton, Inc. common (5,000 shares)	$215,000	$200,000
Monty, Inc. preferred (3,500 shares)	133,000	140,000
Oakwood Corp. common (1,000 shares)	180,000	179,000

On October 10, 2014, the Horton shares were sold at a price of $54 per share. In addition, 3,000 shares of Patriot common stock were acquired at $54.50 per share on November 2, 2014. The December 31, 2014, fair values were Monty $106,000, Patriot $132,000, and the Oakwood common $193,000. All the securities are classified as trading.

Instructions

(a) Prepare the journal entries to record the sale, purchase, and adjusting entries related to the trading securities in the last quarter of 2014.

(b) How would the entries in part (a) change if the securities were classified as available-for-sale?

2 **P17-7 (Available-for-Sale and Held-to-Maturity Debt Securities Entries)** The following information relates to the debt securities investments of Wildcat Company.

1. On February 1, the company purchased 10% bonds of Gibbons Co. having a par value of $300,000 at 100 plus accrued interest. Interest is payable April 1 and October 1.
2. On April 1, semiannual interest is received.
3. On July 1, 9% bonds of Sampson, Inc. were purchased. These bonds with a par value of $200,000 were purchased at 100 plus accrued interest. Interest dates are June 1 and December 1.
4. On September 1, bonds with a par value of $60,000, purchased on February 1, are sold at 99 plus accrued interest.
5. On October 1, semiannual interest is received.
6. On December 1, semiannual interest is received.
7. On December 31, the fair value of the bonds purchased February 1 and July 1 are 95 and 93, respectively.

Instructions

(a) Prepare any journal entries you consider necessary, including year-end entries (December 31), assuming these are available-for-sale securities.

(b) If Wildcat classified these as held-to-maturity investments, explain how the journal entries would differ from those in part (a).

3 **4** **5** **P17-8 (Fair Value and Equity Methods)** Brooks Corp. is a medium-sized corporation specializing in quarrying stone for building construction. The company has long dominated the market, at one time achieving a 70% market penetration. During prosperous years, the company's profits, coupled with a conservative dividend policy, resulted in funds available for outside investment. Over the years, Brooks has had a policy of investing idle cash in equity securities. In particular, Brooks has made periodic investments in the company's principal supplier, Norton Industries. Although the firm currently owns 12% of the outstanding common stock of Norton Industries, Brooks does not have significant influence over the operations of Norton Industries.

Cheryl Thomas has recently joined Brooks as assistant controller, and her first assignment is to prepare the 2014 year-end adjusting entries for the accounts that are valued by the "fair value" rule for financial reporting purposes. Thomas has gathered the following information about Brooks' pertinent accounts.

1. Brooks has trading securities related to Delaney Motors and Patrick Electric. During this fiscal year, Brooks purchased 100,000 shares of Delaney Motors for $1,400,000; these shares currently have a fair value of $1,600,000. Brooks' investment in Patrick Electric has not been profitable; the company acquired 50,000 shares of Patrick in April 2014 at $20 per share, a purchase that currently has a value of $720,000.
2. Prior to 2014, Brooks invested $22,500,000 in Norton Industries and has not changed its holdings this year. This investment in Norton Industries was valued at $21,500,000 on December 31, 2013. Brooks' 12% ownership of Norton Industries has a current fair value of $22,225,000.

Instructions

(a) Prepare the appropriate adjusting entries for Brooks as of December 31, 2014, to reflect the application of the "fair value" rule for both classes of securities described above.

(b) For both classes of securities presented above, describe how the results of the valuation adjustments made in (a) would be reflected in the body of and notes to Brooks' 2014 financial statements.

(c) Prepare the entries for the Norton investment, assuming that Brooks owns 25% of Norton's shares. Norton reported income of $500,000 in 2014 and paid cash dividends of $100,000.

3 **6** **P17-9 (Financial Statement Presentation of Available-for-Sale Investments)** Kennedy Company has the following portfolio of available-for-sale securities at December 31, 2014.

Security	Quantity	Percent Interest	Per Share Cost	Per Share Price
Frank, Inc.	2,000 shares	8%	$11	$16
Ellis Corp.	5,000 shares	14%	23	19
Mendota Company	4,000 shares	2%	31	24

Instructions

(a) What should be reported on Kennedy's December 31, 2014, balance sheet relative to these long-term available-for-sale securities?

On December 31, 2015, Kennedy's portfolio of available-for-sale securities consisted of the following common stocks.

Security	Quantity	Percent Interest	Per Share Cost	Per Share Price
Ellis Corp.	5,000 shares	14%	$23	$28
Mendota Company	4,000 shares	2%	31	23
Mendota Company	2,000 shares	1%	25	23

At the end of 2015, Kennedy Company changed its intent relative to its investment in Frank, Inc. and reclassified the shares to trading securities status when the shares were selling for $8 per share.

(b) What should be reported on the face of Kennedy's December 31, 2015, balance sheet relative to available-for-sale securities investments? What should be reported to reflect the transactions above in Kennedy's 2015 income statement?

3 **5** **P17-10 (Gain on Sale of Investments and Comprehensive Income)** On January 1, 2014, Acker Inc. had the following balance sheet.

ACKER INC.
BALANCE SHEET
AS OF JANUARY 1, 2014

Assets		Equity	
Cash	$ 50,000	Common stock	$260,000
Equity investments (available-for-sale)	240,000	Accumulated other comprehensive income	30,000
Total	$290,000	Total	$290,000

The accumulated other comprehensive income related to unrealized holding gains on available-for-sale securities. The fair value of Acker Inc.'s available-for-sale securities at December 31, 2014, was $190,000; its cost was $140,000. No securities were purchased during the year. Acker Inc.'s income statement for 2014 was as follows. (Ignore income taxes.)

ACKER INC.
INCOME STATEMENT
FOR THE YEAR ENDED DECEMBER 31, 2014

Dividend revenue	$ 5,000
Gain on sale of investments	30,000
Net income	$35,000

Instructions

(Assume all transactions during the year were for cash.)

(a) Prepare the journal entry to record the sale of the available-for-sale securities in 2014.
(b) Prepare a statement of comprehensive income for 2014.
(c) Prepare a balance sheet as of December 31, 2014.

3 **P17-11 (Equity Investments—Available-for-Sale)** Castleman Holdings, Inc. had the following available-for-sale investment portfolio at January 1, 2014.

Evers Company	1,000 shares @ $15 each	$15,000
Rogers Company	900 shares @ $20 each	18,000
Chance Company	500 shares @ $9 each	4,500
Equity investments (available-for-sale) @ cost		37,500
Fair value adjustment (available-for-sale)		(7,500)
Equity investments (available-for-sale) @ fair value		$30,000

During 2014, the following transactions took place.

1. On March 1, Rogers Company paid a $2 per share dividend.
2. On April 30, Castleman Holdings, Inc. sold 300 shares of Chance Company for $11 per share.
3. On May 15, Castleman Holdings, Inc. purchased 100 more shares of Evers Co. stock at $16 per share.
4. At December 31, 2014, the stocks had the following price per share values: Evers $17, Rogers $19, and Chance $8.

During 2015, the following transactions took place.

5. On February 1, Castleman Holdings, Inc. sold the remaining Chance shares for $8 per share.
6. On March 1, Rogers Company paid a $2 per share dividend.
7. On December 21, Evers Company declared a cash dividend of $3 per share to be paid in the next month.
8. At December 31, 2015, the stocks had the following price per share values: Evers $19 and Rogers $21.

Instructions
(a) Prepare journal entries for each of the above transactions.
(b) Prepare a partial balance sheet showing the investment-related amounts to be reported at December 31, 2014 and 2015.

3 **5** **P17-12 (Available-for-Sale Securities—Statement Presentation)** Fernandez Corp. invested its excess cash in available-for-sale securities during 2014. As of December 31, 2014, the portfolio of available-for-sale securities consisted of the following common stocks.

Security	Quantity	Cost	Fair Value
Lindsay Jones, Inc.	1,000 shares	$ 15,000	$ 21,000
Poley Corp.	2,000 shares	40,000	42,000
Arnold Aircraft	2,000 shares	72,000	60,000
	Totals	$127,000	$123,000

Instructions
(a) What should be reported on Fernandez's December 31, 2014, balance sheet relative to these securities? What should be reported on Fernandez's 2014 income statement?

On December 31, 2015, Fernandez's portfolio of available-for-sale securities consisted of the following common stocks.

Security	Quantity	Cost	Fair Value
Lindsay Jones, Inc.	1,000 shares	$ 15,000	$20,000
Lindsay Jones, Inc.	2,000 shares	33,000	40,000
Duff Company	1,000 shares	16,000	12,000
Arnold Aircraft	2,000 shares	72,000	22,000
	Totals	$136,000	$94,000

During the year 2015, Fernandez Corp. sold 2,000 shares of Poley Corp. for $38,200 and purchased 2,000 more shares of Lindsay Jones, Inc. and 1,000 shares of Duff Company.

(b) What should be reported on Fernandez's December 31, 2015, balance sheet? What should be reported on Fernandez's 2015 income statement?

On December 31, 2016, Fernandez's portfolio of available-for-sale securities consisted of the following common stocks.

Security	Quantity	Cost	Fair Value
Arnold Aircraft	2,000 shares	$72,000	$82,000
Duff Company	500 shares	8,000	6,000
	Totals	$80,000	$88,000

During the year 2016, Fernandez Corp. sold 3,000 shares of Lindsay Jones, Inc. for $39,900 and 500 shares of Duff Company at a loss of $2,700.

(c) What should be reported on the face of Fernandez's December 31, 2016, balance sheet? What should be reported on Fernandez's 2016 income statement?

(d) What would be reported in a statement of comprehensive income at (1) December 31, 2014, and (2) December 31, 2015?

7 *P17-13 (Derivative Financial Instrument)** The treasurer of Miller Co. has read on the Internet that the stock price of Wade Inc. is about to take off. In order to profit from this potential development, Miller Co. purchased a call option on Wade common shares on July 7, 2014, for $240. The call option is for 200 shares (notional value), and the strike price is $70. (The market price of a share of Wade stock on that date is $70.) The option expires on January 31, 2015. The following data are available with respect to the call option.

Date	Market Price of Wade Shares	Time Value of Call Option
September 30, 2014	$77 per share	$180
December 31, 2014	75 per share	65
January 4, 2015	76 per share	30

Instructions

Prepare the journal entries for Miller Co. for the following dates.

(a) July 7, 2014—Investment in call option on Wade shares.
(b) September 30, 2014—Miller prepares financial statements.
(c) December 31, 2014—Miller prepares financial statements.
(d) January 4, 2015—Miller settles the call option on the Wade shares.

7 *P17-14 (Derivative Financial Instrument)** Johnstone Co. purchased a put option on Ewing common shares on July 7, 2014, for $240. The put option is for 200 shares, and the strike price is $70. (The market price of a share of Ewing stock on that date is $70.) The option expires on January 31, 2015. The following data are available with respect to the put option.

Date	Market Price of Ewing Shares	Time Value of Put Option
September 30, 2014	$77 per share	$125
December 31, 2014	75 per share	50
January 31, 2015	78 per share	0

Instructions

Prepare the journal entries for Johnstone Co. for the following dates.

(a) July 7, 2014—Investment in put option on Ewing shares.
(b) September 30, 2014—Johnstone prepares financial statements.
(c) December 31, 2014—Johnstone prepares financial statements.
(d) January 31, 2015—Put option expires.

7 *P17-15 (Free-Standing Derivative)** Warren Co. purchased a put option on Echo common shares on January 7, 2014, for $360. The put option is for 400 shares, and the strike price is $85 (which equals the price of an Echo share on the purchase date). The option expires on July 31, 2014. The following data are available with respect to the put option.

Date	Market Price of Echo Shares	Time Value of Put Option
March 31, 2014	$80 per share	$200
June 30, 2014	82 per share	90
July 6, 2014	77 per share	25

Instructions

Prepare the journal entries for Warren Co. for the following dates.

(a) January 7, 2014—Investment in put option on Echo shares.
(b) March 31, 2014—Warren prepares financial statements.
(c) June 30, 2014—Warren prepares financial statements.
(d) July 6, 2014—Warren settles the put option on the Echo shares.

8 *P17-16 (Fair Value Hedge Interest Rate Swap)** On December 31, 2014, Mercantile Corp. had a $10,000,000, 8% fixed-rate note outstanding, payable in 2 years. It decides to enter into a 2-year swap with Chicago First Bank to convert the fixed-rate debt to variable-rate debt. The terms of the swap indicate that Mercantile will receive interest at a fixed rate of 8.0% and will pay a variable rate equal to the 6-month LIBOR rate, based on the $10,000,000 amount. The LIBOR rate on December 31, 2014, is 7%. The LIBOR rate will be reset every 6 months and will be used to determine the variable rate to be paid for the following 6-month period.

Mercantile Corp. designates the swap as a fair value hedge. Assume that the hedging relationship meets all the conditions necessary for hedge accounting. The 6-month LIBOR rate and the swap and debt fair values are as follows.

Date	6-Month LIBOR Rate	Swap Fair Value	Debt Fair Value
December 31, 2014	7.0%	—	$10,000,000
June 30, 2015	7.5%	(200,000)	9,800,000
December 31, 2015	6.0%	60,000	10,060,000

Instructions

(a) Present the journal entries to record the following transactions.
  (1) The entry, if any, to record the swap on December 31, 2014.
  (2) The entry to record the semiannual debt interest payment on June 30, 2015.
  (3) The entry to record the settlement of the semiannual swap amount receivables at 8%, less amount payable at LIBOR, 7%.
  (4) The entry to record the change in the fair value of the debt on June 30, 2015.
  (5) The entry to record the change in the fair value of the swap at June 30, 2015.
(b) Indicate the amount(s) reported on the balance sheet and income statement related to the debt and swap on December 31, 2014.
(c) Indicate the amount(s) reported on the balance sheet and income statement related to the debt and swap on June 30, 2015.
(d) Indicate the amount(s) reported on the balance sheet and income statement related to the debt and swap on December 31, 2015.

9 *P17-17 (Cash Flow Hedge)** LEW Jewelry Co. uses gold in the manufacture of its products. LEW anticipates that it will need to purchase 500 ounces of gold in October 2014, for jewelry that will be shipped for the holiday shopping season. However, if the price of gold increases, LEW's cost to produce its jewelry will increase, which would reduce its profit margins.

To hedge the risk of increased gold prices, on April 1, 2014, LEW enters into a gold futures contract and designates this futures contract as a cash flow hedge of the anticipated gold purchase. The notional amount of the contract is 500 ounces, and the terms of the contract give LEW the right and the obligation to purchase gold at a price of $300 per ounce. The price will be good until the contract expires on October 31, 2014.

Assume the following data with respect to the price of the futures contract and the gold inventory purchase.

Date	Spot Price for October Delivery
April 1, 2014	$300 per ounce
June 30, 2014	310 per ounce
September 30, 2014	315 per ounce

Instructions
Prepare the journal entries for the following transactions.

(a) April 1, 2014—Inception of the futures contract, no premium paid.
(b) June 30, 2014—LEW Co. prepares financial statements.
(c) September 30, 2014—LEW Co. prepares financial statements.
(d) October 10, 2014—LEW Co. purchases 500 ounces of gold at $315 per ounce and settles the futures contract.
(e) December 20, 2014—LEW sells jewelry containing gold purchased in October 2014 for $350,000. The cost of the finished goods inventory is $200,000.
(f) Indicate the amount(s) reported on the balance sheet and income statement related to the futures contract on June 30, 2014.
(g) Indicate the amount(s) reported in the income statement related to the futures contract and the inventory transactions on December 31, 2014.

8 *P17-18 (Fair Value Hedge)** On November 3, 2014, Sprinkle Co. invested $200,000 in 4,000 shares of the common stock of Pratt Co. Sprinkle classified this investment as available-for-sale. Sprinkle Co. is considering making a more significant investment in Pratt Co. at some point in the future but has decided to wait and see how the stock does over the next several quarters.

To hedge against potential declines in the value of Pratt stock during this period, Sprinkle also purchased a put option on the Pratt stock. Sprinkle paid an option premium of $600 for the put option, which gives Sprinkle the option to sell 4,000 Pratt shares at a strike price of $50 per share. The option expires on July 31, 2015. The following data are available with respect to the values of the Pratt stock and the put option.

Date	Market Price of Pratt Shares	Time Value of Put Option
December 31, 2014	$50 per share	$375
March 31, 2015	45 per share	175
June 30, 2015	43 per share	40

Instructions

(a) Prepare the journal entries for Sprinkle Co. for the following dates.
   (1) November 3, 2014—Investment in Pratt stock and the put option on Pratt shares.
   (2) December 31, 2014—Sprinkle Co. prepares financial statements.
   (3) March 31, 2015—Sprinkle prepares financial statements.
   (4) June 30, 2015—Sprinkle prepares financial statements.
   (5) July 1, 2015—Sprinkle settles the put option and sells the Pratt shares for $43 per share.

(b) Indicate the amount(s) reported on the balance sheet and income statement related to the Pratt investment and the put option on December 31, 2014.

(c) Indicate the amount(s) reported on the balance sheet and income statement related to the Pratt investment and the put option on June 30, 2015.

PROBLEMS SET B

See the book's companion website, at **www.wiley.com/college/kieso**, for an additional set of problems.

CONCEPTS FOR ANALYSIS

CA17-1 (Issues Raised about Investment Securities) You have just started work for Warren Co. as part of the controller's group involved in current financial reporting problems. Jane Henshaw, controller for Warren, is interested in your accounting background because the company has experienced a series of financial reporting surprises over the last few years. Recently, the controller has learned from the company's auditors that there is authoritative literature that may apply to its investment in securities. She assumes that you are familiar with this pronouncement and asks how the following situations should be reported in the financial statements.

Situation 1: Trading securities in the current assets section have a fair value that is $4,200 lower than cost.

Situation 2: A trading security whose fair value is currently less than cost is transferred to the available-for-sale category.

Situation 3: An available-for-sale security whose fair value is currently less than cost is classified as noncurrent but is to be reclassified as current.

Situation 4: A company's portfolio of available-for-sale securities consists of the common stock of one company. At the end of the prior year, the fair value of the security was 50% of original cost, and this reduction in fair value was reported as an other than temporary impairment. However, at the end of the current year, the fair value of the security had appreciated to twice the original cost.

Situation 5: The company has purchased some convertible debentures that it plans to hold for less than a year. The fair value of the convertible debentures is $7,700 below its cost.

Instructions

What is the effect upon carrying value and earnings for each of the situations above? Assume that these situations are unrelated.

CA17-2 (Equity Securities) Lexington Co. has the following available-for-sale securities outstanding on December 31, 2014 (its first year of operations).

	Cost	Fair Value
Greenspan Corp. Stock	$20,000	$19,000
Summerset Company Stock	9,500	8,800
Tinkers Company Stock	20,000	20,600
	$49,500	$48,400

During 2015, Summerset Company stock was sold for $9,200, the difference between the $9,200 and the "fair value" of $8,800 being recorded as a "Gain on Sale of Investments." The market price of the stock on December 31, 2015, was Greenspan Corp. stock $19,900; Tinkers Company stock $20,500.

Instructions

(a) What justification is there for valuing available-for-sale securities at fair value and reporting the unrealized gain or loss as part of stockholders' equity?

(b) How should Lexington Company apply this rule on December 31, 2014? Explain.

(c) Did Lexington Company properly account for the sale of the Summerset Company stock? Explain.

(d) Are there any additional entries necessary for Lexington Company at December 31, 2015, to reflect the facts on the financial statements in accordance with generally accepted accounting principles? Explain.

(AICPA adapted)

CA17-3 (Financial Statement Effect of Equity Securities) Presented below are three unrelated situations involving equity securities.

Situation 1: An equity security, whose fair value is currently less than cost, is classified as available-for-sale but is to be reclassified as trading.

Situation 2: A noncurrent portfolio with an aggregate fair value in excess of cost includes one particular security whose fair value has declined to less than one-half of the original cost. The decline in value is considered to be other than temporary.

Situation 3: The portfolio of trading securities has a cost in excess of fair value of $13,500. The available-for-sale portfolio has a fair value in excess of cost of $28,600.

Instructions

What is the effect upon carrying value and earnings for each of the situations above?

CA17-4 (Investment Accounted for under the Equity Method) On July 1, 2015, Fontaine Company purchased for cash 40% of the outstanding capital stock of Knoblett Company. Both Fontaine Company and Knoblett Company have a December 31 year-end. Knoblett Company, whose common stock is actively traded in the over-the-counter market, reported its total net income for the year to Fontaine Company and also paid cash dividends on November 15, 2015, to Fontaine Company and its other stockholders.

Instructions

How should Fontaine Company report the above facts in its December 31, 2015, balance sheet and its income statement for the year then ended? Discuss the rationale for your answer.

(AICPA adapted)

CA17-5 (Equity Investment) On July 1, 2014, Selig Company purchased for cash 40% of the outstanding capital stock of Spoor Corporation. Both Selig and Spoor have a December 31 year-end. Spoor Corporation, whose common stock is actively traded on the American Stock Exchange, paid a cash dividend on November 15, 2014, to Selig Company and its other stockholders. It also reported its total net income for the year of $920,000 to Selig Company.

Instructions

Prepare a one-page memorandum of instructions on how Selig Company should report the above facts in its December 31, 2014, balance sheet and its 2014 income statement. In your memo, identify and describe the method of valuation you recommend. Provide rationale where you can. Address your memo to the chief accountant at Selig Company.

CA17-6 (Fair Value) Addison Manufacturing holds a large portfolio of debt and equity securities as an investment. The fair value of the portfolio is greater than its original cost, even though some securities have decreased in value. Sam Beresford, the financial vice president, and Angie Nielson, the controller, are near year-end in the process of classifying for the first time this securities portfolio in accordance with GAAP. Beresford wants to classify those securities that have increased in value during the period as trading securities in order to increase net income this year. He wants to classify all the securities that have decreased in value as available-for-sale (the equity securities) and as held-to-maturity (the debt securities).

Nielson disagrees. She wants to classify those securities that have decreased in value as trading securities and those that have increased in value as available-for-sale (equity) and held-to-maturity (debt). She contends that the company is having a good earnings year and that recognizing the losses will help to smooth the income this year. As a result, the company will have built-in gains for future periods when the company may not be as profitable.

Instructions

Answer the following questions.

(a) Will classifying the portfolio as each proposes actually have the effect on earnings that each says it will?

(b) Is there anything unethical in what each of them proposes? Who are the stakeholders affected by their proposals?

(c) Assume that Beresford and Nielson properly classify the entire portfolio into trading, available-for-sale, and held-to-maturity categories. But then each proposes to sell just before year-end the securities with gains or with losses, as the case may be, to accomplish their effect on earnings. Is this unethical?

USING YOUR JUDGMENT

FINANCIAL REPORTING

Financial Reporting Problem

The Procter & Gamble Company (P&G)

The financial statements of P&G are presented in Appendix 5B. The company's complete annual report, including the notes to the financial statements, can be accessed at the book's companion website, **www.wiley.com/college/kieso**.

Instructions

Refer to P&G's financial statements and the accompanying notes to answer the following questions.

(a) What investments does P&G report in 2011, and how are these investments accounted for in its financial statements?

(b) How are P&G's investments valued? How does P&G determine fair value?

(c) How does P&G use derivative financial instruments?

Comparative Analysis Case

The Coca-Cola Company and PepsiCo, Inc.

Instructions

Go to the book's companion website and use information found there to answer the following questions related to The Coca-Cola Company and PepsiCo, Inc.

(a) Based on the information contained in these financial statements, determine each of the following for each company.

    (1) Cash used in (for) investing activities during 2011 (from the statement of cash flows).

    (2) Cash used for acquisitions and investments in unconsolidated affiliates (or principally bottling companies) during 2011.

    (3) Total investment in unconsolidated affiliates (or investments and other assets) at the end of 2011.

(b) (1) Briefly identify from Coca-Cola's December 31, 2011, balance sheet the investments it reported as being accounted for under the equity method. (2) What is the amount of investments that Coca-Cola reported in its 2011 balance sheet as "cost method investments," and what is the nature of these investments?

(c) In its Note 2 on Investments, what total amounts did Coca-Cola report at December 31, 2011, as: (1) trading securities, (2) available-for-sale securities, and (3) held-to-maturity securities?

Financial Statement Analysis Case

Union Planters

Union Planters is a Tennessee bank holding company (that is, a corporation that owns banks). (Union Planters is now part of Regions Bank.) Union Planters manages $32 billion in assets, the largest of which is its loan portfolio of $19 billion. In addition to its loan portfolio, however, like other banks it has significant debt investments. The nature of these investments varies from short-term in nature to long-term in nature. As a consequence, consistent with the requirements of accounting rules, Union Planters reports its investments in two different categories—trading and available-for-sale. The following facts were found in a recent Union Planters' annual report.

(all dollars in millions)	Amortized Cost	Gross Unrealized Gains	Gross Unrealized Losses	Fair Value
Trading account assets	$ 275	—	—	$ 275
Securities available for sale	8,209	$108	$15	8,302
Net income				224
Net securities gains (losses)				(9)

Instructions

(a) Why do you suppose Union Planters purchases investments, rather than simply making loans? Why does it purchase investments that vary in nature both in terms of their maturities and in type (debt versus stock)?

(b) How must Union Planters account for its investments in each of the two categories?

(c) In what ways does classifying investments into two different categories assist investors in evaluating the profitability of a company like Union Planters?

(d) Suppose that the management of Union Planters was not happy with its net income for the year. What step could it have taken with its investment portfolio that would have definitely increased reported profit? How much could it have increased reported profit? Why do you suppose it chose not to do this?

Accounting, Analysis, and Principles

Instar Company has several investments in the securities of other companies. The following information regarding these investments is available at December 31, 2014.

1. Instar holds bonds issued by Dorsel Corp. The bonds have an amortized cost of $320,000 and their fair value at December 31, 2014, is $400,000. Instar intends to hold the bonds until they mature on December 31, 2022.

2. Instar has invested idle cash in the equity securities of several publicly traded companies. Instar intends to sell these securities during the first quarter of 2015, when it will need the cash to acquire seasonal inventory. These equity securities have a cost basis of $800,000 and a fair value of $920,000 at December 31, 2014.

3. Instar has a significant ownership stake in one of the companies that supplies Instar with various components Instar uses in its products. Instar owns 6% of the common stock of the supplier, does not have any representation on the supplier's board of directors, does not exchange any personnel with the supplier, and does not consult with the supplier on any of the supplier's operating, financial, or strategic decisions. The cost basis of the investment in the supplier is $1,200,000 and the fair value of the investment at December 31, 2014, is $1,550,000. Instar does not intend to sell the investment in the foreseeable future. The supplier reported net income of $80,000 for 2014 and paid no dividends.

4. Instar owns some common stock of Forter Corp. The cost basis of the investment in Forter is $200,000 and the fair value at December 31, 2014, is $50,000. Instar believes the decline in the value of its investment in Forter is other than temporary, but Instar does not intend to sell its investment in Forter in the foreseeable future.

5. Instar purchased 25% of the stock of Slobbaer Co. for $900,000. Instar has significant influence over the operating activities of Slobbaer Co. During 2014, Slobbaer Co. reported net income of $300,000 and paid a dividend of $100,000.

Accounting

(a) Determine whether each of the investments described above should be classified as available-for-sale, held-to-maturity, trading, or equity method.

(b) Prepare any December 31, 2014, journal entries needed for Instar relating to Instar's various investments in other companies. Assume 2014 is Instar's first year of operations.

Analysis

What is the effect on Instar's 2014 net income (as reported on Instar's income statement) of Instar's investments in other companies?

Principles
Briefly explain the different rationales for the different accounting and reporting rules for different types of investments in the securities of other companies.

BRIDGE TO THE PROFESSION

 ## Professional Research: FASB Codification

Your client, Cascade Company, is planning to invest some of its excess cash in 5-year revenue bonds issued by the county and in the stock of one of its suppliers, Teton Co. Teton's shares trade on the over-the-counter market. Cascade plans to classify these investments as available-for-sale. They would like you to conduct some research on the accounting for these investments.

Instructions
- If your school has a subscription to the FASB Codification, go to *http://aaahq.org/ascLogin.cfm* to log in and prepare responses to the following. Provide Codification references for your responses.
  - **(a)** Since the Teton shares do not trade on one of the large stock markets, Cascade argues that the fair value of this investment is not readily available. According to the authoritative literature, when is the fair value of a security "readily determinable"?
  - **(b)** How is an impairment of a security accounted for?
  - **(c)** To avoid volatility in their financial statements due to fair value adjustments, Cascade debated whether the bond investment could be classified as held-to-maturity; Cascade is pretty sure it will hold the bonds for 5 years. How close to maturity could Cascade sell an investment and still classify it as held-to-maturity?
  - **(d)** What disclosures must be made for any sale or transfer from securities classified as held-to-maturity?

Additional Professional Resources

See the book's companion website, at **www.wiley.com/college/kieso**, for professional simulations as well as other study resources.

 IFRS INSIGHTS

LEARNING OBJECTIVE **13**

Compare the accounting for investments under GAAP and IFRS.

The accounting for investments is discussed in *IAS 27* ("Consolidated and Separate Financial Statements"), *IAS 28* ("Accounting for Investments in Associates"), *IAS 39* ("Financial Instruments: Recognition and Measurement"), and *IFRS 9* ("Financial Instruments"). Until recently, when the IASB issued *IFRS 9*, the accounting and reporting for investments under IFRS and GAAP were for the most part very similar. However, *IFRS 9* introduces new investment classifications and increases the situations when investments are accounted for at fair value, with gains and losses recorded in income.

RELEVANT FACTS

Following are the key similarities and differences between GAAP and IFRS related to investments.

Similarities

- GAAP and IFRS use similar classifications for trading investments.
- The accounting for trading investments is the same between GAAP and IFRS. Held-to-maturity (GAAP) and held-for-collection (IFRS) investments are accounted for at

amortized cost. Gains and losses on some investments are reported in other comprehensive income.

- Both GAAP and IFRS use the same test to determine whether the equity method of accounting should be used, that is, significant influence with a general guideline of over 20 percent ownership.
- GAAP and IFRS are similar in the accounting for the fair value option. That is, the option to use the fair value method must be made at initial recognition, the selection is irrevocable, and gains and losses are reported as part of income.
- The measurement of impairments is similar under GAAP and IFRS.

Differences

- While GAAP classifies investments as trading, available-for-sale (both debt and equity investments), and held-to-maturity (only for debt investments), IFRS uses held-for-collection (debt investments), trading (both debt and equity investments), and non-trading equity investment classifications.
- The basis for consolidation under IFRS is control. Under GAAP, a bipolar approach is used, which is a risk-and-reward model (often referred to as a variable-entity approach, discussed in Appendix 17B) and a voting-interest approach. However, under both systems, for consolidation to occur, the investor company must generally own 50 percent of another company.
- While the measurement of impairments is similar under GAAP and IFRS, GAAP does not permit the reversal of an impairment charge related to available-for-sale debt and equity investments. IFRS allows reversals of impairments of held-for-collection investments.
- While GAAP and IFRS are similar in the accounting for the fair value option, one difference is that GAAP permits the fair value option for equity method investments; IFRS does not.

ABOUT THE NUMBERS
Accounting for Financial Assets

A **financial asset** is cash, an equity investment of another company (e.g., ordinary or preference shares), or a contractual right to receive cash from another party (e.g., loans, receivables, and bonds). The accounting for cash is relatively straightforward and is discussed in Chapter 7. The accounting and reporting for equity and debt investments, as discussed in the opening story, is extremely contentious, particularly in light of the credit crisis in the latter part of 2008.

IFRS requires that companies determine how to measure their financial assets based on two criteria:

- The company's business model for managing its financial assets; and
- The contractual cash flow characteristics of the financial asset.

If a company has (1) a business model whose objective is to hold assets in order to collect contractual cash flows and (2) the contractual terms of the financial asset provides specified dates to cash flows that are solely payments of principal and interest on the principal amount outstanding, then the company should use amortized cost.

For example, assume that Mitsubishi purchases a bond investment that it intends to hold to maturity. Its business model for this type of investment is to collect interest and then principal at maturity. The payment dates for the interest rate and principal are stated on the bond. In this case, Mitsubishi accounts for the investment at amortized cost. If, on the other hand, Mitsubishi purchased the bonds as part of a trading strategy to speculate on interest rate changes (a trading investment), then the debt investment is reported at fair value. As a result, only debt investments such as receivables, loans, and bond investments that meet the two criteria above are recorded at amortized cost. All other debt investments are recorded and reported at fair value.

Equity investments are generally recorded and reported at fair value. Equity investments do not have a fixed interest or principal payment schedule and therefore cannot be accounted for at amortized cost. In summary, companies account for investments based on the type of security, as indicated in Illustration IFRS17-1.

ILLUSTRATION IFRS17-1
Summary of Investment Accounting Approaches

Type of Investment	Assessment of Accounting Criteria	Valuation Approach
Debt	Meets business model (held-for-collection) and contractual cash flow tests.	Amortized cost
	Does not meet the business model test (not held-for-collection).	Fair value
Equity	Does not meet contractual cash flow test.	Fair value
	Exercises some control.	Equity method

Debt Investments

Debt Investments—Amortized Cost

Only debt investments can be measured at amortized cost. If a company like **Carrefour** makes an investment in the bonds of **Nokia**, it will receive contractual cash flows of interest over the life of the bonds and repayment of the principal at maturity. If it is Carrefour's strategy to hold this investment in order to receive these cash flows over the life of the bond, it has a held-for-collection strategy and it will measure the investment at amortized cost.[44]

Example: Debt Investment at Amortized Cost. To illustrate the accounting for a debt investment at amortized cost, assume that Robinson Company purchased $100,000 of 8 percent bonds of Evermaster Corporation on January 1, 2014, at a discount, paying $92,278. The bonds mature January 1, 2019, and yield 10 percent; interest is payable each July 1 and January 1. Robinson records the investment as follows.

January 1, 2014

Debt Investments	92,278	
Cash		92,278

As indicated in Chapter 14, companies must amortize premiums or discounts using the **effective-interest method**. They apply the effective-interest method to bond investments in a way similar to that for bonds payable. To compute interest revenue, companies compute the effective-interest rate or yield at the time of investment and apply that rate to the beginning carrying amount (book value) for each interest period. The investment carrying amount is increased by the amortized discount or decreased by the amortized premium in each period.

Illustration IFRS17-2 shows the effect of the discount amortization on the interest revenue that Robinson records each period for its investment in Evermaster bonds.

---

[44]Classification as held-for-collection does not mean the security must be held to maturity. For example, a company may sell an investment before maturity if (1) the security does not meet the company's investment strategy (e.g., the company has a policy to invest in only AAA-rated bonds but the bond investment has a decline in its credit rating), (2) a company changes its strategy to invest only in securities within a certain maturity range, or (3) the company needs to sell a security to fund certain capital expenditures. However, if a company begins trading held-for-collection investments on a regular basis, it should assess whether such trading is consistent with the held-for-collection classification.

		8% BONDS PURCHASED TO YIELD 10%		
Date	Cash Received	Interest Revenue	Bond Discount Amortization	Carrying Amount of Bonds
1/1/14				$ 92,278
7/1/14	$ 4,000[a]	$ 4,614[b]	$ 614[c]	92,892[d]
1/1/15	4,000	4,645	645	93,537
7/1/15	4,000	4,677	677	94,214
1/1/16	4,000	4,711	711	94,925
7/1/16	4,000	4,746	746	95,671
1/1/17	4,000	4,783	783	96,454
7/1/17	4,000	4,823	823	97,277
1/1/18	4,000	4,864	864	98,141
7/1/18	4,000	4,907	907	99,048
1/1/19	4,000	4,952	952	100,000
	$40,000	$47,722	$7,722	

[a]$4,000 = $100,000 × .08 × $^6/_{12}$
[b]$4,614 = $92,278 × .10 × $^6/_{12}$
[c]$614 = $4,614 − $4,000
[d]$92,892 = $92,278 + $614

Robinson records the receipt of the first semiannual interest payment on July 1, 2014 (using the data in Illustration IFRS17-2), as follows.

July 1, 2014

Cash	4,000	
Debt Investments	614	
Interest Revenue		4,614

Because Robinson is on a calendar-year basis, it accrues interest and amortizes the discount at December 31, 2014, as follows.

December 31, 2014

Interest Receivable	4,000	
Debt Investments	645	
Interest Revenue		4,645

Again, Illustration IFRS17-2 shows the interest and amortization amounts. Thus, the accounting for held-for-collection investments in IFRS is the same as held-to-maturity investments under GAAP.

Debt Investments—Fair Value

In some cases, companies both manage and evaluate investment performance on a fair value basis. In these situations, these investments are managed and evaluated based on a documented risk-management or investment strategy based on fair value information. For example, some companies often hold debt investments with the intention of selling them in a short period of time. These debt investments are often referred to as **trading investments** because companies frequently buy and sell these investments to generate profits in short-term differences in price.

Companies that account for and report debt investments at fair value follow the same accounting entries as debt investments held-for-collection during the reporting period. That is, they are recorded at amortized cost. However, **at each reporting date, companies adjust the amortized cost to fair value, with any unrealized holding gain or loss reported as part of net income (fair value method).** An **unrealized holding gain or loss** is the net change in the fair value of a debt investment from one period to another.

Example: Debt Investment at Fair Value. To illustrate the accounting for debt investments using the fair value approach, assume the same information as in our previous illustration for Robinson Company. Recall that Robinson Company purchased $100,000 of 8 percent bonds of Evermaster Corporation on January 1, 2014, at a discount, paying $92,278.[45] The bonds mature January 1, 2019, and yield 10 percent; interest is payable each July 1 and January 1.

The journal entries in 2014 are exactly the same as those for amortized cost. These entries are as follows.

January 1, 2014

Debt Investments	92,278	
Cash		92,278

July 1, 2014

Cash	4,000	
Debt Investments	614	
Interest Revenue		4,614

December 31, 2014

Interest Receivable	4,000	
Debt Investments	645	
Interest Revenue		4,645

Again, Illustration IFRS17-2 shows the interest and amortization amounts. If the debt investment is held-for-collection, no further entries are necessary. To apply the fair value approach, Robinson determines that, due to a decrease in interest rates, the fair value of the debt investment increased to $95,000 at December 31, 2014. Comparing the fair value with the carrying amount of these bonds at December 31, 2014, Robinson has an unrealized holding gain of $1,463, as shown in Illustration IFRS17-3.

ILLUSTRATION IFRS17-3
Computation of Unrealized Gain on Fair Value Debt Investment (2014)

Fair value at December 31, 2014	$95,000
Amortized cost at December 31, 2014 (per Illustration IFRS17-2)	93,537
Unrealized holding gain or (loss)	$ 1,463

Robinson therefore makes the following entry to record the adjustment of the debt investment to fair value at December 31, 2014.

Fair Value Adjustment	1,463	
Unrealized Holding Gain or Loss—Income		1,463

Robinson uses a valuation account (**Fair Value Adjustment**) instead of debiting Debt Investments to record the investment at fair value. The use of the Fair Value Adjustment account enables Robinson to maintain a record at amortized cost in the accounts. Because the valuation account has a debit balance, in this case the fair value of Robinson's debt investment is higher than its amortized cost.

The Unrealized Holding Gain or Loss—Income account is reported in the other income and expense section of the income statement as part of net income. This account is closed to net income each period. The Fair Value Adjustment account is not closed each period and is simply adjusted each period to its proper valuation. The Fair Value Adjustment balance is not shown on the statement of financial position but is simply used to restate the debt investment account to fair value.

---

[45]Companies may incur brokerage and transaction costs in purchasing securities. For investments accounted for at fair value (both debt and equity), IFRS requires that these costs be recorded in net income as other income and expense and not as an adjustment to the carrying value of the investment.

Robinson reports its investment in Evermaster bonds in its December 31, 2014, financial statements as shown in Illustration IFRS17-4.

Statement of Financial Position	
Current assets	
Interest receivable	$ 4,000
Debt investments (trading)	95,000
Income Statement	
Other income and expense	
Interest revenue ($4,614 + $4,645)	$ 9,259
Unrealized holding gain or (loss)	1,463

As you can see from this example, the accounting for trading debt investments under IFRS is the same as GAAP.

Equity Investments

As in GAAP, under IFRS, the degree to which one corporation (**investor**) acquires an interest in the shares of another corporation (**investee**) generally determines the accounting treatment for the investment subsequent to acquisition. To review, the classification of such investments depends on the percentage of the investee voting shares that is held by the investor:

1. Holdings of less than 20 percent (**fair value method**)—investor has passive interest.
2. Holdings between 20 percent and 50 percent (**equity method**)—investor has significant influence.
3. Holdings of more than 50 percent (**consolidated statements**)—investor has controlling interest.

The accounting and reporting for equity investments therefore depend on the level of influence and the type of security involved, as shown in Illustration IFRS17-5.

Category	Valuation	Unrealized Holding Gains or Losses	Other Income Effects
Holdings less than 20%			
1. Trading	Fair value	Recognized in net income	Dividends declared; gains and losses from sale.
2. Non-Trading	Fair value	Recognized in "Other comprehensive income" (OCI) and as separate component of equity	Dividends declared; gains and losses from sale.
Holdings between 20% and 50%	Equity	Not recognized	Proportionate share of investee's net income.
Holdings more than 50%	Consolidation	Not recognized	Not applicable.

Equity Investments at Fair Value

When an investor has an interest of less than 20 percent, it is presumed that the investor has little or no influence over the investee. As indicated in Illustration IFRS17-5, there are two classifications for holdings less than 20 percent. Under IFRS, the presumption is that equity investments are held-for-trading. That is, companies hold these securities to profit from price changes. As with debt investments that are held-for-trading, the general accounting and reporting rule for these investments is to value the securities at fair value and record unrealized gains and losses in net income (**fair value method**).[46]

However, some equity investments are held for purposes other than trading. For example, a company may be required to hold an equity investment in order to sell its products in a particular area. In this situation, the recording of unrealized gains and losses in income, as is required for trading investments, is not indicative of the company's performance with respect to this investment. As a result, IFRS allows companies to classify some equity investments as non-trading. **Non-trading equity investments** are recorded at fair value on the statement of financial position, with unrealized gains and losses reported in other comprehensive income.

Example: Equity Investment (Income). Upon acquisition, companies record equity investments at fair value. To illustrate, assume that on November 3, 2014, Republic Corporation purchased ordinary shares of three companies, each investment representing less than a 20 percent interest.

	Cost
Burberry	$259,700
Nestlé	317,500
St. Regis Pulp Co.	141,350
Total cost	$718,550

Republic records these investments as follows.

November 3, 2014

Equity Investments	718,550	
Cash		718,550

On December 6, 2014, Republic receives a cash dividend of $4,200 on its investment in the ordinary shares of Nestlé. It records the cash dividend as follows.

December 6, 2014

Cash	4,200	
Dividend Revenue		4,200

All three of the investee companies reported net income for the year, but only Nestlé declared and paid a dividend to Republic. But, recall that when an investor owns less than 20 percent of the shares of another corporation, it is presumed that the investor has relatively little influence on the investee. As a result, **net income of the investee is not a proper basis for recognizing income from the investment by the investor**. Why? Because the increased net assets resulting from profitable operations may be permanently retained for use in the investee's business. Therefore, **the investor recognizes net income only when the investee declares cash dividends**.

At December 31, 2014, Republic's equity investment portfolio has the carrying value and fair value shown in Illustration IFRS17-6.

[46]Fair value at initial recognition is the transaction price (exclusive of brokerage and other transaction costs). Subsequent fair value measurements should be based on market prices, if available. For non-traded investments, a valuation technique based on discounted expected cash flows can be used to develop a fair value estimate. While IFRS requires that all equity investments be measured at fair value, in certain limited cases, cost may be an appropriate estimate of fair value for an equity investment.

EQUITY INVESTMENT PORTFOLIO DECEMBER 31, 2014			
Investments	Carrying Value	Fair Value	Unrealized Gain (Loss)
Burberry	$259,700	$275,000	$ 15,300
Nestlé	317,500	304,000	(13,500)
St. Regis Pulp Co.	141,350	104,000	(37,350)
Total of portfolio	$718,550	$683,000	(35,550)
Previous fair value adjustment balance			–0–
Fair value adjustment—Cr.			$(35,550)

ILLUSTRATION IFRS17-6
Computation of Fair Value Adjustment—Equity Investment Portfolio (2014)

For Republic's equity investment portfolio, the gross unrealized gains are $15,300, and the gross unrealized losses are $50,850 ($13,500 + $37,350), resulting in a net unrealized loss of $35,550. The fair value of the equity investment portfolio is below cost by $35,550.

As with **debt** investments, Republic records the net unrealized gains and losses related to changes in the fair value of **equity** investments in an Unrealized Holding Gain or Loss—Income account. Republic reports this amount as other income and expense. In this case, Republic prepares an adjusting entry debiting the Unrealized Holding Gain or Loss—Income account and crediting the Fair Value Adjustment account to record the decrease in fair value and to record the loss as follows.

December 31, 2014

Unrealized Holding Gain or Loss—Income	35,550	
Fair Value Adjustment		35,550

On January 23, 2015, Republic sold all of its Burberry ordinary shares, receiving $287,220. Illustration IFRS17-7 shows the computation of the realized gain on the sale.

Net proceeds from sale	$287,220
Cost of **Burberry** shares	259,700
Gain on sale of shares	$ 27,520

ILLUSTRATION IFRS17-7
Computation of Gain on Sale of Burberry Shares

Republic records the sale as follows.

January 23, 2015

Cash	287,220	
Equity Investments		259,700
Gain on Sale of Equity Investment		27,520

As indicated in this example, the fair value method accounting for trading equity investments under IFRS is the same as GAAP for trading equity investments. As shown in the next section, the accounting for *non-trading* equity investments under IFRS is similar to the accounting for available-for-sale equity investments under GAAP.

Example: Equity Investments (OCI). The accounting entries to record non-trading equity investments are the same as for trading equity investments, except for recording the unrealized holding gain or loss. For non-trading equity investments, companies **report the unrealized holding gain or loss as other comprehensive income (OCI)**. Thus, the account titled Unrealized Holding Gain or Loss—Equity is used.

To illustrate, assume that on December 10, 2014, Republic Corporation purchased $20,750 of 1,000 ordinary shares of Hawthorne Company for $20.75 per share (which represents less than a 20 percent interest). Hawthorne is a distributor for Republic products in certain locales, the laws of which require a minimum level of share ownership of a company in that region. The investment in Hawthorne meets this regulatory requirement. As a result, Republic accounts for this investment at fair value, with unrealized gains and losses recorded in OCI.[47] Republic records this investment as follows.

December 10, 2014

Equity Investments	20,750	
Cash		20,750

On December 27, 2014, Republic receives a cash dividend of $450 on its investment in the ordinary shares of Hawthorne Company. It records the cash dividend as follows.

December 27, 2014

Cash	450	
Dividend Revenue		450

Similar to the accounting for trading investments, when an investor owns less than 20 percent of the ordinary shares of another corporation, it is presumed that the investor has relatively little influence on the investee. Therefore, **the investor earns income when the investee declares cash dividends**.

At December 31, 2014, Republic's investment in Hawthorne has the carrying value and fair value shown in Illustration IFRS17-8.

ILLUSTRATION IFRS17-8
Computation of Fair Value Adjustment— Non-Trading Equity Investment (2014)

Non-Trading Equity Investment	Carrying Value	Fair Value	Unrealized Gain (Loss)
Hawthorne Company	$20,750	$24,000	$3,250
Previous fair value adjustment balance			0
Fair value adjustment (Dr.)			$3,250

For Republic's non-trading investment, the unrealized gain is $3,250. That is, the fair value of the Hawthorne investment exceeds cost by $3,250. Because Republic has classified this investment as non-trading, Republic records the unrealized gains and losses related to changes in the fair value of this non-trading **equity** investment in an Unrealized Holding Gain or Loss—Equity account. Republic reports this amount as **a part of other comprehensive income and as a component of other accumulated comprehensive income (reported in equity) until realized**. In this case, Republic prepares an adjusting entry crediting the Unrealized Holding Gain or Loss—Equity account and debiting the Fair Value Adjustment account to record the decrease in fair value and to record the loss as follows.

December 31, 2014

Fair Value Adjustment	3,250	
Unrealized Holding Gain or Loss—Equity		3,250

Republic reports its equity investments in its December 31, 2014, financial statements as shown in Illustration IFRS17-9.

ILLUSTRATION IFRS17-9
Financial Statement Presentation of Equity Investments at Fair Value (2014)

Statement of Financial Position	
Investments	
Equity investments (non-trading)	$24,000
Equity	
Accumulated other comprehensive gain	$ 3,250
Statement of Comprehensive Income	
Other income and expense	
Dividend revenue	$ 450
Other comprehensive income	
Unrealized holding gain	$ 3,250

[47]The classification of an equity investment as non-trading is irrevocable. This approach is designed to provide some discipline to the application of the non-trading classification, which allows unrealized gains and losses to bypass net income.

During 2015, sales of Republic products through Hawthorne as a distributor did not meet management's goals. As a result, Republic withdrew from these markets and on December 20, 2015, Republic sold all of its Hawthorne Company ordinary shares, receiving net proceeds of $22,500. Illustration IFRS17-10 shows the computation of the realized gain on the sale.

Net proceeds from sale	$22,500	
Cost of Hawthorne shares	20,750	
Gain on sale of shares	$ 1,750	

ILLUSTRATION IFRS17-10
Computation of Gain on Sale of Shares

Republic records the sale as follows.

December 20, 2015

Cash	22,500	
Equity Investments		20,750
Gain on Sale of Equity Investment		1,750

Because Republic no longer holds any equity investments, it makes the following entry to eliminate the Fair Value Adjustment account.

December 31, 2015

Unrealized Holding Gain or Loss—Equity	3,250	
Fair Value Adjustment		3,250

In summary, the accounting for non-trading equity investments deviates from the general provisions for equity investments. The IASB noted that while fair value provides the most useful information about investments in equity investments, recording unrealized gains or losses in other comprehensive income is more representative for non-trading equity investments.

Impairments

A company should evaluate every held-for-collection investment, at each reporting date, to determine if it has suffered **impairment**—a loss in value such that the fair value of the investment is below its carrying value.[48] For example, if an investee experiences a bankruptcy or a significant liquidity crisis, the investor may suffer a permanent loss. **If the company determines that an investment is impaired, it writes down the amortized cost basis of the individual security to reflect this loss in value.** The company accounts for the write-down as a realized loss, and it includes the amount in net income.

For debt investments, a company uses the impairment test to determine whether "it is probable that the investor will be unable to collect all amounts due according to the contractual terms." If an investment is impaired, the company should measure the loss due to the **impairment**. This impairment loss is calculated as the difference between the carrying amount plus accrued interest and the expected future cash flows discounted at the investment's historical effective-interest rate.

Example: Impairment Loss

At December 31, 2013, Mayhew Company has a debt investment in Bellovary Inc., purchased at par for $200,000. The investment has a term of four years, with annual interest payments at 10 percent, paid at the end of each year (the historical effective-interest rate is 10 percent). This debt investment is classified as held-for-collection. Unfortunately, Bellovary is experiencing significant financial difficulty and indicates that it will be unable

---

[48]Note that impairments tests are conducted only for debt investments that are held-for-collection (which are accounted for at amortized cost). Other debt and equity investments are measured at fair value each period; thus, an impairment test is not needed.

to make all payments according to the contractual terms. Mayhew uses the present value method for measuring the required impairment loss. Illustration IFRS17-11 shows the cash flow schedule prepared for this analysis.

ILLUSTRATION IFRS17-11
Investment Cash Flows

Dec. 31	Contractual Cash Flows	Expected Cash Flows	Loss of Cash Flows
2014	$ 20,000	$ 16,000	$ 4,000
2015	20,000	16,000	4,000
2016	20,000	16,000	4,000
2017	220,000	216,000	4,000
Total cash flows	$280,000	$264,000	$16,000

As indicated, the expected cash flows of $264,000 are less than the contractual cash flows of $280,000. The amount of the impairment to be recorded equals the difference between the recorded investment of $200,000 and the present value of the expected cash flows, as shown in Illustration IFRS17-12.

ILLUSTRATION IFRS17-12
Computation of Impairment Loss

Recorded investment			$200,000
Less: Present value of $200,000 due in 4 years at 10%			
(Table 6-2); FV(PVF$_{4,10\%}$); ($200,000 × .68301)		$136,602	
Present value of $16,000 interest receivable annually			
for 4 years at 10% (Table 6-4); R(PVF-OA$_{4,10\%}$);			
($16,000 × 3.16986)		50,718	187,320
Loss on impairment			$ 12,680

The loss due to the impairment is $12,680. Why isn't it $16,000 ($280,000 − $264,000)? A loss of $12,680 is recorded because Mayhew must measure the loss at a present value amount, not at an undiscounted amount. Mayhew recognizes an impairment loss of $12,680 by debiting Loss on Impairment for the expected loss. At the same time, it reduces the overall value of the investment. The journal entry to record the loss is therefore as follows.

Loss on Impairment	12,680	
Debt Investments		12,680

Recovery of Impairment Loss

Subsequent to recording an impairment, events or economic conditions may change such that the extent of the impairment loss decreases (e.g., due to an improvement in the debtor's credit rating). In this situation, some or all of the previously recognized impairment loss shall be reversed with a debit to the Debt Investments account and a credit to Recovery of Impairment Loss. Similar to the accounting for impairments of receivables shown in Chapter 7, the reversal of impairment losses shall not result in a carrying amount of the investment that exceeds the amortized cost that would have been reported had the impairment not been recognized.

ON THE HORIZON

At one time, both the FASB and IASB have indicated that they believe that all financial instruments should be reported at fair value and that changes in fair value should be reported as part of net income. However, the recently issued IFRS indicates that the IASB believes that certain debt investments should not be reported at fair value. The IASB's decision to issue new rules on investments, prior to the FASB's completion of its deliberations on financial instrument accounting, could create obstacles for the Boards in converging the accounting in this area.

IFRS SELF-TEST QUESTIONS

1. All of the following are key similarities between GAAP and IFRS with respect to accounting for investments **except**:
   (a) IFRS and GAAP have a held-to-maturity investment classification.
   (b) IFRS and GAAP apply the equity method to significant influence equity investments.
   (c) IFRS and GAAP have a fair value option for financial instruments.
   (d) the accounting for impairment of investments is similar, although IFRS allows recovery of impairment losses.

2. Which of the following statements is **correct**?
   (a) GAAP has a held-for-collection investment classification.
   (b) GAAP permits recovery of impairment losses.
   (c) Under IFRS, non-trading equity investments are accounted for at amortized cost.
   (d) IFRS and GAAP both have a trading investment classification.

3. IFRS requires companies to measure their financial assets at fair value based on:
   (a) the company's business model for managing its financial assets.
   (b) whether the financial asset is a debt investment.
   (c) whether the financial asset is an equity investment.
   (d) All of the choices are IFRS requirements.

4. Select the investment accounting approach with the correct valuation approach:

	Not Held-for-Collection	Held-for-Collection
(a)	Amortized cost	Amortized cost
(b)	Fair value	Fair value
(c)	Fair value	Amortized cost
(d)	Amortized cost	Fair value

5. Under IFRS, a company:
   (a) should evaluate only equity investments for impairment.
   (b) accounts for an impairment as an unrealized loss, and includes it as a part of other comprehensive income and as a component of other accumulated comprehensive income until realized.
   (c) calculates the impairment loss on debt investments as the difference between the carrying amount plus accrued interest and the expected future cash flows discounted at the investment's historical effective-interest rate.
   (d) All of the above.

IFRS CONCEPTS AND APPLICATION

IFRS17-1 Where can authoritative IFRS be found related to investments?

IFRS17-2 Briefly describe some of the similarities and differences between GAAP and IFRS with respect to the accounting for investments.

IFRS17-3 Describe the two criteria for determining the valuation of financial assets.

IFRS17-4 Which types of investments are valued at amortized cost? Explain the rationale for this accounting.

IFRS17-5 Lady Gaga Co. recently made an investment in the bonds issued by Chili Peppers Inc. Lady Gaga's business model for this investment is to profit from trading in response to changes in market interest rates. How should this investment be classified by Lady Gaga? Explain.

IFRS17-6 Consider the bond investment by Lady Gaga in IFRS17-5. Discuss the accounting for this investment if Lady Gaga's business model is to hold the investment to collect interest while outstanding and to receive the principal at maturity.

IFRS17-7 Indicate how unrealized holding gains and losses should be reported for investments classified as trading and held for-collection.

IFRS17-8 Ramirez Company has a held-for-collection investment in the 6%, 20-year bonds of Soto Company. The investment was originally purchased for $1,200,000 in 2013. Early in 2014, Ramirez recorded an impairment of $300,000 on the Soto investment, due to Soto's financial distress. In 2015, Soto returned to profitability and the Soto investment was no longer impaired. What entry does Ramirez make in 2015 under (a) GAAP and (b) IFRS?

IFRS17-9 Carow Corporation purchased, as a held-for-collection investment, $60,000 of the 8%, 5-year bonds of Harrison, Inc. for $65,118, which provides a 6% return. The bonds pay interest semiannually. Prepare Carow's journal entries for (a) the purchase of the investment, and (b) the receipt of semiannual interest and premium amortization.

IFRS17-10 Fairbanks Corporation purchased 400 ordinary shares of Sherman Inc. as a trading investment for $13,200. During the year, Sherman paid a cash dividend of $3.25 per share. At year-end, Sherman shares were selling for $34.50 per share. Prepare Fairbanks' journal entries to record (a) the purchase of the investment, (b) the dividends received, and (c) the fair value adjustment.

IFRS17-11 Use the information from IFRS17-10 but assume the shares were purchased to meet a non-trading regulatory requirement. Prepare Fairbanks' journal entries to record (a) the purchase of the investment, (b) the dividends received, and (c) the fair value adjustment.

IFRS17-12 On January 1, 2014, Roosevelt Company purchased 12% bonds, having a maturity value of $500,000, for $537,907.40. The bonds provide the bondholders with a 10% yield. They are dated January 1, 2014, and mature January 1, 2019, with interest receivable December 31 of each year. Roosevelt's business model is to hold these bonds to collect contractual cash flows.

Instructions
(a) Prepare the journal entry at the date of the bond purchase.
(b) Prepare a bond amortization schedule.
(c) Prepare the journal entry to record the interest received and the amortization for 2014.
(d) Prepare the journal entry to record the interest received and the amortization for 2015.

IFRS17-13 Assume the same information as in IFRS17-12 except that Roosevelt has an active trading strategy for these bonds. The fair value of the bonds at December 31 of each year-end is as follows.

2014	$534,200	2017	$517,000
2015	$515,000	2018	$500,000
2016	$513,000		

Instructions
(a) Prepare the journal entry at the date of the bond purchase.
(b) Prepare the journal entries to record the interest received and recognition of fair value for 2014.
(c) Prepare the journal entry to record the recognition of fair value for 2015.

IFRS17-14 On December 21, 2014, Zurich Company provided you with the following information regarding its trading investments.

December 31, 2014

Investments (Trading)	Cost	Fair Value	Unrealized Gain (Loss)
Stargate Corp. shares	$20,000	$19,000	$(1,000)
Carolina Co. shares	10,000	9,000	(1,000)
Vectorman Co. shares	20,000	20,600	600
Total of portfolio	$50,000	$48,600	$(1,400)
Previous fair value adjustment balance	–0–		
Fair value adjustment—Cr.	$ (1,400)		

During 2015, Carolina Company shares were sold for $9,500. The fair value of the shares on December 31, 2015, was Stargate Corp. shares—$19,300; Vectorman Co. shares—$20,500.

Instructions
(a) Prepare the adjusting journal entry needed on December 31, 2014.
(b) Prepare the journal entry to record the sale of the Carolina Company shares during 2015.
(c) Prepare the adjusting journal entry needed on December 31, 2015.

IFRS17-15 Komissarov Company has a debt investment in the bonds issued by Keune Inc. The bonds were purchased at par for $400,000 and, at the end of 2014, have a remaining life of 3 years with annual interest payments at 10%, paid at the end of each year. This debt investment is classified as held-for-collection. Keune is facing a tough economic environment and informs all of its investors that it will be unable to make all payments according to the contractual terms. The controller of Komissarov has prepared the following revised expected cash flow forecast for this bond investment.

Dec. 31	Expected Cash Flows
2015	$ 35,000
2016	35,000
2017	385,000
Total cash flows	$455,000

Instructions

(a) Determine the impairment loss for Komissarov at December 31, 2014.

(b) Prepare the entry to record the impairment loss for Komissarov at December 31, 2014.

(c) On January 15, 2015, Keune receives a major capital infusion from a private equity investor. It informs Komissarov that the bonds now will be paid according to the contractual terms. Briefly describe how Komissarov would account for the bond investment in light of this new information.

Professional Research

IFRS17-16 Your client, Cascade Company, is planning to invest some of its excess cash in 5-year revenue bonds issued by the county and in the shares of one of its suppliers, Teton Co. Teton's shares trade on the over-the-counter market. Cascade plans to classify these investments as trading. They would like you to conduct some research on the accounting for these investments.

Instructions

Access the IFRS authoritative literature at the IASB website (*http://eifrs.iasb.org/*). (Click on the IFRS tab and then register for free eIFRS access if necessary.) When you have accessed the documents, you can use the search tool in your Internet browser to respond to the following questions. (Provide paragraph citations.)

(a) Since the Teton shares do not trade on one of the large securities exchanges, Cascade argues that the fair value of this investment is not readily available. According to the authoritative literature, when is the fair value of a security "readily determinable"?

(b) How is an impairment of a debt investment accounted for?

(c) To avoid volatility in their financial statements due to fair value adjustments, Cascade debated whether the bond investment could be classified as held-for-collection; Cascade is pretty sure it will hold the bonds for 5 years. What criteria must be met for Cascade to classify it as held-for-collection?

International Financial Reporting Problem
Marks and Spencer plc

IFRS17-17 The financial statements of Marks and Spencer plc (M&S) are available at the book's companion website or can be accessed at *http://annualreport.marksandspencer.com/_assets/downloads/Marks-and-Spencer-Annual-report-and-financial-statements-2012.pdf*.

Instructions

Refer to M&S's financial statements and the accompanying notes to answer the following questions.

(a) What investments does M&S report in 2012, and where are these investments reported in its financial statements?

(b) How are M&S's investments valued? How does M&S determine fair value?

(c) How does M&S use derivative financial instruments?

ANSWERS TO IFRS SELF-TEST QUESTIONS

1. a **2.** d **3.** a **4.** c **5.** c

Remember to check the book's companion website to find additional resources for this chapter.

It's Back

Several years after passage, the accounting world continues to be preoccupied with the Sarbanes-Oxley Act of 2002 (SOX). Unfortunately, SOX did not solve one of the classic accounting issues—how to properly account for revenue. In fact, revenue recognition practices are the most prevalent reason for accounting restatements. A number of revenue recognition issues relate to possible fraudulent behavior by company executives and employees.

As a result of such revenue recognition problems, the SEC has increased its enforcement actions in this area. In some of these cases, companies made significant adjustments to previously issued financial statements. As Lynn Turner, a former chief accountant of the SEC, indicated, "When people cross over the boundaries of legitimate reporting, the Commission will take appropriate action to ensure the fairness and integrity that investors need and depend on every day."

Consider some SEC actions:

- The SEC charged the former co-chairman and CEO of **Qwest Communications International Inc.** and eight other former Qwest officers and employees with fraud and other violations of the federal securities laws. Three of these people fraudulently characterized nonrecurring revenue from one-time sales as revenue from recurring data and Internet services. The SEC release notes that internal correspondence likened Qwest's dependence on these transactions to fill the gap between actual and projected revenue to an addiction.

- The SEC filed a complaint against three former senior officers of **iGo Corp.**, alleging that the defendants collectively caused iGo to improperly recognize revenue on consignment sales and products that were not shipped or that were shipped after the end of a fiscal quarter.

- The SEC filed a complaint against the former CEO and chairman of **Homestore Inc.** and its former executive vice president of business development, alleging that they engaged in a fraudulent scheme to overstate advertising and subscription revenues. The scheme involved a complex structure of "round-trip" transactions using various third-party companies that, in essence, allowed Homestore to recognize its own cash as revenue.

- The SEC claims that **Lantronix** deliberately sent excessive product to distributors and granted them generous return rights and extended payment terms. In addition, as part of its alleged channel stuffing and to prevent product returns, Lantronix loaned funds to a third party to purchase Lantronix products from one of its distributors. The third party later returned the products. The SEC also asserted that Lantronix engaged in other improper revenue recognition practices, including shipping without a purchase order and recognizing revenue on a contingent sale.

Revenue numbers are attracting more attention from investors these days. For example, in a recent quarter, revenue for the S&P 500 actually decreased by a small percentage. A concern expressed recently is that revenue growth is not robust, and increases in net income (the bottom line) are caused by factors such as low financing costs and lower labor costs which in the long run may not be sustainable. So more attention is now being given to a company's top-line revenue number as many believe strong revenue growth suggests a more profitable company in the future.

Recently, the FASB and IASB issued a new standard on revenue recognition that hopefully will improve the reporting of revenue transactions. This new standard provides a set of guidelines to follow in determining when revenue should be reported and how it should be measured. The new standard is comprehensive and applies to all companies. As a result, comparability and consistency in reporting revenue should be enhanced. After studying this chapter, you should have a good understanding of the new revenue recognition concepts.

Sources: Cheryl de Mesa Graziano, "Revenue Recognition: A Perennial Problem," *Financial Executive* (July 14, 2005), *www.fei.org/mag/ articles/7-2005_revenue.cfm;* and S. Taub, "SEC Accuses Ex-CFO of Channel Stuffing," *CFO.com* (September 30, 2006).

CONCEPTUAL FOCUS

> See the **Underlying Concepts** on pages 1043 and 1049.
> Read the **Evolving Issue** on page 1070 for a discussion of the implementation of the recently issued revenue recognition standard.

INTERNATIONAL FOCUS

> With the issuance of the new standard ("Revenue from Contracts with Customers"), the accounting for revenue recognition is now converged under U.S. GAAP and IFRS.
> See the **International Perspective** on page 1042.

PREVIEW OF CHAPTER 18

As indicated in the opening story, the issue of when revenue should be recognized is complex. The many methods of marketing products and services make it difficult to develop guidelines that will apply to all situations. This chapter provides you with general guidelines used in most business transactions. The content and organization of the chapter are as follows.

Revenue Recognition

Overview of Revenue Recognition	The Five-Step Process	Other Revenue Recognition Issues	Presentation and Disclosure
• Background • New revenue recognition standard	• Contract with customer • Separate performance obligations • Determining the transaction price • Allocating the transaction price • Satisfying performance obligations	• Right of return • Repurchase agreements • Bill-and-hold arrangements • Principal-agent relationships • Consignments • Warranties • Nonrefundable upfront fees	• Presentation • Disclosure

OVERVIEW OF REVENUE RECOGNITION
Background

LEARNING OBJECTIVE
Understand revenue recognition issues.

Most revenue transactions pose few problems for revenue recognition. This is because, in many cases, the transaction is initiated and completed at the same time. However, not all transactions are that simple. For example, consider a cell phone contract between a company such as **Verizon** and a customer. The customer is often provided with a package that may include a handset, free minutes of talk time, data downloads, and text messaging service. In addition, some providers will bundle that with a fixed-line broadband service. At the same time, the customer may pay for these services in a variety of ways, possibly receiving a discount on the handset and then paying higher prices for connection fees and so forth. In some cases, depending on the package purchased, the company may provide free applications in subsequent periods. How, then, should the various pieces of this sale be reported by Verizon? The answer is not obvious.

It is therefore not surprising that a recent survey of financial executives noted that the revenue recognition process is increasingly more complex to manage, more prone to error, and more material to financial statements compared to any other area in financial reporting. The report went on to note that revenue recognition is a top fraud risk and that regardless of the accounting rules followed (GAAP or IFRS), the risk of errors and inaccuracies in revenue reporting is significant.[1]

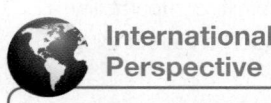

International Perspective

The converged revenue recognition standard represents a significant milestone in the FASB/IASB convergence project.

Both the FASB and the IASB have indicated that the state of reporting for revenue was unsatisfactory. IFRS was criticized because it lacked guidance in a number of areas. For example, IFRS had one basic standard on revenue recognition—*IAS 18*—plus some limited guidance related to certain minor topics. In contrast, GAAP had numerous standards related to revenue recognition (by some counts, well over 100), but many believed the standards were often inconsistent with one another. Thus, the accounting for revenues provided a most fitting contrast of the principles-based (IFRS) and rules-based (GAAP) approaches. While both sides had their advocates, the FASB and IASB recognized a number of deficiencies in this area.[2]

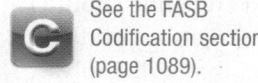

See the FASB Codification section (page 1089).

Recently, the FASB and IASB issued a converged standard on revenue recognition entitled *Revenue from Contracts with Customers*. **[1]** To address the inconsistencies and weaknesses of the previous approaches, a comprehensive revenue recognition standard now applies to a wide range of transactions and industries. The Boards believe this new standard will improve GAAP and IFRS by:

(a) Providing a more robust framework for addressing revenue recognition issues.

(b) Improving comparability of revenue recognition practices across entities, industries, jurisdictions, and capital markets.

---

[1]See *www.softrax.com/resources/pdf/intlriskrevreporting*.

[2]See, for example, "Preliminary Views on Revenue Recognition in Contracts with Customers," *IASB/FASB Discussion Paper* (December 19, 2008). Some noted that GAAP has so many standards that at times they are inconsistent with each other in applying basic principles. In addition, even with the many standards, no comprehensive guidance was provided for service transactions. Conversely, IFRS lacked guidance in certain fundamental areas such as multiple-deliverable arrangements. In addition, there were inconsistencies in applying revenue recognition principles to long-term contracts versus other elements of revenue recognition.

(c) Simplifying the preparation of financial statements by reducing the number of requirements to which companies must refer.

(d) Requiring enhanced disclosures to help financial statement users better understand the amount, timing, and uncertainty of revenue that is recognized. **[2]**

New Revenue Recognition Standard

The new standard, *Revenue from Contracts with Customers*, adopts an **asset-liability approach** as the basis for revenue recognition. The asset-liability approach recognizes and measures revenue based on changes in assets and liabilities. The Boards decided that focusing on (a) the recognition and measurement of assets and liabilities and (b) changes in those assets or liabilities over the life of the contract brings more discipline to the measurement of revenue, compared to the "earned and realized" criteria in prior standards.

Under the asset-liability approach, companies account for revenue based on the asset or liability arising from contracts with customers. Companies analyze contracts with customers because contracts are the lifeblood of most businesses. Contracts indicate the terms of the transaction, provide the measurement of the consideration, and specify the promises that must be met by each party. Without contracts, companies cannot know whether promises will be met.

Illustration 18-1 shows the key concepts related to this new standard on revenue recognition. The new standard first identifies the key objective of revenue recognition, followed by a five-step process that companies should use to ensure that revenue is measured and reported correctly. The culmination of the process is the **revenue recognition principle**, that is, recognition of revenue when the performance obligation is satisfied. We examine all steps in more detail in the following section.

 Underlying Concepts

The asset-liability approach is consistent with the conceptual framework approach to recognition.

ILLUSTRATION 18-1
Key Concepts of Revenue Recognition

KEY OBJECTIVE

Recognize revenue to depict the transfer of goods or services to customers in an amount that reflects the consideration that the company receives, or expects to receive, in exchange for these goods or services.

FIVE-STEP PROCESS FOR REVENUE RECOGNITION

1. Identify the contract with customers.
2. Identify the separate performance obligations in the contract.
3. Determine the transaction price.
4. Allocate the transaction price to the separate performance obligations.
5. Recognize revenue when each performance obligation is satisfied.

REVENUE RECOGNITION PRINCIPLE

Recognize revenue in the accounting period when the performance obligation is satisfied.

THE FIVE-STEP PROCESS

Assume that **Boeing Corporation** signs a contract to sell airplanes to **Delta Air Lines** for $100 million. Illustration 18-2 (page 1044) shows the five steps that Boeing follows to recognize revenue.

2 LEARNING OBJECTIVE
Identify the five steps in the revenue recognition process.

ILLUSTRATION 18-2
Five Steps of Revenue
Recognition

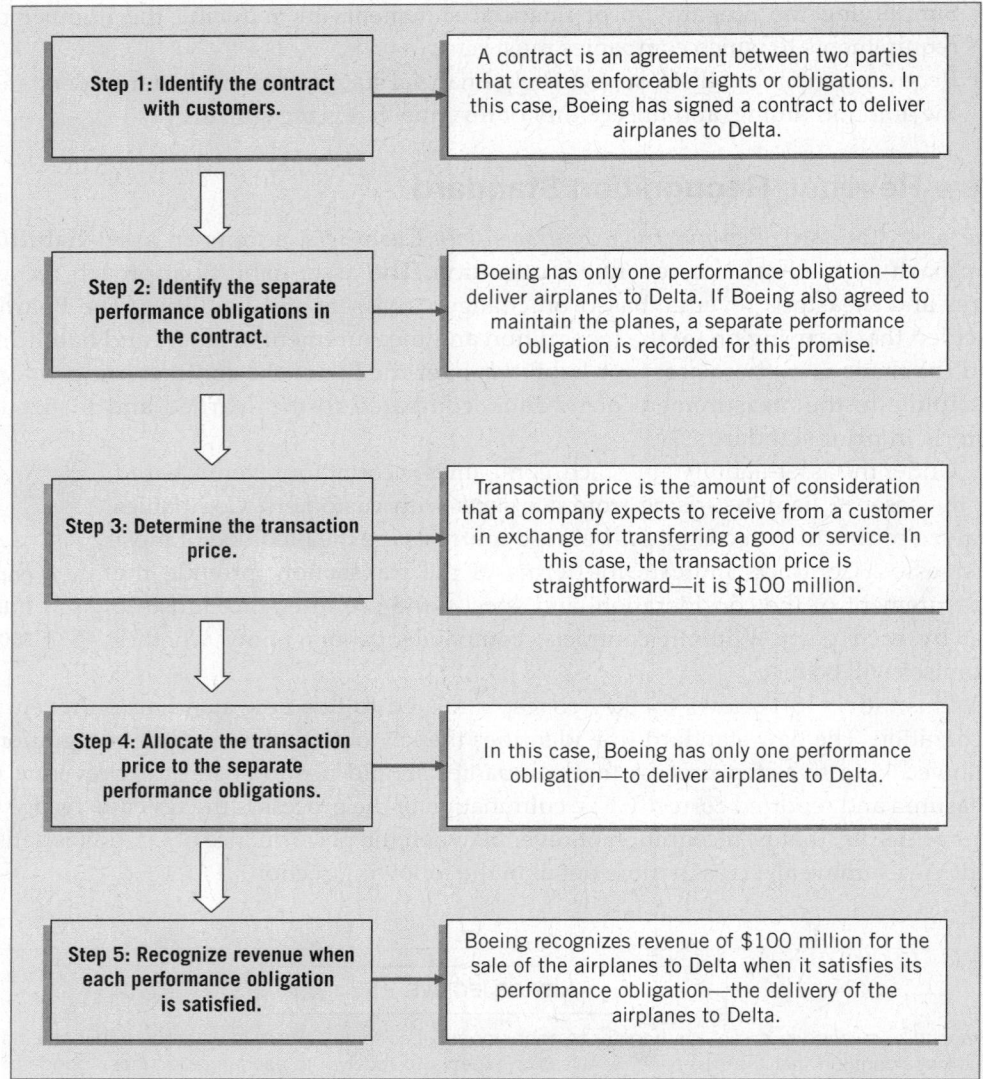

Illustration 18-2 highlights the five-step process used to recognize revenue. Step 5 is when Boeing recognizes revenue related to the sale of the airplanes to Delta. At this point, Boeing delivers the airplanes to Delta and satisfies its performance obligation. In essence, a change in control from Boeing to Delta occurs. Delta now controls the assets because it has the ability to direct the use of and obtain substantially all the remaining benefits from the airplanes. Control also includes Delta's ability to prevent other companies from directing the use of, or receiving the benefits from, the airplanes. In the following sections, we provide an expanded discussion of this five-step process.

Identifying the Contract with Customers—Step 1

LEARNING OBJECTIVE 3
Identify the contract with customers.

A **contract** is an agreement between two or more parties that creates enforceable rights or obligations. Contracts can be written, oral, or implied from customary business practice. A company applies the revenue guidance to a contract according to the following criteria in Illustration 18-3. **[3]**

In some cases, there are multiple contracts related to the transaction, and accounting for each contract may or may not occur, depending on the circumstances. These situations often develop when not only a product is provided but some type of service is performed as well.

Apply Revenue Guidance to Contracts If:	Disregard Revenue Guidance to Contracts If:
• The contract has commercial substance; • The parties to the contract have approved the contract and are committed to perform their respective obligations; • The company can identify each party's rights regarding the goods or services to be transferred; and • The company can identify the payment terms for the goods and services to be transferred. • It is probable that the company will collect the consideration to which it will be entitled.[3]	• The contract is wholly unperformed, and • Each party can unilaterally terminate the contract without compensation.

ILLUSTRATION 18-3
Contract Criteria for
Revenue Guidance

In some cases, a company should combine contracts and account for them as one contract.

Basic Accounting

Revenue from a contract with a customer cannot be recognized until a contract exists. On entering into a contract with a customer, a company obtains rights to receive consideration from the customer and assumes obligations to transfer goods or services to the customer (performance obligations). The combination of those rights and performance obligations gives rise to an (net) asset or (net) liability. If the measure of the remaining rights exceeds the measure of the remaining performance obligations, the contract is an asset (a contract asset). Conversely, if the measure of the remaining performance obligations exceeds the measure of the remaining rights, the contract is a liability (a contract liability). However, **a company does not recognize contract assets or liabilities until one or both parties to the contract perform.** The basic accounting for a contract in which both parties perform is shown in Illustration 18-4.

CONTRACTS AND RECOGNITION

Facts: On March 1, 2014, Margo Company enters into a contract to transfer a product to Soon Yoon on July 31, 2014. The contract is structured such that Soon Yoon is required to pay the full contract price of $5,000 on August 31, 2014. The cost of the goods transferred is $3,000. Margo delivers the product to Soon Yoon on July 31, 2014.

Question: **What journal entries should Margo Company make in regards to this contract in 2014?**

Solution: No entry is required on March 1, 2014, because neither party has performed on the contract. On July 31, 2014, Margo delivers the product and therefore should recognize revenue on that date as it satisfies its performance obligation by delivering the product to Soon Yoon.

The journal entry to record the sale and related cost of goods sold is as follows.

July 31, 2014

Accounts Receivable	5,000	
Sales Revenue		5,000
Cost of Goods Sold	3,000	
Inventory		3,000

After receiving the cash payment on August 31, 2014, Margo makes the following entry.

August 31, 2014

Cash	5,000	
Accounts Receivable		5,000

ILLUSTRATION 18-4
Basic Revenue
Transaction

[3]The FASB included this criterion (which acts like a collectibility threshold) because the Board concluded that the assessment of a customer's credit risk was an important part of determining whether a contract is valid. That is, under the revenue standard (and discussed later in the chapter), collectibility is not a consideration for determining whether revenue is recognized. However, collectibility may be a consideration in assessing whether parties to the contract are committed to perform. In determining whether it is probable that a company will collect the amount of consideration to which it is entitled, the company assesses both the customer's ability and intent to pay as amounts become due. **[4]**

A key feature of the revenue arrangement is that the signing of the contract by the two parties is not recorded (does not result in a journal entry) until one or both of the parties *perform under the contract*. **Until performance occurs, no net asset or net liability occurs.**

Contract Modifications

Companies sometimes change the contract terms while it is ongoing; this is referred to as a contract modification. When a contract modification occurs, companies determine whether a new contract (and performance obligations) results or whether it is a modification of the existing contract.

Separate Performance Obligation   A company accounts for a contract modification as a new contract if **both** of the following conditions are satisfied:

- The promised **goods or services are distinct** (i.e., the company sells them separately and they are not interdependent with other goods and services), and
- The company has the right to receive an amount of **consideration that reflects the standalone selling price** of the promised goods or services. **[5]**

For example, Crandall Co. has a contract to sell 100 products to a customer for $10,000 ($100 per product) at various points in time over a six-month period. After 60 products have been delivered, Crandall modifies the contract by promising to deliver 20 more products for an additional $1,900, or $95 per product (which is the standalone selling price of the products at the time of the contract modification). Crandall regularly sells the products separately. In this situation, the contract modification for the additional 20 products is, in effect, a **new and separate contract** because it meets both of the conditions above. That is, it does not affect the accounting for the original contract.

Given a new contract, Crandall recognizes an additional $4,000 [(100 units − 60 units) × $100] related to the original contract terms and $1,900 (20 units × $95) related to the new products. Total revenue after the modification is therefore $5,900 ($4,000 + $1,900).

Prospective Modification   What if Crandall Co. determines that the additional products are not a separate performance obligation? This might arise if the new products are not priced at the proper standalone selling price or if they are not distinct. In this situation, companies generally account for the modification using a prospective approach.

Under the prospective approach, Crandall should account for the effect of the change in the period of change as well as future periods if the change affects both. Crandall should not change previously reported results. Thus, for Crandall, the amount recognized as revenue for each of the remaining products would be a blended price of $98.33, computed as shown in Illustration 18-5.

ILLUSTRATION 18-5
Revenue Under
Prospective Modification

Consideration for products not yet delivered under original contract ($100 × 40)	$4,000
Consideration for products to be delivered under the contract modification ($95 × 20)	1,900
Total remaining revenue	$5,900
Revenue per remaining unit ($5,900 ÷ 60) = $98.33	

Therefore, under the prospective approach, this computation differs from that in the separate performance obligation approach in that revenue on the remaining units is recognized at the blended price. Total revenue after the modification is therefore $5,900

(60 units × $98.33). Illustration 18-6 shows the revenue reported under the two contract modification approaches for Crandall Co.

	Revenue Recognized Prior to Modification	Revenue Recognized After Modification	Total Revenue Recognized
Separate performance obligation	$6,000	$5,900	$11,900
No separate performance obligation—prospectively	$6,000	$5,900	$11,900

ILLUSTRATION 18-6
Comparison of Contract Modification Approaches

As indicated, whether a modification is treated as a separate performance obligation or prospectively, the same amount of revenue is recognized before and after the modification. However, under the prospective approach, a blended price ($98.33) is used for sales in the periods after the modification.[4]

Identifying Separate Performance Obligations—Step 2

A **performance obligation** is a promise in a contract to provide a product or service to a customer. This promise may be explicit, implicit, or possibly based on customary business practice. To determine whether a performance obligation exists, **the company must provide a distinct product or service**. Illustration 18-7 summarizes some classic situations when revenue is recognized as a result of providing a distinct product or service, therefore satisfying a performance obligation.

4 LEARNING OBJECTIVE
Identify the separate performance obligations in the contract.

ILLUSTRATION 18-7
Revenue Recognition Situations

Type of transaction	Sale of product from inventory	Rendering a service	Permitting use of an asset	Sale of asset other than inventory
Description of revenue	Revenue from sales	Revenue from fees or services	Revenue from interest, rents, and royalties	Gain or loss on disposition
Timing of revenue recognition	Date of sale (date of delivery)	Services performed and billable	As time passes or assets are used	Date of sale or trade-in

[4]Another approach to account for a contract modification is to report the information in a cumulative catch-up manner. In other words, assuming that these new products are part of the original contract, companies adjust the revenue account to reflect the cumulative effect for periods prior to when the modification occurred. An example of a catch-up situation is a long-term construction contract, which is discussed in more detail in Appendix 18A. Use of the prospective approach avoids the complexity of opening up the accounting for previously satisfied performance obligations. However, it ignores any adjustments to revenue that have already been recognized. **[6]** *For homework purposes, unless instructed otherwise, use the prospective approach for modifications that do not result in a separate performance obligation.* Expanded discussion of the prospective and cumulative catch-up (retrospective) approaches to accounting changes is provided in Chapter 22.

The accounting for the transactions in Illustration 18-7 is straightforward as only one performance obligation exists. However, many revenue arrangements may have more than one performance obligation. To determine whether a company has to account for multiple performance obligations, it evaluates a second condition. That is, **whether the product is distinct within the contract**. In other words, if the performance obligation is not highly dependent on, or interrelated with, other promises in the contract, then each performance obligation should be accounted for separately. Conversely, if each of these services is interdependent and interrelated, these services are combined and reported as one performance obligation.

To illustrate, assume that General Motors sells an automobile to Marquart Auto Dealers at a price that includes six months of telematics services such as navigation and remote diagnostics. These telematics services are regularly sold on a standalone basis by General Motors for a monthly fee. After the six-month period, the consumer can renew these services on a fee basis with General Motors. In this case, two performance obligations exist, one related to providing the automobile and the other related to the telematics services. **Both are distinct (they can be sold separately) and are not interdependent.**

Illustration 18-8 provides additional case examples of issues related to identifying performance obligations.

ILLUSTRATION 18-8
Identifying Performance
Obligations

Case 1: Single Performance Obligation

SoftTech Inc. licenses customer-relationship software to Lopez Company. In addition to providing the software itself, SoftTech promises to perform consulting services by extensively customizing the software to Lopez's information technology environment, for a total consideration of $600,000. In this case, SoftTech is providing a significant service by integrating the goods and services (the license and the consulting service) into one combined item for which Lopez has contracted. In addition, the software is significantly customized by SoftTech in accordance with specifications negotiated by Lopez. As a result, **the license and the consulting services are distinct but interdependent, and therefore should be accounted for as one performance obligation**.

Case 2: Separate Performance Obligation

Chen Computer Inc. manufactures and sells computers that include a warranty to make good on any defect in its computers for 120 days (often referred to as an assurance warranty). In addition, it sells separately an extended warranty, which provides protection from defects for three years beyond the 120 days (often referred to as a service warranty). In this case, two performance obligations exist, one related to the sale of the computer and the assurance warranty, and the other to the extended warranty (service warranty). In this case, **the sale of the computer and related assurance warranty are one performance obligation as they are interdependent and interrelated with each other. However, the extended warranty is separately sold and is not interdependent**.

Determining the Transaction Price—Step 3

LEARNING OBJECTIVE 5
Determine the transaction price.

The transaction price is the amount of consideration that a company expects to receive from a customer in exchange for transferring goods and services. The transaction price in a contract is often easily determined because the customer agrees to pay a fixed amount to the company over a short period of time. In other contracts, companies must consider the following factors. **[7]**

- Variable consideration
- Time value of money
- Noncash consideration
- Consideration paid or payable to the customer

Variable Consideration

In some cases, the price of a good or service is dependent on future events. These future events might include discounts, rebates, credits, performance bonuses, or royalties. In these cases, the company estimates the amount of variable consideration it will receive from the contract to determine the amount of revenue to recognize. Companies use either the **expected value,** which is a probability-weighted amount, or the **most likely amount** in a range of possible amounts to estimate variable consideration. Companies select among these two methods based on which approach better predicts the amount of consideration to which a company is entitled. **[8]** Illustration 18-9 highlights the issues to be considered in selecting the appropriate method.

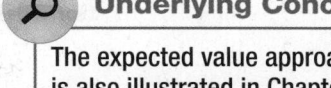

Underlying Concepts

The expected value approach is also illustrated in Chapter 6 to determine the liability for warranties.

Expected Value: Probability-weighted amount in a range of possible consideration amounts.	**Most Likely Amount:** The single most likely amount in a range of possible consideration outcomes.
• May be appropriate if a company has a large number of contracts with similar characteristics. • Can be based on a limited number of discrete outcomes and probabilities.	• May be appropriate if the contract has only two possible outcomes.

ILLUSTRATION 18-9
Estimating Variable Consideration

Illustration 18-10 provides an application of the two estimation methods.

ILLUSTRATION 18-10
Transaction Price—
Variable Consideration

ESTIMATING VARIABLE CONSIDERATION

Facts: Peabody Construction Company enters into a contract with a customer to build a warehouse for $100,000, with a performance bonus of $50,000 that will be paid based on the timing of completion. The amount of the performance bonus decreases by 10% per week for every week beyond the agreed-upon completion date. The contract requirements are similar to contracts that Peabody has performed previously, and management believes that such experience is predictive for this contract. Management estimates that there is a 60% probability that the contract will be completed by the agreed-upon completion date, a 30% probability that it will be completed 1 week late, and only a 10% probability that it will be completed 2 weeks late.

Question: How should Peabody account for this revenue arrangement?

Solution: The transaction price should include management's estimate of the amount of consideration to which Peabody will be entitled. Management has concluded that the **probability-weighted method** is the most predictive approach for estimating the variable consideration in this situation:

60% chance of $150,000 [$100,000 + ($50,000 × 1.0)] =	$ 90,000
30% chance of $145,000 [$100,000 + ($50,000 × .90)] =	43,500
10% chance of $140,000 [$100,000 + ($50,000 × .80)] =	14,000
	$147,500

Thus, the total transaction price is $147,500 based on the probability-weighted estimate. Management should update its estimate at each reporting date. Using a most likely outcome approach may be more predictive if a performance bonus is binary (Peabody either will or will not earn the performance bonus), such that Peabody earns either $50,000 for completion on the agreed-upon date or nothing for completion after the agreed-upon date. In this scenario, if management believes that Peabody will meet the deadline and estimates the consideration using the **most likely outcome**, the total transaction price would be $150,000 (the outcome with 60% probability).

A word of caution—a company only **allocates variable consideration if it is reasonably assured that it will be entitled to that amount**. Companies therefore may only recognize variable consideration if (1) they have experience with similar contracts and are able to estimate the cumulative amount of revenue, and (2) based on experience, it is highly probable that there will not be a significant reversal of revenue previously recognized.[5] If these criteria are not met, revenue recognition is constrained. **[10]** Illustration 18-11 provides an example of how the revenue constraint works.

ILLUSTRATION 18-11
Transaction Price—
Revenue Constraint

REVENUE CONSTRAINT

Facts: On January 1, Shera Company enters into a contract with Hornung Inc. to perform asset-management services for 1 year. Shera receives a quarterly management fee based on a percentage of Hornung's assets under management at the end of each quarter. In addition, Shera receives a performance-based incentive fee of 20% of the fund's return in excess of the return of an observable index at the end of the year.

Shera accounts for the contract as a single performance obligation to perform investment-management services for 1 year because the services are interdependent and interrelated. To recognize revenue for satisfying the performance obligation over time, Shera selects an output method of measuring progress toward complete satisfaction of the performance obligation. Shera has had a number of these types of contracts with customers in the past.

Question: At what point should Shera recognize the management fee and the performance-based incentive fee related to Hornung?

Solution: Shera should record the management fee each quarter as it is performs the management of the fund over the year. However, Shera should not record the incentive fee until the end of the year. Although Shera has experience with similar contracts, that experience is not predictive of the outcome of the current contract because the amount of consideration is highly susceptible to volatility in the market. In addition, the incentive fee has a large number and high variability of possible consideration amounts. Thus, revenue related to the incentive fee is constrained (not recognized) until the incentive fee is known at the end of the year.

Time Value of Money

Timing of payment to the company sometimes does not match the transfer of the goods or services to the customer. In most situations, companies receive consideration after the product is provided or the service performed. In essence, the company provides financing for the customer.

Companies account for the time value of money if the contract **involves a significant financing component**. When a sales transaction involves a significant financing component (i.e., interest is accrued on consideration to be paid over time), the fair value is determined either by measuring the consideration received or by discounting the payment using an imputed interest rate. The imputed interest rate is the more clearly determinable of either (1) the prevailing rate for a similar instrument of an issuer with a similar credit rating, or (2) a rate of interest that discounts the nominal amount of the instrument to the current sales price of the goods or services. The company

---

[5]Conditions such as one of the following would indicate that the revenue is constrained (or not recognized):

1. The amount of consideration is highly susceptible to factors outside the company's influence. Factors include volatility in a market, the judgment of third parties, weather conditions, and a high risk of obsolescence of the promised good or service.
2. The uncertainty about the amount of consideration is not expected to be resolved for a long period of time.
3. The company's experience (or other evidence) with similar types of performance obligations is limited.
4. The contract has a large number and broad range of possible consideration amounts. **[9]**

will report the effects of the financing either as interest expense or interest revenue. Illustration 18-12 provides an example of a financing transaction.

ILLUSTRATION 18-12
Transaction Price—
Extended Payment Terms

EXTENDED PAYMENT TERMS

Facts: On July 1, 2014, SEK Company sold goods to Grant Company for $900,000 in exchange for a 4-year, zero-interest-bearing note with a face amount of $1,416,163. The goods have an inventory cost on SEK's books of $590,000.

Questions: (a) How much revenue should SEK Company record on July 1, 2014? (b) How much revenue should it report related to this transaction on December 31, 2014?

Solution:
(a) SEK should record revenue of $900,000 on July 1, 2014, which is the fair value of the inventory in this case.

(b) SEK is also financing this purchase and records interest revenue on the note over the 4-year period. In this case, the interest rate is imputed and is determined to be 12%. SEK records interest revenue of $54,000 (12% × ½ × $900,000) at December 31, 2014.

The entry to record SEK's sale to Grant Company is as follows.

July 1, 2014

Notes Receivable	1,416,163	
Discount on Notes Receivable		516,163
Sales Revenue		900,000

The related entry to record the cost of goods sold is as follows.

July 1, 2014

Cost of Goods Sold	590,000	
Inventory		590,000

SEK makes the following entry to record interest revenue at the end of the year.

December 31, 2014

Discount on Notes Receivable	54,000	
Interest Revenue (12% × ½ × $900,000)		54,000

As a practical expedient, companies are not required to reflect the time value of money to determine the transaction price if the time period for payment is less than a year. **[11]**

Noncash Consideration

Companies sometimes receive consideration in the form of goods, services, or other noncash consideration. When these situations occur, **companies generally recognize revenue on the basis of the fair value of what is received.** For example, assume that Raeylinn Company receives common stock of Monroe Company in payment for consulting services. In that case, Raeylinn Company recognizes revenue in the amount of the fair value of the common stock received. If Raeylinn cannot determine this amount, then it should estimate the selling price of the services performed and recognize this amount as revenue.

In addition, companies sometimes receive contributions (e.g., donations and gifts). A contribution is often some type of asset (e.g., securities, land, buildings, or use of facilities) but it could be the forgiveness of debt. In these cases, companies recognize revenue for the fair value of the consideration received. Similarly, customers sometimes contribute goods or services, such as equipment or labor, as consideration for goods provided or services performed. This consideration should be recognized as revenue based on the fair value of the consideration received.

Consideration Paid or Payable to Customers

Companies often make payments to their customers as part of a revenue arrangement. Consideration paid or payable may include discounts, volume rebates, coupons, free products, or services. In general, these elements reduce the consideration received and the revenue to be recognized. Illustration 18-13 provides an example of this type of transaction.

ILLUSTRATION 18-13
Transaction Price—
Volume Discount

VOLUME DISCOUNT

Facts: Sansung Company offers its customers a 3% volume discount if they purchase at least $2 million of its product during the calendar year. On March 31, 2014, Sansung has made sales of $700,000 to Artic Co. In the previous 2 years, Sansung sold over $3,000,000 to Artic in the period April 1 to December 31.

> *Question:* How much revenue should Sansung recognize for the first 3 months of 2014?

Solution: In this case, Sansung should reduce its revenue by $21,000 ($700,000 × 3%) because it is probable that it will provide this rebate. Revenue is therefore $679,000 ($700,000 − $21,000). To not recognize this volume discount overstates Sansung's revenue for the first 3 months of 2014. In other words, the appropriate revenue is $679,000, not $700,000.

Given these facts, Sansung makes the following entry on March 31, 2014, to recognize revenue.

Accounts Receivable	679,000	
Sales Revenue		679,000

Assuming that Sansung's customer **meets the discount threshold**, Sansung makes the following entry.

Cash	679,000	
Accounts Receivable		679,000

If Sansung's customer **fails to meet the discount threshold**, Sansung makes the following entry upon payment.

Cash	700,000	
Accounts Receivable		679,000
Sales Discounts Forfeited		21,000

As indicated in Chapter 7 (pages 351–352), Sales Discounts Forfeited is reported in the "Other revenues and gains" section of the income statement.

In many cases, companies provide cash discounts to customers for a short period of time (often referred to as prompt settlement discounts). For example, assume that terms are payment due in 60 days, but if payment is made within five days, a two percent discount is given (referred to as 2/5, net 60). These prompt settlement discounts should reduce revenues, if material. In most cases, companies record the revenue at full price (gross) and record a sales discount if payment is made within the discount period.

Allocating the Transaction Price to Separate Performance Obligations—Step 4

LEARNING OBJECTIVE 6
Allocate the transaction price to the separate performance obligations.

Companies often have to allocate the transaction price to more than one performance obligation in a contract. If an allocation is needed, the transaction price allocated to the various performance obligations is based on their relative fair values. The best measure of fair value is what the company could sell the good or service for on a standalone basis, referred to as the **standalone selling price**. If this information is not available, companies should use their best estimate of what the good or service might sell for as a standalone unit. Illustration 18-14 summarizes the approaches that companies follow (in preferred order of use).

ILLUSTRATION 18-14
Transaction Price
Allocation

Allocation Approach	Implementation
Adjusted market assessment approach	Evaluate the market in which it sells goods or services and estimate the price that customers in that market are willing to pay for those goods or services. That approach also might include referring to prices from the company's competitors for similar goods or services and adjusting those prices as necessary to reflect the company's costs and margins.
Expected cost plus a margin approach	Forecast expected costs of satisfying a performance obligation and then add an appropriate margin for that good or service.
Residual approach	If the standalone selling price of a good or service is highly variable or uncertain, then a company may estimate the standalone selling price by reference to the total transaction price less the sum of the observable standalone selling prices of other goods or services promised in the contract.[6]

Illustrations 18-15 and 18-16 (on page 1054) are examples of the measurement issues involved in allocating the transaction price.

ILLUSTRATION 18-15
Allocation—Multiple
Performance Obligations

MULTIPLE PERFORMANCE OBLIGATIONS—EXAMPLE 1

Facts: Lonnie Company enters into a contract to build, run, and maintain a highly complex piece of electronic equipment for a period of 5 years, commencing upon delivery of the equipment. There is a fixed fee for each of the build, run, and maintenance deliverables, and any progress payments made are nonrefundable. All the deliverables have a standalone value. There is verifiable evidence of the selling price for the building and maintenance but not for running the equipment. It is determined that the transaction price must be allocated to the three performance obligations: building, running, and maintaining the equipment.

Question: **What procedure should Lonnie Company use to allocate the transaction price to the three performance obligations?**

Solution: The performance obligations relate to building the equipment, running the equipment, and maintaining the equipment. As indicated, Lonnie can determine standalone values for the equipment and the maintenance agreements. The company then can make a best estimate of the selling price for running the equipment, using the adjusted market assessment approach or expected cost plus a margin approach. Lonnie next applies the relative fair value method at the inception of the transaction to determine the proper allocation to each performance obligation. Once the allocation is performed, Lonnie recognizes revenue independently for each performance obligation using regular revenue recognition criteria.

If, on the other hand, Lonnie is unable to estimate the standalone selling price for running the equipment because such an estimate is highly variable or uncertain, Lonnie may use a residual approach. In this case, Lonnie uses the fair values of the equipment and maintenance agreements and subtracts their fair value from the total transaction price to arrive at a residual value for running the equipment.

[6]A selling price is highly variable when a company sells the same good or service to different customers (at or near the same time) for a broad range of amounts. A selling price is uncertain when a company has not yet established a price for a good or service and the good or service has not previously been sold. **[12]**

ILLUSTRATION 18-16
Multiple Performance
Obligations—Product,
Installation, and Service

MULTIPLE PERFORMANCE OBLIGATIONS—EXAMPLE 2

Facts: Handler Company is an experienced manufacturer of equipment used in the construction industry. Handler's products range from small to large individual pieces of automated machinery to complex systems containing numerous components. Unit selling prices range from $600,000 to $4,000,000 and are quoted inclusive of installation and training. The installation process does not involve changes to the features of the equipment and does not require proprietary information about the equipment in order for the installed equipment to perform to specifications. Handler has the following arrangement with Chai Company.

- Chai purchases equipment from Handler for a price of $2,000,000 and chooses Handler to do the installation. Handler charges the same price for the equipment irrespective of whether it does the installation or not. (Some companies do the installation themselves because they either prefer their own employees to do the work or because of relationships with other customers.) The price of the installation service is estimated to have a fair value of $20,000.
- The fair value of the training sessions is estimated at $50,000. Other companies can also perform these training services.
- Chai is obligated to pay Handler the $2,000,000 upon the delivery and installation of the equipment.
- Handler delivers the equipment on September 1, 2014, and completes the installation of the equipment on November 1, 2014 (transfer of control is complete). Training related to the equipment starts once the installation is completed and lasts for 1 year. The equipment has a useful life of 10 years.

Questions: (a) What are the performance obligations for purposes of accounting for the sale of the equipment? (b) If there is more than one performance obligation, how should the payment of $2,000,000 be allocated to various components?

Solution:
(a) The first condition for separation into a standalone unit for the equipment is met. That is, the equipment, installation, and training are distinct and not interdependent. That is, the equipment, installation, and training are three separate products or services. Each of these items has a standalone selling price and therefore is not interdependent.
(b) The total revenue of $2,000,000 should be allocated to the three components based on their relative fair values. In this case, the fair value of the equipment should be considered $2,000,000, the installation fee is $20,000, and the training is $50,000. The total fair value to consider is $2,070,000 ($2,000,000 + $20,000 + $50,000). The allocation is as follows.

Equipment	$1,932,367 [($2,000,000 ÷ $2,070,000) × $2,000,000]
Installation	$19,324 [($20,000 ÷ $2,070,000) × $2,000,000]
Training	$48,309 [($50,000 ÷ $2,070,000) × $2,000,000]

Handler makes the following entry on November 1, 2014, to record both sales revenue and service revenue on the installation, as well as unearned service revenue.

November 1, 2014

Cash	2,000,000	
Service Revenue (installation)		19,324
Unearned Service Revenue		48,309
Sales Revenue		1,932,367

Assuming the cost of the equipment is $1,500,000, the entry to record cost of goods sold is as follows.

November 1, 2014

Cost of Goods Sold	1,500,000	
Inventory		1,500,000

As indicated by these entries, Handler recognizes revenue from the sale of the equipment once the installation is completed on November 1, 2014. In addition, it recognizes revenue for the installation fee because these services have been performed.

Handler recognizes the training revenues on a straight-line basis starting on November 1, 2014, or $4,026 ($48,309 ÷ 12) per month for one year (unless a more appropriate method such as the percentage-of-completion method is warranted). The journal entry to recognize the training revenue for two months in 2014 is as follows.

December 31, 2014

Unearned Service Revenue	8,052	
Service Revenue (training) ($4,026 × 2)		8,052

Therefore, Handler recognizes revenue at December 31, 2014, in the amount of $1,959,743 ($1,932,367 + $19,324 + $8,052). Handler makes the following journal entry to recognize the training revenue in 2015, assuming adjusting entries are made at year-end.

December 31, 2015

Unearned Service Revenue	40,257	
Service Revenue (training) ($48,309 − $8,052)		40,257

When a company sells a bundle of goods or services, the selling price of the bundle is often less than the sum of the individual standalone prices. In this case, the company should allocate the discount to the product (or products) that is causing the discount and not to the entire bundle. Illustration 18-17 indicates how a discount should be allocated.

DISCOUNTED TRANSACTION PRICE

ILLUSTRATION 18-17
Allocating Transaction
Price with a Discount

Facts: Colorado Joe's Golf Shop provides the following information related to three items that are often sold as a package.

Item	Standalone Selling Price	Price When Bundled
Lessons (per session)	$100	$100
Custom irons	525	500
Putter	125	25
Total	$750	$625

Question: How should the discount be allocated to the elements of the revenue arrangement?

Solution: As indicated, the standalone price for the lesson, custom irons, and putter is $750, but the bundled price for all three is $625. In this case, the discount applies to the performance obligations related to the providing of the custom irons and putter. As a result, Colorado Joe's allocates the discount solely to the custom irons and putter, and not to the lessons, as follows.

	Allocated Amounts
Lessons	$100
Custom irons and putter	525
Total	$625

Recognizing Revenue When (or as) Each Performance Obligation Is Satisfied—Step 5

7 LEARNING OBJECTIVE
Recognize revenue when the company satisfies its performance obligation.

A company satisfies its performance obligation when the customer obtains control of the good or service. As indicated earlier, the concept of change in control is the deciding factor in determining when a performance obligation is satisfied. The customer controls the product or service when it has the ability to direct the use of and obtain substantially all the remaining benefits from the asset or service. Control also includes the customer's ability to prevent other companies from directing the use of, or receiving the benefits, from the asset or service. Illustration 18-18 summarizes the indicators that the customer has obtained control. [13]

ILLUSTRATION 18-18
Change in Control
Indicators

1. The company has a right to payment for the asset.
2. The company has transferred legal title to the asset.
3. The company has transferred physical possession of the asset.
4. The customer has significant risks and rewards of ownership.
5. The customer has accepted the asset.

Companies satisfy performance obligations either at a point in time or over a period of time. Companies recognize revenue over a period of time if the customer receives and consumes the benefits as the seller performs and one of the following two criteria is met.

1. The customer controls the asset as it is created or enhanced (e.g., a builder constructs a building on a customer's property).
2. The company does not have an alternative use for the asset created or enhanced (e.g., an aircraft manufacturer builds specialty jets to a customer's specifications) and either (a) the customer receives benefits as the company performs and therefore the task would not need to be re-performed, or (b) the company has a right to payment and this right is enforceable.

Illustration 18-19 provides an example of the point in time when revenue should be recognized.

ILLUSTRATION 18-19
Satisfying a Performance Obligation

TIMING OF REVENUE RECOGNITION

Facts: Gomez Software Company enters into a contract with Hurly Company to develop and install customer relationship management (CRM) software. Progress payments are made upon completion of each stage of the contract. If the contract is terminated, then the partly completed CRM software passes to Hurly Company. Gomez Software is prohibited from redirecting the software to another customer.

Question: **At what point should Gomez Software Company recognize revenue related to its contract with Hurly Company?**

Solution: Gomez Software does not create an asset with an alternative use because it is prohibited from redirecting the software to another customer. In addition, Gomez Software is entitled to payments for performance to date and expects to complete the project. Therefore, Gomez Software concludes that the contract meets the criteria for recognizing revenue over time.

A company recognizes revenue from a performance obligation over time by measuring the progress toward completion. The method selected for measuring progress should depict the transfer of control from the company to the customer. Companies use various methods to determine the extent of progress toward completion. The most common are the cost-to-cost and units-of-delivery methods. The objective of all these methods is to measure the extent of progress in terms of costs, units, or value added. Companies identify the various measures (costs incurred, labor hours worked, tons produced, floors completed, etc.) and classify them as input or output measures.

Input measures (e.g., costs incurred and labor hours worked) are efforts devoted to a contract. Output measures (with units of delivery measured as tons produced, floors of a building completed, miles of a highway completed, etc.) track results. Neither is universally applicable to all long-term projects. Their use requires the exercise of judgment and careful tailoring to the circumstances.

The most popular input measure used to determine the progress toward completion is the cost-to-cost basis. Under this basis, a company measures the percentage of completion by comparing costs incurred to date with the most recent estimate of the total costs required to complete the contract. The percentage-of-completion method is discussed more fully in Appendix 18A, which examines the accounting for long-term contracts.

Summary

Illustration 18-20 provides a summary of the five-step revenue recognition process.

Step in Process	Description	Implementation
1. Identify the contract with customers.	A contract is an agreement that creates enforceable rights or obligations.	A company applies the revenue guidance to contracts with customers and must determine if new performance obligations are created by a contract modification.
2. Identify the separate performance obligations in the contract.	A performance obligation is a promise in a contract to provide a product or service to a customer. A performance obligation exists if the customer can benefit from the good or service on its own or together with other readily available resources.	A contract may be comprised of multiple performance obligations. The accounting for multiple performance obligations is based on evaluation of whether the product or service is distinct within the contract. If each of the goods or services is distinct, but is interdependent and interrelated, these goods and services are combined and reported as one performance obligation.
3. Determine the transaction price.	The transaction price is the amount of consideration that a company expects to receive from a customer in exchange for transferring goods and services.	In determining the transaction price, companies must consider the following factors: (1) variable consideration, (2) time value of money, (3) noncash consideration, and (4) consideration paid or payable to customer.
4. Allocate the transaction price to the separate performance obligations.	If more than one performance obligation exists, allocate the transaction price based on relative fair values.	The best measure of fair value is what the good or service could be sold for on a standalone basis (standalone selling price). Estimates of standalone selling price can be based on (1) adjusted market assessment, (2) expected cost plus a margin approach, or (3) a residual approach.
5. Recognize revenue when each performance obligation is satisfied.	A company satisfies its performance obligation when the customer obtains control of the good or service.	Companies satisfy performance obligations either at a point in time or over a period of time. Companies recognize revenue over a period of time if (1) the customer controls the asset as it is created or (2) the company does not have an alternative use for the asset.

ILLUSTRATION 18-20
Summary of the Five-Step Revenue Recognition Process

OTHER REVENUE RECOGNITION ISSUES

The revenue recognition principle and the concept of control are illustrated for the following situations.

8 LEARNING OBJECTIVE
Identify other revenue recognition issues.

- Right of return
- Repurchase agreements
- Bill and hold
- Principal-agent relationships
- Consignments
- Warranties
- Nonrefundable upfront fees

Right of Return

Sales with rights of return have long been a challenge in the area of revenue recognition. For example, assume that Hogland Glass Works transfers control of hurricane glass to Henlo Builders. Hogland grants Henlo the **right of return** for the product for various reasons (e.g., dissatisfaction with the product) and to receive any combination of the following.

1. A full or partial refund of any consideration paid.
2. A credit that can be applied against amounts owed, or that will be owed, to the seller.
3. Another product in exchange.

To account for the transfer of this glass with a right of return (and for some services that are performed subject to a refund), Hogland should recognize all of the following.

(a) Revenue for the transferred products in the amount of consideration to which Hogland is reasonably assured to be entitled (considering the products expected to be returned).

(b) A refund liability.

(c) An asset (and corresponding adjustment to cost of sales) for its right to recover glass from Henlo on settling the refund liability.

An example of a return situation is presented in Illustration 18-21.[7]

ILLUSTRATION 18-21
Recognition—Right of Return

RIGHT OF RETURN

Facts: Venden Company sells 100 products for $100 each to Amaya Inc. for cash. Venden allows Amaya to return any unused product within 30 days and receive a full refund. The cost of each product is $60. To determine the transaction price, Venden decides that the approach that is most predictive of the amount of consideration to which it will be entitled is the most likely amount. Using the most likely amount, Venden estimates that:

1. Three products will be returned.
2. The costs of recovering the products will be immaterial.
3. The returned products are expected to be resold at a profit.

Question: How should Venden record this sale?

Solution: Upon transfer of control of the products, Venden recognizes (a) revenue of $9,700 ($100 × 97 products expected not to be returned), (b) a refund liability for $300 ($100 refund × 3 products expected to be returned), and (c) an asset of $180 ($60 × 3 products) for its right to recover products from customers on settling the refund liability. Hence, the amount recognized in cost of sales for 97 products is $5,820 ($60 × 97).

Venden records the sale as follows.

Cash	10,000	
Sales Revenue		9,700
Refund Liability		300

Venden also records the related cost of goods sold with the following entry.

Cost of Goods Sold	5,820	
Estimated Inventory Returns	180	
Inventory		6,000

When a return occurs, Venden should reduce the Refund Liability and Estimated Inventory Returns accounts. In addition, Venden recognizes the returned inventory in a Returned Inventory account as shown in the following entries for the return of two products.

Refund Liability (2 × $100)	200	
Accounts Payable		200
Returned Inventory (2 × $60)	120	
Estimated Inventory Returns		120

Companies record the returned asset in a separate account from inventory to provide transparency. The carrying value of the returned asset is subject to impairment testing, separate from the inventory. If a company is unable to estimate the level of returns with any reliability, it should not report any revenue until the returns become predictive.

---

[7]Adapted from "Revenue from Contracts with Customers," *Proposed Accounting Standards Update (Revised)* (Norwalk, Conn.: FASB, November 14, 2011, and January 4, 2012), p. 58.

Repurchase Agreements

In some cases, companies enter into **repurchase agreements**, which allow them to transfer an asset to a customer but have an obligation or right to repurchase the asset at a later date. In these situations, the question is whether the company sold the asset.[8] Generally, companies report these transactions as a financing (borrowing). That is, if the company has an obligation or right to repurchase the asset for an amount **greater than or equal to its selling price,** then the transaction is a financing transaction by the company. Illustration 18-22 examines the issues related to a repurchase agreement.

ILLUSTRATION 18-22
Recognition—
Repurchase Agreement

REPURCHASE AGREEMENT

Facts: Morgan Inc., an equipment dealer, sells equipment on January 1, 2014, to Lane Company for $100,000. It agrees to repurchase this equipment from Lane Company on December 31, 2015, for a price of $121,000.

Question: Should Morgan Inc. record a sale for this transaction?

Solution: For a sale and repurchase agreement, the terms of the agreement need to be analyzed to determine whether Morgan Inc. has transferred control to the customer, Lane Company. As indicated earlier, control of an asset refers to the ability to direct the use of and obtain substantially all the benefits from the asset. Control also includes the ability to prevent other companies from directing the use of and receiving the benefit from a good or service. In this case, Morgan Inc. continues to have control of the asset. Therefore, this agreement is a financing transaction and not a sale. Thus, the asset is not removed from the books of Morgan Inc.

Assuming that an interest rate of 10 percent is imputed from the agreement, Morgan Inc. makes the following entries to record this agreement. Morgan Inc. records the financing on January 1, 2014, as follows.

January 1, 2014

Cash	100,000	
Liability to Lane Company		100,000

Morgan Inc. records interest on December 31, 2014, as follows.

December 31, 2014

Interest Expense	10,000	
Liability to Lane Company		10,000
($100,000 × 10%)		

Morgan Inc. records interest and retirement of its liability to Lane Company as follows.

December 31, 2014

Interest Expense	11,000	
Liability to Lane Company		11,000
($110,000 × 10%)		
Liability to Lane Company	121,000	
Cash ($100,000 + $10,000 + $11,000)		121,000

Rather than Morgan Inc. having the obligation or right to repurchase the asset, assume that Lane Company **has the option** to require Morgan Inc. to repurchase the asset at December 31, 2015. This option is a put option; that is, Lane Company has the option to put the asset back to Morgan Inc. Recall from the discussion in Appendix 17A

[8]Beyond financing motivations, a company may transfer inventory to another party on a short-term basis to avoid inventory taxes. If the counterparty is able to use the inventory during the transfer period, the transaction may more appropriately be accounted for as a rental agreement.

that the value of a put option increases when the value of the underlying asset (in this case, the equipment) decreases. In determining how to account for this transaction, Morgan Inc. has to determine whether Lane Company will have an economic incentive to exercise this put option at the end of 2015.

Specifically, Lane Company has a significant economic incentive to exercise its put option if the value of the equipment declines. In this case, the transaction is reported as a financing transaction as shown in Illustration 18-22. That is, Lane Company will return (put) the equipment back to Morgan Inc. if the repurchase price exceeds the fair value of the equipment. For example, if the repurchase price of the equipment is $150,000 but its fair value is $125,000, Lane Company is better off returning the equipment to Morgan Inc.

Conversely, if Lane Company does not have a significant economic incentive to exercise its put option, then the transaction should be reported as a sale of a product with a right of return.

What do the numbers mean? NO TAKE-BACKS

Investors in Lucent Technologies were negatively affected when Lucent violated one of the fundamental criteria for revenue recognition—the "no take-back" rule. This rule holds that revenue should not be booked on inventory that is shipped if the customer can return it at some point in the future. In this particular case, Lucent agreed to take back shipped inventory from its distributors if the distributors were unable to sell the items to their customers.

In essence, Lucent was "stuffing the channel." By booking sales when goods were shipped, even though they most likely would get them back, Lucent was able to report continued sales growth. However, Lucent investors got a nasty surprise when distributors returned those goods and Lucent had to restate its financial results. The restatement erased $679 million in revenues, turning an operating profit into a loss. In response to this bad news, Lucent's share price

declined $1.31 per share, or 8.5 percent. Lucent is not alone in this practice. Sunbeam got caught stuffing the sales channel with barbeque grills and other outdoor items, which contributed to its troubles when it was forced to restate its earnings.

Investors can be tipped off to potential channel stuffing by carefully reviewing a company's revenue recognition policy for generous return policies or use of cash incentives to encourage distributors to buy products (as was done at Monsanto) and by watching inventory and receivables levels. When sales increase along with receivables, that's one sign that customers are not paying for goods shipped on credit. And growing inventory levels are an indicator that customers have all the goods they need. Both scenarios suggest a higher likelihood of goods being returned and revenues and income being restated. So remember, no take-backs!

Sources: Adapted from S. Young, "Lucent Slashes First Quarter Outlook, Erases Revenue from Latest Quarter," *Wall Street Journal Online* (December 22, 2000); Tracey Byrnes, "Too Many Thin Mints: Spotting the Practice of Channel Stuffing," *Wall Street Journal Online* (February 7, 2002); and H. Weitzman, "Monsanto to Restate Results After SEC Probe," *Financial Times* (October 5, 2011).

Bill-and-Hold Arrangements

A bill-and-hold arrangement is a contract under which an entity bills a customer for a product but the entity retains physical possession of the product until it is transferred to the customer at a point in time in the future. Bill-and-hold sales result when the buyer is not yet ready to take delivery but does take title and accepts billing. For example, a customer may request a company to enter into such an arrangement because of (1) lack of available space for the product, (2) delays in its production schedule, or (3) more than sufficient inventory in its distribution channel.[9] Illustration 18-23 provides an example of a bill-and-hold arrangement.

[9]"Revenue from Contracts with Customers," *Proposed Accounting Standards Update* (Stamford, Conn.: FASB, June 24, 2010), p. 54.

BILL AND HOLD

ILLUSTRATION 18-23
Recognition—Bill and
Hold

Facts: Butler Company sells $450,000 (cost $280,000) of fireplaces on March 1, 2014, to a local coffee shop, Baristo, which is planning to expand its locations around the city. Under the agreement, Baristo asks Butler to retain these fireplaces in its warehouses until the new coffee shops that will house the fireplaces are ready. Title passes to Baristo at the time the agreement is signed.

Question: When should Butler recognize the revenue from this bill-and-hold arrangement?

Solution: When to recognize revenue in a bill-and-hold arrangement depends on the circumstances. Butler determines when it has satisfied its performance obligation to transfer a product by evaluating when Baristo obtains control of that product. For Baristo to have obtained control of a product in a bill-and-hold arrangement, all of the following criteria should be met:

(a) The reason for the bill-and-hold arrangement must be substantive.
(b) The product must be identified separately as belonging to Baristo.
(c) The product currently must be ready for physical transfer to Baristo.
(d) Butler cannot have the ability to use the product or to direct it to another customer.

In this case, it appears that the above criteria were met, and therefore revenue recognition should be permitted at the time the contract is signed. Butler has transferred control to Baristo; that is, Butler has a right to payment for the fireplaces and legal title has transferred.

Butler makes the following entry to record the bill-and-hold sale and related cost of goods sold.

March 1, 2014

Accounts Receivable	450,000	
Sales Revenue		450,000
Cost of Goods Sold	280,000	
Inventory		280,000

Principal-Agent Relationships

In a **principal-agent relationship**, the principal's performance obligation is to provide goods or perform services for a customer. The agent's performance obligation is to arrange for the principal to provide these goods or services to a customer. Examples of principal-agent relationships are as follows.

- Preferred Travel Company (agent) facilitates the booking of cruise excursions by finding customers for Regency Cruise Company (principal).
- Priceline (agent) facilitates the sale of various services such as car rentals at Hertz (principal).

In these types of situations, amounts collected on behalf of the principal are not revenue of the agent. Instead, revenue for the agent is the amount of the commission it receives (usually a percentage of total revenue). Illustration 18-24 provides an example of the issues related to principal-agent relationships.

PRINCIPAL-AGENT RELATIONSHIP

ILLUSTRATION 18-24
Recognition—Principal-
Agent Relationship

Facts: Fly-Away Travel sells airplane tickets for British Airways (BA) to various customers.

Question: What are the performance obligations in this situation and how should revenue be recognized for both the principal and agent?

Solution: The principal in this case is BA and the agent is Fly-Away Travel. Because BA has the performance obligation to provide air transportation to the customer, it is the principal. Fly-Away Travel facilitates the sale of the airline ticket to the customer in exchange for a fee or commission. Its performance obligation is to arrange for BA to provide air transportation to the customer.

Although Fly-Away collects the full airfare from the customer, it then remits this amount to BA less the commission. Fly-Away therefore should not record the full amount of the fare as revenue on its books—to do so overstates revenue. Its revenue is the commission, not the full price. Control of performing the air transportation is with BA, not Fly-Away Travel.

Some might argue that there is no harm in letting Fly-Away record revenue for the full price of the ticket and then charging the cost of the ticket against the revenue (often referred to as the **gross method** of recognizing revenue). Others note that this approach overstates the agent's revenue and is misleading. The revenue received is the commission for providing the travel services, not the full fare price (often referred to as the **net approach**). The profession believes the net approach is the correct method for recognizing revenue in a principal-agent relationship. As a result, the FASB has developed specific criteria to determine when a principal-agent relationship exists.[10] An important feature in deciding whether Fly-Away is acting as an agent is whether the amount it earns is predetermined, being either a fixed fee per transaction or a stated percentage of the amount billed to the customer.

What do the numbers mean? GROSSED OUT

As you learned in Chapter 4, many corporate executives obsess over the bottom line. However, analysts on the outside look at the big picture, which includes examination of both the top line and the important subtotals in the income statement, such as gross profit. Recently, the top line is causing some concern, with nearly all companies in the S&P 500 reporting a 2 percent decline in the bottom line while the top line saw revenue decline by 1 percent. This is troubling because it is the first decline in revenues since we crawled out of the recession following the financial crisis. McDonald's gave an ominous preview—it saw its first monthly sales decline in nine years. And the United States, rather than foreign markets, led the drop.

What about income subtotals like gross margin? These metrics too have been under pressure. There is concern that struggling companies may employ a number of manipulations to mask the impact of gross margin declines on the bottom line. In fact, Rite Aid prepares an income statement that omits the gross margin subtotal. That is not surprising when you consider that Rite Aid's gross margin has steadily declined from 28 percent in 2010 to 26 percent in 2012. Rite Aid has used a number of suspect accounting adjustments related to tax allowances and inventory gains to offset its weak gross margin.

Or, consider the classic case of Priceline.com, the company made famous by William Shatner's ads about "naming your own price" for airline tickets and hotel rooms. In one quarter, Priceline reported that it earned $152 million in revenues. But, that included the full amount customers paid for tickets, hotel rooms, and rental cars. Traditional travel agencies call that amount "gross bookings," not revenues. And, much like regular travel agencies, Priceline keeps only a small portion of gross bookings—namely, the spread between the customers' accepted bids and the price it paid for the merchandise. The rest, which Priceline calls "product costs," it pays to the airlines and hotels that supply the tickets and rooms.

However, Priceline's product costs came to $134 million, leaving Priceline just $18 million of what it calls "gross profit" and what most other companies would call revenues. And that's before all of Priceline's other costs—like advertising and salaries—which netted out to a loss of $102 million. The difference isn't academic. Priceline shares traded at about 23 times its reported revenues but at a mind-boggling 214 times its "gross profit." This and other aggressive recognition practices explain the stricter revenue recognition guidance, indicating that if a company performs as an agent or broker without assuming the risks and rewards of ownership of the goods, the company should report sales on a net (fee) basis.

Sources: Jeremy Kahn, "Presto Chango! Sales Are Huge," *Fortune* (March 20, 2000), p. 44; A. Catanach and E. Ketz, "RITE AID: Is Management Selling Drugs or Using Them?" *Grumpy Old Accountants* (August 22, 2011); and S. Jakab, "Weak Revenue Is New Worry for Investors," *Wall Street Journal* (November 25, 2012).

Consignments

A common principal-agent relationship involves consignments. In these cases, manufacturers (or wholesalers) deliver goods but retain title to the goods until they are sold. This specialized method of marketing certain types of products makes use of

---

[10] Indicators that the company's performance obligation is to arrange for the providing of goods or the performing of services by another party (i.e., the company is an agent and should recognize revenue in the net amount) include the following: (a) the other party is primarily responsible for fulfilling the contract; (b) the company does not have inventory risk before or after the customer order, during shipping, or on return; (c) the company does not have latitude in establishing prices for the other party's goods or services and, hence, the benefit that the company can receive from those goods or services is constrained; (d) the company's consideration is in the form of a commission; and (e) the company does not have customer credit risk for the amount receivable in exchange for the other party's goods or services. **[14]**

an agreement known as a **consignment**. Under this arrangement, the **consignor** (manufacturer or wholesaler) ships merchandise to the **consignee** (dealer), who is to act as an agent for the consignor in selling the merchandise. Both consignor and consignee are interested in selling—the former to make a profit or develop a market, the latter to make a commission on the sale.

The consignee accepts the merchandise and agrees to exercise due diligence in caring for and selling it. The consignee remits to the consignor cash received from customers, after deducting a sales commission and any chargeable expenses. In consignment sales, the consignor uses a modified version of the point-of-sale basis of revenue recognition. That is, the consignor recognizes revenue only after receiving notification of the sale and the cash remittance from the consignee.

The consignor carries the merchandise as inventory throughout the consignment, separately classified as Inventory (consignments). **The consignee does not record the merchandise as an asset on its books**. Upon sale of the merchandise, the consignee has **a liability for the net amount due the consignor**. The consignor periodically receives from the consignee a report called **account sales** that shows the merchandise received, merchandise sold, expenses chargeable to the consignment, and the cash remitted. Revenue is then recognized by the consignor. Analysis of a consignment arrangement is provided in Illustration 18-25.

SALES ON CONSIGNMENT

ILLUSTRATION 18-25
Recognition—Sales on Consignment

Facts: Nelba Manufacturing Co. ships merchandise costing $36,000 on consignment to Best Value Stores. Nelba pays $3,750 of freight costs, and Best Value pays $2,250 for local advertising costs that are reimbursable from Nelba. By the end of the period, Best Value has sold two-thirds of the consigned merchandise for $40,000 cash. Best Value notifies Nelba of the sales, retains a 10% commission, and remits the cash due Nelba.

Question: What are the journal entries that the consignor (Nelba) and the consignee (Best Value) make to record this transaction?

Solution:

NELBA MFG. CO. (CONSIGNOR)			BEST VALUE STORES (CONSIGNEE)		
Shipment of consigned merchandise					
Inventory (consignments)	36,000		No entry (record memo of merchandise		
Finished Goods Inventory		36,000	received).		
Payment of freight costs by consignor					
Inventory (consignments)	3,750		No entry.		
Cash		3,750			
Payment of advertising by consignee					
No entry until notified.			Receivable from Consignor	2,250	
			Cash		2,250
Sales of consigned merchandise					
No entry until notified.			Cash	40,000	
			Payable to Consignor		40,000
Notification of sales and expenses and remittance of amount due					
Cash	33,750		Payable to Consignor	40,000	
Advertising Expense	2,250		Receivable from		
Commission Expense	4,000		Consignor		2,250
Revenue from			Commission Revenue		4,000
Consignment Sales		40,000	Cash		33,750
Adjustment of inventory on consignment for cost of sales					
Cost of Goods Sold	26,500		No entry.		
Inventory (consignments)		26,500			
[2/3 ($36,000 + $3,750) = $26,500]					

Under the consignment arrangement, the consignor accepts the risk that the merchandise might not sell and relieves the consignee of the need to commit part of its working capital to inventory. Consignors use a variety of systems and account titles to record consignments, but they all share the common goal of postponing the recognition of revenue until it is known that a sale to a third party has occurred. **Consignees only recognize revenue associated with commissions.**

Warranties

Companies often provide one of two types of **warranties** to customers:

1. Warranties that the product **meets agreed-upon specifications in the contract at the time the product is sold**. This type of warranty is included in the sales price of a company's product and is often referred to as an **assurance-type warranty**.

2. Warranties that provide an **additional service beyond the assurance-type warranty**. This warranty is not included in the sales price of the product and is referred to as a **service-type warranty**. As a consequence, it is recorded as a separate performance obligation.

Companies do not record a separate performance obligation for assurance-type warranties. This type of warranty is nothing more than a quality guarantee that the good or service is free from defects at the point of sale. These types of obligations should be expensed in the period the goods are provided or services performed (in other words, at the point of sale). In addition, the company should record a warranty liability. The estimated amount of the liability includes all the costs that the company will incur after sale due to the correction of defects or deficiencies required under the warranty provisions.

In addition, companies sometimes provide customers with an option to purchase a warranty separately. In most cases, these extended warranties provide the customer a service beyond fixing defects that existed at the time of sale. For example, when you purchase a TV, you are entitled to the company's warranty. You will also undoubtedly be offered an extended warranty on the product at an additional cost. These service-type warranties represent a **separate service and are an additional performance obligation**. As a result, companies should allocate a portion of the transaction price to this performance obligation. The company recognizes revenue in the period that the service-type warranty is in effect. Illustration 18-26 presents an example of both an assurance-type and a service-type warranty.

ILLUSTRATION 18-26
Recognition—
Performance Obligations
and Warranties

WARRANTIES

Facts: Maverick Company sold 1,000 Rollomatics during 2014 at a total price of $6,000,000, with a warranty guarantee that the product was free of any defects. The cost of Rollomatics sold is $4,000,000. The term of the assurance warranty is two years, with an estimated cost of $30,000. In addition, Maverick sold extended warranties related to 400 Rollomatics for 3 years beyond the 2-year period for $12,000.

Question: **What are the journal entries that Maverick Company should make in 2014 related to the sale and the related warranties?**

Solution: To record the revenue and liabilities related to the warranties:

Cash ($6,000,000 + $12,000)	6,012,000	
Warranty Expense	30,000	
Warranty Liability		30,000
Unearned Warranty Revenue		12,000
Sales Revenue		6,000,000

To reduce inventory and recognize cost of goods sold:

Cost of Goods Sold	4,000,000	
Inventory		4,000,000

Similar to that illustrated in Chapter 13 (pages 720–721), Maverick Company reduces the Warranty Liability account over the first two years as the actual warranty costs are incurred. The company also recognizes revenue related to the service-type warranty over the three-year period that extends beyond the assurance warranty period (two years). In most cases, the unearned warranty revenue is recognized on a straight-line basis. The costs associated with the service-type warranty are expensed as incurred.

Nonrefundable Upfront Fees

Companies sometimes receive payments (**upfront fees**) from customers before they deliver a product or perform a service. Upfront payments generally relate to the initiation, activation, or setup of a good or service to be provided or performed in the future. In most cases, these upfront payments are nonrefundable. Examples include fees paid for membership in a health club or buying club, and activation fees for phone, Internet, or cable.

Companies must determine whether these nonrefundable advance payments are for products or services in the current period. In most situations, these payments are for future delivery of products and services and should therefore not be recorded as revenue at the time of payment. In some cases, the upfront fee is viewed similar to a renewal option for future products and services at a reduced price. An example would be a health club where once the initiation fee is paid, no additional fee is necessary upon renewal. Illustration 18-27 provides an example of an upfront fee payment.

ILLUSTRATION 18-27
Transaction Price—
Upfront Fee
Considerations

UPFRONT FEE CONSIDERATIONS

Facts: Erica Felise signs a 1-year contract with Bigelow Health Club. The terms of the contract are that Erica is required to pay a nonrefundable initiation fee of $200 and an annual membership fee of $50 per month. Bigelow determines that its customers, on average, renew their annual membership two times before terminating their membership.

Question: **What is the amount of revenue Bigelow Health Club should recognize in the first year?**

Solution: In this case, the membership fee arrangement may be viewed as a single performance obligation (similar services are provided in all periods). That is, Bigelow is providing a discounted price in the second and third years for the same services, and this should be reflected in the revenue recognized in those periods. Bigelow determines the total transaction price to be $2,000—the upfront fee of $200 and the three years of monthly fees of $1,800 ($50 × 36)—and allocates it over the three years. In this case, Bigelow would report revenue of $55.56 ($2,000 ÷ 36) each month for three years. *Unless otherwise instructed, use this approach for homework problems.*[11]

Summary

Illustration 18-28 (page 1066) provides a summary of the additional issues related to transfer of control and revenue recognition.

---

[11] The initiation fee might be viewed as a separate performance obligation (it provides a renewal option at a lower price than normally charged, perhaps with different sevices). In this situation, in the first period, Bigelow would report revenue of $600 ($50 × 12). The initiation fee would then be allocated to years two and three ($100 in each year) unless forfeited earlier.

Issue	Description	Implementation
Right of return	Return of product by customer (e.g., due to dissatisfaction with the product) in exchange for refunds, a credit against amounts owed or that will be owed, and/or another product in exchange.	Seller may recognize (a) an adjustment to revenue for the products expected to be returned, (b) a refund liability, and (c) an asset for the right to recover the product.
Repurchase agreements	Seller has an obligation or right to repurchase the asset at a later date.	Generally, if the company has an obligation or right to repurchase the asset for an amount greater than its selling price, then the transaction is a financing transaction.
Bill and hold	Result when the buyer is not yet ready to take delivery but does take title and accept billing.	Revenue is recognized depending on when the customer obtains control of that product.
Principal-agent	Arrangement in which the principal's performance obligation is to provide goods or perform services for a customer. The agent's performance obligation is to arrange for the principal to provide these goods or services to a customer.	Amounts collected on behalf of the principal are not revenue of the agent. Instead, revenue for the agent is the amount of the commission it receives. The principal recognizes revenue when the goods or services are sold to a third-party customer.
Consignments	A principal-agent relationship in which the consignor (manufacturer or wholesaler) ships merchandise to the consignee (dealer), who is to act as an agent for the consignor in selling the merchandise.	The consignor recognizes revenue only after receiving notification of the sale and the cash remittance from the consignee (consignor carries the merchandise as inventory throughout the consignment). The consignee records commission revenue (usually some percentage of the selling price).
Warranties	Warranties can be assurance-type (product meets agreed-upon specifications) or service-type (provides additional service beyond the assurance-type warranty).	A separate performance obligation is not recorded for assurance-type warranties (considered part of the product). Service-type warranties are recorded as a separate performance obligation. Companies should allocate a portion of the transaction price to service type-warranties, when present.
Nonrefundable upfront fees	Upfront payments generally relate to initiation, activation, or setup activities for a good or service to be delivered in the future.	The upfront payment should be allocated over the periods benefited.

ILLUSTRATION 18-28
Summary—Other
Revenue Recognition
Issues

PRESENTATION AND DISCLOSURE

Presentation

LEARNING OBJECTIVE 9
Describe presentation and disclosure regarding revenue.

Companies now use an asset-liability approach to recognize revenue. For example, when **General Mills** delivers cereal to **Whole Foods Market** (satisfying its performance obligation), it has a right to consideration from Whole Foods and therefore has a contract asset. If, on the other hand, Whole Foods Market performs first, by prepaying for this cereal, General Mills has a contract liability. Companies must present these contract assets and contract liabilities on their balance sheets.

Contract Assets and Liabilities

Contract assets are of two types: (1) unconditional rights to receive consideration because the company has satisfied its performance obligation with a customer, and (2) conditional rights to receive consideration because the company has satisfied one performance obligation but must satisfy another performance obligation in the contract before it can bill the customer. Companies should report unconditional rights to receive consideration as a receivable on the balance sheet. Conditional rights on the balance sheet should be reported separately as contract assets. Illustration 18-29 provides an example of the accounting and reporting for a contract asset.

CONTRACT ASSET

Facts: On January 1, 2014, Finn Company enters into a contract to transfer Product A and Product B to Obermine Co. for $100,000. The contract specifies that payment of Product A will not occur until Product B is also delivered. In other words, payment will not occur until both Product A and Product B are transferred to Obermine. Finn determines that standalone prices are $30,000 for Product A and $70,000 for Product B. Finn delivers Product A to Obermine on February 1, 2014. On March 1, 2014, Finn delivers Product B to Obermine.

Question: What journal entries should Finn Company make in regards to this contract in 2014?

Solution: No entry is required on January 1, 2014, because neither party has performed on the contract. On February 1, 2014, Finn records the following entry.

February 1, 2014

Contract Asset	30,000	
Sales Revenue		30,000

On February 1, Finn has satisfied its performance obligation and therefore reports revenue of $30,000. However, it does not record an accounts receivable at this point because it does not have an unconditional right to receive the $100,000 unless it also transfers Product B to Obermine. In other words, a contract asset occurs generally when a company must satisfy another performance obligation before it is entitled to bill the customer. When Finn transfers Product B on March 1, 2014, it makes the following entry.

March 1, 2014

Accounts Receivable	100,000	
Contract Asset		30,000
Sales Revenue		70,000

ILLUSTRATION 18-29
Contract Asset
Recognition and
Presentation

As indicated above, a **contract liability** is a company's obligation to transfer goods or services to a customer for which the company has received consideration from the customer. A contract liability is generally referred to as Unearned Sales Revenue, Unearned Service Revenue, or another appropriate account title. Illustration 18-30 provides an example of the recognition and presentation of a contract liability.

CONTRACT LIABILITY

Facts: On March 1, 2014, Henly Company enters into a contract to transfer a product to Propel Inc. on July 31, 2014. It is agreed that Propel will pay the full price of $10,000 in advance on April 15, 2014. Henly delivers the product on July 31, 2014. The cost of the product is $7,500.

Question: What journal entries are required in 2014?

Solution: No entry is required on March 1, 2014, because neither party has performed on the contract. On receiving the cash on April 15, 2014, Henly records the following entry.

April 15, 2014

Cash	10,000	
Unearned Sales Revenue		10,000

On satisfying the performance obligation on July 31, 2014, Henly records the following entry to record the sale.

July 31, 2014

Unearned Sales Revenue	10,000	
Sales Revenue		10,000

In addition, Henly records cost of goods sold as follows.

Cost of Goods Sold	7,500	
Inventory		7,500

ILLUSTRATION 18-30
Contract Liability
Recognition and
Presentation

Companies are not required to use the terms "contract assets" and "contract liabilities" on the balance sheet. For example, contract liabilities are performance obligations and therefore more descriptive titles (as noted earlier) such as unearned service revenue, unearned sales revenue, repurchase liability, and return liability may be used where appropriate. For contract assets, it is important that financial statement users can differentiate between unconditional and conditional rights through appropriate account presentation.

Costs to Fulfill a Contract

Companies may also report assets associated with fulfillment costs related to a revenue arrangement. Companies divide fulfillment costs (contract acquisition costs) into two categories:

1. Those that give rise to an asset.

2. Those that are expensed as incurred.

Companies recognize an asset for the incremental costs if these costs are incurred to obtain a contract with a customer. In other words, incremental costs are those that a company would not incur if the contract had not been obtained (e.g., selling commissions). Additional examples are as follows.

(a) Direct labor, direct materials, and allocation of costs that relate directly to the contract (e.g., costs of contract management and supervision, insurance, and depreciation of tools and equipment).

(b) Costs that generate or enhance resources of the company that will be used in satisfying performance obligations in the future. Such costs include intangible design or engineering costs that will continue to give rise to benefits in the future.

Other costs that are expensed as incurred include general and administrative costs (unless those costs are explicitly chargeable to the customer under the contract) as well as costs of wasted materials, labor, or other resources to fulfill the contract that were not reflected in the price of the contract. That is, **companies only capitalize costs that are direct, incremental, and recoverable** (assuming that the contract period is more than one year). Illustration 18-31 provides an example of costs capitalized to fulfill a contract.

ILLUSTRATION 18-31
Recognition—Contract Costs

CONTRACT COSTS

Facts: Rock Integrators enters into a contract to operate Dello Company's information technology data center for 5 years. Rock Integrators incurs selling commission costs of $10,000 to obtain the contract. Before performing the services, Rock Integrators designs and builds a technology platform that interfaces with Dello's systems. That platform is not transferred to Dello. Dello promises to pay a fixed fee of $20,000 per month. Rock Integrators incurs the following costs: design services for the platform $40,000, hardware for the platform $120,000, software $90,000, and migration and testing of data center $100,000.

Question: What are Rock Integrators' costs for fulfilling the contract to Dello Company?

Solution: The $10,000 selling commission costs related to obtaining the contract are recognized as an asset. The design services cost of $40,000 and the hardware for the platform of $120,000 are also capitalized. As the technology platform is independent of the contract, the pattern of amortization of this platform may not be related to the terms of the contract. The migration and testing costs are expensed as incurred; in general, these costs are not recoverable.

As a practical expedient, a company recognizes the incremental costs of obtaining a contract as an expense when incurred if the amortization period of the asset that the company otherwise would have recognized is one year or less.

Collectibility

As indicated earlier, if it is probable that the transaction price will not be collected, this is an indication that the parties are not committed to their obligations. As a result, one of the criteria for the existence of a contract is not met and therefore revenue is not recognized.

Any time a company sells a product or performs a service on account, a collectibility issue occurs. **Collectibility** refers to a customer's credit risk, that is, the risk that a customer will be unable to pay the amount of consideration in accordance with the contract. Under the revenue guidance—as long as a contract exists (it is probable that the customer will pay)—the amount recognized as revenue is not adjusted for customer credit risk.

Thus, companies report the revenue gross (without consideration of credit risk) and then present an allowance for any impairment due to bad debts (recognized initially and subsequently in accordance with the respective bad debt guidance). An impairment related to bad debts is reported as an operating expense in the income statement. Whether a company will get paid for satisfying a performance obligation is not a consideration in determining revenue recognition. **[15]**

Disclosure

The disclosure requirements for revenue recognition are designed to help financial statement users understand the nature, amount, timing, and uncertainty of revenue and cash flows arising from contracts with customers. To achieve that objective, companies disclose qualitative and quantitative information about all of the following:

- *Contracts with customers.* These disclosures include the disaggregation of revenue, presentation of opening and closing balances in contract assets and contract liabilities, and significant information related to their performance obligations.
- *Significant judgments.* These disclosures include judgments and changes in these judgments that affect the determination of the transaction price, the allocation of the transaction price, and the determination of the timing of revenue.
- *Assets recognized from costs incurred to fulfill a contract.* These disclosures include the closing balances of assets recognized to obtain or fulfill a contract, the amount of amortization recognized, and the method used for amortization.

To implement these requirements and meet the disclosure objectives, companies provide a range of disclosures, as summarized in Illustration 18-32.[12]

ILLUSTRATION 18-32
Revenue Disclosures

Disclosure Type	Requirements
Disaggregation of revenue	Disclose disaggregated revenue information in categories that depict how the nature, amount, timing, and uncertainty of revenue and cash flows are affected by economic factors. Reconcile disaggregated revenue to revenue for reportable segments.
Reconciliation of contract balances	Disclose opening and closing balances of contract assets (e.g., unbilled receivables) and liabilities (e.g., deferred revenue) and provide a qualitative description of significant changes in these amounts. Disclose the amount of revenue recognized in the current period relating to performance obligations satisfied in a prior period (e.g., from contracts with variable consideration). Disclose the opening and closing balances of trade receivables if not presented elsewhere.
Remaining performance obligations	Disclose the amount of the transaction price allocated to performance obligations of any remaining performance obligations not subject to significant revenue reversal. Provide a narrative discussion of potential additional revenue in constrained arrangements.
Costs to obtain or fulfill contracts	Disclose the closing balances of capitalized costs to obtain and fulfill a contract and the amount of amortization in the period. Disclose the method used to determine amortization for each reporting period.
Other qualitative disclosures	Disclose significant judgments and changes in judgments that affect the amount and timing of revenue from contracts with customers. Disclose how management determines the minimum amount of revenue not subject to the variable consideration constraint.

[12]See *PricewaterhouseCoopers Dataline 2013–2014; FASB ASC 605-10-50-1 through 19.* **[16]**

Evolving Issue   *CH, CH, CH CHANGES IN REVENUE RECOGNITION*

As you have learned in this chapter, the recently issued revenue recognition standard provides a comprehensive and general framework for recognizing revenue and should result in improvements in the reporting of revenue. However, these new rules reflect significant change relative to the prior revenue guidance and are expected to create implementation challenges, especially for companies that:

- Currently recognize revenue using industry-specific guidance.
- Have customer contracts with diverse terms and conditions.
- Have arrangements with goods or services delivered over long periods.
- Have systems or processes that do not easily provide new data requirements.

Among the companies that are likely to experience significant changes are those in the telecommunications, aerospace, construction, asset management, real estate, and software industries.

In the months after issuance of the new guidance, the FASB (and IASB) plans to issue documents that will address common questions posed by these industries. In addition, the Boards have created a joint transition resource group that is responsible for informing the FASB and IASB about interpretive issues that could arise when companies, institutions, and other organizations implement the revenue recognition standard. The transition group is comprised of specialists representing financial statement preparers, auditors, regulators, users, and other stakeholders, as well as members of the FASB and IASB.

The resource group solicits, analyzes, and discusses stakeholder issues that apply to common transactions that could reasonably create diversity in practice. In addition to providing a forum to discuss the application of the requirements, the transition group provides information that will help the Boards determine what, if any, action will be needed to resolve that diversity. The group itself will not issue guidance.

As noted by Russ Golden, chairman of the FASB:

> "Effective implementation of the revenue recognition standard is critical to its success in providing financial statement users with the information they need to make the right decisions about how to allocate their capital. The Boards are committed to ensuring a smooth transition to the new standard, and the transition resource group is an important tool for determining any areas that will need additional guidance before the standard becomes effective in 2017."

So change is necessary to achieve improvements in revenue recognition accounting. Hopefully, the extended transition period and expanded support by the transition group will make the change a bit less painful.

Sources: Executive Accounting Update: "Changes to Revenue Recognition," KPMG (January 22, 2014); and *Defining Issues No. 14-9*: "Implementing the Forthcoming Revenue Recognition Standard," KPMG (February 2014).

KEY TERMS

asset-liability approach, *1043*

assurance-type warranty, *1064*

bill-and-hold arrangement, *1060*

collectibility, *1069*

consignee, *1063*

consignment, *1063*

consignor, *1063*

contract, *1044*

contract assets, *1066*

contract liability, *1067*

contract modification, *1046*

performance obligation, *1047*

principal-agent relationship, *1061*

repurchase agreements, *1059*

SUMMARY OF LEARNING OBJECTIVES

1 **Understand revenue recognition issues.** Most revenue transactions pose few problems for revenue recognition. This is because, in many cases, the transaction is initiated and completed at the same time. Increasing complexity of business and revenue arrangements have resulted in revenue recognition practices being identified as the most prevalent reasons for accounting restatements. A number of the revenue recognition issues relate to possible fraudulent behavior by company executives and employees, but are also due to sometimes incomplete and inconsistent accounting guidelines for revenue recognition. A recent new standard provides a set of guidelines to follow in determining when revenue should be reported and how it should be measured. The standard is comprehensive and applies to all companies. As a result, comparability and consistency in reporting revenue should be enhanced.

2 **Identify the five steps in the revenue recognition process.** The five steps in the revenue recognition process are (1) identify the contract with customers, (2) identify the separate performance obligations in the contract, (3) determine the transaction price, (4) allocate the transaction price to the separate performance obligations, and (5) recognize revenue when each performance obligation is satisfied.

3 **Identify the contract with customers.** A contract is an agreement that creates enforceable rights or obligations. A company applies the revenue guidance to contracts with customers and must determine if new performance obligations are created by a contract modification.

4 **Identify the separate performance obligations in the contract.** A performance obligation is a promise in a contract to provide a product or service to a customer. A contract may be comprised of multiple performance obligations. The accounting for multiple performance obligations is based on evaluation of whether the product or service is distinct within the contract. If each of the goods or services is distinct, but is interdependent and interrelated, these goods and services are combined and reported as one performance obligation.

5 **Determine the transaction price.** The transaction price is the amount of consideration that a company expects to receive from a customer in exchange for transferring goods and services. In determining the transaction price, companies must consider the following factors: (1) variable consideration, (2) time value of money, (3) noncash consideration, and (4) consideration paid or payable to a customer.

6 **Allocate the transaction price to the separate performance obligations.** If more than one performance obligation exists in a contract, allocate the transaction price based on relative fair values. The best measure of fair value is what the good or service could be sold for on a standalone basis (standalone selling price). Estimates of standalone selling price can be based on (1) adjusted market assessment, (2) expected cost plus a margin approach, or (3) a residual approach.

7 **Recognize revenue when the company satisfies its performance obligation.** A company satisfies its performance obligation when the customer obtains control of the good or service. Companies satisfy performance obligations either at a point in time or over a period of time. Companies recognize revenue over a period of time if (1) the customer controls the asset as it is created or the company does not have an alternative use for the asset, and (2) the company has a right to payment.

8 **Identify other revenue recognition issues.** Refer to Illustration 18-28 (page 1066) for a summary of the accounting for (a) right of return, (b) repurchase agreements, (c) bill-and-hold sales, (d) principal-agent relationships, (e) consignments, (f) warranties, and (g) nonrefundable upfront fees.

9 **Describe presentation and disclosure regarding revenue.** Under the asset-liability approach, to recognize revenue, companies present contract assets and contract liabilities on their balance sheets. Contract assets are rights to receive consideration. A contract liability is a company's obligation to transfer goods or services to a customer for which the company has received consideration from the customer. Companies may also report assets associated with fulfillment costs and contract acquisition costs related to a revenue arrangement. Companies disclose qualitative and quantitative information about (a) contracts with customers with disaggregation of revenue, presentation of opening and closing balances in contract assets and contract liabilities, and significant information related to their performance obligations; (b) significant judgments that affect the determination of the transaction price, the allocation of the transaction price, and the determination of the timing of revenue; and (c) assets recognized from costs incurred to fulfill a contract.

revenue recognition
    principle, *1043*

right of return, *1057*

service-type warranty,
    1064

transaction price, *1048*

upfront fees, *1065*

warranties, *1064*

APPENDIX **18A**	**LONG-TERM CONSTRUCTION CONTRACTS**

REVENUE RECOGNITION OVER TIME

For the most part, companies recognize revenue at the point of sale because that is when the performance obligation is satisfied. However, as indicated in the chapter, under certain circumstances companies recognize revenue over time. The most

10 **LEARNING OBJECTIVE**

Apply the percentage-of-completion method for long-term contracts.

notable context in which revenue is recognized over time is long-term construction contract accounting.

Long-term contracts frequently provide that the seller (builder) may bill the purchaser at intervals, as it reaches various points in the project. Examples of long-term contracts are construction-type contracts, development of military and commercial aircraft, weapons-delivery systems, and space exploration hardware. When the project consists of separable units, such as a group of buildings or miles of roadway, contract provisions may provide for delivery in installments. In that case, the seller would bill the buyer and transfer title at stated stages of completion, such as the completion of each building unit or every 10 miles of road. The accounting records should record sales when installments are "delivered."

A company satisfies a performance obligation and recognizes revenue over time if at least one of the following two criteria is met: **[17]**

1. The company's performance creates or enhances an asset (for example, work in process) that the customer controls as the asset is created or enhanced; or

2. The company's performance does not create an asset with an alternative use. For example, the asset cannot be used by another customer. In addition to this alternative use element, at least *one* of the following criteria must be met:
   (a) The customer simultaneously receives and consumes the benefits of the entity's performance as the entity performs.
   (b) Another company would not need to substantially re-perform the work the company has completed to date if that other company were to fulfill the remaining obligation to the customer.
   (c) The company has a right to payment for its performance completed to date, and it expects to fulfill the contract as promised.[13]

Therefore, if criterion 1 or 2 is met, then a company recognizes revenue over time *if* **it can reasonably estimate its progress toward satisfaction of the performance obligations**. That is, it recognizes revenues and gross profits each period based upon the progress of the construction—referred to as the **percentage-of-completion method**. The company accumulates construction costs plus gross profit recognized to date in an inventory account (Construction in Process), and it accumulates progress billings in a contra inventory account (Billings on Construction in Process).

The rationale for using percentage-of-completion accounting is that under most of these contracts the buyer and seller have enforceable rights. The buyer has the legal right to require specific performance on the contract. The seller has the right to require progress payments that provide evidence of the buyer's ownership interest. As a result, a continuous sale occurs as the work progresses. Companies should recognize revenue according to that progression.

Alternatively, if the criteria for recognition over time are not met (e.g., the company cannot reasonably estimate its progress toward meeting a performance obligation), the company recognizes revenues and gross profit at a point in time, that is, when the contract is completed. This approach is referred to as the **completed-contract method**.[14]

---

[13] The right to payment for performance completed to date does not need to be for a fixed amount. However, the company must be entitled to an amount that would compensate the company for performance completed to date (even if the customer can terminate the contract for reasons other than the company's failure to perform as promised). Compensation for performance completed to date includes payment that approximates the selling price of the goods or services transferred to date (for example, recovery of the company's costs plus a reasonable profit margin).

[14] *Accounting Trends and Techniques—2012* reports that of the 83 of its 500 sample companies that referred to long-term construction contracts, 75 used the percentage-of-completion method and 8 used the completed-contract method. In some circumstances (e.g., in the early stages of a contract), a company may not be able to reasonably measure the outcome of a performance obligation, but it expects to recover the costs incurred in satisfying the performance obligation. In these situations, companies recognize revenue only to the extent of the costs incurred until such time that they can reasonably measure the outcome of the performance obligation. This is referred to as the cost-recovery method.

The company accumulates construction costs in an inventory account (Construction in Process), and it accumulates progress billings in a contra inventory account (Billings on Construction in Process).

Percentage-of-Completion Method

The **percentage-of-completion method** recognizes revenues, costs, and gross profit as a company makes progress toward completion on a long-term contract. To defer recognition of these items until completion of the entire contract is to misrepresent the efforts (costs) and accomplishments (revenues) of the accounting periods during the contract. In order to apply the percentage-of-completion method, a company must have some basis or standard for measuring the progress toward completion at particular interim dates.

Measuring the Progress Toward Completion

As one practicing accountant wrote, "The big problem in applying the percentage-of-completion method . . . has to do with the ability to make reasonably accurate estimates of completion and the final gross profit." Companies use various methods to determine the **extent of progress toward completion**. The most common are the *cost-to-cost* and *units-of-delivery* methods.

As indicated in the chapter, the objective of all these methods is to measure the extent of progress in terms of costs, units, or value added. Companies identify the various measures (costs incurred, labor hours worked, tons produced, floors completed, etc.) and classify them as input or output measures. **Input measures** (costs incurred, labor hours worked) are efforts devoted to a contract. **Output measures** (with units of delivery measured as tons produced, floors of a building completed, miles of a highway completed) track results. Neither measure is universally applicable to all long-term projects. Their use requires the exercise of judgment and careful tailoring to the circumstances.

Both input and output measures have certain disadvantages. The input measure is based on an established relationship between a unit of input and productivity. If inefficiencies cause the productivity relationship to change, inaccurate measurements result. Another potential problem is front-end loading, in which significant upfront costs result in higher estimates of completion. To avoid this problem, companies should disregard some early-stage construction costs—for example, costs of uninstalled materials or costs of subcontracts not yet performed—if they do not relate to contract performance.

Similarly, output measures can produce inaccurate results if the units used are not comparable in time, effort, or cost to complete. For example, using floors (stories) completed can be deceiving. Completing the first floor of an eight-story building may require more than one-eighth the total cost because of the substructure and foundation construction.

The most popular input measure used to determine the progress toward completion is the **cost-to-cost basis**. Under this basis, a company like **EDS** measures the percentage of completion by comparing costs incurred to date with the most recent estimate of the total costs required to complete the contract. Illustration 18A-1 shows the formula for the cost-to-cost basis.

$$\frac{\text{Costs incurred to date}}{\text{Most recent estimate of total costs}} = \text{Percent complete}$$

ILLUSTRATION 18A-1
Formula for Percentage-of-Completion, Cost-to-Cost Basis

Once EDS knows the percentage that costs incurred bear to total estimated costs, it applies that percentage to the total revenue or the estimated total gross profit on the contract. The resulting amount is the revenue or the gross profit to be recognized to date. Illustration 18A-2 shows this computation.

$$\text{Percent complete} = \begin{array}{c}\text{Estimated} \\ \text{total revenue} \\ \text{(or gross profit)}\end{array} = \begin{array}{c}\text{Revenue (or gross} \\ \text{profit) to be} \\ \text{recognized to date}\end{array}$$

ILLUSTRATION 18A-2
Formula for Total Revenue (or Gross Profit) to Be Recognized to Date

To find the amounts of revenue and gross profit recognized each period, EDS subtracts total revenue or gross profit recognized in prior periods, as shown in Illustration 18A-3.

ILLUSTRATION 18A-3
Formula for Amount of
Current-Period Revenue
(or Gross Profit) Cost-to-
Cost Basis

Revenue (or gross profit) to be recognized to date	−	Revenue (or gross profit) recognized in prior periods	=	Current-period revenue (or gross profit)

Because **the cost-to-cost method is widely used** (without excluding other bases for measuring progress toward completion), we have adopted it for use in our examples.

Example of Percentage-of-Completion Method—Cost-to-Cost Basis

To illustrate the percentage-of-completion method, assume that Hardhat Construction Company has a contract to construct a $4,500,000 bridge at an estimated cost of $4,000,000. The contract is to start in July 2014, and the bridge is to be completed in October 2016. The following data pertain to the construction period. (Note that by the end of 2015, Hardhat has revised the estimated total cost from $4,000,000 to $4,050,000.)

	2014	2015	2016
Costs to date	$1,000,000	$2,916,000	$4,050,000
Estimated costs to complete	3,000,000	1,134,000	—
Progress billings during the year	900,000	2,400,000	1,200,000
Cash collected during the year	750,000	1,750,000	2,000,000

Hardhat would compute the percent complete as shown in Illustration 18A-4.

ILLUSTRATION 18A-4
Application of
Percentage-of-
Completion Method,
Cost-to-Cost Basis

	2014	2015	2016
Contract price	$4,500,000	$4,500,000	$4,500,000
Less estimated cost:			
Costs to date	1,000,000	2,916,000	4,050,000
Estimated costs to complete	3,000,000	1,134,000	—
Estimated total costs	4,000,000	4,050,000	4,050,000
Estimated total gross profit	$ 500,000	$ 450,000	$ 450,000
Percent complete	25%	72%	100%
	($1,000,000 / $4,000,000)	($2,916,000 / $4,050,000)	($4,050,000 / $4,050,000)

On the basis of the data above, Hardhat would make the following entries to record (1) the costs of construction, (2) progress billings, and (3) collections. These entries appear as summaries of the many transactions that would be entered individually as they occur during the year.

ILLUSTRATION 18A-5
Journal Entries—
Percentage-of-
Completion Method,
Cost-to-Cost Basis

	2014		2015		2016	
To record costs of construction:						
Construction in Process	1,000,000		1,916,000		1,134,000	
Materials, Cash, Payables, etc.		1,000,000		1,916,000		1,134,000
To record progress billings:						
Accounts Receivable	900,000		2,400,000		1,200,000	
Billings on Construction in Process		900,000		2,400,000		1,200,000
To record collections:						
Cash	750,000		1,750,000		2,000,000	
Accounts Receivable		750,000		1,750,000		2,000,000

In this example, the costs incurred to date are a measure of the extent of progress toward completion. To determine this, Hardhat evaluates the costs incurred to date as a proportion of the estimated total costs to be incurred on the project. The estimated revenue and gross profit that Hardhat will recognize for each year are calculated as shown in Illustration 18A-6.

	To Date	Recognized in Prior Years	Recognized in Current Year
2014			
Revenues ($4,500,000 × 25%)	$1,125,000		$1,125,000
Costs	1,000,000		1,000,000
Gross profit	$ 125,000		$ 125,000
2015			
Revenues ($4,500,000 × 72%)	$3,240,000	$1,125,000	$2,115,000
Costs	2,916,000	1,000,000	1,916,000
Gross profit	$ 324,000	$ 125,000	$ 199,000
2016			
Revenues ($4,500,000 × 100%)	$4,500,000	$3,240,000	$1,260,000
Costs	4,050,000	2,916,000	1,134,000
Gross profit	$ 450,000	$ 324,000	$ 126,000

ILLUSTRATION 18A-6
Percentage-of-Completion Revenue, Costs, and Gross Profit by Year

Illustration 18A-7 shows Hardhat's entries to recognize revenue and gross profit each year and to record completion and final approval of the contract.

	2014		2015		2016	
To recognize revenue and gross profit:						
Construction in Process (gross profit)	125,000		199,000		126,000	
Construction Expenses	1,000,000		1,916,000		1,134,000	
Revenue from Long-Term Contracts		1,125,000		2,115,000		1,260,000
To record completion of the contract:						
Billings on Construction in Process					4,500,000	
Construction in Process						4,500,000

ILLUSTRATION 18A-7
Journal Entries to Recognize Revenue and Gross Profit and to Record Contract Completion—Percentage-of-Completion Method, Cost-to-Cost Basis

Note that **Hardhat debits gross profit (as computed in Illustration 18A-6) to Construction in Process**. Similarly, it credits Revenue from Long-Term Contracts for the amounts computed in Illustration 18A-6. Hardhat then debits the difference between the amounts recognized each year for revenue and gross profit to a nominal account, Construction Expenses (similar to Cost of Goods Sold in a manufacturing company). It reports that amount in the income statement as the actual cost of construction incurred in that period. For example, in 2014 Hardhat uses the actual costs of $1,000,000 to compute both the gross profit of $125,000 and the percent complete (25 percent).

Hardhat continues to accumulate costs in the Construction in Process account, in order to maintain a record of total costs incurred (plus recognized gross profit) to date. Although theoretically a series of "sales" takes place using the percentage-of-completion method, the selling company cannot remove the inventory cost until the construction is completed and transferred to the new owner. Hardhat's Construction in Process account for the bridge would include the following summarized entries over the term of the construction project.

ILLUSTRATION 18A-8
Content of Construction in Process Account—Percentage-of-Completion Method

Construction in Process				
2014 construction costs	$1,000,000	12/31/16	to close completed project	$4,500,000
2014 recognized gross profit	125,000			
2015 construction costs	1,916,000			
2015 recognized gross profit	199,000			
2016 construction costs	1,134,000			
2016 recognized gross profit	126,000			
Total	$4,500,000	Total		$4,500,000

Recall that the Hardhat Construction Company example contained a **change in estimated costs**: In the second year, 2015, it increased the estimated total costs from $4,000,000 to $4,050,000. The change in estimate is accounted for in a **cumulative catch-up manner**, as indicated in the chapter. This is done by first adjusting the percent completed to the new estimate of total costs. Next, Hardhat deducts the amount of revenues and gross profit recognized in prior periods from revenues and gross profit computed for progress to date. That is, it accounts for the change in estimate in the period of change. That way, the balance sheet at the end of the period of change and the accounting in subsequent periods are as they would have been if the revised estimate had been the original estimate.

Financial Statement Presentation—Percentage-of-Completion

Generally, when a company records a receivable from a sale, it reduces the Inventory account. Under the percentage-of-completion method, however, the company continues to carry both the receivable and the inventory. Subtracting the balance in the **Billings account** from Construction in Process avoids double-counting the inventory. During the life of the contract, Hardhat reports in the balance sheet the difference between the Construction in Process and the Billings on Construction in Process accounts. If that amount is a debit, Hardhat reports it **as a current asset**; if it is a credit, it reports it **as a current liability**.

At times, the costs incurred plus the gross profit recognized to date (the balance in Construction in Process) exceed the billings. In that case, Hardhat reports this excess as a current asset entitled "Costs and recognized profit in excess of billings." Hardhat can at any time calculate the unbilled portion of revenue recognized to date by subtracting the billings to date from the revenue recognized to date, as illustrated for 2014 for Hardhat Construction in Illustration 18A-9.

ILLUSTRATION 18A-9
Computation of Unbilled Contract Price at 12/31/14

Contract revenue recognized to date: $4,500,000 $\times$	$\dfrac{\$1,000,000}{\$4,000,000}$		$1,125,000
Billings to date			(900,000)
Unbilled revenue			$ 225,000

At other times, the billings exceed costs incurred and gross profit to date. In that case, Hardhat reports this excess as a current liability entitled "Billings in excess of costs and recognized profit."

What happens, as is usually the case, when companies have more than one project going at a time? When a company has a number of projects, costs exceed billings on some contracts and billings exceed costs on others. In such a case, the company segregates the contracts. The asset side includes only those contracts on which costs and recognized profit exceed billings. The liability side includes only those on which billings exceed costs and recognized profit. Separate disclosures of the dollar volume of billings and costs are preferable to a summary presentation of the net difference.

Using data from the bridge example, Hardhat Construction Company would report the status and results of its long-term construction activities under the percentage-of-completion method as shown in Illustration 18A-10.

HARDHAT CONSTRUCTION COMPANY		
Income Statement (from Illustration 18A-6)		2014
Revenue from long-term contracts		$1,125,000
Costs of construction		1,000,000
Gross profit		$ 125,000

HARDHAT CONSTRUCTION COMPANY		
Balance Sheet (12/31)		2014
Current assets		
Accounts receivable ($900,000 − $750,000)		$ 150,000
Inventory		
Construction in process	$1,125,000	
Less: Billings	900,000	
Costs and recognized profit in excess of billings		225,000

ILLUSTRATION 18A-10
Financial Statement Presentation—Percentage-of-Completion Method (2014)

In 2015, its financial statement presentation is as follows.

HARDHAT CONSTRUCTION COMPANY		
Income Statement (from Illustration 18A-6)		2015
Revenue from long-term contracts		$2,115,000
Costs of construction		1,916,000
Gross profit		$ 199,000

HARDHAT CONSTRUCTION COMPANY		
Balance Sheet (12/31)		
Current assets		
Accounts receivable ($150,000 + $2,400,000 − $1,750,000)		$ 800,000
Current liabilities		
Billings	$3,300,000	
Less: Construction in process	3,240,000	
Billings in excess of costs and recognized profits		60,000

ILLUSTRATION 18A-11
Financial Statement Presentation—Percentage-of-Completion Method (2015)

In 2016, Hardhat's financial statements only include an income statement because the bridge project was completed and settled.

HARDHAT CONSTRUCTION COMPANY		
Income Statement (from Illustration 18A-6)		2016
Revenue from long-term contracts		$1,260,000
Costs of construction		1,134,000
Gross profit		$ 126,000

ILLUSTRATION 18A-12
Financial Statement Presentation—Percentage-of-Completion Method (2016)

In addition, Hardhat should disclose the following information in each year.

ILLUSTRATION 18A-13
Percentage-of-Completion
Method Note Disclosure

> **Note 1.   Summary of significant accounting policies.**
> **Long-Term Construction Contracts.**   The company recognizes revenues and reports profits from long-term construction contracts, its principal business, under the percentage-of-completion method of accounting. These contracts generally extend for periods in excess of one year. The amounts of revenues and profits recognized each year are based on the ratio of costs incurred to the total estimated costs. Costs included in construction in process include direct materials, direct labor, and project-related overhead. Corporate general and administrative expenses are charged to the periods as incurred and are not allocated to construction contracts.

Completed-Contract Method

LEARNING OBJECTIVE 11

Apply the completed-contract method for long-term contracts.

Under the **completed-contract method**, companies recognize revenue and gross profit only at point of sale—that is, when the contract is completed. Under this method, companies accumulate costs of long-term contracts in process, but they make no interim charges or credits to income statement accounts for revenues, costs, or gross profit.

The principal advantage of the completed-contract method is that reported revenue reflects final results rather than *estimates* of unperformed work. Its major disadvantage is that it does not reflect current performance when the period of a contract extends into more than one accounting period. Although operations may be fairly uniform during the period of the contract, the company will not report revenue until the year of completion, creating a distortion of earnings.

Under the completed-contract method, the company would make the same **annual entries** to record costs of construction, progress billings, and collections from customers as those illustrated under the percentage-of-completion method. The significant difference is that the company **would not make entries to recognize revenue and gross profit**.

For example, under the completed-contract method for the bridge project illustrated on the preceding pages, Hardhat Construction Company would make the following entries in 2016 to recognize revenue and costs and to close out the inventory and billing accounts.

Billings on Construction in Process	4,500,000	
Revenue from Long-Term Contracts		4,500,000
Costs of Construction	4,050,000	
Construction in Process		4,050,000

Illustration 18A-14 compares the amount of gross profit that Hardhat Construction Company would recognize for the bridge project under the two revenue recognition methods.

ILLUSTRATION 18A-14
Comparison of Gross
Profit Recognized under
Different Methods

	Percentage-of-Completion	Completed-Contract
2014	$125,000	$ 0
2015	199,000	0
2016	126,000	450,000

Under the completed-contract method, Hardhat Construction would report its long-term construction activities as follows.

ILLUSTRATION 18A-15
Financial Statement
Presentation—Completed-
Contract Method

HARDHAT CONSTRUCTION COMPANY				
		2014	2015	2016
Income Statement				
Revenue from long-term contracts		—	—	$4,500,000
Costs of construction		—	—	4,050,000
Gross profit		—	—	$ 450,000

Balance Sheet (12/31)				
Current assets				
Accounts receivable		$150,000	$800,000	$ –0–
Inventory				
Construction in process	$1,000,000			
Less: Billings	900,000			
Costs in excess of billings		100,000		–0–
Current liabilities				
Billings ($3,300,000) in excess of				
costs ($2,916,000)			384,000	–0–

Note 1. Summary of significant accounting policies.
Long-Term Construction Contracts.   The company recognizes revenues and reports profits from long-term construction contracts, its principal business, under the completed-contract method. These contracts generally extend for periods in excess of one year. Contract costs and billings are accumulated during the periods of construction, but no revenues or profits are recognized until completion of the contract. Costs included in construction in process include direct material, direct labor, and project-related overhead. Corporate general and administrative expenses are charged to the periods as incurred.

Long-Term Contract Losses

Two types of losses can become evident under long-term contracts:

12 LEARNING OBJECTIVE

Identify the proper accounting for losses on long-term contracts.

1. *Loss in the current period on a profitable contract.* This condition arises when, during construction, there is a significant increase in the estimated total contract costs but the increase does not eliminate all profit on the contract. Under the percentage-of-completion method only, the estimated cost increase requires a current-period adjustment of excess gross profit recognized on the project in prior periods. The company records this adjustment as a loss in the current period because it is a change in accounting estimate (discussed in Chapter 22).

2. *Loss on an unprofitable contract.* Cost estimates at the end of the current period may indicate that a loss will result on completion of the *entire* contract. Under both the percentage-of-completion and the completed-contract methods, the company must recognize in the current period the entire expected contract loss.

The treatment described for unprofitable contracts is consistent with the accounting custom of anticipating foreseeable losses to avoid overstatement of current and future income (conservatism). **[18]**

Loss in Current Period

To illustrate a loss in the current period on a contract expected to be profitable upon completion, we'll continue with the Hardhat Construction Company bridge project. Assume that on December 31, 2015, Hardhat estimates the costs to complete the bridge contract at $1,468,962 instead of $1,134,000 (refer to page 1074). Assuming all other data are the same as before, Hardhat would compute the percentage complete and recognize the loss as shown in Illustration 18A-16. Compare these computations with those for 2015 in Illustration 18A-4 (page 1074). The "percent complete" has dropped, from 72 percent to 66½ percent, due to the increase in estimated future costs to complete the contract.

ILLUSTRATION 18A-16
Computation of Recognizable Loss, 2015—Loss in Current Period

Cost to date (12/31/15)	$2,916,000
Estimated costs to complete (revised)	1,468,962
Estimated total costs	$4,384,962
Percent complete ($2,916,000 ÷ $4,384,962)	66½%
Revenue recognized in 2015	
($4,500,000 × 66½%) − $1,125,000	$1,867,500
Costs incurred in 2015	1,916,000
Loss recognized in 2015	$ (48,500)

The 2015 loss of $48,500 is a cumulative adjustment of the "excessive" gross profit recognized on the contract in 2014. Instead of restating the prior period, the company absorbs the prior period misstatement entirely in the current period. In this illustration, the adjustment was large enough to result in recognition of a loss.

Hardhat Construction would record the loss in 2015 as follows.

Construction Expenses	1,916,000	
Construction in Process (loss)		48,500
Revenue from Long-Term Contracts		1,867,500

Hardhat will report the loss of $48,500 on the 2015 income statement as the difference between the reported revenue of $1,867,500 and the costs of $1,916,000.[15] **Under the completed-contract method, the company does not recognize a loss in 2015.** Why not? Because the company still expects the contract **to result in a profit**, to be recognized in the year of completion.

Loss on an Unprofitable Contract

To illustrate the accounting for an **overall loss on a long-term contract**, assume that at December 31, 2015, Hardhat Construction Company estimates the costs to complete the bridge contract at $1,640,250 instead of $1,134,000. Revised estimates for the bridge contract are as follows.

	2014	2015
	Original Estimates	Revised Estimates
Contract price	$4,500,000	$4,500,000
Estimated total cost	4,000,000	4,556,250*
Estimated gross profit	$ 500,000	
Estimated loss		$ (56,250)

*($2,916,000 + $1,640,250)

[15] In 2016, Hardhat Construction will recognize the remaining 33½ percent of the revenue ($1,507,500), with costs of $1,468,962 as expected, and will report a gross profit of $38,538. The total gross profit over the three years of the contract would be $115,038 [$125,000 (2014) − $48,500 (2015) + $38,538 (2016)]. This amount is the difference between the total contract revenue of $4,500,000 and the total contract costs of $4,384,962.

Under the percentage-of-completion method, Hardhat recognized $125,000 of gross profit in 2014 (see Illustration 18A-6 on page 1075). This amount must be offset in 2015 because it is no longer expected to be realized. In addition, since losses must be recognized as soon as estimable, the company must recognize the total estimated loss of $56,250 in 2015. Therefore, Hardhat must recognize a total loss of $181,250 ($125,000 + $56,250) in 2015.

Illustration 18A-17 shows Hardhat's computation of the revenue to be recognized in 2015.

Revenue recognized in 2015:		
Contract price		$4,500,000
Percent complete		× 64%*
Revenue recognizable to date		2,880,000
Less: Revenue recognized prior to 2015		1,125,000
Revenue recognized in 2015		$1,755,000
*Cost to date (12/31/15)	$2,916,000	
Estimated cost to complete	1,640,250	
Estimated total costs	$4,556,250	
Percent complete: $2,916,000 ÷ $4,556,250 = 64%		

ILLUSTRATION 18A-17
Computation of Revenue Recognizable, 2015—Unprofitable Contract

To compute the construction costs to be expensed in 2015, Hardhat adds the total loss to be recognized in 2015 ($125,000 + $56,250) to the revenue to be recognized in 2015. Illustration 18A-18 shows this computation.

Revenue recognized in 2015 (computed above)		$1,755,000
Total loss recognized in 2015:		
Reversal of 2014 gross profit	$125,000	
Total estimated loss on the contract	56,250	181,250
Construction cost expensed in 2015		$1,936,250

ILLUSTRATION 18A-18
Computation of Construction Expense, 2015—Unprofitable Contract

Hardhat Construction would record the long-term contract revenues, expenses, and loss in 2015 as follows.

Construction Expenses	1,936,250	
Construction in Process (loss)		181,250
Revenue from Long-Term Contracts		1,755,000

At the end of 2015, Construction in Process has a balance of $2,859,750 as shown below.[16]

Construction in Process			
2014 Construction costs	1,000,000		
2014 Recognized gross profit	125,000		
2015 Construction costs	1,916,000	2015 Recognized loss	181,250
Balance	**2,859,750**		

ILLUSTRATION 18A-19
Content of Construction in Process Account at End of 2015—Unprofitable Contract

[16] If the costs in 2016 are $1,640,250 as projected, at the end of 2016 the Construction in Process account will have a balance of $1,640,250 + $2,859,750, or $4,500,000, equal to the contract price. When the company matches the revenue remaining to be recognized in 2016 of $1,620,000 [$4,500,000 (total contract price) − $1,125,000 (2014) − $1,755,000 (2015)] with the construction expense to be recognized in 2016 of $1,620,000 [total costs of $4,556,250 less the total costs recognized in prior years of $2,936,250 (2014, $1,000,000; 2015, $1,936,250)], a zero profit results. Thus, the total loss has been recognized in 2015, the year in which it first became evident.

Under the completed-contract method, Hardhat also would recognize the contract loss of $56,250 through the following entry in 2015 (the year in which the loss first became evident).

Loss from Long-Term Contracts	56,250	
Construction in Process (loss)		56,250

Just as the Billings account balance cannot exceed the contract price, neither can the balance in Construction in Process exceed the contract price. In circumstances where the Construction in Process balance exceeds the billings, the company can deduct the recognized loss from such accumulated costs on the balance sheet. That is, under both the percentage-of-completion and the completed-contract methods, the provision for the loss (the credit) may be combined with Construction in Process, thereby reducing the inventory balance. In those circumstances, however (as in the 2015 example above), where the billings exceed the accumulated costs, Hardhat must report separately on the balance sheet, as a current liability, the amount of the estimated loss. That is, under both the percentage-of-completion and the completed-contract methods, Hardhat would take the $56,250 loss, as estimated in 2015, from the Construction in Process account and report it separately as a current liability titled "Estimated liability from long-term contracts."

KEY TERMS

Billings account, *1076*

completed-contract method, *1078*

cost-to-cost basis, *1073*

input measures, *1073*

output measures, *1073*

percentage-of-completion method, *1073*

SUMMARY OF LEARNING OBJECTIVES FOR APPENDIX 18A

10 **Apply the percentage-of-completion method for long-term contracts.** To apply the percentage-of-completion method to long-term contracts, a company must have some basis for measuring the progress toward completion at particular interim dates. One of the most popular input measures used to determine the progress toward completion is the cost-to-cost basis. Using this basis, a company measures the percentage of completion by comparing costs incurred to date with the most recent estimate of the total costs to complete the contract. The company applies that percentage to the total revenue or the estimated total gross profit on the contract, to arrive at the amount of revenue or gross profit to be recognized to date.

11 **Apply the completed-contract method for long-term contracts.** Under this method, companies recognize revenue and gross profit only at point of sale—that is, when the company completes the contract. The company accumulates costs of long-term contracts in process and current billings. It makes no interim charges or credits to income statement accounts for revenues, costs, and gross profit. The annual journal entries to record costs of construction, progress billings, and collections from customers would be identical to those for the percentage-of-completion method—with the significant exclusion of the recognition of revenue and gross profit.

12 **Identify the proper accounting for losses on long-term contracts.** Two types of losses can become evident under long-term contracts. (1) *Loss in current period on a profitable contract:* Under the percentage-of-completion method only, the estimated cost increase requires a current-period adjustment of excess gross profit recognized on the project in prior periods. The company records this adjustment as a loss in the current period because it is a change in accounting estimate. (2) *Loss on an unprofitable contract:* Under both the percentage-of-completion and the completed-contract methods, the company must recognize the entire expected contract loss in the current period.

APPENDIX 18B — REVENUE RECOGNITION FOR FRANCHISES

In this appendix, we cover a common yet unique type of business transaction—franchises. As indicated throughout this chapter, companies recognize revenue when performance obligations in a revenue arrangement are satisfied. **Franchises** represent a challenging area because a variety of performance obligations may exist in a given franchise agreement. As a result, companies must carefully analyze franchise agreements to identify the separate performance obligations, determine when performance obligations are met, and, therefore, when revenue should be recognized.[17]

13 LEARNING OBJECTIVE
Explain revenue recognition for franchises.

Four types of franchising arrangements have evolved: (1) manufacturer-retailer, (2) manufacturer-wholesaler, (3) service sponsor-retailer, and (4) wholesaler-retailer. The fastest-growing category of franchising, and the one that has given rise to accounting challenges, is the third category, **service sponsor-retailer**. Included in this category are such industries and businesses as:

- Soft ice cream/frozen yogurt stores (**Tastee Freez, TCBY, Dairy Queen**)
- Food drive-ins (**McDonald's, KFC, Burger King**)
- Restaurants (**TGI Friday's, Pizza Hut, Denny's**)
- Motels (**Holiday Inn, Marriott, Best Western**)
- Auto rentals (**Avis, Hertz, National**)
- Others (**H & R Block, Meineke Mufflers, 7-Eleven Stores, Kelly Services**)

Franchise companies derive their revenue from one or both of two sources: (1) from the sale of initial franchises and related assets or services, and (2) from continuing fees based on the operations of franchises. The **franchisor** (the party who grants business rights under the franchise) normally provides the **franchisee** (the party who operates the franchised business) with the following services.

1. Assistance in site selection: (a) analyzing location and (b) negotiating lease.
2. Evaluation of potential income.
3. Supervision of construction activity: (a) obtaining financing, (b) designing building, and (c) supervising contractor while building.
4. Assistance in the acquisition of signs, fixtures, and equipment.
5. Bookkeeping and advisory services: (a) setting up franchisee's records; (b) advising on income, real estate, and other taxes; and (c) advising on local regulations of the franchisee's business.
6. Employee and management training.
7. Quality control.
8. Advertising and promotion.

In the past, it was standard practice for franchisors to recognize the entire franchise fee at the date of sale, whether the fee was received then or was collectible over a long

---

[17]Franchises are an example of a license or similar rights to use intellectual property. In such arrangements, a company grants a customer the right to use, but not own, intellectual property of the company. Other examples of intellectual property include (1) software and technology; (2) motion pictures, music, and other forms of media and entertainment; and (3) patents, trademarks, and copyrights. Generally, revenue is recognized in these situations when the customer obtains control of the rights. In some cases, a license is a promise to provide a right, which transfers to the customer at a point in time. In other cases, a license is a promise to provide access to an entity's intellectual property, which transfers benefits to the customer over time. **[19]**

period of time. Frequently, franchisors recorded the entire amount as revenue in the year of sale, even though many of the services were yet to be performed and uncertainty existed regarding the collection of the entire fee. (In effect, the franchisors were counting their fried chickens before they were hatched.) However, a **franchise agreement** may provide for refunds to the franchisee if certain conditions are not met, and franchise fee profit can be reduced sharply by future costs of obligations and services to be rendered by the franchisor.

FRANCHISE ACCOUNTING

As indicated, the performance obligations in a franchise arrangement relate to the right to open a business, use of the trade name or other intellectual property of the franchisor, and continuing services, such as marketing help, training, and in some cases supplying inventory and inventory management. Franchisors commonly charge an initial franchise fee as well as continuing franchise fees. The **initial franchise fee** is payment for establishing the franchise relationship and providing some initial services. **Continuing franchise fees** are received in return for the continuing rights granted by the franchise agreement and for providing such services as management training, advertising and promotion, legal assistance, and other support. Illustration 18B-1 provides an example of a franchise arrangement.

ILLUSTRATION 18B-1
Recognition—Franchise
Arrangement

FRANCHISE

Facts: Tum's Pizza Inc. enters into a franchise agreement on December 31, 2014, giving Food Fight Corp. the right to operate as a franchisee of Tum's Pizza for 5 years. Tum's charges Food Fight an initial franchise fee of $50,000 for the right to operate as a franchisee. Of this amount, $20,000 is payable when Food Fight signs the agreement, and the note balance is payable in five annual payments of $6,000 each on December 31. As part of the arrangement, Tum's helps locate the site, negotiate the lease or purchase of the site, supervise the construction activity, and provide employee training and the equipment necessary to be a distributor of its products. Similar training services and equipment are sold separately.

Food Fight also promises to pay ongoing royalty payments of 1% of its annual sales (payable each January 31 of the following year) and is obliged to purchase products from Tum's at its current standalone selling prices at the time of purchase. The credit rating of Food Fight indicates that money can be borrowed at 8%. The present value of an ordinary annuity of five annual receipts of $6,000 each discounted at 8% is $23,957. The discount of $6,043 represents the interest revenue to be accrued by Tum's over the payment period.

Question: **What are the performance obligations in this arrangement and the point in time at which the performance obligations for Tum's are satisfied and revenue is recognized?**

Solution: To identify the performance obligations, Tum's must determine whether the promised rights, site selection and construction services, training services, and equipment are distinct.

- Rights to the trade name, market area, and proprietary know-how for 5 years are not individually distinct because each one is not sold separately and cannot be used with other goods or services that are readily available to the franchisee. Therefore, those combined rights give rise to a single performance obligation. Tum's satisfies the performance obligation to grant those rights at the point in time when Food Fight obtains control of the rights. That is, once Food Fight begins operating the store, Tum's has no further obligation with respect to these rights.
- Training services and equipment are distinct because similar services and equipment are sold separately. Tum's satisfies those performance obligations when it transfers the services and equipment to Food Fight.
- Tum's cannot recognize revenue for the royalty payments because it is not reasonably assured to be entitled to those sales-based royalty amounts. That is, these payments represent variable consideration. Therefore, Tum's recognizes revenue for the royalties when (or as) the uncertainty is resolved.

Tum's promise to stand ready to provide products to the franchisee in the future at standalone selling prices is not accounted for as a separate performance obligation in the contract because it does not provide Food Fight with a material right. Thus, revenue from those sales is recorded in the future when the sales are made.

To illustrate the accounting for this franchise, consider the following values for allocation of the transaction price at December 31, 2014.

Rights to the trade name, market area, and proprietary know-how	$20,000
Training services	9,957
Equipment (cost of $10,000)	14,000
Total transaction price	$ 43,957

Training is completed in January 2015, the equipment is installed in January 2015, and Food Fight holds a grand opening on February 2, 2015. The entries for the Tum's franchise arrangement are summarized in Illustration 18B-2.

ILLUSTRATION 18B-2
Franchise Entries—
Inception and
Commencement of
Operations

Tum's signs the agreement and receives upfront payment and note.		
December 31, 2014		
Cash	20,000	
Notes Receivable	30,000	
Discount on Notes Receivable		6,043
Unearned Franchise Revenue		20,000
Unearned Service Revenue (training)		9,957
Unearned Sales Revenue (equipment)		14,000

Franchise opens. Tum's satisfies the performance obligations related to the franchise rights, training, and equipment. That is, Tum's has no further obligations related to these elements of the franchise.		
February 2, 2015		
Unearned Franchise Revenue	20,000	
Franchise Revenue		20,000
Unearned Service Revenue (training)	9,957	
Service Revenue (training)		9,957
Unearned Sales Revenue (equipment)	14,000	
Sales Revenue		14,000
Cost of Goods Sold	10,000	
Inventory		10,000

As indicated, when Food Fight begins operations, Tum's satisfies the performance obligations related to the franchise rights, training, and equipment under the franchise agreement. That is, Tum's has no further obligations related to these elements of the franchise.

During 2015, Food Fight does well, recording $525,000 of sales in its first year of operations. The entries for Tum's related to the first year of operations of the franchise are summarized in Illustration 18B-3.

ILLUSTRATION 18B-3
Franchise Entries—First Year of Franchise Operations

To record continuing franchise fees		
December 31, 2015		
Accounts Receivable ($525,000 × 1%)	5,250	
Franchise Revenue		5,250

To record payment received and interest revenue on note		
December 31, 2015		
Cash	6,000	
Notes Receivable		6,000
Discount on Notes Receivable ($23,957 × 8%)	1,917	
Interest Revenue		1,917

Tum's will make similar entries in subsequent years of the franchise agreement.

RECOGNITION OF FRANCHISE RIGHTS REVENUE OVER TIME

In the franchise example presented in Illustration 18B-1, Tum's transferred control of the franchise rights at a point in time—that is, when the franchisee began operations and could benefit from control of the rights—with no further involvement by Tum's. In other situations, depending on the economic substance of the rights, the franchisor may be providing **access to the right** rather than transferring control of the franchise rights. In this case, **the franchise revenue is recognized over time**, rather than at a point in time. The franchise arrangement presented in Illustration 18B-4 provides an example of a franchise agreement with revenue recognized over time.

ILLUSTRATION 18B-4
Revenue Recognition over Time—Franchise

FRANCHISE REVENUE OVER TIME

Facts: Tech Solvers Corp. is a franchisor in the emerging technology consulting service business. Tech Solvers' stores provide a range of computing services (hardware/software installation, repairs, data backup, device syncing, and network solutions) on popular Apple and PC devices. Each franchise agreement gives a franchisee the right to open a Tech Solvers store and sell Tech Solvers' products and services in the area for 5 years. Under the contract, Tech Solvers also provides the franchisee with a number of services to support and enhance the franchise brand, including (a) advising and consulting on the operations of the store; (b) communicating new hardware and software developments, and service techniques; (c) providing business and training manuals; and (d) advertising programs and training. As an almost entirely service operation (all parts and other supplies are purchased as needed by customers), Tech Solvers provides few upfront services to franchisees. Instead, the franchisee recruits service technicians, who are given Tech Solvers' training materials (online manuals and tutorials), which are updated for technology changes, on a monthly basis at a minimum.

Tech Solvers enters into a franchise agreement on December 15, 2014, giving a franchisee the rights to operate a Tech Solvers franchise in eastern Indiana for 5 years. Tech Solvers charges an initial franchise fee of $5,000 for the right to operate as a franchisee, payable upon signing the contract. Tech Solvers also receives ongoing royalty payments of 7% of the franchisee's annual sales (payable each January 15 of the following year).

Question: What are the performance obligations in this arrangement and the point in time at which the performance obligations will be satisfied and revenue will be recognized?

Solution: To identify the performance obligations, Tech Solvers must determine whether the promised rights and the ongoing franchisee technology support and training services are distinct.

- Rights to the trade name, market area, and proprietary know-how for 5 years are not individually distinct because each one is not sold separately and cannot be used with other goods or services that are readily available to the franchisee. In addition, these licensed rights have a close connection with the underlying Tech Solvers' intellectual property (its ability to keep its service and training materials up-to-date). Therefore, those combined rights and the ongoing training materials are a single performance obligation. Tech Solvers satisfies the performance obligation over time. That is, once the franchisee begins operating a Tech Solvers franchise, Tech Solvers is providing access to the rights and must continue to perform updates and services.

- Tech Solvers cannot recognize revenue for the royalty payments because it is not reasonably assured to be entitled to those revenue-based royalty amounts. That is, these payments represent variable consideration. Therefore, Tech Solvers recognizes revenue for the royalties when (or as) the uncertainty is resolved.

The entries for Tech Solvers related to the franchise are summarized in Illustration 18B-5.

ILLUSTRATION 18B-5
Franchise Entries—
Revenue Recognized
over Time

Franchise agreement signed and receipt of upfront payment and note		
December 15, 2014		
Cash	5,000	
Unearned Franchise Revenue		5,000
Franchise begins operations in January 2015 and records $85,000 of revenue for the year ended December 31, 2015		
December 31, 2015		
Unearned Franchise Revenue	1,000	
Franchise Revenue ($5,000 ÷ 5)		1,000
Accounts Receivable	5,950	
Franchise Revenue ($85,000 × 7%)		5,950
To record payment received from franchisee		
January 31, 2016		
Cash	5,950	
Accounts Receivable		5,950

As indicated, Tech Solvers satisfies the performance obligation related to access to the franchise rights and training materials over time (in this case, on a straight-line basis). Continuing franchise fees are recognized when uncertainty related to the variable consideration is resolved.

In summary, analysis of the characteristics of the Tech Solvers' franchise indicates that it does not reflect a right that is transferred at a point in time. That is, Tech Solvers has a continuing obligation to provide updated materials and ongoing support, suggesting the control of the right has not been transferred to the franchisee. Thus, revenue from the franchise rights is recognized over time.

KEY TERMS

continuing franchise
  fees, *1084*
franchisee, *1083*
franchises, *1083*
franchisor, *1083*
initial franchise fee, *1084*

SUMMARY OF LEARNING OBJECTIVE FOR APPENDIX 18B

13 **Explain revenue recognition for franchises.** In a franchise arrangement, the franchisor satisfies its performance obligation for a franchise license when control of the franchise rights is transferred, generally when the franchisee begins operations of the franchise. In situations where the franchisor provides *access to the rights* rather than transferring control of the franchise rights, the franchise rights' revenue is recognized over time rather than at a point in time. Franchisors recognize continuing franchise fees as uncertainty related to the variable consideration is resolved, that is, over time.

DEMONSTRATION PROBLEM

Outback Industries manufactures emergency power equipment. Its most popular generator is a model called the E-Booster, which has a retail price of $1,500 and costs Outback $740 to manufacture. It sells the E-Booster on a standalone basis directly to businesses, as well as provides installation services. Outback also distributes the E-Booster through a consignment agreement with Home Depot. Income data for Outback's first quarter of 2014 from operations other than the E-Booster generator are as follows.

Revenues	$6,500,000
Expenses	4,350,000

Outback has the following information related to four E-Booster revenue arrangements during the first quarter of 2014.

1. Outback entered into an arrangement with the Grocers Co-op in eastern Minnesota to deliver E-Boosters for the meat lockers in the grocers' stores. Outback provides a 5% volume discount for E-Boosters purchased by Grocers if at least $450,000 of E-Boosters are purchased during 2014. By March 31, 2014, Outback has made sales of $360,000 to Grocers Co-op. Based on prior experience with this promotion in two neighboring states, Outback met the discount threshold for the year if more than one-half of the target had been met by mid-year.
2. On January 1, 2014, Outback sells 20 E-Boosters to Nick's Liquors. Nick's signs a 6-month note due in 6 months at an annual interest rate of 12%. Outback allows Nick's to return any E-Booster that it cannot use within 60 days and receive a full refund. Based on prior experience, Outback estimates that three units will be returned (using the most likely outcome approach). Outback's costs to recover the products will be immaterial, and the returned generators are expected to be resold at a profit.
3. Outback sells 30 E-Boosters to a community bank in the Florida Keys, to provide uninterrupted power for bank branches with ATMs, for a total contract price of $50,000. In addition to the E-Boosters, Outback also provides installation (at a cost of $150 per E-Booster) on a standalone basis; the fair value of this service is $200 per unit installed. The E-Boosters are delivered and installed on March 1, 2014, and full payment is made to Outback.
4. Outback ships 300 E-Boosters to Home Depot on consignment. By March 31, 2014, Home Depot has sold three-fourths of the consigned merchandise at the listed price of $1,500 per unit. Home Depot notifies Outback of the sales, retains an 8% commission, and remits the cash due to Outback.

Instructions
(a) Determine net income for Outback Industries for the first quarter of 2014. (Ignore taxes.)
(b) In reviewing the credit history of Nick's Liquors, Outback has some concerns about the collectibility of the full amount due on the note. Briefly discuss how collectibility of the note affects revenue recognition and income measurement for Outback.

Solution

(a) The amount of revenue and expense recognized on each of the arrangements is as follows.

1.

Sales revenue [95% × ($1,500 × 240)]	$342,000	
Cost of goods sold ($740 × 240)	177,600	
Gross profit		$164,400

2.

Sales revenue (20 × $1,500)	30,000	
Less: Estimated returns (3 × $1,500)	4,500	
Net sales	25,500	
Cost of goods sold (17 × $740)	12,580	
Gross profit	12,920	
Interest revenue ($30,000 × 12% × 3/12)	900	
Net income on this arrangement		13,820

3. The total transaction price of $50,000 is allocated between the equipment and installation. The transaction price for the equipment and installation is allocated based on relative fair values:

Equipment: $44,118 = ($45,000 ÷ $51,000) × $50,000
Installation: $5,882 = ($6,000 ÷ $51,000) × $50,000

Sales revenue	$44,118	
Cost of goods sold (30 × $740)	22,000	
Gross profit	$22,118	
Installation revenue	5,882	
Installation expense (30 × $150)	4,500	
Net profit	1,382	
Net income on this arrangement		$23,500

4.

Sales revenue (225 × $1,500)	337,500	
Cost of goods sold (225 × $740)	166,500	
Gross profit	171,000	
Commission expense ($337,500 × 8%)	27,000	
Net income on this arrangement		144,000
Net income on E-Booster		$345,720

Income for the quarter: $6,500,000 − $4,350,000 + $345,720 = $2,495,720.

(b) Whether a company will get paid for satisfying a performance obligation is not a consideration in determining revenue recognition. That is, the amount recognized is not adjusted for customer credit risk. If significant doubt exists at contract inception about collectibility, Outback reports the revenue gross and then presents an allowance for any impairment due to bad debts, which will reduce net income and which is reported as an operating expense in the income statement.

FASB CODIFICATION

FASB Codification References

[1] FASB ASC 606. [Predecessor literature: None.]

[2] FASB Accounting Standards Update No. 2014-09, *Revenue from Contracts with Customers* (Topic 606) (May 2014), Summary.

[3] FASB ASC 606-10-25-1 to 4. [Predecessor literature: None.]

[4] FASB ASC 606-10-25-1 (e). [Predecessor literature: None.]

[5] FASB ASC 606-10-25-12. [Predecessor literature: None.]

[6] FASB ASC 606-10-25-13. [Predecessor literature: None.]

[7] FASB ASC 606-10-32-2 to 4. [Predecessor literature: None.]

[8] FASB ASC 606-10-32-5 to 9. [Predecessor literature: None.]

[9] FASB ASC 606-10-32-12. [Predecessor literature: None.]

[10] FASB ASC 606-10-32-11. [Predecessor literature: None.]

[11] FASB ASC 606-10-32-18. [Predecessor literature: None.]

[12] FASB ASC 606-10-32-34. [Predecessor literature: None.]

[13] FASB Accounting Standards Update No. 2014-09, *Revenue from Contracts with Customers* (Topic 606) (May 2014), pp. 5–6.

[14] FASB ASC 606-10-55-38. [Predecessor literature: None.]

[15] FASB Accounting Standards Update No. 2014-09, *Revenue from Contracts with Customers* (Topic 606) (May 2014), par. BC261.

[16] FASB ASC 606-10-50-1 to 21. [Predecessor literature: None.]

[17] FASB ASC 606-10-25-27 to 29. [Predecessor literature: None.]

[18] FASB ASC 450 *(Contingencies)*.

[19] FASB ASC 606-10-55-54 to 64. [Predecessor literature: None.]

Exercises

If your school has a subscription to the FASB Codification, go to *http://aaahq.org/asclogin.cfm* to log in and prepare responses to the following. Provide Codification references for your responses.

CE18-1 Access the glossary ("Master Glossary") to answer the following.

    (a) What is the definition of a customer?
    (b) What is a performance obligation?
    (c) How is standalone selling price defined?
    (d) What is a transaction price?

CE18-2 Briefly explain the conditions when a contract modification shall be accounted for as a separate performance obligation.

CE18-3 Describe the accounting for refund liabilities.

CE18-4 What procedures are followed in the allocation of a discount?

Be sure to check the book's companion website for a Review and Analysis Exercise, with solution.

WileyPLUS

Brief Exercises, Exercises, Problems, and many more learning and assessment tools and resources are available for practice in WileyPLUS.

Note: All asterisked Questions, Exercises, and Problems relate to material in the appendices to the chapter.

QUESTIONS

1. Explain the current environment regarding revenue recognition.

2. What was viewed as a major criticism of GAAP as regards revenue recognition?

3. Describe the revenue recognition principle.

4. Identify the five steps in the revenue recognition process.

5. Describe the critical factor in evaluating whether a performance obligation is satisfied.

6. When is revenue recognized in the following situations? (a) Revenue from selling products, (b) revenue from services performed, (c) revenue from permitting others to use company assets, and (d) revenue from disposing of assets other than products.

7. Explain the importance of a contract in the revenue recognition process.

8. On October 10, 2014, Executor Co. entered into a contract with Belisle Inc. to transfer Executor's specialty products (sales value of $10,000, cost of $6,500) on December 15, 2014. Belisle agrees to make a payment of $5,000 upon delivery and signs a promissory note to pay the remaining balance on January 15, 2015. What entries does Executor make in 2014 on this contract? Ignore time value of money considerations.

9. Explain the accounting for contract modifications.

10. What is a performance obligation? Under what conditions does a performance obligation exist?

11. When must multiple performance obligations in a revenue arrangement be accounted for separately?

12. Engelhart Implements Inc. sells tractors to area farmers. The price for each tractor includes GPS positioning service for 9 months (which facilitates field settings for planting and harvesting equipment). The GPS service is regularly sold on a standalone basis by Engelhart for a monthly fee. After the 9-month period, the consumer can renew the service on a fee basis. Does Engelhart have one or multiple performance obligations? Explain.

13. What is the transaction price? What additional factors related to the transaction price must be considered in determining the transaction price?

14. What are some examples of variable consideration? What are the two approaches for estimating variable consideration?

15. Allee Corp. is evaluating a revenue arrangement to determine proper revenue recognition. The contract is for construction of 10 speedboats for a contract price of $400,000. The customer needs the boats in its show-rooms by February 1, 2015, for the boat purchase season; the customer provides a bonus payment of $21,000 if all boats are delivered by the February 1 deadline. The bonus is reduced by $7,000 each week that the boats are delivered after the deadline until no bonus is paid if the boats are delivered after February 15, 2015. Allee frequently includes such bonus terms in it contracts and thus has good historical data for estimating the probabilities of completion at different dates. It estimates an equal probability (25%) for each full delivery outcome. What approach should Allee use to determine the transaction price for this contract? Explain.

16. Refer to the information in Question 15. Assume that Allee has limited experience with a construction project on the same scale as the 10 speedboats. How does this affect the accounting for the variable consideration?

17. In measuring the transaction price, explain the accounting for (a) time value of money, and (b) noncash consideration.

18. What is the proper accounting for volume discounts on sales of products?

19. On what basis should the transaction price be allocated to various performance obligations? Identify the approaches for allocating the transaction price.

20. Fuhremann Co. is a full-service manufacturer of surveillance equipment. Customers can purchase any combination of equipment, installation services, and training as part of Fuhremann's security services. Thus, each of these performance obligations are separate with individual standalone values. Laplante Inc. purchased cameras, installation, and training at a total price of $80,000. Estimated standalone fair values of the equipment, installation, and training are $90,000, $7,000, and $3,000, respectively. How should the transaction price be allocated to the equipment, installation, and training?

21. When does a company satisfy a performance obligation? Identify the indicators of satisfaction of a performance obligation.

22. Under what conditions does a company recognize revenue over a period of time?

23. How do companies recognize revenue from a performance obligation over time?

24. Explain the accounting for sales with right of return.

25. What are the reporting issues in a sale with a repurchase agreement?

26. Explain a bill-and-hold sale. When is revenue recognized in these situations?

27. Explain a principal-agent relationship and its significance to revenue recognition.

28. What is the nature of a sale on consignment?

29. What are the two types of warranties? Explain the accounting for each type.

30. Campus Cellular provides cell phones and 1 year of cell service to students for an upfront, nonrefundable fee of $300 and a usage fee of $5 per month. Students may renew the service for each year they are on campus (on average, students renew their service one time). What amount of revenue should Campus Cellular recognize in the first year of the contract?

31. Describe the conditions when contract assets and liabilities are recognized and presented in financial statements.

32. Explain the reporting for (a) costs to fulfill a contract and (b) collectibility.

33. What qualitative and quantitative disclosures are required related to revenue recognition?

*34. What are the two basic methods of accounting for long-term construction contracts? Indicate the circumstances that determine when one or the other of these methods should be used.

*35. For what reasons should the percentage-of-completion method be used over the completed-contract method whenever possible?

*36. What methods are used in practice to determine the extent of progress toward completion? Identify some "input measures" and some "output measures" that might be used to determine the extent of progress.

*37. What are the two types of losses that can become evident in accounting for long-term contracts? What is the nature of each type of loss? How is each type accounted for?

*38. Why in franchise arrangements may it not be proper to recognize the entire franchise fee as revenue at the date of sale?

*39. How should a franchisor account for continuing franchise fees and routine sales of equipment and supplies to franchisees?

BRIEF EXERCISES

3 **BE18-1** On May 10, 2014, Cosmo Co. enters into a contract to deliver a product to Greig Inc. on June 15, 2014. Greig agrees to pay the full contract price of $2,000 on July 15, 2014. The cost of the goods is $1,300. Cosmo delivers the product to Greig on June 15, 2014, and receives payment on July 15, 2014. Prepare the journal entries for Cosmo related to this contract.

3 **BE18-2** Stengel Co. enters into a 3-year contract to perform maintenance service to Laplante Inc. Laplante promises to pay $100,000 at the beginning of each year (the standalone selling price of the service at contract inception is $100,000 per year). At the end of the second year, the contract is modified and the fee for third year of service, which reflects a reduced menu of maintenance services to be performed at Laplante locations, is reduced to $80,000 (the standalone selling price of the services at the beginning of the third year is $80,000 per year). Briefly describe the accounting for this contract modification.

4 **BE18-3** Ismail Construction enters into a contract to design and build a hospital. Ismail is responsible for the overall management of the project and identifies various goods and services to be provided, including engineering, site clearance, foundation, procurement, construction of the structure, piping and wiring, installation of equipment, and finishing. Does Ismail have a single performance obligation to the customer in this revenue arrangement? Explain.

4 **BE18-4** Mauer Company licenses customer-relationship software to Hedges Inc. for 3 years. In addition to providing the software, Mauer promises to provide consulting services over the life of the license to maintain operability within Hedges' computer system. The total transaction price is $200,000. Based on standalone values, Mauer estimates the consulting services have a value of $75,000 and the software license has a value of $125,000. Upon installation of the software on July 1, 2014, Hedges pays $100,000; the contract balance is due on December 31, 2014. Identify the performance obligations and the revenue in 2014, assuming (a) the performance obligations are interdependent and (b) the performance obligations are not interdependent.

5 **BE18-5** Nair Corp. enters into a contract with a customer to build an apartment building for $1,000,000. The customer hopes to rent apartments at the beginning of the school year and provides a performance bonus of $150,000 to be paid if the building is ready for rental beginning August 1, 2015. The bonus is reduced by $50,000 each week that completion is delayed. Nair commonly includes these completion bonuses in its contracts and, based on prior experience, estimates the following completion outcomes:

Completed by	Probability
August 1, 2015	70%
August 8, 2015	20
August 15, 2015	5
After August 15, 2015	5

Determine the transaction price for this contract.

5 **BE18-6** Referring to the revenue arrangement in BE18-5, determine the transaction price for the contract, assuming (a) Nair is only able to estimate whether the building can be completed by August 1, 2015, or not (Nair estimates that there is a 70% chance that the building will be completed by August 1, 2015), and (b) Nair has limited information with which to develop a reliable estimate of completion by the August 1, 2015, deadline.

5 **BE18-7** On January 2, 2014, Adani Inc. sells goods to Geo Company in exchange for a zero-interest-bearing note with face value of $11,000, with payment due in 12 months. The fair value of the goods at the date of sale is $10,000 (cost $6,000). Prepare the journal entry to record this transaction on January 2, 2014. How much total revenue should be recognized in 2014?

5 **BE18-8** On March 1, 2014, Parnevik Company sold goods to Goosen Inc. for $660,000 in exchange for a 5-year, zero-interest-bearing note in the face amount of $1,062,937. The goods have an inventory cost on

Parnevik's books of $400,000. Prepare the journal entries for Parnevik on (a) March 1, 2014, and (b) December 31, 2014.

5 **BE18-9** Telephone Sellers Inc. sells prepaid telephone cards to customers. Telephone Sellers then pays the telecommunications company, TeleExpress, for the actual use of its telephone lines related to the prepaid telephone cards. Assume that Telephone Sellers sells $4,000 of prepaid cards in January 2014. It then pays TeleExpress based on usage, which turns out to be 50% in February, 30% in March, and 20% in April. The total payment by Telephone Sellers for TeleExpress lines over the 3 months is $3,000. Indicate how much income Telephone Sellers should recognize in January, February, March, and April.

5 **BE18-10** Manual Company sells goods to Nolan Company during 2014. It offers Nolan the following rebates based on total sales to Nolan. If total sales to Nolan are 10,000 units, it will grant a rebate of 2%. If it sells up to 20,000 units, it will grant a rebate of 4%. If it sells up to 30,000 units, it will grant a rebate of 6%. In the first quarter of the year, Manual sells 11,000 units to Nolan at a sales price of $110,000. Manual, based on past experience, has sold over 40,000 units to Nolan, and these sales normally take place in the third quarter of the year. Prepare the journal entry that Manual should make to record the sale of the 11,000 units in the first quarter of the year.

6 **BE18-11** Geraths Windows manufactures and sells custom storm windows for three-season porches. Geraths also provides installation service for the windows. The installation process does not involve changes in the windows, so this service can be performed by other vendors. Geraths enters into the following contract on July 1, 2014, with a local homeowner. The customer purchases windows for a price of $2,400 and chooses Geraths to do the installation. Geraths charges the same price for the windows irrespective of whether it does the installation or not. The price of the installation service is estimated to have a fair value of $600. The customer pays Geraths $2,000 (which equals the fair value of the windows, which have a cost of $1,100) upon delivery and the remaining balance upon installation of the windows. The windows are delivered on September 1, 2014, Geraths completes installation on October 15, 2014, and the customer pays the balance due. Prepare the journal entries for Geraths in 2014. (Round amounts to nearest dollar.)

6 **7** **BE18-12** Refer to the revenue arrangement in BE18-11. Repeat the requirements, assuming (a) Geraths estimates the standalone value of the installation based on an estimated cost of $400 plus a margin of 20% on cost, and (b) given uncertainty of finding skilled labor, Geraths is unable to develop a reliable estimate for the fair value of the installation. (Round amounts to nearest dollar.)

8 **BE18-13** On July 10, 2014, Amodt Music sold CDs to retailers on account and recorded sales revenue of $700,000 (cost $560,000). Amodt grants the right to return CDs that do not sell in 3 months following delivery. Past experience indicates that the normal return rate is 15%. By October 11, 2014, retailers returned CDs to Amodt and were granted credit of $78,000. Prepare Amodt's journal entries to record (a) the sale on July 10, 2014, and (b) $78,000 of returns on October 11, 2014.

8 **BE18-14** Kristin Company sells 300 units of its products for $20 each to Logan Inc. for cash. Kristin allows Logan to return any unused product within 30 days and receive a full refund. The cost of each product is $12. To determine the transaction price, Kristin decides that the approach that is most predictive of the amount of consideration to which it will be entitled is the probability-weighted amount. Using the probability-weighted amount, Kristin estimates that (1) 10 products will be returned and (2) the returned products are expected to be resold at a profit. Prepare the journal entry for Kristin at the time of the sale to Logan.

8 **BE18-15** On June 1, 2014, Mills Company sells $200,000 of shelving units to a local retailer, ShopBarb, which is planning to expand its stores in the area. Under the agreement, ShopBarb asks Mills to retain the shelving units at its factory until the new stores are ready for installation. Title passes to ShopBarb at the time the agreement is signed. The shelving units are delivered to the stores on September 1, 2014, and ShopBarb pays in full. Prepare the journal entries for this bill-and-hold arrangement (assuming that conditions for recognizing the sale have been met) for Mills on June 1 and September 1, 2014. The cost of the shelving units to Mills is $110,000.

8 **BE18-16** Travel Inc. sells tickets for a Caribbean cruise on ShipAway Cruise Lines to Carmel Company employees. The total cruise package price to Carmel Company employees is $70,000. Travel Inc. receives a commission of 6% of the total price. Travel Inc. therefore remits $65,800 to ShipAway. Prepare the journal entry to record the remittance and revenue recognized by Travel Inc. on this transaction.

8 **BE18-17** Jansen Corporation shipped $20,000 of merchandise on consignment to Gooch Company. Jansen paid freight costs of $2,000. Gooch Company paid $500 for local advertising, which is reimbursable from Jansen. By year-end, 60% of the merchandise had been sold for $21,500. Gooch notified Jansen, retained a

10% commission, and remitted the cash due to Jansen. Prepare Jansen's journal entry when the cash is received.

8 **BE18-18** Talarczyk Company sold 10,000 Super-Spreaders on July 1, 2014, at a total price of $1,000,000, with a warranty guarantee that the product was free of any defects. The cost of the spreaders sold is $550,000. The assurance warranties extend for a 2-year period and are estimated to cost $40,000. Talarczyk also sold extended warranties (service-type warranties) related to 2,000 spreaders for 2 years beyond the 2-year period for $12,000. Prepare the journal entries that Talarczyk should make in 2014 related to the sale and the related warranties.

9 **BE18-19** On May 1, 2014, Mount Company enters into a contract to transfer a product to Eric Company on September 30, 2014. It is agreed that Eric will pay the full price of $25,000 in advance on June 15, 2014. Eric pays on June 15, 2014, and Mount delivers the product on September 30, 2014. Prepare the journal entries required for Mount in 2014.

8 **BE18-20** Nate Beggs signs a 1-year contract with BlueBox Video. The terms of the contract are that Nate is required to pay a nonrefundable initiation fee of $100. After the first year, membership can be renewed by paying an annual membership fee of $5 per month. BlueBox determines that its customers, on average, renew their annual membership three times after the first year before terminating their membership. What amount of revenue should BlueBox recognize in its first year?

10 *BE18-21** Turner, Inc. began work on a $7,000,000 contract in 2014 to construct an office building. During 2014, Turner, Inc. incurred costs of $1,700,000, billed its customers for $1,200,000, and collected $960,000. At December 31, 2014, the estimated future costs to complete the project total $3,300,000. Prepare Turner's 2014 journal entries using the percentage-of-completion method.

11 *BE18-22** Guillen, Inc. began work on a $7,000,000 contract in 2014 to construct an office building. Guillen uses the completed-contract method. At December 31, 2014, the balances in certain accounts were Construction in Process $1,715,000; Accounts Receivable $240,000; and Billings on Construction in Process $1,000,000. Indicate how these accounts would be reported in Guillen's December 31, 2014, balance sheet.

12 *BE18-23** Archer Construction Company began work on a $420,000 construction contract in 2014. During 2014, Archer incurred costs of $278,000, billed its customer for $215,000, and collected $175,000. At December 31, 2014, the estimated future costs to complete the project total $162,000. Prepare Archer's journal entry to record profit or loss, if any, using (a) the percentage-of-completion method and (b) the completed-contract method.

13 *BE18-24** Frozen Delight, Inc. charges an initial franchise fee of $75,000 for the right to operate as a franchisee of Frozen Delight. Of this amount, $25,000 is collected immediately. The remainder is collected in four equal annual installments of $12,500 each. These installments have a present value of $41,402. As part of the total franchise fee, Frozen Delight also provides training (with a fair value of $2,000) to help franchisees get the store ready to open. The franchise agreement is signed on April 1, 2014, training is completed, and the store opens on July 1, 2014. Prepare the journal entries required by Frozen Delight in 2014.

EXERCISES

3 **5** **E18-1 (Sales with Discounts)** Jupiter Company sells goods to Danone Inc. on account on January 1, 2014. The goods have a sales price of $610,000 (cost $500,000). The terms of the sale are net 30. If Danone pays within 5 days, it receives a cash discount of $10,000. Past history indicates the cash discount will be taken.

Instructions
(a) Prepare the journal entries for Jupiter for January 1, 2014.
(b) Prepare the journal entries for Jupiter for January 31, 2014, assuming Danone does not make payment until January 31, 2014.

3 **5** **E18-2 (Transaction Price)** Presented below are three revenue recognition situations.
(a) Grupo sells goods to MTN for $1,000,000, payment due at delivery.
(b) Grupo sells goods on account to Grifols for $800,000, payment due in 30 days.
(c) Grupo sells goods to Magnus for $500,000, payment due in two installments: the first installment payable in 18 months and the second payment due 6 months later. The present value of the future payments is $464,000.

Instructions

Indicate the transaction price for each of these transactions and when revenue will be recognized.

3 ▶ **E18-3 (Contract Modification)** In September 2014, Gaertner Corp. commits to selling 150 of its iPhone-compatible docking stations to Better Buy Co. for $15,000 ($100 per product). The stations are delivered to Better Buy over the next 6 months. After 90 stations are delivered, the contract is modified and Gaertner promises to deliver an additional 45 products for an additional $4,275 ($95 per station). All sales are cash on delivery.

Instructions

(a) Prepare the journal entry for Gaertner for the sale of the first 90 stations. The cost of each station is $54.

(b) Prepare the journal entry for the sale of 10 more stations after the contract modification, assuming that the price for the additional stations reflects the standalone selling price at the time of the contract modification. In addition, the additional stations are distinct from the original products as Gaertner regularly sells the products separately.

(c) Prepare the journal entry for the sale of 10 more stations (as in (b)), assuming that the pricing for the additional products *does not* reflect the standalone selling price of the additional products and the prospective method is used.

3 ▶ **E18-4 (Contract Modification)** Tyler Financial Services performs bookkeeping and tax-reporting services to startup companies in the Oconomowoc area. On January 1, 2014, Tyler entered into a 3-year service contract with Walleye Tech. Walleye promises to pay $10,000 at the beginning of each year, which at contract inception is the standalone selling price for these services. At the end of the second year, the contract is modified and the fee for the third year of services is reduced to $8,000. In addition, Walleye agrees to pay an additional $20,000 at the beginning of the third year to cover the contract for 3 additional years (i.e., 4 years remain after the modification). The extended contract services are similar to those provided in the first 2 years of the contract.

Instructions

(a) Prepare the journal entries for Tyler in 2014 and 2015 related to this service contract.

(b) Prepare the journal entries for Tyler in 2016 related to the modified service contract, assuming a prospective approach.

(c) Repeat the requirements for part (b), assuming Tyler and Walleye agree on a revised set of services (fewer bookkeeping services but more tax services) in the extended contract period and the modification results in a separate performance obligation.

5 ▶ **E18-5 (Variable Consideration)** Blair Biotech enters into a licensing agreement with Pang Pharmaceutical for a drug under development. Blair will receive a payment of $10,000,000 if the drug receives regulatory approval. Based on prior experience in the drug-approval process, Blair determines it is 90% likely that the drug will gain approval and a 10% chance of denial.

Instructions

(a) Determine the transaction price of the arrangement for Blair Biotech.

(b) Assuming that regulatory approval was granted on December 20, 2014, and that Blair received the payment from Pang on January 15, 2015, prepare the journal entries for Blair.

5 ▶ **E18-6 (Trailing Commission)** Aaron's Agency sells an insurance policy offered by Capital Insurance Company for a commission of $100. In addition, Aaron will receive an additional commission of $10 each year for as long as the policyholder does not cancel the policy. After selling the policy, Aaron does not have any remaining performance obligations. Based on Aaron's significant experience with these types of policies, it estimates that policyholders on average renew the policy for 4.5 years. It has no evidence to suggest that previous policyholder behavior will change.

Instructions

(a) Determine the transaction price of the arrangement for Aaron, assuming 100 policies are sold.

(b) Prepare the journal entries, assuming that the 100 policies are sold in January 2014 and that Aaron receives commissions from Capital.

5 ▶ **E18-7 (Sales with Discounts)** On June 3, 2014, Hunt Company sold to Ann Mount merchandise having a sales price of $8,000 (cost $5,600) with terms of 2/10, n/60, f.o.b. shipping point. Hunt estimates that merchandise with a sales value of $800 will be returned. An invoice totaling $120, terms n/30, was received by Mount on June 8 from Olympic Transport Service for the freight cost. Upon receipt of the goods, on June 5, Mount notified Hunt that $300 of merchandise contained flaws. The same day, Hunt issued a credit memo covering the defective merchandise and asked that it be returned at Hunt's expense.

Hunt estimates the returned items to have a fair value of $120. The freight on the returned merchandise was $24, paid by Hunt on June 7. On June 12, the company received a check for the balance due from Mount.

Instructions

(a) Prepare journal entries for Hunt Company to record all the events noted above assuming sales and receivables are entered at gross selling price.

(b) Prepare the journal entry assuming that Ann Mount did not remit payment until August 5.

5 ▶ **E18-8 (Sales with Discounts)** Taylor Marina has 300 available slips that rent for $800 per season. Payments must be made in full at the start of the boating season, April 1, 2015. The boating season ends October 31, and the marina has a December 31 year-end. Slips for future seasons may be reserved if paid for by December 31, 2015. Under a new policy, if payment for 2016 season slips is made by December 31, 2015, a 5% discount is allowed. If payment for 2017 season slips is made by December 31, 2015, renters get a 20% discount (this promotion hopefully will provide cash flow for major dock repairs).

On December 31, 2014, all 300 slips for the 2015 season were rented at full price. On December 31, 2015, 200 slips were reserved and paid for the 2016 boating season, and 60 slips were reserved and paid for the 2017 boating season.

Instructions

(a) Prepare the appropriate journal entries for December 31, 2014, and December 31, 2015.

(b) Assume the marina operator is unsophisticated in business. Explain the managerial significance of the above accounting to this person.

5 ▶ **6** ▶ **E18-9 (Allocate Transaction Price)** Sanchez Co. enters into a contract to sell Product A and Product B on January 2, 2014, for an upfront cash payment of $150,000. Product A will be delivered in 2 years (January 2, 2016) and Product B will be delivered in 5 years (January 2, 2019). Sanchez Co. allocates the $150,000 to Products A and B on a relative standalone selling price basis as follows.

	Standalone Selling Prices	Percent Allocated	Allocated Amounts
Product A	$ 40,000	25%	$ 37,500
Product B	120,000	75%	112,500
	$160,000		$150,000

Sanchez Co. uses an interest rate of 6%, which is its incremental borrowing rate.

Instructions

(a) Prepare the journal entries necessary on January 2, 2014, and December 31, 2014.

(b) Prepare the journal entries necessary on December 31, 2015.

(c) Prepare the journal entries necessary on January 2, 2016.

6 ▶ **E18-10 (Allocate Transaction Price)** Shaw Company sells goods that cost $300,000 to Ricard Company for $410,000 on January 2, 2014. The sales price includes an installation fee, which is valued at $40,000. The fair value of the goods is $370,000. The installation is considered a separate performance obligation and is expected to take 6 months to complete.

Instructions

(a) Prepare the journal entries (if any) to record the sale on January 2, 2014.

(b) Shaw prepares an income statement for the first quarter of 2014, ending on March 31, 2014 (installation was completed on June 18, 2014). How much revenue should Shaw recognize related to its sale to Ricard?

5 ▶ **E18-11 (Allocate Transaction Price)** Crankshaft Company manufactures equipment. Crankshaft's products range from simple automated machinery to complex systems containing numerous components. Unit selling prices range from $200,000 to $1,500,000 and are quoted inclusive of installation. The installation process does not involve changes to the features of the equipment and does not require proprietary information about the equipment in order for the installed equipment to perform to specifications. Crankshaft has the following arrangement with Winkerbean Inc.

- Winkerbean purchases equipment from Crankshaft for a price of $1,000,000 and contracts with Crankshaft to install the equipment. Crankshaft charges the same price for the equipment irrespective of whether it does the installation or not. Using market data, Crankshaft determines installation service is estimated to have a fair value of $50,000. The cost of the equipment is $600,000.

- Winkerbean is obligated to pay Crankshaft the $1,000,000 upon the delivery and installation of the equipment.

Crankshaft delivers the equipment on June 1, 2014, and completes the installation of the equipment on September 30, 2014. The equipment has a useful life of 10 years. Assume that the equipment and the installation are two distinct performance obligations which should be accounted for separately.

Instructions
- (a) How should the transaction price of $1,000,000 be allocated among the service obligations?
- (b) Prepare the journal entries for Crankshaft for this revenue arrangement in 2014 assuming Crankshaft receives payment when installation is completed.

6 **E18-12 (Allocate Transaction Price)** Refer to the revenue arrangement in E18-11.

Instructions
Repeat requirements (a) and (b) assuming Crankshaft does not have market data with which to determine the standalone selling price of the installation services. As a result, an expected cost plus margin approach is used. The cost of installation is $36,000; Crankshaft prices these services with a 25% margin relative to cost.

6 **E18-13 (Allocate Transaction Price)** Appliance Center is an experienced home appliance dealer. Appliance Center also offers a number of services together with the home appliances that it sells. Assume that Appliance Center sells ovens on a standalone basis. Appliance Center also sells installation services and maintenance services for ovens. However, Appliance Center does not offer installation or maintenance services to customers who buy ovens from other vendors. Pricing for ovens is as follows.

Oven only	$ 800
Oven with installation service	850
Oven with maintenance services	975
Oven with installation and maintenance services	1,000

In each instance in which maintenance services are provided, the maintenance service is separately priced within the arrangement at $175. Additionally, the incremental amount charged by Appliance Center for installation approximates the amount charged by independent third parties. Ovens are sold subject to a general right of return. If a customer purchases an oven with installation and/or maintenance services, in the event Appliance Center does not complete the service satisfactorily, the customer is only entitled to a refund of the portion of the fee that exceeds $800.

Instructions
- (a) Assume that a customer purchases an oven with both installation and maintenance services for $1,000. Based on its experience, Appliance Center believes that it is probable that the installation of the equipment will be performed satisfactorily to the customer. Assume that the maintenance services are priced separately. Identify the separate performance obligations related to the Appliance Center revenue arrangement.
- (b) Indicate the amount of revenue that should be allocated to the oven, the installation, and to the maintenance contract.

8 **E18-14 (Sales with Returns)** Organic Growth Company is presently testing a number of new agricultural seeds that it has recently harvested. To stimulate interest, it has decided to grant to five of its largest customers the unconditional right of return to these products if not fully satisfied. The right of return extends for 4 months. Organic Growth sells these seeds on account for $1,500,000 (cost $800,000) on January 2, 2014. Customers are required to pay the full amount due by March 15, 2014.

Instructions
- (a) Prepare the journal entry for Organic Growth at January 2, 2014, assuming Organic Growth estimates returns of 20% based on prior experience.
- (b) Assume that one customer returns the seeds on March 1, 2014, due to unsatisfactory performance. Prepare the journal entry to record this transaction, assuming this customer purchased $100,000 of seeds from Organic Growth.
- (c) Briefly describe the accounting for these sales if Organic Growth is unable to reliably estimate returns.

8 **E18-15 (Sales with Returns)** Uddin Publishing Co. publishes college textbooks that are sold to bookstores on the following terms. Each title has a fixed wholesale price, terms f.o.b. shipping point, and payment is due 60 days after shipment. The retailer may return a maximum of 30% of an order at the retailer's expense. Sales are made only to retailers who have good credit ratings. Past experience indicates that the normal return rate is 12%, and the average collection period is 72 days.

Instructions
(a) Identify the revenue recognition criteria that Uddin could employ concerning textbook sales.
(b) Briefly discuss the reasoning for your answers in (a) above.
(c) On July 1, 2014, Uddin shipped books invoiced at $15,000,000 (cost $12,000,000). Prepare the journal entry to record this transaction.
(d) On October 3, 2014, $1.5 million of the invoiced July sales were returned according to the return policy, and the remaining $13.5 was paid. Prepare the journal entries for the return and payment.

8 **E18-16 (Sales with Repurchase)** Cramer Corp. sells idle machinery to Enyart Company on July 1, 2014, for $40,000. Cramer agrees to repurchase this equipment from Enyart on June 30, 2015, for a price of $42,400 (an imputed interest rate of 6%).

Instructions
(a) Prepare the journal entry for Cramer for the transfer of the asset to Enyart on July 1, 2014.
(b) Prepare any other necessary journal entries for Cramer in 2014.
(c) Prepare the journal entry for Cramer when the machinery is repurchased on June 30, 2015.

8 **E18-17 (Repurchase Agreement)** Zagat Inc. enters into an agreement on March 1, 2014, to sell Werner Metal Company aluminum ingots in 2 months. As part of the agreement, Zagat also agrees to repurchase the ingots in 60 days at the original sales price of $200,000 plus 2%. (Because Zagat has an unconditional obligation to repurchase the ingots at an amount greater than the original sales price, the transaction is treated as a financing.)

Instructions
(a) Prepare the journal entry necessary on March 1, 2014.
(b) Prepare the journal entry for the repurchase of the ingots on May 1, 2014.

8 **E18-18 (Bill and Hold)** Wood-Mode Company is involved in the design, manufacture, and installation of various types of wood products for large construction projects. Wood-Mode recently completed a large contract for Stadium Inc., which consisted of building 35 different types of concession counters for a new soccer arena under construction. The terms of the contract are that upon completion of the counters, Stadium would pay $2,000,000. Unfortunately, due to the depressed economy, the completion of the new soccer arena is now delayed. Stadium has therefore asked Wood-Mode to hold the counters for 2 months at its manufacturing plant until the arena is completed. Stadium acknowledges in writing that it ordered the counters and that they now have ownership. The time that Wood-Mode Company must hold the counters is totally dependent on when the arena is completed. Because Wood-Mode has not received additional progress payments for the arena due to the delay, Stadium has provided a deposit of $300,000.

Instructions
(a) Explain this type of revenue recognition transaction.
(b) What factors should be considered in determining when to recognize revenue in this transaction?
(c) Prepare the journal entry(ies) that Wood-Mode should make, assuming it signed a valid sales contract to sell the counters and received at the time the $300,000 deposit.

8 **E18-19 (Consignment Sales)** On May 3, 2014, Eisler Company consigned 80 freezers, costing $500 each, to Remmers Company. The cost of shipping the freezers amounted to $840 and was paid by Eisler Company. On December 30, 2014, a report was received from the consignee, indicating that 40 freezers had been sold for $750 each. Remittance was made by the consignee for the amount due after deducting a commission of 6%, advertising of $200, and total installation costs of $320 on the freezers sold.

Instructions
(a) Compute the inventory value of the units unsold in the hands of the consignee.
(b) Compute the profit for the consignor for the units sold.
(c) Compute the amount of cash that will be remitted by the consignee.

8 ▶ E18-20 (Warranty Arrangement) On December 31, 2014, Grando Company sells production equipment to Fargo Inc. for $50,000. Grando includes a 1-year assurance warranty service with the sale of all its equipment. The customer receives and pays for the equipment on December 31, 2014. Grando estimates the prices to be $48,800 for the equipment and $1,200 for the cost of the warranty.

Instructions
   (a) Prepare the journal entry to record this transaction on December 31, 2014.
   (b) Repeat the requirements for (a), assuming that in addition to the assurance warranty, Grando sold an extended warranty (service-type warranty) for an additional 2 years (2016–2017) for $800.

8 ▶ E18-21 (Warranties) Celic Inc. manufactures and sells computers that include an assurance-type warranty for the first 90 days. Celic offers an optional extended coverage plan under which it will repair or replace any defective part for 3 years from the expiration of the assurance-type warranty. Because the optional extended coverage plan is sold separately, Celic determines that the 3 years of extended coverage represent a separate performance obligation. The total transaction price for the sale of a computer and the extended warranty is $3,600 on October 1, 2014, and Celic determines the standalone selling price of each is $3,200 and $400, respectively. Further, Celic estimates, based on historical experience, it will incur $200 in costs to repair defects that arise within the 90-day coverage period for the assurance-type warranty. The cost of the equipment is $1,440.

Instructions
   (a) Prepare the journal entry (ies) to record the sale of the computer, cost of goods sold, and liabilities related to the warranties.
   (b) Briefly describe the accounting for the service-type warranty after the 90-day assurance-type warranty period.

9 ▶ E18-22 (Existence of a Contract) On January 1, 2014, Gordon Co. enters into a contract to sell a customer a wiring base and shelving unit that sits on the base in exchange for $3,000. The contract requires delivery of the base first but states that payment for the base will not be made until the shelving unit is delivered. Gordon identifies two performance obligations and allocates $1,200 of the transaction price to the wiring base and the remainder to the shelving unit. The cost of the wiring base is $700; the shelves have a cost of $320.

Instructions
   (a) Prepare the journal entry on January 1, 2014, for Gordon.
   (b) Prepare the journal entry on February 5, 2014, for Gordon when the wiring base is delivered to the customer.
   (c) Prepare the journal entry on February 25, 2014, for Gordon when the shelving unit is delivered to the customer and Gordon receives full payment.

9 ▶ E18-23 (Existence of a Contract) On May 1, 2014, Richardson Inc. entered into a contract to deliver one of its specialty mowers to Kickapoo Landscaping Co. The contract requires Kickapoo to pay the contract price of $900 in advance on May 15, 2014. Kickapoo pays Richardson on May 15, 2014, and Richardson delivers the mower (with cost of $575) on May 31, 2014.

Instructions
   (a) Prepare the journal entry on May 1, 2014, for Richardson.
   (b) Prepare the journal entry on May 15, 2014, for Richardson.
   (c) Prepare the journal entry on May 31, 2014, for Richardson.

9 ▶ E18-24 (Contract Costs) Rex's Reclaimers entered into a contract with Dan's Demolition to manage the processing of recycled materials on Dan's various demolition projects. Services for the 3-year contract include collecting, sorting, and transporting reclaimed materials to recycling centers or contractors who will reuse them. Rex's incurs selling commission costs of $2,000 to obtain the contract. Before performing the services, Rex's also designs and builds specialty receptacles and loading equipment that interfaces with Dan's demolition equipment at a cost of $27,000. These receptacles and equipment are retained by Rex's. Dan's promises to pay a fixed fee of $12,000 per year, payable every 6 months for the services under the contract. Rex's incurs the following costs: design services for the receptacles to interface with Dan's equipment $3,000, loading equipment controllers $6,000, and special testing and OSHA inspection fees $2,000 (some of Dan's projects are on government property).

Instructions

(a) Determine the costs that should be capitalized as part of Rex's Reclaimers revenue arrangement with Dan's Demolition.

(b) Dan's also expects to incur general and administrative costs related to this contract, as well as costs of wasted materials and labor that likely cannot be factored into the contract price. Can these costs be capitalized? Explain.

9 **E18-25 (Contract Costs, Collectibility)** Refer to the information in E18-24.

Instructions

(a) Does the accounting for capitalized costs change if the contract is for 1 year rather than 3 years? Explain.

(b) Dan's Demolition is a startup company; as a result, there is more than insignificant uncertainty about Dan's ability to make the 6-month payments on time. Does this uncertainty affect the amount of revenue to be recognized under the contract? Explain.

10 **11** *E18-26 (Recognition of Profit on Long-Term Contracts)** During 2014, Nilsen Company started a construction job with a contract price of $1,600,000. The job was completed in 2016. The following information is available.

	2014	2015	2016
Costs incurred to date	$400,000	$825,000	$1,070,000
Estimated costs to complete	600,000	275,000	–0–
Billings to date	300,000	900,000	1,600,000
Collections to date	270,000	810,000	1,425,000

Instructions

(a) Compute the amount of gross profit to be recognized each year, assuming the percentage-of-completion method is used.

(b) Prepare all necessary journal entries for 2015.

(c) Compute the amount of gross profit to be recognized each year, assuming the completed-contract method is used.

10 *E18-27 (Analysis of Percentage-of-Completion Financial Statements)** In 2014, Steinrotter Construction Corp. began construction work under a 3-year contract. The contract price was $1,000,000. Steinrotter uses the percentage-of-completion method for financial accounting purposes. The income to be recognized each year is based on the proportion of cost incurred to total estimated costs for completing the contract. The financial statement presentations relating to this contract at December 31, 2014, are shown below.

Balance Sheet

Accounts receivable	$18,000
Construction in process	65,000
Less: Billings	61,500
Costs and recognized profit in excess of billings	3,500

Income Statement

Income (before tax) on the contract recognized in 2014	$19,500

Instructions

(a) How much cash was collected in 2014 on this contract?

(b) What was the initial estimated total income before tax on this contract?

(AICPA adapted)

10 *E18-28 (Gross Profit on Uncompleted Contract)** On April 1, 2014, Dougherty Inc. entered into a cost plus fixed fee contract to construct an electric generator for Altom Corporation. At the contract date, Dougherty estimated that it would take 2 years to complete the project at a cost of $2,000,000. The fixed fee stipulated in the contract is $450,000. Dougherty appropriately accounts for this contract under the percentage-of-completion method. During 2014, Dougherty incurred costs of $800,000 related to the project. The estimated cost at December 31, 2014, to complete the contract is $1,200,000. Altom was billed $600,000 under the contract.

Instructions

Prepare a schedule to compute the amount of gross profit to be recognized by Dougherty under the contract for the year ended December 31, 2014. Show supporting computations in good form.

(AICPA adapted)

10 **11** *E18-29 (**Recognition of Revenue on Long-Term Contract and Entries**) Hamilton Construction Company uses the percentage-of-completion method of accounting. In 2014, Hamilton began work under contract #E2-D2, which provided for a contract price of $2,200,000. Other details follow:

	2014	2015
Costs incurred during the year	$640,000	$1,425,000
Estimated costs to complete, as of December 31	960,000	–0–
Billings during the year	420,000	1,680,000
Collections during the year	350,000	1,500,000

Instructions

(a) What portion of the total contract price would be recognized as revenue in 2014? In 2015?

(b) Assuming the same facts as those above except that Hamilton uses the completed-contract method of accounting, what portion of the total contract price would be recognized as revenue in 2015?

(c) Prepare a complete set of journal entries for 2014 (using the percentage-of-completion method).

10 **11** *E18-30 (**Recognition of Profit and Balance Sheet Amounts for Long-Term Contracts**) Yanmei Construction Company began operations on January 1, 2014. During the year, Yanmei Construction entered into a contract with Lundquist Corp. to construct a manufacturing facility. At that time, Yanmei estimated that it would take 5 years to complete the facility at a total cost of $4,500,000. The total contract price for construction of the facility is $6,000,000. During the year, Yanmei incurred $1,185,800 in construction costs related to the construction project. The estimated cost to complete the contract is $4,204,200. Lundquist Corp. was billed and paid 25% of the contract price.

Instructions

Prepare schedules to compute the amount of gross profit to be recognized for the year ended December 31, 2014, and the amount to be shown as "costs and recognized profit in excess of billings" or "billings in excess of costs and recognized profit" at December 31, 2014, under each of the following methods. Show supporting computations in good form.

(a) Completed-contract method.

(b) Percentage-of-completion method.

(AICPA adapted)

13 *E18-31 (**Franchise Entries**) Pacific Crossburgers Inc. charges an initial franchise fee of $70,000. Upon the signing of the agreement (which covers 3 years), a payment of $28,000 is due. Thereafter, three annual payments of $14,000 are required. The credit rating of the franchisee is such that it would have to pay interest at 10% to borrow money. The franchise agreement is signed on May 1, 2014, and the franchise commences operation on July 1, 2014.

Instructions

Prepare the journal entries in 2014 for the franchisor under the following assumptions. (Round to the nearest dollar.)

(a) No future services are required by the franchisor once the franchise starts operations.

(b) The franchisor has substantial services to perform, once the franchise begins operations, to maintain the value of the franchise.

(c) The total franchise fee includes training services (with a value of $2,400) for the period leading up to the franchise opening and for 2 months following opening.

13 *E18-32 (**Franchise Fee, Initial Down Payment**) On January 1, 2014, Lesley Benjamin signed an agreement, covering 5 years, to operate as a franchisee of Campbell Inc. for an initial franchise fee of $50,000. The amount of $10,000 was paid when the agreement was signed, and the balance is payable in five annual payments of $8,000 each, beginning January 1, 2015. The agreement provides that the down payment is nonrefundable and that no future services are required of the franchisor once the franchise commences operations on April 1, 2014. Lesley Benjamin's credit rating indicates that she can borrow money at 11% for a loan of this type.

Instructions

(a) Prepare journal entries for Campbell for 2014-related revenue for this franchise arrangement.

(b) Prepare journal entries for Campbell for 2014-related revenue for this franchise arrangement, assuming that in addition to the franchise rights, Campbell also provides 1 year of operational consulting and training services, beginning on the signing date. These services have a value of $3,600.

(c) Repeat the requirements for part (a), assuming that Campbell must provide services to Benjamin throughout the franchise period to maintain the franchise value.

EXERCISES SET B

See the book's companion website, at **www.wiley.com/college/kieso**, for an additional set of exercises.

PROBLEMS

4 5 6 7 P18-1 (Allocate Transaction Price, Upfront Fees) Tablet Tailors sells tablet PCs combined with Internet service (Tablet Bundle A) that permits the tablet to connect to the Internet anywhere (set up a Wi-Fi hot spot). The price for the tablet and a 4-year Internet connection service contract is $500. The standalone selling price of the tablet is $250 (cost to Tablet Tailors $175). Tablet Tailors sells the Internet access service independently for an upfront payment of $100, plus $72 payments at the beginning of years 2–4 of the contract. With an imputed interest rate of 8%, the standalone value of the service is $286. On January 2, 2014, Tablet Tailors signed 100 contracts, receiving a total of $31,445 in cash (full payment of $500 each in cash, less the upfront fee for Internet service, less the present value of the note for the future service plan payments), delivered tablets, and started service for 100 tablet packages.

Instructions

(a) Prepare any journal entries to record this revenue arrangement on January 2, 2014.

(b) Prepare any journal entries to record this revenue arrangement on December 31, 2015.

(c) Prepare any journal entries to record this revenue arrangement on December 31, 2016.

(d) Repeat the requirements for part (a), assuming that Tablet Tailors has no reliable data with which to estimate the standalone selling price for the Internet service.

3 4 5 6 7 P18-2 (Modification of Contract, Allocate Transaction Price) Refer to the revenue arrangement in P18-1.

Instructions

Consider the following information and respond to the requirements indicated.

(a) In response to competitive pressures for the Internet access service for Bundle A, at the end of the second year of the 4-year contract, Tablet Tailors offers a modified contract and extension incentive. The extended contract services are similar to those provided in the first 2 years of the contract. Signing the extension and paying $120 (which equals the fair value of the revised service package) extends access for 2 more years of Internet connection. Assuming 40 Bundle A customers sign up for this offer, prepare the journal entries when the contract is signed in January 2, 2016, and at December 31, 2016, for those contracts. Assume the modification does not result in a separate performance obligation.

(b) Tablet Tailors offers a second package (Tablet Bundle B) which includes a service plan for the tablet PC covering the 4-year contract period. That product bundle sells for $600. Tablet Tailors provides the tablet service as a separate product with a standalone selling price of $160. Prepare any journal entries to record the sale of 200 of these packages on January 2, 2014.

4 5 6 7 P18-3 (Allocate Transaction Price, Discounts, Time Value) Grill Master Company sells total outdoor grilling solutions, providing gas and charcoal grills, accessories, and installation services for custom patio grilling stations.

Instructions

Respond to the requirements related to the following independent revenue arrangements for Grill Master products and services.

(a) Grill Master offers contract GM205, which is comprised of a free-standing gas grill for small patio use plus installation to a customer's gas line for a total price $800. On a standalone basis, the grill sells for $700 (cost $425), and Grill Master estimates that the fair value of the installation service (based on cost-plus estimation) is $150. Grill Master signed 10 GM205 contracts on April 20, 2014, and customers paid the contract price in cash. The grills were delivered and installed on May 15, 2014. Prepare journal entries for Grill Master for GM205 in April and May 2014.

(b) The State of Kentucky is planning major renovations in its parks during 2014 and enters into a contract with Grill Master to purchase 400 durable, easy maintenance, standard charcoal grills during 2014. The grills are priced at $200 each (with a cost of $160 each), and Grill Master provides a 6% volume discount if Kentucky purchases at least 300 grills during 2014. On April 17, 2014, Grill Master delivered and received payment for 280 grills. Based on prior experience with the State of Kentucky renovation projects, the delivery of this many grills makes it certain that Kentucky will meet the discount threshold. Prepare the journal entries for Grill Master for grills sold on April 17, 2014.

(c) Grill Master sells its specialty combination gas/wood-fired grills to local restaurants. Each grill is sold for $1,000 (cost $550) on credit with terms 3/30, net/90. Prepare the journal entries for the sale of 20 grills on September 1, 2014, and upon payment, assuming the customer paid on (1) September 25, 2014, and (2) October 15, 2014. Assume the company records sales net.

(d) On October 1, 2014, Grill Master sold one of its super deluxe combination gas/charcoal grills to a local builder. The builder plans to install it in one of its "Parade of Homes" houses. Grill Master accepted a 3-year, zero-interest-bearing note with face amount of $5,324. The grill has an inventory cost of $2,700. An interest rate of 10% is an appropriate market rate of interest for this customer. Prepare the journal entries on October 1, 2014, and December 31, 2014.

 P18-4 (Allocate Transaction Price, Discounts, Time Value) Economy Appliance Co. manufactures low-price, no-frills appliances that are in great demand for rental units. Pricing and cost information on Economy's main products are as follows.

Item	Standalone Selling Price (Cost)
Refrigerator	$500 ($260)
Range	$560 ($275)
Stackable washer/dryer unit	$700 ($400)

Customers can contract to purchase either individually at the stated prices or a three-item bundle with a price of $1,800. The bundle price includes delivery and installation. Economy provides delivery and installation as a standalone service for any of its products for a price of $100.

Instructions

Respond to the requirements related to the following independent revenue arrangements for Economy Appliance Co.

(a) On June 1, 2014, Economy sold 100 washer/dryer units without installation to Laplante Rentals for $70,000. Laplante is a newer customer and is unsure how this product will work in its older rental units. Economy offers a 60-day return privilege and estimates, based on prior experience with sales on this product, 4% of the units will be returned. Prepare the journal entries for the sale and related cost of goods sold on June 1, 2014.

(b) YellowCard Property Managers operates upscale student apartment buildings. On May 1, 2014, Economy signs a contract with YellowCard for 300 appliance bundles to be delivered and installed in one of its new buildings. YellowCard pays 20% cash at contract signing and will pay the balance upon delivery and installation no later than August 1, 2014. Prepare journal entries for Economy on (1) May 1, 2014, and (2) August 1, 2014, when all appliances are delivered and installed.

(c) Refer to the arrangement in part (b). It would help YellowCard secure lease agreements with students if the delivery and installation of the appliance bundles can be completed by July 1, 2014. YellowCard offers a 10% bonus payment if Economy can complete delivery and installation by July 1, 2014. Economy estimates its chances of meeting the bonus deadline to be 60%, based on a number of prior contracts of similar scale. Repeat the requirement for part (b), given this bonus provision. Assume installation is completed by July 1, 2014.

(d) Epic Rentals would like to take advantage of the bundle price for its 400-unit project; on February 1, 2014, Economy signs a contract with Epic for delivery and installation of 400 bundles. Under the agreement, Economy will hold the appliance bundles in its warehouses until the new rental units are ready for installation. Epic pays 10% cash at contract signing. On April 1, 2014, Economy completes manufacture of the appliances in the Epic bundle order and places them in the warehouse. Economy and Epic have documented the warehouse arrangement and identified the units designated for Epic. The units are ready to ship, and Economy may not sell these units to other customers. Prepare journal entries for Economy on (1) February 1, 2014, and (2) April 1, 2014.

6 8 **P18-5 (Allocate Transaction Price, Returns, and Consignments)** Ritt Ranch & Farm is a distributor of ranch and farm equipment. Its products range from small tools, power equipment for trench-digging and fencing, grain dryers, and barn winches. Most products are sold direct via its company catalog and Internet site. However, given some of its specialty products, select farm implement stores carry Ritt's products. Pricing and cost information on three of Ritt's most popular products are as follows.

Item	Standalone Selling Price (Cost)
Mini-trencher	$ 3,600 ($2,000)
Power fence hole auger	1,200 ($800)
Grain/Hay dryer	14,000 ($11,000)

Instructions

Respond to the requirements related to the following independent revenue arrangements for Ritt Ranch & Farm.

(a) On January 1, 2014, Ritt sells augers to Mills Farm & Fleet for $48,000. Mills signs a 6-month note at an annual interest rate of 12%. Ritt allows Mills to return any auger that it cannot use within 60 days and receive a full refund. Based on prior experience, Ritt estimates that 5% of units sold to customers like Mills will be returned (using the most likely outcome approach). Ritt's costs to recover the products will be immaterial, and the returned augers are expected to be resold at a profit. Prepare the journal entry for Ritt on January 1, 2014.

(b) On August 10, 2014, Ritt sells 16 mini-trenchers to a farm co-op in western Minnesota. Ritt provides a 4% volume discount on the mini-trenchers if the co-op has a 15% increase in purchases from Ritt compared to the prior year. Given the slowdown in the farm economy, sales to the co-op have been flat, and it is highly uncertain that the benchmark will be met. Prepare the journal entry for Ritt on August 10, 2014.

(c) Ritt sells three grain/hay dryers to a local farmer at a total contract price of $45,200. In addition to the dryers, Ritt provides installation, which has a standalone sales value of $1,000 per unit installed. The contract payment also includes a $1,200 maintenance plan for the dryers for 3 years after installation. Ritt signs the contract on June 20, 2014, and receives a 20% down payment from the farmer. The dryers are delivered and installed on October 1, 2014, and full payment is made to Ritt. Prepare the journal entries for Ritt in 2014 related to this arrangement.

(d) On April 25, 2014, Ritt ships 100 augers to Farm Depot, a farm supply dealer in Nebraska, on consignment. By June 30, 2014, Farm Depot has sold 60 of the consigned augers at the listed price of $1,200 per unit. Farm Depot notifies Ritt of the sales, retains a 10% commission, and remits the cash due Ritt. Prepare the journal entries for Ritt and Farm Depot for the consignment arrangement.

8 **P18-6 (Warranty, Customer Loyalty Program)** Hale Hardware takes pride as the "shop around the corner" that can compete with the big-box home improvement stores by providing good service from knowledgeable sales associates (many of whom are retired local handymen). Hale has developed the following two revenue arrangements to enhance its relationships with customers and increase its bottom line.

1. Hale sells a specialty portable winch that is popular with many of the local customers for use at their lake homes (putting docks in and out, launching boats, etc.). The Hale winch is a standard manufacture winch that Hale modifies so the winch can be used for a variety of tasks. Hale sold 70 of these winches during 2014 at a total price of $21,000, with a warranty guarantee that the product was free of any defects. The cost of winches sold is $16,000. The assurance warranties extend for a 3-year period with an estimated cost of $2,100. In addition, Hale sold extended warranties related to 20 Hale winches for 2 years beyond the 3-year period for $400 each.

2. To bolster its already strong customer base, Hale implemented a customer loyalty program that rewards a customer with 1 loyalty point for every $10 of purchases on a select group of Hale products. Each point is redeemable for a $1 discount on any purchases of Hale merchandise in

the following 2 years. During 2014, customers purchased select group products for $100,000 (all products are sold to provide a 45% gross profit) and earned 10,000 points redeemable for future purchases. The standalone selling price of the purchased products is $100,000. Based on prior experience with incentives programs like this, Hale expects 9,500 points to be redeemed related to these sales (Hale appropriately uses this experience to estimate the value of future consideration related to bonus points).

Instructions

(a) Identify the separate performance obligations in the Hale warranty and bonus point programs, and briefly explain the point in time when the performance obligations are satisfied.

(b) Prepare the journal entries for Hale related to the sales of Hale winches with warranties.

(c) Prepare the journal entries for the bonus point sales for Hale in 2014.

(d) How much additional sales revenue is recognized by Hale in 2015, assuming 4,500 bonus points are redeemed?

8 **P18-7 (Customer Loyalty Program)** Martz Inc. has a customer loyalty program that rewards a customer with 1 customer loyalty point for every $10 of purchases. Each point is redeemable for a $3 discount on any future purchases. On July 2, 2014, customers purchase products for $300,000 (with a cost of $171,000) and earn 30,000 points redeemable for future purchases. Martz expects 25,000 points to be redeemed (based on its past experience, which is predictive of the amount of consideration to which it will be entitled). Martz estimates a standalone selling price of $2.50 per point (or $75,000 total) on the basis of the likelihood of redemption. The points provide a material right to customers that they would not receive without entering into a contract. As a result, Martz concludes that the points are a separate performance obligation.

Instructions

(a) Determine the transaction price for the product and the customer loyalty points.

(b) Prepare the journal entries to record the sale of the product and related points on July 2, 2014.

(c) At the end of the first reporting period (July 31, 2014), 10,000 loyalty points are redeemed. Martz continues to expect 25,000 loyalty points to be redeemed in total. Determine the amount of loyalty point revenue to be recognized at July 31, 2014.

  P18-8 (Comprehensive Three-Part Revenue Recognition) Van Hatten Consolidated has three operating divisions: DeMent Publishing Division, Ankiel Securities Division, and Depp Advisory Division. Each division maintains its own accounting system.

DeMent Publishing Division

The DeMent Publishing Division sells large volumes of novels to a few book distributors, which in turn sell to several national chains of bookstores. DeMent allows distributors to return up to 30% of sales, and distributors give the same terms to bookstores. While returns from individual titles fluctuate greatly, the returns from distributors have averaged 20% in each of the past 5 years. A total of $7,000,000 of paperback novel sales were made to distributors during fiscal 2014. On November 30, 2014 (the end of the fiscal year), $1,500,000 of fiscal 2014 sales were still subject to return privileges over the next 6 months. The remaining $5,500,000 of fiscal 2014 sales had actual returns of 21%. Sales from fiscal 2013 totaling $2,000,000 were collected in fiscal 2014 less 18% returns. This division records revenue according to the revenue recognition method when the right of return exists.

Ankiel Securities Division

The Ankiel Securities Division works through manufacturers' agents in various cities. Orders for alarm systems and down payments are forwarded from agents, and the division ships the goods f.o.b. factory directly to customers (usually police departments and security guard companies). Customers are billed directly for the balance due plus actual shipping costs. The company received orders for $6,000,000 of goods during the fiscal year ended November 30, 2014. Down payments of $600,000 were received, and $5,200,000 of goods were billed and shipped. Actual freight costs of $100,000 were also billed. Commissions of 10% on product price are paid to manufacturing agents after goods are shipped to customers. Such goods are warranted for 90 days after shipment, and warranty returns have been about 1% of sales. Revenue is recognized at the point of sale by this division.

Depp Advisory Division

The Depp Advisory Division provides asset management services. This division grew out of Van Hatten's own treasury and asset management operations that several of its customers asked to have access to. On January 1, 2014, Depp entered into a contract with Scutaro Co. to perform asset management services for

1 year. Depp receives a quarterly management fee of 0.25% of Scutaro's assets under management at the end of each quarter. In addition, Depp receives a performance-based incentive fee of 20% of the fund's annual return in excess of the return of the S&P 500 index at the end of the quarter (multiplied by the assets under management at quarter-end). At the end of the first quarter of 2014, Depp was managing $2,400,000 of Scutaro assets. The annualized return on the portfolio was 6.2% (the S&P 500 index had an annualized return of 5.7%).

Instructions

(a) For each division's revenue arrangements, identify the separate performance obligations, briefly explain allocation of the transaction process to each performance obligation, and indicate when the performance obligations are satisfied.

(b) Compute the revenue to be recognized in fiscal year 2014 for each of the three operating divisions of Van Hatten in accordance with generally accepted accounting principles.

5 8 P18-9 (Time Value, Gift Cards, Discounts) Presented below are three independent revenue arrangements for Colbert Company.

Instructions

Respond to the requirements related to each revenue arrangement.

(a) Colbert sells 3-D printer systems. Recently, Colbert provided a special promotion of zero-interest financing for 2 years on any new 3-D printer system. Assume that Colbert sells Lyle Cartright a 3-D system receiving a $5,000 zero-interest-bearing note on January 1, 2014. The cost of the 3-D printer system is $4,000. Colbert imputes a 6% interest rate on this zero-interest note transaction. Prepare the journal entry to record the sale on January 1, 2014, and compute the total amount of revenue to be recognized in 2014.

(b) Colbert sells 20 nonrefundable $100 gift cards for 3-D printer paper on March 1, 2014. The paper has a standalone selling price of $100 (cost $80). The gift cards expiration date is June 30, 2014. Colbert estimates that customers will not redeem 10% of these gift cards. The pattern of redemption is as follows.

	Redemption Total
March 31	50%
April 30	80%
June 30	85%

Prepare the 2014 journal entries related to the gift cards at March 1, March 31, April 30, and June 30.

(c) Colbert sells 3-D printers along with a number of retail items. The package price and standalone selling prices of each item are as follows

Item	Standalone Selling Price	Price When Bundled	Bundling Discount
3-D printer (cost $4,000)	$5,000	$4,500	$500
Custom stand (cost $200)	450	450	0
Special 3-D paper (cost $135)	175	175	0
Total for bundle	$5,625	$5,125	$500

Due to the timing of delivery—the paper is delivered 6 months after the printer is delivered to the customer—Colbert chooses to account for two performance obligations: (1) the printer and stand, and (2) the paper. Prepare the journal entries for Colbert on (a) March 1, 2014, when Colbert receives $51,250 for the sale of 10 printer bundles, and (b) September 1, 2014, when the paper is delivered to customers.

10 11 *P18-10 (Recognition of Profit on Long-Term Contract) Shanahan Construction Company has entered into a contract beginning January 1, 2014, to build a parking complex. It has been estimated that the complex will cost $600,000 and will take 3 years to construct. The complex will be billed to the purchasing company at $900,000. The following data pertain to the construction period.

	2014	2015	2016
Costs to date	$270,000	$450,000	$610,000
Estimated costs to complete	330,000	150,000	–0–
Progress billings to date	270,000	550,000	900,000
Cash collected to date	240,000	500,000	900,000

Instructions

(a) Using the percentage-of-completion method, compute the estimated gross profit that would be recognized during each year of the construction period.

(b) Using the completed-contract method, compute the estimated gross profit that would be recognized during each year of the construction period.

10 ***P18-11 (Long-Term Contract with Interim Loss)** On March 1, 2014, Pechstein Construction Company
11 contracted to construct a factory building for Fabrik Manufacturing Inc. for a total contract price of
12 $8,400,000. The building was completed by October 31, 2016. The annual contract costs incurred, estimated costs to complete the contract, and accumulated billings to Fabrik for 2014, 2015, and 2016 are given below.

	2014	2015	2016
Contract costs incurred during the year	$2,880,000	$2,230,000	$2,190,000
Estimated costs to complete the contract at 12/31	3,520,000	2,190,000	–0–
Billings to Fabrik during the year	3,200,000	3,500,000	1,700,000

Instructions

(a) Using the percentage-of-completion method, prepare schedules to compute the profit or loss to be recognized as a result of this contract for the years ended December 31, 2014, 2015, and 2016. (Ignore income taxes.)

(b) Using the completed-contract method, prepare schedules to compute the profit or loss to be recognized as a result of this contract for the years ended December 31, 2014, 2015, and 2016. (Ignore incomes taxes.)

10 ***P18-12 (Long-Term Contract with an Overall Loss)** On July 1, 2014, Torvill Construction Company Inc.
11 contracted to build an office building for Gumbel Corp. for a total contract price of $1,900,000. On July 1,
12 Torvill estimated that it would take between 2 and 3 years to complete the building. On December 31, 2016, the building was deemed substantially completed. Following are accumulated contract costs incurred, estimated costs to complete the contract, and accumulated billings to Gumbel for 2014, 2015, and 2016.

	At 12/31/14	At 12/31/15	At 12/31/16
Contract costs incurred to date	$ 300,000	$1,200,000	$2,100,000
Estimated costs to complete the contract	1,200,000	800,000	–0–
Billings to Gumbel	300,000	1,100,000	1,850,000

Instructions

(a) Using the percentage-of-completion method, prepare schedules to compute the profit or loss to be recognized as a result of this contract for the years ended December 31, 2014, 2015, and 2016. (Ignore income taxes.)

(b) Using the completed-contract method, prepare schedules to compute the profit or loss to be recognized as a result of this contract for the years ended December 31, 2014, 2015, and 2016. (Ignore income taxes.)

13 ***P18-13 (Franchise Revenue)** Amigos Burrito Inc. sells franchises to independent operators throughout the northwestern part of the United States. The contract with the franchisee includes the following provisions.

1. The franchisee is charged an initial fee of $120,000. Of this amount, $20,000 is payable when the agreement is signed, and a $20,000 zero-interest-bearing note is payable at the end of each of the 5 subsequent years.

2. All of the initial franchise fee collected by Amigos is to be refunded and the remaining obligation canceled if, for any reason, the franchisee fails to open his or her franchise.

3. In return for the initial franchise fee, Amigos agrees to (a) assist the franchisee in selecting the location for the business, (b) negotiate the lease for the land, (c) obtain financing and assist with building design, (d) supervise construction, (e) establish accounting and tax records, and (f) provide expert advice over a 5-year period relating to such matters as employee and management training, quality control, and promotion. This continuing involvement by Amigos helps maintain the brand value of the franchise.

4. In addition to the initial franchise fee, the franchisee is required to pay to Amigos a monthly fee of 2% of sales for menu planning, recipe innovations, and the privilege of purchasing ingredients from Amigos at or below prevailing market prices.

XLS

Management of Amigos Burrito estimates that the value of the services rendered to the franchisee at the time the contract is signed amounts to at least $20,000. All franchisees to date have opened their locations at the scheduled time, and none have defaulted on any of the notes receivable. The credit ratings of all franchisees would entitle them to borrow at the current interest rate of 10%. The present value of an ordinary annuity of five annual receipts of $20,000 each discounted at 10% is $75,816.

Instructions

(a) Discuss the alternatives that Amigos Burrito Inc. might use to account for the franchise fees.

(b) Prepare the journal entries for the initial and continuing franchise fees, assuming:

(1) Franchise agreement is signed on January 5, 2014.

(2) Amigos completes franchise startup tasks and the franchise opens on July 1, 2014.

(3) The franchisee records $260,000 in sales in the first 6 months of operations and remits the monthly franchise fee on December 31, 2014.

(c) Briefly describe the accounting for unearned franchise fees, assuming that Amigos has little or no involvement with the franchisee related to expert advice on employee and management training, quality control, and promotion, once the franchise opens.

PROBLEMS SET B

See the book's companion website, at **www.wiley.com/college/kieso**, for an additional set of problems.

CONCEPTS FOR ANALYSIS

CA18-1 (Five-Step Revenue Process) Revenue is recognized based on a five-step process that is applied to a company's revenue arrangements.

Instructions

(a) Briefly describe the five-step process.

(b) Explain the importance of contracts when analyzing revenue arrangements.

(c) How are fair value measurement concepts applied in implementation of the five-step process?

(d) How does the five-step process reflect application of the definitions of assets and liabilities?

CA18-2 (Satisfying Performance Obligations) Judy Schaeffer is getting up to speed on the new guidance on revenue recognition. She is trying to understand the revenue recognition principle as it relates to the five-step revenue recognition process.

Instructions

(a) Describe the revenue recognition principle.

(b) Briefly discuss how the revenue recognition principle relates to the definitions of assets and liabilities. What is the importance of control?

(c) Judy recalls that previous revenue recognition guidance required that revenue not be recognized unless the revenue was realized or realizable (also referred to as collectibility). Is collectibility a consideration in the recognition of revenue? Explain.

CA18-3 (Recognition of Revenue—Theory) Revenue is usually recognized at the point of sale (a point in time). Under special circumstances, however, bases other than the point of sale are used for the timing of revenue recognition.

Instructions

(a) Why is the point of sale usually used as the basis for the timing of revenue recognition?

(b) Disregarding the special circumstances when bases other than the point of sale are used, discuss the merits of each of the following objections to the point-of-sale basis of revenue recognition:

(1) It is too conservative because revenue is earned throughout the entire process of production.

(2) It is not conservative enough because accounts receivable do not represent disposable funds, sales returns and allowances may be made, and collection and bad debt expenses may be incurred in a later period.

(c) Revenue may also be recognized over time. Give an example of the circumstances in which revenue is recognized over time and accounting merits of its use instead of the point-of-sale basis.

(AICPA adapted)

CA18-4 (Recognition of Revenue—Theory) Revenue is recognized for accounting purposes when a performance obligation is satisfied. In some situations, revenue is recognized over time as the fair values of assets and liabilities change. In other situations, however, accountants have developed guidelines for recognizing revenue at the point of sale.

Instructions
(Ignore income taxes.)

(a) Explain and justify why revenue is often recognized at time of sale.
(b) Explain in what situations it would be appropriate to recognize revenue over time.

CA18-5 (Discounts) Fahey Company sells Stairmasters to a retailer, Physical Fitness, Inc., for $2,000,000. Fahey has a history of providing price concessions on this product if the retailer has difficulty selling the Stairmasters to customers. Fahey has experience with sales like these in the past and estimates that the maximum amount of price concessions is $300,000.

Instructions

(a) Determine the amount of revenue that Fahey should recognize at the date of the sale of Stairmasters to Physical Fitness, Inc.
(b) According to GAAP, in some situations, the amount of revenue recognized may be constrained. Explain how the accounting for the Stairmasters sales might be affected by the revenue constraint due to variable consideration or returns.
(c) Some believe that revenue recognition should be constrained by collectibility. Is such a view consistent with GAAP? Explain.

CA18-6 (Recognition of Revenue from Subscriptions) *Cutting Edge* is a monthly magazine that has been on the market for 18 months. It currently has a circulation of 1.4 million copies. Negotiations are underway to obtain a bank loan in order to update the magazine's facilities. *Cutting Edge* is producing close to capacity and expects to grow at an average of 20% per year over the next 3 years.

After reviewing the financial statements of *Cutting Edge*, Andy Rich, the bank loan officer, had indicated that a loan could be offered to *Cutting Edge* only if it could increase its current ratio and decrease its debt to equity ratio to a specified level. Jonathan Embry, the marketing manager of *Cutting Edge*, has devised a plan to meet these requirements. Embry indicates that an advertising campaign can be initiated to immediately increase circulation. The potential customers would be contacted after the purchase of another magazine's mailing list. The campaign would include:

1. An offer to subscribe to *Cutting Edge* at three-fourths the normal price.
2. A special offer to all new subscribers to receive the most current world atlas whenever requested at a guaranteed price of $2.
3. An unconditional guarantee that any subscriber will receive a full refund if dissatisfied with the magazine.

Although the offer of a full refund is risky, Embry claims that few people will ask for a refund after receiving half of their subscription issues. Embry notes that other magazine companies have tried this sales promotion technique and experienced great success. Their average cancellation rate was 25%. On average, each company increased its initial circulation threefold and in the long run increased circulation to twice that which existed before the promotion. In addition, 60% of the new subscribers are expected to take advantage of the atlas premium. Embry feels confident that the increased subscriptions from the advertising campaign will increase the current ratio and decrease the debt to equity ratio.

You are the controller of *Cutting Edge* and must give your opinion of the proposed plan.

Instructions

(a) When should revenue from the new subscriptions be recognized?
(b) How would you classify the estimated sales returns stemming from the unconditional guarantee?
(c) How should the atlas premium be recorded? Is the estimated premium claims a liability? Explain.
(d) Does the proposed plan achieve the goals of increasing the current ratio and decreasing the debt to equity ratio?

CA18-7 (Recognition of Revenue—Bonus Points) Griseta & Dubel Inc. was formed early this year to sell merchandise credits to merchants, who distribute the credits free to their customers. For example, customers can earn additional credits based on the dollars they spend with a merchant (e.g., airlines and hotels). Accounts for accumulating the credits and catalogs illustrating the merchandise for which the credits may be exchanged are maintained online. Centers with inventories of merchandise premiums have been established for redemption of the credits. Merchants may not return unused credits to Griseta & Dubel.

The following schedule expresses Griseta & Dubel's expectations as to the percentages of a normal month's activity that will be attained. For this purpose, a "normal month's activity" is defined as the level of operations expected when expansion of activities ceases or tapers off to a stable rate. The company expects that this level will be attained in the third year and that sales of credits will average $6,000,000 per month throughout the third year.

Month	Actual Credit Sales Percent	Merchandise Premium Purchases Percent	Credit Redemptions Percent
6th	30%	40%	10%
12th	60	60	45
18th	80	80	70
24th	90	90	80
30th	100	100	95

Griseta & Dubel plans to adopt an annual closing date at the end of each 12 months of operation.

Instructions
   (a) Discuss the factors to be considered in determining when revenue should be recognized.
   (b) Apply the revenue recognition factors to the Griseta & Dubel Inc. revenue arrangement.
   (c) Provide balance sheet accounts that should be used and indicate how each should be classified.

(AICPA adapted)

CA18-8 (Revenue Recognition—Membership Fees) Midwest Health Club (MHC) offers 1-year memberships. Membership fees are due in full at the beginning of the individual membership period. As an incentive to new customers, MHC advertised that any customers not satisfied for any reason could receive a refund of the remaining portion of unused membership fees. As a result of this policy, Richard Nies, corporate controller, recognized revenue ratably over the life of the membership. MHC is in the process of preparing its year-end financial statements. Rachel Avery, MHC's treasurer, is concerned about the company's lackluster performance this year. She reviews the financial statements Nies prepared and tells Nies to recognize membership revenue when the fees are received.

Instructions
Answer the following questions.

   (a) What are the ethical issues involved?
   (b) What should Nies do?

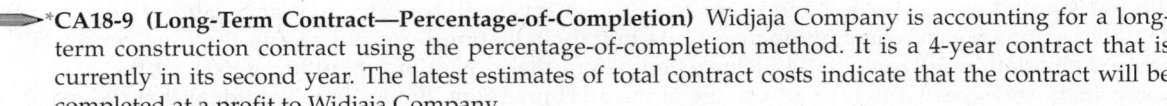

*CA18-9 (Long-Term Contract—Percentage-of-Completion)** Widjaja Company is accounting for a long-term construction contract using the percentage-of-completion method. It is a 4-year contract that is currently in its second year. The latest estimates of total contract costs indicate that the contract will be completed at a profit to Widjaja Company.

Instructions
   (a) What theoretical justification is there for Widjaja Company's use of the percentage-of-completion method?
   (b) How would progress billings be accounted for? Include in your discussion the classification of progress billings in Widjaja Company financial statements.
   (c) How would the income recognized in the second year of the 4-year contract be determined using the cost-to-cost method of determining percentage of completion?
   (d) What would be the effect on earnings per share in the second year of the 4-year contract of using the percentage-of-completion method instead of the completed-contract method? Discuss.

(AICPA adapted)

USING YOUR JUDGMENT

As the new revenue recognition guidance is not yet implemented, note that the financial statements and notes for Procter & Gamble, Coca-Cola, PepsiCo, and Westinghouse reflect revenue recognition under prior standards.

FINANCIAL REPORTING

Financial Reporting Problem

P&G **The Procter & Gamble Company (P&G)**

The financial statements of **P&G** are presented in Appendix 5B. The company's complete annual report, including the notes to the financial statements, can be accessed at the book's companion website, **www.wiley.com/college/kieso.**

Instructions

Refer to P&G's financial statements and the accompanying notes to answer the following questions.

(a) What were P&G's net sales for 2011?
(b) What was the percentage of increase or decrease in P&G's net sales from 2010 to 2011? From 2009 to 2010? From 2009 to 2011?
(c) In its notes to the financial statements, what criteria does P&G use to recognize revenue?
(d) How does P&G account for trade promotions? Does the accounting conform to accrual accounting concepts? Explain.

Comparative Analysis Case

The Coca-Cola Company and PepsiCo, Inc.

Instructions

Go to the book's companion website and use information found there to answer the following questions related to **The Coca-Cola Company** and **PepsiCo, Inc.**

(a) What were Coca-Cola's and PepsiCo's net revenues (sales) for the year 2011? Which company increased its revenue more (dollars and percentage) from 2010 to 2011?

(b) Are the revenue recognition policies of Coca-Cola and PepsiCo similar? Explain.

(c) In which foreign countries (geographic areas) did Coca-Cola and PepsiCo experience significant revenues in 2011? Compare the amounts of foreign revenues to U.S. revenues for both Coca-Cola and PepsiCo.

Financial Statement Analysis Case

Westinghouse Electric Corporation

The following note appears in the "Summary of Significant Accounting Policies" section of the Annual Report of **Westinghouse Electric Corporation**.

> **Note 1 (in part): Revenue Recognition.** Sales are primarily recorded as products are shipped and services are rendered. The percentage-of-completion method of accounting is used for nuclear steam supply system orders with delivery schedules generally in excess of five years and for certain construction projects where this method of accounting is consistent with industry practice.
>
> WFSI revenues are generally recognized on the accrual method. When accounts become delinquent for more than two payment periods, usually 60 days, income is recognized only as payments are received. Such delinquent accounts for which no payments are received in the current month, and other accounts on which income is not being recognized because the receipt of either principal or interest is questionable, are classified as nonearning receivables.

Instructions

(a) Identify the revenue recognition methods used by Westinghouse Electric as discussed in its note on significant accounting policies.

(b) Under what conditions are the revenue recognition methods identified in the first paragraph of Westinghouse's note above acceptable?

(c) From the information provided in the second paragraph of Westinghouse's note, identify the type of operation being described and defend the acceptability of the revenue recognition method.

Accounting, Analysis, and Principles

Diversified Industries manufactures sump-pumps. Its most popular product is called the Super Soaker, which has a retail price of $1,200 and costs $540 to manufacture. It sells the Super Soaker on a stand-alone basis directly to businesses. Diversified also provides installation services for these commercial customers, who want an emergency pumping capability (with regular and back-up generator power) at their businesses. Diversified also distributes the Super Soaker through a consignment agreement with Menards. Income data for the first quarter of 2014 from operations other than the Super Soaker are as follows.

Revenues	$9,500,000
Expenses	7,750,000

Diversified has the following information related to two Super Soaker revenue arrangements during the first quarter of 2014.

1. Diversified sells 30 Super Soakers to businesses in flood-prone areas for a total contract price of $54,600. In addition to the pumps, Diversified also provides installation (at a cost of $150 per pump). On a standalone basis, the fair value of this service is $200 per unit installed. The contract payment also includes a $10 per month service plan for the pumps for 3 years after installation (Diversified's cost to provide this service is $7 per month). The Super Soakers are delivered and installed on March 1, 2014, and full payment is made to Diversified. Any discount is applied to the pump/installation bundle.

2. Diversified ships 300 Super Soakers to Menards on consignment. By March 31, 2014, Menards has sold two-thirds of the consigned merchandise at the listed price of $1,200 per unit. Menards notifies Diversified of the sales, retains a 5% commission, and remits the cash due Diversified.

Accounting

Determine Diversified Industries' 2014 first-quarter net income. (Ignore taxes.)

Analysis

Determine free cash flow (see Chapter 5) for Diversified Industries for the first quarter of 2014. In the first quarter, Diversified had depreciation expense of $175,000 and a net increase in working capital (change in accounts receivable and accounts payable) of $250,000. In the first quarter, capital expenditures were $500,000; Diversified paid dividends of $120,000.

Principles

Explain how the five-step revenue recognition process, when applied to Diversified's two revenue arrangements, reflects the concept of control in the definition of an asset and trade-offs between relevance and faithful representation.

BRIDGE TO THE PROFESSION

Professional Research: FASB Codification

Employees at your company disagree about the accounting for sales returns. The sales manager believes that granting more generous return provisions can give the company a competitive edge and increase sales revenue. The controller cautions that, depending on the terms granted, loose return provisions might lead to non-GAAP revenue recognition. The company CFO would like you to research the issue to provide an authoritative answer.

Instructions

If your school has a subscription to the FASB Codification, go to *http://aaahq.org/ascLogin.cfm* to log in and prepare responses to the following. Provide Codification references for your responses. (Provide paragraph citations.)

(a) What is the authoritative literature addressing revenue recognition when right of return exists?

(b) What is meant by "right of return"? "Bill and hold"?

(c) Describe the accounting when there is a right of return.

(d) When goods are sold on a bill-and-hold basis, what conditions must be met to recognize revenue upon receipt of the order?

Additional Professional Resources

See the book's companion website, at **www.wiley.com/college/kieso**, for professional simulations as well as other study resources.

Remember to check the book's companion website to find additional resources for this chapter.

Notes

Notes

How Much Is Enough?

In the wake of the economic downturn due to the financial crisis, a number of companies and numerous banks reported operating losses. As you will learn in this chapter, the tax code allows companies that report operating losses to claim a tax credit related to these losses for taxes paid in the past (referred to as "carrybacks") and to offset taxable income in periods following the operating loss (referred to as "carryforwards"). When companies use these offsets, they reduce income tax expense, which increases net income. For tax carryforwards, companies also record a deferred tax asset, which measures the expected future net cash inflows from lower taxable income in future periods.

Citigroup is a good example of a company that has used operating loss credits to reduce its tax bill. In 2008, it had deferred tax assets (DTAs) of $28.5 billion, which represented 80 percent of stockholders' equity and nearly eclipsed the bank's market value of equity. Some analysts have raised concerns about Citi's DTAs and whether these assets will ever be realized by Citi. Why the concerns?

Well, in order to receive the tax deductions in future years, a company like Citigroup needs to be reasonably sure it will have taxable income in the future. In Citi's case, analysts predict that the struggling bank will need to earn $99 billion in taxable income over the next 20 years. Given that Citigroup recorded operating losses of $60 billion in 2008 and 2009, some are skeptical that the DTAs will be realized. As a result, market watchers are debating whether Citi should set up an allowance to reduce its deferred tax assets due to the possibility that the assets will not be realized. Not surprisingly, Citigroup has resisted setting up an allowance as it would reduce its DTAs and increase its income tax expense.

This accounting does not sit well with some market observers. As one critic noted, "Why should auditors, investors, regulators and others rely on Citigroup's projections . . . to justify the use (realizability) of their DTAs?" Former SEC chief accountant, Lynn Turner, agrees: "Citi's position defies imagination and logic. Instead of talking about making money, what Citi ought to do is to reserve for at least part of the deferred tax assets and reap the benefit of reducing the reserves once it actually makes money."

CONCEPTUAL FOCUS

> Read the **Evolving Issue** on page 1143 for a discussion of uncertain tax positions.

INTERNATIONAL FOCUS

> See the **International Perspectives** on pages 1119, 1128, 1137, 1140, and 1145.
> Read the **IFRS Insights** on pages 1175–1181 for a discussion of:
 —Deferred tax asset (non-recognition)
 —Statement of financial position classification

In response, Citigroup, which accumulated deferred tax assets partly because of its huge losses during the financial crisis, said it was "very comfortable with the recording of our deferred tax assets." And some market analysts sided with the bank, remarking that Citi's accounts were not out of order due to a misstatement of its DTAs. The Citigroup debate has arisen because accounting standards on DTAs are vague, stating that an allowance is not needed if management believes it is "more likely than not" the company will earn enough taxable income in the future.

This debate over Citigroup's accounting highlights the extent to which management judgment plays an important role in the accounting for taxes. After studying this chapter, you should be better able to evaluate Citigroup's accounting as well as the other judgments inherent in the accounting for income taxes.

Sources: Adapted from J. Weil, "Citigroup's Capital Was All Casing, No Meat," *www.bloomberg.net* (November 24, 2008); and F. Guerra and J. Eaglesham, "Citi Under Fire Over Deferred Tax Assets," *Financial Times* (September 6, 2010).

PREVIEW OF CHAPTER   19

As our opening story indicates, the accounting for income taxes involves significant judgment. Investors need to be knowledgeable of the accounting provisions related to taxes to be able to evaluate these judgments. Thus, companies must present financial information to the investment community that provides a clear picture of present and potential tax obligations and tax benefits. In this chapter, we discuss the basic guidelines that companies must follow in reporting income taxes. The content and organization of the chapter are as follows.

Accounting for Income Taxes

Fundamentals of Accounting for Income Taxes	Accounting for Net Operating Losses	Financial Statement Presentation	Review of the Asset-Liability Method
• Future taxable amounts and deferred taxes • Future deductible amounts and deferred taxes • Valuation allowance • Income statement presentation • Specific differences • Rate considerations	• Loss carryback • Loss carryforward • Loss carryback example • Loss carryforward example	• Balance sheet • Income statement	

FUNDAMENTALS OF ACCOUNTING FOR INCOME TAXES

Up to this point, you have learned the basic guidelines that corporations use to report information to investors and creditors. Corporations also must file income tax returns following the guidelines developed by the Internal Revenue Service (IRS). Because GAAP and tax regulations differ in a number of ways, so frequently do pretax financial income and taxable income. Consequently, the amount that a company reports as tax expense will differ from the amount of taxes payable to the IRS. Illustration 19-1 highlights these differences.

ILLUSTRATION 19-1
Fundamental Differences between Financial and Tax Reporting

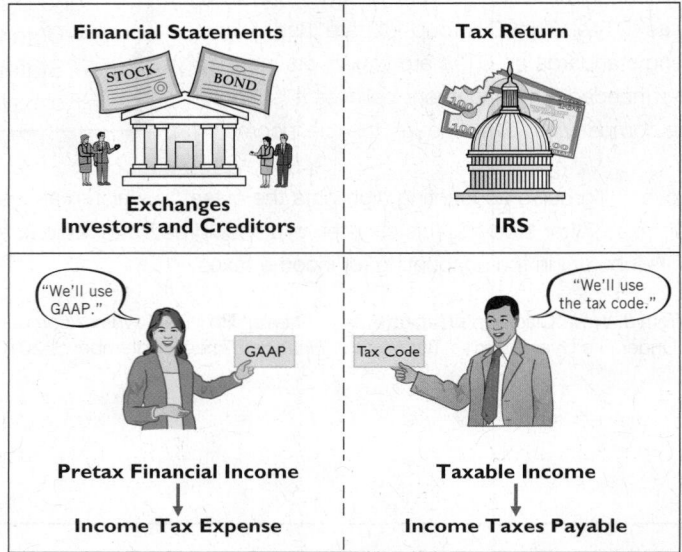

Pretax financial income is a **financial reporting** term. It also is often referred to as income before taxes, income for financial reporting purposes, or income for book purposes. Companies determine pretax financial income according to GAAP. They measure it with the objective of providing useful information to investors and creditors.

Taxable income (income for tax purposes) is a **tax accounting** term. It indicates the amount used to compute income taxes payable. Companies determine taxable income according to the Internal Revenue Code (the tax code). Income taxes provide money to support government operations.

To illustrate how differences in GAAP and IRS rules affect financial reporting and taxable income, assume that Chelsea Inc. reported revenues of $130,000 and expenses of $60,000 in each of its first three years of operations. Illustration 19-2 shows the (partial) income statement over these three years.

ILLUSTRATION 19-2
Financial Reporting Income

CHELSEA INC. GAAP REPORTING				
	2014	2015	2016	Total
Revenues	$130,000	$130,000	$130,000	
Expenses	60,000	60,000	60,000	
Pretax financial income	$ 70,000	$ 70,000	$ 70,000	$210,000
Income tax expense (40%)	$ 28,000	$ 28,000	$ 28,000	$ 84,000

For tax purposes (following the tax code), Chelsea reported the same expenses to the IRS in each of the years. But, as Illustration 19-3 shows, Chelsea reported taxable revenues of $100,000 in 2014, $150,000 in 2015, and $140,000 in 2016.

CHELSEA INC. TAX REPORTING				
	2014	2015	2016	Total
Revenues	$100,000	$150,000	$140,000	
Expenses	60,000	60,000	60,000	
Taxable income	$ 40,000	$ 90,000	$ 80,000	$210,000
Income taxes payable (40%)	$ 16,000	$ 36,000	$ 32,000	$ 84,000

ILLUSTRATION 19-3
Tax Reporting Income

Income tax expense and income taxes payable differed over the three years but were equal **in total**, as Illustration 19-4 shows.

CHELSEA INC. INCOME TAX EXPENSE AND INCOME TAXES PAYABLE				
	2014	2015	2016	Total
Income tax expense	$28,000	$28,000	$28,000	$84,000
Income taxes payable	16,000	36,000	32,000	84,000
Difference	$12,000	$ (8,000)	$ (4,000)	$ 0

ILLUSTRATION 19-4
Comparison of Income Tax Expense to Income Taxes Payable

The differences between income tax expense and income taxes payable in this example arise for a simple reason. For financial reporting, companies use the full accrual method to report revenues. For tax purposes, they use a modified cash basis. As a result, Chelsea reports pretax financial income of $70,000 and income tax expense of $28,000 for each of the three years. However, taxable income fluctuates. For example, in 2014 taxable income is only $40,000, so Chelsea owes just $16,000 to the IRS that year. Chelsea classifies the income taxes payable as a current liability on the balance sheet.

As Illustration 19-4 indicates, for Chelsea the $12,000 ($28,000 − $16,000) difference between income tax expense and income taxes payable in 2014 reflects taxes that it will pay in future periods. This $12,000 difference is often referred to as a **deferred tax amount**. In this case, it is a **deferred tax liability**. In cases where taxes will be lower in the future, Chelsea records a **deferred tax asset**. We explain the measurement and accounting for deferred tax liabilities and assets in the following two sections.[1]

International Perspective

In some countries, taxable income equals pretax financial income. As a consequence, accounting for differences between tax and book income is insignificant.

Future Taxable Amounts and Deferred Taxes

The example summarized in Illustration 19-4 shows how income taxes payable can differ from income tax expense. This can happen when there are temporary differences between the amounts reported for tax purposes and those reported for

2 LEARNING OBJECTIVE
Describe a temporary difference that results in future taxable amounts.

---

[1]Determining the amount of tax to pay the IRS is a costly exercise for both individuals and companies. Individuals and businesses must pay not only the taxes owed but also the costs of their own time spent filing and complying with the tax code, including (1) the tax collection costs of the IRS, and (2) the tax compliance outlays that individuals and businesses pay to help them file their taxes. One study estimated this cost to be 30 cents on every dollar sent to the government. Another study noted how big the tax compliance industry has become. According to the research, the tax compliance industry employs more people than all the workers at Wal-Mart, UPS, McDonald's, IBM, and Citigroup combined. *Source:* A. Laffer, "The 30-Cent Tax Premium," *Wall Street Journal* (April 18, 2011).

book purposes. A **temporary difference** is the difference between the tax basis of an asset or liability and its reported (carrying or book) amount in the financial statements, which will result in taxable amounts or deductible amounts in future years. **Taxable amounts** increase taxable income in future years. **Deductible amounts** decrease taxable income in future years.

In Chelsea's situation, the only difference between the book basis and tax basis of the assets and liabilities relates to accounts receivable that arose from revenue recognized for book purposes. Illustration 19-5 indicates that Chelsea reports accounts receivable at $30,000 in the December 31, 2014, GAAP-basis balance sheet. However, the receivables have a zero tax basis.

ILLUSTRATION 19-5
Temporary Difference, Sales Revenue

Per Books	12/31/14	Per Tax Return	12/31/14
Accounts receivable	$30,000	Accounts receivable	$–0–

What will happen to the $30,000 temporary difference that originated in 2014 for Chelsea? Assuming that Chelsea expects to collect $20,000 of the receivables in 2015 and $10,000 in 2016, this collection results in future taxable amounts of $20,000 in 2015 and $10,000 in 2016. These future taxable amounts will cause taxable income to exceed pretax financial income in both 2015 and 2016.

An assumption inherent in a company's GAAP balance sheet is that companies recover and settle the assets and liabilities at their reported amounts (carrying amounts). This assumption creates a requirement under accrual accounting to recognize **currently** the deferred tax consequences of temporary differences. That is, companies recognize the amount of income taxes that are payable (or refundable) when they recover and settle the reported amounts of the assets and liabilities, respectively. Illustration 19-6 shows the reversal of the temporary difference described in Illustration 19-5 and the resulting taxable amounts in future periods.

ILLUSTRATION 19-6
Reversal of Temporary Difference, Chelsea Inc.

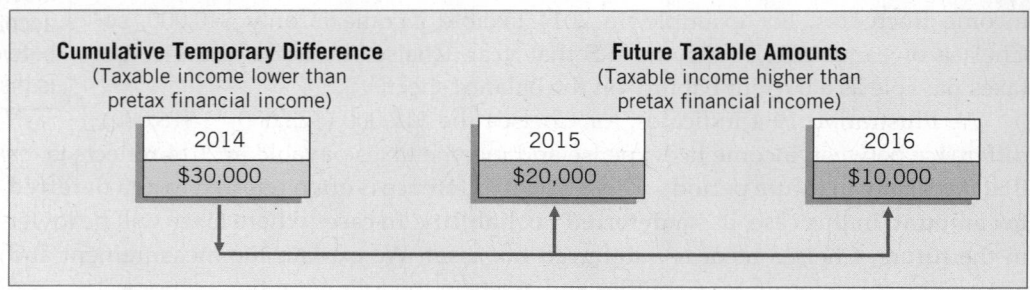

Chelsea assumes that it will collect the accounts receivable and report the $30,000 collection as taxable revenues in future tax returns. A payment of income tax in both 2015 and 2016 will occur. Chelsea should therefore record in its books in 2014 the deferred tax consequences of the revenue and related receivables reflected in the 2014 financial statements. Chelsea does this by recording a deferred tax liability.

Deferred Tax Liability

A **deferred tax liability** is the deferred tax consequences attributable to taxable temporary differences. In other words, **a deferred tax liability represents the increase in taxes payable in future years as a result of taxable temporary differences existing at the end of the current year**.

Recall from the Chelsea example that income taxes payable is $16,000 ($40,000 × 40%) in 2014 (Illustration 19-4 on page 1119). In addition, a temporary difference exists at year-end because Chelsea reports the revenue and related accounts receivable differently for book and tax purposes. The book basis of accounts receivable is $30,000, and the tax basis is zero. Thus, the total deferred tax liability at the end of 2014 is $12,000, computed as shown in Illustration 19-7.

Book basis of accounts receivable	$30,000
Tax basis of accounts receivable	–0–
Cumulative temporary difference at the end of 2014	30,000
Tax rate	40%
Deferred tax liability at the end of 2014	$12,000

ILLUSTRATION 19-7
Computation of Deferred
Tax Liability, End of 2014

Companies may also compute the deferred tax liability by preparing a schedule that indicates the future taxable amounts due to existing temporary differences. Such a schedule, as shown in Illustration 19-8, is particularly useful when the computations become more complex.

	Future Years		
	2015	2016	Total
Future taxable amounts	$20,000	$10,000	$30,000
Tax rate	40%	40%	
Deferred tax liability at the end of 2014	$ 8,000	$ 4,000	$12,000

ILLUSTRATION 19-8
Schedule of Future
Taxable Amounts

Because it is the first year of operations for Chelsea, there is no deferred tax liability at the beginning of the year. Chelsea computes the income tax expense for 2014 as shown in Illustration 19-9.

Deferred tax liability at end of 2014	$12,000
Deferred tax liability at beginning of 2014	–0–
Deferred tax expense for 2014	12,000
Current tax expense for 2014 (income taxes payable)	16,000
Income tax expense (total) for 2014	$28,000

ILLUSTRATION 19-9
Computation of Income
Tax Expense, 2014

This computation indicates that income tax expense has two components—**current tax expense** (the amount of income taxes payable for the period) and deferred tax expense. **Deferred tax expense** is the increase in the deferred tax liability balance from the beginning to the end of the accounting period.

Companies credit taxes due and payable to Income Taxes Payable, and credit the increase in deferred taxes to Deferred Tax Liability. They then debit the sum of those two items to Income Tax Expense. For Chelsea, it makes the following entry at the end of 2014.

Income Tax Expense	28,000	
Income Taxes Payable		16,000
Deferred Tax Liability		12,000

At the end of 2015 (the second year), the difference between the book basis and the tax basis of the accounts receivable is $10,000. Chelsea multiplies this difference by the applicable tax rate to arrive at the deferred tax liability of $4,000 ($10,000 × 40%), which it reports at the end of 2015. Income taxes payable for 2015 is $36,000 (Illustration 19-3 on page 1119), and the income tax expense for 2015 is as shown in Illustration 19-10 (page 1122).

ILLUSTRATION 19-10
Computation of Income
Tax Expense, 2015

Deferred tax liability at end of 2015	$ 4,000
Deferred tax liability at beginning of 2015	12,000
Deferred tax expense (benefit) for 2015	(8,000)
Current tax expense for 2015 (income taxes payable)	36,000
Income tax expense (total) for 2015	$28,000

Chelsea records income tax expense, the change in the deferred tax liability, and income taxes payable for 2015 as follows.

Income Tax Expense	28,000	
Deferred Tax Liability	8,000	
Income Taxes Payable		36,000

The entry to record income taxes at the end of 2016 reduces the Deferred Tax Liability by $4,000. The Deferred Tax Liability account appears as follows at the end of 2016.

ILLUSTRATION 19-11
Deferred Tax Liability
Account after Reversals

Deferred Tax Liability			
2015	8,000	2014	12,000
2016	4,000		

The Deferred Tax Liability account has a zero balance at the end of 2016.

What do the numbers mean? "REAL LIABILITIES"

Some analysts dismiss deferred tax liabilities when assessing the financial strength of a company. But the FASB indicates that the deferred tax liability meets the definition of a liability established in *Statement of Financial Accounting Concepts No. 6,* "Elements of Financial Statements" because:

1. *It results from a past transaction.* In the Chelsea example, the company performed services for customers and recognized revenue in 2014 for financial reporting purposes but deferred it for tax purposes.

2. *It is a present obligation.* Taxable income in future periods will exceed pretax financial income as a result of this temporary difference. Thus, a present obligation exists.

3. *It represents a future sacrifice.* Taxable income and taxes due in future periods will result from past events. The payment of these taxes when they come due is the future sacrifice.

A study by B. Ayers indicates that the market views deferred tax assets and liabilities similarly to other assets and liabilities. Further, the study concludes that the FASB rules in this area increased the usefulness of deferred tax amounts in financial statements.

Source: B. Ayers, "Deferred Tax Accounting Under *SFAS No. 109*: An Empirical Investigation of Its Incremental Value-Relevance Relative to APB No. 11," *The Accounting Review* (April 1998).

Summary of Income Tax Accounting Objectives

One objective of accounting for income taxes is to recognize the amount of taxes payable or refundable for the current year. In Chelsea's case, income taxes payable is $16,000 for 2014.

A **second objective** is to recognize deferred tax liabilities and assets for the future tax consequences of events already recognized in the financial statements or tax returns. For example, Chelsea sold services to customers that resulted in accounts receivable of $30,000 in 2014. It reported that amount on the 2014 income statement, but not on the tax return as income. That amount will appear on future tax returns as income for the period **when collected**. As a result, a $30,000 temporary difference exists at the end of 2014, which will cause future taxable amounts. Chelsea reports a deferred tax liability of $12,000 on the balance sheet at the end of 2014, which represents the increase in taxes payable in future years ($8,000 in 2015 and $4,000 in 2016) as a result of a temporary difference existing at the end of the current year. The related deferred tax liability is reduced by $8,000 at the end of 2015 and by another $4,000 at the end of 2016.

In addition to affecting the balance sheet, deferred taxes impact income tax expense in each of the three years affected. In 2014, taxable income ($40,000) is less than pretax financial income ($70,000). Income taxes payable for 2014 is therefore $16,000 (based on taxable income). Deferred tax expense of $12,000 results from the increase in the Deferred Tax Liability account on the balance sheet. Income tax expense is then $28,000 for 2014.

In 2015 and 2016, however, taxable income will exceed pretax financial income, due to the reversal of the temporary difference ($20,000 in 2015 and $10,000 in 2016). Income taxes payable will therefore exceed income tax expense in 2015 and 2016. Chelsea will debit the Deferred Tax Liability account for $8,000 in 2015 and $4,000 in 2016. It records credits for these amounts in Income Tax Expense. These credits are often referred to as a **deferred tax benefit** (which we discuss again later on).

Future Deductible Amounts and Deferred Taxes

Assume that during 2014, Cunningham Inc. estimated its warranty costs related to the sale of microwave ovens to be $500,000, paid evenly over the next two years. For book purposes, in 2014 Cunningham reported warranty expense and a related estimated liability for warranties of $500,000 in its financial statements. For tax purposes, **the warranty tax deduction is not allowed until paid**. Therefore, Cunningham recognizes no warranty liability on a tax-basis balance sheet. Illustration 19-12 shows the balance sheet difference at the end of 2014.

3 LEARNING OBJECTIVE

Describe a temporary difference that results in future deductible amounts.

Per Books	12/31/14	Per Tax Return	12/31/14
Estimated liability for warranties	$500,000	Estimated liability for warranties	$–0–

ILLUSTRATION 19-12
Temporary Difference, Warranty Liability

When Cunningham pays the warranty liability, it reports an expense (deductible amount) for tax purposes. Because of this temporary difference, Cunningham should recognize in 2014 the tax benefits (positive tax consequences) for the tax deductions that will result from the future settlement of the liability. Cunningham reports this future tax benefit in the December 31, 2014, balance sheet as a **deferred tax asset**.

We can think about this situation another way. Deductible amounts occur in future tax returns. These **future deductible amounts** cause taxable income to be less than pretax financial income in the future as a result of an existing temporary difference. Cunningham's temporary difference originates (arises) in one period (2014) and reverses over two periods (2015 and 2016). Illustration 19-13 diagrams this situation.

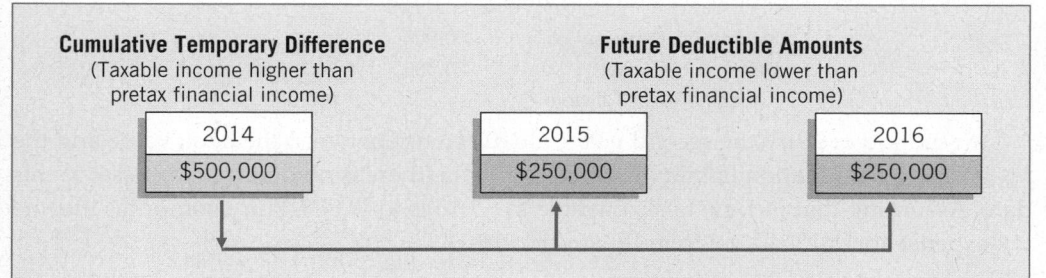

ILLUSTRATION 19-13
Reversal of Temporary Difference, Cunningham Inc.

Deferred Tax Asset

A **deferred tax asset** is the deferred tax consequence attributable to deductible temporary differences. In other words, a **deferred tax asset represents the increase in taxes refundable (or saved) in future years as a result of deductible temporary differences existing at the end of the current year.**

To illustrate, assume that Hunt Co. accrues a loss and a related liability of $50,000 in 2014 for financial reporting purposes because of pending litigation. Hunt cannot deduct this amount for tax purposes until the period it pays the liability, expected in 2015. As a result, a deductible amount will occur in 2015 when Hunt settles the liability (Estimated Litigation Liability), causing taxable income to be lower than pretax financial income. Illustration 19-14 shows the computation of the deferred tax asset at the end of 2014 (assuming a 40 percent tax rate).

ILLUSTRATION 19-14
Computation of Deferred
Tax Asset, End of 2014

Book basis of litigation liability	$50,000
Tax basis of litigation liability	–0–
Cumulative temporary difference at the end of 2014	50,000
Tax rate	40%
Deferred tax asset at the end of 2014	$20,000

Hunt can also compute the deferred tax asset by preparing a schedule that indicates the future deductible amounts due to deductible temporary differences. Illustration 19-15 shows this schedule.

ILLUSTRATION 19-15
Schedule of Future
Deductible Amounts

	Future Years
Future deductible amounts	$50,000
Tax rate	40%
Deferred tax asset at the end of 2014	$20,000

Assuming that 2014 is Hunt's first year of operations and income taxes payable is $100,000, Hunt computes its income tax expense as follows.

ILLUSTRATION 19-16
Computation of Income
Tax Expense, 2014

Deferred tax asset at end of 2014	$ 20,000
Deferred tax asset at beginning of 2014	–0–
Deferred tax expense (benefit) for 2014	(20,000)
Current tax expense for 2014 (income taxes payable)	100,000
Income tax expense (total) for 2014	$ 80,000

The **deferred tax benefit** results from the increase in the deferred tax asset from the beginning to the end of the accounting period (similar to the Chelsea example earlier). The deferred tax benefit is a negative component of income tax expense. The total income tax expense of $80,000 on the income statement for 2014 thus consists of two elements—current tax expense of $100,000 and a deferred tax benefit of $20,000. For Hunt, it makes the following journal entry at the end of 2014 to record income tax expense, deferred income taxes, and income taxes payable.

Income Tax Expense	80,000	
Deferred Tax Asset	20,000	
Income Taxes Payable		100,000

At the end of 2015 (the second year), the difference between the book value and the tax basis of the litigation liability is zero. Therefore, there is no deferred tax asset at this date. Assuming that income taxes payable for 2015 is $140,000, Hunt computes income tax expense for 2015 as shown in Illustration 19-17.

ILLUSTRATION 19-17
Computation of Income
Tax Expense, 2015

Deferred tax asset at the end of 2015	$ –0–
Deferred tax asset at the beginning of 2015	20,000
Deferred tax expense (benefit) for 2015	20,000
Current tax expense for 2015 (income taxes payable)	140,000
Income tax expense (total) for 2015	$160,000

The company records income taxes for 2015 as follows.

Income Tax Expense	160,000	
Deferred Tax Asset		20,000
Income Taxes Payable		140,000

The total income tax expense of $160,000 on the income statement for 2015 thus consists of two elements—current tax expense of $140,000 and deferred tax expense of $20,000. Illustration 19-18 shows the Deferred Tax Asset account at the end of 2015.

Deferred Tax Asset			
2014	20,000	2015	20,000

ILLUSTRATION 19-18
Deferred Tax Asset
Account after Reversals

What do the numbers mean?   *"REAL ASSETS"*

A key issue in accounting for income taxes is whether a company should recognize a deferred tax asset in the financial records. Based on the conceptual definition of an asset, a deferred tax asset meets the three main conditions for an item to be recognized as an asset:

1. *It results from a past transaction.* In the Hunt example, the accrual of the loss contingency is the past event that gives rise to a future deductible temporary difference.
2. *It gives rise to a probable benefit in the future.* Taxable income exceeds pretax financial income in the current year (2014). However, in the next year the exact opposite occurs. That is, taxable income is lower than pretax financial income. Because this deductible temporary difference reduces taxes payable in the future, a probable future benefit exists at the end of the current period.
3. *The entity controls access to the benefits.* Hunt can obtain the benefit of existing deductible temporary differences by reducing its taxes payable in the future. Hunt has the exclusive right to that benefit and can control others' access to it.

Market analysts' reactions to the **write-off** of deferred tax assets also supports their treatment as assets. When Bethlehem Steel reported a $1 billion charge to write off a deferred tax asset, analysts believed that Bethlehem was signaling that it would not realize the future benefits of the tax deductions. Thus, Bethlehem should write down the asset like other assets.

Source: J. Weil and S. Liesman, "Stock Gurus Disregard Most Big Write-Offs but They Often Hold Vital Clues to Outlook," *Wall Street Journal Online* (December 31, 2001).

Deferred Tax Asset—Valuation Allowance

Companies recognize a deferred tax asset for all deductible temporary differences. However, a company should reduce a deferred tax asset by a **valuation allowance** if, based on available evidence, **it is more likely than not** that it **will not realize** some portion or all of the deferred tax asset. **"More likely than not"** means a level of likelihood of at least slightly more than 50 percent.

Assume that Jensen Co. has a deductible temporary difference of $1,000,000 at the end of its first year of operations. Its tax rate is 40 percent, which means it records a deferred tax asset of $400,000 ($1,000,000 × 40%). Assuming $900,000 of income taxes payable, Jensen records income tax expense, the deferred tax asset, and income taxes payable as follows.

4 LEARNING OBJECTIVE
Explain the purpose of a deferred tax asset valuation allowance.

Income Tax Expense	500,000	
Deferred Tax Asset	400,000	
Income Taxes Payable		900,000

After careful review of all available evidence, Jensen determines that it is more likely than not that it will not realize $100,000 of this deferred tax asset. Jensen records this reduction in asset value as follows.

Income Tax Expense	100,000	
Allowance to Reduce Deferred Tax Asset to Expected Realizable Value		100,000

This journal entry increases income tax expense in the current period because Jensen does not expect to realize a favorable tax benefit for a portion of the deductible temporary difference. Jensen **simultaneously establishes a valuation allowance to recognize the reduction in the carrying amount of the deferred tax asset.** This valuation account is a contra account. Jensen reports it on the financial statements in the following manner.

ILLUSTRATION 19-19
Balance Sheet
Presentation of Valuation
Allowance Account

Deferred tax asset	$400,000
Less: Allowance to reduce deferred tax asset to expected realizable value	100,000
Deferred tax asset (net)	$300,000

Jensen then evaluates this allowance account at the end of each accounting period. If, at the end of the next period, the deferred tax asset is still $400,000 but now the company expects to realize $350,000 of this asset, Jensen makes the following entry to adjust the valuation account.

Allowance to Reduce Deferred Tax Asset to Expected Realizable Value	50,000	
Income Tax Expense		50,000

Jensen should consider all available evidence, both positive and negative, to determine whether, based on the weight of available evidence, it needs a valuation allowance. For example, if Jensen has been experiencing a series of loss years, it reasonably assumes that these losses will continue. Therefore, Jensen will lose the benefit of the future deductible amounts. We discuss the use of a valuation account under other conditions later in the chapter.

Income Statement Presentation

LEARNING OBJECTIVE
Describe the presentation of income tax expense in the income statement.

Circumstances dictate whether a company should add or subtract the change in deferred income taxes to or from income taxes payable in computing income tax expense. For example, a company adds an increase in a deferred tax liability to income taxes payable. On the other hand, it subtracts an increase in a deferred tax asset from income taxes payable. The formula in Illustration 19-20 is used to compute income tax expense (benefit).

ILLUSTRATION 19-20
Formula to Compute
Income Tax Expense

Income Taxes Payable or Refundable	±	Change in Deferred Income Taxes	=	Total Income Tax Expense or Benefit

In the income statement or in the notes to the financial statements, a company should disclose the significant components of income tax expense attributable to continuing operations. Given the information related to Chelsea on page 1121, Chelsea reports its income statement as follows.

ILLUSTRATION 19-21
Income Statement
Presentation of Income
Tax Expense

CHELSEA INC.		
INCOME STATEMENT		
FOR THE YEAR ENDING DECEMBER 31, 2014		
Revenues		$130,000
Expenses		60,000
Income before income taxes		70,000
Income tax expense		
Current	$16,000	
Deferred	12,000	28,000
Net income		$ 42,000

As illustrated, Chelsea reports both the current portion (amount of income taxes payable for the period) and the deferred portion of income tax expense. Another option is to simply report the total income tax expense on the income statement and then indicate in the notes to the financial statements the current and deferred portions. Income tax expense is often referred to as "Provision for income taxes." Using this terminology, the current provision is $16,000, and the provision for deferred taxes is $12,000.

Specific Differences

Numerous items create differences between pretax financial income and taxable income. For purposes of accounting recognition, these differences are of two types: (1) temporary, and (2) permanent.

6 LEARNING OBJECTIVE
Describe various temporary and permanent differences.

Temporary Differences

Taxable temporary differences are temporary differences that will result in taxable amounts in future years when the related assets are recovered. **Deductible temporary differences** are temporary differences that will result in deductible amounts in future years, when the related book liabilities are settled. As discussed earlier, taxable temporary differences give rise to recording deferred tax liabilities. Deductible temporary differences give rise to recording deferred tax assets. Illustration 19-22 provides examples of temporary differences.

ILLUSTRATION 19-22
Examples of Temporary Differences

Revenues or gains are taxable after they are recognized in financial income.
An asset (e.g., accounts receivable or investment) may be recognized for revenues or gains that will result in **taxable amounts in future years** when the asset is recovered. Examples: 1. Sales accounted for on the accrual basis for financial reporting purposes and on the installment (cash) basis for tax purposes. 2. Contracts accounted for under the percentage-of-completion method for financial reporting purposes and a portion of related gross profit deferred for tax purposes. 3. Investments accounted for under the equity method for financial reporting purposes and under the cost method for tax purposes. 4. Gain on involuntary conversion of nonmonetary asset which is recognized for financial reporting purposes but deferred for tax purposes. 5. Unrealized holding gains for financial reporting purposes (including use of the fair value option), but deferred for tax purposes.

Expenses or losses are deductible after they are recognized in financial income.
A liability (or contra asset) may be recognized for expenses or losses that will result in **deductible amounts in future years** when the liability is settled. Examples: 1. Product warranty liabilities. 2. Estimated liabilities related to discontinued operations or restructurings. 3. Litigation accruals. 4. Bad debt expense recognized using the allowance method for financial reporting purposes; direct write-off method used for tax purposes. 5. Stock-based compensation expense. 6. Unrealized holding losses for financial reporting purposes (including use of the fair value option), but deferred for tax purposes.

Revenues or gains are taxable before they are recognized in financial income.
A liability may be recognized for an advance payment for goods or services to be provided in future years. For tax purposes, the advance payment is included in taxable income upon the receipt of cash. Future sacrifices to provide goods or services (or future refunds to those who cancel their orders) that settle the liability will result in **deductible amounts in future years**. Examples: 1. Subscriptions received in advance. 2. Advance rental receipts. 3. Sales and leasebacks for financial reporting purposes (income deferral) but reported as sales for tax purposes. 4. Prepaid contracts and royalties received in advance.

Expenses or losses are deductible before they are recognized in financial income.
The cost of an asset may have been deducted for tax purposes faster than it was expensed for financial reporting purposes. Amounts received upon future recovery of the amount of the asset for financial reporting (through use or sale) will exceed the remaining tax basis of the asset and thereby result in **taxable amounts in future years**. Examples: 1. Depreciable property, depletable resources, and intangibles. 2. Deductible pension funding exceeding expense. 3. Prepaid expenses that are deducted on the tax return in the period paid.

Determining a company's temporary differences may prove difficult. A company should prepare a balance sheet for tax purposes that it can compare with its GAAP balance sheet. Many of the differences between the two balance sheets are temporary differences.

Originating and Reversing Aspects of Temporary Differences. An **originating temporary difference** is the initial difference between the book basis and the tax basis of an asset or liability, regardless of whether the tax basis of the asset or liability exceeds or is exceeded by the book basis of the asset or liability. A **reversing difference**, on the other hand, occurs when eliminating a temporary difference that originated in prior periods and then removing the related tax effect from the deferred tax account.

For example, assume that Sharp Co. has tax depreciation in excess of book depreciation of $2,000 in 2012, 2013, and 2014. Further, it has an excess of book depreciation over tax depreciation of $3,000 in 2015 and 2016 for the same asset. Assuming a tax rate of 30 percent for all years involved, the Deferred Tax Liability account reflects the following.

ILLUSTRATION 19-23
Tax Effects of Originating and Reversing Differences

	Deferred Tax Liability				
Tax Effects of Reversing Differences	{2015	900	2012	600 }	Tax Effects of Originating Differences
	{2016	900	2013	600 }	
			2014	600 }	

The originating differences for Sharp in each of the first three years are $2,000. The related tax effect of each originating difference is $600. The reversing differences in 2015 and 2016 are each $3,000. The related tax effect of each is $900.

Permanent Differences

International Perspective

If companies switch to IFRS, the impact on tax accounting methods will require consideration. For example, in cases in which GAAP and tax rules are the same, what happens if IFRS is different from GAAP? Should the tax method change to IFRS? And what might happen at the state level, due to changes in the financial reporting rules?

Some differences between taxable income and pretax financial income are permanent. **Permanent differences** result from items that (1) enter into pretax financial income but **never** into taxable income, or (2) enter into taxable income but **never** into pretax financial income.

Congress has enacted a variety of tax law provisions to attain certain political, economic, and social objectives. Some of these provisions exclude certain revenues from taxation, limit the deductibility of certain expenses, and permit the deduction of certain other expenses in excess of costs incurred. A corporation that has tax-free income, nondeductible expenses, or allowable deductions in excess of cost has an effective tax rate that differs from its statutory (regular) tax rate.

Since permanent differences affect only the period in which they occur, they do not give rise to future taxable or deductible amounts. As a result, **companies recognize no deferred tax consequences**. Illustration 19-24 shows examples of permanent differences.

ILLUSTRATION 19-24
Examples of Permanent Differences

Items are recognized for financial reporting purposes but not for tax purposes.

Examples:
1. Interest received on state and municipal obligations.
2. Expenses incurred in obtaining tax-exempt income.
3. Proceeds from life insurance carried by the company on key officers or employees.
4. Premiums paid for life insurance carried by the company on key officers or employees (company is beneficiary).
5. Fines and expenses resulting from a violation of law.

Items are recognized for tax purposes but not for financial reporting purposes.

Examples:
1. "Percentage depletion" of natural resources in excess of their cost.
2. The deduction for dividends received from U.S. corporations, generally 70% or 80%.

Examples of Temporary and Permanent Differences

To illustrate the computations used when both temporary and permanent differences exist, assume that Bio-Tech Company reports pretax financial income of $200,000 in each of the years 2012, 2013, and 2014. The company is subject to a 30 percent tax rate and has the following differences between pretax financial income and taxable income.

1. Bio-Tech reports gross profit of $18,000 from an installment sale in 2012 for tax purposes over an 18-month period at a constant amount per month beginning January 1, 2013. It recognizes the entire amount for book purposes in 2012.

2. It pays life insurance premiums for its key officers of $5,000 in 2013 and 2014. Although not tax-deductible, Bio-Tech expenses the premiums for book purposes.

The installment sale is a temporary difference, whereas the life insurance premium is a permanent difference. Illustration 19-25 shows the reconciliation of Bio-Tech's pretax financial income to taxable income and the computation of income taxes payable.

	2012	2013	2014
Pretax financial income	$200,000	$200,000	$200,000
Permanent difference			
Nondeductible expense		5,000	5,000
Temporary difference			
Installment sale	(18,000)	12,000	6,000
Taxable income	182,000	217,000	211,000
Tax rate	30%	30%	30%
Income taxes payable	$ 54,600	$ 65,100	$ 63,300

ILLUSTRATION 19-25
Reconciliation and Computation of Income Taxes Payable

Note that Bio-Tech **deducts** the installment-sales gross profit from pretax financial income to arrive at taxable income. The reason: Pretax financial income includes the installment-sales gross profit; taxable income does not. Conversely, it **adds** the $5,000 insurance premium to pretax financial income to arrive at taxable income. The reason: Pretax financial income records an expense for this premium, but for tax purposes the premium is not deductible. As a result, pretax financial income is lower than taxable income. Therefore, the life insurance premium must be added back to pretax financial income to reconcile to taxable income.

Bio-Tech records income taxes for 2012, 2013, and 2014 as follows.

December 31, 2012

Income Tax Expense ($54,600 + $5,400)	60,000	
Deferred Tax Liability ($18,000 × 30%)		5,400
Income Taxes Payable ($182,000 × 30%)		54,600

December 31, 2013

Income Tax Expense ($65,100 − $3,600)	61,500	
Deferred Tax Liability ($12,000 × 30%)	3,600	
Income Taxes Payable ($217,000 × 30%)		65,100

December 31, 2014

Income Tax Expense ($63,300 − $1,800)	61,500	
Deferred Tax Liability ($6,000 × 30%)	1,800	
Income Taxes Payable ($211,000 × 30%)		63,300

Bio-Tech has one temporary difference, which originates in 2012 and reverses in 2013 and 2014. It recognizes a deferred tax liability at the end of 2012 because the temporary difference causes future taxable amounts. As the temporary difference reverses,

Bio-Tech reduces the deferred tax liability. There is no deferred tax amount associated with the difference caused by the nondeductible insurance expense because it is a permanent difference.

Although an enacted tax rate of 30 percent applies for all three years, the effective rate differs from the enacted rate in 2013 and 2014. Bio-Tech computes the **effective tax rate** by dividing total income tax expense for the period by pretax financial income. The effective rate is 30 percent for 2012 ($60,000 ÷ $200,000 = 30%) and 30.75 percent for 2013 and 2014 ($61,500 ÷ $200,000 = 30.75%).

Tax Rate Considerations

LEARNING OBJECTIVE 7
Explain the effect of various tax rates and tax rate changes on deferred income taxes.

In our previous illustrations, the enacted tax rate did not change from one year to the next. Thus, to compute the deferred income tax amount to report on the balance sheet, a company simply multiplies the cumulative temporary difference by the current tax rate. Using Bio-Tech as an example, it multiplies the cumulative temporary difference of $18,000 by the enacted tax rate, 30 percent in this case, to arrive at a deferred tax liability of $5,400 ($18,000 × 30%) at the end of 2012.

Future Tax Rates

What happens if tax rates are expected to change in the future? In this case, a company should use the **enacted tax rate** expected to apply. Therefore, a company must consider presently enacted changes in the tax rate that become effective for a particular future year(s) when determining the tax rate to apply to existing temporary differences. For example, assume that Warlen Co. at the end of 2011 has the following cumulative temporary difference of $300,000, computed as shown in Illustration 19-26.

ILLUSTRATION 19-26
Computation of Cumulative Temporary Difference

Book basis of depreciable assets	$1,000,000
Tax basis of depreciable assets	700,000
Cumulative temporary difference	$ 300,000

Furthermore, assume that the $300,000 will reverse and result in taxable amounts in the future, with the enacted tax rates shown in Illustration 19-27.

ILLUSTRATION 19-27
Deferred Tax Liability Based on Future Rates

	2012	2013	2014	2015	2016	Total
Future taxable amounts	$80,000	$70,000	$60,000	$50,000	$40,000	$300,000
Tax rate	40%	40%	35%	30%	30%	
Deferred tax liability	$32,000	$28,000	$21,000	$15,000	$12,000	$108,000

The total deferred tax liability at the end of 2011 is $108,000. Warlen may only use tax rates other than the current rate when the future tax rates have been enacted, as is the case in this example. **If new rates are not yet enacted for future years, Warlen should use the current rate.**

In determining the appropriate enacted tax rate for a given year, companies must use the **average tax rate**. The Internal Revenue Service and other taxing jurisdictions tax income on a graduated tax basis. For a U.S. corporation, the IRS taxes the first $50,000 of taxable income at 15 percent, the next $25,000 at 25 percent, with higher incremental levels of income at rates as high as 39 percent. In computing deferred income taxes, companies for which graduated tax rates are a significant factor must therefore **determine the average tax rate and use that rate.**

If you are concerned about your tax rate and the taxes you pay, you might want to consider moving to Switzerland, which has a personal tax rate of anywhere from zero percent to 13.2 percent. You don't want to move to Denmark though. Yes, the people of Denmark are regularly voted to be the happiest people on Earth but it's uncertain how many of these polls take place at tax time. The government in Denmark charges income tax rates ranging from 38 percent to 59 percent. So, taxes are a major item to many individuals, wherever they reside.

Taxes are also a big deal to corporations. For example, the Organisation for Economic Co-operation and Development (OECD) is an international organization of 30 countries that accepts the principles of a free-market economy. Most OECD members are high-income economies and are regarded as developed countries. However, companies in the OECD can be subject to significant tax levies, as indicated in the following list of the ten highest corporate income tax rates for the OECD countries.

United States	40.0%	Germany	29.5%
Japan	38.0	Luxembourg	28.8
Belgium	33.9	New Zealand	28.0
France	33.3	Spain	28.0
Australia	30.0	Canada	26.0

On the low end of the tax rate spectrum are Iceland and Ireland, with tax rates of 15 percent and 12.5 percent, respectively. Indeed, corporate tax rates have been dropping around the world as countries attempt to spur capital investment, which in turn spurs international tax competition. However, with stagnant global economic growth, there is concern that governments will target increases in corporate tax rates as a source of revenues to address budget shortfalls. In addition, further expansion of value-added taxes (VAT) is being considered. Indirect taxes such as VAT are charged on consumption of goods and services, which is much more stable than the corporate tax.

If these tax proposals result in changes in the tax rates applied to future deductible and taxable amounts, be prepared for significant remeasurement of deferred tax assets and liabilities.

Source: The rates reported reflect the base corporate rate in effect in 2012. Effective rates paid may vary depending on country-specific additional levies for such items as unemployment and local taxes, and, in the case of Japan, earthquake damage assessments. Effective rates may be lower due to credits for investments and capital gains. See *http://www.kpmg.com/global/en/services/tax/tax-tools-and-resources/pages/tax-rates-online.aspx.* See also P. Toscano, "The World's Highest Tax Rates," *http://www.cnbc.com/id/30727913* (May 13, 2009).

Revision of Future Tax Rates

When a change in the tax rate is enacted, companies should record its effect on the existing deferred income tax accounts immediately. **A company reports the effect as an adjustment to income tax expense in the period of the change.**

Assume that on December 10, 2011, a new income tax act is signed into law that lowers the corporate tax rate from 40 percent to 35 percent, effective January 1, 2013. If Hostel Co. has one temporary difference at the beginning of 2011 related to $3 million of excess tax depreciation, then it has a Deferred Tax Liability account with a balance of $1,200,000 ($3,000,000 × 40%) at January 1, 2011. If taxable amounts related to this difference are scheduled to occur equally in 2012, 2013, and 2014, the deferred tax liability at the end of 2011 is $1,100,000, computed as follows.

	2012	2013	2014	Total
Future taxable amounts	$1,000,000	$1,000,000	$1,000,000	$3,000,000
Tax rate	40%	35%	35%	
Deferred tax liability	$ 400,000	$ 350,000	$ 350,000	$1,100,000

ILLUSTRATION 19-28
Schedule of Future Taxable Amounts and Related Tax Rates

Hostel, therefore, recognizes the decrease of $100,000 ($1,200,000 − $1,100,000) at the end of 2011 in the deferred tax liability as follows.

Deferred Tax Liability	100,000	
Income Tax Expense		100,000

Corporate tax rates do not change often. Therefore, companies usually employ the current rate. However, state and foreign tax rates change more frequently, and they require adjustments in deferred income taxes accordingly.[2]

ACCOUNTING FOR NET OPERATING LOSSES

LEARNING OBJECTIVE 8
Apply accounting procedures for a loss carryback and a loss carryforward.

Every management hopes its company will be profitable. But hopes and profits may not materialize. For a start-up company, it is common to accumulate operating losses while expanding its customer base but before realizing economies of scale. For an established company, a major event such as a labor strike, rapidly changing regulatory and competitive forces, a disaster such as 9/11, or a general economic recession can cause expenses to exceed revenues—a net operating loss.

A **net operating loss (NOL)** occurs for tax purposes in a year when tax-deductible expenses exceed taxable revenues. An inequitable tax burden would result if companies were taxed during profitable periods without receiving any tax relief during periods of net operating losses. Under certain circumstances, therefore, the federal tax laws permit taxpayers to use the losses of one year to offset the profits of other years.

Companies accomplish this income-averaging provision through the **carryback and carryforward of net operating losses**. Under this provision, a company pays no income taxes for a year in which it incurs a net operating loss. In addition, it may select one of the two options discussed below and on the following pages.

Loss Carryback

Through use of a **loss carryback**, a company may carry the net operating loss back two years and receive refunds for income taxes paid in those years. The company must apply the loss to the earlier year first and then to the second year. It may **carry forward** any loss remaining after the two-year carryback up to 20 years to offset future taxable income. Illustration 19-29 diagrams the loss carryback procedure, assuming a loss in 2014.

ILLUSTRATION 19-29
Loss Carryback Procedure

Loss Carryforward

A company may forgo the loss carryback and use only the **loss carryforward** option, offsetting future taxable income for up to 20 years. Illustration 19-30 shows this approach.

[2]Tax rate changes nearly always will substantially impact income numbers and the reporting of deferred income taxes on the balance sheet. As a result, you can expect to hear an economic consequences argument every time that Congress decides to change the tax rates. For example, when Congress raised the corporate rate from 34 percent to 35 percent in 1993, companies took an additional "hit" to earnings if they were in a deferred tax liability position. Thus, corporate America is following closely the recent budget and deficit-reduction negotiations. Some proposals will eliminate certain corporate deductions (or loopholes) in order to "broaden the tax base" and therefore allow for lower tax rates. Depending on a company's deferred tax position, a change in tax rates can have a positive or negative effect on net income.

ILLUSTRATION 19-30
Loss Carryforward
Procedure

Operating losses can be substantial. For example, Yahoo! at one time had net operating losses of approximately $5.4 billion. That amount translates into tax savings of $1.4 billion if Yahoo! is able to generate taxable income before the NOLs expire.

Loss Carryback Example

To illustrate the accounting procedures for a net operating loss carryback, assume that Groh Inc. has no temporary or permanent differences. Groh experiences the following.

Year	Taxable Income or Loss	Tax Rate	Tax Paid
2011	$ 50,000	35%	$17,500
2012	100,000	30%	30,000
2013	200,000	40%	80,000
2014	(500,000)	—	–0–

In 2014, Groh incurs a net operating loss that it decides to carry back. Under the law, Groh must apply the carryback first to the **second year preceding the loss year**. Therefore, it carries the loss back first to 2012. Then, Groh carries back any unused loss to 2013. Accordingly, Groh files amended tax returns for 2012 and 2013, receiving refunds for the $110,000 ($30,000 + $80,000) of taxes paid in those years.

For accounting as well as tax purposes, the $110,000 represents the **tax effect (tax benefit)** of the loss carryback. Groh should recognize this tax effect in 2014, the loss year. Since the tax loss gives rise to a refund that is both measurable and currently realizable, Groh should recognize the associated tax benefit in this loss period.

Groh makes the following journal entry for 2014.

Income Tax Refund Receivable	110,000	
Benefit Due to Loss Carryback (Income Tax Expense)		110,000

Groh reports the account debited, Income Tax Refund Receivable, on the balance sheet as a current asset at December 31, 2014. It reports the account credited on the income statement for 2014 as shown in Illustration 19-31.

ILLUSTRATION 19-31
Recognition of Benefit of
the Loss Carryback in the
Loss Year

GROH INC.	
INCOME STATEMENT (PARTIAL) FOR 2014	
Operating loss before income taxes	$(500,000)
Income tax benefit	
Benefit due to loss carryback	110,000
Net loss	$(390,000)

Since the $500,000 net operating loss for 2014 exceeds the $300,000 total taxable income from the 2 preceding years, Groh carries forward the remaining $200,000 loss.

Loss Carryforward Example

If a carryback fails to fully absorb a net operating loss, or if the company decides not to carry the loss back, then it can carry forward the loss for up to 20 years.[3] Because companies use carryforwards to offset future taxable income, the **tax effect of a loss carryforward** represents **future tax savings**. Realization of the future tax benefit depends on future earnings, an uncertain prospect.

The key accounting issue is whether there should be different requirements for recognition of a deferred tax asset for (a) deductible temporary differences, and (b) operating loss carryforwards. The FASB's position is that in substance these items are the same—both are tax-deductible amounts in future years. As a result, the Board concluded that there **should not be different requirements** for recognition of a deferred tax asset from deductible temporary differences and operating loss carryforwards.[4]

Carryforward without Valuation Allowance

To illustrate the accounting for an operating loss carryforward, return to the Groh example from the preceding section. In 2014, the company records the tax effect of the $200,000 loss carryforward as a deferred tax asset of $80,000 ($200,000 × 40%), assuming that the enacted future tax rate is 40 percent. Groh records the benefits of the carryback and the carryforward in 2014 as follows.

To recognize benefit of loss carryback

Income Tax Refund Receivable	110,000	
Benefit Due to Loss Carryback (Income Tax Expense)		110,000

To recognize benefit of loss carryforward

Deferred Tax Asset	80,000	
Benefit Due to Loss Carryforward (Income Tax Expense)		80,000

Groh realizes the income tax refund receivable of $110,000 immediately as a refund of taxes paid in the past. It establishes a Deferred Tax Asset account for the benefits of future tax savings. The two accounts credited are contra income tax expense items, which Groh presents on the 2014 income statement shown in Illustration 19-32.

ILLUSTRATION 19-32
Recognition of the Benefit of the Loss Carryback and Carryforward in the Loss Year

GROH INC.		
INCOME STATEMENT (PARTIAL) FOR 2014		
Operating loss before income taxes		$(500,000)
Income tax benefit		
Benefit due to loss carryback	$110,000	
Benefit due to loss carryforward	80,000	190,000
Net loss		$(310,000)

The **current tax benefit** of $110,000 is the income tax refundable for the year. Groh determines this amount by applying the carryback provisions of the tax law to the taxable loss for 2014. The $80,000 is the **deferred tax benefit** for the year, which results from an increase in the deferred tax asset.

[3]The length of the carryforward and carryback periods has varied. The carryforward period has increased from 7 years to 20 years over a period of time. As part of the Economic Recovery Act of 2009, Congress enacted a temporary extension of the carryback period from 2 to 5 years for operating losses incurred in 2008 and 2009. It is estimated that the companies in the S&P 500 will reap a refund of $5 billion due to this change. See D. Zion, A. Varshney, and C. Cornett, "Spinning Losses into Gold," *Equity Research—Accounting and Tax*, Credit Suisse (November 12, 2009).

[4]This requirement is controversial because many believe it is inappropriate to recognize deferred tax assets except when assured beyond a reasonable doubt. Others argue that companies should never recognize deferred tax assets for loss carryforwards until realizing the income in the future.

For 2015, assume that Groh returns to profitable operations and has taxable income of $250,000 (prior to adjustment for the NOL carryforward), subject to a 40 percent tax rate. Groh then realizes the benefits of the carryforward for tax purposes in 2015, which it recognized for accounting purposes in 2014. Groh computes the income taxes payable for 2015 as shown in Illustration 19-33.

Taxable income prior to loss carryforward	$ 250,000
Loss carryforward deduction	(200,000)
Taxable income for 2015	50,000
Tax rate	40%
Income taxes payable for 2015	$ 20,000

ILLUSTRATION 19-33
Computation of Income Taxes Payable with Realized Loss Carryforward

Groh records income taxes in 2015 as follows.

Income Tax Expense	100,000	
Deferred Tax Asset		80,000
Income Taxes Payable		20,000

The benefits of the NOL carryforward, realized in 2015, reduce the Deferred Tax Asset account to zero.

The 2015 income statement that appears in Illustration 19-34 does **not report** the tax effects of either the loss carryback or the loss carryforward because Groh had reported both previously.

GROH INC.
INCOME STATEMENT (PARTIAL) FOR 2015

Income before income taxes		$250,000
Income tax expense		
Current	$20,000	
Deferred	80,000	100,000
Net income		$150,000

ILLUSTRATION 19-34
Presentation of the Benefit of Loss Carryforward Realized in 2015, Recognized in 2014

Carryforward with Valuation Allowance

Let us return to the Groh example. Assume that it is more likely than not that Groh will *not* realize the entire NOL carryforward in future years. In this situation, Groh records the tax benefits of $110,000 associated with the $300,000 NOL carryback, as we previously described. In addition, it records Deferred Tax Asset of $80,000 ($200,000 × 40%) for the potential benefits related to the loss carryforward, and an allowance to reduce the deferred tax asset by the same amount. Groh makes the following journal entries in 2014.

To recognize benefit of loss carryback

Income Tax Refund Receivable	110,000	
Benefit Due to Loss Carryback (Income Tax Expense)		110,000

To recognize benefit of loss carryforward

Deferred Tax Asset	80,000	
Benefit Due to Loss Carryforward (Income Tax Expense)		80,000

To record allowance amount

Benefit Due to Loss Carryforward (Income Tax Expense)	80,000	
Allowance to Reduce Deferred Tax Asset		
to Expected Realizable Value		80,000

The latter entry indicates that because positive evidence of sufficient quality and quantity is unavailable to counteract the negative evidence, Groh needs a valuation allowance.

Illustration 19-35 shows Groh's 2014 income statement presentation.

ILLUSTRATION 19-35
Recognition of Benefit of
Loss Carryback Only

GROH INC.	
INCOME STATEMENT (PARTIAL) FOR 2014	
Operating loss before income taxes	$(500,000)
Income tax benefit	
Benefit due to loss carryback	110,000
Net loss	$(390,000)

In 2015, assuming that Groh has taxable income of $250,000 (before considering the carryforward) subject to a tax rate of 40 percent, it realizes the deferred tax asset. It thus no longer needs the allowance. Groh records the following entries.

To record current and deferred income taxes

Income Tax Expense	100,000	
Deferred Tax Asset		80,000
Income Taxes Payable		20,000

To eliminate allowance and recognize loss carryforward

Allowance to Reduce Deferred Tax Asset to		
Expected Realizable Value	80,000	
Benefit Due to Loss Carryforward (Income Tax Expense)		80,000

Groh reports the $80,000 Benefit Due to the Loss Carryforward on the 2015 income statement. The company did not recognize it in 2014 because it was more likely than not that it would not be realized. Assuming that Groh derives the income for 2015 from continuing operations, it prepares the income statement as shown in Illustration 19-36.

ILLUSTRATION 19-36
Recognition of Benefit of
Loss Carryforward When
Realized

GROH INC.		
INCOME STATEMENT (PARTIAL) FOR 2015		
Income before income taxes		$250,000
Income tax expense		
Current	$ 20,000	
Deferred	80,000	
Benefit due to loss carryforward	(80,000)	20,000
Net income		$230,000

Another method is to report only one line for total income tax expense of $20,000 on the face of the income statement and disclose the components of income tax expense in the notes to the financial statements.

Valuation Allowance Revisited

A company should consider all positive and negative information in determining whether it needs a valuation allowance. Whether the company will realize a deferred tax asset depends on whether sufficient taxable income exists or will exist within the carryforward period available under tax law. Illustration 19-37 shows possible sources of taxable income that may be available under the tax law to realize a tax benefit for deductible temporary differences and carryforwards.[5]

[5]Companies implement a tax-planning strategy to realize a tax benefit for an operating loss or tax credit carryforward before it expires. Companies consider tax-planning strategies when assessing the need for and amount of a valuation allowance for deferred tax assets.

Possible Sources of
Taxable Income

Taxable Income Sources

a. Future reversals of existing taxable temporary differences.

b. Future taxable income exclusive of reversing temporary differences and carryforwards.

c. Taxable income in prior carryback year(s) if carryback is permitted under the tax law.

d. **Tax-planning strategies** that would, if necessary, be implemented to:
(1) Accelerate taxable amounts to utilize expiring carryforwards.
(2) Change the character of taxable or deductible amounts from ordinary income or loss to capital gain or loss.
(3) Switch from tax-exempt to taxable investments. [1]

 See the FASB
Codification section
(page 1156).

If any one of these sources is sufficient to support a conclusion that a valuation allowance is unnecessary, a company need not consider other sources.

Forming a conclusion that a valuation allowance is not needed is difficult when there is negative evidence such as cumulative losses in recent years. Companies may also cite positive evidence indicating that a valuation allowance is not needed. Illustration 19-38 presents examples (not prerequisites) of evidence to consider when determining the need for a valuation allowance.[6]

ILLUSTRATION 19-38
Evidence to Consider in
Evaluating the Need for
a Valuation Account

Negative Evidence

a. A history of operating loss or tax credit carryforwards expiring unused.

b. Losses expected in early future years (by a presently profitable entity).

c. Unsettled circumstances that, if unfavorably resolved, would adversely affect future operations and profit levels on a continuing basis in future years.

d. A carryback, carryforward period that is so brief that it would limit realization of tax benefits if (1) a significant deductible temporary difference is expected to reverse in a single year or (2) the enterprise operates in a traditionally cyclical business.

Positive Evidence

a. Existing contracts or firm sales backlog that will produce more than enough taxable income to realize the deferred tax asset based on existing sale prices and cost structures.

b. An excess of appreciated asset value over the tax basis of the entity's net assets in an amount sufficient to realize the deferred tax asset.

c. A strong earnings history exclusive of the loss that created the future deductible amount (tax loss carryforward or deductible temporary difference) coupled with evidence indicating that the loss is an aberration rather than a continuing condition (for example, the result of an unusual, infrequent, or extraordinary item). [2]

The use of a valuation allowance provides a company with an opportunity to manage its earnings. As one accounting expert notes, "The 'more likely than not' provision is perhaps the most judgmental clause in accounting." Some companies may set up a valuation account and then use it to increase income as needed. Others may take the income immediately to increase capital or to offset large negative charges to income.

International Perspective

> Under IFRS (*IAS 12*), a company may not recognize a deferred tax asset unless realization is "probable." However, "probable" is not defined in the standard, leading to diversity in the recognition of deferred tax assets.

[6]In contrast to the valuation allowance issue for **Citigroup** in the opening story, **Sony Corp.** announced a $3.2 billion net loss, blaming a $4.4 billion write-off on a certain portion of deferred tax assets in Japan, in what would be the company's third straight year of red ink. The write-off is an admission that the March 2011 earthquake and tsunami have shattered its expectations for a robust current fiscal year. In the wake of the disaster, Sony temporarily shut 10 plants in and around the quake-hit region. Like other Japanese auto and electronics makers, Sony faced uncertainties because its recovery prospects are partially dependent on parts and materials suppliers, many of which have also been affected by the quake. Thus, the post-quake outlook put Sony in a position where it had to set aside reserves of ¥360 billion on certain deferred tax assets in its fiscal fourth quarter. See J. Osawa, "Sony Expects Hefty Loss: Electronics Giant Reverses Prediction for Full-Year Profit, Blaming Earthquake," *Wall Street Journal* (May 24, 2011).

Here are some net operating loss numbers reported by several notable companies.

NOLs ($ in millions)

Company	Income (Loss)	Operating Loss Carryforward	Tax Benefit (Deferred Tax Asset)	Comment
Delta Air Lines, Inc.	$(5,198.00)	$7,500.00	$2,848.00	Begins to expire in 2022. Valuation allowance recorded.
Goodyear	114.80	1,306.60	457.30	Begins to expire in next year. Full valuation allowance.
Kodak	556.00	509.00	234.00	Begins to expire in next year. Valuation allowance on foreign credits only.
Yahoo!	42.82	5,400.00	1,443.50	State and federal carryforwards. Begins to expire in next year. Valuation allowance recorded.

All of these companies are using the carryforward provisions of the tax code for their NOLs. For many of them, the NOL is an amount far exceeding their reported profits. Why carry forward the loss to get the tax deduction? First, the company may have already used up the carryback provision, which allows only a two-year carryback period. (Carryforwards can be claimed up to 20 years in the future.) In some cases, management expects the tax rates in the future to be higher. This difference in expected rates provides a bigger tax benefit if the losses are carried forward and matched against future income. Is there a downside? To realize the benefits of carryforwards, a company must have future taxable income in the carryforward period in order to claim the NOL deductions. As we learned, if it is more likely than not that a company will not have taxable income, it must record a valuation allowance (and increased tax expense). As the data above indicate, recording a valuation allowance to reflect the uncertainty of realizing the tax benefits has merit. But for some, the NOL benefits begin to expire in the following year, which may be not enough time to generate sufficient taxable income in order to claim the NOL deduction.

Source: Company annual reports.

FINANCIAL STATEMENT PRESENTATION
Balance Sheet

LEARNING OBJECTIVE 9
Describe the presentation of deferred income taxes in financial statements.

Deferred tax accounts are reported on the balance sheet as assets and liabilities. Companies should classify these accounts as a net current amount and a net non-current amount. **An individual deferred tax liability or asset is classified as current or noncurrent based on the classification of the related asset or liability for financial reporting purposes.**

A company considers a deferred tax asset or liability to be related to an asset or liability if reduction of the asset or liability causes the temporary difference to reverse or turn around. A company should classify a deferred tax liability or asset that is unrelated to an asset or liability for financial reporting, including a deferred tax asset related to a loss carryforward, according to the expected reversal date of the temporary difference.

To illustrate, assume that Morgan Inc. records bad debt expense using the allowance method for accounting purposes and the direct write-off method for tax purposes. It currently has Accounts Receivable and Allowance for Doubtful Accounts balances of $2 million and $100,000, respectively. In addition, given a 40 percent tax rate, Morgan has a debit balance in the Deferred Tax Asset account of $40,000 (40% × $100,000). It considers the $40,000 debit balance in the Deferred Tax Asset account to be related to the Accounts Receivable and the Allowance for Doubtful Accounts balances because collection or write-off of the receivables will cause the temporary difference to reverse. Therefore,

Morgan classifies the Deferred Tax Asset account as current, the same as the Accounts Receivable and Allowance for Doubtful Accounts balances.

In practice, most companies engage in a large number of transactions that give rise to deferred taxes. Companies should classify the balances in the deferred tax accounts on the balance sheet in two categories: one for the **net current amount**, and one for the **net noncurrent amount**. We summarize this procedure as follows.

1. *Classify the amounts as current or non-current.* If related to a specific asset or liability, classify the amounts in the same manner as the related asset or liability. If not related, classify them on the basis of the expected reversal date of the temporary difference.

2. *Determine the net current amount* by summing the various deferred tax assets and liabilities classified as current. If the net result is an asset, report it on the balance sheet as a current asset; if a liability, report it as a current liability.

3. *Determine the net non-current amount* by summing the various deferred tax assets and liabilities classified as noncurrent. If the net result is an asset, report it on the balance sheet as a noncurrent asset; if a liability, report it as a long-term liability.

To illustrate, assume that K. Scott Company has four deferred tax items at December 31, 2014. Illustration 19-39 shows an analysis of these four temporary differences as current or noncurrent.

Temporary Difference	Resulting Deferred Tax (Asset)	Liability	Related Balance Sheet Account	Classification
1. Rent collected in advance: recognized when earned for accounting purposes and when received for tax purposes.	$(42,000)		Unearned Rent	Current
2. Use of straight-line depreciation for accounting purposes and accelerated depreciation for tax purposes.		$214,000	Equipment	Noncurrent
3. Recognition of profits on installment sales during period of sale for accounting purposes and during period of collection for tax purposes.		45,000	Installment Accounts Receivable	Current
4. Warranty liabilities: recognized for accounting purposes at time of sale; for tax purpose at time paid.	(12,000)		Estimated Liability under Warranties	Current
Totals	$(54,000)	$259,000		

ILLUSTRATION 19-39
Classification of Temporary Differences as Current or Noncurrent

K. Scott classifies as current a deferred tax asset of $9,000 ($42,000 + $12,000 − $45,000). It also reports as noncurrent a deferred tax liability of $214,000. Consequently, K. Scott's December 31, 2014, balance sheet reports deferred income taxes as shown in Illustration 19-40.

Current assets	
Deferred tax asset	$ 9,000
Long-term liabilities	
Deferred tax liability	$214,000

ILLUSTRATION 19-40
Balance Sheet Presentation of Deferred Income Taxes

As we indicated earlier, a deferred tax asset or liability **may not be related** to an asset or liability for financial reporting purposes. One example is an operating loss carryforward. In this case, a company records a deferred tax asset, but there is no related, identifiable asset or liability for financial reporting purposes. In these limited situations, deferred income taxes are classified according to the **expected reversal date** of the temporary difference. That is, a company should report the tax effect of any temporary difference reversing next year as current, and the remainder as noncurrent. If a deferred tax asset is noncurrent, a company should classify it in the "Other assets" section.

The total of all deferred tax liabilities, the total of all deferred tax assets, and the total valuation allowance should be disclosed. In addition, companies should disclose the following: (1) any net change during the year in the total valuation allowance, and (2) the types of temporary differences, carryforwards, or carrybacks that give rise to significant portions of deferred tax liabilities and assets.

International Perspective

IFRS requires that deferred tax assets and liabilities be classified as noncurrent, regardless of the classification of the underlying asset or liability.

Income taxes payable is reported as a current liability on the balance sheet. Corporations make estimated tax payments to the Internal Revenue Service quarterly. They record these estimated payments by a debit to Prepaid Income Taxes. As a result, the balance of the Income Taxes Payable offsets the balance of the Prepaid Income Taxes account when reporting income taxes on the balance sheet.

What do the numbers mean?   IMAGINATION AT WORK

Here's one thing you can say that's true about U.S. corporate taxes: The statutory rate (35 percent at the federal level, 39.2 percent when you average in state rates) is the highest on earth (see the "What Do the Numbers Mean?" box on page 1131). Here's another thing you can say that's true about U.S. corporate taxes: The average effective tax rate is more like 25 percent, and many corporations generally pay much less than that. How do they do it? Take Apple, for example. It uses a tax structure known as the "Double Irish with a Dutch Sandwich," which reduces taxes by routing profits through Irish subsidiaries and the Netherlands and then to the Caribbean. As a result of using this tactic, Apple paid cash taxes of $3.3 billion around the world on its reported profits of $34.2 billion in a recent year, a tax rate of just 9.8 percent. Google uses the same strategy to reduce its overseas tax rate to 2.4 percent, the lowest of the top five U.S. technology companies by market capitalization, according to regulatory filings in six countries.

General Electric (GE) is generally viewed as the most skilled at reducing its tax burden. GE uses a maze of shelters, tax credits, and subsidiaries to pay far less than the stated tax rate. In a recent year, it reported worldwide profits of $14.2 billion, and said $5.1 billion of the total came from its operations in the United States. Its American tax bill? Zero. In fact, GE claimed a tax benefit of $3.2 billion. GE's giant tax department is viewed by some as the world's best tax law firm. Indeed, the company's slogan, "Imagination at Work," fits this department well. The team includes former officials not just from the Treasury, but also from the IRS and virtually all the tax-writing committees in Congress. The strategies employed by Apple, Google, and GE, as well as changes in tax laws that encouraged some businesses and professionals to file as individuals, have pushed down the corporate share of the nation's tax receipts from 30 percent of all federal revenue in the mid-1950s to 6.6 percent in 2009.

One IRS provision designed to curb excessive tax avoidance is the alternative minimum tax (AMT). Companies compute their potential tax liability under the AMT, adjusting for various preference items that reduce their tax bills under the regular tax code. (Examples of such preference items are accelerated depreciation methods and the installment method for revenue recognition.) Companies must pay the higher of the two tax obligations computed under the AMT and the regular tax code. But, as indicated by the cases above, some profitable companies avoid high tax bills, even in the presence of the AMT. Indeed, a recent study by the Government Accounting Office found that roughly two-thirds of U.S. and foreign corporations paid no federal income taxes from 1998–2005. Many citizens and public-interest groups cite corporate avoidance of income taxes as a reason for more tax reform.

Sources: D. Kocieniewski, "G.E.'s Strategies Let It Avoid Taxes Altogether," *The New York Times* (March 24, 2011); and J. Fox, "Why Some Multinationals Pay Such Low Taxes," *HBR Blog Network* (March 27, 2012).

Income Statement

Companies should allocate income tax expense (or benefit) to continuing operations, discontinued operations, extraordinary items, and prior period adjustments. This approach is referred to as intraperiod tax allocation.

In addition, companies should disclose the significant components of income tax expense attributable to continuing operations:

1. Current tax expense or benefit.

2. Deferred tax expense or benefit, exclusive of other components listed below.

3. Investment tax credits.

4. Government grants (if recognized as a reduction of income tax expense).

5. The benefits of operating loss carryforwards (resulting in a reduction of income tax expense).

6. Tax expense that results from allocating tax benefits either directly to paid-in capital or to reduce goodwill or other noncurrent intangible assets of an acquired entity.

7. Adjustments of a deferred tax liability or asset for enacted changes in tax laws or rates or a change in the tax status of a company.

8. Adjustments of the beginning-of-the-year balance of a valuation allowance because of a change in circumstances that causes a change in judgment about the realizability of the related deferred tax asset in future years.

In the notes, companies must also reconcile (using percentages or dollar amounts) income tax expense attributable to continuing operations with the amount that results from applying domestic federal statutory tax rates to pretax income from continuing significant reconciling items. Illustration 19-41 (page 1142) presents an example from the 2011 annual report of **PepsiCo, Inc.**

These income tax disclosures are required for several reasons:

1. *Assessing quality of earnings.* Many investors seeking to assess the quality of a company's earnings are interested in the reconciliation of pretax financial income to taxable income. Analysts carefully examine earnings that are enhanced by a favorable tax effect, particularly if the tax effect is nonrecurring. For example, the tax disclosure in Illustration 19-41 indicates that PepsiCo's effective tax rate increased from 23 percent in 2010 to 26.8 percent in 2011 (due to acquisitions of PBG and PAS and "other"). This decrease in the effective tax rate increased income for 2011.

2. *Making better predictions of future cash flows.* Examination of the deferred portion of income tax expense provides information as to whether taxes payable are likely to be higher or lower in the future. In PepsiCo's case, analysts expect future taxable amounts and higher tax payments, primarily from lower depreciation and amortization in the future. PepsiCo expects future deductible amounts and lower tax payments due to deductions for carryforwards, employee benefits, and state taxes. These deferred tax items indicate that actual tax payments for PepsiCo will be higher than the tax expense reported on the income statement in the future.[7]

---

[7]An article by R. P. Weber and J. E. Wheeler, "Using Income Tax Disclosures to Explore Significant Economic Transactions," *Accounting Horizons* (September 1992), discusses how analysts use deferred tax disclosures to assess the quality of earnings and to predict future cash flows.

ILLUSTRATION 19-41
Disclosure of Income
Taxes—PepsiCo, Inc.

PepsiCo, Inc.
(in millions)

Note 5—Income Taxes (in part)	2011	2010
Income before income taxes		
U.S.	$3,964	$4,008
Foreign	4,870	4,224
	$8,834	$8,232
Provision for income taxes		
Current: U.S. Federal	611	932
Foreign	882	728
State	124	137
	1,617	1,797
Deferred: U.S. Federal	789	78
Foreign	(88)	18
State	54	1
	755	97
	$2,372	$1,894
Tax rate reconciliation		
U.S. Federal statutory tax rate	35.0%	35.0%
State income tax, net of U.S. Federal tax benefit	1.3	1.1
Lower taxes on foreign results	(8.7)	(9.4)
Acquisitions of PBG and PAS	0	(3.1)
Other, net	(0.8)	(0.6)
Annual tax rate	26.8%	23.0%
Deferred tax liabilities		
Investments in noncontrolled affiliates	$ 41	$ 74
Debt guarantee of wholly owned subsidiary	828	828
Property, plant and equipment	2,466	1,984
Intangible assets other than nondeductible goodwill	4,297	3,726
Other	184	647
Gross deferred tax liabilities	7,816	7,259
Deferred tax assets		
Net carryforwards	1,373	1,264
Stock-based compensation	429	455
Retiree medical benefits	504	579
Other employee-related benefits	695	527
Pension benefits	545	291
Deductible state tax and interest benefits	339	320
Long-term debt obligations acquired	223	291
Other	822	904
Gross deferred tax assets	4,930	4,631
Valuation allowances	(1,264)	(875)
Deferred tax assets, net	3,666	3,756
Net deferred tax liabilities (assets)	$4,150	$3,503
Deferred taxes included within:		
Assets:		
Prepaid expenses and other current assets	$ 845	$ 554
Liabilities:		
Deferred income taxes	$4,995	$4,057
Analysis of valuation allowances		
Balance, beginning of year	$ 875	$ 586
(Benefit/provision)	464	75
Other additions/(deductions)	(75)	214
Balance, end of year	$1,264	$ 875

The labels in the left margin of the illustration: "Current and deferred tax expense", "Tax rate reconciliation", "Deferred tax liabilities and deferred tax assets", "Valuation allowance adjustments".

Carryforwards and allowances
Operating loss carryforwards totaling $10.0 billion at year-end 2011 are being carried forward in a number of foreign and state jurisdictions where we are permitted to use tax operating losses from prior periods to reduce future taxable income. These operating losses will expire as follows: $0.1 billion in 2012, $8.2 billion between 2013 and 2031 and $1.7 billion may be carried forward indefinitely. We establish valuation allowances for our deferred tax assets if, based on the available evidence, it is more likely than not that some portion or all of the deferred tax assets will not be realized.

3. *Predicting future cash flows for operating loss carryforwards.* Companies should disclose the amounts and expiration dates of any operating loss carryforwards for tax purposes. From this disclosure, analysts determine the amount of income that the company may recognize in the future on which it will pay no income tax. For example, the PepsiCo disclosure in Illustration 19-41 indicates that PepsiCo has $10.0 billion in net operating loss carryforwards that it can use to reduce future taxes. However, the valuation allowance indicates that $1.264 million of deferred tax assets may not be realized in the future.

Loss carryforwards can be valuable to a potential acquirer. For example, as mentioned earlier, **Yahoo!** has a substantial net operating loss carryforward. A potential acquirer would find Yahoo! more valuable as a result of these carryforwards. That is, the acquirer may be able to use these carryforwards to shield future income. However the acquiring company has to be careful because the structure of the deal may lead to a situation where the deductions will be severely limited.

Much the same issue arises in companies emerging from bankruptcy. In many cases, these companies have large NOLs but the value of the losses may be limited. This is because any gains related to the cancellation of liabilities in bankruptcy must be offset against the NOLs. For example, when **Kmart Holding Corp.** emerged from bankruptcy in early 2004, it disclosed NOL carryforwards approximating $3.8 billion. At the same time, Kmart disclosed cancellation of debt gains that reduced the value of the NOL carryforward. These reductions soured the merger between Kmart and **Sears Roebuck** because the cancellation of the indebtedness gains reduced the value of the Kmart carryforwards to the merged company by $3.74 billion.[8]

Evolving Issue   UNCERTAIN TAX POSITIONS

Whenever there is a contingency, companies determine if the contingency is **probable** and can be reasonably estimated. If both of these criteria are met, the company records the contingency in the financial statements. These guidelines also apply to uncertain tax positions. **Uncertain tax positions** are tax positions for which the tax authorities may disallow a deduction in whole or in part. Uncertain tax positions often arise when a company takes an aggressive approach in its tax planning. Examples are instances in which the tax law is unclear or the company may believe that the risk of audit is low. Uncertain tax positions give rise to tax benefits either by reducing income tax expense or related payables or by increasing an income tax refund receivable or deferred tax asset.

Unfortunately, companies have not applied these provisions consistently in accounting and reporting of uncertain tax positions. Some companies have not recognized a tax benefit unless it is probable that the benefit will be realized and can be reasonably estimated. Other companies have used a lower threshold, such as that found in the existing authoritative literature. As we have learned, the lower threshold—described as "**more likely than not**"—means that the company believes it has at least a 51 percent chance that the uncertain tax position will pass muster with the taxing authorities. Thus, there has been diversity in practice concerning the accounting and reporting of uncertain tax positions.

As a result, the FASB has issued rules for companies to follow to determine whether it is "more likely than not" that tax positions will be sustained upon audit. **[3]** If the probability is more than 50 percent, companies may reduce their liability or increase their assets. If the probability is less than 50 percent, companies may not record the tax benefit. In determining "more likely than not," companies must assume that they will be audited by the tax authorities. If the recognition threshold is passed, companies must then estimate the amount to record as an adjustment to their tax assets and

[8]P. McConnell, J. Pegg, C. Senyak, and D. Mott, "The ABCs of NOLs," *Accounting Issues*, Bear Stearns Equity Research (June 2005). In addition, some U.S. banks hope to cash in tax credits by acquiring weaker banks with operating losses and housing credits, arising from the credit crisis. See D. Palletta, "Goldman Looks to Buy Fannie Tax Credits," *Wall Street Journal* (November 2, 2009). The IRS frowns on acquisitions done solely to obtain operating loss carryforwards. If it determines that the merger is solely tax-motivated, the IRS disallows the deductions. But because it is very difficult to determine whether a merger is or is not tax-motivated, the "purchase of operating loss carryforwards" continues.

liabilities. (This estimation process is complex and is beyond the scope of this textbook.)

Companies will experience varying financial statement effects upon adoption of these rules. Those with a history of conservative tax strategies may have their tax liabilities decrease or their tax assets increase. For example, PepsiCo recorded a $7 million increase to retained earnings upon adoption of the guidelines. Others that followed more aggressive tax planning may have to increase their liabilities or reduce their assets, with a resulting negative effect on net income.

REVIEW OF THE ASSET-LIABILITY METHOD

LEARNING OBJECTIVE **10**

Indicate the basic principles of the asset-liability method.

The FASB believes that the **asset-liability method** (sometimes referred to as the **liability approach**) is the most consistent method for accounting for income taxes. One objective of this approach is to recognize the amount of taxes payable or refundable for the current year. A second objective is to recognize **deferred tax liabilities and assets** for the **future tax consequences** of events that have been recognized in the financial statements or tax returns.

To implement the objectives, companies apply some basic principles in accounting for income taxes at the date of the financial statements, as listed in Illustration 19-42. **[4]**

ILLUSTRATION 19-42
Basic Principles of the Asset-Liability Method

Basic Principles
a. A current tax liability or asset is recognized for the estimated taxes payable or refundable on the tax return for the current year.
b. A deferred tax liability or asset is recognized for the estimated future tax effects attributable to temporary differences and carryforwards.
c. The measurement of current and deferred tax liabilities and assets is based on provisions of the enacted tax law; the effects of future changes in tax laws or rates are not anticipated.
d. The measurement of deferred tax assets is reduced, if necessary, by the amount of any tax benefits that, based on available evidence, are not expected to be realized.

Illustration 19-43 diagrams the procedures for implementing the asset-liability method.

ILLUSTRATION 19-43
Procedures for Computing and Reporting Deferred Income Taxes

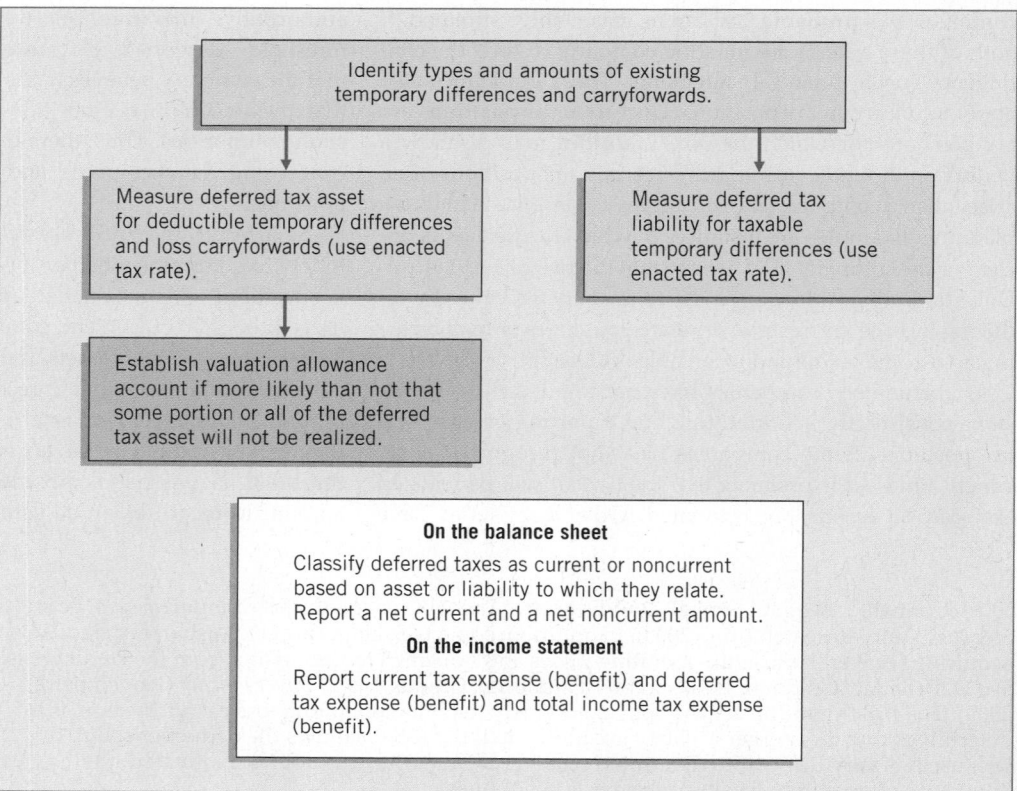

Gateway to the Profession

Discussion of Conceptual Approaches to Interperiod Tax Allocation

As an aid to understanding deferred income taxes, we provide the following glossary.

KEY DEFERRED INCOME TAX TERMS

CARRYBACKS. Deductions or credits that cannot be utilized on the tax return during a year and that may be carried back to reduce taxable income or taxes paid in a prior year. An **operating loss carryback** is an excess of tax deductions over gross income in a year. A **tax credit carryback** is the amount by which tax credits available for utilization exceed statutory limitations.

CARRYFORWARDS. Deductions or credits that cannot be utilized on the tax return during a year and that may be carried forward to reduce taxable income or taxes payable in a future year. An **operating loss carryforward** is an excess of tax deductions over gross income in a year. A **tax credit carryforward** is the amount by which tax credits available for utilization exceed statutory limitations.

CURRENT TAX EXPENSE (BENEFIT). The amount of income taxes paid or payable (or refundable) for a year as determined by applying the provisions of the enacted tax law to the taxable income or excess of deductions over revenues for that year.

DEDUCTIBLE TEMPORARY DIFFERENCE. Temporary differences that result in deductible amounts in future years when recovering or settling the related asset or liability, respectively.

DEFERRED TAX ASSET. The deferred tax consequences attributable to deductible temporary differences and carryforwards.

DEFERRED TAX CONSEQUENCES. The future effects on income taxes as measured by the enacted tax rate and provisions of the enacted tax law resulting from temporary differences and carryforwards at the end of the current year.

DEFERRED TAX EXPENSE (BENEFIT). The change during the year in a company's deferred tax liabilities and assets.

DEFERRED TAX LIABILITY. The deferred tax consequences attributable to taxable temporary differences.

INCOME TAXES. Domestic and foreign federal (national), state, and local (including franchise) taxes based on income.

INCOME TAXES CURRENTLY PAYABLE (REFUNDABLE). Refer to current tax expense (benefit).

INCOME TAX EXPENSE (BENEFIT). The sum of current tax expense (benefit) and deferred tax expense (benefit).

TAXABLE INCOME. The excess of taxable revenues over tax-deductible expenses and exemptions for the year as defined by the governmental taxing authority.

TAXABLE TEMPORARY DIFFERENCE. Temporary differences that result in taxable amounts in future years when recovering or settling the related asset or liability, respectively.

TAX-PLANNING STRATEGY. An action that meets certain criteria and that a company implements to realize a tax benefit for an operating loss or tax credit carryforward before it expires. Companies consider tax-planning strategies when assessing the need for and amount of a valuation allowance for deferred tax assets.

TEMPORARY DIFFERENCE. A difference between the tax basis of an asset or liability and its reported amount in the financial statements that will result in taxable or deductible amounts in future years when recovering or settling the reported amount of the asset or liability, respectively.

VALUATION ALLOWANCE. The portion of a deferred tax asset for which it is more likely than not that a company will not realize a tax benefit.

International Perspective

IFRS on income taxes is based on the same principles as GAAP—comprehensive recognition of deferred tax assets and liabilities.

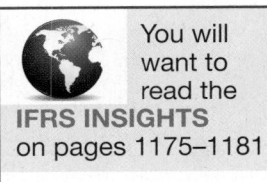 You will want to read the **IFRS INSIGHTS** on pages 1175–1181 for discussion of IFRS related to income taxes.

KEY TERMS

alternative minimum tax (AMT), *1140*

asset-liability method, *1144*

average tax rate, *1130*

current tax expense (benefit), *1121, 1134*

deductible amounts, *1120*

deductible temporary difference, *1127*

deferred tax asset, *1123*

deferred tax expense (benefit), *1121, 1124*

deferred tax liability, *1120*

effective tax rate, *1130*

enacted tax rate, *1130*

Income Tax Refund Receivable, *1133*

loss carryback, *1132*

loss carryforward, *1132*

more likely than not, *1125*

net current amount, *1139*

net noncurrent amount, *1139*

net operating loss (NOL), *1132*

originating temporary difference, *1128*

permanent difference, *1128*

pretax financial income, *1118*

reversing difference, *1128*

taxable amounts, *1120*

taxable income, *1118*

taxable temporary difference, *1127*

tax effect (tax benefit), *1133*

temporary difference, *1120*

uncertain tax positions, *1143*

valuation allowance, *1125*

SUMMARY OF LEARNING OBJECTIVES

1 **Identify differences between pretax financial income and taxable income.** Companies compute pretax financial income (or income for book purposes) in accordance with generally accepted accounting principles. They compute taxable income (or income for tax purposes) in accordance with prescribed tax regulations. Because tax regulations and GAAP differ in many ways, so frequently do pretax financial income and taxable income. Differences may exist, for example, in the timing of revenue recognition and the timing of expense recognition.

2 **Describe a temporary difference that results in future taxable amounts.** Revenue recognized for book purposes in the period earned but deferred and reported as revenue for tax purposes when collected results in future taxable amounts. The future taxable amounts will occur in the periods the company recovers the receivable and reports the collections as revenue for tax purposes. This results in a deferred tax liability.

3 **Describe a temporary difference that results in future deductible amounts.** An accrued warranty expense that a company pays for and deducts for tax purposes, in a period later than the period in which it incurs and recognizes it for book purposes, results in future deductible amounts. The future deductible amounts will occur in the periods during which the company settles the related liability for book purposes. This results in a deferred tax asset.

4 **Explain the purpose of a deferred tax asset valuation allowance.** A deferred tax asset should be reduced by a valuation allowance if, based on all available evidence, it is more likely than not (a level of likelihood that is at least slightly more than 50 percent) that it will not realize some portion or all of the deferred tax asset. The company should carefully consider all available evidence, both positive and negative, to determine whether, based on the weight of available evidence, it needs a valuation allowance.

5 **Describe the presentation of income tax expense in the income statement.** Significant components of income tax expense should be disclosed in the income statement or in the notes to the financial statements. The most commonly encountered components are the current expense (or benefit) and the deferred expense (or benefit).

6 **Describe various temporary and permanent differences.** Examples of temporary differences are (1) revenues or gains that are taxable after recognition in financial income; (2) expenses or losses that are deductible after recognition in financial income; (3) revenues or gains that are taxable before recognition in financial income; and (4) expenses or losses that are deductible before recognition in financial income. Examples of permanent differences are (1) items recognized for financial reporting purposes but not for tax purposes, and (2) items recognized for tax purposes but not for financial reporting purposes.

7 **Explain the effect of various tax rates and tax rate changes on deferred income taxes.** Companies may use tax rates other than the current rate only after enactment of the future tax rates. When a change in the tax rate is enacted, a company should immediately recognize its effect on the deferred income tax accounts. The company reports the effects as an adjustment to income tax expense in the period of the change.

8 **Apply accounting procedures for a loss carryback and a loss carryforward.** A company may carry a net operating loss back two years and receive refunds for income taxes paid in those years. The loss is applied to the earlier year first and then to the second year. Any loss remaining after the two-year carryback may be carried forward up to 20 years to offset future taxable income. A company may forgo the loss carryback and use the loss carryforward, offsetting future taxable income for up to 20 years.

9 **Describe the presentation of deferred income taxes in financial statements.** Companies report deferred tax accounts on the balance sheet as assets and liabilities. These deferred tax accounts are classified as a net current and a net noncurrent amount. Companies classify an individual deferred tax liability or asset as current or noncurrent based on the classification of the related asset or liability for financial reporting. A deferred tax liability or asset that is not related to an asset or liability for financial reporting, including a deferred tax asset related to a loss carryforward, is classified according to the expected reversal date of the temporary difference.

10 **Indicate the basic principles of the asset-liability method.** Companies apply the following basic principles in accounting for income taxes at the date of the financial statements. (1) Recognize a current tax liability or asset for the estimated taxes payable or refundable on the tax return for the current year. (2) Recognize a deferred tax liability or asset for the estimated future tax effects attributable to temporary differences and carryforwards using the enacted tax rate. (3) Base the measurement of current and deferred tax liabilities and assets on provisions of the enacted tax law. (4) Reduce the measurement of deferred tax assets, if necessary, by the amount of any tax benefits that, based on available evidence, companies do not expect to realize.

APPENDIX 19A | **COMPREHENSIVE EXAMPLE OF INTERPERIOD TAX ALLOCATION**

This appendix presents a comprehensive illustration of a deferred income tax problem with several temporary and permanent differences. The example follows one company through two complete years (2013 and 2014). **Study it carefully.** It should help you understand the concepts and procedures presented in the chapter.

11 **LEARNING OBJECTIVE**
Understand and apply the concepts and procedures of interperiod tax allocation.

FIRST YEAR—2013

Allman Company, which began operations at the beginning of 2013, produces various products on a contract basis. Each contract generates a gross profit of $80,000. Some of Allman's contracts provide for the customer to pay on an installment basis. Under these contracts, Allman collects one-fifth of the contract revenue in each of the following four years. For financial reporting purposes, the company recognizes gross profit in the year of completion (accrual basis); for tax purposes, Allman recognizes gross profit in the year cash is collected (installment basis).

Presented below is information related to Allman's operations for 2013.

1. In 2013, the company completed seven contracts that allow for the customer to pay on an installment basis. Allman recognized the related gross profit of $560,000 for financial reporting purposes. It reported only $112,000 of gross profit on installment sales on the 2013 tax return. The company expects future collections on the related installment receivables to result in taxable amounts of $112,000 in each of the next four years.

2. At the beginning of 2013, Allman Company purchased depreciable assets with a cost of $540,000. For financial reporting purposes, Allman depreciates these assets using the straight-line method over a six-year service life. For tax purposes, the assets fall in the five-year recovery class, and Allman uses the MACRS system. The depreciation schedules for both financial reporting and tax purposes are shown on page 1148.

Year	Depreciation for Financial Reporting Purposes	Depreciation for Tax Purposes	Difference
2013	$ 90,000	$108,000	$(18,000)
2014	90,000	172,800	(82,800)
2015	90,000	103,680	(13,680)
2016	90,000	62,208	27,792
2017	90,000	62,208	27,792
2018	90,000	31,104	58,896
	$540,000	$540,000	$ –0–

3. The company warrants its product for two years from the date of completion of a contract. During 2013, the product warranty liability accrued for financial reporting purposes was $200,000, and the amount paid for the satisfaction of warranty liability was $44,000. Allman expects to settle the remaining $156,000 by expenditures of $56,000 in 2014 and $100,000 in 2015.

4. In 2013, nontaxable municipal bond interest revenue was $28,000.

5. During 2013, nondeductible fines and penalties of $26,000 were paid.

6. Pretax financial income for 2013 amounts to $412,000.

7. Tax rates enacted before the end of 2013 were:

2013	50%
2014 and later years	40%

8. The accounting period is the calendar year.

9. The company is expected to have taxable income in all future years.

Taxable Income and Income Taxes Payable—2013

The first step is to determine Allman Company's income taxes payable for 2013 by calculating its taxable income. Illustration 19A-1 shows this computation.

ILLUSTRATION 19A-1
Computation of Taxable Income, 2013

Pretax financial income for 2013	$412,000
Permanent differences:	
Nontaxable revenue—municipal bond interest	(28,000)
Nondeductible expenses—fines and penalties	26,000
Temporary differences:	
Excess gross profit per books ($560,000 − $112,000)	(448,000)
Excess depreciation per tax ($108,000 − $90,000)	(18,000)
Excess warranty expense per books ($200,000 − $44,000)	156,000
Taxable income for 2013	$100,000

Allman computes income taxes payable on taxable income for $100,000 as follows.

ILLUSTRATION 19A-2
Computation of Income Taxes Payable, End of 2013

Taxable income for 2013	$100,000
Tax rate	50%
Income taxes payable (current tax expense) for 2013	$ 50,000

Computing Deferred Income Taxes—End of 2013

The schedule in Illustration 19A-3 summarizes the temporary differences and the resulting future taxable and deductible amounts.

	Future Years					
	2014	2015	2016	2017	2018	Total
Future taxable (deductible) amounts:						
Installment sales	$112,000	$112,000	$112,000	$112,000		$448,000
Depreciation	(82,800)	(13,680)	27,792	27,792	$58,896	18,000
Warranty costs	(56,000)	(100,000)				(156,000)

ILLUSTRATION 19A-3
Schedule of Future
Taxable and Deductible
Amounts, End of 2013

Allman computes the amounts of deferred income taxes to be reported at the end of 2013 as shown in Illustration 19A-4.

Temporary Difference	Future Taxable (Deductible) Amounts	Tax Rate	Deferred Tax (Asset)	Liability
Installment sales	$448,000	40%		$179,200
Depreciation	18,000	40%		7,200
Warranty costs	(156,000)	40%	$(62,400)	
Totals	$310,000		$(62,400)	$186,400*

*Because only a single tax rate is involved in all relevant years, these totals can be reconciled:
$310,000 × 40% = ($62,400) + $186,400.

ILLUSTRATION 19A-4
Computation of Deferred
Income Taxes, End of
2013

A temporary difference is caused by the use of the accrual basis for financial reporting purposes and the installment method for tax purposes. This temporary difference will result in future taxable amounts and hence a deferred tax liability. Because of the installment contracts completed in 2013, a temporary difference of $448,000 originates that will reverse in equal amounts over the next four years. The company expects to have taxable income in all future years, and there is only one enacted tax rate applicable to all future years. Allman uses that rate (40 percent) to compute the entire deferred tax liability resulting from this temporary difference.

The temporary difference caused by different depreciation policies for books and for tax purposes originates over three years and then reverses over three years. This difference will cause deductible amounts in 2014 and 2015 and taxable amounts in 2016, 2017, and 2018. These amounts sum to a net future taxable amount of $18,000 (which is the cumulative temporary difference at the end of 2013). Because the company expects to have taxable income in all future years and because there is only one tax rate enacted for all of the relevant future years, Allman applies that rate to the net future taxable amount to determine the related net deferred tax liability.

The third temporary difference is caused by different methods of accounting for warranties. This difference will result in deductible amounts in each of the two future years it takes to reverse. Because the company expects to report a positive income on all future tax returns and because there is only one tax rate enacted for each of the relevant future years, Allman uses that 40 percent rate to calculate the resulting deferred tax asset.

Deferred Tax Expense (Benefit) and the Journal Entry to Record Income Taxes—2013

To determine the deferred tax expense (benefit), we need to compare the beginning and ending balances of the deferred income tax accounts. Illustration 19A-5 (on page 1150) shows that computation.

ILLUSTRATION 19A-5
Computation of Deferred
Tax Expense (Benefit),
2013

Deferred tax asset at the end of 2013	$ 62,400
Deferred tax asset at the beginning of 2013	–0–
Deferred tax expense (benefit)	$ (62,400)
Deferred tax liability at the end of 2013	$186,400
Deferred tax liability at the beginning of 2013	–0–
Deferred tax expense (benefit)	$186,400

The $62,400 increase in the deferred tax asset causes a deferred tax benefit to be reported in the income statement. The $186,400 increase in the deferred tax liability during 2013 results in a deferred tax expense. These two amounts **net** to a deferred tax expense of $124,000 for 2013.

ILLUSTRATION 19A-6
Computation of Net
Deferred Tax Expense,
2013

Deferred tax expense (benefit)	$ (62,400)
Deferred tax expense (benefit)	186,400
Net deferred tax expense for 2013	$124,000

Allman then computes the total income tax expense as follows.

ILLUSTRATION 19A-7
Computation of Total
Income Tax Expense,
2013

Current tax expense for 2013	$ 50,000
Deferred tax expense for 2013	124,000
Income tax expense (total) for 2013	$174,000

Allman records income taxes payable, deferred income taxes, and income tax expense as follows.

Income Tax Expense	174,000	
Deferred Tax Asset	62,400	
Income Taxes Payable		50,000
Deferred Tax Liability		186,400

Financial Statement Presentation—2013

Companies should classify deferred tax assets and liabilities as current and noncurrent on the balance sheet based on the classifications of related assets and liabilities. Multiple categories of deferred taxes are classified into a net current amount and a net noncurrent amount. Illustration 19A-8 shows the classification of Allman's deferred tax accounts at the end of 2013.

ILLUSTRATION 19A-8
Classification of Deferred
Tax Accounts, End of
2013

Temporary Difference	Resulting Deferred Tax (Asset)	Liability	Related Balance Sheet Account	Classification
Installment sales		$179,200	Installment Receivable	Current
Depreciation		7,200	Plant Assets	Noncurrent
Warranty costs	$(62,400)		Warranty Obligation	Current
Totals	$(62,400)	$186,400		

For the first temporary difference, there is a related asset on the balance sheet, installment accounts receivable. Allman classifies that asset as current because it has a trade practice of selling to customers on an installment basis. Allman therefore classifies the resulting deferred tax liability as a current liability.

Certain assets on the balance sheet are related to the depreciation difference—the property, plant, and equipment being depreciated. Allman would classify the plant assets as noncurrent. Therefore, it also classifies the resulting deferred tax liability as noncurrent. Since the company's operating cycle is at least four years in length, Allman classifies the entire $156,000 warranty obligation as a current liability. Thus, it also classifies the related deferred tax asset of $62,400 as current.[9]

The balance sheet at the end of 2013 reports the following amounts.

Current liabilities		
Income taxes payable		$ 50,000
Deferred tax liability ($179,200 − $62,400)		116,800
Long-term liabilities		
Deferred tax liability		$ 7,200

ILLUSTRATION 19A-9
Balance Sheet
Presentation of Deferred
Taxes, 2013

Allman's income statement for 2013 reports the following.

Income before income taxes		$412,000
Income tax expense		
Current	$ 50,000	
Deferred	124,000	174,000
Net income		$238,000

ILLUSTRATION 19A-10
Income Statement
Presentation of Income
Tax Expense, 2013

SECOND YEAR—2014

1. During 2014, Allman collected $112,000 from customers for the receivables arising from contracts completed in 2013. The company expects recovery of the remaining receivables to result in taxable amounts of $112,000 in each of the following three years.

2. In 2014, the company completed four new contracts that allow for the customer to pay on an installment basis. These installment sales created new installment receivables. Future collections of these receivables will result in reporting gross profit of $64,000 for tax purposes in each of the next four years.

3. During 2014, Allman continued to depreciate the assets acquired in 2013 according to the depreciation schedules appearing on page 1148. Thus, depreciation amounted to $90,000 for financial reporting purposes and $172,800 for tax purposes.

4. An analysis at the end of 2014, of the product warranty liability account, showed the following details.

Balance of liability at beginning of 2014	$156,000
Expense for 2014 income statement purposes	180,000
Amount paid for contracts completed in 2013	(56,000)
Amount paid for contracts completed in 2014	(50,000)
Balance of liability at end of 2014	$230,000

[9]If Allman's operating cycle were less than one year in length, the company would expect to settle $56,000 of the warranty obligation within one year of the December 31, 2013, balance sheet and would use current assets to do so. Thus, $56,000 of the warranty obligation would be a current liability and the remaining $100,000 warranty obligation would be a long-term (noncurrent) liability. This would mean that Allman would classify $22,400 ($56,000 × 40%) of the related deferred tax asset as a current asset, and $40,000 ($100,000 × 40%) of the deferred tax asset as a noncurrent asset. *In doing homework problems, unless it is evident otherwise, assume a company's operating cycle is not longer than one year.*

The balance of the liability is expected to require expenditures in the future as follows.

> $100,000 in 2015 due to 2013 contracts
> $ 50,000 in 2015 due to 2014 contracts
> $ 80,000 in 2016 due to 2014 contracts
>
> $230,000

5. During 2014, nontaxable municipal bond interest revenue was $24,000.
6. Allman accrued a loss of $172,000 for financial reporting purposes because of pending litigation. This amount is not tax-deductible until the period the loss is realized, which the company estimates to be 2022.
7. Pretax financial income for 2014 amounts to $504,800.
8. The enacted tax rates still in effect are:

2013	50%
2014 and later years	40%

Taxable Income and Income Taxes Payable—2014

Allman computes taxable income for 2014 as follows.

ILLUSTRATION 19A-11
Computation of Taxable Income, 2014

Pretax financial income for 2014	$504,800
Permanent difference:	
Nontaxable revenue—municipal bond interest	(24,000)
Reversing temporary differences:	
Collection on 2013 installment sales	112,000
Payments on warranties from 2013 contracts	(56,000)
Originating temporary differences:	
Excess gross profit per books—2014 contracts	(256,000)
Excess depreciation per tax	(82,800)
Excess warranty expense per books—2014 contracts	130,000
Loss accrual per books	172,000
Taxable income for 2014	$500,000

Income taxes payable for 2014 are as follows.

ILLUSTRATION 19A-12
Computation of Income Taxes Payable, End of 2014

Taxable income for 2014	$500,000
Tax rate	40%
Income taxes payable (current tax expense) for 2014	$200,000

ILLUSTRATION 19A-13
Schedule of Future Taxable and Deductible Amounts, End of 2014

Computing Deferred Income Taxes—End of 2014

The schedule in Illustration 19A-13 summarizes the temporary differences existing at the end of 2014 and the resulting future taxable and deductible amounts.

	Future Years					
	2015	2016	2017	2018	2022	Total
Future taxable (deductible) amounts:						
Installment sales—2013	$112,000	$112,000	$112,000			$336,000
Installment sales—2014	64,000	64,000	64,000	$64,000		256,000
Depreciation	(13,680)	27,792	27,792	58,896		100,800
Warranty costs	(150,000)	(80,000)				(230,000)
Loss accrual					$(172,000)	(172,000)

Allman computes the amounts of deferred income taxes to be reported at the end of 2014 as follows.

Temporary Difference	Future Taxable (Deductible) Amounts	Tax Rate	Deferred Tax (Asset)	Liability
Installment sales	$592,000*	40%		$236,800
Depreciation	100,800	40%		40,320
Warranty costs	(230,000)	40%	$ (92,000)	
Loss accrual	(172,000)	40%	(68,800)	
Totals	$290,800		$(160,800)	$277,120**

*Cumulative temporary difference = $336,000 + $256,000
**Because of a flat tax rate, these totals can be reconciled: $290,800 × 40% = $(160,800) + $277,120

ILLUSTRATION 19A-14
Computation of Deferred Income Taxes, End of 2014

Deferred Tax Expense (Benefit) and the Journal Entry to Record Income Taxes—2014

To determine the deferred tax expense (benefit), Allman must compare the beginning and ending balances of the deferred income tax accounts, as shown in Illustration 19A-15.

Deferred tax asset at the end of 2014	$160,800
Deferred tax asset at the beginning of 2014	62,400
Deferred tax expense (benefit)	$ (98,400)
Deferred tax liability at the end of 2014	$277,120
Deferred tax liability at the beginning of 2014	186,400
Deferred tax expense (benefit)	$ 90,720

ILLUSTRATION 19A-15
Computation of Deferred Tax Expense (Benefit), 2014

The deferred tax expense (benefit) and the total income tax expense for 2014 are, therefore, as follows.

Deferred tax expense (benefit)	$ (98,400)
Deferred tax expense (benefit)	90,720
Deferred tax benefit for 2014	(7,680)
Current tax expense for 2014	200,000
Income tax expense (total) for 2014	$192,320

ILLUSTRATION 19A-16
Computation of Total Income Tax Expense, 2014

The deferred tax expense of $90,720 and the deferred tax benefit of $98,400 net to a deferred tax benefit of $7,680 for 2014.

Allman records income taxes for 2014 with the following journal entry.

Income Tax Expense	192,320	
Deferred Tax Asset	98,400	
Income Taxes Payable		200,000
Deferred Tax Liability		90,720

Financial Statement Presentation—2014

Illustration 19A-17 (on page 1154) shows the classification of Allman's deferred tax accounts at the end of 2014.

ILLUSTRATION 19A-17
Classification of Deferred Tax Accounts, End of 2014

Temporary Difference	Resulting Deferred Tax (Asset)	Liability	Related Balance Sheet Account	Classification
Installment sales		$236,800	Installment Receivables	Current
Depreciation		40,320	Plant Assets	Noncurrent
Warranty costs	$ (92,000)		Warranty Obligation	Current
Loss accrual	(68,800)		Litigation Obligation	Noncurrent
Totals	$(160,800)	$277,120		

The new temporary difference introduced in 2014 (due to the litigation loss accrual) results in a litigation obligation that is classified as a long-term liability. Thus, the related deferred tax asset is noncurrent.

Allman's balance sheet at the end of 2014 reports the following amounts.

ILLUSTRATION 19A-18
Balance Sheet Presentation of Deferred Taxes, End of 2014

Other assets (noncurrent)	
Deferred tax asset ($68,800 − $40,320)	$ 28,480
Current liabilities	
Income taxes payable	$200,000
Deferred tax liability ($236,800 − $92,000)	144,800

The income statement for 2014 reports the following.

ILLUSTRATION 19A-19
Income Statement Presentation of Income Tax Expense, 2014

Income before income taxes		$504,800
Income tax expense		
Current	$200,000	
Deferred	(7,680)	192,320
Net income		$312,480

SUMMARY OF LEARNING OBJECTIVE FOR APPENDIX 19A

11 **Understand and apply the concepts and procedures of interperiod tax allocation.** Accounting for deferred taxes involves the following steps. (1) Calculate taxable income and income taxes payable for the year. (2) Compute deferred income taxes at the end of the year. (3) Determine deferred tax expense (benefit) and make the journal entry to record income taxes. (4) Classify deferred tax assets and liabilities as current or noncurrent in the financial statements.

DEMONSTRATION PROBLEM

Johnny Bravo Company began operations in 2014 and has provided the following information.

1. Pretax financial income for 2014 is $100,000.
2. The tax rate enacted for 2014 and future years is 40%.
3. Differences between the 2014 income statement and tax return are listed below.
   (a) Warranty expense accrued for financial reporting purposes amounts to $5,000. Warranty deductions per the tax return amount to $2,000.

(b) Gross profit on construction contracts using the percentage-of-completion method for books amounts to $92,000. Gross profit on construction contracts for tax purposes amounts to $62,000.

(c) Depreciation of property, plant, and equipment for financial reporting purposes amounts to $60,000. Depreciation of these assets amounts to $80,000 for the tax return.

(d) A $3,500 fine paid for violation of pollution laws was deducted in computing pretax financial income.

(e) Interest revenue earned on an investment in tax-exempt municipal bonds amounts to $1,400.

Assume (a) is short-term in nature; assume (b) and (c) are long-term in nature.

4. Taxable income is expected for the next few years.

Instructions

(a) Compute taxable income for 2014.

(b) Compute the deferred taxes at December 31, 2014, that relate to the temporary differences described above.

(c) Prepare the journal entry to record income tax expense, deferred taxes, and income taxes payable for 2014.

(d) Draft the income tax expense section of the income statement, beginning with "Income before income taxes."

(e) Assume that in 2015 Johnny Bravo reported a pretax operating loss of $100,000. There were no other temporary or permanent differences in tax and book income for 2015. Prepare the journal entry to record income tax expense for 2015. Johnny Bravo expects to return to profitability in 2016.

Solution

(a)

Pretax financial income	$100,000
Permanent differences	
Fine for pollution	3,500
Tax-exempt interest	(1,400)
Originating temporary differences	
Excess warranty expense per books ($5,000 − $2,000)	3,000
Excess construction profits per books ($92,000 − $62,000)	(30,000)
Excess depreciation per tax ($80,000 − $60,000)	(20,000)
Taxable income	$ 55,100

(b)

			Deferred Tax	
Temporary Difference	Future Taxable (Deductible) Amounts	Tax Rate	(Asset)	Liability
Warranty costs	$ (3,000)	40%	$(1,200)	
Construction contracts	30,000	40%		$12,000
Depreciation	20,000	40%		8,000
Totals	$47,000		$(1,200)	$20,000*

(c)

Income Tax Expense	40,840	
Deferred Tax Asset	1,200	
Deferred Tax Liability		20,000
Income Taxes Payable		22,040

Taxable income for 2014 [from part (a)]	$55,100
Tax rate	40%
Income taxes payable for 2014	$22,040
Deferred tax liability at the end of 2014 [from part (b)]	$20,000
Deferred tax liability at the beginning of 2014	–0–
Deferred tax expense for 2014	$20,000
Deferred tax asset at the end of 2014 [from part (b)]	$ 1,200
Deferred tax asset at the beginning of 2014	–0–
Deferred tax benefit for 2014	$ (1,200)

(d)

Income before income taxes		$100,000
Income tax expense		
Current	$22,040	
Deferred	18,800	40,840
Net income		$ 59,160

(e)

Income Tax Refund Receivable*	22,040	
Deferred Tax Asset**	17,960	
Benefit from Operating Loss Carryback		22,040
Benefit from Operating Loss Carryforward		17,960

2015 Loss	$100,000
*Carryback	(55,100) × 40% = $22,040 refund
**Carryforward	$ 44,900 × 40% = $17,960 deferred tax asset

No valuation allowance is needed since Johnny Bravo is expected to return to profitability in 2016. This is positive evidence that the deferred tax asset will be realized.

FASB CODIFICATION

FASB Codification References

[1] FASB ASC 740-10-30-18. [Predecessor literature: "Accounting for Income Taxes," *Statement of Financial Accounting Standards No. 109* (Norwalk, Conn.: FASB, 1992).]

[2] FASB ASC 740-10-30-21 & 22. [Predecessor literature: "Accounting for Income Taxes," *Statement of Financial Accounting Standards No. 109* (Norwalk, Conn.: FASB, 1992), paras. 23 and 24.]

[3] FASB ASC 740-10-25-6. [Predecessor literature: "Accounting for Uncertainty in Income Taxes," *FASB Interpretation No. 48* (Norwalk, Conn.: FASB, 2006).]

[4] FASB ASC 740-10-05. [Predecessor literature: "Accounting for Income Taxes," *Statement of Financial Accounting Standards No. 109* (Norwalk, Conn.: FASB, 1992), paras. 6 and 8.]

Exercises

If your school has a subscription to the FASB Codification, go to *http://aaahq.org/ascLogin.cfm* to log in and prepare responses to the following. Provide Codification references for your responses.

CE19-1 Access the glossary ("Master Glossary") to answer the following.

    (a) What is a deferred tax asset?
    (b) What is taxable income?
    (c) What is the definition of valuation allowance?
    (d) What is a deferred tax liability?

CE19-2 What are the two basic requirements applied to the measurement of current and deferred income taxes at the date of the financial statements?

CE19-3 A company wishes to conduct business in a foreign country that attracts businesses by granting "holidays" from income taxes for a certain period of time. Would the company have to disclose this "holiday" to the SEC? If so, what information must be disclosed?

CE19-4 When is a company allowed to initially recognize the financial statement effects of a tax position?

An additional Codification case can be found in the Using Your Judgment section, on page 1174.

Be sure to check the book's companion website for a **Review and Analysis Exercise,** with solution.

 Brief Exercises, Exercises, Problems, and many more learning and assessment tools and resources are available for practice in WileyPLUS.

QUESTIONS

1. Explain the difference between pretax financial income and taxable income.

2. What are the two objectives of accounting for income taxes?

3. Interest on municipal bonds is referred to as a permanent difference when determining the proper amount to report for deferred taxes. Explain the meaning of permanent differences, and give two other examples.

4. Explain the meaning of a temporary difference as it relates to deferred tax computations, and give three examples.

5. Differentiate between an originating temporary difference and a reversing difference.

6. The book basis of depreciable assets for Erwin Co. is $900,000, and the tax basis is $700,000 at the end of 2015. The enacted tax rate is 34% for all periods. Determine the amount of deferred taxes to be reported on the balance sheet at the end of 2015.

7. Roth Inc. has a deferred tax liability of $68,000 at the beginning of 2015. At the end of 2015, it reports accounts receivable on the books at $90,000 and the tax basis at zero (its only temporary difference). If the enacted tax rate is 34% for all periods, and income taxes payable for the period is $230,000, determine the amount of total income tax expense to report for 2015.

8. What is the difference between a future taxable amount and a future deductible amount? When is it appropriate to record a valuation account for a deferred tax asset?

9. Pretax financial income for Lake Inc. is $300,000, and its taxable income is $100,000 for 2015. Its only temporary difference at the end of the period relates to a $70,000 difference due to excess depreciation for tax purposes. If the tax rate is 40% for all periods, compute the amount of income tax expense to report in 2015. No deferred income taxes existed at the beginning of the year.

10. How are deferred tax assets and deferred tax liabilities reported on the balance sheet?

11. Describe the procedures involved in segregating various deferred tax amounts into current and noncurrent categories.

12. How is it determined whether deferred tax amounts are considered to be "related" to specific asset or liability amounts?

13. At the end of the year, Falabella Co. has pretax financial income of $550,000. Included in the $550,000 is $70,000 interest income on municipal bonds, $25,000 fine for dumping hazardous waste, and depreciation of $60,000. Depreciation for tax purposes is $45,000. Compute income taxes payable, assuming the tax rate is 30% for all periods.

14. Addison Co. has one temporary difference at the beginning of 2014 of $500,000. The deferred tax liability established for this amount is $150,000, based on a tax rate of 30%. The temporary difference will provide the following taxable amounts: $100,000 in 2015, $200,000 in 2016, and $200,000 in 2017. If a new tax rate for 2017 of 20% is enacted into law at the end of 2014, what is the journal entry necessary in 2014 (if any) to adjust deferred taxes?

15. What are some of the reasons that the components of income tax expense should be disclosed and a reconciliation between the effective tax rate and the statutory tax rate be provided?

16. Differentiate between "loss carryback" and "loss carryforward." Which can be accounted for with the greater certainty when it arises? Why?

17. What are the possible treatments for tax purposes of a net operating loss? What are the circumstances that determine the option to be applied? What is the proper treatment of a net operating loss for financial reporting purposes?

18. What controversy relates to the accounting for net operating loss carryforwards?

19. What is an uncertain tax position, and what are the general guidelines for accounting for uncertain tax positions?

BRIEF EXERCISES

BE19-1 In 2014, Amirante Corporation had pretax financial income of $168,000 and taxable income of $120,000. The difference is due to the use of different depreciation methods for tax and accounting purposes. The effective tax rate is 40%. Compute the amount to be reported as income taxes payable at December 31, 2014.

BE19-2 Oxford Corporation began operations in 2014 and reported pretax financial income of $225,000 for the year. Oxford's tax depreciation exceeded its book depreciation by $40,000. Oxford's tax rate for 2014 and years thereafter is 30%. In its December 31, 2014, balance sheet, what amount of deferred tax liability should be reported?

9 **BE19-3** Using the information from BE19-2, assume this is the only difference between Oxford's pretax financial income and taxable income. Prepare the journal entry to record the income tax expense, deferred income taxes, and income taxes payable, and show how the deferred tax liability will be classified on the December 31, 2014, balance sheet.

2 **5** **BE19-4** At December 31, 2014, Appaloosa Corporation had a deferred tax liability of $25,000. At December 31, 2015, the deferred tax liability is $42,000. The corporation's 2015 current tax expense is $48,000. What amount should Appaloosa report as total 2015 income tax expense?

1 **3** **BE19-5** At December 31, 2014, Suffolk Corporation had an estimated warranty liability of $105,000 for accounting purposes and $0 for tax purposes. (The warranty costs are not deductible until paid.) The effective tax rate is 40%. Compute the amount Suffolk should report as a deferred tax asset at December 31, 2014.

3 **5** **BE19-6** At December 31, 2014, Percheron Inc. had a deferred tax asset of $30,000. At December 31, 2015, the deferred tax asset is $59,000. The corporation's 2015 current tax expense is $61,000. What amount should Percheron report as total 2015 income tax expense?

4 **BE19-7** At December 31, 2014, Hillyard Corporation has a deferred tax asset of $200,000. After a careful review of all available evidence, it is determined that it is more likely than not that $60,000 of this deferred tax asset will not be realized. Prepare the necessary journal entry.

5 **BE19-8** Mitchell Corporation had income before income taxes of $195,000 in 2014. Mitchell's current income tax expense is $48,000, and deferred income tax expense is $30,000. Prepare Mitchell's 2014 income statement, beginning with Income before income taxes.

2 **3** **BE19-9** Shetland Inc. had pretax financial income of $154,000 in 2014. Included in the computation of that amount is insurance expense of $4,000 which is not deductible for tax purposes. In addition, depreciation for tax purposes exceeds accounting depreciation by $10,000. Prepare Shetland's journal entry to record 2014 taxes, assuming a tax rate of 45%.

2 **BE19-10** Clydesdale Corporation has a cumulative temporary difference related to depreciation of $580,000 at December 31, 2014. This difference will reverse as follows: 2015, $42,000; 2016, $244,000; and 2017, $294,000. Enacted tax rates are 34% for 2015 and 2016, and 40% for 2017. Compute the amount Clydesdale should report as a deferred tax liability at December 31, 2014.

7 **BE19-11** At December 31, 2014, Fell Corporation had a deferred tax liability of $680,000, resulting from future taxable amounts of $2,000,000 and an enacted tax rate of 34%. In May 2015, a new income tax act is signed into law that raises the tax rate to 40% for 2015 and future years. Prepare the journal entry for Fell to adjust the deferred tax liability.

8 **BE19-12** Conlin Corporation had the following tax information.

Year	Taxable Income	Tax Rate	Taxes Paid
2012	$300,000	35%	$105,000
2013	$325,000	30%	$ 97,500
2014	$400,000	30%	$120,000

In 2015, Conlin suffered a net operating loss of $480,000, which it elected to carry back. The 2015 enacted tax rate is 29%. Prepare Conlin's entry to record the effect of the loss carryback.

8 **BE19-13** Rode Inc. incurred a net operating loss of $500,000 in 2014. Combined income for 2012 and 2013 was $350,000. The tax rate for all years is 40%. Rode elects the carryback option. Prepare the journal entries to record the benefits of the loss carryback and the loss carryforward. Rode expects to return to profitability in 2015.

4 **8** **BE19-14** Use the information for Rode Inc. given in BE19-13. Assume that it is more likely than not that the entire net operating loss carryforward will not be realized in future years. Prepare all the journal entries necessary at the end of 2014.

9 **BE19-15** Youngman Corporation has temporary differences at December 31, 2014, that result in the following deferred taxes.

Deferred tax liability—current	$38,000
Deferred tax asset—current	$62,000
Deferred tax liability—noncurrent	$96,000
Deferred tax asset—noncurrent	$27,000

Indicate how these balances would be presented in Youngman's December 31, 2014, balance sheet.

EXERCISES

2 5 **E19-1 (One Temporary Difference, Future Taxable Amounts, One Rate, No Beginning Deferred Taxes)** South Carolina Corporation has one temporary difference at the end of 2014 that will reverse and cause taxable amounts of $55,000 in 2015, $60,000 in 2016, and $65,000 in 2017. South Carolina's pretax financial income for 2014 is $300,000, and the tax rate is 30% for all years. There are no deferred taxes at the beginning of 2014.

Instructions
(a) Compute taxable income and income taxes payable for 2014.
(b) Prepare the journal entry to record income tax expense, deferred income taxes, and income taxes payable for 2014.
(c) Prepare the income tax expense section of the income statement for 2014, beginning with the line "Income before income taxes."

2 **E19-2 (Two Differences, No Beginning Deferred Taxes, Tracked through 2 Years)** The following information is available for Wenger Corporation for 2013 (its first year of operations).

1. Excess of tax depreciation over book depreciation, $40,000. This $40,000 difference will reverse equally over the years 2014–2017.
2. Deferral, for book purposes, of $20,000 of rent received in advance. The rent will be recognized in 2014.
3. Pretax financial income, $300,000.
4. Tax rate for all years, 40%.

Instructions
(a) Compute taxable income for 2013.
(b) Prepare the journal entry to record income tax expense, deferred income taxes, and income taxes payable for 2013.
(c) Prepare the journal entry to record income tax expense, deferred income taxes, and income taxes payable for 2014, assuming taxable income of $325,000.

2 5 **E19-3 (One Temporary Difference, Future Taxable Amounts, One Rate, Beginning Deferred Taxes)** Bandung Corporation began 2014 with a $92,000 balance in the Deferred Tax Liability account. At the end of 2014, the related cumulative temporary difference amounts to $350,000, and it will reverse evenly over the next 2 years. Pretax accounting income for 2014 is $525,000, the tax rate for all years is 40%, and taxable income for 2014 is $405,000.

Instructions
(a) Compute income taxes payable for 2014.
(b) Prepare the journal entry to record income tax expense, deferred income taxes, and income taxes payable for 2014.
(c) Prepare the income tax expense section of the income statement for 2014 beginning with the line "Income before income taxes."

2 3 **5 6** **E19-4 (Three Differences, Compute Taxable Income, Entry for Taxes)** Zurich Company reports pretax financial income of $70,000 for 2014. The following items cause taxable income to be different than pretax financial income.

1. Depreciation on the tax return is greater than depreciation on the income statement by $16,000.
2. Rent collected on the tax return is greater than rent recognized on the income statement by $22,000.
3. Fines for pollution appear as an expense of $11,000 on the income statement.

Zurich's tax rate is 30% for all years, and the company expects to report taxable income in all future years. There are no deferred taxes at the beginning of 2014.

Instructions
(a) Compute taxable income and income taxes payable for 2014.
(b) Prepare the journal entry to record income tax expense, deferred income taxes, and income taxes payable for 2014.
(c) Prepare the income tax expense section of the income statement for 2014, beginning with the line "Income before income taxes."
(d) Compute the effective income tax rate for 2014.

2 3 **E19-5 (Two Temporary Differences, One Rate, Beginning Deferred Taxes)** The following facts relate to
5 Krung Thep Corporation.

1. Deferred tax liability, January 1, 2014, $40,000.
2. Deferred tax asset, January 1, 2014, $0.
3. Taxable income for 2014, $95,000.
4. Pretax financial income for 2014, $200,000.
5. Cumulative temporary difference at December 31, 2014, giving rise to future taxable amounts, $240,000.
6. Cumulative temporary difference at December 31, 2014, giving rise to future deductible amounts, $35,000.
7. Tax rate for all years, 40%.
8. The company is expected to operate profitably in the future.

Instructions
(a) Compute income taxes payable for 2014.
(b) Prepare the journal entry to record income tax expense, deferred income taxes, and income taxes payable for 2014.
(c) Prepare the income tax expense section of the income statement for 2014, beginning with the line "Income before income taxes."

6 **E19-6 (Identify Temporary or Permanent Differences)** Listed below are items that are commonly accounted for differently for financial reporting purposes than they are for tax purposes.

Instructions
For each item below, indicate whether it involves:

(1) A temporary difference that will result in future deductible amounts and, therefore, will usually give rise to a deferred income tax asset.
(2) A temporary difference that will result in future taxable amounts and, therefore, will usually give rise to a deferred income tax liability.
(3) A permanent difference.

Use the appropriate number to indicate your answer for each.

(a) _____ The MACRS depreciation system is used for tax purposes, and the straight-line depreciation method is used for financial reporting purposes for some plant assets.
(b) _____ A landlord collects some rents in advance. Rents received are taxable in the period when they are received.
(c) _____ Expenses are incurred in obtaining tax-exempt income.
(d) _____ Costs of guarantees and warranties are estimated and accrued for financial reporting purposes.
(e) _____ Installment sales of investments are accounted for by the accrual method for financial reporting purposes and the installment method for tax purposes.
(f) _____ For some assets, straight-line depreciation is used for both financial reporting purposes and tax purposes but the assets' lives are shorter for tax purposes.
(g) _____ Interest is received on an investment in tax-exempt municipal obligations.
(h) _____ Proceeds are received from a life insurance company because of the death of a key officer. (The company carries a policy on key officers.)
(i) _____ The tax return reports a deduction for 80% of the dividends received from U.S. corporations. The cost method is used in accounting for the related investments for financial reporting purposes.
(j) _____ Estimated losses on pending lawsuits and claims are accrued for books. These losses are tax deductible in the period(s) when the related liabilities are settled.
(k) _____ Expenses on stock options are accrued for financial reporting purposes.

2 3 **E19-7 (Terminology, Relationships, Computations, Entries)**
4 6 **Instructions**
Complete the following statements by filling in the blanks.

(a) In a period in which a taxable temporary difference reverses, the reversal will cause taxable income to be _____ (less than, greater than) pretax financial income.
(b) If a $76,000 balance in Deferred Tax Asset was computed by use of a 40% rate, the underlying cumulative temporary difference amounts to $_____.
(c) Deferred taxes _____ (are, are not) recorded to account for permanent differences.
(d) If a taxable temporary difference originates in 2014, it will cause taxable income for 2014 to be _____ (less than, greater than) pretax financial income for 2014.
(e) If total tax expense is $50,000 and deferred tax expense is $65,000, then the current portion of the expense computation is referred to as current tax _____ (expense, benefit) of $_____.

(f) If a corporation's tax return shows taxable income of $100,000 for Year 2 and a tax rate of 40%, how much will appear on the December 31, Year 2, balance sheet for "Income taxes payable" if the company has made estimated tax payments of $36,500 for Year 2? $_____.

(g) An increase in the Deferred Tax Liability account on the balance sheet is recorded by a _____ (debit, credit) to the Income Tax Expense account.

(h) An income statement that reports current tax expense of $82,000 and deferred tax benefit of $23,000 will report total income tax expense of $_____.

(i) A valuation account is needed whenever it is judged to be _____ that a portion of a deferred tax asset _____ (will be, will not be) realized.

(j) If the tax return shows total taxes due for the period of $75,000 but the income statement shows total income tax expense of $55,000, the difference of $20,000 is referred to as deferred tax _____ (expense, benefit).

2 3 5 9   **E19-8 (Two Temporary Differences, One Rate, 3 Years)** Button Company has the following two temporary differences between its income tax expense and income taxes payable.

	2014	2015	2016
Pretax financial income	$840,000	$910,000	$945,000
Excess depreciation expense on tax return	(30,000)	(40,000)	(10,000)
Excess warranty expense in financial income	20,000	10,000	8,000
Taxable income	$830,000	$880,000	$943,000

The income tax rate for all years is 40%.

Instructions

(a) Assuming there were no temporary differences prior to 2014, prepare the journal entry to record income tax expense, deferred income taxes, and income taxes payable for 2014, 2015, and 2016.

(b) Indicate how deferred taxes will be reported on the 2016 balance sheet. Button's product warranty is for 12 months.

(c) Prepare the income tax expense section of the income statement for 2016, beginning with the line "Pretax financial income."

8   **E19-9 (Carryback and Carryforward of NOL, No Valuation Account, No Temporary Differences)** The pretax financial income (or loss) figures for Jenny Spangler Company are as follows.

2009	$160,000
2010	250,000
2011	80,000
2012	(160,000)
2013	(380,000)
2014	120,000
2015	100,000

Pretax financial income (or loss) and taxable income (loss) were the same for all years involved. Assume a 45% tax rate for 2009 and 2010 and a 40% tax rate for the remaining years.

Instructions

Prepare the journal entries for the years 2011 to 2015 to record income tax expense and the effects of the net operating loss carrybacks and carryforwards assuming Jenny Spangler Company uses the carryback provision. All income and losses relate to normal operations. (In recording the benefits of a loss carryforward, assume that no valuation account is deemed necessary.)

8   **E19-10 (Two NOLs, No Temporary Differences, No Valuation Account, Entries and Income Statement)** Felicia Rashad Corporation has pretax financial income (or loss) equal to taxable income (or loss) from 2006 through 2014 as follows.

	Income (Loss)	Tax Rate
2006	$ 29,000	30%
2007	40,000	30%
2008	17,000	35%
2009	48,000	50%
2010	(150,000)	40%
2011	90,000	40%
2012	30,000	40%
2013	105,000	40%
2014	(60,000)	45%

Pretax financial income (loss) and taxable income (loss) were the same for all years since Rashad has been in business. Assume the carryback provision is employed for net operating losses. In recording the benefits of a loss carryforward, assume that it is more likely than not that the related benefits will be realized.

Instructions
(a) What entry(ies) for income taxes should be recorded for 2010?
(b) Indicate what the income tax expense portion of the income statement for 2010 should look like. Assume all income (loss) relates to continuing operations.
(c) What entry for income taxes should be recorded in 2011?
(d) How should the income tax expense section of the income statement for 2011 appear?
(e) What entry for income taxes should be recorded in 2014?
(f) How should the income tax expense section of the income statement for 2014 appear?

2 3 9 **E19-11 (Three Differences, Classify Deferred Taxes)** At December 31, 2013, Belmont Company had a net deferred tax liability of $375,000. An explanation of the items that compose this balance is as follows.

Temporary Differences	Resulting Balances in Deferred Taxes
1. Excess of tax depreciation over book depreciation	$200,000
2. Accrual, for book purposes, of estimated loss contingency from pending lawsuit that is expected to be settled in 2014. The loss will be deducted on the tax return when paid.	(50,000)
3. Accrual method used for book purposes and installment method used for tax purposes for an isolated installment sale of an investment.	225,000
	$375,000

In analyzing the temporary differences, you find that $30,000 of the depreciation temporary difference will reverse in 2014, and $120,000 of the temporary difference due to the installment sale will reverse in 2014. The tax rate for all years is 40%.

Instructions
Indicate the manner in which deferred taxes should be presented on Belmont Company's December 31, 2013, balance sheet.

2 3 5 **E19-12 (Two Temporary Differences, One Rate, Beginning Deferred Taxes, Compute Pretax Financial Income)** The following facts relate to Duncan Corporation.

1. Deferred tax liability, January 1, 2014, $60,000.
2. Deferred tax asset, January 1, 2014, $20,000.
3. Taxable income for 2014, $105,000.
4. Cumulative temporary difference at December 31, 2014, giving rise to future taxable amounts, $230,000.
5. Cumulative temporary difference at December 31, 2014, giving rise to future deductible amounts, $95,000.
6. Tax rate for all years, 40%. No permanent differences exist.
7. The company is expected to operate profitably in the future.

Instructions
(a) Compute the amount of pretax financial income for 2014.
(b) Prepare the journal entry to record income tax expense, deferred income taxes, and income taxes payable for 2014.
(c) Prepare the income tax expense section of the income statement for 2014, beginning with the line "Income before income taxes."
(d) Compute the effective tax rate for 2014.

2 7 **E19-13 (One Difference, Multiple Rates, Effect of Beginning Balance versus No Beginning Deferred Taxes)** At the end of 2013, Lucretia McEvil Company has $180,000 of cumulative temporary differences that will result in reporting future taxable amounts as shown on the next page.

2014	$ 60,000
2015	50,000
2016	40,000
2017	30,000
	$180,000

Tax rates enacted as of the beginning of 2012 are:

2012 and 2013	40%
2014 and 2015	30%
2016 and later	25%

McEvil's taxable income for 2013 is $320,000. Taxable income is expected in all future years.

Instructions
(a) Prepare the journal entry for McEvil to record income taxes payable, deferred income taxes, and income tax expense for 2013, assuming that there were no deferred taxes at the end of 2012.
(b) Prepare the journal entry for McEvil to record income taxes payable, deferred income taxes, and income tax expense for 2013, assuming that there was a balance of $22,000 in a Deferred Tax Liability account at the end of 2012.

E19-14 (Deferred Tax Asset with and without Valuation Account) Jennifer Capriati Corp. has a deferred tax asset account with a balance of $150,000 at the end of 2013 due to a single cumulative temporary difference of $375,000. At the end of 2014, this same temporary difference has increased to a cumulative amount of $450,000. Taxable income for 2014 is $820,000. The tax rate is 40% for all years. No valuation account related to the deferred tax asset is in existence at the end of 2013.

Instructions
(a) Record income tax expense, deferred income taxes, and income taxes payable for 2014, assuming that it is more likely than not that the deferred tax asset will be realized.
(b) Assuming that it is more likely than not that $30,000 of the deferred tax asset will not be realized, prepare the journal entry at the end of 2014 to record the valuation account.

E19-15 (Deferred Tax Asset with Previous Valuation Account) Assume the same information as E19-14, except that at the end of 2013, Jennifer Capriati Corp. had a valuation account related to its deferred tax asset of $45,000.

Instructions
(a) Record income tax expense, deferred income taxes, and income taxes payable for 2014, assuming that it is more likely than not that the deferred tax asset will be realized in full.
(b) Record income tax expense, deferred income taxes, and income taxes payable for 2014, assuming that it is more likely than not that none of the deferred tax asset will be realized.

E19-16 (Deferred Tax Liability, Change in Tax Rate, Prepare Section of Income Statement) Novotna Inc.'s only temporary difference at the beginning and end of 2013 is caused by a $3 million deferred gain for tax purposes for an installment sale of a plant asset, and the related receivable (only one-half of which is classified as a current asset) is due in equal installments in 2014 and 2015. The related deferred tax liability at the beginning of the year is $1,200,000. In the third quarter of 2013, a new tax rate of 34% is enacted into law and is scheduled to become effective for 2015. Taxable income for 2013 is $5,000,000, and taxable income is expected in all future years.

Instructions
(a) Determine the amount reported as a deferred tax liability at the end of 2013. Indicate proper classification(s).
(b) Prepare the journal entry (if any) necessary to adjust the deferred tax liability when the new tax rate is enacted into law.
(c) Draft the income tax expense portion of the income statement for 2013. Begin with the line "Income before income taxes." Assume no permanent differences exist.

E19-17 (Two Temporary Differences, Tracked through 3 Years, Multiple Rates) Taxable income and pretax financial income would be identical for Huber Co. except for its treatments of gross profit on installment sales and estimated costs of warranties. The income computations shown on page 1164 have been prepared.

Taxable income	2013	2014	2015
Excess of revenues over expenses (excluding two temporary differences)	$160,000	$210,000	$90,000
Installment gross profit collected	8,000	8,000	8,000
Expenditures for warranties	(5,000)	(5,000)	(5,000)
Taxable income	$163,000	$213,000	$93,000

Pretax financial income	2013	2014	2015
Excess of revenues over expenses (excluding two temporary differences)	$160,000	$210,000	$90,000
Installment gross profit earned	24,000	–0–	–0–
Estimated cost of warranties	(15,000)	–0–	–0–
Income before taxes	$169,000	$210,000	$90,000

The tax rates in effect are 2013, 40%; 2014 and 2015, 45%. All tax rates were enacted into law on January 1, 2013. No deferred income taxes existed at the beginning of 2013. Taxable income is expected in all future years.

Instructions

Prepare the journal entry to record income tax expense, deferred income taxes, and income taxes payable for 2013, 2014, and 2015.

E19-18 (Three Differences, Multiple Rates, Future Taxable Income) During 2014, Kate Holmes Co.'s first year of operations, the company reports pretax financial income at $250,000. Holmes's enacted tax rate is 45% for 2014 and 40% for all later years. Holmes expects to have taxable income in each of the next 5 years. The effects on future tax returns of temporary differences existing at December 31, 2014, are summarized as follows.

	Future Years					
	2015	2016	2017	2018	2019	Total
Future taxable (deductible) amounts:						
Installment sales	$32,000	$32,000	$32,000			$ 96,000
Depreciation	6,000	6,000	6,000	$6,000	$6,000	30,000
Unearned rent	(50,000)	(50,000)				(100,000)

Instructions

(a) Complete the schedule below to compute deferred taxes at December 31, 2014.
(b) Compute taxable income for 2014.
(c) Prepare the journal entry to record income taxes payable, deferred taxes, and income tax expense for 2014.

	Future Taxable		December 31, 2014	
	(Deductible)	Tax	Deferred Tax	
Temporary Difference	Amounts	Rate	(Asset)	Liability
Installment sales	$ 96,000			
Depreciation	30,000			
Unearned rent	(100,000)			
Totals	$_____		_____	_____

E19-19 (Two Differences, One Rate, Beginning Deferred Balance, Compute Pretax Financial Income) Andy McDowell Co. establishes a $100 million liability at the end of 2014 for the estimated site-cleanup costs at two of its manufacturing facilities. All related closing costs will be paid and deducted on the tax return in 2015. Also, at the end of 2014, the company has $50 million of temporary differences due to excess depreciation for tax purposes, $7 million of which will reverse in 2015.

The enacted tax rate for all years is 40%, and the company pays taxes of $64 million on $160 million of taxable income in 2014. McDowell expects to have taxable income in 2015.

Instructions

(a) Determine the deferred taxes to be reported at the end of 2015.
(b) Indicate how the deferred taxes computed in (a) are to be reported on the balance sheet.

(c) Assuming that the only deferred tax account at the beginning of 2014 was a deferred tax liability of $10,000,000, draft the income tax expense portion of the income statement for 2014, beginning with the line "Income before income taxes." (*Hint:* You must first compute (1) the amount of temporary difference underlying the beginning $10,000,000 deferred tax liability, then (2) the amount of temporary differences originating or reversing during the year, and then (3) the amount of pretax financial income.)

2 3
9
E19-20 (Two Differences, No Beginning Deferred Taxes, Multiple Rates) Teri Hatcher Inc., in its first year of operations, has the following differences between the book basis and tax basis of its assets and liabilities at the end of 2013.

	Book Basis	Tax Basis
Equipment (net)	$400,000	$340,000
Estimated warranty liability	$200,000	$ –0–

It is estimated that the warranty liability will be settled in 2014. The difference in equipment (net) will result in taxable amounts of $20,000 in 2014, $30,000 in 2015, and $10,000 in 2016. The company has taxable income of $520,000 in 2013. As of the beginning of 2013, the enacted tax rate is 34% for 2013–2015, and 30% for 2016. Hatcher expects to report taxable income through 2016.

Instructions
(a) Prepare the journal entry to record income tax expense, deferred income taxes, and income taxes payable for 2013.
(b) Indicate how deferred income taxes will be reported on the balance sheet at the end of 2013.

2 3
7 9
E19-21 (Two Temporary Differences, Multiple Rates, Future Taxable Income) Nadal Inc. has two temporary differences at the end of 2013. The first difference stems from installment sales, and the second one results from the accrual of a loss contingency. Nadal's accounting department has developed a schedule of future taxable and deductible amounts related to these temporary differences as follows.

	2014	2015	2016	2017
Taxable amounts	$40,000	$50,000	$60,000	$80,000
Deductible amounts		(15,000)	(19,000)	
	$40,000	$35,000	$41,000	$80,000

As of the beginning of 2013, the enacted tax rate is 34% for 2013 and 2014, and 38% for 2015–2018. At the beginning of 2013, the company had no deferred income taxes on its balance sheet. Taxable income for 2013 is $500,000. Taxable income is expected in all future years.

Instructions
(a) Prepare the journal entry to record income tax expense, deferred income taxes, and income taxes payable for 2013.
(b) Indicate how deferred income taxes would be classified on the balance sheet at the end of 2013.

2 3
9
E19-22 (Two Differences, One Rate, First Year) The differences between the book basis and tax basis of the assets and liabilities of Castle Corporation at the end of 2013 are presented below.

	Book Basis	Tax Basis
Accounts receivable	$50,000	$–0–
Litigation liability	30,000	–0–

It is estimated that the litigation liability will be settled in 2014. The difference in accounts receivable will result in taxable amounts of $30,000 in 2014 and $20,000 in 2015. The company has taxable income of $350,000 in 2013 and is expected to have taxable income in each of the following 2 years. Its enacted tax rate is 34% for all years. This is the company's first year of operations. The operating cycle of the business is 2 years.

Instructions
(a) Prepare the journal entry to record income tax expense, deferred income taxes, and income taxes payable for 2013.
(b) Indicate how deferred income taxes will be reported on the balance sheet at the end of 2013.

4 7 8 **E19-23 (NOL Carryback and Carryforward, Valuation Account versus No Valuation Account)** Spamela Hamderson Inc. reports the following pretax income (loss) for both financial reporting purposes and tax purposes. (Assume the carryback provision is used for a net operating loss.)

Year	Pretax Income (Loss)	Tax Rate
2012	$120,000	34%
2013	90,000	34%
2014	(280,000)	38%
2015	220,000	38%

The tax rates listed were all enacted by the beginning of 2012.

Instructions

(a) Prepare the journal entries for the years 2012–2015 to record income tax expense (benefit) and income taxes payable (refundable) and the tax effects of the loss carryback and carryforward, assuming that at the end of 2014 the benefits of the loss carryforward are judged more likely than not to be realized in the future.

(b) Using the assumption in (a), prepare the income tax section of the 2014 income statement beginning with the line "Operating loss before income taxes."

(c) Prepare the journal entries for 2014 and 2015, assuming that based on the weight of available evidence, it is more likely than not that one-fourth of the benefits of the loss carryforward will not be realized.

(d) Using the assumption in (c), prepare the income tax section of the 2014 income statement beginning with the line "Operating loss before income taxes."

4 7 8 **E19-24 (NOL Carryback and Carryforward, Valuation Account Needed)** Beilman Inc. reports the following pretax income (loss) for both book and tax purposes. (Assume the carryback provision is used where possible for a net operating loss.)

Year	Pretax Income (Loss)	Tax Rate
2012	$120,000	40%
2013	90,000	40%
2014	(280,000)	45%
2015	120,000	45%

The tax rates listed were all enacted by the beginning of 2012.

Instructions

(a) Prepare the journal entries for years 2012–2015 to record income tax expense (benefit) and income taxes payable (refundable), and the tax effects of the loss carryback and loss carryforward, assuming that based on the weight of available evidence, it is more likely than not that one-half of the benefits of the loss carryforward will not be realized.

(b) Prepare the income tax section of the 2014 income statement beginning with the line "Operating loss before income taxes."

(c) Prepare the income tax section of the 2015 income statement beginning with the line "Income before income taxes."

4 7 8 **E19-25 (NOL Carryback and Carryforward, Valuation Account Needed)** Meyer reported the following pretax financial income (loss) for the years 2012–2016.

2012	$240,000
2013	350,000
2014	120,000
2015	(570,000)
2016	180,000

Pretax financial income (loss) and taxable income (loss) were the same for all years involved. The enacted tax rate was 34% for 2012 and 2013, and 40% for 2014–2016. Assume the carryback provision is used first for net operating losses.

Instructions

(a) Prepare the journal entries for the years 2014–2016 to record income tax expense, income taxes payable (refundable), and the tax effects of the loss carryback and loss carryforward, assuming that based on the weight of available evidence, it is more likely than not that one-fifth of the benefits of the loss carryforward will not be realized.

(b) Prepare the income tax section of the 2015 income statement beginning with the line "Income (loss) before income taxes."

EXERCISES SET B

See the book's companion website, at **www.wiley.com/college/kieso**, for an additional set of exercises.

PROBLEMS

  P19-1 (Three Differences, No Beginning Deferred Taxes, Multiple Rates) The following information is available for Remmers Corporation for 2014.

1. Depreciation reported on the tax return exceeded depreciation reported on the income statement by $120,000. This difference will reverse in equal amounts of $30,000 over the years 2015–2018.
2. Interest received on municipal bonds was $10,000.
3. Rent collected in advance on January 1, 2014, totaled $60,000 for a 3-year period. Of this amount, $40,000 was reported as unearned at December 31, 2014, for book purposes.
4. The tax rates are 40% for 2014 and 35% for 2015 and subsequent years.
5. Income taxes of $320,000 are due per the tax return for 2014.
6. No deferred taxes existed at the beginning of 2014.

Instructions

(a) Compute taxable income for 2014.

(b) Compute pretax financial income for 2014.

(c) Prepare the journal entries to record income tax expense, deferred income taxes, and income taxes payable for 2014 and 2015. Assume taxable income was $980,000 in 2015.

(d) Prepare the income tax expense section of the income statement for 2014, beginning with "Income before income taxes."

 P19-2 (One Temporary Difference, Tracked for 4 Years, One Permanent Difference, Change in Rate) The pretax financial income of Truttman Company differs from its taxable income throughout each of 4 years as follows.

Year	Pretax Financial Income	Taxable Income	Tax Rate
2014	$290,000	$180,000	35%
2015	320,000	225,000	40%
2016	350,000	260,000	40%
2017	420,000	560,000	40%

Pretax financial income for each year includes a nondeductible expense of $30,000 (never deductible for tax purposes). The remainder of the difference between pretax financial income and taxable income in each period is due to one depreciation temporary difference. No deferred income taxes existed at the beginning of 2014.

Instructions

(a) Prepare journal entries to record income taxes in all 4 years. Assume that the change in the tax rate to 40% was not enacted until the beginning of 2015.

(b) Prepare the income statement for 2015, beginning with Income before income taxes.

2 5 6 9 **P19-3 (Second Year of Depreciation Difference, Two Differences, Single Rate, Extraordinary Item)** The following information has been obtained for the Gocker Corporation.

1. Prior to 2014, taxable income and pretax financial income were identical.
2. Pretax financial income is $1,700,000 in 2014 and $1,400,000 in 2015.
3. On January 1, 2014, equipment costing $1,200,000 is purchased. It is to be depreciated on a straight-line basis over 5 years for tax purposes and over 8 years for financial reporting purposes. (*Hint:* Use the half-year convention for tax purposes, as discussed in Appendix 11A.)
4. Interest of $60,000 was earned on tax-exempt municipal obligations in 2015.
5. Included in 2015 pretax financial income is an extraordinary gain of $200,000, which is fully taxable.
6. The tax rate is 35% for all periods.
7. Taxable income is expected in all future years.

Instructions
(a) Compute taxable income and income taxes payable for 2015.
(b) Prepare the journal entry to record 2015 income tax expense, income taxes payable, and deferred taxes.
(c) Prepare the bottom portion of Gocker's 2015 income statement, beginning with "Income before income taxes and extraordinary item."
(d) Indicate how deferred income taxes should be presented on the December 31, 2015, balance sheet.

2 3 5 **P19-4 (Permanent and Temporary Differences, One Rate)** The accounting records of Shinault Inc. show the following data for 2014 (its first year of operations).

1. Life insurance expense on officers was $9,000.
2. Equipment was acquired in early January for $300,000. Straight-line depreciation over a 5-year life is used, with no salvage value. For tax purposes, Shinault used a 30% rate to calculate depreciation.
3. Interest revenue on State of New York bonds totaled $4,000.
4. Product warranties were estimated to be $50,000 in 2014. Actual repair and labor costs related to the warranties in 2014 were $10,000. The remainder is estimated to be paid evenly in 2015 and 2016.
5. Gross profit on an accrual basis was $100,000. For tax purposes, $75,000 was recorded on the installment-sales method.
6. Fines incurred for pollution violations were $4,200.
7. Pretax financial income was $750,000. The tax rate is 30%.

Instructions
(a) Prepare a schedule starting with pretax financial income in 2014 and ending with taxable income in 2014.
(b) Prepare the journal entry for 2014 to record income taxes payable, income tax expense, and deferred income taxes.

5 7 8 9 **P19-5 (NOL without Valuation Account)** Jennings Inc. reported the following pretax income (loss) and related tax rates during the years 2010–2016.

	Pretax Income (loss)	Tax Rate
2010	$ 40,000	30%
2011	25,000	30%
2012	50,000	30%
2013	80,000	40%
2014	(180,000)	45%
2015	70,000	40%
2016	100,000	35%

Pretax financial income (loss) and taxable income (loss) were the same for all years since Jennings began business. The tax rates from 2013–2016 were enacted in 2013.

Instructions
(a) Prepare the journal entries for the years 2014–2016 to record income taxes payable (refundable), income tax expense (benefit), and the tax effects of the loss carryback and carryforward. Assume that Jennings elects the carryback provision where possible and expects to realize the benefits of any loss carryforward in the year that immediately follows the loss year.
(b) Indicate the effect the 2014 entry(ies) has on the December 31, 2014, balance sheet.
(c) Prepare the portion of the income statement, starting with "Operating loss before income taxes," for 2014.
(d) Prepare the portion of the income statement, starting with "Income before income taxes," for 2015.

2 3 9 **P19-6 (Two Differences, Two Rates, Future Income Expected)** Presented below are two independent situations related to future taxable and deductible amounts resulting from temporary differences existing at December 31, 2014.

1. Mooney Co. has developed the following schedule of future taxable and deductible amounts.

	2015	2016	2017	2018	2019
Taxable amounts	$300	$300	$300	$ 300	$300
Deductible amount	—	—	—	(1,600)	—

2. Roesch Co. has the following schedule of future taxable and deductible amounts.

	2015	2016	2017	2018
Taxable amounts	$300	$300	$ 300	$300
Deductible amount	—	—	(2,300)	—

Both Mooney Co. and Roesch Co. have taxable income of $4,000 in 2014 and expect to have taxable income in all future years. The tax rates enacted as of the beginning of 2014 are 30% for 2014–2017 and 35% for years thereafter. All of the underlying temporary differences relate to noncurrent assets and liabilities.

Instructions

For each of these two situations, compute the net amount of deferred income taxes to be reported at the end of 2014, and indicate how it should be classified on the balance sheet.

2 5 7 **P19-7 (One Temporary Difference, Tracked 3 Years, Change in Rates, Income Statement Presentation)** Crosley Corp. sold an investment on an installment basis. The total gain of $60,000 was reported for financial reporting purposes in the period of sale. The company qualifies to use the installment-sales method for tax purposes. The installment period is 3 years; one-third of the sale price is collected in the period of sale. The tax rate was 40% in 2014, and 35% in 2015 and 2016. The 35% tax rate was not enacted in law until 2015. The accounting and tax data for the 3 years is shown below.

	Financial Accounting	Tax Return
2014 (40% tax rate)		
Income before temporary difference	$ 70,000	$70,000
Temporary difference	60,000	20,000
Income	$130,000	$90,000
2015 (35% tax rate)		
Income before temporary difference	$ 70,000	$70,000
Temporary difference	–0–	20,000
Income	$ 70,000	$90,000
2016 (35% tax rate)		
Income before temporary difference	$ 70,000	$70,000
Temporary difference	–0–	20,000
Income	$ 70,000	$90,000

Instructions

(a) Prepare the journal entries to record the income tax expense, deferred income taxes, and the income taxes payable at the end of each year. No deferred income taxes existed at the beginning of 2014.

(b) Explain how the deferred taxes will appear on the balance sheet at the end of each year. (Assume Installment Accounts Receivable is classified as a current asset.)

(c) Draft the income tax expense section of the income statement for each year, beginning with "Income before income taxes."

2 3 5 9 **P19-8 (Two Differences, 2 Years, Compute Taxable Income and Pretax Financial Income)** The information shown below and on page 1170 was disclosed during the audit of Elbert Inc.

1.

Year	Amount Due per Tax Return
2014	$130,000
2015	104,000

2. On January 1, 2014, equipment costing $600,000 is purchased. For financial reporting purposes, the company uses straight-line depreciation over a 5-year life. For tax purposes, the company uses the elective straight-line method over a 5-year life. (*Hint:* For tax purposes, the half-year convention as discussed in Appendix 11A must be used.)

3. In January 2015, $225,000 is collected in advance rental of a building for a 3-year period. The entire $225,000 is reported as taxable income in 2015, but $150,000 of the $225,000 is reported as unearned revenue in 2015 for financial reporting purposes. The remaining amount of unearned revenue is to be recognized equally in 2016 and 2017.

4. The tax rate is 40% in 2014 and all subsequent periods. (*Hint:* To find taxable income in 2014 and 2015, the related income taxes payable amounts will have to be "grossed up.")

5. No temporary differences existed at the end of 2013. Elbert expects to report taxable income in each of the next 5 years.

Instructions

(a) Determine the amount to report for deferred income taxes at the end of 2014, and indicate how it should be classified on the balance sheet.

(b) Prepare the journal entry to record income taxes for 2014.

(c) Draft the income tax section of the income statement for 2014, beginning with "Income before income taxes." (*Hint:* You must compute taxable income and then combine that with changes in cumulative temporary differences to arrive at pretax financial income.)

(d) Determine the deferred income taxes at the end of 2015, and indicate how they should be classified on the balance sheet.

(e) Prepare the journal entry to record income taxes for 2015.

(f) Draft the income tax section of the income statement for 2015, beginning with "Income before income taxes."

P19-9 (Five Differences, Compute Taxable Income and Deferred Taxes, Draft Income Statement) Wise Company began operations at the beginning of 2015. The following information pertains to this company.

1. Pretax financial income for 2015 is $100,000.

2. The tax rate enacted for 2015 and future years is 40%.

3. Differences between the 2015 income statement and tax return are listed below:

   (a) Warranty expense accrued for financial reporting purposes amounts to $7,000. Warranty deductions per the tax return amount to $2,000.

   (b) Gross profit on construction contracts using the percentage-of-completion method per books amounts to $92,000. Gross profit on construction contracts for tax purposes amounts to $67,000.

   (c) Depreciation of property, plant, and equipment for financial reporting purposes amounts to $60,000. Depreciation of these assets amounts to $80,000 for the tax return.

   (d) A $3,500 fine paid for violation of pollution laws was deducted in computing pretax financial income.

   (e) Interest revenue recognized on an investment in tax-exempt municipal bonds amounts to $1,500.

4. Taxable income is expected for the next few years. (Assume (a) is short-term in nature; assume (b) and (c) are long-term in nature.)

Instructions

(a) Compute taxable income for 2015.

(b) Compute the deferred taxes at December 31, 2015, that relate to the temporary differences described above. Clearly label them as deferred tax asset or liability.

(c) Prepare the journal entry to record income tax expense, deferred taxes, and income taxes payable for 2015.

(d) Draft the income tax expense section of the income statement, beginning with "Income before income taxes."

PROBLEMS SET B

See the book's companion website, at **www.wiley.com/college/kieso**, for an additional set of problems.

CONCEPTS FOR ANALYSIS

CA19-1 (Objectives and Principles for Accounting for Income Taxes) The amount of income taxes due to the government for a period of time is rarely the amount reported on the income statement for that period as income tax expense.

Instructions

(a) Explain the objectives of accounting for income taxes in general-purpose financial statements.

(b) Explain the basic principles that are applied in accounting for income taxes at the date of the financial statements to meet the objectives discussed in (a).

(c) List the steps in the annual computation of deferred tax liabilities and assets.

CA19-2 (Basic Accounting for Temporary Differences) Dexter Company appropriately uses the asset-liability method to record deferred income taxes. Dexter reports depreciation expense for certain machinery purchased this year using the modified accelerated cost recovery system (MACRS) for income tax purposes and the straight-line basis for financial reporting purposes. The tax deduction is the larger amount this year.

Dexter received rent revenues in advance this year. These revenues are included in this year's taxable income. However, for financial reporting purposes, these revenues are reported as unearned revenues, a current liability.

Instructions

(a) What are the principles of the asset-liability approach?

(b) How would Dexter account for the temporary differences?

(c) How should Dexter classify the deferred tax consequences of the temporary differences on its balance sheet?

CA19-3 (Identify Temporary Differences and Classification Criteria) The asset-liability approach for recording deferred income taxes is an integral part of generally accepted accounting principles.

Instructions

(a) Indicate whether each of the following independent situations should be treated as a temporary difference or as a permanent difference, and explain why.

(1) Estimated warranty costs (covering a 3-year warranty) are expensed for financial reporting purposes at the time of sale but deducted for income tax purposes when paid.

(2) Depreciation for book and income tax purposes differs because of different bases of carrying the related property, which was acquired in a trade-in. The different bases are a result of different rules used for book and tax purposes to compute the basis of property acquired in a trade-in.

(3) A company properly uses the equity method to account for its 30% investment in another company. The investee pays dividends that are about 10% of its annual earnings.

(4) A company reports a gain on an involuntary conversion of a nonmonetary asset to a monetary asset. The company elects to replace the property within the statutory period using the total proceeds so the gain is not reported on the current year's tax return.

(b) Discuss the nature of the deferred income tax accounts and possible classifications in a company's balance sheet. Indicate the manner in which these accounts are to be reported.

CA19-4 (Accounting and Classification of Deferred Income Taxes)

Part A: This year, Gumowski Company has each of the following items in its income statement.

1. Gross profits on installment sales.
2. Revenues on long-term construction contracts.
3. Estimated costs of product warranty contracts.
4. Premiums on officers' life insurance policies with Gumowski as beneficiary.

Instructions

(a) Under what conditions would deferred income taxes need to be reported in the financial statements?

(b) Specify when deferred income taxes would need to be recognized for each of the items above, and indicate the rationale for such recognition.

Part B: Gumowski Company's president has heard that deferred income taxes can be classified in different ways in the balance sheet.

Instructions

Identify the conditions under which deferred income taxes would be classified as a noncurrent item in the balance sheet. What justification exists for such classification?

(AICPA adapted)

CA19-5 (Explain Computation of Deferred Tax Liability for Multiple Tax Rates) At December 31, 2014, Higley Corporation has one temporary difference which will reverse and cause taxable amounts in 2015. In 2014, a new tax act set taxes equal to 45% for 2014, 40% for 2015, and 34% for 2016 and years thereafter.

Instructions

Explain what circumstances would call for Higley to compute its deferred tax liability at the end of 2014 by multiplying the cumulative temporary difference by:

(a) 45%.
(b) 40%.
(c) 34%.

CA19-6 (Explain Future Taxable and Deductible Amounts, How Carryback and Carryforward Affects Deferred Taxes) Maria Rodriquez and Lynette Kingston are discussing accounting for income taxes. They are currently studying a schedule of taxable and deductible amounts that will arise in the future as a result of existing temporary differences. The schedule is as follows.

	2014	Future Years			
		2015	2016	2017	2018
Taxable income	$850,000				
Taxable amounts		$375,000	$375,000	$375,000	$375,000
Deductible amounts				(2,400,000)	
Enacted tax rate	50%	45%	40%	35%	30%

Instructions
(a) Explain the concept of future taxable amounts and future deductible amounts as illustrated in the schedule.
(b) How do the carryback and carryforward provisions affect the reporting of deferred tax assets and deferred tax liabilities?

CA19-7 (Deferred Taxes, Income Effects) Stephanie Delaney, CPA, is the newly hired director of corporate taxation for Acme Incorporated, which is a publicly traded corporation. Ms. Delaney's first job with Acme was the review of the company's accounting practices on deferred income taxes. In doing her review, she noted differences between tax and book depreciation methods that permitted Acme to realize a sizable deferred tax liability on its balance sheet. As a result, Acme paid very little in income taxes at that time.

Delaney also discovered that Acme has an explicit policy of selling off plant assets before they reversed in the deferred tax liability account. This policy, coupled with the rapid expansion of its plant asset base, allowed Acme to "defer" all income taxes payable for several years, even though it always has reported positive earnings and an increasing EPS. Delaney checked with the legal department and found the policy to be legal, but she's uncomfortable with the ethics of it.

Instructions
Answer the following questions.

(a) Why would Acme have an explicit policy of selling plant assets before the temporary differences reversed in the deferred tax liability account?
(b) What are the ethical implications of Acme's "deferral" of income taxes?
(c) Who could be harmed by Acme's ability to "defer" income taxes payable for several years, despite positive earnings?
(d) In a situation such as this, what are Ms. Delaney's professional responsibilities as a CPA?

USING YOUR JUDGMENT

FINANCIAL REPORTING

Financial Reporting Problem

The Procter & Gamble Company (P&G)

The financial statements of P&G are presented in Appendix 5B. The company's complete annual report, including the notes to the financial statements, can be accessed at the book's companion website, **www.wiley.com/college/kieso**.

Instructions

Refer to P&G's financial statements and the accompanying notes to answer the following questions.

(a) What amounts relative to income taxes does P&G report in its:
- **(1)** 2011 income statement?
- **(2)** June 30, 2011, balance sheet?
- **(3)** 2011 statement of cash flows?

(b) P&G's income taxes in 2009, 2010, and 2011 were computed at what effective tax rates? (See the notes to the financial statements.)

(c) How much of P&G's 2011 total income taxes was current tax expense, and how much was deferred tax expense?

(d) What did P&G report as the significant components (the details) of its June 30, 2011, deferred tax assets and liabilities?

Comparative Analysis Case

The Coca-Cola Company and PepsiCo, Inc.

Instructions

Go to the book's companion website and use information found there to answer the following questions related to The Coca-Cola Company and PepsiCo, Inc.

(a) What are the amounts of Coca-Cola's and PepsiCo's provision for income taxes for the year 2011? Of each company's 2011 provision for income taxes, what portion is current expense and what portion is deferred expense?

(b) What amount of cash was paid in 2011 for income taxes by Coca-Cola and by PepsiCo?

(c) What was the U.S. federal statutory tax rate in 2011? What was the effective tax rate in 2011 for Coca-Cola and PepsiCo? Why might their effective tax rates differ?

(d) For year-end 2011, what amounts were reported by Coca-Cola and PepsiCo as (1) gross deferred tax assets and (2) gross deferred tax liabilities?

(e) Do either Coca-Cola or PepsiCo disclose any net operating loss carrybacks and/or carryforwards at year-end 2011? What are the amounts, and when do the carryforwards expire?

Financial Statement Analysis Case

Homestake Mining Company

Homestake Mining Company is a 120-year-old international gold mining company with substantial gold mining operations and exploration in the United States, Canada, and Australia. At year-end, Homestake reported the following items related to income taxes (thousands of dollars).

Total current taxes	$ 26,349
Total deferred taxes	(39,436)
Total income and mining taxes (the provision for taxes per its income statement)	(13,087)
Deferred tax liabilities	$303,050
Deferred tax assets, net of valuation allowance of $207,175	95,275
Net deferred tax liability	$207,775

Note 6: The classification of deferred tax assets and liabilities is based on the related asset or liability creating the deferred tax. Deferred taxes not related to a specific asset or liability are classified based on the estimated period of reversal.

Tax loss carryforwards (U.S., Canada, Australia, and Chile)	$71,151
Tax credit carryforwards	$12,007

Instructions

(a) What is the significance of Homestake's disclosure of "Current taxes" of $26,349 and "Deferred taxes" of $(39,436)?

(b) Explain the concept behind Homestake's disclosure of gross deferred tax liabilities (future taxable amounts) and gross deferred tax assets (future deductible amounts).

(c) Homestake reported tax loss carryforwards of $71,151 and tax credit carryforwards of $12,007. How do the carryback and carryforward provisions affect the reporting of deferred tax assets and deferred tax liabilities?

Accounting, Analysis, and Principles

DeJohn Company, which began operations at the beginning of 2012, produces various products on a contract basis. Each contract generates a gross profit of $80,000. Some of DeJohn's contracts provide for the customer to pay on an installment basis. Under these contracts, DeJohn collects one-fifth of the contract revenue in each of the following four years. For financial reporting purposes, the company recognizes gross profit in the year of completion (accrual basis). For tax purposes, DeJohn recognizes gross profit in the year cash is collected (installment basis).

Presented below is information related to DeJohn's operations for 2014:

1. In 2014, the company completed seven contracts that allow for the customer to pay on an installment basis. DeJohn recognized the related gross profit of $560,000 for financial reporting purposes. It reported only $112,000 of gross profit on installment sales on the 2014 tax return. The company expects future collections on the related installment receivables to result in taxable amounts of $112,000 in each of the next four years.
2. In 2014, nontaxable municipal bond interest revenue was $28,000.
3. During 2014, nondeductible fines and penalties of $26,000 were paid.
4. Pretax financial income for 2014 amounts to $500,000.
5. Tax rates (enacted before the end of 2014) are 50% for 2014 and 40% for 2015 and later.
6. The accounting period is the calendar year.
7. The company is expected to have taxable income in all future years.
8. The company has no deferred tax assets or liabilities at the end of 2013.

Accounting

Prepare the journal entry to record income taxes for 2014.

Analysis

Classify deferred income taxes on the balance sheet at December 31, 2014, and indicate, starting with Income before income taxes, how income taxes are reported on the income statement. What is DeJohn's effective tax rate?

Principles

Explain how the conceptual framework is used as a basis for determining the proper accounting for deferred income taxes.

BRIDGE TO THE PROFESSION

 ## Professional Research: FASB Codification

Kleckner Company started operations in 2010. Although it has grown steadily, the company reported accumulated operating losses of $450,000 in its first four years in business. In the most recent year (2014), Kleckner appears to have turned the corner and reported modest taxable income of $30,000. In addition to a deferred tax asset related to its net operating loss, Kleckner has recorded a deferred tax asset related to product warranties and a deferred tax liability related to accelerated depreciation.

Given its past operating results, Kleckner has established a full valuation allowance for its deferred tax assets. However, given its improved performance, Kleckner management wonders whether the company can now reduce or eliminate the valuation allowance. They would like you to conduct some research on the accounting for its valuation allowance.

Instructions

If your school has a subscription to the FASB Codification, go to *http://aaahq.org/ascLogin.cfm* to log in and prepare responses to the following. Provide Codification references for your responses.

(a) Briefly explain to Kleckner management the importance of future taxable income as it relates to the valuation allowance for deferred tax assets.

(b) What are the sources of income that may be relied upon to remove the need for a valuation allowance?

(c) What are tax-planning strategies? From the information provided, does it appear that Kleckner could employ a tax-planning strategy to support reducing its valuation allowance?

Additional Professional Resources

See the book's companion website, at **www.wiley.com/college/kieso**, for professional simulations as well as other study resources.

The accounting for income taxes in IFRS is covered in *IAS 12* ("Income Taxes"), which is based on an asset-liability approach to measurement of deferred taxes.

12 LEARNING OBJECTIVE

Compare the accounting for income taxes under GAAP and IFRS.

RELEVANT FACTS

Following are the key similarities and differences between GAAP and IFRS related to accounting for taxes.

Similarities

- Similar to GAAP, IFRS uses the asset and liability approach for recording deferred taxes.

Differences

- The classification of deferred taxes under IFRS is always non-current. As indicated in the chapter, GAAP classifies deferred taxes based on the classification of the asset or liability to which it relates.
- Under IFRS, an affirmative judgment approach is used, by which a deferred tax asset is recognized up to the amount that is probable to be realized. GAAP uses an impairment approach. In this approach, the deferred tax asset is recognized in full. It is then reduced by a valuation account if it is more likely than not that all or a portion of the deferred tax asset will not be realized.
- IFRS uses the enacted tax rate or substantially enacted tax rate. ("Substantially enacted" means virtually certain.) For GAAP, the enacted tax rate must be used.
- The tax effects related to certain items are reported in equity under IFRS. That is not the case under GAAP, which charges or credits the tax effects to income.
- GAAP requires companies to assess the likelihood of uncertain tax positions being sustainable upon audit. Potential liabilities must be accrued and disclosed if the position is "more likely than not" to be disallowed. Under IFRS, all potential liabilities must be recognized. With respect to measurement, IFRS uses an expected-value approach to measure the tax liability, which differs from GAAP.

ABOUT THE NUMBERS

Deferred Tax Asset (Non-Recognition)

Under IFRS, companies recognize a deferred tax asset for all deductible temporary differences. However, based on available evidence, a company should reduce a deferred tax asset if it is probable that it **will not realize** some portion or all of the deferred tax asset. "**Probable**" means a level of likelihood of at least slightly more than 50 percent.

Assume that Jensen Co. has a deductible temporary difference of $1,000,000 at the end of its first year of operations. Its tax rate is 40 percent, which means it records a deferred tax asset of $400,000 ($1,000,000 × 40%). Assuming $900,000 of income taxes payable, Jensen records income tax expense, the deferred tax asset, and income taxes payable as follows.

Income Tax Expense	500,000	
Deferred Tax Asset	400,000	
Income Taxes Payable		900,000

After careful review of all available evidence, Jensen determines that it is probable that it will not realize $100,000 of this deferred tax asset. Jensen records this reduction in asset value as follows.

Income Tax Expense	100,000	
Deferred Tax Asset		100,000

This journal entry increases income tax expense in the current period because Jensen does not expect to realize a favorable tax benefit for a portion of the deductible temporary difference. Jensen **simultaneously recognizes a reduction in the carrying amount of the deferred tax asset**. Jensen then reports a deferred tax asset of $300,000 in its statement of financial position.

Jensen evaluates the deferred tax asset account at the end of each accounting period. If, at the end of the next period, it expects to realize $350,000 of this deferred tax asset, Jensen makes the following entry to adjust this account.

Deferred Tax Asset ($350,000 − $300,000)	50,000	
Income Tax Expense		50,000

Jensen should consider all available evidence, both positive and negative, to determine whether, based on the weight of available evidence, it needs to adjust the deferred tax asset. For example, if Jensen has been experiencing a series of loss years, it reasonably assumes that these losses will continue. Therefore, Jensen will lose the benefit of the future deductible amounts.

Generally, sufficient taxable income arises from temporary taxable differences that will reverse in the future or from a tax-planning strategy that will generate taxable income in the future. Illustration IFRS19-1 shows how **Ahold** describes its reporting of deferred assets.

ILLUSTRATION IFRS19-1
Deferred Tax Asset Disclosure

Ahold

Note 11. Significant judgment is required in determining whether deferred tax assets are realizable. Ahold determines this on the basis of expected taxable profits arising from recognized deferred tax liabilities and on the basis of budgets, cash flow forecasts, and impairment models. Where utilization is not considered probable, deferred taxes are not recognized.

Carryforward (Non-Recognition)

To illustrate non-recognition of a loss carryforward, assume that Groh Inc. has tax benefits of $110,000 associated with a NOL carryback and a potential deferred tax asset of $80,000 associated with an operating loss carryforward of $200,000, assuming a future tax rate of 40% ($200,000 × 40%). However, if it is probable that Groh will *not* realize the entire NOL carryforward in future years, it does not recognize this deferred tax asset. To illustrate, Groh makes the following journal entry in 2014 to record only the tax refund receivable.

To recognize benefit of loss carryback

Income Tax Refund Receivable	110,000	
Benefit Due to Loss Carryback (Income Tax Expense)		110,000

Illustration IFRS19-2 shows Groh's 2014 income statement presentation.

GROH INC. INCOME STATEMENT (PARTIAL) FOR 2014	
Operating loss before income taxes	$(500,000)
Income tax benefit	
Benefit due to loss carryback	110,000
Net loss	$(390,000)

ILLUSTRATION IFRS19-2
Recognition of Benefit of Loss Carryback Only

In 2015, assuming that Groh has taxable income of $250,000 (before considering the carryforward), subject to a tax rate of 40 percent, it realizes the deferred tax asset. Groh records the following entries.

To recognize deferred tax asset and loss carryforward

Deferred Tax Asset	80,000	
Benefit Due to Loss Carryforward (Income Tax Expense)		80,000

To record current and deferred income taxes

Income Tax Expense	100,000	
Deferred Tax Asset		80,000
Income Taxes Payable		20,000

Groh reports the $80,000 Benefit Due to the Loss Carryforward on the 2015 income statement. The company did not recognize it in 2014 because it was probable that it would not be realized. Assuming that Groh derives the income for 2015 from continuing operations, it prepares the income statement as shown in Illustration IFRS19-3.

GROH INC. INCOME STATEMENT (PARTIAL) FOR 2015		
Income before income taxes		$250,000
Income tax expense		
Current	$ 20,000	
Deferred	80,000	
Benefit due to loss carryforward	(80,000)	20,000
Net income		$230,000

ILLUSTRATION IFRS19-3
Recognition of Benefit of Loss Carryforward When Realized

Another method is to report only one line for total income tax expense of $20,000 on the face of the income statement and disclose the components of income tax expense in the notes to the financial statements.

Statement of Financial Position Classification

Companies classify taxes receivable or payable as current assets or current liabilities. Although current tax assets and liabilities are separately recognized and measured, they are often offset in the statement of financial position. The offset occurs because companies normally have a legally enforceable right to offset a current tax asset (Taxes Receivable) against a current tax liability (Taxes Payable) when they relate to income taxes levied by the same taxation authority. Deferred tax assets and deferred tax liabilities are also separately recognized and measured but may be offset in the statement of financial position. Companies are permitted to offset deferred tax assets and deferred tax liabilities if, and only if (1) the company has a legally enforceable right to offset current tax assets against current tax liabilities, and (2) the deferred tax assets and the deferred tax liabilities relate to income taxes levied by the same tax authority and for the same company.

The net deferred tax asset or net deferred tax liability is reported in the non-current section of the statement of financial position. Deferred tax amounts should not be discounted. The IASB apparently considers discounting to be an unnecessary complication even if the effects are material. To illustrate, assume that K. Scott Company has four deferred tax items at December 31, 2014, as shown in Illustration IFRS19-4.

ILLUSTRATION IFRS19-4
Classification of Temporary Differences

Temporary Difference	Resulting Deferred Tax (Asset)	Liability
1. Rent collected in advance: recognized when earned for accounting purposes and when received for tax purposes.	$(42,000)	
2. Use of straight-line depreciation for accounting purposes and accelerated depreciation for tax purposes.		$214,000
3. Recognition of profits on installment sales during period of sale for accounting purposes and during period of collection for tax purposes.		45,000
4. Warranty liabilities: recognized for accounting purposes at time of sale; for tax purposes at time paid.	(12,000)	
Totals	$(54,000)	$259,000

As indicated, K. Scott has a total deferred tax asset of $54,000 and a total deferred tax liability of $259,000. Assuming these two items can be offset, K. Scott reports a deferred tax liability of $205,000 ($259,000 − $54,000) in the non-current liability section of its statement of financial position.

ON THE HORIZON

The IASB and the FASB have been working to address some of the differences in the accounting for income taxes. Some of the issues under discussion are the term "probable" under IFRS for recognition of a deferred tax asset, which might be interpreted to mean "more likely than not." If the term is changed, the reporting for impairments of deferred tax assets will be essentially the same between GAAP and IFRS. In addition, the IASB is considering adoption of the classification approach used in GAAP for deferred assets and liabilities. Also, GAAP will likely continue to use the enacted tax rate in computing deferred taxes, except in situations where the taxing jurisdiction is not involved. In that case, companies should use IFRS, which is based on enacted rates or substantially enacted tax rates. Finally, the issue of allocation of deferred income taxes to equity for certain transactions under IFRS must be addressed in order to converge with GAAP, which allocates the effects to income. At the time of this printing, deliberations on the income tax project have been suspended indefinitely.

IFRS SELF-TEST QUESTIONS

1. Which of the following is **false**?
   (a) Under GAAP, deferred taxes are reported based on the classification of the asset or liability to which it relates.
   (b) Under IFRS, some potential liabilities are not recognized.
   (c) Under GAAP, the enacted tax rate is used to measure deferred tax assets and liabilities.
   (d) Under IFRS, all deferred tax assets and liabilities are classified as non-current.
2. Which of the following statements is **correct** with regard to IFRS and GAAP?
   (a) Under GAAP, all potential liabilities related to uncertain tax positions must be recognized.
   (b) The tax effects related to certain items are reported in equity under GAAP; under IFRS, the tax effects are charged or credited to income.

(c) IFRS uses an affirmative judgment approach for deferred tax assets, whereas GAAP uses an impairment approach for deferred tax assets.

(d) IFRS classifies deferred taxes based on the classification of the asset or liability to which it relates.

3. Under IFRS:

(a) "probable" is defined as a level of likelihood of at least slightly more than 60%.

(b) a company should reduce a deferred tax asset when it is likely that some or all of it will not be realized by using a valuation allowance.

(c) a company considers only positive evidence when determining whether to recognize a deferred tax asset.

(d) deferred tax assets must be evaluated at the end of each accounting period.

4. Stephens Company has a deductible temporary difference of $2,000,000 at the end of its first year of operations. Its tax rate is 40 percent. Stephens has $1,800,000 of income taxes payable. After a careful review of all available evidence, Stephens determines that it is probable that it will not realize $200,000 of this deferred tax asset. On Stephens Company's statement of financial position at the end of its first year of operations, what is the amount of deferred tax asset?

(a) $2,000,000.   (c) $800,000.
(b) $1,800,000.   (d) $600,000.

5. Lincoln Company has the following four deferred tax items at December 31, 2014. The deferred tax assets and the deferred tax liabilities relate to income taxes levied by the same tax authority.

Temporary Difference	Deferred Tax Asset	Deferred Tax Liability
Rent collected in advance: recognized when earned for accounting purposes and when received for tax purposes.	$652,000	
Use of straight-line depreciation for accounting purposes and accelerated depreciation for tax purposes.		$330,000
Recognition of profits on installment sales during period of sale for accounting purposes and during period of collection for tax purposes.		64,000
Warranty liabilities: recognized for accounting purposes at time of sale; for tax purposes at time paid.	37,000	

On Lincoln's December 31, 2014, statement of financial position, it will report:

(a) $394,000 non-current deferred tax liability and $689,000 non-current deferred tax asset.

(b) $330,000 non-current liability and $625,000 current deferred tax asset.

(c) $295,000 non-current deferred tax asset.

(d) $295,000 current tax receivable.

IFRS CONCEPTS AND APPLICATION

IFRS19-1 Where can authoritative IFRS related to the accounting for taxes be found?

IFRS19-2 Briefly describe some of the similarities and differences between GAAP and IFRS with respect to income tax accounting.

IFRS19-3 Describe the current convergence efforts of the FASB and IASB in the area of accounting for taxes.

IFRS19-4 How are deferred tax assets and deferred tax liabilities reported on the statement of financial position under IFRS?

IFRS19-5 Describe the procedure(s) involved in classifying deferred tax amounts on the statement of financial position under IFRS.

IFRS19-6 At December 31, 2014, Hillyard Corporation has a deferred tax asset of $200,000. After a careful review of all available evidence, it is determined that it is probable that $60,000 of this deferred tax asset will not be realized. Prepare the necessary journal entry.

IFRS19-7 Rode Inc. incurred a net operating loss of $500,000 in 2014. Combined income for 2012 and 2013 was $350,000. The tax rate for all years is 40%. Rode elects the carryback option. Prepare the journal entries to record the benefits of the loss carryback and the loss carryforward.

IFRS19-8 Use the information for Rode Inc. given in IFRS19-7. Assume that it is probable that the entire net operating loss carryforward will not be realized in future years. Prepare the journal entry(ies) necessary at the end of 2014.

IFRS19-9 Youngman Corporation has temporary differences at December 31, 2014, that result in the following deferred taxes.

Deferred tax asset	$24,000
Deferred tax liability	$69,000

Indicate how these balances would be presented in Youngman's December 31, 2014, statement of financial position.

IFRS19-10 At December 31, 2014, Cascade Company had a net deferred tax liability of $450,000. An explanation of the items that compose this balance is as follows.

Temporary Differences in Deferred Taxes	Resulting Balances
1. Excess of tax depreciation over book depreciation.	$200,000
2. Accrual, for book purposes, of estimated loss contingency from pending lawsuit that is expected to be settled in 2015. The loss will be deducted on the tax return when paid.	$ (50,000)
3. Accrual method used for book purposes and installment method used for tax purposes for an isolated installment sale of an investment.	$300,000

In analyzing the temporary differences, you find that $30,000 of the depreciation temporary difference will reverse in 2015, and $120,000 of the temporary difference due to the installment sale will reverse in 2015. The tax rate for all years is 40%.

Instructions

Indicate the manner in which deferred taxes should be presented on Cascade Company's December 31, 2014, statement of financial position.

IFRS19-11 Callaway Corp. has a deferred tax asset account with a balance of $150,000 at the end of 2014 due to a single cumulative temporary difference of $375,000. At the end of 2015, this same temporary difference has increased to a cumulative amount of $500,000. Taxable income for 2015 is $850,000. The tax rate is 40% for all years.

Instructions

(a) Record income tax expense, deferred income taxes, and income taxes payable for 2015, assuming that it is probable that the deferred tax asset will be realized.

(b) Assuming that it is probable that $30,000 of the deferred tax asset will not be realized, prepare the journal entry at the end of 2015 to recognize this probability.

Professional Research

IFRS19-12 Kleckner Company started operations in 2010. Although it has grown steadily, the company reported accumulated operating losses of $450,000 in its first four years in business. In the most recent year (2014), Kleckner appears to have turned the corner and reported modest taxable income of $30,000. In addition to a deferred tax asset related to its net operating loss, Kleckner has recorded a deferred tax asset related to product warranties and a deferred tax liability related to accelerated depreciation. Given its past operating results, Kleckner has determined that it is not probable that it will realize any of the deferred tax assets. However, given its improved performance, Kleckner management wonders whether there are any accounting consequences for its deferred tax assets. They would like you to conduct some research on the accounting for recognition of its deferred tax asset.

Instructions

Access the IFRS authoritative literature at the IASB website (*http://eifrs.iasb.org/*). (Click on the IFRS tab and then register for free eIFRS access if necessary.) When you have accessed the documents, you can use the search tool in your Internet browser to respond to the following questions. (Provide paragraph citations.)

(a) Briefly explain to Kleckner management the importance of future taxable income as it relates to the recognition of deferred tax assets.

(b) What are the sources of income that may be relied upon in assessing realization of a deferred tax asset?

(c) What are tax-planning strategies? From the information provided, does it appear that Kleckner could employ a tax-planning strategy in evaluating its deferred tax asset?

International Financial Reporting Problem
Marks and Spencer plc

IFRS19-13 The financial statements of **Marks and Spencer plc (M&S)** are available at the book's companion website or can be accessed at *http://annualreport.marksandspencer.com/_assets/downloads/Marks-and-Spencer-Annual-report-and-financial-statements-2012.pdf.*

Instructions

Refer to M&S's financial statements and the accompanying notes to answer the following questions.

(a) What amounts relative to income taxes does M&S report in its:
  (1) 2012 income statement?
  (2) 31 March 2012 statement of financial position?
  (3) 2012 statement of cash flows?

(b) M&S's provision for income taxes in 2011 and 2012 was computed at what effective tax rates? (See the notes to the financial statements.)

(c) How much of M&S's 2012 total provision for income taxes was current tax expense, and how much was deferred tax expense?

(d) What did M&S report as the significant components (the details) of its 31 March 2012 deferred tax assets and liabilities?

ANSWERS TO IFRS SELF-TEST QUESTIONS

1. b **2.** c **3.** d **4.** d **5.** c

Remember to check the book's companion website to find additional resources for this chapter.

20 Accounting for Pensions and Postretirement Benefits

Where Have All the Pensions Gone?

Many companies have benefit plans that promise income and other benefits to retired employees in exchange for services during their working years. However, a shift is on from traditional defined benefit plans, in which employers bear the risk of meeting the benefit promises, to plans in which employees bear more of the risk. In some cases, employers are dropping retirement plans altogether. Here are some of the reasons for the shift.

- **Competition.** Newer and foreign competitors do not have the same retiree costs that older U.S. companies do. **Southwest Airlines** does not offer a traditional pension plan, but **United** has a pension deficit exceeding $100,000 per employee.

- **Cost.** Retirees are living longer, and the costs of retirement are higher. Combined with annual retiree healthcare costs, retirement benefits are costing the S&P 500 companies over $25 billion a year and are rising at double-digit rates.

- **Insurance.** Pensions are backed by premiums paid to the **Pension Benefit Guarantee Corporation (PBGC)**. When a company fails, the PBGC takes over the plan. But due to a number of significant company failures, the PBGC is running a deficit, and healthy companies are subsidizing the weak.

- **Accounting.** To bring U.S. standards in line with international rules, accounting rule-makers are considering rules that will require companies to "mark their pensions to market" (value them at market rates). Such a move would increase the reported volatility of the retirement plan and of company financial statements. When Great Britain made this shift, 25 percent of British companies closed their plans to new entrants.

As a result of such factors, it is understandable that experts can think of no major company that has instituted a traditional pension plan in the past decade. What does this mean for you as you evaluate job offers and benefit packages? To start, you should begin building *your own* retirement nest egg,

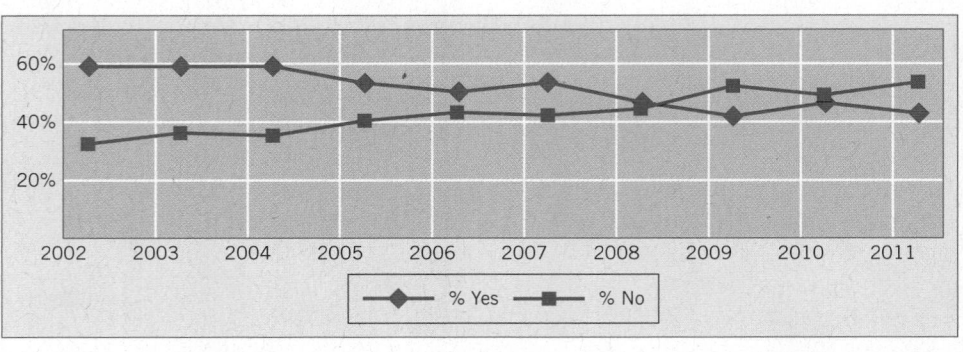

rather than relying on your employer to provide postretirement income and healthcare benefits. Recently, a sample of Americans was asked the following question: When you retire, do you think you will have enough money to live comfortably, or not?

The graph on the previous page shows a substantial change in responses from nonretired adults from 2002 to 2011.

In 2002, adults were nearly twice as likely to say they would have enough money to live comfortably (59%) as to say they would not (32%). Those views changed as time passed. By 2011, a majority said they would not have enough money to live comfortably in retirement.

General economic conditions affect how Americans look at retirement. Americans were more positive about the overall economy—and retirement—prior to the recent recession than they are now. The continuing political discussion about the fragility of the country's Social Security and Medicare programs may also reduce nonretired Americans' comfort with projections of their monetary resources in their retirement. In addition, many are beginning to realize that retirement at the age of 65 may no longer be possible given the possible extension of social benefits to later ages.

This means that retirement accounts, including individual retirement accounts and defined contribution pensions such as 401(k) plans, will need to become a bigger piece of the pie to fill the gap left by smaller government and employer-sponsored benefits. So get started now with a personal savings strategy to ensure an adequate nest egg at your retirement.

Sources: Story adapted from Nanette Byrnes with David Welch, "The Benefits Trap," *BusinessWeek* (July 19, 2004), pp. 54–72; and F. Newport, "In U.S., 53% Worry About Having Enough Money in Retirement," *http://www.gallup.com/poll/147254/%20-americans-biggest-financial-worry.aspx* (April 25, 2011).

CONCEPTUAL FOCUS

> See the **Underlying Concepts** on pages 1189, 1208, 1209, and 1213.
> Read the **Evolving Issue** on page 1202 for a discussion of the corridor approach.

INTERNATIONAL FOCUS

> See the **International Perspectives** on pages 1186 and 1207.
> Read the **IFRS Insights** on pages 1250–1266 for a discussion of:
  —Accounting for pensions
  —Using a pension worksheet

PREVIEW OF CHAPTER | **20**

As our opening story indicates, the cost of retirement benefits is steep. For example, **British Airways'** pension and healthcare costs for retirees in a recent year totaled $195 million, or approximately $6 per passenger carried. Many other companies are also facing substantial pension and other postretirement expenses and obligations. In this chapter, we discuss the accounting issues related to these benefit plans. The content and organization of the chapter are as follows.

Accounting for Pensions and Postretirement Benefits

Nature of Pension Plans	Accounting for Pensions	Using a Pension Worksheet	Reporting Pension Plans in Financial Statements
• Defined contribution plan • Defined benefit plan • Role of actuaries	• Alternative measures of liability • Recognition of net funded status • Components of pension expense	• 2014 entries and worksheet • Amortization of prior service cost • 2015 entries and worksheet • Gain or loss • Corridor amortization • 2016 entries and worksheet	• Within the financial statements • Within the notes to the financial statements • Pension note disclosure • 2017 entries and worksheet—a comprehensive example • Special issues

NATURE OF PENSION PLANS

LEARNING OBJECTIVE 1

Distinguish between accounting for the employer's pension plan and accounting for the pension fund.

A **pension plan** is an arrangement whereby an employer provides benefits (payments) to retired employees for services they provided in their working years. Pension accounting may be divided and separately treated as **accounting for the employer** and **accounting for the pension fund**. The *company* or *employer* is the organization sponsoring the pension plan. It incurs the cost and makes contributions to the pension fund. The *fund* or *plan* is the entity that receives the contributions from the employer, administers the pension assets, and makes the benefit payments to the retired employees (pension recipients). Illustration 20-1 shows the three entities involved in a pension plan and indicates the flow of cash among them.

ILLUSTRATION 20-1
Flow of Cash among
Pension Plan Participants

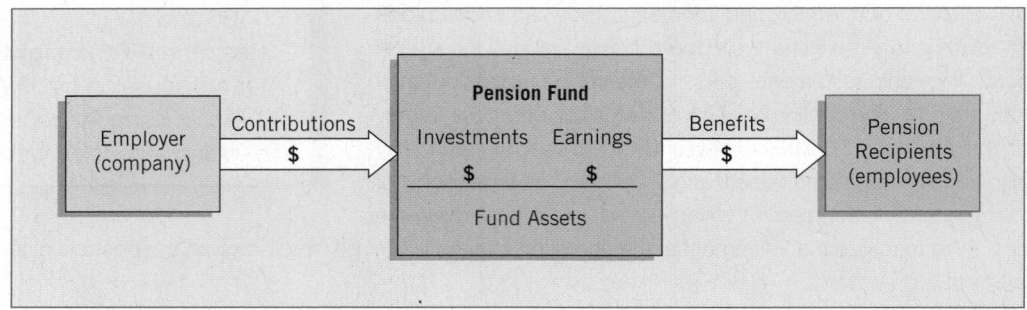

A pension plan is **funded** when the employer makes payments to a funding agency.[1] That agency accumulates the assets of the pension fund and makes payments to the recipients as the benefits come due.

Some pension plans are **contributory**. In these, the employees bear part of the cost of the stated benefits or voluntarily make payments to increase their benefits. Other plans are **noncontributory**. In these plans, the employer bears the entire cost. Companies generally design their pension plans so as to take advantage of federal income tax benefits. Plans that offer tax benefits are called **qualified pension plans**. They permit **deductibility of the employer's contributions to the pension fund and tax-free status of earnings from pension fund assets**.

The pension fund should be a separate legal and accounting entity. The pension fund, as a separate entity, maintains a set of books and prepares financial statements. Maintaining records and preparing financial statements for the fund, an activity known as "accounting for employee benefit plans," is not the subject of this chapter.[2] Instead, this chapter explains the pension accounting and reporting problems **of the employer** as the sponsor of a pension plan.

The need to properly administer and account for pension funds becomes apparent when you understand the size of these funds. Listed in Illustration 20-2 are the pension fund assets and pension expenses of six major companies.

ILLUSTRATION 20-2
Pension Funds and
Pension Expense

Company ($ in millions)	Size of Pension Fund	2011 Pension Expense (Income)	Pension Expense as % of Pretax Income
General Motors	$108,980	$(490)	−8.19%
Hewlett-Packard	10,662	280	3.12%
Deere & Company	9,552	91	2.15%
Merck	12,481	543	7.40%
The Coca-Cola Company	6,171	249	2.18%
Molson Coors Brewing	3,139	19	2.45%

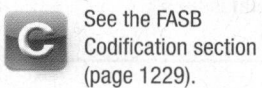

See the FASB
Codification section
(page 1229).

[1]When used as a verb, **fund** means to pay to a funding agency (as to fund future pension benefits or to fund pension cost). Used as a noun, it refers to assets accumulated in the hands of a funding agency (trustee) for the purpose of meeting pension benefits when they become due.

[2]The FASB issued a separate standard covering the accounting and reporting for employee benefit plans. **[1]**

As Illustration 20-2 indicates, pension expense is a substantial percentage of total pretax income for many companies.[3] The two most common types of pension plans are **defined contribution plans** and **defined benefit plans**, and we look at each of them in the following sections.

Defined Contribution Plan

In a defined contribution plan, the employer agrees to contribute to a pension trust a certain sum each period, based on a formula. This formula may consider such factors as age, length of employee service, employer's profits, and compensation level. **The plan defines only the employer's contribution.** It makes no promise regarding the ultimate benefits paid out to the employees. A common form of this plan is a **401(k) plan.**

2 **LEARNING OBJECTIVE**
Identify types of pension plans and their characteristics.

The size of the pension benefits that the employee finally collects under the plan depends on several factors: the amounts originally contributed to the pension trust, the income accumulated in the trust, and the treatment of forfeitures of funds caused by early terminations of other employees. A company usually turns over to an **independent third-party trustee** the amounts originally contributed. The trustee, acting on behalf of the beneficiaries (the participating employees), assumes ownership of the pension assets and is accountable for their investment and distribution. The trust is separate and distinct from the employer.

The accounting for a defined contribution plan is straightforward. The employee gets the benefit of gain (or the risk of loss) from the assets contributed to the pension plan. The employer simply contributes each year based on the formula established in the plan. As a result, the employer's annual cost (pension expense) is simply the amount that it is obligated to contribute to the pension trust. The employer reports a liability on its balance sheet only if it does not make the contribution in full. The employer reports an asset only if it contributes more than the required amount.

In addition to pension expense, the employer must disclose the following for a defined contribution plan: a plan description, including employee groups covered; the basis for determining contributions; and the nature and effect of significant matters affecting comparability from period to period. **[2]**

Defined Benefit Plan

A defined benefit plan outlines the benefits that employees will receive when they retire. These benefits typically are a function of an employee's years of service and of the compensation level in the years approaching retirement.

To meet the defined benefit commitments that will arise at retirement, a company must determine what the contribution should be today (a time value of money computation). Companies may use many different contribution approaches. However, the funding method should provide enough money at retirement to meet the benefits defined by the plan.

The **employees** are the beneficiaries of a defined **contribution** trust, but the **employer** is the beneficiary of a defined **benefit** trust. Under a defined benefit plan, the trust's primary purpose is to safeguard and invest assets so that there will be enough to pay the employer's obligation to the employees. **In form**, the trust is a separate entity. **In substance**, the trust assets and liabilities belong to the employer. That is, **as long as**

[3]Retirement assets in the 13 major global markets increased 4 percent to a record $27.5 trillion in 2011. The United States accounts for 59 percent of total pension assets, followed by Japan at 12 percent and the United Kingdom at 9 percent. Defined contribution assets for the seven largest markets—United States, United Kingdom, Japan, Netherlands, Canada, Australia, and Switzerland—now make up 43 percent of global retirement assets, up from 41 percent in 2005 and 38 percent in 2001. The United States, Australia, and Switzerland are the only countries with more defined contribution assets than defined benefit ones. See K. Olsen, "Global Pension Market Hits $27.5T," *http://www.pionline.com/article/20120206/PRINTSUB/302069986#* (February 6, 2012).

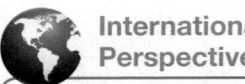

International Perspective

Outside the United States, private pension plans are less common because many other nations rely on government-sponsored pension plans. Consequently, accounting for defined benefit pension plans is typically a less important issue elsewhere in the world.

the plan continues, the employer is responsible for the payment of the defined benefits **(without regard to what happens in the trust)**. The employer must make up any shortfall in the accumulated assets held by the trust. On the other hand, the employer can recapture any excess accumulated in the trust, either through reduced future funding or through a reversion of funds.

Because a defined benefit plan specifies benefits in terms of uncertain future variables, a company must establish an appropriate funding pattern to ensure the availability of funds at retirement in order to provide the benefits promised. This funding level depends on a number of factors such as turnover, mortality, length of employee service, compensation levels, and interest earnings.

Employers are at risk with defined benefit plans because they must contribute enough to meet the cost of benefits that the plan defines. The expense recognized each period is not necessarily equal to the cash contribution. Similarly, the liability is controversial because its measurement and recognition relate to unknown future variables. Thus, the accounting issues related to this type of plan are complex. **Our discussion in the following sections deals primarily with defined benefit plans.**[4]

What do the numbers mean? WHICH PLAN IS RIGHT FOR YOU?

Defined contribution plans have become much more popular with employers than defined benefit plans, as indicated in the chart below. One reason is that they are cheaper. Defined contribution plans often cost no more than 3 percent of payroll, whereas defined benefit plans can cost 5 to 6 percent of payroll.

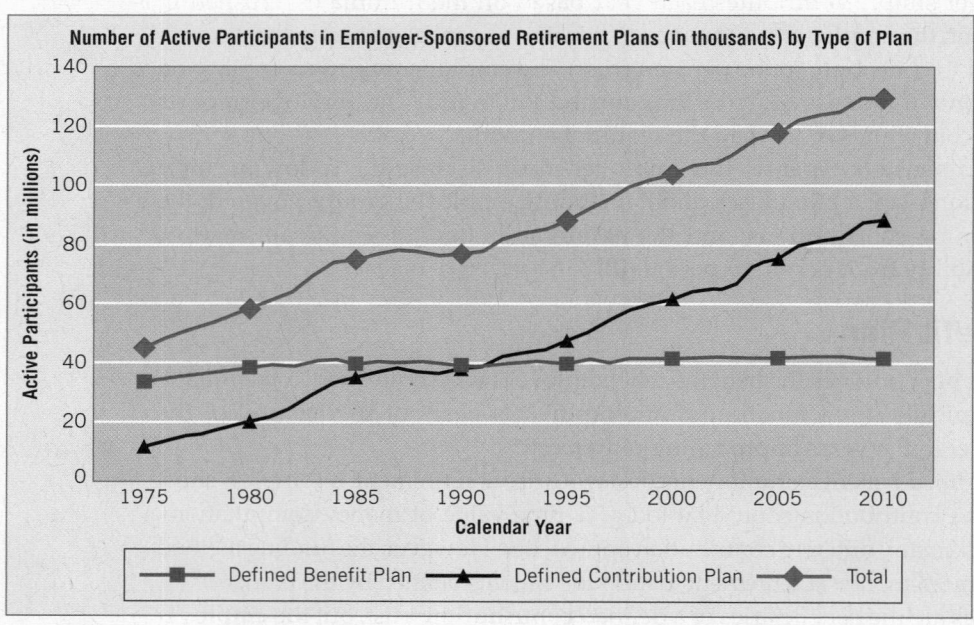

Source: Form 5500 filings with U.S. Department of Labor, November 2012, "Private Pension Plan Bulletin."

The total amount of assets held by pension plans increased 14 percent to $6.3 trillion in 2010. Defined benefit plan assets increased 12 percent to $2.4 trillion, while defined contribution plans increased 16 percent to $3.8 trillion.

---

[4]A recent federal law requires employees to explicitly opt out of an employer-sponsored defined contribution plan. This should help employees build their own nest eggs (as suggested in the opening story) and will contribute to further growth in defined contribution plans. However, note the following three warnings: (1) low-income workers will still not be able to stash enough away, (2) it leaves each participant alone to manage risk, and (3) companies establish a minimum contribution, which too many participants choose to use, instead of a larger contribution.

The Role of Actuaries in Pension Accounting

The problems associated with pension plans involve complicated mathematical considerations. Therefore, companies engage actuaries to ensure that a pension plan is appropriate for the employee group covered.[5] Actuaries are individuals trained through a long and rigorous certification program to assign probabilities to future events and their financial effects. The insurance industry employs actuaries to assess risks and to advise on the setting of premiums and other aspects of insurance policies. Employers rely heavily on actuaries for assistance in developing, implementing, and funding pension funds.

Actuaries make predictions (called *actuarial assumptions*) of mortality rates, employee turnover, interest and earnings rates, early retirement frequency, future salaries, and any other factors necessary to operate a pension plan. They also compute the various pension measures that affect the financial statements, such as the pension obligation, the annual cost of servicing the plan, and the cost of amendments to the plan. In summary, accounting for defined benefit pension plans relies heavily upon information and measurements provided by actuaries.

ACCOUNTING FOR PENSIONS

In accounting for a company's pension plan, two questions arise. (1) What is the pension obligation that a company should report in the financial statements? (2) What is the pension expense for the period? Attempting to answer the first question has produced much controversy.

3 LEARNING OBJECTIVE

Explain alternative measures for valuing the pension obligation.

Alternative Measures of the Liability

Most agree that an employer's **pension obligation** is the deferred compensation obligation it has to its employees for their service under the terms of the pension plan. Measuring that obligation is not so simple, though, because there are alternative ways of measuring it.[6]

One measure of the pension obligation is to base it only on the benefits vested to the employees. Vested benefits are those that the employee is entitled to receive even if he or she renders no additional services to the company. Most pension plans require a certain minimum number of years of service to the employer before an employee achieves vested benefits status. Companies compute the vested benefit obligation using only vested benefits, at current salary levels.

Another way to measure the obligation uses both vested and nonvested years of service. On this basis, the company computes the deferred compensation amount on all years of employees' service—both vested and nonvested—using current salary levels. This measurement of the pension obligation is called the accumulated benefit obligation.

---

[5]An actuary's primary purpose is to ensure that the company has established an appropriate funding pattern to meet its pension obligations. This computation involves developing a set of assumptions and continued monitoring of these assumptions to ensure their realism. That the general public has little understanding of what an actuary does is illustrated by the following excerpt from the *Wall Street Journal*: "A polling organization once asked the general public what an actuary was, and received among its more coherent responses the opinion that it was a place where you put dead actors."

[6]One measure of the pension obligation is to determine the amount that the Pension Benefit Guaranty Corporation would require the employer to pay if it defaulted. (This amount is limited to 30 percent of the employer's net worth.) The accounting profession rejected this approach for financial reporting because it is too hypothetical and ignores the going concern concept.

A third measure bases the deferred compensation amount on both vested and nonvested service **using future salaries**. This measurement of the pension obligation is called the projected benefit obligation. Because future salaries are expected to be higher than current salaries, this approach results in the largest measurement of the pension obligation.

The choice between these measures is critical. The choice affects the amount of a company's pension liability and the annual pension expense reported. The diagram in Illustration 20-3 presents the differences in these three measurements.

ILLUSTRATION 20-3
Different Measures of the Pension Obligation

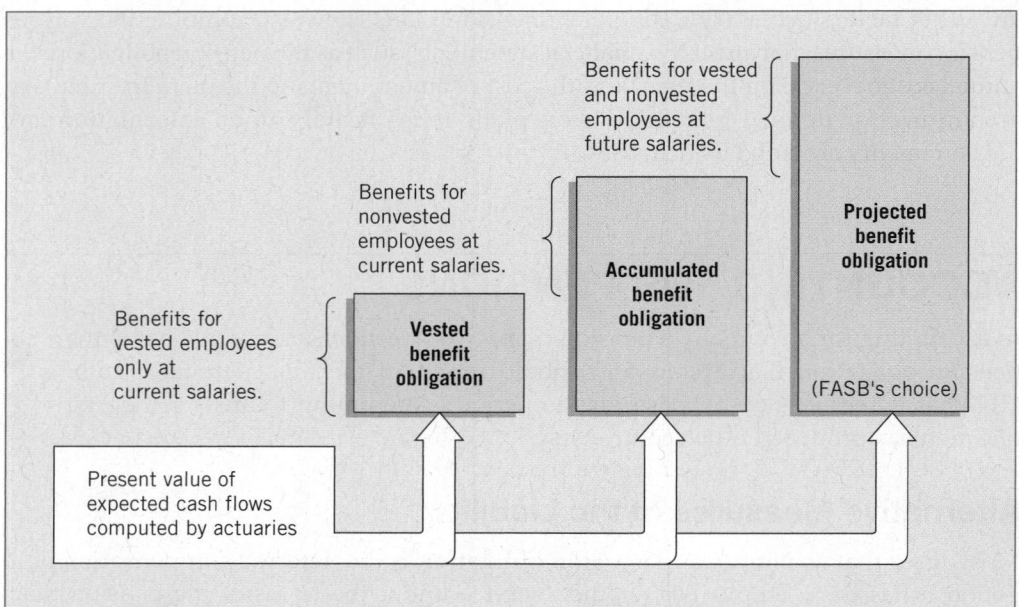

Which of these alternative measures of the pension liability does the profession favor? **The profession adopted the projected benefit obligation—the present value of vested and nonvested benefits accrued to date, based on employees' future salary levels.**[7] Those in favor of the projected benefit obligation contend that a promise by an employer to pay benefits based on a percentage of the employees' future salaries is far greater than a promise to pay a percentage of their current salary, and such a difference should be reflected in the pension liability and pension expense.

Moreover, companies discount to present value the estimated future benefits to be paid. Minor changes in the interest rate used to discount pension benefits can dramatically affect the measurement of the employer's obligation. For example, a 1 percent decrease in the discount rate can increase pension liabilities 15 percent. Accounting rules require that at each measurement date, a company must determine the appropriate discount rate used to measure the pension liability, based on current interest rates.

---

[7]When we use the term "present value of benefits" throughout this chapter, we really mean the *actuarial* present value of benefits. **Actuarial present value** is the amount payable adjusted to reflect the time value of money *and* the probability of payment (by means of decrements for events such as death, disability, withdrawals, or retirement) between the present date and the expected date of payment. For simplicity, though, we use the term "present value" instead of "actuarial present value" in our discussion.

Recognition of the Net Funded Status of the Pension Plan

Companies must recognize on their balance sheet the full overfunded or underfunded status of their defined benefit pension plan.[8] **[3]** The overfunded or underfunded status is measured as the difference between the fair value of the plan assets and the projected benefit obligation.

To illustrate, assume that Coker Company has a projected benefit obligation of $300,000, and the fair value of its plan assets is $210,000. In this case, Coker Company's pension plan is underfunded, and therefore it reports a pension liability of $90,000 ($300,000 − $210,000) on its balance sheet. If instead the fair value of Coker's plan assets were $430,000, it would report a pension asset of $130,000 ($430,000 − $300,000).

In 2007, by slowing the growth of pension liabilities and increasing contributions to pension funds, the S&P 500 companies reported aggregate overfunding (assets exceeded liabilities) of $47.2 billion. However, by 2011, these same pension plans were underfunded by $358.4 billion.[9]

Components of Pension Expense

There is broad agreement that companies should account for pension cost on the **accrual basis**.[10] The profession recognizes that **accounting for pension plans requires measurement of the cost and its identification with the appropriate time periods**. The determination of pension cost, however, is extremely complicated because it is a function of the following components.

> **4 LEARNING OBJECTIVE**
>
> List the components of pension expense.

1. *Service cost.* Service cost is the expense caused by the increase in pension benefits payable (the **projected benefit obligation**) to employees because of their services rendered during the current year. Actuaries compute **service cost** as the present value of the new benefits earned by employees during the year.

2. *Interest on the liability.* Because a pension is a deferred compensation arrangement, there is a time value of money factor. As a result, companies record the pension liability on a discounted basis. **Interest expense accrues each year on the projected benefit obligation just as it does on any discounted debt.** The actuary helps to select the interest rate, referred to as the **settlement rate**.

3. *Actual return on plan assets.* The return earned by the accumulated pension fund assets in a particular year is relevant in measuring the net cost to the employer of sponsoring an employee pension plan. Therefore, **a company should adjust annual pension expense for interest and dividends that accumulate within the fund, as well as increases and decreases in the fair value of the fund assets.**

4. *Amortization of prior service cost.* Pension plan amendments (including initiation of a pension plan) often include provisions to increase benefits (or in rare situations, to decrease benefits) for employee service provided in prior years. A company grants plan amendments with the expectation that it will realize economic benefits in future periods. Thus, **it allocates the cost (prior service cost) of providing these**

> **Underlying Concepts** 🔍
>
> The expense recognition principle and the definition of a liability justify accounting for pension cost on the accrual basis. This requires recording an expense when employees earn the future benefits, and recognizing an existing obligation to pay pensions later based on current services received.

---

[8]Recognize that GAAP applies to pensions as well as other postretirement benefit plans (OPEBs). Appendix 20A addresses the accounting for OPEBs.

[9]J. Ciesielski, "State of the Pension Promise: The S&P 500 in 2011," *The Analyst's Accounting Observer* (May 29, 2012).

[10]At one time, companies applied the **cash basis** of accounting to pension plans by recognizing the amount paid in a particular accounting period as the pension expense for the period. The problem was that the amount paid or funded in a fiscal period depended on financial management and was too often discretionary. For example, funding could depend on the availability of cash, the level of earnings, or other factors unrelated to the requirements of the plan. Application of the cash basis made it possible to manipulate the amount of pension expense appearing in the income statement simply by varying the cash paid to the pension fund.

retroactive benefits to pension expense in the future, specifically to the remaining service-years of the affected employees.

5. *Gain or loss.* Volatility in pension expense can result from sudden and large changes in the fair value of plan assets and by changes in the projected benefit obligation (which changes when actuaries modify assumptions or when actual experience differs from expected experience). Two items comprise this gain or loss: (1) the difference between the actual return and the expected return on plan assets, and (2) amortization of the net gain or loss from previous periods. We will discuss this complex computation later in the chapter.

Illustration 20-4 shows the **components of pension expense** and their effect on total pension expense (increase or decrease).

ILLUSTRATION 20-4
Components of Annual
Pension Expense

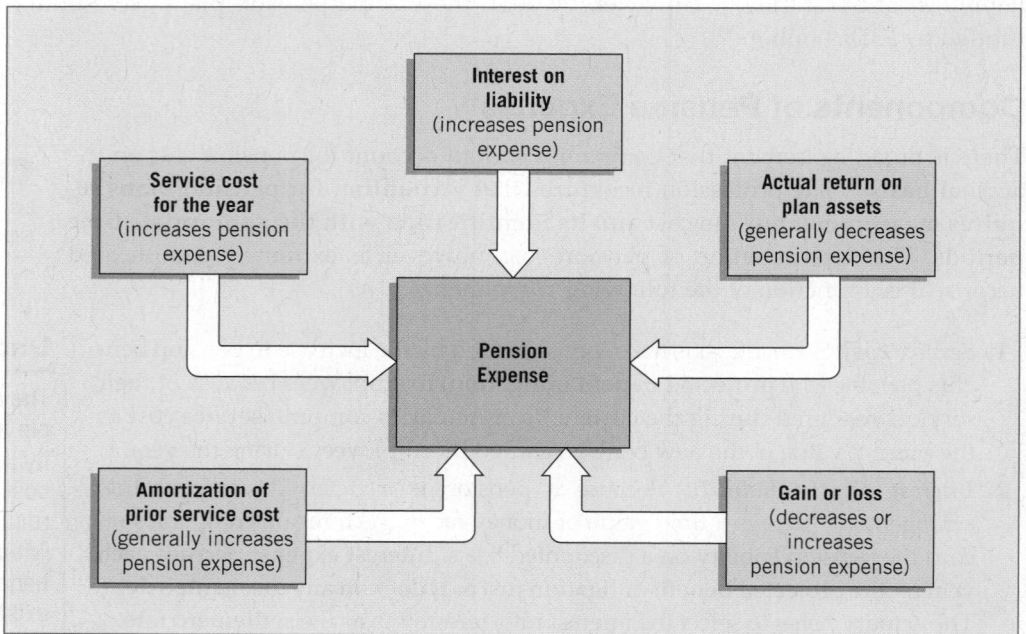

Service Cost

The service cost is the **actuarial present value of benefits attributed by the pension benefit formula to employee service during the period.** That is, the actuary predicts the additional benefits that an employer must pay under the plan's benefit formula as a result of the employees' current year's service, and then discounts the cost of those future benefits back to their present value.

The Board concluded that **companies must consider future compensation levels in measuring the present obligation and periodic pension expense if the plan benefit formula incorporates them.** In other words, the present obligation resulting from a promise to pay a benefit of 1 percent of an employee's **final pay** differs from the promise to pay 1 percent of **current pay.** To overlook this fact is to ignore an important aspect of pension expense. Thus, the FASB adopts the **benefits/years-of-service actuarial method, which determines pension expense based on future salary levels.**

Some object to this determination, arguing that a company should have more freedom to select an expense recognition pattern. Others believe that incorporating future salary increases into current pension expense is accounting for events that have not yet happened. They argue that if a company terminates the plan today, it pays only liabilities for accumulated benefits. **Nevertheless, the FASB indicates that the projected benefit obligation provides a more realistic measure of the employer's obligation under the** plan on a going concern basis and, therefore, companies should use it as the basis for determining service cost.

Interest on the Liability

The second component of pension expense is interest on the liability, or interest expense. Because a company defers paying the liability until maturity, the company records it on a discounted basis. The liability then accrues interest over the life of the employee. **The interest component is the interest for the period on the projected benefit obligation outstanding during the period.** The FASB did not address the question of how often to compound the interest cost. To simplify our illustrations and problem materials, we use a simple interest computation, applying it to the beginning-of-the-year balance of the projected benefit liability.

How do companies determine the interest rate to apply to the pension liability? The Board states that the assumed discount rate should **reflect the rates at which companies can effectively settle pension benefits**. In determining these settlement rates, companies should look to rates of return on high-quality fixed-income investments currently available, whose cash flows match the timing and amount of the expected benefit payments. The objective of selecting the assumed discount rates is to measure a single amount that, if invested in a portfolio of high-quality debt instruments, would provide the necessary future cash flows to pay the pension benefits when due.

Actual Return on Plan Assets

Pension plan assets are usually investments in stocks, bonds, other securities, and real estate that a company holds to earn a reasonable return, generally at minimum risk. Employer contributions and actual returns on pension plan assets increase pension plan assets. Benefits paid to retired employees decrease them. As we indicated, the actual return earned on these assets increases the fund balance and correspondingly reduces the employer's net cost of providing employees' pension benefits. That is, the higher the actual return on the pension plan assets, the less the employer has to contribute eventually and, therefore, the less pension expense that it needs to report.

The actual return on the plan assets is the increase in pension funds from interest, dividends, and realized and unrealized changes in the fair value of the plan assets. Companies compute the actual return by adjusting the change in the plan assets for the effects of contributions during the year and benefits paid out during the year. The equation in Illustration 20-5, or a variation thereof, can be used to compute the actual return.

$$\text{Actual Return} = \left(\begin{array}{c} \text{Plan} \\ \text{Assets} \\ \text{Ending} \\ \text{Balance} \end{array} - \begin{array}{c} \text{Plan} \\ \text{Assets} \\ \text{Beginning} \\ \text{Balance} \end{array} \right) - (\text{Contributions} - \text{Benefits Paid})$$

ILLUSTRATION 20-5
Equation for Computing Actual Return

Stated another way, the actual return on plan assets is the difference between the fair value of the plan assets at the beginning of the period and at the end of the period, adjusted for contributions and benefit payments. Illustration 20-6 uses the equation above to compute the actual return, using some assumed amounts.

Fair value of plan assets at end of period		$5,000,000
Deduct: Fair value of plan assets at beginning of period		4,200,000
Increase in fair value of plan assets		800,000
Deduct: Contributions to plan during period	$500,000	
Less benefits paid during period	300,000	200,000
Actual return on plan assets		$ 600,000

ILLUSTRATION 20-6
Computation of Actual Return on Plan Assets

If the actual return on the plan assets is positive (a gain) during the period, a company subtracts it when computing pension expense. If the actual return is negative (a loss) during the period, the company adds it when computing pension expense.[11]

USING A PENSION WORKSHEET

We will now illustrate the basic computation of pension expense using the first three components: (1) service cost, (2) interest on the liability, and (3) actual return on plan assets. We discuss the other pension expense components (amortization of prior service cost, and gains and losses) in later sections.

Companies often use a worksheet to record pension-related information. As its name suggests, the worksheet is a working tool. A worksheet is **not** a permanent accounting record. It is neither a journal nor part of the general ledger. The worksheet is merely a device to make it easier to prepare entries and the financial statements.[12] Illustration 20-7 shows the format of the **pension worksheet**.

ILLUSTRATION 20-7
Basic Format of Pension Worksheet

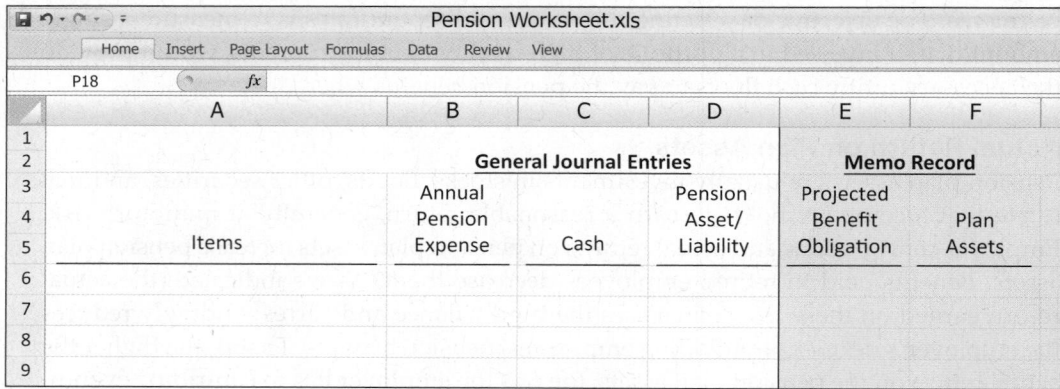

The "General Journal Entries" columns of the worksheet (near the left side) determine the entries to record in the formal general ledger accounts. The "Memo Record" columns (on the right side) maintain balances in the projected benefit obligation and the plan assets. The difference between the projected benefit obligation and the fair value of the plan assets is the **pension asset/liability**, which is shown in the balance sheet. If the projected benefit obligation is greater than the plan assets, a pension liability occurs. If the projected benefit obligation is less than the plan assets, a pension asset occurs.

On the first line of the worksheet, a company records the beginning balances (if any). It then records subsequent transactions and events related to the pension plan using debits and credits, using both sets of columns as if they were one. For each transaction or event, the debits must equal the credits. **The ending balance in the Pension Asset/Liability column should equal the net balance in the memo record.**

2014 Entries and Worksheet

To illustrate the use of a worksheet and how it helps in accounting for a pension plan, assume that on January 1, 2014, Zarle Company provides the following information related to its pension plan for the year 2014.

[11]At this point, we use the actual rate of return. Later, for purposes of computing pension expense, we use the expected rate of return.

[12]The use of a pension entry worksheet is recommended and illustrated by Paul B. W. Miller, "The New Pension Accounting (Part 2)," *Journal of Accountancy* (February 1987), pp. 86–94.

Plan assets, January 1, 2014, are $100,000.

Projected benefit obligation, January 1, 2014, is $100,000.

Annual service cost is $9,000.

Settlement rate is 10 percent.

Actual return on plan assets is $10,000.

Funding contributions are $8,000.

Benefits paid to retirees during the year are $7,000.

Using this data, the worksheet in Illustration 20-8 presents the beginning balances and all of the pension entries recorded by Zarle in 2014. Zarle records the beginning balances for the projected benefit obligation and the pension plan assets on the first line of the worksheet in the memo record. Because the projected benefit obligation and the plan assets are the same at January 1, 2014, the Pension Asset/Liability account has a zero balance at January 1, 2014.

ILLUSTRATION 20-8
Pension
Worksheet—2014

Pension Worksheet—2014.xls

Home   Insert   Page Layout   Formulas   Data   Review   View

P18   fx

	A	B	C	D	E	F
1						
2		**General Journal Entries**			**Memo Record**	
3		Annual		Pension	Projected	
4		Pension		Asset/	Benefit	Plan
5	Items	Expense	Cash	Liability	Obligation	Assets
6	Balance, Jan. 1, 2014			—	100,000 Cr.	100,000 Dr.
7	(a) Service cost	9,000 Dr.			9,000 Cr.	
8	(b) Interest cost	10,000 Dr.			10,000 Cr.	
9	(c) Actual return	10,000 Cr.				10,000 Dr.
10	(d) Contributions		8,000 Cr.			8,000 Dr.
11	(e) Benefits				7,000 Dr.	7,000 Cr.
12						
13						
14	Journal entry for 2014	9,000 Dr.	8,000 Cr.	1,000 Cr.*		
15	Balance, Dec. 31, 2014			1,000 Cr.**	112,000 Cr.	111,000 Dr.
16						
17	*$9,000 – $8,000 = $1,000					
18	**$112,000 – $111,000 = $1,000					

Entry (a) in Illustration 20-8 records the service cost component, which increases pension expense by $9,000 and increases the liability (projected benefit obligation) by $9,000. Entry (b) accrues the interest expense component, which increases both the liability and the pension expense by $10,000 (the beginning projected benefit obligation multiplied by the settlement rate of 10 percent). Entry (c) records the actual return on the plan assets, which increases the plan assets and decreases the pension expense. Entry (d) records Zarle's contribution (funding) of assets to the pension fund, thereby decreasing cash by $8,000 and increasing plan assets by $8,000. Entry (e) records the benefit payments made to retirees, which results in equal $7,000 decreases to the plan assets and the projected benefit obligation.

Zarle makes the "formal journal entry" on December 31, which records the pension expense in 2014, as follows.

2014

Pension Expense	9,000	
Cash		8,000
Pension Asset/Liability		1,000

The credit to Pension Asset/Liability for $1,000 represents the difference between the 2014 pension expense of $9,000 and the amount funded of $8,000. Pension Asset/Liability (credit) is a liability because Zarle underfunds the plan by $1,000. The Pension Asset/Liability account balance of $1,000 also equals the net of the balances in the memo accounts. Illustration 20-9 shows that the projected benefit obligation exceeds the plan assets by $1,000, which reconciles to the pension liability reported in the balance sheet.

ILLUSTRATION 20-9
Pension Reconciliation Schedule—December 31, 2014

Projected benefit obligation (Credit)	$(112,000)
Plan assets at fair value (Debit)	111,000
Pension asset/liability (Credit)	$ (1,000)

If the net of the memo record balances is a credit, the reconciling amount in the pension asset/liability column will be a credit equal in amount. If the net of the memo record balances is a debit, the pension asset/liability amount will be a debit equal in amount. The worksheet is designed to produce this reconciling feature, which is useful later in the preparation of the financial statements and required note disclosure related to pensions.

In this illustration (for 2014), the debit to Pension Expense exceeds the credit to Cash, resulting in a credit to Pension Asset/Liability—the recognition of a liability. If the credit to Cash exceeded the debit to Pension Expense, Zarle would debit Pension Asset/Liability—the recognition of an asset.

Amortization of Prior Service Cost (PSC)

LEARNING OBJECTIVE 6
Describe the amortization of prior service costs.

When either initiating (adopting) or amending a defined benefit plan, a company often provides benefits to employees for years of service before the date of initiation or amendment. As a result of this prior service cost, the projected benefit obligation is increased to recognize this additional liability. In many cases, the increase in the projected benefit obligation is substantial.

Should a company report an expense for these prior service costs (PSC) at the time it initiates or amends a plan? The FASB says no. The Board's rationale is that the employer would not provide credit for past years of service unless it expects to receive benefits in the future. As a result, a company should not recognize the retroactive benefits as pension expense in the year of amendment. Instead, **the employer initially records the prior service cost as an adjustment to other comprehensive income. The employer then recognizes the prior service cost as a component of pension expense over the remaining service lives of the employees who are expected to benefit from the change in the plan.**

The cost of the retroactive benefits (including any benefits provided to existing retirees) is the increase in the projected benefit obligation at the date of the amendment. An actuary computes the amount of the prior service cost. Amortization of the prior service cost is also an accounting function performed with the assistance of an actuary.

The Board prefers a years-of-service method that is similar to a units-of-production computation. First, the company computes the total number of service-years to be worked by all of the participating employees. Second, it divides the prior service cost by the total number of service-years, to obtain a cost per service-year (the unit cost). Third, the company multiplies the number of service-years consumed each year by the cost per service-year, to obtain the annual amortization charge.

To illustrate the amortization of the prior service cost under the years-of-service method, assume that Zarle Company's defined benefit pension plan covers 170 employees. In its negotiations with the employees, Zarle Company amends its pension plan on January 1, 2015, and grants $80,000 of prior service costs to its employees. The employees are grouped according to expected years of retirement, as shown on the next page.

Group	Number of Employees	Expected Retirement on Dec. 31
A	40	2015
B	20	2016
C	40	2017
D	50	2018
E	20	2019
	170	

Illustration 20-10 shows computation of the service-years per year and the total service-years.

			Service-Years			
Year	A	B	C	D	E	Total
2015	40	20	40	50	20	170
2016		20	40	50	20	130
2017			40	50	20	110
2018				50	20	70
2019					20	20
	40	40	120	200	100	500

ILLUSTRATION 20-10
Computation of Service-Years

Computed on the basis of a prior service cost of $80,000 and a total of 500 service-years for all years, the cost per service-year is $160 ($80,000 ÷ 500). The annual amount of amortization based on a $160 cost per service-year is computed as follows.

Year	Total Service-Years	×	Cost per Service-Year	=	Annual Amortization
2015	170		$160		$27,200
2016	130		160		20,800
2017	110		160		17,600
2018	70		160		11,200
2019	20		160		3,200
	500				$80,000

ILLUSTRATION 20-11
Computation of Annual Prior Service Cost Amortization

An alternative method of computing amortization of **prior service cost is permitted. Employers may use straight-line amortization over the average remaining service life of the employees.** In this case, with 500 service-years and 170 employees, the average would be 2.94 years (500 ÷ 170). The annual expense would be $27,211 ($80,000 ÷ 2.94). Using this method, Zarle Company would charge cost to expense in 2015, 2016, and 2017 as follows.

Year	Expense
2015	$27,211
2016	27,211
2017	25,578*
	$80,000

*.94 × $27,211

2015 Entries and Worksheet

Continuing the Zarle Company illustration into 2015, we note that the company amends the pension plan on January 1, 2015, to grant employees prior service benefits with a present value of $80,000. Zarle uses the annual amortization amounts, as computed in the previous section using the years-of-service approach ($27,200 for 2015). The following additional facts apply to the pension plan for the year 2015.

> Annual service cost is $9,500.
>
> Settlement rate is 10 percent.
>
> Actual return on plan assets is $11,100.
>
> Annual funding contributions are $20,000.
>
> Benefits paid to retirees during the year are $8,000.
>
> Amortization of prior service cost (PSC) using the years-of-service method is $27,200.
>
> Accumulated other comprehensive income (hereafter referred to as accumulated OCI) on December 31, 2014, is zero.

Illustration 20-12 presents a worksheet of all the pension entries and information recorded by Zarle in 2015. We now add an additional column to the worksheet to record the prior service cost adjustment to other comprehensive income. In addition, as shown in rows 19, 21, and 22, the other comprehensive income amount related to prior service cost is added to accumulated other comprehensive income ("Accumulated OCI") to arrive at a debit balance of $52,800 at December 31, 2015.

	Pension Worksheet—2015.xls						
	Home Insert Page Layout Formulas Data Review View						
	P18 *fx*						
	A	B	C	D	E	F	G
1							
2				General Journal Entries		Memo Record	
3							
4				Other Comprehensive			
5		Annual		Income	Pension	Projected	
6		Pension		Prior Service	Asset/	Benefit	
7	Items	Expense	Cash	Cost	Liability	Obligation	Plan Assets
8	Balance, Dec. 31, 2014				1,000 Cr.	112,000 Cr.	111,000 Dr.
9	(f) Prior service cost			80,000 Dr.		80,000 Cr.	0
10							
11	Balance, Jan. 1, 2015					192,000 Cr.	111,000 Dr.
12	(g) Service cost	9,500 Dr.				9,500 Cr.	
13	(h) Interest cost	19,200 Dr.				19,200 Cr.	
14	(i) Actual return	11,100 Cr.					11,100 Dr.
15	(j) Amortization of PSC	27,200 Dr.		27,200 Cr.			
16	(k) Contributions		20,000 Cr.				20,000 Dr.
17	(l) Benefits					8,000 Dr.	8,000 Cr.
18							
19	Journal entry for 2015	44,800 Dr.	20,000 Cr.	52,800 Dr.	77,600 Cr.		
20							
21	Accumulated OCI, Dec. 31, 2014			0			
22	Balance, Dec. 31, 2015			52,800 Dr.	78,600 Cr.	212,700 Cr.	134,100 Dr.
23							

ILLUSTRATION 20-12
Pension
Worksheet—2015

The first line of the worksheet shows the beginning balances of the Pension Asset/ Liability account and the memo accounts. Entry (f) records Zarle's granting of prior service cost, by adding $80,000 to the projected benefit obligation and decreasing other comprehensive income—prior service cost by the same amount. Entries (g), (h), (i), (k), and (l) are similar to the corresponding entries in 2014. To compute the interest cost on the projected benefit obligation for entry (h), we use the beginning projected benefit balance of $192,000, which has been adjusted for the prior service cost amendment on January 1, 2015. Entry (j) records the 2015 amortization of prior service cost by debiting Pension Expense for $27,200 and crediting **Other Comprehensive Income (PSC)** for the same amount.

Zarle makes the following journal entry on December 31 to formally record the 2015 pension expense (the sum of the annual pension expense column), and related pension information.

	2015		
Pension Expense	44,800	
Other Comprehensive Income (PSC)	52,800	
Cash		20,000
Pension Asset/Liability		77,600

Because the debits to Pension Expense and to Other Comprehensive Income (PSC) exceed the funding, Zarle credits the Pension Asset/Liability account for the $77,600 difference. That account is a liability. In 2015, as in 2014, the balance of the Pension Asset/Liability account ($78,600) is equal to the net of the balances in the memo accounts, as shown in Illustration 20-13.

Projected benefit obligation (Credit)	$(212,700)
Plan assets at fair value (Debit)	134,100
Pension asset/liability (Credit)	$ (78,600)

ILLUSTRATION 20-13
Pension Reconciliation
Schedule—December 31,
2015

The reconciliation is the formula that makes the worksheet work. It relates the components of pension accounting, recorded and unrecorded, to one another.

Gain or Loss

Of great concern to companies that have pension plans are the uncontrollable and unexpected swings in pension expense that can result from (1) sudden and large changes in the fair value of plan assets, and (2) changes in actuarial assumptions that affect the amount of the projected benefit obligation. If these gains or losses impact fully the financial statements in the period of realization or incurrence, substantial fluctuations in pension expense result.

7 LEARNING OBJECTIVE
Explain the accounting for unexpected gains and losses.

Therefore, the FASB decided to reduce the volatility associated with pension expense by using **smoothing techniques** that dampen and in some cases fully eliminate the fluctuations.

Smoothing Unexpected Gains and Losses on Plan Assets

One component of pension expense, actual return on plan assets, reduces pension expense (assuming the actual return is positive). A large change in the actual return can substantially affect pension expense for a year. Assume a company has a 40 percent return in the stock market for the year. Should this substantial, and perhaps one-time, event affect current pension expense?

Actuaries ignore current fluctuations when they develop a funding pattern to pay expected benefits in the future. They develop an **expected rate of return** and multiply it by an asset value weighted over a reasonable period of time to arrive at an **expected return on plan assets**. They then use this return to determine a company's funding pattern.

The FASB adopted the actuary's approach to dampen wide swings that might occur in the actual return. That is, a company includes the **expected return** on the plan assets as a component of pension expense, not the actual return in a given year. To achieve this goal, the company multiplies the expected rate of return by the market-related value of the plan assets. The **market-related asset value** of the plan assets is either the fair value of plan assets or a calculated value that recognizes changes in fair value in a systematic and rational manner. **[4]**[13]

The difference between the expected return and the actual return is referred to as the **unexpected gain or loss**; the FASB uses the term **asset gains and losses**. **Asset gains** occur when actual return exceeds expected return; **asset losses** occur when actual return is less than expected return.

What happens to unexpected gains or losses in the accounting for pensions? Companies record asset gains and asset losses in an account, **Other Comprehensive Income (G/L)**, combining them with gains and losses accumulated in prior years. This treatment is similar to prior service cost. The Board believes this treatment is consistent with the practice of including in other comprehensive income certain changes in value that have not been recognized in net income (for example, unrealized gains and losses on available-for-sale securities). **[5]** In addition, the accounting is simple, transparent, and symmetrical.

To illustrate the computation of an unexpected gain or loss and its related accounting, assume that in 2016, Zarle Company has an actual return on plan assets of $12,000 when the expected return is $13,410 (the expected rate of return of 10% on plan assets times the beginning-of-the-year plan assets). The unexpected asset loss of $1,410 ($12,000 − $13,410) is debited to Other Comprehensive Income (G/L) and credited to Pension Expense.

What do the numbers mean? PENSION COSTS UPS AND DOWNS

For some companies, pension plans generated real profits in 2011. The plans not only paid for themselves but also increased earnings. This happens when the expected return on pension assets exceed the company's annual costs. At Mead-Westvaco, pension income amounted to approximately 27 percent of operating profit. It tallied 11 percent of operating profit at CenturyTel and 9.5 percent at Sun Trust Banks. The issue is important because in these cases management is not driving the operating income—pension income is. And as a result, income can change quickly.

Unfortunately, when the stock market stops booming, pension expense substantially increases for many companies. The reason: Expected return on a smaller asset base no longer offsets pension service costs and interest on the projected benefit obligation. As a result, many companies find it difficult to meet their earnings targets, and at a time when meeting such targets is crucial to maintaining the stock price.

Smoothing Unexpected Gains and Losses on the Pension Liability

In estimating the projected benefit obligation (the liability), actuaries make assumptions about such items as mortality rate, retirement rate, turnover rate, disability rate, and salary amounts. Any change in these actuarial assumptions affects the amount of the projected benefit obligation. Seldom does actual experience coincide exactly with actuarial predictions. These unexpected gains or losses from changes in the projected benefit obligation are called **liability gains and losses**.

[13]Companies may use different ways of determining the calculated market-related value for different classes of assets. For example, an employer might use fair value for bonds and a five-year moving-average for equities. But companies should consistently apply the manner of determining market-related value from year to year for each asset class. Throughout our Zarle illustrations, we assume that market-related values based on a calculated value and the fair value of plan assets are equal. *For homework purposes, use the fair value of plan assets as the measure for the market-related value.*

Companies report liability gains (resulting from unexpected decreases in the liability balance) and liability losses (resulting from unexpected increases) in Other Comprehensive Income (G/L). Companies combine the liability gains and losses in the same Other Comprehensive Income (G/L) account used for asset gains and losses. They accumulate the asset and liability gains and losses from year to year that are not amortized in Accumulated Other Comprehensive Income. This amount is reported on the balance sheet in the stockholders' equity section.

Corridor Amortization

The asset gains and losses and the liability gains and losses can offset each other. As a result, the Accumulated OCI account related to gains and losses may not grow very large. But, it is possible that no offsetting will occur and that the balance in the Accumulated OCI account related to gains and losses will continue to grow.

To limit the growth of the Accumulated OCI account, the FASB invented the **corridor approach** for amortizing the account's accumulated balance when it gets too large. How large is too large? The FASB set a limit of 10 percent of the larger of the beginning balances of the projected benefit obligation or the market-related value of the plan assets. **Above that size, the Accumulated OCI account related to gains and losses is considered too large and must be amortized.**

To illustrate the corridor approach, data for Callaway Co.'s projected benefit obligation and plan assets over a period of six years are shown in Illustration 20-14.

ILLUSTRATION 20-14
Computation of the Corridor

Beginning-of-the-Year Balances	Projected Benefit Obligation	Market-Related Asset Value	Corridor* +/− 10%
2013	$1,000,000	$ 900,000	$100,000
2014	1,200,000	1,100,000	120,000
2015	1,300,000	1,700,000	170,000
2016	1,500,000	2,250,000	225,000
2017	1,700,000	1,750,000	175,000
2018	1,800,000	1,700,000	180,000

*The corridor becomes 10% of the larger (in red type) of the projected benefit obligation or the market-related plan asset value.

How the corridor works becomes apparent when we portray the data graphically, as in Illustration 20-15.

ILLUSTRATION 20-15
Graphic Illustration of the Corridor

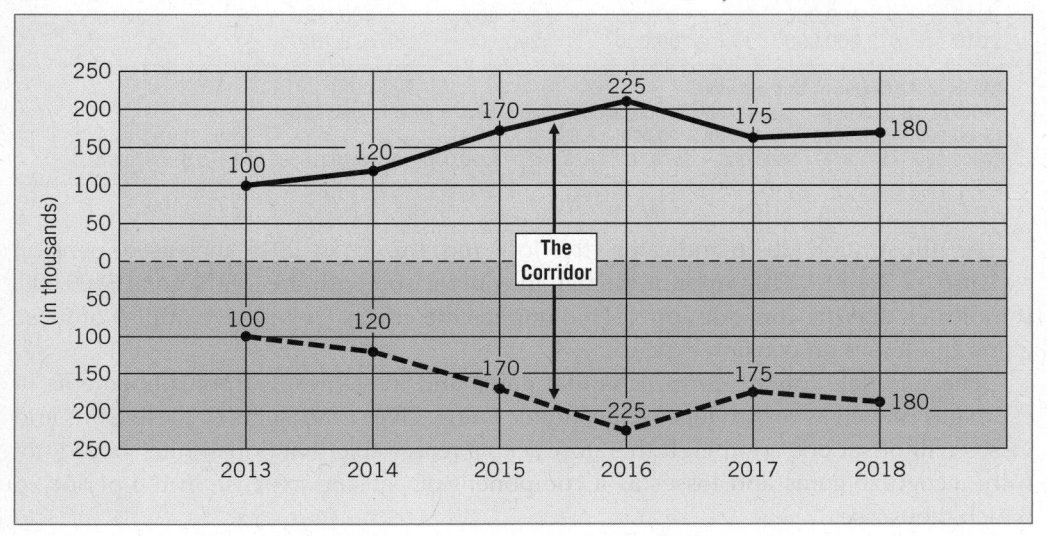

If the balance in the Accumulated OCI account related to gains and losses stays within the upper and lower limits of the corridor, no amortization is required. In that case, Callaway carries forward unchanged the accumulated OCI related to gains and losses.

If amortization is required, the minimum amortization is the excess divided by the average remaining service period of active employees who are expected to receive benefits under the plan. Callaway may use any systematic method of amortization of gains and losses in lieu of the minimum, provided it is greater than the minimum. It must use the method consistently for both gains and losses, and must disclose the amortization method used.

Example of Gains/Losses

In applying the corridor, companies should include amortization of the net gain or loss as a component of pension expense only if, at the **beginning of the year**, the net gain or loss in Accumulated OCI exceeded the corridor. That is, if no net gain or loss exists in Accumulated OCI at the beginning of the period, the company cannot recognize pension expense gains or losses in that period.

To illustrate the amortization of net gains and losses, assume the following information for Soft-White, Inc.

	2014	2015	2016
		(beginning of the year)	
Projected benefit obligation	$2,100,000	$2,600,000	$2,900,000
Market-related asset value	2,600,000	2,800,000	2,700,000

Soft-White recorded in Other Comprehensive Income actuarial losses of $400,000 in 2014 and $300,000 in 2015.

If the average remaining service life of all active employees is 5.5 years, the schedule to amortize the net gain or loss is as shown in Illustration 20-16.

ILLUSTRATION 20-16
Corridor Test and
Gain/Loss Amortization
Schedule

Year	Projected Benefit Obligation[a]	Plan Assets[a]	Corridor[b]	Accumulated OCI (G/L)[a]	Minimum Amortization of Loss (For Current Year)
2014	$2,100,000	$2,600,000	$260,000	$ –0–	$ –0–
2015	2,600,000	2,800,000	280,000	400,000	21,818[c]
2016	2,900,000	2,700,000	290,000	678,182[d]	70,579[d]

[a]All as of the beginning of the period.
[b]10% of the greater of projected benefit obligation or plan assets' market-related value.
[c]$400,000 − $280,000 = $120,000; $120,000 ÷ 5.5 = $21,818.
[d]$400,000 − $21,818 + $300,000 = $678,182; $678,182 − $290,000 = $388,182; $388,182 ÷ 5.5 = $70,579.

As Illustration 20-16 indicates, the loss recognized in 2015 increased pension expense by $21,818. This amount is small in comparison with the total loss of $400,000. It indicates that the corridor approach dampens the effects (reduces volatility) of these gains and losses on pension expense.

The rationale for the corridor is that gains and losses result from refinements in estimates as well as real changes in economic value. Over time, some of these gains and losses will offset one another. It therefore seems reasonable that Soft-White should not fully recognize gains and losses as a component of pension expense in the period in which they arise.

However, Soft-White should immediately recognize in net income certain gains and losses—if they arise from a single occurrence not directly related to the operation of the pension plan and not in the ordinary course of the employer's business. For example, a gain or loss that is directly related to a plant closing, a disposal of a business component, or a similar event that greatly affects the size of the employee work force should be recognized as a part of the gain or loss associated with that event.

For example, at one time, Bethlehem Steel reported a quarterly loss of $477 million. A great deal of this loss was attributable to future estimated benefits payable to workers who were permanently laid off. In this situation, the loss should be treated as an adjustment to the gain or loss on the plant closing and should not affect pension cost for the current or future periods.

Summary of Calculations for Asset Gain or Loss

The difference between the actual return on plan assets and the expected return on plan assets is the **unexpected asset gain or loss** component. This component defers the difference between the actual return and expected return on plan assets in computing current-year pension expense. Thus, after considering this component, **it is really the expected return on plan assets (not the actual return) that determines current pension expense**.

Companies determine the amortized net gain or loss by amortizing the Accumulated OCI amount related to net gain or loss at the beginning of the year subject to the corridor limitation. In other words, **if the accumulated gain or loss is greater than the corridor, these net gains and losses are subject to amortization**. Soft-White computed this minimum amortization by dividing the net gains or losses subject to amortization by the average remaining service period. When the current-year unexpected gain or loss is combined with the amortized net gain or loss, we determine the current-year gain or loss. Illustration 20-17 summarizes these gain and loss computations.

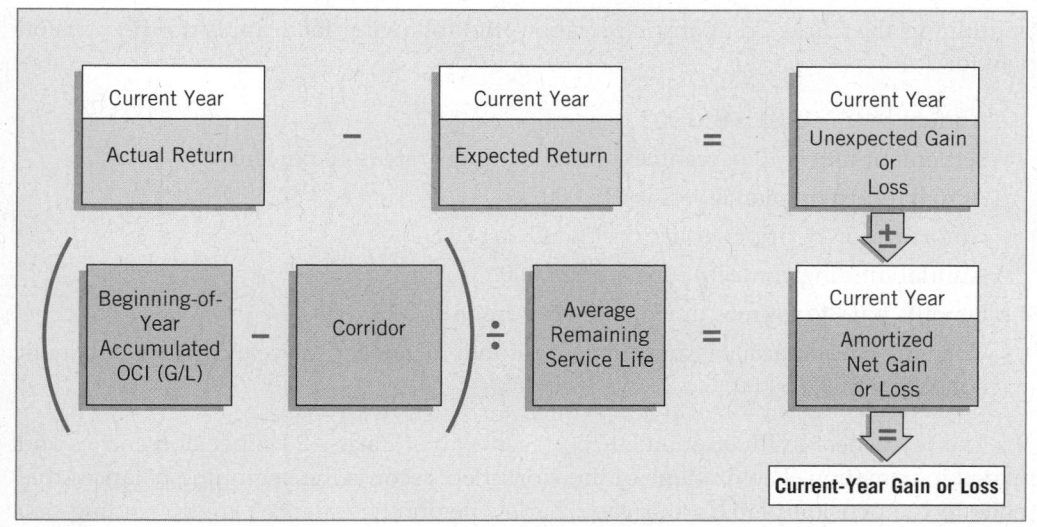

ILLUSTRATION 20-17
Graphic Summary of Gain or Loss Computation

In essence, these gains and losses are subject to *triple* smoothing. That is, companies first smooth the asset gain or loss by using the expected return. Second, they do not amortize the accumulated gain or loss at the beginning of the year unless it is greater than the corridor. Finally, they spread the excess over the remaining service life of existing employees.

Evolving Issue BYE BYE CORRIDOR

Many companies have significant actuarial losses in their pension plans, which are presently deferred through use of the corridor approach. However, companies do have a choice—they may select any method of accounting for these deferred losses as long as it is systematic, rational, and consistently applied, and meets a minimum for recognition in the income statement.

Some companies are now shifting away from the corridor approach and recognizing actuarial losses immediately. For example, AT&T, Verizon Communications, and Honeywell International have recently changed accounting principles from smoothing these losses to recognizing them in the year incurred.

Companies argue this approach provides more transparency for these losses that will directly affect pension expense in the current period (and this accounting is also more similar to IFRS). However, there is a silver lining for these companies—they can charge many of these deferred losses to past years. For example, the table at the top of the right-hand column indicates deferred losses as of 2009 for three major companies.

	Deferred Losses as of 2009 (in billions)	Losses as % of Pension Assets
AT&T	$23.04	49%
Verizon	$12.20	43
Honeywell	$7.57	55

When AT&T changed to immediate recognition in 2010, it restated its previous years. In 2008, for example, AT&T increased its pension cost by $24.9 billion, which led to a net loss in 2008 of $2.6 billion instead of a profit of $12.9 billion. As a result, in 2010 it recognized a much smaller pension cost of $3 billion. Skeptics suggest that AT&T made this change to charge these losses to prior periods. In other words, does anyone in 2011 care that the profit in 2008 was changed to a loss? In addition, once these losses are charged to prior periods, they no longer affect current and future earnings.

Although earnings in the future will probably be more volatile due to fluctuations in pension expense, more companies are willing to move in the direction of immediate expensing to eliminate large deferred losses which would be a drag on future income.

Source: Michael Rapoport, "Rewriting Pension History," *Wall Street Journal* (March 9, 2011).

2016 Entries and Worksheet

Continuing the Zarle Company illustration, the following facts apply to the pension plan for 2016.

> Annual service cost is $13,000.
>
> Settlement rate is 10 percent; expected earnings rate is 10 percent.
>
> Actual return on plan assets is $12,000.
>
> Amortization of prior service cost (PSC) is $20,800.
>
> Annual funding contributions are $24,000.
>
> Benefits paid to retirees during the year are $10,500.
>
> Changes in actuarial assumptions resulted in an end-of-year projected benefit obligation of $265,000.

The worksheet in Illustration 20-18 presents all of Zarle's 2016 pension entries and related information. The first line of the worksheet records the beginning balances that relate to the pension plan. In this case, Zarle's beginning balances are the ending balances from its 2015 pension worksheet in Illustration 20-12 (page 1196).

Entries (m), (n), (o), (q), (r), and (s) are similar to the corresponding entries in 2014 or 2015.

Entries (o) and (p) are related. We explained the recording of the actual return in entry (o) in both 2014 and 2015; it is recorded similarly in 2016. In both 2014 and 2015, Zarle assumed that the actual return on plan assets was equal to the expected return on plan assets. In 2016, the expected return of $13,410 (the expected rate of return of

	A	B	C	D	E	F	G	H
1								
2		General Journal Entries					Memo Record	
3								
4				Other Comprehensive Income				
5		Annual				Pension	Projected	
6		Pension		Prior Service		Asset/	Benefit	
7	Items	Expense	Cash	Cost	Gains/Losses	Liability	Obligation	Plan Assets
8	Balance, Jan. 1, 2016					78,600 Cr.	212,700 Cr.	134,100 Dr.
9	(m) Service cost	13,000 Dr.					13,000 Cr.	
10	(n) Interest cost	21,270 Dr.					21,270 Cr.	
11	(o) Actual return	12,000 Cr.						12,000 Dr.
12	(p) Unexpected loss	1,410 Cr.			1,410 Dr.			
13	(q) Amortization of PSC	20,800 Dr.		20,800 Cr.				
14	(r) Contributions		24,000 Cr.					24,000 Dr.
15	(s) Benefits						10,500 Dr.	10,500 Cr.
16	(t) Liability increase				28,530 Dr.		28,530 Cr.	
17								
18	Journal entry for 2016	41,660 Dr.	24,000 Cr.	20,800 Cr.	29,940 Dr.	26,800 Cr.		
19								
20	Accumulated OCI, Dec. 31, 2015			52,800 Dr.	0			
21	Balance, Dec. 31, 2016*			32,000 Dr.	29,940 Dr.	105,400 Cr.	265,000 Cr.	159,600 Dr.
22								
23	*Accumulated OCI (PSC)	$32,000 Dr.						
24	Accumulated OCI (G/L)	29,940 Dr.						
25	Accumulated OCI, Dec. 31, 2016	$61,940 Dr.						
26								

ILLUSTRATION 20-18
Pension Worksheet—2016

10 percent times the beginning-of-the-year plan assets' balance of $134,100) is higher than the actual return of $12,000. To smooth pension expense, Zarle defers the unexpected loss of $1,410 ($13,410 − $12,000) by debiting the Other Comprehensive Income (G/L) account and crediting Pension Expense. **As a result of this adjustment, the expected return on the plan assets is the amount actually used to compute pension expense.**

Entry (t) records the change in the projected benefit obligation resulting from the change in the actuarial assumptions. As indicated, the actuary has now computed the ending balance to be $265,000. Given the PBO balance at December 31, 2015, and the related transactions during 2016, the PBO balance to date is computed as shown in Illustration 20-19.

December 31, 2015, PBO balance	$212,700
Service cost [entry (m)]	13,000
Interest cost [entry (n)]	21,270
Benefits paid [entry (s)]	(10,500)
December 31, 2016, PBO balance (before liability increases)	$236,470

ILLUSTRATION 20-19
Projected Benefit
Obligation Balance
(Unadjusted)

The difference between the ending balance of $265,000 and the balance of $236,470 before the liability increase is $28,530 ($265,000 − $236,470). This $28,530 increase in the employer's liability is an unexpected loss. The journal entry on December 31, 2016, to record the pension information is as follows.

Pension Expense	41,660	
Other Comprehensive Income (G/L)	29,940	
Cash		24,000
Other Comprehensive Income (PSC)		20,800
Pension Asset/Liability		26,800

As the 2016 worksheet indicates, the $105,400 balance in the Pension Asset/Liability account at December 31, 2016, is equal to the net of the balances in the memo accounts. Illustration 20-20 shows this computation.

ILLUSTRATION 20-20
Pension Reconciliation
Schedule—December 31,
2016

Projected benefit obligation (Credit)	$(265,000)
Plan assets at fair value (Debit)	159,600
Pension asset/liability	$(105,400)

What do the numbers mean? ROLLER COASTER

The chart below shows what has happened to the financial health of pension plans over the last few years. It is a real roller coaster.

At the turn of the century, when the stock market was strong, pension plans were overfunded. However, the bubble burst, and by 2002 companies in the S&P 500 saw their pension plans funded at just 85 percent of reported liabilities. Then, plans bounced back, and by 2007 pension plans were overfunded again. However, due to recent downturns,

plans are now underfunded again and the future is highly uncertain.

A number of factors cause a fund to change from being overfunded to underfunded. First, low interest rates decimate returns on pension plan assets. Second, using low interest rates to discount the projected benefit payments leads to a higher pension liability. Finally, more individuals are retiring, which leads to a depletion of the pension plan assets.

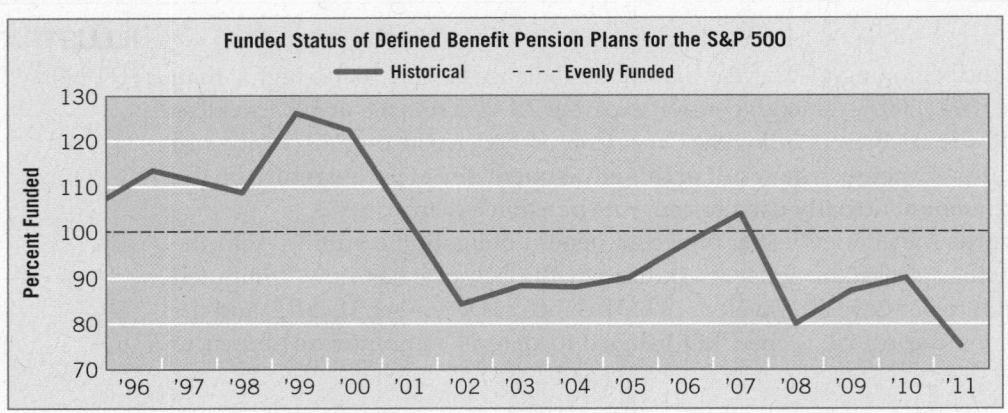

Source: D. Zion, A. Varshay, and N. Burnap, "From Bad to Worse," *Credit Suisse Equity Research* (October 10, 2011).

REPORTING PENSION PLANS IN FINANCIAL STATEMENTS

LEARNING OBJECTIVE 9
Describe the requirements for reporting pension plans in financial statements.

As you might suspect, a phenomenon as significant and complex as pensions involves extensive reporting and disclosure requirements. We will cover these requirements in two categories: (1) those within the financial statements, and (2) those within the notes to the financial statements.

Within the Financial Statements

Recognition of the Net Funded Status of the Pension Plan

Companies must recognize on their balance sheet the overfunded (pension asset) or underfunded (pension liability) status of their defined benefit pension plan. The overfunded or underfunded status is measured as the difference between the fair value of the plan assets and the projected benefit obligation.

Classification of Pension Asset or Pension Liability

No portion of a pension asset is reported as a current asset. The excess of the fair value of the plan assets over the benefit obligation is classified as a noncurrent asset. The rationale for noncurrent classification is that the pension plan assets are restricted. That is, these assets are used to fund the projected benefit obligation, and therefore noncurrent classification is appropriate.

The current portion of a net pension liability represents the amount of benefit payments to be paid in the next 12 months (or operating cycle, if longer), if that amount cannot be funded from existing plan assets. Otherwise, the pension liability is classified as a noncurrent liability.[14]

Aggregation of Pension Plans

Some companies have two or more pension plans. In such instances, a question arises as to whether these multiple plans should be combined and shown as one amount on the balance sheet. The Board takes the position that **all overfunded plans should be combined** and shown as a pension asset on the balance sheet. Similarly, if the company has two or more underfunded plans, the **underfunded plans are combined and shown as one amount** on the balance sheet.

The FASB rejected the alternative of combining *all* plans and representing the net amount as a single net asset or net liability. The rationale: A company does not have the ability to offset excess assets of one plan against underfunded obligations of another plan. Furthermore, netting all plans is inappropriate because offsetting assets and liabilities is not permitted under GAAP unless a right of offset exists.

To illustrate, assume that Cresci Company has three pension plans as shown in Illustration 20-21.

	Pension Assets (at Fair Value)	Projected Benefit Obligation	Pension Asset/Liability
Plan A	$400,000	$300,000	$100,000 Asset
Plan B	600,000	720,000	120,000 Liability
Plan C	550,000	700,000	150,000 Liability

ILLUSTRATION 20-21
Multiple Pension Plans' Funded Status

In this case, Cresci reports a pension plan asset of $100,000 and a pension plan liability of $270,000 ($120,000 + $150,000).

Actuarial Gains and Losses/Prior Service Cost

Actuarial gains and losses not recognized as part of pension expense are recognized as increases and decreases in other comprehensive income. The same type of accounting is also used for prior service cost. The Board requires that the prior service cost arising in the year of the amendment (which increases the projected benefit obligation) be recognized

[14]Recently, the FASB required more extensive disclosures related to pension plan assets. At a minimum, companies must disclose the amount of assets allocated to equities, government and corporate bonds, mortgage-backed securities, derivatives, and real estate. Also, information on concentrations of risk must be explained. Finally, fair value disclosures would be required, including classification of amounts into levels of the fair value hierarchy. **[6]**

by an offsetting debit to other comprehensive income. By recognizing both actuarial gains and losses and prior service cost as part of other comprehensive income, the Board believes that the usefulness of financial statements is enhanced.

To illustrate the presentation of other comprehensive income and related accumulated OCI, assume that Obey Company provides the following information for the year 2014. None of the Accumulated OCI on January 1, 2014, should be amortized in 2014.

Net income for 2014	$100,000
Actuarial liability loss for 2014	60,000
Prior service cost adjustment to provide additional benefits in December 2014	15,000
Accumulated OCI, January 1, 2014	40,000

Both the actuarial liability loss and the prior service adjustment decrease the funded status of the plan on the balance sheet. This results because the projected benefit obligation increases. However, neither the actuarial liability loss nor the prior service cost adjustment affects pension expense in 2014. In subsequent periods, these items will impact pension expense through amortization.

For Obey Company, the computation of "Other comprehensive loss" for 2014 is as follows.

ILLUSTRATION 20-22
Computation of Other Comprehensive Income

Actuarial liability loss	$60,000
Prior service cost benefit adjustment	15,000
Other comprehensive loss	$75,000

The computation of "Comprehensive income" for 2014 is as follows.

ILLUSTRATION 20-23
Computation of Comprehensive Income

Net income	$100,000
Other comprehensive loss	75,000
Comprehensive income	$ 25,000

The components of other comprehensive income must be reported in one of two ways: (1) in a second income statement, or (2) in a combined statement of comprehensive income. Regardless of the format used, net income must be added to other comprehensive income to arrive at comprehensive income. *For homework purposes, use the second income statement approach unless stated otherwise.* Earnings per share information related to comprehensive income is not required.

To illustrate the second income statement approach, assume that Obey Company has reported a traditional income statement. The comprehensive income statement is shown in Illustration 20-24.

ILLUSTRATION 20-24
Comprehensive Income Reporting

OBEY COMPANY COMPREHENSIVE INCOME STATEMENT FOR THE YEAR ENDED DECEMBER 31, 2014		
Net income		$100,000
Other comprehensive loss		
Actuarial liability loss	$60,000	
Prior service cost	15,000	75,000
Comprehensive income		$ 25,000

The computation of "Accumulated other comprehensive income" as reported in stock-holders' equity at December 31, 2014, is as follows.

Accumulated other comprehensive income, January 1, 2014	$40,000
Other comprehensive loss	75,000
Accumulated other comprehensive loss, December 31, 2014	$35,000

ILLUSTRATION 20-25
Computation of Accumulated Other Comprehensive Income

Regardless of the display format for the income statement, the accumulated other comprehensive loss is reported in the stockholders' equity section of the balance sheet of Obey Company as shown in Illustration 20-26. (Illustration 20-26 uses assumed data for the common stock and retained earnings information.)

OBEY COMPANY
BALANCE SHEET
AS OF DECEMBER 31, 2014
(STOCKHOLDERS' EQUITY SECTION)

Stockholders' equity	
Common stock	$100,000
Retained earnings	60,000
Accumulated other comprehensive loss	35,000
Total stockholders' equity	$125,000

ILLUSTRATION 20-26
Reporting of Accumulated OCI

By providing information on the components of comprehensive income as well as total accumulated other comprehensive income, the company communicates all changes in net assets.

In this illustration, it is assumed that the accumulated other comprehensive income at January 1, 2014, is not adjusted for the amortization of any prior service cost or actuarial gains and losses that would change pension expense. As discussed in the earlier examples, these items will be amortized into pension expense in future periods.

Within the Notes to the Financial Statements

Pension plans are frequently important to understanding a company's financial position, results of operations, and cash flows. Therefore, a company discloses the following information, either in the body of the financial statements or in the notes. **[7]**

1. A schedule showing all the major components of pension expense.
   Rationale: Information provided about the components of pension expense helps users better understand how a company determines pension expense. It also is useful in forecasting a company's net income.
2. A **reconciliation** showing how the projected benefit obligation and the fair value of the plan assets changed from the beginning to the end of the period. *Rationale:* Disclosing the projected benefit obligation, the fair value of the plan assets, and changes in them should help users understand the economics underlying the obligations and resources of these plans. Explaining the changes in the projected benefit obligation and fair value of plan assets in the form of a reconciliation provides a more complete disclosure and makes the financial statements more understandable.

International Perspective

The IASB and FASB are studying whether the various components of pension expense, such as interest cost and investment earnings on plan assets, should be presented separately in the income statement along with other interest expense and investment earnings.

3. A disclosure of the rates used in measuring the benefit amounts (discount rate, expected return on plan assets, rate of compensation).
   Rationale: Disclosure of these rates permits users to determine the reasonableness of the assumptions applied in measuring the pension liability and pension expense.

4. A table indicating the allocation of pension plan assets by category (equity securities, debt securities, real estate, and other assets), and showing the percentage of the fair value to total plan assets. In addition, a company must include a narrative description of investment policies and strategies, including the target allocation percentages (if used by the company).
   Rationale: Such information helps financial statement users evaluate the pension plan's exposure to market risk and possible cash flow demands on the company. It also will help users better assess the reasonableness of the company's expected rate of return assumption.

5. The **expected benefit payments** to be paid to current plan participants for each of the next five fiscal years and in the aggregate for the five fiscal years thereafter. Also required is disclosure of a company's best **estimate of expected contributions** to be paid to the plan during the next year.
   Rationale: These disclosures provide information related to the cash outflows of the company. With this information, financial statement users can better understand the potential cash outflows related to the pension plan. They can better assess the liquidity and solvency of the company, which helps in assessing the company's overall financial flexibility.

6. The nature and amount of changes in plan assets and benefit obligations recognized in net income and in other comprehensive income of each period.
   Rationale: This disclosure provides information on pension elements affecting the projected benefit obligation and plan assets and on whether those amounts have been recognized in income or deferred to future periods.

7. The accumulated amount of changes in plan assets and benefit obligations that have been recognized in other comprehensive income and that will be recycled into net income in future periods.
   Rationale: This information indicates the pension-related balances recognized in stockholders' equity, which will affect future income.

Underlying Concepts

Does it make a difference to users of financial statements whether companies recognize pension information in the financial statements or disclose it only in the notes? The FASB was unsure, so in accord with the full disclosure principle, it decided to provide extensive pension plan disclosures.

8. The amount of estimated net actuarial gains and losses and prior service costs and credits that will be amortized from accumulated other comprehensive income into net income over the next fiscal year.
   Rationale: This information helps users predict the impact of deferred pension expense items on next year's income.

In summary, the disclosure requirements are extensive, and purposely so. One factor that has been a challenge for useful pension reporting has been the lack of consistent terminology. Furthermore, a substantial amount of offsetting is inherent in the measurement of pension expense and the pension liability. These disclosure requirements are designed to address these concerns and take some of the mystery out of pension reporting.

Example of Pension Note Disclosure

In the following sections, we provide examples and explain the key pension disclosure elements.

Components of Pension Expense

The FASB requires disclosure of the individual pension expense components (derived from the information in the pension expense worksheet column): (1) service cost,

(2) interest cost, (3) expected return on assets, (4) other gains or losses component, and (5) prior service cost component. The purpose of such disclosure is to clarify to more sophisticated readers how companies determine pension expense. Providing information on the components should also be useful in predicting future pension expense.

Illustration 20-27 presents an example of this part of the disclosure. It uses the information from the Zarle illustration, specifically the expense component information from the worksheets in Illustrations 20-8 (page 1193), 20-12 (page 1196), and 20-18 (page 1203).

ILLUSTRATION 20-27
Summary of Expense Components—2014, 2015, 2016

ZARLE COMPANY			
	2014	2015	2016
Components of Pension Expense			
Service cost	$ 9,000	$ 9,500	$13,000
Interest cost	10,000	19,200	21,270
Expected return on plan assets	(10,000)	(11,100)	(13,410)*
Amortization of prior service cost	–0–	27,200	20,800
Pension expense	$ 9,000	$44,800	$41,660

*Note that the expected return must be disclosed, not the actual return. In 2016, the expected return is $13,410, which is the actual gain ($12,000) adjusted by the unrecognized loss ($1,410).

Funded Status of Plan

Having a reconciliation of the changes in the assets and liabilities from the beginning of the year to the end of the year, statement readers can better understand the underlying economics of the plan. In essence, this disclosure contains the information in the pension worksheet for the projected benefit obligation and plan asset columns. Using the information for Zarle, the schedule in Illustration 20-28 provides an example of the reconciliation.

Underlying Concepts 🔍

This represents another compromise between relevance and faithful representation. Disclosure attempts to balance these objectives.

ILLUSTRATION 20-28
Pension Disclosure for Zarle Company—2014, 2015, 2016

ZARLE COMPANY PENSION DISCLOSURE			
	2014	2015	2016
Change in benefit obligation			
Benefit obligation at beginning of year	$100,000	$112,000	$ 212,700
Service cost	9,000	9,500	13,000
Interest cost	10,000	19,200	21,270
Amendments (Prior service cost)	–0–	80,000	–0–
Actuarial loss	–0–	–0–	28,530
Benefits paid	(7,000)	(8,000)	(10,500)
Benefit obligation at end of year	112,000	212,700	265,000
Change in plan assets			
Fair value of plan assets at beginning of year	100,000	111,000	134,100
Actual return on plan assets	10,000	11,100	12,000
Contributions	8,000	20,000	24,000
Benefits paid	(7,000)	(8,000)	(10,500)
Fair value of plan assets at end of year	111,000	134,100	159,600
Funded status (Pension asset/liability)	$ (1,000)	$ (78,600)	$(105,400)

The 2014 column reveals that Zarle underfunds the projected benefit obligation by $1,000. The 2015 column reveals that Zarle reports the underfunded liability of $78,600 in the balance sheet. Finally, the 2016 column indicates that Zarle recognizes the underfunded liability of $105,400 in the balance sheet.

2017 Entries and Worksheet—A Comprehensive Example

Incorporating the corridor computation and the required disclosures, we continue the Zarle Company pension plan accounting based on the following facts for 2017.

> Service cost is $16,000.
>
> Settlement rate is 10 percent; expected rate of return is 10 percent.
>
> Actual return on plan assets is $22,000.
>
> Amortization of prior service cost is $17,600.
>
> Annual funding contributions are $27,000.
>
> Benefits paid to retirees during the year are $18,000.
>
> Average service life of all covered employees is 20 years.

Zarle prepares a worksheet to facilitate accumulation and recording of the components of pension expense and maintenance of amounts related to the pension plan. Illustration 20-29 shows that worksheet, which uses the basic data presented above. Beginning-of-the-year 2017 account balances are the December 31, 2016, balances from Zarle's revised 2016 pension worksheet in Illustration 20-18 (on page 1203).

Comprehensive Pension Worksheet—2017.xls

	A	B	C	D	E	F	G	H
1				**General Journal Entries**			**Memo Record**	
2								
3								
4					Other Comprehensive Income			
5		Annual		Prior Service		Pension Asset/	Projected Benefit	
6		Pension						
7	Items	Expense	Cash	Cost	Gains/Losses	Liability	Obligation	Plan Assets
8	Balance, Dec. 31, 2016					105,400 Cr.	265,000 Cr.	159,600 Dr.
9	(aa) Service cost	16,000 Dr.					16,000 Cr.	
10	(bb) Interest cost	26,500 Dr.					26,500 Cr.	
11	(cc) Actual return	22,000 Cr.						22,000 Dr.
12	(dd) Unexpected gain	6,040 Dr.			6,040 Cr.			
13	(ee) Amortization of PSC	17,600 Dr.		17,600 Cr.				
14	(ff) Contributions		27,000 Cr.					27,000 Dr.
15	(gg) Benefits						18,000 Dr.	18,000 Cr.
16	(hh) Amortization of loss	172 Dr.			172 Cr.			
17								
18	Journal entry for 2017	44,312 Dr.	27,000 Cr.	17,600 Cr.	6,212 Cr.	6,500 Dr.		
19								
20	Accumulated OCI, Dec. 31, 2016			32,000 Dr.	29,940 Dr.			
21	Balance, Dec. 31, 2017*			14,400 Dr.	23,728 Dr.	98,900 Cr.	289,500 Cr.	190,600 Dr.
22								
23	*Accumulated OCI (PSC)	$14,400 Dr.						
24	Accumulated OCI (G/L)	23,728 Dr.						
25	Accumulated OCI, Dec. 31, 2017	$38,128 Dr.						
26								

ILLUSTRATION 20-29
Comprehensive Pension Worksheet—2017

Worksheet Explanations and Entries

Entries (aa) through (gg) are similar to the corresponding entries previously explained in the prior years' worksheets, with the exception of entry (dd). In 2016, the expected return on plan assets exceeded the actual return, producing an unexpected loss. In 2017, the actual return of $22,000 exceeds the expected return of $15,960 ($159,600 × 10%), resulting in an unexpected gain of $6,040, entry (dd). By netting the gain of $6,040 against the actual return of $22,000, pension expense is affected only by the expected return of $15,960.

A new entry (hh) in Zarle's worksheet results from application of the corridor test on the accumulated balance of net gain or loss in accumulated other comprehensive income. Zarle Company begins 2017 with a balance in the net loss account of $29,940. The company applies the corridor criterion in 2017 to determine whether the balance is excessive and should be amortized. In 2017, the corridor is 10 percent of the larger of the beginning-of-the-year projected benefit obligation of $265,000 or the plan asset's $159,600 market-related asset value (assumed to be fair value). The corridor for 2017 is $26,500 ($265,000 × 10%). Because the balance in Accumulated OCI is a net loss of $29,940, the excess (outside the corridor) is $3,440 ($29,940 − $26,500). Zarle amortizes the $3,440 excess over the average remaining service life of all employees. Given an average remaining service life of 20 years, the amortization in 2017 is $172 ($3,440 ÷ 20). In the 2017 pension worksheet, Zarle debits Pension Expense for $172 and credits that amount to Other Comprehensive Income (G/L). Illustration 20-30 shows the computation of the $172 amortization charge.

2017 Corridor Test	
Net (gain) or loss at beginning of year in accumulated OCI	$29,940
10% of larger of PBO or market-related asset value of plan assets	(26,500)
Amortizable amount	$ 3,440
Average service life of all employees	20 years
2017 amortization ($3,440 ÷ 20 years)	$172

ILLUSTRATION 20-30
Computation of 2017 Amortization Charge (Corridor Test)

Zarle formally records pension expense for 2017 as follows.

2017		
Pension Expense	44,312	
Pension Asset/Liability	6,500	
Cash		27,000
Other Comprehensive Income (G/L)		6,212
Other Comprehensive Income (PSC)		17,600

Note Disclosure

Illustration 20-31 (page 1212) shows the note disclosure of Zarle's pension plan for 2017. Note that this example assumes that the pension liability is noncurrent and that the 2018 adjustment for amortization of the net gain or loss and amortization of prior service cost are the same as 2017.

Special Issues

The Pension Reform Act of 1974

A classic example of the unfortunate consequences of an underfunded pension plan is the 1963 shutdown of the Studebaker Automobile operations in South Bend, Indiana, in which 4,500 workers lost 85 percent of their vested benefits. As a result of such situations, the Employee Retirement Income Security Act of 1974—ERISA—was passed. The legislation affects virtually every private retirement plan in the United States. It attempts

ILLUSTRATION 20-31
Minimum Note
Disclosure of Pension
Plan, Zarle Company,
2017

ZARLE COMPANY
NOTES TO THE FINANCIAL STATEMENTS

Note D. The company has a pension plan covering substantially all of its employees. The plan is noncontributory and provides pension benefits that are based on the employee's compensation during the three years immediately preceding retirement. The pension plan's assets consist of cash, stocks, and bonds. The company's funding policy is consistent with the relevant government (ERISA) and tax regulations.

Pension expense for 2017 is comprised of the following components of pension cost.

Components of pension expense

Service cost	$16,000	
Interest on projected benefit obligation	26,500	
Expected return on plan assets	(15,960)	
Amortization of prior service cost	17,600	
Amortization of net loss	172	
Pension expense		$44,312

Other changes in plan assets and benefit obligations recognized in other comprehensive income

Amounts recognized in other comprehensive income

Net actuarial gain	$ 6,212	
Amortization of prior service cost	17,600	
Total recognized in other comprehensive income		(23,812)
Total recognized in pension expense and other comprehensive income		$20,500

The estimated net actuarial loss and prior service cost for the defined benefit pension plan that will be amortized from accumulated other comprehensive into pension expense over the next year are estimated to be the same as this year.

The amount recognized as a long-term liability in the balance sheet is as follows:

Amounts recognized in the balance sheet

Noncurrent liability

Pension liability	$98,900

The amounts recognized in accumulated other comprehensive income related to pensions consist of:

Net actuarial loss	$23,728
Prior service cost	14,400
Total	$38,128

Change in benefit obligation

Reconciliations of pension liability and plan assets

Benefit obligation at beginning of year	$265,000
Service cost	16,000
Interest cost	26,500
Amendments (Prior service cost)	–0–
Actuarial gain	–0–
Benefits paid	(18,000)
Benefit obligation at end of year	289,500

Change in plan assets

Fair value of plan assets at beginning of year	159,600
Actual return on plan assets	22,000
Contributions	27,000
Benefits paid	(18,000)
Fair value of plan assets at end of year	190,600

Funded status of plan

Funded status (liability)	$ 98,900

Rates used to estimate plan elements

The weighted-average discount rate used in determining the 2017 projected benefit obligation was 10 percent. The rate of increase in future compensation levels used in computing the 2017 projected benefit obligation was 4.5 percent. The weighted-average expected long-term rate of return on the plan's assets was 10 percent.

to safeguard employees' pension rights by mandating many pension plan requirements, including minimum funding, participation, and vesting.

These requirements can influence the employers' cash flows significantly. Under this legislation, annual funding is no longer discretionary. An employer now must fund the plan in accordance with an actuarial funding method that over time will be sufficient to pay for all pension obligations. If companies do not fund their plans in a reasonable manner, they may be subject to fines and/or loss of tax deductions.[15]

The law requires plan administrators to publish a comprehensive description and summary of their plans, along with detailed annual reports that include many supplementary schedules and statements.

Another important provision of the act is the creation of the **Pension Benefit Guaranty Corporation (PBGC)**. **The PBGC's purpose is to administer terminated plans** and to impose liens on an employer's assets for certain unfunded pension liabilities. If a company terminates its pension plan, the PBGC can effectively impose a lien against the employer's assets for the excess of the present value of guaranteed vested benefits over the pension fund assets. This lien generally has had the status of a tax lien; it takes priority over most other creditorship claims. This section of the act gives the PBGC the power to force an involuntary termination of a pension plan whenever the risks related to nonpayment of the pension obligation seem too great. Because ERISA restricts to 30 percent of net worth the lien that the PBGC can impose, the PBGC must monitor all plans to ensure that net worth is sufficient to meet the pension benefit obligations.

A large number of terminated plans have caused the PBGC to pay out substantial benefits. Currently the PBGC receives its funding from employers, who contribute a certain dollar amount for each employee covered under the plan.[16]

Underlying Concepts

Many plans are underfunded but still quite viable. For example, at one time Loews Corp. had a $159 million shortfall, but also had earnings of $594 million and a good net worth. Thus, the going concern assumption permits us to ignore pension underfundings in some cases because in the long run they are not significant.

What do the numbers mean? WHO GUARANTEES THE GUARANTOR?

The **Pension Benefit Guaranty Corporation (PBGC)** in its 2012 annual report indicates that its primary mission is to encourage the continuation and maintenance of voluntary private pension plans. It's an obligation which the PBGC takes seriously. However, the trends are ominous:

- Americans today are spending more years in retirement. They're healthier and more active, which is great news. Unfortunately, pensions haven't kept up.

- Many businesses, for competitive and other reasons, continue to reduce their support for retirement plans. Some have switched from a defined benefit plan to a defined contribution plan which costs less and comes with fewer obligations. Others offer lump-sum cash payments to employees or retirees to settle the employer's obligations.

- Left on their own, many people save less, as well as invest and plan less well. They also pay higher fees and they get lower returns.

- Many people defer retirement but still don't have enough money for retirement—and they're worried. One poll cited by the Senate Health, Education, Labor, and Pensions Committee says that 92 percent of people think there's a retirement crisis. They're right to be concerned.

Add to these concerns that obligations in pension plans today greatly exceed pension assets. Finally, the PBGC has a problem as well—a large deficit in its accounts. The chart on page 1214 indicates that downward spiral in the net worth of the PBGC over the last 10 years.

[15]In 2006, Congress passed the Pension Protection Act. This law has many provisions. One important aspect of the act is that it forced many companies to expedite their contributions to their pension plans. One group estimates that companies in the S&P 500 would have had to contribute $47 billion to their pension plans if the new rules were fully phased in for 2006. That amount is about 57 percent more than the $30 billion that companies were expecting to contribute to their plans that year. Subsequently, Congress continues to provide pension funding relief. For example, in the "Moving Ahead for Progress in the 21st Century" Act (enacted July 6, 2012), companies can use a higher discount rate based on high-grade bond yields averaged over 25 years, which helps reduce the pension liability and required contributions.

[16]**Pan American Airlines** is a good illustration of how difficult it is to assess when to terminate. When Pan Am filed for bankruptcy in 1991, it had a pension liability of $900 million. From 1983 to 1991, the IRS gave it six waivers so it did not have to make contributions. When Pan Am terminated the plan, there was little net worth left upon which to impose a lien. An additional accounting problem relates to the manner of disclosing the possible termination of a plan. For example, should Pan Am have disclosed a contingent liability for its struggling plan? At present this issue is unresolved, and considerable judgment is needed to analyze a company with these contingent liabilities.

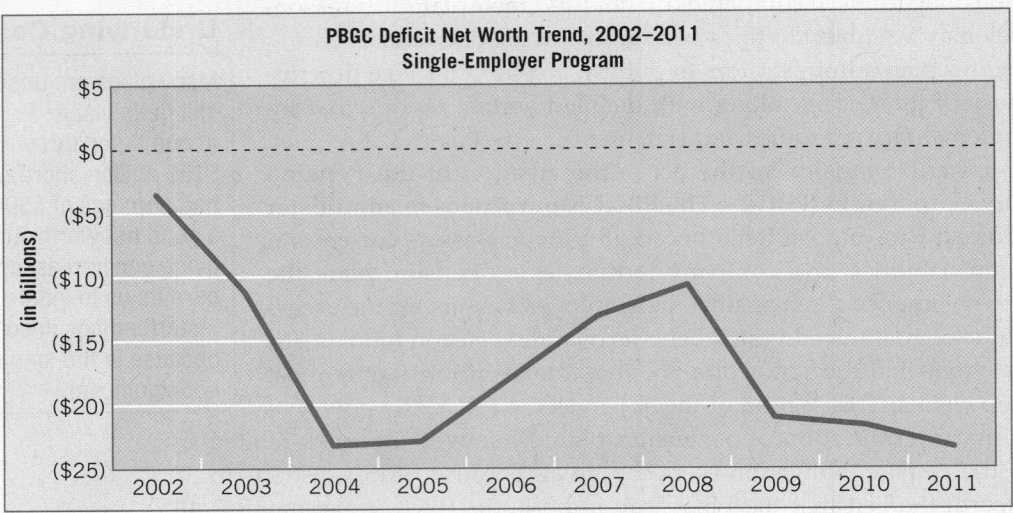

In February 2012, **American Airlines** announced that it is ending its defined benefit plans, which would result in the PBGC having to increase its deficit even more to an estimated $35 billion. The result is a growing deficit problem which is likely to continue. Who has the risk? You guessed it, the American taxpayer.

Source: Alex Pollock, "The Pension Benefit Guaranty Corporation: Who Will Guarantee This Guarantor?" *2012 Annual Report of the Pension Benefit Guarantee Corporation* (June 26, 2012).

Pension Terminations

A congressman at one time noted, "Employers are simply treating their employee pension plans like company piggy banks, to be raided at will." What this congressman was referring to is the practice of paying off the projected benefit obligation and pocketing any excess. ERISA prevents companies from recapturing excess assets unless they pay participants what is owed to them and then terminate the plan. As a result, companies were buying *annuities* to pay off the pension claimants and then used the excess funds for other corporate purposes.[17]

For example, at one time, pension plan terminations netted $363 million for **Occidental Petroleum Corp.**, $95 million for **Stroh's Brewery Co.**, $58 million for **Kellogg Co.**, and $29 million for **Western Airlines**. Recently, many large companies have terminated their pension plans and captured billions in surplus assets. The U.S. Treasury also benefits: Federal legislation requires companies to pay an excise tax of anywhere from 20 percent to 50 percent on the gains. All of this is quite legal.[18]

---

[17]A question exists as to whose money it is. Some argue that the excess funds belong to the employees, not the employer. In addition, given that the funds have been reverting to the employer, critics charge that cost-of-living increases and the possibility of other increased benefits are reduced because companies will be reluctant to use those remaining funds to pay for such increases.

[18]Another way that companies have reduced their pension obligations is through adoption of **cash-balance plans**. These are *hybrid* plans combining features of defined benefit and defined contribution plans. Although these plans permit employees to transfer their pension benefits when they change employers (like a defined contribution plan), they are controversial because the change to a cash-balance plan often reduces benefits to older workers.

The accounting for cash-balance plans is similar to that for defined benefit plans, because employers bear the investment risk in cash-balance plans. When an employer adopts a cash-balance plan, the measurement of the future benefit obligation to employees generally is lower, compared to a traditional defined benefit plan. See A. T. Arcady and F. Mellors, "Cash-Balance Conversions," *Journal of Accountancy* (February 2000), pp. 22–28.

The accounting issue that arises from these terminations is whether a company should recognize a gain when pension plan assets revert back to the company (often called **asset reversion** transactions). The issue is complex. In some cases, a company starts a new defined benefit plan after it eliminates the old one. Thus, some contend that there has been no change in substance but merely a change in form. However, the FASB disagrees. It requires recognition in earnings of a gain or loss when the employer settles a pension obligation either by lump-sum cash payments to participants or by purchasing nonparticipating annuity contracts. **[8]**[19]

Concluding Observations

Hardly a day goes by without the financial press analyzing in depth some issue related to pension plans in the United States. This is not surprising, since pension funds exceed over $22 trillion in assets globally. As you have seen, the accounting issues related to pension plans are complex. Recent changes to GAAP have clarified many of these issues and should help users understand the financial implications of a company's pension plans on its financial position, results of operations, and cash flows.

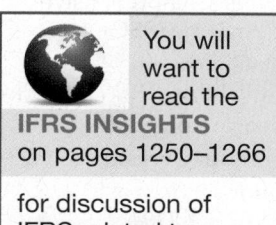

You will want to read the **IFRS INSIGHTS** on pages 1250–1266

for discussion of IFRS related to pension accounting.

SUMMARY OF LEARNING OBJECTIVES

KEY TERMS

accumulated benefit obligation, *1187*

actual return on plan assets, *1191*

actuarial present value, *1188(n)*

actuaries, *1187*

asset gains and losses, *1198*

cash-balance plans, *1214(n)*

components of pension expense, *1190*

contributory pension plan, *1184*

corridor approach, *1199*

defined benefit plan, *1185*

defined contribution plan, *1185*

ERISA, *1211*

expected rate of return, *1197*

expected return on plan assets, *1197*

fair value of plan assets, *1191*

funded pension plan, *1184*

funded status (overfunded or underfunded), *1189*

interest on the liability (interest expense), *1191*

1 **Distinguish between accounting for the employer's pension plan and accounting for the pension fund.** The company or employer is the organization sponsoring the pension plan. It incurs the cost and makes contributions to the pension fund. The fund or plan is the entity that receives the contributions from the employer, administers the pension assets, and makes the benefit payments to the pension recipients (retired employees). The fund should be a separate legal and accounting entity; it maintains a set of books and prepares financial statements.

2 **Identify types of pension plans and their characteristics.** The two most common types of pension arrangements are as follows. (1) *Defined contribution plans:* The employer agrees to contribute to a pension trust a certain sum each period based on a formula. This formula may consider such factors as age, length of employee service, employer's profits, and compensation level. Only the employer's contribution is defined; no promise is made regarding the ultimate benefits paid out to the employees. (2) *Defined benefit plans:* These plans define the benefits that the employee will receive at the time of retirement. The formula typically provides for the benefits to be a function of the employee's years of service and the compensation level when he or she nears retirement.

3 **Explain alternative measures for valuing the pension obligation.** One measure bases the pension obligation only on the benefits vested to the employees. Vested benefits are those that the employee is entitled to receive even if he or she renders no additional services under the plan. Companies compute the *vested benefit pension obligation* using current salary levels; this obligation includes only vested benefits. Another measure of the obligation, called the *accumulated benefit obligation*, computes the deferred compensation amount based on all years of service performed by employees

[19]Some companies have established *pension poison pills* as an anti-takeover measure. These plans require asset reversions from termination of a plan to benefit employees and retirees rather than the acquiring company. For a discussion of pension poison pills, see Eugene E. Comiskey and Charles W. Mulford, "Interpreting Pension Disclosures: A Guide for Lending Officers," *Commercial Lending Review* (Winter 1993–94), Vol. 9, No. 1.

liability gains and losses, *1198*

market-related asset value, *1198*

noncontributory pension plan, *1184*

Other Comprehensive Income (G/L), *1198*

Other Comprehensive Income (PSC), *1197*

pension asset/ liability, *1192*

pension plan, *1184*

pension worksheet, *1192*

prior service cost (PSC), *1194*

projected benefit obligation, *1188*

qualified pension plan, *1184*

reconciliation, *1207*

retroactive benefits, *1194*

service cost, *1190*

settlement rate, *1191*

unexpected gain or loss, *1198*

vested benefit obligation, *1187*

vested benefits, *1187*

years-of-service method, *1194*

under the plan—both vested and nonvested—using current salary levels. A third measure, called the *projected benefit obligation*, bases the computation of the deferred compensation amount on both vested and nonvested service using future salaries.

4 **List the components of pension expense.** Pension expense is a function of the following components: (1) service cost, (2) interest on the liability, (3) return on plan assets, (4) amortization of prior service cost, and (5) gain or loss.

5 **Use a worksheet for employer's pension plan entries.** Companies may use a worksheet unique to pension accounting. This worksheet records both the formal entries and the memo entries to keep track of all the employer's relevant pension plan items and components.

6 **Describe the amortization of prior service costs.** An actuary computes the amount of the prior service cost, and the company then records it as an adjustment to the projected benefit obligation and other comprehensive income. It then amortizes it, generally using a "years-of-service" amortization method, similar to a units-of-production computation. First, the company computes total estimated number of service-years to be worked by all of the participating employees. Second, it divides the accumulated prior service cost by the total number of service-years, to obtain a cost per service-year (the unit cost). Third, the company multiplies the number of service-years consumed each year times the cost per service-year, to obtain the annual amortization charge.

7 **Explain the accounting for unexpected gains and losses.** In estimating the projected benefit obligation (the liability), actuaries make assumptions about such items as mortality rate, retirement rate, turnover rate, disability rate, and salary amounts. Any change in these actuarial assumptions affects the amount of the projected benefit obligation. These unexpected gains or losses from changes in the projected benefit obligation are liability gains and losses. Liability gains result from unexpected decreases in the liability balance; liability losses result from unexpected increases. Companies also incur asset gains or losses. Both types of actuarial gains and losses are recorded in other comprehensive income and adjust either the projected benefit obligation or the plan assets.

8 **Explain the corridor approach to amortizing gains and losses.** The FASB set a limit for the size of an accumulated net gain or loss balance. That arbitrarily selected limit (called a *corridor*) is 10 percent of the larger of the beginning balances of the projected benefit obligation or the market-related value of the plan assets. Beyond that limit, an accumulated net gain or loss balance is considered too large and must be amortized. If the balance of the accumulated net gain or loss account stays within the upper and lower limits of the corridor, no amortization is required.

9 **Describe the requirements for reporting pension plans in financial statements.** Currently, companies must disclose the following pension plan information in their financial statements. (1) The components of pension expense for the period. (2) A schedule showing changes in the benefit obligation and plan assets during the year. (3) The amount of prior service cost and net gains and losses in accumulated OCI, including the estimated prior service cost and gains and losses that will affect net income in the next year. (4) The weighted-average assumed discount rate, the rate of compensation increase used to measure the projected benefit obligation, and the weighted-average expected long-term rate of return on plan assets. (5) A table showing the allocation of pension plan assets by category and the percentage of the fair value to total plan assets. (6) The expected benefit payments for current plan participants for each of the next five fiscal years and for the following five years in aggregate, along with an estimate of expected contributions to the plan during the next year.

APPENDIX **20A**	ACCOUNTING FOR POSTRETIREMENT BENEFITS

IBM's adoption of the GAAP requirements on postretirement benefits resulted in a $2.3 billion charge and a historical curiosity—IBM's first-ever quarterly loss. General Electric disclosed that its charge for adoption of the same GAAP rules would be $2.7 billion. AT&T absorbed a $2.1 billion pretax hit for postretirement benefits upon adoption. What is GAAP in this area, and how could its adoption have so grave an impact on companies' earnings?

10 LEARNING OBJECTIVE

Identify the differences between pensions and postretirement healthcare benefits.

ACCOUNTING GUIDANCE

After a decade of study, the FASB in December 1990 issued GAAP for "Employers' Accounting for Postretirement Benefits Other Than Pensions." **[9]** It alone was the cause for the large charges to income cited above. These rules cover for healthcare and other "welfare benefits" provided to retirees, their spouses, dependents, and beneficiaries.[20] These other welfare benefits include life insurance offered outside a pension plan; medical, dental, and eye care; legal and tax services; tuition assistance; day care; and housing assistance.[21] Because healthcare benefits are the largest of the other postretirement benefits, we use this item to illustrate accounting for postretirement benefits.

For many employers (about 95 percent), these GAAP rules required a change from the predominant practice of accounting for postretirement benefits on a pay-as-you-go (cash) basis to an accrual basis. Similar to pension accounting, the accrual basis necessitates measuring the employer's obligation to provide future benefits and accrual of the cost during the years that the employee provides service.

One of the reasons companies had not prefunded these benefit plans was that payments to prefund healthcare costs, unlike excess contributions to a pension trust, are not tax-deductible. Another reason was that postretirement healthcare benefits were once perceived to be a low-cost employee benefit that could be changed or eliminated at will and therefore were not a legal liability. Now, the accounting definition of a liability goes beyond the notion of a legally enforceable claim; the definition now encompasses equitable or constructive obligations as well, making it clear that the postretirement benefit promise is a liability.[22]

---

[20]*Accounting Trends and Techniques* recently reported that of its 500 surveyed companies, 317 reported benefit plans that provide postretirement healthcare benefits. In response to rising healthcare costs and higher premiums on healthcare insurance, companies are working to get their postretirement benefit costs under control.

[21]"OPEB" is the acronym frequently used to describe postretirement benefits other than pensions. This term came into being before the scope of guidance was narrowed from "other postemployment benefits" to "other postretirement benefits," thereby excluding postemployment benefits related to severance pay or wage continuation to disabled, terminated, or laid-off employees.

[22]"Elements of Financial Statements," *Statement of Financial Accounting Concepts No. 6* (Stamford, Conn.: 1985), p. 13, footnote 21.

DIFFERENCES BETWEEN PENSION BENEFITS AND HEALTHCARE BENEFITS

The FASB used the GAAP rules on pensions as a reference for the accounting prescribed for healthcare and other nonpension postretirement benefits.[23] Why didn't the FASB cover these other types of postretirement benefits in the earlier pension accounting statement? Because the apparent similarities between the two benefits mask some significant differences. Illustration 20A-1 shows these differences.[24]

ILLUSTRATION 20A-1

Differences between Pensions and Postretirement Healthcare Benefits

Item	Pensions	Healthcare Benefits
Funding	Generally funded.	Generally **not** funded.
Benefit	Well-defined and level dollar amount.	Generally uncapped and great variability.
Beneficiary	Retiree (maybe some benefit to surviving spouse).	Retiree, spouse, and other dependents.
Benefit payable	Monthly.	As needed and used.
Predictability	Variables are reasonably predictable.	Utilization difficult to predict. Level of cost varies geographically and fluctuates over time.

Two of the differences in Illustration 20A-1 highlight why measuring the future payments for healthcare benefit plans is so much more difficult than for pension plans.

1. Many postretirement plans do not set a limit on healthcare benefits. No matter how serious the illness or how long it lasts, the benefits continue to flow. (Even if the employer uses an insurance company plan, the premiums will escalate according to the increased benefits provided.)

2. The levels of healthcare benefit use and healthcare costs are difficult to predict. Increased longevity, unexpected illnesses (e.g., AIDS, SARS, and avian flu), along with new medical technologies and cures, cause changes in healthcare utilization.

Additionally, although the fiduciary and reporting standards for employee benefit funds under government regulations generally cover healthcare benefits, the stringent minimum vesting, participation, and funding standards that apply to pensions do not apply to healthcare benefits. Nevertheless, as you will learn, many of the basic concepts of pensions, and much of the related accounting terminology and measurement methodology, do apply to other postretirement benefits. Therefore, in the following discussion and illustrations, we point out the similarities and differences in the accounting and reporting for these two types of postretirement benefits.

[23]Other postemployment (but before retirement) benefits include, but are not limited to, salary continuation, disability-related benefits, severance benefits, and continuance of healthcare benefits and life insurance for inactive or former (e.g., terminated, disabled, or deceased) employees or their beneficiaries. These benefits are accounted for similar to accounting for compensated absences (see Chapter 13). **[10]**

[24]D. Gerald Searfoss and Naomi Erickson, "The Big Unfunded Liability: Postretirement Health-Care Benefits," *Journal of Accountancy* (November 1988), pp. 28–39.

For many companies, *other postretirement benefit obligations* (OPEBs) are substantial. Generally, OPEBs are not well funded because companies are not permitted a tax deduction for contributions to the plan assets, as is the case with pensions.

That is, the company may not claim a tax deduction until it makes a payment to the participant (pay-as-you-go).

Presented below are companies with the largest OPEB obligations, indicating their relationship with other financial items.

For year ended 12/31/2011 ($ in millions)	Obligation	% Underfunded	Obligation as a % of Stockholders' Equity
General Motors	$ 7,312	100.00%	18.75%
AT&T Inc.	34,963	71.70%	33.04%
Verizon Communications	27,369	90.40%	81.86%
General Electric	11,637	27.98%	9.85%
Boeing Company	7,997	98.72%	221.65%
Alcatel-Lucent	4,541	85.22%	76.08%

So, how big are OPEB obligations? REALLY big.

Source: Company reports.

POSTRETIREMENT BENEFITS ACCOUNTING PROVISIONS

Healthcare and other postretirement benefits for current and future retirees and their dependents are forms of deferred compensation. They are earned through employee service and are subject to accrual during the years an employee is working.

The period of time over which the postretirement benefit cost accrues is called the **attribution period**. It is the period of service during which the employee earns the benefits under the terms of the plan. The attribution period, shown in Illustration 20A-2 for a hypothetical employee, generally begins when an employee is hired and ends on the date the employee is eligible to receive the benefits and ceases to earn additional benefits by performing service, the vesting date.[25]

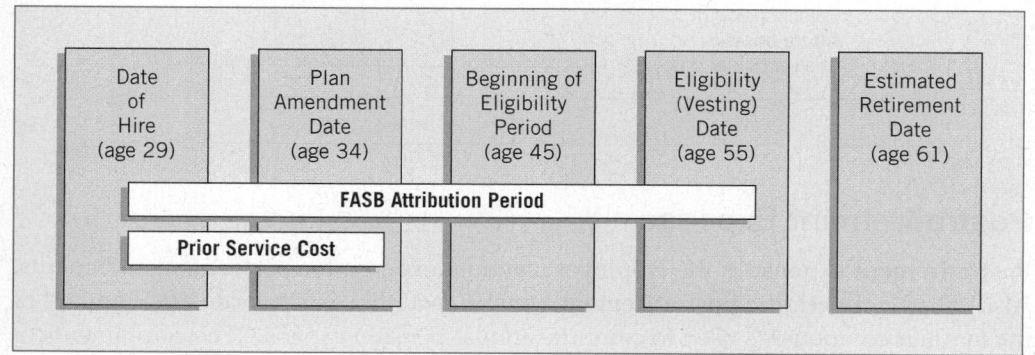

ILLUSTRATION 20A-2
Range of Possible Attribution Periods

[25]This is a benefit-years-of-service approach (the projected unit credit actuarial cost method). The FASB found no compelling reason to switch from the traditional pension accounting approach. It rejected the employee's full service period (i.e., to the estimated retirement date) because it was unable to identify any approach that would appropriately attribute benefits beyond the date when an employee attains full eligibility for those benefits. Employees attain full eligibility by meeting specified age, service, or age and service requirements of the plan.

Obligations Under Postretirement Benefits

In defining the obligation for postretirement benefits, the FASB maintained many concepts similar to pension accounting. It also designed some new and modified terms specifically for postretirement benefits. Two of the most important of these specialized terms are (a) expected postretirement benefit obligation and (b) accumulated postretirement benefit obligation.

The **expected postretirement benefit obligation (EPBO)** is the actuarial present value as of a particular date of **all benefits a company expects to pay after retirement to employees and their dependents**. Companies do not record the EPBO in the financial statements, but they do use it in measuring periodic expense.

The **accumulated postretirement benefit obligation (APBO)** is the actuarial present value of **future benefits attributed to employees' services rendered to a particular date**. The APBO is equal to the EPBO for retirees and active employees fully eligible for benefits. Before the date an employee achieves full eligibility, the APBO is only a portion of the EPBO. Or stated another way, the difference between the APBO and the EPBO is the future service costs of active employees who are not yet fully eligible.

Illustration 20A-3 contrasts the EPBO and the APBO. At the date an employee is fully eligible (the end of the attribution period), the APBO and the EPBO for that employee are equal.

ILLUSTRATION 20A-3
APBO and EPBO
Contrasted

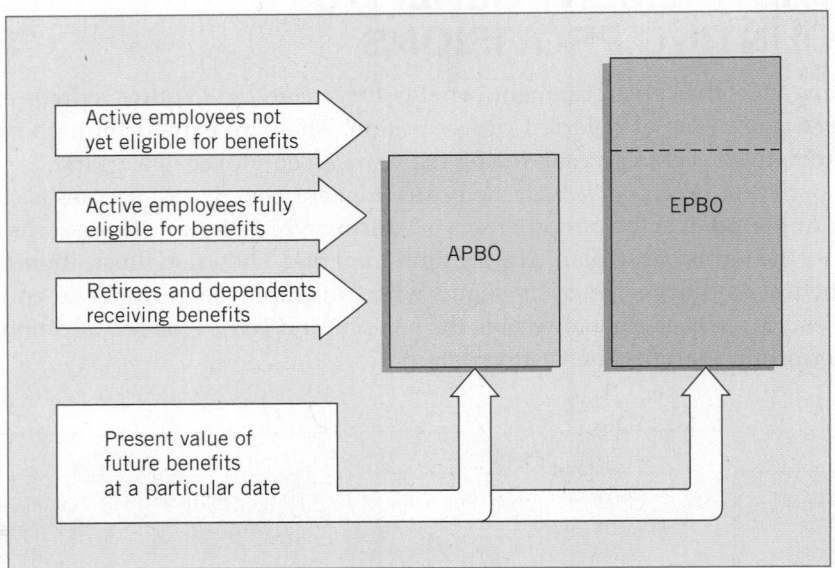

Postretirement Expense

Postretirement expense is the employer's annual expense for postretirement benefits. Also called **net periodic postretirement benefit cost**, this expense consists of many of the familiar components used to compute annual pension expense. The components of net periodic postretirement benefit cost are as follows. **[11]**[26]

1. *Service cost.* The portion of the EPBO attributed to employee service during the period.
2. *Interest cost.* The increase in the APBO attributable to the passage of time. Companies compute interest cost by applying the beginning-of-the-year discount rate to

[26]See James R. Wilbert and Kenneth E. Dakdduk, "The New FASB 106: How to Account for Postretirement Benefits," *Journal of Accountancy* (August 1991), pp. 36–41.

the beginning-of-the-year APBO, adjusted for benefit payments to be made during the period. The discount rate is based on the rates of return on high-quality, fixed-income investments that are currently available.[27]

3. *Actual return on plan assets.* The change in the fair value of the plan's assets adjusted for contributions and benefit payments made during the period. Because companies charge or credit the postretirement expense for the gain or loss on plan assets (the difference between the actual and the expected return), this component is actually the expected return.

4. *Amortization of prior service cost.* The amortization of the cost of retroactive benefits resulting from plan amendments. The typical amortization period, beginning at the date of the plan amendment, is the remaining service periods through the full eligibility date.

5. *Gains and losses.* In general, changes in the APBO resulting from changes in assumptions or from experience different from that assumed. For funded plans, this component also includes the difference between actual return and expected return on plan assets.

ILLUSTRATIVE ACCOUNTING ENTRIES

Like pension accounting, the accounting for postretirement plans must recognize in the accounts and in the financial statements effects of several significant items. These items are:

11 LEARNING OBJECTIVE

Contrast accounting for pensions to accounting for other postretirement benefits.

1. Expected postretirement benefit obligation (EPBO).
2. Accumulated postretirement benefit obligation (APBO).
3. Postretirement benefit plan assets.
4. Prior service cost.
5. Net gain or loss.

The EPBO is not recognized in the financial statements or disclosed in the notes. Companies recompute it each year, and the actuary uses it in measuring the annual service cost. Because of the numerous assumptions and actuarial complexity involved in measuring annual service cost, we have omitted these computations of the EPBO.

Similar to pensions, companies must recognize in the financial statements items 2 through 5 listed above. In addition, as in pension accounting, companies must know the exact amount of these items in order to compute postretirement expense. Therefore, companies use the worksheet like that for pension accounting to record both the formal general journal entries and the memo entries.

2014 Entries and Worksheet

To illustrate the use of a worksheet in accounting for a postretirement benefits plan, assume that on January 1, 2014, Quest Company adopts a healthcare benefit plan. The following facts apply to the postretirement benefits plan for the year 2014.

Plan assets at fair value on January 1, 2014, are zero.

Actual and expected returns on plan assets are zero.

Accumulated postretirement benefit obligation (APBO), January 1, 2014, is zero.

---

[27]The FASB concluded that the discount rate for measuring the present value of the postretirement benefit obligation and the service cost component should be the same as that applied to pension measurements. It chose not to label it the *settlement rate*, in order to clarify that the objective of the discount rate is to measure the time value of money.

Service cost is $54,000.

No prior service cost exists.

Interest cost on the APBO is zero.

Funding contributions during the year are $38,000.

Benefit payments to employees from plan are $28,000.

ILLUSTRATION 20A-4
Postretirement
Worksheet—2014

Using that data, the worksheet in Illustration 20A-4 presents the postretirement entries for 2014.

		General Journal Entries			Memo Record	
	Items	Annual Postretirement Expense	Cash	Postretirement Asset/Liability	APBO	Plan Assets
6	Balance, Jan. 1, 2014					
7	(a) Service cost	54,000 Dr.			54,000 Cr.	
8	(b) Contributions		38,000 Cr.			38,000 Dr.
9	(c) Benefits				28,000 Dr.	28,000 Cr.
10						
11	Journal entry for 2014	54,000 Dr.	38,000 Cr.	16,000 Cr.*		
12	Balance, Dec. 31, 2014			16,000 Cr.**	26,000 Cr.	10,000 Dr.
13						
14	*$54,000 − $38,000 = $16,000					
15	**$26,000 − $10,000 = $16,000					
16						

Postretirement Worksheet—2014.xls

Entry (a) records the service cost component, which increases postretirement expense $54,000 and increases the liability (APBO) $54,000. Entry (b) records Quest's funding of assets to the postretirement fund. The funding decreases cash $38,000 and increases plan assets $38,000. Entry (c) records the benefit payments made to retirees, which results in equal $28,000 decreases to the plan assets and the liability (APBO).

Quest's December 31 adjusting entry formally records the postretirement expense in 2014, as follows.

December 31, 2014

Postretirement Expense	54,000	
Cash		38,000
Postretirement Asset/Liability		16,000

The credit to Postretirement Asset/Liability for $16,000 represents the difference between the APBO and the plan assets. The $16,000 credit balance is a liability because the plan is underfunded. The Postretirement Asset/Liability account balance of $16,000 also equals the net of the balances in the memo accounts.

Illustration 20A-5 shows the funded status reported in the balance sheet. (Notice its similarity to the pension schedule.)

ILLUSTRATION 20A-5
Postretirement
Reconciliation Schedule—
December 31, 2014

Accumulated postretirement benefit obligation (Credit)	$(26,000)
Plan assets at fair value (Debit)	10,000
Postretirement asset/liability (Credit)	$(16,000)

Recognition of Gains and Losses

Gains and losses represent changes in the APBO or the value of plan assets. These changes result either from actual experience different from that expected or from changes in actuarial assumptions. The amortization of these gains and losses follows the approach used for pensions. That is, the gains and losses are recorded in other comprehensive income.

The Corridor Approach

Consistent with pension accounting, companies amortize the gains and losses in accumulated other comprehensive income as a component of postretirement expense if, at the beginning of the period, they exceed a "corridor" limit. The corridor is measured as the greater of 10 percent of the APBO or 10 percent of the market-related value of plan assets.

The intent of the corridor approach is to reduce volatility of postretirement expense by providing a reasonable opportunity for gains and losses to offset over time without affecting net periodic expense.

Amortization Methods

If the company must amortize gains and losses (beyond the corridor) on postretirement benefit plans, the **minimum amortization amount** is the excess gain or loss divided by the average remaining service life to expected retirement of all active employees. Companies may use any systematic method of amortization provided that: (1) the amount amortized in any period is equal to or greater than the minimum amount, (2) the company applies the method consistently, and (3) the company applies the method similarly for gains and losses.

The company must recompute the amount of gain or loss in accumulated other comprehensive income each year and amortize the gain or loss over the average remaining service life if the net amount exceeds the "corridor."

2015 Entries and Worksheet

Continuing the Quest Company illustration into 2015, the following facts apply to the postretirement benefits plan for the year 2015.

> Actual return on plan assets is $600.
>
> Expected return on plan assets is $800.
>
> Discount rate is 8 percent.
>
> Increase in APBO due to change in actuarial assumptions is $60,000.
>
> Service cost is $26,000.
>
> Funding contributions during the year are $18,000.
>
> Benefit payments to employees during the year are $5,000.
>
> Average remaining service to expected retirement: 25 years.

The worksheet in Illustration 20A-6 (on page 1224) presents all of Quest's postretirement benefit entries and information for 2015. The beginning balances on the first line of the worksheet are the ending balances from Quest's 2014 postretirement benefits worksheet in Illustration 20A-4 (on page 1222).

Entries (d), (h), and (i) are similar to the corresponding entries previously explained for 2014. Entry (e) accrues the interest expense component, which increases both the liability and the postretirement expense by $2,080 (the beginning APBO multiplied by the discount rate of 8%). Entries (f) and (g) are related. The expected return of $800 is higher than the actual return of $600. To smooth postretirement expense,

	Postretirement Benefits Worksheet—2015.xls						
Home	Insert	Page Layout	Formulas	Data	Review	View	

P18   fx

	A	B	C	D	E	F	G
1		General Journal Entries				Memo Record	
2							
3		Annual		Other			
4		Postretirement		Comprehensive	Postretirement		
5	Items	Expense	Cash	Income (G/L)	Asset/Liability	APBO	Plan Assets
6	Balance, Jan. 1, 2015				16,000 Cr.	26,000 Cr.	10,000 Dr.
7	(d) Service cost	26,000 Dr.				26,000 Cr.	
8	(e) Interest cost	2,080 Dr.				2,080 Cr.	
9	(f) Actual return	600 Cr.					600 Dr.
10	(g) Unexpected loss	200 Cr.		200 Dr.			
11	(h) Contributions		18,000 Cr.				18,000 Dr.
12	(i) Benefits					5,000 Dr.	5,000 Cr.
13	(j) Increase in APBO (Loss)			60,000 Dr.		60,000 Cr.	
14	Journal entry for 2015	27,280 Dr.	18,000 Cr.	60,200 Dr.	69,480 Cr.		
15							
16	Accumulated OCI, Dec. 31, 2014			0			
17	Balance, Dec. 31, 2015			60,200 Dr.	85,480 Cr.	109,080 Cr.	23,600 Dr.
18							

ILLUSTRATION 20A-6
Postretirement Benefits
Worksheet—2015

Quest defers the unexpected loss of $200 ($800 − $600) by debiting Other Comprehensive Income (G/L) and crediting Postretirement Expense. As a result of this adjustment, the expected return on the plan assets is the amount actually used to compute postretirement expense.

Entry (j) records the change in the APBO resulting from a change in actuarial assumptions. This $60,000 increase in the employer's accumulated liability is an unexpected loss. Quest debits this loss to Other Comprehensive Income (G/L).

On December 31 Quest formally records net periodic expense for 2015 as follows.

December 31, 2015		
Postretirement Expense	27,280	
Other Comprehensive Income (G/L)	60,200	
Cash		18,000
Postretirement Asset/Liability		69,480

The balance of the Postretirement Asset/Liability account at December 31, 2015, is $85,480. This balance is equal to the net of the balances in the memo accounts as shown in the reconciliation schedule in Illustration 20A-7.

ILLUSTRATION 20A-7
Postretirement Benefits
Reconciliation Schedule—
December 31, 2015

Accumulated postretirement benefit obligation (Credit)	$(109,080)
Plan assets at fair value (Debit)	23,600
Postretirement asset/liability (Credit)	$ (85,480)

Amortization of Net Gain or Loss in 2016

Quest has a beginning balance in Accumulated OCI related to losses of $60,200. Therefore, Quest must apply the corridor test for amortization of the balance for 2016. Illustration 20A-8 shows the computation of the amortization charge for the loss.

2016 Corridor Test	
Accumulated OCI at beginning of year	$60,200
10% of greater of APBO or market-related value of plan assets ($109,080 × .10)	(10,908)
Amortizable amount	$49,292
Average remaining service to expected retirement	25 years
2016 amortization of loss ($49,292 ÷ 25)	$1,972

ILLUSTRATION 20A-8
Computation of Amortization Charge (Corridor Test)—2016

DISCLOSURES IN NOTES TO THE FINANCIAL STATEMENTS

The disclosures required for other postretirement benefit plans are similar to and just as detailed and extensive as those required for pensions. The note disclosure for Tootsie Roll, Inc. in Illustration 20A-9 (page 1226) provides a good example of the extensive disclosure required for other postretirement benefit plans.

As indicated in Illustration 20A-9, Tootsie Roll shows the impact of the postretirement benefit plan on income, the balance sheet, and the cash flow statement, and it provides information on important assumptions used in the measurement of the postretirement benefit obligation. Also note that given no tax incentives for funding, Tootsie Roll (like many companies) does not have any assets set aside for its other postretirement benefit obligations.

While Tootsie Roll has only an other postretirement benefit plan, many companies sponsor both defined benefit pension and other postretirement plans. Given the similarities in accounting for these plans, companies can combine pension and other postretirement benefit disclosures.

ACTUARIAL ASSUMPTIONS AND CONCEPTUAL ISSUES

Measurement of the EPBO, the APBO, and the net periodic postretirement benefit cost is involved and complex. Due to the uncertainties in forecasting healthcare costs, rates of use, changes in government health programs, and the differences employed in non-medical assumptions (e.g., discount rate, employee turnover, rate of pre-65 retirement, spouse-age difference), estimates of postretirement benefit costs may have a large margin of error. Is the information relevant, reliable, or verifiable? The FASB concluded that "the obligation to provide postretirement benefits meets the definition of a liability, is representationally faithful, is relevant to financial statement users, and can be measured with sufficient reliability at a justifiable cost." **[12]** Failure to accrue an obligation and an expense prior to payment of benefits would result in an unfaithful representation of what financial statements should represent.

The FASB took a momentous step by requiring recognition of a postretirement liability. Many opposed the requirement, warning that the GAAP rules would devastate earnings. Others argued that putting these numbers on the balance sheet was inappropriate. Others noted that the requirement would force companies to curtail postretirement benefits to employees.

The authors believe that the FASB deserves special praise. Because the Board addressed this issue, companies now recognize the magnitude of these costs. This recognition has

ILLUSTRATION 20A-9
Postretirement Benefit
Disclosure

Tootsie Roll Industries, Inc.

Notes to Financial Statements

Note 7   Employee Benefit Plans (partial)
Postretirement health care and life insurance benefit plans:

The Company provides certain postretirement health care and life insurance benefits for corporate office and management employees based upon their age, years of service, date of hire and if they agree to contribute a portion of the cost as determined by the Company. The Company has the right to modify or terminate these benefits and does not fund postretirement health care and life insurance benefits in advance of payments for benefit claims. The Company is currently contemplating changes to its postretirement health care and life insurance benefits with the intention of reducing the Company's cost of providing such benefits. These changes are likely to include increasing retiree premium contributions, reducing and eliminating certain benefits, and taking steps to ensure that the Company does not become subject to the excise tax on high value coverage instituted by the Patient Protection and Affordability Act. The Company is not presently able to determine the effects of such changes on its financial statements.

Amounts recognized in accumulated other comprehensive loss (pre-tax) at December 31, 2011 are as follows:

Amounts recognized in other comprehensive income

Prior service credit	$ (626)
Net actuarial loss	8,255
Net amount recognized in accumulated other comprehensive loss	$7,629

The estimated actuarial loss and prior service credit to be amortized from accumulated other comprehensive income into net periodic benefit cost during 2012 are $1,146 and $(125), respectively.

The changes in the accumulated postretirement benefit obligation at December 31, 2011 and 2010 consist of the following:

Reconciliation of OPEB liability

	December 31,	
	2011	2010
Benefit obligation, beginning of year	$20,689	$16,674
Service cost	831	696
Interest cost	1,117	958
Actuarial loss	3,898	2,714
Benefits paid	(427)	(353)
Benefit obligation, end of year	$26,108	$20,689

Net periodic postretirement benefit cost included the following components:

Components of OPEB expense

	2011	2010	2009
Service cost—benefits attributed to service during the period	$ 831	$ 696	$ 704
Interest cost on the accumulated postretirement benefit obligation	1,117	958	853
Net amortization	501	128	140
Net periodic postretirement benefit cost	$2,449	$1,782	$1,697

Rates used to estimate plan elements

For measurement purposes, the 2012 annual rate of increase in the per capita cost of covered health care benefits was assumed to be 8.2% for pre-age 65 retirees, post 65 retirees and for prescription drugs; these rates were assumed to decrease gradually to 5.0% for 2019 and remain at that level thereafter. The health care cost trend rate assumption has a significant effect on the amounts reported. The weighted-average discount rate used in determining the accumulated postretirement benefit obligation was 4.31% and 5.47% at December 31, 2011 and 2010, respectively.

Increasing or decreasing the health care trend rates by one percentage point in each year would have the following effect:

	1% Increase	1% Decrease
Postretirement benefit obligation	$6,247	$(4,277)
Total of service and interest cost components	$ 484	$ (320)

The Company estimates future benefit payments will be $574, $710, $882, $993 and $1,095 in 2012 through 2016, respectively, and a total of $7,002 in 2017 through 2020. The future benefit payments are net of the annual Medicare Part D subsidy of approximately $1,094 beginning in 2012.

led to efforts to control escalating healthcare costs. As John Ruffle, a former president of the Financial Accounting Foundation noted, "The Board has done American industry a gigantic favor. Over the long term, industry will look back and say thanks."

What do the numbers mean?   WANT SOME BAD NEWS?

Many companies have underfunded pension and other post-retirement plans. Unfortunately, many governmental entities also have the same problem but on a much larger scale. Here are some examples.

- The actual liabilities of the federal government—including Social Security, Medicare, and federal employees' future retirement benefits—is estimated to be $86.8 trillion or 550 percent of GDP at the end of 2011. When the accrued expenses of the government's entitled programs are counted, we need to collect over $8 trillion in tax revenues annually. Even if you take all the taxable income of corporations and of individuals earning over approximately $66,000, that still falls short of the $8 trillion.

- A State Budget Crisis Task Force recently declared underfunded retirement promises as one of the six major threats to states' "fiscal sustainability."

- According to the Milliman's Public Pension Fund Study and the Pew Center for the States Report, an $859 billion gap exists between obligations for the country's 100 largest public pension plans and the funding of these plans. Nine states were 60 percent funded or less. In Illinois, just

45 percent of the state's pension liabilities were funded. California alone had $113 billion in unfunded liability.

So what does all this have to do with accounting? Similar to the FASB, there is an organization called the Governmental Accounting Standards Board (GASB), which establishes standards of financial accounting and reporting for state and local governmental agencies.

Until recently, the GASB went about its work in relative obscurity. How did the GASB get everyone's attention? It recently required that governmental units recognize postretirement benefits on their balance sheets on an accrual basis. Some states do not like this requirement and have proposed legislation that will allow them to ignore GASB standards. However, the GASB, with the support of users of government reports, has pushed for the change. They are concerned that without the new requirements, governments will continue to misrepresent the true cost of their retirement-related promises to public employees. In their view, the new accounting rules are in the best interests of municipal bondholders and the public in general. Thus, it appears that the FASB is not the only standard-setter subject to political pressure.

Sources: R. H. Attmore, "Who Do Texas Elected Officials Think They Are Fooling?" *The Bond Buyer* (June 18, 2007); Chris Cox and Bill Archer, "Why $16 Trillion Only Hints at the True U.S. Debt," *Wall Street Journal* (November 27, 2012); and "More Bad News for Public Pensions," *Wall Street Journal* (July 12, 2012). For more information on the GASB, go to *www.gasb.org/*.

SUMMARY OF LEARNING OBJECTIVES FOR APPENDIX 20A

KEY TERMS

accumulated postretirement benefit obligation (APBO), *1220*

attribution period, *1219*

corridor approach, *1223*

expected postretirement benefit obligation (EPBO), *1220*

10   **Identify the differences between pensions and postretirement healthcare benefits.** Pension plans are generally funded, but healthcare benefit plans are not. Pension benefits are generally well-defined and level in amount; healthcare benefits are generally uncapped and variable. Pension benefits are payable monthly; healthcare benefits are paid as needed and used. Pension plan variables are reasonably predictable, whereas healthcare plan variables are difficult to predict.

11   **Contrast accounting for pensions to accounting for other postretirement benefits.** Many of the basic concepts, accounting terminology, and measurement methodology that apply to pensions also apply to other postretirement benefit accounting. Because other postretirement benefit plans are unfunded, large obligations can occur. Two significant concepts peculiar to accounting for other postretirement benefits are (1) expected postretirement benefit obligation (EPBO), and (2) accumulated postretirement benefit obligation (APBO).

DEMONSTRATION PROBLEM

Jablonski Corp. sponsors a defined benefit pension plan for its employees. On January 1, 2014, the following balances related to this plan.

Plan assets (market-related value)	$170,000
Projected benefit obligation	340,000
Pension asset/liability	170,000 Cr.
Prior service cost	100,000
OCI—Loss	39,000

As a result of the operation of the plan during 2014, the actuary provided the following additional data at December 31, 2014.

Service cost for 2014	$45,000
Actual return on plan assets in 2014	27,000
Amortization of prior service cost	20,000
Contributions in 2014	85,000
Benefits paid retirees in 2014	51,000
Settlement rate	7%
Expected return on plan assets	8%
Average remaining service life of active employees	10 years

Instructions

(a) Compute pension expense for Jablonski Corp. for the year 2014 by preparing a pension worksheet that shows the journal entry for pension expense.

(b) Indicate the pension amounts reported in the financial statements.

Solution

(a)

Jablonski Corp.xls

Home   Insert   Page Layout   Formulas   Data   Review   View

P18   fx

JABLONSKI CORP.
Pension Worksheet—2014
General Journal Entries

Memo Record

Items	Annual Pension Expense	Cash	Other Comprehensive Income — Prior Service Cost	Other Comprehensive Income — Gain/Loss	Pension Asset/ Liability	Projected Benefit Obligation	Plan Assets
Balance, Jan. 1, 2014					170,000 Cr.	340,000 Cr.	170,000 Dr.
Service cost	45,000 Dr.					45,000 Cr.	
Interest cost*	23,800 Dr.					23,800 Cr.	
Actual return	27,000 Cr.						27,000 Dr.
Unexpected gain**	13,400 Dr.			13,400 Cr.			
Amortization of PSC	20,000 Dr.		20,000 Cr.				
Amortization of loss***	500 Dr.			500 Cr.			
Contributions		85,000 Cr.					85,000 Dr.
Benefits						51,000 Dr.	51,000 Cr.
Journal entry for 2014	75,700 Dr.	85,000 Cr.	20,000 Cr.	13,900 Cr.	43,200 Dr.		
Accumulated OCI, Dec. 31, 2014			100,000 Dr.	39,000 Dr.			
Balance, Dec. 31, 2014			80,000 Dr.	25,100 Dr.	126,800 Cr.	357,800 Cr.	231,000 Dr.

*$23,800 = $340,000 × .07

**$13,400 = ($170,000 × .08) − $27,000

***

Year	1/1 Projected Benefit Obligation	Value of 1/1 Plan Assets	10% Corridor	Accumulated OCI (G/L), 1/1	Minimum Amortization of Loss for 2013
2014	$340,000	$170,000	$34,000	$39,000	$500****

**** ($39,000 − $34,000) = $5,000 ÷ 10 = $500

<u>**2014**</u>

Pension Expense	75,700	
Pension Asset/Liability	43,200	
Other Comprehensive Income (PSC)		20,000
Other Comprehensive Income (G/L)		13,400
Cash		85,000

(b) The pension amounts reported in the 2014 financial statements are as follows.

Income Statement

Pension expense	$ 75,700

Comprehensive Income Statement

Net Income		$ XXXX
Other comprehensive income		
Asset gain	$13,900	
Amortization of loss	500	
Prior service cost amortization	20,000	34,400
Comprehensive income		$ XXXX

Balance Sheet

Liabilities	
Pension liability	$126,800
Stockholders' equity	
Accumulated other comprehensive loss (PSC)	$ 80,000
Accumulated other comprehensive loss (G/L)	25,100

FASB CODIFICATION

FASB Codification References

[1] FASB ASC 960. [Predecessor literature: "Accounting and Reporting by Defined Benefit Pension Plans," *Statement of Financial Accounting Standards No. 35* (Stamford, Conn.: FASB, 1979).]

[2] FASB ASC 715-70-50-1. [Predecessor literature: "Employers' Accounting for Pension Plans," *Statement of Financial Accounting Standards No. 87* (Stamford, Conn.: FASB, 1985), paras. 63–66.]

[3] FASB ASC 715-30-25-1. [Predecessor literature: "Employers' Accounting for Defined Benefit Pension and Other Postretirement Plans: An Amendment to SFAS Nos. 87, 88, 106, and 132(R)," *Statement of Financial Accounting Standards No. 158* (Norwalk, Conn.: FASB, 2006).]

[4] FASB ASC 715-30-35-22. [Predecessor literature: "Employers' Accounting for Pension Plans," *Statement of Financial Accounting Standards No. 87* (Stamford, Conn.: FASB, 1985), par. 30.]

[5] FASB ASC 220-10-45-13. [Predecessor literature: "Employers' Accounting for Defined Benefit Pension and Other Postretirement Plans: An Amendment of SFAS Nos. 87, 88, 106, and 132(R)," *Statement of Financial Accounting Standards No. 158* (Norwalk, Conn.: FASB, 2006), par. B41.]

[6] FASB ASC 715-20-50-1. [Predecessor literature: None.]

[7] FASB ASC 715-20-50-1. [Predecessor literature: "Employers' Disclosure about Pensions and Other Postretirement Benefits," *Statement of Financial Accounting Standards No. 132* (Stamford, Conn.: FASB, 1998; revised 2003); and "Employers' Accounting for Defined Benefit Pension and Other Postretirement Plans: An Amendment of SFAS Nos. 87, 88, 106, and 132(R)," *Statement of Financial Accounting Standards No. 158* (Norwalk, Conn.: FASB, 2006).]

[8] FASB ASC 715-30-05-9. [Predecessor literature: "Employers' Accounting for Settlements and Curtailments of Defined Benefit Pension Plans and for Termination Benefits," *Statement of Financial Accounting Standards No. 88* (Stamford, Conn.: FASB, 1985).]

[9] FASB ASC 715-60. [Predecessor literature: "Employers' Accounting for Postretirement Benefits Other Than Pensions," *Statement of Financial Accounting Standards No. 106* (Norwalk, Conn.: FASB, 1990).]

[10] FASB ASC 712-10-05. [Predecessor literature: "Employers' Accounting for Postemployment Benefits," *Statement of Financial Accounting Standards No. 112* (Norwalk, Conn.: FASB, 1992).]

[11] FASB ASC 715-60-35-9. [Predecessor literature: "Employers' Accounting for Postretirement Benefits Other Than Pensions," *Statement of Financial Accounting Standards No. 106* (Norwalk, Conn.: FASB, 1990), paras. 46–66.]

[12] FASB ASC 715-60-25. [Predecessor literature: "Employers' Accounting for Postretirement Benefits Other Than Pensions," *Statement of Financial Accounting Standards No. 106* (Norwalk, Conn.: FASB, 1990), par. 163.]

Exercises

If your school has a subscription to the FASB Codification, go to *http://aaahq.org/ascLogin.cfm* to log in and prepare responses to the following. Provide Codification references for your responses.

CE20-1 Access the glossary ("Master Glossary") to answer the following.

    (a) What is an accumulated benefit obligation?
    (b) What is a defined benefit postretirement plan?
    (c) What is the definition of "actuarial present value"?
    (d) What is a prior service cost?

CE20-2 In general, how can an employer choose an appropriate discount rate for its pension plan? What information could an employer use in choosing a discount rate?

CE20-3 If an employer has a defined benefit pension plan, what components would make up its net periodic pension cost?

CE20-4 What information about its pension plan must a publicly traded company disclose in its interim financial statements?

An additional Codification case can be found in the Using Your Judgment section, on page 1250.

Be sure to check the book's companion website for a Review and Analysis Exercise, with solution.

WileyPLUS

Brief Exercises, Exercises, Problems, and many more learning and assessment tools and resources are available for practice in WileyPLUS.

Note: All asterisked Questions, Exercises, and Problems relate to material in the appendix to the chapter.

QUESTIONS

1. What is a private pension plan? How does a contributory pension plan differ from a noncontributory plan?

2. Differentiate between a defined contribution pension plan and a defined benefit pension plan. Explain how the employer's obligation differs between the two types of plans.

3. Differentiate between "accounting for the employer" and "accounting for the pension fund."

4. The meaning of the term "fund" depends on the context in which it is used. Explain its meaning when used as a noun. Explain its meaning when it is used as a verb.

5. What is the role of an actuary relative to pension plans? What are actuarial assumptions?

6. What factors must be considered by the actuary in measuring the amount of pension benefits under a defined benefit plan?

7. Name three approaches to measuring benefit obligations from a pension plan and explain how they differ.

8. Explain how cash-basis accounting for pension plans differs from accrual-basis accounting for pension plans. Why is cash-basis accounting generally considered unacceptable for pension plan accounting?

9. Identify the five components that comprise pension expense. Briefly explain the nature of each component.

10. What is service cost, and what is the basis of its measurement?

11. In computing the interest component of pension expense, what interest rates may be used?

12. Explain the difference between service cost and prior service cost.

13. What is meant by "prior service cost"? When is prior service cost recognized as pension expense?

14. What are "liability gains and losses," and how are they accounted for?

15. If pension expense recognized in a period exceeds the current amount funded by the employer, what kind of account arises, and how should it be reported in the financial statements? If the reverse occurs—that is, current funding by the employer exceeds the amount recognized as pension expense—what kind of account arises, and how should it be reported?

16. Given the following items and amounts, compute the actual return on plan assets: fair value of plan assets at the beginning of the period $9,500,000; benefits paid during the period $1,400,000; contributions made during the period $1,000,000; and fair value of the plan assets at the end of the period $10,150,000.

17. How does an "asset gain or loss" develop in pension accounting? How does a "liability gain or loss" develop in pension accounting?

18. What is the meaning of "corridor amortization"?

19. At the end of the current period, Agler Inc. had a projected benefit obligation of $400,000 and pension plan assets (at fair value) of $350,000. What are the accounts and amounts that will be reported on the company's balance sheet as pension assets or pension liabilities?

20. At the end of the current year, Pociek Co. has prior service cost of $9,150,000. Where should the prior service cost be reported on the balance sheet?

21. Describe the accounting for actuarial gains and losses.

22. Boey Company reported net income of $25,000 in 2015. It had the following amounts related to its pension plan in 2015: Actuarial liability gain $10,000; Unexpected asset loss $14,000; Accumulated other comprehensive income (G/L) (beginning balance), zero. Determine for 2015 (a) Boey's other comprehensive income, and (b) comprehensive income.

23. Describe the reporting of pension plans for a company with multiple plans, some of which are underfunded and some of which are overfunded.

24. Determine the meaning of the following terms.
   (a) Contributory plan.
   (b) Vested benefits.
   (c) Retroactive benefits.
   (d) Years-of-service method.

25. A headline in the *Wall Street Journal* stated, "Firms Increasingly Tap Their Pension Funds to Use Excess Assets." What is the accounting issue related to the use of these "excess assets" by companies?

*26. What are postretirement benefits other than pensions?

*27. Why didn't the FASB cover both types of postretirement benefits—pensions and healthcare—in the earlier pension accounting rules?

*28. What are the major differences between postretirement healthcare benefits and pension benefits?

*29. What is the difference between the APBO and the EPBO? What are the components of postretirement expense?

BRIEF EXERCISES

4 **BE20-1** AMR Corporation (parent company of American Airlines) reported the following for 2011 (in millions).

Service cost	$366
Interest on P.B.O.	737
Return on plan assets	593
Amortization of prior service cost	13
Amortization of net loss	154

Compute AMR Corporation's 2011 pension expense.

4 **BE20-2** For Warren Corporation, year-end plan assets were $2,000,000. At the beginning of the year, plan assets were $1,780,000. During the year, contributions to the pension fund were $120,000, and benefits paid were $200,000. Compute Warren's actual return on plan assets.

5 **BE20-3** At January 1, 2014, Hennein Company had plan assets of $280,000 and a projected benefit obligation of the same amount. During 2014, service cost was $27,500, the settlement rate was 10%, actual and expected return on plan assets were $25,000, contributions were $20,000, and benefits paid were $17,500. Prepare a pension worksheet for Hennein Company for 2014.

4 **BE20-4** For 2012, Campbell Soup Company had pension expense of $73 million and contributed $71 million to the pension fund. Prepare Campbell Soup Company's journal entry to record pension expense and funding.

6 **BE20-5** Mancuso Corporation amended its pension plan on January 1, 2014, and granted $160,000 of prior service costs to its employees. The employees are expected to provide 2,000 service years in the future, with 350 service years in 2014. Compute prior service cost amortization for 2014.

9 **BE20-6** At December 31, 2014, Besler Corporation had a projected benefit obligation of $560,000, plan assets of $322,000, and prior service cost of $127,000 in accumulated other comprehensive income. Determine the pension asset/liability at December 31, 2014.

8 **BE20-7** Shin Corporation had a projected benefit obligation of $3,100,000 and plan assets of $3,300,000 at January 1, 2014. Shin also had a net actuarial loss of $465,000 in accumulated OCI at January 1, 2014. The average remaining service period of Shin's employees is 7.5 years. Compute Shin's minimum amortization of the actuarial loss.

9 **BE20-8** Hawkins Corporation has the following balances at December 31, 2014.

Projected benefit obligation	$2,600,000
Plan assets at fair value	2,000,000
Accumulated OCI (PSC)	1,100,000

How should these balances be reported on Hawkins's balance sheet at December 31, 2014?

9 **BE20-9** Norton Co. had the following amounts related to its pension plan in 2014.

Actuarial liability loss for 2014	$28,000
Unexpected asset gain for 2014	18,000
Accumulated other comprehensive income (G/L) (beginning balance)	7,000 Cr.

Determine for 2014: (a) Norton's other comprehensive income (loss), and (b) comprehensive income. Net income for 2014 is $26,000; no amortization of gain or loss is necessary in 2014.

9 **BE20-10** Lahey Corp. has three defined benefit pension plans as follows.

	Pension Assets (at Fair Value)	Projected Benefit Obligation
Plan X	$600,000	$500,000
Plan Y	900,000	720,000
Plan Z	550,000	700,000

How will Lahey report these multiple plans in its financial statements?

10 **11** *BE20-11** Manno Corporation has the following information available concerning its postretirement benefit plan for 2014.

Service cost	$40,000
Interest cost	47,400
Actual and expected return on plan assets	26,900

Compute Manno's 2014 postretirement expense.

10 **11** *BE20-12** For 2014, Sampsell Inc. computed its annual postretirement expense as $240,900. Sampsell's contribution to the plan during 2014 was $180,000. Prepare Sampsell's 2014 entry to record postretirement expense.

EXERCISES

4 **6** **E20-1 (Pension Expense, Journal Entries)** The following information is available for the pension plan of Radcliffe Company for the year 2014.

Actual and expected return on plan assets	$ 15,000
Benefits paid to retirees	40,000
Contributions (funding)	90,000
Interest/discount rate	10%
Prior service cost amortization	8,000
Projected benefit obligation, January 1, 2014	500,000
Service cost	60,000

Instructions

(a) Compute pension expense for the year 2014.

(b) Prepare the journal entry to record pension expense and the employer's contribution to the pension plan in 2014.

4 6 E20-2 (Computation of Pension Expense) Veldre Company provides the following information about its defined benefit pension plan for the year 2014.

Service cost	$ 90,000
Contribution to the plan	105,000
Prior service cost amortization	10,000
Actual and expected return on plan assets	64,000
Benefits paid	40,000
Plan assets at January 1, 2014	640,000
Projected benefit obligation at January 1, 2014	700,000
Accumulated OCI (PSC) at January 1, 2014	150,000
Interest/discount (settlement) rate	10%

Instructions

Compute the pension expense for the year 2014.

5 E20-3 (Preparation of Pension Worksheet) Using the information in E20-2, prepare a pension worksheet inserting January 1, 2014, balances, showing December 31, 2014, balances, and the journal entry recording pension expense.

5 E20-4 (Basic Pension Worksheet) The following facts apply to the pension plan of Boudreau Inc. for the year 2014.

Plan assets, January 1, 2014	$490,000
Projected benefit obligation, January 1, 2014	490,000
Settlement rate	8%
Service cost	40,000
Contributions (funding)	25,000
Actual and expected return on plan assets	49,700
Benefits paid to retirees	33,400

Instructions

Using the preceding data, compute pension expense for the year 2014. As part of your solution, prepare a pension worksheet that shows the journal entry for pension expense for 2014 and the year-end balances in the related pension accounts.

6 E20-5 (Application of Years-of-Service Method) Andrews Company has five employees participating in its defined benefit pension plan. Expected years of future service for these employees at the beginning of 2014 are as follows.

Employee	Future Years of Service
Jim	3
Paul	4
Nancy	5
Dave	6
Kathy	6

On January 1, 2014, the company amended its pension plan, increasing its projected benefit obligation by $72,000.

Instructions

Compute the amount of prior service cost amortization for the years 2014 through 2019 using the years-of-service method, setting up appropriate schedules.

4 E20-6 (Computation of Actual Return) Gingrich Importers provides the following pension plan information.

Fair value of pension plan assets, January 1, 2014	$2,400,000
Fair value of pension plan assets, December 31, 2014	2,725,000
Contributions to the plan in 2014	280,000
Benefits paid retirees in 2014	350,000

Instructions

From the data above, compute the actual return on the plan assets for 2014.

5 6 **E20-7 (Basic Pension Worksheet)** The following defined pension data of Rydell Corp. apply to the year 2014.

Projected benefit obligation, 1/1/14 (before amendment)	$560,000
Plan assets, 1/1/14	546,200
Pension liability	13,800
On January 1, 2014, Rydell Corp., through plan amendment, grants prior service benefits having a present value of	120,000
Settlement rate	9%
Service cost	58,000
Contributions (funding)	65,000
Actual (expected) return on plan assets	52,280
Benefits paid to retirees	40,000
Prior service cost amortization for 2014	17,000

Instructions

For 2014, prepare a pension worksheet for Rydell Corp. that shows the journal entry for pension expense and the year-end balances in the related pension accounts.

8 **E20-8 (Application of the Corridor Approach)** Kenseth Corp. has the following beginning-of-the-year present values for its projected benefit obligation and market-related values for its pension plan assets.

	Projected Benefit Obligation	Plan Assets Value
2013	$2,000,000	$1,900,000
2014	2,400,000	2,500,000
2015	2,950,000	2,600,000
2016	3,600,000	3,000,000

The average remaining service life per employee in 2013 and 2014 is 10 years and in 2015 and 2016 is 12 years. The net gain or loss that occurred during each year is as follows: 2013, $280,000 loss; 2014, $90,000 loss; 2015, $11,000 loss; and 2016, $25,000 gain. (In working the solution, the gains and losses must be aggregated to arrive at year-end balances.)

Instructions

Using the corridor approach, compute the amount of net gain or loss amortized and charged to pension expense in each of the four years, setting up an appropriate schedule.

9 **E20-9 (Disclosures: Pension Expense and Other Comprehensive Income)** Taveras Enterprises provides the following information relative to its defined benefit pension plan.

Balances or Values at December 31, 2014	
Projected benefit obligation	$2,737,000
Accumulated benefit obligation	1,980,000
Fair value of plan assets	2,278,329
Accumulated OCI (PSC)	210,000
Accumulated OCI—Net loss (1/1/14 balance, –0–)	45,680
Pension liability	458,671
Other pension plan data for 2014:	
Service cost	94,000
Prior service cost amortization	42,000
Actual return on plan assets	130,000
Expected return on plan assets	175,680
Interest on January 1, 2014, projected benefit obligation	253,000
Contributions to plan	93,329
Benefits paid	140,000

Instructions

   (a) Prepare the note disclosing the components of pension expense for the year 2014.

   (b) Determine the amounts of other comprehensive income and comprehensive income for 2014. Net income for 2014 is $35,000.

   (c) Compute the amount of accumulated other comprehensive income reported at December 31, 2014.

5 **E20-10 (Pension Worksheet)** Webb Corp. sponsors a defined benefit pension plan for its employees. On January 1, 2014, the following balances relate to this plan.

Plan assets	$480,000
Projected benefit obligation	600,000
Pension asset/liability	120,000
Accumulated OCI (PSC)	100,000 Dr.

As a result of the operation of the plan during 2014, the following additional data are provided by the actuary.

Service cost	$90,000
Settlement rate, 9%	
Actual return on plan assets	55,000
Amortization of prior service cost	19,000
Expected return on plan assets	52,000
Unexpected loss from change in projected benefit obligation, due to change in actuarial predictions	76,000
Contributions	99,000
Benefits paid retirees	85,000

Instructions

(a) Using the data above, compute pension expense for Webb Corp. for the year 2014 by preparing a pension worksheet.

(b) Prepare the journal entry for pension expense for 2014.

4 9 **E20-11 (Pension Expense, Journal Entries, Statement Presentation)** Henning Company sponsors a defined benefit pension plan for its employees. The following data relate to the operation of the plan for the year 2014 in which no benefits were paid.

1. The actuarial present value of future benefits earned by employees for services rendered in 2014 amounted to $56,000.
2. The company's funding policy requires a contribution to the pension trustee amounting to $145,000 for 2014.
3. As of January 1, 2014, the company had a projected benefit obligation of $900,000, an accumulated benefit obligation of $800,000, and a debit balance of $400,000 in accumulated OCI (PSC). The fair value of pension plan assets amounted to $600,000 at the beginning of the year. The actual and expected return on plan assets was $54,000. The settlement rate was 9%. No gains or losses occurred in 2014 and no benefits were paid.
4. Amortization of prior service cost was $50,000 in 2014. Amortization of net gain or loss was not required in 2014.

Instructions

(a) Determine the amounts of the components of pension expense that should be recognized by the company in 2014.

(b) Prepare the journal entry or entries to record pension expense and the employer's contribution to the pension trustee in 2014.

(c) Indicate the amounts that would be reported on the income statement and the balance sheet for the year 2014.

4 6 7 8 9 **E20-12 (Pension Expense, Journal Entries, Statement Presentation)** Ferreri Company received the following selected information from its pension plan trustee concerning the operation of the company's defined benefit pension plan for the year ended December 31, 2014.

	January 1, 2014	December 31, 2014
Projected benefit obligation	$1,500,000	$1,527,000
Market-related and fair value of plan assets	800,000	1,130,000
Accumulated benefit obligation	1,600,000	1,720,000
Accumulated OCI (G/L)—Net gain	–0–	(200,000)

The service cost component of pension expense for employee services rendered in the current year amounted to $77,000 and the amortization of prior service cost was $120,000. The company's actual funding (contributions) of the plan in 2014 amounted to $250,000. The expected return on plan assets and the actual rate were both 10%; the interest/discount (settlement) rate was 10%. Accumulated other comprehensive income (PSC) had a balance of $1,200,000 on January 1, 2014. Assume no benefits paid in 2014.

Instructions

(a) Determine the amounts of the components of pension expense that should be recognized by the company in 2014.

(b) Prepare the journal entry to record pension expense and the employer's contribution to the pension plan in 2014.

(c) Indicate the pension-related amounts that would be reported on the income statement and the balance sheet for Ferreri Company for the year 2014.

4 6 7 8 9 **E20-13 (Computation of Actual Return, Gains and Losses, Corridor Test, and Pension Expense)** Erickson Company sponsors a defined benefit pension plan. The corporation's actuary provides the following information about the plan.

	January 1, 2014	December 31, 2014
Vested benefit obligation	$1,500	$1,900
Accumulated benefit obligation	1,900	2,730
Projected benefit obligation	2,500	3,300
Plan assets (fair value)	1,700	2,620
Settlement rate and expected rate of return		10%
Pension asset/liability	800	?
Service cost for the year 2014		400
Contributions (funding in 2014)		700
Benefits paid in 2014		200

Instructions

(a) Compute the actual return on the plan assets in 2014.

(b) Compute the amount of the other comprehensive income (G/L) as of December 31, 2014. (Assume the January 1, 2014, balance was zero.)

(c) Compute the amount of net gain or loss amortization for 2014 (corridor approach).

(d) Compute pension expense for 2014.

5 **E20-14 (Worksheet for E20-13)** Using the information in E20-13 about Erickson Company's defined benefit pension plan, prepare a 2014 pension worksheet with supplementary schedules of computations. Prepare the journal entries at December 31, 2014, to record pension expense and related pension transactions. Also, indicate the pension amounts reported in the balance sheet.

4 **E20-15 (Pension Expense, Journal Entries)** Latoya Company provides the following selected information related to its defined benefit pension plan for 2014.

Pension asset/liability (January 1)	$ 25,000 Cr.
Accumulated benefit obligation (December 31)	400,000
Actual and expected return on plan assets	10,000
Contributions (funding) in 2014	150,000
Fair value of plan assets (December 31)	800,000
Settlement rate	10%
Projected benefit obligation (January 1)	700,000
Service cost	80,000

Instructions

(a) Compute pension expense and prepare the journal entry to record pension expense and the employer's contribution to the pension plan in 2014. Preparation of a pension worksheet is not required. Benefits paid in 2014 were $35,000.

(b) Indicate the pension-related amounts that would be reported in the company's income statement and balance sheet for 2014.

8 **E20-16 (Amortization of Accumulated OCI (G/L), Corridor Approach, Pension Expense Computation)** The actuary for the pension plan of Gustafson Inc. calculated the following net gains and losses.

Incurred during the Year	(Gain) or Loss
2014	$300,000
2015	480,000
2016	(210,000)
2017	(290,000)

Other information about the company's pension obligation and plan assets is as follows.

As of January 1,	Projected Benefit Obligation	Plan Assets (market-related asset value)
2014	$4,000,000	$2,400,000
2015	4,520,000	2,200,000
2016	5,000,000	2,600,000
2017	4,240,000	3,040,000

Gustafson Inc. has a stable labor force of 400 employees who are expected to receive benefits under the plan. The total service-years for all participating employees is 5,600. The beginning balance of accumulated

OCI (G/L) is zero on January 1, 2014. The market-related value and the fair value of plan assets are the same for the 4-year period. Use the average remaining service life per employee as the basis for amortization.

Instructions
(Round to the nearest dollar.)

Prepare a schedule which reflects the minimum amount of accumulated OCI (G/L) amortized as a component of net periodic pension expense for each of the years 2014, 2015, 2016, and 2017. Apply the "corridor" approach in determining the amount to be amortized each year.

8 **E20-17 (Amortization of Accumulated OCI Balances)** Keeton Company sponsors a defined benefit pension plan for its 600 employees. The company's actuary provided the following information about the plan.

	January 1, 2014	December 31, 2014	December 31, 2015
Projected benefit obligation	$2,800,000	$3,650,000	$4,195,000
Accumulated benefit obligation	1,900,000	2,430,000	2,900,000
Plan assets (fair value and market-related asset value)	1,700,000	2,900,000	3,790,000
Accumulated net (gain) or loss (for purposes of the corridor calculation)	–0–	198,000	(24,000)
Discount rate (current settlement rate)		9%	8%
Actual and expected asset return rate		10%	10%
Contributions		1,030,000	600,000

The average remaining service life per employee is 10.5 years. The service cost component of net periodic pension expense for employee services rendered amounted to $400,000 in 2014 and $475,000 in 2015. The accumulated OCI (PSC) on January 1, 2014, was $1,260,000. No benefits have been paid.

Instructions
(Round to the nearest dollar.)

(a) Compute the amount of accumulated OCI (PSC) to be amortized as a component of net periodic pension expense for each of the years 2014 and 2015.

(b) Prepare a schedule which reflects the amount of accumulated OCI (G/L) to be amortized as a component of pension expense for 2014 and 2015.

(c) Determine the total amount of pension expense to be recognized by Keeton Company in 2014 and 2015.

5 **8** **E20-18 (Pension Worksheet—Missing Amounts)** The accounting staff of Usher Inc. has prepared the following pension worksheet. Unfortunately, several entries in the worksheet are not decipherable. The company has asked your assistance in completing the worksheet and completing the accounting tasks related to the pension plan for 2014.

	Pension Worksheet—Usher Inc.xls							
	Home Insert Page Layout Formulas Data Review View							
	P18	fx						
	A	B	C	D	E	F	G	H
1				**General Journal Entries**				**Memo Record**	
2								
3		Annual				Pension	Projected	
4		Pension		OCI—Prior	OCI—	Asset/	Benefit	
5	Items	Expense	Cash	Service Cost	Gain/Loss	Liability	Obligation	Plan Assets
6	Balance, Jan. 1, 2014					1,100 Cr.	2,800	1,700
7	Service cost	(1)					500	
8	Interest cost	(2)					280	
9	Actual return	(3)						220
10	Unexpected gain	150			(4)			
11	Amortization of PSC	(5)		55				
12	Contributions		800					800
13	Benefits						200	200
14	Liability increase				(6)		365	
15	Journal entry	(7)	(8)	(9)	(10)	(11)		
16								
17	Accumulated OCI, Dec. 31, 2013			1,100	0			
18	Balance, Dec. 31, 2014			1,045	215	1,225	3,745	2,520
19								

Instructions

(a) Determine the missing amounts in the 2014 pension worksheet, indicating whether the amounts are debits or credits.

(b) Prepare the journal entry to record 2014 pension expense for Usher Inc.

(c) The accounting staff has heard of a pension accounting procedure called "corridor amortization." Is Usher required to record any amounts for corridor amortization in (1) 2014? In (2) 2015? Explain.

10 11 *E20-19 **(Postretirement Benefit Expense Computation)** Kreter Co. provides the following information about its postretirement benefit plan for the year 2014.

Service cost	$ 45,000
Contribution to the plan	10,000
Actual and expected return on plan assets	11,000
Benefits paid	20,000
Plan assets at January 1, 2014	110,000
Accumulated postretirement benefit obligation	
at January 1, 2014	330,000
Discount rate	8%

Instructions

Compute the postretirement benefit expense for 2014.

10 11 *E20-20 **(Postretirement Benefit Worksheet)** Using the information in E20-19, prepare a worksheet inserting January 1, 2014, balances, and showing December 31, 2014, balances. Prepare the journal entry recording postretirement benefit expense.

10 11 *E20-21 **(Postretirement Benefit Expense Computation)** Garner Inc. provides the following information related to its postretirement benefits for the year 2014.

Accumulated postretirement benefit obligation at January 1, 2014	$710,000
Actual and expected return on plan assets	34,000
Prior service cost amortization	21,000
Discount rate	10%
Service cost	83,000

Instructions

Compute postretirement benefit expense for 2014.

10 11 *E20-22 **(Postretirement Benefit Expense Computation)** Englehart Co. provides the following information about its postretirement benefit plan for the year 2014.

Service cost	$ 90,000
Prior service cost amortization	3,000
Contribution to the plan	56,000
Actual and expected return on plan assets	62,000
Benefits paid	40,000
Plan assets at January 1, 2014	710,000
Accumulated postretirement benefit obligation at January 1, 2014	760,000
Accumulated OCI (PSC) at January 1, 2014	100,000 Dr.
Discount rate	9%

Instructions

Compute the postretirement benefit expense for 2014.

10 11 *E20-23 **(Postretirement Benefit Worksheet)** Using the information in E20-22, prepare a worksheet inserting January 1, 2014, balances, showing December 31, 2014, balances, and the journal entry recording postretirement benefit expense.

10 11 *E20-24 **(Postretirement Benefit Worksheet—Missing Amounts)** The accounting staff of Holder Inc. has prepared the following postretirement benefit worksheet. Unfortunately, several entries in the worksheet are not decipherable. The company has asked your assistance in completing the worksheet and completing the accounting tasks related to the pension plan for 2014.

| | Postretirement Benefit Worksheet—Holder Inc.xls | | | | | | |

Home Insert Page Layout Formulas Data Review View

P18 *fx*

	A	B	C	D	E	F	G
1							
2			**General Journal Entries**			**Memo Record**	
3				Other			
4		Annual		Comprehensive	Postretirement		
5	Items	Expense	Cash	Income—PSC	Asset/Liability	APBO	Plan Assets
6	Balance, Jan. 1, 2014				290,000	410,000	120,000
7	Service cost	(1)				56,000	
8	Interest cost	(2)				36,900	
9	Actual/Expected return	(3)					2,000
10	Contributions		66,000				(4)
11	Benefits					5,000	5,000
12	Amortization of PSC	3,000		(5)			
13	Journal entry for 2014	(6)	(7)	(8)	(9)		
14							
15	Accumulated OCI, Dec. 31, 2013			30,000 Dr.			
16	Balance, Dec. 31, 2014			27,000 Dr.	314,900 Cr.	497,900 Cr.	183,000 Dr.
17							

Instructions

(a) Determine the missing amounts in the 2014 postretirement worksheet, indicating whether the amounts are debits or credits.

(b) Prepare the journal entry to record 2014 postretirement expense for Holder Inc.

(c) What discount rate is Holder using in accounting for the interest on its other postretirement benefit plan? Explain.

EXERCISES SET B

See the book's companion website, at **www.wiley.com/college/kieso**, for an additional set of exercises.

PROBLEMS

P20-1 (2-Year Worksheet) On January 1, 2014, Harrington Company has the following defined benefit pension plan balances.

Projected benefit obligation	$4,500,000
Fair value of plan assets	4,200,000

The interest (settlement) rate applicable to the plan is 10%. On January 1, 2015, the company amends its pension agreement so that prior service costs of $500,000 are created. Other data related to the pension plan are as follows.

	2014	2015
Service cost	$150,000	$180,000
Prior service cost amortization	–0–	90,000
Contributions (funding) to the plan	240,000	285,000
Benefits paid	200,000	280,000
Actual return on plan assets	252,000	260,000
Expected rate of return on assets	6%	8%

Instructions

(a) Prepare a pension worksheet for the pension plan for 2014 and 2015.

(b) For 2015, prepare the journal entry to record pension-related amounts.

 P20-2 (3-Year Worksheet, Journal Entries, and Reporting) Jackson Company adopts acceptable accounting for its defined benefit pension plan on January 1, 2013, with the following beginning balances: plan assets $200,000; projected benefit obligation $250,000. Other data relating to 3 years' operation of the plan are as follows.

	2013	2014	2015
Annual service cost	$16,000	$ 19,000	$ 26,000
Settlement rate and expected rate of return	10%	10%	10%
Actual return on plan assets	18,000	22,000	24,000
Annual funding (contributions)	16,000	40,000	48,000
Benefits paid	14,000	16,400	21,000
Prior service cost (plan amended, 1/1/14)		160,000	
Amortization of prior service cost		54,400	41,600
Change in actuarial assumptions establishes a December 31, 2015, projected benefit obligation of:			520,000

Instructions

(a) Prepare a pension worksheet presenting all 3 years' pension balances and activities.

(b) Prepare the journal entries (from the worksheet) to reflect all pension plan transactions and events at December 31 of each year.

(c) Indicate the pension-related amounts reported in the financial statements for 2015.

 P20-3 (Pension Expense, Journal Entries, Amortization of Loss) Gottschalk Company sponsors a defined benefit plan for its 100 employees. On January 1, 2014, the company's actuary provided the following information.

Accumulated other comprehensive loss (PSC)	$150,000
Pension plan assets (fair value and market-related asset value)	200,000
Accumulated benefit obligation	260,000
Projected benefit obligation	380,000

The average remaining service period for the participating employees is 10 years. All employees are expected to receive benefits under the plan. On December 31, 2014, the actuary calculated that the present value of future benefits earned for employee services rendered in the current year amounted to $52,000; the projected benefit obligation was $490,000; fair value of pension assets was $276,000; the accumulated benefit obligation amounted to $365,000. The expected return on plan assets and the discount rate on the projected benefit obligation were both 10%. The actual return on plan assets is $11,000. The company's current year's contribution to the pension plan amounted to $65,000. No benefits were paid during the year.

Instructions

(a) Determine the components of pension expense that the company would recognize in 2014. (With only one year involved, you need not prepare a worksheet.)

(b) Prepare the journal entry to record the pension expense and the company's funding of the pension plan in 2014.

(c) Compute the amount of the 2014 increase/decrease in gains or losses and the amount to be amortized in 2014 and 2015.

(d) Indicate the pension amounts reported in the financial statement as of December 31, 2014.

 P20-4 (Pension Expense, Journal Entries for 2 Years) Gordon Company sponsors a defined benefit pension plan. The following information related to the pension plan is available for 2014 and 2015.

	2014	2015
Plan assets (fair value), December 31	$699,000	$849,000
Projected benefit obligation, January 1	700,000	800,000
Pension asset/liability, January 1	140,000 Cr.	?
Prior service cost, January 1	250,000	240,000
Service cost	60,000	90,000
Actual and expected return on plan assets	24,000	30,000
Amortization of prior service cost	10,000	12,000
Contributions (funding)	115,000	120,000
Accumulated benefit obligation, December 31	500,000	550,000
Interest/settlement rate	9%	9%

Instructions

(a) Compute pension expense for 2014 and 2015.

(b) Prepare the journal entries to record the pension expense and the company's funding of the pension plan for both years.

7 8 **P20-5 (Computation of Pension Expense, Amortization of Net Gain or Loss–Corridor Approach, Journal Entries for 3 Years)** Hiatt Toothpaste Company initiates a defined benefit pension plan for its 50 employees on January 1, 2014. The insurance company which administers the pension plan provided the following selected information for the years 2014, 2015, and 2016.

	For Year Ended December 31,		
	2014	2015	2016
Plan assets (fair value)	$50,000	$ 85,000	$180,000
Accumulated benefit obligation	45,000	165,000	292,000
Projected benefit obligation	60,000	200,000	324,000
Net (gain) loss (for purposes of corridor calculation)	–0–	78,400	86,121
Employer's funding contribution (made at end of year)	50,000	60,000	105,000

There were no balances as of January 1, 2014, when the plan was initiated. The actual and expected return on plan assets was 10% over the 3-year period, but the settlement rate used to discount the company's pension obligation was 13% in 2014, 11% in 2015, and 8% in 2016. The service cost component of net periodic pension expense amounted to the following: 2014, $60,000; 2015, $85,000; and 2016, $119,000. The average remaining service life per employee is 12 years. No benefits were paid in 2014, $30,000 of benefits were paid in 2015, and $18,500 of benefits were paid in 2016 (all benefits paid at end of year).

Instructions

(Round to the nearest dollar.)

(a) Calculate the amount of net periodic pension expense that the company would recognize in 2014, 2015, and 2016.

(b) Prepare the journal entries to record net periodic pension expense, employer's funding contribution, and related pension amounts for the years 2014, 2015, and 2016.

6 7 **P20-6 (Computation of Prior Service Cost Amortization, Pension Expense, Journal Entries, and Net**
8 **Gain or Loss)** Aykroyd Inc. has sponsored a noncontributory, defined benefit pension plan for its employees since 1991. Prior to 2014, cumulative net pension expense recognized equaled cumulative contributions to the plan. Other relevant information about the pension plan on January 1, 2014, is as follows.

1. The company has 200 employees. All these employees are expected to receive benefits under the plan. The average remaining service life per employee is 12 years.
2. The projected benefit obligation amounted to $5,000,000 and the fair value of pension plan assets was $3,000,000. The market-related asset value was also $3,000,000. Unrecognized prior service cost was $2,000,000.

On December 31, 2014, the projected benefit obligation and the accumulated benefit obligation were $4,850,000 and $4,025,000, respectively. The fair value of the pension plan assets amounted to $4,100,000 at the end of the year. A 10% settlement rate and a 10% expected asset return rate were used in the actuarial present value computations in the pension plan. The present value of benefits attributed by the pension benefit formula to employee service in 2014 amounted to $200,000. The employer's contribution to the plan assets amounted to $775,000 in 2014. This problem assumes no payment of pension benefits.

Instructions

(Round all amounts to the nearest dollar.)

(a) Prepare a schedule, based on the average remaining life per employee, showing the prior service cost that would be amortized as a component of pension expense for 2014, 2015, and 2016.

(b) Compute pension expense for the year 2014.

(c) Prepare the journal entries required to report the accounting for the company's pension plan for 2014.

(d) Compute the amount of the 2014 increase/decrease in net gains or losses and the amount to be amortized in 2014 and 2015.

5 6 **P20-7 (Pension Worksheet)** Hanson Corp. sponsors a defined benefit pension plan for its employees. On
7 January 1, 2014, the following balances related to this plan.

Plan assets (market-related value)	$520,000
Projected benefit obligation	700,000
Pension asset/liability	180,000 Cr.
Prior service cost	81,000
Net gain or loss (debit)	91,000

As a result of the operation of the plan during 2014, the actuary provided the following additional data for 2014.

Service cost	$108,000
Settlement rate, 9%; expected return rate, 10%	
Actual return on plan assets	48,000
Amortization of prior service cost	25,000
Contributions	133,000
Benefits paid retirees	85,000
Average remaining service life of active employees	10 years

Instructions

Using the preceding data, compute pension expense for Hanson Corp. for the year 2014 by preparing a pension worksheet that shows the journal entry for pension expense. Use the market-related asset value to compute the expected return and for corridor amortization.

P20-8 (Comprehensive 2-Year Worksheet) Lemke Company sponsors a defined benefit pension plan for its employees. The following data relate to the operation of the plan for the years 2014 and 2015.

	2014	2015
Projected benefit obligation, January 1	$600,000	
Plan assets (fair value and market-related value), January 1	410,000	
Pension asset/liability, January 1	190,000 Cr.	
Prior service cost, January 1	160,000	
Service cost	40,000	$ 59,000
Settlement rate	10%	10%
Expected rate of return	10%	10%
Actual return on plan assets	36,000	61,000
Amortization of prior service cost	70,000	50,000
Annual contributions	97,000	81,000
Benefits paid retirees	31,500	54,000
Increase in projected benefit obligation due to changes in actuarial assumptions	87,000	–0–
Accumulated benefit obligation at December 31	721,800	789,000
Average service life of all employees		20 years
Vested benefit obligation at December 31		464,000

Instructions

(a) Prepare a pension worksheet presenting both years 2014 and 2015 and accompanying computations and amortization of the loss (2015) using the corridor approach.

(b) Prepare the journal entries (from the worksheet) to reflect all pension plan transactions and events at December 31 of each year.

(c) For 2015, indicate the pension amounts reported in the financial statements.

P20-9 (Comprehensive 2-Year Worksheet) Hobbs Co. has the following defined benefit pension plan balances on January 1, 2014.

Projected benefit obligation	$4,600,000
Fair value of plan assets	4,600,000

The interest (settlement) rate applicable to the plan is 10%. On January 1, 2015, the company amends its pension agreement so that prior service costs of $600,000 are created. Other data related to the pension plan are:

	2014	2015
Service cost	$150,000	$170,000
Prior service cost amortization	–0–	90,000
Contributions (funding) to the plan	200,000	184,658
Benefits paid	220,000	280,000
Actual return on plan assets	252,000	350,000
Expected rate of return on assets	6%	8%

Instructions

(a) Prepare a pension worksheet for the pension plan in 2014.

(b) Prepare any journal entries related to the pension plan that would be needed at December 31, 2014.

(c) Prepare a pension worksheet for 2015 and any journal entries related to the pension plan as of December 31, 2015.

(d) Indicate the pension-related amounts reported in the 2015 financial statements.

5 **6** **7** **P20-10 (Pension Worksheet—Missing Amounts)** Kramer Co. has prepared the following pension worksheet. Unfortunately, several entries in the worksheet are not decipherable. The company has asked your assistance in completing the worksheet and completing the accounting tasks related to the pension plan for 2014.

	Pension Worksheet—Kramer Co.xls							
Home Insert Page Layout Formulas Data Review View								
P18	fx							
	A	B	C	D	E	F	G	H
1								
2				**General Journal Entries**			**Memo Record**	
3		Annual				Pension	Projected	
4		Pension		OCI—Prior	OCI—	Asset/	Benefit	
5	Items	Expense	Cash	Service Cost	Gain/Loss	Liability	Obligation	Plan Assets
6	Balance, Jan. 1, 2014					120,000	325,000	205,000 Dr.
7	Service cost	(1)					20,000	
8	Interest cost	(2)					26,000	
9	Actual return	(3)						18,000 Dr.
10	Unexpected loss	2,500			(4)			
11	Amortization of PSC	(5)		35,000				
12	Contributions		41,000					41,000 Dr.
13	Benefits						15,000	15,000 Cr.
14	Increase in PBO				(6)		43,500	
15	Journal entry for 2014	(7)	(8)	(9)	(10)	(11)		
16	Accumulated OCI, Dec. 31, 2013			80,000	0			
17	Balance, Dec. 31, 2014			45,000	46,000	150,500 Cr.	399,500 Cr.	249,000 Dr.
18								

Instructions

(a) Determine the missing amounts in the 2014 pension worksheet, indicating whether the amounts are debits or credits.

(b) Prepare the journal entry to record 2014 pension expense for Kramer Co.

(c) Determine the following for Kramer for 2014: (1) settlement rate used to measure the interest on the liability and (2) expected return on plan assets.

5 **6** **7** **8** **9** **P20-11 (Pension Worksheet)** The following data relate to the operation of Kramer Co.'s pension plan in 2015. The pension worksheet for 2014 is provided in P20-10.

Service cost	$59,000
Actual return on plan assets	32,000
Amortization of prior service cost	28,000
Annual contributions	51,000
Benefits paid retirees	27,000
Average service life of all employees	25 years

For 2015, Kramer will use the same assumptions as 2014 for the expected rate of returns on plan assets. The settlement rate for 2015 is 10%.

Instructions

(a) Prepare a pension worksheet for 2015 and accompanying computations and amortization of the loss, if any, in 2015 using the corridor approach.

(b) Prepare the journal entries (from the worksheet) to reflect all pension plan transactions and events at December 31.

(c) Indicate the pension amounts reported in the financial statements.

5 **6** **7** **8** **9** **P20-12 (Pension Worksheet)** Larson Corp. sponsors a defined benefit pension plan for its employees. On January 1, 2015, the following balances related to this plan.

Plan assets (market-related value)	$270,000
Projected benefit obligation	340,000
Pension asset/liability	70,000 Cr.
Prior service cost	90,000
OCI—Loss	39,000

As a result of the operation of the plan during 2015, the actuary provided the following additional data for 2015.

Service cost	$45,000
Actual return on plan assets	27,000
Amortization of prior service cost	12,000
Contributions	65,000
Benefits paid retirees	41,000
Settlement rate	7%
Expected return on plan assets	8%
Average remaining service life of active employees	10 years

Instructions

(a) Compute pension expense for Larson Corp. for the year 2015 by preparing a pension worksheet that shows the journal entry for pension expense.

(b) Indicate the pension amounts reported in the financial statements.

 *P20-13 (Postretirement Benefit Worksheet) Hollenbeck Foods Inc. sponsors a postretirement medical and dental benefit plan for its employees. The following balances relate to this plan on January 1, 2014.

Plan assets	$200,000
Expected postretirement benefit obligation	820,000
Accumulated postretirement benefit obligation	200,000
No prior service costs exist.	

As a result of the plan's operation during 2014, the following additional data are provided by the actuary.

Service cost is $70,000
Discount rate is 10%
Contributions to plan are $65,000
Expected return on plan assets is $10,000
Actual return on plan assets is $15,000
Benefits paid to employees are $44,000
Average remaining service to full eligibility: 20 years

Instructions

(a) Using the preceding data, compute the net periodic postretirement benefit cost for 2014 by preparing a worksheet that shows the journal entry for postretirement expense and the year-end balances in the related postretirement benefit memo accounts. (Assume that contributions and benefits are paid at the end of the year.)

(b) Prepare any journal entries related to the postretirement plan for 2014 and indicate the postretirement amounts reported in the financial statements for 2014.

10 **11** *P20-14 (Postretirement Benefit Worksheet—2 Years) Elton Co. has the following postretirement benefit plan balances on January 1, 2014.

Accumulated postretirement benefit obligation	$2,250,000
Fair value of plan assets	2,250,000

The interest (settlement) rate applicable to the plan is 10%. On January 1, 2015, the company amends the plan so that prior service costs of $175,000 are created. Other data related to the plan are:

	2014	2015
Service costs	$ 75,000	$ 85,000
Prior service costs amortization	–0–	12,000
Contributions (funding) to the plan	45,000	35,000
Benefits paid	40,000	45,000
Actual return on plan assets	140,000	120,000
Expected rate of return on assets	8%	6%

Instructions

(a) Prepare a worksheet for the postretirement plan in 2014.

(b) Prepare any journal entries related to the postretirement plan that would be needed at December 31, 2014.

(c) Prepare a worksheet for 2015 and any journal entries related to the postretirement plan as of December 31, 2015.

(d) Indicate the postretirement-benefit–related amounts reported in the 2015 financial statements.

PROBLEMS SET B

See the book's companion website, at **www.wiley.com/college/kieso**, for an additional set of problems.

CONCEPTS FOR ANALYSIS

CA20-1 (Pension Terminology and Theory) Many business organizations have been concerned with providing for the retirement of employees since the late 1800s. During recent decades, a marked increase in this concern has resulted in the establishment of private pension plans in most large companies and in many medium- and small-sized ones.

The substantial growth of these plans, both in numbers of employees covered and in amounts of retirement benefits, has increased the significance of pension costs in relation to the financial position, results of operations, and cash flows of many companies. In examining the costs of pension plans, a CPA encounters certain terms. The components of pension costs that the terms represent must be dealt with appropriately if generally accepted accounting principles are to be reflected in the financial statements of entities with pension plans.

Instructions

(a) Define a private pension plan. How does a contributory pension plan differ from a noncontributory plan?

(b) Differentiate between "accounting for the employer" and "accounting for the pension fund."

(c) Explain the terms "funded" and "pension liability" as they relate to:
   (1) The pension fund.
   (2) The employer.

(d) (1) Discuss the theoretical justification for accrual recognition of pension costs.
   (2) Discuss the relative objectivity of the measurement process of accrual versus cash (pay-as-you-go) accounting for annual pension costs.

(e) Distinguish among the following as they relate to pension plans.
   (1) Service cost.
   (2) Prior service costs.
   (3) Vested benefits.

CA20-2 (Pension Terminology) The following items appear on Brueggen Company's financial statements.
   1. Under the caption Assets:
      Pension asset/liability.
   2. Under the caption Liabilities:
      Pension asset/liability.
   3. Under the caption Stockholders' Equity:
      Prior service cost as a component of Accumulated Other Comprehensive Income.
   4. On the income statement:
      Pension expense.

Instructions

Explain the significance of each of the items above on corporate financial statements. (*Note:* All items set forth above are not necessarily to be found on the statements of a single company.)

CA20-3 (Basic Terminology) In examining the costs of pension plans, Helen Kaufman, CPA, encounters certain terms. The components of pension costs that the terms represent must be dealt with appropriately if generally accepted accounting principles are to be reflected in the financial statements of entities with pension plans.

Instructions

(a) (1) Discuss the theoretical justification for accrual recognition of pension costs.
   (2) Discuss the relative objectivity of the measurement process of accrual versus cash (pay-as-you-go) accounting for annual pension costs.

(b) Explain the following terms as they apply to accounting for pension plans.
   (1) Market-related asset value.
   (2) Projected benefit obligation.
   (3) Corridor approach.

(c) What information should be disclosed about a company's pension plans in its financial statements and its notes?

(AICPA adapted)

CA20-4 (Major Pension Concepts) Davis Corporation is a medium-sized manufacturer of paperboard containers and boxes. The corporation sponsors a noncontributory, defined benefit pension plan that covers its 250 employees. Sid Cole has recently been hired as president of Davis Corporation. While reviewing last year's financial statements with Carol Dilbeck, controller, Cole expressed confusion about several of the items in the footnote to the financial statements relating to the pension plan. In part, the footnote reads as follows.

> **Note J.** The company has a defined benefit pension plan covering substantially all of its employees. The benefits are based on years of service and the employee's compensation during the last four years of employment. The company's funding policy is to contribute annually the maximum amount allowed under the federal tax code. Contributions are intended to provide for benefits expected to be earned in the future as well as those earned to date.

The net periodic pension expense on Davis Corporation's comparative income statement was $72,000 in 2014 and $57,680 in 2013.

The following are selected figures from the plan's funded status and amounts recognized in the Davis Corporation's Statement of Financial Position at December 31, 2014 ($000 omitted).

Actuarial present value of benefit obligations:	
Accumulated benefit obligation	
(including vested benefits of $636)	$ (870)
Projected benefit obligation	$(1,200)
Plan assets at fair value	1,050
Projected benefit obligation in	
excess of plan assets	$ (150)

Given that Davis Corporation's work force has been stable for the last 6 years, Cole could not understand the increase in the net periodic pension expense. Dilbeck explained that the net periodic pension expense consists of several elements, some of which may increase or decrease the net expense.

Instructions
(a) The determination of the net periodic pension expense is a function of five elements. List and briefly describe each of the elements.
(b) Describe the major difference and the major similarity between the accumulated benefit obligation and the projected benefit obligation.
(c) (1) Explain why pension gains and losses are not recognized on the income statement in the period in which they arise.
    (2) Briefly describe how pension gains and losses are recognized.

(CMA adapted)

CA20-5 (Implications of GAAP Rules on Pensions) Jill Vogel and Pete Dell have to do a class presentation on GAAP rules for reporting pension information. In developing the class presentation, they decided to provide the class with a series of questions related to pensions and then discuss the answers in class. Given that the class has all read the rules related to pension accounting and reporting, they felt this approach would provide a lively discussion. Here are the questions:

1. In an article in *BusinessWeek* prior to new rules related to pensions, it was reported that the discount rates used by the largest 200 companies for pension reporting ranged from 5% to 11%. How can such a situation exist, and does GAAP alleviate this problem?
2. An article indicated that when new GAAP rules were issued related to pensions, it caused an increase in the liability for pensions for approximately 20% of companies. Why might this situation occur?
3. A recent article noted that while "smoothing" is not necessarily an accounting virtue, pension accounting has long been recognized as an exception—an area of accounting in which at least some dampening of market swings is appropriate. This is because pension funds are managed so that their performance is insulated from the extremes of short-term market swings. A pension expense that reflects the volatility of market swings might, for that reason, convey information of little relevance. Are these statements true?

4. Understanding the impact of the changes required in pension reporting requires detailed information about its pension plan(s) and an analysis of the relationship of many factors, particularly the:
   (a) Type of plan(s) and any significant amendments.
   (b) Plan participants.
   (c) Funding status.
   (d) Actuarial funding method and assumptions currently used.
   What impact does each of these items have on financial statement presentation?

5. An article noted "You also need to decide whether to amortize gains and losses using the corridor method, or to use some other systematic method. Under the corridor approach, only gains and losses in excess of 10% of the greater of the projected benefit obligation or the plan assets would have to be amortized." What is the corridor method and what is its purpose?

Instructions
What answers do you believe Jill and Pete gave to each of these questions?

CA20-6 (Gains and Losses, Corridor Amortization) Vickie Plato, accounting clerk in the personnel office of Streisand Corp., has begun to compute pension expense for 2016 but is not sure whether or not she should include the amortization of unrecognized gains/losses. She is currently working with the following beginning-of-the-year present values for the projected benefit obligation and market-related values for the pension plan:

	Projected Benefit Obligation	Plan Assets Value
2013	$2,200,000	$1,900,000
2014	2,400,000	2,500,000
2015	2,900,000	2,600,000
2016	3,900,000	3,000,000

The average remaining service life per employee in 2013 and 2014 is 10 years and in 2015 and 2016 is 12 years. The net gain or loss that occurred during each year is as follows.

2013	$280,000 loss
2014	85,000 loss
2015	12,000 loss
2016	25,000 gain

(In working the solution, you must aggregate the unrecognized gains and losses to arrive at year-end balances.)

Instructions
You are the manager in charge of accounting. Write a memo to Vickie Plato, explaining why in some years she must amortize some of the net gains and losses and in other years she does not need to. In order to explain this situation fully, you must compute the amount of net gain or loss that is amortized and charged to pension expense in each of the 4 years listed above. Include an appropriate amortization schedule, referring to it whenever necessary.

CA20-7 (Nonvested Employees—An Ethical Dilemma) Thinken Technology recently merged with College Electronix (CE), a computer graphics manufacturing firm. In performing a comprehensive audit of CE's accounting system, Gerald Ott, internal audit manager for Thinken Technology, discovered that the new subsidiary did not record pension assets and liabilities, subject to GAAP.

The net present value of CE's pension assets was $15.5 million, the vested benefit obligation was $12.9 million, and the projected benefit obligation was $17.4 million. Ott reported this audit finding to Julie Habbe, the newly appointed controller of CE. A few days later, Habbe called Ott for his advice on what to do. Habbe started her conversation by asking, "Can't we eliminate the negative income effect of our pension dilemma simply by terminating the employment of nonvested employees before the end of our fiscal year?"

Instructions
How should Ott respond to Habbe's remark about firing nonvested employees?

USING YOUR JUDGMENT

FINANCIAL REPORTING

Financial Reporting Problem

P&G

The Procter & Gamble Company (P&G)

The financial statements of **P&G** are presented in Appendix 5B. The company's complete annual report, including the notes to the financial statements, can be accessed at the book's companion website, **www.wiley.com/college/kieso**.

Instructions

Refer to P&G's financial statements and the accompanying notes to answer the following questions.

(a) What kind of pension plan does P&G provide its employees in the United States?

(b) What was P&G's pension expense for 2011, 2010, and 2009 for the United States?

(c) What is the impact of P&G's pension plans for 2011 on its financial statements?

(d) What information does P&G provide on the target allocation of its pension assets? (Compare the asset allocation for "Pensions and Other Retiree Benefits.") How do the allocations relate to the expected returns on these assets?

Comparative Analysis Case

The Coca-Cola Company and PepsiCo, Inc.

Instructions

Go to the book's companion website and use information found there to answer the following questions related to **The Coca-Cola Company** and **PepsiCo, Inc.**

(a) What kind of pension plans do Coca-Cola and PepsiCo provide their employees?

(b) What net periodic pension expense (cost) did Coca-Cola and PepsiCo report in 2011?

(c) What is the year-end 2011 funded status of Coca-Cola's and PepsiCo's U.S. plans?

(d) What relevant rates were used by Coca-Cola and PepsiCo in computing their pension amounts?

(e) Compare the expected benefit payments and contributions for Coca-Cola and PepsiCo.

*Financial Statement Analysis Case

General Electric

A *Wall Street Journal* article discussed a $1.8 billion charge to income made by **General Electric** for post-retirement benefit costs. It was attributed to previously unrecognized healthcare and life insurance cost. As financial vice president and controller for Peake, Inc., you found this article interesting because the president recently expressed interest in adopting a postemployment benefit program for Peake's employees, to complement the company's existing defined benefit plan. The president, Martha Beyerlein, wants to know how the expense on the new plan will be determined and what impact the accounting for the plan will have on Peake's financial statements.

Instructions

(a) As financial vice president and controller of Peake, Inc., explain the calculation of postemployment benefit expense under GAAP, and indicate how the accounting for the plan will affect Peake's financial statements.

(b) Discuss the similarities and differences in the accounting for the other postemployment benefit plan relative to the accounting for the defined benefit plan.

Accounting, Analysis, and Principles

PENCOMP's balance sheet at December 31, 2014, is as follows.

PENCOMP, INC.
BALANCE SHEET
AS OF DECEMBER 31, 2014

Assets		*Liabilities*	
Cash	$ 438	Notes payable	$1,000
Inventory	1,800	Pension liability	344
Total current assets	2,238	Total liabilities	1,344
Plant and equipment	2,000	*Stockholders' equity*	
Accumulated depreciation	(240)	Common stock	2,000
	1,760	Retained earnings	896
Total assets	$3,998	Accumulated other comprehensive income	(242)
		Total stockholders' equity	2,654
		Total liabilities and stockholders' equity	$3,998

Additional information concerning PENCOMP's defined benefit pension plan is as follows.

Projected benefit obligation at 12/31/14	$ 820.5
Plan assets (fair value) at 12/31/14	476.5
Unamortized past service cost at 12/31/14	150.0
Amortization of past service cost during 2015	15.0
Service cost for 2015	42.0
Discount rate	10%
Expected rate of return on plan assets in 2015	12%
Actual return on plan assets in 2015	10.4
Contributions to pension fund in 2015	70.0
Benefits paid during 2015	40.0
Unamortized net loss due to changes in actuarial assumptions and deferred net losses on plan assets at 12/31/14	92.0
Expected remaining service life of employees	15.0
Average period to vesting of prior service costs	10.0

Other information about PENCOMP is as follows.

Salary expense, all paid with cash during 2015	$ 700.0
Sales, all for cash	3,000.0
Purchases, all for cash	2,000.0
Inventory at 12/31/15	1,800.0

Property originally cost $2,000 and is depreciated on a straight-line basis over 25 years with no residual value.

Interest on the note payable is 10% annually and is paid in cash on 12/31 of each year.

Dividends declared and paid are $200 in 2015.

Accounting

Prepare an income statement for 2015 and a balance sheet as of December 31, 2015. Also, prepare the pension expense journal entry for the year ended December 31, 2015. Round to the nearest tenth (e.g., round 2.87 to 2.9).

Analysis

Compute return on equity for PENCOMP for 2015 (assume stockholders' equity is equal to year-end average stockholders' equity). Do you think an argument can be made for including some or even all of the change in accumulated other comprehensive income (due to pensions) in the numerator of return on equity? Illustrate that calculation.

Principles

Explain a rationale for why the FASB has (so far) decided to exclude from the current period income statement the effects of pension plan amendments and gains and losses due to changes in actuarial assumptions.

BRIDGE TO THE PROFESSION

 ## Professional Research: FASB Codification

Monat Company has grown rapidly since its founding in 2004. To instill loyalty in its employees, Monat is contemplating establishment of a defined benefit plan. Monat knows that lenders and potential investors will pay close attention to the impact of the pension plan on the company's financial statements, particularly any gains or losses that develop in the plan. Monat has asked you to conduct some research on the accounting for gains and losses in a defined benefit plan.

Instructions

If your school has a subscription to the FASB Codification, go to *http://aaahq.org/ascLogin.cfm* to log in and prepare responses to the following. Provide Codification references for your responses.

(a) Briefly describe how pension gains and losses are accounted for.

(b) Explain the rationale behind the accounting method described in part (a).

(c) What is the related pension asset or liability that will show up on the balance sheet? When will each of these situations occur?

Additional Professional Resources

See the book's companion website, at **www.wiley.com/college/kieso**, for professional simulations as well as other study resources.

 IFRS INSIGHTS

LEARNING OBJECTIVE **12**
Compare the accounting for pensions under GAAP and IFRS.

The accounting for various forms of compensation plans under IFRS is found in *IAS 19* ("Employee Benefits") and *IFRS 2* ("Share-Based Payment"). *IAS 19* addresses the accounting for a wide range of compensation elements—wages, bonuses, postretirement benefits, and compensated absences. The underlying concepts for the accounting for postretirement benefits are similar between GAAP and IFRS—both GAAP and IFRS view pensions and other postretirement benefits as forms of deferred compensation. At present, there are significant differences in the specific accounting provisions as applied to these plans.

RELEVANT FACTS

Following are the key similarities and differences between GAAP and IFRS related to pensions.

Similarities

- IFRS and GAAP separate pension plans into defined contribution plans and defined benefit plans. The accounting for defined contribution plans is similar.

- IFRS and GAAP recognize a pension asset or liability as the funded status of the plan (i.e., defined benefit obligation minus the fair value of plan assets). (Note that defined benefit obligation is referred to as the projected benefit obligation in GAAP.)

- IFRS and GAAP compute unrecognized past service cost (PSC) (referred to as prior service cost in GAAP) in the same manner. However, IFRS recognizes past service cost as a component of pension expense in income immediately. GAAP amortizes PSC over the remaining service lives of employees.

Differences

- IFRS and GAAP include interest expense on the liability in pension expense. Regarding asset returns, IFRS reduces pension expense by the amount of interest revenue (based on the discount rate times the beginning value of pension assets). GAAP includes an asset return component based on the expected return on plan assets.

- Under IFRS, companies recognize both liability and asset gains and losses (referred to as remeasurements) in other comprehensive income. These gains and losses are not "recycled" into income in subsequent periods. GAAP recognizes liability and asset gains and losses in "Accumulated other comprehensive income" and amortizes these amounts to income over remaining service lives, using the "corridor approach."

- The accounting for pensions and other postretirement benefit plans is the same under IFRS. GAAP has separate standards for these types of benefits, and significant differences exist in the accounting.

ABOUT THE NUMBERS

Accounting for Pensions

Net Defined Benefit Obligation (Asset)

As in GAAP, under IFRS the **net defined benefit liability** (asset) is the deficit or surplus related to a defined benefit pension plan. The deficit or surplus is measured as follows.

Defined Benefit Obligation − Fair Value of Plan Assets (if any)

The deficit or surplus is often referred to as the **funded status** of the plan.

If the defined benefit obligation is greater than the plan assets, the pension plan has a deficit. Conversely, if the defined pension obligation is less than the plan assets, the pension plan has a surplus. Illustration IFRS20-1 shows these relationships.

Deficit		Surplus	
Defined benefit obligation	$1,000,000	Defined benefit obligation	$150,000
Plan assets	900,000	Plan assets	200,000
Net defined benefit obligation	$ 100,000	Net defined benefit asset	$ 50,000

ILLUSTRATION IFRS20-1
Presentation of Funded Status

The net defined benefit obligation (asset) is often referred to simply as the pension liability or the pension asset on the statement of financial position.

As indicated, companies should report either a pension asset or pension liability related to a pension plan on the statement of financial position (often referred to as the **net approach**). To illustrate, assume that at year-end Acer Company has a defined pension obligation of $4,000,000 and plan assets of $3,700,000. In this case, Acer reports $300,000 ($4,000,000 − $3,700,000) as a pension liability on its statement of financial position.

Some believe that companies should report separately both the defined benefit obligation and the plan assets on the statement of financial position. This approach (often referred to as the **gross approach**) would report Acer's defined benefit obligation of $4,000,000 and its plan assets of $3,700,000 on the statement of financial position. The IASB disagrees, indicating that offsetting these amounts is consistent with its standard on when assets and liabilities should be netted.[28]

[28]*IAS 32* states that a financial asset and a financial liability should be offset and the net amount reported in the statement of financial position when a company (a) has a legally enforceable right to set off the recognized amounts and (b) intends either to settle on a net basis, or to realize the asset and settle it simultaneously.

Reporting Changes in the Defined Benefit Obligation (Asset)

The IASB requires that all changes in the defined benefit obligation and plan assets in the current period be recognized in comprehensive income. The Board believes that immediate recognition of the effects of these changes in the statement of comprehensive income provides the most understandable and useful information to financial statement users. The IASB requires that companies report changes arising from different elements of pension liabilities and assets in different sections of the statement of comprehensive income, depending on their nature.

In the past, companies often reported only a single pension expense number in the comprehensive income statement. Providing additional segmentation of the **components of pension cost** provides additional transparency about the nature of these costs. The three components are as follows.

- *Service cost.* **Service cost** is either current service cost or past service cost. Current service cost is the increase in the present value of the defined benefit obligation from employee service in the current period. Past service cost is the change in the present value of the defined benefit obligation for employee service for prior periods—generally resulting from a plan amendment (e.g., changes to the plan). This component is reported in the statement of comprehensive income in the operating section of the statement and affects net income.

- *Net interest.* Net interest is computed by multiplying the discount rate by the funded status of the plan (defined benefit obligation minus plan assets). If the plan has a net defined benefit obligation at the end of the period, the company reports interest expense. Conversely, if it has a net defined benefit asset, it reports interest revenue. This approach is justified on the basis of its simplicity and that any financing costs should be based on the funded status of the plan. This amount is often shown below the operating section of the income statement in the financing section and affects net income.

- *Remeasurements.* Remeasurements are gains and losses related to the defined benefit obligation (changes in discount rate or other actuarial assumptions) and gains or losses on the fair value of the plan assets (actual rate of return less interest revenue included in the finance component). This component is reported in other comprehensive income, net of tax. **These remeasurement gains or losses therefore affect comprehensive income but not net income.**

Illustration IFRS20-2 shows the components of changes in the pension liability (asset) and their placement on the statement of comprehensive income.

ILLUSTRATION IFRS20-2

Reporting Changes in the Pension Obligation (Assets)

As indicated in Illustration IFRS20-2, service cost and net interest are reported in net income. We discuss determination of each of these components in the following section. Remeasurements, which are reported in other comprehensive income, are discussed in a later section.

Service Cost. To determine current service cost and the related increase in the defined benefit obligation, companies must:

1. Apply an actuarial valuation method.
2. Assign benefits to period of service.
3. Make actuarial assumptions.[29]

In applying an actuarial valuation method, the IASB concluded that **companies must consider future compensation levels in measuring the present obligation and periodic pension expense if the plan benefit formula incorporates them.** In other words, the present obligation resulting from a promise to pay a benefit of 1 percent of an employee's **final pay** differs from the promise to pay 1 percent of **current pay**. To overlook this fact is to ignore an important aspect of pension expense. Thus, the Board adopts the *projected unit credit method* (**often referred to as the** *benefits/years-of-service method*), **which determines pension expense based on future salary levels.**

Some object to this determination, arguing that a company should have more freedom to select an expense recognition pattern. Others believe that incorporating future salary increases into current pension expense is accounting for events that have not yet happened. They argue that if a company terminates the plan today, it pays only liabilities for accumulated benefits. **Nevertheless, the IASB indicates that the defined benefit obligation provides a more realistic measure of the employer's obligation under the plan on a going concern basis and, therefore, companies should use it as the basis for determining service cost.**

The assignment of benefits to periods of service is based on the actuarial valuation method. The actuary then allocates the cost of the pension benefits over the expected service life of the company's employees. In determining the proper service cost for a period, the actuary makes actuarial assumptions related to such factors as mortality; rates of employee turnover, disability, and early retirement; discount rate; benefit levels; and future salary levels. While *IAS 19* does not require use of an actuary, given the complexity of these estimates, just about all companies rely on an actuary to determine service cost and related other defined benefit measures.

Net Interest. In computing net interest, companies assume that the discount rate, the net defined benefit obligation, and the pension asset are determined at the beginning of the year.[30] The **discount rate** is based on the yields of high-quality bonds with terms consistent with the company's pension obligation. Net interest is then computed as indicated in the following equation.

Net Interest = (Defined Benefit Obligation × Discount Rate) − (Plan Assets × Discount Rate)

---

[29] As indicated earlier, service cost is comprised of current and past service cost. Determination of past service cost is based on the same actuarial valuation model as that used for current service cost. We discuss recognition of past service cost in a later section.

[30] The IASB indicates that if the beginning of the year amount changes materially (due to contributions to or payments out of the plan), an adjustment to the beginning balances should be made. *For homework purposes, unless information indicates that balances have changed materially, use the beginning of the year balances.*

That is, net interest is determined by multiplying the net defined pension obligation (asset) by the discount rate.

Because payment of the pension obligation is deferred, companies record the pension liability on a discounted basis. As a result, the liability accrues interest over the service life of the employee (passage of time), which is essentially interest expense (**interest on the liability**). Similarly, companies earn a return on their plan assets. That is, a company assumes that it earns interest based on multiplying the discount rate by the plan assets. While the IASB recognizes that the actual return on plan assets may differ from the assumed interest revenue computed, it believes that the change in plan assets can be divided into an amount that arises from the passage of time and amounts that arise from other changes. As we discuss in the next section, changes not related to the passage of time are reported in other comprehensive income as remeasurements. Thus, the growth in the plan assets should mirror the growth in the defined benefit obligation. In other words, the assumed interest revenue on the plan assets based on the passage of time offsets the interest expense on the defined benefit obligation.

In summary, pension expense is comprised of two components: (1) service cost and (2) net interest. Companies report each of these components in the statement of comprehensive income. In some cases, companies may choose to report these components in one section of the statement of comprehensive income and report total pension expense. Other companies may choose to report the service cost component in operating income and the net interest in a separate section related to financing.[31]

Plan Assets and Actual Return

Pension **plan assets** are usually investments in shares, bonds, other securities, and real estate that a company holds to earn a reasonable rate of return. Plan assets are reported at fair value. Companies generally hold these assets in a separate legal entity (a pension fund) that exists only to administer the employee benefit plan. These assets held by the pension fund are therefore not available to the company's own creditors (even in bankruptcy). Employer contributions and the actual return on plan assets increase pension plan assets. **Actual return on plan assets** is the increase in the pension fund assets arising from interest, dividends, and realized and unrealized changes in the fair value of the plan. Benefits paid to retired employees decrease plan assets.

To illustrate, assume that Hasbro Company has pension plan assets of $4,200,000 on January 1, 2014. During 2014, Hasbro contributed $300,000 to the plan and paid out retirement benefits of $250,000. Its actual return on plan assets was $210,000 for the year. Hasbro's plan assets at December 31, 2014, are $4,460,000, computed as shown in Illustration IFRS20-3.

ILLUSTRATION IFRS20-3
Determination of Pension Assets

Plan assets, January 1, 2014	$4,200,000
Contributions by Hasbro to plan	300,000
Actual return	210,000
Benefits paid to employees	(250,000)
Plan assets, December 31, 2014	$4,460,000

In some cases, companies compute the actual return by adjusting the change in plan assets for the effect of contributions during the year and benefits paid during the year. The equation in Illustration IFRS20-4, or a variation thereof, can be used to compute the actual return.

[31]The IASB does not provide guidance on which of these two approaches is preferred. *For homework purposes, report pension expense as a single total in income from operations in the statement of comprehensive income.*

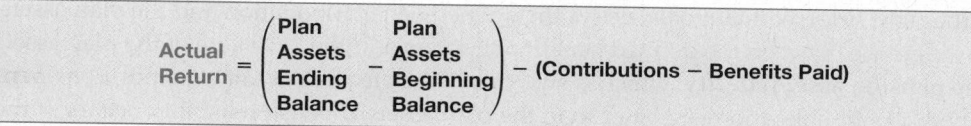

ILLUSTRATION
IFRS20-4
Equation for Computing
Actual Return

Stated another way, the actual return on plan assets is the difference between the fair value of the plan assets at the beginning of the period and at the end of the period, adjusted for contributions and benefit payments. Illustration IFRS20-5 uses the equation above to compute actual return, using the information provided in Illustration IFRS20-3.

Plan assets, December 31, 2014		$4,460,000
Plan assets, January 1, 2014		(4,200,000)
Increase in fair value of plan assets		260,000
Deduct: Contributions to plan	$300,000	
Add: Benefit payments to employees	250,000	(50,000)
Actual return		$ 210,000

ILLUSTRATION
IFRS20-5
Computation of Actual
Return on Plan Assets

In this case, Hasbro has a positive actual return on plan assets. Recently, some pension plans have experienced negative actual returns due to the increased volatility in global securities markets.

Using a Pension Worksheet

We will now illustrate the basic computation of pension expense using the first two components: (1) service cost and (2) net interest. We discuss remeasurements in later sections.

Companies often use a worksheet to record pension-related information. As its name suggests, the worksheet is a working tool. A worksheet is **not** a permanent accounting record: It is neither a journal nor part of the general ledger. The worksheet is merely a device to make it easier to prepare entries and the financial statements.[32] Illustration IFRS20-6 shows the format of the **pension worksheet**.

ILLUSTRATION
IFRS20-6
Basic Format of Pension
Worksheet

	General Journal Entries			Memo Record	
Items	Annual Pension Expense	Cash	Pension Asset/ Liability	Defined Benefit Obligation	Plan Assets

The "General Journal Entries" columns of the worksheet (near the left side) determine the entries to record in the formal general ledger accounts. The "Memo Record" columns

[32]The use of a pension entry worksheet is recommended and illustrated by Paul B. W. Miller, "The New Pension Accounting (Part 2)," *Journal of Accountancy* (February 1987), pp. 86–94.

(on the right side) maintain balances in the defined benefit obligation and the plan assets. The difference between the defined benefit obligation and the fair value of the plan assets is the **pension asset/liability**, which is shown in the statement of financial position. If the defined benefit obligation is greater than the plan assets, a pension liability occurs. If the defined benefit obligation is less than the plan assets, a pension asset occurs.

On the first line of the worksheet, a company enters the beginning balances (if any). It then records subsequent transactions and events related to the pension plan using debits and credits, using both sets of columns as if they were one. For each transaction or event, the debits must equal the credits. **The ending balance in the Pension Asset/ Liability column should equal the net balance in the memo record.**

2014 Entries and Worksheet

To illustrate the use of a worksheet and how it helps in accounting for a pension plan, assume that on January 1, 2014, Zarle Company provides the following information related to its pension plan for the year 2014.

> Plan assets, January 1, 2014, are $100,000.
>
> Defined benefit obligation, January 1, 2014, is $100,000.
>
> Annual service cost is $9,000.
>
> Discount rate is 10 percent.
>
> Funding contributions are $8,000.
>
> Benefits paid to retirees during the year are $7,000.

Using the data presented above, the worksheet in Illustration IFRS20-7 presents the beginning balances and all of the pension entries recorded by Zarle in 2014. Zarle records the beginning balances for the defined benefit obligation and the pension plan assets on the first line of the worksheet in the memo record. Because the defined benefit obligation and the plan assets are the same at January 1, 2014, the Pension Asset/Liability account has a zero balance at January 1, 2014.

Entry (a) in Illustration IFRS20-7 records the service cost component, which increases pension expense by $9,000 and increases the liability (defined benefit obligation)

ILLUSTRATION IFRS20-7
Pension Worksheet—2014

	General Journal Entries			Memo Record	
Items	Annual Pension Expense	Cash	Pension Asset/ Liability	Defined Benefit Obligation	Plan Assets
Balance, Jan. 1, 2014			—	100,000 Cr.	100,000 Dr.
(a) Service cost	9,000 Dr.			9,000 Cr.	
(b) Interest expense	10,000 Dr.			10,000 Cr.	
(c) Interest revenue	10,000 Cr.				10,000 Dr.
(d) Contributions		8,000 Cr.			8,000 Dr.
(e) Benefits				7,000 Dr.	7,000 Cr.
Journal entry for 2014	9,000 Dr.	8,000 Cr.	1,000 Cr.*		
Balance, Dec. 31, 2014			1,000 Cr.**	112,000 Cr.	111,000 Dr.
*$9,000 − $8,000 = $1,000					
**$112,000 − $111,000 = $1.000					

by $9,000. Entry (b) accrues the interest expense component, which increases both the liability and the pension expense by $10,000 (the beginning defined benefit obligation multiplied by the discount rate of 10 percent). Entry (c) records the interest revenue component, which increases plan assets and decreases pension expense by $10,000. This is computed by multiplying the beginning plan assets by the discount rate of 10 percent. As a result, net interest expense (income) is zero in 2014. Entry (d) records Zarle's contribution (funding) of assets to the pension fund, thereby decreasing cash by $8,000 and increasing plan assets by $8,000. Entry (e) records the benefit payments made to retirees, which results in equal $7,000 decreases to the plan assets and the defined benefit obligation.

Zarle makes the "formal journal entry" on December 31, which records the pension expense in 2014, as follows.

2014

Pension Expense	9,000	
Cash		8,000
Pension Asset/Liability		1,000

The credit to Pension Asset/Liability for $1,000 represents the difference between the 2014 pension expense of $9,000 and the amount funded of $8,000. Pension Asset/Liability (credit) is a liability because Zarle underfunds the plan by $1,000. The Pension Asset/Liability account balance of $1,000 also equals the net of the balances in the memo accounts. Illustration IFRS20-8 shows that the defined benefit obligation exceeds the plan assets by $1,000, which reconciles to the pension liability reported in the statement of financial position.

Defined benefit obligation (Credit)	$(112,000)
Plan assets at fair value (Debit)	111,000
Pension asset/liability (Credit)	$ (1,000)

ILLUSTRATION IFRS20-8
Pension Reconciliation Schedule—December 31, 2014

If the net of the memo record balances is a credit, the reconciling amount in the Pension Asset/Liability column will be a credit equal in amount. If the net of the memo record balances is a debit, the Pension Asset/Liability amount will be a debit equal in amount. The worksheet is designed to produce this reconciling feature, which is useful later in the preparation of the financial statements and required note disclosure related to pensions.

In this illustration (for 2014), the debit to Pension Expense exceeds the credit to Cash, resulting in a credit to Pension Asset/Liability—the recognition of a liability. If the credit to Cash exceeded the debit to Pension Expense, Zarle would debit Pension Asset/Liability—the recognition of an asset.[33]

Past Service Cost

Past service cost is the change in the present value of the defined benefit obligation resulting from a plan amendment or a curtailment.[34] For example, a plan amendment arises when a company decides to provide additional benefits to existing employees

[33]The IASB in *IAS 19* limits the amount of a pension asset that is recognized, based on a recoverability test. This test, which has been further clarified in *IFRIC 14*, limits the amount of the pension asset to the sum of unrecognized actuarial gains and losses (discussed later) and amounts that will be received by the company in the form of refunds or reduction of future contributions. *For purposes of homework, assume that a pension asset, if present, meets the criteria for full recognition.*

[34]The IASB also indicates that gains and losses on non-routine settlements are considered past service costs. A **settlement** is a payment of benefits that is not set out in the terms of the plan.

for past service. Conversely, the company may decide that it is necessary to reduce its benefit package retroactively for existing employees, thereby reducing their pension benefit. A **curtailment** occurs when the company has a significant reduction in the number of employees covered by the plan. Because a curtailment has the same effect as a reduction in benefits due to an amendment to the plan, these situations are accounted for in the same way. Illustration IFRS20-9 summarizes the nature of past service costs.

ILLUSTRATION IFRS20-9
Types of Past Service Costs

PAST SERVICE COSTS (EXPENSE IN CURRENT PERIOD)	
Plan Amendments	Curtailments
• Introduction of a plan. • Withdrawal of a plan. • Changes to a plan.	• Significant reduction in the number of employees covered by the plan.

The accounting for past service cost is straightforward—expense past service cost in the period of the amendment or curtailment. As a result, a substantial increase (decrease) in pension expense and the defined benefit obligation often results when a plan amendment or curtailment occurs. Because current and past service costs relate directly to employment, they are reported in the operating section of the statement of comprehensive income.

Some disagree with the IASB position of expensing these costs in the year a plan is amended or curtailed. They argue that a company would not provide these additional benefits for past years of service unless it expects to receive benefits in the future. According to this reasoning, a company should not recognize the full past service cost in the year of the amendment. Instead, the past service cost should be spread out over the remaining service life of employees who are expected to benefit from the changes in the plan. Others believe that if they are truly past service costs, they should be treated retroactively as an adjustment made to prior periods.

However, the IASB decided that any changes in the defined benefit obligation or plan assets should be recognized in the current period. To do otherwise is not informative and leads to delayed recognition of costs or reduced benefits which are neither assets nor liabilities.

It is also possible to decrease past service costs by decreasing the defined benefit obligation (referred to as negative past service cost). Negative past service cost arises when an entity changes the benefits attributable to past service cost so that the present value of the defined benefit obligation decreases. In that case, pension expense is decreased. Both positive (increased pension expense) and negative (decreased pension expense) past service cost adjustments are handled in the same manner; that is, adjust pension expense immediately.

2015 Entries and Worksheet

Continuing the Zarle Company illustration into 2015, we note that the company amends the pension plan on January 1, 2015, to grant employees past service benefits with a present value of $81,600. The following additional facts apply to the pension plan for the year 2015.

Annual service cost is $9,500.

Discount rate is 10 percent.

Annual funding contributions are $20,000.

Benefits paid to retirees during the year are $8,000.

Illustration IFRS20-10 presents a worksheet of all the pension entries and information recorded by Zarle in 2015.

Pension Worksheet—2015.xls					
	General Journal Entries			**Memo Record**	
Items	Annual Pension Expense	Cash	Pension Asset/ Liability	Defined Benefit Obligation	Plan Assets
Balance, Dec. 31, 2014			1,000 Cr.	112,000 Cr.	111,000 Dr.
(f) Additional PSC, 1/1/2015	81,600 Dr.			81,600 Cr.	
Balance, Jan. 1, 2015				193,600 Cr.	
(g) Service cost	9,500 Dr.			9,500 Cr.	
(h) Interest expense	19,360 Dr.			19,360 Cr.	
(i) Interest revenue	11,100 Cr.				11,100 Dr.
(j) Contributions		20,000 Cr.			20,000 Dr.
(k) Benefits				8,000 Dr.	8,000 Cr.
Journal entry for 2015	99,360 Dr.	20,000 Cr.	79,360 Cr.		
Balance, Dec. 31, 2015			80,360 Cr.	214,460 Cr.	134,100 Dr.

The first line of the worksheet shows the beginning balances of the Pension Asset/ Liability account and the memo accounts. Entry (f) records Zarle's granting of past service cost, by adding $81,600 to the defined benefit obligation and to Pension Expense. Entry (g) records the current service cost; entry (h) records interest expense for the period. Because the past service cost occurred at the beginning of the year, interest is computed on the January 1, 2015, balance of the defined benefit obligation, adjusted for the past service cost. Interest expense is therefore $19,360 ($193,600 × 10%). Entry (i) records interest revenue for the period of $11,100 ($111,000 × 10%). Entries (j) and (k) are similar to the corresponding entries in 2014.

Zarle makes the following journal entry on December 31 to formally record the 2015 pension expense—the sum of the annual pension expense column.

2015		
Pension Expense	99,360	
Cash		20,000
Pension Asset/Liability		79,360

Because the expense exceeds the funding, Zarle credits the Pension Asset/Liability account for the $79,360 difference. That account is a liability. In 2015, as in 2014, the balance of the Pension Asset/Liability account ($80,360) is equal to the net of the balances in the memo accounts, as shown in Illustration IFRS20-11.

Defined benefit obligation (Credit)	$(214,460)
Plan assets at fair value (Debit)	134,100
Pension asset/liability (Credit)	$ (80,360)

The **reconciliation** is the formula that makes the worksheet work. It relates the components of pension accounting, recorded and unrecorded, to one another.

Remeasurements

Of great concern to companies that have pension plans are the uncontrollable and unexpected swings that can result from (1) sudden and large changes in the fair value of plan assets and (2) changes in actuarial assumptions that affect the amount of the defined benefit obligation. How should these changes (referred to as **remeasurements**) affect the financial statements, most notably pension expense? The IASB believes that the most informative way is to recognize the remeasurement in other comprehensive income. The rationale for this reporting is that the predictive nature of remeasurements is much different than the other two components of pension benefit cost—service cost and net interest.

Remeasurements are generally of two types:

1. Gains and losses on plan assets.
2. Gains and losses on the defined benefit obligation.

Asset Gains and Losses. The gains and losses on plan assets (referred to as **asset gains and losses**) is the difference between the actual return and the interest revenue computed in determining net interest. Asset gains occur when actual returns exceed the interest revenue. Asset losses occur when the actual returns are less than interest revenue. To illustrate, assume that Shopbob Company has plan assets at January 1, 2014, of $100,000. The discount rate for the year is 6 percent, and the actual return on the plan assets for 2014 is $8,000. In 2014, Shopbob should record an asset gain of $2,000, computed as follows.

ILLUSTRATION IFRS20-12
Computation of Asset Gain

Actual return	$8,000
Less: Interest revenue ($100,000 × 6%)	6,000
Asset gain	$2,000

Shopbob therefore debits plan assets for the asset gain of $2,000 and credits Other Comprehensive Income (G/L) for the same amount. If interest revenue exceeds the actual return, Shopbob debits Other Comprehensive Income (G/L) for the asset loss and credits plan assets.

Liability Gains and Losses. In estimating the defined benefit obligation (the liability), actuaries make assumptions about such items as mortality rate, retirement rate, turnover rate, disability rate, and salary amounts. Any change in these actuarial assumptions affects the amount of the defined benefit obligation. Seldom does actual experience coincide exactly with actuarial predictions. These gains or losses from changes in the defined benefit obligation are called **liability gains and losses**.

Companies report liability gains (resulting from unexpected decreases in the liability balance) and liability losses (resulting from unexpected increases in the liability balance) in Other Comprehensive Income (G/L). Companies combine the liability gains and losses in the same Other Comprehensive Income (G/L) account used for asset gains and losses. They accumulate the asset and liability gains and losses from year to year in Accumulated Other Comprehensive Income.[35] This amount is reported on the statement of financial position in the equity section.

---

[35]The IASB is silent as to whether the account "Accumulated Other Comprehensive Income" should be used instead of another equity account, like Retained Earnings. *For homework purposes, use an Accumulated Other Comprehensive Income account.* The IASB also permits the transfer of the balance in the Accumulated Other Comprehensive Income account to other equity accounts at a later date.

2016 Entries and Worksheet

Continuing the Zarle Company illustration, the following facts apply to the pension plan for 2016.

  Annual service cost is $13,000.

  Discount rate is 10 percent.

  Actual return on plan assets is $12,000.

  Annual funding contributions are $24,000.

  Benefits paid to retirees during the year are $10,500.

  Changes in actuarial assumptions establish the end-of-year defined benefit obligation at $265,000.

The worksheet in Illustration IFRS20-13 presents all of Zarle's 2016 pension entries and related information. The first line of the worksheet records the beginning balances that relate to the pension plan. In this case, Zarle's beginning balances are the ending balances from its 2015 pension worksheet in Illustration IFRS20-10.

	Pension Worksheet—2016.xls						
Home	Insert	Page Layout	Formulas	Data	Review	View	
P18		*fx*					
	A	B	C	D	E	F	G
1							
2		**General Journal Entries**				**Memo Record**	
3		Annual			Pension	Defined	
4		Pension		OCI—	Asset/	Benefit	
5	Items	Expense	Cash	Gain/Loss	Liability	Obligation	Plan Assets
6	Balance, Jan. 1, 2016				80,360 Cr.	214,460 Cr.	134,100 Dr.
7	(l) Service cost	13,000 Dr.				13,000 Cr.	
8	(m) Interest expense	21,446 Dr.				21,446 Cr.	
9	(n) Interest revenue	13,410 Cr.					13,410 Dr.
10	(o) Contributions		24,000 Cr.				24,000 Dr.
11	(p) Benefits					10,500 Dr.	10,500 Cr.
12	(q) Asset loss			1,410 Dr.			1,410 Cr.
13	(r) Liability loss			26,594 Dr.		26,594 Cr.	
14	Journal entry for 2016	21,036 Dr.	24,000 Cr.	28,004 Dr.	25,040 Cr.		
15							
16	Accumulated OCI, Dec. 31, 2015			0			
17	Balance, Dec. 31, 2016			28,004 Dr.	105,400 Cr.	265,000 Cr.	159,600 Dr.
18							

ILLUSTRATION IFRS20-13
Pension Worksheet—2016

Entries (l), (m), (n), (o), and (p) are similar to the corresponding entries in 2014 or 2015. Entries (m) and (n) are related. Entry (m) records the interest expense of $21,446 ($214,460 × 10%). Entry (n) records interest revenue of $13,410 ($134,100 × 10%). Therefore, net interest expense is $8,036 ($21,446 − $13,410). Entries (o) and (p) are recorded similarly in 2016 as those in 2014 and 2015.

Entries (q) and (r) need additional explanation. As indicated, the actual return on plan assets for 2016 was $12,000. However, as indicated in entry (n), pension expense was decreased $13,410 as a result of multiplying the beginning plan assets by the discount rate to arrive at an assumed interest revenue of $13,410. As a result, Zarle has an asset loss of $1,410 ($13,410 − $12,000) because the assumed interest revenue is greater than the actual return. This asset loss is debited to Other Comprehensive Income (G/L) and credited to plan assets. Pension plan assets are then properly stated at their fair value.

Entry (r) records the change in the defined benefit obligation resulting from the changes in the actuarial assumptions related to this obligation. As indicated in the facts on page 1261, the actuary has determined that the ending balance in the defined benefit obligation should be $265,000 at December 31, 2016. However, the balance at December 31, 2016, before any adjustment for actuarial gains and losses related to the defined benefit obligation is $238,406, as shown in Illustration IFRS20-14.

ILLUSTRATION IFRS20-14
Defined Benefit Obligation Balance (Unadjusted)

December 31, 2015, DBO balance	$214,460
Service cost [entry (l)]	13,000
Interest expense [entry (m)]	21,446
Benefits paid [entry (p)]	(10,500)
December 31, 2016, DBO balance (before liability increases)	$238,406

The difference between the ending balance of $265,000 as determined by the actuary and the present balance of $238,406 is $26,594 (a liability loss on the defined benefit liability). This liability loss is debited to Other Comprehensive Income (G/L) and credited to the defined benefit obligation. After this worksheet adjustment, the defined benefit obligation is stated at its actuarial value of $265,000. The journal entry to record the information related to the pension plan at December 31, 2016, based on the pension worksheet in Illustration IFRS20-13, is as follows.

Pension Expense	21,036	
Other Comprehensive Income (G/L)	28,004	
Cash		24,000
Pension Asset/Liability		25,040

As the 2016 worksheet indicates, the $105,400 balance in the Pension Asset/Liability account at December 31, 2016, is equal to the net of the balances in the memo accounts. Illustration IFRS20-15 shows this computation.

ILLUSTRATION IFRS20-15
Pension Reconciliation Schedule—December 31, 2016

Defined benefit obligation (Credit)	$(265,000)
Plan assets at fair value (Debit)	159,600
Pension asset/liability	$(105,400)

Zarle carries the 2016 ending balances for Pension Asset/Liability and Accumulated Other Comprehensive Income forward as the beginning balances for pension plan accounting in 2017. These balances will be adjusted by changes in the defined benefit obligation and plan assets as shown in the prior examples. For example, assume that Zarle's pension plan had the following activity in 2017:

Service cost	$10,072	Contributions	$32,000
Pension expense	17,450	Benefits	11,000
Asset gain	13,150	Decrease in Pension Asset/Liability	27,700
Discount rate	7%		

The ending balances for the defined benefit obligation and plan assets are $282,622 and $204,922, respectively. These elements are summarized in the partial 2017 pension worksheet shown in Illustration IFRS20-16.

	General Journal Entries				Memo Record	
Items	Annual Pension Expense	Cash	OCI— Gain/Loss	Pension Asset/ Liability	Defined Benefit Obligation	Plan Assets
Balance, Jan. 1, 2017			28,004 Dr.	105,400 Cr.	265,000 Cr.	159,600 Dr.
Journal entry for 2017	17,450 Dr.	32,000 Cr.	13,150 Cr.	27,700 Dr.		
Accumulated OCI, Jan. 1, 2017			28,004 Dr.			
Balance, Dec. 31, 2017			14,854 Dr.	77,700 Cr.	282,622 Cr.	204,922 Dr.

ILLUSTRATION IFRS20-16
Partial Pension Worksheet—2017

Focusing on the "Journal Entry" row, in 2017 Zarle records pension expense of $17,450 and a decrease in Pension Asset/Liability of $27,700. The reduction in Pension Asset/Liability is due in part to the asset gain of $13,150 recorded in 2017. As a result, Zarle's 2017 ending balances (which become the 2018 beginning balances) are $77,700 for Pension Asset/Liability and Accumulated Other Comprehensive Income $14,854 (beginning Accumulated OCI of $28,004 − gain of $13,150).

ON THE HORIZON

The IASB and the FASB have been working collaboratively on a postretirement benefit project. The recent amendments issued by the IASB moves IFRS closer to GAAP with respect to recognition of the funded status on the statement of financial position. However, as illustrated in the *About the Numbers* section above, significant differences remain in the components of pension expense. The FASB is expected to begin work on a project that will reexamine expense measurement of postretirement benefit plans. The FASB likely will consider the recent IASB amendments in this area, which could lead to a converged standard.

IFRS SELF-TEST QUESTIONS

1. At the end of the current period, Oxford Ltd. has a defined benefit obligation of $195,000 and pension plan assets with a fair value of $110,000. The amount of the vested benefits for the plan is $105,000. What amount related to its pension plan will be reported on the company's statement of financial position?
   (a) $5,000.   (c) $85,000.
   (b) $90,000.   (d) $20,000.

2. At the end of the current year, Kennedy Co. has a defined benefit obligation of $335,000 and pension plan assets with a fair value of $245,000. The amount of the vested benefits for the plan is $225,000. Kennedy has an actuarial gain of $8,300. What account and amount(s) related to its pension plan will be reported on the company's statement of financial position?
   (a) Pension Liability and $74,300.   (c) Pension Asset and $233,300.
   (b) Pension Liability and $90,000.   (d) Pension Asset and $110,000.

3. For 2014, Carson Majors Inc. had pension expense of $77 million and contributed $55 million to the pension fund. Which of the following is the journal entry that Carson Majors would make to record pension expense and funding?

(a)
Pension Expense	77,000,000	
Pension Asset/Liability		22,000,000
Cash		55,000,000

(b)
Pension Expense	77,000,000	
Pension Asset/Liability	22,000,000	
Cash		99,000,000

(c)
Pension Expense	55,000,000	
Pension Asset/Liability	22,000,000	
Cash		77,000,000

(d)
Pension Expense	22,000,000	
Pension Asset/Liability	55,000,000	
Cash		77,000,000

4. At January 1, 2014, Wembley Company had plan assets of $250,000 and a defined benefit obligation of the same amount. During 2014, service cost was $27,500, the discount rate was 10%, actual return on plan assets was $25,000, contributions were $20,000, and benefits paid were $17,500. Based on this information, what would be the defined benefit obligation for Wembley Company at December 31, 2014?

(a) $277,500.   (c) $27,500.

(b) $285,000.   (d) $302,500.

5. Towson Company has experienced tough competition for its talented workforce, leading it to enhance the pension benefits provided to employees. As a result, Towson amended its pension plan on January 1, 2014, and granted past service costs of $250,000. Current service cost for 2014 is $52,000. Interest expense is $18,000, and interest revenue is $5,000. Actual return on assets in 2014 is $3,000. What is Towson's pension expense for 2014?

(a) $65,000.   (c) $317,000.

(b) $302,000.   (d) $315,000.

IFRS CONCEPTS AND APPLICATION

IFRS20-1 What is net interest? Identify the elements of net interest and explain how they are computed.

IFRS20-2 What is service cost, and what is the basis of its measurement?

IFRS20-3 What is meant by "past service cost"? When is past service cost recognized as pension expense?

IFRS20-4 Bill Haley is learning about pension accounting. He is convinced that in years when companies record liability gains and losses, total comprehensive income will not be affected. Is Bill correct? Explain.

IFRS20-5 At the end of the current year, Joshua Co. has a defined benefit obligation of $335,000 and pension plan assets with a fair value of $345,000. The amount of the vested benefits for the plan is $225,000. Joshua has a liability gain of $8,300 (beginning accumulated OCI is zero). What amount and account(s) related to its pension plan will be reported on the company's statement of financial position?

IFRS20-6 Villa Company has experienced tough competition, leading it to seek concessions from its employees in the company's pension plan. In exchange for promises to avoid layoffs and wage cuts, the employees agreed to receive lower pension benefits in the future. As a result, Villa amended its pension plan on January 1, 2014, and recorded negative past service cost of $125,000. Current service cost for 2014 is $26,000. Interest expense is $9,000, and interest revenue is $2,500. Actual return on assets in 2012 is $1,500. Compute Villa's pension expense in 2014.

IFRS20-7 Tevez Company experienced an actuarial loss of $750 in its defined benefit plan in 2014. For 2014, Tevez's revenues are $125,000, and expenses (excluding pension expense of $14,000, which does not include the actuarial loss) are $85,000. Prepare Tevez's statement of comprehensive income for 2014.

IFRS20-8 The following defined pension data of Doreen Corp. apply to the year 2014.

Defined benefit obligation, 1/1/14 (before amendment)	$560,000
Plan assets, 1/1/14	546,200
Pension asset/liability	13,800 Cr.
On January 1, 2014, Doreen Corp., through plan amendment,	
grants past service benefits having a present value of	120,000
Discount rate	9%
Service cost	58,000
Contributions (funding)	65,000
Actual return on plan assets	49,158
Benefits paid to retirees	40,000

Instructions

For 2014, prepare a pension worksheet for Doreen Corp. that shows the journal entry for pension expense and the year-end balances in the related pension accounts.

IFRS20-9 Buhl Corp. sponsors a defined benefit pension plan for its employees. On January 1, 2014, the following balances relate to this plan.

Plan assets	$480,000
Defined benefit obligation	600,000
Pension asset/liability	120,000

As a result of the operation of the plan during 2014, the following additional data are provided by the actuary.

Service cost for 2014	$90,000
Discount rate, 6%	
Actual return on plan assets in 2014	55,000
Unexpected loss from change in defined benefit obligation,	
due to change in actuarial predictions	76,000
Contributions in 2014	99,000
Benefits paid retirees in 2014	85,000

Instructions

(a) Using the data above, compute pension expense for Buhl Corp. for the year 2014 by preparing a pension worksheet.

(b) Prepare the journal entry for pension expense for 2014.

IFRS20-10 Linda Berstler Company sponsors a defined benefit pension plan. The corporation's actuary provides the following information about the plan.

	January 1, 2014	December 31, 2014
Defined benefit obligation	$2,500	$3,300
Plan assets (fair value)	1,700	2,620
Discount rate		10%
Pension asset/liability	800	?
Service cost for the year 2014		400
Contributions (funding in 2014)		700
Benefits paid in 2014		200

Instructions

(a) Compute the actual return on the plan assets in 2014.

(b) Compute the amount of other comprehensive income (G/L) as of December 31, 2014. (Assume the January 1, 2014, balance was zero.)

Professional Research

IFRS20-11 Jack Kelly Company has grown rapidly since its founding in 2004. To instill loyalty in its employees, Kelly is contemplating establishment of a defined benefit plan. Kelly knows that lenders and potential investors will pay close attention to the impact of the pension plan on the company's financial statements, particularly any gains or losses that develop in the plan. Kelly has asked you to conduct some research on the accounting for gains and losses in a defined benefit plan.

Instructions

Access the IFRS authoritative literature at the IASB website (*http://eifrs.iasb.org/*). (Click on the IFRS tab and then register for free eIFRS access if necessary.) When you have accessed the documents, you can use the search tool in your Internet browser to respond to the following questions. (Provide paragraph citations.)

(a) Briefly describe how pension gains and losses are accounted for.
(b) Explain the rationale behind the accounting method described in part (a).
(c) What is the related pension asset or liability that may show up on the statement of financial position? When will each of these situations occur?

International Financial Reporting Problem
Marks and Spencer plc

IFRS20-12 The financial statements of **Marks and Spencer plc (M&S)** are available at the book's companion website or can be accessed at *http://annualreport.marksandspencer.com/_assets/downloads/ Marks-and-Spencer-Annual-report-and-financial-statements-2012.pdf.*

Instructions

Refer to M&S's financial statements and the accompanying notes to answer the following questions.

(a) What kind of pension plan does M&S provide its employees?
(b) What was M&S's pension expense for 2012 and 2011?
(c) What is the impact of M&S's pension plans for 2012 on its financial statements?
(d) What information does M&S provide on the target allocation of its pension assets? How do the allocations relate to the expected returns on these assets?

ANSWERS TO IFRS SELF-TEST QUESTIONS

1. c **2.** b **3.** a **4.** b **5.** d

Remember to check the book's companion website to find additional resources for this chapter.

21 Accounting for Leases

LEARNING OBJECTIVES

After studying this chapter, you should be able to:

1 Explain the nature, economic substance, and advantages of lease transactions.

2 Describe the accounting criteria and procedures for capitalizing leases by the lessee.

3 Contrast the operating and capitalization methods of recording leases.

4 Explain the advantages and economics of leasing to lessors and identify the classifications of leases for the lessor.

5 Describe the lessor's accounting for direct-financing leases.

6 Identify special features of lease arrangements that cause unique accounting problems.

7 Describe the effect of residual values, guaranteed and unguaranteed, on lease accounting.

8 Describe the lessor's accounting for sales-type leases.

9 List the disclosure requirements for leases.

More Companies Ask, "Why Buy?"

Leasing has grown tremendously in popularity. Today, it is the fastest growing form of capital investment. Instead of borrowing money to buy an airplane, computer, nuclear core, or satellite, a company makes periodic payments to lease these assets. Even gambling casinos lease their slot machines. Of the 500 companies surveyed by the AICPA in 2011, more than half disclosed lease data.*

A classic example is the airline industry. Many travelers on airlines such as **United**, **Delta**, and **Southwest** believe these airlines own the planes on which they are flying. Often, this is not the case. Airlines lease many of their airplanes due to the favorable accounting treatment they receive if they lease rather than purchase. Presented below are the lease percentages for the major U.S. airlines.

The Phantom Fleets: Number of Aircraft and Percent Carried Off the Balance Sheet

American — 26%
UAL — 12%
Delta — 12%
Southwest — 28%
Republic — 43%

Number of planes: 200 400 600 800 1000

Fleet Under Operating Leases
Fleet Owned

Source: Company reports, 2011.

What about other companies? They are also exploiting the existing lease accounting rules to keep assets and liabilities off the books. For example, **Krispy Kreme**, a chain of 217 doughnut shops, had been showing good growth and profitability using a relatively small bit of capital. That's an impressive feat if you care about return on capital. But there's a hole in this doughnut. The company explained that it was building a $30 million new mixing plant and warehouse in Effingham, Illinois.

*AICPA, *Accounting Trends and Techniques—2011*. 277 out of 500 surveyed companies reported leased assets. Companies that lease tend to be smaller, are high growth, and are in technology-oriented industries (see *www.techlease.com*).

Yet the financial statements failed to disclose the investments and obligations associated with that $30 million. By financing through a synthetic lease, Krispy Kreme kept the investment and obligation off the books.

In a synthetic lease, a financial institution like **Bank of America** sets up a special-purpose entity (SPE) that borrows money to build the plant and then leases it to Krispy Kreme. For accounting purposes, Krispy Kreme reports only rent expense. For tax purposes, however, Krispy Kreme can be considered the owner of the asset and gets depreciation tax deductions. This is a pretty good deal for Krispy Kreme. But for investors? Not so good. This is because the Krispy Kreme financial statements failed to disclose the investments and obligations associated with that $30 million.

Another example is struggling drug store chain **Rite Aid**. Its balance sheet is in shambles. While its current assets exceed current liabilities, that's the end of any good news in the balance sheet. Total assets are $7,364 million, while total liabilities are $9,951 million, thereby yielding a shareholders' deficit of $(2,587) million. Things are even worse once you consider Rite Aid's large off-balance-sheet lease obligations. Using the data in note 10 of the financial statements, analysts estimate the company's lease liabilities to be $5,939 million. This adjustment increases total liabilities to $15,890 million, causing the stockholders' deficit to worsen to $(8,526) million.

As you will learn in this chapter, due to lease accounting rules, users of financial statements must make an educated guess on the real-but-hidden leverage of leasing only by using the information disclosed in the notes and by applying a rule-of-thumb multiple. As the chairperson for the IASB noted, "It seems odd to expect an analyst to guess the liabilities associated with leases when management already has this information at its fingertips." This concern explains why the FASB and IASB are working on a new standard on leasing, so that assets and liabilities avoid on-balance-sheet treatment simply by calling a loan a "lease."

Sources: Adapted from Seth Lubore and Elizabeth MacDonald, "Debt? Who, Me?" *Forbes* (February 18, 2002), p. 56; A. Catanach and E. Ketz, "Still Searching for the 'Rite' Stuff," *Grumpy Old Accountants* (April 30, 2012), at *http://blogs.smeal.psu.edu/grumpyoldaccountants/archives/643*; and Hans Hoogervorst, "Harmonisation and Global Economic Consequences," Public lecture at the London School of Economics (November 6, 2012).

 CONCEPTUAL FOCUS

> See the **Underlying Concepts** on pages 1274 and 1307.
> Read the **Evolving Issues** on pages 1283 and 1303 for discussions of off-balance-sheet reporting of leases.

INTERNATIONAL FOCUS

> See the **International Perspectives** on pages 1272, 1276, 1285, and 1303.
> Read the **IFRS Insights** on pages 1331–1341 for a discussion of:
   —Lessee accounting
   —Lessor accounting

| PREVIEW OF CHAPTER | 21 |

Our opening story indicates the increased significance and prevalence of lease arrangements. As a result, the need for uniform accounting and informative reporting of these transactions has intensified. In this chapter, we look at the accounting issues related to leasing. The content and organization of this chapter are as follows.

Accounting for Leases

Leasing Environment	Accounting by Lessee	Accounting by Lessor	Special Lease Accounting Problems
• Who are players? • Advantages of leasing • Conceptual nature of a lease	• Capitalization criteria • Accounting differences • Capital lease method • Operating method • Comparison	• Economics of leasing • Classification • Direct-financing method • Operating method	• Residual values • Sales-type leases • Bargain-purchase option • Initial direct costs • Current versus noncurrent • Disclosure • Unresolved problems

THE LEASING ENVIRONMENT

Aristotle once said, "Wealth does not lie in ownership but in the use of things"! Clearly, many U.S. companies have decided that Aristotle is right, as they have become heavily involved in leasing assets rather than owning them. For example, according to the Equipment Leasing Association (ELA), the global equipment-leasing market is a $600–$700 billion business, with the United States accounting for about one-third of the global market. The ELA estimates that of the $1.3 trillion in total fixed investment expected from domestic businesses in 2012, $654 billion (50 percent) will be financed through leasing. Remember that these statistics are just for equipment leasing. Add in real estate leasing, which is probably larger, and we are talking about a very large and growing business, one that is at least in part driven by the accounting.

What types of assets are being leased? As the opening story indicated, any type of equipment can be leased, such as railcars, helicopters, bulldozers, barges, CT scanners, computers, and so on.

Illustration 21-1 summarizes, in their own words, what several major companies are leasing.

ILLUSTRATION 21-1
What Do Companies Lease?

Company (Ticker)	Description
Gap (GPS)	"We lease most of our store premises and some of our headquarters facilities and distribution centers."
ExxonMobil Corp. (XOM)	"Minimum commitments for operating leases, shown on an undiscounted basis, cover drilling equipment, tankers, service stations, and other properties."
JPMorgan Chase (JPM)	"JPMorgan Chase and its subsidiaries were obligated under a number of noncancelable operating leases for premises and equipment used primarily for banking purposes."
Maytag Corp. (MYG)	"The Company leases real estate, machinery, equipment, and automobiles under operating leases, some of which have renewal options."
McDonald's Corp. (MCD)	"The Company was the lessee at 15,235 restaurant locations through ground leases (the Company leases the land and the Company or franchisee owns the building) and through improved leases (the Company leases land and buildings)."
Starbucks Corp. (SBUX)	"Starbucks leases retail stores, roasting and distribution facilities, and office space under operating leases."
TXU Corp. (TXU)	"TXU Energy Holdings and TXU Electric Delivery have entered into operating leases covering various facilities and properties including generation plant facilities, combustion turbines, transportation equipment, mining equipment, data processing equipment, and office space."
Viacom Inc. (VIA.B)	"The Company has long-term non-cancelable operating lease commitments for office space and equipment, transponders, studio facilities, and vehicles. The Company also enters into capital leases for satellite transponders."

Source: Company 10-K filings.

The largest group of leased equipment involves information technology equipment, followed by assets in the transportation area (trucks, aircraft, rail), and then construction and agriculture.

Who Are the Players?

A **lease** is a contractual agreement between a lessor and a lessee. This arrangement gives the **lessee** the right to use specific property, owned by the **lessor**, for a specified period of time. In return for the use of the property, the lessee makes rental payments over the lease term to the lessor.

Who are the lessors that own this property? They generally fall into one of three categories:

1. Banks.
2. Captive leasing companies.
3. Independents.

Banks

Banks are the largest players in the leasing business. They have low-cost funds, which give them the advantage of being able to purchase assets at less cost than their competitors. Banks also have been more aggressive in the leasing markets. Deciding that there is money to be made in leasing, banks have expanded their product lines in this area. Finally, leasing transactions are now more standardized, which gives banks an advantage because they do not have to be as innovative in structuring lease arrangements. Thus, banks like **Wells Fargo**, **Chase**, **Citigroup**, and **PNC** have substantial leasing subsidiaries.

Captive Leasing Companies

Captive leasing companies are subsidiaries whose primary business is to perform leasing operations for the parent company. Companies like **Caterpillar Financial Services Corp.** (for Caterpillar), **Ford Motor Credit** (for Ford), and **IBM Global Financing** (for IBM) facilitate the sale of products to consumers. For example, suppose that **Sterling Construction Co.** wants to acquire a number of earthmovers from Caterpillar. In this case, Caterpillar Financial Services Corp. will offer to structure the transaction as a lease rather than as a purchase. Thus, Caterpillar Financial provides the financing rather than an outside financial institution.

Captive leasing companies have the point-of-sale advantage in finding leasing customers. That is, as soon as Caterpillar receives a possible order, its leasing subsidiary can quickly develop a lease-financing arrangement. Furthermore, the captive lessor has product knowledge that gives it an advantage when financing the parent's product.

The current trend is for captives to focus primarily on their companies' products rather than do general lease financing. For example, **Boeing Capital** and **UPS Capital** are two captives that have left the general finance business to focus exclusively on their parent companies' products.

Independents

Independents are the final category of lessors. Independents have not done well over the last few years. Their market share has dropped fairly dramatically as banks and captive leasing companies have become more aggressive in the lease-financing area. Independents do not have point-of-sale access, nor do they have a low cost of funds advantage. What they *are* often good at is developing innovative contracts for lessees. In addition, they are starting to act as captive finance companies for some companies that do not have a leasing subsidiary. For example, **International Lease Finance Corp.** is one of the world's largest independent lessors.

According to recent data at *www.ficinc.com* on new business volume by lessor type, banks hold about 49 percent of the market, followed by captives at 32 percent. Independents had the remaining 19 percent of new business. Data on changes in market share show that both captives and independents have increased business at the expense of the banks. That is, from 2009 to 2010, captives' and independents' market shares had grown by 11.3 percent and 5.3 percent, respectively, while the banks' market share declined by 0.9 percent.

Advantages of Leasing

The growth in leasing indicates that it often has some genuine advantages over owning property, such as:

1. *100% financing at fixed rates.* Leases are often signed without requiring any money down from the lessee. This helps the lessee conserve scarce cash—an especially desirable feature for new and developing companies. In addition, lease payments often remain fixed, which protects the lessee against inflation and increases in the cost of money. The following comment explains why companies choose a lease instead of a conventional loan: "Our local bank finally came up to 80 percent of the purchase price but wouldn't go any higher, and they wanted a floating interest rate. We just couldn't afford the down payment, and we needed to lock in a final payment rate we knew we could live with."

2. *Protection against obsolescence.* Leasing equipment reduces risk of obsolescence to the lessee and in many cases passes the risk of residual value to the lessor. For example, Merck (a pharmaceutical maker) leases computers. Under the lease agreement, Merck may turn in an old computer for a new model at any time, canceling the old lease and writing a new one. The lessor adds the cost of the new lease to the balance due on the old lease, less the old computer's trade-in value. As one treasurer remarked, "Our instinct is to purchase." But if a new computer is likely to come along in a short time, "then leasing is just a heck of a lot more convenient than purchasing." Naturally, the lessor also protects itself by requiring the lessee to pay higher rental payments or provide additional payments if the lessee does not maintain the asset.

3. *Flexibility.* Lease agreements may contain less restrictive provisions than other debt agreements. Innovative lessors can tailor a lease agreement to the lessee's special needs. For instance, the duration of the lease—the lease term—may be anything from a short period of time to the entire expected economic life of the asset. The rental payments may be level from year to year, or they may increase or decrease in amount. The payment amount may be predetermined or may vary with sales, the prime interest rate, the Consumer Price Index, or some other factor. In most cases, the rent is set to enable the lessor to recover the cost of the asset plus a fair return over the life of the lease.

4. *Less costly financing.* Some companies find leasing cheaper than other forms of financing. For example, start-up companies in depressed industries or companies in low tax brackets may lease to claim tax benefits that they might otherwise lose. Depreciation deductions offer no benefit to companies that have little if any taxable income. Through leasing, the leasing companies or financial institutions use these tax benefits. They can then pass some of these tax benefits back to the user of the asset in the form of lower rental payments.

5. *Tax advantages.* In some cases, companies can "have their cake and eat it too" with tax advantages that leases offer. That is, for financial reporting purposes, companies do not report an asset or a liability for the lease arrangement. For tax purposes, however, companies can capitalize and depreciate the leased asset. As a result, a company takes deductions earlier rather than later and also reduces its taxes. A common vehicle for this type of transaction is a "synthetic lease" arrangement, such as that described in the opening story for Krispy Kreme.

6. *Off-balance-sheet financing.* Certain leases do not add debt on a balance sheet or affect financial ratios. In fact, they may add to borrowing capacity.[1] Such off-balance-sheet financing is critical to some companies.

---

[1]As demonstrated later in this chapter, certain types of lease arrangements are not capitalized on the balance sheet. The liabilities section is thereby relieved of large future lease commitments that, if recorded, would adversely affect the debt to equity ratio. The reluctance to record lease obligations as liabilities is one of the primary reasons some companies resist capitalized lease accounting.

As shown in our opening story, airlines use lease arrangements extensively. This results in a great deal of off-balance-sheet financing. The following chart indicates that many airlines that lease aircraft understate debt levels by a substantial amount.

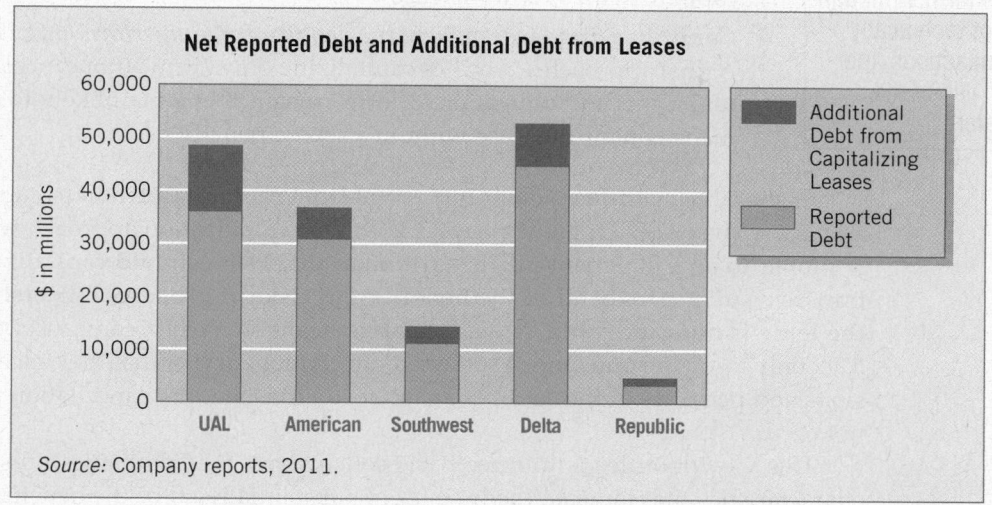

Source: Company reports, 2011.

Airlines are not the only ones playing the off-balance-sheet game. A recent study estimates that for S&P 500 companies, off-balance-sheet lease obligations total more than one-half trillion dollars, or roughly three percent of market value. Thus, analysts must adjust reported debt levels for the effects of non-capitalized leases. A methodology for making this adjustment is discussed in Eugene A. Imhoff, Jr., Robert C. Lipe, and David W. Wright, "Operating Leases: Impact of Constructive Capitalization," *Accounting Horizons* (March 1991).

Source: D. Zion and A. Varshney, "Leases Landing on Balance Sheets," *Credit Suisse Equity Research* (August 17, 2010).

Conceptual Nature of a Lease

If Delta borrows $47 million on a 10-year note from Bank of America to purchase a Boeing 737 jet plane, Delta should clearly report an asset and related liability at that amount on its balance sheet. Similarly, if Delta purchases the 737 for $47 million directly from Boeing through an installment purchase over 10 years, it should obviously report an asset and related liability (i.e., it should "capitalize" the installment transaction).

However, what if Delta **leases** the Boeing 737 for 10 years from International Lease Finance Corp. (ILFC)—the world's largest lessor of airplanes—through a noncancelable lease transaction with payments of the same amount as the installment purchase transaction? In that case, opinion differs over how to report this transaction. The various views on capitalization of leases are as follows.

1. *Do not capitalize any leased assets.* This view considers capitalization inappropriate because Delta does not own the property. Furthermore, a lease is an "**executory**" **contract** requiring continuing performance by both parties. Because companies do not currently capitalize other executory contracts (such as purchase commitments and employment contracts), they should not capitalize leases either.

2. *Capitalize leases that are similar to installment purchases.* This view holds that companies should report transactions in accordance with their economic substance. Therefore, if companies capitalize installment purchases, they should also capitalize leases that have similar characteristics. For example, Delta makes the same payments over a 10-year period for either a lease or an installment purchase. Lessees make rental payments, whereas owners make mortgage payments.

Underlying Concepts

> The issue of how to report leases is the classic case of substance versus form. Although legal title does not technically pass in lease transactions, the benefits from the use of the property do transfer.

Why should the financial statements not report these transactions in the same manner?

3. *Capitalize all long-term leases.* This approach requires only the long-term right to use the property in order to capitalize. This property-rights approach capitalizes all long-term leases.[2]

4. *Capitalize firm leases where the penalty for nonperformance is substantial.* A final approach advocates capitalizing only "firm" (noncancelable) contractual rights and obligations. "Firm" means that it is unlikely to avoid performance under the lease without a severe penalty.

In short, the various viewpoints range from no capitalization to capitalization of all leases. The FASB apparently agrees with the capitalization approach when the lease is similar to an installment purchase. It notes that Delta **should capitalize a lease that transfers substantially all of the benefits and risks of property ownership, provided the lease is noncancelable**. Noncancelable means that Delta can cancel the lease contract only upon the outcome of some remote contingency, or that the cancellation provisions and penalties of the contract are so costly to Delta that cancellation probably will not occur.

This viewpoint leads to three basic conclusions. (1) Companies must identify the characteristics that indicate the transfer of substantially all of the benefits and risks of ownership. (2) The same characteristics should apply consistently to the lessee and the lessor. (3) Those leases that do **not** transfer substantially all the benefits and risks of ownership are operating leases. Companies should not capitalize operating leases. Instead, companies should account for them as rental payments and receipts.

ACCOUNTING BY THE LESSEE

LEARNING OBJECTIVE 2

Describe the accounting criteria and procedures for capitalizing leases by the lessee.

If Delta Airlines (the lessee) **capitalizes** a lease, it records an asset and a liability generally equal to the present value of the rental payments. ILFC (the lessor), having transferred substantially all the benefits and risks of ownership, recognizes a sale by removing the asset from the balance sheet and replacing it with a receivable. The typical journal entries for Delta and ILFC, assuming leased and capitalized equipment, appear as shown in Illustration 21-2.

ILLUSTRATION 21-2
Journal Entries for Capitalized Lease

Delta (Lessee)			ILFC (Lessor)		
Leased Equipment	XXX		Lease Receivable	XXX	
Lease Liability		XXX	Equipment		XXX

Having capitalized the asset, Delta records depreciation on the leased asset. Both ILFC and Delta treat the lease rental payments as consisting of interest and principal.

If Delta does not capitalize the lease, it does not record an asset, nor does ILFC remove one from its books. When Delta makes a lease payment, it records rental expense; ILFC recognizes rental revenue.

---

[2]Capitalization of most leases (based on either a right of use or on noncancelable rights and obligations) has the support of financial analysts. See Peter H. Knutson, "Financial Reporting in the 1990s and Beyond," Position Paper (Charlottesville, Va.: AIMR, 1993); and Warren McGregor, "Accounting for Leases: A New Approach," Special Report (Norwalk, Conn.: FASB, 1996). The joint FASB/IASB project on lease accounting is based on a right-of-use model, which will require expanded capitalization of lease assets and liabilities. See *http://www.fasb.org* (click on the "Projects" tab).

In order to record a lease as a **capital lease**, the lease must be noncancelable. Further, it must meet one or more of the four criteria listed in Illustration 21-3.

Capitalization Criteria (Lessee)
• The lease transfers ownership of the property to the lessee. • The lease contains a bargain-purchase option.[3] • The lease term is equal to 75 percent or more of the estimated economic life of the leased property. • The present value of the minimum lease payments (excluding executory costs) equals or exceeds 90 percent of the fair value of the leased property. [1]

ILLUSTRATION 21-3
Capitalization Criteria for Lessee

See the FASB Codification section (page 1313).

Delta classifies and accounts for leases that **do not meet any of the four criteria** as **operating leases**. Illustration 21-4 shows that a lease meeting any one of the four criteria results in the lessee having a capital lease.

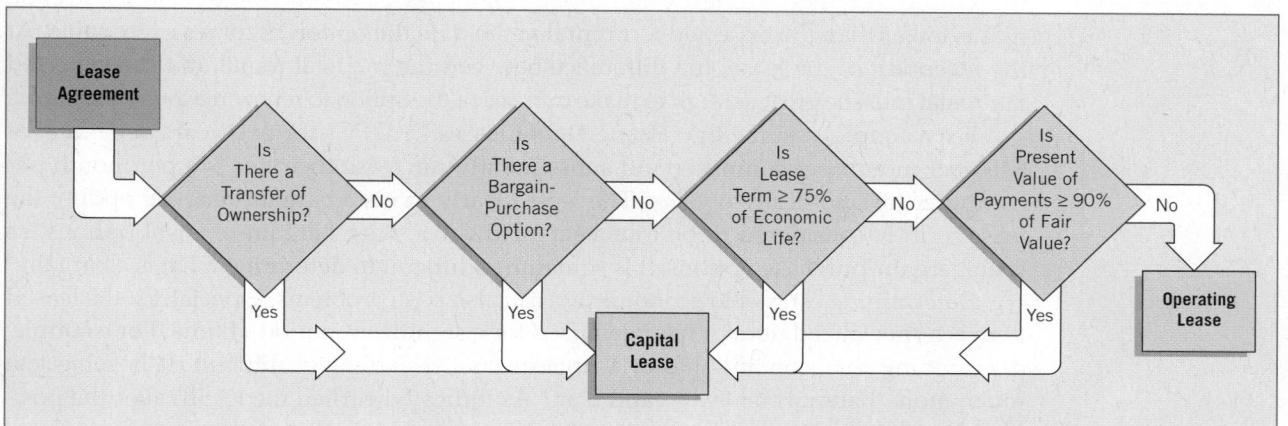

ILLUSTRATION 21-4
Diagram of Lessee's Criteria for Lease Classification

In keeping with the FASB's reasoning that a company consumes a significant portion of the value of the asset in the first 75 percent of its life, the lessee applies neither the third nor the fourth criterion when the inception of the lease occurs during the last 25 percent of the asset's life.

Capitalization Criteria

Three of the four **capitalization criteria** that apply to lessees are controversial and can be difficult to apply in practice. We discuss each of the criteria in detail on the following pages.

Transfer of Ownership Test

If the lease transfers ownership of the asset to the lessee, it is a capital lease. This criterion is not controversial and easily implemented in practice.

Bargain-Purchase Option Test

A **bargain-purchase option** allows the lessee to purchase the leased property for a price that is **significantly lower** than the property's expected fair value at the date the option becomes exercisable. At the inception of the lease, the difference between the option price and the expected fair value must be large enough to make exercise of the option reasonably assured.

[3]We define a bargain-purchase option in the next section.

For example, assume that Brett's Delivery Service was to lease a Honda Accord for $599 per month for 40 months, with an option to purchase for $100 at the end of the 40-month period. If the estimated fair value of the Honda Accord is $3,000 at the end of the 40 months, the $100 option to purchase is clearly a bargain. Therefore, Brett must capitalize the lease. In other cases, the criterion may not be as easy to apply, and determining *now* that a certain *future* price is a bargain can be difficult.

Economic Life Test (75% Test)

If the lease period equals or exceeds 75 percent of the asset's economic life, the lessor transfers most of the risks and rewards of ownership to the lessee. Capitalization is therefore appropriate. However, determining the lease term and the economic life of the asset can be troublesome.

The **lease term** is generally considered to be the fixed, noncancelable term of the lease. However, a bargain-renewal option, if provided in the lease agreement, can extend this period. A **bargain-renewal option** allows the lessee to renew the lease for a rental that is lower than the expected fair rental at the date the option becomes exercisable. At the inception of the lease, the difference between the renewal rental and the expected fair rental must be great enough to make exercise of the option to renew reasonably assured.

For example, assume that Home Depot leases Dell PCs for two years at a rental of $100 per month per computer and subsequently can lease them for $10 per month per computer for another two years. The lease clearly offers a bargain-renewal option; the lease term is considered to be four years. However, with bargain-renewal options, as with bargain-purchase options, it is sometimes difficult to determine what is a bargain.[4]

Determining estimated economic life can also pose problems, especially if the leased item is a specialized item or has been used for a significant period of time. For example, determining the economic life of a nuclear core is extremely difficult. It is subject to much more than normal "wear and tear." As indicated earlier, the FASB takes the position that if the lease starts during the last 25 percent of the life of the asset, companies cannot use the economic life test to classify a lease as a capital lease.

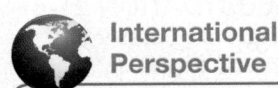

International Perspective

IFRS does not specify an exact percentage, such as 90%. Instead, it uses the term "substantially all." This difference illustrates the distinction between rules-based and principles-based standards.

Recovery of Investment Test (90% Test)

If the present value of the minimum lease payments equals or exceeds 90 percent of the fair value of the asset, then a lessee like Delta should capitalize the leased asset. Why? If the present value of the minimum lease payments is reasonably close to the fair value of the aircraft, Delta is effectively purchasing the asset.

Determining the present value of the minimum lease payments involves three important concepts: (1) minimum lease payments, (2) executory costs, and (3) discount rate.

Minimum Lease Payments. Delta is obligated to make, or expected to make, **minimum lease payments** in connection with the leased property. These payments include the following.

1. *Minimum rental payments.* Minimum rental payments are those that Delta must make to ILFC under the lease agreement. In some cases, the minimum rental payments may equal the minimum lease payments. However, the minimum lease payments may also include a guaranteed residual value (if any), penalty for failure to renew, or a bargain-purchase option (if any), as we note on the next page.

---

[4]The original lease term is also extended for leases having the following: substantial penalties for nonrenewal, periods for which the lessor has the option to renew or extend the lease, renewal periods preceding the date a bargain-purchase option becomes exercisable, and renewal periods in which any lessee guarantees of the lessor's debt are expected to be in effect or in which there will be a loan outstanding from the lessee to the lessor. The lease term, however, can never extend beyond the time a bargain-purchase option becomes exercisable. **[2]**

2. *Guaranteed residual value.* The residual value is the estimated fair (market) value of the leased property at the end of the lease term. ILFC may transfer the risk of loss to Delta or to a third party by obtaining a guarantee of the estimated residual value. The **guaranteed residual value** is either (1) the certain or determinable amount that Delta will pay ILFC at the end of the lease to purchase the aircraft at the end of the lease, or (2) the amount Delta or the third party guarantees that ILFC will realize if the aircraft is returned. (**Third-party guarantors** are, in essence, insurers who for a fee assume the risk of deficiencies in leased asset residual value.) If not guaranteed in full, the **unguaranteed residual value** is the estimated residual value exclusive of any portion guaranteed.[5]

3. *Penalty for failure to renew or extend the lease.* The amount Delta must pay if the agreement specifies that it must extend or renew the lease, and it fails to do so.

4. *Bargain-purchase option.* As we indicated earlier (in item 1), an option given to Delta to purchase the aircraft at the end of the lease term at a price that is fixed sufficiently below the expected fair value, so that, at the inception of the lease, purchase is reasonably assured.

Delta excludes executory costs (defined below) from its computation of the present value of the minimum lease payments.

Executory Costs. Like most assets, leased tangible assets incur insurance, maintenance, and tax expenses—called **executory costs**—during their economic life. If ILFC retains responsibility for the payment of these "ownership-type costs," **it should exclude**, in computing the present value of the minimum lease payments, a portion of each lease payment that represents executory costs. Executory costs do not represent payment on or reduction of the obligation.

Many lease agreements specify that the lessee directly pays executory costs to the appropriate third parties. In these cases, the lessor can use the rental payment **without adjustment** in the present value computation.

Discount Rate. A lessee like Delta generally computes the present value of the minimum lease payments using its **incremental borrowing rate**. This rate is defined as: "The rate that, at the inception of the lease, the lessee would have incurred to borrow the funds necessary to buy the leased asset on a secured loan with repayment terms similar to the payment schedule called for in the lease." **[4]**

To determine whether the present value of these payments is less than 90 percent of the fair value of the property, Delta discounts the payments using its incremental borrowing rate. Determining the incremental borrowing rate often requires judgment because the lessee bases it on a hypothetical purchase of the property.

However, there is one exception to this rule. If (1) Delta knows the **implicit interest rate computed by ILFC** and (2) it is less than Delta's incremental borrowing rate, then Delta **must use ILFC's implicit rate**. What is the **interest rate implicit in the lease**? It is the discount rate that, when applied to the minimum lease payments and any unguaranteed residual value accruing to the lessor, causes the aggregate present value to equal the fair value of the leased property to the lessor. **[5]**

The purpose of this exception is twofold. First, **the implicit rate of ILFC is generally a more realistic rate** to use in determining the amount (if any) to report as the asset and related liability for Delta. Second, the guideline ensures that Delta **does not use an artificially high incremental borrowing rate** that would cause the present value of the minimum lease payments to be less than 90 percent of the fair value of the aircraft. Use of such a rate would thus make it possible to avoid capitalization of the asset and related liability.

---

[5]A lease provision requiring the lessee to make up a residual value deficiency that is attributable to damage, extraordinary wear and tear, or excessive usage is not included in the minimum lease payments. Lessees recognize such costs as period costs when incurred. **[3]**

Delta may argue that it cannot determine the implicit rate of the lessor and therefore should use the higher rate. However, in most cases, Delta can approximate the implicit rate used by ILFC. The determination of whether or not a reasonable estimate could be made will require judgment, particularly where the result from using the incremental borrowing rate comes close to meeting the 90 percent test. Because Delta **may not capitalize the leased property at more than its fair value** (as we discuss later), it cannot use an excessively low discount rate.

Asset and Liability Accounted for Differently

In a capital lease transaction, Delta uses the lease as a source of financing. ILFC finances the transaction (provides the investment capital) through the leased asset. Delta makes rent payments, which actually are installment payments. Therefore, over the life of the aircraft rented, **the rental payments to ILFC constitute a payment of principal plus interest**.

Asset and Liability Recorded

Under the capital lease method, Delta treats the lease transaction as if it purchases the aircraft in a financing transaction. That is, Delta acquires the aircraft and creates an obligation. Therefore, it records a capital lease as an asset and a liability at the lower of (1) the present value of the minimum lease payments (excluding executory costs) or (2) the fair value of the leased asset at the inception of the lease. The rationale for this approach is that companies should not record a leased asset for more than its fair value.

Depreciation Period

One troublesome aspect of accounting for the depreciation of the capitalized leased asset relates to the period of depreciation. If the lease agreement transfers ownership of the asset to Delta (criterion 1) or contains a bargain-purchase option (criterion 2), Delta depreciates the aircraft consistent with its normal depreciation policy for other aircraft, **using the economic life of the asset**.

On the other hand, if the lease does not transfer ownership or does not contain a bargain-purchase option, then Delta depreciates it over the **term of the lease**. In this case, the aircraft reverts to ILFC after a certain period of time.

Effective-Interest Method

Throughout the term of the lease, Delta uses the effective-interest method to allocate each lease payment between principal and interest. This method produces a periodic interest expense equal to a constant percentage of the carrying value of the lease obligation. When applying the effective-interest method to capital leases, Delta must use the same discount rate that determines the present value of the minimum lease payments.

Depreciation Concept

Although Delta computes the amounts initially capitalized as an asset and recorded as an obligation at the same present value, the **depreciation of the aircraft and the discharge of the obligation are independent accounting processes** during the term of the lease. It should depreciate the leased asset by applying conventional depreciation methods: straight-line, sum-of-the-years'-digits, declining-balance, units of production, etc. The FASB uses the term "amortization" more frequently than "depreciation" to recognize intangible leased property rights. We prefer "depreciation" to describe the write-off of a tangible asset's expired services.

Capital Lease Method (Lessee)

To illustrate a capital lease, assume that Caterpillar Financial Services Corp. (a subsidiary of Caterpillar) and Sterling Construction Corp. sign a lease agreement dated January 1,

2014, that calls for Caterpillar to lease a front-end loader to Sterling beginning January 1, 2014. The terms and provisions of the lease agreement, and other pertinent data, are as follows.

- The term of the lease is five years. The lease agreement is noncancelable, requiring equal rental payments of $25,981.62 at the beginning of each year (annuity-due basis).
- The loader has a fair value at the inception of the lease of $100,000, an estimated economic life of five years, and no residual value.
- Sterling pays all of the executory costs directly to third parties except for the property taxes of $2,000 per year, which is included as part of its annual payments to Caterpillar.
- The lease contains no renewal options. The loader reverts to Caterpillar at the termination of the lease.
- Sterling's incremental borrowing rate is 11 percent per year.
- Sterling depreciates, on a straight-line basis, similar equipment that it owns.
- Caterpillar sets the annual rental to earn a rate of return on its investment of 10 percent per year; Sterling knows this fact.

The lease meets the criteria for classification as a capital lease for the following reasons.

1. The lease term of five years, being equal to the equipment's estimated economic life of five years, satisfies the 75 percent test.
2. The present value of the minimum lease payments ($100,000 as computed below) exceeds 90 percent of the fair value of the loader ($100,000).

The minimum lease payments are $119,908.10 ($23,981.62 × 5). Sterling computes the amount capitalized as leased assets as the present value of the minimum lease payments (excluding executory costs—property taxes of $2,000) as shown in Illustration 21-5.

<table>
<tr><td>Capitalized amount = ($25,981.62 − $2,000) × Present value of an annuity due of 1 for
5 periods at 10% (Table 6-5)
= $23,981.62 × 4.16986
= $100,000</td></tr>
</table>

ILLUSTRATION 21-5
Computation of Capitalized Lease Payments

Sterling uses Caterpillar's implicit interest rate of 10 percent instead of its incremental borrowing rate of 11 percent because (1) it is lower and (2) it knows about it.[6]
Sterling records the capital lease on its books on January 1, 2014, as:

| Leased Equipment (under capital leases) | 100,000 | |
| Lease Liability | | 100,000 |

Note that the entry records the obligation at the net amount of $100,000 (the present value of the future rental payments) rather than at the gross amount of $119,908.10 ($23,981.62 × 5).
Sterling records the **first lease payment on January 1, 2014**, as follows.

Property Tax Expense	2,000.00	
Lease Liability	23,981.62	
Cash		25,981.62

[6]If Sterling has an incremental borrowing rate of, say, 9 percent (lower than the 10 percent rate used by Caterpillar) and it did not know the rate used by Caterpillar, the present value computation would yield a capitalized amount of $101,675.35 ($23,981.62 × 4.23972). And, because this amount exceeds the $100,000 fair value of the equipment, Sterling should capitalize the $100,000 and use 10 percent as its effective rate for amortization of the lease obligation.

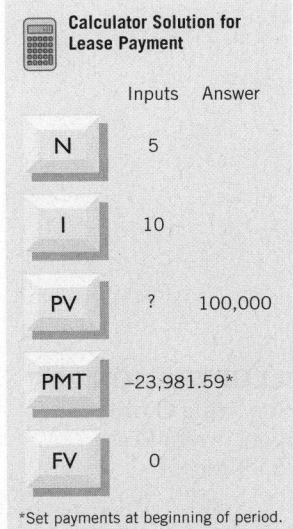

Calculator Solution for Lease Payment

	Inputs	Answer
N	5	
I	10	
PV	?	100,000
PMT	−23,981.59*	
FV	0	

*Set payments at beginning of period.

Each lease payment of $25,981.62 consists of three elements: (1) a reduction in the lease liability, (2) a financing cost (interest expense), and (3) executory costs (property taxes). The total financing cost (interest expense) over the term of the lease is $19,908.10. This amount is the difference between the present value of the lease payments ($100,000) and the actual cash disbursed, net of executory costs ($119,908.10). Therefore, the annual interest expense, applying the effective-interest method, is a function of the outstanding liability, as Illustration 21-6 shows.

ILLUSTRATION 21-6
Lease Amortization
Schedule for Lessee—
Annuity-Due Basis

	STERLING CONSTRUCTION				
	LEASE AMORTIZATION SCHEDULE				
	ANNUITY-DUE BASIS				
Date	Annual Lease Payment	Executory Costs	Interest (10%) on Liability	Reduction of Lease Liability	Lease Liability
	(a)	(b)	(c)	(d)	(e)
1/1/14					$100,000.00
1/1/14	$ 25,981.62	$ 2,000	$ –0–	$ 23,981.62	76,018.38
1/1/15	25,981.62	2,000	7,601.84	16,379.78	59,638.60
1/1/16	25,981.62	2,000	5,963.86	18,017.76	41,620.84
1/1/17	25,981.62	2,000	4,162.08	19,819.54	21,801.30
1/1/18	25,981.62	2,000	2,180.32*	21,801.30	–0–
	$129,908.10	$10,000	$19,908.10	$100,000.00	

(a) Lease payment as required by lease.
(b) Executory costs included in rental payment.
(c) Ten percent of the preceding balance of (e) except for 1/1/14; since this is an annuity due, no time has elapsed at the date of the first payment and no interest has accrued.
(d) (a) minus (b) and (c).
(e) Preceding balance minus (d).

*Rounded by 19 cents.

At the end of its fiscal year, December 31, 2014, Sterling records **accrued interest** as follows.

Interest Expense	7,601.84	
Interest Payable		7,601.84

Depreciation of the leased equipment over its five-year lease term, applying Sterling's normal depreciation policy (straight-line method), results in the following entry on December 31, 2014.

Depreciation Expense (capital leases)	20,000	
Accumulated Depreciation—Capital Leases		20,000
($100,000 ÷ 5 years)		

At December 31, 2014, Sterling separately identifies the assets recorded under capital leases on its balance sheet. Similarly, it separately identifies the related obligations. Sterling classifies the portion due within one year or the operating cycle, whichever is longer, with current liabilities, and the rest with noncurrent liabilities. For example, the current portion of the December 31, 2014, total obligation of $76,018.38 in Sterling's amortization schedule is the amount of the reduction in the obligation in 2015, or $16,379.78. Illustration 21-7 shows the liabilities section as it relates to lease transactions at December 31, 2014.

ILLUSTRATION 21-7
Reporting Current and
Noncurrent Lease
Liabilities

Current liabilities	
Interest payable	$ 7,601.84
Lease liability	16,379.78
Noncurrent liabilities	
Lease liability	59,638.60

Sterling records the lease payment of January 1, 2015, as follows.

Property Tax Expense	2,000.00	
Interest Payable	7,601.84	
Lease Liability	16,379.78	
Cash		25,981.62

Entries through 2018 follow the pattern above. Sterling records its other executory costs (insurance and maintenance) in a manner similar to how it records any other operating costs incurred on assets it owns.

Upon expiration of the lease, Sterling has fully amortized the amount capitalized as leased equipment. It also has fully discharged its lease obligation. If Sterling does not purchase the loader, it returns the equipment to Caterpillar. Sterling then removes the leased equipment and related accumulated depreciation accounts from its books.[7]

If Sterling purchases the equipment at termination of the lease, at a price of $5,000, and the estimated life of the equipment changes from five to seven years, it makes the following entry.

Equipment ($100,000 + $5,000)	105,000	
Accumulated Depreciation—Capital Leases	100,000	
Leased Equipment (under capital leases)		100,000
Accumulated Depreciation—Equipment		100,000
Cash		5,000

Operating Method (Lessee)

Under the **operating method**, rent expense (and the associated liability) accrues day by day to the lessee as it uses the property. **The lessee assigns rent to the periods benefiting from the use of the asset and ignores, in the accounting, any commitments to make future payments.** The lessee makes appropriate accruals or deferrals if the accounting period ends between cash payment dates.

For example, assume that the capital lease illustrated in the previous section did not qualify as a capital lease. Sterling therefore accounts for it as an operating lease. The first-year charge to operations is now $25,981.62, the amount of the rental payment. Sterling records this payment on January 1, 2014, as follows.

Rent Expense	25,981.62	
Cash		25,981.62

Sterling does not report the loader, as well as any long-term liability for future rental payments, on the balance sheet. Sterling reports rent expense on the income statement. And, as discussed later in the chapter, **Sterling must disclose all operating leases that have noncancelable lease terms in excess of one year**.

What do the numbers mean? RESTATEMENTS ON THE MENU

Accounting for operating leases would appear routine, so it is unusual for a bevy of companies in a single industry—restaurants—to get caught up in the accounting rules for operating leases. Getting the accounting right is particularly important for restaurant chains because they make extensive use of leases for their restaurants and equipment.

The problem stems from the way most property (and equipment) leases cover a specific number of years (the so-called *primary lease term*) as well as renewal periods (sometimes referred to as the *option term*). In some cases, companies were calculating their lease expense for the primary term but depreciating lease-related assets over

---

[7]If Sterling purchases the front-end loader during the term of a "capital lease," it accounts for it like a renewal or extension of a capital lease. "Any difference between the purchase price and the carrying amount of the lease obligation shall be recorded as an adjustment of the carrying amount of the asset." **[6]**

both the primary and option terms. This practice resulted in understating the total cost of the lease and thus boosted earnings.

For example, the CFO at CKE Restaurants Inc., owner of the Hardee's and Carl's Jr. chains, noted that CKE ran into trouble because it was not consistent in calculating the lease and depreciation expense. Correcting the error at CKE reduced earnings by nine cents a share in fiscal 2002, nine cents a share in fiscal 2003, and 10 cents a share in fiscal 2004. The company now uses the shorter, primary lease terms for

calculating both lease expense and depreciation. The change increases depreciation annually, which in turn decreases total assets.

CKE was not alone in improper operating lease accounting. Notable restaurateurs who ran afoul of the lease rules included Brinker International Inc., operator of Chili's; Darden Restaurants Inc., which operates Red Lobster and Olive Garden; and Jack in the Box. To correct their operating lease accounting, these restaurants reported restatements that resulted in lower earnings and assets.

Source: Steven D. Jones and Richard Gibson, *Wall Street Journal* (January 26, 2005), p. C3.

Comparison of Capital Lease with Operating Lease

LEARNING OBJECTIVE

Contrast the operating and capitalization methods of recording leases.

As we indicated, if accounting for the lease as an operating lease, the first-year charge to operations is $25,981.62, the amount of the rental payment. Treating the transaction as a capital lease, however, results in a first-year charge of $29,601.84: depreciation of $20,000 (assuming straight-line), interest expense of $7,601.84 (per Illustration 21-6), and executory costs of $2,000. Illustration 21-8 shows that **while the total charges to operations are the same over the lease term whether accounting for the lease as a capital lease or as an operating lease, under the capital lease treatment the charges are higher in the earlier years and lower in the later years.**[8]

ILLUSTRATION 21-8
Comparison of Charges to Operations—Capital vs. Operating Leases

		STERLING CONSTRUCTION SCHEDULE OF CHARGES TO OPERATIONS CAPITAL LEASE VERSUS OPERATING LEASE				
		Capital Lease			Operating Lease	
Year	Depreciation	Executory Costs	Interest	Total Charge	Lease Charge	Difference
2014	$ 20,000	$ 2,000	$ 7,601.84	$ 29,601.84	$ 25,981.62	$3,620.22
2015	20,000	2,000	5,963.86	27,963.86	25,981.62	1,982.24
2016	20,000	2,000	4,162.08	26,162.08	25,981.62	180.46
2017	20,000	2,000	2,180.32	24,180.32	25,981.62	(1,801.30)
2018	20,000	2,000	—	22,000.00	25,981.62	(3,981.62)
	$100,000	$10,000	$19,908.10	$129,908.10	$129,908.10	$ –0–

If using an accelerated method of depreciation, the differences between the amounts charged to operations under the two methods would be even larger in the earlier and later years.

In addition, using the capital lease approach results in an asset and related liability of $100,000 initially reported on the balance sheet. The lessee would not report any asset

---

[8]The higher charges in the early years is one reason lessees are reluctant to adopt the capital lease accounting method. Lessees (especially those of real estate) claim that it is really no more costly to operate the leased asset in the early years than in the later years. Thus, they advocate an even charge similar to that provided by the operating method.

or liability under the operating method. Therefore, the following differences occur if using a capital lease instead of an operating lease.

1. An increase in the amount of reported debt (both short-term and long-term).

2. An increase in the amount of total assets (specifically long-lived assets).

3. A lower income early in the life of the lease and, therefore, lower retained earnings.

Thus, many companies believe that capital leases negatively impact their financial position: Their debt to total equity ratio increases, and their rate of return on total assets decreases. As a result, the business community resists capitalizing leases.

Whether this resistance is well founded is debatable. From a cash flow point of view, the company is in the same position whether accounting for the lease as an operating or a capital lease. Managers often argue against capitalization for several reasons. First, capitalization can more easily lead to **violation of loan covenants**. It also can affect the **amount of compensation received by owners** (for example, a stock compensation plan tied to earnings). Finally, capitalization can **lower rates of return** and **increase debt to equity relationships**, making the company less attractive to present and potential investors.[9]

Evolving Issue   ARE YOU LIABLE?

Under current accounting rules, companies can keep the obligations associated with operating leases off the balance sheet. (For example, see the "What Do the Numbers Mean?" box on page 1273 for the effects of this approach for airlines.) This approach may change if the FASB and IASB are able to craft a new lease accounting rule. The current plans for a new rule in this area should result in many more operating leases on balance sheets. Analysts are beginning to estimate the expected impact of a new rule. As shown in the table below, if the FASB (and IASB) issue a new rule on operating leases, a company like Walgreen could see its liabilities jump a whopping 216 percent.

Retailer	Estimated Off-Balance-Sheet Lease Liabilities	Jump in Liabilities If They Were on the Balance Sheet
McDonald's	$ 7.996 billion	149%
Walgreen	23.212	216
Home Depot	5.846	27
Starbucks	3.685	146
CVS	26.913	104

And it is not just retailers who would be impacted. A PricewaterhouseCoopers survey of 3,000 international companies indicated the following impacts for several industries.

	Average Increase in Interest-Bearing Debt	Companies with over 25% Increase	Average Increase in Leverage
Retail and trade	213%	71%	64%
Other services	51	35	34
Transportation and warehousing	95	38	31
Professional services	158	52	19
Accommodation	101	41	18
All companies	58	24	13

As indicated, the expected effects are significant, with all companies expecting a 58 percent increase in their debt levels and a 13 percent increase in leverage ratios.

This is not a pretty picture, but investors need to see it if they are to fully understand a company's lease obligations.

Sources: Nanette Byrnes, "You May Be Liable for That Lease," *BusinessWeek* (June 5, 2006), p. 76; PricewaterhouseCoopers, *The Future of Leasing: Research of Impact on Companies' Financial Ratios* (2009); and J. E. Ketz, "Operating Lease Obligations to Be Capitalized," *Smartpros* (August 2010), *http://accounting.smartpros.com/x70304.xml.*

[9]One study indicates that management's behavior did change as a result of the leasing rules. For example, many companies restructure their leases to avoid capitalization. Others increase their purchases of assets instead of leasing. Still others, faced with capitalization, postpone their debt offerings or issue stock instead. However, note that the study found no significant effect on stock or bond prices as a result of capitalization of leases. See A. Rashad Abdel-khalik, "The Economic Effects on Lessees of *FASB Statement No. 13*, Accounting for Leases," Research Report (Stamford, Conn.: FASB, 1981).

ACCOUNTING BY THE LESSOR

Earlier in this chapter, we discussed leasing's advantages to the lessee. Three important benefits are available to the lessor:

1. *Interest revenue.* Leasing is a form of financing. Banks, captives, and independent leasing companies find leasing attractive because it provides competitive interest margins.

2. *Tax incentives.* In many cases, companies that lease cannot use the tax benefit of the asset, but leasing allows them to transfer such tax benefits to another party (the lessor) in return for a lower rental rate on the leased asset. To illustrate, Boeing Aircraft might sell one of its 737 jet planes to a wealthy investor who needed only the tax benefit. The investor then leased the plane to a foreign airline, for whom the tax benefit was of no use. Everyone gained. Boeing sold its airplane, the investor received the tax benefit, and the foreign airline cheaply acquired a 737.[10]

3. *High residual value.* Another advantage to the lessor is the return of the property at the end of the lease term. Residual values can produce very large profits. Citigroup at one time estimated that the commercial aircraft it was leasing to the airline industry would have a residual value of 5 percent of their purchase price. It turned out that they were worth 150 percent of their cost—a handsome profit. At the same time, if residual values decline, lessors can suffer losses when less-valuable leased assets are returned at the conclusion of the lease. At one time, automaker Ford took a $2.1 billion write-down on its lease portfolio, when rising gas prices spurred dramatic declines in the resale values of leased trucks and SUVs. Such residual value losses led Chrysler to get out of the leasing business altogether.

Economics of Leasing

A lessor, such as Caterpillar Financial in our earlier example, determines the amount of the rental, basing it on the rate of return—the implicit rate—needed to justify leasing the front-end loader. In establishing the rate of return, Caterpillar considers the credit standing of Sterling Construction, the length of the lease, and the status of the residual value (guaranteed versus unguaranteed).

In the Caterpillar/Sterling example on pages 1278–1281, Caterpillar's implicit rate was 10 percent, the cost of the equipment to Caterpillar was $100,000 (also fair value), and the estimated residual value was zero. Caterpillar determines the amount of the lease payment as follows.

ILLUSTRATION 21-9
Computation of Lease Payments

Fair value of leased equipment	$100,000.00
Less: Present value of the residual value	–0–
Amount to be recovered by lessor through lease payments	$100,000.00
Five beginning-of-the-year lease payments to yield a 10% return ($100,000 ÷ 4.16986[a])	$ 23,981.62

[a]PV of an annuity due of 1 for 5 years at 10% (Table 6-5).

If a residual value is involved (whether guaranteed or not), Caterpillar would not have to recover as much from the lease payments. Therefore, the lease payments would be less. (Illustration 21-16, on page 1291, shows this situation.)

[10]Some would argue that there is a loser—the U.S. government. The tax benefits enable the profitable investor to reduce or eliminate taxable income.

Classification of Leases by the Lessor

For accounting purposes, the **lessor** may classify leases as one of the following:

1. Operating leases.
2. Direct-financing leases.
3. Sales-type leases.

Illustration 21-10 presents two groups of capitalization criteria for the lessor. If at the date of inception the lessor agrees to a lease that meets **one or more** of the Group I criteria (1, 2, 3, and 4) and **both** of the Group II criteria (1 and 2), the lessor shall classify and account for the arrangement as a direct-financing lease or as a sales-type lease. **[7]** Note that the Group I criteria are identical to the criteria that must be met in order for a lessee to classify a lease as a capital lease, as shown in Illustration 21-3 (on page 1275).

ILLUSTRATION 21-10
Capitalization Criteria
for Lessor

Capitalization Criteria (Lessor)

Group I
1. The lease transfers ownership of the property to the lessee.
2. The lease contains a bargain-purchase option.
3. The lease term is equal to 75 percent or more of the estimated economic life of the leased property.
4. The present value of the minimum lease payments (excluding executory costs) equals or exceeds 90 percent of the fair value of the leased property.

Group II
1. Collectibility of the payments required from the lessee is reasonably predictable.
2. No important uncertainties surround the amount of unreimbursable costs yet to be incurred by the lessor under the lease (lessor's performance is substantially complete or future costs are reasonably predictable).

International Perspective

GAAP is consistent with *International Accounting Standard No. 17* (Accounting for Leases). However, the international standard is a relatively simple statement of basic principles, whereas the U.S. rules on leases are more prescriptive and detailed.

Why the Group II requirements? The profession wants to ensure that the lessor has really transferred the risks and benefits of ownership. If collectibility of payments is not predictable or if performance by the lessor is incomplete, then the criteria for revenue recognition have not been met. The lessor should therefore account for the lease as an operating lease.

For example, computer leasing companies at one time used to buy **IBM** equipment, lease the equipment, and remove the leased assets from their balance sheets. In leasing the assets, the computer lessors stated that they would substitute new IBM equipment if obsolescence occurred. However, when IBM introduced a new computer line, IBM refused to sell it to the computer leasing companies. As a result, a number of the lessors could not meet their contracts with their customers and had to take back the old equipment. The computer leasing companies therefore had to reinstate the assets they had taken off the books. Such a case demonstrates one reason for the Group II requirements.

The distinction for the lessor between a direct-financing lease and a sales-type lease is the presence or absence of a manufacturer's or dealer's profit (or loss). A sales-type lease involves a manufacturer's or dealer's profit, and a direct-financing lease does not. The profit (or loss) to the lessor is evidenced by the difference between the fair value of the leased property at the inception of the lease and the lessor's cost or carrying amount (book value).

Normally, sales-type leases arise when manufacturers or dealers use leasing as a means of marketing their products. For example, a computer manufacturer will lease its computer equipment (possibly through a captive) to businesses and institutions. Direct-financing leases generally result from arrangements with lessors that are primarily engaged in financing operations (e.g., banks). However, a lessor need not be a manufacturer or dealer to recognize a profit (or loss) at the inception of a lease that requires application of sales-type lease accounting.

Lessors classify and account for all leases that do not qualify as direct-financing or sales-type leases as operating leases. Illustration 21-11 shows the circumstances under which a lessor classifies a lease as operating, direct-financing, or sales-type.

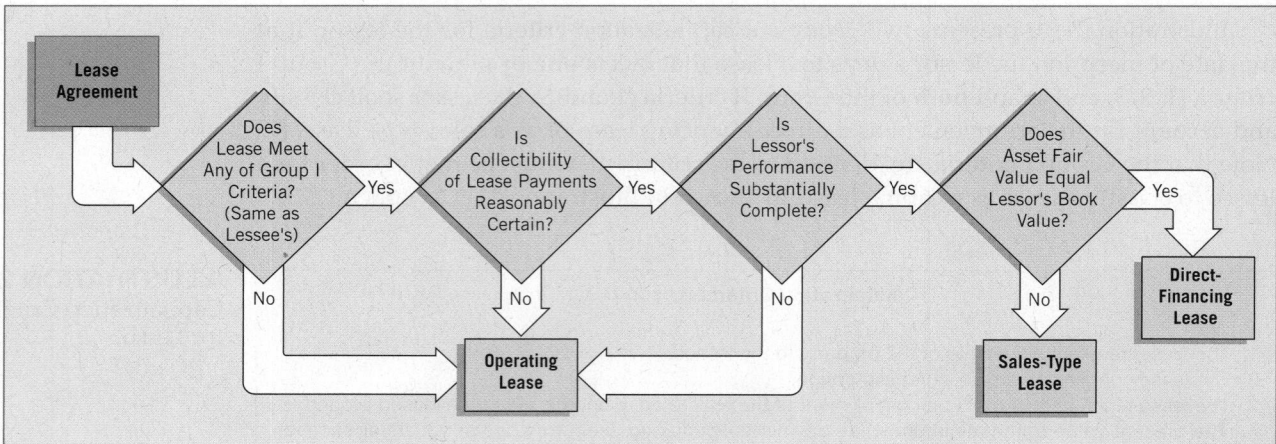

ILLUSTRATION 21-11
Diagram of Lessor's Criteria for Lease Classification

As a consequence of the additional Group II criteria for lessors, a lessor may classify a lease as an **operating** lease but the lessee may classify the same lease as a **capital** lease. In such an event, both the lessor and lessee will carry the asset on their books, and both will depreciate the capitalized asset.

For purposes of comparison with the lessee's accounting, we will illustrate only the operating and direct-financing leases in the following section. We will discuss the more complex sales-type lease later in the chapter.

Direct-Financing Method (Lessor)

LEARNING OBJECTIVE **5**

Describe the lessor's accounting for direct-financing leases.

Direct-financing leases are in substance the financing of an asset purchase by the lessee. In this type of lease, the lessor records a **lease receivable** instead of a leased asset. The lease receivable is the present value of the minimum lease payments. Remember that "minimum lease payments" include:

1. Rental payments (excluding executory costs).

2. Bargain-purchase option (if any).

3. Guaranteed residual value (if any).

4. Penalty for failure to renew (if any).

Thus, the lessor records the residual value, whether guaranteed or not. Also, recall that if the lessor pays any executory costs, then it should reduce the rental payment by that amount in computing minimum lease payments.

The following presentation, using the data from the preceding Caterpillar/Sterling example on page 1279, illustrates the accounting treatment for a direct-financing lease. We repeat here the information relevant to Caterpillar in accounting for this lease transaction.

1. The term of the lease is five years beginning January 1, 2014, noncancelable, and requires equal rental payments of $25,981.62 at the beginning of each year. Payments include $2,000 of executory costs (property taxes).

2. The equipment (front-end loader) has a cost of $100,000 to Caterpillar, a fair value at the inception of the lease of $100,000, an estimated economic life of five years, and no residual value.

3. Caterpillar incurred no initial direct costs in negotiating and closing the lease transaction.

4. The lease contains no renewal options. The equipment reverts to Caterpillar at the termination of the lease.

5. Collectibility is reasonably assured and Caterpillar incurs no additional costs (with the exception of the property taxes being collected from Sterling).

6. Caterpillar sets the annual lease payments to ensure a rate of return of 10 percent (implicit rate) on its investment as shown in Illustration 21-12.

Fair value of leased equipment	$100,000.00
Less: Present value of residual value	–0–
Amount to be recovered by lessor through lease payments	$100,000.00
Five beginning-of-the-year lease payments to yield a 10% return ($100,000 ÷ 4.16986ª)	$ 23,981.62

ªPV of an annuity due of 1 for 5 years at 10% (Table 6-5).

ILLUSTRATION 21-12
Computation of Lease Payments

The lease meets the criteria for classification as a direct-financing lease for several reasons. (1) The lease term exceeds 75 percent of the equipment's estimated economic life. (2) The present value of the minimum lease payments exceeds 90 percent of the equipment's fair value. (3) Collectibility of the payments is reasonably assured. (4) Caterpillar incurs no further costs. It is not a sales-type lease because there is no difference between the fair value ($100,000) of the loader and Caterpillar's cost ($100,000).

The Lease Receivable is the present value of the minimum lease payments (excluding executory costs which are property taxes of $2,000). Caterpillar computes it as follows.

Lease receivable = ($25,981.62 − $2,000) × Present value of an annuity due of 1 for 5 periods at 10% (Table 6-5)

= $23,981.62 × 4.16986
= $100,000

ILLUSTRATION 21-13
Computation of Lease Receivable

Caterpillar records the lease of the asset and the resulting receivable on January 1, 2014 (the inception of the lease), as follows.

Lease Receivable	100,000	
Equipment		100,000

Companies often **report** the lease receivable in the balance sheet as "Net investment in capital leases." Companies classify it either as current or noncurrent, depending on when they recover the net investment.[11]

Caterpillar replaces its investment (the leased front-end loader, a cost of $100,000), with a lease receivable. In a manner similar to Sterling's treatment of interest, Caterpillar applies the effective-interest method and recognizes interest revenue as a function of the lease receivable balance, as Illustration 21-14 (page 1288) shows.

---

[11]In the notes to the financial statements (see Illustration 21-32, pages 1301–1302, for lessor disclosures by **Hewlett-Packard**), the lease receivable is reported at its gross amount (minimum lease payments plus the unguaranteed residual value). In addition, the lessor also reports total unearned interest related to the lease. As a result, some lessors record lease receivable on a gross basis and record the unearned interest in a separate account. We illustrate the net approach here because it is consistent with the accounting for the lessee.

ILLUSTRATION 21-14
Lease Amortization
Schedule for Lessor—
Annuity-Due Basis

			CATERPILLAR FINANCIAL		
			LEASE AMORTIZATION SCHEDULE		
			ANNUITY-DUE BASIS		
Date	Annual Lease Payment	Executory Costs	Interest (10%) on Lease Receivable	Lease Receivable Recovery	Lease Receivable
	(a)	(b)	(c)	(d)	(e)
1/1/14					$100,000.00
1/1/14	$ 25,981.62	$ 2,000.00	$ –0–	$ 23,981.62	76,018.38
1/1/15	25,981.62	2,000.00	7,601.84	16,379.78	59,638.60
1/1/16	25,981.62	2,000.00	5,963.86	18,017.76	41,620.84
1/1/17	25,981.62	2,000.00	4,162.08	19,819.54	21,801.30
1/1/18	25,981.62	2,000.00	2,180.32*	21,801.30	–0–
	$129,908.10	$10,000.00	$19,908.10	$100,000.00	

(a) Annual rental that provides a 10% return on net investment.
(b) Executory costs included in rental payment.
(c) Ten percent of the preceding balance of (e) except for 1/1/14.
(d) (a) minus (b) and (c).
(e) Preceding balance minus (d).

*Rounded by 19 cents.

On January 1, 2014, Caterpillar records receipt of the first year's lease payment as follows.

Cash	25,981.62	
Lease Receivable		23,981.62
Property Tax Expense/Property Taxes Payable		2,000.00

On December 31, 2014, Caterpillar recognizes the interest revenue during the first year through the following entry.

Interest Receivable	7,601.84	
Interest Revenue (leases)		7,601.84

At December 31, 2014, Caterpillar reports the lease receivable in its balance sheet among current assets or noncurrent assets, or both. It classifies the portion due within one year or the operating cycle, whichever is longer, as a current asset, and the rest with noncurrent assets.

Illustration 21-15 shows the assets section as it relates to lease transactions at December 31, 2014.

ILLUSTRATION 21-15
Reporting Lease
Transactions by Lessor

Current assets	
Interest receivable	$ 7,601.84
Lease receivable	16,379.78
Noncurrent assets (investments)	
Lease receivable	$59,638.60

The following entries record receipt of the second year's lease payment and recognition of the interest.

January 1, 2015

Cash	25,981.62	
Lease Receivable		16,379.78
Interest Receivable		7,601.84
Property Tax Expense/Property Taxes Payable		2,000.00

December 31, 2015

Interest Receivable	5,963.86	
Interest Revenue (leases)		5,963.86

Journal entries through 2018 follow the same pattern except that Caterpillar records no entry in 2018 (the last year) for interest revenue. Because it fully collects the receivable by January 1, 2018, no balance (investment) is outstanding during 2018. Caterpillar **recorded no depreciation**. If Sterling buys the loader for $5,000 upon expiration of the lease, Caterpillar recognizes disposition of the equipment as follows.

Cash	5,000	
Gain on Disposal of Equipment		5,000

Operating Method (Lessor)

Under the **operating method**, the lessor records each rental receipt as rental revenue. It **depreciates the leased asset in the normal manner**, with the depreciation expense of the period matched against the rental revenue. The amount of revenue recognized in each accounting period is a level amount (straight-line basis) regardless of the lease provisions, unless another systematic and rational basis better represents the time pattern in which the lessor derives benefit from the leased asset.

In addition to the depreciation charge, the lessor expenses maintenance costs and the cost of any other services performed under the provisions of the lease that pertain to the current accounting period. The lessor **amortizes over the life of the lease** any costs paid to independent third parties, such as appraisal fees, finder's fees, and costs of credit checks, usually on a straight-line basis.

To illustrate the operating method, assume that the direct-financing lease illustrated in the previous section does not qualify as a capital lease. Therefore, Caterpillar accounts for it as an operating lease. It records the cash rental receipt, assuming the $2,000 was for property tax expense, as follows.

Cash	25,981.62	
Rent Revenue		25,981.62

Caterpillar records depreciation as follows (assuming a straight-line method, a cost basis of $100,000, and a five-year life).

Depreciation Expense (leased equipment)	20,000	
Accumulated Depreciation—Equipment		20,000

If Caterpillar pays property taxes, insurance, maintenance, and other operating costs during the year, it records them as expenses chargeable against the gross rental revenues.

If Caterpillar owns plant assets that it uses in addition to those leased to others, the company **separately classifies the leased equipment and accompanying accumulated depreciation** as Equipment Leased to Others or Investment in Leased Property. If significant in amount or in terms of activity, Caterpillar separates the rental revenues and accompanying expenses in the income statement from sales revenue and cost of goods sold.

SPECIAL LEASE ACCOUNTING PROBLEMS

The features of lease arrangements that cause unique accounting problems are:

1. Residual values.

2. Sales-type leases (lessor).

3. Bargain-purchase options.

6 LEARNING OBJECTIVE

Identify special features of lease arrangements that cause unique accounting problems.

4. Initial direct costs.

5. Current versus noncurrent classification.

6. Disclosure.

We discuss each of these features on the following pages.

Residual Values

LEARNING OBJECTIVE

Describe the effect of residual values, guaranteed and unguaranteed, on lease accounting.

Up to this point, in order to develop the basic accounting issues related to lessee and lessor accounting, we have generally ignored residual values. Accounting for residual values is complex and will probably provide you with the greatest challenge in understanding lease accounting.

Meaning of Residual Value

The residual value is the estimated fair value of the leased asset at the end of the lease term. Frequently, a significant residual value exists at the end of the lease term, especially when the economic life of the leased asset exceeds the lease term. If title does not pass automatically to the lessee (criterion 1) and if a bargain-purchase option does not exist (criterion 2), the lessee returns physical custody of the asset to the lessor at the end of the lease term.[12]

Guaranteed versus Unguaranteed

The residual value may be unguaranteed or guaranteed by the lessee. Sometimes the lessee agrees to make up any deficiency below a stated amount that the lessor realizes in residual value at the end of the lease term. In such a case, that stated amount is the guaranteed residual value.

The parties to a lease use guaranteed residual value in lease arrangements for two reasons. The first is a business reason: It protects the lessor against any loss in estimated residual value, thereby ensuring the lessor of the desired rate of return on investment. The second reason is an accounting benefit that you will learn from the discussion at the end of this chapter.

Lease Payments

A guaranteed residual value—by definition—has more assurance of realization than does an unguaranteed residual value. As a result, the lessor may adjust lease payments because of the increased certainty of recovery. After the lessor establishes this rate, it makes no difference from an accounting point of view whether the residual value is guaranteed or unguaranteed. The net investment that the lessor records (once the rate is set) will be the same.

Assume the same data as in the Caterpillar/Sterling illustrations except that Caterpillar estimates a residual value of $5,000 at the end of the five-year lease term. In addition, Caterpillar assumes a 10 percent return on investment (ROI),[13] whether the residual value is guaranteed or unguaranteed. Caterpillar would compute the amount of the lease payments as follows.

---

[12]When the lease term and the economic life are not the same, the residual value and the salvage value of the asset will probably differ. For simplicity, we will assume that residual value and salvage value are the same, even when the economic life and lease term vary.

[13]Technically, the rate of return Caterpillar demands would differ depending upon whether the residual value was guaranteed or unguaranteed. To simplify the illustrations, we are ignoring this difference in subsequent sections.

ILLUSTRATION 21-16
Lessor's Computation of
Lease Payments

CATERPILLAR'S COMPUTATION OF LEASE PAYMENTS (10% ROI) GUARANTEED OR UNGUARANTEED RESIDUAL VALUE ANNUITY-DUE BASIS, INCLUDING RESIDUAL VALUE	
Fair value of leased asset to lessor	$100,000.00
Less: Present value of residual value ($5,000 × .62092, Table 6-2)	3,104.60
Amount to be recovered by lessor through lease payments	$ 96,895.40
Five periodic lease payments ($96,895.40 ÷ 4.16986, Table 6-5)	$ 23,237.09

Contrast the foregoing lease payment amount to the lease payments of $23,981.62 as computed in Illustration 21-9 (on page 1284), where no residual value existed. In the second example, the payments are less, because the present value of the residual value reduces Caterpillar's total recoverable amount from $100,000 to $96,895.40.

Lessee Accounting for Residual Value

Whether the estimated residual value is guaranteed or unguaranteed has both economic and accounting consequence to the lessee. We saw the economic consequence—lower lease payments—in the preceding example. The accounting consequence is that the **minimum lease payments**, the basis for capitalization, include the guaranteed residual value but exclude the unguaranteed residual value.

Guaranteed Residual Value (Lessee Accounting). A guaranteed residual value affects the lessee's computation of minimum lease payments. Therefore, it also affects the amounts capitalized as a leased asset and a lease obligation. In effect, the guaranteed residual value **is an additional lease payment that the lessee will pay in property or cash, or both, at the end of the lease term**.

Using the rental payments as computed by the lessor in Illustration 21-16, the minimum lease payments are $121,185.45 ([$23,237.09 × 5] + $5,000). Illustration 21-17 shows the capitalized present value of the minimum lease payments (excluding executory costs) for Sterling Construction.

STERLING'S CAPITALIZED AMOUNT (10% RATE) ANNUITY-DUE BASIS, INCLUDING **GUARANTEED** RESIDUAL VALUE	
Present value of five annual rental payments ($23,237.09 × 4.16986, Table 6-5)	$ 96,895.40
Present value of guaranteed residual value of $5,000 due five years after date of inception: ($5,000 × .62092, Table 6-2)	3,104.60
Lessee's capitalized amount	$100,000.00

Sterling prepares a schedule of interest expense and amortization of the $100,000 lease liability. That schedule, shown in Illustration 21-18 (page 1292), is based on a $5,000 final guaranteed residual value payment at the end of five years.

Sterling records the leased asset (front-end loader) and liability, depreciation, interest, property tax, and lease payments on the basis of a guaranteed residual value. (These journal entries are shown in Illustration 21-23, on page 1294.) The format of these entries is the same as illustrated earlier, although the amounts are different because of the guaranteed residual value. Sterling records the loader at $100,000 and depreciates it over five years. To compute depreciation, it subtracts the guaranteed

ILLUSTRATION 21-18
Lease Amortization
Schedule for Lessee—
Guaranteed Residual
Value

	Lease Payment Plus GRV	Executory Costs	Interest (10%) on Liability	Reduction of Lease Liability	Lease Liability
Date	(a)	(b)	(c)	(d)	(e)
1/1/14					$100,000.00
1/1/14	$ 25,237.09	$ 2,000	–0–	$ 23,237.09	76,762.91
1/1/15	25,237.09	2,000	$ 7,676.29	15,560.80	61,202.11
1/1/16	25,237.09	2,000	6,120.21	17,116.88	44,085.23
1/1/17	25,237.09	2,000	4,408.52	18,828.57	25,256.66
1/1/18	25,237.09	2,000	2,525.67	20,711.42	4,545.24
12/31/18	5,000.00*		454.76**	4,545.24	–0–
	$131,185.45	$10,000	$21,185.45	$100,000.00	

STERLING CONSTRUCTION
LEASE AMORTIZATION SCHEDULE
ANNUITY-DUE BASIS, GUARANTEED RESIDUAL VALUE—GRV

(a) Annual lease payment as required by lease.
(b) Executory costs included in rental payment.
(c) Preceding balance of (e) × 10%, except 1/1/14.
(d) (a) minus (b) and (c).
(e) Preceding balance minus (d).

*Represents the guaranteed residual value.
**Rounded by 24 cents.

residual value from the cost of the loader. Assuming that Sterling uses the straight-line method, the depreciation expense each year is $19,000 ([$100,000 − $5,000] ÷ 5 years).

At the end of the lease term, before the lessee transfers the asset to Caterpillar, the lease asset and liability accounts have the following balances.

ILLUSTRATION 21-19
Account Balances on
Lessee's Books at End of
Lease Term—Guaranteed
Residual Value

Leased equipment (under capital leases)	$100,000.00	Interest payable	$ 454.76
Less: Accumulated depreciation— capital leases	95,000.00	Lease liability	4,545.24
	$ 5,000.00		$5,000.00

If at the end of the lease the fair value of the residual value is less than $5,000, Sterling will have to record a loss. Assume that Sterling depreciated the leased asset down to its residual value of $5,000 but that the fair value of the residual value at December 31, 2018, was $3,000. In this case, Sterling would have to report a loss of $2,000. Assuming that it pays cash to make up the residual value deficiency, Sterling would make the following journal entry.

Loss on Capital Lease	2,000.00	
Interest Expense (or Interest Payable)	454.76	
Lease Liability	4,545.24	
Accumulated Depreciation—Capital Leases	95,000.00	
Leased Equipment (under capital leases)		100,000.00
Cash		2,000.00

If the fair value *exceeds* $5,000, a gain may be recognized. Caterpillar and Sterling may apportion gains on guaranteed residual values in whatever ratio the parties initially agree.

When there is a guaranteed residual value, the lessee must be careful not to depreciate the total cost of the asset. For example, if Sterling mistakenly depreciated the total cost of the loader ($100,000), a misstatement would occur. That is, the carrying amount of the asset at the end of the lease term would be zero, but Sterling would show the liability under the capital lease at $5,000. In that case, if the asset was worth $5,000, Sterling would end up reporting a gain of $5,000 when it transferred the asset back to

Caterpillar. As a result, Sterling would overstate depreciation and would understate net income in 2014–2017; in the last year (2018) net income would be overstated.

Unguaranteed Residual Value (Lessee Accounting). From the lessee's viewpoint, an **unguaranteed residual value** is the same as no residual value in terms of its effect upon the lessee's method of computing the minimum lease payments and the capitalization of the leased asset and the lease liability.

Assume the same facts as those above except that the $5,000 residual value is **unguaranteed** instead of guaranteed. The amount of the annual lease payments would be the same—$23,237.09. Whether the residual value is guaranteed or unguaranteed, Caterpillar will recover the same amount through lease rentals—that is, $96,895.40. The minimum lease payments are $116,185.45 ($23,237.09 × 5). Sterling would capitalize the amount shown in Illustration 21-20.

STERLING'S CAPITALIZED AMOUNT (10% RATE) ANNUITY-DUE BASIS, INCLUDING UNGUARANTEED RESIDUAL VALUE	
Present value of 5 annual rental payments of $23,237.09 × 4.16986 (Table 6-5)	$96,895.40
Unguaranteed residual value of $5,000 (not capitalized by lessee)	–0–
Lessee's capitalized amount	$96,895.40

ILLUSTRATION 21-20
Computation of Lessee's Capitalized Amount—Unguaranteed Residual Value

Illustration 21-21 shows Sterling's schedule of interest expense and amortization of the lease liability of $96,895.40, assuming an unguaranteed residual value of $5,000 at the end of five years.

ILLUSTRATION 21-21
Lease Amortization Schedule for Lessee—Unguaranteed Residual Value

	STERLING CONSTRUCTION LEASE AMORTIZATION SCHEDULE (10%) ANNUITY-DUE BASIS, UNGUARANTEED RESIDUAL VALUE				
Date	Annual Lease Payments	Executory Costs	Interest (10%) on Liability	Reduction of Lease Liability	Lease Liability
	(a)	(b)	(c)	(d)	(e)
1/1/14					$96,895.40
1/1/14	$ 25,237.09	$ 2,000	–0–	$23,237.09	73,658.31
1/1/15	25,237.09	2,000	$ 7,365.83	15,871.26	57,787.05
1/1/16	25,237.09	2,000	5,778.71	17,458.38	40,328.67
1/1/17	25,237.09	2,000	4,032.87	19,204.22	21,124.45
1/1/18	25,237.09	2,000	2,112.64*	21,124.45	–0–
	$126,185.45	$10,000	$19,290.05	$96,895.40	

(a) Annual lease payment as required by lease.
(b) Executory costs included in rental payment.
(c) Preceding balance of (e) × 10%.
(d) (a) minus (b) and (c).
(e) Preceding balance minus (d).

*Rounded by 19 cents.

Sterling records the leased asset and liability, depreciation, interest, property tax, and lease payments on the basis of an unguaranteed residual value. (These journal entries are shown in Illustration 21-23 on page 1294.) The format of these capital lease entries is the same as illustrated earlier. Note that Sterling records the leased asset at $96,895.40 and depreciates it over five years. Assuming that it uses the straight-line method, the depreciation expense each year is $19,379.08 ($96,895.40 ÷ 5 years). At the end of the lease term, before Sterling transfers the asset to Caterpillar, the lease asset and liability accounts have the following balances.

ILLUSTRATION 21-22
Account Balances on
Lessee's Books at
End of Lease Term—
Unguaranteed Residual
Value

Leased equipment (under capital leases)	$96,895	Lease liability	$–0–
Less: Accumulated depreciation—capital leases	96,895		
	$ –0–		

Assuming that Sterling has fully depreciated the leased asset and has fully amortized the lease liability, no entry is required at the end of the lease term, except to remove the asset from the books.

If Sterling depreciated the asset down to its unguaranteed residual value, a misstatement would occur. That is, the carrying amount of the leased asset would be $5,000 at the end of the lease, but the liability under the capital lease would be stated at zero before the transfer of the asset. Thus, Sterling would end up reporting a loss of $5,000 when it transferred the asset back to Caterpillar. Sterling would understate depreciation and would overstate net income in 2014–2017; in the last year (2018), net income would be understated because of the recorded loss.

Lessee Entries Involving Residual Values. Illustration 21-23 shows, in comparative form, Sterling's entries for both a guaranteed and an unguaranteed residual value.

ILLUSTRATION 21-23
Comparative Entries
for Guaranteed and
Unguaranteed Residual
Values, Lessee Company

Guaranteed Residual Value			Unguaranteed Residual Value		
Capitalization of lease (January 1, 2014):					
Leased Equipment (under capital leases)	100,000.00		Leased Equipment (under capital leases)	96,895.40	
Lease Liability		100,000.00	Lease Liability		96,895.40
First payment (January 1, 2014):					
Property Tax Expense	2,000.00		Property Tax Expense	2,000.00	
Lease Liability	23,237.09		Lease Liability	23,237.09	
Cash		25,237.09	Cash		25,237.09
Adjusting entry for accrued interest (December 31, 2014):					
Interest Expense	7,676.29		Interest Expense	7,365.83	
Interest Payable		7,676.29	Interest Payable		7,365.83
Entry to record depreciation (December 31, 2014):					
Depreciation Expense (capital leases)	19,000.00		Depreciation Expense (capital leases)	19,379.08	
Accumulated Depreciation—Capital Leases ([$100,000 – $5,000] ÷ 5 years)		19,000.00	Accumulated Depreciation—Capital Leases ($96,895.40 ÷ 5 years)		19,379.08
Second payment (January 1, 2015):					
Property Tax Expense	2,000.00		Property Tax Expense	2,000.00	
Lease Liability	15,560.80		Lease Liability	15,871.26	
Interest Expense (or Interest Payable)	7,676.29		Interest Expense (or Interest Payable)	7,365.83	
Cash		25,237.09	Cash		25,237.09

Lessor Accounting for Residual Value

As we indicated earlier, the lessor will recover the same net investment whether the residual value is guaranteed or unguaranteed. That is, the lessor works on the assumption that it will realize **the residual value at the end of the lease term whether guaranteed or unguaranteed**. The lease payments required in order for the company to earn a certain return on investment are the same (e.g., $23,237.09 in our example) whether the residual value is guaranteed or unguaranteed.

To illustrate, we again use the Caterpillar/Sterling data and assume classification of the lease as a direct-financing lease. With a residual value (either guaranteed or unguaranteed) of $5,000, Caterpillar determines the payments as shown in Illustration 21-24.

Fair value of leased equipment	$100,000.00
Less: Present value of residual value ($5,000 × .62092, Table 6-2)	3,104.60
Amount to be recovered by lessor through lease payments	$ 96,895.40
Five beginning-of-the-year lease payments to yield a 10% return ($96,895.40 ÷ 4.16986, Table 6-5)	$ 23,237.09

ILLUSTRATION 21-24
Computation of Direct-Financing Lease Payments

The amortization schedule is the same for guaranteed or unguaranteed residual value, as Illustration 21-25 shows.

CATERPILLAR FINANCIAL
LEASE AMORTIZATION SCHEDULE
ANNUITY-DUE BASIS, **GUARANTEED OR UNGUARANTEED** RESIDUAL VALUE

Date	Annual Lease Payment Plus Residual Value (a)	Executory Costs (b)	Interest (10%) on Lease Receivable (c)	Lease Receivable Recovery (d)	Lease Receivable (e)
1/1/14					$100,000.00
1/1/14	$ 25,237.09	$ 2,000.00	$ –0–	$ 23,237.09	76,762.91
1/1/15	25,237.09	2,000.00	7,676.29	15,560.80	61,202.11
1/1/16	25,237.09	2,000.00	6,120.21	17,116.88	44,085.23
1/1/17	25,237.09	2,000.00	4,408.52	18,828.57	25,256.66
1/1/18	25,237.09	2,000.00	2,525.67	20,711.42	4,545.24
12/31/18	5,000.00	–0–	454.76*	4,545.24	–0–
	$131,185.45	$10,000.00	$21,185.45	$100,000.00	

(a) Annual lease payment as required by lease.
(b) Executory costs included in rental payment.
(c) Preceding balance of (e) × 10%, except 1/1/14.
(d) (a) minus (b) and (c).
(e) Preceding balance minus (d).

*Rounded by 24 cents.

ILLUSTRATION 21-25
Lease Amortization Schedule, for Lessor— Guaranteed or Unguaranteed Residual Value

Using the amounts computed above, Caterpillar would make the following entries for this direct-financing lease in the first year. Note the similarity to Sterling's entries in Illustration 21-23.

Inception of lease (January 1, 2014):		
Lease Receivable	100,000.00	
Equipment		100,000.00
First payment received (January 1, 2014):		
Cash	25,237.09	
Lease Receivable		23,237.09
Property Tax Expense/Property Taxes Payable		2,000.00
Adjusting entry for accrued interest (December 31, 2014):		
Interest Receivable	7,676.29	
Interest Revenue		7,676.29

ILLUSTRATION 21-26
Entries for Either Guaranteed or Unguaranteed Residual Value, Lessor Company

Sales-Type Leases (Lessor)

As already indicated, the primary difference between a direct-financing lease and a **sales-type lease** is the manufacturer's or dealer's gross profit (or loss). The diagram in Illustration 21-27 presents the distinctions between direct-financing and sales-type leases.

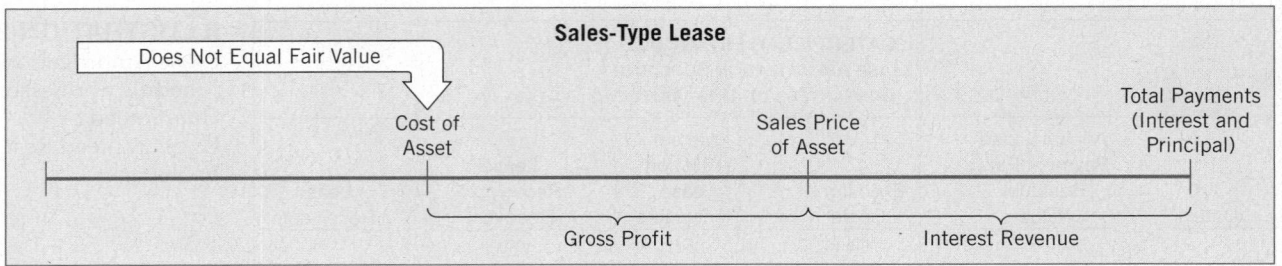

ILLUSTRATION 21-27
Direct-Financing versus
Sales-Type Leases

In a sales-type lease, the lessor records the sales price of the asset, the cost of goods sold and related inventory reduction, and the lease receivable. The information necessary to record the sales-type lease is as follows.

SALES-TYPE LEASE TERMS

LEASE RECEIVABLE (also referred to as **NET INVESTMENT**). The present value of the minimum lease payments plus the present value of any unguaranteed residual value. The lease receivable therefore includes the present value of the residual value, whether guaranteed or not.

SALES PRICE OF THE ASSET. The present value of the minimum lease payments.

COST OF GOODS SOLD. The cost of the asset to the lessor, less the present value of any unguaranteed residual value.

When recording sales revenue and cost of goods sold, there is a difference in the accounting for guaranteed and unguaranteed residual values. The guaranteed residual value can be considered part of sales revenue because the lessor knows that the entire asset has been sold. But there is less certainty that the unguaranteed residual portion of the asset has been "sold" (i.e., will be realized). Therefore, the lessor recognizes sales and cost of goods sold only for the portion of the asset for which realization is assured. However, **the gross profit amount on the sale of the asset is the same whether a guaranteed or unguaranteed residual value is involved**.

To illustrate a sales-type lease with a guaranteed residual value and with an unguaranteed residual value, assume the same facts as in the preceding direct-financing lease situation (pages 1286–1287). The estimated residual value is $5,000 (the present value of which is $3,104.60), and the leased equipment has an $85,000 cost to the dealer, Caterpillar. Assume that the fair value of the residual value is $3,000 at the end of the lease term.

Illustration 21-28 shows computation of the amounts relevant to a sales-type lease.

	Sales-Type Lease	
	Guaranteed Residual Value	Unguaranteed Residual Value
Lease receivable	$100,000 [$23,237.09 × 4.16986 (Table 6-5) + $5,000 ×.62092 (Table 6-2)]	Same
Sales price of the asset	$100,000	$96,895.40 ($100,000 − $3,104.60)
Cost of goods sold	$85,000	$81,895.40 ($85,000 − $3,104.60)
Gross profit	$15,000 ($100,000 − $85,000)	$15,000 ($96,895.40 − $81,895.40)

ILLUSTRATION 21-28
Computation of Lease Amounts by Caterpillar Financial—Sales-Type Lease

Caterpillar records the same profit ($15,000) at the point of sale whether the residual value is guaranteed or unguaranteed. The difference between the two is that **the sales revenue and cost of goods sold amounts are different**.

In making this computation, we deduct the present value of the unguaranteed residual value from sales revenue and cost of goods sold for two reasons. (1) The criteria for revenue recognition have not been met. (2) It is improper to record an expense against revenue not yet recognized. The revenue recognition criteria have not been met **because of the uncertainty surrounding the realization of the unguaranteed residual value**.

Caterpillar makes the following entries to record this transaction on January 1, 2014, and the receipt of the residual value at the end of the lease term.

ILLUSTRATION 21-29
Entries for Guaranteed and Unguaranteed Residual Values, Lessor Company—Sales-Type Lease

Guaranteed Residual Value			Unguaranteed Residual Value		
To record sales-type lease at inception (January 1, 2014):					
Cost of Goods Sold	85,000.00		Cost of Goods Sold	81,895.40	
Lease Receivable	100,000.00		Lease Receivable	100,000.00	
Sales Revenue		100,000.00	Sales Revenue		96,895.40
Inventory		85,000.00	Inventory		85,000.00
To record receipt of the first lease payment (January 1, 2014):					
Cash	25,237.09		Cash	25,237.09	
Lease Receivable		23,237.09	Lease Receivable		23,237.09
Property Tax Exp./Pay.		2,000.00	Property Tax Exp./Pay.		2,000.00
To recognize interest revenue during the first year (December 31, 2014):					
Interest Receivable	7,676.29		Interest Receivable	7,676.29	
Interest Revenue		7,676.29	Interest Revenue		7,676.29
(See lease amortization schedule, Illustration 21-25 on page 1295)					
To record receipt of the second lease payment (January 1, 2015):					
Cash	25,237.09		Cash	25,237.09	
Interest Receivable		7,676.29	Interest Receivable		7,676.29
Lease Receivable		15,560.80	Lease Receivable		15,560.80
Property Tax Exp./Pay.		2,000.00	Property Tax Exp./Pay.		2,000.00
To recognize interest revenue during the second year (December 31, 2015):					
Interest Receivable	6,120.21		Interest Receivable	6,120.21	
Interest Revenue		6,120.21	Interest Revenue		6,120.21
To record receipt of residual value at end of lease term (December 31, 2018):					
Inventory	3,000		Inventory	3,000	
Cash	2,000		Loss on Capital Lease	2,000	
Lease Receivable		5,000	Lease Receivable		5,000

**Gateway to
the Profession**

*Expanded Discussion of
Real Estate Leases and
Leveraged Leases*

Companies must periodically review the **estimated unguaranteed residual value in a sales-type lease**. If the estimate of the unguaranteed residual value declines, the company must revise the accounting for the transaction using the changed estimate. The decline represents a reduction in the lessor's lease receivable (net investment). The lessor recognizes the decline as a loss in the period in which it reduces the residual estimate. Companies do not recognize upward adjustments in estimated residual value.

What do the numbers mean? XEROX TAKES ON THE SEC

Xerox derives much of its income from leasing equipment. Reporting such leases as sales leases, Xerox records a lease contract as a sale, thereby recognizing income immediately. One problem is that each lease receipt consists of payments for items such as supplies, services, financing, and equipment.

The SEC *accused* Xerox of inappropriately allocating lease receipts, which affects the timing of income that it reports. If Xerox applied SEC guidelines, it would report income in different time periods. Xerox contended that its methods were correct. It also noted that when the lease term is up, the bottom line is the same using either the SEC's recommended allocation method or its current method.

Although Xerox can refuse to change its method, the SEC has the right to prevent a company from selling stock or bonds to the public if the agency rejects financial filings of the company.

Apparently, being able to access public markets is very valuable to Xerox. The company agreed to change its accounting according to SEC wishes, and Xerox will pay $670 million to settle a shareholder lawsuit related to its lease transactions. Its former auditor, **KPMG LLP**, will pay $80 million.

Sources: Adapted from "Xerox Takes on the SEC," *Accounting Web* (January 9, 2002), *www.account-ingweb.com*; and K. Shwiff and M. Maremont, "Xerox, KPMG Settle Shareholder Lawsuit," *Wall Street Journal Online* (March 28, 2008), p. B3.

Bargain-Purchase Option (Lessee)

As stated earlier, a bargain-purchase option allows the lessee to purchase the leased property for a future price that is substantially lower than the property's expected future fair value. The price is so favorable at the lease's inception that the future exercise of the option appears to be reasonably assured. If a bargain-purchase option exists, **the lessee must increase the present value of the minimum lease payments by the present value of the option price**.

For example, assume that Sterling Construction (see Illustration 21-18 on page 1292) had an option to buy the leased equipment for $5,000 at the end of the five-year lease term. At that point, Sterling and Caterpillar expect the fair value to be $18,000. The significant difference between the option price and the fair value creates a bargain-purchase option, and the exercise of that option is reasonably assured.

A bargain-purchase option affects the accounting for leases in essentially the same way as a guaranteed residual value. In other words, with a guaranteed residual value, the lessee must pay the residual value at the end of the lease. Similarly, a purchase option that is a bargain will almost certainly be paid by the lessee. Therefore, the computations, amortization schedule, and entries that would be prepared for this $5,000 bargain-purchase option are identical to those shown for the $5,000 guaranteed residual value (see Illustrations 21-16, 21-17, and 21-18 on pages 1291 and 1292).

The only difference between the accounting treatment for a bargain-purchase option and a guaranteed residual value of identical amounts and circumstances is in the **computation of the annual depreciation**. In the case of a guaranteed residual value, Sterling depreciates the asset over the lease term. In the case of a bargain-purchase option, it uses the **economic life** of the asset.

Initial Direct Costs (Lessor)

Initial direct costs are of two types: incremental and internal. **[8] Incremental direct costs** are paid to independent third parties for originating a lease arrangement. Examples include the cost of independent appraisal of collateral used to secure a lease, the cost of an outside credit check of the lessee, or a broker's fee for finding the lessee.

Internal direct costs are directly related to specified activities performed **by the lessor** on a given lease. Examples are evaluating the prospective lessee's financial condition; evaluating and recording guarantees, collateral, and other security arrangements; negotiating lease terms and preparing and processing lease documents; and closing the transaction. The costs directly related to an employee's time spent on a specific lease transaction are also considered initial direct costs.

However, initial direct costs should **not** include **internal indirect costs**. Such costs are related to activities the lessor performs for advertising, servicing existing leases, and establishing and monitoring credit policies. Nor should the lessor include the costs for supervision and administration or for expenses such as rent and depreciation.

The accounting for initial direct costs depends on the type of lease:

- For **operating leases**, the lessor should defer initial direct costs and **allocate them over the lease term** in proportion to the recognition of rental revenue.
- For **sales-type leases**, the lessor expenses the initial direct costs **in the period** in which it recognizes the profit on the sale.
- For a **direct-financing lease**, the lessor adds initial direct costs to the net investment in the lease and **amortizes them over the life of the lease as a yield adjustment**.

In a direct-financing lease, the lessor must disclose the unamortized deferred initial direct costs that are part of its investment in the direct-financing lease. For example, if the carrying value of the asset in the lease is $4,000,000 and the lessor incurs initial direct costs of $35,000, then the lease receivable (net investment in the lease) would be $4,035,000. The yield would be lower than the initial rate of return, and the lessor would adjust the yield to ensure proper amortization of the amount over the life of the lease.

Current versus Noncurrent

Earlier in the chapter, we presented the classification of the lease liability/receivable in an annuity-due situation. Illustration 21-7 (on page 1280) indicated that Sterling's current liability is the payment of $23,981.62 (excluding $2,000 of executory costs) to be made on January 1 of the next year. Similarly, as shown in Illustration 21-15 (on page 1288), Caterpillar's current asset is the $23,981.62 (excluding $2,000 of executory costs) it will collect on January 1 of the next year. In these annuity-due instances, the balance sheet date is December 31 and the due date of the lease payment is January 1 (less than one year), so the present value ($23,981.62) of the payment due the following January 1 is the same as the rental payment ($23,981.62).

What happens if the situation is an ordinary annuity rather than an annuity due? For example, assume that the rent is due at the **end of the year** (December 31) rather than at the beginning (January 1). GAAP does not indicate how to measure the current and noncurrent amounts. It requires that for the lessee the "obligations shall be separately identified on the balance sheet as obligations under capital leases and shall be subject to the same considerations as other obligations in classifying them with current and noncurrent liabilities in classified balance sheets." **[9] The most common method of measuring the current liability portion in ordinary annuity leases is the change-in-the-present-value method.**[14]

---

[14]For additional discussion on this approach and possible alternatives, see R. J. Swieringa, "When Current Is Noncurrent and Vice Versa!" *The Accounting Review* (January 1984), pp. 123–30; and A. W. Richardson, "The Measurement of the Current Portion of the Long-Term Lease Obligations—Some Evidence from Practice," *The Accounting Review* (October 1985), pp. 744–52.

To illustrate the change-in-the-present-value method, assume an ordinary-annuity situation with the same facts as the Caterpillar/Sterling case, excluding the $2,000 of executory costs. Because Sterling pays the rents at the end of the period instead of at the beginning, Caterpillar sets the five rents at $26,379.73, to have an effective-interest rate of 10 percent. Illustration 21-30 shows the ordinary-annuity amortization schedule.

ILLUSTRATION 21-30
Lease Amortization Schedule—Ordinary-Annuity Basis

		STERLING/CATERPILLAR		
		LEASE AMORTIZATION SCHEDULE		
		ORDINARY-ANNUITY BASIS		
Date	Annual Lease Payment	Interest 10%	Reduction of Lease Liability/Receivable	Balance of Lease Liability/Receivable
1/1/14				$100,000.00
12/31/14	$ 26,379.73	$10,000.00	$ 16,379.73	83,620.27
12/31/15	26,379.73	8,362.03	18,017.70	65,602.57
12/31/16	26,379.73	6,560.26	19,819.47	45,783.10
12/31/17	26,379.73	4,578.31	21,801.42	23,981.68
12/31/18	26,379.73	2,398.05*	23,981.68	–0–
	$131,898.65	$31,898.65	$100,000.00	

*Rounded by 12 cents.

The current portion of the lease liability/receivable under the **change-in-the-present-value method** as of December 31, 2014, would be $18,017.70 ($83,620.27 − $65,602.57). At December 31, 2014, Caterpillar classifies $65,602.57 of the receivable as noncurrent. As of December 31, 2015, the current portion would be $19,819.47 ($65,602.57 − $45,783.10).

Thus, both the annuity-due and the ordinary-annuity situations report the reduction of principal for the next period as a current liability/current asset. In the annuity-due situation, Caterpillar accrues interest during the year but is not paid until the next period. As a result, **a current asset arises for the receivable reduction and for the interest** that was recognized in the preceding period.

In the ordinary-annuity situation, the interest accrued during the period is also paid in the same period. Consequently, the lessor shows as a current asset only the principal reduction.

Disclosing Lease Data

The FASB requires **lessees** and **lessors** to disclose certain information about leases in their financial statements or in the notes. These requirements vary based upon the type of lease (capital or operating) and whether the issuer is the lessor or lessee. These disclosure requirements provide investors with the following information.

• General description of the nature of leasing arrangements.
• The nature, timing, and amount of cash inflows and outflows associated with leases, including payments to be paid or received for each of the five succeeding years.
• The amount of lease revenues and expenses reported in the income statement each period.
• Description and amounts of leased assets by major balance sheet classification and related liabilities.
• Amounts receivable and unearned revenues under lease agreements. **[10]**

Illustration 21-31 presents financial statement excerpts from the annual report of Wal-Mart Stores, Inc. dated January 31, 2012. These excerpts represent the statement and note disclosures typical of a lessee having both capital leases and operating leases.

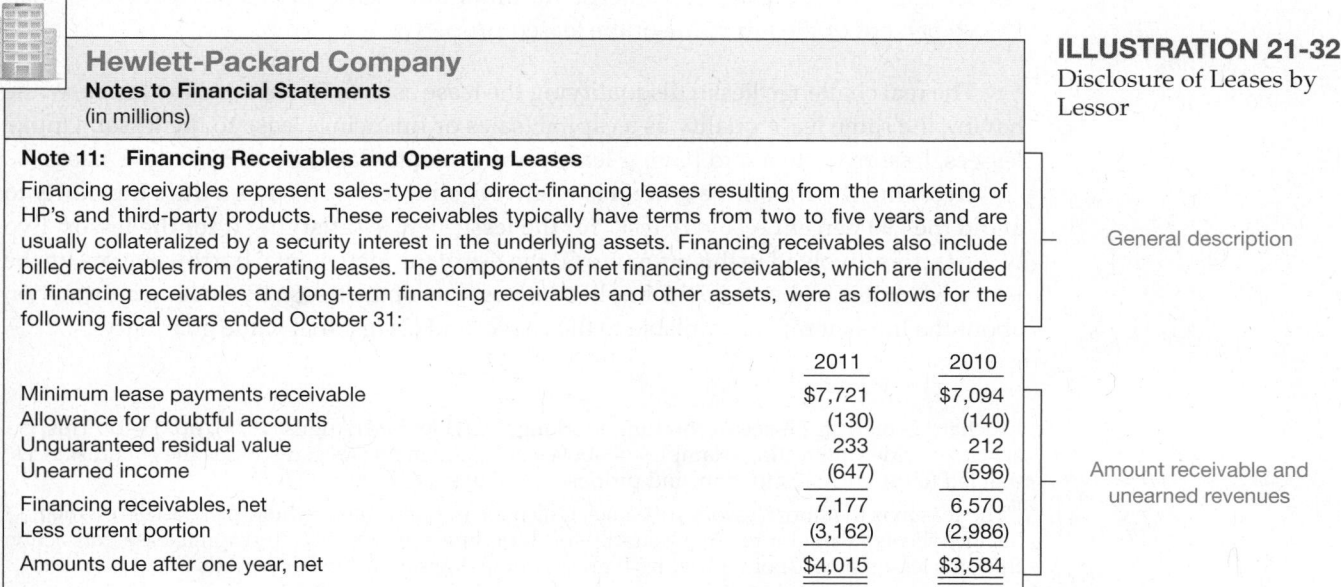

Wal-Mart Stores, Inc.
(dollar amounts in millions)

	Jan. 31, 2012	Jan. 31, 2011
Current Liabilities		
Obligations under capital leases due within one year	$ 326	$ 336
Noncurrent Liabilities		
Long-term obligations under capital leases	$3,009	$3,150

ILLUSTRATION 21-31
Disclosure of Leases by Lessee

Description and amount of lease obligations

Note 12: Commitments

The Company and certain of its subsidiaries have long-term leases for stores and equipment. Aggregate minimum annual rentals at January 31, 2012, under non-cancelable leases are as follows (dollar amounts in millions):

General description

	Operating Leases	Capital Leases
2013	$1,644	$ 608
2014	1,590	580
2015	1,525	532
2016	1,428	497
2017	1,312	457
Thereafter	8,916	3,261
Total minimum rentals		$5,935
Less estimated executory costs		50
Net minimum lease payments		$5,885
Less imputed interest		2,550
Present value of minimum lease payments		$3,335

Description and amounts of leased assets

Rental expense was approximately $2.4 billion in 2012 and $2 billion in 2011.

Certain of the Company's leases provide for the payment of contingent rentals based on a percentage of sales. Such contingent rentals were immaterial for fiscal 2012 and 2011. Substantially all of the Company's store leases have renewal options, some of which may trigger an escalation in rentals. The Company has future lease commitments for land and buildings for approximately 425 future locations. These lease commitments have lease terms ranging from 4 to 50 years and provide for certain minimum rentals. If executed, payments under operating leases would increase by $92 million for fiscal 2013, based on current cost estimates.

Nature, timing, and amounts of cash outflows

Amount of lease rental expense

Illustration 21-32 presents the lease note disclosure from the 2011 annual report of Hewlett-Packard Company. The disclosure highlights required lessor disclosures.

Hewlett-Packard Company
Notes to Financial Statements
(in millions)

ILLUSTRATION 21-32
Disclosure of Leases by Lessor

Note 11: Financing Receivables and Operating Leases

Financing receivables represent sales-type and direct-financing leases resulting from the marketing of HP's and third-party products. These receivables typically have terms from two to five years and are usually collateralized by a security interest in the underlying assets. Financing receivables also include billed receivables from operating leases. The components of net financing receivables, which are included in financing receivables and long-term financing receivables and other assets, were as follows for the following fiscal years ended October 31:

General description

	2011	2010
Minimum lease payments receivable	$7,721	$7,094
Allowance for doubtful accounts	(130)	(140)
Unguaranteed residual value	233	212
Unearned income	(647)	(596)
Financing receivables, net	7,177	6,570
Less current portion	(3,162)	(2,986)
Amounts due after one year, net	$4,015	$3,584

Amount receivable and unearned revenues

ILLUSTRATION 21-32
(Continued)

Nature, timing, and
amounts of cash inflows

Description of leased
assets

Amount of future
rentals

As of October 31, 2011, scheduled maturities of HP's minimum lease payments receivable were as follows for the following fiscal years ended October 31:

	2012	2013	2014	2015	Thereafter	Total
Scheduled maturities of minimum lease payments receivable	$3,518	$2,256	$1,257	$517	$173	$7,721

Equipment leased to customers under operating leases was $4.0 billion at October 31, 2011 and $3.5 billion at October 31, 2010 and is included in machinery and equipment. Accumulated depreciation on equipment under lease was $1.3 billion at October 31, 2011 and $1.0 billion at October 31, 2010. As of October 31, 2011, minimum future rentals on non-cancelable operating leases related to leased equipment were as follows for the following fiscal years ended October 31:

	2012	2013	2014	2015	Thereafter	Total
Minimum future rentals on non-cancelable operating leases	$1,273	$801	$414	$152	$42	$2,682

Unresolved Lease Accounting Problems

As we indicated at the beginning of this chapter, lease accounting is subject to abuse. Companies make strenuous efforts to circumvent GAAP in this area. In practice, the strong desires of lessees to resist capitalization have rendered the accounting rules for capitalizing leases partially ineffective. Leasing generally involves large dollar amounts that, when capitalized, materially increase reported liabilities and adversely affect the debt to equity ratio. Lessees also resist lease capitalization because charges to expense made in the early years of the lease term are higher under the capital lease method than under the operating method, frequently without tax benefit. As a consequence, "let's beat the lease standard" is one of the most popular games in town.[15]

To avoid leased asset capitalization, companies design, write, and interpret lease agreements to prevent satisfying any of the four capitalized lease criteria. Companies can easily devise lease agreements in such a way, by meeting the following specifications.

1. Ensure that the lease does not specify the transfer of title of the property to the lessee.
2. Do not write in a bargain-purchase option.
3. Set the lease term at something less than 75 percent of the estimated economic life of the leased property.
4. Arrange for the present value of the minimum lease payments to be less than 90 percent of the fair value of the leased property.

The real challenge lies in disqualifying the lease as a capital lease to the lessee, while having the same lease qualify as a capital (sales or financing) lease to the lessor. Unlike lessees, lessors try to avoid having lease arrangements classified as operating leases.[16]
Avoiding the first three criteria is relatively simple, but it takes a little ingenuity to avoid the "90 percent recovery test" for the lessee while satisfying it for the lessor. Two of the factors involved in this effort are (1) the use of the incremental borrowing rate by the lessee when it is higher than the implicit interest rate of the lessor, by making information about the implicit rate unavailable to the lessee, and (2) residual value guarantees.

---

[15]Richard Dieter, "Is Lessee Accounting Working?" *CPA Journal* (August 1979), pp. 13–19. This article provides interesting examples of abuses of GAAP in this area, discusses the circumstances that led to the current situation, and proposes a solution.

[16]The reason is that most lessors are banks, which are not permitted to hold these assets on their balance sheets except for relatively short periods of time. Furthermore, the capital lease transaction from the lessor's standpoint provides higher income flows in the earlier periods of the lease life.

The lessee's use of the higher interest rate is probably the more popular subterfuge. Lessees are knowledgeable about the fair value of the leased property and, of course, the rental payments. However, they generally are unaware of the estimated residual value used by the lessor. Therefore, the lessee who does not know exactly the lessor's implicit interest rate might use a different (higher) incremental borrowing rate.

The residual value guarantee is the other unique, yet popular, device used by lessees and lessors. In fact, a whole new industry has emerged to circumvent symmetry between the lessee and the lessor in accounting for leases. The residual value guarantee has spawned numerous companies whose principal, or even sole, function is to guarantee the residual value of leased assets.

Because the minimum lease payments include the guaranteed residual value for the lessor, this satisfies the 90 percent recovery of the fair value test. The lease is a nonoperating lease to the lessor. **But because a third-party guarantees the residual value, the minimum lease payments of the lessee exclude the guarantee.** Thus, by merely transferring some of the risk to a third party, lessees can alter substantially the accounting treatment by converting what would otherwise be capital leases to operating leases.[17]

International Perspective

> The IASB and the FASB are working on a joint project to reconsider lease accounting standards.

The nature of the criteria encourages much of this circumvention, stemming from weaknesses in the basic objective of the lease accounting guidelines. Accounting rule-makers continue to have poor experience with arbitrary break points or other size and percentage criteria—such as rules like "90 percent of" and "75 percent of." Some believe that a more workable solution is to require capitalization of all leases that have noncancelable payment terms in excess of one year. Under this approach, the lessee acquires an asset (a property right) and a corresponding liability, rather than on the basis that the lease transfers substantially all the risks and rewards of ownership.

> **You will want to read the IFRS INSIGHTS** on pages 1331–1341 for discussion of IFRS related to lease accounting.

Evolving Issue LEASE ACCOUNTING—IF IT QUACKS LIKE A DUCK

Three years after it issued a lease accounting pronouncement, a majority of the FASB expressed "the tentative view that, if the lease accounting rules were to be reconsidered, they would support a property right approach in which all leases are included as 'rights to use property' and as 'lease obligations' in the lessee's balance sheet." The FASB and IASB have issued a proposal on lease accounting to address off-balance-sheet reporting of leases. As summarized in the adjacent table, early analysis of the potential impact of the proposed leasing rules indicates significant impacts.

As indicated, over $1.1 trillion of operating leases will come on-balance-sheet if the rules are adopted. In addition,

> **A quick look at the current leasing market, and some possible effects of the proposed rules:**
>
> - *$600 billion.* Annual volume of leased equipment.
> - *70%.* Volume of real estate leases as a percentage of all leases held by U.S. public companies.
> - *$1.3 trillion.* Amount of operating lease payments that U.S. public companies will bring back on balance sheets as capital leases under the proposed rule.
> - *7%.* Potential first-year average increase in lease expense for a 3-year lease.
> - *21%.* Potential first-year average increase in lease expense for a 10-year lease.
>
> *Source:* Equipment Leasing and Finance Association, 2009; PricewaterhouseCoopers and Rotterdam School of Management, 2009.

---

[17]As an aside, third-party guarantors have experienced some difficulty. Lloyd's of London, at one time, insured the fast-growing U.S. computer leasing industry in the amount of $2 billion against revenue losses, and losses in residual value, for canceled leases. Because of "overnight" technological improvements and the successive introductions of more efficient and less expensive computers, lessees in abundance canceled their leases. As the market for secondhand computers became flooded, residual values plummeted, and third-party guarantor Lloyd's of London projected a loss of $400 million. The lessees' and lessors' desire to circumvent GAAP stimulated much of the third-party guarantee business.

there will be a significant negative impact on lessee income statements in the early years of leases.

As shown below, the frontloading of lease expenses will be felt by lessees in several industry sectors.

Lease Expense Impacts by Industry Sector

Sector	Typical Lease Term (Years)	First-Year % Increase Prompted by New Rules*	Cumulative % Increase Through Peak Year*
Airline	17	26%	128%/yr. 9
Automotive fleet	3	4	N/A
Banking	10	21	64%/yr. 5
Copier/office equipment	3	7	7%/yr. 3
Equipment manufacturers	5	11	17%/yr. 2
Health-care equipment	5	11	17%/yr. 2
Information technology	3	7	7%/yr. 2
Rail	22	26	200%/yr. 12
Real estate	10	21	64%/yr. 5
Trucking	7	16	33%/yr. 4

*As compared with the straight-line method of accounting.

Source: Equipment Leasing and Finance Association, 2009.

Given these effects—increased reported debt and lower income—as a consequence of these proposed rules, it is not surprising that the FASB (and IASB) are receiving numerous comments opposing changes in lease accounting rules. At the same time, an analysis of the new rules and how they might impact the advantages of leasing presented in the following table suggests that many of the advantages of leases will remain after implementation of the new rules.

Reason for Leasing	Details	Status After Proposed New Rules Implemented
Funding source	Additional capital source, 100% financing, fixed rate, level payments, longer terms.	Still a major benefit versus a purchase—money loan financing, fixed rate, level payments—especially for smaller companies with limited sources of capital.
Low-cost capital	Low payments/rate due to tax benefits, residual and lessor's comparatively low cost of funds.	Still a benefit versus a loan.
Tax benefits	Lessee cannot use tax benefits and lease versus buy shows lease option offers lowest after tax cost.	Still a benefit.
Manage need for assets/ residual risk transfer	Lessee has flexibility to return asset.	Still a benefit.
Convenience	Quick and convenient financing process often available at point-of-sale.	Still a benefit.
Regulatory	Can help in meeting capital requirements.	Still a partial benefit if the capitalized amount is less than the cost of the asset as it is in many leases due to residuals assumed and tax benefits.
Accounting	Asset and liability off-balance-sheet.	Still a partial benefit if the capitalized amount is less than the cost of the asset as it is in many leases due to residuals assumed and tax benefits.

Source: Equipment Leasing & Finance Foundation, *2011 State of the Equipment Finance Industry Report.*

So while concerns about changes in lease accounting may be valid, accounting standard-setters are resolved to address lease accounting deficiencies. As the chairperson of the IASB remarked, ". . . a financing, in the form of a loan to purchase an asset, then it would be recorded. Call it a lease and miraculously it does not show up in your books. In my book, if it looks like a duck, swims like a duck, and quacks like a duck, then it probably is a duck. So is the case with debt— leasing or otherwise."

We hope that new accounting rules can be developed so that financial statements provide relevant and representationally faithful information about leasing arrangements.

Sources: M. Leone, "Taking the 'Ease' Out of 'Lease'?" *CFO Magazine* (December 1, 2010); and Hans Hoogervorst, "Harmonisation and Global Economic Consequences," Public lecture at the London School of Economics (November 6, 2012). For the latest on the lease project, go to *www.fasb.org* (click on Leases under the Projects tab).

SUMMARY OF LEARNING OBJECTIVES

1 **Explain the nature, economic substance, and advantages of lease transactions.** A lease is a contractual agreement between a lessor and a lessee that conveys to the lessee the right to use specific property (real or personal), owned by the lessor, for a specified period of time. In return, the lessee periodically pays cash (rent) to the lessor. The advantages of lease transactions are (1) 100 percent financing, (2) protection against obsolescence, (3) flexibility, (4) less costly financing, (5) possible tax advantages, and (6) off-balance-sheet financing.

2 **Describe the accounting criteria and procedures for capitalizing leases by the lessee.** A lease is a capital lease if it meets one or more of the following criteria. (1) The lease transfers ownership of the property to the lessee. (2) The lease contains a bargain-purchase option. (3) The lease term is equal to 75 percent or more of the estimated economic life of the leased property. (4) The present value of the minimum lease payments (excluding executory costs) equals or exceeds 90 percent of the fair value of the leased property. For a capital lease, the lessee records an asset and a liability at the lower of (1) the present value of the minimum lease payments, or (2) the fair value of the leased asset at the inception of the lease.

3 **Contrast the operating and capitalization methods of recording leases.** The total charges to operations are the same over the lease term whether accounting for the lease as a capital lease or as an operating lease. Under the capital lease treatment, the charges are higher in the earlier years and lower in the later years. If using an accelerated method of depreciation, the differences between the amounts charged to operations under the two methods would be even larger in the earlier and later years. If using a capital lease instead of an operating lease, the following occurs: (1) an increase in the amount of reported debt (both short-term and long-term), (2) an increase in the amount of total assets (specifically long-lived assets), and (3) lower income early in the life of the lease and, therefore, lower retained earnings.

4 **Explain the advantages and economics of leasing to lessors and identify the classifications of leases for the lessor.** Three important benefits available to the lessor are (1) interest revenue, (2) tax incentives, and (3) residual value profits. Lessors are essentially renting or selling assets, and in many cases are providing financing for the purchase of the asset. The lessor determines the amount of the rental, basing it on the rate of return—the implicit rate—needed to justify leasing the asset, taking into account the credit standing of the lessee, the length of the lease, and the status of the residual value (guaranteed versus unguaranteed).

A lessor may classify leases for accounting purposes as follows: (1) operating leases, (2) direct-financing leases, and (3) sales-type leases. The lessor should classify and account for an arrangement as a direct-financing lease or a sales-type lease if, at the date of the lease agreement, the lease meets one or more of the Group I criteria (as shown in Learning Objective 2 for lessees) and *both* of the following Group II criteria: (1) collectibility of the payments required from the lessee is reasonably predictable, and (2) no important uncertainties surround the amount of unreimbursable costs yet to be incurred by the lessor under the lease. The lessor classifies and accounts for all leases that fail to meet the criteria as operating leases.

5 **Describe the lessor's accounting for direct-financing leases.** Leases that are in substance the financing of an asset purchase by a lessee require the lessor to substitute a "lease receivable" for the leased asset. "Lease receivable" is the present value of the minimum lease payments plus the present value of the unguaranteed residual value. Therefore, lessors include the residual value, whether guaranteed or unguaranteed, as part of the lease receivable.

KEY TERMS

bargain-purchase option, *1275*

bargain-renewal option, *1276*

capitalization criteria, *1275*

capitalization of leases, *1273*

capital lease, *1275*

direct-financing lease, *1286*

effective-interest method, *1278*

executory costs, *1277*

guaranteed residual value, *1277, 1290*

implicit interest rate, *1277*

incremental borrowing rate, *1277*

initial direct costs, *1298*

lease, *1270*

lease receivable, *1286*

lease term, *1272*

lessee, *1270*

lessor, *1270*

manufacturer's or dealer's profit (or loss), *1285*

minimum lease payments, *1276*

noncancelable, *1274*

off-balance-sheet financing, *1272*

operating lease, *1275*

residual value, *1290*

sales-type lease, *1296*

third-party guarantors, *1277*

unguaranteed residual value, *1293*

6 **Identify special features of lease arrangements that cause unique accounting problems.** The features of lease arrangements that cause unique accounting problems are (1) residual values, (2) sales-type leases (lessor), (3) bargain-purchase options, (4) initial direct costs, (5) current versus noncurrent, and (6) disclosures.

7 **Describe the effect of residual values, guaranteed and unguaranteed, on lease accounting.** Whether the estimated residual value is guaranteed or unguaranteed is of both economic and accounting consequence to the lessee. The accounting consequence is that the minimum lease payments, the basis for capitalization, include the guaranteed residual value but exclude the unguaranteed residual value. A guaranteed residual value affects the lessee's computation of minimum lease payments and the amounts capitalized as a leased asset and a lease obligation. In effect, the guaranteed residual value is an additional lease payment that the lessee will pay in property or cash, or both, at the end of the lease term. An unguaranteed residual value from the lessee's viewpoint is the same as no residual value in terms of its effect upon the lessee's method of computing the minimum lease payments and the capitalization of the leased asset and the lease liability.

8 **Describe the lessor's accounting for sales-type leases.** A sales-type lease recognizes interest revenue like a direct-financing lease. It also recognizes a manufacturer's or dealer's profit. In a sales-type lease, the lessor records at the inception of the lease the sales price of the asset, the cost of goods sold and related inventory reduction, and the lease receivable. Sales-type leases differ from direct-financing leases in terms of the cost and fair value of the leased asset, which results in gross profit. Lease receivable and interest revenue are the same whether a guaranteed or an unguaranteed residual value is involved. The accounting for guaranteed and for unguaranteed residual values requires recording sales revenue and cost of goods sold differently. The guaranteed residual value can be considered part of sales revenue because the lessor knows that the entire asset has been sold. There is less certainty that the unguaranteed residual portion of the asset has been "sold." Therefore, lessors recognize sales and cost of goods sold only for the portion of the asset for which realization is assured. However, the gross profit amount on the sale of the asset is the same whether a guaranteed or unguaranteed residual value is involved.

9 **List the disclosure requirements for leases.** The disclosure requirements for the lessees and lessors vary based upon the type of lease (capital or operating) and whether the issuer is the lessor or lessee. These disclosure requirements provide investors with the following information: (1) general description of the nature of leasing arrangements; (2) the nature, timing, and amount of cash inflows and outflows associated with leases, including payments to be paid or received for each of the five succeeding years; (3) the amount of lease revenues and expenses reported in the income statement each period; (4) description and amounts of leased assets by major balance sheet classification and related liabilities; and (5) amounts receivable and unearned revenues under lease agreements.

APPENDIX 21A | **SALE-LEASEBACKS**

LEARNING OBJECTIVE 10
Describe the lessee's accounting for
sale-leaseback transactions.

The term **sale-leaseback** describes a transaction in which the owner of the property (seller-lessee) sells the property to another and simultaneously leases it back from the new owner. The use of the property is generally continued without interruption.

Sale-leasebacks are common. Financial institutions (e.g., **Bank of America** and **First Chicago**) have used this technique for their administrative offices, public utilities (**Ohio Edison** and **Pinnacle West Corporation**) for their generating plants, and airlines (**Continental** and **Alaska Airlines**) for their aircraft. The advantages of a sale-leaseback from the seller's viewpoint usually involve two primary considerations:

1. *Financing.* If the purchase of equipment has already been financed, a sale-leaseback can allow the seller to refinance at lower rates, assuming rates have dropped. In addition, a sale-leaseback can provide another source of working capital, particularly when liquidity is tight.
2. *Taxes.* At the time a company purchased equipment, it may not have known that it would be subject to an alternative minimum tax and that ownership might increase its minimum tax liability. By selling the property, the seller-lessee may deduct the entire lease payment, which is not subject to alternative minimum tax considerations.

DETERMINING ASSET USE

To the extent the **seller-lessee continues to use** the asset after the sale, the sale-leaseback is really a form of financing. Therefore, the lessor **should not recognize a gain or loss** on the transaction. In short, the seller-lessee is simply borrowing funds.

On the other hand, if the **seller-lessee gives up the right to the use** of the asset, the transaction is in substance a sale. In that case, **gain or loss recognition** is appropriate. Trying to ascertain when the lessee has given up the use of the asset is difficult, however, and the FASB has formulated complex rules to identify this situation.[18] To understand the profession's position in this area, we discuss the basic accounting for the lessee and lessor below.

Underlying Concepts 🔍

A sale-leaseback is similar in substance to the parking of inventories (discussed in Chapter 8). The ultimate economic benefits remain under the control of the "seller," thus satisfying the definition of an asset.

Lessee

If the lease meets one of the four criteria for treatment as a capital lease (see Illustration 21-3 on page 1275), the **seller-lessee accounts for the transaction as a sale and the lease as a capital lease**. The seller-lessee should defer any profit or loss it experiences from the sale of the assets that are leased back under a capital lease; it should **amortize that profit over the lease term** (or the economic life if either criterion 1 or 2 is satisfied) in proportion to the amortization of the leased assets.

For example, assume **Scott Paper** sells equipment having a book value of $580,000 and a fair value of $623,110 to **General Electric Credit** for $623,110 and leases the equipment back for $50,000 a year for 20 years. Scott should amortize the profit of $43,110 over the 20-year period at the same rate that it depreciates the $623,110. **[12]** It credits the $43,110 ($623,110 − $580,000) to **Unearned Profit on Sale-Leaseback**.

If none of the capital lease criteria are satisfied, **the seller-lessee accounts for the transaction as a sale and the lease as an operating lease**. Under an operating lease, the lessee defers such profit or loss and amortizes it in proportion to the rental payments over the period when it expects to use the assets.

---

[18]Sales and leasebacks of real estate are often accounted for differently. A discussion of the issues related to these transactions is beyond the scope of this textbook. **[11]**

There are exceptions to these two general rules. They are:

1. *Losses recognized.* When the fair value of the asset is **less than the book value** (carrying amount), the lessee must recognize a loss immediately, up to the amount of the difference between the book value and fair value. For example, if Lessee, Inc. sells equipment having a book value of $650,000 and a fair value of $623,110, it should charge the difference of $26,890 to a loss account.[19]

2. *Minor leaseback.* Leasebacks in which the present value of the rental payments are 10 percent or less of the fair value of the asset are minor leasebacks. In this case, the seller-lessee gives up most of the rights to the use of the asset sold. Therefore, the transaction is a sale, and full gain or loss recognition is appropriate. It is not a financing transaction because the risks of ownership have been transferred.[20]

Lessor

If the lease meets one of the criteria in Group I and both of the criteria in Group II (see Illustration 21-10 on page 1285), the **purchaser-lessor** records the transaction as a purchase and a direct-financing lease. If the lease does not meet the criteria, the purchaser-lessor records the transaction as a purchase and an operating lease.

SALE-LEASEBACK EXAMPLE

To illustrate the accounting treatment accorded a sale-leaseback transaction, assume that American Airlines on January 1, 2014, sells a used Boeing 757 having a carrying amount on its books of $75,500,000 to CitiCapital for $80,000,000. American immediately leases the aircraft back under the following conditions:

1. The term of the lease is 15 years, noncancelable, and requires equal rental payments of $10,487,443 at the beginning of each year.
2. The aircraft has a fair value of $80,000,000 on January 1, 2014, and an estimated economic life of 15 years.
3. American pays all executory costs.
4. American depreciates similar aircraft that it owns on a straight-line basis over 15 years.
5. The annual payments assure the lessor a 12 percent return.
6. American's incremental borrowing rate is 12 percent.

This lease is a capital lease to American because the lease term exceeds 75 percent of the estimated life of the aircraft and because the present value of the lease payments exceeds 90 percent of the fair value of the aircraft to CitiCapital. Assuming that collectibility of the lease payments is reasonably predictable and that no important uncertainties exist

---

[19]There can be two types of losses in sale-leaseback arrangements. One is a real economic loss that results when the carrying amount of the asset is higher than the fair value of the asset. In this case, the loss should be recognized. An artificial loss results when the sales price is below the carrying amount of the asset but the fair value is above the carrying amount. In this case, the loss is more in the form of prepaid rent, and the lessee should defer the loss and amortize it in the future.

[20]In some cases, the seller-lessee retains more than a minor part but less than substantially all. The computations to arrive at these values are complex and beyond the scope of this textbook.

in relation to unreimbursable costs yet to be incurred by CitiCapital, it should classify this lease as a direct-financing lease.

Illustration 21A-1 presents the typical journal entries to record the sale-leaseback transactions for American and CitiCapital for the first year.

ILLUSTRATION 21A-1
Comparative Entries for
Sale-Leaseback for Lessee
and Lessor

American Airlines (Lessee)			CitiCapital (Lessor)		
Sale of Aircraft by American to CitiCapital (January 1, 2014):					
Cash	80,000,000		Aircraft	80,000,000	
Aircraft		75,500,000	Cash		80,000,000
Unearned Profit on Sale-Leaseback		4,500,000	Lease Receivable	80,000,000	
Leased Aircraft (under capital leases)	80,000,000		Aircraft		80,000,000
Lease Liability		80,000,000			
First Lease Payment (January 1, 2014):					
Lease Liability	10,487,443		Cash	10,487,443	
Cash		10,487,443	Lease Receivable		10,487,443
Incurrence and Payment of Executory Costs by American Corp. throughout 2014:					
Insurance, Maintenance, Taxes, etc.	XXX		(No entry)		
Cash or Accounts Payable		XXX			
Depreciation Expense on the Aircraft (December 31, 2014):					
Depreciation Expense	5,333,333		(No entry)		
Accumulated Depr.—Capital Leases		5,333,333			
($80,000,000 ÷ 15)					
Amortization of Profit on Sale-Leaseback by American (December 31, 2014):					
Unearned Profit on Sale-Leaseback	300,000		(No entry)		
Depreciation Expense		300,000			
($4,500,000 ÷ 15)					
(*Note:* A case might be made for crediting Sales Revenue instead of Depreciation Expense.)					
Interest for 2014 (December 31, 2014):					
Interest Expense	8,341,507[a]		Interest Receivable	8,341,507	
Interest Payable		8,341,507	Interest Revenue		8,341,507[a]

[a]Partial Lease Amortization Schedule:

Date	Annual Rental Payment	Interest 12%	Reduction of Balance	Balance
1/1/14				$80,000,000
1/1/14	$10,487,443	$ –0–	$10,487,443	69,512,557
1/1/15	10,487,443	8,341,507	2,145,936	67,366,621

KEY TERMS

minor leaseback, *1308*
sale-leaseback, *1306*

SUMMARY OF LEARNING OBJECTIVE FOR APPENDIX 21A

10 Describe the lessee's accounting for sale-leaseback transactions. If the lease meets one of the four criteria for treatment as a capital lease, the seller-lessee accounts for the transaction as a sale and the lease as a capital lease. The seller-lessee defers any profit it experiences from the sale of the assets that are leased back under a capital lease. The seller-lessee amortizes any profit over the lease term (or the economic life if either criterion 1 or 2 is satisfied) in proportion to the amortization of the leased assets. If the lease satisfies none of the capital lease criteria, the seller-lessee accounts for the transaction as a sale and the lease as an operating lease. Under an operating lease, the lessee defers such profit and amortizes it in proportion to the rental payments over the period of time that it expects to use the assets.

DEMONSTRATION PROBLEM

Morgan Bakeries is involved in four different lease situations. Each of these leases is noncancelable, and in no case does Morgan receive title to the properties leased during or at the end of the lease term. All leases start on January 1, 2014, with the first rental due at the beginning of the year. Additional information is shown in the following table.

	(a) Harmon, Inc.	(b) Arden's Oven Co.	(c) Mendota Truck Co.	(d) Appleland Computer
Type of property	Cabinets	Oven	Truck	Computer
Yearly rental	$6,000	$15,000	$5,582.62	$3,557.25
Lease term	20 years	10 years	3 years	3 years
Estimated economic life	30 years	25 years	7 years	5 years
Purchase option	None	$75,000 at end of 10 years $4,000 at end of 15 years	None	$3,000 at end of 3 years, which approximates fair value
Renewal option	None	5-year renewal option at $15,000 per year	None	1 year at $1,500; no penalty for nonrenewal; standard renewal clause
Fair value at inception of lease	$60,000	$120,000	$20,000	$10,000
Cost of asset to lessor	$60,000	$120,000	$15,000	$10,000
Residual value				
Guaranteed	–0–	–0–	$7,000	–0–
Unguaranteed	$5,000	–0–	–0–	$3,000
Incremental borrowing rate of lessee	12%	12%	12%	12%
Executory costs paid by	*Lessee* $300 per year	*Lessee* $1,000 per year	*Lessee* $500 per year	*Lessor* Estimated to be $500 per year, included in lease payment
Present value of minimum lease payments				
Using incremental borrowing rate of lessee	$50,194.68	$115,153.35	$20,000	$8,224.16
Using implicit rate of lessor	Not known	Not known	Not known	Known by lessee, $8,027.48
Estimated fair value at end of lease	$5,000	$80,000 at end of 10 years $60,000 at end of 15 years	Not available	$3,000

Instructions

For each lease arrangement, determine the correct classification of the lease and prepare the journal entry at its inception.

Solution

(a) Analysis of the Harmon, Inc. lease:

1. **Transfer of title?** No.
2. **Bargain-purchase option?** No.
3. **Economic life test (75% test).** The lease term is 20 years and the estimated economic life is 30 years. Thus, it **does not** meet the 75 percent test.
4. **Recovery of investment test (90% test):**

Fair value	$60,000	Rental payments	$ 6,000
Rate	× 90%	PV of annuity due for	
90% of fair value	$54,000	20 years at 12%	× 8.36578
		PV of rental payments	$50,194.68

Because the present value of the minimum lease payments is less than 90 percent of the fair value, the lease does not meet the 90 percent test.

Both Morgan and Harmon should account for this lease as an operating lease, as indicated by the following January 1, 2014, entries.

Morgan Bakeries (Lessee)		Harmon, Inc. (Lessor)	
Rent Expense	6,000	Cash	6,000
Cash	6,000	Rent Revenue	6,000

(b) Analysis of the Arden's Oven Co. lease:

1. **Transfer of title?** No.
2. **Bargain-purchase option?** The $75,000 option at the end of 10 years does not appear to be sufficiently lower than the expected fair value of $80,000 to make it reasonably assured that it will be exercised. However, the $4,000 at the end of 15 years when the fair value is $60,000 does appear to be a bargain. From the information given, criterion 2 is therefore met. Note that both the guaranteed and the unguaranteed residual values are assigned zero values because the lessor does not expect to repossess the leased asset.
3. **Economic life test (75% test):** Given that a bargain-purchase option exists, the lease term is the initial lease period of 10 years plus the five-year renewal option since it precedes a bargain-purchase option. Even though the lease term is now considered to be 15 years, this test is still not met because 75 percent of the economic life of 25 years is 18.75 years.
4. **Recovery of investment test (90% test):**

Fair value	$120,000	Rental payments	$ 15,000.00
Rate	× 90%	PV of annuity due for	
90% of fair value	$108,000	15 years at 12%	× 7.62817
		PV of rental payments	$114,422.55

PV of bargain-purchase option: = $4,000 × $(PVF_{15,12\%})$ = $4,000 × .18270 = $730.80

PV of rental payments	$114,422.55
PV of bargain-purchase option	730.80
PV of minimum lease payments	$115,153.35

The present value of the minimum lease payments is greater than 90 percent of the fair value. Therefore, the lease does meet the 90 percent test.

Morgan Bakeries should account for this as a capital lease because the lease meets both criteria 2 and 4. Assuming that Arden's implicit rate is less than Morgan's incremental borrowing rate, the following entries are made on January 1, 2014.

Morgan Bakeries (Lessee)		Arden's Oven Co. (Lessor)	
Leased Equipment (oven)	115,153.35	Lease Receivable	120,000
Lease Liability	115,153.35	Equipment (oven)	120,000

Morgan Bakeries would depreciate the leased asset over its economic life of 25 years, given the bargain-purchase option. Arden's Oven Co. does not use sales-type accounting because the fair value and the cost of the asset are the same at the inception of the lease.

(c) Analysis of the Mendota Truck Co. lease:

1. **Transfer of title?** No.
2. **Bargain-purchase option?** No.
3. **Economic life test (75% test):** The lease term is three years and the estimated economic life is seven years. Thus, it **does not** meet the 75 percent test.
4. **Recovery of investment test (90% test):**

Fair value	$20,000	Rental payments	$ 5,582.62
Rate	× 90%	PV of annuity due for	
90% of fair value	$18,000	3 years at 12%	× 2.69005
		PV of rental payments	$15,017.54

(*Note:* Adjusted for $0.01 due to rounding.)

PV of guaranteed residual value: $= \$7,000 \times (PVF_{3,12\%}) = \$7,000 \times .71178 = \$4,982.46$

PV of rental payments	$15,017.54
PV of guaranteed residual value	4,982.46
PV of minimum lease payments	$20,000.00

The present value of the minimum lease payments is greater than 90 percent of the fair value. Therefore, the lease meets the 90 percent test.

Assuming that Mendota's implicit rate is the same as Morgan's incremental borrowing rate, the following entries are made on January 1, 2014.

Morgan Bakeries			Mendota Truck Co.		
(Lessee)			(Lessor)		
Leased Equipment (truck)	20,000		Lease Receivable	20,000	
Lease Liability		20,000	Cost of Goods Sold	15,000	
			Trucks		15,000
			Sales Revenue		20,000

Because the cost of the truck is less than the fair value, this is a sales-type lease for Mendota. Morgan depreciates the leased asset over three years to its guaranteed residual value.

(d) Analysis of the Appleland Computer lease:

1. **Transfer of title?** No.
2. **Bargain-purchase option?** No. The option to purchase at the end of three years at approximate fair value is clearly not a bargain.
3. **Economic life test (75% test):** The lease term is three years, and no bargain-renewal period exists. Therefore, the 75 percent test **is not** met.
4. **Recovery of investment test (90% test):**

Fair value	$10,000	Rental payments	$3,557.25
Rate	× 90%	Less executory costs	500.00
90% of fair value	$ 9,000		3,057.25
		PV of annuity-due factor	
		for 3 years at 12%	× 2.69005
		PV of minimum lease payments	
		using incremental borrowing rate	$8,224.16

The present value of the minimum lease payments using the incremental borrowing rate is $8,224.16. Using the implicit rate, it is $8,027.48. The lessor's implicit rate is therefore higher than the incremental borrowing rate. Given this situation, the lessee uses the $8,224.16 (lower interest rate when discounting) when comparing with the 90 percent of fair value. Because the present value of the minimum lease payments is lower than 90 percent of the fair value, the lease does **not** meet the recovery of investment test.

The following entries are made on January 1, 2014, indicating an operating lease.

Morgan Bakeries (Lessee)			Appleland Computer (Lessor)		
Rent Expense	3,557.25		Cash	3,557.25	
Cash		3,557.25	Rent Revenue		3,557.25

If the lease payments had been $3,557.25 with no executory costs involved, this lease arrangement would have qualified for capital-lease accounting treatment.

FASB CODIFICATION

FASB Codification References

[1] FASB ASC 840-10-25-1. [Predecessor literature: "Accounting for Leases," *FASB Statement No. 13* as amended and interpreted through May 1980 (Stamford, Conn.: FASB, 1980), par. 7.]

[2] FASB ASC 840-10-25. [Predecessor literature: "Accounting for Leases: Sale-Leaseback Transactions Involving Real Estate; Sales-Type Leases of Real Estate; Definition of the Lease Term; Initial Direct Costs of Direct Financing Leases," *Statement of Financial Accounting Standards No. 98* (Stamford, Conn.: FASB, 1988).]

[3] FASB ASC 840-10-25-9. [Predecessor literature: "Lessee Guarantee of the Residual Value of Leased Property," *FASB Interpretation No. 19* (Stamford, Conn.: FASB, 1977), par. 3.]

[4] FASB ASC 840-10-25-22. [Predecessor literature: "Accounting for Leases," *FASB Statement No. 13* as amended and interpreted through May 1980 (Stamford, Conn.: FASB, 1980), par. 5 (l).]

[5] FASB ASC 840-10-25-31. [Predecessor literature: "Accounting for Leases," *FASB Statement No. 13* as amended and interpreted through May 1980 (Stamford, Conn.: FASB, 1980), par. 5 (k).]

[6] FASB ASC 840-30-35-14. [Predecessor literature: "Accounting for Purchase of a Leased Asset by the Lessee During the Term of the Lease," *FASB Interpretation No. 26* (Stamford, Conn.: FASB, 1978), par. 5.]

[7] FASB ASC 840-10-25-43. [Predecessor literature: "Accounting for Leases," *FASB Statement No. 13* as amended and interpreted through May 1980 (Stamford, Conn.: FASB, 1980), paras. 6, 7, and 8.]

[8] FASB ASC 840-30-30-12. [Predecessor literature: "Accounting for Nonrefundable Fees and Costs Associated with Originating or Acquiring Loans and Initial Direct Costs of Leases," *Statement of Financial Accounting Standards No. 91* (Stamford: Conn.: FASB, 1987).]

[9] FASB ASC 840-30-50-1. [Predecessor literature: "Accounting for Leases," *FASB Statement No. 13* as amended and interpreted through May 1980 (Stamford, Conn.: FASB, 1980), par. 16.]

[10] FASB ASC 840-30-50-4. [Predecessor literature: "Accounting for Leases," *FASB Statement No. 13* as amended and interpreted through May 1980 (Stamford, Conn.: FASB, 1980), paras. 16 and 23.]

[11] FASB ASC 840-40. [Predecessor literature: "Accounting for Leases: Sale-Leaseback Transactions Involving Real Estate; Sales-Type Leases of Real Estate; Definition of the Lease Term; Initial Direct Costs of Direct Financing Leases," *Statement of Financial Accounting Standards No. 98* (Stamford, Conn.: FASB, 1988).]

[12] FASB ASC 840-40. [Predecessor literature: *Statement of Financial Accounting Standards No. 28*, "Accounting for Sales with Leasebacks" (Stamford, Conn.: FASB, 1979).]

Exercises

If your school has a subscription to the FASB Codification, go to *http://aaahq.org/ascLogin.cfm* to log in and prepare responses to the following. Provide Codification references for your responses.

CE21-1 Access the glossary ("Master Glossary") to answer the following.

(a) What is a bargain-purchase option?
(b) What is the definition of "incremental borrowing rate"?
(c) What is the definition of "estimated residual value"?
(d) What is an unguaranteed residual value?

CE21-2 What comprises a lessee's minimum lease payments? What is excluded?

CE21-3 What information should a lessee disclose about its capital leases in its financial statements and footnotes?

CE21-4 How should a lessor measure its initial gross investment in either a sales-type lease or a direct-financing lease?

An additional Codification case can be found in the Using Your Judgment section, on page 1331.

WileyPLUS

Brief Exercises, Exercises, Problems, and many more learning and assessment tools and resources are available for practice in WileyPLUS.

Note: All asterisked Questions, Exercises, and Problems relate to material in the appendix to the chapter. (*Unless instructed otherwise, round all amounts to the nearest dollar.*)

QUESTIONS

1. What are the major lessor groups in the United States? What advantage does a captive have in a leasing arrangement?

2. Bradley Co. is expanding its operations and is in the process of selecting the method of financing this program. After some investigation, the company determines that it may (1) issue bonds and with the proceeds purchase the needed assets or (2) lease the assets on a long-term basis. Without knowing the comparative costs involved, answer these questions:

    (a) What might be the advantages of leasing the assets instead of owning them?

    (b) What might be the disadvantages of leasing the assets instead of owning them?

    (c) In what way will the balance sheet be differently affected by leasing the assets as opposed to issuing bonds and purchasing the assets?

3. Identify the two recognized lease accounting methods for lessees and distinguish between them.

4. Ballard Company rents a warehouse on a month-to-month basis for the storage of its excess inventory. The company periodically must rent space whenever its production greatly exceeds actual sales. For several years, the company officials have discussed building their own storage facility, but this enthusiasm wavers when sales increase sufficiently to absorb the excess inventory. What is the nature of this type of lease arrangement, and what accounting treatment should be accorded it?

5. Distinguish between minimum rental payments and minimum lease payments, and indicate what is included in minimum lease payments.

6. Explain the distinction between a direct-financing lease and a sales-type lease for a lessor.

7. Outline the accounting procedures involved in applying the operating method by a lessee.

8. Outline the accounting procedures involved in applying the capital lease method by a lessee.

9. Identify the lease classifications for lessors and the criteria that must be met for each classification.

10. Outline the accounting procedures involved in applying the direct-financing method.

11. Outline the accounting procedures involved in applying the operating method by a lessor.

12. Walker Company is a manufacturer and lessor of computer equipment. What should be the nature of its lease arrangements with lessees if the company wishes to account for its lease transactions as sales-type leases?

13. Metheny Corporation's lease arrangements qualify as sales-type leases at the time of entering into the transactions. How should the corporation recognize revenues and costs in these situations?

14. Alice Foyle, M.D. (lessee), has a noncancelable 20-year lease with Brownback Realty, Inc. (lessor) for the use of a medical building. Taxes, insurance, and maintenance are paid by the lessee in addition to the fixed annual payments, of which the present value is equal to the fair value of the leased property. At the end of the lease period, title becomes the lessee's at a nominal price. Considering the terms of the lease described above, comment on the nature of the lease transaction and the accounting treatment that should be accorded it by the lessee.

15. The residual value is the estimated fair value of the leased property at the end of the lease term.

    (a) Of what significance is (1) an unguaranteed and (2) a guaranteed residual value in the lessee's accounting for a capitalized-lease transaction?

    (b) Of what significance is (1) an unguaranteed and (2) a guaranteed residual value in the lessor's accounting for a direct-financing lease transaction?

16. How should changes in the estimated unguaranteed residual value be handled by the lessor?

17. Describe the effect of a "bargain-purchase option" on accounting for a capital lease transaction by a lessee.

18. What are "initial direct costs" and how are they accounted for?

19. What disclosures should be made by lessees and lessors related to future lease payments?

*20. What is the nature of a "sale-leaseback" transaction?

BRIEF EXERCISES

2 **BE21-1** Callaway Golf Co. leases telecommunication equipment. Assume the following data for equipment leased from Photon Company. The lease term is 5 years and requires equal rental payments of $31,000 at the beginning of each year. The equipment has a fair value at the inception of the lease of $138,000, an estimated useful life of 8 years, and no residual value. Callaway pays all executory costs directly to third parties. Photon set the annual rental to earn a rate of return of 10%, and this fact is known to Callaway. The lease does not transfer title or contain a bargain-purchase option. How should Callaway classify this lease?

2 **BE21-2** Waterworld Company leased equipment from Costner Company. The lease term is 4 years and requires equal rental payments of $43,019 at the beginning of each year. The equipment has a fair value at the inception of the lease of $150,000, an estimated useful life of 4 years, and no salvage value. Waterworld pays all executory costs directly to third parties. The appropriate interest rate is 10%. Prepare Waterworld's January 1, 2014, journal entries at the inception of the lease.

2 **BE21-3** Rick Kleckner Corporation recorded a capital lease at $300,000 on January 1, 2014. The interest rate is 12%. Kleckner Corporation made the first lease payment of $53,920 on January 1, 2014. The lease requires eight annual payments. The equipment has a useful life of 8 years with no salvage value. Prepare Kleckner Corporation's December 31, 2014, adjusting entries.

2 **BE21-4** Use the information for Rick Kleckner Corporation from BE21-3. Assume that at December 31, 2014, Kleckner made an adjusting entry to accrue interest expense of $29,530 on the lease. Prepare Kleckner's January 1, 2015, journal entry to record the second lease payment of $53,920.

3 **BE21-5** Jana Kingston Corporation enters into a lease on January 1, 2014, that does not transfer ownership or contain a bargain-purchase option. It covers 3 years of the equipment's 8-year useful life, and the present value of the minimum lease payments is less than 90% of the fair value of the asset leased. Prepare Jana Kingston's journal entry to record its January 1, 2014, annual lease payment of $35,000.

4 **5** **BE21-6** Assume that IBM leased equipment that was carried at a cost of $150,000 to Sharon Swander Company. The term of the lease is 6 years beginning January 1, 2014, with equal rental payments of $30,044 at the beginning of each year. All executory costs are paid by Swander directly to third parties. The fair value of the equipment at the inception of the lease is $150,000. The equipment has a useful life of 6 years with no salvage value. The lease has an implicit interest rate of 8%, no bargain-purchase option, and no transfer of title. Collectibility is reasonably assured with no additional cost to be incurred by IBM. Prepare IBM's January 1, 2014, journal entries at the inception of the lease.

4 **5** **BE21-7** Use the information for IBM from BE21-6. Assume the direct-financing lease was recorded at a present value of $150,000. Prepare IBM's December 31, 2014, entry to record interest.

4 **BE21-8** Jennifer Brent Corporation owns equipment that cost $80,000 and has a useful life of 8 years with no salvage value. On January 1, 2014, Jennifer Brent leases the equipment to Donna Havaci Inc. for one year with one rental payment of $15,000 on January 1. Prepare Jennifer Brent Corporation's 2014 journal entries.

6 **7** **BE21-9** Indiana Jones Corporation enters into a 6-year lease of equipment on January 1, 2014, which requires 6 annual payments of $40,000 each, beginning January 1, 2014. In addition, Indiana Jones guarantees the lessor a residual value of $20,000 at lease-end. The equipment has a useful life of 6 years. Prepare Indiana Jones' January 1, 2014, journal entries assuming an interest rate of 10%.

6 **7** **BE21-10** Use the information for Indiana Jones Corporation from BE21-9. Assume that for Lost Ark Company, the lessor, collectibility is reasonably predictable, there are no important uncertainties concerning costs, and the carrying amount of the equipment is $202,921. Prepare Lost Ark's January 1, 2014, journal entries.

8 **BE21-11** Geiberger Corporation manufactures replicators. On January 1, 2014, it leased to Althaus Company a replicator that had cost $110,000 to manufacture. The lease agreement covers the 5-year useful life of the replicator and requires 5 equal annual rentals of $40,800 payable each January 1, beginning January 1, 2014. An interest rate of 12% is implicit in the lease agreement. Collectibility of the rentals is reasonably assured, and there are no important uncertainties concerning costs. Prepare Geiberger's January 1, 2014, journal entries.

10 *BE21-12 On January 1, 2014, Irwin Animation sold a truck to Peete Finance for $33,000 and immediately leased it back. The truck was carried on Irwin's books at $28,000. The term of the lease is 5 years, and title transfers to Irwin at lease-end. The lease requires five equal rental payments of $8,705 at the end of each year. The appropriate rate of interest is 10%, and the truck has a useful life of 5 years with no salvage value. Prepare Irwin's 2014 journal entries.

EXERCISES

2 **E21-1 (Lessee Entries; Capital Lease with Unguaranteed Residual Value)** On January 1, 2014, Burke Corporation signed a 5-year noncancelable lease for a machine. The terms of the lease called for Burke to make annual payments of $8,668 at the beginning of each year, starting January 1, 2014. The machine has an estimated useful life of 6 years and a $5,000 unguaranteed residual value. The machine reverts back to the lessor at the end of the lease term. Burke uses the straight-line method of depreciation for all of its plant assets. Burke's incremental borrowing rate is 10%, and the Lessor's implicit rate is unknown.

Instructions

(a) What type of lease is this? Explain.
(b) Compute the present value of the minimum lease payments.
(c) Prepare all necessary journal entries for Burke for this lease through January 1, 2015.

2 **E21-2 (Lessee Computations and Entries; Capital Lease with Guaranteed Residual Value)** Pat Delaney Company leases an automobile with a fair value of $8,725 from John Simon Motors, Inc., on the following terms:

1. Noncancelable term of 50 months.
2. Rental of $200 per month (at end of each month). (The present value at 1% per month is $7,840.)
3. Estimated residual value after 50 months is $1,180. (The present value at 1% per month is $715.) Delaney Company guarantees the residual value of $1,180.
4. Estimated economic life of the automobile is 60 months.
5. Delaney Company's incremental borrowing rate is 12% a year (1% a month). Simon's implicit rate is unknown.

Instructions

(a) What is the nature of this lease to Delaney Company?
(b) What is the present value of the minimum lease payments?
(c) Record the lease on Delaney Company's books at the date of inception.
(d) Record the first month's depreciation on Delaney Company's books (assume straight-line).
(e) Record the first month's lease payment.

2 **7** **E21-3 (Lessee Entries; Capital Lease with Executory Costs and Unguaranteed Residual Value)** Assume that on January 1, 2014, Kimberly-Clark Corp. signs a 10-year noncancelable lease agreement to lease a storage building from Sheffield Storage Company. The following information pertains to this lease agreement.

1. The agreement requires equal rental payments of $72,000 beginning on January 1, 2014.
2. The fair value of the building on January 1, 2014 is $440,000.
3. The building has an estimated economic life of 12 years, with an unguaranteed residual value of $10,000. Kimberly-Clark depreciates similar buildings on the straight-line method.
4. The lease is nonrenewable. At the termination of the lease, the building reverts to the lessor.
5. Kimberly-Clark's incremental borrowing rate is 12% per year. The lessor's implicit rate is not known by Kimberly-Clark.
6. The yearly rental payment includes $2,471 of executory costs related to taxes on the property.

Instructions

Prepare the journal entries on the lessee's books to reflect the signing of the lease agreement and to record the payments and expenses related to this lease for the years 2014 and 2015. Kimberly-Clark's corporate year-end is December 31.

5 **E21-4 (Lessor Entries; Direct-Financing Lease with Option to Purchase)** Castle Leasing Company signs a lease agreement on January 1, 2014, to lease electronic equipment to Jan Way Company. The term of the noncancelable lease is 2 years, and payments are required at the end of each year. The following information relates to this agreement:

1. Jan Way has the option to purchase the equipment for $16,000 upon termination of the lease.
2. The equipment has a cost and fair value of $160,000 to Castle Leasing Company. The useful economic life is 2 years, with a salvage value of $16,000.
3. Jan Way Company is required to pay $5,000 each year to the lessor for executory costs.
4. Castle Leasing Company desires to earn a return of 10% on its investment.
5. Collectibility of the payments is reasonably predictable, and there are no important uncertainties surrounding the costs yet to be incurred by the lessor.

Instructions

   (a) Prepare the journal entries on the books of Castle Leasing to reflect the payments received under the lease and to recognize income for the years 2014 and 2015.

   (b) Assuming that Jan Way Company exercises its option to purchase the equipment on December 31, 2015, prepare the journal entry to reflect the sale on Castle's books.

2 **3** **E21-5 (Type of Lease; Amortization Schedule)** Mike Macinski Leasing Company leases a new machine that has a cost and fair value of $95,000 to Sharrer Corporation on a 3-year noncancelable contract. Sharrer Corporation agrees to assume all risks of normal ownership including such costs as insurance, taxes, and maintenance. The machine has a 3-year useful life and no residual value. The lease was signed on January 1, 2014. Mike Macinski Leasing Company expects to earn a 9% return on its investment. The annual rentals are payable on each December 31.

Instructions

   (a) Discuss the nature of the lease arrangement and the accounting method that each party to the lease should apply.

   (b) Prepare an amortization schedule that would be suitable for both the lessor and the lessee and that covers all the years involved.

8 **E21-6 (Lessor Entries; Sales-Type Lease)** Crosley Company, a machinery dealer, leased a machine to Dexter Corporation on January 1, 2014. The lease is for an 8-year period and requires equal annual payments of $35,013 at the beginning of each year. The first payment is received on January 1, 2014. Crosley had purchased the machine during 2013 for $160,000. Collectibility of lease payments is reasonably predictable, and no important uncertainties surround the amount of costs yet to be incurred by Crosley. Crosley set the annual rental to ensure an 11% rate of return. The machine has an economic life of 10 years with no residual value and reverts to Crosley at the termination of the lease.

Instructions

   (a) Compute the amount of the lease receivable.

   (b) Prepare all necessary journal entries for Crosley for 2014.

8 **E21-7 (Lessee-Lessor Entries; Sales-Type Lease)** On January 1, 2014, Bensen Company leased equipment to Flynn Corporation. The following information pertains to this lease.

  1. The term of the noncancelable lease is 6 years, with no renewal option. The equipment reverts to the lessor at the termination of the lease.

  2. Equal rental payments are due on January 1 of each year, beginning in 2014.

  3. The fair value of the equipment on January 1, 2014, is $150,000, and its cost is $120,000.

  4. The equipment has an economic life of 8 years, with an unguaranteed residual value of $10,000. Flynn depreciates all of its equipment on a straight-line basis.

  5. Bensen set the annual rental to ensure an 11% rate of return. Flynn's incremental borrowing rate is 12%, and the implicit rate of the lessor is unknown.

  6. Collectibility of lease payments is reasonably predictable, and no important uncertainties surround the amount of costs yet to be incurred by the lessor.

Instructions

(Both the lessor and the lessee's accounting period ends on December 31.)

   (a) Discuss the nature of this lease to Bensen and Flynn.

   (b) Calculate the amount of the annual rental payment.

   (c) Prepare all the necessary journal entries for Flynn for 2014.

   (d) Prepare all the necessary journal entries for Bensen for 2014.

8 **E21-8 (Lessee Entries with Bargain-Purchase Option)** The following facts pertain to a noncancelable lease agreement between Mooney Leasing Company and Rode Company, a lessee.

Inception date:	May 1, 2014
Annual lease payment due at the beginning of each year, beginning with May 1, 2014	$21,227.65
Bargain-purchase option price at end of lease term	$ 4,000.00
Lease term	5 years
Economic life of leased equipment	10 years
Lessor's cost	$65,000.00
Fair value of asset at May 1, 2014	$91,000.00
Lessor's implicit rate	10%
Lessee's incremental borrowing rate	10%

The collectibility of the lease payments is reasonably predictable, and there are no important uncertainties surrounding the costs yet to be incurred by the lessor. The lessee assumes responsibility for all executory costs.

Instructions

(Round all numbers to the nearest cent.)

  (a) Discuss the nature of this lease to Rode Company.
  (b) Discuss the nature of this lease to Mooney Company.
  (c) Prepare a lease amortization schedule for Rode Company for the 5-year lease term.
  (d) Prepare the journal entries on the lessee's books to reflect the signing of the lease agreement and to record the payments and expenses related to this lease for the years 2014 and 2015. Rode's annual accounting period ends on December 31. Reversing entries are used by Rode.

8 **E21-9 (Lessor Entries with Bargain-Purchase Option)** A lease agreement between Mooney Leasing Company and Rode Company is described in E21-8.

Instructions

(Round all numbers to the nearest cent.)
Refer to the data in E21-8 and do the following for the lessor.

  (a) Compute the amount of the lease receivable at the inception of the lease.
  (b) Prepare a lease amortization schedule for Mooney Leasing Company for the 5-year lease term.
  (c) Prepare the journal entries to reflect the signing of the lease agreement and to record the receipts and income related to this lease for the years 2014, 2015, and 2016. The lessor's accounting period ends on December 31. Reversing entries are not used by Mooney.

5 **E21-10 (Computation of Rental; Journal Entries for Lessor)** Morgan Leasing Company signs an agreement on January 1, 2014, to lease equipment to Cole Company. The following information relates to this agreement.

  1. The term of the noncancelable lease is 6 years with no renewal option. The equipment has an estimated economic life of 6 years.
  2. The cost of the asset to the lessor is $245,000. The fair value of the asset at January 1, 2014, is $245,000.
  3. The asset will revert to the lessor at the end of the lease term, at which time the asset is expected to have a residual value of $43,622, none of which is guaranteed.
  4. Cole Company assumes direct responsibility for all executory costs.
  5. The agreement requires equal annual rental payments, beginning on January 1, 2014.
  6. Collectibility of the lease payments is reasonably predictable. There are no important uncertainties surrounding the amount of costs yet to be incurred by the lessor.

Instructions

(Round all numbers to the nearest cent.)

  (a) Assuming the lessor desires a 10% rate of return on its investment, calculate the amount of the annual rental payment required. (Round to the nearest dollar.)
  (b) Prepare an amortization schedule that would be suitable for the lessor for the lease term.
  (c) Prepare all of the journal entries for the lessor for 2014 and 2015 to record the lease agreement, the receipt of lease payments, and the recognition of income. Assume the lessor's annual accounting period ends on December 31.

2 **E21-11 (Amortization Schedule and Journal Entries for Lessee)** Laura Leasing Company signs an agreement on January 1, 2014, to lease equipment to Plote Company. The following information relates to this agreement.

  1. The term of the noncancelable lease is 5 years with no renewal option. The equipment has an estimated economic life of 5 years.
  2. The fair value of the asset at January 1, 2014, is $80,000.
  3. The asset will revert to the lessor at the end of the lease term, at which time the asset is expected to have a residual value of $7,000, none of which is guaranteed.
  4. Plote Company assumes direct responsibility for all executory costs, which include the following annual amounts: (1) $900 to Rocky Mountain Insurance Company for insurance and (2) $1,600 to Laclede County for property taxes.
  5. The agreement requires equal annual rental payments of $18,142.95 to the lessor, beginning on January 1, 2014.

6. The lessee's incremental borrowing rate is 12%. The lessor's implicit rate is 10% and is known to the lessee.
7. Plote Company uses the straight-line depreciation method for all equipment.
8. Plote uses reversing entries when appropriate.

Instructions

(Round all numbers to the nearest cent.)

(a) Prepare an amortization schedule that would be suitable for the lessee for the lease term.
(b) Prepare all of the journal entries for the lessee for 2014 and 2015 to record the lease agreement, the lease payments, and all expenses related to this lease. Assume the lessee's annual accounting period ends on December 31.

3 4 E21-12 (Accounting for an Operating Lease) On January 1, 2014, Doug Nelson Co. leased a building to Patrick Wise Inc. The relevant information related to the lease is as follows.

1. The lease arrangement is for 10 years.
2. The leased building cost $4,500,000 and was purchased for cash on January 1, 2014.
3. The building is depreciated on a straight-line basis. Its estimated economic life is 50 years with no salvage value.
4. Lease payments are $275,000 per year and are made at the end of the year.
5. Property tax expense of $85,000 and insurance expense of $10,000 on the building were incurred by Nelson in the first year. Payment on these two items was made at the end of the year.
6. Both the lessor and the lessee are on a calendar-year basis.

Instructions

(a) Prepare the journal entries that Nelson Co. should make in 2014.
(b) Prepare the journal entries that Wise Inc. should make in 2014.
(c) If Nelson paid $30,000 to a real estate broker on January 1, 2014, as a fee for finding the lessee, how much should be reported as an expense for this item in 2014 by Nelson Co.?

3 4 E21-13 (Accounting for an Operating Lease) On January 1, 2014, a machine was purchased for $900,000 by Young Co. The machine is expected to have an 8-year life with no salvage value. It is to be depreciated on a straight-line basis. The machine was leased to St. Leger Inc. on January 1, 2014, at an annual rental of $210,000. Other relevant information is as follows.

1. The lease term is for 3 years.
2. Young Co. incurred maintenance and other executory costs of $25,000 in 2014 related to this lease.
3. The machine could have been sold by Young Co. for $940,000 instead of leasing it.
4. St. Leger is required to pay a rent security deposit of $35,000 and to prepay the last month's rent of $17,500.

Instructions

(a) How much should Young Co. report as income before income tax on this lease for 2014?
(b) What amount should St. Leger Inc. report for rent expense for 2014 on this lease?

3 4 E21-14 (Operating Lease for Lessee and Lessor) On February 20, 2014, Barbara Brent Inc., purchased a machine for $1,500,000 for the purpose of leasing it. The machine is expected to have a 10-year life, no residual value, and will be depreciated on the straight-line basis. The machine was leased to Rudy Company on March 1, 2014, for a 4-year period at a monthly rental of $19,500. There is no provision for the renewal of the lease or purchase of the machine by the lessee at the expiration of the lease term. Brent paid $30,000 of commissions associated with negotiating the lease in February 2014.

Instructions

(a) What expense should Rudy Company record as a result of the facts above for the year ended December 31, 2014? Show supporting computations in good form.
(b) What income or loss before income taxes should Brent record as a result of the facts above for the year ended December 31, 2014? (*Hint:* Amortize commissions over the life of the lease.)

(AICPA adapted)

10 *E21-15 (Sale-Leaseback) Assume that on January 1, 2014, Elmer's Restaurants sells a computer system to Liquidity Finance Co. for $680,000 and immediately leases the computer system back. The relevant information is as follows.

1. The computer was carried on Elmer's books at a value of $600,000.
2. The term of the noncancelable lease is 10 years; title will transfer to Elmer.
3. The lease agreement requires equal rental payments of $110,666.81 at the end of each year.

4. The incremental borrowing rate for Elmer is 12%. Elmer is aware that Liquidity Finance Co. set the annual rental to insure a rate of return of 10%.

5. The computer has a fair value of $680,000 on January 1, 2014, and an estimated economic life of 10 years.

6. Elmer pays executory costs of $9,000 per year.

Instructions

Prepare the journal entries for both the lessee and the lessor for 2014 to reflect the sale and leaseback agreement. No uncertainties exist, and collectibility is reasonably certain.

10 *E21-16 (Lessee-Lessor, Sale-Leaseback) Presented below are four independent situations.

(a) On December 31, 2014, Zarle Inc. sold computer equipment to Daniell Co. and immediately leased it back for 10 years. The sales price of the equipment was $520,000, its carrying amount is $400,000, and its estimated remaining economic life is 12 years. Determine the amount of deferred revenue to be reported from the sale of the computer equipment on December 31, 2014.

(b) On December 31, 2014, Wasicsko Co. sold a machine to Cross Co. and simultaneously leased it back for one year. The sale price of the machine was $480,000, the carrying amount is $420,000, and it had an estimated remaining useful life of 14 years. The present value of the rental payments for the one year is $35,000. At December 31, 2014, how much should Wasicsko report as deferred revenue from the sale of the machine?

(c) On January 1, 2014, McKane Corp. sold an airplane with an estimated useful life of 10 years. At the same time, McKane leased back the plane for 10 years. The sales price of the airplane was $500,000, the carrying amount $379,000, and the annual rental $73,975.22. McKane Corp. intends to depreciate the leased asset using the sum-of-the-years'-digits depreciation method. Discuss how the gain on the sale should be reported at the end of 2014 in the financial statements.

(d) On January 1, 2014, Sondgeroth Co. sold equipment with an estimated useful life of 5 years. At the same time, Sondgeroth leased back the equipment for 2 years under a lease classified as an operating lease. The sales price (fair value) of the equipment was $212,700, the carrying amount is $300,000, the monthly rental under the lease is $6,000, and the present value of the rental payments is $115,753. For the year ended December 31, 2014, determine which items would be reported on its income statement for the sale-leaseback transaction.

EXERCISES SET B

See the book's companion website, at **www.wiley.com/college/kieso**, for an additional set of exercises.

PROBLEMS

2 8 P21-1 (Lessee-Lessor Entries, Sales-Type Lease) Glaus Leasing Company agrees to lease machinery to Jensen Corporation on January 1, 2014. The following information relates to the lease agreement.

1. The term of the lease is 7 years with no renewal option, and the machinery has an estimated economic life of 9 years.

2. The cost of the machinery is $525,000, and the fair value of the asset on January 1, 2014, is $700,000.

3. At the end of the lease term, the asset reverts to the lessor and has a guaranteed residual value of $100,000. Jensen depreciates all of its equipment on a straight-line basis.

4. The lease agreement requires equal annual rental payments, beginning on January 1, 2014.

5. The collectibility of the lease payments is reasonably predictable, and there are no important uncertainties surrounding the amount of costs yet to be incurred by the lessor.

6. Glaus desires a 10% rate of return on its investments. Jensen's incremental borrowing rate is 11%, and the lessor's implicit rate is unknown.

Instructions

(Assume the accounting period ends on December 31.)

(a) Discuss the nature of this lease for both the lessee and the lessor.

(b) Calculate the amount of the annual rental payment required.

(c) Compute the present value of the minimum lease payments.

(d) Prepare the journal entries Jensen would make in 2014 and 2015 related to the lease arrangement.

(e) Prepare the journal entries Glaus would make in 2014 and 2015.

 P21-2 (Lessee-Lessor Entries, Operating Lease) Cleveland Inc. leased a new crane to Abriendo Construction under a 5-year noncancelable contract starting January 1, 2014. Terms of the lease require payments of $33,000 each January 1, starting January 1, 2014. Cleveland will pay insurance, taxes, and maintenance charges on the crane, which has an estimated life of 12 years, a fair value of $240,000, and a cost to Cleveland of $240,000. The estimated fair value of the crane is expected to be $45,000 at the end of the lease term. No bargain-purchase or renewal options are included in the contract. Both Cleveland and Abriendo adjust and close books annually at December 31. Collectibility of the lease payments is reasonably certain, and no uncertainties exist relative to unreimbursable lessor costs. Abriendo's incremental borrowing rate is 10%, and Cleveland's implicit interest rate of 9% is known to Abriendo.

Instructions

(a) Identify the type of lease involved and give reasons for your classification. Discuss the accounting treatment that should be applied by both the lessee and the lessor.

(b) Prepare all the entries related to the lease contract and leased asset for the year 2014 for the lessee and lessor, assuming the following amounts.

   (1) Insurance $500.

   (2) Taxes $2,000.

   (3) Maintenance $650.

   (4) Straight-line depreciation and salvage value $15,000.

(c) Discuss what should be presented in the balance sheet, the income statement, and the related notes of both the lessee and the lessor at December 31, 2014.

 P21-3 (Lessee-Lessor Entries, Balance Sheet Presentation, Sales-Type Lease) Winston Industries and Ewing Inc. enter into an agreement that requires Ewing Inc. to build three diesel-electric engines to Winston's specifications. Upon completion of the engines, Winston has agreed to lease them for a period of 10 years and to assume all costs and risks of ownership. The lease is noncancelable, becomes effective on January 1, 2014, and requires annual rental payments of $413,971 each January 1, starting January 1, 2014.

Winston's incremental borrowing rate is 10%. The implicit interest rate used by Ewing Inc. and known to Winston is 8%. The total cost of building the three engines is $2,600,000. The economic life of the engines is estimated to be 10 years, with residual value set at zero. Winston depreciates similar equipment on a straight-line basis. At the end of the lease, Winston assumes title to the engines. Collectibility of the lease payments is reasonably certain; no uncertainties exist relative to unreimbursable lessor costs.

Instructions

(a) Discuss the nature of this lease transaction from the viewpoints of both lessee and lessor.

(b) Prepare the journal entry or entries to record the transaction on January 1, 2014, on the books of Winston Industries.

(c) Prepare the journal entry or entries to record the transaction on January 1, 2014, on the books of Ewing Inc.

(d) Prepare the journal entries for both the lessee and lessor to record the first rental payment on January 1, 2014.

(e) Prepare the journal entries for both the lessee and lessor to record interest expense (revenue) at December 31, 2014. (Prepare a lease amortization schedule for 2 years.)

(f) Show the items and amounts that would be reported on the balance sheet (not notes) at December 31, 2014, for both the lessee and the lessor.

 P21-4 (Balance Sheet and Income Statement Disclosure—Lessee) The following facts pertain to a noncancelable lease agreement between Alschuler Leasing Company and McKee Electronics, a lessee, for a computer system.

Inception date	October 1, 2014
Lease term	6 years
Economic life of leased equipment	6 years
Fair value of asset at October 1, 2014	$300,383
Residual value at end of lease term	–0–
Lessor's implicit rate	10%
Lessee's incremental borrowing rate	10%
Annual lease payment due at the beginning of each year, beginning with October 1, 2014	$62,700

The collectibility of the lease payments is reasonably predictable, and there are no important uncertainties surrounding the costs yet to be incurred by the lessor. The lessee assumes responsibility for all executory costs, which amount to $5,500 per year and are to be paid each October 1, beginning October 1, 2014. (This $5,500 is not included in the rental payment of $62,700.) The asset will revert to the lessor at the end of the lease term. The straight-line depreciation method is used for all equipment.

The following amortization schedule has been prepared correctly for use by both the lessor and the lessee in accounting for this lease. The lease is to be accounted for properly as a capital lease by the lessee and as a direct-financing lease by the lessor.

Date	Annual Lease Payment/ Receipt	Interest (10%) on Unpaid Liability/Receivable	Reduction of Lease Liability/Receivable	Balance of Lease Liability/Receivable
10/01/14				$300,383
10/01/14	$ 62,700		$ 62,700	237,683
10/01/15	62,700	$23,768	38,932	198,751
10/01/16	62,700	19,875	42,825	155,926
10/01/17	62,700	15,593	47,107	108,819
10/01/18	62,700	10,882	51,818	57,001
10/01/19	62,700	5,699*	57,001	–0–
	$376,200	$75,817	$300,383	

*Rounding error is $1.

Instructions

(a) Assuming the lessee's accounting period ends on September 30, answer the following questions with respect to this lease agreement.

    (1) What items and amounts will appear on the lessee's income statement for the year ending September 30, 2015?

    (2) What items and amounts will appear on the lessee's balance sheet at September 30, 2015?

    (3) What items and amounts will appear on the lessee's income statement for the year ending September 30, 2016?

    (4) What items and amounts will appear on the lessee's balance sheet at September 30, 2016?

(b) Assuming the lessee's accounting period ends on December 31, answer the following questions with respect to this lease agreement.

    (1) What items and amounts will appear on the lessee's income statement for the year ending December 31, 2014?

    (2) What items and amounts will appear on the lessee's balance sheet at December 31, 2014?

    (3) What items and amounts will appear on the lessee's income statement for the year ending December 31, 2015?

    (4) What items and amounts will appear on the lessee's balance sheet at December 31, 2015?

5 **9** **P21-5 (Balance Sheet and Income Statement Disclosure—Lessor)** Assume the same information as in P21-4.

Instructions

(a) Assuming the lessor's accounting period ends on September 30, answer the following questions with respect to this lease agreement.

    (1) What items and amounts will appear on the lessor's income statement for the year ending September 30, 2015?

    (2) What items and amounts will appear on the lessor's balance sheet at September 30, 2015?

    (3) What items and amounts will appear on the lessor's income statement for the year ending September 30, 2016?

    (4) What items and amounts will appear on the lessor's balance sheet at September 30, 2016?

(b) Assuming the lessor's accounting period ends on December 31, answer the following questions with respect to this lease agreement.

    (1) What items and amounts will appear on the lessor's income statement for the year ending December 31, 2014?

    (2) What items and amounts will appear on the lessor's balance sheet at December 31, 2014?

    (3) What items and amounts will appear on the lessor's income statement for the year ending December 31, 2015?

    (4) What items and amounts will appear on the lessor's balance sheet at December 31, 2015?

2 **7** **P21-6 (Lessee Entries with Residual Value)** The following facts pertain to a noncancelable lease agreement between Faldo Leasing Company and Vance Company, a lessee.

Inception date	January 1, 2014
Annual lease payment due at the beginning of each year, beginning with January 1, 2014	$124,798
Residual value of equipment at end of lease term, guaranteed by the lessee	$50,000
Lease term	6 years
Economic life of leased equipment	6 years
Fair value of asset at January 1, 2014	$600,000
Lessor's implicit rate	12%
Lessee's incremental borrowing rate	12%

The lessee assumes responsibility for all executory costs, which are expected to amount to $5,000 per year. The asset will revert to the lessor at the end of the lease term. The lessee has guaranteed the lessor a residual value of $50,000. The lessee uses the straight-line depreciation method for all equipment.

Instructions
(a) Prepare an amortization schedule that would be suitable for the lessee for the lease term.
(b) Prepare all of the journal entries for the lessee for 2014 and 2015 to record the lease agreement, the lease payments, and all expenses related to this lease. Assume the lessee's annual accounting period ends on December 31 and reversing entries are used when appropriate.

2 **9** **P21-7 (Lessee Entries and Balance Sheet Presentation, Capital Lease)** Ludwick Steel Company as lessee signed a lease agreement for equipment for 5 years, beginning December 31, 2014. Annual rental payments of $40,000 are to be made at the beginning of each lease year (December 31). The taxes, insurance, and the maintenance costs are the obligation of the lessee. The interest rate used by the lessor in setting the payment schedule is 9%; Ludwick's incremental borrowing rate is 10%. Ludwick is unaware of the rate being used by the lessor. At the end of the lease, Ludwick has the option to buy the equipment for $1, considerably below its estimated fair value at that time. The equipment has an estimated useful life of 7 years, with no salvage value. Ludwick uses the straight-line method of depreciation on similar owned equipment.

Instructions
(a) Prepare the journal entry or entries, with explanations, that should be recorded on December 31, 2014, by Ludwick.
(b) Prepare the journal entry or entries, with explanations, that should be recorded on December 31, 2015, by Ludwick. (Prepare the lease amortization schedule for all five payments.)
(c) Prepare the journal entry or entries, with explanations, that should be recorded on December 31, 2016, by Ludwick.
(d) What amounts would appear on Ludwick's December 31, 2016, balance sheet relative to the lease arrangement?

2 **9** **P21-8 (Lessee Entries and Balance Sheet Presentation, Capital Lease)** On January 1, 2014, Cage Company contracts to lease equipment for 5 years, agreeing to make a payment of $137,899 (including the executory costs of $6,000) at the beginning of each year, starting January 1, 2014. The taxes, the insurance, and the maintenance, estimated at $6,000 a year, are the obligations of the lessee. The leased equipment is to be capitalized at $550,000. The asset is to be depreciated on a double-declining-balance basis, and the obligation is to be reduced on an effective-interest basis. Cage's incremental borrowing rate is 12%, and the implicit rate in the lease is 10%, which is known by Cage. Title to the equipment transfers to Cage when the lease expires. The asset has an estimated useful life of 5 years and no residual value.

Instructions
(a) Explain the probable relationship of the $550,000 amount to the lease arrangement.
(b) Prepare the journal entry or entries that should be recorded on January 1, 2014, by Cage Company.
(c) Prepare the journal entry to record depreciation of the leased asset for the year 2014.
(d) Prepare the journal entry to record the interest expense for the year 2014.
(e) Prepare the journal entry to record the lease payment of January 1, 2015, assuming reversing entries are not made.
(f) What amounts will appear on the lessee's December 31, 2014, balance sheet relative to the lease contract?

2 **P21-9 (Lessee Entries, Capital Lease with Monthly Payments)** Shapiro Inc. was incorporated in 2013 to operate as a computer software service firm with an accounting fiscal year ending August 31. Shapiro's primary product is a sophisticated online inventory-control system; its customers pay a fixed fee plus a usage charge for using the system.

Shapiro has leased a large, Alpha-3 computer system from the manufacturer. The lease calls for a monthly rental of $40,000 for the 144 months (12 years) of the lease term. The estimated useful life of the computer is 15 years.

Each scheduled monthly rental payment includes $3,000 for full-service maintenance on the computer to be performed by the manufacturer. All rentals are payable on the first day of the month beginning with August 1, 2014, the date the computer was installed and the lease agreement was signed. The lease is non-cancelable for its 12-year term, and it is secured only by the manufacturer's chattel lien on the Alpha-3 system.

This lease is to be accounted for as a capital lease by Shapiro, and it will be depreciated by the straight-line method with no expected salvage value. Borrowed funds for this type of transaction would cost Shapiro 12% per year (1% per month). Following is a schedule of the present value of $1 for selected periods discounted at 1% per period when payments are made at the beginning of each period.

Periods (months)	Present Value of $1 per Period Discounted at 1% per Period
1	1.000
2	1.990
3	2.970
143	76.658
144	76.899

Instructions

Prepare all entries Shapiro should have made in its accounting records during August 2014 relating to this lease. Give full explanations and show supporting computations for each entry. Remember, August 31, 2014, is the end of Shapiro's fiscal accounting period and it will be preparing financial statements on that date. Do not prepare closing entries.

(AICPA adapted)

4 **7** **P21-10 (Lessor Computations and Entries, Sales-Type Lease with Unguaranteed Residual Value)** George
8 Company manufactures a check-in kiosk with an estimated economic life of 12 years and leases it to
 National Airlines for a period of 10 years. The normal selling price of the equipment is $278,072, and its unguaranteed residual value at the end of the lease term is estimated to be $20,000. National will pay annual payments of $40,000 at the beginning of each year and all maintenance, insurance, and taxes. George incurred costs of $180,000 in manufacturing the equipment and $4,000 in negotiating and closing the lease. George has determined that the collectibility of the lease payments is reasonably predictable, that no additional costs will be incurred, and that the implicit interest rate is 10%.

Instructions

(a) Discuss the nature of this lease in relation to the lessor and compute the amount of each of the following items.
  (1) Lease receivable.
  (2) Sales price.
  (3) Cost of sales.
(b) Prepare a 10-year lease amortization schedule.
(c) Prepare all of the lessor's journal entries for the first year.

2 **6** **P21-11 (Lessee Computations and Entries, Capital Lease with Unguaranteed Residual Value)** Assume
7 the same data as in P21-10 with National Airlines Co. having an incremental borrowing rate of 10%.

Instructions

(a) Discuss the nature of this lease in relation to the lessee, and compute the amount of the initial lease liability.
(b) Prepare a 10-year lease amortization schedule.
(c) Prepare all of the lessee's journal entries for the first year.

2 **6** **P21-12 (Basic Lessee Accounting with Difficult PV Calculation)** In 2013, Grishell Trucking Company negotiated and closed a long-term lease contract for newly constructed truck terminals and freight storage facilities. The buildings were erected to the company's specifications on land owned by the company. On January 1, 2014, Grishell Trucking Company took possession of the lease properties. On

January 1, 2014 and 2015, the company made cash payments of $948,000 that were recorded as rental expenses.

Although the terminals have a composite useful life of 40 years, the noncancelable lease runs for 20 years from January 1, 2014, with a bargain-purchase option available upon expiration of the lease.

The 20-year lease is effective for the period January 1, 2014, through December 31, 2033. Advance rental payments of $800,000 are payable to the lessor on January 1 of each of the first 10 years of the lease term. Advance rental payments of $320,000 are due on January 1 for each of the last 10 years of the lease. The company has an option to purchase all of these leased facilities for $1 on December 31, 2033. It also must make annual payments to the lessor of $125,000 for property taxes and $23,000 for insurance. The lease was negotiated to assure the lessor a 6% rate of return.

Instructions

(a) Prepare a schedule to compute for Grishell Trucking Company the present value of the terminal facilities and related obligation at January 1, 2014.

(b) Assuming that the present value of terminal facilities and related obligation at January 1, 2014, was $7,600,000, prepare journal entries for Grishell Trucking Company to record the:

 (1) Cash payment to the lessor on January 1, 2016.

 (2) Amortization of the cost of the leased properties for 2016 using the straight-line method and assuming a zero salvage value.

 (3) Accrual of interest expense at December 31, 2016.

Selected present value factors are as follows.

Periods	For an Ordinary Annuity of $1 at 6%	For $1 at 6%
1	.943396	.943396
2	1.833393	.889996
8	6.209794	.627412
9	6.801692	.591898
10	7.360087	.558395
19	11.158117	.330513
20	11.469921	.311805

(AICPA adapted)

 P21-13 (Lessor Computations and Entries, Sales-Type Lease with Guaranteed Residual Value) Amirante Inc. manufactures an X-ray machine with an estimated life of 12 years and leases it to Chambers Medical Center for a period of 10 years. The normal selling price of the machine is $411,324, and its guaranteed residual value at the end of the noncancelable lease term is estimated to be $15,000. The hospital will pay rents of $60,000 at the beginning of each year and all maintenance, insurance, and taxes. Amirante Inc. incurred costs of $250,000 in manufacturing the machine and $14,000 in negotiating and closing the lease. Amirante Inc. has determined that the collectibility of the lease payments is reasonably predictable, that there will be no additional costs incurred, and that the implicit interest rate is 10%.

Instructions

(a) Discuss the nature of this lease in relation to the lessor and compute the amount of each of the following items.

 (1) Lease receivable at inception of the lease.

 (2) Sales price.

 (3) Cost of sales.

(b) Prepare a 10-year lease amortization schedule.

(c) Prepare all of the lessor's journal entries for the first year.

P21-14 (Lessee Computations and Entries, Capital Lease with Guaranteed Residual Value) Assume the same data as in P21-13 and that Chambers Medical Center has an incremental borrowing rate of 10%.

Instructions

(a) Discuss the nature of this lease in relation to the lessee, and compute the amount of the initial lease liability.

(b) Prepare a 10-year lease amortization schedule.

(c) Prepare all of the lessee's journal entries for the first year.

P21-15 (Operating Lease vs. Capital Lease) You are auditing the December 31, 2014, financial statements of Hockney, Inc., manufacturer of novelties and party favors. During your inspection of the company garage, you discovered that a used automobile not listed in the equipment subsidiary ledger is parked there. You ask Stacy Reeder, plant manager, about the vehicle, and she tells you that the company did not list the automobile because the company was only leasing it. The lease agreement was entered into on January 1, 2014, with Crown New and Used Cars.

You decide to review the lease agreement to ensure that the lease should be afforded operating lease treatment, and you discover the following lease terms.

1. Noncancelable term of 4 years.
2. Rental of $3,240 per year (at the end of each year). (The present value at 8% per year is $10,731.)
3. Estimated residual value after 4 years is $1,100. (The present value at 8% per year is $809.) Hockney guarantees the residual value of $1,100.
4. Estimated economic life of the automobile is 5 years.
5. Hockney's incremental borrowing rate is 8% per year.

Instructions

You are a senior auditor writing a memo to your supervisor, the audit partner in charge of this audit, to discuss the above situation. Be sure to include (a) why you inspected the lease agreement, (b) what you determined about the lease, and (c) how you advised your client to account for this lease. Explain every journal entry that you believe is necessary to record this lease properly on the client's books. (It is also necessary to include the fact that you communicated this information to your client.)

  P21-16 (Lessee-Lessor Accounting for Residual Values) Goring Dairy leases its milking equipment from King Finance Company under the following lease terms.

1. The lease term is 10 years, noncancelable, and requires equal rental payments of $30,300 due at the beginning of each year starting January 1, 2014.
2. The equipment has a fair value and cost at the inception of the lease (January 1, 2014) of $220,404, an estimated economic life of 10 years, and a residual value (which is guaranteed by Goring Dairy) of $20,000.
3. The lease contains no renewable options, and the equipment reverts to King Finance Company upon termination of the lease.
4. Goring Dairy's incremental borrowing rate is 9% per year. The implicit rate is also 9%.
5. Goring Dairy depreciates similar equipment that it owns on a straight-line basis.
6. Collectibility of the payments is reasonably predictable, and there are no important uncertainties surrounding the costs yet to be incurred by the lessor.

Instructions

(a) Evaluate the criteria for classification of the lease, and describe the nature of the lease. In general, discuss how the lessee and lessor should account for the lease transaction.
(b) Prepare the journal entries for the lessee and lessor at January 1, 2014, and December 31, 2014 (the lessee's and lessor's year-end). Assume no reversing entries.
(c) What would have been the amount capitalized by the lessee upon the inception of the lease if:
   (1) The residual value of $20,000 had been guaranteed by a third party, not the lessee?
   (2) The residual value of $20,000 had not been guaranteed at all?
(d) On the lessor's books, what would be the amount recorded as the Net Investment (Lease Receivable) at the inception of the lease, assuming:
   (1) The residual value of $20,000 had been guaranteed by a third party?
   (2) The residual value of $20,000 had not been guaranteed at all?
(e) Suppose the useful life of the milking equipment is 20 years. How large would the residual value have to be at the end of 10 years in order for the lessee to qualify for the operating method? (Assume that the residual value would be guaranteed by a third party.) (*Hint:* The lessee's annual payments will be appropriately reduced as the residual value increases.)

PROBLEMS SET B

See the book's companion website, at **www.wiley.com/college/kieso**, for an additional set of problems.

CONCEPTS FOR ANALYSIS

CA21-1 (Lessee Accounting and Reporting) On January 1, 2014, Evans Company entered into a noncancelable lease for a machine to be used in its manufacturing operations. The lease transfers ownership of the machine to Evans by the end of the lease term. The term of the lease is 8 years. The minimum lease payment made by Evans on January 1, 2014, was one of eight equal annual payments. At the inception of the lease, the criteria established for classification as a capital lease by the lessee were met.

Instructions
- **(a)** What is the theoretical basis for the accounting standard that requires certain long-term leases to be capitalized by the lessee? Do not discuss the specific criteria for classifying a specific lease as a capital lease.
- **(b)** How should Evans account for this lease at its inception and determine the amount to be recorded?
- **(c)** What expenses related to this lease will Evans incur during the first year of the lease, and how will they be determined?
- **(d)** How should Evans report the lease transaction on its December 31, 2014, balance sheet?

CA21-2 (Lessor and Lessee Accounting and Disclosure) Sylvan Inc. entered into a noncancelable lease arrangement with Breton Leasing Corporation for a certain machine. Breton's primary business is leasing; it is not a manufacturer or dealer. Sylvan will lease the machine for a period of 3 years, which is 50% of the machine's economic life. Breton will take possession of the machine at the end of the initial 3-year lease and lease it to another, smaller company that does not need the most current version of the machine. Sylvan does not guarantee any residual value for the machine and will not purchase the machine at the end of the lease term.

Sylvan's incremental borrowing rate is 10%, and the implicit rate in the lease is 9%. Sylvan has no way of knowing the implicit rate used by Breton. Using either rate, the present value of the minimum lease payments is between 90% and 100% of the fair value of the machine at the date of the lease agreement.

Sylvan has agreed to pay all executory costs directly, and no allowance for these costs is included in the lease payments.

Breton is reasonably certain that Sylvan will pay all lease payments. Because Sylvan has agreed to pay all executory costs, there are no important uncertainties regarding costs to be incurred by Breton. Assume that no indirect costs are involved.

Instructions
- **(a)** With respect to Sylvan (the lessee), answer the following.
  - **(1)** What type of lease has been entered into? Explain the reason for your answer.
  - **(2)** How should Sylvan compute the appropriate amount to be recorded for the lease or asset acquired?
  - **(3)** What accounts will be created or affected by this transaction, and how will the lease or asset and other costs related to the transaction be matched with earnings?
  - **(4)** What disclosures must Sylvan make regarding this leased asset?
- **(b)** With respect to Breton (the lessor), answer the following.
  - **(1)** What type of leasing arrangement has been entered into? Explain the reason for your answer.
  - **(2)** How should this lease be recorded by Breton, and how are the appropriate amounts determined?
  - **(3)** How should Breton determine the appropriate amount of earnings to be recognized from each lease payment?
  - **(4)** What disclosures must Breton make regarding this lease?

(AICPA adapted)

CA21-3 (Lessee Capitalization Criteria) On January 1, Santiago Company, a lessee, entered into three noncancelable leases for brand-new equipment, Lease L, Lease M, and Lease N. None of the three leases transfers ownership of the equipment to Santiago at the end of the lease term. For each of the three leases, the present value at the beginning of the lease term of the minimum lease payments, excluding that portion of the payments representing executory costs such as insurance, maintenance, and taxes to be paid by the lessor, is 75% of the fair value of the equipment.

The following information is peculiar to each lease.

1. Lease L does not contain a bargain-purchase option. The lease term is equal to 80% of the estimated economic life of the equipment.
2. Lease M contains a bargain-purchase option. The lease term is equal to 50% of the estimated economic life of the equipment.
3. Lease N does not contain a bargain-purchase option. The lease term is equal to 50% of the estimated economic life of the equipment.

Instructions

(a) How should Santiago Company classify each of the three leases above, and why? Discuss the rationale for your answer.

(b) What amount, if any, should Santiago record as a liability at the inception of the lease for each of the three leases above?

(c) Assuming that the minimum lease payments are made on a straight-line basis, how should Santiago record each minimum lease payment for each of the three leases above?

(AICPA adapted)

CA21-4 (Comparison of Different Types of Accounting by Lessee and Lessor)

Part 1: Capital leases and operating leases are the two classifications of leases described in FASB pronouncements from the standpoint of the **lessee**.

Instructions

(a) Describe how a capital lease would be accounted for by the lessee both at the inception of the lease and during the first year of the lease, assuming the lease transfers ownership of the property to the lessee by the end of the lease.

(b) Describe how an operating lease would be accounted for by the lessee both at the inception of the lease and during the first year of the lease, assuming equal monthly payments are made by the lessee at the beginning of each month of the lease. Describe the change in accounting, if any, when rental payments are not made on a straight-line basis.

Do **not** discuss the criteria for distinguishing between capital leases and operating leases.

Part 2: Sales-type leases and direct-financing leases are two of the classifications of leases described in FASB pronouncements from the standpoint of the **lessor**.

Instructions

Compare and contrast a sales-type lease with a direct-financing lease as follows.

(a) Lease receivable.

(b) Recognition of interest revenue.

(c) Manufacturer's or dealer's profit.

Do **not** discuss the criteria for distinguishing between the leases described above and operating leases.

(AICPA adapted)

CA21-5 (Lessee Capitalization of Bargain-Purchase Option) Albertsen Corporation is considering proposals for either leasing or purchasing aircraft. The proposed lease agreement involves a twin-engine turboprop Viking that has a fair value of $1,000,000. This plane would be leased for a period of 10 years beginning January 1, 2014. The lease agreement is cancelable only upon accidental destruction of the plane. An annual lease payment of $141,780 is due on January 1 of each year; the first payment is to be made on January 1, 2014. Maintenance operations are strictly scheduled by the lessor, and Albertsen Corporation will pay for these services as they are performed. Estimated annual maintenance costs are $6,900. The lessor will pay all insurance premiums and local property taxes, which amount to a combined total of $4,000 annually and are included in the annual lease payment of $141,780. Upon expiration of the 10-year lease, Albertsen Corporation can purchase the Viking for $44,440. The estimated useful life of the plane is 15 years, and its salvage value in the used plane market is estimated to be $100,000 after 10 years. The salvage value probably will never be less than $75,000 if the engines are overhauled and maintained as prescribed by the manufacturer. If the purchase option is not exercised, possession of the plane will revert to the lessor, and there is no provision for renewing the lease agreement beyond its termination on December 31, 2023.

Albertsen Corporation can borrow $1,000,000 under a 10-year term loan agreement at an annual interest rate of 12%. The lessor's implicit interest rate is not expressly stated in the lease agreement, but this rate appears to be approximately 8% based on 10 net rental payments of $137,780 per year and the initial fair value of $1,000,000 for the plane. On January 1, 2014, the present value of all net rental payments and the purchase option of $44,440 is $888,890 using the 12% interest rate. The present value of all net rental payments and the $44,440 purchase option on January 1, 2014, is $1,022,226 using the 8% interest rate implicit in the lease agreement. The financial vice president of Albertsen Corporation has established that this lease agreement is a capital lease as defined in GAAP.

Instructions

(a) What is the appropriate amount that Albertsen Corporation should recognize for the leased aircraft on its balance sheet after the lease is signed?

(b) Without prejudice to your answer in part (a), assume that the annual lease payment is $141,780 as stated in the question, that the appropriate capitalized amount for the leased aircraft is $1,000,000 on January 1, 2014, and that the interest rate is 9%. How will the lease be reported in the December 31, 2014, balance sheet and related income statement? (Ignore any income tax implications.)

(CMA adapted)

CA21-6 (Lease Capitalization, Bargain-Purchase Option) Baden Corporation entered into a lease agreement for 10 photocopy machines for its corporate headquarters. The lease agreement qualifies as an operating lease in all terms except there is a bargain-purchase option. After the 5-year lease term, the corporation can purchase each copier for $1,000, when the anticipated fair value is $2,500.

Jerry Suffolk, the financial vice president, thinks the financial statements must recognize the lease agreement as a capital lease because of the bargain-purchase option. The controller, Diane Buchanan, disagrees: "Although I don't know much about the copiers themselves, there is a way to avoid recording the lease liability." She argues that the corporation might claim that copier technology advances rapidly and that by the end of the lease term the machines will most likely not be worth the $1,000 bargain price.

Instructions

Answer the following questions.

(a) What ethical issue is at stake?

(b) Should the controller's argument be accepted if she does not really know much about copier technology? Would it make a difference if the controller were knowledgeable about the pace of change in copier technology?

(c) What should Suffolk do?

*CA21-7 (Sale-Leaseback)** On January 1, 2014, Perriman Company sold equipment for cash and leased it back. As seller-lessee, Perriman retained the right to substantially all of the remaining use of the equipment.

The term of the lease is 8 years. There is a gain on the sale portion of the transaction. The lease portion of the transaction is classified appropriately as a capital lease.

Instructions

(a) What is the theoretical basis for requiring lessees to capitalize certain long-term leases? **Do not discuss the specific criteria for classifying a lease as a capital lease**.

(b) (1) How should Perriman account for the sale portion of the sale-leaseback transaction at January 1, 2014?

   (2) How should Perriman account for the leaseback portion of the sale-leaseback transaction at January 1, 2014?

(c) How should Perriman account for the gain on the sale portion of the sale-leaseback transaction during the first year of the lease? Why?

(AICPA adapted)

USING YOUR JUDGMENT

FINANCIAL REPORTING

Financial Reporting Problem

P&G **The Procter & Gamble Company (P&G)**

The financial statements of P&G are presented in Appendix 5B. The company's complete annual report, including the notes to the financial statements, can be accessed at the book's companion website, **www.wiley.com/college/kieso**.

Instructions

Refer to P&G's financial statements, accompanying notes, and management's discussion and analysis to answer the following questions.

(a) What types of leases are used by P&G?

(b) What amount of capital leases was reported by P&G in total and for less than one year?

(c) What minimum annual rental commitments under all noncancelable leases at June 30, 2011, did P&G disclose?

Comparative Analysis Case

UAL, Inc. and Southwest Airlines

Instructions

Go to the book's companion website or the company websites and use information found there to answer the following questions related to UAL, Inc. and Southwest Airlines.

(a) What types of leases are used by Southwest and on what assets are these leases primarily used?

(b) How long-term are some of Southwest's leases? What are some of the characteristics or provisions of Southwest's (as lessee) leases?

(c) What did Southwest report in 2011 as its future minimum annual rental commitments under noncancelable leases?

(d) At year-end 2011, what was the present value of the minimum rental payments under Southwest's capital leases? How much imputed interest was deducted from the future minimum annual rental commitments to arrive at the present value?

(e) What were the amounts and details reported by Southwest for rental expense in 2011, 2010, and 2009?

(f) How does UAL's use of leases compare with Southwest's?

Financial Statement Analysis Case

Wal-Mart Stores, Inc.

Presented in Illustration 21-31 are the financial statement disclosures from the January 31, 2012, annual report of Wal-Mart Stores, Inc.

Instructions

Answer the following questions related to these disclosures.

(a) What is the total obligation under capital leases at January 31, 2012, for Wal-Mart?

(b) What is the total rental expense reported for leasing activity for the year ended January 31, 2012, for Wal-Mart?

(c) Estimate the off-balance-sheet liability due to Wal-Mart's operating leases at January 31, 2012.

Accounting, Analysis, and Principles

Salaur Company is evaluating a lease arrangement being offered by TSP Company for use of a computer system. The lease is noncancelable, and in no case does Salaur receive title to the computers during or at the end of the lease term. The lease starts on January 1, 2014, with the first rental payment due on January 1, 2014. Additional information related to the lease is as follows.

Yearly rental	$3,557.25
Lease term	3 years
Estimated economic life	5 years
Purchase option	$3,000 at end of 3 years, which approximates fair value
Renewal option	1 year at $1,500; no penalty for nonrenewal; standard renewal clause
Fair value at inception of lease	$10,000
Cost of asset to lessor	$10,000
Residual value:	
Guaranteed	–0–
Unguaranteed	$3,000
Lessor's implicit rate (known by the lessee)	12%
Executory costs paid by:	Lessor; estimated to be $500 per year (included in rental equipment)
Estimated fair value at end of lease	$3,000

Accounting

Analyze the lease capitalization criteria for this lease for Salaur Company. Prepare the journal entry for Salaur on January 1, 2014.

Analysis

Briefly discuss the impact of the accounting for this lease for two common ratios: return on assets and debt to total assets.

Principles

What element of faithful representation (completeness, neutrality, free from error) is being addressed when a company like Salaur evaluates lease capitalization criteria?

BRIDGE TO THE PROFESSION

 ## Professional Research: FASB Codification

Daniel Hardware Co. is considering alternative financing arrangements for equipment used in its warehouses. Besides purchasing the equipment outright, Daniel is also considering a lease. Accounting for the outright purchase is fairly straightforward, but because Daniel has not used equipment leases in the past, the accounting staff is less informed about the specific accounting rules for leases.

The staff is aware of some lease rules related to a "90 percent of fair value," "75 percent of useful life," and "residual value deficiencies," but they are unsure about the meanings of these terms in lease accounting. Daniel has asked you to conduct some research on these items related to lease capitalization criteria.

Instructions

If your school has a subscription to the FASB Codification, go to *http://aaahq.org/ascLogin.cfm* to log in and prepare responses to the following. Provide Codification references for your responses.

(a) What is the objective of lease classification criteria?

(b) An important element of evaluating leases is determining whether substantially all of the risks and rewards of ownership are transferred in the lease. How is "substantially all" defined in the authoritative literature?

(c) Besides the noncancelable term of the lease, name at least three other considerations in determining the "lease term."

(d) A common issue in the accounting for leases concerns lease requirements that the lessee make up a residual value deficiency that is attributable to damage, extraordinary wear and tear, or excessive usage (e.g., excessive mileage on a leased vehicle). Do these features constitute a lessee guarantee of the residual value such that the estimated residual value of the leased property at the end of the lease term should be included in minimum lease payments? Explain.

Additional Professional Resources

See the book's companion website, at **www.wiley.com/college/kieso**, for professional simulations as well as other study resources.

 IFRS INSIGHTS

Leasing is a global business. Lessors and lessees enter into arrangements with one another without regard to national boundaries. Although GAAP and IFRS for leasing are similar, both the FASB and the IASB have decided that the existing accounting does not provide the most useful, transparent, and complete information about leasing transactions that should be provided in the financial statements.

11 LEARNING OBJECTIVE

Compare the accounting for leases under GAAP and IFRS.

RELEVANT FACTS

Following are the key similarities and differences between GAAP and IFRS related to the accounting for leases.

Similarities

- Both GAAP and IFRS share the same objective of recording leases by lessees and lessors according to their economic substance—that is, according to the definitions of assets and liabilities.
- Much of the terminology for lease accounting in IFRS and GAAP is the same.
- Under IFRS, lessees and lessors use the same general lease capitalization criteria to determine if the risks and rewards of ownership have been transferred in the lease.

Differences

- One difference in lease terminology is that finance leases are referred to as capital leases in GAAP.
- GAAP for leases uses bright-line criteria to determine if a lease arrangement transfers the risks and rewards of ownership; IFRS is more general in its provisions.
- GAAP has additional lessor criteria: payments are collectible and there are no additional costs associated with a lease.
- IFRS requires that lessees use the implicit rate to record a lease unless it is impractical to determine the lessor's implicit rate. GAAP requires use of the incremental rate unless the implicit rate is known by the lessee and the implicit rate is lower than the incremental rate.
- Under GAAP, extensive disclosure of future non-cancelable lease payments is required for each of the next five years and the years thereafter. Although some international companies (e.g., Nokia) provide a year-by-year breakout of payments due in years 1 through 5, IFRS does not require it.
- The FASB standard for leases was originally issued in 1976. The standard (*SFAS No. 13*) has been the subject of more than 30 interpretations since its issuance. The IFRS leasing standard is *IAS 17*, first issued in 1982. This standard is the subject of only three interpretations. One reason for this small number of interpretations is that IFRS does not specifically address a number of leasing transactions that are covered by GAAP. Examples include lease agreements for natural resources, sale-leasebacks, real estate leases, and leveraged leases.

ABOUT THE NUMBERS

Accounting by the Lessee

If Air France (the lessee) **capitalizes** a lease, it records an asset and a liability generally equal to the present value of the rental payments. ILFC (the lessor), having transferred substantially all the benefits and risks of ownership, recognizes a sale by removing the asset from the statement of financial position and replacing it with a receivable.

Under IFRS, a lease is classified as a **finance lease** if it transfers substantially all the risks and rewards incidental to ownership. In order to record a lease as a finance lease, the lease must be non-cancelable. The IASB identifies the four criteria listed in Illustration IFRS21-1 for assessing whether the risks and rewards have been transferred in the lease arrangement.

Capitalization Criteria (Lessee)

1. The lease transfers ownership of the property to the lessee.
2. The lease contains a bargain-purchase option.
3. The lease term is for the major part of the economic life of the asset.
4. The present value of the minimum lease payments amounts to substantially all of the fair value of the leased asset.

Air France classifies and accounts for leases that **do not meet any of the four criteria** as **operating leases**. Illustration IFRS21-2 shows that a lease meeting any one of the four criteria results in the lessee having a finance lease.

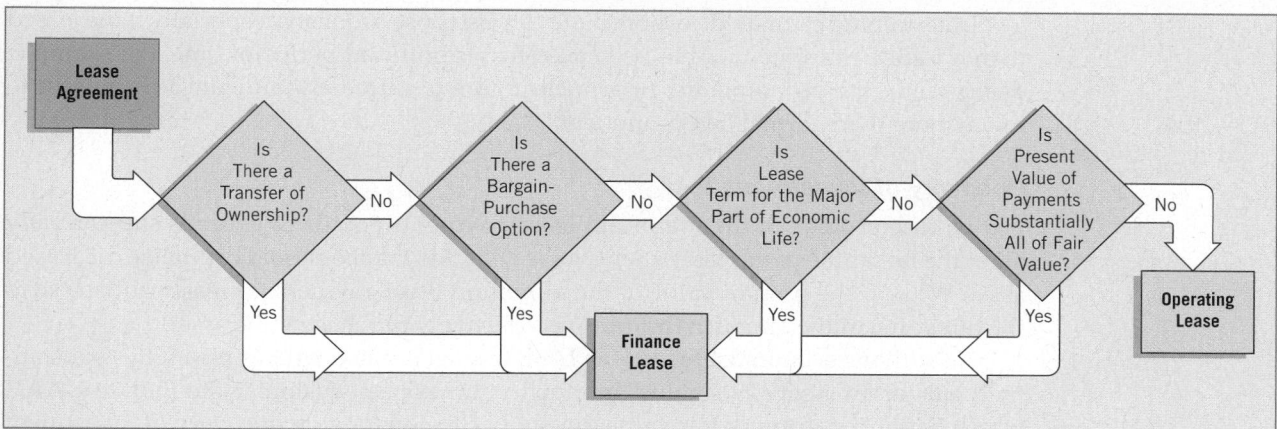

Thus, the proper classification of a lease is determined based on the substance of the lease transaction rather than on its mere form. This determination often requires the use of professional judgment of whether the risks and rewards of ownership are transferred.

As indicated, the capitalization criteria for finance leases are similar to those used in GAAP for capital leases (see Illustration 21-3 on page 1275). The main differences relate to the economic life and recoverability tests, which we describe in the following sections.

Economic Life Test

If the lease period is for a major part of the asset's economic life, the lessor transfers most of the risks and rewards of ownership to the lessee. Capitalization is therefore appropriate. However, determining the lease term and what constitutes the major part of the economic life of the asset can be troublesome.

The IASB has not defined what is meant by the "major part" of an asset's economic life. In practice, following the IASB Hierarchy, it has been customary to look to GAAP, which has a 75 percent of economic life threshold for evaluating the economic life test. While the 75 percent guideline may be a useful reference point, it does not represent an automatic cutoff point. Rather, lessees and lessors should consider all relevant factors when assessing whether substantially all the risks and rewards of ownership have been transferred in the lease.[21] *For purposes of homework, assume a 75 percent threshold for the economic life test, unless otherwise stated.*

---

[21]See KPMG, *Insights into IFRS*, Fifth Edition (Thomson Reuters: London, 2008), p. 1011; and The International Financial Reporting Group of Ernst and Young, *International GAAP, 2009* (John Wiley and Sons: New York, 2009), p. 1356.

The **lease term** is generally considered to be the fixed, non-cancelable term of the lease. However, a bargain-renewal option, if provided in the lease agreement, can extend this period. A **bargain-renewal option** allows the lessee to renew the lease for a rental that is lower than the expected fair rental at the date the option becomes exercisable. At the inception of the lease, the difference between the renewal rental and the expected fair rental must be great enough to make exercise of the option to renew reasonably assured.

For example, assume that Carrefour leases Lenovo PCs for two years at a rental of $100 per month per computer and subsequently can lease them for $10 per month per computer for another two years. The lease clearly offers a bargain-renewal option; the lease term is considered to be four years. However, with bargain-renewal options, as with bargain-purchase options, it is sometimes difficult to determine what is a bargain.

Determining estimated economic life can also pose problems, especially if the leased item is a specialized item or has been used for a significant period of time. For example, determining the economic life of a nuclear core is extremely difficult. It is subject to much more than normal "wear and tear."

Recovery of Investment Test

If the present value of the minimum lease payments equals or exceeds substantially all of the fair value of the asset, then a lessee like Air France should capitalize the leased asset. Why? If the present value of the minimum lease payments is reasonably close to the fair value of the aircraft, Air France is effectively purchasing the asset.

As with the economic life test, the IASB has not defined what is meant by "substantially all" of an asset's fair value. In practice, it has been customary to look to GAAP, which has a 90 percent of fair value threshold for assessing the recovery of investment test. Again, rather than focusing on any single element of the lease classification indicators, lessees and lessors should consider all relevant factors when evaluating lease classification criteria.[22] *For purposes of homework, assume a 90 percent threshold for the recovery of investment test.*

Determining the present value of the minimum lease payments involves three important concepts: (1) minimum lease payments, (2) executory costs, and (3) discount rate. The IFRS guidelines for minimum lease payments and executory costs are the same as that of GAAP.

Discount Rate. A lessee, like Air France, computes the present value of the minimum lease payments using the **implicit interest rate**. This rate is defined as the discount rate that, at the inception of the lease, causes the aggregate present value of the minimum lease payments and the unguaranteed residual value to be equal to the fair value of the leased asset.

While Air France may argue that it cannot determine the implicit rate of the lessor, in most cases Air France can approximate the implicit rate used by ILFC. In the event that it is impracticable to determine the implicit rate, Air France should use its incremental borrowing rate. The incremental borrowing rate is the rate of interest the lessee would have to pay on a similar lease or the rate that, at the inception of the lease, the lessee would incur to borrow over a similar term the funds necessary to purchase the asset.

---

[22]*Ibid.* The 75 percent of useful life and 90 percent of fair value "bright-line" cutoffs in GAAP have been criticized. Many believe that lessees structure leases so as to just miss the 75 and 90 percent cutoffs, thereby avoiding classifying leases as finance leases and keeping leased assets and the related liabilities off the statement of financial position. See Warren McGregor, "Accounting for Leases: A New Approach," Special Report (Norwalk, Conn.: FASB, 1996).

If known or practicable to estimate, use of the implicit rate is preferred. This is because **the implicit rate of ILFC is generally a more realistic rate** to use in determining the amount (if any) to report as the asset and related liability for Air France. In addition, use of the implicit rate avoids use of **an artificially high incremental borrowing rate** that would cause the present value of the minimum lease payments to be lower, supporting an argument that the lease does not meet the recovery of investment test. Use of such a rate would thus make it more likely that the lessee avoids capitalization of the leased asset and related liability.

The determination of whether or not a reasonable estimate could be made will require judgment, particularly where the result from using the incremental borrowing rate comes close to meeting the fair value test. Because Air France **may not capitalize the leased property at more than its fair value** (as we discuss later), it cannot use an excessively low discount rate.

Finance Lease Method (Lessee)

To illustrate a finance lease, assume that CNH Capital (a subsidiary of CNH Global) and Ivanhoe Mines Ltd. sign a lease agreement dated January 1, 2014, that calls for CNH to lease a front-end loader to Ivanhoe beginning January 1, 2014. The terms and provisions of the lease agreement, and other pertinent data, are as follows.

- The term of the lease is five years. The lease agreement is non-cancelable, requiring equal rental payments of $25,981.62 at the beginning of each year (annuity-due basis).
- The loader has a fair value at the inception of the lease of $100,000, an estimated economic life of five years, and no residual value.
- Ivanhoe pays all of the executory costs directly to third parties except for the property taxes of $2,000 per year, which is included as part of its annual payments to CNH.
- The lease contains no renewal options. The loader reverts to CNH at the termination of the lease.
- Ivanhoe's incremental borrowing rate is 11 percent per year.
- Ivanhoe depreciates similar equipment that it owns on a straight-line basis.
- CNH sets the annual rental to earn a rate of return on its investment of 10 percent per year; Ivanhoe knows this fact.

The lease meets the criteria for classification as a finance lease for the following reasons:

1. The lease term of five years, being equal to the equipment's estimated economic life of five years, satisfies the economic life test.
2. The present value of the minimum lease payments ($100,000 as computed below) equals the fair value of the loader ($100,000).

The minimum lease payments are $119,908.10 ($23,981.62 × 5). Ivanhoe computes the amount capitalized as leased assets as the present value of the minimum lease payments (excluding executory costs—property taxes of $2,000) as shown in Illustration IFRS21-3.

Capitalized amount	= ($25,981.62 − $2,000) × Present value of an annuity due of 1 for 5 periods at 10% (Table 6-5)
	= $23,981.62 × 4.16986
	= $100,000

ILLUSTRATION IFRS21-3
Computation of Capitalized Lease Payments

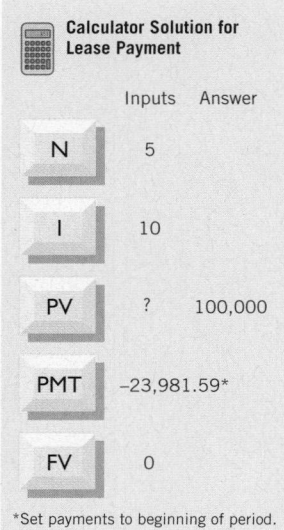

Calculator Solution for Lease Payment

	Inputs	Answer
N	5	
I	10	
PV	?	100,000
PMT	−23,981.59*	
FV	0	

*Set payments to beginning of period.

Ivanhoe uses CNH's implicit interest rate of 10 percent instead of its incremental borrowing rate of 11 percent because it knows about it.[23] Ivanhoe records the finance lease on its books on January 1, 2014, as:

Leased Equipment (under finance leases)	100,000	
Lease Liability		100,000

Note that the entry records the obligation at the net amount of $100,000 (the present value of the future rental payments) rather than at the gross amount of $119,908.10 ($23,981.62 × 5).

Ivanhoe records the **first lease payment on January 1, 2014**, as follows.

Property Tax Expense	2,000.00	
Lease Liability	23,981.62	
Cash		25,981.62

Each lease payment of $25,981.62 consists of three elements: (1) a reduction in the lease liability, (2) a financing cost (interest expense), and (3) executory costs (property taxes). The total financing cost (interest expense) over the term of the lease is $19,908.10. This amount is the difference between the present value of the lease payments ($100,000) and the actual cash disbursed, net of executory costs ($119,908.10). The annual interest expense, applying the effective-interest method, is a function of the outstanding liability, as Illustration IFRS21-4 shows.

ILLUSTRATION IFRS21-4

Lease Amortization Schedule for Lessee—Annuity-Due Basis

IVANHOE MINES
LEASE AMORTIZATION SCHEDULE
ANNUITY-DUE BASIS

Date	Annual Lease Payment	Executory Costs	Interest (10%) on Liability	Reduction of Lease Liability	Lease Liability
	(a)	(b)	(c)	(d)	(e)
1/1/14					$100,000.00
1/1/14	$ 25,981.62	$ 2,000	$ −0−	$ 23,981.62	76,018.38
1/1/15	25,981.62	2,000	7,601.84	16,379.78	59,638.60
1/1/16	25,981.62	2,000	5,963.86	18,017.76	41,620.84
1/1/17	25,981.62	2,000	4,162.08	19,819.54	21,801.30
1/1/18	25,981.62	2,000	2,180.32*	21,801.30	−0−
	$129,908.10	$10,000	$19,908.10	$100,000.00	

(a) Lease payment as required by lease.
(b) Executory costs included in rental payment.
(c) Ten percent of the preceding balance of (e) except for 1/1/14; since this is an annuity due, no time has elapsed at the date of the first payment and no interest has accrued.
(d) (a) minus (b) and (c).
(e) Preceding balance minus (d).

*Rounded by 19 cents.

At the end of its fiscal year, December 31, 2014, Ivanhoe records **accrued interest** as follows.

Interest Expense	7,601.84	
Interest Payable		7,601.84

Depreciation of the leased equipment over its five-year lease term, applying Ivanhoe's normal depreciation policy (straight-line method), results in the following entry on December 31, 2014.

[23]If it is impracticable for Ivanhoe to determine the implicit rate and it has an incremental borrowing rate of, say, 9 percent (lower than the 10 percent rate used by CNH), the present value computation would yield a capitalized amount of $101,675.35 ($23,981.62 × 4.23972). Thus, use of an unrealistically low discount rate could lead to a lessee recording a leased asset at an amount exceeding the fair value of the equipment, which is generally prohibited in IFRS. This explains why the implicit rate should be used to capitalize the minimum lease payments.

Depreciation Expense (finance leases)	20,000	
Accumulated Depreciation—Finance Leases		20,000
($100,000 ÷ 5 years)		

At December 31, 2014, Ivanhoe separately identifies the assets recorded under finance leases on its statement of financial position. Similarly, it separately identifies the related obligations. Thus, once a lessee capitalizes a finance lease, the accounting under IFRS is the same as that applied for capital leases under GAAP.

Accounting by the Lessor

For accounting purposes, under IFRS the **lessor** also classifies leases as operating or finance leases. Finance leases may be further subdivided into direct-financing and sales-type leases.

As with lessee accounting, if the lease transfers substantially all the risks and rewards incidental to ownership, the lessor shall classify and account for the arrangement as a finance lease. Lessors evaluate the same criteria shown in Illustration IFRS21-1 to make this determination.

The distinction for the lessor between a direct-financing lease and a sales-type lease is the presence or absence of a manufacturer's or dealer's profit (or loss). A sales-type lease involves a manufacturer's or dealer's profit, and a direct-financing lease does not. The profit (or loss) to the lessor is evidenced by the difference between the fair value of the leased property at the inception of the lease and the lessor's cost or carrying amount (book value).

Normally, sales-type leases arise when manufacturers or dealers use leasing as a means of marketing their products. For example, a computer manufacturer will lease its computer equipment (possibly through a captive) to businesses and institutions. Direct-financing leases generally result from arrangements with lessors that are primarily engaged in financing operations (e.g., banks).

Lessors classify and account for all leases that do not qualify as direct-financing or sales-type leases as operating leases. Illustration IFRS21-5 shows the circumstances under which a lessor classifies a lease as operating, direct-financing, or sales-type.

ILLUSTRATION IFRS21-5
Diagram of Lessor's Criteria for Lease Classification

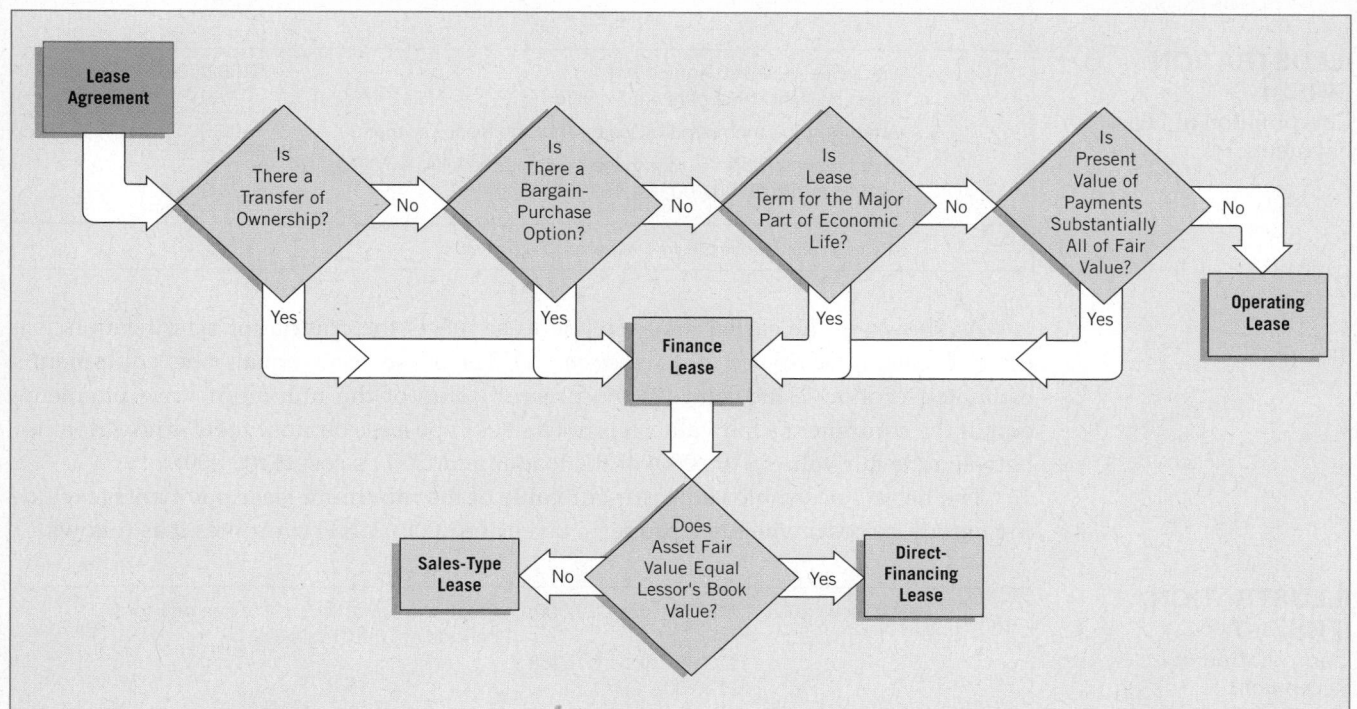

For purposes of comparison with the lessee's accounting, we will illustrate only the operating and direct-financing leases in the following section.

Direct-Financing Method (Lessor)

Direct-financing leases are in substance the financing of an asset purchase by the lessee. In this type of lease, the lessor records a **lease receivable** instead of a leased asset. The lease receivable is the present value of the minimum lease payments plus the present value of the unguaranteed residual value. Remember that "minimum lease payments" include (1) rental payments (excluding executory costs), (2) bargain-purchase option (if any), (3) guaranteed residual value (if any), and (4) penalty for failure to renew (if any).

Thus, the lessor records the residual value, whether guaranteed or not. Also, recall that if the lessor pays any executory costs, then it should reduce the rental payment by that amount in computing minimum lease payments.

The following presentation, using the data from the preceding CNH/Ivanhoe example on pages 1335–1337, illustrates the accounting treatment for a direct-financing lease. We repeat here the information relevant to CNH in accounting for this lease transaction.

1. The term of the lease is five years beginning January 1, 2014, non-cancelable, and requires equal rental payments of $25,981.62 at the beginning of each year. Payments include $2,000 of executory costs (property taxes).

2. The equipment (front-end loader) has a cost of $100,000 to CNH, a fair value at the inception of the lease of $100,000, an estimated economic life of five years, and no residual value.

3. CNH incurred no initial direct costs in negotiating and closing the lease transaction.

4. The lease contains no renewal options. The equipment reverts to CNH at the termination of the lease.

5. CNH sets the annual lease payments to ensure a rate of return of 10 percent (implicit rate) on its investment, as shown in Illustration IFRS21-6.

ILLUSTRATION IFRS21-6
Computation of Lease Payments

Fair value of leased equipment	$100,000.00
Less: Present value of residual value	–0–
Amount to be recovered by lessor through lease payments	$100,000.00
Five beginning-of-the-year lease payments to yield a 10% return ($100,000 ÷ 4.16986[a])	$ 23,981.62

[a]PV of an annuity due of 1 for 5 years at 10% (Table 6-5).

As shown in the earlier analysis, the lease meets the criteria for classification as a direct-financing lease for two reasons. (1) The lease term equals the equipment's estimated economic life, and (2) the present value of the minimum lease payments equals the equipment's fair value. It is not a sales-type lease because there is no difference between the fair value ($100,000) of the loader and CNH's cost ($100,000).

The Lease Receivable is the present value of the minimum lease payments (excluding executory costs which are property taxes of $2,000). CNH computes it as follows.

ILLUSTRATION IFRS21-7
Computation of Lease Receivable

Lease receivable = ($25,981.62 − $2,000) × Present value of an annuity due of 1 for 5 periods at 10% (Table 6-5)

= $23,981.62 × 4.16986

= $100,000

CNH records the lease of the asset and the resulting receivable on January 1, 2014 (the inception of the lease), as follows.

Lease Receivable	100,000	
Equipment		100,000

Companies often **report** the lease receivable in the statement of financial position as "Net investment in finance leases." Companies classify it either as current or non-current, depending on when they recover the net investment.

Under IFRS, once a lessor determines classification of a lease as either direct-financing or sales-type, the accounting for the lease arrangement is the same as GAAP (as shown on pages 1286–1289 and 1296–1298).

ON THE HORIZON

Lease accounting is one of the areas identified in the IASB/FASB Memorandum of Understanding. The Boards have issued proposed rules based on "right of use," which requires that all leases, regardless of their terms, be accounted for in a manner similar to how finance leases are treated today. That is, the notion of an operating lease will be eliminated, which will address the concerns under current rules in which no asset or liability is recorded for many operating leases. A final standard is expected in 2013. You can follow the lease project at either the FASB (*http://www.fasb.org*) or IASB (*http://www.iasb.org*) websites.

IFRS SELF-TEST QUESTIONS

1. Which of the following is **not** a criterion for a lease to be recorded as a finance lease?
  (a) There is transfer of ownership.
  (b) The lease is cancelable.
  (c) The lease term is for the major part of the economic life of the asset.
  (d) There is a bargain-purchase option.

2. Under IFRS, in computing the present value of the minimum lease payments, the lessee should:
  (a) use its incremental borrowing rate in all cases.
  (b) use either its incremental borrowing rate or the implicit rate of the lessor, whichever is higher, assuming that the implicit rate is known to the lessee.
  (c) use either its incremental borrowing rate or the implicit rate of the lessor, whichever is lower, assuming that the implicit rate is known to the lessee.
  (d) use the implicit rate of the lessor, unless it is impracticable to determine the implicit rate.

3. A lease that involves a manufacturer's or dealer's profit is a(an):
  (a) direct financing lease.   **(c)** operating lease.
  (b) finance lease.   **(d)** sales-type lease.

4. Which of the following statements is **true** when comparing the accounting for leasing transactions under GAAP with IFRS?
  (a) IFRS for leases is more "rules-based" than GAAP and includes many bright-line criteria to determine ownership.
  (b) IFRS requires that companies provide a year-by-year breakout of future non-cancelable lease payments due in years 1 through 5.
  (c) The IFRS leasing standard is the subject of over 30 interpretations since its issuance in 1982.
  (d) IFRS does not provide detailed guidance for leases of natural resources, sale-leasebacks, and leveraged leases.

5. All of the following statements about lease accounting under IFRS and GAAP are true **except**:
  (a) IFRS requires a year-by-year breakout of payments related to leasing arrangements.
  (b) IFRS is more general in its lease accounting provisions than is GAAP.
  (c) The IFRS leasing standard, *IAS 17*, is the subject of only three interpretations.
  (d) Finance leases under IFRS are referred to as capital leases under GAAP.

IFRS CONCEPTS AND APPLICATION

IFRS21-1 Where can authoritative IFRS related to the accounting for leases be found?

IFRS21-2 Briefly describe some of the similarities and differences between GAAP and IFRS with respect to the accounting for leases.

IFRS21-3 Briefly discuss the IASB and FASB efforts to converge their accounting guidelines for leases.

IFRS21-4 Outline the accounting procedures involved in applying the operating lease method by a lessee.

IFRS21-5 Outline the accounting procedures involved in applying the finance lease method by a lessee.

IFRS21-6 Identify the lease classifications for lessors and the criteria that must be met for each classification.

IFRS21-7 Rick Kleckner Corporation recorded a finance lease at $300,000 on January 1, 2014. The interest rate is 12%. Kleckner Corporation made the first lease payment of $53,920 on January 1, 2014. The lease requires eight annual payments. The equipment has a useful life of 8 years with no residual value. Prepare Kleckner Corporation's December 31, 2014, adjusting entries.

IFRS21-8 Use the information for Rick Kleckner Corporation from IFRS21-7. Assume that at December 31, 2014, Kleckner made an adjusting entry to accrue interest expense of $29,530 on the lease. Prepare Kleckner's January 1, 2015, journal entry to record the second lease payment of $53,920.

IFRS21-9 Brecker Company leases an automobile with a fair value of $10,906 from Emporia Motors, Inc., on the following terms:

1. Non-cancelable term of 50 months.
2. Rental of $250 per month (at end of each month). (The present value at 1% per month is $9,800.)
3. Estimated residual value after 50 months is $1,180. (The present value at 1% per month is $715.) Brecker Company guarantees the residual value of $1,180.
4. Estimated economic life of the automobile is 60 months.
5. Brecker Company's incremental borrowing rate is 12% a year (1% a month). It is impracticable to determine Emporia's implicit rate.

Instructions
(a) What is the nature of this lease to Brecker Company?
(b) What is the present value of the minimum lease payments?
(c) Record the lease on Brecker Company's books at the date of inception.
(d) Record the first month's depreciation on Brecker Company's books (assume straight-line).
(e) Record the first month's lease payment.

IFRS21-10 The following facts pertain to a non-cancelable lease agreement between Lennox Leasing Company and Gill Company, a lessee. (Round all numbers to the nearest cent.)

Inception date: May 1, 2014

Annual lease payment due at the beginning of each year, beginning with May 1, 2014: $18,829.49

Bargain-purchase option price at end of lease term: $4,000.00

Lease term: 5 years

Economic life of leased equipment: 10 years

Lessor's cost: $65,000.00; fair value of asset at May 1, 2014, $81,000.00

Lessor's implicit rate: 10%; lessee's incremental borrowing rate 10%

The lessee assumes responsibility for all executory costs.

Instructions
(a) Discuss the nature of this lease to Gill Company.
(b) Discuss the nature of this lease to Lennox Company.
(c) Prepare a lease amortization schedule for Gill Company for the 5-year lease term.
(d) Prepare the journal entries on the lessee's books to reflect the signing of the lease agreement and to record the payments and expenses related to this lease for the years 2014 and 2015. Gill's annual accounting period ends on December 31. Reversing entries are used by Gill.

IFRS21-11 A lease agreement between Lennox Leasing Company and Gill Company is described in IFRS21-10. Refer to the data in IFRS21-10 and do the following for the lessor. (Round all numbers to the nearest cent.)

Instructions

(a) Compute the amount of the lease receivable at the inception of the lease.
(b) Prepare a lease amortization schedule for Lennox Leasing Company for the 5-year lease term.
(c) Prepare the journal entries to reflect the signing of the lease agreement and to record the receipts and income related to this lease for the years 2014, 2015, and 2016. The lessor's accounting period ends on December 31. Reversing entries are not used by Lennox.

Professional Research

IFRS21-12 Daniel Hardware Co. is considering alternative financing arrangements for equipment used in its warehouses. Besides purchasing the equipment outright, Daniel is also considering a lease. Accounting for the outright purchase is fairly straightforward, but because Daniel has not used equipment leases in the past, the accounting staff is less informed about the specific accounting rules for leases. The staff is aware of some general lease rules related to "risks and rewards," but they are unsure about the meanings of these terms in lease accounting. Daniel has asked you to conduct some research on these items related to lease capitalization criteria.

Instructions

Access the IFRS authoritative literature at the IASB website (*http://eifrs.iasb.org/*). (Click on the IFRS tab and then register for free eIFRS access if necessary.) When you have accessed the documents, you can use the search tool in your Internet browser to respond to the following questions. (Provide paragraph citations.)

(a) What is the objective of lease classification criteria?
(b) An important element of evaluating leases is determining whether substantially all of the risks and rewards of ownership are transferred in the lease. How is "substantially all" defined in the authoritative literature?
(c) Besides the non-cancelable term of the lease, name at least three other considerations in determining the "lease term."

International Financial Reporting Problem
Marks and Spencer plc

IFRS21-13 The financial statements of **Marks and Spencer plc (M&S)** are available at the book's companion website or can be accessed at *http://annualreport.marksandspencer.com/_assets/downloads/Marks-and-Spencer-Annual-report-and-financial-statements-2012.pdf*.

Instructions

Refer to M&S's financial statements and the accompanying notes to answer the following questions.

(a) What types of leases are used by M&S?
(b) What amount of finance leases was reported by M&S in total and for less than one year?
(c) What minimum annual rental commitments under all non-cancelable leases at 31 March 2012 did M&S disclose?

ANSWERS TO IFRS SELF-TEST QUESTIONS

1. b **2.** d **3.** d **4.** d **5.** a

Remember to check the book's companion website to find additional resources for this chapter.

22 Accounting Changes and Error Analysis

In the Dark

The FASB's conceptual framework describes comparability (including consistency) as one of the qualitative characteristics that contribute to the usefulness of accounting information. Unfortunately, companies are finding it difficult to maintain comparability and consistency due to the numerous changes in accounting principles mandated by the FASB. In addition, a number of companies have faced restatements due to errors in their financial statements. For example, the table below shows types and numbers of recent accounting changes.

Business combinations	49	Debt–equity financial instruments	18
Noncontrolling interests	38	Transfers of financial instruments	12
Fair value measurements	32	Earnings per share	6
Defined benefit pension and postretirement plans	21	Other, including depreciation, stock-based compensation, derivatives, inventory, and revenue	75

Although the percentage of companies reporting material changes or errors is small, readers of financial statements still must be careful. The reason: The amounts in the financial statements may have changed due to changing accounting principles and/or restatements. The chart below indicates the recent trends in restatements.

There is much good news in the chart. In 2007, restatements declined by 32.2 percent (from 1,790 to 1,213). In 2008, restatements declined another 24 percent (from 1,213 to 922). The declining trend continued in 2009, with restatements stabilized at pre-crisis levels in 2010 and 2011. However, investors can be in the dark when a company has an error that requires restatement. It may take some time for companies to sort out the source of an error, prepare corrected statements, and get auditor sign-off. Recent data indicate it takes on average about 3 months to resolve a restatement. The following table reports the range of periods when investors are in the dark due to a restatement.

Time to File Restated Financial Statements	% of All Restatements
Up to 3 Months	77
3–9 Months	11
Greater than 9 Months	12

While most companies (77%) resolve their errors within 3 months, 12 percent (or over 200 companies) take more than 9 months to file corrected statements.

These lengthy "dark periods" have caught the attention of policy-setters and were a topic of discussion of the Committee for Improvements in Financial Reporting (CIFR). As one member of CIFR noted, "The dark period is bad for users." As a result, the committee is proposing that for some errors, companies might not need to go through the pain of restatement, but enhanced disclosures about errors are needed.

Sources: Accounting change data from *Accounting Trends and Techniques—2011–2012* (New York: AICPA, 2011–2012). Restatement data from *2011 Financial Restatements: A Nine Year Comparison*, Audit Analytics (April 2012), p. 3; M. Leone, "Materiality Debate Emerges from the Dark," *CFO.com* (July 14, 2008); and B. Badertscher and J. Burks, "Accounting Restatements and the Timeliness of Disclosures," *Accounting Horizons* (December 2011), pp. 609–629.

CONCEPTUAL FOCUS

> See the **Underlying Concepts** on pages 1344, 1346, and 1366.

INTERNATIONAL FOCUS

> See the **International Perspectives** on pages 1345 and 1355.
> Read the **IFRS Insights** on pages 1404–1408 for a discussion of:
—Direct and indirect effects of changes
—Impracticability

PREVIEW OF CHAPTER 22

As our opening story indicates, changes in accounting principles and errors in financial information have increased substantially in recent years. When these changes occur, companies must follow specific accounting and reporting requirements. In addition, to ensure comparability among companies, the FASB has standardized reporting of accounting changes, accounting estimates, error corrections, and related earnings per share information. In this chapter, we discuss these reporting standards, which help investors better understand a company's financial condition. The content and organization of the chapter are as follows.

Accounting Changes and Error Analysis

Accounting Changes	Changes in Principle	Changes in Estimates	Changes in Entity	Accounting Errors	Error Analysis
	• Retrospective • Direct and indirect effects • Impracticability	• Prospective • Disclosures		• Example • Summary • Motivations	• Balance sheet errors • Income statement errors • Balance sheet and income statement errors • Comprehensive example • Preparation of statements with error corrections

ACCOUNTING CHANGES

LEARNING OBJECTIVE

Identify the types of accounting changes.

Accounting alternatives diminish the comparability of financial information between periods and between companies; they also obscure useful historical trend data. For example, if **Ford** revises its estimates for equipment useful lives, depreciation expense for the current year will not be comparable to depreciation expense reported by Ford in prior years. Similarly, if **OfficeMax** changes to FIFO inventory pricing while **Staples** uses LIFO, it will be difficult to compare these companies' reported results. A reporting framework helps preserve comparability when there is an accounting change.

 See the FASB Codification section (page 1381).

The FASB has established a reporting framework, which involves three types of accounting changes. **[1]** The three types of accounting changes are:

1. *Change in accounting principle.* A change from one generally accepted accounting principle to another one. For example, a company may change its inventory valuation method from LIFO to average-cost.

2. *Change in accounting estimate.* A change that occurs as the result of new information or additional experience. For example, a company may change its estimate of the useful lives of depreciable assets.

3. *Change in reporting entity.* A change from reporting as one type of entity to another type of entity. As an example, a company might change the subsidiaries for which it prepares consolidated financial statements.

Underlying Concepts

While changes in accounting may enhance the qualitative characteristic of *usefulness*, these changes may adversely affect the enhancing characteristics of *comparability* and *consistency*.

A fourth category necessitates changes in accounting, though it is not classified as an accounting change.

4. *Errors in financial statements.* Errors result from mathematical mistakes, mistakes in applying accounting principles, or oversight or misuse of facts that existed when preparing the financial statements. For example, a company may incorrectly apply the retail inventory method for determining its final inventory value.

The FASB classifies changes in these categories because each category involves different methods of recognizing changes in the financial statements. In this chapter, we discuss these classifications. We also explain how to report each item in the accounts and how to disclose the information in comparative statements.

CHANGES IN ACCOUNTING PRINCIPLE

LEARNING OBJECTIVE

Describe the accounting for changes in accounting principles.

By definition, a **change in accounting principle** involves **a change from one generally accepted accounting principle to another**. For example, a company might change the basis of inventory pricing from average-cost to LIFO. Or, it might change its method of revenue recognition for long-term construction contracts from the completed-contract to the percentage-of-completion method.

Companies must carefully examine each circumstance to ensure that a change in principle has actually occurred. **Adoption of a new principle** in recognition of events that have occurred for the first time or that were previously immaterial is not an accounting change. For example, a change in accounting principle has not occurred when a company adopts an inventory method (e.g., FIFO) for **newly** acquired items of inventory, even if FIFO differs from that used for **previously recorded** inventory. Another example is certain marketing expenditures that were previously immaterial and expensed in the period incurred. It would not be considered a change in accounting principle if they become material and so may be acceptably deferred and amortized.

Finally, what if a company previously followed an accounting principle that was not acceptable? Or what if the company applied a principle incorrectly? In such cases, the profession considers a change to a generally accepted accounting principle **a correction of an error**. For example, a switch from the cash (income tax) basis of accounting to the accrual basis is a correction of an error. Or, if a company deducted salvage value when computing double-declining depreciation on plant assets and later recomputed depreciation without deducting estimated salvage value, it has corrected an error.

There are three possible approaches for reporting changes in accounting principles:

1. *Report changes currently.* In this approach, companies report the cumulative effect of the change in the current year's income statement as an irregular item. The cumulative effect is the difference in prior years' income between the newly adopted and prior accounting method. Under this approach, the effect of the change on prior years' income appears only in the current-year income statement. The company does not change **prior year financial statements**.

   Advocates of this position argue that changing prior years' financial statements results in a loss of confidence in financial reports. How do investors react when told that the earnings computed three years ago are now entirely different? Changing prior periods, if permitted, also might upset contractual arrangements based on the old figures. For example, profit-sharing arrangements computed on the old basis might have to be recomputed and completely new distributions made, creating numerous legal problems. Many practical difficulties also exist. The cost of changing prior period financial statements may be excessive, or determining the amount of the prior period effect may be impossible on the basis of available data.

2. *Report changes retrospectively.* Retrospective application refers to the application of a different accounting principle to recast previously issued financial statements— **as if the new principle had always been used**. In other words, the company "goes back" and adjusts **prior years' statements** on a basis consistent with the newly adopted principle. The company shows any cumulative effect of the change as an adjustment to beginning retained earnings of the earliest year presented.

   Advocates of this position argue that retrospective application ensures comparability. Think for a moment what happens if this approach is not used. The year *previous* to the change will be on the old method, the year *of the change* will report the entire cumulative adjustment, and the *following* year will present financial statements on the new basis without the cumulative effect of the change. Such lack of consistency fails to provide meaningful earnings-trend data and other financial relationships necessary to evaluate the business.

3. *Report changes prospectively (in the future).* In this approach, previously reported results remain. As a result, companies do not adjust opening balances to reflect the change in principle. Advocates of this position argue that once management presents financial statements based on acceptable accounting principles, they are final. Management cannot change prior periods by adopting a new principle. According to this line of reasoning, the current-period cumulative adjustment is not appropriate because that approach includes amounts that have little or no relationship to the current year's income or economic events.

Given these three possible approaches, which does the accounting profession prefer? The FASB **requires that companies use the retrospective approach.** Why? Because it provides financial statement users with more useful information than

International Perspective

IFRS (*IAS 8*) generally requires retrospective application to prior years for accounting changes. However, *IAS 8* permits the prospective method if a company cannot reasonably determine the amounts to which to restate prior periods.

the cumulative-effect or prospective approaches. **[2]** The rationale is that changing the prior statements to be on the same basis as the newly adopted principle results in greater consistency across accounting periods. Users can then better compare results from one period to the next.[1]

What do the numbers mean?   QUITE A CHANGE

The cumulative-effect approach results in a loss of comparability. Also, reporting the cumulative adjustment in the period of the change can significantly affect net income, resulting in a misleading income figure. For example, at one time **Chrysler Corporation** changed its inventory accounting from LIFO to FIFO. If Chrysler had used the cumulative-effect approach, it would have reported a $53,500,000 adjustment to net income. That adjustment would have resulted in net income of $45,900,000, instead of a net loss of $7,600,000.

A second case: In the early 1980s, the railroad industry switched from the retirement-replacement method of depreciating railroad equipment to more generally used methods such as straight-line depreciation. Using cumulative treatment, railroad companies would have made substantial adjustments to income in the period of change. Many in the industry argued that including such large cumulative-effect adjustments in the current year would distort the information and make it less useful.

Such situations lend support to retrospective application so that comparability is maintained.

Retrospective Accounting Change Approach

LEARNING OBJECTIVE
Understand how to account for retrospective accounting changes.

 Underlying Concepts

Retrospective application contributes to comparability.

A presumption exists that once a company adopts an accounting principle, it should not change. That presumption is understandable, given the idea that consistent use of an accounting principle enhances the usefulness of financial statements. However, the environment continually changes, and companies change in response. Recent standards on such subjects as stock options, exchanges of nonmonetary assets, and derivatives indicate that changes in accounting principle will continue to occur.

When a company changes an accounting principle, it should report the change using retrospective application. In general terms, here is what it must do:

1. *It adjusts its financial statements for each prior period presented.* Thus, financial statement information about prior periods is on the same basis as the new accounting principle.

2. *It adjusts the carrying amounts of assets and liabilities as of the beginning of the first year presented.* By doing so, these accounts reflect the cumulative effect on periods prior to those presented of the change to the new accounting principle. The company also makes an offsetting adjustment to the opening balance of retained earnings or other appropriate component of stockholders' equity or net assets as of the beginning of the first year presented.

For example, assume that **Target** decides to change its inventory valuation method in 2014 from the retail inventory method (FIFO) to the retail inventory method (average-cost). It provides comparative information for 2012 and 2013 based on the new method. Target would adjust its assets, liabilities, and retained earnings for periods prior to 2012 and report these amounts in the 2012 financial statements, when it prepares comparative financial statements.

---

[1]Adoption of the retrospective approach contributes to international accounting convergence. As discussed throughout the textbook, the FASB and the IASB are collaborating on a project in which they have agreed to converge around high-quality solutions to resolve differences between GAAP and IFRS. By adopting the retrospective approach, which is the method used in IFRS, the FASB agreed that this approach is superior to the current approach.

Retrospective Accounting Change: Long-Term Contracts

To illustrate the retrospective approach, assume that Denson Company has accounted for its income from long-term construction contracts using the completed-contract method. In 2014, the company changed to the percentage-of-completion method. Management believes this approach provides a more appropriate measure of the income earned. For tax purposes, the company uses the completed-contract method and plans to continue doing so in the future. (We assume a 40% enacted tax rate.)

Illustration 22-1 shows portions of three income statements for 2012–2014—for both the completed-contract and percentage-of-completion methods (2012 was Denson's first year of operations in the construction business).

COMPLETED-CONTRACT METHOD
DENSON COMPANY
INCOME STATEMENT (PARTIAL)
FOR THE YEARS ENDED DECEMBER 31

	2012	2013	2014
Income before income tax	$400,000	$160,000	$190,000
Income tax (40%)	160,000	64,000	76,000
Net income	$240,000	$ 96,000	$114,000

PERCENTAGE-OF-COMPLETION METHOD
DENSON COMPANY
INCOME STATEMENT (PARTIAL)
FOR THE YEARS ENDED DECEMBER 31

	2012	2013	2014
Income before income tax	$600,000	$180,000	$200,000
Income tax (40%)	240,000	72,000	80,000
Net income	$360,000	$108,000	$120,000

ILLUSTRATION 22-1
Comparative Income Statements for Completed-Contract versus Percentage-of-Completion Methods

To record a change from the completed-contract to the percentage-of-completion method, we analyze the various effects, as Illustration 22-2 shows.

Year	Pretax Income from		Difference in Income		
	Percentage-of-Completion	Completed-Contract	Difference	Tax Effect 40%	Income Effect (net of tax)
Prior to 2013	$600,000	$400,000	$200,000	$80,000	$120,000
In 2013	180,000	160,000	20,000	8,000	12,000
Total at beginning of 2014	$780,000	$560,000	$220,000	$88,000	$132,000
Total in 2014	$200,000	$190,000	$ 10,000	$ 4,000	$ 6,000

ILLUSTRATION 22-2
Data for Retrospective Change Example

The entry to record the change at the beginning of 2014 would be:

Construction in Process	220,000	
Deferred Tax Liability		88,000
Retained Earnings		132,000

The Construction in Process account increases by $220,000 (as indicated in the first column under "Difference in Income" in Illustration 22-2). The credit to Retained Earnings of $132,000 reflects the cumulative income effects prior to 2014 (third column under "Difference in Income" in Illustration 22-2). The company credits Retained Earnings because prior years' income is closed to this account each year. The credit to Deferred Tax Liability represents the adjustment to prior years' tax expense. The company now recognizes that amount, $88,000, as a tax liability for future taxable amounts. That is, in future periods, taxable income will be higher than book income as a result of current temporary differences. Therefore, Denson must report a deferred tax liability in the current year.

What do the numbers mean?   CHANGE MANAGEMENT

Halliburton offers a case study in the importance of good reporting of an accounting change. Note that Halliburton uses percentage-of-completion accounting for its long-term construction-services contracts. The SEC questioned the company about its change in accounting for disputed claims.

Prior to the year of the change, Halliburton took a very conservative approach to its accounting for disputed claims. That is, the company waited until all disputes were resolved before recognizing associated revenues. In contrast, in the year of the change, the company recognized revenue for disputed claims *before* their resolution, using estimates of amounts expected to be recovered. Such revenue and its related profit are more tentative and subject to possible later adjustment. The accounting method adopted is more aggressive than the company's former policy but is within the boundaries of GAAP.

It appears that the problem with Halliburton's accounting stems more from how the company handled its accounting change than from the new method itself. That is, Halliburton did not provide in its annual report in the year of the change an explicit reference to its change in accounting method. In fact, rather than stating its new policy, the company simply deleted the sentence that described how it accounted for disputed claims. Then later, in its next year's annual report, the company stated its new accounting policy.

When companies make such changes in accounting, investors need to be informed about the change and about its effects on the financial results. With such information, investors and analysts can compare current results with those of prior periods and can make a more informed assessment about the company's future prospects.

Source: Adapted from "Accounting Ace Charles Mulford Answers Accounting Questions," *Wall Street Journal Online* (June 7, 2002).

Reporting a Change in Principle. The disclosure of accounting changes is particularly important. Financial statement readers want consistent information from one period to the next. Such consistency ensures the usefulness of financial statements. The major disclosure requirements are as follows.

1. The nature of and reason for the change in accounting principle. This must include an explanation of why the newly adopted accounting principle is preferable.
2. The method of applying the change, and:
   (a) A description of the prior period information that has been retrospectively adjusted, if any.
   (b) The effect of the change on income from continuing operations, net income (or other appropriate captions of changes in net assets or performance indicators), any other affected line item, and any affected per share amounts for the current period and for any prior periods retrospectively adjusted.
   (c) The cumulative effect of the change on retained earnings or other components of equity or net assets in the statement of financial position as of the beginning of the earliest period presented.[2]

To illustrate, Denson will prepare comparative financial statements for 2013 and 2014 using the percentage-of-completion method (the new construction accounting method). Illustration 22-3 indicates how Denson presents this information.

---

[2]Presentation of the effect on financial statement subtotals and totals other than income from continuing operations and net income (or other appropriate captions of changes in the applicable net assets or performance indicator) is not required. **[3]**

ILLUSTRATION 22-3
Comparative Information
Related to Accounting
Change (Percentage-of-
Completion)

DENSON COMPANY
INCOME STATEMENT (PARTIAL)
FOR THE YEAR ENDED

	2014	2013
		As Adjusted (Note A)
Income before income tax	$200,000	$180,000
Income tax (40%)	80,000	72,000
Net income	$120,000	$108,000

Note A: Change in Method of Accounting for Long-Term Contracts. The company has accounted for revenue and costs for long-term construction contracts by the percentage-of-completion method in 2014, whereas in all prior years, revenue and costs were determined by the completed-contract method. The new method of accounting for long-term contracts was adopted to recognize . . . [state justification for change in accounting principle] . . . and financial statements of prior years have been restated to apply the new method retrospectively. For income tax purposes, the completed-contract method has been continued. The effect of the accounting change on income of 2014 was an increase of $6,000 net of related taxes and on income of 2013 as previously reported was an increase of $12,000 net of related taxes. The balances of retained earnings for 2013 and 2014 have been adjusted for the effect of applying retroactively the new method of accounting. As a result of the accounting change, retained earnings as of January 1, 2013, increased by $120,000 compared to that reported using the completed-contract method.

As Illustration 22-3 shows, Denson Company reports net income under the newly adopted percentage-of-completion method for both 2013 and 2014. The company retrospectively adjusted the 2013 income statement to report the information on a percentage-of-completion basis. Also, the note to the financial statements indicates the nature of the change, why the company made the change, and the years affected.

In addition, companies are required to provide data on important differences between the amounts reported under percentage-of-completion versus completed-contract. When identifying the significant differences, some companies show the *entire* financial statements and line-by-line differences between percentage-of-completion and completed-contract. However, most companies will show only line-by-line differences. For example, Denson would show the differences in construction in process, retained earnings, gross profit, and net income for 2013 and 2014 under the completed-contract and percentage-of-completion methods.

Retained Earnings Adjustment. As indicated earlier, one of the disclosure requirements is to show the cumulative effect of the change on retained earnings as of the beginning of the earliest period presented. For Denson Company, that date is January 1, 2013. Denson disclosed that information by means of a narrative description (see Note A in Illustration 22-3). Denson also would disclose this information in its retained earnings statement. Assuming a retained earnings balance of $1,360,000 at the beginning of 2012, Illustration 22-4 shows Denson's retained earnings statement under the completed-contract method—that is, before giving effect to the change in accounting principle. (The income information comes from Illustration 22-1 on page 1347.)

ILLUSTRATION 22-4
Retained Earnings
Statement before
Retrospective Change

DENSON COMPANY
RETAINED EARNINGS STATEMENT
FOR THE YEAR ENDED

	2014	2013	2012
Retained earnings, January 1	$1,696,000	$1,600,000	$1,360,000
Net income	114,000	96,000	240,000
Retained earnings, December 31	$1,810,000	$1,696,000	$1,600,000

If Denson presents comparative statements for 2013 and 2014 under percentage-of-completion, then it must change the beginning balance of retained earnings at

January 1, 2013. The difference between the retained earnings balances under completed-contract and percentage-of-completion is computed as follows.

Retained earnings, January 1, 2013 (percentage-of-completion)	$1,720,000
Retained earnings, January 1, 2013 (completed-contract)	(1,600,000)
Cumulative-effect difference	$ 120,000

The $120,000 difference is the cumulative effect. Illustration 22-5 shows a comparative retained earnings statement for 2013 and 2014, giving effect to the change in accounting principle to percentage-of-completion.

ILLUSTRATION 22-5
Retained Earnings
Statement after
Retrospective Application

DENSON COMPANY RETAINED EARNINGS STATEMENT FOR THE YEAR ENDED		
	2014	2013
Retained earnings, January 1, as reported	—	$1,600,000
Add: Adjustment for the cumulative effect on prior years of applying retrospectively the new method of accounting for construction contracts		120,000
Retained earnings, January 1, as adjusted	$1,828,000	1,720,000
Net income	120,000	108,000
Retained earnings, December 31	$1,948,000	$1,828,000

Denson adjusted the beginning balance of retained earnings on January 1, 2013, for the excess of percentage-of-completion net income over completed-contract net income in 2012. This comparative presentation indicates the type of adjustment that a company needs to make. It follows that this adjustment would be much larger if a number of prior periods were involved.

Retrospective Accounting Change: Inventory Methods

As a second illustration of the retrospective approach, assume that Lancer Company has accounted for its inventory using the LIFO method. In 2014, the company changes to the FIFO method because management believes this approach provides a more appropriate reporting of its inventory costs. Illustration 22-6 provides additional information related to Lancer Company.

ILLUSTRATION 22-6
Lancer Company
Information

1. Lancer Company started its operations on January 1, 2012. At that time, stockholders invested $100,000 in the business in exchange for common stock.
2. All sales, purchases, and operating expenses for the period 2012–2014 are cash transactions. Lancer's cash flows over this period are as follows.

	2012	2013	2014
Sales	$300,000	$300,000	$300,000
Purchases	90,000	110,000	125,000
Operating expenses	100,000	100,000	100,000
Cash flow from operations	$110,000	$ 90,000	$ 75,000

3. Lancer has used the LIFO method for financial reporting since its inception.
4. Inventory determined under LIFO and FIFO for the period 2012–2014 is as follows.

	LIFO Method	FIFO Method	Difference
January 1, 2012	$ 0	$ 0	$ 0
December 31, 2012	10,000	12,000	2,000
December 31, 2013	20,000	25,000	5,000
December 31, 2014	32,000	39,000	7,000

ILLUSTRATION 22-6
(Continued)

5. Cost of goods sold under LIFO and FIFO for the period 2012–2014 are as follows.

	Cost of Goods Sold LIFO	Cost of Goods Sold FIFO	Difference
2012	$ 80,000	$ 78,000	$2,000
2013	100,000	97,000	3,000
2014	113,000	111,000	2,000

6. Earnings per share information is not required on the income statement.
7. All tax effects for this illustration should be ignored.

Given the information about Lancer Company, Illustration 22-7 shows its income statement, retained earnings statement, balance sheet, and statement of cash flows for 2012–2014 under LIFO.

ILLUSTRATION 22-7
Lancer Financial
Statements (LIFO)

LANCER COMPANY
INCOME STATEMENT
FOR THE YEAR ENDED DECEMBER 31

	2012	2013	2014
Sales	$300,000	$300,000	$300,000
Cost of goods sold (LIFO)	80,000	100,000	113,000
Operating expenses	100,000	100,000	100,000
Net income	$120,000	$100,000	$ 87,000

LANCER COMPANY
RETAINED EARNINGS STATEMENT
FOR THE YEAR ENDED DECEMBER 31

	2012	2013	2014
Retained earnings (beginning)	$ 0	$120,000	$220,000
Add: Net income	120,000	100,000	87,000
Retained earnings (ending)	$120,000	$220,000	$307,000

LANCER COMPANY
BALANCE SHEET
AT DECEMBER 31

	2012	2013	2014
Cash	$210,000	$300,000	$375,000
Inventory (LIFO)	10,000	20,000	32,000
Total assets	$220,000	$320,000	$407,000
Common stock	$100,000	$100,000	$100,000
Retained earnings	120,000	220,000	307,000
Total liabilities and stockholders' equity	$220,000	$320,000	$407,000

LANCER COMPANY
STATEMENT OF CASH FLOWS
FOR THE YEAR ENDED DECEMBER 31

	2012	2013	2014
Cash flows from operating activities			
Sales	$300,000	$300,000	$300,000
Purchases	90,000	110,000	125,000
Operating expenses	100,000	100,000	100,000
Net cash provided by operating activities	110,000	90,000	75,000
Cash flows from financing activities			
Issuance of common stock	100,000	—	—
Net increase in cash	210,000	90,000	75,000
Cash at beginning of year	0	210,000	300,000
Cash at end of year	$210,000	$300,000	$375,000

As Illustration 22-7 indicates, under LIFO Lancer Company reports $120,000 net income in 2012, $100,000 net income in 2013, and $87,000 net income in 2014. The amount of inventory reported on Lancer's balance sheet reflects LIFO costing.

Illustration 22-8 shows Lancer's income statement, retained earnings statement, balance sheet, and statement of cash flows for 2012–2014 under **FIFO**. You can see that **the cash flow statement under FIFO is the same as under LIFO**. Although the net incomes are different in each period, there is no cash flow effect from these differences in net income. (If we considered income taxes, a cash flow effect would result.)

ILLUSTRATION 22-8
Lancer Financial
Statements (FIFO)

LANCER COMPANY
INCOME STATEMENT
FOR THE YEAR ENDED DECEMBER 31

	2012	2013	2014
Sales	$300,000	$300,000	$300,000
Cost of goods sold (FIFO)	78,000	97,000	111,000
Operating expenses	100,000	100,000	100,000
Net income	$122,000	$103,000	$ 89,000

LANCER COMPANY
RETAINED EARNINGS STATEMENT
FOR THE YEAR ENDED DECEMBER 31

	2012	2013	2014
Retained earnings (beginning)	$ 0	$122,000	$225,000
Add: Net income	122,000	103,000	89,000
Retained earnings (ending)	$122,000	$225,000	$314,000

LANCER COMPANY
BALANCE SHEET
AT DECEMBER 31

	2012	2013	2014
Cash	$210,000	$300,000	$375,000
Inventory (FIFO)	12,000	25,000	39,000
Total assets	$222,000	$325,000	$414,000
Common stock	$100,000	$100,000	$100,000
Retained earnings	122,000	225,000	314,000
Total liabilities and stockholders' equity	$222,000	$325,000	$414,000

LANCER COMPANY
STATEMENT OF CASH FLOWS
FOR THE YEAR ENDED DECEMBER 31

	2012	2013	2014
Cash flows from operating activities			
Sales	$300,000	$300,000	$300,000
Purchases	90,000	110,000	125,000
Operating expenses	100,000	100,000	100,000
Net cash provided by operating activities	110,000	90,000	75,000
Cash flows from financing activities			
Issuance of common stock	100,000	—	—
Net increase in cash	210,000	90,000	75,000
Cast at beginning of year	0	210,000	300,000
Cash at end of year	$210,000	$300,000	$375,000

Compare the financial statements reported in Illustration 22-7 and Illustration 22-8. You can see that under retrospective application, the change to FIFO inventory valuation affects reported inventories, cost of goods sold, net income, and retained earnings. In the following sections, we discuss the accounting and reporting of Lancer's accounting change from LIFO to FIFO.

Given the information provided in Illustrations 22-6, 22-7, and 22-8, we now are ready to account for and report on the accounting change.

Our first step is to adjust the financial records for the change from LIFO to FIFO. To do so, we perform the analysis in Illustration 22-9.

Year	Net Income		Difference in Income
	LIFO	FIFO	
2012	$120,000	$122,000	$2,000
2013	100,000	103,000	3,000
Total at beginning of 2014	$220,000	$225,000	$5,000
Total in 2014	$ 87,000	$ 89,000	$2,000

ILLUSTRATION 22-9
Data for Recording Change in Accounting Principle

The entry to record the change to the FIFO method at the beginning of 2014 is as follows.

Inventory	5,000	
Retained Earnings		5,000

The change increases the Inventory account by $5,000. This amount represents the difference between the ending inventory at December 31, 2013, under LIFO ($20,000) and the ending inventory under FIFO ($25,000). The credit to Retained Earnings indicates the amount needed to change the prior year's income, assuming that Lancer had used FIFO in previous periods.

Reporting a Change in Principle. Lancer Company will prepare comparative financial statements for 2013 and 2014 using FIFO (the new inventory method). Illustration 22-10 indicates how Lancer might present this information.

LANCER COMPANY
INCOME STATEMENT
FOR THE YEAR ENDED DECEMBER 31

	2014	2013
		As adjusted (Note A)
Sales	$300,000	$300,000
Cost of goods sold	111,000	97,000
Operating expenses	100,000	100,000
Net income	$ 89,000	$103,000

ILLUSTRATION 22-10
Comparative Information Related to Accounting Change (FIFO)

Note A

Change in Method of Accounting for Inventory Valuation On January 1, 2014, Lancer Company elected to change its method of valuing its inventory to the FIFO method; in all prior years, inventory was valued using the LIFO method. The Company adopted the new method of accounting for inventory to better report cost of goods sold in the year incurred. Comparative financial statements of prior years have been adjusted to apply the new method retrospectively. The following financial statement line items for years 2014 and 2013 were affected by the change in accounting principle.

Nature and reason for change; description of prior period information adjusted

	2014			2013		
Balance Sheet	LIFO	FIFO	Difference	LIFO	FIFO	Difference
Inventory	$ 32,000	$ 39,000	$7,000	$ 20,000	$ 25,000	$5,000
Retained earnings	307,000	314,000	7,000	220,000	225,000	5,000
Income Statement						
Cost of goods sold	$113,000	$111,000	$2,000	$100,000	$ 97,000	$3,000
Net income	87,000	89,000	2,000	100,000	103,000	3,000
Statement of Cash Flows						
(no effect)						

Effect of change on key performance indicators

As a result of the accounting change, retained earnings as of January 1, 2013, increased from $120,000, as originally reported using the LIFO method, to $122,000 using the FIFO method.

Cumulative effect on retained earnings

As Illustration 22-10 shows, Lancer Company reports net income under the newly adopted FIFO method for both 2013 and 2014. The company retrospectively adjusted the 2013 income statement to report the information on a FIFO basis. In addition, the note to the financial statements indicates the nature of the change, why the company made the change, and the years affected. The note also provides data on important differences between the amounts reported under LIFO versus FIFO. (When identifying the significant differences, some companies show the *entire* financial statements and line-by-line differences between LIFO and FIFO.)

Retained Earnings Adjustment. As indicated earlier, one of the disclosure requirements is to show the cumulative effect of the change on retained earnings as of the beginning of the earliest period presented. For Lancer Company, that date is January 1, 2013. Lancer disclosed that information by means of a narrative description (see Note A in Illustration 22-10). Lancer also would disclose this information in its retained earnings statement. Illustration 22-11 shows Lancer's retained earnings statement under LIFO—that is, before giving effect to the change in accounting principle. (This information comes from Illustration 22-7 on page 1351.)

ILLUSTRATION 22-11
Retained Earnings
Statements (LIFO)

	2014	2013	2012
Retained earnings, January 1	$220,000	$120,000	$ 0
Net income	87,000	100,000	120,000
Retained earnings, December 31	$307,000	$220,000	$120,000

If Lancer presents comparative statements for 2013 and 2014 under FIFO, then it must change the beginning balance of retained earnings at January 1, 2013. The difference between the retained earnings balances under LIFO and FIFO is computed as follows.

Retained earnings, January 1, 2013 (FIFO)	$122,000
Retained earnings, January 1, 2013 (LIFO)	(120,000)
Cumulative effect difference	$ 2,000

The $2,000 difference is the cumulative effect. Illustration 22-12 shows a comparative retained earnings statement for 2013 and 2014, giving effect to the change in accounting principle to FIFO.

ILLUSTRATION 22-12
Retained Earnings
Statements after
Retrospective Application

	2014	2013
Retained earnings, January 1, as reported		$120,000
Add: Adjustment for the cumulative effect on prior years of applying retrospectively the new method of accounting for inventory		2,000
Retained earnings, January 1, as adjusted	$225,000	122,000
Net income	89,000	103,000
Retained earnings, December 31	$314,000	$225,000

Lancer adjusted the beginning balance of retained earnings on January 1, 2013, for the excess of FIFO net income over LIFO net income in 2012. This comparative presentation indicates the type of adjustment that a company needs to make. It follows that the amount of this adjustment would be much larger if a number of prior periods were involved.

Direct and Indirect Effects of Changes

Are there other effects that a company should report when it makes a change in accounting principle? For example, what happens when a company like Lancer has a bonus plan based on net income and the prior year's net income changes when FIFO is retrospectively applied? Should Lancer also change the reported amount of bonus expense? Or what happens if we had not ignored income taxes in the Lancer example? Should Lancer adjust net income, given that taxes will be different under LIFO and FIFO in prior periods? The answers depend on whether the effects are direct or indirect.

Direct Effects

The FASB takes the position that companies should retrospectively apply the **direct effects of a change in accounting principle**. An example of a **direct effect** is an adjustment to an inventory balance as a result of a change in the inventory valuation method. For example, Lancer Company should change the inventory amounts in prior periods to indicate the change to the FIFO method of inventory valuation. Another inventory-related example would be an impairment adjustment resulting from applying the lower-of-cost-or-market test to the adjusted inventory balance. Related changes, such as deferred income tax effects of the impairment adjustment, are also considered direct effects. This entry was illustrated in the Denson example, in which the change to percentage-of-completion accounting resulted in recording a deferred tax liability.

Indirect Effects

In addition to direct effects, companies can have **indirect effects related to a change in accounting principle**. An **indirect effect** is any change to current or future cash flows of a company that result from making a change in accounting principle that is applied retrospectively. An example of an indirect effect is a change in profit-sharing or royalty payment that is based on a reported amount such as revenue or net income. **Indirect effects do not change prior period amounts.**

For example, let's assume that Lancer has an employee profit-sharing plan based on net income. As Illustration 22-9 showed (on page 1353), Lancer would report higher income in 2012 and 2013 if it used the FIFO method. In addition, let's assume that the profit-sharing plan requires that Lancer pay the incremental amount due based on the FIFO income amounts. In this situation, Lancer reports this additional expense **in the current period**; it would not change prior periods for this expense. If the company prepares comparative financial statements, it follows that it does not recast the prior periods for this additional expense.[3]

If the terms of the profit-sharing plan indicate that *no payment is necessary* in the current period due to this change, then the company need not recognize additional profit-sharing expense in the current period. Neither does it change amounts reported for prior periods.

When a company recognizes the indirect effects of a change in accounting principle, it includes in the financial statements a description of the indirect effects. In doing so, it discloses the amounts recognized in the current period and related per share information.

International Perspective

IFRS does not explicitly address the accounting and disclosure of indirect effects.

---

[3]The rationale for this approach is that companies should recognize, in the period the adoption occurs (not the prior period), the effect on the cash flows that is caused by the adoption of the new accounting principle. That is, the accounting change is a necessary "past event" in the definition of an asset or liability that gives rise to the accounting recognition of the indirect effect in the current period. **[4]**

Impracticability

LEARNING OBJECTIVE **4**
Understand how to account for impracticable changes.

It is not always possible for companies to determine how they would have reported prior periods' financial information under retrospective application of an accounting principle change. Retrospective application is considered **impracticable** if a company cannot determine the prior period effects using every reasonable effort to do so.

Companies should not use retrospective application if one of the following conditions exists:

1. The company cannot determine the effects of the retrospective application.
2. Retrospective application requires assumptions about management's intent in a prior period.
3. Retrospective application requires significant estimates for a prior period, and the company cannot objectively verify the necessary information to develop these estimates.

If any of the above conditions exists, it is deemed impracticable to apply the retrospective approach. In this case, the company **prospectively applies** the new accounting principle as of the earliest date it is practicable to do so. **[5]**

For example, assume that Williams Company changed its inventory method from FIFO to LIFO, effective January 1, 2015. Williams prepares statements on a calendar-year basis and has used the FIFO method since its inception. Williams judges it impracticable to retrospectively apply the new method. Determining prior period effects would require subjective assumptions about the LIFO layers established in prior periods. These assumptions would ordinarily result in the computation of a number of different earnings figures.

As a result, the only adjustment necessary may be to restate the beginning inventory to a cost basis from a lower-of-cost-or-market approach (which establishes the beginning LIFO layer). Williams must disclose only the effect of the change on the results of operations in the period of change. Also, the company should explain the reasons for omitting the computations of the cumulative effect for prior years. Finally, it should disclose the justification for the change to LIFO. **[6]**[4] Illustration 22-13, from the annual report of **The Quaker Oats Company**, shows the type of disclosure needed.

ILLUSTRATION 22-13
Disclosure of Change to LIFO

The Quaker Oats Company

Note 1 (In Part): Summary of Significant Accounting Policies

Inventories. Inventories are valued at the lower of cost or market, using various cost methods, and include the cost of raw materials, labor and overhead. The percentage of year-end inventories valued using each of the methods is as follows:

June 30	Current Year	Prior Year
Average quarterly cost	21%	54%
Last-in, first-out (LIFO)	65%	29%
First-in, first-out (FIFO)	14%	17%

Effective July 1, the Company adopted the LIFO cost flow assumption for valuing the majority of remaining U.S. Grocery Products inventories. The Company believes that the use of the LIFO method better matches current costs with current revenues. The cumulative effect of this change on retained earnings at the beginning of the year is not determinable, nor are the pro-forma effects of retroactive application of LIFO to prior years. The effect of this change on current-year fiscal results was to decrease net income by $16.0 million, or $.20 per share.

If the LIFO method of valuing certain inventories were not used, total inventories would have been $60.1 million higher in the current year, and $24.0 million higher in the prior year.

[4]In practice, many companies defer the formal adoption of LIFO until year-end. Management thus has an opportunity to assess the impact that a change to LIFO will have on the financial statements and to evaluate the desirability of a change for tax purposes. As indicated in Chapter 8, many companies use LIFO because of the advantages of this inventory valuation method in a period of inflation.

CHANGES IN ACCOUNTING ESTIMATES

To prepare financial statements, companies must estimate the effects of future conditions and events. For example, the following items require estimates.

1. Uncollectible receivables.
2. Inventory obsolescence.
3. Useful lives and salvage values of assets.
4. Periods benefited by deferred costs.
5. Liabilities for warranty costs and income taxes.
6. Recoverable mineral reserves.
7. Change in depreciation methods.

A company cannot perceive future conditions and events and their effects with certainty. Therefore, estimation requires the exercise of judgment. Accounting estimates will change as new events occur, as a company acquires more experience, or as it obtains additional information.

Prospective Reporting

Companies report prospectively changes in accounting estimates. That is, companies should not adjust previously reported results for changes in estimates. Instead, they account for the effects of all changes in estimates in (1) the period of change if the change affects that period only, or (2) the period of change and future periods if the change affects both. The FASB views changes in estimates as **normal recurring corrections and adjustments**, the natural result of the accounting process. It prohibits retrospective treatment.

The circumstances related to a change in estimate differ from those for a change in accounting principle. If companies reported changes in estimates retrospectively, continual adjustments of prior years' income would occur. It seems proper to accept the view that, because new conditions or circumstances exist, the revision fits the new situation (not the old one). Companies should therefore handle such a revision in the current and future periods.

To illustrate, Underwriters Labs Inc. purchased for $300,000 a building that it originally estimated to have a useful life of 15 years and no salvage value. It recorded depreciation for 5 years on a straight-line basis. On January 1, 2014, Underwriters Labs revises the estimate of the useful life. It now considers the asset to have a total life of 25 years. (Assume that the useful life for financial reporting and tax purposes and depreciation method are the same.) Illustration 22-14 shows the accounts at the beginning of the sixth year.

Buildings	$300,000
Less: Accumulated depreciation—buildings (5 × $20,000)	100,000
Book value of building	$200,000

ILLUSTRATION 22-14
Book Value after Five Years' Depreciation

Underwriters Labs records depreciation for the year 2014 as follows.

Depreciation Expense	10,000	
Accumulated Depreciation—Buildings		10,000

The company computes the $10,000 depreciation charge as shown in Illustration 22-15.

$$\text{Depreciation Charge} = \frac{\text{Book Value of Asset}}{\text{Remaining Service Life}} = \frac{\$200,000}{25 \text{ years} - 5 \text{ years}} = \$10,000$$

ILLUSTRATION 22-15
Depreciation after Change in Estimate

Companies sometime find it difficult to differentiate between a change in estimate and a change in accounting principle. Is it a change in principle or a change in estimate when a company changes from deferring and amortizing marketing costs to expensing them as incurred because future benefits of these costs have become doubtful? If it is impossible to determine whether a change in principle or a change in estimate has occurred, the rule is this: **Consider the change as a change in estimate.** This is often referred to as a change in estimate effected by a change in accounting principle.

Another example of a change in estimate effected by a change in principle is a change in depreciation (as well as amortization or depletion) methods. Because companies change depreciation methods based on changes in estimates about future benefits from long-lived assets, it is not possible to separate the effect of the accounting principle change from that of the estimates. **As a result, companies account for a change in depreciation methods as a change in estimate effected by a change in accounting principle. [7]**

A similar problem occurs in differentiating between a change in estimate and a correction of an error, although here the answer is more clear-cut. How does a company determine whether it overlooked the information in earlier periods (an error), or whether it obtained new information (a change in estimate)? Proper classification is important because the accounting treatment differs for corrections of errors versus changes in estimates. The general rule is this: **Companies should consider careful estimates that later prove to be incorrect as changes in estimate.** Only when a company obviously computed the estimate incorrectly because of lack of expertise or in bad faith should it consider the adjustment an error. There is no clear demarcation line here. Companies must use good judgment in light of all the circumstances.[5]

Disclosures

Illustration 22-16 shows disclosure of a change in estimated useful lives, which appeared in the annual report of **Ampco–Pittsburgh Corporation.**

ILLUSTRATION 22-16
Disclosure of Change in Estimated Useful Lives

Ampco–Pittsburgh Corporation

Note 11: Change in Accounting Estimate. The Corporation revised its estimate of the useful lives of certain machinery and equipment. Previously, all machinery and equipment, whether new when placed in use or not, were in one class and depreciated over 15 years. The change principally applies to assets purchased new when placed in use. Those lives are now extended to 20 years. These changes were made to better reflect the estimated periods during which such assets will remain in service. The change had the effect of reducing depreciation expense and increasing net income by approximately $991,000 ($.10 per share).

For the most part, companies need not disclose changes in accounting estimates made as part of normal operations, such as bad debt allowances or inventory obsolescence, unless such changes are material. However, for a change in estimate that affects several periods (such as a change in the service lives of depreciable assets), companies should disclose the effect on income from continuing operations and related per share

[5]In evaluating reasonableness, the auditor should use one or a combination of the following approaches.
    (a) Review and test the process used by management to develop the estimate.
    (b) Develop an independent expectation of the estimate to corroborate the reasonableness of management's estimate.
    (c) Review subsequent events or transactions occurring prior to completion of fieldwork.
"Auditing Accounting Estimates," *Statement on Auditing Standards No. 57* (New York: AICPA, 1988).

amounts of the current period. When a company has a change in estimate effected by a change in accounting principle, it must indicate why the new method is preferable. In addition, companies are subject to all other disclosure guidelines established for changes in accounting principle.

CHANGES IN REPORTING ENTITY

Occasionally, companies make changes that result in different reporting entities. In such cases, companies report the change by **changing the financial statements of all prior periods presented**. The revised statements show the financial information for the **new reporting entity** for all periods.

6 LEARNING OBJECTIVE
Identify changes in a reporting entity.

Examples of a change in reporting entity are:

1. Presenting consolidated statements in place of statements of individual companies.
2. Changing specific subsidiaries that constitute the group of companies for which the entity presents consolidated financial statements.
3. Changing the companies included in combined financial statements.
4. Changing the cost, equity, or consolidation method of accounting for subsidiaries and investments.[6] In this case, a change in the reporting entity does not result from creation, cessation, purchase, or disposition of a subsidiary or other business unit.

In the year in which a company changes a reporting entity, it should disclose in the financial statements the nature of the change and the reason for it. It also should report, for all periods presented, the effect of the change on income before extraordinary items, net income, and earnings per share. These disclosures need not be repeated in subsequent periods' financial statements.

Illustration 22-17 shows a note disclosing a change in reporting entity, from the annual report of **Hewlett-Packard Company**.

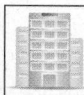

Hewlett-Packard Company

Note: Accounting and Reporting Changes (In Part)

Consolidation of Hewlett-Packard Finance Company. The company implemented a new accounting pronouncement on consolidations. With the adoption of this new pronouncement, the company consolidated the accounts of Hewlett-Packard Finance Company (HPFC), a wholly owned subsidiary previously accounted for under the equity method, with those of the company. The change resulted in an increase in consolidated assets and liabilities but did not have a material effect on the company's financial position. Since HPFC was previously accounted for under the equity method, the change did not affect net earnings. Prior years' consolidated financial information has been restated to reflect this change for comparative purposes.

ILLUSTRATION 22-17
Disclosure of Change in Reporting Entity

ACCOUNTING ERRORS

No business, large or small, is immune from errors. As the opening story discusses, the number of accounting errors that lead to restatement are beginning to decline. However, without accounting and disclosure guidelines for the reporting of errors, investors can be left in the dark about the effects of errors.

7 LEARNING OBJECTIVE
Describe the accounting for correction of errors.

Certain errors, such as misclassifications of balances within a financial statement, are not as significant to investors as other errors. Significant errors would be those resulting in overstating assets or income, for example. However, investors should know

---

[6]An exception to retrospective application occurs when changing from the equity method. We provide an expanded illustration of the accounting for a change from or to the equity method in Appendix 22A.

the potential impact of all errors. Even "harmless" misclassifications can affect important ratios. Also, some errors could signal important weaknesses in internal controls that could lead to more significant errors.

In general, accounting errors include the following types:

1. A change from an accounting principle that is **not** generally accepted to an accounting principle that is acceptable. The rationale is that the company incorrectly presented prior periods because of the application of an improper accounting principle. For example, a company may change from the cash (income tax) basis of accounting to the accrual basis.

2. Mathematical mistakes, such as incorrectly totaling the inventory count sheets when computing the inventory value.

3. Changes in estimates that occur because a company did not prepare the estimates in good faith. For example, a company may have adopted a clearly unrealistic depreciation rate.

4. An oversight, such as the failure to accrue or defer certain expenses and revenues at the end of the period.

5. A misuse of facts, such as the failure to use salvage value in computing the depreciation base for the straight-line approach.

6. The incorrect classification of a cost as an expense instead of an asset, and vice versa.

ILLUSTRATION 22-18
Accounting-Error Types

Accounting errors occur for a variety of reasons. Illustration 22-18 indicates 11 major categories of accounting errors that drive restatements.

Accounting Category	Type of Restatement
Expense recognition	Recording expenses in the incorrect period or for an incorrect amount.
Revenue recognition	Improper revenue accounting. This category includes instances in which revenue was improperly recognized, questionable revenues were recognized, or any other number of related errors that led to misreported revenue.
Misclassification	Misclassifying significant accounting items on the balance sheet, income statement, or statement of cash flows. These include restatements due to misclassification of short- or long-term accounts or those that impact cash flows from operations.
Equity—other	Improper accounting for EPS, restricted stock, warrants, and other equity instruments.
Reserves/Contingencies	Errors involving bad debts related to accounts receivable, inventory reserves, income tax allowances, and loss contingencies.
Long-lived assets	Asset impairments of property, plant, and equipment; goodwill; or other related items.
Taxes	Errors involving correction of tax provision, improper treatment of tax liabilities, and other tax-related items.
Equity—other comprehensive income	Improper accounting for comprehensive income equity transactions including foreign currency items, unrealized gains and losses on certain investments in debt, equity securities, and derivatives.
Inventory	Inventory costing valuations, quantity issues, and cost of sales adjustments.
Equity—stock options	Improper accounting for employee stock options.
Other	Any restatement not covered by the listed categories including those related to improper accounting for acquisitions or mergers.

Source: T. Baldwin and D. Yoo, "Restatements—Traversing Shaky Ground," *Trend Alert*, Glass Lewis & Co. (June 2, 2005), p. 8.

As soon as a company discovers an error, it must correct the error. Companies record **corrections of errors** from prior periods as an adjustment to the beginning balance of retained earnings in the current period. Such corrections are called **prior period adjustments**.[7] **[8]**

[7]See Mark L. Defond and James Jiambalvo, "Incidence and Circumstances of Accounting Errors," *The Accounting Review* (July 1991) for examples of different types of errors and why these errors might have occurred.

If it presents comparative statements, a company should restate the prior statements affected, to correct for the error.[8] The company need not repeat the disclosures in the financial statements of subsequent periods.

Example of Error Correction

To illustrate, in 2015 the bookkeeper for Selectro Company discovered an error. In 2014, the company failed to record $20,000 of depreciation expense on a newly constructed building. This building is the only depreciable asset Selectro owns. The company correctly included the depreciation expense in its tax return and correctly reported its income taxes payable. Illustration 22-19 presents Selectro's income statement for 2014 (starting with income before depreciation expense) with and without the error.

ILLUSTRATION 22-19
Error Correction Comparison

SELECTRO COMPANY
INCOME STATEMENT
FOR THE YEAR ENDED, DECEMBER 31, 2014

		Without Error		With Error
Income before depreciation expense		$100,000		$100,000
Depreciation expense		20,000		0
Income before income tax		80,000		100,000
Current income tax expense	$32,000		$32,000	
Deferred income tax expense	–0–	32,000	8,000	40,000
Net income		$ 48,000		$ 60,000

Illustration 22-20 shows the entries that Selectro should have made and did make for recording depreciation expense and income taxes.

ILLUSTRATION 22-20
Error Entries

Entries Company Should Have Made (Without Error)			Entries Company Did Make (With Error)		
Depreciation Expense	20,000		No entry made for depreciation		
Accumulated Depreciation—Buildings		20,000			
Income Tax Expense	32,000		Income Tax Expense	40,000	
Income Taxes Payable		32,000	Deferred Tax Liability		8,000
			Income Taxes Payable		32,000

As Illustration 22-20 indicates, the $20,000 omission error in 2014 results in the following effects.

Income Statement Effects
Depreciation expense (2014) is understated $20,000.
Income tax expense (2014) is overstated $8,000 ($20,000 × 40%).
Net income (2014) is overstated $12,000 ($20,000 − $8,000).

Balance Sheet Effects
Accumulated depreciation—buildings is understated $20,000.
Deferred tax liability is overstated $8,000 ($20,000 × 40%).

To make the proper correcting entry in 2015, Selectro should recognize that net income in 2014 is overstated by $12,000, the Deferred Tax Liability is overstated by $8,000,

[8]The term **restatement** is used for the process of revising previously issued financial statements to reflect the correction of an error. This distinguishes an error correction from a change in accounting principle. **[9]**

and Accumulated Depreciation—Buildings is understated by $20,000. The entry to correct this error in 2015 is as follows.

Retained Earnings	12,000	
Deferred Tax Liability	8,000	
Accumulated Depreciation—Buildings		20,000

The debit to Retained Earnings results because net income for 2014 is overstated. The debit to Deferred Tax Liability is made to remove this account, which was caused by the error. The credit to Accumulated Depreciation—Buildings reduces the book value of the building to its proper amount. Selectro will make the same journal entry to record the correction of the error in 2015 whether it prepares single-period (noncomparative) or comparative financial statements.

Single-Period Statements

To demonstrate how to show this information in a single-period statement, assume that Selectro Company has a beginning retained earnings balance at January 1, 2015, of $350,000. The company reports net income of $400,000 in 2015. Illustration 22-21 shows Selectro's retained earnings statement for 2015.

ILLUSTRATION 22-21
Reporting an Error—
Single-Period Financial
Statement

SELECTRO COMPANY RETAINED EARNINGS STATEMENT FOR THE YEAR ENDED DECEMBER 31, 2015		
Retained earnings, January 1, as reported		$350,000
Correction of an error (depreciation)	$20,000	
Less: Applicable income tax reduction	8,000	(12,000)
Retained earnings, January 1, as adjusted		338,000
Add: Net income		400,000
Retained earnings, December 31		$738,000

The balance sheet in 2015 would not have any deferred tax liability related to the building, and Accumulated Depreciation—Buildings is now restated at a higher amount. The income statement would not be affected.

Comparative Statements

If preparing comparative financial statements, a company should make adjustments to correct the amounts for all affected accounts reported in the statements for **all periods** reported. The company should restate the data to the correct basis for each year presented. It should **show any catch-up adjustment as a prior period adjustment to retained earnings for the earliest period it reported**. These requirements are essentially the same as those for reporting a change in accounting principle.

For example, in the case of Selectro, the error of omitting the depreciation of $20,000 in 2014, discovered in 2015, results in the restatement of the 2014 financial statements. Illustration 22-22 shows the accounts that Selectro restates in the 2014 financial statements.

ILLUSTRATION 22-22
Reporting an Error—
Comparative Financial
Statements

In the balance sheet:	
Accumulated depreciation—buildings	$20,000 increase
Deferred tax liability	$ 8,000 decrease
Retained earnings, ending balance	$12,000 decrease
In the income statement:	
Depreciation expense—buildings	$20,000 increase
Income tax expense	$ 8,000 decrease
Net income	$12,000 decrease
In the retained earnings statement:	
Retained earnings, ending balance (due to lower net income for the period)	$12,000 decrease

Selectro prepares the 2015 financial statements in comparative form with those of 2014 **as if the error had not occurred**. In addition, Selectro must disclose that it has restated its previously issued financial statements, and it describes the nature of the error. Selectro also must disclose the following.

1. The effect of the correction on each financial statement line item and any per share amounts affected for each prior period presented.
2. The cumulative effect of the change on retained earnings or other appropriate components of equity or net assets in the statement of financial position, as of the beginning of the earliest period presented. **[10]**

Summary of Accounting Changes and Correction of Errors

Having guidelines for reporting accounting changes and corrections has helped resolve several significant and long-standing accounting problems. Yet, because of diversity in situations and characteristics of the items encountered in practice, use of professional judgment is of paramount importance. In applying these guidelines, the primary objective is to serve the users of the financial statements. Achieving this objective requires accuracy, full disclosure, and an absence of misleading inferences.

Illustration 22-23 summarizes the main distinctions and treatments presented in the discussion in this chapter.

ILLUSTRATION 22-23
Summary of Guidelines for Accounting Changes and Errors

Changes in accounting principle

Employ the retrospective approach by:
a. Changing the financial statements of all prior periods presented.
b. Disclosing in the year of the change the effect on net income and earnings per share for all prior periods presented.
c. Reporting an adjustment to the beginning retained earnings balance in the retained earnings statement in the earliest year presented.

If impracticable to determine the prior period effect (e.g., change to LIFO):
a. Do not change prior years' income.
b. Use opening inventory in the year the method is adopted as the base-year inventory for all subsequent LIFO computations.
c. Disclose the effect of the change on the current year, and the reasons for omitting the computation of the cumulative effect and pro forma amounts for prior years.

Changes in accounting estimate

Employ the current and prospective approach by:
a. Reporting current and future financial statements on the new basis.
b. Presenting prior period financial statements as previously reported.
c. Making no adjustments to current-period opening balances for the effects in prior periods.

Changes in reporting entity

Employ the retrospective approach by:
a. Restating the financial statements of all prior periods presented.
b. Disclosing in the year of change the effect on net income and earnings per share data for all prior periods presented.

Changes due to error

Employ the restatement approach by:
a. Correcting all prior period statements presented.
b. Restating the beginning balance of retained earnings for the first period presented when the error effects occur in a period prior to the first period presented.

Changes in accounting principle are appropriate **only** when a company demonstrates that the newly adopted generally accepted accounting principle is **preferable** to the existing one. Companies and accountants determine preferability on the basis of whether the new principle constitutes an **improvement in financial reporting**, not on the basis of the income tax effect alone.[9]

But it is not always easy to determine an improvement in financial reporting. **How does one measure preferability or improvement?** Such measurement varies from company to company. Quaker Oats Company, for example, argued that a change in accounting principle to LIFO inventory valuation "better matches current costs with current revenues" (see Illustration 22-13, page 1356). Conversely, another company might change from LIFO to FIFO because it wishes to report a more realistic ending inventory. How do you determine which is the better of these two arguments? Determining the preferable method requires some "standard" or "objective." Because no universal standard or objective is generally accepted, the problem of determining preferability continues to be difficult.

Initially, the SEC took the position that the auditor should indicate whether a change in accounting principle was preferable. The SEC has since modified this approach, noting that greater reliance may be placed on management's judgment in assessing preferability. Even though the preferability criterion is difficult to apply, the general guidelines have acted as a deterrent to capricious changes in accounting principles.[10] **If a FASB rule creates a new principle, expresses preference for, or rejects a specific accounting principle, a change is considered clearly acceptable.**

What do the numbers mean?   CAN I GET MY MONEY BACK?

When companies report restatements, investors usually lose money. What should investors do if a company misleads them by misstating its financial results? Join other investors in a class-action suit against the company and in some cases, the auditor.

Class-action activity has picked up in recent years, and settlements can be large. To find out about class actions, investors can go online to see if they are eligible to join any class actions. Below are some recent examples.

Company	Settlement Amount	Contact for Claim
Samsung	$1 billion	www.lawyersandsettlements.com
Merck	$950 million	www.lawyersandsettlements.com
Wal-Mart	$13.5 million	www.lawyersandsettlements.com

The amounts reported are *before* attorney's fees, which can range from 15 to 30 percent of the total. Also, investors may owe taxes if the settlement results in a capital gain on the investment. Thus, investors can get back some of the money they lost due to restatements, but they should be prepared to pay an attorney and the government first.

Sources: Adapted from C. Coolidge, "Lost and Found," *Forbes* (October 1, 2001), pp. 124–125; data from *www.lawyersandsettlements.com* as of 11/13/12.

[9]A change in accounting principle, a change in the reporting entity (special type of change in accounting principle), and a correction of an error require an explanatory paragraph in the auditor's report discussing lack of consistency from one period to the next. A change in accounting estimate does not affect the auditor's opinion relative to consistency. However, if the change in estimate has a material effect on the financial statements, disclosure may still be required. Error correction not involving a change in accounting principle does not require disclosure relative to consistency.

[10]If management has not provided reasonable justification for the change in accounting principle, the auditor should express a qualified opinion. Or, if the effect of the change is sufficiently material, the auditor should express an adverse opinion on the financial statements. "Reports on Audited Financial Statements," *Statement on Auditing Standards No. 58* (New York: AICPA, 1988).

Motivations for Change of Accounting Method

Difficult as it is to determine which accounting standards have the strongest conceptual support, other complications make the process even more complex. These complications stem from the fact that managers have self-interest in how the financial statements make the company look. They naturally wish to show their financial performance in the best light. A **favorable profit picture** can influence investors, and a strong liquidity position can influence creditors. **Too favorable a profit picture**, however, can provide union negotiators and government regulators with ammunition during bargaining talks. Hence, managers might have varying motives for reporting income numbers.

8 **LEARNING OBJECTIVE**
Identify economic motives for changing accounting methods.

Research has provided additional insight into why companies may prefer certain accounting methods.[11] Some of these reasons are as follows.

1. *Political costs.* As companies become larger and more politically visible, politicians and regulators devote more attention to them. The larger the firm, the more likely it is to become subject to regulation such as antitrust, and the more likely it is to be required to pay higher taxes. Therefore, companies that are politically visible may seek to report low income numbers, to avoid the scrutiny of regulators. In addition, other constituents, such as labor unions, may be less willing to ask for wage increases if reported income is low. Researchers have found that the larger the company, the more likely it is to adopt income-decreasing approaches in selecting accounting methods.

2. *Capital structure.* A number of studies have indicated that the capital structure of the company can affect the selection of accounting methods. For example, a company with a high debt to equity ratio is more likely to be constrained by debt covenants. The debt covenant may indicate that the company cannot pay dividends if retained earnings fall below a certain level. As a result, such a company is more likely to select accounting methods that will increase net income.

3. *Bonus payments.* Studies have found that if compensation plans tie managers' bonus payments to income, management will select accounting methods that maximize their bonus payments.

4. *Smooth earnings.* Substantial earnings increases attract the attention of politicians, regulators, and competitors. In addition, large increases in income are difficult to achieve in following years. Further, executive compensation plans would use these higher numbers as a baseline and make it difficult for managers to earn bonuses in subsequent years. Conversely, investors and competitors might view large decreases in earnings as a signal that the company is in financial trouble. Also, substantial decreases in income raise concerns on the part of stockholders, lenders, and other interested parties about the competency of management. For all these reasons, companies have an incentive to "manage" or "smooth" earnings. In general, management tends to believe that a steady 10 percent growth a year is much better than a 30 percent growth one year and a 10 percent decline the next.[12] In other words, managers usually prefer a gradually increasing income report and sometimes change accounting methods to ensure such a result.

[11]See Ross L. Watts and Jerold L. Zimmerman, "Positive Accounting Theory: A Ten-Year Perspective," *The Accounting Review* (January 1990) for an excellent review of research findings related to management incentives in selecting accounting methods.

[12]O. Douglas Moses, "Income Smoothing and Incentives: Empirical Tests Using Accounting Changes," *The Accounting Review* (April 1987). The findings provide evidence that earnings smoothing is associated with firm size, the existence of bonus plans, and the divergence of actual earnings from expectations.

Management pays careful attention to the accounting it follows and often changes accounting methods, not for conceptual reasons, but for economic reasons. As indicated throughout this textbook, such arguments have come to be known as **economic consequences** arguments. These arguments focus on the supposed impact of the accounting method on the behavior of investors, creditors, competitors, governments, or managers of the reporting companies themselves.[13]

 Underlying Concepts

Neutrality is an important element of faithful representation.

To counter these pressures, standard-setters such as the FASB have declared, as part of their conceptual framework, that they will assess the merits of proposed standards from a position of **neutrality**. That is, they evaluate the soundness of standards on the basis of conceptual soundness, not on the grounds of possible impact on behavior. It is not the FASB's place to choose standards according to the kinds of behavior it wishes to promote and the kinds it wishes to discourage. At the same time, it must be admitted that some standards often **will have** the effect of influencing behavior. Yet their justification should be conceptual, and not viewed in terms of their economic impact.

ERROR ANALYSIS

LEARNING OBJECTIVE 9

Analyze the effect of errors.

In this section, we show some additional types of accounting errors. Companies generally do not correct for errors that do not have a significant effect on the presentation of the financial statements. For example, should a company with a total annual payroll of $1,750,000 and net income of $940,000 correct its financial statements if it finds it failed to record accrued wages of $5,000? No—it would not consider this error significant or material.

Obviously, defining materiality is difficult, and managers and auditors must use experience and judgment to determine whether adjustment is necessary for a given error. We assume **all errors discussed in this section to be material and to require adjustment**. (Also, we ignore all tax effects in this section.)

Companies must answer three questions in error analysis:

1. What type of error is involved?
2. What entries are needed to correct for the error?
3. After discovery of the error, how are financial statements to be restated?

As indicated earlier, companies treat errors **as prior period adjustments and report them in the current year as adjustments to the beginning balance of Retained Earnings**. If a company presents comparative statements, it restates the prior affected statements to correct for the error.

Balance Sheet Errors

Balance sheet errors affect only the presentation of an asset, liability, or stockholders' equity account. Examples are the classification of a short-term receivable as part of the investment section, the classification of a note payable as an account payable, and the classification of plant assets as inventory.

When the error is discovered, the company reclassifies the item to its proper position. If the company prepares comparative statements that include the error year, it should correctly restate the balance sheet for the error year.

[13]Lobbyists use economic consequences arguments—and there are many of them—to put pressure on standard-setters. We have seen examples of these arguments in the oil and gas industry about successful-efforts versus full-cost in the technology area, with the issue of mandatory expensing of research and developmental costs and stock options.

Income Statement Errors

Income statement errors involve the improper classification of revenues or expenses. Examples include recording interest revenue as part of sales, purchases as bad debt expense, and depreciation expense as interest expense. An income statement classification error has no effect on the balance sheet and **no effect on net income**.

A company must make a reclassification entry when it discovers the error, if it makes the discovery in the same year in which the error occurs. If the error occurred in prior periods, the company does not need to make a reclassification entry at the date of discovery because the accounts for the current year are correctly stated. (Remember that the company has closed the income statement accounts from the prior period to retained earnings.) If the company prepares comparative statements that include the error year, it restates the income statement for the error year.

Balance Sheet and Income Statement Errors

The third type of error involves both the balance sheet and income statement. For example, assume that the bookkeeper overlooked accrued wages payable at the end of the accounting period. The effect of this error is to understate expenses, understate liabilities, and overstate net income for that period of time. This type of error affects both the balance sheet and the income statement. We classify this type of error in one of two ways—counterbalancing or noncounterbalancing.

Counterbalancing errors are those that will be offset or corrected over two periods. For example, the failure to record accrued wages is a counterbalancing error because over a two-year period the error will no longer be present. In other words, the failure to record accrued wages in the previous period means: (1) net income for the first period is overstated, (2) accrued wages payable (a liability) is understated, and (3) wages expense is understated. In the next period, net income is understated, accrued wages payable (a liability) is correctly stated, and wages expense is overstated. For the two **years combined**: (1) net income is correct, (2) wages expense is correct, and (3) accrued wages payable at the end of the second year is correct. Most errors in accounting that affect both the balance sheet and income statement are counterbalancing errors.

Noncounterbalancing errors are those that are not offset in the next accounting period. An example would be the failure to capitalize equipment that has a useful life of five years. If we expense this asset immediately, expenses will be overstated in the first period but understated in the next four periods. At the end of the second period, the effect of the error is not fully offset. Net income is correct in the aggregate only at the end of five years because the asset is fully depreciated at this point. Thus, **noncounterbalancing errors are those that take longer than two periods to correct themselves**.

Only in rare instances is an error never reversed. An example would be if a company initially expenses land. Because land is not depreciable, theoretically the error is never offset, unless the land is sold.

Counterbalancing Errors

We illustrate the usual types of counterbalancing errors on the following pages. In studying these illustrations, keep in mind a couple of points.

First, determine whether the company has closed the books for the period in which the error is found:

1. **If the company has closed the books in the current year:**
   (a) If the error is already counterbalanced, no entry is necessary.
   (b) If the error is not yet counterbalanced, make an entry to adjust the present balance of retained earnings.

2. If the company has not closed the books in the current year:
   (a) If the error is already counterbalanced, make an entry to correct the error in the current period and to adjust the beginning balance of Retained Earnings.
   (b) If the error is not yet counterbalanced, make an entry to adjust the beginning balance of Retained Earnings.

Second, if the company presents comparative statements, it must restate the amounts for comparative purposes. **Restatement is necessary even if a correcting journal entry is not required.**

To illustrate, assume that Sanford's Cement Co. failed to accrue revenue in 2012 when it fulfilled its performance obligation, but recorded the revenue in 2013 when it received payment. The company discovered the error in 2015. It does not need to make an entry to correct for this error because the effects have been counterbalanced by the time Sanford discovered the error in 2015. However, if Sanford presents comparative financial statements for 2012 through 2015, it must **restate the accounts and related amounts for the years 2012 and 2013 for financial reporting purposes**.

The sections that follow demonstrate the accounting for the usual types of counterbalancing errors.

Failure to Record Accrued Wages. On December 31, 2014, Hurley Enterprises did not accrue wages in the amount of $1,500. The entry in 2015 to correct this error, assuming Hurley has not closed the books for 2015, is:

Retained Earnings	1,500	
Salaries and Wages Expense		1,500

The rationale for this entry is as follows. (1) When Hurley pays the 2014 accrued wages in 2015, it makes an additional debit of $1,500 to 2015 Salaries and Wages Expense. (2) Salaries and Wages Expense—2015 is overstated by $1,500. (3) Because the company did not record 2014 accrued wages as Salaries and Wages Expense in 2014, the net income for 2014 was overstated by $1,500. (4) Because 2014 net income is overstated by $1,500, the Retained Earnings account is overstated by $1,500 (because net income is closed to Retained Earnings).

If Hurley has closed the books for 2015, it makes no entry because the error is counterbalanced.

Failure to Record Prepaid Expenses. In January 2014, Hurley Enterprises purchased a two-year insurance policy costing $1,000. It debited Insurance Expense, and credited Cash. The company made no adjusting entries at the end of 2014.

The entry on December 31, 2015, to correct this error, assuming Hurley has not closed the books for 2015, is:

Insurance Expense	500	
Retained Earnings		500

If Hurley has closed the books for 2015, it makes no entry because the error is counterbalanced.

Understatement of Unearned Revenue. On December 31, 2014, Hurley Enterprises received $50,000 as a prepayment for renting certain office space for the following year. At the time of receipt of the rent payment, the company recorded a debit to Cash and a credit to Rent Revenue. It made no adjusting entry as of December 31, 2014. The entry on December 31, 2015, to correct for this error, assuming that Hurley has not closed the books for 2015, is:

Retained Earnings	50,000	
Rent Revenue		50,000

If Hurley has closed the books for 2015, it makes no entry because the error is counterbalanced.

Overstatement of Accrued Revenue. On December 31, 2014, Hurley Enterprises accrued as interest revenue $8,000 that applied to 2015. On that date, the company recorded a debit to Interest Receivable and a credit to Interest Revenue. The entry on December 31, 2015, to correct for this error, assuming that Hurley has not closed the books for 2015, is:

Retained Earnings	8,000	
Interest Revenue		8,000

If Hurley has closed the books for 2015, it makes no entry because the error is counterbalanced.

Overstatement of Purchases. Hurley's accountant recorded a purchase of merchandise for $9,000 in 2014 that applied to 2015. The physical inventory for 2014 was correctly stated. The company uses the periodic inventory method. The entry on December 31, 2015, to correct for this error, assuming that Harley has not closed the books for 2015, is:

Purchases	9,000	
Retained Earnings		9,000

If Hurley has closed the books for 2015, it makes no entry because the error is counterbalanced.

Noncounterbalancing Errors

The entries for noncounterbalancing errors are more complex. Companies must make correcting entries, even if they have closed the books.

Failure to Record Depreciation. Assume that on January 1, 2014, Hurley Enterprises purchased a machine for $10,000 that had an estimated useful life of five years. The accountant incorrectly expensed this machine in 2014, but discovered the error in 2015. If we assume that Hurley uses straight-line depreciation on this asset, the entry on December 31, 2015, to correct for this error, given that Hurley has not closed the books, is:

Equipment	10,000	
Depreciation Expense	2,000	
Retained Earnings		8,000*
Accumulated Depreciation—Equipment (20% × $10,000 × 2)		4,000

*Computations:
Retained Earnings

Overstatement of expense in 2014	$10,000
Proper depreciation for 2014 (20% × $10,000)	(2,000)
Retained earnings understated as of Dec. 31, 2014	$ 8,000

If Hurley has closed the books for 2015, the entry is:

Equipment	10,000	
Retained Earnings		6,000*
Accumulated Depreciation—Equipment		4,000

*Computations:
Retained Earnings

Retained earnings understated as of Dec. 31, 2014	$ 8,000
Proper depreciation for 2015 (20% × $10,000)	(2,000)
Retained earnings understated as of Dec. 31, 2015	$ 6,000

Failure to Adjust for Bad Debts. Companies sometimes use a specific charge-off method in accounting for bad debt expense when a percentage of sales is more appropriate. They then make adjustments to change from the specific write-off to some type of allowance method. For example, assume that Hurley Enterprises has recognized bad debt expense when it has the following uncollectible debts.

	2014	2015
From 2014 sales	$550	$690
From 2015 sales		700

Hurley estimates that it will charge off an additional $1,400 in 2016, of which $300 is applicable to 2014 sales and $1,100 to 2015 sales. The entry on December 31, 2015, assuming that Hurley **has not closed the books for 2015**, is:

Bad Debt Expense	410	
Retained Earnings	990	
Allowance for Doubtful Accounts		1,400

Allowance for doubtful accounts: Additional $300 for 2014 sales and $1,100 for 2015 sales.

Bad debts and retained earnings balance:

	2014	2015
Bad debts charged for	$1,240*	$ 700
Additional bad debts anticipated in 2016	300	1,100
Proper bad debt expense	1,540	1,800
Charges currently made to each period	(550)	(1,390)
Bad debt adjustment	$ 990	$ 410

*$550 + $690 = $1,240

If Hurley **has closed the books for 2015**, the entry is:

Retained Earnings	1,400	
Allowance for Doubtful Accounts		1,400

Comprehensive Example: Numerous Errors

In some circumstances a combination of errors occurs. The company therefore prepares a worksheet to facilitate the analysis. The following problem demonstrates use of the worksheet. The mechanics of its preparation should be obvious from the solution format. The income statements of Hudson Company for the years ended December 31, 2013, 2014, and 2015, indicate the following net incomes.

2013	$17,400
2014	20,200
2015	11,300

An examination of the accounting records for these years indicates that Hudson Company made several errors in arriving at the net income amounts reported:

1. The company consistently omitted from the records wages earned by workers but not paid at December 31. The amounts omitted were:

December 31, 2013	$1,000
December 31, 2014	$1,400
December 31, 2015	$1,600

When paid in the year following that in which they were earned, Hudson recorded these amounts as expenses.

2. The company overstated merchandise inventory on December 31, 2013, by $1,900 as the result of errors made in the footings and extensions on the inventory sheets.

3. On December 31, 2014, Hudson expensed prepaid insurance of $1,200, applicable to 2015.

4. The company did not record on December 31, 2014, interest receivable in the amount of $240.

5. On January 2, 2014, Hudson sold for $1,800 a piece of equipment costing $3,900. At the date of sale, the equipment had accumulated depreciation of $2,400. The company recorded the cash received as Miscellaneous Income in 2014. In addition, the company continued to record depreciation for this equipment in both 2014 and 2015 at the rate of 10 percent of cost.

The first step in preparing the worksheet is to prepare a schedule showing the corrected net income amounts for the years ended December 31, 2013, 2014, and 2015. Each correction of the amount originally reported is clearly labeled. The next step is to indicate the balance sheet accounts affected as of December 31, 2015. Illustration 22-24 shows the completed worksheet for Hudson Company.

ILLUSTRATION 22-24
Worksheet to Correct Income and Balance Sheet Errors

	🖫 ⤺ ⤻ ≡					$f\!x$	HUDSON COMPANY.xls			

Home	Insert	Page Layout	Formulas	Data	Review	View

P18		$f\!x$

	A	B	C	D	E	F	G	H
1		**HUDSON COMPANY**						
2		**Worksheet to Correct Income and**						
3		**Balance Sheet Errors**						
4		Worksheet Analysis of Changes in Net Income				Balance Sheet Correction at December 31, 2015		
5		2013	2014	2015	Totals	Debit	Credit	Account
6	Net income as reported	$17,400	$20,200	$11,300	$48,900			
7	Wages unpaid, 12/31/13	(1,000)	1,000		–0–			
8	Wages unpaid, 12/31/14		(1,400)	1,400	–0–			
9	Wages unpaid, 12/31/15			(1,600)	(1,600)		$1,600	Salaries and Wages Payable
10	Inventory overstatement, 12/31/13	(1,900)	1,900		–0–			
11	Prepaid insurance, 12/31/14		1,200	(1,200)	–0–			
12	Interest receivable, 12/31/14		240	(240)	–0–			
13	Correction for entry made upon sale of equipment, 1/2/14ᵃ		(1,500)		(1,500)	$2,400	3,900	Accumulated Depreciation—Equipment Equipment
14	Overcharge of depreciation, 2014		390		390	390		Accumulated Depreciation—Equipment
15	Overcharge of depreciation, 2015			390	390	390		Accumulated Depreciation—Equipment
16	Corrected net income	$14,500	$22,030	$10,050	$46,580			
17	ᵃCost	$ 3,900						
18	Less: Accumulated depreciation	2,400						
19	Book value	1,500						
20	Less: Proceeds from sale	1,800						
21	Gain on sale	300						
22	Income reported	(1,800)						
23	Adjustment	$(1,500)						

Assuming that Hudson Company **has not closed the books**, correcting entries on December 31, 2015, are:

Retained Earnings	1,400	
Salaries and Wages Expense		1,400
(To correct improper charge to Salaries and Wages Expense for 2015)		
Salaries and Wages Expense	1,600	
Salaries and Wages Payable		1,600
(To record proper wages expense for 2015)		

Insurance Expense	1,200	
Retained Earnings		1,200
(To record proper insurance expense for 2015)		
Interest Revenue	240	
Retained Earnings		240
(To correct improper credit to Interest Revenue in 2015)		
Retained Earnings	1,500	
Accumulated Depreciation—Equipment	2,400	
Equipment		3,900
(To record write-off of equipment in 2014 and adjustment		
of Retained Earnings)		
Accumulated Depreciation—Equipment	780	
Depreciation Expense		390
Retained Earnings		390
(To correct improper charge for depreciation expense		
in 2014 and 2015)		

If Hudson Company has closed the books for 2015, the correcting entries are:

Retained Earnings	1,600	
Salaries and Wages Payable		1,600
(To record proper wage expense for 2015)		
Retained Earnings	1,500	
Accumulated Depreciation—Equipment	2,400	
Equipment		3,900
(To record write-off of equipment in 2014 and		
adjustment of Retained Earnings)		
Accumulated Depreciation—Equipment	780	
Retained Earnings		780
(To correct improper charge for depreciation expense		
in 2014 and 2015)		

What do the numbers mean?   GUARD THE FINANCIAL STATEMENTS!

Restatements sometimes occur because of financial fraud. Financial frauds involve the intentional misstatement or omission of material information in the organization's financial reports. Common methods of financial fraud manipulation include recording fictitious revenues, concealing liabilities or expenses, and artificially inflating reported assets. Financial frauds made up around 8 percent of the frauds in a recent study on occupational fraud but caused a median loss of more than $1 million in 2012 ($4 million in 2010)—by far the most costly category of fraud. The following chart compares loss amounts for 2012 versus 2010 for financial statement fraud, corruption, and asset misappropriation.

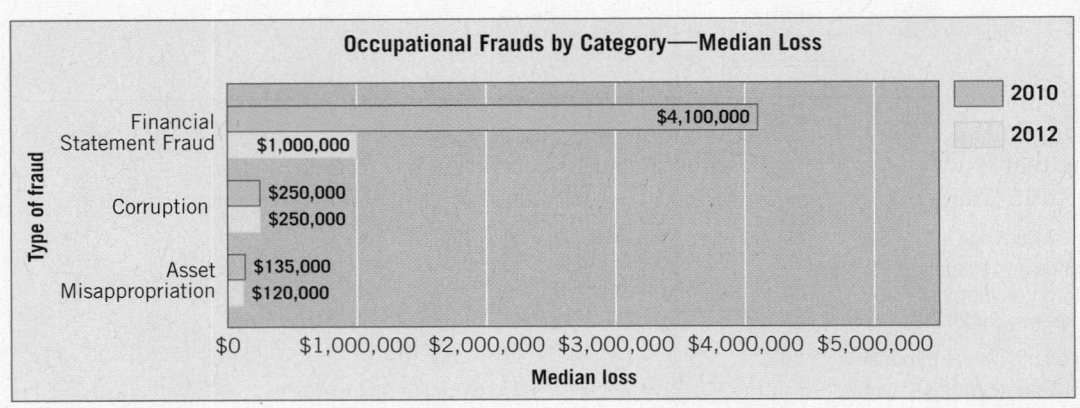

While the trend in the dollar amount of losses is going in the right direction, another study indicates that the number of fraud reports at 1,400 companies in the "Quarterly Corporate Fraud Index" is on the climb—with 2,348 reported frauds in the 2nd quarter of 2005 to over 7,800 in the 2nd quarter of 2012. While there is some debate about whether the reporting of fraud has increased with regulation that provides whistle-blower protections (i.e., the incidence of fraud is not increasing as much as the reporting of fraud), companies must increase their efforts to protect their statements from the negative effects of fraud.

Sources: Report to the Nations on Occupational Fraud and Abuse, 2012 Global Fraud Study, Association of Certified Fraud Examiners (2012), p. 11; and C. McDonald, "Fraud Reports Climb Still Higher," *CFO.com* (September 26, 2012).

Preparation of Financial Statements with Error Corrections

Up to now, our discussion of error analysis has focused on identifying the type of error involved and accounting for its correction in the records. We have noted that companies must present the correction of the error on comparative financial statements.

The following example illustrates how a company would restate a typical year's financial statements, given many different errors.

Dick & Wally's Outlet is a small retail outlet in the town of Holiday. Lacking expertise in accounting, the company does not keep adequate records, and numerous errors occurred in recording accounting information.

1. The bookkeeper inadvertently failed to record a cash receipt of $1,000 on the sale of merchandise in 2015.

2. Accrued wages expense at the end of 2014 was $2,500; at the end of 2015, $3,200. The company does not accrue for wages; all wages are charged to Administrative Expenses.

3. The company had not set up an allowance for estimated uncollectible receivables. Dick and Wally decided to set up such an allowance for the estimated probable losses, as of December 31, 2015, for 2014 accounts of $700, and for 2015 accounts of $1,500. They also decided to correct the charge against each year so that it shows the losses (actual and estimated) relating to that year's sales. The company has written off accounts to bad debt expense (selling expense) as follows.

	In 2014	In 2015
2014 accounts	$400	$2,000
2015 accounts		1,600

4. Prepaid insurance not recorded at the end of 2014 was $600, and at the end of 2015, $400. All insurance is charged to Administrative Expenses.

5. An account payable of $6,000 should have been a note payable.

6. During 2014, the company sold for $7,000 an asset that cost $10,000 and had a book value of $4,000. At the time of sale, Cash was debited and Miscellaneous Income was credited for $7,000.

7. As a result of the last transaction, the company overstated depreciation expense (an administrative expense) in 2014 by $800 and in 2015 by $1,200.

Illustration 22-25 (page 1374) presents a worksheet that begins with the unadjusted trial balance of Dick & Wally's Outlet. You can determine the correcting entries and their effect on the financial statements by examining the worksheet.

	DICK & WALLY'S OUTLET.xls								
Home Insert Page Layout Formulas Data Review View									
P18	fx								

DICK & WALLY'S OUTLET
Worksheet Analysis to Adjust Financial
Statements for the Year 2015

	Trial Balance Unadjusted		Adjustments				Income Statement Adjusted		Balance Sheet Adjusted	
	Dr.	Cr.		Dr.		Cr.	Dr.	Cr.	Dr.	Cr.
Cash	3,100		(1)	1,000					4,100	
Accounts Receivable	17,600								17,600	
Notes Receivable	8,500								8,500	
Inventory	34,000								34,000	
Property, Plant, and Equipment	112,000				(6)	10,000ᵃ			102,000	
Accumulated Depreciation— Equipment		83,500	(6) (7)	6,000ᵃ 2,000						75,500
Investments	24,300								24,300	
Accounts Payable		14,500	(5)	6,000						8,500
Notes Payable		10,000			(5)	6,000				16,000
Capital Stock		43,500								43,500
Retained Earnings		20,000	(3) (6) (2)	2,700ᵇ 4,000ᵃ 2,500	(4) (7)	600 800				12,200
Sales Revenue		94,000			(1)	1,000		95,000		
Cost of Goods Sold	21,000						21,000			
Selling Expenses	22,000				(3)	500ᵇ	21,500			
Administrative Expenses	23,000		(2) (4)	700 600	(4) (7)	400 1,200	22,700			
Totals	265,500	265,500								
Salaries and Wages Payable					(2)	3,200				3,200
Allowance for Doubtful Accounts					(3)	2,200ᵇ				2,200
Prepaid Insurance			(4)	400					400	
Net Income							29,800			29,800
Totals				25,900		25,900	95,000	95,000	190,900	190,900

Computations:

ᵃMachinery			ᵇBad Debts	2014	2015
Proceeds from sale	$ 7,000		Bad debts charged for	$2,400	$1,600
Book value of machinery	(4,000)		Additional bad debts anticipated	700	1,500
Gain on sale	3,000			3,100	3,100
Less: Income credited	7,000		Charges currently made to each year	(400)	(3,600)
Retained earnings adjustment	$(4,000)		Bad debt adjustment	$2,700	$ (500)

ILLUSTRATION 22-25
Worksheet to Analyze
Effect of Errors in
Financial Statements

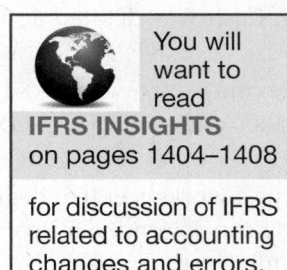

You will want to read
IFRS INSIGHTS
on pages 1404–1408

for discussion of IFRS related to accounting changes and errors.

SUMMARY OF LEARNING OBJECTIVES

1 **Identify the types of accounting changes.** The three different types of accounting changes are as follows. (1) *Change in accounting principle:* a change from one generally accepted accounting principle to another generally accepted accounting principle. (2) *Change in accounting estimate:* a change that occurs as the result of new information or as additional experience is acquired. (3) *Change in reporting entity:* a change from reporting as one type of entity to another type of entity.

2 **Describe the accounting for changes in accounting principles.** A change in accounting principle involves a change from one generally accepted accounting principle to another. A change in accounting principle is not considered to result from the adoption of a new principle in recognition of events that have occurred for the first time or that were previously immaterial. If the accounting principle previously followed was not acceptable or if the principle was applied incorrectly, a change to a generally accepted accounting principle is considered a correction of an error.

3 **Understand how to account for retrospective accounting changes.** The general requirement for changes in accounting principle is retrospective application. Under retrospective application, companies change prior years' financial statements on a basis consistent with the newly adopted principle. They treat any part of the effect attributable to years prior to those presented as an adjustment of the earliest retained earnings presented.

4 **Understand how to account for impracticable changes.** Retrospective application is impracticable if the prior period effect cannot be determined using every reasonable effort to do so. For example, in changing to LIFO, the base-year inventory for all subsequent LIFO calculations is generally the opening inventory in the year the company adopts the method. There is no restatement of prior years' income because it is often too impractical to do so.

5 **Describe the accounting for changes in estimates.** Companies report changes in estimates prospectively. That is, companies should make no changes in previously reported results. They do not adjust opening balances nor change financial statements of prior periods.

6 **Identify changes in a reporting entity.** An accounting change that results in financial statements that are actually the statements of a different entity should be reported by restating the financial statements of all prior periods presented, to show the financial information for the new reporting entity for all periods.

7 **Describe the accounting for correction of errors.** Companies must correct errors as soon as they discover them, by proper entries in the accounts, and report them in the financial statements. The profession requires that a company treat corrections of errors as prior period adjustments, record them in the year in which it discovered the errors, and report them in the financial statements in the proper periods. If presenting comparative statements, a company should restate the prior statements affected to correct for the errors. The company need not repeat the disclosures in the financial statements of subsequent periods.

8 **Identify economic motives for changing accounting methods.** Managers might have varying motives for income reporting, depending on economic times and whom they seek to impress. Some of the reasons for changing accounting methods are (1) political costs, (2) capital structure, (3) bonus payments, and (4) smoothing of earnings.

KEY TERMS

change in accounting
  estimate, *1344, 1357*
change in accounting
  estimate effected by a
  change in accounting
  principle, *1358*
change in accounting
  principle, *1344*
change in reporting
  entity, *1344*
correction of an
  error, *1360*
counterbalancing
  errors, *1367*
cumulative effect, *1345*
direct effects of change
  in accounting
  principle, *1355*
economic
  consequences, *1366*
errors in financial
  statements, *1344*
impracticable, *1356*
indirect effects of change
  in accounting
  principle, *1355*
noncounterbalancing
  errors, *1367*
prior period
  adjustments, *1360*
prospectively, *1345*
restatement, *1361(n)*
retrospective
  application, *1345*

9 **Analyze the effect of errors.** Three types of errors can occur. (1) *Balance sheet errors*, which affect only the presentation of an asset, liability, or stockholders' equity account. (2) *Income statement errors*, which affect only the presentation of revenue, expense, gain, or loss accounts in the income statement. (3) *Balance sheet and income statement errors*, which involve both the balance sheet and income statement. Errors are classified into two types. (1) *Counterbalancing errors* are offset or corrected over two periods. (2) *Noncounterbalancing errors* are not offset in the next accounting period and take longer than two periods to correct themselves.

As an aid to understanding accounting changes, we provide the following glossary.

KEY TERMS RELATED TO ACCOUNTING CHANGES

ACCOUNTING CHANGE. A change in (1) an accounting principle, (2) an accounting estimate, or (3) the reporting entity. The correction of an error in previously issued financial statements is not an accounting change.

CHANGE IN ACCOUNTING PRINCIPLE. A change from one generally accepted accounting principle to another generally accepted accounting principle when two or more generally accepted accounting principles apply or when the accounting principle formerly used is no longer generally accepted.

CHANGE IN ACCOUNTING ESTIMATE. A change that has the effect of adjusting the carrying amount of an existing asset or liability or altering the subsequent accounting for existing or future assets or liabilities. Changes in accounting estimates result from new information.

CHANGE IN ACCOUNTING ESTIMATE EFFECTED BY A CHANGE IN ACCOUNTING PRINCIPLE. A change in accounting estimate that is inseparable from the effect of a related change in accounting principle.

CHANGE IN THE REPORTING ENTITY. A change that results in financial statements that, in effect, are those of a different reporting entity (see page 1359).

DIRECT EFFECTS OF A CHANGE IN ACCOUNTING PRINCIPLE. Those recognized changes in assets or liabilities necessary to effect a change in accounting principle.

ERROR IN PREVIOUSLY ISSUED FINANCIAL STATEMENTS. An error in recognition, measurement, presentation, or disclosure in financial statements resulting from mathematical mistakes, mistakes in the application of GAAP, or oversight or misuse of facts that existed at the time the financial statements were prepared. A change from an accounting principle that is not generally accepted to one that is generally accepted is a correction of an error.

INDIRECT EFFECTS OF A CHANGE IN ACCOUNTING PRINCIPLE. Any changes to current or future cash flows of an entity that result from making a change in accounting principle that is applied retrospectively.

RESTATEMENT. The process of revising previously issued financial statements to reflect the correction of an error in those financial statements.

RETROSPECTIVE APPLICATION. The application of a different accounting principle to one or more previously issued financial statements, or to the statement of financial position at the beginning of the current period, as if that principle had always been used, or a change to financial statements of prior accounting periods to present the financial statements of a new reporting entity as if it had existed in those prior years. **[11]**

APPENDIX **22A**	**CHANGING FROM OR TO THE EQUITY METHOD**

As noted in the chapter, companies generally should report an accounting change that results in financial statements for a different entity by **changing the financial statements of all prior periods presented**.

An example of a change in reporting entity is when a company's level of ownership or influence changes, such as when it changes from or to the equity method. When changing **to** the equity method, companies use retrospective application. Companies treat a change **from** the equity method prospectively. We present examples of these changes in entity in the following two sections.

◄ **10 LEARNING OBJECTIVE**
Make the computations and prepare the entries necessary to record a change from or to the equity method of accounting.

CHANGE FROM THE EQUITY METHOD

If the investor level of influence or ownership falls below that necessary for continued use of the equity method, a company must change from the equity method to the fair value method. The earnings or losses that the investor previously recognized under the equity method should **remain as part of the carrying amount** of the investment, with no retrospective application to the new method.

When a company changes **from the equity method to the fair value method, the cost basis for accounting purposes is the carrying amount of the investment at the date of the change**. The investor applies the new method in its entirety once the equity method is no longer appropriate. At the next reporting date, the investor should record the unrealized holding gain or loss to recognize the difference between the carrying amount and fair value.[14]

Dividends in Excess of Earnings

In subsequent periods, dividends received by the investor company may exceed its share of the investee's earnings for such periods (all periods following the change in method). To the extent that they do so, the investor company should account for such dividends as a **reduction of the investment carrying amount**, rather than as revenue. The reason: Dividends in excess of earnings are viewed as a liquidating dividend, with this excess then accounted for as a reduction of the equity investment.

To illustrate, assume that on January 1, 2013, Investor Company purchased 250,000 shares of Investee Company's 1,000,000 shares of outstanding stock for $8,500,000. Investor correctly accounted for this investment using the equity method. After accounting for dividends received and investee net income, in 2013 Investor reported its investment in Investee Company at $8,780,000 at December 31, 2013. On January 2, 2014, Investee Company sold 1,500,000 additional shares of its own common stock to the public, thereby reducing Investor Company's ownership from 25 percent to 10 percent. Illustration 22A-1 (page 1378) shows the net income (or loss) and dividends of Investee Company for the years 2014 through 2016.

---

[14]A retrospective application for this type of change is impracticable in many cases. Determining fair values on a portfolio basis for securities in previous periods may be quite difficult. As a result, prospective application is used.

ILLUSTRATION 22A-1
Income Earned and
Dividends Received

Year	Investor's Share of Investee Income (Loss)	Investee Dividends Received by Investor
2014	$600,000	$ 400,000
2015	350,000	400,000
2016	–0–	210,000
Totals	$950,000	$1,010,000

Assuming a change from the equity method to the fair value method as of January 2, 2014, Investor Company's reported investment in Investee Company and its reported income would be as shown in Illustration 22A-2.

ILLUSTRATION 22A-2
Impact on Investment
Carrying Amount

Year	Dividend Revenue Recognized	Cumulative Excess of Share of Earnings over Dividends Received	Investment at December 31
2014	$400,000	$200,000[a]	$8,780,000
2015	400,000	150,000[b]	8,780,000
2016	150,000	(60,000)[c]	$8,780,000 − $60,000 = $8,720,000

[a]$600,000 − $400,000 = $200,000
[b]($350,000 − $400,000) + $200,000 = $150,000
[c]$150,000 − $210,000 = $(60,000)

Investor Company would record the dividends and earnings data for the three years subsequent to the change in methods as shown by the following entries.

2014 and 2015

Cash	400,000	
Dividend Revenue		400,000
(To record dividend received from Investee Company)		

2016

Cash	210,000	
Equity Investments (available-for-sale)		60,000
Dividend Revenue		150,000
(To record dividend revenue from Investee Company in 2016 and to recognize cumulative excess of dividends received over share of Investee earnings in periods subsequent to change from equity method)		

CHANGE TO THE EQUITY METHOD

When converting to the equity method, companies use retrospective application. Such a change involves adjusting the carrying amount of the investment, results of current and prior operations, and retained earnings of the investor **as if the equity method has been in effect during all of the previous periods in which this investment was held**. [12] When changing from the fair value method to the equity method, companies also must eliminate any balances in the Unrealized Holding Gain or Loss—Equity account and the Fair Value Adjustment account. In addition, they eliminate the available-for-sale classification for this investment, and they record the investment under the equity method.

For example, on January 2, 2014, Amsted Corp. purchased, for $500,000 cash, 10 percent of the outstanding shares of Cable Company common stock. On that date, the net identifiable assets of Cable Company had a fair value of $3,000,000. The excess of cost over the underlying equity in the net identifiable assets of Cable Company is goodwill.

On January 2, 2016, Amsted Corp. purchased an additional 20 percent of Cable Company's stock for $1,200,000 cash when the fair value of Cable's net identifiable assets was $4,000,000. The excess of cost over fair value related to this additional investment is goodwill. Now having a 30 percent interest, Amsted Corp. must use the equity method.

From January 2, 2014, to January 2, 2016, Amsted Corp. used the fair value method and categorized these securities as available-for-sale. At January 2, 2016, Amsted has a credit balance of $92,000 in its Unrealized Holding Gain or Loss—Equity account and a debit balance in its Fair Value Adjustment account of the same amount. This change in fair value occurred in 2014. (Income tax effects are ignored.) Illustration 22A-3 shows the net income reported by Cable Company and the Cable Company dividends received by Amsted during the period 2014 through 2016.

Year	Cable Company Net Income	Cable Co. Dividends Paid to Amsted
2014	$ 500,000	$ 20,000
2015	1,000,000	30,000
2016	1,200,000	120,000

ILLUSTRATION 22A-3
Income Earned and
Dividends Received

Amsted makes the following journal entries from January 2, 2014, through December 31, 2016, relative to Amsted Corp.'s investment in Cable Company, reflecting the data above and a change from the fair value method to the equity method.[15]

January 2, 2014

Equity Investments (available-for-sale)	500,000	
Cash		500,000
(To record the purchase of a 10% interest in Cable Company)		

December 31, 2014

Cash	20,000	
Dividend Revenue		20,000
(To record the receipt of cash dividends from Cable Company)		
Fair Value Adjustment (available-for-sale)	92,000	
Unrealized Holding Gain or Loss—Equity		92,000
(To record increase in fair value of securities)		

December 31, 2015

Cash	30,000	
Dividend Revenue		30,000
(To record the receipt of cash dividends from Cable Company)		

January 2, 2016

Equity Investments (Cable Company)	1,300,000	
Cash		1,200,000
Retained Earnings		100,000
(To record the purchase of an additional interest in Cable Company and to reflect retrospectively a change from the fair value method to the equity method of accounting for the investment. The $100,000 adjustment is computed as follows:)		

	2014	2015	Total
Amsted Corp. equity in earnings of Cable Company (10%)	$50,000	$100,000	$150,000
Dividend received	(20,000)	(30,000)	(50,000)
Retrospective application	$30,000	$ 70,000	$100,000

[15]Adapted from Paul A. Pacter, "Applying APB Opinion No. 18—Equity Method," *Journal of Accountancy* (September 1971), pp. 59–60.

January 2, 2016

Equity Investments (Cable Company)	500,000	
Equity Investments (available-for-sale)		500,000
(To reclassify initial 10% interest to equity method)		

January 2, 2016

Unrealized Holding Gain or Loss—Equity	92,000	
Fair Value Adjustment (available-for-sale)		92,000
(To eliminate fair value accounts for change to equity method)		

December 31, 2016

Equity Investments (Cable Company)	360,000	
Investment Revenue		360,000
[To record equity in earnings of Cable Company (30% of $1,200,000)]		
Cash	120,000	
Equity Investments (Cable Company)		120,000
(To record the receipt of cash dividends from Cable Company)		

Companies change to the equity method by placing the accounts related to and affected by the investment on the same basis **as if the equity method had always been the basis of accounting for that investment**. Thus, they report the effects of this accounting change using the retrospective approach.[16]

SUMMARY OF LEARNING OBJECTIVE FOR APPENDIX 22A

10 **Make the computations and prepare the entries necessary to record a change from or to the equity method of accounting.** When changing *from* the equity method to the fair value method, the cost basis for accounting purposes is the carrying amount used for the investment at the date of change. The investor company applies the new method in its entirety once the equity method is no longer appropriate. When changing *to* the equity method, the company adjusts the accounts to be on the same basis as if the equity method had always been used for that investment.

DEMONSTRATION PROBLEM

Wangerin Company is in the process of adjusting and correcting its books at the end of 2014. In reviewing its records, the following information is compiled.

1. At December 31, 2014, Wangerin decided to change the depreciation method on its office equipment from double-declining-balance to straight-line. The equipment had an original cost of $200,000 when purchased on January 1, 2012. It has a 10-year useful life and no salvage value. Depreciation expense recorded prior to 2014 under the double-declining-balance method was $72,000. Wangerin has already recorded 2014 depreciation expense of $25,600 using the double-declining-balance method.

---

[16]The change to the equity method illustration assumes that the fair value and the book value of the net identifiable assets of the investee are the same. However, the fair value of the net identifiable assets of the investee may be greater than their book value. In this case, this excess (if depreciable or amortizable) reduces the net income reported by the investor from the investee. For example, assume that the fair value of an investee's building is $1,000,000 and its book value is $800,000 at the time of change to the equity method. In that case, this difference of $200,000 is depreciated over the useful life of the building, thereby reducing the amount of investee's net income reported on the investor's books.

2. Before 2014, Wangerin accounted for its income from long-term construction contracts on the completed-contract basis. Early in 2014, Wangerin changed to the percentage-of-completion basis for accounting purposes. It continues to use the completed-contract method for tax purposes. Income for 2014 has been recorded using the percentage-of-completion method. The following information is available.

	Pretax Income	
	Percentage-of-Completion	Completed-Contract
Prior to 2014	$450,000	$315,000
2014	180,000	60,000

3. Insurance for a 12-month period purchased on November 1 of this year was charged to insurance expense in the amount of $3,300 because "the amount of the check is about the same every year."

4. Reported sales revenue for the year is $1,908,000. This includes all sales taxes collected for the year. The sales tax rate is 6%. Because the sales tax is forwarded to the state's Department of Revenue, the Sales Tax Expense account is debited. The bookkeeper thought that "the sales tax is a selling expense." At the end of the current year, the balance in the Sales Tax Expense account is $103,400.

Instructions

Prepare the journal entries necessary at December 31, 2014, to record the above corrections and changes. The books are still open for 2014. The income tax rate is 40%. Wangerin has not yet recorded its 2014 income tax expense and payable amounts so current-year tax effects may be ignored. Prior-year tax effects must be considered in item 2.

Solution

1.

Accumulated Depreciation—Equipment	9,600	
Depreciation Expense		9,600*

*Equipment cost	$200,000
Depreciation before 2012	(72,000)
Book value	$128,000
Depreciation recorded	$ 25,600
Depreciation to be taken ($128,000/8)	(16,000)
Difference	$ 9,600

2.

Construction in Process	135,000	
Deferred Tax Liability		54,000*
Retained Earnings		81,000
*($450,000 − $315,000) × 40%		

3.

Prepaid Insurance ($3,300 × 10/12)	2,750	
Insurance Expense		2,750

4.

Sales Revenue [$1,908,000 ÷ (1.00 + .06) × 6%]	108,000	
Sales Taxes Payable		108,000
Sales Taxes Payable	103,400	
Sales Tax Expense		103,400

FASB CODIFICATION

FASB Codification References

[1] FASB ASC 250-10-05-1. [Predecessor literature: "Accounting Changes and Error Corrections," *Statement of Financial Accounting Standards No. 154* (Stamford, Conn.: FASB, 2005).]

[2] FASB ASC 250-10-05-2. [Predecessor literature: "Accounting Changes and Error Corrections," *Statement of Financial Accounting Standards No. 154* (Stamford, Conn.: FASB, 2005).]

[3] FASB ASC 250-10-50-1. [Predecessor literature: "Accounting Changes and Error Corrections," *Statement of Financial Accounting Standards No. 154* (Stamford, Conn.: FASB, 2005), par. 17.]

[4] FASB ASC 250-10-50-1. [Predecessor literature: "Accounting Changes and Error Corrections," *Statement of Financial Accounting Standards No. 154* (Stamford, Conn.: FASB, 2005), par. B19.]

[5] FASB ASC 250-10-45-6. [Predecessor literature: "Accounting Changes and Error Corrections," *Statement of Financial Accounting Standards No. 154* (Stamford, Conn.: FASB, 2005), paras. 8–11.]

[6] FASB ASC 250-10-50-1. [Predecessor literature: "Accounting Changes and Error Corrections," *Statement of Financial Accounting Standards No. 154* (Stamford, Conn.: FASB, 2005), par. 17.]

[7] FASB ASC 250-10-45-18. [Predecessor literature: "Accounting Changes and Error Corrections," *Statement of Financial Accounting Standards No. 154* (Stamford, Conn.: FASB, 2005), par. 20.]

[8] FASB ASC 250-10-45-24. [Predecessor literature: "Prior Period Adjustments," *Statement of Financial Accounting Standards No. 16* (Stamford, Conn.: FASB, 1977), p. 5.]

[9] FASB ASC 250-10-50-4. [Predecessor literature: "Accounting Changes and Error Corrections," *Statement of Financial Accounting Standards No. 154* (Stamford, Conn.: FASB, 2005), par. 2.]

[10] FASB ASC 250-10-50-7. [Predecessor literature: "Accounting Changes and Error Corrections," *Statement of Financial Accounting Standards No. 154* (Stamford, Conn.: FASB, 2005), par. 26.]

[11] FASB ASC 250-10-50-1. [Predecessor literature: "Accounting Changes and Error Corrections," *Statement of Financial Accounting Standards No. 154* (Stamford, Conn.: FASB, 2005), par. 2.]

[12] FASB ASC 323-10-35-33. [Predecessor literature: "The Equity Method of Accounting for Investments in Common Stock," *Opinions of the Accounting Principles Board No. 18* (New York: AICPA, 1971), par. 17.]

Exercises

If your school has a subscription to the FASB Codification, go to *http://aaahq.org/ascLogin.cfm* to log in and prepare responses to the following. Provide Codification references for your responses.

CE22-1 Access the glossary ("Master Glossary") to answer the following.
   (a) What is a change in accounting estimate?
   (b) What is a change in accounting principle?
   (c) What is a restatement?
   (d) What is the definition of "retrospective application"?

CE22-2 When a company has to restate its financial statements to correct an error, what information must the company disclose?

CE22-3 What reporting requirements does retrospective application require?

CE22-4 If a company registered with the SEC justifies a change in accounting method as preferable under the circumstances, and the circumstances change, can that company switch back to its prior method of accounting before the change? Why or why not?

An additional Codification case can be found in the Using Your Judgment section, on page 1404.

Be sure to check the book's companion website for a Review and Analysis Exercise, with solution.

WileyPLUS

Brief Exercises, Exercises, Problems, and many more learning and assessment tools and resources are available for practice in WileyPLUS.

Note: All asterisked Questions, Exercises, and Problems relate to material in the appendix to the chapter.

QUESTIONS

1. In recent years, the *Wall Street Journal* has indicated that many companies have changed their accounting principles. What are the major reasons why companies change accounting methods?

2. State how each of the following items is reflected in the financial statements.

(a) Change from FIFO to LIFO method for inventory valuation purposes.

(b) Charge for failure to record depreciation in a previous period.

(c) Litigation won in current year, related to prior period.

(d) Change in the realizability of certain receivables.

(e) Write-off of receivables.

(f) Change from the percentage-of-completion to the completed-contract method for reporting net income.

3. Discuss briefly the three approaches that have been suggested for reporting changes in accounting principles.

4. Identify and describe the approach the FASB requires for reporting changes in accounting principles.

5. What is the indirect effect of a change in accounting principle? Briefly describe the reporting of the indirect effects of a change in accounting principle.

6. Define a change in estimate and provide an illustration. When is a change in accounting estimate effected by a change in accounting principle?

7. Lenexa State Bank has followed the practice of capitalizing certain marketing costs and amortizing these costs over their expected life. In the current year, the bank determined that the future benefits from these costs were doubtful. Consequently, the bank adopted the policy of expensing these costs as incurred. How should the bank report this accounting change in the comparative financial statements?

8. Indicate how the following items are recorded in the accounting records in the current year of Coronet Co.

(a) Impairment of goodwill.

(b) A change in depreciating plant assets from accelerated to the straight-line method.

(c) Large write-off of inventories because of obsolescence.

(d) Change from the cash basis to accrual basis of accounting.

(e) Change from LIFO to FIFO method for inventory valuation purposes.

(f) Change in the estimate of service lives for plant assets.

9. Whittier Construction Co. had followed the practice of expensing all materials assigned to a construction job without recognizing any salvage inventory. On December 31, 2014, it was determined that salvage inventory should be valued at $52,000. Of this amount, $29,000 arose during the current year. How does this information affect the financial statements to be prepared at the end of 2014?

10. Parsons Inc. has proposed a change from the completed-contract to the percentage-of-completion method for financial reporting purposes. The auditor indicates that a change would be permitted only if it is to a preferable method. What difficulties develop in assessing preferability?

11. Discuss how a change to the LIFO method of inventory valuation is handled when it is impracticable to determine previous LIFO inventory amounts.

12. How should consolidated financial statements be reported this year when statements of individual companies were presented last year?

13. Simms Corp. controlled four domestic subsidiaries and one foreign subsidiary. Prior to the current year, Simms Corp. had excluded the foreign subsidiary from consolidation. During the current year, the foreign subsidiary was included in the financial statements. How should this change in accounting entity be reflected in the financial statements?

14. Distinguish between counterbalancing and noncounterbalancing errors. Give an example of each.

15. Discuss and illustrate how a correction of an error in previously issued financial statements should be handled.

16. Prior to 2014, Heberling Inc. excluded manufacturing overhead costs from work in process and finished goods inventory. These costs have been expensed as incurred. In 2014, the company decided to change its accounting methods for manufacturing inventories to full costing by including these costs as product costs. Assuming that these costs are material, how should this change be reflected in the financial statements for 2013 and 2014?

17. Elliott Corp. failed to record accrued salaries for 2013, $2,000; 2014, $2,100; and 2015, $3,900. What is the amount of the overstatement or understatement of Retained Earnings at December 31, 2016?

18. In January 2014, installation costs of $6,000 on new machinery were charged to Maintenance and Repairs Expense. Other costs of this machinery of $30,000 were correctly recorded and have been depreciated using the straight-line method with an estimated life of 10 years and no salvage value. At December 31, 2015, it is decided that the machinery has a remaining useful life of 20 years, starting with January 1, 2015. What entry(ies) should be made in 2015 to correctly record transactions related to machinery, assuming the machinery has no salvage value? The books have not been closed for 2015 and depreciation expense has not yet been recorded for 2015.

19. On January 2, 2014, $100,000 of 11%, 10-year bonds were issued for $97,000. The $3,000 discount was charged to Interest Expense. The bookkeeper, Mark Landis, records interest only on the interest payment dates of January 1 and July 1. What is the effect on reported net income for 2014 of this error, assuming straight-line amortization of the discount? What entry is necessary to correct for this error, assuming that the books are not closed for 2014?

20. An entry to record Purchases and related Accounts Payable of $13,000 for merchandise purchased on December 23, 2015, was recorded in January 2016. This merchandise was not included in inventory at December 31, 2015. What effect does this error have on reported net income for 2015? What entry should be made to correct for this error, assuming that the books are not closed for 2015?

21. Equipment was purchased on January 2, 2014, for $24,000, but no portion of the cost has been charged to depreciation. The corporation wishes to use the straight-line method for these assets, which have been estimated to have a life of 10 years and no salvage value. What effect does this error have on net income in 2014? What entry is necessary to correct for this error, assuming that the books are not closed for 2014?

BRIEF EXERCISES

3 **BE22-1** Wertz Construction Company decided at the beginning of 2014 to change from the completed-contract method to the percentage-of-completion method for financial reporting purposes. The company will continue to use the completed-contract method for tax purposes. For years prior to 2014, pretax income under the two methods was as follows: percentage-of-completion $120,000, and completed-contract $80,000. The tax rate is 35%. Prepare Wertz's 2014 journal entry to record the change in accounting principle.

3 **BE22-2** Refer to the accounting change by Wertz Construction Company in BE22-1. Wertz has a profit-sharing plan, which pays all employees a bonus at year-end based on 1% of pretax income. Compute the indirect effect of Wertz's change in accounting principle that will be reported in the 2014 income statement, assuming that the profit-sharing contract explicitly requires adjustment for changes in income numbers.

3 **BE22-3** Shannon, Inc., changed from the LIFO cost flow assumption to the FIFO cost flow assumption in 2014. The increase in the prior year's income before taxes is $1,200,000. The tax rate is 40%. Prepare Shannon's 2014 journal entry to record the change in accounting principle.

5 **BE22-4** Tedesco Company changed depreciation methods in 2014 from double-declining-balance to straight-line. Depreciation prior to 2014 under double-declining-balance was $90,000, whereas straight-line depreciation prior to 2014 would have been $50,000. Tedesco's depreciable assets had a cost of $250,000 with a $40,000 salvage value, and an 8-year remaining useful life at the beginning of 2014. Prepare the 2014 journal entries, if any, related to Tedesco's depreciable assets.

5 **BE22-5** Sesame Company purchased a computer system for $74,000 on January 1, 2013. It was depreciated based on a 7-year life and an $18,000 salvage value. On January 1, 2015, Sesame revised these estimates to a total useful life of 4 years and a salvage value of $10,000. Prepare Sesame's entry to record 2015 depreciation expense.

7 **BE22-6** In 2014, Bailey Corporation discovered that equipment purchased on January 1, 2012, for $50,000 was expensed at that time. The equipment should have been depreciated over 5 years, with no salvage value. The effective tax rate is 30%. Prepare Bailey's 2014 journal entry to correct the error.

7 **BE22-7** At January 1, 2014, Beidler Company reported retained earnings of $2,000,000. In 2014, Beidler discovered that 2013 depreciation expense was understated by $400,000. In 2014, net income was $900,000 and dividends declared were $250,000. The tax rate is 40%. Prepare a 2014 retained earnings statement for Beidler Company.

7 **BE22-8** Indicate the effect—Understate, Overstate, No Effect—that each of the following errors has on 2014 net income and 2015 net income.

	2014	2015
(a) Equipment purchased in 2012 was expensed.	___	___
(b) Wages payable were not recorded at 12/31/14.	___	___
(c) Equipment purchased in 2014 was expensed.	___	___
(d) 2014 ending inventory was overstated.	___	___
(e) Patent amortization was not recorded in 2015.	___	___

3 **5** **BE22-9** Roundtree Manufacturing Co. is preparing its year-end financial statements and is considering the accounting for the following items.

1. The vice president of sales had indicated that one product line has lost its customer appeal and will be phased out over the next 3 years. Therefore, a decision has been made to lower the estimated lives on related production equipment from the remaining 5 years to 3 years.
2. The Hightone Building was converted from a sales office to offices for the Accounting Department at the beginning of this year. Therefore, the expense related to this building will now appear as an administrative expense rather than a selling expense on the current year's income statement.
3. Estimating the lives of new products in the Leisure Products Division has become very difficult because of the highly competitive conditions in this market. Therefore, the practice of deferring and amortizing preproduction costs has been abandoned in favor of expensing such costs as they are incurred.

Identify and explain whether each of the above items is a change in principle, a change in estimate, or an error.

3 **7** BE22-10 Palmer Co. is evaluating the appropriate accounting for the following items.

1. Management has decided to switch from the FIFO inventory valuation method to the LIFO inventory valuation method for all inventories.
2. When the year-end physical inventory adjustment was made for the current year, the controller discovered that the prior year's physical inventory sheets for an entire warehouse were mislaid and excluded from last year's count.
3. Palmer's Custom Division manufactures large-scale, custom-designed machinery on a contract basis. Management decided to switch from the completed-contract method to the percentage-of-completion method of accounting for long-term contracts.

Identify and explain whether each of the above items is a change in accounting principle, a change in estimate, or an error.

10 *BE22-11 Simmons Corporation owns stock of Armstrong, Inc. Prior to 2014, the investment was accounted for using the equity method. In early 2014, Simmons sold part of its investment in Armstrong, and began using the fair value method. In 2014, Armstrong earned net income of $80,000 and paid dividends of $95,000. Prepare Simmons's entries related to Armstrong's net income and dividends, assuming Simmons now owns 10% of Armstrong's stock.

10 *BE22-12 Oliver Corporation has owned stock of Conrad Corporation since 2011. At December 31, 2014, its balances related to this investment were:

Equity Investments	$185,000
Fair Value Adjustment (AFS)	34,000 Dr.
Unrealized Holding Gain or Loss—Equity	34,000 Cr.

On January 1, 2015, Oliver purchased additional stock of Conrad Company for $475,000 and now has significant influence over Conrad. If the equity method had been used in 2011–2014, Oliver's share of income would have been $33,000 greater than dividends received. Prepare Oliver's journal entries to record the purchase of the investment and the change to the equity method.

EXERCISES

3 **E22-1 (Change in Principle—Long-Term Contracts)** Pam Erickson Construction Company changed from the completed-contract to the percentage-of-completion method of accounting for long-term construction contracts during 2015. For tax purposes, the company employs the completed-contract method and will continue this approach in the future. (*Hint:* Adjust all tax consequences through the Deferred Tax Liability account.) The appropriate information related to this change is as follows.

	Pretax Income from:		
	Percentage-of-Completion	Completed-Contract	Difference
2014	$780,000	$590,000	$190,000
2015	700,000	480,000	220,000

Instructions
(a) Assuming that the tax rate is 35%, what is the amount of net income that would be reported in 2015?
(b) What entry(ies) are necessary to adjust the accounting records for the change in accounting principle?

3 **E22-2 (Change in Principle—Inventory Methods)** Holder-Webb Company began operations on January 1, 2012, and uses the average-cost method of pricing inventory. Management is contemplating a change in inventory methods for 2015. The following information is available for the years 2012–2014.

	Net Income Computed Using		
	Average-Cost Method	FIFO Method	LIFO Method
2012	$15,000	$19,000	$12,000
2013	18,000	23,000	14,000
2014	20,000	25,000	17,000

Instructions

(Ignore all tax effects.)

(a) Prepare the journal entry necessary to record a change from the average-cost method to the FIFO method in 2015.

(b) Determine net income to be reported for 2012, 2013, and 2014, after giving effect to the change in accounting principle.

(c) Assume Holder-Webb Company used the LIFO method instead of the average-cost method during the years 2012–2014. In 2015, Holder-Webb changed to the FIFO method. Prepare the journal entry necessary to record the change in principle.

3 **E22-3 (Accounting Change)** Taveras Co. decides at the beginning of 2014 to adopt the FIFO method of inventory valuation. Taveras had used the LIFO method for financial reporting since its inception on January 1, 2012, and had maintained records adequate to apply the FIFO method retrospectively. Taveras concluded that FIFO is the preferable inventory method because it reflects the current cost of inventory on the balance sheet. The following table presents the effects of the change in accounting principles on inventory and cost of goods sold.

	Inventory Determined by		Cost of Goods Sold Determined by	
Date	LIFO Method	FIFO Method	LIFO Method	FIFO Method
January 1, 2012	$ 0	$ 0	$ 0	$ 0
December 31, 2012	100	80	800	820
December 31, 2013	200	240	1,000	940
December 31, 2014	320	390	1,130	1,100

Other information:

1. For each year presented, sales are $3,000 and operating expenses are $1,000.
2. Taveras provides two years of financial statements. Earnings per share information is not required.

Instructions

(a) Prepare income statements under LIFO and FIFO for 2012, 2013, and 2014.

(b) Prepare income statements reflecting the retrospective application of the accounting change from the LIFO method to the FIFO method for 2014 and 2013.

(c) Prepare the note to the financial statements describing the change in method of inventory valuation. In the note, indicate the income statement line items for 2014 and 2013 that were affected by the change in accounting principle.

(d) Prepare comparative retained earnings statements for 2013 and 2014 under FIFO. Retained earnings reported under LIFO are as follows:

	Retained Earnings Balance
December 31, 2012	$1,200
December 31, 2013	2,200
December 31, 2014	3,070

3 **E22-4 (Accounting Change)** Gordon Company started operations on January 1, 2009, and has used the FIFO method of inventory valuation since its inception. In 2015, it decides to switch to the average-cost method. You are provided with the following information.

	Net Income		Retained Earnings (Ending Balance)
	Under FIFO	Under Average-Cost	Under FIFO
2009	$100,000	$ 90,000	$100,000
2010	70,000	65,000	160,000
2011	90,000	80,000	235,000
2012	120,000	130,000	340,000
2013	300,000	290,000	590,000
2014	305,000	310,000	780,000

Instructions

(a) What is the beginning retained earnings balance at January 1, 2011, if Gordon prepares comparative financial statements starting in 2011?

(b) What is the beginning retained earnings balance at January 1, 2014, if Gordon prepares comparative financial statements starting in 2014?

(c) What is the beginning retained earnings balance at January 1, 2015, if Gordon prepares single-period financial statements for 2015?

(d) What is the net income reported by Gordon in the 2014 income statement if it prepares comparative financial statements starting with 2012?

3 **E22-5 (Accounting Change)** Presented below are income statements prepared on a LIFO and FIFO basis for Kenseth Company, which started operations on January 1, 2013. The company presently uses the LIFO method of pricing its inventory and has decided to switch to the FIFO method in 2014. The FIFO income statement is computed in accordance with the requirements of GAAP. Kenseth's profit-sharing agreement with its employees indicates that the company will pay employees 10% of income before profit-sharing. Income taxes are ignored.

	LIFO Basis		FIFO Basis	
	2014	2013	2014	2013
Sales	$3,000	$3,000	$3,000	$3,000
Cost of goods sold	1,130	1,000	1,100	940
Operating expenses	1,000	1,000	1,000	1,000
Income before profit-sharing	870	1,000	900	1,060
Profit-sharing expense	87	100	96	100
Net income	$ 783	$ 900	$ 804	$ 960

Instructions

Answer the following questions.

(a) If comparative income statements are prepared, what net income should Kenseth report in 2013 and 2014?

(b) Explain why, under the FIFO basis, Kenseth reports $100 in 2013 and $96 in 2014 for its profit-sharing expense.

(c) Assume that Kenseth has a beginning balance of retained earnings at January 1, 2014, of $8,000 using the LIFO method. The company declared and paid dividends of $500 in 2014. Prepare the retained earnings statement for 2014, assuming that Kenseth has switched to the FIFO method.

5 **E22-6 (Accounting Changes—Depreciation)** Kathleen Cole Inc. acquired the following assets in January of 2012.

Equipment, estimated service life, 5 years; salvage value, $15,000	$525,000
Building, estimated service life, 30 years; no salvage value	$693,000

The equipment has been depreciated using the sum-of-the-years'-digits method for the first 3 years for financial reporting purposes. In 2015, the company decided to change the method of computing depreciation to the straight-line method for the equipment, but no change was made in the estimated service life or salvage value. It was also decided to change the total estimated service life of the building from 30 years to 40 years, with no change in the estimated salvage value. The building is depreciated on the straight-line method.

Instructions

(a) Prepare the general journal entry to record depreciation expense for the equipment in 2015.

(b) Prepare the journal entry to record depreciation expense for the building in 2015. (Round all computations to two decimal places.)

5 **7** **E22-7 (Change in Estimate and Error; Financial Statements)** Presented below are the comparative income and retained earnings statements for Denise Habbe Inc. for the years 2014 and 2015.

	2015	2014
Sales	$340,000	$270,000
Cost of sales	200,000	142,000
Gross profit	140,000	128,000
Expenses	88,000	50,000
Net income	$ 52,000	$ 78,000
Retained earnings (Jan. 1)	$125,000	$ 72,000
Net income	52,000	78,000
Dividends	(30,000)	(25,000)
Retained earnings (Dec. 31)	$147,000	$125,000

The following additional information is provided:

1. In 2015, Denise Habbe Inc. decided to switch its depreciation method from sum-of-the-years'-digits to the straight-line method. The assets were purchased at the beginning of 2014 for $100,000 with an estimated useful life of 4 years and no salvage value. (The 2015 income statement contains depreciation expense of $30,000 on the assets purchased at the beginning of 2014.)

2. In 2015, the company discovered that the ending inventory for 2014 was overstated by $24,000; ending inventory for 2015 is correctly stated.

Instructions

Prepare the revised retained earnings statement for 2014 and 2015, assuming comparative statements. (Ignore income taxes.)

3 5 7 E22-8 (Accounting for Accounting Changes and Errors) Listed below are various types of accounting changes and errors.

_____ **1.** Change in a plant asset's salvage value.
_____ **2.** Change due to overstatement of inventory.
_____ **3.** Change from sum-of-the-years'-digits to straight-line method of depreciation.
_____ **4.** Change from presenting unconsolidated to consolidated financial statements.
_____ **5.** Change from LIFO to FIFO inventory method.
_____ **6.** Change in the rate used to compute warranty costs.
_____ **7.** Change from an unacceptable accounting principle to an acceptable accounting principle.
_____ **8.** Change in a patent's amortization period.
_____ **9.** Change from completed-contract to percentage-of-completion method on construction contracts.
_____ **10.** Change from FIFO to average-cost inventory method.

Instructions

For each change or error, indicate how it would be accounted for using the following code letters:

(a) Accounted for prospectively.
(b) Accounted for retrospectively.
(c) Neither of the above.

5 7 E22-9 (Error and Change in Estimate—Depreciation) Joy Cunningham Co. purchased a machine on January 1, 2012, for $550,000. At that time, it was estimated that the machine would have a 10-year life and no salvage value. On December 31, 2015, the firm's accountant found that the entry for depreciation expense had been omitted in 2013. In addition, management has informed the accountant that the company plans to switch to straight-line depreciation, starting with the year 2015. At present, the company uses the sum-of-the-years'-digits method for depreciating equipment.

Instructions

Prepare the general journal entries that should be made at December 31, 2015, to record these events. (Ignore tax effects.)

5 E22-10 (Depreciation Changes) On January 1, 2011, Jackson Company purchased a building and equipment that have the following useful lives, salvage values, and costs.

> Building, 40-year estimated useful life, $50,000 salvage value, $800,000 cost
> Equipment, 12-year estimated useful life, $10,000 salvage value, $100,000 cost

The building has been depreciated under the double-declining-balance method through 2014. In 2015, the company decided to switch to the straight-line method of depreciation. Jackson also decided to change the total useful life of the equipment to 9 years, with a salvage value of $5,000 at the end of that time. The equipment is depreciated using the straight-line method.

Instructions

(a) Prepare the journal entry(ies) necessary to record the depreciation expense on the building in 2015.
(b) Compute depreciation expense on the equipment for 2015.

5 E22-11 (Change in Estimate—Depreciation) Peter M. Dell Co. purchased equipment for $510,000 which was estimated to have a useful life of 10 years with a salvage value of $10,000 at the end of that time. Depreciation has been entered for 7 years on a straight-line basis. In 2015, it is determined that the total estimated life should be 15 years with a salvage value of $5,000 at the end of that time.

Instructions

(a) Prepare the entry (if any) to correct the prior years' depreciation.
(b) Prepare the entry to record depreciation for 2015.

5 E22-12 (Change in Estimate—Depreciation) Gerald Englehart Industries changed from the double-declining-balance to the straight-line method in 2015 on all its plant assets. There was no change in the assets' salvage values or useful lives. Plant assets, acquired on January 2, 2012, had an original cost of $1,600,000, with a $100,000 salvage value and an 8-year estimated useful life. Income before depreciation expense was $270,000 in 2014 and $300,000 in 2015.

Instructions

(a) Prepare the journal entry(ies) to record depreciation expense in 2015.

(b) Starting with income before depreciation expense, prepare the remaining portion of the income statement for 2014 and 2015.

3 **E22-13 (Change in Principle—Long-Term Contracts)** Cullen Construction Company, which began operations in 2014, changed from the completed-contract to the percentage-of-completion method of accounting for long-term construction contracts during 2015. For tax purposes, the company employs the completed-contract method and will continue this approach in the future. The appropriate information related to this change is as follows.

	Pretax Income		
	Percentage-of-Completion	Completed-Contract	Difference
2014	$880,000	$590,000	$290,000
2015	900,000	480,000	420,000

Instructions

(a) Assuming that the tax rate is 40%, what is the amount of net income that would be reported in 2015?

(b) What entry(ies) are necessary to adjust the accounting records for the change in accounting principle?

3 **E22-14 (Various Changes in Principle—Inventory Methods)** Below is the net income of Anita Ferreri Instrument Co., a private corporation, computed under the three inventory methods using a periodic system.

	FIFO	Average-Cost	LIFO
2012	$26,000	$24,000	$20,000
2013	30,000	25,000	21,000
2014	28,000	27,000	24,000
2015	34,000	30,000	26,000

Instructions

(Ignore tax considerations.)

(a) Assume that in 2015 Ferreri decided to change from the FIFO method to the average-cost method of pricing inventories. Prepare the journal entry necessary for the change that took place during 2015, and show net income reported for 2012, 2013, 2014, and 2015.

(b) Assume that in 2015 Ferreri, which had been using the LIFO method since incorporation in 2012, changed to the FIFO method of pricing inventories. Prepare the journal entry necessary to record the change in 2015 and show net income reported for 2012, 2013, 2014, and 2015.

7 **E22-15 (Error Correction Entries)** The first audit of the books of Bruce Gingrich Company was made for the year ended December 31, 2015. In examining the books, the auditor found that certain items had been overlooked or incorrectly handled in the last 3 years. These items are:

1. At the beginning of 2013, the company purchased a machine for $510,000 (salvage value of $51,000) that had a useful life of 6 years. The bookkeeper used straight-line depreciation, but failed to deduct the salvage value in computing the depreciation base for the 3 years.

2. At the end of 2014, the company failed to accrue sales salaries of $45,000.

3. A tax lawsuit that involved the year 2013 was settled late in 2015. It was determined that the company owed an additional $85,000 in taxes related to 2013. The company did not record a liability in 2013 or 2014 because the possibility of loss was considered remote, and charged the $85,000 to a loss account in 2015.

4. Gingrich Company purchased a copyright from another company early in 2013 for $45,000. Gingrich had not amortized the copyright because its value had not diminished. The copyright has a useful life at purchase of 20 years.

5. In 2015, the company wrote off $87,000 of inventory considered to be obsolete; this loss was charged directly to Retained Earnings.

Instructions

Prepare the journal entries necessary in 2015 to correct the books, assuming that the books have not been closed. Disregard effects of corrections on income tax.

7 **E22-16 (Error Analysis and Correcting Entry)** You have been engaged to review the financial statements of Gottschalk Corporation. In the course of your examination, you conclude that the bookkeeper hired during the current year is not doing a good job. You notice a number of irregularities as follows.

1. Year-end wages payable of $3,400 were not recorded because the bookkeeper thought that "they were immaterial."

2. Accrued vacation pay for the year of $31,100 was not recorded because the bookkeeper "never heard that you had to do it."

3. Insurance for a 12-month period purchased on November 1 of this year was charged to insurance expense in the amount of $2,640 because "the amount of the check is about the same every year."

4. Reported sales revenue for the year is $2,120,000. This includes all sales taxes collected for the year. The sales tax rate is 6%. Because the sales tax is forwarded to the state's Department of Revenue, the Sales Tax Expense account is debited. The bookkeeper thought that "the sales tax is a selling expense." At the end of the current year, the balance in the Sales Tax Expense account is $103,400.

Instructions
Prepare the necessary correcting entries, assuming that Gottschalk uses a calendar-year basis.

7 E22-17 (Error Analysis and Correcting Entry) The reported net incomes for the first 2 years of Sandra Gustafson Products, Inc., were as follows: 2014, $147,000; 2015, $185,000. Early in 2016, the following errors were discovered.

1. Depreciation of equipment for 2014 was overstated $17,000.
2. Depreciation of equipment for 2015 was understated $38,500.
3. December 31, 2014, inventory was understated $50,000.
4. December 31, 2015, inventory was overstated $16,200.

Instructions
Prepare the correcting entry necessary when these errors are discovered. Assume that the books are closed. (Ignore income tax considerations.)

7 9 E22-18 (Error Analysis) Peter Henning Tool Company's December 31 year-end financial statements contained the following errors.

	December 31, 2014	December 31, 2015
Ending inventory	$9,600 understated	$8,100 overstated
Depreciation expense	$2,300 understated	—

An insurance premium of $66,000 was prepaid in 2014 covering the years 2014, 2015, and 2016. The entire amount was charged to expense in 2014. In addition, on December 31, 2015, fully depreciated machinery was sold for $15,000 cash, but the entry was not recorded until 2016. There were no other errors during 2014 or 2015, and no corrections have been made for any of the errors. (Ignore income tax considerations.)

Instructions
(a) Compute the total effect of the errors on 2015 net income.
(b) Compute the total effect of the errors on the amount of Henning's working capital at December 31, 2015.
(c) Compute the total effect of the errors on the balance of Henning's retained earnings at December 31, 2015.

7 9 E22-19 (Error Analysis; Correcting Entries) A partial trial balance of Julie Hartsack Corporation is as follows on December 31, 2015.

	Dr.	Cr.
Supplies	$ 2,700	
Salaries and wages payable		$ 1,500
Interest receivable	5,100	
Prepaid insurance	90,000	
Unearned rent		–0–
Interest payable		15,000

Additional adjusting data:
1. A physical count of supplies on hand on December 31, 2015, totaled $1,100.
2. Through oversight, the Salaries and Wages Payable account was not changed during 2015. Accrued salaries and wages on December 31, 2015, amounted to $4,400.
3. The Interest Receivable account was also left unchanged during 2015. Accrued interest on investments amounts to $4,350 on December 31, 2015.
4. The unexpired portions of the insurance policies totaled $65,000 as of December 31, 2015.
5. $28,000 was received on January 1, 2015, for the rent of a building for both 2015 and 2016. The entire amount was credited to rent revenue.
6. Depreciation on equipment for the year was erroneously recorded as $5,000 rather than the correct figure of $50,000.
7. A further review of depreciation calculations of prior years revealed that equipment depreciation of $7,200 was not recorded. It was decided that this oversight should be corrected by a prior period adjustment.

Instructions

(a) Assuming that the books have not been closed, what are the adjusting entries necessary at December 31, 2015? (Ignore income tax considerations.)

(b) Assuming that the books have been closed, what are the adjusting entries necessary at December 31, 2015? (Ignore income tax considerations.)

(c) Repeat the requirements for items 6 and 7, taking into account income tax effects (40% tax rate) and assuming that the books have been closed.

7 9 **E22-20 (Error Analysis)** The before-tax income for Lonnie Holdiman Co. for 2014 was $101,000 and $77,400 for 2015. However, the accountant noted that the following errors had been made:

1. Sales for 2014 included amounts of $38,200 which had been received in cash during 2014, but for which the related products were delivered in 2015. Title did not pass to the purchaser until 2015.
2. The inventory on December 31, 2014, was understated by $8,640.
3. The bookkeeper in recording interest expense for both 2014 and 2015 on bonds payable made the following entry on an annual basis.

Interest Expense	15,000	
Cash		15,000

The bonds have a face value of $250,000 and pay a stated interest rate of 6%. They were issued at a discount of $15,000 on January 1, 2014, to yield an effective-interest rate of 7%. (Assume that the effective-yield method should be used.)

4. Ordinary repairs to equipment had been erroneously charged to the Equipment account during 2014 and 2015. Repairs in the amount of $8,500 in 2014 and $9,400 in 2015 were so charged. The company applies a rate of 10% to the balance in the Equipment account at the end of the year in its determination of depreciation charges.

Instructions

Prepare a schedule showing the determination of corrected income before taxes for 2014 and 2015.

7 9 **E22-21 (Error Analysis)** When the records of Debra Hanson Corporation were reviewed at the close of 2015, the errors listed below were discovered. For each item, indicate by a check mark in the appropriate column whether the error resulted in an overstatement, an understatement, or had no effect on net income for the years 2014 and 2015.

	2014			2015		
Item	**Over-statement**	**Under-statement**	**No Effect**	**Over-statement**	**Under-statement**	**No Effect**
1. Failure to record amortization of patent in 2015.						
2. Failure to record the correct amount of ending 2014 inventory. The amount was understated because of an error in calculation.						
3. Failure to record merchandise purchased in 2014. Merchandise was also omitted from ending inventory in 2014 but was not yet sold.						
4. Failure to record accrued interest on notes payable in 2014; that amount was recorded when paid in 2015.						
5. Failure to reflect supplies on hand on balance sheet at end of 2014.						

10 *E22-22 (Change from Fair Value to Equity)** On January 1, 2014, Beyonce Co. purchased 25,000 shares (a 10% interest) in Elton John Corp. for $1,400,000. At the time, the book value and the fair value of John's net assets were $13,000,000.

On July 1, 2015, Beyonce paid $3,040,000 for 50,000 additional shares of John common stock, which represented a 20% investment in John. The fair value of John's identifiable assets net of liabilities was equal to their carrying amount of $14,200,000. As a result of this transaction, Beyonce owns 30% of John and can exercise significant influence over John's operating and financial policies.

John reported the following net income and declared and paid the following dividends.

	Net Income	Dividend per Share
Year ended 12/31/14	$700,000	None
Six months ended 6/30/15	500,000	None
Six months ended 12/31/15	815,000	$1.55

Instructions

(Any excess fair value is attributed to goodwill.)

Determine the ending balance that Beyonce Co. should report as its investment in John Corp. at the end of 2015.

10 *E22-23 (Change from Equity to Fair Value)** Dan Aykroyd Corp. was a 30% owner of Steve Martin Company, holding 210,000 shares of Martin's common stock on December 31, 2013. The investment account had the following entries.

Investment in Martin			
1/1/12 Cost	$3,180,000	12/6/12 Dividend received	$150,000
12/31/12 Share of income	390,000	12/5/13 Dividend received	240,000
12/31/13 Share of income	510,000		

On January 2, 2014, Aykroyd sold 126,000 shares of Martin for $3,440,000, thereby losing its significant influence. During the year 2014, Martin experienced the following results of operations and paid the following dividends to Aykroyd.

	Martin Income (Loss)	Dividends Paid to Aykroyd
2014	$300,000	$50,400

At December 31, 2014, the fair value of Martin shares held by Aykroyd is $1,570,000. This is the first reporting date since the January 2 sale.

Instructions

(a) What effect does the January 2, 2014, transaction have upon Aykroyd's accounting treatment for its investment in Martin?

(b) Compute the carrying amount of the investment in Martin as of December 31, 2014 (prior to any fair value adjustment).

(c) Prepare the adjusting entry on December 31, 2014, applying the fair value method to Aykroyd's long-term investment in Martin Company securities.

EXERCISES SET B

See the book's companion website, at **www.wiley.com/college/kieso**, for an additional set of exercises.

PROBLEMS

2 5 7 **P22-1 (Change in Estimate and Error Correction)** Holtzman Company is in the process of preparing its financial statements for 2014. Assume that no entries for depreciation have been recorded in 2014. The following information related to depreciation of fixed assets is provided to you.

1. Holtzman purchased equipment on January 2, 2011, for $85,000. At that time, the equipment had an estimated useful life of 10 years with a $5,000 salvage value. The equipment is depreciated on a

straight-line basis. On January 2, 2014, as a result of additional information, the company determined that the equipment has a remaining useful life of 4 years with a $3,000 salvage value.

2. During 2014, Holtzman changed from the double-declining-balance method for its building to the straight-line method. The building originally cost $300,000. It had a useful life of 10 years and a salvage value of $30,000. The following computations present depreciation on both bases for 2012 and 2013.

	2013	2012
Straight-line	$27,000	$27,000
Declining-balance	48,000	60,000

3. Holtzman purchased a machine on July 1, 2012, at a cost of $120,000. The machine has a salvage value of $16,000 and a useful life of 8 years. Holtzman's bookkeeper recorded straight-line depreciation in 2012 and 2013 but failed to consider the salvage value.

Instructions

(a) Prepare the journal entries to record depreciation expense for 2014 and correct any errors made to date related to the information provided. (Ignore taxes.)

(b) Show comparative net income for 2013 and 2014. Income before depreciation expense was $300,000 in 2014, and was $310,000 in 2013. (Ignore taxes.)

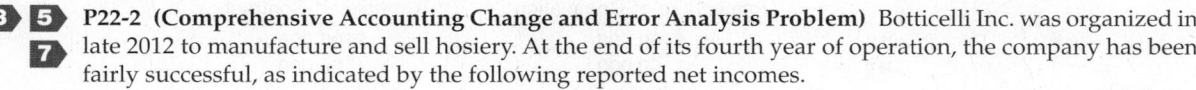 **P22-2 (Comprehensive Accounting Change and Error Analysis Problem)** Botticelli Inc. was organized in late 2012 to manufacture and sell hosiery. At the end of its fourth year of operation, the company has been fairly successful, as indicated by the following reported net incomes.

2012	$140,000[a]	2014	$205,000
2013	160,000[b]	2015	276,000

[a]Includes a $10,000 increase because of change in bad debt experience rate.
[b]Includes extraordinary gain of $30,000.

The company has decided to expand operations and has applied for a sizable bank loan. The bank officer has indicated that the records should be audited and presented in comparative statements to facilitate analysis by the bank. Botticelli Inc. therefore hired the auditing firm of Check & Doublecheck Co. and has provided the following additional information.

1. In early 2013, Botticelli Inc. changed its estimate from 2% of sales to 1% on the amount of bad debt expense to be charged to operations. Bad debt expense for 2012, if a 1% rate had been used, would have been $10,000. The company therefore restated its net income for 2012.

2. In 2015, the auditor discovered that the company had changed its method of inventory pricing from LIFO to FIFO. The effect on the income statements for the previous years is as follows.

	2012	2013	2014	2015
Net income unadjusted—LIFO basis	$140,000	$160,000	$205,000	$276,000
Net income unadjusted—FIFO basis	155,000	165,000	215,000	260,000
	$ 15,000	$ 5,000	$ 10,000	$ (16,000)

3. In 2015, the auditor discovered that:

(a) The company incorrectly overstated the ending inventory (under both LIFO and FIFO) by $14,000 in 2014.

(b) A dispute developed in 2013 with the Internal Revenue Service over the deductibility of entertainment expenses. In 2012, the company was not permitted these deductions, but a tax settlement was reached in 2015 that allowed these expenses. As a result of the court's finding, tax expenses in 2015 were reduced by $60,000.

Instructions

(a) Indicate how each of these changes or corrections should be handled in the accounting records. (Ignore income tax considerations.)

(b) Present comparative income statements for the years 2012 to 2015, starting with income before extraordinary items. (Ignore income tax considerations.)

P22-3 (Error Corrections and Accounting Changes) Penn Company is in the process of adjusting and correcting its books at the end of 2014. In reviewing its records, the following information is compiled.

1. Penn has failed to accrue sales commissions payable at the end of each of the last 2 years, as follows.

December 31, 2013	$3,500
December 31, 2014	$2,500

2. In reviewing the December 31, 2014, inventory, Penn discovered errors in its inventory-taking procedures that have caused inventories for the last 3 years to be incorrect, as follows.

December 31, 2012	Understated	$16,000
December 31, 2013	Understated	$19,000
December 31, 2014	Overstated	$ 6,700

Penn has already made an entry that established the incorrect December 31, 2014, inventory amount.

3. At December 31, 2014, Penn decided to change the depreciation method on its office equipment from double-declining-balance to straight-line. The equipment had an original cost of $100,000 when purchased on January 1, 2012. It has a 10-year useful life and no salvage value. Depreciation expense recorded prior to 2014 under the double-declining-balance method was $36,000. Penn has already recorded 2014 depreciation expense of $12,800 using the double-declining-balance method.

4. Before 2014, Penn accounted for its income from long-term construction contracts on the completed-contract basis. Early in 2014, Penn changed to the percentage-of-completion basis for accounting purposes. It continues to use the completed-contract method for tax purposes. Income for 2014 has been recorded using the percentage-of-completion method. The following information is available.

	Pretax Income	
	Percentage-of-Completion	Completed-Contract
Prior to 2014	$150,000	$105,000
2014	60,000	20,000

Instructions

Prepare the journal entries necessary at December 31, 2014, to record the above corrections and changes. The books are still open for 2014. The income tax rate is 40%. Penn has not yet recorded its 2014 income tax expense and payable amounts so current-year tax effects may be ignored. Prior-year tax effects must be considered in item 4.

 P22-4 (Accounting Changes) Aston Corporation performs year-end planning in November of each year before its calendar year ends in December. The preliminary estimated net income is $3 million. The CFO, Rita Warren, meets with the company president, J. B. Aston, to review the projected numbers. She presents the following projected information.

ASTON CORPORATION
PROJECTED INCOME STATEMENT
FOR THE YEAR ENDED DECEMBER 31, 2014

Sales		$29,000,000
Cost of goods sold	$14,000,000	
Depreciation	2,600,000	
Operating expenses	6,400,000	23,000,000
Income before income tax		6,000,000
Income tax		3,000,000
Net income		$ 3,000,000

ASTON CORPORATION
SELECTED BALANCE SHEET INFORMATION
AT DECEMBER 31, 2014

Estimated cash balance	$ 5,000,000
Available-for-sale securities (at cost)	10,000,000
Fair value adjustment (1/1/14)	—0—

Estimated fair value at December 31, 2014:

Security	Cost	Estimated Fair Value
A	$ 2,000,000	$ 2,200,000
B	4,000,000	3,900,000
C	3,000,000	3,100,000
D	1,000,000	1,800,000
Total	$10,000,000	$11,000,000

Other information at December 31, 2014:

Equipment	$3,000,000
Accumulated depreciation (5-year SL)	1,200,000
New robotic equipment (purchased 1/1/14)	5,000,000
Accumulated depreciation (5-year DDB)	2,000,000

The corporation has never used robotic equipment before, and Warren assumed an accelerated method because of the rapidly changing technology in robotic equipment. The company normally uses straight-line depreciation for production equipment.

Aston explains to Warren that it is important for the corporation to show a $7,000,000 income before taxes because Aston receives a $1,000,000 bonus if the income before taxes and bonus reaches $7,000,000. Aston also does not want the company to pay more than $3,000,000 in income taxes to the government.

Instructions
(a) What can Warren do within GAAP to accommodate the president's wishes to achieve $7,000,000 in income before taxes and bonus? Present the revised income statement based on your decision.
(b) Are the actions ethical? Who are the stakeholders in this decision, and what effect do Warren's actions have on their interests?

3 **P22-5 (Change in Principle—Inventory—Periodic)** The management of Utrillo Instrument Company had concluded, with the concurrence of its independent auditors, that results of operations would be more fairly presented if Utrillo changed its method of pricing inventory from last-in, first-out (LIFO) to average-cost in 2014. Given below is the 5-year summary of income under LIFO and a schedule of what the inventories would be if stated on the average-cost method.

UTRILLO INSTRUMENT COMPANY
STATEMENT OF INCOME AND RETAINED EARNINGS
FOR THE YEARS ENDED MAY 31

	2010	2011	2012	2013	2014
Sales—net	$13,964	$15,506	$16,673	$18,221	$18,898
Cost of goods sold					
Beginning inventory	1,000	1,100	1,000	1,115	1,237
Purchases	13,000	13,900	15,000	15,900	17,100
Ending inventory	(1,100)	(1,000)	(1,115)	(1,237)	(1,369)
Total	12,900	14,000	14,885	15,778	16,968
Gross profit	1,064	1,506	1,788	2,443	1,930
Administrative expenses	700	763	832	907	989
Income before taxes	364	743	956	1,536	941
Income taxes (50%)	182	372	478	768	471
Net income	182	371	478	768	470
Retained earnings—beginning	1,206	1,388	1,759	2,237	3,005
Retained earnings—ending	$ 1,388	$ 1,759	$ 2,237	$ 3,005	$ 3,475
Earnings per share	$1.82	$3.71	$4.78	$7.68	$4.70

SCHEDULE OF INVENTORY BALANCES USING AVERAGE-COST METHOD
FOR THE YEARS ENDED MAY 31

2009	2010	2011	2012	2013	2014
$1,010	$1,124	$1,101	$1,270	$1,500	$1,720

Instructions
Prepare comparative statements for the 5 years, assuming that Utrillo changed its method of inventory pricing to average-cost. Indicate the effects on net income and earnings per share for the years involved. Utrillo Instruments started business in 2009. (All amounts except EPS are rounded up to the nearest dollar.)

5 **7** **9** **P22-6 (Accounting Change and Error Analysis)** On December 31, 2014, before the books were closed, the management and accountants of Madrasa Inc. made the following determinations about three pieces of equipment.

1. Equipment A was purchased January 2, 2011. It originally cost $540,000 and, for depreciation purposes, the straight-line method was originally chosen. The asset was originally expected to be

useful for 10 years and have a zero salvage value. In 2014, the decision was made to change the depreciation method from straight-line to sum-of-the-years'-digits, and the estimates relating to useful life and salvage value remained unchanged.

2. Equipment B was purchased January 3, 2010. It originally cost $180,000 and, for depreciation purposes, the straight-line method was chosen. The asset was originally expected to be useful for 15 years and have a zero residual value. In 2014, the decision was made to shorten the total life of this asset to 9 years and to estimate the residual value at $3,000.

3. Equipment C was purchased January 5, 2010. The asset's original cost was $160,000, and this amount was entirely expensed in 2010. This particular asset has a 10-year useful life and no residual value. The straight-line method was chosen for depreciation purposes.

Additional data:

1. Income in 2014 before depreciation expense amounted to $400,000.
2. Depreciation expense on assets other than A, B, and C totaled $55,000 in 2014.
3. Income in 2013 was reported at $370,000.
4. Ignore all income tax effects.
5. 100,000 shares of common stock were outstanding in 2013 and 2014.

Instructions

(a) Prepare all necessary entries in 2014 to record these determinations.
(b) Prepare comparative retained earnings statements for Madrasa Inc. for 2013 and 2014. The company had retained earnings of $200,000 at December 31, 2012.

 P22-7 (Error Corrections) You have been assigned to examine the financial statements of Zarle Company for the year ended December 31, 2014. You discover the following situations.

1. Depreciation of $3,200 for 2014 on delivery vehicles was not recorded.
2. The physical inventory count on December 31, 2013, improperly excluded merchandise costing $19,000 that had been temporarily stored in a public warehouse. Zarle uses a periodic inventory system.
3. A collection of $5,600 on account from a customer received on December 31, 2014, was not recorded until January 2, 2015.
4. In 2014, the company sold for $3,700 fully depreciated equipment that originally cost $25,000. The company credited the proceeds from the sale to the Equipment account.
5. During November 2014, a competitor company filed a patent-infringement suit against Zarle claiming damages of $220,000. The company's legal counsel has indicated that an unfavorable verdict is probable and a reasonable estimate of the court's award to the competitor is $125,000. The company has not reflected or disclosed this situation in the financial statements.
6. Zarle has a portfolio of trading securities. No entry has been made to adjust to market. Information on cost and fair value is as follows.

	Cost	Fair Value
December 31, 2013	$95,000	$95,000
December 31, 2014	$84,000	$82,000

7. At December 31, 2014, an analysis of payroll information shows accrued salaries of $12,200. The Salaries and Wages Payable account had a balance of $16,000 at December 31, 2014, which was unchanged from its balance at December 31, 2013.
8. A large piece of equipment was purchased on January 3, 2014, for $40,000 and was charged to Maintenance and Repairs Expense. The equipment is estimated to have a service life of 8 years and no residual value. Zarle normally uses the straight-line depreciation method for this type of equipment.
9. A $12,000 insurance premium paid on July 1, 2013, for a policy that expires on June 30, 2016, was charged to insurance expense.
10. A trademark was acquired at the beginning of 2013 for $50,000. No amortization has been recorded since its acquisition. The maximum allowable amortization period is 10 years.

Instructions

Assume the trial balance has been prepared but the books have not been closed for 2014. Assuming all amounts are material, prepare journal entries showing the adjustments that are required. (Ignore income tax considerations.)

 P22-8 (Comprehensive Error Analysis) On March 5, 2015, you were hired by Hemingway Inc., a closely held company, as a staff member of its newly created internal auditing department. While reviewing the company's records for 2013 and 2014, you discover that no adjustments have yet been made for the items listed on the next page.

Items

1. Interest income of $14,100 was not accrued at the end of 2013. It was recorded when received in February 2014.

2. A computer costing $4,000 was expensed when purchased on July 1, 2013. It is expected to have a 4-year life with no salvage value. The company typically uses straight-line depreciation for all fixed assets.

3. Research and development costs of $33,000 were incurred early in 2013. They were capitalized and were to be amortized over a 3-year period. Amortization of $11,000 was recorded for 2013 and $11,000 for 2014.

4. On January 2, 2013, Hemingway leased a building for 5 years at a monthly rental of $8,000. On that date, the company paid the following amounts, which were expensed when paid.

Security deposit	$20,000
First month's rent	8,000
Last month's rent	8,000
	$36,000

5. The company received $36,000 from a customer at the beginning of 2013 for services that it is to perform evenly over a 3-year period beginning in 2013. None of the amount received was reported as unearned revenue at the end of 2013.

6. Merchandise inventory costing $18,200 was in the warehouse at December 31, 2013, but was incorrectly omitted from the physical count at that date. The company uses the periodic inventory method.

Instructions

Indicate the effect of any errors on the net income figure reported on the income statement for the year ending December 31, 2013, and the retained earnings figure reported on the balance sheet at December 31, 2014. Assume all amounts are material, and ignore income tax effects. Using the following format, enter the appropriate dollar amounts in the appropriate columns. Consider each item independent of the other items. It is not necessary to total the columns on the grid.

	Net Income for 2013		Retained Earnings at 12/31/14	
Item	Understated	Overstated	Understated	Overstated

(CIA adapted)

7 9 P22-9 (Error Analysis) Lowell Corporation has used the accrual basis of accounting for several years. A review of the records, however, indicates that some expenses and revenues have been handled on a cash basis because of errors made by an inexperienced bookkeeper. Income statements prepared by the bookkeeper reported $29,000 net income for 2013 and $37,000 net income for 2014. Further examination of the records reveals that the following items were handled improperly.

1. Rent was received from a tenant in December 2013. The amount, $1,000, was recorded as revenue at that time even though the rental pertained to 2014.

2. Salaries and wages payable on December 31 have been consistently omitted from the records of that date and have been entered as expenses when paid in the following year. The amounts of the accruals recorded in this manner were:

December 31, 2012	$1,100
December 31, 2013	1,200
December 31, 2014	940

3. Invoices for supplies purchased have been charged to expense accounts when received. Inventories of supplies on hand at the end of each year have been ignored, and no entry has been made for them.

December 31, 2012	$1,300
December 31, 2013	940
December 31, 2014	1,420

Instructions

Prepare a schedule that will show the corrected net income for the years 2013 and 2014. All items listed should be labeled clearly. (Ignore income tax considerations.)

7 **9** **P22-10 (Error Analysis and Correcting Entries)** You have been asked by a client to review the records of Roberts Company, a small manufacturer of precision tools and machines. Your client is interested in buying the business, and arrangements have been made for you to review the accounting records. Your examination reveals the following information.

1. Roberts Company commenced business on April 1, 2012, and has been reporting on a fiscal year ending March 31. The company has never been audited, but the annual statements prepared by the bookkeeper reflect the following income before closing and before deducting income taxes.

Year Ended March 31	Income Before Taxes
2013	$ 71,600
2014	111,400
2015	103,580

2. A relatively small number of machines have been shipped on consignment. These transactions have been recorded as ordinary sales and billed as such. On March 31 of each year, machines billed and in the hands of consignees amounted to:

2013	$6,500
2014	none
2015	5,590

Sales price was determined by adding 25% to cost. Assume that the consigned machines are sold the following year.

3. On March 30, 2014, two machines were shipped to a customer on a C.O.D. basis. The sale was not entered until April 5, 2014, when cash was received for $6,100. The machines were not included in the inventory at March 31, 2014. (Title passed on March 30, 2014.)

4. All machines are sold subject to a 5-year warranty. It is estimated that the expense ultimately to be incurred in connection with the warranty will amount to ½ of 1% of sales. The company has charged an expense account for warranty costs incurred.

  Sales per books and warranty costs were as follows.

Year Ended March 31	Sales	Warranty Expense for Sales Made in 2013	2014	2015	Total
2013	$ 940,000	$760			$ 760
2014	1,010,000	360	$1,310		1,670
2015	1,795,000	320	1,620	$1,910	3,850

5. Bad debts have been recorded on a direct write-off basis. Experience of similar enterprises indicates that losses will approximate ¼ of 1% of sales. Bad debts written off were:

	Bad Debts Incurred on Sales Made in 2013	2014	2015	Total
2013	$750			$ 750
2014	800	$ 520		1,320
2015	350	1,800	$1,700	3,850

6. The bank deducts 6% on all contracts financed. Of this amount, ½% is placed in a reserve to the credit of Roberts Company that is refunded to Roberts as finance contracts are paid in full. (Thus, Roberts should have a receivable for these payments and should record revenue when the net balance is remitted each year.) The reserve established by the bank has not been reflected in the books of Roberts. The excess of credits over debits (net increase) to the reserve account with Roberts on the books of the bank for each fiscal year were as follows.

2013	$ 3,000
2014	3,900
2015	5,100
	$12,000

7. Commissions on sales have been entered when paid. Commissions payable on March 31 of each year were as follows.

2013	$1,400
2014	900
2015	1,120

8. A review of the corporate minutes reveals the manager is entitled to a bonus of 1% of the income before deducting income taxes and the bonus. The bonuses have never been recorded or paid.

Instructions

(a) Present a schedule showing the revised income before income taxes for each of the years ended March 31, 2013, 2014, and 2015. (Make computations to the nearest whole dollar.)

(b) Prepare the journal entry or entries you would give the bookkeeper to correct the books. Assume the books have not yet been closed for the fiscal year ended March 31, 2015. Disregard correction of income taxes.

(AICPA adapted)

10 *P22-11 (Fair Value to Equity Method with Goodwill)** On January 1, 2014, Millay Inc. paid $700,000 for 10,000 shares of Genso Company's voting common stock, which was a 10% interest in Genso. At that date, the net assets of Genso totaled $6,000,000. The fair values of all of Genso's identifiable assets and liabilities were equal to their book values. Millay does not have the ability to exercise significant influence over the operating and financial policies of Genso. Millay received dividends of $1.50 per share from Genso on October 1, 2014. Genso reported net income of $550,000 for the year ended December 31, 2014.

On July 1, 2015, Millay paid $2,325,000 for 30,000 additional shares of Genso Company's voting common stock which represents a 30% investment in Genso. The fair values of all of Genso's identifiable assets net of liabilities were equal to their book values of $6,550,000. As a result of this transaction, Millay has the ability to exercise significant influence over the operating and financial policies of Genso. Millay received dividends of $2.00 per share from Genso on April 1, 2015, and $2.50 per share on October 1, 2015. Genso reported net income of $650,000 for the year ended December 31, 2015, and $350,000 for the 6 months ended December 31, 2015.

Instructions

(For both purchases, assume any excess of cost over book value is due to goodwill.)

(a) Prepare a schedule showing the income or loss before income taxes for the year ended December 31, 2014, that Millay should report from its investment in Genso in its income statement issued in March 2015.

(b) During March 2016, Millay issues comparative financial statements for 2014 and 2015. Prepare schedules showing the income or loss before income taxes for the years ended December 31, 2014 and 2015, that Millay should report from its investment in Genso.

(AICPA adapted)

10 *P22-12 (Change from Fair Value to Equity Method)** On January 3, 2013, Martin Company purchased for $500,000 cash a 10% interest in Renner Corp. On that date, the net assets of Renner had a book value of $3,700,000. The excess of cost over the underlying equity in net assets is attributable to undervalued depreciable assets having a remaining life of 10 years from the date of Martin's purchase.

The fair value of Martin's investment in Renner securities is as follows: December 31, 2013, $560,000, and December 31, 2014, $515,000.

On January 2, 2015, Martin purchased an additional 30% of Renner's stock for $1,545,000 cash when the book value of Renner's net assets was $4,150,000. The excess was attributable to depreciable assets having a remaining life of 8 years.

During 2013, 2014, and 2015, the following occurred.

	Renner Net Income	Dividends Paid by Renner to Martin
2013	$350,000	$15,000
2014	450,000	20,000
2015	550,000	70,000

Instructions

On the books of Martin Company, prepare all journal entries in 2013, 2014, and 2015 that relate to its investment in Renner Corp., reflecting the data above and a change from the fair value method to the equity method.

PROBLEMS SET B

See the book's companion website, at **www.wiley.com/college/kieso**, for an additional set of problems.

CONCEPTS FOR ANALYSIS

CA22-1 (Analysis of Various Accounting Changes and Errors) Mathys Inc. has recently hired a new independent auditor, Karen Ogleby, who says she wants "to get everything straightened out." Consequently, she has proposed the following accounting changes in connection with Mathys Inc.'s 2014 financial statements.

1. At December 31, 2013, the client had a receivable of $820,000 from Hendricks Inc. on its balance sheet. Hendricks Inc. has gone bankrupt, and no recovery is expected. The client proposes to write off the receivable as a prior period item.

2. The client proposes the following changes in depreciation policies.
   (a) For office furniture and fixtures, it proposes to change from a 10-year useful life to an 8-year life. If this change had been made in prior years, retained earnings at December 31, 2013, would have been $250,000 less. The effect of the change on 2014 income alone is a reduction of $60,000.
   (b) For its new equipment in the leasing division, the client proposes to adopt the sum-of-the-years'-digits depreciation method. The client had never used SYD before. The first year the client operated a leasing division was 2014. If straight-line depreciation were used, 2014 income would be $110,000 greater.

3. In preparing its 2013 statements, one of the client's bookkeepers overstated ending inventory by $235,000 because of a mathematical error. The client proposes to treat this item as a prior period adjustment.

4. In the past, the client has spread preproduction costs in its furniture division over 5 years. Because its latest furniture is of the "fad" type, it appears that the largest volume of sales will occur during the first 2 years after introduction. Consequently, the client proposes to amortize preproduction costs on a per-unit basis, which will result in expensing most of such costs during the first 2 years after the furniture's introduction. If the new accounting method had been used prior to 2014, retained earnings at December 31, 2013, would have been $375,000 less.

5. For the nursery division, the client proposes to switch from FIFO to LIFO inventories because it believes that LIFO will provide a better matching of current costs with revenues. The effect of making this change on 2014 earnings will be an increase of $320,000. The client says that the effect of the change on December 31, 2013, retained earnings cannot be determined.

6. To achieve an appropriate recognition of revenues and expenses in its building construction division, the client proposes to switch from the completed-contract method of accounting to the percentage-of-completion method. Had the percentage-of-completion method been employed in all prior years, retained earnings at December 31, 2013, would have been $1,075,000 greater.

Instructions
(a) For each of the changes described above, decide whether:
   (1) The change involves an accounting principle, accounting estimate, or correction of an error.
   (2) Restatement of opening retained earnings is required.
(b) What would be the proper adjustment to the December 31, 2013, retained earnings?

CA22-2 (Analysis of Various Accounting Changes and Errors) Various types of accounting changes can affect the financial statements of a business enterprise differently. Assume that the following list describes changes that have a material effect on the financial statements for the current year of your business enterprise.

1. A change from the completed-contract method to the percentage-of-completion method of accounting for long-term construction-type contracts.

2. A change in the estimated useful life of previously recorded fixed assets as a result of newly acquired information.

3. A change from deferring and amortizing preproduction costs to recording such costs as an expense when incurred because future benefits of the costs have become doubtful. The new accounting method was adopted in recognition of the change in estimated future benefits.

4. A change from including the employer share of FICA taxes with payroll tax expenses to including it with "Retirement benefits" on the income statement.

5. Correction of a mathematical error in inventory pricing made in a prior period.

6. A change from presentation of statements of individual companies to presentation of consolidated statements.

7. A change in the method of accounting for leases for tax purposes to conform with the financial accounting method. As a result, both deferred and current taxes payable changed substantially.

8. A change from the FIFO method of inventory pricing to the LIFO method of inventory pricing.

Instructions

Identify the type of change that is described in each item above and indicate whether the prior year's financial statements should be recast when presented in comparative form with the current year's financial statements.

CA22-3 (Analysis of Three Accounting Changes and Errors) The following are three independent, unrelated sets of facts relating to accounting changes.

Situation 1: Sanford Company is in the process of having its first audit. The company has used the cash basis of accounting for revenue recognition. Sanford president, B. J. Jimenez, is willing to change to the accrual method of revenue recognition.

Situation 2: Hopkins Co. decides in January 2015 to change from FIFO to weighted-average pricing for its inventories.

Situation 3: Marshall Co. determined that the depreciable lives of its fixed assets are too long at present to fairly match the cost of the fixed assets with the revenue produced. The company decided at the beginning of the current year to reduce the depreciable lives of all of its existing fixed assets by 5 years.

Instructions

For each of the situations described, provide the information indicated below.

(a) Type of accounting change.
(b) Manner of reporting the change under current generally accepted accounting principles, including a discussion where applicable of how amounts are computed.
(c) Effect of the change on the balance sheet and income statement.

CA22-4 (Analysis of Various Accounting Changes and Errors) Katherine Irving, controller of Lotan Corp., is aware of a pronouncement on accounting changes. After reading the pronouncement, she is confused about what action should be taken on the following items related to Lotan Corp. for the year 2014.

1. In 2014, Lotan decided to change its policy on accounting for certain marketing costs. Previously, the company had chosen to defer and amortize all marketing costs over at least 5 years because Lotan believed that a return on these expenditures did not occur immediately. Recently, however, the time differential has considerably shortened, and Lotan is now expensing the marketing costs as incurred.

2. In 2014, the company examined its entire policy relating to the depreciation of plant equipment. Plant equipment had normally been depreciated over a 15-year period, but recent experience has indicated that the company was incorrect in its estimates and that the assets should be depreciated over a 20-year period.

3. One division of Lotan Corp., Hawthorne Co., has consistently shown an increasing net income from period to period. On closer examination of its operating statement, it is noted that bad debt expense and inventory obsolescence charges are much lower than in other divisions. In discussing this with the controller of this division, it has been learned that the controller has increased his net income each period by knowingly making low estimates related to the write-off of receivables and inventory.

4. In 2014, the company purchased new machinery that should increase production dramatically. The company has decided to depreciate this machinery on an accelerated basis, even though other machinery is depreciated on a straight-line basis.

5. All equipment sold by Lotan is subject to a 3-year warranty. It has been estimated that the expense ultimately to be incurred on these machines is 1% of sales. In 2014, because of a production breakthrough, it is now estimated that $\frac{1}{2}$ of 1% of sales is sufficient. In 2012 and 2013, warranty expense was computed as $64,000 and $70,000, respectively. The company now believes that these warranty costs should be reduced by 50%.

6. In 2014, the company decided to change its method of inventory pricing from average-cost to the FIFO method. The effect of this change on prior years is to increase 2012 income by $65,000 and increase 2013 income by $20,000.

Instructions

Katherine Irving has come to you, as her CPA, for advice about the situations above. Prepare a report, indicating the appropriate accounting treatment that should be given for each of these situations.

CA22-5 (Change in Principle, Estimate) As a certified public accountant, you have been contacted by Joe Davison, CEO of Sports-Pro Athletics, Inc., a manufacturer of a variety of athletic equipment. He has asked you how to account for the following changes.

1. Sports-Pro appropriately changed its depreciation method for its machinery from the double-declining-balance method to the units-of-production method effective January 1, 2014.
2. Effective January 1, 2014, Sports-Pro appropriately changed the salvage values used in computing depreciation for its office equipment.
3. On December 31, 2014, Sports-Pro appropriately changed the specific subsidiaries constituting the group of companies for which consolidated financial statements are presented.

Instructions
Write a 1–1.5 page letter to Joe Davison explaining how each of the above changes should be presented in the December 31, 2014, financial statements.

 CA22-6 (Change in Estimate) Mike Crane is an audit senior of a large public accounting firm who has just been assigned to the Frost Corporation's annual audit engagement. Frost has been a client of Crane's firm for many years. Frost is a fast-growing business in the commercial construction industry. In reviewing the fixed asset ledger, Crane discovered a series of unusual accounting changes, in which the useful lives of assets, depreciated using the straight-line method, were substantially lowered near the midpoint of the original estimate. For example, the useful life of one dump truck was changed from 10 to 6 years during its fifth year of service. Upon further investigation, Mike was told by Kevin James, Frost's accounting manager, "I don't really see your problem. After all, it's perfectly legal to change an accounting estimate. Besides, our CEO likes to see big earnings!"

Instructions
Answer the following questions.

(a) What are the ethical issues concerning Frost's practice of changing the useful lives of fixed assets?
(b) Who could be harmed by Frost's unusual accounting changes?
(c) What should Crane do in this situation?

USING YOUR JUDGMENT

FINANCIAL REPORTING

Financial Reporting Problem
P&G **The Procter & Gamble Company (P&G)**
The financial statements of P&G are presented in Appendix 5B. The company's complete annual report, including the notes to the financial statements, can be accessed at the book's companion website, **www.wiley.com/college/kieso**.

Instructions
Refer to P&G's financial statements and the accompanying notes to answer the following questions.

(a) Were there changes in accounting principles reported by P&G during the three years covered by its income statements (2009–2011)? If so, describe the nature of the change and the year of change.
(b) What types of estimates did P&G discuss in 2011?

Comparative Analysis Case
The Coca-Cola Company and PepsiCo, Inc.

Instructions
Go to the book's companion website and use information found there to answer the following questions related to The Coca-Cola Company and PepsiCo, Inc.

(a) Identify the changes in accounting principles reported by Coca-Cola during the 3 years covered by its income statements (2009–2011). Describe the nature of the change and the year of change.
(b) Identify the changes in accounting principles reported by PepsiCo during the 3 years covered by its income statements (2009–2011). Describe the nature of the change and the year of change.
(c) For each change in accounting principle by Coca-Cola and PepsiCo, identify, if possible, the cumulative effect of each change on prior years and the effect on operating results in the year of change.

Accounting, Analysis, and Principles

In preparation for significant expansion of its international operations, ABC Co. has adopted a plan to gradually shift to the same accounting methods as used by its international competitors. Part of this plan includes a switch from LIFO inventory accounting to FIFO (recall that IFRS does not allow LIFO). ABC decides to make the switch to FIFO at January 1, 2014. The following data pertains to ABC's 2014 financial statements (in millions of dollars).

Sales	$550
Inventory purchases	350
12/31/14 inventory (using FIFO)	580
Compensation expense	17

All sales and purchases were with cash. All of 2014's compensation expense was paid with cash. (Ignore taxes.) ABC's property, plant, and equipment cost $400 million and has an estimated useful life of 10 years with no salvage value.

ABC Co. reported the following for fiscal 2013 (in millions of dollars):

ABC CO.
BALANCE SHEET AT DECEMBER 31, 2013

	2013	2012		2013	2012
Cash	$ 365	$ 200	Common stock	$ 500	$ 500
Inventory	500	480	Retained earnings	685	540
Property, plant, and equipment	400	400			
Accumulated depreciation	(80)	(40)			
Total assets	$1,185	$1,040	Total equity	$1,185	$1,040

ABC CO.
INCOME STATEMENT
FOR THE YEAR ENDED DECEMBER 31, 2013

	2013
Sales	$ 500
Cost of goods sold	(300)
Depreciation expense	(40)
Compensation expense	(15)
Net income	$ 145

Summary of Significant Accounting Policies

Inventory: The company accounts for inventory by the LIFO method. The current cost of the company's inventory, which approximates FIFO, was $60 and $50 higher at the end of fiscal 2013 and 2012, respectively, than those reported in the balance sheet.

Accounting

Prepare ABC's December 31, 2014, balance sheet and an income statement for the year ended December 31, 2014. In columns beside 2014's numbers, include 2013's numbers *as they would appear in the 2014 financial statements* for comparative purposes.

Analysis

Compute ABC's inventory turnover for 2013 and 2014 under both LIFO and FIFO. Assume averages are equal to year-end balances where necessary. What causes the differences in this ratio between LIFO and FIFO?

Principles

Briefly explain, in terms of the principles discussed in Chapter 2, why GAAP requires that companies that change accounting methods recast prior year's financial statement data.

BRIDGE TO THE PROFESSION

 ## Professional Research: FASB Codification

As part of the year-end accounting process and review of operating policies, Cullen Co. is considering a change in the accounting for its equipment from the straight-line method to an accelerated method. Your supervisor wonders how the company will report this change in principle. He read in a newspaper article that the FASB has issued a standard in this area and has changed GAAP for a "change in estimate that is effected by a change in accounting principle." (Thus, the accounting may be different from what he learned in intermediate accounting.) Your supervisor wants you to research the authoritative guidance on a change in accounting principle related to depreciation methods.

Instructions

If your school has a subscription to the FASB Codification, go to *http://aaahq.org/ascLogin.cfm* to log in and prepare responses to the following. Provide Codification references for your responses.

(a) What are the accounting and reporting guidelines for a change in accounting principle related to depreciation methods?

(b) What are the conditions that justify a change in depreciation method, as contemplated by Cullen Co.?

(c) What guidance does the SEC provide concerning the impact that recently issued accounting standards will have on the financial statements in a future period?

Additional Professional Resources

See the book's companion website, at **www.wiley.com/college/kieso**, for professional simulations as well as other study resources.

ACCOUNTING CHANGES AND ERRORS

LEARNING OBJECTIVE **11**
Compare the procedures for accounting changes and error analysis under GAAP and IFRS.

The IFRS addressing accounting and reporting for changes in accounting principles, changes in estimates, and errors is *IAS 8* ("Accounting Policies, Changes in Accounting Estimates and Errors"). Various presentation issues related to restatements are addressed in *IAS 1* ("Presentation of Financial Statements"). As indicated in the chapter, the FASB has issued guidance on changes in accounting principles, changes in estimates, and corrections of errors, which essentially converges GAAP to *IAS 8*.

RELEVANT FACTS

Following are the key similarities and differences between GAAP and IFRS related to the procedures for accounting changes.

Similarities

• The accounting for changes in estimates is similar between GAAP and IFRS.

• Under GAAP and IFRS, if determining the effect of a change in accounting policy is considered impracticable, then a company should report the effect of the change in the period in which it believes it practicable to do so, which may be the current period.

Differences

• One area in which GAAP and IFRS differ is the reporting of error corrections in previously issued financial statements. While both sets of standards require restatement, GAAP is an absolute standard—that is, there is no exception to this rule.

- Under IFRS, the impracticality exception applies both to changes in accounting principles and to the correction of errors. Under GAAP, this exception applies only to changes in accounting principle.
- IFRS (*IAS 8*) does not specifically address the accounting and reporting for indirect effects of changes in accounting principles. As indicated in the chapter, GAAP has detailed guidance on the accounting and reporting of indirect effects.

ABOUT THE NUMBERS

Direct and Indirect Effects of Changes

Are there other effects that a company should report when it makes a change in accounting policy? For example, what happens when a company like Lancer (see pages 1350–1354) has a bonus plan based on net income and the prior year's net income changes when FIFO is retrospectively applied? Should Lancer also change the reported amount of bonus expense? Or, what happens if we had not ignored income taxes in the Lancer example? Should Lancer adjust net income, given that taxes will be different under average-cost and FIFO in prior periods? The answers depend on whether the effects are direct or indirect.

Direct Effects

Similar to GAAP, IFRS indicates that companies should retrospectively apply the **direct effects of a change in accounting policy**. An example of a **direct effect** is an adjustment to an inventory balance as a result of a change in the inventory valuation method. For example, referring to Lancer Company on pages 1350–1354, Lancer should change the inventory amounts in prior periods to indicate the change to the FIFO method of inventory valuation. Another inventory-related example would be an impairment adjustment resulting from applying the lower-of-cost-or-net realizable value test to the adjusted inventory balance. Related changes, such as deferred income tax effects of the impairment adjustment, are also considered direct effects. This entry was illustrated in the Denson example on page 1349, in which the change to percentage-of-completion accounting resulted in recording a deferred tax liability.

Indirect Effects

In addition to direct effects, companies can have **indirect effects related to a change in accounting policy**. An **indirect effect** is any change to current or future cash flows of a company that results from making a change in accounting policy that is applied retrospectively. An example of an indirect effect is a change in profit-sharing or royalty payment that is based on a reported amount such as revenue or net income. The IASB is silent on what to do in this situation. GAAP (likely because its standard in this area was issued after *IAS 8*) requires that indirect effects do not change prior period amounts.

For example, let's assume that Lancer Company has an employee profit-sharing plan based on net income and it changed from the weighted-average inventory method to FIFO in 2014. Lancer reports higher income in 2013 and 2014 if it used the FIFO method. In addition, let's assume that the profit-sharing plan requires that Lancer pay the incremental amount due based on the FIFO income amounts. In this situation, Lancer reports this additional expense **in the current period**; it would not change prior periods for this expense. If the company prepares comparative financial statements, it follows that it does not recast the prior periods for this additional expense. If the terms of the profit-sharing plan indicate that *no payment is necessary* in the current period due to this change, then the company need not recognize additional profit-sharing expense in the current period. Neither does it change amounts reported for prior periods.

When a company recognizes the indirect effects of a change in accounting policy, it includes in the financial statements a description of the indirect effects. In doing so, it discloses the amounts recognized in the current period and related per share information.

Impracticability

It is not always possible for companies to determine how they would have reported prior periods' financial information under retrospective application of an accounting policy change. Retrospective application is considered **impracticable** if a company cannot determine the prior period effects using every reasonable effort to do so.

Companies should not use retrospective application if one of the following conditions exists:

1. The company cannot determine the effects of the retrospective application.

2. Retrospective application requires assumptions about management's intent in a prior period.

3. Retrospective application requires significant estimates for a prior period, and the company cannot objectively verify the necessary information to develop these estimates.

If any of the above conditions exists, it is deemed impracticable to apply the retrospective approach. In this case, the company **prospectively applies** the new accounting policy as of the earliest date it is practicable to do so.

For example, assume that Williams Company changed its accounting policy for depreciable assets so as to more fully apply component depreciation under revaluation accounting. Unfortunately, the company does not have detailed accounting records to establish a basis for the components of these assets. As a result, Williams determines it is not practicable to account for the change to full component depreciation using the retrospective application approach. It therefore applies the policy prospectively, starting at the beginning of the current year.

Williams must disclose only the effect of the change on the results of operations in the period of change. Also, the company should explain the reasons for omitting the computations of the cumulative effect for prior years. Finally, it should disclose the justification for the change to component depreciation.

ON THE HORIZON

For the most part, IFRS and GAAP are similar in the area of accounting changes and reporting the effects of errors. Thus, there is no active project in this area. A related development involves the presentation of comparative data. Under IFRS, when a company prepares financial statements on a new basis, two years of comparative data are reported. GAAP requires comparative information for a three-year period. Use of the shorter comparative data period must be addressed before U.S. companies can adopt IFRS.

IFRS SELF-TEST QUESTIONS

1. Which of the following is **false**?
   (a) GAAP and IFRS have the same absolute standard regarding the reporting of error corrections in previously issued financial statements.
   (b) The accounting for changes in estimates is similar between GAAP and IFRS.
   (c) Under IFRS, the impracticability exception applies both to changes in accounting principles and to the correction of errors.
   (d) GAAP has detailed guidance on the accounting and reporting of indirect effects; IFRS does not.

2. Which of the following is **not** classified as an accounting change by IFRS?
   (a) Change in accounting policy.   (c) Errors in financial statements.
   (b) Change in accounting estimate.   (d) None of the above.
3. IFRS requires companies to use which method for reporting changes in accounting policies?
   (a) Cumulative effect approach.   (c) Prospective approach.
   (b) Retrospective approach.   (d) Averaging approach.
4. Under IFRS, the retrospective approach should **not** be used if:
   (a) retrospective application requires assumptions about management's intent in a prior period.
   (b) the company does not have trained staff to perform the analysis.
   (c) the effects of the change have counterbalanced.
   (d) the effects of the change have not counterbalanced.
5. Which of the following is **true** regarding whether IFRS specifically addresses the accounting and reporting for effects of changes in accounting policies?

	Direct effects	Indirect effects
(a)	Yes	Yes
(b)	No	No
(c)	No	Yes
(d)	Yes	No

IFRS CONCEPTS AND APPLICATION

IFRS22-1 Where can authoritative IFRS related to accounting changes be found?

IFRS22-2 Briefly describe some of the similarities and differences between GAAP and IFRS with respect to reporting accounting changes.

IFRS22-3 How might differences in presentation of comparative data under GAAP and IFRS affect adoption of IFRS by U.S. companies?

IFRS22-4 What is the indirect effect of a change in accounting policy? Briefly describe the approach to reporting the indirect effects of a change in accounting policy under IFRS.

IFRS22-5 Discuss how a change in accounting policy is handled when it is impracticable to determine previous amounts.

IFRS22-6 Joblonsky Inc. has recently hired a new independent auditor, Karen Ogleby, who says she wants "to get everything straightened out." Consequently, she has proposed the following accounting changes in connection with Joblonsky Inc.'s 2014 financial statements.

1. At December 31, 2013, the client had a receivable of $820,000 from Hendricks Inc. on its statement of financial position. Hendricks Inc. has gone bankrupt, and no recovery is expected. The client proposes to write off the receivable as a prior period item.
2. The client proposes the following changes in depreciation policies.
   (a) For office furniture and fixtures, it proposes to change from a 10-year useful life to an 8-year life. If this change had been made in prior years, retained earnings at December 31, 2013, would have been $250,000 less. The effect of the change on 2014 income alone is a reduction of $60,000.
   (b) For its new equipment in the leasing division, the client proposes to adopt the sum-of-the-years'-digits depreciation method. The client had never used SYD before. The first year the client operated a leasing division was 2014. If straight-line depreciation were used, 2014 income would be $110,000 greater.
3. In preparing its 2013 statements, one of the client's bookkeepers overstated ending inventory by $235,000 because of a mathematical error. The client proposes to treat this item as a prior period adjustment.
4. In the past, the client has spread preproduction costs in its furniture division over 5 years. Because its latest furniture is of the "fad" type, it appears that the largest volume of sales will occur during the first 2 years after introduction. Consequently, the client proposes to amortize preproduction costs on a per-unit basis, which will result in expensing most of such costs during the first 2 years after the furniture's introduction. If the new accounting method had been used prior to 2014, retained earnings at December 31, 2013, would have been $375,000 less.

5. For the nursery division, the client proposes to switch from FIFO to average-cost inventories because it believes that average-cost will provide a better income measure. The effect of making this change on 2014 earnings will be an increase of $320,000. The client says that the effect of the change on December 31, 2013, retained earnings cannot be determined.

6. To achieve an appropriate recognition of revenues and expenses in its building construction division, the client proposes to switch from the cost-recovery method of accounting to the percentage-of-completion method. Had the percentage-of-completion method been employed in all prior years, retained earnings at December 31, 2013, would have been $1,075,000 greater.

Instructions

(a) For each of the changes described above, decide whether:
   (1) The change involves an accounting policy, accounting estimate, or correction of an error.
   (2) Restatement of opening retained earnings is required.
(b) What would be the proper adjustment to the December 31, 2013, retained earnings?

Professional Research

IFRS22-7 As part of the year-end accounting process and review of operating policies, Cullen Co. is considering a change in the accounting for its equipment from the straight-line method to an accelerated method. Your supervisor wonders how the company will report this change in accounting. It has been a few years since he took intermediate accounting, and he cannot remember whether this change would be treated in a retrospective or prospective manner. Your supervisor wants you to research the authoritative guidance on a change in accounting policy related to depreciation methods.

Instructions

Access the IFRS authoritative literature at the IASB website (*http://eifrs.iasb.org/*). (Click on the IFRS tab and then register for free eIFRS access if necessary.) When you have accessed the documents, you can use the search tool in your Internet browser to respond to the following questions. (Provide paragraph citations.)

(a) What are the accounting and reporting guidelines for a change in accounting policy related to depreciation methods?
(b) What are the conditions that justify a change in depreciation method, as contemplated by Cullen Co.?

International Financial Reporting Problem
Marks and Spencer plc

IFRS22-8 The financial statements of Marks and Spencer plc (M&S) are available at the book's companion website or can be accessed at *http://annualreport.marksandspencer.com/assets/downloads/Marks-and-Spencer-Annual-report-and-financial-statements-2012.pdf*.

Instructions

Refer to M&S's financial statements and the accompanying notes to answer the following questions.

(a) Were there changes in accounting policies reported by M&S during the two years covered by its income statements (2011–2012)? If so, describe the nature of the change and the year of change.
(b) What types of estimates did M&S discuss in 2012?

ANSWERS TO IFRS SELF-TEST QUESTIONS

1. a 2. c 3. b 4. a 5. d

Remember to check the book's companion website to find additional resources for this chapter.

LEARNING OBJECTIVES

After studying this chapter, you should be able to:

1 Describe the purpose of the statement of cash flows.

2 Identify the major classifications of cash flows.

3 Prepare a statement of cash flows.

4 Differentiate between net income and net cash flow from operating activities.

5 Determine net cash flows from investing and financing activities.

6 Identify sources of information for a statement of cash flows.

7 Contrast the direct and indirect methods of calculating net cash flow from operating activities.

8 Discuss special problems in preparing a statement of cash flows.

9 Explain the use of a worksheet in preparing a statement of cash flows.

Show Me the Money!

Investors usually look to net income as a key indicator of a company's financial health and future prospects. The following graph shows the net income of one company over a seven-year period.

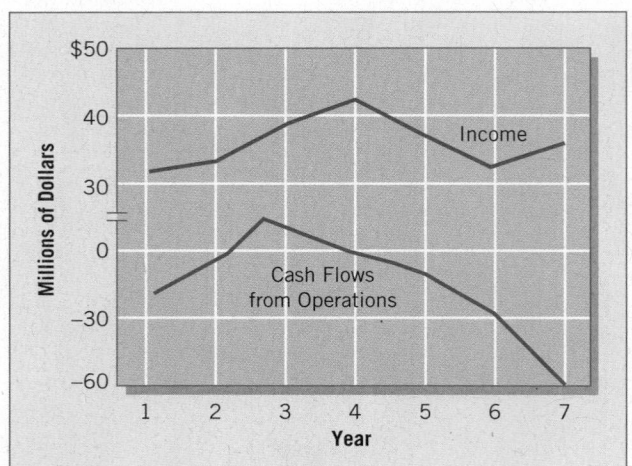

The company showed a pattern of consistent profitability and even some periods of income growth. Between years 1 and 4, net income for this company grew by 32 percent, from $31 million to $41 million. Would you expect its profitability to continue? The company had consistently paid dividends and interest. Would you expect it to continue to do so? Investors answered these questions by buying the company's stock. Eighteen months later, this company—**W. T. Grant**—filed for bankruptcy, in what was then the largest bankruptcy filing in the United States.

How could this happen? As indicated by the second line in the graph, the company had experienced several years of negative cash flow from its operations, even though it reported profits. How can a company have negative cash flows while reporting profits? The answer lays partly in the fact that W. T. Grant was having trouble collecting the receivables from its credit sales, causing cash flow to be less than net income. Investors who analyzed the cash flows would have been likely to find an early warning signal of W. T. Grant's operating problems.

Investors can also look to cash flow information to sniff out companies that can be good buys. As one analyst stated when it comes to valuing stocks: "Show me the money!" Here's the thinking behind that statement. Start with the "cash flows from operations" reported in the statement of cash flows, which (as you will learn in this chapter) consists of net income with non-cash charges (like depreciation and deferred taxes) added back and cash-draining events (like an inventory pile-up) taken out. Now subtract capital expenditures and dividends. What you're left with is free cash flow (as discussed in Chapter 5).

Many analysts like companies trading at low multiples of their free cash flow—low, that is, in relation to rivals today or the same company in past years. Why? They know that reported earnings can be misleading. Case in point: Computer-game firm **Activision Blizzard** reported net income of $113 million in a recent year. But it did better than that. It took in an additional $300 million, mostly for subscriptions to online multiplayer games. It gets the cash now but records the revenue only over time, as the subscriptions run out. A couple of investment houses put this stock on their buy list on the strength of its cash flows. So watch cash flow—to get an indicator of companies headed for trouble, as well as companies that may be undervalued.

Sources: Adapted from James A. Largay III and Clyde P. Stickney, "Cash Flows, Ratio Analysis, and the W. T. Grant Company Bankruptcy," *Financial Analysts Journal* (July–August 1980), p. 51; and D. Fisher, "Cash Doesn't Lie," *Forbes* (April 12, 2010), pp. 52–55.

CONCEPTUAL FOCUS

> See the **Underlying Concepts** on pages 1412 and 1437.
> Read the **Evolving Issue** on page 1433 for a discussion of the direct versus indirect method.

INTERNATIONAL FOCUS

> See the **International Perspectives** on pages 1413, 1415, and 1434.
> Read the **IFRS Insights** on pages 1480–1485 for a discussion of:
  — Significant non-cash transactions
  — Special disclosures

PREVIEW OF CHAPTER	23

As the opening story indicates, examination of **W. T. Grant's** cash flows from operations would have shown the financial inflexibility that eventually caused the company's bankruptcy. This chapter explains the main components of a statement of cash flows and the types of information it provides. The content and organization of the chapter are as follows.

Statement of Cash Flows

Preparation of the Statement	Illustrations—Tax Consultants	Special Problems in Statement Preparation	Use of a Worksheet
• Usefulness of statement • Classification of cash flows • Format of statement • Steps in preparation	• Change in cash • Operating cash flows • Cash flows from investing and financing • Statement of cash flows—2013 • Illustrations—2014 and 2015 • Sources of information • Indirect vs. direct method	• Adjustments to net income • Accounts receivable (net) • Other working capital changes • Net losses • Significant non-cash transactions	• Preparation of worksheet • Analysis of transactions • Preparation of final statement

PREPARATION OF THE STATEMENT OF CASH FLOWS

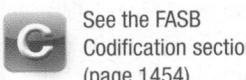

LEARNING OBJECTIVE **1**

Describe the purpose of the statement of cash flows.

The primary purpose of the **statement of cash flows** is to provide information about a company's cash receipts and cash payments during a period. A secondary objective is to provide cash-basis information about the company's operating, investing, and financing activities. The statement of cash flows therefore reports cash receipts, cash payments, and net change in cash resulting from a company's operating, investing, and financing activities during a period. Its format reconciles the beginning and ending cash balances for the period.

Usefulness of the Statement of Cash Flows

See the FASB Codification section (page 1454).

The statement of cash flows provides information to help investors, creditors, and others assess the following [1]:

1. *The entity's ability to generate future cash flows.* A primary objective of financial reporting is to provide information with which to predict the amounts, timing, and uncertainty of future cash flows. By examining relationships between items such as sales and net cash flow from operating activities, or net cash flow from operating activities and increases or decreases in cash, it is possible to better predict the future cash flows than is possible using accrual-basis data alone.

Underlying Concepts

Reporting information in the statement of cash flows contributes to meeting the objective of financial reporting.

2. *The entity's ability to pay dividends and meet obligations.* Simply put, cash is essential. Without adequate cash, a company cannot pay employees, settle debts, pay out dividends, or acquire equipment. A statement of cash flows indicates where the company's cash comes from and how the company uses its cash. Employees, creditors, stockholders, and customers should be particularly interested in this statement, because it alone shows the flows of cash in a business.

3. *The reasons for the difference between net income and net cash flow from operating activities.* The net income number is important: It provides information on the performance of a company from one period to another. But some people are critical of accrual-basis net income because companies must make estimates to arrive at it. Such is not the case with cash. Thus, as the opening story showed, financial statement readers can benefit from knowing why a company's net income and net cash flow from operating activities differ, and can assess for themselves the reliability of the income number.

4. *The cash and noncash investing and financing transactions during the period.* Besides operating activities, companies undertake investing and financing transactions. *Investing* activities include the purchase and sale of assets other than a company's products or services. *Financing* activities include borrowings and repayments of borrowings, investments by owners, and distributions to owners. By examining a company's investing and financing activities, a financial statement reader can better understand why assets and liabilities increased or decreased during the period. For example, by reading the statement of cash flows, the reader might find answers to the following questions:

   - Why did cash decrease for **Home Depot** when it reported net income for the period?
   - How much did **Southwest Airlines** spend on property, plant, and equipment last year?
   - Did dividends paid by **Campbell's Soup** increase?
   - How much money did **Coca-Cola** borrow last year?
   - How much cash did **Hewlett-Packard** use to repurchase its common stock?

Classification of Cash Flows

The statement of cash flows classifies cash receipts and cash payments by operating, investing, and financing activities.[1] Transactions and other events characteristic of each kind of activity are as follows.

2 LEARNING OBJECTIVE

Identify the major classifications of cash flows.

1. **Operating activities** involve the cash effects of transactions that enter into the determination of net income, such as cash receipts from sales of goods and services, and cash payments to suppliers and employees for acquisitions of inventory and expenses.

2. **Investing activities** generally involve long-term assets and include (a) making and collecting loans, and (b) acquiring and disposing of investments and productive long-lived assets.

3. **Financing activities** involve liability and stockholders' equity items and include (a) obtaining cash from creditors and repaying the amounts borrowed, and (b) obtaining capital from owners and providing them with a return on, and a return of, their investment.

Illustration 23-1 classifies the typical cash receipts and payments of a company according to operating, investing, and financing activities. The operating activities category is the most important. It shows the cash provided by company operations. This source of cash is generally considered to be the best measure of a company's ability to generate enough cash to continue as a going concern.

Operating
  Cash inflows
    From sales of goods or services.
    From returns on loans (interest) and on equity
      securities (dividends).
  Cash outflows
    To suppliers for inventory.
    To employees for services.
    To government for taxes.
    To lenders for interest.
    To others for expenses.

          Income Statement Items

Investing
  Cash inflows
    From sale of property, plant, and equipment.
    From sale of debt or equity securities of other entities.
    From collection of principal on loans to other entities.
  Cash outflows
    To purchase property, plant, and equipment.
    To purchase debt or equity securities of other entities.
    To make loans to other entities.

          Generally Long-Term Asset Items

Financing
  Cash inflows
    From sale of equity securities.
    From issuance of debt (bonds and notes).
  Cash outflows
    To stockholders as dividends.
    To redeem long-term debt or reacquire capital stock.

          Generally Long-Term Liability and Equity Items

ILLUSTRATION 23-1
Classification of Typical Cash Inflows and Outflows

[1]The basis recommended by the FASB for the statement of cash flows is actually "cash and cash equivalents." **Cash equivalents** are short-term, highly liquid investments that are both (a) readily convertible to known amounts of cash, and (b) so near their maturity that they present insignificant risk of changes in interest rates. Generally, only investments with original maturities of three months or less qualify under this definition. Examples of cash equivalents are Treasury bills, commercial paper, and money market funds purchased with cash that is in excess of immediate needs.

Although we use the term "cash" throughout our discussion and illustrations, we mean cash and cash equivalents when reporting the cash flows and the net increase or decrease in cash.

International Perspective

According to IFRS, companies can define "cash and cash equivalents" as "net monetary assets"—that is, as "cash and demand deposits and highly liquid investments less short-term borrowings."

Note the following general guidelines about the classification of cash flows.

1. Operating activities involve income statement items.
2. Investing activities involve cash flows resulting from changes in investments and long-term asset items.
3. Financing activities involve cash flows resulting from changes in long-term liability and stockholders' equity items.

Companies classify some cash flows relating to investing or financing activities as operating activities.[2] For example, companies classify receipts of investment income (interest and dividends) and payments of interest to lenders as operating activities. Why are these considered operating activities? Companies report these items in the income statement, where the results of operations are shown.

Conversely, companies classify some cash flows relating to operating activities as investing or financing activities. For example, a company classifies the cash received from the sale of property, plant, and equipment at a gain, although reported in the income statement, as an investing activity. It excludes the effects of the related gain in net cash flow from operating activities. Likewise, a gain or loss on the payment (extinguishment) of debt is generally part of the cash outflow related to the repayment of the amount borrowed. It therefore is a financing activity.

What do the numbers mean?   HOW'S MY CASH FLOW?

To evaluate overall cash flow, it is useful to understand where in the product life cycle a company is. Generally, companies move through several stages of development, which have implications for cash flow. As the following graph shows, the pattern of cash flows from operating, financing, and investing activities will vary depending on the stage of the product life cycle.

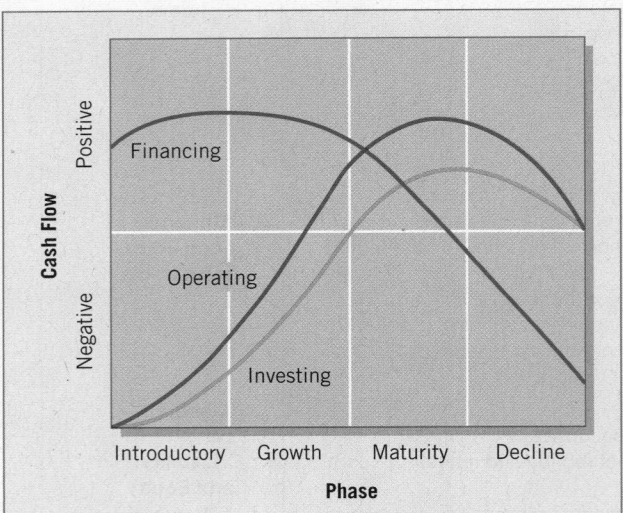

In the introductory phase, the product is likely not generating much revenue (operating cash flow is negative). Because the company is making heavy investments to get a product off the ground, cash flow from investment is negative, and financing cash flows are positive.

[2]Banks and brokers must classify cash flows from purchases and sales of loans and securities specifically for resale and carried at fair value **as operating activities**. This requirement recognizes that for these firms these assets are similar to inventory in other businesses. **[2]**

As the product moves to the growth and maturity phases, these cash flow relationships reverse. The product generates more cash flow from operations, which can be used to cover investments needed to support the product, and less cash is needed from financing. So is a negative operating cash flow bad? Not always. It depends on the product life cycle.

Source: Adapted from Paul D. Kimmel, Jerry J. Weygandt, and Donald E. Kieso, *Financial Accounting: Tools for Business Decision Making*, 6th ed. (New York: John Wiley & Sons, 2011), p. 628.

Format of the Statement of Cash Flows

The three activities we discussed above constitute the general format of the statement of cash flows. The operating activities section always appears first. It is followed by the investing activities section and then the financing activities section.

A company reports the individual inflows and outflows from investing and financing activities separately. That is, a company reports them gross, not netted against one another. Thus, a cash outflow from the purchase of property is reported separately from the cash inflow from the sale of property. Similarly, a cash inflow from the issuance of debt is reported separately from the cash outflow from its retirement.

The net increase or decrease in cash reported during the period should reconcile the beginning and ending cash balances as reported in the comparative balance sheets. The general format of the statement of cash flows presents the results of the three activities discussed previously—operating, investing, and financing. Illustration 23-2 shows a widely used form of the statement of cash flows.

ILLUSTRATION 23-2
Format of the Statement of Cash Flows

COMPANY NAME STATEMENT OF CASH FLOWS PERIOD COVERED		
Cash flows from operating activities		
Net income		XXX
Adjustments to reconcile net income to net cash provided (used) by operating activities:		
(List of individual items)	XX	XX
Net cash provided (used) by operating activities		XXX
Cash flows from investing activities		
(List of individual inflows and outflows)	XX	
Net cash provided (used) by investing activities		XXX
Cash flows from financing activities		
(List of individual inflows and outflows)	XX	
Net cash provided (used) by financing activities		XXX
Net increase (decrease) in cash		XXX
Cash at beginning of period		XXX
Cash at end of period		XXX

International Perspective

Both IFRS and GAAP specify that companies must classify cash flows as operating, investing, or financing.

Steps in Preparation

Companies prepare the statement of cash flows differently from the three other basic financial statements. For one thing, it is not prepared from an adjusted trial balance. The cash flow statement requires detailed information concerning the changes in account balances that occurred between two points in time. An adjusted trial balance will not provide the necessary data. Second, the statement of cash flows deals with cash receipts and payments. As a result, the company must adjust the effects of the use of accrual accounting to determine cash flows. The information to prepare this statement usually comes from three sources:

1. **Comparative balance sheets** provide the amount of the changes in assets, liabilities, and equities from the beginning to the end of the period.
2. **Current income statement data** help determine the amount of cash provided by or used by operations during the period.
3. **Selected transaction data** from the general ledger provide additional detailed information needed to determine how the company provided or used cash during the period.

Preparing the statement of cash flows from the data sources above involves three major steps:

Step 1. *Determine the change in cash.* This procedure is straightforward. A company can easily compute the difference between the beginning and the ending cash balance from examining its comparative balance sheets.

Step 2. *Determine the net cash flow from operating activities.* This procedure is complex. It involves analyzing not only the current year's income statement but also comparative balance sheets as well as selected transaction data.

Step 3. *Determine net cash flows from investing and financing activities.* A company must analyze all other changes in the balance sheet accounts to determine their effects on cash.

On the following pages, we work through these three steps in the process of preparing the statement of cash flows for Tax Consultants Inc. over several years.

ILLUSTRATIONS—TAX CONSULTANTS INC.

LEARNING OBJECTIVE **3**

Prepare a statement of cash flows.

We show the steps in preparing the statement of cash flows using data for Tax Consultants Inc. To begin, we use the **first year of operations** for Tax Consultants Inc. The company started on January 1, 2013, when it issued 60,000 shares of $1 par value common stock for $60,000 cash. The company rented its office space, furniture, and equipment, and performed tax consulting services throughout the first year. The comparative balance sheets at the beginning and end of the year 2013 appear in Illustration 23-3.

ILLUSTRATION 23-3

Comparative Balance Sheets, Tax Consultants Inc., Year 1

TAX CONSULTANTS INC. COMPARATIVE BALANCE SHEETS			
Assets	Dec. 31, 2013	Jan. 1, 2013	Change Increase/Decrease
Cash	$49,000	$-0-	$49,000 Increase
Accounts receivable	36,000	-0-	36,000 Increase
Total	$85,000	$-0-	
Liabilities and Stockholders' Equity			
Accounts payable	$ 5,000	$-0-	$ 5,000 Increase
Common stock ($1 par)	60,000	-0-	60,000 Increase
Retained earnings	20,000	-0-	20,000 Increase
Total	$85,000	$-0-	

Illustration 23-4 shows the income statement and additional information for Tax Consultants.

TAX CONSULTANTS INC.
INCOME STATEMENT
FOR THE YEAR ENDED DECEMBER 31, 2013

Revenues	$125,000
Operating expenses	85,000
Income before income taxes	40,000
Income tax expense	6,000
Net income	$ 34,000

Additional Information
Examination of selected data indicates that a dividend of $14,000 was declared and paid during the year.

ILLUSTRATION 23-4
Income Statement, Tax
Consultants Inc., Year 1

Step 1: Determine the Change in Cash

To prepare a statement of cash flows, the first step is to **determine the change in cash**. This is a simple computation. Tax Consultants had no cash on hand at the beginning of the year 2013. It had $49,000 on hand at the end of 2013. Thus, cash changed (increased) in 2013 by $49,000.

Step 2: Determine Net Cash Flow from Operating Activities

To determine net cash flow from operating activities,[3] companies adjust net income in numerous ways. A useful starting point is to understand why net income must be converted to net cash provided by operating activities.

4 LEARNING OBJECTIVE
Differentiate between net income and net cash flow from operating activities.

Under generally accepted accounting principles, most companies use the accrual basis of accounting. As you have learned, this basis requires that companies record revenue when a performance obligation is met and record expenses when incurred. Revenues may include credit sales for which the company has not yet collected cash. Expenses incurred may include some items that the company has not yet paid in cash. Thus, under the accrual basis of accounting, net income is not the same as net cash flow from operating activities.

To arrive at net cash flow from operating activities, a company must determine revenues and expenses on a **cash basis**. **It does this by eliminating the effects of income statement transactions that do not result in an increase or decrease in cash.** Illustration 23-5 shows the relationship between net income and net cash flow from operating activities.

ILLUSTRATION 23-5
Net Income versus Net
Cash Flow from
Operating Activities

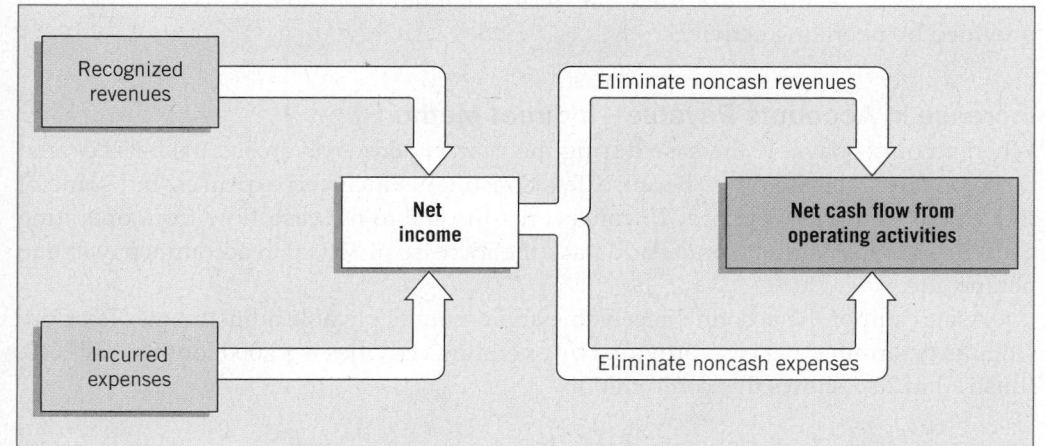

[3]"Net cash flow from operating activities" is a generic phrase, replaced in the statement of cash flows with either "Net cash **provided by** operating activities" if operations increase cash, or "Net cash **used by** operating activities" if operations decrease cash.

In this chapter, we use the term net income to refer to accrual-based net income. A company may convert net income to net cash flow from operating activities through either a direct method or an indirect method. Due to its widespread use in practice, in the following sections we illustrate use of the indirect method. Later in the chapter, we describe the direct method and discuss the advantages and disadvantages of the two methods.[4]

The **indirect method** (or **reconciliation method**) starts with net income and converts it to net cash flow from operating activities. In other words, **the indirect method adjusts net income for items that affected reported net income but did not affect cash**. To compute net cash flow from operating activities, a company adds back noncash charges in the income statement to net income and deducts noncash credits. We explain the two adjustments to net income for Tax Consultants, namely, the increases in accounts receivable and accounts payable, as follows.

Increase in Accounts Receivable—Indirect Method

Tax Consultants' accounts receivable increased by $36,000 (from $0 to $36,000) during the year. For Tax Consultants, this means that cash receipts were $36,000 lower than revenues. The Accounts Receivable account in Illustration 23-6 shows that Tax Consultants had $125,000 in revenues (as reported on the income statement), but it collected only $89,000 in cash.

ILLUSTRATION 23-6
Analysis of Accounts
Receivable

Accounts Receivable				
1/1/13	Balance	–0–	Receipts from customer	89,000
	Revenues	125,000		
12/31/13	Balance	36,000		

As shown in Illustration 23-7, to adjust net income to net cash provided by operating activities, Tax Consultants must deduct the increase of $36,000 in accounts receivable from net income. When the Accounts Receivable balance *decreases*, cash receipts are higher than revenue recognized under the accrual basis. Therefore, the company adds to net income the amount of the decrease in accounts receivable to arrive at net cash provided by operating activities.

Increase in Accounts Payable—Indirect Method

When accounts payable increase during the year, expenses on an accrual basis exceed those on a cash basis. Why? Because Tax Consultants incurred expenses, but some of the expenses are not yet paid. To convert net income to net cash flow from operating activities, Tax Consultants must add back the increase of $5,000 in accounts payable to net income.

As a result of the accounts receivable and accounts payable adjustments, Tax Consultants determines net cash provided by operating activities is $3,000 for the year 2013. Illustration 23-7 shows this computation.

---

[4]*Accounting Trends and Techniques—2012* reports that out of its 500 surveyed companies, 495 (99 percent) used the indirect method, and only 5 used the direct method. *In doing homework assignments, you should follow instructions for use of either the direct or indirect method.*

Net income		$ 34,000
Adjustments to reconcile net income to net		
cash provided by operating activities:		
Increase in accounts receivable	$(36,000)	
Increase in accounts payable	5,000	(31,000)
Net cash provided by operating activities		$ 3,000

ILLUSTRATION 23-7
Computation of Net
Cash Flow from
Operating Activities,
Year 1—Indirect Method

What do the numbers mean? EARNINGS AND CASH FLOW MANAGEMENT?

Investors must be vigilant in their monitoring of management incentives to manipulate both earnings and cash flows. That is, financial success is dependent not only on a company's ability to generate revenues and earnings, but also cash flow. A company that shows profits but is unable to generate cash will also experience waning investor enthusiasm.

Thus, management has an incentive to make operating cash flow look good because Wall Street has paid a premium for companies that generate a lot of cash from operations, rather than through borrowings. However, similar to earnings, companies have ways to pump up cash flow from operations.

One way that companies can boost their operating cash flow is by "securitizing" receivables. That is, companies can speed up cash collections by selling their receivables. For example, Federated Department Stores reported a $2.2 billion increase in cash flow from operations. This seems impressive until you read the fine print, which indicates that a big part of the increase was due to the sale of receivables. As

discussed in this section, decreases in accounts receivable increase cash flow from operations. So while it appeared that Federated's core operations had improved, the company really did little more than accelerate collections of its receivables. In fact, the cash flow from the securitizations represented more than half of Federated's operating cash flow.

Similarly, companies may time the recognition of noncash gains to mask cash flow problems. Take the example of Chesapeake Energy Corp. In a recent quarter, Chesapeake, the second-largest U.S. gas producer, reported a $929 million net profit, nearly double from a year earlier. These results seem pretty good until you take a closer look. Falling commodity prices for natural gas resulted in a 45 percent decrease in Chesapeake's operating cash flow. To plug the hole in its bottom line, the company sold pipeline assets. As a result, all but $3 million of its net income came from these sales and other noncash gains. Thus, in evaluating the quality of accounting, investors must keep an eye on the quality of earnings and cash flows.

Source: Adapted from Ann Tergesen, "Cash Flow Hocus Pocus," *BusinessWeek* (July 16, 2002), pp. 130–131. See also C. Mulford and A. Lopez de Mesa, *Cash Flow Trends and Their Fundamental Drivers: Comprehensive Industry Review*, Georgia Tech Financial Analysis Lab (October 2, 2012); and D. Gilbert, "Chesapeake Plans Increase in Asset Sales as Net Rises," *Wall Street Journal* (August 6, 2012).

Step 3: Determine Net Cash Flows from Investing and Financing Activities

After Tax Consultants has computed the net cash provided by operating activities, the next step is to determine whether any other changes in balance sheet accounts caused an increase or decrease in cash.

For example, an examination of the remaining balance sheet accounts for Tax Consultants shows increases in both common stock and retained earnings. The common stock increase of $60,000 resulted from the issuance of common stock for cash. The issuance of common stock is reported in the statement of cash flows as a receipt of cash from a financing activity.

Two items caused the retained earnings increase of $20,000:

5 LEARNING OBJECTIVE
Determine net cash flows from investing and financing activities.

1. Net income of $34,000 increased retained earnings.
2. Declaration of $14,000 of dividends decreased retained earnings.

Tax Consultants has converted net income into net cash flow from operating activities, as explained earlier. The additional data indicate that it paid the dividend. Thus, the company reports the dividend payment as a cash outflow, classified as a financing activity.

Statement of Cash Flows—2013

We are now ready to prepare the statement of cash flows. The statement starts with the operating activities section. Tax Consultants uses the indirect method to report net cash flow from operating activities.

Illustration 23-8 shows the statement of cash flows for Tax Consultants Inc., for year 1 (2013).

ILLUSTRATION 23-8
Statement of Cash Flows, Tax Consultants Inc., Year 1

TAX CONSULTANTS INC.		
STATEMENT OF CASH FLOWS		
FOR THE YEAR ENDED DECEMBER 31, 2013		
Cash flows from operating activities		
Net income		$ 34,000
Adjustments to reconcile net income to net cash provided by operating activities:		
Increase in accounts receivable	$(36,000)	
Increase in accounts payable	5,000	(31,000)
Net cash provided by operating activities		3,000
Cash flows from financing activities		
Issuance of common stock	60,000	
Payment of cash dividends	(14,000)	
Net cash provided by financing activities		46,000
Net increase in cash		49,000
Cash, January 1, 2013		–0–
Cash, December 31, 2013		$ 49,000

As indicated, the $60,000 increase in common stock results in a financing activity cash inflow. The payment of $14,000 in cash dividends is a financing activity outflow of cash. The $49,000 increase in cash reported in the statement of cash flows agrees with the increase of $49,000 shown in the comparative balance sheets as the change in the Cash account.

Illustration—2014

Tax Consultants Inc. continued to grow and prosper in its second year of operations. The company purchased land, building, and equipment, and revenues and net income increased substantially over the first year. Illustrations 23-9 and 23-10 present information related to the second year of operations for Tax Consultants Inc.

Step 1: Determine the Change in Cash

To prepare a statement of cash flows from the available information, the first step is to determine the change in cash. As indicated from the information presented, cash decreased $12,000 ($49,000 − $37,000).

ILLUSTRATION 23-9
Comparative Balance Sheets, Tax Consultants Inc., Year 2

TAX CONSULTANTS INC.
COMPARATIVE BALANCE SHEETS
AS OF DECEMBER 31

Assets	2014	2013	Change Increase/Decrease
Cash	$ 37,000	$ 49,000	$ 12,000 Decrease
Accounts receivable	26,000	36,000	10,000 Decrease
Prepaid expenses	6,000	-0-	6,000 Increase
Land	70,000	-0-	70,000 Increase
Buildings	200,000	-0-	200,000 Increase
Accumulated depreciation—buildings	(11,000)	-0-	11,000 Increase
Equipment	68,000	-0-	68,000 Increase
Accumulated depreciation—equipment	(10,000)	-0-	10,000 Increase
Total	$386,000	$ 85,000	
Liabilities and Stockholders' Equity			
Accounts payable	$ 40,000	$ 5,000	$ 35,000 Increase
Bonds payable	150,000	-0-	150,000 Increase
Common stock ($1 par)	60,000	60,000	-0-
Retained earnings	136,000	20,000	116,000 Increase
Total	$386,000	$ 85,000	

ILLUSTRATION 23-10
Income Statement, Tax Consultants Inc., Year 2

TAX CONSULTANTS INC.
INCOME STATEMENT
FOR THE YEAR ENDED DECEMBER 31, 2014

Revenues		$492,000
Operating expenses (excluding depreciation)	$269,000	
Depreciation expense	21,000	290,000
Income from operations		202,000
Income tax expense		68,000
Net income		$134,000

Additional Information
(a) The company declared and paid an $18,000 cash dividend.
(b) The company obtained $150,000 cash through the issuance of long-term bonds.
(c) Land, building, and equipment were acquired for cash.

Step 2: Determine Net Cash Flow from Operating Activities—Indirect Method

Using the indirect method, we adjust net income of $134,000 on an accrual basis to arrive at net cash flow from operating activities. Explanations for the adjustments to net income follow.

Decrease in Accounts Receivable. Accounts receivable decreased during the period because cash receipts (cash-basis revenues) are higher than revenues reported on an accrual basis. To convert net income to net cash flow from operating activities, the decrease of $10,000 in accounts receivable must be added to net income.

Increase in Prepaid Expenses. When prepaid expenses (assets) increase during a period, expenses on an accrual-basis income statement are lower than they are on a cash-basis income statement. The reason: Tax Consultants has made cash payments in the current period, but expenses (as charges to the income statement) have been deferred to future periods. To convert net income to net cash flow from operating activities, the company must deduct from net income the increase of $6,000 in prepaid expenses. An increase in prepaid expenses results in a decrease in cash during the period.

Increase in Accounts Payable. Like the increase in 2013, Tax Consultants must add the 2014 increase of $35,000 in accounts payable to net income, to convert to net cash flow from operating activities. The company incurred a greater amount of expense than the amount of cash it disbursed.

Depreciation Expense (Increase in Accumulated Depreciation). The purchase of depreciable assets is a use of cash, shown in the investing section in the year of acquisition. Tax Consultants' depreciation expense of $21,000 (also represented by the increase in accumulated depreciation) is a noncash charge; the company adds it back to net income, to arrive at net cash flow from operating activities. The $21,000 is the sum of the $11,000 depreciation on the building plus the $10,000 depreciation on the equipment.

Certain other periodic charges to expense do not require the use of cash. Examples are the amortization of intangible assets and depletion expense. Such charges are treated in the same manner as depreciation. Companies frequently list depreciation and similar noncash charges as the first adjustments to net income in the statement of cash flows.

As a result of the foregoing items, net cash provided by operating activities is $194,000 as shown in Illustration 23-11.

ILLUSTRATION 23-11
Computation of Net Cash Flow from Operating Activities, Year 2—Indirect Method

Net income		$134,000
Adjustments to reconcile net income to		
net cash provided by operating activities:		
Depreciation expense	$21,000	
Decrease in accounts receivable	10,000	
Increase in prepaid expenses	(6,000)	
Increase in accounts payable	35,000	60,000
Net cash provided by operating activities		$194,000

Step 3: Determine Net Cash Flows from Investing and Financing Activities

After you have determined the items affecting net cash provided by operating activities, the next step involves analyzing the remaining changes in balance sheet accounts. Tax Consultants Inc. analyzed the following accounts.

Increase in Land. As indicated from the change in the Land account, the company purchased land of $70,000 during the period. This transaction is an investing activity, reported as a use of cash.

Increase in Buildings and Related Accumulated Depreciation. As indicated in the additional data and from the change in the Buildings account, Tax Consultants acquired an office building using $200,000 cash. This transaction is a cash outflow, reported in the investing section. The $11,000 increase in accumulated depreciation results from recording depreciation expense on the building. As indicated earlier, the reported depreciation expense has no effect on the amount of cash.

Increase in Equipment and Related Accumulated Depreciation. An increase in equipment of $68,000 resulted because the company used cash to purchase equipment. This transaction is an outflow of cash from an investing activity. The depreciation expense entry for the period explains the increase in Accumulated Depreciation—Equipment.

Increase in Bonds Payable. The Bonds Payable account increased $150,000. Cash received from the issuance of these bonds represents an inflow of cash from a financing activity.

Increase in Retained Earnings. Retained earnings increased $116,000 during the year. Two factors explain this increase. (1) Net income of $134,000 increased retained earnings, and (2) dividends of $18,000 decreased retained earnings. As indicated earlier, the company adjusts net income to net cash provided by operating activities in the operating activities section. Payment of the dividends is a financing activity that involves a cash outflow.

Statement of Cash Flows—2014

Combining the foregoing items, we get a statement of cash flows for 2014 for Tax Consultants Inc., using the indirect method to compute net cash flow from operating activities.

TAX CONSULTANTS INC.
STATEMENT OF CASH FLOWS
FOR THE YEAR ENDED DECEMBER 31, 2014

Cash flows from operating activities		
Net income		$ 134,000
Adjustments to reconcile net income to		
net cash provided by operating activities:		
Depreciation expense	$ 21,000	
Decrease in accounts receivable	10,000	
Increase in prepaid expenses	(6,000)	
Increase in accounts payable	35,000	60,000
Net cash provided by operating activities		194,000
Cash flows from investing activities		
Purchase of land	(70,000)	
Purchase of building	(200,000)	
Purchase of equipment	(68,000)	
Net cash used by investing activities		(338,000)
Cash flows from financing activities		
Issuance of bonds	150,000	
Payment of cash dividends	(18,000)	
Net cash provided by financing activities		132,000
Net decrease in cash		(12,000)
Cash, January 1, 2014		49,000
Cash, December 31, 2014		$ 37,000

ILLUSTRATION 23-12
Statement of Cash Flows, Tax Consultants Inc., Year 2

Illustration—2015

Our third example, covering the 2015 operations of Tax Consultants Inc., is more complex. It again uses the indirect method to compute and present net cash flow from operating activities.

Tax Consultants Inc. experienced continued success in 2015 and expanded its operations to include the sale of computer software used in tax-return preparation and tax planning. Thus, inventory is a new asset appearing in the company's December 31, 2015, balance sheet. Illustrations 23-13 and 23-14 (on page 1424) show the comparative balance sheets, income statements, and selected data for 2015.

Step 1: Determine the Change in Cash

The first step in the preparation of the statement of cash flows is to determine the change in cash. As the comparative balance sheets show, cash increased $17,000 in 2015.

ILLUSTRATION 23-13
Comparative Balance
Sheets, Tax Consultants
Inc., Year 3

TAX CONSULTANTS INC.
COMPARATIVE BALANCE SHEETS
AS OF DECEMBER 31

Assets	2015	2014	Change Increase/Decrease
Cash	$ 54,000	$ 37,000	$ 17,000 Increase
Accounts receivable	68,000	26,000	42,000 Increase
Inventory	54,000	–0–	54,000 Increase
Prepaid expenses	4,000	6,000	2,000 Decrease
Land	45,000	70,000	25,000 Decrease
Buildings	200,000	200,000	–0–
Accumulated depreciation—buildings	(21,000)	(11,000)	10,000 Increase
Equipment	193,000	68,000	125,000 Increase
Accumulated depreciation—equipment	(28,000)	(10,000)	18,000 Increase
Totals	$569,000	$386,000	
Liabilities and Stockholders' Equity			
Accounts payable	$ 33,000	$ 40,000	$ 7,000 Decrease
Bonds payable	110,000	150,000	40,000 Decrease
Common stock ($1 par)	220,000	60,000	160,000 Increase
Retained earnings	206,000	136,000	70,000 Increase
Totals	$569,000	$386,000	

ILLUSTRATION 23-14
Income Statement, Tax
Consultants Inc., Year 3

TAX CONSULTANTS INC.
INCOME STATEMENT
FOR THE YEAR ENDED DECEMBER 31, 2015

Revenues		$890,000
Cost of goods sold	$465,000	
Operating expenses	221,000	
Interest expense	12,000	
Loss on sale of equipment	2,000	700,000
Income from operations		190,000
Income tax expense		65,000
Net income		$125,000

Additional Information
(a) Operating expenses include depreciation expense of $33,000 and expiration of prepaid expenses of $2,000.
(b) Land was sold at its book value for cash.
(c) Cash dividends of $55,000 were declared and paid.
(d) Interest expense of $12,000 was paid in cash.
(e) Equipment with a cost of $166,000 was purchased for cash. Equipment with a cost of $41,000 and a book value of $36,000 was sold for $34,000 cash.
(f) Bonds were redeemed at their book value for cash.
(g) Common stock ($1 par) was issued for cash.

Step 2: Determine Net Cash Flow from Operating Activities—Indirect Method

We explain the adjustments to net income of $125,000 as follows.

Increase in Accounts Receivable. The increase in accounts receivable of $42,000 represents recorded accrual-basis revenues in excess of cash collections in 2015. The company deducts this increase from net income to convert from the accrual basis to the cash basis.

Increase in Inventory. The $54,000 increase in inventory represents an operating use of cash, not an expense. Tax Consultants therefore deducts this amount from net income, to arrive at net cash flow from operations. In other words, when inventory purchased exceeds inventory sold during a period, cost of goods sold on an accrual basis is lower than on a cash basis.

Decrease in Prepaid Expenses. The $2,000 decrease in prepaid expenses represents a charge to the income statement for which Tax Consultants made no cash payment in the current period. The company adds back the decrease to net income, to arrive at net cash flow from operating activities.

Decrease in Accounts Payable. When accounts payable decrease during the year, cost of goods sold and expenses on a cash basis are higher than they are on an accrual basis. To convert net income to net cash flow from operating activities, the company must deduct the $7,000 in accounts payable from net income.

Depreciation Expense (Increase in Accumulated Depreciation). Accumulated Depreciation—Buildings increased $10,000 ($21,000 − $11,000). The Buildings account did not change during the period, which means that Tax Consultants recorded depreciation expense of $10,000 in 2015.

Accumulated Depreciation—Equipment increased by $18,000 ($28,000 − $10,000) during the year. But Accumulated Depreciation—Equipment decreased by $5,000 as a result of the sale during the year. Thus, depreciation for the year was $23,000. The company reconciled Accumulated Depreciation—Equipment as follows.

Beginning balance	$10,000
Add: Depreciation for 2015	23,000
	33,000
Deduct: Sale of equipment	5,000
Ending balance	$28,000

The company must add back to net income the total depreciation of $33,000 ($10,000 + $23,000) charged to the income statement, to determine net cash flow from operating activities.

Loss on Sale of Equipment. Tax Consultants Inc. sold for $34,000 equipment that cost $41,000 and had a book value of $36,000. As a result, the company reported a loss of $2,000 on its sale. To arrive at net cash flow from operating activities, it must add back to net income the loss on the sale of the equipment. The reason is that the loss is a noncash charge to the income statement. The loss did not reduce cash, but it did reduce net income.[5]

From the foregoing items, the company prepares the operating activities section of the statement of cash flows, as shown in Illustration 23-15.

Cash flows from operating activities		
Net income		$125,000
Adjustments to reconcile net income to		
net cash provided by operating activities:		
Depreciation expense	$ 33,000	
Loss on sale of equipment	2,000	
Increase in accounts receivable	(42,000)	
Increase in inventory	(54,000)	
Decrease in prepaid expenses	2,000	
Decrease in accounts payable	(7,000)	(66,000)
Net cash provided by operating activities		59,000

ILLUSTRATION 23-15
Operating Activities Section of Cash Flow Statement

---

[5]A similar adjustment is required for unrealized gains or losses recorded on trading security investments or other financial assets and liabilities accounted for under the fair value option. Marking these assets and liabilities to fair value results in an increase or decrease in income, but there is no effect on cash flows.

Step 3: Determine Net Cash Flows from Investing and Financing Activities

By analyzing the remaining changes in the balance sheet accounts, Tax Consultants identifies cash flows from investing and financing activities.

Land. Land decreased $25,000 during the period. As indicated from the information presented, the company sold land for cash at its book value. This transaction is an investing activity, reported as a $25,000 source of cash.

Equipment. An analysis of the Equipment account indicates the following.

Beginning balance	$ 68,000
Purchase of equipment	166,000
	234,000
Deduct: Sale of equipment	41,000
Ending balance	$193,000

The company used cash to purchase equipment with a fair value of $166,000—an investing transaction reported as a cash outflow. The sale of the equipment for $34,000 is also an investing activity, but one that generates a cash inflow.

Bonds Payable. Bonds payable decreased $40,000 during the year. As indicated from the additional information, the company redeemed the bonds at their book value. This financing transaction used $40,000 of cash.

Common Stock. The Common Stock account increased $160,000 during the year. As indicated from the additional information, Tax Consultants issued common stock of $160,000 at par. This financing transaction provided cash of $160,000.

Retained Earnings. Retained earnings changed $70,000 ($206,000 − $136,000) during the year. The $70,000 change in retained earnings results from net income of $125,000 from operations and the financing activity of paying cash dividends of $55,000.

Statement of Cash Flows—2015

Tax Consultants Inc. combines the foregoing items to prepare the statement of cash flows shown in Illustration 23-16.

Sources of Information for the Statement of Cash Flows

LEARNING OBJECTIVE 6

Identify sources of information for a statement of cash flows.

Important points to remember in the preparation of the statement of cash flows are these:

1. Comparative balance sheets provide the basic information from which to prepare the report. Additional information obtained from analyses of specific accounts is also included.
2. An analysis of the Retained Earnings account is necessary. The net increase or decrease in Retained Earnings without any explanation is a meaningless amount in the statement. Without explanation, it might represent the effect of net income, dividends declared, or prior period adjustments.
3. The statement includes all changes that have passed through cash or have resulted in an increase or decrease in cash.
4. Write-downs, amortization charges, and similar "book" entries, such as depreciation of plant assets, represent neither inflows nor outflows of cash because they have no effect on cash. To the extent that they have entered into the determination of net income, however, the company must add them back to or subtract them from net income, to arrive at net cash provided (used) by operating activities.

TAX CONSULTANTS INC.
STATEMENT OF CASH FLOWS
FOR THE YEAR ENDED DECEMBER 31, 2015

Cash flows from operating activities		
Net income		$ 125,000
Adjustments to reconcile net income to		
net cash provided by operating activities:		
Depreciation expense	$ 33,000	
Loss on sale of equipment	2,000	
Increase in accounts receivable	(42,000)	
Increase in inventory	(54,000)	
Decrease in prepaid expenses	2,000	
Decrease in accounts payable	(7,000)	(66,000)
Net cash provided by operating activities		59,000
Cash flows from investing activities		
Sale of land	25,000	
Sale of equipment	34,000	
Purchase of equipment	(166,000)	
Net cash used by investing activities		(107,000)
Cash flows from financing activities		
Redemption of bonds	(40,000)	
Sale of common stock	160,000	
Payment of dividends	(55,000)	
Net cash provided by financing activities		65,000
Net increase in cash		17,000
Cash, January 1, 2015		37,000
Cash, December 31, 2015		$ 54,000

ILLUSTRATION 23-16
Statement of Cash Flows,
Tax Consultants Inc.,
Year 3

Indirect Method—Additional Adjustments

For consistency and comparability and because it is the most widely used method in practice, we used the indirect method in the Tax Consultants' illustrations. We determined net cash flow from operating activities by adding back to or deducting from net income those items that had no effect on cash. Illustration 23-17 presents a more complete set of common adjustments that companies make to net income to arrive at net cash flow from operating activities.

ILLUSTRATION 23-17
Adjustments Needed to
Determine Net Cash
Flow from Operating
Activities—Indirect
Method

The additions and deductions in Illustration 23-17 reconcile net income to net cash flow from operating activities, illustrating why the indirect method is also called the reconciliation method.

Net Cash Flow from Operating Activities—Direct Method

Two different methods are available to adjust income from operations on an accrual basis to net cash flow from operating activities. We showed the indirect method in the Tax Consultants' illustrations in the prior sections.

The **direct method** reports cash receipts and cash disbursements from operating activities. The difference between these two amounts is the net cash flow from operating activities. In other words, the direct method deducts operating cash disbursements from operating cash receipts. The direct method results in the presentation of a condensed cash receipts and cash disbursements statement.

As indicated from the accrual-based income statement (see Illustration 23-4 on page 1417), Tax Consultants reported revenues of $125,000. However, because the company's accounts receivable increased during 2013 by $36,000, the company collected only $89,000 ($125,000 − $36,000) in cash from these revenues. Similarly, Tax Consultants reported operating expenses of $85,000. However, accounts payable increased during the period by $5,000. Assuming that these payables relate to operating expenses, cash operating expenses were $80,000 ($85,000 − $5,000). Because no taxes payable exist at the end of the year, the company must have paid $6,000 income tax expense for 2013 in cash during the year. Tax Consultants computes net cash flow from operating activities as shown in Illustration 23-18.

ILLUSTRATION 23-18
Computation of Net Cash Flow from Operating Activities, Year 1—Direct Method

Cash collected from revenues	$89,000
Cash payments for expenses	80,000
Income before income taxes	9,000
Cash payments for income taxes	6,000
Net cash provided by operating activities	$ 3,000

"Net cash provided by operating activities" is the equivalent of cash basis net income. ("Net cash used by operating activities" is equivalent to cash basis net loss.)

The FASB encourages use of the direct method and permits use of the indirect method. Yet, if the direct method is used, the Board requires that companies provide in a separate schedule a reconciliation of net income to net cash flow from operating activities. Therefore, under either method, companies must prepare and report information from the indirect (reconciliation) method.

Direct Method—Expanded Example

Under the direct method, the statement of cash flows reports net cash flow from operating activities as major classes of *operating cash receipts* (e.g., cash collected from customers and cash received from interest and dividends) and *cash disbursements* (e.g., cash paid to suppliers for goods, to employees for services, to creditors for interest, and to government authorities for taxes).

We illustrate the direct method here in more detail to help you understand the difference between accrual-based income and net cash flow from operating activities. This example also illustrates the data needed to apply the direct method. Emig Company, which began business on January 1, 2014, has the following selected balance sheet information.

ILLUSTRATION 23-19
Balance Sheet Accounts,
Emig Co.

	December 31, 2014	January 1, 2014
Cash	$159,000	-0-
Accounts receivable	15,000	-0-
Inventory	160,000	-0-
Prepaid expenses	8,000	-0-
Property, plant, and equipment (net)	90,000	-0-
Accounts payable	60,000	-0-
Accrued expenses payable	20,000	-0-

Emig Company's December 31, 2014, income statement and additional information are as follows.

ILLUSTRATION 23-20
Income Statement,
Emig Co.

Sales revenue		$780,000
Cost of goods sold		450,000
Gross profit		330,000
Operating expenses	$160,000	
Depreciation	10,000	170,000
Income before income taxes		160,000
Income tax expense		48,000
Net income		$112,000

Additional Information
(a) Dividends of $70,000 were declared and paid in cash.
(b) The accounts payable increase resulted from the purchase of merchandise.
(c) Prepaid expenses and accrued expenses payable relate to operating expenses.

Under the **direct method**, companies compute net cash provided by operating activities by **adjusting each item in the income statement** from the accrual basis to the cash basis. To simplify and condense the operating activities section, only major classes of operating cash receipts and cash payments are reported. As Illustration 23-21 shows, the difference between these major classes of cash receipts and cash payments is the net cash provided by operating activities.

ILLUSTRATION 23-21
Major Classes of Cash
Receipts and Payments

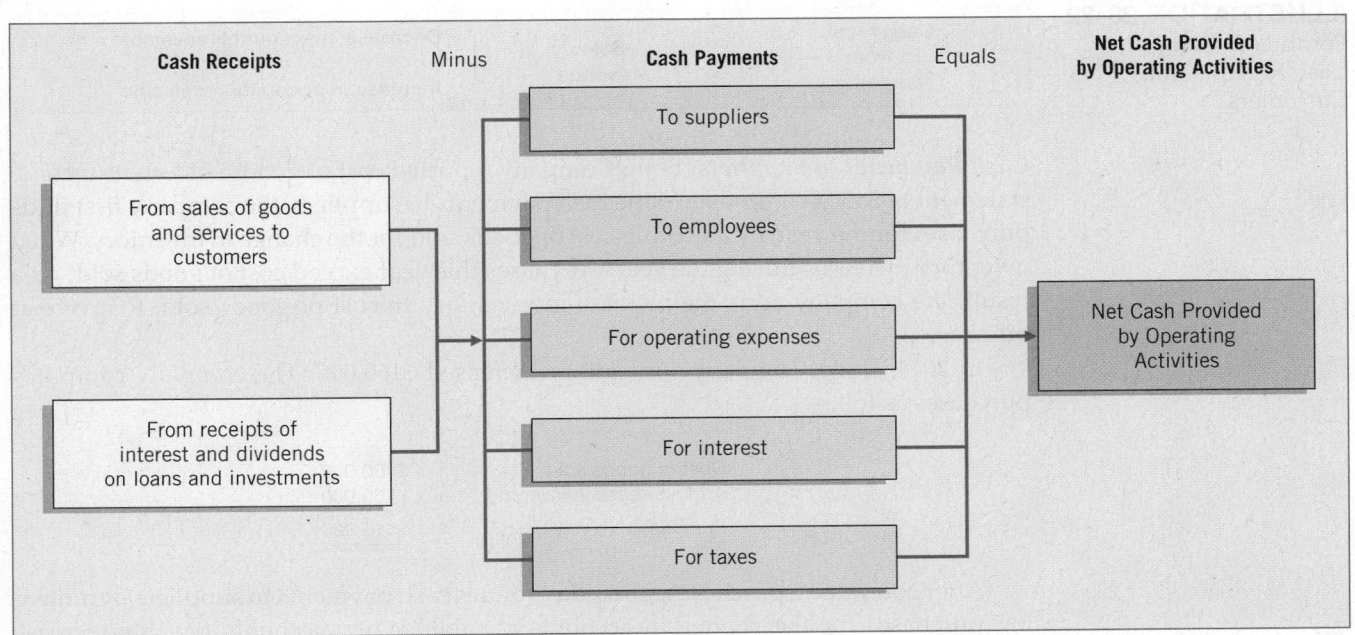

An efficient way to apply the direct method is to analyze the revenues and expenses reported in the income statement in the order in which they are listed. The company then determines cash receipts and cash payments related to these revenues and expenses. In the following sections, we present the direct method adjustments for Emig Company in 2014, to determine net cash provided by operating activities.

Cash Receipts from Customers. The income statement for Emig Company reported revenues from customers of $780,000. To determine cash receipts from customers, the company considers the change in accounts receivable during the year.

When accounts receivable increase during the year, revenues on an accrual basis are higher than cash receipts from customers. In other words, operations led to increased revenues, but not all of these revenues resulted in cash receipts. To determine the amount of increase in cash receipts, deduct the amount of the increase in accounts receivable from the total sales revenue. Conversely, a decrease in accounts receivable is added to sales revenue because cash receipts from customers then exceed sales revenue.

For Emig Company, accounts receivable increased $15,000. Thus, cash receipts from customers were $765,000, computed as follows.

Sales revenue	$780,000
Deduct: Increase in accounts receivable	15,000
Cash receipts from customers	$765,000

Emig could also determine cash receipts from customers by analyzing the Accounts Receivable account as shown below.

Accounts Receivable				
1/1/14	Balance	–0–	Receipts from customers	765,000
	Sales revenue	780,000		
12/31/14	Balance	15,000		

Illustration 23-22 shows the relationships between cash receipts from customers, sales revenue, and changes in accounts receivable.

ILLUSTRATION 23-22
Formula to Compute
Cash Receipts from
Customers

Cash receipts from customers	=	Sales revenue	{ + **Decrease in accounts receivable** or – **Increase in accounts receivable**

Cash Payments to Suppliers. Emig Company reported cost of goods sold on its income statement of $450,000. To determine cash payments to suppliers, the company first finds purchases for the year, by adjusting cost of goods sold for the change in inventory. When inventory increases during the year, purchases this year exceed cost of goods sold. As a result, the company adds the increase in inventory to cost of goods sold, to arrive at purchases.

In 2014, Emig Company's inventory increased $160,000. The company computes purchases as follows.

Cost of goods sold	$450,000
Add: Increase in inventory	160,000
Purchases	$610,000

After computing purchases, Emig determines cash payments to suppliers by adjusting purchases for the change in accounts payable. When accounts payable increase during the year, purchases on an accrual basis are higher than they are on a cash basis. As a result, the company deducts from purchases the increase in accounts payable to arrive at cash payments to suppliers. Conversely, if cash payments to suppliers exceed purchases, Emig adds to purchases the decrease in accounts payable. Cash payments to suppliers were $550,000, computed as follows.

Purchases	$610,000
Deduct: Increase in accounts payable	60,000
Cash payments to suppliers	$550,000

Emig also can determine cash payments to suppliers by analyzing Accounts Payable, as shown below.

Accounts Payable

Payments to suppliers	550,000	1/1/14	Balance		–0–
			Purchases		610,000
		12/31/14	Balance		60,000

Illustration 23-23 shows the relationships between cash payments to suppliers, cost of goods sold, changes in inventory, and changes in accounts payable.

ILLUSTRATION 23-23
Formula to Compute Cash Payments to Suppliers

Cash Payments for Operating Expenses. Emig reported operating expenses of $160,000 on its income statement. To determine the cash paid for operating expenses, it must adjust this amount for any changes in prepaid expenses and accrued expenses payable.

For example, when prepaid expenses increased $8,000 during the year, cash paid for operating expenses was $8,000 higher than operating expenses reported on the income statement. To convert operating expenses to cash payments for operating expenses, the company adds to operating expenses the increase of $8,000. Conversely, if prepaid expenses decrease during the year, it deducts from operating expenses the amount of the decrease.

Emig also must adjust operating expenses for changes in accrued expenses payable. When accrued expenses payable increase during the year, operating expenses on an accrual basis are higher than they are on a cash basis. As a result, the company deducts from operating expenses an increase in accrued expenses payable, to arrive at cash payments for operating expenses. Conversely, it adds to operating expenses a decrease in accrued expenses payable, because cash payments exceed operating expenses.

Emig's cash payments for operating expenses were $148,000, computed as follows.

Operating expenses	$160,000
Add: Increase in prepaid expenses	8,000
Deduct: Increase in accrued expenses payable	20,000
Cash payments for operating expenses	$148,000

The relationships among cash payments for operating expenses, changes in prepaid expenses, and changes in accrued expenses payable are shown in Illustration 23-24 (page 1432).

ILLUSTRATION 23-24
Formula to Compute
Cash Payments for
Operating Expenses

Cash payments for operating expenses	=	Operating expenses	+ Increase in prepaid expense or − Decrease in prepaid expense	+ Decrease in accrued expenses payable or − Increase in accrued expenses payable

Note that the company did not consider depreciation expense because it is a noncash charge.

Cash Payments for Income Taxes. The income statement for Emig shows income tax expense of $48,000. This amount equals the cash paid. How do we know that? Because the comparative balance sheet indicated no income taxes payable at either the beginning or end of the year.

Summary of Net Cash Flow from Operating Activities—Direct Method
The following schedule summarizes the computations illustrated above.

ILLUSTRATION 23-25
Accrual Basis to Cash
Basis

Accrual Basis		Adjustment	Add (Subtract)	Cash Basis
Sales revenue	$780,000	− Increase in accounts receivable	$ (15,000)	$765,000
Cost of goods sold	450,000	+ Increase in inventory	160,000	
		− Increase in accounts payable	(60,000)	550,000
Operating expenses	160,000	+ Increase in prepaid expenses	8,000	
		− Increase in accrued expenses payable	(20,000)	148,000
Depreciation expense	10,000	− Depreciation expense	(10,000)	–0–
Income tax expense	48,000			48,000
Total expense	668,000			746,000
Net income	$112,000	Net cash provided by operating activities		$ 19,000

Illustration 23-26 shows the presentation of the direct method for reporting net cash flow from operating activities for the Emig Company illustration.

ILLUSTRATION 23-26
Operating Activities
Section—Direct Method,
2014

EMIG COMPANY
STATEMENT OF CASH FLOWS (PARTIAL)

Cash flows from operating activities		
Cash received from customers		$765,000
Cash payments:		
To suppliers	$550,000	
For operating expenses	148,000	
For income taxes	48,000	746,000
Net cash provided by operating activities		$ 19,000

If Emig Company uses the direct method to present the net cash flow from operating activities, it must provide in a separate schedule the reconciliation of net income to net cash provided by operating activities. The reconciliation assumes the identical form and content of the indirect method of presentation, as the following shows.

ILLUSTRATION 23-27
Reconciliation of Net
Income to Net Cash
Provided by Operating
Activities

EMIG COMPANY		
RECONCILIATION		
Net income		$112,000
Adjustments to reconcile net income to net cash		
provided by operating activities:		
Depreciation expense	$ 10,000	
Increase in accounts receivable	(15,000)	
Increase in inventory	(160,000)	
Increase in prepaid expenses	(8,000)	
Increase in accounts payable	60,000	
Increase in accrued expense payable	20,000	(93,000)
Net cash provided by operating activities		$ 19,000

When the direct method is used, the company may present this reconciliation at the bottom of the statement of cash flows or in a separate schedule.

Evolving Issue   DIRECT VERSUS INDIRECT

The most contentious decision that the FASB faced related to cash flow reporting was choosing between the direct method and the indirect method of determining net cash flow from operating activities. Companies lobbied *against* the direct method, urging adoption of the indirect method. Commercial lending officers expressed to the FASB a strong preference in favor of the direct method. What are the arguments in favor of each of the methods?

In Favor of the Direct Method
The principal advantage of the direct method is that **it shows operating cash receipts and payments**. Thus, it is more consistent with the objective of a statement of cash flows—to provide information about cash receipts and cash payments—than the indirect method, which does not report operating cash receipts and payments.

Supporters of the direct method contend that knowledge of the specific sources of operating cash receipts and the purposes for which operating cash payments were made in past periods is useful in estimating future operating cash flows. Furthermore, information about amounts of major classes of operating cash receipts and payments is more useful than information only about their arithmetic sum (the net cash flow from operating activities). Such information is more revealing of a company's ability (1) to generate sufficient cash from operating activities to pay its debts, (2) to reinvest in its operations, and (3) to make distributions to its owners. **[3]**

Many companies indicate that they do not currently collect information in a manner that allows them to determine amounts such as cash received from customers or cash paid to suppliers directly from their accounting systems. But supporters of the direct method contend that the incremental cost of determining operating cash receipts and payments is not significant.

In Favor of the Indirect Method
The principal advantage of the indirect method is that **it focuses on the differences between net income and net cash flow from operating activities**. That is, it provides a useful link between the statement of cash flows and the income statement and balance sheet.

Many companies contend that it is less costly to adjust net income to net cash flow from operating activities (indirect) than it is to report gross operating cash receipts and payments (direct). Supporters of the indirect method also state that the direct method, which effectively reports income statement information on a cash rather than an accrual basis, may erroneously suggest that net cash flow from operating activities is as good as, or better than, net income as a measure of performance.

In their joint financial statement presentation project, the FASB and the IASB have proposed to allow only the direct method. However, there has been significant pushback on this proposal, which suggests that the choice of either the direct or indirect method will continue to be available.

Source: See *http://www.fasb.org*; click on Projects and then on Inactive Joint FASB/IASB Projects.

Special Reporting Rules Applying to Direct and Indirect Methods
Companies that use the direct method are required, at a minimum, to report separately the following classes of operating cash receipts and payments:

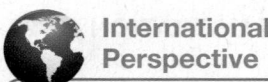

International Perspective

Consolidated statements of cash flows may be of limited use to analysts evaluating multinational companies. Without disaggregation, users of such statements are not able to determine "where in the world" the funds are sourced and used.

Receipts

1. Cash collected from customers (including lessees, licensees, etc.).

2. Interest and dividends received.

3. Other operating cash receipts, if any.

Payments

1. Cash paid to employees and suppliers of goods or services (including suppliers of insurance, advertising, etc.).

2. Interest paid.

3. Income taxes paid.

4. Other operating cash payments, if any.

The FASB encourages companies to provide further breakdowns of operating cash receipts and payments that they consider meaningful.

Companies using the indirect method must disclose separately changes in inventory, receivables, and payables in order to reconcile net income to net cash flow from operating activities. In addition, they must disclose, elsewhere in the financial statements or in accompanying notes, interest paid (net of amount capitalized) and income taxes paid.[6] The FASB requires these separate and additional disclosures so that users may approximate the direct method. Also, an acceptable alternative presentation of the indirect method is to report net cash flow from operating activities as a single line item in the statement of cash flows and to present the reconciliation details elsewhere in the financial statements.

Finally, the FASB **encourages** the use of the direct method over the indirect method. If a company uses the direct method of reporting net cash flow from operating activities, the FASB **requires** that the company provide in a separate schedule a reconciliation of net income to net cash flow from operating activities. If a company uses the indirect method, it can either report the reconciliation within the statement of cash flows or can provide it in a separate schedule, with the statement of cash flows reporting only the **net** cash flow from operating activities. **[4]**

SPECIAL PROBLEMS IN STATEMENT PREPARATION

LEARNING OBJECTIVE 8

Discuss special problems in preparing a statement of cash flows.

We discussed some of the special problems related to preparing the statement of cash flows in connection with the preceding illustrations. Other problems that arise with some frequency in the preparation of this statement include the following.

1. Adjustments to net income.

2. Accounts receivable (net).

3. Other working capital changes.

4. Net losses.

5. Significant noncash transactions.

---

[6]*Accounting Trends and Techniques—2012* reports that of the 500 companies surveyed, 207 disclosed interest paid in notes to the financial statements, 257 disclosed interest paid at the bottom of the statement of cash flows, 7 disclosed interest paid within the statement of cash flows, and 29 reported no separate amount. Income taxes paid during the year were disclosed in a manner similar to interest payments.

Adjustments to Net Income

Depreciation and Amortization

Depreciation expense is the most common adjustment to net income that companies make to arrive at net cash flow from operating activities. But there are numerous other noncash expense or revenue items. Examples of expense items that companies must add back to net income are the **amortization of limited-life intangible assets** such as patents, and the **amortization of deferred costs** such as bond issue costs. These charges to expense involve expenditures made in prior periods that a company amortizes currently. These charges reduce net income without affecting cash in the current period.

Also, **amortization of bond discount or premium** on long-term bonds payable affects the amount of interest expense. However, neither affects cash. As a result, a company should add back discount amortization and subtract premium amortization from net income to arrive at net cash flow from operating activities.

Postretirement Benefit Costs

If a company has postretirement costs such as an employee pension plan, chances are that the pension expense recorded during a period will either be higher or lower than the cash funded. It will be higher when there is an unfunded liability and will be lower when there is a pension asset. When the expense is higher or lower than the cash paid, **the company must adjust net income by the difference between cash paid and the expense reported** in computing net cash flow from operating activities.

Changes in Deferred Income Taxes

Changes in deferred income taxes affect net income but have no effect on cash. For example, Delta Airlines reported an increase in its liability for deferred taxes of approximately $1.2 billion. This change in the liability increased tax expense and decreased net income, but did not affect cash. Therefore, Delta added back $1.2 billion to net income on its statement of cash flows.

Equity Method of Accounting

Another common adjustment to net income is **a change related to an investment in common stock** when recording income or loss under the equity method. Recall that under the equity method, the investor (1) debits the investment account and credits revenue for its share of the investee's net income, and (2) credits dividends received to the investment account. Therefore, the net increase in the investment account does not affect cash flow. A company must deduct the net increase from net income to arrive at net cash flow from operating activities.

Assume that Victor Co. owns 40 percent of Milo Inc. During the year, Milo reports net income of $100,000 and pays a cash dividend of $30,000. Victor reports this in its statement of cash flows as a deduction from net income in the following manner—Equity in earnings of Milo, net of dividends, $28,000 [($100,000 − $30,000) × 40%].

Losses and Gains

Realized Losses and Gains. In the illustration for Tax Consultants, the company experienced a loss of $2,000 from the sale of equipment. The company added this loss to net income to compute net cash flow from operating activities because **the loss is a noncash charge in the income statement**.

If Tax Consultants experiences a **gain** from a sale of equipment, it too requires an adjustment to net income. Because a company reports the gain in the statement of cash flows as part of the cash proceeds from the sale of equipment under investing activities, **it deducts the gain from net income to avoid double-counting**—once as part of net income and again as part of the cash proceeds from the sale.

To illustrate, assume that Tax Consultants had land with a carrying value of $200,000, which was condemned by the state government for a highway project. The condemnation proceeds received were $205,000, resulting in a gain of $5,000. In the statement of cash flows (indirect method), the company would deduct the $5,000 gain from net income in the operating activities section. It would report the $205,000 cash inflow from the condemnation as an investing activity, as follows.

Cash flows from investing activities	
Condemnation of land	$205,000

Unrealized Losses and Gains. Unrealized losses and gains generally occur for debt investments and for equity investments. For example, assume that **Target** purchases the following two investments on January 10, 2014.

1. Debt investment for $1 million that is classified as trading. During 2014, the debt investment has an unrealized holding gain of $110,000 (recorded in net income).
2. Equity investment for $600,000 that is classified as available-for-sale. During 2014, the available-for-sale equity investment has an unrealized holding loss of $50,000 (recorded in other comprehensive income).

For Target, the unrealized holding gain of $110,000 on the debt investment increases net income but does not increase net cash flow from operating activities. As a result, the unrealized holding gain of $110,000 is deducted from net income to compute net cash flow from operating activities.

On the other hand, the unrealized holding loss of $50,000 that Target incurs on the available-for-sale equity investment does not affect net income or cash flows—this loss is reported in the other comprehensive income section. As a result, no adjustment to net income is necessary in computing net cash flow from operating activities.

Thus, the general rule is that unrealized holding gains or losses that affect net income must be adjusted to determine net cash flow from operating activities. Conversely, unrealized holding gains or losses that do not affect net income are not adjusted to determine net cash flow from operating activities.

Stock Options

Recall for share-based compensation plans that companies are required to use the fair value method to determine total compensation cost. The compensation cost is then recognized as an expense in the periods in which the employee provides services. When Compensation Expense is debited, Paid-in Capital—Stock Options is often credited. Cash is not affected by recording the expense. **Therefore, the company must increase net income by the amount of compensation expense from stock options in computing net cash flow from operating activities.**

To illustrate how this information should be reported on a statement of cash flows, assume that First Wave Inc. grants 5,000 options to its CEO, Ann Johnson. Each option entitles Johnson to purchase one share of First Wave's $1 par value common stock at $50 per share at any time in the next two years (the service period). The fair value of the options is $200,000. First Wave records compensation expense in the first year as follows.

Compensation Expense ($200,000 ÷ 2)	100,000	
Paid-in Capital—Stock Options		100,000

In addition, if we assume that First Wave has a 35 percent tax rate, it would recognize a deferred tax asset of $35,000 ($100,000 × 35%) in the first year as follows.

Deferred Tax Asset	35,000	
Income Tax Expense		35,000

Therefore, on the statement of cash flows for the first year, First Wave reports the following (assuming a net income of $600,000).

Net income	$600,000
Adjustments to reconcile net income to net cash provided by operating activities:	
Share-based compensation expense	100,000
Increase in deferred tax asset	(35,000)

As shown in First Wave's statement of cash flows, it adds the share-based compensation expense to net income because it is a noncash expense. The increase in the deferred tax asset and the related reduction in income tax expense increase net income. Although the negative income tax expense increases net income, it does not increase cash. Therefore, it should be deducted.

Subsequently, if Ann Johnson exercises her options, First Wave reports "Cash provided by exercise of stock options" in the financing section of the statement of cash flows.[7]

Extraordinary Items

Companies should report **either as investing activities or as financing activities** cash flows from extraordinary transactions and other events whose effects are included in net income, but which are not related to operations.

For example, assume that Tax Consultants had land with a carrying value of $200,000, which was condemned by the state of Maine for a highway project. The condemnation proceeds received were $205,000, resulting in an extraordinary gain of $5,000 less $2,000 of taxes. In the statement of cash flows (indirect method), the company would deduct the $5,000 gain from net income in the operating activities section. It would report the $205,000 cash inflow from the condemnation as an investing activity, as follows.

Cash flows from investing activities	
Condemnation of land	$205,000

Note that Tax Consultants handles the gain at its **gross** amount ($5,000), not net of tax. The company reports the cash received in the condemnation as an investing activity at $205,000, also exclusive of the tax effect.

The FASB requires companies to classify **all income taxes paid as operating cash outflows**. Some suggested that income taxes paid be allocated to investing and financing transactions. But the Board decided that allocation of income taxes paid to operating, investing, and financing activities would be so complex and arbitrary that the benefits, if any, would not justify the costs involved. Under both the direct method and the indirect method, companies must disclose the total amount of income taxes paid.[8]

> **Underlying Concepts**
>
> By rejecting the requirement to allocate taxes to the various activities, the FASB invoked the cost constraint. The information would be beneficial, but the cost of providing such information would exceed the benefits of providing it.

---

[7]Companies receive a tax deduction related to share-based compensation plans at the time employees exercise their options. The amount of the deduction is equal to the difference between the market price of the stock and the exercise price at the date the employee purchases the stock, which in most cases is much larger than the total compensation expense recorded. When the tax deduction exceeds the total compensation recorded, this provides an additional cash inflow to the company. For example, in a recent year Cisco Systems reported an additional cash inflow related to its stock-option plans equal to $537 million. Under GAAP, this tax-related cash inflow is reported in the financing section of the statement of cash flows. **[5]**

[8]For an insightful article on some weaknesses and limitations in the statement of cash flows, see Hugo Nurnberg, "Inconsistencies and Ambiguities in Cash Flow Statements Under *FASB Statement No. 95*," *Accounting Horizons* (June 1993), pp. 60–73. Nurnberg identifies the inconsistencies caused by the three-way classification of all cash receipts and cash payments, gross versus net of tax, the ambiguous disclosure requirements for noncash investing and financing transactions, and the ambiguous presentation of third-party financing transactions. See also Paul B. W. Miller and Bruce P. Budge, "Nonarticulation in Cash Flow Statements and Implications for Education, Research, and Practice," *Accounting Horizons* (December 1996), pp. 1–15; and Charles Mulford and Michael Ely, "Calculating Sustainable Cash Flow: A Study of the S&P 100," *Georgia Tech Financial Analysis Lab* (October 2004).

Accounts Receivable (Net)

Up to this point, we assumed no allowance for doubtful accounts—a contra account—to offset accounts receivable. However, if a company needs an allowance for doubtful accounts, how does that allowance affect the company's determination of net cash flow from operating activities? For example, assume that Redmark Co. reports net income of $40,000. It has the accounts receivable balances as shown in Illustration 23-28.

ILLUSTRATION 23-28
Accounts Receivable
Balances, Redmark Co.

	2014	2013	Change Increase/Decrease
Accounts receivable	$105,000	$90,000	$15,000 Increase
Allowance for doubtful accounts	(10,000)	(4,000)	6,000 Increase
Accounts receivable (net)	$ 95,000	$86,000	9,000 Increase

Indirect Method

Because an increase in Allowance for Doubtful Accounts results from a charge to bad debt expense, a company should add back an increase in Allowance for Doubtful Accounts to net income to arrive at net cash flow from operating activities. Illustration 23-29 shows one method for presenting this information in a statement of cash flows.

ILLUSTRATION 23-29
Presentation of
Allowance for Doubtful
Accounts—Indirect
Method

REDMARK CO.
STATEMENT OF CASH FLOWS (PARTIAL)
FOR THE YEAR 2014

Cash flows from operating activities		
Net income		$40,000
Adjustments to reconcile net income to net cash provided by operating activities:		
Increase in accounts receivable	$(15,000)	
Increase in allowance for doubtful accounts	6,000	(9,000)
		$31,000

As we indicated, the increase in the Allowance for Doubtful Accounts balance results from a charge to bad debt expense for the year. Because bad debt expense is a noncash charge, a company must add it back to net income in arriving at net cash flow from operating activities.

Instead of separately analyzing the allowance account, a short-cut approach is to net the allowance balance against the receivable balance and compare the change in accounts receivable on a net basis. Illustration 23-30 shows this presentation.

ILLUSTRATION 23-30
Net Approach to
Allowance for Doubtful
Accounts—Indirect
Method

REDMARK CO.
STATEMENT OF CASH FLOWS (PARTIAL)
FOR THE YEAR 2014

Cash flows from operating activities	
Net income	$40,000
Adjustments to reconcile net income to net cash provided by operating activities:	
Increase in accounts receivable (net)	(9,000)
	$31,000

This short-cut procedure works also if the change in the allowance account results from a write-off of accounts receivable. This reduces both Accounts Receivable and Allowance for Doubtful Accounts. No effect on cash flows occurs. *Because of its simplicity, use the net approach for your homework assignments.*

Direct Method

If using the direct method, a company **should not net** Allowance for Doubtful Accounts against Accounts Receivable. To illustrate, assume that Redmark Co.'s net income of $40,000 consisted of the items shown in Illustration 23-31.

REDMARK CO. INCOME STATEMENT FOR THE YEAR 2014		
Sales revenue		$100,000
Expenses		
Salaries	$46,000	
Utilities	8,000	
Bad debts	6,000	60,000
Net income		$ 40,000

ILLUSTRATION 23-31
Income Statement,
Redmark Co.

If Redmark deducts the $9,000 increase in accounts receivable (net) from sales for the year, it would report cash sales at $91,000 ($100,000 − $9,000) and cash payments for operating expenses at $60,000. Both items would be misstated: Cash sales should be reported at $85,000 ($100,000 − $15,000), and total cash payments for operating expenses should be reported at $54,000 ($60,000 − $6,000). Illustration 23-32 shows the proper presentation.

REDMARK CO. STATEMENT OF CASH FLOWS (PARTIAL) FOR THE YEAR 2014		
Cash flows from operating activities		
Cash received from customers		$85,000
Salaries paid	$46,000	
Utilities paid	8,000	54,000
Net cash provided by operating activities		$31,000

ILLUSTRATION 23-32
Bad Debts—Direct
Method

An added complication develops when a company writes off accounts receivable. Simply adjusting sales for the change in accounts receivable will not provide the proper amount of cash sales. The reason is that the write-off of the accounts receivable is not a cash collection. Thus, an additional adjustment is necessary.

What do the numbers mean? NOT WHAT IT SEEMS

The controversy over direct and indirect methods highlights the importance that the market attributes to operating cash flow. By showing an improving cash flow, a company can give a favorable impression of its ongoing operations. For example, WorldCom concealed declines in its operations by capitalizing certain operating expenses—to the tune of $3.8 billion! This practice not only "juiced up" income but also made it possible to report the cash payments in the investing section of the cash flow statement rather than as a deduction from operating cash flow.

The SEC recently addressed a similar cash flow classification issue with automakers like Ford, GM, and Chrysler. For years, automakers classified lease receivables and other dealer-financing arrangements as investment cash flows. Thus, they reported an increase in lease or loan receivables from cars sold as a use of cash in the investing section of the statement of cash flows. The SEC objected and now requires automakers to report these receivables as operating cash flows, since the leases and loans are used to facilitate car sales. At GM, these reclassifications reduced its operating cash flows from $7.6 billion to $3 billion in the year before the change.

In the banking industry, how banks classify their investments, deposits, and cash flow from acquisitions results in huge swings in operating cash flows, both downward (Bank of America) and upward (KeyCorp). According to one analyst, "As it stands now, banks can't be reliably compared to each other by their recorded cash flow from operations . . . operating cash flow for a bank is basically meaningless." Another questionable cash flow classification for banks is the characterization of increases and decreases in deposits as financing cash flow. Many analysts believe customer-driven deposits should be accounted for under operating cash flow (rather than as a financing cash flow) since "the very health of a bank's operations depends on its deposit base and its ability to attract a growing stream of deposits." So while the overall cash flow—from operations, investing, and financing—remained the same, operating cash flow at these companies looked better than it really was.

Sources: Peter Elstrom, "How to Hide $3.8 Billion in Expenses," *BusinessWeek Online* (July 8, 2002); Judith Burns, "SEC Tells US Automakers to Retool Cash-Flow Accounting," *Wall Street Journal Online* (February 28, 2005); and Sarah Johnson, "Cash Flow: A Better Way to Know Your Bank?" *CFO.com* (July 9, 2009).

Other Working Capital Changes

Up to this point, we showed how companies handled all of the changes in working capital items (current asset and current liability items) as adjustments to net income in determining net cash flow from operating activities. You must be careful, however, because **some changes in working capital, although they affect cash, do not affect net income**. Generally, these are investing or financing activities of a current nature.

One activity is the purchase of **short-term available-for-sale securities**. For example, the purchase of short-term available-for-sale securities for $50,000 cash has no effect on net income but it does cause a $50,000 decrease in cash. A company reports this transaction as a cash flow from investing activities as follows. **[6]**

Cash flows from investing activities	
Purchase of short-term available-for-sale securities	$(50,000)

What about **trading securities?** Because companies hold these investments principally for the purpose of selling them in the near term, companies should classify the cash flows from purchases and sales of trading securities as cash flows from **operating activities**. **[7]**[9]

Another example is the issuance of a **short-term nontrade note payable** for cash. This change in a working capital item has no effect on income from operations but it increases cash by the amount of the note payable. For example, a company reports the issuance of a $10,000 short-term note payable for cash in the statement of cash flows as follows.

Cash flows from financing activities	
Issuance of short-term note	$10,000

Another change in a working capital item that has no effect on income from operations or on cash is a **cash dividend payable**. Although a company will report the cash dividends when paid as a financing activity, it does not report the declared but unpaid dividend on the statement of cash flows.

Net Losses

If a company reports a net loss instead of a net income, it must adjust the net loss for those items that do not result in a cash inflow or outflow. The net loss, after adjusting for

[9]If the basis of the statement of cash flows is **cash and cash equivalents** and the short-term investment is considered a cash equivalent, then a company reports nothing in the statement because the transaction does not affect the balance of cash and cash equivalents. The Board notes that cash purchases of short-term investments generally are part of the company's cash management activities rather than part of its operating, investing, or financing activities.

the charges or credits not affecting cash, may result in a negative or a positive cash flow from operating activities.

For example, if the net loss is $50,000 and the total amount of charges to add back is $60,000, then net cash provided by operating activities is $10,000. Illustration 23-33 shows this computation.

Net loss		$(50,000)
Adjustments to reconcile net income to net cash provided by operating activities:		
Depreciation of plant assets	$55,000	
Amortization of patents	5,000	60,000
Net cash provided by operating activities		$ 10,000

ILLUSTRATION 23-33
Computation of Net Cash Flow from Operating Activities—Cash Inflow

If the company experiences a net loss of $80,000 and the total amount of the charges to add back is $25,000, the presentation appears as follows.

Net loss	$(80,000)
Adjustments to reconcile net income to net cash used by operating activities:	
Depreciation of plant assets	25,000
Net cash used by operating activities	$(55,000)

ILLUSTRATION 23-34
Computation of Net Cash Flow from Operating Activities—Cash Outflow

Although not illustrated in this chapter, a negative cash flow may result even if the company reports a net income.

Significant Noncash Transactions

Because the statement of cash flows reports only the effects of operating, investing, and financing activities in terms of cash flows, it omits some **significant noncash transactions** and other events that are investing or financing activities. Among the more common of these noncash transactions that a company should report or disclose in some manner are the following.

1. Acquisition of assets by assuming liabilities (including capital lease obligations) or by issuing equity securities.
2. Exchanges of nonmonetary assets.
3. Refinancing of long-term debt.
4. Conversion of debt or preferred stock to common stock.
5. Issuance of equity securities to retire debt.

A company does not incorporate these noncash items in the statement of cash flows. If material in amount, these disclosures may be either narrative or summarized in a separate schedule at the bottom of the statement, or they may appear in a separate note or supplementary schedule to the financial statements.[10] Illustration 23-35 (page 1442) shows the presentation of these significant noncash transactions or other events in a separate schedule at the bottom of the statement of cash flows.

---

[10]Some noncash investing and financing activities are part cash and part noncash. Companies should report only the cash portion on the statement of cash flows. The noncash component should be reported at the bottom of the statement or in a separate note.

ILLUSTRATION 23-35
Schedule Presentation of Noncash Investing and Financing Activities

Net increase in cash	$3,717,000
Cash at beginning of year	5,208,000
Cash at end of year	$8,925,000
Noncash investing and financing activities	
Purchase of land and building through issuance of 250,000 shares of common stock	$1,750,000
Exchange of Steadfast, NY, land for Bedford, PA, land	$2,000,000
Conversion of 12% bonds to 50,000 shares of common stock	$500,000

Or, companies may present these noncash transactions in a separate note, as shown in Illustration 23-36.

ILLUSTRATION 23-36
Note Presentation of Noncash Investing and Financing Activities

Note G: Significant noncash transactions. During the year, the company engaged in the following significant noncash investing and financing transactions:	
Issued 250,000 shares of common stock to purchase land and building	$1,750,000
Exchanged land in Steadfast, NY, for land in Bedford, PA	$2,000,000
Converted 12% bonds to 50,000 shares of common stock	$500,000

Companies do not generally report certain other significant noncash transactions or other events in conjunction with the statement of cash flows. Examples of these types of transactions are **stock dividends, stock splits, and restrictions on retained earnings**. Companies generally report these items, neither financing nor investing activities, in conjunction with the statement of stockholders' equity or schedules and notes pertaining to changes in capital accounts.

What do the numbers mean? CASH FLOW TOOL

By understanding the relationship between cash flow and income measures, analysts can gain better insights into company performance. Because earnings altered through creative accounting practices generally do not change operating cash flows, analysts can use the relationship between earnings and operating cash flow to detect suspicious accounting practices. Also, by monitoring the ratio between cash flow from operations and operating income, they can get a clearer picture of developing problems in a company.

For example, the following chart plots the ratio of operating cash flows to earnings for **Xerox Corp.** in the years leading up to the SEC singling it out in 2000 for aggressive revenue recognition practices on its leases.

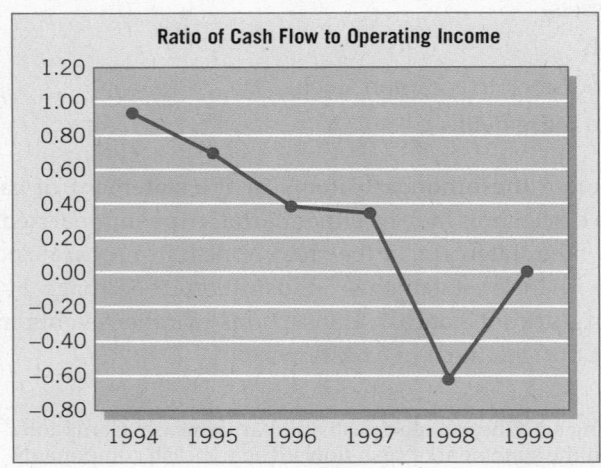

Ratio of Cash Flow to Operating Income

Similar to **W. T. Grant** in the opening story, Xerox was reporting earnings growth in the years leading up to its financial breakdown in 2000 but teetering near bankruptcy in 2001. However, Xerox's ratio of cash flow to earnings showed a declining trend and became negative well before its revenue recognition practices were revealed. The trend revealed in the graph should have given any analyst reason to investigate Xerox further. As one analyst noted, "Earnings growth that exceeds the growth in operating cash flow cannot continue for extended periods and should be investigated."

Source: Adapted from Charles Mulford and Eugene Comiskey, *The Financial Numbers Game: Detecting Creative Accounting Practices* (New York: John Wiley & Sons, 2002), Chapter 11, by permission.

USE OF A WORKSHEET

When numerous adjustments are necessary or other complicating factors are present, companies often use **a worksheet to assemble and classify the data that will appear on the statement of cash flows**. The worksheet is merely a device that aids in the preparation of the statement. Its use is optional. Illustration 23-37 shows the skeleton format of the worksheet for preparation of the statement of cash flows using the indirect method.

9 LEARNING OBJECTIVE
Explain the use of a worksheet in preparing a statement of cash flows.

ILLUSTRATION 23-37
Format of Worksheet for Preparation of Statement of Cash Flows

	XYZ COMPANY.xls				
	Home Insert Page Layout Formulas Data Review View				
	P18 *fx*				
	A	B	C	D	E
1	XYZ COMPANY				
2					
3	Statement of Cash Flows for the Year Ended...				
4	Balance Sheet Accounts	End of Prior Year Balances	Reconciling Items Debits	Reconciling Items Credits	End of Current Year Balances
5	Debit balance accounts	XX	XX	XX	XX
6		XX	XX	XX	XX
7	Totals	XXX			XXX
8	Credit balance accounts	XX	XX	XX	XX
9		XX	XX	XX	XX
10	Totals	XXX			XXX
11	Statement of Cash Flows Effects				
12	Operating activities				
13	Net income		XX		
14	Adjustments		XX	XX	
15	Investing activities				
16	Receipts and payments		XX	XX	
17	Financing activities				
18	Receipts and payments		XX	XX	
19	Totals		XXX	XXX	
20	Increase (decrease) in cash		(XX)	XX	
21	Totals		XXX	XXX	
22					

The following guidelines are important in using a worksheet.

1. In the balance sheet accounts section, **list accounts with debit balances separately from those with credit balances**. This means, for example, that Accumulated Depreciation is listed under credit balances and not as a contra account under debit balances. Enter the beginning and ending balances of each account in the appropriate columns. Then, enter the transactions that caused the change in the account balance during the year as reconciling items in the two middle columns.

After all reconciling items have been entered, each line pertaining to a balance sheet account should foot across. That is, the beginning balance plus or minus the reconciling item(s) must equal the ending balance. When this agreement exists for all balance sheet accounts, all changes in account balances have been reconciled.

2. The bottom portion of the worksheet consists of the operating, investing, and financing activities sections. Accordingly, it provides the information necessary to prepare the formal statement of cash flows. **Enter inflows of cash as debits in the reconciling columns, and outflows of cash as credits in the reconciling columns.** Thus, in this section, a company would enter the sale of equipment for cash at book value as a debit under inflows of cash from investing activities. Similarly, it would enter the purchase of land for cash as a credit under outflows of cash from investing activities.

3. **Do not enter in any journal or post to any account the reconciling items shown in the worksheet.** These items do not represent either adjustments or corrections of the balance sheet accounts. They are used only to facilitate the preparation of the statement of cash flows.

Preparation of the Worksheet

The preparation of a worksheet involves the following steps.

Step 1. Enter the balance sheet accounts and their beginning and ending balances in the balance sheet accounts section.

Step 2. Enter the data that explain the changes in the balance sheet accounts (other than cash) and their effects on the statement of cash flows in the reconciling columns of the worksheet.

Step 3. Enter the increase or decrease in cash on the cash line and at the bottom of the worksheet. This entry should enable the totals of the reconciling columns to be in agreement.

To illustrate the preparation and use of a worksheet and to illustrate the reporting of some of the special problems discussed in the prior section, we present a comprehensive example for Satellite Corporation. Again, the indirect method serves as the basis for the computation of net cash provided by operating activities. Illustrations 23-38 and 23-39 (page 1446) present the balance sheet, combined statement of income and retained earnings, and additional information for Satellite Corporation.

The discussion that follows provides additional explanations related to the preparation of the worksheet.

Analysis of Transactions

The following discussion explains the individual adjustments that appear on the worksheet in Illustration 23-40 (page 1450). Because cash is the basis for the analysis, Satellite reconciles the Cash account last. Because income is the first item that appears on the statement of cash flows, it is handled first.

Change in Retained Earnings

Net income for the period is $117,000. The entry for it on the worksheet is as follows.

(1)

Operating—Net Income	117,000	
Retained Earnings		117,000

ILLUSTRATION 23-38
Comparative Balance
Sheet, Satellite
Corporation

A	B	C	D
SATELLITE CORPORATION			
Comparative Balance Sheet–December 31, 2014 and 2013			
Assets	2014	2013	Increase or (Decrease)
Cash	$ 59,000	$ 66,000	$ (7,000)
Accounts receivable (net)	104,000	51,000	53,000
Inventory	493,000	341,000	152,000
Prepaid expenses	16,500	17,000	(500)
Investment in Porter Co. (equity method)	18,500	15,000	3,500
Land	131,500	82,000	49,500
Equipment	187,000	142,000	45,000
Accumulated depreciation—equipment	(29,000)	(31,000)	(2,000)
Buildings	262,000	262,000	–
Accumulated depreciation—buildings	(74,100)	(71,000)	3,100
Trademarks	7,600	10,000	(2,400)
Total assets	$1,176,000	$884,000	
Liabilities			
Accounts payable	$ 132,000	$ 131,000	$ 1,000
Accrued liabilities	43,000	39,000	4,000
Income taxes payable	3,000	16,000	(13,000)
Notes payable (long-term)	60,000	–	60,000
Bonds payable	100,000	100,000	–
Premium on bonds payable	7,000	8,000	(1,000)
Deferred tax liability (long-term)	9,000	6,000	3,000
Total liabilities	354,000	300,000	
Stockholders' Equity			
Common stock ($1 par)	60,000	50,000	10,000
Paid-in capital in excess of par—common stock	187,000	38,000	149,000
Retained earnings	592,000	496,000	96,000
Treasury stock	(17,000)	–	17,000
Total stockholders' equity	822,000	584,000	
Total liabilities and stockholders' equity	$1,176,000	$884,000	

Satellite reports net income on the bottom section of the worksheet. This **is the starting point for preparation of the statement of cash flows (under the indirect method).**

A stock dividend and a cash dividend also affected retained earnings. The retained earnings statement reports a stock dividend of $15,000. The worksheet entry for this transaction is as follows.

(2)

Retained Earnings	15,000	
Common Stock		1,000
Paid-in Capital in Excess of Par—Common Stock		14,000

The issuance of stock dividends is not a cash operating, investing, or financing item. Therefore, **although the company enters this transaction on the worksheet for reconciling purposes, it does not report it in the statement of cash flows**.

ILLUSTRATION 23-39
Income and Retained
Earnings Statements,
Satellite Corporation

SATELLITE CORPORATION
COMBINED STATEMENT OF INCOME AND RETAINED EARNINGS
FOR THE YEAR ENDED DECEMBER 31, 2014

Net sales		$526,500
Other revenue		3,500
Total revenues		530,000
Expense		
Cost of goods sold		310,000
Selling and administrative expenses		47,000
Other expenses and losses		12,000
Total expenses		369,000
Income before income tax and extraordinary item		161,000
Income tax		
Current	$47,000	
Deferred	3,000	50,000
Income before extraordinary item		111,000
Gain on condemnation of land (net of $2,000 tax)		6,000
Net income		117,000
Retained earnings, January 1		496,000
Less:		
Cash dividends	6,000	
Stock dividend	15,000	21,000
Retained earnings, December 31		$592,000
Per share:		
Income before extraordinary item		$2.02
Extraordinary item		.11
Net income		$2.13

Additional Information

(a) Other revenue of $3,500 represents Satellite's equity share in the net income of Porter Co., an equity investee. Satellite owns 22% of Porter Co.

(b) An analysis of the equipment account and related accumulated depreciation indicates the following:

	Equipment Dr./(Cr.)	Accum. Dep. Dr./(Cr.)	Gain or (Loss)
Balance at end of 2013	$142,000	$(31,000)	
Purchases of equipment	53,000		
Sale of equipment	(8,000)	2,500	$(1,500)
Depreciation for the period		(11,500)	
Major repair charged to accumulated depreciation		11,000	
Balance at end of 2014	$187,000	$(29,000)	

(c) Land in the amount of $60,000 was purchased through the issuance of a long-term note; in addition, certain parcels of land costing $10,500 were condemned. The state government paid Satellite $18,500, resulting in an $8,000 gain which has a $2,000 tax effect.

(d) The change in the Accumulated Depreciation—Buildings, Trademarks, and Premium on Bonds Payable accounts resulted from depreciation and amortization entries.

(e) An analysis of the paid-in capital accounts in stockholders' equity discloses the following.

	Common Stock	Paid-In Capital in Excess of Par—Common Stock
Balance at end of 2013	$50,000	$ 38,000
Issuance of 2% stock dividend	1,000	14,000
Sale of stock for cash	9,000	135,000
Balance at end of 2014	$60,000	$187,000

(f) Interest paid (net of amount capitalized) is $9,000; income taxes paid is $62,000.

The $6,000 cash dividend paid represents a financing activity cash outflow. Satellite makes the following worksheet entry:

(3)

Retained Earnings	6,000	
Financing—Cash Dividends		6,000

The company reconciles the beginning and ending balances of retained earnings by entry of the three items above.

Accounts Receivable (Net)

The increase in accounts receivable (net) of $53,000 represents adjustments that did not result in cash inflows during 2014. As a result, the company would deduct from net income the increase of $53,000. Satellite makes the following worksheet entry.

(4)

Accounts Receivable (net)	53,000	
Operating—Increase in Accounts Receivable (net)		53,000

Inventory

The increase in inventory of $152,000 represents an operating use of cash. The incremental investment in inventory during the year reduces cash without increasing the cost of goods sold. Satellite makes the following worksheet entry.

(5)

Inventory	152,000	
Operating—Increase in Inventory		152,000

Prepaid Expense

The decrease in prepaid expenses of $500 represents a charge in the income statement for which there was no cash outflow in the current period. Satellite should add that amount back to net income through the following entry.

(6)

Operating—Decrease in Prepaid Expenses	500	
Prepaid Expenses		500

Investment in Stock

Satellite's investment in the stock of Porter Co. increased $3,500. This amount reflects Satellite's share of net income earned by Porter (its equity investee) during the current year. Although Satellite's revenue and therefore its net income increased $3,500 by recording Satellite's share of Porter Co.'s net income, no cash (dividend) was provided. Satellite makes the following worksheet entry.

(7)

Equity Investments (Porter Co.)	3,500	
Operating—Equity in Earnings of Porter Co.		3,500

Land

Satellite purchased land in the amount of $60,000 through the issuance of a long-term note payable. This transaction did not affect cash. It is a significant noncash investing/financing transaction that the company would disclose either in a separate schedule below the statement of cash flows or in the accompanying notes. Satellite makes the following entry to reconcile the worksheet.

(8)

Land	60,000	
Notes Payable		60,000

In addition to the noncash transaction involving the issuance of a note to purchase land, the Land account was decreased by the condemnation proceedings. The following worksheet entry records the receipt of $18,500 for land having a book value of $10,500.

(9)

Investing—Proceeds from Condemnation of Land	18,500	
Land		10,500
Operating—Gain on Condemnation of Land		8,000

In reconciling net income to net cash flow from operating activities, Satellite deducts from net income the extraordinary gain of $8,000. The reason is that the transaction that gave rise to the gain is an item whose cash effect is already classified as an investing cash inflow. The Land account is now reconciled.

Equipment and Accumulated Depreciation

An analysis of Equipment and Accumulated Depreciation—Equipment shows that a number of transactions have affected these accounts. The company purchased equipment in the amount of $53,000 during the year. Satellite records this transaction on the worksheet as follows.

(10)

Equipment	53,000	
Investing—Purchase of Equipment		53,000

In addition, Satellite sold at a loss of $1,500 equipment with a book value of $5,500. It records this transaction as follows.

(11)

Investing—Sale of Equipment	4,000	
Operating—Loss on Sale of Equipment	1,500	
Accumulated Depreciation—Equipment	2,500	
Equipment		8,000

The proceeds from the sale of the equipment provided cash of $4,000. In addition, the loss on the sale of the equipment has reduced net income but did not affect cash. Therefore, the company adds back to net income the amount of the loss, in order to accurately report cash provided by operating activities.

Satellite reported depreciation on the equipment at $11,500 and recorded it on the worksheet as follows.

(12)

Operating—Depreciation Expense—Equipment	11,500	
Accumulated Depreciation—Equipment		11,500

The company adds depreciation expense back to net income because that expense reduced income but did not affect cash.

Finally, the company made a major repair to the equipment. It charged this expenditure, in the amount of $11,000, to Accumulated Depreciation—Equipment. This expenditure required cash, and so Satellite makes the following worksheet entry.

(13)

Accumulated Depreciation—Equipment	11,000	
Investing—Major Repairs of Equipment		11,000

After adjusting for the foregoing items, Satellite has reconciled the balances in the Equipment and related Accumulated Depreciation—Equipment accounts.

Building Depreciation and Amortization of Trademarks

Depreciation expense on the buildings of $3,100 and amortization of trademarks of $2,400 are both expenses in the income statement that reduced net income but did not require cash outflows in the current period. Satellite makes the following worksheet entry.

(14)

Operating—Depreciation Expense—Buildings	3,100	
Operating—Amortization of Trademarks	2,400	
Accumulated Depreciation—Buildings		3,100
Trademarks		2,400

Other Noncash Charges or Credits

Analysis of the remaining accounts indicates that changes in the Accounts Payable, Accrued Liabilities, Income Taxes Payable, Premium on Bonds Payable, and Deferred Tax Liability balances resulted from charges or credits to net income that did not affect cash. The company should individually analyze each of these items and enter them in the worksheet. The following compound entry summarizes these noncash, income-related items.

(15)

Income Taxes Payable	13,000	
Premium on Bonds Payable	1,000	
Operating—Increase in Accounts Payable	1,000	
Operating—Increase in Accrued Liabilities	4,000	
Operating—Increase in Deferred Tax Liability	3,000	
Operating—Decrease in Income Taxes Payable		13,000
Operating—Amortization of Bond Premium		1,000
Accounts Payable		1,000
Accrued Liabilities		4,000
Deferred Tax Liability		3,000

Common Stock and Related Accounts

Comparison of the Common Stock balances and the Paid-in Capital in Excess of Par—Common Stock balances shows that transactions during the year affected these accounts. First, Satellite issues a stock dividend of 2 percent to stockholders. As the discussion of worksheet entry (2) indicated, no cash was provided or used by the stock dividend transaction. In addition to the shares issued via the stock dividend, Satellite sold shares of common stock at $16 per share. The company records this transaction as follows.

(16)

Financing—Sale of Common Stock	144,000	
Common Stock		9,000
Paid-in Capital in Excess of Par—Common Stock		135,000

Also, the company purchased shares of its common stock in the amount of $17,000. It records this transaction on the worksheet as follows.

(17)

Treasury Stock	17,000	
Financing—Purchase of Treasury Stock		17,000

Final Reconciling Entry

The final entry to reconcile the change in cash and to balance the worksheet is shown below. The $7,000 amount is the difference between the beginning and ending cash balance.

(18)

Decrease in Cash	7,000	
Cash		7,000

Once the company has determined that the differences between the beginning and ending balances per the worksheet columns have been accounted for, it can total the reconciling transactions columns, and they should balance. Satellite can prepare the statement of cash flows entirely from the items and amounts that appear at the bottom of the worksheet under "Statement of Cash Flows Effects," as shown in Illustration 23-40.

ILLUSTRATION 23-40
Completed Worksheet for Preparation of Statement of Cash Flows, Satellite Corporation

SATELLITE CORPORATION.xls

Home Insert Page Layout Formulas Data Review View

P18

SATELLITE CORPORATION
Worksheet for Preparation of Statement of Cash Flows
for the Year Ended December 31, 2014

	A	B	C	D	E	F	G
5		Balance 12/31/13		Reconciling Items–2014 Dr.		Cr.	Balance 12/31/14
6	Debits						
7	Cash	$ 66,000			(18)	$ 7,000	$ 59,000
8	Accounts receivable (net)	51,000	(4)	$ 53,000			104,000
9	Inventory	341,000	(5)	152,000			493,000
10	Prepaid expenses	17,000			(6)	500	16,500
11	Investment in Porter Co. (equity method)	15,000	(7)	3,500			18,500
12	Land	82,000	(8)	60,000	(9)	10,500	131,500
13	Equipment	142,000	(10)	53,000	(11)	8,000	187,000
14	Buildings	262,000					262,000
15	Trademarks	10,000			(14)	2,400	7,600
16	Treasury stock		(17)	17,000			17,000
17	Total debits	$986,000					$1,296,100
18	Credits						
19	Accum. depr.–equipment	$ 31,000	(11)	2,500	(12)	11,500	
20			(13)	11,000			$ 29,000
21	Accum. depr.–buildings	71,000			(14)	3,100	74,100
22	Accounts payable	131,000			(15)	1,000	132,000
23	Accrued liabilities	39,000			(15)	4,000	43,000
24	Income taxes payable	16,000	(15)	13,000			3,000
25	Notes payable	-0-			(8)	60,000	60,000
26	Bonds payable	100,000					100,000
27	Premium on bonds payable	8,000	(15)	1,000			7,000
28	Deferred tax liability	6,000			(15)	3,000	9,000
29	Common stock	50,000			(2)	1,000	
30					(16)	9,000	60,000
31	Paid-in capital in excess of	38,000			(2)	14,000	
32	par—common stock				(16)	135,000	187,000
33	Retained earnings	496,000	(2)	15,000	(1)	117,000	
34			(3)	6,000			592,000
35	Total credits	$986,000					$1,296,100
36	Statement of Cash Flows Effects						
37	Operating activities						
38	Net income		(1)	117,000			
39	Increase in accounts receivable (net)				(4)	53,000	
40	Increase in inventory				(5)	152,000	
41	Decrease in prepaid expenses		(6)	500			
42	Equity in earnings of Porter Co.				(7)	3,500	
43	Gain on condemnation of land				(9)	8,000	
44	Loss on sale of equipment		(11)	1,500			
45	Depr. expense–equipment		(12)	11,500			
46	Depr. expense–buildings		(14)	3,100			
47	Amortization of trademarks		(14)	2,400			
48	Increase in accounts payable		(15)	1,000			
49	Increase in accrued liabilities		(15)	4,000			
50	Increase in deferred tax liability		(15)	3,000			
51	Decrease in income taxes payable				(15)	13,000	
52	Amortization of bond premium				(15)	1,000	
53	Investing activities						
54	Proceeds from condemnation of land		(9)	18,500			
55	Purchase of equipment				(10)	53,000	
56	Sale of equipment		(11)	4,000			
57	Major repairs of equipment				(13)	11,000	
58	Financing activities						
59	Payment of cash dividend				(3)	6,000	
60	Issuance of common stock		(16)	144,000			
61	Purchase of treasury stock				(17)	17,000	
62	Totals			697,500		704,500	
63	Decrease in cash		(18)	7,000			
64	Totals			$704,500		$704,500	
65							

Preparation of Final Statement

Illustration 23-41 presents a formal statement of cash flows prepared from the data compiled in the lower portion of the worksheet.

ILLUSTRATION 23-41
Statement of Cash Flows,
Satellite Corporation

SATELLITE CORPORATION
STATEMENT OF CASH FLOWS
FOR THE YEAR ENDED DECEMBER 31, 2014

Cash flows from operating activities		
Net income		$117,000
Adjustments to reconcile net income to net		
cash used by operating activities:		
Depreciation expense	$ 14,600	
Amortization of trademarks	2,400	
Amortization of bond premium	(1,000)	
Equity in earnings of Porter Co.	(3,500)	
Gain on condemnation of land	(8,000)	
Loss on sale of equipment	1,500	
Increase in deferred tax liability	3,000	
Increase in accounts receivable (net)	(53,000)	
Increase in inventory	(152,000)	
Decrease in prepaid expenses	500	
Increase in accounts payable	1,000	
Increase in accrued liabilities	4,000	
Decrease in income taxes payable	(13,000)	(203,500)
Net cash used by operating activities		(86,500)
Cash flows from investing activities		
Proceeds from condemnation of land	18,500	
Purchase of equipment	(53,000)	
Sale of equipment	4,000	
Major repairs of equipment	(11,000)	
Net cash used by investing activities		(41,500)
Cash flows from financing activities		
Payment of cash dividend	(6,000)	
Issuance of common stock	144,000	
Purchase of treasury stock	(17,000)	
Net cash provided by financing activities		121,000
Net decrease in cash		(7,000)
Cash, January 1, 2014		66,000
Cash, December 31, 2014		$ 59,000

Supplemental Disclosures of Cash Flow Information:
Cash paid during the year for:

Interest (net of amount capitalized)		$ 9,000
Income taxes		$ 62,000

Supplemental Schedule of Noncash Investing and Financing Activities:
Purchase of land for $60,000 in exchange for a $60,000 long-term note.

**Gateway to
the Profession**

*Discussion of the
T-Account Approach
to Preparation of
the Statement of
Cash Flows*

You will
want to
read
IFRS INSIGHTS
on pages 1480–1485

for discussion of
IFRS related to
the statement of
cash flows.

SUMMARY OF LEARNING OBJECTIVES

KEY TERMS

cash equivalents, *1413(n)*
direct method, *1428*
financing activities, *1413*
indirect method, *1418*
investing activities, *1413*
operating activities, *1413*

1 **Describe the purpose of the statement of cash flows.** The primary purpose of the statement of cash flows is to provide information about cash receipts and cash payments of an entity during a period. A secondary objective is to report the entity's operating, investing, and financing activities during the period.

significant noncash transactions, *1441*

statement of cash flows, *1412*

2 **Identify the major classifications of cash flows.** Companies classify cash flows as follows. (1) *Operating activities*—transactions that result in the revenues, expenses, gains, and losses that determine net income. (2) *Investing activities*—lending money and collecting on those loans, and acquiring and disposing of investments, plant assets, and intangible assets. (3) *Financing activities*—obtaining cash from creditors and repaying loans, issuing and reacquiring capital stock, and paying cash dividends.

3 **Prepare a statement of cash flows.** Preparing the statement involves three major steps. (1) *Determine the change in cash*. This is the difference between the beginning and the ending cash balance shown on the comparative balance sheets. (2) *Determine the net cash flow from operating activities*. This procedure is complex; it involves analyzing not only the current year's income statement but also the comparative balance sheets and the selected transaction data. (3) *Determine cash flows from investing and financing activities*. Analyze all other changes in the balance sheet accounts to determine the effects on cash.

4 **Differentiate between net income and net cash flow from operating activities.** Companies must adjust net income on an accrual basis to determine net cash flow from operating activities because some expenses and losses do not cause cash outflows, and some revenues and gains do not provide cash inflows.

5 **Determine net cash flows from investing and financing activities.** Once a company has computed the net cash flow from operating activities, the next step is to determine whether any other changes in balance sheet accounts caused an increase or decrease in cash. Net cash flows from investing and financing activities can be determined by examining the changes in noncurrent balance sheet accounts.

6 **Identify sources of information for a statement of cash flows.** The information to prepare the statement usually comes from three sources. (1) *Comparative balance sheets*: Information in these statements indicates the amount of the changes in assets, liabilities, and equities during the period. (2) *Current income statement*: Information in this statement is used in determining the cash provided by operations during the period. (3) *Selected transaction data*: These data from the general ledger provide additional detailed information needed to determine how cash was provided or used during the period.

7 **Contrast the direct and indirect methods of calculating net cash flow from operating activities.** Under the direct approach, companies calculate the major classes of operating cash receipts and cash disbursements. Companies summarize the computations in a schedule of changes from the accrual- to the cash-basis income statement. Presentation of the direct approach of reporting net cash flow from operating activities takes the form of a condensed cash-basis income statement. The indirect method adds back to net income the noncash expenses and losses and subtracts the noncash revenues and gains.

8 **Discuss special problems in preparing a statement of cash flows.** These special problems are (1) adjustments to income (depreciation and amortization, postretirement benefit costs, change in deferred income taxes, equity method of accounting, losses and gains, stock options, extraordinary items); (2) accounts receivable (net); (3) other working capital changes; (4) net losses; and (5) significant noncash transactions.

9 **Explain the use of a worksheet in preparing a statement of cash flows.** When numerous adjustments are necessary or other complicating factors are present, companies often use a worksheet to assemble and classify the data that will appear on the statement of cash flows. The worksheet is merely a device that aids in the preparation of the statement. Its use is optional.

DEMONSTRATION PROBLEM

Data presented below are from the records of Antonio Brasileiro Company.

	December 31, 2014	December 31, 2013
Cash	$ 15,000	$ 8,000
Current assets other than cash	85,000	60,000
Long-term investments	10,000	53,000
Plant assets	335,000	215,000
	$445,000	$336,000
Accumulated depreciation	$ 20,000	$ 40,000
Current liabilities	40,000	22,000
Bonds payable	75,000	–0–
Common stock	254,000	254,000
Retained earnings	56,000	20,000
	$445,000	$336,000

Additional information:

1. In 2014, the company sold for $34,000 available-for-sale investments carried at a cost of $43,000 on December 31, 2014. The loss (not extraordinary) was incorrectly charged directly to Retained Earnings.
2. In 2014, the company sold for $8,000 plant assets that cost $50,000 and were 80% depreciated. The loss (not extraordinary) was incorrectly charged directly to Retained Earnings.
3. Net income as reported on the income statement for the year was $57,000.
4. The company paid dividends totaling $10,000.
5. Depreciation charged for the year was $20,000.

Instructions

Prepare a statement of cash flows for the year 2014 using the indirect method.

Solution

ANTONIO BRASILEIRO COMPANY
STATEMENT OF CASH FLOWS
FOR THE YEAR ENDED DECEMBER 31, 2014
INDIRECT METHOD

Cash flows from operating activities		
Net income ($57,000 − $9,000 − $2,000)		$ 46,000
Adjustments to reconcile net income to net cash provided by operating activities:		
Depreciation expense	$ 20,000	
Loss on sale of investments	9,000	
Loss on sale of plant assets	2,000	
Increase in current assets other than cash	(25,000)	
Increase in current liabilities	18,000	24,000
Net cash provided by operating activities		70,000
Cash flows from investing activities		
Sale of plant assets	8,000	
Sale of held-to-maturity investments	34,000	
Purchase of plant assets*	(170,000)	
Net cash used by investing activities		(128,000)
Cash flows from financing activities		
Issuance of bonds payable	75,000	
Payment of dividends	(10,000)	
Net cash provided by financing activities		65,000
Net increase in cash		7,000
Cash balance, January 1, 2014		8,000
Cash balance, December 31, 2014		$ 15,000

*Supporting computation (purchase of plant assets):

Plant assets, December 31, 2014	$335,000
Less: Plant assets, December 31, 2013	215,000
Net change	120,000
Plant assets sold	50,000
Plant assets purchased	$170,000

FASB CODIFICATION

FASB Codification References

[1] FASB ASC 230-10-10-2. [Predecessor literature: "The Statement of Cash Flows," *Statement of Financial Accounting Standards No. 95* (Stamford, Conn.: FASB, 1987), paras. 4 and 5.]

[2] FASB ASC 230-10-45-18 through 21. [Predecessor literature: "Statement of Cash Flows—Exemption of Certain Enterprises and Classification of Cash Flows from Certain Securities Acquired for Resale (amended)," *Statement of Financial Accounting Standards No. 102* (February 1989).]

[3] FASB ASC 230-10-45-25. [Predecessor literature: "Statement of Cash Flows," *Statement of Financial Accounting Standards No. 95* (Stamford, Conn.: FASB, 1987), paras. 107 and 111.]

[4] FASB ASC 230-10-45-31. [Predecessor literature: "The Statement of Cash Flows," *Statement of Financial Accounting Standards No. 95* (Stamford, Conn.: FASB, 1987), paras. 27 and 30.]

[5] FASB ASC 230-10-45-14. [Predecessor literature: "Share-Based Payment," *Statement of Financial Accounting Standard No. 123(R)* (Norwalk, Conn.: FASB, 2004), par. 68.]

[6] FASB ASC 320-10-45-11. [Predecessor literature: "Accounting for Certain Investments in Debt and Equity Securities," *Statement of Financial Accounting Standards No. 115* (Norwalk, Conn.: 1993), par. 118.]

[7] FASB ASC 320-10-45-11. [Predecessor literature: "Accounting for Certain Investments in Debt and Equity Securities," *Statement of Financial Accounting Standards No. 115* (Norwalk, Conn.: 1993), par. 118.]

Exercises

If your school has a subscription to the FASB Codification, go to *http://aaahq.org/ascLogin.cfm* to log in and prepare responses to the following. Provide Codification references for your responses.

CE23-1 Access the glossary ("Master Glossary") to answer the following.

   (a) What are cash equivalents?
   (b) What are financing activities?
   (c) What are investing activities?
   (d) What are operating activities?

CE23-2 Name five cash inflows that would qualify as a "financing activity."

CE23-3 How should cash flows from purchases, sales, and maturities of available-for-sale securities be classified and reported in the statement of cash flows?

CE23-4 Do companies need to disclose information about investing and financing activities that do not affect cash receipts or cash payments? If so, how should such information be disclosed?

An additional codification case can be found in the Using Your Judgment section, on page 1479.

Be sure to check the book's companion website for a Review and Analysis Exercise, with solution.

WileyPLUS

Brief Exercises, Exercises, Problems, and many more learning and assessment tools and resources are available for practice in WileyPLUS.

QUESTIONS

1. What is the purpose of the statement of cash flows? What information does it provide?

2. Of what use is the statement of cash flows?

3. Differentiate between investing activities, financing activities, and operating activities.

4. What are the major sources of cash (inflows) in a statement of cash flows? What are the major uses (outflows) of cash?

5. Identify and explain the major steps involved in preparing the statement of cash flows.

6. Identify the following items as (1) operating, (2) investing, or (3) financing activities: purchase of land, payment of dividends, cash sales, and purchase of treasury stock.

7. Unlike the other major financial statements, the statement of cash flows is not prepared from the adjusted trial balance. From what sources does the information to prepare this statement come, and what information does each source provide?

8. Why is it necessary to convert accrual-based net income to a cash basis when preparing a statement of cash flows?

9. Differentiate between the direct method and the indirect method by discussing each method.

10. Broussard Company reported net income of $3.5 million in 2014. Depreciation for the year was $520,000; accounts receivable increased $500,000; and accounts payable increased $300,000. Compute net cash flow from operating activities using the indirect method.

11. Collinsworth Co. reported sales on an accrual basis of $100,000. If accounts receivable increased $30,000 and the allowance for doubtful accounts increased $9,000 after a write-off of $2,000, compute cash sales.

12. Your roommate is puzzled. During the last year, the company in which she is a stockholder reported a net loss of $675,000, yet its cash increased $321,000 during the same period of time. Explain to your roommate how this situation could occur.

13. The board of directors of Gifford Corp. declared cash dividends of $260,000 during the current year. If dividends payable was $85,000 at the beginning of the year and $90,000 at the end of the year, how much cash was paid in dividends during the year?

14. Explain how the amount of cash payments to suppliers is computed under the direct method.

15. The net income for Letterman Company for 2014 was $320,000. During 2014, depreciation on plant assets was $124,000, amortization of patent was $40,000, and the company incurred a loss on sale of plant assets of $21,000. Compute net cash flow from operating activities.

16. Each of the following items must be considered in preparing a statement of cash flows for Blackwell Inc. for the year ended December 31, 2014. State where each item is to be shown in the statement, if at all.

(a) Plant assets that had cost $18,000 6½ years before and were being depreciated on a straight-line basis

over 10 years with no estimated scrap value were sold for $4,000.

(b) During the year, 10,000 shares of common stock with a stated value of $20 a share were issued for $41 a share.

(c) Uncollectible accounts receivable in the amount of $22,000 were written off against Allowance for Doubtful Accounts.

(d) The company sustained a net loss for the year of $50,000. Depreciation amounted to $22,000, and a gain of $9,000 was realized on the sale of available-for-sale securities for $38,000 cash.

17. Classify the following items as (1) operating, (2) investing, (3) financing, or (4) significant non-cash investing and financing activities, using the direct method.

(a) Cash payments to employees.
(b) Redemption of bonds payable.
(c) Sale of building at book value.
(d) Cash payments to suppliers.
(e) Exchange of equipment for furniture.
(f) Issuance of preferred stock.
(g) Cash received from customers.
(h) Purchase of treasury stock.
(i) Issuance of bonds for land.
(j) Payment of dividends.
(k) Purchase of equipment.
(l) Cash payments for operating expenses.

18. Stan Conner and Mark Stein were discussing the presentation format of the statement of cash flows of Bombeck Co. At the bottom of Bombeck's statement of cash flows was a separate section entitled "Noncash investing and financing activities." Give three examples of significant non-cash transactions that would be reported in this section.

19. During 2014, Simms Company redeemed $2,000,000 of bonds payable for $1,880,000 cash. Indicate how this transaction would be reported on a statement of cash flows, if at all.

20. What are some of the arguments in favor of using the indirect (reconciliation) method as opposed to the direct method for reporting a statement of cash flows?

21. Why is it desirable to use a worksheet when preparing a statement of cash flows? Is a worksheet required to prepare a statement of cash flows?

BRIEF EXERCISES

5 **BE23-1** Wainwright Corporation had the following activities in 2014.

1. Sale of land $180,000.
2. Purchase of inventory $845,000.
3. Purchase of treasury stock $72,000.
4. Purchase of equipment $415,000.
5. Issuance of common stock $320,000.
6. Purchase of available-for-sale securities $59,000.

Compute the amount Wainwright should report as net cash provided (used) by investing activities in its 2014 statement of cash flows.

5 **BE23-2** Stansfield Corporation had the following activities in 2014.

1. Payment of accounts payable $770,000.
2. Issuance of common stock $250,000.
3. Payment of dividends $350,000.
4. Collection of note receivable $100,000.
5. Issuance of bonds payable $510,000.
6. Purchase of treasury stock $46,000.

Compute the amount Stansfield should report as net cash provided (used) by financing activities in its 2014 statement of cash flows.

2 **BE23-3** Novak Corporation is preparing its 2014 statement of cash flows, using the indirect method. Presented below is a list of items that may affect the statement. Using the code below, indicate how each item will affect Novak's 2014 statement of cash flows.

Code Letter	Effect
A	Added to net income in the operating section
D	Deducted from net income in the operating section
R-I	Cash receipt in investing section
P-I	Cash payment in investing section
R-F	Cash receipt in financing section
P-F	Cash payment in financing section
N	Noncash investing and financing activity

Items

____ (a) Purchase of land and building.
____ (b) Decrease in accounts receivable.
____ (c) Issuance of stock.
____ (d) Depreciation expense.
____ (e) Sale of land at book value.
____ (f) Sale of land at a gain.
____ (g) Payment of dividends.
____ (h) Increase in accounts receivable.
____ (i) Purchase of available-for-sale investment.

____ (j) Increase in accounts payable.
____ (k) Decrease in accounts payable.
____ (l) Loan from bank by signing note.
____ (m) Purchase of equipment using a note.
____ (n) Increase in inventory.
____ (o) Issuance of bonds.
____ (p) Redemption of bonds payable.
____ (q) Sale of equipment at a loss.
____ (r) Purchase of treasury stock.

4 **7** **BE23-4** Bloom Corporation had the following 2014 income statement.

Sales revenue	$200,000
Cost of goods sold	120,000
Gross profit	80,000
Operating expenses (includes depreciation of $21,000)	50,000
Net income	$ 30,000

The following accounts increased during 2014: Accounts Receivable $12,000; Inventory $11,000; Accounts Payable $13,000. Prepare the cash flows from operating activities section of Bloom's 2014 statement of cash flows using the direct method.

4 **7** **BE23-5** Use the information from BE23-4 for Bloom Corporation. Prepare the cash flows from operating activities section of Bloom's 2014 statement of cash flows using the indirect method.

7 **BE23-6** At January 1, 2014, Eikenberry Inc. had accounts receivable of $72,000. At December 31, 2014, accounts receivable is $54,000. Sales revenue for 2014 total $420,000. Compute Eikenberry's 2014 cash receipts from customers.

7 **BE23-7** Moxley Corporation had January 1 and December 31 balances as follows.

	1/1/14	12/31/14
Inventory	$95,000	$113,000
Accounts payable	61,000	69,000

For 2014, cost of goods sold was $500,000. Compute Moxley's 2014 cash payments to suppliers.

3 **BE23-8** In 2014, Elbert Corporation had net cash provided by operating activities of $531,000; net cash used by investing activities of $963,000; and net cash provided by financing activities of $585,000. At January 1, 2014, the cash balance was $333,000. Compute December 31, 2014, cash.

4 **7** **BE23-9** Loveless Corporation had the following 2014 income statement.

Revenues	$100,000
Expenses	60,000
	$ 40,000

In 2014, Loveless had the following activity in selected accounts.

	Accounts Receivable					Allowance for Doubtful Accounts			
1/1/14	20,000							1,200	1/1/14
Revenues	100,000	1,000	Write-offs		Write-offs	1,000		1,840	Bad debt expense
		90,000	Collections						
12/31/14	29,000							2,040	12/31/14

Prepare Loveless's cash flows from operating activities section of the statement of cash flows using (a) the direct method and (b) the indirect method.

4 **BE23-10** Hendrickson Corporation reported net income of $50,000 in 2014. Depreciation expense was $17,000. The following working capital accounts changed.

Accounts receivable	$11,000 increase
Available-for-sale securities	16,000 increase
Inventory	7,400 increase
Nontrade note payable	15,000 decrease
Accounts payable	12,300 increase

Compute net cash provided by operating activities.

4 **BE23-11** In 2014, Wild Corporation reported a net loss of $70,000. Wild's only net income adjustments were depreciation expense $81,000, and increase in accounts receivable $8,100. Compute Wild's net cash provided (used) by operating activities.

8 **BE23-12** In 2014, Leppard Inc. issued 1,000 shares of $10 par value common stock for land worth $40,000.

(a) Prepare Leppard's journal entry to record the transaction.
(b) Indicate the effect the transaction has on cash.
(c) Indicate how the transaction is reported on the statement of cash flows.

9 **BE23-13** Indicate in general journal form how the items below would be entered in a worksheet for the preparation of the statement of cash flows.

(a) Net income is $317,000.
(b) Cash dividends declared and paid totaled $120,000.
(c) Equipment was purchased for $114,000.
(d) Equipment that originally cost $40,000 and had accumulated depreciation of $32,000 was sold for $10,000.

EXERCISES

2 **E23-1 (Classification of Transactions)** Red Hot Chili Peppers Co. had the following activity in its most recent year of operations.

(a)	Purchase of equipment.	(g)	Amortization of intangible assets.
(b)	Redemption of bonds payable.	(h)	Purchase of treasury stock.
(c)	Sale of building.	(i)	Issuance of bonds for land.
(d)	Depreciation.	(j)	Payment of dividends.
(e)	Exchange of equipment for furniture.	(k)	Increase in interest receivable on notes receivable.
(f)	Issuance of capital stock.	(l)	Pension expense exceeds amount funded.

Instructions

Classify the items as (1) operating—add to net income; (2) operating—deduct from net income; (3) investing; (4) financing; or (5) significant non-cash investing and financing activities. Use the indirect method.

2 **4** **E23-2 (Statement Presentation of Transactions—Indirect Method)** Each of the following items must be considered in preparing a statement of cash flows (indirect method) for Turbulent Indigo Inc. for the year ended December 31, 2014.

(a) Plant assets that had cost $20,000 6 years before and were being depreciated on a straight-line basis over 10 years with no estimated scrap value were sold for $5,300.

(b) During the year, 10,000 shares of common stock with a stated value of $10 a share were issued for $43 a share.

(c) Uncollectible accounts receivable in the amount of $27,000 were written off against Allowance for Doubtful Accounts.

(d) The company sustained a net loss for the year of $50,000. Depreciation amounted to $22,000, and a gain of $9,000 was realized on the sale of land for $39,000 cash.

(e) A 3-month U.S. Treasury bill was purchased for $100,000. The company uses a cash and cash equivalent basis for its cash flow statement.

(f) Patent amortization for the year was $20,000.

(g) The company exchanged common stock for a 70% interest in Tabasco Co. for $900,000.

(h) During the year, treasury stock costing $47,000 was purchased.

Instructions

State where each item is to be shown in the statement of cash flows, if at all.

 E23-3 (Preparation of Operating Activities Section—Indirect Method, Periodic Inventory) The income statement of Vince Gill Company is shown below.

VINCE GILL COMPANY		
INCOME STATEMENT		
FOR THE YEAR ENDED DECEMBER 31, 2014		

Sales revenue		$6,900,000
Cost of goods sold		
Beginning inventory	$1,900,000	
Purchases	4,400,000	
Goods available for sale	6,300,000	
Ending inventory	1,600,000	
Cost of goods sold		4,700,000
Gross profit		2,200,000
Operating expenses		
Selling expenses	450,000	
Administrative expenses	700,000	1,150,000
Net income		$1,050,000

Additional information:

1. Accounts receivable decreased $360,000 during the year.
2. Prepaid expenses increased $170,000 during the year.
3. Accounts payable to suppliers of merchandise decreased $275,000 during the year.
4. Accrued expenses payable decreased $100,000 during the year.
5. Administrative expenses include depreciation expense of $60,000.

Instructions

 Prepare the operating activities section of the statement of cash flows for the year ended December 31, 2014, for Vince Gill Company, using the indirect method.

 E23-4 (Preparation of Operating Activities Section—Direct Method) Data for the Vince Gill Company are presented in E23-3.

Instructions

Prepare the operating activities section of the statement of cash flows using the direct method.

 E23-5 (Preparation of Operating Activities Section—Direct Method) Krauss Company's income statement for the year ended December 31, 2014, contained the following condensed information.

Service revenue		$840,000
Operating expenses (excluding depreciation)	$624,000	
Depreciation expense	60,000	
Loss on sale of equipment	26,000	710,000
Income before income taxes		130,000
Income tax expense		40,000
Net income		$ 90,000

Krauss's balance sheet contained the following comparative data at December 31.

	2014	2013
Accounts receivable	$37,000	$54,000
Accounts payable	41,000	31,000
Income taxes payable	4,000	8,500

(Accounts payable pertains to operating expenses.)

Instructions
Prepare the operating activities section of the statement of cash flows using the direct method.

4 7 E23-6 (Preparation of Operating Activities Section—Indirect Method) Data for Krauss Company are presented in E23-5.

Instructions
Prepare the operating activities section of the statement of cash flows using the indirect method.

4 7 E23-7 (Computation of Operating Activities—Direct Method) Presented below are two independent situations.

Situation A: Annie Lennox Co. reports revenues of $200,000 and operating expenses of $110,000 in its first year of operations, 2014. Accounts receivable and accounts payable at year-end were $71,000 and $29,000, respectively. Assume that the accounts payable related to operating expenses. (Ignore income taxes.)

Instructions
Using the direct method, compute net cash provided by operating activities.

Situation B: The income statement for Blues Traveler Company shows cost of goods sold $310,000 and operating expenses (exclusive of depreciation) $230,000. The comparative balance sheet for the year shows that inventory increased $26,000, prepaid expenses decreased $8,000, accounts payable (related to merchandise) decreased $17,000, and accrued expenses payable increased $11,000.

Instructions
Compute (a) cash payments to suppliers and (b) cash payments for operating expenses.

4 7 E23-8 (Schedule of Net Cash Flow from Operating Activities—Indirect Method) Ballard Co. reported $145,000 of net income for 2014. The accountant, in preparing the statement of cash flows, noted the following items occurring during 2014 that might affect cash flows from operating activities.

1. Ballard purchased 100 shares of treasury stock at a cost of $20 per share. These shares were then resold at $25 per share.
2. Ballard sold 100 shares of IBM common at $200 per share. The acquisition cost of these shares was $145 per share. This investment was shown on Ballard's December 31, 2013, balance sheet as an available-for-sale security.
3. Ballard revised its estimate for bad debts. Before 2014, Ballard's bad debt expense was 1% of its net sales. In 2014, this percentage was increased to 2%. Net sales for 2014 were $500,000, and net accounts receivable decreased by $12,000 during 2014.
4. Ballard issued 500 shares of its $10 par common stock for a patent. The market price of the shares on the date of the transaction was $23 per share.
5. Depreciation expense is $39,000.
6. Ballard Co. holds 40% of the Nirvana Company's common stock as a long-term investment. Nirvana Company reported $27,000 of net income for 2014.
7. Nirvana Company paid a total of $2,000 of cash dividends to all investees in 2014.
8. Ballard declared a 10% stock dividend. One thousand shares of $10 par common stock were distributed. The market price at date of issuance was $20 per share.

Instructions
Prepare a schedule that shows the net cash flow from operating activities using the indirect method. Assume no items other than those listed above affected the computation of 2014 net cash flow from operating activities.

7 E23-9 (SCF—Direct Method) Los Lobos Corp. uses the direct method to prepare its statement of cash flows. Los Lobos's trial balances at December 31, 2014 and 2013, are as follows.

	December 31	
	2014	2013
Debits		
Cash	$ 35,000	$ 32,000
Accounts receivable	33,000	30,000
Inventory	31,000	47,000
Property, plant, and equipment	100,000	95,000
Unamortized bond discount	4,500	5,000
Cost of goods sold	250,000	380,000
Selling expenses	141,500	172,000
General and administrative expenses	137,000	151,300
Interest expense	4,300	2,600
Income tax expense	20,400	61,200
	$756,700	$976,100
Credits		
Allowance for doubtful accounts	$ 1,300	$ 1,100
Accumulated depreciation—plant assets	16,500	15,000
Accounts payable	25,000	15,500
Income taxes payable	21,000	29,100
Deferred tax liability	5,300	4,600
8% callable bonds payable	45,000	20,000
Common stock	50,000	40,000
Paid-in capital in excess of par	9,100	7,500
Retained earnings	44,700	64,600
Sales revenue	538,800	778,700
	$756,700	$976,100

Additional information:

1. Los Lobos purchased $5,000 in equipment during 2014.
2. Los Lobos allocated one-third of its depreciation expense to selling expenses and the remainder to general and administrative expenses.
3. Bad debt expense for 2014 was $5,000, and write-offs of uncollectible accounts totaled $4,800.

Instructions

Determine what amounts Los Lobos should report in its statement of cash flows for the year ended December 31, 2014, for the following items.

(a) Cash collected from customers.
(b) Cash paid to suppliers.
(c) Cash paid for interest.

(d) Cash paid for income taxes.
(e) Cash paid for selling expenses.

2 8 **E23-10 (Classification of Transactions)** Following are selected balance sheet accounts of Allman Bros. Corp. at December 31, 2014 and 2013, and the increases or decreases in each account from 2013 to 2014. Also presented is selected income statement information for the year ended December 31, 2014, and additional information.

Selected balance sheet accounts	2014	2013	Increase (Decrease)
Assets			
Accounts receivable	$ 34,000	$ 24,000	$ 10,000
Property, plant, and equipment	277,000	247,000	30,000
Accumulated depreciation—plant assets	(178,000)	(167,000)	(11,000)
Liabilities and stockholders' equity			
Bonds payable	$ 49,000	$ 46,000	$ 3,000
Dividends payable	8,000	5,000	3,000
Common stock, $1 par	22,000	19,000	3,000
Additional paid-in capital	9,000	3,000	6,000
Retained earnings	104,000	91,000	13,000

Selected income statement information for the year ended December 31, 2014

Sales revenue	$ 155,000
Depreciation	33,000
Gain on sale of equipment	14,500
Net income	31,000

Additional information:

1. During 2014, equipment costing $45,000 was sold for cash.
2. Accounts receivable relate to sales of merchandise.
3. During 2014, $20,000 of bonds payable were issued in exchange for property, plant, and equipment. There was no amortization of bond discount or premium.

Instructions

Determine the category (operating, investing, or financing) and the amount that should be reported in the statement of cash flows for the following items.

(a) Payments for purchase of property, plant, and equipment.
(b) Proceeds from the sale of equipment.
(c) Cash dividends paid.
(d) Redemption of bonds payable.

3 **E23-11 (SCF—Indirect Method)** Condensed financial data of Pat Metheny Company for 2014 and 2013 are presented below.

PAT METHENY COMPANY
COMPARATIVE BALANCE SHEET
AS OF DECEMBER 31, 2014 AND 2013

	2014	2013
Cash	$1,800	$1,150
Receivables	1,750	1,300
Inventory	1,600	1,900
Plant assets	1,900	1,700
Accumulated depreciation	(1,200)	(1,170)
Long-term investments (held-to-maturity)	1,300	1,420
	$7,150	$6,300
Accounts payable	$1,200	$ 900
Accrued liabilities	200	250
Bonds payable	1,400	1,550
Capital stock	1,900	1,700
Retained earnings	2,450	1,900
	$7,150	$6,300

PAT METHENY COMPANY
INCOME STATEMENT
FOR THE YEAR ENDED DECEMBER 31, 2014

Sales revenue	$6,900
Cost of goods sold	4,700
Gross margin	2,200
Selling and administrative expense	930
Income from operations	1,270
Other revenues and gains	
Gain on sale of investments	80
Income before tax	1,350
Income tax expense	540
Net income	810
Cash dividends	260
Income retained in business	$ 550

Additional information:

During the year, $70 of common stock was issued in exchange for plant assets. No plant assets were sold in 2014.

Instructions

Prepare a statement of cash flows using the indirect method.

3 **E23-12 (SCF—Direct Method)** Data for Pat Metheny Company are presented in E23-11.

Instructions
Prepare a statement of cash flows using the direct method. (Do not prepare a reconciliation schedule.)

3 **E23-13 (SCF—Direct Method)** Brecker Inc., a greeting card company, had the following statements prepared as of December 31, 2014.

BRECKER INC.
COMPARATIVE BALANCE SHEET
AS OF DECEMBER 31, 2014 AND 2013

	12/31/14	12/31/13
Cash	$ 6,000	$ 7,000
Accounts receivable	62,000	51,000
Short-term investments (available-for-sale)	35,000	18,000
Inventory	40,000	60,000
Prepaid rent	5,000	4,000
Equipment	154,000	130,000
Accumulated depreciation—equipment	(35,000)	(25,000)
Copyrights	46,000	50,000
Total assets	$313,000	$295,000
Accounts payable	$ 46,000	$ 40,000
Income taxes payable	4,000	6,000
Salaries and wages payable	8,000	4,000
Short-term loans payable	8,000	10,000
Long-term loans payable	60,000	69,000
Common stock, $10 par	100,000	100,000
Contributed capital, common stock	30,000	30,000
Retained earnings	57,000	36,000
Total liabilities and stockholders' equity	$313,000	$295,000

BRECKER INC.
INCOME STATEMENT
FOR THE YEAR ENDING DECEMBER 31, 2014

Sales revenue		$338,150
Cost of goods sold		175,000
Gross profit		163,150
Operating expenses		120,000
Operating income		43,150
Interest expense	$11,400	
Gain on sale of equipment	2,000	9,400
Income before tax		33,750
Income tax expense		6,750
Net income		$ 27,000

Additional information:
1. Dividends in the amount of $6,000 were declared and paid during 2014.
2. Depreciation expense and amortization expense are included in operating expenses.
3. No unrealized gains or losses have occurred on the investments during the year.
4. Equipment that had a cost of $20,000 and was 70% depreciated was sold during 2014.

Instructions
Prepare a statement of cash flows using the direct method. (Do not prepare a reconciliation schedule.)

3 **E23-14 (SCF—Indirect Method)** Data for Brecker Inc. are presented in E23-13.

Instructions
Prepare a statement of cash flows using the indirect method.

3 **E23-15 (SCF—Indirect Method)** Presented below are data taken from the records of Alee Company.

	December 31, 2014	December 31, 2013
Cash	$ 15,000	$ 8,000
Current assets other than cash	85,000	60,000
Long-term investments	10,000	53,000
Plant assets	335,000	215,000
	$445,000	$336,000
Accumulated depreciation	$ 20,000	$ 40,000
Current liabilities	40,000	22,000
Bonds payable	75,000	–0–
Capital stock	254,000	254,000
Retained earnings	56,000	20,000
	$445,000	$336,000

Additional information:

1. Held-to-maturity securities carried at a cost of $43,000 on December 31, 2013, were sold in 2014 for $34,000. The loss (not extraordinary) was incorrectly charged directly to Retained Earnings.
2. Plant assets that cost $50,000 and were 80% depreciated were sold during 2014 for $8,000. The loss (not extraordinary) was incorrectly charged directly to Retained Earnings.
3. Net income as reported on the income statement for the year was $57,000.
4. Dividends paid amounted to $10,000.
5. Depreciation charged for the year was $20,000.

Instructions
Prepare a statement of cash flows for the year 2014 using the indirect method.

2 **4** **E23-16 (Cash Provided by Operating, Investing, and Financing Activities)** The balance sheet data of
5 Brown Company at the end of 2014 and 2013 follow.

	2014	2013
Cash	$ 30,000	$ 35,000
Accounts receivable (net)	55,000	45,000
Inventory	65,000	45,000
Prepaid expenses	15,000	25,000
Equipment	90,000	75,000
Accumulated depreciation—equipment	(18,000)	(8,000)
Land	70,000	40,000
	$307,000	$257,000
Accounts payable	$ 65,000	$ 52,000
Accrued expenses	15,000	18,000
Notes payable—bank, long-term	–0–	23,000
Bonds payable	30,000	–0–
Common stock, $10 par	189,000	159,000
Retained earnings	8,000	5,000
	$307,000	$257,000

Land was acquired for $30,000 in exchange for common stock, par $30,000, during the year; all equipment purchased was for cash. Equipment costing $10,000 was sold for $3,000; book value of the equipment was $6,000. Cash dividends of $10,000 were declared and paid during the year.

Instructions
Compute net cash provided (used) by:

(a) Operating activities.
(b) Investing activities.
(c) Financing activities.

3 **E23-17** (SCF—Indirect Method and Balance Sheet) Jobim Inc. had the following condensed balance sheet at the end of operations for 2013.

	JOBIM INC.		
	BALANCE SHEET		
	DECEMBER 31, 2013		
Cash	$ 8,500	Current liabilities	$ 15,000
Current assets other than cash	29,000	Long-term notes payable	25,500
Investments	20,000	Bonds payable	25,000
Plant assets (net)	67,500	Capital stock	75,000
Land	40,000	Retained earnings	24,500
	$165,000		$165,000

During 2014, the following occurred.

1. A tract of land was purchased for $9,000.
2. Bonds payable in the amount of $15,000 were redeemed at par.
3. An additional $10,000 in capital stock was issued at par.
4. Dividends totaling $9,375 were paid to stockholders.
5. Net income was $35,250 after allowing depreciation of $13,500.
6. Land was purchased through the issuance of $22,500 in bonds.
7. Jobim Inc. sold part of its investment portfolio for $12,875. This transaction resulted in a gain of $2,000 for the company. The company classifies the investments as available-for-sale.
8. Both current assets (other than cash) and current liabilities remained at the same amount.

Instructions

(a) Prepare a statement of cash flows for 2014 using the indirect method.
(b) Prepare the condensed balance sheet for Jobim Inc. as it would appear at December 31, 2014.

3 **8** **E23-18** (Partial SCF—Indirect Method) The accounts below appear in the ledger of Anita Baker Company.

	Retained Earnings	Dr.	Cr.	Bal.
Jan. 1, 2014	Credit Balance			$ 42,000
Aug. 15	Dividends (cash)	$15,000		27,000
Dec. 31	Net Income for 2014		$40,000	67,000

	Equipment	Dr.	Cr.	Bal.
Jan. 1, 2014	Debit Balance			$140,000
Aug. 3	Purchase of Equipment	$62,000		202,000
Sept. 10	Cost of Equipment Constructed	48,000		250,000
Nov. 15	Equipment Sold		$56,000	194,000

	Accumulated Depreciation—Equipment	Dr.	Cr.	Bal.
Jan. 1, 2014	Credit Balance			$ 84,000
Apr. 8	Extraordinary Repairs	$21,000		63,000
Nov. 15	Accum. Depreciation on Equipment Sold	25,200		37,800
Dec. 31	Depreciation for 2014		$16,800	54,600

Instructions

From the postings in the accounts above, indicate how the information is reported on a statement of cash flows by preparing a partial statement of cash flows using the indirect method. The loss on sale of equipment (November 15) was $5,800.

9 **E23-19** (Worksheet Analysis of Selected Accounts) Data for Anita Baker Company are presented in E23-18.

Instructions

Prepare entries in journal form for all adjustments that should be made on a worksheet for a statement of cash flows.

9 **E23-20 (Worksheet Analysis of Selected Transactions)** The transactions below took place during the year 2014.

1. Convertible bonds payable with a par value of $300,000 were exchanged for unissued common stock with a par value of $300,000. The market price of both types of securities was par.
2. The net income for the year was $410,000.
3. Depreciation expense for the building was $90,000.
4. Some old office equipment was traded in on the purchase of some dissimilar office equipment, and the following entry was made.

Equipment	50,000	
Accum. Depreciation—Equipment	30,000	
Equipment		40,000
Cash		34,000
Gain on Disposal of Plant Assets		6,000

The Gain on Disposal of Plant Assets was credited to current operations as ordinary income.

5. Dividends in the amount of $123,000 were declared. They are payable in January of next year.

Instructions

Show by journal entries the adjustments that would be made on a worksheet for a statement of cash flows.

9 **E23-21 (Worksheet Preparation)** Below is the comparative balance sheet for Stevie Wonder Corporation.

	Dec. 31, 2014	Dec. 31, 2013
Cash	$ 16,500	$ 21,000
Short-term investments	25,000	19,000
Accounts receivable	43,000	45,000
Allowance for doubtful accounts	(1,800)	(2,000)
Prepaid expenses	4,200	2,500
Inventory	81,500	65,000
Land	50,000	50,000
Buildings	125,000	73,500
Accumulated depreciation—buildings	(30,000)	(23,000)
Equipment	53,000	46,000
Accumulated depreciation—equipment	(19,000)	(15,500)
Delivery equipment	39,000	39,000
Accumulated depreciation—delivery equipment	(22,000)	(20,500)
Patents	15,000	—0—
	$379,400	$300,000

	Dec. 31, 2014	Dec. 31, 2013
Accounts payable	$ 26,000	$ 16,000
Short-term notes payable (trade)	4,000	6,000
Accrued payables	3,000	4,600
Mortgage payable	73,000	53,400
Bonds payable	50,000	62,500
Capital stock	140,000	102,000
Paid-in capital in excess of par	10,000	4,000
Retained earnings	73,400	51,500
	$379,400	$300,000

Dividends in the amount of $15,000 were declared and paid in 2014.

Instructions

From this information, prepare a worksheet for a statement of cash flows. Make reasonable assumptions as appropriate. The short-term investments are considered available-for-sale and no unrealized gains or losses have occurred on these securities.

PROBLEMS

3 4 8 **P23-1 (SCF—Indirect Method)** The following are Sullivan Corp.'s comparative balance sheet accounts at December 31, 2014 and 2013, with a column showing the increase (decrease) from 2013 to 2014.

COMPARATIVE BALANCE SHEETS

	2014	2013	Increase (Decrease)
Cash	$ 815,000	$ 700,000	$115,000
Accounts receivable	1,128,000	1,168,000	(40,000)
Inventory	1,850,000	1,715,000	135,000
Property, plant, and equipment	3,307,000	2,967,000	340,000
Accumulated depreciation	(1,165,000)	(1,040,000)	(125,000)
Investment in Myers Co.	310,000	275,000	35,000
Loan receivable	250,000	—	250,000
Total assets	$6,495,000	$5,785,000	$710,000
Accounts payable	$1,015,000	$ 955,000	$ 60,000
Income taxes payable	30,000	50,000	(20,000)
Dividends payable	80,000	100,000	(20,000)
Lease liability	400,000	—	400,000
Common stock, $1 par	500,000	500,000	—
Paid-in capital in excess of par—common stock	1,500,000	1,500,000	—
Retained earnings	2,970,000	2,680,000	290,000
Total liabilities and stockholders' equity	$6,495,000	$5,785,000	$710,000

Additional information:

1. On December 31, 2013, Sullivan acquired 25% of Myers Co.'s common stock for $275,000. On that date, the carrying value of Myers's assets and liabilities, which approximated their fair values, was $1,100,000. Myers reported income of $140,000 for the year ended December 31, 2014. No dividend was paid on Myers's common stock during the year.
2. During 2014, Sullivan loaned $300,000 to TLC Co., an unrelated company. TLC made the first semi-annual principal repayment of $50,000, plus interest at 10%, on December 31, 2014.
3. On January 2, 2014, Sullivan sold equipment costing $60,000, with a carrying amount of $38,000, for $40,000 cash.
4. On December 31, 2014, Sullivan entered into a capital lease for an office building. The present value of the annual rental payments is $400,000, which equals the fair value of the building. Sullivan made the first rental payment of $60,000 when due on January 2, 2015.
5. Net income for 2014 was $370,000.
6. Sullivan declared and paid the following cash dividends for 2014 and 2013.

	2014	2013
Declared	December 15, 2014	December 15, 2013
Paid	February 28, 2015	February 28, 2014
Amount	$80,000	$100,000

Instructions
Prepare a statement of cash flows for Sullivan Corp. for the year ended December 31, 2014, using the indirect method.

(AICPA adapted)

P23-2 (SCF—Indirect Method) The comparative balance sheets for Hinckley Corporation show the following information.

	December 31	
	2014	2013
Cash	$ 33,500	$13,000
Accounts receivable	12,250	10,000
Inventory	12,000	9,000
Investments	–0–	3,000
Buildings	–0–	29,750
Equipment	45,000	20,000
Patents	5,000	6,250
	$107,750	$91,000
Allowance for doubtful accounts	$ 3,000	$ 4,500
Accumulated depreciation—equipment	2,000	4,500
Accumulated depreciation—building	–0–	6,000
Accounts payable	5,000	3,000
Dividends payable	–0–	5,000
Notes payable, short-term (nontrade)	3,000	4,000
Long-term notes payable	31,000	25,000
Common stock	43,000	33,000
Retained earnings	20,750	6,000
	$107,750	$91,000

Additional data related to 2014 are as follows.

1. Equipment that had cost $11,000 and was 40% depreciated at time of disposal was sold for $2,500.
2. $10,000 of the long-term note payable was paid by issuing common stock.
3. Cash dividends paid were $5,000.
4. On January 1, 2014, the building was completely destroyed by a flood. Insurance proceeds on the building were $30,000 (net of $2,000 taxes).
5. Investments (available-for-sale) were sold at $1,700 above their cost. The company has made similar sales and investments in the past.
6. Cash was paid for the acquisition of equipment.
7. A long-term note for $16,000 was issued for the acquisition of equipment.
8. Interest of $2,000 and income taxes of $6,500 were paid in cash.

Instructions
Prepare a statement of cash flows using the indirect method. Flood damage is unusual and infrequent in that part of the country.

P23-3 (SCF—Direct Method) Mortonson Company has not yet prepared a formal statement of cash flows for the 2014 fiscal year. Comparative balance sheets as of December 31, 2013 and 2014, and a statement of income and retained earnings for the year ended December 31, 2014, are presented as follows.

MORTONSON COMPANY
STATEMENT OF INCOME AND RETAINED EARNINGS
FOR THE YEAR ENDED DECEMBER 31, 2014
($000 OMITTED)

Sales revenue		$3,800
Expenses		
Cost of goods sold	$1,200	
Salaries and benefits	725	
Heat, light, and power	75	
Depreciation	80	
Property taxes	19	
Patent amortization	25	
Miscellaneous expenses	10	
Interest	30	2,164

MORTONSON COMPANY
STATEMENT OF INCOME AND RETAINED EARNINGS
FOR THE YEAR ENDED DECEMBER 31, 2014
(CONTINUED)

Income before income taxes	1,636
Income taxes	818
Net income	818
Retained earnings—Jan. 1, 2014	310
	1,128
Stock dividend declared and issued	600
Retained earnings—Dec. 31, 2014	$ 528

MORTONSON COMPANY
COMPARATIVE BALANCE SHEETS
AS OF DECEMBER 31
($000 OMITTED)

Assets	2014	2013
Current assets		
Cash	$ 333	$ 100
U.S. Treasury notes (available-for-sale)	10	50
Accounts receivable	780	500
Inventory	720	560
Total current assets	1,843	1,210
Long-term assets		
Land	150	70
Buildings and equipment	910	600
Accumulated depreciation—buildings and equipment	(200)	(120)
Patents (less amortization)	105	130
Total long-term assets	965	680
Total assets	$2,808	$1,890

Liabilities and Stockholders' Equity	2014	2013
Current liabilities		
Accounts payable	$ 420	$ 330
Income taxes payable	40	30
Notes payable	320	320
Total current liabilities	780	680
Long-term notes payable—due 2016	200	200
Total liabilities	980	880
Stockholders' equity		
Common stock	1,300	700
Retained earnings	528	310
Total stockholders' equity	1,828	1,010
Total liabilities and stockholders' equity	$2,808	$1,890

Instructions

Prepare a statement of cash flows using the direct method. Changes in accounts receivable and accounts payable relate to sales and cost of goods sold. Do not prepare a reconciliation schedule.

(CMA adapted)

 P23-4 (SCF—Direct Method) Michaels Company had available at the end of 2014 the information shown on the next page.

MICHAELS COMPANY
COMPARATIVE BALANCE SHEETS
AS OF DECEMBER 31, 2014 AND 2013

	2014	2013
Cash	$ 10,000	$ 4,000
Accounts receivable	20,500	12,950
Short-term investments	22,000	30,000
Inventory	42,000	35,000
Prepaid rent	3,000	12,000
Prepaid insurance	2,100	900
Supplies	1,000	750
Land	125,000	175,000
Buildings	350,000	350,000
Accumulated depreciation—buildings	(105,000)	(87,500)
Equipment	525,000	400,000
Accumulated depreciation—equipment	(130,000)	(112,000)
Patents	45,000	50,000
Total assets	$910,600	$871,100
Accounts payable	$ 22,000	$ 32,000
Income taxes payable	5,000	4,000
Salaries and wages payable	5,000	3,000
Short-term notes payable	10,000	10,000
Long-term notes payable	60,000	70,000
Bonds payable	400,000	400,000
Premium on bonds payable	20,303	25,853
Common stock	240,000	220,000
Paid-in capital in excess of par—common stock	25,000	17,500
Retained earnings	123,297	88,747
Total liabilities and stockholders' equity	$910,600	$871,100

MICHAELS COMPANY
INCOME STATEMENT AND DIVIDEND INFORMATION
FOR THE YEAR ENDED DECEMBER 31, 2014

Sales revenue		$1,160,000
Cost of goods sold		748,000
Gross margin		412,000
Operating expenses		
Selling expenses	$ 79,200	
Administrative expenses	156,700	
Depreciation/Amortization expense	40,500	
Total operating expenses		276,400
Income from operations		135,600
Other revenues/expenses		
Gain on sale of land	8,000	
Gain on sale of short-term investment	4,000	
Dividend revenue	2,400	
Interest expense	(51,750)	(37,350)
Income before taxes		98,250
Income tax expense		39,400
Net income		58,850
Dividends to common stockholders		(24,300)
To retained earnings		$ 34,550

Instructions

Prepare a statement of cash flows for Michaels Company using the direct method accompanied by a reconciliation schedule. Assume the short-term investments are classified as available-for-sale.

3 6 8 **P23-5 (SCF—Indirect Method)** You have completed the field work in connection with your audit of Alexander Corporation for the year ended December 31, 2014. The balance sheet accounts at the beginning and end of the year are shown below.

	Dec. 31, 2014	Dec. 31, 2013	Increase or (Decrease)
Cash	$ 277,900	$ 298,000	($20,100)
Accounts receivable	469,424	353,000	116,424
Inventory	741,700	610,000	131,700
Prepaid expenses	12,000	8,000	4,000
Investment in subsidiary	110,500	–0–	110,500
Cash surrender value of life insurance	2,304	1,800	504
Machinery	207,000	190,000	17,000
Buildings	535,200	407,900	127,300
Land	52,500	52,500	–0–
Patents	69,000	64,000	5,000
Copyrights	40,000	50,000	(10,000)
Bond discount and issue costs	4,502	–0–	4,502
	$2,522,030	$2,035,200	$486,830
Income taxes payable	$ 90,250	$ 79,600	$ 10,650
Accounts payable	299,280	280,000	19,280
Dividends payable	70,000	–0–	70,000
Bonds payable—8%	125,000	–0–	125,000
Bonds payable—12%	–0–	100,000	(100,000)
Allowance for doubtful accounts	35,300	40,000	(4,700)
Accumulated depreciation—buildings	424,000	400,000	24,000
Accumulated depreciation—machinery	173,000	130,000	43,000
Premium on bonds payable	–0–	2,400	(2,400)
Common stock—no par	1,176,200	1,453,200	(277,000)
Paid-in capital in excess of par—common stock	109,000	–0–	109,000
Retained earnings—unappropriated	20,000	(450,000)	470,000
	$2,522,030	$2,035,200	$486,830

STATEMENT OF RETAINED EARNINGS
FOR THE YEAR ENDED DECEMBER 31, 2014

January	1, 2014	Balance (deficit)	$(450,000)
March	31, 2014	Net income for first quarter of 2014	25,000
April	1, 2014	Transfer from paid-in capital	425,000
		Balance	–0–
December	31, 2014	Net income for last three quarters of 2014	90,000
		Dividend declared—payable January 21, 2015	(70,000)
		Balance	$ 20,000

Your working papers from the audit contain the following information:

1. On April 1, 2014, the existing deficit was written off against paid-in capital created by reducing the stated value of the no-par stock.
2. On November 1, 2014, 29,600 shares of no-par stock were sold for $257,000. The board of directors voted to regard $5 per share as stated capital.
3. A patent was purchased for $15,000.
4. During the year, machinery that had a cost basis of $16,400 and on which there was accumulated depreciation of $5,200 was sold for $9,000. No other plant assets were sold during the year.
5. The 12%, 20-year bonds were dated and issued on January 2, 2002. Interest was payable on June 30 and December 31. They were sold originally at 106. These bonds were redeemed at 100.9 plus accrued interest on March 31, 2014.
6. The 8%, 40-year bonds were dated January 1, 2014, and were sold on March 31 at 97 plus accrued interest. Interest is payable semiannually on June 30 and December 31. Expense of issuance was $839.
7. Alexander Corporation acquired 70% control in Crimson Company on January 2, 2014, for $100,000. The income statement of Crimson Company for 2014 shows a net income of $15,000.
8. Extraordinary repairs to buildings of $7,200 were charged to Accumulated Depreciation—Buildings.
9. Interest paid in 2014 was $10,500 and income taxes paid were $34,000.

Instructions

From the information given, prepare a statement of cash flows using the indirect method. A worksheet is not necessary, but the principal computations should be supported by schedules or general ledger accounts. The company uses straight-line amortization for bond interest.

 P23-6 (SCF—Indirect Method, and Net Cash Flow from Operating Activities, Direct Method) Comparative balance sheet accounts of Marcus Inc. are presented below.

MARCUS INC.
COMPARATIVE BALANCE SHEET ACCOUNTS
AS OF DECEMBER 31, 2014 AND 2013

	December 31	
Debit Accounts	2014	2013
Cash	$ 42,000	$ 33,750
Accounts Receivable	70,500	60,000
Inventory	30,000	24,000
Investments (available-for-sale)	22,250	38,500
Machinery	30,000	18,750
Buildings	67,500	56,250
Land	7,500	7,500
	$269,750	$238,750
Credit Accounts		
Allowance for Doubtful Accounts	$ 2,250	$ 1,500
Accumulated Depreciation—Machinery	5,625	2,250
Accumulated Depreciation—Buildings	13,500	9,000
Accounts Payable	35,000	24,750
Accrued Payables	3,375	2,625
Long-Term Notes Payable	21,000	31,000
Common Stock, no-par	150,000	125,000
Retained Earnings	39,000	42,625
	$269,750	$238,750

Additional data (ignoring taxes):

1. Net income for the year was $42,500.
2. Cash dividends declared and paid during the year were $21,125.
3. A 20% stock dividend was declared during the year. $25,000 of retained earnings was capitalized.
4. Investments that cost $25,000 were sold during the year for $28,750.
5. Machinery that cost $3,750, on which $750 of depreciation had accumulated, was sold for $2,200.

Marcus's 2014 income statement follows (ignoring taxes).

Sales revenue		$540,000
Less: Cost of goods sold		380,000
Gross margin		160,000
Less: Operating expenses (includes $8,625 depreciation and $5,400 bad debts)		120,450
Income from operations		39,550
Other: Gain on sale of investments	$3,750	
Loss on sale of machinery	(800)	2,950
Net income		$ 42,500

Instructions

(a) Compute net cash flow from operating activities using the direct method.
(b) Prepare a statement of cash flows using the indirect method.

 P23-7 (SCF—Direct and Indirect Methods from Comparative Financial Statements) Chapman Company, a major retailer of bicycles and accessories, operates several stores and is a publicly traded company. The comparative balance sheet and income statement for Chapman as of May 31, 2014, are as follows. The company is preparing its statement of cash flows.

CHAPMAN COMPANY
COMPARATIVE BALANCE SHEET
AS OF MAY 31

	2014	2013
Current assets		
Cash	$ 28,250	$ 20,000
Accounts receivable	75,000	58,000
Inventory	220,000	250,000
Prepaid expenses	9,000	7,000
Total current assets	332,250	335,000
Plant assets		
Plant assets	600,000	502,000
Less: Accumulated depreciation—plant assets	150,000	125,000
Net plant assets	450,000	377,000
Total assets	$782,250	$712,000
Current liabilities		
Accounts payable	$123,000	$115,000
Salaries and wages payable	47,250	72,000
Interest payable	27,000	25,000
Total current liabilities	197,250	212,000
Long-term debt		
Bonds payable	70,000	100,000
Total liabilities	267,250	312,000
Stockholders' equity		
Common stock, $10 par	370,000	280,000
Retained earnings	145,000	120,000
Total stockholders' equity	515,000	400,000
Total liabilities and stockholders' equity	$782,250	$712,000

CHAPMAN COMPANY
INCOME STATEMENT
FOR THE YEAR ENDED MAY 31, 2014

Sales revenue	$1,255,250
Cost of goods sold	722,000
Gross profit	533,250
Expenses	
Salaries and wages expense	252,100
Interest expense	75,000
Depreciation expense	25,000
Other expenses	8,150
Total expenses	360,250
Operating income	173,000
Income tax expense	43,000
Net income	$ 130,000

The following is additional information concerning Chapman's transactions during the year ended May 31, 2014.

1. All sales during the year were made on account.
2. All merchandise was purchased on account, comprising the total accounts payable account.
3. Plant assets costing $98,000 were purchased by paying $28,000 in cash and issuing 7,000 shares of stock.
4. The "other expenses" are related to prepaid items.
5. All income taxes incurred during the year were paid during the year.
6. In order to supplement its cash, Chapman issued 2,000 shares of common stock at par value.
7. Cash dividends of $105,000 were declared and paid at the end of the fiscal year.

Instructions

(a) Compare and contrast the direct method and the indirect method for reporting cash flows from operating activities.

(b) Prepare a statement of cash flows for Chapman Company for the year ended May 31, 2014, using the direct method. Be sure to support the statement with appropriate calculations. (A reconciliation of net income to net cash provided is not required.)

(c) Using the indirect method, calculate only the net cash flow from operating activities for Chapman Company for the year ended May 31, 2014.

3 6 **P23-8 (SCF—Direct and Indirect Methods)** Comparative balance sheet accounts of Sharpe Company are
8 presented below.

<table>
<tr><td colspan="3" align="center">SHARPE COMPANY
COMPARATIVE BALANCE SHEET ACCOUNTS
AS OF DECEMBER 31</td></tr>
<tr><td>Debit Balances</td><td>2014</td><td>2013</td></tr>
<tr><td>Cash</td><td>$ 70,000</td><td>$ 51,000</td></tr>
<tr><td>Accounts Receivable</td><td>155,000</td><td>130,000</td></tr>
<tr><td>Inventory</td><td>75,000</td><td>61,000</td></tr>
<tr><td>Investments (available-for-sale)</td><td>55,000</td><td>85,000</td></tr>
<tr><td>Equipment</td><td>70,000</td><td>48,000</td></tr>
<tr><td>Buildings</td><td>145,000</td><td>145,000</td></tr>
<tr><td>Land</td><td>40,000</td><td>25,000</td></tr>
<tr><td>Totals</td><td>$610,000</td><td>$545,000</td></tr>
<tr><td>Credit Balances</td><td></td><td></td></tr>
<tr><td>Allowance for Doubtful Accounts</td><td>$ 10,000</td><td>$ 8,000</td></tr>
<tr><td>Accumulated Depreciation—Equipment</td><td>21,000</td><td>14,000</td></tr>
<tr><td>Accumulated Depreciation—Buildings</td><td>37,000</td><td>28,000</td></tr>
<tr><td>Accounts Payable</td><td>66,000</td><td>60,000</td></tr>
<tr><td>Income Taxes Payable</td><td>12,000</td><td>10,000</td></tr>
<tr><td>Long-Term Notes Payable</td><td>62,000</td><td>70,000</td></tr>
<tr><td>Common Stock</td><td>310,000</td><td>260,000</td></tr>
<tr><td>Retained Earnings</td><td>92,000</td><td>95,000</td></tr>
<tr><td>Totals</td><td>$610,000</td><td>$545,000</td></tr>
</table>

Additional data:

1. Equipment that cost $10,000 and was 60% depreciated was sold in 2014.
2. Cash dividends were declared and paid during the year.
3. Common stock was issued in exchange for land.
4. Investments that cost $35,000 were sold during the year.
5. There were no write-offs of uncollectible accounts during the year.

Sharpe's 2014 income statement is as follows.

Sales revenue		$950,000
Less: Cost of goods sold		600,000
Gross profit		350,000
Less: Operating expenses (includes depreciation expense and bad debt expense)		250,000
Income from operations		100,000
Other revenues and expenses		
Gain on sale of investments	$15,000	
Loss on sale of equipment	(3,000)	12,000
Income before taxes		112,000
Income taxes		45,000
Net income		$ 67,000

Instructions

(a) Compute net cash provided by operating activities under the direct method.

(b) Prepare a statement of cash flows using the indirect method.

P23-9 (Indirect SCF) Dingel Corporation has contracted with you to prepare a statement of cash flows. The controller has provided the following information.

	December 31	
	2014	2013
Cash	$ 38,500	$13,000
Accounts receivable	12,250	10,000
Inventory	12,000	10,000
Investments	–0–	3,000
Buildings	–0–	29,750
Equipment	40,000	20,000
Copyrights	5,000	5,250
Totals	$107,750	$91,000
Allowance for doubtful accounts	$ 3,000	$ 4,500
Accumulated depreciation—equipment	2,000	4,500
Accumulated depreciation—buildings	–0–	6,000
Accounts payable	5,000	4,000
Dividends payable	–0–	5,000
Notes payable, short-term (nontrade)	3,000	4,000
Long-term notes payable	36,000	25,000
Common stock	38,000	33,000
Retained earnings	20,750	5,000
	$107,750	$91,000

Additional data related to 2014 are as follows.

1. Equipment that had cost $11,000 and was 30% depreciated at time of disposal was sold for $2,500.
2. $5,000 of the long-term note payable was paid by issuing common stock.
3. Cash dividends paid were $5,000.
4. On January 1, 2014, the building was completely destroyed by a flood. Insurance proceeds on the building were $33,000 (net of $4,000 taxes).
5. Investments (available-for-sale) were sold at $1,500 above their cost. The company has made similar sales and investments in the past.
6. Cash and long-term note for $16,000 were given for the acquisition of equipment.
7. Interest of $2,000 and income taxes of $5,000 were paid in cash.

Instructions

(a) Use the indirect method to analyze the above information and prepare a statement of cash flows for Dingel. Flood damage is unusual and infrequent in that part of the country.

(b) What would you expect to observe in the operating, investing, and financing sections of a statement of cash flows of:

(1) A severely financially troubled firm?

(2) A recently formed firm that is experiencing rapid growth?

PROBLEMS SET B

See the book's companion website, at **www.wiley.com/college/kieso**, for an additional set of problems.

CONCEPTS FOR ANALYSIS

CA23-1 (Analysis of Improper SCF) The following statement was prepared by Maloney Corporation's accountant.

MALONEY CORPORATION
STATEMENT OF SOURCES AND APPLICATION OF CASH
FOR THE YEAR ENDED SEPTEMBER 30, 2014

Sources of cash	
Net income	$111,000
Depreciation and depletion	70,000
Increase in long-term debt	179,000
Changes in current receivables and inventories, less current	
liabilities (excluding current maturities of long-term debt)	14,000
	$374,000
Application of cash	
Cash dividends	$ 60,000
Expenditure for property, plant, and equipment	214,000
Investments and other uses	20,000
Change in cash	80,000
	$374,000

The following additional information relating to Maloney Corporation is available for the year ended September 30, 2014.

1. Salaries and wages expense attributable to stock option plans was $25,000 for the year.
2. Expenditures for property, plant, and equipment $250,000
   Proceeds from retirements of property, plant, and equipment   36,000
   Net expenditures $214,000

3. A stock dividend of 10,000 shares of Maloney Corporation common stock was distributed to common stockholders on April 1, 2014, when the per share market price was $7 and par value was $1.
4. On July 1, 2014, when its market price was $6 per share, 16,000 shares of Maloney Corporation common stock were issued in exchange for 4,000 shares of preferred stock.
5. Depreciation expense $ 65,000
   Depletion expense   5,000
        $ 70,000

6. Increase in long-term debt $620,000
   Less: Redemption of debt   441,000
   Net increase $179,000

Instructions
(a) In general, what are the objectives of a statement of the type shown above for Maloney Corporation? Explain.
(b) Identify the weaknesses in the form and format of Maloney Corporation's statement of cash flows without reference to the additional information. (Assume adoption of the indirect method.)
(c) For each of the six items of additional information for the statement of cash flows, indicate the preferable treatment and explain why the suggested treatment is preferable.

(AICPA adapted)

 CA23-2 (SCF Theory and Analysis of Improper SCF) Teresa Ramirez and Lenny Traylor are examining the following statement of cash flows for Pacific Clothing Store's first year of operations.

PACIFIC CLOTHING STORE
STATEMENT OF CASH FLOWS
FOR THE YEAR ENDED JANUARY 31, 2014

Sources of cash	
From sales of merchandise	$ 382,000
From sale of capital stock	380,000
From sale of investment	120,000
From depreciation	80,000
From issuance of note for truck	30,000
From interest on investments	8,000
Total sources of cash	1,000,000

PACIFIC CLOTHING STORE
STATEMENT OF CASH FLOWS
FOR THE YEAR ENDED JANUARY 31, 2014
(CONTINUED)

Uses of cash	
For purchase of fixtures and equipment	330,000
For merchandise purchased for resale	253,000
For operating expenses (including depreciation)	170,000
For purchase of investment	95,000
For purchase of truck by issuance of note	30,000
For purchase of treasury stock	10,000
For interest on note	3,000
Total uses of cash	891,000
Net increase in cash	$ 109,000

Teresa claims that Pacific's statement of cash flows is an excellent portrayal of a superb first year, with cash increasing $109,000. Lenny replies that it was not a superb first year—that the year was an operating failure, the statement was incorrectly presented, and $109,000 is not the actual increase in cash.

Instructions

(a) With whom do you agree, Teresa or Lenny? Explain your position.

(b) Using the data provided, prepare a statement of cash flows in proper indirect method form. The only noncash items in income are depreciation and the gain from the sale of the investment (purchase and sale are related).

CA23-3 (SCF Theory and Analysis of Transactions) Ashley Company is a young and growing producer of electronic measuring instruments and technical equipment. You have been retained by Ashley to advise it in the preparation of a statement of cash flows using the indirect method. For the fiscal year ended October 31, 2014, you have obtained the following information concerning certain events and transactions of Ashley.

1. The amount of reported earnings for the fiscal year was $700,000, which included a deduction for an extraordinary loss of $110,000 (see item 5 below).
2. Depreciation expense of $315,000 was included in the income statement.
3. Uncollectible accounts receivable of $40,000 were written off against the allowance for doubtful accounts. Also, $51,000 of bad debt expense was included in determining income for the fiscal year, and the same amount was added to the allowance for doubtful accounts.
4. A gain of $6,000 was realized on the sale of a machine. It originally cost $75,000, of which $30,000 was undepreciated on the date of sale.
5. On April 1, 2014, lightning caused an uninsured building loss of $110,000 ($180,000 loss, less reduction in income taxes of $70,000). This extraordinary loss was included in determining income as indicated in item 1 above.
6. On July 3, 2014, building and land were purchased for $700,000. Ashley gave in payment $75,000 cash, $200,000 market price of its unissued common stock, and signed a $425,000 mortgage note payable.
7. On August 3, 2014, $800,000 face value of Ashley's 10% convertible debentures was converted into $150,000 par value of its common stock. The bonds were originally issued at face value.

Instructions

Explain whether each of the seven numbered items above is a cash inflow or outflow, and explain how it should be disclosed in Ashley's statement of cash flows for the fiscal year ended October 31, 2014. If any item is neither an inflow nor an outflow of cash, explain why it is not, and indicate the disclosure, if any, that should be made of the item in Ashley's statement of cash flows for the fiscal year ended October 31, 2014.

CA23-4 (Analysis of Transactions' Effect on SCF) Each of the following items must be considered in preparing a statement of cash flows for Cruz Fashions Inc. for the year ended December 31, 2014.

1. Fixed assets that had cost $20,000 6½ years before and were being depreciated on a 10-year basis, with no estimated scrap value, were sold for $4,750.
2. During the year, goodwill of $15,000 was considered impaired and was completely written off to expense.
3. During the year, 500 shares of common stock with a stated value of $25 a share were issued for $32 a share.
4. The company sustained a net loss for the year of $2,100. Depreciation amounted to $2,000 and patent amortization was $400.
5. Uncollectible accounts receivable in the amount of $2,000 were written off against Allowance for Doubtful Accounts.

6. Investments (available-for-sale) that cost $12,000 when purchased 4 years earlier were sold for $10,600. The loss was considered ordinary.

7. Bonds payable with a par value of $24,000 on which there was an unamortized bond premium of $2,000 were redeemed at 101. The gain was credited to ordinary income.

Instructions

For each item, state where it is to be shown in the statement and then how you would present the necessary information, including the amount. Consider each item to be independent of the others. Assume that correct entries were made for all transactions as they took place.

CA23-5 (Purpose and Elements of SCF) GAAP requires the statement of cash flows be presented when financial statements are prepared.

Instructions

(a) Explain the purposes of the statement of cash flows.

(b) List and describe the three categories of activities that must be reported in the statement of cash flows.

(c) Identify and describe the two methods that are allowed for reporting cash flows from operations.

(d) Describe the financial statement presentation of noncash investing and financing transactions. Include in your description an example of a noncash investing and financing transaction.

CA23-6 (Cash Flow Reporting) Brockman Guitar Company is in the business of manufacturing top-quality, steel-string folk guitars. In recent years, the company has experienced working capital problems resulting from the procurement of factory equipment, the unanticipated buildup of receivables and inventories, and the payoff of a balloon mortgage on a new manufacturing facility. The founder and president of the company, Barbara Brockman, has attempted to raise cash from various financial institutions, but to no avail because of the company's poor performance in recent years. In particular, the company's lead bank, First Financial, is especially concerned about Brockman's inability to maintain a positive cash position. The commercial loan officer from First Financial told Barbara, "I can't even consider your request for capital financing unless I see that your company is able to generate positive cash flows from operations."

Thinking about the banker's comment, Barbara came up with what she believes is a good plan: With a more attractive statement of cash flows, the bank might be willing to provide long-term financing. To "window dress" cash flows, the company can sell its accounts receivables to factors and liquidate its raw materials inventories. These rather costly transactions would generate lots of cash. As the chief accountant for Brockman Guitar, it is your job to tell Barbara what you think of her plan.

Instructions

Answer the following questions.

(a) What are the ethical issues related to Barbara Brockman's idea?

(b) What would you tell Barbara Brockman?

USING YOUR JUDGMENT

FINANCIAL REPORTING

Financial Reporting Problem

The Procter & Gamble Company (P&G)

The financial statements of P&G are presented in Appendix 5B. The company's complete annual report, including the notes to the financial statements, can be accessed at the book's companion website, **www.wiley.com/college/kieso**.

Instructions

Refer to P&G's financial statements and the accompanying notes to answer the following questions.

(a) Which method of computing net cash provided by operating activities does P&G use? What were the amounts of net cash provided by operating activities for the years 2009, 2010, and 2011? Which two items were most responsible for the decrease in net cash provided by operating activities in 2011?

(b) What was the most significant item in the cash flows used for investing activities section in 2011? What was the most significant item in the cash flows used for financing activities section in 2011?

(c) Where is "deferred income taxes" reported in P&G's statement of cash flows? Why does it appear in that section of the statement of cash flows?

(d) Where is depreciation reported in P&G's statement of cash flows? Why is depreciation added to net income in the statement of cash flows?

Comparative Analysis Case

The Coca-Cola Company and PepsiCo, Inc.

Instructions

Go to the book's companion website and use information found there to answer the following questions related to The Coca-Cola Company and PepsiCo, Inc.

(a) What method of computing net cash provided by operating activities does Coca-Cola use? What method does PepsiCo use? What were the amounts of cash provided by operating activities reported by Coca-Cola and PepsiCo in 2011?

(b) What was the most significant item reported by Coca-Cola and PepsiCo in 2011 in their investing activities sections? What is the most significant item reported by Coca-Cola and PepsiCo in 2011 in their financing activities sections?

(c) What were these two companies' trends in net cash provided by operating activities over the period 2009 to 2011?

(d) Where is "depreciation and amortization" reported by Coca-Cola and PepsiCo in their statements of cash flows? What is the amount and why does it appear in that section of the statement of cash flows?

(e) Based on the information contained in Coca-Cola's and PepsiCo's financial statements, compute the following 2011 ratios for each company. These ratios require the use of statement of cash flows data. (These ratios were covered in Chapter 5.)

    (1) Current cash debt coverage.

    (2) Cash debt coverage.

(f) What conclusions concerning the management of cash can be drawn from the ratios computed in (e)?

Financial Statement Analysis Case

Vermont Teddy Bear Co.

Founded in the early 1980s, the Vermont Teddy Bear Co. designs and manufactures American-made teddy bears and markets them primarily as gifts called Bear-Grams or Teddy Bear-Grams. Bear-Grams are personalized teddy bears delivered directly to the recipient for special occasions such as birthdays and anniversaries. The Shelburne, Vermont, company's primary markets are New York, Boston, and Chicago. Sales have jumped dramatically in recent years. Such dramatic growth has significant implications for cash flows. Provided below are the cash flow statements for two recent years for the company.

	Current Year	Prior Year
Cash flows from operating activities:		
Net income	$ 17,523	$ 838,955
Adjustments to reconcile net income to net cash provided by operating activities		
Deferred income taxes	(69,524)	(146,590)
Depreciation and amortization	316,416	181,348
Changes in assets and liabilities:		
Accounts receivable, trade	(38,267)	(25,947)
Inventories	(1,599,014)	(1,289,293)
Prepaid and other current assets	(444,794)	(113,205)
Deposits and other assets	(24,240)	(83,044)
Accounts payable	2,017,059	(284,567)
Accrued expenses	61,321	170,755
Accrued interest payable, debentures	—	(58,219)
Other	—	(8,960)
Income taxes payable	—	117,810
Net cash provided by (used for) operating activities	236,480	(700,957)
Net cash used for investing activities	(2,102,892)	(4,422,953)
Net cash (used for) provided by financing activities	(315,353)	9,685,435
Net change in cash and cash equivalents	(2,181,765)	4,561,525

Other information:

Current liabilities	$ 4,055,465	$ 1,995,600
Total liabilities	4,620,085	2,184,386
Net sales	20,560,566	17,025,856

Instructions

(a) Note that net income in the current year was only $17,523 compared to prior-year income of $838,955, but net cash flow from operating activities was $236,480 in the current year and a negative $700,957 in the prior year. Explain the causes of this apparent paradox.

(b) Evaluate Vermont Teddy Bear's liquidity, solvency, and profitability for the current year using cash flow-based ratios.

Accounting, Analysis, and Principles

The income statement for the year ended December 31, 2014, for Laskowski Manufacturing Company contains the following condensed information.

LASKOWSKI CO. INCOME STATEMENT		
Revenues		$6,583,000
Operating expenses (excluding depreciation)	$4,920,000	
Depreciation expense	880,000	5,800,000
Income before income tax		783,000
Income tax expense		353,000
Net income		$ 430,000

Included in operating expenses is a $24,000 loss resulting from the sale of machinery for $270,000 cash. The company purchased machinery at a cost of $750,000.

Laskowski reports the following balances on its comparative balance sheets at December 31.

LASKOWSKI CO. COMPARATIVE BALANCE SHEETS (PARTIAL)		
	2014	2013
Cash	$672,000	$130,000
Accounts receivable	775,000	610,000
Inventory	834,000	867,000
Accounts payable	521,000	501,000

Income tax expense of $353,000 represents the amount paid in 2014. Dividends declared and paid in 2014 totaled $200,000.

Accounting
Prepare the statement of cash flows using the indirect method.

Analysis
Laskowski has an aggressive growth plan, which will require significant investments in plant and equipment over the next several years. Preliminary plans call for an investment of over $500,000 in the next year. Compute Laskowski's free cash flow (from Chapter 5) and use it to evaluate the investment plans with the use of only internally generated funds.

Principles
How does the statement of cash flows contribute to achieving the objective of financial reporting?

BRIDGE TO THE PROFESSION

 ## Professional Research: FASB Codification

As part of the year-end accounting process for your company, you are preparing the statement of cash flows according to GAAP. One of your team, a finance major, believes the statement should be prepared to report the change in working capital, because analysts many times use working capital in ratio analysis. Your supervisor would like research conducted to verify the basis for preparing the statement of cash flows.

Instructions

If your school has a subscription to the FASB Codification, go to *http://aaahq.org/ascLogin.cfm* to log in and prepare responses to the following. Provide Codification references for your responses.

(a) What is the primary objective for the statement of cash flows? Is working capital the basis for meeting this objective?

(b) What information is provided in a statement of cash flows?

(c) List some of the typical cash inflows and outflows from operations.

Additional Professional Resources

See the book's companion website, at **www.wiley.com/college/kieso**, for professional simulations as well as other study resources.

 IFRS INSIGHTS

LEARNING OBJECTIVE 10
Compare the statement of cash flows under GAAP and IFRS.

As in GAAP, the statement of cash flows is a required statement for IFRS. In addition, the content and presentation of a U.S. statement of cash flows is similar to one used for IFRS. However, the disclosure requirements related to the statement of cash flows are more extensive under GAAP. *IAS 7* ("Cash Flow Statements") provides the overall IFRS requirements for cash flow information.

RELEVANT FACTS

Following are the key similarities and differences between GAAP and IFRS related to the statement of cash flows.

Similarities

• Both GAAP and IFRS require that companies prepare a statement of cash flows.

• Both IFRS and GAAP require that the statement of cash flows should have three major sections—operating, investing, and financing—along with changes in cash and cash equivalents.

• Similar to GAAP, the cash flow statement can be prepared using either the indirect or direct method under IFRS. For both IFRS and GAAP, most companies use the indirect method for reporting net cash flow from operating activities.

• The definition of cash equivalents used in IFRS is similar to that used in GAAP.

Differences

• A major difference in the definition of cash and cash equivalents is that in certain situations, bank overdrafts are considered part of cash and cash equivalents under IFRS (which is not the case in GAAP). Under GAAP, bank overdrafts are classified as financing activities.

• IFRS requires that non-cash investing and financing activities be excluded from the statement of cash flows. Instead, these non-cash activities should be reported elsewhere. This requirement is interpreted to mean that non-cash investing and financing activities should be disclosed in the notes to the financial statements instead of in the financial statements. Under GAAP, companies may present this information in the cash flow statement.

- One area where there can be substantive differences between IFRS and GAAP relates to the classification of interest, dividends, and taxes. IFRS provides more alternatives for disclosing these items, while GAAP requires that except for dividends paid (which are classified as a financing activity), these items are all reported as operating activities.

ABOUT THE NUMBERS

Significant Non-Cash Transactions

Because the statement of cash flows reports only the effects of operating, investing, and financing activities in terms of cash flows, it omits some **significant non-cash transactions** and other events that are investing or financing activities. Among the more common of these non-cash transactions that a company should report or disclose in some manner are the following.

1. Acquisition of assets by assuming liabilities (including finance lease obligations) or by issuing equity securities.
2. Exchanges of non-monetary assets.
3. Refinancing of long-term debt.
4. Conversion of debt or preference shares to ordinary shares.
5. Issuance of equity securities to retire debt.

Investing and financing transactions that do not require the use of cash are excluded from the statement of cash flows. If material in amount, these disclosures may be either narrative or summarized in a separate schedule. This schedule may appear in a separate note or supplementary schedule to the financial statements.

Illustration IFRS23-1 shows the presentation of these significant non-cash transactions or other events in a separate schedule in the notes to the financial statements.

<table>
<tr><td colspan="2">**Note G: Significant non-cash transactions.**   During the year, the company engaged in the following significant non-cash investing and financing transactions:</td></tr>
<tr><td>Issued 250,000 ordinary shares to purchase land and building</td><td>$1,750,000</td></tr>
<tr><td>Exchanged land in Steadfast, New York, for land in Bedford, Pennsylvania</td><td>$2,000,000</td></tr>
<tr><td>Converted 12% bonds to 50,000 ordinary shares</td><td>$ 500,000</td></tr>
</table>

ILLUSTRATION IFRS23-1
Note Presentation of Non-Cash Investing and Financing Activities

Companies do not generally report certain other significant non-cash transactions or other events in conjunction with the statement of cash flows. Examples of these types of transactions are **share dividends, share splits, and restrictions on retained earnings**. Companies generally report these items, neither financing nor investing activities, in conjunction with the statement of changes in equity or schedules and notes pertaining to changes in equity accounts.

Special Disclosures

IAS 7 indicates that cash flows related to interest received and paid, and dividends received and paid, should be separately disclosed in the statement of cash flows. IFRS allows flexibility in how these items are classified in the statement of cash flows. However, each item should be classified in a consistent manner from period to period as operating, investing, or financing cash flows. *For homework purposes, classify interest received and paid and dividends received as part of cash flows from operating activities and dividends paid as cash flows from financing activities.* The justification for reporting the first three items in cash flows from operating activities is that each item affects net income. Dividends paid, however, do not affect net income and are often considered a cost of financing.

Companies should also disclose income taxes paid separately in the cash flows from operating activities unless they can be separately identified as part of investing or financing activities. While tax expense may be readily identifiable with investing or financing activities, the related tax cash flows are often impracticable to identify and may arise in a different period from the cash flows of the underlying transaction. Therefore, taxes paid are usually classified as cash flows from operating activities. IFRS requires that the cash paid for taxes, as well as cash flows from interest and dividends received and paid, be disclosed. The category (operating, investing, or financing) that each item was included in must be disclosed as well.

An example of such a disclosure from the notes to **Daimler**'s financial statements is provided in Illustration IFRS23-2.

ILLUSTRATION IFRS23-2
Note Disclosure of Interest, Taxes, and Dividends

Daimler

Cash provided by operating activities includes the following cash flows:

(in millions of €)	2012	2011	2010
Interest paid	(894)	(651)	(1,541)
Interest received	471	765	977
Income taxes paid, net	(358)	(898)	(1,020)
Dividends received	109	67	69

Other companies choose to report these items directly in the statement of cash flows. In many cases, companies start with income before income taxes and then show income taxes paid as a separate item. In addition, they often add back interest expense on an accrual basis and then subtract interest paid. Reporting these items in the operating activities section is shown for Mermel Company in Illustration IFRS23-3.

ILLUSTRATION IFRS23-3
Reporting of Interest, Taxes, and Dividends in the Operating Section

MERMEL COMPANY STATEMENT OF CASH FLOWS ($000,000) (OPERATING ACTIVITIES SECTION ONLY)		
Income before income tax		$ 4,000
Adjustments to reconcile income before income tax to net cash provided by operating activities:		
Depreciation expense	$1,000	
Interest expense	500	
Investment revenue (dividends)	(650)	
Decrease in inventories	1,050	
Increase in trade receivables	(310)	1,590
Cash generated from operations		5,590
Interest paid	(300)	
Income taxes paid	(760)	(1,060)
Net cash provided by operating activities		$ 4,530

Companies often provide a separate section to identify interest and income taxes paid.

ON THE HORIZON

Presently, the IASB and the FASB are involved in a joint project on the presentation and organization of information in the financial statements. With respect to the cash flow statement specifically, the notion of *cash equivalents* will probably not be retained. The definition of cash in the existing literature would be retained, and the statement of cash flows would present information on changes in cash only. In addition, the IASB and FASB favor presentation of operating cash flows using the direct method only. This approach is generally opposed by the preparer community.

IFRS SELF-TEST QUESTIONS

1. Which of the following is **true** regarding the statement of cash flows under IFRS?
   (a) The statement of cash flows has two major sections—operating and non-operating.
   (b) The statement of cash flows has two major sections—financing and investing.
   (c) The statement of cash flows has three major sections—operating, investing, and financing.
   (d) The statement of cash flows has three major sections—operating, non-operating, and financing.
2. In the case of a bank overdraft:
   (a) GAAP typically includes the amount in cash and cash equivalents.
   (b) IFRS typically includes the amount in cash equivalents but not in cash.
   (c) GAAP typically treats the overdraft as a liability, and reports the amount in the financing section of the statement of cash flows.
   (d) IFRS typically treats the overdraft as a liability, and reports the amount in the investing section of the statement of cash flows.
3. Under IFRS, significant non-cash transactions:
   (a) are classified as operating, if they are related to income items.
   (b) are excluded from the statement of cash flows and disclosed in a narrative form or summarized in a separate schedule.
   (c) are classified as an investing or financing activity.
   (d) are classified as an operating activity, unless they can be specifically identified with financing or investing activities.
4. For purposes of the statement of cash flows, under IFRS interest paid is treated as:
   (a) an operating activity in all cases.
   (b) an investing or operating activity, depending on use of the borrowed funds.
   (c) either a financing or investing activity.
   (d) either an operating or financing activity, but treated consistently from period to period.
5. For purposes of the statement of cash flows, under IFRS income taxes paid are treated as:
   (a) cash flows from operating activities unless they can be separately identified as part of investing or financing activities.
   (b) an operating activity in all cases.
   (c) an investing or operating activity, depending on whether a refund is received.
   (d) either operating, financing, or investing activity, but treated consistently to other companies in the same industry.

IFRS CONCEPTS AND APPLICATION

IFRS23-1 Where can authoritative IFRS related to the statement of cash flows be found?

IFRS23-2 Briefly describe some of the similarities and differences between GAAP and IFRS with respect to cash flow reporting.

IFRS23-3 What are some of the key obstacles for the FASB and IASB within their accounting guidance in the area of cash flow reporting? Explain.

IFRS23-4 Stan Conner and Mark Stein were discussing the statement of cash flows of Bombeck Co. In the notes to the statement of cash flows was a schedule entitled "Non-cash investing and financing activities." Give three examples of significant non-cash transactions that would be reported in this schedule.

IFRS23-5 Springsteen Co. had the following activity in its most recent year of operations.

(a) Pension expense exceeds amount funded.	(g) Amortization of intangible assets.
(b) Redemption of bonds payable.	(h) Purchase of treasury shares.
(c) Sale of building at book value.	(i) Issuance of bonds for land.
(d) Depreciation.	(j) Payment of dividends.
(e) Exchange of equipment for furniture.	(k) Increase in interest receivable on notes receivable.
(f) Issuance of ordinary shares.	(l) Purchase of equipment.

Instructions

Classify the items as (1) operating—add to net income, (2) operating—deduct from net income, (3) investing, (4) financing, or (5) significant non-cash investing and financing activities. Use the indirect method.

IFRS23-6 Following are selected statement of financial position accounts of Sander Bros. Corp. at December 31, 2014 and 2013, and the increases or decreases in each account from 2013 to 2014. Also presented is selected income statement information for the year ended December 31, 2014, and additional information.

Selected statement of financial position accounts	2014	2013	Increase (Decrease)
Assets			
Property, plant, and equipment	$277,000	$247,000	$30,000
Accumulated depreciation	(178,000)	(167,000)	(11,000)
Accounts receivable	34,000	24,000	10,000
Equity and liabilities			
Share capital—ordinary, $1 par	$ 22,000	$ 19,000	$ 3,000
Share premium—ordinary	9,000	3,000	6,000
Retained earnings	104,000	91,000	13,000
Bonds payable	49,000	46,000	3,000
Dividends payable	8,000	5,000	3,000

Selected income statement information for the year ended December 31, 2014	
Sales revenue	$155,000
Depreciation	38,000
Gain on sale of equipment	14,500
Net income	31,000

Additional information:

1. During 2014, equipment costing $45,000 was sold for cash.
2. Accounts receivable relate to sales of merchandise.
3. During 2014, $25,000 of bonds payable were issued in exchange for property, plant, and equipment.

There was no amortization of bond discount or premium.

Instructions

Determine the category (operating, investing, or financing) and the amount that should be reported in the statement of cash flows for the following items.

(a) Payments for purchase of property, plant, and equipment.
(b) Proceeds from the sale of equipment.
(c) Cash dividends paid.
(d) Redemption of bonds payable.

IFRS23-7 Dingel Corporation has contracted with you to prepare a statement of cash flows. The controller has provided the following information.

	December 31	
	2014	2013
Buildings	$ –0–	$29,750
Equipment	45,000	20,000
Patents	5,000	6,250
Investments	–0–	3,000
Inventory	12,000	9,000
Accounts receivable	12,250	10,000
Cash	33,500	13,000
	$107,750	$91,000
Share capital—ordinary	$ 43,000	$33,000
Retained earnings	20,750	6,000
Allowance for doubtful accounts	3,000	4,500
Accumulated depreciation on equipment	2,000	4,500
Accumulated depreciation on buildings	–0–	6,000
Accounts payable	5,000	3,000
Dividends payable	–0–	5,000
Long-term notes payable	31,000	25,000
Notes payable, short-term (non-trade)	3,000	4,000
	$107,750	$91,000

Additional data related to 2014 are as follows.

1. Equipment that had cost $11,000 and was 40% depreciated at time of disposal was sold for $2,500.
2. $10,000 of the long-term notes payable was paid by issuing ordinary shares.
3. Cash dividends paid were $5,000.
4. On January 1, 2014, the building was completely destroyed by a flood. Insurance proceeds on the building were $32,000.
5. Equity investments (non-trading) were sold at $1,700 above their cost.
6. Cash was paid for the acquisition of equipment.
7. A long-term note for $16,000 was issued for the acquisition of equipment.
8. Interest of $2,000 and income taxes of $6,500 were paid in cash.

Instructions

Prepare a statement of cash flows using the indirect method.

Professional Research

IFRS23-8 As part of the year-end accounting process for your company, you are preparing the statement of cash flows according to IFRS. One of your team, a finance major, believes the statement should be prepared to report the change in working capital because analysts many times use working capital in ratio analysis. Your supervisor would like research conducted to verify the basis for preparing the statement of cash flows.

Instructions

Access the IFRS authoritative literature at the IASB website (*http://eifrs.iasb.org/*). (Click on the IFRS tab and then register for free eIFRS access if necessary.) When you have accessed the documents, you can use the search tool in your Internet browser to respond to the following questions. (Provide paragraph citations.)

(a) What is the primary objective for the statement of cash flows? Is working capital the basis for meeting this objective?
(b) What information is provided in a statement of cash flows?
(c) List some of the typical cash inflows and outflows from operations.

International Financial Reporting Problem
Marks and Spencer plc

IFRS23-9 The financial statements of **Marks and Spencer plc (M&S)** are available at the book's companion website or can be accessed at *http://annualreport.marksandspencer.com/_assets/downloads/Marks-and-Spencer-Annual-report-and-financial-statements-2012.pdf.*

Instructions

Refer to M&S's financial statements and the accompanying notes to answer the following questions.

(a) Which method of computing net cash provided by operating activities does M&S use? What were the amounts of net cash provided by operating activities for the years 2011 and 2012? Which two items were most responsible for the increase in net cash provided by operating activities in 2012?
(b) What was the most significant item in the cash flows used for investing activities section in 2012? What was the most significant item in the cash flows used for financing activities section in 2012?
(c) Where is "deferred income taxes" reported in M&S's statement of cash flows? Why does it appear in that section of the statement of cash flows?
(d) Where is depreciation reported in M&S's statement of cash flows? Why is depreciation added to net income in the statement of cash flows?

ANSWERS TO IFRS SELF-TEST QUESTIONS

1. c **2.** c **3.** b **4.** d **5.** a

Remember to check the book's companion website to find additional resources for this chapter.

24 Full Disclosure in Financial Reporting

After studying this chapter, you should be able to:

1 Review the full disclosure principle and describe implementation problems.

2 Explain the use of notes in financial statement preparation.

3 Discuss the disclosure requirements for related-party transactions, post-balance-sheet events, and major business segments.

4 Describe the accounting problems associated with interim reporting.

5 Identify the major disclosures in the auditor's report.

6 Understand management's responsibilities for financials.

7 Identify issues related to financial forecasts and projections.

8 Describe the profession's response to fraudulent financial reporting.

High-Quality Financial Reporting—Always in Fashion

Here are excerpts from leading experts regarding the importance of high-quality financial reporting:

Warren E. Buffett, Chairman and Chief Executive Officer, **Berkshire Hathaway Inc.**:

> Financial reporting for Berkshire Hathaway, and for me personally, is the beginning of every decision that we make around here in terms of capital. I'm punching out 10-Ks and 10-Qs every single day. We look at the numbers and try to evaluate the quality of the financial reporting, and then we try to figure out what that means for the bonds and stocks that we're looking at, and thinking of either buying or selling.

Judy Lewent, Executive Vice President and Chief Financial Officer, **Merck & Co., Inc.**:

> Higher standards, when properly implemented, drive excellence. I can make a parallel to the pharmaceutical industry. If you look around the world at where innovations come from, economists have studied and seen that where regulatory standards are the highest is where innovation is also the highest.

Floyd Norris, Chief Financial Correspondent, **New York Times**:

> We are in a situation now in our society where the temptations to provide "bad" financial reporting are probably greater than they used to be. The need to get the stock price up, or to keep it up, is intense. So, the temptation to play games, the temptation to manage earnings—some of which can be legitimate and some of which cannot be—is probably greater than it used to be.

Abby Joseph Cohen, Chair, Investment Policy Committee, **Goldman, Sachs & Co.**:

> High-quality financial reporting is perhaps the most important thing we can expect from companies. For investors to make good decisions—whether those investors are buying stocks or bonds or making private investments—they need to know the truth. And we think that when information is as clear as possible and is reported as frequently as makes sense, investors can do their jobs as best they can.

We can also get insight into the importance of high-quality reporting based on the market assessment of companies perceived to have poor-quality reporting. In a recent quarter, **Coach, Inc.** stopped reporting as separate items sales from regular stores (full price) and factory outlets. As a result, readers of its financial statements have a hard time determining the source of Coach's sales growth. Analysts are especially concerned that the less-transparent reporting may obscure slowing sales at its regular stores, as consumers cut down on luxury goods in the sluggish economy. Did Coach's stock price suffer as a result of this lower-quality reporting? You bet, as shown in the price graph on the next page.

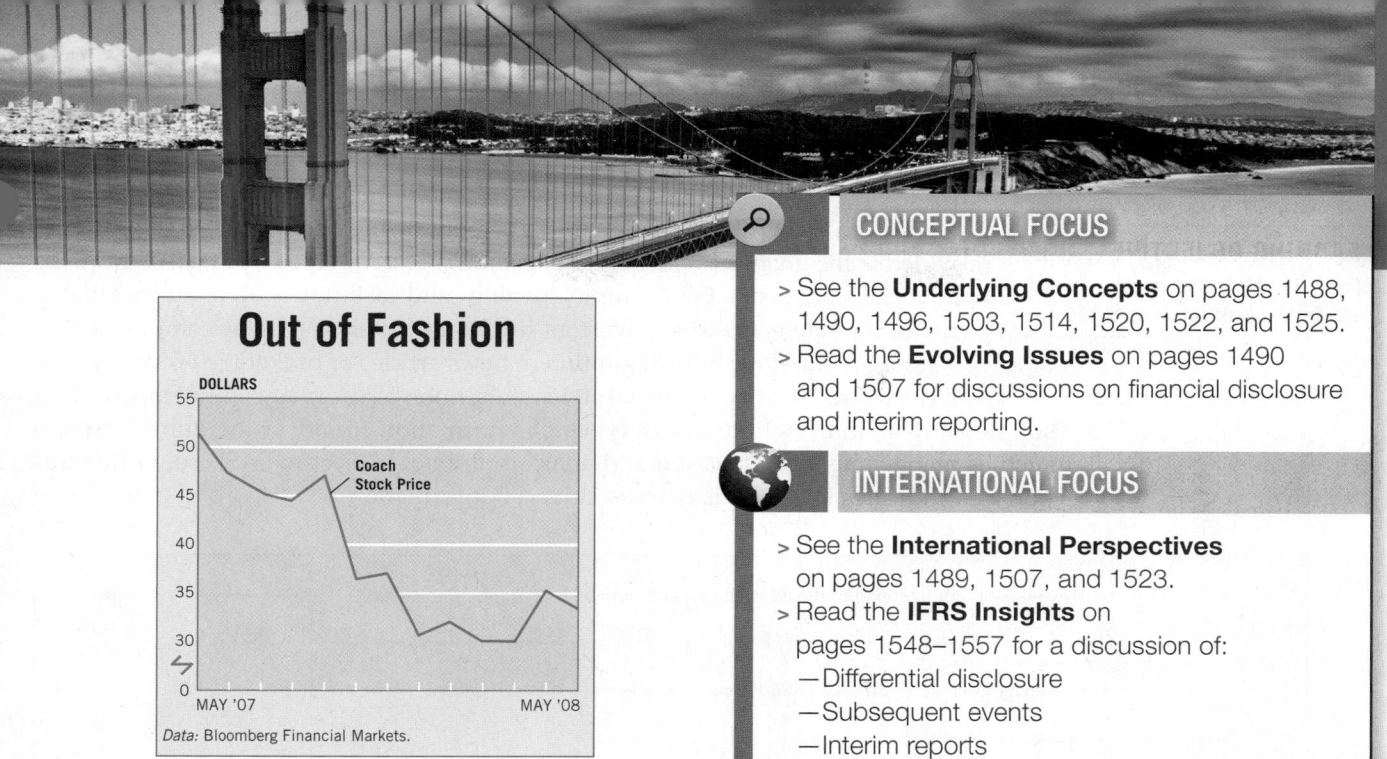

Out of Fashion

DOLLARS

Coach Stock Price

MAY '07 — MAY '08

Data: Bloomberg Financial Markets.

CONCEPTUAL FOCUS

> See the **Underlying Concepts** on pages 1488, 1490, 1496, 1503, 1514, 1520, 1522, and 1525.
> Read the **Evolving Issues** on pages 1490 and 1507 for discussions on financial disclosure and interim reporting.

INTERNATIONAL FOCUS

> See the **International Perspectives** on pages 1489, 1507, and 1523.
> Read the **IFRS Insights** on pages 1548–1557 for a discussion of:
> — Differential disclosure
> — Subsequent events
> — Interim reports

In the year following the change in reporting, Coach's stock price was down 34 percent. As one analyst noted, "It's never a good sign when you reduce transparency . . . It's a sign of weakness."

In short, the analyst's comments above illustrate why high-quality reporting is always in fashion—for companies, investors, and the capital markets. And, as the Coach example illustrates, full disclosure is at the heart of high-quality reporting.

Sources: Excerpts taken from video entitled "Financially Correct with Ben Stein," Financial Accounting Standards Board (Norwalk, Conn.: FASB, 2002). By permission. See also J. Porter, "As Belts Tighten, Coach Feels the Pinch," *BusinessWeek* (May 29, 2008), p. 66.

PREVIEW OF CHAPTER 24

As the opening story indicates, our markets will not function properly without transparent, complete, and truthful reporting of financial performance. Investors and other interested parties need to read and understand all aspects of financial reporting—the financial statements, the notes, the president's letter, and management's discussion and analysis. In this chapter, we cover the full disclosure principle in more detail and examine disclosures that must accompany financial statements so that they are not misleading. The content and organization of this chapter are as follows.

Full Disclosure in Financial Reporting

Full Disclosure Principle	Notes to Financial Statements	Disclosure Issues	Auditor's and Management's Reports	Current Reporting Issues
• Increase in reporting requirements • Differential disclosure	• Accounting policies • Common notes	• Special transactions or events • Post-balance-sheet events • Diversified companies • Interim reports	• Auditor's report • Management's reports	• Reporting on forecasts and projections • Internet financial reporting • Fraudulent financial reporting • Criteria for accounting and reporting choices

FULL DISCLOSURE PRINCIPLE

According to the FASB Conceptual Framework, some useful information is best provided in the financial statements, and some is best provided by means other than in financial statements. For example, earnings and cash flows are readily available in financial statements—but investors might do better to look at comparisons to other companies in the same industry, found in news articles or brokerage house reports.

FASB rules directly affect financial statements, notes to the financial statements, and supplementary information. Other types of information found in the annual report, such as management's discussion and analysis, are not subject to FASB rules. Illustration 24-1 indicates the various types of financial information.

ILLUSTRATION 24-1
Types of Financial
Information

As Chapter 2 indicated, the profession has adopted a **full disclosure principle**. The full disclosure principle calls for financial reporting of any **financial facts significant enough to influence the judgment of an informed reader**. In some situations, the benefits of disclosure may be apparent but the costs uncertain. In other instances, the costs may be certain but the benefits of disclosure not as apparent.

Underlying Concepts

Here is a good example of the trade-off between cost considerations and the benefits of full disclosure.

For example, the SEC required companies to provide expanded disclosures about their contractual obligations. In light of the off-balance-sheet accounting frauds at companies like Enron, the benefits of these expanded disclosures seem fairly obvious to the investing public. While no one has documented the exact costs of disclosure in these situations, they would appear to be relatively small.

On the other hand, the cost of disclosure can be substantial in some cases and the benefits difficult to assess. For example, at one time the *Wall Street Journal* reported that if segment reporting were adopted, a company like Fruehauf would have had to increase its accounting staff 50 percent, from 300 to 450 individuals. In this case, the cost of disclosure can be measured, but the benefits are less well defined.

Some even argue that the reporting requirements are so detailed and substantial that users have a difficult time absorbing the information. These critics charge the profession with engaging in **information overload**.

Financial disasters at **Microstrategy**, **PharMor**, **WorldCom**, and **Lehman** highlight the difficulty of implementing the full disclosure principle. They raise the issue of why investors were not aware of potential problems. Was the information these companies presented not comprehensible? Was it buried? Was it too technical? Was it properly presented and fully disclosed as of the financial statement date, but the situation later deteriorated? Or was it simply not there? In the following sections, we describe the elements of high-quality disclosure that will enable companies to avoid these disclosure pitfalls.

Increase in Reporting Requirements

Disclosure requirements have increased substantially. One survey showed that the size of many companies' annual reports is growing in response to demands for increased transparency. For example, annual report page counts ranged from 70 pages for **Gateway** up to a whopping 244 pages in **Eastman Kodak**'s annual report. And annual report lengths continue to grow in the post-Sarbanes-Oxley environment, with the number of companies producing reports over 100 pages increasing from 19 percent to 37 percent—almost double.[1] This result is not surprising. As illustrated throughout this textbook, the FASB has issued many pronouncements in recent years that have substantial disclosure provisions.

The reasons for this increase in disclosure requirements are varied. Some of them are:

- *Complexity of the business environment.* The increasing complexity of business operations magnifies the difficulty of distilling economic events into summarized reports. Such areas as derivatives, leasing, business combinations, pensions, financing arrangements, revenue recognition, and deferred taxes are complex. As a result, companies extensively use **notes to the financial statements** to explain these transactions and their future effects.

- *Necessity for timely information.* Today, more than ever before, users are demanding information that is current and predictive. For example, users want more complete **interim data**. Also, the SEC recommends published financial forecasts, long avoided and even feared by management.

- *Accounting as a control and monitoring device.* The government has recently sought public disclosure of such phenomena as management compensation, off-balance-sheet financing arrangements, and related-party transactions. An "Enronitis" concern is expressed in many of these newer disclosure requirements, and the SEC has selected accountants and auditors as the agents to assist in controlling and monitoring these concerns.

Differential Disclosure

A trend toward **differential disclosure** is also occurring. For example, the SEC requires that companies report to it certain substantive information that is not found in annual reports to stockholders. Likewise, the FASB, recognizing that certain disclosure requirements are costly and unnecessary for certain companies, has eliminated reporting requirements for nonpublic enterprises in such areas as fair value of financial instruments and segment reporting.

International Perspective

IFRS allows different accounting rules for small- and medium-sized entities.

---

[1] MWW Group, *MWW White Paper: Annual Report* (Winter 2012). See also *Final Report of the Advisory Committee on Improvements to Financial Reporting to the United States Securities and Exchange Commission* (August 1, 2008) for discussion of the need to address the growing volume and complexity of the financial reports and disclosures.

Underlying Concepts

Surveys indicate that users differ in their needs for information and that not all companies should report all elements of information. Thus, some contend that companies should report only information that users and preparers agree is needed in the particular circumstances.

Some still complain that the FASB has not gone far enough. They note that certain types of companies (small or nonpublic) should not have to follow complex GAAP requirements such as those for deferred income taxes, leases, or pensions. This issue, often referred to as **"big GAAP versus little GAAP,"** continues to be controversial.[2]

The FASB has traditionally taken the position that there should be one set of GAAP. However, due to the growing concern about differential costs and benefits of a "one size fits all" reporting package, the FASB is working with an advisory committee to explore ways that its standards can be more cost-effective for all companies, regardless of size. The Board is studying such areas as fair value measurement disclosures, and the accounting for consolidations, financial instruments, presentation of comprehensive income, and leases. In addition, the FASB has initiated a project to develop a framework, including a set of decision criteria, for determining whether and when to adjust the requirements for recognition, measurement, presentation, disclosure, effective dates, and transition methods for financial accounting standards that apply to private companies.[3]

 Evolving Issue DISCLOSURE—QUANTITY AND QUALITY

There is no better illustration of the adage that both quality and quantity are important than the issue of financial disclosure. While the full disclosure principle holds that more is better, how much more and of what form? An evaluation of this issue requires careful analysis of costs and benefits. Furthermore, as noted by one FASB member, the usefulness of expanded required disclosure also depends on users' ability to distinguish between the form of reporting (i.e., disclosed versus recognized items in financial statements). Research to date is inconclusive on this matter. So it is not just the amount but the quality.

Indeed, the SEC Committee on Improvement in Financial Reporting recommended the development of a disclosure framework that integrates existing SEC and FASB disclosure requirements into a cohesive whole to ensure meaningful communication and logical presentation of disclosures, based on consistent objectives and principles. This would eliminate redundancies and provide a single source of disclosure guidance across all financial reporting standards. Adopting such a framework should lead to disclosure of the principal assumptions, estimates, and sensitivity analyses that may impact a company's business, as well as a qualitative discussion of the key risks and uncertainties that could significantly change these amounts over time. This would encompass transactions recognized and measured in the financial statements, as well as events and uncertainties that are not recorded.

The FASB (and IASB) have responded to this recommendation by initiating a project with the objective and primary focus of improving the effectiveness of disclosures in notes to financial statements by clearly communicating the information that is most important to users of each company's financial statements. Achieving the objective of improving effectiveness will require development of a framework that promotes consistent decisions about disclosure requirements by standard-setters and the appropriate exercise of discretion by reporting companies. The FASB has issued an invitation to comment, seeking input on whether and, if so, how to provide guidance to improve the organization, formatting, and style of notes to financial statements. The FASB notes that while reducing the volume of the notes to financial statements is not the primary focus, the Board hopes that a sharper focus on important information will result in reduced volume in most cases. That is, get the quantity as well as the quality of disclosure right.

Sources: K. Schipper, "Required Disclosures in Financial Reports," Presidential Address to the American Accounting Association Annual Meeting (San Francisco, Calif., August 2005); *Final Report of the Advisory Committee on Improvements to Financial Reporting to the United States Securities and Exchange Commission* (August 1, 2008); and FASB, *Invitation to Comment: Disclosure Framework* (July 12, 2012).

[2]In response to cost-benefit concerns, the SEC has exempted some small public companies from certain rules implemented in response to the Sarbanes-Oxley Act. For example, smaller companies have more time to comply with the internal control rules required by the Sarbanes-Oxley law and have more time to file annual and interim reports.

[3]See "Private Company Decision-Making Framework: A Framework for Evaluating Financial Accounting and Reporting Guidance for Private Companies," *FASB Invitation to Comment* (July 31, 2012).

NOTES TO THE FINANCIAL STATEMENTS

As you know from your study of this textbook, notes are an integral part of the financial statements of a business enterprise. However, readers of financial statements often overlook them because they are highly technical and often appear in small print. **Notes are the means of amplifying or explaining the items presented in the main body of the statements.** They can explain in qualitative terms information pertinent to specific financial statement items. In addition, they can provide supplementary data of a quantitative nature to expand the information in the financial statements. Notes also can explain restrictions imposed by financial arrangements or basic contractual agreements. Although notes may be technical and difficult to understand, they provide meaningful information for the user of the financial statements.

2 LEARNING OBJECTIVE

Explain the use of notes in financial statement preparation.

Accounting Policies

Accounting policies are the specific accounting principles and methods a company currently uses and considers most appropriate to present fairly its financial statements. GAAP states that information about the accounting policies adopted by a reporting entity is essential for financial statement users in making economic decisions. It recommends that companies should present **as an integral part of the financial statements a statement identifying the accounting policies adopted and followed by the reporting entity**. Companies should present the disclosure as the first note or in a separate Summary of Significant Accounting Policies section preceding the notes to the financial statements.

The Summary of Significant Accounting Policies answers such questions as: What method of depreciation is used on plant assets? What valuation method is employed on inventories? What amortization policy is followed in regard to intangible assets? How are marketing costs handled for financial reporting purposes?

Refer to the financial statements and notes to the financial statements for The Procter & Gamble Company (available at the book's companion website, **www.wiley.com/college/kieso**) for an illustration of note disclosure of accounting policies (Note 1) and other notes accompanying the audited financial statements.

Analysts examine carefully the summary of accounting policies to determine whether a company is using conservative or liberal accounting practices. For example, depreciating plant assets over an unusually long period of time is considered liberal. Using LIFO inventory valuation in a period of inflation is generally viewed as conservative.

Companies that fail to adopt high-quality reporting policies may be heavily penalized by the market. For example, when Microstrategy disclosed that it would restate prior-year results due to use of aggressive revenue recognition policies, its share price dropped over 60 percent in one day. Investors viewed Microstrategy's quality of earnings as low.

Common Notes

We have discussed many of the notes to the financial statements throughout this textbook, and will discuss others more fully in this chapter. The more common are as follows.

MAJOR DISCLOSURES

INVENTORY. Companies should report the basis upon which inventory amounts are stated (lower-of-cost-or-market) and the method used in determining cost (LIFO, FIFO, average-cost, etc.). Manufacturers should report, either in the balance sheet or in a separate schedule in the notes, the inventory composition (finished goods, work in process, raw materials). Unusual or significant financing arrangements relating to inventories that may require disclosure include transactions with related parties, product financing arrangements, firm purchase commitments, involuntary liquidation of LIFO inventories, and pledging of inventories as collateral. Chapter 9 (pages 494–495) illustrates these disclosures.

PROPERTY, PLANT, AND EQUIPMENT. Companies should state the basis of valuation for property, plant, and equipment. It is usually historical cost. Companies also should disclose pledges, liens, and other commitments related to these assets. In the presentation of depreciation, companies should disclose the following in the financial statements or in the notes: (1) depreciation expense for the period; (2) balances of major classes of depreciable assets, by nature and function, at the balance sheet date; (3) accumulated depreciation, either by major classes of depreciable assets or in total, at the balance sheet date; and (4) a general description of the method or methods used in computing depreciation with respect to major classes of depreciable assets. Finally, companies should explain any major impairments. Chapter 11 (pages 609–611) illustrates property, plant, and equipment.

CREDITOR CLAIMS. Investors normally find it extremely useful to understand the nature and cost of creditor claims. However, the liabilities section in the balance sheet can provide the major types of liabilities only in the aggregate. Note schedules regarding such obligations provide additional information about how a company is financing its operations, the costs that it will bear in future periods, and the timing of future cash outflows. Financial statements must disclose for each of the five years following the date of the statements the aggregate amount of maturities and sinking fund requirements for all long-term borrowings. Chapter 14 (pages 785–787) illustrates these disclosures.

EQUITYHOLDERS' CLAIMS. Many companies present in the body of the balance sheet information about equity securities: the number of shares authorized, issued, and outstanding and the par value for each type of security. Or, companies may present such data in a note. Beyond that, a common equity note disclosure relates to contracts and senior securities outstanding that might affect the various claims of the residual equityholders. An example would be the existence of outstanding stock options, outstanding convertible debt, redeemable preferred stock, and convertible preferred stock. In addition, it is necessary to disclose certain types of restrictions currently in force. Generally, these types of restrictions involve the amount of earnings available for dividend distribution. Examples of these types of disclosures are illustrated in Chapter 15 (pages 847–848) and Chapter 16 (pages 909–910).

CONTINGENCIES AND COMMITMENTS. A company may have gain or loss contingencies that are not disclosed in the body of the financial statements. These contingencies include litigation, debt and other guarantees, possible tax assessments, renegotiation of government contracts, and sales of receivables with recourse. In addition, companies should disclose in the notes commitments that relate to dividend restrictions, purchase agreements (through-put and take-or-pay), hedge contracts, and employment contracts. Disclosures of such items are illustrated in Chapter 7 (page 372), Chapter 9 (page 483), and Chapter 13 (pages 728–729).

FAIR VALUES. Companies that have assets or liabilities measured at fair value must disclose both the cost and the fair value of all financial instruments in the notes to the financial statements. Fair value measurements may be used for many financial assets and liabilities, investments, impairments of long-lived assets, and some contingencies. Companies also provide disclosure of information that enables users to determine the extent of usage of fair value and the inputs used to implement fair value measurement. This fair value hierarchy identifies three broad levels related to the measurement of fair values (Levels 1, 2, and 3). The levels indicate the reliability of the measurement of fair value information. Appendix 17C (pages 999–1003) discusses in detail fair value disclosures.

DEFERRED TAXES, PENSIONS, AND LEASES. The FASB also requires extensive disclosure in the areas of deferred taxes, pensions, and leases. Chapter 19 (pages 1138–1144), Chapter 20 (pages 1204–1215), and Chapter 21 (pages 1300–1302) discuss in detail each of these disclosures. Users of financial statements should carefully read notes to the financial statements for information about off-balance-sheet commitments, future financing needs, and the quality of a company's earnings.

CHANGES IN ACCOUNTING PRINCIPLES. The profession defines various types of accounting changes and establishes guides for reporting each type. Companies discuss, either in the summary of significant accounting policies or in the other notes, changes in accounting principles (as well as material changes in estimates and corrections of errors). See Chapter 22 (pages 1363–1364).

In earlier chapters, we discussed the disclosures listed above. The following sections of this chapter illustrate four additional disclosures of significance—special transactions or events, subsequent events, segment reporting, and interim reporting.

What do the numbers mean? FOOTNOTE SECRETS

Often, note disclosures are needed to give a complete picture of a company's financial position. A good example of such disclosures is the required disclosure of debt triggers that may be buried in financing arrangements. These triggers can require a company to pay off a loan immediately if the debt rating collapses; they are one of the reasons Enron crumbled so quickly. But few Enron stockholders knew about the debt triggers until the gun had gone off. Companies are also disclosing more about their bank credit lines, liquidity, and any special-purpose entities. (The latter were major villains in the Enron drama.)

How can you get better informed about note disclosures that may contain important information related to your investments? Beyond your study in this class, a good Web resource for understanding the contents of note disclosures is *http://www.footnoted.org/*. This site highlights "the things companies bury in their SEC filings." It notes that company reports are more complete of late, but only the largest companies are preparing documents that are readable. As the editor of the site noted, "[some companies] are being dragged kicking and screaming into plain English."

Sources: Gretchen Morgenson, "Annual Reports: More Pages, but Better?" *The New York Times* (March 17, 2002); and D. Stead, "The Secrets in SEC Filings," *BusinessWeek* (August 25, 2008), p. 12.

DISCLOSURE ISSUES
Disclosure of Special Transactions or Events

Related-party transactions, errors and fraud, and illegal acts pose especially sensitive and difficult problems. The accountant/auditor who has responsibility for reporting on these types of transactions must take care to properly balance the rights of the reporting company and the needs of users of the financial statements.

3 LEARNING OBJECTIVE

Discuss the disclosure requirements for related-party transactions, post-balance-sheet events, and major business segments.

Related-party transactions arise when a company engages in transactions in which one of the parties has the ability to significantly influence the policies of the other. They may also occur when a nontransacting party has the ability to influence the policies of the two transacting parties.[4] Competitive, free-market dealings may not exist

[4]Examples of related-party transactions include transactions between (a) a parent company and its subsidiaries; (b) subsidiaries of a common parent; (c) a company and trusts for the benefit of employees (controlled or managed by the enterprise); and (d) a company and its principal owners, management, or members of immediate families, and affiliates. Two classic cases of related-party transactions were Enron, with its misuse of special-purpose entities, and Tyco International, which forgave loans to its management team.

in related-party transactions, and so an "arm's-length" basis cannot be assumed. Transactions such as borrowing or lending money at abnormally low or high interest rates, real estate sales at amounts that differ significantly from appraised value, exchanges of nonmonetary assets, and transactions involving enterprises that have no economic substance ("shell corporations") suggest that related parties may be involved.

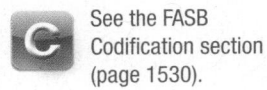

See the FASB Codification section (page 1530).

In order to make adequate disclosure, companies should report the economic substance, rather than the legal form, of these transactions. GAAP requires the following disclosures of material related-party transactions. **[1]**

1. The nature of the relationship(s) involved.

2. A description of the transactions (including transactions to which no amounts or nominal amounts were ascribed) for each of the periods for which income statements are presented.

3. The dollar amounts of transactions for each of the periods for which income statements are presented.

4. Amounts due from or to related parties as of the date of each balance sheet presented.

Illustration 24-2, from the annual report of **Harley-Davidson, Inc.**, shows disclosure of related-party transactions.

ILLUSTRATION 24-2
Disclosure of Related-Party Transactions

Harley-Davidson, Inc.

22. Related Party Transactions

The Company has the following material related party transactions. A director of the Company is Chairman and Chief Executive Officer and an equity owner of Fred Deeley Imports Ltd. (Deeley Imports), the exclusive distributor of the Company's motorcycles in Canada. The Company recorded motorcycles and related products revenue and financial services revenue from Deeley Imports during 2011, 2010 and 2009 of $155.2 million, $158.7 million and $177.2 million, respectively, and had finance receivables balances due from Deeley Imports of $14.5 million, $21.0 million and $13.9 million at December 31, 2011, 2010 and 2009, respectively. All such products were provided in the ordinary course of business at prices and on terms and conditions that the Company believes are the same as those that would result from arm's-length negotiations between unrelated parties.

Many companies are involved in related-party transactions. Errors, fraud (sometimes referred to as irregularities), and illegal acts, however, are the exception rather than the rule. Accounting **errors** are **unintentional** mistakes, whereas **fraud** (misappropriation of assets and fraudulent financial reporting) involves **intentional** distortions of financial statements.[5] As indicated earlier, companies should correct the financial statements when they discover errors. The same treatment should be given fraud. The discovery of fraud, however, gives rise to a different set of procedures and responsibilities for the accountant/auditor.[6]

Illegal acts encompass such items as illegal political contributions, bribes, kickbacks, and other violations of laws and regulations.[7] In these situations, the accountant/auditor

[5]"Consideration of Fraud in a Financial Statement Audit," *Statement on Auditing Standards No. 99* (New York: AICPA, 2002). We have an expanded discussion of fraudulent financial reporting later in this chapter. Since passage of the Sarbanes-Oxley Act, auditors of public companies are regulated by the Public Company Accounting Oversight Board (PCAOB). The PCAOB is now the audit standard-setter for auditors of public companies. It has adopted much of the prior auditing standards issued by the Auditing Standards Board of the AICPA.

[6]The profession became so concerned with certain management frauds that affect financial statements that it established a National Commission on Fraudulent Financial Reporting. The major purpose of this organization was to determine how fraudulent reporting practices could be constrained. Fraudulent financial reporting is discussed later in this chapter.

[7]"Illegal Acts by Clients," *Statement on Auditing Standards No. 54* (New York: AICPA, 1988).

must evaluate the adequacy of disclosure in the financial statements. For example, if a company derives revenue from an illegal act that is considered material in relation to the financial statements, this information should be disclosed. The Sarbanes-Oxley Act is intended to deter these illegal acts. This law adds significant fines and longer jail time for those who improperly sign off on the correctness of financial statements that include willing and knowing misstatements.

Disclosure plays a very important role in these types of transactions because the events are more qualitative than quantitative and involve more subjective than objective evaluation. Users of the financial statements need some indication of the existence and nature of these transactions, through disclosures, modifications in the auditor's report, or reports of changes in auditors.

Post-Balance-Sheet Events (Subsequent Events)

Notes to the financial statements should explain any significant financial events that took place after the formal balance sheet date, but before the statement is issued. These events are referred to as post-balance-sheet events, or just plain subsequent events. Illustration 24-3 shows a time diagram of the subsequent events period.

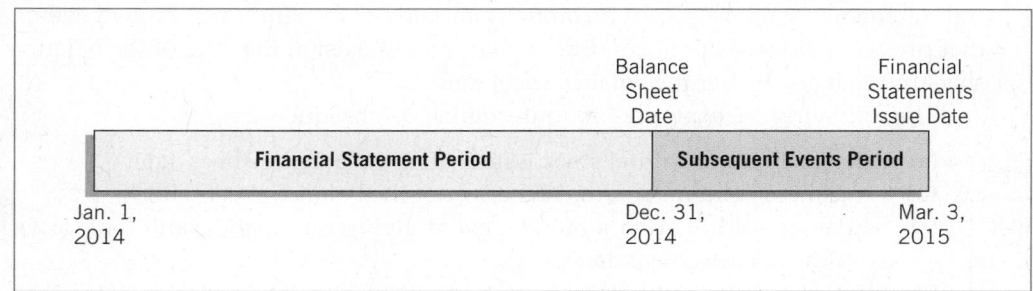

ILLUSTRATION 24-3
Time Periods for
Subsequent Events

A period of several weeks, and sometimes months, may elapse after the end of the fiscal year but before the company issues financial statements. Various activities involved in closing the books for the period and issuing the statements all take time: taking and pricing the inventory, reconciling subsidiary ledgers with controlling accounts, preparing necessary adjusting entries, ensuring that all transactions for the period have been entered, obtaining an audit of the financial statements by independent certified public accountants, and printing the annual report. During the period between the balance sheet date and its distribution to stockholders and creditors, important transactions or other events may occur that materially affect the company's financial position or operating situation.

Many who read a balance sheet believe the balance sheet condition is constant, and they project it into the future. However, readers must be told if the company has experienced a significant change—e.g., sold one of its plants, acquired a subsidiary, suffered extraordinary losses, settled significant litigation, or experienced any other important event in the post-balance-sheet period. Without an explanation in a note, the reader might be misled and draw inappropriate conclusions.

Two types of events or transactions occurring after the balance sheet date may have a material effect on the financial statements or may need disclosure so that readers interpret these statements accurately:

1. Events that provide additional evidence about conditions **that existed** at the balance sheet date, including the estimates inherent in the process of preparing financial statements. These events are referred to as recognized subsequent events and require adjustments to the financial statements. All information available prior to the issuance of the financial statements helps investors and creditors evaluate estimates previously made. To ignore these subsequent events is to pass up an opportunity to improve the accuracy of the financial statements. This first type of event encompasses information that an accountant would have recorded in the accounts had the information been known at the balance sheet date.

For example, if a loss on an account receivable results from a customer's bankruptcy subsequent to the balance sheet date, the company adjusts the financial statements before their issuance. The bankruptcy stems from the customer's poor financial health existing at the balance sheet date.

The same criterion applies to settlements of litigation. The company must adjust the financial statements if the events that gave rise to the litigation, such as personal injury or patent infringement, took place prior to the balance sheet date.

2. Events that provide evidence about conditions that **did not exist** at the balance sheet date but arise subsequent to that date. These events are referred as **nonrecognized subsequent events** and do not require adjustment of the financial statements. To illustrate, a loss resulting from a customer's fire or flood *after* the balance sheet date does not reflect conditions existing at that date. Thus, adjustment of the financial statements is not necessary. A company should not recognize subsequent events that provide evidence about conditions that did not exist at the date of the balance sheet but that arose after the balance sheet date.

The following are examples of nonrecognized subsequent events:

<table>
<tr><td>(a)</td><td>Sale of a bond or capital stock issued after the balance sheet date.</td></tr>
<tr><td>(b)</td><td>A business combination that occurs after the balance sheet date.</td></tr>
<tr><td>(c)</td><td>Settlement of litigation when the event giving rise to the claim took place after the balance sheet date.</td></tr>
<tr><td>(d)</td><td>Loss of plant or inventories as a result of fire or natural disaster that occurred after the balance sheet date.</td></tr>
<tr><td>(e)</td><td>Losses on receivables resulting from conditions (such as a customer's major casualty) arising after the balance sheet date.</td></tr>
<tr><td>(f)</td><td>Changes in the quoted market prices of securities or foreign exchange rates after the balance sheet date.</td></tr>
<tr><td>(g)</td><td>Entering into significant commitments or contingent liabilities, for example, by issuing significant guarantees after the balance sheet date. [2][8]</td></tr>
</table>

> ### Underlying Concepts
>
> A company also should consider supplementing the historical financial statements with pro forma financial data. Occasionally, a nonrecognized subsequent event may be so significant that disclosure can best be made by means of pro forma financial data.

Some nonrecognized subsequent events may have to be disclosed to keep the financial statements from being misleading. For such events, a company discloses the nature of the event and an estimate of its financial effect.

Illustration 24-4 presents an example of subsequent events disclosure, excerpted from the annual report of **Commercial Metals Company**.

Many subsequent events or developments do not require adjustment of or disclosure in the financial statements. Typically, these are nonaccounting events or conditions

---

[8]The effects from natural disasters, like hurricanes Katrina, Rita, and Sandy, which occurred after the year-end for companies with August fiscal years, require disclosure in order to keep the statements from being misleading. Some companies may have to consider whether these disasters affect their ability to continue as going concerns. *Accounting Trends and Techniques—2012* listed the following types of subsequent events and their frequency of occurrence among the 500 companies surveyed: acquisitions, 32; debt incurred, reduced, or refinanced, 31; business combinations pending or effected, 29; capital stock issued or purchased, 18; discontinued operations or asset disposals, 15; litigation, 14; and restructuring/bankruptcy, 13.

Commercial Metals Company

NOTE 22. SUBSEQUENT EVENTS (August 31 Fiscal Year End)
On October 7, 2011, The Company announced its decision to exit the business in CMCS by way of sale and/or closure. During 2011, the Company made operational improvements in the business but not to a level which would restore profitability for the long run. Additionally, delayed entry in the European Union, cyclical demand for tubular products, unsustainable losses and increased demand for capital resources resulted in the decision to exit the business. The operation will service any existing customer commitments and the Company expects to wind down operations and liquidate inventory over the next several months. In connection with this decision, the Company expects to incur severance and other closure costs between $25 million and $40 million in fiscal 2012.

ILLUSTRATION 24-4
Disclosure of Subsequent Events

that management normally communicates by other means. These events include legislation, product changes, management changes, strikes, unionization, marketing agreements, and loss of important customers.

Reporting for Diversified (Conglomerate) Companies

In certain business climates, companies have a tendency to diversify their operations. Take the case of conglomerate General Electric (GE), whose products include locomotives and jet engines, credit card services, and water purification systems. Or, consider cable giant Comcast; its NBC Universal subsidiary owns NBC TV, Telemundo, Universal Pictures, and Universal Parks and Resorts. When businesses are so diversified, investors and investment analysts want more information about the details behind conglomerate financial statements. Particularly, they want income statement, balance sheet, and cash flow information on the **individual segments** that compose the total income figure.

Illustration 24-5 shows **segmented** (disaggregated) financial information of an office equipment and auto parts company.

ILLUSTRATION 24-5
Segmented Income Statement

OFFICE EQUIPMENT AND AUTO PARTS COMPANY			
INCOME STATEMENT DATA			
(IN MILLIONS)			
	Consolidated	Office Equipment	Auto Parts
Net sales	$78.8	$18.0	$60.8
Manufacturing costs			
Inventories, beginning	12.3	4.0	8.3
Materials and services	38.9	10.8	28.1
Wages	12.9	3.8	9.1
Inventories, ending	(13.3)	(3.9)	(9.4)
	50.8	14.7	36.1
Selling and administrative expenses	12.1	1.6	10.5
Total operating expenses	62.9	16.3	46.6
Income before taxes	15.9	1.7	14.2
Income taxes	(9.3)	(1.0)	(8.3)
Net income	$ 6.6	$ 0.7	$ 5.9

Much information is hidden in the aggregated totals. If the analyst has only the consolidated figures, he/she cannot tell the extent to which the differing product lines **contribute to the company's profitability, risk, and growth potential**. For example, in Illustration 24-5, the office equipment segment looks like a risky venture. Segmented reporting would provide useful information about the two business segments and would be useful for making an informed investment decision regarding the whole company.

In addition to the example of Coach, Inc. in the opening story, a classic situation that demonstrates the need for segmented data involved Caterpillar, Inc. The SEC cited Caterpillar because it failed to tell investors that nearly a quarter of its income in one year came from a Brazilian unit and was nonrecurring in nature. The company knew that different economic policies in the next year would probably greatly affect earnings of the Brazilian unit. But Caterpillar presented its financial results on a consolidated basis, not disclosing the Brazilian operations. The SEC found that Caterpillar's failure to include information about Brazil left investors with an incomplete picture of the company's financial results and denied investors the opportunity to see the company "through the eyes of management."

Companies have always been somewhat hesitant to disclose segmented data for various reasons:

1. Without a thorough knowledge of the business and an understanding of such important factors as the competitive environment and capital investment requirements, the investor may find the segmented information meaningless or may even draw improper conclusions about the reported earnings of the segments.

2. Additional disclosure may be helpful to competitors, labor unions, suppliers, and certain government regulatory agencies, and thus harm the reporting company.

3. Additional disclosure may discourage management from taking intelligent business risks because segments reporting losses or unsatisfactory earnings may cause stockholder dissatisfaction with management.

4. The wide variation among companies in the choice of segments, cost allocation, and other accounting problems limits the usefulness of segmented information.

5. The investor is investing in the company as a whole and not in the particular segments, and it should not matter how any single segment is performing if the overall performance is satisfactory.

6. Certain technical problems, such as classification of segments and allocation of segment revenues and costs (especially "common costs"), are formidable.

On the other hand, the advocates of segmented disclosures offer these reasons in support of the practice:

1. Investors need segmented information to make an intelligent investment decision regarding a diversified company.
   (a) Sales and earnings of individual segments enable investors to evaluate the differences between segments in growth rate, risk, and profitability, and to forecast consolidated profits.
   (b) Segmented reports help investors evaluate the company's investment worth by disclosing the nature of a company's businesses and the relative size of the components.

2. The absence of segmented reporting by a diversified company may put its unsegmented, single product-line competitors at a competitive disadvantage because the conglomerate may obscure information that its competitors must disclose.

The advocates of segmented disclosures appear to have a much stronger case. Many users indicate that segmented data are the most useful financial information provided, aside from the basic financial statements. As a result, the FASB has issued extensive reporting guidelines in this area.

Objective of Reporting Segmented Information

The objective of reporting segmented financial data is to provide information about the **different types of business activities** in which an enterprise engages and the **different economic environments** in which it operates. Meeting this objective will help users of financial statements do the following.

(a) Better understand the enterprise's performance.

(b) Better assess its prospects for future net cash flows.

(c) Make more informed judgments about the enterprise as a whole.

Basic Principles

Financial statements can be disaggregated in several ways. For example, they can be disaggregated by products or services, by geography, by legal entity, or by type of customer. However, it is not feasible to provide all of that information in every set of financial statements. GAAP requires that general-purpose financial statements include selected information on a single basis of segmentation. Thus, a company can meet the segmented reporting objective by providing financial statements segmented based on how the company's operations are managed. The method chosen is referred to as the management approach. **[3] The management approach reflects how management segments the company for making operating decisions.** The segments are evident from the components of the company's organization structure. These components are called **operating segments**.

Identifying Operating Segments

An **operating segment** is a component of an enterprise:

(a) That engages in business activities from which it earns revenues and incurs expenses.

(b) Whose operating results are regularly reviewed by the company's chief operating decision-maker to assess segment performance and allocate resources to the segment.

(c) For which discrete financial information is available that is generated by or based on the internal financial reporting system.

Companies may aggregate information about two or more operating segments only if the segments have the same basic characteristics in each of the following areas.

(a) The nature of the products and services provided.

(b) The nature of the production process.

(c) The type or class of customer.

(d) The methods of product or service distribution.

(e) If applicable, the nature of the regulatory environment.

After the company decides on the possible segments for disclosure, it makes a quantitative materiality test. This test determines whether the segment is significant enough to warrant actual disclosure. An operating segment is deemed significant, and therefore a reportable segment, if it satisfies **one or more** of the following quantitative thresholds.

1. Its **revenue** (including both sales to external customers and intersegment sales or transfers) is 10 percent or more of the combined revenue of all the company's operating segments.

2. The absolute amount of its **profit or loss** is 10 percent or more of the greater, in absolute amount, of (a) the combined operating profit of all operating segments that did not incur a loss, or (b) the combined loss of all operating segments that did report a loss.

3. Its **identifiable assets** are 10 percent or more of the combined assets of all operating segments.

In applying these tests, the company must consider two additional factors. First, segment data must explain a significant portion of the company's business. Specifically, the segmented results must equal or exceed 75 percent of the combined sales to unaffiliated customers for the entire company. This test prevents a company from providing limited information on only a few segments and lumping all the rest into one category.

Second, the profession recognizes that reporting too many segments may overwhelm users with detailed information. The FASB decided that 10 is a reasonable upper limit for the number of segments that a company must disclose.

To illustrate these requirements, assume a company has identified six possible reporting segments, as shown in Illustration 24-6 (000s omitted).

ILLUSTRATION 24-6

Data for Different Possible Reporting Segments

Segments	Total Revenue (Unaffiliated)	Operating Profit (Loss)	Identifiable Assets
A	$ 100	$10	$ 60
B	50	2	30
C	700	40	390
D	300	20	160
E	900	18	280
F	100	(5)	50
	$2,150	$85	$970

The company would apply the respective tests as follows.

Revenue test: 10% × $2,150 = $215; C, D, and E meet this test.

Operating profit (loss) test: 10% × $90 = $9 (note that the $5 loss is ignored because the test is based on non-loss segments); A, C, D, and E meet this test.

Identifiable assets tests: 10% × $970 = $97; C, D, and E meet this test.

The reporting segments are therefore A, C, D, and E, assuming that these four segments have enough sales to meet the 75 percent of combined sales test. The 75 percent test is computed as follows.

75% of combined sales test: 75% × $2,150 = $1,612.50. The sales of A, C, D, and E total $2,000 ($100 + $700 + $300 + $900); therefore, the 75 percent test is met.

Measurement Principles

The accounting principles that companies use for segment disclosure need not be the same as the principles they use to prepare the consolidated statements. This flexibility may at first appear inconsistent. But, preparing segment information in accordance with generally accepted accounting principles would be difficult because some principles are not expected to apply at a segment level. Examples are accounting for the cost of company-wide employee benefit plans, accounting for income taxes in a company that files a consolidated tax return, and accounting for inventory on a LIFO basis if the pool includes items in more than one segment.

The FASB does not require allocations of joint, common, or company-wide costs solely for external reporting purposes. Common costs are those incurred for the benefit of more than one segment and whose interrelated nature prevents a completely objective division of costs among segments. For example, the company president's salary is difficult to allocate to various segments. Allocations of common costs are inherently arbitrary and may not be meaningful. There is a presumption that if companies allocate common costs to segments, these allocations are either directly attributable or reasonably allocable.

Segmented Information Reported

The FASB requires that an enterprise report the following.

1. *General information about its operating segments.* This includes factors that management considers most significant in determining the company's operating segments, and the types of products and services from which each operating segment derives its revenues.

2. *Segment profit and loss and related information.* Specifically, companies must report the following information about each operating segment if the amounts are included in determining segment profit or loss.
   (a) Revenues from transactions with external customers.
   (b) Revenues from transactions with other operating segments of the same enterprise.
   (c) Interest revenue.
   (d) Interest expense.
   (e) Depreciation, depletion, and amortization expense.
   (f) Unusual items.
   (g) Equity in the net income of investees accounted for by the equity method.
   (h) Income tax expense or benefit.
   (i) Extraordinary items.
   (j) Significant noncash items other than depreciation, depletion, and amortization expense.

3. *Segment assets.* A company must report each operating segment's total assets.

4. *Reconciliations.* A company must provide a reconciliation of the total of the segments' revenues to total revenues, a reconciliation of the total of the operating segments' profits and losses to its income before income taxes, and a reconciliation of the total of the operating segments' assets to total assets.

5. *Information about products and services and geographic areas.* For each operating segment not based on geography, the company must report (unless it is impracticable): (1) revenues from external customers, (2) long-lived assets, and (3) expenditures during the period for long-lived assets. This information, if material, must be reported (a) in the enterprise's country of domicile and (b) in each other country.

6. *Major customers.* If 10 percent or more of company revenue is derived from a single customer, the company must disclose the total amount of revenue from each such customer by segment.

Illustration of Disaggregated Information

Illustration 24-7 (page 1502) shows the segment disclosure for Johnson & Johnson.

Interim Reports

Another source of information for the investor is interim reports. As noted earlier, interim reports cover periods of less than one year. The stock exchanges, the SEC, and the accounting profession have an active interest in the presentation of interim information.

4 **LEARNING OBJECTIVE**
Describe the accounting problems associated with interim reporting.

The SEC mandates that certain companies file a **Form 10-Q**, in which a company discloses quarterly data similar to that disclosed in the annual report. It also requires

Johnson & Johnson
(notes excluded)

Segments of Business and Geographic Areas

	Sales to Customers		
(Dollars in Millions)	2011	2010	2009
Consumer—United States	$ 5,151	$ 5,519	$ 6,837
International	9,732	9,071	8,966
Total	14,883	14,590	15,803
Pharmaceutical—United States	12,386	12,519	13,041
International	11,982	9,877	9,479
Total	24,368	22,396	22,520
Medical Devices and Diagnostics—United States	11,371	11,412	11,011
International	14,408	13,189	12,563
Total	25,779	24,601	23,574
Worldwide total	$65,030	$61,587	$ 61,897

	Operating Profit			Identifiable Assets		
(Dollars in Millions)	2011	2010	2009	2011	2010	2009
Consumer	$ 2,096	$ 2,342	$ 2,475	$ 24,210	$ 23,753	$24,671
Pharmaceutical	6,406	7,086	6,413	23,747	19,961	21,460
Medical Devices and Diagnostics	5,263	8,272	7,694	23,609	23,277	22,853
Total	13,765	17,700	16,582	71,566	66,991	68,984
Less: Expense not allocated to segments	1,404	753	827			
General corporate				42,078	35,917	25,698
Worldwide total	$12,361	$16,947	$15,755	$113,644	$102,908	$94,682

	Additions to Property, Plant & Equipment			Depreciation and Amortization		
(Dollars in Millions)	2011	2010	2009	2011	2010	2009
Consumer	$ 670	$ 526	$ 439	$ 631	$ 532	$ 513
Pharmaceutical	729	508	535	958	912	922
Medical Devices and Diagnostics	1,095	1,113	1,114	1,331	1,270	1,124
Segments total	2,494	2,147	2,088	2,920	2,714	2,559
General corporate	399	237	277	238	225	215
Worldwide total	$2,893	$2,384	$2,365	$3,158	$2,939	$2,774

	Sales to Customers			Long-Lived Assets		
(Dollars in Millions)	2011	2010	2009	2011	2010	2009
United States	$28,908	$29,450	$30,889	$ 23,529	$ 23,315	$22,399
Europe	17,129	15,510	15,934	19,056	16,791	17,347
Western Hemisphere excluding U.S.	6,418	5,550	5,156	3,517	3,653	3,540
Asia-Pacific, Africa	12,575	11,077	9,918	2,163	2,089	1,868
Segments total	65,030	61,587	61,897	48,265	45,848	45,154
General corporate				750	715	790
Other non long-lived assets				64,629	56,345	48,738
Worldwide total	$65,030	$61,587	$61,897	$113,644	$102,908	$94,682

ILLUSTRATION 24-7
Segment Disclosure

those companies to disclose selected quarterly information in notes to the annual financial statements. Illustration 24-8 presents the selected quarterly disclosure of Tootsie Roll Industries, Inc. In addition to Form 10-Q, GAAP narrows the reporting alternatives related to interim reports. **[4]**

Because of the short-term nature of the information in these reports, there is considerable controversy as to the general approach companies should employ. One group,

Tootsie Roll Industries, Inc.

For the Year Ended December 31, 2011

	First	Second	Third	Fourth	Total
	(Thousands of dollars except per share data)				
Net product sales	$108,323	$104,884	$186,784	$128,378	$528,369
Product gross margin	34,799	33,898	54,554	39,893	163,144
Net earnings	8,330	6,486	18,855	10,267	43,938
Net earnings per share	0.14	0.11	0.33	0.18	0.76

	Stock Prices 2011		Dividends 2011
	High	Low	
1st Qtr	$29.45	$27.06	$0.08
2nd Qtr	$29.68	$27.78	$0.08
3rd Qtr	$29.80	$23.52	$0.08
4th Qtr	$25.95	$22.85	$0.08

ILLUSTRATION 24-8
Disclosure of Selected Quarterly Data

which favors the **discrete approach**, believes that companies should treat each interim period as a separate accounting period. Using that treatment, companies would follow the principles for deferrals and accruals used for annual reports. In this view, companies should report accounting transactions as they occur, and expense recognition should not change with the period of time covered.

Another group, which favors the **integral approach**, believes that the interim report is an integral part of the annual report and that deferrals and accruals should take into consideration what will happen for the entire year. In this approach, companies should assign estimated expenses to parts of a year on the basis of sales volume or some other activity base.

At present, many companies follow the discrete approach for certain types of expenses and the integral approach for others, because the standards currently employed in practice are vague and lead to differing interpretations.

Interim Reporting Requirements

Generally, companies should use the same accounting principles for interim reports and for annual reports. They should recognize revenues in interim periods on the same basis as they are for annual periods. For example, if Cedars Corp. uses the installment-sales method as the basis for recognizing revenue on an annual basis, then it should use the installment basis for interim reports as well. Also, Cedars should treat costs directly associated with revenues (product costs, such as materials, labor and related fringe benefits, and manufacturing overhead) in the same manner for interim reports as for annual reports.

Companies should use the same inventory pricing methods (FIFO, LIFO, etc.) for interim reports and for annual reports. However, the following exceptions are appropriate at interim reporting periods.

1. Companies may use the gross profit method for interim inventory pricing. But they must disclose the method and adjustments to reconcile with annual inventory.

2. When a company liquidates LIFO inventories at an interim date and expects to replace them by year-end, cost of goods sold should include the expected cost of replacing the liquidated LIFO base, rather than give effect to the interim liquidation.

Underlying Concepts

For information to be relevant, it must be available to decision-makers before it loses its capacity to influence their decisions (timeliness). Interim reporting is an excellent example of this concept.

3. Companies should not defer inventory market declines beyond the interim period unless they are temporary and no loss is expected for the fiscal year.

4. Companies ordinarily should defer planned variances under a standard cost system; such variances are expected to be absorbed by year-end.

Companies often charge to the interim period, as incurred, costs and expenses other than product costs (often referred to as **period costs**). But companies may allocate these costs among interim periods on the basis of an estimate of time expired, benefit received, or activity associated with the periods. Companies display considerable latitude in accounting for these costs in interim periods, and many believe more definitive guidelines are needed.

Regarding disclosure, companies should report the following interim data at a minimum.

1. Sales or gross revenues, provision for income taxes, extraordinary items, and net income.

2. Basic and diluted earnings per share where appropriate.

3. Seasonal revenue, cost, or expenses.

4. Significant changes in estimates or provisions for income taxes.

5. Disposal of a component of a business and extraordinary, unusual, or infrequently occurring items.

6. Contingent items.

7. Changes in accounting principles or estimates.

8. Significant changes in financial position.

The FASB encourages, but does not require, companies to publish an interim balance sheet and statement of cash flows. If a company does not present this information, it should disclose significant changes in such items as liquid assets, net working capital, long-term liabilities, and stockholders' equity.

Unique Problems of Interim Reporting

GAAP reflects a preference for the integral approach. However, within this broad guideline, a number of unique reporting problems develop related to the following items.

Advertising and Similar Costs. The general guidelines are that companies should defer in an interim period costs such as advertising if the benefits extend beyond that period; otherwise, the company should expense those costs as incurred. But such a determination is difficult, and even if the company defers the costs, how should it allocate them between quarters?

Because of the vague guidelines in this area, accounting for advertising varies widely. At one time, some companies in the food industry, such as RJR Nabisco and Pillsbury, charged advertising costs as a percentage of sales and adjusted to actual at year-end, whereas General Foods and Kellogg expensed these costs as incurred.

The same type of problem relates to such items as Social Security taxes, research and development costs, and major repairs. For example, should the company expense Social Security costs (payroll taxes) on highly paid personnel early in the year, or allocate and spread them to subsequent quarters? Should a major repair that occurs later in the year be anticipated and allocated proportionately to earlier periods?

Expenses Subject to Year-End Adjustment. Companies often do not know with a great deal of certainty amounts of bad debts, executive bonuses, pension costs, and inventory shrinkage until year-end. **They should estimate these costs and allocate them to interim periods as best they can.** Companies use a variety of allocation techniques to accomplish this objective.

Income Taxes. Not every dollar of corporate taxable income is taxed at the same rate; the tax rate is progressive. This aspect of business income taxes poses a problem in preparing interim financial statements. Should the company use the **annualized approach**, which is to annualize income to date and accrue the proportionate income tax for the period to date? Or should it follow the **marginal principle approach**, which is to apply the lower rate of tax to the first amount of income earned? At one time, companies generally followed the latter approach and accrued the tax applicable to each additional dollar of income.

The profession now, however, uses the annualized approach. This requires that "at the end of each interim period the company should make its best estimate of the effective tax rate expected to be applicable for the full fiscal year. The rate so determined should be used in providing for income taxes on income for the quarter." **[5]**[9]

Because businesses did not uniformly apply this guideline in accounting for similar situations, the FASB issued authoritative guidance. GAAP now requires companies, when computing the year-to-date tax, to apply the **estimated annual effective tax rate** to the year-to-date "ordinary" income at the end of each interim period. Further, the **interim period tax** related to "ordinary" income shall be the difference between the amount so computed and the amounts reported for previous interim periods of the fiscal period. **[6]**[10]

Extraordinary Items. Extraordinary items consist of unusual and nonrecurring material gains and losses. In the past, companies handled them in interim reports in one of three ways: (1) absorbed them entirely in the quarter in which they occurred, (2) prorated them over four quarters, or (3) disclosed them only by note. **The required approach now is to charge or credit the loss or gain in the quarter in which it occurs,** instead of attempting some arbitrary multiple-period allocation. This approach is consistent with the way in which companies must handle extraordinary items on an annual basis. No attempt is made to prorate the extraordinary items over several years.

Some favor the omission of extraordinary items from the quarterly net income. They believe that inclusion of extraordinary items that may be large in proportion to interim results distorts the predictive value of interim reports. Many, however, consider such an omission inappropriate because it deviates from actual results.

Earnings per Share. Interim reporting of earnings per share has all the problems inherent in computing and presenting annual earnings per share, and then some. If a company issues shares in the third period, EPS for the first two periods will not reflect year-end EPS. If an extraordinary item is present in one period and the company sells new equity shares in another period, the EPS figure for the extraordinary item will change for the year. On an annual basis, only one EPS figure can be associated with an extraordinary item and that figure does not change; the interim figure is subject to change.

For purposes of computing earnings per share and making the required disclosure determinations, each interim period should stand alone. That is, all applicable tests should be made for that single period.

---

[9]The estimated annual effective tax rate should reflect anticipated tax credits, foreign tax rates, percentage depletion, capital gains rates, and other available tax-planning alternatives.

[10]"Ordinary" income (or loss) refers to "income (or loss) from continuing operations before income taxes (or benefits)" excluding extraordinary items and discontinued operations.

Seasonality. Seasonality occurs when most of a company's sales occur in one short period of the year while certain costs are fairly evenly spread throughout the year. For example, the natural gas industry has its heavy sales in the winter months. In contrast, the beverage industry has its heavy sales in the summer months.

The problem of seasonality is related to the expense recognition principle in accounting. Generally, expenses are associated with the revenues they create. In a seasonal business, wide fluctuations in profits occur because off-season sales do not absorb the company's fixed costs (for example, manufacturing, selling, and administrative costs that tend to remain fairly constant regardless of sales or production).

To illustrate why seasonality is a problem, assume the following information.

ILLUSTRATION 24-9
Data for Seasonality
Example

Selling price per unit	$1
Annual sales for the period (projected and actual)	
100,000 units @ $1	$100,000
Manufacturing costs	
Variable	10¢ per unit
Fixed	20¢ per unit or $20,000 for the year
Nonmanufacturing costs	
Variable	10¢ per unit
Fixed	30¢ per unit or $30,000 for the year

Sales for four quarters and the year (projected and actual) were:

ILLUSTRATION 24-10
Sales Data for Seasonality
Example

		Percent of Sales
1st Quarter	$ 20,000	20%
2nd Quarter	5,000	5
3rd Quarter	10,000	10
4th Quarter	65,000	65
Total for the year	$100,000	100%

Under the present accounting framework, the income statements for the quarters might be as shown in Illustration 24-11.

ILLUSTRATION 24-11
Interim Net Income for
Seasonal Business—
Discrete Approach

	1st Qtr	2nd Qtr	3rd Qtr	4th Qtr	Year
Sales	$20,000	$ 5,000	$10,000	$65,000	$100,000
Manufacturing costs					
Variable	(2,000)	(500)	(1,000)	(6,500)	(10,000)
Fixed[a]	(4,000)	(1,000)	(2,000)	(13,000)	(20,000)
	14,000	3,500	7,000	45,500	70,000
Nonmanufacturing costs					
Variable	(2,000)	(500)	(1,000)	(6,500)	(10,000)
Fixed[b]	(7,500)	(7,500)	(7,500)	(7,500)	(30,000)
Net income	$ 4,500	$(4,500)	$ (1,500)	$31,500	$ 30,000

[a]The fixed manufacturing costs are inventoried, so that equal amounts of fixed costs do not appear during each quarter.
[b]The fixed nonmanufacturing costs are not inventoried, so equal amounts of fixed costs appear during each quarter.

An investor who uses the first quarter's results might be misled. If the first quarter's earnings are $4,500, should this figure be multiplied by four to predict annual earnings of $18,000? Or, if first-quarter sales of $20,000 are 20 percent of the predicted sales for the year, would the net income for the year be $22,500 ($4,500 × 5)? Both figures are obviously wrong, and after the second quarter's results occur, the investor may become even more confused.

The problem with the conventional approach is that the fixed nonmanufacturing costs are not charged in proportion to sales. Some enterprises have adopted a way of avoiding this problem by making all fixed nonmanufacturing costs follow the sales pattern, as shown in Illustration 24-12.

	1st Qtr	2nd Qtr	3rd Qtr	4th Qtr	Year
Sales	$20,000	$ 5,000	$10,000	$65,000	$100,000
Manufacturing costs					
Variable	(2,000)	(500)	(1,000)	(6,500)	(10,000)
Fixed	(4,000)	(1,000)	(2,000)	(13,000)	(20,000)
	14,000	3,500	7,000	45,500	70,000
Nonmanufacturing costs					
Variable	(2,000)	(500)	(1,000)	(6,500)	(10,000)
Fixed	(6,000)	(1,500)	(3,000)	(19,500)	(30,000)
Net income	$ 6,000	$ 1,500	$ 3,000	$19,500	$ 30,000

ILLUSTRATION 24-12
Interim Net Income for Seasonal Business—
Integral Approach

This approach solves some of the seasonality problems of interim reporting. Sales in the first quarter are 20 percent of total sales for the year, and net income in the first quarter is 20 percent of total income. In this case, as in the previous example, the investor cannot rely on multiplying any given quarter by four but can use comparative data or rely on some estimate of sales in relation to income for a given period.

The greater the degree of seasonality experienced by a company, the greater the possibility of distortion. Because there are no definitive guidelines for handling such items as the fixed nonmanufacturing costs, variability in income can be substantial. To alleviate this problem, the profession recommends that companies subject to material seasonal variations disclose the seasonal nature of their business and consider supplementing their interim reports with information for 12-month periods ended at the interim date for the current and preceding years.

The two illustrations highlight the difference between the **discrete** and **integral** approaches. Illustration 24-11 represents the discrete approach, in which the fixed nonmanufacturing expenses are expensed as incurred. Illustration 24-12 shows the integral approach, in which expenses are charged to expense on the basis of some measure of activity.

International
Perspective

IFRS requires that interim financial statements use the discrete method, except for tax expenses.

Evolving Issue   *IT'S FASTER BUT IS IT BETTER?*

The profession has developed some rules for interim reporting, but much still has to be done. As yet, it is unclear whether the discrete or the integral method, or some combination of the two, will be settled on.

Discussion also persists about the independent auditor's involvement in interim reports. Many auditors are reluctant to express an opinion on interim financial information, arguing that the data are too tentative and subjective. On the other hand, more people are advocating some examination of interim reports. As a compromise, the SEC currently requires that auditors perform a review of interim financial information. Such a review, which is much more limited in

its procedures than the annual audit, provides some assurance that the interim information appears to be in accord with GAAP. (See "Interim Financial Information," *Statement on Auditing Standards No. 101* (New York: AICPA, 2002).)

Analysts and investors want financial information as soon as possible, before it's old news. We may not be far from a continuous database system in which corporate financial records can be accessed via the Internet. Investors might be able to access a company's financial records whenever they wish and put the information in the format they need. Thus, they could learn about sales slippage, cost increases, or earnings changes as they happen, rather than waiting until after the quarter has ended.

A step in this direction is the SEC's mandate for companies to file their financial statements electronically with the SEC. The system, called EDGAR (electronic data gathering and retrieval), provides interested parties with computer access to financial information such as periodic filings, corporate prospectuses, and proxy materials.

The SEC also believes that timeliness of information is of extreme importance. First, the SEC has said that large public companies will have only 60 days to complete their annual reports, down from 90 days. Quarterly reports must be done within 40 days of the close of the quarter, instead of 45. In addition, corporate executives and shareholders with more than 10 percent of a company's outstanding stock now have two days to disclose their sale or purchase of stock.

Finally, in a bid to increase Internet disclosure, the SEC encourages companies to post current, quarterly, and annual reports on their websites—or explain why they don't. The Internet postings would have to be made by the day the company submits the information to the SEC, rather than within 24 hours as current rules allow.

A steady stream of information from the company to the investor could be very positive because it might alleviate management's continual concern with short-run interim numbers. Today, many contend that U.S. management is too oriented to the short-term. The truth of this statement is echoed by the words of the president of a large company who decided to retire early: "I wanted to look forward to a year made up of four seasons rather than four quarters."

AUDITOR'S AND MANAGEMENT'S REPORTS
Auditor's Report

Another important source of information, which is often overlooked, is the **auditor's report**. An **auditor** is an accounting professional who conducts an independent examination of a company's accounting data.

If satisfied that the financial statements present the financial position, results of operations, and cash flows fairly in accordance with generally accepted accounting principles, the auditor expresses an **unqualified opinion**. An example is shown in Illustration 24-13.[11]

In preparing the report, the auditor follows these reporting standards.

1. The report states whether the financial statements are in accordance with generally accepted accounting principles.

2. The report identifies those circumstances in which the company has not consistently observed such principles in the current period in relation to the preceding period.

3. Users are to regard the informative disclosures in the financial statements as reasonably adequate unless the report states otherwise.

4. The report contains either an expression of opinion regarding the financial statements taken as a whole or an assertion to the effect that an opinion cannot be expressed. When the auditor cannot express an overall opinion, the report should state the reasons. In all cases where an auditor's name is associated with financial statements, the report should contain a clear-cut indication of the character of the auditor's examination, if any, and the degree of responsibility being taken.

In most cases, the auditor issues a standard **unqualified** or **clean opinion**. That is, the auditor expresses the opinion that the financial statements present fairly, in all material respects, the financial position, results of operations, and cash flows of the entity in conformity with generally accepted accounting principles.

[11]This auditor's report is in exact conformance with the specifications contained in "Reports on Audited Financial Statements," *Statement on Auditing Standards No. 58* (New York: AICPA, 1988). The last paragraph refers to the assessment of the company's internal controls, as required by the PCAOB.

ILLUSTRATION 24-13
Auditor's Report

Best Buy Co., Inc.

Report of Independent Registered Public Accounting Firm

To the Board of Directors and Shareholders of Best Buy Co., Inc.:

We have audited the accompanying consolidated balance sheets of Best Buy Co., Inc. and subsidiaries (the "Company") as of March 3, 2012 and February 26, 2011 and the related consolidated statements of earnings, cash flows, and changes in shareholders' equity for each of the three fiscal years in the period ended March 3, 2012. Our audits also included the financial statement schedule listed in the Index at Item 15(a). These financial statements and financial statement schedule are the responsibility of the Company's management. Our responsibility is to express an opinion on these financial statements and financial statement schedule based on our audits.

We conducted our audits in accordance with the standards of the Public Company Accounting Oversight Board (United States). Those standards require that we plan and perform the audit to obtain reasonable assurance about whether the financial statements are free of material misstatement. An audit includes examining, on a test basis, evidence supporting the amounts and disclosures in the financial statements. An audit also includes assessing the accounting principles used and significant estimates made by management, as well as evaluating the overall financial statement presentation. We believe that our audits provide a reasonable basis for our opinion.

In our opinion, such consolidated financial statements present fairly, in all material respects, the financial position of Best Buy Co., Inc. and subsidiaries as of March 3, 2012 and February 26, 2011, and the results of their operations and their cash flows for each of the three fiscal years in the period ended March 3, 2012, in conformity with accounting principles generally accepted in the United States of America. Also, in our opinion, such financial statement schedule, when considered in relation to the basic consolidated financial statements taken as a whole, presents fairly, in all material respects, the information set forth therein. We have also audited, in accordance with the standards of the Public Company Accounting Oversight Board (United States), the Company's internal control over financial reporting as of March 3, 2012, based on the criteria established in *Internal Control-Integrated Framework* issued by the Committee of Sponsoring Organizations of the Treadway Commission and our report dated May 1, 2012, expressed an unqualified opinion on the Company's internal control over financial reporting.

Deloitte & Touche LLP

Minneapolis, Minnesota
May 1, 2012

Certain circumstances, although they do not affect the auditor's unqualified opinion, may require the auditor to add an explanatory paragraph to the audit report. Some of the more important circumstances are as follows.

1. *Going concern.* The auditor must evaluate whether there is substantial doubt about the entity's **ability to continue as a going concern** for a reasonable period of time, taking into consideration all available information about the future. (The future is at least, but not limited to, 12 months from the end of the reporting period.) If substantial doubt exists about the company continuing as a going concern, the auditor adds to the report an explanatory note describing the potential problem. **[7]**[12]

---

[12]The FASB has a project requiring certain disclosures when management concludes it is *more likely than not* that the company will not be able to meet its obligations in the ordinary course of business for a reasonable period of time. When management concludes it is *probable* that the entity will not be able to meet its obligations in the ordinary course of business for a reasonable period of time, a statement that there is substantial doubt about the entity's ability to continue as a going concern would also be required. Similar to auditing standards, the Board defines a *reasonable period of time* as 12 months from the balance sheet date. However, management would also consider events that are probable of resulting in an entity's potential inability to meet its obligations beyond 12 months. The combined assessment period would not exceed 24 months. See *http://www.fasb.org/*; click on the Projects tab and scroll down to the Going Concern link. See also the project on liquidation accounting.

2. *Lack of consistency.* If a company has changed accounting principles or the method of their application in a way that has a material effect on the comparability of its financial statements, the auditor should refer to the change in an explanatory paragraph of the report. Such an explanatory paragraph should identify the nature of the change and refer readers to the note in the financial statements that discusses the change in detail. The auditor's concurrence with a change is implicit unless the auditor takes exception to the change in expressing an opinion as to fair presentation in conformity with generally accepted accounting principles.

3. *Emphasis of a matter.* The auditor may wish to emphasize a matter regarding the financial statements but nevertheless intends to express an unqualified opinion. For example, the auditor may wish to emphasize that the entity is a component of a larger business enterprise or that it has had significant transactions with related parties. The auditor presents such explanatory information in a separate paragraph of the report.

In some situations, however, the auditor is required to express (1) a **qualified** opinion or (2) an **adverse** opinion, or (3) to **disclaim** an opinion.

A qualified opinion contains an exception to the standard opinion. Ordinarily, the exception is not of sufficient magnitude to invalidate the statements as a whole; if it were, an adverse opinion would be rendered. The usual circumstances in which the auditor may deviate from the standard unqualified short-form report on financial statements are as follows.

1. The scope of the examination is limited or affected by conditions or restrictions.
2. The statements do not fairly present financial position or results of operations because of:
   (a) Lack of conformity with generally accepted accounting principles and standards.
   (b) Inadequate disclosure.

If confronted with one of the situations noted above, the auditor must offer a qualified opinion. A qualified opinion states that, except for the effects of the matter to which the qualification relates, the financial statements present fairly, in all material respects, the financial position, results of operations, and cash flows in conformity with generally accepted accounting principles.

Illustration 24-14 shows an example of an auditor's report with a qualified opinion. The auditor qualified the opinion because the company used an accounting principle at variance with generally accepted accounting principles.

ILLUSTRATION 24-14
Qualified Auditor's
Report

Helio Company

Independent Auditor's Report

(Same first and second paragraphs as the standard report)

Helio Company has excluded, from property and debt in the accompanying balance sheets, certain lease obligations that, in our opinion, should be capitalized in order to conform with generally accepted accounting principles. If these lease obligations were capitalized, property would be increased by $1,500,000 and $1,300,000, long-term debt by $1,400,000 and $1,200,000, and retained earnings by $100,000 and $50,000 as of December 31, in the current and prior year, respectively. Additionally, net income would be decreased by $40,000 and $30,000 and earnings per share would be decreased by $.06 and $.04, respectively, for the years then ended.

In our opinion, except for the effects of not capitalizing certain lease obligations as discussed in the preceding paragraph, the financial statements referred to above present fairly, in all material respects, the financial position of Helio Company, and the results of its operations and its cash flows for the years then ended in conformity with generally accepted accounting principles.

An **adverse opinion** is required in any report in which the exceptions to fair presentation are so material that in the independent auditor's judgment, a qualified opinion is not justified. In such a case, the financial statements taken as a whole are not presented in accordance with generally accepted accounting principles. Adverse opinions are rare, because most companies change their accounting to conform with GAAP. The SEC will not permit a company listed on an exchange to have an adverse opinion.

A **disclaimer of an opinion** is appropriate when the auditor has gathered so little information on the financial statements that no opinion can be expressed.

The audit report should provide useful information to the investor. One investment banker noted, "Probably the first item to check is the auditor's opinion to see whether or not it is a clean one—'in conformity with generally accepted accounting principles'—or is qualified in regard to differences between the auditor and company management in the accounting treatment of some major item, or in the outcome of some major litigation."

What do the numbers mean?   *HEART OF THE MATTER*

As we discussed in the opening story, financial disclosure is one of a number of institutional features that contribute to vibrant security markets. In fact, a recent study of disclosure and other mechanisms (such as civil lawsuits and criminal sanctions) found that good disclosure is the most important contributor to a vibrant market. The study, which compared disclosure and other legal and regulatory elements across 49 countries, found that countries with the best disclosure laws have the biggest stock markets.

Countries with more successful market environments also tend to have regulations that make it relatively easy for private investors to sue corporations that provide bad information. That is, while criminal sanctions can be effective in some circumstances, disclosure and other legal and regulatory elements encouraging good disclosure are the most important determinants of highly liquid and deep securities markets.

These findings hold for nations in all stages of economic development, with particular importance for nations that are in the early stages of securities regulation. In addition, countries with fewer market protections likely will benefit the most from adoption of international standards for market regulation and disclosure. The lesson: Disclosure is good for your market.

Sources: Rebecca Christie, "Study: Disclosure at Heart of Effective Securities Laws," *Wall Street Journal Online* (August 11, 2003); and L. Hail, C. Leuz, and P. Wysocki, "Global Accounting Convergence and the Potential Adoption of IFRS by the U.S. (Part I): Conceptual Underpinnings and Economic Analysis," *Accounting Horizons* (September 2010).

Management's Reports

Management's Discussion and Analysis

The SEC mandates inclusion of **management's discussion and analysis (MD&A)**. This section covers three financial aspects of an enterprise's business—liquidity, capital resources, and results of operations. In it, management highlights favorable or unfavorable trends and identifies significant events and uncertainties that affect these three factors. This approach obviously involves subjective estimates, opinions, and soft data. However, the SEC believes that the relevance of this information exceeds the potential lack of faithful representation.

6   LEARNING OBJECTIVE
Understand management's responsibilities for financials.

Illustration 24-15 (page 1512) presents an excerpt from the MD&A section (2009 "Business Risks" only) of **PepsiCo**'s annual report.

The MD&A section also must provide information about the effects of inflation and changing prices, if they are material to financial statement trends. The SEC has not required specific numerical computations, and companies have provided little analysis on changing prices.

An additional disclosure provided in the MD&A of many companies is discussion of the company's critical accounting policies. This disclosure identifies accounting

ILLUSTRATION 24-15
Management's
Discussion and Analysis

PepsiCo, Inc.

MD&A Our business risks (in part)

Risk Management Framework

The achievement of our strategic and operating objectives will necessarily involve taking risks. Our risk management process is intended to ensure that risks are taken knowingly and purposefully. As such, we leverage an integrated risk management framework to identify, assess, prioritize, manage, monitor and communicate risks across the Company. This framework includes:

- The PepsiCo Risk Committee (PRC), comprised of a cross-functional, geographically diverse, senior management group which meets regularly to identify, assess, prioritize and address strategic and reputational risks;

- Division Risk Committees (DRCs), comprised of cross-functional senior management teams which meet regularly to identify, assess, prioritize and address division-specific operating risks;

- PepsiCo's Risk Management Office, which manages the overall risk management process, provides ongoing guidance, tools and analytical support to the PRC and the DRCs, identifies and assesses potential risks, and facilitates ongoing communication between the parties, as well as to PepsiCo's Audit Committee and Board of Directors;

- PepsiCo Corporate Audit, which evaluates the ongoing effectiveness of our key internal controls through periodic audit and review procedures; and

- PepsiCo's Compliance Department, which leads and coordinates our compliance policies and practices.

Market Risks

We are exposed to market risks arising from adverse changes in:

- commodity prices, affecting the cost of our raw materials and energy,
- foreign exchange rates, and
- interest rates.

In the normal course of business, we manage these risks through a variety of strategies, including productivity initiatives, global purchasing programs and hedging strategies. Ongoing productivity initiatives involve the identification and effective implementation of meaningful cost saving opportunities or efficiencies. Our global purchasing programs include fixed-price purchase orders and pricing agreements.

**Gateway to
the Profession**

*Expanded Discussion
of Accounting for
Changing Prices*

policies that require management to make subjective judgments regarding uncertainties, resulting in potentially significant effects on the financial results.[13] For example, in its critical accounting policy disclosure, PepsiCo showed the impact on stock-based compensation expense in response to changes in estimated interest rates and stock return volatility. Through this voluntary disclosure, companies can expand on the information contained in the notes to the financial statements to indicate the sensitivity of the financial results to accounting policy judgments.

Management's Responsibilities for Financial Statements

The Sarbanes-Oxley Act requires the SEC to develop guidelines for *all* publicly traded companies to report on management's responsibilities for, and assessment of, the internal control system. An example of the type of disclosure that public companies are now making is shown in Illustration 24-16.[14]

---

[13]See *Cautionary Advice Regarding Disclosure about Critical Accounting Policies,* Release Nos. 33-8040; 34-45149; FR-60 (Washington, D.C.: SEC); and *Proposed Rule: Disclosure in Management's Discussion and Analysis about the Application of Critical Accounting Policies,* Release Nos. 33-8098; 34-45907; International Series Release No. 1258; File No. S7-16-02 (Washington, D.C.: SEC).

[14]As indicated in this disclosure, management is responsible for preparing the financial statements and establishing and maintaining an effective system of internal controls. The auditor provides an independent assessment of whether the financial statements are prepared in accordance with GAAP, and for public companies, whether the internal controls are effective (see the audit opinion in Illustration 24-13 on page 1509).

ILLUSTRATION 24-16
Report on Management's
Responsibilities

Home Depot

Management's Responsibility for Financial Statements

The financial statements presented in this Annual Report have been prepared with integrity and objectivity and are the responsibility of the management of The Home Depot, Inc. These financial statements have been prepared in conformity with U.S. generally accepted accounting principles and properly reflect certain estimates and judgments based upon the best available information.

The financial statements of the Company have been audited by KPMG LLP, an independent registered public accounting firm. Their accompanying report is based upon an audit conducted in accordance with the standards of the Public Company Accounting Oversight Board (United States).

The Audit Committee of the Board of Directors, consisting solely of independent directors, meets five times a year with the independent registered public accounting firm, the internal auditors and representatives of management to discuss auditing and financial reporting matters. In addition, a telephonic meeting is held prior to each quarterly earnings release. The Audit Committee retains the independent registered public accounting firm and regularly reviews the internal accounting controls, the activities of the independent registered public accounting firm and internal auditors and the financial condition of the Company. Both the Company's independent registered public accounting firm and the internal auditors have free access to the Audit Committee.

Management's Report on Internal Control over Financial Reporting

Our management is responsible for establishing and maintaining adequate internal control over financial reporting, as such term is defined in Rule 13a-15(f) promulgated under the Securities Exchange Act of 1934, as amended (the "Exchange Act"). Under the supervision and with the participation of our management, including our Chief Executive Officer and Chief Financial Officer, we conducted an evaluation of the effectiveness of our internal control over financial reporting as of January 29, 2012 based on the framework in *Internal Control—Integrated Framework* issued by the Committee of Sponsoring Organizations of the Treadway Commission (COSO). Based on our evaluation, our management concluded that our internal control over financial reporting was effective as of January 29, 2012 in providing reasonable assurance regarding the reliability of financial reporting and the preparation of financial statements for external purposes in accordance with U.S. generally accepted accounting principles. The effectiveness of our internal control over financial reporting as of January 29, 2012 has been audited by KPMG LLP, an independent registered public accounting firm, as stated in their report which is included on page 28 in this Form 10-K.

Francis S. Blake
Chairman & Chief Executive Officer

Carol B. Tomé
Chief Financial Officer &
Executive Vice President—Corporate Services

CURRENT REPORTING ISSUES
Reporting on Financial Forecasts and Projections

In recent years, the investing public's demand for more and better information has focused on disclosure of corporate expectations for the future.[15] These disclosures take one of two forms:[16]

7 LEARNING OBJECTIVE
Identify issues related to financial forecasts and projections.

- *Financial forecasts.* A **financial forecast** is a set of prospective financial statements that present, to the best of the responsible party's knowledge and belief, a company's expected financial position, results of operations, and cash flows. The

---

[15]Some areas in which companies are using financial information about the future are equipment lease-versus-buy analysis, analysis of a company's ability to successfully enter new markets, and examination of merger and acquisition opportunities. In addition, companies also prepare forecasts and projections for use by third parties in public offering documents (requiring financial forecasts), tax-oriented investments, and financial feasibility studies. Use of forward-looking data has been enhanced by the increased capability of microcomputers to analyze, compare, and manipulate large quantities of data.

[16]"Financial Forecasts and Projections" and "Guide for Prospective Financial Information," *Codification of Statements on Standards for Attestation Engagements* (New York: AICPA 2006), paras. 3.04 and 3.05.

responsible party bases a financial forecast on conditions it expects to exist and the course of action it expects to take.

- *Financial projections.* Financial projections are prospective financial statements that present, to the best of the responsible party's knowledge and belief, given one or more *hypothetical assumptions*, an entity's expected financial position, results of operations, and cash flows. The responsible party bases a financial projection on conditions it expects *would* exist and the course of action it expects *would* be taken, given one or more hypothetical assumptions.

The difference between a financial forecast and a financial projection is clear-cut. A forecast provides information on what is **expected** to happen, whereas a projection provides information on what **might** take place but is not necessarily expected to happen.

Whether companies should be required to provide financial forecasts is the subject of intensive discussion with journalists, corporate executives, the SEC, financial analysts, accountants, and others. Predictably, there are strong arguments on either side. Listed below are some of the arguments.

Arguments for requiring published forecasts:

1. Investment decisions are based on future expectations. Therefore, information about the future facilitates better decisions.
2. Companies already circulate forecasts informally. This situation should be regulated to ensure that the forecasts are available to all investors.
3. Circumstances now change so rapidly that historical information is no longer adequate for prediction.

Arguments against requiring published forecasts:

1. No one can foretell the future. Therefore, forecasts will inevitably be wrong. Worse, they may mislead, if they convey an impression of precision about the future.
2. Companies may strive only to meet their published forecasts, thereby failing to produce results that are in the stockholders' best interest.
3. If forecasts prove inaccurate, there will be recriminations and probably legal actions.[17]
4. Disclosure of forecasts will be detrimental to organizations, because forecasts will inform competitors (foreign and domestic) as well as investors.

Underlying Concepts

The profession indicates that the legal environment discourages companies from disclosing forward-looking information. Companies should not have to expand reporting of forward-looking information unless there are more effective deterrents to unwarranted litigation.

The AICPA has issued a statement on standards for accountants' services on prospective financial information. This statement establishes guidelines for the preparation and presentation of financial forecasts and projections.[18] It requires accountants to provide (1) a summary of significant assumptions used in the forecast or projection and (2) guidelines for minimum presentation.

To encourage management to disclose prospective financial information, the SEC has a safe harbor rule. It provides protection to a company that presents an erroneous forecast, as long as the company prepared the forecast on a reasonable basis

---

[17]The issue is serious. Over a recent three-year period, 8 percent of the companies on the NYSE were sued because of an alleged lack of financial disclosure. Companies complain that they are subject to lawsuits whenever the stock price drops. And as one executive noted, "You can even be sued if the stock price goes up—because you did not disclose the good news fast enough."

[18]*Op. cit.*, par. 1.02.

and disclosed it in good faith.[19] However, many companies note that the safe harbor rule does not work in practice, since it does not cover oral statements, nor has it kept them from investor lawsuits.

What do the numbers mean? GLOBAL FORECASTS

Great Britain permits financial forecasts, and the results have been fairly successful. Some significant differences do exist between the English and the U.S. business and legal environments. The British system, for example, does not permit litigation on forecasted information, and the solicitor (lawyer) is not permitted to work on a contingent-fee basis.

But such differences probably could be overcome if influential interests in this country cooperated to produce an atmosphere conducive to quality forecasting. A typical British forecast adapted from a construction company's report to support a public offering of stock is as follows.

> Profits have grown substantially over the past 10 years and directors are confident of being able to continue this expansion. . . . While the rate of expansion will be dependent on the level of economic activity in Ireland and England, the group is well structured to avail itself of opportunities as they arise, particularly in the field of property development, which is expected to play an increasingly important role in the group's future expansion.
>
> Profits before taxation for the half year ended 30th June were 402,000 pounds. On the basis of trading experiences since that date and the present level of sales and completions, the directors expect that in the absence of unforeseen circumstances, the group's profits before taxation for the year to 31st December will be not less than 960,000 pounds.
>
> No dividends will be paid in respect of the current year. In a full financial year, on the basis of above forecasts (not including full year profits) it would be the intention of the board, assuming current rates of tax, to recommend dividends totaling 40% (of after-tax profits), which will be payable in the next two years.

A general narrative-type forecast issued by a U.S. corporation might appear as follows.

> On the basis of promotions planned by the company for the second half of the fiscal year, net earnings for that period are expected to be approximately the same as those for the first half of the fiscal year, with net earnings for the third quarter expected to make the predominant contribution to net earnings for the second half of the year.

As indicated, the U.S. version is much less specific in its forecasted information.

Source: See "A Case for Forecasting—The British Have Tried It and Find That It Works," *World* (New York: Peat, Marwick, Mitchell & Co., Autumn 1978), pp. 10–13. In a recent survey, U.K. companies remain stubbornly backward-looking. Just 5 percent of FTSE 100 companies address the future of the business in their discussion and analysis. See PricewaterhouseCoopers, "Guide to Forward-looking Information: Don't Fear the Future" (2006).

Questions of Liability

What happens if a company does not meet its forecasts? Can the company and the auditor be sued? If a company, for example, projects an earnings increase of 15 percent and achieves only 5 percent, should stockholders be permitted to have some judicial recourse against the company?

One court case involving **Monsanto Chemical Corporation** set a precedent. In this case, Monsanto predicted that sales would increase 8 to 9 percent and that earnings would rise 4 to 5 percent. In the last part of the year, the demand for Monsanto's products dropped as a result of a business turndown. Instead of increasing, the company's earnings declined. Investors sued the company because the projected earnings figure was erroneous, but a judge dismissed the suit because the forecasts were the best estimates of qualified people whose intents were honest.

As indicated earlier, the SEC's safe harbor rules are intended to protect companies that provide good-faith projections. However, much concern exists as to how the SEC

[19]"Safe-Harbor Rule for Projections," *Release No. 5993* (Washington, D.C.: SEC, 1979). The Private Securities Litigation Reform Act of 1995 recognizes that some information that is useful to investors is inherently subject to less certainty or reliability than other information. By providing safe harbor for forward-looking statements, Congress has sought to facilitate access to this information by investors.

and the courts will interpret such terms as "good faith" and "reasonable assumptions" when erroneous forecasts mislead users of this information.

Internet Financial Reporting

Most companies now use the power and reach of the Internet to provide more useful information to financial statement readers. All large companies have Internet sites, and a large proportion of companies' websites contain links to their financial statements and other disclosures. The popularity of such reporting is not surprising since it reduces the companies' costs of printing and disseminating paper reports.

Does Internet financial reporting improve the usefulness of a company's financial reports? Yes, in several ways. First, dissemination of reports via the Web allows firms **to communicate more easily and quickly with users** than do traditional paper reports. In addition, **Internet reporting allows users to take advantage of tools** such as search engines and hyperlinks to quickly find information about the firm and to download the information for analysis. Finally, **Internet reporting can help make financial reports more relevant** by allowing companies to report expanded disaggregated data and more timely data than is possible through paper-based reporting. For example, some companies voluntarily report weekly sales data and segment operating data on their websites.

Given the widespread use of the Internet by investors and creditors, it is not surprising that organizations are developing new technologies and standards to further enable and enhance Internet financial reporting. An example is the increasing use of eXtensible Business Reporting Language (XBRL). **XBRL** is a computer language adapted from the code of the Internet. It "tags" accounting data to correspond to financial reporting items that are reported in the balance sheet, income statement, and the cash flow statement. Once tagged, any company's XBRL data can be easily processed using spreadsheets and other computer programs. In fact, the SEC is phasing in requirements for all companies and mutual funds to prepare their financial reports using XBRL, thereby allowing users to more easily search a company's reports, extract and analyze data, and perform financial comparisons within industries.[20]

To complement the implementation of XBRL use, the SEC has also announced a major upgrade to its EDGAR database. The new system is called IDEA (short for Interactive Data Electronic Applications). This replacement of EDGAR marks the SEC's transition from collecting forms and documents to making the information itself freely available to investors in a timely form they can readily use. With IDEA, investors will be able to quickly collate information from thousands of companies and forms and create reports and analyses on the fly, in any way they choose. It is hoped that IDEA will open the door for both the SEC and investors to the new world of financial disclosure in interactive data (XBRL) format.[21]

---

[20]See *SEC Interactive Data Rules for Operating Companies* (*http://www.sec.gov/rules/final/2009/33-9002. pdf*); and C. Twarowski, "Financial Data 'on Steroids'," *Washington Post* (August 19, 2008), p. D01. See also *www.xbrl.org/us/us/BusinessCaseForXBRL.pdf* for additional information on XBRL. The IASB and the FASB are collaborating to implement XBRL with their standards. See *http://www. ifrs.org/XBRL/XBRL/htm.*

[21]See *http://www.sec.gov/edgar/aboutedgar.htm*. The SEC has implemented other regulations to ensure that investors get high-quality disclosures. For example, as discussed in Chapter 4, the SEC was concerned that companies may use pro forma reporting to deflect investor attention from bad news. In response, the SEC issued Regulation G, which requires companies to reconcile non-GAAP financial measures to GAAP. This regulation provides investors with a roadmap to analyze adjustments companies make to their GAAP numbers to arrive at pro forma results. [See SEC Regulation G, "Conditions for Use of Non-GAAP Financial Measures," Release No. 33-8176 (March 28, 2003).] Regulation FD (Release Nos. 33-7881) was issued in 2000 to address the concern that some analysts were receiving information sooner than the general public (e.g., during conference calls with analysts when earnings releases were discussed). Regulation FD requires that when relevant information is released, all have equal access to it.

What do the numbers mean?   *NEW FORMATS, NEW DISCLOSURE*

As indicated in earlier chapters in the *IFRS Insights* discussions, the FASB and the IASB are exploring better ways to present information in the financial statements. Recently, these two standard-setters have issued a discussion paper that requests input on a proposed reformatting of the financial statements. The table below provides a "snapshot" of the proposed changes (go to *http://www.fasb.org* to learn more about this joint international project).

Statement of Financial Position	Statement of Comprehensive Income	Statement of Cash Flows
Business	Business	Business
• Operating assets and liabilities	• Operating income and expenses	• Operating cash flows
• Investing assets and liabilities	• Investing income and expenses	• Investing cash flows
Financing	Financing	Financing
• Financing assets	• Financing asset income	• Financing asset cash flows
• Financing liabilities	• Financing liability expenses	• Financing liability cash flows
Income Taxes	Income Taxes	Income Taxes

As indicated, each statement will use the same format. While the proposed changes will not affect the measurement of individual financial statement elements, the use of a consistent format (e.g., Business, Financing, Income Taxes) will help users understand the interrelationships in the financial statements. In addition, a new schedule reconciling cash flows to comprehensive income will be provided. As part of this schedule, changes in fair value will be included. It is a good thing the timeline for the project is lengthy, as these changes in presentation are significant.

Fraudulent Financial Reporting

Economic crime is on the rise around the world. A recent global survey of over 3,000 executives from 54 countries documented the types of economic crimes, as shown in Illustration 24-17 and Illustration 24-18 (page 1518).

8 **LEARNING OBJECTIVE**

Describe the profession's response to fraudulent financial reporting.

ILLUSTRATION 24-17
Types of Economic Crime

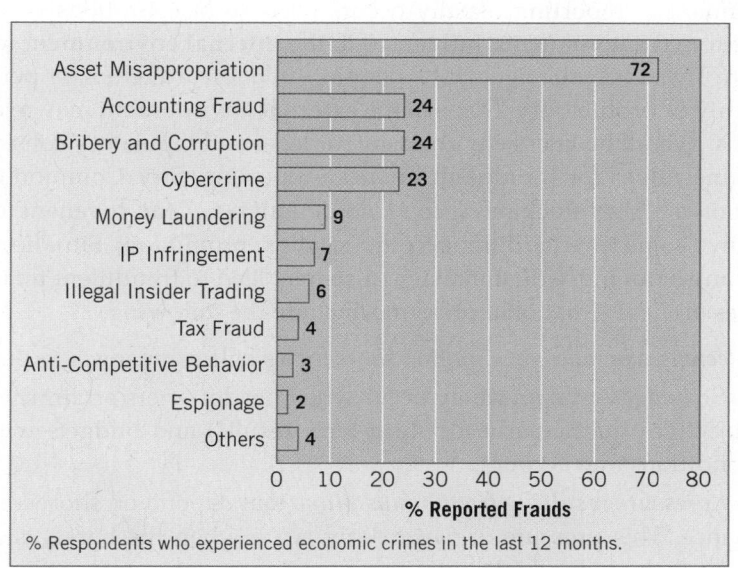

As indicated, a wide range of economic crimes are reported. As shown in Illustration 24-18, while the trend for the top three areas is improving, accounting fraud consistently is in the top three.

Fraudulent financial reporting is defined as "intentional or reckless conduct, whether act or omission, that results in materially misleading financial statements."[22] Fraudulent

---

[22]"Report of the National Commission on Fraudulent Financial Reporting" (Washington, D.C., 1987), page 2. Unintentional errors as well as corporate improprieties (such as tax fraud, employee embezzlements, and so on) which do not cause the financial statements to be misleading are excluded from the definition of fraudulent financial reporting.

ILLUSTRATION 24-18
Trends in Reported Fraud

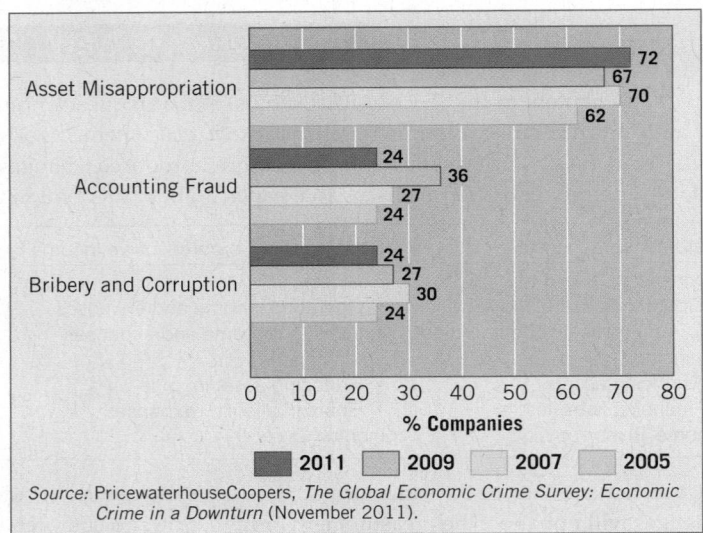

Source: PricewaterhouseCoopers, *The Global Economic Crime Survey: Economic Crime in a Downturn* (November 2011).

reporting can involve gross and deliberate distortion of corporate records (such as inventory count tags), or misapplication of accounting principles (failure to disclose material transactions). Although frauds are unusual, recent events involving such well-known companies as Enron, WorldCom, Adelphia, and Tyco indicate that more must be done to address this issue.

Causes of Fraudulent Financial Reporting

Fraudulent financial reporting usually occurs because of conditions in a company's internal or external environment. Influences in the **internal environment** relate to poor internal control systems, management's poor attitude toward ethics, or perhaps a company's liquidity or profitability. Those in the **external environment** may relate to industry conditions, overall business environment, or legal and regulatory considerations.

General incentives for fraudulent financial reporting vary. Common ones are the desire to obtain a higher stock price, to avoid default on a loan covenant, or to make a personal gain of some type (additional compensation, promotion). Situational pressures on the company or an individual manager also may lead to fraudulent financial reporting. Examples of these situational pressures include the following.

- *Sudden decreases in revenue or market share* for a single company or an entire industry.
- *Unrealistic budget pressures* may occur when headquarters arbitrarily determines profit objectives (particularly for short-term results) and budgets without taking actual conditions into account.
- *Financial pressure resulting from bonus plans* that depend on short-term economic performance. This pressure is particularly acute when the bonus is a significant component of the individual's total compensation.

Opportunities for fraudulent financial reporting are present in circumstances when the fraud is easy to commit and when detection is difficult. Frequently, these opportunities arise from:

1. *The absence of a board of directors or audit committee* that vigilantly oversees the financial reporting process.
2. *Weak or nonexistent internal accounting controls.* This situation can occur, for example, when a company's revenue system is overloaded as a result of a rapid

expansion of sales, an acquisition of a new division, or the entry into a new, unfamiliar line of business.

3. *Unusual or complex transactions* such as the consolidation of two companies, the divestiture or closing of a specific operation, and the purchase and sale of derivative instruments.

4. *Accounting estimates requiring significant subjective judgment* by company management, such as the allowance for loan losses and the estimated liability for warranty expense.

5. *Ineffective internal audit staffs* resulting from inadequate staff size and severely limited audit scope.

A weak corporate ethical climate contributes to these situations. Opportunities for fraudulent financial reporting also increase dramatically when the accounting principles followed in reporting transactions are nonexistent, evolving, or subject to varying interpretations.[23]

The AICPA has issued numerous auditing standards in response to concerns of the accounting profession, the media, and the public.[24] For example, the standard on fraudulent financial reporting "raises the bar" on the performance of financial statement audits by explicitly requiring auditors to assess the risk of material financial misstatement due to fraud.[25] As indicated earlier, the Sarbanes-Oxley Act now raises the penalty substantially for executives who are involved in fraudulent financial reporting.

What do the numbers mean? DISCLOSURE OVERLOAD

As we discussed in Chapter 1 and throughout the textbook, IFRS is gaining popularity around the world. The U.S. Securities and Exchange Commission is still studying whether and how to incorporate IFRS in the accounting rules used by publicly traded companies in the United States. There is some debate on U.S. readiness to make the switch. For example, there are several areas in which the FASB and the IASB must iron out a number of technical accounting issues before they reach a substantially converged set of accounting standards. Here is a list of six important areas yet to be converged.

1. *Error correction.* According to *IAS 8*, it's not always necessary to retrospectively restate financial results when a company corrects errors, especially if the adjustment is impractical or too costly. GAAP, on the other hand, requires restatements in many error-correction cases.

2. *Death of LIFO.* Last-in, first-out (LIFO) inventory accounting is prohibited under *IAS 2*, so any U.S. company using the method will have to abandon it (and the tax benefits) and move to another methodology. Although LIFO is permitted under GAAP, the repeal of LIFO for tax purposes is an ongoing debate.

3. *Reversal of impairments.* IAS 36 permits companies to reverse impairment losses up to the amount of the original impairment when the reason for the charge decreases or no longer exists. However, GAAP bans reversal.

4. *PP&E revaluation.* IAS 16 allows for the revaluation of property, plant, and equipment, but the entire asset class must be revalued. That means a company can choose to use the revaluation model if the asset class's fair value can be measured reliably. But, it must choose to use one

---

[23]The discussion in this section is based on the Report of the National Commission on Fraudulent Financial Reporting, pp. 23–24 (2004). See also "2012 Report to the Nation on Occupational Fraud and Abuse, Association of Certified Fraud Examiners" (*http://www.acfe.com/uploadedFiles/ ACFE_Website/Content/rttn/2012-report-to-nations.pdf*), for fraudulent financial reporting causes and consequences.

[24]Because the profession believes that the role of the auditor is not well understood outside the profession, much attention has been focused on the expectation gap. The **expectation gap** is the gap between (1) the expectation of financial statement users concerning the level of assurance they believe the independent auditor provides, and (2) the assurance that the independent auditor actually does provide under generally accepted auditing standards.

[25]"Consideration of Fraud in a Financial Statement Audit," *Statement on Auditing Standards No. 99* (New York: AICPA, 2002).

model or the other; both cannot be used at the same time. GAAP does not allow revaluation.

5. *Component depreciation.* Also under *IAS 16*, companies must recognize and depreciate equipment components separately if the components can be physically separated from the asset and have different useful life spans. In practical terms, that means controllers will have to rely on the operations side of the business to help assess equipment components. GAAP allows component depreciation, but it is not required.

6. *Development costs.* Based on *IAS 38*, companies are permitted to capitalize development costs as long as they meet six criteria. However, research costs are still expensed. GAAP requires that all R&D costs be charged to expense when incurred.

Some are already debating what will happen if and when U.S. companies adopt these new standards. It is almost certain that expanded disclosure will be needed to help users navigate accounting reports upon adoption of IFRS. As one accounting analyst remarked, "Get ready for an avalanche of footnotes." Since using IFRS requires more judgment than using GAAP, two to three times as many footnotes will be needed to explain the rationales for accounting approaches. So while principles-based standards should promote more comparability, they require investors to dig into the disclosures in the footnotes.

Source: Marie Leone, "GAAP and IFRS: Six Degrees of Separation," *CFO.com* (June 30, 2010).

Criteria for Making Accounting and Reporting Choices

Underlying Concepts

The FASB concept statements on the objective of financial reporting, elements of financial statements, qualitative characteristics of accounting information, and recognition and measurement are important steps in the right direction.

Throughout this textbook, we have stressed the need to provide information that is useful to predict the amounts, timing, and uncertainty of future cash flows. To achieve this objective, companies must make judicious choices between alternative accounting concepts, methods, and means of disclosure. You are probably surprised by the large number of choices that exist among acceptable alternatives.

You should recognize, however, as indicated in Chapter 1, that accounting is greatly influenced by its environment. It does not exist in a vacuum. Therefore, it is unrealistic to assume that the profession can entirely eliminate alternative presentations of certain transactions and events. Nevertheless, we are hopeful that the profession, by adhering to the conceptual framework, will be able to focus on the needs of financial statement users and eliminate diversity where appropriate. The SEC's and FASB's projects on principles-based standards are directed at these very issues. They seek to develop guidance that will result in accounting and financial reporting that reflects the economic substance of the transactions, not the desired financial result of management. The profession must continue its efforts to develop a sound foundation upon which to build financial standards and practice. As Aristotle said, "The correct beginning is more than half the whole."

You will want to read
IFRS INSIGHTS
on pages 1548–1557
for discussion of IFRS related to disclosure.

KEY TERMS

accounting policies, *1491*

adverse opinion, *1511*

auditor, *1508*

auditor's report, *1508*

common costs, *1500*

differential
    disclosure, *1489*

disclaimer of an
    opinion, *1511*

discrete approach, *1503*

errors, *1494*

financial forecast, *1513*

SUMMARY OF LEARNING OBJECTIVES

1 **Review the full disclosure principle and describe implementation problems.** The full disclosure principle calls for financial reporting of any financial facts significant enough to influence the judgment of an informed reader. Implementing the full disclosure principle is difficult because the cost of disclosure can be substantial and the benefits difficult to assess. Disclosure requirements have increased because of (1) the growing complexity of the business environment, (2) the necessity for timely information, and (3) the use of accounting as a control and monitoring device.

2 **Explain the use of notes in financial statement preparation.** Notes are the accountant's means of amplifying or explaining the items presented in the main body of the statements. Notes can explain in qualitative terms information pertinent to specific financial statement items, and can provide supplementary data of a quantitative nature. Common note disclosures relate to such items as accounting policies; inventories; property, plant, and equipment; creditor claims; contingencies and commitments; and subsequent events.

3 **Discuss the disclosure requirements for related-party transactions, post-balance-sheet events, and major business segments.** In related-party transactions, one party has the ability to significantly influence the policies of the other. As a result, GAAP requires disclosure of the relationship(s) involved, a description and dollar amounts of the transactions, and amounts due from or to related parties. For post-balance-sheet events, companies should disclose recognized subsequent events as well as nonrecognized subsequent events. Finally, aggregated figures hide much information about the composition of these consolidated figures. There is no way to tell from the consolidated data the extent to which the differing product lines contribute to the company's profitability, risk, and growth potential. As a result, the profession requires segment information in certain situations.

4 **Describe the accounting problems associated with interim reporting.** Interim reports cover periods of less than one year. Two viewpoints exist regarding interim reports. The discrete approach holds that each interim period should be treated as a separate accounting period. The integral approach is that the interim report is an integral part of the annual report and that deferrals and accruals should take into consideration what will happen for the entire year.

Companies should use the same accounting principles for interim reports that they use for annual reports. A number of unique reporting problems develop related to the following items: (1) advertising and similar costs, (2) expenses subject to year-end adjustment, (3) income taxes, (4) extraordinary items, (5) earnings per share, and (6) seasonality.

5 **Identify the major disclosures in the auditor's report.** The auditor expresses an unqualified opinion if satisfied that the financial statements present the financial position, results of operations, and cash flows fairly in accordance with generally accepted accounting principles. A qualified opinion contains an exception to the standard opinion; ordinarily the exception is not of sufficient magnitude to invalidate the statements as a whole.

An adverse opinion is required when the exceptions to fair presentation are so material that a qualified opinion is not justified. A disclaimer of an opinion is appropriate when the auditor has so little information on the financial statements that no opinion can be expressed.

6 **Understand management's responsibilities for financials.** Management's discussion and analysis (MD&A) section covers three financial aspects of an enterprise's business: liquidity, capital resources, and results of operations. Management's responsibility for the financial statements is often indicated in a letter to stockholders in the annual report.

7 **Identify issues related to financial forecasts and projections.** The SEC has indicated that companies are permitted (not required) to include profit forecasts in their reports. To encourage management to disclose such information, the SEC issued a safe harbor rule. The rule provides protection to a company that presents an erroneous forecast, as long as it prepared the projection on a reasonable basis and disclosed it in good faith. However, the safe harbor rule has not worked well in practice.

8 **Describe the profession's response to fraudulent financial reporting.** Fraudulent financial reporting is intentional or reckless conduct, whether through act or omission, that results in materially misleading financial statements. Fraudulent financial reporting usually occurs because of poor internal control, management's poor attitude toward ethics, poor performance, and so on. The Sarbanes-Oxley Act has numerous provisions intended to help prevent fraudulent financial reporting.

financial projection, *1514*

fraud, *1494*

fraudulent financial reporting, *1517*

full disclosure principle, *1488*

illegal acts, *1494*

integral approach, *1503*

interim reports, *1501*

management approach, *1499*

management's discussion and analysis (MD&A), *1511*

nonrecognized subsequent event, *1496*

notes to financial statements, *1491*

operating segment, *1499*

post-balance-sheet events, *1495*

qualified opinion, *1510*

recognized subsequent event, *1495*

related-party transactions, *1493*

safe harbor rule, *1514*

seasonality, *1506*

subsequent events, *1495*

unqualified or clean opinion, *1508*

XBRL, *1516*

| APPENDIX **24A** | BASIC FINANCIAL STATEMENT ANALYSIS |

LEARNING OBJECTIVE
Understand the approach to financial statement analysis.

What would be important to you in studying a company's financial statements? The answer depends on your particular interest—whether you are a creditor, stockholder, potential investor, manager, government agency, or labor leader. For example, **short-term creditors** such as banks are primarily interested in the ability of the firm to pay its currently maturing obligations. In that case, you would examine the current assets and their relation to short-term liabilities to evaluate the short-run solvency of the firm.

Bondholders, on the other hand, look more to long-term indicators, such as the enterprise's capital structure, past and projected earnings, and changes in financial position. **Stockholders**, present or prospective, also are interested in many of the features considered by a long-term creditor. As a stockholder, you would focus on the earnings picture, because changes in it greatly affect the market price of your investment. You also would be concerned with the financial position of the company, because it affects indirectly the stability of earnings.

The **managers** of a company are concerned about the composition of its capital structure and about the changes and trends in earnings. This financial information has a direct influence on the type, amount, and cost of external financing that the company can obtain. In addition, the company managers find financial information useful on a day-to-day operating basis in such areas as capital budgeting, break-even analysis, variance analysis, gross margin analysis, and for internal control purposes.

PERSPECTIVE ON FINANCIAL STATEMENT ANALYSIS

Readers of financial statements can gather information by examining relationships between items on the statements and identifying trends in these relationships. The relationships are expressed numerically in ratios and percentages, and trends are identified through comparative analysis.

 Underlying Concepts

Because financial statements report on the past, they emphasize the *qualitative characteristic of feedback value*. This feedback value is useful because it can be used to better achieve the *qualitative characteristic of predictive value*.

A problem with learning how to analyze statements is that the means may become an end in itself. Analysts could identify and calculate thousands of possible relationships and trends. If one knows only how to calculate ratios and trends without understanding how such information can be used, little is accomplished. Therefore, a logical approach to financial statement analysis is necessary, consisting of the following steps.

1. *Know the questions for which you want to find answers.* As indicated earlier, various groups have different types of interest in a company.
2. *Know the questions that particular ratios and comparisons are able to help answer.* These will be discussed in this appendix.
3. *Match 1 and 2 above.* By such a matching, the statement analysis will have a logical direction and purpose.

Several caveats must be mentioned. **Financial statements report on the past.** Thus, analysis of these data is an examination of the past. When using such information in a decision-making (future-oriented) process, analysts assume that the past is a reasonable basis for predicting the future. This is usually a reasonable approach, but its limitations should be recognized.

Also, ratio and trend analyses will help identify a company's present strengths and weaknesses. They may serve as "red flags" indicating problem areas. In many cases, however, such analyses will not reveal **why** things are as they are. Finding answers about "why" usually requires an in-depth analysis and an awareness of many factors about a company that are not reported in the financial statements.

Another caveat is that a **single ratio by itself is not likely to be very useful**. For example, analysts may generally view a current ratio of 2 to 1 (current assets are twice current liabilities) as satisfactory. However, if the industry average is 3 to 1, such a conclusion may be invalid. Even given this industry average, one may conclude that the particular company is doing well if one knows the previous year's ratio was 1.5 to 1. Consequently, to derive meaning from ratios, analysts need some standard against which to compare them. Such a standard may come from industry averages, past years' amounts, a particular competitor, or planned levels.

Finally, **awareness of the limitations of accounting numbers used in an analysis** is important. We will discuss some of these limitations and their consequences later in this appendix.

International Perspective

> Some companies outside the United States provide "convenience" financial statements for U.S. readers. These financial statements have been translated into English, and they may also translate the currency units into U.S. dollars. However, the statements are *not restated* using U.S. accounting principles; financial statement analysis needs to take this fact into account.

RATIO ANALYSIS

In analyzing financial statement data, analysts use various devices to bring out the comparative and relative significance of the financial information presented. These devices include ratio analysis, comparative analysis, percentage analysis, and examination of related data. No one device is more useful than another. Every situation is different, and analysts often obtain the needed answers only upon close examination of the interrelationships among all the data provided. Ratio analysis is the starting point. Ratios can be classified as follows.

10 LEARNING OBJECTIVE

Identify major analytic ratios and describe their calculation.

MAJOR TYPES OF RATIOS

LIQUIDITY RATIOS. Measures of the company's short-run ability to pay its maturing obligations.

ACTIVITY RATIOS. Measures of how effectively the company is using the assets employed.

PROFITABILITY RATIOS. Measures of the degree of success or failure of a given company or division for a given period of time.

COVERAGE RATIOS. Measures of the degree of protection for long-term creditors and investors.[26]

We have integrated discussions and illustrations about the computation and use of these financial ratios throughout this book. Illustration 24A-1 (page 1524) summarizes all of the ratios presented in the book and identifies the specific chapters that presented that material.

---

[26]Some analysts use other terms to categorize these ratios. For example, liquidity ratios are sometimes referred to as *solvency* ratios; activity ratios as *turnover* or *efficiency* ratios; and coverage ratios as *leverage* or *capital structure* ratios.

ILLUSTRATION 24A-1
Summary of Financial
Ratios

Ratio	Formula for Computation	Reference
SUMMARY OF RATIOS PRESENTED IN EARLIER CHAPTERS		
I. Liquidity		
1. **Current ratio**	$\dfrac{\text{Current assets}}{\text{Current liabilities}}$	Chapter 13, p. 729
2. **Quick or acid-test ratio**	$\dfrac{\text{Cash, short-term investments, and net receivables}}{\text{Current liabilities}}$	Chapter 13, p. 730
3. **Current cash debt coverage**	$\dfrac{\text{Net cash provided by operating activities}}{\text{Average current liabilities}}$	Chapter 5, p. 234
II. Activity		
4. **Accounts receivable turnover**	$\dfrac{\text{Net sales}}{\text{Average trade receivables (net)}}$	Chapter 7, p. 373
5. **Inventory turnover**	$\dfrac{\text{Cost of goods sold}}{\text{Average inventory}}$	Chapter 9, p. 496
6. **Asset turnover**	$\dfrac{\text{Net sales}}{\text{Average total assets}}$	Chapter 11, p. 611
III. Profitability		
7. **Profit margin on sales**	$\dfrac{\text{Net income}}{\text{Net sales}}$	Chapter 11, p. 612
8. **Return on assets**	$\dfrac{\text{Net income}}{\text{Average total assets}}$	Chapter 11, p. 612
9. **Return on common stock equity**	$\dfrac{\text{Net income minus preferred dividends}}{\text{Average common stockholders' equity}}$	Chapter 15, p. 849
10. **Earnings per share**	$\dfrac{\text{Net income minus preferred dividends}}{\text{Weighted-average number of shares outstanding}}$	Chapter 16, p. 900
11. **Payout ratio**	$\dfrac{\text{Cash dividends}}{\text{Net income}}$	Chapter 15, p. 850
IV. Coverage		
12. **Debt to assets ratio**	$\dfrac{\text{Total liabilities}}{\text{Total assets}}$	Chapter 14, p. 787
13. **Times interest earned**	$\dfrac{\text{Income before income taxes and interest expense}}{\text{Interest expense}}$	Chapter 14, p. 787
14. **Cash debt coverage**	$\dfrac{\text{Net cash provided by operating activities}}{\text{Average total liabilities}}$	Chapter 5, p. 234
15. **Book value per share**	$\dfrac{\text{Common stockholders' equity}}{\text{Outstanding shares}}$	Chapter 15, p. 850

**Gateway to
the Profession**

Financial Analysis Primer

You can find additional coverage of these ratios, accompanied by assignment material, at the book's companion website, at **www.wiley.com/college/kieso**. This supplemental coverage takes the form of a comprehensive case adapted from the annual report of a large international chemical company that we have disguised under the name of Anetek Chemical Corporation.

Limitations of Ratio Analysis

LEARNING OBJECTIVE 11
Explain the limitations of ratio analysis.

The reader of financial statements must understand the basic limitations associated with ratio analysis. As analytical tools, ratios are attractive because they are simple and convenient. But too frequently, decision-makers base their decisions on only these simple computations. The ratios are only as good as the data upon which they are based and the information with which they are compared.

One important limitation of ratios is that they generally are **based on historical cost, which can lead to distortions in measuring performance**. Inaccurate assessments of the enterprise's financial condition and performance can result from failing to incorporate fair value information.

Also, investors must remember that **where estimated items (such as depreciation and amortization) are significant, income ratios lose some of their credibility**. For example, income recognized before the termination of a company's life is an approximation. In analyzing the income statement, users should be aware of the uncertainty surrounding the computation of net income. As one writer aptly noted, "The physicist has long since conceded that the location of an electron is best expressed by a probability curve. Surely an abstraction like earnings per share is even more subject to the rules of probability and risk."[27]

Probably the greatest limitation of ratio analysis is the **difficult problem of achieving comparability among firms in a given industry**. Achieving comparability requires that the analyst (1) identify basic differences in companies' accounting principles and procedures, and (2) adjust the balances to achieve comparability. Basic differences in accounting usually involve one of the following areas.

Underlying Concepts

Consistency and comparability are important concepts for financial statement analysis. If the principles and assumptions used to prepare the financial statements are continually changing, accurate assessments of a company's progress become difficult.

1. Inventory valuation (FIFO, LIFO, average-cost).
2. Depreciation methods, particularly the use of straight-line versus accelerated depreciation.
3. Capitalization versus expensing of certain costs.
4. Capitalization of leases versus noncapitalization.
5. Investments in common stock carried at equity versus fair value.
6. Differing treatments of postretirement benefit costs.
7. Questionable practices of defining discontinued operations, impairments, and extraordinary items.

The use of these different alternatives can make a significant difference in the ratios computed. For example, at one time Anheuser-Busch InBev noted that if it had used average-cost for inventory valuation instead of LIFO, inventories would have increased approximately $33,000,000. Such an increase would have a substantive impact on the current ratio. Several studies have analyzed the impact of different accounting methods on financial statement analysis. The differences in income that can develop are staggering in some cases. Investors must be aware of the potential pitfalls if they are to be able to make the proper adjustments.[28]

Finally, analysts should recognize that a **substantial amount of important information** is not included in a company's financial statements. Events involving such things as industry changes, management changes, competitors' actions, technological developments, government actions, and union activities are often critical to a company's successful operation. These events occur continuously, and information about them must come from careful analysis of financial reports in the media and other sources. Indeed many argue, in what is known as the **efficient-market hypothesis**, that financial statements contain "no surprises" to those engaged in market activities. They contend that the effect of these events is known in the marketplace—and the price of the company's stock adjusts accordingly—well before the issuance of such reports.

---

[27]Richard E. Cheney, "How Dependable Is the Bottom Line?" *The Financial Executive* (January 1971), p. 12.

[28]See, for example, Eugene A. Imhoff, Jr., Robert C. Lipe, and David W. Wright, "Operating Leases: Impact of Constructive Capitalization," *Accounting Horizons* (March 1991).

COMPARATIVE ANALYSIS

LEARNING OBJECTIVE **12**
Describe techniques of comparative analysis.

Comparative analysis presents the same information for two or more different dates or periods, so that like items may be compared. Ratio analysis provides only a single snapshot, for one given point or period in time. In a comparative analysis, an investment analyst can concentrate on a given item and determine whether it appears to be growing or diminishing year by year and the proportion of such change to related items. Generally, companies present comparative financial statements. They typically include two years of balance sheet information and three years of income statement information.

In addition, many companies include in their annual reports five- or ten-year summaries of pertinent data that permit readers to examine and analyze trends. As indicated in GAAP, "the presentation of comparative financial statements in annual and other reports enhances the usefulness of such reports and brings out more clearly the nature and trends of current changes affecting the enterprise." Illustration 24A-2 presents a five-year condensed statement, with additional supporting data, of Anetek Chemical Corporation.

ILLUSTRATION 24A-2
Condensed Comparative
Financial Information

ANETEK CHEMICAL CORPORATION CONDENSED COMPARATIVE STATEMENTS (000,000 OMITTED)							
	2014	2013	2012	2011	2010	10 Years Ago 2004	20 Years Ago 1994
Sales and other revenue:							
Net sales	$1,600.0	$1,350.0	$1,309.7	$1,176.2	$1,077.5	$636.2	$170.7
Other revenue	75.0	50.0	39.4	34.1	24.6	9.0	3.7
Total	1,675.0	1,400.0	1,349.1	1,210.3	1,102.1	645.2	174.4
Costs and other charges:							
Cost of sales	1,000.0	850.0	827.4	737.6	684.2	386.8	111.0
Depreciation and amortization	150.0	150.0	122.6	115.6	98.7	82.4	14.2
Selling and administrative expenses	225.0	150.0	144.2	133.7	126.7	66.7	10.7
Interest expense	50.0	25.0	28.5	20.7	9.4	8.9	1.8
Income taxes	100.0	75.0	79.5	73.5	68.3	42.4	12.4
Total	1,525.0	1,250.0	1,202.2	1,081.1	987.3	587.2	150.1
Net income for the year	$ 150.0	$ 150.0	$ 146.9	$ 129.2	$ 114.8	$ 58.0	$ 24.3
Other Statistics							
Earnings per share on common stock (in dollars)[a]	$ 5.00	$ 5.00	$ 4.90	$ 3.58	$ 3.11	$ 1.66	$ 1.06
Cash dividends per share on common stock (in dollars)[a]	2.25	2.15	1.95	1.79	1.71	1.11	0.25
Cash dividends declared on common stock	67.5	64.5	58.5	64.6	63.1	38.8	5.7
Stock dividend at approximate market value				46.8		27.3	
Taxes (major)	144.5	125.9	116.5	105.6	97.8	59.8	17.0
Wages paid	389.3	325.6	302.1	279.6	263.2	183.2	48.6
Cost of employee benefits	50.8	36.2	32.9	28.7	27.2	18.4	4.4
Number of employees at year end (thousands)	47.4	36.4	35.0	33.8	33.2	26.6	14.6
Additions to property	306.3	192.3	241.5	248.3	166.1	185.0	49.0

[a]Adjusted for stock splits and stock dividends.

PERCENTAGE (COMMON-SIZE) ANALYSIS

Analysts also use percentage analysis to help them evaluate and compare companies. **Percentage analysis** consists of reducing a series of related amounts to a series of percentages of a given base. For example, analysts frequently express all items in an income statement as a percentage of sales or sometimes as a percentage of cost of goods sold. They may analyze a balance sheet on the basis of total assets. Percentage analysis facilitates comparison and is helpful in evaluating the relative size of items or the relative change in items. A conversion of absolute dollar amounts to percentages may also facilitate comparison between companies of different size.

13 LEARNING OBJECTIVE

Describe techniques of percentage analysis.

Illustration 24A-3 shows a comparative analysis of the expense section of Anetek for the last two years.

ANETEK CHEMICAL CORPORATION HORIZONTAL COMPARATIVE ANALYSIS (000,000 OMITTED)				
	2014	2013	Difference	% Change Inc. (Dec.)
Cost of sales	$1,000.0	$850.0	$150.0	17.6%
Depreciation and amortization	150.0	150.0	0	0
Selling and administrative expenses	225.0	150.0	75.0	50.0
Interest expense	50.0	25.0	25.0	100.0
Income taxes	100.0	75.0	25.0	33.3

ILLUSTRATION 24A-3
Horizontal Percentage Analysis

This approach, normally called **horizontal analysis**, indicates the proportionate change over a period of time. It is especially useful in evaluating trends, because absolute changes are often deceiving.

Another comparative approach, called **vertical analysis**, is the proportional expression of each financial statement item in a given period to a base figure. For example, Anetek Chemical's income statement using this approach appears in Illustration 24A-4.

ANETEK CHEMICAL CORPORATION INCOME STATEMENT (000,000 OMITTED)		
	Amount	Percentage of Total Revenue
Net sales	$1,600.0	96%
Other revenue	75.0	4
Total revenue	1,675.0	100
Less:		
Cost of sales	1,000.0	60
Depreciation and amortization	150.0	9
Selling and administrative expenses	225.0	13
Interest expense	50.0	3
Income taxes	100.0	6
Total expenses	1,525.0	91
Net income	$ 150.0	9%

ILLUSTRATION 24A-4
Vertical Percentage Analysis

Vertical analysis is frequently called **common-size analysis** because it reduces all of the statement items to a "common size." That is, all of the elements within each statement are expressed in percentages of some common number and always add up to 100 percent. Common-size (percentage) analysis reveals the composition of each of the financial statements.

In the analysis of the balance sheet, common-size analysis answers such questions as: What percentage of the capital structure is stockholders' equity, current liabilities, and long-term debt? What is the mix of assets (percentage-wise) with which the company has chosen to conduct business? What percentage of current assets is in inventory, receivables, and so forth?

Common-size analysis of the income statement typically relates each item to sales. It is instructive to know what proportion of each sales dollar is absorbed by various costs and expenses incurred by the enterprise.

Analysts may use common-size statements to compare one company's statements from different years, to detect trends not evident from comparing absolute amounts. Also, common-size statements provide intercompany comparisons regardless of size because they recast financial statements into a comparable common-size format.

KEY TERMS

accounts receivable
  turnover, *1524*
acid-test ratio, *1524*
activity ratios, *1523*
asset turnover, *1524*
book value per share, *1524*
cash debt coverage, *1524*
common-size
  analysis, *1527*
comparative
  analysis, *1526*
coverage ratios, *1523*
current cash debt
  coverage, *1524*
current ratio, *1524*
debt to assets ratio, *1524*
earnings per share, *1524*
horizontal analysis, *1527*
inventory turnover, *1524*
liquidity ratios, *1523*
payout ratio, *1524*
percentage analysis, *1527*
profit margin on
  sales, *1524*
profitability ratios, *1523*
quick ratio, *1524*
return on assets, *1524*
return on common stock
  equity, *1524*
times interest
  earned, *1524*
vertical analysis, *1527*

SUMMARY OF LEARNING OBJECTIVES FOR APPENDIX 24A

9 **Understand the approach to financial statement analysis.** Basic financial statement analysis involves examining relationships between items on the statements (ratio and percentage analysis) and identifying trends in these relationships (comparative analysis). Analysis is used to predict the future, but ratio analysis is limited because the data are from the past. Also, ratio analysis identifies present strengths and weaknesses of a company, but it may not reveal *why* they are as they are. Although single ratios are helpful, they are not conclusive. For maximum usefulness, analysts must compare them with industry averages, past years, planned amounts, and the like.

10 **Identify major analytic ratios and describe their calculation.** Ratios are classified as liquidity ratios, activity ratios, profitability ratios, and coverage ratios. (1) *Liquidity ratio analysis* measures the short-run ability of a company to pay its currently maturing obligations. (2) *Activity ratio analysis* measures how effectively a company is using its assets. (3) *Profitability ratio analysis* measures the degree of success or failure of a company to generate revenues adequate to cover its costs of operation and provide a return to the owners. (4) *Coverage ratio analysis* measures the degree of protection afforded long-term creditors and investors.

11 **Explain the limitations of ratio analysis.** Ratios are based on historical cost, which can lead to distortions in measuring performance. Also, where estimated items are significant, income ratios lose some of their credibility. In addition, comparability problems exist because companies use different accounting principles and procedures. Finally, analysts must recognize that a substantial amount of important information is not included in a company's financial statements.

12 **Describe techniques of comparative analysis.** Companies present comparative data, which generally includes two years of balance sheet information and three years of income statement information. In addition, many companies include in their annual reports five- to ten-year summaries of pertinent data that permit the reader to analyze trends.

13 **Describe techniques of percentage analysis.** Percentage analysis consists of reducing a series of related amounts to a series of percentages of a given base. Analysts use two approaches. *Horizontal analysis* indicates the proportionate change in financial statement items over a period of time; such analysis is most helpful in evaluating trends. *Vertical analysis* (common-size analysis) is a proportional expression of each item on the financial statements in a given period to a base amount. It analyzes the composition of each of the financial statements from different years (a) to detect trends not evident from the comparison of absolute amounts and (b) to make intercompany comparisons of different-sized enterprises.

DEMONSTRATION PROBLEM

Konetzke Corporation, a publicly traded company, is preparing the interim financial data which it will issue to its stockholders and the Securities and Exchange Commission (SEC) for the fiscal year ending December 31, 2014. Your job as a member of the accounting team is to help determine the appropriate disclosures and any other potential year-end adjustments. You have collected the following information.

1. Konetzke is involved in four separate industries. The following information is available for each of the four industries. Konetzke wonders which segments are reportable.

Operating Segment	Total Revenue	Operating Profit (Loss)	Identifiable Assets
Badger	$ 60,000	$15,000	$167,000
Spartan	10,000	1,500	83,000
Cornhusker	23,000	(2,000)	21,000
Hawkeye	9,000	1,000	19,000
	$102,000	$15,500	$290,000

2. On February 3, 2015, one of Konetzke's customers declared bankruptcy. At December 31, 2014, this company owed Konetzke $15,000, of which $3,000 was paid in January 2015.
3. On January 18, 2015, one of the three major plants of the client burned down.
4. On January 23, 2015, a strike was called at one of Konetzke's largest plants, which halted 30% of its production. As of today (February 13), the strike has not been settled.
5. On February 1, 2013, the board of directors adopted a resolution accepting the offer of an investment banker to guarantee the marketing of $1,200,000 of preferred stock.

Instructions
(a) State in each case how the 2014 financial statements would be affected, if at all.
(b) Moving ahead to the first quarter of 2015, your team has compiled the following summarized revenue and expense data for the first quarter of the year.

Sales revenue	$30,000
Cost of goods sold	18,000
Variable selling expenses	500
Fixed selling expenses	1,500

Included in the fixed selling expenses was the single lump-sum payment of $800 for Internet advertisements for the entire year. Address the following with respect to the first quarter report. (1) Explain whether Konetzke should report its operating results for the quarter as if the quarter were a separate reporting period in and of itself, or as if the quarter were an integral part of the annual reporting period. (2) State how the sales revenue, cost of goods sold, and fixed selling expenses would be reflected in Konetzke's quarterly report prepared for the first quarter of 2015.

Solution

(a) 1. Konetzke first conducts the following three tests:

Revenue test: 10% × $102,000 = $10,200. The Badger ($23,000) and Cornhusker ($60,000) segments both meet this test.

Operating profit (loss) test: 10% × ($15,000 + $1,500 + $1,000) = $1,750. The Badger ($15,000) and Cornhusker ($2,000 absolute amount) segments both meet this test.

Identifiable assets test: 10% × $290,000 = $29,000. The Badger ($167,000) and Spartan ($83,000) segments both meet this test.

Thus, Konetzke has three reportable segments for which segment information should be disclosed.

Regarding the post-balance-sheet events:

2. The financial statements should be adjusted for the expected loss pertaining to the remaining receivable of $12,000. Such adjustment should reduce accounts receivable to their realizable value as of December 31, 2015.

3. Report the fire loss in a footnote to the balance sheet and refer to it in connection with the income statement, since earnings power is presumably affected.

4. Strikes are considered general knowledge and therefore disclosure is not required. Many auditors, however, would encourage disclosure in all cases.

5. Report the action of the new stock issue in a footnote to the balance sheet.

(b) 1. The company should report its quarterly results as if each interim period is an integral part of the annual period.

2. The company's revenue and expenses would be reported as follows on its quarterly report prepared for the first quarter of 2015:

Sales revenue	$30,000
Cost of goods sold	18,000
Variable selling expenses	500
Fixed selling expenses	
Advertising ($800 ÷ 4)	200
Other ($1,500 − $800)	700

Sales revenue and cost of goods sold receive the same treatment as if this were an annual report. Costs and expenses other than product costs should be charged to expense in interim periods as incurred or allocated among interim periods. Consequently, the variable selling expenses and the portion of fixed selling expenses not related to Internet advertising should be reported in full. One-fourth of the Internet advertising is reported as an expense in the first quarter, assuming the advertising is constant throughout the year. These costs can be deferred within the fiscal period if the benefits of the expenditure clearly extend beyond the interim period in which the expenditure is made.

FASB CODIFICATION

FASB Codification References

[1] FASB ASC 850-10-05 [Predecessor literature: "Related Party Disclosures," *Statement of Financial Accounting Standards No. 57* (Stamford, Conn.: FASB, 1982).]

[2] FASB ASC 855-10-05 [Predecessor literature: "Subsequent Events," *Statement on Auditing Standards No. 1* (New York: AICPA, 1973), pp. 123–124.]

[3] FASB ASC 280-10-05-3. [Predecessor literature: "Disclosures about Segments of an Enterprise and Related Information," *Statement of Financial Accounting Standards No. 131* (Norwalk, Conn.: FASB, 1997).]

[4] FASB ASC 270-10. [Predecessor literature: "Interim Financial Reporting," *Opinions of the Accounting Principles Board No. 28* (New York: AICPA, 1973).]

[5] FASB ASC 740-270-30-2 through 3. [Predecessor literature: "Interim Financial Reporting," *Opinions of the Accounting Principles Board No. 28* (New York: AICPA, 1973), par. 19.]

[6] FASB ASC 740-270-35-4. [Predecessor literature: "Accounting for Income Taxes in Interim Periods," *FASB Interpretation No. 18* (Stamford, Conn.: FASB, March 1977), par. 9.]

[7] FASB ASC 205-30 [Predecessor literature: "The Auditor's Consideration of an Entity's Ability to Continue as a Going Concern," *Statement on Auditing Standards No. 59* (New York: AICPA, 1988).]

Exercises

If your school has a subscription to the FASB Codification, go to *http://aaahq.org/ascLogin.cfm* to log in and prepare responses to the following. Provide Codification references for your responses.

CE24-1 Access the glossary ("Master Glossary") to answer the following.

(a) What is the definition of "ordinary income" (loss)?

(b) What is an error in previously issued financial statements?

(c) What is the definition of "earnings per share"?

(d) What is a publicly traded company?

CE24-2 What are some examples of related parties?

CE24-3 What are the quantitative thresholds that would require a public company to report separately information about an operating segment?

CE24-4 If an SEC-registered company uses the gross profit method to determine cost of goods sold for interim periods, would it be acceptable for the company to state that it's not practicable to determine components of inventory at interim periods? Why or why not?

An additional Codification case can be found in the Using Your Judgment section, on page 1548.

Be sure to check the book's companion website for a Review and Analysis Exercise, with solution.

WileyPLUS Brief Exercises, Exercises, Problems, and many more learning and assessment tools and resources are available for practice in WileyPLUS.

Note: All asterisked Questions, Exercises, and Problems relate to material in the appendix to the chapter.

QUESTIONS

1. What are the major advantages of notes to the financial statements? What types of items are usually reported in notes?

2. What is the full disclosure principle in accounting? Why has disclosure increased substantially in the last 10 years?

3. The FASB requires a reconciliation between the effective tax rate and the federal government's statutory rate. Of what benefit is such a disclosure requirement?

4. What type of disclosure or accounting do you believe is necessary for the following items?

(a) Because of a general increase in the number of labor disputes and strikes, both within and outside the industry, there is an increased likelihood that a company will suffer a costly strike in the near future.

(b) A company reports an extraordinary item (net of tax) correctly on the income statement. No other mention is made of this item in the annual report.

(c) A company expects to recover a substantial amount in connection with a pending refund claim for a prior year's taxes. Although the claim is being contested, counsel for the company has confirmed the client's expectation of recovery.

5. The following information was described in a note of Canon Packing Co.

"During August, Holland Products Corporation purchased 311,003 shares of the Company's common stock which constitutes approximately 35% of the stock outstanding. Holland has since obtained representation on the Board of Directors."

"An affiliate of Holland Products Corporation acts as a food broker for Canon Packing in the greater New York City marketing area. The commissions for such services after August amounted to approximately $20,000."

Why is this information disclosed?

6. What are the major types of subsequent events? Indicate how each of the following "subsequent events" would be reported.

(a) Collection of a note written off in a prior period.

(b) Issuance of a large preferred stock offering.

(c) Acquisition of a company in a different industry.

(d) Destruction of a major plant in a flood.

(e) Death of the company's chief executive officer (CEO).

(f) Additional wage costs associated with settlement of a four-week strike.

(g) Settlement of a federal income tax case at considerably more tax than anticipated at year-end.

(h) Change in the product mix from consumer goods to industrial goods.

7. What are diversified companies? What accounting problems are related to diversified companies?

8. What quantitative materiality test is applied to determine whether a segment is significant enough to warrant separate disclosure?

9. Identify the segment information that is required to be disclosed by GAAP.

10. What is an operating segment, and when can information about two operating segments be aggregated?

11. The controller for Lafayette Inc. recently commented, "If I have to disclose our segments individually, the only people who will gain are our competitors and the only people that will lose are our present stockholders." Evaluate this comment.

12. An article in the financial press entitled "Important Information in Annual Reports This Year" noted that annual reports include a management's discussion and analysis section. What would this section contain?

13. "The financial statements of a company are management's, not the accountant's." Discuss the implications of this statement.

14. Olga Conrad, a financial writer, noted recently, "There are substantial arguments for including earnings projections in annual reports and the like. The most compelling is that it would give anyone interested something now available to only a relatively select few—like large stockholders, creditors, and attentive bartenders." Identify some arguments against providing earnings projections.

15. The following comment appeared in the financial press: "Inadequate financial disclosure, particularly with respect to how management views the future and its role in the marketplace, has always been a stone in the shoe. After all, if you don't know how a company views the future, how can you judge the worth of its corporate strategy?" What are some arguments for reporting earnings forecasts?

16. What are interim reports? Why are balance sheets often not provided with interim data?

17. What are the accounting problems related to the presentation of interim data?

18. Dierdorf Inc., a closely held corporation, has decided to go public. The controller, Ed Floyd, is concerned with presenting interim data when a LIFO inventory valuation is used. What problems are encountered with LIFO inventories when quarterly data are presented?

19. What approaches have been suggested to overcome the seasonality problem related to interim reporting?

20. What is the difference between a CPA's unqualified opinion or "clean" opinion and a qualified one?

21. Jane Ellerby and Sam Callison are discussing the recent fraud that occurred at LowRental Leasing, Inc. The fraud involved the improper reporting of revenue to ensure that the company would have income in excess of $1 million. What is fraudulent financial reporting, and how does it differ from an embezzlement of company funds?

*22. "The significance of financial statement data is not in the amount alone." Discuss the meaning of this statement.

*23. A close friend of yours, who is a history major and who has not had any college courses or any experience in business, is receiving the financial statements from companies in which he has minor investments (acquired for him by his now-deceased father). He asks you what he needs to know to interpret and to evaluate the financial statement data that he is receiving. What would you tell him?

*24. Distinguish between ratio analysis and percentage analysis relative to the interpretation of financial statements. What is the value of these two types of analyses?

*25. In calculating inventory turnover, why is cost of goods sold used as the numerator? As the inventory turnover increases, what increasing risk does the business assume?

*26. What is the relationship of the asset turnover to the return on assets?

*27. Explain the meaning of the following terms: (a) common-size analysis, (b) vertical analysis, (c) horizontal analysis, and (d) percentage analysis.

*28. Presently, the profession requires that earnings per share be disclosed on the face of the income statement. What are some disadvantages of reporting ratios on the financial statements?

BRIEF EXERCISES

2 **BE24-1** An annual report of Crestwood Industries states, "The company and its subsidiaries have long-term leases expiring on various dates after December 31, 2014. Amounts payable under such commitments, without reduction for related rental income, are expected to average approximately $5,711,000 annually for the next 3 years. Related rental income from certain subleases to others is estimated to average $3,094,000 annually for the next 3 years." What information is provided by this note?

2 **BE24-2** An annual report of Ford Motor Corporation states, "Net income a share is computed based upon the average number of shares of capital stock of all classes outstanding. Additional shares of common stock may be issued or delivered in the future on conversion of outstanding convertible debentures, exercise of outstanding employee stock options, and for payment of defined supplemental compensation. Had such additional shares been outstanding, net income a share would have been reduced by 10¢ in the current year and 3¢ in the previous year. . . . As a result of capital stock transactions by the company during the current year (primarily the purchase of Class A Stock from Ford Foundation), net income a share was increased by 6¢." What information is provided by this note?

3 **BE24-3** Morlan Corporation is preparing its December 31, 2014, financial statements. Two events that occurred between December 31, 2014, and March 10, 2015, when the statements were issued, are described below.

  1. A liability, estimated at $160,000 at December 31, 2014, was settled on February 26, 2015, at $170,000.
  2. A flood loss of $80,000 occurred on March 1, 2015.

What effect do these subsequent events have on 2014 net income?

3 **BE24-4** Tina Bailey, a student of intermediate accounting, was heard to remark after a class discussion on segment reporting, "All this is very confusing to me. First we are told that there is merit in presenting the consolidated results, and now we are told that it is better to show segmental results. I wish they would make up their minds." Evaluate this comment.

3 **BE24-5** Foley Corporation has seven industry segments with total revenues as follows.

Penley	$600	Cheng	$225
Konami	650	Takuhi	200
KSC	250	Molina	700
Red Moon	275		

Based only on the revenues test, which industry segments are reportable?

3 **BE24-6** Operating profits and losses for the seven industry segments of Foley Corporation are:

Penley	$ 90	Cheng	$ (20)
Konami	(40)	Takuhi	34
KSC	25	Molina	150
Red Moon	50		

Based only on the operating profit (loss) test, which industry segments are reportable?

3 **BE24-7** Identifiable assets for the seven industry segments of Foley Corporation are:

Penley	$500	Cheng	$200
Konami	550	Takuhi	150
KSC	250	Molina	475
Red Moon	400		

Based only on the identifiable assets test, which industry segments are reportable?

10 *BE24-8 Answer each of the questions in the following unrelated situations.

  (a) The current ratio of a company is 5:1 and its acid-test ratio is 1:1. If the inventories and prepaid items amount to $500,000, what is the amount of current liabilities?
  (b) A company had an average inventory last year of $200,000 and its inventory turnover was 5. If sales volume and unit cost remain the same this year as last and inventory turnover is 8 this year, what will average inventory have to be during the current year?
  (c) A company has current assets of $90,000 (of which $40,000 is inventory and prepaid items) and current liabilities of $40,000. What is the current ratio? What is the acid-test ratio? If the company borrows $15,000 cash from a bank on a 120-day loan, what will its current ratio be? What will the acid-test ratio be?
  (d) A company has current assets of $600,000 and current liabilities of $240,000. The board of directors declares a cash dividend of $180,000. What is the current ratio after the declaration but before payment? What is the current ratio after the payment of the dividend?

10 *BE24-9 Heartland Company's budgeted sales and budgeted cost of goods sold for the coming year are $144,000,000 and $99,000,000, respectively. Short-term interest rates are expected to average 10%. If Heartland can increase inventory turnover from its present level of 9 times a year to a level of 12 times per year, compute its expected cost savings for the coming year.

EXERCISES

3 **E24-1 (Post-Balance-Sheet Events)** Madrasah Corporation issued its financial statements for the year ended December 31, 2014, on March 10, 2015. The following events took place early in 2015.

  (a) On January 10, 10,000 shares of $5 par value common stock were issued at $66 per share.
  (b) On March 1, Madrasah determined after negotiations with the Internal Revenue Service that income taxes payable for 2014 should be $1,270,000. At December 31, 2014, income taxes payable were recorded at $1,100,000.

Instructions

Discuss how the preceding post-balance-sheet events should be reflected in the 2014 financial statements.

3 ▶ **E24-2 (Post-Balance-Sheet Events)** For each of the following subsequent (post-balance-sheet) events, indicate whether a company should (a) adjust the financial statements, (b) disclose in notes to the financial statements, or (c) neither adjust nor disclose.

_____ 1. Settlement of federal tax case at a cost considerably in excess of the amount expected at year-end.
_____ 2. Introduction of a new product line.
_____ 3. Loss of assembly plant due to fire.
_____ 4. Sale of a significant portion of the company's assets.
_____ 5. Retirement of the company president.
_____ 6. Prolonged employee strike.
_____ 7. Loss of a significant customer.
_____ 8. Issuance of a significant number of shares of common stock.
_____ 9. Material loss on a year-end receivable because of a customer's bankruptcy.
_____ 10. Hiring of a new president.
_____ 11. Settlement of prior year's litigation against the company (no loss was accrued).
_____ 12. Merger with another company of comparable size.

3 ▶ **E24-3 (Segmented Reporting)** Carlton Company is involved in four separate industries. The following information is available for each of the four industries.

Operating Segment	Total Revenue	Operating Profit (Loss)	Identifiable Assets
W	$ 60,000	$15,000	$167,000
X	10,000	3,000	83,000
Y	23,000	(2,000)	21,000
Z	9,000	1,000	19,000
	$102,000	$17,000	$290,000

Instructions

Determine which of the operating segments are reportable based on the:

(a) Revenue test.
(b) Operating profit (loss) test.
(c) Identifiable assets test.

10 ▶ *E24-4 (Ratio Computation and Analysis; Liquidity)** As loan analyst for Utrillo Bank, you have been presented the following information.

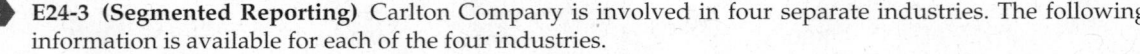

	Toulouse Co.	Lautrec Co.
Assets		
Cash	$ 120,000	$ 320,000
Receivables	220,000	302,000
Inventories	570,000	518,000
Total current assets	910,000	1,140,000
Other assets	500,000	612,000
Total assets	$1,410,000	$1,752,000
Liabilities and Stockholders' Equity		
Current liabilities	$ 305,000	$ 350,000
Long-term liabilities	400,000	500,000
Capital stock and retained earnings	705,000	902,000
Total liabilities and stockholders' equity	$1,410,000	$1,752,000
Annual sales	$ 930,000	$1,500,000
Rate of gross profit on sales	30%	40%

Each of these companies has requested a loan of $50,000 for 6 months with no collateral offered. Because your bank has reached its quota for loans of this type, only one of these requests is to be granted.

Instructions

Which of the two companies, as judged by the information given above, would you recommend as the better risk and why? Assume that the ending account balances are representative of the entire year.

10 *E24-5 (Analysis of Given Ratios)** Picasso Company is a wholesale distributor of professional equipment and supplies. The company's sales have averaged about $900,000 annually for the 3-year period 2012–2014. The firm's total assets at the end of 2014 amounted to $850,000.

The president of Picasso Company has asked the controller to prepare a report that summarizes the financial aspects of the company's operations for the past 3 years. This report will be presented to the board of directors at their next meeting.

In addition to comparative financial statements, the controller has decided to present a number of relevant financial ratios which can assist in the identification and interpretation of trends. At the request of the controller, the accounting staff has calculated the following ratios for the 3-year period 2012–2014.

	2012	2013	2014
Current ratio	1.80	1.89	1.96
Acid-test (quick) ratio	1.04	0.99	0.87
Accounts receivable turnover	8.75	7.71	6.42
Inventory turnover	4.91	4.32	3.42
Debt to assets	51.0%	46.0%	41.0%
Long-term debt to assets	31.0%	27.0%	24.0%
Sales to fixed assets (fixed asset turnover)	1.58	1.69	1.79
Sales as a percent of 2012 sales	1.00	1.03	1.07
Gross margin percentage	36.0%	35.1%	34.6%
Net income to sales	6.9%	7.0%	7.2%
Return on assets	7.7%	7.7%	7.8%
Return on common stock equity	13.6%	13.1%	12.7%

In preparation of the report, the controller has decided first to examine the financial ratios independent of any other data to determine if the ratios themselves reveal any significant trends over the 3-year period.

Instructions

(a) The current ratio is increasing while the acid-test (quick) ratio is decreasing. Using the ratios provided, identify and explain the contributing factor(s) for this apparently divergent trend.

(b) In terms of the ratios provided, what conclusion(s) can be drawn regarding the company's use of financial leverage during the 2012–2014 period?

(c) Using the ratios provided, what conclusion(s) can be drawn regarding the company's net investment in plant and equipment?

10 *E24-6 (Ratio Analysis)** Edna Millay Inc. is a manufacturer of electronic components and accessories with total assets of $20,000,000. Selected financial ratios for Millay and the industry averages for firms of similar size are presented below.

	Edna Millay			2014 Industry Average
	2012	2013	2014	
Current ratio	2.09	2.27	2.51	2.24
Quick ratio	1.15	1.12	1.19	1.22
Inventory turnover	2.40	2.18	2.02	3.50
Net sales to stockholders' equity	2.71	2.80	2.99	2.85
Return on common stock equity	0.14	0.15	0.17	0.11
Total liabilities to stockholders' equity	1.41	1.37	1.44	0.95

Millay is being reviewed by several entities whose interests vary, and the company's financial ratios are a part of the data being considered. Each of the parties listed below must recommend an action based on its evaluation of Millay's financial position.

Archibald MacLeish Bank. The bank is processing Millay's application for a new 5-year term note. Archibald MacLeish has been Millay's banker for several years but must reevaluate the company's financial position for each major transaction.

Robert Lowell Company. Lowell is a new supplier to Millay and must decide on the appropriate credit terms to extend to the company.

Robert Penn Warren. A brokerage firm specializing in the stock of electronics firms that are sold over-the-counter, Robert Penn Warren must decide if it will include Millay in a new fund being established for sale to Robert Penn Warren's clients.

Working Capital Management Committee. This is a committee of Millay's management personnel chaired by the chief operating officer. The committee is charged with the responsibility of periodically reviewing the company's working capital position, comparing actual data against budgets, and recommending changes in strategy as needed.

Instructions

(a) Describe the analytical use of each of the six ratios presented on page 1535.

(b) For each of the four entities described above, identify two financial ratios, from the ratios presented on page 1535, that would be most valuable as a basis for its decision regarding Millay.

(c) Discuss what the financial ratios presented in the question reveal about Millay. Support your answer by citing specific ratio levels and trends as well as the interrelationships between these ratios.

(CMA adapted)

EXERCISES SET B

See the book's companion website, at **www.wiley.com/college/kieso**, for an additional set of exercises.

PROBLEMS

3 **P24-1 (Subsequent Events)** Your firm has been engaged to examine the financial statements of Almaden Corporation for the year 2014. The bookkeeper who maintains the financial records has prepared all the unaudited financial statements for the corporation since its organization on January 2, 2009. The client provides you with the following information.

ALMADEN CORPORATION
BALANCE SHEET
DECEMBER 31, 2014

Assets		Liabilities	
Current assets	$1,881,100	Current liabilities	$ 962,400
Other assets	5,171,400	Long-term liabilities	1,439,500
		Capital	4,650,600
	$7,052,500		$7,052,500

An analysis of current assets discloses the following.

Cash (restricted in the amount of $300,000 for plant expansion)	$ 571,000
Investments in land	185,000
Accounts receivable less allowance of $30,000	480,000
Inventories (LIFO flow assumption)	645,100
	$1,881,100

Other assets include:

Prepaid expenses	$ 62,400
Plant and equipment less accumulated depreciation of $1,430,000	4,130,000
Cash surrender value of life insurance policy	84,000
Unamortized bond discount	34,500
Notes receivable (short-term)	162,300
Goodwill	252,000
Land	446,200
	$5,171,400

Current liabilities include:

Accounts payable	$ 510,000
Notes payable (due 2017)	157,400
Estimated income taxes payable	145,000
Premium on common stock	150,000
	$ 962,400

Long-term liabilities include:

Unearned revenue	$ 489,500
Dividends payable (cash)	200,000
8% bonds payable (due May 1, 2019)	750,000
	$1,439,500

Capital includes:

Retained earnings	$2,810,600
Common stock, par value $10; authorized 200,000 shares, 184,000 shares issued	1,840,000
	$4,650,600

The supplementary information below is also provided.

1. On May 1, 2014, the corporation issued at 95.4, $750,000 of bonds to finance plant expansion. The long-term bond agreement provided for the annual payment of interest every May 1. The existing plant was pledged as security for the loan. Use the straight-line method for discount amortization.
2. The bookkeeper made the following mistakes.
   (a) In 2012, the ending inventory was overstated by $183,000. The ending inventories for 2013 and 2014 were correctly computed.
   (b) In 2014, accrued wages in the amount of $225,000 were omitted from the balance sheet, and these expenses were not charged on the income statement.
   (c) In 2014, a gain of $175,000 (net of tax) on the sale of certain plant assets was credited directly to retained earnings.
3. A major competitor has introduced a line of products that will compete directly with Almaden's primary line, now being produced in a specially designed new plant. Because of manufacturing innovations, the competitor's line will be of comparable quality but priced 50% below Almaden's line. The competitor announced its new line on January 14, 2015. Almaden indicates that the company will meet the lower prices that are high enough to cover variable manufacturing and selling expenses, but permit recovery of only a portion of fixed costs.
4. You learned on January 28, 2015, prior to completion of the audit, of heavy damage because of a recent fire to one of Almaden's two plants; the loss will not be reimbursed by insurance. The newspapers described the event in detail.

Instructions

Analyze the above information to prepare a corrected balance sheet for Almaden in accordance with proper accounting and reporting principles. Prepare a description of any notes that might need to be prepared. The books are closed and adjustments to income are to be made through retained earnings.

3 **P24-2 (Segmented Reporting)** Cineplex Corporation is a diversified company that operates in five different industries: A, B, C, D, and E. The following information relating to each segment is available for 2015.

	A	B	C	D	E
Sales revenue	$40,000	$ 75,000	$580,000	$35,000	$55,000
Cost of goods sold	19,000	50,000	270,000	19,000	30,000
Operating expenses	10,000	40,000	235,000	12,000	18,000
Total expenses	29,000	90,000	505,000	31,000	48,000
Operating profit (loss)	$11,000	$ (15,000)	$ 75,000	$ 4,000	$ 7,000
Identifiable assets	$35,000	$ 80,000	$500,000	$65,000	$50,000

Sales of segments B and C included intersegment sales of $20,000 and $100,000, respectively.

Instructions

(a) Determine which of the segments are reportable based on the:
   (1) Revenue test.
   (2) Operating profit (loss) test.
   (3) Identifiable assets test.
(b) Prepare the necessary disclosures required by GAAP.

10 **12** *P24-3 (Ratio Computations and Additional Analysis)** Bradburn Corporation was formed 5 years ago through a public subscription of common stock. Daniel Brown, who owns 15% of the common stock, was one of the organizers of Bradburn and is its current president. The company has been successful, but it currently is experiencing a shortage of funds. On June 10, 2014, Daniel Brown approached the Topeka National Bank, asking for a 24-month extension on two $35,000 notes, which are due on June 30, 2015, and September 30, 2015. Another note of $6,000 is due on March 31, 2016, but he expects no difficulty in paying this note on its due date. Brown explained that Bradburn's cash flow problems are due primarily to the company's desire to finance a $300,000 plant expansion over the next 2 fiscal years through internally generated funds.

The commercial loan officer of Topeka National Bank requested the following financial reports for the last 2 fiscal years.

BRADBURN CORPORATION
BALANCE SHEET
MARCH 31

Assets	2015	2014
Cash	$ 18,200	$ 12,500
Notes receivable	148,000	132,000
Accounts receivable (net)	131,800	125,500
Inventories (at cost)	105,000	50,000
Plant & equipment (net of depreciation)	1,449,000	1,420,500
Total assets	$1,852,000	$1,740,500
Liabilities and Stockholders' Equity		
Accounts payable	$ 79,000	$ 91,000
Notes payable	76,000	61,500
Accrued liabilities	9,000	6,000
Common stock (130,000 shares, $10 par)	1,300,000	1,300,000
Retained earnings[a]	388,000	282,000
Total liabilities and stockholders' equity	$1,852,000	$1,740,500

[a]Cash dividends were paid at the rate of $1 per share in fiscal year 2014 and $2 per share in fiscal year 2015.

BRADBURN CORPORATION
INCOME STATEMENT
FOR THE FISCAL YEARS ENDED MARCH 31

	2015	2014
Sales revenue	$3,000,000	$2,700,000
Cost of goods sold[a]	1,530,000	1,425,000
Gross margin	1,470,000	1,275,000
Operating expenses	860,000	780,000
Income before income taxes	610,000	495,000
Income taxes (40%)	244,000	198,000
Net income	$ 366,000	$ 297,000

[a]Depreciation charges on the plant and equipment of $100,000 and $102,500 for fiscal years ended March 31, 2014 and 2015, respectively, are included in cost of goods sold.

Instructions

(a) Compute the following items for Bradburn Corporation.
  (1) Current ratio for fiscal years 2014 and 2015.
  (2) Acid-test (quick) ratio for fiscal years 2014 and 2015.
  (3) Inventory turnover for fiscal year 2015.
  (4) Return on assets for fiscal years 2014 and 2015. (Assume total assets were $1,688,500 at 3/31/13.)
  (5) Percentage change in sales, cost of goods sold, gross margin, and net income after taxes from fiscal year 2014 to 2015.

(b) Identify and explain what other financial reports and/or financial analyses might be helpful to the commercial loan officer of Topeka National Bank in evaluating Daniel Brown's request for a time extension on Bradburn's notes.

(c) Assume that the percentage changes experienced in fiscal year 2015 as compared with fiscal year 2014 for sales and cost of goods sold will be repeated in each of the next 2 years. Is Bradburn's desire to finance the plant expansion from internally generated funds realistic? Discuss.

(d) Should Topeka National Bank grant the extension on Bradburn's notes considering Daniel Brown's statement about financing the plant expansion through internally generated funds? Discuss.

13 *P24-4 (Horizontal and Vertical Analysis)** Presented below is the comparative balance sheet for Gilmour Company.

GILMOUR COMPANY
COMPARATIVE BALANCE SHEET
AS OF DECEMBER 31, 2015 AND 2014

	December 31	
	2015	2014
Assets		
Cash	$ 180,000	$ 275,000
Accounts receivable (net)	220,000	155,000
Short-term investments	270,000	150,000
Inventories	1,060,000	980,000
Prepaid expenses	25,000	25,000
Plant & equipment	2,585,000	1,950,000
Accumulated depreciation	(1,000,000)	(750,000)
	$3,340,000	$2,785,000
Liabilities and Stockholders' Equity		
Accounts payable	$ 50,000	$ 75,000
Accrued expenses	170,000	200,000
Bonds payable	450,000	190,000
Capital stock	2,100,000	1,770,000
Retained earnings	570,000	550,000
	$3,340,000	$2,785,000

Instructions
(Round to two decimal places.)
  (a) Prepare a comparative balance sheet of Gilmour Company showing the percent each item is of the total assets or total liabilities and stockholders' equity.
  (b) Prepare a comparative balance sheet of Gilmour Company showing the dollar change and the percent change for each item.
  (c) Of what value is the additional information provided in part (a)?
  (d) Of what value is the additional information provided in part (b)?

10 *P24-5 (Dividend Policy Analysis)** Matheny Inc. went public 3 years ago. The board of directors will be meeting shortly after the end of the year to decide on a dividend policy. In the past, growth has been financed primarily through the retention of earnings. A stock or a cash dividend has never been declared. Presented below is a brief financial summary of Matheny Inc. operations.

	($000 omitted)				
	2015	2014	2013	2012	2011
Sales revenue	$20,000	$16,000	$14,000	$6,000	$4,000
Net income	2,400	1,400	800	700	250
Average total assets	22,000	19,000	11,500	4,200	3,000
Current assets	8,000	6,000	3,000	1,200	1,000
Working capital	3,600	3,200	1,200	500	400
Common shares:					
Number of shares outstanding (000)	2,000	2,000	2,000	20	20
Average market price	$9	$6	$4	—	—

Instructions
  (a) Suggest factors to be considered by the board of directors in establishing a dividend policy.
  (b) Compute the return on assets, profit margin on sales, earnings per share, price-earnings ratio, and current ratio for each of the 5 years for Matheny Inc.
  (c) Comment on the appropriateness of declaring a cash dividend at this time, using the ratios computed in part (b) as a major factor in your analysis.

PROBLEMS SET B

See the book's companion website, at **www.wiley.com/college/kieso**, for an additional set of problems.

CONCEPTS FOR ANALYSIS

CA24-1 (General Disclosures; Inventories; Property, Plant, and Equipment) Koch Corporation is in the process of preparing its annual financial statements for the fiscal year ended April 30, 2015. Because all of Koch's shares are traded intrastate, the company does not have to file any reports with the Securities and Exchange Commission. The company manufactures plastic, glass, and paper containers for sale to food and drink manufacturers and distributors.

Koch Corporation maintains separate control accounts for its raw materials, work in process, and finished goods inventories for each of the three types of containers. The inventories are valued at the lower-of-cost-or-market.

The company's property, plant, and equipment are classified in the following major categories: land, office buildings, furniture and fixtures, manufacturing facilities, manufacturing equipment, and leasehold improvements. All fixed assets are carried at cost. The depreciation methods employed depend on the type of asset (its classification) and when it was acquired.

Koch Corporation plans to present the inventory and fixed asset amounts in its April 30, 2015, balance sheet as shown below.

Inventories	$4,814,200
Property, plant, and equipment (net of depreciation)	6,310,000

Instructions
What information regarding inventories and property, plant, and equipment must be disclosed by Koch Corporation in the audited financial statements issued to stockholders, either in the body or the notes, for the 2014–2015 fiscal year?

(CMA adapted)

CA24-2 (Disclosures Required in Various Situations) Ace Inc. produces electronic components for sale to manufacturers of radios, television sets, and digital sound systems. In connection with her examination of Ace's financial statements for the year ended December 31, 2015, Gloria Rodd, CPA, completed field work 2 weeks ago. Ms. Rodd now is evaluating the significance of the following items prior to preparing her auditor's report. Except as noted, none of these items have been disclosed in the financial statements or notes.

Item 1: A 10-year loan agreement, which the company entered into 3 years ago, provides that dividend payments may not exceed net income earned after taxes subsequent to the date of the agreement. The balance of retained earnings at the date of the loan agreement was $420,000. From that date through December 31, 2015, net income after taxes has totaled $570,000 and cash dividends have totaled $320,000. On the basis of these data, the staff auditor assigned to this review concluded that there was no retained earnings restriction at December 31, 2015.

Item 2: Recently Ace interrupted its policy of paying cash dividends quarterly to its stockholders. Dividends were paid regularly through 2014, discontinued for all of 2015 to finance purchase of equipment for the company's new plant, and resumed in the first quarter of 2016. In the annual report, dividend policy is to be discussed in the president's letter to stockholders.

Item 3: A major electronics firm has introduced a line of products that will compete directly with Ace's primary line, now being produced in the specially designed new plant. Because of manufacturing innovations, the competitor's line will be of comparable quality but priced 50% below Ace's line. The competitor announced its new line during the week following completion of field work. Ms. Rodd read the announcement in the newspaper and discussed the situation by telephone with Ace executives. Ace will meet the lower prices that are high enough to cover variable manufacturing and selling expenses but will permit recovery of only a portion of fixed costs.

Item 4: The company's new manufacturing plant building, which cost $2,400,000 and has an estimated life of 25 years, is leased from Wichita National Bank at an annual rental of $600,000. The company is obligated to pay property taxes, insurance, and maintenance. At the conclusion of its 10-year noncancelable lease, the company has the option of purchasing the property for $1. In Ace's income statement, the rental payment is reported on a separate line.

Instructions

For each of the above items, discuss any additional disclosures in the financial statements and notes that the auditor should recommend to her client. (The cumulative effect of the four items should not be considered.)

CA24-3 (Disclosures, Conditional and Contingent Liabilities) Presented below are three independent situations.

Situation 1: A company offers a one-year warranty for the product that it manufactures. A history of warranty claims has been compiled, and the probable amounts of claims related to sales for a given period can be determined.

Situation 2: Subsequent to the date of a set of financial statements but prior to the issuance of the financial statements, a company enters into a contract that will probably result in a significant loss to the company. The amount of the loss can be reasonably estimated.

Situation 3: A company has adopted a policy of recording self-insurance for any possible losses resulting from injury to others by the company's vehicles. The premium for an insurance policy for the same risk from an independent insurance company would have an annual cost of $4,000. During the period covered by the financial statements, there were no accidents involving the company's vehicles that resulted in injury to others.

Instructions

Discuss the accrual or type of disclosure necessary (if any) and the reason(s) why such disclosure is appropriate for each of the three independent sets of facts above.

(AICPA adapted)

 CA24-4 (Post-Balance-Sheet Events) At December 31, 2014, Coburn Corp. has assets of $10,000,000, liabilities of $6,000,000, common stock of $2,000,000 (representing 2,000,000 shares of $1 par common stock), and retained earnings of $2,000,000. Net sales for the year 2014 were $18,000,000, and net income was $800,000. As auditors of this company, you are making a review of subsequent events on February 13, 2015, and you find the following.

1. On February 3, 2015, one of Coburn's customers declared bankruptcy. At December 31, 2014, this company owed Coburn $300,000, of which $60,000 was paid in January 2015.
2. On January 18, 2015, one of the three major plants of the client burned.
3. On January 23, 2015, a strike was called at one of Coburn's largest plants, which halted 30% of its production. As of today (February 13), the strike has not been settled.
4. A major electronics enterprise has introduced a line of products that would compete directly with Coburn's primary line, now being produced in a specially designed new plant. Because of manufacturing innovations, the competitor has been able to achieve quality similar to that of Coburn's products but at a price 50% lower. Coburn officials say they will meet the lower prices, which are high enough to cover variable manufacturing and selling costs but which permit recovery of only a portion of fixed costs.
5. Merchandise traded in the open market is recorded in the company's records at $1.40 per unit on December 31, 2014. This price had prevailed for 2 weeks, after release of an official market report that predicted vastly enlarged supplies; however, no purchases were made at $1.40. The price throughout the preceding year had been about $2, which was the level experienced over several years. On January 18, 2015, the price returned to $2, after public disclosure of an error in the official calculations of the prior December, correction of which destroyed the expectations of excessive supplies. Inventory at December 31, 2015, was on a lower-of-cost-or-market basis.
6. On February 1, 2015, the board of directors adopted a resolution accepting the offer of an investment banker to guarantee the marketing of $1,200,000 of preferred stock.

Instructions

State in each case how the 2014 financial statements would be affected, if at all.

CA24-5 (Segment Reporting) You are compiling the consolidated financial statements for Winsor Corporation International. The corporation's accountant, Anthony Reese, has provided you with the segment information shown on the next page.

Note 7: Major Segments of Business

WCI conducts funeral service and cemetery operations in the United States and Canada. Substantially all revenues of WCI's major segments of business are from unaffiliated customers. Segment information for fiscal 2015, 2014, and 2013 follows.

	Funeral	Floral	Cemetery	(thousands) Real Estate	Dried Whey	Limousine	Consolidated
Revenues							
2015	$302,000	$10,000	$ 73,000	$ 2,000	$7,000	$12,000	$406,000
2014	245,000	6,000	61,000	4,000	4,000	4,000	324,000
2013	208,000	3,000	42,000	3,000	1,000	3,000	260,000
Operating Income							
2015	74,000	1,500	18,000	(36,000)	500	2,000	60,000
2014	64,000	200	12,000	(28,000)	200	400	48,800
2013	54,000	150	6,000	(21,000)	100	350	39,600
Capital Expenditures							
2015	26,000	1,000	9,000	400	300	1,000	37,700
2014	28,000	2,000	60,000	1,500	100	700	92,300
2013	14,000	25	8,000	600	25	50	22,700
Depreciation and Amortization							
2015	13,000	100	2,400	1,400	100	200	17,200
2014	10,000	50	1,400	700	50	100	12,300
2013	8,000	25	1,000	600	25	50	9,700
Identifiable Assets							
2015	334,000	1,500	162,000	114,000	500	8,000	620,000
2014	322,000	1,000	144,000	52,000	1,000	6,000	526,000
2013	223,000	500	78,000	34,000	500	3,500	339,500

Instructions

Determine which of the above segments must be reported separately and which can be combined under the category "Other." Then, write a one-page memo to the company's accountant, Anthony Reese, explaining the following.

(a) What segments must be reported separately and what segments can be combined.

(b) What criteria you used to determine reportable segments.

(c) What major items for each must be disclosed.

CA24-6 (Segment Reporting—Theory) Presented below is an excerpt from the financial statements of H. J. Heinz Company.

Segment and Geographic Data

The company is engaged principally in one line of business—processed food products—which represents over 90% of consolidated sales. Information about the business of the company by geographic area is presented in the table below.

There were no material amounts of sales or transfers between geographic areas or between affiliates, and no material amounts of United States export sales.

(in thousands of U.S. dollars)	Domestic	United Kingdom	Canada	Foreign Western Europe	Other	Total	Worldwide
Sales	$2,381,054	$547,527	$216,726	$383,784	$209,354	$1,357,391	$3,738,445
Operating income	246,780	61,282	34,146	29,146	25,111	149,685	396,465
Identifiable assets	1,362,152	265,218	112,620	294,732	143,971	816,541	2,178,693
Capital expenditures	72,712	12,262	13,790	8,253	4,368	38,673	111,385
Depreciation expense	42,279	8,364	3,592	6,355	3,606	21,917	64,196

Instructions

(a) Why does H. J. Heinz not prepare segment information on its products or services?

(b) What are export sales, and when should they be disclosed?

(c) Why are sales by geographical area important to disclose?

CA24-7 (Segment Reporting—Theory) The following article appeared in the *Wall Street Journal*.

WASHINGTON—The Securities and Exchange Commission staff issued guidelines for companies grappling with the problem of dividing up their business into industry segments for their annual reports.

An industry segment is defined by the Financial Accounting Standards Board as a part of an enterprise engaged in providing a product or service or a group of related products or services primarily to unaffiliated customers for a profit.

Although conceding that the process is a "subjective task" that "to a considerable extent, depends on the judgment of management," the SEC staff said companies should consider . . . various factors . . . to determine whether products and services should be grouped together or reported as segments.

Instructions
    (a) What does financial reporting for segments of a business enterprise involve?
    (b) Identify the reasons for requiring financial data to be reported by segments.
    (c) Identify the possible disadvantages of requiring financial data to be reported by segments.
    (d) Identify the accounting difficulties inherent in segment reporting.

CA24-8 (Interim Reporting) Snider Corporation, a publicly traded company, is preparing the interim financial data which it will issue to its stockholders and the Securities and Exchange Commission (SEC) at the end of the first quarter of the 2014–2015 fiscal year. Snider's financial accounting department has compiled the following summarized revenue and expense data for the first quarter of the year.

Sales revenue	$60,000,000
Cost of goods sold	36,000,000
Variable selling expenses	1,000,000
Fixed selling expenses	3,000,000

Included in the fixed selling expenses was the single lump-sum payment of $2,000,000 for television advertisements for the entire year.

Instructions
    (a) Snider Corporation must issue its quarterly financial statements in accordance with generally accepted accounting principles regarding interim financial reporting.
       (1) Explain whether Snider should report its operating results for the quarter as if the quarter were a separate reporting period in and of itself, or as if the quarter were an integral part of the annual reporting period.
       (2) State how the sales revenue, cost of goods sold, and fixed selling expenses would be reflected in Snider Corporation's quarterly report prepared for the first quarter of the 2014–2015 fiscal year. Briefly justify your presentation.
    (b) What financial information, as a minimum, must Snider Corporation disclose to its stockholders in its quarterly reports?

                                                                               (CMA adapted)

 CA24-9 (Treatment of Various Interim Reporting Situations) The following statement is an excerpt from the FASB pronouncement related to interim reporting.

Interim financial information is essential to provide investors and others with timely information as to the progress of the enterprise. The usefulness of such information rests on the relationship that it has to the annual results of operations. Accordingly, the Board has concluded that each interim period should be viewed primarily as an integral part of an annual period.

In general, the results for each interim period should be based on the accounting principles and practices used by an enterprise in the preparation of its latest annual financial statements unless a change in an accounting practice or policy has been adopted in the current year. The Board has concluded, however, that certain accounting principles and practices followed for annual reporting purposes may require modification at interim reporting dates so that the reported results for the interim period may better relate to the results of operations for the annual period.

Instructions
Listed on the next page are six independent cases on how accounting facts might be reported on an individual company's interim financial reports. For each of these cases, state whether the method proposed to be used for interim reporting would be acceptable under generally accepted accounting principles applicable to interim financial data. Support each answer with a brief explanation.

(a) J. D. Long Company takes a physical inventory at year-end for annual financial statement purposes. Inventory and cost of sales reported in the interim quarterly statements are based on estimated gross profit rates, because a physical inventory would result in a cessation of operations. Long Company does have reliable perpetual inventory records.

(b) Rockford Company is planning to report one-fourth of its pension expense each quarter.

(c) Republic Company wrote inventory down to reflect lower-of-cost-or-market in the first quarter. At year-end, the market exceeds the original acquisition cost of this inventory. Consequently, management plans to write the inventory back up to its original cost as a year-end adjustment.

(d) Gansner Company realized a large gain on the sale of investments at the beginning of the second quarter. The company wants to report one-third of the gain in each of the remaining quarters.

(e) Fredonia Company has estimated its annual audit fee. It plans to pro rate this expense equally over all four quarters.

(f) LaBrava Company was reasonably certain it would have an employee strike in the third quarter. As a result, it shipped heavily during the second quarter but plans to defer the recognition of the sales in excess of the normal sales volume. The deferred sales will be recognized as sales in the third quarter when the strike is in progress. LaBrava Company management thinks this is more representative of normal second- and third-quarter operations.

CA24-10 (Financial Forecasts) An article in *Barron's* noted the following.

Okay. Last fall, someone with a long memory and an even longer arm reached into that bureau drawer and came out with a moldy cheese sandwich and the equally moldy notion of corporate forecasts. We tried to find out what happened to the cheese sandwich—but, rats!, even recourse to the Freedom of Information Act didn't help. However, the forecast proposal was dusted off, polished up and found quite serviceable. The SEC, indeed, lost no time in running it up the old flagpole—but no one was very eager to salute. Even after some of the more objectionable features—compulsory corrections and detailed explanations of why the estimates went awry—were peeled off the original proposal.

Seemingly, despite the Commission's smiles and sweet talk, those craven corporations were still afraid that an honest mistake would lead them down the primrose path to consent decrees and class action suits. To lay to rest such qualms, the Commission last week approved a "Safe Harbor" rule that, providing the forecasts were made on a reasonable basis and in good faith, protected corporations from litigation should the projections prove wide of the mark (as only about 99% are apt to do).

Instructions
(a) What are the arguments for preparing profit forecasts?
(b) What is the purpose of the "safe harbor" rule?
(c) Why are corporations concerned about presenting profit forecasts?

CA24-11 (Disclosure of Estimates) Nancy Tercek, the financial vice president, and Margaret Lilly, the controller, of Romine Manufacturing Company are reviewing the financial ratios of the company for the years 2014 and 2015. The financial vice president notes that the profit margin on sales ratio has increased from 6% to 12%, a hefty gain for the 2-year period. Tercek is in the process of issuing a media release that emphasizes the efficiency of Romine Manufacturing in controlling cost. Margaret Lilly knows that the difference in ratios is due primarily to an earlier company decision to reduce the estimates of warranty and bad debt expense for 2015. The controller, not sure of her supervisor's motives, hesitates to suggest to Tercek that the company's improvement is unrelated to efficiency in controlling cost. To complicate matters, the media release is scheduled in a few days.

Instructions
(a) What, if any, is the ethical dilemma in this situation?
(b) Should Lilly, the controller, remain silent? Give reasons.
(c) What stakeholders might be affected by Tercek's media release?
(d) Give your opinion on the following statement and cite reasons: "Because Tercek, the vice president, is most directly responsible for the media release, Lilly has no real responsibility in this matter."

CA24-12 (Reporting of Subsequent Events) In June 2014, the board of directors for McElroy Enterprises Inc. authorized the sale of $10,000,000 of corporate bonds. Jennifer Grayson, treasurer for McElroy Enterprises Inc., is concerned about the date when the bonds are issued. The company really needs the cash, but she is worried that if the bonds are issued before the company's year-end (December 31, 2014) the additional liability will have an adverse effect on a number of important ratios. In July, she explains to company president William McElroy that if they delay issuing the bonds until after December 31 the bonds will not affect the ratios until December 31, 2015. They will have to report the issuance as a subsequent event which

requires only footnote disclosure. Grayson expects that with expected improved financial performance in 2015, ratios should be better.

Instructions

(a) What are the ethical issues involved?

(b) Should McElroy agree to the delay?

 ***CA24-13 (Effect of Transactions on Financial Statements and Ratios)** The transactions listed below relate to Wainwright Inc. You are to assume that on the date on which each of the transactions occurred, the corporation's accounts showed only common stock ($100 par) outstanding, a current ratio of 2.7:1, and a substantial net income for the year to date (before giving effect to the transaction concerned). On that date, the book value per share of stock was $151.53.

Each numbered transaction is to be considered completely independent of the others, and its related answer should be based on the effect(s) of that transaction alone. Assume that all numbered transactions occurred during 2015 and that the amount involved in each case is sufficiently material to distort reported net income if improperly included in the determination of net income. Assume further that each transaction was recorded in accordance with generally accepted accounting principles and, where applicable, in conformity with the all-inclusive concept of the income statement.

For each of the numbered transactions you are to decide whether it:

(a) Increased the corporation's 2015 net income.

(b) Decreased the corporation's 2015 net income.

(c) Increased the corporation's total retained earnings directly (i.e., not via net income).

(d) Decreased the corporation's total retained earnings directly.

(e) Increased the corporation's current ratio.

(f) Decreased the corporation's current ratio.

(g) Increased each stockholder's proportionate share of total stockholders' equity.

(h) Decreased each stockholder's proportionate share of total stockholders' equity.

(i) Increased each stockholder's equity per share of stock (book value).

(j) Decreased each stockholder's equity per share of stock (book value).

(k) Had none of the foregoing effects.

Instructions

List the numbers 1 through 9. Select as many letters as you deem appropriate to reflect the effect(s) of each transaction as of the date of the transaction by printing beside the transaction number the letter(s) that identifies that transaction's effect(s).

Transactions

_____ 1. In January, the board directed the write-off of certain patent rights that had suddenly and unexpectedly become worthless.

_____ 2. The corporation sold at a profit land and a building that had been idle for some time. Under the terms of the sale, the corporation received a portion of the sales price in cash immediately, the balance maturing at 6-month intervals.

_____ 3. Treasury stock originally repurchased and carried at $127 per share was sold for cash at $153 per share.

_____ 4. The corporation wrote off all of the unamortized discount and issue expense applicable to bonds that it refinanced in 2015.

_____ 5. The corporation called in all its outstanding shares of stock and exchanged them for new shares on a 2-for-1 basis, reducing the par value at the same time to $50 per share.

_____ 6. The corporation paid a cash dividend that had been recorded in the accounts at time of declaration.

_____ 7. Litigation involving Wainwright Inc. as defendant was settled in the corporation's favor, with the plaintiff paying all court costs and legal fees. In 2012, the corporation had appropriately established a special contingency for this court action. (Indicate the effect of reversing the contingency only.)

_____ 8. The corporation received a check for the proceeds of an insurance policy from the company with which it is insured against theft of trucks. No entries concerning the theft had been made previously, and the proceeds reduce but do not cover completely the loss.

_____ 9. Treasury stock, which had been repurchased at and carried at $127 per share, was issued as a stock dividend. In connection with this distribution, the board of directors of Wainwright Inc. had authorized a transfer from retained earnings to permanent capital of an amount equal to the aggregate market value ($153 per share) of the shares issued. No entries relating to this dividend had been made previously.

(AICPA adapted)

USING YOUR JUDGMENT

FINANCIAL REPORTING

Financial Reporting Problem

P&G **The Procter & Gamble Company (P&G)**

As stated in the chapter, notes to the financial statements are the means of explaining the items presented in the main body of the statements. Common note disclosures relate to such items as accounting policies, segmented information, and interim reporting. The financial statements of **P&G** are presented in Appendix 5B. The company's complete annual report, including the notes to the financial statements, can be accessed at the book's companion website, **www.wiley.com/college/kieso**.

Instructions

Refer to P&G's financial statements and the accompanying notes to answer the following questions.

(a) What specific items does P&G discuss in its Note 1—Summary of Significant Accounting Policies? (List the headings only.)

(b) For what segments did P&G report segmented information? Which segment is the largest? Who is P&G's largest customer?

(c) What interim information was reported by P&G?

Comparative Analysis Case

The Coca-Cola Company and PepsiCo, Inc.

Instructions

Go to the book's companion website and use information found there to answer the following questions related to The Coca-Cola Company and PepsiCo, Inc.

(a) **(1)** What specific items does Coca-Cola discuss in its Note 1—Accounting Policies? (Prepare a list of the headings only.)

   (2) What specific items does PepsiCo discuss in its Note 2—Our Summary of Significant Accounting Policies? (Prepare a list of the headings only.)

(b) For what lines of business or segments do Coca-Cola and PepsiCo present segmented information?

(c) Note and comment on the similarities and differences between the auditors' reports submitted by the independent auditors of Coca-Cola and PepsiCo for the year 2011.

*Financial Statement Analysis Case

RNA Inc. manufactures a variety of consumer products. The company's founders have run the company for 30 years and are now interested in retiring. Consequently, they are seeking a purchaser who will continue its operations, and a group of investors, Morgan Inc., is looking into the acquisition of RNA. To evaluate its financial stability and operating efficiency, RNA was requested to provide the latest financial statements and selected financial ratios. Summary information provided by RNA is as follows.

RNA INC.
INCOME STATEMENT
FOR THE YEAR ENDED NOVEMBER 30, 2015
(IN THOUSANDS)

Sales (net)	$30,500
Interest income	500
Total revenue	31,000
Costs and expenses	
Cost of goods sold	17,600
Selling and administrative expenses	3,550
Depreciation and amortization expense	1,890
Interest expense	900
Total costs and expenses	23,940
Income before taxes	7,060
Income taxes	2,800
Net income	$ 4,260

RNA INC.
BALANCE SHEET
AS OF NOVEMBER 30
(IN THOUSANDS)

	2015	2014
Cash	$ 400	$ 500
Short-term investments (at cost)	300	200
Accounts receivable (net)	3,200	2,900
Inventory	6,000	5,400
Total current assets	9,900	9,000
Property, plant, & equipment (net)	7,100	7,000
Total assets	$17,000	$16,000
Accounts payable	$ 3,700	$ 3,400
Income taxes payable	900	800
Accrued expenses	1,700	1,400
Total current liabilities	6,300	5,600
Long-term debt	2,000	1,800
Total liabilities	8,300	7,400
Common stock ($1 par value)	2,700	2,700
Paid-in capital in excess of par	1,000	1,000
Retained earnings	5,000	4,900
Total stockholders' equity	8,700	8,600
Total liabilities and stockholders' equity	$17,000	$16,000

SELECTED FINANCIAL RATIOS

	RNA INC. 2014	RNA INC. 2013	Current Industry Average
Current ratio	1.61	1.62	1.63
Acid-test ratio	.64	.63	.68
Times interest earned	8.55	8.50	8.45
Profit margin on sales	13.2%	12.1%	13.0%
Asset turnover	1.84	1.83	1.84
Inventory turnover	3.17	3.21	3.18

Instructions
(a) Calculate a new set of ratios for the fiscal year 2015 for RNA based on the financial statements presented.
(b) Explain the analytical use of each of the six ratios presented, describing what the investors can learn about RNA's financial stability and operating efficiency.
(c) Identify two limitations of ratio analysis.

(CMA adapted)

Accounting, Analysis, and Principles

Savannah, Inc. is a company that manufactures and sells a single product. Unit sales for each of the four quarters of 2014 are projected as follows.

Quarter	Units
First	80,000
Second	150,000
Third	550,000
Fourth	120,000
Annual Total	900,000

Savannah incurs variable manufacturing costs of $0.40 per unit and variable nonmanufacturing costs of $0.35 per unit. Savannah will incur fixed manufacturing costs of $720,000 and fixed nonmanufacturing costs of $1,080,000. Savannah will sell its product for $4.00 per unit.

Accounting

Determine the amount of net income Savannah will report in each of the four quarters of 2014, assuming actual sales are as projected and employing the integral approach to interim financial reporting. (Ignore income taxes.)

Analysis

Compute Savannah's profit margin on sales for each of the four quarters of 2014 under both the integral and discrete approaches. What effect does employing the integral approach instead of the discrete approach have on the degree to which Savannah's profit margin on sales varies from quarter to quarter?

Principles

Explain the conceptual rationale behind the integral approach to interim financial reporting.

BRIDGE TO THE PROFESSION

 ## Professional Research: FASB Codification

As part of the year-end audit, you are discussing the disclosure checklist with your client. The checklist identifies the items that must be disclosed in a set of GAAP financial statements. The client is surprised by the disclosure item related to accounting policies. Specifically, since the audit report will attest to the statements being prepared in accordance with GAAP, the client questions the accounting policy checklist item. The client has asked you to conduct some research to verify the accounting policy disclosures.

Instructions

If your school has a subscription to the FASB Codification, go to *http://aaahq.org/ascLogin.cfm* to log in and prepare responses to the following. Provide Codification references for your responses.

(a) In general, what should disclosures of accounting policies encompass?

(b) List some examples of the most commonly required disclosures.

Additional Professional Resources

See the book's companion website, at **www.wiley.com/college/kieso**, for professional simulations as well as other study resources.

 IFRS ▸ INSIGHTS

LEARNING OBJECTIVE 14
Compare the disclosure requirements under GAAP and IFRS.

IFRS and GAAP disclosure requirements are similar in many regards. The IFRS addressing various disclosure issues are *IAS 24* ("Related Party Disclosures"), disclosure and recognition of post-statement of financial position events in *IAS 10* ("Events after the Balance Sheet Date"), segment reporting IFRS provisions in *IFRS 8* ("Operating Segments"), and interim reporting requirements in *IAS 34* ("Interim Financial Reporting").

RELEVANT FACTS

Following are the key similarities and differences between GAAP and IFRS related to disclosures.

Similarities

- GAAP and IFRS have similar standards on post-statement of financial position (subsequent) events. That is, under both sets of standards, events that occurred after the statement of financial position date, and which provide additional evidence of conditions that existed at the statement of financial position date, are recognized in the financial statements.
- Like GAAP, IFRS requires that for transactions with related parties, companies disclose the amounts involved in a transaction; the amount, terms, and nature of the outstanding balances; and any doubtful amounts related to those outstanding balances for each major category of related parties.
- Following the recent issuance of *IFRS 8*, "Operating Segments," the requirements under IFRS and GAAP are very similar. That is, both standards use the management approach to identify reportable segments, and similar segment disclosures are required.
- Neither GAAP nor IFRS require interim reports. Rather, the SEC and securities exchanges outside the United States establish the rules. In the United States, interim reports generally are provided on a quarterly basis; outside the United States, six-month interim reports are common.

Differences

- Due to the broader range of judgments allowed in more principles-based IFRS, note disclosures generally are more expansive under IFRS compared to GAAP.
- Subsequent (or post-statement of financial position) events under IFRS are evaluated through the date that financial instruments are "authorized for issue." GAAP uses the date when financial statements are "issued." Also, for share dividends and splits in the subsequent period, IFRS does not adjust but GAAP does.
- Under IFRS, there is no specific requirement to disclose the name of the related party, which is this case under GAAP.
- Under IFRS, interim reports are prepared on a discrete basis; GAAP generally follows the integral approach.

ABOUT THE NUMBERS

Differential Disclosure

A trend toward **differential disclosure** is occurring. The IASB has developed IFRS for small- and medium-sized entities (SMEs). SMEs are entities that publish general-purpose financial statements for external users but do not issue shares or other securities in a public market. Many believe a simplified set of standards makes sense for these companies because they do not have the resources to implement full IFRS. Simplified IFRS for SMEs is a single standard of fewer than 230 pages. It is designed to meet the needs and capabilities of SMEs, which are estimated to account for over 95 percent of all companies around the world. Compared with full IFRS (and many national accounting standards), simplified IFRS for SMEs is less complex in a number of ways:

- Topics not relevant for SMEs are omitted. Examples are earnings per share, interim financial reporting, and segment reporting.
- Simplified IFRS for SMEs allows fewer accounting policy choices. Examples are no option to revalue property, equipment, or intangibles, and no corridor approach for actuarial gains and losses.
- Many principles for recognizing and measuring assets, liabilities, revenue, and expenses are simplified. For example, goodwill is amortized (as a result, there is no annual impairment test), and all borrowing and R&D costs are expensed.

- Significantly fewer disclosures are required (roughly 300 versus 3,000).
- To further reduce standard overload, revisions to the IFRS for SMEs will be limited to once every three years.

Thus, the option of using simplified IFRS helps SMEs meet the needs of their financial statement users while balancing the costs and benefits from a preparer perspective.[29]

Events after the Reporting Period (Subsequent Events)

Notes to the financial statements should explain any significant financial events that took place after the formal statement of financial position date, but before the statements are authorized for issuance (hereafter referred to as the authorization date). These events are referred to as **events after the reporting date**, or **subsequent events**. Illustration IFRS24-1 shows a time diagram of the subsequent events period.

ILLUSTRATION IFRS24-1
Time Periods for Subsequent Events

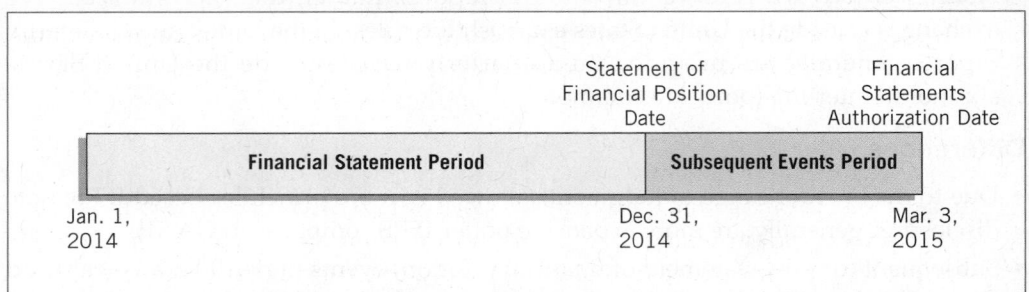

A period of several weeks, and sometimes months, may elapse after the end of the fiscal year but before the management or the board of directors authorizes issuance of the financial statements. Various activities involved in closing the books for the period and issuing the statements all take time: taking and pricing the inventory, reconciling subsidiary ledgers with controlling accounts, preparing necessary adjusting entries, ensuring that all transactions for the period have been entered, obtaining an audit of the financial statements by independent certified public accountants, and printing the annual report. During the period between the statement of financial position date and its authorization date, important transactions or other events may occur that materially affect the company's financial position or operating situation.

Many who read a statement of financial position believe the financial condition is constant, and they project it into the future. However, readers must be told if the company has experienced a significant change—e.g., sold one of its plants, acquired a subsidiary, suffered unusual losses, settled significant litigation, or experienced any other important event in the post-statement of financial position period. Without an explanation in a note, the reader might be misled and draw inappropriate conclusions.

Two types of events or transactions occurring after the statement of financial position date may have a material effect on the financial statements or may need disclosure so that readers interpret these statements accurately:

---

[29]In the United States, there has been a preference for one set of GAAP except in unusual situations. With the advent of simplified IFRS for SMEs, this position is under review. Both the FASB and the AICPA are studying the big GAAP/little GAAP issue to ensure that any kind of differential reporting is conceptually sound and meets the needs of users. As discussed in the chapter, the FASB has formed a Private Company Financial Reporting Committee, whose primary objectives are to provide recommendations on FASB standard-setting for privately held enterprises (see *http://www.pcfr.org/*).

1. Events that provide additional evidence about conditions **that existed** at the statement of financial position date, including the estimates inherent in the process of preparing financial statements. These events are referred to as **adjusted subsequent events** and require adjustments to the financial statements. All information available prior to the authorization date of the financial statements helps investors and creditors evaluate estimates previously made. To ignore these subsequent events is to pass up an opportunity to improve the accuracy of the financial statements. This first type of event encompasses information that an accountant would have recorded in the accounts had the information been known at the statement of financial position date.

For example, if a loss on an account receivable results from a customer's bankruptcy subsequent to the statement of financial position date, the company adjusts the financial statements before their issuance. The bankruptcy stems from the customer's poor financial health existing at the statement of financial position date.

The same criterion applies to settlements of litigation. The company must adjust the financial statements if the events that gave rise to the litigation, such as personal injury or patent infringement, took place prior to the statement of financial position date.

2. Events that provide evidence about conditions that **did not exist** at the statement of financial position date but arise subsequent to that date. These events are referred to as **non-adjusted subsequent events** and do not require adjustment of the financial statements. To illustrate, a loss resulting from a customer's fire or flood *after* the statement of financial position date does not reflect conditions existing at that date.

Thus, adjustment of the financial statements is not necessary. A company should not recognize subsequent events that provide evidence about conditions that did not exist at the date of the statement of financial position but that arose after the statement of financial position date.

The following are examples of non-adjusted subsequent events:

- A major business combination after the reporting period or disposing of a major subsidiary.
- Announcing a plan to discontinue an operation or commencing the implementation of a major restructuring.
- Major purchases of assets, other disposals of assets, or expropriation of major assets by government.
- The destruction of a major production plant or inventories by a fire or natural disaster after the reporting period.
- Major ordinary share transactions and potential ordinary share transactions after the reporting period.
- Abnormally large changes after the reporting period in asset prices, foreign exchange rates, or taxes.
- Entering into significant commitments or contingent liabilities, for example, by issuing significant guarantees after the statement date.[30]

---

[30]The effects from natural disasters, like the recent eruption of the Icelandic volcano, which occurred after the year-end for companies with March fiscal years, require disclosure in order to keep the statements from being misleading. Some companies may have to consider whether these disasters affect their ability to continue as going concerns.

Some non-adjusted subsequent events may have to be disclosed to keep the financial statements from being misleading. For such events, a company discloses the nature of the event and an estimate of its financial effect. Illustration IFRS24-2 presents an example of subsequent events disclosure, excerpted from the annual report of Magyar Telecom plc.

ILLUSTRATION IFRS24-2
Disclosure of Subsequent Events

Magyar Telecom plc

Note 37. Events After the Reporting Period (in part)

On March 1, 2011 the Hungarian Government announced that as part of its long-term effort to reduce the Hungarian budget deficit it intends to amend existing law that provides for a reduction in corporate tax rates from the current 19% to 10% starting in 2013. When the law reducing future corporate tax rates was enacted in 2010, the Group recalculated its deferred tax balances, resulting in the reversal of net deferred tax liabilities of HUF 14.5 billion (see Note 9.3) in the 2010 income statement of comprehensive income. The recent announcement of the intended cancellation of the scheduled reduction of the tax rate from 2013 is expected to cause the recognition of a substantially higher amount of net deferred tax liabilities in 2011 and result in a negative impact on deferred tax expense in 2011 equivalent in magnitude to the positive impact on net deferred tax expense in 2010.

Many subsequent events or developments do not require adjustment of or disclosure in the financial statements. Typically, these are non-accounting events or conditions that management normally communicates by other means. These events include legislation, product changes, management changes, strikes, unionization, marketing agreements, and loss of important customers.

Interim Reports

Another source of information for the investor is interim reports. As noted earlier, **interim reports** cover periods of less than one year. The securities exchanges, market regulators, and the accounting profession have an active interest in the presentation of interim information.

Because of the short-term nature of the information in these reports, there is considerable controversy as to the general approach companies should employ. One group, which favors the **discrete approach**, believes that companies should treat each interim period as a separate accounting period. Using that treatment, companies would follow the principles for deferrals and accruals used for annual reports. In this view, companies should report accounting transactions as they occur, and expense recognition should not change with the period of time covered.

Another group, which favors the **integral approach**, believes that the interim report is an integral part of the annual report and that deferrals and accruals should take into consideration what will happen for the entire year. In this approach, companies should assign estimated expenses to parts of a year on the basis of sales volume or some other activity base. In general, IFRS requires companies to follow the discrete approach.

Interim Reporting Requirements

Under IFRS, companies should use the same accounting policies for interim reports and for annual reports. They should recognize revenues in interim periods on the same basis as they are for annual periods. For example, if Cedars Corp. uses the percentage-of-completion method as the basis for recognizing revenue on an annual basis, it should use the percentage-of-completion method for interim reports as well. Also, Cedars should treat costs directly associated with revenues (product costs, such as materials, labor and related fringe benefits, and manufacturing overhead) in the same manner for interim reports as for annual reports.

Companies should use the same inventory pricing methods (FIFO, average-cost, etc.) for interim reports and for annual reports. However, companies may use the gross profit method for interim inventory pricing. But, they must disclose the method and adjustments to reconcile with annual inventory.

Discrete Approach. Following the discrete approach, companies record in interim reports revenues and expenses according to the revenue and expense recognition principles. This includes costs and expenses other than product costs (often referred to as period costs). No accruals or deferrals in anticipation of future events during the year should be reported. For example, the cost of a planned major periodic maintenance or overhaul for a company like Airbus or other seasonal expenditure that is expected to occur late in the year is not anticipated for interim reporting purposes. The mere intention or necessity to incur expenditure related to the future is not sufficient to give rise to an obligation.

Or, a company like Carrefour may budget certain costs expected to be incurred irregularly during the financial year, such as advertising and employee training costs. Those costs generally are discretionary even though they are planned and tend to recur from year to year. However, recognizing an obligation at the end of an interim financial reporting period for such costs that have not yet been incurred generally is not consistent with the definition of a liability.

While year-to-date measurements may involve changes in estimates of amounts reported in prior interim periods of the current financial year, the principles for recognizing assets, liabilities, income, and expenses for interim periods are the same as in annual financial statements. For example, Wm Morrison Supermarkets plc records losses from inventory write-downs, restructurings, or impairments in an interim period similar to how it would treat these items in the annual financial statements (when incurred). However, if an estimate from a prior interim period changes in a subsequent interim period of that year, the original estimate is adjusted in the subsequent interim period.

Interim Disclosures. IFRS does not require a complete set of financial statements at the interim reporting date. Rather, companies may comply with the requirements by providing condensed financial statements and selected explanatory notes. Because users of interim financial reports also have access to the most recent annual financial report, companies only need provide explanation of significant events and transactions since the end of the last annual reporting period. Companies should report the following interim data at a minimum.

1. Statement that the same accounting policies and methods of computation are followed in the interim financial statements as compared with the most recent annual financial statements or, if those policies or methods have been changed, a description of the nature and effect of the change.
2. Explanatory comments about the seasonality or cyclicality of interim operations.
3. The nature and amount of items affecting assets, liabilities, equity, net income, or cash flows that are unusual because of their nature, size, or incidence.
4. The nature and amount of changes in accounting policies and estimates of amounts previously reported.
5. Issuances, repurchases, and repayments of debt and equity securities.
6. Dividends paid (aggregate or per share) separately for ordinary shares and other shares.

7. Segment information, as required by *IFRS 8,* "Operating Segments."

8. Changes in contingent liabilities or contingent assets since the end of the last annual reporting period.

9. Effect of changes in the composition of the company during the interim period, such as business combinations, obtaining or losing control of subsidiaries and long-term investments, restructurings, and discontinued operations.

10. Other material events subsequent to the end of the interim period that have not been reflected in the financial statements for the interim period.

If a complete set of financial statements is provided in the interim report, companies comply with the provisions of *IAS 1,* "Presentation of Financial Statements."

ON THE HORIZON

Hans Hoogervorst, chairperson of the IASB, recently noted: "High quality financial information is the lifeblood of market-based economies. If the blood is of poor quality, then the body shuts down and the patient dies. It is the same with financial reporting. If investors cannot trust the numbers, then financial markets stop working. For market-based economies, that is really bad news. It is an essential public good for market-based economies. . . . And in the past 10 years, most of the world's economies—developed and emerging—have embraced IFRSs." While the United States has yet to adopt IFRS, there is no question that IFRS and GAAP are converging quickly. We have provided expanded discussion in the *International Perspectives* and *IFRS Insights* to help you understand the issues surrounding convergence as they relate to intermediate accounting. After reading these discussions, you should realize that IFRS and GAAP are very similar in many areas, with differences in those areas revolving around some minor technical points. In other situations, the differences are major; for example, IFRS does not permit LIFO inventory accounting. Our hope is that the FASB and IASB can quickly complete their convergence efforts, resulting in a single set of high-quality accounting standards for use by companies around the world.

IFRS SELF-TEST QUESTIONS

1. Which of the following is **false**?
   (a) In general, IFRS note disclosures are more expansive compared to GAAP.
   (b) GAAP and IFRS have similar standards on subsequent events.
   (c) Both IFRS and GAAP require interim reports although the reporting frequency varies.
   (d) Segment reporting requirements are very similar under IFRS and GAAP.

2. Differential reporting for small- and medium-sized entities:
   (a) is required for all companies less than a certain size.
   (b) omits accounting topics not relevant for SMEs, such as earnings per share, and interim and segment reporting.
   (c) has different rules for topics such as earnings per share, and interim and segment reporting.
   (d) requires significantly more disclosures, since more items are not recognized in the financial statements.

3. Subsequent events are reviewed through which date under IFRS?
   (a) Statement of financial position date.
   (b) Sixty days after the year-end date.
   (c) Date of independent auditor's opinion.
   (d) Authorization date of the financial statements.

4. Under IFRS, share dividends declared after the statement of financial position date but before the end of the subsequent events period are:
   (a) accounted for similar to errors as a prior period adjustment.
   (b) adjusted subsequent events, because they are paid from prior year earnings.
   (c) not adjusted in the current year's financial statements.
   (d) recognized on a prospective basis from the date of declaration.
5. Interim reporting under IFRS:
   (a) is prepared using the discrete approach.
   (b) is prepared using a combination of the discrete and integral approach.
   (c) requires a complete set of financial statements for each interim period.
   (d) permits companies to omit disclosure of material events subsequent to the interim reporting date.

IFRS CONCEPTS AND APPLICATION

IFRS24-1 Where can authoritative IFRS be found related to the various disclosure issues discussed in the chapter?

IFRS24-2 What are the major types of subsequent events? Indicate how each of the following "subsequent events" would be reported.

(a) Collection of a note written off in a prior period.
(b) Issuance of a large preference share offering.
(c) Acquisition of a company in a different industry.
(d) Destruction of a major plant in a flood.
(e) Death of the company's chief executive officer (CEO).
(f) Additional wage costs associated with settlement of a four-week strike.
(g) Settlement of an income tax case at considerably more tax than anticipated at year-end.
(h) Change in the product mix from consumer goods to industrial goods.

IFRS24-3 Morlan Corporation is preparing its December 31, 2014, financial statements. Two events that occurred between December 31, 2014, and March 10, 2015, when the statements were authorized for issue, are described below.

1. A liability, estimated at $160,000 at December 31, 2014, was settled on February 26, 2015, at $170,000.
2. A flood loss of $80,000 occurred on March 1, 2015.

Instructions
What effect do these subsequent events have on 2014 net income?

IFRS24-4 Keystone Corporation's financial statements for the year ended December 31, 2014, were authorized for issue on March 10, 2015. The following events took place early in 2015.

(a) On January 10, 10,000 ordinary shares of $5 par value were issued at $66 per share.
(b) On March 1, Keystone determined after negotiations with the taxing authorities that income taxes payable for 2014 should be $1,320,000. At December 31, 2014, income taxes payable were recorded at $1,100,000.

Instructions
Discuss how the preceding subsequent events should be reflected in the 2014 financial statements.

IFRS24-5 For each of the following subsequent events, indicate whether a company should (a) adjust the financial statements, (b) disclose in notes to the financial statements, or (c) neither adjust nor disclose.

_____ 1. Settlement of a tax case at a cost considerably in excess of the amount expected at year-end.
_____ 2. Introduction of a new product line.
_____ 3. Loss of assembly plant due to fire.
_____ 4. Sale of a significant portion of the company's assets.
_____ 5. Retirement of the company president.

_____ **6.** Issuance of a significant number of ordinary shares.

_____ **7.** Loss of a significant customer.

_____ **8.** Prolonged employee strike.

_____ **9.** Material loss on a year-end receivable because of a customer's bankruptcy.

_____ **10.** Hiring of a new president.

_____ **11.** Settlement of prior year's litigation against the company (no loss was accrued).

_____ **12.** Merger with another company of comparable size.

IFRS24-6 What are interim reports? Why is a complete set of financial statements often not provided with interim data? What are the accounting problems related to the presentation of interim data?

IFRS24-7 Dierdorf Inc., a closely held corporation, has decided to go public. The controller, Ed Floyd, is concerned with presenting interim data when an inventory write-down is recorded. What problems are encountered with inventories when quarterly data are presented?

IFRS24-8 Bill Novak is working on an audit of an IFRS client. In his review of the client's interim reports, he notes that the reports are prepared on a discrete basis. That is, each interim report is viewed as a distinct period. Is this acceptable under IFRS? If so, explain how that treatment could affect comparisons to a GAAP company.

IFRS24-9 Snider Corporation, a publicly traded company, is preparing the interim financial data which it will issue to its shareholders at the end of the first quarter of the 2014–2015 fiscal year. Snider's financial accounting department has compiled the following summarized revenue and expense data for the first quarter of the year.

Sales revenue	$60,000,000
Cost of goods sold	36,000,000
Variable selling expenses	1,000,000
Fixed selling expenses	3,000,000

Included in the fixed selling expenses was the single lump-sum payment of $2,000,000 for television advertisements for the entire year.

Instructions

(a) Snider Corporation must issue its quarterly financial statements in accordance with IFRS regarding interim financial reporting.

   (1) Explain whether Snider should report its operating results for the quarter as if the quarter were a separate reporting period in and of itself, or as if the quarter were an integral part of the annual reporting period.

   (2) State how the sales revenue, cost of goods sold, and fixed selling expenses would be reflected in Snider Corporation's quarterly report prepared for the first quarter of the 2014–2015 fiscal year. Briefly justify your presentation.

(b) What financial information, as a minimum, must Snider Corporation disclose to its shareholders in its quarterly reports?

Professional Research

IFRS24-10 As part of the year-end audit, you are discussing the disclosure checklist with your client. The checklist identifies the items that must be disclosed in a set of IFRS financial statements. The client is surprised by the disclosure item related to accounting policies. Specifically, since the audit report will attest to the statements being prepared in accordance with IFRS, the client questions the accounting policy checklist item. The client has asked you to conduct some research to verify the accounting policy disclosures.

Instructions

Access the IFRS authoritative literature at the IASB website (_http://eifrs.iasb.org/_). (Click on the IFRS tab and then register for free eIFRS access if necessary.) When you have accessed the documents, you can use the search tool in your Internet browser to respond to the following questions. (Provide paragraph citations.)

(a) In general, what should disclosures of accounting policies encompass?

(b) List some examples of the most commonly required disclosures.

International Financial Reporting Problem
Marks and Spencer plc

IFRS24-11 The financial statements of **Marks and Spencer plc (M&S)** are available at the book's companion website or can be accessed at *http://annualreport.marksandspencer.com/_assets/downloads/ Marks-and-Spencer-Annual-report-and-financial-statements-2012.pdf.*

Instructions

Refer to M&S's financial statements and the accompanying notes to answer the following questions.

- **(a)** What specific items does M&S discuss in its Note 1—Summary of Significant Accounting Policies? (List the headings only.)
- **(b)** For what segments did M&S report segmented information? Which segment is the largest? Who is M&S's largest customer?
- **(c)** What interim information was reported by M&S?

ANSWERS TO IFRS SELF-TEST QUESTIONS

1. c **2.** b **3.** d **4.** c **5.** a

Remember to check the book's companion website to find additional resources for this chapter.

A

A. C. Nielsen Company, 721*n*.17
Abbott Laboratories, 219–220, 967
Abdel-khalik, A. Rashad, 1283*n*.9
Abnormal shortages, 493
Absences, compensated, 712–714
Accelerated Cost Recovery System
    (ACRS), 614
Accountability, 54
Accounting:
    ethics in, 21
    principles of, 56–61
Accounting changes, *see* Change(s) in
    accounting *entries*
Accounting cycle, 89–114
    adjusted trial balance, 108
    adjusting entries, 96–108
    closing, 110–113
    journalizing, 91–92
    post-closing trial balance, 113
    posting, 92–96
    preparing financial statements, 108–110
    reversing entries, 113
    steps of, 114
    transactions and other events,
        identifying/recording, 89–91
    trial balance, 96
Accounting information system, 84–89
Accounting policies:
    accounting for changes in, 1404–1406
    on balance sheets, 236, 237
    disclosure of, 1491
    MD&A of, 1511–1512
Accounting principle, changes in,
    see Change(s) in accounting principle
Accounting Principles Board (APB), 9, 27.
    *See also Opinions of the Accounting
    Principles Board*
Accounting Research Bulletins, 9
Accounting Research Study No. 13
    ("The Accounting Basis of Inventories"),
    481*n*.5
Accounting standards:
    economic consequences of, 17
    need for development of, 7
    politicization of, 26–27
Accounting Standards Executive
    Committee (AcSEC), 10, 541*n*.2, 557*n*.6,
    559*n*.12
Accounting Standards Updates, 11, 12,
    57*n*.16
Accounting theory, cash basis accounting
    and, 118–120
Accounts payable(s), 703
    decrease in, 1425
    increase in, 1422
    indirect method of analyzing,
        1418–1419

Accounts receivable(s), 349–358
    days to collect, 374
    decrease in, 1421
    disposition of, 365–370
    increase in, 1424
    indirect method of analyzing, 1418
    net, accounts receivable, 1438–1440, 1447
    recognition of, 351–352
    trade, 363
    uncollectible, 353–358
    valuation of, 352–358
Accounts receivable turnover, 372
Accruals:
    adjusting entries for, 102–108
    as class of adjusting entries, 97
    in reversing entries illustration,
        124–125
Accrual basis accounting, 6–7
    cash basis accounting vs., 118–123
    conversion to cash basis accounting,
        120–123
    for warranties, 719–720
Accrued expenses:
    adjusting entries for, 104–108
    as class of adjusting entries, 97
Accrued interest, adjusting entries
    for, 105
Accrued revenue(s):
    adjusting entries for, 103–104
    as class of adjusting entries, 97
    overstatement of, 1369
Accrued salaries, adjusting entries for,
    106–107
Accrued wages, failure to record, 1368
Accumulated benefit obligation, 1187
Accumulated depreciation, 1422, 1425,
    1448–1449
Accumulated other comprehensive
    income, 280
Accumulated other comprehensive loss,
    847*n*.21
Accumulated postretirement benefit
    obligation (APBO), 1220
Accumulated rights, 713
Acid-test ratio, 730
Acquisition costs, 556–560, 605
ACRS (Accelerated Cost Recovery
    System), 614
AcSEC, *see* Accounting Standards
    Executive Committee
Activision Blizzard, 1411
Activity method for depreciation, 593
Activity ratios, 245, 1523, 1524
Actually refinancing, 706
Actual return on plan assets, 1191–1192,
    1221, 1254–1255
Actuarial present value, 1188*n*.7
Actuaries, 1187

Adaptec, 911
ADC Telecommunications, 347
Additions, 558
Additional paid-in capital, 826
Adecco, 83
Adelphia Communications, 54, 783, 1518
Adjunct account, 774
Adjustable-rate mortgage, 782
Adjusted subsequent events, 1551
Adjusted trial balance, 85, 108, 113, 129
Adjustments, 96–108
    for accruals, 102–108
    for bad debts, 107–108
    for deferrals, 97–102
    defined, 85
    for depreciation, 100–101
    for insurance, 99–100
    prior period, 181
    for statement presentation, 101–102
    types of, 97
    for unearned revenues, 102
    on worksheet, 127–129
Adjustments columns, 127
Administrative expenses, on income
    statement, 164
Adverse opinion, 1511
Advertising costs, 669, 1504
AES, 176
After-closing trial balance, 85
Aging schedule, 357
Agricultural inventory, 530–532
Agricultural produce, 530
Ahold NV, 1109, 1176
AICPA, *see* American Institute of Certified
    Public Accountants
AICPA Task Force on LIFO Inventory
    Problems, 479*n*.3
AIG, 2, 31, 48, 364, 984
Airbus, 1553
Air France, 1332–1335
Airline industry, 215, 591*n*.2
Air Products & Chemicals, 979*n*.14
Airtran, 215
Alaska Airlines, 1307
Alberto-Culver Company, 240
Alcatel-Lucent, 1111, 1219
Allied Products Corporation, 835
Allowance accounts:
    for multiple periods, 480
    and net realizable value adjustments, 529
    use of, 479–480
Allowance method, 353–358
Alltel Corp., 707
Almost Family, Inc., 107
Altera International, 965
Alternative minimum tax (AMT), 1140
Alterra Healthcare Corp., 217–218
Altman, E. I., 226

Amazon.com, 158, 159, 214, 224, 276, 427, 657, 821, 885, 899, 933–934, 955, 965–966
Ameren, 611
American Airlines, 102, 215, 708, 822, 1231, 1273, 1308–1309
American Bar Association, 822
American Express, 366
American Home Mortgage Investment Corp., 1041
American Institute of Certified Public Accountants (AICPA), 9–10, 597n.6
  and APB, 9
  and big GAAP/little GAAP issue, 1550n.29
  changing role of, 10
  and Committee on Accounting Procedure, 9, 26, 27
  and GAAP standards development, 9
  and government intervention, 29
  and SEC, 7
  Task Force on LIFO Inventory Problems, 479n.3
American Maize-Products Company, 433
America Online, 650
Amgen, 831
AM International, 425
Amortization:
  adjustment to net income for, 1434–1435
  of bonds, 314–315, 769–770
  corridor, 1199–1200, 1210–1211, 1223
  defined, 590
  effective-interest method, 314–315
  of intangible assets, 651–653
  on postretirement benefit plans, 1223
  of prior service costs, 1194–1195, 1221
  straight-line, 1195
  of trademark, 1448–1449
  on units-of-production basis, 657n.3
  years-of-service, 1194–1195
Amortization policies, 55
Amortized cost, 953, 1028–1029
Ampco-Pittsburgh Corporation, 596, 1358
AMR Corporation, 1231
AMT (alternative minimum tax), 1140
Anadarko Petroleum Corporation, 546, 999
Anheuser-Busch, 1525
Anixter Bros., Inc., 425
Annual interest rate, in compound interest tables, 292–293
Annualized approach, 1505
Annual reports:
  content and organization of, 247
  on the Internet, 19
Annuity(-ies), 299–313
  deferred, 311–313
  due, future value of, 303–306
  due, present value of, 308–311
  ordinary, 291–292, 306–307, 309–311
  ordinary, future value of, 300–302, 304–306
  present value of, 306–311
Annuity due, 303–306
  future value of, 303–306
  present value of, 308–311
Ante, S. E., 480
Antidilutive securities, 904, 908–909, 921n.22

APB (Accounting Principles Board), 9, 27
APBO (accumulated postretirement benefit obligation), 1220
APB Opinions (*Opinions of the Accounting Principles Board*), 9, 11–13
Apple Inc. (Apple Computer), 189, 241, 349, 358, 488, 654, 657, 670, 718, 822, 1054, 1140
April-Marcus, Inc., 422
Arbitrageurs, 979
Arcady, A. T., 1214n.18
AROs (asset retirement obligations), 723–724
Arrears:
  dividend in, 835
  preferred dividends in, 707
Articulation, 52
Artificial loss, 1308n.19
Artistic-related intangible assets, 655
Assessments, 718–719
Asset(s):
  on balance sheet, 216
  biological, 530
  contingent, 758
  current, 217–220
  defined, 52, 53, 79
  depreciable base for, 590
  fixed, 538, 599
  held for disposal, 603–604
  in lessee accounting, 1278
  noncurrent, 221–222
  of pension plans, 1197–1198, 1260
  recognition of, 1125
  sales price of, 1296
  soft, 19
  transfer of, 791
Asset expenditures, 557
Asset gains and losses, with pension plans, 1197–1198, 1260
Asset-liability method, 1144
Asset-linked bonds, 765
Asset retirement obligations (AROs), 723–724
Asset turnover ratio, 611
Asset valuation, 556
Assumptions, 54–56
Astra Zeneca Plc., 657–658
Atlantic Richfield, 608
AT&T Inc., 90, 595, 888–889, 1202, 1217, 1219
Attmore, R. H., 1227
Attribution period, 1219
Audit and Accounting Guides (AdSEC), 10
Auditor's report, 1508–1511
  emphasis of matter in, 1510
  and expectation gap, 1519n.24
  on going concern of entity, 1509
  and lack of consistency, 1510
  and management's responsibilities for financial statements, 1512n.14
  qualified/adverse/disclaimer opinion, 1510–1511
  standards for, 1508
  unqualified/clean opinion, 1508–1510
Automatic Data Processing, 768
Available-for-sale securities, 182n.21, 218, 952, 955–959, 962–964, 968

Average-cost method:
  for cost flow assumption, 429–430
  for security purchases, 962n.6
Average days to sell inventory, 496
Avis, 1081
Avon Products, 236
AXA, 32
Ayers, B., 1122

B

Baan NV, 1109
Bad debts:
  adjusting entries for, 107–108
  failure to adjust for, 1369–1370
Bahree, B., 607
Baker Hughes, Inc., 537
Balance sheet(s), 85, 214–227, 243
  accounting policies on, 236, 237
  assets on, 216
  and cash flows statement, 1415, 1421, 1423, 1429
  classification in, 215–226
  classified, 215
  columns on, 129
  comparative, 1445
  contingencies on, 236, 237
  contractual situations on, 236, 237
  current assets on, 217–218
  debit vs. credit balances on, 1443–1444
  deferred tax reporting on, 1138–1140
  elements of, 216
  equity on, 216
  errors on, 1366–1370
  events after preparation of, 1495–1496
  example, 115–116
  fair values on, 236, 238–239
  format of, 226–228
  liabilities on, 216, 222–225
  limitations of, 214–215
  noncurrent assets on, 221–222
  owner's equity on, 225–226
  presentation of, 185
  stockholders' equity on, 88, 225–226, 847–850
  usefulness of, 214
Balance sheet (percentage-of-receivables) approach, 356–357
Ball, J., 607
Banks:
  as lessors, 1271, 1302n.16
  loan losses, 344–345
  operating cash flows in, 1439–1440
  treatment of purchases/sales of loans/securities by, 1414n.2
Bank, David, 709
Bank accounts, 376–377
Bank charges, reconciling, 378–381
Bank credits, reconciling, 379
Bank errors, reconciling, 379
Bankers Trust, 979
Bankia Group, 364
Bank of America, 5, 83, 822, 984, 1269, 1273, 1307, 1440
BankOne, 897, 899
Bank overdrafts, 348
Bank reconciliation, 378–381
Bankruptcy-prediction model, 226

Bank statements, 378–381
Barclays, 984
Bargain purchases, 1083–1084
Bargain purchase option, 1277, 1298, 1338
Bargain purchase option test, 1275–1276
Bargain renewal option, 1334
Barnesandnoble.com, 657
Barrick Gold Corporation, 523–524
Barth, Mary, 890n.6
Barth Industries, 716
Basic elements, 52–53
Basis Technology, 965
Basket purchase, 482
Bearer (coupon) bonds, 765
Bear Stearns & Co., 224
Beaver, W. H., 161n.2
Beijing Lenovo Parasaga Information
    Technology, 966–967
Benchmark, verifiable, 56
Benefits/years-of-service actuarial method,
    1189–1190, 1219n.25
Beresford, Dennis R., 972n.11
Berkshire Hathaway Inc., 32, 822, 1486
Bernanke, Ben S., 316
Beru AG Corporation, 700
Best Buy, 68, 114, 134, 352, 373, 419,
    472–474, 489, 727, 730, 785, 823,
    849, 1509
Best Western, 1081
Bethlehem Steel, 1125, 1201
Bhamornsiri, Sak, 1064n.19
Biddle, Gary C., 445n.20
"Big GAAP versus little GAAP" issue,
    1490, 1550n.29
Biggs, Stanley F., 484n.8
Bill and hold sales, 1050
Biological assets, 530
Birchall, J., 420
Black & Decker, 68
Bloom, R., 445
Bloomingdale's, 488
BLS (Bureau of Labor Statistics), 440n.9
Blumenstein, Rebecca, 557
BMC Industries, Inc., 716
BMW, 875
Boeing Capital, 1271
Boeing Corporation, 58, 100, 216, 416, 538,
    556, 1067–1068, 1219, 1273, 1284
Boise Cascade, 484
Bonds, 763. *See also specific types,*
    e.g.: Discount bonds
    between-interest-date issuance of, 770
    convertible, 765, 884–886, 890, 919–920,
        944–946
    corporate listings, 765–766
    effective-interest method for, 770–774
    and extinguishment of debt, 775–776
    face value of, 766–767
    and interest date, 768–770
    issuance of, 764, 768–770, 816
    monitoring investments in, 765–766
    notes vs., 777
    par on interest date, issuance at, 768
    premium, 766–770, 1435
    types of, 765
Bond amortization, effective-interest
    method of, 314–315

Bond discount, amortization of, 1435
Bondholders, 1522
Bond indenture, 765
Bonds payable, 764–776
    and contra accounts, 774
    decrease in, 1426
    discount, 774
    increase in, 1422
Bond premium:
    amortization of, 1435
    valuation of, 766–770
Bonus agreements, 714–715
Bonus payments, and change in accounting
    method, 1365–1366
Book depreciation, tax depreciation vs., 617
Book of original entry, 85, 91
Book value, 836
    bonds, 101
    for preference shares, 876
Book value per share, 850, 853–854
BOP Clothing Co., 751–753
Borrowing rate, 1335
Borrus, A., 768
Boston Scientific, 166
BP, 32
Brand images, 670
Briggs & Stratton, 715, 799
"Bright line" cutoffs, 1334n.22
Brinker International Inc., 1282
British Airways, 1050, 1183
Broadcom, 831, 911
Brokers, 1414n.2
Brokerage costs, 1030n.44
Brown, K., 48
Brown, K. L., 1058n.18
Brown, Robert Moren, 443n.18
Brown Group, Inc., 845
Brown Shoe Company, 433
Budge, Bruce P., 1437n.8
Buffet, Warren E., 1486
Building depreciation, 1422, 1448–1449
Burberry, 1032, 1033
Burden, 540
Bureau of Labor Statistics (BLS), 440n.9
Burger King, 1081
Burlington Industries, 481n.4
Burnap, N., 1204
Burton, John C., 8n.4
Business combinations:
    intangible assets acquired in, 650n.1
    as present value-based measurement, 289
Business-method patents, 656
Business organization, *see* Corporate form
Buyback(s), 830–831
    of outstanding stock, 837n.12
    sales with, 1049
    of treasury stock, 837n.12
Buyback agreements, 422–423
Byrnes, Nanette, 1183, 1283
Byrnes, Tracey, 1053

C

Cablevision Systems, 836
Calhoun, Charles H., III, 1083n.31
Callable bonds, 765, 775n.8
Callable preferred stock, 835
Callaway Golf Co., 1315

Call option, 980
Calpine, 785
Campbell Soup Company, 621, 962–963,
    1231, 1412
Cannondale Corporation, 68
Canon, 666
CAP, *see* Committee on Accounting
    Procedure
Capettini, Robert, 554n.10
Capital:
    contributed, 875
    earned, 875
    paid-in, 875
Capital allocation, 4–5
Capital assets errors, 1360
Capital expenditures, 536–537, 557
Capitalization criteria:
    avoiding, 1302–1303
    for lessee, 1275–1278
    for lessor, 1285
Capitalization period, 542
Capitalized lease accounting, 1272n.1,
    1273–1278
    bargain purchase option test in,
        1275–1276
    economic life test in, 1276
    recovery of investment test in, 1276–1278
    transfer of ownership test in, 1275
Capital leases, 1275–1278, 1333
Capital lease method, 1278–1281
Capital maintenance approach, 163n.4
Capital markets, integration of, 32
Capital One Financial, 236
Capital stock, 823–824, 830
Capital structure, 1365–1366
Capital structure ratios, 1523n.26
Captive leasing companies, 1271
Carcache, B., 614n.15
Cargill, 822
Carrefour, 756, 1028, 1334, 1553
Carrybacks, 1116, 1132–1133, 1145
Carryforward(s), 1116, 1145, 1176–1177.
    See also Loss carryforwards
Carrying value (bonds), 770n.3, 816
Cash and cash equivalents, 217–218,
    346–349, 1413n.1, 1437n.7
    alternate terminology for, 346n.2
    on balance sheets, 217–218
    basis of valuation of, 217
    determining change in, 1416, 1417,
        1420, 1423
    internal control over, 376
    from operating activities, 231
    reporting, 346–348
    restricted cash vs., 347–348
    and statement of cash flows, 1480, 1481
Cash balances, physical protection of, 378
Cash-balance pension plans, 1214n.18
Cash basis accounting, 6
    and accounting theory, 118–120
    accrual-basis accounting vs., 118–123
    conversion to accrual basis, 120–123
    financial statements, 119
    modified cash basis, 120
    of pension plan, 1189n.10
    theoretical weaknesses of, 123
    warranties, 719

Cash controls, 376–381
 and bank balances reconciliation, 378–381
 and imprest petty cash system, 377–378
 and physical protection of cash balances, 378
 using bank accounts, 376–377
Cash crunch, 233
Cash debt coverage, 234
Cash deposits, returnable, 707
Cash discounts, 351–352, 427, 547
Cash dividends, 839–840
Cash dividends payable, 1440
Cash flows, 7n.2
 classification of, 1413–1415
 determining future change of, 550n.7
 evaluating, 1414–1415
 free, 234–235
 net income vs., 232–233
Cash flow hedge, 987–989
Cash flow risk, 987
Cash flow statement, see Statement of cash flows
Cash funds, 346
Cash-generating units, 696
Cash over account, 377–378
Cash payments:
 classes of, 1429
 and direct method, 1432–1433
 for income taxes, 1432
 for operating expenses, 1431–1432
 special rules applying to, 1434
 to suppliers, 1430–1431
Cash rebates, 721
Cash receipts:
 classes of, 1429
 from customers, 1430
 and direct method, 1432–1433
 special rules applying to, 1434
Cash-related items, 348–349
Catanach, A., 1051
Caterpillar Financial Services Corp., 1271, 1278–1281, 1284, 1286–1289
Caterpillar Inc., 100, 442, 970, 979, 1271, 1291–1295, 1298–1300, 1498
CBS, 656, 830
CDs (certificates of deposit), 346n.1
CECL ("Current Expected Credit Loss") model, 374
Ceiling (upper), 475–476
Cendant, 17
Cenker, W., 445
CenturyTel, 1198
Certificates of deposit (CDs), 346n.1
Change(s) due to error, 1363
Change(s) in accounting (general), 1344
 guidelines for, 1363–1364
 motivations for, 1365–1366
 from or to equity method, 1377–1380
Change(s) in accounting estimate, 180, 1357–1359, 1363, 1404
Change(s) in accounting policies, 1404–1406
Change(s) in accounting principle, 179–180, 1344–1366
 accounting for/reporting of, 179–180, 1353–1354

 direct/indirect effects of, 1355
 disclosure of, 1493
 and impracticability, 1356
 prospective reporting of, 1345
 and retained earnings adjustment, 1354
 retrospective, 1345–1354
Change in cash, determining, 1416, 1417, 1420, 1423
Changes in equity, statement of, 877–878
Change(s) in reporting entity, 1359, 1363
Change-in-the-present-value method, 1299–1300
Channel stuffing, 1053
Checks:
 outstanding, 379
 paper, 378n.17
 postdated, 346
Check fraud, 378n.17
Checking accounts, 377
Cheney, Richard E., 1525n.27
Chesapeake Corporation, 237
Chesapeake Energy Corp., 785, 1419
Chevron, 32
ChevronTexaco, 608n.10
China National Petroleum, 32
Chipotle, 166
Choice Point, Inc., 999
Christie, Rebecca, 1511
Chrysler Corporation, 31, 54, 444, 600n.8, 1284, 1346
Ciba-Geigy, 469
Ciesielski, J., 883, 1189n.9
CIFR (Committee for Improvements in Financial Reporting), 1343
Cinergy, 899
Cintas, 537
Cisco Systems, 61, 110, 161, 480, 654, 783, 979, 1437n.7
CitiCapital, 1308–1309
Citicorp, 170n.12
Cities Service Company, 729
Citigroup, 49, 170n.12, 344, 345, 358, 364, 788, 979, 998, 1116–1117, 1119n.1, 1137n.6, 1271, 1284
CKE Restaurants Inc., 1282
Claims, 718–719, 1492
Clarcor Inc., 713
Class B common stock, 836
Classification:
 of financial instruments, 975–976
 in statement of financial position, 278–280
Classified balance sheets, 215
Clean opinion (unqualified opinion), 1508–1510
Clorox Co., 648, 649, 839
Closing, 110–113
Closing entries, 85, 111–113, 117
Closing prices, 110–113
CMCS (Commercial Metals Company), 1496–1497
CNG (Consolidated Natural Gas Company), 332–333
CNH Capital, 1335–1339
CNH Global, 1335–1339
Coach, Inc., 166, 1486–1487, 1498

The Coca-Cola Company, 20, 31, 76, 97, 151, 176, 203, 274, 404–405, 522, 559, 635, 650, 658, 670, 690, 750, 813, 822, 843n.17, 872, 897, 899, 940, 952, 979, 984, 997, 1024, 1107, 1173, 1184, 1248, 1402, 1412, 1478, 1546
"The Codification," 14, 22
Codification Research System (CRS), 14
Cohen, A. J., 911, 1486
Cohesiveness of reporting, 185–186
Collaterized receivables, 366n.11
Collection float, 376
Columbia Sportswear Company, 677
Combination methods for depreciation, 597
Comcast, 1497
Comiskey, Eugene E., 1215n.19, 1443
Commercial Metals Company (CMCS), 1496–1497
Commercial paper, 346n.1
Commercial substance, 550–554
Commitments, disclosure of, 1492
Committee for Improvements in Financial Reporting (CIFR), 1343
Committee on Accounting Procedure (CAP), 9, 27, 842n.15
Commodity-backed bonds, 765
Common costs, 1500–1501
Common-size analysis, 1527–1528
Common stock, 824, 836, 875. See also Preferred stock
 adjustment to net income for change related to, 1435
 cash dividend paid for, 838n.13
 increase in, 1426
 rate of return on, 849
 in treasury at cost, 831n.8
 as worksheet entry, 1449
Commonwealth Edison Company, 295, 813
Company names (intangible asset), 654
Comparability, 51, 57
Comparative analysis, 1526
Comparative balance sheets, 1416, 1421, 1424, 1445
Comparative financial statements, correcting errors on, 1362–1363
Compensated absences, 712–714
Compensating balances, 347
Compensation plans:
 dilutive securities issuance in, 904n.15
 effective, 891
 stock compensation plans, 891–892
Completed-contract accounting method, 1057, 1063–1064, 1067
Completeness, 49
Completion-of-production basis, 1068
Complex capital structure EPS, 904–912
 antidilution, 908–909
 contingent issue agreement, 908
 convertible securities—diluted EPS, 905–907
 options and warrants—diluted EPS, 907–908
 presentation and disclosure of, 909–910
 simple vs., 900
Components, 170
Component depreciation, 597n.6, 638–639, 1520

Composite depreciation rate, 596
Composite life, 596
Composite methods for depreciation, 595–597
Composite rate, 357
Compounded continuously, 293n.4
Compounded daily, 293
Compound instrument, 942
Compound interest, 290–293
  future value as variable in, 294
  on IRAs, 302–303
  number of time periods, 294
  present value as variable in, 294
  rate of interest as variable in, 294
  and Social Security, 291
  tables for, 291–293, 334–343
  variables fundamental to, 294
Comprehensive dollar-value LIFO method, 437–438
Comprehensive income, 182–186, 971–972
  defined, 53
  display requirements of, 183n.22
  errors in, 1360
  and IFRS, 205–206
  one-statement approach, 183
  two-statement approach, 183, 184
Computer Associates, 899
ConAgra Foods, Inc., 511, 848
Conceptual framework, 42–63
  basic assumptions, 54–56
  basic elements, 52–53
  basic principles, 56–61
  constraints, 61–63
  defined, 42
  development of, 43–44
  and IFRS, 78–80
  need for, 42–43
  objective of financial reporting, 45
  qualitative characteristics of information, 45–52
Condensed income statements, 166–167
Conditional expenses, 715
Confirmatory value, 47
Conglomerate (diversified) companies reporting, 1497–1501
ConocoPhillips, 32, 829, 830
Conservatism, 49n.8
Consigned goods, 422
Consignments, 1051–1053
Consignment shipment, 422
Consistency, 51, 57
Consolidated Edison, 539
Consolidated financial statements, 967
Consolidated Natural Gas Company (CNG), 332–333
Consolidated statements of cash flows, 1434
Consolidations, 1027, 1359
Constant-currency financial reports, 55
Constraints, 61–63
Construction contracts, 1110–1111
Continental Airlines, 215, 1307
Continental Trucking, 963
Contingencies, 757–758
  on balance sheets, 236, 237
  defined, 237
  disclosure of, 1492

errors in, 1360
  gain, 715–716
  loss, 716–725
  presentation of, 728–729
Contingent assets, 758
Contingent liabilities, 700–701, 754, 757.
    See also Loss contingencies
Contingent shares, 908
Continuing franchise fees, 1083
Continuously compounded, 293n.4
Contra accounts, and bonds payable, 774
Contracts, onerous, 757
Contract provisions, 757
Contract-related intangible assets, 655–656
Contractual situations, on balance sheets, 236, 237
Contra items, 241
Contributed capital, 875
Contributions, accounting for, 555–556
Contributory pension plans, 1184
Control device, 489
Controlling interest, 967
Convenience financial statements, 1523
Convergence, of U.S. and international standards, 21, 36–38, 414–415, 1346n.1, 1554
Conversion, involuntary, 561
Convertible bonds, 765, 884–886, 890, 919–920, 944–946
Convertible debt, 942–946
Convertible debt accounting, 884–886
Convertible preferred stock, 835, 886–887, 920
Convertible securities, 905–907
Coolidge, C., 1364
Coon, William R., 437n.7
Copel CIA, 776
Copyrights, 655
Cornett, C., 1134n.3
Corning, 911
Corporate bond listings, 765–766
Corporate capital, 824–834
Corporate form, 822–824
  capital stock/share system, 823–824
  and ownership interests, 824
  state laws, 822
Corporate taxes, 710n.6. *See also* Income taxes, accounting for
Corporations:
  bonds issued by, 763
  international accounting standards for, 31
Corrections of errors:
  in income statement, 180–181
  reporting, 1359–1366
Corridor amortization, 1199–1200, 1202, 1210–1211, 1223
Cost, 474, 527
Cost allocation, 429n.4, 590–601.
    See also Depreciation
Cost approach, for valuation, 549n.5
Cost-benefit analysis, 62
Cost-benefit relationship, 61
Cost constraint, 61–63
Cost flow assumption, 421
  average-cost method for, 429–430
  and first-in, first-out, 430–431

identification, 428–429
  and last-in, first-out, 431–432
Costs included in inventory, 421
  period costs, 426
  product costs, 426
  and treatment of purchase discounts, 426–428
Cost method, 489, 831, 961n.5
Costs of financing, 426
Cost of goods available for sales or use, 420
Cost of goods sold, 420, 1296
  multiple pools contributing to, 437n.7
  in periodic inventory system, 418
  section of income statement, 164
Cost-of-goods-sold method, 478–479, 528
Cost per unit of product, 606–607
Cost-recovery accounting method, 1077–1078, 1110–1112
Cost-to-cost basis, 1059–1061
Coughlan, J. D., 591n.1
Counterbalancing errors, 1367–1369
Counterparty, 981n.18
Countrywide Financial Corp., 371
Coupons, 721–722
Coupon bonds, 765
Coupon rate, 766
Coverage ratios, 245, 1523, 1524
CPC International, 358
Craig, Susanne, 959
Credits (Cr.), 85–86
Credit balance, 85
Credit cards, 367n.12
Credit crisis, 12, 588, 601
Creditors, 5–6, 232, 233
  disclosure of claims by, 1492
  short-term, 1522
Creditor calculations, 794
Credit quality, 768
Credit risk, disclosure of, 372
Credit risk rate of interest, 316
Creswell, J., 176, 657
Cron, William R., 441n.10
Cross-reference items, 241
CRS (Codification Research System), 14
Cummins, C., 607
Cumulative catch-up, 1061
Cumulative-effect approach, 1345
Cumulative preferred stock, 835
Current assets, 217–220
  on balance sheets, 217–220
  cash, 217–218
Current cash debt coverage, 234
"Current Expected Credit Loss" (CECL) model, 374
Current liability(-ies), 702–715. *See also specific types, e.g.:* Accounts payable(s)
  analysis of, 729–730
  on balance sheets, 222–223
  declared cash dividends as, 840
  defined, 702
  presentation of, 726–729
Current maturities of long-term debt, 705
Current operating performance approach, 168
Current ratios, 729–730
Current receivables, 349
Current tax expense (benefit), 1121, 1145

Curtailment, 1258
Cushing, Barry E., 443n.17
Customary form, of balance sheets, 226n.9
Customer-related intangible assets, 654–655
CVS, 1283
CVS/Caremark Corp., 846
Cycle, accounting, see Accounting cycle

D
Daily compounding, 293
Daimler, 666, 1482
DaimlerChrysler, 1439
Dairy Queen, 1081
Dakdduk, Kenneth E., 1220n.26
Darden Restaurants Inc., 1282
Date of declaration (stock dividends), 839
Date of payment (stock dividends), 839
Date of record (stock dividends), 839
Days outstanding, 374
Days to collect accounts receivable, 374
Debenture bonds, 765
Debits (Dr.), 85–86
Debit balance, 85
Debt(s), 762–763
  bad, failure to adjust for, 1369–1370
  continuation of, 792–796
  current maturities of, 705
  extinguishment of, 775–776
  issue cost (SFAS No. 6), 774n.5
  long-term, see Long-term debt
  settlement of, 791–792
Debt investments, 1028–1031
Debtor accounting, 792n.16
Debtor calculations, 793
Debt ratings, 768
Debt-rating triggers, 1493
Debt securities, 884
  available-for-sale, 218, 952, 955–959,
    962–964, 968
  convertible, 942–946
  held-to-maturity, 218, 953–955
  trading, 953, 959–960, 964, 1440
Debt to assets ratio, 787
Debt triggers, 1493
Decision-usefulness approach, 6–7, 45–46
Declaration, date of (stock dividends), 839
Declared cash dividends, 839–840
Declining-balance method, 595
Decreasing-charge methods for
  depreciation, 594–595
Deductible amounts, 1120
Deductible temporary differences,
  1127–1128, 1145
Deep-discount bonds, 765
Deere and Company, 505
Defaults, 1073–1075
Deferrals:
  adjusting entries for, 97–102
  defined, 97
  in reversing entries illustration, 124–125
Deferred annuities, 311–313
Deferred costs, amortization of, 1434–1435
Deferred income taxes, 1119–1126
  adjustment to net income for, 1435
  and changes in tax rate, 1130–1132
  Congressional acts affecting, 1131n.2
  on income statements, 1125–1126

in interperiod tax allocation (example),
  1149–1150, 1152–1153
Deferred payment, 1047
Deferred-payment contracts, 547–548
Deferred taxes, disclosure of, 1493
Deferred tax amount, 1119
Deferred tax assets (DTAs), 1116–1117,
  1119, 1123–1126, 1145
  asset recognition for, in company
    records, 1125
  non-recognition of, 1175–1177
  recognized as loss carryforwards, 1134n.4
  valuation allowance for, 1125–1126
Deferred tax benefits, 1124
Deferred tax consequences, 1145
Deferred tax expense (benefit), 1121, 1145,
  1149–1150, 1152–1153
Deferred tax liabilities, 1119–1122, 1145
  in company assessments, 1122
  Congressional acts affecting, 1131n.2
  and SFAS No. 6, 1122
  and SFAS No. 109, 1122
Defined-benefit plans, 1185–1186
Defined-contribution plans, 1185
DeFord, Mark L., 1360n.7
Delhaize Group, 280
Dell Computer, 52, 215, 977–978, 1276
Delta Airlines, 58, 102, 215, 979, 1138, 1268,
  1273–1278, 1435
De Mesa Graziano, Cheryl, 1041
Denny's, 1081
Depletion, 604–607
  acquisition costs of, 605
  defined, 590
  development costs of, 605
  exploration costs of, 605
  and liquidating dividends, 607–608
  in oil and gas industry, 608–609
  and recoverable reserves, 607
  restoration costs of, 605–606
Depletion base, 604–606
Deposits:
  legally restricted, 348
  in transit, 379
Deposit method, 1078–1079
Depositor errors, reconciling, 379
Depreciable assets, revaluation of, 642
Depreciable base, for assets, 590
Depreciable tax life (recovery periods), 614
Depreciation, 590–601, 637, 638
  activity method for, 593
  adjusting entries for, 100–101
  and asset vs. liability accounting, 1278
  changes in method of, 1358
  decreasing-charge methods for,
    594–595, 611
  defined, 590
  factors involved in process of, 590
  failure to record, 1369
  group and composite methods for,
    595–597
  hybrid or combination methods for, 597
  issues in airline industry, 591n.2
  under partial periods, 598–599
  post-September 11, 2001 measures,
    614n.15
  rate revision for, 600

and replacement of fixed assets, 599
  straight-line method for, 593–594
  tax methods for, 614–617
Depreciation expense, 1422, 1425,
  1434–1435
Depreciation policies, 55
Derivatives, 977–995
  basic accounting principles for, 980–984
  cash flow hedge, 987–989
  characteristics of, 983
  defined, 977–978
  disclosures for, 991
  embedded, 989
  and fair hedge value, 984–987
  hedging, 984–989
Designated market value, 476
Detachable stock warrant, 888, 890
Development costs, 605, 694, 1520
Devon Energy Corporation, 238–239
Dieter, Richard, 1302n.15
Differential disclosure, 1489–1490,
  1549–1550
Diluted earnings per share, 904–908
  convertible securities, 905–907
  factors in, 906–907
  illustration of, 918–921
  options and warrants, 907–908
  reconciliation for basic and, 910
Dilutive securities, 884–892, 904, 941–947
Diners Club, 366
Dingell, John, 29
Direct costs, incremental vs. internal,
  1298–1299
Direct effects (accounting changes), 1405
Direct-financing leases, 1286–1289,
  1337–1339
  initial direct costs in, 1299
  sales-type vs., 1296
Direct method:
  for accounts receivable (net), 1439
  for determining net cash flow from
    operating activities, 1427–1433
  indirect vs., 1427–1428, 1433–1434
  special rules applying to, 1433–1434
Direct verification, 51
Direct write-off method, 353
Disclaimer of an opinion, 1511
Disclosure(s), 372n.15
  of change in accounting estimate,
    1358–1359
  for derivatives, 991
  of fair value, 999–1003
  in financial statements, 1067
  of franchisors, 1084
  full disclosure principle, 60–61. See also
    Full disclosure in financial reporting
  of interest rates, 289n.2
  for investment securities, 964
  of lease data, 1300–1302
  of LIFO inventory liquidations, 442n.13
  of operating activities, 1434
  as present value-based measurement,
    289
  quality and quantity of, 1490
  of restrictions on retained earnings,
    846–847
  and Sarbanes-Oxley Act of 2002, 726

and *Statement of Position* 94-6, 278
  techniques of, 239–243
Discontinued operations, 164, 170–173,
  921*n*.21
Discounts:
  cash, 351–352
  sales with, 1046–1047
  volume, 1046
Discount bonds, 766, 767, 774, 782*n*.13, 816
Discounting, 296–297
Discount notes, 779
Discount rate:
  leases, 1334
  postretirement benefit obligations,
  1221*n*.27
Discover, 366
Discrete approach, 1503, 1507, 1552, 1553
Distributions to owners, 53
Diversified (conglomerate) companies
  reporting, 1497–1501
Dividends. *See also* Stock dividends
  cash, 839–840, 1440
  date determining receipt of, 839*n*.14
  and economic recovery, 846
  liquidating, 839–840
  number of companies paying, 846
  property, 840
  types of, 838–843
Dividend in arrears, 835
Dividends payable, 707
Dividend policy, 837–847
Dividend preferences, 852–853
Dollar-value LIFO method, 435–440, 489,
  498–500
  and AICPA Task Force on LIFO
   Inventory Problems, 479*n*.3
  comprehensive, 437–438
  for determining cost of single item,
   478*n*.1
  example, 436
  and price index selection, 438–440
  specific-goods pooled approach vs.,
   435–440
Dollar-value retail method, 436*n*.5
Double-declining-balance method, 595
"Double dipping," 1272
Double-entry accounting system, 86, 154
Double-extension method, 439
Dow Chemical, 821
Dow Jones & Co., 836
Dr. (debits), 85–86
Dr. Pepper, 488
Dresser Industries, 203–204
Drugs.com, 654
Drugstore.com, 50, 427–428, 965
DTAs, *see* Deferred tax assets
Dudley, Lola W., 899*n*.12
Due process system, 11–12
Duffy, Wendy A., 543*n*.3
DuPont, 840
Durham, Timothy S., 822
Dynegy, 785

E
E. F. Hutton, 348*n*.3
Eagle Clothes, Inc., 422
Eaglesham, J., 1117

Earned capital, 824, 875
Earned revenues, 1043
Earnings:
  claim by stockholders, 824
  retained, *see* Retained earnings
  smooth, and changes in accounting
   method, 1365–1366
Earnings before interest, taxes,
  depreciation, and amortization
  (EBITDA), 592
Earnings management, 161
Earnings per common share, 177–179
Earnings per share (EPS), 177–179, 899
  for complex capital structure, 904–912
  computations, 899–912
  diluted, 904–908
  illustration of, 916–921
  on income statement, 164, 165*n*.7
  interim reporting of, 1505
  International Financial Reporting
   Standards for, 941–947
  for simple capital structure, 900–904
Eastman Kodak Company, 68, 170*n*.12, 358,
  1138, 1489
Eavis, P., 228, 984
eBay, 999
Ebbers, Bernie, 28
EBITDA (earnings before interest, taxes,
  depreciation, and amortization), 592
Ecolab, 236
Economic consequences, 17, 17*n*.9, 591,
  842*n*.15
Economic crime, 82–83
Economic entity assumption, 54, 79
Economic life, 1290*n*.12
Economic life test (75% test), 1276,
  1333–1334
Economic Recovery Act, 1134*n*.3
Economic Recovery Tax Act of 1981, 614
EDGAR (electronic data gathering and
  retrieval), 1516
Effective-interest method, 361, 778, 779
  and accruing interest, 773
  asset vs. liability accounting with, 1278
  of bond amortization, 314–315
  for bonds, 770–774
  for bonds issued at discount, 771–772
  for bonds issued at premium, 772–773
  and IFRS, 815–818
Effective interest rate, 359*n*.9
Effective yield, 359*n*.9, 767
Efficiency ratios, 1523*n*.26
Efficient-market hypothesis, 1525
EITF (Emerging Issues Task Force),
  12–13, 176
Elective straight-line method, 616–617
Electronic data gathering and retrieval
  (EDGAR), 1516
Electronic dissemination of financial
  reports, 1516
Eli Lilly, 658*n*.4
Elliott, J., 170*n*.12
Elmer's Restaurants, 1319–1320
El Paso Corporation, 607
Elstrom, P., 428
Ely, Michael, 1437*n*.8
Embedded derivatives, 989

Emerging Issues Task Force (EITF),
  12–13, 176
Emerging market IPOs, 820–821
Employees, as pension beneficiaries,
  1185–1186
Employee discounts, 493
Employee payroll deductions, 712
Employee-related liabilities, 710–715
Employee Retirement Income Security Act
  (ERISA) (1974), 1211–1212
Employee stock purchase plans (ESPPs),
  896, 946
Employer(s):
  payroll taxes paid by, 712
  and pension plan risks, 1185–1186
Employer-sponsored defined contribution
  pension plans, 1186*n*.4
Enacted tax rate, 1130
Ending inventory, misstated, 424
Enhancing qualitative characteristics,
  50–52
Enron Corp., 5, 9, 17, 43, 48, 215, 364, 726,
  776, 783–785, 829, 959, 979*n*.14, 996,
  1488, 1493, 1493*n*.4, 1518
Entity:
  economic entity assumption, 54, 79
  as going concern, 1509
  in reporting, 1359
Entity perspective, 6
Entries:
  adjusting, *see* Adjustments
  reversing, *see* Reversing entries
Environmental liabilities, 289, 722–726
EPBO (expected postretirement benefit
  obligation), 1220
Epictetus, 706
EPS, *see* Earnings per share
Equipment:
  depreciation of, 1422
  loss on sale of, 1425
  purchase of, 1426
  as worksheet entry, 1448
Equipment lease-versus buy analysis,
  1513*n*.15
Equity:
  on balance sheets, 216
  defined, 53, 79
  IFRS for, 875
  owner's, 225–226
  presentation of, 877–878
  statement of changes in, 877–878
  on statement of financial position,
   280–281
Equity awards, share-based, 914
Equity classifications (securities), 884
Equity errors, 1360
Equity holders' claims, disclosure of, 1492
Equity interest, 791–792
Equity investments, 1031–1035
Equity investors, 5–6
Equity method, 965–967, 1377–1380, 1435
  changing from, 1377–1378
  changing to, 1378–1380
  and fair value options, 967–968
  and retrospective application, 1359*n*.6
Equity securities, 960–967
Erickson, Naomi, 1218*n*.24

ERISA (Employee Retirement Income Security Act of 1974), 1211–1212

Ernst and Young, 821

Error, information items free from, 49–50

Errors, accounting, 1366–1374
  on balance sheet and income statement, 1366–1370
  correction of, 180–181, 1359–1366, 1519
  counterbalancing, 1367–1369
  example of, 1361–1363, 1370–1373
  fraud vs., 1494
  noncounterbalancing, 1369–1370
  preparation of financial statements with corrections to, 1373–1374
  reporting correction of, 1359–1364
  types of, 1360

ESPPs (employee stock purchase plans), 896, 946

Estée Lauder, 836

Estimates:
  changes in, see Change(s) in accounting estimate
  judgments and, 215

Estimated annual effective tax rate, 1505

E-tailers, 427–428

Ethics, 21

eToys.com, 427

E*Trade Financial, 691

Euronext, 820

European Union, 950

Event, defined, 84

Exchange for noncash consideration, 962n.6

Exchanges–gain situation, 552–554

Exchanges–loss situation, 551–552

Exchange price, 351

Exchange rate risk, 984

Excise tax, 1214

Ex-dividend date, 839n.14

Executory contract, lease as, 1273

Executory costs, 1277, 1334

Exercise price, 980

Expectations gap, 18, 1519n.24

Expected cash flow approach, 315–317

Expected inflation rate of interest, 316

Expected postretirement benefit obligation (EPBO), 1220

Expected rate of return, 1197, 1201

Expected reversal date, 1140

Expense(s):
  classification of, 206–208
  conditional, 715
  defined, 53, 79
  on financial statements, 163
  on income statement, 164
  pension, 1189–1192
  postretirement, 1221
  prepaid, see Prepaid expenses

Expense expenditures, 557

Expense recognition errors, 1360

Expense recognition principle, 58–60

Expenses subject to year-end-adjustment, 1504–1505

Expense warranty approach, 719–720

Exploration costs of depletion, 605

eXtensible Business Reporting Language (XBLR), 19, 1516

External environment, fraud and, 1518

External events, 84, 90–91

External indexes, 438n.8, 440n.9

Extinguishment of debt, 775–776

Extractive industries, R&D costs of, 667n.12

Extraordinary items:
  adjustment to net income for, 1437
  determining, 174n.15
  frequency of, 174n.14
  on income statement, 164, 173–176
  interim reporting of, 1505
  net-of-tax treatment for, 175n.17
  reporting, after September 11, 2001, 175–176

Extraordinary losses, 175

ExxonMobil Company, 32, 90, 349, 416, 605, 607, 608n.10, 768, 821, 830, 979, 984, 1270

Eziba.com, 966

F

Facebook, 5, 836, 911

Face rate (interest), 293

Face value (bonds), 766

Factors, 366–367

Factoring arrangement, 367n.12

Factoring receivables, 366–367

FAF (Financial Accounting Foundation), 10

Failure to adjust for bad debts, 1369–1370

Failure to record accrued wages, 1368

Failure to record prepaid expenses, 1368

Faircloth, Lauch, 29

Fair hedge value, 984–987

Fair presentation, 281

Fair value(s), 56–58, 78, 79, 409, 411
  of asset, 555
  of asset given up, 552
  of asset received, 552
  on balance sheets, 236, 238–239
  debt investments held at, 1029–1031
  of derivatives, 980n.16
  disclosure of, 999–1003
  equity investments at, 1032–1035
  and GAAP/IFRS, 78–79, 1026–1027
  hierarchy of, 57, 238, 980n.16, 1000
  of liabilities, 788
  and long-term liabilities, 782–783
  and monetary exchanges, 553n.9
  of security, 953, 959, 969, 974–975
  of stock in lump-sum exchange, 826–827
  of stock issued, 841
  of stock options, 892

Fair value accounting, economic consequences and, 17

Fair Value Adjustment account, 957

Fair value controversy, 969

Fair value hedge, 992–993

Fair value hierarchy, 57, 238, 980n.16, 1000

Fair value information, disclosure of, 19

Fair value less costs to sell, 639

Fair value method:
  changing from, 1378
  changing from equity method to, 1377–1378
  of stock compensation, 892, 897–899
  for unrealized gains/losses, 1425n.5

Fair value options, 57, 967–968

Fair value principle, 56–57

Fair-value tests:
  for indefinite-life intangible impairment, 662–663
  for limited-life intangible impairment, 662

Faithful representation, 48–50

Falconbridge Ltd. Nickel Mines, 601

Family Dollar Stores Inc., 846

Fannie Mae, 32, 899, 979n.14

FASAC (Financial Accounting Standards Advisory Council), 11

FASB, see Financial Accounting Standards Board

FASB Codification Research System (CRS), 14

FASB Concepts, see Statements of Financial Accounting Concepts

FASB Statements, see Statements of Financial Accounting Standards

Federal Insurance Contribution Act (F.I.C.A.), 710–711

Federal Reserve Bank, 316

Federal Unemployment Tax Act (F.U.T.A.), 711

Federated Department Stores, 1419

FedEx Corporation, 68

Feedback value, 1522

FFO (funds from operations), 597n.7

Fiat, 31

F.I.C.A. (Federal Insurance Contribution Act), 710–711

FIFO, see First-in, first-out

Final reconciling entry, 1451

Finance leases, 1332

Financial accounting, as discipline, 4

Financial Accounting Foundation (FAF), 10

Financial Accounting Standards Advisory Council (FASAC), 11

Financial Accounting Standards Board (FASB), 10–13
  on accounting changes, 1344
  Accounting Standards Codification, 14, 22
  Accounting Standards Updates of, 11
  allowance method, 353–354
  APB vs., 10–12
  on basis for statement of cash flows, 1413n.1
  and capitalization of interest costs, 426
  and cash and cash equivalents, 228n.10
  Codification Research System, 14
  Concepts of, 13. See also Statements of Financial Accounting Concepts
  conceptual framework, 42, 78–80
  convergence, 1554
  and cost constraint, 61, 62
  on differential disclosure, 1489–1490
  on direct method on statement of cash flows, 1420
  disclosure of receivables, 372
  disclosure requirements, 1550n.29
  disclosures effectiveness project of, 1490
  due process system of, 11–12
  and fair value, 17, 56–58, 788, 969
  and financial engineering, 785n.14
  on financial instruments, 975–976
  financial statement presentation, 159, 179, 281–282, 411

and financial statements, 215–216
and GAAP, 10–13, 1490
and goodwill measurement, 660*n*.6
and guarantees, 729*n*.21
and held-to-maturity requirement,
    953*n*.2
and IFRS, 31
improved financial statement
    presentation, 1517
and investments, 950–951, 1037
and irregular items, 168
and key elements of financial
    statements, 153
and lease accounting, 1274*n*.2, 1283,
    1303–1304, 1331–1332, 1339
on leased property, 1278
and liabilities, 818
on loan loss allowances, 374
and loss contingencies, 716
on offsetting, 243
on operating cash receipts/payments,
    1433–1434
on pension plans, 1190–1191, 1205*n*.14
on postretirement benefits accounting,
    1217, 1221*n*.27, 1225, 1227, 1263
Proposed Standards Updates, 55*n*.15,
    58*n*.17, 790*n*.15
and qualitative characteristics of
    accounting information, 45–46
and revenue recognition, 1042
and sales, 369–370
and SEC, 7, 8*n*.4
and securities, 884*n*.1
Standards of. *See also Statements of
    Financial Accounting Standards*
and statement of cash flows, 1482
and technical accounting issues, 1519
and transactions, 90–91
on uncertain tax positions, 1143
Financial assets, IFRS and, 1027–1028
Financial components approach, 368
Financial crisis, 370*n*.14, 1189
Financial engineering, 785*n*.14
Financial Executives Institute, 39
Financial flexibility, 214, 229, 234
Financial forecasts, 1513–1516
Financial fraud, 1372–1373
Financial income, 1118, 1127–1130
Financial information, types of, 1488
Financial instruments, 238, 884*n*.1, 975–976.
    See also specific instruments
Financial liquidity, 234
Financial markets, 31
Financial position, statement of, 877.
    See also Balance sheet(s)
Financial projections, 1513–1516
Financial reporting, 4. *See also* Reporting
    accuracy of, 2
    ethics in, 21
    and expectations gap, 18
    full disclosure in, 1487–1520
    general-purpose, 45
    of international accounting
        standards, 20
    objective of, 5–7, 45
    and politically-influenced standard
        setting, 16–17

Financial statement(s), 4. *See also specific
    types of statements*
    and change, 158–159
    correcting errors on, 1361–1363
    elements of, 162–163
    with error corrections, 1373–1374
    example of, 247–252
    general-purpose, 7
    installment-sales transactions
        presentation, 1075–1077
    interest rate swap presentation, 994–995
    in interperiod tax allocation (example),
        1150–1151, 1153–1154
    inventory accounting for, 478*n*.2
    maintaining monthly vs. quarterly, 117
    management's responsibilities for,
        1512–1513
    for merchandising company, 114–117
    notes to, *see* Notes to the financial
        statements
    and ownership structure, 88–89
    pension plan reporting in, *see* Pension
        plan reporting
    percentage-of-completion presentation,
        1061–1063
    preparing, 108–110, 1373–1374
    presenting, 958–959
    timeliness of, 19
    worksheet preparation of, 130
Financial statement analysis, 1522–1528
    comparative analysis, 1526
    percentage analysis, 1527–1528
    perspective on, 1522–1523
    ratio analysis, 1523–1525
Financing activities, 229, 231, 1412, 1414
    extraordinary items, 1437
    on statement of cash flows,
        1480, 1481–1482
Financing agreement, 706
Finished goods inventory, 416
Firm (as concept), 484*n*.8
"Firm" contractual rights and
    obligations, 1274
Firm purchase commitments, 484*n*.8
First Chicago, 1307
First-in, first-out (FIFO), 51
    accounting for, 474
    for assigning investment costs, 962*n*.6
    and cost flow assumption, 430–431
    and LIFO, 432–433
Fisher, D., 1411
Fixed assets, 538, 599
Fixed percentage of book value method
    (declining balance), 595
Fixed-rate mortgage, 782
Fleming, Sir Alexander, 656*n*.4
Flexibility, financial, 214, 229, 234
Float, collection, 376
Floating-rate mortgage, 782
Floor (lower), 475–476
f.o.b. (free on board) destination, 421
Footstar, 176
Ford, 891, 1271
Ford Motor Company, 4, 18, 51, 54, 160,
    236, 239–240, 366, 416, 450, 600*n*.8,
    714, 715, 821, 822, 836, 891, 1219, 1284,
    1344, 1439

Ford Motor Credit, 366, 1271
Foreign companies, SOX compliance
    by, 154
Foreign Corrupt Practices Act, 82
Foreign currency hedging, 984*n*.23
Form 10-Q, 1501, 1502
Fortune Brands, Inc., 495
Foster, Taylor W., III, 842*n*.16, 845*n*.18
401(k) plan, 1185
Forward-looking information, 19
Fox (network), 656
Fox, J., 1140
*Framework for the Preparation and
    Presentation of Financial Statements*, 34
Franchise(s), 655–656, 1081–1084
Franchise agreement, 1082
Franchise fees, continuing, 1083
Franchisor's cost, 1084
Fraud, check, 378*n*.17
Fraudulent financial reporting, 1517–1520
    accounting errors vs., 1494
    causes of, 1518–1519
    National Commission on, 1494*n*.6
Free cash flow, 234–235, 245
Free on board (f.o.b.) destination, 421
Freight costs, 493
Frequent-flyer programs, 722
Frito Lay, 45
Fruehauf, 1488
Fujitsu Limited, 588
Full-cost concept, 608
Full-costing approach, 540
Full disclosure in financial reporting,
    1487–1520
    of auditor's reports, 1508–1511
    criteria for accounting/reporting choices
        in, 1520
    current reporting issues with, 1513–1520
    and differential disclosure, 1489–1490
    of diversified companies, 1497–1501
    on financial forecasts/projections,
        1513–1516
    and fraudulent reporting, 1517–1520
    increase in reporting requirements, 1489
    of interim reports, 1501–1508
    on Internet, 1516–1517
    issues with, 1493–1508
    of management's reports, 1511–1513
    and notes to financial statements,
        1491–1493
    of post-balance-sheet events, 1495–1496
    as principle, 1488–1489
    of special transactions/events, 1493–1495
    and stock markets, 1511
Full disclosure principle, 60–61
Functional expense classification, 164
Function-of-expense method, 207
Fund (term), 1184*n*.1
Fundamental qualities, 46–50
Funds from operations (FFO), 597*n*.7
Fuqua Industries, 441
F.U.T.A. (Federal Unemployment
    Tax Act), 711
Future deductible amounts, 1123–1126
Future tax consequences, 1144
Future tax rates, 1130–1132
Future tax savings, 1134

Future value:
  of annuity due, 303–306
  of an ordinary annuity of 1 (table), 291
  computing for unknown, 294
  of deferred annuity, 311–312
  of 1 (table), 291, 292
  of ordinary annuity, 300–302, 304–306
  of single sum, 295–296
  as variable in compound interest, 294

G
GAAP, *see* Generally accepted accounting principles
Gains:
  adjustment to net income for, 1435–1436
  defined, 53
  from discontinued operations, 172–173
  on financial statements, 163
  on income statements, 164
  on pension plans, 1197–1202, 1260
  and postretirement expense, 1221, 1223
  smoothing unexpected, 1260
Gain contingencies, 715–716
Gains trading, 969
The Gap, Inc., 493, 506, 650, 709, 1270
Gap fillers, 658
GASB (Governmental Accounting Standards Board), 1227
Gates, Bill, 895n.10
Gateway, 1489
GE, *see* General Electric
Genentech, 649
General checking account, 377
General Electric (GE), 32, 48, 68, 160, 170, 349, 358, 670, 707, 765, 766, 821, 822, 897, 899, 979, 984, 1140, 1217, 1219, 1248, 1497
General Electric Capital Corp., 707
General Electric Credit, 1307
General expenses, 164
General Foods, 1504
General indexes, 438n.8
General journal entry, 91–92
General ledger, 85, 91–92
Generally accepted accounting principles (GAAP), 7, 13–16
  accounting changes and error analysis, 1404–1406
  and actual interest capitalization, 542
  balance sheet and statement of cash flows, 277–278
  "big GAAP versus little GAAP" issue, 1490, 1550n.29
  codification of, 22
  comparability of changes, 51n.9
  conceptual framework, 78–79
  convergence of IFRS and, 156, 1554
  depreciation, 637, 638
  development costs, 1520
  disclosure requirements, 1548–1549, 1550n.29
  earnings per share disclosures, 910n.20
  and fair value, 56–58, 989n.32
  hierarchy, 14n.6
  and historical cost, 56

  and IFRS, 31, 205–206, 243, 278, 408–409, 525, 693–694, 700, 753–754, 815, 874–875, 942, 1026–1027, 1109–1110, 1175, 1250–1251, 1346n.1, 1404–1405, 1480–1481, 1549
  income statements, 205–206
  income tax reporting, 1175
  intangible assets and impairments, 693–694
  inventory accounting, 525
  investments, 1026–1037
  lease accounting, 1331–1332, 1337, 1339
  liabilities, 753–754
  major sources of, 13
  for offsetting, 243
  and OPEBs, 1189n.8
  organizations settings standards for, 7–13
  pensions and postretirement benefits, 1250–1251
  receivables, 408–409
  recovery of impairment loss, 410
  and Regulation G, 61
  and revaluation equity, 281
  revenue recognition, 1042, 1109–1110
  share-based compensation, 892
  share issuances accounting, 875
  statement of cash flows, 1480–1481
  stock-based compensation plans, 910n.20
  stockholders' equity, 874–875
  straight-line method, 815
  transaction analysis under, 153
  using judgment in applying, 14
  and variable interest entities, 996–999
General Mills, Inc., 107, 388
General Motors (GM), 32, 49, 51, 54, 539, 600n.8, 817, 840, 899, 911, 1184, 1219, 1439
General-purpose financial reporting, 45
General-purpose financial statements, 5
General Tire and Rubber, 443n.14
Georgia-Pacific, 214, 484, 561
Gerth, J., 607
GHGs (greenhouse gases), 730–731
Gibson, Richard, 1282
Gift cards, 1045
Gilbert, D., 1419
GlaxoSmithKline plc, 666
Glencore International, 32
Global Crossing, 48, 555
Global tax rates, 1131–1132
GM, *see* General Motors
Going concern assumption, 55
Going concern concept, 1509
Goldman Sachs, 5, 1486
Golf Digest, 708
Goods in transit, 421–422
Goodwill, 658–661
  impairment of, 663–665, 696–697
  recording, 659–661
  as write-off, 661
Goodyear Tire and Rubber, 590, 776, 1138
Google, 52, 117, 650, 670, 822, 836, 977–978, 1140
Gore, Richard, 597n.7
Gotham Utility Company, 713
Governmental Accounting Standards Board (GASB), 1227
Government debt, 762–763

Government grant approach, 731
Granof, Michael H., 443n.15, 445n.20
Grant date, 893
The Great Atlantic & Pacific Tea Company, 224–225
Greenberg, Herb, 76, 592
Greenhouse gases (GHGs), 730–731
Gross approach, 1251
Gross margin percentage, 486n.11
Gross method of revenue recognition, 1051
Gross profit method (gross margin method), 485–488
Gross profit on selling price, 486–487
Gross profit percentage, 486–487
Group methods for depreciation, 595–597
Groupon, 5, 158, 159, 836, 911
Guarantees, 719–721, 729n.21. *See also* Warranties
Guaranteed residual value, 1277, 1338
  in capitalization of lease, 1303
  in lessee accounting, 1291–1293
  in lessor accounting, 1294–1295
  for sales-type lease, 1297
Guerra, F., 1117
Gujarathi, Mahendra R., 484n.8

H
H. J. Heinz Company, 1542
Half-year convention, 599, 615
Hall, Ben, 17
Halliburton Company, 223, 1067–1068, 1348
Halperin, Alex, 836
Hanna, D., 170n.12
Harley-Davidson, Inc., 1494
Hasbro, Inc., 220, 1254–1255
Hayes, Randall, 437n.7, 441n.10
Healthcare benefits, 1217n.20, 1218–1219
Hedging, 979, 984–989
Held-for-collection classification, 1028
Held-to-maturity debt securities, 218, 953–955
Henry, David, 844
The Hershey Company, 5, 6, 444
Hershey Foods, 204, 825
Hertz, 1081
Herz, Bob, 21, 364
Hewitt, Conrad W., 3
Hewlett-Packard Company (HP), 372, 481n.4, 670, 1184, 1287n.11, 1301–1302, 1359, 1412
Hickok, Richard S., 1058n.17
Hierarchy, 35
Historical cost, 56, 57, 78, 214, 638
Holiday Inn, 1081
The Home Depot, 54, 539, 1276, 1283, 1412, 1513
Homestake Mining Company, 1173
Homestore Inc., 1040
Honda, 51
Honeywell Inc., 830, 911
Honeywell International, 1202
Hoogervorst, Hans, 1304, 1554
Horizontal percentage analysis, 1527
Horngren, C., 42n.2
Host security, 989
HP, *see* Hewlett-Packard Company
H & R Block, 1081

HTC, 657
Hudson, M., 371
Huffy Corp., 790
Hurricanes, 1496n.8
Hybrid methods for depreciation, 597
Hybrid plans, 1214n.18
Hybrid securities, 989
Hypo Real Estate, 588

I

IAASB (International Auditing and
    Assurance Standards Board), 156
IASs, *see International Accounting Standards*
IASB, *see International Accounting
    Standards Board*
IASCF (International Accounting Standards
    Committee Foundation), 33
IBM Corporation, 4, 5, 20, 48, 160, 216, 245,
    256, 416, 424, 670, 821, 1119n.1, 1217,
    1271, 1285, 1315, 1489
IBM Global Financing, 1271
IDEA (Interactive Data Electronic
    Applications), 1516
If-converted method, 905–906, 918–919
IFRIC (International Financial Reporting
    Interpretations Committee), 34–35
IFRIC No. 14, 1257n.33
IFRS, *see International Financial Reporting
    Standards*
IGo Corp., 1040
Ijiri, Yuji, 484n.8
ILFC (International Lease Finance Corp.),
    1271, 1273–1278
Illegal acts, 1494–1495
Imhoff, Eugene A., Jr., 1525n.28
Impaired note receivable, 364
Impairments, 601–604
    GAAP/IFRS standards, 602, 603
    of goodwill, 696–697
    and IFRS, 638–640, 1035–1036
    of indefinite-life intangibles, 696
    of intangible assets, 695–696
    International Financial Reporting
        Standards for, 693–699
    of limited-life tangibles, 695
    measuring, 382–383, 602–603
    of receivables, 381–383
    recognizing, 381–382, 601–602
    recoverability tests for, 602, 662
    and restructuring, 792n.17
    reversal of, 1519
    risk of, 665
    of value, 969–970
Impairment evaluation process, 409–410
Impairment loss, 382–383, 410, 603, 695–696
    recovery of, 1036
    reversal of, 640–641
Impairment test, 652
Implicit interest rate, 360–361, 1277–1278
Implicit rate, 1332, 1334, 1335
Impracticability, 1356, 1406
Imprest bank accounts, 377–378
Imprest system for petty cash, 377–378
Improvements, 558–559
Imputation, 363, 780
Imputed interest rate, 363, 780
Inadequacy, 591

Incentives, monitoring, 1419
Income, defined, 79
Income approach, 549n.5
Income available to common
    stockholders, 904
Income before taxes, *see* Pretax financial
    income
Income bonds, 765
Income statement(s), 85, 160–168
    and accounting principle changes,
        179–180
    alternate terminology for, 160n.1
    and cash flows statement, 1416–1417,
        1421, 1424, 1429
    and changes in estimates, 180
    columns on, 129
    and comprehensive income, 182–186
    condensed, 166–167
    and corrections of errors, 180–181
    deferred tax reporting on, 1126–1127,
        1141–1143
    and discontinued operations, 170–173
    and earnings per share, 177–179
    errors on, 1367–1370
    example, 115
    and extraordinary items, 173–176
    and extraordinary losses, 175
    format of, 162–168
    illustration of, 1446
    intermediate components of, 164–166
    irregular items reported on, 168–179
    limitations of, 160–161
    and quality of earnings, 161–162
    and retained earnings statement, 181–182
    segmented, 1498
    single-step, 167–168
    and unusual gains and losses, 169–170
Income statement (percentage-of-sales)
    approach, 356
Income statement method,
    see Direct method
Income tax(es):
    deferred, adjustment to net income
        for, 1435
    defined, 1145
    as operating cash outflows, 1437
    payable, in interperiod tax allocation
        (example), 1147–1154
    on statement of cash flows, 1481–1482
Income taxes, accounting for, 1116–1145,
    1434n.6
    accounting objectives, 1122–1123
    asset-liability method, 1144
    on balance sheet, 1138–1140
    deferred taxes, 1119–1126, 1145
    depreciation, 614–617
    differences between pretax and taxable
        income, 1127–1130
    and future deductible amounts,
        1123–1126
    and future taxable amounts, 1119–1123
    on income statement, 164, 1126–1127,
        1141–1143
    interim reporting, 1505
    interperiod tax allocation (example),
        1147–1154
    intraperiod tax allocation, 171–172

LIFO, 441n.11
    and net operating losses, 1132–1138
    tax rate considerations in, 1130–1132
    and uncertain tax positions, 1143–1144
    and withholding, 711–712
Income tax benefit, 1145
Income taxes currently payable, 1145
Income tax expense, 1145
Income taxes payable, 709–710
Income taxes refundable, 1145
Incorporation acts, 822
Increasing-charge method,
    of depreciation, 597
Incremental borrowing rate, 1277, 1279n.6
Incremental direct costs, 1298–1299
Incremental method, 827, 889–890, 919–920
Indefinite-life intangibles, 652, 662–663, 696
Independent lessors, 1271
Independent third-party trustee, 1185
Indexes, computing, 438
Indirect effects (accounting changes),
    1405–1406
Indirect method:
    for accounts receivable (net), 1438
    for determining net cash flow from
        operating activities, 1418–1419, 1428
    direct vs., 1433–1434
    special rules applying to, 1433–1434
Indirect verification, 51
Induced conversions, 885–886
Indy Mac Bank, 9
Inflation, monetary unit assumption
    and, 55
Inflows, cash, 1444
Information, financial, 1488
Information overload, 1488
Information technology, international
    accounting standards for, 31
ING Group, 32
Initial direct costs (lessor accounting), 1299
Initial franchise fee, 1082–1083
Initial operating-losses, 669
Inland Steel, 593
In-process research and development
    (IPR&D), 693–694
Input:
    in depreciation, 593
    measures of, 1058
Installment-sales accounting method,
    1068–1077
Instruments, financial, *see* Financial
    instruments
In-substance defeasance, 775n.7
Insurance, adjusting entries for, 99–100
Intangible assets, 648–653, 670–672.
    See also specific types, e.g.: Limited-life
        intangibles
    amortization of, 651–653
    on balance sheets, 222
    characteristics of, 650
    defined, 650
    impairment of, 652, 662–664, 694
    International Financial Reporting
        Standards for, 693–697
    presentation of, 670–672
    recognition of, 673
    valuation of, 650–651

Integral approach, 1503, 1507, 1552
Integrated reports, 649
Intel, 31, 59, 102, 215, 256, 289, 480, 560, 670, 821, 997
Interactive Data Electronic Applications (IDEA), 1516
Interbrand Corp., 670
Interest. *See also* Compound interest
  accruing with effective-interest method, 773
  capitalization of, 426n.3, 543–544
  components of, 316
  computation of, 289–293
  costs of, 426
  as pension expense, 1191
  as period cost, 426
  as postretirement expense, 1220–1221
  residual, 875
  and time value concepts, 289–293
  variables in computation of, 289
Interest-bearing notes, 359, 361–363, 703–704, 778–779
Interest costs, incurred during construction, 638
Interest rate(s), 543–544
  in capitalization of lease, 1303
  choosing, 316, 363
  computation of, 310
  disclosure requirement, 289n.2
  implicit, 360–361
  imputed, 363
  as variable in interest computation, 289
Interest rate risk, 984
Interest rate swap, 994–995
Interest revenue, 352, 546–547
Interest tables, 291–293
Interim period tax, 1505
Interim reports, 1501–1508
  continuing controversy about, 1507–1508
  and IFRS, 1549, 1552–1554
  requirements for, 1503–1504, 1552–1554
  unique problems of, 1503–1508
Internal controls, 18, 154, 376
Internal direct costs, 1299
Internal environment, fraud and, 1518
Internal events, 91
Internal indexes, 438n.8
Internally created goodwill, 659
Internally created intangibles, 650–651, 673
Internal Revenue Code, 1118–1119, 1145
Internal Revenue Service (IRS):
  and indexes, 440n.9
  and LIFO conformity rule, 444
  and purchases-only-approach, 501n.16
International accounting convergence, *see* Convergence, of U.S. and international standards
International Accounting Standards (IASs), 20, 34
  No. 1 ("Presentation of Financial Statements"), 408, 753, 874, 1404, 1554
  No. 2 ("Inventories"), 525, 1519
  No. 7 ("Cash Flow Statements"), 1480, 1481
  No. 8 ("Accounting Policies, Changes in Accounting Estimates and Errors"), 1404, 1405, 1519

No. 10 ("Events after the Balance Sheet Date"), 1548
No. 12 ("Income Taxes"), 1175
No. 13, 1110
No. 16, 1519, 1520
No. 17 ("Accounting and Leases"), 1285, 1332
No. 18 ("Revenue"), 525, 1042, 1109
No. 19 ("Employee Benefits"), 1250, 1253, 1257n.33
No. 24 ("Related Party Disclosures"), 1548
No. 27 ("Consolidated and Separate Financial Statements"), 1026
No. 32 ("Financial Instruments: Presentation"), 874, 1251n.28
No. 33 ("Earnings per Share"), 904, 941
No. 34 ("Interim Financial Reporting"), 1548
No. 36 ("Impairment of Assets"), 753, 1519
No. 37 ("Provisions, Contingent Liabilities, and Contingent Assets"), 753
No. 38 ("Intangible Assets"), 712, 1520
No. 39 ("Financial Instruments: Recognition and Measurement"), 408, 409, 874, 941, 995, 1026
No. 41 ("Agriculture"), 525
International Accounting Standards Board (IASB), 20, 31, 901, 904, 1346n.1, 1517
  adoption of IFRS, 155–156
  classified financial statements, 278–280
  conceptual framework, 78–80
  contingent liabilities, 700–701
  convergence, 1554
  definition of entity, 54n.13
  development of standards, 81
  disclosures effectiveness project of, 1490
  and fair value, 788
  and fair value accounting, 17
  fair values, 969
  on financial instruments, 975–976
  financial statement presentation, 159, 179, 281–282, 411
  and IFRIC, 35
  investments, 950–951, 1037
  key elements of financial statements, 153
  lease accounting, 1274n.2, 1283, 1303–1304, 1333, 1334, 1339
  on lease accounting, 1303, 1304
  liabilities, 818
  on loan loss allowances, 374
  on offsetting, 243
  and postretirement benefits, 1263
  provisions in, 716
  receivables, 409
  recognition of pension assets, 1257n.33
  revenue recognition, 1109–1110, 1113
  as standard-setting organization, 32–33
  in standard-setting structure, 33–34
  statement of cash flows, 1482
  technical accounting issues, 1519
International Accounting Standards Committee Foundation (IASCF), 33
International Auditing and Assurance Standards Board (IAASB), 156
International companies, 153

International Financial Reporting Interpretations Committee (IFRIC), 34–35
International Financial Reporting Standards (IFRS), 20, 1109–1113, 1346n.1
  No. 2 ("Share-Based Payment"), 941, 1250
  No. 7 ("Financial Instruments: Disclosure"), 408
  No. 8 ("Operating Segments"), 1548, 1549, 1554
  No. 9 ("Financial Instruments"), 411, 950, 976, 1026
  accounting by the lessee, 1332–1337
  accounting by the lessor, 1337–1339
  accounting changes and error analysis, 1404–1406
  accounting for financial assets, 1027–1028
  accounting for leases, 1331–1339
  accounting for property, plant, and equipment, 637–638
  accounting information system, 153–156
  adoption of, by U.S., 36–38
  agricultural products, 482
  balance sheet and statement of cash flows, 277–282
  cash and cash equivalents, 1412
  component depreciation, 638–639
  conceptual framework, 78–80
  and CPA exam, 10
  debt investments, 1028–1031
  development of, 31–38
  dilutive securities, 941–947
  disclosure requirements, 1548–1554
  earnings per share, 941–947
  employee stock-purchase plans, 896
  equity investments, 1031–1035
  GAAP comparison to, 31, 205–206, 243, 278, 408–409, 525, 693–694, 700, 753–754, 815, 874–875, 942, 1026–1027, 1109–1110, 1175, 1250–1251, 1346n.1, 1404–1405, 1480–1481, 1549
  hierarchy of, 35
  impairments, 693–699, 1035–1036
  income statements, 205–208
  income taxes, 1145
  income tax reporting, 1175–1178
  intangible assets, 693–697
  inventory under, 525–532
  issuing of, 32–34
  liabilities, 753–758, 815–818
  long-term debt, 706
  markets, 474, 475
  mineral products, 482
  offsetting, 243
  pensions and postretirement benefits, 1250–1263
  receivables, 408–411
  recognizing impairments, 639–640
  revaluations, 638, 642–643
  revenue recognition, 1042
  reversal of impairment loss, 640–641
  share-based compensation, 892
  statement of cash flows, 1480–1482
  stockholders' equity, 874–878
  technical accounting issues, 1519–1520

International GAAP (iGAAP),
   see Convergence, of U.S. and
   international standards
International Lease Finance Corp. (ILFC),
   1271, 1273–1278
International Organization of Securities
   Commissions (IOSCO), 33
International Paper Co., 240, 600,
   610–611, 911
International stock exchanges, 820
International Thoroughbred Breeders, 347
Internet:
   annual reports published on, 19
   full disclosure in financial reporting on,
     1516–1517
Interperiod tax allocation, 1147–1154
Intraperiod tax allocation, 171–172
Intrinsic value, 981
Intuit Inc., 219
Inventory(-ies), 416–420. *See also related
   headings, e.g.:* Periodic inventory system
   alternative method for estimating,
     486n.11
   analysis of, 495–496
   average days to sell, 496
   on balance sheets, 219–220
   basis of valuation of, 217
   comparable information about, 472–473
   control, 419–420
   costs included in, 425–428
   defined, 416
   disclosure of, 1491–1492
   estimating, using gross profit percentage,
     486n.11
   gross profit method for, 485–488
   increase in, 1424–1425
   International Financial Reporting
     Standards for, 525–532
   land as, 539
   management of, 472–473
   method selection for, 443–446
   misstated, 424–425
   at net realizable value, 481–482
   obsolete, 495
   presentation of, 494–496
   pricing methods, 1553
   purchases of, 441n.10
   recovery of loss to, 529–530
   slow moving, 495
   valuation of, 420, 445–446, 481–485
   as worksheet entry, 1447
Inventory cost flow, 417
Inventory errors, 423–425, 1360
Inventory methods, 420n.1, 443n.16
Inventory turnover, 496
Investing activities, 229, 231, 1412, 1414
   extraordinary items, 1437
   on statement of cash flows, 1480,
     1481–1482
Investment(s), 950–976
   available-for-sale securities, 955–959,
     962–964
   debt securities, 952–960
   derivatives, 979–995
   equity method for accounting, 965–966
   equity securities, 960–967
   fair value controversy, 969

held-to-maturity securities, 953–955
holdings of less than 20%, 961–964
impairment of value, 969–970
long-term, 221
measurement issues, 967–970
by owners, 53
reclassification adjustments, 970–974
security, 952n.1
short-term, 218–219
stock, as worksheet entry, 1447
trading securities, 959–960, 964
transfers between categories, 974–975
variable-interest entities, 996–999
Investment carrying amount, 1377–1378
Investment in Debt Securities, 952–960
Investors, equity, 5–6
Investors Technical Advisory Committee
   (ITAC), 11n.5
Involuntary conversion, 561
IOSCO (International Organization of
   Securities Commissions), 33
I.O.U.s, 346
Ip, Greg, 154n.4, 224
iPhone, 654
IPR&D (in-process research and
   development), 693–694
Irregular items:
   analyzing, 169
   categories of, 169
   and FASB, 168
   on income statement, 168–179
IRS, *see* Internal Revenue Service
Issuance, accounting at time of, 943–944
Issue costs, 828
ITAC (Investors Technical Advisory
   Committee), 11n.5
Ivanhoe Mines Ltd., 1335–1339

J
Jack in the Box, 48, 1282
Jaenicke, Henry R., 1044n.8
Jakab, S., 1051
Japan, 51
Japan Post Holdings, 32
JCPenney Company, 415, 765
Jet Blue Airways, 537
Jiambalvo, James, 1360n.7
Jiffy Lube International, 1082n.30
Jim Walter's Corporation, 546
Job Creation and Worker Assistance Act of
   2002, 614n.15
John Deere and Company, 203, 275, 366,
   444, 1184
John Deere Credit, 366
Johnson, L. Todd, 972n.11
Johnson, Todd, 41
Johnson & Johnson, 584–585, 611, 612, 666,
   690–691, 768, 829, 979, 1501, 1502
Jones, S. D., 48, 1282
Journal(s), 85, 91–92
Journal entry, general, 91–92
Journalizing, 91–92
JP Morgan, 788, 999
JPMorgan Chase & Co., 49, 224, 822,
   839, 1270
Judgments and estimates, 215
Junk bonds, 768

K
Kahn, Jeremy, 1051
Kapner, S., 345
Kardous, D., 488
Kazenski, Paul M., 543n.3
Kellogg Company, 45, 151–152, 496, 538,
   825, 872, 1214, 1504
Kelly, Kate, 224
Kelly Services, 1081
Ketz, E., 1051
Ketz, J. E., 1283
KeyCorp, 1440
KFC, 1081
Kiley, David, 658
Kimberly-Clark Corp., 999, 1316
Kimco Realty, 597
King, Thomas E., 554n.10
Klinke Cleaners, 58
Kmart Holding, 1143
Knutson, Peter H., 1274n.2
Kocieniewski, D., 1140
Kohl's, 347
Kraft Foods, 414
Krispy Kreme, 235–236, 783,
   1268–1269, 1272
Kroger, 236, 611
Kurzweil Applied Intelligence Inc., 423

L
Labaton, S., 607
Laffer, A., 1119n.1
Land:
   cost of, 539
   decrease in, 1426
   expenditures for, 546
   increase in, 1422
   revaluation of, 641–642
   as worksheet entry, 1447–1448
Landsman, Wayne, 890n.6
Lantronix, 1040
Largay, James A., III, 1411
Large stock dividends, 842n.16
Larson, R. K., 1058n.18
Last-in, first-out (LIFO). *See also*
   LIFO *entries*
   adoption of, for inventory valuation,
     1356n.4
   advantages of, 441–442
   approach comparisons, 440–441
   and cost flow assumption, 431–432
   disadvantages of, 442–443
   external indexes computations, 440n.9
   and FIFO, 432–433
   and future earning hedge, 442
   and international convergence, 414–415
   prohibition of, 1519, 1554
   repeal of, 445
   specific-goods, 434–435
   tax benefits, 441–442, 444
Las Vegas Sands Corporation, 225–226
Lavelle, Louis, 883
Lawsuits, 1514n.17
Layers, 434
LBO (leveraged buyout), 830
LCM, *see* Lower-of-cost-or-market
LCM rule, *see* Lower-of-cost-or-market
   (LCM) rule

LCNRV (lower-of-cost-or-net realizable value), 526–529
Leach, Jim, 29
Lease accounting:
  and bargain purchase option, 1298
  current vs. noncurrent classification in, 1299–1300
  and disclosing lease data, 1300–1302
  and initial direct costs, 1298–1299
  by lessee, 1274–1283
  by lessor, 1284–1289
  and residential values, 1290
  for sales-type leases, 1296–1298
  special problems in, 1289–1302
  unresolved problems in, 1302–1304
Leases and leasing, 1268–1304
  accounting for, see Lease accounting
  advantages of, 1272–1273
  classifications of, 1285–1286
  conceptual nature of, 1273–1274
  and disclosure, 1493
  economics of, 1284
  environment for, 1270–1274
  lessor types in, 1270–1271
  operating leases, 784
  and present value-based measurement, 288
  term of lease, 1272, 1276, 1290n.12, 1334
Lease receivable, 1286–1289, 1296
LeClere, Marc J., 443n.17
Ledger, 85
Legally restricted deposits, 348
Lehman Brothers, 2, 31, 43, 370, 1489
Lennard, A., 1303
Lenovo Group, 642, 966–967, 1334
Leone, M., 213, 1304, 1343, 1520
LePeep Restaurants, Inc., 1082n.30
Leslie Fay (company), 425
Lessee accounting, 1274–1283, 1332–1337
  of assets vs. liabilities, 1278
  for bargain purchase option, 1298
  capitalization criteria for, 1275–1278
  capital lease method of, 1278–1281
  capital vs. operating, 1282–1283
  operating method of, 1281–1282
  for residual value, 1291–1294
  for sale-leasebacks, 1307–1308
Lessor accounting, 1284–1289, 1337–1339
  benefits of, 1284
  and classification of leases, 1285–1286
  direct-financing method of, 1286–1289
  and economics of leasing, 1284
  for initial direct costs, 1299
  operating method of, 1289
  for residual value, 1294–1295
  for sale-leasebacks, 1308
  for sales-type leases, 1296–1298
Level 8 Systems, 61
Leveraged buyout (LBO), 830
Leverage ratios, 1523n.26
Levitt, A., 161n.3
Lewent, Judy, 1486
Liability(-ies), 702
  on balance sheets, 216, 222–225
  contingent, 700–701, 754, 757.
    See also Loss contingencies
  current vs. noncurrent lease, 1299–1300

defined, 53, 79, 702
  employee-related, 710–715
  environmental, 722–726
  and historical cost, 56
  International Financial Reporting Standards for, 753–758
  in lessee accounting, 1278, 1283
  long-term, see Long-term liabilities
  not fairly valued, 969
  pension, 1198–1199
Liability approach, 1144
Liability awards, share-based, 914–915
Liability gains and losses, 1260
Liability valuation account, 774
Liberty International, 645–646
Licenses, 656
Liesman, S., 14, 1125
LIFO, see Last-in, first-out
LIFO conformity rule, 444
LIFO liquidations, 434–435, 479n.3
LIFO matches, 441
LIFO method, dollar-value, 435–440
LIFO reserve, 432–433
LIFO retail methods, 489, 497–502
  changing from conventional retail method to, 501–502
  and stable prices, 497–498
Limited-life intangibles, 651–652
  accounting treatment for, 653
  amortization of, 1434–1435
  fair value tests for, 662
  impairment of, 662
Limited-life tangibles, impairment of, 695
LinkedIn, 836, 911
Lipe, Robert C., 1525n.28
Liquidating dividends, 607–608, 840–841
Liquidity, 214, 229
Liquidity evaluation, 435
Liquidity ratios, 245, 1523, 1524
Litigation, 718–719, 1514–1516, 1551
Lloyd's of London, 1303n.17
Loans, 374, 381n.18, 408, 1414n.2
Loans.com, 654
Lobbyists, 1366n.13
Lockbox accounts, 376–377
Loews Corporation, 1211
Long-term assets, 288
Long-term bonds, valuation of, 313–314
Long-term borrowing, 348
Long-term construction contracts, 1110–1111
Long-term contract losses, 1064–1067
Long-term debt, 764
  analysis of, 787
  current maturities of, 705
  on financial statements, 764
  International Financial Reporting Standards for, 706
  off-balance-sheet financing, 783–785
  presentation of, 786
  reporting, 783–787
  and SAF Opinion No. 5, 783
  and SAF Opinion No. 6, 783
Long-term investments, 221
Long-term liabilities, 762–787
  on balance sheets, 224–225
  bonds payable, 764–776

long-term notes payable, 776–783
  and reporting and analysis of debt, 783–787
Long-term notes payable, 776–783
Lopez de Mesa, A., 1419
Loss(es):
  accumulated other comprehensive loss, 847n.21
  adjustment to net income for, 1435–1436
  from continuing operations, 921n.22
  defined, 53
  from discontinued operations, 173
  on financial statements, 163
  impairment, 695–696
  on income statement, 164
  loan, 374
  on pension plans, 1197–1202, 1260
  and postretirement expense, 1221
  on sale-leasebacks, 1308
  on sale of equipment, 1425
  smoothing unexpected, 1260
Loss carrybacks, 1132–1133
Loss carryforwards, 1134–1137
  deferred tax assets recognized as, 1134n.4
  example, 1134–1137
  operating, 1134–1135
  period length for, 1134n.3
  with valuation allowance, 1135–1136
  without valuation allowance, 1134–1135
Loss contingencies, 381, 716–725
  coupons, 721–722
  environmental liabilities, 722–726
  guarantee and warranty costs, 719–721
  and likelihood of loss, 716–718
  litigations, claims, and assessments, 718–719
  of no-par stock, 825–826
  premiums, 721–722
  self-insurance, 725
Loss in current period, 1064–1065
Loss measurement, 169–170
Loss method, 478–479, 528
Loten, A., 359
Lower (floor), 475–476
Lower-of-cost-or-market (LCM):
  applying, 477–478
  with IFRS, 525
  and net realized value, 474
  in practice, 481n.5
  and recording market instead of cost, 478–479
Lower-of-cost-or-market (LCM) rule, 475, 476–477, 481
Lower-of-cost-or-net realizable value (LCNRV), 526–529
Lowe's, 54
LTV Corporation, 835
Lubore, Seth, 1269
Lucent Technologies, 844, 911, 1053
Lump-sum exchange, 827
Lump-sum price, 548–549
Lump-sum purchases, 548–549

M

McConnell, Pat, 1143n.8
McDermott, D., 168n.10
MacDonald, Elizabeth, 1269

McDonald, Robert A., 248

McDonald's Corporation, 4, 31, 48, 96, 163, 635–636, 670, 821, 978–979, 1051, 1081, 1119*n*.1, 1270, 1283

McGregor, Warren, 1274*n*.2

MacKay, Archibald E., 1082*n*.29

McNamee, M., 768

MACRS, *see* Modified Accelerated Cost Recovery System

McTauge, R., 48

Magyar Telecom plc, 1552

Mahoney, Jeff, 364

Major repair, 559

Maker, 359

Management, 1511–1513, 1522

Management incentives, monitoring of, 1419

Management's discussion and analysis (MD&A), 1511–1512

Managerial accounting, 4

Mannesmann, 31

Manufacturers Hanover Trust Co., 376

Manufacturing, 416–417, 426

Maremont, M., 1298

Marginal principle approach, 1505

Markdowns, 488–490

Markdown cancellations, 490

Marketable securities, 346*n*.2

Market approach, 549*n*.5

Marketing-related intangible assets, 653–654

Market rate, 359*n*.9, 767

Market-related asset value, 1198

Marks and Spencer plc, 39, 81, 157, 211, 284, 412, 534, 646, 699, 758, 761, 820, 880, 949, 1039, 1115, 1181, 1266, 1341, 1408, 1485, 1557

Markup, 489

Marriott, 655, 1081

Martha Stewart Living, 836

MasterCard, 310, 366, 367*n*.12

Master valuation accounts, 658

Master valuation approach, 660

Matching principle, 59*n*.18

Materiality, 47, 48

Mattel, Inc., 221–222

Maturing spirits, 495

Maturity value (bonds), 766

Maxwell House, 351

Maytag Corp., 1270

MD&A (management's discussion and analysis), 1511–1512

MDAs (multiple-deliverable arrangements), 1054–1056

Mead-Westvaco, 1198

Means, Kathryn, 543*n*.3

Measurements:
  of financial instruments, 975–976
  nonfinancial, 18–19
  in valuation, 286–287

Measurement principle, 56–58, 79

Medicare, 710–711

Medtronic, 763

Meineke Mufflers, 1081

Mellors, F., 1214*n*.18

Memorandum of understanding (MOU), 33

Merchandising concerns, 416–417

Merck & Co., Inc., 656, 672, 690–691, 715, 831, 940, 1184, 1272, 1364, 1486

Meredith, 836

Mergers and acquisitions, 904*n*.15
  international accounting standards for, 31
  tax-motivated, 1143*n*.8

Merit rating, 711

Mermin, G., 1183

Merrill Lynch, 899

Mesa Limited Partnerships, 609*n*.12

Metallgesellschaft, 979*n*.14

M&I Bank, 979

Microsoft Corporation, 4, 19, 20, 161, 289, 349, 405–406, 537, 665, 670, 708, 709, 768, 831, 883

MicroStrategy, 1489, 1491

Miller, Paul B. W., 1192*n*.12, 1437*n*.8

MillerCoors, 966–967

Millward Brown, 670

Minimum lease payments, 1276, 1291, 1334, 1338

Minimum rental payments, 1276

Minority interest, 280

Minor leasebacks, 1308

Misclassification errors, 1360

Mitsubishi, 1027–1028

Model Business Corporate Act, 822

Modification of terms, 817–818

Modified Accelerated Cost Recovery System (MACRS), 614–616
  example of, 615
  optional straight-line method vs., 616–617
  property classes, 615
  and tax depreciation methods, 615

Modified cash basis, 120

Modified perpetual inventory system, 419

Mohican Company, 751

Molson Coors Brewing Company, 350, 725, 966–967, 1184

Monetary assets, 550*n*.6

Monetary exchange, 553*n*.9

Monetary unit assumption, 55, 79

Money-market funds, 346*n*.1

Money-market savings certificates, 346*n*.1

Monsanto Chemical Corporation, 358, 1515

Montavon Winery, 706

Monthly financial statements, 117

Moody's Investors Service, 768

Moran, M., 911

"More likely than not," 1125

Morgan Stanley, 959

Morgenson, Gretchen, 50, 61, 1493

Mortgages, 782

Mortgage-backed securities, 984

Mortgage notes payable, 782

Moses, O. Douglas, 1365*n*.12

Moto Photo, Inc., 1082*n*.30

Motorola Inc., 59, 68, 221, 416

Mott, D., 1143*n*.8

MOU (memorandum of understanding), 33

Moving-average method, 430

Mulford, Charles W., 1215*n*.19, 1419, 1437*n*.8, 1443

Multinational corporations, international accounting standards for, 31

Multiple-deliverable arrangements (MDAs), 1054–1056

Multiple periods, 480

Mumford of Wyoming, 495

Myers, David, 28

N

NAC (Not-for-Profit Advisor Committee), 11*n*.5

Nailor, H., 1303

Nakheel, 817

NASDAQ, 820

National Car Rental, 1081

National Commission on Fraudulent Financial Reporting, 1494*n*.6, 1517*n*.22

Natural disasters, 1551*n*.30

Natural expense classification, 164

Natural resources, 609–611, 638

Nature-of-expense method, 207

Navistar, 654

NBC TV, 656, 1497

NBC Universal, 1497

NEC, 1109

Nesco Holdings, Inc., 716

Nestlé, 31, 1032, 1033

Net approach, 1051, 1251

Net cash flow:
  direct method of determining, 1427–1428
  indirect method of determining, 1418–1419, 1434
  from investing/financing activities, 1416, 1419, 1422–1423, 1426, 1427
  from operating activities, 231, 1417–1419, 1421–1422, 1424–1425, 1427–1434, 1436, 1440–1441

Net current amount, 1139

Net defined benefit liability, 1251–1255

Net income:
  accrual-basis accounting for determining, 7
  adjustments to, 1434–1437
  cash flows vs., 233–234
  and IFRS, 205–206
  and indirect method, 1434

Net increase in cash, 231

Net interest, 1252–1254

Net liability approach, 730–731

Net losses, 165*n*.7, 1440–1441

Net method, 427

Net noncurrent amount, 1139

Net of cash discounts, 427

Net operating loss (NOL), 1132–1138

Net periodic postretirement benefit cost, 1220

Net realizable value (NRV), 353, 475–476, 481–482
  of agricultural inventory, 530–532
  allowance account for adjustments to, 529
  and cost, 526–529
  lower-of-cost-or-, 526–529

Net settlement, 982

Net working capital, 223

Network Rail, 641

Neutrality, 49, 1366

New allowance account, 480
New average unit cost, 430
New Century, 58
New York Stock Exchange (NYSE), 820, 844
The New York Times, 836, 1486
NFL, 656
Nicholaisen, Don, 48
Nike, 488, 821
90% test, *see* Recovery of investment test
Nissan (formerly Datsun), 654
Nokia, 592, 638, 657, 666, 694, 1028, 1332
NOL (net operating loss), 1132–1138
NOL carrybacks, *see* Loss carrybacks
NOL carryforwards, *see* Loss carryforwards
Nominal accounts, 85
Nominal rate, 293, 766
Non-adjusted subsequent events, 1551
Noncalculable purchase commitments, 484n.8
Noncancelable leases, 1274
Noncash charges/credits, 1449
Non-cash investing, 1480
Noncash transactions, 1441–1442, 1481
Non-consolidated subsidiary, 784
Noncontributory pension plans, 1184
Non-controlling interest, 176, 280
Noncounterbalancing errors, 1367, 1369–1370
Noncurrent assets, 221–222
Noncurrent liabilities, 782
Noncurrent receivables, 349
Nondetachable stock warrants, 890
Nonfinancial measurements, 18–19
Non-interest bearing notes, *see* Zero-interest-bearing notes
Nonmonetary assets, 550–555, 561
Nonpublic enterprise, 899n.13
Nonqualified stock-option plans, 913
Nonreciprocal transfers, 555
Non-recognition, of deferred tax assets, 1175–1177
Nonrecognized subsequent events, 1496
Nontrade receivables, 350
Non-trading equity investments, 1032
No-par stock, 825–826
Norby, William C., 44n.4
Nordstrom, 474
Norfolk Southern Corporation, 68, 537
Normal shortages, 493
Normand, Troy, 28–29
Norris, F., 17, 383–384, 887, 1486
Nortel Networks Corp., 83
Northern Trust Company, 295
Northland Cranberries, 750–751
Northrup Grumman, 648, 649
Northwest Airlines, 215
Northwest Industries, Inc., 962–963
Note(s):
    accounting for, 777
    bonds vs., 777
    choice of interest rate for, 780–781
    common, 1491–1493
    discount, 779
    interest-bearing, 359, 361–363, 778–779

issuance of, at face value, 359–360, 777
issuance of, for property, goods, and services, 363, 779–780
of noncash investing/financing activities, 1441–1442
not issued at face value, 360–363, 777–779
as present value-based measurement, 288
Notes payable, 703–705, 777n.10, 779–781, 1440
Notes receivable, 350, 359–364
    disposition of, 365–370
    fair value option for, 365
    impaired, 364
    recognition of, 359–360
    valuation of, 363–364
Notes to the financial statements, 224n.8
    accounting policies in, 1491
    defined, 60
    as disclosure technique, 240–241
    pension plan reporting within, 1207–1208, 1211
    postretirement benefits reporting within, 1225, 1226
Not-for-Profit Advisor Committee (NAC), 11n.5
Notional amount, 981
Not-sufficient funds (NSF) checks, 379
Novartis, 756
Noven Pharmaceuticals, Inc., 469–470
NRV, *see* Net realizable value
NSF (not-sufficient funds) checks, 379
Nurnberg, Hugo, 1437n.8
NYSE (New York Stock Exchange), 820, 844
NYSE Eurotext, 820

O

O.A.S.D.I (old age, survivor, and disability insurance), 710–711
"Objectives of Financial Reporting by Nonbusiness Organizations," 43n.3
Obligations (postretirement benefits), 1220
Obsolescence, 591
Occidental Petroleum, 405, 1214
OECD (Organisation for Economic Co-operation and Development), 1131
Off-balance-sheet financing, 783–785
    forms of, 784–785
    and leases, 1272–1273, 1283
    rationale for, 785
    and SEC stance on, 785
OfficeMax, 1344
Offsetting, 243
Ohio Edison, 1307
Oil and gas industry, depletion issues in, 608–609
Old age, survivor, and disability insurance (O.A.S.D.I), 710–711
Olofson, Roy, 555
OMX, 820
On-balance-sheet financing, 785
1-800-Flowers, 836
Onerous contracts, 757
One-time items, 170n.12
OPEB, *see* Other postretirement benefits

Operating activities:
    net cash flow computation from, 1417–1419, 1421–1422, 1424–1425, 1427–1434, 1436, 1441
    net cash provided by, 231
    net income vs. net cash flow from, 1417–1419
    and securitizing receivables, 1419
    on statement of cash flows, 229, 1412, 1414, 1425, 1480
Operating cycle, 702
Operating expense computation, 122–123
Operating leases, 784, 1286, 1289, 1299, 1333, 1339
Operating lease method, 1281–1283, 1289
Operating losses, 1116–1117
Operating loss carryforwards, 1134–1135
Operating segments, 1499–1500
Opinions of the Accounting Principles Board (APB Opinions), 9, 11–13
Options, *see* Stock options
Optional straight-line method, 615
Option term, 1281
Option to purchase (franchises), 1084
Oracle Corporation, 68, 405–406
Ordinary annuity, 291–292, 306–311
Ordinary stock dividends, 842
Orenstein, E., 17
Organisation for Economic Co-operation and Development (OECD), 1131
Original entry, book of, 85, 91
Originating temporary difference, 1128
Osawa, J., 1137n.6
Other postretirement benefits (OPEB), 1189n.8, 1217n.21, 1219
Outdoor Channel Holdings, 653
Outflows, cash, 1444
Output:
    in depreciation, 593
    measures of, 1058
Outstanding checks, 379
Outstanding stock, 830, 837n.12
Overfunded pension plans, 1205
Overhead, 540
Overseas National Airways, 841
Overstatement of accrued revenue, 1369
Overstatement of purchases, 1369
Overstock.com, 449
Owens Corning, Inc., 218
Owens-Illinois, 166
Owners:
    distributions to, 53
    investments by, 53
Owners' equity, *see* Stockholders' equity
Ownership structure, 88–89

P

Pacific Lighting, 609n.12
Pacter, Paul A., 1379n.15
Paid-in capital, 825, 847n.20, 875
Paid-in Capital–Expired Stock Warrants, 889
Paid-in capital in excess of par, 825
Paid-in Capital in Excess of Par–Common Stock, 832, 836, 886, 891, 896
Paid-in Capital in Excess of Par–Preferred Stock, 886

Palletta, D., 1143*n*.8
Pan American Airlines, 1213*n*.16
Panera Bread Company, 54
Paper checks, 378*n*.17
Parent company, 967
Parenthetical explanations, 239–240
Parking transactions, 423
Parmalat, 31, 817
Partial period depreciation, 598–599
Participating preferred stock, 835
Par value:
  as basis for fair value, 826
  of bonds, 766
  of stock issued, 841, 844–845
Par value method, 831
Par value stock, 825
Passage of title rule, 421
"Past event," 1355*n*.3
Past service cost (PSC), 1257–1258
Patents, business-method, 656
Payee, 359
Payment:
  date of (stock dividends), 839
  deferred, 1047
Payout ratio, 849–850
Payroll deductions:
  example of, 712
  income tax withholding, 711–712
  Social Security taxes, 710–711
  unemployment taxes, 711
Payroll taxes, 712
PBGC, *see* Pension Benefit Guaranty
  Corporation
PCAOB (Public Company Accounting
  Oversight Board), 18, 1494*n*.5
Pegg, Janet, 1143*n*.8
Penalty for failure to renew/extend
  lease, 1277
Penn Central Railroad, 705–706
Pensions, 288, 1493
Pension Benefit Guaranty Corporation
  (PBGC), 1182, 1187*n*.6, 1213
Pension obligations, 1187–1188
Pension plan(s), 1182–1215
  accounting for, *see* Pension plan
    accounting
  defined-benefit, 1185–1186
  defined-contribution, 1185
  financial health of, 1204
  funding of, 1184–1185, 1227
  nature of, 1184–1187
  net funded status of, 1189
  reporting, *see* Pension plan reporting
  trends in, 1182–1183
  worksheet for, 1192–1204
Pension plan accounting, 1187–1192
  actual return on plan assets, 1191–1192
  actuaries' role in, 1187
  employer's obligation in, 1187
  expense components in, 1189–1192
  under IFRS, 1251–1263
  interest on liability, 1191
  pension obligation measures in, 1187–1188
  service cost in, 1190–1191
Pension plan assets, 1254
  actual return on, 1191–1192, 1221,
    1254–1255

smoothing unexpected gains/losses on,
  1197–1198, 1260
Pension plan gains/losses, 1197–1202
  calculations for, 1201
  corridor amortization, 1199–1200
  example of unrecognized, 1200–1201
  IFRS for, 1260
  smoothing, 1197–1198, 1260
Pension plan liabilities, smoothing
  unexpected gains/losses on,
  1198–1199, 1260
Pension plan reporting:
  ERISA, 1211–1212
  within financial statements, 1205–1215
  within notes to financial statements,
    1207–1208, 1211
  terminations, pension, 1214–1215
  2017 entries/worksheet example,
    1210–1211
Pension poison pills, 1215*n*.19
Pension Protection Act, 1213*n*.15
Pension Reform Act (1974), 1211–1213
Pension terminations, 1214–1215
Pension worksheet, 1192–1204
  amortization of unrecognized prior
    service costs, 1194–1195
  gain or loss, 1197–1202
  IFRS for, 1255–1263
  2014 entries, 1192–1194
  2015 entries, 1195–1197, 1258–1259
  2016 entries, 1202–1204, 1261–1263
  2017 entries, 1210–1211
Pep Boys, 999
PepsiCo, Inc., 51, 76, 151, 169–170, 203, 222,
  274, 404–405, 522, 635, 669, 690, 705,
  750, 813, 825, 872, 940, 952, 1024, 1107,
  1141–1143, 1173, 1248, 1402, 1478,
  1512, 1546
PepsiCo Beverages, 45
PepsiCo International, 45
Percentage analysis, 1527–1528
Percentage markup, 486*n*.11
Percentage-of-completion accounting
  method, 1057–1063, 1066, 1110–1111
Percentage-of-receivables approach, 356–357
Percentage-of-sales approach, 356
Performance approach, current
  operating, 168
Periods, compounding, 292–293
Period costs, 60, 1504
  interest as, 426
  in inventory, 426
Periodic inventory system, 418–419
Periodicity assumption, 55–56
Periodic rent, 310–311
Permanent accounts, 85, 112
Permanent differences, 1128
Permits, 656
Perpetual inventory system, 418–419, 478
Petrone, Kim, 41
Petty cash disbursements, imprest system
  for, 377–378
Petty cash funds, 346, 377–378
Pfizer, 349, 831
PharMor, 1489
Phillip Morris, 763
Phillips, Michael M., 224

Physical factors, of depreciation, 591
Physical goods included in inventory,
  421–425
  consigned goods, 422
  goods in transit, 421–422
  and sales agreements, 422–423
Physical inventory count, 419
Pillsbury, 1504
Pinnacle West Corporation, 1307
Pizza Hut, 1081
Plains All American Pipelines, 763
Plan assets, *see* Pension plan assets
Plant assets, 538
  dispositions of, 560–561
  and involuntary conversion, 561
  problems with, 561
  sale of, 560–561
Pledge, 366*n*.10
Plugs, 658
PNC, 1271
Points (note), 782
Polaroid, 656
Political costs, 1365–1366
Politicization, 26
Polo Ralph Lauren, 836
Polymer Group Inc., 649
Pools, 435, 436*nn*.6–7, 441*n*.11
Porter, J., 1487
Positive intent, 953
Postage stamps on hand, 346
Post-balance-sheet events (subsequent
  events), 1495–1496, 1550–1552
Post-closing trial balance, 85, 113
Postdated checks, 346
Postemployment benefits, 712*n*.9
Posting, 92–96
  closing entries, 111–113
  defined, 85
Postretirement benefits, 288, 714*n*.10
  disclosures of, 1225, 1226
  eligibility for, 1219*n*.25
  obligations under, 1220
  pension vs. healthcare, 1218–1219
  underfunded, 1227
Postretirement benefits accounting,
  1217–1227
  actuarial assumptions/conceptual issues
    of, 1225, 1227
  adjustment to net income for costs of
    benefits, 1435
  expense under, 1220–1221
  FASB on, 1217
  gains/losses recognition, 1223
  illustrative entries of, 1221–1225
  provisions of, 1219–1221
  2014 entries and worksheet, 1221–1222
  2015 entries and worksheet, 1223–1224
  2016 amortization of unrecognized net
    gain/loss, 1224–1225
Postretirement expense, 1220–1221
Potlatch Corporation, 799
PPE, *see* Property, plant, and equipment
Prab Command, Inc., 522–523
Prab Limited (U.K.), 523
Prab Robots, Inc., 522–523
Practice Bulletins (AdSEC), 10
Predictive value, 47

Preemptive privilege, 890
Preemptive right, 823
Preference shares, 280, 876
Preferred dividends in arrears, 707
Preferred stock, 824, 825, 834–835, 918.
    See also Common stock; *specific types,*
    e.g.: Convertible preferred stock
    accounting and reporting of, 836
    convertible bonds vs., 836
    dividends from, 900–901
    features of, 834–835
    participating, 834–835, 852*n*.24
    redeemable, 835
Preferred stock outstanding, 834*n*.10, 836
Premiums, 721–722
Premium amortization, of bonds, 769–770
Premium bonds, 766–770
Prepaid expenses:
    adjusting entries for, 98–102
    on balance sheets, 220
    basis of valuation of, 217
    as class of adjusting entries, 97
    decrease in, 1425
    failure to record, 1368
    increase in, 1421
    as worksheet entry, 1447
Preparing financial statements, 108–110
Prepayments:
    as class of adjusting entries, 97
    in reversing entries illustration, 129
Present value:
    of annuity, 306–311
    of annuity due, 308–311
    of annuity due of 1 (table), 291
    of an ordinary annuity, 306–307,
        309–311
    of an ordinary annuity of 1 (table), 291
    of benefits, 1188*n*.7
    computing for unknown, 294
    of deferred annuity, 312–313
    measurement, 315–317
    of 1 (table), 291
    of single sum, 296–298
    solving for, 295
    as variable in compound interest, 294
Present value amortization,
    see Effective-interest method
Present value-based measurements,
    288–289
Pretax financial income, 1118, 1127–1130
Price index selection, 438–440
Priceline.com, 50, 166, 1051
PricewaterhouseCoopers, 1045
Primary lease term, 1281
Prime Motor Inn, 233
Primerica (formerly American Can), 654
Principal, 289
Principal-agent relationships, 1050–1053
Principal amount (bonds), 766
Principle-based accounting standards,
    rule-based vs., 14
Principles of accounting, 56–61
    expense recognition principle, 58–60
    full disclosure principle, 60–61
    measurement principle, 56–58
    revenue recognition principle, 58
Principles-based rules, 43

Prior period adjustments, 181, 1359
Prior service costs (PSC), 1194–1195, 1221
Private Company Financial Reporting
    Committee (PCFRC), 11*n*.5
Probability, degree of, 718
"Probable" tax assets, 1175–1176
The Procter & Gamble Company, 19, 76,
    133, 151, 202–203, 238, 247–252, 274,
    332, 404, 416, 522, 635, 666, 690, 750,
    812, 849, 871–872, 899, 939, 979*n*.14,
    1024, 1107, 1172–1173, 1248, 1329,
    1402, 1477, 1491, 1546
Produce, agricultural, 530
Product costs, 60, 426
Product guarantees, *see* Guarantees
Production variable method, 597
Profitability ratios, 245, 1523, 1524
Profit margin on sales ratio, 612
Pro-forma measures, 61
Projected benefit obligation, 1188
Project financing arrangement, 784
Promissory note, 359
Property, goods, or services, 363
Property, plant, and equipment
        (PPE), 560
    acquisition of, 538–547
    analysis of, 611–612
    on balance sheets, 221
    and cost of buildings, 539–540
    and cost of equipment, 540
    and cost of land, 539
    disclosure of, 1492
    and IFRS, 206, 637–638
    and interest costs during construction,
        541–547
    and limited-life intangibles, 695
    observations for, 547
    presentation of, 609–611
    and self-constructed assets, 540–541
    valuation of, 547–556, 1519–1520
Property dividends, 840
Property-rights approach, 1274–1283,
    1302–1303
Proportional method, 827, 888–889
Proprietary perspective, 6
Pro rata portion, 540
Prorating, 773
Proved reserves, 607
Provisions, 408, 716, 755–757
Prudence, 49*n*.8
Prudent cost, 556
PSC (past service cost), 1257–1258
PSC (prior service costs), 1194–1195, 1221
Public Company Accounting Oversight
    Board (PCAOB), 18, 1494*n*.5
Purchases, misstatement/overstatement of,
    425, 1369
Purchase allowances, 493
Purchase commitments, valuation of,
    483–485
Purchased goodwill, 659–661
Purchased intangibles, 650
Purchase discounts, 426–427, 493
Purchases-only-approach, 501*n*.16
Purchase returns, 493
Pure rate of interest, 316
Put option, 980*n*.17

Q
Quaker Foods, 45
Quaker Oats Company, 1356, 1364
Quaker State Oil Refining Corp., 716–717
Qualcomm Inc., 656, 843, 911
Qualified opinion, 1508–1510
Qualified pension plans, 1184
Qualifying assets, 542
Qualitative characteristics, of accounting
    information, 45–52
Quality of earnings, 161–162
Quality ratings (bonds), 768
Quantum Corporation, 372
Quarterly financial statements, 117
Questcor Pharmaceuticals Inc., 840
Qwest Communications, 555, 1040

R
R. G. Barry & Co., 90
R. J. Reynolds, 49
Radioshack, 730
Ranchers Exploration and Development
    Corp., 840
Rapoport, M., 345
Rate of gross profit, 486*n*.11
Rate of interest, 294
Ratios, 245–246. *See also specific ratios,*
    e.g.: Cash debt coverage
    activity, 1523, 1524
    coverage, 1523, 1524
    liquidity, 1523, 1524
    profitability, 1523, 1524
Ratio analysis, 245–246, 1523–1525
Raw materials inventory, 416–417
Raymark Corporation, 728
R&D, *see* Research and development
    (R&D)
R&D costs, *see* Research and development
    (R&D) costs
Reacquisition price, 775–776
Real accounts, 85
Real economic loss, 1308*n*.19
Real estate investment trusts (REITs), 597*n*.7
Realizable revenues, 1043
Realized losses and gains, adjustment to
    net income for, 1435
Realized revenues, 1043
Really Useful Group, 655
Rearrangements, costs of, 559
Reason, Tim, 213
Reasonableness test, 1358*n*.5
Receivables, 349–374. *See also* Accounts
    receivable(s)
    analysis of, 372–374
    on balance sheets, 219
    basis of valuation of, 217
    classifying, 372
    defined, 349
    disappearing, 829
    impairment of, 381–383
    presentation of, 372
    with recourse, 368–369
    sales of, 366–370
    securitizing, 1419
    trade, 350
    without recourse, 368
Reclassification adjustments, 970–975

Recognition, 53–54
expense recognition principle, 58–60
revenue recognition principle, 58
Recognized subsequent events, 1495–1496
Reconciliation, 1259
Reconciliation method, *see* Indirect method
Reconciling entry, final, 1451
Reconciling items, 379
Record, date of (stock dividends), 839
Recourse:
defined, 368*n*.13
receivables with, 368–369
receivables without, 368
Recoverability tests, 602, 662, 663
Recoverable amounts, 639, 695
Recoverable reserves, 607
Recovery of investment test (90% test), 1276–1278, 1302, 1334–1335
Recovery periods, 614
Redeemable preferred stock, 835
Reed, Jack, 364
Reeve, James M., 436*n*.5, 441*n*.11
Refinancing, 706, 754–755
Refunding, 776
Regions Bank, 1024–1025
Registered bonds, 765
Registrars, 824
Reilly, David, 364
Reinstallation costs, 559
Reither, Cheri L., 972*n*.11
REITs (real estate investment trusts), 597*n*.7
Related-party transactions, disclosure of, 1493–1494
Relative sales value, 482–483
Relevance, of financial information, 46–48, 56
Remeasurement(s), 1252, 1260
Rendleman, Richard, Jr., 890*n*.6
Rental payments, 1338
Repairs, 559
Replacements, 492*n*.12, 558–559
Reported amounts, 1119–1120
Reporting, 4, 1513–1520
change in entity, 1359
change in estimate, 180, 1357–1358
change in principle, 179–180, 1348–1349
correction of error, 180–181, 1359–1374
criteria for accounting/reporting choices, 1520
on financial forecasts/projections, 1513–1516
fraudulent financial reporting, 1517–1520
income, 185–186
integrated, 649
Internet financial reporting, 1516–1517
of offsetting on balance sheet, 243
requirements, 1489
Repossessions (installment sales), 1073–1075
Republic Airlines, 1273
Repurchase agreements, 370
Research and development (R&D):
IFRS requirements for, 693–697
in-process, 693–694
Research and development (R&D) costs, 650–651
accounting for, 666–667
under contractual arrangements, 667*n*.13

of extractive industries, 667*n*.12
identifying, 665–666
presentation of, 670–672
recognition of, 673
Reserves, 242–243, 278, 280, 607
Reserves errors, 1360
Residual interest, 825, 875
Residual value, 1284, 1290–1295
guaranteed vs. unguaranteed, 1290
and lease payments, 1290–1291
lessee accounting for, 1291–1294
lessor accounting for, 1294–1295
meaning of, 1290
Restatement, 1361*n*.8, 1368
Restaurant chains, 1281–1282
Restoration costs, of depletion, 605–606
Restricted cash, 347–348
Restricted-stock plans, 894–896
Restricted-stock units, 896*n*.11
Restrictions on retained earnings, 846–847, 1442
Restructuring, 170*n*.12, 790–796, 815
continuation of debt, 792–796
settlement of debt, 791–792
Restructuring charge, 170
Retail inventory methods, 488–494
concepts of, 489–490
with conventional method, 490–492
evaluation of, 493–494
special items relating to, 493–494
Retail methods, 497–502
Retained earnings, 875
change in, 1426, 1444, 1445
defined, 280
disclosures of restrictions on, 846–847
illustration of statement of, 1446
increase in, 1423
reporting restrictions on, 1442
restrictions on, 182, 846–847
statement of, 115
on statement of stockholders' equity, 182*n*.20
as worksheet entry, 1444, 1445
Retained earnings adjustment, 1354
Retained earnings statement, 181–182
Retired shares, 834
Retirement benefits, *see* Postretirement benefits
Retirement of convertible debt, 886
Retirement savings, 302–303
Retrospective adjustment, 179
Retrospective application, of IFRS, 155
Retrospective changes in accounting principle, 1345–1354
accounting for, 1353
and equity method, 1359*n*.6
example of, 1350–1352
and IFRS, 1406
impracticability of, 1356
inventory methods, 1350–1355
long-term contracts, 1347–1350
reporting of, 1348–1349
Return, 423
on common stock equity, 849
on sales, 612
Returnable cash deposits, 707
Return on assets (ROA), 612

Revaluations, IFRS and, 638, 642–643
Revaluation equity, 281
Revell, Janice, 204
Revenue(s):
defined, 53
on financial statements, 163
in income statement, 164
overstatement of accrued, 1369
understatement of unearned, 1368–1369
Revenue bonds, 765
Revenue expenditures, 557
Revenue recognition, 1040–1079
after delivery, 1068–1079
before delivery, 1057–1068
errors, 1360
for franchises, 1081–1084
at point of sale (delivery), 1045–1056
and SFAC No. 3, 1043*n*.4
and SFAC No. 5, 1043*nn*.4–5, 1057*n*.15, 1068*nn*.22–23
for special sales transactions, 1081–1084
steps of, 59
Revenue recognition principle, 58
Reverse stock splits, 844–845
Reversing differences, 1128
Reversing entries, 113, 124–127
Rhone-Poulenc Rorer (RPR), 469
Ribson, R., 48
Richard, Christine, 776
Richardson, A. W., 1299*n*.14
Right of return, 1047–1049
Risk, 214*n*.1
cash flow, 987
exchange rate, 984
of impairment, 665
interest rate, 984
Risk management (derivatives), 977–995
Rite-Aid, 17, 153, 1051, 1269
RJR Nabisco, 764, 1504
ROA (return on assets), 612
Roche Group, 666, 943–945
Rohde, L., 657
Royal Ahold, 31
Royal Dutch Shell, 32, 607, 655
Rule-based accounting standards, 14
Ryder System, 236

S
S. C. Johnson, 170
SAC (Standards Advisory Council), 33
Sack, Robert J., 21
Safe harbor rule, 1514–1515
Safeway, 489
St. Regis Pulp Co., 962–963, 1032, 1033
Sales:
bill and hold, 1050
with buybacks, 422–423, 1049
conditions for, 369–370
consignments, 1051–1053
with discounts, 1046–1047
and FASB, 369–370
with high rates of return, 423
with recourse, 368–369
with right of return, 1047–1049
secured borrowing vs., 369–370
of treasury stock, 832–833
without recourse, 368

Sales agreements, 422–423
Sales discounts, 351–352, 493
Sale-leasebacks, 1306–1309
  asset use determination in, 1307–1308
  example of, 1308–1309
  as term, 1306–1307
Sales price of asset, 1296
Sales tax payable, 709
Sales transactions, 1044
Sales-type leases, 1285–1286, 1296–1298, 1337
Sales-warranty approach, 720–721
Salvage value, 590
Sampling, statistical, 420n.1
Samsung, 666, 1364
Sandberg, Jared, 557
San Diego Gas and Electric (SDGE), 999
SARs, see Stock appreciation rights
Sarbanes-Oxley Act of 2002 (SOX), 17–18,
      62, 153, 154, 1494n.5, 1512, 1519
  and "big GAAP versus little GAAP,"
      1490n.2
  companies' views of, 84n.1
  and disclosure, 726
  with non-U.S. companies, 31
  and SEC, 726
  Section 404 of, 18
Sarkozy, Nicolas, 17
SAS, 649
Satyam Computer Services, 31
Savings certificates, money-market, 346n.1
Scannel, Kara, 154n.4
Schipper, K., 1490
Schlumberger Ltd., 846
Scott, Richard A., 1069n.24
Scott, Rita K., 1069n.24
Scott Paper, 1307
Scribner, Edmund, 845n.18
SDGE (San Diego Gas and Electric), 999
Seaboard Corporation, 350
Searfoss, D., 1218n.24
Sears Holdings, 419, 488
Sears Roebuck, 1143
Seasonality, 1506–1507
SEC, see Securities and Exchange
      Commission
Secret reserves, 828
Secured bonds, 765
Secured borrowing, 366, 367, 369–370
Securities, 952n.1
  available-for-sale, 182n.21, 218, 952,
      955–959, 962–964, 968
  convertible debt accounting, 884–886
  convertible preferred stock, 886–887
  debt and equity classifications of, 884
  equity, 960–967
  held-to-maturity, 953–955
  holdings between 20% and 50%,
      964–966
  holdings of less than 20%, 961–964
  holdings of more than 50%, 967
  short-term available-for-sale, 1440
  on statement of cash flows, 1414n.2
  stock warrants, 887–892
  trading, 959–960, 964, 1440
Securities and Exchange Commission
      (SEC), 7–9, 27–28
  action against Suntrust Banks, 358

and adoption of IFRS, 1519
and American Institute of Certified
    Public Accountants, 7
and Caterpillar, 1498
on differential disclosure, 1489
and earnings management, 161
enforcement by, 9
and FASB, 8
and GAAP standards development, 8
IDEA database, 1516
and IFRS, 36–37
on interim reporting, 1507–1508
and management's responsibilities for
    financial statements, 1512
on MD&A, 1511
and off-balance-sheet financing, 785
in private sector, 8
Regulation G, 61, 159
rules on materiality issued by, 48
and Sarbanes-Oxley Act of 2002, 726
staff Work Plan of, 36
on timeliness of information, 1508
Securitization, 308, 368
Securitizing receivables, 1419
Segment disclosures, 1498–1501
  disadvantages of, 1498
  identifying operating segments for,
      1499–1500
  illustration of, 1502
  measurement principles for,
      1500–1501
  objectives of, 1499
  principles of, 1499
  types of information in, 1501
Self-insurance, 725
Sender, Henny, 555
Senyak, C., 1143n.8
September 11, 2001 terrorist attacks:
  depreciation measures taken after,
      614n.15
  effect on airlines, 215
  reporting extraordinary items after,
      175–176
Serial bonds, 765
Service costs, 1190–1191, 1220,
      1252, 1253
Service lives, 591
Service period, 893
Service revenue, 120–121
Settlement of debt, 791–792
7-Eleven Stores, 1081
75% test, 1276, 1333–1334
Sewer, Andy, 836
SFAC, see Statements of Financial
      Accounting Concepts
SFAS, see Statements of Financial
      Accounting Standards
Shares, reacquisition of, 829–834
Share-based compensation, 892
Share capital, 280, 875–876
Shareholders, entity perspective and, 6
Shareholders' equity, see Equity
Share premium, 280, 876
Share price appreciation, 914
Share system, 823–824
Shatner, William, 1051
Shaustyuk, K., 911

Sherwin-Williams Company, 275, 416, 417,
      444, 445
Short, Daniel G., 443n.15, 445n.20
Short account, 377–378
Shortages, normal/abnormal, 493
Short-term available-for-sale securities, 1440
Short-term borrowing, 348
Short-term creditors, 1522
Short-term financing, 352n.4
Short-term investments, 217–219
Short-term nontrade notes payable, 1440
Short-term obligations, 705n.5, 754
Short-term paper, 346n.1
Short-term receivables, 349
Showa Shell Sekiyu, 979n.14
Shwiff, K., 1298
Sick pay, 713
Sidel, Robin, 224
Siebel Systems, 1489
Siemens AG, 755
Siemens Group, 641
Significant influence, 964
Significant noncash activities, 232
Significant noncash transactions, 1441–1442
Simon Property Group, 763
Simple capital structure EPS, 900–904, 911
  complex vs., 900
  comprehensive example of, 903–904
  preferred stock dividends, 900–901
  stock dividends/stock splits, 902–903
  weighted-average number of shares
      outstanding, 901–903
Simple interest, 290
Single-period statements, correcting errors
      on, 1362
Single-step income statements, 167–168
Single sum:
  future value of, 295–296
  present value of, 296–298
Single-sum problems, 294–299
  and future values of an annuity, 300–306
  and present value of annuity due, 308–311
  and present value of ordinary annuity,
      306–311
  solving for unknown in, 298–299
Sinopec, 32
Small- and medium-sized entities (SMEs),
      358, 1549–1550
Small stock dividends, 842
Smith, Alison, 488
Smooth earnings, and change in
      accounting method, 1365–1366
Smoothing unexpected gains/losses,
      1197–1198, 1260
Social Security, 291, 710–711
Société Générale, 281
Soft assets, 19
Software costs, 669–670
Solectron Corporation, 68
Solomon, Deborah, 154n.4, 557
Solvency, 214, 229
Solvency ratios, 1523n.26
Sonic Foundry Corporation, 326
Sony Corp., 31, 1137n.6
SOPs (Statements of Position), 10
Sotheby's Holdings, 422
South American countries, 55

Southern California Edison, 835

Southwest Airlines, 102, 215, 559, 648, 979, 1182, 1268, 1273, 1330, 1412

SOX, *see* Sarbanes-Oxley Act of 2002

SPEs, *see* Special purpose entities

Special assessments, 539

Special journals, 92

Special purpose entities (SPEs), 371, 784, 996, 1269

Specific-goods LIFO approach, 435

Specific-goods pooled approach, 435

Specific-goods pooled LIFO approach, 435

Specific identification, 429, 962*n*.6

Specific indexes, 438*n*.8

Speculators, and derivatives, 979

Spirits, maturing, 495

Sprint Nextel, 691

Standard account form, 92–93

Standardized cost system, 481*n*.4

Standard & Poor's Corporation, 768

Standards Advisory Council (SAC), 33

Standards setting:
  government intervention in, 29
  in political environment, 16–17

Standard-setting organizations, international, 32–35

Stanga, Keith G., 436*n*.5, 441*n*.11

Stanley Black & Decker, 219

Staples, 475, 1344

Starbucks Corp., 68, 538, 953, 1008, 1270, 1283

Start-up costs, 668–669

State corporate law, 822

Stated interest rate, 293, 359*n*.9, 766

Stated value method, 831

State Grid, 32

Statement of cash flows, 85, 228–236, 1410–1451
  accounts receivable (net), 1438–1440
  adjustments to net income, 1434–1437
  analysis of transactions, 1444–1450
  change in cash, 1417, 1420, 1423
  classification of cash flows, 1413–1415
  content and format of, 229–230
  format of, 1415
  illustrations, 1416–1434
  indirect vs. direct method, 1427–1434
  net cash flow from operating activities, 1417–1419, 1421–1422, 1424–1425, 1427–1434
  net cash flows from investing and financing activities, 1419, 1422–1423, 1426, 1427
  net losses, 1440–1441
  preparation of, 230–232, 1415–1416. *See also* Statement of cash flows worksheet
  purpose of, 228–229, 1412
  significant noncash transactions, 1441–1442
  sources of information for, 1426
  usefulness of, 232–236, 1412
  working capital changes, 1440
  worksheets for, 1443–1451

Statement of cash flows worksheet, 1443–1451
  accounts receivable (net), 1447
  building depreciation and amortization of trademark, 1448–1449

change in retained earnings, 1444, 1445

common stock/related accounts, 1449

equipment and accumulated depreciation, 1448

final reconciling entry, 1449–1450

guidelines for using, 1443–1444

illustration of completed, 1451

inventories, 1447

investment in stock, 1447

land, 1447–1448

noncash charges/credits, 1449

prepaid expense, 1447

preparing, 1444, 1445

reasons for using, 1443–1444

Statement of changes in equity, 877–878

Statements of Financial Accounting Concepts (SFAC), 13, 43–44, 73
  No. 1 ("Objectives of Financial Reporting by Business Enterprises"), 43, 1488
  No. 2 ("Qualitative Characteristics of Accounting Information"), 43
  No. 3 ("Elements of Financial Statements of Business Enterprises"), 43, 1043*n*.4
  No. 5 ("Recognition and Measurement in Financial Statements of Business Enterprises"), 43, 53–55, 784, 1043*nn*.4–5, 1046*n*.10, 1057*n*.15, 1068*nn*.22–23
  No. 6 ("Elements of Financial Statements"), 43, 52, 54, 163*n*.6, 485, 774*n*.5, 784, 825*n*.3
  No. 7 ("Using Cash Flow Information and Present Value in Accounting Measurements"), 44
  No. 8 ("Conceptual Framework for Financial Reporting"), 42*n*.1, 43, 44, 45*nn*.5–6
  No. 54 ("Illegal Acts by Clients"), 1494*n*.7
  No. 109 ("An Empirical Investigation of Its Incremental Value-Relevance Relative to APB No. 11"), 1122
  No. 141–Revised, 693

Statements of Financial Accounting Standards (SFAS):
  No. 6 ("Elements of Financial Statements"), 1217*n*.22
  No. 13 ("Accounting for Leases"), 1283*n*.9
  No. 34 ("Capitalization of Interest Cost"), 543*n*.3
  No. 58 ("Reports on Audited Financial Statements"), 1364*n*.10
  No. 114 ("Accounting by Creditors for Impairment of a Loan"), 792*n*.16, 792*n*.17
  No. 145 ("Rescission of FASH Statements No. 4, 44, and 64, and Technical Corrections"), 776*n*.9

Statement of financial position, 212–213, 877. *See also* Balance sheet(s)

Statement of retained earnings, 115

Statement of stockholders' equity, 182*n*.20, 184–185, 848

Statement on Auditing Standards:
  No. 58 ("Reports on Audited Financial Statements"), 1508*n*.11

No. 99 ("Consideration of Fraud in a Financial Statement Audit"), 1494*n*.5, 1519*n*.25

Statements of Position (SOPs), 10

Statistical sampling, 420*n*.1

Stauffer Chemical Company, 441

Stead, D., 1493

Sterling Construction Corp., 1271, 1278–1281, 1286–1289, 1291–1295, 1298–1300

Sternstein, Aliya, 1489*n*.1

Stewardship, 6

Stickney, Clyde P., 1411

Stires, David, 899

STMicroelectronics (STM), 887

Stock. *See also specific types, e.g.:* Preferred stock
  buybacks, *see* Buyback(s)
  costs of issuing, 828
  dividend distributions, 837–838
  issuance of, 549, 825–829
  issued below par value, 825*n*.4
  issued in noncash transaction, 827–828
  issued with other securities, 826–827
  rights and privileges of, 823–824
  as worksheet entry, 1449

Stock appreciation rights (SARs), 913–916
  equity awards, 914
  example of, 915–916
  liability awards, 914–915

Stock-based compensation plans, 891–892
  accounting for, 893–899
  debate over stock option accounting, 897–899
  disclosure of, 897
  employee stock purchase plans, 896
  and fair value, 289
  reporting issue with, 892
  restricted-stock, 894–896
  stock appreciation rights, 913–916
  stock-option plans, 893–894

Stock dividends, 707, 841–843
  in EPS computation, 902–903
  and par value, 844–845
  reporting, 1442
  stock splits vs., 844–845

Stockholders, 823, 1522

Stockholders' equity, 88–89, 225, 820–850
  analysis of, 849–850
  on balance sheet, 225–226, 847–848
  and corporate capital, 824–834
  and corporate form of organization, 822–824
  dividend policy, 837–847
  International Financial Reporting Standards for, 874–878
  preferred stock, 834–836
  presentation of, 847–848
  and SFAS No. 6, 825*n*.3
  statement of, *see* Statement of stockholders' equity

Stock investment, as worksheet entry, 1447

Stock markets, 1511

Stock-option plans, 893–894

Stock options, 891
   adjustment to net income for, 1436–1437
   in diluted EPS computation, 907–908
   errors in, 1360
   reduced use of, 882–883
Stock right, 823n.2, 890
Stock splits, 843–845
   in 1990s, 844
   in EPS computation, 902–903
   reporting, 1442
   reverse, 844–845
   stock dividends vs., 844–845
Stock warrants, 823n.2, 887–892
   conceptual questions regarding, 889–890
   in diluted EPS computation, 907–908
   incremental method, 889–890
   issued with other securities, 889–891
   proportional method, 888–889–911
   rights to subscribe to additional shares, 890–891
Stott, David, 597n.7
Straight-line amortization, 815, 1195
Straight-line depreciation, 593–594
Strand, W. K., 591n.1
TheStreet.com, 776
Strict cash basis, 118–119
Strike price, 980
Stroh's Brewery Co., 1214
Studebaker Automobile, 1211
Study Group on Establishment of Accounting Principles, 9
Subprime mortgage crisis, 371
Subsequent events (post-balance-sheet events), 1495–1496, 1550–1552
Subsidiaries, 967
Subsidiary ledger, 85
Substitution approach, 558–559
Subway, 655
Successful-efforts concept, 608
Sullivan, Scott, 28
Summary of Significant Accounting, 237
Summers, Lawrence, 20
Sum-of-the-years'-digits method, 594
Sunbeam, 17, 48, 153, 1053
Sunder, Shyam, 443n.18
Sunshine Mining, 42–43, 765
Suntrust Banks, 18, 358n.8, 1198
Supersession, 591
SUPERVALU Inc., 470
Supplementary information, 60–61
Supplies, adjusting entries for, 98–99
Supporting schedules, 242
Surplus (term), 243
Sustainability issues, 648–649
Swensen's, Inc., 1082n.30
Swieringa, R. J., 1299n.14
Synthetic lease, 1269, 1272

T
Tait, Nikki, 17
Take-or-pay contract, 784
Takeover protection covenants, 885n.2
Target Corporation, 69, 228, 419, 474, 488, 497, 538, 620, 786–787, 1346, 1436
Tastee Freeze, 1081

Taxes. See also Income taxes, accounting for
   allocation of, 1437
   corporate, 710n.6, 1140
   disclosure of, 1493
   employer payroll, 712
   errors in, 1360
   and leasing, 1284
   Social Security, 710–711
   uncertain tax positions, 1143–1144
   unemployment, 711
Taxable amounts, 1120
Taxable income, 1118–1119, 1127–1130, 1145, 1148–1149, 1152
Taxable temporary differences, 1127, 1145
Tax depreciation, book depreciation vs., 617
Tax expense, deferred (benefit), 1149–1150
Tax-planning strategy, 1145
Tax rates, 1130–1132
TCBY, 1081
Technology-related intangible assets, 656–658
Teco Energy, 236
Telemundo, 1497
Temporary accounts, 112
Temporary differences, 1120, 1127–1130, 1145
   examples of, 1129–1130
   originating, 1128
   originating/reversing aspects of, 1128
   and SFAS No. 6, 1122
Tenet Healthcare, 844
Tenneco, Inc., 888
Tergesen, Ann, 1419
Term bonds, 765
Terminations, pension, 1214–1215
Terminology of financial statements, as disclosure technique, 242
Texaco, 358
TGI Friday's, 1081
Third-party guarantors, 1277, 1303
3M, 849
Three-bucket model, 374
Three-column form of account, 92–93
Timberland, 236
Time diagram, 294
Timeliness, 19, 51–52
Time period assumption (periodicity assumption), 55–56
Times interest earned, 787
Time value concepts, 288–294
   applications of, 288–289
   and compound interest, 290–293
   and interest, 289–293
   and simple interest, 290
   variables fundamental to, 294
Timex, 474
Timmons, H., 768
T J International, 468–469
Tootsie Roll Industries, 204, 626–627, 839, 1225, 1226, 1502, 1503
Toscano, P., 1132
Total-inventory approach, 527–528
Total S.A., 32, 756
Townsend, Leah, 18n.11
Toyota, 31, 32, 51, 160, 655, 756

Trade accounts payable, 703, see Accounts payable(s)
Trade accounts receivable, 363
Trade discounts, 351
Trade loading, 1053
Trademark (trade name), 653, 1448–1449
Trade notes payable, see Notes payable
Trade receivables, 350
Trading, 218
   debt securities, 953, 959–960, 964, 1440
   on the equity, 849
Trading investments, 1029
Trading securities, 953, 959–960, 964, 1440
Traditional LIFO, 434
Transactions, 84, 91
   and cash flows statement, 1416
   identifying and recording, 89–91
Transaction analysis, 153
Transaction approach, 162–163
Transaction costs, 1030n.44
Transfer agents, 824
Transfers between investment categories, 974–975
Transfers-in, 493
Transfer of ownership test, 1275
Transwitch, 480
Travel advances, 346
Treasury bills, 346n.1
Treasury stock (shares), 280, 830
   acquisitions of, 831n.9
   as assets, 830n.7
   buyback of, 837n.12
   and capital stock, 830
   cash dividends on, 839
   purchase of, 831–832
   retiring, 834
   sale of, 832–833
Treasury-stock method, 908, 918
Trial balance, 96, 153. See also specific types, e.g.: Adjusted trial balance
Trial balance columns, 127
Triggers, debt-rating, 1493
Triple smoothing, 1201
Troubled debt:
   accounting for, 790–798
   restructuring, 790–796, 815
"True and fair view," 35
Trusts, 1185, 1186
Trustees, 1185
Tucker, Reed, 658
Turner, Lynn, 61, 829, 1116
Turner, Ted, 830
Turnover ratios, 1523n.26
Tweedle, Sir D., 21
TXU Corp., 1270
Tyco International, 1493n.4, 1518

U
UAL, Inc., 1273, 1330
Unamortized bond issue costs, 774
Uncertain tax positions, 1143–1144
Uncollectible accounts receivable, 50, 353–358, 1073
Underfunded pension plans, 1189, 1205
Understandability, 19, 52
Understatement of unearned revenue, 1368–1369

Underwriters Labs Inc., 1357
Unearned revenues, 708
    adjusting entries for, 102
    as class of adjusting entries, 97
    understatement of, 1368–1369
Unemployment taxes, 711
Unexpected (deferred) asset gain or
    loss, 1201
Unfiled suits, 718
Unguaranteed residual value, 1277
    in lessee accounting, 1293–1294
    in lessor accounting, 1294–1295
    for sales-type lease, 1297–1298
Uniform Commercial Code, 824
Uniform Stock Transfer Act, 824
Union Planters, 1024–1025
Uniroyal Technology Corporation (UTC),
    274–275
Unit approach, AcSEC and, 597n.6
United Airlines, 215, 979, 1182, 1268
United Continental Holdings, 722
United Kingdom, 1515
United Parcel Service (UPS), 47, 602
United States, 51
U.S. Congress, 17
U.S. Forest Service, 484
Unit LIFO, 434
Units-of-production approach, 606
Universal Parks and Resorts, 1497
Universal Pictures, 1497
Unqualified opinion (clean option),
    1508–1510
Unrealized gains/losses, 1436
Unrealized holding gain/loss,
    365, 782–783
Unrecognized gains/losses:
    in pension plan, 1200–1201
    in postretirement benefits,
    1224–1225
Unsecured bonds, 765
Unusual gains or losses, 169–170
Upper (ceiling), 475–476
UPS, 47, 602, 707, 1119n.1
UPS Capital, 1271
Upton, Wayne, Jr., 215n.4
Urban Outfitters, 891
US Airways, 215
USX Corp., 358
UTC (Uniroyal Technology Corporation),
    274–275

V

Valuation:
    of accounts receivable, 352–358
    of agricultural inventory, 530–532
    of inventories, 420, 481–485
    measurement issues in, 286–287
    at net realizable value, 481–482
    and purchase commitments, 483–485
    and SFAS No. 15X, 549n.5
    using relative sales value, 482–483
Valuation allowance, 1135–1136, 1145
    for deferred tax asset, 1125–1126
    evidence for, 1135–1136
    loss carryforward with, 1135–1136

loss carryforward without, 1134–1135
Valuation Resource Group (VRG),
    11n.5, 286–287
Value-added taxes, 1132
Value-in-use, 639, 693
Vames, Steven, 707, 776
Variable-interest entities (VIEs), 996–999
Variable-rate mortgage, 782
Varshney, A., 1134n.3, 1204, 1273
Vatter, William J., 353n.5
Verifiability, 51
Verifiable benchmark, 56
VeriFone, 5
Verizon, 1042
Verizon Communications Inc., 1202, 1219
Vermont Teddy Bear Co., 1478–1479
Vertical percentage analysis, 1527
Vested (term), 893n.8
Vested benefits, 1187, 1188
Vested rights, 713
Viacom Inc., 1270
Vickrey, Don, 842n.16
VIEs (variable-interest entities), 996–999
Vincent, Linda, 597n.7
VISA, 366, 367n.12
Vishay Intertechnology, 480
Visteon, 18
Vodafone, 31
Volkswagen, 32
Volume discount, 1046
VRG (Valuation Resource Group),
    286–287

W

W. R. Grace, 54
W. T. Grant Company, 228, 233,
    1410–1411, 1443
Wachovia, 897
Wages, 106–107, 1368
Walgreen Company, 68, 98, 134, 203, 216,
    421, 828–829, 1283
Wal-Mart Stores, Inc., 19, 32, 77, 328, 345,
    358, 416, 420, 489, 497, 537, 539, 709,
    765, 766, 821, 822, 829, 891, 1119n.1,
    1300–1301, 1330, 1364
Walt Disney Company, 45, 651, 655, 670,
    824–825, 891
Warrants, *see* Stock warrants
Warranties, 719–721. *See also* Guarantees
    accrual method for, 719–721
    cash-basis method for, 719
    tax deduction for, 1123
Washington Mutual, 691
The Washington Post, 897, 899
Watered stock, 828
Watts, Ross L., 1365n.11
Webber, Andrew Lloyd, 655
Webber Inc., 38
Weber, R. P., 1141n.7
Webvan, 844
Weighted-average accumulated
    expenditures, 543–544
Weighted-average method, 429
Weighted-average number of shares
    outstanding, 901–903, 917

Weil, J., 48, 829, 951, 959, 1117, 1125
Welch, David, 1183
"Welfare benefits," 1217
Wells Fargo, 344, 1271
Western Airlines, 1214
Westinghouse Electric Corporation,
    1107–1108
Weyerhaeuser Company, 174,
    220, 484
Wheat, Francis, 9
Wheat Committee, 9, 10
Wheeler, J. E., 1141n.7
Wherehouse Entertainment Inc., 885n.2
WHX Corporation, 597
Wiebold, Incorporated, 873
Wilbert, James, R., 1220n.26
Willamette Industries, 241, 601
Williams Companies, 785
Williams-Sonoma Inc., 999
William Wrigley Jr. (company), 474
Wingfield, Nick, 654n.3
Wisconsin, 308
"With-and-without" method,
    942–943
Wm Morrison Supermarkets, 1553
Wolverton, Troy, 899
Working capital, 223, 1440
Working capital ratio, 729
Work in process inventory, 416
Worksheet(s):
    adjustments entered on, 127–129
    pension, *see* Pension worksheet
    preparation of, 130
    statement of cash flows, *see* Statement of
    cash flows worksheet
WorldCom, 2, 17, 28, 31, 153, 557, 1439,
    1489, 1518
World markets, 32
Wright, David W., 1525n.28
Write-offs, 168, 355, 588, 601, 1125

X

XBRL, *see* eXtensible Business Reporting
    Language
Xerox Corp., 17, 153, 656, 1298, 1442–1443

Y

Yahoo Inc., 61, 68, 883, 1133, 1138, 1143
Year-end-adjustment, expenses subject to,
    1504–1505
Years-of-service amortization, 1194–1195
Year-to-date measurements, 1553
Young, S., 1053

Z

Zeff, Stephen A., 17n.9, 842n.15
Zero-interest-bearing notes, 359, 360–361,
    704–705, 777–778
Zero-interest debenture bonds, 765
Zero-profit method, 1110–1112
Zimmerman, Jerold L., 1365n.11
Zion, D., 614n.15, 1134n.3, 1204, 1273
Z-scores, 226
Zuckerberg, Mark, 836
Zynga, 5, 836, 911

The Wiley Faculty Network

The Place Where Faculty Connect ...

The Wiley Faculty Network is a global community of faculty connected by a passion for teaching and a drive to learn and share. Connect with the Wiley Faculty Network to collaborate with your colleagues, find a mentor, attend virtual and live events, and view a wealth of resources all designed to help you grow as an educator. Embrace the art of teaching—great things happen where faculty connect!

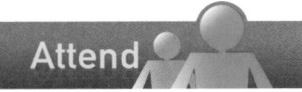

Attend

Discover innovative ideas and gain knowledge you can use.

- Training
- Virtual Guest Lectures
- Live Events

View

Explore your resources and development opportunities.

- Teaching Resources
- Archived Guest Lectures
- Recorded Presentations
- Professional Development Modules

Collaborate

Connect with colleagues— your greatest resource.

- Find a Mentor
- Interest Groups
- Blog

Find out more at
www.WHEREFACULTYCONNECT.com

WILEY FACULTY NETWORK

Virtual Guest Lectures

Connect with recognized leaders across disciplines and collaborate with your peers on timely topics and discipline specific issues, many of which offer CPE credit.

Live and Virtual Events

These invitation-only, discipline-specific events are organized through a close partnership between the WFN, Wiley, and the academic community near the event location.

Technology Training

Discover a wealth of topic- and technology-specific training presented by subject matter experts, authors, and faculty where and when you need it.

Teaching Resources

Propel your teaching and student learning to the next level with quality peer-reviewed case studies, testimonials, classroom tools, and checklists.

Connect with Colleagues

Achieve goals and tackle challenges more easily by enlisting the help of your peers. Connecting with colleagues through the WFN can help you improve your teaching experience.

KIESO INTERMEDIATE ACCOUNTING 15E: LIST OF ACCOUNTS

A

Accounts Payable
Accounts Receivable
Accrued Liabilities
Accumulated Depreciation
Accumulated Depreciation—Buildings
Accumulated Depreciation—Capital
 Leases
Accumulated Depreciation—Equipment
Accumulation Depreciation—Machinery
Accumulated Depreciation—Plant Assets
Accumulated Depreciation—Trucks
Adjustment to Record Inventory at Cost
Administrative Expenses
Admissions Revenue
Advances to Employees
Advertising Expense
Allowance for Doubtful Accounts
Allowance for Expropriation
Allowance for Sales Returns and
 Allowances
Allowance to Reduce Deferred Tax Asset
 to Expected Realizable Value
Allowance to Reduce Inventory to LIFO
Allowance to Reduce Inventory to Market
Amortization Expense
Asset Retirement Obligation

B

Bad Debt Expense
Benefit Due to Loss Carryback
Benefit Due to Loss Carryforward
Billings on Construction in Process
Bond Issue Expense
Bond Sinking Fund
Bonds Payable
Buildings

C

Call Option
Cash
Cash Over and Short
Cash Surrender Value of Life Insurance
Coal Mine
Commission Expense
Commission Payable
Common Stock
Common Stock Dividend Distributable
Compensation Expense
Computer Software Costs
Construction Expenses
Construction in Process
Contribution Expense
Contribution Revenue
Convertible Preferred Stock
Copyrights
Cost of Goods Sold
Cost of Installment Sales
Costs of Construction
Current Maturity of Long-Term Debt

D

Dealer's Fund Reserve
Debt Conversion Expense
Debt Investments
Deferred Gross Profit
Deferred Tax Asset
Deferred Tax Liability
Delivery Expense
Depreciation Expense
Direct Labor
Discount on Bonds Payable
Discount on Notes Payable
Discount on Notes Receivable
Dividend Receivable
Dividend Revenue
Dividends
Dividends Payable
Due to Customer
Due from Factor
Dues Revenue

E

Entertainment Expense
Equipment
Equity Investments
Estimated Liability on Purchase
 Commitments
Executory Costs
Executory Costs Payable
Extraordinary Items—Gain
Extraordinary Items—Loss

F

Factory Overhead
Fair Value Adjustment
FICA Taxes Payable
Finance Charge
Finance Expense
Finance Revenue
Finished Goods Inventory
Franchises
Freight-In
Freight-Out
FUTA Taxes Payable
Futures Contract

G

Gain on Disposal of Equipment
Gain on Disposal of Land
Gain on Disposal of Machinery
Gain on Disposal of Plant Assets
Gain on Disposal of Trucks
Gain on Redemption of Bonds
Gain on Repossession
Gain on Restructuring of Debt
Gain on Sale of Investments
Gain on Sale of Land
Gain on Sale of Machinery
Gain on Sale of Plant Assets

Gain on Settlement of ARO
Goodwill
Green Fees Revenue

I

Income Summary
Income Tax Expense
Income Taxes Payable
Income Taxes Receivable
Installment Accounts Receivable
Installment Sales Revenue
Insurance Expense
Insurance Premium Payable
Insurance Revenue
Intangible Assets
Interest Expense
Interest Payable
Interest Receivable
Interest Revenue
Inventory
Inventory of Premiums
Inventory on Consignment
Inventory Over and Short
Investment Income
Investment Loss
Investments
Investments in Common Stock
Investments in Stocks and Bonds

L

Land
Land Improvements
Lawsuit Liability
Lawsuit Loss
Lease Liability
Lease Receivable
Leased Buildings
Leased Equipment
Liability under Stock-Appreciation Plan
Litigation Expense or Loss
Litigation Liability
Loss Due to Market Decline
 of Inventory
Loss from Expropriation
Loss from Long-Term Contracts
Loss on ARO Settlement
Loss on Capital Lease
Loss on Disposal of Equipment
Loss on Disposal of Machinery
Loss on Disposal of Plant Assets
Loss on Disposal of Trucks
Loss on Disposal of Land
Loss on Impairment
Loss on Investments
Loss on Redemption of Bonds
Loss on Repossession
Loss on Sale of Investments
Loss on Sale of Receivables
Loss on Settlement of Call Option
Loss on Settlement of Put Option

M

Machinery
Maintenance and Repairs Expense
Materials
Memo entry
Miscellaneous Expense
Mortgage Payable

N

No entry
Noncontrolling Interest
Notes Payable
Notes Receivable

O

Office Expense
Oil Platform
Operating Expenses
Organization Expense
Other Comprehensive Income (G/L)
Other Comprehensive Income (PSC)
Other Expense
Other Revenue
Owner's Capital
Owner's Drawings

P

Paid-in Capital from Treasury Stock
Paid-in Capital in Excess of Par—
   Common Stock
Paid-in Capital in Excess of Par—
   Preferred Stock
Paid-in Capital in Excess of Stated
   Value—Common Stock
Paid-in Capital—Expired Stock Options
Paid-in Capital—Stock Options
Paid-in Capital—Stock Warrants
Patents
Payroll Tax Expense
Payroll Taxes Payable
Pension Asset/Liability
Pension Expense
Petty Cash
Plant Assets
Postage Expense
Postretirement Asset/Liability
Postretirement Expense

Preferred Stock
Premium Expense
Premium Liability
Premium on Bonds Payable
Prepaid Advertising
Prepaid Expenses
Prepaid Insurance
Prepaid Lease Executory Costs
Prepaid Rent
Property Dividends Payable
Property Tax Expense
Property Taxes Payable
Purchase Discounts
Purchase Discounts Lost
Purchase Returns and Allowances
Purchases
Put Option

R

Raw Materials
Recourse Liability
Realized Gross Profit
Recovery of Loss from Impairment
Rent Expense
Rent Payable
Rent Receivable
Rent Revenue
Repossessed Merchandise
Research and Development Expense
Restricted Cash
Retained Earnings
Returnable Deposit
Revenue from Consignment Sales
Revenue from Franchise Fees
Revenue from Long-Term Contracts

S

Salaries and Wages Expense
Salaries and Wages Payable
Sales Commission Expense
Sales Commissions Payable
Sales Discounts
Sales Discounts Forfeited
Sales Returns and Allowances
Sales Revenue
Sales Tax Expense
Sales Taxes Payable
Selling Expenses
Service Revenue

Shipping Expense
Supplies
Supplies Expense
SUTA Taxes Payable
Swap Contract

T

Telephone and Internet Expense
Timber
Timberland
Trademarks
Trade Names
Trading Securities
Travel Expense
Treasury Stock
Trucks

U

Unamortized Bond Issue Costs
Unearned Admissions Revenue
Unearned Advertising Revenue
Unearned Compensation
Unearned Dues Revenue
Unearned Football Ticket Revenue
Unearned Franchise Fees
Unearned Profit on Sale-Leaseback
Unearned Rent Revenue
Unearned Revenue
Unearned Sales Revenue
Unearned Service Revenue
Unearned Subscriptions Revenue
Unearned Warranty Revenue
Union Dues Payable
Unrealized Holding Gain or
   Loss—Equity
Unrealized Holding Gain or
   Loss—Income
Utilities Expenses

W

Warranty Expense
Warranty Liability
Warranty Payable
Warranty Revenue
Withholding Taxes Payable
Work-in-Process
Write-Off of Goodwill
Write-Off of Inventory

Laurie Mauro, Pharm. D.

Laurie Mauro, Pharm. D.

Sixth Edition

Applied Therapeutics:

The Clinical Use of Drugs

Edited By

Lloyd Yee Young, Pharm.D.
Adjunct, Associate Professor of Clinical Pharmacy,
Washington State University,
Pullman/Vancouver, Washington

Mary Anne Koda-Kimble, Pharm.D.
Professor, Chairwoman, Division of Clinical Pharmacy,
School of Pharmacy, University of California at
San Francisco, San Francisco, California

Assistant Editors

Wayne A. Kradjan, Pharm.D.
Professor, Associate Dean, University of
Washington, School of Pharmacy,
Seattle, Washington

B. Joseph Guglielmo, Pharm.D.
Professor, Division of Clinical Pharmacy,
School of Pharmacy, University of California
at San Francisco, San Francisco, California

Applied Therapeutics, Inc.
Vancouver, WA

Applied Therapeutics, Inc.
P.O. Box 5077
Vancouver, WA 98668-5077
Phone: (360) 253-7123
FAX: (360) 253-8475

Previous editions of *Applied Therapeutics: The Clinical Use of Drugs:*
© 1992 fifth edition; © 1988 fourth edition; © 1983 third edition; the
first and second editions were entitled Applied Therapeutics for
Clinical Pharmacists © 1975 and © 1978 by Applied Therapeutics, Inc.

Library of Congress Card Catalog #95-075490
ISBN 0-915486-23-7

First Printing August 1995

PREFACE TO THE SIXTH EDITION

As this sixth edition of Applied Therapeutics goes to press, unprecedented change is occurring in the delivery of health care. Managed care increasingly dictates how care will be delivered; hospitals are closing or consolidating as the number of admissions diminish and patient stays become more abbreviated; primary care providers are taking center stage, while specialists struggle to find their niche; wellness and prevention programs intended to keep patients out of health care systems are growing; and medical information systems are beginning to provide "outcomes" information for large populations. Drugs comprise approximately 7% to 9% of the total health costs and are considered by many to be one of the most cost-effective modes of treatment. Nevertheless, because drug benefits are often "carved out" of the medical reimbursement, benefit managers tend to treat these agents as commodities. Price and efficient delivery are often foremost on the minds of decision makers even though neither guarantees the desired therapeutic outcome.

This text amply demonstrates the complexity of pharmaceutical care. A good therapeutic outcome relies on the appropriate selection, use, and evaluation of drug therapy and requires thoughtful attention to the individual characteristics of the patient. As the managed care system produces an increasing number of therapeutic guidelines and clinical pathways, we urge clinicians to keep a watchful eye for the exception to the rule and to continually incorporate new data from the literature into their thinking.

Many changes have been made to this sixth edition. As in past editions, we have urged our authors to present cases which stimulate the reader to integrate and apply therapeutic principles to the specific patient described. Generous feedback from our readers caused us to expand substantially the oncology, psychiatric, dermatology, drug abuse, pediatric, and geriatric sections. New chapters addressing a problem-oriented approach to drug therapy and biotechnology have been added as well. For our readers outside of the United States, equivalent international units have been added, where appropriate, to the end of each case history. In addition, commonly abbreviated terms are spelled out on first usage to help familiarize practitioners with standard terminology. All chapters have been revised and updated, many of them substantially, to reflect changes in the field. We believe we have upgraded the quality of the text significantly through the critical reviews and guidance of our section editors.

Ultimately, we have added more at a time when the health care world cries for less. Nevertheless, we feel this is justified as drug therapy becomes more complex and patients previously treated in hospitals are cared for in intermediate-care facilities, the home, and other ambulatory settings. We continue to abide by the philosophies and principles set forth in the prefaces of our first and fifth editions: to provide students and practitioners with a glimpse into the minds of clinicians who are assessing and solving therapeutic problems on a daily basis so that they too can begin modeling their own problem-solving skills. The "Update Sections" we have included at the end of some chapters reaffirm our commitment to bring you a text that is as current as possible. As always, we welcome and value your comments so that we can continue to improve our product.

Lloyd Yee Young
Mary Anne Koda-Kimble
August 1995

PREFACE TO THE FIFTH EDITION

Two decades have passed since the publication of the first edition of this textbook. As we reflect on this fifth edition, we remain enthused about our original intent: to provide students and young practitioners with a glimpse into the minds of experienced clinicians who are assessing and solving therapeutic problems on a daily basis. We continue to use the case-history-based, question-and-answer format which encourages readers to utilize specific patient data to identify, assess, and solve therapeutic problems. We have also encouraged the authors to expand the introductory portions of their chapters to provide the overview which is needed to integrate and apply information from a variety of sources to the solution of a specific problem.

Health care educators across the country are becoming increasingly concerned about the *amount* of information which seems important to include in their curriculums. As faculty have begun to reach the realization that they cannot continue to "stuff their students like sausages" with the volume of facts that seem important—but which are ever changing—they have begun to turn to the competencies that students will need to practice throughout their careers. The ability to learn on one's own, think critically, communicate effectively, and to identify, assess, and solve problems are competencies that have received most attention. Now, faculty are beginning to focus on *how* they can provide an environment in which these skills can be nurtured, practiced, and refined.

We view this textbook as a tool that can be used by the reader to begin modeling his or her own therapeutic problem-solving skills. Although each of the responses has been carefully researched and well thought out, we emphasize that any given response represents a *single approach* to the solution of a problem. As all of us in practice know, therapeutic solutions are seldom black or white—they are gray. Furthermore, each of us brings with us our own sets of biases and experiences to the solution of a problem. That is why it is often useful to collaborate with others in the solution of particularly complex and difficult issues, to welcome different viewpoints, and—in the end—to do what is absolutely best for the patient. This is all to say that the essential feature of this text is that it serves as a model of how one might begin to approach common therapeutic problems which arise in the treatment of patients with various diseases. One's own interpretation of the original data and consideration of new information that has become available must always be incorporated into the solution of a problem that involves an actual patient.

We are committed to offering you a text that is as up-to-date as possible. Thus, we have given our authors the opportunity to add "last minute" information in an Update section which appears at the end of selected chapters. For example, you will find information on sumitriptan for managing migraine headaches, the effects of enalapril on mortality from congestive heart failure, ticlopidine for stroke, and other new drugs that were approved by the FDA since the original writing of these chapters. Each chapter has been thoroughly revised and updated, and we have added new chapters addressing solid organ transplantation and cerebrovascular disorders as well. To facilitate the use of this text as a reference source, the outlines which appear at the beginning of each chapter have be revised to reflect the order in which the material actually appears and the index has been expanded to facilitate retrieval of specific information from text. Many of these features have been added in response to our readers who have taken the time to tell us how we can make this textbook better. We always welcome your comments.

Mary Anne Koda-Kimble
Lloyd Yee Young
January 1992

In the past decade, new roles for the pharmacist have emerged. More and more frequently the pharmacist is placed in increasingly responsible positions within the health care delivery system. In this capacity (s)he is able to have a significant influence on the quality of health care delivered to the patient. M. Silverman and P. Lee have skillfully assessed the current and future role of the pharmacist in *Pills, Profits and Politics*.[1]

"...It is the pharmacist who can play a vital role in assisting physicians to prescribe rationally, who can help see to it that the right drug is ordered for the right patient at the right time, in the right amounts and with due consideration of costs and that the patient knows how, when and why to use both prescription and non-prescription products.

It is the pharmacist who has been most highly trained as an expert in drug products, who has the best opportunity to keep up-date on developments in this field and who can serve both physician and patient as a knowledgeable advisor. It is the pharmacist who can take a key part in preventing drug misuse, drug abuse and irrational prescribing."

Many schools of pharmacy have made substantial curriculum changes to prepare their graduates for these responsibilities. Although traditional pharmacy courses have imparted factual information about drugs, they have not enabled the students too apply these facts to the drug therapy of patients. Similarly, traditional pharmacology and medical text books do not provide the professional with sufficient information to make a judgment regarding the selection and dosing of a particular product for a specific patient. To arrive at this decision, the clinician must consider a number of patient factors, including age, renal and hepatic function, concurrent disease states and medications and allergies. (S)he must also consider drug product factors, including bioavailability, pharmacokinetics, efficacy, toxicity, risk to benefit ratio, and cost.

We have found that students have most difficulty in *integrating* and *applying* the multiple components of their eduction to formulate the safest, most rational drug regimen for a given patient. We have also observed that although the student is able to enumerate the adverse effects of a drug, (s)he is unable to recognize or monitor for these effects should they occur in his/her patient.

This text is an outgrowth of the clinical pharmacy courses taught at the University of California and at Washington State University. The major objective of these courses is to enable the student to practice effectively in the clinical setting. Lectures on the pathophysiology and medical management of disease states are supplemented with conferences where students are challenged with drug therapy questions frequently asked by physicians and by case histories which require drug therapy assessment and the selection of appropriate alternatives. The objective of these conferences and this text is to enable the student to identify relevant factors in drug treatment, such as the probability of whether or not a specific drug is responsible for a patient's symptoms; the clinical significance of a drug interaction; why a specific drug is not achieving therapeutic blood levels; the dose for a patient with multiple disease states.

The success of the conference portion of our courses was a major determinant of the format used for this text; case histories which simulate the actual practice situations and frequently asked therapeutic questions are followed by well-referenced responses.

The authors have drawn much information from their clinical experiences. *It remains the responsibility of every practitioner to evaluate the appropriateness of a particular opinion in the context of the actual clinical situation and with due consideration of any new developments in the field.* Although the authors have been careful to recommend dosages that are in agreement with current standards and responsible literature, we suggest the student or practitioner consult several appropriate information sources when dealing with new and unfamiliar drugs.

---

1   Silverman, M. and Lee, PR.: Pills, Profits and Politics, University of California Press, Berkeley, 1975, p. 192.

ACKNOWLEDGMENTS

The effort needed to produce the sixth edition was prodigious. It could not have occurred without the diligence, dedication, and commitments of time from many people. As always, we are indebted to our contributing authors who struggled with deadlines and our format. To Wayne A. Kradjan and B. Joseph Guglielmo, our sincere appreciation for their cheerful cooperation, genuine thoughtfulness, and high professionalism as they worked with us on new and revised chapters. Thank you to the section editors for their commitment, patience, and expertise, they are sincerely appreciated: Rebecca S. Finley and Celeste M. Lindley, Neoplastic Disorders; Mark D. Watanabe, Psychiatric Disorders; Jeffrey N. Baldwin, Substance Abuse; Brian K. Alldredge, Neurological Disorders and Cerebrovascular Disorders; C. A. Bond, Skin Disorders; Bradley R. Williams, Geriatric Therapy; Curtis A. Johnson, Renal Disorders. Also, thank you to Ann M. Bolinger and Alvin F. Wong who graciously stepped in to rescue Pediatric Considerations. This edition required more than the usual commitment and sacrifice of personal time from our dedicated staff. Thank you to everyone on the ATI team and to the following in particular: Nannette Naught, Pam Uthe, Rick Walsh, Amy Davidson, Michele Jobes, Shanna Jacobson, Allison Wilson, Nick Welsh, Linda McCarley, Deron Kosoff, and Dianne Ellis. Producing the sixth edition in six months was a tremendous feat.

I (LYY) also am especially appreciative of Adda Alexander who taught me about learning organizations and learning styles; and Jeff Robert who insisted upon fiscally responsible pharmaceutical care. To our spouses, Linda and Don, and our children, Steve and Chris, Loren, Christopher, and Kiyomi, thank you for your loving understanding and sacrifice of many evenings and weekends of family time.

Lloyd Yee Young
Mary Anne Koda-Kimble

NOTICE TO READER

Drug therapy information is constantly evolving. Our ever changing knowledge and experience with drugs and the continual development of new drugs necessitates changes in treatment and drug therapy. The editors, authors, and the publisher of this work have made every effort to ensure the information provided herein was accurate at the time of publication. *It remains the responsibility of every practitioner to evaluate the appropriateness of a particular opinion or therapy in the context of the actual clinical situation and with due consideration of any new developments in the field.* Although the authors have been careful to recommend dosages that are in agreement with current standards and responsible literature, the student or practitioner should consult several appropriate information sources when dealing with new and unfamiliar drugs.

CONTRIBUTORS

Steven R. Abel, Pharm.D.
Assistant Director of Pharmacy, Clinical, and Educational Services, Indiana University Medical Center, Indianapolis, Indiana

Brian K. Alldredge, Pharm.D.
Associate Professor of Clinical Pharmacy and Neurology, Division of Clinical Pharmacy, Department of Neurology, School of Pharmacy and Medicine, University of California at San Francisco, San Francisco, California

J. V. Anandan, Pharm.D.
Adjunct Associate Professor, College of Pharmacy and Allied Health Professionals, Wayne State University, Detroit; Assistant Director of Pharmacy, Henry Ford Hospital, Detroit, Michigan

Laura E. Arrigoni, Pharm.D.
Clinical Assistant Professor, Department of Pharmacy, Harborview Medical Center, University of Washington, Seattle, Washington

Arasb Ateshkadi, Pharm.D.
Assistant Professor of Pharmacy Practice, College of Pharmacy, University of Utah, Salt Lake City, Utah

Francesca T. Aweeka, Pharm.D.
Associate Clinical Professor of Pharmacy, Division of Clinical Pharmacy, University of California at San Francisco, San Francisco, California

LaGenia Bailey, Pharm.D.
Clinical Assistant Professor, Department of Pharmacy Practice, College of Pharmacy, University of Illinois at Chicago, Chicago, Illinois

George R. Bailie, Pharm.D., Ph.D.
Professor of Pharmacy Practice, Albany College of Pharmacy, Albany, New York

Jeffrey N. Baldwin, Pharm.D.
Associate Professor of Pharmacy Practice and Pediatrics, Colleges of Pharmacy and Medicine, University of Nebraska Medical Center, Omaha, Nebraska

Terri L. Barton, Pharm.D.
Assistant Professor and Director of Drug Information Service, College of Pharmacy, University of Oklahoma Health Sciences Center, Oklahoma City, Oklahoma

William H. Benefield, Jr., Pharm.D.
FASCP; Clinical Pharmacologist, San Antonio State School; Clinical Assistant Professor of Pharmacy, College of Pharmacy, University of Texas at Austin, Austin; Clinical Assistant Professor of Pharmacology, Department of Pharmacology, University of Texas Health Science Center at San Antonio, San Antonio, Texas

Blaine (Jess) Benson, Pharm.D.
ABAT; Managing Director, The Poison Center, Children's Hospital, Omaha; Clinical Instructor, University of Nebraska College of Pharmacy, Omaha; Adjunct Assistant Professor, Creighton University School of Pharmacy, Omaha, Nebraska

Paul M. Beringer, Pharm.D.
Assistant Professor of Clinical Pharmacy, Department of Pharmacy, University of Southern California University Hospital, Los Angeles, California

Ann M. Bolinger, Pharm.D.
Associate Professor of Clinical Pharmacy, University of California at San Francisco School of Pharmacy, San Francisco, California

C. A. (CAB) Bond, Pharm.D.
FASHP; FCCP; Professor of Pharmacy Practice, Associate Dean for Clinical Affairs, School of Pharmacy, Texas Tech University Health Sciences Center, Amarillo, Texas

Laurie L. Briceland, Pharm.D.
Associate Professor of Pharmacy, Albany College of Pharmacy, Albany, New York

Gerald G. Briggs, B.Pharm.
Clinical Coordinator, Women's Hospital, Long Beach Memorial Medical Center, Long Beach; Adjunct Associate Professor of Pharmacy, University of Southern California, Los Angeles; Assistant Clinical Professor of Pharmacy, University of California at San Francisco, San Francisco, California

Glen Brown, Pharm.D.
Pharmacy Department, St. Paul's Hospital, Vancouver, B.C., Canada

Keith D. Campagna, Pharm.D.
BCPS; Associate Professor and Head, Department of Clinical Pharmacy Practice, Auburn University, Auburn, Alabama

Betsy A. Carlisle, Pharm.D.
Clinical Specialist, Ambulatory Care, Veterans Affairs Outpatient Clinic, Austin; Clinical Assistant Professor, University of Texas at Austin, Austin, Texas

Barry C. Carter, Pharm.D.
Professor and Chairman, Department of Pharmacy Practice, School of Pharmacy, University of Colorado, Denver, Colorado

Peggy L. Carver, Pharm.D.
Associate Professor of Pharmacy, University of Michigan College of Pharmacy, and Clinical Pharmacist, Infectious Diseases, University of Michigan Medical Center, Ann Arbor, Michigan

Connie L. Celum, M.D.
Medical Director, Harborview STD Clinic, Assistant Professor of Medicine, Division of Infectious Diseases, University of Washington, Seattle, Washington

C. Y. Jennifer Chan, Pharm.D.
Clinical Assistant Professor, College of Pharmacy, University of Texas at Austin, Austin; Clinical Assistant Professor of Pediatrics and Pharmacology, University of Texas Health Science Center at San Antonio, San Antonio, Texas

Stanley W. Chapman, M.D.
Professor of Medicine and Associate Professor of Microbiology, Director of Infectious Diseases, University of Mississippi Medical Center, Jackson, Mississippi

Moses S. S. Chow, Pharm.D.
Professor of Clinical Pharmacy and Pharmaceutics, School of Pharmacy, University of Connecticut; Director of Drug Information Service, Hartford Hospital, Hartford, Connecticut

Tom Christian, B.S.
Staff Pharmacist, Southwest Washington Medical Center, Vancouver, Washington

Alice M. Clark, Ph.D.
Department of Pharmacognosy, University of Mississippi Medical Center, School of Pharmacy, Jackson, Mississippi

John D. Cleary, Pharm.D.
Associate Professor of Clinical Pharmacy Practice, School of Pharmacy, University of Mississippi, Jackson, Mississippi

Michael A. Clotz, Pharm.D.
Clinical Pharmacist, Critical Care, Children's Hospital, Columbus; Assistant Clinical Professor, College of Pharmacy and Medicine, Ohio State University, Columbus, Ohio

Pamala A. Colburn-Jacobson, Pharm.D.
Clinical Pharmacist, Bone Marrow Transplantation, University of Michigan Medical Center and Clinical Assistant Professor of Pharmacy, University of Michigan College of Pharmacy, Ann Arbor, Michigan

Thomas J. Comstock, Pharm.D.
Associate Professor, Department of Pharmacy and Pharmaceutics, Virginia Commonwealth University/Medical College of Virginia, Richmond, Virginia

Marcus D. Cook, Pharm.D., M.B.A.
CAC; Assistant Professor of Pharmacy, Idaho State University, College of Pharmacy, Boise, Idaho

Laurie J. Cooksey, Pharm.D.
Staff Pharmacist, part-time, Department of Pharmacy Services, Medical College of Virginia Hospitals, Richmond, Virginia

Robin L. Corelli, Pharm.D.
Assistant Clinical Professor of Pharmacy, School of Pharmacy, University of California at San Francisco, San Francisco, California

Judy L. Curtis, Pharm.D.
Assistant Professor, Department of Pharmacy Practice and Science, University of Maryland at Baltimore, Baltimore; Director of Pharmacy Services, Rosewood Center, Owings Mills, Maryland

Stephen L. Dahl, Pharm.D.
BCPS; Associate Professor of Medicine, University of Missouri, Kansas City, School of Medicine; Gold IV Unit, Kansas City, Missouri

Larry H. Danziger, Pharm.D.
Associate Professor of Pharmacy Practice, College of Pharmacy, University of Illinois at Chicago, Chicago, Illinois

Edward M. DeSimone II, Ph.D.
Associate Professor, Department of
Pharmaceutical and Administrative Sciences,
Creighton University, School of Pharmacy
and Allied Health Professions, Omaha,
Nebraska

Betty J. Dong, Pharm.D.
Professor of Clinical Pharmacy, Division of
Clinical Pharmacy, Clinical Professor of Family
and Community Medicine, University of
California Schools of Pharmacy and Medicine,
University of California at San Francisco, San
Francisco, California

Andrew J. Donnelly, Pharm.D., M.B.A.
Assistant Director of Pharmacy and
Clinical Pharmacist, Operating Room/
Anesthesiology, Rush-Presbyterian-St.
Luke's Medical Center, Clinical Assistant
Professor, Department of Pharmacy
Practice, University of Illinois at Chicago
College of Pharmacy, Chicago; Associate
Professor, Chicago College of Pharmacy,
Midwestern University, Downers Grove,
Illinois

Julie A. Dopheide, Pharm.D.
Assistant Professor of Clinical Pharmacy
(Psychiatry), University of Southern
California School of Pharmacy, Los Angeles,
California

George E. Dukes, Jr., Pharm.D.
Professor and Chairman, Department of
Pharmacy Practice and Science, School of
Pharmacy, University of Maryland, Baltimore,
Maryland

Babette S. Duncan, Pharm.D.
BCPS; Director, Medical Information, Advance
Paradigm Clinical Services, Inc., Hunt Valley,
Maryland; Assistant Professor, Department of
Pharmacy Practice and Science, University of
Maryland School of Pharmacy, Baltimore,
Maryland

Robert E. Dupuis, Pharm.D.
BCPS; Assistant Professor of Pharmacy,
School of Pharmacy, University of North
Carolina at Chapel Hill, Chapel Hill, North
Carolina

Allan J. Ellsworth, Pharm.D.
Associate Professor, Departments of Pharmacy
and Family Medicine, Schools of Pharmacy and
Medicine, University of Washington, Seattle,
Washington

Rebecca S. Finley, Pharm.D.
Associate Professor of Clinical Pharmacy,
School of Pharmacy, University of Maryland,
Baltimore; Associate Professor of Oncology,
University of Maryland Cancer Center,
Baltimore, Maryland

John F. Flaherty, Pharm.D.
BCPS; Associate Professor of Clinical Pharmacy,
School of Pharmacy, University of California at
San Francisco, San Francisco; Clinical
Pharmacist, Infectious Diseases, Mt. Zion
Medical Center of UCSF, San Francisco,
California

Robin H. Fuerst, Pharm.D.
St. Joseph Regional Medical Center,
Clinical Pharmacy Coordinator, Lewiston,
Idaho; Adjunct Clinical Assistant Professor,
Washington State University, Pullman,
Washington

Elaine M. Furmaga, Pharm.D.
Clinical Pharmacist Ambulatory Care, Veterans
Affairs West Side Medical Center, Chicago;
Clinical Assistant Professor, Department of
Pharmacy Practice, College of Pharmacy,
University of Illinois at Chicago, Chicago,
Illinois

Kevin M. Furmaga, Pharm.D.
Clinical Assistant Professor, Department of
Pharmacy Practice, The University of Illinois at
Chicago, Chicago, Illinois

Teri L. Gabel, Pharm.D.
Assistant Professor, Department of Pharmacy
Practice, College of Pharmacy, University
of Nebraska Medical Center, Omaha,
Nebraska

Joseph P. Gee, Pharm.D.
Associate Professor of Pharmacy and Clinical
Pharmacist in Pulmonary Medicine, King Khalid
University Hospital, King Saud University,
Riyadh, Kingdom of Saudi Arabia

Milo Gibaldi, Ph.D.
Dean, School of Pharmacy, Professor,
Department of Pharmaceutics, University of
Washington, Seattle, Washington

Barry E. Gidal, Pharm.D.
Assistant Professor, University of Wisconsin
School of Pharmacy and Department of
Neurology, Madison, Wisconsin

Sara R. Grimsley, Pharm.D.
Assistant Professor of Pharmacy Practice,
Mercer University School of Pharmacy, Atlanta,
Georgia

Dale R. Grothe, Pharm.D.
Clinical Mental Health Specialist, National
Institutes of Health Pharmacy
Department/National Institute of Mental Health,
Bethesda, Maryland

B. Joseph Guglielmo, Pharm.D.
Professor, Division of Clinical Pharmacy,
School of Pharmacy, University of
California at San Francisco, San Francisco,
California

Thomas G. Hall, Pharm.D.
Manager-Clinical Services, Department of
Pharmacy, Barnes and Jewish Hospitals, St.
Louis, Missouri

Philip D. Hansten, Pharm.D.
Professor of Pharmacy, School of
Pharmacy, University of Washington, Seattle,
Washington

Fotini K. Hatzopoulos, Pharm.D.
Neonatal Pharmacotherapist, University
of Illinois Hospital, Chicago; Clinical
Assistant Professor, Department of Pharmacy
Practice, College of Pharmacy, University of
Illinois at Chicago Medical Center, Chicago,
Illinois

Daniel P. Healy, Pharm.D.
Associate Professor, University of Southern
California, School of Pharmacy, Los Angeles,
California

David W. Henry, M.S.
FASHP; Associate Professor and Pharmacy
Specialist in Pediatric Hematology/Oncology,
Department of Pharmacy Practice, University
of Kansas Medical Center, Kansas City,
Kansas

Beverly J. Holcombe, Pharm.D.
BCNSP; Clinical Specialist, Nutrition Support,
Department of Pharmacy, University of North
Carolina Hospitals, Chapel Hill; Clinical
Associate Professor, Division of Pharmacy
Practice, School of Pharmacy, University of
North Carolina at Chapel Hill, Chapel Hill,
North Carolina

Mark T. Holdsworth, Pharm.D.
Assistant Professor, College of Pharmacy,
University of New Mexico, Albuquerque, New
Mexico

Eileen G. Holland, Pharm.D.
BCPS; Assistant Professor Clinical Pharmacy
Practice, Auburn University School of Pharmacy,
Auburn; Adjunct Assistant Professor, Department
of Family Practice and Community Medicine,
University of Southern Alabama, College of
Medicine, Mobile, Alabama

David M. Hunnicutt, Ph.D.
Director, Applied Health Research, Inc., Lincoln,
Nebraska

Gail S. Itokazu, Pharm.D.
Clinical Assistant Professor of Pharmacy in
Medicine, Cook County Hospital and Medical
Center, University of Illinois at Chicago,
Chicago, Illinois

George S. Jaresko, Pharm.D.
Assistant Professor of Clinical Pharmacy, School
of Pharmacy, University of Southern California
at Los Angeles, Los Angeles, California

Lucia K. Jim, Pharm.D.
Associate Professor of Pharmacy and Vice
Chairwoman, Department of Clinical Pharmacy,
King Saud University College of Pharmacy,
Riyadh; Clinical Pharmacist, Hematology and
Oncology, King Khalid University Hospital,
Riyadh, Kingdom of Saudi Arabia

Martin J. Jinks, Pharm.D.
Professor and Chair, Department of Pharmacy
Practice, Washington State University College of
Pharmacy, Pullman, Washington

Curtis A. Johnson, Pharm.D.
Professor of Pharmacy and Medicine, University
of Wisconsin, Madison, Wisconsin

James W. Jones, Pharm.D.
Clinical Pharmacist, Division of Pulmonary
Medicine, Columbus Children's Hospital,
Columbus; Assistant Clinical Professor, College
of Pharmacy, Ohio State University, Columbus,
Ohio

Paul W. Jungnickel, Ph.D.
Assistant Professor of Pharmacy Practice,
Coordinator of Experiential Education, Clinical
Pharmacist - Internal Medicine and
Gastroenterology, University of Nebraska
Medical Center, Omaha, Nebraska

H. William Kelly, Pharm.D.
College of Pharmacy, University of New Mexico
Health Sciences Center, Albuquerque, New
Mexico

Heather R. Kertland, Pharm.D.
Assistant Clinical Professor, College of
Pharmacy, University of Connecticut, Storrs,
Connecticut

Rachel L. Kleiman-Wexler, Pharm.D.
Director, Department of Pharmacy, All Saints
Health Systems, Fort Worth, Texas

Mary Anne Koda-Kimble, Pharm.D.
Professor, Chairwoman, Division of Clinical Pharmacy, School of Pharmacy, University of California at San Francisco, San Francisco, California

Jim M. Koeller, M.S.
Professor, University of Texas at Austin and Health Science Center San Antonio, Texas

Peter J. S. Koo, Pharm.D.
Associate Clinical Professor of Pharmacy, Division of Clinical Pharmacy, Pharmacy Specialist, University of California at San Francisco, San Francisco Medical Center, San Francisco, California

Karen Kostiuk, Pharm.D.
Assistant Clinical Professor, Division of Clinical Pharmacy, University of California at San Francisco, San Francisco, California

Wayne A. Kradjan, Pharm.D.
Professor, Associate Dean, University of Washington, School of Pharmacy, Seattle, Washington

Donna M. Kraus, Pharm.D.
Associate Professor of Pharmacy Practice, Departments of Pharmacy Practice and Pediatrics, Colleges of Pharmacy and Medicine, University of Illinois at Chicago, Chicago, Illinois

Cynthia L. LaCivita, Pharm.D.
Assistant Professor of Oncology and Clinical Pharmacy, School of Pharmacy, University of Maryland Cancer Center, Baltimore, Maryland

Lyle Knight Laird, Pharm.D.
Clinical Pharmacologist, San Antonio State Hospital and Clinical Assistant Professor, University of Texas College of Pharmacy, Austin; Departments of Pharmacology and Psychiatry, UTHSCSA, San Antonio, Texas

Alan H. Lau, Pharm.D.
College of Pharmacy, University of Illinois at Chicago, Chicago, Illinois

David B. Lawrence, Pharm.D.
Director of Clinical Services, Pharmaceutical Care Management, Inc., Charleston, South Carolina

Nancy A. Letassy, Pharm.D.
Ambulatory Clinical Specialist, Department of Veterans Affairs Medical Center, Oklahoma City; Clinical Assistant Professor of Pharmacy Practice, University of Oklahoma Health Sciences Center, College of Pharmacy, Oklahoma City, Oklahoma

Celeste M. Lindley, Pharm.D.
FCCP; FASHP; Associate Professor of Pharmacy, Clinical Associate Professor of Medicine, University of North Carolina at Chapel Hill, Chapel Hill, North Carolina

Rex S. Lott, Pharm.D.
Clinical Pharmacist, Fircrest School, Clinical Associate Professor of Pharmacy, University of Washington, School of Pharmacy, Seattle, Washington

Raymond C. Love, Pharm.D.
Vice Chair and Assistant Professor, School of Pharmacy, University of Maryland at Baltimore, Baltimore, Maryland

Helen L. Lucia, M.D.
Professor of Pathology, School of Medicine, Saba University, Saba, Netherlands-Antilles

Allan T. Mailloux, Pharm.D.
Assistant Professor, School of Pharmacy, University of Wisconsin, Madison, Wisconsin

Hilary D. Mandler, Pharm.D.
Clinical Specialist, Infectious Diseases, Hahnemann University Hospital, Clinical Assistant Professor of Medicine, Medical College of Pennsylvania and Hahnemann University; Clinical Associate Professor of Pharmacy, Philadelphia College of Pharmacy and Science; Adjunct Associate Professor of Pharmacy, Temple University School of Pharmacy, Philadelphia, Pennsylvania

Patricia A. Marken, Pharm.D.
University of Missouri-Kansas City Schools of Pharmacy and Medicine, Assistant Professor of Pharmacy Practice and Psychiatry, Psychopharmacy Specialist, Western Missouri Mental Health Center, Kansas City, Missouri

Dayna L. McCauley, Pharm.D.
Senior Pharmacist, Specialist, Bone Marrow Transplantation and Clinical Coordinator, University Hospital, State University of New York at Stony Brook, Stony Brook, New York

Patrick L. McCollam, Pharm.D.
Assistant Professor, College of Pharmacy, Medical University of South Carolina, Charleston, South Carolina

James P. McCormack, Pharm.D.
Associate Professor, Faculty of Pharmaceutical Sciences, Clinical Pharmacist, St. Paul's Hospital, Vancouver, B.C., Canada

James M. McKenney, Pharm.D.
Professor and Chairman, Division of Clinical Pharmacy, School of Pharmacy, Medical College of Virginia, Virginia Commonwealth University, Richmond, Virginia

Robert Michocki, Pharm.D.
Professor, Pharmacy Practice and Science, and Clinical Professor Family Medicine, University of Maryland Schools of Pharmacy and Medicine, Baltimore, Maryland

Robert K. Middleton, Pharm.D.
Drug Information Pharmacist, Kaiser Foundation Hospitals, Northern California Pharmacy Operations/Professional Services, Oakland, California

Gene D. Morse, Pharm.D.
FCCP; BCPS; Associate Professor of Pharmacy, Research Associate Professor of Medicine, State University of New York at Buffalo, Buffalo, New York

Christine M. Murphy, Pharm.D.
Clinical Assistant Professor, Department of Pharmacy Practice, University of Illinois College of Pharmacy, Chicago; Clinical Pharmacist, West Side Veterans Administration, Chicago, Illinois

Milap C. Nahata, Pharm.D.
Professor of Pharmacy and Pediatrics, Colleges of Pharmacy and Medicine, Ohio State University, Columbus; Director, Infectious Disease Research Laboratory, Wexner Institute for Pediatric Research, Children's Hospital, Columbus, Ohio

Jean M. Nappi, Pharm.D.
FCCP; BCPS; Professor and Vice Chair for Academic Affairs, Department of Hospital Pharmacy Practice and Administration, Medical University of South Carolina, Charleston, South Carolina

Warren A. Narducci, Pharm.D.
Associate Professor and Chairman, Department of Pharmacy Practice, University of Nebraska Medical Center College of Pharmacy, Omaha, Nebraska

Alice M. O'Donnell, Pharm.D.
Center for Clinical Pharmacy Research, School of Pharmacy, State University of New York at Buffalo, Buffalo, New York

Christopher M. Paap, Pharm.D.
Assistant Professor, University of Colorado School of Pharmacy, Denver; Clinical Specialist, The Children's Hospital, Denver, Colorado

Carl W. Peterson, Pharm.D.
BCPS; Florida District Clinical Manager, Owen Healthcare, Inc., Houston, Texas

Ralph H. Raasch, Pharm.D.
Associate Professor, School of Pharmacy, The University of North Carolina at Chapel Hill, Chapel Hill, North Carolina

Cynthia L. Raehl, Pharm.D.
Professor of Pharmacy Practice Chair, Department of Pharmacy Practice, School of Pharmacy, Texas Tech University Health Sciences Center, Amarillo, Texas

Deborah K. Rogers, Pharm.D.
Clinical Assistant Professor, Harborview Medical Center, School of Pharmacy, University of Washington, Seattle, Washington

Carol J. Rollins, Pharm.D.
R.D.; BCNSP; Coordinator, Nutrition Support Service, Department of Pharmacy Services, University Medical Center, and Adjunct Assistant Professor, College of Pharmacy, University of Arizona, Tucson, Arizona

Ronald J. Ruggiero, Pharm.D.
Clinical Professor, Division of Clinical Pharmacy and Department of Obstetrics, Gynecology, and Reproductive Sciences, U.C.S.F. Pharmacist Specialist in Obstetrics and Gynecology, Department of Pharmaceutical Services, University of California at San Francisco, San Francisco, California

Rosalie Sagraves, Pharm.D.
Professor and Assistant Dean for Academic Affairs, College of Pharmacy, University of Oklahoma Health Sciences Center, Oklahoma City, Oklahoma

Jan Sahai, Pharm.D.
Assistant Professor of Medicine and Pharmacology, Clinical Investigation Unit, Ottawa General Hospital, Ottawa, Ontario, Canada

Judith J. Saklad, Pharm.D.
Clinical Pharmacologist, San Antonio State School, Clinical Assistant Professor of Pharmacy, University of Texas at Austin, Austin; Clinical Assistant Professor of Pharmacology, University of Texas Health Science Center at San Antonio, San Antonio, Texas

David M. Scott, Ph.D.
Assistant Professor, Department of Pharmacy Practice, University of Nebraska Medical Center, Omaha, Nebraska

Terry L. Seaton, Pharm.D.
BCPS; Assistant Professor, Division of Pharmacy Practice, St. Louis College of Pharmacy, St. Louis, Missouri

Timothy H. Self, Pharm.D.
Professor of Clinical Pharmacy, University of Tennessee, Memphis, Tennessee

Amy L. Shafer, Pharm.D.
Assistant Director of Pharmacy, Beth Israel Hospital, Boston, Massachusetts

Mark Joel Shelton, Pharm.D.
ACCP Infectious Diseases Fellowship, Center for Clinical Pharmacy Research, School of Pharmacy State University of New York at Buffalo, Buffalo, New York

Pamela A. Simon, Pharm.D.
Clinical Assistant Professor, Department of Pharmacy Practice, University of Illinois at Chicago, Chicago, Illinois

Ralph E. Small, Pharm.D.
Professor of Pharmacy and Pharmaceutics, Professor of Medicine (Rheumatology, Allergy, and Immunology), Medical College of Virginia, Virginia Commonwealth University, Richmond, Virginia

Candace J. Smith, Pharm.D.
Associate Clinical Professor, Clinical Pharmacy Practice, College of Pharmacy and Allied Health Professions, St. John's University, Jamaica, New York

Steve W. Stanislav, Pharm.D.
Psychopharmacologist, The Healthcare Rehabilitation Center, Austin, Texas

Ignatius Y. S. Tang, Pharm.D.
BCPS; Clinical Assistant Professor, Department of Pharmacy Practice, College of Pharmacy and Clinical Assistant Professor of Pharmacy Practice in Medicine, Department of Medicine, College of Medicine, University of Illinois at Chicago, Chicago; Pharmacotherapist, Outpatient Dialysis Unit and Inpatient Nephrology Consult Service, University of Illinois Hospital and Clinics, Chicago, Illinois

Teresa Tartaglione, Pharm.D.
Infectious Diseases Pharmacotherapy, Seattle, Washington

Paula A. Teichner, Pharm.D.
Clinical Assistant Professor of Pharmacy Practice, University of Illinois at Chicago, Chicago; Pharmacotherapist, Adult Internal Medicine, Michael Reese Hospital and Medical Center, Chicago, Illinois

John F. Thompson, Pharm.D.
FCP; Associate Professor of Clinical Pharmacy and Clinical Gerontology, University of Southern California, Los Angeles, California

Carla Van Den Berg, Pharm.D.
Clinical Instructor and Research Fellow of Divisions of Oncology and Pharmacy, University of Texas Health Science Center at San Antonio, San Antonio, Texas

Jon C. Wagner, Pharm.D.
Associate Dean for Student and Professional Affairs, Assistant Professor of Pharmacy Practice, University of Nebraska Medical Center College of Pharmacy, Omaha, Nebraska

Earl S. Ward, Jr., Pharm.D.
FASHP; Associate Dean and Professor, Department of Pharmacy Practice, Mercer University School of Pharmacy, Atlanta, Georgia

Mark D. Watanabe, Pharm.D., Ph.D.
Clinical Assistant Professor of Pharmacy Practice, University of Illinois at Chicago and Clinical Consultant, Illinois Department of Mental Health and Developmental Disabilities, Chicago, Illinois

William A. Watson, Pharm.D
ABAT; Clinical Professor, Departments of Emergency Medicine and Pharmacy Practice, Schools of Medicine and Pharmacy, University of Missouri-Kansas City, and Truman Medical Center, Kansas City, Missouri

C. Wayne Weart, Pharm.D.
Professor of Community Pharmacy Practice and Administration, Associate Professor of Family Medicine, Department of Family Medicine, Medical University of South Carolina, Charleston, South Carolina

Timothy E. Welty, Pharm.D.
Clinical Associate Professor, Clinical Pharmacy Practitioner, University of Cincinnati, Director of Publishing, Harvey Whitney Books Company, Cincinnati, Ohio

Bradley R. Williams, Pharm.D.
Associate Professor, Clinical Pharmacy and Clinical Gerontology, University of Southern California School of Pharmacy, and Andrus Gerontology Center, Los Angeles, California

Dennis M. Williams, Pharm.D.
BCPS; Assistant Professor, Vice Chairman of Professional Education, University of North Carolina at Chapel Hill, Chapel Hill, North Carolina

Michael E. Winter, Pharm.D.
Professor of Clinical Pharmacy, Director Clinical Pharmacokinetics Consulting Service, Division of Clinical Pharmacy, School of Pharmacy, University of California at San Francisco, San Francisco, California

Ann K. Wittkowsky, Pharm.D.
Clinical Associate Professor, University of Washington School of Pharmacy, Seattle; Clinical Pharmacist, Cardiology/Anticoagulation Specialist, University of Washington Medical Center, Seattle, Washington

Alvin F. Wong, Pharm.D.
Associate Clinical Professor, Division of Clinical Pharmacy, School of Pharmacy, University of California at San Francisco, San Francisco, California

Annie Wong-Beringer, Pharm.D.
University of California Los Angeles, Department of Pharmaceutical Services, Infectious Diseases Pharmacist Specialist, Los Angeles, California

Lloyd Yee Young, Pharm.D.
Adjunct Associate Professor of Clinical Pharmacy, College of Pharmacy, Washington State University, Spokane/Vancouver, Washington

CONTENTS

Preface to Sixth Edition. v
Preface to Fifth Edition vi
Preface to First Edition vii
Acknowledgments viii
Notice to Reader ix
Contributors x
Other publications xvii

General Principles

1. Assessments of Therapy and Pharmaceutical Care 1-1
   *Lloyd Yee Young, Wayne A. Kradjan, B. Joseph Guglielmo,
   and Mary Anne Koda-Kimble*
2. Clinical Pharmacokinetics 2-1
   Michael E. Winter
3. Drug Interactions 3-1
   Philip D. Hansten
4. Interpretation of Clinical Laboratory Tests 4-1
   Lloyd Yee Young and Eileen G. Holland
5. Implications of Biotechnology for Clinical Practice 5-1
   Milo Gibaldi

General Care

6. Anaphylaxis and Drug Allergy 6-1
   Paul M. Beringer and Robert K. Middleton
7. Pain 7-1
   Peter J. S. Koo
8. Perioperative Care 8-1
   Andrew J. Donnelly and Amy L. Shafer

Cardiac and Vascular Disorders
Wayne A. Kradjan, Section Editor
9. Dyslipidemias 9-1
   James M. McKenney
10. Essential Hypertension 10-1
    *Barry C. Carter, Elaine M. Furmaga, and
    Christine M. Murphy*
11. Peripheral Vascular Disorders 11-1
    David B. Lawrence and C. Wayne Weart
12. Thrombosis 12-1
    Ann K. Wittkowsky
13. Ischemic Heart Disease 13-1
    Cynthia L. Raehl
14. Myocardial Infarction 14-1
    Jean M. Nappi and Patrick L. McCollam
15. Congestive Heart Failure 15-1
    Wayne A. Kradjan
16. Cardiac Arrhythmias 16-1
    Moses S. S. Chow and Heather R. Kertland
17. Hypertensive Emergencies. 17-1
    Robert Michocki
18. Intensive Care Therapeutics. 18-1
    Laura E. Arrigoni and Deborah K. Rogers

Respiratory Disorders

19. Asthma 19-1
    Timothy H. Self and H. William Kelly
20. Chronic Obstructive Airways Disease 20-1
    Dennis M. Williams
21. Acute and Chronic Rhinitis 21-1
    Pamela A. Simon
22. Drug-Induced Pulmonary Disorders. 22-1
    H. William Kelly, Wendy Wilkinson, and Baxi Dang

Gastrointestinal Disorders

23. Upper Gastrointestinal Disorders. 23-1
    Candace J. Smith
24. Inflammatory Bowel Disease. 24-1
    George E. Dukes, Jr. and Babette S. Duncan

Hepatic Disorders

25. Alcoholic Cirrhosis 25-1
    Paula A. Teichner, Lucia K. Jim, and Joseph P. Gee
26. Adverse Effects of Drugs on the Liver. 26-1
    Lucia K. Jim and Joseph P. Gee

Renal Disorders
Curtis A. Johnson, Section Editor
27. Acid-Base Disorders 27-1
    Thomas G. Hall and Rachel L. Kleiman-Wexler
28. Fluid and Electrolyte Disorders 28-1
    Ignatius Y. S. Tang and Alan H. Lau
29. Acute Renal Failure. 29-1
    George R. Bailie
30. Chronic Renal Failure 30-1
    Arasb Ateshkadi and Curtis A. Johnson
31. Renal Dialysis. 31-1
    Thomas J. Comstock
32. Dosing of Drugs in Renal Failure 32-1
    Francesca T. Aweeka
33. Solid Organ Transplantation 33-1
    Robert E. Dupuis

Nutritional Disorders

34. Adult Enteral Nutrition 34-1
    Carol J. Rollins
35. Adult Parenteral Nutrition 35-1
    Beverly J. Holcombe

Skin Disorders
C. A. Bond, Section Editor
36. Dermatotherapy. 36-1
    C. A. Bond
37. Acne 37-1
    Terry L. Seaton
38. Psoriasis 38-1
    Allan J. Ellsworth
39. Photosensitivity and Burns 39-1
    Allan T. Mailloux

Joint and Connective Tissue Disorders

40. Gout and Hyperuricemia 40-1
    Lloyd Yee Young and Keith D. Campagna
41. Rheumatic Disorders. 41-1
    Stephen L. Dahl
42. Connective Tissue Disorders:
    The Clinical Use of Corticosteroids 42-1
    Ralph E. Small and Laurie J. Cooksey

Women's Health

43. Contraception 43-1
    Ronald J. Ruggiero
44. Obstetrics 44-1
    Rosalie Sagraves, Nancy A. Letassy, and Terri L. Barton
45. Teratogenicity and Drugs in Breast Milk 45-1
    Gerald G. Briggs
46. Gynecological Disorders 46-1
    Rosalie Sagraves and Nancy A. Letassy

Endocrine Disorders

47. Thyroid Disorders 47-1
    Betty J. Dong
48. Diabetes Mellitus 48-1
    Mary Anne Koda-Kimble and Betsy A. Carlisle

Ocular Disorders

49. Eye Disorders 49-1
    Steven R. Abel

Neurological Disorders

Brian K. Alldredge, Section Editor

50. Headache 50-1
    Brian K. Alldredge
51. Parkinson's Disease 51-1
    John F. Flaherty and Barry E. Gidal
52. Seizure Disorders 52-1
    Rex S. Lott

Cerebrovascular Disorders

Brian K. Alldredge, Section Editor

53. Cerebrovascular Disorders 53-1
    Timothy E. Welty

Infectious Diseases

B. Joseph Guglielmo, Section Editor

54. Principles of Infectious Diseases 54-1
    B. Joseph Guglielmo
55. Antimicrobial Prophylaxis for Surgical Procedures 55-1
    Laurie L. Briceland and B. Joseph Guglielmo
56. Central Nervous System Infections 56-1
    John F. Flaherty
57. Endocarditis 57-1
    Daniel P. Healy and Annie Wong-Beringer
58. Respiratory Tract Infections 58-1
    George S. Jaresko
59. Tuberculosis 59-1
    Earl S. Ward, Jr.
60. Gastrointestinal Infections 60-1
    Larry H. Danziger and Gail S. Itokazu
61. Intra-Abdominal Infections 61-1
    Peggy L. Carver and Karen Kostiuk
62. Acute and Chronic Hepatitis 62-1
    Robin L. Corelli
63. Urinary Tract Infections 63-1
    Jan Sahai
64. Sexually Transmitted Diseases 64-1
    Teresa A. Tartaglione and Connie L. Celum
65. Osteomyelitis/Septic Arthritis 65-1
    Ralph H. Raasch
66. Traumatic Skin and Soft Tissue Infections 66-1
    James P. McCormack and Glen Brown
67. Infections in Immunocompromised Hosts 67-1
    Hilary D. Mandler
68. Human Immunodeficiency Virus (HIV) Infection 68-1
    Gene D. Morse, Alice M. O'Donnell,
    and Mark Joel Shelton
69. Fungal Infections 69-1
    John D. Cleary, Stanley W. Chapman, Alice M. Clark,
    and Helen L. Lucia
70. Viral Infections 70-1
    Milap C. Nahata
71. Parasitic Infections 71-1
    J. V. Anandan
72. Lyme Disease 72-1
    Tom Christian

Psychiatric Disorders

Mark D. Watanabe, Section Editor

73. Anxiety Disorders 73-1
    Sara R. Grimsley
74. Sleep Disorders 74-1
    Julie A. Dopheide
75. Schizophrenia 75-1
    Patricia A. Marken and Steve W. Stanislav
76. Mood Disorders I: Major Depressive Disorders 76-1
    Lyle Knight Laird and William H. Benefield, Jr.
77. Mood Disorders II: Bipolar Affective Disorders 77-1
    Raymond C. Love and Dale R. Grothe
78. Psychiatric Disorders in Children, Adolescents, and
    People with Developmental Disabilities 78-1
    Judith J. Saklad and Judy L. Curtis
79. Secondary Neuropsychiatric Disorders 79-1
    Kevin M. Furmaga and Mark D. Watanabe
80. Eating Disorders 80-1
    LaGenia Bailey

Substance Abuse

Jeffrey N. Baldwin, Section Editor

81. Issues: Psychoactive Substance Use Disorders 81-1
    Jeffrey N. Baldwin and Marcus D. Cook
82. Alcohol Abuse 82-1
    Paul W. Jungnickel and David M. Hunnicutt
83. Depressant and Inhalant Abuse 83-1
    Jeffrey N. Baldwin and Blaine (Jess) Benson
84. CNS Stimulant Abuse 84-1
    David M. Scott and Teri L. Gabel
85. Nicotine and Caffeine Abuse 85-1
    Edward M. DeSimone II and David M. Scott
86. Entactogen and Phencyclidine Abuse 86-1
    Paul W. Jungnickel
87. Drug Abuse in Athletics 87-1
    Jon C. Wagner and Warren A. Narducci

Hematopoietic Disorders

88. Anemias 88-1
    Jim M. Koeller and Carla Van Den Berg
89. Drug-Induced Blood Disorders 89-1
    Carl W. Peterson

Neoplastic Disorders

Rebecca S. Finley and Celeste M. Lindley, Section Editors

90. Neoplastic Disorders and Their Treatment:
    General Principles 90-1
    Rebecca S. Finley
91. Adverse Effects of Chemotherapy 91-1
    Celeste M. Lindley, Rebecca S. Finley, and
    Cynthia L. LaCivita
92. Hematological Malignancies 92-1
    Celeste M. Lindley, Rebecca S. Finley, Cynthia L. LaCivita,
    David W. Henry, and Mark T. Holdsworth
93. Solid Tumors 93-1
    Celeste M. Lindley, Rebecca S. Finley, Cynthia L. LaCivita,
    and David W. Henry
94. Bone Marrow Transplantation 94-1
    Dayna L. McCauley and Pamala A. Colburn-Jacobson

Special Age Group: Pediatric Therapy

95. Pediatric Considerations 95-1
    Ann M. Bolinger and C. Y. Jennifer Chan
96. Neonatal Therapy 96-1
    Donna M. Kraus and Fotini K. Hatzopoulos
97. Pediatric Infectious Diseases 97-1
    Christopher M. Paap
98. Bronchopulmonary Dysplasia 98-1
    Michael A. Clotz

99. Pediatric Nutrition 99-1
     Alvin F. Wong and Ann M. Bolinger

Cystic Fibrosis

100. Cystic Fibrosis 100-1
     James W. Jones

Special Age Group: Geriatric Therapy
Bradley R. Williams, Section Editor

101. Geriatric Rehabilitation and Drug Use 101-1
     Martin J. Jinks and Robin H. Fuerst

102. Geriatric Dementias 102-1
     Bradley R. Williams

103. Geriatric Urological Disorders 103-1
     John F. Thompson

Clinical Toxicology

104. Clinical Toxicology 104-1
     William A. Watson

Nausea and Vomiting

105. Nausea and Vomiting 105-1
     Mary Anne Koda-Kimble and Lloyd Yee Young

Other Publications by Applied Therapeutics, Inc.

Handbook of Applied Therapeutics, 6th edition
by Lloyd Yee Young, Mary Anne Koda-Kimble, Wayne A. Kradjan, and B. Joseph Guglielmo
ISBN 0-915486-24-5

Drug Interactions & Updates Quarterly
by Philip D. Hansten and John R. Horn
ISSN 0271-8707

Applied Pharmacokinetics: Principles of Therapeutic Drug Monitoring, 3rd Edition
edited by William E. Evans, Jerome J. Schentag, and William J. Jusko
ISBN 0-915486-15-6

Basic Clinical Pharmacokinetics, 3rd Edition
by Michael E. Winter
ISBN 0-915486-22-9

Basic Clinical Pharmacokinetics Handbook
by John R. White, Jr. and Mark W. Garrison
ISBN 0-915486-21-0

A Short Course in Clinical Pharmacokinetics
by Dennis A. Noe
ISBN 0-915486-19-9

Clinical Clerkship Manual
edited by Larry E. Boh
ISBN 0-915486-17-2

Physical Assessment: A Guide For Evaluating Drug Therapy
by R. Leon Longe and Jon C. Calvert
ISBN 0-915486-20-2

Extemporaneous Ophthalmic Preparations
edited by Lois A. Reynolds and Richard G. Closson
ISBN 0-915486-18-0

Sixth Edition

Applied Therapeutics:

The Clinical Use of Drugs

Assessment of Therapy and Pharmaceutical Care

Wayne A Kradjan
Mary Anne Koda-Kimble
Lloyd Y Young
B Joseph Guglielmo

Establishing the Patient Record 1-1
  Knowledge 1-2
  Sources of Patient Information 1-2
    Data-rich environment 1-2
    Data-poor environment 1-2
  Interviewing the Patient (See Table 1.1) 1-2
Organizing the Patient Record 1-2
  Medical History 1-2
  Drug History 1-3
    Drug identification and use 1-3
    Assessment of therapeutic response 1-3
    Assessment of adverse effects 1-4
  Social History 1-4
    Work 1-4
    Exercise 1-4
    Diet 1-4
    Support systems 1-4
    Attitude 1-4
Systematic Approaches to Patient Therapy
Assessment 1-4
  Problem-Oriented Medical Record (POMR) Approach
  (See Table 1.2) 1-4
    Problem list 1-4
    Subjective and objective data 1-5
    Assessment 1-6
    Plan 1-6
      Diagnostic 1-6
      Pharmaceutical care 1-6

    Therapeutic objectives 1-6
    Patient education 1-8
  Illustration of SOAP (Also see Table 1.6) 1-8
  Pharmacist's Work-Up of Drug Therapy (PWDT)
  (Also see Question 16) 1-8
Drug Therapy Assessment 1-8
  Previously Prescribed Drug Therapy 1-9
    Community pharmacy setting
    (See Tables 1.4 and 1.5) 1-9
    Inpatient pharmacy setting 1-11
  Initiating Over-the-Counter (OTC) Treatment 1-11
  Establishing Priorities 1-12
    Age and gender 1-12
    Number of medications prescribed or number
    of doses per day 1-12
    Drugs with a high risk for adverse drug effects
    or drug interactions 1-12
    Target diseases 1-12
    High-cost drugs 1-12
    Altered drug clearance 1-12
    Allergy 1-12
    Prescriber contact 1-12
  Example of the PWDT 1-13
  Evaluating a Possible Adverse Drug Effect 1-14
    Subjective and objective data 1-14
    Assessment 1-15
    Therapeutic goals 1-15
    Plan 1-15
Writing a Consult Note (See Table 1.6) 1-16

This chapter presents several approaches to the assessment of therapy and to the provision of basic pharmaceutical care. The illustrations used in this chapter focus on the pharmacist; however, the principles to assess the response of patients to drug therapy are of value to all who have responsibility for the health and well-being of the patients they serve. Although the *philosophy* of pharmaceutical care has been embraced only recently by pharmacy organizations, numerous physicians, nurses, physician assistants, nurse practitioners, and pharmacists have been applying the principles of pharmaceutical care for a long time without using this specific terminology.

Pharmaceutical care has been described as "the responsible provision of drug therapy to achieve definite outcomes that are intended to improve a patient's quality of life."[1] Several key concepts form the basis of pharmaceutical care. The first is a belief and commitment by the practitioner that she or he shares *equal responsibility* with the patient and prescriber for optimal drug therapy outcomes and is willing to make this belief be the driving force of practice. Secondly, the practitioner must be able to establish a trusting *professional-patient relationship*. This allows him or her to gather the essential medical and social history needed to identify therapeutic problems, assess the patient's knowledge about drug

therapy, and establish and evaluate therapeutic outcomes. This information is essential to the design and implementation of a pharmaceutical care plan that is specific to the needs of the individual patient. The provision of such ongoing, individualized care also encourages patients to utilize the pharmacist as a resource for drug therapy dilemmas. The third critical component of pharmaceutical care is the *formal documentation* not only of the pharmaceutical care plan, but also of all clinical interventions and therapeutic outcomes. These records enhance the continuity of care and can be used to communicate with other providers involved in the care of the patient.

Establishing the Patient Record

The purpose of the patient record is to have readily available information that is needed to identify and assess medical problems. The patient record is needed to design patient-specific care plans and document pharmaceutical care.

Pharmaceutical care has not progressed as readily in the community setting as it has in the institutional setting for several reasons. One explanation for this slow progress is attributed to the inaccessibility of patient "data" and the lack of easy communication between community practitioners and the other providers of care to their patients. In the ideal situation, all practitioners providing care to a patient would have access to, and communicate through, a common patient record. Although computer technology is making patient records more readily available to all practitioners who are responsible for the care of a patient, practitioners within each practice site currently establish and maintain their own patient records. Community pharmacists, therefore, must do the same. The development of a patient database by community pharmacists primarily entails taking a detailed history from the patient and supplementing this history with direct observations (e.g., physical appearance, mental acuity, insulin injection technique), physical examination [e.g., blood pressure (BP), pulse], and laboratory tests (e.g., blood glucose or cholesterol).

Knowledge

To establish an accurate patient record, the practitioner should have a good understanding of the pathophysiology and clinical presentation of commonly encountered medical conditions so that she or he can correlate certain signs and symptoms with diseases. Pharmacists and other providers also must have a clear understanding of the appropriate use of drugs that are prescribed commonly to manage these diseases, including a thorough knowledge of pharmacology, how drugs are used to treat disease, and most importantly, the expected outcome of the therapy.

Sources of Patient Information

Successful patient assessment and monitoring requires the gathering and organizing of all available information. The patient (or a family member or other representative) always is the primary source of information. The primary care provider asks the patient a series of questions to obtain subjective information that is helpful in making a diagnosis or evaluating ongoing therapy. Likewise, pharmacists, home care nurses, and other providers without direct access to patient data also must observe or measure objective physical data to guide their recommendations for therapy or to prospectively monitor previously prescribed therapy.

Data-Rich Environment

In a "data-rich environment" such as a hospital or long-term care facility, a wealth of information is available to practitioners from the medical chart, pharmacy patient profile, and nursing medication administration record. Easy access to physicians, nurses, and patient (or patient representative if the patient is unresponsive) facilitates timely, effective communication among those involved in the success of drug therapy. Objective data regarding diagnosis, physical examination, laboratory and other test results, vital signs, weight, drug dosing, intravenous (IV) flow rates, and fluid balance (also called "ins and outs" or "I and O's") are available readily. Likewise, the cases presented throughout this text usually provide considerable data on which to make more thorough assessments and therapeutic decisions.

Data-Poor Environment

In reality, pharmacists and other home care providers often are required to make assessments from a limited database. Even in a relatively "data-poor environment," such as a community pharmacy, there still are two valuable sources of information: the medication profile and the patient. In addition, it usually is possible to consult with the physician (or the physician's office staff); however, there may be a delay in making contact with the physician and, in some cases, the response may be adversarial. As illustrated later in this chapter, the successful practitioner is able to make assessments and intervene on the patient's behalf even in the absence of all of the available information.

Interviewing the Patient

An ability to use communication principles (e.g., listening, body language, voice intonation) and history-taking skills is crucial to a successful patient interaction. Ideally, the initial patient interaction should occur by appointment in a private, professional, and unhurried environment; however, the ideal often is not an option. To the extent possible, the practitioner should ask open-ended questions which cannot be answered by a "yes" or a "no," but require the patient to explain and elaborate. Skilled use of these questions puts the practitioner in the role of observer, listener, recorder, and prompter and the patient in the role of storyteller. This technique also allows the practitioner to quickly assess the patient's depth of knowledge and understanding of his medications and health situation. Close-ended questions (e.g., those that can be simply answered "yes" or "no") can be used to prompt patients who know little about their health situation and to systematically minimize inadvertent omissions. For example, many practitioners use a "head-to-toe" organ systems approach at the conclusion of the interview: "Just to be sure we haven't missed anything important, can you tell me if you have ever had any problems with your head? Eyes? Heart? Lungs? Gastrointestinal (GI) tract? Liver? Kidney? Urinary tract? or Legs?" As the practitioner gains experience and becomes more sophisticated in interviewing patients, subtle clues (e.g., unusual information, observation, body language) can be used to pursue a line of questioning that could elucidate an unexpected problem or clarify an existing problem.

In all interactions, the health care provider must treat the patient with respect and must make every effort to ask questions and receive information in a nonjudgmental way (e.g., "Please tell me how you take your medications" as opposed to "Do you take your medications as prescribed by your physician?"). Practitioners providing pharmaceutical care also must keep in mind that patients hold them in trust and often share intimate details of their medical and social histories. Thus, practitioners must maintain the confidentiality of that information and share it only with those who also are directly involved in the patient's care, and then only when it is for the purpose of improving the patient's quality of life. The process of interviewing the patient, setting the stage for the interview, and the essential information to be gleaned from the interview are outlined in Table 1.1.

Organizing the Patient Record

Those who provide pharmaceutical care should develop standardized forms to record patient information. Standardization facilitates quick retrieval of information, minimizes the inadvertent omission of data, and enhances the ability of other practitioners to use shared records.

For convenience, the patient record can be divided into sections such as the history (medical history, the drug history, and the social history), assessment, and plan (including expected outcomes). In some situations, these histories can be supplemented by the generation of flow chart diagrams to monitor changes in specific parameters (e.g., blood glucose concentrations, weight) over time.

Medical History

The medical history is essential to the provision of pharmaceutical care. It can be as extensive as the medical records that are maintained in an institution or in a physician's office, or it can be a simple (but well-designed) patient profile that is maintained in a community pharmacy. The purpose of the medical history is to: identify significant past medical conditions or procedures; identify, characterize, and assess current acute and chronic medical conditions and symptoms; and gather all relevant health information that could influence drug selection or dosing (e.g., function of major

Table 1.1	Interviewing the Patient[a]

Importance of Interviewing the Patient
- Establishes professional relationship with patient
- Can get subjective data on medical problems
- Can obtain patient-specific information on drug efficacy and toxicity
- Can assess patient's knowledge, attitudes toward, and pattern of medication use
- Helps formulate problem list
- Helps to formulate plans for medication teaching and pharmaceutical care

Setting the Stage for the Interview
- Introduce yourself
- Make setting as private as possible
- No friends or relatives without permission of patient
- Do not appear rushed
- Be polite
- Be attentive
- Maintain eye contact
- Listen more than you talk
- Be nonjudgmental
- Encourage patient to be descriptive
- Clarify by restatement or patient demonstration (e.g., of a technique)

General Interview Rules
- Read chart or patient profile first
- Ask for patient's permission or make an appointment
- Begin with open-ended questions
- Move to close-ended questions
- Document interaction

Information to Be Obtained
- History of allergies
- History of adverse drug reactions
- Weight and height
- Drugs: dose, route, frequency, and reason for use
- Perceived efficacy of each drug
- Perceived side effects
- Compliance to drug regimens
- Nonprescription medication use
- Possibility of pregnancy in women of child-bearing age
- Family or other support systems

[a] Adapted from work by Teresa O'Sullivan, Pharm D, University of Washington.

organs such as the GI tract, liver, and kidney that are involved in the absorption and elimination of drugs; height and weight, including recent changes in either; age and gender; pregnancy and lactation status; and special diets).

1. P.J., a 45-year-old female of normal height and weight, states that she has diabetes. What questions might the practitioner ask of P.J. to determine whether Type I or Type II disease should be documented in her medical history?

Patients usually can enumerate their medical problems in a general way, but the practitioner often will have to probe more specifically to refine the diagnosis and assess the severity of the condition. The following questioning of P.J. should generate information to assist in the determination of whether she has Type I or Type II diabetes mellitus.

- How old were you when you were told you had diabetes?
- Do any of your relatives have diabetes mellitus? What do you know of their diabetes?
- Do you remember your symptoms? Please describe them to me.
- What medications were used to treat your diabetes?

When questions such as these are combined with good knowledge of the pathophysiology of diabetes, good appreciation of the typical presenting signs and symptoms of the disease, and good understanding of the drugs generally used to treat both forms of diabetes, meaningful pharmaceutical care can be provided. Even simple assessments such as the observation of a patient's body size can provide information useful for therapeutic interventions.

Drug History

After the initial visit, patients often present themselves to community pharmacists in one of three ways: 1) with a self-diagnosed condition for which nonprescription drug therapy is sought; 2) with a newly diagnosed condition for which a drug has been prescribed; or 3) with a chronic condition which requires refill of a previously prescribed drug or the preparation of a new drug. In the first and second situations, the practitioner must confirm the diagnosis using disease-specific questions as illustrated in Question 1. In the third situation, the practitioner uses the same type of questioning as in the first two situations; however, this time the practitioner needs to evaluate whether or not therapeutic outcomes have been achieved. The information gleaned during follow-up visits must be evaluated in the context of the current history and incorporated into the practitioner's assessment and pharmaceutical care plan. The goals of the therapeutic history are to obtain and assess the following information: the specific prescription and nonprescription drugs the patient is taking [the latter includes over-the-counter (OTC) medications, vitamins and other dietary or nutritional supplements, recreational drugs, alcohol, cigarettes, herbs, and home remedies]; the intended purpose or indications for each of these medications; how (e.g., route, ingestion in relation to meals), how much, and how often these medications are used; how long these agents have been taken or used (start and stop dates); whether the patient is achieving any therapeutic benefit from each of these agents; whether the patient is or has experienced any adverse effects that could be caused by each of these agents (idiosyncratic reactions, toxic effects, adverse effects); and allergic reactions and any history of hypersensitivity or other severe reactions to drugs. This information should be as specific as possible including a description of the reaction, the treatment, and the date of its occurrence.

2. P.J. has indicated that she is injecting insulin to treat her diabetes. What questions might be asked to evaluate P.J.'s use of and response to insulin?

The following types of questions when asked of P.J. should provide the practitioner with information on P.J.'s use of, and response to, insulin.

Drug Identification and Use

- What type of insulin do you use?
- How many units of insulin do you use?
- When do you inject your insulin in relationship to meals?
- Where do you inject your insulin? (Rather than the more judgmental question: "Do you rotate your injection sites?")
- Please show me how you usually prepare your insulin for injection. (This request of the patient requires the patient to demonstrate a skill.)

Assessment of Therapeutic Response

- How do you evaluate your response to insulin?
- What glucose levels are you aiming for?
- How often and when during the day do you test your blood glucose concentration?

- Do you have any blood glucose records that you could share with me?
- Would you show me how you test your blood glucose concentration?

Assessment of Adverse Effects

- Do you ever experience low blood sugar reactions?
- What symptoms warn you of such a reaction?
- When do these typically occur during the day?
- How often?
- What circumstances seem to make them occur more frequently?
- *Examine* injection sites

The patient's responses to these questions on drug usage, therapeutic response, and adverse effects will allow a quick assessment of the patient's knowledge of insulin and whether she is using it in a way that is likely to result in blood glucose concentrations that are neither too high nor too low. The responses to these questions also should provide the practitioner with insight as to the extent to which the patient has been involved in establishing and monitoring therapeutic outcomes. Based upon this information the practitioner can begin to formulate the patient's educational needs.

Social History

The purpose of the social history is to determine the patient's: occupation and lifestyle; important family relationships or other support systems; any particular circumstances (e.g., a disability) or stresses in her life that could influence the pharmaceutical care plan that is developed to achieve the agreed upon therapeutic outcome; and attitudes, values, and feelings about health, illness, and treatments.

3. A patient's occupation, lifestyle, and attitudes often can determine the success or failure of drug therapy. Therefore, P.J.'s nutritional history, her level of activity or exercise in a typical day or week, the family dynamics, and any particular stresses that may affect glucose control need to be documented and assessed. What questions might be asked of P.J. to gain this information?

Work. Describe a typical work day and a typical weekend day for me.

Exercise. Do you exercise? What type of exercise is it? How often, how long, and when during the day do you exercise? Do you change your meals or insulin when you exercise? If so, how?

Diet. What do you usually eat for each of your main meals and snacks? Are you able to eat at the same time each day? What do you do if a meal is delayed or missed? Who cooks the meals at home? Does this person understand your dietary needs? How often do you eat meals in a restaurant? How do you order meals in a restaurant to maintain a proper diet for your diabetes?

Support Systems. Do you live with anyone? What do they know about diabetes? How do they respond to the fact that you have diabetes? Does it ever strain your relationship? What are the issues that seem to be most troublesome? (*Note:* These questions apply equally to the workplace or school setting. Often, the biggest barrier to multiple daily injections is refusal of the patient to inject insulin while at work or school.)

Attitude. How do you feel about having diabetes? What worries or bothers you the most about having diabetes? (*Note:* The patient's demeanor and response to this and other questions will cue the history taker to the issues the patient considers most important. By addressing these concerns first, one can begin to build a long-standing professional relationship.)

Systematic Approaches to Patient Therapy Assessment

Patient therapy assessment is the process whereby a practitioner integrates his knowledge of medical and drug-related facts with information about a specific patient's medical and social history to develop an optimal therapeutic plan for that patient. At first, the process seems overwhelming because of the multiple steps involved and the difficulty in transcending from generalities to specifics. Abnormal *laboratory values* must be placed into perspective as to what is clinically relevant and what is considered normal variation. When *doses* are recommended, they must be specific for the patient's needs and not generalities based upon the package insert, the Physicians Desk Reference, or Facts and Comparisons.[1] When faced with multiple treatment options, one must decide which one is the preferred intervention. Terms such as ''frequent monitoring'' must be translated to specific time points such as hourly, daily, weekly, or annually based upon the severity of the patient's problem. When another practitioner has prescribed a treatment regimen that you do not consider optimal, a decision must be made to either accept the plan or advocate for a change on the patient's behalf. With time and practice, the process of assessing patient therapy becomes second nature and does not require a concerted effort to mentally check off each step after it has been performed. Recall of prior clinical experience helps make assessments easier. Time constraints and the amount of patient information available in certain practice environments may dictate the level of assessment that can be undertaken and the need to prioritize certain patient situations over others, but the need to intervene on the patient's behalf should never be abdicated.

Implementing pharmaceutical care entails integrating, assessing, and applying the information from the patient's record or database to the identification and solution of therapeutic problems. This requires an organized thought process for evaluating information. A systematic approach, therefore, is needed for analyzing a case history, setting priorities as to which patients require more in-depth intervention, monitoring drug therapy, and communicating information to other health care providers in an organized and concise format.

Problem-Oriented Medical Record (POMR) Approach

The organization of information according to medical problems (e.g., diseases) helps to break down a complex situation (e.g., a patient with multiple medical problems requiring multiple drugs) into its individual parts.[2] The medical community has long used a *problem-oriented medical record* or *SOAP note* to record information in the medical record or chart using a standardized format (see Table 1.2). Each medical problem is identified, listed sequentially, and assigned a number. *Subjective* data and *objective* data in support of each problem are delineated; an *assessment* is made; and a *plan* of action identified. The first letter of the four key words (subjective, objective, assessment, and plan) serve as the basis for the SOAP acronym.

Problem List

Problems are listed in order of importance and supported by the subjective and objective evidence gathered during the patient encounter. This list of problems can then be given a number and all subsequent references to specific problems can be identified merely with that number (e.g., ''problem #1'' or simply ''#1''). For the purpose of assessing a patient's drug therapy, two categories of problems exist. The first are *medical problems*. These generally are thought of in terms of a diagnosed disease, but they also may be a symptom complex that is being evaluated, a preventive measure

Table 1.2	Elements of the Problem-Oriented Medical Record[a]

Problem name: Each "problem" is listed separately and given an identifying number. Problems may be a patient complaint (e.g., headache), a laboratory abnormality (e.g., hypokalemia), or a specific disease name if prior diagnosis is known. When monitoring previously described drug therapy, more than one drug-related problem may be considered (e.g., noncompliance, a suspected adverse drug reaction or drug interaction, or an inappropriate dose). Under each problem name, the following information is identified:

Subjective	Information that explains or delineates the reason for the encounter. Information that the patient reports concerning symptoms, treatments tried, medications used, and adverse effects encountered. These are considered nonreproducible data since the information is based upon the patient's interpretation and recall of past events
Objective	Information from physical examination, laboratory results, diagnostic tests, pill counts, and pharmacy patient profile information. Objective data are reproducible
Assessment	A brief, but complete, description of the problem including a conclusion or diagnosis that is supported logically by the above subjective and objective data. The assessment should not include a problem/diagnosis that is not defined above
Plan	A detailed description of recommended or intended further work-up (laboratory, radiology, consultation), treatment (e.g., continued observation, physiotherapy, diet, medications, surgery), patient education (self-care, goals of therapy, medication use and monitoring), monitoring and follow-up relative to the above assessment

[a] Sometimes referred to as the SOAP (subjective, objective, assessment, plan) note.

(e.g., contraception), or a cognitive problem (e.g., noncompliance). Problems should be identified based upon your level of understanding. For example, the symptoms of "difficulty breathing at night" or "two-pillow orthopnea" are consistent with the symptom complex of congestive heart failure (CHF); however, these symptoms could be assessed as individual problems if the student or practitioner is unaware of the association of these symptoms with CHF. Any condition that requires a unique management plan should be identified as a problem to serve as a reminder to the practitioner that a solution or remedy is needed for that problem.

The second type of problem refers to *drug-related problems* such as prescribing errors, dosing errors, adverse drug effects, compliance issues, and the need for medication counseling. Drug-related problems may be definite (i.e., you are certain the problem exists) or possible (i.e., require further investigation to establish if the problem really exists). The most frequently encountered types of drug-related problems are listed in Table 1.3.[4]

The distinction between medical problems and drug-related problems sometimes is unclear and considerable overlap exists. For example, a medical problem (i.e., a disease, syndrome, symptom, or health condition such as pregnancy) can be prevented, cured, alleviated, or exacerbated by medications. When assessing drug therapy, several situations could exist: treatment is appropriate and therapeutic outcomes have been achieved; drugs that have been selected are ineffective or therapeutic outcomes are partially achieved; doses are subtherapeutic or medication is taken improperly; an inappropriate drug for the medical condition under treatment has been prescribed or is being used; or the condition is not being treated.

Likewise, a drug-related problem can cause or aggravate a medical problem. Such drug-related problems could include: hypersen-

sitivity reactions; idiosyncratic reactions; toxic reactions secondary to excessive doses; adverse reactions (e.g., insulin-induced hypoglycemia or weight gain); or drug-drug, drug-disease, drug-laboratory test, and drug-lifestyle interactions.

Furthermore, medical problems can alter the selection of drugs or the manner in which drugs are dosed or administered. Avoid spending inordinate amounts of time trying to categorize a problem as being a "medical problem" or a "drug-related problem;" rather, use these two terms to help identify the problems that require a management plan to achieve the therapeutic objective.

Subjective and Objective Data

Subjective and objective data in support of a problem are important because assessment of patients and therapies requires the gathering of specific information to verify that a problem continues to exist or that therapeutic objectives are being achieved. Subjective data refer to information provided by the patient which cannot be confirmed independently. Subjective assessments by the practitioner (e.g., "patient appears to be in pain") are objective because the assessment can be confirmed independently by another individual. Objective data refer to information observed or measured by the practitioner (e.g., laboratory tests).

4. P.N., a 28-year-old male, has a BP of 140/100 mm Hg. What is the primary problem? What subjective and objective data support the problem and what additional subjective and objective data are not provided, but usually are needed to define this particular problem?

Table 1.3	Drug-Related Problems

Drug Indicated
- A medical problem has been diagnosed, but there is no indication that treatment has been prescribed (maybe it is not needed)
- Correct drug prescribed, but not taken (noncompliance)

Wrong/Inappropriate Drug
- No apparent medical problem justifying the use of the drug
- Drug not indicated for the medical problem for which it has been prescribed
- Medical problem no longer exists
- Duplication of other therapy
- Less expensive alternative available
- Drug not covered by formulary
- Failure to account for pregnancy status, age of patient, other contraindications
- Incorrect OTC[a] self-prescribed by the patient
- Recreational drug use

Wrong Dose
- Prescribed dose too high (includes adjustments for kidney and liver function, age, body size)
- Correct prescribed dose, but overuse by patient (overcompliance)
- Prescribed dose too low (includes adjustments for age, body size)
- Correct prescribed dose, but underuse by patient (undercompliance)
- Incorrect, inconvenient, or less than optimal dosing interval (consider use of sustained-release dosage forms)

Adverse Drug Reaction
- Side effects
- Allergy
- Drug-induced disease
- Drug-induced laboratory change

Drug Interaction
- Drug-drug interaction
- Drug-food interaction
- Drug-laboratory test interaction

[a] OTC = Over the counter.

The primary problem is hypertension. No subjective data are given. The objective data are the patient's age, gender, and blood pressure of 140/100 mm Hg. Each of these are important in designing a patient-specific therapy plan. Since hypertension often is an asymptomatic disease (see Chapter 10: Essential Hypertension), subjective complaints such as headache, tiredness or anxiety, shortness of breath (SOB), chest pain, and visual changes usually are absent. If long-term complications such as rupturing of blood vessels in the eye, glomerular damage, or encephalopathy were present, then subjective complaints might be blurring or loss of vision, fatigue, or confusion. Objective data would include a report by the physician on the findings of the chest examination (abnormal heart or lung sounds if secondary CHF has developed), an ocular examination (e.g., presence of retinal hemorrhages), and laboratory data on renal function [blood urea nitrogen (BUN), creatinine, or creatinine clearance]. To place these complications in better perspective, the rate of change should be stated. For example, the serum creatinine has increased from a level of 1.0 mg/dL six months ago to a value of 3.0 mg/dL today. Vague descriptions such as ''eye changes'' or ''kidney damage'' are of little value because progressive damage to these end-organs is a consequence of uncontrolled high blood pressure and progress of the disease needs to be monitored more precisely.

5. D.L., a 36-year-old construction worker, tripped on a board at the construction site 2 days ago, sustaining an abrasion of his left shin. He presents today to the emergency room (ER) with pain, redness, and swelling in the area of the injury. He is diagnosed as having cellulitis. What is the primary problem? What subjective and objective data support the problem? What additional subjective and objective data are not provided, but usually are needed to define this particular problem?

The primary problem is cellulitis of the left leg. Useful subjective information is D.L.'s description of how he injured his shin during his work as a construction worker and his current complaints of pain, redness, and swelling. The fact that he was at a construction site is indirect evidence of a possible dirty wound. Further information must be obtained as to how he cleaned the wound following the injury and whether he has received a booster dose of tetanus immunization within the past ten years. Objectively, the wound is on the left shin. No other objective data are given. Additional data to obtain would be to document the intensity of the redness on a one-to-four-plus scale, the size of the inflamed area as described by an area of demarcation, the circumference of his left shin compared to his right shin, the presence or absence of pus and any lymphatic involvement, his temperature, white blood cell (WBC) count with differential, and any available blood culture and sensitivity data.

6. C.S., a 58-year-old female, has complaints of fatigue, ankle swelling, and SOB, especially when lying down for the past week. Physical examination shows distended neck veins, bilateral rales, an S_3 gallop rhythm, and lower extremity edema. A chest x-ray shows an enlarged heart. She is diagnosed as having CHF and is being treated with furosemide and digoxin. What is the primary problem? What subjective and objective data support the problem? What additional subjective and objective data are not provided but usually are needed to define this particular problem?

The primary problem is congestive heart failure. Subjectively, C.S. claims fatigue, ankle swelling, and shortness of breath, especially when lying down. She claims to have been taking furosemide and digoxin. An expanded description of these symptoms and of her use of medications would be helpful. The findings on physical examination and the enlarged heart on chest x-ray are objective data in support of the primary problem of CHF. In addition, other objective findings that would help in assessment would be the pulse rate, blood pressure, serum creatinine, serum potassium concentration, digoxin blood level, and a more thorough description of the rales on lung examination, extent of neck vein distention, and degree of leg edema. Pharmacy records could be screened to find out current doses and refill patterns of the medications.

Assessment

After the subjective and objective data have been gathered in support of specific listed problems, the acuity, severity, and importance of these problems need to be assessed. All factors that could be causing or contributing to the problem should be identified. The assessment of the severity and acuity is important because the patient expects relief from the symptoms that are of particular concern at this point in time. At the initial encounter with a patient, the medical problem might be only a symptom complex with an assessment that a diagnosis is needed to more accurately identify the problem and further define its severity. When a possible drug-related problem is detected during follow-up or monitoring, the assessment also should include an evaluation of the potential severity of this problem.

Plan

After generating the problem list, reviewing subjective and objective data, and assessing the severity and acuity of the problems, the next step in the problem-oriented (i.e., the SOAP) approach is to create a plan. The plan, at the very minimum, should consist of a diagnostic plan and a pharmaceutical care plan which includes patient education.

Diagnostic. The diagnostic plan could include further diagnostic tests, evaluation of drug-induced problems, or referral to another health care provider. The extent of the diagnostic plan, of course, would differ with different specialists. For example, primary care providers would have a more general diagnostic plan, medical subspecialists would have a more narrowly focused diagnostic plan, and pharmacists would have a more drug-induced component to their diagnostic plan and would likely defer to the diagnostic plan of other practitioners.

Pharmaceutical Care: Therapeutic Objectives. The pharmaceutical care plan describes desired clinical outcomes or therapeutic objectives. Well-conceived targets of desired clinical outcomes must be patient-specific and should be established in collaboration with the patient and, if appropriate, with other members of the healthcare team. These clinical outcomes also must be clearly defined and either measurable (e.g., laboratory test) or observable (e.g., task performance) by the patient and the practitioner within a specified time-line such that both know whether progress is being made toward the targeted objective. The therapeutic objectives should be realistic (i.e., what can be accomplished reasonably) and should begin with interventions which are essential to the patient's acute well-being or those which the patient perceives to be most important. Examples of clinical outcomes or therapeutic objectives are as follows: Cure of a disease (e.g., treatment of an infection); elimination or reduction of a patient's symptoms (e.g., pain control); arresting or slowing of a disease process (e.g., lowering a patient's cholesterol or blood pressure to reduce the risk of coronary heart disease); preventing a disease or other unwanted condition (e.g., contraception, prophylactic antibiotics, avoiding the complications of diabetes or hypertension); or improving the quality of life.

In a patient with multiple medical problems, the therapeutic objective for each problem should be considered separately, as well as in the aggregate. Ideally, a single treatment that achieves the targeted clinical outcome of more than one problem concomitantly is desirable. Conversely, care must be taken to assure that the therapy given for one problem does not make another problem worse or create a new problem. Furthermore, more than one therapeutic objective may be needed for each of the patient's problems recognizing the ideal clinical outcome may have to be achieved through a series of intermediate step-wise goals. In some situations, an intermediate goal may be that which is realistic within the context of the patient's situation. For example, with peptic ulcer disease, there is a short-term goal of symptomatic relief, an intermediate goal of healing the ulcer, and a long-term goal of preventing recurrence of the disease.

These examples all relate to achieving a positive outcome (i.e., assuring that the therapy is effective). However, there are other concurrent goals related to drug therapy: avoidance of adverse effects, convenience (to improve compliance), and cost effectiveness. While these latter three elements of the therapeutic goal may not always be articulated, they are part of every desired clinical outcome and must be considered when evaluating a pharmaceutical care plan. The potential benefits always should be balanced against the risks of therapy. This becomes particularly relevant when considering drug doses. In some cases, higher-than-average doses may be acceptable if the patient is not responding to "usual doses" and side effects have not been experienced yet. The interventions necessary to achieve the specified clinical outcomes also are integral to the pharmaceutical care plan. The following are examples of interventions in a pharmaceutical care plan: reinstituting correct use of a prescription medication when it is being taken or used improperly; educating and working with the patient to self-diagnose, evaluate, and solve therapeutic problems; instituting nonprescription drugs, nondrug therapies, administration aids, or monitoring tools; recommending or prescribing prescription medications; reinforcing continuation of already prescribed medications; alerting physicians to potential drug-related problems that can be solved only through an alteration of the original prescription (these include discontinuing the medication, prescribing an alternative drug, altering the dose or route of the current medications, and adding other medications); and referring the patient back to her primary care provider.

7. In Question 4, the subjective and objective data were considered for P.N., who has a BP of 140/100 mm Hg. What would be some therapeutic objectives or desired clinical outcomes of P.N.'s treatment?

Eradication or cure of the disease is not a realistic goal for hypertension (see Chapter 10: Essential Hypertension). Symptomatic control also is not relevant since blood pressure often is an asymptomatic disease. To simply state that the therapeutic objective is to control his blood pressure technically is correct, but it is not specific enough to define how attainment of this therapeutic objective will be measured. Thus, a starting therapeutic objective may be to "achieve a diastolic blood pressure of less than 90 mm Hg, but greater than 65 mm Hg within the next three months." This objective clearly is measurable, has a timeline, and hopefully is realistic. It also addresses both efficacy and, to a lesser extent, a side effect (i.e., avoidance of hypotension). Another short-term objective for this patient is for him "to be able to explain the long-term risks of untreated hypertension" and "the importance of complying to his treatment."

The pharmacist's interventions in the effort to attain these therapeutic objectives would be to educate the patient on both of these issues. The pharmacist also would assess medication refill patterns and measure the patient's blood pressure to determine whether these short-term therapeutic objectives have been met within the

established time-lines. A long-term therapeutic objective is to "prevent the long-term complications of hypertension such as kidney damage, loss of eyesight, and the development of congestive heart failure or other cardiovascular complications." This latter objective is better defined than simply stating that the goal is to "prevent complications of his disease." As always, unstated objectives are to avoid side effects and to make the treatment regimen as simple and cost effective as possible.

8. D.L. (see Question 5) presented to the ER with subjective and objective data sufficient to support a diagnosis of cellulitis. What would be some therapeutic objectives or desired clinical outcomes of his treatment?

Unlike the hypertension case above, a simple statement of objective such as "to cure his infection" technically is correct, but in terms of specifics, it leaves much to be desired. In this case, the therapeutic objectives or desired clinical outcomes are to eradicate the infection, provide symptomatic relief, and prevent spread of the infection to adjacent tissues (see Chapter 66: Traumatic Skin and Soft Tissue Infections). When faced with an infectious disease case and the need to choose or evaluate antibiotic choices, the practitioner must know usual causative organisms for a particular site or type of infection, the bacterial coverage of available antibiotics, and the patient's drug allergy history (see Chapter 54: Principles of Infectious Diseases). When available, culture and sensitivity data specific for the patient should be obtained. The most likely causative organisms for cellulitis are streptococci or staphylococci. Thus, a therapeutic objective could be "to eradicate a probable streptococcal or staphylococcal cellulitis; prevent bacteremia and spread to lymphatics; and reduce pain and swelling" within a specific time. In this case, the inclusion of the type of infection and probable organisms helps to define the antibiotic of choice (e.g., a penicillinase-resistant penicillin or a first-generation cephalosporin). Culture and sensitivity data would not be available at the time of initial treatment and a Gram's stain of the involved tissue seldom provides accurate data for this type of skin infection. D.L. should be asked about possible allergies to penicillins or cephalosporins. As always, other implied therapeutic objectives are to avoid side effects and to prescribe a regimen that is convenient and cost-effective. The education of the patient is an intervention that usually helps patients and practitioners achieve their mutually developed therapeutic objectives.

9. C.S. (see Question 6) presented with subjective and objective data sufficient to support a diagnosis of CHF and is being treated with furosemide and digoxin. What would be the therapeutic objective in this case?

Short of a heart transplant, cure or eradication of the disease is out of the question. A very narrow therapeutic objective might be "to increase cardiac output." Obviously, there is more to treating CHF than increasing cardiac output (see Chapter 15: Congestive Heart Failure). Also, this stated objective implies that there is an ability to perform invasive procedures to actually measure cardiac output. This would be beyond the scope of most practitioners. A more realistic statement of a therapeutic objective is "to provide symptomatic relief of congestive heart failure including increased exercise capacity, decreased shortness of breath, and reduced ankle swelling." A long-range objective is to prolong survival of the patient. The physician's objectives may be more specific and include reduction of neck vein distention, elimination of the S_3 gallop rhythm, and minimizing pulmonary and ankle edema. The specificity of the goal is determined by the practitioner's knowledge of the pathophysiology, signs, and symptoms of congestive heart failure and by his prior experience in treating such patients. Once again, other goals are to minimize toxicity and strive for a convenient, cost-effective regimen.

Patient Education. Education of the patient to better understand her medical problem(s) and treatment also is an implied goal of all treatment plans and is of sufficient importance to categorize this process as the development of a *patient education plan.* The level of teaching will have to be tailored to the patient's educational background, willingness to learn, and her general state of health and mind. The patient should be taught the knowledge and skills needed to achieve and evaluate her therapeutic outcome. An important component of the patient education plan emphasizes the need for patients to follow their prescribed treatment regimens.

Illustration of SOAP

10. Based upon the data presented in Questions 1–3, the practitioner believes P.J. is experiencing frequent hypoglycemic reactions. What SOAP note could be developed for P.J.?

The following example of a SOAP note illustrates the importance of integrating the patient's medical, therapeutic, and social history into the design of a pharmaceutical care plan (also see Chapter 48: Diabetes Mellitus).

Problem #1: Patient has been experiencing frequent hypoglycemia reactions.

Subjective: Patient reports episodes characterized by severe hunger, tremors, and profuse sweating that are relieved by orange juice. Episodes occur twice weekly, generally in the late afternoon. Patient often skips lunch to exercise. Patient states that she uses 30 U of NPH insulin every morning mixed with 30 U of regular insulin. She claims to never miss a dose and takes her insulin at 8 a.m. each day.

Objective: Occasional blood glucose values of 30 to 60 mg/dL in the late afternoon, often followed by values greater than 300 mg/dL before dinner and at bedtime.

Assessment: Total daily dose of insulin is high (1.2 U/kg). Morning dose of NPH insulin may be excessive.

Plan: *Therapeutic objectives:*

- Fasting blood glucose less than 140 mg/dL, postprandial blood glucose less than 180 mg/dL, all blood glucose greater than 70 mg/dL.

- No symptoms of hypoglycemia such as those noted above under ''S.''

- Patient to eat more regularly and carbohydrate intake to be distributed appropriately throughout the day.

- Patient to be able to predict time of peak NPH insulin activity and the relationship between carbohydrate intake and insulin dose.

- Patient and family members can describe symptoms of hypoglycemia and its treatment.

- Patient can make appropriate insulin and dietary adjustments for exercise.

- Patient can demonstrate correct blood glucose testing procedure; bring in records of blood glucose test results that reflect appropriate testing frequency.

Education plan:

- Teach patient and key family members about dangers of hypoglycemia, symptoms of hypoglycemia, relationship between insulin action and food intake (insulin pharmacodynamics), and treatment of hypoglycemia.

- Ask patient to demonstrate blood glucose testing technique. Correct as necessary. Institute more frequent glucose testing (before meals and at bedtime) to document patterns of glucose response to insulin therapy. Instruct patient to perform additional tests whenever she experiences symptoms of hypoglycemia to verify reaction.

- Educate patient about effect of exercise on blood glucose.

- Refer to dietitian. Objective is to emphasize importance of eating regularly and spreading out carbohydrate content of meals.

- Review and evaluate patient glucose records, signs, symptoms, and dietary and exercise history weekly. Help patient interpret and adjust insulin doses accordingly until target is achieved. Then evaluate quarterly.

- Call and write primary care provider regarding hypoglycemic reactions.

- Recommend how to decrease and reallocate doses based upon glucose test results.

It is easy to see in the above example of a SOAP note that pharmaceutical care is an iterative process and has the potential for a high level of sophistication and complexity. Each time the practitioner interacts with the patient, he monitors and evaluates the patient's progress toward the designated therapeutic outcome or target. This, along with any new information, is used to redefine or refine the problem list, clarify the assessment, or modify the therapeutic targets or plan. Thus, a continuous readjustment occurs with the overall goal of improving therapeutic outcomes and the patient's quality of life.

Pharmacist's Work-Up of Drug Therapy (PWDT)

The pharmacist's work-up of drug therapy[3,4,5] is an alternative to the SOAP approach for problem-solving clinical problems in that it focuses specifically on the identification of drug-related problems. The PWDT utilizes the following six interrelated steps: 1) establishing a comprehensive patient-specific database; 2) identifying patient-specific, drug-related problems; 3) describing desired therapeutic outcomes; 4) listing all therapeutic alternatives that might produce the desired outcomes; 5) selecting the drug recommendation(s) that most likely will result in the desired outcomes; and 6) establishing a plan for therapeutic drug monitoring that documents that desired effects occur and undesired effects are minimized.

The key to both the PWDT and the SOAP techniques is a *systematic approach to assessing and monitoring drug therapy.* Although the PWDT is preferred by some pharmacists for monitoring continuing drug therapy, the SOAP approach should be used when communicating in writing with other health providers (e.g., chart notes, formal letters) because it is recognized universally by physicians, nurses, and other health care professionals. Regardless of whether the PWDT or the SOAP technique is used, in the final analysis, it is more important to develop an organized thought process for identifying and solving clinical problems than to make every situation fit a specific mnemonic.

Drug Therapy Assessment

A responsibility of the practitioner is to monitor the response of patients to prescribed therapeutic regimens. This responsibility does not fall solely within the purview of physicians, physician assistants, and nurses: it also is the responsibility of pharmacists, especially when dispensing or refilling prescriptions in the community pharmacy, when assessing a patient's therapy on the medical ward during hospitalization, or as part of routine monthly evaluations of patients in a long-term care facility. The extent of monitoring is governed by the individual patient's need (this should be the primary determinant), time constraints, the working environment (which is a determinant of the amount of patient information that is available), and the individual practitioner's comfort level. Similarly, the exact steps used to monitor therapy and the order in which they are executed need to be adapted to a practitioner's personal style. Thus, the examples given in this chapter should be used by the reader as a guide, rather than as a recipe in a cookbook.

The purpose of drug therapy monitoring is to identify and solve drug-related problems and to assure that all therapeutic objectives are being achieved. Unless proven otherwise, the medical diagnosis should be assumed to be correct. On occasion, the diagnosis may not be readily apparent, or a drug-induced problem may have been diagnosed incorrectly as being a disease entity.

Previously Prescribed Drug Therapy

Community Pharmacy Setting

11. T.M. has requested a refill of a previously dispensed prescription from her community pharmacy. This particular pharmacy has a computerized patient profile system that can display all drugs that the patient has taken in the last 2 years, including the date and quantity of each drug refill. What actions should be expected of the pharmacist before dispensing this medication for T.M.?

The problem-oriented medical record approach (i.e., SOAP) begins the process of problem-solving with the development of a problem list; however, in reality, the medical record of most patients begins with demographic data (e.g., age, address) followed by a medical history which contains a history of present illness, past medical history, physical examination findings, and the results of laboratory tests. In essence, problem-solving must begin first with the accumulation of a database. Since the community pharmacist seldom has access to such data, the pharmacist also must *upgrade and update the patient's database* (i.e., the patient profile). The community pharmacist could begin by carefully reviewing the patient profile for all drugs currently being taken by the patient; for drugs that have been taken previously, but are now discontinued; and for the apparent refill frequency rates for regularly scheduled, routine medications as well as for those medications with the potential for abuse.

The pharmacist should be ready now to generate a problem list by *identifying patient-specific, drug-related problems*. The order of problems listed should be prioritized with the most important problem or the patient's current complaint (chief complaint) ranked first, followed in an order based upon the pharmacist's personal assessment of the severity of the problems. The order of the pharmacist's problem list may be markedly different from that of the physician or nurse since each has a different perspective when evaluating a patient. In some cases, an abbreviated problem list can be developed that includes only the currently active problems or even a single problem that is being given priority (e.g., specific suspected adverse drug effect). The risk of an abbreviated problem list is that confounding variables from other problems may be overlooked, thus affecting the practitioner's ability to accurately assess the current problem.

Although the community pharmacist in this scenario is not likely to have access to the patient's medical records, the pharmacist can formulate a problem list predicated upon the most likely indications for the drugs that the patient is taking. When in doubt, the most valuable source of information can be accessed (i.e., the patient can be interviewed). In a tactful way, the patient can be asked about current medical problems or why medical help was sought. One example is to say: "I see that you are taking digoxin. Do you know why this medicine was started?" or "Are you taking this to help regulate your heart beat or for congestive heart failure?" The exact phrasing of these sample questions needs to be adapted to the patient and the professional "style" of the pharmacist. Questions also should be asked to determine how well the patient feels

the drug is working and if the patient has experienced any problems. At the same time, the patient can be asked about medications that are obtained from another pharmacy, nonprescription medications being used, and if previous drug allergies have been experienced. Gathering of information may be expedited by using written history forms for the patient to complete, but the importance of talking directly to the patient at the time of the initial filling of a prescription or when they are obtaining refills cannot be overestimated. Note that at this point the practitioner is gathering *subjective data* (i.e., information gleaned from the patient) while preparing a problem list for the patient.

A helpful intermediate step in gathering *objective data* is to link the patient's drugs to one or more of her medical problems (see Table 1.4). This process aids in identifying drugs that may have been prescribed for more than one indication or drugs that are inappropriate (i.e., have no apparent indication). Drugs with multiple indications should be listed separately under each relevant problem. Some medications such as vitamins, analgesics, sedatives, antacids, and laxatives may be difficult to categorize. These nonprescription medications can be grouped under a general category such as "general care," but these should not be ignored because overuse or side effects can occur with these drugs as well. Alternatively, a term such as "medication issues" can be used as a generic term for issues such as compliance, need for medication counseling, and other possible drug-related problems.

If a *drug-related problem* is suspected, but objective (e.g., physical findings, laboratory tests) data are needed to confirm this suspicion, the patient can be asked if she has knowledge of these clinical or laboratory test results. Alternatively, the physician's office can be called (to find out the values or suggest laboratory tests that may be needed). It also is appropriate for the pharmacist to perform minor physical assessments such as monitoring the pulse rate (e.g., digoxin by slowing conduction through the AV node should decrease the pulse rate); measuring the blood pressure (e.g., antihypertensives); or observing the patient for obvious dermatologic conditions (e.g., skin color, rashes, presence of edema, insulin injection sites). Pharmacists also can perform simple laboratory tests (e.g., measure lipid, theophylline, glucose serum concentrations).

The monitoring of the patient's drug list for drug-related problems can be facilitated by a series of questions. These questions are summarized in Table 1.5 and elaborated below:

- Is the treatment working? If this question identifies a possible drug-related problem (i.e., the therapeutic objective is not being achieved), the problem list must be expanded accordingly. Relative to the drug-related problems in Ta-

Table 1.4	Example Problem List
Problem[a]	**Drugs Prescribed**
Medical problem #1 (usually the chief complaint)	Drug A
Medical problem #2	Drug B Drug C
Medical problem #3	Drug B Drug D Drug E
Medical problem #4	No drug therapy
Drug-related problem #1	
Drug-related problem #2	

[a] Identify problem name.

ble 1.3, this could provide a clue to one of several problems: a compliance problem; an ineffective drug has been prescribed ("wrong drug"); the prescribed dose is too low; or a drug interaction has led to lower-than-desired blood levels of the drug.

- Is there evidence of actual or potential side effects, drug interactions or duplications within the same therapeutic category? If this question identifies a possible drug-related problem, the problem should be labeled and added to the problem list.

- Are there any contraindications that need to be considered? If the profile indicates prior allergies, the current regimen should be screened for possible cross-reacting drugs. For women of child-bearing age, the possibility of pregnancy should be considered and the profile reviewed to see if contraceptives are being taken. When possible teratogenic drugs are prescribed, women should be asked if they currently are pregnant or considering pregnancy, and counseled about the risks of becoming pregnant.

- Are the doses correct? For all drugs that a patient is on, the pharmacist should evaluate the appropriateness of the dose, schedule, and the dosage form considering ease of use, reliability of the drug product, the patient's renal and hepatic function, the patient's age (especially pediatric and geriatric patients) and body size, and possible interactions with food or other drugs that are being taken. If this question identifies one or more possible drug-related problems, they should be added to the problem list.

- Is the patient taking the medications as prescribed (i.e., is there evidence of noncompliance, underuse, or overuse)? If this question identifies a possible drug-related problem, it should be added to the problem list.

- Are there more cost-effective alternatives for any of the treatments? If this question identifies a possible drug-related problem, the problem list should be expanded.

- Are there any drugs prescribed for the patient with no apparent indication (i.e., when constructing the problem list, there is a prescribed drug that does not match with any of the medical diagnoses)? If the answer is yes, one of the patient's problems may have been overlooked, an unusual use of a drug specific to this patient's needs has been missed, or the drug has been prescribed inappropriately. Each of these possibilities should be investigated and the problem list modified accordingly. This may involve adding a new medical problem to the list, linking the drug to an existing problem, or adding a new drug-related problem (wrong drug, inappropriate use) to the list.

- Are there any medical problems (diagnoses) listed for which no drug therapy has been prescribed? If the answer is yes, it may be appropriate (e.g., a patient with a past medical history of hypertension who has achieved acceptable blood pressure control with weight loss alone). Other possible explanations include: 1) failure by the pharmacist to identify a drug that was prescribed for the patient; 2) the patient is getting a drug from another pharmacy; 3) a drug is being given for one problem and the pharmacist thought it was being used for something else; or 4) the prescriber has inadvertently forgotten to order something for that patient. Each of these possibilities should be investigated further and the problem list modified accordingly.

- Could any of the medical problems or abnormal laboratory values be drug-induced? If so, a new drug-related problem should be added to the list.

- Are there any other obvious drug-related problems of the types listed in Table 1.3?

The above questions will identify suspected drug-related problems that might need to be substantiated by additional data. The challenge at this stage is to *clarify the problem*. While this task may sound simple, it is the most difficult component of patient assessment. In some cases, the signs and symptoms of diseases or adverse drug effects are similar to those found in textbooks; more often, some of the classic signs may be absent or the patient presents with unusual symptoms that require further observation. There generally is a need to obtain more data, but a recognition that time is limited. With experience and continual expansion of one's own knowledge base, this process becomes easier.

The problem list for both medical problems and drug-related problems now has been finalized and considerable subjective and objective data have been reviewed. After the listed problems have been assessed for severity and acuity, *a plan can now be developed*. As previously presented, the plan should include both therapeutic objectives and an educational component for each of the defined medical or drug-related problems. The immediate emphasis may be on short-term therapeutic objectives, but intermediate and long-term objectives also should be formulated from the beginning.

The therapeutic objectives of course would include the correction of possible drug-related problems. After *considering all potential corrective actions*, the pharmacist ultimately must choose the one option that is best for the patient. The process of merely identifying several possible solutions to a problem without being able to prioritize and select what seems to be the one best option does not really benefit the patient. If a change in therapy is necessary, or if there is sufficient concern to warrant contacting the prescriber, the recommended solution to the problem must be specific and include a specific alternative drug, route of administration, dose, and frequency of administration. Furthermore, the pharmacist must be prepared to justify the reasoning behind her recommendations (i.e., provide supporting evidence). If there are more cost-effective alternatives, the pharmacist will need to work with both the patient and the prescriber to change the therapy.

Table 1.5	Monitoring Questions

1) Is the treatment working? (i.e., is the therapeutic objective being achieved?)
2) Is there evidence of actual or potential side effects?
3) How compliant is the patient to the prescribed therapy?
4) Is there evidence of actual or potential drug interactions or duplications within the same therapeutic category?
5) Are there any contraindications or allergies that need to be considered?
6) Is the patient pregnant?
7) Are the doses, dosage regimens, and dosage forms correct? Have adjustments been made for renal function, hepatic function, age, and body size?
8) Could a less expensive or more convenient dosage form be used?
9) Are they any drugs prescribed for the patient with no apparent indication?
10) Are there any medical problems (diagnoses) listed for which no drug therapy has been prescribed?
11) Are there any of the medical problems or abnormal laboratory values that could be drug-induced?

A plan for further ongoing monitoring also needs to be established for the patient. The ongoing plan should contain specifics as to what parameters will continue to be monitored for efficacy, side effects, appropriateness of dose, and compliance. The pharmacist will have to decide how often monitoring for these parameters will be necessary. It also is helpful to anticipate possible future complications (e.g., changes in disease control, future complications of the disease) that may necessitate a change in the dose or drug of choice. For example, if a diabetic patient develops decreased visual acuity or worsening of renal function, the therapeutic plan may have to be altered by using larger print on labels, recommending a magnifying attachment for the patient's insulin syringes, or adjusting the dose of one or more of the patient's drugs. Finally, issues for future counseling also need to be considered, taking into consideration the level of sophistication of the individual patient (i.e., education plan).

Inpatient Pharmacy Setting

12. W.G. has just been hospitalized in a large medical center where the pharmacist has access to the medical chart, nursing record, medication administration record, and a computer that directly links to the clinical laboratory. The pharmacists at this facility assess the patients' drug therapy and routinely provide clinical pharmacokinetic monitoring. How would the pharmacist approach W.G. differently in this clinical setting compared to the pharmacist in Question 11 who worked in a community pharmacy?

The drug therapy monitoring process is similar in both situations, and the same SOAP or PWDT formats should be used. In the medical center setting, a problem list can be generated more easily because objective data (i.e., diagnoses, laboratory tests) are readily available. On the other hand, a hospitalized patient usually has more acute medical problems that often are superimposed on previous chronic problems. As a result, new therapies are being added and home medications may or may not be continued. For this reason, the problem list development step needs to be modified. Instead of making a two-column matrix of medical diagnoses and drug therapy as previously described, a multiple-column matrix is created. For each medical problem, drugs previously taken at home are compared to those prescribed while in the hospital. Later, an additional column can be added listing discharge medications. If the lists are not the same, an explanation should be sought. Many times the reasons are obvious (e.g., if a patient is changed from oral to parenteral therapy, or if a side effect of one of the home medications was the cause for the admission). At other times, this process helps to identify a home medication that the prescriber has forgotten to reorder. Discharge medication counseling is more effective when the pharmacist can differentiate between drugs that are new for the patient and those that are continuations of prior therapy. This also makes it easier to alert the patient to changes in dosage and give instructions about medications at home that should be discarded.

The assessment of appropriateness of drug doses requires knowledge of basic pharmacokinetic parameters (e.g., route of elimination). For hospitalized patients or those in nursing homes, the patient's renal function (BUN and serum creatinine) and liver function (transferase enzymes, bilirubin, albumin) should be reviewed. If either of these organs is not functioning properly, the prescribed drugs should be reviewed to determine whether rates of elimination would be altered. Then the ideal dose for the patient should be calculated for those drugs that have well-described pharmacokinetic models (e.g., aminoglycosides, antidysrhythmics, digoxin, phenytoin, theophylline). If serum drug concentrations are to be monitored, the cost effectiveness of obtaining serum levels now or in the physician's office should be determined and can be influenced by insurance reimbursements for hospital versus outpatient services. Appropriate timing and frequency of obtaining drug levels also should be suggested. If plasma levels have been reported previously, they should be reviewed for validity. Pharmacokinetic assessments should use actual patient data, rather than theoretical models whenever possible. If a serum drug concentration seems unusually high or low, all of the various factors that may influence the serum concentration of the drug in that particular patient should be considered (e.g., assess patient compliance and question the reliability of the laboratory). When there is no apparent explanation as to why the serum drug concentration is abnormal, the test should be repeated rather than recommending a dose that may cause toxic or subtherapeutic concentrations because of spurious data.

Initiating Over-the-Counter (OTC) Treatment

13. S.F., a female who appears to be about 25 years of age, asks her community pharmacist whether Gyne-Lotrimin Cream is better than Monistat-7 suppositories. How does the pharmacist's work-up of drug therapy principles presented in this chapter apply to S.F.?

First, it is important to identify the real question being asked. Superficially, the question relates to choosing one type of vaginal antifungal product versus another. S.F.'s question is confusing because two different chemicals are involved (clotrimazole versus miconazole) and the dosage forms are different (a cream versus suppository). S.F. may be asking the question because she simply is curious, but more likely she is indirectly asking the pharmacist to diagnose a problem and to recommend a therapy. Moreover, the treatment may be for her, or it may be for someone else. The pharmacist should ask several questions and mentally develop a problem list before recommending therapy.

The only approved indication for nonprescription vaginal antifungal products is the treatment of a recurrent candidal vaginal infection. Therefore, the pharmacist needs to gather subjective and objective data to verify the existence of this problem in S.F. or in whomever she is buying the product for. As a minimum, the pharmacist should inquire about symptoms (e.g., include vaginal itching or burning, inflammation, a cottage-cheese-like discharge) and confirm that previous symptoms were diagnosed by a physician. Possible questions to ask are: "Will you be using this product or will someone else?" "What symptoms are you having?" "Describe the discharge" "Have you been treated for this problem before?" "How were you treated before?" "Have you ever used either of these two products?" and "Was the drug effective last time?"

At least two other important questions should be asked: "What other medications are you taking?" and "Is it possible that you are pregnant?" The answer to the first question will help identify other possible medical problems to add to the problem list as well as possible drugs that could be the cause of her infection (e.g., antibiotics, oral contraceptives). If she is pregnant, referral to her doctor is indicated.

14. At this point, an initial assessment can be made as to whether or not S.F. has a recurrent vaginal yeast infection. Assume for the moment that the diagnosis is confirmed and S.F. is not taking any other medications and has no other medical problems. What is the therapeutic goal of her treatment and what is the next step for the pharmacist to take?

The goal is to eliminate the current vaginal yeast infection by educating S.F. how to treat this infection and prevent future infections.

The next step for the pharmacist is to consider all of the therapeutic options. Possibilities include referral to a physician for prescription therapy, use of nondrug therapies (e.g., avoiding occlusive clothing, daily ingestion of cultured yogurt), and nonprescription clotrimazole or miconazole. Note that this list of options is for illustrative purposes only and is not meant to be an exhaustive review of treatment modalities.

From these options, one or more specific recommendations must be given to the patient. Clotrimazole and miconazole generally are considered equally effective; therefore, the selection of one drug over the other can be based upon cost. The choice of a cream versus a suppository will be based upon whether or not there is external vaginal involvement, patient convenience, and patient preference. Counseling as to how to apply the medication, how long to use it, and hygienic precautions to avoid future infections also should be part of the plan.

The recommendations obviously will be different if the pharmacist determines that the patient does not have a vaginal yeast infection (e.g., the discharge is more characteristic of bacterial vaginosis); the patient has not had a previous diagnosis of a yeast infection; she has a drug-induced cause; or she is pregnant. Discussion of treatment options for each of these possibilities is beyond the scope of this chapter (also see Chapters 46: Gynecological Disorders and 69: Fungal Infections).

This case illustrates a pharmacist prescribing nonprescription drugs. The same thought process is followed when working under preapproved prescriptive authority protocols.

Establishing Priorities

15. How are priorities decided upon as to which patients should be monitored and when the pharmacist should intervene?

Ideally, all patients should be monitored closely and interventions made in every instance that an actual or potential problem is identified. For the pharmacist working in a specialized unit (e.g., a bone marrow transplant unit), it may be feasible to monitor all patients with the same level of intensity since the numbers of patients may be relatively small and the underlying problem is similar for all of the patients. On the other hand, pharmacists consulting on a general medicine ward, a nursing home, or in a busy retail pharmacy have a greater diversity and larger volume of patients, making universal monitoring impractical. Thus, criteria need to be established to determine which patients need to be monitored more extensively. While there are no absolute rules on how to set priorities, the following guidelines might be helpful:

Age and Gender. The doses of medications should be reviewed for children under the age of 12 and adults over the age of 65 because of smaller body size and possible impaired drug clearance or enhanced sensitivity to drug effects. Women of child-bearing age should be evaluated more closely if possible teratogenic drugs are ordered.

Number of Medications Prescribed or Number of Doses per Day. People receiving more than three medications should be monitored more closely for duplication of therapy, potential adverse drug effects, and possible drug interactions. Complicated drug regimens should be evaluated for the possibility of using sustained-release preparations or combination products to improve compliance.

Drugs with a High Risk for Adverse Drug Effects or Drug Interactions. Pharmacists should develop a list of key drugs within their practice that trigger a more in-depth review every time they are encountered. This could include drugs such as anticoagulants, digoxin, theophylline, metered-dose inhalers, oral corticosteroids, insulin or oral hypoglycemics, aminoglycosides, and anticonvulsants. Drugs with a high potential for triggering drug interactions include enzyme inhibitors and inducers, especially anticonvulsants, cimetidine, macrolide antibiotics, fluoroquinolones, and fluoxetine.

Target Diseases. As with the drug examples listed above, the drug therapy of some patient populations needs to be monitored more closely. This will have to be tailored to an individual's specific practice site and also may change over time. For example, one may wish to develop a specialty interest in patients with asthma, diabetes, hypertension, or lipid disorders. For six months or a year, a pharmacist could target all patients with asthma using more than one canister of a metered-dose beta-agonist inhaler per month to receive special counseling and intervention. In some cases, protocols can be developed with local prescribers to help the target population treat their disease more effectively. During the following year, different screening criteria could be established such as all patients with hypertension who fail to refill their prescriptions within two weeks of their next scheduled refill.

High-Cost Drugs. The most cost-effective therapy always should be considered. A common example is the use of cephalosporins or amoxicillin/clavulanic acid (Augmentin) for the treatment of otitis media. A more general guideline might be to review all regimens that cost the patient more than $100 to $150 per month.

Altered Drug Clearance. In practice settings where laboratory values are available for monitoring, all patients with an elevated serum creatinine, bilirubin, or transferase concentration should be monitored closely for drugs that may need dosage adjustment. Similarly, drugs with well-established pharmacokinetic monitoring parameters such as antiarrhythmics, aminoglycosides, anticonvulsants, digoxin, and theophylline should be monitored closely.

Allergy. Patients whose drug profile indicates a drug allergy should be screened closely to make sure that no cross-reacting drugs have been ordered. If at all possible, the patient should be consulted to ascertain the nature of the allergy and a notation made in their medical or pharmacy record as to the clinical presentation of the allergy.

Prescriber Contact. The next level of priority setting is to determine when to contact a prescriber. This requires establishing a balance between patient safety, convenience, and the time available for both the pharmacist and physician. Any situation which represents potential harm to the patient (e.g., a newly identified adverse drug effect, a well-documented drug interaction, a dosing error) must be acted upon immediately. Switching to less costly drugs or more convenient regimens also should have a high priority but sometimes can be postponed until a more convenient time. If the pharmacist practices in the patient care area, it is easier to sense when the physician is stressed and, thus, postpone an intervention until a more convenient time. The physician should not be confronted in front of her peers, so it is prudent to make an intervention during a private one-on-one consultation as opposed to during rounds or in a crowded room. If the same physician has several potential problem patients, it may be best to intervene on the most pressing issues and leave the others to another time. When a good working relationship has been established with the physician, it may be possible to schedule a time to review all of his or her patients in a very collegial fashion. Interventions over the telephone are less desirable since it is difficult to judge how busy the physician is at the time of the phone call. Nonurgent communications to inform the physician of an intervention or to make suggestions for change can be made by written notes in the chart or formal letters. Getting to know the physician on a personal basis by visiting her office or going to lunch together helps promote a more collegial and less adversarial relationship. Finally, many problems can be resolved between the pharmacist and the patient without having to actively involve the physician, although the physician should be informed as soon as possible.

Example of the PWDT

16. M.B. practices in the outpatient pharmacy of a community hospital. V.C., a 30-year-old female, comes to the pharmacy with a prescription for nitrofurantoin sustained-release (Macrobid) 100 mg BID for 7 days. The computer profile shows that the only other medicine V.C. is taking is metronidazole (Flagyl) 500 mg BID × 7 days which she received 7 days prior. Both of the prescriptions were written by the same general practitioner in the hospital's medical clinic. No other information is available at this time. Based upon the information given, what medical problems does V.C. have? Develop a tentative problem list with corresponding drug therapy.

The data given are insufficient to definitively state the diagnoses at this time. The most likely use for the nitrofurantoin is a urinary tract infection, probably cystitis or urethritis. The metronidazole could have been prescribed for a trichomonal infection, bacterial vaginosis, or as an adjunct for anaerobic bacterial coverage. Given the dose prescribed and the general circumstances, the most likely indication is bacterial vaginosis. Upon questioning V.C., these conclusions are confirmed. She claims good compliance to the metronidazole (she will take her last dose tonight), notes no side effects, and states that her vaginal itching and discharge are decreased, but now she has some burning on urination. Thus the problem list is as follows:

	Problem	Drugs
1	New onset urinary tract infection	Nitrofurantoin 100 mg BID
2	Bacterial vaginosis	Metronidazole 500 mg BID

17. Are there any drug-related problems illustrated by V.C.?

No. The indications and doses are appropriate. It is too early to determine if the therapy is effective. V.C. claims no adverse effects and there is no evidence of a compliance problem. There are no obvious drug interactions. V.C. should be counseled about the GI effects of the nitrofurantoin.

18. Three days later, V.C. presents to the ER with a chief complaint of nausea and vomiting of mixed coffee-ground-appearing material and bright red blood. She states that she was in her usual state of health until 2 days ago when the nausea and vomiting began soon after dinner. Blood appeared in the vomitus after the first several episodes and she has continued to vomit intermittently since then to the point where she has vomited "more times than she can count." V.C. also states that her stools turned black yesterday and appear to be tarry. She has had no oral intake since the vomiting began and now has some dizziness. She denies fever, chills, abdominal pain, or diarrhea. Her urinary tract infection symptoms have subsided. Past medical history includes a "nervous stomach" since childhood, occasional heartburn when lying down after a large meal, and endometriosis diagnosed 2 years ago. She has no previous history of ulcer disease. Her only current medication is the nitrofurantoin identified previously. She completed her metronidazole treatment course 3 nights ago. V.C. reports occasional alcohol use; she did not ingest any alcohol while taking the metronidazole per her pharmacist's directions, but she drank 2 glasses of wine with dinner on the night her vomiting began. She denies use of aspirin or nonsteroidal agents.

Physical examination shows a temperature of 37.3 °C; respiration 20 breaths/min; BP 114/74 mm Hg, without a postural drop; and a pulse 64 beats/min lying down, increasing to 100 beats/min on standing. The rest of the examination is unremarkable except for dry oral mucous membranes. Bowel sounds are normal.

Laboratory results are sodium (Na) 140 mEq/L, potassium (K) 3.3 mEq/L, chloride (Cl) 109 mEq/L, total carbon dioxide (CO_2) 24 mEq/L, glucose 94 mg/dL, BUN 15 mg/dL, creatinine 0.9 mg/dL, hematocrit (Hct) 36%, WBC count 9600 cells/mm^3, platelets 249,000/mm^3, prothrombin time 11.6 seconds, International Normalized Ratio (INR) 0.9. Urine and blood cultures are pending. Nasogastric aspirate is now negative for blood, but the stool sample is hemoccult positive. The physician's assessment is GI bleed, volume depletion, and hypokalemia. Admission orders are for ranitidine 50 mg IV Q 8 hr, prochlorperazine 5–10 mg IV Q 4–6 hr PRN nausea, nitrofurantoin SR 100 mg BID, and 1 L of dextrose 5% in 0.45% normal saline with 40 mEq KCl at 125 mL/hr. Based upon this information, develop an updated medical problem list: [SI units: Na 140 mmol/L; K 3.3 mmol/L; Cl 109 mmol/L; total CO_2 24 mmol/L; glucose 5.2 mmol/L; BUN 5.35 mmol/L; creatinine 68.6 μmol/L; Hct 0.36; WBC count 9600 × 10^6 cells/L; platelets 249 × 10^9/L]

	Problem	Drugs
1	Nausea, vomiting, GI bleeding	Ranitidine
2	Volume depletion, hypokalemia	D5 ½ NS, KCl
3	Resolving urinary tract infection	Nitrofurantoin 100 mg BID
4	Bacterial vaginosis (resolved)	None
5	History of endometriosis	None

It is possible that V.C. also has underlying gastroesophageal reflux. This is not listed as a separate problem, although it may contribute to her primary problem.

19. Are there any drug-related problems that should be added to this list? Make an assessment as to the likelihood of any of the problems that could be drug-induced.

There is a distinct possibility that V.C.'s GI distress and bleeding may be drug-related. The most common side effect of nitrofurantoin is nausea and abdominal distress. She took the drug for several days without difficulty, but this could represent a cumulative effect or a combined effect with the factors below. Metronidazole generally is well tolerated, but when taken with alcohol, it can cause a disulfiram-like reaction with severe nausea, vomiting, and flushing. V.C. drank alcohol the afternoon following her last evening dose of metronidazole. While this may raise a suspicion that she is having an disulfiram-like reaction, the possibility is unlikely since the half-life of metronidazole is relatively short (4 to 6 hours). Thus, most, if not all, of the drug would have been out of the system at the time she ingested the alcohol. Finally, alcohol is a GI irritant itself, but she has continued to have symptoms for several days despite no further alcohol ingestion. Any of these factors could help to explain the initial GI distress, but frank ulceration and bleeding as a result of her drugs are not as easy to explain. Of the three drugs, the one most likely to cause bleeding would be the alcohol, but only with chronic ingestion. She denies alcohol abuse. Of course, other factors such as a coincident viral gastroenteritis cannot be ruled out. As a final assessment, it cannot be said with certainty that any of her drugs played a direct role in her admission. Nonetheless, she should be cautioned about future combinations of alcohol with metronidazole and the importance of taking nitrofurantoin with food.

An endoscopic examination the following day showed gastritis and an esophageal tear (Mallory Weiss tear) from retching. The actual cause of the gastroenteritis remains unknown. She was discharged home on ranitidine and as-needed antacids. This case illustrates how a possible incorrect assessment (e.g., metronidazole-alcohol interaction with a disulfiram-like effect) could be made if one does not take into account all facts known about the patient's history and the drug's pharmacokinetic properties.

Evaluating a Possible Adverse Drug Effect

20. D.G., a 41-year-old female, is admitted to the hospital after presenting to the ER with a chief complaint of fatigue for 2 weeks. One week before admission, she experienced blurred vision, which caused her to miss work, and over the past few days, she has noted increasing ataxia. One day before admission, D.G. became dizzy and fell in the shower, sustaining a head injury. She has had a history of a seizure disorder (grand mal/generalized tonic-clonic and petit mal/absence) since childhood, but she has been seizure-free for 10 years. She also has a history of adenocarcinoma of the sigmoid colon with metastases to the liver diagnosed 3 years ago. Medication history includes phenytoin (Dilantin) 100 mg PO Q AM and 200 mg PO Q PM; phenobarbital 30 mg PO Q AM and 60 mg PO Q PM; and prochlorperazine 10 mg tablets up to Q 6 hr PRN for nausea. She has undergone chemotherapy with 5FU 1000 mg IV 1 month ago and 500 mg IV plus leucovorin 30 mg IV 5 days before admission. She has no known allergies. Family history and social history are noncontributory. Upon questioning, D.G. states she has been taking anticonvulsants "as usual" and has taken no extra doses. She denies recent nausea or vomiting, but she has been taking the prochlorperazine prophylactically Q 6 hr since her last chemotherapy because she had experienced nausea and vomiting with the chemotherapy in the past. D.G. has had chills recently, but denies fever. Her appetite is good and, in fact, she has gained 4 pounds over the last week. Her sleep pattern has been good, but she awakens feeling "drugged."

Physical examination revealed the following: weight 57.5 kg, height unknown, BP 136/85 mm Hg, pulse 78 beats/min, respiration 16 breaths/min, and temperature 37 °C. There is a bruise on the left side of the forehead, 3+ bilateral nystagmus, and gingival hyperplasia. A staggering gait is confirmed on the neurological examination. Admission laboratory results are unremarkable with normal electrolytes, liver function tests, renal function tests, and complete blood count. A stat phenytoin concentration at 1:45 p.m. when she was admitted is 49.6 µg/mL; albumin is 4.4 mg/dL. A repeat phenytoin concentration at 8:00 the next morning is still 42.7 µg/mL. Of note, a phenytoin concentration measured 1 month ago was 10.5 µg/mL. The tentative diagnosis is phenytoin toxicity. Based upon this information, develop a medical problem list and corresponding drug therapies.

Problem	Drugs
1 Possible phenytoin toxicity	Phenytoin
2 Head injury (bruise, fall and dizziness probably secondary to #1)	Prochlor-perazine (?)
3 Seizure disorder	Phenytoin, phenobarbital
4 Adenocarcinoma of sigmoid colon with liver metastases	5 FU; leucovorin
5 Nausea and vomiting	Prochlor-perazine
6 Gingival hyperplasia secondary to long-term phenytoin use	Phenytoin (none for treatment)

The order of this problem list is prioritized based upon the pharmacist's primary interest; therefore, possible phenytoin toxicity is listed as the first problem. The patient's oncologist may have listed her colon cancer as the number one problem and other practitioner specialists may have other priorities as well. If the diagnosis of phenytoin toxicity had not been established, the problem list would have included ataxia and blurred vision as separate medical problems or as a complex of symptoms that needed further assessment. A practitioner seeing these side effects in a patient with anticonvulsant therapy would have to be suspicious of possible phenytoin or phenobarbital toxicity.

21. Which of the problems on the list require further intervention or consideration?

Predisposing factors to the possible phenytoin toxicity should be explored further. For the moment, the seizure disorder and adenocarcinoma of the colon appear to be stable problems and do not require any immediate intervention. The seizures are well controlled symptomatically, meeting the primary therapeutic objective of this problem. The therapeutic objective for the cancer may either be cure or palliation. Not enough information is provided to assess the current status of this problem, but for the moment, it does not appear to be the most immediate problem. The nausea and vomiting are not bothering D.G. at this time and she should reconsider the necessity for the continuation of the prophylactic prochlorperazine. A secondary objective may be to counsel D.G. on the most effective way to use the prochlorperazine. The gingival hyperplasia may be an unavoidable consequence of her phenytoin therapy. It is not appropriate to discontinue the phenytoin since her seizures are well controlled. She should be questioned about her dental hygiene and counseled about proper mouth care.

The tentative diagnosis is phenytoin toxicity; however, additional data are needed to confirm the diagnosis of this drug-related problem.

Subjective and Objective Data

22. What subjective and objective data are given to help verify the diagnosis of phenytoin toxicity in D.G.? What other information is needed? Do you agree with the assessment?

Subjectively, D.G.'s complaints are classic for phenytoin toxicity (e.g., blurred vision, staggering when walking, dizziness). The latter problem led to her fall. Objectively, she has nystagmus, ataxia, and an obvious supratherapeutic phenytoin serum concentration of 49.6 µg/mL that was verified by a subsequent measurement the following day of 42.7 µg/mL. A free (unbound) serum phenytoin concentration could be measured, but it is not necessary since her albumin level is normal. The gingival hyperplasia is a sign of chronic phenytoin side effects, but it is not relevant to her current problem. The assessment of phenytoin toxicity is appropriate. However, it would be desirable to also obtain a phenobarbital level to rule out possible concurrent phenobarbital toxicity.

23. Which of the drug-related problem types in Table 1.3 does D.G.'s case illustrate? What factors could have contributed to the problem?

This is an example of a patient getting too much of the correct drug. In other words, phenytoin is indicated for D.G.'s seizure disorder and, for a long time, has provided the desired therapeutic objective of good seizure control. Possible causes for the new onset of toxicity include an inappropriately prescribed dose, overcompliance, possible purposeful overdose (e.g., suicidal gesture), changes in drug metabolism, or a possible drug interaction. A laboratory error can be ruled out because a subsequent phenytoin serum concentration also was high and D.G.'s clinical complaints are compatible with phenytoin toxicity. Finally, it is possible that the symptoms are related to another cause (e.g., a cerebrovascular accident, brain metastases from her cancer or phenobarbital toxicity). None of these latter possibilities can be ruled out absolutely with the present data.

Assessment

24. Which of the factors above are the most likely explanation for D.G.'s problem?

D.G. claims good compliance and says she has not taken any extra doses. It is possible that she is an unreliable historian but she has taken the drug at the same dose for many years without previous complications. Her history of liver metastases raises a suspicion of impaired metabolism, but her liver function tests are all normal and she has no evidence of jaundice. Her recent course of cancer chemotherapy may have inactivated enough of her P450 enzyme system to decrease the clearance of phenytoin and increase its serum concentrations. Phenytoin pharmacokinetics are nonlinear and rise rapidly when hepatic metabolism is saturated by increased drug or decreased liver function. The slow rate of decline of D.G.'s blood levels of phenytoin after admission is consistent with a decreased clearance and saturation of her cytochrome P450 enzyme system. There are no obvious drug interactions accounting for the increase in phenytoin serum concentrations with the possible exception of prochlorperazine. In one anecdotal case report,[6] prochlorperazine seemed to ''impair'' phenytoin metabolism. The report provided minimal information regarding the patient's medical history making if difficult to evaluate the validity of this interaction. D.G.'s other drug, phenobarbital, should not be contributing to the phenytoin toxicity since she has taken it for many years and it is an enzyme-inducer which would tend to lower her serum phenytoin concentration, not increase it. However, phenobarbital toxicity still may be contributing to D.G.'s clinical syndrome.

Therapeutic Goals

25. What is the desired therapeutic outcome relative to D.G.'s phenytoin toxicity?

The short-term goal is to provide symptomatic relief with cessation of her ataxia, dizziness, and blurred vision. The long-term goal is continued seizure control and avoidance of future phenytoin toxicity.

26. Identify the therapeutic alternatives to help solve this potential problem.

For the short-term, phenytoin should be discontinued until the plasma level returns to the therapeutic range. No definitive therapy or antidotes are needed. Long-term alternatives include: 1) deletion of phenytoin (and possibly phenobarbital), with the substitution of an alternative anticonvulsant such as carbamazepine or sodium valproate; 2) restarting the phenytoin at a lower dose; 3) deletion of phenytoin with no other therapy being started; or 4) no change in drug therapy.

Plan

27. Which of the above alternatives should be recommended?

There is no one right answer to this question. Factors to consider are efficacy, risk for side effects, patient acceptance, and cost. Recommendations must be specific including drug name, dosing, and timing of monitoring. Contingency plans need to be available in case the primary plan fails.

It is not the purpose of this example to exhaustively examine the rationale for the best recommendations. For illustrative purposes, assume that the recommendation was that phenytoin concentrations be measured every other morning with the plan to restart phenytoin at a dose of 100 mg/day orally when the serum concentration of phenytoin had decreased to 10 to 12 μg/mL. It

may take several days for the serum concentration of phenytoin to decrease to this range because of its nonlinear pharmacokinetics. A phenobarbital serum concentration also should be recommended and the results compared to the last known serum phenobarbital concentration. The dose of phenobarbital then can be adjusted accordingly. These recommendations would be reasonable because both phenobarbital and phenytoin have been effective in D.G. and her phenytoin toxicity may be attributable to a temporary change in metabolism. She will need to be counseled extensively and further questioned to make sure she, in fact, did not take extra doses.

28. What follow-up monitoring is required?

After phenytoin is restarted, a new serum concentration can be obtained at day three and day seven. D.G. should be observed for further signs of toxicity (ataxia, nystagmus, dizziness) and for sei-

Table 1.6	Sample Chart Note[a]

9/13; 5 p.m.

Problem #1: **Possible phenytoin toxicity**

S   41-year-old WF admitted with 2-week history of fatigue and 1-week history of blurred vision and dizziness ("drugged feeling") likely due to phenytoin toxicity. PMH significant for seizure disorder since childhood (seizure-free for 10 years) and metastatic adenocarcinoma of sigmoid colon (biopsy 3/90). Patient taking Dilantin 100 mg Q AM, 200 mg Q PM; phenobarbital 32 mg Q AM, 64 mg Q PM; and prochlorperazine 10 mg Q 6 hr to prevent nausea. Has not taken any extra doses. Denies use of any OTC medications or other nonprescribed drugs. Also receives intermittent 5 FU (1000 mg on 8/14; 500 mg on 9/6; and leucovorin 30 mg IV on 9/6)

O   *Weight:* 57.5 kg; NKDA

     PE: Bruise on left side of forehead; (+) gingival hyperplasia; (+) nystagmus, otherwise nonfocal neurological exam; remaining exam WNL

     Lab: Admission phenytoin concentration = 49.6 μg/mL (therapeutic: 10–20 μg/mL); previous phenytoin concentration on 8/16 was 10.5 with an albumin of 4.4 gm/dL

A   There are no likely drug interactions accounting for the increase in phenytoin serum concentrations with the possible exception of prochlorperazine. 1 paper (JAMA 1968; 203:969) noted in 1 instance that it seemed to "impair" phenytoin metabolism. Since there is minimal information regarding the patient, extent of metabolism impairment, disease status, or concomitant medications/disease, it is impossible to evaluate the validity of this report and its significance to this case

     Phenytoin pharmacokinetics are nonlinear and rise rapidly when hepatic metabolism is saturated by increased drug or decreased liver function. Given the timing of the chemotherapy medications, it is likely that the chemotherapy has inactivated enough of her metabolizing cells (P450 enzyme system), to decrease clearance and account for the increase in phenytoin serum concentrations

R   Consider discontinuing phenytoin and monitoring for further seizure activity. Given her long seizure-free period, this may be reasonable. Phenobarbital should be continued for now, but considered for discontinuation at a later time. If maintenance phenytoin is preferred, hold phenytoin now, measuring serum concentration QOD, until the concentration falls below 15 μg/mL, then reinstate phenytoin at 100 mg PO Q HS. Measure serum concentrations in the morning at 3 and 7 days post-initiation of new dose, then weekly while on chemotherapy regimen and monthly thereafter if she is doing well. Measure phenobarbital level now. May produce similar toxicity. Monitor for dizziness, blurred vision, ataxia, lateral gaze nystagmus. Feel free to call should you have further questions. Will follow. Thank you for the consult

Signature, R.Ph.

[a] A = Assessment; NKDA = No known drug allergies; O = Objective; OTC = Over the counter; PE = Physical examination; PMH = Past medical history; R = Recommendation; S = Subjective; WF = White female; WNL = Within normal limits.

zure control. Weekly monitoring of phenytoin serum concentrations may be needed for the next month until steady state is achieved. If phenytoin serum concentrations on 100 mg/day orally are still above 10 to 20 µg/mL or D.G. still is experiencing toxicity, the dose can be decreased to 30 mg/day or discontinuation should be considered. If seizures recur, the dose should be increased or another therapy started.

Writing a Consult Note

Practitioners must be able to communicate patient information effectively both verbally and in writing. Written consults may take the form of notes in the patient's medical record or a formal letter for corresponding through the mail. Brevity and clarity are important; recommendations should be complete and specific. Elements to include in the consult are a brief overview of patient data necessary to show your thought process and assessment of the problem. Recommendations for drugs should include the specific dose for the patient, the route, and the dosage frequency. Include parameters you would recommend for monitoring to ensure efficacy of the treatment regimen, prevention of toxicity, and the assessment of compliance. Be sure to include how often you recommend the parameters should be monitored. The SOAP format is desirable for the medical record, although you might change the P (plan) to R (recommend) if it seems more logical.

29. Using D.G.'s case, how would you formulate your consult note for D.G.'s medical record?

At the top of your note, include the current date, time, and name of the problem being addressed. The body of the note should be in the SOAP format and you should sign your name at the end. Common abbreviations and incomplete sentences often are used to keep the length of the note manageable. A formal consult written as a letter may be more formal, including full sentences and fewer abbreviations. See Table 1.6 for the note written in D.G.'s chart.

Acknowledgments

The authors appreciate the valuable contributions of Drs. Allan Ellsworth and Teresa O'Sullivan for their help in writing portions of the cases and consult notes found in this chapter. They, along with Dr. Danial Baker, Karan Dawson, Nathan Lawless, Dr. Peggy Odegard, and other pharmacy faculty at the University of Washington, Washington State University, and the University of California, contributed their clinical insights and creative energies.

References

1 **Facts and Comparisons.** St. Louis, MO: Facts and Comparisons Inc; 1993.
2 **Weed LL.** Medical Records, Medical Education and Patient Care. Cleveland, OH: Case Western Reserve Press; 1971.
3 **Strand L et al.** Pharmaceutical Care: An Introduction. Current Concepts. The Upjohn Co.; 1992.
4 **Strand L et al.** Drug related problems: their structure and function. DICP Ann Pharmacother. 1990;24:1093.
5 **Kishi D, Watanabe A.** A systematic approach to drug therapy for the pharmacist. Am J Hosp P. 1974;31:494.
6 **JAMA** 1968;203:969.

Clinical Pharmacokinetics

Michael E Winter

Basic Principles	2-1
Plasma Concentration (Cp)	2-2
Cp as calculated or reported	2-2
Protein binding	2-2
Adjustment for alterations in plasma binding	2-2
Absorption	2-3
Bioavailability (F)	2-3
Factors influencing bioavailability	2-3
Solubility	2-3
Dosage form and route of administration	2-3
First-pass effect	2-3
Salt form (S)	2-3
Rate of Administration (R_A)	2-3
Volume of Distribution (Vd)	2-3
Loading dose	2-4
Two-compartment model	2-4
Clearance (Cl)	2-5
Maintenance dose	2-5
Routes of elimination	2-5
Half-Life (t½)	2-5
Elimination Rate Constant (Kd)	2-5
Clinical Use of Equations	2-6
Time to Sample	2-6
After starting or changing a regimen	2-6
Nonsteady-state plasma concentrations	2-6
At steady state	2-7
Evaluation of Renal Function	2-7
Clinical Application Calculations	2-8
Loading Dose	2-8–9
Two-Compartment Distribution	2-8
Target organ located in Vi	2-8
Target organ located in Vt	2-4, 2-7
Loading Dose Followed by Infusion	2-8–9
Clearance	2-8–9, 2-11, 2-13–14, 2-16–19
Estimate from the literature	2-8, 2-11, 2-14, 2-16–17, 2-19

Revision from maintenance dose and average steady-state level	2-9
Revision from plasma concentrations	2-13, 2-18
Volume of Distribution	2-8–9, 2-11, 2-13–17, 2-19
Estimate from the literature	2-8–9, 2-11, 2-14–17, 2-19
Revision from plasma concentrations	2-13, 2-16
Maintenance Dose	2-8, 2-10
Estimate from the literature	2-8
Adjustment based on measured plasma concentrations	2-10
Conversion from parenteral to oral route of administration	2-10
Sustained-release product	2-10
Elimination Rate Constant (Kd)	2-10–11, 2-13–19
Estimate of Kd from Cl and Vd	2-10–11, 2-15–17, 2-19
Estimate of Kd from two plasma concentrations	2-13–15, 2-18
Estimate of time required for plasma concentration to decay	2-10, 2-14
Influence of Vd on Measured Plasma Concentration	2-8, 2-18
Influence of Cl on Measured Plasma Concentration	2-9, 2-18
Plasma Sample	2-9–11, 2-13–14, 2-16–18
Time to obtain sample	2-9, 2-11, 2-13–14, 2-16–17
Interpretation of nonsteady-state plasma concentrations	2-9
Interpretation of steady-state plasma concentrations	2-9–10, 2-13–14, 2-16–18
Half-Life (t½)	2-9, 2-11, 2-13, 2-15–19
Estimate of t½	2-9, 2-11, 2-13, 2-15–19
Estimate of time required to achieve steady state	2-9
Steady-State Intermittent Dose Administration	2-10–12, 2-15–19
Short infusion model	2-11–12, 2-16–17
Bolus dose model	2-10, 2-12, 2-15, 2-18–19

Basic Principles

Plasma drug concentrations commonly are used in both the acute and ambulatory care settings to evaluate the adequacy or potential toxicity of a prescribed dosage regimen. Pharmacokinetic calculations which are based upon a patient's plasma drug concentrations can be used to modify dosing regimens in an attempt to maximize the therapeutic response while minimizing the risk of toxicity.

A complete presentation of this topic is beyond the scope of this chapter. A basic introduction to key pharmacokinetic principles and illustrations of their clinical application is presented in **Basic Clinical Pharmacokinetics,** 3rd edition[1] and several other pharmacokinetics texts.[2–4] In this chapter, pharmacokinetic parameters will be presented briefly. This will be followed by typical situations which demonstrate the clinical application of these parameters. Other examples of the clinical use of pharmacokinetics appear in various chapters of this book. Because of space constraints, the primary focus of this chapter will be on the prediction of loading and maintenance doses and the evaluation of steady-state plasma drug concentrations.

Reported or calculated plasma levels are useful tools in the initial estimation and evaluation of a drug regimen; however, they should never be used as the sole criterion for determination of dosage regimens because laboratory errors or inappropriate sampling methods can limit the value of reported results. Furthermore, if a calculated regimen appears unreasonable, there is always the possibility of a mathematical error. Perhaps the formula being used is inappropriate for the situation at hand or in some cases, the pharmacokinetic parameters utilized in the calculations may be inappropriate for the patient in question.[5,6] This last point is an important one. Because many of the pharmacokinetic parameters available in the literature are based upon a relatively small number of patients or normal volunteers,[7–12] values obtained from experimental data are, at best, only estimates for those of any given patient. This problem, as well as the variations which exist among subjects, emphasizes the need to obtain accurate plasma level measurements and to individualize pharmacokinetic parameters for each patient. Review articles which list pharmacokinetic parameters for a number of drugs may be used as a starting point,[8–10,13–16] but the clinician is strongly encouraged to seek out original literature to determine the degree of intersubject variability and to evaluate the methodology used to generate data quoted in these reviews.

Plasma Concentration (Cp)

Cp as Calculated or Reported

The plasma concentration which is reported by the laboratory or calculated from a formula represents the sum of drug that is bound to plasma protein plus drug that is unbound or free. However, it is the free or unbound drug that is in equilibrium with the receptor site and is the pharmacologically active moiety. Alterations in plasma protein binding can present a problem in the interpretation of Cp for drugs which are highly protein-bound because the usual ratio of free (active) drug to total drug concentration will be changed. In patients with altered protein binding, an increased or decreased pharmacologic effect can be expected for any given Cp.

In most cases, the unbound fraction of drug is independent of total drug concentration as long as saturation of the binding sites is not approached. Valproic acid[17,18] and salicylates[19] are important exceptions because plasma concentrations which exceed protein binding capacity are commonly achieved with therapeutic doses of these drugs.

Protein Binding

Two factors determine the degree of plasma protein binding. One is the binding affinity of the drug for plasma proteins, and the second is the number of available binding sites. In most cases, plasma protein concentration will be proportional to the number of binding sites.

Acidic drugs tend to bind extensively to serum albumin,[20-22] and albumin concentrations are frequently decreased but seldom, if ever, significantly increased. Since serum albumin concentrations are readily available in the clinical setting, the majority of research on plasma binding of drugs relates to acidic compounds such as phenytoin, salicylates, and valproic acid in clinical settings of decreased serum albumin.

Unlike acidic drugs, the plasma binding for basic drugs (e.g., lidocaine, quinidine) can be markedly increased or decreased. For example, the plasma binding of basic drugs is increased in inflammatory disease processes, and decreased in severe liver disease. Unlike albumin, plasma concentrations of α_1-acid glycoprotein are not measured in the clinical setting, and because basic drugs tend to bind to α_1-acid glycoprotein and to multiple plasma proteins, there are relatively few clinical tools available to help the clinician adjust for alterations in plasma binding of basic drugs.

Alterations in plasma binding seldom change the patient's response to a given dose of a drug. If the plasma protein binding is decreased, drug molecules that are released will not remain in the plasma compartment exclusively but will re-equilibrate with the tissue compartment. As long as the drug's volume of distribution is relatively large, the free concentration (Cp free) and tissue concentration (Ct free), as well as the drug binding to the pharmacologically active receptor sites, will remain relatively constant. Any slight increase in unbound drug concentration would be eliminated by the normal clearance mechanisms. When a drug with significant plasma protein binding has an alteration in its binding characteristics, however, the therapeutic range for that drug will be altered. A decrease in plasma binding will decrease the therapeutic range and an increase in plasma binding will increase the therapeutic range. (See Figure 2.1.)

Adjustments for Alterations in Plasma Binding

The fraction of drug that is free is usually expressed as alpha (α):

$$\alpha = \frac{\text{Free Drug Concentration}}{\text{Total Drug Concentration}} \qquad Eq\ 2.1$$

The smaller the alpha value, the greater will be the significance of altered plasma protein binding on the total drug concentration. As a general rule, if a drug's alpha is ≤ 0.1 (i.e., 10% or less free), there is a good possibility that protein binding changes will be significant. In such cases, the plasma concentration which will produce a given therapeutic effect should be reassessed. In contrast, if a drug's alpha is 0.5 or more, less than one-half of the drug concentration is bound to plasma protein and protein binding changes are unlikely to be clinically significant. Take, for example, a situation in which another highly protein-bound drug is added to the regimen. Because it is unlikely that more than one-half of the bound drug will ever be displaced from plasma protein binding sites, a maximum decrease of 25% in the therapeutic range would be anticipated. Therefore, plasma protein displacement is unlikely to be of clinical significance if a drug's alpha is greater than 0.5.

In order to evaluate a measured plasma concentration which has been altered by protein binding, either adjust the normal therapeutic range to reflect changes in plasma protein binding *or* convert the measured plasma concentration to that concentration which would have been measured if plasma binding were normal. The unbound or free plasma concentration (Cp free) can be calculated by multiplying the total plasma concentration (bound plus free) by alpha:

$$\text{Cp free} = (\text{Cp total})(\alpha) \qquad Eq\ 2.2$$

Assuming the goal is to achieve the same therapeutic *free* plasma concentration whether or not protein binding is altered, a measured plasma concentration (Cp') in the presence of altered plasma protein binding (α') would have the following relationship to a comparable drug concentration (Cp) in the absence of protein binding alteration (α).

$$(\alpha')(\text{Cp}') = \text{Cp free} = (\text{Cp total})(\alpha) \qquad Eq\ 2.3$$

Therefore, the "patient's therapeutic range" will be equal to the usual therapeutic range adjusted for altered protein binding.

$$\text{``Patient's Therapeutic Range''} = \left(\frac{\alpha}{\alpha'}\right)\left(\text{Usual Therapeutic Range}\right) \qquad Eq\ 2.4$$

In other words, the "patient's therapeutic range" represents the plasma concentrations that will result in a normal unbound or free

Fig 2.1 Equilibrium Between Free and Bound Drug Concentrations
It is assumed that only Cp Free can cross into the tissue compartment or site of pharmacologic activity.

plasma concentration. Even though these adjusted concentrations will be higher or lower than the usual therapeutic concentrations, a normal therapeutic response to the drug would be expected.

Alternatively, the observed plasma concentration for a patient with abnormal binding (Cp') can be used to calculate the plasma concentration which would have been observed if plasma binding had been normal ($Cp_{Normal\ Binding}$).

$$Cp_{Normal\ Binding} = \left(\frac{\alpha'}{\alpha}\right)\left(Cp'\right) \qquad Eq\ 2.5$$

This concentration can then be interpreted on the basis of the usual therapeutic range.

While it would be ideal to have the capability of measuring free or unbound plasma drug concentrations, this capability is not routinely available in the clinical setting. When these assay procedures are available to measure free or unbound drug levels, they are more expensive than the traditional assays that measure total drug concentration. In addition, little clinical data or studies support the concept that monitoring free or unbound drug concentrations improves patient care. This may be in part due to the fact that most patients do not have alterations in plasma binding and it is only a relatively few patients for whom free drug concentrations would be required. In some specific clinical settings, it is a common practice to measure free or unbound drug concentrations; however, these are usually limited to specific compounds, the most common of which is phenytoin. When highly bound drugs are administered to patients whose concentration of serum binding proteins is altered, a first approximation of the equivalent plasma concentration which would be expected if plasma protein binding were normal, can be made using a ratio of the patient's binding protein concentration to the normal protein concentration value. For example, if this technique is applied to drugs which are bound to serum albumin, a $Cp_{Normal\ Binding}$ can be calculated using the following equation:

$$Cp_{Normal\ Binding} = \left(Cp'\right)\left(\frac{4.4\ gm/dL}{Patient's\ Albumin\ Concentration}\right) \qquad Eq\ 2.6$$

The value 4.4 gm/dL represents the average serum albumin concentration, Cp' is the patient's measured or reported drug concentration, and $Cp_{Normal\ Binding}$ is the value which would be compared to the usual therapeutic range to assess the probability of drug efficacy or toxicity. Equation 2.6 can only be used for those drugs which are significantly bound to albumin when abnormal albumin concentrations are the primary cause of binding alterations. It cannot be used when drug displacing agents are present, when the affinity of drugs to proteins has been altered (e.g., renal failure), or when plasma proteins other than albumin bind a significant amount of drug.

Absorption

Bioavailability (F)

Bioavailability is the fraction of the parent compound which reaches the systemic circulation. Several factors influence the bioavailability of a drug.

Solubility. A drug must be both lipid and water soluble to be absorbed from the gastrointestinal (GI) tract. If a drug is too water soluble (e.g., aminoglycosides), it cannot pass through the lipid membrane of the gastrointestinal tract and will not be absorbed following oral administration. Other drugs that are more lipid than water soluble (e.g., griseofulvin, phenytoin) may have diminished or delayed absorption because they must first dissolve in the aqueous fluids of the GI tract before they can be absorbed.[14,25,26] Drugs

with intermediate lipid-water solubilities are more likely to be completely bioavailable by the oral route if properly formulated (e.g., theophylline).

Dosage Form and Route of Administration. The dosage form and route of administration may be important factors in determining the bioavailability of a drug. For example, the fraction of orally-administered digoxin (Lanoxin) that is absorbed can vary not only with the manufacturer, but also with the dosage form. The average F for tablets is 0.7, while the F for digoxin elixir is 0.8, and the F for the soft gelatin capsule is 1.0.[27–29] Generally, drugs administered by the intravenous or parenteral route are completely bioavailable (F = 1.0) because all of the drug is assumed to reach the circulation. Intramuscular administration is associated with slower, but eventually complete, absorption. There are a few exceptions to the assumption that parenterally administered drugs have an F of 1.0. One example is intravenously administered chloramphenicol succinate which has a bioavailability as low as 50% because some of the chloramphenicol succinate is eliminated by the kidney before it is converted to the active compound.[30]

First-Pass Effect

If a drug which is absorbed from the GI tract is metabolized by the liver to a great extent before it reaches the systemic circulation (first-pass effect), oral bioavailability will be decreased. Lidocaine (Xylocaine) and propranolol (Inderal) are examples of drugs which undergo a large first-pass effect.[31,32]

Some drugs have such a large first-pass effect that their use is essentially limited to the parenteral route (e.g., lidocaine). In other instances, the dose of such drugs administered orally is substantially larger than the usual parenteral dose (e.g., propranolol).

Salt Form (S)

The salt form of a drug is another factor which determines how much drug will reach the systemic circulation. For example, theophylline has an F of 1.0; however, it is often administered as aminophylline, which is 80% theophylline. The fraction of the drug salt or ester that is the parent compound is represented by the letter S. The S for aminophylline is, therefore, 0.8. S can be determined by dividing the molecular weight of the parent drug by the molecular weight of the salt or ester form of the drug.

Rate of Administration (R_A)

The rate of drug administration is expressed by the following equation:

$$Rate\ of\ Administration\ (R_A) = \frac{(S)(F)(Dose)}{\tau} \qquad Eq\ 2.7$$

where S and F are the salt form and bioavailability, respectively, and tau (τ) is the dosing interval.

Equation 2.7 is most commonly used when drugs are administered as a continuous infusion. However, it also represents the *average* rate of drug administration even when the drug is administered intermittently at regular intervals.

Volume of Distribution (Vd)

At steady state, drugs are distributed unequally between plasma and the various other fluids and tissues that make up the body. The actual nature of the distribution is dependent upon the physico-chemical properties of each drug. However, for practical purposes, it is often assumed that the body is a single compartment in which drugs are uniformly distributed. Therefore, it is also assumed that the concentration of drug throughout the body is the same as that of the plasma sample. Volumes of distribution for drugs vary considerably; in fact, a drug may have such extensive tissue distribution that its ''apparent volume of distribution'' greatly exceeds any conceivable volume in the body. The practical value of this fictitious ''apparent volume of distribution'' is that it allows the clinician to estimate the loading dose of a drug that would be required to rapidly achieve a desired plasma concentration.

Loading Dose

The relationship between plasma concentration and volume of distribution is as follows:

$$Cp = \frac{Ab}{Vd} \qquad \qquad Eq\ 2.8$$

where Cp is the plasma concentration of the drug, Ab is the amount of drug in the body, and Vd is the apparent volume of distribution of the drug. Since Vd accounts for all of the drug in the body, it can be used to calculate the loading dose which would rapidly result in a desired plasma concentration (Cp):

$$Loading\ Dose = \frac{(Vd)(Cp)}{(S)(F)} \qquad \qquad Eq\ 2.9$$

where (S)(F) represents the fraction of the administered dose that will be absorbed or reach the systemic circulation.

For example, to calculate the loading dose of digoxin required to obtain a plasma concentration of 1.5 µg/L for a 70 kg patient, the previous formula would be used as follows. The apparent volume of digoxin is ≈7.3 L/kg,[33] or 511 L for a 70 kg individual (7.3 L/kg × 70 kg = 511 L). Assuming that digoxin tablets are to be used (F = 0.7, S = 1.0), the calculated loading dose using Equation 2.9 would be as follows:

$$Loading\ Dose = \frac{(Vd)(Cp)}{(S)(F)}$$

$$= \frac{(511\ L)(1.5\ µg/L)}{(1.0)(0.7)}$$

$$= 1095\ µg = 1.095\ mg\ or\ ≈1\ mg$$

The usual clinical approach would be to give the loading dose in divided doses (0.25–0.5 mg/dose) every six hours and observe the patient before each successive dose is administered. Some clinicians use a bioavailability factor greater than 0.7 for digoxin tablets to guard against overshooting the desired level.

If a patient has been taking digoxin and an initial plasma concentration is known (Cp observed), the previous equation can be modified to calculate a loading dose which will produce a higher concentration (Cp desired):

$$Loading\ Dose = \frac{(Vd)(Cp\ desired - Cp\ observed)}{(S)(F)} \qquad Eq\ 2.10$$

For example, if this same patient had a measured digoxin level of 1.0 µg/L, and 1.5 µg/L was desired, an additional loading dose would be calculated as follows:

$$Loading\ Dose = \frac{(511\ L)(1.5\ µg/L - 1\ µg/L)}{(1)(0.7)}$$

$$= 365\ µg = 0.365\ mg\ or\ ≈0.375\ mg$$

$$(0.25 + 0.125\ mg\ tablets)$$

Two-Compartment Model

Most pharmacokinetic calculations are based upon the premise that drugs are distributed into and eliminated from the body as though it were a single compartment. However, the pharmacokinetic behavior of many drugs does not lend itself to this model; for these drugs, it is more accurate to divide the body into two or more compartments.

The first compartment has a volume referred to as Vi or $V_{initial}$. This compartment equilibrates rapidly with administered drug and is usually made up of blood or plasma and those organs or tissues that have a high blood flow. The second compartment has a volume referred to as Vt or V_{tissue}. Administered drug distributes into Vt from Vi and eventually, equilibrium between the first and second compartments is achieved. The half-time for the distribution phase (i.e., the time for one-half of the drug to distribute from Vi into Vt) is referred to as the alpha (α) half-life, and the half-time for drug elimination from the body is referred to as the beta (β) half-life. The sum of Vi and Vt is the apparent volume of distribution (Vd). (See Figure 2.2.)

If a drug does behave as though it distributes into two compartments, one could err in the calculation of a rapidly administered loading dose if the one-compartment model volume of distribution, Vd, is used. A loading dose calculated on the basis of Vd would result in an initial plasma concentration much higher than predicted because Vd is large relative to the initial volume of distribution (Vi).

If a drug's target organ behaves as though it is located in the first compartment, then toxicity may occur. This can be circumvented by first calculating a loading dose based upon Vd. This dose can then be administered slowly to allow the drug to distribute from Vi into Vt. Alternatively, the loading dose can be given in sufficiently small increments to prevent the Cp in Vi from exceeding some critical concentration. Examples of drugs that behave in this fashion are lidocaine and procainamide.[32,34]

When a drug's target organ behaves as though it were located in the second compartment, toxicity is not a consequence of the initially high Cp. However, if plasma samples for these drugs are obtained before distribution into Vt is complete, the reported level will not reflect the drug concentration at the target organ and cannot be used to predict therapeutic or toxic effects of the drug. An example of a drug that behaves in this fashion is digoxin.[36]

The initially high plasma concentrations of digoxin are not toxic; however, the loading dose of digoxin is still divided to minimize

Fig 2.2 Two-Compartment Model Volumes of distribution for a two-compartment model. Vi is the initial volume of distribution. Note that drug administration (R_A) and elimination (R_E) are assumed to occur in Vi. The lower graph shows how a drug administered into Vi follows a biphasic decay pattern. The initial decay half-life (αt½) usually is due to drug being distributed into Vt. The second decay half-life (βt½) is usually due to drug being eliminated from the body.

the probability of over-shooting the therapeutic effect and to decrease the probability of drug-induced toxicities. The usual practice is to divide the loading dose of digoxin into three or four portions and to carefully evaluate the patient for both clinical efficacy and toxicity before administering each successive part of the loading dose. This gradual approach allows clinicians to withhold the remaining portion of the loading dose if the patient develops either a satisfactory therapeutic response or toxicity.

Clearance (Cl)

Maintenance Dose

Drugs are usually eliminated from the body at a rate which is proportional to their plasma concentration. Clearance may be thought of as the proportionality constant which makes the rate of drug elimination equal to the rate of drug administration at steady state. Clearance is the volume of blood or plasma which is completely cleared of a drug per unit of time. When the clearance of a drug is known, the maintenance dose required to sustain an average steady-state plasma concentration can be calculated as follows:

$$\text{Maintenance Dose} = \frac{(Cl)(Cpss\ ave)(\tau)}{(S)(F)} \qquad Eq\ 2.11$$

where Cl is clearance, Cpss ave is the average plasma concentration at steady state, and tau (τ) is the dosing interval. S and F represent the fraction of the dose which reaches the systemic circulation.

For example, to calculate the maintenance dose of phenobarbital required to produce an average steady-state plasma concentration of 20 mg/L in a 65 kg individual, Equation 2.11 would be used as follows. First, one needs to know that the usual clearance of phenobarbital is 0.1 L/kg/day, or 6.5 L/day for this 65 kg individual (0.1 L/kg/day × 65 kg = 6.5 L/day). S and F can both be considered equal to 1.0 because the sodium in sodium phenobarbital is negligible and the drug is 100% absorbed. Therefore, using Equation 2.11, the calculation can be made as follows:

$$\begin{aligned}
\text{Maintenance Dose} &= \frac{(Cl)(Cpss\ ave)(\tau)}{(S)(F)} \\
&= \frac{(6.5\ L/day)(20\ mg/L)(1\ day)}{(1)(1)} \\
&= 130\ mg
\end{aligned}$$

This concept of clearance is applicable to most drugs. The rate of drug removal is proportional to the plasma concentration, and the concentration of drug diminishes logarithmically with time (see Elimination Rate Constant). Drugs which behave in this way are described as following first-order kinetics. (See Figure 2.3.) However, a few drugs (phenytoin and salicylate being important examples) do not behave in this way. For these drugs, clearance or volume of distribution changes with the plasma concentration and are not fixed parameters. Therefore, equations which utilize clearance or volume of distribution as constant parameters are not applicable to these few drugs.

Routes of Elimination

The two primary routes of drug elimination are metabolism (usually hepatic) and renal clearance. A drug's clearance (Cl_{total}) can then be broken down into its two primary components: clearance metabolic (Cl_m) and clearance renal (Cl_r).

$$Cl_{Total} = Cl_m + Cl_r \qquad Eq\ 2.12$$

For drugs that are eliminated through the renal pathway to a significant extent, adjustments in maintenance doses will be re-

quired in patients with altered renal function. For those drugs that are primarily metabolized, a reduction in the maintenance dose will be required if a patient's metabolizing enzymes are inhibited or the patient has serious hepatic disease. Patients receiving drugs known to increase hepatic metabolism through enzyme induction may require an increase in maintenance dose of drugs eliminated hepatically.

Half-life (t½)

For drugs that follow a first-order elimination process, the half-life is the time required for the plasma concentration or the total amount of drug in the body to decline by one-half. The half-life of a drug is important when considering questions involving time, such as "How long will it take a patient to reach steady state on a constant dosage regimen?" or "How long will it take for all of the drug to be eliminated from the body?"

Half-life may also be used to estimate the appropriate dosing interval or tau (τ) during maintenance therapy or to estimate whether steady state has been reached. It takes one half-life to reach 50% of steady state, two half-lives to reach 75%, three half-lives to reach 87.5%, and four half-lives to reach 93.75% of steady state. In most clinical situations, steady-state conditions can be assumed after three or four half-lives.

The half-life of a drug is dependent upon its volume of distribution and clearance. This relationship is expressed by the following formula:

$$t\tfrac{1}{2} = \frac{(0.693)(Vd)}{Cl} \qquad Eq\ 2.13$$

Elimination Rate Constant (Kd)

The elimination rate constant is the fraction of the volume of distribution which is cleared of drug per unit of time. Like half-life, it is a function of the drug's volume of distribution and its clearance:

$$Kd = \frac{Cl}{Vd} \qquad Eq\ 2.14$$

The elimination rate constant is utilized to predict how the plasma concentration varies with time, assuming no additional drug is added. For example, if Cp_1 is the initial plasma concentration and Cp_2 is the plasma concentration after an interval of decay, Cp_2 can be calculated using the elimination rate constant:

$$Cp_2 = (Cp_1)(e^{-Kdt}) \qquad Eq\ 2.15$$

In this equation, (e^{-Kdt}) is the fraction of the initial plasma concentration which is remaining at the end of the time interval.

In Equation 2.15 there are essentially four variables: Kd, t, Cp_1, and Cp_2. Equation 2.15 can be rearranged to solve for any of the

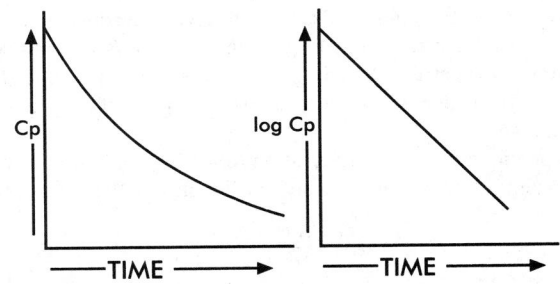

Fig 2.3   First-Order Elimination When Cp or log Cp Is Plotted Versus Time

variables if the other three are known. For example, Equation 2.15 could be rearranged to solve for the elimination rate constant (Kd):

$$Kd = \frac{\ln\left(\dfrac{Cp_1}{Cp_2}\right)}{t} \qquad Eq\ 2.16$$

or, the time interval (t) between any two plasma concentrations.

$$t = \frac{\ln\left(\dfrac{Cp_1}{Cp_2}\right)}{Kd} \qquad Eq\ 2.17$$

Equation 2.15 can also be rearranged to calculate an initial plasma concentration (Cp_1) sometime before a measured plasma concentration (Cp_2):

$$Cp_1 = \frac{Cp_2}{e^{-Kdt}} \qquad Eq\ 2.18$$

Clinical Use of Equations

As previously discussed, Equation 2.9 can be used to calculate a loading dose, and Equation 2.11 can be used to calculate a maintenance dose which will achieve and then maintain a desired plasma concentration.

$$\text{Loading Dose} = \frac{(Vd)(Cp)}{(S)(F)}$$

$$\text{Maintenance Dose} = \frac{(Cl)(Cpss\ ave)(\tau)}{(S)(F)}$$

In cases where drugs are administered on an intermittent basis and the time required for absorption is relatively short, an intermittent steady-state bolus model can be used to predict the plasma concentrations.

$$Cpss\ t_1 = \frac{\dfrac{(S)(F)(Dose)}{Vd}}{(1 - e^{-Kd\tau})}(e^{-Kdt_1}) \qquad Eq\ 2.19$$

Where $(S)(F)(Dose)/Vd$ represents the change in concentration which will be observed following the administration of each dose, $(1 - e^{-Kd\tau})$ represents the fraction lost within a dosing interval, and (e^{-Kdt_1}) is the fraction remaining at t_1 hours from the peak concentration (see Figure 2.4). Equation 2.19 should be used for those drugs administered at a dosing interval which is approximately equal to or longer than the drug's half-life. When a drug is administered at a dosing interval (τ) which is equal to or less than one-half its half-life, the plasma concentration can be approximated using Equation 2.20.

$$Cpss\ ave = \frac{(S)(F)(Dose/\tau)}{Cl} \qquad Eq\ 2.20$$

The previous equation is an appropriate pharmacokinetic model when there are small changes in concentration within a dosing interval; that is, Equation 2.20 can be used when the dosing interval is much less than the half-life, a drug is given as a continuous infusion, or when the drug is given as a sustained-release (SR) dosage form which allows continuous absorption throughout the dosing interval.

To predict a plasma concentration following the administration of a loading dose, a rearrangement of Equation 2.9 can be used:

$$Cp = \frac{(S)(F)(Dose)}{Vd} \qquad Eq\ 2.21$$

Note that Equation 2.21 is analogous to Equation 2.8 except that (S)(F)(Dose) has replaced the amount of drug in the body. If a

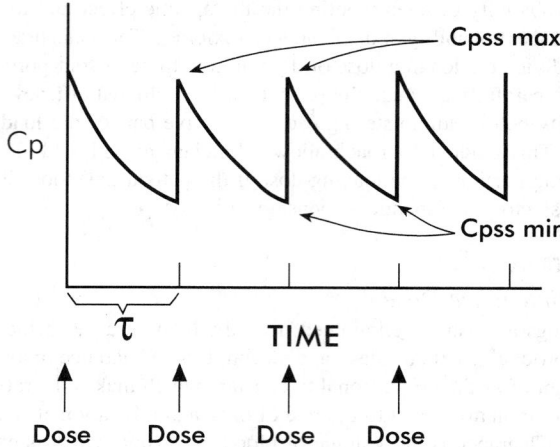

Fig 2.4 Graphical Representation of the Steady-State Plasma Concentration Versus Time Curve Which Occurs When Drugs Are Given Intermittently at Regular Dosing Intervals   Note that any maximum concentration (Cpss max) is interchangeable with another maximum and any minimum concentration (Cpss min) is interchangeable with another minimum as would be any concentration (Cpss t_1) at (t_1) hours after a steady-state peak. The peak can be calculated by using Equation 2.19.

patient has been taking the drug and has a pre-existing plasma concentration, then Cp will represent the change in concentration which results following the dose administration (ΔCp).

Time to Sample

After Starting or Changing a Regimen

After starting or changing a dosing regimen, the ideal time to obtain a plasma sample for routine monitoring is at steady state (after 3–5 t½s). This minimizes the potential interpretation problems which can occur as a result of minor alterations in the volume of distribution, clearance, or the measured plasma concentration.

Nonsteady-State Plasma Concentrations

While waiting three to five half-lives may be ideal from a pharmacokinetic standpoint, it is possible for a patient with an unusually low clearance to develop excessively high plasma concentrations before steady state is reached (see Figure 2.5). Therefore, it may be clinically appropriate to obtain a plasma concentration before steady state is achieved. However, one should recognize that plasma levels obtained within the first two half-lives of starting or changing a dosing regimen offer little information about eventual steady-state concentrations. (See Figure 2.5.) Unusually low plasma concentrations obtained within the first two half-lives may indicate a need for additional bolus or partial loading doses, while exceedingly high levels may alert the clinician to adjust or discontinue the maintenance regimen.

Plasma concentrations obtained within the first two to four half-lives can help the clinician discriminate between those patients with a normal clearance and normal half-life and those patients with a low clearance and prolonged drug half-life. When plasma concentrations obtained between two and four half-lives are significantly greater than expected, the patient most likely has a lower-than-average clearance; therefore, some downward adjustment in the maintenance regimen might be indicated. Additional plasma concentration monitoring is usually appropriate for these patients because they tend to have longer half-lives, and this leads to greater uncertainty regarding their final steady-state concentrations.

At Steady State

Once steady state has been achieved, the sampling time is dictated by the relationship between the dosing interval and the drug's half-life. For those drugs which are administered at a dosing interval that is much less than a half-life, the time of sampling within the dosing interval is not critical. The same would be true for drugs administered as SR drug products or continuous infusions. However, trough concentrations are generally recommended to avoid sampling during the distribution phase. This is particularly important following the intravenous administration of almost all drugs and following the oral administration of a limited number of drugs such as digoxin and lithium.

For drugs which are administered at a dosing interval that is approximately equal to the drug's half-life, the recommended time of sampling is again at the trough or just before the next dose. This sampling time results in the most reproducible levels because it avoids sampling during the distribution phase for drugs administered intravenously. In addition, when drugs are given orally, enhanced or delayed absorption rates can alter the time at which peak concentrations will occur. (See Figure 2.6.)

When trough concentrations (Cpss min) are obtained, a peak concentration (Cpss max) can be estimated using Equation 2.22.

$$\text{Cpss max} = \text{Cpss min} + \frac{(S)(F)(\text{Dose})}{Vd} \qquad Eq\ 2.22$$

The above equation does not apply to the patient receiving an SR drug product because concentrations would not be expected to vary considerably within the dosing interval. Also, if the peak concentration is significantly greater than (two times) the trough concentration, an accurate volume of distribution value will be critical to the prediction of the peak concentration. For this reason, when drugs are administered at a dosing interval which is significantly greater than the drug's half-life, it is usually necessary to obtain both peak and trough concentrations. For example, it is common

Fig 2.6   Schematic Representation of the Effect of Delayed Absorption (– – –) on Plasma Level Measurements   Note the magnitude of error at one hour (theoretical time to reach Cpss max) as compared to six hours (Cpss min).

practice to obtain both peak and trough concentrations for aminoglycosides which are typically administered at a dosing interval (8 hr) which greatly exceeds their half-life (2 hr). However, as stated previously, peak concentrations must be obtained with care to avoid the distribution phase.

Evaluation of Renal Function

Since many drugs are eliminated by the kidney to a significant extent, evaluation of a patient's renal function is integral to the application of pharmacokinetic principles to drug dosing. The daily production of creatinine, creatinine clearance, and serum creatinine is analogous to the relationship between maintenance dose, drug clearance, and drug plasma concentration as expressed in Equation 2.11.

$$\text{Maintenance Dose} = \frac{(Cl)(\text{Cpss ave})(\tau)}{(S)(F)}$$

In the above equation, maintenance dose would be equivalent to the daily production of creatinine, Cl would correspond to the creatinine clearance (Cl_{Cr}), and Cpss ave would correspond to the steady-state serum creatinine concentration (SrCr).

The usual Cl_{Cr} for a 70 kg young adult is 100 to 120 mL/min, and the average creatinine production rate is 20 mg/kg/day. This clearance and production rate results in an average serum creatinine concentration of 1 mg/dL. As patients age, both the production and clearance of creatinine decrease. Therefore, elderly patients who have a normal serum creatinine concentration of 1 mg/dL may have a creatinine clearance which is much less than 100 mL/min.

There are a number of methods used to calculate creatinine clearance. Many of these consider factors such as age, weight, and gender to determine the expected production rate of creatinine. This value is then divided by the measured serum creatinine concentration to estimate the patient's creatinine clearance. One such method was developed by Cockcroft and Gault:[37]

$$\underset{\text{(mL/min)}}{Cl_{Cr}\text{ for Males}} = \frac{(140 - \text{Age})(\text{Weight})}{(72)(\text{SrCr})} \qquad Eq\ 2.23$$

$$\underset{\text{(mL/min)}}{Cl_{Cr}\text{ for Females}} = \frac{(0.85)(140 - \text{Age})(\text{Weight})}{(72)(\text{SrCr})} \qquad Eq\ 2.24$$

The units for the above equation are as follows: weight in kg, age in years, SrCr in mg/dL, and Cl_{Cr} in mL/min. Equations 2.23 and 2.24 are reasonably accurate in predicting the creatinine clearance if the patient under consideration has a normal ratio of muscle mass

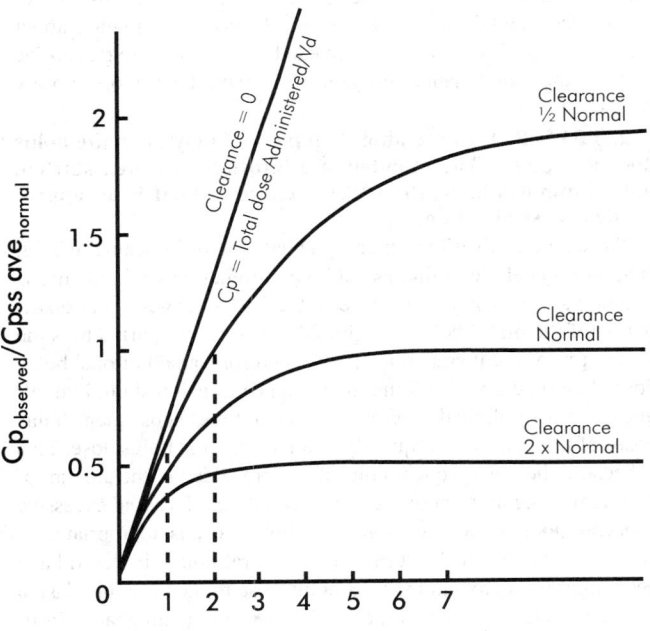

Fig 2.5   Relationship Between Observed Plasma Concentrations (Cp observed) and the Normal Steady-State Concentrations (Cpss ave normal) Following the Initiation of a Maintenance Regimen at Various Clearance Values   At steady state, the plasma concentrations are inversely proportional to clearance. Note that plasma concentrations obtained at or before one normal half-life are all very similar regardless of clearance. After two half-lives, alterations in a patient's clearance and ultimately steady-state concentrations can be detected by unexpectedly high or low plasma drug concentrations. After three half-lives, more confident predictions of steady-state concentrations can be made.

to total body weight. The predicted creatinine clearance for obese or emaciated patients tends to be greater than the true value since these individuals have a lower-than-average production of creatinine per kg of body weight.

For obese patients, most clinicians use an estimate of nonobese or ideal body weight (IBW):[38]

$$\begin{array}{c}\text{IBW for} \\ \text{Males in kg}\end{array} = 50 \text{ kg} + 2.3(\text{Height in Inches} > 60) \qquad Eq\ 2.25$$

$$\begin{array}{c}\text{IBW for} \\ \text{Females in kg}\end{array} = 45 \text{ kg} + 2.3(\text{Height in Inches} > 60) \qquad Eq\ 2.26$$

While the above equations are commonly used, there is considerable error in estimating the ideal body weight or "nonobese weight" for obese patients. In addition, for patients who are greater than 100% over their ideal body weight, an "adjusted" body weight should be used when calculating their creatinine clearance.[39,40]

$$\begin{array}{c}\text{Adjusted Body Weight} \\ \text{in kg}\end{array} = \text{IBW} + 0.4(\text{TBW} - \text{IBW}) \qquad Eq\ 2.27$$

In the above equation, IBW is the ideal body weight as calculated by either Equations 2.25 or 2.26, and TBW is the patient's total body weight. It is the adjusted body weight in kg that would then be used in Equations 2.23 or 2.24 to calculate the patient's creatinine clearance.

Also, when renal function is unstable and the serum creatinine is changing (i.e., nonsteady state), the creatinine clearance may be under- or overestimated depending upon whether the serum creatinine is rising or falling.

Clinical Application Calculations

1. T.M., a 50-year-old, 60 kg woman, was admitted to the coronary care unit with multiple premature ventricular contractions (PVCs) which occurred as the result of an acute myocardial infarction. She has a history of congestive heart failure (CHF) and asthma.

Using the following pharmacokinetic parameters for lidocaine,[41] calculate an appropriate loading and maintenance dose for T.M.

	Normal	Heart Failure	Liver Disease
$\alpha t\frac{1}{2}$ (min)	8.3	7.3	8.8
$\beta t\frac{1}{2}$ (hr)	1.8	2.0	3.0
Vi (L/kg)	0.53	0.30	0.61
Vd (L/kg)	1.3	0.88	2.31
Cl (mL/kg/min)	10.0	6.3	6.0

The distribution of lidocaine follows a two-compartment model. Since the myocardium responds as though it is in the first compartment (Vi), the loading dose of lidocaine should be administered in a way which avoids toxic plasma levels in the first compartment before distribution is complete. This goal can be achieved by using the initial volume of distribution (Vi) to calculate the bolus dose. However, it is likely that additional bolus doses will be required because the plasma concentration produced by this initial bolus dose will decline rapidly to subtherapeutic concentrations as the drug distributes into the larger, final volume of distribution (Vd).

Using the value of 0.30 L/kg for T.M.'s initial volume of distribution, Vi would be 18.0 L in this 60 kg individual. The usual therapeutic range for lidocaine is 1 to 5 mg/L (µg/mL); for the purpose of calculating the initial bolus dose, a plasma concentration of 3 mg/L will be used. S and F can be assumed to be 0.87 and 1.0, respectively. By substituting Vi for Vd in Equation 2.9, Equation 2.28 can be derived, which can be used to calculate an initial bolus dose.

$$\text{Bolus Dose} = \frac{(Vi)(Cp)}{(S)(F)} \qquad Eq\ 2.28$$

$$= \frac{(18 \text{ L})(3 \text{ mg/L})}{(0.87)(1)}$$

$$= 62 \text{ mg}$$

This bolus dose is compatible with the usual recommended dose of 1 to 2 mg/kg.[42]

Equation 2.11 can be used to calculate the maintenance dose. Since T.M. has CHF, her lidocaine clearance will be assumed to be 6.3 mL/kg/min or, expressed as L/min for her 60 kg of body weight, 0.378 L/min. Therefore, her maintenance infusion would be calculated as follows using Equation 2.11:

$$\text{Maintenance Dose} = \frac{(Cl)(Cpss\ ave)(\tau)}{(S)(F)}$$

$$= \frac{(0.378 \text{ L/min})(3 \text{ mg/L})(1 \text{ min})}{(0.87)(1)}$$

$$= 1.3 \text{ mg}$$

This maintenance infusion rate is compatible with the usual recommended rate of 1 to 4 mg/min.[32,42] If more information about the severity of T.M.'s heart failure had been provided (e.g., cardiac output), the maintenance infusion could have been more closely adjusted.[43]

2. T.M.'s PVCs were abolished immediately after the bolus dose was given. The maintenance infusion was then started, but 15 minutes later, the PVCs recurred. What is an appropriate course of action?

The expected distribution or alpha half-life of lidocaine in T.M. is approximately ten minutes, and the elimination or β half-life is two hours. This early recurrence of the PVCs suggests that distribution of the initial bolus dose into the second compartment is the reason for loss of therapeutic effect. Therefore, an additional bolus dose should be given and the maintenance infusion should be left unchanged. In clinical practice, the second and subsequent bolus doses of lidocaine are frequently one-half the first bolus dose. This is because these subsequent bolus doses are added to the amount of drug remaining in the body from previous doses. To avoid excessive concentrations, some reduction in the bolus dose is appropriate.

If T.M.'s PVCs had returned after several hours, it would have been appropriate to administer a bolus dose to increase the plasma concentrations rapidly and then to increase the maintenance infusion as well. The latter would assure that the plasma concentrations would remain within the therapeutic range.

3. On the following day, T.M. developed wheezing which required aminophylline therapy. She was given a 350 mg loading dose and was started on a maintenance infusion of 40 mg/hr. Two hours after the loading dose had been given, a theophylline level of 12 mg/L was obtained. Therapeutic concentrations of theophylline are 10–20 mg/L. Does this suggest that the maintenance infusion of 40 mg/hr is appropriate?

The usual half-life of theophylline in healthy, nonsmoking patients is approximately eight hours. Because T.M.'s theophylline level was obtained only two hours after the initial loading dose (nonsteady state), it is much too early to determine whether or not the maintenance infusion will result in an acceptable steady-state concentration. As stated previously, plasma concentrations reported from samples obtained within the first two half-lives after a drug regimen has been started or changed cannot be used to evaluate steady-state concentrations. Since T.M.'s theophylline concentration is within the usual therapeutic range of 10 to 20 mg/L, it is unnecessary to administer an additional loading dose. If the observed plasma concentration had been unusually low, Equation 2.10 could have been used to calculate an additional loading dose.

$$\text{Loading Dose} = \frac{(Vd)(Cp \text{ desired} - Cp \text{ observed})}{(S)(F)}$$

It is also unnecessary to withhold the maintenance infusion at this point since the observed plasma concentration does not exceed the therapeutic range. Since only a small fraction of the administered theophylline (aminophylline) has been eliminated, no conclusion can be drawn from the reported plasma level regarding the ultimate steady-state concentration which will be achieved by her maintenance dose of 40 mg/hr. As patients with congestive heart failure are likely to have theophylline half-lives that are twice the normal value (16 hr), the theophylline plasma concentration of 12 mg/L obtained two hours after the dose primarily reflects the initial loading dose and T.M.'s volume of distribution. The theophylline concentration expected from the initial 350 mg loading dose can be calculated using Equation 2.21 with a theophylline volume of distribution of 30 L (0.5 L/kg × 60 kg); a bioavailability of 1.0; and an S of 0.8 to account for the fact that aminophylline represents approximately 80% theophylline.[16,44]

$$Cp = \frac{(S)(F)(Dose)}{Vd}$$

$$= \frac{(0.8)(1)(350 \text{ mg})}{30 \text{ L}}$$

$$= 9.3 \text{ or } \approx 9 \text{ mg/L}$$

The difference in the observed concentration (12 mg/L) and the calculated concentration (9 mg/L) may represent the additional theophylline T.M. has received from the maintenance infusion (40 mg/hr) for the past two hours; a slightly smaller-than-average volume of distribution, or assay error. Based upon the information available, it would not be possible to determine which one or combination of the above factors is responsible for this difference.

4. Forty-eight hours after the initiation of aminophylline therapy, T.M. was doing well, and a second theophylline concentration was obtained. The reported concentration was 19 mg/L. Does this reported concentration indicate that the infusion rate of 40 mg/hr is appropriate? [SI units: 105.45 µmol/L]

Although the reported theophylline concentration of 19 mg/L falls within the usual therapeutic range of 10 to 20 mg/L, it is important to establish whether or not this concentration represents a steady-state value. To determine this, the patient's theophylline half-life will have to be calculated using Equation 2.13.

$$t^{1/2} = \frac{(0.693)(Vd)}{Cl}$$

If T.M. has been receiving the infusion of 40 mg/hr for longer than three to five half-lives, then it would be safe to as-

sume that the concentration of 19 mg/L is at, or very close to, the steady-state concentration.

From previous calculations, it has been confirmed that T.M.'s volume of distribution is ≈30 L, which is close to the average literature value. To calculate T.M.'s half-life, we will first assume the level of 19 mg/L is at steady state and calculate an apparent clearance value. We will then use this clearance to calculate an apparent half-life. If we determine steady state could not have been achieved using this half-life, we know that our initial assumption that 19 mg/L represents a steady-state concentration and the calculated clearance is incorrect. If we can establish that steady state could have been achieved, this would tend to confirm our initial assumption and the calculated clearance value. To calculate T.M.'s clearance, Equation 2.20 can be rearranged to Equation 2.29.

$$Cpss \text{ ave} = \frac{(S)(F)(Dose/\tau)}{Cl}$$

$$Cl = \frac{(S)(F)(Dose/\tau)}{Cpss \text{ ave}} \qquad Eq \ 2.29$$

Substituting the appropriate values in Equation 2.29 yields a clearance value of ≈1.7 L/hr (assuming for now that 19 mg/L represents a steady-state concentration).

$$Cl = \frac{(0.8)(1)(40 \text{ mg/1 hr})}{19 \text{ mg/L}}$$

$$= 1.68 \text{ or } \approx 1.7 \text{ L/hr}$$

Based on T.M.'s volume of distribution (30 L) and a clearance value of 1.7 L/hr, a theophylline half-life of approximately 12.2 or 12 hours is calculated using Equation 2.13:

$$t^{1/2} = \frac{(0.693)(Vd)}{Cl}$$

$$= \frac{(0.693)(30 \text{ L})}{1.7 \text{ L/hr}}$$

$$= 12.2 \text{ hr}$$

Because the apparent half-life is ≈12 hours and T.M. has been receiving her aminophylline infusion for 48 hours (i.e., >3–4 t½s), it is probable that the reported theophylline concentration of 19 mg/L is a steady-state level. Therefore, our original assumption has been confirmed.

If there had been no prior estimate of T.M.'s volume of distribution, a literature value would have been used. While this is an appropriate technique, one must recognize that estimation of the patient's half-life would be more uncertain. Also, if it had been determined that the plasma concentration of 19 mg/L was not a steady-state level (i.e., the drug was still accumulating), it would have been clinically appropriate to *reduce* the maintenance infusion and obtain additional theophylline levels to confirm the patient's steady-state concentration on the prescribed regimen. It must be re-emphasized that the full impact of any dose adjustment cannot be evaluated until an additional three to five half-lives have passed.

5. T.M. complains of nausea and her pulse is 110/min. Based on these findings, it is decided to decrease her theophylline level from 19 mg/L to 12 mg/L. How long should the maintenance infusion be withheld? Calculate a new infusion rate to maintain the new desired steady-state theophylline concentration of 12 mg/L. [SI units: theophylline levels 105.45 µmol/L to 66.6 µmol/L; steady-state theophylline concentration 66.6 µmol/L]

Using Equation 2.14 and the previously calculated values for clearance and volume of distribution, an elimination rate constant of 0.057 hr^{-1} is calculated.

$$Kd = \frac{Cl}{Vd}$$

$$= \frac{1.7 \text{ L/hr}}{30 \text{ L}}$$

$$= 0.057 \text{ hr}^{-1}$$

Using this elimination rate constant of 0.057 hr^{-1} in a rearranged version of the decay equation (Equations 2.15 to 2.17), the time required for the theophylline concentration to decline from 19 mg/L (Cp_1) to 12 mg/L (Cp_2) is calculated to be approximately eight hours.

$$(Cp_2)(e^{-Kdt}) = Cp_1$$

$$e^{-Kdt} = \frac{(Cp_2)}{(Cp_1)}$$

$$-Kdt = \ln\left(\frac{Cp_2}{Cp_1}\right)$$

$$Kdt = \ln\left(\frac{Cp_1}{Cp_2}\right)$$

$$t = \frac{\ln\left(\dfrac{Cp_1}{Cp_2}\right)}{Kd}$$

$$t = \frac{\ln\left(\dfrac{19}{12}\right)}{0.057 \text{ hr}^{-1}}$$

$$= \frac{0.46}{0.057 \text{ hr}^{-1}}$$

$$= 8 \text{ hr}$$

After the aminophylline infusion is withheld for approximately eight hours, one would expect the theophylline concentration to be 12 mg/L. At that time, a new maintenance infusion would be reinstituted at a rate of 25 mg/hr as calculated from Equation 2.11.

$$\text{Maintenance Dose} = \frac{(Cl)(Cpss\ ave)(\tau)}{(S)(F)}$$

$$= \frac{(1.7 \text{ L/hr})(12 \text{ mg/L})(1 \text{ hr})}{(0.8)(1)}$$

$$= 25.5 \text{ or} \approx 25 \text{ mg}$$

6. Three days later, it is decided to discontinue parenteral therapy. Calculate an oral dose of aminophylline for T.M. that would maintain a theophylline concentration of 12 mg/L. [SI units: 66.6 µmol/L]

To minimize the fluctuations in the plasma levels between doses, the dosing interval of aminophylline should be equal to or shorter than the drug's half-life. As previously calculated, T.M.'s theophylline half-life is approximately 12 hours, indicating that a dosing interval of 12 hours could be appropriate. However, if one wished to further minimize fluctuations in the plasma levels, a shorter dosing interval (τ) of approximately eight hours could be used. T.M.'s maintenance dose can be calculated using Equation 2.11:

$$\text{Maintenance Dose} = \frac{(Cl)(Cpss\ ave)(\tau)}{(S)(F)}$$

$$= \frac{(1.7 \text{ L/hr})(12 \text{ mg/L})(8 \text{ hr})}{(0.8)(1)}$$

$$= 204 \text{ or} \approx 200 \text{ mg}$$

This dose of 200 mg (to be given every eight hours) could be administered as a sustained-released product or as an immediate-release drug product because T.M. has an unusually long half-life.

If a nonsustained-release drug product is administered, Equation 2.19 (which represents intermittent dosing situations) can be used to determine the peak and trough theophylline concentrations which will result. T.M.'s previously calculated pharmacokinetic values for theophylline should be used. Assuming peak concentrations will occur approximately one hour after administration of an oral dose, Equation 2.19 would predict a peak level of 13.5 mg/L.

$$Cpss\ t_1 = \frac{\dfrac{(S)(F)(Dose)}{Vd}}{(1 - e^{-Kdt})}(e^{-Kdt_1})$$

$$= \frac{\dfrac{(0.8)(1)(200 \text{ mg})}{30 \text{ L}}}{(1 - e^{-(0.057)(8 \text{ hr})})}(e^{-(0.057)(1 \text{ hr})})$$

$$= \frac{(5.33 \text{ mg/L})}{(1 - 0.63)}(0.94)$$

$$= (14.4 \text{ mg/L})(0.94)$$

$$= 13.5 \text{ mg/L}$$

The trough concentration of 9 mg/L can be calculated from Equation 2.19 by using a value of eight hours for t_1:

$$Cpss\ t_1 = \frac{\dfrac{(0.8)(1)(200 \text{ mg})}{30 \text{ L}}}{(1 - e^{-(0.057)(8 \text{ hr})})}(e^{-(0.057)(8 \text{ hr})})$$

$$= 9.1 \text{ or} \approx 9 \text{ mg/L}$$

Sustained-Release (SR) Product. Although it is unnecessary, T.M. might receive an SR drug product such as Theo-Dur. If this occurs, Equation 2.19, which represents an intermittent dosing situation, should not be used because a much smaller fluctuation in plasma concentration would result following the administration of a sustained-release drug product. Plasma concentrations produced by SR drug products can be approximated using Equation 2.20 as long as the dosing interval does not greatly exceed the absorption duration of the sustained-release drug product.

If Theo-Dur were to be administered to T.M., a 12-hour dosing interval would be more convenient. Furthermore, because she has a long half-life, it is unlikely that any significant fluctuations in the plasma concentrations would occur. If the bioavailability and salt form of Theo-Dur are both assumed to be 1.0, then a maintenance dose of $\approx$250 mg given every 12 hours can be calculated using Equation 2.11:

$$\text{Maintenance Dose} = \frac{(Cl)(Cpss\ ave)(\tau)}{(S)(F)}$$

$$= \frac{(1.7 \text{ L/hr})(12 \text{ mg/L})(12 \text{ hr})}{(1)(1)}$$

$$= 244.8 \text{ or} \approx 250 \text{ mg}$$

This maintenance dose could be achieved by administering one-half of a 300 mg (150 mg) tablet plus a 100 mg Theo-Dur tablet. Alternatively, one could administer one 300 mg tablet every 12 hours and accept a slightly higher steady-state level. While SR theophylline products are commonly used, they are most appropriate for patients with unusually short theophylline half-lives. A number of reviews[45-47] indicate that absorption characteristics of various sustained-release drug products differ from one another. Therefore, some care should be taken in selecting drug products and dosing intervals. In addition, there is increasing evidence that the absorption from the sustained-release drug products may be more variable than once believed. Thus, the assumption that plasma concentrations vary relatively little within a dosing interval may, in some cases, be incorrect.[48,49]

7. When should a plasma sample for theophylline be obtained to evaluate T.M.'s oral aminophylline regimen? Can a plasma sample be drawn one hour after the dose to determine a peak concentration?

Since the oral maintenance dose calculated for T.M. was based upon the parenteral maintenance dose, she is theoretically at steady state, and a level can be drawn after approximately one half-life or more on the oral regimen. If the oral maintenance dose had been substantially different from that used parenterally, a level would best be drawn after four or more half-lives.

In general, plasma samples which are obtained at a time which theoretically corresponds to peak levels are difficult to interpret as they are subject to error if the actual peak occurs earlier or later than anticipated. Trough levels, on the other hand, will be affected by absorption rate to a much lesser degree (see Figure 2.6). Trough levels obtained just before the next dose, therefore, are more useful in plasma level evaluation. One should avoid drawing levels at other times unless there is a specific reason to do so (e.g., in the case of acute toxicity).

8. T.M. did well for the next three days but then developed a fever. She had blood cultures taken and was started on 100 mg of tobramycin (infused over 30 min) Q 8 hr. T.M. still weighs 60 kg and has a SrCr of 2.1 mg/dL. Calculate the expected steady-state "peak" concentration one hour after the initiation of a half-hour infusion and the steady-state trough concentration. [SI units: SrCr 186 μmol/L]

In patients with normal renal function, the half-life for the aminoglycosides is usually about two hours; therefore, a significant amount of the drug may be eliminated from the body over the 30-minute infusion period. To predict a Cpss max for the aminoglycosides, it is more appropriate to use Equation 2.30 which is based upon an intermittent infusion model rather than Equation 2.19 which is based upon a bolus model of administration.

$$\text{Cpss } t_2 = \frac{\dfrac{(S)(F)(Dose/t_{in})}{Cl}(1 - e^{-Kdt_{in}})}{(1 - e^{-Kd\tau})}(e^{-Kdt_2}) \qquad Eq\ 2.30$$

Where τ is the time interval between each infusion, t_{in} is the actual duration of the intermittent infusion, t_2 is the number of hours since the end of the infusion, and Cpss t_2 is the drug concentration t_2 hours following the completion of the infusion.

Equation 2.30 is most appropriately used when the duration of the intermittent infusion approaches the half-life of the drug. As a general rule, however, Equation 2.19 can be used whenever the duration of the infusion is less than one-sixth of half-life; the intermittent infusion model, or Equation 2.30, should be used when the duration of infusion exceeds one-sixth of the drug's half-life. In this case, the intermittent infusion model, or Equation 2.30, will be used.

Conceptually, Equation 2.30 can be broken down into several different components. $(S)(F)(Dose/t_{in})(1 - e^{-Kdt_{in}})/Cl$ represents the plasma concentration at the conclusion of a single infusion (i.e., 30 minutes after the initiation of the infusion). Dividing this value by $(1 - e^{-Kd\tau})$ provides a steady-state peak concentration produced by several intermittent infusion doses administered at τ intervals. Finally, multiplying this concentration by (e^{-Kdt_2}) provides the steady state concentration any time after the infusion has ended (in this case 0.5 hr following completion of the infusion).

Before Equation 2.30 can be used, a variety of pharmacokinetic parameters for the aminoglycoside, tobramycin, must be calcu-

lated. The expected volume of distribution for the aminoglycosides is 0.25 L/kg[50,51] or 15 L for T.M. (0.25 L/kg × 60 kg). The clearance of aminoglycosides is approximately equal to the creatinine clearance.[51,52] The creatinine clearance can be estimated for T.M. using Equation 2.24.

$$\begin{aligned}\text{Cl}_{Cr}\text{ for Females} \atop \text{(mL/min)} &= \frac{(0.85)(140 - Age)(Weight)}{(72)(SrCr)} \\[6pt] &= \frac{(0.85)(140 - 50)(60)}{(72)(2.1)} \\[6pt] &= 30\text{ mL/min or }1.8\text{ L/hr}\end{aligned}$$

The half-life of tobramycin in T.M. can be estimated using Equation 2.13:

$$\begin{aligned}t^{1/2} &= \frac{(0.693)(Vd)}{Cl} \\[6pt] &= \frac{(0.693)(15\text{ L})}{1.8\text{ L/hr}} \\[6pt] &= 5.8\text{ hr}\end{aligned}$$

The elimination rate constant can be estimated using Equation 2.14:

$$\begin{aligned}Kd &= \frac{Cl}{Vd} \\[6pt] &= \frac{1.8\text{ L/hr}}{15\text{ L}} \\[6pt] &= 0.12\text{ hr}^{-1}\end{aligned}$$

Using these calculated pharmacokinetic parameters and Equation 2.30, the "peak" concentration of tobramycin one hour after the initiation of the infusion can be calculated as follows:

$$\begin{aligned}\text{Cpss } t_2 &= \frac{\dfrac{(1)(1)(100\text{ mg}/0.5\text{ hr})}{1.8\text{ L/hr}}(1 - e^{-(0.12)(0.5)})}{(1 - e^{-(0.12)(8\text{ hr})})}(e^{-(0.12)(0.5)}) \\[6pt] &= \frac{(111.1\text{ mg/L})(0.058)}{(1 - 0.38)}(0.94) \\[6pt] &= \left(\frac{6.5\text{ mg/L}}{0.62}\right)(0.94) \\[6pt] &= (10.5\text{ mg/L})(0.94) \\[6pt] &= 9.9\text{ mg/L}\end{aligned}$$

Note that the true peak concentration would be at the end of the half-hour infusion, where t_2 would be 0 hr. However, most clinical studies define the "peak" concentration as that which occurs one hour after the dose or, in this case, one half-hour after the end of a half-hour infusion. If the plasma sample were obtained at the end of the half-hour infusion, the measured concentration could be much higher than the predicted concentration of 10.5 mg/L because not all of the drug would be fully distributed from Vi into Vt in this two-compartment model.

The trough concentration would be equal to the peak concentration decayed to the time of the trough. In this case, with a dosing interval of eight hours, the theoretical concentration of 10.5 mg/L could be decayed by the use of Equation 2.15 for 7.5 hours:

$$\begin{aligned}Cp_2 &= (Cp_1)(e^{-Kdt}) \\[6pt] &= (10.5\text{ mg/L})(e^{-(0.12)(7.5)}) \\[6pt] &= (10.5\text{ mg/L})(0.41) \\[6pt] &= 4.3\text{ mg/L}\end{aligned}$$

The trough concentration could also have been calculated by using Equation 2.30 where t_2 would have been 7.5 hours.

9. Assuming that the current dosing regimen of tobramycin (100 mg Q 8 hr) and the expected drug levels are unacceptable, calculate a dosing regimen that will achieve peak concentrations in the range of 6 mg/L and trough concentrations of <2 mg/L.

Since the usual dosing interval for aminoglycosides is two or more half-lives, the tobramycin for T.M. should be dosed at ≈12-hour intervals. This dosing interval is based upon an expected half-life of 5.8 hours and that at least two half-lives will be required for the initial peak concentration to decline to a value of <2 mg/L. That is, the peak concentration of ≈6 mg/L will decline to a value of 3 mg/L in one half-life and to 1.5 mg/L in the second half-life. While a trial-and-error method could be used to select an appropriate dose, Equation 2.30 could be rearranged so that a dose could be calculated.

$$Cpss\ t_2 = \frac{\frac{(S)(F)(Dose/t_{in})}{Cl}(1 - e^{-Kdt_{in}})}{(1 - e^{-Kd\tau})}(e^{-Kdt_2})$$

$$Dose = \frac{(Cpss\ t_2)(t_{in})(Cl)(1 - e^{-Kd\tau})}{(S)(F)(1 - e^{-Kdt_{in}})(e^{-Kdt_2})} \qquad Eq\ 2.31$$

In the above equation, Cpss t_2 is any plasma concentration within the dosing interval. However, for clinical purposes, it is most rational to target the peak concentration and, therefore, the value of t_2 will be the time from the end of the infusion until the desired clinical peak concentration of 6 mg/L. Assuming the "clinical peak" is one half-hour after the end of a half-hour infusion and making the other appropriate substitutions in Equation 2.31, a dose of ≈75 mg can be calculated as follows:

$$\begin{aligned}
Dose &= \frac{(Cpss\ t_2)(t_{in})(Cl)(1 - e^{-Kd\tau})}{(S)(F)(1 - e^{-Kdt_{in}})(e^{-Kdt_2})} \\
&= \frac{(6\ mg/L)(0.5\ hr)(1.8\ L/hr)(1 - e^{-(0.12)(12)})}{(1)(1)(1 - e^{-(0.12)(0.5)})(e^{-(0.12)(0.5)})} \\
&= \frac{(5.4\ mg)(1 - 0.24)}{(1)(1)(1 - 0.94)(0.94)} \\
&= 72.8\ or\ ≈75\ mg
\end{aligned}$$

Using a dose of 75 mg given every 12 hours, Equation 2.30 can be used to confirm that the trough concentration would be <2 mg/L.

$$\begin{aligned}
Cpss\ t_2 &= \frac{\frac{(S)(F)(Dose/t_{in})}{Cl}(1 - e^{-Kdt_{in}})}{(1 - e^{-Kd\tau})}(e^{-Kdt_2}) \\
&= \frac{\frac{(1)(1)(75\ mg/0.5\ hr)}{1.8\ L/hr}(1 - e^{-(0.12)(0.5)})}{(1 - e^{-(0.12)(12)})}(e^{-(0.12)(11.5)}) \\
&= \frac{(83.3\ mg/L)(1 - 0.94)}{(1 - 0.24)}(0.25) \\
&= 1.6\ mg/L
\end{aligned}$$

Although the short infusion model, or Equations 2.30 and 2.31, was used to estimate this dose, very similar results could have been obtained using the bolus model. In this case, the bolus model would have been satisfactory because the aminoglycoside half-life for T.M. is relatively long and very little tobramycin would have been eliminated during the infusion process. In a manner similar to that used for the short infusion model, the bolus dose model (Equation 2.19) can be rearranged to calculate a dose as follows:

$$Cpss\ t_1 = \frac{\frac{(S)(F)(Dose)}{Vd}}{(1 - e^{-Kd\tau})}(e^{-Kdt_1})$$

$$Dose = \frac{(Cpss\ t_1)(Vd)(1 - e^{-Kd\tau})}{(S)(F)(e^{-Kdt_1})} \qquad Eq\ 2.32$$

By making the appropriate substitutions, where Cpss t_1 is the clinical peak concentration of 6 mg/L, and t_1 is the interval from the start of the infusion until the clinical peak (i.e., 1 hr), a dose of ≈75 mg can be calculated again.

$$\begin{aligned}
Dose &= \frac{(Cpss\ t_1)(Vd)(1 - e^{-Kd\tau})}{(S)(F)(e^{-Kdt_1})} \\
&= \frac{(6\ mg/L)(15\ L)(1 - e^{-(0.12)(12)})}{(1)(1)(e^{-(0.12)(1)})} \\
&= \frac{(90\ mg)(1 - 0.24)}{(1)(1)(0.89)} \\
&= 76.8\ or\ ≈75\ mg
\end{aligned}$$

Using the dose of 75 mg in Equation 2.19, a trough concentration of <2 mg/L is calculated again.

$$\begin{aligned}
Cpss\ t_1 &= \frac{\frac{(S)(F)(Dose)}{Vd}}{(1 - e^{-Kd\tau})}(e^{-Kdt_1}) \\
&= \frac{\frac{(1)(1)(75\ mg)}{15\ L}}{(1 - e^{-(0.12)(12)})}(e^{-(0.12)(12)}) \\
&= \frac{(5\ mg/L)}{(1 - 0.24)}(0.24) \\
&= 1.6\ mg/L
\end{aligned}$$

Although the short infusion model and the bolus dose model resulted in slightly different doses, both equations calculated doses that are clinically equivalent. As a general rule, if the infusion time for t_{in} is less than or equal to one-sixth of a half-life (i.e., $t_{in} \leq t\frac{1}{2}$), the bolus dose model and short infusion model are essentially equivalent. Because the bolus dose model is simpler and easier to use, it would be the preferred method for pharmacokinetic calculations.

10. T.M.'s tobramycin dose was adjusted to 75 mg IV over one half-hour Q 12 hr. A trough level was obtained just before the infusion of the third dose of 75 mg, and a peak level was obtained one half-hour after the end of this infusion. The peak and trough levels were reported as 5.0 mg/L and 1.2 mg/L, respectively. Using the dosing history and reported tobramycin concentrations, calculate T.M.'s patient-specific pharmacokinetic parameters of t½, Kd, Cl, and Vd.

In order to calculate T.M.'s tobramycin pharmacokinetic parameters, the first step would be to estimate her elimination rate constant by transposing the peak concentration of 5 mg/L, obtained one hour after the infusion was begun, to the previous interval so that both the peak and trough concentrations are considered to be within the same interval. This process of transposing the peak into the previous interval is appropriate only if the dosing regimen is at steady state (i.e., the dose and dosing interval have been consistent for at least three to five half-lives). Using Equation 2.16 and inserting 5.0 mg/L for Cp_1, 1.2 mg/L for Cp_2, and 11 hr for t (i.e., the interval between the peak and trough concentration), an elimination rate constant of 0.13 hr^{-1} can be calculated.

$$Kd = \frac{\ln\left(\frac{Cp_1}{Cp_2}\right)}{t}$$

$$= \frac{\ln\left(\dfrac{5.0 \text{ mg/L}}{1.2 \text{ mg/L}}\right)}{11 \text{ hr}}$$

$$= \frac{\ln(4.17)}{11 \text{ hr}}$$

$$= \frac{1.43}{11 \text{ hr}}$$

$$= 0.13 \text{ hr}^{-1}$$

By using a combination of Equations 2.13 and 2.14, a new Equation 2.33 can be used to calculate T.M.'s tobramycin half-life.

$$t\tfrac{1}{2} = \frac{(0.693)(Vd)}{Cl}$$

$$Kd = \frac{Cl}{Vd}$$

$$t\tfrac{1}{2} = \frac{0.693}{Kd} \qquad Eq.\ 2.33$$

$$= \frac{0.693}{0.13 \text{ hr}^{-1}}$$

$$= 5.3 \text{ hr}$$

Since the revised tobramycin half-life for T.M. is approximately five hours and the infusion time is one-half hour, the criterion of having the infusion time be less than one-sixth of the drug half-life ($t_{in} \leq \tfrac{1}{6}t\tfrac{1}{2}$) has been met. Therefore, the results from using a bolus dose model will be equivalent to the results obtained from using the short infusion model in calculating the patient specific pharmacokinetic parameters of T.M. and in predicting new doses and plasma concentrations. Although the bolus dose model is simpler and, therefore, the preferred approach, both models will be used to calculate pharmacokinetic parameters. Equation 2.30 can be rearranged to solve for clearance.

$$Cpss\ t_2 = \frac{\dfrac{(S)(F)(Dose/t_{in})}{Cl}(1 - e^{-Kdt_{in}})}{(1 - e^{-Kd\tau})}(e^{-Kdt_2})$$

$$Cl = \frac{\dfrac{(S)(F)(Dose/t_{in})}{Cpss\ t_2}(1 - e^{-Kdt_{in}})}{(1 - e^{-Kd\tau})}(e^{-Kdt_2}) \qquad Eq\ 2.34$$

By making the appropriate substitutions in Equation 2.34 a clearance can be calculated. Either the peak or trough concentration can be substituted for Cpss t_2; however, the appropriately corresponding t_2 would have to be used. For example, if the trough concentration of 1.2 mg/L were used, t_2 would be 11.5 hr, as that is the time from the end of the half-hour infusion to the trough concentration at the end of the 12-hour dosing interval. Making this substitution, a clearance can be calculated as follows:

$$Cl = \frac{\dfrac{(S)(F)(Dose/t_{in})}{Cpss\ t_2}(1 - e^{-Kdt_2})}{(1 - e^{-Kd\tau})}(e^{-Kdt_{in}})$$

$$= \frac{\dfrac{(1)(1)(75 \text{ mg}/0.5 \text{ hr})}{1.2 \text{ mg/L}}(1 - e^{-(0.13)(0.5)})}{(1 - e^{-(0.13)(12)})}(e^{-(0.13)(11.5)})$$

$$= \frac{(125 \text{ L/hr})(1 - 0.94)}{(1 - 0.21)}(0.22)$$

$$= 2.1 \text{ L/hr}$$

Alternatively, the peak concentration of 5.0 mg/L and a t_2 of 0.5 hours could have been used in Equation 2.34 to calculate the revised clearance of 2.1 L/hr. While some practitioners may prefer to use either the peak or the trough, both values will result in similar patient-specific pharmacokinetic parameters because both the peak and the trough were used in Equation 2.16 to calculate the elimination rate constant. Therefore, the revised Cl became fixed and will be the same when either the peak or the trough is used.

By rearranging Equation 2.14 and substituting the previously calculated elimination rate constant of 0.13 hr^{-1} and the clearance value of 2.1 L/hr, a volume of distribution can be calculated as shown below:

$$Kd = \frac{Cl}{Vd}$$

$$Vd = \frac{Cl}{Kd} \qquad Eq\ 2.35$$

$$= \frac{2.1 \text{ L/hr}}{0.13 \text{ hr}^{-1}}$$

$$= 16.2 \text{ L}$$

Very similar results are also obtained by using the bolus dose model. Initially, the process is the same. One would start with the observed peak and trough concentrations and Equation 2.16 to calculate the elimination rate constant and Equation 2.33 to calculate the corresponding half-life. Now instead of using Equation 2.34 to solve for Cl, the steady-state bolus dose model (Equation 2.19) will be rearranged to solve for Vd.

$$Cpss\ t_1 = \frac{\dfrac{(S)(F)(Dose)}{Vd}}{(1 - e^{-Kd\tau})}(e^{-Kdt_1})$$

$$Vd = \frac{\dfrac{(S)(F)(Dose)}{Cpss\ t_1}}{(1 - e^{-Kd\tau})}(e^{-Kdt_1}) \qquad Eq\ 2.36$$

In Equation 2.36, as with the short infusion model, either the peak or the trough concentration can be used; however, t_1 now represents the time from the beginning of the infusion until the time the plasma sample was obtained. In this case, using the trough concentration of 1.2 mg/L, t_1 would be 12 hr or the entire dosing interval. Making the appropriate substitutions, a Vd can be calculated as follows:

$$Vd = \frac{\dfrac{(S)(F)(Dose)}{Cpss\ t_1}}{(1 - e^{-Kd\tau})}(e^{-Kdt_1})$$

$$= \frac{\dfrac{(1)(1)(75 \text{ mg})}{1.2 \text{ mg/L}}}{(1 - e^{-(0.13)(12)})}(e^{-(0.13)(12)})$$

$$= \frac{62.5 \text{ L}}{(1 - 0.21)}(0.21)$$

$$= 16.6 \text{ L}$$

Equation 2.14 can be rearranged to calculate the corresponding clearance by using the revised elimination rate constant and the volume of distribution.

$$Kd = \frac{Cl}{Vd}$$

$$Cl = (Kd)(Vd) \qquad Eq\ 2.37$$

$$= (0.13 \text{ hr}^{-1})(16.6 \text{ L})$$

$$= 2.2 \text{ L/hr}$$

Note that the revised elimination rate constant and half-life are equivalent when the short infusion or bolus dose revision process is used. The clearance and volume of distribution obtained by each of these methods is slightly different. This difference is not clinically important so long as the infusion time is less than or equal to one-sixth of a half-life (i.e., $t_{in} \leq t\frac{1}{2}$). If T.M.'s observed peak and trough concentrations were considered to be clinically unacceptable, a new dose could be calculated by following the process described in Question 9.

11. A.B., a 41-year-old, 70 kg male with an SrCr of 1 mg/dL, was placed on gentamicin 140 mg IV Q 8 hr. After steady state had been achieved, a trough concentration of 0.7 mg/L was obtained just before a dose and a peak level of 4 mg/L was obtained two hours after the end of the infusion which lasted for one half-hour. Does A.B.'s dose or dosing interval need to be adjusted since the peak concentration was at the lower end of the usual target of 4 to 8 mg/L?

This peak gentamicin serum concentration was obtained 2.5 hours after the start of the infusion, and the "clinical peak" is normally attained one hour after the start of the infusion. Therefore, the plasma concentration at the normal time possibly would have been within the usual therapeutic range. In order to estimate A.B.'s plasma concentration at this earlier time, his elimination rate constant should be estimated by using Equation 2.16. The time between Cp_1 (4 mg/L) and Cp_2 (0.7 mg/L) is 5.5 hours based upon calculations obtained by transposing the peak that was obtained 2.5 hours after starting the infusion to the previous interval so that both the peak and trough are in the same dosing interval with no intervening dose. Then the time "t" from the peak to the observed trough concentration, or 5.5 hours, can be calculated. Alternatively, some clinicians calculate "t" by subtracting the time interval between the trough and the subsequent peak (2.5 hr in this case) from the dosing interval (8 hr − 2.5 hr = 5.5 hr).

An elimination rate constant can be calculated using Equation 2.16 as follows:

$$Kd = \frac{\ln\left(\dfrac{Cp_1}{Cp_2}\right)}{t}$$

$$= \frac{\ln\left(\dfrac{4\ mg/L}{0.7\ mg/L}\right)}{5.5\ hr}$$

$$= \frac{\ln(5.7)}{5.5\ hr}$$

$$= \frac{1.74}{5.5\ hr}$$

$$= 0.32\ hr^{-1}$$

Now, by using the elimination rate constant and Equation 2.18, the plasma concentration 1.5 hours earlier (i.e., the peak concentration one hour after the start of the infusion) can be calculated.

$$Cp_1 = \frac{Cp_2}{e^{-Kdt}}$$

$$= \frac{4\ mg/L}{(e^{-(0.32)(1.5)})}$$

$$= \frac{4\ mg/L}{(e^{-(0.32)(1.5)})}$$

$$= \frac{4\ mg/L}{0.62}$$

$$= 6.4\ mg/L$$

This back-extrapolated concentration of 6.4 mg/L appears to be well within the usual therapeutic range and, therefore, no dose adjustment would be indicated for A.B. based upon the measured plasma concentrations.

12. T.T., a 45-year-old, 100 kg, obese male (5′10″), is receiving tobramycin and piperacillin for a suspected Pseudomonas pneumonia. T.T. does not have any edema or third spacing of fluid and SrCr is 1.4 mg/dL. Calculate a tobramycin dosing regimen that should achieve peak concentrations of 6–8 mg/L and trough concentrations of <2 mg/L. [SI units: SrCr 124 µmol/L]

In order to calculate T.T.'s tobramycin regimen, begin by estimating his ideal or nonobese weight (Equation 2.25). His height, which corresponds to 70 inches (i.e., ten inches >60) would be substituted into this equation to calculate his IBW as follows:

$$\text{Ideal Body Weight for Males in kg} = 50\ kg + 2.3(\text{Height in Inches} > 60)$$

$$= 50\ kg + 2.3(10)$$

$$= 50\ kg + 23$$

$$= 73\ kg$$

Using his calculated ideal body weight of 73 kg, his SrCr of 1.4 mg/dL and Equation 2.23, a creatinine clearance for T.T. can be calculated as shown below.

$$\text{Cl}_{Cr}\text{ for Males (mL/min)} = \frac{(140 - \text{Age})(\text{Weight})}{(72)(\text{SrCr})}$$

$$= \frac{(140 - 45)(73)}{(72)(1.4\ mg/dL)}$$

$$= 68.8\ mL/min$$

$$= 68.8\ mL/min\left(\frac{60\ min/hr}{1000\ mL/L}\right)$$

$$= 4.1\ L/hr$$

Calculating T.T.'s volume of distribution is more problematic. Since aminoglycoside antibiotics appear to distribute primarily into the extracellular fluid compartment, excess adipose tissue should make a smaller than average volume of distribution, and excess third-spacing fluid (ascites or edema) should make a larger volume of distribution for the aminoglycoside antibiotics. Although it is difficult to estimate accurately the volume of distribution for patients with unusual body compositions, the following equation has been developed from the literature based upon the premise that aminoglycoside antibiotics distribute primarily into extracellular fluid.[40,53,54]

$$\begin{aligned}\text{Vd}_{Aminoglycoside}\text{ in Obese and Patients with Third-Space Fluid (L)} &= 0.25\ L/kg\left(\begin{array}{c}\text{Nonobese,}\\\text{Nonthird-}\\\text{Space Fluid}\\\text{Weight in kg}\end{array}\right) + 0.1\ L/kg\left(\begin{array}{c}\text{Excess}\\\text{Adipose}\\\text{Weight}\\\text{in kg}\end{array}\right)\\ &+ 1\ L/kg\left(\begin{array}{c}\text{Excess}\\\text{Third-Space}\\\text{Fluid Weight}\\\text{in kg}\end{array}\right)\end{aligned}$$

Eq 2.38

In the above equation, the nonobese, nonthird-space fluid weight is usually estimated to be the ideal body weight, and the excess adipose weight is assumed to be the difference between the patient's ideal body weight and total body weight without excess third-space fluid weight. Estimation of excess fluid weight is difficult and usually is a "clinical estimate" based upon a physical examination of the patient and the extent of edema or ascites. Because patients cannot rapidly change their nonfluid weight, their excess third-space fluid is often estimated to be their weight gain in kg when a patient is noted to have an increase in weight that occurs over only a few days. Assuming T.T. has no excess third-space fluid and his IBW is 73 kg, his excess adipose weight would be 27 kg (100 kg − 73 kg). Using these weights in Equation 2.38, a volume of distribution can be calculated.

$$\begin{aligned}
\text{Vd}_{\text{Aminoglycoside}} \text{ in} \\
\text{Obese and Patients} \\
\text{with Third-Space} \\
\text{Fluid (L)}
\end{aligned} = 0.25 \text{ L/kg} \begin{pmatrix} \text{Nonobese,} \\ \text{Nonthird-Space} \\ \text{Fluid Weight} \\ \text{in kg} \end{pmatrix} + 0.1 \text{ L/kg} \begin{pmatrix} \text{Excess} \\ \text{Adipose} \\ \text{Weight} \\ \text{in kg} \end{pmatrix}$$

$$+ 1 \text{ L/kg} \begin{pmatrix} \text{Excess} \\ \text{Third-Space} \\ \text{Fluid Weight} \\ \text{in kg} \end{pmatrix}$$

$$= 0.25 \text{ L/kg}(73 \text{ kg})$$

$$+ 0.1 \text{ L/kg}(27 \text{ kg}) + 1 \text{ L/kg}(0)$$

$$= 18.2 \text{ L} + 2.7 \text{ L} + 0$$

$$= 20.9 \text{ L}$$

Using our estimates for clearance and volume of distribution, the elimination rate constant and half-life can be calculated by using Equations 2.14 and 2.13.

$$Kd = \frac{Cl}{Vd}$$

$$= \frac{4.1 \text{ L/hr}}{20.9 \text{ L}}$$

$$= 0.2 \text{ hr}^{-1}$$

$$t\tfrac{1}{2} = \frac{0.693(Vd)}{Cl}$$

$$= \frac{0.693(20.9 \text{ L})}{4.1 \text{ L/hr}}$$

$$= 3.5 \text{ hr}$$

To calculate a dose that will achieve a peak concentration of 7 mg/L, the bolus dose model would be appropriate considering T.T.'s half-life of 3.5 hours and assuming an infusion time ≈0.5 hours for the tobramycin dose ($t_{in} \leq \tfrac{1}{6} t\tfrac{1}{2}$). Using Equation 2.32 and a dosing interval of eight hours (≈2 × t½), a dose can be calculated.

$$\text{Dose} = \frac{(\text{Cpss t}_1)(\text{Vd})(1 - e^{-Kd\tau})}{(S)(F)(e^{-Kdt_1})}$$

$$= \frac{(7 \text{ mg/L})(20.9 \text{ L})(1 - e^{-(0.2)(8)})}{(1)(1)(e^{-(0.2)(1)})}$$

$$= \frac{(146.3 \text{ mg})(1 - 0.2)}{(1)(1)(0.82)}$$

$$= 142.7 \text{ mg or} \approx 140 \text{ mg}$$

This dose of 140 mg given every eight hours would be expected to result in a trough concentration of approximately 1.7 mg/L. The trough concentration can be calculated by using Equation 2.15 and decaying the peak concentration of 7 mg/L for an additional seven hours.

$$Cp_2 = (Cp_1)(e^{-Kdt})$$

$$= 7 \text{ mg/L}(e^{-(0.2)(7)})$$

$$= 7 \text{ mg/L}(0.25)$$

$$= 1.75 \text{ mg/L}$$

The trough tobramycin serum concentration also can be calculated by using Equation 2.19 and assuming t_1 to be 8 hr (i.e., the entire dosing interval).

$$Cpss \, t_1 = \frac{\dfrac{(S)(F)(Dose)}{Vd}}{(1 - e^{-Kd\tau})} (e^{-Kdt_1})$$

$$= \frac{\dfrac{(1)(1)(140 \text{ mg})}{20.9 \text{ L}}}{(1 - e^{-(0.2)(8)})} (e^{-(0.2)(8)})$$

$$= \frac{6.7 \text{ mg/L}}{(1 - 0.2)} (0.2)$$

$$= 1.7 \text{ mg/L}$$

Although the peak concentration falls within the usual range accepted for therapeutic efficacy (i.e., peaks of 4–8 mg/L), and the trough concentration is less than 2 mg/L, it would be appropriate to obtain steady state tobramycin peak and trough concentrations to confirm the accuracy of assumptions and calculations.

13. T.T. was started on tobramycin 140 mg IV over one half-hour Q 8 hr. A trough tobramycin level of 1.5 mg/L was obtained just before the start of the fourth dose and a subsequent peak level was reported as 3 mg/L obtained one half-hour after the end of the half-hour infusion. What are the revised pharmacokinetic parameters for T.T. and are the revised parameters reasonable?

It should be obvious from the predicted peak and trough concentrations of 7 mg/L and 1.7 mg/L that, although the observed trough concentration of 1.5 mg/L is similar, the peak concentration of 3 mg/L is much lower than expected. The revised tobramycin pharmacokinetic parameters, therefore, will be substantially different from those predicted.

The first step in revising T.T.'s pharmacokinetic parameters would be to transpose the peak tobramycin concentration to one hour after the previous dose so that the peak and trough levels are within the same dosing interval. Equation 2.16 would then be used with the corresponding peak and trough concentrations (Cp_1 and Cp_2) and the time interval (t) between the peak and trough of seven hours to calculate an elimination rate constant (Kd).

$$Kd = \frac{\ln\left(\dfrac{Cp_1}{Cp_2}\right)}{t}$$

$$= \frac{\ln\left(\dfrac{3 \text{ mg/L}}{1.5 \text{ mg/L}}\right)}{7 \text{ hr}}$$

$$= 0.099 \text{ hr}^{-1}$$

Equation 2.33 can then be used to calculate T.T.'s revised half-life of 7 hours.

$$t\tfrac{1}{2} = \frac{0.693}{Kd}$$

$$= \frac{0.693}{0.099 \text{ hr}^{-1}}$$

$$= 7 \text{ hr}$$

The time criterion of one half-life between Cp_1 and Cp_2 as the time interval for calculating a revised half-life or elimination rate constant has been met.

Because T.T. has a long tobramycin half-life ($t_{in} \leq t\tfrac{1}{2}$), the bolus dose model (Equation 2.36) can be used to calculate a revised volume of distribution for T.T. Inserting 1.5 mg/L as Cpss t_1, eight hours as t_1, and the corresponding values for the other parameters, a volume of distribution is calculated as follows:

$$Vd = \frac{\frac{(S)(F)(Dose)}{Cpss\ t_1}}{(1 - e^{-Kd\tau})}\ (e^{-Kdt_1})$$

$$= \frac{\frac{(1)(1)(140\ mg)}{1.5\ mg/L}}{(1 - e^{-(0.099)(8)})}\ (e^{-(0.099)(8)})$$

$$= \frac{93.3\ L}{(1 - 0.45)}\ (0.45)$$

$$= 76.3\ L$$

This volume of distribution is very large and would seem unreasonable given that T.T. has no third-spacing of fluid. For this reason, the measured plasma concentrations would not be considered useful in making clinical decisions. If dose adjustments are felt to be necessary on a clinical basis, it would be appropriate to do so, but the observed peak and trough concentrations should not be the basis for making this decision. It would also be appropriate to repeat the plasma concentrations if necessary. One possible explanation for the unusually large Vd in T.T. is the peak concentration may be spuriously low because of an assay error, late sampling, or a penicillin-aminoglycoside interaction that can occur *in vivo,* as well as *in vitro.*[55–57] Because T.T.'s renal function is expected to be good, it is doubtful that this interaction has *in vivo* significance; however, if the sample was stored improperly the interaction could have occurred in the test tube before the assay procedure.

Comparing the revised and expected pharmacokinetic parameters and plasma concentrations is an important part of the pharmacokinetic revision process. Any time the measured plasma concentrations and revised pharmacokinetic parameters appear to be unreasonable, patient care decisions based upon pharmacokinetic manipulations must be undertaken cautiously.

14. C.D., a 40-year-old, 60 kg, nonobese female with a SrCr of 1 mg/dL, is started on gentamicin 300 mg infused over one hour daily for postoperative fever. Calculate the expected steady-state peak concentration at the end of the one-hour infusion, at 12 hours after starting the infusion, and at the trough. [SI units: SrCr 88 μmol/L]

In order to calculate C.D.'s gentamicin pharmacokinetic parameters, begin by estimating her renal function using Equation 2.24 and the corresponding weight, age, and serum creatinine.

$$\begin{aligned}\frac{Cl_{Cr}\ for\ Females}{(mL/min)} &= \frac{(0.85)(140 - Age)(Weight)}{(72)(SrCr)} \\[6pt] &= \frac{(0.85)(140 - 40)(60)}{(72)(1)} \\[6pt] &= 70.8\ mL/min \\[6pt] &= 70.8\ mL/min\left(\frac{60\ min/hr}{1000\ mL/L}\right) \\[6pt] &= 4.2\ L/hr\end{aligned}$$

A volume of distribution of 15 L (0.25 L/kg $\times$ 60 kg) can be estimated for C.D. assuming she is not obese and does not have excess third spacing of fluid. C.D.'s elimination rate constant and corresponding half-life can be calculated using Equations 2.14 and 2.33.

$$\begin{aligned}Kd &= \frac{Cl}{Vd} \\[6pt] &= \frac{4.2\ L/hr}{15\ L} \\[6pt] &= 0.28\ hr^{-1}\end{aligned}$$

$$\begin{aligned}t\tfrac{1}{2} &= \frac{0.693}{Kd} \\[6pt] &= \frac{0.693}{0.28\ hr^{-1}} \\[6pt] &= 2.5\ hr\end{aligned}$$

Because the infusion time of one hour is greater than one-sixth of C.D.'s aminoglycoside half-life, the short infusion model would be most appropriate for calculating the expected gentamicin concentrations ($t_{in} > \tfrac{1}{6}t\tfrac{1}{2}$). Using Equation 2.30 where the peak concentration at the end of the one hour infusion will be calculated by using zero for t_2 and inserting the appropriate dose, time, and pharmacokinetic parameters, a peak concentration can be calculated.

$$\begin{aligned}Cpss\ t_2 &= \frac{\frac{(S)(F)(Dose/t_{in})}{Cl}(1 - e^{-Kdt_{in}})}{(1 - e^{-Kd\tau})}\ (e^{-Kdt_2}) \\[6pt] &= \frac{\frac{(1)(1)(300\ mg/1\ hr)}{4.2\ L/hr}(1 - e^{-(0.28)(1)})}{(1 - e^{-(0.28)(24)})}\ (e^{-(0.28)(0)}) \\[6pt] &= \frac{71.4\ mg/L(1 - 0.76)}{(1 - 0.0012)}\ (1) \\[6pt] &= 17.1\ mg/L\end{aligned}$$

Although the peak concentration was calculated at the end of a one-hour infusion, plasma samples should not be obtained at the end of the infusion due to the distribution phase. As a general rule, peak aminoglycoside samples should be obtained approximately half an hour after the end of the infusion. In patients with extensive third spacing of fluid, an even longer time period may be required to ensure the distribution phase is complete. Plasma concentrations at 12 and 24 hours can be estimated by using Equation 2.15 and decaying the peak concentration for an additional 11 and 23 hours, respectively.

$$\begin{aligned}Cp_2 &= (Cp_1)(e^{-Kdt}) \\[6pt] &= (17.1\ mg/L)(e^{-(0.28)(11)}) \\[6pt] &= (17.1\ mg/L)(0.046) \\[6pt] &= 0.79\ mg/L\ at\ 12\ hours\ after\ starting\ the\ infusion\end{aligned}$$

$$\begin{aligned}Cpss\ t_2 &= (Cp_1)(e^{-Kdt}) \\[6pt] &= (17.1\ mg/L)(e^{-(0.28)(23)}) \\[6pt] &= (17.1\ mg/L)(0.0016) \\[6pt] &= 0.027\ mg/L\ at\ the\ trough\end{aligned}$$

The plasma concentration at the midpoint of the interval in C.D. is <1 mg/L and virtually nondetectable at the end of the 24-hour interval.

While there is literature to support once-daily dosing of aminoglycosides,[58–60] it is unclear whether there are specific patient populations that are likely to fail this type of regimen. The support for once-daily dosing of aminoglycoside antibiotics is based upon the advantage of concentration-dependent killing as well as upon the postantibiotic effect of aminoglycosides.[59–61] Although animal data suggest the immunocompromised host may be at some risk for therapeutic failure from once-a-day dosing of aminoglycosides, clinical studies suggest that when aminoglycosides are combined with other antibiotics this may not be the case.[58,60,62]

As can be seen from the calculations above, the anticipated peak and trough concentrations are quite different from those normally associated with a therapeutic response. Tobramycin and gentamicin peak levels of 4 to 8 mg/L are usually associated with efficacy and trough levels of <2 mg/L with minimizing the risk of toxicity.[63-65]

The value of plasma concentrations in monitoring once-daily dosing of aminoglycosides is unknown. Trough concentrations probably will be of little use because they will be nondetectable in the majority of patients. Conjecturally, midinterval samples might be useful in identifying those patients with unusual aminoglycoside disposition. In any case, while the use of once-daily aminoglycoside antibiotics is increasing, the amount of clinical data available to assess this type of drug therapy, especially in patients with altered aminoglycoside disposition (e.g., decreased renal function, obesity, third spacing of fluid), are limited.

15. B.Q., a 30-year-old, 65 kg, nonobese male with a SrCr of 1 mg/dL, was started on 1 gm of vancomycin IV Q 12 hr for nafcillin-resistant *Staphylococcus aureus*. Calculate B.Q.'s expected steady-state peak, vancomycin concentration two hours after starting the one-hour infusion, and trough concentration just before his next dose. [SI units: SrCr 88 μmol/L]

Vancomycin is cleared primarily by the renal route, therefore, B.Q.'s creatinine clearance should be estimated first by using Equation 2.23, which has been modified to calculate Cl_{Cr} in mL/kg/min.

$$Cl_{Cr} \text{ for Males (mL/min)} = \frac{(140 - Age)(Weight)}{(72)(SrCr)}$$

$$Cl_{Cr} \text{ for Males (mL/kg/min)} = \frac{(140 - Age)}{(72)(SrCr)}$$

$$= \frac{(140 - 30)}{(72)(1)}$$

$$= 1.5 \text{ mL/kg/min}$$

$$= 1.5 \text{ mL/kg/min}\left(\frac{60 \text{ min/hr}}{1000 \text{ mL/L}}\right)$$

$$= 0.09 \text{ L/kg/hr}$$

Vancomycin clearance is approximately 65% of creatinine clearance and appears to be estimated best by using total body weight (TBW) in patients who have a normal body weight and in patients who are obese.[66-69] B.Q.'s vancomycin clearance ($Cl_{vancomycin}$) can be estimated by using Equation 2.39 as follows:

$$Cl_{Vancomycin} \text{ (L/hr)} = 0.65(Cl_{Cr} \text{ in L/kg/hr})(TBW) \quad Eq\ 2.39$$

$$= 0.65(0.09 \text{ L/kg/hr})(65 \text{ kg})$$

$$= 3.8 \text{ L/hr}$$

In Equation 2.39 TBW represents total body weight, even if patients are obese, unless excess third spacing of fluid is present.

While the usual estimates of vancomycin clearance are considerably less than creatinine clearance (i.e., ≈65%), the clearance of vancomycin may approach that of creatinine in some patients.[70]

The volume of distribution for vancomycin is ≈0.7 L/kg and should be based upon total body weight[66-69] even when patients are obese and third-spacing fluid weight is present.

$$Vd_{Vancomycin} \text{ (L)} = (0.7 \text{ L/kg})(TBW) \quad Eq\ 2.40$$

$$= (0.7 \text{ L/kg})(65 \text{ kg})$$

$$= 45.5 \text{ L}$$

Equations 2.14 and 2.33 would be used to calculate the corresponding elimination rate constant and half-life, respectively.

$$Kd = \frac{Cl}{Vd}$$

$$= \frac{3.8 \text{ L/hr}}{45.5 \text{ L}}$$

$$= 0.084 \text{ hr}^{-1}$$

$$t^{1}/_{2} = \frac{0.693}{Kd}$$

$$= \frac{0.693}{0.084 \text{ hr}^{-1}}$$

$$= 8.2 \text{ hr}$$

Equation 2.19 can be used to calculate the expected peak and trough concentrations of vancomycin. Since a sample would be obtained two hours after the start of the infusion, the peak concentration of t_1 would be two hours. The trough concentration would be at 12 hours because that sample would be obtained just before the start of the next infusion or 12 hours after start of the infusion for the previous dose.

$$Cpss\ t_1 = \frac{\frac{(S)(F)(Dose)}{Vd}}{(1 - e^{-Kd\tau})}(e^{-Kdt_1})$$

$$= \frac{\frac{(1)(1)(1000 \text{ mg})}{45.5 \text{ L}}}{(1 - e^{-(0.084)(12)})}(e^{-(0.084)(2)})$$

$$= \frac{22 \text{ mg/L}}{(1 - 0.36)}(0.84)$$

$$= 34.4 \text{ mg/L}(0.84)$$

$$= 28.9 \text{ mg/L}$$

$$Cpss\ t_1 = \frac{\frac{(S)(F)(Dose)}{Vd}}{(1 - e^{-Kd\tau})}(e^{-Kdt_1})$$

$$= \frac{\frac{(1)(1)(1000 \text{ mg})}{45.5 \text{ mL}}}{(1 - e^{-(0.084)(12)})}(e^{-(0.084)(12)})$$

$$= \frac{22 \text{ mg/L}}{(1 - 0.36)}(0.36)$$

$$= 34.4 \text{ mg/L}(0.36)$$

$$= 12.4 \text{ mg/L}$$

As can be seen from the calculations, the expected peak concentration of approximately 29 mg/L is within an acceptable range in order to avoid toxicity. Most clinicians accept peak vancomycin levels of less than 50 mg/L as being nontoxic but generally target levels of ≈30 mg/L. For efficacy, trough concentrations in the range of 5 to 15 mg/L are usually considered appropriate because the minimum inhibitory concentrations are less than 5 mg/L for most susceptible organisms.[71-73] While it is important to consider the peak concentrations in calculations, it is probably not necessary to obtain actual peak samples. In most clinical settings, trough samples will be sufficient to guide therapy because the therapeutic goal is to maintain trough levels that are adequate for efficacy but not unnecessarily high. As long as individual doses of vancomycin are limited to ≤15 mg/kg and trough levels are 5 to 15 mg/L, it is unlikely that peak levels of vancomycin will be excessive.[73] In addition, if peak samples are to be obtained, care should be taken to ensure at least one hour after the end of the infusion be allowed to elapse before sampling in order to accommodate the distribution phase.

16. B.Q.'s vancomycin trough concentration just before the next dose at steady state was 20 mg/L. What would be an appropriate dosing regimen for B.Q. to achieve a trough concentration of 5–15 mg/L?

One approach that could be taken would be to simply reduce B.Q.'s vancomycin dose in proportion to the desired change in the trough concentration. Since B.Q. is currently receiving 1000 mg every 12 hours and has a trough concentration of 20 mg/L, one would expect that reducing the dose by one-half to 500 mg every 12 hours would result in a halving of the steady-state trough concentration to 10 mg/L. This adjustment of the maintenance dose in proportion to the desired concentration change assumes that the dosing intervals remain unchanged and that the measured concentration was at steady state and obtained at the appropriate time within the dosing interval.

An alternative approach would be to use Equation 2.22 to calculate the expected Cpss max. Using B.Q.'s volume of distribution of 45.5 L and the dose of 1000 mg, a peak concentration can be calculated.

$$\text{Cpss max} = \text{Cpss min} + \frac{(S)(F)(\text{Dose})}{Vd}$$

$$= 20 \text{ mg/L} + \frac{(1)(1)(1000 \text{ mg})}{45.5 \text{ L}}$$

$$= 20 \text{ mg/L} + 22 \text{ mg/L}$$

$$= 42 \text{ mg/L}$$

Then, using Equation 2.16 and inserting the calculated peak concentration of 42 mg/L for Cp_1, the trough value of 20 mg/L for Cp_2, and using the entire dosing interval or 12 hr for t, an elimination rate constant can be calculated.

$$Kd = \frac{\ln\left(\dfrac{Cp_1}{Cp_2}\right)}{t}$$

$$= \frac{\ln\left(\dfrac{42 \text{ mg/L}}{20 \text{ mg/L}}\right)}{12 \text{ hr}}$$

$$= \frac{\ln(2.1)}{12 \text{ hr}}$$

$$= \frac{0.74}{12 \text{ hr}}$$

$$= 0.062 \text{ hr}^{-1}$$

B.Q.'s vancomycin half-life can also be calculated using Equation 2.33.

$$t\tfrac{1}{2} = \frac{0.693}{Kd}$$

$$= \frac{0.693}{0.062 \text{ hr}^{-1}}$$

$$= 11.2 \text{ hr}$$

Using Equation 2.37, the revised elimination rate constant, and the assumed volume of distribution, the vancomycin clearance for B.Q. can be calculated.

$$Cl = (Kd)(Vd)$$

$$= (0.062 \text{ hr}^{-1})(45.5 \text{ L})$$

$$= 2.8 \text{ L/hr}$$

Using the revised pharmacokinetic parameters for B.Q. and assuming a bolus dose model would be satisfactory, a new dose could be calculated using Equation 2.32. If the current dosing interval of 12 hours is maintained at 12 hours and a desired trough concentration of 10 mg/L is inserted into Equation 2.32, the new dose will be proportional to the desired change in the plasma concentration because all of the factors in Equation 2.32 have remained the same with the exception of the steady-state trough concentration.

$$\text{Dose} = \frac{(\text{Cpss } t_1)(Vd)(1 - e^{-Kd\tau})}{(S)(F)(e^{-Kdt_1})}$$

$$= \frac{(10 \text{ mg/L})(45.5 \text{ L})(1 - e^{-(0.062)(12)})}{(1)(1)(e^{-(0.062)(12)})}$$

$$= \frac{(455 \text{ mg})(1 - 0.475)}{(1)(1)(0.475)}$$

$$= 503 \text{ mg or} \approx 500 \text{ mg}$$

If Equation 2.32 is used and the dosing interval is extended to 24 hours, and a trough concentration of 10 mg/L is desired, the new dose is not proportional to the desired change in the plasma concentration and would have to be calculated as follows:

$$\text{Dose} = \frac{(\text{Cpss } t_1)(Vd)(1 - e^{-Kd\tau})}{(S)(F)(e^{-Kdt_1})}$$

$$= \frac{(10 \text{ mg/L})(45.5 \text{ L})(1 - e^{-(0.062)(24)})}{(1)(1)(e^{-(0.062)(24)})}$$

$$= \frac{(455 \text{ mg})(1 - 0.226)}{(1)(1)(0.226)}$$

$$= 1558 \text{ mg or} \approx 1500 \text{ mg}$$

As a practical approach, administering 1000 mg every 24 hours, the calculated peak concentration two hours after the start of the infusion, and the trough concentration, would be approximately 25 mg/L and 6 mg/L, respectively (Equation 2.19).

$$\text{Cpss } t_1 = \frac{\dfrac{(S)(F)(\text{Dose})}{Vd}}{(1 - e^{-Kd\tau})} (e^{-Kdt_1})$$

$$= \frac{\dfrac{(1)(1)(1000 \text{ mg})}{45.5 \text{ L}}}{(1 - e^{-(0.062)(24)})} (e^{-(0.062)(2)})$$

$$= \frac{22 \text{ mg/L}}{(1 - 0.226)} (0.88)$$

$$= 28.4 \text{ mg/L}(0.88)$$

$$= 25 \text{ mg/L}$$

Using Equation 2.15 to calculate the trough level 22 hours later:

$$Cp_2 = (Cp_1)(e^{-Kdt})$$

$$= (25 \text{ mg/L})(e^{-(0.062)(22)})$$

$$= 25 \text{ mg/L}(0.26)$$

$$= 6.5 \text{ mg/L}$$

While it may be desirable to increase the dosing interval to 24 hours for convenience, the vancomycin dose of 1500 mg is more than the usual 15 mg/kg/dose. However, the 1000 mg dose given every 24 hours appears to result in trough concentrations at the lower end of the therapeutic range. One would have to choose between the options available, based upon the necessity for achieving a convenient interval and the desire to ensure that therapeutic trough concentrations are achieved. For example, if B.Q. were to receive his vancomycin at home, once-daily dosing would be a high priority given the cost of providing home therapy. The calculation of the trough concentration with the every-24-hours schedule, however, is less reliable than the every-12-hours schedule because the dosing interval was extended beyond one half-life based, in part, upon literature estimates of Vd. If the change in the dosing interval did not extend beyond one half-life, the usual errors in the literature estimate of Vd would only minimally influence the trough concentration.

17. E.W., a 30-year-old, 120 kg, obese male with a SrCr of 1 mg/dL, was to be started on vancomycin for a suspected cellulitis. What dose would be appropriate for E.W.? [SI units: SrCr 88 µmol/L]

The pharmacokinetic parameters for vancomycin appear to correlate more closely with total body weight in obese patients. Again, begin by calculating a creatinine clearance in units of mL/kg/min by modifying Equation 2.23 for this obese male.

$$\frac{\text{Cl}_{\text{Cr}} \text{ for Males}}{(\text{mL/min})} = \frac{(140 - \text{Age})(\text{Weight})}{(72)(\text{SrCr})}$$

$$\frac{\text{Cl}_{\text{Cr}} \text{ for Males}}{(\text{mL/kg/min})} = \frac{(140 - \text{Age})}{(72)(\text{SrCr})}$$

$$= \frac{(140 - 30)}{(72)(1)}$$

$$= 1.53 \text{ mL/kg/min}$$

$$\doteq 1.53 \text{ mL/kg/min}\left(\frac{60 \text{ min/hr}}{1000 \text{ mL/L}}\right)$$

$$= 0.092 \text{ L/kg/hr}$$

This creatinine clearance of 0.092 L/kg/hr can now be used in Equation 2.39 to calculate the $\text{Cl}_{\text{vancomycin}}$ as follows:

$$\text{Cl}_{\text{Vancomycin}} \text{ (L/hr)} = (0.65)(\text{Cl}_{\text{Cr}} \text{ L/kg/hr})(\text{TBW})$$

$$= (0.65)(0.092 \text{ L/hr/kg})(120 \text{ kg})$$

$$= 7.2 \text{ L/hr}$$

The corresponding volume of distribution would be calculated based upon E.W.'s total body weight and Equation 2.40.

$$\text{Vd}_{\text{Vancomycin}} \text{ (L)} = 0.7 \text{ L/kg(TBW)}$$

$$= 0.7 \text{ L/kg}(120 \text{ kg})$$

$$= 84 \text{ L}$$

Using Equations 2.14 and 2.33, E.W.'s vancomycin elimination rate constant and half-life are calculated as follows:

$$\text{Kd} = \frac{\text{Cl}}{\text{Vd}}$$

$$= \frac{7.2 \text{ L/hr}}{84 \text{ L}}$$

$$= 0.086 \text{ hr}^{-1}$$

$$\text{t}\frac{1}{2} = \frac{0.693}{\text{Kd}}$$

$$= \frac{0.693}{0.086 \text{ hr}^{-1}}$$

$$= 8.06 \text{ hr}$$

Assuming a desired trough concentration of 10 mg/L, a τ of 12 hours, and using Equation 2.32, a dose can be calculated:

$$\text{Dose} = \frac{(\text{Cpss t}_1)(\text{Vd})(1 - e^{-\text{Kd}\tau})}{(\text{S})(\text{F})(e^{-\text{Kdt}_1})}$$

$$= \frac{(10 \text{ mg/L})(84 \text{ L})(1 - e^{-(0.086)(12)})}{(1)(1)(e^{-(0.086)(12)})}$$

$$= \frac{(840 \text{ mg})(1 - 0.36)}{(0.36)}$$

$$= 1493.3 \text{ mg or} \approx 1500 \text{ mg}$$

The corresponding peak concentration two hours after starting the one-hour infusion as calculated by Equation 2.19 would be ≈ 23 mg/L.

$$\text{Cpss t}_1 = \frac{\dfrac{(\text{S})(\text{F})(\text{Dose})}{\text{Vd}}}{(1 - e^{-\text{Kd}\tau})} (e^{-\text{Kdt}_1})$$

$$= \frac{\dfrac{(1)(1)(1500 \text{ mg})}{84 \text{ L}}}{(1 - e^{-(0.086)(12)})} (e^{-(0.086)(2)})$$

$$= \frac{17.86 \text{ mg/L}}{(1 - 0.36)} (0.84)$$

$$= 23.4 \text{ mg/L}$$

Many clinicians are concerned about the vancomycin side effects (e.g., flushing, tachycardia, and hypotension) that are associated with the infusion of doses greater than 1000 mg. Therefore, it might also be rational to consider giving the same total daily dose of 3000 mg on a three-times-daily divided dose, or 1000 mg every eight hours. Again, using Equation 2.19 and making the appropriate substitutions for the 1000 mg dose and the dosing interval of eight hours, the corresponding peak at two hours and trough concentration at eight hours can be calculated as follows:

$$\text{Cpss t}_1 = \frac{\dfrac{(\text{S})(\text{F})(\text{Dose})}{\text{Vd}}}{(1 - e^{-\text{Kd}\tau})} (e^{-\text{Kdt}_1})$$

$$= \frac{\dfrac{(1)(1)(1000 \text{ mg})}{84 \text{ L}}}{(1 - e^{-(0.086)(8)})} (e^{-(0.086)(2)})$$

$$= \frac{11.9 \text{ mg/L}}{(1 - 0.5)} (0.84)$$

$$= 20.2 \text{ mg/L}$$

$$\text{Cpss t}_1 = \frac{\dfrac{(\text{S})(\text{F})(\text{Dose})}{\text{Vd}}}{(1 - e^{-\text{Kd}\tau})} (e^{-\text{Kdt}_1})$$

$$= \frac{\dfrac{(1)(1)(1000 \text{ mg})}{84 \text{ L}}}{(1 - e^{-(0.086)(8)})} (e^{-(0.086)(8)})$$

$$= \frac{11.9 \text{ mg/L}}{(1 - 0.5)} (0.5)$$

$$= 11.9 \text{ mg/L}$$

As with the previous example, the decision to prescribe smaller doses more often, or to increase the dosing interval and prescribe larger doses less frequently, is essentially a clinical decision. The decision should be based upon the risks of having low vancomycin trough concentrations and, if the dose is large, infusion-related side effects versus the convenience of a less frequent dosing schedule.

Update

U1. What type of patients are candidates for once-daily high-dose aminoglycoside therapy?

Many patients who receive aminoglycoside therapy are potential candidates for once-a-day dosing regimens consisting of 5 to 7 mg/kg of gentamicin or tobramycin and amikacin 20 mg/kg.[58,74] Although the optimal use of once-daily high-dose aminoglycoside therapy is still being explored, this method of administration seems to be at least as effective and perhaps less toxic than the traditional method of administering tobramycin or gentamicin 1 to 2 mg/kg every 8 hours or amikacin 5 to 7.5 mg/kg every 12 hours.

Almost all of the patients receiving once-daily high-dose aminoglycoside therapy have had normal renal function and normal muscle mass, adipose tissue, and third spacing of fluid. Probably the most common criterion used for dosing once-daily aminoglycoside is creatinine clearance. While ranges have been suggested, a creatinine clearance of at least 60 mL/minute/70 kg should be the minimum renal function appropriate for once-daily aminoglycoside therapy.[74] Clinical experience in patients with unusual body composition (obesity, edema, or ascites) or any other physical characteristic that would result in an alteration in the volume of distribution and, therefore, half-life of the aminoglycoside is inadequate. As a result, some patients have been excluded from receiving once-a-day aminoglycoside therapy based upon their disease state or clinical condition (e.g., pediatrics or pregnancy). Although more experience is being gained with immunocompromised patients, many clinicians are still concerned about the potential for therapeutic failure with once-a-day aminoglycoside regimens in this high-risk patient population.

Given the uncertainty as to the efficacy and potential for toxicity in limited or untested patient populations, the use of once-daily high-dose aminoglycoside therapy should be restricted to adult patients with a creatinine clearance of greater than 60 mL/minute/70 kg and who have relatively normal body composition (e.g., absence of third spacing fluid, nonobese).

U2. In patients receiving once-daily high-dose aminoglycoside therapy, when should blood samples be obtained to assay for serum concentrations?

While the use of serum drug concentrations in once-daily high-dose aminoglycoside therapy is still being studied, the optimal peak concentrations with this type of therapy to insure efficacy or avoid toxicity have not been established. As discussed previously (see Question 14), concentrations of about 20 mg/L appear to be target with no data suggesting the limits of this approximate range. Therefore, peak levels should not be obtained. Trough concentrations (see Question 14) are unlikely to be detectable in patients with a creatinine clearance greater than 60 mL/minute/70 kg and, therefore, trough levels should not be obtained.

When to measure aminoglycoside serum concentrations within a dosing interval is problematic, but sampling 6 to 12 hours after the single-daily dose has been administered would seem logical as these levels should be detectable. The decision to monitor aminoglycoside serum concentrations would rest in part on the confidence with which renal function and body composition have been estimated. Those patients in whom the renal function would appear to be near the lower range at which once-daily aminoglycoside therapy would be acceptable are potentially candidates for aminoglycoside drug level monitoring. If creatinine clearance is greater than 60 mL/minute/70 kg aminoglycoside drug levels are not recommended.[74]

A nomogram based upon high serum aminoglycoside concentrations, is available for patients who require increased dosing intervals of more than 24 hours.[74] There are no data to suggest what to do if the aminoglycoside level is not detectable at 6, 8, or 12 hours after the single-daily dose has been administered. An area under the curve (AUC) approach might be useful,[75] but would require at least two measurable drug concentrations. In addition, the AUC approach would seem less rational because AUC is a function of clearance and AUC defines the Cpss ave rather than the Cpss peak and Cpss trough.

At this time, drug toxicity and efficacy have not been correlated to aminoglycoside serum concentrations that have been obtained from patients treated with the once-a-day high dose regimen. High peak aminoglycoside serum concentrations would be expected to improve efficacy, and low trough serum concentrations would be expected to lessen toxicity. However, whether the total time of exposure above some critical serum concentration results in a higher (or lower) potential for toxicity, or whether the total amount of time below a specific minimum concentration is more (or less) desirable still needs to be determined. When this information becomes available, regimens that allow for a drug "holiday" could perhaps be created to minimize the potential for toxicity. The issue of aminoglycoside efficacy is equally perplexing because the optimal peak serum concentration and duration of time above some critical concentration have yet to be determined.

When single dose therapy has to be extended beyond 24 hours, it becomes problematic as to what would be an appropriate aminoglycoside regimen. The nomogram by Nicolau[74] provides some guidelines for increasing the dosing interval from 24 to 36 or 48 hours; however, the number of patients who have been treated with extended dosing intervals beyond 24 hours is still relatively small. When the dosing interval is extended, the absolute time while the drug concentrations are below the MIC increases. Even though there is a postantibiotic effect for the aminoglycosides, in most studies the postantibiotic effect lasts for only three hours and there is little information that the postantibiotic effect would last much longer than nine hours even with the increased concentrations achieved with high-dose aminoglycoside therapy.[76]

Until more data become available as to the safety and efficacy of extending the dosing interval beyond 24 hours, aminoglycosides should be used in a more traditional fashion for patients who do not meet the standard criteria for once-daily high-dose aminoglycoside therapy (i.e., target tobramycin and gentamicin peak concentrations of 4 to 10 mg/L and trough concentrations of less than 2 mg/L).

References

1 **Winter ME.** Basic Clinical Pharmacokinetics. 3rd ed. Vancouver, WA: Applied Therapeutics, Inc.; 1994.

2 **Evans WE et al, eds.** Applied Pharmacokinetics: Principles of Therapeutic Drug Monitoring. 3rd ed. Vancouver, WA: Applied Therapeutics, Inc.; 1992.

3 **Gibaldi M et al.** Pharmacokinetics. New York, NY: Marcel Dekker, Inc.; 1980.

4 **Roland M, Tozer TN.** Clinical Pharmacokinetics: Concepts and Applications. 2nd ed. Philadelphia, PA: Lea and Febiger; 1989.

5 **Woo WE, Greenblatt DJ.** Pharmacokinetics and clinical implications of quinidine protein binding. J Pharm Sci. 1979;68:466.

6 **Saal AK et al.** Effects of amiodarone on serum quinidine and procainamide levels. Am J Cardiol. 1984;53:1264.

7 **Mitenko PA et al.** Rational intravenous doses of theophylline. N Engl J Med. 1973;289:600.

8 **Pagliaro LA et al.** Critical compilation of terminal half-lives, percent excreted unchanged, and changes of half-life in renal and hepatic dysfunction from studies in humans, with references. J Pharmacokinet Biopharm. 1975;3:333.

9 **Welling PG et al.** Predictions of drug dosage in patients with renal failure us-

ing data derived from normal subjects. Clin Pharmacol Ther. 1975;18:45.

10 Benet LA, Sheiner LB. Design and optimization of dosage regimens; pharmacokinetic data. In: Gilman AG et al., eds. The Pharmacologic Basis of Therapeutics. 7th ed. New York: Macmillan Publishing Company; 1985.

11 Vlasses PH et al. Immediate release and sustained release procainamide: bioavailability at steady state in cardiac patients. Ann Intern Med. 1983;89:613.

12 Liponi DL et al. Renal function and therapeutic concentrations of phenytoin. Neurology (NY). 1984;34:395.

13 Chow MS et al. Pharmacokinetic data and drug monitoring: antibiotics and antiarrhythmics. J Clin Pharmacol. 1975;15:405.

14 Cacek AT. Review of alterations in oral phenytoin bioavailability associated with formulation, antacids and food. Ther Drug Monit. 1986;8:166.

15 Ochs HR. Clinical pharmacokinetics of quinidine. Clin Pharmacokinet. 1980; 5:150.

16 Hendeles L, Weinberger M. Theophylline: "A state of the art" review. Pharmacotherapy. 1983;3:2.

17 Bowdle TA et al. Valproic acid dosage and plasma protein binding and clearance. Clin Pharmacol Ther. 1980;28:486.

18 Gugler R, Unruh GE. Clinical pharmacokinetics of valproic acid. Clin Pharmacokinet. 1980;5:67.

19 Furst DE et al. Salicylate clearance, the result of protein binding and metabolism. Clin Pharmacol Ther. 1979; 26:380.

20 Koch-Weser J et al. Binding of drugs to serum albumin. N Engl J Med. 1974; 290:706.

21 Odər-Cedarlof I et al. Kinetics of diphenylhydantoin in uremic patients: consequence of decreased protein binding. Eur J Clin Pharmacol. 1974; 7:31.

22 Levy R, Shand D, eds. Clinical implications of drug-protein binding. Clin Pharmacokinet. 1984;9(Suppl).:1.

23 Piafsky KM. Disease-induced changes in the plasma binding of basic drugs. Clin Pharmacokinet. 1980;5:246.

24 Rutledge PA et al. Increased alpha1-acid glycoprotein and lidocaine disposition in myocardial infarction. Ann Intern Med. 1980;93:701.

25 Lin C et al. Absorption, metabolism and excretion of 14C-griseofulvin in man. J Pharmacol Exp Ther. 1973;187:415.

26 Jung O et al. Effect of dose on phenytoin absorption. Clin Pharmacol Ther. 1980;28:479.

27 Huffman DG et al. Absorption of digoxin from different oral preparations in normal subjects during steady-state. Clin Pharmacol Ther. 1974;16:310.

28 Johnson BE et al. A completely absorbed oral preparation of digoxin. Clin Pharmacol Ther. 1976;19:746.

29 Mallis GI et al. Superior bioavailability of digoxin solution in capsules. Clin Pharmacol Ther. 1975;18:761.

30 Nahata NC, Powell DA. Bioavailability and clearance of chloramphenicol after intravenous chloramphenicol succinate. Clin Pharmacol Ther. 1981; 30:368.

31 Rowland M. Drug administration and regimens. In: Melon KL, Morrelli HF, eds. Clinical Pharmacology: Basic Principles in Therapeutics. New York: Macmillan Publishing Co.; 1987.

32 Benowitz N. Clinical application of the pharmacokinetics of lidocaine. In: Melmon K, Davis FM, eds. Cardiovascular Drug Therapy. Philadelphia: FA Davis Co.; 1974:77.

33 Reuning RH et al. Role of pharmacokinetics in drug dosage adjustment: pharmacologic effect kinetics and apparent volume of distribution of digoxin. J Clin Pharmacol. 1973;13:127.

34 Koch-Weser J. Pharmacokinetics of procainamide in man. Ann N Y Acad Sci. 1971;169:370.

35 Mitenko PA et al. Rapidly achieved plasma concentration plateaus with observations on theophylline. Clin Pharmacol Ther. 1972;13:329.

36 Walsh FM et al. Significance of non-steady-state serum digoxin concentrations. Am J Clin Pathol. 1975;63:446.

37 Cockcroft DW, Gault MH. Prediction of creatinine clearance from serum creatinine. Nephron. 1976;16:31.

38 Devine BJ. Gentamicin therapy. Drug Intell Clin Pharm. 1974;7:650–55.

39 Dionne RE et al. Estimating creatinine clearance in morbidly obese patients. Am J Hosp Pharm. 1981;38:841–44.

40 Bauer LA et al. Estimating creatinine clearance in morbidly obese patients. Eur J Clin Pharmacol. 1983;24:643–47.

41 Thompson PD et al. Lidocaine pharmacokinetics in advanced heart failure, liver disease, and renal failure in humans. Ann Intern Med. 1973;78:499.

42 Anderson JL et al. Anti-arrhythmic drugs: clinical pharmacology and therapeutic uses. Drugs. 1978;15:271.

43 Zito RA et al. Lidocaine kinetics predicted by indocyanine green clearance. N Engl J Med. 1978;298:1160.

44 Powell JR et al. Theophylline disposition in acutely ill hospitalized patients. Am Rev Respir Dis. 1978;118:229.

45 Hendeles L et al. A clinical and pharmacokinetic basis for the selection and use of slow release theophylline products. Clin Pharmacokinet. 1984;9:95.

46 Upton RA et al. Evaluation of the absorption from some commercial sustained release theophylline products. J Pharmacokinet Biopharm. 1980;80:131.

47 Weinberger MM. Theophylline: QID, TID, BID, QD. Pharmacotherapy. 1984; 4:181.

48 Hendeles L et al. Food induced dose dumping from a "once a day" theophylline product as a cause of theophylline toxicity. Chest. 1985;87:758.

49 Karim A et al. Food induced changes in theophylline absorption from controlled released formulations. Part I. Substantial increased and decreased absorption with Uniphyl tablets and Theo-Dur Sprinkle. Clin Pharmacol Ther. 1985;38:77.

50 Sawchuk RJ et al. Pharmacokinetics of dosing regimens which utilize multiple intravenous infusions: gentamicin in burn patients. J Pharmacokinet Biopharm. 1976;4:183.

51 Regamay C et al. Comparative pharmacokinetics of tobramycin and gentamicin. Clin Pharmacol Ther. 1973; 14:396.

52 Gyselynek AM et al. Pharmacokinetics of gentamicin: distribution and plasma and renal clearance. J Infect Dis. 1971; 124(Suppl).:70.

53 Sampliner R et al. Influence of ascites on tobramycin pharmacokinetics. J Clin. Pharmacol. 1984;24:43.

54 Hodgman T et al. Tobramycin disposition into ascitic fluid. Clin Pharm. 1984;3:203.

55 Ervin FR et al. Inactivation of gentamicin by penicillins in patients with renal failure. Antimicrob Agents Chemother. 1976;9:1004.

56 Weibert RT, Keane WF. Carbenicillin-gentamicin interaction in acute renal failure. Am J Hosp Pharm. 1977; 34:1137.

57 Pickering LK, Gerahart P. Effect of time and concentration upon interaction between gentamicin, tobramycin, netilmicin, or amikacin, and carbenicillin or ticarcillin. Antimicrob Agents Chemother. 1979;15:592.

58 Calandra T et al. (The International Antimicrobial Therapy Cooperative Group of the European Organization for Research and Treatment of Cancer). Efficacy and toxicity of single daily doses of amikacin and ceftriaxone versus multiple daily doses of amikacin and ceftazidime for infection in patients with cancer and granulocytopenia. Ann Intern Med. 1993;119:584–93.

59 Moore RD et al. Clinical response to aminoglycoside therapy: importance of the ratio of peak concentration to minimal inhibitory concentration. J Infect Dis. 1987;155:93–9.

60 Kapusnik JE et al. Single, large, daily dosing versus intermittent dosing of tobramycin for treating experimental pseudomonas pneumonia. J Infect Dis. 1988;158:7–22.

61 Craig WA, Vogelman B. The post-antibiotic effect. Ann Intern Med. 1987; 106:900–02.

62 Fan ST et al. Once daily administration of netilmicin compared with thrice daily, both in combination with metronidazole, in gangrenous and perforated appendicitis. J Antimicrob Chemother. 1988;22:69–74.

63 Noone P et al. Experience in monitoring gentamicin therapy during treatment of serious gram-negative sepsis. Br Med J. 1974;1:477.

64 Jackson GG, Riff LF. Pseudomonas bacteremia: pharmacologic and other basis for failure of treatment with gentamicin. J Infect Dis. 1971:124 (Suppl): 185.

65 Klastersky J et al. Antibacterial activity in serum and urine as a therapeutic guide in bacterial infections. J Infect Dis. 1974;129:187.

66 Krogstad DJ et al. Single dose kinetics of intravenous vancomycin. J Clin Pharm. 1980;20:197.

67 Nielsen HE et al. Renal excretion of vancomycin in kidney disease. Acta Med Scand. 1975;197:261.

68 Blouin RA et al. Vancomycin pharmacokinetics in normal and morbidly obese subjects. Antimicrob Agents Chemother. 1982;21:575.

69 Vance-Bryan K et al. Effect of obesity on vancomycin pharmacokinetics as determined by a bayesian forecasting technique. Antimicrob Agents Chemother. 1993;37:436–40.

70 Leonard AE, Boro MS. Vancomycin pharmacokinetic parameters in middle-aged and elderly men. Am J Hosp Pharm. 1994;51:798–800.

71 Alexander MB. A review of vancomycin. Drug Intell Clin Pharm. 1974; 8:520.

72 Banner WN Jr, Ray CG. Vancomycin in perspective. Am J Dis Child. 1984;183:14.

73 Fitzsimmons WE, Posteinick MJ. Rational use of vancomycin serum concentrations: update on infectious disease for the hospital pharmacist. Macmillan Health Care Information Florham Park; 1988:1.

74 Nicolau DP, Belliveau PP et al. Experience with a once-daily aminoglycoside program administered to 2184 adult patients. Antimicrob Agents Chemother. 1995;39:650–55.

75 Barclay ML et al. What is the evidence for once-daily aminoglycoside therapy? Clin Pharmacokinet. 1994;27:32–48.

76 Zhanel GG, Craig WA. Pharmacokinetic contributions to postantibiotic effect. Clin Pharmacokinet. 1994;27:337–92.

Drug Interactions

Philip D Hansten

Drug Interaction Mechanisms 3-1
  Pharmacokinetic Mechanisms 3-1
    Absorption 3-1
    Distribution 3-1
    Metabolism 3-2
    Renal excretion 3-2
  Pharmacodynamic Mechanism 3-2
Evaluation of Drug Interaction Literature 3-3
  Time Course of the Interaction 3-3
    Measurements taken too soon 3-3
    Measurements taken too late 3-3
  Drug Interaction Studies in Normal Subjects 3-3
  Extrapolation of an Interaction from One Member
    of a Drug Class to Other Members of that Class 3-3
  Significance of Case Reports 3-4
  Sequence of Drug Administration 3-4
  Importance of Dose in the Outcome of Drug
    Interactions 3-4
  The Significance of ''Mean'' Changes Due to Drug
    Interactions 3-4

  Importance of the Indication for Which the Drug
    is Used 3-5
  Titrated versus Non-Titrated Drug Therapy 3-5
  Value of Personal Clinical Experience 3-5
Clinical Outcome of Drug Interactions—High
  Variability 3-5
  Sequence of Administration 3-5
  Duration of Therapy 3-5
  Dose of Drugs 3-6
  Other Drugs Taken by the Patient 3-6
  Subtherapeutic Pre-Existing Serum Digoxin Level 3-6
  Increases Within Therapeutic Range 3-6
  Toxic Levels of Digoxin Without Adverse Effects 3-6
  Minor Digoxin Toxicity 3-6
  Severe Digoxin Toxicity 3-7
Assessment of Risk in Specific Patients 3-7
Clinical Management of Patients at Risk 3-8
Decision Support Systems for Drug Interactions 3-8

Drug-drug interactions represent a difficult dilemma for the clinician. On the one hand, there is ample evidence that drug interactions may lead to adverse outcomes in patients. It is equally clear, however, that most patients receiving potentially interacting drugs do not manifest adverse consequences. Thus, one must be alert for those situations in which the patient is truly at risk, without overreacting every time a patient receives a potentially interacting combination of drugs. Unfortunately, it is not possible for the clinician to remember all of the necessary details for every drug interaction. Nevertheless, knowledge of the interactive properties of drugs can enable one to predict many adverse drug interactions before they occur.

Drug Interaction Mechanisms

Drugs interact with each other through a variety of mechanisms, but most can be classified as pharmacokinetic, pharmacodynamic, or combined toxicity. In this discussion and in Table 3.1, the terms ''object drug'' and ''precipitant drug'' are used. The *object drug's* action is altered by the interaction, and the *precipitant drug* causes the altered action.[1]

Pharmacokinetic Mechanisms

Drugs may affect the absorption, distribution, metabolism, or renal excretion of other drugs. It is important to note that these pharmacokinetic changes may or may not result in an altered pharmacologic response or therapeutic outcome. (See Table 3.1 for additional information on some common pharmacokinetic mechanisms.)

Absorption

The gastrointestinal (GI) absorption of drugs may be inhibited by: 1) drugs with large surface areas such as antacids, 2) binding resins such as cholestyramine, and occasionally by 3) drugs which affect GI motility or 4) drugs that alter gastrointestinal pH. In a few cases, absorption may be reduced to the extent that therapeutic response is impaired, but in many other instances, only small reductions in the serum concentration of the object drug occur.

It is important to distinguish between a reduced *rate* of absorption and a reduced *extent* of absorption. Since reduction in absorption *rate* does not decrease overall bioavailability nor alter steady-state serum concentrations of the affected drug, the drug response should not be reduced. Nevertheless, a slowed rate of absorption could be clinically important if a rapid drug response is desired (e.g., an analgesic or hypnotic). In contrast, if the *extent* of absorption is reduced, bioavailability and the steady-state serum concentration will be reduced. If the magnitude or impaired absorption is large enough, the therapeutic response may be diminished. Examples of drugs that inhibit the gastrointestinal absorption of other drugs are found in Table 3.1.

Distribution

Drugs may compete with each other for binding sites on plasma proteins or tissues. When this occurs, the unbound or free serum concentration of one or both drugs may increase; this may theoretically increase drug response. In practice, however, protein-binding displacement interactions generally do not produce clinically important changes in drug response. Displacement interactions are usually not important unless the displaced drug is highly bound, has a limited distribution in the body, is slowly eliminated, and has a low therapeutic index. Even when a displaced drug possesses these properties, the enhanced pharmacologic effect only occurs transiently (i.e., for a few days) because more unbound drug is available for elimination in the liver and/or kidney. For this reason, protein-binding displacement interactions may assume greater importance when the displacing drug (or some other drug given concurrently) also reduces the elimination of the object drug. For example, the dramatic increase in hypoprothrombinemia seen when phenylbutazone (Butazolidin) is added to warfarin (Coumadin) therapy results from the combined effects of displacement

Table 3.1

Common Pharmacokinetic Mechanisms

Mechanism	Effect[a]	Time Course[b]	Precipitant Drug Examples[c]
Reduced extent of GI absorption (binding)	↓ serum concentration of object drug	Interaction begins as soon as the two drugs are given together	Antacids, iron, kaolin-pectin, cholestyramine, colestipol
Displacement from plasma protein binding	Transient ↑ in free serum concentration of 1 or both drugs. Generally not clinically significant unless precipitant drug also has enzyme inhibition properties	Begins quickly but usually dissipates after several days, even if both drugs continue to be given	Sulfonamides, phenytoin, NSAIDs, sulfonylureas
Enzyme induction	↓ serum concentration of object drug (e.g., warfarin or theophylline)	Gradual onset over 1–2 weeks. Dissipation may take even longer	Barbiturates, carbamazepine, phenytoin, primidone, rifampin
Enzyme inhibition	↑ serum concentration of object drug (e.g., warfarin or theophylline)	Usually rapid (i.e., within first 1–2 doses of inhibitor). Erythromycin effect may be delayed by several days	Amiodarone, chloramphenicol, cimetidine, ciprofloxacin, disulfiram, diltiazem,[d] erythromycin, fluoxetine, isoniazid, ketoconazole, propoxyphene, quinidine, sulfonamides, valproic acid, verapamil[d]
Reduced renal elimination (active tubular secretion)	↑ serum concentration of 1 or both drugs	Usually rapid (i.e., by the time maximal serum concentrations of precipitant drug are achieved)	Amphotericin B, cephalosporins, methotrexate, NSAIDs, penicillins, probenecid, salicylates, sulfinpyrazone, thiazides

[a] Object drug = Drug whose effect is altered by the interaction.

[b] "Time course" in this table refers to the time until the precipitant drug is exerting its maximal interacting effect. The actual onset of any adverse effects from the interaction is dependent upon many factors in addition to the time until maximal interacting effect and can vary widely from patient to patient.

[c] Precipitant drug = Drug which causes the altered effect.

[d] Verapamil is a more predictable enzyme inhibitor than diltiazem. These drugs also may alter hepatic blood flow.

of warfarin from plasma protein binding sites as well as inhibition of hepatic warfarin metabolism. (See Table 3.1 for examples of drugs that are involved in plasma protein-binding displacement interactions.)

Metabolism

Drug metabolism can be enhanced or reduced by the concurrent administration of other drugs. Alterations in the metabolism of one drug by another probably cause more clinically important drug interactions than any other type of pharmacokinetic mechanism. Enhanced drug metabolism usually results from the administration of "enzyme-inducing" agents (examples of which are listed in Table 3.1). The onset and offset of enzyme induction is gradual, since onset depends upon the accumulation of the inducing agent and the synthesis of new enzyme, while offset depends upon elimination of enzyme-inducing drug and decay of the increased enzyme stores. Thus, enzyme inducers with long half-lives (e.g., phenobarbital) would be expected to have a longer onset and offset than inducers with shorter half-lives, such as rifampin (Rimactane).

Inhibition of drug metabolism can increase plasma drug concentrations and drug response with possible toxicity. Most clinically important inhibition interactions result from inhibition of the hepatic mixed-function oxidase system in which cytochrome P450 plays an important role. Cytochrome P450 is not one enzyme, but rather a group of related isozymes. Inhibitors of drug metabolism tend to affect some isozymes and not others. For example, the metabolism of terfenadine by cytochrome P4503A4 is inhibited by erythromycin and ketoconazole, but apparently not by cimetidine. The inhibition of drug metabolism tends to begin fairly quickly and is usually maximal by the time steady-state concentrations of the inhibitor are achieved in the plasma. Examples of drugs that inhibit metabolism are found in Table 3.1.

Renal Excretion

Most renal excretion drug interactions involve *reduced* excretion of one drug by another, leading to increased plasma levels and possible toxicity. Although some mechanisms of drug-induced alteration in renal excretion have been elucidated, in many cases the

precise mechanism is unknown. Some drugs are excreted by the kidneys by active tubular secretion. When a patient receives two drugs that are actively secreted by the same process, one or both drugs may interfere with the renal elimination of the other. Examples of drugs which interact by this mechanism are found in Table 3.1.

Another mechanism by which drugs can alter renal excretion is through alteration of the urinary pH. For example, alkalinization of the urine reduces ionization of drugs that are weak bases. As a consequence, lipid solubility and reabsorption of drug from the renal tubule into the blood stream are increased as is the plasma drug concentration. Examples of weak bases that are affected by changes in urinary pH are quinidine, methadone, and many sympathomimetics (e.g., phenylpropanolamine, pseudoephedrine, and amphetamines). The opposite is true for drugs that are weak acids (e.g., salicylates); urinary alkalinization enhances renal excretion and reduces plasma levels. Fortunately, relatively few commonly used drugs undergo pH-dependent renal excretion, so this is not a common mechanism for adverse drug interactions. Also, this mechanism is sometimes used to advantage in overdose situations, as described in Chapter 104: Clinical Toxicology.

Finally, some drugs can produce nephrotoxicity, thus reducing the renal elimination of other drugs eliminated by glomerular filtration. For example, a patient on chronic digoxin therapy who develops aminoglycoside-induced renal failure is likely to develop marked increases in digoxin serum concentrations. Other drugs that often produce nephrotoxicity include amphotericin B and pentamidine. (See Chapter 29: Acute Renal Failure for a discussion of drug-induced nephrotoxicity.)

Pharmacodynamic Mechanisms

The majority of the known pharmacodynamic drug interactions, sometimes called "pharmacologic drug interactions," occur when drugs with additive or antagonistic pharmacodynamic effects are combined. Although such drug combinations often are used therapeutically (e.g., combinations of antihypertensive agents, cancer chemotherapy, or pain management), in other situations the additive or antagonistic response may produce adverse effects (e.g., the patient receiving several drugs with anticholinergic effects). Some pharmacodynamic drug interactions involve mechanisms other than additive or antagonistic pharmacologic effects. For example, tricyclic antidepressants tend to reduce blood pressure when given alone but are likely to *increase* blood pressure in patients stabilized on clonidine (Catapres).

Pharmacodynamic drug interactions occur commonly in clinical medicine and, when anticipated, usually do not cause serious clinical difficulties. Nevertheless, it is difficult to anticipate all such interactions in a patient receiving up to 10 or 15 drugs, each of which may have two or three secondary pharmacologic effects. Indeed, it seems likely that most such additive or antagonistic drug interactions that occur in the clinical setting are recognized only after the adverse effect has occurred. Clinicians should try to anticipate these drug interactions so the adverse effects can either be prevented or recognized early by monitoring the clinical response and/or laboratory results.

Evaluation of Drug Interaction Literature

Numerous perils await those who attempt to assess the scientific validity and clinical importance of drug interaction reports and then attempt to apply this information to specific patient situations. Some of the more important principles of evaluating drug interaction studies and case reports are described below.

Time Course of the Interaction

Some drug interactions occur almost immediately, while others may take days, weeks, or even months to develop. Still others tend to dissipate with time even though the two interacting drugs continue to be given. Thus, if the drug interaction is evaluated at the wrong time, one may falsely conclude that an interaction does not exist. If the mechanism is known, the likely time course of many interactions can be estimated so the patient can be monitored at the appropriate time. If there is no proposed mechanism for an interaction, some guesswork may be involved in deciding when the effects of the interaction should be measured.

Measurements Taken Too Soon

Many interactions take longer than expected to become manifest; in this instance, one may attempt to detect the interaction before it occurs.

Example: The inhibitory effect of tricycle antidepressants on the antihypertensive response to guanethidine (Ismelin) takes a day or two to develop.[2] In early studies of this interaction, blood pressure measurements were stopped after eight to ten hours. This led to the erroneous conclusion that tricyclic antidepressants have no effect on the guanethidine response.

Measurements Taken Too Late

If an interaction has a rapid onset and offset, measurements must be taken soon enough so the interaction is not missed.

Example: In a study of the effect of famotidine on procainamide pharmacokinetics in eight healthy subjects, famotidine (40 mg HS for 5 days) was found to have no effect on the serum concentrations of procainamide or N-acetylprocainamide (NAPA).[3] However, the famotidine was given at 8 p.m., and the procainamide was given the following morning. Thus, it is likely that famotidine serum concentrations were minimal by the time the procainamide was given. Theoretically, one would not expect famotidine to interact significantly with procainamide; to establish this, however, the interaction needs to be studied when serum famotidine concentrations are higher.

Example: Epinephrine-induced increases in blood pressure in patients receiving noncardioselective β-adrenergic blockers occur within a few minutes.[4,5] Thus, if measurement of the blood pressure is begun 15 minutes after epinephrine administration, one can underestimate the hypertensive response of this drug combination.

Example: The ability of chloral hydrate (Noctec) to increase the hypoprothrombinemic response to warfarin is due to displacement of warfarin from plasma protein-binding sites.[6,7] Such interactions tend to be self-limited; that is, the prothrombin time returns to prechloral hydrate levels even if chloral hydrate is continued. A spirited debate ensued between those who found the interaction by measuring the prothrombin time within the first few days of chloral hydrate administration and those who failed to find an interaction because they monitored the prothrombin time after the interaction had already run its course.

Drug Interaction Studies in Normal Subjects

Drug interaction studies in healthy subjects are vital to the characterization of drug interactions. Such studies can control for many of the factors that may interfere with the results of studies performed in a patient population. Nevertheless, studies in healthy subjects may fail to reveal the presence and/or the magnitude of some clinically important interactions.

Example: Study in healthy subjects indicates that erythromycin inhibits the elimination of warfarin only slightly;[8] yet, marked increases in warfarin response due to erythromycin have been noted in many patients.[9] It is likely that the patients developed greater increases because predisposing factors were present. Examples of these factors include hyperpyrexia (fever increases the catabolism of clotting factors) and concurrent drug therapy (e.g., sulfonamides can displace warfarin from plasma protein binding).

Example: In healthy subjects, nonsteroidal anti-inflammatory drugs (NSAIDs) inhibit the natriuretic effect of diuretics to a small extent.[10] Patients with congestive heart failure, however, may be acutely affected by the addition of NSAIDs to diuretic therapy.[11] One possible explanation for this difference is that prostaglandins exert an important compensatory influence in patients with severe heart failure. Thus, NSAIDs may reduce the protective influence of the prostaglandins, causing decompensation. Prostaglandins are probably far less important to the maintenance of cardiovascular homeostasis in healthy subjects; thus, studies of the interaction of NSAIDs and diuretics in normals are likely to underestimate the potential magnitude of the interaction in some patients.

Extrapolation of an Interaction from One Member of a Drug Class to Other Members of that Class

Some drug classes are relatively homogeneous, and all members of the class probably interact with other drugs in essentially the same way. One example of a relatively homogeneous drug class would be the thiazide diuretics. For most drug classes, however, pharmacokinetic or pharmacologic differences exist which result in differing interaction patterns for individual members of the class.

Example (Fluoroquinolones): Fluoroquinolone antibiotics differ in their ability to inhibit hepatic drug metabolism.[12] For example, enoxacin markedly inhibits the metabolism of theophylline, resulting in theophylline toxicity in a majority of patients. Ciprofloxacin also inhibits theophylline metabolism, but the effect usually is not as marked as with enoxacin. Ofloxacin and lomefloxacin appear to have minimal effects on theophylline metabolism in most patients.

Example (H₂-Receptor Antagonists): Cimetidine (Tagamet) inhibits the metabolism of numerous other drugs, while ranitidine (Zantac), nizatidine (Axid), and famotidine (Pepcid) are unlikely to do so.[13,14]

Example (Calcium Channel Blockers): Verapamil (Isoptin, Calan) and diltiazem (Cardizem) tend to inhibit the hepatic metabolism of other drugs, while nifedipine (Procardia) appears unlikely to do so.[15]

Example (NSAIDs): Some NSAIDs, such as phenylbutazone (Butazolidin) and meclofenamate (Meclomen), are more likely to enhance the hypoprothrombinemic effect of warfarin than other NSAIDs such as naproxen (Anaprox, Naprosyn) or ibuprofen (Motrin).[16] On the other hand, sulindac appears less likely than other NSAIDs to increase serum lithium concentrations or inhibit the antihypertensive response to captopril (Capoten).[17,18]

Significance of Case Reports

The inappropriate evaluation of case reports has resulted in both over- and underestimations of the clinical importance of certain drug interactions. It is important to remember that enormous differences exist in the quality of case reports. Some case reports represent poorly controlled casual observations and often can be challenged by one or more logical alternative explanations. Often, the effects are inconsistent with the known interactive properties of the drugs involved. Conversely, other cases involve carefully controlled observations which may include measurements of serum drug concentrations; a positive dechallenge; and a positive rechallenge. In these well-controlled cases, the effect observed is more likely to be consistent with the known interactive properties of the drugs involved. Thus, some cases only confuse the issue, while others may, in and of themselves, be sufficient to prove with reasonable certainty the existence of a particular drug interaction.

Sequence of Drug Administration

The order in which the interacting drugs are given may have an important bearing on the likelihood that an adverse effect from the interaction will occur. Often, when the object drug (i.e., the drug whose effect is altered) is titrated in the presence of the precipitant drug (i.e., the drug that induces the interaction), no adverse clinical response occurs since the titration process mitigates the interaction. Conversely, when the precipitant drug is added to chronic therapy with the object drug, a clinically important adverse interaction is more likely due to perturbation in the response to the object drug. The sequence of administration must be taken into account when evaluating the results of clinical drug interaction studies and case reports.

Example: Thyroid function influences the response to oral anticoagulants. Clinically hypothyroid patients tend to be resistant to the hypoprothrombinemic effect of warfarin, while those who are hyperthyroid are particularly sensitive. Thus, any change in a patient's thyrometabolic status is likely to affect the warfarin response. Most patients are stabilized on chronic thyroid therapy when the oral anticoagulant is begun and thus are at little or no risk of adverse effects from this interaction. Occasionally, a patient on chronic warfarin therapy is found to be hypothyroid and is started on thyroid replacement therapy. Such patients are at very high risk of over anticoagulation, since the thyroid hormones will increase the warfarin response.[19]

Importance of Dose in the Outcome of Drug Interactions

The magnitude of virtually all drug interactions varies depending upon the dose of the drugs involved. Some drug interaction studies involve smaller-than-usual doses of one or both drugs, thus substantially reducing the likelihood of detecting an interaction. This is occasionally done intentionally by those interested in demonstrating a lack of interaction. Conversely, larger than usual doses sometimes are used in order to increase the possibility of observing an interaction. This is sometimes done intentionally by those who feel that a positive result will increase the chances that the study will be published or by those interested in casting an unfavorable light on a competitor's drug. In addition to the general tendency of drug interactions to be more pronounced with increasing doses, some drug interactions are unlikely to be clinically important unless the dose is above a certain level.

Example: When salicylates are given in small or occasional doses (e.g., <2 gm/day), the majority of the salicylate is eliminated by hepatic metabolism, and relatively little is excreted unchanged by the kidneys. Thus, drugs that increase urinary excretion of unchanged salicylate by increasing urinary pH have little effect on serum salicylate concentrations. Conversely, in a patient receiving 5 mg/day of salicylate for rheumatoid arthritis, some of the hepatic pathways of salicylate elimination become saturated, and the renal excretion of unchanged salicylate becomes much more important. In this situation, alkalinization of the urine can produce substantial reductions in plasma salicylate concentrations by enhancing renal salicylate excretion.[20]

Example: Omeprazole, in a dose of 40 mg/day, appears to inhibit the hepatic metabolism of drugs such as diazepam and phenytoin. However, when the more commonly used omeprazole dose of 20 mg/day was studied, it had minimal effects on the metabolism of these drugs.[38,39] Thus, it appears that in most people omeprazole will not produce clinically important inhibition of hepatic drug metabolism. Dose-dependent inhibition of drug metabolism also has been observed with several other inhibitors such as cimetidine, fluconazole, isoniazid, and verapamil.

The Significance of "Mean" Changes Due to Drug Interactions

For some drug interactions, there may be no mean change in the response and/or serum concentration of Drug A with or without concurrent administration of Drug B. If one looks at the data for the individual subjects, however, one may find that perhaps 2 of 12 subjects manifested a marked change, while no effect was seen in the other ten. This might result from the presence of a predisposing factor (e.g., genetic make-up) in the two reacting subjects. Thus, the investigators may conclude that no significant interaction exists even though the interaction actually may occur in an important subgroup of individuals.

Example: Antibiotics such as erythromycin may enhance the gastrointestinal absorption of digoxin by reducing the bacterial degradation of digoxin in the gut.[21,22] However, it appears that only a small proportion of the population is susceptible to this interaction because digoxin undergoes significant gastrointestinal bacterial degradation in only about 10% of the population. Thus, this interaction is unlikely to be identified in a study of a large group of individuals if one looks at mean values only.

Even when a drug interaction is known to exist, there is a tendency to place excessive importance on the mean changes reported in the clinical studies. In drug interaction studies there is almost always considerable variation around the mean, so even when mean changes are very small, a particular patient may manifest large changes due to the interaction. The same principle applies in reverse as well: a drug interaction that generally produces a very large change may produce no change at all in a given patient.

Example: Most studies indicate that diltiazem (Cardizem) produces only modest increases in mean serum digoxin concentrations (usually 20% to 30%).[23] Even though such increases are unlikely to be clinically important, an occasional patient may be much more susceptible to this interaction and may develop a clinically significant increase in serum digoxin level.

Importance of the Indication for Which the Drug Is Used

Some drug interactions may occur when a drug is being used for one purpose, but not when it is being used for another. This should always be considered when drugs are used for more than one disorder, especially when the drug in question has more than one mechanism of action.

Example: When methotrexate is given in the large doses necessary to treat malignancies, concurrent use of nonsteroidal anti-inflammatory drugs may increase methotrexate toxicity.[24] On the other hand NSAIDs frequently are used successfully with smaller doses of methotrexate to treat rheumatoid arthritis. Although isolated examples of toxicity have been reported with low-dose methotrexate plus NSAIDs, the risk appears to be greater in patients receiving methotrexate as an antineoplastic agent.

Example: Large doses of salicylate tend to inhibit the uricosuric effect of probenecid, but do not appear to affect the ability of probenecid to inhibit the renal elimination of penicillins.[25]

Titrated versus Non-Titrated Drug Therapy

Some drugs may be administered in both a titrated manner (where interacting drugs may interfere with this titration), but also may be given in a non-titrated manner (where interacting drugs may not interact in a clinically important way).

Example: Patients receiving corticosteroids for chronic diseases such as asthma, rheumatoid arthritis, and systemic lupus erythematous generally are receiving the lowest possible dose of corticosteroid that provides adequate control of their disease. The addition of an enzyme-inducing drug such as a barbiturate, carbamazepine (Tegretol), phenytoin (Dilantin), primidone (Mysoline), or rifampin (Rifadin, Rimactane) is likely to reduce the serum concentration of the corticosteroid sufficiently to result in an exacerbation of disease symptoms.[26,27] Conversely, patients receiving high-dose, short-term corticosteroids for an acute disorder are less likely to manifest adverse effects from the interaction since excess doses of corticosteroids often are used. In these individuals, a modest reduction in corticosteroid serum concentration is unlikely to significantly reduce the therapeutic response.

Value of Personal Clinical Experience

Drug interactions are notoriously difficult to detect in the clinical setting, making personal clinical impressions one of the least reliable methods of making decisions on the clinical importance of a given drug interaction. Nevertheless, personal clinical impressions are one of the most popular methods of making such decisions. Clinical experience can provide valuable information, but only if it is applied in the context of clinical studies and reports. To illustrate, assume that a particular interaction tends to produce adverse effects in 20% of the patients who receive the combination. If it is assumed that in this group of 20% only one out of five is correctly diagnosed as having manifested a drug interaction (probably a liberal figure), that means only 4% of patients on that drug combination will develop an adverse drug interaction that is recognized as such. Thus, it is easy to understand how one might conclude, based upon clinical experience alone, that a given drug interaction has virtually no clinical importance. Alternatively, if a severe adverse response to a given drug interaction is observed, there is a tendency to completely avoid that combination of drugs (even if such reactions are actually exceedingly rare).

Example: Even though enzyme-inducing agents such as barbiturates and phenytoin markedly enhance the hepatic metabolism of quinidine, quinidine was used together with enzyme inducers for several decades before the interaction was detected.[28] The clinical impression of virtually all clinicians during that period was that no interaction existed between quinidine and enzyme-inducing agents, even though it is likely that many patients had subtherapeutic serum quinidine concentrations as a result of the interaction.

Drug interaction clinical studies and case reports are the "life blood" of the efforts to reduce the incidence of adverse effects from drug interactions. Nevertheless, the path from the publication of such reports to the appropriate application of the information to specific patients is plagued with errors and misinterpretations. Avoiding the pitfalls outlined above may enhance the appropriate use of the information.

Clinical Outcome of Drug Interactions—High Variability

As described previously, it is not uncommon for individuals to under- or overestimate the clinical importance of specific drug interactions, since such assessments often are based upon personal clinical experience with use of the particular drug combination. Underestimation of the clinical importance of specific drug interactions is more common than overestimation because most patients who receive potentially interacting drugs do not develop observable adverse consequences. If one generalizes regarding the clinical importance of a drug interaction, the degree of risk in specific patients can be miscalculated because the clinical outcome of a drug interaction can vary dramatically from one patient to another. It has become clear that the same pair of interacting drugs can produce no adverse effects in one patient and a life-threatening reaction in another. Thus, the clinical outcome of most drug interactions is highly situational. It is seldom possible to say that a given drug interaction is dangerous or not dangerous without considering the specific patient in question.

To demonstrate the situational nature of the risk of adverse effects from drug interactions, let us consider a group of patients receiving quinidine and digoxin. Although undetected for half a century, this interaction has now been verified and intensively studied by numerous investigators.[29-36] These studies have demonstrated that quinidine substantially increases serum digoxin concentrations in almost all subjects who receive the combination. Digoxin is a drug with a narrow therapeutic index which can produce significant toxicity when serum levels rise above the therapeutic range. Why, then, did it take so long for the interaction to be detected, and why do we continue to see patients receive the combination without apparent ill effects? The following patient examples of the digoxin-quinidine interaction represent a composite of the outcomes actually observed in clinical studies and individual cases. These examples may provide some insight into the questions posed above.

Sequence of Administration

If a patient is receiving quinidine chronically and is then started on therapy with digoxin, the digoxin is titrated in the presence of the quinidine, and the appropriate digoxin level will be achieved even if the prescriber is unaware of the interaction. Of course, there is the danger that subtherapeutic digoxin concentrations will occur if the quinidine is later discontinued. (See Figure 3.1.)

Duration of Therapy

In a patient receiving digoxin who is then given quinidine, it takes approximately one week for the serum digoxin concentration to reach a new steady state.[33] The patient illustrated in Figure 3.2 developed an adverse reaction to the quinidine, resulting in its discontinuation after two days of treatment. Thus, the serum digoxin concentration, although somewhat increased, did not reach the toxic range.

Fig 3.1   Chronic Quinidine Therapy

Fig 3.2   Short-Term Quinidine

Fig 3.3   Low Quinidine Dose

Fig 3.4   On Enzyme Inducer

Dose of Drugs

The dose of quinidine is important in determining the magnitude of the increased serum digoxin concentrations; quinidine doses of ≤500 mg/day tend to produce relatively small increases.[29] The patient in Figure 3.3 received a low dose of quinidine (550 mg/day) while receiving chronic digoxin therapy. This low dose of quinidine produced only a small increase in serum digoxin concentration.

Other Drugs Taken by the Patient

The patient illustrated in Figure 3.4 was receiving chronic therapy with phenytoin (Dilantin) and phenobarbital for seizures when quinidine was added to the digoxin therapy. Since the hepatic metabolism of quinidine is enhanced by enzyme induction,[28,35] serum quinidine levels are often quite low in a patient receiving phenytoin and phenobarbital. Thus, the quinidine-induced increase in serum digoxin concentration was small. If the enzyme inducer is stopped in this situation, the rise in the quinidine serum concentration may then result in considerable increases in the serum digoxin concentration. This sequence of events has been observed clinically.[36]

Subtherapeutic Pre-Existing Serum Digoxin Level

The patients shown in Figure 3.5 had subtherapeutic serum digoxin concentrations before quinidine therapy was initiated. This nudged the digoxin concentrations into the therapeutic range. Thus, the interaction had a beneficial effect in these two patients, assuming that digoxin was the appropriate therapy for their conditions. On the other hand, patients whose pre-existing serum digoxin lev-

els are at the high end of the therapeutic range are probably at a higher-than-average risk of developing adverse effects from this interaction.

Increases Within the Therapeutic Range

The patients illustrated in Figure 3.6 had serum digoxin concentrations that were at the low end of the therapeutic range. The initiation of quinidine therapy increased digoxin levels into the high therapeutic range. Theoretically, this change would have no beneficial or detrimental effect on the patients.

Toxic Levels of Digoxin Without Adverse Effects

The patients illustrated in Figure 3.7 developed digoxin concentrations which fall in the "toxic" range after quinidine was started. However, they did not manifest any clinical evidence of digoxin toxicity. Although subtherapeutic, therapeutic, and toxic ranges are usually depicted as adjoining, the ranges actually overlap. Thus, one patient may develop toxicity while in the "therapeutic" range while another will show no evidence of toxicity even though he or she is well into the "toxic" range. Moreover, it is possible that quinidine protects the patient against the adverse cardiac effects of digoxin.

Minor Digoxin Toxicity

In the patients illustrated in Figure 3.8, serum digoxin concentrations increased into the toxic range, producing minor signs of toxicity, such as gastrointestinal distress. Mild toxicity usually can be managed by reducing the digoxin dose.

Severe Digoxin Toxicity

The patient illustrated in Figure 3.9 developed a serious cardiac arrhythmia as a result of the quinidine-induced increase in serum digoxin concentration. Such adverse effects generally can be prevented by closely monitoring the serum digoxin concentration after starting the quinidine, since the digoxin level rises gradually over a period of five to seven days. Alternatively, some clinicians prefer to prophylactically lower the digoxin dose when quinidine is begun. The preventative measure used would depend upon the clinical situation.

Although the patients previously described are fictional, all the outcomes described have been documented in clinical studies of this interaction and have been observed by those of us who have followed patients receiving this combination. The examples also help explain why it took so long to detect this interaction. Although beyond the scope of this chapter, the digoxin-quinidine drug interaction is further complicated by complex interactions of the two drugs on AV node conduction in the heart (see Chapter 15: Congestive Heart Failure). Finally, the quinidine-digoxin interaction is not atypical; the clinical outcomes of most other drug interactions are similarly affected by a variety of factors, including some not mentioned previously in this chapter. The decision support systems described later in this chapter represent an effort to present the factors that are likely to affect the risk of adverse effects to specific interacting drug combinations.

In conclusion, most patients who receive interacting drug combinations do not develop observable adverse effects; moreover, when adverse drug interactions do occur, they often are not recognized. Consequently, many clinicians have the impression that drug interactions are of limited clinical importance. Conversely, when adverse drug interactions are recognized, especially if severe, there is a tendency to place more importance on the interactions than they deserve. As a result of these phenomena, clinicians commonly under- and overestimate the potential harm of drug interactions to their patients. Since the risk of a given drug interaction to a specific patient usually depends upon the situation, more emphasis must be placed on those factors that increase or decrease the patient's risk rather than dwelling on the purported clinical importance of the interaction itself.

Assessment of Risk in Specific Patients

There is a common misconception that once one is aware that a patient is receiving a potentially interacting drug combination, one only needs to take the appropriate precautions that will prevent the adverse effects of the interaction. Thus, avoiding adverse drug interactions often is perceived as a two-step process: 1) identify those patients who are receiving potentially interacting drugs, and 2) take steps to prevent any adverse effects. Although this two-step method may sound reasonable, it omits a critical, albeit difficult, step in the process of efficiently minimizing the adverse effects of drug interactions in the clinical setting. This missing step involves identifying those patients who are actually at significant risk and who would thus benefit from appropriate preventative measures. Failure to assess risk before taking action often results in the institution of unnecessary precautions that may not be in the best interest of the patient or inefficiently use health care resources. These unnecessary precautions may produce the following undesirable results:

Fig 3.5   Subtherapeutic to Therapeutic

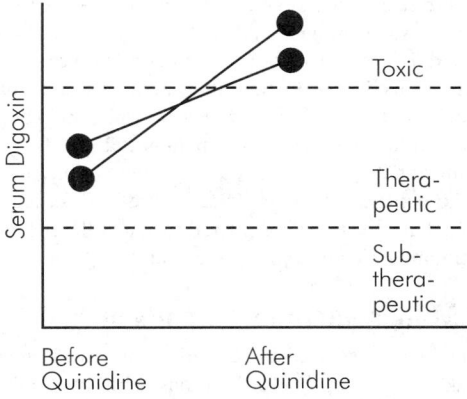

Fig 3.7   "Toxic" Levels Without Observable Adverse Effects

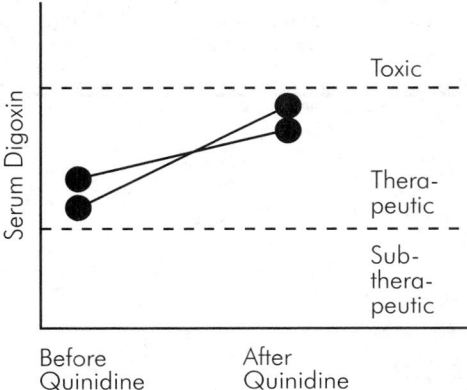

Fig 3.6   Low Therapeutic to High Therapeutic

Fig 3.8   Minor Toxicity

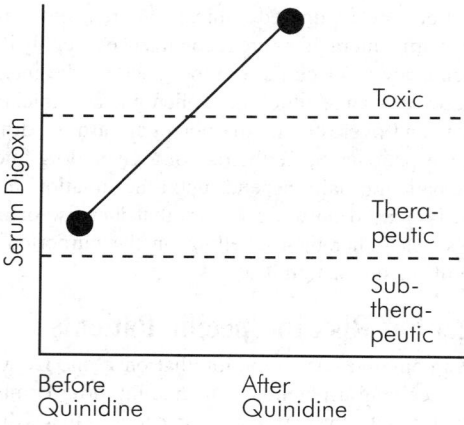

Fig 3.9   Serious Toxicity

- Discontinuation of one or more drugs that are important in the patient's treatment.

- An unnecessary increase or decrease in a drug's dose resulting in an excessive or inadequate response to that drug.

- The inconvenience and expense of more frequent medical visits to monitor the potential interaction.

- The added expense of performing unnecessary drug serum concentration determinations and/or other clinical laboratory tests.

- A lack of patient confidence in the prescriber, and possibly, an increased likelihood of litigation if the patient assumes that a "mistake" has been made.

For some drug interactions, assessment of risk is a relatively simple process. An example would be the interaction between warfarin (Coumadin) and thyroid hormones described previously. The interaction presents little problem if the patient is already stabilized on an appropriate dose of thyroid when the warfarin is begun, but the risk is high if thyroid is added to a patient stabilized on warfarin therapy. Unfortunately, the risk of most interactions in specific patients is more difficult to assess. See Figure 3.10 for an example of the factors that need to be considered to assess the risk of giving erythromycin and carbamazepine concurrently.

Clinical Management of Patients at Risk

Once a patient is assessed to be at risk for a drug interaction, one must take the appropriate precautions to minimize the likelihood of an adverse consequence. The management may differ depending upon the type of drug interaction. Some drug combinations are contraindicated (Table 3.2, InteractionType A). Here, the decision is simple: the combination should not be used. Other interactions can be circumvented easily by, for example, separating the doses of the interacting drugs (Table 3.2, Interaction Type B). For still other interactions, an alternative drug is available that is therapeutically equivalent, but is less likely to interact adversely with the drug the patient currently is receiving (Table 3.2, Interaction Type C). In other words, the combination is not contraindicated, but there may be safer alternatives. This situation occurs most often when a precipitant drug is being added in the presence of stabilized object drug therapy.

For interaction Types A, B, and C, the interaction is avoided either by not using the combination, or by administering the drugs in a way that the interaction does not occur. Some would consider such interactions "no-brainers" in that the problem is solved by *avoiding* the problem. Many drug interactions, however, do not fall into categories A, B, or C. In these cases, it is necessary to assess the risk of the interaction and take appropriate precautions when there is a risk (Table 3.2, Interaction Type D).

Decision Support Systems for Drug Interactions

Since so many factors must be considered to estimate the risk of a drug interaction in a specific patient and to determine the optimal management strategy, it is difficult for the clinician to remember all the necessary information. Moreover, it is often difficult to obtain the needed information from texts or computer systems. There are two reasons for this. First, these information sources often do not address the items of information needed for the decision-making process. Secondly, the information is not arranged in a way that facilitates the decision-making process. Complex situations such as this can be more readily addressed by decision support systems, which focus on the factors that affect the action taken by the clinician.[37] It is important to keep in mind, however, that such systems only *support* the decision-making process. The judgment of the clinician is still the most important factor minimizing the occurrence of adverse drug interactions.

Figure 3.10 is an example of a decision support algorithm for erythromycin and carbamazepine.

Table 3.2	Management of Different Types of Interactions	
Type of Interactions	**Management**	**Example**
A. Contraindicated combination	Avoid using the combination	MAO inhibitor + fluoxetine (Never use together)
B. Interaction easily circumvented	Take necessary steps to circumvent interaction	Ciprofloxacin + sucralfate (Give ciprofloxacin 2 hr before sucralfate)
C. Alternative drug available with lower risk of interaction	It is generally preferable to use the alternate drug	Cimetidine + warfarin (Use H_2-receptor antagonist other than cimetidine)
D. Interactions that do not fall into categories A, B, or C	Assess risk to patient and take precautions to avoid adverse outcome	Antihypertensive + NSAID (monitor blood pressure; adjust doses as needed)

Erythromycin + Carbamazepine

Summary: Erythromycin markedly inhibits the hepatic metabolism of carbamazepine, resulting in substantial increases in serum carbamazepine concentrations in many patients[40-50]

Step 1: The patient is NOT likely to be at risk if any of the following conditions apply. Skip Step 2.

◆ A suitable alternative to erythromycin can be used.[a]
◆ The patient is stabilized on both drugs with appropriate carbamazepine response.[b,c]
    (Usual effective carbamazepine concentration: 4–10 μg/mL)
◆ Erythromycin is being used by a nonsystemic route (e.g., topical, on skin, eye, etc.)

Step 2: Select the sequence of administration that best fits the patient's situation, and follow the arrows

Sequence of Administration	Expected Clinical Consequences	Management Options (Risk Reduction)
Starting erythromycin in the presence of carbamazepine therapy.	Carbamazepine toxicity is likely to occur.[d,e]	Monitor for carbamazepine toxicity and measure carbamazepine serum level.[f] Reduce carbamazepine dose if necessary. Advise patient about the risk of stopping erythromycin.[b,c]
Starting carbamazepine in the presence of erythromycin therapy.	Serum carbamazepine levels are likely to be higher than expected.[e,g]	Dose carbamazepine conservatively. Monitor for carbamazepine toxicity.[f] Advise patient about the risk of stopping erythromycin.[b,c]
Starting therapy with both erythromycin and carbamazepine.	Serum carbamazepine levels are likely to be higher than expected.[e,h]	Dose carbamazepine conservatively. Monitor for carbamazepine toxicity.[f] Advise patient about the risk of stopping erythromycin.[b,c]
Taking both erythromycin and carbamazepine, AND the response to carbamazepine is excessive[f] and/or carbamazepine level is in the toxic range.	Risk of continued carbamazepine toxicity.	Reduce dose or discontinue carbamazepine as necessary and continue to monitor. Reconsider alternative drugs.[a] Advise patient about the risk of stopping erythromycin.[b,c]
Taking both erythromycin and carbamazepine, AND the response to carbamazepine is inadequate and/or carbamazepine levels are subtherapeutic.	Risk of continued inadequate carbamazepine response.	Consider increasing carbamazepine dose. Advise patient about the risk of stopping erythromycin.[b,c]

Fig 3.10 Decision Support Algorithm for Erythromycin + Carbamazepine [a] Due to the high risk of carbamazepine toxicity, erythromycin should be avoided whenever possible. Effect of other anti-infective agents on carbamazepine. Serum carbamazepine levels do not appear to be affected: Azithramycin (preliminary data). *Increased serum carbamazepine levels have been reported:* Clarithromycin (Biaxin), isoniazid, troleandomycin. *Increased serum carbamazepine levels theoretically may occur (e.g., anti-infectives known to inhibit hepatic drug metabolism):* Ciprofloxacin, chloramphenicol, co-trimoxazole, enoxacin, fluconazole, itraconazole, ketoconazole, miconazole, nalidixic acid, norfloxacin.

[b] Advise patient not to discontinue erythromycin before completing the full course of therapy or alter erythromycin dose without prescriber approval; such changes can alter the response to carbamazepine.

[c] When erythromycin is discontinued, the new steady-state carbamazepine concentration will usually be achieved within 24–48 hr, but in some patients it occurred in as few as 8–12 hr.[45] Monitor the patient for inadequate carbamazepine effects (e.g., seizures) especially if the carbamazepine dose was reduced in anticipation of the erythromycin interaction.

[d] Carbamazepine serum levels tend to increase rapidly; symptoms of carbamazepine toxicity often appear within the first 24 hours of erythromycin therapy (usual range: 8–48 hr, but occasionally may take 3–4 days).

[e] Factors that may increase the risk of this interaction include large doses of erythromycin and/or carbamazepine, and when the two drugs are ordered by different physicians.

[f] Symptoms of carbamazepine toxicity include dizziness, drowsiness, lethargy, weakness, slurred speech, headache, nausea, vomiting, ataxia, nystagmus, tremor, and movement disorders. (Note that some of these symptoms may be confused with alcohol intoxication.) Syndrome of inappropriate antidiuretic hormone secretion (SIADH) has also been reported, with symptoms of water intoxication (e.g., irritability, lethargy, confusion, seizures).

[g] The time to reach toxic levels of carbamazepine is likely to be variable, depending upon the initial carbamazepine doses and the titration schedule; in one case, toxicity occurred two days after starting carbamazepine (600 mg on first day, 900 mg on second day).[43]

[h] The time to reach toxic levels of carbamazepine is likely to be variable, depending upon the initial carbamazepine doses and the titration schedule; in one case, toxicity occurred 5 days after starting carbamazepine (200 mg/day for 3 days, then 400 mg/day).[46]

References

1   **Aronson JK et al.** Adverse drug interactions. Br J Med. 1981;282:288.

2   **Mitchell JR et al.** Guanethidine and related agents. III. Antagonism by drugs which inhibit the norepinephrine pump in man. J Clin Invest. 1970;49:1596.

3   **Klotz U et al.** Interaction study of diazepam and procainamide with the new H₂-receptor antagonist famotidine. Clin Pharmacol Ther. 1985;37:205.

4   **Yasue H et al.** Prinzmetal's variant form of angina as manifestation of alpha-adrenergic receptor-mediated coronary artery spasm: documentation by coronary arteriography. Am Heart J. 1976;91:148.

5   **Hansbrough JF, Near A.** Propranolol-epinephrine antagonism with hypertension and stroke. Ann Intern Med. 1980;92:717.

6   **Sellers EM, Koch-Weser J.** Potentia-tion of warfarin-induced hypoprothrombinemia by chloral hydrate. N Engl J Med. 1970;283:827.

7   **Sellers EM, Koch-Weser J.** Kinetics and clinical importance of displacement of warfarin from albumin by acidic drugs. Ann N Y Acad Sci. 1971;179:213.

8   **Bachmann K et al.** The effect of erythromycin on the disposition kinetics of warfarin. Pharmacology. 1984;28:171.

9   **Hansten PD et al.** Erythromycin and warfarin. Drug Interactions Newslet. 1985;5:37.

10 **Brater DC et al.** Interaction studies with bumetanide and furosemide. Effects of probenecid and of indomethacin on response to bumetanide in man. J Clin Pharmacol. 1981;21:647.

11 **Dzau VJ et al.** Prostaglandins in severe congestive heart failure in relation to activation for the renin-angiotensin

system and hyponatremia. N Engl J Med. 1984;310:347.

12 **Marchbanks CR.** Drug-drug interactions with fluoroquinolones. Pharmacotherapy. 1993;13(Suppl. 2):23S.

13 **Powell JR et al.** Histamine H_2-antagonist drug interactions in perspective: mechanistic concepts and clinical implications. Am J Med. 1984;77(Suppl. 5B):57.

14 **Staiger CH et al.** Comparative effects of famotidine and cimetidine on antipyrine kinetics in healthy volunteers. Br J Clin Pharmacol. 1984;18:105.

15 **Hansten PD et al.** Calcium channel blocker-induced drug interactions: evidence for metabolic inhibition. Drug Interactions Newslet. 1987;7:7.

16 **Hansten PD et al.** All nonsteroidal anti-inflammatory drugs are not alike with regard to drug interactions. Drug Interactions Newslet. 1987;7:7.

17 **Furnell MM et al.** The effect of sulindac on lithium therapy. Drug Intell Clin Pharm. 1985;19:374.

18 **Salvetti A et al.** Differential effects of selective and non-selective prostaglandin-synthesis inhibition on the pharmacological responses to captopril in patients with essential hypertension. Clin Sci. 1982;63:261s.

19 **Costigan DC et al.** Potentiation of oral anticoagulant effect by L-thyroxine. Clin Pediatr. 1984;23:172.

20 **Hansten PD et al.** Effect of antacid and ascorbic acid on serum salicylate concentration. J Clin Pharmacol. 1980; 20:326.

21 **Lindenbaum J et al.** Inactivation of digoxin by the gut flora: reversal by antibiotic therapy. N Engl J Med. 1981; 305:789.

22 **Doherty JE.** A digoxin-antibiotic drug interaction. N Engl J Med. 1981;305:827.

23 **Kayser SR.** Drug increasing digoxin serum concentrations. Drug Interactions Newslet. 1985;5:1.

24 **Frenia ML, Long KS.** Methotrexate and nonsteroidal antiinflammatory drug interactions. Ann Pharmacother. 1992;26:234.

25 **Boger WP et al.** Probenecid and salicylates: the question of interaction in terms of penicillin excretion. J Lab Clin Med. 1955;45:478.

26 **Petereit LB et al.** Effectiveness of prednisolone during phenytoin therapy. Clin Pharmacol Ther. 1977;22:912.

27 **Brooks SM et al.** Adverse effects of phenobarbital on corticosteroid metabolism in patients with bronchial asthma. N Engl J Med. 1972;286:1125.

28 **Data JL et al.** Interaction of quinidine with anticonvulsant drugs. N Engl J Med. 1976;294:699.

29 **Doering W.** Quinidine-digoxin interaction. N Engl J Med. 1979;301:400.

30 **Fichtl B et al.** The quinidine-digoxin interaction in perspective. Clin Pharmacokinet. 1983;8:137.

31 **Schenck-Gustafsson K et al.** Cardiac effects of treatment with quinidine and digoxin, alone and in combination. Am J Cardiol. 1983;51:777.

32 **Fenster PE et al.** Digoxin-quinidine interaction: pharmacokinetic evaluation. Ann Intern Med. 1980;93:698.

33 **Leahey EB et al.** Quinidine-digoxin interaction: time course and pharmacokinetics. Am J Cardiol. 1981;48:1141.

34 **Mordel A et al.** Quinidine enhances digitalis toxicity at therapeutic serum digoxin levels. Clin Pharmacol Ther. 1993;53:457.

35 **Bussey HI et al.** The influence of rifampin on quinidine and digoxin. Arch Intern Med. 1984;144:1021.

36 **Chapron DJ et al.** Apparent quinidine-induced digoxin toxicity after withdrawal of pentobarbital. A case of sequential drug interactions. Arch Intern Med. 1979;139:363.

37 **Hansten PD.** Drug Interactions Decision Support Tables. Vancouver, WA: Applied Therapeutics; 1986.

38 **Andersson T.** Omeprazole drug interaction studies. Clin Pharmacokinet. 1991;21:195.

39 **Massoomi F et al.** Omeprazole: a comprehensive review. Pharmacotherapy. 1993;13:46.

40 **Vajda FJE et al.** Carbamazepine-erythromycin base interaction. Med J Aust. 1984;140:81. Letter.

41 **Caranco E et al.** Carbamazepine toxicity induced by concurrent erythromycin therapy. Arch Neurol. 1985;42:187–88.

42 **Kessler JM et al.** Erythromycin-carbamazepine interaction. S Afr Med J. 1985;67:1038. Letter.

43 **Jaster PJ et al.** Erythromycin-carbamazepine interaction. Neurology. 1986; 36:594–95. Letter.

44 **Wroblewski BA et al.** Carbamazepine-erythromycin interaction: case studies and clinical significance. JAMA. 1986;255:1165–167.

45 **Goulden KJ et al.** Severe carbamazepine intoxication after coadministration of erythromycin. J Pediatr. 1986;109:135–37.

46 **Berrettini WH.** A case of erythromycin-induced carbamazepine toxicity. J Clin Psychiatry. 1986;47:147.

47 **Zetelli BJ et al.** Erythromycin-induced drug interactions: an illustrative case and review of the literature. Clin Pediatr. 1987;26:117–19.

48 **Mitsch RA.** Carbamazepine toxicity precipitated by intravenous erythromycin. DICP Ann Pharmacother. 1989; 23:878–79.

49 **Wong YY et al.** Effect of erythromycin on carbamazepine kinetics. Clin Pharmacol Ther. 1983;33:460–64.

50 **Turner PV et al.** The interaction between carbamazepine and erythromycin. Can J Physiol Pharmacol. 1989;67:582–86.

Chapter 4

Interpretation of Clinical Laboratory Tests

Lloyd Y Young
Eileen G Holland

General Principles 4-1
  Normal Values 4-2
  Laboratory Error 4-2
    Spoiled specimen 4-2
    Specimen taken at wrong time 4-2
    Incomplete specimen 4-2
    Faulty reagents 4-2
    Technical errors 4-2
    Diagnostic and therapeutic procedures 4-2
    Diet 4-2
    Medication 4-2
  Units of Measure (See Table 4.1) 4-2

Electrolytes 4-3
  Sodium 4-3
    Hyponatremia 4-3
    Hypernatremia 4-3
  Potassium 4-3
    Hypokalemia 4-3
    Hyperkalemia 4-5
  Carbon Dioxide Content (See Equations 4.1 and 4.2) 4-5
  Chloride 4-6
    Hyper- and hypochloremia (See Equation 4.3) 4-6
  Anion Gap 4-6
  Osmolality (See Equations 4.4 and 4.5) 4-6

Blood Chemistry (See Table 4.2) 4-7
  SMA-6, SMA-12, and Chem Profile-20 4-7
  Calcium 4-7
    Hypocalcemia 4-8
    Hypercalcemia 4-8
  Phosphate 4-8
    Hyper- and hypophosphatemia 4-8
  Glucose 4-8
    Hyper- and hypoglycemia 4-8
  Uric Acid 4-8
  Blood Urea Nitrogen (BUN) 4-9
  Creatinine 4-9
  Creatinine Clearance (Cl_{Cr}) (See Equations 4.6 to 4.9
    and Table 4.3) 4-9
  Lactic Dehydrogenase (LD) 4-10
  Creatine Kinase (CK) 4-10
  Albumin 4-11
  Globulin 4-11
  Aspartate Aminotransferase (AST) 4-11

Alanine Aminotransferase (ALT) 4-11
Alkaline Phosphatase 4-11
Gamma-Glutamyl Transferase (GGT) 4-12
Bilirubin (See Figure 4.1) 4-12
  Causes of increased bilirubin 4-12
    Hepatocellular damage 4-12
    Cholestasis (posthepatic) 4-12
    Hemolysis (prehepatic) 4-12
Acid Phosphatase 4-12
Prostate-Specific Antigen (PSA) 4-12

Hematology (See Table 4.4) 4-13
  Complete Blood Count (CBC) 4-13
    Red Blood Cells (RBCs) 4-14
    Hematocrit (Hct) 4-14
    Hemoglobin (Hgb) 4-14
    Red Cell Indices (Wintrobe Indices) 4-14
      MCV (See Equation 4.10) 4-14
      MCH (See Equation 4.11) 4-14
      MCHC (See Equation 4.12) 4-14
    Reticulocytes 4-14
    Erythrocyte Sedimentation Rate (ESR) 4-14
    White Blood Cells (WBCs) 4-15
      Neutrophils 4-15
      Agranulocytosis and absolute neutrophil
        count (ANC) 4-16
      Tissue injury (See Table 4.5) 4-16
      Lymphocytes 4-16
      Monocytes 4-16
      Eosinophils 4-16
      Basophils 4-16
  Coagulation Studies 4-17
    Activated partial thromboplastin time (aPPT) 4-17
    Prothrombin time (PT) 4-17
    International normalized ratio (INR;
      See Equation 4.13) 4-17

Urinalysis (UA) 4-18
  Gross Appearance of Specimen 4-18
  Specimen pH 4-18
  Specific Gravity 4-18
  Protein 4-18
  Microscopic Examination 4-18
  Urine Drug Screening (See Table 4.7) 4-19

Serum Drug Concentrations (See Table 4.8) 4-19

This chapter will introduce the reader to some of the most frequently encountered laboratory tests utilized in clinical medicine. Specialized laboratory tests that commonly are used to monitor specific disease states or specific drug therapy will be integrated into the case histories, questions, and answers in subsequent chapters of this book rather than in this introductory chapter.

Students will find Richard Ravel's *Clinical Laboratory Medicine* (Yearbook Medical Publishers, Inc.), Frances Fischbach's *A Manual of Laboratory and Diagnostic Tests* (J.B. Lippincott Company), or Scott L. Traub's *Basic Skills in Interpreting Laboratory Data* (American Society of Hospital Pharmacists) essential in the clinical setting. If a more comprehensive review of clinical labo-

ratory tests is needed, the reader is referred to the most recent edition of *Clinical Diagnosis and Management by Laboratory Methods* published by W.B. Saunders (Philadelphia). The major pharmacokinetic and pharmacodynamic principles governing the clinical use of specific drugs are reviewed critically in *Applied Pharmacokinetics: Principles of Therapeutic Drug Monitoring* (Applied Therapeutics, Inc.).

General Principles

The serum, urine, and other fluids of patients are analyzed routinely; however, the economic cost of obtaining these data always must be balanced by benefits to patient outcomes. Generally, laboratory tests only should be ordered if the results of the test will affect decisions on the therapeutic management of the patient. There is little justification for frequent multiorgan baseline studies in the absence of a suspected problem or diagnosis.

Normal Values

The results of clinical laboratory tests falling within a predetermined range of values are termed ''normal'' and those outside this range are called ''abnormal.'' Abnormal laboratory values are not always of diagnostic significance (see Question 1); and normal values sometimes can be interpreted as being abnormal in some diseases (see Question 2). Various factors (e.g., age, sex, weight, height, time since last meal, drugs) can affect the range of normal values for a given test.

Clinical laboratories may analyze sample specimens by different laboratory methods; therefore, each laboratory has its own set of normal values. When a laboratory department changes its analytical procedures or equipment, normal values also will change accordingly. Consequently, clinicians should use the normal values listed by their own clinical laboratory facility when interpreting laboratory test results in preference to those published in reference texts.

Laboratory Error

The possibility of laboratory error always must be considered when laboratory results do not correlate with clinical expectations. Common sources of laboratory error are as follows:

Spoiled Specimen. Improper handling, improper preservation, or undue delay in analyzing the specimen may invalidate test results. For example, if a blood sample is allowed to hemolyze, a spurious hyperkalemia may be noted because potassium concentrations are higher within erythrocytes than in plasma.

Specimen Taken at Wrong Time. The concentrations of substances in biological fluids can be influenced by time of day and relationship to meals, as well as other factors. Thus, specimens obtained at improper times can yield misleading test results.

Incomplete Specimen. Studies requiring 24-hour collections (e.g., urine) can be a source of error because of the difficulty inherent in the collection of every sample specimen throughout the 24-hour period.

Faulty Reagents. Reagents which are prepared improperly or those which have deteriorated (more likely with infrequently ordered tests) may produce erroneous results.

Technical Errors. Laboratory personnel may make an error in reading an instrument or making a calculation. Patient names and samples might be interchanged, or results can be transcribed incorrectly.

Diagnostic and Therapeutic Procedures. Some diagnostic and therapeutic procedures can alter laboratory test results. For example, digital examination of the prostate can increase the serum concentration of acid phosphatase, and electrocardioversion can increase the serum concentration of creatine kinase (CK).

Diet. Certain foods contain substances which can appear in biological fluids and interfere with various laboratory tests.

Medication. Drugs can alter laboratory results by:

- Interfering with the testing procedure. For example, spironolactone can interfere with some digoxin assays, resulting in false increases in the serum concentration of digoxin. Digoxin assays utilizing sheep antibodies may be less likely to be affected by spironolactone than digoxin assays using rabbit antibodies.[1]

- Altering laboratory values by virtue of their pharmacological or toxicological properties. For example, thiazide diuretics can increase uric acid serum concentrations by inhibiting the tubular secretion of urate.

Units of Measure

The Systeme International (SI) units of measure is a method of reporting clinical laboratory values in a standard metric format. The basic unit of mass for the SI system is the mole which is not influenced by the added weight of salt or ester formulations. It is technically and pharmacologically more meaningful than the gram because each physiologic reaction occurs on a molecular level.

When substances are expressed in mass concentration units (e.g., mg), the amount of the substance relative to others in the body is unclear. For example, a substance of a high molecular weight can react with a substance of low molecular weight on a molar to molar basis. Yet, the number of moles of these substances relative to each other is not readily apparent to most clinicians. The use of SI units, therefore, would make it possible to better appreciate the influence of albumin concentrations on the binding of drugs. The SI system is based upon fundamental units for measuring quantity from which derivations are made (see Table 4.1).

Efforts to implement the SI system internationally began in the 1970s and resulted in the adoption of full-SI transition policies by several major medical and pharmaceutical journals in the late 1980s.[2,3] However, acceptance of this system has met resistance among many American clinicians. In January 1992, in recognition of this resistance, two major medical journals announced adjustments to their former policies and compromised by reporting both the SI units and conventional U.S. units or a method for conversion between the two.[4,5] The most appropriate method to report clinical laboratory values remains controversial. Proponents of further implementation of the SI system argue that its adoption by the U.S. would further enhance international collaboration in the medical field. Proponents of continuing the use of conventional units claim that conversion to SI units offers little benefit in daily use and its adoption would require learning unfamiliar reference ranges, with the possibility for errors. For an effective conversion to the SI reporting system in the U.S., there must be a concerted effort within the medical community to implement the change. During the transition period, many journals will compromise and report

Table 4.1	SI Units and Symbols	
Physical Quantity Measured	Unit	Symbol
Length	Meter	m
Mass	Kilogram	kg
Time	Second	s
Amount of substance	Mole	mol
Temperature	Kelvin	K
Electric current	Ampere	A
Luminous intensity	Candela	Cd
Area	Square meter	m^2
Volume	Cubic meter	m^3
Force	Newton	N
Pressure	Pascal	Pa
Work energy	Joule	J
Density	Kilogram per cubic meter	kg/m^3
Frequency	Hertz	Hz

both figures or conversion factors, and clinicians and students should be aware of these figures.

In this chapter, laboratory values will be expressed in traditional units and the comparable SI units will be placed at the end of a question. Table 4.1 lists the units and corresponding SI symbols. Conversion factors for changing common individual laboratory values from the traditional units to SI units can be found in Table 4.2 (Blood Chemistry Reference Values), Table 4.4 (Hematologic Laboratory Values), and Table 4.7 (Drug Concentrations). Comprehensive conversion tables and guides are available.[6]

Electrolytes

Sodium

Sodium (135 to 147 mEq/L or mmol/L) is the predominant cation of the extracellular fluid. Along with chloride, potassium, and water, sodium is important in establishing osmotic pressure relationships between intracellular and extracellular fluids. An increase in the serum sodium concentration may signify impaired sodium excretion or dehydration. Conversely, a decrease in the serum sodium concentration to less than normal values may reflect over-hydration, abnormal sodium losses, or sodium starvation. Healthy individuals are able to maintain their sodium balance without difficulty; however, patients with kidney failure, heart failure, or pulmonary disease often have problems with sodium and water balance. In adults, changes in serum sodium concentration most often represent water imbalances and not salt imbalances. Hence, the serum sodium concentration often is a reliable indicator of a patient's fluid status rather than sodium balance.

Hyponatremia

Hyponatremia may be related to dilution of serum sodium or to total body depletion of sodium. Since water moves freely across cell membranes in response to oncotic pressures, hyponatremia simply means that sodium is diluted throughout all body fluids. Dilutional hyponatremia occurs whenever the extracellular fluid compartment expands without an equivalent increase in sodium. Clinical conditions such as cirrhosis, congestive heart failure (CHF), and nephrosis, or the administration of osmotically active solutes such as albumin or mannitol, commonly are associated with dilutional hyponatremia.

Hyponatremia which results from sodium depletion presents as a low serum sodium concentration in the absence of edema. Sodium depletion hyponatremia might be due to mineralocorticoid deficiencies, sodium-wasting renal disease, or replacement of sodium-containing fluid losses with nonsaline solutions.

Hypernatremia

Hypernatremia represents a state of relative water deficiency and hence excessive concentrations of sodium in all body fluids (hypertonicity). Therefore, hypernatremia can be caused by the loss of free water, loss of hypotonic fluid, or excessive sodium intake. Free water loss is uncommon except in the presence of diabetes insipidus. Fluid loss which occurs with gastroenteritis is the most common cause of hypotonic fluid loss in infants and the elderly (the "nursing home prune syndrome"). Excessive salt intoxication usually is accidental or iatrogenic resulting from intravenous administration of hypertonic salt solutions. In addition, some beta-lactam antibiotics (e.g., ticarcillin) contain a modest sodium load and can cause fluid overload when high doses are administered.

The primary defense against hypertonicity is thirst and subsequent fluid intake. Therefore, hypernatremic syndromes usually occur in patients who are unable to drink sufficient fluids. Infants who cannot demand fluid or patients who are vomiting, comatose, or not allowed oral fluids are at greatest risk for the development of hypernatremia.

1. T.T., a 75-year-old woman, was hospitalized with a chief complaint of increasing shortness of breath (SOB) and orthopnea over the past week. She had been treated previously for CHF, but has not taken any medication over the past 2 weeks. T.T. was noted to have severe (4+) pedal edema and to be in severe respiratory distress. An SMA-6 was ordered and revealed the following blood chemistries: sodium (Na) 123 mEq/L (Normal: 135–147); potassium (K) 4.1 mEq/L (Normal: 3.5–5.0); chloride (Cl) 90 mEq/L (Normal: 95–105); carbon dioxide (CO_2) 28 mEq/L (Normal: 22–28); blood urea nitrogen (BUN) 30 mg/dL (Normal: 8–18); and glucose 100 mg/dL (Normal: 70–110). Why should T.T., with a serum sodium concentration of 123 mEq/L, not be given sodium chloride to return her serum sodium concentration to normal values? [SI units: Na 123 mmol/L; K 4.1 mmol/L; Cl 90 mmol/L; CO_2 28 mmol/L; BUN 10.7 mmol/L UREA; glucose 5.5 mmol/L]

All body fluids are in osmotic equilibrium and changes in serum sodium concentration are associated with shifts of water into and out of cells. The serum sodium concentration should not be used as an index of sodium need because cell membranes are freely permeable to water. The serum sodium concentration does not reflect total body sodium content. The serum sodium concentration, however, does detect water balance disturbances because the serum sodium concentration is a significant component of body osmolality.

In T.T. with 4+ pedal edema and CHF, the serum concentration of sodium probably is low because the plasma volume is increased relative to sodium. The usual treatment of this type of hyponatremia is salt and water restriction plus diuretics. (See Chapters 15: Congestive Heart Failure and 28: Fluid and Electrolyte Disorders for further discussion.)

Potassium

The major intracellular cation in the body is potassium (3.5 to 5.0 mEq/L or mmol/L); approximately 3500 mEq of potassium are contained in the body of a 70 kg person. Only about 10% of this total body concentration of potassium is extracellular, and only about 50 mEq are in the extracellular fluid. The potassium ion is filtered freely at the glomerulus of the kidney; reabsorbed in the proximal tubule; and secreted into the distal segments of the renal nephron.

The serum potassium concentration is not a good measure of total body potassium because most of the potassium is sequestered within cells. Intracellular potassium, however, cannot be measured easily. Fortunately, the clinical manifestations of potassium deficiency (fatigue, drowsiness, dizziness, confusion, electrocardiographic changes, muscle weakness, and pain) correlate well with serum concentrations.

The serum potassium concentration is buffered and may be within normal limits despite abnormalities in total body potassium. During potassium depletion, potassium moves from the intracellular fluid (ICF) into the extracellular fluid (ECF) to maintain the serum concentration. There is about a 100 mEq total body potassium deficit when the serum concentration decreases by only 0.3 mEq/L. Consequently, serum potassium concentrations may be misleading and no assumptions may be made as to the status of total body potassium concentrations.

Hypokalemia

The renal system is responsible for about 90% of daily potassium losses (about 40 to 90 mEq/day). The gastrointestinal (GI) system and sweating account for the remainder of potassium losses.

The kidney has a limited ability to conserve potassium. Even when potassium intake is reduced to zero, the urine will contain at

Table 4.2				Blood Chemistry Reference Values
Laboratory Test[a]	**Normal Reference Values**		**Conversion Factor**	**Comments**
	Conventional Units	**SI Units**		
Acid Phosphatase	0–3 KA units[a]	0–5.5 U/L	1	From prostate; different form in erythrocytes and platelets. ↑ in prostatic carcinoma or vigorous prostatic massage
ALT	0–3.5 U/L	0–3.5 U/L[b]	1	From heart, liver, muscle, kidney, pancreas. ↑ negligible unless parenchymal liver disease. More liver-specific than AST
Albumin	4–6 gm/dL	40–60 gm/L	10	Produced in liver; important for intravascular osmotic pressure. ↓ in liver disease, malnutrition, ascites, hemorrhage, protein-wasting nephropathy
Alk Phos	30–120 U/L	30–120 U/L	1	Large amounts in bile ducts, placenta, bone. ↑ in bile duct obstruction, obstructive liver disease, rapid bone growth (e.g., Paget's)
AST	0–35 U/L	0–35 U/L	1	High in heart and liver; moderate in muscle, kidney, and pancreas. ↑ with myocardial infarction and liver injury
Bilirubin				Breakdown product of hemoglobin, bound to albumin, conjugated (direct) in liver. ↑ with hemolysis, cholestasis, liver injury
Total	0.1–1 mg/dL	2–18 μmol/L	17.1	
Direct	0–0.2 mg/dL	0–4 μmol/L	17.1	
BUN	8–18 mg/dL	3–6.5 mmol/L	0.357	End product of protein metabolism, produced by liver, transported in blood, excreted renally. ↑ in renal dysfunction, high protein intake, GI bleeding, esophageal varices, dehydration
Calcium				Regulated by body skeleton redistribution, parathyroid hormone, vitamin D, calcitonin. Plasma level affected by changes in albumin concentration (40% bound to albumin)
Total	8.8–10.2 mg/dL	2.20–2.56 mmol/L	0.250	
	4.4–5.1 mEq/L	2.20–2.56 mmol/L	0.250	
Unbound	4–4.6 mg/dL	1.0–1.15 mmol/L	0.250	Physiologically active form. Unbound "free" calcium unchanged as albumin fluctuates. Total calcium ↓ when albumin ↓
	2.0–2.3 mEq/L	1.0–1.15 mmol/L	0.250	
CO_2 Content	22–28 mEq/L	22–28 mmol/L	1	Sum of HCO_3 and dissolved CO_2. Reflects acid-base balance and compensatory pulmonary (CO_2) and renal (HCO_3) mechanisms. Primarily reflects HCO_3
Chloride	95–105 mEq/L	95–105 mmol/L	1	Important for acid-base balance. ↓ by GI loss of chloride-rich fluid (vomiting, diarrhea, GI suction, intestinal fistulas, overdiuresis)
Cholesterol				Desirable = Total <200; LDL <130; HDL >50 mg/dL; ↑ LDL or ↓ HDL equals risk factor for cardiovascular disease. High in hypothyroid, nephrotic syndrome, systemic lupus erythematosus, multiple myeloma, obstructive liver disease
Total	<200 mg/dL	<5.2 mmol/L	0.02586	
LDL[a]	<130 mg/dL	<3.362 mmol/L	0.02586	
HDL[a]	>50 mg/dL	>1.29 mmol/L	0.02586	
CK	0–150 U/L	0–150 U/L	1	In tissues that use high energy (skeletal muscle, myocardium, brain). ↑ by IM injections, myocardial infarction, acute psychotic episodes. Isoenzyme CK-MM in skeletal muscle; CK-MB in myocardium; CK-BB in brain. MB Fraction >5% in MI[a]
Creatinine	0.6–1.2 mg/dL	50–110 μmol/L	88.4	Major constituent of muscle; rate of formation constant; affected by muscle mass; excreted renally. ↑ in renal dysfunction. Cimetidine and trimethoprim interfere
Cl_{Cr}	75–125 mL/min	1.24–2.08 mL/s	0.01667	Reflects glomerular filtration rate; ↓ in renal dysfunction
GGT	0–30 U/L	0–30 U/L	1	Sensitive test reflecting hepatocellular injury; not helpful in differentiating liver disorders. Usually high in chronic alcoholics
Globulin	2.3–3.5 gm/dL	23–35 gm/L	10	Active role in immunological mechanisms. Immunoglobulins ↑ in chronic infection, rheumatoid arthritis, multiple myeloma
Glucose	70–110 mg/dL	3.9–6.1 mmol/L	0.05551	↑ in diabetes or by adrenal corticosteroids
Iron				Body stores 2/3 in hemoglobin; 1/3 in bone marrow, spleen, liver; only small amount present in plasma. Blood loss major cause of deficiency. ↑ needs in pregnancy and lactation
Male	80–180 μg/dL	14–32 μmol/L	0.1791	
Female	60–160 μg/dL	11–29 μmol/L	0.1791	
TIBC	250–460 μg/dL	45–82 μmol/L	0.1791	↑ capacity to bind iron with iron deficiency
LD	50–150 U/L	50–150 U/L	1	High in heart, kidney, liver, and skeletal muscle. 5 isoenzymes — LD_1 mostly in heart, LD_5 mostly liver and skeletal muscle. Pleural fluid to serum LD ratio >0.6 suggests exudative rather than transudative effusion
Magnesium	1.6–2.4 mEq/L	0.8–1.20 mmol/L	0.5 1	Malabsorption, severe diarrhea, alcoholism, pancreatitis, diuretics, hyperaldosteronism causes for hypomagnesemia (symptoms of weakness, depression, agitation, seizures, hypokalemia, and arrhythmias). Renal failure can cause hypermagnesemia
	1.8–3.0 mg/dL	0.8–1.20 mmol/L	0.5 1	

Continued

Table 4.2	Blood Chemistry Reference Values (Continued)			
	Normal Reference Values		Conversion	
Laboratory Test[a]	Conventional Units	SI Units	Factor	Comments
Phosphate[c]	2.5–5 mg/dL	8.8–1.60 mmol/L	0.3229	↑ with renal dysfunction, hypervitaminosis D, and hypoparathyroidism. ↓ with excess aluminum antacids, malabsorption, renal losses
Potassium	3.5–5 mEq/L	3.5–5 mmol/L	1	↑ by renal dysfunction, acidosis, hemolysis, burns, crush injuries. ↓ by diuretics, alkalosis, protracted vomiting, severe diarrhea
Sodium	135–147 mEq/L	135–147 mmol/L	1	Low sodium usually because of dilution with water (e.g., excess serum antidiuretic hormone) and treated with water restriction
SGOT	See AST			
SGPT	See ALT			
Triglycerides	<160 mg/dL	<1.80 mmol/L	0.01129	↑ by alcohol, saturated fats, drugs (propranolol, diuretics, oral contraceptives)
Uric acid	2–7 mg/dL	120–420 μmol/L	59.48	↑ in gout, neoplastic, or myeloproliferative disorders, and drugs (diuretics, niacin, low-dose salicylate, cyclosporine)

[a] Alk Phos = Alkaline phosphatase; AST = Aspartate aminotransferase; BUN = Blood urea nitrogen; CO_2 = Carbon dioxide; CK = Creatine kinase, formerly known as creatine phosphokinase (CPK); Cl $_{Cr}$= Creatinine clearance; GGT = Gamma glutamyl transferase; KA units = King-Armstrong units; LD = Lactate dehydrogenase, formerly known as LDH; LDL = Low-density lipoprotein; HDL = High-density lipoprotein; MI = Myocardial infarction; SGOT = Serum glutamate axaloacetic transaminase; SGPT = Serum glutamate pyruvate transaminase; TIBC = Total iron binding capacity.

[b] Enzyme activity can be reported as U/L where 1 unit equals the amount of enzyme generating 1 μmol of product per minute, or as a katal (kat) unit which reports product formation in moles per second. The U/L will be used in this book rather than the katal.

[c] Phosphate as inorganic phosphorus.

least 5 to 20 mEq of potassium per 24 hours. Therefore, prolonged intravenous therapy with potassium-free solutions in a patient who is unable to eat can result in hypokalemia. Hypokalemia also can be induced by osmotic diuretics (e.g., mannitol) or by substantial glucosuria. Thiazide or loop diuretics commonly cause hypokalemia, as does excessive mineralocorticoid activity.

Protracted vomiting is another common cause of potassium depletion. Although the fluid secreted along most of the upper GI tract contains only 5 to 20 mEq/L of potassium, vomiting of this fluid in conjunction with decreased food intake, loss of acid, loss of sodium, and the development of alkalosis all combine to produce hypokalemia. Severe diarrhea especially leads to potassium depletion because of the loss of large volumes of colonic fluid containing 30 to 40 mEq/L of potassium. Stimulation of β_2-adrenergic receptors and insulin are other causes of hypokalemia because these processes facilitate the intracellular movement of potassium.

Hyperkalemia

Hyperkalemia most often results from decreased renal excretion of potassium, excessive exogenous potassium administration, or excessive cellular breakdown (e.g., hemolysis, burns, crush injuries, surgery, infections). Additionally, metabolic acidosis may induce hyperkalemia as hydrogen ions move into the cell in exchange for potassium and sodium.

Potassium excesses or deficits primarily affect the excitability of nerve and muscle tissue. As a result, cardiac function can be affected adversely. Potassium also affects certain enzyme systems, acid-base balance, and carbohydrate and protein metabolism.

2. K.C., a 27-year-old male with insulin dependent diabetes mellitus (IDDM), was hospitalized for ketoacidosis. His blood sugar was 918 mg/dL (Normal: 70–110); urine output was 135 mL/hr (Normal: 50); urine was positive (4+) for sugar and ketones. K.C.'s blood pH was 7.1 and his serum potassium concentration was 4.1 mEq/L. Why should the clinician monitoring K.C. be concerned about the ''normal'' potassium serum concentration? [SI units: sugar 51.0 mmol/L, (Normal: 3.9–6.1) K 4.1 mmol/L]

Treatment of K.C.'s diabetic ketoacidosis without supplemental potassium could result in life-threatening hypokalemia. When the pH of the blood is acidic, potassium shifts out of cells in response to increased concentrations of intracellular hydrogen ion. Although K.C.'s total body potassium concentration is decreased as a result of glycosuria and polyuria, the serum potassium concentration appears ''normal'' because acidosis has shifted potassium from intracellular storage sites into the circulating plasma volume. When the acidosis and hyperglycemia are corrected, the serum potassium concentration will decrease dramatically if potassium supplementation is not provided. As a very general guideline, every 0.1 unit pH change from 7.4 will alter the serum potassium concentration by about 0.6 mEq/L. Since K.C.'s pH is 7.1 (i.e., 0.3 units <7.4), his serum potassium concentration will be about 2.3 mEq/L when the acidosis is corrected and potassium returns intracellularly (i.e., three 0.1 units × 0.6 mEq/L = 1.8 mEq/L; and 4.1 mEq/L − 1.8 mEq/L = 2.3 mEq/L). (See Chapter 28: Fluid and Electrolyte Disorders for a thorough presentation on the treatment of fluid and electrolyte disorders.)

Carbon Dioxide Content

The carbon dioxide content (22 to 28 mEq/L or mmol/L) in the serum represents the sum of the bicarbonate concentration and the concentration of dissolved carbon dioxide in the serum. Although there are several buffer systems in the body (including hemoglobin, phosphate, and protein), the carbonic acid-sodium bicarbonate system is the most important in regulating pH within physiological limits. From a clinical standpoint, most disturbances of acid-base balance can be considered in terms of imbalances in this system.

Combinations of weak acids and strong bases are called buffer systems because they resist changes in hydrogen ion concentration by binding and releasing H^+. For example, the bicarbonate ions bind hydrogen ions to form carbonic acid as follows:

$$HCO_3^- + H^+ \leftrightarrows H_2CO_3 \leftrightarrows H_2O + CO_2 \qquad \text{Eq 4.1}$$

Normally a ratio of one part carbonic acid to 20 parts bicarbonate is present in the extracellular fluid. This ratio is uniquely important and can be appreciated best when viewed in the context of the Henderson-Hasselbalch equation (Eq 4.2).

$$pH = pKa + \log \frac{[Salt]}{[Acid]} \qquad Eq\ 4.2$$

$$= pKa + \log \frac{HCO_3^-}{H_2CO_3}$$

$$= 6.1 + \log \frac{20}{1}$$

$$= 7.4$$

This equation unequivocally states that it is the *ratio* of HCO_3^- to H_2CO_3 (or pCO_2) and *not* the absolute value of either one which defines the pH or acid-base status of the patient. To assess the acid-base status of the patient accurately, two of the three variables (pH, pCO_2, bicarbonate) must be known. The bicarbonate concentration, by itself, does not determine a patient's acid-base balance and neither does the pH.

Decreases in blood pH (acidosis) may be compensated for by either "blowing off" CO_2 from the lungs or by excreting H^+ in the urine. Increases in pH (alkalosis) result in compensatory retention of CO_2 by the lungs.

In clinical practice, the serum bicarbonate concentration is measured because the acid-base balance can be inferred if a patient has normal pulmonary function based upon past medical history and present bedside evaluation. For example, if a clinician reasonably can conclude that a patient's pCO_2 would not be greatly altered because of normal pulmonary function, an increase in measured serum bicarbonate concentration most likely would indicate alkalosis based upon the Henderson-Hasselbalch equation. (See Chapter 27: Acid-Base Disorders for additional clinical examples.)

Chloride

Hyper- and Hypochloremia

Chloride (95 to 105 mEq/L or mmol/L) is the principal inorganic anion of the extracellular fluid and is important in the maintenance of acid-base balance. A decreased serum chloride concentration often accompanies metabolic alkalosis, whereas an increased serum chloride concentration may be indicative of a hyperchloremic metabolic acidosis. The serum chloride, however, also may be slightly decreased in acidosis if organic acids or other acids are the primary cause of the acidosis. Clinically, hyperchloremia in the absence of metabolic acidosis seldom is encountered because chloride retention usually is accompanied by sodium and water retention. Hypochloremia may result from excessive gastrointestinal loss of chloride-rich fluid (e.g., vomiting, diarrhea, gastric suctioning, intestinal fistulas). Since chloride ions are excreted renally with cations, hypochloremia also may result from significant diuresis.

Generally, alteration in the serum concentration of chloride seldom is the primary indicator of a major medical problem. The serum chloride level *per se* has no real diagnostic significance. In fact, the only real reason for measuring the serum chloride is to validate the serum sodium concentration. The relationship between serum concentrations of sodium, bicarbonate, and chloride can be described by Equation 4.3 as follows (where R is the anion gap):

$$Cl^- + HCO_3^- + R = Na^+ \qquad Eq\ 4.3$$

Anion Gap

The R factor (or anion gap) represents the contribution of unmeasured acids. Although it may vary widely under different clinical conditions, it normally has a value of 10. If the anion gap is established for a given patient by measuring the serum concentrations of chloride, bicarbonate, and sodium at the same time, sub-sequent electrolyte measurements can be checked against each other because the anion gap should remain fairly constant or at least change in a predictable manner.[7]

An elevated anion gap may result from metabolic acidosis (e.g., caused by lactic acids, ketoacids, salicylic acids, methanol, ethylene glycol); sodium salts of strong acids with "unmeasured anions" (e.g., sodium citrate, sodium acetate); or certain antibiotics (e.g., carbenicillin) in high doses. A low anion gap may be the result of reduced concentrations of unmeasured anions (e.g., hypoalbuminemia), or from systematic underestimation of serum sodium (e.g., hyperviscosity of myeloma). (See Chapter 27: Acid-Base Disorders for a discussion of the clinical use of the anion gap.)

3. The electrolyte values for K.C. (the patient in Question 2) were as follows: Na 130 mEq/L; Cl 100 mEq/L; and HCO_3^- 20 mEq/L. The following evening's laboratory results were: Na 140 mEq/L; Cl 100 mEq/L; and HCO_3^- 20 mEq/L. Why is this second set of laboratory results suspicious? [SI units: Na 130 and 140 mmol/L; Cl 100 mmol/L; HCO_3^- 20 mmol/L]

K.C.'s R fraction has increased from 10 to 20 and the R fraction should be fairly constant. There is either a laboratory error in reporting these electrolyte values, or organic acids and/or other acids are accumulating in K.C. In this particular case, the possibility of ketoacidosis should be considered because K.C. is diabetic. Otherwise, one would have to question the validity of these electrolyte values.

Osmolality

The osmolality (280 to 300 mOsm/kg or mmol/kg) of a solution is a measure of the osmotic strength, or number of osmotically active ions (i.e., particles present) per unit of solution. It is the total number of particles in the solution, not the weight of the particle or the nature of the particle, that determines osmolality. Since one mole of a substance contains 6×10^{23} molecules, equimolar concentrations of all substances in the undissociated state exert the same osmotic pressure. A mole of an ionized compound such as NaCl contributes twice as many particles in solution as one mole of an undissociated compound such as glucose.

The principle determinants of serum osmolality in most situations are sodium (and its accompanying anions), glucose, and urea. If one corrects for the concentrations of glucose and urea, the serum concentration of sodium closely mirrors the serum osmolality. The serum osmolality can be calculated as follows:

$$Osmolality^* = 1.86\,[Na^+] + \frac{[Glucose]}{18} + \frac{[BUN]}{2.8} \qquad Eq\ 4.4$$

*Osmolality is measured in mOsm/kg H_2O

Under normal physiological conditions, only about 93% of sodium chloride dissociates in plasma; hence, the osmolality for sodium chloride in plasma is $1.86 \times$ molality. The glucose and BUN concentrations are divided by 18 and 2.8 respectively in order to convert the units from mg/dL to mmol/L. A more simplified formula useful for rule of thumb calculations is:

$$Osmolality^* = 2\,[Na^+] + \frac{[Glucose]}{20} + \frac{[BUN]}{2.8} \qquad Eq\ 4.5$$

*Osmolality is measured in mOsm/kg H_2O

If the measured serum osmolality exceeds the calculated serum osmolality by more than 10 mOsm/kg H_2O, then clinicians must consider the possibility of decreased water content in the serum because of hyperlipidemia or hypoproteinemia; the presence of substantial amounts of low-molecular weight substances (e.g., ethanol, methanol, isopropyl alcohol, acetone, paraldehyde, ethyl ether, ethylene glycol); or laboratory error. The difference between the measured serum osmolality and the calculated serum osmolality commonly is referred to as the "osmol gap."

Although the serum osmolality commonly is measured to evaluate hyponatremia, it is of limited usefulness in this disorder. Tonicity is more important than osmolality in the clinical assessment of hydration because tonicity measures the movement of water across a semipermeable membrane. Some solutes, such as urea and alcohol, freely enter cells, and thereby, can increase the measured osmolality without affecting tonicity. These solutes do not shift water out of cells, and, therefore, do not affect water balance or the serum sodium concentration. However, impermeable solutes such as sodium or mannitol, in the extracellular fluid increase tonicity and pull water out of cells. As a result, measurement of serum osmolality is unnecessary for the evaluation of hyponatremia unless the diagnosis of hyperlipidemia or hypoproteinemia is a consideration.[8]

Osmolality also can be used in the evaluation of renal function by comparing the ratio of urine to plasma (or serum) osmolality (U/P osmol ratio). The ratio of urine to serum osmolality ranges from 1:1 to 3:1. This ratio validates the clinical finding that urine usually is more concentrated than plasma. If the kidney loses its ability to concentrate urine, the ratio of urine to serum osmolality cannot increase beyond a ratio of 1.2:1. For example, in acute and chronic renal dysfunction, the urine sodium is greater than 20 mEq/L and the U/P ratio is ≤1.2:1. In cases of prerenal azotemia, the U/P ratio is greater than 1.2:1 and urinary sodium is less than 20 mEq/L.[9–11]

In summary, measurement of serum osmolality assists in the determination of whether there are large deviations in water content and also whether low molecular weight substances are present in substantial amounts in the plasma.

4. Q.P., a 35-year-old male, was seen in the emergency room (ER) after complaining of a peculiar whiteness to his vision like a "snow field." He also reported being restless and short of breath with mild exertion. He had been watching television and drinking alcohol. He was afebrile, his blood pressure (BP) was 170/105 mm Hg, pulse 110 beats/min, and respiration 30/min. Physical examination was unremarkable, including a thorough eye examination. Routine laboratory studies showed: Na 135 mEq/L, K 4.7 mEq/L, Cl 107 mEq/L, HCO_3^- 9 mEq/L, pH 7.10, pCO_2 11 mm Hg, blood glucose 100 mg/dL, BUN 12 mg/dL, and serum osmolality 335 mOsm/kg H_2O. Blood ethanol level was 100 mg/dL and blood methanol was 50 mg/dL. Calculate the serum osmol gap and explain why it is high. Why was the osmolality measured? [SI units: Na 135 mmol/L; K 4.7 mmol/L; Cl 107 mmol/L; HCO_3^- 9 mmol/L; pCO_2 1.5 kPa; glucose 5.5 mmol/L; BUN 4.3 mmol/L UREA; osmolality 335 mmol/kg; ethanol 21.7 mmol/L; methanol 15.6 mmol/L]

Patients presenting to an emergency room with a recent history of alcohol consumption complaining of whitish vision concurrent with restlessness and shortness of breath are highly suspect for methanol ingestion. The patient's calculated osmolality is determined from Equation 4.5 to be 279 mOsm/kg H_2O (2 × 135 + 100/20 + 12/3). The osmol gap is 335 − 279 or 56 mOsm/kg H_2O. An osmol gap greater than ten is suggestive of the presence of osmotically active substances in addition to the normal contributors to osmolality. Methanol, as indicated by a level of 50 mg/dL, is the osmotically active substance in this case which caused the osmol gap.[10,12]

Blood Chemistry
SMA-6, SMA-12, and Chem Profile-20

5. What are the advantages and disadvantages of biochemical profiles such as the Chem profile-20, SMA-12, or the SMA-6 ordered for T.T. (from Question 1)?

The SMA-6, SMA-12, and Chem profile-20 are compilations of 6, 12, or 20 biochemical tests that analyze blood chemistries on large-volume, automated instruments. Such tests have become increasingly "routine" procedures because they quickly provide basic information concerning organ function at relatively low cost. If abnormal values are noted, additional tests can be ordered to further investigate specific organ function. Nevertheless, the routine use of biochemical profiles is controversial. When biochemical profiles are ordered without regard to the clinical evidence in an individual patient (i.e., routine testing is done on all patients upon admission to a hospital), there is no evidence that such batteries of tests have improved patient care, lessened hospital costs, or shortened lengths of stay.

The SMA-6 blood chemistry panel typically analyzes the sodium, potassium, chloride, CO_2, BUN, and glucose concentrations. This particular blood chemistry panel rapidly provides insights into the nature of T.T.'s serum electrolytes, acid-base status, renal function, and metabolic state. If an SMA-12 is ordered instead of the SMA-6 panel, six additional blood chemistry tests are performed. These six additional tests usually include a determination of the serum concentrations of albumin, total protein, bilirubin, alkaline phosphatase, calcium, and creatinine. The creatinine provides a more specific evaluation of renal function than the BUN, and some of the other added tests provide an evaluation of liver function.

An abbreviated method to report the SMA-6 and serum creatinine which is used commonly by clinicians is as follows.

Na	Cl	BUN	Glucose
K	CO_2	Creatinine	

A Chem profile-20 provides an additional eight tests: phosphorus, cholesterol, triglycerides, uric acid, iron, lactic dehydrogenase (LD), aspartate aminotransferase (AST), and alanine aminotransferase (ALT). These eight tests provide additional information for a general evaluation of metabolism, cardiovascular risk factors, and liver function which are not provided by some SMA-6 or SMA-12 automated biochemical profiles. The cost of a Chem profile-20 seldom is much greater than that of an SMA-6 or SMA-12 because of the automated nature of these tests. Costs and the particular grouping of tests into an SMA-6, SMA-12, or chem profile-20 panel vary with different clinical laboratories.

Although additional automated blood chemistry tests are relatively inexpensive, the probability of obtaining a false "abnormal" test result increases with the number of tests. For example, an estimated 65% of patients would have at least one abnormal test result if 20 tests were performed. When faced with an unexpected abnormal test result, the clinician has the choice of ignoring it, repeating the test, or obtaining further tests for confirmation. The induced costs, inconvenience, and potential risk of further investigations may more than offset the initial benefits ascribed to profile testing. Although clinicians often state that they should follow-up on the unexpected abnormality, in practice most often they do not.[13] Therefore, laboratory abnormalities based upon routine biochemical profiles should be interpreted with appropriate caution.

Calcium

The total calcium (8.8 to 10.2 mg/dL or 2.20 to 2.56 mmol/L) content of normal adult humans is 20 to 25 gm/kg of fat-free tissue, and about 44% of this calcium is in the body skeleton. About 1% of the skeletal calcium is freely exchangeable with that in the extracellular fluid. This reservoir of calcium in bones maintains the concentration of calcium in the plasma constant despite pronounced changes in the external balance of calcium. If the homeostatic factors (i.e., parathyroid hormone, vitamin D, calcitonin) which regulate the calcium content of body fluid are intact, a patient may lose 25% to 30% of total body calcium without a change in the concentration of calcium ion in the plasma.

About 40% of the calcium in the extracellular fluid is bound to plasma proteins (especially with albumin); 5% to 15% is complexed with phosphate and citrate; and about 45% to 55% is in the unbound, ionized form. Most laboratories measure the total calcium concentration, although it is the free, ionized calcium level that is important physiologically and the form that is regulated closely.

Hypocalcemia

A reduced calcium concentration, or hypocalcemia, usually implies a deficiency in either the production or response to parathyroid hormone or vitamin D. The abnormality in the parathyroid hormone system may be due to hypoparathyroidism, pseudohypoparathyroidism, or hypomagnesemia. The abnormality in the vitamin D system may be caused by decreased nutritional intake; decreased absorption of vitamin D because of gastrectomy, chronic pancreatitis, or small bowel disease; decreased production of 25-hydroxycholecalciferol because of liver disease; increased metabolism of 25-hydroxycholecalciferol because of enzyme stimulating drugs (e.g., phenobarbital, phenytoin, rifampin); or decreased production of 1,25-dihydroxycholecalciferol because of chronic renal disease.

Hypercalcemia

An elevated calcium concentration commonly is associated with malignancy or metastatic diseases. Other causes of hypercalcemia include: hyperparathyroidism, Paget's disease, milk-alkali syndrome, granulomatous disorders, thiazide diuretics, or vitamin D intoxication.

6. V.C., a 38-year-old male, was hospitalized because of obtundation, somnolence, and severe alcohol intoxication. Laboratory tests revealed the following: albumin 2.0 gm/dL (Normal: 4–6), Ca 6.8 mg/dL (Normal: 8.8–10.2), total bilirubin 10.8 mg/dL (Normal: 0.1–1.0), serum AST 280 U/mL (Normal: 0–35 U/L), and alkaline phosphatase 240 IU/L (Normal: 30–120 U/L). Why should V.C. not be treated with calcium despite his apparently low serum concentration of calcium? [SI units: albumin 20 gm/L; Ca 1.7 mmol/L; total bilirubin 184.6 µmol/L; AST 280 U/L; Alkaline phosphatase 240 U/L]

This case presentation provides insufficient patient data to make a conclusion concerning treatment. Clinicians should not become so engrossed in the patient's ''numbers'' that the patient himself is overlooked. Always remember to *treat* the patient and *observe* laboratory tests; do not treat laboratory values. Furthermore, remember that serum calcium is partially bound to plasma proteins and the serum concentration is dependent upon the concentration of these plasma proteins, particularly albumin. If the concentration of plasma proteins is low, the reported serum calcium generally will be less than the lower limit of normal. Although it would be best to measure ionized calcium, available instrumentation and methodology make such measurement difficult on a routine basis. In the absence of a direct measurement of ionized calcium, a useful method to estimate a corrected value for serum calcium in the presence of a low serum albumin is to use the following rule: the total serum calcium will fall by 0.8 mg/dL for each 1.0 gm/dL decrease in serum albumin concentration. V.C.'s serum albumin concentration is about 3.0 mg/dL less than ''normal'' (5.0 mg/dL − 2.0 mg/dL = 3.0 mg/dL). Therefore, the amount of available ionized calcium in V.C. is comparable to that available if his serum calcium were 9.2 mg/dL (i.e., calculated ionized calcium = 3.0 × 0.8 = 2.4 mg/dL; ''corrected'' serum calcium = 2.4 + 6.8 = 9.2 mg/dL). The ''corrected'' serum calcium concentration is

within the normal range, therefore, V.C. should not be treated with calcium based upon the available data.

Phosphate

The extracellular concentration of phosphate, as inorganic phosphorus, (2.5 to 5.0 mg/dL or 0.80 to 1.60 mmol/L) is the prime determinant of the intracellular concentration, which in turn is the source of phosphate for adenosine triphosphate (ATP) and phospholipid synthesis. Intracellular phosphate also is important in the regulation of nucleotide degradation.

Hyper- and Hypophosphatemia

The extracellular fluid concentration of phosphate is influenced by parathyroid hormone, intestinal absorption, renal function, bone metabolism, and nutrition. Hyperphosphatemia most commonly is caused by renal insufficiency, although hypervitaminosis D and hypoparathyroidism also are significant causes. Moderate hypophosphatemia appears in malnourished patients, especially when anabolism is induced; in patients with excessive use of aluminum-containing antacids which bind phosphorus in the GI tract; in chronic alcoholics; and in septic patients. Clinical consequences of severe hypophosphatemia involve nervous system dysfunction, muscle weakness, rhabdomyolysis, cardiac irregularities, and dysfunction of leukocytes and erythrocytes.

Glucose

The glucose (70 to 110 mg/dL or 3.9 to 6.1 mmol/L) concentration in extracellular fluid is regulated closely by homeostatic mechanisms to provide body tissues with a ready source of energy. The plasma glucose concentration usually is measured in either the fasting or postprandial state depending upon the type of information desired. Generally, normal glucose values refer to the plasma glucose concentration in the fasting state. The specific laboratory assay of blood sugar determinations also must be considered, because different assay methods vary in specificity and sensitivity to glucose.

Hyper- and Hypoglycemia

Hyperglycemia and hypoglycemia are nonspecific signs of abnormal glucose metabolism. Diabetes mellitus is the most common cause of hyperglycemia, and insufficient carbohydrate intake because of a missed meal in a patient receiving insulin or another hypoglycemic medication is the most common cause of hypoglycemia. (See Chapter 48: Diabetes Mellitus for an in-depth presentation of laboratory tests associated with abnormal glucose metabolism.)

Uric Acid

Uric acid (2.0 to 7.0 mg/dL or 120 to 420 µmol/L) is an end-product of nucleoprotein metabolism. It serves no biological function, is not metabolized, and must be excreted renally. Gout usually is associated with increased serum concentrations of uric acid and deposits of monosodium urates.

Increased serum uric acid concentrations can result either from a decrease in renal urate excretion or from excessive urate production (e.g., from the nucleoprotein turnover that accompanies neoplastic or myeloproliferative disorders). Low serum uric acid concentrations are inconsequential and usually are reflective of drugs that have hypouricemic activity (e.g., high doses of salicylates). The determinants of the serum concentration of uric acid, the clinical implications of hyperuricemia, and the therapeutic management of uric acid disorders are presented in Chapter 40: Gout and Hyperuricemia.

Blood Urea Nitrogen (BUN)

Urea nitrogen (8 to 18 mg/dL or 3.0 to 6.5 mmol/L) is an end-product of protein metabolism. It is produced solely by the liver; is transported in the blood; and is excreted by the kidneys. The concentration of BUN reflects renal function because the urea nitrogen in blood is filtered completely at the glomerulus of the kidney, then reabsorbed and tubularly secreted within nephrons. Acute or chronic renal failure is the most common cause of an elevated BUN. Although the BUN is an excellent "screening" test for renal dysfunction, it is not sufficiently selective for quantifying the extent of renal disease. A number of factors other than renal function can affect the serum BUN concentration. For example, unusually high protein intake or conditions which increase protein catabolism tend to increase the BUN. Gastrointestinal bleeding or esophageal varices can increase the BUN because blood is converted by bacteria in the bowel to ammonia and urea nitrogen. The hydrational status of a patient may either increase or decrease the BUN because a water deficit would tend to concentrate the urea nitrogen and a water excess would dilute the urea nitrogen. Finally, the BUN may be decreased in the terminal stages of liver disease because of the inability of the liver to form urea.

7. Why is the BUN abnormal for T.T. (from Question 1)?

The BUN serum concentration in T.T. is somewhat increased perhaps due to inadequate renal perfusion secondary to her heart failure. Her renal function also could be more severely compromised than one would anticipate from her slightly increased BUN value because of dilution by increased extracellular fluid volume. Therefore, T.T.'s renal status should be evaluated.

Creatinine

Creatinine (0.6 to 1.2 mg/dL or 50 to 110 μmol/L) is derived from creatine and phosphocreatine, a major constituent of muscle. Its rate of formation for a given individual is remarkably constant and is determined primarily by an individual's muscle mass or lean body weight. Therefore, the serum creatinine concentration is slightly higher in muscular subjects, but unlike the BUN, it is less affected by exogenous factors. Once creatinine is released from muscle into plasma, it is excreted renally almost exclusively by glomerular filtration. A decrease in the glomerular filtration rate would result in an increase in the serum creatinine concentration. Thus, determination and careful interpretation of the serum creatinine concentration is used widely in the clinical evaluation of patients with suspected renal disease.

A doubling of the serum creatinine (SrCr) roughly corresponds to a 50% reduction in the glomerular filtration rate. This general rule of thumb only holds for steady-state creatinine levels.[14]

8. T.T. was given digoxin 0.25 mg/day, and a SrCr was ordered to further assess her renal function. The clinical laboratory determined that her SrCr was 1.2 mg/dL. Since this laboratory test result is within normal limits, does it indicate normal renal function for T.T.? [SI unit: SrCr 106 μmol/L]

A serum creatinine of 1.2 mg/dL in T.T. does not necessarily reflect normal renal function. As patients become older, muscle mass represents a smaller proportion of total weight and creatinine production is decreased. Furthermore, the serum creatinine concentration in female patients generally is 0.2 to 0.4 mg/dL (85% to 90%) less than for males, due to relatively smaller kidneys. Since T.T. is a 75-year-old female, a creatinine clearance determination would reflect more accurately her renal function status.

Creatinine Clearance (Cl$_{Cr}$)

The clearance of any substance that is filtered freely at the glomerulus and is not absorbed, secreted, synthesized, or metabolized by the kidney is equal to the glomerular filtration rate. Creatinine meets these criteria; therefore, creatinine clearance should reflect the glomerular filtration rate.

An accurate estimation of creatinine clearance is crucial to rational drug therapy because many drugs are partially or totally eliminated by the kidney. Although creatinine clearance is a more specific measure of renal function than the serum creatinine concentration, an accurate creatinine clearance is difficult to obtain clinically. Twenty-four hour urine collections often are unreliable because a portion of urine may be discarded accidentally, or the time period of collection is shorter or longer than requested. An incomplete urine collection could result in a substantial underestimation of renal function. Urine should be collected over a 24-hour period rather than over a shorter time interval because of the possibility of a daily cyclical pattern in the clearance of creatinine. Nevertheless, in critically ill, trauma, or postsurgical patients, the 24-hour creatinine clearance can be estimated from an eight-hour urine collection if a deviation of up to 20% from the 24-hour value is clinically acceptable.[15] No significant cyclical variation in creatinine excretion was found over the 24-hour period of this latter study.

Urine collections are time consuming and expensive. As a result, several nomograms and formulas have been developed to provide estimates of creatinine clearances by utilizing measured serum creatinine values. The following formula created by Jelliffe is used commonly:[16]

$$\begin{array}{c} Cl_{Cr} \\ \text{for Males} \\ (mL/min/1.73\ m^2) \end{array} = \frac{98 - [(0.8)(Age - 20)]}{SrCr_{ss}} \qquad Eq\ 4.6$$

This Jelliffe formula must be multiplied by 90% to calculate creatinine clearances for females.

An evaluation of various formulas which estimate creatinine clearance noted that all methods of calculation appeared to be equally reliable for patients with a serum creatinine in the 1.5 to 5.0 mg/dL range.[17] The above formula by Jelliffe, however, substantially underestimated the creatinine clearance in patients with a serum creatinine of less than 1.5 mg/dL. The Cockcroft and Gault[18] formula below uses age, body weight, and serum creatinine and has the highest correlation and the greatest accuracy in patients with serum creatinine concentrations less than 1.5 mg/dL.[19]

$$\begin{array}{c} Cl_{Cr} \\ \text{for Males} \\ (mL/min) \end{array} = \frac{(140 - Age)(\text{Body Weight in kg})}{(SrCr)(72\ kg)} \qquad Eq\ 4.7$$

The Cockcroft and Gault formula must be multiplied by 85% to calculate creatinine clearance for females.

For patients with liver dysfunction, all methods of calculating creatinine clearance from a serum creatinine value are associated with significant overprediction of creatinine clearance.[17] Thus, methods for predicting creatinine clearance should not be used in patients with liver disease as a basis for the adjustment of drug dosages.

9. A 24-hour Cl$_{Cr}$ determination was ordered for B.J., a 44-year-old, 50 kg male. The following data were returned from the clinical laboratory:[13] total collection time 24 hours; urine volume 1200 mL; urine creatinine concentration 42 mg/dL; SrCr 1.5 mg/dL; Cl$_{Cr}$ 23 mL/min (uncorrected) and 30 mL/min (corrected). Why should B.J.'s reported Cl$_{Cr}$ be viewed with considerable suspicion? [SI units: SrCr 132.6 mmol/L; Cl$_{Cr}$ 0.38 and 0.50 mL/s, respectively]

Whenever creatinine clearance determinations are reported, clinicians always should verify the reliability of the test result before altering drug dosing schedules. First of all, it would be appropriate to determine whether the urine collection was complete. The total amount of creatinine actually collected in the 24-hour period should be compared to the calculated amount of creatinine that is expected to be produced.

$$\begin{array}{l} \text{Creatinine} \\ \text{Excreted} \end{array} = \left(\text{Urine Volume/24 hr}\right)\left(\begin{array}{l}\text{Urine Creatinine}\\\text{Concentration}\end{array}\right) \quad Eq\ 4.8$$

$$= (1200\ mL/24\ hr)(42\ mg/100\ mL)$$

$$= 504\ mg\ Creatinine/24\ hr$$

The total amount of creatinine excreted per 24 hours can be divided by the patient's body weight to determine the apparent creatinine production per day.

$$\begin{array}{l}\text{Apparent Rate}\\\text{of Creatinine}\\\text{Production}\\\text{per Day}\end{array} = \frac{\text{Amount of Creatinine Excreted}}{\text{Patient's Weight}} \quad Eq\ 4.9$$

$$= \frac{504\ mg\ Creatinine/24\ hr}{50\ kg}$$

$$= 10.08\ mg/kg/day$$

This apparent rate of creatinine production of approximately 10 mg/kg/day is considerably less than the expected 20 mg/kg/day creatinine production for a 44-year-old male (see Table 4.3). Therefore, this collection of urine for B.J. probably was incomplete, and the reported creatinine clearance probably is much less than his actual creatinine clearance. However, if B.J. has a very small muscle mass because of atrophy, cachexia, or age, the urine collection could be adequate and the reported creatinine clearance accurate.

As shown in B.J.'s laboratory test results, both uncorrected and corrected creatinine clearance values are reported by clinical laboratories. The "uncorrected" value usually represents the patient's actual creatinine clearance and the "corrected" value predicts what the patient's creatinine clearance would be if he or she were 1.73 m^2 or 70 kg.[13] (See Chapter 29: Acute Renal Failure for a more thorough description of renal function assessments.)

Lactate Dehydrogenase
(LD; Previously Abbreviated LDH)

The glycolytic enzyme, lactate dehydrogenase (50 to 150 Units/L or U/L) catalyzes the interconversion of lactate and pyruvate and is present in most tissues. It is present in especially high concentrations in heart, kidney, liver, and skeletal muscle, although it also is abundantly present in erythrocytes and lung tissue. Since increased serum concentrations of LD can be associated with diseases in many different organs and tissues, the diagnostic useful-

Table 4.3	Expected Daily Creatinine Production for Males[a]
Age (yr)	Daily Creatinine Production (mg/kg/day)
20–29	24
30–39	22
40–49	20
50–59	19
60–69	17
70–79	14
80–89	12
90–99	9

[a] Reprinted with permission of Reference 14.

ness of an LD determination is somewhat limited. There are, however, five isoenzymes of LD, and there are striking differences in the isoenzyme content of different tissues. Most tissues contain all five isoenzymes, but LD$_1$ and, to a lesser extent, LD$_2$ predominate in the heart. Skeletal muscle and the liver have mostly LD$_5$. Red blood cells, kidneys, brain, stomach, and pancreas are other important sources of LD$_1$. Consequently, chemical or electrophoretic separation of these isoenzymes can increase the diagnostic usefulness of serum LD determinations. For example, the elevated serum LD associated with myocardial infarction (MI) consists mostly of LD$_1$ and LD$_2$; whereas with acute liver disease, there is a greater proportion of LD$_4$ and LD$_5$. Unfortunately, these isoenzyme patterns are not necessarily typical of all myocardial or liver diseases.

The lactate dehydrogenase isoenzymes are removed from the serum at different rates. The biological half-life of LD$_5$ is eight to ten hours, while the biological half-life of LD$_1$ is estimated to be from 48 to 113 hours. The liver will liberate LD quickly when damaged by physical trauma, infection, or ischemia. If the insult is an isolated event and not an ongoing process, the released lactate dehydrogenase will be cleared from the serum within a day.

Creatine Kinase (CK)

The creatine kinase (0 to 130 Units/L or U/L) enzyme (formerly known as creatine phosphokinase) catalyzes the transfer of high-energy phosphate groups in tissues that consume large amounts of energy (e.g., skeletal muscle, myocardium, brain). Therefore, total creatine kinase can be increased by strenuous exercise, intramuscular injections of drugs that are irritating to tissue (e.g., diazepam, phenytoin), acute psychotic episodes, or myocardial injury.

Creatine kinase is composed of M and B subunits which are further divided into three isoenzymes: MM, BB, and MB. The CK-MM isoenzyme is found predominantly in skeletal muscle, the CK-BB in the brain, and the CK-MB in the myocardium. Myocardial CK activity consists of 80% to 85% CK-MM and 15% to 20% CK-MB. Noncardiac tissues that contain large amounts of CK have either CK-MM or CK-BB. The MB fraction is either absent or present in trace amounts in tissues other than the myocardium.

After a myocardial infarction, the CK-MB fraction accounts for about 5% or more of the total CK.[20] Myocardial damage appears to be directly correlated with the amount of CK-MB released into the serum (i.e., the higher the amount of CK-MB, the more extensive the myocardial injury). Although CK-MB levels greater than 25 U/L usually are associated with a myocardial infarction,[21] the absolute amount may vary depending upon assay technique. Generally, if the amount of CK-MB exceeds 6% of the total, myocardial injury presumably has occurred. Analysis of CK-MB provides a rapid, sensitive, specific, cost-effective, and definitive means of detecting myocardial infarction.[22]

10. O.D., a 55-year-old male, presents to the ER with sudden onset of acute chest pain, diaphoresis, and nausea that began about 1 hour ago. He describes his pain as severe and not relieved by position, antacids, or nitroglycerin. An electrocardiogram (ECG) reveals changes consistent with an acute evolving MI. The total CK serum concentration is 118 U/L and the CK-MB is 5 U/L. O.D. was admitted to the coronary care unit to rule out an acute MI. Why are the total CK and CK-MB serum concentrations within the normal range in O.D. who presents with strong evidence of an MI? [SI units: CK 1.97 μkat/L; CK-MB 0.08 μkat/L]

The total creatine kinase and CK-MB are both within the normal range for O.D.; however, a myocardial infarction cannot be excluded. CK serum concentrations usually do not rise above normal values until four to eight hours after myocardial injury, and usually peak in about 12 to 24 hours. Therefore, it is important to measure

CK and CK-MB serum concentrations 12 to 24 hours after the initial determination to be assured that subsequent increases in the serum concentrations of these myocardial enzymes will be detected. About 10% of patients with suspected myocardial infarctions will fail to demonstrate an increase in the total CK, although serial CK-MB fractions will be increased. Therefore, when CK-MB is greater than 6% of total CK, a myocardial infarction probably has occurred even if the total CK is not elevated.[20]

11. How can myocardial enzymes be detected earlier than 4-8 hours after myocardial injury?

The CK-MM in normal patients usually is composed of approximately 34%, 30%, and 37%, respectively of three CK-MM isoforms, MM_A, MM_B, and MM_C. These isoforms of CK-MM change their distribution characteristics significantly during the first hours after onset of symptoms of a myocardial infarction. The average ratio of subform A to C normally is 0.31 to 3.1. In patients with infarction, the concentration of MM_A is higher and the ratio of MM_A to MM_C always is greater than 2.5. These early changes in the isoforms occur after the onset of infarction at a time when CK-MB and total CK still are within the normal range. The laboratory assay for the CK-MM isoforms is not readily available in many clinical laboratories.[23,24]

Albumin

Albumin (4.0 to 6.0 gm/dL or 40 to 60 gm/L) is produced by the liver and contributes approximately 80% of serum colloid osmotic pressure. Hypoalbuminemic states, therefore, commonly are associated with edema and transudation of extracellular fluid. A lack of essential amino acids, either due to malnutrition or malabsorption, or impaired synthesis by the liver can result in decreased serum albumin concentrations. Most forms of hepatic insufficiency are associated with decreased synthesis of albumin. Albumin can be lost directly from the blood because of hemorrhage, burns, or exudates, or may be lost directly into the urine because of nephrosis. Serum albumin concentrations seldom increase, but may be noted in volume depletion, shock, or immediately after the administration of large amounts of intravenous albumin. In addition to its diagnostic value, the serum albumin concentration is an important consideration in the therapeutic monitoring of drugs and electrolytes that are highly protein bound (e.g., phenytoin, digoxin, calcium). In cases of severe hypoalbuminemia, determination of the ''free'' or unbound concentration of these entities may be required for an accurate assessment.

Globulin

The plasma proteins primarily consist of albumin, globulin (2.3 to 3.5 gm/dL or 23 to 35 gm/L), and fibrinogen fractions. While albumin principally functions to maintain serum oncotic pressure, globulins play an active role in some immunological processes. The globulins can be separated into several subgroups (e.g., alpha, beta, gamma). The gamma globulins can be separated further into various immunoglobulins (e.g., IgA, IgM, IgG). Chronic infection or rheumatoid arthritis can increase immunoglobulin levels, and fractionation of immunoglobulins can provide useful information in the evaluation of immune disorders. When the immunoglobulins are separated by electrophoresis, elevations of one or several of the immunoglobulins in a specific pattern can suggest a diagnosis of multiple myeloma, a plasma cell malignancy.

Since globulin is not manufactured solely by the liver, the ratio of albumin to globulin (the A/G ratio) is changed in patients with liver disease. Changes in this ratio are due to decreased albumin concentration and a compensatory increase in globulin concentration.

Aspartate Aminotransferase (AST)

The aspartate aminotransferase enzyme (0 to 35 Units/L or U/L), formerly called serum glutamic oxaloacetic transaminase (SGOT), is abundant in heart and liver tissue, and moderately present in skeletal muscle, kidney, and pancreas. In cases of acute cellular injury to the heart or liver, the enzyme is released into the blood from the damaged cells and presumably is metabolized within the body. In clinical practice, AST determinations are used to evaluate myocardial injury and to diagnose and assess the prognosis of liver disease resulting from hepatocellular injury.

The serum concentration of AST activity is increased in about 96% to 98% of patients following a myocardial infarction. However, the serum concentrations do not become abnormal until four to six hours after the onset of myocardial injury. The AST activity in serum peaks after 24 to 36 hours and the activity returns to the normal range in about four to five days. The peak values of AST approximate the extent of myocardial damage. (See Chapter 14: Myocardial Infarction.)

Serum AST values are elevated markedly in patients with acute hepatic necrosis whether caused by viral hepatitis (see Chapter 62: Acute and Chronic Hepatitis) or a hepatotoxin such as carbon tetrachloride. In these situations, the serum concentrations of both AST and ALT (see below) will be increased, even before the appearance of clinical symptoms (e.g., jaundice). The AST and ALT serum concentrations may be increased by as much as 100 times the usual upper limits of normal in the presence of parenchymal liver disease. Patients with intrahepatic cholestasis, post-hepatic jaundice, or cirrhosis usually experience more moderate elevations of AST depending upon the extent of cell necrosis. The AST serum concentration usually is higher than that of ALT in patients with cirrhosis and the AST increase usually is about four to five times the upper limit of normal.

Alanine Aminotransferase (ALT)

The enzyme, alanine aminotransferase (ALT) (0 to 35 Units/L or U/L), formerly called serum glutamic pyruvic transaminase (SGPT), is found in essentially the same tissues that have high concentrations of AST. In liver diseases, serum ALT elevations parallel those of AST, although slightly more acute hepatocellular parenchymal damage must occur to produce abnormal values. The ALT is relatively more abundant in hepatic tissue versus cardiac tissue than AST; however, the liver still contains 3.5 times more AST than ALT. Although serum concentrations of both AST and ALT increase whenever disease processes affect liver cell structure, the ALT is the more liver-specific enzyme. ALT serum concentrations rarely are increased except in parenchymal liver disease. The ALT activity is increased only marginally by a myocardial infarction because the ALT activity in heart muscle is only a small fraction of the quantity of AST present. Furthermore, elevations of ALT persist longer than those of AST.

Alkaline Phosphatase

The alkaline phosphatases (30 to 120 Units/L or U/L) constitute a large group of isoenzymes which play important roles in the transport of sugar and phosphate. These isoenzymes of alkaline phosphatase have different physiochemical properties and originate from different tissues (e.g., liver, bone, placenta, intestine).

In normal adults, the circulating alkaline phosphatase is derived primarily from liver and bone. Although only small amounts of alkaline phosphatase are present in the liver, this enzyme is secreted into the bile, and its serum concentration increases substantially with mild intrahepatic or extrahepatic biliary obstruction.

Thus, the presence of early bile duct abnormalities can result in alkaline phosphatase elevations before increases in the serum bilirubin are observed. Drug-induced cholestatic jaundice (e.g., chlorpromazine or sulfonamides) can increase the serum concentration of alkaline phosphate. The serial evaluation of serum concentrations of alkaline phosphatase determinations are not particularly useful in assessing the degree of hepatic impairment. In mild cases of acute liver cell damage, the alkaline phosphatase seldom is elevated, and even in cirrhosis, the alkaline phosphatase serum concentration is variable and depends upon the degree of hepatic decompensation and obstruction. The serum alkaline phosphatase concentration is an excellent indicator of space-occupying lesions in the liver primarily because of disruption of biliary canaliculi within the liver.[26]

The osteoblasts in bone produce large amounts of alkaline phosphatase. Thus, alkaline phosphatase concentrations in serum are increased markedly in Paget's disease, hyperparathyroidism, osteogenic sarcoma, osteoblastic cancer metastatic to bone, and other conditions of pronounced osteoblastic activity. The serum alkaline phosphatase is increased during periods of rapid bone growth (e.g., infancy, early childhood, healing bone fractures) and during pregnancy because of the contributions of the placenta and fetal bones.

Gamma-Glutamyl Transferase (GGT)

Although the enzyme, gamma-glutamyl transferase (0 to 30 Units/L or U/L), is found in the kidney, liver, and pancreas, its major clinical value is in the evaluation of hepatobiliary disease. An increase in the serum concentration of gamma-glutamyl transferase parallels the increase of alkaline phosphatase in obstructive jaundice and infiltrative disease of the liver. Since GGT is a hepatic microsomal enzyme, tissue concentrations increase in response to microsomal enzyme induction by alcohol and other drugs (e.g., phenobarbital, phenytoin). As a result, gamma-glutamyl transferase is a sensitive indicator of recent alcohol exposure.

Bilirubin

Bilirubin (0.1 to 1.0 mg/dL or 2 to 18 μmol/L for total bilirubin; 0 to 0.2 mg/dL or 0 to 4 μmol/L for direct conjugated bilirubin) primarily is a breakdown product of hemoglobin and is formed in the reticuloendothelial system (Step 1 of Figure 4.1). It is transferred then into the blood (Step 2) where it is almost completely bound to serum albumin (Step 3). When the bilirubin arrives at the sinusoidal surface of the liver cells, the free fraction rapidly is taken up into the cell (Step 4) and converted primarily to bilirubin diglucuronide (Step 5). A monoglucuronide also is formed that is metabolized predominantly to the diglucuronide. The conjugated bilirubin diglucuronide then is excreted into the bile (Step 6) and appears in the intestine where bacteria convert the majority of it to urobilinogen (Step 7). Most of the urobilinogen is destroyed or excreted in the feces (Step 13), but some is reabsorbed into the blood (Step 8). A portion of this small amount of urobilinogen in the blood is then reabsorbed into the liver (Step 9) and subsequently excreted into the bile (Step 12); the other portion is excreted into the urine (Step 10). The mechanism by which conjugated bilirubin in the liver cell is transferred to the blood (Step 14) is not well understood. However, in many types of liver disease, the conjugated form of bilirubin (direct-acting) is present in increased concentrations in the blood. When this concentration exceeds 0.2 to 0.4 mg/dL, bilirubin will begin to appear in the urine (Step 11). Unconjugated bilirubin (indirect-acting) is water insoluble and is highly bound to serum albumin; both of these factors account for its lack of excretion in the urine.[27]

Causes of Increased Bilirubin

12. A.R., a 42-year-old male with a 2-year history of hypertension controlled with hydrochlorothiazide and methyldopa, is hospitalized following an episode of orthostatic hypotension. Admitting laboratory results show a Hct of 27%. Liver function tests (LFTs) were obtained because A.R. had a long history of alcoholism and because of concern for methyldopa hepatotoxicity. His bilirubin (total) was 3.5 mg/dL, bilirubin (direct) 0.5 mg/dL, alkaline phosphatase 40 U/L, AST 32 U/L, and ALT 27 U/L. Based upon the above information and Figure 4.1, what are 3 major causes of increased bilirubin in adults, and what might be the most logical cause of increased bilirubin in A.R.? [SI units: Hct 0.27; bilirubin 59.8 and 8.6 μmol/L, respectively; alkaline phosphatase 40 U/L; AST 32 U/L; ALT 27 U/L]

Hepatocellular Damage. When the liver is unable to conjugate bilirubin, the serum concentration of total bilirubin will increase out of proportion to the direct bilirubin (i.e., the indirect bilirubin will be increased). A.R.'s normal AST and ALT values, however, indicate that hepatocellular damage is not likely. Therefore, in this situation, a diagnosis of hepatocellular damage cannot be confirmed by the serum bilirubin concentrations alone.

Cholestasis (Posthepatic). When bile flow is obstructed in the absence of severe liver impairment, the increase in the total bilirubin serum concentration can be attributed primarily to an increase in the direct or conjugated bilirubin. A determination of the alkaline phosphatase serum concentration is useful in differentiating cholestasis from other forms of jaundice. In this case, the normal serum concentrations of alkaline phosphatase and direct bilirubin indicate that there is not a cholestatic component to A.R.'s problem.

Hemolysis (Prehepatic). When erythrocytes are hemolyzed rapidly, the serum concentration of indirect bilirubin increases. If the liver is conjugating and eliminating bilirubin normally, the total bilirubin will increase out of proportion to the direct bilirubin. This is evident in the above case. Thus, A.R.'s increased indirect bilirubin concentration probably is caused by hemolysis.

Acid Phosphatase

The function of acid phosphatase (0 to 3 KA units or 0 to 5.5 U/L) is not well understood. This enzyme is present in high concentrations in prostatic tissue, although a different acid phosphatase also can be found in erythrocytes and platelets. Acid phosphatase is measured to detect the presence of metastatic carcinoma of the prostate and to monitor its response to therapy. Patients with benign prostatic hyperplasia or prostatitis do not have increased serum concentrations of acid phosphatase, although slight elevations sometimes may be noticed after vigorous prostatic massage.[26] The usefulness of acid phosphatase as a marker for carcinoma of the prostate has been challenged by the new organ-specific marker, prostate-specific antigen (PSA).[28]

Prostate-Specific Antigen (PSA)

Prostate-specific antigen is a protease glycoprotein produced almost exclusively by prostate epithelial cells. Serum concentrations of PSA are increased when the normal prostate glandular structure is disrupted by benign or malignant tumor or inflammation. In fact, the serum concentration of PSA is elevated in 55% to 83% of men with benign prostatic hyperplasia. Nevertheless, the PSA is most useful for the staging of cancer and for monitoring the progression and response to therapy of prostate cancer.[48,49]

PSA serum concentrations increase following prostatic manipulation such as digital rectal examination (DRE), transrectal ultrasound, cystoscopy, or biopsy of the prostate. Although elevated

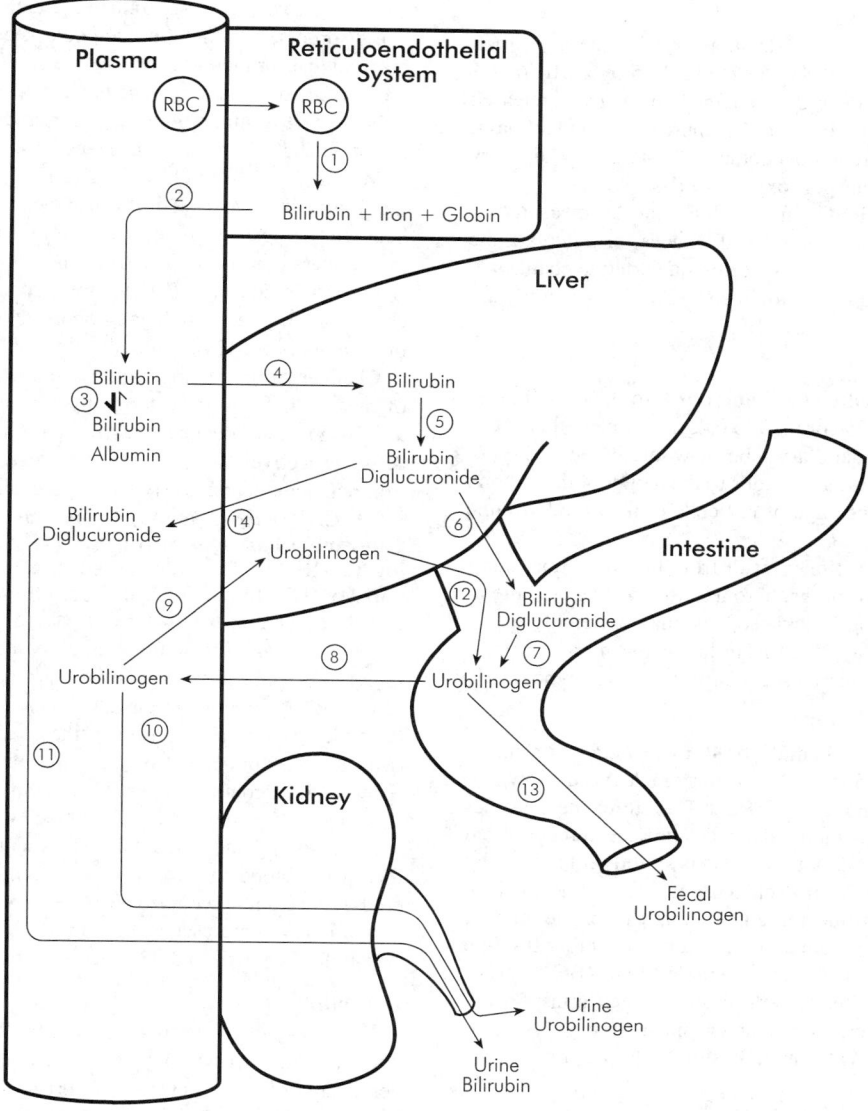

Fig 4.1   Bilirubin Metabolism.

serum concentrations of PSA can occur in men with benign prostatic hyperplasia, these concentrations are higher and encountered more frequently in men with cancer. As a result, the American Cancer Society[50] and the American Urological Association[51] recommended in 1992 that an annual digital rectal examination should be accompanied by a blood test for PSA. These tests should begin by age 50 for most men, and even earlier for blacks or sons of men with prostate cancer.[52] After reviewing the test results of more than 6300 men, a U.S. Food and Drug Administration (FDA) panel noted that PSA blood testing when combined with a DRE was much more effective in detecting prostate cancer than either a DRE or a PSA test alone. Subsequently, the FDA approved Hybritech Corporation's PSA assay for early diagnosis of prostate cancer.

The serum half-life of PSA is two to three days, but serum PSA concentrations can remain high for several weeks after manipulation of the prostate. When PSA levels from blood samples of men in the Physician's Health Study (an ongoing, randomized trial that enrolled 22,071 men 40 to 84 years of age in 1982) were analyzed, high sensitivities and specificities for the entire 10-year follow-up were detected.[53] This group concluded that "PSA has the highest validity of any circulating cancer screening marker discovered thus

far, and that intensive effort to identify cost-effective screening strategies incorporating PSA testing are warranted."[53] Therefore, the optimal "cutoff" serum PSA concentrations for delineation of aggressive cancers versus nonaggressive cancers, the estimated relative risks of prostate cancer within given ranges of PSA, and the predictive value of PSA screening relative to costs and benefits will be clarified further in the near future. An aggressive approach to localize prostate cancer for men with life expectancies more than ten years is now favored.[54] (Prostate cancer and its treatment are presented in Chapter 93: Solid Tumors.)

Hematology
Complete Blood Count (CBC)

The CBC is one of the most common clinical laboratory tests ordered in medical practice. A complete blood count measures the hemoglobin (Hgb), hematocrit (Hct), total white blood cells (WBCs), red blood cells (RBCs), mean cell volume (MCV), and mean cell hemoglobin concentration (MCHC). Depending upon the laboratory, an order for a CBC may or may not include a platelet count, reticulocyte count, or leukocyte differential count.

Red Blood Cells (RBCs)

Red blood cells (4.3 to 5.9 × 10^6/mm³ or 4.3 to 5.9 × 10^{12}/L for males and 3.5 to 5.0 × 10^6/mm³ or 3.5 to 5.0 × 10^{12}/L for females) or erythrocytes are produced in the bone marrow, released into the peripheral blood, circulate for approximately 120 days, and are cleared by the reticuloendothelial system. The primary function of RBCs is to transport oxygen to tissues.

The concentration of RBCs in the blood can be measured to detect anemia, calculate red blood cell indices, or calculate the hematocrit. For the purpose of monitoring quantitative changes in RBCs, the hematocrit and hemoglobin concentration generally are used.

Hematocrit (Hct)

The hematocrit [packed cell volume (39% to 49% or 0.39 to 0.49 for males; 33% to 43% or 0.33 to 0.43 for females)] is determined by centrifuging a capillary tube of whole blood and comparing the height of the settled red cells to the height of the column of whole blood. The percentage of red cells to the blood volume is the hematocrit.

A decrease in hematocrit may result from bleeding, bone marrow suppressant effects of drugs, chronic diseases, genetic alterations in red cell morphology (sickle cell anemia), or hemolysis. An increase in hematocrit may result from hemoconcentration, polycythemia vera, or polycythemia secondary to chronic hypoxia.

Hemoglobin (Hgb)

Hemoglobin (14.0 to 18.0 gm/dL or 40 to 180 gm/L for males; 11.5 to 15.5 gm/dL or 115 to 155 gm/L for females) is the oxygen-carrying compound contained in RBCs. Therefore, the total hemoglobin concentration primarily depends upon the number of red cells in the blood sample, although it also is slightly influenced by the amount of hemoglobin in each red cell. The same medical conditions that increase or decrease the hematocrit or the number of RBCs affect the hemoglobin concentration in a similar fashion.

A hemoglobin determination is preferable to an RBC determination because it most directly reflects the oxygen transport capability of blood; however, the hematocrit most commonly is utilized clinically because it is technically simpler to perform.[30]

Red Cell Indices (Wintrobe Indices)

Red cell indices are useful in the classification of anemias. These indices include the mean cell volume (MCV), the mean cell hemoglobin (MCH), and the mean cell hemoglobin concentration (MCHC). These indices are calculated as follows:

$$MCV = \frac{Hct \times 1000}{RBC \ (in \ millions/\mu L)} = 76 - 100 \ (in \ \mu m^3 \ or \ fL)$$

Eq 4.10

$$MCH = \frac{Hgb \ (in \ gm/L)}{RBC \ (in \ millions/\mu L)} = 27 - 33 \ (in \ pg)$$

Eq 4.11

$$MCHC = \frac{Hgb \ (in \ gm/dL)}{Hct} = 33 - 37 \ (in \ gm/dL)$$

Eq 4.12

MCV. The MCV detects changes in cell size. Therefore, descriptive terms such as macro- or microcytosis can be used for abnormal MCV values. For example, a decreased MCV would suggest a microcytic cell which can result from iron deficiency anemia. A large MCV would suggest a macrocytic cell which can be caused by a vitamin B_{12} or folic acid deficiency. The MCV can be normal in a patient with a "mixed" (micro- and macrocytic) anemia. Red cell indices cannot take the place of direct observation of a blood smear.

An increased MCV has been correlated with a variety of disease states (e.g., alcoholism, habitual drinking, chronic liver disease, anorexia nervosa, hypothyroidism, reticulocytosis, and hematological disorders).[31] Although one could speculate as to whether the macrocytosis or increased MCV noted in these disorders represents preclinical folate or B_{12} deficiencies, an increased MCV may be indicative of an underlying disorder, and an MCV determination might be useful as a screening tool for occult disease.[31]

MCHC. The MCHC is a more reliable index of red cell hemoglobin than the MCH. The former measures the concentration of hemoglobin whereas the latter measures the weight of hemoglobin in the average red cell. In normochromic anemias, changes in the size of red blood cells (MCV) are associated with corresponding changes in the weight of hemoglobin (MCH), but the concentration of hemoglobin (MCHC) remains normal.[9]

Changes in the hemoglobin content of red cells alter the color of these cells. Thus, the terms hypo- and normochromic can be used to indicate, decreased or normal amounts of hemoglobin in cells, respectively. Hypochromic red cells are characteristic of an iron deficiency anemia. Hyperchromic cells are very rare.[14]

13. C.U., a 58-year-old chronic alcoholic, was hospitalized following a barroom brawl. A CBC was ordered and the following RBC indices were noted: MCV 108 mm³, MCH 38 pg, and MCHC 34 gm/dL. How should these indices be interpreted in C.U.? [SI Units: MCV 108 fL; MCH 38 pg; MCHC 340 gm/L]

The MCH and MCV are both increased and the MCHC usually is normal in macrocytic anemias associated with vitamin B_{12} or folic acid deficiency. The MCH is increased because the RBCs have increased in size; however, the concentration of hemoglobin (MCHC) has not been changed. This characteristic picture is illustrated in the alcoholic patient, C.U., who is likely to have a dietary folic acid deficiency. If C.U.'s indices were normal (normocytic, normochromic) and if anemia was present (decreased Hgb or Hct), then acute blood loss from his barroom brawl should be considered. If the anemia seems to be more chronic in nature, then alcohol bone marrow suppression should be considered (see Chapters 25: Alcoholic Cirrhosis and 82: Alcohol Abuse).

Reticulocytes

Reticulocytes (0.1% to 2.4% of red cells or 0.001 to 0.024 l) are young, immature erythrocytes. The reticulocyte count measures the percentage of these new corpuscles in the circulating blood. An increase in the number of reticulocytes suggests that an increased number of erythrocytes are being released into the blood in response to a stimulus. Reticulocytosis can be noted after hemolysis (e.g., sickle cell anemia) or after a hemorrhagic episode within three to five days because erythrocytes regenerate rapidly. The reticulocyte count can be as high as 40% during rapid erythrocyte regeneration. Appropriate treatment of anemias caused by iron, vitamin B_{12}, or folic acid deficiencies should result in an increased reticulocyte count as well. If a properly functioning bone marrow is present and the reticulocyte count does not increase in response to replacement therapy, then the diagnosis or the treatment should be re-evaluated. Furthermore, caution must be exercised in the interpretation of reticulocyte counts. Changes in the number of red blood cells will result in proportional changes in the reticulocyte count because the reticulocyte count is reported as a percentage of the number of red blood cells.

Erythrocyte Sedimentation Rate (ESR)

The sedimentation rate (0 to 20 mm/hour for males and 0 to 30 mm/hour for females) is the rate at which erythrocytes settle to the bottom of a test tube through the forces of gravity. The ESR is nonspecific and seldom is the sole clue to disease in asymptomatic persons.

The sedimentation rate is increased abnormally in acute and chronic inflammatory processes, acute and chronic infections, neo-

Table 4.4			Hematologic Laboratory Values[b]
	Normal Reference Values		
Laboratory Test[a]	Conventional Units	SI Units	Comments
ESR			Nonspecific; ↑ with inflammation, infection, neoplasms, connective tissue disorders, pregnancy, nephritis. Useful monitor of temporal arteritis and polymyalgia rheumatica
Male	0–20 mm/hr	0–20 mm/hr	
Female	0–30 mm/hr	0–30 mm/hr	
Hct			↓ with anemias, bleeding, hemolysis. ↑ with polycythemia, chronic hypoxia
Male	39%–49%	0.39–0.49 l[b]	
Female	33%–43%	0.33–0.43 l[b]	
Hgb			Similar to hematocrit
Male	14–18 gm/dL	140–180 gm/L	
Female	11.5–15.5 gm/dL	115–155 gm/L	
MCH	27–33 pg	27–32 pg	Measures weight of Hgb in average RBC
MCHC	33–37 gm/dL	330–370 gm/L	More reliable index of red cell hemoglobin than MCH. Measures concentration of Hgb in average RBC. Concentration will not change with weight or size of RBC
MCV	76–100 μm^3	76–100 fL[c]	Describes cell size (macrocytic and microcytic)
Platelets	130,000–400,000/mm^3	$1.3–1.4 \times 10^{11}$/L	$<1.0 \times 10^{11}$/L = thrombocytopenia; $<0.2 \times 10^{11}$/L = ↑ risk for bleeding
RBC count			
Male	$4.3–5.9 \times 10^6$/mm^3	$4.3–5.9 \times 10^{12}$/L	
Female	$3.5–5 \times 10^6$/mm^3	$3.5–5 \times 10^{12}$/L	
Reticulocyte count (adults)	0.1%–2.4%	0.001–0.024 l[b]	An ↑ suggests ↑ number of erythrocytes released in response to stimulus (e.g., iron in iron-deficiency anemia)
WBC count	3200–9800/mm^3	$3.2–9.8 \times 10^9$/L	Consists of neutrophils, lymphocytes, monocytes, eosinophils, and basophils
Bands	3%–5%	0.03–0.05 l[b]	An ↑ in neutrophils suggests bacterial or fungal infection. ↑ in bands and immature neutrophils suggests bacterial infection. Absolute neutrophil count (% neutrophils × WBC count) <100 ↑ risk of bacteremia; >1000 = low risk of infection.
Neutrophils	54%–62%	0.54–0.62 l[b]	
Lymphocytes	25%–33%	0.25–0.33 l[b]	
Monocytes	3%–7%	0.03–0.07 l[b]	
Eosinophils	1%–3%	0.01–0.03 l[b]	Eosinophils ↑ with allergies and parasitic infections
Basophils	<1%	<0.01 l[b]	

[a] ESR = Erythrocyte sedimentation rate; MCH = Mean corpuscular hemoglobin; MCHC = Mean corpuscular hemoglobin concentration; MCV = Mean corpuscular volume; RBC = Red blood cell; WBC = White blood cell.

[b] With the SI, the concept of number fraction replaces %. Thus for mass fraction, volume fraction, and relative quantities, the unit "l" is used to replace former units.

[c] fL = Femtoliter; femto = 10^{-15}; pico = 10^{-12}; nano = 10^{-9}; micro = 10^{-6}; milli = 10^{-3}.

plasms, infarction, tissue necrosis, rheumatoid-collagen disease, dysproteinemias, nephritis, and pregnancy. On the other hand, it sometimes is normal in diseases where it usually is abnormal, and laboratory technique can affect the sedimentation rate substantially.[26] Since many factors can enhance the settling rate of RBCs, moderate to marked elevation of the erythrocyte sedimentation rate merely indicates a disease state. An increased ESR in the setting of a normal physical examination usually is transitory and infrequently is the harbinger of serious occult disease.[32]

The ESR is useful, however, in the diagnosis and monitoring of temporal arteritis and polymyalgia rheumatica. A normal ESR excludes the diagnosis of temporal arteritis; however, if the ESR is normal despite other strong evidence of temporal arteritis, the disease still must be treated aggressively. When monitoring patients with rheumatoid arthritis, the ESR principally is utilized to help resolve conflicting clinical evidence and to evaluate response to therapy.[32] The ESR has been correlated with the severity of illness in patients with chronic congestive heart failure, however, the test is of limited value in the clinical management of CHF because of its lack of discriminatory specificity.[55] The ESR also has been identified as one of the most important pretherapy prognostic factors in patients with early-stage Hodgkin's disease; an unexplained increase in the ESR after treatment suggests the presence of ag-

gressive, resistant Hodgkin's disease, early relapse, and poor prognosis.[56] The ESR also is useful in differentiating organic diseases from those of psychosomatic origin in symptomatic patients.

White Blood Cells (WBCs)

White blood cells (3200 to 9800/mm^3 or 3.2 to 9.8×10^9/L), unlike red blood cells and platelets, perform no physiological function within the vascular system. The blood merely serves as a transportation network which allows white cells to move from their site of origin, the bone marrow, into various body tissues and cavities.

Neutrophils are the most abundant of the circulating white blood cells, followed in order of frequency by lymphocytes, monocytes, eosinophils, and basophils. The neutrophils, eosinophils, basophils, and monocytes are formed from stem cells in the bone marrow. Some lymphocytes are formed in the bone marrow, but most are formed in lymph nodes, thymus, and spleen. Also in the bone marrow, another type of leukocyte, the plasma cell, is observed. The entire system of white blood cells contributes to the host defense mechanisms; however, each of these types of cells has unique functions. Therefore, it is best to think of these cell types as individual types of cells rather than collectively as "leukocytes."[33]

Neutrophils. The terms "polys," "segs," "PMNs," and sometimes "granulocytes" are synonymous with the term "neutrophil" in clinical practice. The normal maturation sequence of the neutrophil in the bone marrow is as follows: the stem cell gives rise to the myeloblast, which then matures progressively into a promyelocyte, myelocyte, metamyelocyte, band neutrophil, and finally into a polymorphonuclear segmented neutrophil. Segmented neutrophils constitute 54% to 62% of circulating leukocytes and band neutrophils usually represent about 3% to 5%. Normally about 35% of the polymorphonuclear segmented neutrophils have two lobes, 41% have three lobes, and 20% have four or more lobes. At one time, the maturation of neutrophils was depicted with the more immature neutrophils on the left and the more mature forms on the right. Therefore, a ''shift to the left'' occurred when band neutrophils and other immature neutrophils increased and a lower average number of lobes of segmented neutrophils appeared in the blood.[9]

The number of neutrophils commonly is increased during bacterial or fungal infections because these cells are essential in killing invading micro-organisms, and a ''shift to the left'' is associated commonly with a bacterial infection. Neutrophils, however, also are important in the pathogenesis of tissue damage in some noninfectious diseases.[34]

The same processes that are so important to the destruction of microbes also can induce tissue injury in diseases such as rheumatoid arthritis, inflammatory bowel disease, asthma, or myocardial infarction (see Table 4.5). Neutrophilia also can be encountered during metabolic toxic states (e.g., diabetic ketoacidosis, uremia, eclampsia) and during physiological response to stress (e.g., physical exercise, childbirth). Drugs (e.g., epinephrine, corticosteroids) also can cause significant neutrophilia primarily by demargination from blood vessel walls.

Agranulocytosis and Absolute Neutrophil Count (ANC). Decreased neutrophils or neutropenia is defined as a neutrophil count of less than 2000 cells/mm^3; agranulocytosis refers to severe neutropenia. The degree of neutropenia often is expressed by the absolute neutrophil count. The ANC is defined as the total number of granulocytes (polymorphonuclear leukocytes and band-forms) present in the circulating pool of WBCs. Generally, the risk of infection is low when the ANC exceeds 1000/mm^3; however, the risk of infection increases substantively when the ANC drops below 500/mm^3. The risk of developing bacteremia is increased further as the ANC drops to less than 100/mm^3. The most common causes of neutropenia are metastatic carcinoma, lymphoma, and chemotherapeutic agents.

Lymphocytes constitute the second most common white cell in circulating blood. These leukocytes respond to foreign antigens by initiating the immune defense system. The vast majority of the lymphocytes are located in the spleen, lymph nodes, and other organized lymphatic tissue. The lymphocytes circulating in blood represent less than 5% of the total body pool.

There are two major types of lymphocytes. *T-lymphocytes* (thymic dependent) participate in cell-mediated immune responses, and *B-lymphocytes* (bone marrow derived) are responsible for humoral antibody responses. Therefore, diseases affecting lymphocytes primarily manifest themselves as immune deficiency disorders which render the patient unable to defend against normal pathogens [see Chapter 68: Human Immunodeficiency Virus (HIV) Infection] or as autoimmune diseases in which immune responses are directed against the body's own cells.[33]

Increased numbers of lymphocytes on a white count differential sometimes accompany viral infections such as infectious mononucleosis, mumps, and rubella. A relative lymphocytosis sometimes is encountered when the total lymphocytes have remained constant despite a decline in the total neutrophils.

Monocytes are formed in the bone marrow and transported by the blood to tissues where they mature into macrophages.[35] Monocytosis may be observed in subacute bacterial endocarditis, malaria, tuberculosis, and during the recovery phase of some infections.

Eosinophils have surface receptors that bind IgG and IgE and, as a result, eosinophils can modify reactions associated with IgG- and IgE-mediated degranulation of mast cells. These receptors are responsible for damaging larval-tissue states of some helminth parasites, especially *Schistosoma mansoni.*[36,37] Primary lysosomal granules, small dense granules, and specific or secondary granules are the three types of granules found within eosinophils. The specific granules account for most of the biologic activity of eosinophils and consist of three basic polypeptides: major basic protein (MBP), eosinophil cationic protein (ECP), and eosinophil-derived neurotoxin (EDN). These basic polypeptides are toxic to parasites, tumor cells, and some epithelial cells.[38]

Investigations have focused on this white blood cell because of the fatalities associated with tryptophan-induced eosinophilic-myalgia syndrome;[39] however, little is known about the natural function of eosinophils. Eosinophils have phagocytic activity, catalyze the oxidation of many substances, facilitate killing of micro-organisms, initiate mast cell secretion, protect against various parasites, and play some role in host defense. A high serum concentration of eosinophils (i.e., eosinophilia) probably is associated most commonly with allergic reactions to drugs, allergic disorders (e.g., hay fever, asthma, eczema), invasive parasitic infections (e.g., hookworm, schistosomiasis, trichinosis), collagen vascular diseases (e.g., rheumatoid arthritis, eosinophilic fasciitis, eosinophilic-myalgia syndrome), and malignancies (e.g., Hodgkin's disease).[37–40]

Basophils are poorly understood. An increase in basophils commonly accompanies chronic myeloid leukemia, myelofibrosis, and polycythemia vera. A decrease in the number of basophils generally is not readily apparent because of the paucity of these cells in the blood.[33]

14. R.L., a 45-year-old male, is hospitalized with a sustained high fever of 39.4 °C, SOB, and pleurisy. He is coughing up rusty sputum and appears to be in acute distress. The results of the CBC and leukocyte differential are as follows: total WBC count 18,000; neutrophils (''polys'') 76%; bands (stabs) 13%; lymphocytes 10%; monocytes 0; eosinophils 1%; and basophils 0. On the basis of this laboratory report and other findings, a diagnosis of pneumococcal pneumonia is suspected. How is R.L.'s laboratory report consistent with bacterial infection? [SI units: neutrophils 0.76; bands 0.13; lymphocytes 0.10; eosinophils 0.01]

White blood cells are the host's chief defense system, and the neutrophil is the main component of that system. During bacterial

Table 4.5	Diseases in Which Tissue Injury or Symptoms May be Mediated by Neutrophils[34]

Adult respiratory distress syndrome
Asthma
Emphysema
Glomerulonephritis
Gout
Immune vasculitis
Inflammatory bowel disease
Malignant neoplasms at sites of chronic inflammation
Myocardial infarction
Neutrophil dermatoses
Rheumatoid arthritis
Thermal injury-associated hemolysis

infections, the leukocyte count and the neutrophils generally are increased and a "shift to the left" may be noticeable. The percentage of other types of white cells is decreased proportionately because the number of neutrophils is increased.

As the infection progresses, the percentage of band cells may decrease, due to an increase in the number of neutrophils that have a longer half-life. This decrease in bands does not necessarily indicate improvement. A decrease in the percentage of neutrophils with a decrease in the total WBC count is characteristic of effective antibiotic therapy.

15. S.Q., a 35-year-old female, was treated for 7 days with dicloxacillin for a cellulitis of the left leg. On the 8th day, an allergic urticarial rash developed. The CBC noted a total leukocyte count of 10,000 with 6% eosinophils. What is the significance of this eosinophil count? [SI unit: eosinophils 0.06]

Eosinophils usually are increased in allergic reactions; therefore, a drug-induced hypersensitivity reaction is a strong probability in S.Q. with 600 eosinophils/mm^3 (i.e., 6% of 10,000 leukocytes). Clinicians should become suspicious of an allergic drug reaction whenever the absolute eosinophil count exceeds 300 cells. Eosinophils may increase before, after, or concurrent with other evidence of allergy (e.g., rash). Eosinophilia without evidence of allergy is not sufficient cause to discontinue a suspected medication unless the eosinophilia is massive (i.e., >2000 cells).

Coagulation Studies

The control of bleeding depends upon the formation of a platelet plug and the formation of a stable fibrin clot. The formation of this clot, the complex interactions of plasma proteins and clotting factors, and the clinical application of laboratory tests of coagulation are described in Chapter 12: Thrombosis. The prothrombin time (PT), international normalized ratio (INR), and activated partial thromboplastin time (aPTT) are commonly used laboratory tests of coagulation to assist clinicians in localizing the specific factor or factors responsible for a coagulation abnormality. These tests are described briefly in this chapter with the understanding that the reader will need to refer to Chapter 12: Thrombosis to gain the appropriate perspective on the clinical applicability of these tests.

Activated Partial Thromboplastin Time (aPTT)

The activated partial thromboplastin time measures the intrinsic clotting system which is dependent upon factors VIII, IX, XI, and XII and the factors involved in the final common pathway of the clotting cascade (factors II, X, and V). The aPTT is a modified PTT which is a more sensitive test than the PTT. The typical control ranges from 35 to 45 seconds. The aPTT commonly is used to monitor heparin therapy.

Prothrombin Time (PT)

Prothrombin is synthesized in the liver and is converted to thrombin during the blood clotting process. Thrombin formation is the critical event in the hemostatic process because thrombin creates fibrin monomers that ultimately assemble into a clot and thrombin stimulates platelet activation. The prothrombin time test directly measures the clotting activity of Factors V, VII, X, prothrombin (Factor II), and fibrinogen. Automated laboratory instruments measure and record the time in seconds required for the blood to clot (i.e., the prothrombin time) after tissue thromboplastin has been added to the patient's blood sample. The reference range will depend upon the specific laboratory, but usually is between 10 to 12 seconds when rabbit brain thromboplastin is used. The PT in combination with the PT ratio has been used to monitor warfarin (Coumadin) therapy. Traditionally, the PT ratio had been calculated as the patient's PT divided by a mean normal PT.

International Normalized Ratio (INR)

The laboratory testing procedures of the prothrombin time in the U.S. commonly use rabbit brain thromboplastin; however, rabbit thromboplastins from different manufacturers differ in their sensitivity and precision. In an effort to standardize the PT, the use of the international normalized ratio (INR) has been proposed. The INR is the PT ratio that would result if the World Health Organization's international reference thromboplastin were used to test the patient's blood sample. The first proposed guidelines for anticoagulant therapy based upon INR ranges were published in 1984. In 1992, the American College of Chest Physicians recommended that all laboratories convert to the INR for monitoring warfarin therapy, and the American Society of Health-Systems Pharmacists issued a position statement on the use of the INR in 1995.[57,58,62] Institutions are in various stages in this conversion process.

In order for the INR to function as proposed, however, the following four points must be clearly understood.[59–61]

- The INR should be used only for monitoring patients who have been receiving long-term (i.e., >6 weeks) stable doses of warfarin.

- The patient's prothrombin time for calculating the INR should be assayed as soon as possible after the sample of blood has been obtained from the patient, and preferably within four hours.

- The International Sensitivity Index (ISI) is thromboplastin- and instrument-specific (i.e., it is determined for a particular combination of thromboplastin and clotting instrument). Changes in either can result in significant changes in the calculated INR.

- The INR is intended for use with prothrombin time test systems which use sensitive thromboplastins with international sensitivity indices (ISI) of about 2.0. In America, commercially available thromboplastins commonly have ISIs in the range of 1.0 to 2.88. The insensitive thromboplastins introduce considerable error into the calculation of the INR, particularly in the therapeutic, and the above-therapeutic, range for anticoagulation.

Until more sensitive, standardized thromboplastins become available in America, clinicians in the U.S. should continue to rely upon the prothrombin time ratio (i.e., the patient's prothrombin time divided by the mean prothrombin time of the normal population) rather than upon the INR. Since the INR is the exponential product of the prothrombin ratio and the ISI (see Equation 4.13 below), considerable error can be introduced by the various "insensitive" thromboplastins.

The INR is calculated as in Equation 4.13 where the prothrombin ratio (PTR) is the ratio between the patient's PT and the laboratory's control PT, and the ISI is the international sensitivity index. The commercial manufacturer of the thromboplastin reagent calculates the ISI and includes it in the product package insert. The ISI is specific for each lot.

$$INR = \left\{ \frac{PT_{(Patient)}}{PT_{(Control)}} \right\}^{ISI} = PTR^{ISI} \qquad Eq\ 4.13$$

When guidelines for oral anticoagulation therapy are based upon INR ranges, one can "back calculate" the desired prothrombin ratio range based upon the ISI that is applicable to the specific test system that is in use within a clinical laboratory. For example, when a clinical laboratory has a test system with an ISI of 2.17 and a mean normal prothrombin time of 12 seconds, the therapeutic ranges for anticoagulation listed in Table 4.6 would be targeted.

Clinicians must be careful when interpreting prothrombin times that have been obtained for a patient by more than one clinical laboratory because the INR and prothrombin times are specific to each institution.[45-47] For a thorough review on the monitoring of anticoagulant therapy, see Chapter 12: Thrombosis.

Urinalysis (UA)

A standard urinalysis begins with simple observation of the color and the gross general appearance of the urine specimen. The urine pH and specific gravity then are recorded. Formed elements in the urine are examined microscopically, and the urine is searched routinely for pathologically significant substances that normally are not present (e.g., glucose, blood, ketones, and bile pigments).

Gross Appearance of Specimen

The concentrated, first-morning urine specimen usually is analyzed to rule out effects of undue dilution due to water intake. The color should be slightly yellow depending upon the degree of dilution and the appearance should be clear. The appearance of the urine may reveal clouds of crystals, bilirubin, blood, porphyrins, proteins, food or drug colorings, or melanin. Red, brown, or dark orange urine is abnormal. A red coloration may be imparted by blood, porphyria, or ingestion of phenolphthalein. A brown urine color may be caused by the acid hematin of blood or from melanin pigments. A dark orange color may be caused by the excessive excretion of urobilinogen or the effects of drugs such as rifampin or phenazopyridine.

Specimen pH

Urine normally is acidic (pH 4.6 to 8) when freshly produced. Alkaline urine may indicate an aged specimen, systemic alkalosis, failure of renal acidifying mechanisms, or infection in the urinary tract.

Specific Gravity

A normal morning urine specimen should have a specific gravity of 1.020 to 1.025. The upper end of this range is close to the maximal concentrating ability of the kidney. Glomerular filtrate has a specific gravity of 1.010, and a urine of such a low specific gravity, under conditions of restricted water intake, would suggest failure of renal concentrating mechanisms. When water intake is not restricted, specific gravity readings are difficult to interpret.

Protein

A positive test for urine protein is common (e.g., 1+) and often is a transient and insignificant laboratory finding. Proteinuria, however, is a classic sign of renal injury and a matter of concern. If proteinuria is found during the evaluation of a patient with a nonrenal illness, it suggests that the disease also may involve the kid-

Table 4.7	Detection Times in Urine with Enzyme Multiplied Immunoassay Technique (EMIT) Methods[44]
Drug	**Detection Time in Urine**
Amphetamines	Within 24–48 hr after ingestion. Oral decongestants (ephedrine, pseudoephedrine, or phenylpropanolamine) may give positive results
Barbiturates	1 dose of 250 mg phenobarbital detectable for up to 9 days. Others detectable for up to 1–2 days
Benzodiazepines	1 dose usually not detectable. Up to 5–7 days in chronic users
Cocaine	Up to 48 hr after a single dose
Codeine	1 dose of 120 mg detectable for up to 48 hr. Excreted and detected as morphine
Heroin	1 dose of 10 mg detectable for up to 24 hr. 4–5 days for chronic users
Marijuana	≤5 days after occasional use. 21–32 days after last dose in chronic users
Methadone	≈3 days. Possible interference from high levels of chlorpromazine, promethazine, and dextromethorphan
Methaqualone	Typical dose ≥ 5 days
Morphine	1 dose of 10 mg detectable for 24–48 hr
Phencyclidine	1 dose detectable for 7 days. Up to 14 days in chronic users
Propoxyphene	Up to 48 hr after a single dose

neys (i.e., hypertension, diabetes).[41] A healthy adult generally excretes 30 to 130 mg/day of protein into the urine.

The protein in a urine sample generally is tested qualitatively on a random urine sample by a dipstick method and usually is reported on a scale of 0 (<30 mg/dL); 1+ (30 to 100 mg/dL); 2+ (100 to 300 mg/dL); 3+ (300 to 1000 mg/dL); and 4+ (>1000 mg/dL). A positive qualitative test for urine protein should be repeated after a few days because transient proteinuria can accompany various physiologic and pathologic states even when kidney function is normal. Therefore, patients with congestive heart failure, seizures, or febrile illnesses and normal renal function need not undergo invasive renal function tests if the proteinuria is modest and likely to be transient. Another qualitative evaluation of proteinuria can be repeated in about two weeks to confirm the diagnosis of transient proteinuria.[42] If subsequent qualitative test results are positive, a 24-hour urine should be collected to *quantitatively* test for protein and creatinine. In patients with a normal 24-hour urinary protein concentration, previous positive qualitative test results probably represent either false-positive results or the transient phenomenon.[41] This approach should minimize unwarranted risks and costs without overlooking serious and treatable conditions.

Microscopic Examination

The urine sediment is examined for red cells, white cells, casts, yeast, crystals, and epithelial cells. *Red blood cells* should be absent in normal urine, although one to two RBC per high powered field (HPF) still would be considered in the normal range of acceptability. Bleeding or clotting disorders, some collagen diseases, and various bladder, urethral, and prostatic conditions may cause microscopic hematuria. In females, vaginal blood occasionally contaminates the urine specimen, but the presence of numerous squamous epithelial cells should be sufficient to alert clinicians to this artifact. *White blood cells* should be virtually absent in normal urine, although up to five WBCs/HPF still would be in the normal

Table 4.6	Therapeutic Ranges for Anticoagulation[a]		
Clinical Use	**Recommended INR**	**Corresponding PT (sec)**	**Corresponding PTR**
Prophylaxis DVT	2.0–2.5	16.8–18.0	1.4–1.5
Treatment of DVT, PE	2.0–3.0	16.8–20.4	1.4–1.7
Recurrent DVT	3.0–4.5	20.4–24.0	1.7–2.0

[a] DVT = Deep vein thrombosis; INR = International normalized ratio; PE = Pulmonary embolism; PT = Prothrombin time; PTR = Prothrombin ratio.

range. The presence of white cells in the urine usually suggests an acute infection in the urinary tract (see Chapter 63: Urinary Tract Infections). Some noninfectious inflammatory diseases of the kidney, ureter, or bladder also may contribute white cells to the urine sediment. *Casts* basically are composed of proteinaceous or fatty material which outline the shape of the renal tubules where they were deposited. The presence of casts in the urine must be interpreted in light of other factors related to the kidney and its function; however, fatty casts, RBC casts, and WBC casts always are significant. Red cell casts usually suggest glomerular injury, and white cell casts suggest tubular or interstitial injury. Lipid casts with proteinuria are characteristic findings in patients with the nephrotic syndrome.[43] The finding of hyaline casts alone in the presence of proteinuria suggests a renal origin for the protein. Hyaline or granular casts alone, however, only suggest some defect in factors that affect cast formation, and are, therefore, difficult to interpret. *Crystals* originally may appear as a cloud in the urine. Their formation is pH-dependent and they frequently appear only as the urine cools to room temperature or in concentrated urine. In acid urine, crystals may be uric acid or calcium oxalate; in alkaline urine they may be phosphates. Crystals *per se* are not highly significant, although they may reflect a tendency toward the formation of renal calculi (see Chapter 29: Acute Renal Failure).

16. R.C. is a 23-year-old male diagnosed with insulin-dependent diabetes mellitus about 10 years ago who, up until now, has been well-controlled with an aggressive insulin regimen. His sister brings him to the ER with a 3-day history of fever, chills, dysuria, malaise, and some confusion. He also complains of nausea and vomiting and a poor appetite. Because he has not been able to keep any food down for about 48 hours, he has not taken his insulin. A finger-stick blood glucose is 545 mg/dL and a stat midstream UA and Gram's stain indicate the following: pH 5.2; appearance cloudy; specific gravity 1.033; urine protein 3+; urine glucose 4+; urine ketones positive; urine bacteria 4+; urine WBC too numerous to count (TNTC); squamous epithelial few/HPF; urine nitrite positive; and Gram's stain numerous gram-negative rods. What objective data from the UA indicate that R.C. is critically ill? [SI unit: glucose 30.3 mmol/L]

The cloudy appearance of R.C.'s urine indicates the presence of bacteria, protein, and WBCs which is substantiated by the data (4+ bacteria, 3+ protein, and TNTC WBCs). The lack of a significant amount of squamous epithelial cells, the presence of a significant amount of nitrite-producing bacteria, and the Gram's stain, indicate a clean-catch urine specimen and a urinary tract infection (UTI) due to gram-negative organisms. Because the renal threshold of glucose is typically 180 mg/dL, the presence of 4+ glucose in the urine indicates that the blood glucose concentration significantly exceeds this figure (substantiated by blood glucose of 545 mg/dL). Acidification of the urine and ketonuria occurs following the release of ketone bodies into the bloodstream after the

Table 4.8	Therapeutic Drug Concentrations[a]		
	Normal Reference Values		
Laboratory Test	Conventional Units	SI Units	Conversion Factor
Amitriptyline	50–200 ng/mL	180–820 nmol/L	3.61
Carbamazepine	4–12 µg/mL	17–51 µmol/L	4.23
Desipramine	50–200 ng/mL	170–200 nmol/L	3.75
Digoxin	0.5–2 ng/mL	0.6–2.6 nmol/L	1.28
Disopyramide	2–6 µg/L	6–18 µmol/L	2.946
Ethosuximide	40–110 µg/mL	280–780 µmol/L	7.084
Imipramine	50–200 ng/mL	180–710 nmol/L	3.566
Iron			
male	80–180 µg/dL	14–32 µmol/L	0.179
female	60–160 µg/dL	11–29 µmol/L	0.179
Lidocaine	1–5 µg/mL	4.5–21.5 µmol/L	4.267
Lithium	0.5–1.5 mEq/L	0.5–1.5 mmol/L	1
Phenobarbital	15–50 µg/mL	65–215 µmol/L	4.34
Phenytoin	5–20 µg/mL	20–80 µmol/L[b]	4
Procainamide	4–10 µg/mL	17–42 µmol/L	4.25
Quinidine	1.2–4 µg/mL	3.7–12.3 µmol/L	3.08
Salicylate	20–25 mg/dL	1.4–1.8 mmol/L	0.07
Theophylline	5–15 µg/mL	28–83 µmol/L	5.55
Valproic acid	50–100 µg/mL	350–700 µmol/L	7.0

[a] Drug concentrations of antibiotics are presented in the Infectious Disorders chapters.
[b] Unbound phenytoin = 0.5–2 µg/mL = 2–8 mmol/L.

breakdown of fatty acids for energy utilization. It is likely that R.C. has a severe UTI and, probably, diabetic ketoacidosis. (See Chapters 48: Diabetes Mellitus and 63: Urinary Tract Infections for thorough discussions of diabetes, diabetic ketoacidosis, and UTIs.)

Urine Drug Screening

With one exception, urine drug screening is the preferred method to screen for an unknown drug. The exception is ethyl alcohol, which is most reliably detected in the blood. Administration of drugs that occurred days to weeks before the test may be detectable because drug concentrations are higher in the urine and drug metabolites are excreted for a longer period of time through urine (see Table 4.7). There are several indications for toxicology screening including: to confirm the clinical diagnosis and contributing diagnoses and to test for drug abuse/use in the workplace or as a pre-employment screen. It is important to recognize the psychological, social, and legal implications associated with urine drug screening. (See Chapter 81: Issues: Psychoactive Substance Use Disorders.)

References

1   **Hansten PD, Horn JR.** Drug Interactions & Updates Quarterly. Vancouver, WA: Applied Therapeutics, Inc. 1993.

2   **Evans PC, Cleary JD.** SI units—are we leaders or followers? Ann Pharmacother. 1993;27:97. Editorial.

3   **Vaughan LM.** SI units: is it pass the mass but hold the mole? Ann Pharmacother. 1993;29:99. Editorial.

4   **Making it easier.** Ann Intern Med. 1992;117:87. Editorial.

5   **Campion EW.** A retreat from SI units. N Engl J Med. 1992;327:49. Editorial.

6   **The New England Journal of Medicine SI Unit Conversion Guide.** Waltham, MA: Massachusetts Medical Society; 1992:56.

7   **Scully RE et al.** Normal reference values. N Engl J Med. 1986;314:39.

8   **Gennari FJ.** Serum osmolality—use and limitations. N Engl J Med. 1984; 310:102.

9   **Henry JB ed.** Clinical Diagnosis and Management by Laboratory Methods. 18th ed. Philadelphia, PA: WB Saunders; 1991.

10 **Tintinali JE.** Of anions, osmols, and methanol poisoning. JACEP. 1977;6:417.

11 **Kassirer J.** Clinical evaluation of kidney function-glomerular function. N Engl J Med. 1971;285:385.

12 **Becker CE.** Methanol poisoning. J Emerg Med. 1983;1:51.

13 **Cebul RD, Beck JR.** Biochemical profiles. Ann Intern Med. 1987;106:403.

14 **Winter ME et al.** Basic Clinical Pharmacokinetics. 3rd ed. Applied Therapeutics. Vancouver: 1994;93.

15 **Baumann TJ et al.** Minimum urine collection periods for accurate determination of creatinine clearance in critically ill patients. Clin Pharm. 1987;6: 393.

16 **Jelliffe RW.** Creatinine clearance: bed-

side estimate. Ann Intern Med. 1973; 79:604.

17 **Hull JH et al.** Influence of range of renal function and liver disease on predictability of creatinine clearance. Clin Pharmacol Ther. 1981;29:516.

18 **Cockcroft DW, Gault MH.** Prediction of creatinine clearance from serum creatinine. Nephron. 1976;16:31.

19 **Rhodes PJ et al.** Evaluation of eight methods for estimating creatinine clearance in men. Clin Pharm. 1987;6:399.

20 **Lee TH, Goldman L.** Serum enzyme assays on the diagnosis of acute myocardial infarction. Ann Intern Med. 1986;105:221.

21 **White RD et al.** Diagnostic and prognostic significance of minimally elevated creatine kinase-MB in suspected acute myocardial infarction. Am J Cardiol. 1985;55:1478.

22 **Roberts R.** Where, oh where has the MB gone? N Engl J Med. 1985;313: 1081.

23 **Hong RA et al.** Elevated CK-MB with normal total creatine kinase in suspected myocardial infarction: associated clinical findings and early prognosis. Am Heart J. 1986;111:1041.

24 **Jaffe AS et al.** Diagnostic changes in plasma creatine kinase isoforms early after the onset of acute myocardial infarction. Circulation. 1986;74:105.

25 **Friedman LS et al.** Evaluation of blood donors with elevated serum alanine aminotransferase levels. Ann Intern Med. 1987;107:137.

26 **Ravel R.** Clinical Laboratory Medicine: Clinical Application of Laboratory Data. 5th ed. Chicago, IL: Yearbook Medical Publishers; 1989.

27 **Schmid R.** Bilirubin metabolism in man. N Engl J Med. 1972;285:703.

28 **Stamey TA et al.** Prostate-specific antigen as a serum marker for adenocarcinoma of the prostate. N Engl J Med. 1987;317:909.

29 **Gittes RF.** Prostate-specific antigen. N Engl J Med. 1987;317:954.

30 **Hillman RS, Finch CA.** Red Cell Manual. 6th ed. Philadelphia, PA: F.A. Davis Company, 1992.

31 **Keenan WF.** Macrocytosis as an indicator of human disease. J Am Board Fam Pract. 1989;2:252–56.

32 **Sox HC, Liang MH.** The erythrocyte sedimentation rate. Ann Intern Med. 1986;104:515.

33 **Boggs DR, Winkelstein A.** White Cell Manual. 3rd ed. Philadelphia, PA: F.A. Davis Company; 1974.

34 **Malech HL, Gallin JI.** Neutrophils in human diseases. N Engl J Med. 1987; 317:687.

35 **Cline MG et al.** Monocytes and macrophages: functions and diseases. Ann Intern Med. 1978;88:78.

36 **Enright T et al.** Pulmonary eosinophilic syndromes. Ann Allergy. 1989; 62:277–83.

37 **Butterworth AE, David JR.** Eosinophil function. N Engl J Med. 1981;304: 154.

38 **Beeson PB.** Cancer and eosinophilia. N Engl J Med. 1983;309:792.

39 **Clauw DJ et al.** Tryptophan-associated eosinophilic connective-tissue disease. JAMA. 1990;263:1502–506.

40 **Maddox DE.** Eosinophils. Clin Rev Allergy. 1988;6:163–90.

41 **Abuelo JG.** Proteinuria: diagnostic principles and procedures. Ann Intern Med. 1983;98:186.

42 **Reuben DB et al.** Transient proteinuria in emergency medical admissions. N Engl J Med. 1982;306:1031.

43 **Morrin PAF.** Urinary sediment in the interpretation of proteinuria. Ann Intern Med. 1983;98:254.

44 **Wilson J.** Clinical Chemistry News Laboratory Guide to Abused Drugs (for Roche Diagnostic Systems). Washington: AACC Press, 1990.

45 **Force RW et al.** Comment: warfarin and the international normalized ratio. DICP, Ann Pharmacother. 1992;26: 430. Editorial.

46 **Vanscoy GJ, Krause JR.** Warfarin and the international normalized ratio: reducing the inter-laboratory effects. DICP, Ann Pharmacother. 1991;25: 1190.

47 **Triplett DA, Brandt J.** International normalized ratios; has their time come? Arch Pathol Lab Med. 1993;117:590. Editorial.

48 **Oesterling JE.** Prostate-specific antigen: a valuable clinical tool. Oncology. 1991;5:107.

49 **Garnick MB.** Prostate cancer: screening, diagnosis, and management. Ann Intern Med. 1993;118:804.

50 **Mettlin C et al.** Defining and updating the American Cancer Society guidelines for cancer-related check-up. CA Cancer J Clin. 1993;43:42.

51 **American Urological Association Executive Committee Report, 1992.** Baltimore, MD. American Urological Association; May 1992.

52 **Anon.** New prostate screening guidelines. Harvard Health Lett. 1993;18:2.

53 **Gan PH et al.** Prospective evaluation of plasma prostate-specific antigen for detection of prostate cancer. JAMA. 1995;273:289.

54 **Lange PH.** New information about prostate-specific antigen and the paradoxes of prostate cancer. JAMA. 1995; 273:336.

55 **Haber HL et al.** The erythrocyte sedimentation rate in congestive heart failure. N Engl J Med. 1991;324:353.

56 **Henry-Amar M et al.** Erythrocyte sedimentation rate predicts early relapse and survival in early-stage Hodgkin disease. Ann Intern Med. 1991; 114:361.

57 **British Committee for Standards in Haematology; Haemostasis and Thrombosis Task Force.** Guidelines on oral anticoagulation. 2nd ed. J Clin Path. 1990;43:177.

58 **Third ACCP Consensus Conference on Antithrombotic Therapy.** Chest. 1992;102(Suppl.):303S.

59 **Comparison of thromboplastins using the ISI and the INR systems.** Path. 1990;22:71.

60 **Taberner DA et al.** Effect of international sensitivity index (ISI) of thromboplastins on precision of international normalized ratios (INR). J Clin Path. 1989;42:92.

61 **Howard PA.** Monitoring warfarin therapy with the international normalized ratio. Ann Pharmacother. 1984;28:242.

62 **Anon.** ASHP therapeutic position statement on the use of the international normalized ratio system to monitor oral anticoagulant therapy. Am J Health-Syst Pharm. 1995;52:529.

Implications of Biotechnology for Clinical Practice

Milo Gibaldi

Recombinant Proteins 5-1
Monoclonal Antibodies (MABs) 5-1
   Some Clinical Applications 5-2
   Radioimmunoconjugates 5-2
   Immunotoxins 5-2
   Monoclonal Antibodies and Killer Cells 5-3
   Site-Directed Monoclonal Antibodies 5-3

Monoclonal Antibodies Accelerate Breakdown of Toxic
   and Addictive Drugs 5-4
Monoclonal Antibodies in the Treatment of
   Septic Shock 5-4
Gene Therapy 5-5
Regulating Biotechnology 5-7
Future Directions 5-7

The science of biotechnology emanates from two critical discoveries: the determination in 1944 that a nucleic acid called deoxyribose nucleic acid (DNA) plays a key role in inheritance[1] and the elucidation in 1953 of the double-helical structure of DNA.[2] This new paradigm joins and complements morphology and chemistry as means for describing, diagnosing, and treating disease.

Recombinant Proteins

In 1973 scientists reduced theory to practice by carrying out the first DNA recombination experiment.[3] They inserted a mammalian gene (a specific segment of DNA) coding for a particular protein into a bacterial vector and found replication of the gene and expression of the desired protein. The new technology had provided a mechanism to "copy" naturally occurring proteins, and in large amounts.

The first proteins to be made by recombinant DNA technology were human insulin and human growth hormone, peptides whose physiological roles and medical importance were recognized widely. Soon thereafter, however, investigators were producing proteins that previously had been difficult or impossible to obtain by isolation in quantities sufficient to treat disease.

About 20 human recombinant proteins currently are registered as drugs. They include interferons, colony-stimulating factors, and peptide hormones. Some, such as tissue plasminogen activator (tPA), hepatitis B vaccine, and erythropoietin, have achieved therapeutic prominence. Therapeutic recombinant proteins also have had a substantial economic impact. Erythropoietin is the first product of biotechnology to exceed one billion dollars in annual worldwide sales and hepatitis B vaccine is not far behind. Human insulin, human growth hormone, alpha-interferon, and granulocyte colony-stimulating factor (G-CSF) each had total sales in 1992 of more than $500 million.

Among the more recently approved recombinant human proteins are interleukin-2, for the treatment of metastatic renal cell carcinoma; beta-interferon, which modulates the course of multiple sclerosis; and DNase, an enzyme that may help in the treatment of lung congestion in patients with cystic fibrosis. Tumor necrosing factor (TNF), a small natural protein, secreted primarily by activated macrophages, which kills tumor cells in experimental animals is another potential product. TNF, however, causes devastating toxicity when given systemically and developers must resolve this problem before TNF can be considered a candidate for treating cancer.

Another recombinant protein under investigation is interleukin-1 receptor antagonist (ILRA). ILRA, a naturally occurring protein, binds to a widely distributed plasma membrane glycoprotein that regulates the actions of interleukin-1 (IL-1). ILRA, thereby, blocks the effects of this important cytokine.[4] If, as many believe, IL-1 is a key mediator of septic shock, the administration of ILRA (Antril) may limit the extensive tissue damage that is part of the syndrome.[5]

Early, uncontrolled (Phase II) studies were encouraging, suggesting that Antril reduced mortality associated with septic shock by as much as 60%, but a subsequent well-controlled (Phase III) trial with nearly 900 patients found no difference in mortality between patients treated with Antril and those receiving placebo. The startlingly different outcomes in the Phase II and III trials are a textbook example of why blinded and randomized clinical trials to evaluate new drugs are needed. Despite the general disappointment, Antril did show some activity in the most seriously ill patients and a second Phase III trial with Antril in this limited population is under way.

Monoclonal Antibodies (MABs)

Antibodies are large protein molecules produced by lymphocytes after exposure to an antigen. They are designed to attack foreign invaders. In nature, an "antibody" is polyclonal because it consists of a mixture of antibodies, derived from different cells, all of which have some activity against a specific antigen. Monoclonal antibodies to a specific antigen derived from a single cell line may be much more specific and safer.

Monoclonal antibodies do not exist in nature. Their production begins with the harvesting from mouse spleen of B-lymphocytes stimulated by introducing an antigen. Only a few of the B-lymphocytes recovered from the spleen, however, actually secrete the desired specific antibody. To increase the yield and enrich the population of antibody-secreting cells, investigators mix the lymphocytes with myeloma cells. This results in the membranes of the two cell types fusing together. The fused myeloma-B-lymphocyte is called a hybridoma and is capable of mass producing large quantities of identical antibody molecules.

As a result of the development of cell fusion technology, it is possible to produce large quantities of MABs to virtually any antigen. Now available are MABs that can react with proteins, carbohydrates, or nucleic acids. Investigators also have developed MABs that perform enzymatic functions by enhancing reactivity with intermediary products of chemical reactions.[6]

The Food and Drug Administration (FDA) has approved two therapeutic products based upon MABs: murine monoclonal antibody (OKT3) to prevent rejection in kidney transplantation and Digibind to remove tissue stores of digoxin from patients who exhibit digitalis toxicity. The agency also has given approval to a monoclonal antibody-based *in vivo* imaging agent incorporating indium[111] for the detection of colorectal and ovarian cancer. About 40 other MABs are in investigational clinical trials. Many of these, if safe and effective, will be used to stop or slow the growth of malignant tissues.

A monoclonal antibody derived from a tumor cell surface antigen, while not tumor-specific, will have a greater affinity for tumor tissue than for normal tissue. Binding to the antigen on the cell surface alone, however, rarely results in cell kill. Therapy with an unmodified antibody must rely upon the ability of the agent to trigger host effector mechanisms.

Since antibodies have at least two binding sites, the site not involved in binding to antigen can recruit monocytes, macrophages, granulocytes, and other cells to increase cytotoxicity at the tumor cell surface. The ability of unconjugated MABs to exert cytotoxic effects depends upon both the nature of the antibody and its capacity to activate endogenous cytotoxic mechanisms. Different classes of antibodies have different abilities to activate both complement and human effector cells.

Despite their ability to orchestrate an attack on tumor cells, unconjugated MABs are not as effective as had been hoped and investigators have sought other ways to increase cytotoxicity. One approach has been to link cytotoxic agents to the free binding site of the antibody. Radionuclides were the first conjugates considered. Early results, however, were disappointing. Drug and toxin conjugates also ran into obstacles.

Investigators identified several problems. Only a small percentage of the injected dose localized in the tumor; other organs showed evidence of uptake. Radionuclides came off the MAB and distributed in normal tissue. Toxin conjugates often caused toxicity at low doses with less than adequate delivery to the tumor. Drugs were bound either so tightly to the antibody that they were no longer toxic to the tumor cell or so loosely that they dissociated prematurely.[7] There was a limit to the number of doses that could be given because the MAB came from mice cells and often provoked an immune response. Today, biotechnology scientists have solved many of those problems.

Investigators now use banks of tissue specimens to select more specific MABs. They have developed stable-labeling techniques to prevent radionuclides from dissociating, without harming the ability of the protein to bind to its target antigen. Improved drug-antibody linkages with the appropriate degree of stability have been designed, allowing drugs to be released selectively within the target cell. Scientists also developed techniques to remove some regions of toxin molecules and improve the safety/effectiveness profile of immunotoxins. They have circumvented the problem of immunogenicity of mouse monoclonals by developing completely human monoclonals and by using genetic engineering techniques to replace a large percentage of the mouse monoclonal sequences with human protein.[7]

Some Clinical Applications

Progress in the development of safer and more effective MABs opened the floodgates to clinical research. Scientists learned that antibodies to surface markers on lymphocytes, particularly T-cells, are effective in blocking clinical rejection of grafts. These discoveries led to the development of OKT3.

Clinical investigators also gave attention to the treatment of autoimmune and inflammatory disease. They showed that monoclonal antibody therapy in patients with intractable systemic vasculitis may result in long-lasting remission. Working with a single patient, investigators used a combination of two MABs: CAMPATH-1H, a genetically engineered "humanized" form of a rat antibody capable of depleting human lymphocytes, and a rat antibody to the human CD4 molecule on T-helper cells that interferes with the function of this cell-surface adhesion receptor.[8]

Three courses of CAMPATH-1H therapy at monthly intervals resulted each time in dramatic improvement of the patient's skin rash and resolution of his fever. Remission, however, was short lived. The investigators then gave the patient CAMPATH-1H followed by rat CD4 antibody. Complete remission of fever and other symptoms, persisting for more than three years, followed the sequential administration of the two antibodies. The patient presented no immune response to antibody therapy.

A follow-up report described the outcome of MAB therapy in three additional patients.[9] Although two patients had a good response, one patient had an antiglobulin reaction against CAMPATH-1H, despite "humanization" and failed to achieve a long-term remission.

CAMPATH-1H also has shown benefit in rheumatoid arthritis.[10] There is compelling evidence that T-lymphocytes have a vital role in the pathogenesis of RA. Investigators gave a daily intravenous (IV) dose of CAMPATH-1H to eight patients with rheumatoid arthritis for ten days. Seven patients showed significant clinical benefit, lasting for eight months in one case. After one course of therapy, there was no measurable adverse reaction to the drug. On retreatment of four patients, however, three became sensitized. The investigators concluded that "humanization" reduces the immunogenicity of rodent antibodies but immune responses that reduce the therapeutic effect may occur on repeated therapy.

Radioimmunoconjugates

As a consequence of the improvements in the design of MABs, radioimmunotherapy has gained a new lease on life. In this form of treatment, radioisotope-labeled monoclonal antibodies that can recognize and bind tumor-associated antigens are given systemically with the hope that the antibodies will preferentially target lethal radioactivity to tumor sites, sparing normal tissues. Leukemias and lymphomas are particularly good targets for radioimmunotherapy because of their sensitivity to radionuclides.

Clinical scientists recently reported on the antitumor effects and toxicity of ^{131}I-labeled antiB$_1$ antibody in patients with non-Hodgkin's lymphoma.[11] AntiB$_1$ is a mouse monoclonal antibody directed against the CD20 B-lymphocyte-associated surface membrane antigen, widely expressed by normal and malignant B-cells. Six of nine treated patients had favorable tumor responses; four patients had complete remissions and remained free of disease for at least eight months. There was little or no toxicity.

Immunotoxins

Immunotoxins (i.e., antibody-toxin conjugates) are another therapeutic option for the treatment of cancer. Scientists typically have used highly potent protein toxins to design immunotoxins. Toxins used clinically are ricin, a natural material purified from the seeds of the castor bean; diphtheria toxin, derived from *Corynebacterium diphtheriae*; and *Pseudomonas* exotoxin, derived from *Pseudomonas aeruginosa*. Ricin consists of an A-chain linked by a disulfide bond to a B-chain. Immunotoxins made of whole ricin are very potent, but they lack specificity because the B-chain binds to galactosyl residues of glycoproteins and glycolipids found on the surface of many cells. Coupling the A-chain alone seems to decrease the nonspecific binding and substantial toxicity of conjugates based upon whole ricin.[12]

Ricin A-based toxins are potent inhibitors of protein synthesis and possess a mechanism of cytotoxicity different from standard anticancer drugs so they circumvent usual mechanisms of resistance. If given directly to patients, these toxins also are lethal, but, by altering molecular structure, chemists can further eliminate nonspecific binding and thereby attenuate nonspecific toxicity.

One review described the findings of clinical trials with ricin-based immunotoxins in patients with colorectal and breast cancers, and malignant melanomas.[13] These trials have identified serious problems requiring attention: 1) A single MAB seldom reacts with more than a small fraction of cells within a tumor. Investigators now believe a cocktail of at least three antibodies recognizing different tumor antigens is needed in the treatment of colorectal cancer and at least two antibodies are required to adequately target ovarian cancer cells. 2) Immunotoxins are not sufficiently sparing of normal tissue, resulting in serious side effects. 3) Simple access to a solid tumor may be a major problem because tumors are poorly perfused and because the high molecular weight of the antibody-toxin conjugate limits diffusion.

An immunotoxin consisting of chemically modified ricin A-chain and RFB4, an antiCD22 mouse MAB targeting B-lymphocytes, is effective in treating B-cell lymphoma. This immunotoxin produced a 50% partial response rate when more than half of the tumor cells in a patient carried the targeted antigen.

The most successful immunotoxin to date, H65-RTA, also uses the ricin A-chain as the toxic entity. The antibody acts against T-lymphocytes and is effective in patients with graft-versus-host disease (GVHD). Its success in GVHD is largely the consequence of the indication itself, which bypasses many of the problems that have arisen with other indications. Patients who are to receive a bone marrow graft are deliberately and severely immunosuppressed, to avoid graft rejection, so the anti-immunotoxin responses are low in incidence and titer. Furthermore, only one course of immunotoxin is needed to destroy the majority of mature lymphocytes producing the disease.

H65-RTA also has shown activity against rheumatoid arthritis. A five-day course produced a greater than 50% overall decrease in joint point and swelling in patients with rheumatoid arthritis. In some cases, improvement persisted for more than one year. Circulating T-lymphocytes decreased sharply within 24 hours of the start of treatment, to about 20% of baseline. However, the counts returned to baseline within a few days after completion of therapy, even though joint scores remained substantially improved for many months.

Other investigators have studied the use of a monoclonal immunotoxin in Hodgkin's disease.[14] Its characteristic histology features the presence of Reed-Sternberg cells. In Hodgkin's disease, these cells consistently express the antigen CD30. A newly developed monoclonal antibody, Ber-H2, directed against an antigenic determinant of CD30, binds avidly to Reed-Sternberg cells but exerts no antitumor effect. Investigators gave an immunotoxin prepared by chemically linking Ber-H2 to saporin, a potent cytotoxic protein derived from plant sources, to patients with advanced Hodgkin's disease resistant to conventional treatment.

All four patients showed a measurable decrease in tumor mass within one week of injection, and in three of them tumor size decreased by 50% to 100%. Clinical responses, however, lasted only six to ten weeks and antibodies to both parts of the immunotoxin developed in all patients, precluding further treatment. Combining Ber-H2 to a different cytotoxic protein may prevent the antibody response. In the meantime, the investigators suggested that Ber-H2/saporin immunotoxin may have a role in the treatment of minimum residual disease in certain forms of Hodgkin's disease where a single administration might be very useful.

Monoclonal Antibodies and Killer Cells

Scientists have demonstrated that one can target human cytotoxic T-lymphocytes to a tumor by conjugating them with MABs to a tumor cell antigen. Their work holds promise for the treatment of colon cancer.[15] Killer cells are a subset of T-cells capable of lysing virus-infected, foreign, or cancerous cells. Culturing killer cells in a media containing interleukin-2 markedly enhances their cytotoxicity. These cells are called lymphokine-activated killer cells (LAK cells). LAK cells are cytotoxic to colon cancer cells in vitro but, in clinical trials, human colon cancer has been refractory to immunotherapy with LAK cells.

When the investigators gave antibody-directed LAK cells to severely immunodeficient mice with established human colon cancer tumors there was both increased uptake into the tumor and increased suppression of tumor growth compared with the administration of LAK cells alone. There also were significant improvements in the survival of tumor-bearing mice. The investigators concluded that, as a result of their work, "It will be possible to test genetically modified effector cells by conjugating the cells with tumor-specific antibodies to further increase their antitumor effects."[15]

One of the most interesting drug-antibody conjugates in development is BR96-doxorubicin (BR96-DOX). BR96 is a "humanized" variant of a mouse MAB.[16] It binds to a tumor-associated antigen abundantly expressed on many human carcinoma lines. It offers advantages over most other MABs to human tumors because it is more tumor-selective and is rapidly internalized after binding to cells expressing the antigen. BR96-DOX induced complete regressions and cures of grafted human lung, breast, and colon carcinomas growing subcutaneously in mice and cured 70% of mice bearing extensive metastases of a human lung carcinoma.

Site-Directed Monoclonal Antibodies

Scientists also have used MABs to direct therapeutic agents to sites other than tumors. Improved access to the central nervous system (CNS) is of particular interest. The typical products of biotechnology are so large, water-soluble, and biologically unstable that their administration poses major challenges. How does one get these molecules across cell membranes to the brain, lungs, or other target tissues?

A recent report on nerve growth factor (NGF) provides an example of the ingenuity applied to the task of delivering therapeutic agents. Survival of cholinergic neurons of the basal forebrain, which degenerate in patients with Alzheimer's disease, depends upon an adequate supply of NGF. Direct administration of nerve growth factor to the brain in rats with experimental brain lesions rescues degenerating cholinergic neurons and leads to functional recovery.[17] Given that direct injection into the brain is not practical or safe in humans, investigators interested in the therapeutic application of NGF in patients with Alzheimer's dementia must first find a way to get the protein across the blood-brain barrier.

The blood-brain barrier consists of specialized capillary endothelial cells joined by highly restrictive tight junctions. It prevents the passage of large, water-soluble molecules from the blood to the central nervous system. However, investigators have demonstrated facilitated transport of some biologically active proteins across the blood-brain barrier. For example, after intravenous injection of certain antibodies to brain-receptor protein, one can find the antibodies in the central nervous system bound to brain capillary endothelial cells.[18] More recently, investigators reported that drugs conjugated to these antibodies also can cross the blood-brain barrier.[19,20]

Others have shown that nerve growth factor, conjugated to a brain-receptor-protein antibody, also crosses the blood-brain barrier. The conjugated NGF, given by intravenous injection, increased survival of both cholinergic and noncholinergic neurons in brain tissue. As a result of their findings, the investigators suggested: "The ability to deliver proteins to the brain will facilitate a critical examination of the efficacy of neurotrophic factors on the amelioration of neurodegenerative disorders."[59]

Monoclonal Antibodies Accelerate Breakdown of Toxic and Addictive Drugs

One of the most novel applications of MAB therapy is in the treatment of cocaine intoxications. Among the common drug dependencies, cocaine addiction is the most difficult to treat. Currently, there are no drugs that block uptake of cocaine at brain receptors, but scientists have made progress in interrupting the delivery of cocaine to its receptors.

Enzymes hydrolyze cocaine via a high-energy, unstable tetrahedral intermediate to form inactive products. Although hydrolysis is rapid, it is not sufficiently rapid to prevent some cocaine from reaching the brain. One report described the development of anti-cocaine antibodies that catalyze the hydrolysis of cocaine and may effectively prevent the delivery of cocaine to the brain.[21]

Scientists raised antibodies by injecting mice with an immunogenic compound whose structure resembles that of the tetrahedral intermediate. They found that these antibodies bind and stabilize the tetrahedral intermediate and catalyze the hydrolysis of cocaine. Monoclonal antibodies derived from the polyclonal pool increased the rate of cocaine hydrolysis by a factor of 100 to 1000. A commentary on this work notes that such antibodies are a form of passive immunization, preventing cocaine from reaching the brain and causing the "rush" that makes it so addictive.[22]

Monoclonal Antibodies in the Treatment of Septic Shock

The most controversial application of MAB therapy is in the treatment of sepsis. Sepsis syndrome or septic shock (sepsis syndrome with hypotension) is a frequently fatal, inflammatory response to infections usually involving endotoxin-producing gram-negative bacteria and sometimes other organisms. *Escherichia coli*, *Klebsiella* species, and *Staphylococcus* species are the most commonly encountered organisms. Sepsis affects hundreds of thousands of people in the U.S. each year. In more than 50% of cases, sepsis syndrome leads to major organ damage, often involving the lungs, and, depending upon the patient population, from 20% to 90% die, despite treatment.[23] Septic shock is among the most dreaded complications of surgery and in critically ill patients.

The use of immunologic therapy for the prevention and treatment of septic shock currently is under investigation. Scientists have identified endotoxin, a component of the outer membrane of gram-negative bacilli, as a mediator of septic shock. Interventions directed at endotoxin appear to be protective in experimental and clinical sepsis.[24] Two endotoxin-targeted MABs have received attention: E5, a monoclonal mouse antibody to the endotoxin from clinically important gram-negative organisms; and HA-1A, a human IgM antibody that binds to the lipid A components of endotoxin. Both E5 and HA-1A bind to endotoxin from a wide variety of gram-negative bacteria.

A team of investigators reported results from a well-controlled trial evaluating HA-1A.[25] In this study, the investigators gave a single dose of HA-1A to 262 patients with sepsis and suspected gram-negative infection; 281 patients received placebo. The protocol called for following the patients for 28 days or until death. Twenty-eight days after the start of the study, mortality rate was 49% in patients with gram-negative bacteremia treated with placebo and 30% in those treated with antibody. For patients with gram-negative bacteremia and shock at study entry, mortality was 57% in the placebo group and 33% in the HA-1A group. HA-1A seemed to have no effect in patients with gram-negative infection but no bacteremia. All patients tolerated HA-1A well, and the investigators detected no antiHA-1A antibodies.

In another multicenter clinical trial, nearly 500 patients received two intravenous doses of E5 or placebo, 24 hours apart.[26] Thirty-day mortality in the entire panel was 17% and there was no difference between the treated and untreated groups. Among those with confirmed gram-negative sepsis, who made up about two-thirds of all patients, 30-day mortality was about 25%, and again there was little difference between treated and placebo groups. More than half of the patients with confirmed gram-negative sepsis were in shock refractory to usual treatment. Mortality in this subgroup was 50% among those randomized to E5 and 45% among those assigned placebo. The only subgroup in which E5 was significantly more effective than placebo consisted of patients with confirmed gram-negative sepsis who were not in shock. Mortality was 41% in the treated group and 68% in the placebo group.

Neither E5 nor HA-1A decreased mortality in a general population of patients presumed to have gram-negative septic shock, but each benefited some patients. E5 was effective in sepsis patients with gram-negative infection who were not in shock, regardless of the presence of bacteremia. HA-1A provided benefit to patients with gram-negative bacteremia regardless of whether shock was present.

The clinical implications of both studies are clouded by the fact that one cannot clinically identify the patient with gram-negative (compared with gram-positive or fungal) sepsis at the onset of the septic syndrome when therapy must be initiated.[27] In both trials, the investigators demonstrated effectiveness in only a relatively small fraction of the study population. E5 showed benefit in 29% of the patients, while HA-1A benefited 37% of the patients. In both cases, identification of the patients who would benefit depended upon knowing the results of bacteriological cultures, which would only be available some 18 hours after the patient became acutely ill. This means that only about one-third of the at-risk population would benefit from an antisepsis antibody given empirically before microbiological confirmation to those thought to have gram-negative sepsis. While this approach may not cause harm, it would be very expensive.

The FDA's advisory panel on vaccines and other biological products agreed that HA-1A was safe and effective for the treatment of septic patients with a presumptive diagnosis of gram-negative bacteremia, including those with shock. The panel expressed concern, however, as to appropriate patient selection criteria.[28] At the same meeting, the FDA asked the panel to defer recommendations on E5.[29] Following this request, the drug's sponsor presented published findings as well as preliminary data from a second Phase III study.

The first trial showed E5 was effective in improving survival among patients with gram-negative sepsis who were not in shock. The second trial, however, failed to demonstrate a survival advantage in the same type of patients. In addition, E5 did not improve survival in the group of patients with major morbidities as it had in the first trial. Although the sponsor argued that collectively its clinical data showed a clear benefit with E5 in certain patients, the advisory panel unanimously concluded that the data were insufficient to support a claim of efficacy and voiced reservations about the use of subset analysis to isolate a benefit in a relatively small number of patients.

A few months later, to the surprise of many observers, the FDA announced it wanted to see the results of a second clinical trial before resuming the review of HA-1A.[30] The agency stated that since the advisory committee meeting, its staff learned that the drug's sponsor had revised the protocol for analyzing the data in the middle of the trial after looking at interim results, an action the FDA said could have introduced bias into the results.[31]

Another severe blow to the fortunes of the antiendotoxin monoclonal antibodies, particularly HA-1A, was a critical commentary published by Warren et al.[32] Warren's critique raised important questions as to the reliability of the data supporting the effectiveness of HA-1A. At the heart of the matter, independent investigators could not reproduce the results of preclinical studies showing very high binding between the antibody and the endotoxin receptor on the surface of gram-negative organisms and protection of laboratory animals from experimental gram-negative septic shock, purported findings which served as the catalyst for the clinical development of HA-1A.[33]

Warren et al. also pointed out that clinicians most likely would use antiendotoxin monoclonal antibodies as adjunctive therapy and would not expect benefit in patients who receive inadequate antimicrobial therapy. Among patients with gram-negative bacteremia in the placebo group of the HA-1A trial, the investigators saw a strong association between inappropriate antimicrobial therapy and death. The mortality rate was 69% with inappropriate therapy but only 27% with appropriate therapy.[34]

In the large clinical trial evaluating HA-1A, the investigators included patients who had received inadequate therapy in the analysis of the HA-1A clinical study, and considerably more patients in the placebo group than in the active treatment group received inappropriate antimicrobial therapy. When data analysis included only patients who received adequate chemotherapy, HA-1A had no significant effect on mortality rate in patients with gram-negative bacteremia.[35]

The most damaging news of all for HA-1A came in early 1993. The news media reported that an outside review of interim data from a second Phase III trial found a higher mortality rate in patients treated with HA-1A who turned out not to have gram-negative bacteremia than in similar patients who received placebo. Consequently, the drug's sponsor halted the trial.[36] No one knows at this time the ultimate fates of E5 and HA-1A.

Gene Therapy

After almost a decade of expectation that the technology to isolate and purify human genes would lead rapidly to gene therapies, the first human trial, involving administration of cells containing a foreign gene to mark the distribution of the cells, began in May 1989. The National Institutes of Health (NIH), in September 1990, approved the first gene therapy treatment plan to correct a genetic deficiency in adenosine deaminase (ADA). The next three years saw an explosion of clinical testing to find gene-based treatments for genetic diseases and cancer.

The treatment of genetic diseases by replacing affected genes with functioning ones almost is intuitively obvious. Writing on the treatment of inherited disorders, a leading expert observed: "The ability to introduce genetic information that would directly correct or replace the function of the affected genes would be the ultimate form of therapy."[37] Delivering functional genes to the appropriate site, however, is a formidable challenge.

One of the earliest disease targets for human gene therapy was ADA deficiency. After speculation on the use of viruses as gene-transfer vectors, investigators selected retroviruses for the first attempts at gene therapy in humans. Two fundamental approaches to gene therapy guided early efforts and continue to be applied: the *in vivo* approach (i.e., the introduction of a functioning gene into a cell that lacks the gene or contains a defective gene) and the *ex vivo* approach (i.e., the removal of cells from a patient, the introduction of a gene into the cells, and the return of the modified cells to the patient).[38]

Viral vectors have the advantage of infecting multiple cell types with efficiencies up to 100%. These altered viruses can infect cells and insert foreign genes but they cannot replicate and produce more infectious viruses because their own genetic material is removed and replaced by the "therapeutic" gene.[39] By replacing the viral gene with the therapeutic gene and counting on the efficient viral infection process, investigators have shown that the therapeutic gene penetrates the target cell as if it were a viral gene.

Retroviruses are a class of viruses that contain reverse transcriptase, an enzyme required for replication. Retroviral-mediated gene transfer takes place only in target cells that are actively synthesizing DNA. This requirement can be exploited to limit gene delivery to proliferating tumor cells present in an organ in which the resident normal cells are not proliferating. Retroviral vectors have a broad host range, enabling the introduction of genes not only into adherent cells (e.g., solid tumor cells) but also into many suspension cells (e.g., lymphoid, myeloid) and hematopoietic stems cells in the bone marrow.[40]

Gene delivery by means of replication-deficient adenovirus vectors also is of interest. Adenoviruses are capable of efficiently infecting nondividing cells. Less well-developed viral vectors that also may have applications in gene therapy are adeno-associated virus, herpes virus, and vaccina virus.[41]

Investigators designed the first gene transfer protocol to mark infused tumor-infiltrating lymphocytes (TILs) with a DNA tag that would not alter cellular physiology but would enable them to determine the fate of these cells when given to patients receiving adoptive immunotherapy for cancer. They used the bacterial antibiotic resistance gene for neomycin phosphotransferase as the marker gene.[42] Although this protocol produced little information of direct clinical interest, it was very important because it demonstrated the safety (no side effects or pathology of any kind have been attributable to the gene transfer) and feasibility of gene transfer (marked cells could be recovered both from the blood stream and from tumors).[42] It also showed that at least some TILs, if not all, have the ability to target the tumor.

The next step in this series of investigations involved the introduction of unmarked genes into TIL cells. The investigators selected genes coding for proteins that either can directly kill tumor cells or induce a strong local immune response and indirectly produce an antitumor effect. If the gene-modified TIL cells targeted tumor deposits, they could deliver cytotoxic agents locally and avoid the toxicity associated with systemic administration of such agents. The first protocol in this line of research called for insertion of the gene for tumor necrosing factor. There now is ample evidence of the safety of this procedure but the effectiveness of the approach has not been demonstrated.[43]

Another potential approach to treating cancer is the introduction of lymphokine genes into transplantable tumor cells. Animal studies indicate these cells can destroy the ability of tumor cells to become established as tumors. Protocols involving the use of TNF-modified[44] or IL-2-modified[45] tumor cells returned to the patient by means of intramuscular or subcutaneous injection are under investigation. Insertion of genes for making interleukins, TNF, or interferons into tumor cells also may increase the immune recognition of tumors and lead to their rejection. In a similar vein, melanoma cells are being treated to induce them to produce foreign HLA antigens so that once reincorporated in the tumor they become targets for immune rejection.[46]

Another protocol, approved for investigational treatment of patients with metastatic renal cell cancer, calls for modifying patients' own tumor cells to secrete granulocyte-macrophage colony stimulating factor (GM-CSF), a hematological growth hormone. GM-CSF stimulates the functional activities of some white blood cells and macrophages, including their antitumor cytotoxic activities. Investigators have shown that insertion of the gene coding for GM-CSF into tumor cells greatly enhances the interaction between tumor-specific antigens and the tumor cell surface, resulting in a rapid antitumor effect mediated by T-lymphocytes.[47]

A novel and creative approach to the treatment of gliobastoma and other brain tumors using mouse fibroblasts "infected" with a retroviral vector containing a "suicide gene" also is under investigation. The "suicide gene" exists in herpes simplex virus and codes for thymidine kinase, an enzyme highly sensitive to ganciclovir, a potent antiviral agent. After injection of infected fibroblasts directly into the brain tumor, the transplanted cells generate the retrovirus and it transduces the rapidly dividing tumor cells while not affecting normal cells because they are mitotically inactive. After several days, injection of ganciclovir kills all cells containing the thymidine kinase gene including the mice fibroblasts. The NIH approved a protocol for transferring a viral gene into human brain tumor cells, making them susceptible to destruction by ganciclovir, in June 1992 and the study currently is under way.[48]

The NIH also approved the first gene therapy protocols to use the multidrug resistance (MDR) gene in patients with cancer to protect the bone marrow from the toxic effects of chemotherapy and, thereby, permit the administration of higher doses of anticancer agents. The protocol calls for introducing, by means of a retroviral vector, the MDR gene into stem cells harvested from the bone marrow of patients with advanced ovarian cancer. After receiving usual chemotherapy, the patients will be reinfused with the modified cells and treated with increasing doses of anticancer drugs. The hope is that the glycoprotein pump encoded by the MDR gene will remove cytotoxic agents from marrow cells and avoid dose-limiting myelosuppression.

Despite the popular emphasis on therapeutic gene protocols, marker gene protocols continue to command interest. Of particular importance are studies using the neomycin resistance gene to label a portion of collected bone marrow and determine the origins of relapse in leukemias and other cancers after bone marrow transplantation. The usual procedure calls for ablative chemotherapy and subsequent salvage with autologous bone marrow. Relapses, however, are common. The outcome of these gene marker studies has clinical importance because it would tell us whether *ex vivo* bone marrow purging of residual disease or more stringent ablative therapy is the appropriate course of treatment to minimize recurrence. In one study, the first two patients with acute myeloid leukemia who suffered a relapse had gene-marked cells in the leukemic-relapsed cells. As a result of this information, experts in bone marrow transplantation now are focusing their efforts on improving bone marrow purging techniques.

The first therapeutic gene transfer protocol proposed isolating lymphocytes from a patient with ADA deficiency, introducing a human ADA gene by means of a retroviral vector *in vitro*, expanding the altered lymphocytes in culture, and returning the lymphocytes to the patient. The expectation was that this would initiate the synthesis of ADA and jump-start the functions of the cellular and antibody immune systems.

The protocol began in Fall 1990 with a four-year old; the investigators enrolled a second patient a few months later. The results so far have been encouraging, showing improved immune functions and the presence of a substantial number of gene-corrected circulating T-cells. Both children attend regular public schools and now have no more than the average number of infections for children their age. There have been no significant side effects from the cell infusions and no detected side effects from the presence of the transferred ADA gene itself.

Patients with cystic fibrosis (CF) lack the CF transmembrane conductance regulator (CFTR) gene, essential for the regulation of chloride channels in the airway epithelial cells. The lack of this gene in patients with cystic fibrosis results in the buildup of viscid mucus in the lungs and the development of pulmonary infections sometimes impossible to eradicate.

The NIH has approved three separate protocols to deliver the normal chloride transport gene missing in patients with cystic fibrosis. In one study, the investigators will place the gene in the nostrils, in another in the lungs, and in the third in both the nostrils and lungs. All three studies will use a recombinant adenovirus vector for gene delivery for the first time. The retroviral vectors ordinarily used in gene therapy can only "infect" dividing cells and are unlikely to be efficient in transducing the target cells in the lungs, which divide slowly.[49]

Another gene therapy protocol approved by the NIH seeks to treat patients with an inherited form of elevated cholesterol. These people lack the gene expressing low-density lipoprotein (LDL) receptors in the liver, which are essential to keep blood levels of cholesterol in check. This project already has met with some success.

The first patient to be treated had baseline cholesterol levels ranging from 500 to 650 mg/dL resistant to lipid-lowering drugs. After surgically removing a small part of her liver and infecting the harvested hepatocytes in culture with a modified retrovirus that contained an LDL-receptor gene, the investigators returned the cells to the patient. Soon after, a liver biopsy showed that the LDL-receptor gene was functioning and serum LDL cholesterol levels fell by 20% to 40%.[50] The next step will be to give the patient cholesterol-lowering drugs, hoping to further reduce cholesterol levels. These agents had no effect on lipid levels before gene therapy because they work by stimulating the activity of LDL receptors, which the patient lacked.

Another protocol seeks to correct Hemophilia B, a blood coagulation disorder arising from a deficiency or absence of Factor IX, a blood-clotting protein. Patients have received autologous fibroblasts modified with a retroviral vector containing the gene for human Factor IX. Results are not yet available.

Also approved is a treatment protocol for Gaucher's disease, a rare inherited disorder now treated by enzyme replacement therapy using a modified form of glucocerebrosidase. Gene therapy promises to provide a more permanent replacement of the enzyme than the current treatment in which the missing enzyme is administered by periodic injections.

Several approaches to the treatment of human immunodeficiency virus (HIV) infection by means of gene therapy are being considered, none of which are generating encouraging results. Many believe it is unlikely gene therapy will ever be a practical form of therapy because it is too costly and cumbersome to treat the millions of individuals worldwide with HIV infection.[51]

Nonviral means of introducing DNA into cells also are under study. One approach for *in vivo* gene transfer involves encapsulation of DNA in liposomes.[52] Investigators have administered a marker gene packaged in liposomes to rats by means of a nebulizer. They measured significant levels of gene activity throughout the airways and alveoli of the lungs for at least 21 days. They saw no expression of the marker gene in tissues other than the lungs. Histological evaluation showed no apparent damage to the lung epithelial tissue after exposure.[53] The results have important implications for the development of human gene therapy.

Although experience suggests that insertion of foreign DNA into cells requires elaborate genetic-engineering tricks (e.g., the use of disarmed viral vectors) or promoters (e.g., liposomes), direct injection of DNA also may lead to uptake and expression of DNA, particularly in muscle tissue. This discovery came about when industrial scientists were trying to get mice to make new proteins by chemically coercing their muscle cells into taking up foreign DNA.

As a control, they left out the chemical promoter and found that muscle cells took up the DNA anyway and produced even higher levels of the foreign protein.[54]

More recently, investigators have shown that naked DNA can work as a vaccine to protect mice from influenza virus.[55] The researchers focused on the nucleoprotein (NP) component of influenza A virus. They stitched the DNA that codes for NP into a circular piece of bacterial DNA called a plasmid. Injecting the plasmid carrying the viral gene into the muscles of mice produced NP-specific antibodies and primary cytotoxic T-lymphocytes (CTLs) directed against NP. Challenged with a lethal dose of influenza, 90% of the protected mice survived, compared with only 20% of the controls.

This unusual vaccine may provide powerful cross-strain protection against influenza. Ordinary flu vaccines elicit antibodies against surface proteins on the virus. These surface proteins mutate rather easily and mutations render the vaccine inactive. In contrast, core pieces of the virus, such as the nucleoprotein used in this study, rarely change and can activate the production of killer cells as well as protein-specific antibodies. This technique also may work for other infectious pathogens.

Regulating Biotechnology

In the U.S., all drugs and biologics intended for human use require review, approval, and regulation. Most of the responsibility falls to the FDA. Gene therapy protocols must undergo multiple levels of review. The National Institutes of Health's Recombinant DNA Advisory Committee (RAC) plays a key role in this process. The NIH established the RAC in 1991 to review protocols concerned with recombinant DNA. Sometime later, the NIH asked the committee to assume the responsibility of reviewing gene therapy protocols as well. The NIH requires review for any protocol involving investigators or institutions in receipt of federal funding. While not required, biotechnology companies often ask the RAC to review recombinant DNA and gene therapy protocols.

The Recombinant DNA Advisory Committee reports its recommendations directly to the Director of the NIH whose approval is needed before any protocol can be initiated. A specialist journal, *Human Gene Therapy*, publishes every protocol approved by the RAC. The advisory committee's principal responsibility in reviewing clinical protocols is safeguarding individuals and society. Final approval for recombinant DNA and gene therapy protocols rests with the FDA.

Future Directions

What does the future hold? One observer estimates that about 150 new recombinant proteins, some of which have no precedent in nature, now are in some stage of clinical evaluation. Looking into the future, he predicts that drug companies will market 30 to 40 of these proteins successfully over the next five years.[56] He also forecasts that during this period at least 10% to 15% of revenues and profits derived from new drugs will stem from recombinant proteins.

The biotechnology industry is now moving beyond proteins to develop a more balanced menu of genetically engineered drugs. Drugs based upon the other major types of biologically active molecules (nucleic acids, sugars, and fats) now are in development. New technologies are revealing new vistas.

According to one observer, some companies are focusing on the genetic code in an effort to design drugs that block it from giving instructions for making disease-causing proteins such as oncogenes. Some are seeking to block protein synthesis at its first stage: the transcription of DNA into messenger RNA. Their first target is likely to be viruses (e.g., herpes). Others see advantages in blocking protein synthesis after the messenger RNA is made. One approach is the "antisense" method. It involves the development of short pieces of nucleic acid that recognize and bind to specific messenger RNAs long enough to prevent protein synthesis.[57]

Other biotechnology laboratories are finding targets for new drugs in the receptors located on the cell surface. By binding to a surface receptor, a drug may prevent the binding of molecules that interact with the receptor and initiate a cellular response. Some companies are designing small organic molecules that bind with receptors while others are customizing novel peptides.

In 1991 most observers considered gene therapy an experimental and unproved technology. Things have changed dramatically. According to one expert today, nearly a dozen companies are in the gene therapy business. To date, the NIH and/or the FDA review panels have approved 50 proposals to put foreign genes into patients. Therapies aimed at cancer, AIDS and other infectious diseases, Gaucher's disease, blood and brain diseases, and arthritis are among them.[58] Most current or planned applications, however, involve intensive individual patient-based therapies. For the long-term, major efforts are needed "to make gene therapy straightforward and routine before it can fulfill its promise as a broadly enabling therapeutic technique."[38]

References

1   Avery AT. Studies on the chemical nature of the substance inducing transformation of pneumococcal types. J Exp Med. 1994;79:137.

2   Watson JD, Crick FHC. Molecular structure of nucleic acids: a structure for deoxyribose nucleic acid. Nature. 1953;171:737.

3   Cohen SN et al. Construction of biologically functional bacterial plasmids in vitro. Proc Natl Acad Sci USA. 1973;70:3240–244.

4   Hannum CH et al. Interleukin-1 receptor antagonist activity of a human interleukin-1 inhibitor. Nature. 1990; 343:336.

5   Bone RC. A critical evaluation of new agents for the treatment of sepsis. JAMA. 1991;266:1686.

6   Kummer U, Staerz UD. Concepts of antibody-mediated cancer therapy. Cancer Invest. 1993;11:174.

7   Abrams P. Have monoclonals fulfilled their promise? Biotechnology. 1993; 11(No. 2):156.

8   Mathieson PW et al. Monoclonal-antibody therapy in systemic vasculitis. N Engl J Med. 1990;323:250.

9   Lockwood CM et al. Long-term remission of intractable systemic vasculitis with monoclonal antibody therapy. Lancet. 1993;341:1620.

10   Isaacs JD et al. Humanized monoclonal antibody therapy for rheumatoid arthritis. Lancet. 1992;340:748.

11   Kaminski MS et al. Radioimmunotherapy of B-cell lymphoma with [^{131}I] anti-B1 (anti-CD20) antibody. N Engl J Med. 1993;329:459.

12   Pai LH, Pastan I. Immunotoxin therapy for cancer. JAMA. 1993;269:78.

13   Byers VS, Baldwin RW. Target kill: from umbrellas to monoclonal antibodies. J Clin Immunol. 1992;12:391.

14   Falini B et al. Response of refractory Hodgkin's disease to monoclonal anti-CD30 immunotoxin. Lancet. 1992; 339:1195.

15   Takahashi H et al. Inhibition of human colon cancer growth by antibody-directed human LAK cells in SCID mice. Science. 1993;259:1460.

16   Trail PA et al. Cure of xenografted human carcinomas by BR96-doxorubicin immunoconjugates. Science. 1993;261: 212.

17   Hefti F. Nerve growth factor promotes survival of septal cholinergic neurons after fimbrial transactions. J Neurosci. 1986;6:2155.

18   Jefferies WA et al. Transferrin receptor on endothelium of brain capillaries. Nature. 1984;312:162.

19   Friden PM et al. Anti-transferrin receptor antibody and antibody-drug conjugates cross the blood-brain barrier. Proc Natl Acad Sci USA. 1991;88: 4771.

20   Pardridge WM et al. Selective transport of an anti-transferrin receptor antibody through the blood-brain barrier. J Pharmacol Exp Ther. 1991;259:66.

21   Landry DW et al. Antibody-catalyzed degradation of cocaine. Science. 1993; 259:1899.

22   Mortell V. Enzyme may blunt cocaine's action. Science. 1993;259: 1828.

23   Skolnick A. Inflammation-mediator blockers may be weapons against sepsis syndrome. JAMA. 1990;263:930.

24 **Teng N et al.** Protection against gram-negative bacteremia with human monoclonal IgM antibodies. Proc Natl Acad Sci USA. 1985;82:1790.

25 **Ziegler EJ et al.** Treatment of gram-negative bacteremia and septic shock with HA-1A human monoclonal antibody against endotoxin. N Engl J Med. 1991;324:429.

26 **Greenman RL et al.** A controlled clinical trial of E5 murine monoclonal IgM antibody to endotoxin in the treatment of gram-negative sepsis. JAMA. 1991; 266:1097.

27 **Parillo JE.** Management of septic shock: present and future. Ann Intern Med. 1991;115:491.

28 **Anon.** Centocor's *Centoxin* for presumptive gram-negative bacteremia, including shock, safe and effective, FDA advisory committee agrees, but ''reservations'' voiced. FDC Reports (The Pink Sheet). 1991;53(No. 36):14.

29 **Anon.** Xoma's E5 approval review put on hold for addition analyses; committee stop short of seeking further clinicals but suggests comparison to Centoxin. FDC Reports (The Pink Sheet). 1991;53(No. 36):17.

30 **Anon.** Centocor must perform second trial of Centoxin. FDC Reports (The Pink Sheet). 1992;54(No. 16):T&G 1.

31 **Winslow R.** Centocor shares fall 41% on FDA move. The Wall Street Journal. 1992 Apr 16:B6.

32 **Warren HS et al.** Anti-endotoxin monoclonal antibodies. N Engl J Med. 1992;326:1153.

33 **Baumgartner JD et al.** The HA-1A monoclonal antibody for gram-negative sepsis. N Engl J Med. 1991;325:281.

34 **Open Meeting of the Vaccines and Related Biological Products Advisory Committee, September 4, 1991.** Vol 1. Bethesda, MD: Food and Drug Administration; 1991:111–12.

35 **Open Meeting of the Vaccines and Related Biological Products Advisory Committee, September 4, 1991.** Vol. 1. Bethesda, MD: Food and Drug Administration; 1991:99–124.

36 **Fisher LM.** Investors punish Centocor for more bad news. The New York Times. 1993 Jan 19:C1,C5.

37 **Cournoyer D et al.** Gene therapy: a new approach for the treatment of genetic disorders. Clin Pharmacol Ther. 1990;47:1.

38 **Tolstoshev P.** Gene therapy, concepts, current trials and future directions. Annu Rev Pharmacol Toxicol. 1993; 32:573.

39 **Anderson WF.** Human gene therapy. Science. 1992;256:808.

40 **Gansbacher B et al.** Retroviral vector-mediated cytokine-gene transfer into tumor cells. Cancer Invest. 1993;11: 345.

41 **Mulligan RC.** The basic science of gene therapy. Science 1993;260:926.

42 **Fisher B et al.** Tumor localization of adoptively transferred indium-111 labeled tumor infiltrating lymphocytes in patients with metastatic melanoma. Clin Oncol. 1989;7:250.

43 **Anon.** TNF/TIL human gene therapy clinical protocol. Hum Gene Ther. 1990;1:443.

44 **Anon.** Immunization of cancer patients using autologous cancer cells modified by insertion of the gene for tumor necrosis factor. Hum Gene Ther. 1992;3: 57.

45 **Anon.** Immunization of cancer patients using autologous cancer cells modified by insertion of the gene for Interleukin-2. Hum Gene Ther. 1992;3:75.

46 **Shapiro LJ.** Gene therapy: possibilities and promise. Pediatr Res. 1993;33: 321.

47 **Pardoll DM et al.** Molecular engineering of the antitumor immune response. Bone Marrow Transplant. 1992; 9(Suppl. 1):182.

48 **Stone R.** Cancer therapy. Molecular ''surgery'' for brain tumors. Science. 1992;256:1513.

49 **Siegfried W.** Perspectives in gene therapy with recombinant adenoviruses. Exp Clin Endocrinol. 1993;101:7.

50 **Randall T.** First gene therapy for inherited hypercholesterolemia a partial success. JAMA. 1993;269:837.

51 **Buchschacher GL.** Molecular targets of gene transfer therapy for HIV infection. JAMA. 1993;269:2880.

52 **Nabel EG et al.** Site-specific gene expression in vivo by direct gene transfer into the arterial wall. Science. 1990; 249:1285.

53 **Stribling R et al.** Aerosol gene delivery *in vivo*. Proc Natl Acad Sci USA. 1992;89:11277.

54 **Wolff JA et al.** Direct gene transfer into mouse muscle cells in vivo. Science. 1990;247:1465.

55 **Ulmer JB et al.** Heterologous protection against influenza by injection of DNA encoding a viral protein. Science. 1993;259:1745.

56 **Drews J.** Into the 21st century. Biotechnology and the pharmaceutical industry in the next ten years. Biotechnology. 1993;11(March):S16.

57 **Gibbons A.** Biotech's second generation. Science. 1992;256:766.

58 **Culotta E.** New startups move in as gene therapy goes commercial. Science. 1993;260:914.

59 **Friden PM et al.** Blood-brain barrier penetration and in vivo activity of an NGF conjugate. Science. 1993;259:373.

Anaphylaxis and Drug Allergies

Paul M Beringer
Robert K Middleton

Epidemiology 6-1
Definition 6-1
Predisposing Factors 6-1
    Age and gender 6-1
    Genetic factors 6-1
    Associated illness 6-1
    Previous drug administration 6-1
    Drug-related factors 6-2
Pathogenesis 6-2
    Drugs as allergens and immunological classification
    (See Table 6.1) 6-2
        Type I: Anaphylactic reactions 6-2
        Type II: Cytotoxic reactions 6-2
        Type III: Immune complex mediated reactions 6-2
        Type IV: Cell mediated (delayed) reactions 6-2
Diagnosis 6-2
    Distinctive features of allergic reactions
    (See Table 6.2) 6-2
    Skin testing (See Table 6.4) 6-3
    Cross-reactivity 6-4
Generalized Reactions 6-4

Anaphylaxis (See Table 6.5) 6-4
Serum Sickness (See Tables 6.6 and 6.7) 6-8
Drug Fever (See Tables 6.8 and 6.9) 6-8
Hypersensitivity Vasculitis (HSV) (See Table 6.10) 6-8
Drug-Induced Vasculitis (See Tables 6.10 to 6.12) 6-10
Autoimmune Drug Reactions
    (See Tables 6.13 and 6.14) 6-10
Organ Specific Reactions 6-11
    Blood: Immune Cytopenias 6-11
    Liver 6-11
    Lung 6-11
    Kidney 6-11
    Skin 6-13
Pseudoallergic Reactions
(See Tables 6.15 and 6.16) 6-13
Prevention and Management of Allergic
Reactions 6-14
    Desensitization 6-17
        Beta-lactams (See Tables 6.17 and 6.18) 6-17
        Other drugs 6-19

Epidemiology

Allergic drug reactions account for 5% to 20% of all observed adverse drug reactions.[1-3] Adverse drug reactions have been reported to occur in as many as 30% of hospitalized patients, and 3% of all hospitalizations are a result of adverse drug reactions.[4] In a computerized surveillance study of over 36,000 hospitalized patients, 731 adverse events were identified. Of those, 1% were categorized as severe, life threatening, and allergic in nature.[5] The potential morbidity and mortality associated with allergic drug reactions is potentially great even though they occur infrequently.

Definition

In order to appropriately diagnose and treat a patient experiencing an allergic reaction, it is necessary to be able to differentiate allergic reactions from other closely related adverse drug reactions. One method of classification divides adverse reactions into those that are "predictable, usually dose-dependent, and related to the pharmacologic actions of the drug," and those that are "unpredictable, often dose independent, and are related to the individual's immunologic response or to genetic differences in susceptible patients."[1] Under this classification scheme, drug allergy or drug hypersensitivity is an unpredictable adverse drug reaction that is immunologically mediated.[1,2,6]

Predisposing Factors

Factors known to affect the incidence of allergic reactions can be categorized as being drug or patient related.[7]

Age and Gender. Children are less likely to become sensitized than adults, presumably because younger age is likely to be associated with less cumulative drug exposure.[6-9] A concurrent evaluation of over 15,000 patients revealed a significantly higher incidence (35%) of cutaneous reactions in females than in males.[10]

Genetic Factors. Patients with histories of allergic rhinitis, asthma, or atopic dermatitis who develop a systemic drug reaction tend to react more severely than others.[7,8,11] A patient's ability to metabolize a drug may affect the incidence of allergic reactions. Patients who are slow acetylators are more likely to develop antinuclear antibodies (ANAs) and symptoms of systemic lupus erythematosus (SLE) when treated with procainamide or hydralazine. (Drug-induced lupus reactions may be considered allergic in nature since they are associated with an immune response, as evidenced by an increase in antinuclear antibodies.) In addition, a link between certain histocompatibility types and a few allergic reactions has been identified.[7]

Associated Illness. The incidence of maculopapular rash with ampicillin therapy is markedly higher in patients with Epstein-Barr infections (e.g., infectious mononucleosis), lymphocytic leukemia, or gout.[2,7] About 64% of acquired immunodeficiency syndrome (AIDS) patients affected by *Pneumocystis carinii* pneumonia develop adverse reactions to medications (e.g., skin rash to sulfonamides). In addition, a higher incidence of skin eruptions with amoxicillin-clavulanate therapy has been found in human immunodeficiency virus (HIV)-positive patients with CD4+ cell counts below 200 cells/mm^3 compared with those with higher counts (62% versus 11%). One explanation for this increased susceptibility is thought to be due to impaired T-cell regulation of IgE production.[7]

Previous Drug Administration. A previous history of allergic reaction to a drug being considered for treatment, or one that is immunochemically similar, is the most reliable risk factor for development of a subsequent allergic reaction.[6,7] A commonly encountered example is the patient with a prior history of penicillin allergy, in whom all structurally related penicillin compounds should be avoided, and in whom the possibility of a reaction when using other beta-lactam antibiotics should be considered.[7]

Drug-Related Factors. The dose, frequency of exposure, and route of administration influence the incidence of drug allergy. For example, penicillin-induced hemolytic anemia requires high and sustained drug concentrations.[9] In beta-lactam antibiotic IgE sensitivity, frequent intermittent courses rather than continuous therapy are more likely to result in drug sensitization.[21] The route of administration is important both in terms of risk of sensitization and risk of allergic reaction in a previously sensitized individual. Topical administration carries the greatest risk of sensitization, while the oral route is the least sensitizing. Intramuscular (IM) administration is more sensitizing than the intravenous (IV) route. In a patient who is already sensitized to a specific medication, the risk of an allergic reaction to that medication is greatest when given intravenously and least when given orally. This is thought to be a function of the rate of drug delivery.[7]

Pathogenesis

The immunopathological mechanisms which lead to an allergic drug reaction occur in two phases: initial sensitization and subsequent elicitation.[12] Sensitization occurs as a result of binding of a drug or a metabolite to a carrier protein in a process referred to as haptenization.[2,3,6,11,12] This drug-protein (or drug metabolite-protein) complex induces the production of drug specific T- or B-lymphocytes and IgM, IgG, and IgE. Upon re-exposure to the drug, the patient is likely to present with allergic symptoms.[12]

Drugs as Allergens and Immunological Classification

Allergic drug reactions can be classified into one of four different types (see Table 6.1).[6,7]

Type I: anaphylactic reactions are acute generalized reactions which occur when a previously sensitized individual is re-exposed to a particular antigen. Reactions range in severity from pruritus and urticaria, to bronchospasm, respiratory distress, laryngeal edema, circulatory collapse, and death. Anaphylactic reactions to antibiotics and radiographic contrast media reportedly occur in 1 in every 5000 exposures, 10% of which are fatal.[13] Initial exposure to an antigen results in production of specific IgE antibodies. Upon re-exposure, antigen interacts with antibodies bound to the surface of mast cells or basophils causing the release of histamine and other mediators.[12] A period of several weeks is required after initial exposure and sensitization before an anaphylactic reaction can be elicited; once sensitized, however, an anaphylactic response can be elicited within minutes as a result of existing antibodies. In addition, an anaphylactic response can occur upon re-exposure to small amounts of drug administered by any route.[12-15] Reactions that clinically resemble anaphylaxis, but do not involve immunological mediators (antibodies), are termed anaphylactoid reactions.

Type II: cytotoxic reactions involve the interaction of IgG or IgM and can occur by three different mechanisms (see Table 6.1). Common clinical manifestations of cytotoxic reactions include: hemolytic anemia, thrombocytopenia, and granulocytopenia. Penicillin-induced hemolytic anemia is the most well-known example of a cytotoxic drug reaction. This reaction typically appears after seven days of high-dose therapy.[9,17,18]

Type III: immune-complex mediated reactions result from the formation of drug-antibody complexes in serum which often deposit in blood vessel walls resulting in activation of complement and endothelial cell injury.[16] Also referred to as serum sickness, these reactions typically manifest as fever, urticaria, arthralgia, and lymphadenopathy 7 to 21 days after exposure.[9,16]

Type IV: Cell-Mediated (Delayed) Reactions. In type IV reactions, antigen binds with sensitized T-lymphocytes. Contact dermatitis is the most common manifestation of cell-mediated reactions, although systemic reactions can occur.

An understanding of the immunological mechanism can be helpful in the diagnosis and treatment of an allergic reaction; however, the exact immunological mechanism is unknown for many allergic reactions to drugs. In addition, patients often present with a number of symptoms characteristic of more than one of the reactions described above. The use of many drugs concurrently in hospitalized patients also makes it difficult to identify the drug responsible for the reaction. Therefore, a careful drug history, as well as diagnostic tests (e.g., wheal and flare, in vitro detection of drug-specific IgE antibodies), often are necessary to appropriately diagnose and treat a patient.

Diagnosis

Distinctive Features of Allergic Reactions

The first step in the diagnosis of an allergic drug reaction is to recognize and differentiate it from other adverse drug reactions. This can be accomplished by having a good understanding of the distinctive features of allergic drug reactions (see Table 6.2).[2,6]

1. J.A., a 73-year-old female, is admitted from a nursing home with an infected decubitus ulcer. Cultures reveal *Staphylococcus aureus* which is sensitive to oxacillin, cefazolin, and vancomycin. Upon questioning, J.A. reports having experienced a rash to penicillin in the past. Her current medications include: docusate 100 mg PO BID, enalapril 5 mg PO Q AM, prednisone 20 mg PO QD, and ibuprofen 800 mg PO TID. What information should be obtained in order to determine if J.A.'s rash represents an allergic drug reaction?

The single most informative diagnostic procedure for allergic drug reactions is a detailed drug history (see Table 6.3). A detailed drug history is helpful in obtaining the information necessary to

Table 6.1		Immunopathologic Classification of Allergic Drug Reactions[a]	
Immunological Class	Antibody	Mechanism	Common Clinical Manifestations
Type I (Anaphylactic)	IgE	Drug-hapten reacts with IgE antibody on the surface of mast cells and basophils resulting in the release of mediators	Anaphylaxis
Type II (Cytotoxic)	IgG IgM	*Hapten-Cell Reaction:* Drug interacts with cell surfaces resulting in the formation of an immunogenic complex and the production of antibodies *Immune Complex Reaction:* Drug reacts with antibody in circulation forming a complex, which with complement, binds to the cell resulting in injury (Hematologic reactions only) *Autoimmune Reaction:* Drug induces autoantibody production against red blood cells	Hemolytic anemia, granulocytopenia, thrombocytopenia
Type III (Immune Complex)	IgG	Same as type II immune complex reactions (Nonhematologic reactions)	Serum sickness
Type IV (Cell Mediated)		Interaction of sensitized T-lymphocytes with drug antigen	Contact dermatitis

[a] Adapted from reference 6.

Table 6.2	Clinical Features of Allergic Drug Reactions[a]

- Have no correlation with known pharmacological properties of the drug
- Require an induction period on primary exposure but not on readministration
- Can occur with doses far below therapeutic range
- Often include a rash, angioedema, serum sickness syndrome, anaphylaxis, and asthma
- Occur in a small proportion of the population
- Disappear on cessation of therapy and reappear after readministration of a small dose of the suspected drug(s) of similar chemical structure
- Desensitization may be possible

[a] Adapted from reference 2.

determine if a reaction represents drug allergy and to identify the culprit drug. Inquiring about prior allergic and medication encounters is important to document the drugs to which the patient has or has not previously reacted. This can sometimes alert the clinician as to certain types of compounds the patient is likely to react to. In addition, the acquired information allows the clinician to characterize the drug reaction and to appreciate how such a reaction might be manifested in the patient upon exposure to the same, or immunologically similar, compound in the future.

The temporal relationship between drugs and reactions often is the strongest piece of evidence implicating an allergic reaction to a particular agent. Drugs that the patient has received for long continuous periods of time before the onset of a reaction are less likely to be implicated than drugs that have been recently initiated or restarted.[19] Equally important is to determine when an adverse reaction occurred. Many compounds have been reformulated over the years resulting in removal of sensitizing impurities (e.g., penicillin, vancomycin). Therefore, it is possible that re-exposure to the agent will not result in an adverse event. Inquiring about whether the patient has received the drug since the first episode by asking the patient about other brands or names of other drugs in the same class (e.g., amoxicillin, ampicillin) will assist in determining if the patient is likely to react to the drug upon re-exposure. It usually is helpful to chart all the drugs the patient is currently taking with their dose and start and stop dates of use for comparison with the onset and disappearance of the reaction.

2. Upon further questioning, J.A. reports having experienced an urticarial rash in the past when given ampicillin for a kidney infection approximately 2 years ago. The rash developed over her entire body less than a day after starting the antibiotic and disappeared 2 days after discontinuation. Her treatment course was completed with ciprofloxacin. She denies having had a viral infection at the time of the rash to ampicillin. She does not recall having experienced any adverse effects when she received penicillin before this reaction. No other recent changes in her treatment regimen were made before the occurrence of the rash. Why is it likely that J.A. is allergic to penicillin?

A number of useful pieces of information were gleaned from the drug history obtained from J.A. that can be used in determining the likelihood of an allergic reaction to penicillin. Since J.A.'s rash appeared less than a day after initiation of ampicillin and no other recent changes in her treatment regimen had been made, it is likely that the rash is due to ampicillin.

Another important method of identifying a potential drug-induced allergic reaction is to examine the patient's medication list to determine if the patient is receiving an agent that commonly is implicated in causing the exhibited allergic manifestation. In an

evaluation of drug-induced cutaneous reactions, amoxicillin and ampicillin were identified as two of the top three drugs implicated in drug rash.[10]

J.A. received penicillin in the past without any adverse effects until an urticarial rash (a relatively common allergic manifestation) developed upon subsequent exposure. This sequence of events follows the typical pattern of an allergic reaction. Allergic reactions require an induction period to sensitize the individual to the antigen; however, these allergic reactions typically occur immediately upon re-exposure.[19] Therefore, any history of prior exposures to the same or structurally related compounds needs to be documented.

Finally, it is important to evaluate other medical problems that may elicit or mimic a reaction resembling drug allergy. Rashes to ampicillin occur in 69% to 100% of patients with concurrent Epstein-Barr virus infection.[17] Since J.A. denies having a viral infection during her rash, it further strengthens her reaction as being a true allergic reaction.

Skin Testing

3. Why would skin testing for penicillin allergy be appropriate for J.A.?

Based upon J.A.'s elicited medication history, allergy to penicillin is highly suggestive. However, skin testing and drug rechallenge are the most definitive methods of diagnosing drug allergy. Although skin testing procedures have been described for local anesthetics, penicillin, beta-lactams, and sulfamethoxazole, skin test antigens are currently available commercially for penicillin only.[9] Metabolism of penicillin results in the production of penicilloyl, penicillate, and penicillate derivatives of benzylpenicillin. The penicilloyl derivative is the primary metabolite, and is, thus, referred to as the "major determinant." The other derivatives including the parent compound (penicillin) are referred to as "minor determinants." When combined to proteins, penicillin and its metabolites become antigenic and can precipitate a hypersensitivity reaction in a patient upon re-exposure.

The terms "major determinant" and "minor determinant" refer to the frequency of antibody formation to these antigenic penicillin metabolite-protein complexes. These terms do *not* describe the severity of the allergic reaction. Indeed, the "major determinant" is thought to be responsible for accelerated reactions, but not anaphylaxis. The "minor determinants" are responsible for anaphylaxis and immediate systemic reactions.

Penicillin skin testing is a safe and effective procedure (see Table 6.4) with less than 1% of positive responders developing systemic reactions.[18] In those individuals in whom a false-negative response occurred, reactions were mild and in most cases did not

Table 6.3	Detailed Drug History[a]

- Prior allergic and medication encounters
- Nature and severity of reaction
- Temporal relationships between drugs and reaction (dose, date initiated, duration)
- Prior exposure to the same or structurally-related medications subsequent to the reaction
- Effect of drug discontinuation
- Response to treatment
- Prior diagnostic testing or rechallenge
- Route of administration (e.g., preservatives in formulations)
- Other medical problems if any

[a] From references 3,19.

Table 6.4   Penicillin Skin Testing Procedure[a]

Agent	Procedure	Interpretation
Penicilloyl penicillin (Pre-Pen) major determinant	Scratch test 1 drop of full strength solution (6×10^{-5} mol/L)[b]	*No wheal or erythema after 10 min:* proceed with intradermal test. *Wheal or erythema within 10 min:* choose alternative agent, desensitization if no other alternatives exist
Penicilloyl penicillin (Pre-Pen)	*Intradermal test:* 0.01–0.02 mL PPL (Pre-Pen)[b] *Saline:* negative control *Histamine:* positive control (optional; useful if it is suspected that patient may be anergic)	*Negative response:* induration size similar or less than saline control *Positive response:* induration 1–4 mm or more greater than saline control with or without erythema: choose alternative agent, desensitization if no other alternatives exist
Penicillin G potassium (<1 week old) most important of the minor determinants	Scratch test 1 drop of 10,000 U/mL solution	Same as scratch test with PPL (see above)
Penicillin G potassium	*Intradermal test:* 0.002 mL 10,000 U/mL solution. *Serial testing* with 10,100 or 1000 U/mL solutions can be performed in individuals with strong history/serious reactions.	Same as intradermal test with PPL (see above)

[a] Schwarz Pharma, Kremers Urban Company, Milwaukee, Wis.
[b] The penicilloyl derivative of penicillin conjugated to polylysine (PPL) is administered initially as a scratch test. If no wheal or erythema develops, then intradermal testing is performed.

require drug discontinuation.[17,18] Administration of the penicilloyl derivative, benzylpenicillin-polylysine (Pre-Pen), identifies 80% of patients allergic to penicillin. When the penicilloyl derivative is supplemented with skin tests for the minor determinants of penicillin,[17] 99.5% of penicillin-allergic patients can be identified. The "minor determinants" are found not only *in vivo*, but also in the penicillin G solutions formulated for intravenous administration. Therefore, some investigators have recommended utilizing the penicilloyl-polylysine (Pre-Pen) product to test for the "major determinants" and penicillin G to test for the "minor determinants."

In patients with a history of penicillin hypersensitivity, skin test reactivity is affected by the length of time since the allergic reaction and by the nature of the past reaction. Skin test positivity is greatest 6 to 12 months after a reaction and decreases with time. Skin test positivity in one study was found to be only 40% of patients with a history of anaphylaxis, 17% with urticaria, and 7% for maculopapular rashes.[17] Skin testing should not be performed in patients receiving antihistamines since they will block the response to the antigen and result in misinterpretation. In patients receiving antihistamines (i.e., H_1- or H_2-receptor antagonists) or where skin testing is not possible due to severe skin disease, *in vitro* assays to detect drug specific IgE antibodies have been developed for major and minor determinants of penicillin and sulfamethoxazole.

In order to determine whether skin testing is appropriate for J.A., the risks and benefits must be weighed. Since the time of the last reaction was approximately two years ago, J.A. may still retain some skin test positivity if the previous reaction was truly an allergic reaction to ampicillin (skin test positivity is greatest 6 to 12 months after a reaction). Testing with PPL (major determinant) and penicillin (minor determinant) could be useful in determining if J.A. is likely to develop an urticarial or anaphylactic reaction to penicillin or its derivatives. The fact that J.A. is currently receiving prednisone should not alter the interpretation of the skin test results since the corticosteroids do not interfere with the IgE mediated immediate hypersensitivity reactions. The risks of developing serious systemic reactions to penicillin skin testing are minimal. The benefit of penicillin skin testing J.A., however, is questionable because she could be treated with an antibiotic other than a penicillin. The most practical approach to penicillin-allergic patients is to simply avoid the drug. Therefore, the patient's drug history should always be evaluated carefully. In the unlikely situation where treatment with a penicillin is essential, penicillin skin testing would be useful.

Cross-Reactivity

4. J.A. received a scratch test with PPL which was negative, however, an intradermal test was positive. What treatment options are available to J.A. for her infection?

Since J.A. exhibited a positive skin test reaction, all penicillin derivatives should be avoided. Since the specific antigenic determinants for allergy to cephalosporins and other beta-lactams are unknown, skin tests currently are not available for these other beta-lactam antibiotics. Therefore, the clinician must rely on data on cross-reactivity to determine whether a cephalosporin, or other nonpenicillin beta-lactam antibiotic, can be used for J.A. In one study, about 50% of patients with a history of penicillin allergy exhibited hypersensitivity reactions to the beta-lactam carbapenem antibiotic, imipenem (Primaxin).[17] Cross-reactivity (i.e., cross-antigenicity) occurs between penicillin and cephalosporins in 5% to 15% of patients;[17,18] however, the true incidence of cross-reactivity may be considerably less because these percentages are based upon the patient's recollection of an allergic history rather than by objective skin tests. Some patients also have multiple drug allergies and may manifest an allergic reaction to these drugs (and others which are not beta-lactams) in a manner similar to their penicillin reaction.[17] Desensitization with an appropriate cephalosporin is a potential option for J.A.; however, her infection is not life-threatening and probably is sensitive to other antimicrobial agents. In this case, it would be more prudent to treat J.A. with a nonbeta-lactam antibiotic. If J.A.'s skin tests had been negative, she may have been able to receive a cephalosporin or other beta-lactam despite her positive history; however, it would be prudent in this situation to use a small (i.e., "test") initial dose.[17]

Generalized Reactions

Drug allergies can be grouped into three categories: generalized reactions, organ-specific reactions, and pseudoallergic reactions. Generalized reactions involve multiple organ systems and variable clinical manifestations. Anaphylactic reactions, serum sickness reactions, drug-induced fever, drug-induced vasculitis, and autoimmune drug reactions comprise the generalized drug reactions presented in this chapter.

Anaphylaxis

5. L.P., a 43-year-old male, is brought to the emergency room with a chief complaint of a hand wound received while defending himself during an attempted robbery. Physical ex-

amination reveals a male in moderate distress with a 3.5″ laceration on the palm of his right hand requiring sutures. L.P.'s history is notable for migraine headaches, which are managed with atenolol 25 mg QD; adult-onset diabetes, controlled with diet; and multiple scars from wounds obtained during a barroom brawl 2 years before admission. He has no known allergies. The wound is cleansed and 1% lidocaine infiltrated around the laceration in preparation for suturing. Four minutes after the lidocaine injections, L.P. notes tingling and pruritus of both his hands and feet, and appears flushed. Three minutes later he complains of light-headedness, difficulty breathing, and a "lump" in his throat. His vital signs at that time were as follows: blood pressure (BP) 80/40 mm Hg; heart rate 75 beats/min; and respiratory rate of 27 breaths/min. Chest auscultation reveals restrictive air flow and stridor. A diagnosis of anaphylaxis is made and emergency treatment is started. What subjective and objective evidence support the diagnosis of anaphylaxis in L.P.?

Anaphylaxis is an acute, clinical syndrome that results from the rapid release of immunological mediators from tissue mast cells and peripheral blood basophils. The symptoms of anaphylaxis vary widely, depending upon the route of exposure, rate of exposure, and dose of allergen.[13,14,175,176] Symptoms usually begin within minutes of exposure, as in L.P., and most reactions occur within one hour; however, anaphylaxis can appear several hours after exposure on rare occasions. In general, the severity of the anaphylaxis is directly proportional to the speed of onset. L.P. displays symptoms in many of the organs commonly involved in anaphylaxis. Although almost any organ system can be affected, the cutaneous, gastrointestinal (GI), respiratory, and cardiovascular systems are involved most frequently, either singly or in combination.[13,14,175,176] Not surprisingly, these "shock organs" contain the largest number of mast cells and are, thus, the most highly affected. L.P. exhibits erythema (flushed appearance) and complains of pruritus of his hands and feet, both common initial symptoms of anaphylaxis: the groin also is frequently affected. These symptoms may progress to urticaria and angioedema, especially of the palms, soles, periorbital tissue, and mucous membranes. L.P. describes the early manifestations of angioedema (laryngeal edema) with complaints of a "lump" in his throat; this also may be described as throat tightness or constriction by some patients. The upper and/or lower respiratory tracts also can be involved during an anaphylactic event. L.P. exhibits stridor, indicating upper airway involvement. Hoarseness is another sign of upper respiratory tract involvement. Additionally L.P. is tachypneic with poor air flow, suggesting his lower airway also is affected. Although not displayed by L.P., wheezing and acute emphysema are further clues to lower airway involvement.

Table 6.5		Drug Therapy of Anaphylaxis[a,b]	
Drug	Indication	Adult Dosage	Complications
Initial Therapy			
Epinephrine	Hypotension, bronchospasm, laryngeal edema, urticaria, angioedema	0.3–0.5 mL of 1:1000 SQ or IM Q 10–20 min PRN. 3–5 mL of 1:10,000 IV over 5 min Q 10–20 min PRN. 1 mL of 1:1000 in 500 mL of dextrose 5% IV at a rate of 0.5–5 µg/min. 3–5 mL of 1:10,000 intratracheally Q 10–20 min PRN	Arrhythmias, hypertension, nervousness, tremor
Oxygen	Hypoxemia	40%–100%	None
Metaproterenol OR	Bronchospasm	0.3 mL of 5% solution in 2.5 mL of saline via nebulizer	Arrhythmias, hypertension, nervousness, tremor
Albuterol OR		0.5 mL of 0.5% solution in 2.5 mL of saline via nebulizer	
Isoetharine		0.5 mL of 1% solution in 2 mL of saline via nebulizer	
IV fluids	Hypotension	1 L of crystalloid or colloid Q 20–30 min PRN	Pulmonary edema, CHF
Secondary Therapy[c]			
Antihistamines H₁-receptor antagonists	Hypotension, urticaria	Diphenhydramine or hydroxyzine 25–50 mg IV/IM/PO Q 6–8 hr PRN	Drowsiness, dry mouth, urinary retention; may obscure symptoms of continuing reaction
H₂-receptor antagonists		Cimetidine 300 mg IV over 3–5 min or PO Q 6–8 hr PRN OR Ranitidine 50 mg IV over 3–5 min Q 8 hr PRN or 150 mg PO BID PRN	
Corticosteroids	Bronchospasm; patients undergoing prolonged resuscitation or severe reaction	Hydrocortisone sodium succinate 100 mg IM/IV Q 3–6 hr for 2–4 doses OR Methylprednisolone sodium succinate 40–125 mg IV Q 6 hr for 2–4 doses	Hyperglycemia, fluid retention
Aminophylline	Bronchospasm	6 mg/kg loading dose (if necessary) IV over 30 min followed by 0.3–0.9 mg/kg/hr as a maintenance dose[d]	Arrhythmias, nausea, vomiting, nervousness, seizures
Norepinephrine	Hypotension	4 mg in 1 L dextrose 5% IV at a rate of 2–12 µg/min	Arrhythmias, hypertension, nervousness, tremor
Glucagon[e]	Refractory hypotension	1 mg in 1 L of dextrose 5% IV at a rate of 5–15 µg/min	

[a] Adapted from references 13, 175, 176. Choice of agent and starting doses should be patient specific weighing safety and efficacy.

[b] CHF = Congestive heart failure; IM = Intramuscularly; IV = Intravenously; PO = Orally; PRN = As needed; SQ = Subcutaneously.

[c] Although not effective during acute anaphylaxis, these agents may reduce or prevent recurrent or prolonged reactions.

[d] Doses are for aminophylline; to convert to theophylline, multiply by 0.8. Lower rates may be required in elderly patients, those taking medications which reduce aminophylline metabolism, those with hepatic dysfunction, and those with CHF. Higher doses may be required in younger patients or cigarette smokers.

[e] Glucagon may be particularly useful in patients taking beta-adrenergic blockers, since it can increase both cardiac rate and contractility regardless of beta-adrenergic blockade.

Respiratory symptoms can lead to suffocation and death.[175] The principal event in 25% of the cases in one autopsy series was laryngeal edema, and in another 25% of cases, acute emphysema was the cause of death.[177] Cardiovascular symptoms also are ominous. Cardiovascular collapse and hypotensive shock (anaphylactic shock) are caused by peripheral vasodilation, enhanced vascular permeability, leakage of plasma, low cardiac output, and intravascular volume depletion. Thus, hypotension, as seen with L.P., is a common cardiac manifestation. Tachycardia also is commonly seen in patients with cardiac complications of anaphylaxis. L.P. does not show a significant increase in heart rate, however, since he is taking the beta blocker, atenolol. Other cardiac manifestations include a direct cardiodepressant effect as well as a variety of electrocardiographic changes including arrhythmias and ischemia. Lastly, although not demonstrated by L.P., common gastrointestinal manifestations such as abdominal cramping, diarrhea (which may be bloody), and nausea and vomiting also are manifested during an anaphylactic reaction.[13,14,175] In summary, L.P.'s rapid onset and progression of symptoms involving multiple organ systems (i.e., cutaneous, respiratory, and cardiovascular systems) are consistent with an anaphylactic reaction. L.P.'s anaphylaxis is a severe reaction given its speed of onset, the number of organ systems involved, and the degree of involvement. In particular, his respiratory and cardiovascular symptoms indicate a potentially life-threatening reaction is occurring.

6. What is the likely etiology of L.P.'s anaphylactic event?

Anaphylaxis occurs through one of three mechanisms.[13] In the first type of reaction, exposure to a foreign protein, either in its native state or as a hapten conjugated to a carrier protein, causes IgE-antibody formation. The IgE antibodies then bind to receptors on mast cells and basophils. Upon re-exposure, the antigen stimulates cellular degranulation through antigen-IgE antibody formation and cross-linking, thus causing massive release of preformed immunologic mediators from the mast cells and basophils. Histamine is the major mediator of anaphylaxis and the primary preformed cellular constituent. Histamine has multiple effects and is likely responsible for vasodilation, urticaria, angioedema, hypotension, vomiting, abdominal cramping, and changes in coronary flow.[14] Leukotrienes [e.g., leukotrienes C_4 and D, also known as slow reacting substance of anaphylaxis (SRS-A)], platelet acti-

vating factor, and prostaglandins are generated rapidly as a result of cellular degranulation, and other mediators of anaphylaxis (e.g., tryptase, chymase, heparin, and chondroitin sulfate) are released as well.[13,175] Anaphylactic reactions to Hymenoptera venom (e.g., bee stings), insulin, streptokinase, penicillins, cephalosporins, local anesthetics, and sulfonamides occur through this IgE mediated mechanism.

Anaphylaxis also can occur via a second mechanism involving formation of immune complexes that activate the complement system, and the subsequent formation of anaphylatoxins C3a, C4a, and C5a. Such anaphylatoxins can directly stimulate mast cell and basophil degranulation and mediator release. The third mechanism by which substances such as radiocontrast media and other hyperosmolar agents can cause anaphylaxis is by the direct stimulation of mediator release (primarily histamine) through an as yet unknown pathway which is independent of IgE and complement. Lastly, anaphylaxis can occur in which no distinct mechanism is identified; such cases are described as idiopathic recurrent anaphylaxis.[13,176]

The etiology of L.P.'s anaphylactic episode most likely is related to the first mechanism (i.e., IgE-antibody formation). Specifically, L.P. probably received lidocaine for the suturing of wounds he received two years ago in the barroom brawl. Exposure to lidocaine at that time probably stimulated IgE-antibody formation. Following re-exposure to lidocaine during this admission, antibody-antigen complexes were formed, resulting in cellular degranulation and anaphylaxis. The temporal relationship of L.P.'s anaphylactic reaction to the administration of lidocaine also strongly implicates lidocaine as the precipitating agent. Additionally, L.P. was not exposed to agents known to cause anaphylaxis by one of the other known mechanisms.

7. Given L.P.'s signs and symptoms and the presumed etiology of his anaphylactic reaction, how should L.P. be treated?

Effective management of anaphylaxis requires quick recognition and aggressive therapeutic interventions because of the immediate life-threatening nature of the reaction, as evidenced by L.P. The severity of the anaphylactic reaction must be assessed quickly; the probable causative agent determined; the administration of the offending substance discontinued; and the absorption of the offending agent minimized. All of these interventions must be undertaken promptly and the clinical status of the patient closely monitored. Vital signs, cardiac and pulmonary function, oxygenation, cardiac output, and tissue perfusion in particular must be immediately and continuously assessed.[13,175] Since lidocaine infiltrated around the wound is the probable cause of L.P.'s reaction, attempts should be made to prevent its further systemic absorption. Thus, the wound should be thoroughly flushed with normal saline.

Since L.P. is showing signs of anaphylactic shock and peripheral vasodilation, these effects must be countered immediately. Epinephrine is the drug of choice for the pharmacologic management of anaphylaxis and for all major or severe allergic reactions. Epinephrine also can be used for the symptomatic relief of minor adverse allergic reactions. The α-adrenergic effects of epinephrine will increase systemic vascular resistance and maintain blood pressure to overcome the vasodilating and hypotensive effects of histamine and the other mediators of anaphylaxis. Additionally, the β-adrenergic effects of epinephrine promote bronchodilation and increase cardiac rate and contractility. Epinephrine also inhibits further release of mediators from basophils and mast cells.

The selection of the route of epinephrine administration is also important. In the presence of anaphylactic shock, epinephrine should be administered intravenously because the low cardiac output and intravascular volume depletion from shock decrease tissue

Table 6.6	Hypersensitivity Reactions to Drugs: Serum Sickness[a,21–23]
Clinical manifestations	Fever, cutaneous eruptions (95% of cases), lymphadenopathy, and joint systems (10%–50%).[21–23] Onset 1–2 weeks after exposure, 2–4 days in sensitized individuals. Laboratory data relatively nonspecific: elevated ESR and circulating immune complexes. Complements C_3 and C_4 are often low while activation products C_{3a}, and C_{3a} des-arginine are elevated. RF sometimes present. UA may reveal proteinuria, hematuria, or an occasional cast[21–23]
Prognosis	Usually mild and self-limiting. Most resolve within a few days to weeks after withdrawal of inciting agent
Treatment	Aspirin and antihistamines can relieve arthralgias and pruritus. Corticosteroids may be required for severe cases and tapered over 10–14 days[21–23]

[a] ESR = Erythrocyte sedimentation rate; RF = Rheumatoid factor; UA = Urinalysis

Table 6.7		Serum Sickness Reactions
Drugs	Frequency	Clinical Remarks[a]
Antithymocyte globulin [24,26–28]	Common	Serum sickness reactions occurred in 30 of 35 patients treated with ATG for bone marrow failure. Clinical symptoms included: fever, malaise, cutaneous eruptions (primarily morbilliform eruptions), arthralgias, GI complaints, and lymphadenopathy that began from day 7–9 and lasted 10–14 days. An erythematous eruption on the sides of the fingers, toes, palms, and soles occurred in the majority of patients 12–48 hours before manifestation of morbilliform eruption. A single case report of a serum sickness reaction with glomerulonephritis occurred in a renal transplant recipient. After 14 days of therapy the patient exhibited fever, myalgias, arthralgias, and periorbital edema which resolved 14 days after discontinuation of ATG. Manufacturers' package information reports an incidence of serum sickness reactions of 5%–10%
Carbamazepine [36]	Rare	Fever, maculopapular rash, and lymphadenopathy developed in an 8-year-old girl 37 days after initiating carbamazepine for treatment of complex partial seizures. Anticarbamazepine antibodies subsequently were identified
Ciprofloxacin [45,46]	Rare	2 cases describe serum sickness reactions to ciprofloxacin. Symptoms included: arthralgias, myalgias, fever, rash (macular in 1 and urticarial in the other), and lymphadenopathy in 1. Onset of symptoms occurred after 4 days and 10 days of treatment. Hydrocortisone was administered and tapered over 7 days without any recurrence in 1 patient. The other patient responded to discontinuation of the drug alone
Fluoxetine [43,44]	Rare	2 cases describe serum sickness induced by fluoxetine. Symptoms in both cases were consistent with serum sickness and included: rash, fever, lymphadenopathy, arthralgias, and myalgias. 1 patient was treated with antihistamines and topical corticosteroids after which the rash and pruritus resolved over several weeks. In the 2nd case, prednisone was prescribed and tapered over 4 weeks. Symptoms in this patient resolved in 2 days. An additional 32 cases in 2.5 million patients treated with fluoxetine have been reported to the manufacturer [54]
Furazolidone [49]	Rare	In 2 cases, patients experienced rash, arthralgias, and fever. Symptoms arose 6 and 9 days after completion of the therapeutic course. A combination of antihistamine and corticosteroids in both cases resulted in resolution of symptoms
Hemophilus B vaccine [50]	Rare	10 cases of serum sickness-like reactions were reported to the FDA within the 1st year after the vaccine became available
Indomethacin [48]	Rare	A serum sickness reaction due to indomethacin is described in a 58-year-old female with a knee effusion. 2 weeks after beginning therapy, a diffuse urticarial rash, polyarthritis, and lymphadenopathy developed. Laboratory data were significant for an elevated ESR, and 6% eosinophilia. Symptoms resolved after discontinuation of indomethacin
Intravenous immune globulin [42]	Rare	The presence of fever, urticaria, angioedema, lymphadenopathy, pruritus, and vomiting led to the diagnosis of serum sickness in a 9-month-old boy 14 days after initiation of IVIG for the treatment of Kawasaki disease. Symptoms responded to antihistamines, aspirin, and prednisone
Iron dextran [47]	Rare	A 37-year-old female developed arthralgia, headaches, fever, and cutaneous eruptions 11 days after administration of iron dextran. ESR was elevated; all other labs were within normal limits. Prednisone was initiated: the patient improved within 24 hr and was discharged a day later with tapering steroids
Minocycline [25]	Rare	Skin and joint symptoms, fever and lymphadenopathy developed in a 19-year-old male 8 days after initiation of minocycline for treatment of acne. The drug was discontinued and antiallergic drugs were administered. Symptoms resolved within 6 days
Pentoxifylline [41]	Rare	A single case report describes a 62-year-old man who developed fever, malaise, myalgias, arthralgias, an erythematous rash, and lymphadenopathy 6 days after initiation of pentoxifylline. Laboratory data revealed an elevated ESR, hematuria, proteinuria, and hyaline casts. The patient also was receiving cefoxitin which was initiated 15 days before onset of symptoms and also could have been the etiological agent. Several doses of indomethacin were administered and acute symptoms resolved within 72 hr of discontinuation of both agents
Phenytoin [38–40]	Uncommon	In a retrospective review of phenytoin hypersensitivity reactions, 2/38 reactions were identified as serum sickness reactions. Reactions were characterized by fever, rash, and arthritis. Anemia, lymphadenopathy, abnormal LFTs, and albuminuria also were present in both cases. A similar but often more severe form of hypersensitivity referred to as the "phenytoin syndrome" is characterized by fever, erythematous maculopapular morbilliform rash that progresses to exfoliation, hepatitis, lymphadenopathy, myalgia, and arthralgia. Onset is typically several weeks after initiation of the drug
Rabies vaccine [25]	Uncommon	5% of patients receiving booster injections or postexposure primary immunization develop serum sickness reactions characterized by urticaria, fever, malaise, arthralgias, arthritis, nausea, and vomiting. Onset typically from 2–21 days after administration

[a] ATG = Antithymocyte globulin; ESR = Erythrocyte sedimentation rate; FDA = Food and Drug Administration; GI = Gastrointestinal; IVIG = Intravenous immune globulin; LFTs = Liver function tests.

perfusion and possibly the absorption of subcutaneously administered epinephrine. In cases of anaphylaxis where shock is not present, subcutaneous epinephrine is acceptable. Since L.P. presents with symptoms of shock, an IV line should be placed rapidly and 5 mL of 1:10,000 epinephrine administered over five minutes. At the same time, another IV line should be established and 1 L of normal saline infused at a rate sufficient to maintain perfusion to vital organs (e.g., every 30 minutes until his blood pressure is stabilized). Cerebral perfusion, as evidenced by adequate mentation, must always take precedence over blood pressure readings when managing shock.

The effect of L.P.'s atenolol also must be anticipated. If L.P.'s blood pressure and heart rate do not substantially improve shortly after the initial dose of epinephrine, intravenous glucagon, which can stimulate heart rate and cardiac contractility independent of β-adrenergic blockade, should be given as outlined in Table 6.5. Medications commonly used to augment the actions of epinephrine include H_1- and H_2-receptor antagonists, inhaled beta-agonists, corticosteroids, and aminophylline. In light of L.P.'s severe pulmonary reaction, he should receive oxygen as well as a nebulized beta-agonist, such as albuterol. Nebulized ipratropium bromide also may be a useful bronchodilator, although its use in anaphylaxis has not been documented. If L.P.'s respiratory status fails to improve after pharmacologic intervention, intubation must be considered. The presence of atenolol would not be expected to diminish the effect of albuterol because atenolol is a β_1 cardioselective beta blocker and the dose is low. Since histamine is the primary mediator of anaphylaxis, IV administration of an antihistamine such as diphenhydramine, 50 mg every six hours until the reaction resolves, is warranted. Similarly, giving an H_2-receptor antagonist is reasonable. Since L.P. is not receiving any drugs known to interact with cimetidine and has no diseases which require dose adjustment, cimetidine may be given as outlined in Table 6.5. Lastly, given the severity of his reaction and his pulmonary involvement, L.P. is also a candidate for IV corticosteroids. Methylprednisolone 125 mg every six hours for four doses may be beneficial and is of minimal relative risk. The effect of methylprednisolone on L.P.'s diabetes should be considered, but the severity of L.P.'s clinical status certainly does not preclude its administration. Once stabilized, L.P. should be transferred to a critical care setting and monitored for a minimum of 24 hours, since relapses of the anaphylactic reaction may occur.[13,14,175,176]

Serum Sickness

Serum sickness is a type III hypersensitivity reaction which results from the production of antibodies directed against heterologous protein or drug haptens with subsequent tissue deposition. The typical presentation of serum sickness (see Table 6.6) includes: fever, cutaneous eruptions (95%), lymphadenopathy, and joint symptoms (10% to 50%).[22–24] Onset of symptoms usually occurs one to two weeks after exposure. Accelerated reactions may occur within two to four days in previously sensitized individuals. Laboratory data are relatively nonspecific and offer little to the diagnosis. The erythrocyte sedimentation rate (ESR) is usually slightly elevated. The serum concentration of circulating immune complexes usually is increased. Complements C3 and C4 are often low while activation products C3a, and C3a des-arginine are elevated. Occasionally rheumatoid factor is present. Urinalysis may reveal proteinuria, hematuria, or an occasional cast.[22–24]

In most cases serum sickness reactions are mild and self-limiting and resolve within a few days to weeks after withdrawal of the inciting agent. Use of antihistamines and aspirin can relieve pru-

Table 6.8	Hypersensitivity Reactions to Drugs: Drug-Induced Fever[187–194]
Frequency	True frequency unknown, since fever is a common manifestation and almost any drug may cause fever. However, it has been estimated that 3%–5% of hospitalized patients experiencing adverse drug reaction suffer from drug fever alone or as part of multiple symptoms
Clinical manifestations	Temperatures may be ≥38 °C and do not follow a consistent pattern. Although patients may have high fevers with shaking chills, patients generally have few symptoms or serious systemic illness. Skin rash (18%), eosinophilia (22%), chills (53%), headache (16%), myalgias (25%), and bradycardia (11%) may occur in patients with drug fever. Onset of fever after exposure to the offending agent highly variable, ranging from an average of 6 days for antineoplastics to 45 days for cardiovascular agents. Occurrence of fever independent of the dose of the offending agent
Treatment	Although drug fever may be treated symptomatically (e.g., with antipyretics, cooling blankets), stopping the offending agent is the only therapy that will eliminate fevers completely. Patients generally defervescence within 48–72 hr of stopping the suspect drug
Prognosis	Drug fever usually benign, although 1 review found a mean of increased length of hospitalization of 9 days per episode of drug fever. Rechallenge with the offending drug will usually result in rapid return of the fever. Although reexposure to the suspect drug was previously thought to be potentially hazardous, there is little risk of serious sequelae

ritus and arthralgias. In severe cases corticosteroids may be required and can be tapered over 10 to 14 days.[22–24] Serum sickness reactions are very rare because of the infrequent use of foreign serum today;[24] however, reactions to specific agents continue to be reported (see Table 6.7).

Drug Fever

Drug fever may be caused by a variety of mechanisms, although it is ascribed most commonly to a hypersensitivity reaction. Other mechanisms include tissue injury (e.g., from antineoplastic agents), increased metabolic rate (e.g., from thyroid hormone), decreased sweating (e.g., from anticholinergic agents such as atropine), or idiosyncratic reactions (e.g., neuroleptic malignant syndrome from haloperidol).[190] The majority of the information available on drug fever is based upon case reports or small case series, and the only critical appraisal of the literature[192] is not consistent with information in other reports. Additionally, the literature is inconsistent regarding descriptions of the frequency of drug fever (e.g., very common, common, uncommon), and not supported by good clinical data. The reader is referred to a more extensive discussion of drug fever for further information.[190] The characteristics of hypersensitivity drug-induced fever are presented in Table 6.8 and the reactions to specific drugs are described in Table 6.9.

Hypersensitivity Vasculitis (HSV)

Hypersensitivity vasculitis is characterized by inflammation of the small blood vessel walls. These reactions occur as a result of immune complex deposition within the small veins and arterioles resulting in complement activation and release of chemotactic factors which attract polymorphonuclear cells causing vessel damage.[52–54]

Table 6.9		Drug Fever
Drugs[a],[187–194]	Frequency	Clinical Remarks[b]
Allopurinol	Occasional	May cause fever without other manifestations, or as part of a severe hypersensitivity reaction involving dermatitis, hepatic dysfunction, eosinophilia, and renal insufficiency
Aminoglycosides	Uncommon	
Amphotericin B	Common	May cause fever alone, without other manifestations. Fever due to release of endogenous pyrogens from leukocytes
Antacids	Rare	
Antihistamines	Common	Fever may be result of altered thermoregulation. *Note:* some references state that diphenhydramine rarely, if ever, causes drug fever
Antineoplastics	Common	Fever commonly due to release of endogenous pyrogen from rapid destruction of neoplastic cells. One study found antineoplastics accounted for 8% of all cases of drug fever[192]
Azathioprine	Occasional	Fever due to drug hypersensitivity
Barbiturates	Common	Although barbiturates commonly cause drug fever, mechanism is unknown
Carbamazepine	Uncommon	1 study found that 2% of the reported cases of drug fever were due to carbamazepine[192]
Cephalosporins	Occasional	1 trial found drug fever to occur approximately one-half as often with cephalosporins as with penicillins.[192] As with penicillins, fever most commonly due to a hypersensitivity reaction, although may also be administration related
Chloramphenicol	Uncommon	
Cimetidine	Uncommon	Fever may be a true allergic reaction in some patients (i.e., IgE-mediated)
Clindamycin	Uncommon	
Clofibrate	Uncommon	Fever due to drug hypersensitivity
Corticosteroids	Rare	
Diazoxide	Uncommon	May cause fever alone, without other manifestations
Digoxin	Rare	
Erythromycin	Uncommon	
Folate	Uncommon	
Griseofulvin	Uncommon	
Heparin	Uncommon	
Hydralazine	Uncommon	Fever may be due to an immunologic reaction resembling serum sickness (early reaction occurring within 10–20 days of starting therapy) or SLE (late reaction)
Hydroxyurea	Uncommon	
Ibuprofen	Occasional	Fever most likely due to drug hypersensitivity
Insulin	Rare	
Iodides	Occasional	May cause fever alone, without other manifestations
Isoniazid	Occasional	Drug fever occurred in 0.8% of patients in 1 series; fever as the only indication of a reaction occurred in 0.1% of patients.[191] Fever may occur within 1–7 weeks of starting therapy and may be associated with myalgias and repeated chills. Alternatively, isoniazid may cause fever alone, without other manifestations
Iron dextran	Occasional	May cause fever alone, without other manifestations
Mebendazole	Uncommon	
Metoclopramide	Uncommon	
Methyldopa	Very common	Fever occurs in 1%–6% of patients taking methyldopa. Although methyldopa may cause fever without other manifestations, most patients also experience malaise, chills, and diarrhea and 30% may have abnormal LFTs
Neuroleptics	Occasional	1 study found this class of agents to account for 3.4% of all cases of drug fever, and 17% of the cases involving CNS-active drugs
Nifedipine	Uncommon	Fever due to drug hypersensitivity
Nitrofurantoin	Occasional	Fever may be a manifestation of pulmonary toxicity from nitrofurantoin
Oral contraceptives	Rare	
Para-aminosalicyclic acid	Common	Fever occurred in 3.8% of cases in 1 series[190]
Penicillins	Very common	Fever usually occurs within 1 week of starting therapy and commonly due to drug hypersensitivity
Phenytoin	Common	High fever may be accompanied by generalized lymphadenopathy and hepatosplenomegaly, a syndrome called pseudolymphoma. Fever also may occur as the sole manifestation of a drug reaction. Onset may be from 2–6 weeks after starting phenytoin (Also see Chapter 52: Seizure Disorders)

Continued

Table 6.9		Drug Fever (Continued)
Drugs[a,187–194]	Frequency	Clinical Remarks[b]
Procainamide	Common	Fever develops after about 2 weeks of therapy and may be associated with a maculopapular rash, splenomegaly, arthralgias, malaise, and eosinophilia (drug-induced lupus)
Propylthiouracil	Occasional	May cause fever alone, without other manifestations
Quinidine	Very common	Most reactions occur within 3 weeks of starting therapy, but cases occurring after 1 year of use also have been reported. Leukocytosis with a left shift also may occur during high fevers, simulating sepsis. Fever not dose related
Quinine	Common	
Ranitidine	Rare	Fever may be a true allergic reaction in some patients (i.e., IgE-mediated)
Rifampin	Occasional	Fever due to drug hypersensitivity
Salicylates	Rare	May cause fever in overdosage
Streptomycin	Occasional	Fever occurred in 2.7% of cases in 1 series.[190] May cause fever alone, without other manifestations
Sulfonamides	Common	Fever usually occurs within 1 week of starting therapy
Sulindac	Occasional	Fever most likely due to drug hypersensitivity
Tetracyclines	Rare	Fever, when occurring, most likely represents drug hypersensitivity
Tolmetin	Uncommon	Fever most likely represents drug hypersensitivity
Triamterene	Uncommon	
Trimethoprim	Uncommon	
Vancomycin	Occasional	Fever represents drug hypersensitivity
Vitamins	Rare	

[a] The majority of the information available on drug fever is based upon case reports or small case series; there is only one critical appraisal of the literature,[192] and the information presented in this review often contradicted other authors. Additionally, there is very little consistency in the literature regarding descriptions of the frequency of drug fever (e.g., very common, common, uncommon), and little clinical data to support the descriptions. Lastly, there are many causes of drug-induced fever (e.g., drug hypersensitivity, altered thermoregulation). The reader is referred to a more extensive discussion of drug fever for further information.[190]

[b] CNS = Central nervous system; LFTs = Liver function tests; SLE = Systemic lupus erythematosus.

Drug-Induced Vasculitis

Vasculitis secondary to drug use occurs infrequently. Among 10,000 cases of vasculitis, 8.8% were identified as drug related.[52] The diagnosis of HSV is based upon five clinical criteria (see Table 6.10). The presence of any three of the five criteria is suggestive of hypersensitivity vasculitis.[51]

Onset of symptoms typically occurs seven to ten days after initiation of drug therapy but can occur sooner upon re-exposure. Purpuric papules and macular eruptions, the most common observed finding, are usually symmetrical and occur on the extremities (see Table 6.11).[52] Hypersensitivity vasculitis often involves multiple organ systems. Renal damage ranging from microscopic hematuria to nephrotic syndrome and acute renal failure is common in patients with disseminated disease.[52] An enlarged liver with elevated enzymes is indicative of hepatocellular involvement. Although the lung and ear also often are involved, clinical manifestations are usually mild.[52] Arthralgia also is commonly observed. Laboratory examinations usually show nonspecific abnormalities of inflammation such as an elevated ESR and leukocytosis. Peripheral eosinophilia sometimes is present. Serum complement concentrations can be low. Histological findings upon biopsy typically reveal granulocytes in the wall of a venule or arteriole and eosinophils at any location.[51] Numerous drugs have been implicated in hypersensitivity vasculitis (see Table 6.12).

Autoimmune Drug Reactions

Some drugs may produce a state of autoimmunity characterized by the presence of autoantibodies and in some instances clinical features of an autoimmune disorder. A syndrome resembling systemic lupus erythematosus has been associated with a number of drugs and the characteristics of this drug-induced syndrome are described in Table 6.13. Drug-induced SLE was first recognized over 40 years ago in a group of patients receiving hydralazine for antihypertensive therapy.[83] Subsequent reports of drug-induced lupus have implicated hydralazine and procainamide most frequently. Other drugs causing drug-induced lupus include isoniazid, chlorpromazine, anticonvulsants, β-adrenergic blockers, quinidine, methyldopa, penicillamine, and sulfasalazine.[84–87] The exact incidence of drug-induced lupus for each drug is difficult to ascertain due to the changing pattern of usage and emergence of new lupus-inducing drugs.

In contrast to idiopathic systemic lupus erythematosus, drug-induced lupus is less likely to affect females and blacks.[84] Individuals with slow acetylator phenotype have a higher tendency to develop drug-induced lupus; and antinuclear antibodies following exposure to lupus-inducing drugs also appear more rapidly.[88,89] In general, drug-induced lupus is a milder disease than idiopathic systemic lupus erythematosus. However, many patients with drug-induced lupus would fulfill the diagnostic criteria for systemic lupus erythematosus according to the revised American Rheumatism Association.[90] Arthralgias or myalgias accompanied by a positive ANA test may be the only clinical features for some patients with drug-induced lupus. The onset of drug-induced lupus usually is abrupt and appears several months to years after continuous therapy with the offending drug. Common complaints include fever, malaise, arthralgias, myalgias, pleurisy, and slight weight loss. Mild splenomegaly and lymphadenopathy have been reported occasionally. The classic butterfly malar rash, discoid lesions, oral mucosal ulcers, Raynaud's phenomenon, and alopecia are unusual features in drug-induced lupus as opposed to idiopathic systemic lupus erythematosus. In addition, the central nervous system and kidneys rarely are affected.[84] Laboratory abnormalities commonly include anemia and an elevated erythrocyte sedimentation rate.

Table 6.10	1990 Criteria for the Classification of Hypersensitivity Vasculitis[a]
Criteria[b]	Definition
Age at disease onset >16 yr	Development of symptoms after age 16
Medication at disease onset	Medication was taken at the onset of symptoms that may have been a precipitating factor
Palpable purpura	Slightly elevated purpuric rash over 1 or more areas of the skin; does not blanch with pressure and not related to thrombocytopenia
Maculopapular rash	Flat and raised lesions of various sizes over one or more areas of the skin
Biopsy including arteriole and venule	Histologic changes showing granulocytes in a perivascular or extravascular location

[a] Adapted from reference 50.
[b] The diagnosis of hypersensitivity vasculitis can be made if a patient exhibits ≥3 of these criteria.

All patients with symptomatic drug-induced lupus test positive for ANAs, consisting predominantly of single-stranded DNA and antihistone antibodies.[84] However, many patients who received lupus-inducing drugs may demonstrate the presence of ANAs without development of lupus disease. In procainamide-treated patients, about 50% to 75% of patients are positive for ANAs after 12 months and 90% after two years or more of continuous therapy; only 10% to 20% of those patients actually develop lupus symptoms.[91–93] Similarly, up to 44% of patients are ANA-positive after receiving three years of hydralazine therapy but the incidence of drug-induced lupus occurs in only 6.7% of patients after three years of treatment.[94] It is not necessary to discontinue therapy in asymptomatic patients with positive ANAs since most of them will never develop clinical symptoms.[84] Musculoskeletal complaints can be managed by aspirin or nonsteroidal anti-inflammatory drugs. More severe symptoms from pleuropulmonary or pericardial involvement may require the use of corticosteroids.[85] Clinical features of drug-induced lupus usually subside and disappear in days to weeks with discontinuation of the offending drug. Occasionally, these symptoms may linger or recur over a course of several months before eventually disappearing. Serologic tests tend to resolve more slowly; ANAs may persist for a year or longer.[84,95] Drug-induced lupus is not considered a predisposition to subsequent development of idiopathic systemic lupus erythematosus.[96] In most instances, lupus-inducing drugs do not increase the risk of exacerbation of idiopathic systemic lupus erythematosus;[97] however, long term treatment with interferon-gamma therapy may worsen pre-existing systemic lupus erythematosus.[98] The clinical characteristics of specific drug-induced lupus reactions are described in Table 6.14.

Organ Specific Reactions

The drug allergies in this chapter are grouped into categories of generalized reactions, organ-specific reactions, and pseudoallergic reactions. The organ-specific hypersensitivity drug reactions affecting the blood, liver, lung, kidney, and skin are described below.

Blood: Immune Cytopenias

Drug-induced immune cytopenias such as granulocytopenia, thrombocytopenia, and hemolytic anemia result from type II mediated allergic reactions (see Table 6.1). A drug or drug metabolite binds to the surface of blood elements such as granulocytes, plate-

lets, and red blood cells. IgG or IgM antibodies are formed and are directed against the drug/drug metabolite bound to the cell (i.e., hapten-cell reaction).[9] The immune complex and autoimmune mechanisms for hemolytic anemia are presented in Chapter 89: Drug-Induced Blood Disorders. Typical symptoms associated with immune thrombocytopenia include: chills, fever, petechiae, and mucous membrane bleeding. Granulocytopenia manifests with chills, fever, arthralgias, and a precipitous drop in leukocyte count. Symptoms of hemolytic anemia may be subacute or acute and may be sufficiently severe to cause renal failure in some instances. The Coombs' test is useful in identifying antibodies bound to red cells or the presence of circulating immune complexes directed against red cells. Antibiotics are the most frequently implicated class of drugs causing either neutropenia or hemolytic anemia (see Chapter 89: Drug-Induced Blood Disorders for a more complete description of the immune cytopenias).

Liver

Hypersensitivity reactions involving the liver can be classified as cholestatic or cytotoxic. Jaundice is usually the first sign of a cholestatic reaction in addition to pruritus, pale stools, and dark urine. Cholestatic reactions usually are reversible upon discontinuation of the offending agent.

Cytotoxic reactions can involve hepatocellular necrosis or steatosis and may result in irreversible damage if not recognized early. (See Chapter 26: Adverse Effects of Drugs on the Liver for a discussion of hypersensitivity reactions involving the liver.)

Lung

Pulmonary manifestations of drug hypersensitivity include asthma and infiltrative reactions. Asthma typically occurs as part of a generalized systemic reaction. Most reactions to drugs which involve asthma alone represent a pharmacologic side effect rather than a true allergic reaction.

Infiltrative reactions typically develop two to ten days after exposure and manifest with: cough, dyspnea, fever, chills, and malaise.[6] Infiltrative reactions vary in presentation from eosinophilic pneumonitis to acute pulmonary edema. (See Chapter 22: Drug-Induced Pulmonary Disorders for a discussion of hypersensitivity reactions to specific drugs.)

Kidney

The most common hypersensitivity reaction involving the kidney is interstitial nephritis. Typical findings include fever, rash, and eosinophilia. Methicillin is the most frequently reported drug implicated as a causative agent. Other agents that have been iden-

Table 6.11	Hypersensitivity Reactions to Drugs: Clinical Manifestations of Drug-Induced Vasculitis[a,50–53]

- Palpable purpura and maculopapular rash occurring symmetrically on the extremities
- Multiple organ systems may be involved:
  - *Renal:* microscopic hematuria to nephrotic syndrome and acute renal failure
  - *Liver:* enlarged liver, elevated enzymes, and arthralgias
- Laboratory data usually show nonspecific abnormalities of inflammation: elevated ESR and leukocytosis. Peripheral eosinophilia may be present and serum complement concentrations can be low. Histologic findings upon biopsy reveal granulocytes in venule or arteriole walls
- Onset typically 7–10 days after initiation therapy

[a] ESR = Erythrocyte sedimentation rate.

Table 6.12		Hypersensitivity Reactions to Drugs: Drug-Induced Vasculitis[a]
Drugs[57,60]	Frequency	Clinical Remarks
Allopurinol[57,60]	Infrequent	≈100 cases of AHS have been described. Fever and skin rash were the most common clinical findings (95% of patients). Complications were common among the 101 cases consisting of renal failure, infections and a high mortality rate (27%). Treatment consists of drug withdrawal and supportive therapy. Use of corticosteroids appears not to have impacted on the high rate of mortality observed
Azathioprine[55]	Rare	2 patients with end-stage renal disease receiving azathioprine as part of a pretransplant transfusion protocol developed HSV. Onset of symptoms occurred 1–2 weeks after initiation of therapy. Symptoms included: fever and maculopapular rash. Treatment consisted of drug withdrawal and topical corticosteroids in one and oral corticosteroids in the other
Carbamazepine[51]	Rare	2 cases have been reported (1 resulted in death)
Cimetidine[56]	Rare	Urticarial rash developed in a patient 4 days after initiation of cimetidine. Biopsy confirmed that the reaction was HSV. After drug withdrawal and administration of 7-day course of prednisone and hydroxyzine the rash resolved
Ciprofloxacin[64–66]	Rare	4 cases of HSV have been described with ciprofloxacin. Symptoms involved primarily fever and maculopapular rash in all cases. Renal impairment developed in 1 individual and elevations in liver enzymes in another. Treatment included drug withdrawal and corticosteroids (1 patient). Fever and rash resolved in about 1 week
Furosemide[81]	Rare	A purpuric maculopapular rash developed in a 75-year-old male taking furosemide. The rash recurred upon rechallenge and he developed renal dysfunction as evidenced by a rise in SrCr to 10.4 mg/dL. Treatment consisted of drug discontinuation and oral corticosteroids to which the patient responded
Hydralazine[71]	Rare	A case report of cutaneous vasculitis after receiving iopamidol is described. 60-year-old female received iopamidol for a urogram and within 24 hr developed a maculopapular rash. A skin biopsy confirmed the diagnosis of HSV. Upon review of the literature, the authors identified 2 case reports of HSV following injection of nonionic contrast agents. In both cases there was a link with SLE or hydralazine which is known to induce a SLE-like syndrome. Based upon these observations, the authors recommend avoidance of IV contrast agents in patients receiving hydralazine or patients with SLE
Hydrochlorothiazide[75]	Rare	A pruritic eruption suggestive of HSV is described in a 63-year-old female who was receiving HCTZ for 2 years. A skin biopsy confirmed the diagnosis of HSV and a mast cell degranulation test implicated HCTZ as the causative agent. The rash disappeared over a few weeks after drug discontinuation
L-Tryptophan[72]	Rare	A single case of hypersensitivity pneumonitis and pulmonary vasculitis is described in a 70-year-old female. She had taken L-tryptophan for a period of 3 months before onset of symptoms (fatigue, weakness, cough, and dyspnea). Diagnosis was confirmed by open lung biopsy which showed lymphocytic infiltration. Treatment consisted of IV corticosteroids to which she showed dramatic improvement
Mefloquine[70]	Rare	A single case report is described in a 44-year-old male. Symptoms began 3 weeks after initiation of therapy and consisted of a purpuric maculopapular rash on lower extremities. No skin biopsy was obtained. The rash healed after drug discontinuation over a few weeks
Naproxen[54]	Rare	A 52-year-old male developed a maculopapular rash over both legs 3 days after initiation of naproxen. He also developed renal failure. Naproxen was discontinued and the skin lesions healed over 10–15 days. Renal biopsy confirmed vasculitic process. He was treated with prednisone 60 mg/day and was discharged on the 26th hospital day
Ofloxacin[62,63]	Rare	A 67-year-old patient developed HSV as evidenced by diffuse papular purpuric rash and leukocytoclastic angiitis on biopsy. Symptoms developed 3 days after initiation of ofloxacin. Renal and liver involvement was present as demonstrated by elevated enzyme and serum creatinine levels. Symptoms resolved with drug discontinuation and administration of prednisone for 17 days. 4 additional cases have been reported, however, not enough data exist to evaluate these cases [11]
Penicillin[76]	Rare	≈30 cases of HSV associated with penicillins have been described. Causative agents include: penicillin, methicillin, and ampicillin
Phenytoin[51]	Rare	13 cases have been described. Occurs mostly in elderly black males. Skin rash, fever, and peripheral eosinophilia (71%) were the most common signs and symptoms. Histology revealed involvement of many organs. 4 patients died of cardiac or cerebrovascular complications. Treatment included withdrawal of phenytoin and administration of corticosteroids
Phenylbutazone[79]	Rare	2 cases of systemic vasculitis secondary to phenylbutazone are described. Both patients presented with oliguric renal failure 4 weeks after initiation of phenylbutazone. Renal function recovered after treatment with cyclophosphamide, prednisone, and hemodialysis for 3 months in 1 patient. Renal function failed to improve in 2nd patient who was placed on continuous ambulatory peritoneal dialysis
Procainamide[80]	Rare	Hypersensitivity vasculitis is described in 2 patients on procainamide for 7 months in one and 3 years in the other. Both presented with urticarial pruritic lesions. Diagnosis was confirmed by skin biopsy. Rashes resolved after drug discontinuation and oral corticosteroids in one patient and drug discontinuation in the other
Propylthiouracil[67–69]	Rare	3 cases of HSV have been described in recent years. In 2 of the 3 cases the patients presented with

Continued

Table 6.12		Hypersensitivity Reactions to Drugs: Drug-Induced Vasculitis[a] (Continued)
Drugs[57,60]	Frequency	Clinical Remarks
Propylthiouracil (Continued)		cutaneous manifestations; the 3rd presented with respiratory failure. The onset of symptoms was 15 days, 2 months, and over 1 year after initiation of PTU. Treatment consisted of antihistamines and corticosteroids in one patient, no treatment in another, and NSAIDs in the 3rd. Symptoms resolved within 2–3 weeks after drug discontinuation in all cases
Ritodrine[74]	Rare	A 30-year-old women developed HSV after administration of IV ritodrine for 5 weeks for treatment of premature contractions. She developed a petechial rash and prolonged bleeding time. A biopsy confirmed the diagnosis. IV corticosteroids were begun postpartum with subsequent improvement in the rash
Sulfadiazine[59]	Rare	A 76-year-old man is described who developed fever and a diffuse exanthematous and palpable purpuric eruption over both legs. Arthralgias and renal failure also developed. The drug was withdrawn and he was treated with methylprednisolone for 24 hours after which his symptoms improved
Terbutaline[75]	Rare	A single case report is described in a 73-year-old female 6 days after initiation of therapy. Her only symptom was a maculopapular eruption. Diagnosis was verified by skin biopsy. She was treated by drug discontinuation after which the rash faded over a few days
Trimethadione[51]	Rare	A single case has been reported
Valproate[77]	Rare	2 cases of HSV associated with valproate are described. Red purpuric lesions developed in the 1st patient 3 years after initiation of drug therapy. The lesions disappeared on drug discontinuation and reappeared on rechallenge. A similar reaction occurred in the 2nd patient after 3 days of therapy. Diagnosis was confirmed by skin biopsy in both cases. Both patients responded to drug discontinuation
Vitamins[59]	Rare	HSV is described in a 52-year-old female secondary to ingesting large doses of multiple vitamin tablets over a 4-month period. Symptoms included: fever and generalized maculopapular rash. Renal involvement also occurred as evidenced by a decrease in Cl_{Cr} and necrotizing vasculitis on renal biopsy. After drug withdrawal she was treated with cyclophosphamide and prednisone for 1 month with rapid clinical improvement
Warfarin[78]	Rare	A 65-year-old patient developed nonpruritic purpuric skin eruptions 10 days after initiation of warfarin therapy. Diagnosis was confirmed by skin biopsy. Warfarin was implicated as the causative agent by drug rechallenge which resulted in reappearance of the skin eruptions as well as by indirect mast cell degranulation test. Skin eruptions resolved within 5 days after drug discontinuation
Zidovudine[61]	Rare	2 cases of HSV associated with zidovudine use in patients infected with HIV are described. Symptoms of fever and pruritic papular eruptions developed within 2–4 weeks after initiation of zidovudine. Biopsy confirmed HSV in both individuals. 1 patient was treated by drug withdrawal and antihistamines, the second by drug withdrawal and prednisone. Symptoms resolved within 36 hours in one and 10 days in the second

a AHS = Allopurinol hypersensitivity syndrome; Cl_{Cr} Creatinine clearance; HCTZ = Hydrochlorothiazide; HIV = Human immunodeficiency virus; HSV = Hypersensitivity vasculitis; IV = Intravenous; NSAIDs = Nonsteroidal anti-inflammatory drugs; PTU = Propylthiouracil; SLE = Systemic lupus erythematosus; SrCr = Serum creatinine.

tified include: other penicillins, sulfonamides, and cimetidine.[6,9] (See Chapter 29: Acute Renal Failure for an analysis of hypersensitivity reactions to specific drugs that adversely affect the kidney.)

Skin

Adverse reactions involving the skin are the most common clinical manifestation of drug allergy. Although a number of different types of cutaneous reactions are possible, most drug-induced skin eruptions can be classified as erythematous, morbilliform, or maculopapular in nature.[9] A surveillance study of drug-induced skin reactions identified amoxicillin as the most common cause followed by trimethoprim-sulfamethoxazole and ampicillin. Overall allergic skin reactions were identified in 2% of hospitalized patients.[10]

Treatment of skin reactions includes discontinuation of the offending drug and general supportive care. (See Chapter 36: Dermatotherapy for a discussion of causative agents and specific treatments of various cutaneous reactions.)

Pseudoallergic Reactions

8. C.C., a 37-year-old male with no known allergies, is hospitalized for treatment of methicillin-resistant *S. aureus* (MRSA) bacteremia associated with an infected central line. His medical history is significant for short-bowel syndrome requiring parenteral nutrition and one previous episode of MRSA line infection successfully treated with vancomycin. Similar to his last admission, vancomycin 750 mg IV over 60 min Q 12 hr is begun. A trough level taken after the fifth dose, however, is 5 mg/L and the vancomycin dose is doubled to 1500 mg IV Q 12 hr, to be administered at the same rate. Fifteen minutes after the new dose of vancomycin is begun, C.C. experienced hypotension (100/70 mm Hg), tachycardia (85 beats/min), generalized pruritus, and facial flushing. C.C. is diagnosed as having a pseudoallergic reaction to vancomycin. What subjective and objective data in C.C. are important in differentiating vancomycin pseudoallergic reaction from a true allergic reaction?

Pseudoallergic reactions are drug reactions that exhibit clinical signs and symptoms of an allergic response, but are not immunologically mediated.[178] They may manifest as relatively benign symptoms or as severe, life-threatening events indistinguishable from anaphylaxis (see Table 6.15).[178] The latter response is described as an *anaphylactoid* reaction, since it resembles true anaphylaxis but does not involve IgE antibody formation.[9,178] Unlike true allergic reactions, which require an induction period during which a patient becomes sensitized to an antigen, pseudoallergic

Table 6.13	Hypersensitivity Reactions to Drugs: Autoimmune Drug-Induced Lupus[a,82–97]
Frequency	Less likely to affect females and blacks than idiopathic SLE. Drug-induced lupus is more common in individuals with slow acetylator phenotype
Clinical manifestations	Milder disease than idiopathic SLE. Arthralgias, myalgias, fever, malaise, pleurisy, and slight weight loss. Mild splenomegaly and lymphadenopathy. *Onset:* usually abrupt occurring several months to years after continuous therapy with the offending drug. Classic butterfly malar rash, discoid lesions, oral mucosal ulcers, Raynaud's phenomenon, and alopecia are unusual features with DIL as opposed to idiopathic SLE. *Laboratory studies:* positive ANA (predominantly single-stranded DNA and antihistone antibodies), anemia, and elevated ESR. Many patients demonstrate presence of ANAs **without** development of lupus disease. It is, therefore, not necessary to discontinue therapy in asymptomatic patients with positive ANAs
Treatment	Clinical features subside and disappear days to weeks after discontinuation of the offending drug. Serologic tests resolve more slowly. ANAs may persist for a year or longer
Prognosis	DIL does not predispose to development of idiopathic SLE. Lupus-inducing drugs do not appear to ↑ the risk of exacerbation of idiopathic SLE. However, long-term treatment with interferon-gamma may worsen pre-existing SLE

[a] ANA = Antinuclear antibody; DIL = Drug-induced lupus; ESR = Erythrocyte sedimentation rate; SLE = Systemic lupus erythematosus.

reactions can occur on the first exposure to a drug. The development of pseudoallergic reactions may be dose related and become manifested only when large doses of the drug are administered, when the dose is increased, or only when the rate of intravenous administration is increased.[6]

C.C. has experienced a common pseudoallergic reaction to vancomycin, usually referred to as the ''Red Man Syndrome'' or ''Red Neck Syndrome,'' that primarily occurs when large doses of vancomycin are administered rapidly. Differentiating between a true allergic response and a pseudoallergic response can be difficult since clinically the signs and symptoms can be indistinguishable. For example, each of the symptoms experienced by C.C. (flushing, tachycardia, pruritus, and hypotension) is caused by histamine release and can occur during an anaphylactic episode. To conclusively determine the etiology of the reaction would require immunologic testing for the presence or absence of antibodies to the suspect drug or agent, which is not always possible or practical. In this case, C.C. has uneventfully received vancomycin previously and has tolerated five doses during this hospitalization; therefore, it is unlikely that the reaction is immunologically mediated (i.e., a true allergic reaction). Furthermore, the reaction occurred after an increase in his vancomycin dose, which further supports a diagnosis of a pseudoallergic reaction.

9. Why did vancomycin cause a pseudoallergic reaction in C.C.?

Two general mechanisms have been proposed for pseudoallergic reactions: complement activation and direct histamine release.[13] Complement activation is secondary to immune complex formation, leading to the production of C3a, C4a, and C5a. These *anaphylatoxins* directly stimulate tissue mast cell and basophil degranulation, and the subsequent release of neurochemical me-

diators. Radiocontrast media, whole blood and blood products, and protamine cause pseudoallergic reactions via this mechanism of complement activation.[178] Pseudoallergic reactions from direct drug-induced histamine release occurs through an as yet unknown pathway. Direct drug-induced release of histamine does not involve complement activation or IgE antibody formation. Several drugs are known to directly stimulate histamine release: vancomycin, protamine, radiocontrast media, opiates, pentamidine, phytonadione, and deferoxamine.[6,178] Some drugs (e.g., radiocontrast media and protamine) cause pseudoallergic reactions via both mechanisms. Furthermore, some drugs (e.g., vancomycin, quaternary ammonium muscle relaxants, and ciprofloxacin) can cause both true allergic reactions as well as pseudoallergic reactions.[3] Table 6.16 characterizes the pseudoallergic reactions to specific drugs.

10. How should C.C.'s pseudoallergic reaction be managed? Does treatment of pseudoallergic reactions differ from that of true allergic reactions?

The first step in treating C.C.'s reaction is to eliminate the underlying cause. Thus, his vancomycin infusion should be held until the reaction resolves. Since the reaction is histamine mediated, administration of an antihistamine such as diphenhydramine, 50 mg IV, is warranted. Observation of his blood pressure and heart rate is mandatory. IV fluids should be administered if his blood pressure continues to fall or fails to stabilize. Patients with allergic reactions should be treated based upon their clinical signs and symptoms, regardless of the mechanism behind the reaction. Thus, for all intents and purposes, pseudoallergic reactions are treated in the same manner as true allergic reactions.

11. Can C.C. continue to receive vancomycin? How can future reactions be prevented?

It is not necessary to discontinue vancomycin therapy in C.C. This reaction can be prevented by administering smaller doses of the drug more frequently (e.g., 1000 mg Q 8 hr rather than 1500 mg Q 12 hr) and/or infusing the dose over a longer interval, typically two hours. Alternatively, pretreatment with an antihistamine one hour before vancomycin administration is effective. Additionally, tachyphylaxis to vancomycin-induced Red Man Syndrome is independent of pretreatment with antihistamine and is another characteristic which differentiates a pseudoallergic reaction from a true allergic reaction.

Pretreatment regimens to prevent pseudoallergic reactions to a variety of other drugs, in particular radiocontrast media, also are well described and can be very effective. For example, 32 mg of oral methylprednisolone given 12 and 2 hours before a procedure involving high osmolality radiocontrast media can reduce the reaction rate by up to 45% in some patients.[180] Another pretreatment regimen uses oral prednisone 50 mg taken 13 hours, 7 hours, and 1 hour before the procedure plus diphenhydramine 50 mg orally or intramuscularly one hour before the examination.[181] This regimen successfully lowers the occurrence of pseudoallergic reactions to high osmolality contrast media, even in high-risk patients (i.e., those with a prior history of severe anaphylactoid reactions).

Prevention and
Management of Allergic Reactions

12. A.M., a 40-year-old female, is hospitalized with a diagnosis of community-acquired pneumonia. Her medical history is noncontributory except for an uneventful course of ampicillin 6 months before admission for an ear infection. A.M. is empirically treated with IV cefuroxime 0.75 gm IV Q 8 hr. On day 2 of therapy, however, she develops a raised pruritic maculopapular rash on her back, abdomen, and upper extremities. Antacid, docusate sodium, albuterol by metered-dose inhaler,

Table 6.14		Autoimmune Drug Reactions
Drugs	**Frequency**	**Clinical Remarks[a]**
Anticonvulsants[51,127–133]	Infrequent	Frequency of positive ANAs with chronic treatment far exceeds that of clinical symptoms of SLE; about 60% of patients on phenytoin, primidone, or carbamazepine and 20% on phenobarbital have positive ANAs. Most cases of DIL related to anticonvulsants were due to phenytoin; majority were children, symptoms occurred 4 weeks to 2 years after start of therapy with quick resolution upon discontinuation. At least 80 cases of carbamazepine-induced DIL have been reported to Ciba-Geigy. Less commonly reported anticonvulsants include valproate (2 cases) and primidone (1 case). The only anticonvulsants never implicated in DIL on monotherapy were phenobarbital and benzodiazepines. Few reports suggested a higher tendency to develop DIL even when therapy is switched to a different class of anticonvulsant in patients who have developed DIL to 1 anticonvulsant in the past, thus limiting therapeutic option
Beta blockers[83,123]	Rare	Only few reported cases with symptomatic lupus. One study examining over 1500 patients on antihypertensive therapy prospectively found ANA positivity in 33% of patients receiving acebutolol, 11% atenolol, 13% labetalol, and 3% propranolol. Practolol was withdrawn from the market because of the frequency of DIL
Chlorpromazine[105–108]	Rare	Only 5 cases documented met the ARA diagnostic criteria for lupus. Chlorpromazine is the most implicated phenothiazine. ANA positivity is observed in 30%–50% of patients receiving a daily dose of ≥400 mg for ≥7 weeks
Hydralazine[83,96,98]	Common	No female predominance. Risk factors associated with development of DIL include: prolonged treatment with high daily dose (>400 mg), slow acetylator phenotype, family history of autoimmune disease, HLA-DRw4 phenotype (suggesting a genetic predisposition). *Usual symptoms:* musculoskeletal predominance such as nondeforming polyarthritis, rare reports of glomerulonephritis
Interferon[86,97,124,125]	Infrequent	1 study described 11% (n = 15) of patients developed positive ANAs and lupus symptoms while receiving interferon-alpha and/or interferon-gamma therapy for chronic myelogenous leukemia and essential thrombocythemia. 3 patients met the ARA criteria for SLE and required discontinuation of treatment. *Common symptoms:* myalgia, arthralgia, Raynaud's phenomenon, and arthritis. Long-term treatment with interferons has exacerbated pre-existing SLE
Isoniazid[102–104]	Infrequent	20 reported cases. 1 study showed ANA positivity in 19% of patients receiving isoniazid therapy for pulmonary tuberculosis; none developed DIL. *Risk factor:* slow acetylator phenotype more likely to develop ANA positivity and clinical symptoms of DIL. *Usual symptoms:* arthritis, arthralgias, fever (most common); others reported pleuritis, pericarditis, and cardiac tamponade
Methyldopa[119–122]	Rare	<5 reported cases of DIL. ANA positivity in up to 24% of patients treated. *Usual symptoms:* arthritis, arthralgias, pleurocarditis, hemolytic anemia
Penicillamine[118]	Infrequent	*Incidence of DIL:* 0.4%–2%. One study showed 2% of patients receiving treatment for RA for >6 months developed DIL with the following symptoms: pleurisy, rashes, nephritis, and neurologic abnormalities. *Unusual features compared to other DIL:* antibodies to double-stranded DNA and low complement levels, glomerulonephritis, neurologic abnormalities, Sjögren's syndrome, and positive lupus band test
Procainamide[83,84,88,99–101]	Common	No female predominance. *Risk factors:* slow acetylator phenotype likely to develop DIL after shorter duration of therapy and lower cumulative dose. DIL can be prevented by giving N-acetylprocainamide, the major acetylated metabolite of procainamide, instead of the parent drug. Remission of DIL also has been shown in patients who switched therapy from procainamide to N-acetylprocainamide. *Usual symptoms:* pleuropericardial involvement more common (pleurisy, pleural effusions, pulmonary infiltrates, pericarditis, pericardial effusions)
Quinidine[109–112]	Infrequent	Only few cases (<15) met the ARA criteria for lupus. *Usual symptoms:* fever, arthritis, pleurisy
Sulfasalazine[85,113–117]	Infrequent	*Usual symptoms* (in order of frequency): arthralgias, arthritis or pleuritis, fever, skin rash, adenopathy, pericarditis. Less common lupus manifestations include pulmonary infiltrate; CNS involvement, Raynaud's phenomenon, and renal disease

[a] ANA = Antinuclear antibody; ARA = American Rheumatological Association; DIL = Drug-induced lupus; RA = Rheumatoid arthritis; SLE = Systemic lupus erythematosus.

and multivitamins were initiated on the same day as the cefuroxime. How should A.M.'s allergic reaction be managed? How might her allergic reaction have been prevented?

When examining methods to prevent allergic reactions, three possibilities exist: 1) the patient has unknowingly been sensitized to a drug and experiences an allergic reaction upon receiving the same or similar drug again; 2) the patient has a history of an allergic reaction to a medication and mistakenly receives the same or a similar medication a second time and again develops an allergic reaction; and 3) the patient has a history of an allergic reaction to a medication and intentionally receives the same or similar medication again. As in the first situation, the allergic reaction of A.M., was unpredictable and, therefore, could not be prevented. However, to prevent future allergic reactions (i.e., the second situation), A.M.'s reaction should be well documented in the medical chart

and pharmacy records. In addition all patients should undergo a thorough drug history upon hospitalization. Careful attention should be paid to differentiating drug intolerance (e.g., stomach upset) from true allergic reactions and any allergic reactions elicited during an interview should be documented appropriately. Adequate communication of allergic reactions is the single most important method of preventing their occurrence.

As described earlier, the first step in managing an allergic reaction is to determine its etiology. Given A.M.'s history of exposure to ampicillin, the timing of the reaction, and the low frequency of allergic reactions to her other medications, cefuroxime is the most likely candidate. Secondly, a decision as to whether or not to stop the suspect drug should be made. This decision must be based upon the severity of the reaction, the condition being treated, and the availability of suitable alternatives. Whenever possible, an

Table 6.15 Hypersensitivity Reactions to Drugs: Pseudoallergic Reactions[5,9,126,178–180,182–186,196–199]

Frequency	Highly variable, depending upon the agent involved. For example, up to 30% of patients taking aspirin develop a cutaneous pseudoallergic response. On the other hand, pseudoallergic reactions to other agents, such as phytonadione and thiamine, are rare
Clinical manifestations	Range from benign reactions (e.g., pruritus and flushing) to a life-threatening clinical syndrome indistinguishable from anaphylaxis
Treatment	Pseudoallergic reactions treated the same as true allergic reactions (i.e., according to the clinical presentations of the patient). Thus, some reactions simply may require removal of the suspect agent, while some anaphylactoid reactions may require aggressive therapy (e.g., epinephrine, antihistamines, corticosteroids)
Prognosis	As with true allergic reactions, patients who have experienced a pseudoallergic drug reaction may have a similar reaction upon re-exposure. However, the severity of response may lessen with repeated administration. Furthermore, for some drugs, the frequency and severity of the reaction also may be influenced by the dose and/or rate of IV administration. Pretreatment regimens to reduce the frequency as well as the severity of responses have been developed for some drugs well known to cause pseudoallergic reactions (e.g., radiocontrast media)

equally effective alternative drug should be substituted for the suspect agent, preferably one that is immunologically distinct to avoid cross-sensitivity (see Question 4 for a discussion of cross-reactivity).[134] If a suitable alternative exists, the offending agent should be stopped and the reaction treated symptomatically, if needed. In the case of A.M., another antimicrobial such as trimethoprim-sulfamethoxazole could be substituted for cefuroxime (see Chapter 58: Respiratory Tract Infections), and her symptoms treated with an oral or parenteral antihistamine, as well as a low potency topical corticosteroid if necessary.

Lastly, there are some cases described by the third situation: a patient develops an allergic reaction (or has a well-documented history of drug allergy), and it is inappropriate or not possible to change to an alternative drug. If the sensitivity reaction is severe or life-threatening desensitization should be considered (see Questions 13 to 16): premedication to prevent or minimize anaphylaxis is not effective.[3] If the reaction is minor (e.g., pruritus, rash, or GI symptoms), premedication or management of the reaction with antiallergy medications (e.g., antihistamines) may be sufficient to allow completion of therapy. It is rare in such cases for the reaction to progress to more serious allergic symptoms such as anaphylaxis;[134] however, suppression of allergic symptoms should be undertaken cautiously because many immunologic reactions are not IgE-mediated and may progress to serious reactions, in spite of treatment.[134] In general, allergy suppression should be reserved for prevention of mild reactions that are known or strongly suspected to be IgE mediated.[3,134]

Table 6.16 Pseudoallergic Reactions[a]

Drugs	Frequency	Clinical Remarks
Acetylcysteine[196]	Uncommon	Anaphylactoid reactions, including flushing, chest pain, tachycardia, and fever have been reported in up to 3% of patients receiving IV acetylcysteine. Mechanism appears to be by direct histamine release
ACE inhibitors[182]	*Cough:* Occasional *Angioneurotic edema:* Rare	Cough may occur in up to 39% of patients after 1 week to 6 months of therapy. More common in women than men. Angioneurotic edema can be life-threatening and usually occurs within 1 hr of starting therapy; rare cases have occurred after 1 week of therapy
Aspirin[183,186]	*Bronchospasm with rhinoconjunctivitis:* Uncommon to very common, depending upon the population studied *Urticaria and angioedema:* Occasional	The prevalence of bronchospasm with rhinoconjunctivitis occurs in up to 28% of children with aspirin sensitivity. In adult asthmatics, the prevalence of aspirin sensitivity ranges from 5%–20%. The prevalence of aspirin sensitivity during aspirin challenge in adult asthmatics with a prior history of aspirin-induced respiratory reaction ranges from 66%–97%. Symptoms usually occur within 3 hours of ingestion. The aspirin triad seen in many sensitive patients consists of aspirin sensitivity, nasal polyps, and asthma. The prevalence of cutaneous reactions to aspirin ranges from 21%–30%, although disease activity at the time of aspirin challenge plays an important role. In 1 study, 70% of patients with urticaria at the time of challenge reacted to aspirin, compared to only 6.6% of patients whose urticaria was not active at the time of challenge
Beta blockers[178]	Occasional	This class of drugs may aggravate or provoke asthma in susceptible patients; 1 early study found 2.6% of outpatients treated with propranolol developed significant bronchospasm. Cardioselective β-adrenergic blockers may be safer in susceptible patients (See Chapter 22: Drug-Induced Pulmonary Disorders)
Ciprofloxacin[5,184,197,198]	Uncommon	A 1988 review of reports to the FDA found 1.2 cases of anaphylactoid reactions occurred per 100,000 prescriptions. The onset of the reaction ranged from 5–60 min; 14 of 15 reactions occurred after the 1st dose. 1 death has since been reported; 1/3 of cases have occurred in HIV-infected patients.
Deferoxamine[178]	Uncommon if by IM or slow IV/SQ administration	Flushing, urticaria, and hypotension may occur with rapid IV administration. IM is the preferred route, although slow IV or SQ administration also may be used
Immune globulin[178]	Rare	Pseudoallergic reactions occur by direct activation of the classical complement pathway. Rapid IV administration can cause hypotension and symptoms similar to true anaphylaxis. IM administration rarely results in an allergic response. True allergic reactions also may occur with immune globulins particularly in patients who have anti-IgA antibodies
Narcotic analgesics[178]	Occasional	Morphine and meperidine produce symptoms of histamine release both *in vitro* and *in vivo*; fentanyl, sufentanil, methadone, and oxymorphone do not. Histamine release from meperidine may be more common than from morphine

Continued

Table 6.16		Pseudoallergic Reactions[a] (Continued)
Drugs	Frequency	Clinical Remarks
NSAIDs[183]	See Aspirin	All NSAIDs cross-react with aspirin with respect to respiratory and cutaneous pseudoallergic reactions. Furthermore, all NSAIDs that cross-react with aspirin also participate in cross-desensitization (i.e., if a patient is desensitized to aspirin, they also will be desensitized to NSAIDs)
Ondansetron[185,199]	Rare	26 cases of anaphylactoid-anaphylactic reactions to IV ondansetron have been reported in the literature. Most reactions occurred after the 1st dose during the 2nd or 3rd course of chemotherapy
Pentamidine[178]	Common	Facial flushing, pruritus, tachycardia, syncope, nausea, and hypotension may occur in up to 75% of recipients following rapid IV administration. Thus, it should be infused slowly
Phytonadione[178]	Rare	IV administration of this colloidal form of vitamin K has caused severe anaphylactoid reactions, including shock, respiratory arrest, and death in some cases. These reactions have occurred despite precautions to dilute the injection and administer it slowly. These pseudoallergic reactions may be due to the emulsifying agent rather than the vitamin itself. Administer IM or SQ if possible. If phytonadione must be given IV, the rate should not exceed 1 mg/min
Protamine[9]	Occasional	Protamine sulfate is a component of some insulin preparations and is used extensively to neutralize heparin during cardiac procedures. In 1 study, 11% of patients receiving protamine during cardiac surgery experienced an adverse reaction, including angioedema, wheezing, erythema, and urticaria. There also are reports of shock leading to death. The mechanism of these severe reactions is unknown, but may be pseudoallergic as well as IgE-mediated
Pyrethrin with piperonyl butoxide[126]	Rare	Over a period of ≈8 hr a patient developed periorbital edema, wheezing, SOB, numbness in the extremities, chest tightness, dysphagia, hypotension, and loss of consciousness. Given the time course, the reaction appeared to be anaphylactoid, although an immunologic cross-reactivity to ragweed could not be ruled out
Quaternary ammonium muscle relaxants[5,178]	Uncommon to common, depending upon dose	All such agents produce a wheal-and-erythema reaction after intradermal administration if the dose is high enough, indicating direct histamine release. However, only d-tubocurarine and atracurium produce histamine levels that may be clinically relevant. These agents may cause both pseudoallergic and immunologically mediated reactions. D-tubocurarine is the most potent histamine releasing quaternary ammonium muscle relaxant; atracurium is ≈1/3 as potent as d-tubocurarine
Radiocontrast media[180]	Uncommon to common	Overall incidence of reaction to radiocontrast media is 3%–13%, depending upon the type of agent selected and if the patient was pretreated before administration of the radiocontrast media. The mortality rate varies widely from 1:15,000 to 1:117,000
Reserpine[178]	Common	Reserpine produces a dose-related increase in nasal stuffiness, discharge, or both that may aggravate bronchospasm at high doses
Thiamine	Rare	Urticaria, pruritus, weakness, nausea, throat tightening, angioneurotic edema, cardiovascular collapse, and death have all been reported following thiamine administration. In patients with suspected sensitivity to thiamine, an intradermal skin test may be useful before administering a therapeutic dose. The route of administration does not appear to be significant
Vancomycin[9,179]	Common	The "red man" syndrome is a pseudoallergic response to vancomycin, that is characterized by pruritis, erythema of the face/neck and/or torso, hypotension, occasionally angioedema, and rarely cardiovascular shock. The dose and rate of vancomycin infusion affect histamine release and development of signs and symptoms. Vancomycin also may cause immune-mediated reactions

[a] ACE = Angiotensin-converting enzyme; FDA = Food and Drug Administration; HIV = Human immunodeficiency virus; IM = Intramuscular; IV = Intravenous; NSAIDs = Nonsteroidal anti-inflammatory drugs; SOB = Shortness of breath; SQ = Subcutaneous.

Desensitization

Beta-Lactams

13. K.A. is a 24-year-old primigravida in her eighth week of pregnancy with a history of angioedema secondary to penicillin. Her initial pregnancy screening revealed a positive Venereal Disease Research Laboratory (VDRL) reaction and a Fluorescent Treponemal Antibody Absorption (FTA-Abs) titer of 1:64. K.A. denies a history of genital lesions, currently does not exhibit clinical signs or symptoms of syphilis, and denies previous treatment for syphilis. Based upon the serological evidence and her history, a diagnosis of early latent syphilis is made. Current treatment guidelines indicate penicillin is the drug of choice for K.A. How can a possible reaction to penicillin be prevented in K.A.? Is premedication an alternative to preventing a reaction?

Acute desensitization (or hyposensitization) is the process of administering gradually increasing doses of a drug over hours or days in an effort to develop clinical tolerance.[1,3,6,18,134] This process has been used successfully to reintroduce drugs to patients with known allergic reactions in situations where no alternatives exist: it is most commonly used in patients with IgE-mediated hypersensitivity and is well described for penicillin-allergic patients. Desensitization, however, is not useful in preventing late penicillin reactions, and should not be attempted in patients who have experienced severe dermatological reactions such as exfoliative dermatitis.[18] Since K.A.'s reaction to penicillin may be potentially severe, premedication is not an option and desensitization to penicillin should be started. (See Chapter 64: Sexually Transmitted Diseases for a discussion of alternative therapy.)

Table 6.17		Beta-Lactam Oral Desensitization Protocol[a]		
Stock Drug Concentration (mg/mL)[b]	Dose No.	Amount (mL)	Drug Dose (mg)	Cumulative Drug (mg)
0.5	1[c]	0.05	0.025	0.025
	2	0.10	0.05	0.075
	3	0.20	0.10	0.175
	4	0.40	0.20	0.375
	5	0.80	0.40	0.775
5.0	6	0.15	0.75	1.525
	7	0.30	1.50	3.025
	8	0.60	3.00	6.025
	9	1.20	6.00	12.025
	10	2.40	12.00	24.025
50	11	0.50	25.00	49.025
	12	1.20	60.00	109.025
	13	2.50	125.00	234.025
	14	5.00	250.00	484.025

[a] Adapted from references 135 and 137. Dosing for the oral protocol is arbitrary and should be adjusted for individual patients based upon the clinical sensitivity and the desired drug dose end point.
[b] Dilutions using 250 mg/5 mL of pediatric suspension.
[c] Oral dose doubled approximately every 15–30 minutes.

14. How should K.A. be desensitized? Why should she be skin tested before desensitization?

Before desensitization is begun, K.A. should be skin tested (see Questions 3 to 4) to confirm her penicillin allergy.[3,18,134] Patients who give a positive history of penicillin allergy, but are skin test negative, can receive full therapeutic doses without desensitization with little risk of developing an allergic reaction. One author, for example, reported only one case of acute anaphylaxis in a skin test negative patient given full therapeutic doses of penicillin in over 1500 skin tests: similar results have been reported by other investigators.[18,134] If K.A.'s skin test is positive, desensitization should be initiated. Acute oral desensitization to penicillin and other beta-lactam antibiotics is well established; one such protocol is outlined in Table 6.17, although others have been used successfully.[135–138] The oral route for beta-lactam desensitization is preferred to the parenteral route because: 1) exposure by the oral route is less likely to cause a systemic allergic reaction than parenteral exposure; 2) fatal anaphylaxis from oral beta-lactam drug therapy is rare; 3) preformed polymers and conjugates of penicillin major and minor determinants to penicillium proteins are not well absorbed after oral administration; 4) blood levels rise gradually, favoring univalent haptenation (appearance of multivalent hapten-carrier conjugates, on the other hand, is gradual); and 5) fatal or life-endangering reactions have not occurred using current methods. In addition, oral desensitization can be accomplished over several hours.[3] In cases where oral desensitization is not possible, for example if oral absorption is questionable, parenteral desensitization can be instituted. Although the subcutaneous and intramuscular routes have been used, the intravenous route is quicker, allows better control over the rate and concentration of drug administered, and any untoward reaction can be detected promptly and treated rapidly.[3,6,9] Table 6.18 outlines an intravenous beta-lactam desensitization protocol. Unfortunately, oral and parenteral desensitization methods have not been compared formally. Patients should not be premedicated before desensitization, since this may prevent detection of minor allergic responses which may precede more

serious reactions. In addition, desensitization should be performed in a setting where emergency resuscitative equipment and personnel are readily available.[134] Thus, K.A. should undergo oral desensitization as outlined in Table 6.17 if her skin test is positive.

15. Is K.A. at risk for an allergic reaction during desensitization? If desensitization is successful, is she at risk for a reaction during full-dose penicillin therapy?

Acute beta-lactam desensitization, regardless of the route or protocol chosen, is not without risk. Approximately 5% of patients will experience mild cutaneous reactions during desensitization, although one study reported reactions in 20% of patients during oral desensitization.[3,138] In cases when a reaction occurs during the desensitization procedure itself, the reaction may be treated and desensitization continued using either lower doses, increased intervals between doses, or both, after the reaction has abated. Severe, fatal reactions during desensitization are rare.[3]

Uneventful beta-lactam desensitization, however, does not guarantee patients will be without reaction during full-dose therapy. Approximately 25% to 30% of patients will experience a mild reaction during therapy, while 5% experience more severe reactions including drug-induced serum sickness, hemolytic anemia, or nephritis.[3] Reaction rates are no different in severely ill or pregnant patients compared to stable or nonpregnant patients, although those with cystic fibrosis may be more difficult to desensitize because of their high frequency of allergic reactions.[3,138,140,141] Despite the occurrence of reactions, full-dose therapy is possible for the majority of desensitizations, although suppression of the reaction (for example by diphenhydramine) may be required.[3]

16. If K.A. requires penicillin at a later date, will she need to undergo desensitization at that time? What is chronic desensitization?

The desensitized state, once achieved, will persist for approximately 48 hours after the last full dose of antibiotic. After this time, drug sensitivity will return.[3] Thus, if K.A. requires future courses of penicillin, she will need to undergo desensitization once again.

Table 6.18		IV Beta-Lactam Desensitization Protocol[a]	
Stock Drug Concentration (mg/mL)[b]	Dose No.[c]	Amount per 50 mL (mg/mL)[d]	Cumulative Drug (mg)
0.005	1[b]	0.0001	0.005
0.025	2	0.0005	0.030
0.125	3	0.0025	0.155
0.625	4	0.0125	0.780
3.125	5	0.0625	3.905
15.625	6[b]	0.3125	19.530
31.25	7	0.625	50.780
62.50	8	1.25	113.280
125.00	9	2.5	238.280
250.00	10[e]	5.0	488.280

[a] Adapted from reference 195. Dosing for the IV protocol is arbitrary and should be adjusted for individual patients based upon the clinical sensitivity and the desired drug dose end point.
[b] Stock drug solutions are prepared using serial dilutions of the desired goal (e.g., 500 mg of beta-lactam). Doses 1–5 represent fivefold dilutions; doses 6–10 represent twofold dilutions.
[c] Interval between doses is 15–30 minutes. If desensitization is interrupted for >2 half-lives of the beta-lactam, desensitization should be repeated.
[d] Mix 1 mL of stock drug solution in 50 mL 5% dextrose/0.225 normal saline or other compatible solution. Infuse each dose over 20–45 minutes. Dilution volume may vary with patient age and weight.
[e] If all 10 doses are administered and tolerated, the remainder of a full therapeutic dose of the beta-lactam should be administered.

Table 6.19	Oral Trimethoprim-Sulfamethoxazole Desensitization Protocol[a,b]		
Day	Sulfamethoxazole mg/mL of Suspension or Tablet[c]	Daily Dose Administered	Sulfamethoxazole Dose per Day (mg)
1	2 mg/mL	0.5 mL	1
2	2 mg/mL	1 mL	2
3	2 mg/mL	2 mL	4
4	2 mg/mL	4 mL	8
5	2 mg/mL	5 mL	10
6	2 mg/mL	8 mL	16
7	40 mg/mL	0.6 mL	24
8	40 mg/mL	1 mL	40
9	40 mg/mL	2 mL	80
10	40 mg/mL	2.5 mL	100
11	40 mg/mL	3 mL	120
12	40 mg/mL	4 mL	160
13	40 mg/mL	5 mL	200
14	40 mg/mL	7.5 mL	300
15	80 mg trimethoprim/ 400 mg sulfamethoxazole	1 tablet	400
16–22	80 mg trimethoprim/ 400 mg sulfamethoxazole	2 tablets (1 tablet BID)	800
≥23	80 mg trimethoprim/ 400 mg sulfamethoxazole	4 tablets (2 tablets BID)	1600

[a] Adapted from reference 165. This protocol should serve as a guide only since it has not been validated in a controlled fashion. Obtaining informed consent from the patient before initiating desensitization may be advisable.

[b] Although this protocol takes ≈3 weeks to complete, protocols for more rapid desensitization (e.g., ≤8 days) have been described.[171–173] In addition, some authors prescribe antihistamines during desensitization.[170]

[c] Stock solution of trimethoprim-sulfamethoxazole may be prepared by appropriate dilutions of the commercially available suspension (8 mg trimethoprim and 40 mg sulfamethoxazole) with simple syrup or distilled water.

In some cases, those requiring long-term antibiotic therapy (e.g., for endocarditis), those who may require beta-lactams at a future date (e.g., those with cystic fibrosis), or those who have occupational exposure to beta-lactams, maintenance of the desensitized state can be considered. Chronic twice daily dosing of oral penicillin has safely resulted in ''chronic desensitization.'' However, similar to acute desensitization, once therapy is interrupted, the allergic state returns.[3,9]

Other Drugs

17. Have patients allergic to drugs besides beta-lactams been desensitized successfully?

Although the majority of experience with desensitization is with penicillin and other beta-lactams, desensitization also has been accomplished with a variety of other drugs including rifampin,[141] isoniazid,[141] acyclovir,[142] sulfasalazine,[143–148] aminoglycosides,[140] vancomycin,[149–150] and several others.[151–164] Interestingly, not all of these cases represent IgE-mediated hypersensitivity reactions. Acute desensitization, which has until recently been used to manage only IgE-mediated reactions, appears to be effective in other forms of immunopathology.[3] For example, reactions to trimethoprim-sulfamethoxazole (TMP/SMX) commonly occur in HIV-infected patients and may not be IgE mediated. Yet, successful desensitization to TMP/SMX is increasingly common given its role in treating and preventing *Pneumocystis carinii* pneumonia.[3] One procedure for TMP/SMX desensitization is outlined in Table 6.19, although a number of other protocols have been used successfully.[9,165–173] Although mild to moderate reactions may occur (e.g., fever, mild skin rash), patients may complete desensitization successfully by suppressing the reaction with antihistamines, reducing the dose to the highest level previously taken without a reaction until the reaction subsides, or both.[165,167,168] As with the beta-lactams, before desensitization for any medication is undertaken, alternative therapies should be sought and used if possible. Furthermore, desensitization is contraindicated if the reaction is a serious dermatologic response such as toxic epidermal necrolysis or Stevens-Johnson syndrome. Lastly, desensitization should be undertaken only in an appropriate setting by experienced personnel, as severe reactions can develop.[174]

References

1 **DeSwarte RD.** Drug allergy: problems and strategies. J Allergy Clin Immunol. 1984;74(Pt. 1):209.

2 **Assem E-S K.** Drug allergy and tests for its detection. In: Davies DM, ed. Textbook of Adverse Drug Reactions. 3rd ed. New York: Oxford University Press; 1985:689.

3 **Sullivan TJ.** Drug allergy. In: Middleton E Jr et al., eds. Allergy. Principles and Practices. 4th ed. St. Louis: Mosby; 1993:1726.

4 **Jick H.** Adverse drug reactions: the magnitude of the problem. J Allergy Clin Immunol. 1984;74:555.

5 **Classen DC et al.** Computerized surveillance of adverse drug events in hospital patients. JAMA. 1991;266:2847.

6 **Van Arsdel PP Jr.** Drug hypersensitivity. In: Bierman CW, Pearlman DS, eds. Allergic Diseases From Infancy to Adulthood. 2nd ed. Philadelphia: WB Saunders; 1988:684.

7 **Van Arsdel PP Jr.** Classification and risk factors for drug allergy. Immunol Allergy Clin North Am. 1991;11:475.

8 **Adkinson NF Jr.** Risk factors for drug allergy. J Allergy Clin Immunol. 1984; 74:567.

9 **Anderson JA.** Allergic reactions to drugs and biological agents. JAMA. 1992;268:2845.

10 **Bigby M et al.** Drug-induced cutaneous reactions. JAMA. 1986;256:3358.

11 **Parker CW.** Drug allergy. N Engl J Med. 1975;292(Pt. 1–3):511,732,957.

12 **de Weck AL.** Pharmacological and immunochemical mechanisms of drug hypersensitivity. Immunol Allergy Clin North Am. 1991;11:461.

13 **Bochner BS, Lichtenstein LM.** Anaphylaxis. N Engl J Med. 1991;324:1785.

14 **Marquardt DL, Wasserman SI.** Anaphylaxis. In: Middleton E Jr et al., eds. Allergy. Principles and Practices. 4th ed. St. Louis: Mosby; 1993:1365.

15 **Yunginger JW.** Anaphylaxis. Ann Allergy. 1992;69:87.

16 **Gruchalla RS, Sullivan TJ.** In vivo and in vitro diagnosis of drug allergy. Immunol Allergy Clin North Am. 1991; 11:595.

17 **Shepherd GM.** Allergy to β-lactam antibiotics. Immunol Allergy Clin North Am. 1991;11:611.

18 **Lin RY.** A perspective on penicillin allergy. Arch Intern Med. 1992;152:930.

19 **Weiss ME.** Drug allergy. Med Clin North Am. 1992;76:857.

20 **Sogn DD et al.** Results of the National Institute of Allergy and Infectious Diseases Collaborative Clinical Trial to test the predictive value of skin testing with major and minor penicillin derivatives in hospitalized adults. Arch Intern Med. 1992;152:1025.

21 **Buhner D, Grant JA.** Serum sickness. Dermatol Clin. 1985;3:107.

22 **Lin RY.** Serum sickness syndrome. Am Fam Physician. 1986;33:157.

23 **Erffmeyer JE.** Serum sickness. Ann Allergy. 1986;56:105.

24 **Lawley TJ et al.** A study of human serum sickness. J Invest Dermatol. 1985;85(Suppl.):129s.

25 **Dukes MNG, ed.** Myelers Side Effects of Drugs. 12th ed. Amsterdam: Elsevier Science Publishers; 1992.

26 **Cunningham E et al.** Acute serum sickness with glomerulonephritis induced by antithymocyte globulin. Transplantation. 1987;43:309.

27 **Bielory L et al.** Human serum sickness: a prospective analysis of 35 patients treated with equine anti-thymocyte globulin for bone marrow failure. Medicine. 1988;67:40.

28 **Bielory L et al.** Cutaneous manifestations of serum sickness in patients receiving antithymocyte globulin. J Am Acad Dermatol. 1985;13:411.

29 **Yen MC et al.** Serum sickness-like syndrome associated with propranolol therapy. Postgrad Med. 1983;74:291.

30 **Totty WG et al.** Serum sickness following streptokinase therapy. Am J Rheum. 1982;138:143.

31 **Clesham GJ et al.** Serum sickness and purpura following intravenous streptokinase. J R Soc Med. 1992;85:638.

32 **Patel A et al.** Serum sickness-like illness and leukocytoclastic vasculitis after intravenous streptokinase. J Am Acad Dermatol. 1991;24:652.

33 **Schweitzer DH et al.** Serum-sickness-like illness as a complication after streptokinase therapy for acute myocardial infarction. Cardiology. 1991; 78:68.

34 **Stricker BH, Tijssen JG.** Serum sickness-like reactions to cefaclor. J Clin Epidemiol. 1992;45:1177.

35 **Platt R et al.** Serum sickness-like reactions to amoxicillin, cefaclor, cephalexin, and trimethoprim-sulfamethoxazole. J Infect Dis. 1988;158:474.

36 **Igarashi M et al.** An immunodominant haptenic epitope of carbamazepine detected in serum from patients given long-term treatment with carbamazepine without allergic reaction. J Clin Immunol. 1992;12:335.

37 **Weart CW, Hyman LC.** Serum sickness associated with metronidazole. South Med J. 1983;76:410.

38 **Haruda F.** Phenytoin hypersensitivity. Neurology. 1979;29:1480.

39 **Josephs SH et al.** Phenytoin hypersensitivity. J Allergy Clin Immunol. 1980; 66:166.

40 **Tomsick RS.** The phenytoin syndrome. Cutis. 1983;32:535.

41 **Panwalker AP et al.** Serum sickness associated with cefoxitin and pentoxifylline therapy. Drug Intell Clin Pharm. 1986;20:953.

42 **Comenzo RL et al.** Immune hemolysis, disseminated intravascular coagulation, and serum sickness after large doses of immune globulin given intravenously for Kawasaki disease. J Pediatr. 1992;120:926.

43 **Vincent A et al.** Serum sickness induced by fluoxetine. Am J Psychiatry. 1991;148:1602.

44 **Miller LG et al.** A case of fluoxetine-induced serum sickness. Am J Psychiatry. 1989;146:1616.

45 **Tomas S et al.** Ciprofloxacin and immunocomplex-mediated disease. J Intern Med. 1991;230:550.

46 **Slama TG.** Serum sickness-like illness associated with ciprofloxacin. Antimicrob Agents Chemother. 1990;34: 904.

47 **Bielory L.** Serum sickness from iron-dextran administration. Acta Haematol. 1990;83:166.

48 **Ferraccioli G et al.** Indomethacin-related serum sickness-like illness with IgM lambda cryoparaprotein? Acta Haematol. 1985;73:45.

49 **Wolfe MS, Moede AL.** Serum sickness with furazolidone. Am J Trop Med Hyg. 1978;27:762.

50 **Calabrese LH et al.** The American College of Rheumatology 1990 criteria for the classification of hypersensitivity vasculitis. Arthritis Rheum. 1990;33: 1108.

51 **Drory VE, Korczyn AD.** Hypersensitivity vasculitis and systemic lupus erythematosus induced by anticonvulsants. Clin Neuropharmacol. 1993;16: 19.

52 **Calabrese LH.** Differential diagnosis of hypersensitivity vasculitis. Cleve Clin J Med. 1990;57:506.

53 **Semble EL et al.** Vasculitis: a practical approach to management. Postgrad Med. 1991;90:161.

54 **Singhal PC et al.** Hypersensitivity angiitis associated with naproxen. Ann Allergy. 1989;63:107.

55 **Bergman SM et al.** Azathioprine and hypersensitivity vasculitis. Ann Intern Med. 1988;109:83.

56 **Mitchell GG et al.** Cimetidine-induced cutaneous vasculitis. Am J Med. 1983; 75:875.

57 **Arellano F, Sacristan JA.** Allopurinol hypersensitivity syndrome. Ann Pharmacother. 1993;27:337.

58 **Volckaert A et al.** Systemic hypersensitivity reaction due to sulfadiazine. Acta Clin Belg. 1987;42:381.

59 **Bear RA et al.** Vasculitis and vitamin abuse. Arch Pathol Lab Med. 1982; 106:48.

60 **Steinmetz JC et al.** Hypersensitivity vasculitis associated with 2-deoxycoformycin and allopurinol therapy. Am J Med. 1989;86:499.

61 **Torres RA et al.** Zidovudine-induced leukocytoclastic vasculitis. Arch Intern Med. 1992;152:850.

62 **Huminer D et al.** Hypersensitivity vasculitis due to ofloxacin. BMJ. 1989; 299:303.

63 **Jungst G, Mohr R.** Side effects of ofloxacin in clinical trials and in postmarketing surveillance. Drugs. 1987; 34(Suppl. 1):144.

64 **Kanuga J et al.** Ciprofloxacin induced leukocytoclastic vasculitis with cryoglobulinemia. Ann Allergy. 1991;66: 76. Abstract.

65 **Choe U et al.** Ciprofloxacin-induced vasculitis. N Engl J Med. 1989;320: 257.

66 **Stubbings J et al.** Cutaneous vasculitis due to ciprofloxacin. BMJ. 1992;305: 29.

67 **Stankus SJ, Johnson NT.** Propylthiouracil-induced hypersensitivity vasculitis presenting as respiratory failure. Chest. 1992;102:1595.

68 **Wolf D et al.** Nodular vasculitis associated with propylthiouracil. Cutis. 1992;49:253.

69 **Carrasco MD et al.** Cutaneous vasculitis associated with propylthiouracil therapy. Arch Intern Med. 1987;147: 1677.

70 **Scerri L, Pace JL.** Mefloquine-associated cutaneous vasculitis. Int J Dermatol. 1993;32:517.

71 **Reynolds NJ et al.** Hydralazine predisposes to acute cutaneous vasculitis following urography with iopamidol. Br J Dermatol. 1993;129:82.

72 **Travis WD et al.** Hypersensitivity pneumonitis and pulmonary vasculitis with eosinophilia in a patient taking a L-tryptophan preparation. Ann Intern Med. 1990;112:301.

73 **Bosnyak S et al.** Acute cutaneous vasculitis associated with prolonged intravenous ritodrine hydrochloride therapy. Am J Obstet Gynecol. 1991;165: 427.

74 **Enat R et al.** Hypersensitivity vasculitis induced by terbutaline sulfate. Ann Allergy. 1988;61:275.

75 **Grunwald MH et al.** Allergic vasculitis induced by hydrochlorothiazide: confirmation by mast cell degranulation test. Isr J Med Sci. 1989;25:572.

76 **Hannedouche T, Fillastre JP.** Penicillin-induced hypersensitivity vasculitides. J Antimicrob Chemother. 1987; 20:3.

77 **Kamper AM et al.** Cutaneous vasculitis induced by sodium valproate. Lancet. 1991;337:497.

78 **Tanay A et al.** Dermal vasculitis due to coumadin hypersensitivity. Dermatologica. 1982;165:178.

79 **Leung AC et al.** Phenylbutazone-induced systemic vasculitis with crescentic glomerulo-nephritis. Arch Intern Med. 1985;145:685.

80 **Knox JP et al.** Procainamide-induced urticarial vasculitis. Cutis. 1988;42:469.

81 **Lin RY.** Unusual autoimmune manifestations in furosemide-associated hypersensitivity angiitis. N Y State J Med. 1988;88:439.

82 **Morrow JD et al.** Studies on the control of hypertension by hyphex. II. Toxic reactions and side effects. Circulation. 1953;8:829.

83 **Gilliland BC.** Drug-induced autoimmune and hematologic disorders. Drug Allergy. 1991;11:525.

84 **Skaer TL.** Medication-induced systemic lupus erythematosus. Clin Ther. 1992;14:496.

85 **Vyse T, So AKL.** Sulphasalazine induced autoimmune syndrome. Br J Rheumatol. 1992;31:115.

86 **Wandl UB et al.** Lupus-like autoimmune disease induced by interferon therapy for myeloproliferative disorders. Clin Immunol Immunopathol. 1992;65:70.

87 **Perry HJ et al.** Relationship of acetyltransferase activity to antinuclear antibodies and toxic symptoms in hypertensive patients treated with hydralazine. J Lab Clin Med. 1970;76:114.

88 **Woosley RL et al.** Effect of acetylator phenotype on the rate at which procainamide induces antinuclear antibodies and the lupus syndrome. N Engl J Med. 1978;298:1157.

89 **Tan EM et al.** The 1982 revised criteria for the classification of systemic lupus erythematosus. Arthritis Rheum. 1982;25:1271.

90 **Blomgren SE et al.** Antinuclear antibody induced by procainamide. N Engl J Med. 1969;281:64.

91 **Henningsen NC et al.** Effects of long-term treatment with procainamide. Acta Med Scand. 1975;198:475.

92 **Kowsowsky BC et al.** Long-term use of procainamide following acute myocardial infarction. Circulation. 1973; 47:1204.

93 **Cameron HA, Ramsay LE.** The lupus syndrome induced by hydralazine: a common complication with low dose treatment. Br Med J. 1984;189:410.

94 **Anderson JA, Adkinson NF Jr.** Allergic reactions to drugs and biologic agents. JAMA. 1987;258:2891.

95 **Blombgren SE et al.** Procainamide-induced lupus erythematosus: clinical and laboratory observations. Am J Med. 1972;52:338.

96 **Solinger AM.** Drug-related lupus. Clinical and etiologic considerations. Rheum Dis Clin North Am. 1988;14: 187.

97 **Machold KP, Smolen JS.** Interferon-gamma induced exacerbation of systemic lupus erythematosus. J Rheumatol. 1990;17:831.

98 **Alarcon-Segovia D et al.** Clinical and experimental studies on the hydralazine syndrome and its relation to SLE. Medicine. 1967;46:1.

99 **Lahita R et al.** Antibodies to nuclear antigens in patients treated with procainamide or acetylprocainamide. N Engl J Med. 1979;301:1382.

100 **Roden DM et al.** Antiarrhythmic efficacy, pharmacokinetics and safety of N-acetylprocainamide in human subjects: comparison with procainamide. Am J Cardiol. 1980;46:463.

101 **Stec GP et al.** Remission of procainamide-induced lupus erythematosus with N-acetylprocainamide therapy. Ann Intern Med. 1979;90:799.

102 **Greenberg JH, Lutcher CL.** Drug-induced systemic lupus erythematosus. JAMA. 1972;222:191.

103 **Lee SL, Chase PH.** Drug-induced systemic lupus erythematosus. A critical review. Semin Arthritis Rheum. 1975; 6:83.

104 **Perry HM.** Late toxicity to hydralazine resembling systemic lupus erythematosus or rheumatoid arthritis. Am J Med. 1973;54:58.

105 **Dubois EL et al.** Chlorpromazine-induced systemic lupus erythematosus. JAMA. 1972;221:595.

106 **Fabius AJM, Faulhofer WK.** Systemic lupus erythematosus induced by psychotropic drugs. Acta Rheumatol Scand. 1971;17:137.

107 **Goldman LS et al.** Lupus-like illness associated with chlorpromazine. Am J Psychiatry. 1980;137:1613.

108 **Quismorio FP et al.** Antinuclear antibodies in chronic psychotic patients treated with chlorpromazine. Am J Psychiatry. 1975;132:1204.

109 **Kendall MJ, Hawkins CF.** Quinidine-induced systemic lupus erythematosus. Postgrad Med J. 1970;46:729.

110 **Cohen MG et al.** Two distinct quinidine-induced rheumatic syndromes. Ann Intern Med. 1988;108:369.

111 **West SG et al.** Quinidine-induced lupus erythematosus. Ann Intern Med. 1984;100:840.

112 **Burlingame RW, Rubin RL.** Antihistone antibody induction by drugs implicates autoimmunization with nucleohistone. Arthritis Rheum. 1980;32 (Suppl. 4):S22. Abstract.

113 **Griffiths ID, Kane SP.** Sulphasalazine-induced lupus syndrome in ulcerative colitis. Br Med J. 1977;2:1188.

114 **Crisp AJ, Hoffbrand BI.** Sulphasalazine-induced systemic lupus erythematosus in a patient with Sjogren's syndrome. J R Soc Med. 1980;73:60.

115 **Carr-Locke D.** Sulfasalazine-induced lupus syndrome in a patient with Crohn's disease. Am J Gastroenterol. 1982;77:614.

116 **Clementz GL, Doli BJ.** Sulfasalazine-induced lupus erythematosus. Am J Med. 1988;84:535.

117 **Rafferty P et al.** Sulphasalazine-induced cerebral lupus erythematosus. Postgrad Med J. 1982;58:98.

118 **Chalmer A et al.** Systemic lupus erythematosus during penicillamine therapy for rheumatoid arthritis. Ann Intern Med. 1982;97:659.

119 **Harrington TM, Davis DE.** Systemic lupus-like syndrome induced by methyldopa therapy. Chest. 1981;79:696.

120 **Dupont A, Six R.** Lupus-like syndrome induced by methyldopa. Br Med J. 1982;285:693.

121 **Perry HM Jr et al.** Immunologic findings in patients receiving methyldopa: a prospective study. J Lab Clin Med. 1971;78:905.

122 **Nordstrom DM et al.** Methyldopa-induced systemic lupus erythematosus. Arthritis Rheum. 1989;32:205.

123 **Booth RJ et al.** Beta-adrenergic-receptor blockers and antinuclear antibodies in hypertension. Clin Pharmacol Ther. 1982;31:555.

124 **Ronnblom LE et al.** Possible induction of systemic lupus erythematosus by interferon-alpha treatment in a patient with a malignant carcinoid tumour. J Intern Med. 1990;227:207.

125 **Schilling PJ et al.** Development of systemic lupus erythematosus after interferon therapy for chronic myelogenous leukemia. Cancer. 1991;68:1536.

126 **Culver CA et al.** Probable anaphylactoid reaction to a pyrethrin pediculicide shampoo. Clin Pharm. 1988;7:846.

127 **Alarcon-Segovia D et al.** Antinuclear antibodies in patients on anticonvulsant therapy. Clin Exp Immunol. 1972;12: 39.

128 **Jacobs JC.** Systemic lupus erythematosus in childhood. Report of 35 cases, with discussion of 7 apparently induced by anticonvulsant medication, and of prognosis and treatment. Pediatrics. 1963;32:257.

129 **Bleck TP, Smith MC.** Possible induction of systemic lupus erythematosus syndrome by valproate. Epilepsia. 1990; 31:343.

130 **Ahuja GK, Schumacher GA.** Drug-induced SLE: primidone as a possible cause. JAMA. 1966;198:201.

131 **Drory VE et al.** Carbamazepine-induced systemic lupus erythematosus. Clin Neuropharmacol. 1989;12:115.

132 **Livingston S et al.** Carbamazepine in epilepsy. Nine year follow-up with special emphasis on untoward reactions. Dis Nerv Syst. 1974;35:103.

133 **Livingston S et al.** Systemic lupus erythematosus. Occurrence in association with ethosuximide therapy. JAMA. 1968;204:185.

134 **Wedner HJ.** Drug allergy prevention and treatment. Immunol Allergy Clin North Am. 1991;11:679–94.

135 **Sullivan TJ et al.** Desensitization of patients allergic to penicillin using orally administered β-lactam antibiotics. J Allergy Clin Immunol. 1982;69: 275.

136 **Sullivan TJ.** Antigen-specific desensitization of patients allergic to penicillin. J Allergy Clin Immunol. 1982;69: 500.

137 **Wendel GD Jr et al.** Penicillin allergy and desensitization in serious infections during pregnancy. N Engl J Med. 1985;312:1229.

138 **Stark BJ et al.** Acute and chronic desensitization of penicillin-allergic patients using oral penicillin. J Allergy Clin Immunol. 1987;79:523.

139 **Brown LA et al.** Long-term ticarcillin desensitization by the continuous oral administration of penicillin. J Allergy Clin Immunol. 1982;69:51.

140 **Earl HS, Sullivan TJ.** Acute desensitization of a patient with cystic fibrosis allergic to both beta-lactam and aminoglycoside antibiotics. J Allergy Clin Immunol. 1987;79:477.

141 **Holland CL et al.** Rapid oral desensitization to isoniazid and rifampin. Chest. 1990;98:1518.

142 **Henry RE et al.** Successful oral acy-clovir desensitization. Ann Allergy. 1993;70:386.

143 **Farr M et al.** Sulphasalazine desensitization in rheumatoid arthritis. Br Med J. 1982;284:118. Letter.

144 **Bax DE, Amos RS.** Sulphasalazine in rheumatoid arthritis: desensitizing the patient with a skin rash. Ann Rheum Dis. 1986;45:139.

145 **Purdy BH et al.** Desensitization for sulfasalazine skin rash. Ann Intern Med. 1984;100:512.

146 **Toila V.** Sulfasalazine desensitization in children and adolescents with chronic inflammatory bowel disease. Am J Gastroenterol. 1992;87:1029.

147 **Taffet SL, Das KM.** Desensitization of patients with inflammatory bowel disease to sulfasalazine. Am J Med. 1982;73:520.

148 **Holdsworth CD.** Sulfasalazine desensitization. Br Med J. 1982;282:110. Letter.

149 **Lerner A, Dwyer JM.** Desensitization to vancomycin. Ann Intern Med. 1984; 100:157. Letter.

150 **Lin RY.** Desensitization in the management of vancomycin hypersensitivity. Arch Intern Med. 1990;150:2197.

151 **Bell ET et al.** Sulphadiazine desensitization in AIDS patients. Lancet. 1985;1:163. Letter.

152 **Tenant-Flowers M et al.** Sulphadiazine desensitization in patients with AIDS and cerebral toxoplasmosis. AIDS. 1991;5:311.

153 **de la Hoz Caballer B et al.** Management of sulfadiazine allergy in patients with acquired immunodeficiency syndrome. J Allergy Clin Immunol. 1991; 88:137.

154 **Greenberger PA, Patterson R.** Management of drug allergy in patients with acquired immunodeficiency syndrome. J Allergy Clin Immunol. 1987; 79:484.

155 **Walz-LeBlanc BAE et al.** Allopurinol sensitivity in a patient with chronic tophaceous gout: success of intravenous desensitization after failure of oral desensitization. Arthritis Rheum. 1991; 34:1329.

156 **Fasm AG et al.** Desensitization to allopurinol in patients with gout and cutaneous reactions. Am J Med. 1992;93: 299.

157 **Pleskow WW et al.** Aspirin desensitization in aspirin-sensitive asthmatic patients: clinical manifestations and characterization of the refractory period. J Allergy Clin Immunol. 1982;69: 11.

158 **Knight A.** Desensitization to aspirin in aspirin-sensitive patients with rhino-sinusitis and asthma: a review. J Otolaryngol. 1989;18:165.

159 **Lumry WR et al.** Aspirin-sensitive asthma and rhinosinusitis: current concepts and recent advances. Ear Nose Throat J. 1984;63:102.

160 **Smith H, Newton R.** Adverse reactions to carbamazepine managed by desensitization. Lancet. 1985;1:753. Letter.

161 **Carr A et al.** Allergy and desensitization to zidovudine in patients with acquired immunodeficiency syndrome.

J Allergy Clin Immunol. 1993;91:683.

162 **Kurohara ML et al.** Metronidazole hypersensitivity and oral desensitization. J Allergy Clin Immunol. 1991;88: 279.

163 **Rassiga AL et al.** Cytarabine-induced anaphylaxis. Demonstration of antibody and successful desensitization. Arch Intern Med. 1980;140:425.

164 **Thompson DM, Ronco JJ.** Prolonged desensitization required for treatment of generalized allergy to human insulin. Diabetes Care. 1993;16:957. Letter.

165 **Smith RM et al.** Trimethoprim-sulfamethoxazole desensitization in the acquired immunodeficiency syndrome. Ann Intern Med. 1987;106:335. Letter.

166 **Hughes TE et al.** Co-trimoxazole desensitization in bone marrow transplant. Ann Intern Med. 1986;105:148. Letter.

167 **Torgovnick J, Arsura E.** Desensitization to sulfonamides in patients with HIV infection. Am J Med. 1990;88: 548. Letter.

168 **Kletzel M et al.** Trimethoprim-sulfamethoxazole oral desensitization in hemophiliacs infected with human immunodeficiency virus with a history of hypersensitivity reactions. Am J Dis Child. 1991;145:1428.

169 **Finegold I.** Oral desensitization to trimethoprim-sulfamethoxazole in a patient with acquired immunodeficiency syndrome. J Allergy Clin Immunol. 1986;78:905.

170 **White MV et al.** Desensitization to trimethoprim sulfamethoxazole in patients with acquired immune deficiency syndrome and *Pneumocystis carinii* pneumonia. Ann Allergy. 1989;62:177.

171 **Gluckstein D, Ruskin J.** Trimethoprim-sulfamethoxazole (TS) desensitization (D) permits long-term Pneumocystis prophylaxis in AIDS patients (pts) with prior TS intolerance. Interscience Conference on Antimicrobial Agents and Chemotherapy. Los Angeles, CA: 1992 Oct. Abstract 1475.

172 **Rich JD et al.** Successful oral desensitization to TMP/SMX in persons with HIV infection and prior hypersensitive reactions. Int Conf AIDS. Boston, MA: 1993 Jun 6–11. Abstract PO-810-1482.

173 **Moreno JN, Maggio CM.** Oral desensitization to sulfadiazine and trimethoprim-sulfamethoxazole (TMP-SMZ) in 4 patients with acquired immunodeficiency syndrome. Int Conf AIDS. Miami, FL: 1989 Jun 4–9. Abstract T.B.P. 320.

174 **Sher MR et al.** Anaphylactic shock induced by oral desensitization to trimethoprim/sulfamethoxazole (TMP-SMZ). J Allergy Clin Immunol. 1986; 77:133. Abstract.

175 **Fath JJ, Cerra FB.** The therapy of anaphylactic shock. Drug Intell Clin Pharm. 1984;18:14.

176 **Atkinson TP, Kaliner MA.** Anaphylaxis. Med Clin North Am. 1992;76: 841.

177 **Delage C, Irey NA.** Anaphylactic deaths: a clinicopathologic study of 43 cases. J Forensic Sci. 1972;17:525.

178 **Van Arsdel PP Jr.** Pseudoallergic drug reactions. Introduction and general review. Immunol Allergy Clin North Am. 1991;11:635.

179 **Polk RE.** Anaphylactoid reactions to glycopeptide antibiotics. J Antimicrob Chemother. 1991;27(Suppl. B):17.

180 **Lasser EC.** Pseudoallergic drug reactions. Radiographic contrast media. Immunol Allergy Clin North Am. 1991;11:645.

181 **Greenberger PA et al.** Two pretreatment regimens for high-risk patients receiving radiographic contrast media. J Allergy Clin Immunol. 1984;74:540.

182 **Israili ZH, Hall WD.** Cough and angioneurotic edema associated with angiotensin-converting enzyme inhibitor therapy. A review of the literature and pathophysiology. Ann Intern Med. 1992;117:234.

183 **Manning ME, Stevenson DD.** Pseudoallergic drug reactions. Aspirin, nonsteroidal anti-inflammatory drugs, dyes, additives, and preservatives. Immunol Allergy Clin North Am. 1991; 11:659.

184 **Davis H et al.** Anaphylactoid reactions reported after treatment with ciprofloxacin. Ann Intern Med. 1989;111:1041.

185 **Chen M et al.** Anaphylactoid-anaphylactic reactions associated with ondansetron. Ann Intern Med. 1993;119:862. Letter.

186 **Stevenson DD, Simon RA.** Sensitivity to aspirin and nonsteroidal anti-inflammatory drugs. In: Middleton E Jr et al., eds. Allergy. Principles and Practices. 4th ed. St. Louis: Mosby; 1993:1747.

187 **Young EJ et al.** Drug-induced fever: cases seen in the evaluation of unexplained fever in a general hospital population. Rev Infect Dis. 1982;4:69.

188 **Lipsky BA, Hirschmann JV.** Drug fever. JAMA. 1981;245:851.

189 **Kumar KL, Reuler JB.** Drug fever. West J Med. 1986;144:753.

190 **Tabor PA.** Drug-induced fever. Drug Intell Clin Pharm. 1986;20:413.

191 **Cunha BA.** Drug fever. Postgrad Med. 1986;80:123.

192 **Mackowiak PA, LeMaistre CF.** Drug fever: a critical appraisal of conventional concepts. Ann Intern Med. 1987; 106:728.

193 **Hofland SL.** Drug fever: is your patient's fever drug-related? Crit Care Nurse. 1985;5:29.

194 **Hiraide A et al.** IgE-mediated drug fever due to histamine H$_2$-receptor blockers. Drug Saf. 1990;5:455.

195 **Borish L et al.** Intravenous desensitization to beta-lactam antibiotics. J Allergy Clin Immunol. 1987;80:314.

196 **Bonfiglio MF et al.** Anaphylactoid reaction to intravenous acetylcysteine associated with electrocardiographic abnormalities. Ann Pharmacother. 1992; 26:22.

197 **Deamer RL et al.** Hypersensitivity and anaphylactoid reactions to ciprofloxacin. Ann Pharmacother. 1992;26:1081.

198 **Soetikno RM et al.** Ciprofloxacin-induced anaphylactoid reaction in a patient with AIDS. Ann Pharmacother. 1993;27:1404. Letter.

199 **Kossey JL, Kwok KK.** Anaphylactoid reactions associated with ondansetron. Ann Pharmacother. 1994;28:1029.

Chapter 7

Pain

Peter J. S. Koo

Mechanisms of Pain 7-2
  Transmission 7-2
  Peripheral nociception, transduction,
    and inflammation 7-2
  Central mechanism for chronic pain 7-2
Mode of Analgesic Action 7-2
  Nonsteroidal Anti-Inflammatory Drugs (NSAIDs) ...7-2
  Opiates 7-2
  Analgesic adjunctive agents 7-3
Classification of Pain 7-3
  Acute pain 7-3
  Chronic pain 7-3
    Pain associated with malignancy
      (chronic malignant pain) 7-4
    Chronic nonmalignant pain 7-4
General Treatment Principles 7-4
  Differentiate clinical opioid use and drug abuse 7-5
  Analgesic selection 7-5
Mild Analgesics 7-5
Opioid Analgesics 7-5

Acute Pain 7-6
Analgesic Goals 7-6
Combination Analgesics 7-7
Equianalgesic Dosing of Opioid Analgesics 7-7
Ketorolac 7-7
Nonsteroidal Anti-Inflammatory Drugs (NSAIDs) 7-7
  Selection 7-7
  Use in Renal Disease 7-8
Analgesic Nephrotoxicity 7-8
Opioids 7-8
  Managing side effects 7-8
  Patient controlled analgesia (PCA) 7-9
    Opioid selection for use in PCA 7-10
    PCA prescriptions 7-10
    PCA selection criteria 7-11
    Dose conversion between opioid analgesics 7-11
    Conversion from PCA to oral opioids 7-11
  Tapering of opioid analgesics 7-11
  Pain Management in the opioid dependent patient ... 7-11
  Use of opioids in recovering addicts 7-12
  Use of opioids in renal disease 7-12
  Obstetrical pain: special considerations
    for opioid analgesia 7-12
    Epidurals 7-12
      In opioid dependent patients 7-12
      Clonidine for opioid withdrawal symptoms 7-13
    Systemic opioids during labor 7-13
  Variability in intramuscular (IM)
    meperidine absorption 7-13
  Special consideration for using partial agonist
    and antagonist opioid analgesics 7-13

  Tramadol 7-14
Chronic Malignant Pain 7-14
  Goal of Malignant Pain Management 7-14
  Indications for Use of Fentanyl Patches 7-14
  Morphine 7-14
    Use of oral morphine 7-14
    Tolerance, dependence, and addiction 7-15
    Use of sustained-release (SR) morphine 7-15
    Rectal use of suppositories and SR tablets 7-15
    Oral infusion 7-16
    Continuous intravenous (IV) infusion
      (See Question 39) 7-16
  Tricyclic Antidepressants (TCAs) 7-16
  Methadone 7-16
    Guidelines 7-16
    Dosing 7-16
  Brompton's Mixture 7-17
  Pentazocine 7-17
  Hydroxyzine or Phenothiazine 7-17
  Adrenal Corticosteroids 7-17
  Nonsteroidal anti-inflammatory drugs (NSAIDs) 7-17
Chronic Nonmalignant Pain 7-18
  Goal of Therapy 7-18
  Analgesic Consolidation 7-18
  Opioid Tapering and Withdrawal 7-18
  Managing Opioid Overdose 7-18
Neuropathic Pain 7-19
  α_2-Agonists 7-19
  Tricyclic Antidepressants (TCAs) 7-19
  Mexiletine 7-19
Head Injury and Opioid Analgesia 7-19
Myocardial Pain 7-20
Colic Pain 7-20
  Biliary Colic 7-20
  Renal Colic 7-20
Liver Disease and Analgesia 7-20
Respiratory Disease and Analgesia 7-21
Opioids in Special Age Groups 7-21
  Advanced Age 7-21
  Neonates and Children 7-21
Morphine Induced Nausea and Vomiting 7-21
Use of Central Nervous System Stimulants 7-22
Important Drug Interactions 7-22
  Phenytoin and Methadone 7-22
  Cimetidine and Methadone 7-22
Primary Dysmenorrhea 7-22
Headaches 7-23
Procedural Pain 7-23
Topical Anesthetics 7-23

Pain is an unpleasant sensation disturbing a patient's comfort, thought, sleep, emotion, or normal daily activity and is only symptomatic of an underlying disease process. It is influenced by the patient's anxiety, perceptions, fatigue, prior conditioning, and other psychological variables as well as the extent of tissue damage. Pain is the net effect of complex interactions of ascending and descending neurosystems with biochemical, physiological, psychological, and neocortical processes. By the time an individual perceives pain, the stimulus for pain has already been subjected to the processes within these neurosystems.

Pain is a subjective experience. Therefore, it is the patient, not the clinician, who can best describe the intensity of pain. Pain is whatever the experiencing person says it is, existing wherever he says it does. Thus, the patient's description of pain must be believed if clinicians wish to alleviate their patient's discomfort.

Pain serves the useful purpose of alerting an individual to an injury, but persistent pain serves no additional purpose. Sometimes pain can be referred to sites other than the apparent source. This type of pain is typical of neuropathy, nerve injury, or visceral pain. For example, myocardial ischemic pain can be referred to the chest, back, arms, neck, jaw, or midepigastric area. Sometimes radicular pain can present as gastrointestinal complaints due to its referring nature. Therefore, the source of referred pain often is difficult to find.

Mechanisms of Pain

Transmission. Since Melzack and Wall proposed the "Gate Theory" in the 1960s, progress has been made in the areas of neurointegration, modulation, and nociception. Pain mechanisms are complex and influenced by several peripheral and central neurochemical processes. The physiological mechanism of pain starts with a noxious stimuli at the receptor or a tissue site. Receptors translate the noxious stimuli into an electrical impulse which is then transmitted via the afferent nerve to the spinal cord at the dorsal horn. Noxious stimuli evoked receptor action potentials are transmitted through two nerve types: myelinated A-δ nerves and unmyelinated C-fibers. The larger diameter myelinated A-δ nerves conduct electrical impulses rapidly to the spinal cord, resulting in the subject perceiving an injury or insult to the receptor tissue. In response to the painful stimuli, the central nervous system (CNS) can produce other spinal cord effects such as reflex musculoskeletal withdrawal from the pain stimulus. The unmyelinated C-fibers, on the other hand, conduct impulses much slower to the spinal cord at the dorsal horn. These slowed electrical impulses are processed in the CNS and interpreted as pain by the subject. C-fiber pain often is described by the subject as second wave pain, because of its slower onset and longer duration. In addition, the slow excitatory postsynaptic potentials generated within C-fibers are now believed to be responsible for the central sensitization of chronic pain.

Peripheral Nociception, Transduction, and Inflammation.[1] The process of nociception (stimulation of peripheral nerve endings) and pain transduction is complex and not completely understood. A variety of inflammatory mediators are released from the terminal nerve endings of both primary afferent and sympathetic postganglionic neurons at peripheral sensory sites. The primary afferent neurons release the neurogenic inflammatory mediators, substance P along with calcitonin-gene-related peptide (CGRP), galanin, and somatostatin. Some of the effects of these peptides may be mediated through sympathetic postganglionic neurons. The sympathetic postganglionic neurons release prostaglandins, purines, neuropeptide Y, and norepinephrine. These various neuropeptides interact in a very complex fashion. Some of the neuropeptides have proinflammatory effects through their action on mast cells, lymphocytes, and other leukocytes. Other neuropeptides, such as substance P and calcitonin-gene-related peptides, directly potentiate inflammatory activity. These inflammatory producing neuropeptides possibly are responsible for some of the persistent chronic painful diseases. For example, the postganglionic neurons are responsible for maintaining the inflammation of the joints in patients with rheumatoid arthritis.[2] On the other hand, some of the mediators produce the

opposite effect. For example, galanin and somatostatin may have an anti-inflammatory effect by presynaptically inhibiting the release of substance P and CGRP. Similarly, postganglionic sympathetic neurogenic inflammatory mediators such as norepinephrine, neuropeptide Y, and adenosine also may have a neuron terminal anti-inflammatory effect.

Central Mechanism for Chronic Pain[3]. Prolonged and cumulative stimulation of the central neurons by primary unmyelinated C-fibers can result in summation and excessive sensitivity to pain. This pathophysiological pain has been associated with the action of glutamate at both the N-methyl-d-aspartate (NMDA) receptor and the α-Amino-3-hydroxy-5-methylisoxazole-4-propionic acid (AMPA) receptor.[4] The combined action of central NMDA receptor stimulation and substance P-mediated inflammation at peripheral neurokinin receptors (nociceptors) can lower the activation threshold and spontaneously activate the postsynaptic nociceptive transmission neuron. The areas adjacent to the nociceptors can activate the neuron, leading to exaggerated responses to thermal or mechanical stimuli. These hyperresponsive receptors are thought to be responsible for the pain radiation and pathophysiologic hypersensitivity that is observed clinically. Drugs such as 6-cyno-7-dinitro-quinoxaline-2,3-dione (CNQX) and ketamine are effective in blocking the central sensitization at the AMPA and NMDA receptors, respectively.[5]

Mode of Analgesic Action

Nonsteroidal Anti-Inflammatory Drugs (NSAIDs). Nonsteroidal anti-inflammatory drugs presumably exert their analgesic effects by inhibiting prostaglandin synthesis in the periphery; however, this probably is an over-simplistic view of their action. Various chemical mediators such as 5-HT, substance-P, bradykinin, and histamine are released in addition to prostaglandins in response to tissue injury and the physiologic response to these chemicals is complex. These substances do not all produce pain when experimentally injected as individual substances. Instead, the combined effects of multiple chemicals are required before a pain response is produced. For example, when either histamine, prostaglandin E_2, or bradykinin is given alone, they do not produce pain; but when all of the agents are given together, they produce intense pain. Prostaglandins, therefore, probably cause hyperalgesia (excessive sensitivity to pain) in the local sensory nerve receptors when combined with the effects of the other chemical mediators. The analgesic capability of an NSAID does not correlate with its capacity for prostaglandin inhibition in the periphery. Acetaminophen and salicylate also can produce analgesia at concentrations that do not inhibit cyclooxygenase and prostaglandins. Therefore, the exact mechanism of NSAID analgesia has yet to be elucidated; however, their analgesic effect probably is central in origin and involves substance-P receptors of the neurokinin-1 type and glutamate receptors of the NMDA type. Since spinal NSAIDs reduce the hyperalgesia evoked by spinal substance-P and NMDA, the action of the NSAIDs appears to be independent of peripheral inflammation. NSAID actions through gamma-aminobutyric acid (GABA)ergic pathways, arachidonic acids, and AMPA receptor are the subject of additional research.

Opiates can attach to one or more of five opioid receptors: the mu, delta, epsilon, kappa, and sigma receptors. These receptors can be differentiated further into subtypes (e.g., mu_1, mu_2, $delta_1$, $delta_2$, $kappa_1$, $kappa_2$, and $kappa_3$). Stimulation of the mu_1 receptors may be responsible for the desired effects of supraspinal analgesia; and stimulation of mu_2 receptors may lead to unwanted consequences such as respiratory depression, euphoria, constipation, and physical dependence. Delta, epsilon, and some kappa receptors also mediate analgesic response. Sigma receptors may cause autonomic stimulation, dysphoria, and hallucinations. The effect of opiates on these receptor subtypes is gradually being discovered. Morphine can stimulate both mu_1, mu_2 and kappa receptors and perhaps this capability to stimulate multiple receptors can account for morphine's mixed analgesic and side effect profile. Pure opiate antagonists (e.g., naloxone) occupy opiate receptors without eliciting a direct response and block the access of naturally occurring opiates and drugs such as morphine to these receptors. As a result, narcotic antagonists block both the desired and undesired opiate effect. Pentazocine and butorphanol (both mixed agonist/antagonists) produce analgesia through stimulation of kappa receptors, but cause unwanted dysphoria and hallucinations through their effect on sigma receptors. Pentazocine and butorphanol also block access of morphine to mu receptors leading to withdrawal symptoms in individuals physically dependent upon morphine.

In the spinal cord the highest concentration of opioid receptors is located around the C-fiber terminal zones in the lamina 1 and the substantia gelatinosa. The mu opioid receptors constitute about 70% of the total receptor population; delta and kappa receptors account for 24% and 6% of the population, respectively. Mu receptors also are located in the afferent terminals. Since the pharmacological action of opioids depends upon the availability of opioid receptors, the cutting of peripheral nerves will lead to degeneration and loss of opioid receptors in the nerve itself. This may explain the clinical observation of opioid resistance that occurs in postamputation pain.[6] Morphine has a 50-fold higher affinity for the mu receptor than the delta or the kappa receptors; however, nonselective physiological effects can occur at very high doses.

There are three main mechanisms by which opioids produce analgesia:[7]

- Presynaptically, opioids reduce the release of inflammatory transmitters (e.g., tachykinin, excitatory amino acids, and peptides) from the terminals of afferent C-fiber neurons after activation of opioid receptors. This presynaptic action is achieved by opening of potassium channels and closing of calcium channels, which reduce calcium influx into the C-fiber terminal. The mu and delta opioid receptors respond to the opening of potassium channels and the kappa opioid receptors respond to closing of calcium channels.

- Opioids also can reduce the activity of output neurons, interneurons, or dendrites in the neuronal pathways by means of postsynaptic hyperpolarization. The postsynaptic hyperpolarization is achieved by a mechanism similar to the opening of the potassium channels and closing of the calcium channels of the nerve terminal.

- Opioids also inhibit neuronal activity via GABA and enkephalin neurons in the substantia gelatinosa.

Analgesic Adjunctive Agents. Tricyclic antidepressants are commonly utilized as adjunctive analgesics in the treatment of neuropathic pain (e.g., diabetic neuropathy, postherpetic neuralgia). The precise mechanism of action of the tricyclic antidepressants, amitriptyline, desipramine, and imipramine, is unclear but is postulated to involve blockade of norepinephrine and 5-HT reuptake, antagonism of histamine and muscarinic cholinergic receptors, α-adrenergic blockade, or depression of C-fiber afferent evoked activity in the spinal cord.[8,9] Antidepressants also have membrane-stabilizing properties in the peripheral nerves of animal models. Other membrane-stabilizing drugs such as mexiletine and carbamazepine also are effective for the management of neuropathic pain.

Classification of Pain

Acute Pain. Pain immediately following an injury to the body is considered to be acute pain, and pain lasting for more than a few months is labeled as chronic pain. Acute pain serves a useful purpose in helping identify the site of injury. In most cases, the objective physical findings associated with acute pain can be localized directly to the site of injury. Injury to nerves on visceral organ systems, however, can present as diffuse, poorly differentiated, referred pain.

Acute pain is usually, but not always, self-limiting and typically subsides when the injury heals. Untreated or inadequately treated pain can evoke physiological hormonal responses that alter circulation and tissue metabolism, and produce physical findings such as tachypnea, tachycardia, widening of the pulse pressure, and increased sympathetic nervous system activity. In addition, inadequately treated pain can produce major psychological stress responses and compromise the body's immune system. Decreased range of motion, diminished vital pulmonary capacity, and compromise in the overall well-being of the patient secondary to poorly treated pain may delay recovery from tissue injury following surgery or trauma. Acute pain often is exacerbated by anxiety and secondary reflex musculoskeletal spasms.

Acute pain always should be aggressively managed, even before a definitive cause is known, except for pain from acute abdominal or traumatic head injuries.[10] When pain is relieved, the patient will be more comfortable and better able to cooperate with physical examinations and procedures. Unfortunately, postoperative and other acute pain syndromes often are ignored or inadequately treated. Part of the tendency to undertreat pain is the reluctance of caregivers to unduly prescribe opiates. However, addiction to opioids is essentially nonexistent when these drugs are prescribed for acute pain and withholding appropriate pain treatment causes unneeded patient suffering.

Chronic Pain. The origins of chronic pain may be neurogenic, nociceptic, psychiatric, or idiopathic. As presented later, it is important to further differentiate chronic pain syndromes into those that are associated with malignancy and those that are not. However, there are certain characteristics that all forms of chronic pain have in common. Unlike acute pain which instructs the afflicted individual to avoid further injury or seek help, chronic pain usually serves no benefit to the individual. Often the original source of the chronic pain has apparently healed, yet the pain persists. Chronic pain can be episodic or continuous, and chronic pain patients frequently describe both forms of pain at various stages of their disease. As an analogy, chronic pain is nonlinear; like a circle it has no beginning or end. Chronic pain often is destructive to the host by deteriorating quality of life, functional ability, spiritual and psychological well-being, interpersonal relationships, and financial status.[12–14] Besides frequent sleep disturbances, chronic pain also can cause changes in appetite, psychomotor retardation, irritability, social withdrawal, and depression. The patient often cannot remember an existence free of pain and is convinced that the pain will be present until death. In short, chronic pain can become an all consuming focus of the patient's life.

The key to successful chronic pain management rests on prevention and elimination of unnecessary suffering and despair. Chronic pain management should consider the applicability of cognitive interventions (relaxation technique, self hypnosis, and/or psychiatric therapy), physical manipulations (local application of heat, cold massage, electrical nerve stimulation, and physical therapy), pharmacological agents (antidepressants, antiarrhythmics, anticonvulsants, major tranquilizers, and the use of longer-acting opioids), regional anesthesia (local anesthetic blocks with or without corticosteroids), and spinal analgesia (intraspinal opioids and/or local anesthetic agents).[15,16]

Pain Associated with Malignancy (Chronic Malignant Pain). Chronic malignant pain can have a combination of acute, intermittent, or constant components. Although the pain is chronic in nature, it has elements of acute pain if there is continuing evidence of tissue damage by tumor infiltration. Other contributors to malignant pain are nerve destruction, chemotherapy, radiation therapy, and surgery. Occasionally, chronic malignant pain has only minimal or no associated objective clinical physical findings, and may be erroneously dismissed by inexperienced clinicians.[11]

Anticipation by the patient that malignant pain will be continuous leads to anxiety, depression, and insomnia.[17] These destructive feelings can accentuate the patient's perception of pain. Inadequately treated chronic malignant pain can become progressively more severe and cause relentless suffering. Persistent pain can accelerate the deterioration of the patient's physical and psychological condition more than the malignant disease itself.

Some cancer patients, when confronted with a dreaded disease and the possibility of impending death, respond with fear not only for themselves, but for their loved ones as well, especially when young children are involved. Their anxiety is heightened by the fear of loss of social position, possible surgical mutilation, loss of self-control, and fear of uncontrollable pain. These fears and anxieties can be projected as resentment, anger, isolation, depression, and frustration. A full discussion of the psychological and emotional aspects of chronic malignant pain is beyond the scope of this chapter, but successful treatment of a large percentage of these patients[18] requires a comprehensive multidisciplinary approach.[19,20] The most important aspect of chronic malignant pain management is for the clinician to use a logical and systematic approach. The goal of chronic malignant pain management should be pain alleviation and prevention. The most important element of chronic malignant pain management for the patient is to have access to healthcare and pain management information. It is the duty of all healthcare providers to effectively assess their patients' pain management needs and to make the appropriate referrals.

Chronic Nonmalignant Pain. Pain not associated with a malignant disease and lasting longer than several weeks is considered to be chronic nonmalignant pain. Unfortunately this pain also has been called chronic benign pain; an obvious misrepresentation since pain is never benign when it causes patient suffering. The treatment of chronic nonmalignant pain is difficult and frustrating because there is no consensus on its treatment. The use of opiates in this patient population is controversial; however, there are increasing data to support their use in psychologically healthy patients.[21] Although often difficult or frustrating to accomplish, alleviation of pain can be extremely rewarding because it offers instant gratification for both the patient and the clinician. Much of the difficulty encountered in chronic pain management arises when clinicians are not sufficiently educated or trained in dealing with the complex pharmacological and psychosocial problems associated with chronic pain. Often the clinician fails to listen to the patient or recognize clues to the subtle nature of their patient's pain complaints. Drug selection often is irrational and doses are frequently inadequate. The unfortunate tragedy, however, occurs when clinicians occasionally withhold adequate analgesia because of a misunderstood fear of addiction.[22–28]

General Treatment Principles

Table 7.1 lists eight common causes of failure when using analgesics to treat pain.[29] In general the reasons relate to a lack of understanding of pain management principles or the pharmaco-

logic properties of the drugs, an overestimation of the risk of addiction by both patients and caregivers, or poor communication between the patient and medical personnel. A number of steps are described below to overcome these barriers.

Effective analgesic therapy should start with an accurate pain history that characterizes the date of onset (i.e., duration of the pain syndrome), a description of the pain, association of the pain with movement, as well as the names and amounts of all analgesics the patient is taking. A patient fearful of being accused of analgesic abuse might be reluctant to give an accurate drug use history unless a trusting relationship can be established.

Effective treatment of pain requires that the pain be eliminated or reduced to the lowest manageable intensity and prevented from recurring, rather than waiting to treat the pain when it becomes unbearable. Therefore, knowing the cause of the pain is helpful. For example, it would be irrational to treat the severe abdominal cramping pain of constipation with morphine which may serve only to worsen the constipation. If pain is the result of a fracture, then stabilization and immobilization in addition to appropriate analgesics will reduce the pain of the affected bone.

The elimination and prevention of recurring chronic pain are best accomplished by using analgesics at fixed time intervals (a "time-contingent" basis) rather than on an "as needed" basis. The traditional "on demand" or PRN analgesic dosing schedule is inadequate at least 34% of the time, leading to greater 24-hour drug intake and a pattern of step-wise increases in dosage. Therefore, most pain management specialists now administer or at least offer analgesics to their patients on a time-contingent basis. However, in patients with severe acute or malignant pain, scheduled analgesics alone may not be adequate without additional analgesics for "breakthrough" episodes. Until the dosage is stabilized, all patients who are receiving analgesics should be monitored closely for efficacy of analgesia as well as untoward side-effects.

When pain is prevented by the continual administration of analgesics, the fear and memory of pain diminish in the patient's mind, and she becomes less anxious and more comfortable. If possible, the amount of analgesic should then be decreased gradually.[30]

Anxiety and guilt often complicate the management of pain. Patients sometimes become anxious for fear that their pain will become uncontrollable or that they will become addicted to opiates. Also, patients sometimes feel guilty that they have to take opioids for their pain because of the negative social connotations associated with the use of opioids. They may feel that they have failed their clinicians' expectations. Therefore, it is imperative that patients are educated about the rational use of analgesics.

Pain can be managed best when there is trust and communication between the caregiver and the patient. Patients must feel com-

Table 7.1	Common Causes of Analgesic Failure

- Overestimating the analgesic efficacy of a drug
- Underestimating the analgesic requirement of the patient
- Prejudice against the use of analgesics that may prevent objective therapy
- Lack of knowledge in analgesic pharmacology
- Patient noncompliance because of fear of addiction
- Patient not communicating with caregivers for fear of being labeled as a drug addict
- Patient wants to please by not complaining
- Patient does not know how or is afraid to communicate with caregiver

fortable telling caregivers whenever their pain needs arise, and caregivers must respond appropriately and in a timely fashion. Good communication between caregivers and patients can alleviate anxiety and guilt regarding patients' pain needs.

Differentiate Clinical Opioid Use and Drug Abuse. The patient and the caregiver must differentiate between clinical opioid use and opioid abuse. When an opioid is administered for the purpose of alleviating pain, it is considered appropriate clinical use; but when opioids are used for purposes other than alleviation of pain, the term "opioid abuse" can be applied. Patients should expect aggressive management of their acute pain. Acute pain often will require very large opioid doses during the first few days after the injury, but the need for such doses will decrease rapidly. Chronic malignant pain usually requires escalating opioid doses because of the progression of the disease rather than the development of tolerance. Increasing requirements of opioid analgesics do not represent opioid abuse, but rather require careful clinical evaluation.

Analgesic Selection. The selection of the analgesic of choice must be individualized for each patient depending upon the cause and chronicity of the pain as well as the patient's age and other medical conditions that may alter drug response. Furthermore, the clinical response of the patient will dictate the dose, route, or desired dosing interval.[31] The selection of the most appropriate drug should be based upon pharmacological data as well as clinical experience. The selection of an opioid for the management of severe acute and chronic malignant pain must always include consideration of morphine which is the "gold standard" against which other opioids need to be compared; however, the role of NSAIDs should not be overlooked. Adjunctive analgesic medications often are chosen instead of opioids for the management of chronic nonmalignant pain because this type of pain often is associated with sympathetic dysfunction and neuropathies. The NSAIDs are the analgesic agents of choice in the management of mild to moderate pain involving the musculoskeletal tissues; and also are extremely effective in the management of pain from bony neoplastic metastasis. Neurogenic pain responds better to tricyclic antidepressants than to either opioids or NSAIDs: neurogenic pain often will not be relieved by opioids until the dose is large enough to cause significant side effects.

If the maintenance dose of an opioid analgesic is too high, the patient can be over sedated and less functional. In extreme cases, patients may become bed ridden from excessive opiate use. When given the choice of eliminating the last trace of discomfort at the cost of some sensorium clouding, patients will almost invariably select full alertness and the continued presence of some pain.[32,33] Patients who are receiving opioids also need to be monitored for deterioration in vital signs (pulse and respiratory rate), constipation, and urinary retention. Stool softeners and other prophylactic measures may be required. Similarly, a patient who is receiving NSAIDs or adjunctive analgesics also should be monitored for possible untoward side effects.

Orally administered analgesics allow a patient a greater degree of independence and control over their daily activities than parenteral administration. Similar advantages can be obtained with an intravenous infusion device. Regular parenteral administration by other routes can be difficult and painful in cachectic patients.

Every patient has the inherent right to expect their pain to be controlled and clinicians should discuss pain management before surgical procedures or following an unexpected trauma or injury. The pain management team should be involved before surgery if severe pain is anticipated or if pain relief is less than satisfactory.[34]

Mild Analgesics

The nonsteroidal anti-inflammatory analgesics tend to have a relatively flat dose-response effect, reaching maximum analgesia with relatively few doses. These drugs, however, are frequently given at doses that exceed the effective maximum analgesic dose because the duration of analgesia tends to increase at higher doses. Patients can be dosed less frequently with a higher dose. For example, ibuprofen can be given as either 600 mg every six hours or 400 mg every four hours, but the side effects increase as the dose is increased. Although the NSAIDs have both analgesic and anti-inflammatory properties, it is often difficult to differentiate these two effects in published studies or during clinical use in patients.

All of the nonsteroidal anti-inflammatory drugs including ibuprofen (Motrin), naproxen (Naprosyn), naproxen sodium (Anaprox), diflunisal (Dolobid), diclofenac (Voltaren), diclofenac potassium (Cataflam), nabumetone (Relafen), ketoprofen (Orudis), flurbiprofen (Ansaid), ketorolac (Toradol), and others, provide analgesia equivalent or superior to that of aspirin,[55-60] or acetaminophen combined with codeine 60 mg in a variety of mild to moderate painful conditions.[61-65] Like the opioid analgesics, the duration of action of the NSAID does not correlate well with the serum half-life of the drug. Patient response always should be used to guide the clinician in selecting dosing intervals of these agents, especially when used in combination with opioids for the treatment of pain.

In many clinical trials peripheral analgesics were as effective as opioid analgesics; however, most of these studies failed to take into account the anti-inflammatory effects of the NSAIDs or used pain models that were not sufficiently sensitive to differentiate between a potent and a weak analgesic.[47-50] Despite these and other study-design flaws, the NSAIDs and the combination of aspirin or acetaminophen with 32 mg of codeine were superior to either aspirin, acetaminophen, or codeine used alone.[51]

Opioid Analgesics

An intramuscular (IM) dose of 10 mg/70 kg of morphine sulfate can provide significant analgesia in approximately 70% of patients with severe pain. The other 30% of patients will require higher doses[35] which not only increase the intensity and duration of analgesia, but also the incidence of side effects.[36] Morphine dosage requirements also vary with the severity of pain, individual perceptions of pain, age, weight, opioid tolerance, and the presence of concomitant diseases.[37-42] Thus, single parenteral analgesic doses of morphine ranging from 4 mg to more than 20 mg are used for treating acute pain; and parenteral doses as high as 200 mg/hour have been needed to treat end-stage malignant pain.

A 10 mg dose of morphine is the reference standard by which all other opioid analgesics are compared. Therefore, morphine equivalents often are used when calculating other opioid analgesic doses. The duration of analgesia of an opioid correlates partially with its serum half-life, but also with the dose, route of administration, and the distribution characteristics of the drug.[43] For example, methadone has a very long serum half-life of 24 hours, but its duration of analgesia is only about six hours. However, single daily doses of methadone are retained on opiate receptors in the brain long enough to satisfy the craving for opiates in substance abusers. Also, the long half-life of methadone may contribute to cumulative effects and drug toxicity. When methadone is administered epidurally, its duration of analgesia is extremely short due to its high lipophilicity and rapid redistribution from the epidural space. Conversely, morphine has a relatively short duration of analgesia when administered systemically, but when it is administered epidurally it has an exceptionally long duration of analgesia because of its low lipophilicity that prevents its redistribution from the epidural space.

The administration of opioid analgesics frequently is complicated by the need to convert between different routes of administration or different opioid formulations. The approximate equianalgesic doses of parenteral and oral opioid analgesics are listed in Table 7.2. The specific oral to parenteral ratios of these drugs also are listed in Table 7.2, however, the preciseness of these ratios is controversial. For example, some investigators maintain that the oral to parenteral ratio for morphine is 6:1, but other clinicians practicing in hospices maintain that the oral to parenteral ratio for morphine is closer to 2:1. This confusion may be the result of differences in the design of single dose versus multiple dose clinical trials. First pass hepatic metabolism may be greater in single-dose clinical studies than in multiple-dose studies because first-pass metabolic pathways can become saturated with multiple doses. Furthermore, the accumulation of the active metabolite morphine-6-glucuronide after chronic dosing may contribute to the

clinically observed differences. When all of the factors are taken into account, the bioavailability of oral morphine varies from 17% to 70% of a dose; therefore, it is reasonable to expect individual patient response to be highly variable.[44,45] No matter which ratio the clinician uses, the dosing must guided by the patient's clinical response and frequent clinical reassessment.

If an opioid analgesic is to be substituted with another opioid, the equivalent doses as listed in Table 7.2 can be used as an approximate guide to dosage conversions unless the patient has developed tolerance. Cross-tolerance between opioid analgesics exists, but it may not be complete. Therefore, doses may be reduced by as much as 50% when interchanging different opioids. This is especially true when switching to methadone from other opioids.[46] Patient comfort is the goal and the response of the patient should always be the basis for dosage adjustments. Whenever a new opioid analgesic is initiated, the patient's response to the new analgesic should be assessed within the first few hours because the initial dose of the new analgesic is only correctly estimated about half of the time. Frequent reassessment of clinical responses should facilitate dosage adjustments and bring the patient's pain under control more quickly.

The analgesic efficacy of propoxyphene and combinations of acetaminophen with propoxyphene 65 mg remains controversial. Most double-blind studies demonstrate no advantage of propoxyphene alone over aspirin, acetaminophen, or codeine in relieving various types of pain.[52] This lack of benefit is seemingly in conflict with the observation that propoxyphene in combination with acetaminophen remains one of most frequently prescribed drug regimens in the U.S. This may be partially explained by an additive effect when the two drugs are used in combination. Another possible explanation is the tendency of many patients to take more than the prescribed doses. Because propoxyphene has a 13 hour half-life, repeated doses taken on an every four to six hour regimen for several days can result in significant drug accumulation. Furthermore, analgesic assessments of propoxyphene efficacy have been based primarily upon single dose studies[53] in spite of the fact that patients take as many as 10 to 12 tablets daily. Propoxyphene has mild CNS depressant effects and like other opioid analgesics, propoxyphene can produce physical dependency.[54] As with all opioid analgesics, patients taking propoxyphene need to be warned about the risks of concurrent alcohol use, the operation of equipment or machinery requiring mental acuity, and the potential of agitation and sleeplessness when the medication is discontinued abruptly after prolonged use.

Acute Pain
Analgesic Goals

1. E.T., a 36-year-old female with no drug allergies or history of recreational drug use, had been taking ibuprofen 400 mg PO Q 6 hr PRN for menstrual cramps. She is now recovering from the surgical repair of a left tibia fracture that resulted from a motor vehicle accident. E.T. was treated with acetaminophen 325 mg with codeine 30 mg 2 tablets PO Q 3 hr for postoperative pain, however, this analgesic regimen has not controlled her pain adequately. After extensive complaints, E.T.'s analgesic medication was replaced with hydrocodone 5 mg with acetaminophen 500 mg 2 tablets Q 4–6 hr. In spite of these changes, E.T. continues to complain of pain. She rates the intensity of her pain as 8 on a 1–10 point scale. What is your assessment of E.T.'s pain and what are reasonable analgesia goals for E.T.?

The current analgesic regimen has not provided E.T. with adequate relief of pain based upon her pain evaluation rating of 8 on a 10-point scale. The apparent analgesic failure in E.T. can be

Table 7.2	Equianalgesic Doses[a,b]	
Drug	IM/SQ	PO/PR/Transdermal
Buprenorphine (Buprenex)	0.4 mg	
Butorphanol[c] (Stadol)	3.0 mg	
Codeine (various)	60 mg	180 mg; 120 mg PR
Dezocine[c] (Dalgan)	50 mg	
Fentanyl (Sublimaze, Duragesic)	0.15 mg	0.05 mg/hr transdermal[d]
Hydrocodeine (DHC, various)[e]		20 mg
Hydrocodone (Vicodin, Lorcet, Lortab, others)[e]		20 mg
Hydromorphone (Dilaudid)	2 mg	8 mg; 6 mg PR
Levorphanol (Levo-Dromoran)	2 mg	4 mg
Meperidine (Demerol)	100 mg	200 mg
Methadone (Dolophine, various)	10 mg (2.5 mg)[f]	10 mg (2.5 mg)[f]
Morphine (various)	10 mg	60 mg (30 mg);[f] 30 mg PR
Nalbuphine[c] (Nubain)	20 mg	
Oxycodone (Percocet, Percodan, Tylox)[e]		20 mg
Oxymorphone (Numorphan)	1.5 mg	10 mg PR
Pentazocine[c] (Talwin)	60 mg	200 mg

[a] Equivalent doses are provided only as a guide; individual patient variations may exist.
[b] IM = Intramuscular; PO = Oral; PR = Rectal; SQ = Subcutaneous.
[c] Mixed agonist/antagonist analgesics can precipitate opioid withdrawal symptoms in patients who are dependent upon opioid agonists.
[d] Equivalent transdermal dose is based upon an average intravenous dosing interval of 3 hr.
[e] Combination products; aspirin and acetaminophen content may vary significantly.
[f] Equianalgesic dose is based upon single dose studies. With repeated administration, the equivalent dose may be much lower, in parentheses.

attributed to several factors. First, she may simply require more analgesics than anticipated. Standard analgesic dosage recommendations only are conservative estimates of average initial doses. Ultimately, analgesic dosing must be tailored to the needs of specific patients. Patients with small body size or compromised metabolic function may need smaller doses, whereas larger patients, or those with extensive injury may require larger doses. After an initial analgesic has been administered, the patient should be assessed frequently and doses should be adjusted quickly in response to inadequate pain control or excessive sedation. The dose of an analgesic should be modified before a patient feels the need to express significant discomfort from pain. E.T.'s complaints of significant pain intensity probably are commensurate with a high level of anxiety that commonly accompanies inadequate pain relief. Acute pain always should be aggressively treated.[66] Furthermore, E.T.'s possible anxiety over the current surgical outcome could intensify her pain because pain and anxiety are reinforcing phenomena. For most patients, pain is synonymous with injury. When an injury has been repaired and the patient continues to experience pain, the patient's anxiety and fear can intensify pain sensations. The goal for managing acute pain is to keep the patient as comfortable as possible while minimizing possible untoward adverse effects from the analgesic. This analgesia goal for E.T. can be accomplished only by careful follow-up evaluations and rational analgesic dosage adjustments.

Combination Analgesics

2. Why is the choice of acetaminophen with hydrocodone for E.T. appropriate?

NSAIDs and opioid analgesics provide pain relief by different mechanisms of action and it is reasonable to use both for their additive effects when managing pain. The acetaminophen with hydrocodone, however, is a fixed-dose combination and these combination drug formulations decrease dosing flexibility and frequently can lead to unintended toxic side effects. For example, the combination of acetaminophen 500 mg and hydrocodone 5 mg given two tablets every four hours can result in the patient receiving 6 gm of acetaminophen in a 24 hour period. Chronic administration of acetaminophen in excess of 5 gm/day has been associated with hepatic enzyme changes. Short-term use of 6 gm of acetaminophen daily for a few days in patients without risk factors (e.g., alcoholism, malnutrition) usually is safe.[67] Several NSAIDs also have been associated with hepatotoxicity.[68] Acetaminophen and NSAIDs should be avoided in patients who have severe liver disease, as evidenced by elevated liver enzymes, a low serum albumin, or a prolonged prothrombin time. If acetaminophen is to be used at all in patients with impaired hepatic function, doses have to be limited to less than 3 gm/24 hours.

E.T. should have been started on more potent analgesics initially to bring the pain under control. Analgesic combinations of acetaminophen with either codeine 30 mg or hydrocodone 5 mg are effective for mild pain, but these combinations are less than adequate for moderate pain, unless the opioid dose is increased. It would have been reasonable to start her on oral morphine 30 mg and acetaminophen 650 mg every four hours.

An NSAID such as ibuprofen or naproxen also may be used adjunctively for E.T.'s pain. Although NSAIDs alone usually are inadequate for controlling moderate pain, they have additive analgesic effects when combined with opiates. In E.T., one also must consider the risk of bleeding from the incisional site due to the antiplatelet effect of NSAIDs.

Equianalgesic Dosing of Opioid Analgesics

3. How should E.T.'s hydrocodone dose be converted to oral morphine?

Hydrocodone 20 mg orally is about equal to morphine 30 mg (see Table 7.2). Therefore, the 10 mg of hydrocodone as originally ordered for E.T. is equal to an oral morphine dose of about 15 mg or 5 mg of morphine by injection. For the reasons discussed in Question 1, this dose of morphine probably would be inadequate for E.T. because only about 70% of patients obtain effective relief following a 10 mg morphine injection. Thus, E. T. should be started on oral morphine 30 mg every four hours around-the-clock for the first 24 hours, then changed to ''as needed'' dosing afterwards.

Ketorolac

4. Could IM ketorolac (Toradol) be given to E.T. instead of the morphine?

Short-term use of opioids for acute pain, even at very large doses, does not cause dependency or abuse and, therefore, should not be withheld because of fear of addiction. E.T. will be receiving the opioids only during the immediate postoperative period, and the opioid can be rapidly tapered after the acute pain has subsided. The acute clinical use of opioids in hospitalized patients does not cause drug addiction in an otherwise psychologically healthy individual.[90] For patients like E.T. with acute moderate pain, an intermediate-acting opioid such as oral or parenteral morphine or hydromorphone should be the first-line agents for pain management.

Because it is the only available injectable NSAID in the U.S., ketorolac sometimes is used as an alternative to opioids.[92,93] Although ketorolac is effective for many patient's pain, it should not be substituted for appropriate opioid analgesics for the management of acute postoperative pain. Ketorolac is most beneficial in postoperative pain if it is used in combination with the opioids instead of being used as monotherapy. Parenteral formulations of NSAIDs are no more effective than oral formulations given in equivalent doses (e.g., ibuprofen 600 mg PO Q 6 hr is equally as effective as IM ketorolac). Ketorolac also has been associated with several cases of serious postsurgical bleeding. Although ketorolac could be effective in relieving E.T.'s pain, it is no more effective than morphine, costs considerably more, and is not more advantageous for E.T. Patients receiving ketorolac should be monitored for all the nonsteroidal anti-inflammatory side effects, especially postsurgical bleeding.[91] All NSAIDs should be used with caution in patients with compromised hemodynamics such as congestive heart failure or hypovolemia, or any other conditions that compromise renal blood flow and increase the risk of developing renal toxicity.

Nonsteroidal Anti-Inflammatory Drugs (NSAIDs)

Selection

5. Is any one NSAID analgesic superior to the others?

In all probability, all NSAIDs, not just those with an approved indication for the treatment of mild to moderate pain, have analgesic properties. The superiority of any particular NSAID for a particular patient cannot be predicted and no one NSAID has been demonstrated to be superior over any other. Nevertheless, patients who fail to benefit from one NSAID can respond to a different NSAID. Therefore, an NSAID should be selected based upon previous history of response, efficacy, safety, and cost. Ibuprofen and naproxen have a long history of safety and are available as less costly generic products. (See Chapter 41: Rheumatic Disorders for a more detailed discussion of the clinical use of NSAIDs.)

When selecting one of these agents, the clinician must be aware of the considerable risk of systemic side effects. Although gastrointestinal side effects are the most common, these agents have caused undesirable nervous system, otic, ocular, hematological, renal, and hepatic adverse effects. Once an NSAID has been selected, the doses should be increased until pain has been relieved or the maximum tolerable dose has been achieved. Some investigators have used rather large doses with remarkable success.

6. If E.T. had a history of asthma, would NSAIDs be safe to use?

Aspirin can induce bronchospasms in patients who have a history of asthma, allergic rhinitis, and nasal polyps. Although NSAIDs also can precipitate asthma and other allergenic responses,[96,97] the asthma response is not an allergic reaction, but rather a pharmacologic effect associated with prostaglandin inhibition and unopposed leukotriene activity. Acetaminophen does not induce bronchospasms and is safe to give to patients with an asthma history. The risk of using NSAIDs or aspirin in asthmatics without nasal polyps or a history of drug-induced bronchospasm with these drugs is less clear. If E.T. had a history of asthma, then NSAIDs perhaps should be avoided or used cautiously.[98,99]

Analgesic Nephrotoxicity

7. What are the risks of analgesic nephrotoxicity from NSAIDs in E.T.?

Analgesic overuse is a common cause of chronic interstitial nephritis (CIN) and may account for approximately 5% of the cases of chronic renal failure in the U.S. Historically, aspirin and phenacetin in combination were thought to be the causative agent for most cases of chronic interstitial nephritis, however, acetaminophen, aspirin,[100] and the NSAIDs[101,102] also have been implicated. Acetaminophen-induced renal toxicity almost always is accompanied by concomitant serum liver enzyme changes and generally is associated with acute acetaminophen intoxication.[103] Most cases of interstitial nephritis seem to be related to both dose and duration of NSAID therapy.[104,105] (Also see Chapter 29: Acute Renal Failure.)

The NSAIDs effect on the renal function may be twofold. The NSAIDs can directly damage renal tubules, and also can reduce renal blood flow by inhibiting prostacyclin. Prostacyclin modifies renal function in response to the effects of endogenous vasoconstrictors (e.g., norepinephrine and angiotensin II) especially if the patient is volume depleted, has been taking diuretics, or is elderly. Renal insufficiency may occur in 20% of patients with one or more of these identifiable risks who also take NSAIDs.[106,107] Patients with cirrhosis and ascites[108] and patients with significantly altered hemodynamic status can experience as much as a 50% decrease in creatinine clearance (Cl_{Cr}) when treated with indomethacin (Indocin)[109–111] or ibuprofen (Motrin). Some normal subjects have experienced profound changes in glomerular filtration rate when taking indomethacin concurrent with triamterene (Dyrenium).[112]

For E.T., who is fairly young and healthy without risk factors, the risk of developing NSAID-induced renal toxicity is quite low, but her renal function still should be monitored if she is to be placed on NSAIDs for more than a few days because she has recently undergone surgery and may be at risk for volume depletion.

NSAID Use in Renal Disease

8. If E.T. was currently exhibiting renal dysfunction, what NSAID could be used?

Sulindac (Clinoril) and nabumetone (Relafen) have been reported to cause less renal insufficiency because of the absence of active urinary nephrotoxic metabolites. These two NSAIDs can

Table 7.3	NSAID Analgesics
Drug	Availability
Aspirin (numerous)	81, 325, and 500 mg tab; 81, 325, and 500 mg enteric coated tab; 60, 125, 325, and 650 mg suppositories
Choline magnesium trisalicylate (Trilisate)	500 mg tab
Diclofenac [Voltaren (sodium), Cataflam (potassium)]	*Sodium*: 25, 50, and 75 mg tab; *Potassium*: 25 and 50 mg tab
Diflunisal (Dolobid)	500 mg tab
Etodolac (Lodine)	150 and 200 mg cap
Fenoprofen (Nalfon)	200 and 300 mg cap
Flurbiprofen (Ansaid)	50 and 100 mg tab
Ibuprofen (Motrin, Rufen, Advil, Nuprin)	200, 300, 400, 600, and 800 mg tab; 100 mg/5 mL suspension
Indomethacin (Indocin)	25 and 50 mg cap, 75 mg SR capsule; 50 mg suppository; 25 mg/5 mL suspension
Ketoprofen (Orudis, Oruvail)	50 and 75 mg cap; 200 mg SR
Ketorolac (Toradol)	30 and 60 mg injectable syringe; 10 mg tab
Nabumetone (Relafen)	500 and 750 mg tab
Naproxen [Naprosyn, Aleve, Anaprox (sodium)]	250, 375, and 500 mg tab 200, 275, and 350 mg tab (sodium) 125 mg/5 mL suspension
Sulindac (Clinoril)	150, 200 mg
Piroxicam (Feldene)	10 and 20 mg ca
Other (Nonanti-inflammatory) Acetaminophen (Tylenol, numerous others)	81, 325, and 500 mg tab, gel tab, caplets, and gel cap; 60, 125, 325, and 650 mg suppositories; 80 mg/5 cc, 100 mg/5 cc liquid, and infant drops

still decrease renal blood flow in patients at risk and can cause renal dysfunction via hypersensitivity reactions unrelated to their effects on renal blood flow. Although sulindac and nabumetone appear to be preferred over other NSAIDs in patients with renal dysfunction, clinical experience is not as great with these two drugs relative to other NSAIDs and patient satisfaction reportedly is less with these two NSAIDs.

Possible drug-induced nephrotic syndrome has been reported with indomethacin (Indocin), ibuprofen (Motrin), naproxen (Naprosyn), phenylbutazone (Butazolidin), fenoprofen (Nalfon), sulindac (Clinoril), and tolmetin (Tolectin). In particular, fenoprofen has been implicated in 71% of 31 cases.[113] The prognosis for recovery of renal function is excellent although some patients required treatment with corticosteroids.[114] It is unclear if patients with pre-existing renal dysfunction are at any greater risk of developing further drug-induced abnormalities, but most clinicians consider it as a relative contraindication.

Opioids

Managing Side Effects

9. E.T. complains of itching from her morphine, but shows no sign of rash. What can be done to alleviate the problem?

Opioid analgesics can cause pruritic rashes and other true allergic-type reactions. Opioids can stimulate histamine release from mast cells and cause a local wheal, burning, itching, and erythema at the site of injection. Systemic release of histamine after both oral and parenteral administration of opioid can produce either localized or generalized flushing and itching. While these latter reactions occur frequently and may be confused with an allergic reaction, true opioid allergies are infrequent.[115,116] Coadministration of diphenhydramine (Benadryl) or hydroxyzine (Vistaril) prevents histamine-induced itching and anti-anxiety effects that may add to morphine's analgesic benefit.

Chemically there are three distinct structural categories of opioids: the *phenanthrenes* (morphine, codeine, hydrocodone, hydromorphone, hydrocodeine, oxycodone, levorphanol, nalbuphine, butorphanol, dezocine, and dihydrocodeine), the *phenylpiperidines* (meperidine, fentanyl, alfentanil, and sufentanil), and the *phenylheptanones* (methadone and the weak analgesic propoxyphene). Allergic reactions may cross react within the same chemical structural class, but are less likely between classes. Thus, in patients with true allergic reactions, treatment can be switched to a product in one of the other chemical groups. For example, if E.T. was allergic to morphine, she could be switched to meperidine or methadone.

10. What other adverse effects from morphine should be monitored for in E.T.? What preventive measures should be considered?

The most common side effects reported with the use of opioid analgesics are nausea, vomiting, itching, and constipation. These are expected untoward opioid effects, and with some care they can be managed or minimized. These first three symptoms of nausea, vomiting, and itching can all be minimized by antihistamines such as diphenhydramine 25 to 50 mg orally every six hours as needed. If the drowsiness from the antihistamine is excessive when used in combination with the opioid, a nonsedating antihistamine can be substituted. Persistent and more problematic symptoms may require switching to an alternative opioid analgesic. The best method for treating opioid-induced constipation is prevention. Postsurgical patients are especially prone to develop opioid-induced constipation because their gastrointestinal motility already is slowed from decreased physical activity and from anesthetic agents received during surgery.

Morphine and other opioids suppress the propulsive peristaltic action of the colon, increase colonic tone, greatly increase the tone of the anal sphincter, and reduce the reflex relaxation response to rectal distention. These actions, combined with decreased normal sensory stimuli for defecation because of the CNS depressant actions of the opioids contribute to opioid-induced constipation. Stool softeners are effective in keeping the bowel contents moist, but do not stimulate bowel peristaltic propulsion. Only the stimulative laxative and prokinetic agents can increase bowel propulsive activity. When opioid analgesics are initiated, a stimulative laxative also should be initiated. E.T. will be receiving morphine orally around-the-clock and probably would benefit from one senna tablet orally three times daily in addition to docusate 200 mg orally three times daily. For more resistant constipation, one can use oral lactulose 30 mL every hour and/or phospho-soda enemas. Postoperative ileus frequently is exacerbated by opioid analgesics, but opioids rarely produce ileus or bowel obstruction alone without some other underlying physiological causes. Oral naloxone 0.4 to 12 mg every six hours has been used with some success in preventing opioid-induced constipation. Unlike parenteral naloxone, oral naloxone is not absorbed systemically and, therefore, will not interfere with analgesic effect.[117–122] An oral naloxone formulation is not commercially available, but the parenteral preparation can be given orally (in spite of the high cost of this product) if needed.

11. On the third day of her morphine treatment, E.T. appears agitated. Could her agitation be attributed to her morphine?

Although opioids are central nervous system depressants, they can cause CNS excitation, especially if the patient is on a large dose for a prolonged period of time. Anxiety, agitation, irritability, motor restlessness, tremors, involuntary twitching, and myoclonic seizures have been associated with meperidine, morphine, and hydromorphone, but not methadone. For meperidine and morphine, the CNS toxicity correlates best with accumulation of their active metabolites, normeperidine and morphine-6-glucuronate, respectively. Since both of these metabolites are cleared renally, patients with renal insufficiency are at greatest risk, but toxicity can occur when high doses are administered frequently in patients with normal renal function.[123–128] With meperidine, the problem is compounded by the 17-hour half-life of normeperidine in patients with renal failure. In patients with normal renal function, CNS toxicity is minimized by avoiding doses in excess of 60 mg/hour of meperidine, 100 mg/hour of morphine, or 40 mg/hour of hydromorphone.

The treatment of opioid-induced CNS irritability should include discontinuation of the opioid analgesic and treatment with a benzodiazepine. Myoclonic seizures resulting from meperidine administration sometimes are preceded by involuntary twitching in the extremities and can be averted by discontinuing the meperidine. Seizures induced by meperidine are resistant to naloxone, but respond to anticonvulsants such as phenytoin or diazepam. Since E.T. has normal renal function and her morphine dose is not excessive, it is unlikely that she is suffering from morphine-induced CNS effects. It is more likely that she is starting to recover from her surgery and is anxious from her environment. Nonetheless, it may be time to start reducing her morphine dose if her pain is well controlled.

Patient Controlled Analgesia (PCA)

12. T.J., a 52-year-old female, is status-post posterior spinal fusion with instrumentation because of severe scoliosis that had compromised her respiratory function and quality of life. She has just been transferred to the ward from the postanesthetic recovery critical care unit. She is now crying and complaining of severe pain not relieved by meperidine 75 mg IM Q 3 hr. T.J. has no known drug allergies. She has a history of taking acetaminophen 500 mg with hydrocodone 7.5 mg 2 tablets Q 3 hours before admission. Why would a PCA device be useful for T.J.?

Patient controlled analgesia is a technique whereby patients self administer narcotics by using a preprogrammed mechanical infusion device attached to tubing that delivers the drug to the patient through an intravenous or subcutaneous needle or catheter. In basic terms, the patient depresses a button to activate the PCA controller to deliver a preset dose of narcotic medication. This avoids the need to call a nurse or other caregiver when the need for pain relief arises and also obviates the problem of drug doses that are not ordered frequently enough. The controller also is preprogrammed to establish "lock-out" periods that prevent the pump from delivering a dose if the patient presses the button too often. By adjusting the concentration of drug in the controller and the duration of the lockout period, there are safeguards as to the total dose of drug that the patient can receive each hour. Both of these variables can be adjusted to fit the patient's analgesic needs.

Numerous PCA devices are currently available, most of which have the capability of providing continuous infusion of drug or intermittent self-boluses. Some systems utilize syringe pump technology, and others an IV pump system. Some of the more compact

Table 7.4	Recommended Starting Opioid Analgesic Doses[a]	
Drug	Dose Based upon Weight	Average Adult Dose
Phenanthrene Analogs		
Codeine		
IV[b]	0.2–0.4 mg/kg Q 2 hr	15–30 mg Q 2 hr
IM	0.4–0.8 mg/kg Q 3 hr	30–60 mg Q 3 hr
PO	0.8–1.5 mg/kg Q 3 hr	60–120 mg Q 3 hr
PR	0.8–1.5 mg/kg Q 3 hr	60–120 mg Q 3 hr
Morphine Sulfate		
IV	0.05–0.07 mg/kg Q 2 hr	3–5 mg Q 2 hr
IM	0.14–0.17 mg/kg Q 3 hr	10–12 mg Q 3 hr
PO	0.4 mg/kg Q 3 hr	30 mg Q 3 hr
PR	0.4–0.6 mg/kg Q 3 hr	30–40 mg Q 3 hr
PCA		
Concentration	1.0 mg/mL	1.0 mg/mL
Basal	0–0.014 mg/kg/hr	0–1.0 mg/hr
Bolus	0.014 mg/kg/6 min	1.0 mg/6 min
Hydromorphone		
IV	0.01–0.014 mg/kg Q 1 hr	0.75–1.0 mg Q 2 hr
IM	0.02–0.03 mg/kg Q 3 hr	1.5–2.0 mg Q 3 hr
PO	0.05–0.09 mg/kg Q 3 hr	4.0–6.0 mg Q 3 hr
PR	0.04–0.09 mg/kg Q 3 hr	3.0–6.0 mg Q 3 hr
PCA		
Concentration	0.2 mg/mL	0.2 mg/mL
Basal	0–0.003 mg/kg/hr	0–0.2 mg/hr
Bolus	0.003 mg/kg/6 min	0.2 mg/6 min
Levorphanol[c]		
IV	0.014 mg/kg Q 2 hr (Q 3 hr)	1.0 mg Q 2 hr (Q 3 hr)
IM	0.02–0.03 mg/kg Q 4 hr (Q 6 hr)	1.5–2.0 mg Q 4 hr (Q 6 hr)
PO	0.03–0.06 mg/kg Q 4 hr (Q 6 hr)	2.0–4.0 mg Q 4 hr (Q 6 hr)
Oxymorphone		
IV	0.01–0.014 mg/kg Q 2 hr	0.75–1.0 mg Q 2 hr
IM	0.014–0.02 mg/kg Q 3 hr	1.0–1.5 mg Q 3 hr
PR	0.07–0.14 mg/kg Q 3 hr	5–10 mg Q 3 hr
Phenylpiperidine Analogs		
Meperidine		
IV	0.35–0.7 mg/kg Q 2 hr	25–50 mg Q 2 hr
IM	1.0–1.4 mg/kg Q 3 hr	75–100 mg Q 3 hr
PO	1.4–2.0 mg/kg hr Q 3 hr	100–150 mg Q 3 hr
PCA		
Concentration	10 mg/mL	10 mg/mL
Basal	0–0.14 mg/kg/hr	0–10 mg/hr
Bolus	0.14 mg/kg/6 min	10 mg/6 min
Fentanyl		
IV	0.5 µg/kg Q 2 hr	25–50 µg Q 2 hr
IM	1.0 µg/kg Q 3 hr	75–100 µg Q 3 hr
PCA		
Concentration	10 µg/mL	10 µg/mL
Basal	0–0.14 µg/kg/hr	0–10 µg/hr
Bolus	0.14 µg/kg/6 min	10 µg/6 min
Phenylheptanone Analog		
Methadone[c]		
IV	0.03 mg/kg Q 2 hr (Q 3 hr)	2.5 mg Q 2 hr (Q 3 hr)
IM	0.03–0.07 mg/kg Q 4 hr (Q 6 hr)	2.5–5.0 mg Q 4 hr (Q 6 hr)
PO	0.07–0.14 mg/kg Q 4 hr (Q 6 hr)	5–10 mg Q 4 hr (Q 6 hr)

[a] Recommended starting dose for patients without prior opioid exposure. The actual dose must be titrated to the patient's need.
[b] IM = Intramuscular; IV = Intravenous; PO = Oral; PCA = Patient controlled analgesia; PR = Rectal.
[c] The dosing interval should be ↑ with repeated dosages to avoid drug accumulation and toxicity.

devices are convenient for ambulatory use. T.J.'s pain can be managed with a PCA device for as long as she is able to comprehend the operation of the device. Most postoperative patients will require a basal continuous infusion of narcotic in addition to inter-

mittent boluses during the first 48-hour period. The need for continuous basal infusion usually diminishes after 24 to 48 hours. PCA is most useful in the first three to five postoperative days when the patient has the most severe pain. After the initial critical period the pain can readily be managed with oral analgesic doses. The PCA will allow T.J. to have control over her pain. She will determine how often and when the opioid analgesic is dosed, and she can titrate the dose to a level of comfort or side effects that is acceptable to her.

13. Opioid Selection for Use in PCA. **What opioid analgesics could be used in T.J.'s PCA device?**

Most of the commonly prescribed parenteral opioids can be used in a PCA, but fentanyl, hydromorphone, meperidine, and morphine are used most frequently. (See Table 7.4 for dosing guidelines.) Morphine usually is recommended first, followed by hydromorphone, meperidine, and fentanyl. If the patient has a history of morphine intolerance (e.g., itching or nausea), alternative agents such as hydromorphone or meperidine should be initiated. Most of the opioids used for PCA have a broad therapeutic range with the exception of meperidine because the active normeperidine metabolite can accumulate even at normal therapeutic doses. Meperidine also has only a three hour half-life and perhaps an even shorter duration of action as an analgesic.[129,130] Therefore, meperidine is unsuitable for treatment of acute severe pain when the analgesic requirement is exceedingly high or when patients have decreased renal function.

Patient controlled analgesia is most commonly used for administering opioids intravenously, and on rare occasions, subcutaneously. Subcutaneous opioid administration is limited by the fluid volume needed to deliver the drug. A subcutaneous infusion of 1 mL/hour is universally accepted, however, slightly larger volumes can be acceptable in some patients. Highly concentrated morphine solutions (e.g., 60 mg/mL) must be compounded to permit maximal doses for these patients. Alternatively, hydromorphone (Dilaudid HP) at concentrations of 10 mg/mL can be used. When necessary, hydromorphone powder can be purchased and higher concentrations can be prepared, but it is unknown if concentrations that exceed those of commercial products increase local tissue irritation or other untoward effects.[131,132] Since no contraindications exist, T.J. should be started on intravenous morphine in her PCA pump.

14. PCA Prescriptions. **How should T.J.'s PCA prescriptions be ordered?**

A basic PCA prescription for opioid analgesics must include the name of the drug, solution concentration, dose for self-bolus, lockout period, continuous basal dose, and hourly maximum dose limit. Additionally, a "rescue dose" and frequency also should be ordered for breakthrough pain. Monitoring parameters such as respiratory rate, blood pressure, mental status, and frequency of assessment also should be included on the prescription. It is of utmost importance to have the name and telephone or pager number of the person responsible for pain management on the prescription. For example, the IV PCA order for morphine for T.J. would include the following:

Morphine sulfate	1 mg/mL
Self dose	1 mg (1 mL) IV
Lockout time	6 min
Basal dose	1 mg/hr (1 mL/hr) IV
Rescue	1 mg IV Q 20 min PRN pain
1 hr Limit Total	12 mg IV

Hold PCA for respiratory <10
breaths/min or systolic BP <90 mm Hg

Naloxone 0.4 mg 2 ampules by bedside

ª VAS = Verbal or visual analog scale

T.J. should be re-evaluated two hours after starting the PCA, and doses adjusted at that time.

15. PCA Selection Criteria. What general criteria can one use in selecting a PCA device?

A patient controlled analgesia device must first of all be easy to use. If the operation of a device is too complicated patients can easily become confused, especially patients who are recovering from anesthetics and other medications administered during surgery. Patients generally are not interested in learning all the capabilities of a particular device. Most just want to learn the specifics of administering the analgesics. The device selected must have enough programming capability to allow the healthcare providers to increase or decrease the continuous infusion rate as well as the size of the self-bolus dose and lockout interval. Most PCA devices allow programming of the dosage of analgesics in milliliters as well as in micrograms and milligrams. PCA devices which are only capable of administering doses in milligrams increase the risk of medication calculation errors and should be avoided. For ambulatory patients, the PCA pump also must be easily portable. Unlike the devices used for general inpatient postoperative care, the ambulatory PCA devices generally do not need extensive restrictions to patient access. If a patient is unreliable and a locked, tamper-proof PCA device is needed, the patient probably is too unreliable for PCA. Subcutaneous or epidural PCAs can be an alternative for acute and chronic administration of analgesics,[133–136] but are more costly than oral analgesics. PCA use does not replace the need to assess patient response. For example, it is not appropriate to assume that when a patient is on a PCA that her pain is automatically controlled. Some form of measuring tool should be used to assess the patient's pain and appropriate documentation made in the patient's medical records. "Patient on PCA" is not adequate documentation for pain assessment. When assessing pain the clinician should always use either a verbal or visual analog scale as a guide.

16. Dose Conversion Between Opioid Analgesics. T.J. has requested another analgesic agent because of excessive sedation. She currently needs 10 mg of morphine per hour from her PCA. How should T.J. be converted to another PCA opioid analgesic?

The intravenous equivalent of morphine 10 mg/hour is about equal to hydromorphone 2 mg/hour, meperidine 100 mg/hour, or fentanyl 150 µg/hour (see Table 7.2). Meperidine is not a viable alternative for T.J. because the equivalent meperidine dose of 100 mg/hour exceeds the maximum recommended dose of 60 mg/hour. The remaining options are either hydromorphone or fentanyl PCA. Example prescriptions for these two drugs are as follows:

Fentanyl	10 µg/mL
Self dose	10 µg (1 mL) IV
Lockout time	6 min
Basal dose	10 µg/hr (1 mL/hr) IV
Rescue	10 mg IV Q 20 min PRN pain
1 hr Limit Total	120 µg IV

Hold PCA for respiratory <10
breaths/min or systolic BP <90 mm Hg

Naloxone 0.4 mg 2 ampules by bedside

OR

Hydromorphone	0.2 mg/mL
Self dose	0.2 mg (1 mL) IV
Lockout time	6 min
Basal dose	0.2 mg/hr (1 mL/hr) IV
Rescue	0.2 mg IV Q 20 min PRN pain
1 hr Limit Total	2.4 mg IV

Hold PCA for respiratory <10
breaths/min or systolic BP <90 mm Hg

Naloxone 0.4 mg 2 ampules by bedside

As always, T.J. should be re-evaluated in two hours after changing the PCA, and doses adjusted at that time.

17. Conversion From PCA to Oral Opioids. Forty-eight hours later T.J.'s requirement for hydromorphone has decreased significantly. She is now requiring on the average of 0.5 mg hydromorphone/hr in the last 12 hours. How should T.J. be converted to oral opioid analgesics?

PCA is rarely used beyond the first 72-hour postoperative period,[137] and the continuous basal infusions frequently are discontinued after the first 24 hours. Transition to oral opioid analgesics from PCA should occur as soon as the patient is able to tolerate oral intake after the first 24 hours postoperatively. Oral opioid analgesia usually is given every three to four hours for convenience, as well as allowing time for drug absorption. Conversion to oral from parenteral opioids is best achieved based upon the total opioid requirement of the previous 24-hour period. For T.J., the total 24-hour intravenous hydromorphone (0.5 mg/hour) requirement is 12 mg, and that is equal to intravenous morphine 60 mg, methadone 18 mg, and levorphanol 12 mg. Orally, morphine 180 mg, methadone 18 mg, levorphanol 24 mg, and hydromorphone 48 mg are the equivalent to T.J.'s intravenous hydromorphone daily requirement. Levorphanol with its long duration of action and a lower incidence for gastrointestinal intolerance would be a good oral agent to use for T.J. This daily equianalgesic dose can be given in six equally divided doses. The levorphanol dose for T.J. would be 4 mg every four hours. Also, there should be a period of four to six hours of PCA overlapping with oral opioids, but the PCA's continuous basal infusion should be stopped as soon as the oral dose is given.

Tapering of Opioid Analgesics

18. How should T.J.'s opioid analgesics be tapered?

Most patients gradually decrease their activation of a PCA pump as soon as their acute pain begins to subside. In those instances when patients have not decreased their PCA pump use, the dose may safely be reduced by 15% to 20% each day without precipitating symptoms of withdrawal. For T.J., the oral levorphanol regimen should be changed to an as needed schedule once the pain is stabilized. For most patients a scheduled opioid taper is not essential unless the total daily requirement is in excess of 160 mg of oral morphine (or its equivalent) or if opioid use is prolonged. T.J. should be able to be converted to acetaminophen 325 mg with codeine 30 mg after her oral levorphanol has been completely discontinued.

Pain Management in the Opioid Dependent Patient

19. If T.J. had a history of heroin and cocaine abuse, how would her pain treatment be modified?

Pain management in an intravenous drug abuser is not difficult as long as the clinician does not judge the patient's behavior or interject personal values into the decision making process. As with any patient, the goal is to provide as much comfort as possible. Concerns over opiate abuse or addiction are not relevant when treating acute pain.

The first step in the management of a patient with a history of substance abuse is to try to determine the amount of illicit drugs the patient has been using, being alert to the possible abuse of multiple drugs in varying quantities.[138] Patients who have a history of opiate (heroin) and stimulant (cocaine) use are likely to demonstrate a much greater tolerance to opiates than a patient who has been using opiates alone. There is some evidence that cross tolerance can occur between cocaine and some opiates, but not to methadone.[139-142]

The primary goal is to control the patient's pain. A combination of methadone titrated to prevent withdrawal and to provide background analgesia plus a short-acting opioid analgesic dosed adequately to prevent breakthrough pain can be used. In T.J.'s case, if she had a history of substance abuse, she could be started on methadone 20 to 40 mg/day in four equally divided doses depending upon how much heroin had been used (see Chapter 83: Depressant and Inhalant Abuse). The methadone would cover her possible heroin withdrawal and possibly provide additional analgesia. Since her actual pain requirements are unknown, she also would be placed on a hydromorphone PCA. One should always reassess the patient one to two hours after starting the analgesic regimen for signs of withdrawal, clinical response, and toxicity and then titrate the doses of both the methadone and hydromorphone accordingly.[143] The final dose requirement may be higher than those typically used in opioid-naive patients. Conversely, some patients may exaggerate their history of prior drug use and are actually quite sensitive to the prescribed therapy. Long-term management should include offering the patient appropriate referrals to drug treatment centers, but the final responsibility should rest with the patient.[144-149]

Use of Opioids in Recovering Addicts

20. Should opioid analgesics be prescribed to recovering opiate addicts?

Acute opioid use in the hospitalized setting is unlikely to cause opioid addiction: the rate of addiction from clinical opioid use is much less than 1%. Unless it is the patient's choice not to use opioids, there is no rational reason for not using them. Often the patient's fear of addiction can be alleviated by thorough education. The clinician should have a therapeutic contract with the patient that includes pain management as well as opioid tapering upon the resolution of the acute pain. (Also see Chapter 83: Depressant and Inhalant Abuse.)

Use of Opioids in Renal Disease

21. What adjustments in analgesic dosing would be required if T.J. had a Cl$_{Cr}$ of 30 mL/min?

Uremia often can produce CNS changes in renal disease patients and, therefore, make them more sensitive to the opioids' additional CNS depressant effects. As discussed in Question 11, some opioids have active metabolites that are renally excreted, and uremia can lead to their accumulation. For example, the active metabolites of meperidine and morphine (normeperidine and morphine-6-glucuronate) undergo renal excretion. Both of these active metabolites can cause CNS excitation: in particular, normeperidine can precipitate grand mal seizures. Therefore, meperidine should be avoided in uremic patients, but other opioids can be used as long as one is aware of the potential toxicities, the patient is closely monitored,

and dosage is properly titrated. For T.J., hydromorphone PCA could still be a reasonable choice for the management of her acute pain, however, a continuous basal infusion would be unnecessary in this situation. As with all patients receiving opioid analgesics, close monitoring and follow-up care is essential.

Obstetrical Pain: Special Considerations for Opioid Analgesia

22. Epidurals. M.T., a 28-year-old female, has been in labor for 10 hours and is experiencing strong, erratic contractions at 5–15 minute intervals. Her cervix is minimally dilated, suggesting that delivery is still several hours away. Her pain is severe and, if continued, may compromise her ability to assist in the labor and delivery process. A single 50 μg epidural dose of fentanyl is ordered for M.T. by anesthesia. What guidelines are necessary for the safe use of epidural opioids?

Fentanyl and morphine are frequently administered epidurally during labor,[150-152] and during lower extremity surgical procedures (e.g., cesarean delivery, total joint replacements) because of limited systemic effects and exceptionally long duration of analgesic action.[153-155] Occasionally, epidural analgesia also has been used in thoracic surgery.[156] A single dose of 2 to 10 mg morphine given epidurally may provide analgesia for ≥12 hours.[157] Respiratory depression can occur one to three hours after the administration of epidural morphine and can be readily reversed by naloxone. Facial or generalized pruritus also can occur hours after the administration of epidural morphine. If pruritus does occur, it can be controlled by low doses of intramuscular or intravenous naloxone 0.02 to 0.08 mg without reversing the analgesic effect of the epidural morphine. Frequent monitoring of vital signs is essential after the administration of epidural opioids. Besides morphine, fentanyl (Sublimaze),[158-163] sufentanil (Sufenta),[164] and buprenorphine (Buprenex)[165-169] also have been used epidurally. The duration of analgesia of epidurally administered opioids is less dependent upon the serum half-life of the opioid than upon the lipid solubility of the drug. The more lipophilic the opioid, the shorter the duration of epidural analgesia because the lipophilic opioids can rapidly diffuse out of the epidural space. The more hydrophilic opioids remain in the epidural space longer. The highly lipophilic opiate analgesic, methadone, has a very short duration of activity when administered epidurally even though it has a long serum half-life of 24 hours.[170,171] For M.T., fentanyl is a good choice because it has a fairly long duration of analgesia, but will not produce significant systemic effects that might compromise the fetus transplacentally. Also the duration of fentanyl is short enough that it will not unnecessarily delay maternal postpartum recovery. A single dose of 50 μg of epidural fentanyl was given to M.T. through an epidural catheter and complete analgesia was achieved.

23. *Spinal Analgesia in Opioid Dependent Patients.* Why would spinal opioid analgesia still be appropriate if M.T. is opioid dependent?

Previous opioid use has minimal influence in the determination of opioid doses. Opioid dependent patients can achieve adequate analgesia from epidural opioids, but their physical opioid dependency will not be satisfied. In spite of adequate analgesia, the opioid dependent patient may exhibit symptoms of opiate withdrawal. If withdrawal symptoms occur, they can be treated effectively by systemic administration of morphine or other opioids. The dose of the systemic opioids vary with the patient's previous level of opioid dependence and doses will need to be adjusted accordingly. It would be appropriate to start M.T. on a short-acting opioid such as meperidine 10 mg IV every 15 to 20 minutes until the symptoms of withdrawal subside. This may be somewhat hazardous because the incidence of respiratory depression in the first 24 hours may be increased when opioids are administered by simultaneous epidural and systemic routes.[172] Therefore, longer-acting opioids such as methadone or levorphanol should be avoided. The respiratory depression can be treated with the opioid antagonist naloxone, but the dose must be limited to 0.1 mg increments given intravenously to avoid precipitation of an acute withdrawal syndrome. The naloxone dose can be repeated and the dose titrated to the desired clinical response.

24. *Clonidine for Opioid Withdrawal Symptoms.* **If M.T. was opioid dependent, what are alternatives in managing the symptoms of physical withdrawal while she is treated with epidural opioids?**

Clonidine (Catapres) 0.2 to 1.2 mg/day can effectively suppress the signs and symptoms of opioid withdrawal without eliciting other opioid effects.[173–175] The specific dose must be individualized for each patient to avoid hypotension, dry mouth, or drowsiness.[176–179] Clonidine also can be given sublingually or transdermally in equivalent doses. Clonidine transdermal patches of 3.5, 7, and 10.5 cm^2 deliver 0.2, 0.4, and 0.6 mg of clonidine, respectively, over a 24-hour period.[180,181] Approximately 24 hours must elapse before steady-state plasma concentrations of clonidine are attained from the patches.[182,183] Therefore, supplemental oral or sublingual[184] clonidine 0.1 mg every 6 to 12 hours must be administered during the first 24 hours of the application of the transdermal patches. Clonidine transdermal patches should be used to treat the signs of physical opioid withdrawal only when these symptoms are expected to be severe or prolonged. For M.T., who is in labor, clonidine should be avoided due to the risk of hypotension and possible adverse effects on the fetus. A shorter-acting opioid should be used as in Question 23.

25. *Systemic Opioids During Labor.* **Should M.T. be given a systemic analgesic rather than epidural analgesia?**

If possible, central nervous system depressants should be avoided during labor because they can compromise fetal vital functions.[185–188] Nevertheless, if an analgesic is deemed necessary, then an agent should be chosen which meets the following criteria: a) provides adequate pain relief; b) has little effect on the course or duration of labor; and c) affects fetal vital signs minimally during labor, delivery, and postpartum. Meperidine and fentanyl meet these criteria for the most part and, therefore, are frequently preferred over other opioids in obstetrics when given in small, frequent parenteral injections or through a PCA.[189–191] As with all opioid analgesic use, close monitoring of the patient for analgesia and untoward effects is essential. Although meperidine and fentanyl seem to have only minimal residual effects on the neonate at analgesic doses, adverse effects still may occur.[192] For example, 4 of 35 neonates manifested some degree of respiratory depression following maternal analgesia with meperidine.[193] Furthermore, according to an early neonatal neurobehavioral scale, meperidine broadly depressed most measured neonatal activities on the first and second days of life.[194] Nevertheless, if the contractions are very strong, erratic, and prolonged early in the course of labor (e.g., M.T.), a short-acting analgesic (e.g., meperidine) could be useful to blunt the labor pain and calm the mother, so that she may regain control over her contractions and conserve her energy for the actual delivery. Butorphanol (Stadol) also has minimal effects on fetal and neonatal function and is a reasonable alternative to meperidine or fentanyl in this situation.[195–197] All potent analgesics should be administered intramuscularly or subcutaneously because intravenous administration is associated with more neonatal and fetal depression due to the high peak serum concentration achieved by this route.[198,199] Pentazocine has similar effects as butorphanol, but is seldom used because of local tissue reactions at the site of intramuscular or subcutaneous injections. Pentazocine and butorphanol are mixed opiate-agonists/antagonists and can precipitate acute withdrawal reactions in some opiate-dependent individuals. As a result, these drugs need to be used cautiously, if at all, in the opiate-addicted population (see Question 27).

Should neonatal respiratory difficulties be manifested as a result of opioid analgesics administered during labor, they can be reversed with the opioid antagonist, naloxone (Narcan).[200] For M.T., meperidine 50 mg IM was given with good clinical response. As with all opioid analgesics, the dose has to be adjusted after an evaluation of the patient's history and clinical findings. Analgesic doses always should be individualized for the specific patient.

Variability in Intramuscular (IM) Meperidine Absorption

26. M.T. achieved excellent analgesia from the first dose of meperidine 50 mg IM, but she started to complain that subsequent doses produced variable pain relief, and she accused the nurse of giving her placebos. What are some of the explanations for this problem?

The most common cause of variable clinical response after an intramuscular meperidine injection is an erratic bioavailability after repetitive injections at the same site. The absorption of meperidine from an injection may vary by as much as 30% to 50% after repeated intramuscular administrations. Other considerations also should include tachyphylaxis, progression of an underlying disease (e.g., in patients with cancer), and the possibility of opioid diversion by the patient or someone else through dilution or removal of active drug from its container.

Special Consideration for Using Partial Agonist and Antagonist Opioid Analgesics

27. What are precautions for using partial agonist and antagonist opioids for analgesia in M.T.?

Pentazocine, butorphanol, dezocine, and nalbuphine are partial agonist/antagonist opioid analgesics. Besides exhibiting agonist analgesic effects, they all possess opiate antagonist properties as well. Pentazocine can simultaneously produce analgesia and precipitate withdrawals due to the partial agonist/antagonist nature. This property also would apply to other partial agonist/antagonist opioid analgesics such as butorphanol, nalbuphine, and dezocine.[201,202] Pentazocine has an opioid antagonist effect equal to $\frac{1}{50}$ of nalorphine: 80 mg has been known to precipitate abstinence in patients who have been given opioids for chronic pain. If a partial opiate agonist is instituted in a patient previously taking a pure agonist, the dose should be increased gradually and the patient should be observed closely for symptoms of abstinence.[203,204] If possible, the pure agonist opioid should be withdrawn gradually; a drug-free period of two days before the institution of pentazocine also has been suggested, but is impractical for a patient in pain.

When partial agonist/antagonist opioid analgesics are being considered, the risk of unpleasant psychotomimetic side effects must be weighed against the benefits. For example, butorphanol[205,206] dysphoric responses are well documented. A 2 mg dose of butorphanol was associated with an 18% incidence of psychic disturbance and a 4 mg dose with a 33% incidence. Pentazocine (Talwin) is associated with a higher incidence of psychotomimetic reactions than other opioid analgesics. For example, hallucinations occurred in 24 of 65 patients (37%) who received 40 to 50 mg of intramuscular pentazocine. In another trial, psychic changes occurred in 1.7% of patients receiving morphine versus 11.4% of pentazocine-treated patients. In comparison, nalbuphine (Nubain)[207–212] and other analgesics induce much less psychotomimetic effect than butorphanol or pentazocine.[213–218] Therefore, a partial agonist/antagonist opioid analgesic should be used in M.T. only if she cannot tolerate the available shorter acting opioid agonist analgesics.

Tramadol

28. What is the purported advantage of tramadol (Ultram) over other opioid analgesics and NSAIDs?

Tramadol, a centrally-acting analgesic with weak opioid agonist properties, activates monoaminergic spinal inhibition of pain. The O-demethylated metabolite of tramadol has a higher affinity for opioid receptors than the parent drug; however, after a single oral dose, the binding of tramadol to the mu-opioid receptor is overshadowed by its nonopioid analgesic effects.[432] The tolerance and dependence potential of tramadol during treatment for up to six months appear to be low; however, the possibility of dependence with long-term use cannot be excluded entirely.[433] Tramadol is an effective and relatively safe analgesic that may be of value in several painful conditions not requiring treatment with strong opioid drugs.

In a double-blind single dose study conducted in 161 patients with severe pain following cesarean section, tramadol 75 and 150 mg was as effective as the combination of acetaminophen 650 mg with dextropropoxyphene napsylate 100 mg. In another study, oral tramadol was about equal in effectiveness as acetaminophen with codeine 30 mg. The optimal single dose of tramadol for acute pain seems to be 100 mg and tramadol 50 mg is about similar in analgesic efficacy to codeine 60 mg. Steady-state plasma tramadol concentrations after administration of 50 mg oral doses every six hours are similar to those obtained after administration of a 100 mg single oral dose.[140] Tramadol will be made available by Ortho-McNeil in the U.S. initially in 50 mg tablets for oral use; however, this drug has been available in European countries orally, rectally, intravenously, and intramuscularly.

In patients with moderate to severe postoperative pain, intravenous or intramuscular tramadol is about equal in potency to meperidine (Demerol); and tramadol 50 to 150 mg IV is about equivalent in analgesic efficacy to morphine 5 to 15 mg. Tramadol, however, is only about 1/30th as potent as morphine when administered epidurally.[433]

Tramadol is well tolerated in short term use. As would be expected with an opioid, the principal adverse effects are sedation, dizziness, nausea, vomiting, dry mouth, and sweating; however, the potential for respiratory depression is low.[41] Furthermore, tramadol is not likely to induce the gastrointestinal distress that has been associated with the nonsteroidal anti-inflammatory drugs because tramadol does not inhibit the cytoprotective effects of prostaglandins.

Chronic Malignant Pain

Goal of Malignant Pain Management

29. A.J., a 68-year-old male, was diagnosed with metastatic prostatic cancer 6 months ago. Now he is admitted for evaluation of possible accidental opioid overdose. A.J. was started on a fentanyl patch 100 µg/hr 24 hours ago by his physician because of spinal pain not adequately relieved by oral acetaminophen 325 mg and hydrocodone 5 mg Q 3 hr. The fentanyl patch was removed 6 hours ago, and A.J. is again complaining of his spinal pain radiating to his buttocks and left leg. A.J. is currently awake and alert, and relates that his pain level is at 9/10 on the pain scale. What is the goal in managing pain such as A.J.'s?

The goal in treating pain of terminal illness is comfort and an acceptable (to the patient) level of consciousness. Opioids should not be withheld for fear of addiction or that the dose may be too high. The dose should be titrated based upon the patient's clinical response and not on the drug amount. Ideally, the patient should be comfortable and voice no complaints when questioned about his level of activity and alertness. Under these conditions, any dosage reductions or changes in therapy would serve no purpose, even

if the patient was receiving doses several times those typically used to treat acute pain. Clinicians should focus attention on their patients' clinical response rather than on an arbitrary list of doses or ideal number of medications. The immediate goal for A.J. is to break the cycle of pain and to rapidly have him as pain-free as possible.

Indications for Use of Fentanyl Patches

30. What special considerations are necessary for use of fentanyl transdermal patches in patients such as A.J.?

Transdermal fentanyl can be effectively used for the management of chronic cancer pain. Due to the nature of the transdermal delivery system the onset of analgesia may be delayed by 6 to 12 hours after the placement of the patch.[219-221] Upon removal of the patch, the fentanyl deposited in the subcutaneous tissue will continue to release active drug for about another 8 to 12 hours. These delays in onset upon application, and offset after removal, of the transdermal patch, discourage use of the patch except for patients who require a steady maintenance analgesic dose. The transdermal patches do not provide sufficient flexibility in dosing to manage rapidly changing analgesic needs. Even after stabilized on a given drug regimen, cancer pain patients always should be given an immediate-onset opioid analgesic (e.g., morphine elixir) to take as needed for management of breakthrough pain.[222] If the need for breakthrough drugs becomes frequent, the underlying dosage regimen should be reassessed and the doses increased as appropriate. Fentanyl absorption from the patches can be affected by body temperature, and unintentional overdoses can occur with hyperthermia.[224]

A patient given fentanyl patches must be instructed to dispose of used patches appropriately to prevent inadvertent access by children or household animals. Fentanyl patches were thought to be safe from diversion and abuse, but the drug enclosure membrane can be removed and active drug accessed.[223]

Morphine

Use of Oral Morphine

31. What oral dose of morphine should be selected for A.J.?

The usual initial dose for morphine is 30 mg orally every three hours (see Table 7.4), but A.J. has been receiving acetaminophen with oxycodone for an unknown length of time and might have some degree of opioid tolerance. His response to morphine should be monitored carefully one to two hours after his initial dose and the dose adjusted appropriately. If A.J.'s clinical response indicates that the dose is too high, it should be decreased; however, if he is still uncomfortable after the two hours, an additional 30 mg should be given at once, and subsequent doses increased by 10 mg to a total of 40 mg every three hours. A.J.'s response should be the primary criterion for determining the dose, and the pharmacokinetics of the drug should determine the dosing interval. Frequent reassessment of A.J.'s pain status and level of consciousness is essential.

When the pain has been relieved, the dose of morphine often can be decreased. Ideally, only one clinician should assume responsibility for coordinating frequent monitoring of the patient's level of awareness and pain control. Once the pain has been controlled, single day dosage adjustment should be sufficient. If the dose is changed, then it should be reassessed within the first two hours to prevent unnecessary exposure to pain or adverse effects. Most oral opioids reach maximum analgesic effect within the first two hours after administration, but for longer-acting opioid analgesics such as methadone, the patient should be monitored for several days because of possible drug accumulation.

Tolerance, Dependence, and Addiction

32. Should tachyphylaxis, dependence, and addiction to morphine be an issue in A.J.?

Tachyphylaxis or tolerance with chronic opioid use can occur, but addiction is not an issue for patients with a terminal disease. Tolerance occurs when a given dose no longer produces the same effect over time. For patients with a malignant disease, it is very difficult to differentiate between tolerance and increased pain from disease progression. Escalating doses of opioid analgesics should not deter the clinician from continuing with analgesic therapy, but it should serve as a warning that alternative analgesic agents might need to be considered.

Dependence can be physical or psychological. Physical dependency occurs when the patient develops signs and symptoms of physical withdrawal upon the cessation of a drug therapy. Psychological dependency occurs when a "need" state (craving) develops upon the cessation of a drug. The potential for dependency to opioid analgesics should never prevent the clinical use of opioid analgesics in malignant disease.

Addiction should not be confused with dependence or tolerance. Addiction is a compulsive behavior relating to drug procurement and use. Addiction from clinical opioid use for the treatment of pain is rare. Yet, in a survey by Marks and associates, a majority of physicians underestimated the effective dosage range, overestimated the duration of action, and exaggerated the dangers of addiction for medical inpatients receiving meperidine.[225] Another study noted that nurses administered less than the prescribed amounts of opioids to their patients and that 75% of these patients suffered moderate to marked distress.[226]

Further evidence that patients should not suffer pain needlessly comes from data on the incidence of hospitalization for treatment of opioid addiction secondary to medical use of opiates. The Illinois State Drug Abuse Center showed that only 3 of 1900 cases of addiction were possible complications of previous medical treatment; and in a Boston Collaborative Drug Study of almost 12,000 patients, only four patients who received opioids had developed probable addiction.

Twycross, in reporting his experiences with heroin as an analgesic stated: a) there is no single optimal or maximum effective dose; b) the use of diamorphine does not, by itself, impair mental faculties; c) tolerance is not a problem; d) psychological dependence does not occur; and e) physical dependence may occur, but does not prevent the downward adjustment of the dose when considered clinically feasible.

Although these statements pertain to heroin, there is little clinical difference between heroin (diacetylmorphine) and morphine when used for analgesia.[227] The purported craving for opioids, which occasionally is observed in cancer patients, is most likely due to inadequate analgesic doses rather than to addiction. Therefore, clinicians should not exercise undue caution in prescribing opioid analgesics for fear of "addicting" patients in a clinical setting.[228]

The small number of cases of iatrogenic opioid addiction of hospitalized patients does not imply that physical dependence does not occur in this setting. Approximately 50% of patients who receive therapeutic doses of opioid analgesics several times daily for two to three weeks will experience some mild degree of sleep disturbance and irritability after abrupt withdrawal of opioid analgesics. These symptoms usually peak within 8 to 12 hours and usually are not recognized as being a consequence of opioid administration. Therefore, physical dependence to opioids frequently develops during chronic pain management. Physical dependence, however, is not synonymous with addiction. In the hospital, or in a supervised medical setting, opioids are administered in a defined context and the patient does not have the same stimuli for addiction as in the nonmedical social setting. In the latter setting, contact with friends, sights, and sounds associated with drug taking powerfully reinforce the rituals leading to abuse.[229,230] (See Chapter 81: Issues: Psychoactive Substance Use Disorders for additional discussions of addiction and physical dependence.)

When additional pain relief is needed, doses of opioid analgesics should be increased. There is essentially no upper limit to the dose of morphine, methadone, levorphanol, or hydromorphone that can safely be given to patients with physical pain.[231]

Use of Sustained-Release (SR) Morphine

33. A.J.'s pain was controlled on 40 mg of morphine solution orally Q 3 hr, but he is now complaining of the frequency of the morphine dose. He wishes to have the therapy changed to allow fewer daily doses so that he may have longer periods of rest. What can be done about A.J.'s request?

A.J.'s daily morphine requirement of 320 mg can be provided by use of a sustained-release dosage form given every 8 to 12 hours. However, direct conversion of doses from oral morphine solutions or other immediate-release dosage forms to sustained-release tablets often leads to oversedation initially, and particularly during the first hours of the dosing period. Therefore, the SR dose should be reduced by 25% or 240 mg/day (320 mg × 75%) for A.J. This can be given as 90 mg every eight hours or as 120 mg every 12 hours. Sustained-release morphine is available as 30 and 60 mg tablets and as 100 mg tablets. When starting a patient on oral SR preparations, it often is desirable to try an every eight-hour regimen in order to avoid the initial sedation that often is associated with the larger individual doses of the every 12-hour regimen.

The two commercially available sustained-release morphine products differ only in their formulation, but not in clinical efficacy.[232] Careful assessment of the patient's response and toxicity by the clinician is the most essential ingredient between success or failure with either product in managing the patient's pain. When larger doses are needed, eight-hour dosing intervals usually cause less sedation than 12-hour intervals (i.e., during the first 2 hours of the dosing period).[233] Some patients also may have more breakthrough pain at the end of the 12-hour dosing interval.

Rectal Use of Morphine Suppositories and SR Tablets

34. Several weeks later, A.J. is no longer able to swallow his medication because of worsening of an existing esophageal stricture. What are alternatives for giving A.J. his required daily analgesic?

In addition to the parenteral routes already presented, morphine can be administered as an oral solution or via a rectal suppository. The absorption of the rectal suppository is at least comparable or better than that of the morphine solution.[234,235] If A.J. was stabilized on 240 mg/day of sustained-release morphine, the initial morphine suppository dose also should be 240 mg/day. The duration of action of morphine suppositories is similar to that of morphine solution and, therefore, must be administered every three to four hours. In A.J. the starting dose would be 30 mg rectally every three hours. Other agents such as hydromorphone (Dilaudid) and oxymorphone (Numorphan) also are available as suppositories. The equianalgesic doses of these agents for A.J. (see Table 7.2) would be 6 and 10 mg, respectively.[236–238] Sustained-release oral morphine tablets also can be used for rectal administration. The rectal absorption of sustained-release tablets is comparable to the oral route of administration.[239–242] There is no maximum dose for opioid analgesics for the management of pain of a terminal disease, but there is a limit as to how many suppositories or tablets the patient can hold rectally.

Oral Infusion

35. Because A.J. was unable to swallow, he agreed to have a gastrostomy feeding tube placed by a general surgeon. He is now being fed through the tube at a rate of 50 mL/hr. Morphine sulfate solution is added to each feeding bag to deliver 10 mg/hr. He also is receiving amitriptyline (Elavil) 150 mg HS, naproxen suspension 250 mg QID, and lorazepam (Ativan) 4 mg TID via the feeding tube. A.J. is reasonably alert and is only slightly uncomfortable. Are there any problems associated with placing A.J.'s morphine in the feeding formula?

There is no reason why morphine cannot be given in this manner. The obvious questions about drug stability, solubility, and binding to proteins in the feeding formula do not appear to present a problem because A.J. has been receiving the morphine in this manner for the past several days. The dose of morphine (240 mg/day) is apparently not causing undesirable effects. A.J. is, in fact, quite comfortable. Administering morphine as a continuous oral infusion at night while the patient sleeps is perhaps the best method to insure restful, pain-free sleep.

Tricyclic Antidepressants (TCAs)

36. Why would TCAs be beneficial for managing A.J.'s cancer pain?

Tricyclic antidepressants have been used experimentally at low to moderate doses as an adjunct to analgesic for pain control. These agents may alter psychological responses to pain, may have intrinsic analgesic activity, or may potentiate opioid analgesics.[243-247] European investigations noted an 82% overall response rate to these agents.[248] Imipramine (Tofranil) relieved cancer and surgical pain in about 75% to 80% of patients, and doxepin (Sinequan) relieved pain completely in about half of 16 depressed chronic pain patients.[249] Tension headaches also were improved with 25 to 100 mg of doxepin.[250] Imipramine 50 to 200 mg/day or amitriptyline 10 to 40 mg/day alone or in combination with fluphenazine (Prolixin) also have been recommended.[251] Tricyclic antidepressants and methadone combination also have been used successfully for the long-term management of chronic phantom limb pain (see Question 49).[252] For A.J., the choice of tricyclic antidepressants is limited, because of his inability to swallow. However, a few TCAs are available as parenteral formulations (amitriptyline and imipramine) or oral suspensions (doxepin and nortriptyline). Therefore, it would be reasonable to continue A.J.'s present TCA therapy.

Methadone

Guidelines

37. The decision has been made to use oral methadone to treat A.J.'s pain. What are guidelines for the safe use of methadone in treating cancer pain?

Clinical experience with the use of methadone for cancer pain is favorable.[253] The patient's physical and mental condition should be monitored closely, and clinicians should be aware of the long elimination half-life of methadone.[254,255] Repeated dosing with methadone requires decreasing the dose when comfort is achieved to prevent drug accumulation and overdose. Methadone is 85% bound to serum proteins, and its average plasma half-life is about 23 hours with a range of 13 to 47 hours.[256] Therefore, the drug probably is tightly bound and only slowly released from its binding sites. Plasma levels of methadone may continue to rise for up to ten days after an increase in dose.

Unfortunately, analgesia is not related to the serum half-life, and multiple doses must be given each day. The absolute amount of methadone in plasma, although it undoubtedly affects sedation and respiratory depression, is not a factor in the magnitude of analgesic response. Nevertheless, analgesic effects are obtained only while

methadone plasma levels are above a certain individualized concentration. Most patients can be maintained on doses of methadone every six or eight hours after pain control is achieved, but the drug often must be given every four hours or administered with another short-acting opioid analgesic during the first day or two of therapy to control pain.[257,258] Alternatively, methadone loading with higher doses for the first few doses can accomplish rapid analgesia at the onset of methadone administration. Unfortunately this carries a higher risk of rapid drug accumulation and excessive drowsiness. Thus, loading doses must be reduced after the first one to two doses.

The necessity for shorter dosing intervals during the initiation of methadone can cause clinicians unfamiliar with the long half-life of methadone to adjust doses too frequently or to then maintain a patient at an inappropriately high dose after initial pain control is achieved. This can threaten the patient with dangerous drug accumulation. A scenario which often is repeated is one in which analgesia is obtained after two or three days of gradually increasing doses, and the patient is quite comfortable. On days four and five, the patient is increasingly more sedated and on day six alarmingly so. The drug is then discontinued or the opioid antagonist, naloxone (Narcan) is administered. Suddenly, the patient is no longer sedated, but the pain has reappeared. This sudden reversal of sedation may be short lived. Since the half-life of methadone is much longer than that of naloxone, the patient can still slip back into sedation once the naloxone is cleared from the plasma in one to two hours.[259] Elderly and severely debilitated patients may require smaller doses of methadone for pain control; therefore, caution must be exercised when methadone is used in these patients.[260]

Dosing

38. What dose of methadone should be prescribed to treat A.J.'s pain?

In order to convert A.J.'s dose of morphine to an equivalent dose of methadone, one must use Table 7.2 as a standard reference for comparison. A.J.'s 10 mg every hour oral morphine sulfate solution dose is estimated to be about equivalent to 10 mg every three hours of morphine intramuscularly. On a single dose basis, intramuscular doses of methadone and morphine are equally potent; however, with repeated doses on a chronic basis, the duration of methadone activity is about four times longer than that of morphine. Therefore, the total daily parenteral methadone dose will only be one-fourth that of parenteral morphine. In this case, A.J. would require 20 mg/day of intramuscular methadone. Since oral methadone is only 75% as effective as methadone intramuscularly,[261] A.J. should receive about 7.5 mg of methadone orally every six hours.[262] Approximately five to ten days will elapse before the full methadone effect is realized, unless loading doses equal to twice that of the maintenance analgesic dose are used for the first two doses. These two larger doses will accelerate the process of reaching the steady-state concentration.

Continuous Intravenous (IV) Morphine Infusion

39. Three months later, A.J. is again hospitalized because of a compression fracture of his spine. He is cachectic and weighs only 87 pounds. He has been receiving 20 mg of morphine IM Q 3 hr since his admission. His pain is bothersome and his cachectic condition is not conducive to IM injections. What would be a reasonable intravenous analgesic program for A.J.?

Continuous intravenous infusions of morphine are superior to intramuscular injections in maintaining a pain-free condition in cancer and surgical patients.[263-265] In one study, six of eight children with cancer experienced complete pain control with 0.025 to 2.6 mg/kg/hour of morphine for 1 to 16 days.

A.J. has been receiving 160 mg of morphine daily, which is about 7 mg/hour. His initial intravenous infusion dose of morphine should be increased to 8 mg/hour because his pain is still bothersome. When 500 mg of morphine sulfate is added to 500 mL of 5% dextrose in water, the resulting 1 mg/mL solution can be infused intravenously at 8 mL/hour in order to deliver the 8 mg/hour dose. In addition, an order should be written for a 4 mg intravenous bolus of morphine every hour as needed for signs of pain or discomfort.

The supplemental bolus doses of intravenous morphine will facilitate subsequent adjustments of the continuous infusion rate. At the end of a predetermined period of time, the number of milligrams of drug which were administered by constant infusion are added to 1.5 times the number of milligrams of drug used in supplemental bolus doses. This amount of drug is then divided by the elapsed interval of time, thereby calculating the new infusion rate. For example, if at the end of six hours A.J. has received five supplemental doses of 4 mg each, then (6 hours × 8 mg/hour) plus (1.5 × 5 doses of 4 mg) = 78 mg per six hours. The new infusion rate should then be 13 mg/hour, and the new supplemental doses should be 6 mg (approximately equal to the amount of drug normally infused in 30 minutes) every hour as needed. Continual assessment of the patient and hourly adjustments of dose are probably superior to the method outlined above, but the above method may be more practical for the busy clinician.

Brompton's Mixture

40. What is Brompton's mixture? Will heroin (diamorphine) be superior to morphine for managing A.J.'s malignant pain?

An opioid mixture for oral administration in severe pain was formulated at the Brompton Chest Hospital in London in 1926 and was included in the British Pharmaceutical Codex by 1973. The mixture contained diamorphine (heroin) in variable doses, cocaine, alcohol, chloroform water, and syrup. Because clinicians in the U.S. were precluded from using heroin, they formulated their own versions of Brompton's mixture by substituting either morphine or methadone for the heroin, often adding a phenothiazine as well. Since the analgesic effectiveness of heroin and morphine are comparable, cancer pain was successfully treated in approximately 90% of patients using these Brompton's mixtures.[266–269]

A double-blind crossover trial compared a standard Brompton's mixture containing morphine, cocaine, ethanol, syrup, and chloroform water to a flavored aqueous solution of morphine alone.[270] Pain was measured by the pain intensity index of the McGill Pain Questionnaire, and assessments of confusion, drowsiness, and nausea were obtained from the patients, their relatives, and the nurses. Of 44 patients with painful and advanced malignant diseases, no differences in pain relief, drowsiness, or other side effects were observed between the two products.[271–274] Studies in cancer patients have demonstrated that the analgesia claimed to be obtained from heroin is most likely due to its metabolites, morphine and 6-acetyl-morphine. Oral morphine solution should be prescribed for A.J. because Brompton's mixture is not superior.[275–277]

Pentazocine

41. Why should pentazocine (Talwin) not be used in treating cancer pain?

Mild oral analgesics always should be employed first in the treatment of cancer pain, but pentazocine is inferior to aspirin.[278,279] The use of agonist/antagonists also should be avoided because of poor oral efficacy and because of the particularly disturbing nature of the psychotomimetic side effects in patients who are already fearful and anxious. Furthermore, pentazocine is a "ceiling" drug; doses cannot be greatly increased to treat increasing pain without greatly increasing the incidence or severity of side effects.[280]

Hydroxyzine or Phenothiazine

42. Would coadministration of either hydroxyzine or phenothiazine be beneficial for A.J.'s pain?

The addition of hydroxyzine (Vistaril, Atarax) to an analgesic regimen is thought to potentiate the analgesia of the opioid analgesic.[281–283] Whether this is a true analgesic effect or a consequence of its sedating properties is unclear. Two additional benefits related to the antihistamine properties of hydroxyzine are prevention of opiate-induced nausea and itching.

Phenothiazines, like antihistamines, often are administered concomitantly with opioids to "enhance" analgesia. Claims of enhanced analgesia, however, are not supported by well-designed studies. Many of these studies lack double-blinding, a cross-over of patients, placebo control, or appropriate instruments capable of evaluating pain. Another problem in the design of studies evaluating the combination of a phenothiazine or antihistamine with an opioid is the failure to differentiate between analgesia and sedation.[284] Two excellent reviews summarize the studies that demonstrate analgesia with antihistamines and discuss the proposed mechanisms of action.[285,286]

All phenothiazines, except for methotrimeprazine, initially demonstrated anti-analgesic effects in experimental pain studies. Clinicians now realize that experimental pain is not a completely valid model to assess the response of a patient in pain. These studies could not assess the anxiolytic properties of the phenothiazines and the effect a reduction in anxiety has upon pain perception. Furthermore, cancer and chronic pain cause anxiety and anxiety makes pain worse. This reinforcement cannot be overestimated and helps to explain the apparent benefit many patients obtain from the combination of hydroxyzine with an opioid.

Adrenal Corticosteroids

43. Why might corticosteroids be useful for A.J.'s spinal pain?

Patients who have spinal metastatic disease often will obtain pain relief with corticosteroids. This is thought to be due to a combination of direct anti-inflammatory effects and a reduction of pressure from edema around affected nerves. A short-course of dexamethasone at a dose of 10 mg orally or intravenously three times daily with rapid tapering should be considered for A.J. Corticosteroid response may decrease with repeated use, but a single short-course therapy often can produce a significantly prolonged effect. Dexamethasone is most often used because of its long duration of action and lack of mineralocorticoid effects. However, other corticosteroids may be substituted for the dexamethasone using a conversion table to calculate equivalent doses.

Nonsteroidal Anti-Inflammatory Drugs (NSAIDs)

44. Why should the use of an NSAID be considered for A.J.'s spinal pain?

Pain from tumor metastasis to bone is particularly distressing and difficult to treat. Although the most effective therapy for the relief of bone pain is radiation to the site of the pain,[287] prostaglandin inhibitors may be another reasonable alternative to increased doses of opioids. Osseous metastases induce the production of prostaglandins that may cause osteolysis, sensitize free nerve endings, and augment pain perception. The NSAIDs effectively decrease prostaglandin and endoperoxide production and may be useful in treating metastatic bone pain if administered on a scheduled, as opposed to an "as needed" basis.[288–292] Usual analgesic doses of NSAIDs often are effective, but maximum therapeutic doses may be necessary.[293] Some specialists in treating cancer pain advocate doses considerably larger than the manufacturers' recommendations. Sometime intravenous ketorolac is used for this purpose.[294] In extremely painful cases, ketorolac has been used as a continuous infusion for managing metastatic bone pain.

Chronic Nonmalignant Pain

Goal of Therapy

45. W.C., a 38-year-old male, has been disabled for the past 2 years because of an injury to his cervical spine while operating a forklift at a warehouse. He is currently taking oxycodone 5 mg with acetaminophen 325 mg (Percocet) PO 2 tablets QID PRN severe pain, codeine 30 mg with acetaminophen 325 mg (Tylenol #3) or hydrocodone 5 mg with acetaminophen 325 mg (Lorcet-5) 2 tablets PO QID PRN less severe pain, and diazepam 10 mg PO TID for neck spasms. W.C. describes the pain as sharp and stabbing, and the spasms in his neck are his most troublesome problem. The spasms become extremely severe if he stops taking the diazepam, and the pain starts to build 2 hours after taking the opioids. W.C. currently is seeing an internist and an orthopedic surgeon who prescribed his analgesics. W.C. also has undergone several cervical discectomies and fusions with minimal pain relief. What are the treatment goals in W.C.?

Opioid use for chronic nonmalignant pain remains the most controversial issue facing clinical pain management. Not only is opioid efficacy subject to debate, but in addition the potential for opioid dependency creates considerable hesitation on the part of many prescribers.[295,296] There is some indication that neuropathic pain may respond to opioids, but at a much higher dose.[297] Overall, the data supporting opioid use in chronic nonmalignant pain are limited.[298,299] Opioid analgesics should be considered only after the patient has received and failed adequate trials of NSAIDs or other nonopioid agents. As with any chronic pain management, time contingent dosing (fixed dose and interval) is superior to as needed dosing. If an opioid is used to manage chronic pain, a longer-acting agent (e.g., SR morphine, methadone, or levorphanol) should be used to minimize fluctuations in serum concentrations. Patients should be monitored closely both for efficacy and toxicity.

Shorter-acting opioid analgesics often can complicate chronic nonmalignant pain management by exacerbating the pain perception because of fluctuating serum concentrations and the production of opioid withdrawal hyperalgesia when serum concentrations are low. Analogous withdrawal effects can occur with sedative-hypnotics and antispasmodics as well.

A written contract (including provisions for a single prescriber, for monitoring of serum drug concentrations, urine or blood substance abuse screening, agreement to inform all current and future healthcare providers regarding pain management, and termination of service) must be agreed upon between the primary caregiver and the patient before any therapeutic modality can be initiated. There should only be one prescriber for all of W.C.'s medications, and all of his healthcare providers have to be informed of the therapeutic plans. The immediate goal of pain management for W.C. is to consolidate his analgesic regimen to a time contingent longer acting opioid. Longer term goals should include withdrawal of both opioids and diazepam, while alternative analgesic adjuncts (antidepressants, antiarrhythmics, or α_2-agonists) are instituted. Psychological evaluation and support should supplement pharmacologic therapy. The overall therapeutic goal for W.C. is pain control and pain reduction, but not total pain elimination. He should be able to conduct activities of daily life with minimal discomfort, and ideally be able to return to work in some capacity.

Analgesic Consolidation

46. W.C. relates that he has been taking up to 18 tablets of various opioid analgesics daily. How should his pain be managed?

Chronic opiate use can lead to dependency as well as tolerance. The immediate need is to stabilize W.C.'s pain, but a longer term goal should include analgesic tapering and detoxification. However, this is not likely to be achieved quickly. W.C. should be started on an opiate tapering regimen after his pain is stabilized, and this process should occur within 24 hours after the analgesic dose has stabilized. The first step in opiate analgesic tapering is opiate consolidation. As in this case, the patient often is receiving several analgesics unnecessarily. A longer acting opioid analgesic should be used for W.C. to minimize the pain and analgesia fluctuations. One method is to add up his total opioid use per day during the last several weeks and then convert to an equivalent dose of either methadone or sustained-release morphine. Alternatively, an arbitrary dose such as oral methadone 5 mg every six hours could be started and all of his current analgesics could be discontinued. If this dose is insufficient, a temporary dosage increase may be necessary. The long half-life of methadone will be beneficial when instituting opioid tapering. Opioid taper should start as soon as pain control is achieved. Alternative analgesic adjuncts such as antidepressants also should be considered at this time. A second reason for consolidation in W.C. is to reduce his exposure to acetaminophen. He is currently taking three different acetaminophen containing products. While centered use of opioids leads to tolerance and a lack of adverse effects from the opioids, there is the risk of either short-term overdose or cumulative effects from acetaminophen leading to either liver or renal toxicity. W.C. should be instructed not to exceed 5 gm/day of acetaminophen from all sources.

Opioid Tapering and Withdrawal

47. How rapidly can you taper a patient such as W.C. off of opiate analgesics without precipitating withdrawal symptoms?

W.C. is going to need long-term multidisciplinary pain management. That includes behavior therapy as well as adjustment of his drug doses.[300] In most patients the opiate analgesics can be successfully tapered. It is not unusual to successfully reduce a hospitalized patient's acute pain opiate analgesic dose by 20% daily without precipitating opiate withdrawal symptoms; but in a patient such as W.C. who has been taking opiate analgesics for an extended period of time, tapering will have to be much slower. In chronic opiate dependence, tapering can be carried out at about 10% every three to five days without producing withdrawal symptoms. Addition of clonidine also can modify withdrawal symptoms, and improve the overall opioid tapering process.

Managing Opioid Overdose

48. W.C. accidentally received an excessive dose of methadone leading to a respiratory rate of 8 breaths/min and excessive sedation. How should he be managed?

Methadone accumulation can occur when converting from short-acting opioids unless careful attention is paid to the difference in pharmacokinetics between agents. Since methadone has a long half-life it may take two to three days before reaching steady state. In W.C., the challenge is to treat the toxicity without interfering with the desired analgesic effects or even precipitating narcotic withdrawal. Opioid toxicity is not life-threatening if it is attended to immediately. Naloxone will reverse opioid-induced CNS sedation and respiratory depression following overdose of all opiates except buprenorphine. W.C. should be given naloxone 0.1 mg parenterally at two to three minute intervals until the desired effect (improved respiration rate and increased alertness) is achieved. Because methadone has a long half-life, the naloxone dose may need to be repeated every 15 to 20 minutes, sometimes for several hours, until the methadone toxicity dissipates. Over aggressive naloxone dosing only causes the patient to become agitated and elicit enhanced pain responses. The methadone dose will have to be adjusted accordingly.

In the event of a massive overdose of opioid analgesics, naloxone can be given as a continuous infusion of 2.5 µg/kg/hour to 0.4 mg/hour. In light of the low incidence of side effects from naloxone, it might be reasonable to start with a loading dose of 0.8 mg and a higher infusion dose such as 0.4 mg/hour, followed by subsequent titration depending upon clinical response. The duration of naloxone infusion required will vary depending upon the specific opioid and the amount involved.[301-305]

Neuropathic Pain

49. R.L., a 40-year-old generally healthy female, suffered a superficial laceration of her left arm at work from a broken glass window. The initial laceration has since healed without complications, but now she is referred for evaluation of pain management because of persistent intolerable pain in her left arm and hand. Physical examination reveals allodynia (pain resulting from a non-noxious stimulus to normal skin) in her left hand and arm. What caused R.L.'s condition, and how would you manage her pain pharmacologically?

Hyperalgesia following a minor injury is well described, but the mechanism of such pain is not. In these afflicted patients there is a decrease in the pain threshold as well as an increased stimuli-response in the affected region. This persistent pain also may be associated with changes in regional cutaneous blood flow, osteoporosis, swelling, changes in regional temperature, and atrophic musculocutaneous changes in the affected region without demonstrable nerve injury. In the affected areas, pain is elicited by even the slightest mechanical or thermal stimuli. This painful hyperalgesic condition, known as causalgia or reflex sympathetic dystrophy, or sympathetically maintained pain (SMP), results from sympathetic excess. It also can be the result of other central or peripheral mechanisms that are independent of the sympathetic nervous system, referred to as sympathetically independent pain (SIP). SMP will respond to pharmacological agents that interfere with the α-adrenergic function and, therefore, one would expect it to respond to clonidine, prazosin, phenoxybenzamine, or guanethidine. SIP may respond to other classes of pharmacological agents such as steroidal and nonsteroidal anti-inflammatory agents, tricyclic antidepressants, anticonvulsants, or antiarrhythmics. Patients can have both SMP and SIP simultaneously. (See Mechanisms of Pain: Central Mechanism for Chronic Pain.)

α₂-Agonists

50. What doses of α₂-agonist will be required for pain management in R.L.?

α₂-agonists (e.g., clonidine) are useful in the management of sympathetically-mediated pain by reversing the excessive sympathetic adrenergic response at central and peripheral receptors. Clonidine has analgesic effects when administered either systemically or locally at the spinal level. The α₁-blocker, prazosin also has been used in the management of sympathetically maintained pain. The doses for clonidine and prazosin are 0.2 to 0.6 mg and 1 to 6 mg per day, respectively, in two to three equally divided doses. The major disadvantage of these agents is their side-effects, especially hypotension and exacerbation of depression.[306-311] Clonidine 0.1 mg orally four times daily would be a good starting dose for R.L., but the final dose must be titrated based upon the patient's clinical response or side effects.

Tricyclic Antidepressants (TCAs)

51. What is the rationale for using antidepressants to treat pain? What types of pain are most responsive? Is there any advantage of using one antidepressant over another for pain management in patients such as R.L.?

The analgesic properties of tricyclic antidepressants are independent of their antidepressant properties. However, depression frequently accompanies chronic pain, and in turn, depression often potentiates the patient's response to pain.[312,313] Thus, the antidepressant may help to break this cycle of events. The tricyclic antidepressants produce analgesia directly through modulation of the descending inhibitory nerve pathway by either altering serotonin or norepinephrine neurotransmission. Another secondary benefit of some TCAs is their sedative effect, which can aid the patient with sleep.

Antidepressants have been most widely studied in patients with diabetic neuropathy and post-herpetic neuralgia.[314,315] However, they also have shown some value in deafferentation pain (central pain resulting from loss of spinal afferent nerve pathway), phantom limb pain, human immunodeficiency virus (HIV) neuropathy,[316] postsurgical pain,[317,318] and chronic pain associated with depression. They also have limited usefulness in the management of lower back pain, radiation neuropathy, and direct malignant nerve infiltration.

Amitriptyline has the most available clinical data for the management of pain, but other tricyclic antidepressants also have been used for this purpose.[319-321] Data on the use of selective serotonin reuptake inhibitors such as fluoxetine, paroxetine, and sertraline are limited.[322] The major disadvantage of using TCAs is their sedative, anticholinergic, and cardiac (quinidine like effects; widening of QRS on ECG) side effects (also see Question 36). Sedation and anticholinergic effects are less with the secondary amine TCAs (desipramine, nortriptyline) than with the tertiary amine TCAs such as amitriptyline and doxepin. Weight gain can also sometimes be a limiting factor in the use of TCAs for pain.[323-327] In patients such as R.L. who do not have any cardiac history, a TCA can help in the management of pain. Controversy remains for the use of TCA in the elderly population.[328]

Mexiletine

52. What other alternatives are there for the management of R.L.'s neuropathic pain?

The reported use of antiarrhythmics in the management of neuropathic pain is primarily in the form of anecdotal reports or non-controlled trials. These drugs function primarily by stabilizing sodium channel based neuronal activation.[329,330] (See Mode of Analgesic Action.) Mexiletine has been used for diabetic neuropathy, HIV neuropathy, and other neuropathic pain syndromes.[331-335] The total daily dose is approximately 10 mg/kg in three to four equally divided doses. Other antiarrhythmics such as regional application of bretylium and tocainide have been tried, but clinical data are limited.[336]

Head Injury and Opioid Analgesia

53. M.C., a 24-year-old hemophiliac male, is admitted to the emergency room (ER) with several minor lacerations, contusions, and painful hemarthrosis secondary to a bicycle accident. Meperidine 50 mg IV was ordered and he was transferred to the medical ward for further evaluation. There, M.C. was given antihemophilic factor. He also was given meperidine 50–75 mg IV Q 3 hr PRN pain. What is the danger in administering opioid to M.C. in the ER or shortly after he was admitted?

Opioid analgesics generally are avoided in patients with head injury for the following reasons: a) opioid-induced pupillary changes, nausea, and general central nervous system clouding may mask or confuse the neurological evaluation; b) head injury potentiates the respiratory depressant effects of opioids; c) opioids induce carbon dioxide retention which in turn causes vasodilation of cerebral arteries and an increase in cerebrospinal fluid pressure which might already be elevated because of head injury;[337-339] d) opioids in excessive doses can mask internal organ injury; and e) morphine and meperidine can produce further hypotension in patients who have blood loss due to trauma. However, these potential complications should not preclude the use of a short-acting opioid such as fentanyl for pain control in emergency situations especially when the patient's clinical condition and analgesic responses are monitored closely. If fentanyl is to be used, small but frequent intravenous doses are preferred over single large boluses (see Table 7.3 for starting doses) for analgesia titration. The final dose is based upon the patient's analgesic and toxic responses. It would be reasonable to start M.C. on fentanyl 25 to 50 µg IV every 30 to 60 minutes followed by analgesic titration.

Myocardial Pain

54. C.P., a 65-year-old male with a history of angina pectoris, is brought to the ER with a suspected acute myocardial infarction. Pentazocine 45 mg IV is prescribed. Would another analgesic be preferred over pentazocine in C.P.?

This dose of pentazocine (Talwin) would be effective for analgesia;[340,350] however, pentazocine has several hemodynamic effects which increase myocardial workload and oxygen consumption.[341-344] Parenteral pentazocine doses of 30 to 60 mg increase mean arterial pressure, left ventricular end diastolic pressure, and, especially, pulmonary vascular pressure.[345] In one study, the pulmonary artery pressure rose from 17.5 to 23.1 mm Hg in ten acute myocardial infarction patients who received pentazocine.[346] Furthermore, pentazocine can produce idiosyncratic hypotensive episodes, which could be disastrous in these patients. Butorphanol (Stadol) can similarly increase pulmonary vascular resistance and pulmonary artery pressure.[347-349]

Morphine does not increase myocardial wall tension or oxygen consumption and does not affect cardiac dimensions. Morphine also can decrease heart rate and induces only minimal orthostatic changes in blood pressures. Sedative and emetic effects of morphine and pentazocine are comparable. Methadone, meperidine, hydromorphone, buprenorphine, and nalbuphine affect the cardiovascular system in a manner similar to morphine.[350-352]

In summary, although all of the above agents are effective analgesics;[353,354] pentazocine and butorphanol cause greater cardiovascular effects and can exacerbate an acute myocardial infarction by increasing the cardiac workload and oxygen consumption. Therefore, morphine remains the preferred agent. (See Chapter 14: Myocardial Infarction for further discussion.)

Colic Pain

Biliary Colic

55. B.C., a 42-year-old male, is admitted for severe, intermittent right upper quadrant pain accompanied by nausea, vomiting, and clay colored stools. The differential diagnosis is biliary colic versus acute pancreatitis. Two doses of meperidine 100 mg IM 3 hours apart fail to ease the pain. What other potent analgesics are preferred in this situation?

Opioid analgesics can induce smooth muscle spasms in the sphincter of Oddi and thereby increase intrabiliary pressures.[355-357] The resulting intraductal back pressure can aggravate pain symp-

toms, and increase the serum concentrations of amylase five to ten times above the control value.[358] Although it often is claimed that meperidine is less likely than morphine to cause spasm of the sphincter of Oddi, there is no clear evidence of superiority of one agent over the other.[364] Significant increases in intrabiliary pressures of patients receiving fentanyl (Sublimaze), morphine, meperidine, pentazocine (Talwin), butorphanol (Stadol), and oxycodone are documented.[359,360]

In one study,[361] buprenorphine (Buprenex) did not increase biliary pressure, but further controlled investigations are needed to substantiate this finding. Generally, biliary pressures increase and spasms begin within five minutes of parenteral opioid administration. These effects peak within 20 to 60 minutes, and values gradually return to normal over one to two hours.[362,363] Since the reported severity, intensity, and duration of the biliary hypertension vary greatly, it is unlikely that any agent presently available has a clear advantage over another.[364]

Opioid-induced biliary hypertension and sphincter of Oddi spasm can be reversed by parenteral glucagon or naloxone.[365-369] It is still unclear whether orally administered naloxone will have similar effects, although there is a study to show that orally administered naloxone can prevent opioid-induced constipation.[118,122] It is unclear if B.C. is having more pain because of an adverse drug effect or primary failure of meperidine. Since there is no consistent way to clinically measure intraductal pressure, it is recommended that he be given a longer acting opioid methadone 10 mg IM every six hours for pain.

Renal Colic

56. M.J., a 36-year-old female with a history of urolithiasis, comes to the ER because of severe flank pain along with microscopic hematuria. She is diagnosed with renal colic by the ER physician who wishes to treat her pain with meperidine 100 mg IM, but M.J. does not want to take opioids. What can you give to M.J. for her severe pain from her renal colic?

Renal colic is extremely painful, and patients often will require parenteral opioid analgesics. There is no significant clinical difference between any of the opioids for this type of acute analgesic indication. Since M.J. does not want to receive opioids the choice of analgesics is severely limited. The parenteral nonsteroidal analgesic ketorolac is likely to be the best alternative.[370,371] In the U.S. ketorolac is presently approved only for intramuscular and oral use. However, the parenteral ketorolac preparation can be used intravenously. Due to acute toxicity associated with peak serum drug levels, the intravenous dose is reduced to 15 mg, and the use of a large loading dose should be discouraged. It would be appropriate to start M.J. on ketorolac 30 mg IM every six hours as an alternative to the opioids for acute analgesia.

Liver Disease and Analgesia

57. A.A., a 54-year-old male with alcoholic cirrhosis, severe ascites, and mild jaundice, has been hospitalized with severe right upper quadrant abdominal pain. His stools are guaiac positive and he occasionally has bright red blood present at the rectum secondary to hemorrhoids. He was placed on oral lactulose 30 gm QID when the protein content of his diet was increased. Although he has a past history of hepatic encephalopathy, he is currently alert and receiving only spironolactone 200 mg/day and prophylactic lactulose. What problems can arise upon administration of opioid analgesics to patients such as A.A.?

Morphine can induce electroencephalogram (EEG) changes similar to those associated with impending hepatic encephalopathy when administered to patients with hepatic cirrhosis.[372] These morphine-induced EEG changes cannot be correlated with alkalosis, hypokalemia, or increased blood ammonia levels and the mechanism is unknown.

Since most opioid analgesics are significantly metabolized in the liver, their serum levels may accumulate if dosing intervals are not adjusted in patients with decreased hepatic function.[373–379] The oral bioavailability of some of the opioids also may be increased because of a decreased hepatic first-pass effect.[380] The opioids with the greatest first pass effect or a high extraction ratio will have the greatest variability in the bioavailability. For example, morphine and meperidine have a higher extraction ratio than methadone and, therefore, are more likely to produce unpredictable absorption results that can lead to either inadequate analgesia or opioid overdoses in severe liver disease patients. In these patients methadone will most likely give a more consistent absorption and clinical response when administered orally.

It would be reasonable to treat A.A.'s pain with a single modest dose of parenteral morphine, but subsequent doses should await the reappearance of signs of pain to prevent the possible precipitation of hepatic encephalopathy. Careful monitoring of A.A. is essential to minimize risk while maximizing analgesia. The clinician should remember that any central nervous system depressant may trigger significant problems in a patient such as A.A. If an oral opioid is to be used, then methadone will be a good choice due to its more consistent bioavailability. Although methadone has a long half-life, it is still safer to use orally than morphine. All opioid analgesics should be given in small frequent on demand doses in patients such as A.A. Time contingent dosing of opioids should be avoided in patients with liver disease because of the risk of drug accumulation. A.A. can be given methadone 2.5 mg no more often than every six hours as needed accompanied by close monitoring.

Respiratory Disease and Analgesia

58. C.T., a 65-year-old man admitted with a hip fracture, has a history of chronic obstructive airways disease (COAD). On admission, C.T. has a nonpurulent productive cough and wheezing. His past medical history includes several episodes of pneumonia. Morphine sulfate 6–10 mg IM Q 3 hr is ordered for his severe hip pain. What risks are associated with using morphine in C.T.? Are there better alternative potent analgesics?

Systemic opioids remain as the first-line agents in managing pain in COAD patients. However, careful monitoring orders also should be written along with the opioid orders. Morphine and all other opioid analgesics can depress respiration when given in therapeutic doses and should be used cautiously in patients with advanced respiratory disease and decreased respiratory function.[381] Respiratory rate, tidal volume, and sensitivity to hypercapnia or hypoxemia are all decreased by opioid analgesics.[382] Although all opioids and agonists produce respiratory depression at therapeutic doses, there appears to be a ceiling effect to the respiratory depression caused by butorphanol (Stadol), nalbuphine (Nubain), and buprenorphine (Buprenex) at higher doses.[383–385] Increased doses of these compounds do not further depress respiration and will still provide increased analgesia. The antagonist naloxone will reverse the respiratory difficulty (and analgesia) produced by nalbuphine and butorphanol. Although respiratory depression caused by buprenorphine is infrequent, it is not totally responsive to naloxone.[386] Ventilatory support is the only treatment.

Since C.T. is in severe pain, a lower dose of morphine should be used initially. Opioids do not always depress respiration when dosed correctly. In some instances opioids actually may improve respiratory function in patients who have recently undergone tho-

racotomy. These patients often are afraid to deeply breathe because of the pain elicited by such activity. The analgesic phenothiazine methotrimeprazine, nerve block or epidural anesthetic and opioids also can be used with less respiratory effects than systemic morphine.[387–389] Alternatively, morphine PCA should be considered for C.T., because PCA will allow him to self administer small frequent doses, and thereby reduce the possibility of opioid-induced respiratory effect.

Opioids in Special Age Groups
Advanced Age

59. B.V., a 75-year-old female, is in extreme pain due to severe osteoarthritis and osteoporotic vertebral disease. During an episode of acute back pain, a 6 mg IM dose of morphine gave her almost complete relief of the pain. What special considerations are necessary when administering opioid analgesics to aged patients?

Older patients often experience greater pain relief from opioid analgesics than younger patients. Both the extent of analgesia and the duration are enhanced in this group of patients.[390–395] Older patients achieve higher than expected plasma opioid levels (compared to younger patients) after intramuscular or intravenous administration.[396] Physiologic changes such as decreases in lean body mass, renal function, plasma proteins, hepatic blood flow, and hepatic metabolism[397,398] may be responsible for the enhanced activity of opioids in the aged.[399,400] Elderly patients are more sensitive to the opioids' constipating side-effects and, therefore, should be given stimulative laxatives along with the opioid analgesics. When opioid analgesic use is indicated in older patients a somewhat smaller dose (e.g., 4 to 6 mg IM or equivalent) should be used initially, and one should avoid dosing the aged patient on a time contingent or continuous regimen to avoid accidental overdoses. Starting opioid naive aged patients in acute pain with an on demand analgesic regimen is recommended.

Neonates and Children

60. M.M., a 6-month-old 10 kg female, is status postbowel surgery for congenital bowel atresia. What dose of opioid is recommended for M.M.?

Children appear to mature very early with respect to morphine metabolism. Children as young as five months old show very similar pharmacokinetic parameters as adults; however, morphine concentrations in patients younger than 2.4 months are five times higher than in older patients because of slower metabolic clearance and a lower central compartmental volume of distribution.[401] Therefore, the dosing of morphine in children should be similar to adults on a milligram per kilogram basis, but children younger than five months old may require less frequent dosing. Nonetheless, one should always titrate the individual patient when managing pain with analgesics. Since M.M. is six months old, a reasonable starting rectal morphine dose is 0.4 mg/kg as rectal suppositories or a total dose of 4 mg since she weighs 10 kg.

Morphine-Induced Nausea and Vomiting

61. J.J., a 48-year-old female, has advanced inoperable cervical cancer. The physician has ordered 30 mg of oral morphine solution Q 4 hr for pain, but she has vomited after each dose despite seemingly adequate doses of prochlorperazine. She is at home and does not wish to be institutionalized in order to receive parenteral analgesics. What can be done to relieve pain in J.J. who vomits after oral morphine?

Morphine and its derivatives induce nausea and vomiting by stimulation of the chemoreceptor trigger zone. Although the chemoreceptor trigger zone is stimulated initially, subsequent doses of morphine generally suppress the vomiting center. Because the incidence of nausea (40%) and vomiting (15%) increases in ambulatory patients, it generally is agreed that a vestibular component also is involved. If the vomiting is vestibular in origin, instructing J.J. to lie quietly, with as little head motion as possible for an hour or two, often will help. The nausea usually persists for 48 to 72 hours.[402,403]

Levorphanol (Levo-Dromoran) may cause less nausea and vomiting with equianalgesic doses than other potent opioid analgesics and might be an alternative to morphine if the above recommendations are ineffective in modifying J.J.'s nausea and vomiting. An equipotent dose of levorphanol for J.J. according to Table 7.2 would be 4 mg. The reported duration of action of levorphanol is six hours, longer than that of morphine.[404,405]

Adjunctive drugs such as droperidol, prochlorperazine, hydroxyzine, scopolamine, and diphenhydramine have been successfully used for controlling opioid-induced nausea and vomiting. Patients who are extremely sensitive to the opioid-induced nausea and vomiting may have to be placed on concurrent or scheduled antiemetics. Transdermal scopolamine can be used for this purpose.

Use of Central Nervous System Stimulants

62. D.H., a 34-year-old male, is diagnosed with acquired immunodeficiency syndrome and Karposi's sarcoma. He was discharged from the hospital with a prescription for oral morphine solution, 30 mg Q 3 hr. He has been relatively pain-free for about a month, but now returns to the clinic complaining of excessive morning sedation. He cannot reduce his morphine dose because the pain makes him too uncomfortable. What therapeutic intervention can be used to alleviate D.H.'s problem of excessive morning sedation?

Limited clinical data suggest that a morning dose of methylphenidate (Ritalin) or dextroamphetamine (Dexedrine) could relieve not only opioid-induced drowsiness, but also potentiate analgesia.[406] Less sleepiness has been associated with these combinations than with opioid analgesics alone, and a 10 mg dose of amphetamine combined with the opioid analgesic improved pain tolerance more than the analgesic alone in one study.[407,408] Although these studies involved only single doses, these agents should cause enough central nervous system stimulation to obviate morning drowsiness. D.H. should try a morning dextroamphetamine dose of 5 to 20 mg. A somewhat smaller dose may be added around noon if he desires increased alertness in the late afternoon and early evening hours. Another alternative will be to switch D.H. to a different opioid analgesic that is less sedating. Drugs such as hydromorphone, levorphanol, methadone, and fentanyl often will produce the desired clinical response in a patient like D.H.

Important Drug Interactions
Phenytoin and Methadone

63. B.D., a 32-year-old male, has an 18 year history of chronic pain in the right hip as a result of a motor vehicle accident. He has a long problem list that includes grand mal seizures and gastric ulcer disease. In the past he has been treated with a variety of opioid analgesics on a PRN that resulted in escalating drug requirements and a very complex regimen of multiple ingredient drugs (e.g., Percocet, Tylenol #3, and Vicodin). B.D.'s attending physician prescribed methadone 10 mg Q 6 hr several weeks ago. This switch was initially very successful, but B.D. now presents with symptoms suggestive of opioid withdrawal and poor pain control despite good compliance to his methadone regimen. A note in his chart indicates that B.D. saw a neurologist recently who started him on phenytoin therapy. What important drug-drug interactions might explain this rather complex case?

Phenytoin (Dilantin) increases the clearance of methadone, thereby decreasing serum concentrations of methadone and precipitating symptoms of withdrawal.[409] The methadone dose should be increased to 20 mg every six hours and a note should be made in the chart that the doses will need to be reduced if the phenytoin is discontinued for any reason. After raising his dose now, B.D. should be watched closely for the next several days for drug-induced drowsiness from serum level accumulation because of the long half-life of methadone.

Cimetidine and Methadone

64. One week later B.D.'s wife calls and says that he is very drowsy and his speech has started to slur. Upon further questioning, his wife states B.D. had restarted cimetidine 400 mg PO TID for symptoms of gastritis. She confirms that B.D. has been taking methadone 20 mg PO Q 6 hr. What may explain B.D.'s symptoms of apparent opioid toxicity?

Cimetidine (Tagamet) has been shown to decrease the metabolism of methadone, potentially subjecting patients to toxic levels of the methadone. B.D. also could be reaching serum methadone steady-state levels at this time. He should be instructed to withhold the methadone until his mental status returns to baseline, then the dose of methadone needs to be decreased to 10 mg every six hours. When adding cimetidine to existing methadone therapy, methadone doses need to be decreased; methadone should be increased again if cimetidine is subsequently withdrawn.[410]

Primary Dysmenorrhea

65. P.O., a 27-year-old female, is seen in the primary care clinic because of severe abdominal pain secondary to her menstrual periods. She reports having pain-free menstrual periods only once or twice yearly. She has been diagnosed as having primary dysmenorrhea with no other gynecological pathology being found. How should P.O.'s menstrual pain be treated?

Primary dysmenorrhea is a common gynecological disorder effecting 60% to 80% of women sometime in their life.[411,412] Pain usually occurs 2 to 12 hours before the commencement of menstrual flow, but it may occur simultaneously with, or a few hours after, the beginning of menstruation. Pain reaches a maximal intensity at 2 to 24 hours, then decreases over the next few days.[413,414] Primary dysmenorrhea is associated with increases in endometrial and circulatory prostaglandins.[415,416] Thus, the NSAIDs, which alter the production of the prostaglandins, are frequently used for the management of primary dysmenorrhea. The dosages required for the treatment of primary dysmenorrhea are usually higher than those used for analgesia, but frequently a single dose is sufficient to terminate the dysmenorrheic pain. On some occasions, frequent high doses may be required.

The most efficacious time for initiating an NSAID remains controversial. Some clinicians recommend beginning drug therapy a few days before the start of menses; others argue that the prostaglandins are not stored and, therefore, prefer to initiate drug therapy only after the start of menses. Pretreatment with NSAIDs may carry the risk of fetal drug exposure during early pregnancy. Studies comparing pretreatment versus dosing at the onset of menses show no difference in the analgesia by either of the regimens.[417,418] (Also see Chapter 46: Gynecological Disorders.) P.O. should be instructed to take 600 to 800 mg of ibuprofen at the onset of menses or when discomfort begins. Repeat doses of 400 to 600 mg may be taken every four to six hours as needed. If this regimen is ineffective, she can take the first dose one to two days before her expected first day of menses.

Headaches

66. M.K., a 32-year-old male, is complaining of severe headaches at least once every 2 weeks. He relates that he takes 2 Excedrin extra strength tablets (acetaminophen 250 mg, aspirin 250 mg, and caffeine 65 mg) Q 2 hr until the headache starts to ease, sometimes requiring a cumulative dose of up to 16 tablets. Migraine and vascular headaches have been ruled out in M.K. Would one of the nonsalicylate NSAIDs be more efficacious for M.K.? Are there any other considerations for the management of M.K.'s headache? Is caffeine an effective analgesic for headaches?

Headaches are common, afflicting nearly everyone at some time during their life. The incidence of headache is higher in females and increases with age; 10% of the headaches develop into chronic disabling conditions. For M.K. who self medicates chronically with large doses of acetaminophen, one must be concerned with toxicity from the analgesics. Chronic use of both NSAID analgesics and caffeine (either as single agents or in combination) can possibly precipitate withdrawal headaches upon discontinuation. Although NSAIDs are not considered to be habituating, there is accumulating evidence that chronic intake of peripheral acting analgesics may perpetuate the underlying pain syndrome. In the case of M.K., one must consider the possibility of caffeine withdrawal headache as well, since he is taking a caffeine containing combination product. He should be questioned about how much caffeine he is getting from coffee, tea, and other dietary sources. Caffeine is used in analgesic combination because it has both a CNS stimulative effect and a vasoconstrictive effect, which may reverse some of the headaches symptoms. It is controversial if caffeine, especially in the small quantities found in most pain relievers, is of any value. However, a meta-analysis and subsequent study conclude that caffeine does add to the analgesic effect of aspirin and acetaminophen.[430,431] Acute headache can be managed with parenteral ketorolac, but it is not a viable alternative for chronic headache management.[419] M.K.'s headaches may resolve upon gradual withdrawal of NSAID analgesics and caffeine, but this process is slow and requires the clinician's as well as the patient's determination to stay with the treatment plan. (Also see Chapter 50: Headache.)

Procedural Pain

67. C.T., a 26-year-old female, injured her left knee during a fall while skiing. After immobilizing her left knee and using ice therapy, most of her swelling has subsided. She is now seen in the outpatient surgical center for an arthroscopic evaluation of her knee. She is very concerned that the lidocaine used for anesthetizing her knee is going to produce pain, because she had a bad experience in the past with regional lidocaine injections. What can you recommend to reduce the pain associated with lidocaine infiltration?

Lidocaine injection is quite acidic, and can produce local pain during the infiltration procedure before the anesthetic effect takes place. This is a common complaint, so C.T.'s concerns should be taken seriously. The simple solution to reducing the local irritation from the injection is to neutralize the lidocaine injection solution by adding 1 mL of 1 mEq/mL sodium bicarbonate to 9 mL of 1% to 2% lidocaine before injecting C.T.[420-423]

Topical Anesthetics

68. J.G., a 6-year-old male, is being treated for osteomyelitis of his foot as a result of a skate boarding accident. Because of the requirement for long-term antibiotic therapy he requires occasional IV access replacement. He is very fearful of the procedure because of the associated pain. What can you do for J.G. to reduce his discomfort?

Insertion of a venous catheter often can produce significant discomfort and pain, but there is no reason why C.T. has to endure the pain. Topical lidocaine/prilocaine cream (EMLA) can provide good pain relief during catheter insertion as well as during minor surgical procedures such as circumcision and skin graft.[424-427] This topical cream must be applied 30 to 60 minutes before the procedure with an occlusive dressing; the anesthetic effect lasts approximately 60 to 120 minutes.[428] A smaller gauge catheter also may reduce the amount of pain associated with the venopuncture.[429]

References

1 **Heller PH et al.** Peripheral neural contributions to inflammation. Prog Pain Research Manage. IASP Press. 1994;1:31.

2 **Levine JD et al.** Contribution of sensory afferents and sympathetic efferents to joint injury in experimental arthritis. J Neurosci. 1983;6:3423.

3 **Price DP et al.** Central neural mechanisms of normal and abnormal pain state. Prog Pain Research Manage. IASP Press. 1994;1:61.

4 **Dickenson AH.** NMDA Receptor antagonists as analgesics. Prog Pain Research Manage. IASP Press. 1994;1:173.

5 **Woolf CJ.** A new strategy for the treatment of inflammatory pain. Prevention or elimination of central sensitization. Drugs. 1994;47:1.

6 **Jadad AR et al.** Morphine responsiveness of chronic pain: double-blind randomized crossover study with patient-controlled analgesia. Lancet. 1992;339:1367.

7 **Dickenson AH.** Where and how do opioids Act? Proceedings of the 7th world congress on pain. Prog Pain Research Manage. 1994;2:525.

8 **Max MB et al.** Effects of desipramine, amitriptyline, and fluoxetine on pain in diabetic neuropathy. N Engl J Med. 1992;326:1250.

9 **Tanelian DL, MacIver MB.** Analgesic concentrations of lidocaine suppress tonic A-delta and C fiber discharges produced by acute injury. Anesthesiology. 1991;74:934.

10 **Heller MB.** Emergency management of acute pain. New options and strategies. Postgrad Med. 1992;Aug 3:39.

11 **Miaskowski C.** Pain management: quality assurance and changing practice. Proceedings of the 7th world congress on pain. Prog Pain Research Manage. 1994;2:75.

12 **Somerville M.A.** Human rights and medicine: the relief of suffering. In: Cotler I, Eliadis PO, eds. International Human Rights Law: Theory and Practice, Canadian Human Rights Foundation. Montreal. 1992:505.

13 **Clinical Practice Guideline, Cancer Pain Management.** U.S. Department of Health and Human Services, Agency for Health Care Policy and Research. AHCPR Pub. Rockville, MD, 1994.

14 **Somerville MA.** Pain and suffering at the interfaces of medicine and law. University of Toronto Law Journal. 1992;36:286.

15 **Clinical Practice Guideline, Acute Pain Management.** U.S. Department of Health and Human Services, Agency for Health Care Policy and Research. AHCPR Pub. No. 92-0032. Rockville, MD, 1992.

16 **Krames ES.** Intrathecal infusional therapies for intractable pain: patient management guidelines. J Pain Symptom Manage. 1993;8:36.

17 **Skevington SM.** The relationship between pain and depression: a longitudinal study of early synovitis. Proceedings of the 7th world congress on pain. Prog Pain Research Manage. 1994;2:201.

18 **Keefe FJ, Lefebvre J.** Pain behavior concepts: controversies, current status, and future directions. Proceedings of the 7th world congress on pain. Prog Pain Research Manage. 1994;2:127.

19 **Guck TP et al.** Multidisciplinary pain center follow-up study: evaluation with a no treatment control group. Pain. 1985;21:295.

20 **Stieg RL et al.** Cost benefits of interdisciplinary chronic pain treatment. Clin J Pain. 1985;1:189.

21 **Portenoy RK.** Opioid therapy for chronic nonmalignant pain: current status. Prog Pain Research Manage. 1994;1:247.

22 **Weissman DE.** Doctors, opioids, and the law: the effect of controlled substances regulations on cancer pain management. Semin Oncol. 1993;20(2 Suppl. 1):53.

23 **Portenoy RK.** Cancer pain management. Semin Oncol. 1993;20(2 Suppl. 1):19.

24 **Hill CS Jr.** The barriers to adequate pain management with opioid analgesics. Semin Oncol. 1993;20(2 Suppl. 1):1.

25 **Ashburn MA, Lipman AG.** Management of pain in the cancer patient. Anesth Analg. 1993;76:402.

26 **Bushnell TG, Justins DM.** Choosing the right analgesic: a guide to selection. Drugs. 1993;46:394.

27 **McCaffery M.** Pain control. Barriers to the use of available information. World Health Organization Expert Committee on Cancer Pain Relief and

Active Supportive Care. Cancer. 1992; Sep 1, 70(5 Suppl.):1438.

28 Weis OF et al. Attitudes of patients, housestaff, and nurses toward postoperative analgesic care. Anesth Analg. 1983;62:70.

29 Foley KM. The treatment of cancer pain. N Engl J Med. 1985;313:84.

30 Mount BM et al. Use of the Brompton mixture in treating the chronic pain of malignant disease. Can Med Assoc J. 1976;115:122.

31 Ferguson RK, Mitchell CL. Pain as a factor in the development of tolerance to morphine analgesia in man. Clin Pharmacol Ther. 1969;10:372.

32 Claiborne R. A patient looks at pain and analgesia. Hosp Pract. 1982;17:21.

33 Donovan BD. Patient attitudes to postoperative pain relief. Anesth Intensive Care. 1983;11:125.

34 Hanks GW. Pain management in cancer patients. Therapie. 1992;47:489.

35 Lasagna L. Analgesic methodology: a brief history and commentary. J Clin Pharmacol. 1980;20(Pt. 2):373.

36 Twycross RG. Choice of strong analgesic in terminal cancer: diamorphine or morphine. Pain. 1977;3:93.

37 Beyer JE et al. Patterns of postoperative analgesic use with adults and children following cardiac surgery. Pain. 1983;17:71.

38 Kaiko RF et al. Narcotics in the elderly. Med Clin North Am. 1982;66:1079.

39 Kaiko RF et al. Sources of variation in analgesic responses in cancer patients with chronic pain receiving morphine. Pain. 1983;15:191.

40 Schechter NL et al. Status of pediatric pain control: a comparison of hospital analgesic usage in children and adults. Pediatrics. 1986;77:11.

41 Budd K. Chronic pain-challenge and response. Drugs. 1994;47(Suppl 1:33-8).

42 Kaiko RF. Age and morphine analgesia in cancer patients with post-operative pain. Clin Pharmacol Ther. 1980; 22:823.

43 Levine J et al. Relationship of duration of analgesia to opioid pharmacokinetic variables. Brain Res. 1983;289(1–2): 391.

44 Hammack JE, Loprinzi CL. Use of orally administered opioids for cancer-related pain. Mayo Clin Proc. 1994; 69384.

45 Davis T et al. Comparative morphine pharmacokinetics following sublingual, intramuscular, and oral administration in patients with cancer. Hospice. 1993;9:85.

46 Crews JC et al. Clinical efficacy of methadone in patients refractory to other mu-opioid receptor agonist analgesics for management of terminal cancer pain. Case presentations and discussion of incomplete cross-tolerance among opioid agonist analgesics. Cancer. 1993;72:2266.

47 Cooper SA. Comparative analgesic efficacies of aspirin and acetaminophen. Arch Intern Med. 1981;141:282.

48 Gruber CM Jr et al. A multicenter analgesic study using single doses of placebo, propoxyphene and acetaminophen. Am J Med. 1977;8:35.

49 Mehlisch DR. Review of the comparative analgesic efficacy of salicylates, acetaminophen, and pyrazolones. Am J Med. 1983;75(5A):47.

50 Quiding H et al. Paracetamol plus supplementary doses of codeine. An analgesic study of repeated doses. Eur J Clin Pharmacol. 1982;23:315.

51 Beaver WT. Combination analgesics. Am J Med. 1984;77(3A):38.

52 Miller RR. Propoxyphene: a review. Am J Hosp Pharm. 1977;34:413.

53 Beaver WT. Analgesic efficacy of dextropropoxyphene and dextropropoxyphene-containing combinations. a review. Hum Toxicol. 1984;3(Suppl.): 191S.

54 Collins GB, Kiefer KS. Propoxyphene dependence: an update. Postgrad Med. 1981;70:57.

55 Cooper SA et al. Comparative analgesic potency of aspirin and ibuprofen. J Oral Surg. 1977;35:898.

56 Winter L Jr et al. Analgesic activity of ibuprofen (Motrin) in postoperative oral surgical pain. Oral Surg Oral Med Oral Pathol. 1978;45:159.

57 Berry H et al. Antrafenine, naproxen and placebo in osteoarthritis: a comparative study. Br J Rheumatol. 1983; 22:89.

58 Honig S, Murray KA. An appraisal of codeine as an analgesic: single-dose analysis. J Clin Pharmacol. 1984;24: 96.

59 Beaver WT et al. A method for the 12-hour evaluation of analgesic efficacy in outpatients with postoperative oral surgery pain: three studies of diflunisal. Pharmacotherapy. 1983;3:23S.

60 Parkhouse J. Simple analgesics. Drugs. 1975;10(5–6):366.

61 Heidrich G et al. Efficacy and quality of ibuprofen and acetaminophen plus codeine analgesia. Pain. 1985;22:385.

62 Forbes JA et al. A 12-hour evaluation of the analgesic efficacy of diflunisal, acetaminophen, and acetaminophen-codeine combination, and placebo in postoperative pain. Pharmacotherapy. 1983;3:47S.

63 Laska EM, Sunshine A. Fenoprofen and codeine analgesia. Clin Pharmacol Ther. 1981;29:606.

64 Ruedy J. A comparison of the analgesic efficacy of naproxen and acetylsalicylic acid-codeine in patients with pain after dental surgery. Scand J Rheumatol. 1973;(Suppl. 2):60.

65 White P, Strunin L. Post-anaesthetic dental extraction analgesia: a comparison of paracetamol, codeine, caffeine (Solpadeine) and diflunisal (Dolobid). Br J Oral Surg. 1982;20:275.

66 Wallace LM. Surgical patients' expectations of pain and discomfort: does accuracy of expectations minimize postsurgical pain and distress? Pain. 1985; 21:363.

67 Seeff LB et al. Acetaminophen hepatotoxicity in alcoholics. A therapeutic misadventure. Ann Intern Med. 1986; 104:399.

68 Lewis JH. Hepatic toxicity of nonsteroidal anti-inflammatory drugs. Clin Pharm. 1984;3:128.

69 Beaver WT. Mild analgesics: a review of their clinical pharmacology, part I. Am J Med Sci. 1965;250:577.

70 Holt PR. Measurement of GI blood loss in subjects taking aspirin. J Lab Clin Med. 1960;56:717.

71 Hahn KJ et al. Morphology of gastrointestinal effects of aspirin. Clin Pharmacol Ther. 1975;17:330.

72 Lanza FL et al. Endoscopic evaluation of the effects of aspirin, buffered aspirin, and enteric coated aspirin on gastric and duodenal mucosa. N Engl J Med. 1980;303:136.

73 Leonards JR et al. Effect of pharmaceutical formulation on gastrointestinal bleeding from aspirin tablets. Arch Intern Med. 1972;129:457.

74 Beirne JA et al. Gastrointestinal blood loss cause by tolmetin, aspirin, and indomethacin. Clin Pharmacol Ther. 1974;16:821.

75 Leonards JR et al. Gastrointestinal blood loss during prolonged aspirin administration. N Engl J Med. 1973;289: 1020.

76 Leonards JR et al. Gastrointestinal blood loss from aspirin and sodium salicylate tablets in man. Clin Pharmacol Ther. 1973;14:62.

77 Silverstein FE et al. Upper gastrointestinal tract bleeding. Arch Intern Med. 1981;141:322.

78 Scott JT et al. Studies of GI bleeding caused by corticosteroids, salicylates, and other analgesics. Quart J Med. 1961;30:167.

79 Grossman MI et al. Fecal loss produced by oral and IV administration of various salicylates. Gastroenterology. 1961;40:383.

80 Holt PR. Measurement of GI blood loss in subjects taking aspirin. J Lab Clin Med. 1960;56:717.

81 Pierson RN et al. Aspirin and GI bleeding, chromate blood loss studies. Am J Med. 1961;31:259.

82 Farr CM. NSAID-induced ulcers and prophylaxis. A reappraisal [editorial]. J Clin Gastroenterol. 1993;17:187.

83 Stalnikowicz R, Rachmilewitz D. NSAID-induced gastroduodenal damage: is prevention needed? A review and meta-analysis. J Clin Gastroenterol. 1993;17:238.

84 Lanza FL. Gastrointestinal toxicity of newer NSAIDs. Am J Gastroenterol. 1993;88:1318.

85 Goulston K et al. Alcohol, aspirin and GI bleeding. Br Med J. 1968;4:664.

86 Silvoso GR et al. Incidence of gastric lesion in patient with rheumatic disease on chronic aspirin therapy. Ann Intern Med. 1979;91:517.

87 Smith BM et al. Permeability of the human gastric mucosa. Alteration by acetylsalicylic acid and ethanol. N Engl J Med. 1971;285:716.

88 Canada AT et al. The bioavailability of enteric-coated acetylsalicylic acid: a comparative study in rheumatoid arthritis, part I. Curr Ther Res Clin Exp. 1975;18:727.

89 Shambaugh Jr GE. Gastric bleeding and aspirin. JAMA. 1971;218:1573.

90 Marks RM et al. Undertreatment of medical inpatients with narcotic analgesics. Ann Intern Med. 1973;78:173.

91 Newcomb MD. Substance abuse and control in the United States: ethical and legal issues. Soc Sci Med. 1992;35:471.

92 Litvak KM, McEvoy GK. Ketorolac, an injectable nonnarcotic analgesic. Clin Pharm. 1990;9:921.

93 Resman-Targoff BH. Ketorolac: a parenteral nonsteroidal anti-inflammatory drug. DICP Ann Pharmacother. 1990;24:1098.

94 Buttram VC Jr et al. Naproxen sodium vs. a combination of aspirin, phenacetin, caffeine and codeine phosphate for pain after major gynecologic surgery. A multicenter comparison. J Reprod Med. 1984;29:189.

95 Dahl E et al. Acetylsalicylic acid compared with acetylsalicylic acid plus codeine as postoperative analgesics after removal of impacted mandibular third molars. Swed Dent J. 1985;9:207.

96 Nuutinen LS et al. A risk-benefit appraisal of injectable NSAIDs in the management of postoperative pain. Drug Saf. 1993;9:380.

97 Kerr CP. Eight underused prescriptions [see comments]. Am Fam Physician. 1994;50:1497.

98 Hallen H et al. The nasal reactivity in patients with nasal polyps. J Oto-Rhinlaryng. 1994;56:276.

99 Kowalski ML et al. Nasal secretions in response to acetylsalicylic acid. J Allergy Clin Immunol. 1993;91:580.

100 Muther RS et al. Aspirin-induced depression of glomerular filtration rate in normal humans: role of sodium balance. Ann Intern Med. 1981;94:317.

101 Schoch Ph et al. Acute renal failure in an elderly woman following intramuscular ketorolac administration. Ann Pharmacother. 1992;26:1233.

102 Pearce CJ et al. Renal failure and hyperkalemia associated with ketorolac tromethamine. Arch Intern Med. 1993; 153:1000.

103 Epstein M. Renal prostaglandins and the control of renal function in liver disease. Am J Med. 1986;80(Suppl. 1A):46.

104 Zipser RD, Henrich WL. Implication of nonsteroidal anti-inflammatory drug therapy. Am J Med. 1986;80(Suppl. 1A):78.

105 Brater DC. Drug-drug and drug-disease interactions with nonsteroidal anti-inflammatory drugs. Am J Med. 1986;80(Suppl. 1A):62.

106 Dunn MJ, Zambraski EJ. Renal effects of drugs that inhibit prostaglandin synthesis. Kidney Int. 1980;18:609.

107 Blackshear JL et al. NSAID-induced nephrotoxicity, avoidance, detection and treatment. Drug Ther Hosp. Nov. 1983:47.

108 Zipser RD et al. Prostaglandins: modulators of renal function and pressor resistance in chronic liver disease. J Clin Endocrinol Metab. 1979;48:895.

109 Donker AJ et al. The effect of indomethacin on kidney function and plasma renin activity in man. Nephron. 1976;17:288.

110 Speckart P et al. The effect of sodium restriction and prostaglandin inhibition on the renin-angiotensin system in man. J Clin Endocrinol Metab. 1977; 44:832.

111 Walsche JJ, Venuto RC. Acute oliguric renal failure induced by indomethacin. Possible mechanism. Ann Intern Med. 1979;91:47.

112 Favre L et al. Reversible renal failure from combined triamterene and indomethacin. Ann Intern Med. 1982;96: 317.

113 Stillman MT et al. Adverse effects of nonsteroidal anti-inflammatory drugs on the kidney. Med Clin North Am. 1982;68:371.

114 Finkelstein A et al. Fenoprofen ne-

phropathy: lipoid nephrosis and interstitial nephritis. A possible T-lymphocyte disorder. Am J Med. 1982;72:81.

115 **Doenicke A et al.** Histamine liberation and anaphylactic reaction after IV narcotics. Anaesthesist. 1970;19:413.

116 **Cromwell TA et al.** Hypersensitivity to intravenous morphine sulfate. Plast Reconstr Surg. 1974;54:224.

117 **Longo WE, Vernava AM 3rd.** Prokinetic agents for lower gastrointestinal motility disorders. Dis Colon Rectum. 1993;36:696.

118 **Culpepper-Morgan JA et al.** Treatment of opioid-induced constipation with oral naloxone: a pilot study. Clin Pharmacol Ther. 1992;52:90.

119 **Portoghese PS, Edward E.** Smissman-Bristol-Myers Squibb Award Address. The role of concepts in structure-activity relationship studies of opioid ligands. J Med Chem. 1992;35:1927.

120 **Bassotti G et al.** Extensive investigation on colonic motility with pharmacological testing is useful for selecting surgical options in patients with inertia colica. Am J Gastroenterol. 1992;87:143.

121 **Robinson BA et al.** Oral naloxone in opioid-associated constipation [letter; comment]. Lancet. 1991;338:581.

122 **Sykes NP.** Oral naloxone in opioid-associated constipation [letter] [see comments]. Lancet. 1991;15,337(8755):1475.

123 **Szeto HH et al.** Accumulation of normeperidine, an active metabolite of meperidine, in patients with renal failure or cancer. Ann Intern Med. 1977;86:738.

124 **Reidenberg MM.** A metabolite of meperidine that accumulates and causes central nervous system irritability. Hosp Pharm. 1978;13:339.

125 **Mather LE et al.** Meperidine kinetics in man. Intravenous injection in surgical patients and volunteers. Clin Pharmacol Ther. 1975;17:21.

126 **Pond SM et al.** Presystemic metabolism of meperidine to normeperidine in normal and cirrhotic subjects. Clin Pharmacol Ther. 1981;30:183.

127 **Kaiko RF et al.** Central nervous system excitatory effects of meperidine in cancer patients. Ann Neurol. 1983;13:2.

128 **Carrupt PA et al.** Morphine 6-glucuronide and morphine 3-glucuronide as molecular chameleons with unexpected lipophilicity. J Med Chem. 1991;34:1272.

129 **Fung DL et al.** A comparison of alphaprodine and meperidine pharmacokinetics. J Clin Pharmacol. 1980;20:37.

130 **Stambaugh JE et al.** The clinical pharmacology of meperidine-comparison of routes of administration. J Clin Pharmacol. 1976;16:245.

131 **Poniatowski BC.** Continuous subcutaneous infusions for pain control. J Intraven Nurs. 1991;14:30.

132 **Lang AH et al.** Treatment of severe cancer pain by continuous infusion of subcutaneous opioids. Recent Results Cancer Res. 1991;121:51.

133 **Swanson G et al.** Patient-controlled analgesia for chronic cancer pain in the ambulatory setting: a report of 117 patients. J Clin Oncol. 1989;7(12):1903.

134 **Bruera E et al.** Use of the subcutaneous route for the administration of narcotics in patients with cancer pain. Cancer. 1988;15;62:407.

135 **Marlowe S et al.** Epidural patient-controlled analgesia (PCA): an alternative to continuous epidural infusions. Pain. 1989;37:97.

136 **Gambling DR et al.** A comparative study of patient controlled epidural analgesia (PCEA) and continuous infusion epidural analgesia (CIEA) during labour. Can J Anaesth. 1988;35(3):249.

137 **Sawaki Y et al.** Patient and nurse evaluation of patient-controlled analgesia delivery systems for postoperative pain management. J Pain Symptom Manage. 1992;7:443.

138 **Shaffer HJ, LaSalvia TA.** Patterns of substance use among methadone maintenance patients. Indicators of outcome. J Subst Abuse Treat. 1992;9:143.

139 **Gossop M et al.** Severity of dependence and route of administration of heroin, cocaine and amphetamines. Br J Addict. 1992; 87:1527.

140 **Sunshine A.** New clinical experience with tramadol. Drugs. 1994;47(Suppl. 1):8–18.

141 **Kuhns JB 3d et al.** Substance use/misuse among female prostitutes and female arrestees. Int J Addict. 1992;27:1283.

142 **Portenoy RK, Kanner RM.** Patterns of analgesic prescription and consumption in a university-affiliated community hospital. Arch Intern Med. 1985;145:439.

143 **Hoffman M et al.** Pain management in the opioid-addicted patient with cancer. Cancer. 1991;68:1121.

144 **Unnithan S et al.** Factors associated with relapse among opiate addicts in an out-patient detoxification programme. Br J Psychiatry. 1992;161:654.

145 **Miller WR.** The effectiveness of treatment for substance abuse. Reasons for optimism. J Subst Abuse Treat. 1992;9:93.

146 **Pourciau T et al.** Changing trends in treatment of substance abuse: a look at some of the factors involved in third-party providers and treatment planning. J Louisiana Med Soc. 1992;144:321.

147 **Unnithan S et al.** Factors associated with relapse among opiate addicts in an out-patient detoxification programme. Br J Psychiatry. 1992;161:654.

148 **Kaminer Y et al.** Comparison between treatment completers and noncompleters among dually diagnosed substance-abusing adolescents. J Am Acad Child Adolesc Psychiatry. 1992;31:1046.

149 **Cohen J et al.** Problem drug use in a central London general practice. Br Med J. 1992;304:1158.

150 **Aronski A et al.** Remarks on continuous epidural analgesia as a method of controlling pain during labour. Anaesth Resusc Intensive Ther. 1973;1:349.

151 **Gal D et al.** Segmental epidural analgesia for labor and delivery. Acta Obstet Gynecol Scand. 1979;58:429.

152 **Carmichael FJ.** Epidural morphine for analgesia after caesarean section. Can Anaesth Soc J. 1982;29:359.

153 **Aronski A et al.** Remarks on continuous epidural analgesia as a method of controlling pain during labour. Anaesth Resusc Intensive Ther. 1973;1:349.

154 **Gal D et al.** Segmental epidural analgesia for labor and delivery. Acta Obstet Gynecol Scand. 1979;58:429.

155 **Rickford WJ, Reynolds F.** Epidural analgesia in labour and maternal posture. Anaesthesia. 1983;38:1169.

156 **Conacher ID et al.** Epidural analgesia following thoracic surgery. A review of two years' experience. Anaesthesia. 1983;38:546.

157 **Adu-Gyamfi Y et al.** High dose epidural morphine for surgical analgesia. Middle East J Anaesthesiol. 1985;8:165.

158 **Vella LM et al.** Epidural fentanyl in labour. An evaluation of the systemic contribution to analgesia. Anaesthesia. 1985;40:741.

159 **Bailey PW, Smith BE.** Continuous epidural infusion of fentanyl for postoperative analgesia. Anaesthesia. 1980; 35:1002.

160 **Mather LE.** Clinical pharmacokinetics of fentanyl and its newer derivatives. Clin Pharmacokinet. 1983;8:422.

161 **McClain DA, Hug CC Jr.** Intravenous fentanyl kinetics. Clin Pharmacol Ther. 1980;28:106.

162 **McClain DA, Hug CC Jr.** Pharmacodynamics of opiates. Int Anesthesiol Clin. 1984;22:75.

163 **Robertson K et al.** Epidural fentanyl, with and without epinephrine for post-Caesarean section analgesia. Can Anaesth Soc J. 1985;32:502.

164 **Cohen SE et al.** Respiratory effects of epidural sufentanil after Caesarean section. Anesth Analg. 1992;74:677.

165 **Budd K.** High dose buprenorphine for postoperative analgesia. Anaesthesia. 1981;36:900.

166 **Downing JW et al.** Buprenorphine: a new potent long-acting synthetic analgesic. Comparison with morphine. Br J Anaesth. 1977; 49:251.

167 **Heel RC et al.** Buprenorphine: a review of its pharmacological properties and therapeutic efficacy. Drugs. 1979; 17:81.

168 **Lanz E et al.** Epidural buprenorphine—a double-blind study of postoperative analgesia and side effects. Anesth Analg. 1984;63:593.

169 **Murphy DF et al.** Postoperative analgesia in hip surgery. A controlled comparison of epidural buprenorphine with intramuscular morphine. Anaesthesia. 1984;39:181.

170 **Haynes SR et al.** Comparison of epidural methadone with epidural diamorphine for analgesia following caesarean section. Acta Anaesthesiol Scand. 1993;37:375.

171 **Jacobson L et al.** Intrathecal methadone: a dose-response study and comparison with intrathecal morphine 0.5 mg. Pain. 1990;43:141.

172 **Krames ES.** Intrathecal infusional therapies for intractable pain: patient management guidelines. J Pain Symptom Manage. 1993;8:36.

173 **Uhde TW et al.** Clonidine suppresses the opioid abstinence syndrome without clonidine-withdrawal symptoms: a blind inpatient study. Psychiatry Res. 1980;2:37.

174 **Hoder EL et al.** Clonidine treatment of neonatal abstinence syndrome. Psychiatry Res. 1984;13:243.

175 **Fantozzi R et al.** Clonidine and naloxone-induced opiate withdrawal: a comparison between clonidine and morphine in man. Subst Alcohol Actions Misuse. 1980;1:369.

176 **Bond WS.** Psychiatric indications for clonidine: the neuropharmacologic and clinical basis. J Clin Psychopharmacol. 1986;6:81.

177 **Gold MS et al.** Opiate withdrawal using clonidine. A safe, effective and rapid non-opiate treatment. JAMA. 1980;243:343.

178 **Cami J et al.** Efficacy of clonidine and methadone in the rapid detoxification of patients dependent on heroin. Clin Pharmacol Ther. 1985;38:336.

179 **Charney DS et al.** The clinical use of clonidine in abrupt withdrawal from methadone. Arch Gen Psychiatry. 1982;38:1273.

180 **Gosse P et al.** Treatment of hypertension by a new transdermal form of clonidine. 1985;3(Suppl. 4):S65.

181 **Weber MA et al.** Transdermal administration of clonidine for treatment of high blood pressure. Arch Intern Med. 1984;144:1211.

182 **MacGregor TR et al.** Pharmacokinetics of transdermally delivered clonidine. Clin Pharmacol Ther. 1985;38:278.

183 **Arndts D, Arndts K.** Pharmacokinetics and pharmacodynamics of transdermally administered clonidine. Eur J Clin Pharmacol. 1984;26:78.

184 **Clark HW, Longmuir N.** Clonidine transdermal patches: a recovery oriented treatment of opiate withdrawal. Wesson DR et al., eds. Calif Society Treat Alcohol Other Drug Depend. News. 1986;13:1.

185 **Kanto J, Erkkola R.** Obstetric analgesia: pharmacokinetics and its relation to neonatal behavioral and adaptive functions. Biol Res Pregnancy Perinatol. 1984;5:23.

186 **Barrier G, Sureau C.** Effects of anaesthetic and analgesic drugs on labour, fetus and neonate. Clin Obstet Gynaecol. 1982;9:351.

187 **Nation RL.** Drug kinetics in childbirth. Clin Pharmacokinet. 1980;5:340.

188 **Mirkin BL.** Perinatal pharmacology: placental transfer, fetal localization, and neonatal disposition of drugs. Anesthesiology. 1975;43:156.

189 **McIntosh DG, Rayburn WF.** Patient-controlled analgesia in obstetrics and gynecology. Obstet Gynecol. 1991;78:1129.

190 **Jepson HA et al.** The Apgar score: evolution, limitations, and scoring guidelines. Birth. 1991;18:83.

191 **Bardy AH et al.** Objectively measured perinatal exposure to meperidine and benzodiazepines in Finland. Clin Pharmacol Ther. 1994;55:471.

192 **Nimmo WS et al.** Narcotic analgesics and delayed gastric emptying during labour. Lancet. 1975;1(7912):890.

193 **Refstad SO et al.** Ventilatory depressions of the newborn of women receiving pethidine or pentazocine. Br J Anaesth. 1980;52:265.

194 **Atkinson BD et al.** Double-blind comparison of intravenous butorphanol (Stadol) and fentanyl (Sublimaze) for analgesia during labor. Am J Obstet Gynecol. 1994;171:993.

195 **Mowat J et al.** Comparison of pentazocine and pethidine in labour. Br Med J. 1970;2:757.

196 **Clark RB, Seifen AB.** Systemic medication during, labor and delivery. Obstet Gynecol Annu. 1983;12:165.

197 **Isenor L, Penny-MacGillivray T.** Intravenous meperidine infusion for obstetric analgesia. J Obstet Gynecol Neonatal Nurs. 1993;22:349.

198 **Thorp JA et al.** The effect of intrapartum epidural analgesia on nulliparous labor: a randomized, controlled, prospective trial. Am J Obstet Gynecol. 1993;169:851.

199 **Rosaeg OP et al.** Maternal and fetal effects of intravenous patient-controlled fentanyl analgesia during labour in a thrombocytopenic patient. Can J Anaesth. 1992;39:277.

200 **Weiner PC.** Effects of naloxone on pethidine-induced neonatal depression. Part II—intramuscular naloxone. Br Med J. 1977;2:229.

201 **Martin WR.** Role of agonist-antagonist analgesics in medicine. Drug Alcohol Depend. 1985;14:221.

202 **Goldstein A.** Interactions of narcotic antagonists with receptor sites. Adv Biochem Psychopharmacol. 1973;8:471.

203 **Lipman AG.** Clinically relevant differences among the opioid analgesics. Am J Hosp Pharm. 1990;47(8 Suppl.):S7.

204 **Martin WR.** Opioid antagonists. Pharmacol Rev. 1967;19:463.

205 **Galloway FM et al.** Comparison of analgesia by intravenous butorphanol and meperidine in patients with post-operative pain. Can Anaesth Soc J. 1977;24:90.

206 **Ameer B, Salter FJ.** Drug therapy reviews: evaluation of butorphanol tartrate. Am J Hosp Pharm. 1979;36:1683.

207 **Beaver WT et al.** Analgesic effect of intramuscular and oral nalbuphine in postoperative pain. Clin Pharmacol Ther. 1981;29:174.

208 **Sprigge JS, Otton PE.** Nalbuphine versus meperidine for post-operative analgesia: a double-blind comparison using the patient controlled analgesic technique. Can Anaesth Soc J. 1983;30:517.

209 **Beaver WT, Feise GA.** A comparison of the analgesic effect of intramuscular nalbuphine and morphine in patients with post-operative pain. J Pharmacol Exp Ther. 1978;204:487.

210 **Errick JK, Heel RC.** Nalbuphine. A preliminary review of its pharmacological properties and therapeutic efficacy. Drugs. 1983;26:191.

211 **Forbes JA et al.** Nalbuphine, acetaminophen, and their combination in postoperative pain. Clin Pharmacol Ther. 1984;35:843.

212 **Okun R.** Analgesic effects of oral nalbuphine and codeine in patients with postoperative pain. Clin Pharmacol Ther. 1982;32:517.

213 **Delpizzo A.** Butorphanol, a new intravenous analgesic: double-blind comparison with morphine sulfate in postoperative patients with moderate or severe pain. Curr Ther Res. 1976;20:221.

214 **Lewis JR.** Evaluation of new analgesics. Butorphanol and nalbuphine. JAMA. 1980;243:1465.

215 **North WC, Tielens DR.** Comparison of butorphanol and pentazocine as postoperative analgesics. South Med J. 1979;72:578.

216 **Pallasch TJ, Gill CJ.** Butorphanol and nalbuphine: a pharmacologic compari-

son. Oral Surg Oral Med Oral Pathol. 1985;59:15.

217 **Tavakoli M et al.** Butorphanol and morphine: a double-blind comparison of their parenteral analgesic activity. Anesth Analg. 1976;55:394.

218 **Young RE.** Double-blind placebo controlled oral analgesic comparison of butorphanol and pentazocine in patients with moderate to severe post-operative pain. J Int Med Res. 1977;5:422.

219 **Portenoy RK et al.** Transdermal fentanyl for cancer pain. Repeated dose pharmacokinetics. Anesthesiology. 1993;78:36.

220 **Zech DF et al.** Transdermal fentanyl and initial dose-finding with patient-controlled analgesia in cancer pain. A pilot study with 20 terminally ill cancer patients. Pain. 1992;50:293.

221 **Payne R.** Transdermal fentanyl: suggested recommendations for clinical use. J Pain Symptom Manage. 1992;7(3 Suppl.):S40.

222 **Calis KA et al.** Transdermally administered fentanyl for pain management [see comments]. Clin Pharm. 1992;11:22.

223 **DeSio JM et al.** Intravenous abuse of transdermal fentanyl therapy in a chronic pain patient. Anesthesiology. 1993;79:1139.

224 **Rose PG et al.** Fentanyl transdermal system overdose secondary to cutaneous hyperthermia. Anesth Analg. 1993;77:390.

225 **Himmelsbach CK.** Studies of the addiction liability of Demerol. J Pharmacol Exper Ther. 1942;75:64.

226 **Cohen FL.** Postsurgical pain relief: patients' status and nurses' medication choices. Pain. 1980;9:265.

227 **Twycross RG et al.** Long-term use of morphine in advanced cancer. Adv Pain Res Ther. 1976;1:653.

228 **Clark HW.** Policy and medical-legal issues in the prescribing of controlled substances. J Psychoactive Drugs. 1991;23:321.

229 **Robins LN et al.** How permanent was Vietnam drug addiction. Am J Public Health. 1974;64:38.

230 **Newman RG.** The need to redefine "addiction". N Engl J Med. 1983;308:1096.

231 **Porter J, Jick H.** Addiction rare in patients treated with narcotics. N Engl J Med. 1980;302:123.

232 **Finn JW et al.** Placebo-blinded study of morphine sulfate sustained-release tablets and immediate-release morphine sulfate solution in outpatients with chronic pain due to advanced cancer. J Clin Oncol. 1993;11:967.

233 **Vater M et al.** Pharmacokinetics and analgesic effect of slow-release oral morphine sulfate in volunteers. Br J Anaesth. 1984;56:821.

234 **Westerling D et al.** Absorption and bioavailability of rectally administered morphine in women. Eur J Clin Pharmacol. 1982;23:59.

235 **Westerling D.** Rectally administered morphine: plasma concentration in children premedicated with morphine in hydrogel and in solution. Acta Anaesthesiol Scand. 1985;29:653.

236 **Beaver WT et al.** Comparisons of the analgesic effects of oral and intramuscular oxymorphone and of intramus-

cular oxymorphone and morphine in patients with cancer. J Clin Pharmacol. 1977;17:186.

237 **de Boer AG et al.** Rectal drug administration: clinical pharmacokinetic considerations. Clin Pharmacokinet. 1982;7:285.

238 **Beaver WT, Feise GA.** A comparison of the analgesic effect of oxymorphone by rectal suppository and intramuscular injection in patients with postoperative pain. J Clin Pharmacol. 1977;17:276.

239 **Babul N et al.** Pharmacokinetics of two novel rectal controlled-release morphine formulations. J Pain Symptom Manage. 1992;7:400.

240 **Kaiko RF et al.** The bioavailability of morphine in controlled-release 30-mg tablets per rectum compared with immediate-release 30-mg rectal suppositories and controlled-release 30-mg oral tablets. Pharmacother. 1992;12:107.

241 **Babul N, Darke AC.** Disposition of morphine and its glucuronide metabolites after oral and rectal administration: evidence of route specificity. Clin Pharmacol Ther. 1993;54:286.

242 **Wilkinson TJ et al.** Pharmacokinetics and efficacy of rectal versus oral sustained-release morphine in cancer patients. Cancer Chemother Pharmacol. 1992;31:251.

243 **Montgomery BJ.** Psychotropic agents finding analgesic use. JAMA. 1978;240:1225.

244 **Worz R.** Effects and risks of psychotropic and analgesic combinations. Am J Med. 1983;75:139.

245 **Baraldi M et al.** Antidepressants and opiates interactions: pharmacological and biochemical evidences. Pharmacol Res Commun. 1983;15:843.

246 **Lee RL, Spencer PS.** Effect of tricyclic antidepressants on analgesic activity in laboratory animals. Postgrad Med J. 1980;56(Suppl. 1):19.

247 **Feinmann C.** Pain relief by antidepressants: possible modes of action. Pain. 1985;23:1.

248 **Kocher R.** The use of psychotropic drugs in the treatment of chronic, severe pain. Eur Neurol. 1976;14:458.

249 **Ward NG et al.** The effectiveness of tricyclic antidepressants in the treatment of coexisting pain and depression. Pain. 1979;7:331.

250 **Morland TJ et al.** Doxepin in the prophylactic treatment of mixed 'vascular' and tension headache. Headache. 1979;19:382.

251 **Adler RH.** Psychotropic agents in the management of chronic pain. J Human Stress. 1978;4:15.

252 **Urban BJ et al.** Long-term use of narcotic/antidepressant medication in the management of phantom limb pain. Pain. 1986;24:191.

253 **Fainsinger R et al.** Methadone in the management of cancer pain: a review. Pain. 1993;52:137.

254 **Inturrisi CE, Verebely K.** Disposition of methadone in man after a single oral dose. Clin Pharmacol Ther. 1972;13:923.

255 **Nilsson MI et al.** Pharmacokinetics of methadone during maintenance treatment: adaptive changes during the induction phase. Eur J Clin Pharmacol. 1982;22:343.

256 **Ettinger DS et al.** Important clinical

considerations in the use of methadone in cancer patients. Cancer Treat Rep. 1979;63:457.

257 **Grabinski PY et al.** Plasma levels and analgesia following deltoid and gluteal injections of methadone and morphine. J Clin Pharmacol. 1983;23:48.

258 **Fainsinger R et al.** Methadone in the management of cancer pain: a review. Pain. 1993;52:137.

259 **Berkowitz BA.** The relationship of pharmacokinetics to pharmacological activity: morphine, methadone and naloxone. Clin Pharmacokinet. 1976;1:219.

260 **Symonds P.** Methadone and the elderly. Br Med J. 1977;1:512.

261 **Gourlay GK et al.** A comparative study of the efficacy and pharmacokinetics of oral methadone and morphine in the treatment of severe pain in patients with cancer. Pain. 1986;25:297.

262 **Moolenaar F et al.** Preliminary study on the absorption profile after rectal and oral administration of methadone in human volunteers. Pharm Weekbl [Sci]. 1984;6:237.

263 **Miser AW et al.** Continuous intravenous infusion of morphine sulfate for control of severe pain in children with terminal malignancy. J Pediatr. 1980;96:930.

264 **Bryan-Brown CW et al.** Decremental morphine infusion for postoperative pain. Crit Care Med. 1980;8:233.

265 **Church JJ.** Continuous narcotic infusions for relief of postoperative pain. Br Med J. 1979;1:977.

266 **Mount BM.** Narcotic analgesics in the treatment of pain of advanced malignant disease. In: Ajemin I, Mount BM, eds. The RVH Manual on Palliative/Hospice Care. New York: Arno Press; 1980;148.

267 **Weintraub M.** Potentiation of narcotic analgesics with central stimulant: the use of modified Brompton's mixture. Clinical Pharmacology Reports. 1976;5:9.

268 **Davis AJ.** Brompton's cocktail: making goodbyes possible. Am J Nurs. 1978;78:611.

269 **Melzack R et al.** The Brompton mixture: effects on pain in cancer patients. Can Med Assoc J. 1976;155:125.

270 **Melzack R et al.** The Brompton solution versus morphine solution given orally: effects on pain. Can Med Assoc J. 1979;120:435.

271 **Twycross RG.** Choice of a strong analgesic in terminal cancer: diamorphine or morphine? Pain. 1977;3:93.

272 **Inturrisi CE et al.** The pharmacokinetics of heroin in patients with chronic pain. N Engl J Med. 1984;310:1213.

273 **Kaiko RF, Foley KM.** Heroin: facts and comparisons. PRN Forum. 1985;4:1.

274 **Inturrisi CE et al.** Disposition and effects of heroin in pain patients. Adv. Pain Res & Ther. Vol 9. New York: Raven Press; 1985;709.

275 **Twycross RG.** Clinical experience with diamorphine in advanced malignant disease. Int J Clin Pharmacol. 1974;9:184.

276 **Way EL et al.** The biological disposition of morphine and its surrogates—1. Bull World Health Organ. 1961;25:227.

277 **Twycross RG.** The Brompton cocktail. Adv Pain Res Ther. 1979;2:291.

278 **Houde RW et al.** Clinical assessment of narcotic agonist-antagonist analgesics. In: Bonica JJ et al., eds. Advances in Pain Research and Therapy. New York: Raven Press; 1976:647.

279 **Houde RW.** Analgesic effectiveness of the narcotic agonist-antagonists. Br J Clin Pharmacol. 1979;7:297S.

280 **Moertel CG et al.** Relief of pain by oral medications. JAMA. 1974;229:55.

281 **Beaver WT, Feise G.** Comparison of the analgesic effects of morphine, hydroxyzine, and their combination in patients with postoperative pain. In: Bonica JJ et al., eds. Advances in Pain Research and Therapy. New York: Raven Press; 1976:553.

282 **Hupert C et al.** Effect of hydroxyzine on morphine analgesia for the treatment of postoperative pain. Anesth Analg. 1980;59:690.

283 **Stambaugh JE Jr, Lane C.** Analgesic efficacy and pharmacokinetic evaluation of meperidine and hydroxyzine, alone and in combination. Cancer Invest. 1983;1:111.

284 **Halpern LW.** Psychotropics, ataractics and related drugs. In: Bonica JJ, Ventafridda V, eds. Advances in Pain Research and Therapy. New York: Raven Press; 1979;2:275.

285 **Rumore MM, Schlichting DA.** Clinical efficacy of antihistaminics as analgesics. Pain. 1986;25:7.

286 **Rumore MM, Schlichting DA.** Analgesic effects of antihistaminics. Life Sci. 1985;36:403.

287 **Campa JA 3rd, Payne R.** The management of intractable bone pain: a clinician's perspective. Semin Nucl Medicine. 1992;22:3.

288 **Payne R.** Pharmacologic management of bone pain in the cancer patient. Clin J Pain. 1989;5(Suppl. 2):S43.

289 **Weingart WA et al.** Analgesia with oral narcotics and added ibuprofen in cancer patients. Clin Pharm. 1985;4:53.

290 **Koeller JM.** Understanding cancer pain. Am J Hosp Pharm. 1990;47(8 Suppl.):S3.

291 **Brereton HD et al.** Indomethacin-responsive hypercalcemia in a patient with renal-cell adenocarcinoma. N Engl J Med. 1974;291:83.

292 **Galasko CSB.** Mechanisms of bone destruction in the development of skeletal metastases. Nature. 1976;263:507.

293 **Kantor TG.** Control of pain by nonsteroidal anti-inflammatory drugs. Med Clin North Am. 1982;66:1053.

294 **Miller LJ, Kramer MA.** Pain management with intravenous ketorolac. Ann Pharmacother. 1993;27:307.

295 **Terman GW, Loeser JD.** A case of opiate-insensitive pain: malignant treatment of benign pain. Clin J Pain. 1992;8:255.

296 **Goldman B.** Use and abuse of opioid analgesics in chronic pain. Can Fam Physician. Medecin de Famille Canadien. 1993;39:571.

297 **Bowsher D.** Pain syndromes and their treatment. Curr Opin Neurol Neurosurg. 1993;6:257.

298 **Portenoy RK, Foley KM.** Chronic use of opioid analgesics in non-malignant pain: report of 38 cases. Pain. 1986;25:171.

299 **Schug SA et al.** Treatment principles for the use of opioids in pain of non-malignant origin. Drugs. 1991;42:228.

300 **Wells JC, Miles JB.** Pain clinics and pain clinic treatments. Br Med Bull. 1991;47:762.

301 **Romac DR.** Safety of prolonged, high-dose infusion of naloxone hydrochloride for severe methadone overdose. Clin Pharm. 1986;5:251.

302 **Lewis JM et al.** Continuous naloxone infusion in pediatric narcotic overdose. Am J Dis Child. 1984;138:944.

303 **Redfern N.** Dihydrocodeine overdose treated with naloxone infusion. Br Med J (Clin Res Ed). 1983;287(6394):751.

304 **Masoud PJ, Green CD.** Effects of massive overdose of epidural morphine sulphate. Can Anaesth Soc J. 1982;29:377.

305 **Bradberry JC, Raebel MA.** Continuous infusion of naloxone in the treatment of narcotic overdose. Drug Intell Clin Pharm. 1981;15:945.

306 **De Kock M et al.** Intravenous or epidural clonidine for intra- and postoperative analgesia. Anesthesiology. 1993;79:525.

307 **Quan DB et al.** Clonidine in pain management. Ann Pharmacother. 1993;27:313.

308 **Carabine UA et al.** Extradural clonidine infusions for analgesia after total hip replacement. Br J Anaesth. 1992;68:338.

309 **Rochford J et al.** Naloxone potentiation of novelty-induced hypoalgesia: characterization of the alpha-noradrenergic receptor subtype. Pharmacol Biochem Behav. 1993;44:381.

310 **Eisenach J et al.** Hemodynamic and analgesic actions of epidurally administered clonidine. Anesthesiology. 1993;78:277.

311 **Kayser V et al.** Potent antinociceptive effects of clonidine systemically administered in an experimental model of clinical pain, the arthritic rat. Brain Res. 1992;593:7.

312 **Sullivan MJ et al.** The treatment of depression in chronic low back pain: review and recommendations. Pain. 1992;50:5.

313 **Herr KA et al.** Depression and the experience of chronic back pain: a study of related variables and age differences. Clin J Pain. 1993;9:104.

314 **Gonzales GR.** Postherpes simplex type I neuralgia simulating postherpetic neuralgia. J Pain Symptom Manage. 1992;7:320.

315 **Max MB et al.** Effects of desipramine, amitriptyline, and fluoxetine on pain in diabetic neuropathy. N Engl J Med. 1992;326:1250.

316 **Penfold J, Clark AJ.** Pain syndromes in HIV infection. Can J Anaesth. 1992;39:724.

317 **Kerrick JM et al.** Low-dose amitriptyline as an adjunct to opioids for postoperative orthopedic pain: a placebo-controlled trial. Pain. 1993;52:325.

318 **Dillin W, Uppal GS.** Analysis of medications used in the treatment of cervical disk degeneration. Orthop Clin North Am. 1992;23:421.

319 **Richardson PH et al.** Meta-analysis of antidepressant-induced analgesia in chronic pain: comment [letter]. Pain. 1993;52:247.

320 **McQuay HJ et al.** Dose-response for analgesic effect of amitriptyline in chronic pain. Anaesthesia. 1993;48:281.

321 **Onghena P, Van Houdenhove B.** Antidepressant-induced analgesia in chronic non-malignant pain: a meta-analysis of 39 placebo-controlled studies. Pain. 1992;49:205.

322 **Max MB et al.** Effects of desipramine, amitriptyline, and fluoxetine on pain in diabetic neuropathy [see comments]. N Engl J Med. 1992;326:1250.

323 **Acton J et al.** Amitriptyline produces analgesia in the formalin pain test. Exp Neurol. 1992;117:94.

324 **Magni G.** The use of antidepressants in the treatment of chronic pain. A review of the current evidence. Drugs. 1991;42:730.

325 **Sullivan MJ et al.** The treatment of depression in chronic low back pain: review and recommendations. Pain. 1992;50:5.

326 **Max MB et al.** Effects of desipramine, amitriptyline, and fluoxetine on pain in diabetic neuropathy [see comments]. N Engl J Med. 1992;326:1250.

327 **Panerai AE et al.** Antidepressants in cancer pain. J Palliat Care. 1991;7:42.

328 **Conn DK, Goldman Z.** Pattern of use of antidepressants in long-term care facilities for the elderly. J Geriatr Psychiatry Neurol. 1992;5:228.

329 **Tanelian DL, Brose WG.** Neuropathic pain can be relieved by drugs that are use-dependent sodium channel blockers: lidocaine, carbamazepine, and mexiletine. Anesthesiology. 1991;74:949.

330 **Welch SP, Dunlow LD.** Antinociceptive activity of intrathecally administered potassium channel openers and opioid agonists: a common mechanism of action? J Pharmacol Exp Ther. 1993;267:390.

331 **Pfeifer MA et al.** A highly successful and novel model for treatment of chronic painful diabetic peripheral neuropathy. Diabetes Care. 1993;16:1103.

332 **Stracke H et al.** Mexiletine in the treatment of diabetic neuropathy. Diabetes Care. 1992;15:1550.

333 **Chabal C et al.** The use of oral mexiletine for the treatment of pain after peripheral nerve injury. Anesthesiology. 1992;76:513.

334 **Awerbuch GI, Sandyk R.** Mexiletine for thalamic pain syndrome. Int J Neurosci. 1990;55:129.

335 **Davis RW.** Successful treatment for phantom pain. Orthopedics. 1993;16:691.

336 **Hord AH et al.** Intravenous regional bretylium and lidocaine for treatment of reflex sympathetic dystrophy: a randomized, double-blind study. Anesth Analg. 1992;74:818.

337 **Smith AL, Wollman H.** Cerebral blood flow and metabolism: effects of anesthetic drugs and techniques. Anesthesiology. 1972;36:378.

338 **Sperry RJ et al.** Fentanyl and sufentanil increase intracranial pressure in head trauma patients. Anesthesiology. 1992;77:416.

339 **Albanese J et al.** Sufentanil increases intracranial pressure in patients with head trauma. Anesthesiology. 1993;79:493.

340 **Grossman JA et al.** A clinical trial of pentazocine analgesia in acute myocardial infarction and acute coronary insufficiency. Curr Ther Res Clin Exp. 1971;13:505.

341 **Jewitt DE et al.** Increase pulmonary arterial pressures after pentazocine in myocardial infarction. Br Med J. 1970;1:795.

342 **Jewitt DE et al.** Cardiovascular effects of pentazocine in patients with acute myocardial infarction. Br Heart J. 1971;33:145.

343 **Miller HC et al.** Effect of pentazocine on pulmonary circulation. Lancet. 1972;2:1167.

344 **Scott ME et al.** Circulatory effects of IV pentazocine in patients with acute myocardial infarction. Curr Ther Res. 1971;13:81.

345 **Mitaka C et al.** Comparison of hemodynamic effects of morphine, butorphanol, buprenorphine and pentazocine on ICU patients. Bull Tokyo Med Dent Univ. 1985;32:31.

346 **Lee G et al.** Comparative effects of morphine, meperidine and pentazocine on circulatory dynamics in patients with acute myocardial infarction. Am J Med. 1976;60:949.

347 **Popio KA et al.** Hemodynamic and respiratory effects of morphine and butorphanol. Clin Pharmacol Ther. 1978;23:281.

348 **Vandam LD.** Drug therapy: butorphanol. N Engl J Med. 1980;302:381.

349 **Ameer B, Salter FJ.** Drug therapy reviews: evaluation of butorphanol tartrate. Am J Hosp Pharm. 1979;36:1683.

350 **Zola EM, McLeod DC.** Comparative effects and analgesic efficacy of the agonist-antagonist opioids. Drug Intell Clin Pharm. 1983;17:411.

351 **Rosenfeldt FL et al.** Haemodynamic effects of buprenorphine after heart surgery. Br Med J. 1978;2:1602.

352 **Scott DH et al.** Haemodynamic changes following buprenorphine and morphine. Anaesthesia. 1980;35:957.

353 **Laffey DA, Kay NH.** Premedication with butorphanol. A comparison with morphine. Br J Anaesth. 1984;56:363.

354 **Aldrete JA et al.** Comparison of butorphanol and morphine as analgesics for coronary bypass surgery: a double-blind, randomized study. Anesth Analg. 1983;62:78.

355 **Gaensler EA et al.** A comparative study of the action of demerol and opium alkaloids in relation to biliary spasm. Surgery. 1948;23:211.

356 **Levy MH.** Pain management in advanced cancer. Semin Oncol. 1985;12:394.

357 **Radnay PA et al.** The effect of equianalgesic doses of fentanyl, morphine, piperidine and pentazocine on common bile duct pressure. Anaesthesist. 1980;29:26.

358 **Nossell HL.** The effect of morphine on the serum and urine amylase and the sphincter of Oddi. Gastroenterology. 1955;29:409.

359 **Radnay PA et al.** Common bile duct pressure changes after fentanyl, morphine, meperidine, butorphanol, and naloxone. Anesth Analg. 1984;63:441.

360 **Radnay PA et al.** The effect of equianalgesic doses of fentanyl, morphine, meperidine and pentazocine on common bile duct pressure. Anaesthesist. 1980;29:26.

361 **Staritz M et al.** Effect of modern an-

algesic drugs (tramadol, pentazocine, and buprenorphine) on the bile duct sphincter in man. Gut. 1986;27:567.

362 **Economou G et al.** A cross-over comparison of the effect of morphine, pethidine, pentazocine and phenazocine on biliary pressure. Gut. 1971;12:216.

363 **Hopton DS et al.** Action of various new analgesic drugs on the human common bile duct. Gut. 1967;8:296.

364 **Chisholm RJ et al.** Narcotics and spasm of the sphincter of Oddi. A retrospective study of operative cholangiograms. Anaesthesia. 1983;38:689.

365 **McCammon RL et al.** Reversal of fentanyl induced spasm of the sphincter of Oddi. Surg Gynecol Obstet. 1983;156:329.

366 **McCammon RL et al.** Naloxone reversal of choledochoduodenal sphincter spasm associated with narcotic administration. Anesthesiology. 1978;48: 437.

367 **Takahashi T et al.** Pathogenesis of acute cholecystitis after gastrectomy. Br J Surg. 1990;77:536.

368 **Jones RM et al.** Narcotic-induced choledochoduodenal sphincter spasm reversed by glucagon. Anesth Analg. 1980;59:946.

369 **McLean ER Jr et al.** Cholangiographic demonstration of relief of narcotic-induced spasm of the sphincter of Oddi. Am Surg. 1982;48:134.

370 **Larsen LS et al.** The use of intravenous ketorolac for the treatment of renal colic in the emergency department. Am J Emerg Med. 1993;11:197.

371 **Oosterlinck W et al.** A double-blind single dose comparison of intramuscular ketorolac tromethamine and pethidine in the treatment of renal colic. J Clin Pharmacol. 1990;30:336.

372 **Jackson GL et al.** Analgesic properties of mixtures of chlorpromazine with morphine and meperidine. Ann Intern Med. 1956;45:640.

373 **Hoyampa AM Jr et al.** The disposition and effects of sedatives and analgesics in liver disease. Annu Rev Med. 1978;29:205.

374 **Klotz U et al.** The effect of cirrhosis on the disposition and elimination of meperidine in man. Clin Pharmacol Ther. 1974;16:667.

375 **McHorse TS et al.** Effect of acute viral hepatitis in man on the disposition and elimination of meperidine. Gastroenterology. 1975;68:775.

376 **Neal EA et al.** Enhanced bioavailability and decreased clearance of analgesics in patients with cirrhosis. Gastroenterology. 1979;77:96.

377 **Pond SM et al.** Bioavailability and clearance of meperidine in patients with chronic liver disease. Clin Pharmacol Ther. 1979;25:242.

378 **Barre J et al.** Disease-induced modifications of drug pharmacokinetics. Int J Clin Pharmacol Res. 1983;3:215.

379 **Roberts RK et al.** Drug prescribing in hepatobiliary disease. Drugs. 1979;17: 198.

380 **Pond SM et al.** Enhanced bioavailability of pethidine and pentazocine in patients with cirrhosis of the liver. Aust N Z J Med. 1980;10:515.

381 **Catley DM.** Postoperative analgesia and respiratory control. Int Anesthesiol Clin. 1984;22:95.

382 **Lehmann KA et al.** CO_2-response curves as a measure of opiate-induced respiratory depression. Studies with fentanyl. Anaesthesist. 1983;32:242.

383 **Gal TJ et al.** Analgesic and respiratory depressant activity of nalbuphine: a comparison with morphine. Anesthesiology. 1982;57:367.

384 **Harcus AW et al.** Buprenorphine: experience in an elderly population of 975 patients during a year's monitored release. Br J Clin Pract. 1980;34:144.

385 **Nagashima H et al.** Respiratory and circulatory effects of intravenous butorphanol and morphine. Clin Pharmacol Ther. 1976;19:738.

386 **Heel RC et al.** Buprenorphine: a review of its pharmacological properties and therapeutic efficacy. Drugs. 1979; 17:81.

387 **Bailey CJ et al.** Epidural morphine infusion. Continuous pain relief. AORN J. 1984;39:997.

388 **Staren ED, Cullen ML.** Epidural catheter analgesia for the management of postoperative pain. Surg Gynecol Obstet. 1986;162:389.

389 **Jones SF, White A.** Analgesia following femoral neck surgery. Lateral cutaneous nerve block as an alternative to narcotics in the elderly. Anaesthesia. 1985;40:682.

390 **Faherty BS, Grier MR.** Analgesic medication for elderly people post-surgery. Nurs Res. 1984;33:369.

391 **Wall RT 3rd.** Use of analgesics in the elderly. Clin Geriatr Med. 1990;6:345.

392 **Gerbino PP.** Complications of alcohol use combined with drug therapy in the elderly. J Am Geriatr Soc. 1982;30(11 Suppl.):S88.

393 **Sengstaken EA, King SA.** The problems of pain and its detection among geriatric nursing home residents. J Am Geriatr Soc. 1993;41:541.

394 **Yaster M et al.** The pharmacologic management of pain in children. Compr Ther. 1989;15:14.

395 **Patterson KL.** Pain in the pediatric oncology patient. J Pediatr Oncol Nurs. 1992;9:119.

396 **Waldman SD.** Acute and post-operative pain. Management from a primary care perspective. Postgrad Med. 1992; Aug 3:5.

397 **Cohen JL.** Pharmacokinetic changes in aging. Am J Med. 1986;80:31.

398 **Ouslander JG.** Drug therapy in the elderly. Ann Intern Med. 1981;95:711.

399 **McCaffery M.** Narcotic analgesia for the elderly. Am J Nurs. 1985;85: 296,298.

400 **Harkins SW et al.** Pain and the elderly. Adv in Pain Res and Ther. New York: Raven Press; 1984;7:103.

401 **Olkkola KT et al.** Kinetics and dynamics of postoperative intravenous morphine in children. Clin Pharmacol Ther. 1988;44:128.

402 **Anonymous.** Narcotic analgesics—II. Adverse effects. Br Med J. 1970;2:587.

403 **Gutner LB et al.** The effects of potent analgesics upon vestibular function. J Clin Invest. 1952;31:259.

404 **Dixon R et al.** Levorphanol: pharmacokinetics and steady-state plasma concentrations in patients with pain. Res Commun Chem Pathol Pharmacol. 1983;41:3.

405 **Dixon R et al.** Levorphanol: radioimmunoassay and plasma concentration profiles in dog and man. Res Commun Chem Pathol Pharmacol. 1980;29:535.

406 **Forrest WH et al.** Dextroamphetamine with morphine for the treatment of postoperative pain. N Engl J Med. 1977;296:712.

407 **Twycross RG et al.** Long-term use of morphine in advanced cancer. Adv Pain Res Ther. 1976;1:653.

408 **Webb SS et al.** Toward the development of a potent, nonsedating, oral analgesic. Psychopharmacol. 1978;60:25.

409 **Tong TG et al.** Phenytoin-induced methadone withdrawal. Ann Intern Med. 1981;94:349.

410 **Sorkin EM, Ogawa GS.** Cimetidine potentiation of narcotic action. Drug Intell Clin Pharm. 1983;17:60.

411 **Caufriez A.** Menstrual disorders in adolescence: pathophysiology and treatment. Hormone Research. 1991;36 (3–4):156–59.

412 **Dangfelder JR.** Primary dysmenorrhea treatment with prostaglandin inhibitors: a review. Am J Obstet Gynecol. 1981;140:874.

413 **Mackinnon GL, Partker WA.** Current concepts—the management of primary dysmenorrhea. Can Pharm J. 1982;1150:3.

414 **Dandenell L et al.** Clinical experience of naproxen in the treatment of primary dysmenorrhea. Acta Obstet Gynecol Scand. 1979;87(Suppl.):95.

415 **Morrison JC, Jenning S.** Primary dysmenorrhea treated with indomethacin. South Med J. 1979;72:425.

416 **Anderson ABM et al.** Trial of prostaglandin-synthetase inhibitors in primary dysmenorrhea. Lancet. 1978;1: 345.

417 **Mehlisch DR.** Double-blind crossover comparison of ketoprofen, naproxen, and placebo in patients with primary dysmenorrhea. Clinical Therapeutics. 1990;12(5):398–409.

418 **Shapiro SS, Diem K.** The effect of ibuprofen in the treatment of dysmenorrhea. Curr Ther Res Clin Exp. 1981; 30:327.

419 **Harden RN et al.** Ketorolac in acute headache management. Headache. 1991;31:463.

420 **Roberts JE et al.** Improved peribulbar anaesthesia with alkalinization and hyaluronidase. Can J Anaesth. 1993;40: 835.

421 **Lugo-Janer G et al.** Less painful alternatives for local anesthesia. J Dermatol Surg Oncol. 1993;19:237.

422 **Benzon HT et al.** Onset, intensity of blockade and somatosensory evoked potential changes of the lumbosacral dermatomes after epidural anesthesia with alkalinized lidocaine. Anesth Analg. 1993;76:328.

423 **Smith SL et al.** The importance of bicarbonate in large volume anesthetic preparations. Revisiting the tumescent formula. J Dermatol Surg Oncol. 1992; 18:973.

424 **Benini F et al.** Topical anesthesia during circumcision in newborn infants. JAMA. 1993;270:850.

425 **Kaddour HS.** Myringoplasty under local anaesthesia: day case surgery. Clin Otolaryngol. 1992;17:567.

426 **Holm J et al.** Pain control in the surgical debridement of leg ulcers by the use of a topical lidocaine-prilocaine cream, EMLA. Acta Derm Venereol Suppl (Stockh). 1990;70:132.

427 **Buckley MM, Benfield P.** Eutectic lidocaine/prilocaine cream. A review of the topical anaesthetic/analgesic efficacy of a eutectic mixture of local anaesthetics (EMLA). Drugs. 1993;46: 126.

428 **Farrington E.** Lidocaine 2.5%/prilocaine 2.5% EMLA cream. Pediatr Nurs. 1993;19:484–86, 488.

429 **Gershon RY et al.** Intradermal anesthesia and comparison of intravenous catheter gauge. Anesth Analg. 1991; 73:469.

430 **Laska E et al.** Caffeine as an analgesic adjuvant. JAMA. 1984;251:1711.

431 **Migliardi J et al.** Caffeine as an analgesic adjuvant in tension headache. Clin Pharmacal Ther. 1994;56:576.

432 **Dayer P et al.** The pharmacology of tramadol. Drugs. 1994;47(Suppl 1:3-7).

433 **Lee CR et al.** Tramadol: a preliminary review of its pharmacodynamic and pharmacokinetic properties, and therapeutic potential in acute and chronic pain states. Drugs. 1993;46:313-40.

Chapter 8

Perioperative Care

Andrew J Donnelly
Amy L Shafer

Preoperative Medications (See Table 8.1) 8-2
  Medication Classes 8-2
  Goals of Premedication 8-2
  Selection Criteria 8-2
  Timing and Routes of Administration 8-2
  Drug Interactions 8-2
  Aspiration Pneumonitis Prophylaxis 8-4
    Definition 8-4
    Risk factors (Also see Questions 1 and 3) 8-4
    Agents 8-5
      Antacids 8-5
      Gastric motility stimulants 8-5
      H_2-receptor antagonists 8-5
      Omeprazole 8-5
    Choice of agent 8-5
Intravenous (IV) Anesthetic Agents 8-5
  General Anesthesia 8-5
  Characteristics of IV Anesthetic Agents
  (See Table 8.2) 8-6
  Uses of IV Anesthetic Agents (See Table 8.3) 8-6
  Mechanisms of Action 8-6
  Pharmacokinetics (See Table 8.4) 8-6
  Adverse and Beneficial Effects (See Table 8.5) 8-6
  Propofol Use in Ambulatory Surgery: Antiemetic
  Effect and Full Recovery Characteristics 8-7
  Etomidate Use in Cardiovascular Disease 8-7
    Safety profile 8-7
    Myoclonus 8-7
  Ketamine Use in Pediatrics 8-8
Neuromuscular Blocking Agents 8-8
  Uses 8-8
  Mechanism of Action 8-8
  Monitoring Neuromuscular Blockade 8-8
  Classification (See Table 8.6) 8-8
  Adverse Effects (See Table 8.7) 8-9
  Drug Interactions 8-9
  Reversal of Neuromuscular Blockade 8-9
  Pharmacokinetics and Pharmacodynamics
  (See Table 8.8) 8-9
    Depolarizing agent contraindications 8-10
  Routes of Elimination (See Table 8.9) 8-10
Local Anesthetics 8-11
  Local and Regional Anesthesia 8-11
  Uses of Local Anesthetic Agents (See Table 8.10) ... 8-11
  Mechanism of Action 8-11
  Allergic Reactions 8-12
  Physicochemical Properties Affecting Action
  (See Table 8.11) 8-12
  Regional Anesthesia in High-Risk Patients 8-12
  Topical Cocaine 8-13
  Alkalinization of Local Anesthetics 8-13
Cardioplegia Solution 8-13

Use in Cardiac Surgery 8-13
Delivery Methods 8-13
Phases of Cardioplegia 8-13
Goal of Treatment 8-14
Cardioplegia Solution Vehicles (See Table 8.12) 8-14
Common Characteristics 8-14
Additives (See Table 8.13) 8-14
  Calcium channel blockers 8-14
  Oxygen free radical scavengers 8-14
  Amino acids 8-14
    Warm, blood-based cardioplegia solution 8-15
  Adenosine 8-15
  Potassium 8-15
**Antiemetic Agents and Postoperative Nausea
and Vomiting** 8-16
  Incidence of Postoperative Nausea and Vomiting 8-16
  Causes of Postoperative Nausea and Vomiting and
  Mechanism of Action of Antiemetic Agents
  (See Table 8.14) 8-16
  Factors, Complications, and Patient Groups Associated
  with Postoperative Vomiting (See Table 8.15) 8-16
  Choice of Agent (Also see Question 19) 8-16
    Butyrophenones 8-16
    Benzamides 8-17
    Antiserotonin 8-17
    Phenothiazines 8-17
    Antihistamines 8-17
    Anticholinergics 8-17
    Miscellaneous agents 8-18
  Anesthetic Agents with Low Incidence
  of Postoperative Nausea and Vomiting 8-18
**Analgesic Agents and Postoperative Pain
Management** 8-19
  Acute Pain 8-19
  Management Options 8-19
    Patient-controlled analgesia (PCA) 8-19
      Advantages 8-19
      Patient selection 8-19
      Patient instructions 8-19
      Choice of agent 8-19
        Dosing (see Table 8.16) 8-19
      Use of basal infusion 8-20
      Adverse effects 8-20
    Epidural Analgesia 8-20
      Advantages and disadvantages 8-20
      Patient selection 8-20
      Choice of agent and mechanisms of actions 8-20
        Dosing (See Table 8.17) 8-20
        Pharmacokinetics (See Table 8.18) 8-21
      Adverse effects 8-21
      Adjunctive ketorolac use 8-21

The operating room (OR) is one of the most medication-intensive settings in a hospital. A patient, during the perioperative period (broadly defined to include the pre-, intra-, and postoperative periods), may receive a wide variety of medications. Many of these medications are used primarily in the OR setting and have limited use elsewhere in the institution. For those medications employed elsewhere, their use in the OR often may differ from that seen in other patient care areas. Further, the operating room is unique in that a significant number of the medications are administered as single doses. In order to ensure continuity of care of the surgical patient, health care practitioners from all settings (e.g., acute care, home health care, extended care) should have a basic understanding of perioperative drug therapy.

This chapter reviews six major classes of medications used during the perioperative period: preoperative medications, intravenous (IV) anesthetic agents, neuromuscular blocking agents, local anesthetics, antiemetic agents, and analgesic agents. In addition, cardioplegia solution is discussed.

Preoperative Medications

Medication Classes

Administration of preoperative medications (premedicants) to patients can be thought of as the start of their operative course. Many different medications are used preoperatively and can be grouped into the following classes: benzodiazepines, barbiturates, opioids, anticholinergics, dissociative anesthetics, antihistamines, antiemetics, gastric motility stimulants, H_2-receptor antagonists, antacids, and α_2-agonists.

A key point concerning preoperative medication is that not all patients will require premedicants. Patients should be assessed on an individual basis as to their need for these agents; if required, premedicants should be selected based upon patient-specific needs. Administration of a standard preoperative regimen to all patients should be avoided.

Goals of Premedication

A major goal of premedication is to decrease the patient's anxiety about his upcoming surgery. A preoperative visit by the anesthesiologist has been shown to help decrease the patient's anxiety and reduce the need for premedication.[1,2] In addition to reducing anxiety, premedication is used for a variety of other reasons. Medications can be used before surgery to produce sedation, provide analgesia, produce amnesia, ease anesthetic induction, reduce anesthetic requirements, prevent autonomic effects, decrease salivation and secretions, reduce the risk factors for aspiration pneumonitis, and/or prevent or minimize allergic reactions.[3] Table 8.1 lists medications commonly used preoperatively, their major indications, routes of administration, and dosages.[3–17]

Selection Criteria

Factors to consider when selecting a preoperative drug for a patient include his American Society of Anesthesiologists (ASA) physical status class, medical conditions, degree of anxiety, age, surgical procedure to be performed, length and type of procedure (e.g., inpatient versus outpatient), drug allergies, previous experience with medications, and concurrent drug therapy. The ASA physical status classification system classifies patients as I through V. ASA-I patients are healthy with little medical risk while ASA-V patients have little chance of survival. Severe systemic disorders (e.g., uncontrolled diabetes mellitus, coronary artery disease) are present in ASA-III through ASA-V patients. Selection of preoperative medications in this group of patients will be more difficult. These patients generally have limited physiologic reserve and ad-

ministration of depressant agents may be harmful. Further, these patients will be taking a significant number of medications; hence, chances for drug interactions are increased. The patient's other medical conditions are important to consider to prevent the administration of contraindicated medications. For example, the barbiturates are contraindicated in patients with porphyria.[3] A patient's age will play a role in the response seen with premedicant administration. The elderly often are more sensitive to preoperative opioids and the central nervous system (CNS) effects of anticholinergic agents.[3,13] Being familiar with the surgery to be performed will aid in selecting appropriate premedicants. In surgical cases where painful procedures (e.g., line insertion) will be performed on the patient when arriving to the OR suite, for example, an analgesic premedicant may be warranted. The length and type of the procedure is important to consider when selecting premedicants. For example, emergency surgery patients routinely are administered nonparticulate antacids and H_2-receptor antagonists as they are predisposed to aspiration of gastric contents.[3] Likewise, in short-duration, outpatient surgery, agents with a long duration of action should be avoided as residual effects may prolong discharge time. Certain agents should not be administered to patients because of drug allergies. It is important, however, to differentiate between true allergies and adverse reactions resulting from administration of premedicants. Patients often state allergies to opioids, for example, after having experienced nausea and vomiting which is a common adverse reaction of these agents. A patient's previous experience with premedicants can assist in agent selection. If an agent has caused trouble in the past, it should be avoided. Finally, it is important to review the patient's current drug therapy before selecting an agent to prevent potentially harmful drug interactions.

Timing and Routes of Administration

Almost as important as the choice of the agent is its timing and route of administration. For optimal results, the agent's peak effects should occur before the patient arrives in the operating room suite. This will require the agent to be administered at varying times before surgery depending upon the route of administration chosen. Preoperative agents are administered by several routes: IV, intramuscular (IM), oral (PO), rectal (PR), intranasal (IN), oral transmucosal (OTM), and sublingual (SL). As a general rule, agents administered by the IV route produce the fastest onset of action and often are given after the patient arrives in the OR, while medications administered via the intramuscular route usually are administered 30 to 60 minutes before the patient arrives in the OR. Onset of peak effect is the slowest with oral administration of agents; oral medications should be administered 60 to 90 minutes before the patient's scheduled arrival in the OR.[3]

Drug Interactions

Preoperative medications can interact with each other as well as with drugs the patient is receiving currently or will receive in the OR. These drug interactions may be advantageous and intentionally produced or problematic. A potentially serious interaction occurs when meperidine is administered to patients receiving a monoamine-oxidase inhibitor. Central nervous system excitation, hyperpyrexia, and exaggerated depression of ventilation may be seen, with deaths having occurred.[3] The α_2-agonists, on the other hand, can reduce the anesthetic requirements for inhalational anesthetics and opioids.[17] Preoperative administration of ketamine, opioids, and benzodiazepines also may reduce the concentration of inhaled anesthetic required for anesthesia.[3] And finally, hydroxyzine commonly is administered with opioids for its proposed ad-

Table 8.1	Indications, Routes of Administration and Doses[a] of Preoperative Agents[3-17]		
Agent	Indications	Routes of Administration	Doses[b,c]
Benzodiazepines			
Diazepam (Valium)	Anxiolysis, amnesia, sedation	Oral	*Adults:* 5–20 mg; *Peds:* 0.1–0.5 mg/kg
		IV	*Adults:* 2–20 mg (titrate dose); *Peds:* 0.1–0.2 mg/kg
		PR	*Peds:* 0.1–0.75 mg/kg; (max: 20 mg)
Lorazepam (Ativan)	Anxiolysis, amnesia, sedation	Oral	0.025–0.05 mg/kg (range: 1–4 mg for adults)
		IV	*Adults:* 0.025–0.04 mg/kg; *Peds:* 0.03–0.05 mg/kg
Midazolam (Versed)	Anxiolysis, amnesia, sedation	Oral	*Adults:* 15 mg; *Peds:* 0.08–0.75 mg/kg
		IM	*Adults:* 0.05–0.1 mg/kg; *Peds:* 0.08–0.3 mg/kg
		IV	*Adults:* 1–2.5 mg (titrate dose); *Peds:* 0.1–0.15 mg/kg
		PR	*Peds:* 0.3–1 mg/kg
		IN	*Peds:* 0.2–0.3 mg/kg
		SL	*Peds:* 0.2–0.4 mg/kg
Temazepam (Restoril)	Anxiolysis, amnesia, sedation	Oral	*Adults:* 15–30 mg
Triazolam (Halcion)	Anxiolysis, amnesia, sedation	Oral	*Adults:* 0.25–0.5 mg
Barbiturates[d]			
Pentobarbital (Nembutal) & Secobarbital (Seconal)[e]	Anxiolysis, amnesia, sedation	Oral	*Adults:* 50–200 mg; *Peds:* 2–3 mg/kg
		IM	*Adults:* 50–200 mg; *Peds:* 3–5 mg/kg
		PR	*Peds:* 2–4 mg/kg
Methohexital (Brevital)	Anxiolysis, amnesia, sedation	PR[f]	*Peds:* 20–30 mg/kg
Opioids			
Morphine	Analgesia, anxiolysis, sedation	IM	*Adults:* 5–10 mg; *Peds:* 0.1–0.2 mg/kg
		IV	Titrate dose
Meperidine (Demerol)	Analgesia, anxiolysis, sedation	IM	*Adults:* 50–150 mg; *Peds:* 1–2 mg/kg
		IV	Titrate dose
Fentanyl (Sublimaze)	Analgesia, anxiolysis, sedation	IV	*Adults:* 1–2 µg/kg
		OTM[g]	*Adults:* 400 µg ($\geq$50 kg); 2.5–5 µg/kg (>65 years old); *Peds:* 5–15 µg/kg
Sufentanil (Sufenta)	Analgesia, anxiolysis, sedation	IN[h]	*Peds:* 1.5–3 µg/kg
Anticholinergics			
Atropine (A)	Antisialagogue (S>G>A), sedation (S>A)	Oral	*Peds:* 0.02 mg/kg
		IM/IV	*Adults:* 0.3–1 mg; *Peds:* 0.02 mg/kg IM, 0.01 mg/kg IV
Scopolamine (S)	Amnesia, antisialagogue, sedation	IM/IV	*Adults:* 0.2–0.3 mg; *Peds:* 0.02 mg/kg IM, 0.01 mg/kg IV
Glycopyrrolate (G) (Robinul)	Antisialagogue	IM/IV	*Adults:* 0.1–0.3 mg; *Peds:* 0.01 mg/kg
Dissociative Anesthetics			
Ketamine (Ketalar)	Amnesia, analgesia, sedation	Oral	*Peds:* 6 mg/kg
		IM	*Adults:* 2–5 mg/kg; *Peds:* 2–5 mg/kg
		IV	*Adults:* 0.5–1 mg/kg
		PR	*Peds:* 3 mg/kg
		IN	*Peds:* 3 mg/kg
Antihistamines			
Hydroxyzine (Vistaril, Atarax)	Sedation	Oral	*Adults:* 50–100 mg; *Peds:* 0.5–1 mg/kg
		IM	*Adults:* 25–100 mg; *Peds:* 0.5–1 mg/kg
Antiemetics			
Droperidol (Inapsine)	Antiemetic	IV	*Adults:* 0.625–1.25 mg; *Peds:* 0.01–0.02 mg/kg
Ondansetron (Zofran)	Antiemetic	IV	*Adults:* 1–4 mg; *Peds:* 0.05 mg/kg (max 4 mg)
Gastric Motility Stimulants			
Metoclopramide (Reglan)	Reduce gastric volume, antiemetic	Oral	*Adults:* 10 mg; *Peds:* 0.1 mg/kg
		IV	*Adults:* 0.1–0.2 mg/kg (10–20 mg); *Peds:* 0.1 mg/kg
Cisapride (Propulsid)	Reduce gastric volume	Oral	*Adults:* 10 mg

Continued

Table 8.1		Indications, Routes of Administration and Doses[a] of Preoperative Agents[3–17] (Continued)	
Agent	Indications	Routes of Administration	Doses[b,c]
H₂-Receptor Antagonists			
Cimetidine (Tagamet)	↑ gastric pH	Oral	*Adults:* 300 mg; *Peds:* 7.5 mg/kg
		IV	*Adults:* 300 mg; *Peds:* 7.5 mg/kg
Ranitidine (Zantac)	↑ gastric pH	Oral	*Adults:* 150 mg; *Peds:* 2 mg/kg
		IV	*Adults:* 50 mg; *Peds:* 0.5–1 mg/kg
Famotidine (Pepcid)	↑ gastric pH	Oral	*Adults:* 40 mg; *Peds:* 0.5–0.6 mg/kg
		IV	*Adults:* 20 mg; *Peds:* 0.3–0.4 mg/kg
Nizatidine (Axid)	↑ gastric pH	Oral	*Adults:* 150 mg
Nonparticulate Antacids			
Sodium citrate (Citra pH)	↑ gastric pH	Oral	*Adults:* 30 mL
Sodium citrate/citric acid (Bicitra)	↑ gastric pH	Oral	*Adults:* 30 mL
Sodium bicarbonate/ citric acid/potassium bicarbonate (Alka-Seltzer)	↑ gastric pH	Oral	*Adults:* 2 tabs dissolved in minimal fluid
Alpha₂-Agonists			
Clonidine (Catapres)	Anxiolysis, potentiate action of anesthetic agents, sedation	Oral	0.005 mg/kg
Dexmedetomidine[i]	Anxiolysis, potentiate action of anesthetic agents, sedation	IM	0.001 mg/kg
		IV	0.0003–0.0006 mg/kg

[a] General dosage guidelines; doses must be individualized based upon patient specific parameters.

[b] Doses listed are for agents when used as sole premedicant; doses may need to be reduced if premedicants are administered in combination (e.g., opioids and benzodiazepines).

[c] IM = Intramuscular; IN = Intranasal; IV = Intravenous; OTM = Oral transmucosal; PR = Rectal; SL = Sublingual.

[d] Benzodiazepines have largely replaced barbiturates for use as premedication.

[e] Paradoxical responses (e.g., agitation, disorientation) may be seen in children.

[f] Premedication/induction dose which allows child to fall asleep in parent's arms; anesthesiologist should be present and resuscitative/suction equipment available.

[g] Risk of hypoventilation with its use; anesthesiologist should be present and resuscitative/suction equipment available; indicated when an opioid analgesic effect beyond sedation is indicated.

[h] High incidence of apnea and laryngospasm associated with use (close monitoring by anesthesiologist required), should be reserved for patients who receive endotracheal anesthesia, produces less reliable sedation than intranasal midazolam.

[i] Not commercially available.

ditive effect (e.g., greater degree of analgesia and sedation) with these agents.[18]

Aspiration Pneumonitis Prophylaxis

Definition

Aspiration pneumonitis is a potentially fatal condition which occurs as a result of regurgitation and aspiration of gastric contents. It has been estimated to occur in 1 out of 2131 anesthetics.[19] This condition can result in damage to the alveolar and capillary endothelium and progress to adult respiratory distress syndrome.[19] The acidity and volume of the gastric contents appear to influence the morbidity seen if aspiration occurs. A gastric pH less than 2.5 and gastric volume greater than 25 mL (0.4 mL/kg) traditionally have been accepted as the cutoff values which place the patient at greater risk for severe pneumonitis should aspiration occur. However, more recent work has suggested that these values should be changed to a gastric pH less than 3.5 and volume greater than 50 mL; pH appears to be a greater determinant of morbidity than volume.[20]

Risk Factors

Patient risk factors for aspiration include increased gastric volume, increased abdominal pressure, an incompetent lower esophageal sphincter, delayed gastric emptying, and an abnormal airway. Conditions that may result in delayed gastric emptying include obesity, pregnancy, diabetes, peptic ulcer disease, stress, pain, and trauma.[3,21] Narcotic administration also can result in delayed gastric emptying. Obese patients, in addition to having delayed gastric emptying, often will present with increased abdominal pressure and an abnormal airway, both factors predisposing to aspiration. Administration of benzodiazepines, anticholinergics, opioids, thiopental, halothane, nitroprusside, and dopamine may result in a lower esophageal sphincter pressure. Elderly patients have a higher incidence of aspiration, possibly secondary to decreased esophageal sphincter pressure and/or impaired airway reflexes. Pediatric patients tend to have gastric pHs less than 2.5 and high residual gastric volumes. Hormonal changes in pregnant patients account for the delayed gastric emptying as well as relaxation of the lower esophageal sphincter. An increase in intra-abdominal pressure also is seen in pregnant patients. Labor may increase gastrin levels increasing gastric volume and acidity as well as delay gastric emptying. Emergency surgery is associated with an increased incidence of aspiration.[21] Patients undergoing emergency surgery frequently have full stomachs as they have not had time to fast appropriately. In early studies, ambulatory surgery patients had a greater gastric volume (similar gastric acidity) than inpatients secondary to increased anxiety; however, later studies did not note differences in gastric volume or acidity between these groups.[21] As a general rule, patients with the following conditions should routinely be administered an agent to reduce the risk of pneumonitis should aspiration occur: trauma, pregnancy, Type I diabetes, obesity, and history of gastroesophageal reflux. In addition, patients at the extremes of age, those undergoing emergency surgery, and those in whom airway management or intubation is anticipated to be difficult should be administered an agent to reduce the risk of pneumonitis should aspiration occur.

Agents

A variety of medications are used to reduce the risk of pneumonitis should aspiration occur and can be grouped into the following categories: antacids, gastric motility stimulants, and H_2-receptor antagonists. These agents, for the most part, are relatively free of adverse effects and have a favorable risk-benefit profile.

Antacids are quite effective in raising gastric pH above 2.5.[3,22] They should be given as a single dose (30 mL) approximately 15 to 30 minutes before induction of anesthesia. Nonparticulate antacids [e.g., sodium citrate (Citra pH), sodium citrate/citric acid (Bicitra), sodium bicarbonate/citric acid/potassium bicarbonate effervescent tablets (Alka-Seltzer)] are the agents of choice; the suspension particles in particulate antacids can act as foci for an inflammatory reaction if aspirated.[23] Antacids have two major advantages when used for aspiration pneumonitis prophylaxis: there is no "lag time" with regard to onset of activity, and antacids are effective on the fluid already in the stomach. Their major disadvantages are that their effect may not last as long as the surgical procedure and their administration adds fluid volume to the stomach.[24]

Gastric Motility Stimulants. The gastric motility stimulants, metoclopramide (Reglan) and cisapride (Propulsid), have no effects on gastric pH or acid secretion. These agents are used to reduce gastric volume in predisposed patients (e.g., parturients, obese patients) by promoting gastric emptying.[15,16,25] These agents should be given 60 minutes before induction of anesthesia when administered orally; when given by the IV route, metoclopramide should be administered 15 to 30 minutes before induction. Cisapride is available only for oral administration. It differs from metoclopramide in that it has no antidopaminergic actions and should not produce extrapyramidal reactions. Variable effects have been seen with the gastric motility stimulants; gastric emptying is not always seen after their administration, especially when used with other agents. The concomitant administration of atropine or prior administration of opioids, for example, can offset the effects of these agents on the upper gastrointestinal (GI) tract.[26,27]

H_2-receptor antagonists reduce gastric acidity and volume by inhibition of gastric secretion. These agents will reduce, but not completely eliminate, the number of patients with risk factors for aspiration pneumonitis.[28,29] An important point to remember concerning the H_2-receptor antagonists is that they have no action on the gastric contents already present in the stomach. To help circumvent this problem, an oral dose of H_2-receptor antagonist often is given the evening before surgery followed by an oral or parenteral dose on the morning of surgery.[29,30] Unlike antacids, the H_2-receptor antagonists do not produce immediate effects. Onset time for these agents when administered orally is one to three hours; good effects will be seen in 30 to 60 minutes when administered intravenously.[21,24] Oral doses of the H_2-receptor antagonists should not be crushed and given via a nasogastric tube at the time of surgery. As already mentioned, onset of action is not immediate. Furthermore, administration of tablets introduces particulate matter into the stomach which can be detrimental if aspirated. Duration of action of H_2-receptor antagonists also is important, as the risk of aspiration pneumonitis extends into maintenance of and emergence from anesthesia. After IV administration, the effects of cimetidine (Tagamet) last for four to five hours, ranitidine (Zantac) six to eight hours, and famotidine (Pepcid) 10 to 12 hours.[31] Al-

though cimetidine is associated with more adverse reactions than famotidine or ranitidine, this probably is not clinically significant as only one or two doses of the agent are given.[3]

Omeprazole (Prilosec), a proton-pump inhibitor, is effective in suppressing gastric acid secretion. Onset of action after IV administration is approximately 30 minutes.[32] An oral dose of 40 mg administered at bedtime and the morning of surgery consistently raises the gastric pH to a value greater than 2.5.[33]

1. J.G., a 5'4", 95 kg, 38-year-old male, ASA-II, is scheduled to undergo a hernia repair on an outpatient basis under general anesthesia. J.G. is a Type I diabetic. Physical examination is normal except for an abnormal airway which is anticipated to complicate intubation. What factors predispose J.G. to aspiration?

J.G. has several factors that place him at risk for aspiration. He is obese with an abnormal airway and has diabetes. These conditions will predispose J.G. to an increased abdominal pressure and delayed gastric emptying. His abnormal airway may delay intubation increasing the amount of time J.G. is susceptible to aspiration.

Choice of Agent

2. What medication(s) should be ordered for prophylaxis against aspiration pneumonitis for J.G.?

Since J.G.'s surgery is scheduled and not being performed on an emergency basis, an oral regimen for prophylaxis against aspiration pneumonitis can be used. Oral agents, in general, are less expensive than their parenteral counterparts. J.G. should be instructed to take famotidine (Pepcid) 40 mg orally the evening before surgery. On the day of surgery, J.G. should take a second dose of famotidine 40 mg as well as 10 mg of metoclopramide orally with a sip of water approximately one to one and one-half hours before surgery. The H_2-receptor antagonist contained on the institution's formulary or omeprazole could be substituted easily for famotidine, as these agents all produce similar effects. Since obese and diabetic patients tend to have larger gastric fluid volumes secondary to delayed gastric emptying, metoclopramide is added to J.G.'s regimen to reduce his gastric volume. Metoclopramide was chosen instead of cisapride because it is available generically and is less costly than cisapride.

3. C.T., a 28-year-old female, ASA-I, is admitted for an emergency cesarean section under general anesthesia. She is otherwise healthy and currently on no medications. Why is C.T. susceptible to aspiration pneumonitis and what preoperative medications would be appropriate to help prevent this adverse effect from occurring in C.T.?

C.T. is at an increased risk for aspiration and the possible development of pneumonitis because she is pregnant and about to undergo emergency surgery. An appropriate regimen for C.T. would be sodium citrate/citric acid solution (Bicitra) 30 mL orally, famotidine 20 mg IV (or whichever H_2-receptor antagonist is on the institution's formulary), and metoclopramide 10 mg IV. There is not sufficient time to administer famotidine and metoclopramide orally because of their slower onsets of action when administered by this route. Sodium citrate/citric acid solution provides immediate protection by raising gastric pH; metoclopramide will help reduce the increased gastric volume commonly seen in pregnant patients; and famotidine will provide sustained coverage throughout the surgery. These agents have not been shown to have detrimental effects on the fetus.[34]

Intravenous (IV) Anesthetic Agents
General Anesthesia

Intravenous anesthetic agents commonly are used to induce general anesthesia. General anesthesia is described by four character-

Table 8.2	Characteristics of an IV Induction Agent[a]
Desirable Characteristics	**Undesirable Characteristics**
Water soluble	Histamine release
Stable in solution	Hypersensitivity reaction
Small volume required for dose	Local toxicity at injection site
Rapid, smooth onset of action	Pain upon injection
Predictable effect	Adverse CNS effects
High therapeutic index	Adverse cardiovascular effects
Analgesic	Active metabolites
Amnestic	
Short duration to awakening	
Rapid full recovery	
Availability of reversal agent	

[a] CNS = Central nervous system; IV = Intravenous.

istics: unconsciousness, analgesia, muscle relaxation, and depression of reflexes to surgical or other stimulation.[35] The induction of this state and subsequent endotracheal intubation can result in undesirable changes in cardiovascular dynamics, the magnitude of which can be affected by resting sympathetic tone and level of preoperative anxiety, preoperative ventilatory status, vascular volume, pre-existing cardiovascular disease, chronic medications such as beta blockers or diuretics, and premedicants such as atropine, narcotics, or benzodiazepines. Benzodiazepines also can affect systemic vasculature and reduce blood pressure in patients with compromised cardiac function, especially if given with opioids.

Anesthetic induction agents should produce unconsciousness rapidly and smoothly while minimizing any cardiovascular changes. A list of further characteristics of an induction agent is found in Table 8.2. As mentioned, the administration of an IV induction agent is the most common method for initiation of general anesthesia and generally affords the highest patient acceptance and predictability of response over intramuscular, inhalation, or rectal routes of drug administration.[36] Drugs commonly used for IV induction include ultrashort-acting barbiturates (thiopental, methohexital), benzodiazepines (primarily midazolam), etomidate, propofol, ketamine, and narcotic analgesics (primarily fentanyl, sufentanil, and alfentanil). These drugs blunt the stress response to laryngoscopy and intubation, the perioperative events which often mark the point of maximum patient stimulation, even over the initial surgical incision.[37] Several of these agents also can be used for maintenance of general anesthesia, either alone or in combination with inhalation anesthetics; drugs that lack accumulation during repeat or continuous dosing are ideal choices for maintenance therapy. Conscious sedation for monitored anesthesia care, regional anesthesia, or in the intensive care unit (ICU) also can be achieved with selected agents by using doses lower than those necessary for unconsciousness. Table 8.3 lists common clinical uses for IV anesthetic agents.

Mechanisms of Action

Most IV anesthetic agents produce central nervous system depression by action on the gamma-aminobutyric acid (GABA)-receptor complex. Thiopental (Pentothal), the "gold standard" agent, acts nonselectively by inhibiting the presynaptic release of acetylcholine and more selectively to reduce the rate of dissociation of GABA from its postsynaptic receptor, prolonging the duration of ion channel opening, promoting chloride ion transfer, and resulting in nerve cell hyperpolarization and inhibition of nerve impulse transmission.[38-42] Benzodiazepine binding to the GABA receptor is well described.[43-45] The site of action of etomidate (Amidate) and propofol (Diprivan) is postulated to be at the GABA receptor, although little is known about the mechanics of this action. Ketamine (Ketalar) acts at a different site than other induction agents and produces a cataleptic state termed "dissociative anesthesia." It is thought that ketamine produces a dissociation between the thalamus and the limbic system,[46,47] suppresses spinal cord to brain nerve transmission in specific cord lamina to reduce the emotional component of pain transmission,[48] and may have opiate receptor activity.[49]

Pharmacokinetics

The onset and duration of effect are the most important pharmacokinetic properties of IV anesthetic agents when used for induction of anesthesia. Owing to the high rate of blood flow to vessel rich organs and the high lipophilicity of the drugs, thiopental and methohexital undergo maximal brain uptake within 30 seconds of injection, producing a rapid onset of CNS depression.[39] This is followed by a decline over the next five minutes to half of the initial peak brain concentration through drug redistribution.[39] Patients awaken in less than ten minutes after a single induction dose of thiopental despite a half-life of approximately 11 hours. The principal mechanism for early awakening is drug redistribution.[39] Skeletal muscle represents the tissue into which the initial redistribution is most prominent;[50] equilibrium in skeletal muscle is reached within 15 minutes of injection. Fat concentrations slowly accumulate, continuing to rise 30 minutes after injection;[50] slow initial uptake is due to relatively poor perfusion of adipose tissue. Because cumulative effects can be seen after repeat or continuous dosing of barbiturates due to fat deposition and storage, these drugs make poor choices for maintenance of general anesthesia. Distribution and its effect on onset and duration are similar for other induction agents; the degree to which metabolism plays any role is variable and rapid metabolism may be a significant factor in the relatively shorter duration to full recovery of propofol[36] and etomidate.[51] Table 8.4 provides a comparison of the pharmacokinetic properties of IV anesthetic agents.

Adverse and Beneficial Effects

Intravenous anesthetic agents can produce a variety of adverse and beneficial effects other than loss of consciousness. These effects include cardiovascular depression or stimulation, pain upon injection, nausea and vomiting, respiratory depression or stimulation, CNS cerebroprotection or excitation, and adrenocorticoid suppression. Table 8.5 compares the relative significance of these

Table 8.3	Common Clinical Uses of IV Anesthetic Agents[a]	
Etomidate (Amidate)		**Midazolam (Versed)**
IV induction		ICU sedation
		IV induction
Ketamine (Ketalar)		Maintenance of general
Analgesia		anesthesia
IV induction		Preoperative sedation
IM induction		
Maintenance of general		**Propofol (Diprivan)**
anesthesia		ICU sedation
		IV induction
Methohexital (Brevital)		Maintenance of general
IV induction		anesthesia
PR induction		Preoperative sedation
		Thiopental
		IV induction
		PR induction

[a] ICU = Intensive care unit; IM = Intramuscular; IV = Intravenous; PR = Rectal.

Table 8.4	Pharmacokinetic Comparison of Common IV Anesthetic Agents[a,38,39,45,51,63]			
Drug	Half-life (hr)	Onset (sec)	Clinical Duration (min)[b]	Hangover Effect[c]
Thiopental (Pentothal)	11	≤30	5–8	++
Methohexital (Brevital)	4	≤30	4–8	+
Midazolam (Versed)	1–4	30–60	17–20	+++
Etomidate (Amidate)	2–5	≤30	3–12	+
Propofol (Diprivan)	0.5–7	≤30	4–10	0 – +
Ketamine (Ketalar)	1–3	30–40	10–15	++ – +++

[a] IV = Intravenous.
[b] Time from injection of agent to return to conscious state.
[c] Residual psychomotor impairment after awakening.

effects among available agents. Most troublesome are usually cardiovascular effects or CNS excitation reactions. Contribution to postoperative nausea and vomiting and ''hangover'' can be significant and may delay full recovery and patient discharge from the postanesthesia care unit (PACU). Central nervous system effects can be hiccups, myoclonus, or seizure activity, or euphoria, hallucinations, and emergence delirium. The cerebroprotective effect produced by barbiturates, etomidate, and propofol is a reduction in cerebral blood flow through cerebral vasoconstriction. As a result, cerebral metabolic rate, blood flow, and intracranial pressure are reduced.[39,52,53] This effect is useful if these drugs are available in therapeutic concentrations at a time of potential cerebral ischemia. Thiopental, for example, has been given during deep hypothermic circulatory arrest to minimize the possibility of ischemic events.

Finally, the place in therapy of each agent should be determined based upon patient characteristics, circumstances associated with surgery, and cost. Patient characteristics may include history of postoperative nausea or vomiting, allergy profile, psychiatric history, or cardiovascular status. Circumstances associated with surgery that may influence choice of IV anesthetic include inpatient/outpatient status, placement of an IV line, duration of surgery, and extubation status at the end of the procedure. The cost of induction agents varies widely, with older agents usually priced lower per single induction dose. Newer agents, especially if used for maintenance of anesthesia, are more expensive but may offer cost advantages in some situations by reduction in length of PACU stay, fewer postoperative complications, and improved patient well-being. In general, thiopental remains the standard induction agent, and should be chosen unless there is a relative or absolute contraindication to its use.

Propofol Use in Ambulatory Surgery: Antiemetic Effect and Full Recovery Characteristics

4. K.T., a 15-year-old female, ASA-I, is admitted to the day surgery center for strabismus surgery. K.T. is otherwise healthy and all laboratory values obtained before surgery are within normal limits. Which IV induction agent should be used?

Propofol (Diprivan) would make a good choice here for several reasons. Strabismus surgery is considered highly emetogenic sur-

gery, due to a direct effect on CNS emesis centers during operative manipulation of extraocular muscles.[54] Precautions, therefore, should be taken to reduce the possibility of nausea and vomiting postoperatively, including avoiding the use of an induction agent or volatile anesthetic with a high frequency of this effect. Propofol produces little to no nausea or vomiting and actually has been associated with a direct antiemetic effect.[55,56] This effect may not preclude the need for an additional antiemetic but possibly will contribute to the avoidance of emesis in K.T. Furthermore, outpatient surgery demands rapid, full recovery from general anesthesia. Propofol, etomidate, and the barbiturate agents produce less ''hangover'' than other agents; propofol, especially, is associated with a more rapid recovery of psychomotor function and a patient-perceived superior quality of recovery than other agents.[57] Although thiopental certainly could be used for induction at a less direct cost than propofol, propofol offers advantages over most volatile anesthetics for maintenance of anesthesia during the procedure in antiemetic and rapid recovery properties. Propofol does not accumulate during continuous infusion dosing and could be used in K.T. as an induction as well as maintenance anesthetic. The choice of propofol in this situation represents a desire to avoid volatile anesthetics for maintenance of general anesthesia.

Etomidate Use in Cardiovascular Disease

Safety Profile

5. L.M., a 73-year-old male, ASA-IV, is in need of repair of an abdominal aortic aneurysm. During his preoperative evaluation a few days before surgery, his blood pressure (BP) was 160/102 mm Hg, and his medical records reveal hypertension poorly controlled by propranolol 40 mg QID and angina occasionally requiring treatment with SL nitroglycerin (NTG). An exercise tolerance test is performed to work up his underlying ischemic disease. Results from the test showed electrocardiogram (ECG) changes at a moderate exercise load. Although he was then scheduled for an elective aneurysm repair following full cardiac examination, this morning L.M. presented to the emergency room (ER) with a 4-hour history of severe back pain. His surgeon has determined that there is high likelihood that the aneurysm now is leaking and surgery must be performed as soon as possible. L.M. will remain intubated in the ICU for at least 1 day postoperatively. What is the best plan for L.M.'s anesthetic induction and maintenance?

L.M. has significant cardiovascular disease, and care should be taken to minimize any cardiovascular depression or hypertension during intubation and maintenance anesthesia. Of the currently available induction agents, etomidate produces minimal cardiovascular effects;[58] minimal cardiovascular depression also is noted with narcotic anesthetics. Thiopental can cause hemodynamic changes and is best avoided in L.M. Etomidate would be an optimal choice for induction, followed by narcotic maintenance anesthesia with fentanyl. The fentanyl, if given in doses for maintenance anesthesia, will have a prolonged duration of respiratory depression; this effect fits in well with planned extubation for L.M. one day postoperatively.

Myoclonus

6. L.M. receives a 0.3 mg/kg IV dose of etomidate. Before a neuromuscular blocking agent can be administered, the anesthesiologist notes that L.M. appears to be seizing. What is occurring and how can it be prevented?

Etomidate is associated with a 6% to 33% incidence of myoclonus.[59] Prior IV narcotic or benzodiazepine administration may reduce the incidence of these involuntary muscle movements.[60] The movements resemble seizures, but are not associated with electroencephalographic changes. They are thought to be due to

Table 8.5	Adverse Effects and Costs of IV Inductive Agents[a]					
Adverse Effect	Etomidate (Amidate)	Ketamine (Ketalar)	Methohexital (Brevital)	Midazolam (Versed)	Propofol (Diprivan)	Thiopental (Pentothal)
Adrenocorticoid suppression	+[b]	—	—	—	—	—
Cerebral protection	+	—	+	+	+	+
Cardiovascular depression	—	—	++	+	++	++
Emergence delirium or euphoria	—	++	—	—	+	—
Myoclonus	+++	+	++	—	+	+
Nausea/vomiting	+++	++	++	+	—	++
Pain on injection	++	—	+	—	++	+
Respiratory depression	++	—	++	+++	++	++
Relative cost	++++	++	+	+++++	+++	+

[a] + to +++++ = Likelihood of adverse effect relative to other agents; — = No effect.
[b] Not shown to be clinically significant in single dose.

disinhibition of subcortical structures that normally suppress extrapyramidal motor activity[61] and may interfere with intubation or surgical manipulations. Neuromuscular blockade will cause myoclonic movements to cease.

Ketamine Use in Pediatrics

7. R.L., a 4-year-old male, ASA-II, is scheduled for a short suture removal procedure in the OR. He is brought to the OR by his parents and is in distress over parting from them and "being stuck with needles." He currently has no IV line in place. How could anesthesia and/or analgesia be provided to R.L.?

Suture removal is a quick but painful procedure often performed in the operating room setting for pediatric patients. Analgesia ideally should be provided without the need to start an IV line and, for children with a high level of separation anxiety, in the presence of a parent. Ketamine can be given intramuscularly in the preoperative holding area and, unlike other induction agents, provides excellent analgesia. Analgesia occurs with relatively low doses of ketamine that produce a compliant patient who is not heavily sedated. Ketamine causes little to no respiratory depression, so intubation is not necessary in this setting. An anticholinergic drug, such as atropine, must be given along with ketamine to counteract the sialagogue effect produced by ketamine.

An unusual adverse effect of ketamine is the 5% to 30% occurrence of delirium and hallucinations upon awakening.[62] Emergence reactions (e.g., psychiatric reactions during awakening from anesthesia) vary in severity, and occur more often in adults, females, frequent dreamers, patients with personality disorders, and in patients receiving high doses of ketamine (>2 mg/kg) under rapid IV administration.[62] Reactions can be attenuated by prior administration of benzodiazepines.[62] R.L. is at very low risk for an emergence reaction, based upon age, sex, dose of ketamine, and route of administration. Unless necessary for preoperative anxiolysis, benzodiazepines probably are not needed in R.L.

Neuromuscular Blocking Agents

Uses

Neuromuscular blocking agents are one of the most frequently used classes of drugs in the OR, being used primarily as an adjunct to general anesthesia to facilitate endotracheal intubation and to relax skeletal muscle during surgery.[64] Skeletal muscle relaxation optimizes the surgical field for the surgeon and prevents patient movement as a reflex response to surgical stimulation. In addition to their use in the operating room, neuromuscular blocking agents frequently are used in the ICU to paralyze mechanically ventilated patients.[65–67] An important point to keep in mind is that neuromuscular blocking agents have no known effect on consciousness or pain threshold. Consequently, adequate sedation and analgesia must be ensured when neuromuscular blocking agents are administered to ICU patients.

Mechanism of Action

Neuromuscular blocking agents produce muscle relaxation by occupying the acetylcholine subunits of the nicotinic cholinergic receptors located on the motor endplate. Acetylcholine must bind to the subunits for normal neuromuscular transmission to occur.[68] Once occupying the acetylcholine subunits, neuromuscular blocking agents either can activate them (agonist effect) and produce depolarization or do nothing (antagonist effect). Agents that activate the acetylcholine subunits are referred to as depolarizing agents while agents that produce no effect are termed nondepolarizing agents. The nondepolarizing agents act as competitive antagonists to acetylcholine at the acetylcholine subunits. The paralysis produced by depolarizing agents is preceded initially by fasciculations (transient twitching of skeletal muscle).[64]

Monitoring Neuromuscular Blockade

In addition to clinical assessment (e.g., lack of movement) by the anesthesiologist, the degree of neuromuscular blockade produced by neuromuscular blocking agents is monitored by nerve stimulation with a peripheral nerve stimulator. The ulnar nerve is used most often; facial, common peroneal (fibular), or posterior tibial nerves also can be used. Commonly employed tests performed with the peripheral nerve stimulator include train-of-four (TOF) stimulation, single-twitch stimulation, and tetanic stimulation.[64]

Classification

Neuromuscular blocking agents commonly are classified by type of block produced (depolarizing versus nondepolarizing), chemical structure (steroidal compound, acetylcholine derivative, benzylisoquinolinium compound), or duration of action (ultrashort, short, intermediate, long) as listed in Table 8.6.[69]

Adverse Effects

The underlying mechanisms for the cardiovascular adverse effects of neuromuscular blocking agents are listed in Table 8.7 and include blockade of autonomic ganglia (hypotension), blockade of muscarinic receptors (tachycardia), and/or release of histamine from circulating mast cells (hypotension).[69–71] In general, the steroidal compounds are associated with a vagolytic effect while the benzylisoquinolinium compounds are associated with varying degrees of histamine release. Although not reported as a problem when used short-term in the OR, some of the neuromuscular blocking agents can prolong neuromuscular blockade and cause a generalized myopathy in patients receiving them in the ICU for an extended period of time, albeit infrequently.[72–75] Of the currently available neuromuscular blocking agents, vecuronium (Norcuron), pipecuronium (Arduan), and doxacurium (Nuromax) are virtually devoid of clinically significant cardiovascular effects and are the agents of choice for patients with an unstable cardiovascular profile.[76,77] Succinylcholine (Anectine) is associated with a significant number of adverse effects including hyperkalemia; arrhythmias; fasciculations; muscle pain; myoglobinuria; trismus; phase II block; and increased intraocular, intragastric, and intracranial pressure.[64,69,71,78] Although having the potential to produce a significant number of adverse effects, succinylcholine still is unrivaled in terms of onset of neuromuscular blockade.

Drug Interactions

Several classes of drugs and/or individual agents interact with neuromuscular blocking agents. The volatile inhalational agents potentiate the neuromuscular blockade from nondepolarizing agents and allow a lower dose of the neuromuscular blocking agent

to be used when administered concomitantly. Isoflurane, enflurane, and desflurane produce a greater effect than halothane.[69,79] Other agents reported to potentiate the effects of neuromuscular blocking agents include the aminoglycosides, clindamycin, magnesium sulfate, quinidine, furosemide, lidocaine, amphotericin B, and dantrolene. Carbamazepine, phenytoin, steroids (chronic administration), and theophylline antagonize the effects of neuromuscular blocking agents.[67,69] By appropriately monitoring the patient and dosing the neuromuscular blocking agent to effect, significant problems from drug interactions can be minimized.

Reversal of Neuromuscular Blockade

The neuromuscular blocking action of neuromuscular blocking agents ceases either spontaneously as a result of declining plasma concentrations of the agent or by reversal with acetylcholinesterase inhibitors (e.g., neostigmine, edrophonium, pyridostigmine). Acetylcholinesterase inhibitors inhibit the enzyme acetylcholinesterase which degrades acetylcholine; this results in more acetylcholine being available to compete with the neuromuscular blocking agent for available acetylcholine subunits. These agents are used only to reverse paralysis produced by nondepolarizing agents. Anticholinergic agents are administered concurrently (in same syringe) with the acetylcholinesterase inhibitors to minimize other cholinergic effects (e.g., bradycardia, bronchoconstriction, salivation, increased peristalsis, nausea, vomiting) caused by these agents. Atropine is administered routinely with edrophonium, and glycopyrrolate with neostigmine or pyridostigmine to take advantage of similar onset times and durations of action.[80,81] Adequacy of reversal is assessed by the use of a peripheral nerve stimulator and through clinical assessment of the patient (e.g., ability to sustain head lift for five seconds) by the anesthesiologist prior to extubation.[71,82]

Pharmacokinetics and Pharmacodynamics

8. E.D., a 36-year-old male, ASA-I, is admitted through the ER for an emergency appendectomy. E.D. is otherwise healthy, has no drug allergies, and presently is on no medications. All laboratory tests are normal. Admission notes reveal that E.D. ate dinner approximately 30 minutes earlier. Because of this, the anesthesiologist plans on performing a rapid sequence induction employing the Sellick maneuver. Which neuromuscular blocking agent would be most appropriate for E.D.?

Rapid sequence induction is indicated for patients at risk for aspiration of gastric contents should regurgitation occur. Pregnant or morbidly obese patients are at risk for aspiration as well as those with a full stomach or history of gastroesophageal reflux. The goal of rapid sequence induction is to minimize the time during which the airway is unprotected by intubating the patient as fast as possible (e.g., within 30 to 60 seconds). In this technique, the patient is preoxygenated after which an IV induction agent and neuromuscular blocking agent are administered simultaneously. Manual ventilation of the patient is not attempted after administration of these agents. Apnea occurs as the neuromuscular blocking agent takes effect; therefore, a neuromuscular blocking agent with as rapid an onset as possible is required to produce adequate intubating conditions as quickly as possible. The Sellick maneuver frequently is used during rapid sequence induction. It is performed by placing downward pressure on the cricoid cartilage, which compresses and occludes the esophagus and helps prevent passive regurgitation of gastric contents into the trachea.[71]

Table 8.8 lists the onset times of normal intubating doses as well as other information pertaining to the use of neuromuscular block-

Table 8.6	Classification of Neuromuscular Blocking Agents		
Agent	Type of Block[a]	Clinical Duration of Action[b]	Structure
Atracurium (Tracrium)	–	Intermediate	Benzylisoquinolinium
Doxacurium (Nuromax)	–	Long	Benzylisoquinolinium
Gallamine (Flaxedil)	–	Long	Other
Metocurine (Metubine)	–	Long	Benzylisoquinolinium
Mivacurium (Mivacron)	–	Short	Benzylisoquinolinium
Pancuronium (Pavulon)	–	Long	Steroidal
Pipecuronium (Arduan)	–	Long	Steroidal
Rocuronium (Zemuron)	–	Intermediate	Steroidal
Succinylcholine (Anectine, Quelicin)	+	Ultrashort	Acetylcholine-like
Tubocurarine	–	Long	Benzylisoquinolinium
Vecuronium (Norcuron)	–	Intermediate	Steroidal

[a] + = Depolarizing; – = Nondepolarizing.
[b] Time from injection of agent to return to twitch height to 25% of control (time at which another dose of agent will need to be administered to maintain paralysis); in general, clinical duration of a standard intubating dose of ultra-short agents ranges from 3–5 min, short from 15–30 min, intermediate from 30–40 min, and long from 60–120 min.

ing agents.[69–71,83–87] As can be seen, succinylcholine has the fastest onset time and, hence, is considered the agent of choice for use in rapid sequence induction.

Since E.D. is an otherwise healthy male with no contraindications to the use of succinylcholine, this agent should be used.

Depolarizing Agent Contraindications

9. What would be your choice of a neuromuscular blocking agent if E.D. had a historical susceptibility to malignant hyperthermia and why?

Succinylcholine is contraindicated in patients with skeletal muscle myopathies; after the acute phase of injury (i.e., 5 to 70 days postinjury) following major burns, multiple trauma, extensive denervation of skeletal muscle, or upper motor neuron injury; in children and adolescent patients (except when used for emergency tracheal intubation or where the immediate securing of the airway is necessary); and in patients with a hypersensitivity to the drug.[64,69] Succinylcholine also can trigger malignant hyperthermia and is absolutely contraindicated in malignant hyperthermia susceptible patients.[88]

The nondepolarizing neuromuscular blocking agents are safe to use in malignant hyperthermia-susceptible patients.[89] Rocuronium (Zemuron) has the fastest onset of the nondepolarizing agents although still slower than succinylcholine.[90] Although having onsets of action longer than rocuronium, the intermediate- and long-duration agents' onset can be shortened in two ways. Increasing the dose of agent administered results in a faster onset of action; this, however, also results in a longer duration of action.[91] Vecuronium's onset, for example, can be reduced to 90 seconds with an initial dose of 0.4 mg/kg (versus a normal initial dose of 0.1 mg/kg).[92] The onset of action of nondepolarizing agents, with the exception of rocuronium, also can be shortened by the use of the priming principle; with this technique, approximately 10% of the intubating dose is administered two to three minutes before the standard intubating dose. Depending upon the nondepolarizing agent selected, the onset time is reduced from three to five minutes to 90 to 120 seconds.[91,93,94] A low level of neuromuscular blockade is produced with the priming dose; this effect may be detrimental in certain patient groups (e.g., obese patients).

In E.D.'s case, rocuronium, with its fast onset of action, would be a suitable alternative to succinylcholine. Its cost and slightly

longer onset prevent it from being the first-line agent in individuals able to receive succinylcholine.

Routes of Elimination

10. M.M., a 70-year-old female, ASA-IV, is scheduled to undergo a 2-hour GI procedure. Pertinent laboratory findings are as follows: aspartate aminotransferase (AST) 272 U/L (Normal: 5–45), alanine aminotransferase (ALT) 150 U/L (Normal: 5–37), blood urea nitrogen (BUN) 40 mg/dL (Normal: 8–21), serum creatinine (SrCr) 1.8 mg/dL (Normal: 0.5–1.1), albumin 2.6 gm/dL (Normal: 3.5–5.0), and bilirubin 0.74 mg/dL (Normal: 2–18). Which neuromuscular blocking agent would you recommend for M.M.? [SI units: AST 4.5 μkat/L; ALT 2.5 μkat/L; BUN 14.28 mmol/L; SrCr 159 μmol/L; albumin 26 gm/L; bilirubin 12.7 μmol/L]

When selecting a neuromuscular blocking agent, one of the factors that must be considered is the patient's renal and hepatic function. Neuromuscular blocking agents are dependent to varying degrees upon the kidneys and liver for their metabolism and excretion as can be seen in Table 8.9.[64,69–71,83–87] Neuromuscular blocking agents are metabolized by plasma cholinesterase (pseudocholinesterase), Hofmann elimination (a nonbiologic process which does not require renal, hepatic, or enzymatic function), nonspecific esterases, and through hepatic metabolic pathways.

Hofmann elimination is a pH- and temperature-dependent process unique to atracurium (Tracrium). One of the products produced by Hofmann elimination of atracurium, laudanosine, is a CNS stimulant in high concentrations. Laudanosine undergoes renal and hepatic elimination. Due to the short-term use of the agent in the OR, accumulation of laudanosine with resultant seizure activity is not a concern, even in patients with end-stage renal failure.

Plasma cholinesterase levels may be decreased in patients with hepatic dysfunction.[95] The duration of action of agents metabolized by this enzyme (e.g., succinylcholine, mivacurium) may be prolonged in this patient group. The increased duration of action of succinylcholine seen in patients with low levels of normal plasma cholinesterase is not clinically significant; it can, however, be significant with mivacurium.[96,97] Atypical plasma cholinesterase can increase the duration of action of succinylcholine and mivacurium (Mivacron) significantly.[98,99]

Excretion of neuromuscular blocking agents, either unchanged or as metabolites, is by the renal or biliary routes. The duration of action of renally eliminated agents (pancuronium, metocurine, tub-

Table 8.7	Causes of Cardiovascular Adverse Effects of Neuromuscular Blocking Agents[a,b]			
Agent	Histamine Release	Autonomic Ganglia	Vagolytic Activity	Sympathetic Stimulation
Atracurium[b] (Tracrium)	+	—	—	—
Doxacurium (Nuromax)	—	—	—	—
Gallamine (Flaxedil)	—	—	+++	+
Metocurine (Metubine)	++	Weak block	—	—
Mivacurium[b] (Mivacron)	+	—	—	—
Pancuronium (Pavulon)	—	—	++	+
Pipecuronium (Arduan)	—	—	—	—
Rocuronium[c] (Zemuron)	—	—	+	—
Succinylcholine (Anectine, Quelicin)	+	Stimulates	—	—
Tubocurarine	+++	Blocks	—	—
Vecuronium (Norcuron)	—	—	—	—

[a] + – +++ = Likelihood of developing the cardiovascular adverse effect relative to the other agents; — = No effect.
[b] Histamine release is dose and rate related; cardiovascular changes can be lessened by minimizing dose and injecting agent slowly.
[c] Produces an ↑ in heart rate of ≈18% with intubating dose of 0.6 mg/kg; effect usually transient and resolves spontaneously.

Table 8.8								Pharmacokinetic and Pharmacodynamic Parameters of Action of Neuromuscular Blocking Agents[a,69–71,83–87]
Agent	Relative Potency	Cl (mL/kg/min)	Vd_{ss} (L/kg)	Half-life (min)	ED95[b] (mg/kg)	Initial Dose[c,d] (mg/kg)	Onset (min)	Clinical Duration of Action of Initial Dose (min)
Atracurium[e] (Tracrium)	4	5–7	0.2	20	0.2	0.4–0.5	2–3	20–45
Doxacurium (Arduan)	0.4	1–2.5	0.2	100–120	0.025	0.05–0.08	4–6	100–160
Gallamine (Flaxedil)	40	1.2	0.2	135	3	3.0–4.0	3–5	60–100
Metocurine (Metubine)	4	1–2	0.4	80–120	0.28	0.2–0.5	3–5	60–100
Mivacurium[e] (Mivacron)	1.6	50–100[f]	0.2	2[f]	0.07	0.15–0.25	1.5–3	12–20
Pancuronium (Pavulon)	1	1–2	0.3	80–120	0.07	0.04–0.1	3–5	60–100
Pipecuronium (Arduan)	0.9	2.4	0.3	80–120	0.05	0.07–0.085	3–5	60–120
Rocuronium[e] (Zemuron)	7	4.0	0.3	60–70	0.25–0.3	0.5–1.0	1–1.5	20–40
Succinylcholine[e] (Anectine, Quelicin)	2.8	Unknown	Unknown	Unknown	0.2	1.0–1.5	0.5–1	4–6
Tubocurarine	7	1–2	0.3–0.6	80–120	0.5	0.5–0.6	3–5	60–90
Vecuronium[e] (Norcuron)	0.9	4.5	0.4	50–70	0.05	0.08–0.1	2–3	20–35

[a] Cl = Clearance; Vd_{ss} = Steady-state volume of distribution.

[b] ED95 = Effective dose causing 95% muscle paralysis.

[c] Dose when nitrous oxide-opioid technique used.

[d] Intermittent maintenance doses to maintain paralysis, as a general rule, will be approximately 20%–25% of the initial dose.

[e] Also can be administered as a continuous infusion to maintain paralysis; suggested infusion ranges under balanced anesthesia are: succinylcholine 50–100 μg/kg/min; mivacurium 3–12 μg/kg/min (higher in children); atracurium 4–12 μg/kg/min; vecuronium 0.8–2 μg/kg/min; rocuronium 6–14 μg/kg/min.

[f] Values reflect contribution of trans-trans and cis-trans isomers only.

ocurarine, doxacurium, pipecuronium) will be increased in patients with renal failure.[69,70,84] Vecuronium's duration of action can be increased in patients with liver disease when doses greater than 0.2 mg/kg are administered.[100,101]

Since M.M. has evidence of both significant renal and hepatic impairment, atracurium would be an excellent choice for a neuromuscular blocking agent. Its properties are not altered significantly in the presence of renal and hepatic failure due to its unique manner of metabolism. Further, since atracurium has an intermediate duration of action, it can easily be used in a two-hour procedure.

Local Anesthetics

Local and Regional Anesthesia

Selected surgical cases can be performed under local or regional anesthesia rather than by rendering the patient unconscious under general anesthesia. Epidural, intrathecal, intravenous regional, nerve block, topical, and local infiltration anesthesia can be chosen depending upon the surgical site, patient health and physical characteristics, coagulation status, duration of surgery and patient position, and the desires and cooperativeness of the patient. Beyond preserving consciousness, local or regional techniques have several advantages over general anesthesia. Depending upon the technique chosen, these advantages may include a lowered risk of cardiovascular instability,[102] less risk of malignant hyperthermia syndrome,[103] provision of postoperative analgesia and reduction in pain perception,[104] less respiratory depression,[102,105] reduction in stress response to surgery,[106,107] and a shorter length of hospital stay.[108] Disadvantages include additional time and manipulations required, possible complications or pain from invasive catheter placements or injections such as with epidural or nerve plexus anesthesia, slow onset of effect, possible failure of technique, and toxicities from drugs administered.

Uses of Local Anesthetic Agents

Local anesthetics are a mainstay of analgesia through their blocking effects on the spinal cord, spinal nerve roots, and peripheral nerves. These agents can be administered by all routes discussed above, depending upon the drug chosen. Table 8.10 lists the common uses of currently available local anesthetics. Local anesthetics often are given in combination with other agents, such as with sodium bicarbonate (for increased speed of onset of action), epinephrine (for reduced toxicity, increased effectiveness, and prolonged duration of action at site of injection), or narcotics (for additional analgesia by a different mechanism of action).

Mechanism of Action

The two structural classes of local anesthetics are characterized by the linkage between the molecule's lipophilic aromatic group and hydrophilic amine group: aminoamides and aminoesters. Both act to provide analgesia and other effects by entering nerve cells through a membrane sodium channel and attaching to a receptor site on the internal surface of the channel. Axonal membrane blockade that results is selective depending upon the drug, concentration and volume administered, and the depth of nerve penetration. C fibers (pain transmission and autonomic activity) appear to be the most easily blocked, followed by fibers responsible for touch and pressure sensation (A-alpha, A-beta, and A-delta), and motor function (A-alpha and A-beta). At most commonly used local anesthetic doses and concentrations, some nonpain transmitting nerve fibers also are blocked. The blockade of sensory, motor, or autonomic (sympathetic, parasympathetic) fibers may result in adverse effects such as paresthesia, numbness and inability to move extremities, hypotension, and urinary retention. Systemic effects (such as seizures or cardiac dysrhythmias) are related to the inherent cardiac and CNS safety margins of individual drugs and also to the site of injection (vascularity and the presence of tissue and fat cause a high degree of systemic drug absorption from

Table 8.9   Elimination of Neuromuscular Blocking Agents[64,69–71,83–87]

Agent	Renal	Hepatic	Biliary	Plasma
Atracurium (Tracrium)	<5%	—	—	Hofmann elimination, ester hydrolysis
Doxacurium (Nuromax)	60%–90%	—	Yes	—
Gallamine (Flaxedil)	>90%	—	—	—
Metocurine (Metubine)	80%–100%	—	<2%	—
Mivacurium (Mivacron)	<10%	—	Minor	Plasma cholinesterase
Pancuronium (Pavulon)	60%–80%	15%–40%	5%–10%	—
Pipecuronium (Arduan)	60%–90%	—	20%–25%	—
Rocuronium (Zemuron)	up to 30%	Yes	Yes	—
Succinylcholine (Anectine, Quelicin)	—	—	—	Plasma cholinesterase
Tubocurarine	40%–60%	<1%	10%–20%	—
Vecuronium (Norcuron)	20%–30%	20%–30%	30%–50%	—

sites such as intercostal nerves; less absorption is seen with epidural, brachial plexus, or sciatic nerve drug administration).[109] Ropivacaine, an investigational local anesthetic, is a homolog of mepivacaine and bupivacaine. It is thought to have a long duration similar to bupivacaine, with considerably less cardiotoxicity.[110]

Allergic Reactions

Ester-type local anesthetics can produce allergic reactions in some patients, possibly due to their similarity in structure with a known allergen, para-aminobenzoic acid. True allergy to amide-type local anesthetics is extremely rare[111] and reactions often can be traced back to the presence of the preservatives (methylparaben and metabisulfite) or systemic epinephrine administration instead of the drug itself.[112]

Physicochemical Properties Affecting Action

The potency of local anesthetics is related directly to their degree of lipid solubility.[109] Local anesthetics such as tetracaine, bupivacaine, and etidocaine are highly lipid soluble and can be given in concentrations of 0.25% to 0.5%. Less lipid soluble drugs such as lidocaine and mepivacaine require concentrations of 1% to 2% for many techniques. Differences in the clinical activities of local anesthetics also are explained by other physicochemical properties such as protein binding (affects duration of action) and pKa (affects speed of onset).[113]

Table 8.10   Common Uses of Local Anesthetic Agents

Drug	Types of Anesthesia[a]
Bupivacaine (Sensorcaine, Marcaine)	Epidural, intrathecal, nerve block, local infiltration
Chloroprocaine (Nesacaine)	Epidural
Cocaine	Topical
Etidocaine (Duranest)	Epidural
Lidocaine (Xylocaine)	Epidural, intrathecal, nerve block, IV regional, local infiltration, topical
Mepivacaine (Carbocaine, Polocaine)	Epidural, nerve block, local infiltration
Tetracaine (Pontocaine)	Intrathecal, nerve block, topical

[a] IV = Intravenous.

Choice of local anesthetic often is based upon the duration of the surgical procedure (e.g., the duration of analgesia required). Usually, a local anesthetic is chosen that will, at least minimally, outlast the duration of surgery with a single injection; a continuous infusion also can be administered for titration of effect with shorter-acting agents. Important physicochemical and pharmacokinetic properties of local anesthetics are shown in Table 8.11.

Regional Anesthesia in High-Risk Patients

11. M.S., a 52-year-old black male, 105 kg, 5′9″, is undergoing an emergent minor hand repair procedure after a fall-related injury. His past medical history is positive for Type I diabetes mellitus for 41 years, untreated angina, and hypertension. Upon OR admission, laboratory values of note are: plasma glucose 240 mg/dL and BP 145/92 mm Hg. His sister tells the anesthesiologist that he has been having increasing difficulty walking up stairs and often is short of breath of late. The anesthesiologist chooses to provide regional anesthesia via an axillary block; the anticipated duration of surgery is 2 hours. M.S. agrees with this plan. Why is this a good plan for M.S., and which local anesthetic should be chosen? [SI unit: glucose 13.3 mmol/L]

With his currently uncontrolled angina and hypertension, M.S. is at risk for complications from general or regional anesthesia. The emergent nature of his surgery prevents workup of these problems before administration of an anesthetic. General anesthesia is not necessary in this localized surgery, and intubation and drug administration may cause significant untoward cardiovascular effects if this technique were chosen. Patients with ischemic disease having peripheral operations have less hemodynamic instability if peripheral nerve blockade is employed with regional techniques.[102] Regional anesthesia also is beneficial in M.S. because his diabetes and obesity, and possibly full stomach (emergency surgery, diabetic gastroparesis), place him at significant risk for aspiration during induction or emergence from general anesthesia. An axillary block with a local anesthetic could provide M.S. with adequate analgesia for his procedure.

The local anesthetic of choice is one with a duration of action at least that of anticipated surgery time and a good safety profile should systemic administration occur. Epinephrine can be used to increase a local anesthetic's duration and reduce systemic concentrations attained,[114] but is not indicated in M.S. because of his diabetes (peripheral vascular effects) and hypertension (added effect from catecholamine administration). Lidocaine as a single injection without epinephrine has a duration of action which may be too short for M.S.'s procedure. It could be used together with a longer-acting agent to provide a quick onset of action. Mepivacaine, an intermediate-acting local anesthetic, or bupivacaine, a long-acting agent, would be good choices to use alone or in combination with lidocaine in M.S.

Topical Cocaine

12. C.J., a 21-year-old female, ASA-I, is scheduled for rhinoplasty surgery under general anesthesia. The surgeon requests 4% cocaine solution for topical anesthesia. How is cocaine useful in C.J. and what are other alternatives?

Cocaine is unique among local anesthetics in its ability to produce significant vasoconstriction in addition to anesthesia.[115] It is indicated only for topical anesthesia due to its high level of systemic toxicity and has been used commonly for nasal procedures. High abuse and diversion potential exist, and accountability of cocaine topical solutions can be difficult and time-consuming. Cocaine, with sympathomimetic actions of its own, markedly potentiates sympathomimetics.[116] Cocaine affects general anesthetic requirements and the arrhythmogenic properties of some volatile anesthetics.[115] General anesthesia, in turn, modifies cocaine's sympathomimetic effects, leading to increased toxicity.[115] Alternatives to cocaine include topical mixtures of another local anesthetic (for anesthesia) and a sympathomimetic agent (for vasoconstriction), such as lidocaine/phenylephrine. Such combinations have resulted in effects undiscernible from cocaine itself.[117,118]

Alkalinization of Local Anesthetics

13. T.F., a 72-year-old male, ASA-II, is scheduled for a lithotripsy to shatter a left-sided kidney stone. He agrees to lumbar epidural anesthesia for the procedure. He will have his epidural catheter placed just outside the lithotripsy suite; as soon as the epidural is placed and functioning, the procedure can begin. How can the anesthesiologist minimize the time between the initial epidural injection and the onset of the epidural blockade?

Local anesthetics (usually lidocaine) are given immediately upon epidural catheter placement as a first anesthetic dose or to assess the effectiveness of anesthetics (local anesthetics and narcotics) given through the catheter during surgery. The onset of action of local anesthetics is dependent upon the pKa (i.e., the pH at which 50% of the drug is present in the unionized and 50% in the ionized form). Drugs with pKa's closest to body pH (7.4) will have the fastest onset since a high percentage of molecules will be unionized and able to cross nerve membranes to the intracellular site of action. Local anesthetics are formulated in solutions with acidic pHs to optimize their shelf-lives. When sodium bicarbonate is added to local anesthetic solutions, the pH is increased, the percentage of unionized drug is increased, and the onset of local anesthetic action is considerably shortened.[119,120] The amount of bi-

carbonate added to the solution depends upon the pH of the local anesthetic, a target pH is usually 7.0, without precipitate formation.[121] To shorten by approximately half the onset of lidocaine in T.F.'s epidural, 1 mL of sodium bicarbonate 8.4% could be added to the first 10 mL of lidocaine 2% solution.

Cardioplegia Solution
Use in Cardiac Surgery

Hypothermic, hyperkalemic, cardioplegia solution first began being used routinely in open-heart surgery in the 1970s and enjoys widespread clinical use today. Cardioplegia solution is instilled into the coronary vasculature to produce an elective cardiac arrest. Inducing cardiac arrest, or cardioplegia, helps protect the myocardium while providing the surgeon with a still, bloodless operative field and a flaccid heart on which to work. Cardioplegia solution is administered via the cardiopulmonary-bypass pump through specialized circuits.

During open-heart surgery, the heart is excluded from normal circulation by clamping the aorta. Systemic circulation of blood is maintained through the use of the cardiopulmonary-bypass pump; a cannula is placed in the aorta distal to the clamp and carries oxygenated blood from the pump to the patient. The blood circulates through the body and is returned to the cardiopulmonary bypass pump through cannulas inserted into the superior and inferior venae cava.

Delivery Methods

Cardioplegia solution is delivered to the coronary circulation by three approaches: antegrade, retrograde, or a combination antegrade/retrograde. With antegrade administration, the solution is administered via a cannula placed in the aortic root while with retrograde administration, the cannula is placed in the coronary sinus.[122] The combination approach increasingly is being used. Problems such as nonhomogenous distribution of cardioplegia solution which can be seen with the antegrade approach are eliminated while still ensuring a rapid arrest (arrest produced by retrograde administration not as fast as antegrade).[123,124] Utilizing the combination approach to administer blood-based cardioplegia solution has significantly reduced patient morbidity when compared to antegrade administration, especially in high-risk patients requiring reoperation.[125]

Phases of Cardioplegia

Cardioplegia can be divided into three phases: induction of arrest, maintenance of arrest, and reperfusion resulting from aortic unclamping (reversal of arrest). The cardioplegia solution used in each phase may differ in composition and characteristics. Cardioplegia solution is used routinely during the induction and main-

Table 8.11		Physicochemical and Pharmacokinetic Properties of Common Local Anesthetic Agents[109,110,115]				
Agent	pKa	Partition coefficient[a]	% Protein Binding	Onset	Duration (hr)[b]	
Bupivacaine (Sensorcaine, Marcaine)	8.2	27.5	95	Moderate to slow	2–5 (4–12 for nerve blocks)	
Chloroprocaine (Nesacaine)	9.0	0.14	—	Fast	0.5–1	
Etidocaine (Duranest)	7.7	141	94	Fast	2–4	
Lidocaine (Xylocaine)	7.9	2.9	65	Fast	1–2	
Mepivacaine (Carbocaine, Polocaine)	7.8	0.8	77	Fast	1.5–3	
Tetracaine (Pontocaine)	8.5	4.1	95	Fast	2–4	

[a] n-heptane/pH 7.4 buffer.
[b] Depends upon injection site, dose, use of epinephrine, and other factors.

tenance phases and increasingly in the reperfusion phase, in select patient populations, immediately before aortic unclamping.

Goal of Treatment

The goal of cardioplegia solution is to prevent myocardial ischemic damage that can occur during the induction phase and the destructive phenomena that can occur during reperfusion. Myocardial ischemia can result in a number of detrimental changes to the heart including rapid cellular conversion from aerobic to anaerobic metabolism, high-energy phosphate [e.g., adenosine triphosphate (ATP)] depletion, intracellular acidosis, calcium influx, and myocardial cell membrane disruption. Destructive changes that can occur during reperfusion include intracellular calcium accumulation, explosive cell swelling, and inability to use delivered oxygen.[126] Chemical components are added to cardioplegia solution to counteract the specific cellular effects of ischemia as well as the cellular events that can occur during reperfusion.

Cardioplegia Solution Vehicles

The chemical composition of a cardioplegia solution is dependent upon the vehicle used. There are two major cardioplegia solution vehicles: blood and crystalloid. Each has advantages and disadvantages as can be seen in Table 8.12.[122,123,127] Blood, because of its many advantages, is the vehicle most frequently used. More favorable outcomes (e.g., fewer ECG changes, better preservation of high-energy phosphates) are associated with blood-based cardioplegia solution than with crystalloid solution.[128–130] The disadvantages listed for blood have not been shown to occur during clinical use of blood-based cardioplegia solution. With blood-based cardioplegia solution, the patient's own hemodiluted blood from the extracorporeal circuit is used. Blood-based cardioplegia solution delivery systems deliver a fixed ratio of blood with a premixed crystalloid cardioplegia solution. The

concentration of additives in the crystalloid solution must be tailored to the specific delivery ratio used to prevent accidental over- or underdosage. The most commonly used ratio in clinical practice today is 4:1; in other words, the blood-based cardioplegia solution being delivered to the patient contains four parts blood to one part crystalloid solution. Therefore, the concentration of additives contained in the crystalloid solution is five times greater than that actually delivered to the patient. Further, with blood-based cardioplegia solution, there is a reduced need to place additives in the crystalloid component of the solution. For example, calcium and magnesium need not be added to the crystalloid component as sufficient quantities are contained in blood.

Common Characteristics

Most cardioplegia solutions have certain basic characteristics in common. Cardioplegia solutions usually are chilled to a temperature of 4° to 8 °C before being infused into the coronary circulation. Hypothermia decelerates the metabolic activity of the heart, reduces the effects of myocardial ischemia, and helps maintain cardiac arrest.[131,132] Cardioplegia solutions are made hyperosmolar to help minimize myocardial edema associated with cardiac arrest and usually are made slightly basic to compensate for the metabolic acidosis that accompanies myocardial ischemia.[122]

Additives

Table 8.13 presents commonly used cardioplegia solution additives, the reason for their addition to cardioplegia solution, and frequently used concentrations.[122,123] In addition to these additives, several other classes of agents are being examined for their usefulness in cardioplegia solution.

Calcium channel blockers are believed to protect the myocardium by decreasing myocardial contractility and the degradation of high energy phosphates.[133] Nicardipine (250 µg/L), nifedipine (200 to 333 µg/L), verapamil (1000 µg/L), and diltiazem (50 to 150 µg/kg) have been used clinically.[134–137] Although cardiac performance improves with these agents, no evidence of long-term improvement in patient survival and health was noted. Because of the potential for conduction defects or lingering negative inotropic effects after discontinuation of extracorporeal circulation, routine use of calcium channel blockers is not recommended at the present time.

Oxygen Free Radical Scavengers. Oxygen free radicals (e.g., superoxide anion, hydrogen peroxide, free hydroxyl radical) are released during the sudden reintroduction of oxygen to ischemic tissue during reperfusion. They have been implicated in myocyte death, reperfusion-induced arrhythmias, and prolonged left ventricular dysfunction after reperfusion.[126,133] The addition of oxygen free radical scavengers to cardioplegia solution, theoretically, should reduce the damaging effects of the free radicals. Allopurinol (100 mg/L, parenteral formulation not available in U.S.) and mannitol (59.8 mmol/L), when added to cardioplegia solution, have oxygen free radical scavenging effects in humans.[138,139] An advantage of using blood-based cardioplegia solution is that blood contains endogenous oxygen free radical scavengers (e.g., catalase, superoxide dismutase, glutathione). Additional work needs to be performed in this area before the routine addition of extraneous oxygen free radical scavengers to cardioplegia solution can be advocated.

Amino Acids. Glutamate and aspartate, Krebs' cycle precursors, are added to cardioplegia solution to counteract the depletion of Krebs' cycle intermediates during myocardial ischemia and to enhance energy production during reperfusion.[133,140] Beneficial effects of these agents have been demonstrated in select patient

Table 8.12	Advantages and Disadvantages of Cardioplegia Solution Vehicles[122,123,127]	
Vehicle	**Advantages**	**Disadvantages**
Blood	Oxygen-carrying capacity	Possible sludging at low temperatures
	Active resuscitation	
	Reduction in systemic hemodilution	Possible unfavorable shift in oxyhemoglobin association curve
	Avoidance of reperfusion damage	Potential for poor distribution of solution beyond coronary stenoses
	Provision of inherent buffering, oncotic, and rheologic effects	Possible RBC[a] crenation
	Provision of physiologic calcium concentration	
	Presence of endogenous oxygen free radical scavengers	
Crystalloid	History of effectiveness	Minimal oxygen-carrying capacity
	Ease of solution preparation	Possible damage of coronary endothelium
	Low cost	Reduced efficacy (compared to blood) in preserving left ventricular function postoperatively
	Minimal potential for capillary obstruction	Systemic hemodilution
		Possible role in production of late myocardial fibrosis

[a] RBC = Red blood cell.

Table 8.13	Commonly Used Cardioplegia Solution Additives[a]	
Additive	Frequently Used Concentration[b]	Function
Amino acid substrates (glutamate/aspartate[c])	11–12 mL/L[d]	Improves myocardial metabolism. Improves metabolic and functional recovery in energy-depleted hearts
Calcium	At least trace amounts (0.1 mEq/L)	Maintains integrity of myocardial cell membrane. Prevents "calcium paradox[e]"
Chloride	90–110 mEq/L	Establishes a solution similar in composition to extracellular fluid
CPD[f] solution	12 mL/L[g] 45 mL/L[d]	Chelates calcium in blood-based cardioplegia solution to produce safe levels of hypocalcemia for rapid diastolic arrest. Limits postischemic calcium accumulation and improves postischemic performance
Glucose	5–10 gm/L safely used	Helps achieve desired osmolarity of solution. Serves as a metabolic substrate for the heart
Magnesium	32 mEq/L	Reduces magnesium loss during ischemia. Reduces calcium influx and potassium efflux during ischemia. Has a weak arresting action on heart
Potassium	15–30 mEq/L[h]	Induces rapid diastolic arrest
Sodium	120–140 mEq/L	Necessary for protective action of potassium. Establishes a solution similar in composition to extracellular fluid.
Sodium bicarbonate or THAM[f]	Variable; added until desired pH obtained	Provides buffering capacity. Helps maintain physiologically normal pH range. Counters acidosis produced by ischemia

[a] Adapted from references 122 and 123.

[b] Concentration delivered to patient; concentration dependent upon other cardioplegia solution additives (concentration of any 1 additive may be changed by inclusion of other additives).

[c] Not commercially available in parenteral formulation; each mL of solution contains 178.4 mg monosodium L-glutamate and 163.4 mg monosodium L-aspartate (for preparation directions, see reference 122).

[d] Warm, blood-based induction and reperfusion solutions.

[e] Calcium paradox is a condition which results in rapid consumption of high-energy phosphates, extensive ultrastructural damage of myocardial cells, and myocardial contracture; it results from an influx of calcium into the myocardial cells, resulting from the introduction of a calcium-containing perfusate (i.e., blood), into the system during reperfusion after the use of a cardioplegia solution completely lacking in calcium.

[f] CPD = Citrate-phosphate-dextrose; THAM = Trihydroxymethylaminomethane.

[g] Cold, blood-based induction and maintenance solutions.

[h] Lower concentrations (5–10 mEq/L) used during maintenance and reperfusion phases.

groups [e.g., poor left ventricular function, extending myocardial infarction (MI), cardiogenic shock].[141,142] These agents enhance oxidative metabolism optimally at normothermia (37 °C) and should be used only during warm induction and reperfusion.[140]

Adenosine helps preserve endothelial cell structure in ischemic tissue of animals and prevents progressive reduction in microcirculatory flow that occurs after reperfusion.[143,144] Adenosine's beneficial effects may be due to its ability to produce coronary arteriolar vasodilation, inhibit generation of toxic free radical metabolites, and reduce neutrophil-mediated endothelial damage.[126] Studies examining the use of adenosine in humans need to be performed.

14. Potassium. W.D., a 64-year-old male, ASA-III, is scheduled to undergo a coronary artery bypass graft (CABG). A blood-based cardioplegia solution is ordered for the case consisting of the following constituents (per 1000 mL): potassium 96 mEq, calcium 2.4 mEq, magnesium 32 mEq, sodium 120 mEq, chloride 160 mEq, and bicarbonate 10 mEq. Cold induction (e.g., chilled cardioplegia solution) using a four part blood to one part cardioplegia solution (4:1) delivery system will be used. Upon administration of the solution to W.D., cardiac arrest was not achieved. A stat chemical analysis of the solution revealed that it contained no potassium. Why is this consistent with the findings in W.D.?

Failure to see immediate arrest within one to two minutes after the administration of cardioplegia solution can be due to several factors (e.g., incomplete aortic clamping, aortic insufficiency, and failure to add significant potassium to the cardioplegia solution). Since W.D.'s cardioplegia solution contained no potassium, a direct cause-and-effect relationship can be made to the inability to achieve an arrest.

Potassium's major role in cardioplegia solution is to induce a rapid diastolic arrest by blocking the inward sodium current and initial phases of cellular depolarization. This results in cessation of electromechanical activity and helps preserve ATP and creatine phosphate stores for postischemic work. A delivered potassium concentration in the range of 15 to 30 mEq/L is employed most commonly. This concentration consistently has produced asystole while minimizing adverse effects (e.g., tissue damage, systemic hyperkalemia). Potassium concentrations greater than 40 mEq/L alter myocardial cell membranes, allow extracellular calcium to enter the cell, and raise energy demands.[145] In laboratory studies, high concentrations of potassium (>100 mEq/L) increase myocardial contracture and wall tension, a condition referred to as "stone heart syndrome."[146] Varying concentrations of potassium are used in the cardioplegia solution depending upon the phase of cardioplegia. As already discussed, a high concentration of potassium is required to induce arrest while lower concentrations (e.g., 5 to 10 mEq/L) are sufficient to maintain arrest.[147] Although upon first glance the concentration of potassium ordered in W.D.'s blood-based cardioplegia solution appears excessive, the concentration delivered to the coronary circulation is approximately 19 mEq/L (96 mEq/L ÷ 5) because of the delivery system used. This highlights the importance of knowing the delivery ratio being used for the administration of blood-based cardioplegia solution.

15. Amino Acids: Warm, Blood-Based Cardioplegia Solution. T.E., a 55-year-old male, ASA-IV, is admitted to the hospital with an MI. He currently is in the coronary care unit and is scheduled for myocardial revascularization surgery. He has poor left ventricular function [cardiac output 2.2 L/min (Normal: 4–6), pulmonary capillary wedge pressure 25 mm Hg (Normal: 5–12), left ventricular ejection fraction 25% (Normal: >60%)] and is on an intra-aortic balloon pump (IABP) for circulatory support. In addition to being on the IABP, he is receiving dobutamine, IV NTG, and lidocaine. A diagnosis of cardiogenic shock is made. What type of cardioplegia solution should T.E. receive during his revascularization surgery?

Warm (37 °C), blood-based cardioplegia solution containing the amino acids glutamate and aspartate has been advocated for the induction and reperfusion phases of cardioplegia in patients with ischemic hearts (e.g., extending MI, cardiogenic shock, hemodynamic instability) or those with advanced left or right ventricular hypertrophy or dysfunction. With this technique, cardioplegia induction is accomplished with an infusion of the warm, blood-based cardioplegia solution over five minutes. Normothermia optimizes the rate of cellular repair while glutamate and aspartate improve oxygen utilization capacity.[140] The warm solution is immediately followed by a five-minute infusion of hypothermic blood-based cardioplegia solution. Cardioplegia is maintained with hypothermic blood-based solution. Warm cardioplegia solution is administered again for three to five minutes immediately before aortic unclamping (reperfusion). The administration of warm cardioplegia solution at the conclusion of surgery is referred to by some as a "hot shot" and is felt to allow energy supplies to be channelled into cellular recovery rather than electromechanical work. This results in improved hemodynamic and myocardial metabolic recovery.[140,148]

T.E., with his poor myocardial function, is a suitable candidate to receive amino acid-enriched, warm, blood-based cardioplegia solution during the induction and reperfusion phases of cardioplegia.

Antiemetic Agents and
Postoperative Nausea and Vomiting

Incidence of Postoperative Nausea and Vomiting

Postoperative nausea and vomiting occurs in about 20% to 30% of patients when antiemetic agents are not administered prophylactically.[149] Postoperative nausea and vomiting typically lasts less than 24 hours and in most cases is considered a minor postoperative complication. However, severe postoperative nausea and vomiting has been reported to occur in 0.1% of patients.[150]

Causes of Postoperative Nausea and Vomiting
and Mechanism of Action of Antiemetic Agents

Postoperative nausea and vomiting are thought to result from a variety of factors which stimulate the chemoreceptor trigger zone and/or peripheral receptors in the GI tract (results in activation of the vomiting center).[149,151,152] The emetic response appears to be mediated by four major neurotransmitter systems: serotonergic (5HT$_3$), histaminic (H$_1$), dopaminergic (D$_2$), and muscarinic cholinergic.[149,153] The currently available antiemetic agents act at one or more of these receptors. Table 8.14 lists the agents most frequently used for postoperative nausea and vomiting and their actions at these receptors.[149,153] Combining agents that work at different receptor sites may produce an even greater antiemetic action.

Factors, Complications, and Patient
Groups Associated with Postoperative Vomiting

Factors associated with postoperative vomiting are listed in Table 8.15 and can be divided into nonanesthetic factors, anesthetic-related factors, and postoperative factors.[149,151,154,155] Various complications can result from persistent nausea and vomiting and include dehydration, electrolyte imbalance, and hypertension as well as an increased risk of pulmonary aspiration of vomitus, increased bleeding, and increased tension on suture lines.[149] Postoperative nausea and vomiting can result in prolongation of a patient's recovery room stay, delay discharge after outpatient surgery, or result in unanticipated hospital admission following outpatient surgery.

Routine administration of antiemetic agents for prophylaxis of postoperative nausea and vomiting is not recommended. The majority of patients undergoing surgery do not experience postoperative nausea and vomiting; in those who do, the nausea often is transient and the number of emetic episodes minimal (one or two). Further, the antiemetic agents in clinical use today are not without

side effects (e.g., hypotension, extrapyramidal reactions, drowsiness, dysphoria, lethargy). Prophylactic administration of antiemetic agents is indicated in certain groups of patients or in patients undergoing certain surgical procedures. These include children undergoing orchiopexy, strabismus surgery, tonsilloadenoidectomy, and otoplasty; adults undergoing extracorporeal shock wave lithotripsy, head and neck surgery, GI surgery, ocular surgery, and ear surgery; women undergoing gynecologic procedures; patients with a full stomach; and patients with a history of previous postoperative nausea and vomiting or motion sickness.[149,151,152,155]

16. J.E., a 34-year-old, 55 kg female, ASA-I, is scheduled to undergo a gynecologic laparoscopy under general anesthesia (she refuses regional anesthesia) on an outpatient basis. She has no previous surgical history and no known medication allergies. Upon questioning, she reports no history of motion sickness. All laboratory tests are within normal limits and her physical exam is unremarkable. She is not menstruating. Why is J.E. a candidate for prophylactic antiemetic therapy?

J.E. has several risk factors which make her susceptible to postoperative nausea and vomiting. Adult females have a significantly greater incidence of postoperative nausea and vomiting when compared to males.[149,155] The fact that J.E. is not menstruating is important because the incidence of postoperative nausea and vomiting in females undergoing laparoscopy is increased if surgery is performed during menses.[156] The type of procedure J.E. is undergoing places her at risk for postoperative nausea and vomiting. Gynecologic laparoscopy is associated with a high incidence of postoperative nausea and vomiting.[155] Finally, J.E. is scheduled for general anesthesia. General anesthesia is associated with a greater risk of postoperative nausea and vomiting than when regional anesthetic techniques are used.[157,158] Since J.E. is an outpatient, postoperative nausea and vomiting are not desired as they may delay her discharge or result in admission to the hospital. Based upon the combination of these factors, J.E. should be administered a prophylactic antiemetic agent.

Choice of Agent

17. What antiemetic drug would be most appropriate for J.E.?

Butyrophenones, benzamides, antiserotonin agents, phenothiazines, antihistamines, and anticholinergics all have been used for prophylaxis against postoperative nausea and vomiting.

Butyrophenones. Droperidol and haloperidol possess significant antiemetic activity. Haloperidol, in a dose of 0.5 to 4 mg IM, was shown to be an effective prophylactic agent for postoperative nausea and vomiting and did not delay recovery from anesthesia.[159] When used to treat postoperative nausea and vomiting, a 2 mg IM dose was shown to be effective; however, duration of effect was as short as three hours.[160] Although effective, haloperidol is not used routinely in anesthesia today. Droperidol is the most frequently used butyrophenone with doses in the range of 0.005 to 0.07 mg/kg IV effective in preventing postoperative nausea and vomiting.[153] However, high doses are associated with increased drowsiness and can result in a delayed discharge. Lower doses of droperidol (0.01 to 0.02 mg/kg) have been shown to be effective in preventing postoperative nausea and vomiting in procedures with a moderately high incidence of emesis.[161] The dose of droperidol should not exceed 2.5 mg for outpatients; drowsiness becomes more evident as the dose increases above 1.25 mg. Droperidol also may be more effective when administered toward the end of surgery.[162] Droperidol has an onset of action of three to ten minutes with peak effects seen at 30 minutes. The antiemetic effects of droperidol have been demonstrated up to 24 hours after

Table 8.14	Receptor Activity of Antiemetic Agents[a,b]			
Agent	Muscarinic Cholinergic	Dopamine	Histamine	Serotonin (5HT$_3$)
Anticholinergics				
Atropine	++++	+	+	—
Scopolamine	++++	+	+	—
Antihistamines				
Cyclizine (Marezine)	++	+	++++	—
Promethazine (Phenergan)	++	++	++++	—
Antiserotonin				
Ondansetron (Zofran)	—	—	—	++++
Benzamides				
Metoclopramide (Reglan)	—	+++	+	++[c]
Butyrophenones				
Droperidol (Inapsine)	—	++++	+	+
Haloperidol (Haldol)	—	++++	+	—
Phenothiazines				
Prochlorperazine (Compazine)	+	++++	++	—
Chlorpromazine (Thorazine)	++	++++	++++	+

[a] Adapted from references 149 and 153.
[b] + – ++++ = Level of activity relative to the other agents; — = No activity.
[c] Activity at serotonin receptors becomes evident at higher doses.

administration.[160] Adverse effects of droperidol include sedation, extrapyramidal reactions, hypotension, anxiety, and restlessness; however, extrapyramidal reactions are relatively rare.[162] In one study, droperidol was implicated as the cause of restlessness and anxiety in 23% of outpatients after they had been discharged to home. These patients received a 1.25 mg dose of droperidol at induction of anesthesia.[163]

Benzamides. Metoclopramide, in a dose of 0.1 to 0.2 mg/kg, has been used in the prevention and treatment of postoperative nausea and vomiting. Variable results, however, have been seen with this agent.[149] For maximal benefit, it appears that metoclopramide must be administered near the end of surgery (secondary to its rapid redistribution after IV administration). Further, it appears that doses on the higher end of the normal range may be more effective.[162] Adverse effects of metoclopramide include extrapyramidal reactions, drowsiness, and restlessness. The incidence of extrapyramidal reactions and degree of sedation is less than that seen with droperidol. Several case reports have documented significant cardiovascular effects (e.g., hypotension, bradycardia, supraventricular tachycardia) with IV administration of the agent.[162] Metoclopramide should be administered intravenously over at least one to two minutes.

Antiserotonin. Ondansetron is the first antiserotonin (5HT$_3$-antagonist) agent to receive an indication for postoperative nausea and vomiting. Studies have shown it to be effective for both the prevention and treatment of postoperative nausea and vomiting.[164,165] The Food and Drug Administration-approved dose of the agent for adults is 4 mg IV although lower doses (1 to 2 mg) may provide similar results.[166] A single dose of ondansetron provides acute relief and may protect against nausea and vomiting for up to 24 hours. Adverse effects are minimal and include headache and dizziness.[167] Ondansetron is significantly more expensive than the other commercially used agents for postoperative nausea and vomiting (e.g., droperidol, metoclopramide) and should be reserved for patients who have a previous history of intractable postoperative nausea and vomiting, who are undergoing surgery in which other antiemetic agents have been shown to be ineffective, or postoperatively after other agents have failed.

Phenothiazines. Prochlorperazine has been used successfully in the treatment of postoperative nausea and vomiting.[160] Its usefulness in the prevention of postoperative nausea and vomiting is less clear. A study in patients undergoing gynecological laparoscopies showed a significant reduction (73%) in the incidence of postoperative nausea and vomiting.[168] Other studies have not substantiated this effect, however.[162] Doses in the range of 5 to 12.5 mg IM or IV have been employed. Perphenazine also has been shown to be effective for both the prophylaxis and treatment of postoperative nausea and vomiting (5 mg IM or IV).[162] Both prochlorperazine and perphenazine may cause sedation, extrapyramidal reactions, and cardiovascular effects in patients. A greater degree of sedation and a greater incidence of extrapyramidal reactions are felt to occur with perphenazine.[162] Both agents also have short durations of action and may need to be redosed when being used to treat postoperative nausea and vomiting. Chlorpromazine, although effective in the prevention of postoperative nausea and vomiting, is not used routinely because of its numerous adverse effects (e.g., hypotension, sedation).

Antihistamines. Promethazine is effective for the prevention of postoperative nausea and vomiting; its use, however, is limited by its sedative action.[162] Cyclizine is the antihistamine used most frequently worldwide for both the prevention and treatment of postoperative nausea and vomiting, although it does not enjoy widespread use in the U.S.[169,170] For treatment of postoperative nausea and vomiting, an IM dose of 50 mg every four to six hours can be used. Cyclizine's duration of action is approximately four hours with mild sedation and dry mouth being its main side effects. Parenteral administration is limited to the intramuscular route.

Anticholinergics. Atropine and scopolamine have been administered concurrently with opioid premedication to reduce the emetogenic effects of the opioid.[149] Scopolamine appears to be more effective than atropine in preventing emesis; however, patients administered scopolamine tend to be more drowsy and show a delay in recovery from anesthesia.[162] Transdermal scopolamine is effective in decreasing the incidence of postoperative nausea and vomiting after outpatient laparoscopy and epidural morphine administration; there are conflicting reports about its usefulness in strabismus surgery.[149,171,172] Common side effects include drows-

Table 8.15	Factors Associated with Postoperative Vomiting[a,145,151,152,154,155]

Nonanesthetic

Patient-Related

Age (↑ incidence in pediatric patients)

Gender (↑ incidence in females)

Obesity

History of motion sickness

History of previous postoperative vomiting

Preoperative anxiety

Gastroparesis

Phase of menstrual cycle (↑ incidence during menses)

Surgical Procedure

Type

   Adults: ↑ incidence in laparoscopic gynecological procedures, extracorporeal shock-wave lithotripsy, head and neck surgery, ear surgery, GI surgery

   Children: ↑ incidence in middle ear surgery, hernia surgery, orchiopexy, strabismus surgery, tonsilloadenoidectomy, otoplasty

Duration (↑ incidence with ↑ duration)

Anesthetic

Premedication (↑ incidence with use of opioids)

Mask ventilation (secondary to gastric distension)

Anesthetic Technique

↑ incidence with inhalation versus total IV anesthesia

↑ incidence with nitrous oxide-opioid-relaxant technique versus inhalation or total IV anesthesia

↓ incidence with propofol for total IV anesthesia

↑ incidence with ketamine induction/maintenance of anesthesia

↑ incidence with etomidate induction

↓ incidence with intraoperative use of ketorolac

↑ incidence with use of acetylcholinesterase inhibitors

↓ incidence with regional anesthesia versus general anesthesia

Postoperative

Pain

Dizziness

Ambulation/changes in position

Hypotension

Administration of opioids

[a] GI = Gastrointestinal; IV = Intravenous.

iness, dry mouth, dizziness, amblyopia, and mydriasis. It is important to apply the patch several hours before surgery as steady-state concentrations are not achieved for at least five hours.

Miscellaneous Agents. *Ephedrine*, in a dose of 0.5 mg/kg IM, has been reported to be effective in preventing postoperative nausea and vomiting in patients undergoing outpatient gynecologic laparoscopy. It may be especially useful in patients prone to motion sickness or who experience nausea and vomiting upon ambulation (secondary to postural hypotension). Minimal side effects are seen with its use (e.g., mild sedation). Use of ephedrine should be avoided in patients with hypertension or organic heart disease.[173] *Benzquinamide*, a benzquinolizine derivative, has not been shown to be effective in preventing postoperative nausea and vomiting and its clinical use is limited.

For prophylaxis of postoperative nausea and vomiting, J.E. should be administered droperidol 0.6 mg (0.01 mg/kg) approximately 30 to 45 minutes before conclusion of surgery. This dose has been shown to be effective in surgery with a moderately high incidence of emesis (e.g., gynecologic laparoscopy) while producing a minimal degree of sedation. Metoclopramide in a dose of 10 mg (0.02 mg/kg) also could be used but, because of the variable results seen with this agent, may not be as effective as droperidol.

Since ephedrine appears to be most effective in patients with a postural component to their nausea/vomiting or in those with a history of motion sickness, it is not a good choice in J.E. based upon her negative history of motion sickness. Since nothing in J.E.'s history would indicate that she is predisposed to severe postoperative nausea and vomiting, ondansetron should not be used as a first-line agent, especially when one considers its cost. Cyclizine's limitation of intramuscular administration, prochlorperazine's questionable efficacy in the prevention of postoperative nausea and vomiting, and scopolamine's frequent side effects as well as the need to apply the patch several hours before surgery do not make these agents drugs of choice.

Anesthetic Agents with Low Incidence of Postoperative Nausea and Vomiting

18. J.E. is taken to surgery. Anesthesia is induced with thiopental and maintained with isoflurane. Fentanyl is administered intraoperatively for analgesia. A prophylactic dose of droperidol is administered near the end of surgery. Residual neuromuscular blockade produced by vecuronium is reversed with neostigmine and glycopyrrolate. In the recovery room, J.E. becomes nauseated and has several emetic episodes. What do you recommend? How could the anesthetic regimen have been modified to reduce the likelihood of postoperative nausea and vomiting?

Since J.E. is experiencing postoperative nausea and vomiting, it would be logical to administer a repeat dose of droperidol 0.6 mg IV. Droperidol is effective in both preventing and treating postoperative nausea and vomiting.

Several changes could be made in the anesthetic regimen to reduce the likelihood of postoperative nausea and vomiting. Propofol could be used for induction because it produces less postoperative nausea and vomiting when compared to thiopental.[174] Likewise, a total intravenous technique, utilizing propofol, could be used for maintenance of anesthesia; total intravenous anesthesia reduces the incidence of postoperative nausea and vomiting when compared to inhalational anesthesia.[175] Propofol has been postulated to have antiemetic properties.[56] Controversy exists today over the role of nitrous oxide in postoperative nausea and vomiting. Early studies suggested that it may increase the incidence and severity of postoperative nausea and vomiting when used in conjunction with the volatile anesthetic agents. More recent studies in adult patients have shown that nitrous oxide does not significantly affect the incidence of postoperative nausea and vomiting when used with the volatile agents.[149] Many anesthesiologists still will avoid the use of this agent in patients prone to postoperative nausea and vomiting, as in J.E. Ketorolac could be used to provide intraoperative analgesia; less postoperative nausea and vomiting are associated with this agent when compared to the opioids.[176] Finally, a neuromuscular blocking agent with a short duration of action (i.e., mivacurium) could be used in place of vecuronium. Appropriate titration of the mivacurium dose may obviate the need for reversal of residual neuromuscular block. Acetylcholinesterase inhibitors (i.e., neostigmine) have been shown to contribute to postoperative nausea and vomiting.[81]

19. Thirty minutes have passed and J.E. has experienced several more emetic episodes. What would be the most appropriate antiemetic for J.E.?

Since J.E. already has received two doses of droperidol without apparent effect, additional doses are not likely to be effective and will increase the likelihood of side effects. Instead, an agent that works by a different mechanism of action and preferably with a minimal side effect profile should be selected. These criteria eliminate the phenothiazines and benzamides as they have a mechanism of action similar to droperidol (antidopaminergic). The antihistamines and anticholinergics likewise are excluded secondary to their side effect profiles which potentially could delay J.E.'s discharge from the hospital. Ondansetron, because of its activity at the $5HT_3$ receptors and minimal side effect profile, is the most appropriate agent for J.E. A dose of 4 mg should be given IV push over two to five minutes (not less than 30 seconds). The cost of ondansetron (≈ 60 times greater than that for an average dose of droperidol or metoclopramide) will be more than offset if its use allows J.E. to be discharged without a prolonged delay or prevents an unscheduled admission to the hospital.

Analgesic Agents and Postoperative Pain Management

Acute Pain

Acute pain following surgical procedures has limited utility as a marker of tissue injury and contributes significantly to morbidity and patient discontent.[177,178] Pain severity can only be perceived by the patient himself[179] and is dependent upon the surgical site and procedure, previous pain experiences, and the level of fear or anxiety.[180] Postoperative pain can result in catecholamine release and other metabolic activation with subsequent tachycardia, hypertension, vasoconstriction, cardiac ischemia, fluid retention, hypercoagulability, catabolism and protein wasting, immunosuppression, hyperglycemia, and prolongation of ileus.[177,178,180-182] Pain in the thoracic region can restrict pulmonary function and cause acute pulmonary disease.[177,183,184]

Management Options

The management of postoperative pain has moved away from limited prescribing of "as needed" intramuscular injections of narcotics. As many as 75% of patients receiving such intramuscular narcotics remain in moderate to severe pain;[185] this unacceptable rate of efficacy has been attributed to problems inherent to IM drug administration, inappropriate drug orders, wide patient variability in drug requirements, and a fear of narcotic addiction.[177,186] Today, such options as continuous epidural infusion or intravenous patient-controlled analgesia (PCA) with a wider variety of agents can provide more effective pain management. Local anesthetics, narcotics, and nonsteroidal anti-inflammatory drugs (NSAIDs) are used alone or in combination to create the optimal analgesic regimen for each patient based upon factors such as efficacy for an acceptable level of pain, type of surgery, underlying disease, adverse effects, and cost of therapy. (For more information about general pain management see Chapter 7: Pain.)

Patient-Controlled Analgesia (PCA)

20. Advantages. J.G., a 35-year-old female, is immediately postoperative from an open cholecystectomy procedure. Her medical history is remarkable for chronic renal failure for which she receives dialysis twice weekly on an outpatient basis. She has no known medication allergies. She is admitted to the postsurgical floor for a planned stay of 2 to 3 days. What mode of pain management should be chosen for J.G.?

Patient-controlled analgesia narcotic administration has grown tremendously in popularity in the past several years, and offers several advantages over traditional intramuscular narcotic dosing. Intermittent IM dosing is painful in itself, with such problems as delays between patient medication request and drug administration, variability in drug absorption from IM sites, inappropriate subcutaneous injection, and incorrect patient-specific dosing.[187-189] PCA is equal or superior to IM injections for efficacy of pain management,[190,191] with a high level of patient acceptance[192] and small

frequent PCA dosing minimizes the serum concentration peaks and valleys seen with intermittent IM injections.[193] The use of PCA allows the patient to control her own pain therapy and may save nursing assessment and drug administration time; an infusion pump with a programmed drug dose and minimum dosing interval ("lockout interval") is equipped with a button that the patient presses to receive each dose. IV bolus is the most common PCA route, but subcutaneous and epidural routes also have been used in select patients.

If dosed properly, PCA can be used to alleviate anticipated pain before movement or physical therapy. J.G. has undergone a procedure for which moderate to severe pain is expected in the immediate postoperative period. Her pain requirements could be met with PCA narcotic administration until she can take oral analgesics.

21. Patient Selection. J.G.'s surgeon decides to prescribe PCA for postoperative pain management. How should J.G. be evaluated for her ability to appropriately participate in her analgesic administration?

Patients receiving PCA therapy must be able to understand PCA and operate the drug administration button. J.G. must be alert and oriented before being put in control of her own pain management. She must be able to comprehend verbal or written instructions regarding the function and safety features of the infusion pump and how to titrate drug as needed for satisfactory analgesia.

22. Patient Instructions. J.G. is nervous about giving herself an overdose while using PCA. What instructions should be provided to her?

Patients often worry about the safety of PCA, which can lead to a reluctance to provide themselves with adequate pain relief. J.G. should learn that her infusion pump will be programmed with a maximum amount of drug she can receive in a given period, usually four hours. She also should know that each time she presses the button, she receives only one preprogrammed dose and cannot receive another dose within a specified period of time (the lockout interval), such as eight minutes. If she inadvertently rolled over in bed onto her PCA button, she would receive only one dose despite continuous depression of the button. She should understand the possible adverse effects of her PCA medication and what can be done to prevent and treat these effects, as well as the advantages of providing herself with adequate analgesia (i.e., early ambulation). Finally, she should be told of the negligible risk of narcotic addiction from short-term PCA use and be given ample opportunity to ask questions.

23. Choice of Agent. Meperidine is ordered for J.G.'s PCA. Is this a reasonable drug choice for her?

Narcotics ideal for PCA administration have a rapid onset and intermediate duration of action, with no accumulation, ceiling of effect, or adverse reactions.[194] Morphine and meperidine are used most commonly, although the use of other narcotics such as fentanyl and hydromorphone also is well documented.[194] Drug choice is based upon past patient experiences, allergies, adverse effects, and special considerations. J.G. has significant renal insufficiency, and should receive a drug that does not accumulate or exhibit toxicity if renal clearance is diminished. Meperidine should not be chosen based upon possible accumulation of the metabolite, normeperidine, which can cause CNS excitation leading to seizures.[195] Morphine is used commonly in patients with renal insufficiency despite possible accumulation of a metabolite with some parental activity. Morphine would be a better analgesic choice for J.G. Table 8.16 lists common doses and lockout intervals for drugs administered by PCA.

24. Dosing. J.G. is of average height and weight and has not received any narcotics for several years before her surgery to-

Table 8.16	Adult Analgesic Dosing Recommendations for PCA[a,b]		
	Bolus Dose (mg)		
Drug	**Range**	**Usual**	**Lockout Interval (min)**
Fentanyl (as citrate) (Sublimaze)	0.015–0.1	0.05	3–10
Hydromorphone HCl (Dilaudid)	0.1–0.5	0.2	5–10
Meperidine HCl (Demerol)	5–30	10	5–10
Morphine sulfate	0.5–3	1	5–10

[a] Adapted from references 186 and 203.
[b] HCl = Hydrochloride; PCA = Patient-controlled analgesia.

day. What dose of morphine and lockout interval should be prescribed for J.G.'s initial PCA pump settings?

If J.G. is experiencing pain before PCA has been initiated, she should receive a loading dose of intravenous morphine titrated to achieve baseline pain relief. Then, 1 to 1.5 mg doses of morphine with a lockout interval of six to eight minutes would be a good initial choice for this opiate-naive patient. Downward dose adjustments often are necessary in elderly patients or those at risk for respiratory depression. A higher dose would be initiated in narcotic-tolerant or excessively large patients. A four-hour maximum dose commonly is set at 30 mg of morphine for a patient such as J.G.

25. Use of Basal Infusion. After the first postoperative evening, J.G. tells you that she had a terrible time sleeping. She describes waking up in pain frequently and wishes that she did not have to press her PCA button while she was trying to sleep. During waking hours, she rates her pain relief as satisfactory. What can be done about this problem?

Many PCA infusion pumps offer a continuous infusion setting for a basal infusion during intermittent dosing. Use of a basal infusion can be helpful for nocturnal pain management. However, because literature shows no advantage and possible increased risk of adverse effects with infusion use,[196] routine basal infusions are not recommended for acute pain management. A better approach is to increase the size of the bolus dose during nighttime hours. J.G.'s PCA morphine dose could be increased at night to allow her to sleep for longer periods, and returned to the previous amount during the day.

26. Adverse Effects. The next day, J.G. reports adequate pain relief with her PCA, but complains of feeling slightly groggy and having periodic nausea. Bowel sounds are noted upon physical examination, and J.G. plans to try taking clear liquids later that morning. What are the adverse effects of PCA narcotics and how can J.G.'s complaints be addressed?

Narcotics given by PCA can produce adverse effects similar to those given by other parenteral routes. Sedation, confusion, nausea and vomiting, constipation, urinary retention, and pruritus can be experienced, and managed by dose adjustments or pharmacologic intervention. Respiratory depression is extremely rare with PCA narcotic administration.[194] J.G.'s PCA morphine dose could be reduced to manage her sedated feeling and nausea, with pain assessment to assure efficacy of the new dose. An order for an antiemetic could be provided as well. In patients without renal insufficiency, an NSAID (ketorolac IM/IV or other NSAID orally) could be added to the pain regimen for analgesia without sedation. J.G., however, should avoid NSAID therapy. If J.G. can begin to ingest fluids, she could discontinue PCA and receive analgesics by mouth instead. As time passes, her level of pain will lessen, and oral narcotic/acetaminophen products could manage her pain adequately with potentially less sedation or nausea. Switching from

PCA to oral therapy is simple and self-titrating; the PCA can be disconnected and J.G. then can request oral analgesics as needed.

Epidural Analgesia

27. T.M., a 58-year-old obese male, enters the surgical ICU after a lobectomy procedure. His pain is managed through a thoracic epidural catheter. What are the benefits and risks of epidural analgesic therapy and why was this chosen for T.M.?

Advantages and Disadvantages. Epidural analgesia offers superior pain relief over traditional parenteral analgesia when used in conjunction with appropriate surgical procedures.[121] Other proposed advantages of epidural over parenteral analgesia include less sedation and respiratory depression,[121] reduction in the postoperative stress response,[197,198] and decreased overall morbidity and mortality in high-risk surgical patients.[108] Continuous epidural infusions offer an advantage over intermittent epidural injections because peak and trough concentrations of drugs are avoided. Epidural catheter placement is an invasive procedure and can result on rare occasions in unintentional dural puncture, epidural space infection, bleeding complications, and catheter migrations during therapy.[121]

Patient Selection. Epidural analgesia should be chosen based upon the need for superior analgesia after surgery in which pain is localized at an appropriate level for catheter placement in the thoracic, lumbar, or caudal location of the epidural space. Patients undergoing thoracic, upper abdominal, major vascular, or orthopedic lower limb surgery often are good candidates for epidural analgesia.[177,199] In addition, specific high-risk patients may benefit from epidural pain management; patients with severe respiratory disease or morbid obesity are at high risk of postoperative respiratory complications, and epidural analgesia may reduce their risk of prolonged postoperative intubation.[121] Absolute contraindications to epidural therapy include severe systemic infection or infection in the area of catheter insertion, a major coagulation defect, uncorrected hypovolemia, and patient refusal.

T.M. is a good candidate for epidural analgesia based upon the severity of pain associated with his surgery, the surgical site, and his obesity.

28. Choice of Agent and Mechanisms of Action. What drug or drug combination can be used for T.M.'s epidural infusion? What are the mechanisms of action of the analgesics commonly administered in the epidural space?

Narcotics and local anesthetics commonly are administered alone or in combination in epidural infusions. Narcotics enter the epidural space and are transported by passive diffusion and vas-

Table 8.17	Adult Analgesic Dosing Recommendations for Epidural Infusion[121,199,204–210]	
Drug[a]	**Infusion Concentration (mg/mL)**	**Infusion Rate (mg/hr)**
Bupivacaine HCl (Sensorcaine, Marcaine)	1–5	5–37.5
Fentanyl (as citrate) (Sublimaze)	0.005–0.025	0.2–1.5
Hydromorphone HCl (Dilaudid)	0.02–0.05	0.15–0.3
Meperidine HCl (Demerol)	1–2	5–20
Morphine sulfate	0.05–0.25	0.2–1.5
Sufentanil (as citrate) (Sufenta)	0.001	0.05–0.1

[a] HCl = Hydrochloride.

Table 8.18	Pharmacokinetic Comparison of Common Epidural Narcotic Analgesics[a]			
Drug	Partition Coefficient[b]	Onset of Action of Bolus (min)	Duration of Action of Bolus (hr)	Dermatomal Spread
Fentanyl (Sublimaze)	813	5	3–6	Narrow
Hydromorphone (Dilaudid)	1.4	15	10–16	Intermediate-wide
Meperidine (Demerol)	39	5–10	6–8	Intermediate
Morphine	1.4	30	12–20	Wide
Sufentanil (Sufenta)	1778	5	6–8	Narrow

[a] Adapted from references 121, 211, and 212.
[b] Octanol:pH 4 buffer.

culature to the spinal cord; here they act on opiate receptors in the substantia gelatinosa to alter the transmission of nociceptive (pain) information in the CNS. Narcotics selectively block pain transmission and have no effect on nerve transmission responsible for motor, sensory, or autonomic function. Local anesthetics act on axonal nerve membranes crossing through the epidural space to produce analgesia by inhibiting nerve transmission. Depending upon the drug, concentration and depth of nerve penetration, local anesthetics also produce sensory, motor, or autonomic blockade (see Local Anesthetics).

Various narcotics and local anesthetics have been used successfully in epidural drug preparations. Most commonly, drugs from each class have been combined to produce analgesia by two different mechanisms with minimal additive toxicity. Table 8.17 lists the drugs, concentrations, and typical infusion rates for epidural administration. Bupivacaine most commonly is chosen as the local anesthetic agent because it can produce analgesia without significant motor blockade, has less tachyphylaxis, and has a better safety profile over other drugs.[199] The choice of narcotic is based upon pharmacokinetic differences among available agents. Onset, duration, spread of agent in the spinal fluid (dermatomal spread), and systemic absorption are affected by the lipophilicity of the drug.[199] Highly lipophilic narcotics (e.g., fentanyl) have faster onsets of action, shorter durations of action, less dermatomal spread, and more systemic absorption. The characteristics of the surgical incision often determine the best narcotic for a given patient; a long incision may require a drug with a dermatomal spread large enough to cover the appropriate longitudinal area on the spinal cord and corresponding body dermatomes affected by surgical pain. A comparison of the pharmacokinetic properties important to epidural narcotics is found in Table 8.18.

T.M. can receive a combination local anesthetic/narcotic epidural infusion for optimization of his pain management. His surgery should provoke severe pain over relatively few dermatomes depending upon the chest tube placement site. He could receive fentanyl/bupivacaine or meperidine/bupivacaine to be sure of analgesic coverage of both his surgical and chest tube sites. Meperidine would be a better narcotic choice than fentanyl because it provides more dermatomal spread. Morphine would be less likely to be used because dermatomal spread would be unnecessarily large, perhaps enough in a thoracic epidural catheter to risk migration of the drug into the brain and respiratory depression.

29. Meperidine/bupivacaine is chosen for T.M. How should this be prepared and what infusion rate should be chosen?

Meperidine and bupivacaine are relatively evenly matched for dermatomal spread characteristics and dose-effect relationships. They commonly are admixed as 1 mg/mL concentrations of each drug in 0.9% sodium chloride. Preservative-free preparations of each drug should be used, as neurologic effects are possible with inadvertent subdural administration of large amounts of benzyl al-

cohol or other neurotoxic preservatives. Aseptic technique should be used in epidural solution admixture.

The rate of administration is chosen empirically based upon anticipated level of pain and potential for adverse effects. Usually, 5 to 10 mL/hour is adequate; the epidural space can safely handle up to approximately 20 mL/hour of fluid. T.M. may anticipate a significantly high level of pain after a lobectomy, and he is obese. An initial infusion rate of 8 mL/hour would be reasonable, with titration based upon efficacy and adverse effects.

30. Adverse Effects. **Three hours after initiation of his meperidine/bupivacaine epidural infusion, T.M. experiences discomfort in the form of an itchy feeling on his torso and limbs. Is this related to his epidural infusion?**

Epidural narcotics can cause generalized pruritus at a frequency that is significantly greater than that caused by IV administration.[213] The cause is unknown, but the effect usually is seen within the first few hours, and probably is dose related. Pruritus often resolves with dose reduction or substitution of another narcotic;[199] it also subsides with time in many cases.[211] It can be treated with the IV administration of naloxone if necessary.

Other adverse effects possible with epidural narcotics include respiratory depression, urinary retention, and nausea and vomiting. Respiratory depression from epidural narcotics perhaps is the most worrisome adverse effect, although it is rare in occurrence. Two mechanisms contribute to the development of respiratory depression. Early respiratory depression, usually occurring within one hour of narcotic administration, is thought to be due to systemic absorption of the drug, elevated blood levels, and subsequent distribution to the brain respiratory centers. Late depression, occurring typically 3 to 12 hours after drug administration,[200,201] is thought to be secondary to cerebrospinal fluid spread of the drug to the fourth ventricle of the brain. Most reports of delayed respiratory depression involve the more hydrophilic morphine (frequency: 0.09% to 3%[202]); no reports to date have described this complication with fentanyl or meperidine. Adverse effects of epidural local anesthetics include hypotension, urinary retention, lower limb paresthesias and numbness, and lower limb motor block.

31. Adjunctive Ketorolac Use. **On the second postoperative day, T.M. rests comfortably when undisturbed with a thoracic epidural infusion of meperidine 1 mg/mL + bupivacaine 1 mg/mL at a rate of 5 mL/hr. When he is moved each nursing shift, however, he complains of significant pain. Increasing the rate of his epidural infusion was tried but resulted in unacceptable pruritus. How could T.M.'s intermittent pain needs be addressed?**

The use of additional analgesics for breakthrough pain may be necessary in patients receiving epidural continuous infusions. Parenteral narcotics or other respiratory depressant drugs should not be used, however, as they significantly increase a patient's risk of respiratory depression.[121] T.M.'s intermittent pain could be managed by small bolus doses of epidural fentanyl (quick onset, short duration) if the dermatomal spread is adequate for the source of his pain. Another option is the use of IM or IV ketorolac well before each painful insult.

Ketorolac, the first NSAID available for parenteral administration, does not contribute to respiratory depression and is effective in the treatment of moderate to severe pain. Patient selection for ketorolac therapy should consider renal function, GI disease, risk of bleeding, patient age, and cost of added therapy. If patients can take oral medications, an oral NSAID can be chosen for breakthrough pain at a lesser cost than ketorolac.

References

1 **Egbert LD et al.** The value of the preoperative visit by an anesthetist. JAMA. 1963;185:553.

2 **Leigh JM et al.** Effect of preoperative anesthetic visit on anxiety. Br Med J. 1977;2:987.

3 **Moyers JR.** Preoperative medication. In: Barash PG et al., eds. Clinical Anesthesia. Philadelphia: JB Lippincott; 1992:615.

4 **White PF.** Pharmacologic and clinical aspects of preoperative medication. Anesth Analg. 1986;65:963.

5 **Hargreaves J.** Benzodiazepine premedication in minor day-case surgery: comparison of oral midazolam and temazepam with placebo. Br J Anaesth. 1988;61:611.

6 **Greenwood BK, Bradshaw EG.** Preoperative medication for day-case surgery: a comparison between oxazepam and temazepam. Br J Anaesth. 1983; 55:933.

7 **Beebe DS et al.** Effectiveness of preoperative sedation with rectal midazolam, ketamine, or their combination in young children. Anesth Analg. 1992; 75:880.

8 **Kosarussavadi B.** Premedication. In: Bell C et al., eds. The Pediatric Anesthesia Handbook. St. Louis: Mosby Year Book; 1991:71.

9 **Karl HW et al.** Transmucosal administration of midazolam for premedication of pediatric patients. Anesthesiology. 1993;78:885.

10 **Tasi SK et al.** Intranasal ketamine versus sufentanil as premedicant in children. Anesthesiology. 1989;71:A1173. Abstract.

11 **Friesen RH, Lockhart CH.** Oral transmucosal fentanyl citrate for preanesthetic medication of pediatric day surgery patients with and without droperidol as a prophylactic anti-emetic. Anesthesiology. 1992;76:46.

12 **Karl HW et al.** Nasal midazolam or sufentanil for preinduction of anesthesia in pediatric patients: implications for intraoperative management. Anesthesiology. 1989;71:A1169. Abstract.

13 **Stoelting RK.** Pharmacology and Physiology in Anesthetic Practice. Philadelphia, PA: JB Lippincott; 1987: 69.

14 **Gutstein HB et al.** Oral ketamine preanesthetic medication in children. Anesthesiology. 1992;76:28.

15 **Manchikanti L et al.** Ranitidine and metoclopramide for prophylaxis of aspiration pneumonitis in elective surgery. Anesth Analg. 1984;63:903.

16 **Manchikanti L et al.** Bicitra (sodium citrate) and metoclopramide in outpatient anesthesia for prophylaxis against aspiration pneumonitis. Anesthesiology. 1985;63:378.

17 **Maze M.** Clinical uses of alpha 2 agonists. Paper presented to 44th Annual ASA Refresher Course Lecture Program. Washington, DC: 1993 Oct 10.

18 **Hupert C et al.** Effect of hydroxyzine on morphine analgesia for the treatment of postoperative pain. Anesth Analg. 1980;59:690.

19 **Knight PR et al.** Pathogenesis of gastric particulate lung injury: a comparison and interaction with acidic pneumonitis. Anesth Analg. 1993;77:754.

20 **Rocke DA et al.** At risk for aspiration: new critical values of volume and pH? Anesth Analg. 1993;76:666.

21 **Kallar SK, Everett LL.** Potential risks and preventive measures for pulmonary aspiration: new concepts in preoperative fasting guidelines. Anesth Analg. 1993;77:171.

22 **Gibbs CP, Banner TC.** Effectiveness of Bicitra as a preoperative antacid. Anesthesiology. 1984;61:97.

23 **Gibbs CP et al.** Antacid pulmonary aspiration in the dog. Anesthesiology. 1979;51:380.

24 **Rout CC et al.** Intravenous ranitidine reduces the risk of acid aspiration of gastric contents at emergency cesarean section. Anesth Analg. 1993;76:156.

25 **Cohen SE et al.** Does metoclopramide decrease the volume of gastric contents in patients undergoing cesarean section? Anesthesiology. 1984;61:604.

26 **Wyner J, Cohen SE.** Gastric volume in early pregnancy: effect of metoclopramide. Anesthesiology. 1982;57: 209.

27 **Nummo WS.** Drugs, diseases and altered gastric emptying. Clin Pharmacokinet. 1976;1:189.

28 **Morison DH et al.** A double-blind comparison of cimetidine and ranitidine as prophylaxis against gastric aspiration syndrome. Anesth Analg. 1982;61:988.

29 **Dubin SA et al.** Comparison of the effects of oral famotidine and ranitidine on gastric volume and pH. Anesth Analg. 1989;69:680.

30 **Weber L, Hirschman CA.** Cimetidine for prophylaxis of aspiration pneumonitis: comparison of intramuscular and oral dosage schedules. Anesth Analg. 1979;58:426.

31 **Omoigui S.** The Anesthesia Drug Handbook. St. Louis, MO: Mosby Year Book; 1992.

32 **Atanassoff PG et al.** Effects of single-dose intravenous omeprazole and ranitidine on gastric pH during general anesthesia. Anesth Analg. 1992;75:95.

33 **Ewart MC et al.** A comparison of the effects of omeprazole and ranitidine on gastric secretion in women undergoing elective caesarean section. Anaesthesia. 1990;45:527.

34 **Briggs GG et al.** Drugs in Pregnancy and Lactation. Baltimore, MD: Williams & Wilkins; 1990.

35 **Willenkin RL.** Management of general anesthesia. In: Miller RD, ed. Anesthesia. New York: Churchill Livingstone; 1990:1335.

36 **Dripp RD et al., eds.** Introduction to Anesthesia—The Principles of Safe Practice. Philadelphia: WB Saunders; 1988:141.

37 **Glass PSA et al.** Intravenous anesthetic delivery. In: Miller RD, ed. Anesthesia. New York: Churchill Livingstone; 1990:367.

38 **Fragen RJ, Avram MJ.** Barbiturates. In: Miller RD, ed. Anesthesia. New York: Churchill Livingstone; 1990: 225.

39 **Stoelting RK.** Pharmacology and Physiology in Anesthetic Practice. Philadelphia, PA: JB Lippincott; 1987: 102.

40 **Richter J, Waller MB.** Effects of pentobarbital on the regulation of acetylcholine content and release in different regions of rat brain. Biochem Pharmacol. 1977;26:609.

41 **Fragen RJ, Avram MF.** Comparative pharmacology of drugs used for the induction of anesthesia. In: Stoelting RK et al., eds. Advances in Anesthesia. Chicago: Year Book Medical Publishers; 1986:103.

42 **Ranson BR, Barker J.** Pentobarbital selectively enhances GABA-mediated postsynaptic inhibition in tissue cultured mouse spinal neurons. Brain Res. 1976;114:530.

43 **Mohler H, Richards JG.** The benzodiazepine receptor: a pharmacological control element of brain function. Eur J Anaesthesiol. 1988;2:15.

44 **Amrein R et al.** Clinical pharmacology of flumazenil. Eur J Anaesthesiol. 1988;2:65.

45 **Reves JG, Glass PSA.** Nonbarbiturate intravenous anesthetics. In: Miller RD, ed. Anesthesia. New York: Churchill Livingstone; 1990:243.

46 **Miyasaka M, Domino EF.** Neuronal mechanisms of ketamine-induced anesthesia. Int J Neuropharmacol. 1968; 7:557.

47 **Corssen G et al.** Ketamine in the anesthetic management of asthmatic patients. Anesth Analg. 1972;51:588.

48 **Ohtani M et al.** Effects of ketamine on nociceptive cells in the medial medullary reticular formation of the cat. Anesthesiology. 1979;51:414.

49 **Smith DJ et al.** Ketamine interacts with opiate receptors as an agonist. Anesthesiology. 1980;53:S5.

50 **Price HL et al.** The uptake of thiopental by body tissues and its relation to the duration of narcosis. Clin Pharmacol Ther. 1960;1:16.

51 **Stoelting RK.** Pharmacology and Physiology in Anesthetic Practice. Philadelphia, PA: JB Lippincott; 1987: 134.

52 **Renou AM et al.** Cerebral blood flow and metabolism during etomidate anaesthesia in man. Br J Anaesth. 1978; 50:1047.

53 **Vandersteene A et al.** Effect of propofol on cerebral blood flow and metabolism in man. Anaesthesia. 1988;43: 42.

54 **Greenwald MJ et al.** Extraocular muscle surgery. In: Krupin T, Kolker AE, eds. Complications of Ocular Surgery. St. Louis: Mosby; 1993.

55 **Borgeat A et al.** Subhypnotic doses of propofol possess direct antiemetic effects. Anesth Analg. 1992;74:539.

56 **McCollum JSC et al.** The antiemetic effect of propofol. Anaesthesia. 1988; 43:239.

57 **Skues MA, Prys-Roberts C.** The pharmacology of propofol. J Clin Anesth. 1989;1:387.

58 **Colvin MP et al.** Cardiorespiratory changes following induction of anaesthesia with etomidate in patients with cardiac disease. Br J Anaesth. 1979;51: 551.

59 **Fragen RJ et al.** Clinical use of etomidate for anesthesia induction: a preliminary report. Anesth Analg. 1976;55: 730.

60 **Zacharias M et al.** Effect of preanesthetic medication on etomidate. Br J Anaesth. 1979;51:127.

61 **Kugler J et al.** The EEG after etomidate. Anesth Resuscitation. 1977;106: 31.

62 **White PF et al.** Ketamine—its pharmacology and therapeutic uses. Anesthesiology. 1982;56:119.

63 **Rouse EC.** Propofol for electroconvulsive therapy: a comparison with methohexitone. Preliminary report. Anaesthesia. 1988;43(Suppl.):61.

64 **Bevan DR, Donati F.** Muscle relaxants. In: Barash PG et al., eds. Clinical Anesthesia. Philadelphia: JB Lippincott; 1992:481.

65 **Buck ML, Reed MD.** Use of nondepolarizing neuromuscular blocking agents in mechanically ventilated patients. Clin Pharm. 1991;10:32.

66 **Isenstein DA et al.** Neuromuscular blockade in the intensive care unit. Chest. 1992;102:1258.

67 **Susla GM.** Neuromuscular blocking agents in critical care. In: Rafferty KM, Weiner B, eds. Critical Care Nursing Clinics of North America. Philadelphia: WB Saunders; 1993:297.

68 **Rusy BF.** Physiology of neuromuscular transmission: relation to neuromuscular blockade and reversal. Anesth Today. 1989;1(2):1.

69 **Miller RD, Savarese JJ.** Pharmacology of muscle relaxants and their antagonists. In: Miller RD, ed. Anesthesia. New York: Churchill Livingstone; 1990:389.

70 **Mirakhur RK.** Newer neuromuscular blocking drugs. Drugs. 1992;44(2):182.

71 **Shorten G.** Neuromuscular blockade. In: Davison JK et al., eds. Clinical Anesthesia Procedures of the Massachusetts General Hospital. Boston: Little, Brown and Co.; 1993:151.

72 **Segredo V et al.** Persistent paralysis in critically ill patients after long-term administration of vecuronium. N Engl J Med. 1992;327:524.

73 **Vandenbrom RHG, Wierda MKH.** Pancuronium bromide in the intensive care unit: a case of overdose. Anesthesiology. 1988;69:996.

74 **Douglas JA et al.** Myopathy in severe asthma. Am Rev Respir Dis. 1992;146: 517.

75 **Kupfer Y et al.** Prolonged weakness after long-term infusion of vecuronium. Ann Intern Med. 1992;117:484.

76 **Wierda JMKH et al.** Pharmacokinetics and cardiovascular dynamics of pipecuronium bromide during coronary artery surgery. Can J Anaesth. 1990; 37:183.

77 **Emmott RS et al.** Cardiovascular effects of doxacurium, pancuronium and vecuronium in anaesthetized patients presenting for coronary artery bypass surgery. Br J Anaesth. 1990;65:480.

78 **Larijani GE et al.** Clinical pharmacology of the neuromuscular blocking agents. DICP Ann Pharmacother. 1991;25:54.

79 **Caldwell JE et al.** The neuromuscular effects of desflurane, alone and combined with pancuronium or succinylcholine in humans. Anesthesiology. 1991;74:412.

80 **Penn F.** Neuromuscular blockade reversal agents. Anesth Today. 1989; 1(2):12.

81 **King MJ et al.** Influence of neostigmine on postoperative vomiting. Br J Anaesth. 1988;61:403.

82 **Bevan DR et al.** Reversal of neuromuscular blockade. Anesthesiology. 1992;77:785.

83 **Torda TA.** The "new" relaxants: a review of the clinical pharmacology of atracurium and vecuronium. Anaesth Intensive Care. 1987;15:72.

84 **Agoston S et al.** Clinical pharmacokinetics of neuromuscular blocking drugs. Clin Pharmacokinet. 1992;22 (2):94.

85 **Savarese JJ et al.** The clinical neuromuscular pharmacology of mivacurium chloride (BW B1090U). Anesthesiology. 1988;68:723.

86 **Faulds D, Clissold SP.** Doxacurium: a review of its pharmacology and clinical potential in anesthesia. Drugs. 1991; 42(4):673.

87 **Larijani GE et al.** Clinical pharmacology of pipecuronium bromide. Anesth Analg. 1989;68:734.

88 **Strazis KP, Fox AW.** Malignant hyperthermia: a review of published cases. Anesth Analg. 1993;77:297.

89 **Sufit RL et al.** Doxacurium and mivacurium do not trigger malignant hyperthermia in susceptible swine. Anesth Analg. 1990;71:285.

90 **Puhringer FK et al.** Evaluation of the endotracheal intubating conditions of rocuronium (ORG 9426) and succinylcholine in outpatient surgery. Anesth Analg. 1992;75:37.

91 **Miller RD.** Choice of muscle relaxant: does it make a difference? Paper presented to 42nd Annual ASA Refresher Course Lecture Program. San Francisco, CA: 1991 Oct 26.

92 **Ginsberg B et al.** Onset and duration of neuromuscular blockade following high-dose vecuronium administration. Anesthesiology. 1989;71:201.

93 **Schwarz S et al.** Rapid tracheal intubation with vecuronium: the priming principle. Anesthesiology. 1985;62:388.

94 **Mehta MP et al.** Facilitation of rapid endotracheal intubations with divided doses of nondepolarizing neuromuscular blocking drugs. Anesthesiology. 1985;62:392.

95 **Cook DR.** Pharmacokinetics of mivacurium in normal patients and in those with hepatic or renal failure. Br J Anaesth. 1992;69:580.

96 **Viby-Mogensen J.** Correlation of succinylcholine duration of action with plasma cholinesterase activity in subjects with the genotypically normal enzyme. Anesthesiology. 1980;53:517.

97 **Mangar D et al.** Prolonged neuromuscular block after mivacurium in a patient with end-stage renal disease. Anesth Analg. 1993;76:866.

98 **Peterson RS et al.** Prolonged neuromuscular block after mivacurium. Anesth Analg. 1993;76:194.

99 **Viby-Mogensen J.** Succinylcholine neuromuscular blockade in subjects homozygous for atypical plasma cholinesterase. Anesthesiology. 1981;55: 429.

100 **Lebrault C et al.** Pharmacokinetics and pharmacodynamics of vecuronium (ORG NC 45) in patients with cirrhosis. Anesthesiology. 1985;62:601.

101 **Hunter JM et al.** The use of different doses of vecuronium in patients with liver dysfunction. Br J Anaesth. 1985; 57:758.

102 **Modig J.** Respiration and circulation after total hip replacement surgery. Acta Anaesthesiol Scand. 1976;20: 225.

103 **Mulroy MF.** Indications and contraindications for regional anesthesia. Paper presented to 43rd Annual ASA Refresher Course Lecture Program. New Orleans, LA: 1992 Oct 17.

104 **Tverskoy M et al.** Postoperative pain after inguinal heriorraphy with different types of anesthesia. Anesth Analg. 1990;70:29.

105 **Engberg G.** Respiratory performance after upper abdominal surgery. A comparison of pain relief with intercostal blocks and centrally acting analgesics. Acta Anaesthesiol Scand. 1985;29: 427.

106 **Kehlet H.** Epidural analgesia and endocrine-metabolic response to surgery: update and perspectives. Acta Anaesthesiol Scand. 1984;28:25.

107 **Weissman C.** The metabolic response to stress: an overview and update. Anesthesiology. 1990;73:308.

108 **Yeager MP et al.** Epidural anesthesia and analgesia in high-risk surgical patients. Anesthesiology. 1987;66:729.

109 **Tucker GT, Mather LE.** Properties, absorption, and disposition of local anesthetic agents. In: Cousins MJ, Bridenbaugh PO, eds. Neural Blockade in Clinical Anesthesia and Management of Pain. Philadelphia: JB Lippincott; 1988:47.

110 **Reynolds F.** Ropivacaine. Anaesthesia. 1991;46:339.

111 **Carpenter RL, Mackey DC.** Local anesthetics. In: Barash PG et al., eds. Clinical Anesthesia. Philadelphia: JB Lippincott; 1989;371.

112 **Aldrete JA, Johnson DA.** Evaluation of intracutaneous testing for investigation of allergy to local anesthetic agents. Anesth Analg. 1970;49:173.

113 **Datta S.** Pharmacology of local anesthetics. Paper presented to 43rd Annual ASA Refresher Course Lecture Program. New Orleans, LA: 1992 Oct 17.

114 **Covino BG.** Clinical pharmacology of local anesthetic agents. In: Cousins MJ, Bridenbaugh PO, eds. Neural Blockade in Clinical Anesthesia and Management of Pain. Philadelphia: JB Lippincott; 1988:111.

115 **Fleming JA et al.** Pharmacology and therapeutic applications of cocaine. Anesthesiology. 1990;73:518.

116 **Kalsner S, Nickerson M.** Mechanism of cocaine potentiation of responses to amines. Br J Pharmacol. 1969;35:428.

117 **Gross JB et al.** A suitable substitute for 4% cocaine before blind nasotracheal intubation: 3% lidocaine-0.25% phenylephrine nasal spray. Anesth Analg. 1984;63:915.

118 **Goodell JA et al.** Reducing cocaine solution use by promoting the use of a lidocaine-phenylephrine solution. Am J Hosp Pharm. 1988;45:2510.

119 **Morland GH et al.** The effect of pH adjustment of bupivacaine on onset and duration of epidural anaesthesia for caesarean section. Can J Anaesth. 1988;35:457.

120 **DiFazio CA et al.** Comparison of pH-adjusted lidocaine solutions for epidural anesthesia. Anesth Analg. 1986;65: 760.

121 **Shafer AL, Donnelly AJ.** Management of postoperative pain by continuous epidural infusion of analgesics. Clin Pharm. 1991;10:745.

122 **Donnelly AJ, Djuric M.** Cardioplegia solutions. Am J Hosp Pharm. 1991;48: 2444.

123 **Golembiewski J, Bourtsos N.** Cardioplegia solution. J Pharm Pract. 1993; 6:182.

124 **Partington MT et al.** Studies of retrograde cardioplegia. II: advantages of antegrade/retrograde cardioplegia to optimize distribution in jeopardized myocardium. J Thorac Cardiovasc Surg. 1989;97:613.

125 **Loop FD et al.** Myocardial protection during cardiac operations: decreased morbidity and lower cost with blood cardioplegia and coronary sinus perfusion. J Thorac Cardiovasc Surg. 1992;104:608.

126 **Forman MB et al.** Endothelial and myocardial injury during ischemia and reperfusion: pathogenesis and therapeutic implications. J Am Coll Cardiol. 1989;13:450.

127 **Buckberg GD.** Oxygenated cardioplegia: blood is a many splendored thing. Ann Thorac Surg. 1990;50:175.

128 **Follette D et al.** Superiority of blood cardioplegia over asanguinous cardioplegia: experimental and clinical study. Circulation. 1979;60(Suppl. II):36.

129 **Singh AK et al.** Electrolyte versus blood cardioplegia: randomized clinical and myocardial ultrastructural study. Circulation. 1980;62(Suppl. III): 324.

130 **Beyersdorf F et al.** Clinical evaluation of hypothermic ventricular fibrillation, multi-dose blood cardioplegia, and single-dose Bretschneider cardioplegia in coronary surgery. Thorac Cardiovasc Surg. 1990;38:20.

131 **Griepp RB et al.** The superiority of aortic cross-clamping with profound local hypothermia for myocardial protection during aorta-coronary bypass grafting. J Thorac Cardiovasc Surg. 1975;70:995.

132 **Rosenfeldt FL.** Myocardial preservation in 1987: what is the state of the art? Aust N Z J Surg. 1987;57:349.

133 **Ip JH, Levin RI.** Myocardial preservation during ischemia and reperfusion. Am Heart J. 1988;115:1094.

134 **Grondin CM et al.** Cold cardioplegia with diltiazem: a calcium channel blocker, during coronary revascularization. J Cardiovasc Surg. 1983;24: 291. Abstract.

135 **Mori F et al.** Clinical trial of nicardipine cardioplegia in pediatric cardiac surgery. Ann Thorac Surg. 1990;49: 413.

136 **Hicks GL et al.** Calcium channel blockers: an intraoperative and postoperative trial in women. Ann Thorac Surg. 1984;37:319.

137 **Clark RE et al.** Nifedipine cardioplegia experience: results of a 3-year cooperative clinical study. Ann Thorac Surg. 1983;36:654.

138 **Ferreira R et al.** Reduction of reperfusion injury with mannitol cardioplegia. Ann Thorac Surg. 1989;48:77.

139 **Emerit I et al.** Clastogenic factor in ischemia-reperfusion injury during open-heart surgery: protective effect of allopurinol. Ann Thorac Surg. 1988; 46:619.

140 **Buckberg GD.** Strategies and logic of cardioplegic delivery to prevent, avoid, and reverse ischemic and reperfusion damage. J Thorac Cardiovasc Surg. 1987;93:127.

141 **Rosenkranz ER et al.** Warm induction of cardioplegia with glutamate-enriched blood in coronary patients with cardiogenic shock who are dependent on inotropic drugs and intra-aortic balloon support. J Thorac Cardiovasc Surg. 1983;86:507.

142 **Pisarenko OI et al.** Glutamate-blood cardioplegia improves ATP preservation in human myocardium. Biomed Biochem Acta. 1987;46:499.

143 **Olafsson B et al.** Reduction of reperfusion injury in the canine preparation by intracoronary adenosine: importance of the endothelium and the no-reflow phenomenon. Circulation. 1987; 76:1135.

144 **Keller MW et al.** Microcirculatory dysfunction following perfusion with hyperkalemic, hypothermic, cardioplegic solutions and blood reperfusion. Effects of adenosine. Circulation. 1991; 84:2485.

145 **Tyers GFO.** Cardioplegic additives—a critical review. In: Engelman RM, Levitsky S, eds. A Textbook of Clinical Cardioplegia. Mount Kisco: Futura; 1982:139.

146 **Rich TL, Brady AJ.** Potassium contracture and utilization of high-energy phosphates in rabbit heart. Am J Physiol. 1974;226:105.

147 **O'Riordain DS et al.** Low potassium

cardioplegia: its effect on the incidence of complete heart block following cardiac surgery. Ir J Med Sci. 1989;158:257.

148 **Teoh KH et al.** Accelerated myocardial metabolic recovery with terminal warm blood cardioplegia. J Thorac Cardiovasc Surg. 1986;91:888.

149 **Watcha MF, White PF.** Postoperative nausea and vomiting. Anesthesiology. 1992;77:162.

150 **Forrest JB et al.** Multicenter study of general anesthesia. II. Results. Anesthesiology. 1990;72:262.

151 **Palazzo MGA, Strunin L.** Anaesthesia and emesis. I: etiology. Can Anaesth Soc J. 1984;31:178.

152 **Andrews PLR.** Physiology of nausea and vomiting. Br J Anaesth. 1992; 69(Suppl. 1):2S.

153 **Palazzo MGA, Strunin L.** Anaesthesia and emesis II: prevention and management. Can Anaesth Soc J. 1984;31:407.

154 **Rabey PG, Smith G.** Anaesthetic factors contributing to postoperative nausea and vomiting. Br J Anaesth. 1992;69(Suppl. 1):40S.

155 **Lerman J.** Surgical and patient factors involved in postoperative nausea and vomiting. Br J Anaesth. 1992;69(Suppl. 1):24S.

156 **Honkavaara P et al.** Nausea and vomiting after gynaecological laparoscopy depends upon the phase of the menstrual cycle. Can J Anaesth. 1991;38:876.

157 **Bridenbaugh LD, Soderstrom RM.** Lumbar epidural block anesthesia for outpatient laparoscopy. J Reprod Med. 1979;23:85.

158 **Rickford JK et al.** Comparative evaluation of general, epidural and spinal anaesthesia for extracorporeal shockwave lithotripsy. Ann R Coll Surg Engl. 1988;70:69.

159 **Tornetta FJ.** Double-blind evaluation of haloperidol for antiemetic activity. Anesth Analg. 1972;51:964.

160 **Loeser EA et al.** Comparison of droperidol, haloperidol and prochlorperazine as postoperative anti-emetics. Can Anaesth Soc J. 1979;26:125.

161 **Pandit SK.** Dose-response study of droperidol and metoclopramide as antiemetics for outpatient anesthesia. Anesth Analg. 1989;68:798.

162 **Rowbotham DJ.** Current management of postoperative nausea and vomiting. Br J Anaesth. 1992;69(Suppl. 1):46S.

163 **Melnick B et al.** Delayed side effects of droperidol after ambulatory general anesthesia. Anesth Analg. 1989;69:748.

164 **McKenzie R et al.** Comparison of ondansetron versus placebo to prevent postoperative nausea and vomiting in women undergoing ambulatory gynecologic surgery. Anesthesiology. 1993;78:21.

165 **Scuderi P et al.** Treatment of postoperative nausea and vomiting after outpatient surgery with the 5-HT$_3$ antagonist ondansetron. Anesthesiology. 1993;78:15.

166 **Mingus M et al.** Ondansetron effectively treats postoperative nausea and vomiting following ambulatory surgery. 10th World Congress of Anaesthesiologists. 1992:A502.

167 **Smith RN.** Safety of ondansetron. Eur J Cancer Clin Oncol. 1989;25(Suppl. 1):S47.

168 **Ho RT et al.** Electro-acupuncture and postoperative emesis. Anaesthesia. 1989;45:327.

169 **Dundee JW et al.** A comparison of the efficacy of cyclizine and perphenazine in reducing the emetic effects of morphine and pethidine. Br J Clin Pharmacol. 1975;2:81.

170 **Bonica JJ et al.** Post-anesthetic nausea, retching and vomiting: evaluation of cyclizine (Marezine) suppositories for treatment. Anesthesiology. 1958;19:532.

171 **Bailey PL et al.** Transdermal scopolamine reduces nausea and vomiting after outpatient laparoscopy. Anesthesiology. 1990;72:977.

172 **Kotelko DM et al.** Transdermal scopolamine decreases nausea and vomiting following cesarean section in patients receiving epidural morphine. Anesthesiology. 1989;71:675.

173 **Rothenberg DM et al.** Efficacy of ephedrine in the prevention of postoperative nausea and vomiting. Anesth Analg. 1991;72:58.

174 **Kortilla K et al.** Randomized comparison of recovery after propofol-nitrous oxide versus thiopentone-isoflurane-nitrous oxide anaesthesia in patients undergoing ambulatory surgery. Acta Anaesthesiol Scand. 1990;34:400.

175 **Watcha MF et al.** Effect of propofol on the incidence of postoperative vomiting after strabismus surgery in pediatric outpatients. Anesthesiology. 1991; 75:204.

176 **Ding Y et al.** Use of ketorolac and dezocine as alternatives to fentanyl during outpatient laparoscopy. Anesth Analg. 1992;74(Suppl):S67. Abstract.

177 **Brown DL, Carpenter RL.** Perioperative analgesia: a review of risks and benefits. J Cardiothorac Anesth. 1990; 4:368.

178 **Agency for health care policy and research.** Acute pain management: operative or medical procedures and trauma. Part 1. Clin Pharm. 1992;11:309.

179 **American Pain Society.** Principles of analgesic use in the treatment of acute pain and chronic cancer pain. 2nd ed. Clin Pharm. 1990;9:601.

180 **Rhoney DH, Littrell RA.** Techniques for the management of postoperative pain. Hosp Pharm. 1993;28:341.

181 **Kehlet H.** The endocrine-metabolic response to postoperative pain. Acta Anaesthesiol Scand. 1982;74(Suppl.):173.

182 **Wattwil M.** Postoperative pain relief and gastrointestinal motility. Acta Chir Scand. 1989;550(Suppl.):140.

183 **Hewlett AM, Branthwaite MA.** Postoperative pulmonary function. Br J Anaesth. 1975;47:102.

184 **Sydow FW.** The influence of anesthesia and postoperative analgesic management on lung function. Acta Chir Scand. 1989;550(Suppl.):159.

185 **Cohen FL.** Postsurgical pain relief: patient's status and nurses' medication choices. Pain. 1980;9:265.

186 **White PF.** Patient-controlled analgesia: a new approach to the management of postoperative pain. Semin Anesth. 1985;4:255.

187 **Cockshott WP et al.** Intramuscular or intralipomatous injections? N Engl J Med. 1982;307:356.

188 **Rapp RP et al.** Patient-controlled analgesia: a review of effectiveness of therapy and an evaluation of currently available devices. Drug Intell Clin Pharm. 1989;23:899.

189 **Jackson D.** A study of pain management: patient-controlled analgesia versus intramuscular analgesia. J Intraven Nurs. 1989;12:42.

190 **Keeri-Szanto M.** Apparatus for demand analgesia. Can Anaesth Soc J. 1971;18:581.

191 **Keeri-Szanto M, Heaman S.** Postoperative demand analgesia. Surg Gynecol Obstet. 1972;134:647.

192 **Lubenow TR, Ivankovich AD.** Patient-controlled analgesia for postoperative pain. Crit Care Nurs Clin North Am. 1991;3:35.

193 **Loper KA, Ready LB.** Epidural morphine after anterior cruciate ligament repair: a comparison with patient-controlled intravenous morphine. Anesth Analg. 1989;68:350.

194 **White PF.** Use of patient-controlled analgesia for management of acute pain. JAMA. 1988;259:243.

195 **Szeto HH et al.** Accumulation of normeperidine, an active metabolite of meperidine, in patients with renal failure or cancer. Ann Intern Med. 1977; 86:738.

196 **Parker RK et al.** Effects of a nighttime opioid infusion with PCA therapy on patient comfort and analgesic requirements after abdominal hysterectomy. Anesthesiology. 1992;76:362.

197 **Pflug AE, Halter JB.** Effect of spinal anesthesia on adrenergic tone and the neuroendocrine responses to surgical stress in humans. Anesthesiology. 1981;55:120.

198 **Kehlet H.** The modifying effect of general and regional anaesthesia on the endocrine metabolic response to surgery. Reg Anaesth. 1982;7:S38.

199 **Gregg R.** Spinal analgesia. Anesth Clin NA. 1989;7:79.

200 **Bromage PR et al.** Rostral spread of epidural morphine. Anesthesiology. 1982;56:431.

201 **Camporesi EM et al.** Ventilatory CO^2 sensitivity after intravenous and epidural morphine in volunteers. Anesth Analg. 1983;62:633.

202 **Etches RC et al.** Respiratory depression and spinal opioids. Can J Anaesth. 1989;36:165.

203 **Abram SE.** Pain—acute and chronic. In: Barash PG et al., eds. Clinical Anesthesia. Philadelphia: JB Lippincott; 1989:1427.

204 **Scott NB et al.** Continuous thoracic extradural 0.5% bupivacaine with or without morphine: effect on quality of blockade, lung function and the surgical stress response. Br J Anaesth. 1989; 62:253.

205 **Chrubasik J et al.** Relative analgesic potency of epidural fentanyl, alfentanil, and morphine in treatment of postoperative pain. Anesthesiology. 1988;68:929.

206 **Logas WG et al.** Continuous thoracic epidural analgesia for postoperative pain relief following thoracotomy: a randomized prospective study. Anesthesiology. 1987;67:787.

207 **Cullen ML et al.** Continuous epidural infusion for analgesia after major abdominal operations: a randomized, prospective, double-blind study. Surgery. 1985;98:718.

208 **Dyer RA et al.** Postoperative pain control with a continuous infusion of epidural sufentanil in the intensive care unit: a comparison with epidural morphine. Anesth Analg. 1990;71:130.

209 **Fischer RL et al.** Comparison of continuous epidural infusion of fentanyl-bupivacaine and morphine-bupivacaine in management of postoperative pain. Anesth Analg. 1988;67:559.

210 **Hord AH, Kokenes C.** Postoperative pain, a review of management methods. Hosp Formul. 1989;24:28.

211 **Cousins MJ et al.** Acute and chronic pain: use of spinal opioids. In: Cousins MJ, Bridenbaugh PO, eds. Neural Blockade in Clinical Anesthesia and Management of Pain. Philadelphia: JB Lippincott; 1988:955.

212 **Donadoni R et al.** Epidural sufentanil for postoperative pain relief. Anaesthesia. 1985;40:634.

213 **Bromage PR et al.** Nonrespiratory side effects of epidural morphine. Anesth Analg. 1982;61:490.

Dyslipidemias

James M McKenney

Lipid Metabolism and Drug Effects 9-1
  In vivo cholesterol synthesis 9-1
  Lipoproteins 9-2
    Very-low-density lipoproteins (VLDLs) 9-2
    VLDL remnants 9-2
    Low-density lipoproteins (LDLs) 9-2
    High-density lipoproteins (HDLs) 9-2
    Chylomicrons 9-4
  Apolipoproteins 9-4
  LDL receptor 9-4
Abnormalities in Lipid Metabolism 9-5
  Defective clearance 9-5
    Familial hypercholesterolemia (FH) 9-5
    Familial defective apolipoprotein B-100 (FDB) 9-5
    Familial dysbetalipoproteinemia 9-5
    Polygenic hypercholesterolemia 9-6
  Increased production 9-6
    Familial combined hyperlipidemia (FCHL) 9-6
    Familial hyperapobetalipoproteinemia 9-6
  Hypoalphalipoproteinemia 9-6
Rationale for Treating Dyslipidemia 9-6
  Pathogenesis of atherosclerosis 9-7
  Epidemiologic studies 9-7
  Clinical trials in asymptomatic patients:
    primary prevention 9-8
  Clinical trials in patients with established (CHD):
    secondary prevention 9-8
    Angiographic regression trials 9-8
  Other Considerations 9-10
    Total and non-CHD mortality 9-10
    Cost effectiveness 9-10

Hypercholesterolemia 9-10
  Initial Evaluation of Total and HDL Cholesterol 9-10
  Evaluation of the Lipoprotein Profile 9-10
  Secondary Causes of High Blood Cholesterol 9-11
  Familial Forms of Hypercholesterolemia 9-11
  Evaluation of Atherosclerosis and CHD Risk Factors ...9-11
  Therapy for Lowering Cholesterol Levels 9-12
    Diet therapy 9-12
    Effect on LDL-cholesterol 9-13
    Other lifestyle changes 9-13
    Goal of therapy 9-13
    Drug therapy 9-14

  Bile acid resins 9-14
    Mechanism of action 9-14
    Adverse effects 9-14
    Patient instructions on use (See Question 12) ..9-17
  Niacin (Also see Questions 21 and 22) 9-14
    Clinical use 9-14
    Mechanism of action 9-14
    Adverse effects 9-15
  HMG-CoA reductase inhibitors (statins) 9-15
    Clinical use 9-15
    Mechanism of action 9-16
    Adverse effects 9-16
  Selection of a drug regimen 9-16
    Patient Instructions on Resin Use 9-17
  Fiber 9-17
  Fish oils 9-17
  Postmenopausal drug therapy 9-17
    Estrogen replacement therapy 9-17
    Justification for use in hypercholesterolemia ...9-17
    Adverse effects 9-18
    Clinical use 9-18
Familial Hypercholesterolemia 9-18
  Combination drug therapy 9-18
    Initiating therapy 9-19
Alternative Therapy for Severe Hypercholesterolemia 9-19

Mixed Hyperlipidemia 9-19
  Assessing the Lipoprotein Profile 9-19
  Relation of Triglycerides to CHD 9-20
  Familial Forms of 9-20
  Secondary Causes of Hypertriglyceridemia 9-20
  Insulin Resistance Syndrome 9-21
  Hypertension Management with Mixed
    Hyperlipidemia 9-21
  Treatment 9-21
    Treatment goals 9-21
    Cholesterol lowering and weight loss diet 9-21
    Drugs therapy 9-22
    Fibric acid derivatives 9-22
    Clinical use 9-22
    Mechanism of action 9-22
    Adverse effects 9-22
    Drug selection 9-22
    Initiating combination therapy 9-23
    Antioxidant therapy 9-23

Successful management of the dyslipidemic patient requires a thorough understanding of lipid modulating therapies, including nutritional and other lifestyle approaches as well as drug regimens. These therapies will be the principal focus of this chapter. However, successful management of the dyslipidemic patient also must be founded on a good understanding of lipid metabolism and how abnormalities in lipid metabolism result in lipid disorders. There also needs to be a good understanding of how cholesterol is related to coronary heart disease (CHD). A quick review of these issues is provided below.

Lipid Metabolism and Drug Effects

Cholesterol is a naturally occurring alcohol that is essential for life. It is the precursor molecule for the synthesis of bile acids (which are required for absorption of nutrients) and steroid hormones (which provide important modulating effects in the body). It also is used to form cell membranes. Thus it is essential that cholesterol be available to all cells.

In Vivo Cholesterol Synthesis

Cells derive cholesterol from two sources: via intracellular synthesis or extraction from the systemic circulation. Within each cell cholesterol is synthesized through a series of biochemical steps, many of which are catalyzed by enzymes.[1] (See Figure 9.1.) One important step is the conversion of hepatic hydroxymethylglutaryl coenzyme A (HMG CoA) to mevalonic acid, catalyzed by the enzyme HMG CoA reductase. Several important drugs that interfere with this enzyme and thereby reduce cellular synthesis of cholesterol have been developed. Other catalytic enzymes involved in the biosynthesis of cholesterol such as HMG CoA synthase and squalene synthase are being evaluated as potential sites of action for new classes of competitive inhibitors to reduce cholesterol synthesis. A drug released for cholesterol lowering in the 1950s, MER 29, interfered with a late step in cholesterol biosynthesis and effectively reduced cellular cholesterol production, but caused a toxic accumulation of desmosterol and other cholesterol precursors. High blood levels of these steroids resulted in the development of cataracts and myocardial ischemia in patients who took the drug. The lesson of MER 29 is to consider not only the potential benefits, but also the potential harm produced by interference with cholesterol biosynthesis.

Intracellular cholesterol is stored in the esterified form. Free cholesterol is converted to an ester through the action of the enzyme, acetyl CoA acetyl transferase (ACAT). ACAT also is required for the esterification and absorption of dietary cholesterol from the gut. Inhibition of this enzyme should reduce the absorption of dietary cholesterol and the secretion of cholesterol by the liver. Several inhibitors of ACAT have been developed but, none have proven to be clinically effective in lowering plasma cholesterol levels.

Lipoproteins

Cells also obtain cholesterol via extraction from the systemic circulation. Systemically circulating cholesterol is derived primarily from the liver and to a lesser extent from dietary absorption. Liver synthesized cholesterol is unique since only the hepatocyte secretes cholesterol into the systemic circulation for use by other cells. Because cholesterol and other fatty substances are insoluble in water, they are formed into complexes (particles) in the hepatocyte before being secreted into the aqueous media of the blood. These particles contain an oily inner lipid core made up of cholesterol esters and triglycerides (TGs) and an outer hydrophilic coat made up of phospholipids and unesterified cholesterol. The outer coat also contains at least one protein, which provides the ligand for interaction with receptors on cell surfaces. The presence of a central lipid core with an outer protein supports the name given these particles, lipoproteins.

Lipoproteins can be separated by ultracentrifugation techniques based upon particle density or by electrophoresis based upon electrical charge. Categorization by density is the most common method; the greater the fat content of the lipoprotein, the less dense it becomes. Using these techniques, the three major lipoproteins found in the blood of fasting patients are very-low-density lipoproteins (VLDLs), low-density lipoproteins (LDLs), and high-density lipoproteins (HDLs).[2] These particles vary in size and composition as described in Table 9.1.

Very-Low-Density Lipoproteins (VLDLs). VLDL particles are formed in the liver and to a lesser extent in the intestine. (See Figure 9.2.) They contain 15% to 20% of the total blood cholesterol and most of the total triglyceride measured in the systemic circulation of the fasting patient. The concentration of cholesterol in these particles is approximately one-fifth of the total triglyceride concentration; thus, if the total triglyceride concentration is known, the VLDL-cholesterol (VLDL-C) level can be estimated by dividing it by five. VLDL particles are large and do not appear to be involved in the pathogenesis of atherosclerosis.

VLDL Remnants. When first secreted, VLDL particles are rich in triglycerides and low in cholesterol ester. With time, they become progressively smaller as their triglyceride content is removed. This removal occurs through the action of two enzymes; first, lipoprotein lipase and later, hepatic lipase. Drugs which enhance the activity of lipoprotein lipase increase the delipidization process and effectively lower triglyceride levels. As triglycerides are removed,

the lipoprotein becomes progressively smaller and relatively more cholesterol rich. The particles formed through this process include small VLDL particles called remnant VLDL, intermediate-density lipoproteins (IDL) and LDL. (See Figure 9.2.) All of these particles can participate in development of atherosclerosis. Approximately 50% of the remnant VLDL and IDL particles are removed from the systemic circulation by the LDL receptor (described below); the other 50% are converted into LDL particles.

Low-Density Lipoproteins (LDLs). LDL particles carry 60% to 70% to the total blood cholesterol and make the greatest contribution to the development of atherosclerosis. This is why LDL-cholesterol (LDL-C) is the primary target of cholesterol-lowering therapy. Small, more cholesterol-dense LDL particles have been described which appear to be highly atherogenic.[3] Approximately half of the LDL particles formed are removed from the systemic circulation by the liver; the other half are taken up by peripheral cells, including cells in the coronary vessel and other peripheral arteries where atherosclerosis can develop. The probability that atherosclerosis will develop is related directly to the concentration of LDL-C in the systemic circulation. Thus, patient evaluation and cholesterol-lowering treatment plans are based upon LDL-cholesterol levels.

High-Density Lipoproteins (HDLs). HDL particles appear to transport cholesterol from peripheral cells to the liver, a process referred to as reverse cholesterol transport.[4] In contrast to LDL, high HDL-cholesterol concentrations are desirable since this indicates that cholesterol is being removed from vascular tissue where it may participate in the development of atherosclerosis and coronary artery disease. Through mechanisms which have not been defined fully, HDL particles acquire cholesterol from peripheral cells and either transport it directly to the liver or transfer it to circulating remnant VLDL and LDL particles. If the latter occurs, the cholesterol may be returned to the liver or delivered back to other peripheral cells. (See Figure 9.2.)

HDL particles have been further subfractionated. The smaller HDL_3 particle is converted to the larger HDL_2 particle through the acquisition of both triglycerides from triglyceride-rich lipoproteins and cholesterol from peripheral cells. Conversely, HDL_2 particles are converted to HDL_3 particles by hydrolysis of triglycerides through the action of hepatic lipase. HDL_2 levels provide the best estimate of the antiatherogenic effects of HDL. The cholesterol acquired from peripheral cells by HDL particles is converted into an esterified form through the action of the enzyme, lecithin-cholesterol acyl transferase (LCAT). The transfer of cholesterol from HDL particles to circulating triglyceride-rich lipoproteins is catalyzed by the enzyme, cholesteryl ester transfer protein (CETP). (See Figure 9.2.) In the process, triglycerides are exchanged and the HDL particle becomes less cholesterol rich. Patients have been described who have a relative deficiency of the CETP enzyme and a low incidence of coronary heart disease. This suggests that it is best for HDL particles to deliver cholesterol directly to the liver rather than placing it back into the systemic circulation where it may be deposited into coronary vessels and contribute to the development of plaque.

In most settings, a patient's blood sample is analyzed for total cholesterol, triglycerides, and HDL-cholesterol (HDL-C). From these values, the VLDL-cholesterol concentration can be estimated as described above by dividing the triglyceride level by five. Once the cholesterol concentration in HDL and VLDL are known, the concentration in LDL can be estimated by subtracting these values from the total cholesterol level. [VLDL-C = TG/5; LDL-C = Total Cholesterol − (HDL-C + VLDL-C)] This calculation is used widely by laboratories to estimate LDL-C. However, it is not valid when triglyceride levels exceed 400 mg/dL. Methods to di-

Fig 9.1   Biosynthetic Pathway of Cholesterol.

Table 9.1		Classification and Properties of Plasma Lipoproteins[a]		
	Chylomicron	VLDL	LDL	HDL
Density (gm/mL)	<0.94	0.94–1.006	1.006–1.063	1.063–1.210
Composition (%)				
Protein	1–2	6–10	18–22	45–55
Triglyceride	85–95	50–65	4–8	2–7
Cholesterol	3–7	20–30	51–58	18–25
Phospholipid	3–6	15–20	18–24	26–32
Physiologic origin	Intestine	Intestine and liver	Product of VLDL catabolism	Liver and intestine
Physiologic function	Transport dietary TG to liver	Transport endogenous TG and CH	Transport endogenous CH to cells	Transport CH from cells
Plasma appearance	Cream layer	Turbid	Clear	Clear
Electrophoretic mobility	Origin	Prebeta	Beta	Alpha
Apolipoproteins	A-IV, B-48, C-IC-II, C-III	B-100, C-IC-III, C-III, E	B-100, (a)	A-I, A-II, A-IV

[a] CH = Cholesterol; TG = Triglyceride; VLDL = Very low density lipoprotein.

rectly measure LDL-cholesterol have been developed and will become widely available in the near future.

Chylomicrons. Unlike the lipoproteins which transport cholesterol from the liver to peripheral cells and back (endogenous system), chylomicrons transport fatty acids and cholesterol derived from the diet or synthesized in the intestines from the gut to the liver (exogenous system). (See Table 9.1.) Chylomicrons are large, triglyceride-rich lipoproteins. As they pass through capillary beds on the way to the liver, some of the triglyceride content is removed through the action of lipoprotein lipase in a manner similar to that described for VLDL-triglyceride removal. In the rare individual who has a lipoprotein lipase deficiency, this removal process is faulty and triglyceride levels in the blood become very high. Following a fatty meal, the number of chylomicron particles, and therefore the concentration of triglycerides, is high. However, if the patient fasts for 12 to 14 hours, chylomicrons will have time to clear from the blood. Triglyceride concentrations obtained during fasting reflect entirely that which is produced by the liver and carried in VLDL and other remnant particles (unless the patient has a rare chylomicron clearance disorder). This is why patients should be asked to fast before obtaining a lipoprotein profile.

Apolipoproteins

Each lipoprotein particle contains proteins on their outer surface called apolipoproteins. (See Table 9.1.) These proteins have three functions: 1) to provide structure to the lipoprotein; 2) to activate enzyme systems and; 3) to bind with cell receptors.[2] Abnormal metabolism of apolipoproteins, even in the face of seemingly normal blood cholesterol levels, may result in faulty enzyme activity or cholesterol transport and an increased risk of atherosclerosis. Because of this, many lipid specialists feel that blood levels of apolipoproteins should be used to evaluate dyslipidemic patients, especially those who have a family history of premature coronary heart disease. The five most clinically relevant apolipoproteins are A-I, A-II, B-100, C-II, and E.

VLDL particles contain apolipoproteins B-100, E, and C. (See Figure 9.2.) The B and E proteins are ligands for LDL receptors (also called B-E receptors) on the surface of hepatocytes and peripheral cells. Linkage allows the transfer cholesterol from the circulating lipoprotein into the cell through absorptive endocytosis and cellular uptake of VLDL. Defects in these proteins reduce their ability to bind with receptor proteins. This results in defective clearance of lipoproteins from the systemic circulation and increased levels of circulating cholesterol. Apoprotein C-II is a cofactor for lipoprotein lipase and, by activating this enzyme, stim-

ulates the hydrolysis of triglycerides from lipoprotein particles in the capillary beds. Deficiencies of C-II apoproteins result in faulty triglyceride metabolism and hypertriglyceridemia.

Remnant VLDL and IDL particles retain apolipoproteins B and E during the delipidization process; LDL particles contain only apolipoprotein B. (See Figure 9.2.) Each VLDL and LDL particle contains one apolipoprotein B. Thus, the concentration of apolipoprotein B gives an indication of the number of VLDL and LDL particles in the circulation. Ratios of nonHDL-cholesterol (i.e., total cholesterol-HDL-C) to apolipoprotein B levels gives an estimate of the cholesterol contained in VLDL and LDL particles. Some patients have high levels of apolipoprotein B (suggesting an increased number of VLDL and LDL particles in the circulation), even though their cholesterol level is in the desirable range. This increases the risk of atherosclerosis.

Very small LDL-like particles have been identified which contain a plasminogen-like protein called apolipoprotein (a). (See Figure 9.2.) These particles, named LP$_{(a)}$, (pronounced L P little a), appear to increase coronary heart disease risk significantly.[5] However, their role in the development of atherosclerosis has not been defined, nor has the utility of reducing LP$_{(a)}$ levels with drugs or other modalities.

HDL particles contain apolipoproteins A-I, A-II, and C. A-I protein activates LCAT which catalyzes the esterification of free cholesterol in HDL particles. Levels of apolipoprotein A-I have a stronger inverse correlation with coronary heart disease risk than apolipoprotein A-II levels. High-density lipoprotein particles that contain only A-I apolipoproteins (LpA-I) are associated with a lower coronary heart disease risk than are HDL particles containing both A-I and A-II (LpA-I, A-II).[6]

LDL Receptor

The uptake of cholesterol into peripheral and hepatic cells is accomplished by the binding of apolipoproteins on circulating lipoproteins to cell surface LDL protein receptors. The synthesis of LDL receptors is stimulated by a low intracellular cholesterol concentration.[7] Within the cell, the receptor protein travels from the mitochondria, where it is synthesized, to the cell wall where it migrates to an area called the coated pits. Once in this position, it is capable of binding with lipoproteins that contain apolipoproteins E or B-100, including VLDL, remnant VLDL, IDL, and LDL. Because remnant VLDL and IDL particles contain both B and E proteins, they may have a higher affinity for LDL receptors than do LDL particles. Further, drugs that increase the synthesis of LDL receptors may increase the clearance of VLDL remnant particles as well as LDL particles from the circulation. After these proteins are bound, the lipoproteins undergo endocytosis and are taken up by lysosomes where they are broken into elemental substances for use by the cell. The cholesterol is transferred into the intracellular cholesterol pool. The receptor protein may be returned to the cell surface where it can bind with another circulating apolipoprotein E or B-containing lipoprotein. Drugs that reduce the intracellular synthesis of cholesterol upregulate LDL receptors, thereby increasing the removal of cholesterol-carrying lipoproteins from the general circulation.

Abnormalities in Lipid Metabolism

As can be imagined from the above description of lipid synthesis and transport, there are literally hundreds of possible steps that could malfunction and cause lipid disorders. However, there are but a handful of relatively common and important lipid disorders. These disorders, which roughly may be categorized as involving defective lipoprotein clearance or enhanced lipoprotein synthesis, are described below. (See Table 9.2.)

Defective Clearance

Familial hypercholesterolemia (FH) is the classic lipid disorder of defective clearance. Familial hypercholesterolemia is found in one out of 500 people in the U.S. and is associated strongly with premature coronary heart disease. It is an autosomal dominant inheritance disorder which results in a defective LDL receptor.[7,8] Heterozygotes of this disorder inherit one defective LDL receptor gene. Consequently, they possess approximately one-half the number of functioning LDL receptors and double the LDL-cholesterol level of unaffected patients.[9,10] LDL-C levels are usually in the range of 250 to 450 mg/dL. Triglyceride and HDL-cholesterol levels generally are normal. To date, more than 30 mutations of the LDL receptor gene have been described; all result in a lack of expression or the expression of a dysfunctional receptor protein. Clinically, heterozygous FH patients may deposit cholesterol in the iris leading to *arcus senilis*. Cholesterol deposition in tendons, par-

ticularly the Achilles tendon and extensor tendons of the hands, leads to tendon xanthomas. The clinical diagnosis is established by documenting a very high LDL-cholesterol, strong family history of premature coronary heart disease, and the presence of tendon xanthomas. Untreated heterozygous FH patients have, approximately, a 5% chance of a myocardial infarction (MI) by age 30, 50% chance by age 50, and an 85% chance by age 60. The mean age of death in male heterozygotes is the midfifties and for female heterozygotes, it is in the midsixties.[11] Homozygotes for this disorder inherit a defective LDL receptor gene from both parents and generally have LDL-cholesterol levels above 500 mg/dL. This rare disorder results in coronary heart disease by age 10 to 20 years.

Familial defective apolipoprotein B-100 (FDB) is a genetic disorder clinically indistinguishable from heterozygous familial hypercholesterolemia. These patients have normally functioning LDL receptors but a defective apolipoprotein B which results in reduced binding to LDL receptors.[12,13] Like familial hypercholesterolemia, FDB is an autosomal dominant disorder which results in LDL-cholesterol levels between 250 and 450 mg/dL.[12,14,15] Presumably, the apolipoprotein E and half of the apolipoprotein B in FDB patients function normally, providing mechanisms for removal of these lipoproteins from the systemic circulation. Clinical diagnosis of familial defective apolipoprotein B-100, like FH, is based upon identifying a very high LDL-cholesterol, a family history of premature coronary heart disease, and tendon xanthomas. The definitive diagnosis requires molecular screening techniques.

Familial dysbetalipoproteinemia (also called Type III hyperlipidemia and remnant disease) is caused by an apolipoprotein E with low binding affinity on VLDL and chylomicron particles.[16] Apolipoprotein E is necessary for the normal clearance of VLDL and chylomicrons from the systemic circulation. Apolipoprotein E is inherited as an E2, E3, or E4 isoform from each parent. The E2 isoform has a low binding affinity for the LDL receptor. Thus, individuals with an Apolipoprotein E2:E2 phenotype have a delayed clearance of VLDL remnant (and possibly chylomicron) par-

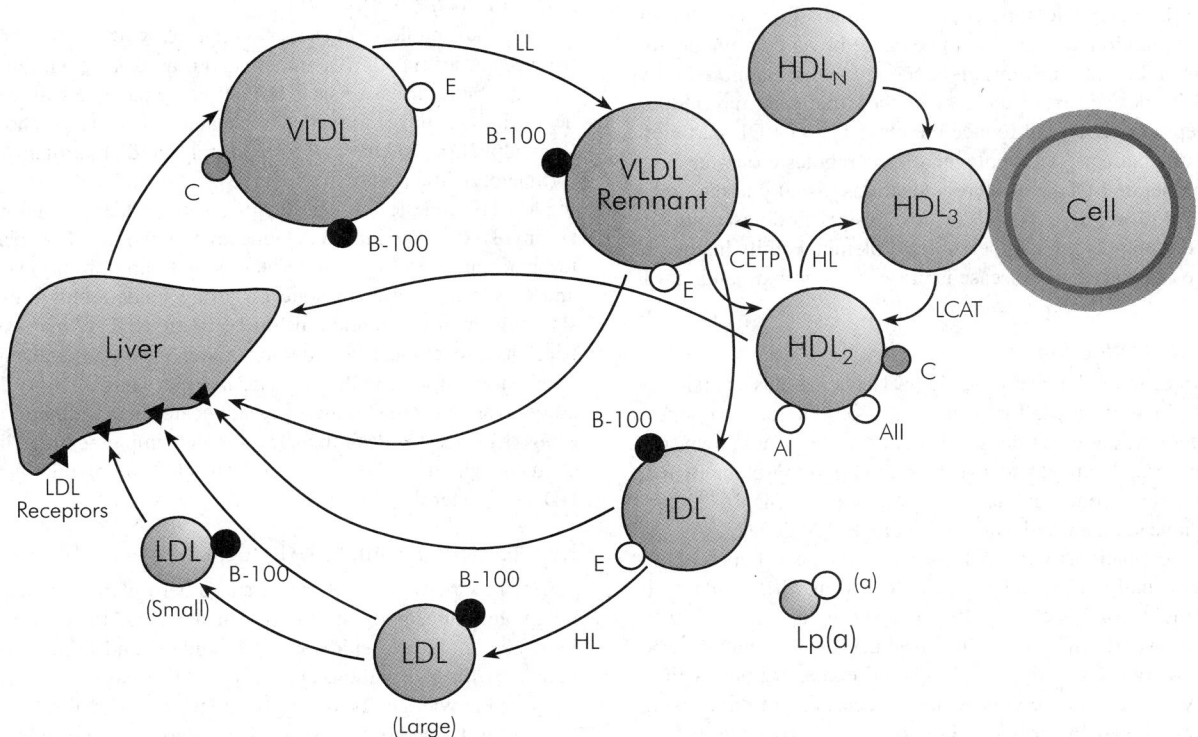

Fig 9.2   The Lipoproteins, Apolipoproteins, and Enzymes Involved in the Transport of Cholesterol and Triglycerides.

Table 9.2		Characteristics of Common Lipid Disorders[a]		
Disorder	Metabolic Defect	Lipid Effect	Main Lipid Parameter	Diagnostic Features
Familial hypercholesterolemia (heterozygous)	Dysfunctional or absent LDL receptors	↑ LDL-C	LDL-C: 250–450 mg/dL	Fam Hx, CHD, tendon xanthomas
Familial defective apoB-100	Defective apoB on LDL and VLDL	↑ LDL-C	LDL-C: 250–450 mg/dL	Fam Hx, CHD, tendon xanthomas
Dysbetalipoproteinemia (Type III hyperlipidemia)	ApoE2:E2 phenotype, ↓ VLDL remnant clearance	↑ remnant VLDL, ↑ IDL	LDL-C: 300–600 mg/dL TG: 400–800 mg/dL	Palmar xanthomas, tuberoeruptive xanthomas
Polygenic hypercholesterolemia	↓ LDL clearance	↑ LDL-C	LDL-C: 160–250 mg/dL	None distinctive
Familial combined hyperlipidemia	↑ ApoB and VLDL production	↑ CH, TG, or both	LDL-C: 250–350 mg/dL TG: 200–800 mg/dL	Fam Hx, CHD Fam Hx, hyperlipidemia
Familial hyperapobetalipoproteinemia	↑ ApoB production	↑ ApoB	ApoB: >125 mg/dL	None distinctive
Hypoalphalipoproteinemia	↑ HDL catabolism	↓ HDL-C	HDL-C: <35 mg/dL	None distinctive

[a] ApoB = Apolipoprotein B; ApoE = Apolipoprotein E; CH = Cholesterol; CHD = Coronary heart disease; Fam Hx = Family history; IDL = Intermediate-density lipoprotein; LDL = Low-density lipoprotein; LDL-C = Low-density lipoprotein-cholesterol; TG = Triglycerides; VLDL = Very low-density lipoprotein.

ticles from the circulation and a reduced conversion of IDL to LDL particles. However, a lipid disorder usually does not result unless accompanied by other metabolic problems such as diabetes, hypothyroidism, and obesity. Clinically, these patients have a high cholesterol (owing to an enrichment of cholesterol esters in VLDL remnant particles); high triglycerides (usually in the range of 400 to 800 mg/dL); and a VLDL cholesterol:triglyceride ratio greater than 0.3.[17] Some patients have palmar xanthomas (yellow-orange discoloration in the creases of the palms and fingers) and tuberoeruptive xanthomas (small raised lesions in areas of pressure, particularly the elbows and knees). A personal and family history of premature atherosclerotic vascular disease frequently is present. In addition, these patients often have diabetes mellitus, hypertension, obesity, and hyperuricemia.

Polygenic hypercholesterolemia is the most prevalent form of dyslipidemia. Polygenic hypercholesterolemia is found in 25% of the U.S. population and appears to be caused by a combination of environmental (e.g., nutrition) and genetic factors. Saturated fatty acids (SFA) derived from the diet of these patients may reduce LDL receptor activity and reduce the clearance of LDL particles. As a result, patients with polygenic hypercholesterolemia have mild to moderate LDL-cholesterol elevations (usually in the range of 160 to 250 mg/dL). There are no physical findings uniquely associated with polygenic hypercholesterolemia. Family history of premature coronary heart disease is present in approximately 20% of cases.

Increased Production

Familial combined hyperlipidemia (FCHL) is the classic example of a dyslipidemia caused by an increased production of lipoproteins. Although the exact cause of this disorder is unknown, patients with FCHL appear to overproduce apolipoprotein B and, apolipoprotein B-containing particles, VLDL and LDL.[18–20] Many patients have an elevated apolipoprotein B-100 level.[21] As the name implies, patients with this disorder may have hypercholesterolemia (usually in the range of 250 to 350 mg/dL) or hypertriglyceridemia (usually between 200 and 800 mg/dL) or both (usually with a low HDL-C). Also, they have first degree relatives who have hypercholesterolemia, hypertriglyceridemia, or both. A family history of premature coronary heart disease is present as well. Familial combined hyperlipidemia patients often are overweight and hypertensive and also may have diabetes or hyperuricemia. A

diagnosis of FCHL is presumed in patients who have increased cholesterol and/or triglyceride levels, a strong family history of premature coronary heart disease, and a family history of dyslipidemia.

Familial hyperapobetalipoproteinemia is a variant of FCHL (or hyperapoB for short). This disorder is characterized by increased hepatic production of apolipoprotein B in the absence of other lipid abnormalities.[22,23] These patients will have acceptable LDL-cholesterol and triglyceride levels with a family history of coronary heart disease. Their apolipoprotein B concentration is usually greater than 125 mg/dL, indicating an increase in the number of cholesterol-carrying lipoprotein particles. It is likely that both FCHL and hyperapoB are related and result from over secretion of apolipoprotein B-containing lipoproteins.[24]

Hypoalphalipoproteinemia

Low HDL-cholesterol (i.e., <35 mg/dL) without an increase in triglyceride level is fairly common and is associated with increased coronary heart disease risk.[25] In fact, many patients with coronary heart disease have so called "isolated" low HDL-cholesterol (hypoalphalipoproteinemia) as their only lipid abnormality.[26] Unfortunately, little is known about the precise molecular defect causing low HDL-cholesterol, although genetic influences undoubtedly are involved.[27] The inherited tendency to low HDL-C also appears to be accentuated by lifestyle factors including obesity, smoking, and lack of exercise. In spite of strong epidemiologic evidence showing an inverse relationship between HDL-C and coronary heart disease, clinical trials demonstrating a benefit of raising "isolated" low HDL-C with drugs are lacking. Until such studies become available, most authorities advocate therapy aimed at lowering LDL-C to desirable levels and implementing lifestyle changes which not only lower LDL-cholesterol but also raise HDL-cholesterol.

Rationale for Treating Dyslipidemia

The link between cholesterol and atherosclerosis is supported by a voluminous body of scientific data derived from animal studies, genetic studies, epidemiologic studies, and clinical trials in patients with and without coronary heart disease. This collective body of knowledge resoundingly supports a critical role for cholesterol in the pathogenesis of atherosclerosis. Even more important, in clinical trials employing cholesterol-lowering therapies, coronary heart disease has been reduced consistently, thus confirming the causal relationship between cholesterol and coronary heart disease. Some of this significant literature is summarized below.

Pathogenesis of Atherosclerosis

One of the most impressive areas of investigation has been the study of the role of cholesterol in the pathogenesis of atherosclerosis. Even the name atherosclerosis depicts the central involvement of cholesterol (athero or porridge-like and sclerosis or fibrous-like). Atherosclerotic lesions begin with the deposition of cholesterol in arteries leading to the development of fatty streaks. The mature atherosclerotic lesion often has an inner lipid core and an outer fibrous cap. This process is depicted in Figure 9.3.

It is now believed that the earliest step in the development of atherosclerosis is the movement of circulating LDL-C into subendothelial space. The reason this occurs has not been defined, but it is related directly to elevated circulating cholesterol levels and to the provocation induced by hypertension, smoking, and stress. An important finding is that native LDL does not contribute to the development of atherosclerosis; instead modified LDL is a key factor in initiating the production of atherogenic plaque. Soon after taking up residence in the subendothelial space following cellular uptake, LDL appears to be modified primarily by oxidation thereby triggering the release of monocyte adherence molecules from endothelial cells.[28,29] This causes some of the circulating monocytes to attach to the intact endothelial surface and then migrate to a junctional space where they squeeze between endothelial cells into the intima. (See Figure 9.3.) This process has been demonstrated in animal models, including primates.[30]

Once recruited, the monocytes are converted to activated macrophage cells which begin to ingest LDL-cholesterol particles. Monocyte-derived macrophage cells do not effectively take up native LDL particles. However, when the polyunsaturated fatty acids in the LDL particles are modified by acetylation or oxidation, the particles may be taken up quickly by special ''scavenger'' or ''acetyl-LDL receptors'' on macrophage cells.[31] In addition, the oxidatively modified LDL is a chemoattractant for circulating monocytes, thus recruiting other monocytes from the systemic circulation. It also inhibits the mobility of resident macrophage cells (thus blocking the egress of these cells from the intima) and is a cytotoxic agent (which may damage the endothelium).[28] As the uptake of modified LDL-C into macrophage cells continues, they become laden with lipid and grow in size. Through this process, they are converted into lipid laden *foam cells*. (See Figure 9.2.) The accumulation of foam cells eventually results in the fatty streak which is widely recognized as the precursor to atherosclerosis. Fatty streaks transform the once smooth endothelial surface of the artery into a lumpy, uneven surface.

During this process, a number of cells (including macrophages, endothelial cells, platelets, and smooth muscle cells) secrete chemoattractant and growth factors which cause smooth muscle cells from the media to migrate and proliferate near the luminal surface.[32] Collagen synthesis also is increased. The lesion that emerges contains a fibrous cap and a lipid core. As the fatty streak expands with accumulation of foam cells, the endothelium becomes stretched and actually may rupture, exposing underlying tissue to circulating blood elements.[33] With this exposure, platelets may adhere and microthrombi may form. This process of fissuring and rehealing appears to lead to the more complicated lesions of atherosclerosis. Evidence suggests that atherosclerotic lesions which result in sudden death or a nonfatal myocardial infarction are not the large lesions which have grown with the recruitment of smooth muscle cells and which prominently appear on a patient's angiogram. Rather, they are the smaller, less stable lesions which have a large lipid core and a thin fibrous cap surrounding the lumen of the vessel.[34] When shear forces or pressure in the artery cause these plaques to fissure, thrombosis may develop quickly leading to the occlusion of the affected vessel and precipitating a clinical event.

Epidemiologic Studies

Epidemiologic studies offer indirect evidence of the link between cholesterol and coronary heart disease. Even though epidemiologic data are observational in nature, they have contributed substantially to our understanding of the frequencies and rate of coronary heart disease in the segments of our population who have elevated blood cholesterol levels.

Many epidemiologic studies have examined the relationship between blood cholesterol and coronary heart disease in cohort and case-controlled populations throughout the world.[35–37] The results of these studies have been very similar. A direct relationship between the total and LDL-cholesterol level in the blood and the prevalence of CHD death and disability has been found consistently. In general, these studies show that for every 1% increase in blood cholesterol levels, there is a 2% increase in the incidence of coronary heart disease. Additionally, for every 1% decrease in HDL-C levels, there is a 2% to 3% increase in CHD.[38]

Epidemiologic trials also have helped to demonstrate the influence of environment on cholesterol levels and coronary heart disease incidence. The observation that Japanese in their native land have very low cholesterol levels and coronary heart disease death rate has been typical of these studies. However, as the Japanese have migrated to Hawaii and subsequently to the west coast of the U.S., cholesterol levels have increased progressively as have deaths due to CHD.[39] Similarly, Mexicans who live close to the U.S. border have a cholesterol level and a CHD incidence similar to that in the U.S., whereas those living in the southern part of the country have a lower cholesterol level and a significantly lower incidence of coronary heart disease.

Women have a very low incidence of CHD during the premenopausal years.[40] Even women with genetic forms of dyslipidemias usually do not develop coronary heart disease before menopause.[41]

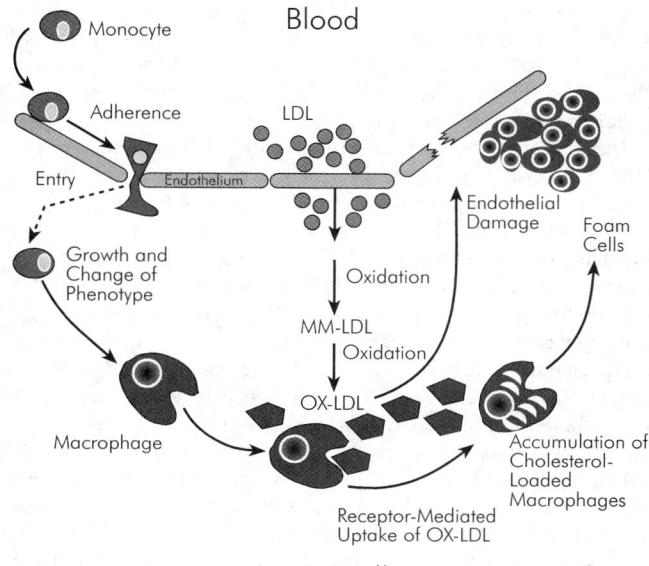

Fig 9.3   Schematic of Some of the Steps Involved in the Development of the Fatty Streak.

After menopause, however, the rate of CHD in women parallels that of men (at least in women who do not receive estrogen replacement therapy). In fact, the prevalence of coronary heart disease in women is similar to that of men; it is just displaced by about ten years.[37,42] While men tend to develop CHD in their 50s and 60s, women develop it in their 60s and 70s. Eventually, coronary heart disease causes nearly as many deaths in women as it does in men.[43] In fact, CHD is the cause of more deaths in women than all forms of cancer, including cancer of the breast, ovary, and cervix. Further, the presence of diabetes in a woman with dyslipidemia negates whatever protection she may have had before menopause and supports aggressive treatment.[44,45] Conversely, a high HDL-C actually may offer the woman more protection from CHD than a similar level offers a man.[38]

Epidemiologic trials also have shown that the relationship between high blood cholesterol levels and an increased risk of coronary heart disease continues at all ages, to at least age 82.[46] Since CHD risk increases with age, most CHD events occur among the elderly. In fact, coronary heart disease is the most common cause of death among the elderly.[47] The relative risk of CHD is nearly twofold greater in elderly patients with elevated cholesterol levels compared to those with normal levels, but this risk level is less than that found in younger populations with similar cholesterol levels. However, the absolute rate of coronary heart disease deaths attributable to high blood cholesterol actually increases in the elderly over that in younger patients.[47,48] In other words, an elevated blood cholesterol level contributes more cases of CHD in the older patient population than in the young, which is due in part to the sheer number of people affected by the disease in the elderly population. Because the problem is so prevalent, it has been estimated that a mere 1% decline in mortality rates due to coronary heart disease in the elderly would translate into 4300 fewer deaths per year in the U.S.[49] Data such as these help us see that targeting interventions at this population may have a substantial impact on reducing the burden of coronary heart disease in our society. It also further underscores the importance of age alone as a predictor of CHD risk.

Clinical Trials in Asymptomatic Patients: Primary Prevention

Proof that a causal relationship exists between blood cholesterol levels and coronary heart disease is provided by several controlled clinical trials in hypercholesterolemic patients.[50–52] The key trials, called primary prevention studies because they were conducted in patients without evidence of CHD initially, are summarized in Table 9.3. These studies evaluated treatment with cholesterol-lowering diet with and without drug therapy for five to seven years in middle-aged men who had elevated cholesterol levels, but no evidence of coronary heart disease. Cholesterol levels in these trials were reduced about 10%, while CHD deaths and nonfatal myocardial infarctions together were reduced 19% to 47%. Analyses of pooled data from these and others trials have shown that interventions to lower blood cholesterol levels are effective in reducing coronary heart disease rates.[53] While epidemiologic trials are important in defining the prevalence of CHD and its relationship to various risk factors, only the primary prevention trials justify the use of cholesterol-lowering therapies in healthy, asymptomatic patients with elevated cholesterol levels to prevent future coronary heart disease events. Since these trials focused primarily on middle-aged men, more data are needed to verify similar benefits in women and geriatric patients. Several ongoing trials now include these populations. Until the results of these trials are available, treatment should be considered in all high risk individuals, regard-

less of gender or age. Based upon epidemiologic and clinical trial data, there is no reason to expect women and geriatric patients to respond differently.

Clinical Trials in Patients with Established CHD: Secondary Prevention

The risk of a myocardial infarction is five to seven times higher in men who have established CHD than in those without coronary heart disease.[54] The level of LDL-cholesterol in these patients helps predict future events. A number of secondary prevention studies (studies in patients who have experienced an MI or have evidence of atherosclerotic vascular disease) have now been carried out which used a variety of cholesterol-lowering therapies including diet, drugs, and partial ileal bypass surgery.[55–58,188] (See Table 9.3.) These studies have shown that cholesterol lowering is associated not only with a reduction in recurrent CHD but also a reduction in total mortality rates, an outcome which has not been achieved in most primary prevention studies. For example, the landmark 4S trial has shown that, compared with placebo treatment, patients receiving simvastatin experienced 30% fewer all-cause deaths, 42% fewer deaths due to coronary heart disease, and 30% less CHD events.[188] A meta-analysis of secondary prevention study data published before the 4S trial concludes that intervention in patients with established coronary disease reduces nonfatal myocardial infarctions by 26%, fatal MI by 14%, and total mortality by 9%.[59]

Angiographic Regression Trials. A second group of studies in patients with established coronary heart disease (secondary prevention trials) have examined the impact of lipid-lowering on atherosclerotic lesions.[55,60–64,187,189–193] (See Table 9.3.) These so called "angiographic studies" have demonstrated that aggressive lipid lowering causes some lesions to progress at a slower rate and, in some cases, to regress (get smaller) to a greater extent than those in placebo-treated patients. These findings were similar regardless of whether the atherosclerosis was found in coronary,[60–64,189–191] carotid,[192,193] or femoral[187] arteries. The therapies used in these trials have included diet and other lifestyle changes alone,[62] diet and drugs,[60,61,63,64] and ileal bypass surgery.[55] Studies included men and women with polygenic and familial hypercholesterolemia. On average, LDL-C was reduced 30% to 50% and HDL-C was increased up to 45% in these studies. As a group, progression of atherosclerosis occurred in 26% of treated patients compared with 53% of control patients and regression of lesions was experienced by 26% of treated patients and 8% of control patients.[34] The average lumen size in treated patients either increased somewhat less than or decreased in placebo-treated patients.

The importance of treatment in patients with angiographically-defined atherosclerotic lesions extends beyond the impressive modification of lipoprotein levels and changes in lumen size. The greatest potential benefit is stabilization of those few lesions which may have otherwise progressed to cause an acute CHD event. As summarized earlier, it currently is thought that the atherosclerotic lesion which causes CHD events is "unstable" by virtue of its large lipid core and a relatively thin fibrous cap.[29,33] Lipid lowering is expected to reduce the lipid core in these lesions and cause other changes which render them more stable and less likely to evolve to a thrombus and produce an acute occlusive event. Since "unstable" lesions represent only 10% to 15% of the all angiographic lesions, treatment-induced changes in average lumen size may not fully reflect the benefit of treatment. Coronary heart disease event rates may be a better marker. While angiographic studies generally were not designed to study event rates, the accumulated experience is that CHD events begin to decline as soon as six months after initiating intensive cholesterol-lowering therapy, resulting in substantially fewer events after as little as two years of treatment.[34]

Table 9.3		Summary of Findings of Key Intervention Trials[a]			
Study	Features	Treatment	Lipid Change	End Point	Change
Primary Prevention Studies					
Oslo Diet and Antismoking[51]	1232, men and women, 5 yr, R, C, P	Diet, reduced smoking	TC = ↓ 10% Smoke = ↓ 24%	Fatal and nonfatal MI and sudden death	↓ 47%
LRC-CPPT[52]	3806 middle-aged men, 7.4 yr, R, DB, C, P	BAR vs diet	TC = ↓ 8.5% LDL-C = ↓ 13%	CHD death + nonfatal MI	↓ 19%
Helsinki Heart Study[50]	4081 middle-aged men, 5 yr, R, DB, C, P	Gemfibrozil vs diet	TC = ↓ 10% LDL-C = ↓ 10% HDL-C = ↑ 10%	CHD death + nonfatal MI	↓ 34%
Secondary Prevention Studies					
Coronary Heart Project[57,58]	3908 men, 6 yr, R, DB, C, P	Niacin vs placebo	TC = ↓ 10% TG = ↓ 26%	Nonfatal MI (6-yr follow-up) Total mortality (15-yr follow-up)	↓ 26% ↓ 11%
POSCH[55]	838 men and women, 9.7 yr, R, C, P	Partial ileal bypass surgery	TC = ↓ 23% LDL-C = ↓ 38%	CHD death + nonfatal MI Total mortality CHD mortality	↓35% ↓22% ↓28%
Stockholm Heart Study[56]	555 men and women, 5 yr, R, C, P	Clofibrate + niacin	TG = ↓ 19% TC = ↓ 13%	Total mortality CHD mortality CHD death + nonfatal MI	↓ 26% ↓ 36% ↓ 41%
4S Trial[188]	444 men and women, 4.5 yr, R, C, P	Simvastatin vs placebo	TC = ↓ 25% LDL-C = ↓ 35% HDL-C = ↑ 8%	Total mortality CHD death CHD events Stroke	↓ 30% ↓ 42% ↓ 30% ↓ 36%
Angiographic Studies					**Rx vs Placebo**
CLAS[60]	188 men, postCABG	Diet, BAR + niacin	LDL-C: –43% HDL-C: +37%	Progression Regression	39% vs 61% 16% vs 2%
FATS[61]	146 men, CAD	Diet, statin + BAR	LDL-C: –46% HDL-C: +15%	Progression Regression	22% vs 46% 32% vs 11%
		Diet, niacin + BAR	LDL-C: –32% HDL-C: +43%	Progression Regression	25% vs 46% 39% vs 11%
Lifestyle[62]	48 men, CAD	Diet, exercise	LDL-C: –37% HDL-C: –3%	Progression Regression	14% vs 32% 41% vs 32%
POSCH[55]	838 men and women, postMI	Partial ileal bypass	LDL-C: –42% HDL-C: +5%	Progression Regression	37% vs 65% 14% vs 6%
SCOR[64]	87 FH	Diet, BAR + niacin + statin	LDL-C: –39% HDL-C: +25%	Progression Regression	20% vs 41% 33% vs 13%
STARS[63]	90 CAD	Diet	LDL-C: –16% HDL-C: 0%	Progression Regression	15% vs 46% 38% vs 46%
		Diet and BAR	LDL-C: –36% HDL-C: –4%	Progression Regression	12% vs 46% 33% vs 4%
MAAS[189]	381 men and women with CAD, 4 yr	Statin	LDL-C: –31% HDL-C: +9%	Progression Regression	21% vs 39% 17% vs 11%
CCAIT[190]	331 men and women with CAD, 2 yr	Statin	LDL-C: –29% HDL-C: +7%	Progression Regression	33% vs 50% 19% vs 13%
SCRIP[191]	300 men and women with CAD, 4 yr	Diet, weight loss, exercise, lipid-lowering drugs	LDL-C: –22% Weight: –4% Exercise: +20% Diet fat: –24%	Progression Cardiac deaths + admissions	47% less with Rx 43% less with Rx
PLACC-II[192]	151 men and women with history of CAD + carotid atherosclerosis	Statin	LDL-C: –29% HDL-C: +7%	Fatal and nonfatal MI	–60%
ACAPS[193]	919 men and women with carotid atherosclerosis	Statin with and without warfarin	LDL-C: –28% HDL-C: +5%	Carotid wall thickness Cardiovascular events	Significant ↓ –64%
Duffield et al[187]	24 men and women with femoral atherosclerosis	Diet + BAR, niacin or clofibrate	LDL-C: –28% Tg: –45%	Progression Regression	7% vs 17% 15% vs 33%

[a] BAR = Bile acid resins; C = Controlled; CABG = Coronary artery bypass surgery; CAD = Coronary artery disease; CHD = Coronary heart disease; DB = Double blind; FH = Familial hypercholesterolemia; HDL-C = High-density lipoprotein-cholesterol; LDL-C = Low-density lipoprotein cholesterol; MI = Myocardial infarction; N = Niacin; P = Parallel; R = Randomized; Rx = Treatment; TC = Total cholesterol; TG = Triglyceride.

These results support the aggressive modification of lipids in patients with angiographic evidence of atherosclerosis to prevent secondary coronary heart disease events.

Other Considerations

Two important issues relative to the treatment of hypercholesterolemia remain unresolved: These are the impact of therapy on total and noncoronary heart disease mortality and the cost effectiveness of drug therapy.

Total and NonCHD Mortality

In the primary prevention trials (see Table 9.3), there was a significant reduction in fatal and nonfatal CHD events in treated patients, but no difference in total mortality. Of note, increases in noncoronary heart disease mortality tended to offset the reductions in CHD mortality. Causes of nonCHD mortality included small, insignificant numerical increases from various causes including cancers, diseases of the biliary tract and intestines, pulmonary diseases, accidents, suicides, and homicides. Because these causes were so diverse, a plausible biological explanation for the lack of a reduction in total mortality is difficult. Meta-analyses of cholesterol-lowering drug studies have found a significant increase in aggregate noncoronary heart disease mortality.[65–67] In contrast to primary prevention trials, secondary prevention trials have reported reductions in both CHD and nonCHD mortality and meta-analyses indicate a favorable trend in total death rates.[68] The 4S trial demonstrated a statistically significant 30% reduction in total mortality with four years of treatment in a population of patients with evidence of coronary heart disease.[188]

The most plausible explanation for the total mortality differences between primary and secondary prevention trials appears to be related to the level of CHD risk in the treated population. In patients with relatively low risk, reductions in coronary heart disease may not be sufficient to offset increases in death from other causes, while in patients with high CHD risk, they are. These results have left in question the wisdom of using drugs to treat patients with relatively low risk of coronary heart disease. While the evidence pointing to cholesterol-lowering drugs as the cause of nonCHD deaths is weak, the possibility exists that adverse drug effects, as yet undefined, may negate reductions in CHD mortality. Until this has been disproven, drug therapy should be employed judiciously in low risk patients, such as young men and premenopausal women. However, in patients with a high coronary heart disease risk, such as in those with established disease or with multiple risk factors, drugs should be considered when nutritional therapy fails to achieve adequate control.

Cost-Effectiveness

Several cost-effectiveness analyses of lipid-lowering therapies have been conducted.[69–72] One variable which often is used in these analyses is the cost per years of life saved. Analyses of other prophylactic measures to reduce coronary heart disease risk, such as the use of aspirin in postMI patients and the treatment of mild hypertension with antihypertensive drugs, indicate that it costs up to $50,000 per year of life saved to treat these patients. Our society has accepted this level of expenditure as cost-effective. Analyses of cholesterol-lowering treatment have found that drug treatment of high-risk patients (i.e., patients who have experienced a CHD event or who have multiple risk factors) is relatively cost-effective (i.e., <$50,000 per year of life saved), while treatment of low risk patients (i.e., asymptomatic premenopausal women and young men) is less cost-effective (i.e., >$300,000 per year of life saved). These analyses support aggressive (i.e., drug and lifestyle) treatment of the highest risk patients and less aggressive (i.e., lifestyle only) treatment of low-risk patients.

Hypercholesterolemia
Initial Evaluation of Total and HDL-Cholesterol

1. T.A., a 43-year old premenopausal female, was screened for cholesterol during a routine medical evaluation. She has never taken cholesterol-lowering medication and has had no symptoms of coronary or peripheral vascular disease. She has a 20-pack-year history of smoking and exercises regularly, without physical limitations. T.A. states that she follows a low-fat, low-cholesterol diet. Her father is alive and well at 71 with a normal cholesterol level. Her mother experienced a heart attack at age 47 and died at age 57 from a second event. Her grandfather died from a heart attack at age 52; a sister has hypercholesterolemia and currently is taking niacin. Pertinent physical findings are a weight of 125 pounds, height 63″, blood pressure (BP) 120/82 mm Hg, pulse 66 and regular, carotid pulses symmetrical bilaterally without bruits, no neck masses, no abdominal bruit, and no evidence of xanthomas in her Achilles tendon. Her nonfasting total and HDL-C levels were 280 mg/dL and 58 mg/dL, respectively. What is your initial assessment of T.A.'s cholesterol level? [SI units: total 7.24 mmol/L; HDL-C 1.50 mmol/L]

T.A.'s physician has followed the guidelines recommended by the National Cholesterol Education Program (NCEP) by obtaining both a total and an HDL-cholesterol level during a routine medical evaluation.[73] These initial screening tests may be made in the nonfasting state since the total and HDL-cholesterol levels are not significantly affected by the intake of dietary cholesterol. The nonfasting results reflect the endogenous production of cholesterol.

NCEP guidelines recommend that a full lipid profile evaluation (i.e., total cholesterol, triglycerides, HDL-cholesterol, and calculated LDL-cholesterol) be obtained in patients who have any one of the following: 1) total cholesterol ≥240 mg/dL whether or not other risk factors (see Table 9.4) are present; total cholesterol between 200 and 239 mg/dL with two or more risk factors for coronary heart disease; HDL-cholesterol less than 35 mg/dL; or established CHD.

Based upon these guidelines, T.A. qualifies for further evaluation since she has a total cholesterol greater than 240 mg/dL. She also has two risk factors, a personal history of smoking and a family history of premature coronary heart disease. Her HDL-C is acceptable [mean HDL-C (women): 55 mg/dL; <35 mg/dL is low].

Evaluation of the Lipoprotein Profile

2. One week later, after fasting for 12 hours, T.A. had the following laboratory test results: total cholesterol 290 mg/dL, triglycerides 55 mg/dL, HDL-C 55 mg/dL, LDL-C 224 mg/dL, plasma glucose 96 mg/dL, thyroid stimulating hormone (TSH) <100 U, alanine aminotransferase (ALT) 11 U (Normal: 0–50), aspartate aminotransferase (AST) 8 U (Normal: 0–50), blood urea nitrogen (BUN) 12 mg/dL, creatinine 1.0 mg/dL, and a negative urinalysis. What is your assessment of these results? [SI units: total cholesterol 7.5 mmol/L; triglycerides 0.62 mmol/L; HDL-C 1.42 mmol/L; LDL-C 5.79 mmol/L; glucose 5.33 mmol/L; TSH<100 U; ALT 0.18 μkat/L; AST 0.13 μkat/L; BUN 4.28 mmol/L UREA; creatinine 88.4 μmol/L]

According to NCEP guidelines, patients who have any one of the following should have a second lipid profile and receive a medical evaluation:

- LDL-C ≥160 mg/dL whether or not other risk factors are present.
- LDL-C between 130 and 159 mg/dL with two or more coronary heart disease risk factors.
- LDL-C greater than 100 mg/dL with established atherosclerotic disease in peripheral, carotid, or coronary vessels.[73]
- HDL-C less than 35 mg/dL.

Table 9.4	Coronary Heart Disease Risk Factors[a]

Positive Risk Factors (↑ Risk)

- Age: Male ≥45 yr
  Female ≥55 yr or premature menopause without estrogen replacement therapy
- Family history of a premature CHD (definite MI), or sudden death before 55 yr in father or other male first-degree relative or before 65 yr in mother or other female first-degree relative
- Current cigarette smoking
- Hypertension (≥140/90 mm Hg or on antihypertensive drugs)
- Low HDL cholesterol (<35 mg/dL)
- Diabetes mellitus

Negative Risk Factor (↓ Risk, Protective)

- High HDL cholesterol (≥60 mg/dL)

[a] CHD = Coronary heart disease; HDLD = High density lipoprotein; MI = Myocardial infarction.

T.A. qualifies for further evaluation because she has an LDL-C greater than 160 mg/dL. However, the decision to establish a diagnosis of hypercholesterolemia should be based upon the mean of at least two lipid profiles obtained one to eight weeks apart. If the two LDL-cholesterol values differ by more than 30 mg/dL, a third lipid profile should be obtained.

T.A.'s lipid and lipoprotein cholesterol levels are valid because she fasted for at least 12 hours. This is required because most laboratories use the triglyceride level to calculate the LDL-C concentration. The calculation requires that the triglycerides derived only from endogenous sources (i.e., VLDL particles) be measured. Having the patient fast for at least 12 hours should provide sufficient time for the exogenous triglycerides, which are carried by chylomicrons, to be cleared from the systemic circulation (provided the patient does not have a hyperchylomicronemia). T.A.'s LDL-cholesterol was determined from the following formula which may be used only when the triglyceride level is less than 400 mg/dL:

$$LDL - C = Total\ Cholesterol - \left(HDL - C + \frac{TG}{5}\right)$$

$$= 280\ mg/dL - \left(55\ mg/dL + \frac{55\ mg/dL}{5}\right)$$

$$= 224\ mg/dL$$

Secondary Causes of High Blood Cholesterol

3. T.A.'s subsequent LDL-C level was 225 mg/dL and the physician proceeded with a medical evaluation. Is there any evidence that T.A.'s elevated LDL-C is secondary to other conditions or concurrent drug therapy? [SI unit: 5.82 mmol/L]

The primary objectives in evaluating a patient who has an increased LDL-C level are to: 1) rule out secondary causes of the high cholesterol level, 2) identify familial disorders, and 3) document the presence of coronary heart disease or risk factors which will guide treatment choices. Conditions that may cause lipid disorders include diabetes mellitus, hypothyroidism, nephrotic syndrome, obstructive liver disease, and selected drugs. Drugs that may induce changes in lipid levels are presented in Table 9.5. When one of these potential causes is identified, it is prudent to treat the secondary disorder first. This often will lead to resolution of the lipid abnormality.

In T.A.'s case, no secondary causes are evident. Her blood glucose does not indicate the presence of diabetes; her TSH does not indicate hypothyroidism; her ALT and AST are within acceptable levels, suggesting normal liver function; and her BUN, creatinine, and urinalysis are acceptable, signifying normal renal function. She is not taking any drugs that could have contributed to her cholesterol elevation.

Familial Forms of Hypercholesterolemia

4. Could T.A. have an inherited form of hyperlipidemia?

T.A.'s history is consistent with polygenic hypercholesterolemia. As described previously, polygenic hypercholesterolemia is suspected when the patient's LDL-cholesterol is between 160 and 250 mg/dL and there is no evidence of tendon xanthomas. (See Table 9.2.) Family history of coronary heart disease is present in about 18% of these patients and is a strong finding in T.A. Polygenic hypercholesterolemia probably is caused by a combination of nutritional and genetic factors which reduce the clearance of LDL particles from the plasma. It is not possible to determine which factor is the main cause of hypercholesterolemia simply by examining the lipoprotein profile in an individual patient. However, if the patient responds to a low-fat diet with a substantial cholesterol reduction, one can assume that nutrition is a major factor in that patient. Conversely, a poor cholesterol response to dietary modification may indicate a primary genetic influence on blood cholesterol levels.

Evaluation of Atherosclerosis and CHD Risk Factors

5. Does T.A. have any evidence of atherosclerosis and associated risk factors?

A search for atherosclerotic vascular disease should not be limited to the coronary artery. Atherosclerosis may be found in any artery bed including the coronary vessels, aorta, arteries of the limbs, and carotid arteries. Wherever atherosclerosis is found, it is associated with a five- to sevenfold higher risk of a myocardial infarction,[89-91] justifying aggressive treatment.

The search for atherosclerotic vascular disease begins with a good clinical history. This is followed by a physical examination of the vascular tree and, when indicated, an imaging procedure of the affected artery. Atherosclerotic disease of the coronary artery can be established with history of myocardial ischemia, clinical and laboratory documentation of a past myocardial infarction [i.e., symptoms of myocardial ischemia, elevated cardiac creatine phosphokinase (CPK), and/or electrocardiographic (ECG) changes], or history of coronary artery surgery or angioplasty. None of these signs are present in T.A. A coronary angiography is indicated only when ischemic symptoms are present. Peripheral arterial disease is established by the presence of an abdominal aortic bruit or clinical signs and symptoms of ischemia to the extremities. T.A. was noted to have no abdominal bruit. The diagnosis is confirmed with angiograms of the suspected vessels, segment-to-arm pressure ratio studies, or flow velocity studies. Carotid atherosclerosis is documented by the presence of a carotid bruit or clinical symptoms of transient ischemic attacks and/or stroke and is confirmed with sono- or angiograms of the carotid vessel. None of these are evident in T.A.

Coronary heart disease risk factors for classifying patients into risk categories and arriving at treatment selections are presented in Table 9.4. Modifiable risk factors should themselves become the target of a risk reduction treatment program. Each risk factor carries an independent risk for coronary heart disease. Thus, one should attempt to modify all of them to reduce the patient's overall CHD risk. T.A. has two of the CHD risk factors on this list: smoking and a family history of premature CHD. These additional risk factors raise T.A.'s potential for a coronary heart disease event up to six times what it would be if they were not present. Clearly, she needs to be advised to stop smoking.

Table 9.5	Drug-Induced Hyperlipidemia[a]			
	Effect on Plasma Lipids			
Drug	Cholesterol	Triglycerides	HDL-C	Comments
Diuretics[74,75]				
Thiazides	↑ 5%–7% initially ↑ 0%–3% later	↑ 30%–50%	↑ 13 mg/dL	Effects transient. Monitor for long-term effects.
Loop	No change	No change	↓ to 15%	
Indapamide	No change	No change	No change	
Metolazone	No change	No change	No change	
Potassium sparing	No change	No change	No change	
Beta Blockers[76–79]				
Nonselective	No change	↑ 20%–50%	↓ 10%–15%	Selective beta blockers have greater effects than
Selective	No change	↑ 15%–30%	↓ 5%–10%	nonselective. Beta blockers with ISA or alpha-blocking
Alpha blocking	No change or ↓	No change	No change	effects are lipid neutral.
Alpha Agonists and Antagonists (e.g., Prazosin and clonidine) [80,81]	↓ 0%–10%	↓ 0%–20%	↓ 0%–15%	In general, drugs which affect alpha receptors ↓ cholesterol and ↑ HDL-C
ACE Inhibitors[82]	No change	No change	No change	
Calcium Channel Blockers	No change	No change	No change	
Oral Contraceptives[83,84]				
Monophasics	↑ 5%–20%	↑ 10%–45%	↑ 15% to ↓ 15%	Effects due to reduced lipolytic activity and/or ↑ VLDL synthesis. Mainly due to progestin component. Estrogen alone protective
Triphasics	↑ 10%–15%	↑ 10%–15%	↑ 5%–10%	
Glucocorticoids[85]	↑ 5%–10%	↑ 15%–20%	——	
Ethanol[86]	No change	↑ up to 50%	——	Marked elevations can occur in hypertriglyceridemic patients
Isotretinoin[87]	↑ 5%–20%	↑ 50%–60%	↓ 10%–15%	Changes may reverse 8 weeks after stopping drug
Cyclosporine[88]	↑ 15%–20%	No change	No change	

[a] ACE = Angiotensin-converting enzyme; HDL-C = High density lipoprotein-cholesterol; ISA = Intrinsic sympathomimetic activity.

Therapy for Lowering Cholesterol Levels

Diet Therapy

6. What dietary changes should be recommended to T.A.?

The centerpiece of treatment for high blood cholesterol is a low-fat, low-cholesterol diet. In fact, the basic, step I NCEP diet is recommended for all people over the age of two years in the U.S., whether or not they have elevated cholesterol levels.[92] The step I diet specifies that total fat intake be restricted to 30% of daily calories, saturated fat be restricted to 10% of daily calories, and dietary cholesterol to 300 mg/day.[73] (See Table 9.6.) The step II, "therapeutic" NCEP diet is advocated for patients like T.A. who do not achieve control with a step I diet. The step II diet still restricts total fat intake to 30% of calories, but further reduces saturated fats to less than 7% of calories and dietary cholesterol to 200 mg/day.[73] (See Table 9.6.) These are minimum goals and some patients will want to exceed them, even to the point of following a "vegetarian" diet. This is permissible, as long as the diet is nutritionally balanced.

A low fat diet should lower total and LDL-cholesterol and triglycerides. It also may reduce weight somewhat, due primarily to the reduction in saturated fats. The significance of HDL-C lowering under these circumstances is unknown.

T.A. is likely to need help in translating dietary recommendations into practical terms and concepts. Two approaches can be used to achieve this: teach her to count calories and provide general guidance in the selection of low fat foods. The more sophisticated patient may want to count calories or grams of total and saturated fat per day. The first step in teaching a patient is to determine their daily caloric requirements, adjusted for their level of activity. The average caloric requirement for women is 1800 calories/day and

for men 2500 calories/day. Based upon this, T.A. should be instructed to restrict total fat intake to 540 calories/day (30% of calories) and saturated fat to 126 calories/day (7% of calories). Using the relationship that there are nine calories generated per gram of fat, T.A.'s total fat intake should be restricted to less than 60 gm/day and saturated fat to less than 14 gm/day. Once these calculations have been made, the next step is to teach T.A. how to determine the grams of saturated and unsaturated fat contained in the foods she eats by reading food labels and referring to reference charts or books that list the nutritional content of foods.

For patients who are not able or willing to count calories (or gm), general instruction on how to select low fat foods can be provided. Principles to teach are:

- Eat less high-fat foods (especially foods high in saturated fats).
- Replace saturated fats with unsaturated fats.
- Eat less high-cholesterol food.
- Choose foods high in complex carbohydrates (starch and fiber).
- Attain and maintain an acceptable weight.

T.A. should be counseled to recognize and minimize the three main sources of saturated fats in her diet: meat products, dairy products, and oils used in processed foods and cooking.

All meat products, including beef, poultry, and fish, contain fat. Much of the fat is visible and may be trimmed off before consumption. The remaining fat is contained within the meat and may be limited by: 1) selecting the leanest meat (e.g., lean beef, skinless chicken, fish), 2) limiting portion size to about the size of a deck of playing cards (no more than 6 oz/day), and 3) cooking the meat in a manner that allows the fat to drip away from the meat (i.e., broiling, grilling).

High-fat dairy products are made with whole milk; low-fat alternatives are made with skim or 1% milk (which contain all of the nutrient value of whole milk products). T.A. should be taught to substitute low fat alternatives for high fat products, for example by choosing soft margarine (or no fatty spread at all) instead of stick butter (note that unsaturated fats exist normally in liquid form and saturated fats in solid form), nonfat creams rather than whole milk creams, low-fat or nonfat soft cheese (i.e., cottage cheese) rather than natural or processed hard cheese (including cream cheese), skim milk rather than whole milk, light or nonfat sour cream rather than regular sour cream, and nonfat frozen yogurt rather than ice cream. She also should avoid or limit cream sauces on meats and vegetables and creamy soups.

Products prepared with coconut, palm, or palm kernel oils as well as lard and bacon fat contain a high concentration of saturated fats and should be restricted. In their place, products made with mono-unsaturated fats (e.g., olive and canola oils) or polyunsaturated fats, (e.g., corn, cottonseed, and soybean oils) may be substituted. The monounsaturated fats have little or no effect on blood lipids and the polyunsaturated fats actually may help to reduce total cholesterol. While unsaturated fats do not elevate cholesterol levels, they are sources of dense calories and so may contribute to the development of obesity and hypertriglyceridemia. Also, when the ''good'' (unsaturated) oils are partially hydrogenated (that is, saturated to make them solid as in some margarine), they take on the character of saturated oils and may raise cholesterol levels. These are called ''trans'' fatty acids. Major sources of saturated and trans fatty acids in our diets include cakes, pies, cookies, chips, and popcorn.

Instruction in good nutrition should not only inform the patient of what not to eat, but what to eat. Good instruction in a low fat diet is not a list of foods to avoid; rather it is how to make good selections. A good model to use in giving T.A. instruction may be the food pyramid described by the National Institutes of Health. The food pyramid prescribes the consumption of the following nutrients each day: lean meat, poultry, and fish: ≤6 ounces/day; low fat dairy products two to three servings per day; breads and cereals ≥6 servings per day; vegetables three to five servings per day; fruits two to four servings per day; and fats and oils ≤6 to 8 teaspoons/day.

T.A. will need to follow a low-fat diet indefinitely to sustain its benefit. For this reason, it would be preferable to have T.A. work with a registered dietitian who understands low fat, low cholesterol diets and can give her personalized instruction. Particularly important is instruction on how to shop for and prepare low-fat foods and how to select low-fat foods in restaurants. Pharmacists and other health professionals should reinforce and support these recommendations.

Table 9.6	Dietary Therapy for High Blood Cholesterol[a,73]	
Nutrient	Step I	Step II
Total fat	30%	30%
Saturated fats	8%–10%	<7%
Polyunsaturated fats	up to 10%	up to 10%
Monounsaturated fats	up to 15%	up to 15%
Carbohydrates	≥55%	≥55%
Protein	≈15%	≈15%
Cholesterol	300 mg/day	200 mg/day

[a] Nutrients expressed as a percent of total daily calories.

7. Effect on LDL-Cholesterol. What changes in T.A.'s LDL-C can be expected if she follows a step II, low-fat diet?

Serum cholesterol is reduced an average of 3% to 14% in males who adhere to a step I diet, although the usual reduction is 5% to 7%.[93,94] A slightly smaller response is attained in women, perhaps because their baseline intake of saturated fats is lower than men.[95] Progression to a step II diet should yield another 3% to 7% average reduction.[63] In some patients, blood cholesterol levels fall substantially, while in others practically no change will occur. Response to a low fat diet depends upon many factors including the patient's dietary habits before implementing the low-fat diet, their compliance with the diet, the degree to which they restrict fats and cholesterol, and the influence of genetic factors.

Since T.A. is a woman and has been following a low-fat diet before her diagnosis, a dramatic reduction in her cholesterol levels would not be expected. However, a low-fat diet should be prescribed because any reduction in cholesterol levels will be beneficial and should have other positive effects on health. Also, the cholesterol lowering that is achieved with diet should be additive with drug therapy, if it becomes necessary. This may allow the use of lower, less toxic doses of lipid altering drugs.

Other Lifestyle Changes

8. What other nondrug (lifestyle) changes can lower T.A.'s cholesterol?

Weight reduction in the overweight patient can reduce LDL-cholesterol. A five to ten pound weight loss, for example, has been reported to double the LDL-C reduction achieved with a low saturated fat diet alone.[93] Weight loss primarily should reduce triglycerides and raise HDL-C.[96] In addition, weight reduction in the obese patient may reduce the risk of developing hypertension and diabetes. Since T.A. has an acceptable weight, these considerations do not apply.

Smoking cessation substantially reduces the risk of CHD, pulmonary disease, and cancer and also may slightly reduce LDL-C. This is an important consideration in T.A. The coronary heart disease risk she has from smoking is greater than the risk she has from the modest LDL-C elevation. By stopping smoking, T.A. will not only reduce her blood cholesterol levels slightly, but substantially alter her risk profile. Since most patients gain weight when they stop smoking, and since weight gain may worsen lipid levels, plans to alter her diet and physical activity to counter these effects should be made.

Increasing physical activity should be a component of the management of any patient with high blood cholesterol. Regular physical exercise may reduce triglycerides and VLDL-cholesterol levels, raise HDL-C levels, promote weight loss or maintenance of desired weight, lower blood pressure, and cause favorable changes in coronary blood flow.[97] Regular aerobic exercise such as brisk walking, jogging, swimming, bicycling, and tennis should be prescribed in terms of amount (e.g., walking 4 miles), intensity (e.g., walking 4 mph), and frequency (walking each day if possible, but at least 3 times a week). T.A. states that she is already physically active. The level of her activity should be documented and enhancements recommended if needed.

Goal of Therapy

9. Lipid profiles obtained 6, 12, and 24 weeks after T.A. had initiated a step II low fat diet and an exercise program and had stopped smoking revealed LDL-C levels of 195, 210, and 200 mg/dL, respectively. What is your assessment of the need for additional lipid-modifying treatment? [SI units: LDL-C 5.40, 5.43, and 5.17 mmol/L, respectively]

According to the NCEP guidelines (see Table 9.7), T.A. should try to achieve an LDL-C less than 160 mg/dL, since she currently

Table 9.7	Treatment Decisions Based upon LDL-C[a,73]		
Goal	Diet Intervention Indicated	Drug Therapy Indicated	LDL-C Treatment Goal
No CHD with <2 risk factors	≥160 mg/dL	≥190 mg/dL	<160 mg/dL
No CHD with ≥2 risk factors	≥130 mg/dL	≥160 mg/dL	<130 mg/dL
With CHD	>100 mg/dL	≥130 mg/dL	≤100 mg/dL

a CHD = Coronary heart disease; LDL-C = Low-density lipoprotein-cholesterol.

has only one CHD risk factor (i.e., family history) and no evidence of coronary heart disease. This represents a 20% reduction from her current level. According to NCEP recommendations, drugs should be considered whenever LDL-cholesterol levels exceed 190 mg/dL in patients who have less than two risk factors and are following a good diet. However, the NCEP guidelines also recommend that the patient's near-term risk of experiencing CHD be considered. Since T.A. is still premenopausal, she has a relatively low risk of coronary heart disease despite her current LDL-C level. Thus, the most prudent approach in managing T.A. is to maximize her lifestyle therapies and periodically monitor her LDL-C. If the LDL-cholesterol remains elevated and especially if it increases further, treatment with a drug that has an established record of safety (e.g., bile acid resins) may be considered.

Drug Therapy

10. B.J., a 53-year-old man, has a mean LDL-C of 200 mg/dL determined on 3 appointments after faithfully following a step II low saturated fat diet for 6 months. He has a normal BP and glucose level. He reports no family history of premature CHD events. He does not smoke. His HDL-C is 45 mg/dL (normal average for a man). There are no secondary or familial causes of his hypercholesterolemia and no evidence of atherosclerosis was found during his initial medical evaluation. He jogs 2 miles 3 times a week. Is B.J. a candidate for cholesterol lowering drug therapy and what drug(s) should be considered for lowering his LDL-C level? [SI unit: LDL-C 5.17 mmol/L]

According to the NCEP guidelines, B.J. has one risk factor for coronary heart disease, male greater than 45 years old, and is a candidate for cholesterol-lowering drug therapy since his LDL-C remains above 190 mg/dL after six months of a low-fat, low-cholesterol diet. (See Table 9.7.) These guidelines indicate that his LDL-cholesterol goal would be less than 160 mg/dL.

The NCEP recognizes bile acid resins, niacin, and the HMG CoA reductase inhibitors (or statins for short) as the "major" drugs for lowering blood cholesterol levels. Therefore, all of the drugs from this list may be considered for treating B.J. (see Table 9.8).

Bile acid resins have appeal in the management of hypercholesterolemia because they have a strong safety record established from years of use, effectively lower LDL-C, and were associated with a reduced CHD risk in the Coronary Primary Prevention Trial.[54,103] Resins are not absorbed from the gastrointestinal (GI) tract and thus lack systemic toxicity. They are available in powder and tablet forms. They reduce total and LDL-C in a dose-dependent manner. (See Table 9.9.) LDL-cholesterol is reduced approximately 15% with 5 gm/day of colestipol powder (equivalent to 4 gm of cholestyramine), 23% with 10 gm/day, and 27% with 15 gm/day.[98] Patients should be initiated on one packet, scoop, or tablet of resin daily. (See Table 9.10.) Even though the maximum recommended daily dose for colestipol is 30 gm of powder, it rarely is necessary

or desirable to increase the daily dose beyond 20 gm of colestipol powder or its equivalent because of intolerable side effects and lack of substantial additional LDL-C lowering efficacy. The reduction achieved is inversely proportional to the baseline, untreated LDL-cholesterol level.[98] Thus, patients with mild to moderate cholesterol elevations (such as T.A. has) will have the greatest relative reduction.

Mechanism of Action. The resins are anion exchange agents which bind bile acids in the intestinal lumen.[104] By disrupting the enterohepatic recirculation of bile acids, the liver is stimulated to convert hepatocellular cholesterol into bile acids. A reduction in the concentration of cholesterol in the hepatocyte prompts the upregulation of LDL receptor synthesis and the uptake of circulating LDL-C, thus lowering blood levels.[7] This mechanism has appeal not only because it leads to effective LDL-cholesterol reduction, but also because it is synergistic with other therapies to lower cholesterol. For example, combining a drug which reduces hepatocellular cholesterol biosynthesis (such as statin, see HMG-CoA Reductase Inhibitors) with a resin which interferes with bile acid recycling can cause a substantial upregulation of LDL receptors and enhanced clearance of cholesterol from the blood.[7]

Adverse Effects. The disadvantage of resins is side effects. Resin therapy frequently causes gastrointestinal symptoms including constipation, bloating, epigastric fullness, nausea, and flatulence.[103] (See Table 9.11.) These may be lessened by using resin therapy in low doses and using appropriate preparation techniques. The patient should be instructed to mix the resin powder in noncarbonated, pulpy juices; to swallow it without engulfing air (administering it through a straw may help avoid air entrapment); and to maintain an adequate intake of fluids and fiber in the diet. Resins also may raise triglyceride levels 3% to 10%, which may be especially problematic in patients with elevated baseline triglyceride levels. Esophageal obstruction has been reported with resin tablets. Reduction in the absorption of fat soluble vitamins and folic acid has been reported with high doses of resins, but this is rarely a clinically relevant problem in otherwise healthy patients. Resins also may reduce the absorption of digitoxin, warfarin, thyroxine, thiazide diuretics, beta blockers, and presumably other anionic drugs. This interaction usually can be minimized by administering other drugs one hour before or four hours after the resin dose.

Based upon this summary, there are no contraindications to the use of resin therapy in B.J. Resins are likely to achieve B.J.'s goal of therapy and are very safe. Proper patient counseling on how to prepare and administer the resins will aid in patient acceptance.

Niacin: Clinical Use. Niacin (or nicotinic acid) is a water-soluble B vitamin which, at high doses, improves all serum lipids. Favorable attributes are low cost, availability as an over-the-counter product, and a demonstrated reduction in recurrent myocardial infarction rate and lower total mortality in the Coronary Drug Project.[57,58] Crystalline niacin lowers total and LDL-C 15% to 25%, lowers triglycerides 30% to 60%, and raises HDL-C 20% to 35%.[57,105,106] (See Table 9.12.) Doses should be started at a low level (e.g., 250 mg in 2 to 3 divided doses daily) and slowly titrated as tolerated (e.g., daily doses increased by 250 mg Q 3 to 7 days) to a maximum of 3000 mg/day. (See Table 9.10.) Doses of niacin often have to be raised to 2000 to 3000 mg/day to lower LDL-C by 20% to 25%, but 1000 to 1500 mg/day may be sufficient to reduce triglycerides and raise HDL-C by 25% to 30%.[105] (See Table 9.9.) Niacin is also the only drug that lowers Lp(a), with reductions being as great as 30%.[107] Its metabolite, nicotinamide, has no effect on cholesterol and should not be used as a substitute to lower side effects.

Mechanism of Action. Niacin produces its effects on cholesterol in part by reducing the production of VLDL particles by the liver.[108] This explains its effectiveness in lowering triglyceride lev-

Table 9.8		Drugs of Choice for Dyslipidemia[a]
Lipid Disorder	Single Drugs of Choice	Combination Drugs of Choice
Polygenic hypercholesterolemia with desirable triglycerides and HDL-C	Bile acid resin, niacin, statin, estrogens (postmenopausal women)	Bile acid resin-niacin, bile acid resin-statin, niacin-statin
Familial hypercholesterolemia with desirable triglycerides and HDL-C	Statin, bile acid resin, niacin	Bile acid resin-niacin, bile acid resin-statin, niacin-statin
Mixed hyperlipidemia in nondiabetics (↑LDL-C and ↑ TG)	Niacin, statin, gemfibrozil	Niacin-statin, statin-gemfibrozil,[b] niacin-bile acid resin, niacin-gemfibrozil
Mixed hyperlipidemia in diabetics (↑ LDL-C and ↑ TG)	Statin, gemfibrozil	Statin-gemfibrozil,[b] statin-bile acid resin, gemfibrozil-bile acid resin
Polygenic hypercholesterolemia with isolated low HDL	Niacin, statin, estrogens (postmenopausal women)	Statin-niacin

[a] HDL = High-density lipoprotein; HDL-c = High-density lipoprotein-cholesterol; LDL-C = Low-density lipoprotein-cholesterol; TG = Triglycerides.
[b] Use cautiously as there is an increased risk of myopathy.

els. Because LDL is a VLDL degradation product, reducing the secretion of VLDL particles also lowers the LDL-cholesterol level.

Adverse Effects. The main drawbacks to niacin therapy are the frequent, bothersome side effects associated with its use.[105,106,109] Vasodilation, leading to flushing, itching and headache, is especially troublesome. (See Table 9.11.) Practically every patient given niacin will experience one of these side effects.[99] These symptoms can be reduced by having patients administer doses with food and by taking 325 mg of aspirin 30 minutes before the morning dose of niacin (to inhibit prostaglandin synthesis which is thought to mediate these side effects).[110] Niacin also can cause fatigue and a variety of gastrointestinal symptoms including nausea, dyspepsia, and activation of peptic ulcer. Doses should be taken with food to minimize GI side effects. It can cause hyperuricemia and gout and worsen the glucose tolerance in diabetics in a dose-dependent manner. (See Table 9.11.)

The most troublesome side effect associated with niacin is hepatotoxicity.[105,111–114] This side effect is associated almost exclusively with the sustained-release (SR) forms of niacin and appears to be dose dependent, occurring in daily doses exceeding 1500 mg. Hepatotoxicity is detected by an elevation in liver transaminase enzymes; in severe cases, this may be accompanied by symptoms including fatigue, anorexia, malaise, and nausea. Rare cases of fulminant hepatitis have been reported. Niacin-induced hepatotoxicity appears to be completely reversible when the drug is discontinued. To detect this problem, patients should be monitored carefully by trained health professionals before treatment begins and every six to eight weeks for the first year with serum transaminase levels. Because of these problems, the crystalline form of niacin is preferred. If sustained-release niacin must be used (e.g., crystalline niacin cannot be tolerated or there are no effective alternatives), doses should not exceed 1500 mg/day.

There are no apparent contraindications to the use of niacin in B.J. Niacin would be expected to effectively lower LDL-C with low daily cost and an established safety profile, if used in a crystalline form.

HMG CoA Reductase Inhibitors (Statins): Clinical Use. One of the most potent groups of drugs available to lower cholesterol are the statins. They lower LDL-C approximately 20% to 25% with initial doses (i.e., 20 mg of lovastatin or its equivalent) and 35% to 45% with maximal daily doses (i.e., lovastatin 80 mg/day or its equivalent).[100,115,116] (See Table 9.9.) Statins also effectively reduce triglyceride levels and increase HDL-C. (See Table 9.12.) The LDL-cholesterol lowering achieved is dose dependent and log-linear, indicating that low doses produce substantial effects and that upward titration of daily doses produces only modest additional reductions. (See Table 9.9.)

The currently available statins including fluvastatin, lovastatin, pravastatin, and simvastatin have similar efficacy at the recommended starting doses and times. Generally, 10 mg of simvastatin and 20 mg of lovastatin, pravastatin, or fluvastatin produce similar LDL-cholesterol lowering (i.e., 20% to 25%). As doses are titrated upward, LDL-cholesterol is reduced by more than 30%, with all statins except fluvastatin which has a flatter dose-response relationship. The efficacy of all statins is greater if administered in the evening rather than in the morning coinciding with the nighttime upturn in endogenous cholesterol biosynthesis; the LDL-C lowering efficacy of twice daily administration is slightly greater (by 2% to 4%) than once daily evening doses. The bioavailability of lovastatin is improved by administration with food.

The greatest concern regarding the use of a statin is the lack of a demonstrated reduction of CHD endpoints in primary prevention studies. However, in trials using a statin alone or in combination with other cholesterol-lowering drugs in patients with established coronary heart disease (secondary prevention) there was less progression of atherosclerotic lesions and fewer CHD events than in placebo-treated patients.[61] This, coupled with their favorable safety

Table 9.9	Dose-Related LDL-C Lowering of Major Drugs[a]	
Drug	Daily Dosage	LDL-C Lowering
Bile acid resins (colestipol)[98]	5 gm	−15%
	10 gm	−23%
	15 gm	−27%
Niacin (crystalline)[99]	1000 mg	−6%
	1500 mg	−13%
	2000 mg	−16%
	3000 mg	−22%
Lovastatin[100]	20 mg	−24%
	40 mg	−34%
	80 mg	−40%
Pravastatin[101]	10 mg	−22%
	20 mg	−32%
	40 mg	−34%
Simvastatin[102]	5 mg	−24%
	10 mg	−33%
	20 mg	−33%
	40 mg	−40%
Fluvastatin	20 mg	−22%
	40 mg	−24%

[a] LDL-C = Low-density lipoprotein-cholesterol.

Table 9.10		Dosages of Selected Lipid Modulating Drugs		
Drug	Initial Dosage	Usual Dosage	Maximum Dosage	Comment
Cholestyramine	4 gm before main meal	4 gm BID before heaviest meals	8 gm BID before heaviest meals	May prescribe 24 gm/day, but few patients can tolerate
Colestipol	5 gm powder or 2 gm tabs QD before main meal	5 gm powder or 4 gm tabs BID before heaviest meals	10 gm powder or 8 gm tabs BID before heaviest meals	May prescribe 30 gm/day powder, but few patients can tolerate
Niacin	100–125 mg BID with food	750–1000 mg BID	1500 mg BID	Doses up to 6 gm/day have been used, but few can tolerate. Dosages may be ↑ 200–250 mg/day Q 3–7 days until desired dosage obtained
Fluvastatin	20 mg with dinner	20 mg with dinner	40 mg with dinner or 20 mg BID with food	Little added benefit with ↑ dosages
Lovastatin	10–20 mg with dinner	20 mg/day with dinner	40 mg BID	Some additional efficacy attained with maximum dosage but side effects may be greater. Administer with food to ↑ bioavailability
Pravastatin	10 mg at bedtime with food	20 mg at bedtime with food	40 mg at bedtime with food	Administer with food to reduce dyspepsia
Simvastatin	5 mg at bedtime with food	10 mg at bedtime with food	40 mg BID with food	Administer with food to reduce dyspepsia
Gemfibrozil	600 mg BID	600 mg BID	600 mg BID	
Probucol	250 mg BID	250 mg BID	500 mg BID	

profile and their potency in lowering LDL-C, supports the NCEP recommendation to consider statins as one of the ''major'' drugs available to lower cholesterol.

Mechanism of Action. Statins competitively inhibit the enzyme responsible for converting HMG CoA to mevalonate in an early, rate-limiting step in the biosynthetic pathway of cholesterol (see Figure 9.1).[7] The reduction in hepatocellular cholesterol prompts an upregulation of LDL receptor proteins, and thus increases the clearance of circulating LDL particles from the blood. The triglyceride lowering effects appear to be produced by an increase in the clearance of VLDL and VLDL remnant particles from the systemic circulation (by the upregulation of LDL receptors) and, to a lesser extent, by a reduced secretion of VLDL particles from the liver.[117–119]

Adverse Effects. Statins are well tolerated by most patients. Side effects are uncommon. Headache and gastrointestinal symptoms (including dyspepsia, flatus, constipation, and abdominal pain) occasionally are experienced.[100,115,116,120] (See Table 9.11.) These symptoms are usually mild and disappear with continued therapy. More serious side effects include hepatotoxicity and myopathy. Hepatotoxicity, manifested as elevations in transaminase enzyme levels three times the upper limit of normal, is seen in 1% to 2% of patients and is dose dependent.[100] Symptoms of hepatic dysfunction are produced rarely. The transaminase level returns to normal when the statin is discontinued. Rechallenge after enzymes are within normal limits is acceptable. If the drug is tolerated upon rechallenge, it can be continued; recurrence of transaminase elevation warrants permanent discontinuation.

Myopathy has been reported in 0.1% of patients who are receiving lovastatin; it also has been reported rarely with the other statins.[100] Myopathy is a clinical diagnosis which is detected by patient symptoms of muscle aches, soreness, or weakness (i.e., myalgia); it is confirmed by an increase in serum creatine phosphokinase levels more than 10 times the upper limit of normal. Routine monitoring of CPK is unnecessary. A few cases of rhabdomyolysis, myoglobinuria, and acute tubular necrosis have been reported in patients receiving statin therapy. Myopathy appears to occur most frequently when lovastatin is combined with cyclosporine, less frequently when it is combined with gemfibrozil, and infrequently when it is used in combination with niacin or erythromycin.[121–123] As with transaminase level elevations, myopathy is quickly reversible when the statin is discontinued.

Lovastatin may prolong the prothrombin time in patients receiving coumarin anticoagulants concurrently; this effect is not caused by pravastatin.[124] Statins should not be used in patients with active liver disease or those who are, or hope to become, pregnant because of potential hazards to the fetus.

Based upon this information, a statin would be an acceptable drug for B.J. He is not receiving a potentially interacting drug and has no apparent contraindication to its use.

11. Selection of a Drug Regimen. **Which one of the three major drugs should be used first to manage B.J.'s lipid disorder?**

The risk of coronary heart disease in B.J. is modest, given the fact that he has no evidence of CHD and only one risk factor. However, he is at the age when CHD events are more likely to occur and meets the NCEP criteria for a cholesterol lowering drug.

The first step in the selection of drug therapy for cholesterol lowering is to determine the average LDL-C reduction needed to achieve the patient's target LDL-C level and which drugs are most likely to achieve it. All three major drugs should effectively lower B.J.'s LDL-cholesterol 20%, the amount required to achieve his treatment goal. (See Table 9.12.) Of the three, however, bile acid resins generally are considered the safest because they are not systemically bioavailable. Therefore, a suitable drug for B.J. would be either colestipol or cholestyramine. Both have equivalent LDL-C lowering efficacy, so the selection between them should be based upon B.J.'s preference (i.e., cost, taste, and texture of the powder). Resin therapy should be initiated as one packet or scoop or four tablets daily, administered with the heaviest meal. If desired reductions have not been achieved after 6 to 12 weeks, the dosage can be advanced to one packet or scoop or four tablets twice daily. At this level, dosages are small enough to avoid bothersome side effects, but large enough to achieve the 20% reduction in LDL-C. (See Table 9.9.) Once resin therapy has been initiated, a lipid profile should be evaluated every four to six weeks. (See Table 9.11.) Control is based upon an average of several readings taken on separate visits.

12. *Patient Instructions on Resin Use.* **How should B.J. be advised to administer bile acid resin therapy?**

Use of resin therapy requires careful patient instruction. The patient needs to know the gastrointestinal side effects that may occur and how to limit them. For example, patients should be instructed to maintain a good fluid and dietary fiber intake to minimize GI symptoms. If needed, a commercial psyllium product may be given to minimize constipation until tolerance develops. Patients also should be allowed to titrate doses to tolerable levels. They should be encouraged to experiment with the vehicle they use to administer resin powder. Many patients find orange and apple juice or apple sauce most preferable. Administration of the powder mixture through a straw may minimize the "grit" feeling in the mouth and the entrapment of air which may reduce flatulence side effects. Preparing the entire next day's dose in the evening and storing it in the refrigerator allows the hygroscopic beads to swell in the liquid and improve its tolerability. Resin doses are best taken just before meals twice to three times a day. Patients taking potentially interacting concurrent drug therapy, should be told to take these doses four hours after a resin dose (i.e., at bedtime). Patients taking resin tablets should be instructed to take each dose with a full glass of water to reduce the risk of esophageal obstruction. Tablets should be taken whole, not cut or crushed.

Fiber

13. Can supplemental fiber be used as an alternative to resins to treat B.J.?

Increasing the fiber intake in the diet or adding supplemental fiber in the form of psyllium (Metamucil), oat bran, gums, or other products, is likely to reduce B.J.'s LDL-C. However, when given to a patient who is following a good low-fat diet, the LDL-C reduction is modest (usually about 5%) and would not be enough to achieve B.J.'s LDL-C goal. Additionally, increased fiber is associated with bothersome gastrointestinal symptoms, including flatulence and bloating.

Fish Oils

14. Can fish oils be used to treat B.J.'s elevated LDL-C?

Fish oils predominantly contain polyunsaturated (omega-3) fatty acids which lower triglyceride levels significantly (i.e., 30% to 60%) but have variable effects on cholesterol levels. Thus, they have no place in the management of B.J. They may be useful in patients who have hypertriglyceridemia who cannot achieve adequate control with conventional triglyceride lowering drugs, niacin and gemfibrozil. Some studies have indicated that fish oils may have a role in preventing re-stenosis after angioplasty.

Postmenopausal Drug Therapy

15. C.M. is a 55-year-old postmenopausal female. Like the last two patients, she continues to have a mean LDL-C of 200 mg/dL after a 6-month trial of diet therapy. Like B.J., she has a strong family history of CHD (i.e., her father died suddenly at age 59 and her 43-year-old brother has had a heart attack). She does not have any other CHD risk factors. Her mean HDL-C is 58 mg/dL and mean triglycerides are 78 mg/dL. C.M. has no evidence of secondary or familial dyslipidemia and no atherosclerosis. She has not had a hysterectomy. She is physically active and has a normal weight. Does C.M. need cholesterol lowering drug therapy and, if so, with which drug? [SI units: LDL-C 5.17 mmol/L; HDL-C 1.5 mmol/L; and triglycerides 0.88 mmol/L]

Being postmenopausal (and not taking hormone replacement therapy) is considered a risk factor for CHD in women. C.M. has two risk factors (postmenopausal status and family history of CHD) and her desirable LDL-C is less than 130 mg/dL. If her mean LDL-cholesterol after diet is 200 mg/dL, she will require a 35% reduction to achieve her goal.

Because C.M. is postmenopausal, consideration should be given to the use of estrogen therapy before (or instead of) other cholesterol-lowering drugs to take advantage of its lipid altering effects as well as its prophylactic value in reducing osteoporosis and perimenopausal symptoms.

16. Estrogen Replacement Therapy: Justification for Use in Hypercholesterolemia **What is the justification for using estrogen therapy in C.M.? What is the ideal dose?**

Epidemiologic studies have reported up to 50% lower CHD rates in women who use estrogens compared to those who do not.[125-127] A recent meta-analysis of 31 case-control, cross-sectional, and cohort studies found an overall relative risk of 0.56; that is, a 44% lower rate of coronary heart disease in estrogen users compared with nonusers.[128] The difference in CHD rates between estrogen users and nonusers is even greater in women who have developed CHD.[127,129] Even though the effect of estrogen therapy on coronary heart disease has not been studied in controlled, clin-

Table 9.11	Monitoring Parameters, Adverse Effects and Drug Interactions with Major Cholesterol-Lowering Drugs[a]		
Drug	Adverse Effects	Drug Interactions	Monitoring Parameters
Bile acid resin	Indigestion, bloating, nausea, constipation, abdominal pain, flatulence	GI binding and reduced absorption of anionic drugs, including warfarin, beta blockers, digitoxin, thyroxine, thiazide diuretics. (Administer drugs 1–2 hr before or 4 hr after bile acid resin)	Lipid profile Q 4–8 wk until control; then TC Q 6–12 months long-term. Check triglyceride level after stable dose achieved, then PRN
Niacin	Flushing, itching, tingling headache, nausea, gas, heartburn, fatigue, rash, worsening of peptic ulcer, elevation in serum glucose and uric acid, hepatitis and elevation in hepatic transaminase levels	Hypotension with BP lowering drugs, such as alpha blockers, possible. Diabetics on insulin or oral agents may require dose adjustment because of ↑ in serum glucose levels	Lipid profile after 1000–1500 mg/day and then after stable dosage achieved; then TC Q 6–12 months long-term. LFTs at baseline and Q 6–8 wk for 1st yr, then PRN symptoms. Uric acid and glucose at baseline and again after stable dose reached (or symptoms produced), more frequently in diabetics. Monitor sitting and standing BP in hypertensive and elderly patients
Statins	Headache, dyspepsia, myositis (myalgia + CPK >10 times normal), elevation in hepatic transaminase levels	↑ myositis with concurrent cyclosporine (use low statin dose) and gemfibrozil. ↑ myositis may occur rarely with concurrent niacin or erythromycin. Lovastatin ↑ protime with concurrent warfarin	Lipid profile Q 4–8 weeks after dose change, then TC Q 6–12 months long-term. LFTs at baseline and Q 6–8 weeks for 1st yr, then PRN symptoms. Measure CPK if patient has symptoms of myalgia

[a] BP = Blood pressure; CPK = Creatine phosphokinase; GI = Gastrointestinal; LFTs = Liver function tests; TC = Total cholesterol.

Table 9.12	Average Effects of Selected Drugs on Lipoprotein Cholesterol and Triglycerides[a]		
Drug	LDL	HDL	TG
Bile acid resins	−14%–30%	±3%	+3%–10%
Niacin	−15%–25%	+20%–35%	−30%–60%
Statin	−25%–45%	+5%–15%	−5%–15%
Estrogens	−15%–25%	+15%–20%	+10%–50%
Gemfibrozil	±10%	+10%–30%	−30%–60%
Probucol	−5%–15%	−20%–30%	No change

[a] HDL = High-density lipoprotein; LDL = Low-density lipoprotein; TG = Triglyceride.

ical trials, the epidemiologic evidence of reduced CHD risk is so impressive and consistent that many authorities believe estrogen replacement therapy should be considered first in dyslipidemic, postmenopausal women, especially if it is otherwise indicated to relieve perimenopausal symptoms or minimize osteoporosis.

The low CHD rates in women taking estrogen are thought to be due to the combined effect of these drugs on lipoprotein levels and on the arterial wall.[130–132] On average, 0.625 mg/day of conjugated estrogen lowers LDL-C 15% to 25% and raises HDL-C 15% to 20%.[130–133] (See Table 9.12.) Estrogens also may increase triglycerides levels significantly, especially in women who have hypertriglyceridemia before estrogen therapy. Doses of 1.25 mg/day appear to provide only small additional effects on LDL-C and HDL-C, but may substantially increase triglyceride levels. Very high doses (i.e., 5 mg/day) may promote thrombosis.[125] Estrogens administered by transcutaneous or percutaneous routes have less effect on cholesterol levels.[134,135]

17. *Adverse Effects.* **C.M. is to be started on 0.625 mg/day of conjugated estrogen. What adverse effects of estrogens should she be monitored for? Is it appropriate to add adjunctive progestin therapy to C.M.'s regimen?**

The adverse effects which commonly occur with estrogens include breast tenderness or enlargement, vaginal bleeding (in women with an intact uterus), GI discomfort, headache, dizziness, fluid retention, and weight gain. The breast tenderness and vaginal bleeding are particularly disturbing to older women (age 60s to 80s) who are started on estrogen several years after the onset of menopause.

The major concern with the use of estrogen therapy is the risk for endometrial hyperplasia, endometrial cancer, and breast cancer. The risk of these problems is quite small compared with the reduction anticipated in CHD. Because the induction of endometrial hyperplasia (and possibly cancer) probably is related to stimulation of estrogen receptors, co-administration of progestins is advised in C.M. and other women who have a uterus. Unfortunately, some progestins derived from C-19 nortestosterone (e.g., norgestrel and levonorgestrel) have opposing effects on blood lipids and may reduce the beneficial effects of estrogens on coronary heart disease.[135] The C-21 progesterone derivative, medroxyprogesterone acetate, has minimal androgenic effects and less adverse effects on LDL-C and HDL-C. Little is known, however, about the effect of combination estrogen-medroxyprogesterone therapy on CHD rates.

Clinical Use. Given these considerations, C.M. appears to be an appropriate candidate for estrogen replacement therapy because she has at least two indications: osteoporosis prevention and dyslipidemia. Before beginning therapy, she should be queried about her family history of endometrial and breast cancer. A strong family history of either would relatively contraindicate estrogen use. Active thrombophlebitis or thromboembolic disorders, liver dis-

ease, migraine headaches, or cholelithiasis also are contraindications to hormone replacement therapy. Otherwise, conjugated estrogens 0.625 mg/day as has been prescribed is appropriate. Continuous daily administration of estrogen is desirable (rather than cyclic administration on the first 25 days of each month) to encourage compliance.

Since C.M. has a uterus, she also should be given progestins concurrently. Medroxyprogesterone is used most commonly. It may be given 5 to 10 mg/day for the last 12 to 13 days of the estrogen therapy each month. One to three days after withdrawal of the progestin, vaginal bleeding should begin. If C.M. objects to continuing menses, 2.5 to 5 mg of medroxyprogesterone may be given every day, continuously. This eventually will create an atrophic endometrium and induce amenorrhea without adversely affecting other estrogen effects. However, spotting may occur for the first three to six months of this continuous regimen.

C.M. should be instructed on self breast examination and seen annually for a pap smear, breast examination, and mammogram. An endometrial biopsy should be taken after one year of continuous therapy to ensure that endometrial hyperplasia is not present. If she chooses to take estrogen without a progestin, endometrial biopsies should be performed annually. She also should have a lipid profile after three to six months and, if still elevated, one of the major cholesterol-lowering drugs may be added to her regimen.

Familial Hypercholesterolemia

18. D.E. is a 45-year-old male with no evidence of CHD. His father and grandfather both died suddenly from an apparent heart attack in their early 50s; he has no other CHD risk factors. He has no evidence of secondary causes of dyslipidemia. On physical examination, he is noted to have bilateral corneal arcus and bilateral Achilles tendon xanthomas; the rest of his exam is normal. Likewise, his laboratory test results are within normal limits, except for the following lipid profile obtained 2 months after initiating a step II diet: total cholesterol 440 mg/dL; triglycerides 55 mg/dL; HDL-C 55 mg/dL; LDL-C 374 mg/dL. What form of hypercholesterolemia does D.E. most likely have? Is he a candidate for drug therapy at this time?
[SI units: total cholesterol 11.38 mmol/L; triglycerides 0.62 mmol/L; HDL-C 1.42 mmol/L; LDL-C 9.67 mmol/L]

The combination of a very high LDL-cholesterol, tendon xanthomas, and a strong family history of premature coronary heart disease is consistent with a diagnosis of familial hypercholesterolemia. In this case, D.E.'s CHD risk is very high and he deserves aggressive treatment with diet and drugs to lower his LDL-C to less than 130 mg/dL, or as close to this level as possible. To achieve this goal, D.E. will require a 65% LDL-C reduction, which almost assuredly will require combination drug therapy in addition to a low-fat diet. Because of the level of risk and the inability of diet to achieve D.E.'s LDL-cholesterol goal, it is acceptable to consider initiating drug treatment even though he has been following a diet for only two months.

Combination Drug Therapy

19. What combinations of cholesterol-lowering drugs would be suitable for D.E.?

Since a substantial LDL-C reduction is needed, a combination of two or more of the NCEP "major" LDL-C lowering drugs should be considered. There are only three possible combinations of these drugs: resin and statin, resin and niacin, and statin and niacin. (See Table 9.8.) All three are very effective in reducing LDL-C. Angiographic studies deploying niacin and resin in combination report that LDL-cholesterol is reduced by 32% to 43% and that a statin and resin combination reduces LDL-C by 46%.[60,61] Clinical trials have documented LDL-C reductions of 50% to 60% when all three drugs are used in combination.[136] Importantly, these reductions may be achieved without deploying maximum doses. For example, the reduction in LDL-C achieved in one study with pravastatin 10 mg/day plus colestipol was 56%, while that achieved with pravastatin 40 mg/day plus colestipol was 53%.[137]

While combinations of the major drugs are very similar with regard to their cholesterol-lowering efficacy, they may differ with respect to side effects. Individually, niacin and resins often cause bothersome side effects to the extent that about 25% of patients cannot tolerate them. When administered together, many patients will find the combination intolerable. The combination of a statin and niacin has been associated with an increased risk of myopathy, although this risk appears to be quite low.[124] Co-administration of a resin and statin may reduce the bioavailability of the statin. However, the efficacy of the combination does not appear to be affected. Given these considerations, a statin and resin combination is selected for D.E.

20. Initiating Therapy. How should combined therapy with a statin and resin be initiated in D.E.?

It is best to initiate combination therapy for D.E. one drug at a time, with careful monitoring of each regimen to establish its efficacy and side effects. Because the statin generally lowers LDL-C more than the resin, it should be started first to determine whether it alone controls D.E.'s LDL-cholesterol. Before initiating therapy, baseline liver function tests and CPK levels should be obtained. (See Table 9.11.) Renal function also should be assessed since reduced function may reduce clearance of the drug and increase the risk of side effects. Initially, 20 mg of lovastatin or its equivalent should be administered once daily in the evening. (See Table 9.10.) Lovastatin should be taken with the evening meal to increase bioavailability. If pravastatin, simvastatin, or fluvastatin are used instead, they would be given at bedtime. As stated previously, statins should be given in the evening or at bedtime to coincide with the increase in cholesterol biosynthesis which occurs in the early morning hours. LDL-C levels should be evaluated in four to six weeks when the maximum effect of the drug is anticipated. If needed to attain D.E.'s LDL-cholesterol goal, the dose may be increased to 40 mg of lovastatin or its equivalent once daily in the evening. If additional cholesterol lowering is required after this dose has been administered for 6 to 12 weeks, either the dose of lovastatin can be increased to 40 mg twice daily (or with other statins its equivalent) or a bile acid resin can be added to the statin. The LDL-C lowering that can be achieved with the combination therapy (i.e., 50% to 60%) is substantially greater than one could anticipate by increasing the dose of lovastatin to 80 mg/day (i.e., 40%). Thus, combination therapy would be the preferred option.

Alternative Therapy for Severe Hypercholesterolemia

21. What should be done if D.E.'s therapeutic goal is not reached using the combined statin and bile acid resin?

If D.E.'s goal of therapy is not reached after two LDL-C lowering drugs have been combined, a third LDL-C lowering drug may be added to the regimen. In this case, the addition of niacin may be considered. Before starting niacin therapy, and regularly at six to eight week intervals for the first year of therapy, liver function tests should be evaluated. (See Table 9.11.) The presence of relative and absolute contraindications to niacin, including active liver disease, gout, peptic ulcer disease, and insulin-dependent diabetes should be assessed before niacin is started. None of these were evident in D.E.'s evaluation. Patients with an active peptic ulcer should not receive niacin, nor should anyone with active liver disease. Niacin may increase glucose levels by an average of 10% to 20% when given to a diabetic necessitating careful monitoring

of glucose control. Since D.E. does not have diabetes, niacin would not be expected to appreciably change his glucose levels.

22. How should niacin dosing be initiated in D.E. and what monitoring is required?

The addition of niacin to D.E.'s current regimen should start with a low dose which is slowly titrated upward to allow tolerance to develop at each dosage level. (See Table 9.10.) As with resin therapy, D.E. should be given as much control over niacin administration as possible. Niacin may be started with 250 mg/day, administered in two or three divided doses. Compliance may be better if D.E. is asked to take it only twice daily. Thereafter, daily dosages may be increased every three to seven days in the following sequence: 500, 1000, 1500, 2000, and 3000 mg. D.E. should be evaluated once the 1000 to 1500 mg/day dose is reached. (See Table 9.11.) If sustained-release niacin is used, further upward dose titration should not be attempted because of the risk of hepatotoxicity. If warranted and tolerated, doses of immediate-release niacin may be increased to 2000 mg and then to 3000 mg daily in two or three divided doses.

D.E. should be warned about the vasodilatory symptoms associated with niacin and reassured that these are not generally dangerous and that tolerance should develop. He should be advised to take 325 mg of ASA or another prostaglandin inhibiting drug 30 minutes before the morning niacin dose to decrease these symptoms. He also should be allowed to back-titrate doses in a manner similar to how the dose was increased if necessary to manage bothersome symptoms. D.E. also should be advised to take doses with food to reduce gastrointestinal symptoms. He should be encouraged to call whenever troublesome symptoms occur and to specifically report symptoms of malaise, lethargy, nausea, and dyspepsia as these may be associated with niacin-induced hepatitis.

Mixed Hyperlipidemia
Assessing the Lipoprotein Profile

23. B.C., a 56-year-old male, experienced an MI 6 months ago. He weighs 220 pounds, is 6′ tall [ideal body weight (IBW): 140–185 pounds], and has a waist:hip ratio of 1.2. He has lost 10 pounds since his MI by following a low-fat diet and an exercise program. He has never taken cholesterol-lowering medication and has had no symptoms of atherosclerotic vascular disease since discharge from the hospital 6 months ago. He currently is taking propranolol 40 mg BID, ASA 325 mg QD, and enalapril 10 mg/day (for high blood pressure). He swims 1 mile 3 times a week without symptoms and he drinks 2 glasses of wine each evening with dinner. His father died at age 58 of an MI (lipids unknown); an uncle has had multiple heart attacks and has hypercholesterolemia; a younger brother has diabetes, hypertriglyceridemia, and had three-vessel bypass surgery 2 years ago; and a postmenopausal sister has hypercholesterolemia which is being treated with estrogen replacement. His only child, a son, has not had a lipid evaluation. Pertinent physical findings include:BP 148/90 mm Hg, arcus senilis, carotid pulses equal without bruits, and a chest clear to auscultation without cardiomegaly. Laboratory tests disclose normal TSH, renal, and liver function and a fasting glucose level of 120 mg/dL. The lipid profile is: total cholesterol 320 mg/dL, triglycerides 300 mg/dL, HDL-C 30 mg/dL, and LDL-C 230 mg/dL. What is your assessment of B.C.'s lipids and lipoprotein cholesterol concentrations? [SI units: glucose 6.66 mmol/L; total cholesterol 8.28 mmol/L; triglycerides 3.39 mmol/L; HDL-C 0.78 mmol/L; LDL-C 5.95 mmol/L]

The first step in interpreting B.C.'s lipid profile is to assess his total and LDL-cholesterol levels. (See Table 9.7.) According to the NCEP guidelines, B.C. has an elevated total cholesterol (>240 mg/dL) and an elevated LDL-C (>100 mg/dL in a patient with a history of CHD).[73] The LDL-C should be confirmed with another lipid profile, although the findings are not likely to substantially change B.C.'s need for treatment; interventions should not be delayed substantially while waiting for the results. B.C. has several risk factors for CHD (i.e., family history, male >45 years old, and low HDL-C). While these factors are important, the risk indicated by his past CHD history is so great that it drives the decision making process. Thus, the treatment goal for B.C. is an LDL-C of less than 100 mg/dL, or a 69% reduction from his baseline of 230 mg/dL.

A second step in evaluating B.C.'s lipid disorder is to assess his HDL-C and triglycerides. (See Table 9.13.) According to the NCEP guidelines, B.C. has a borderline high triglyceride level.[73] (See Table 9.13 for the NCEP's definition of triglycerides.)

As is frequently the case in patients with elevated triglycerides levels, B.C.'s HDL-C is low (i.e., <35 mg/dL). This signals an additional risk of coronary heart disease.

Relation of Triglycerides to CHD

24. Does the increased triglyceride level in B.C. indicate an increased CHD risk?

The exact role that triglycerides play in the pathogenesis of CHD is unclear. In most epidemiologic studies, elevated triglycerides have been identified as an independent risk factor when the data are analyzed by univariant analysis; however, when other lipid abnormalities such as increased LDL-C or low HDL-C are included in the multivariant analysis, triglycerides typically loose their independent predictive power.[138] Part of the reason for this may be the close interrelationship between lipids. Patients with high triglyceride levels almost always have a low HDL-C which predicts CHD risk.[139,140] In addition, elevated triglyceride levels are associated with increased levels of cholesterol-rich remnant VLDL particles and smaller, more cholesterol-dense LDL particles.[3,141] Both of these particles may be more atherogenic and mediate a higher CHD risk.[142,143] These particles are found in familial disorders including dysbetalipoproteinemia and familial combined hyperlipidemia which carry increased CHD risk.[16,144] However, in severe hypertriglyceridemia due to lipoprotein lipase deficiency or familial hypertriglyceridemia, VLDL particles are enriched in triglycerides and do not appear to be atherogenic.[144,145] Hypertriglyceridemia also may induce a procoagulant state which promotes coronary thrombosis.[141] So the issue in B.C.'s case is not whether triglycerides are an independent risk factor for coronary heart disease, but how the presence of an elevated triglyceride level signals other changes which alter CHD risk.

According to an NIH consensus conference, triglyceride levels in the 200 to 400 mg/dL range are likely to be associated with an increased risk of CHD, whereas levels above 1000 mg/dL are likely to be associated with an increased risk of causing pancreatitis.[138] Some patients with triglyceride levels between 400 and 1000 mg/dL have an increased CHD risk.[73] The risk of coronary heart disease is clearly high if the patient has a high LDL-C or low HDL-C level in addition to an elevated triglyceride level, as in B.C.[146] In the Helsinki Heart Study, for example, the risk of CHD in patients with an elevated LDL-cholesterol and triglycerides and

a low HDL-cholesterol was nearly four times greater than the group that had desirable values.[147] In fact, the impact of gemfibrozil treatment was so great in this high-risk group alone that it accounted for 71% of the CHD reduction achieved in the entire study, even though the group represented only 10% of the total study population.

B.C. appears to have a very high risk of CHD based upon this triad of lipid disorders including a triglyceride level between 200 and 400 mg/dL. Of course, the fact that he has already had a heart attack, places him at significant risk of a recurrent event and warrants aggressive treatment.

Familial Forms of Mixed Hyperlipidemia

25. What evidence is there that B.C. has an inherited form of dyslipidemia?

B.C.'s strong family history of premature CHD substantially raises the possibility that his lipid disorder is inherited. The two familial disorders which most commonly produce mixed hyperlipidemia are familial combined hyperlipidemia (FCHL) and dysbetalipoproteinemia. Dysbetalipoproteinemia is not likely to be the cause of B.C.'s lipid disorder because his cholesterol and triglyceride levels are not as high as generally found with this disorder and there is no evidence of tuberous or planar xanthoma which are characteristic.[152] However, if there is access to a specialized lipid laboratory, tests to identify the apoE phenotype (to document the E2 isoform), measure the IDL-C level (which is elevated in these patients), or characterize the triglyceride:cholesterol ratio in the VLDL particles (which is >0.3 in these patients) are advisable.

B.C. probably has FCHL, based upon a strong family history of premature coronary heart disease, the mixture of lipid disorders evident among family members, and the presence of a mixed hyperlipidemia (i.e., both triglyceride and cholesterol elevation). This is a presumptive diagnosis, since there are no unique clinical features of FCHL. Whether or not B.C. has familial combined hyperlipidemia will not appreciably change his need for lipid modulating treatment. However, the suspicion that B.C. has FCHL should prompt the screening of other family members for lipid disorders, especially B.C.'s son. The NCEP has recommended that children over the age of two years who have a parent with a familial lipid disorder or CHD be screened with a lipid profile.

Secondary Causes of Hypertriglyceridemia

26. In addition to an assessment of B.C.'s lipid profile, what other evaluations should be made?

As described previously, the three questions which should be answered routinely when evaluating patients with lipid disorders include: 1) Is there a secondary cause of the patient's lipid disorder? 2) Is there a familial cause of the lipid disorder? 3) Are there accompanying risk factors which should be modified to reduce CHD risk?

Secondary causes of hypertriglyceridemia include chronic renal failure; diabetes mellitus; alcohol abuse; a sedentary lifestyle; obesity; and drugs, including beta blockers, estrogens, and glucocorticoids. (See Table 9.5.) B.C. has a normal TSH, liver function, and renal function tests, but his blood glucose is elevated mildly, suggesting glucose intolerance. In addition, he is overweight with much of the weight distributed around his waist (i.e., a waist-hip ratio >1.0). Patients who have truncal obesity and diabetes often overproduce VLDL particles, thereby raising their triglyceride level. With an increase in triglyceride levels, the HDL-C is inversely reduced. A reduction in weight through an exercise program and low-calorie diet would improve the glucose level, raise HDL-C, and lower the triglyceride level.

Table 9.13	Classification of Triglyceride Serum Concentrations
Normal	<200 mg/dL
Borderline high	200–400 mg/dL
High	400–1000 mg/dL
Very high	>1000 mg/dL

Light to moderate alcohol intake, defined as up to two drinks per day (1 drink = 5 oz wine, 12 oz beer, or 1.5 oz 80 proof liquor), as is practiced by B.C., has been associated with lower CHD rates. The observed reduction in coronary heart disease among light to moderate alcohol drinkers is consistently in the order of 40% to 60% in epidemiologic trials.[148,149] Some studies have reported a particularly strong inverse association between wine intake (but not other spirits) and CHD.[149] The weight of the epidemiologic evidence to date supports arguments of causality. However, until controlled clinical trial evidence is available, alcohol cannot be recommended for CHD prevention.[150,151] From a public health point-of-view, the adverse consequences of alcohol consumption outweigh the benefits gained, if any, from alcohol intake. One known adverse consequence of alcohol consumption is hypertriglyceridemia, especially when alcohol is abused, but it may be seen with only moderate intake as well.

Even though B.C.'s alcohol intake appears moderate, it may be contributing to his hypertriglyceridemia and so a period of abstinence is warranted to determine if this is the case.

Insulin Resistance Syndrome

27. B.C. has a combination of obesity, glucose intolerance, and hypertension in addition to his mild hyperlipidemia. What is the significance of this constellation of findings?

Not only does B.C. have coronary heart disease and a combination of lipid abnormalities which substantially raise his risk of CHD, but he also has a number of nonlipid risk factors which raise it as well.[146] These include obesity, glucose intolerance, and hypertension. Most of B.C.'s excess weight is concentrated around his waist. This central distribution of fat may reflect an excess of intra-abdominal fat which, in turn may influence the development and effect of other risk factors.[153] For example, an increased outflow of fatty acids from intra-abdominal triglyceride stores may provide the substrate for increased hepatic triglyceride synthesis and VLDL secretion. This may explain B.C.'s elevated triglyceride level.

Abdominal obesity also is strongly associated with insulin resistance.[154] Insulin resistance leads to mild hyperglycemia and the pancreas responds by increasing insulin secretion; hyperinsulinemia results.[155,156] Some genetically predisposed patients are not able to secrete enough insulin to overcome this resistance and will develop glucose intolerance or diabetes. The presence of a mildly elevated fasting blood glucose level in B.C. (normal: <100 mg/dL) suggests glucose intolerance and probably insulin resistance (with hyperinsulinemia).

B.C. also has hypertension which currently is treated with a beta blocker and an angiotensin-converting enzyme (ACE) inhibitor. According to the most recent guidelines for high blood pressure, B.C. has a stage 1 blood pressure elevation (i.e., systolic BP >140 mm Hg).[157] Before one can conclude inadequate blood pressure control, however, blood pressure readings should be obtained on at least two other occasions and compliance to therapy documented. Abdominal obesity and insulin resistance also are commonly associated with high blood pressure and could be a factor in B.C.[158,159] The exact mechanisms for this remain speculative.

What emerges from the above discussion is the strong possibility that B.C.'s risk factors are not independent, but represent a constellation of medical problems which have a common pathway. This pathway may be related to insulin resistance.[158,160] The presence of diabetes (or glucose intolerance), hyperinsulinemia, hypertension, low HDL-C, high LDL-C, and high triglycerides in a patient has been called ''syndrome X,'' the ''deadly quadrangle,'' or the ''insulin resistance syndrome.''[156,158,160,161] As these names

suggest, the syndrome is associated with a substantial increase in CHD risk. B.C. may well have this syndrome. However, whether he does or not, his treatment will be similar. Weight loss, especially loss of visceral abdominal adiposity, will be the centerpiece of his treatment program. Weight reduction hopefully will correct, or substantially improve, his blood glucose, triglyceride, and HDL-C levels and blood pressure.

Hypertension Management with Mixed Hyperlipidemia

28. If B.C.'s stage 1 blood pressure elevation persists after lifestyle changes are made, how should he be managed?

Consideration of antihypertensive therapy in a patient with dyslipidemia should take into account how these drugs affect blood lipids. In B.C.'s case, the propranolol he is receiving for postMI prophylaxis may present a problem. This class of drugs is associated with elevated triglyceride levels, reduced HDL-C, and increased small cholesterol-dense LDL particles.[162] (See Table 9.5.) The substantial benefit of beta blockade in postMI prophylaxis warrants its continued use. Fortunately, the adverse lipid effects of these agents usually are small and can be corrected with nondrug therapy. Patients receiving beta blockers should be monitored closely for lipid changes and measures taken to correct the abnormalities identified. Substitution of a beta blocker with intrinsic sympathomimetic activity (e.g., pindolol) or a mixed alpha-beta blocker (e.g., labetalol) may have less effect on lipids (see Table 9.5), but their benefits for postMI prophylaxis are unproven.

The ACE inhibitor B.C. currently is receiving for his hypertension has a neutral effect on serum lipids. If, however, other antihypertensive drugs are required to control his blood pressure, consideration must be given to how they will affect blood lipids. One of the best drugs to reduce systolic blood pressure in elderly patients is a thiazide diuretic.[163] Thiazides also significantly enhance the blood pressure lowering efficacy of ACE inhibitors. However, they may increase blood cholesterol levels. (See Table 9.5.) Fortunately, these effects usually are small, especially with long-term use. Thus, giving B.C. a small dose of a thiazide diuretic should have a negligible effect on his blood lipids. Of course, B.C.'s blood lipids should be monitored closely after the thiazide is initiated. Nonthiazide diuretics such as indapamide and metolazone do not adversely affect blood lipids, but they are more expensive. Calcium channel blockers, like ACE inhibitors, are lipid neutral. Some other antihypertensive drugs such as alpha blockers may lower cholesterol levels, but they are more expensive and do not offer substantial advantage in the management of hypertension.

Treatment

Treatment Goals

29. What are B.C.'s treatment goals?

According to the NCEP guidelines, the primary goal is to lower B.C.'s LDL-cholesterol to less than 100 mg/dL. This aggressive goal is warranted since B.C. has already experienced a heart attack.[73] Secondary goals are to improve the other lipid values by lowering triglycerides to less than 200 mg/dL and raising the HDL-C above 35 mg/dL. Weight loss of 10 to 15 pounds, or better yet, to his ideal body weight, is also an important goal.

Cholesterol Lowering and Weight Loss Diet

30. What nondrug therapies should be implemented to help B.C. achieve his treatment goals?

As discussed previously, B.C. needs to lose weight in addition to lowering his LDL-C level. A diet low in total and saturated fat (such as the NCEP step II diet) may accomplish both goals. For most patients, a reduction in total fat intake also reduces total daily calories, since fats are a source of dense calories (i.e., 9 calories/gm). However, if the patient markedly increases his carbohydrate intake to replace fat, his triglyceride and HDL-C abnormalities may worsen. Thus, in planning B.C.'s diet, attention should be paid to restricting total fats, as well as controlling carbohydrate intake. This level of complexity supports the involvement of a registered dietitian who can provide expert advice and practical meal planning.

Drug Therapy

31. Six months after initiating these lifestyle changes, B.C. has lost 15 pounds and now weighs 205 pounds. His BP is 134/88 mm Hg, fasting blood glucose 98 mg/dL, and the lipid profile is: total cholesterol 280 mg/dL, triglycerides 240 mg/dL, HDL-C 36 mg/dL, and LDL-C 196 mg/dL. If further lifestyle changes will not achieve the goal(s) of therapy, what lipid modulating drugs should be considered? [SI units: glucose 5.40 mmol/L; total cholesterol 5.38 mmol/L; triglycerides 2.71 mmol/L; HDL-C 0.93 mmol/L; LDL-C 5.07 mmol/L]

In patients with FCHL (mixed hyperlipidemia due to an increased VLDL secretion), niacin is the drug of choice. (See Table 9.8.) It inhibits lipoprotein synthesis in the liver and reduces VLDL secretion, lowers triglyceride and LDL-C levels, and increases HDL-C levels. However, in B.C., the goal of reducing his LDL-cholesterol by 50% to less than 100 mg/dL is not likely to be achieved with niacin alone. In addition, niacin can worsen B.C.'s glucose intolerance. Even though B.C.'s glucose level is acceptable while on diet therapy, he has a tendency toward glucose intolerance which may be exacerbated by niacin.

A statin is a second choice to treat mixed hyperlipidemia. (See Table 9.8.) It effectively lowers LDL-C, which is the primary target of treatment. However, it will only lower triglyceride levels and raise HDL-C levels modestly. (See Table 9.12.) It lowers triglycerides by increasing the removal of VLDL remnant particles through the unregulated LDL receptors.[119] It also reduces the secretion of VLDL from the hepatocyte, particularly in patients with hypertriglyceridemia.[118] However, while these effects of the statins are desirable, they are moderate and are unlikely to normalize B.C.'s triglyceride and HDL-C concentrations alone.

Bile acid resins are not indicated in B.C. While they effectively lower LDL-C, they are not likely to achieve the LDL-C goal of therapy. Further, they may raise triglyceride levels by an average of 10% to 15%. This effect is even more pronounced in patients with hypertriglyceridemia. However, if combination therapy is required, bile acid resins may be combined with a drug that counters this triglyceride raising effect, such as niacin or gemfibrozil.

32. Fibric Acid Derivatives. What are the characteristics of gemfibrozil which would qualify it for use in B.C.?

Clinical Use. Gemfibrozil (and the other fibric acid derivative available in the U.S., clofibrate) lowers triglyceride levels by 20% to 50% and, in patients with hypertriglyceridemia, raises HDL-C by 10% to 15%.[164–168] (See Table 9.12.) Fibric acid derivatives generally lower LDL-cholesterol 10% to 15% in patients with isolated hypercholesterolemia.[164,169] However, in patients with a concurrent hypertriglyceridemia, gemfibrozil may have no effect on or actually increase LDL-C levels.[164,165,169]

Gemfibrozil's primary indication is for the reduction of triglyceride levels in patients with hypertriglyceridemia and normal cholesterol levels. In patients who have triglyceride levels above 1000 mg/dL and are at risk for developing pancreatitis, gemfibrozil is one of the drugs of choice.[73] Similarly, in patients with familial dysbetalipoproteinemia, gemfibrozil and clofibrate are highly effective and are considered the drugs of choice. Gemfibrozil also has a place, although limited, in the management of hypercholesterolemia. Support for this comes primarily from the results of the Helsinki Heart Study, in which gemfibrozil combined with diet therapy was associated with a reduction in CHD deaths and nonfatal myocardial infarctions.[52] This beneficial effect was accomplished mainly by a striking reduction in coronary heart disease events in patients who had an abnormal lipid triad (i.e., elevated cholesterol, elevated triglycerides, and low HDL-C).[169] This is B.C.'s lipid profile. Gemfibrozil also is useful in the management of the mixed lipid elevations in diabetic patients. Niacin, the other drug often deployed in these patients, may worsen glucose intolerance. (See Table 9.8.)

Mechanism of Action. The mechanisms through which the fibrates exert their effects are complex and not completely understood. Fibrates increase the activity of the enzyme lipoprotein lipase, thus reducing triglyceride levels by increasing VLDL and IDL catabolism.[170,171] Fibrates also reduce the secretion of VLDL from the liver, reduce the biosynthesis of cholesterol, and promote the secretion of cholesterol in the bile.[171,172]

Adverse Effects. Gemfibrozil usually is well tolerated, although gastrointestinal symptoms are well described. Rarely, myositis, an inflammation of the muscle, is reported.[122] The chance of developing myopathy appears to be increased when gemfibrozil is used in combination with lovastatin, and possibly other statins. Rarely, rhabdomyolysis has been reported in patients receiving this combination. Patients who receive gemfibrozil therapy should be monitored for symptoms of muscle soreness and pain and, if present, with a CPK level. A CPK level greater than ten times the upper limit of normal along with muscle symptoms supports a diagnosis of myositis.

Increased biliary secretion of cholesterol increases the lithogenicity of bile which may lead to the development of cholesterol gallstones, an effect that is well described in fibric acid-treated patients. In fact, some of the deaths reported in the World Health Organization (WHO) study of clofibrate may have been related to gallstone disease.[173]

The results of two major primary prevention trials have raised questions about the safety of these agents. Clofibrate was associated with an increase in total mortality in the World Health Organization trial and, as a result, its use has declined markedly in the U.S.[173,174] While gemfibrozil reduced CHD morbidity and mortality in the Helsinki Heart Study, it increased the nonCHD mortality slightly, so that there was no net reduction in total mortality.[52] In a 3.5 year follow-up to the Helsinki Heart Study, total mortality in the patient group initially treated with gemfibrozil was increased, due to an increase in nonCHD mortality.[175] Based upon a similar follow-up evaluation of niacin therapy in the Coronary Drug Project, one would have expected the beneficial effects of lipid lowering on atherosclerotic events to persist after the trial.[57] At the same time the Helsinki Heart Study was being conducted, a smaller, less carefully constructed five-year trial was implemented which accepted patients who did not qualify for the primary prevention study because they had evidence of probable coronary heart disease at baseline.[176] Patients who were randomly assigned to gemfibrozil therapy experienced a greater total mortality than did placebo-treated patients. These effects are not explained based upon our current understanding of side effects associated with gemfibrozil. Thus, a full interpretation of these trials remains an open question. However, for now, they support a cautious and restricted use of fibric acid derivatives.

33. Drug Selection. Given these considerations, what drugs are indicated for B.C.?

Because he requires a substantial reduction in LDL-C levels to achieve a level less than 100 mg/dL and to maximally reduce his risk of a recurrent myocardial infarction, treatment with a statin is justified. (See Table 9.12.) Any of the statins can be selected since they all effectively lower LDL-C. (See Table 9.9.) As was the case in the first patient, T.A., however, it makes little sense to push the statin to maximal doses, given their relatively flat dose response curve, the increased risk of side effects, and the high costs of larger doses. Also as in T.A., it is unlikely that a statin alone will achieve the LDL-C goal of therapy. If control is not attained with the statin, combining it with a drug which will reduce triglycerides would appear reasonable. These choices are niacin and gemfibrozil. (See Table 9.8.) Both of these drugs lower triglycerides 30% to 60%. (See Table 9.12.) Of the two, niacin lowers cholesterol more and may contribute more to the LDL-C reduction produced by the statin, but it may worsen B.C.'s glucose intolerance. Gemfibrozil would have less LDL-C lowering effect, but would offer complementary triglyceride lowering and would not worsen B.C.'s glucose intolerance. Combined use of either agent with lovastatin has been reported to increase the risk of myositis, but the incidence appears to be greater with gemfibrozil than with niacin combination therapy.[124] The choice of which combination to use is basically a toss up. Given this, niacin will be selected as it is less likely to produce myositis when given with a statin. However, close monitoring of the patient will be required and if glucose intolerance worsens or myopathy occurs, gemfibrozil may be substituted.

34. Initiating Combination Drug Therapy. How should combined therapy with a reductase inhibitor and niacin be initiated in B.C.? What monitoring is required?

As in B.J., one agent, the statin, should be introduced first and titrated to an effective dose. If required, the second agent may then be added and doses titrated.

Patients should be encouraged to remain compliant with the statin to sustain its effects on serum lipids. Withdrawal, even after a long period of consistent cholesterol control, will result in a return of blood lipids to pretreatment levels. Patients should be counseled to call a health professional if they experience any untoward symptoms, especially muscle soreness or discomfort.

Follow-up of patients placed on statin therapy should occur every six to eight weeks during the first year and every 6 to 12 months thereafter. (See Table 9.11.) Liver function tests and efficacy measurements should be obtained at each visit during the first year. Initially, drug efficacy may be judged with lipid profiles. However, after the relationship between total and LDL-cholesterol has been established in B.C.'s profiles (if it is consistent), a nonfasting total cholesterol level may be substituted and the LDL-C estimated based upon previous results. A creatine phosphokinase level should be obtained whenever the patient experiences symptoms of myositis (i.e., muscle soreness and aches). Doses of the statin may be increased after as little as one month of therapy.

Niacin should be initiated slowly and with full participation of the patient as described in Question 10. Patients should be given a thorough explanation on the action and effectiveness of niacin. They should know what effects to expect on their lipid profile to encourage acceptance of the therapy. They also should know about vasodilatory and gastrointestinal side effects and how to reduce or avoid them. Patients should be instructed to administer an adult aspirin 30 minutes before the morning dose of niacin once daily to prevent or diminish vasodilatory side effects. They also should be instructed to administer doses with food to reduce these effects as well as GI irritation. Immediate-release (crystalline) niacin tablets are preferred over sustained-release dosage forms to reduce the risk of hepatic toxicity and costs. Patients should be warned not to switch from an immediate-release to a sustained-release dosage form as this may significantly increase their risk of experiencing liver toxicity. Patients should be given the liberty to initiate and titrate doses on a flexible schedule as tolerance to side effects permits. (See Table 9.10.) With higher doses, periodic evaluation of glucose status and symptoms of peptic ulcer are recommended.

35. Antioxidant Therapy. Should probucol or other antioxidants be considered in the management of hyperlipidemic patients, especially patients who have developed CHD?

Probucol is an enigma among cholesterol-lowering drugs. It lowers LDL-C somewhat, but it also substantially lowers HDL-C in almost all patients who receive it. (See Table 9.12.) Based upon this profile, one would not expect probucol to lower CHD risk; yet, it is one of the few drugs which causes regression of xanthomas in patients with severe hypercholesterolemia.[177]

The greatest potential value of probucol in the prevention of atherosclerosis may be through its potent antioxidant properties.[178–180] As reviewed earlier, only oxidized (or otherwise modified) LDL particles appear to be taken up by macrophage cells to form foam cells. If drugs that have antioxidant properties prevent this from occurring, they may reduce, or block, the development of atherosclerosis. Vitamins E, C and beta carotene (the precursor of vitamin A) also have potent antioxidant properties.[181]

Most of the work available to document the effects of antioxidant therapies has been completed in animals and these have been very encouraging. For example, probucol has been shown to prevent the oxidation of LDL-C *in vivo* and to reduce the development of atherosclerosis in hypercholesterolemic animals.[181,182]

Evaluation of antioxidant therapy in humans has been minimal. Oxidized LDL-cholesterol has been detected in atheromatous lesions and circulating antibodies to oxidized LDL have been detected in human plasma.[183,184] In epidemiologic studies, use of beta carotene and vitamin E has been associated with 35% to 50% fewer CHD events.[185,186] One large prospective, randomized, and blinded clinical trial which deployed probucol in patients with femoral atherosclerosis failed to demonstrate a reduction in CHD events. This has been interpreted to indicate that antioxidants may be useful in preventing atherosclerosis development, but probably do not change already formed lesions.

The evaluation of antioxidant therapy to prevent coronary heart disease is in its formative stage. Clearly, much more needs to be learned about probucol and other antioxidants in atherosclerosis prevention before these drugs can be recommended routinely for clinical use.

36. M.B., an asymptomatic female, is screened with a lipoprotein profile during an annual physical evaluation by her primary care provider. She has noninsulin dependent diabetes which is treated with 60 U/day of NPH insulin . M.B. is about 20% overweight. Her fasting lipoprotein profile is: total cholesterol 234 mg/dL, triglycerides 2300 mg/dL, HDL-C 24 mg/dL, and LDL-C cannot be calculated because triglycerides exceed 400 mg/dL. What is your assessment of M.B.'s CHD risk and what treatment, if any, should she be given? [SI units: total cholesterol 6.05 mmol/L; triglycerides 25.97 mmol/L; and HDL-C 0.62 mmol/L]

Patients with fasting triglycerides exceeding 1000 mg/dL have an increase in triglyceride-rich chylomicron particles. If a whole blood sample were left in the refrigerator overnight, a thick, milky cream layer would appear at the top of the tube confirming the presence of chylomicrons. Triglyceride elevations of this magnitude increase the risk of pancreatitis, but probably not atherosclerosis, unless the patient has a cholesterol disorder in addition to hyperchylomicronemia. Very high triglyceride levels often result from an inherited deficiency of lipoprotein lipase but may be triggered by other causes such as diabetes mellitus; alcohol abuse; obesity; and drugs including estrogens, beta blockers, and steroids. Treatment of these patients should be aggressive because the life-threatening risk is high. Treatment is aimed at removing the underlying cause (weight loss and diabetes control in M.B.) and, if needed, initiation of triglyceride-lowering diet and drugs (i.e., niacin or gemfibrozil) therapy.

References

1   **Russell DW.** Cholesterol biosynthesis and metabolism. Cardiovasc Drugs Ther. 1992;6:103–10.

2   **Eisenberg S.** Metabolism of apolipoproteins and lipoproteins. Curr Opin Lipidol. 1990;1:205–15.

3   **Austin MA et al.** Low-density lipoprotein subclass patterns and risk of myocardial infarction. JAMA. 1988;260:1917–921.

4   **Barter P.** High-density lipoproteins and reverse cholesterol transport. Curr Opin Lipidol. 1993;4:210–17.

5   **Scanu AM.** Update on lipoprotein (a). Curr Opin Lipidol. 1991;2:253–58.

6   **Schmitz G, Williamson E.** High-density lipoprotein metabolism, reverse cholesterol transport and membrane protection. Curr Opin Lipidol. 1991;2:177–89.

7   **Brown MS, Goldstein JL.** A receptor-mediated pathway for cholesterol homeostasis. Science. 1986;232:34–47.

8   **Goldstein JL, Brown MS.** Familial hypercholesterolemia. In: Scriver CR et al., eds. The Metabolic Basis of Inherited Disease. New York: McGraw-Hill; 1989:1215–250.

9   **Hobbs HH et al.** Molecular genetics of the LDL receptor gene in familial hypercholesterolemia. Hum Mutat. 1992;1:445–66.

10 **Hobbs HH et al.** Deletion of the gene for the low-density-lipoprotein receptor in a majority of French Canadians with familial hypercholesterolemia. N Engl J Med. 1987;317:734–37.

11 **Mabuchi H et al.** Development of coronary heart disease in familial hypercholesterolemia. Circulation. 1989;79:225–32.

12 **Soria LF et al.** Association between a specific apolipoprotein B mutation and familial defective apolipoprotein B-100. Proc Natl Acad Sci USA. 1989;86:587–91.

13 **Vega GL, Grundy SM.** In vivo evidence for reduced binding of low density lipoproteins to receptors as a cause of primary moderate hypercholesterolemia. J Clin Invest. 1986;78:1410–414.

14 **Innerarity TL et al.** Familial defective apolipoprotein B-100: a mutation of apolipoprotein B that causes hypercholesterolemia. J Lipid Res. 1990;31:1337–349.

15 **Innerarity TL et al.** Familial defective apolipoprotein B-100: low density lipoproteins with abnormal receptor binding. Proc Natl Acad Sci USA. 1987;84:6919–923.

16 **Mahley RW, Rall SC Jr.** Type III hyperlipoproteinemia (dysbetalipoproteinemia): the role of apolipoprotein E in normal and abnormal lipoprotein metabolism. In: Scriver CR et al., eds. The Metabolic Basis of Inherited Disease. 6th ed. New York: McGraw-Hill; 1991:1195–213.

17 **Brewer HB Jr et al.** Type III hyperlipoproteinemia: diagnosis, molecular defects, pathology, and treatment. Ann Intern Med. 1983;98:623–40.

18 **Kissebah AH et al.** Integrated regulation of very low density lipoprotein triglyceride and apolipoprotein-B kinetics in man: normolipemic subjects, familial hypertriglyceridemia, and familial combined hyperlipidemia. Metabolism. 1981;30:856–68.

19 **Haffner SM et al.** Metabolism of apolipoprotein B in members of a family with accelerated atherosclerosis: influence of apolipoprotein E-3/E-2 pattern. Metabolism. 1992;41(3):241–45.

20 **Cortner JA et al.** Familial combined hyperlipidemia: use of stable isotopes to demonstrate overproduction of very low-density lipoprotein apolipoprotein B by the liver. J Inherit Metab Dis. 1991;14 (6):915–22.

21 **Austin MA et al.** Bimodality of plasma apolipoprotein B levels in familial combined hyperlipidemia. Atherosclerosis. 1992;92:67–77.

22 **Sniderman A, Cianfrone K.** Substrate delivery as a determinant of hepatic ApoB secretion. Arterioscler Thromb. 1993;13:629–36.

23 **Teng B et al.** Composition and distribution of low density lipoprotein fractions in hyperapobetalipoproteinemia, normolipidemia, and familial hypercholesterolemia. Proc Natl Acad Sci USA. 1983;80:6662–666.

24 **Sniderman A et al.** From familial combined hyperlipidemia to hyperapoB: unraveling the overproduction of hepatic apolipoprotein B. Curr Opin Lipidol. 1992;3:137–42.

25 **Rifkind BM.** High-density lipoprotein cholesterol and coronary artery disease: survey of the evidence. Am J Cardiol. 1990;66:3A–6A.

26 **Miller M, Kwiterovich PO Jr.** Isolated low HDL-cholesterol as an important risk factor for coronary heart disease. Eur Heart J. 1990;11(Suppl. H):9–14.

27 **Genest JJ Jr et al.** Prevalence of familial lipoprotein disorders in patients with premature coronary artery disease. Circulation. 1992;85:2025–33.

28 **Steinberg D et al.** Beyond cholesterol: modification of low density lipoprotein that increases its atherogenicity. N Engl J Med. 1989;320:915–25.

29 **Davies MJ et al.** Atherosclerosis: inhibition or regression as therapeutic possibilities. Br Heart J. 1991;65:302–10.

30 **Faggiotto A et al.** Studies of hypercholesterolemia in the nonhuman primate. I. Changes that lead to fatty streak formation. Arterioscler Thromb. 1984;4:323–40.

31 **Witztum JL, Steinberg D.** Role of oxidized low density lipoprotein in atherogenesis. J Clin Invest. 1991;88:1785–792.

32 **Ross R, Agius L.** The process of atherogenesis—cellular and molecular interaction—from experimental animal models to humans. Diabetologia. 1992;35(Suppl. 2):34–40.

33 **Fuster V et al.** The pathogenesis of coronary artery disease and acute coronary syndromes. N Engl J Med. 1992;326:242–50, 310–8.

34 **Brown BG et al.** Lipid lowering and plaque regression. New insights into prevention of plaque disruption and clinical events in coronary disease. Circulation. 1993;87:1781–791.

35 **Neaton JD et al.** Serum cholesterol level and mortality findings for men screened in the Multiple Risk Factor Intervention Trial. Arch Intern Med. 1992;152:1490–500.

36 **Jacobs D et al.** Report of the conference on low blood cholesterol: mortality associations. Circulation. 1992;86:1046–60.

37 **Castelli WP.** Epidemiology of coronary heart disease: the Framingham Study. Am J Med. 1984;76:4–12.

38 **Gordon DJ et al.** High-density lipoprotein cholesterol and cardiovascular disease: four prospective American studies. Circulation. 1989;79:8–15.

39 **Kagan A et al.** Epidemiologic studies of coronary heart disease and stroke in Japanese men living in Japan, Hawaii and California: demographic, physical, dietary and biochemical characteristics. J Chronic Dis. 1974;27:345–64.

40 **Rosenberg L et al.** Myocardial infarction in women under 50 years of age. JAMA. 1983;250:2801–806.

41 **Rosenberg L et al.** Myocardial infarction and cigarette smoking in women younger than 50 years of age. JAMA. 1985;253:2965–969.

42 **Castelli WP et al.** Cardiovascular risk factors in the elderly. Am J Cardiol. 1989;63:12H–19H.

43 **Thom TJ.** Cardiovascular disease mortality among United States women. In: Eaker ED et al., eds. Coronary Heart Disease in Women. New York: Haymarket Doyma; 1987.

44 **Garg A, Grundy SM.** Management of dyslipidemia in NIDDM. Diabetes Care. 1990;13:153–69.

45 **Kannel WB.** Lipids, diabetes, and coronary heart disease: insights from the Framingham Study. Am Heart J. 1985;110:1100–107.

46 **Kannel WB, Gordon T.** Evaluation of cardiovascular risk in the elderly. The Framingham Study. Bull N Y Acad Med. 1978;54:573–91.

47 **Manolio TZ et al.** Cholesterol and heart disease in older persons and women. Review of an NHLBI workshop. Ann Epidemiol. 1992;2:161–76.

48 **Malenka DJ, Baron JA.** Cholesterol and coronary heart disease: the importance of patient-specific attributable risk. Arch Intern Med. 1988;148:2247–253.

49 **LaRosa JC et al.** The cholesterol facts: a summary of the evidence relating dietary fats, serum cholesterol, and coronary heart disease. Circulation. 1990;81:1721–733.

50 **Frick MH et al.** Helsinki Heart Study: primary-prevention trial with gemfibrozil in middle-aged men with dyslipidemia. Safety of treatment, changes in risk factors, and incidence of coronary heart disease. N Engl J Med. 1987;317:1237–245.

51 **Hjermann I et al.** Effect of diet and smoking intervention on the incidence of coronary heart disease. Report from the Oslo Study Group of a randomized trial in healthy men. Lancet. 1981;11:1303–310.

52 **Lipid Research Clinics Program.** The Lipid Research Clinics Coronary Primary Prevention Trial results; I: reduction in incidence of coronary heart disease. JAMA. 1984;251:351–64.

53 **Holme I.** An analysis of randomized trials evaluating the effect of cholesterol reduction on total mortality and coronary heart disease incidence. Circulation. 1990;82:1916–924.

54 **Criqui MH.** Cholesterol, primary and secondary prevention, and all-cause mortality. Ann Intern Med. 1991;115:973–76.

55 **Buchwald H et al.** Effect of partial ileal bypass surgery on mortality and morbidity from coronary heart disease in patients with hypercholesterolemia: report of the Program on the Surgical Control of Hyperlipidemias (POSCH). N Engl J Med. 1990;323:946–55.

56 **Carlson LA, Rosenhamer G.** Reduction of mortality in the Stockholm Ischaemic Heart Disease Secondary Prevention Study by combined treatment with clofibrate and nicotinic acid. Acta Med Scand. 1988;223:405–18.

57 **Coronary Drug Project Research Group.** Clofibrate and niacin in coronary heart disease. JAMA. 1975;231:360–81.

58 **Canner PL et al.** for the Coronary Drug Project Research Group. Fifteen year mortality in coronary drug project patients: long-term benefit with niacin. J Am Coll Cardiol. 1986;8:1245–255.

59 **Rossouw JE et al.** The value of lowering cholesterol after myocardial infarction. N Engl J Med. 1990;323:1112–119.

60 **Blankenhorn DH et al.** Beneficial effects of combined colestipol-niacin therapy on coronary atherosclerosis and coronary venous bypass grafts. JAMA. 1987;257:3233–240.

61 **Brown G et al.** Regression of coronary artery disease as a result of intensive lipid-lowering therapy in men with high levels of apolipoprotein B. N Engl J Med. 1990;323:1289–298.

62 **Ornish D et al.** Can lifestyle changes reverse coronary heart disease: the Lifestyle Heart Trial. Lancet. 1990;336:129–33.

63 **Watts GF et al.** Effects on coronary artery disease of lipid-lowering diet, or diet plus cholestyramine, in the St. Thomas' Atherosclerosis Regression Study (STARS). Lancet. 1992;339:563–69.

64 **Kane JP et al.** Regression of coronary atherosclerosis during treatment of familial hypercholesterolemia with combined drug regimens. JAMA. 1990;264:3007–012.

65 **Muldoon MF et al.** Lowering cholesterol concentrations and mortality: a quantitative review of primary prevention trials. Br Med J. 1990;301:309–14.

66 **Ravnskov U.** Cholesterol lowering trials in coronary heart disease: frequency of citation and outcome. Erratum Br Med J. 1992;305:15–19.

67 **Smith GD, Pekkanen J.** Should there be a moratorium on the use of cholesterol lowering drugs? Br Med J. 1992;304:431–34.

68 **Rossouw JE.** Clinical trials of lipid-lowering drugs. In: Rifkind BM, ed. Drug Treatment of Hyperlipidemia.

New York: Marcel Dekker, Inc. 1991; 67–88.

69 **Schulman KA et al.** Reducing high blood cholesterol level with drugs: cost-effectiveness of pharmacologic management. JAMA. 1990;264:3025–33.

70 **Goldman L et al.** Cost-effectiveness of HMG-CoA reductase inhibition for primary and secondary prevention of coronary heart disease. JAMA. 1991; 265:1145–151.

71 **Weinstein MC et al.** Forecasting coronary heart disease, mortality, and cost: the coronary heart disease policy model. Am J Public Health. 1987;77: 1417–426.

72 **Weissfeld JL et al.** A mathematical representation of the expert panel's guidelines for high blood cholesterol case-finding and treatment. Med Decis Making. 1990;10:135–46.

73 **Expert Panel on Detection, Evaluation, and Treatment of High Blood Cholesterol in Adults.** Summary of the second report of the National Cholesterol Education Program (NCEP) expert panel on detection, evaluation, and treatment of high blood cholesterol in adults (Adult Treatment Panel II). JAMA. 1993;269:3015–23.

74 **Grimm RH et al.** Effects of thiazide diuretics on plasma lipids and lipoproteins in mildly hypertensive patients. Ann Intern Med. 1981;84:7.

75 **Ames RP.** Metabolic disturbances increasing the risk of coronary heart disease during diuretic-based antihypertensive therapy: lipid alteration and glucose intolerance. Am Heart J. 1983; 106:1207.

76 **Lasser NL et al.** Effects of antihypertensive therapy on plasma lipids and lipoproteins in the multiple risk factor intervention trial. Am J Med. 1984;76: 52.

77 **Day JL et al.** Adrenergic mechanisms in the control of plasma lipids in man. Am J Med. 1984;76:94.

78 **Pagman A et al.** Effects of labetalol on lipids and carbohydrate metabolism. Pharmacol Res Commun. 1979;11: 227.

79 **Laren P et al.** Antihypertensive drugs and blood lipids: the Oslo study. Br J Clin Pharmacol. 1982;13:441S.

80 **Lowenstein J.** Effects of prazosin on serum lipids in patients with essential hypertension. Am J Cardiol. 1984;53: 21A.

81 **Ames RP, Hill P.** Antihypertensive therapy and the risk of coronary heart disease. J Cardiovasc Pharmacol. 1982; 5(Suppl. 2):S206.

82 **Weinberger MH.** Comparison of captopril and hydrochlorothiazide alone and in combination in mild to moderate hypertension. Br J Clin Pharmacol. 1982; 14:127S.

83 **Knopp RH et al.** Oral contraceptive and postmenopausal estrogen effects on lipoprotein triglycerides and cholesterol in an adult female population: relationship to estrogen and progestin potency. J Clin Endocrinol Metab. 1981; 53:1123.

84 **Wahl P et al.** Effect of estrogen/progestin potency on lipid/lipoprotein cholesterol. N Engl J Med. 1983;308:862.

85 **Bagdade JD et al.** Steroid-induced hyperlipemia: a complication of high-dose corticosteroid therapy. Arch Intern Med. 1970;125:129.

86 **Ginsburg H et al.** Moderate ethanol ingestion and plasma triglyceride levels. Ann Intern Med. 1974;80:143.

87 **Bershad S et al.** Changes in plasma lipids and lipoproteins during isotretinoin therapy for acne. N Engl J Med. 1985;313:981.

88 **Ballantyne CM et al.** Effects of cyclosporine therapy on plasma lipoprotein levels. JAMA. 1989;262:53.

89 **Pekkanen J et al.** Ten-year mortality from cardiovascular disease in relation to cholesterol level among men with and without preexisting cardiovascular disease. N Engl J Med. 1990;322: 1700–707.

90 **Criqui MH et al.** Mortality over a period of 10 years in patients with peripheral arterial disease. N Engl J Med. 1992;326:381–86.

91 **Salonen JT, Salonen R.** Ultrasonographically assessed carotid morphology and the risk of coronary heart disease. Arterioscler Thromb. 1991;11: 1245–249.

92 **National Cholesterol Education Program.** Report of the expert panel on population strategies for blood cholesterol reduction. Bethesda, MD: National Institutes of Health, National Heart, Lung, and Blood Institute; 1990 Nov. NIH Publication No. 90-3046; 140.

93 **Caggiula AW et al.** The Multiple Risk Factor Intervention Trial (MRFIT), IV: intervention on blood lipids. Prev Med. 1981;10:443–75.

94 **Ramsay LE et al.** Dietary reduction of serum cholesterol concentration: time to think again. Br Med J. 1991;303: 953–57.

95 **Boyd NF et al.** Quantitative changes in dietary fat intake and serum cholesterol in women: results from a randomized, controlled trial. Am J Clin Nutr. 1990; 52:470–76.

96 **Wood PD et al.** Changes in plasma lipids and lipoproteins in overweight men during weight loss through dieting as compared with exercise. N Engl J Med. 1988;319:1173–179.

97 **Wood PD et al.** The effects of plasma lipoproteins of a prudent weight-reducing diet, with or without exercise, in overweight men and women. N Engl J Med. 1991;325:461–66.

98 **Superko HR et al.** Effectiveness of low-dose colestipol therapy in patients with moderate hypercholesterolemia. Am J Cardiol. 1992;70:135–40.

99 **Knopp RH et al.** Contrasting effects of unmodified and time-release forms of niacin on lipoproteins in hyperlipidemic subjects: clues to mechanism of action of niacin. Metabolism. 1985;34: 642–50.

100 **Bradford RH et al.** Expanded Clinical Evaluation of Lovastatin (EXCEL) study results I: efficacy in modifying plasma lipoproteins and adverse event profile in 8245 patients with moderate hypercholesterolemia. Arch Intern Med. 1991;151:43–9.

101 **Jones PH et al.** Once daily pravastatin in patients with primary hypercholesterolemia: a dose response study. Clin Cardiol. 1991;14:146–51.

102 **Zocor package insert, 1991.**

103 **Lipid Research Clinics Program.** The Lipid Research Clinics Coronary Primary Prevention Trial results; II: the relationship of reduction in incidence of coronary heart disease to cholesterol lowering. JAMA. 1984;251:365–74.

104 **Einarsson K et al.** Bile acid sequestrants: mechanisms of action on bile acid and cholesterol metabolism. Eur J Clin Pharm. 1991;40(Suppl. 1):S53–S58.

105 **McKenney JM et al.** A dose response efficacy and safety evaluation of immediate release and sustained nicotinic acid in hypercholesterolemia patients. JAMA. 1994;271:672–77.

106 **Drood JM et al.** Nicotinic acid for the treatment of hyperlipoproteinemia. J Clin Pharmacol. 1991;31:641–50.

107 **Carlson LA et al.** Pronounced lowering of serum levels of lipoprotein Lp(a) in hyperlipidemic subjects treated with nicotinic acid. J Intern Med. 1989;226: 271–76.

108 **Grundy SM et al.** Influence of nicotinic acid on metabolism of cholesterol and triglycerides in man. J Lipid Res. 1981;22–24–36.

109 **Henkin Y et al.** Niacin revisited: clinical observations on an important but underutilized drug. Am J Med. 1991; 91:239–46.

110 **Wilkin J et al.** Aspirin blocks nicotinic acid-induced flushing. Clin Pharmacol Ther. 1982;31:478–82.

111 **Mullin GE et al.** Fulminant hepatic failure after ingestion of sustained-release nicotinic acid. Ann Intern Med. 1989;111:253–55.

112 **Henkin Y et al.** Rechallenge with crystalline niacin after drug-induced hepatitis from sustained-release niacin. JAMA. 1990;264:241–43.

113 **Etchason JA et al.** Niacin-induced hepatitis: a potential side effect with low-dose time-release niacin. Mayo Clin Proc. 1991;66:23–8.

114 **Rader JI et al.** Hepatic toxicity of unmodified and time-release preparations of niacin. Am J Med. 1992;92:77–81.

115 **Hunninghake DB et al.** Efficacy and safety of pravastatin in patients with primary hypercholesterolemia; II: once-daily versus twice-daily dosing. Atherosclerosis. 1990;85:219–27.

116 **Hunninghake DB et al.** Efficacy and safety of pravastatin in patients with primary hypercholesterolemia; I: a dose-response study. Atherosclerosis. 1990;85:81–9.

117 **Grundy SM et al.** Influence of combined therapy with mevinolin and interruption of bile-acid reabsorption on low density lipoproteins in heterozygous familial hypercholesterolemia. Ann Intern Med. 1985;103:339–43.

118 **Ginsberg HN et al.** Suppression of apolipoprotein B production during treatment of cholesteryl ester storage disease with lovastatin: implications for regulation of apolipoprotein B synthesis. J Clin Invest. 1987;80:1692–697.

119 **Arad Y et al.** Effects of lovastatin therapy on very-low-density lipoprotein triglyceride metabolism in subjects with combined hyperlipidemia: evidence for reduced assembly and secretion of triglyceride-rich lipoproteins. Metabolism. 1992;41:487–93.

120 **Dujovne CA et al.** Expanded Clinical Evaluation of Lovastatin (EXCEL) study results. IV. additional perspectives on the tolerability of lovastatin.

Am J Med. 1991;91(Suppl. 1B): 25S–30S.

121 **Corpier CL et al.** Rhabdomyolysis and renal injury with lovastatin use: report of two cases in cardiac transplant recipients. JAMA. 1988;260:239–41.

122 **Pierce LR et al.** Myopathy and rhabdomyolysis associated with lovastatin-gemfibrozil combination therapy. JAMA. 1990;264:71–5.

123 **Reaven P, Witztum JL.** Lovastatin, nicotinic acid, and rhabdomyolysis. Ann Intern Med. 1988;109:597–98. Letter.

124 **Tobert JA et al.** Clinical experience with lovastatin. Am J Cardiol. 1990;65: 23F–26F.

125 **Stampfer MJ et al.** Post-menopausal estrogen therapy and cardiovascular disease: ten-year follow-up from the Nurses Health Study. N Engl J Med. 1991;325:756–62.

126 **Barrett-Connor E, Bush TL.** Estrogen and coronary heart disease in women. JAMA. 1991;265:1861–867.

127 **Grady D et al.** Hormone therapy to prevent disease and prolong life in postmenopausal women. Ann Intern Med. 1992;117:1016–37.

128 **Stampfer MJ, Colditz GA.** Estrogen replacement therapy and coronary heart disease: a quantitative assessment of the epidemiologic evidence. Prev Med. 1991;20:47–63.

129 **Gruchow HW et al.** Postmenopausal use of estrogen and occlusion of arteries. Am Heart J. 1988;115(5):88–94.

130 **Jensen J et al.** Cyclic changes in serum cholesterol and lipoproteins following different doses of combined postmenopausal hormone replacement therapy. Br J Obstet Gynaecol. 1986;93:613–18.

131 **Krauss RM et al.** Effects of estrogen dose and smoking on lipid and lipoprotein levels in postmenopausal women. Am J Obstet Gynecol. 1988;158:1606–611.

132 **Granfone A et al.** Effects of estrogen replacement on plasma lipoproteins and apolipoproteins in postmenopausal, dyslipidemic women. Metabolism. 1992;41:1193–198.

133 **Walsh BW et al.** Effects of postmenopausal estrogen replacement on the concentrations and metabolism of plasma lipoproteins. N Engl J Med. 1991;325:1196–1204.

134 **Elkik F et al.** Effects of percutaneous estradiol and conjugated estrogens on the level of plasma proteins and triglycerides in postmenopausal women. Am J Obstet Gynecol. 1982;143:888–92.

135 **Farhraeus L, Wallentin L.** High density lipoprotein subfractions during oral and cutaneous administration of 17 beta-estradiol to menopausal women. J Clin Endocrinol Metab. 1983;56:797–801.

136 **Illingworth DR.** Clinical implications of new drugs for lowering plasma cholesterol concentrations. Drugs. 1991; 41:151–60.

137 **Pan HY et al.** Pharmacokinetics and pharmacodynamics of pravastatin alone and with cholestyramine in hypercholesterolemia. Clin Pharmacol Ther. 1990;48:201–7.

138 **NIH Consensus Development Panel on Triglyceride, High-Density Lipo-**

protein, and Coronary Heart Disease. Triglyceride, high-density lipoprotein, and coronary heart disease. JAMA. 1993;269:505–10.

139 **Gordon DJ, Rifkind BM.** High-density lipoprotein—the clinical implications of recent studies. N Engl J Med. 1989;321:1311–316.

140 **Grundy SM et al.** The place of HDL in cholesterol management. A perspective from the National Cholesterol Education Program. Arch Intern Med. 1989;149:505–10.

141 **Grundy SM, Vega GL.** Two different views of the relationship of hypertriglyceridemia to coronary heart disease. Implications for treatment. Arch Intern Med. 1992;152:28–34.

142 **Reardon MF et al.** Lipoprotein predictors of the severity of coronary artery disease in men and women. Circulation. 1985;71:881–88.

143 **Steiner G et al.** The association of increased levels of intermediate-density lipoproteins with smoking and with coronary heart disease. Circulation. 1987;75:124–30.

144 **Brunzell JD et al.** Plasma lipoproteins in familial combined hyperlipidemia and monogenic familial hypertriglyceridemia. J Lipid Res. 1983;24:147–55.

145 **Nikkila EA.** Familial lipoprotein lipase deficiency and related disorders of chylomicron metabolism. In: Stanbury JB et al., eds. The Metabolic Basis of Inherited Disease. 5th ed. New York: McGraw-Hill; 1983:622–42.

146 **Assmann G, Schulte H.** Triglycerides and atherosclerosis: results from the Prospective Cardiovascular Munster Study. In: Gotto AM Jr, Paoletti R, eds. Atherosclerosis Reviews. Vol. 22. New York: Raven Press. 1991:51–7.

147 **Manninen V et al.** Joint effects of serum triglyceride and LDL cholesterol and HDL cholesterol concentrations on coronary heart disease risk in the Helsinki Heart Study: implications for treatment. Circulation. 1992;85:37–45.

148 **Marmot M, Brunner E.** Alcohol and cardiovascular disease: the status of the U-shaped curve. Br Med J. 1991;303:565–8.

149 **Jackson R, Beaglehole R.** The relationship between alcohol and coronary heart disease: is there a protective effect? Curr Opin Lipidol. 1993;4:21–6.

150 **Steinberg D et al.** Davis conference, alcohol and atherosclerosis. Ann Intern Med. 1991;114:967–76.

151 **Klatsky AL et al.** Alcohol and mortality: a ten year Kaiser-Permanente experience. Ann Intern Med. 1981;95:139–45.

152 **Brewer HB et al.** Type III hyperlipidemia: diagnosis, molecular defects,

pathology, and treatment. Ann Intern Med. 1983;98(Part 1):623–40.

153 **Fujioka S et al.** Contribution of intra-abdominal fat accumulation to the impairment of glucose and lipid metabolism in human obesity. Metabolism. 1987;36:54–9.

154 **Barakat HA et al.** Influence of obesity, impaired glucose tolerance, and NIDDM on LDL structure and composition. Possible link between hyperinsulinemia and atherosclerosis. Diabetes. 1990;39:1527–533.

155 **Bierman EL.** Atherogenesis in diabetes. Arterioscler Thromb. 1992;12:647–56.

156 **DeFronzo RA, Ferrannini E.** Insulin resistance. A multifaceted syndrome responsible for NIDDM, obesity, hypertension, dyslipidemia, and atherosclerotic cardiovascular disease. Diabetes Care. 1991;14:173–94.

157 **Joint National Committee on Detection, Evaluation and Treatment of High Blood Pressure.** The fifth report of the Joint National Committee on detection, evaluation, and treatment of high blood pressure (JNC V). Arch Intern Med. 1993;153:154–83.

158 **Reaven GM.** Insulin resistance and compensatory hyperinsulinemia: role in hypertension, dyslipidemia, and coronary heart disease. Am Heart J. 1991;121:1283–288.

159 **Gwynne J.** Clinical features and pathophysiology of familial dyslipidemic hypertension syndrome. Curr Opin Lipidol. 1992;3:215–21.

160 **Reaven GM.** Role of insulin resistance in human disease. Diabetes. 1988;37:1595–607.

161 **Kaplan NM.** The deadly quartet. Upper-body obesity, glucose intolerance, hypertriglyceridemia, and hypertension. Arch Intern Med. 1989;149:1514–520.

162 **Campos H et al.** Low density lipoprotein particle size and coronary artery disease. Arteriosclerosis. 1992;12:187–95.

163 **SHEP Cooperative Research Group.** Prevention of stroke by antihypertensive drug treatment in older persons with isolated systolic hypertension: final results of the Systolic Hypertension in the Elderly Program (SHEP). JAMA. 1991;265:3255–254.

164 **Hunninghake DB, Peters JR.** Effect of fibric acid derivatives on blood lipid and lipoprotein levels. Am J Med. 1987;83:44–9.

165 **Manttari M et al.** Effect of gemfibrozil on the concentration and composition of serum lipoproteins: a controlled study with special reference to initial triglyceride levels. Atherosclerosis. 1990;81:11–17.

166 **Rubins HB, Robins SJ.** Effect of reduction of plasma triglycerides with gemfibrozil on high-density-lipoprotein-cholesterol concentrations. J Intern Med. 1992;231:421–26.

167 **Vega GL, Grundy SM.** Comparison of lovastatin and gemfibrozil in normolipidemic patients with hypoalphalipoproteinemia. JAMA. 1989;262:3148–153.

168 **Miller M et al.** Effect of gemfibrozil in men with primary isolated low high-density lipoprotein cholesterol: a randomized, double-blind, placebo-controlled, crossover study. Am J Med. 1993;94:7–12.

169 **Manninen V et al.** Relation between baseline lipid and lipoprotein values and the incidence of coronary heart disease in the Helsinki Heart Study. Am J Cardiol. 1989;63:42H–47H.

170 **Saku K et al.** Mechanism of action of gemfibrozil on lipoprotein metabolism. J Clin Invest. 1985;75:1702–712.

171 **Grundy SM, Vega GL.** Fibric acids: effects on lipids and lipoprotein metabolism. Am J Med. 1987;83:9–20.

172 **Kesaniemi YA, Grundy SM.** Influence of gemfibrozil and clofibrate on metabolism of cholesterol and plasma triglycerides in man. JAMA. 1984;251:2241–246.

173 **Committee of Principal Investigators.** World Health Organization. WHO cooperative trial on primary prevention of ischaemic heart disease using clofibrate to lower serum cholesterol: mortality follow-up. Lancet. 1980;2:379–85.

174 **Committee of Principal Investigators.** A co-operative trial in the primary prevention of ischaemic heart disease using clofibrate. Br Heart J. 1978;40:1069–118.

175 **Lopid package insert.** 1992.

176 **Frick MH et al.** Efficacy of gemfibrozil in dyslipidaemic subjects with suspected heart disease: an ancillary study in the Helsinki Heart Study frame population. Ann Med. 1993;25:41–5.

177 **Yamamoto A et al.** Effects of probucol on xanthomata regression in familial hypercholesterolemia. Am J Cardiol. 1986;57:29H–35H.

178 **Baumstark MW et al.** Probucol, incorporated into LDL particles in vivo, inhibits generation of lipid peroxides more effectively than endogenous antioxidants alone. Clin Biochem. 1992;25:395–97.

179 **Kuzuya M, Kuzuya F.** Probucol as an antioxidant and antiatherogenic drug. Free Radic Biol Med. 1993;14:67–77.

180 **Reaven PD et al.** Effect of probucol dosage on plasma lipid and lipoprotein levels and on protection of low density lipoprotein against in vitro oxidation in

humans. Arterioscler Thromb. 1992;12:318–24.

181 **Parthasarathy S et al.** Probucol inhibits oxidative modification of low density lipoprotein. J Clin Invest. 1986;77:641–44.

182 **Kita T et al.** Probucol prevents the progression of atherosclerosis in watanabe heritable hyperlipidemic rabbits, and animal models for familial hypercholesterolemia. Proc Natl Acad Sci USA. 1987;84:5928–931.

183 **Parums D et al.** Serum antibodies to oxidized low-density lipoprotein and ceroid in chronic periaortitis. Arch Pathol Lab Med. 1990;114:383–87.

184 **Salonen JT et al.** Autoantibody against oxidized LDL and progression of carotid atherosclerosis. Lancet. 1992;339:883–86.

185 **Gaziano JM et al.** Beta carotene therapy for chronic stable angina. Circulation. 1990;82:III–201. Abstract.

186 **Stampfer MJ et al.** A prospective study of vitamin E supplementation and risk of coronary disease in women. Circulation. 1991;86:I-463. Abstract.

187 **Duffield RGM et al.** Treatment of hyperlipidemia retards progression of symptomatic femoral atherosclerosis. A randomized controlled trial. Lancet. 1983;II:639–42.

188 **The Pravastatin Multinational Study Group for Cardiac Risk Patients.** Effects of pravastatin in patients with serum total cholesterol levels from 5.2 to 7.8 mmol/L (200 to 300 mg/dL) plus two additional atherosclerotic risk factors. Amer J Cardiol. 1993;72:1031–37.

189 **MAAS Investigators.** Effect of simvastatin on coronary atheroma: the Multicentre Anti-Atheroma Study (MAAS). Lancet. 1994;344:633–38.

190 **Waters D et al.** Effects of monotherapy with an HMG-CoA reductase inhibitor on the progression of coronary atherosclerosis as assessed by serial quantitative arteriography. The Canadian Coronary Atherosclerosis Intervention Trial. Circulation. 1994;89:959–68.

191 **Haskell WL et al.** Effects of intensive multiple risk factor reduction on coronary atherosclerosis and clinical cardiac events in men and women with coronary heart disease. The Stanford Coronary Risk Intervention Project (SCRIP). Circulation. 1994;89:975–90.

192 **Furberg CD et al.** Pravastatin, lipids, and major coronary events. Amer J Cardiol. 1994;73:1133–134.

193 **Furberg CD et al.** Effect of lovastatin on early carotid atherosclerosis and cardiovascular events. Circulation. 1994;90:1679–687.

Essential Hypertension

Barry L Carter
Elaine M Furmaga
Christine M Murphy

Definitions 10-2
   Blood pressure (BP) 10-2
   Hypertension (See Table 10.1) 10-2
      "Office or white coat hypertension" 10-3
      Hypertensive urgencies and emergencies 10-3
      Isolated systolic hypertension (ISH) 10-3
Blood Pressure Measurements (See Table 10.2) 10-3
Etiology (See Tables 10.3 to 10.5) 10-3
Pathophysiology 10-4

Evaluation 10-5
Clinical Presentation 10-5
Health Beliefs and Patient Education 10-6
Historical Database 10-6
Target Organ Damage 10-6
   Heart 10-6
   Brain 10-7
   Kidney 10-7
   Eye 10-7
Cardiovascular Risk Factors 10-7
   Family history 10-7
   Race 10-8
   Hypertension 10-8
   Cigarette smoking 10-8
   Obesity 10-8
   Dyslipidemia 10-8
   Dietary sodium 10-8

Treatment 10-8
Patient Education (See Table 10.6) 10-8
Patient Benefit (See Table 10.7) 10-8
Goal of Therapy 10-9
Lifestyle Modifications 10-10
   Moderate sodium restriction 10-10
   Weight reduction and dietary fats 10-10
   Exercise 10-10
   Alcohol consumption 10-11
   Stress reduction 10-11
   Smoking cessation 10-11
   Caffeine ingestion 10-11
   Potassium 10-11
   Calcium 10-11
   Magnesium 10-11
Pharmacologic Management (See Tables 10.8 to 10.10
  and Figure 10.1) 10-11
   Appropriate therapy 10-11
   Demographics (See Table 10.9) 10-12
   Co-existing disease states (See Table 10.10) 10-12
   Lifestyle 10-12
   Drug therapy 10-13
      Previous 10-13
      Concomitant 10-13
   Cost 10-13
Categories of Antihypertensive Drugs 10-13
   Diuretics 10-13
   Beta blockers 10-14

ACE inhibitors 10-14
Angiotensin II antagonists 10-28
Calcium antagonists 10-14
Peripheral α_1-antagonists 10-14
Central α_2-agonists 10-14
Adrenergic antagonists 10-14
Direct vasodilators 10-14
Diuretics 10-14
   Therapeutic effect and choice of agent 10-14
      Thiazides 10-14
      Furosemide 10-15
      Potassium-sparing diuretics 10-15
   Patient education 10-15
   Monitoring therapy 10-15
   Adverse effects 10-15
      Diuretic-induced hypokalemia 10-15
         Potassium supplementation 10-16
      Diuretic-induced hyperuricemia and
        hyperglycemia 10-16
         Glucose 10-16
         Uric acid 10-17
      Diuretic-induced alterations in serum lipids 10-17
      Other diuretic-induced metabolic abnormalities ...10-17
         Hypercalcemia 10-17
         Hypomagnesemia 10-17
         Hyponatremia 10-17
Therapeutic Principles for the Selection of the
  Second Antihypertensive Agent (See Table 10.11) 10-17
   Reasons for inadequate control
    (See Table 10.11) 10-18
β-Adrenergic Blockers 10-18
   Role in treatment of hypertension 10-18
   Pharmacologic differences between various agents
    (See Table 10.12) 10-19
      Cardioselectivity 10-19
      Intrinsic sympathomimetic activity (ISA) 10-19
      Lipid solubility 10-19
   Pharmacodynamic properties versus half-life
    (See Table 10.13) 10-20
   Treating hypertension in patients with
    co-existing diseases 10-20
      Angina 10-20
      Hyperkinetic circulation 10-20
      Selected ventricular and supraventricular
        arrhythmias 10-20
      Postmyocardial infarction 10-20
      Other conditions 10-20
      Hyperlipidemia 10-20
      Diabetes 10-21
ACE Inhibitors (See Table 10.14) 10-21
   Mechanism of action 10-21
   Concomitant disorders 10-21
   In black patients 10-22
   Dosing (See Table 10.14) 10-22

(Continued)

Calcium Channel Blockers 10-23
    Efficacy 10-23
    Concomitant disorders and comparison of agents
        (See Table 10.15) 10-23
    Combination of two calcium channel blockers 10-24
α₁-Adrenergic Antagonists 10-24
    Efficacy 10-24
    Dosing 10-24
    Adverse effects and patient education 10-24
    Doxazosin and terazosin 10-25
Alpha-Beta Blockers 10-25
    Mechanism of action 10-25
α₂-Agonists 10-25
    Mechanism of action 10-25
    Efficacy 10-25
    Dosing 10-25

Adverse effects 10-25
Methyldopa 10-26
Guanfacine 10-26
Guanabenz 10-26
Hydralazine 10-26
    Mechanism 10-26
    Adverse reactions: systemic lupus
        erythematosus (SLE) 10-27
Minoxidil 10-27
    Clinical use 10-27
    Adverse effects 10-27
        Hypertrichosis 10-27
Guanethidine and Guanadrel 10-28
Reserpine 10-28
Step-Down Therapy 10-28

Estimates from the 1988 to 1991 National Health and Nutrition Examination Survey suggest that 50 million Americans have hypertension.[1] This is eight million fewer than a previous estimate made in 1978 to 1980. This decline may be due to either differences in sampling techniques or an actual reduction in the prevalence of hypertension as a result of lifestyle changes. Despite these trends, hypertension remains the most frequently encountered chronic medical condition and is one of the most significant risk factors for cardiovascular morbidity and mortality from coronary artery disease (ischemic heart disease, myocardial infarction, sudden death), cardiac disease [left ventricular hypertrophy, congestive heart failure (CHF)], renal failure, stroke, and blindness. The etiology of essential hypertension is unknown and management is generally lifelong.

In 1972, the National Institutes of Health (NIH) funded the development of the National High Blood Pressure Education Program. The purpose of this program was to increase awareness among other health care professionals, and the public about the importance of treating hypertension. This effort appears to have been largely successful. When the program began, only 51% of hypertensive individuals were aware they had elevated blood pressure and only 16% had a pressure below 160/95 mm Hg. By 1988 to 1991, the percentage of individuals who were aware of their hypertension rose to 65% for those with blood pressures greater than 140/90 mm Hg. However, only 21% of these individuals had controlled blood pressures.[1] While these statistics clearly illustrate improvements in the detection and control of hypertension, much work remains to be done.

Coincident with the increased awareness of hypertension, improved treatment and diet, and lifestyle modifications has been a 50% decrease in mortality from coronary heart disease and a 57% decrease in mortality from stroke since 1972.[1] While this favorable trend is apparent in the U.S. and industrialized countries, opposite trends have been noted in third world and former eastern block countries. Moreover, despite the gains being made, cardiovascular disease remains the number one cause of death in the U.S.

Definitions

Blood Pressure (BP)

The heart's primary function is the distribution of blood to the tissues of the body. During systole, the left ventricle contracts causing a peak rise in blood pressure known as the systolic blood pressure (SBP). As the left ventricle relaxes during diastole, the pressure decreases to a trough level, representing the diastolic blood pressure (DBP). When recording blood pressure, the numerator refers to the systolic blood pressure and the denominator refers to the diastolic blood pressure (e.g., 120/80 mm Hg). Both the systolic

and diastolic pressures are important determinants of hypertension control and complications (see Table 10.1). The Fifth Report of the Joint National Committee on Detection, Evaluation, and Treatment of High Blood Pressure (JNC V) has classified blood pressure into stages which represent the degree of risk of nonfatal and fatal cardiovascular disease events and renal disease. The inclusion of target organ disease and major risk factors for hypertension also are important for classification.[1]

In some cases, mean arterial pressure (MAP) is used as a measure of risk or hypertension control.[2,3] MAP is calculated by the following equation:

$$MAP = \left(\frac{\text{Systolic Pressure} - \text{Diastolic Pressure}}{3} \right)$$
$$+ \text{Diastolic Pressure}$$

Hypertension

Hypertension is defined as an elevation of either the systolic blood pressure, the diastolic blood pressure, or both. Although

Table 10.1	Classification of Blood Pressure for Adults Aged 18 Years and Older[1,a]	
Category	Systolic (mm Hg)	Diastolic (mm Hg)
Normal	<130	<85
High Normal	130–139	85–89
Hypertension[b]		
Stage 1 (mild)	140–159	90–99
Stage 2 (moderate)	160–179	100–109
Stage 3 (severe)	180–209	110–119
Stage 4 (very severe)	≥210	≥120

a Not taking antihypertensive drugs and not acutely ill. When systolic and diastolic pressures fall into different categories, the higher category should be selected to classify the individual's blood pressure status. For instance, 160/92 mm Hg should be classified as Stage 2, and 180/120 mm Hg should be classified as Stage 4. Isolated systolic hypertension is defined as a systolic blood pressure of ≥140 mm Hg and a diastolic blood pressure of less than <90 mm Hg and staged appropriately (e.g. 170/85 mm Hg is defined as Stage 2 isolated systolic hypertension). In addition to classifying stages of hypertension on the basis of average blood pressure levels, the clinician should specify presence or absence of target organ disease and additional risk factors. For example, a patient with diabetes and a blood pressure of 142/94 mm Hg, plus left ventricle hypertrophy should be classified as having "Stage 1 hypertension with target organ disease (left ventricular hypertrophy) and with another major risk factor (diabetes)." This specificity is important for risk classification and management.

b Based upon the average of two or more readings taken at each of two or more visits after an initial screening.

cardiovascular risk increases linearly with blood pressures greater than 120/80 mm Hg, blood pressure is not considered elevated unless the systolic pressure exceeds 130 mm Hg or the diastolic pressure exceeds 85 mm Hg (see Table 10.1). Generally, treatment is not initiated unless blood pressure exceeds 140/90 mm Hg. However, in some patients with certain risk factors or the presence of target organ damage, the goal may be to lower blood pressure to below 130/85 mm Hg (see below).[2-4]

"Office or white coat hypertension" refers to an elevated blood pressure reading obtained during a clinic visit which is higher than that obtained either by manual readings or 24-hour ambulatory monitoring.[5,6] This phenomenon was seen in 21 of 292 patients with untreated borderline hypertension who had normal ambulatory pressure readings.[7] This elevation in blood pressure appears to be persistent when the measurement is obtained in the clinic setting. Patients with white coat hypertension need to be monitored closely, preferably with a device for evaluating blood pressure readings outside the physician's office or clinic environment, in order to determine the most appropriate treatment strategy. The accuracy of this device should be checked regularly against the instrument used in the office.

There is growing evidence that blood pressures outside the physician's office, as measured by an ambulatory blood pressure monitor, are a better predictor of cardiovascular damage.[8,9] However, it is important to remember that the major therapeutic trials have relied upon office based pressures. Therefore, the clinician must consider home pressures in the treatment strategy, but definitive recommendations about their use cannot be made at this time.

Hypertensive Urgencies and Emergencies. As introduced previously, hypertension is classified into stages with Stage 4 considered very severe hypertension, requiring immediate evaluation and treatment. Hypertensive crisis is defined as a diastolic blood pressure ≥120 to 130 mm Hg and is subclassified further as hypertensive emergency (with acute or chronic end-organ damage) or urgency (without end-organ damage).[10] An acute increase in DBP (usually >130 mm Hg) without end-organ damage is referred to as accelerated hypertension. Accelerated hypertension associated with end-organ-damage such as encephalopathy, unstable angina, pulmonary edema, severe retinopathy, or renal failure, and a rapidly deteriorating course is classified as malignant hypertension. Hypertensive emergencies require hospitalization in order to immediately lower the blood pressure. Hypertensive urgencies do not require immediate reductions in pressure; instead, pressures should be reduced within 24 hours.[1] (See Chapter 17: Hypertensive Emergencies.)

Isolated systolic hypertension (ISH) is defined as an elevated systolic blood pressure with a normal diastolic blood pressure. The point at which a patient's blood pressure is classified as ISH depends upon the definition used. Isolated systolic hypertension has been defined as a systolic blood pressure ≥160 mm Hg with a diastolic blood pressure of either <95 mm Hg[11] or <90 mm Hg,[12] or as a systolic pressure ≥140 mm Hg with a diastolic pressure <90 mm Hg, according to the JNC V.[1] Thus, the prevalence of ISH depends upon its definition. According to the Framingham Study, the prevalence of ISH increases above the age of 55 years.[11] Also, it is the most frequent type of hypertension in patients over the age of 65 years.[13] In the past, ISH was known to be a risk factor for cardiovascular disease, but there was no evidence that treatment was beneficial. In fact, some argued that older patients required higher pressures and should not be treated for ISH. It has now been clearly established that ISH is a major risk factor for cardiovascular disease and requires treatment.[12,14,15] The Systolic Hypertension in the Elderly Program (SHEP) published a study of

4736 patients aged 60 and over who had ISH with systolic pressures of ≥160 mm Hg. Treatment was initiated with chlorthalidone 12.5 to 25 mg/day and atenolol was added if blood pressures remained elevated. There was a 36% reduction in fatal plus nonfatal stroke, a 27% reduction in myocardial infarction (MI) or coronary death, and a 32% reduction in all major cardiovascular events. This study did not enroll patients with systolic pressures between 140 to 159 mm Hg, thus leaving treatment strategies in this group unanswered. The SHEP trial demonstrated that control of ISH can be readily achieved and the drug of choice is now considered to be a thiazide diuretic.[1,14,15]

Blood Pressure Measurements

Blood pressure readings may vary depending upon the method used by the individual taking the measurement. Therefore, a standardized technique should be used as described in Table 10.2.[16] Correct measurement of blood pressure requires that the clinician listen for the five phases of the Korotkoff sounds. These are:[16]

Phase I	The pressure level at which the first faint, clear tapping sounds are heard. The sounds gradually increase in intensity as the cuff is deflated.
Phase II	That time during cuff deflation when a murmur or swishing sounds are heard.
Phase III	The period during which sound(s) is crisper and increase in intensity.
Phase IV	That time when a distinct, abrupt, muffling of sound (usually of a soft, blowing quality) is heard.
Phase V	That pressure level when the last sound is heard and after which all sound disappears.

When measuring blood pressure, the clinician should consider the possibility of pseudohypertension. In older patients, vessels become stiff and thick due to calcifications and may resist compression from the bladder of the blood pressure cuff. This results in a greater pressure necessary to occlude the artery and it causes an inaccurately high estimation of the systolic pressure. Osler's maneuver can be used to detect pseudohypertension. This is performed by inflating the cuff above the systolic pressure and palpating the brachial and radial arteries to determine if the pulseless artery is still palpable.[17] If the artery is still palpable, the patient may have pseudohypertension. While pseudohypertension has been the subject of numerous discussions, it is thought to be relatively rare.[17]

Etiology

The majority of persons with hypertension have no identifiable cause for the disorder (i.e., primary or essential hypertension). Although the cause of essential hypertension is unknown, a variety of neural and humoral factors are known to influence blood pressure (see Table 10.3).[18-20] Patients are considered to have second-

Table 10.2	Proper Technique for Blood Pressure Measurement[16,a]

1) Patient should be seated for 5 min with arm bared, unrestricted by clothing, and supported at heart level. Smoking or food ingestion should not have occurred within 30 min before the BP measurement

2) The appropriate blood pressure cuff size should be chosen for the patient. The bladder width should be at least 40% and the bladder length at least 80% of the upper arm circumference. The cuff should be wrapped snugly around the arm with the bladder centered over the brachial artery

3) Measurements should be taken with a mercury sphygmomanometer, a recently calibrated aneroid manometer, or a validated electronic device

4) Inflate the cuff to determine the SBP by observing the point at which the radial pulse is no longer palpable. Deflate the cuff and wait 15–30 sec before reinflating

5) Position the stethoscope over the brachial artery and rapidly inflate the cuff to the point determined in Step 4. Deflate the cuff at a rate of 2–3 mm Hg/sec, listening for Phase I and Phase V (Phase IV for children) Korotkoff sounds. Phase V, at the disappearance of sound, is the DBP in adults. Listen for 10–20 mm Hg below Phase V for any further sound, then deflate the cuff completely

6) The BP should be recorded in even numbers with the patient's position, arm used, and cuff size documented

7) Two BP readings should be obtained in the same arm and averaged; 1–2 min should elapse before repeating the BP measurement. If the readings differ by >5 mm Hg, additional measurements should be obtained. The BP should be taken in both arms at the initial visit with the BP taken in the arm with the higher reading at subsequent visits.

a BP = Blood pressure; DBP = Diastolic blood pressure; SBP = Systolic blood pressure.

ary hypertension when a specific cause has been determined (see Table 10.4). Although patients with secondary hypertension only account for approximately 10% of the hypertensive population, patients should be evaluated if physical or laboratory findings are consistent with a secondary cause (see Table 10.5).[21] Further diagnostic work-up also should be considered in patients who do not respond to increasing doses of antihypertensive medication, or who have a sudden increase in blood pressure, or accelerated or malignant hypertension.[1] A thorough review of the patient's prescription and nonprescription medications should be conducted to rule out drug-induced hypertension (see Table 10.4).

Pathophysiology

A number of factors may affect the arterial blood pressure[18–20,22] (see Table 10.3). Blood pressure is normally regulated by compensatory mechanisms that respond to changes in cardiac demand. An increase in cardiac output (CO) normally results in a compensatory decrease in total peripheral resistance (TPR); likewise, an increase in TPR results in a decrease in CO. These events occur in order to maintain mean arterial pressure (MAP) as is evidenced by the following equation:

$$MAP = CO \times TPR$$

When these compensatory mechanisms are not functioning properly, there is a resultant adverse change in blood pressure. It has been suggested that an increase in fluid volume initially results in increases in cardiac output and arterial pressure. Eventually, with long-standing hypertension, total peripheral resistance will increase so that cardiac output returns to normal.[23,24]

The renin-angiotensin-aldosterone system plays an important role in the regulation of arterial pressure. Decreases in blood pres-

sure, blood volume, or sodium concentration result in increased secretion of the enzyme renin from the cells of the juxtaglomerular apparatus. Renin acts on angiotensinogen which results in the formation of angiotensin I. Angiotensin-converting enzyme (ACE) converts angiotensin I to angiotensin II, which is a potent vasoconstrictor acting directly on arteriolar smooth muscle. Angiotensin II also stimulates the production of aldosterone by the adrenal gland which causes sodium and water retention and the excretion of potassium.[25] Many different factors are known to influence renin release, especially those which affect renal perfusion.

Patients can be classified as having low, normal, or high plasma renin activity (PRA). Approximately 20% of patients with essential hypertension have lower than normal renin values, while approximately 15% have levels that are higher than normal. Those with normal to high levels have decreased plasma volume and increased adrenergic activity and should theoretically be more responsive to ACE inhibitors or β-adrenergic blockers. Patients with low PRA have expanded fluid volume and may be more responsive to diuretic therapy. Further research to classify patients into these categories needs to be conducted before measurements of PRA can be advocated as a means for selection of drug therapy.[26,27] Some authors advocate that renin profiling should be performed in all patients as a guide for drug selection.[26] Unfortunately, the profiling is costly and, more importantly, the vast majority of hypertensive patients have renin values in the normal range. Even the proponents of renin profiling acknowledge that drug selection must be empiric for patients with normal plasma renin values. To perform renin profiling for 100 patients when the test will not be helpful in 65 seems to be a poor utilization of health care resources.

Arterial blood pressure also is regulated by the adrenergic nervous system which causes contraction and relaxation of vascular smooth muscle.[28] Stimulation of α-adrenergic receptors in the central nervous system (CNS) results in a decrease in sympathetic outflow causing a decrease in blood pressure. Stimulation of postsynaptic α_1 receptors in the periphery causes vasoconstriction. Alpha receptors are regulated by a negative feedback as norepinephrine is released into the synaptic cleft and stimulates presynaptic α_2 receptors which then inhibit further norepinephrine release. This negative feedback results in a balance between vasoconstriction and vasodilation. Stimulation of postsynaptic β_1 receptors located in the myocardium causes an increase in heart rate and contractility, while stimulation of postsynaptic β_2 receptors in the arterioles and venules results in vasodilation. Baroreceptors are important in the maintenance of blood pressure and are a consideration when

Table 10.3	Mechanisms Involved in Arterial Blood Pressure Control[a]
Hemodynamic	CO, PVR
Adrenergic nervous system	CNS alpha receptors, peripheral alpha and beta receptors
Renin-angiotensin-Aldosterone system	Regulates systemic and renal blood flow via angiotensin II vasoconstriction. Aldosterone stimulates sodium and fluid retention
Renal function and renal blood flow	Fluid and electrolyte balance
Hormonal factors	Adrenal cortical hormones, vasopressin, thyroid, insulin?
Vascular endothelium	EDRF, bradykinin, prostacyclin, endothelin

a CNS = Central nervous system; CO = Cardiac output; EDRF = Endothelium-derived relaxing factor; PVR = Peripheral vascular resistance.

Table 10.4	Causes of Secondary Hypertension

Renal Disease
  Renoparenchymal disease
  Renovascular disease

Coarctation of the Aorta

Primary Aldosteronism

Cushing's Syndrome (Hyperadrenalism)

Pheochromocytoma (Adrenal tumor)

Pregnancy

Drug-Induced[a]
  Adrenocorticosteroids
  Alcohol
  Anorectics (e.g., phenylpropanolamine)
  Appetite suppressants
  Cyclosporine
  Decongestants
  Estrogens
  Licorice
  MAOIs
  NSAIDs
  Oral contraceptives
  Oral decongestants (e.g., phenylpropanolamine, pseudoephedrine)
  Thyroid hormone excess
  TCAs

Increased Intracranial Pressure

[a] MAOIs = Monoamine oxidase inhibitors; NSAIDs = Nonsteroidal anti-inflammatory drugs; TCAs = Tricyclic antidepressants.

determining the efficacy of antihypertensive measures since baroreceptors may reset, interfering with initial blood pressure control.[29]

An association between sodium and blood pressure has been supported by epidemiologic evidence as well as clinical trials.[30,31] Patients with a high dietary sodium intake appear to have a greater prevalence of hypertension than those with a low sodium intake. Restricting sodium intake will result in a lowering of blood pressure in the majority of patients with hypertension.[30] The mechanism by which hypertension is caused by an increase in sodium intake appears to involve natriuretic hormone. In response to an increase in renal sodium retention, and therefore extracellular fluid volume, natriuretic hormone is increased to facilitate sodium and water excretion. However, natriuretic hormone also may cause an increase in intracellular sodium and calcium resulting in increased vascular tone and hypertension.[32]

Epidemiologic evidence and clinical trials have demonstrated an inverse relationship between calcium and blood pressure.[33,34] Calcium supplementation has been shown to decrease blood pressure in certain individuals, but the evidence has been conflicting.[33-38] One proposed mechanism for this relationship involves an alteration in the balance between intracellular and extracellular calcium. Increased intracellular calcium concentrations may cause increases in peripheral vascular resistance, resulting in increased blood pressure.[25]

Potassium also has been found to be inversely related to blood pressure; a decrease in potassium has been associated with an increase in peripheral vascular resistance.[31] Further evidence is necessary before supplementation of potassium is recommended as a therapy for hypertension. In theory, diuretic-induced hypokalemia could contract some of the hypotensive effects. This has not been well studied. It is important, however, that the potassium levels be maintained within the normal range.

Insulin resistance and hyperinsulinemia also have been associated with hypertension.[39-43] Kaplan has suggested that insulin resistance is responsible for the frequent co-existence of diabetes, hyperlipidemia, hypertension, and abdominal obesity.[43] The exact role of insulin resistance in the development of hypertension is still evolving and is the subject of intense investigation.

Finally, studies have determined that the vascular epithelium is not a passive or static system. Rather, it is a very dynamic system in which vascular tone is regulated by numerous substances.[19,20] As noted above, angiotensin II promotes vasoconstriction of the vascular epithelium. However, several other substances regulate vascular tone. Prostacyclin, bradykinin, and endothelium-derived relaxing factor (EDRF) are vasodilatory hormones that relax the vascular epithelium. Hypertensive patients have been found to have impaired EDRF-mediated vasodilation which may contribute to hypertension and/or its vascular complications.[19]

While the factors that regulate blood pressure are becoming better understood, the cause of hypertension is still unknown. Therefore, it is not possible to target therapy to specific abnormalities; therefore, therapy remains largely empiric.

Evaluation

Clinical Presentation

1. D.C., a 50-year-old black male, is referred to the Hypertension Clinic for evaluation of high blood pressure noted on routine screening. D.C. has a chief complaint of a pounding, occipital, morning headache. Hypertension was detected 6 years ago and treated with weight reduction and a low sodium diet. D.C. took medication for 2 years, but stopped it on his own. A gradual 15-pound weight gain is noted over the past 10–12 months. Past medical history is significant for appendectomy 30 years ago and duodenal ulcer 10 years ago. D.C.'s father had hypertension and died of an MI at age 54. His mother had diabetes and hypertension and died of a cerebrovascular accident at the age of 65. D.C. has smoked cigarettes for the past 35 years and believes his elevated blood pressure is caused by job-related stress. He would like medical clearance for his absence from the job during the past week.

Physical examination reveals a well-developed, overweight black male who looks his age and is in no acute distress. He is 5′9″ and weighs 108 kg. BPs are as follows: 164/98 mm Hg (left arm) and 168/96 mm Hg (right arm) while sitting, 162/98 mm Hg (left arm) and 166/98 mm Hg (right arm) while standing. His pulse is 84 beats/min and regular. Funduscopic examination reveals mild arterial narrowing, sharp discs, and no exudates or hemorrhages. The remainder of the physical examination is unremarkable.

Laboratory examination reveals the following: blood urea nitrogen (BUN) 24 mg/dL; serum creatinine (SrCr) 1.7 mg/dL; glucose 95 mg/dL; potassium (K) 4.0 mEq/L; uric acid 8.0 mg/dL; hematocrit (Hct) 42%; total cholesterol 224 mg/dL; and high density lipoprotein (HDL) 37 mg/dL. Urinalysis (UA) reveals 1+ proteinuria with no glucosuria. An electrocardiogram (ECG) and chest x-ray reveal mild left ventricular hypertrophy. What stage of hypertension does D.C. demonstrate?
[SI units: BUN 8.6 mmol/L; glucose 5.3 mmol/L; K 4.0 mmol/L; uric acid 476 μmol/L; Hct 0.42; total cholesterol 5.79 mmol/L; HDL 0.96 mmol/L]

D.C. has a systolic blood pressure consistent with Stage 2 hypertension and a diastolic pressure that would be considered Stage 1.[1] Since the higher of the two stages is used to classify the disorder, D.C. is diagnosed with Stage 2 hypertension. Guidelines also indicate that risk factors and evidence of target organ damage should be included in the classification of hypertension. For D.C., the assessment should be Stage 2 hypertension with evidence of target organ damage (left ventricular hypertrophy, renal impairment, early retinopathy) and three additional risk factors (family history, smoking, elevated cholesterol).

Table 10.5		Clinical Findings Suggestive of Secondary Form of Hypertension	
Correctable Cause	Historical Finding	Physical Examination Finding	Laboratory Finding
Estrogen use	Oral contraceptive use or menopause treatment		
Renovascular disease	Moderate or severe HBP before age 30 or after 55. Rapidly progressive HBP	Abdominal bruits[a] with ↑ systolic and diastolic pressure; funduscopic hemorrhages	Suppressed or stimulated plasma renin activity; IVP (rapid sequence); digital subtraction angiography
Renoparenchymal disease	Dysuria, polyuria, nocturia; urinary tract infections; renal stones (or colic); family history—polycystic kidney disease; renal disease	Edema	Proteinuria; hematuria; bacteriuria
Coarctation of the aorta	Intermittent claudication	Diminished or absent femoral pulses compared to carotids. Lower systolic leg BP compared to arm BP	
Pheochromocytoma	Paroxysmal headaches, palpitations, sweating, dizziness, and pallor (in 30% of patients)	Nervousness, tremor, tachycardia, orthostatic hypotension	Clonidine suppression test[b]; ↑ serum glucose; high urine metanephrine or vanillylmandelic acid
Primary aldosteronism	Weakness, polyuria, polydipsia, intermittent paralysis	Orthostatic hypotension	Hypokalemia
Cushing's syndrome	Menstrual disturbances	Moon face; truncal obesity; buffalo hump; hirsutism; violet striae	↑ serum glucose; ↑ plasma cortisol after suppression with dexamethasone

[a] Majority of abdominal bruits do not originate from the renal artery.
[b] Failure of plasma catecholamines to ↓ by 50% within 3 hr of administration of 0.3 mg clonidine highly suggests pheochromocytoma.

Health Beliefs and Patient Education

2. D.C.'s history demonstrates that he has misconceptions regarding the term "hypertension" and misunderstandings about the disease. Should D.C. be educated about the etiology of hypertension? Why?

Patients like D.C. often correlate their blood pressure elevation with stress or symptoms such as headache.[44,45] As discussed previously, a certain percentage of patients may have an increase in blood pressure due to anxiety as seen in those with office hypertension. However, the majority of patients with essential hypertension will experience an elevated blood pressure reading regardless of their stress level. D.C. requires education as to the etiology of his disease and the lack of correlation between tension or symptoms and high blood pressure. It is vitally important that he understand these concepts and the importance of long-term therapy. Otherwise, the tendency to adhere to the prescribed treatment only when "I feel my blood pressure is high" or during stressful events may occur.

Patients may believe they are able to control their blood pressure by stress management rather than with prescribed therapy. Stress management has not been proven to be of benefit in controlled trials.[46,47] As in the case of D.C., normal daily activities (including work) may be neglected due to hypertension. One study found that patients with recently diagnosed hypertension have an increase in work absenteeism;[48] however, this association has not been seen in other studies.[49] Attitudes regarding a chronic disease state may result in depression or a perceived worsening of health status.[50,51] Therefore, it is important to discuss these issues with patients to determine their health beliefs and attitudes and to educate them about the etiology and management of hypertension to promote blood pressure control.[52]

Historical Database

Target organ damage and other cardiovascular risk factors should be identified when treating hypertensive patients. In addition, secondary causes of hypertension should be considered. Most of these data can be found if a thorough patient history is taken and a complete physical examination with laboratory data is performed.

3. What additional information regarding lifestyle should be obtained from D.C. by interview?

Further information should be obtained from D.C. concerning his weight gain and diet to determine if alterations in the past few months could account for the recent loss of controlled blood pressure. An attempt should be made to quantify his intake of sodium and fat. A more complete social history is needed to determine alcohol consumption and the number of cigarettes smoked per day. In addition, a list of physical activities can be documented to identify means for improving weight control. A complete over-the-counter medication history would be helpful to further assess any secondary causes for elevations in blood pressure. Allergic history to medications also may be necessary if therapy is to be implemented.

Target Organ Damage

Hypertension adversely affects numerous organ systems throughout the body including the heart, brain, kidney, and eye. Damage to these organ systems (specified by terms such as coronary, myocardial, cerebrovascular, renal, or retinal disease) resulting from hypertension is termed cardiovascular disease (CVD). There are often misconceptions about the terms CVD and coronary artery disease (CAD).[53] CVD encompasses the broad scope of cardiovascular complications (including stroke). CAD is a subset of cardiovascular disease and only refers to pathophysiology related to the coronary vasculature, including ischemic heart disease and myocardial infarction.

Heart

Hypertension may affect the heart either indirectly by promoting atherosclerotic changes or directly via pressure related effects. Hypertension can promote cardiovascular disease and increase the risk for ischemic events such as angina and myocardial infarction. Therapy for hypertension has been shown to reduce these coronary events.

Hypertension also may promote the development of left ventricular hypertrophy which is pathologically distinct from coronary artery disease. While left ventricular hypertrophy is a myocardial (cellular) change, and not an arterial change, the two conditions often exist together. It is commonly believed that left ventricular hypertrophy is a compensatory mechanism of the heart to handle the increased resistance caused by elevated blood pressure. However, nonhemodynamic factors also may promote hypertrophy in hypertensive individuals.[53,54] Left ventricular hypertrophy is a potent and independent risk factor for myocardial ischemia, MI, congestive heart failure, arrhythmias, and sudden death.[53,55-60] However, the presence of left ventricular hypertrophy does not necessarily indicate that the patient has CHF.

The third major cardiac manifestation of hypertension is CHF, which may be due to repeated ischemia, excessive ventricular hypertrophy, and/or pressure overload. Uncontrolled hypertension is one of the leading causes of congestive heart failure.[59]

Brain

Hypertension is one of the most frequent causes of transient ischemic attacks (TIAs), ischemic stroke, multiple cerebral infarcts, and hemorrhages.[61-65] A sudden, prolonged increase in systemic blood pressure also can cause hypertensive encephalopathy which is a hypertensive emergency.[62] Clinical signs and symptoms of hypertensive encephalopathy include: blood pressure approximating 250/150 mm Hg, severe headache, altered mental status, vision disturbances, nausea and vomiting, seizures, and retinopathy.[62,66,67] Fortunately, hypertensive encephalopathy is now uncommon since effective antihypertensive therapy is available. Clinical trials have demonstrated that antihypertensive therapy can significantly reduce the risk of stroke (see Treatment: Patient Benefit).[68]

Kidney

Glomerular filtration rate naturally declines with aging. However, hypertension greatly accelerates the rate of decline and coexisting diabetes markedly adds to the risk. While strokes and coronary deaths are declining in the U.S., the rates of renal failure are escalating dramatically.[2,3] Hypertension is associated with nephrosclerosis which is caused by increased intraglomerular pressures. It is still not known if a primary renal lesion with ischemia causes systemic hypertension or whether systemic hypertension directly causes glomerular capillary damage by increasing intraglomerular pressure. Regardless of the mechanism, renal insufficiency frequently progresses to renal failure. Hypertension is responsible for approximately one-third of all cases of end-stage renal disease (ESRD) requiring dialysis. The populations with the highest rates of ESRD are blacks, hispanics, and native Americans; rates are increasing most dramatically in elderly blacks.[3] Although several studies have demonstrated that aggressive blood pressure control is the most important goal to slow the rate of decline in renal function,[3,69-73] it may not be entirely effective in slowing the progression of renal impairment in all patients.[74,75]

Eye

Hypertension causes retinopathies that are evaluated according to the Keith, Wagener, and Barker funduscopic classification system.[76] Grade 1 is characterized by narrowing of the arterial diameter indicative of vasoconstriction. Arteriovenous nicking is the hallmark of Grade 2 and it indicates atherosclerosis. Long-standing untreated hypertension or accelerated hypertension also can cause cotton wool exudates and flame hemorrhages (Grade 3). In severe cases, papilledema occurs and this is classified as Grade 4.[76] Hypertensive patients with diabetes are much more likely to have aggressive retinopathy which may lead to blindness.[4]

4. What evidence of target organ damage is manifested by D.C., and will these target organ changes be reversible upon control of his high blood pressure?

D.C. has several signs of target organ damage from long-standing, poorly controlled hypertension. The funduscopic examination reveals mild arterial narrowing suggesting early retinopathy. He has evidence of left ventricular hypertrophy, indicating cardiac involvement. Finally, D.C.'s serum creatinine of 1.7 mg/dL and his 1+ proteinuria on urinalysis suggest renal insufficiency.

D.C.'s ECG and chest x-ray reveal left ventricular hypertrophy. Both of these tests have low sensitivity for detecting left ventricular hypertrophy (i.e., these tests do not always detect the presence of the disorder).[53,57] However, if left ventricular hypertrophy is detected on an ECG, a very specific test, the condition does exist.[53,77] The best way to detect left ventricular hypertrophy is with echocardiography.[53,77]

All antihypertensive drugs (with the possible exception of direct vasodilators) reduce left ventricular hypertrophy.[54] However, not all drugs act by the same mechanism. Diuretics appear to slowly promote regression over several months via hemodynamic mechanisms. Previous studies that suggested diuretics did not promote regression of left ventricular hypertrophy were not conducted for sufficient lengths of time. Agents such as centrally acting drugs, calcium channel blockers, and angiotensin-converting enzyme (ACE) inhibitors may promote regression by both hemodynamic and nonhemodynamic mechanisms.[54] Evidence suggests that these agents may act directly on myocardial tissue via calcium or angiotensin receptors to promote rapid regression (e.g., 6 to 12 weeks).[54]

While it seems reasonable that regression of left ventricular hypertrophy would be a desirable goal, some controversy surrounds the issue. Some studies have raised concerns that myocardial function might be compromised when hypertrophied muscle regresses in size because of the increased ratio of collagen.[53,54] While active research is ongoing in this speculative area, it appears that regression of left ventricular hypertrophy is a desirable goal.

Once a patient has developed elevations in serum creatinine, significant renal damage has already occurred. D.C. also is spilling protein in his urine which suggests glomerular disease. It does not appear that blood pressure control can halt the decline in D.C.'s renal function, but only reduce the rate of decline. In addition, adequate blood pressure control (e.g., <140/90 mm Hg) does not protect all patients. Many black patients continue to have declining renal function despite ''adequate'' control and this may indicate a greater renal sensitivity in these individuals.[3,74,75] Emerging evidence suggests that some antihypertensive agents, including ACE inhibitors and calcium channel blockers, may be superior to others in their ability to protect the kidneys, but this has not been proven conclusively.[3] It is recommended that the goal blood pressure in patients with established renal insufficiency be less than 130/85 mm Hg in order to slow the decline in renal function.[2]

Reductions in blood pressure can reverse many of the changes associated with retinopathy. In particular, studies have demonstrated that the risk of retinopathy in diabetic patients increases markedly when the diastolic blood pressure is higher than 70 mm Hg and that control of blood pressure can slow this progression.[78,79]

Cardiovascular Risk Factors

5. What risk factors for either hypertension or CVD does D.C. have?

Family History

A family history of hypertension, premature coronary heart disease (CHD), stroke, cardiovascular disease, diabetes mellitus, and dyslipidemia should be obtained in all patients with hypertension.[1] D.C. has a significant family history of hypertension and diabetes, as well as cerebrovascular disease and premature coronary heart disease. Evidence of premature coronary heart disease in a first-degree relative is considered a major risk factor for the development of CHD.[80] Patients with a family history of hypertension appear to be more prone to the development of high blood pressure.[81]

Race

In nearly all age groups, blacks have higher blood pressures than whites.[82] Additionally, the prevalence of hypertension is about 27% among blacks and 20% among whites. Hypertension is more severe and occurs at an earlier age in black patients. This is associated with a 1.8-fold increased risk of fatal stroke, a 1.5-fold increased risk of heart disease death, and a 5-fold greater risk of end-stage renal disease.[1]

Hypertension

Patients with elevated blood pressures ($\geq 140/90$ mm Hg) or those receiving pharmacologic therapy for hypertension are at increased risk of developing coronary heart disease.[80] In addition, patients with high blood pressures that go untreated are at increased risk for coronary heart disease which also is related to the degree of blood pressure increase.[83]

Cigarette Smoking

D.C. has been smoking for 35 years. In addition to increasing the risk for coronary heart disease,[80] cigarette smoking may reduce the efficacy of antihypertensive therapy.[84-86] Although smoking cessation may not lower the patient's blood pressure,[87] it will decrease the risk.[88] In addition, patients should not smoke within approximately 30 minutes of a blood pressure measurement since nicotine acutely increases the blood pressure.[9]

Obesity

Overweight patients are at increased risk of developing hypertension. This relationship is consistent among gender and racial groups and is more prevalent in patients with higher blood pressure readings.[89] D.C. has had a significant weight gain over the past year.

Dyslipidemia

Elevations in blood cholesterol are associated with an increase in cardiovascular risk.[83] Both primary[90,91] and secondary[92,93] intervention trials have shown that reduction of cholesterol levels can decrease the risk of coronary heart disease. Elevations in cholesterol levels in conjunction with hypertension and cigarette smoking demonstrate an additive effect with regard to the risk of coronary heart disease.[83] One study found that it was necessary to lower both cholesterol and blood pressure in order to reduce cardiovascular risk.[94] Since D.C. has an elevation of total cholesterol in conjunction with multiple risk factors for coronary heart disease, a fasting lipid profile for HDL and an LDL cholesterol calculation should be performed.

Dietary Sodium

A diet history should be obtained from patients with elevated blood pressure readings because of the association between dietary sodium intake and hypertension.[21] Although responses to changes in dietary sodium intake vary,[95] patients should be instructed to limit their sodium intake because this lifestyle modification can contribute to blood pressure reduction. Blacks have a higher incidence of salt sensitivity and this appears to be due to racially determined differences in renal handling of sodium.[75]

D.C. has multiple risk factors for the development of hypertension (i.e., family history of hypertension, obesity, a possibility of increased dietary sodium) and cardiovascular disease (i.e., hypertension, cigarette smoking, family history of premature CHD, dyslipidemia). Many of these risk factors are modifiable; therefore, D.C. should be instructed about the implementation of a treatment plan and the benefits of risk factor reduction.

Table 10.6	Patient Education[1]

Patient/Clinician Discussions
- Establish a blood pressure goal
- High blood pressure cannot be cured, only controlled
- Treatment should not be discontinued without medical consultation and chronic treatment usually necessary to control blood pressure
- Blood pressure levels cannot be determined by the way a patient feels
- Potential adverse consequences of poor adherence to antihypertensive therapy and uncontrolled blood pressure
- Patients should verbalize understanding of their diagnosis
- Encourage patients to openly discuss their medications and any problems or side effects

Clinical Responsibilities to Enhance Patient Education and Improve Patient Compliance
- Involve patients' families or caregivers in the treatment process
- Encourage patients to self-monitor blood pressure
- Ask open-ended questions and provide encouragement for achieving goals
- Tailor treatment regimens to maximize compliance (i.e., QD or BID medications, dosage forms)
- Provide oral and written instructions and information on drug regimens and goals
- Provide alternative treatments and be willing to modify the patient's regimen
- Minimize cost of therapy
- Provide assistance to noncompliant patients (i.e., pill boxes, frequent follow-up visits, mail and/or telephone refill reminders)
- Contact patients who fail to attend follow-up appointments
- Collaborate with other health care providers (i.e., pharmacists, physicians, nutritionists, nurses)

Treatment
Patient Education

6. What information about high blood pressure, its treatment, and methods of promoting compliance should be given to D.C.?

Hypertensive patients should be supplied with information on the disease state, treatment, compliance, and hypertension-related morbidity and mortality. Different approaches or strategies can be employed (see Table 10.6). Recommendations should be individualized to each patient's specific needs since not all patients will respond to the same approach. For example, some patients may be able to understand the concept of a controlled blood pressure after reading written materials, whereas others may only understand after self monitoring their own blood pressures. It should be remembered that the educational process needs to continue throughout therapy and not every aspect of hypertension has to be discussed at each office visit. Written and verbal instructions should be selected so as not to overwhelm or scare the patient with too many facts. In addition, a patient's needs may change over time and different strategies may be necessary to enhance education and adherence.

Patient Benefit

7. Can the risks and complications that arise from untreated hypertension be prevented by appropriate therapy?

Numerous studies over the past 25 years clearly have demonstrated that treating hypertension reduces morbidity and mortality.

The first large-scale trial was the Veterans Administration (VA) study in men with diastolic blood pressures between 115 and 129 mm Hg which compared active treatment to placebo.[96] This study was discontinued earlier than originally intended because the benefits of treatment were so dramatic that continuation would have been unethical. Treatment markedly reduced cerebral hemorrhage, MI, CHF, retinopathy, and renal impairment. Other studies have focused on whether treating Stage 1 or Stage 2 hypertension reduces morbidity or mortality. These studies indicate that treatment is beneficial and reduces the risk of stroke, ischemic heart disease, congestive heart failure, progression to more severe hypertension, and death.[1,97-99] In addition to these investigations, several studies in the elderly have noted dramatic benefits (see Table 10.7).

In recent years controversy has arisen concerning the benefits of drug therapy found in clinical trials. This has been generated because epidemiologic evidence would predict that the blood pressure reduction seen in these trials should be able to lower stroke risk by 35% to 40% and coronary heart disease by 20% to 25%.[106] Accordingly, earlier meta-analyses concluded that stroke risk is reduced from 39% to 42%.[97,106] However, these meta-analyses demonstrated only a 14% reduction in coronary heart disease (not statistically significant). This caused many to speculate that the drugs used in these trials (diuretics and beta blockers) were unable to confer full benefits against the risk of coronary heart disease due to the possible metabolic effects of these drugs.

It is now believed that these findings can be explained by the differences in cardiovascular endpoints. Stroke is a readily reversible endpoint and benefits can be observed within a few years. This is consistent with the clinical trials that were only three to five years in length. However, coronary artery disease is not a readily reversible process (although progression can be slowed) and it is not surprising that it was difficult to demonstrate benefit during these relatively short duration trials. It is now clear that antihypertensive therapy can lower coronary risk as evidenced by two additional meta-analyses that include data from newer studies not available during the earlier analyses.[98,99] In one of these analyses, the risk of coronary heart disease was reduced by 16%, which was statistically significant.[98] In contrast to the previous meta-analysis that was not significant (14%), the finding that 16% was significant is probably related to increased numbers of patients and greater power. A meta-analysis of elderly hypertensives revealed a 22% reduction in cardiovascular mortality and a 26% reduction in coronary mortality which were both statistically significant.[99] As more clinical trial data become available concerns about the lack of benefit of drug therapy on coronary risk are being put to rest.

At present, the diuretics and beta blockers are the only antihypertensive agents which have been tested and shown to lower cardiovascular morbidity and mortality.[1] Other categories have not been tested. Studies which are now beginning will not yield data until nearly the year 2000.

The SHEP trial is the only completed study to investigate whether treating elderly patients with isolated systolic hypertension is beneficial (see Table 10.7).[12] Another trial in Europe is currently underway.[107] As discussed previously, in SHEP, patients were randomized to either chlorthalidone 12.5 mg or placebo in a double-blind fashion. The chlorthalidone could be increased to 25 mg and atenolol added for additional blood pressure control if necessary. This study clearly established the benefit of treating isolated systolic hypertension.

Goal of Therapy

8. What is the goal of treating D.C.'s high blood pressure?

The JNC V guidelines state that the goal of therapy is to lower morbidity and mortality by the least intrusive means possible.[1] This statement reflects two major issues. First, a reduction in morbidity and mortality is the ultimate goal of therapy, not a lower blood pressure number. Secondly, the changes in lifestyle necessary to control high blood pressure may interfere with the patient's quality of life, due to inconvenience, adverse reactions, unpalatable diet, or increased costs.

Control of blood pressure is only a surrogate endpoint for the ultimate goal, but it is currently the only endpoint that can be used to guide therapy. While the general goal is to lower the blood pressure to less than 140/90 mm Hg, many other factors need to be considered. For instance, in a patient with no other risk factors and no evidence of target organ damage, it may be acceptable to use only nondrug measures to control blood pressures in the 140/90 to 159/95 mm Hg range. However, in patients like D.C. who have multiple risk factors and/or target organ damage, therapy should be more aggressive. This is especially important for patients with

Table 10.7			Effects of Drug Therapy in Older Hypertensive Patients[15,a]				
Study	Number of Patients	Age	Mean Entry BP (mm Hg)	Stroke Reduction (%)	CAD Reduction (%)	CHF Reduction (%)	Reduction in All CVD (%)
The Management Committee of the National Heart Foundation of Australia[100]	582	60–69	165/101	33	18	—	31
The European Working Party Trial of Hypertension in the Elderly[101]	840	>60	182/101	36	20	22	29[b]
Coope et al.[102]	884	60–79	197/100	42[b]	↑3	32	24[b]
The Swedish Trial in Old Patients with Hypertension[103]	1627	70–84	195/102	47[b]	13	51[b]	40[b]
The Medical Research Council (of Great Britain) Working Party[104]	4396	65–74	185/91	25[b]	19	—	17[b]
The Systolic Hypertension in the Elderly Program[12]	4736	60–80	170/77[c]	33	27	55[b]	32[b]
The Hypertension Detection and Follow-up Program Cooperative Group[105]	2374	60–69	170/101	44[b]	15[b]	—	16[b]

[a] BP = Blood pressure; CAD = Coronary artery disease; CHF = Congestive heart failure; CVD = Cardiovascular disease.
[b] Statistically significant reduction compared to no treatment or placebo.
[c] Isolated systolic hypertension.

renal insufficiency and co-existing diabetes. In these patients, the National High Blood Presssure Education Program recommends that blood pressure should be lowered to less than 130/85 mm Hg.[2,4]

Philosophies regarding the treatment of Stage 1 (mild) hypertension vary between health care professionals in the U.S. and Europe. The British guidelines are less aggressive than those followed in the United States, suggesting that young patients without co-existing risk factors or target organ damage and with diastolic blood pressures from 100 to 109 mm Hg should be treated with nonpharmacologic approaches.[108] If there is a downward trend in the patient's condition, then observation should be continued. The British guidelines do not recommend treating most patients with diastolic blood pressure readings between 90 and 99 mm Hg who have no other risk factors and no evidence of target organ damage. In the U.S., these patients would receive drug therapy for their hypertension.

Considering D.C.'s signs of target organ damage and the presence of additional risk factors, aggressive blood pressure control is indicated. A reasonable blood pressure goal for D.C. would be to maintain diastolic blood pressures between 80 and 85 mm Hg and systolic blood pressure at approximately 130 mm Hg. The general therapeutic goal would be to design a cost effective regimen that minimizes adverse reactions (especially hypotension). A further objective is to ensure that D.C. understands his disease and its complications by providing thorough patient education.

9. Would it be more appropriate to reduce D.C.'s diastolic pressure to 80 mm Hg?

Two papers published in 1987 have generated concern about lowering blood pressure too far.[94,109] These studies found that ischemic heart disease events were decreased as expected when diastolic blood pressure was reduced to approximately 85 mm Hg. However, below this level, the risk of ischemic heart disease actually increased. This has been termed the J-Curve phenomenon.[110] Several other studies have described similar findings. However, several factors must be noted. First, these observations have been made only on retrospective examinations of data; no prospective trial has been designed to look at this question. The J-Curve has been associated only with increased risk of coronary events, not stroke or renal impairment. For stroke and renal impairment, data suggest that the lower the blood pressure the better so long as reductions in pressure are not abrupt. While the J-Curve appears to be a real phenomenon, many believe it is not caused by therapeutic reductions in pressure, but rather that patients with lower blood pressure have other illnesses that predispose them to coronary events (e.g., previous MI or stroke). These questions will not be answered conclusively until a prospective trial is performed.

With these factors in mind, the general goal of therapy should be to lower D.C.'s blood pressure to less than 140/90 mm Hg. In patients with diabetes or renal insufficiency, blood pressure should be lowered cautiously to less than 130/85 mm Hg.

Patients with isolated systolic hypertension also benefit from therapy. Guidelines suggest that when systolic blood pressure is initially greater than 180 mm Hg it should be lowered to less than 160 mm Hg. Patients with initial pressures between 160 and 179 mm Hg should have their blood pressure reduced by 20 mm Hg.[1,15] Patients with systolic blood pressures between 140 and 159 mm Hg have not been studied; therefore, definitive recommendations cannot be made and lifestyle modifications are preferred to drug therapy.[1]

Lifestyle Modifications

10. What nonpharmacologic measures could be used to treat D.C.'s high blood pressure?

Due to the relationships between high blood pressure and various dietary and lifestyle factors, the use of nonpharmacologic interventions has been recognized as an important treatment modality in patients with hypertension.[111] Nondrug measures used to treat hypertension were previously defined as "nonpharmacologic measures." However, the JNC V recognized the importance of behavioral changes that these measures required and changed the term to "lifestyle modifications."[1]

Moderate Sodium Restriction

The JNC V recommends that sodium intake be restricted to less than 100 mmol/day. This is equivalent to less than 6 gm of sodium chloride ($\approx$1 teaspoonful) or 2.3 gm of sodium per day.[1]

Evidence from randomized clinical trials has shown that a 4.9 mm Hg reduction in systolic blood pressure and a 2.6 mm Hg reduction diastolic blood pressure can be achieved with moderate sodium restriction.[112] The response to an alteration in sodium intake will vary depending upon the individual.[95] Certain subgroups of patients appear to be more sensitive to changes in dietary sodium chloride than others. Salt sensitivity is more prevalent in blacks than whites, and also is associated with age and patients with hypertension.[113–115] Although a greater response may be expected from patients in these categories, all patients with hypertension should be instructed to reduce their sodium intake by not adding salt to foods and by avoiding processed or packaged foods, foods with a high salt content, and nonprescription drugs containing sodium. We know that D.C., who is black and thus potentially sensitive to sodium restriction, has not been compliant with salt restriction in the past. Thus further counseling is necessary.

Weight Reduction and Dietary Fats

Significant reductions in blood pressure have been associated with weight loss in overweight patients.[117,118] Therefore, patients with Stage I hypertension should undergo an adequate trial of weight reduction in conjunction with other lifestyle modifications before they are started on drug therapy.[1,116] In a study that included hypertensive patients with or without antihypertensive therapy and normotensive individuals, the mean weight loss was 10.4 kg. This resulted in a 10.3/8.0 mm Hg decrease in blood pressure. In the group of subjects who were obese, hypertensive, and not receiving antihypertensive therapy, the blood pressure reduction was 15.8/13.6 mm Hg.[119] While there is no direct relationship between an alteration in dietary fat consumption and the management of high blood pressure, weight loss is more readily achieved by a low fat diet.[120] In addition, a diet low in cholesterol and saturated fats should be recommended for patients such as D.C. who have dyslipidemia to reduce the risk of coronary heart disease.[80]

Exercise

Individuals who are more physically active have been shown to have lower blood pressures than those who are less physically active.[121,122] Recommended activities for hypertensive patients include aerobic exercise such as walking, running, cycling, swimming, cross-country skiing, and calisthenics.[123] Patients should discuss these activities with their physicians in order to determine the most appropriate exercise as well as the intensity and duration of the activity, taking into consideration the patient's current health status and other risk factors for coronary heart disease. Most patients will benefit from 30 to 45 minutes of brisk walking three to five times a week.[1] Exercise also can be beneficial in losing weight and reducing the risk of cardiovascular disease. D.C. should be questioned about his exercise habits and counseled according to his needs.

Alcohol Consumption

Alcohol consumption has been associated with hypertension. Patients who consumed three to four drinks a day experienced a 3 to 4 mm Hg increase in systolic blood pressure and a 1 to 2 mm Hg increase in diastolic blood pressure over individuals who did not consume alcohol. In patients who consumed more than five to six drinks a day, an increase in systolic blood pressure of 5 to 6 mm Hg and diastolic blood pressure of 2 to 4 mm Hg was seen in comparison to individuals who did not drink alcohol. Therefore patients with hypertension should limit their consumption of alcohol to two drinks or less per day.[124] Patients experiencing withdrawal symptoms from alcohol may demonstrate an elevation in both systolic and diastolic blood pressure.[125] Patients should be instructed not to exceed 1 ounce of ethanol (2 oz 100 proof whiskey, 8 oz wine, 24 oz beer) a day.[1]

Stress Reduction

The results of stress management on blood pressure control have been conflicting;[46,47,126] however such activities may lead to improved quality of life in patients with hypertension.[127]

Smoking Cessation

All patients should be educated about the benefits of smoking cessation because of the association between smoking and increased risk of cardiovascular disease. Cigarette smoking is an independent risk factor for coronary heart disease and has been shown to increase cardiovascular and overall mortality in patients less than 65 years of age.[128] The risk of coronary death increases with the number of cigarettes smoked and is greater in patients with additional risk factors for coronary heart disease.[128] Cigarette smoking carries with it the detrimental effects of decreasing the oxygen-carrying capacity of the blood, increasing platelet adhesiveness, elevating heart rate, acutely increasing catecholamines and fatty acids, and increasing myocardial susceptibility to atrial fibrillation. Chronic atherogenic effects also occur with cigarette smoking. An apparent decrease in the incidence of coronary heart disease has been seen in patients who stopped smoking as compared to those who continued the habit.[129] Although smoking may not be related to chronic alterations in blood pressure, it may interfere with the response to certain antihypertensive medications (e.g., beta blockers).[84,85,130] Therefore, D.C. should be educated about the risks associated with cigarette smoking and available behavior modification programs to assist his smoking cessation efforts.

Caffeine Ingestion

Caffeine has been associated with an acute elevation in blood pressure;[131] however, this appears to be a transient effect and, therefore, does not affect blood pressure control. Limitations on caffeine intake are not recommended unless caffeine ingestion is detrimental for other health reasons (e.g., cardiac arrhythmias).[1]

Potassium

Potassium has been shown to be inversely related to blood pressure;[31] therefore, efforts should be made to maintain the patient's potassium concentration within the normal range. This is particularly important for patients taking potassium wasting diuretics. Further evidence of the relationship between potassium and blood pressure needs to be established before potassium supplementation can be recommended.[1]

Calcium

Evidence from clinical trials on the antihypertensive effect of calcium supplementation through dietary intake or proprietary supplements has been inconclusive.[34–38] Pooled analysis including pa-

tients with hypertension demonstrated a 1.48 mm Hg decrease in systolic blood pressure and a 0.29 mm Hg decrease in diastolic blood pressure with supplementation.[34] There appears to be a subgroup of patients who may respond to calcium supplementation; however, a way to identify these individuals has not been determined.[33] Therefore, the JNC V recommends that patients follow the recommended daily allowance of 800 to 1200 mg calcium intake.[1]

Magnesium

The role of magnesium in hypertension is not well established. An inverse association between magnesium intake and blood pressure appears to exist.[111] Also, there is evidence that low serum magnesium may increase glucose intolerance, lipid abnormalities, and platelet aggregation in diabetic patients.[132,133] Therefore, although the minimum daily allowance should be maintained, there is no indication to recommend an increase in magnesium intake for lowering blood pressure.

There is a considerable amount of literature on nonpharmacologic management for the treatment of hypertension; however only some of the interventions discussed above have been proven to be of benefit. The effects of seven nonpharmacologic modalities were studied in patients with high normal diastolic blood pressure. Both weight and sodium reduction were associated with a significant decrease in both systolic and diastolic blood pressure, whereas stress management or nutritional supplements did not demonstrate a significant benefit.[46] Nonpharmacologic interventions should be initiated in all patients with hypertension, whether or not drug treatment is required. This should be discussed with the patient to set reasonable goals. Patients then need to be committed to making lifestyle changes to improve blood pressure control. They should be monitored for response and provide feedback about their progress. Weight reduction, salt restriction, discontinuation of smoking, and possibly stress management are all appropriate interventions for D.C.

Pharmacologic Management

11. What are the important treatment principles for patients with hypertension?

All antihypertensives can effectively lower blood pressure. This was evidenced in the Treatment of Mild Hypertension Study (TOMHS) which compared a diuretic, a beta blocker, an alpha blocker, an ACE inhibitor, and a calcium antagonist to placebo in a randomized trial in 902 subjects.[134] Decreases in blood pressure were significantly greater in the drug-treated patients than in those receiving the placebo; but, there were no differences between the drugs. The JNC V stated that diuretics and beta blockers are the preferred agents unless there is a specific reason to consider an alternative.[1] The JNC V chose to take this conservative stand because the only scientific evidence for reductions in morbidity and mortality have been with diuretics and beta blockers. The British Hypertension Society has recommended a similar approach.[108] This stand has been criticized primarily because of the metabolic effects of diuretics and beta blockers.[135] However, studies have demonstrated that the lipid effects of these drugs are transient[136] and that diabetic subjects enrolled in therapeutic trials achieved as much benefit from these agents as other subjects.[4,137] Therefore, these theoretical concerns have not held up when examined in rigorous therapeutic trials.

Appropriate Therapy

Table 10.8 and Figure 10.1 list the preferred and alternate agents that can be used as monotherapy for patients with hypertension.

Table 10.8	Agents Acceptable as Monotherapy
Preferred Agents	**Alternative Drugs**
Diuretics	ACE inhibitors
Beta blockers	Calcium channel blockers
	α_1-blockers
	Alpha-beta blocker (labetalol)

All of these drugs can be given alone and are generally well tolerated. Other classes of drugs (e.g., direct vasodilators, α_2-agonists) are not recommended for monotherapy because their long-term benefit is limited by salt and water retention, and because they are associated with more adverse reactions. If for some reason a diuretic or a beta blocker must be avoided, then one of the alternative agents may be selected.

The JNC previously advocated the "stepped care" approach for antihypertensive drug therapy. In this approach, the patient was started on a low dose of an agent which was gradually titrated over weeks or months to at least a moderate dose of the drug. If this was not completely effective, a second agent with a different mechanism of action was then added and the dosage was titrated upwards. This process was continued, if necessary, until the patient was taking three or even four drugs. Some aspects of this approach are still valid for some patients.

The JNC V modified the stepped care approach by suggesting that if the first drug results in adverse reactions or if it proves to be ineffective, then it should be discontinued and another agent substituted. In addition, the JNC V stated that if a diuretic was not the first drug selected for the patient, it should be added as a second drug if there are no contraindications. This is because the vast majority of patients will respond to a two drug regimen if it includes a diuretic.[1] Therefore, by appropriate selection of agents, most patients do not require more than two drugs.

Renin profiling is another method that has been used to select initial therapy for hypertension.[26] However, since the vast majority of patients have normal plasma renin values, renin profiling for all patients is an expensive tool with limited applicability.

12. What is the individualized stepped care approach and could it be used in the management of D.C.'s hypertension?

Many hypertension authorities have advocated an individualized approach to treating hypertension. This approach suggests that several factors be considered before an agent is selected for the patient. These factors include: 1) demographics; 2) co-existing diseases and risk factors; 3) previous therapy; 4) concomitant drug therapy; and 5) cost.[138,139]

Demographics

The two most common demographic variables that have been assessed include age and race. In the past, it was believed that elderly patients responded better to diuretics and calcium channel blockers and poorly to beta blockers and ACE inhibitors. However, numerous studies show that this generally is not the case (see Table 10.9).[140] Most elderly patients respond very well to beta blockers. In one study, the beta blocker was the most effective class in elderly white patients.[136] Also, as seen in Table 10.9, older patients respond very well to ACE inhibitors.

Although blacks may not respond as well as caucasians to beta blockers or ACE inhibitors, many will respond to these drugs. While these two drug classes generally would not be the first choice for blacks, they should not be avoided if they are necessary for secondary therapeutic benefits (e.g., post MI with beta blockers or CHF with ACE inhibitors). If these agents are started in black patients and are not completely effective, the addition of low doses of a thiazide diuretic will control blood pressure in the majority of patients.[1]

Co-Existing Disease States

Many antihypertensives can be used to treat other illnesses in addition to hypertension. Whenever possible, an agent that benefits both conditions should be chosen. Conversely, some antihypertensives may be relatively or absolutely contraindicated because of co-existing disease states and alternatives should be selected. For instance, beta blockers can be used to treat ischemic heart disease, migraine headaches, and some arrhythmias and to prevent re-infarctions in patients who have had an MI. However, beta blockers must be used with caution in patients with asthma, diabetes, or congestive heart failure. Table 10.10 lists some preferred alternatives when individualized therapy is necessary.

Lifestyle

The lifestyles of hypertensive patients often are affected dramatically by therapy. Patients are asked to modify their diets, change their exercise habits, and they may be required to take medication. These changes will likely be lifelong and require that they incorporate them into their daily activities. To help the patient accept these changes, their negative aspects should be minimized.

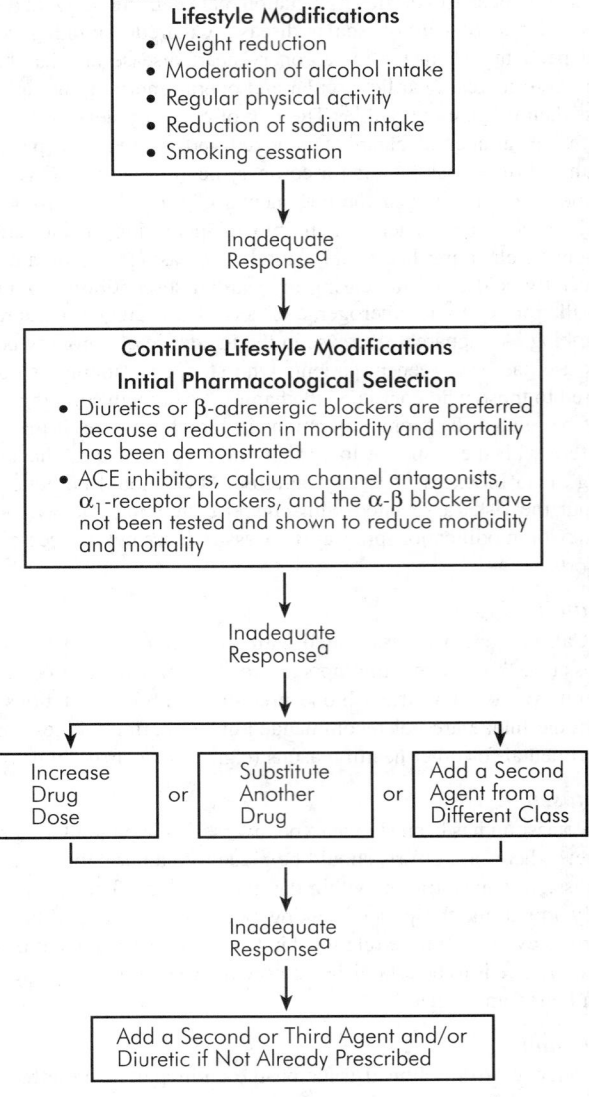

Fig 10.1 JNC V Algorithm for Selecting Hypertension Therapy
ᵃ Response means patient has achieved goal blood pressure or is making considerable progress toward this goal.

Patient Type	Diuretic	Beta Blocker	ACE Inhibitor	Calcium Antagonist	Prazosin	Clonidine
Young caucasian	45–70[a] (32)[b]	50–70 (65)	50–90 (62)	50–60 (58)	(55)	(69)
Elderly caucasian	60–65 (68)	50–70 (72)	50–60 (62)	65–75 (72)	(69)	(73)
Young black	60–70 (48)	36–55 (51)	50–65 (43)	52–75 (70)	(42)	(48)
Elderly black	70–80 (64)	36–53 (45)	50–60 (33)	55–70 (85)	(49)	(58)

Table 10.9   Percentages of Patients Who Can Achieve Blood Pressure Control With Monotherapy as a Function of Demographics[b]

[a] Represents the range responses to monotherapy used in a decision-analysis model.[140]
[b] Values in parentheses are from a VA Cooperative Study.[136,344] The decision analysis did not assess prazosin or clonidine.

Antihypertensive medication has been associated with a wide variety of adverse effects. However, in many cases these side effects may be related to hypertension rather than the drugs. Common symptoms generally thought to be due to drug therapy include sedation, impotence, dizziness, fatigue, and many others. Interestingly, the TOMHS trial and others have found that subjective symptoms of quality of life tend to be better with drug therapy than with placebo.[134] Trials have found that the often-held belief that beta blockers are poorly tolerated is not substantiated with large clinical trials.[136] Therefore, agents listed in Table 10.8 are all generally well tolerated and should not be avoided for theoretical concerns about adverse reactions. If a patient develops a suspected adverse effect, then alternatives may be considered.

The frequency of administration of antihypertensive medications must be considered because it influences patients' lifestyles. Ideally, less frequent administration is desirable. However, this does not necessarily mean that antihypertensive therapy must be given once daily. One study found that compliance with prescribed dosages was 87% with once, 81% with twice, 77% with three, and 39% with four times daily dosing.[141] Another study found compliance to be 86% with once, 78% with twice, 58% with three times, and 46% with four times daily dosing.[142] Only the three times daily dosing had significantly lower compliance rates than once or twice. Neither of these studies found significant differences between once or twice daily dosing. Agents that are sustained-release products are often much more expensive than other alternatives. Therefore, most patients can be treated with less expensive, immediate-release products given once or twice daily. If patients have difficulty adhering to a regimen that is administered twice a day, then once-a-day, sustained-release alternatives, or medications with a 24-hour duration, can be considered.

Nearly all antihypertensives can be given once or twice daily.[1] Many of these are available as generic preparations. The duration of action (pharmacodynamics) is much longer than the serum half-life would predict, making less frequent dosing possible. Numerous studies and clinical practice demonstrate that hydrochlorothiazide (HCTZ) is effective when administered once a day.[1,143] Propranolol has been given once daily successfully, but generally it should be given twice daily.[144–146] Other agents that are traditionally given in multiple daily doses, but which are effective when given twice daily include captopril[147–149] and verapamil.[150–152] Several beta blockers and ACE inhibitors can be given once daily due to their long durations of action.[1]

Drug Therapy

Previous. Patients should be questioned about any previous therapy that may have been ineffective or caused adverse reactions. This may reveal agents that are contraindicated in a given patient. Also patients who have a history of poor compliance to hypertensive therapy should be monitored carefully.

Concomitant. Antihypertensive agents may interact with other drugs.[1] For instance, verapamil and possibly diltiazem can increase serum concentrations of digoxin and carbamazepine. Diuretics may increase lithium serum concentrations. Alternatively, some drugs may increase or decrease the efficacy of antihypertensive drugs (e.g., nonsteroidal anti-inflammatory drugs, sympathomimetics). Therefore, careful drug selection or dosage initiation is essential in these cases.

Cost

The costs of treating hypertension are substantial and include expenses for diagnostic laboratory workups, office visits, and medication. Although the cost of a given drug should not be the primary determining factor in the selection of drug therapy, it is a significant consideration since the costs of blood pressure medications vary widely. Many patients cannot afford costly regimens and some patients may be on other expensive therapies such as lipid lowering drugs. However, it is possible to design an antihypertensive regimen that has a reasonable cost without compromising therapeutic efficacy.

Considering all of these factors, D.C. should be initially started on a low dose diuretic. If the goal blood pressure is not achieved, then a second agent can be added. Alternatively, if D.C. experiences a significant adverse effect with a diuretic, then an agent from another class can be substituted.

Categories of Antihypertensive Drugs

13. What categories of antihypertensive drugs could be used to treat D.C.'s hypertension and how should a drug be selected?

D.C. has Stage 2 hypertension and probably will need antihypertensive medication in addition to lifestyle modifications. The drug of first choice for D.C. would be a diuretic.[1] If this is not completely effective, then a second agent should be added. Available alternatives include beta blockers, ACE inhibitors, calcium antagonists, alpha blockers, alpha-beta blockers, and centrally-acting sympatholytics (e.g., clonidine, guanabenz, guanfacine, methyldopa).

Diuretics

Diuretics have been studied extensively in large clinical trials and have been the drugs most commonly prescribed in the U.S. They are very effective, well tolerated, and most can be given once a day. Concerns have been raised about the biochemical alterations that occur with the diuretics (e.g., hypokalemia, hyperuricemia, hyperglycemia, and hypercholesterolemia). These problems were more prevalent in the past when very high doses were commonly prescribed (e.g., HCTZ 150 to 200 mg/day), but they have been minimized by using lower doses (e.g., HCTZ 12.5 to 25 mg). Additionally, it often is possible to reverse these biochemical changes with dietary modifications. For example, reducing the dietary intake of sodium can reduce hypokalemia. Reducing the intake of fats, especially saturated fat, can counter diuretics' tendency to alter serum lipids. Additionally, the effects of diuretics on lipids appear to be modest and temporary.[134,136] More importantly, diu-

Table 10.10	Individualized Drug Therapy Based Upon Special Patient Characteristics[1,a]		
Clinical Situation	Preferred Agent(s)	Requires Special Monitoring	Relatively or Absolutely Contraindicated
Angina pectoris	Beta blockers; Calcium antagonists		Direct vasodilators
Cardiac failure	Diuretics; ACE inhibitors		Beta blockers; calcium antag- onists; labetalol
Post MI	Beta blocker without ISA		Direct vasodilators
Renal artery stenosis[b]			ACE inhibitors
Renal insufficiency:			
Early renal insufficiency	ACE inhibitors?[c]; calcium antago- nists?[c]		Potassium supplements; potassium sparing agents
Advanced renal insufficiency	Loop diuretics	ACE inhibitors	Potassium supplements; potassium sparing agents
Asthma, COAD			Beta blockers; labetalol
Diabetes mellitus Type I		Beta blockers	
Hyperlipidemia		Diuretics; beta blockers	
Vascular headaches	Beta blockers		Direct vasodilators

a ACE = Angiotensin converting enzyme; COAD = Chronic obstructive airway disease; MI = Myocardial infarction.
b Either bilateral renal arterial disease or severe stenosis in artery to a solitary kidney.
c Encouraging data is emerging for these agents, but it is not known if they are superior to other antihypertensives.

retics are one of only two classes of agents that have been shown to reduce cardiovascular morbidity and mortality. Previous concerns that the diuretics were not able to reduce coronary events have been refuted with the publication of additional large clinical trials.[98,99] Therefore, diuretics are considered the drugs of choice for elderly or black patients who do not have contraindications or other strong reasons to avoid them.

Beta Blockers

Beta blockers are effective antihypertensives and can control blood pressure in the majority of patients (see Table 10.9). Along with diuretics, they are the only agents that have been shown to reduce morbidity and mortality in hypertension. However, they are not as effective in black patients and therefore, would not be the best choice for D.C. Beta blockers should be avoided in patients with asthma, insulin-dependent diabetes, CHF caused by systolic dysfunction, and peripheral vascular disease. The biochemical effects of beta blockers include alterations of lipids and increased glucose concentrations. However, these biochemical changes have been found to generally be temporary or have minimal clinical significance.

Angiotensin-Converting Enzyme (ACE) Inhibitors

Angiotensin-converting enzyme inhibitors also are effective antihypertensive agents when used as monotherapy. They have

been shown to reduce morbidity and mortality in patients with CHF (see Chapter 15: Congestive Heart Failure). However, they have not been subjected to clinical trials to assess their ability to reduce morbidity in hypertension. Generally, they do not cause metabolic effects, but they do require special monitoring to detect hyperkalemia and further progression of renal dysfunction in those patients with prior renal disease or volume depletion. ACE inhibitors are not as effective as diuretics in black patients such as D.C. However, when combined with low doses of a diuretic, ACE inhibitors can effectively lower blood pressure in blacks.

Calcium Antagonists

Calcium antagonists are vasodilators that also are effective in the treatment of ischemic heart disease. As with ACE inhibitors, it is not known if these agents reduce morbidity and mortality in hypertensive patients. Calcium antagonists are effective as monotherapy and they are especially effective in black patients like D.C. They can be combined with a diuretic or a beta blocker; however, since nifedipine and other dihydropyridine derivatives cause a mild natriuresis, the combination with a diuretic may not be additive. The combination of a beta blocker with verapamil or diltiazem should be used cautiously due to additive bradycardia, heart block, and myocardial depressant effects.

Peripheral α₁-Antagonists

Peripheral α_1-antagonists (e.g., doxazosin, prazosin, terazosin) are considered acceptable agents for monotherapy. However, they may cause more adverse reactions than the drugs listed above.[136] In addition, some patients require the addition of a diuretic due to drug-induced fluid retention.

Central α₂-Agonists

Central α_2-agonists (e.g., clonidine, guanabenz, guanfacine, methyldopa) have been used as monotherapy, but they should be reserved for second- or third-line therapy. These drugs cause more frequent side effects such as sedation, dizziness, dry mouth, fatigue, and sexual dysfunction.[136] While these agents have been used alone, they frequently cause fluid retention and loss of blood pressure control. Therefore, in most cases they should be combined with a diuretic.

Adrenergic Antagonists

Adrenergic antagonists (e.g., reserpine, guanadrel, guanethidine) usually are used for third- or fourth-line therapy and generally require concurrent diuretic therapy. Although reserpine is inexpensive and can be given once daily, its acceptance by patients is limited because it causes drowsiness and nasal stuffiness. Guanadrel and guanethidine have numerous significant adverse effects and should be avoided.

Direct Vasodilators

Direct vasodilators (e.g., hydralazine, minoxidil) also are used for third- or fourth-line therapy. These drugs cause fluid retention and reflex tachycardia and generally are combined with both a diuretic and a beta blocker or another agent which slows heart rate (e.g., clonidine, diltiazem, or verapamil).

Diuretics

Therapeutic Effect and Choice of Agent

14. Which diuretic should be selected for D.C. and what would be the expected reduction in the blood pressure?

Thiazides. Thiazide diuretics are the diuretics of choice for hypertension. They are effective in 45% to 80% of patients.[136,140] The two agents that have been used primarily in clinical trials are hydrochlorothiazide and chlorthalidone.[12,96,100–105,153–156] Although there is no reason to choose one of these drugs over the other, hydrochlorothiazide usually is selected. It is inexpensive and can be given once daily.[143] Typically, thiazide diuretics lower systolic blood pressure by 15 to 20 mm Hg and diastolic blood pressure by 8 to 15 mm Hg.[134,136] The usual starting dose for hydrochlorothiazide is 12.5 or 25 mg once daily. At these lower dosages, adverse reactions and metabolic effects are reduced markedly.[157] In fact, the TOMHS trial found that adverse reactions from the diuretic were no different from those experienced with a placebo and the VA Cooperative group found that the diuretics were the best tolerated of six drug classes.[134,136]

D.C. is a good candidate for a diuretic for several reasons. First, as a black patient with Stage 2 hypertension, he should have an excellent response to diuretics. Secondly, D.C. has financial difficulties and the cost of therapy can be a significant factor in adherence to therapy; generic hydrochlorothiazide is the least expensive antihypertensive.

D.C. has no conditions or previous reasons to contraindicate a diuretic. His cholesterol is elevated, but only moderately, and hydrochlorothiazide is unlikely to have a significant effect on his cholesterol levels. He has renal insufficiency, but it is not severe enough to avoid the use of a thiazide. Control of his blood pressure should help stabilize his renal dysfunction.

An appropriate starting dose for D.C. is 25 mg/day. Because of the degree of his pressure elevation and his prior history of difficulty controlling his blood pressure, it is unlikely that 12.5 mg/day would be effective. The final dose that will be effective for D.C. is unpredictable; therefore, he should return in two to four weeks to assess his blood pressure control. The full effects of the diuretic should be achieved within three to four weeks. If the blood pressure is not controlled adequately, the dosage could possibly be titrated upwards. While the maximum recommended dose for hydrochlorothiazide is 50 mg, many clinicians do not use dosages above 25 mg.[1] Alternatively, if there is some response to 25 mg HCTZ, but control remains inadequate, then a second agent can be added. The guidelines suggest that if a diuretic is not the first agent selected, it should be the second drug used in order to improve response.[1]

Furosemide is a more potent diuretic than the thiazides, but it does not have the added property of arterial vasodilation seen with thiazides. HCTZ is consistently more effective at lowering blood pressure.[158–160] Furosemide has a much shorter duration of antihypertensive effect and should be given two or three times daily. The only valid role for furosemide or other loop diuretics is for patients with significant renal insufficiency (e.g., creatinine clearance <30 cc/minute) or when a more potent diuretic is desired (e.g., CHF).

Potassium-sparing diuretics should be reserved for patients who have been treated with a diuretic and then develop hypokalemia. Since most patients do not develop hypokalemia with low dosages of diuretics, it is not rational to start all patients on a combination (e.g., Dyazide, Maxide). Used alone, triamterene (Dyrenium), spironolactone (Aldactone), and amiloride (Midamor) have modest antihypertensive effects,[161] but generally less than those from a thiazide.

Patient Education

15. How should D.C. be counseled about his diuretic therapy?

D.C. should be told that the diuretic is prescribed to lower his blood pressure and that he should try to take it at about the same time each day. Missed doses should be taken as soon as possible within the day (as soon as he remembers), but double doses should be avoided. D.C. should be told that many patients experience in-

creased urination when starting this medicine, but this should diminish with time. He should not take his diuretic in the evening to avoid nocturia and should be encouraged to report any adverse reactions that might result from hypokalemia or other electrolyte abnormalities (e.g., leg cramps, muscle weakness) or anything he thinks may be related to the drug.

Monitoring Therapy

16. After three weeks of HCTZ 25 mg QD, D.C. returns to the clinic for evaluation. He has no complaints and his headache is resolved. His BP is 152/94 mm Hg without orthostasis. His weight is 106 kg, serum potassium is 3.8 mEq/L, uric acid is 9.0 mg/dL, and the other laboratory values are unchanged. What subjective and objective data should be evaluated when assessing efficacy and adverse reactions of thiazide diuretics? What is your assessment from the data given above? [SI units: K 3.8 mmol/L; uric acid 535 mmol/L]

In evaluating D.C.'s response to therapy, the clinician must assess whether the desired therapeutic goal has been achieved and if adverse reactions have occurred. D.C.'s blood pressure should be measured at least twice in the seated position and the values averaged. Ideally, blood pressure measurements should be made in both the seated and standing positions to detect orthostatic changes. Because of renal insufficiency, the goal blood pressure for D.C. is a systolic blood pressure of less than 130 mm Hg and a diastolic blood pressure of less than 85 mm Hg. Progress has been made in lowering D.C.'s pressure, but the goals have not been met. His weight has been reduced by only 2 kg, showing little effect from his diet and diuresis. The inadequate blood pressure response could be due to a lack of compliance, an inadequate time to reach maximal effect, or a suboptimal dose. It must be decided whether to: 1) continue observing D.C.'s response while retaining the current dose for a longer period of time, 2) increase the dose, or 3) add a second drug.

D.C. should be questioned about whether he experienced increased urination which would be an expected pharmacologic effect. Increased urination usually subsides after the first few weeks of therapy, but may be a reason for noncompliance. He should be evaluated for signs or symptoms of metabolic effects such as hypokalemia, hyperglycemia, or hyperuricemia. His serum potassium has dropped slightly and his uric acid has risen. This could be explained by normal variations in laboratory measurements or as a sign of drug-induced abnormalities. D.C. should be questioned about muscle cramps, weakness, or new joint pains. Monitoring for adverse effects is discussed further below.

Adverse Effects

17. Diuretic-Induced Hypokalemia. What is the significance of diuretic-induced hypokalemia and are the changes seen in D.C. of concern?

Serum potassium concentrations commonly are reduced by thiazide and loop diuretics with a reported incidence in ambulatory patients ranging from 14% to 60%.[162,163] Diuretic-induced hypokalemia is dose related and usually noticeable within the first week of therapy.[164] At doses of 25 mg/day or less, only 10% to 15% of patients develop hypokalemia. Most often the diuretic-induced hypokalemia is mild, resulting in a mean decrease in serum potassium of 0.1 to 0.6 mEq/L.[134,165,166] The serum potassium concentrations reach a nadir within the first month of therapy, and generally remain stable thereafter. Although 98% of total body potassium is intracellular, the clinical manifestations of potassium deficiency correlate better with serum concentrations than with total body potassium levels.[166] Therefore, a decrease in the serum potassium concentrations can be important. However, the clinical significance of a decrease of 0.1 to 0.6 mEq/L when serum potassium concentrations are still in the normal range is unknown. D.C.'s potassium has dropped slightly and is at the lower end of the normal range. Since he is not taking digoxin and has no previous history of heart disease, there is no cause for alarm. He can either be advised about dietary modification and seen again in two to four weeks, or he can be given a low dose of a potassium supplement. (Also see Question 18.)

The controversy over diuretic-induced hypokalemia was heightened with the results of the Multiple Risk Factor Intervention Trial (MRFIT). This study documented a nonsignificant decrease in coronary artery disease in hypertensive patients despite "special interventions" to lower blood pressure, decrease tobacco smoking, and decrease high serum lipid concentrations. Therefore, a retrospective analysis of the data was performed.[167] It was discovered that a subgroup of the "special intervention" patients with baseline electrocardiographic abnormalities who then received a diuretic had an increase in coronary artery disease mortality rate, thereby potentially offsetting the results of the other members in the study population. However, these findings were not observed in the HDFP,[168] or SHEP[12] trials, where a better outcome was actually noted in those patients with baseline ECG abnormalities who received a diuretic compared to those receiving placebo. Although adverse cardiac effects have not been substantiated in recent studies, it would be prudent to initiate low doses of diuretics to avoid hypokalemia. If hypokalemia occurs it should be treated. Normal, healthy patients should have their serum potassium checked at baseline and within four weeks of initiating diuretic therapy or following increases in dose. Potassium supplementation and/or potassium-sparing diuretic therapy should be initiated if serum levels fall below 3.5 mEq/L. Hypokalemic patients may experience symptoms of weakness and muscle cramps. Other conditions that may contribute to lower potassium concentrations include chronic diarrhea, high dose corticosteroid use, and hyperaldosteronism; patients with these conditions may need potassium supplementation with diuretic therapy.

As described above, the incidence of hypokalemia is relatively low. For those patients who do develop hypokalemia, the dose of potassium to correct the deficit is highly variable, ranging from 10 to >100 mEq/day. The average replacement dose is 30 to 60 mEq/day.

18. *Potassium Supplementation.* **If potassium supplementation is needed to manage diuretic-induced hypokalemia, what therapeutic options can be used in the ambulatory setting?**

Patients can be encouraged to eat potassium rich foods to help maintain normal potassium concentrations. Dried fruit, bananas, potatoes, and avocados are a few examples of foods containing potassium. However, the use of dietary measures to replenish potassium has the disadvantages of excessive calorie intake and high cost. For instance, one medium size banana, has 11.5 mEq of potassium while the usual replacement dose of potassium is from 20 to 40 mEq/day. Thus, potassium rich foods may help prevent the development of hypokalemia in some patients, but they cannot be used as sole therapy to correct severe hypokalemia (<3.0 mEq/L).

Salt substitutes containing potassium salts may be recommended to hypertensive patients to prevent decreases in potassium concentration while avoiding sodium consumption. One teaspoonful of Morton's Salt Substitute contains 70 mEq of potassium and 0.02 mEq of sodium per teaspoonful. Although tolerable when used modestly, patients often complain about the palatability of these agents. Patients with renal impairment, heart failure, a history of electrolyte imbalance, or patients receiving potassium-sparing diuretics or potassium supplementations must be cautioned concerning the use of salt substitutes because of the increased risk of hyperkalemia.

Asymptomatic diuretic-induced hypokalemia can be corrected with oral potassium chloride preparations. Potassium-sparing diuretics (i.e., spironolactone, triamterene, amiloride) also are prescribed frequently in combination with the thiazide diuretics; however, the potassium-conserving capability of these diuretics is difficult to predict quantitatively in specific patients. Potassium-sparing diuretics may be as effective as potassium supplementation in maintaining serum concentrations of potassium within the normal range.[169] Some patients will require both means of supplementation to maintain normal concentrations. Therefore, monitoring of serum potassium is necessary with potassium-sparing diuretics since hypokalemia or hyperkalemia may occur.

Potassium chloride, bicarbonate, gluconate, acetate, and citrate salts are available as single ingredients and/or components of combination products. The chloride salt is preferred because thiazides can cause hypochloremia along with the hypokalemia to produce a metabolic alkalosis. Potassium salts other than potassium chloride cannot correct hypokalemic, hypochloremic, or metabolic alkalosis.

Oral potassium supplementation is available in liquid, enteric-coated, and slow-release preparations. The slow-release tablets are preferred since they are reported to cause fewer gastrointestinal (GI) adverse effects (e.g., nausea, vomiting, abdominal discomfort, diarrhea) than the liquid and enteric-coated tablets. Small bowel ulcerations have been documented with enteric-coated tablets and these should be avoided. The slow release potassium chloride (KCl) preparations come in a variety of forms including: 1) either sugar-coated (Slow-K, Kaon-Cl) or film coated (K-Tab, Klotrix) tablets; 2) KCl incorporated into a wax matrix, controlled release tablet (K-Dur); or 3) a gelatin capsule containing microencapsulated KCl crystals that are coated with a water polymer (Micro-K). These slow-release tablets and capsule formulations of KCl should not be crushed or chewed and should be taken with food or a large glass of water.

Because D.C.'s potassium is still 3.8 mEq/L, he should be encouraged to continue to improve his low salt diet which may increase his serum potassium. In addition, he should be encouraged to use a salt substitute and to eat more fresh fruits and vegetables to increase his potassium intake. A potassium preparation is not indicated at this time.

19. *Diuretic-Induced Hyperuricemia and Hyperglycemia.* **What is the clinical significance of diuretic-induced hyperuricemia and hyperglycemia? Should these adverse effects, which were evident in D.C.'s last work-up, be treated?**

Glucose. Altered glucose metabolism is a recognized complication of diuretic therapy, but patient response is variable. Patients with diabetes and impaired glucose tolerance are the individuals who most commonly exhibit exaggerated glucose concentrations with diuretic therapy.[170,171] However, this effect also has been observed in nondiabetic patients.[172,173] Diuretic-induced hyperglycemia is dose dependent; therefore, low initial doses of diuretics are recommended.[174,175] Hyperosmolar, nonketotic coma has been documented with 50 to 100 mg of hydrochlorothiazide.[176,177] The TOMHS trial found that serum glucose concentrations actually declined in patients who received chlorthalidone.[134] In the VA Cooperative trial, the fasting blood glucose increased 6.7 mg/dL in patients treated with hydrochlorothiazide.[136] It does not appear that these minor changes are significant in the general population of hypertensive patients. Approximately 20% of SHEP participants had diabetes and they achieved similar reductions in morbidity and mortality as did those patients who did not have diabetes.[137]

The hyperglycemic effect of diuretics appears to be associated with potassium loss. It has been noted that patients with decreased serum potassium concentration are more likely to exhibit impaired glucose tolerance.[172,178] This is supported by a report that potassium supplementation prevented changes in glucose intolerance with thiazides.[179] Therefore, it would be prudent to maintain normal serum potassium concentrations in diabetic patients treated with diuretic therapy.

Diabetes is not a contraindication to the use of diuretics.[1,4] In most patients, diuretic therapy has no perceptible effect on diabetes or the serum concentration of glucose. If hyperglycemia occurs, it can be managed by altering the patient's diet or increasing the dose of insulin or oral antidiabetic agent. D.C. is at increased risk for hyperglycemia due to his family history. Since his initial serum glucose was normal, this should be monitored at least once a year. D.C. should receive patient education regarding signs and symptoms of hyperglycemia and appropriate dietary instruction.

Uric Acid. Thiazide and loop diuretics are known to increase serum uric acid levels in a dose-dependent manner;[180] however, the precise mechanism by which they act is not clear. It has been suggested that increased proximal tubular renal reabsorption, decreased tubular secretion, and/or increased post-secretory reabsorption of uric acid contribute to increases in diuretic-induced hyperuricemia.[181]

In most patients, diuretic-induced hyperuricemia is asymptomatic and does not require treatment. If recurrent, acute gouty attacks occur, treatment is required. Fortunately, the incidence of gout with diuretic therapy is low. In the HDFP study, only 15 of 3693 patients discontinued thiazide diuretic therapy secondary to symptoms associated with gout.[182] A history of gout is not a contraindication to diuretic therapy. If gout develops, uric acid levels will return to pretreatment values after the diuretic is discontinued. D.C.'s elevated serum uric acid concentration is not high enough to require further evaluations and does not require treatment unless he develops repeated acute attacks of gout. Therefore, at the present time the hydrochlorothiazide should be continued.

20. Diuretic-Induced Alterations in Serum Lipids. What is the significance of diuretic-induced alterations in serum lipids and should D.C. receive treatment?

Controversy exists over the significance of the effects of diuretics on the lipid profile. These effects have been implicated as one possible reason for the lack of significant reduction in coronary morbidity in many clinical trials. These alterations can be characterized by increases in total cholesterol of 4% to 13%, low-density lipoprotein cholesterol of 7% to 29%, very low-density lipoprotein (VLDL) cholesterol of 7% to 56%, and total triglycerides of 14% to 37%.[183] Grimm and colleagues[184] have demonstrated that dietary fat restrictions help prevent the hyperlipidemic effects of diuretics. On the other hand, the Multiple Risk Factor Intervention Trial (MRFIT)[185] showed elevated total cholesterol with thiazide diuretic therapy despite dietary modifications. Contrary to other biochemical disturbances, diuretic-induced changes in the lipid profile are not dose related since low dose diuretic therapy has no less of an effect than higher doses.[164,184]

All of these considerations may not be necessary since it has been suggested that diuretic-induced lipid changes may only be transient. Many trials lasting longer than one year have not shown a persistent hyperlipidemic effect with diuretic therapy,[186–188] and in fact, the TOMHS trial found that total and LDL-cholesterol actually decreased in thiazide-treated patients.[134] However, cholesterol reductions with thiazides were less than those achieved with other classes of antihypertensive agents. The VA Cooperative trial found no differences in serum cholesterol between diuretic- and placebo-treated patients after one year of therapy.[136] More importantly, the theoretical concerns about whether diuretics fail to lower coronary heart risk because of lipid effects have been put to rest. One meta-analysis has found that the risk of coronary heart disease

was reduced 16% which was statistically significant.[98] Another meta-analysis found a 26% reduction in coronary mortality.[99] Trials included in these meta-analyses primarily included diuretics and beta blockers.

Diuretic therapy should not be avoided in patients such as D.C. who have normal or borderline lipid profiles. Clinical judgement should be used in patients with significant hyperlipidemia in which the potential for a diuretic-induced rise in LDL-cholesterol or triglycerides would warrant antilipidemic drug therapy. D.C. has a borderline cholesterol value which would not preclude the use of a diuretic. He should be counseled on dietary interventions to lower his blood pressure and cholesterol levels.

21. Other Diuretic-Induced Metabolic Abnormalities. What other metabolic abnormalities should be monitored as a result of D.C.'s diuretic therapy? (See also Chapter 15: Congestive Heart Failure.)

Hypercalcemia. Thiazide diuretics decrease urinary calcium excretion and have been used to prevent stone formation in patients with calcium-related kidney stones.[189] The resulting elevations in serum calcium concentrations usually are asymptomatic and of little clinical significance.[190] In contrast to thiazides, the loop diuretics increase renal clearance of calcium and have been used for acute management of severe hypercalcemia. Baseline serum calcium concentrations should be obtained when diuretic therapy is started and then checked as needed during the course of therapy.

Hypomagnesemia is an often overlooked metabolic complication of diuretic therapy. Both thiazide and loop diuretics increase urinary excretion of magnesium in a dose-dependent manner.[191] The addition of amiloride, a potassium-sparing diuretic, prevents changes in magnesium clearance when used in combination with a thiazide diuretic.[192] Manifestations of magnesium deficiency include muscle weakness, muscle tremor or twitching, mental status changes, and cardiac arrhythmias (including torsades de pointe). Low concentrations of magnesium are common in older, alcoholic, or malnourished patients.

Hypomagnesemia is frequently associated with hypokalemia.[193] Potassium repletion may be refractory in the presence of uncorrected magnesium depletion. Therefore, if management of diuretic-induced hypokalemia is difficult, supplementation of magnesium may be necessary.[194]

Hyponatremia is a metabolic complication associated with diuretic therapy. Changes in sodium concentration are usually small and patients are asymptomatic. Severe hyponatremia (<120 mEq/L) has been reported rarely with diuretic administration. Older, female patients who are underweight are at a higher risk of developing diuretic-induced hyponatremia.[195] Decreased renal excretion of free water, inappropriate antidiuretic hormone secretion, urinary sodium loss, and depletion of magnesium and potassium may all contribute to diuretic-induced hyponatremia.[196]

Therapeutic Principles for the Selection of the Second Antihypertensive Agent

22. D.C.'s systolic blood pressures continue to be 148–152 mm Hg and his diastolic blood pressures are 90–92 mm Hg. He has been taking HCTZ 25 mg/day for 4 weeks. He states that he has only missed 1–2 doses during that time. Today his serum potassium level is 3.6 mEq/L. What treatment principles are important for D.C.?

D.C.'s blood pressures are still elevated. It generally takes at least three to four weeks to be assured that a full antihypertensive effect has been achieved. If he had no other risk factors and no signs of target organ damage, it might be reasonable to attempt continued lifestyle modifications. However, D.C. has renal insufficiency and requires more aggressive therapy. Before considering the therapeutic options, the clinician must examine potential reasons for inadequate success with an antihypertensive (see Table 10.11).

One option would be to increase the dose of hydrochlorothiazide to 50 mg. However, since D.C.'s potassium dropped from 4.0 mEq/L to 3.6 mEq/L, further dosage increases may require potassium supplementation. The second option would be to discontinue the hydrochlorothiazide and substitute a different agent. This would not be reasonable because D.C. has benefited significantly from the diuretic. In addition, other agents may not be completely effective for D.C. without a diuretic. The third option is to add a second agent. The latter option would appear to be preferred.

Tables 10.8 and 10.9 list the agents best suited as additions to D.C.'s diuretic. It is not possible to predict clinical response or adverse reactions in a specific patient. Essentially, drugs from any of these classes could be selected since the efficacy of these agents is very similar when combined with a diuretic. This is even true in black patients where 70% to 80% will respond to a beta blocker or an ACE inhibitor in combination with a diuretic. There is no single agent that could be considered most appropriate for all patients. Each patient must be viewed individually and the drug selected for the specific patient in mind. The clinician should determine which other agents the patient has received. If these were ineffective or caused adverse reactions, they should be avoided. Likewise, the clinician should determine if the patient has relative contraindications to any of the agents listed. Once- or twice-a-day dosing regimens are more likely to be maintained on a regular

Table 10.11	Clinical Causes for Lack of Responsiveness to Therapy[1]

Nonadherence to Therapy
- Cost of medication
- Instructions not clear and/or not given to patient in writing
- Inadequate or no patient education
- Lack of patient involvement in treatment plan
- Side effects of medication
- Organic brain syndrome (e.g., memory deficit)
- Inconvenient dosing

Drug-Related Causes
- Doses too low
- Inappropriate combinations (2 drugs with similar mechanisms)
- *Drug Interactions*
  Nonsteroidal anti-inflammatory drugs
  Oral contraceptives
  Sympathomimetics
  Antidepressants
  Adrenal steroids
  Nasal decongestants
  Licorice-containing substances (e.g., chewing tobacco)
  Cocaine
  Cyclosporine
  Erythropoietin

Associated Conditions
- Increasing obesity
- Alcohol intake >1 oz/day

Secondary Causes (see Table 10.4)

Volume Overload

Inadequate Diuretic Therapy
- Excess sodium intake
- Fluid retention from reduction of blood pressure
- Progressive renal damage

Pseudohypertension

basis. The cost of therapy also must be considered. Finally, many antihypertensives can be used for more than one indication. For instance, a beta blocker may be preferred for a patient who has had a recent MI, while an ACE inhibitor would be preferred for a patient with congestive heart failure (see Table 10.10).

D.C. has no other active diseases that would influence the selection of a second antihypertensive drug. He has a history of peptic ulcer disease that occurred ten years ago. Although reserpine in large doses (i.e., >1 mg/day) is associated with drug-induced peptic ulcer disease, such large doses are not used in the treatment of hypertension. Furthermore, there is no evidence that D.C.'s peptic ulcer disease is active. Chronic obstructive airway disease (COAD), although not noted here, might be a problem in D.C. because of his 35-year history of smoking. COAD would preclude the use of β-adrenergic blocking drugs. Blacks tend to have high volume, low renin hypertension and these patients tend not to respond as favorably to beta blockers and ACE inhibitors as caucasian patients. However, these differences can be overcome with the combined use of a diuretic. Centrally-acting α_2-agonists such as methyldopa, clonidine, guanabenz, and guanfacine are all similar in efficacy. However, they are associated with more frequent adverse reactions that require discontinuation of therapy (e.g., dry mouth, sedation, fatigue, impotence).[136] While it was once thought that only certain agents caused a reversal of left ventricular hypertrophy, recent evidence suggests that all hypertensive drugs share this property.[54,134] Therefore, diuretics, beta blockers, ACE inhibitors, calcium antagonists, and alpha blockers all reverse left ventricular hypertrophy.

The ACE inhibitors have gained a great deal of popularity for patients with renal insufficiency, diabetes, or congestive heart failure. Indeed, they are preferred in patients with CHF, along with diuretics, since they have been documented to reduce morbidity and mortality. However, data supporting their use in hypertensive patients with renal insufficiency and diabetes are limited.[1-4] Continuing research should help determine the role of ACE inhibitors in these patients. Calcium channel blockers also have been shown to be useful in the latter populations.[3]

Based upon all of these considerations, the two most attractive choices for D.C. would be either an ACE inhibitor or a calcium antagonist. ACE inhibitors can cause significant life-threatening hypotension leading to acute renal insufficiency in volume-depleted patients (e.g., those who have been over-diuresed). There is no evidence that D.C. is volume depleted. When this is a concern, one to two doses of the diuretic may be held before initiating the ACE inhibitor. Depending upon the dose, it also may be necessary to lower the diuretic dose.

When agents are combined they should have different mechanisms of action. This often allows for a lower dosage of each agent which may reduce the potential for adverse reactions. If a diuretic is not chosen as the initial agent, it generally should be the second drug in the regimen.[1] Once the patient's blood pressure has been controlled for a year, attempts should be made to reduce the dose(s) or discontinue one agent (step-down therapy).[1,197]

β-Adrenergic Blockers

Role in Treatment of Hypertension

23. What is the role of β-adrenergic blockers in the treatment of hypertension?

Beta blockers are considered the second preferred class of antihypertensive agents for first-line therapy because data support their ability to reduce morbidity and mortality.[1,108] Beta blockers reduce systolic blood pressure by 10 to 20 mm Hg and diastolic pressure by 10 to 15 mm Hg.[134] These agents can control blood pressure in

35% to 70% of patients with some racially determined predictability.[136,140] The lowest response rates have been in elderly black patients.[136] Other studies have found that up to 47% to 60% of black patients can achieve blood pressure control with beta blockers.[198-201] Additionally, all beta blockers have similar activity and patients who fail to respond to one generally fail to respond to others.[1,202-205]

The clinical advantages of beta blockers in the treatment of hypertension include a proven ability to reduce the complications of hypertension; a low incidence of serious adverse reactions; prolonged duration of action (requiring only once- or twice-a-day administration); minimal sexual dysfunction; and low cost when generic products of older agents are chosen. They have fewer CNS effects than centrally-acting drugs. At one time beta blockers were the most widely prescribed agents for hypertension worldwide, but their use diminished after the introduction of ACE inhibitors and calcium antagonists. Despite all of these advantages, beta blockers are associated with numerous adverse metabolic effects and bothersome side effects that limit their universal use in all hypertensive patients.

Pharmacologic Differences Between Various Agents

24. What are the significant pharmacologic differences between the various beta blockers?

Pharmacologic differences between the various beta blockers include cardioselectivity, intrinsic sympathomimetic activity (ISA), and relative lipid solubility (see Table 10.12). These differences have little clinical significance in most situations and generally should not be used for the selection of an agent. Propranolol was the first beta blocker marketed in the U.S. and it is the most widely studied. It continues to be prescribed heavily despite a lack of cardioselectivity or ISA.

Cardioselectivity. β_1-adrenergic receptors are found predominantly in the heart and β_2-adrenergic receptors are located primarily in the lungs, kidneys, and peripheral arteriolar endothelium. Recent evidence also indicates the presence of low affinity β_1 receptors in the lung and low affinity β_2 receptors in the heart. Beta blockers that demonstrate relative cardioselectivity (β_1-blocking activity) include atenolol, betaxolol, metoprolol, and acebutolol. In low doses, these agents predominately antagonize cardiac beta receptors with less activity on β_2 receptors in the lung or bronchial tissue. However, this selectivity is not absolute. For instance, asthma has been precipitated by these drugs when they are used in

higher doses.[206,207] Nonselective beta blockers also may have disadvantages in patients with insulin-dependent diabetes (see Question 31).[208]

β_2 blockade can lead to unopposed alpha-induced vasoconstriction in the periphery and this may lead to patient complaints of cold extremities or worsening of Raynaud's phenomenon.[209] Therefore, selective β_1 blockers may be preferred in patients with peripheral vascular insufficiency or Raynaud's disease.

Intrinsic Sympathomimetic Activity (ISA). Unlike pure beta blockers which completely antagonize the beta receptor, these drugs cause partial stimulation of the receptor which is still much less than a pure agonist.[210,211] When given to a patient with a slow heart rate at rest, partial agonists may increase the heart rate via their agonist properties. In patients with rapid heart rates or during exercise-induced tachycardia, however, these agents may slow heart rate because the beta blocking properties predominate. Theoretically, beta blockers with ISA are less likely to cause bradycardia, bronchospasm, reduced cardiac output, peripheral vasoconstriction, and increased plasma lipids.[210-214] However, these agents can precipitate asthma and worsen CHF. If patients have contraindications or adverse reactions to non-ISA beta blockers, generally the ISA agents also should be avoided. Perhaps, the only role for them is for patients who have severe bradycardia from non-ISA agents. Additionally, they should not be used for myocardial infarction prophylaxis as they may not be protective or may even have detrimental effects due to their agonist properties.[215]

Lipid Solubility. The lipophilic beta blockers include propranolol, metoprolol, acebutolol, penbutolol, and pindolol (see Table 10.12). These drugs tend to have larger volumes of distribution and they undergo more extensive first-pass hepatic metabolism than less lipophilic beta blockers. Therefore, these agents have greater interpatient variability in serum concentrations than less lipophilic beta blockers due to differences in hepatic blood flow between patients. For instance, typical doses of propranolol range from 40 to 480 mg/day. In years past, it was not unusual for research trials to use up to 2000 mg/day of propranolol.

The less lipophilic (more hydrophilic) beta blockers are not influenced as much by hepatic metabolism. This leads to much narrower dosage ranges (e.g., 25 to 100 mg for atenolol). However, beta blockers with low lipophilicity are excreted more in the kidney and may require dosage adjustments with renal impairment (see Table 10.13).

Table 10.12			Pharmacodynamic Properties of Beta Blockers and Dosing Schedules		
Drug	Usual Dosage Range (mg/day)[a]	Daily Dosing Frequency	Relative Selectivity	Intrinsic Sympathomimetic Activity	Lipid Solubility
Atenolol (Tenormin)	25–100	1	++	0	Low
Bisoprolol (Zebeta)	25–200	1	++	0	Low
Betaxolol (Kerlone)	5–20	1	++	0	Low
Metoprolol (Lopressor)	50–200	1 or 2	+	0	Moderate to high
Nadolol (Corgard)	20–240	1	0	0	Low
Propranolol (Inderal)	40–240	2	0	0	High
Timolol (Blocadren)	20–40	2	0	0	Low to moderate
Agents with ISA					
Acebutolol (Sectral)	200–1200	2	++	+	Moderate
Carteolol (Cartrol)	2.5–10	1	0	++	Low
Penbutolol (Levatol)	20–80	1	0	+	High
Pindolol (Visken)	10–60	2	0	+++	Moderate

[a] These dosage ranges are suggested. Higher doses have been used.

Since lipophilic beta blockers theoretically enter the CNS more readily than hydrophilic beta blockers, it has been proposed traditionally that their use may lead to increased side effects such as drowsiness, mental confusion, nightmares, or depression.[216] However, comparative studies have not demonstrated significant differences in adverse reactions between lipophilic and hydrophilic beta blockers.[217] Therefore, beta blockers should not be chosen based upon these theoretical CNS properties. The only reason to consider lipophilicity or hydrophilicity is in patients with renal or hepatic impairment.

Pharmacodynamic Properties Versus Half-Life

25. Since propranolol has a short half-life of only 4 hours, should it be given QID and would long-acting dosage forms (e.g., Inderal-LA) be useful?

While propranolol (and some other beta blockers) have short plasma half-lives, their pharmacodynamic effect lasts much longer. For instance, several studies have demonstrated that immediate-release propranolol can be given twice daily for hypertension and angina.[144,218] There is even data to suggest that immediate-release propranolol may be effective once daily;[145,219] however, its efficacy is not consistently reliable when given once daily.[146]

The long-acting propranolol product produces lower peak concentrations due to slower absorption and increased first pass metabolism.[220] One study found that the long-acting dosage form and regular propranolol were equally effective at lowering blood pressure over 24 hours when each was given once daily.[146] Therefore, there is no reason to use the long-acting dosage form in most patients. The goal should be to initiate therapy with propranolol twice daily. For patients who have difficulty taking medications twice daily (generally <20%),[141,142] therapy with an agent such as atenolol that is effective once daily would be more appropriate.

Treating Hypertension in Patients with Co-Existing Diseases

26. In which patients would beta blockers be particularly useful due to co-existing diseases?

There are several co-existing conditions that may be treated successfully with a beta blocker. Beta blockers should be considered strongly for hypertensive patients with the following co-existing conditions.

Angina. Hypertensive patients who also have angina pectoris should benefit from beta blockers. These drugs reduce heart rate and contractility and, thus, decrease myocardial oxygen requirements.

Hyperkinetic Circulation. Some patients present with hyperkinetic circulation characterized by a rapid heart rate and increased cardiac output and complaints of palpitations and anxiety. These features are much more common in young patients who may particularly benefit from beta blockade.[202,204,221] In general, beta blockers are very useful in treating younger hypertensive patients.

Selected Ventricular and Supraventricular Arrhythmias. Beta blockers are very effective for slowing the rate of cardiac conduction and may be useful in patients with paroxysmal supraventricular tachycardia or atrial fibrillation. Beta blockers commonly are prescribed for patients with mitral valve prolapse who develop tachycardia and anxiety symptoms. Finally, beta blockers are effective in treating ventricular arrhythmias resulting from idiopathic hypertrophic subaortic stenosis (IHSS). This condition is associated with aortic outflow obstruction which leads to arrhythmias in some patients. Beta blockers are used frequently to reduce aortic outflow by reducing cardiac contraction.

Post-Myocardial Infarction. Beta blockers are used in the evolving MI or the immediate post MI phase in order to limit infarct size.[222,223] Therapy generally is initiated with intravenous beta blockers followed by oral therapy. Beta blockers also have been used to prevent recurrent MIs (secondary prevention) in patients who have suffered an MI).[215,222–224] The agents that have been studied most extensively include metoprolol, timolol, and propranolol. One of these agents should be considered strongly in a patient who has hypertension, has had an MI, and has no contraindications to beta blockers. These drugs have been shown to prolong survival and prevent MI recurrence.

Other Conditions. Beta blockers also may be beneficial in hypertensive patients with migraine headaches, tremors, anxiety, hyperthyroidism, pheochromocytoma, stage-fright, and glaucoma.[203,225,226] Since D.C. does not have any of the above conditions, these would not be considerations in his case.

27. Hyperlipidemia. Should beta blockers be avoided in patients like D.C. who have hyperlipidemia?

Nonselective beta blockers have been associated with increased triglycerides and reductions in HDL-cholesterol.[184,214] Agents

Table 10.13			Pharmacokinetic Properties of Beta-Adrenoceptor Blockers		
Drug	Absorption[a] (%)	Bioavailability[a] (%)	Metabolism/Excretion	Protein Binding (%)	Half-Life[b] (hr)
Acebutolol	90	40	Hepatic/renal Biliary/fecal	30–36	3–4
Atenolol	50	40	Renal	6–16	6–7
Betaxolol	100	89	Hepatic/renal	50	14–22
Bisoprolol	90	80	Hepatic/renal	30	9–12
Carteolol	80	85	Hepatic/renal	23–30	6
Labetalol	100	30–40	Hepatic/renal	50	6–8
Metoprolol	95	50	Hepatic/renal	12	3–7
Nadolol	30	30	Renal	30	20–24
Penbutolol	100	100	Hepatic/renal	80–98	5
Pindolol	>95	87–90	Hepatic/renal	40	3–4
Propranolol	90	40	Hepatic/renal	90	4
Timolol	90	61	Hepatic/renal	<10	4

a High absorption drug with low bioavailability indicates high presystemic (first pass) hepatic metabolism which roughly correlates with a more lipid soluble drug. Conversely, less lipid soluble drugs may have poor intrinsic absorption but little presystemic metabolism.
b The duration of antihypertensive effect exceeds the drug's half-life and no more than twice daily dosing is necessary.

with ISA have little or no effects on lipids, while selective beta blockers have intermediate effects.[214] However, the significance of these effects has never been determined. The VA Cooperative trial found no long-term lipid abnormalities from atenolol.[136] Since beta blockers clearly have been shown to lower morbidity and mortality, it is felt that effects on lipids have little clinical significance. Therefore, if a beta blocker is indicated in a patient with hyperlipidemia, it should still be considered and serum lipids should be monitored.[1] Thus, a beta blocker should not be ruled out as a possible agent for D.C. based upon his hyperlipidemia.

28. Diabetes. Why should beta blockers be used cautiously in diabetics and why do cardioselective beta blockers have less risk?

All beta blockers mask many of the symptoms of impending hypoglycemia that are related to epinephrine release (e.g., palpitations, tremor, hunger),[227,228] but they do not prevent hypoglycemia-related sweating. While they do not actually cause hypoglycemia, nonselective beta blockers can potentiate a hypoglycemic episode and prolong the recovery from hypoglycemia.[208] Therefore, these agents generally should be avoided in tightly controlled insulin-dependent diabetic patients. During a hypoglycemic episode, plasma catecholamine levels increase. If β_2 receptors are blocked with a nonselective beta blocker, vasoconstriction and marked increases in blood pressure can occur due to unopposed alpha receptor stimulation. Selective beta blockers are less likely to be associated with a hypertensive response to hypoglycemia. Conversely, beta blockers may inhibit insulin secretion and cause hyperglycemia in some patients.[227,228] If a beta blocker is strongly indicated (e.g., patient has had a previous MI) in an insulin-dependent patient, a selective agent is preferred.

The risk of masking and potentiating hypoglycemia should not be interpreted as an absolute contraindication to beta blocker use in patients with diabetes. While they are best avoided in insulin dependent (Type I) diabetics, they can be used if other agents fail or if concurrent diseases are present to justify the use of a beta blocker. Since hypoglycemia is less common in noninsulin dependent diabetic patients, the beta blockers are less likely to create adverse effects in this population.[1,4,229] Nonetheless, beta blockers should be monitored carefully in all diabetic patients with frequent glucose measurements and targeted patient education about how the signs and symptoms of hypoglycemia may change.

ACE Inhibitors

29. It was decided to treat D.C. with an ACE inhibitor to preserve his renal function. What is the mechanism of action of ACE inhibitors in the management of hypertension and which patients are likely to respond to these drugs?

Mechanism of Action

ACE inhibitors (see Table 10.14 for listing) lower blood pressure by causing peripheral arterial vasodilation without significant changes in cardiac output, heart rate, or glomerular filtration rate.[230,231] The effects on renal blood flow and glomerular filtration can be complex depending upon sodium balance and the presence of renal artery stenosis (see below). The principal activity of ACE inhibitors is believed to be through the inhibition of the renin-angiotensin-aldosterone system.[230]

Renin is an enzyme secreted primarily from the juxtaglomerular cells in the afferent renal artery in response to stimuli such as: 1) reductions in blood pressure; 2) decreased sodium concentrations in renal cells; and 3) pain or stress which lead to sympathetic nervous stimulation.[230–233] Angiotensinogen is released by the liver and renin converts this substance to angiotensin I. Angiotensin I is a decapeptide that is essentially inactive. Angiotensin-converting enzyme cleaves the terminal portion of angiotensin I to form the octapeptide, angiotensin II. Angiotensin II is an extremely potent vasoconstrictor. Angiotensin II also stimulates the adrenal cortex to release aldosterone which increases sodium and water reabsorption, in exchange for potassium excretion, in the distal tubule of the kidney. Angiotensin II then inhibits the further release of renin by negative feedback.

The ACE inhibitors directly inhibit angiotensin-converting enzyme, preventing the formation of angiotensin II. While the primary mechanism of action probably relates to ACE inhibition, there are additional mechanisms. For instance, these drugs increase the formation of vasodilating substances such as bradykinin and prostaglandins.[231] These effects may explain why ACE inhibitors are still effective in some patients who have low renin concentrations. In addition to direct local effects on arterioles of the systemic and renal vasculature, these agents have central ACE inhibiting properties. They also may have direct effects on myocardial tissue to interfere with angiotensin-mediated formation of left ventricular hypertrophy.[53,54]

Concomitant Disorders

The ACE inhibitors are useful for many patients with hypertension, including those who may not adequately respond to diuretics or beta blockers, or those who cannot take these agents (e.g., patients with asthma, gout, diabetes, or congestive heart failure). Patients with low renin hypertension (many black or elderly patients) or primary hyperaldosteronism may not respond as well to ACE inhibitors. However, this is clearly not absolute as many patients with low renin hypertension may respond to ACE inhibitors.

There has been considerable interest in the ability of ACE inhibitors to protect the kidney from the unrelenting deterioration that occurs with renal insufficiency.[2,3,234] Chronic renal insufficiency is characterized by increased intraglomerular pressure and mesangial cell proliferation which leads to proteinuria and a progressive decline in renal function. Reductions in renal blood flow cause the kidney to increase renin release thus activating the angiotensin hormonal system locally. This local action constricts the efferent renal arteriole to preserve glomerular pressure, but this may aggravate further renal impairment. The ACE inhibitors preferentially dilate the efferent arteriole by their ACE inhibiting properties and this relieves intraglomerular pressure. While there is interesting data which suggest that ACE inhibitors may have unique renal preservation properties, it is not known if they are superior to other antihypertensives. However, information is accumulating that ACE inhibitors may be preferred in patients with renal insufficiency.[234] These effects may be unrelated to the systemic blood pressure effects since blood pressure control does not necessarily slow the decline in renal function, especially in black patients.[74,232,234]

ACE inhibitors also are effective in patients with hypertension related to renal artery disease.[235] However, caution must be used in patients who may have bilateral renal artery stenosis or who have stenosis in a solitary kidney following nephrectomy. In these patients, renal blood flow is maintained by high angiotensin levels. Acute renal failure can be precipitated in these patients when ACE inhibitors are started. Many elderly patients have generalized atherosclerosis that leads to renal artery stenosis.[235] There is wide variability in the degree of stenosis and the tendency for patients to develop renal insufficiency from ACE inhibitors.[236,237] It is often not known if a patient has renal artery stenosis. Problems with ACE inhibitors can be minimized by starting with very low doses with careful monitoring of renal function. (Also see Chapter 15: Congestive Heart Failure for further discussion of the relationship between ACE inhibitors and renal function.)

Table 10.14			ACE Inhibitors in Hypertension		
Drug	Dose Range (mg/day)	Daily Doses	Onset (hr)	Duration (hr)	Elimination
Benazepril (Lotensin)	5–80[a]	1–2	1	24	Renal[b]
Captopril (Capoten)	12.5–450[c]	2	0.25–0.5	2–12[d]	50% hepatic
Cilazapril (Inhibace)	2.5–10	1–2	1	24	Renal[b]
Enalapril (Vasotec)	2.5–40[e]	1–2	1	24	Renal[b]
Fosinopril (Monopril)	10–80[f]	1–2	1	24	Hepatic/renal
Lisinopril (Prinivil, Zestril)	5–80[g]	1–2	1	24	Renal
Quinapril (Accupril)	2.5–80[h]	1–2	1	>30	Renal[b]
Ramipril (Altace)	1.25–20[i]	1–2	1–2	24	Renal[b]

[a] Initial dose in patients not on a diuretic is 10 mg QD; usual dose is 20–40 mg QD. A dose of 80 mg gives an increased response, but there is a limited clinical experience with this dose.

[b] Benazepril, cilazapril, enalapril, quinapril, and ramipril are hepatically metabolized to active metabolites (benazeprilat, cilazaprilat, enalaprilat, quinaprilat, ramiprilat) which are eliminated primarily renally.

[c] Initial dose is 12.5–25 mg BID. If blood pressure is not reduced satisfactorily within 1–2 weeks, the dose may be increased to 50 mg BID or TID. The dose seldom exceeds 150 mg/day.

[d] Duration of action is dose related.

[e] Initial dose in patients not on a diuretic is 5 mg QD; usual dose is 10–40 mg/day.

[f] Usual daily maintenance dose is 20–40 mg/day. Since some patients require only 10 mg/day with or without a diuretic, the 10 mg dose may be considered as an appropriate starting dose.

[g] Initial dose in patients not on a diuretic is 10 mg QD; the usual dose is 20–40 mg/day. Doses up to 80 mg/day have been used but do not appear to provide a greater effect.

[h] Initial dose in patients not on a diuretic is 10 mg QD; usual dose is 20–80 mg/day.

[i] Initial dose in patients not on a diuretic is 2.5 mg QD.

In Black Patients

30. Should an ACE inhibitor be avoided in D.C. because he is black?

The ACE inhibitors often have been reported to be more effective in young white patients than in black or elderly patients.[230] Since elderly and black patients are more likely to have low renin hypertension, this may explain some of the differences in response. However, many of these patients will indeed respond to ACE inhibitors as monotherapy (see Table 10.9). For instance, several studies have found that blood pressure can be controlled in 50% to 60% of elderly white patients with an ACE inhibitor.[136,140] Other studies have found that ACE inhibitors can control blood pressure in approximately 50% of black patients.[201,239] However, in a VA Cooperative Trial, ACE inhibitors were effective as monotherapy in the following age and racial groups: 62% of young whites, 62% of elderly whites, 43% of young blacks, and 33% of elderly blacks.[136,344] These findings point to lower efficacy in black patients.

When an antihypertensive agent is being considered in a patient with no other problems or disease states, one would generally not select an ACE inhibitor in a black patient. However, there may be other co-existing conditions that would make an ACE inhibitor desirable. In this case, D.C. has renal insufficiency and many clinicians would prefer an ACE inhibitor to reduce the rate of decline in renal function. Because D.C. is black and needs more aggressive control, an ACE inhibitor will not be reliably effective as monotherapy.

Racial- or age-related differences in response to ACE inhibitors can be overcome with the addition of a diuretic. In patients who do not adequately respond to an ACE inhibitor, the addition of a low dose diuretic (e.g., HCTZ 12.5 mg) can achieve blood pressure control in 80% to 90% of patients.[1] D.C. has responded well to the diuretic but, due to his renal insufficiency, the goal blood pressure should be less than 130/85 mm Hg.[2] In this case it would be better to add an ACE inhibitor to the diuretic than to switch to an ACE inhibitor alone.

At low doses, diuretics may cause hypokalemia and volume depletion. Conversely, ACE inhibitors may increase potassium, especially in patients with renal insufficiency, due to the reduction of aldosterone caused by ACE inhibitors.[240,241] In patients with more severe renal insufficiency, loop diuretics may be needed to relieve edema. Patients who have volume and sodium depletion secondary to diuretics or other causes maintain systemic and renal blood flow by a compensatory increase in renin. If an ACE inhibitor is started under these conditions, sudden drops in pressure and acute renal insufficiency can develop. Therefore, if an ACE inhibitor is added to a diuretic, it is suggested that the diuretic be withheld for one to two days before initiating the ACE inhibitor. Alternatively, low doses of the ACE inhibitor should be initiated (e.g., captopril 6.25 to 12.5 mg twice daily). The dose of hydrochlorothiazide for D.C. is low (25 mg) and not likely to cause problems for him if low ACE inhibitor doses are used and titrated slowly.

31. Are there advantages of newer ACE inhibitors over captopril?

All of the ACE inhibitors are equally effective as antihypertensive agents. However, these compounds differ in terms of potency, pharmacokinetics, adverse reactions, duration of antihypertensive activity, and clinical indication (e.g., CHF).

Dosing

Typical doses of ACE inhibitors are shown in Table 10.14. When captopril was first marketed, large doses commonly were used (e.g., 400 to 600 mg/day). These large doses were associated with several adverse effects such as skin rash (5% to 10%), taste disturbances (5% to 10%), neutropenia (rare), and proteinuria (rare). Currently, much lower doses of captopril are used and these adverse reactions are encountered rarely, but still may be slightly higher in frequency with captopril than with other agents. All of the ACE inhibitors may cause a nonproductive cough in up to 15% of patients.[242,243] The cough may occur more frequently with the long-acting ACE inhibitors and subsides when the drug is discontinued.

The duration of antihypertensive effect is much longer than the serum half-life would predict. Therefore, captopril is effective when administered twice daily.[136,148,244] Other ACE inhibitors usually can be given once, but are sometimes dosed twice-daily in higher dosages.[1] Since most patients can comply with twice-daily dosing, there is no clear advantage of agents that can be given once daily.[141,142] Following the initiation of therapy, it may take several weeks before the full antihypertensive effects of these drugs are observed.

All ACE inhibitors, except captopril, must be hepatically converted to active substances such as enalaprilat. Therefore, the peak antihypertensive activity of a single dose of captopril is seen in 60 to 90 minutes, while the other ACE inhibitors do not achieve peak blood pressure effects until four to six hours after a single dose.[246] In addition, the newer ACE inhibitors have a slower rate of elimination, a longer duration of action, and a slower dissociation from binding sites.[247] However, these differences have not been shown to have major clinical importance.

The newer agents appear to be associated with a slightly lower incidence of some side effects such as rash and taste disturbances. This may relate to the fact that captopril has a sulfhydryl group on its molecule, while the other agents do not. However, as noted above, these reactions diminished in frequency when captopril was used in lower doses. If a patient develops one of these adverse reactions, changing to another ACE inhibitor may be indicated. Captopril increases vasodilating prostaglandins and bradykinins more than enalapril or lisinopril.[231] However, the significance of this finding is unknown. At present, the differences between ACE inhibitors have not been shown to be important in the selection of these agents.

Calcium Channel Blockers

Efficacy

32. How effective are calcium channel blockers as antihypertensive agents and what is their mechanism of action?

The major hemodynamic alteration in most patients with chronic essential hypertension is an increase in peripheral vascular resistance.[18] This increased vascular resistance primarily results from an increase in arteriolar smooth muscle tone that in turn is dependent upon the intracellular free calcium concentrations. Vascular smooth muscle has low intracellular calcium concentrations and smooth muscle contraction depends upon an influx of extracellular calcium through calcium channels located on the cell membrane.[248] The calcium channel blockers inhibit the movement of extracellular calcium through these calcium channels and result in arteriolar dilation and a decrease in blood pressure.

It has been proposed that elderly and black patients have greater blood pressure responses to calcium channel blockers than younger white patients.[249,250] However, this has not been confirmed in all clinical trials.[136,140,251] As seen in Table 10.9, numerous studies have found that young or white patients respond well. If patients do not adequately respond, the addition of a diuretic should be considered. One report found that hydrochlorathiazide was not additive to verapamil, but this has been refuted in other studies.[1,252] The proposed mechanism by which they may not be additive is that both agents have naturetic effects. However, additive effects often are seen in clinical practice.

33. Would a calcium channel blocker be a reasonable choice for D.C. if an ACE inhibitor was ineffective or caused an adverse reaction?

A calcium channel blocker would be a good alternative for D.C. It would actually be more likely to control his blood pressure than an ACE inhibitor, since D.C. is black. Calcium channel blockers will not alter D.C.'s already elevated serum lipids, glucose, or uric acid concentration, nor will they cause further hypokalemia. They do no aggravate asthma or peripheral vascular disease.

The clinician should consider the implications of renal insufficiency in D.C. While information is not as extensive as with ACE inhibitors, calcium channel blockers also appear to slow the progression of renal impairment.[3,234] The exact mechanism for this action is still controversial. Some studies have found that calcium channel blockers dilate the afferent arteriole which would suggest that they would increase glomerular pressure. Other studies suggest equal vasodilatory effects on the afferent and efferent arterioles which would decrease intraglomerular pressure.[234,253,254] Extrarenal effects also may contribute to renal protection with calcium channel blockers.[255] While the prevailing opinion is that the renal protective effects of ACE inhibitors are probably superior to other classes of drugs including the calcium channel blockers, this has not been shown conclusively. Since clinical trials have demonstrated benefits from calcium channel blockers, they are good alternatives for renal protective effects.[3,256,257]

Concomitant Disorders and Comparison of Agents

34. A.P., a 71-year-old white male with a blood pressure of 168/96 on 2 clinic visits, also has a history of angina that is controlled by occasional doses of sublingual nitroglycerin and mild COAD that is managed by inhaled albuterol. Why is a calcium channel blocker appropriate for A.P.? Which one is preferred?

Calcium channel blockers were developed to treat ischemic heart disease and later were used to treat hypertension.[248,258–260] Therefore, they are very effective in treating both conditions. In the case of A.P., calcium channel blockers would be preferred over beta blockers since he has COAD. These agents decrease myocardial oxygen demand and improve myocardial blood flow. They have variable negative inotropic effects, but comparable antihypertensive effects. Table 10.15 lists usual doses of individual agents.

Both verapamil and diltiazem slow AV nodal and conductal tissue velocity since these tissues also contain slow calcium channels.[248] Therefore, they may slow heart rate and cause first or higher degree of heart block. This is the mechanism by which these agents are effective for supraventricular arrhythmias. However, because they also cause vasodilation (the basis for their use in hypertension), patients usually have either no change or a modest

Table 10.15	Calcium Channel Blockers	
Drug	Usual Dosage Range (mg/day)	Dosing Frequency
Diltiazem (Cardizem)	90–360	3
Sustained release (Cardizem SR, Dilacor XR)	120–360	2
Extended release (Cardizem CR)	180–360	1
Verapamil (Calan, Isoptin)	80–480	2
Sustained release (Calan SR, Isoptin SR, Verelan)	120–480	1–2
Dihydropyridines		
Amlodipine (Norvasc)	2.5–10	1
Felodipine (Plendil)	5–20	1
Isradipine (DynaCirc)	2.5–10	2
Nicardipine (Cardene)	60–120	3
Sustained release (Cardene SR)	60–120	2
Nifedipine (Procardia, Adalat)	30–120	3
Sustained release (Procardia XL, Adalat CC)	30–120	1

decrease in heart rate.[258-260] The dihydropyridines do not exhibit nodal blocking activities and they are not effective for arrhythmias. Vasodilation following dihydropyridines may be accompanied by a reflex tachycardia.

Many clinicians have avoided verapamil when treating hypertension because of early concerns about bradycardia, heart block, and cases of asystole. However, most of these reports were with intravenous administration and coadministration with beta blockers.[248] It has since been found that these reactions are rare with oral administration because the potent L-isomer of verapamil is preferentially metabolized on first pass through the liver.[261-263] The L-isomer is 11 times more potent than the d-isomer at AV nodal blockade and the ratio of L:d isomers is much lower with oral therapy. Thus, oral verapamil is a safe and effective antihypertensive. Nonetheless, verapamil and diltiazem should be avoided in patients with congestive heart failure and second or third degree heart block.

Verapamil is an attractive agent for A.P. The regular-release product can be given twice daily for both angina and hypertension and it is the least expensive calcium channel blocker.[150,151,264] Most patients tolerate verapamil well, but the most common problem is constipation which usually can be countered by diet or bulk-forming laxatives. The initial dose should be 80 mg twice daily. The dose can then be slowly titrated at two- to four-week intervals up to 480 mg/day. For patients who have difficulty with twice-daily administration, a sustained-release product may be considered.

If the patient does not tolerate verapamil or there is a contraindication to its use, then diltiazem or a dihydropyridine may be considered. Diltiazem is the best tolerated and would be appropriate. However, for patients with conduction disturbances or those also taking beta blockers, a dihydropyridine would be preferred. The dihydropyridines such as nifedipine and nicardipine have short durations of action and need to be given three times daily unless sustained-release products are used.[1] The dihydropyridines are potent vasodilators which tend to cause more vasodilating adverse reactions such as reflex tachycardia, headache, flushing, and edema.

Combination of Two Calcium Channel Blockers

35. If one calcium channel blocker is not completely effective, is there any rationale to combine two calcium channel blockers?

It is rarely rational to combine two agents from the same therapeutic class. Pharmacists should always question such combinations. However, experimental evidence indicates that calcium channel blockers bind to different sites on the calcium channel.[265,266] Although there is little information on the treatment of hypertension, diltiazem has been combined with dihydropyridines in patients with angina.[267,268] These limited data suggest that the combination may be more effective than the single agents. However, at present, combinations of calcium channel blockers should be considered experimental, especially for the treatment of hypertension.

α₁-Adrenergic Antagonists

Efficacy

36. J.L. is a 60-year-old male with hypertension and dyslipidemia. His blood pressure is currently controlled with enalapril 5 mg QD. He is following a low cholesterol, low fat diet for the management of his dyslipidemia. J.L. has recently experienced frequent nocturia and has been diagnosed as having bladder outlet obstruction due to benign prostatic hypertrophy (BPH). Would J.L. benefit from a switch of his antihypertensive medication to prazosin (Minipress)?

Prazosin is an α₁-adrenergic antagonist which is effective as monotherapy[269] or in combination with other antihypertensive agents[269,270] for the treatment of hypertension. The α₁-inhibitors have been considered to have efficacy comparable to that of the thiazide diuretics and beta blockers.[271,272] The JNC V considered alpha antagonists as acceptable alternatives to beta blockers and diuretics for monotherapy. However, they are not considered first-line therapy for the treatment of hypertension.[1] Their antihypertensive effect is additive when used in combination with diuretics, β-adrenergic blockers, clonidine, methyldopa, and hydralazine.[273] However, in the VA Cooperative Trial, prazosin was not as effective as diltiazem, atenolol, or hydrochlorothiazide (see Table 10.9).[136] In addition, prazosin resulted in significantly more adverse reactions. In the TOMHS trial, doxazosin was as effective as a diuretic, an ACE inhibitor, a beta blocker, and a calcium antagonist.[134] One advantage of the α₁-antagonists for a patient like J.L. is that they do not cause the adverse metabolic effects associated with other agents.[271,274] They have been shown to modestly lower total and LDL cholesterol, and triglycerides, and to increase HDL cholesterol.[272,275-277] The clinical significance of these lipid effects has not been established. Generally, these drugs should not be selected solely on the basis of these minor effects on plasma lipids.

The α₁-antagonists also have been used in the treatment of congestive heart failure,[278] Raynaud's phenomenon,[279] and bladder outlet obstruction.[280,281] Their efficacy in CHF and Raynaud's phenomenon is considered minimal; therefore, the presence of these conditions is not a reason to select one of these drugs. Of importance to J.L., these agents have been shown to improve the symptoms associated with BPH by reducing urethral tone and alleviating the bladder outlet obstruction.[280,281] Prazosin may be a useful alternative in patients who are unable to undergo transurethral resection of the prostate (TURP).

Dosing

37. After discussing the options, J.L. prefers to try prazosin for his symptoms secondary to BPH rather than undergo surgery. What dosing recommendations would you provide?

The initial dose should not exceed 1 mg at bedtime to minimize the risk of first-dose syncope (i.e., profound hypotension, dizziness and possible fainting) which has occurred with this medication.[282] First-dose syncope can be minimized by starting with a low dose, preferably given at bedtime so that if hypotension occurs, the patient will be recumbent. The dosage range is 2 to 20 mg/day in divided doses.[1] Prazosin's antihypertensive effect lasts approximately ten hours; therefore, the drug can be administered twice daily and increased to three times daily if necessary. The hypotensive effect usually is realized within two weeks; however, it may be four to eight weeks before the full therapeutic effect is seen.[269] Doses up to 2 mg administered twice daily have been found to be effective for BPH.[281,283]

Adverse Effects and Patient Education

38. What patient education should be provided about the potential adverse effects of this medication?

Prazosin appears to be relatively well tolerated.[273] Side effects include drowsiness, headache, weakness, palpitations from reflex tachycardia, and nausea. In the VA trial, the following adverse reactions occurred: fatigue (13%), sleepiness (12%), and nonpostural dizziness (12%).[136] Peripheral edema and weight gain, urinary frequency, and aggravation of angina also have been reported.[273] Prazosin is associated with postural hypotension occasionally accompanied by dizziness, palpitations, and syncope.[282] This has been reported to occur in 1% of patients when given an initial dose of 2 mg or more.[273] To help minimize this adverse event, patients should be instructed to take the initial dose at bedtime and to rise more slowly from a seated or supine position.[273]

Doxazosin and Terazosin

39. Would doxazosin (Cardura) or terazosin (Hytrin) be an appropriate alternative for J.L.?

Doxazosin and terazosin are peripheral α_1-adrenergic antagonists similar to prazosin. The initial dose of doxazosin is 1 mg once daily to minimize the possibility of postural hypotension and syncope. Then the drug may be titrated gradually to achieve adequate blood pressure control or to a maximum of 16 mg once daily. The elimination half-life is estimated to be 9 to 22 hours which allows for once daily dosing.[134,284] This would be an advantage for patients unable to adhere to the two or possibly three times daily dosing regimen with prazosin. Patients receiving doxazosin experience side effects similar to those experienced with prazosin including orthostatic hypotension, dizziness, vertigo, drowsiness, edema, and headaches.[284] Dosage increases of greater than 4 mg/day should be avoided to minimize syncopal episodes.

Terazosin initially should be given as a 1 mg dose at bedtime with gradual titration to adequate antihypertensive effect or to a maximum dose of 20 mg/day. Bedtime administration for the first dose is recommended due to the possibility of syncope and postural hypotension which may occur in approximately 1% of patients receiving terazosin.[285] Terazosin's elimination half-life is approximately 12 hours[286] with an antihypertensive effect allowing for once daily administration.[134,287] Side effects include dizziness, weakness, somnolence, peripheral edema, nausea, palpitations, and headache.[285]

Doxazosin has been shown to have a beneficial effect on serum lipids by decreasing total and LDL cholesterol, and triglycerides, and increasing HDL cholesterol.[276] Terazosin also has been shown to decrease total and LDL cholesterol and VLDL cholesterol.[288]

Terazosin has been approved for the treatment of symptoms due to BPH. Studies have demonstrated a dose-related decrease in symptoms with an increase in peak urinary flow rates.[289,290]

Alpha Beta Blocker

40. What is the mechanism for the blood pressure reduction with labetalol and should it be considered for J.L.?

Labetalol is a nonselective beta blocker that also blocks α_1 receptors.[291,292] Thus, its hemodynamic properties are similar to a combination of propranolol and prazosin. Labetalol can be used as monotherapy as an alternative to diuretics and beta blockers;[1] it is effective in both white and black patients and the elderly. However, it tends to cause more adverse reactions than other beta blockers including postural dizziness, lightheadedness, GI reactions, fatigue, and scalp tingling.[291,292] It also must be used with caution in patients with the typical contraindications to beta blockers (e.g., patients with asthma). Labetalol may cause less lipid abnormalities than propranolol and, because it tends to cause vasodilation, it may be safer to use than other beta blockers in patients with peripheral vascular insufficiency. However, because it has no clear advantages over other agents and is associated with more adverse reactions, labetalol is not commonly used and would not be recommended for J.L.

Unlike beta blockers, labetalol is very effective in lowering blood pressure acutely. Therefore, oral and intravenous administration can be used to treat hypertensive urgencies.[293–295]

α_2-Agonists

Mechanism of Action

41. T.M., a 50-year-old male truck driver with a history of hypertension, has been taking HCTZ 25 mg Q AM without complaints or side effects. His blood pressure has not been controlled despite adherence to the medication and nonpharmacologic measures, although T.M. has been unable to quit smoking. Clonidine (Catapres) was chosen to be added to T.M.'s regimen with a dose of 0.2 mg BID for blood pressure control. Why is an α_2-agonist effective in the treatment of hypertension when α-antagonists also are effective? Is there any reason why clonidine may be indicated in particular for T.M.?**

The mechanism of action of the α_2-agonists (clonidine, guanabenz, guanfacine, methyldopa) can be attributed to their central α_2-agonist activity. Stimulation of α_2 receptors in the CNS inhibits sympathetic outflow to the heart, kidneys, and peripheral vasculature.[296] Due to their similar mechanisms of action, the α_2-agonists should not be used together. Peripheral vasodilation occurs by relaxing peripheral arterioles and veins.[297]

The α_2-agonists are effective as monotherapy;[298] however, they are not considered first-line therapy for the treatment of hypertension due to their potential side effects.[1] The α_2-agonists (especially methyldopa) are most effective when used with a diuretic[299] due to their potential for causing fluid retention. Although, the α_2-agonists can be used in combination with any other antihypertensive medications, they should be used with agents that have different mechanisms of action (e.g., diuretics, vasodilators) and do not exert their effects at the adrenergic receptors (e.g., beta blockers).

Clonidine also has been used in smoking cessation to attenuate withdrawal symptoms.[300] Although the results have been variable,[301] there may be an advantage to using clonidine in T.M. as an adjunct to a smoking cessation program.

Dosing

42. How should T.M.'s clonidine dose be adjusted?

Therapy with clonidine should be started with a low dose and gradually increased to achieve optimal efficacy with minimal side effects. The starting dose should be 0.1 mg twice daily which can be increased by 0.1 or 0.2 mg per day or every few days until the desired response is achieved. The manufacturer's recommended maximum daily dose is 2.4 mg; however, most patients will respond with 0.4 to 0.8 mg/day. Oftentimes, patients may not tolerate doses greater than 0.8 mg/day.

Clonidine also is available as a transdermal patch which contains a reservoir of drug that releases the medication at a controlled rate over a period of seven days.[302] This is an option for patients who have difficulty adhering to a daily medication regimen or who have swallowing or absorption difficulties. It also appears to have a lower adverse effect rate over the tablet dosage form.[303] Upon initial application of the patch, the blood pressure effect may be delayed for two to three days.[304] This may result in rebound hypertension if switching from the oral dosage form to the transdermal patch.[305] To prevent this complication, the oral dosage form of the drug may be continued the first day the transdermal patch is initiated. Similarly, the antihypertensive effect may continue for a few days after the patch is removed due to residual drug in the skin.[304] The patch should be changed every seven days; however, the therapeutic benefit will continue if the patch remains on the skin for up to ten days. Skin rash appears to be the most bothersome side effect of the transdermal system.[302]

Adverse Effects

43. T.M.'s blood pressure has been controlled after taking clonidine 0.2 mg BID for several weeks. Since the dose of clonidine was increased to 0.2 mg BID, T.M. has experienced daytime somnolence and dry mouth. Due to T.M.'s occupation, he decided to discontinue the clonidine when he needs to be on the road for an extended period of time. Twenty-four hours after discontinuing the drug, T.M. became restless and agitated

with a severe headache. Upon admission to the emergency room, his blood pressure was 190/116 mm Hg. What is the most likely cause of T.M.'s symptoms?

Sedation and dry mouth are the most frequent and bothersome side effects of the central α_2-agonists. These side effects may be more tolerable in some patients than in others, and may subside with continued use of the drug, or be less bothersome with the transdermal patch. Some patients find it necessary to discontinue the medication, sometimes without notifying their health care providers. This is a concern because rapid discontinuation can lead to rebound hypertension.[306] The patient should be educated about these potential adverse effects and discouraged from discontinuing the medication without medical supervision. A spectrum of effects may occur upon discontinuation, with the severity being at least partially dependent upon both the duration of treatment and the daily dosage. In the least severe case, the blood pressure slowly returns to pretreatment levels over several days without any accompanying subjective symptoms. Other patients may complain of nervousness, agitation, sweating, headache, palpitations, insomnia, and nausea, all related to increased circulating levels of norepinephrine. In extreme cases, the blood pressure rapidly rises to dangerously high levels and is associated with encephalopathic signs of lethargy, confusion, and disorientation. Fortunately, these severe events are rare in patients taking less than 0.8 mg/day. It also should be noted that withdrawal reactions are not unique to clonidine. In particular, patients may experience agitation and rebound increased blood pressure after abrupt discontinuation of other α_2-agonists as well as beta blockers. In general, patients should be counseled to never rapidly discontinue any blood pressure medication.

Although the mechanism by which rebound hypertension occurs has not been fully established, it appears that in patients taking α_2-agonists, norepinephrine release from the adrenergic neuron is decreased and the amount of norepinephrine available to the α_1-receptors in the synaptic cleft is decreased. Thus the α_1-receptors increase their density and/or sensitivity. Withdrawal of the drug leads to an outpouring of norepinephrine (negative feedback is eliminated) and this stimulates the now upregulated α_1-receptor. Even though the risk of rebound hypertension is small at lower doses (<0.6 to 0.8 mg), all patients should be educated about the importance of adherence. The patient should be aware of how to obtain refills and instructed to never abruptly discontinue the medication. If the drug is to be discontinued, it should be tapered over several days depending upon the dose.[307] The transdermal patch also has been associated with rebound hypertension.[308]

An alternative antihypertensive agent from a different class should be chosen for T.M. due to the adverse effects experienced.

44. Why would another α_2-agonist not be appropriate for T.M.?

Methyldopa

The adverse effect profile of the other three α_2-agonists (methyldopa, guanfacine, and guanabenz) are nearly identical to that of clonidine. Although individual tolerances may differ slightly, in general patients who do not tolerate one drug in this class will not tolerate the others. Methyldopa (Aldomet) is not considered first-line therapy and has been replaced with newer antihypertensive agents as the treatment of choice.[1] Patients currently receiving methyldopa for the treatment of hypertension who are controlled and not experiencing side effects usually can be continued on the medication. The usual initial dose is 250 mg administered twice daily up to 2 gm/day.[1] Methyldopa causes side effects similar to those associated with clonidine, including sedation, lethargy, postural hypotension, dizziness, dry mouth, and headache. These side effects generally are well tolerated and may decrease with contin-

ued use. Other significant side effects include hemolytic anemia and hepatitis. Approximately 20% of patients receiving methyldopa may develop a dose-dependent positive direct Coombs' test after 6 to 12 months of continued use.[309] Only a few of these patients will develop hemolytic anemia which, if it occurs, is an indication for discontinuing the medication. If hemolysis is severe, the administration of corticosteroids may be useful.[310] Methyldopa also has been associated with hepatic injury with increases in liver function tests. This reaction is reversible upon discontinuation of the drug; however, progression to hepatic necrosis can occur.[296]

Guanfacine

The adverse effects of guanfacine (Tenex) are similar to those of clonidine and include dry mouth (occurring in up to 60% of patients), sedation, dizziness, orthostatic hypotension, insomnia, constipation, and impotence.[311] A decrease in heart rate also has occurred with the drug.[312] Although complaints of sedation appear to be less common than with clonidine[313] or guanabenz, the dose should be administered at bedtime if given once daily. Rebound hypertension with guanfacine is less common and possibly less severe than that seen with clonidine[313] due to guanfacine's longer duration of action. Its long plasma half-life of approximately 17 to 20 hours allows for once daily administration in most patients.[314]

Guanabenz

The duration of action of guanabenz (Wytensin) is 10 to 12 hours, allowing for twice daily dosing.[315] The usual starting dose for the treatment of hypertension is 4 mg twice daily with the usual effective dose between 8 and 16 mg twice daily.[316] The most common adverse effect of treatment with guanabenz is sedation ($\approx 20\%$)[317] which may decrease with long-term therapy.[318] Sedation appears to be more common with guanabenz than with methyldopa or clonidine. Other common side effects include dizziness and dry mouth.[317] Withdrawal effects appear to be similar to those seen with clonidine; however, the incidence may be less.[319]

Hydralazine

Mechanism

45. C.M. is a 56-year-old white female with a history of new onset hypertension. Due to financial constraints, she was started on hydralazine 50 mg BID. The dose has been increased gradually secondary to inadequate blood pressure control. Currently she is taking hydralazine 150 mg BID and reports good compliance. She has a blood pressure of 172/108 mm Hg and a pulse of 132 beats/min. Her lung fields are clear. Bilateral 3+ pitting edema is present. Serum electrolytes are within normal limits. Why is C.M.'s blood pressure elevated despite increasing doses of hydralazine?

Hydralazine causes direct relaxation of arteriolar smooth muscle with little effect on the venous circulation. As a result, hydralazine is an afterload reducer and has been shown to be beneficial in the treatment of CHF. Vasodilation from hydralazine is associated with stimulation of the sympathetic nervous system, which results in increased heart rate and contractility, increased plasma renin activity, and fluid retention.[320] Following these compensatory cardiovascular responses, the hypotensive effectiveness of direct vasodilators like hydralazine diminishes over time which may explain the inadequate blood pressure control in C.M. Beta blockers and diuretics may counteract the tachyphylaxis associated with hydralazine by blunting the increase in heart rate and reducing fluid retention. Therefore, monotherapy with hydralazine usually is not possible and the drug should be reserved as a third- or fourth-line agent in the management of resistant hypertension.[1]

Another contributor to inadequate control of blood pressure could be a reduction in bioavailability of hydralazine. The administration of hydralazine with food will double or triple its bioavailability.[321] Patient counseling on administration with food may improve response.

Adverse Reactions:

Systemic Lupus Erythematosus (SLE)

46. After 18 months of hydralazine 150 mg BID, propranolol 40 mg BID, and HCTZ 25 mg/day, C.M. presents to clinic for routine follow-up. She complains of a gradual onset of joint pain in both her right and left hands which extends to the wrists and admits to generalized weakness and fever. What is a possible explanation for C.M.'s subjective complaints and what objective data can be obtained to confirm your suspicions?

Hydralazine is a well recognized cause of drug-induced systemic lupus erythematosus (SLE) and C.M.'s symptoms are consistent with this syndrome since they developed after initiation of the drug. The most common symptoms include joint and muscle aches, pleuritic chest pain, and rash. She is receiving a total daily dose of 300 mg which exceeds the dose of 200 mg/day which is usually considered as placing patients at an increased risk for hydralazine-induced SLE.[296,320] In fact, doses as low as 100 mg have resulted in the lupus syndrome.[322]

Depending upon C.M.'s acetylator type, she may have been at further increased risk of developing hydralazine-induced SLE. It has been hypothesized that a slow acetylator will accumulate more of the parent drug which is the mediator of this problem. The U.S. population is divided evenly between slow and rapid acetylators, but pure blood Japanese and native Alaskans are more likely to be rapid acetylators. Since determination of acetylator type is not routinely screened before starting drug therapy, we do not have information on C.M.'s acetylator phenotype.

Several abnormal laboratory findings may be noted with hydralazine-induced SLE and should be evaluated to establish the diagnosis. The presence of antinuclear antibody (ANA) is a common finding in patients taking hydralazine, approaching 70% to 100% in those with long term exposure. However, only a small percentage of these patients become symptomatic. While obtaining baseline titers is recommended by some practitioners, routine monitoring is unnecessary since a positive ANA alone is not an indication for stopping the drug. The typical ANA pattern in drug-induced SLE is diffuse and directed against single stranded DNA (ss-DNA), not against double stranded DNA (ds-DNA) as in idiopathic SLE. Other common laboratory findings include elevated erythrocyte sedimentation rate (ESR), presence of lupus erythematosus cells, and false positive serologic test for syphilis.[323]

Patients with hydralazine-induced SLE may develop blood dyscrasias as part of their clinical picture. Therefore, a complete blood count should be obtained to evaluate for anemia, leukopenia, and, less commonly, thrombocytopenia.

Renal insufficiency, a common complication of idiopathic SLE, is associated infrequently with drug-induced SLE. However, of all drug-induced SLE, hydralazine causes the highest incidence of renal dysfunction.[324,325] A serum creatinine should be obtained to note any elevations and a urinalysis should be conducted to monitor for signs of proteinuria and hematuria.

47. Laboratory findings for C.M. showed a positive ANA (diffuse), a white blood cell count of 3500/mm³, and an ESR of 45 mm/hr. The diagnosis of hydralazine-induced SLE is made. How should this drug-induced toxicity be managed?

Hydralazine should be discontinued. Symptoms should begin to subside within days or weeks and complete resolution of symptoms can be expected.[323] However, a positive ANA may persist for several months. One patient was noted to have an ANA ten years after the onset of hydralazine toxicity.[323] The use of corticosteroids may

be necessary in treating patients with persistent symptoms or more serious manifestations such as lupus nephritis.[324,325]

Minoxidil

Clinical Use

48. C.R. is a 48-year-old white male with a 10-year history of hypertension. Despite therapy with furosemide 40 mg BID, clonidine 0.4 mg BID, and propranolol 160 mg BID, his blood pressure is still 186/112 mm Hg. His compliance to his medication regimen has been good and his prescriptions are refilled consistently. He has experienced previous adverse effects to captopril (increased SrCr) and verapamil (rash). Laboratory findings are unremarkable. His pulse is 60 beats/min and regular. Funduscopic examination reveals grade II Keith-Wagener-Barker changes. Chest x-ray demonstrates borderline cardiomegaly. Minoxidil 5 mg/day is added to his drug regimen and a clinic appointment is made for follow-up in 1 week. Why was minoxidil selected for C.R.?

C.R.'s response to combination therapy with a diuretic, an α_2-agonist, and a beta blocker has not been optimal and the addition of another antihypertensive agent with a different mechanism of action is appropriate. Like hydralazine, minoxidil causes vasodilation of arteriolar resistance vessels resulting in tachycardia, increased cardiac output, increased plasma renin activity (PRA), and fluid retention. Therefore, concomitant beta blocker and diuretic therapy is almost always required with minoxidil therapy. Loop diuretics may be preferred to thiazide diuretics if vigorous diuresis is necessary to alleviate fluid retention.[326] Clonidine also has been used in the place of beta blocker therapy to prevent the compensatory reflex tachycardia produced by minoxidil.[327] Therapy with minoxidil should be reserved for treatment of patients like C.R. with inadequate response to a triple drug regimen or in whom side effects preclude the use of other agents.[328]

Adverse Effects

49. Hypertrichosis. What instructions should C.R. receive concerning hair growth with oral minoxidil administration?

Hypertrichosis is a common adverse effect of oral minoxidil therapy that affects 80% to 100% of patients. The hair growth is not associated with an endocrine abnormality and begins within the first few weeks of therapy. Hair growth usually is noted on the temples, between the eyebrows, on the cheeks, and on the pinna of the ear. With continued use, increased hair growth may extend to the back, legs, arms, and scalp. While hair growth may be controlled with shaving and depilatories,[329] some patients, especially females, find the hypertrichosis so intolerable and that they discontinue therapy.

50. The dosage of minoxidil was increased to 10 mg BID and C.R.'s blood pressure was controlled at 146/88 mm Hg. C.R. admits to thicker beard growth and extension of his eyebrows, but does not find it a significant problem. What other side effects should be monitored in C.R.?

Fluid retention is a common complication of minoxidil therapy and may be evident by signs of edema and weight gain. If adequate diuresis is not achieved, congestive heart failure may be precipitated or worsened.

The compensatory reflex tachycardia after minoxidil may precipitate angina in susceptible patients. There is a report of a nonfatal myocardial infarction in a 75-year-old female after four doses of therapy.[330]

Electrocardiographic changes have been reported in as many as 90% of patients receiving minoxidil treatment.[331] The ECG changes often are nonspecific T-wave changes. Ischemia is not thought to induce the T-wave changes. During long-term treatment, the ECG changes will often resolve.

Guanethidine and Guanadrel

51. What roles do guanethidine and guanadrel have in the treatment of hypertension?

Guanethidine and guanadrel are both guanidine-containing compounds that have similar pharmacologic properties. Both agents inhibit the release of catecholamines produced by sympathetic nerve stimulation, thereby suppressing peripheral sympathetic vasoconstriction.[296,332] The hypotensive effects of these agents are more pronounced in the upright position as compared to the supine position.[332] This explains the orthostatic hypotension commonly noted with administration of guanidine-containing compounds. The difference between these two agents is evident in their pharmacokinetic and side effect profiles. Guanadrel has a shorter duration of action requiring twice-daily administration. Guanethidine has a much longer duration of activity and can be dosed once daily. Although both agents are associated with a high prevalence of distressing adverse effects, guanadrel may have a lower incidence of orthostatic hypotension,[333] diarrhea,[334,335] and sexual dysfunction.[334]

Use of these drugs is reserved for patients with resistant hypertension who do not maintain a blood pressure within the goal range (<140/90 mm Hg) despite therapy with a diuretic, adrenergic inhibitor, and a vasodilator. Due to frequent intolerable side effects, these agents are rarely administered. The development of newer agents (e.g., calcium antagonists and ACE inhibitors) has made quanethidine and quanadrel virtually unnecessary.

Reserpine

52. Is there a role for reserpine in the contemporary management of hypertension?

Reserpine is one of the oldest antihypertensive agents currently available. It is extremely effective when added to a diuretic.[336] Importantly, reserpine is very inexpensive and it can be given once daily. Several of the early key therapeutic trials which demonstrated the importance of treating hypertension used reserpine, including the first VA trials and the HDFP.[96,105] In addition, the SHEP trial used reserpine as a second step agent in patients who could not take atenolol.[12] Because reserpine is no longer patented, there are no pharmaceutical companies that promote its use. Because it has such a long record of success, some authorities still consider it an agent that should be strongly considered.[337–339]

Many other clinicians avoid reserpine because of a common impression that it is a potent inducer of depression. Students often are taught that they should always avoid reserpine in practice. This fear was generated from case reports in the 1950s of depression caused by reserpine.[340–342] Frequently, reserpine doses in these reports were 0.5 to 1.0 mg/day. Many of these patients would not meet current criteria for depression, but rather, were oversedated. In addition, when doses are limited to 0.25 mg/day, depression does not appear to be any more frequent than with any antihypertensive agent.[337] However, due to these historical factors, patients should be monitored carefully and reserpine should be discontinued if depression occurs. The drug should not be used in patients with a history of depression.

Reserpine may cause nasal stuffiness in many patients. In addition, gastrointestinal ulcerations have been reported with parenteral administration or very large doses.[296] In dosages of 0.25 mg/day or less, reserpine does not stimulate gastric secretion significantly. However, since gastric perforation and hemorrhage have occurred, reserpine should be avoided in patients with ulcers.[343]

Step-Down Therapy

53. T.J., a 63-year-old white male, has been treated with HCTZ 25 mg/day and verapamil 180 mg BID for the past 2 years. T.J. has no other risk factors and no evidence of target-organ damage. During this time his blood pressure has been well controlled, he has made significant improvements in his diet and exercise, and he has lost 15 pounds. Today his blood pressures are 128/78 mm Hg and 130/82 mm Hg. His pulse is 68 beats/min. He denies any problems or difficulties with his medication regimen. How should T.J. be managed?

The term step-down was coined when it was observed that, in contrast to rebound hypertension, many patients' blood pressures remain normal for weeks or months following drug discontinuation.[197,238,245] Patients like T.J. whose blood pressure has been well controlled for over a year deserve a trial of step-down therapy.[1] This is particularly true for patients who have lost weight or changed their diets. In this case, step-down would proceed in the reverse of the stepped care approach. The dose of verapamil would be reduced over several weeks. If the blood pressure remained well controlled (<140/90 mm Hg), then verapamil could be stopped. Following additional observation, the dose of hydrochlorothiazide could be reduced and possibly discontinued. Patients who undergo step-down must understand that they still need frequent follow-up assessments of their blood pressures. The majority of patients will continue to need some form of drug therapy. However, using step-down, it may be possible to simplify the regimen, reduce the potential for adverse reactions and lower the cost of therapy. In no case should the patient abruptly discontinue therapy because of the risks of withdrawal symptoms and rebound hypertension discussed in Question 43.

Update

Angiotensin II Receptor Antagonists: Losartan

U1. A.R., a 29-year-old black female with insulin dependent diabetes mellitus since age 18, was first noted to have hypertension 4½ months ago during a routine follow-up for her diabetes. Over the next 3 months she was seen monthly in the clinic during which time her blood pressures were 135–140/95–100 mm Hg despite strict adherence to her diabetic diet. She is not a smoker, her weight is within the desired range for her age and height, and she does not take oral contraceptives. Her fasting blood glucose ranges from 120–150 mg/dL and her latest glycosolated hemoglobin was 8.5% on a regimen of 18 units of NPH mixed with 8 units of regular insulin in the morning and 10 units of NPH with 6 units of regular in the evening. All of her laboratory tests, including renal function, are within normal limits, but she does have microalbuminuria. Six weeks ago she was started on enalapril 10 mg Q AM for blood pressure control and to hopefully slow the progression of her diabetic nephropathy. During today's clinic visit, her blood pressure is well controlled at 128/88 mm Hg, but she notes the development of a persistent dry cough starting about 3 weeks ago. She has no other signs of an upper respiratory infection. Since losartan is associated with a lower incidence of cough than enalapril, should A.R.'s enalapril be replaced with this new antihypertensive?

Losartan potassium (Cozaar) belongs to a new class of antihypertensive drugs known as angiotensin II receptor antagonists.[345–349] Unlike enalapril and the other ACE inhibitors which block the conversion of angiotensin I to angiotensin II, losartan binds to angiotensin II receptors in vascular smooth muscle, adrenal glands, and other tissues. As a result, access of angiotensin II to its receptors is blocked. This selective antagonism of angiotensin II can occur without affecting the metabolism of bradykinin, substance P, or norepinephrine. Blood pressure is reduced by antagonizing angiotensin II mediated vasoconstriction and prevention of aldosterone release. It is postulated that there should be less cough and drug-induced angioedema because both of these adverse effects occur via nonangiotensin pathways. Although the progression of diabetic nephropathy and albuminuria by losartan reduction of intraglomerular pressure has not been studied in controlled clinical trials, these effects are mediated by angiotensin II actions in the efferent arteriole of the kidney. Losartan, therefore, should be of benefit to A.R.

The blood pressure lowering efficacy of 50 mg of losartan is similar to that of 10 to 20 mg of enalapril.[345-349] Daily dosage ranges from 25 to 100 mg, with lower doses recommended for older patients or those with reduced renal function. The drug is well absorbed and extensively metabolized to an active metabolite which is then renally cleared. While the half-life of the parent compound is only 1.5 to 3 hours, the effects of the metabolite are much longer and losartan can be dosed once daily in most patients. Side effects include dizziness and gastrointestinal effects. The incidence of cough was minimal or nonexistent in clinical trials, but further clinical experience is needed to put this side effect in proper perspective. Another possible advantage of losartan is its ability to increase uric acid secretion, a potential benefit to those patients with gout or diuretic-induced hyperuricemia. Because A.R.'s blood pressure has responded well to the enalapril and her cough appears to be drug induced, conversion to losartan at a dose of 50 mg once a day is warranted. If the cough is due to enalapril, it should resolve over several days to two weeks after the enalapril has been discontinued.

References

1 **The Joint National Committee on Detection, Evaluation, and Treatment of High Blood Pressure.** The Fifth Report of the National Committee on Detection, Evaluation, and Treatment of High Blood Pressure (JNC V). Arch Intern Med. 1993;153:154.

2 **National High Blood Pressure Education Program.** National High Blood Pressure Education Program Working Group Report on Hypertension and Chronic Renal Failure. Arch Intern Med. 1991;151:1280.

3 **Brown TER, Carter BL.** Hypertension and end-stage renal disease. Ann Pharmacother. 1994;28:359.

4 **National High Blood Pressure Education Program.** National High Blood Pressure Education Program Working Group Report on Hypertension in Diabetes. Hypertension. 1994;23:145.

5 **White WB.** Assessment of patients with office hypertension by 24-hour noninvasive ambulatory blood pressure monitoring. Arch Intern Med. 1986; 146:2196.

6 **The National High Blood Pressure Education Program Coordinating Committee.** The National High Blood Pressure Education Program Working Group Report on ambulatory blood pressure monitoring. Arch Intern Med. 1990;150:2270.

7 **Pickering TG et al.** How common is white coat hypertension? JAMA. 1988; 259:225.

8 **Perloff D et al.** Prognostic value of ambulatory blood pressure measurements: further analyses. J Hypertens. 1989;7(Suppl. 3):S3.

9 **Pickering TG et al.** Ambulatory monitoring of blood pressure as a predictor of cardiovascular risk. Am Heart J. 1987;114:925.

10 **Calhoun DA et al.** Treatment of hypertensive crisis. N Engl J Med. 1990; 17:1177.

11 **Kannel WB et al.** Perspectives on systolic hypertension. The Framingham Study. Circulation. 1980;61:1179.

12 **SHEP Cooperative Research Group.** Prevention of stroke by antihypertensive drug treatment in older persons with isolated systolic hypertension. Final results of the Systolic Hypertension in the Elderly Program (SHEP). JAMA. 1991;265:3255.

13 **Wilking SVB et al.** Determinants of isolated systolic hypertension. JAMA. 1988;260:341.

14 **Furmaga EM et al.** Isolated systolic hypertension in older patients. Clin Pharm. 1993;12:347.

15 **National High Blood Pressure Education Program.** National High Blood Pressure Education Program Working Group Report on Hypertension in the Elderly. Hypertension. 1993;23:275.

16 **Frohlich ED et al.** Report of a special task force appointed by the Steering Committee, American Heart Association: recommendations for human blood pressure determination by sphygmomanometers. Dallas, TX: American Heart Association; 1987.

17 **Applegate WB.** Hypertension in elderly patients. Ann Intern Med. 1989; 110:901.

18 **Messerli FH, Ventura HO.** Cardiovascular pathophysiology of essential hypertension: a clue to therapy. Drugs. 1985;30(Suppl. 1):25.

19 **Panza JA et al.** Abnormal endothelium-dependent vascular relaxation in patients with essential hypertension. N Engl J Med. 1990;323:22.

20 **Vane JR et al.** Regulatory functions of the vascular endothelium. N Engl J Med. 1990;323:27.

21 **Gifford RW Jr et al.** Office evaluation of hypertension: a statement for health professionals by a Writing Group of the Council for High Blood Pressure Research, American Heart Association. Circulation. 1989;79:721.

22 **Frohlich ED.** Mechanisms contributing to high blood pressure. Ann Intern Med. 1983;98:709.

23 **Guyton AC et al.** Arterial pressure regulation: overriding dominance of the kidneys in long-term regulation and in hypertension. Am J Med. 1972;52:584.

24 **Guyton AC.** Dominant role of the kidneys in long-term regulation of arterial pressure and in hypertension: the integrated system for pressure control. In: Wonsiewicz MJ, ed. Textbook of Medical Physiology. Philadelphia: WB Saunders; 1991:205.

25 **Williams GH et al.** Diseases of the adrenal cortex. In: Wilson JD et al., eds. Harrison's Principles of Internal Medicine. New York: McGraw-Hill; 1991: 1713.

26 **Laragh JH.** Renin profiling for diagnosis, risk assessment, and treatment of hypertension. Kid International. 1993; 44:1163.

27 **Williams GH.** Hypertensive vascular disease. In: Wilson JD et al., eds. Harrison's Principles of Internal Medicine. New York: McGraw-Hill; 1991:1001.

28 **Tarazi RC.** Pathophysiology of essential hypertension: role of the autonomic nervous system. Am J Med. 1983; 7(4A):2.

29 **McCubbin JW et al.** Baroceptor function in chronic renal hypertension. Circ Res. 1956;4:205.

30 **Hunt JC.** Sodium intake and hypertension: a cause for concern. Ann Intern Med. 1983;98:724.

31 **Intersalt Cooperative Research Group.** Intersalt: an international study of electrolyte excretion and blood pressure. Results for 24 hour urinary sodium and potassium excretion. Br Med J. 1988;297:319.

32 **Porter GA.** Chronology of the sodium hypothesis and hypertension. Ann Intern Med. 1983;98:720.

33 **Cutler JA et al.** Calcium and blood pressure: an epidemiologic perspective. Am J Hypertens. 1990;3:137S.

34 **National High Blood Pressure Education Program Working Group.** National High Blood Pressure Education Program Working Group on primary prevention of hypertension. Arch Intern Med. 1993;153:186.

35 **Mikami H et al.** Blood pressure response to dietary calcium intervention in humans. Am J Hypertens. 1990;3: 147S.

36 **Strazzullo P et al.** Controlled trial of long-term oral calcium supplementation in essential hypertension. Hypertension. 1986;8:1084.

37 **McCarron DA et al.** Blood pressure response to oral calcium in persons with mild to moderate hypertension. Ann Intern Med. 1985;103:824.

38 **Cappuccio FP et al.** Does oral calcium supplementation lower high blood pressure?: a double blind study. J Hypertens. 1987;5:67.

39 **Reaven GM.** Role of insulin resistance in human disease. Diabetes. 1988;37: 1595.

40 **Despres J-P et al.** Regional distribution of body fat, plasma lipoproteins, and cardiovascular disease. Arteriosclerosis. 1990;10:497.

41 **Barnard RJ et al.** Role of diet and exercise in the management of hyperinsulinemia and associated atherosclerotic risk factors. Am J Cardiol. 1992; 69:440.

42 **Slater EE.** Insulin resistance and hypertension. Hypertension. 1991;18 (Suppl. I):I-108.

43 **Kaplan NM.** The deadly quartet: upper-body obesity, glucose intolerance, hypertriglyceridemia and hypertension. Arch Intern Med. 1989;149:1514.

44 **Bulpitt CJ et al.** A symptom questionnaire for hypertensive patients. J Chron Dis. 1974;27:309.

45 **Weiss NS.** Relation of high blood pressure to headache, epistaxis, and selected other symptoms: the United States Health Examination Survey of Adults. N Engl J Med. 1972;287:631.

46 **The Trials of Hypertension Prevention Collaborative Research Group.** The effects of nonpharmacologic interventions on blood pressure of persons with high normal levels: results of the Trials of Hypertension Prevention, Phase I. JAMA. 1992;267:1213.

47 **van Montfrans GA et al.** Relaxation therapy and continuous ambulatory blood pressure in mild hypertension: a controlled study. Br Med J. 1990;300: 1368.

48 **Charlson ME et al.** Absenteeism and labelling in hypertensive subjects: prevention of an adverse impact in those at high risk. Am J Med. 1982;73:165.

49 **Croog SH et al.** Work performance, absenteeism and antihypertensive medications. J Hypertens. 1987;5(Suppl. I): S47.

50 **Monk M.** Blood pressure awareness and psychological well-being in the Health and Nutrition Examination Survey. Clin Invest Med. 1981;4:183.

51 **Bloom JR et al.** Hypertension labeling and sense of well-being. Am J Public Health. 1981;71:1228.

52 **Farquhar JW et al.** Effects of community wide education on cardiovascular disease risk factors: the Stanford Five-City Project. JAMA. 1990;264: 359.

53 **Frohlich ED et al.** The heart in hypertension. N Engl J Med. 1992;327:998.

54 **Eselin JA, Carter BL.** Hypertension and left ventricular hypertrophy: is drug therapy beneficial? Pharmacother. 1994;14:60.

55 **Dunn FG et al.** Left ventricular hypertrophy and myocardial ischemia in systemic hypertension. Am J Cardiol. 1987; 60:19I.

56 **Kannel WB et al.** Left ventricular hypertrophy by electrocardiogram: prevalence, incidence, and mortality in the Framingham Study. Ann Intern Med. 1969;71:89.

57 **Levy D et al.** Prognostic implications of echocardiographically determined left ventricular mass in the Framingham Heart Study. N Engl J Med. 1990; 322:1561.

58 **Levy D et al.** Left ventricular mass and incidence of coronary heart disease in an elderly cohort: The Framingham Heart Study. Ann Intern Med. 1989; 110:101.

59 **Kannel WB et al.** Role of blood pressure in the development of congestive heart failure: the Framingham Study. N Engl J Med. 1972;287:781.

60 **Kannel WB et al.** Precursors of sudden coronary death: factors related to the incidence of sudden death. Circulation. 1975;51:606.

61 **Stokes J et al.** Blood pressure as a risk factor for cardiovascular disease. The Framingham study 30 years of follow-up. Hypertension. 1989;13(Suppl. I):I-13.

62 **Phillips SJ, Whisnant JP.** Hypertension and the brain. Arch Intern Med. 1992;152:938.

63 **Dennis MS et al.** A comparison of risk factors and prognosis for transient ischemic attacks and minor ischemic strokes: the Oxfordshire Community Stroke Project. Stroke. 1989;20:1494.

64 **MacMahon S et al.** Blood pressure, stroke, and coronary heart disease, part 1: prolonged differences in blood pressure: prospective observational studies corrected for the regression dilution bias. Lancet. 1990;335:765.

65 **Chobanian AV.** Hypertension, antihypertensive drugs, and atherosclerosis: mechanisms and clinical implications. J Clin Hypertens. 1986;2(Suppl. 3):148.

66 **Chester EM et al.** Hypertensive encephalopathy: a clinicopathologic study of 20 cases. Neurology. 1978;28:928.

67 **Healton EB et al.** Hypertensive encephalopathy and the neurologic manifestations of malignant hypertension. Neurology. 1982;32:127.

68 **Tortorice KL, Carter BL.** Stroke prophylaxis: hypertension management and antithrombotic therapy. Ann Pharmacother. 1992;27:471.

69 **Parving HH et al.** Early aggressive antihypertensive treatment reduces rate of decline in kidney function in diabetic nephropathy. Lancet. 1983;1: 1175.

70 **Shulman NB et al.** Prognostic value of serum creatinine and effect of treatment of hypertension on renal function, results from the Hypertension Detection and Follow-up Program. Hypertension. 1989;13(Suppl. I):I-80.

71 **Bergstrom J et al.** Progression of chronic renal failure in man is retarded with more frequent clinical follow-ups and better blood pressure control. Clin Nephrol. 1986;25:1.

72 **Brazy PC et al.** Progression of renal insufficiency: role of blood pressure. Kid International. 1989;35:670.

73 **Pettinger WA et al.** Long-term improvement in renal function after short-term strict blood pressure control in hypertensive nephrosclerosis. Hypertension. 1989;13:766.

74 **Rostand SG et al.** Renal insufficiency in treated essential hypertension. N Engl J Med. 1989;320:684.

75 **Campese VM et al.** Abnormal renal hemodynamics in black salt-sensitive patients with hypertension. Hypertension. 1991;18:805.

76 **Kaplan NM.** Systemic hypertension: mechanisms and diagnosis. In: Braunwald E, ed. Heart Disease: A Textbook of Cardiovascular Medicine. 3rd ed. Philadelphia: WB Saunders; 1988:819.

77 **Levy D et al.** Determinants of sensitivity and specificity of electrocardiographic criteria for left ventricular hypertrophy. Circulation. 1990;81:815.

78 **Janka HU et al.** Risk factors for progression of background retinopathy in long-standing IDDM. Diabetes. 1989; 38:460.

79 **Tuescher A et al.** Incidence of diabetic retinopathy and relationship to baseline plasma glucose and blood pressure. Diabetes Care. 1988;11:246.

80 **Expert Panel on Detection, Evaluation, and Treatment of High Blood Cholesterol in Adults.** Summary of the second report of the National Cholesterol Education Program (NCEP) Expert Panel on Detection, Evaluation, and Treatment of High Blood Cholesterol in Adults (Adult Treatment Panel II). JAMA. 1993;269:3015.

81 **Zinner SH et al.** Familial aggregation of blood pressure in children. N Engl J Med. 1971;284:401.

82 **Saunders E.** Hypertension in blacks. Primary Care. 1991;18:607.

83 **Kannel WB et al.** Overall and coronary heart disease mortality in relation to major risk factors in 325,348 men screened for the MRFIT. Am Heart J. 1986;112:825.

84 **Materson BJ et al.** The Veterans Administration Cooperative Study Group on Antihypertensive Agents. Cigarette smoking interferes with treatment of hypertension. Arch Intern Med. 1988; 148:2116.

85 **Greenberg G et al.** The relationship between smoking and the response to antihypertensive treatment in mild hypertensives in the Medical Research Council's trial of treatment. Int J Epidemiol. 1987;16:25.

86 **Dollery C et al.** The Medical Research Council Hypertension Trial: the smoking patient. Am Heart J. 1988;115:276.

87 **Green MS et al.** Blood pressure in smokers and nonsmokers: epidemiologic findings. Am Heart J. 1986;111: 932.

88 **Kuller L et al.** Control of cigarette smoking from a medical perspective. Ann Rev Public Health. 1982;3:153.

89 **Stamler R et al.** Weight and blood pressure: findings in hypertension screening of 1 million Americans. JAMA. 1978;240:1607.

90 **Lipid Research Clinics Program.** The Lipid Research Clinics Program Primary Prevention Trial results: I. Reduction in incidence of coronary heart disease. JAMA. 1984;251:351.

91 **Frick MH et al.** Helsinki Heart Study: primary prevention trial with gemfibrozil in middle-aged men with dyslipidemia. N Engl J Med. 1987;317:1237.

92 **Brown G et al.** Regression of coronary artery disease as a result of intensive lipid-lowering therapy in men with high levels of apolipoprotein B. N Engl J Med. 1990;323:1289.

93 **Blankenhorn DH et al.** Beneficial effects of combined colestipol-niacin therapy on coronary atherosclerosis and coronary venous bypass grafts. JAMA. 1987;257:3233.

94 **Samuelsson O et al.** Cardiovascular morbidity in relation to change in blood pressure and serum cholesterol levels in treated hypertension: results from the Primary Prevention Trial in Göteborg, Sweden. JAMA. 1987;258:1768.

95 **Sullivan J.** Salt sensitivity: definition, conception, methodology, and long-term issues. Hypertension. 1991;17(Suppl. I): I-61.

96 **Veterans Administration Cooperative Study Group on Antihypertensive Agents.** Effects of treatment on morbidity in hypertension: results in patients with diastolic blood pressures averaging 115 through 129 mm Hg. JAMA. 1967;202:1028.

97 **Collins R et al.** Blood pressure, stroke, and coronary heart disease: part 2, short-term reductions in blood pressure: overview of randomized drug trials in their epidemiological context. Lancet. 1990;335:827.

98 **Hebert PR et al.** Recent evidence on drug therapy of mild to moderate hypertension and decreased risk of coronary heart disease. Arch Intern Med. 1993;153:578.

99 **Thijs L et al.** A meta-analysis of outcome trials in elderly hypertensives. J Hypertension. 1992;10:1103.

100 **Management Committee of the National Heart Foundation of Australia.** Treatment of mild hypertension in the elderly. Med J Aust. 1981;2:398.

101 **Amery A et al.** Efficacy of antihypertensive drug treatment according to age, sex, blood pressure, and previous cardiovascular disease in patients over the age of 60. Lancet. 1986;2:589.

102 **Coope J et al.** Randomized trial of treatment of hypertension in elderly patients in primary care. Br Med J. 1986; 293:1145.

103 **Dahlöf B et al.** Morbidity and mortality in the Swedish Trial in Old Patients with Hypertension (STOP-Hypertension). Lancet. 1991;338:1281.

104 **MRC Working Party.** Medical Research Council trial of treatment of hypertension in older adults: principal results. Br Med J. 1992;304:405.

105 **Hypertension Detection and Follow-up Program Cooperative Group.** Five-year findings of the Hypertension Detection and Follow-up Program. II. Mortality by race, sex and age. JAMA. 1979;242:2572.

106 **Moser M et al.** An overview of the meta-analyses of the hypertension treatment trials. Arch Intern Med. 1991;151:1277.

107 **Amery A et al.** Syst-Eur: a multicentre trial on the treatment of isolated systolic hypertension in the elderly: objectives, protocol and organization. Aging. 1991;3:287.

108 **Sever P et al.** Management guidelines in essential hypertension: report of the second working party of the British Hypertension Society. Br Med J. 1993; 306:983.

109 **Cruickshank JM et al.** Benefits and potential harm of lowering high blood pressure. Lancet. 1987;1:581.

110 **Farnett L et al.** The J-curve phenomenon and the treatment of hypertension. Is there a point beyond which pressure reduction is dangerous? JAMA. 1991; 265:489.

111 **Joint National Committee.** Nonpharmacological approaches to the control of high blood pressure: final report of the Subcommittee on Nonpharmacological Therapy of the 1984 Joint National Committee on Detection, Evaluation, and Treatment of High Blood Pressure. Hypertension. 1986;8:444.

112 **Cutler JA et al.** An overview of randomized trials of sodium reduction and blood pressure. Hypertension. 1991; 17(Suppl. I):I-27.

113 **Flack JM et al.** Racial and ethnic modifiers of the salt-blood pressure response. Hypertension. 1991;17(Suppl. I):I-115.

114 **Luft FC et al.** Salt sensitivity and resistance of blood pressure: age and race as factors in physiological responses. Hypertension. 1991;17(Suppl. I):I-102.

115 **Grobbee DE.** Methodology of sodium sensitivity assessment: the example of age and sex. Hypertension. 1991;17 (Suppl. I):I-109.

116 **Sims EAH et al.** Obesity and hypertension: mechanisms and implications for management. JAMA. 1982;247:49.

117 **Reisin E et al.** Effect of weight loss without salt restriction on the reduction of blood pressure in overweight hypertensive patients. N Engl J Med. 1978; 298:1.

118 **Reisin E et al.** Effects of weight reduction on arterial hypertension. J Chronic Dis. 1982;35:887.

119 **Schotte DE et al.** The effects of weight reduction on blood pressure in 301 obese patients. Arch Intern Med. 1990; 150:1701.

120 **Sacks FM.** Dietary fats and blood pressure: a critical review of the evidence. Nutr Rev. 1989;47:291.

121 **Gyntelberg F et al.** Relationship between blood pressure and physical fitness, smoking and alcohol consumption in Copenhagen males aged 40–59. Acta Med Scand. 1974;195:375.

122 **Cooper KH et al.** Physical fitness levels vs selected coronary risk factors: a cross-sectional study. JAMA. 1976; 236:166.

123 **World Hypertension League.** Physical exercise in the management of hypertension: a consensus statement by the World Hypertension League. J Hypertens. 1991;9:283.

124 **MacMahon SW et al.** Alcohol and hypertension: implications for prevention and treatment. Ann Intern Med. 1986; 105:124.

125 **Saunders JB et al.** Alcohol-induced hypertension. Lancet. 1981;2:653.

126 **Patel C et al.** Trial of relaxation in reducing coronary risk: four year follow up. Br Med J. 1985;290:1103.

127 **Patel C et al.** Stress management, blood pressure and quality of life. J Hypertens. 1987;5(Suppl.):S21.

128 **Kannel WB.** Update on the role of cigarette smoking in coronary artery disease. Am Heart J. 1981;101:319.

129 **Gordon T et al.** Death and coronary attacks in men after giving up cigarette smoking. A report from the Framingham Study. Lancet. 1974;2:1345.

130 **Bühler FR et al.** Impact of smoking on heart attacks, strokes, blood pressure control, drug dose, and quality of life aspects in the International Pro-

spective Primary Prevention Study in Hypertension. Am Heart J. 1988;11: 282.

131 Robertson D et al. Effects of caffeine on plasma renin activity, catecholamines and blood pressure. N Engl J Med. 1978;298:181.

132 Resnick LM. Hypertension and abnormal glucose homeostasis: possible role of divalent ion metabolism. Am J Med. 1989;87(6A):17S.

133 Nadler J et al. Evidence that intracellular free magnesium deficiency plays a role in increased platelet reactivity in type II diabetes mellitus. Diabetes Care. 1992;15:835.

134 Neaton JD et al. Treatment of Mild Hypertension Study: final results. JAMA. 1993;270:713.

135 Weber MA et al. Hypertension: steps forward and steps backward. The Joint National Committee Fifth Report. Arch Intern Med. 1993;153:149.

136 Materson BJ et al. Single-drug therapy for hypertension in men: a comparison of six antihypertensive agents with placebo. N Engl J Med. 1993;328: 914.

137 Systolic Hypertension in the Elderly Program Cooperative Research Group. Implications of the Systolic Hypertension in the Elderly Program. Hypertension. 1993;21:335.

138 Kaplan NM. Alternating monotherapy is the preferred treatment. Pharmacother. 1985;5:195.

139 Kannel WB et al. Initial drug therapy for hypertensive patients with hyperlipidemia. Amer Heart J. 1989;118: 1012.

140 Carter BL et al. Selected factors that influence responses to antihypertensives. Arch Fam Med. 1994;3:528.

141 Cramer JA et al. How often is medication taken as prescribed? A novel assessment technique. JAMA. 1989;261: 3273.

142 Eisen SA et al. The effect of prescribed daily dose frequency on patient medication compliance. Arch Intern Med. 1990;150:1881.

143 Allen JH et al. Antihypertensive effect of hydrochlorothiazide administered once or twice daily. Clin Pharm. 1982; 1:239.

144 Hornung RS et al. Twice-daily verapamil for hypertension: a comparison with propranolol. Am J Cardiol. 1986; 57:93D.

145 Lopez LM et al. Once-daily propranolol for hypertension. Drug Intell Clin Pharm. 1984;18:812.

146 Carter BL et al. Once-daily propranolol for hypertension: a comparison of regular-release, long-acting, and generic formulations. Pharmacother. 1989;9: 17.

147 Saunders E et al. Comparison of the efficacy and safety of a beta-blocker, a calcium channel blocker, and a converting enzyme inhibitor in hypertensive blacks. Arch Intern Med. 1990; 150:1707.

148 Veterans Administration Cooperative Study Group on Antihypertensive Agents. Low-dose captopril for the treatment of mild to moderate hypertension. I: Results of a 14-week trial. Arch Intern Med. 1984;144:1947.

149 Caralis PV. Hypertension in the Hispanic-American population. Am J Med. 1990;88(Suppl. 3B):9s.

150 Frishman W et al. Twice-daily administration of oral verapamil in the treatment of essential hypertension. Arch Intern Med. 1986;146:561.

151 Carter BL et al. Differences in serum concentrations of and responses to generic verapamil in the elderly. Pharmacother. 1993;13:139.

152 Schwartz JB et al. Prolongation of verapamil elimination kinetics during chronic oral administration. Am Heart J. 1982;104;198.

153 Hypertension Detection and Follow-up Program Cooperative Group. Five-year findings of the Hypertension Detection and Follow-up Program. I. Reduction in mortality of persons with high blood pressure, including mild hypertension. JAMA. 1979;242:2562.

154 The Australian Therapeutic Trial in Mild Hypertension. Report by the management committee. Lancet. 1980; 1:1261.

155 Helgeland A. Treatment of mild hypertension: a 5-year controlled trial. The Oslo Study. Am J Med. 1980;69: 725.

156 Medical Research Council Working Party. MRC trial of treatment of mild hypertension: principal results. Br Med J. 1985;291:97.

157 Vardan S et al. Efficacy and reduced metabolic side effects of a 15 mg chlorthalidone formulation in the treatment of hypertension. JAMA. 1987;258:484.

158 Finnerty FA et al. Long-term effect of furosemide and hydrochlorothiazide in patients with essential hypertension: a two-year comparison of efficacy and safety. Angiology. 1977;28:125.

159 Araoye MA et al. Furosemide compared with hydrochlorothiazide, long-term treatment of hypertension. JAMA. 1978;240:1863.

160 Holland OB et al. Antihypertensive comparisons of furosemide with hydrochlorothiazide for black patients. Arch Intern Med. 1979;139:1015.

161 AHFS Drug Information. Potassium-sparing diuretics. In: McEvoy GK et al., eds. American Hospital Formulary Service, American Society of Hospital Pharmacists. 1993:1638.

162 Morgan DB, Davidson C. Hypokalemia and diuretics: analysis of publications. Br Med J. 1980;280:905.

163 Holland OB et al. Diuretic-induced ventricular ectopic activity. Am J Med. 1981;70:762.

164 McKenney JM et al. The effect of low-dose hydrochlorothiazide on blood pressure, serum potassium and lipoproteins. Pharmacotherapy. 1986;6:179.

165 Schwartz AB, Swartz CD. Dosage of potassium chloride elixir to correct thiazide-induced hypokalemia. JAMA. 1974;230:702.

166 Kosman ME. Management of potassium problems during long-term diuretic therapy. JAMA. 1974;230:743.

167 Multiple Risk Factor Intervention Trial Research Group. Baseline rest electrocardiographic abnormalities, antihypertensive treatment, and mortality in the Multiple Risk Factor Intervention Trial. Am J Cardiol. 1985;55:1.

168 The Hypertension Detection and Follow-up Program Cooperative Research Group. The effect of antihypertensive drug treatment on mortality in the presence of resting electrocardi-

ographic abnormalities at baseline: the HDFP experience. Circulation. 1984; 70:996.

169 Papademetriou V et al. Effectiveness of potassium chloride or triamterene in thiazide hypokalemia. Arch Intern Med. 1985;145:1986.

170 Goldner MG et al. Hyperglycemia and glucosuria due to thiazide derivatives administered in diabetes mellitus. N Engl J Med. 1960;262:403.

171 Hollifiels J. Biochemical consequences of diuretic therapy in hypertension. J Tenn Med Assoc. 1978;71: 757.

172 Amery A et al. Glucose intolerance during diuretic therapy in elderly hypertensive patients. A second report from the European Working Party in High Blood Pressure in the Elderly (EWPHE). Postgrad Med J. 1986;2: 919.

173 Murphy MB et al. Glucose intolerance in hypertensive patients treated with diuretics: a fourteen-year follow-up. Lancet. 1982;2:1293.

174 Carney S et al. Optimal dose of thiazide diuretic. Med J Aust. 1976;2:692.

175 Ram C. Diuretics in the management of hypertension. Postgrad Med. 1982; 71:155.

176 Diamond MT. Hyperglycemic hyperosmolar coma associated with hydrochlorothiazide and pancreatitis. N Y State J Med. 1972;72:1741.

177 Fonseca V et al. Hyperosmolar nonketotic diabetic syndrome precipitated by treatment with diuretics. Br Med J. 1982;284:36.

178 Houston MC. Adverse effects of antihypertensive drug therapy on glucose tolerance. Cardiol Clin. 1986;4:117.

179 Helderman JH et al. Prevention of the glucose intolerance of thiazide diuretics by maintenance of body potassium. Diabetes. 1983;32:1061.

180 Manuel A, Steele TH. Changes in renal urate handling after prolonged thiazide treatment. Am J Med. 1974;57: 741.

181 Boss GR, Seegmiller JE. Hyperuricemia and gout classification, complications and management. New Engl J Med. 1979;300:1459.

182 Langford HG et al. Is thiazide-produced uric acid elevation harmful? Analysis of data from the Hypertension Detection and Follow-up Program. Arch Int Med. 1987;147:645.

183 Ames RP. The effects of antihypertensive drugs on serum lipids and lipoproteins. Diuretics. Drugs. 1986;32:260.

184 Grimm RH et al. Effects of thiazide diuretics on plasma lipids and lipoprotein in mildly hypertensive patients. Ann Int Med. 1981;94:7.

185 Lasser NL et al. Effects of antihypertensive therapy on plasma lipids and lipoprotein in the Multiple Risk Factor Intervention Trial. Am J Med. 1984; 75(2A):52.

186 Amery A et al. Influence of antihypertensive therapy on serum cholesterol in elderly hypertensive patients. Results of trial by the European Working Party on High Blood Pressure in the Elderly (EWPHE). Acta Cardiol. 1982;37:235.

187 Veterans Administration Cooperative Study Group on Antihypertensive Agents. Comparison of propranolol and hydrochlorothiazide for the in-

itial treatment of hypertension. Results of long-term therapy. JAMA. 1982; 248:2004.

188 Helgeland A et al. High-density lipoprotein cholesterol and antihypertensive drugs: the Oslo study. Br Med J. 1978;2:403.

189 Sutton RAL. Diuretics and calcium metabolism. Am J Kidney Dis. 1985; 5:4.

190 Mohamadi M et al. Effect of the thiazides on serum calcium. Clin Pharmacol Ther. 1979;26:390.

191 Hollifield JW. Potassium and magnesium abnormalities: diuretics and arrhythmias in hypertension. Am J Med. 1984;77(5A):28.

192 Leary WP et al. Effects of a combination of hydrochlorothiazide and amiloride on urinary magnesium excretion in healthy adults. Curr Ther Res Clin Exp. 1984;35:293.

193 Whang R et al. Predictors of clinical hypomagnesemia. Arch Int Med. 1984; 144:1794.

194 Whang R. Magnesium deficiency. Causes and clinical implications. Drugs. 1984;28(Suppl. 1):143.

195 Ashouri OS. Severe diuretic-induced hyponatremia in the elderly. Arch Int Med. 1986;146:1355.

196 Freidman E et al. Thiazide-induced hyponatremia: reproducibility by single dose rechallenge and an analysis of pathogenesis. Ann Int Med. 1989;110: 24.

197 Levinson PD et al. Persistence of normal BP after withdrawal of drug treatment in mild hypertension. Arch Intern Med. 1982;142:2265.

198 Freis ED. Age and antihypertensive drugs (hydrochlorothiazide, bendroflumethiazide, nadolol and captopril). Am J Cardiol. 1988;61:117.

199 Massie B et al. Diltiazem and propranolol in mild to moderate essential hypertension as monotherapy or with hydrochlorothiazide. Ann Intern Med. 1987;107:150.

200 Veterans Administration Cooperative Study Group on Antihypertensive Agents. Comparison of propranolol and hydrochlorothiazide for the initial treatment of hypertension: I. Results of short-term titration with emphasis on racial differences in response. JAMA. 1982;248:1996.

201 Saunders E et al. Comparison of the efficacy and safety of a beta-blocker, a calcium channel blocker, and a converting enzyme inhibitor in hypertensive blacks. Arch Intern Med. 1990; 150:1707.

202 Kincaid-Smith P. Beta-adrenergic receptor blocking drugs in hypertension with special reference to their use as initial therapy. Am J Cardiol. 1984;53: 12A.

203 Whipps RG et al. Beta-blockers and hypertension: carbon copies or real choice. Compr Ther. 1984;10:12.

204 Lowenthal DT et al. Mechanisms of action and the clinical pharmacology of beta-adrenergic blocking drugs. Am J Med. 1984;77(4A):119.

205 Gerber JG, Nies AS. Beta-adrenergic blocking drugs. Annu Rev Med. 1985; 36:145.

206 Frishman WH. Atenolol and timolol, two new systemic beta-adrenergic antagonists. N Engl J Med. 1982;306: 1456.

207 **Ellis ME et al.** Cardioselectivity in asthmatic patients. Eur J Clin Pharmacol. 1981;21:173.

208 **Deacon SP et al.** Acebutolol, atenolol, and propranolol and metabolic responses to acute hypoglycaemia in diabetics. Br Med J. 1977;2:1255.

209 **Wallin DJ, Shah SV.** Beta-adrenergic blocking agents in the treatment of hypertension: choices based on pharmacologic properties and patient characteristics. Arch Intern Med. 1987;147:654.

210 **Taylor SH.** Intrinsic sympathomimetic activity: clinical fact or fiction? Am J Cardiol. 1983;52(Suppl.):16D.

211 **Black CD, Mann HJ.** Intrinsic sympathomimetic activity: physiologic reality or marketing phenomenon. Drug Intell Clin Pharm. 1984;18:554.

212 **Frishman WH.** Pindolol: a new beta-adrenoceptor antagonist with partial agonist activity. N Engl J Med. 1983;308:940.

213 **Hansson L.** Hemodynamics of metoprolol and pindolol in systemic hypertension with particular reference to reversal of structural vascular changes. Am J Cardiol. 1986;57(Suppl.):29C.

214 **van Brummelen P.** The relevance of intrinsic sympathomimetic activity for beta-blocker-induced changes in plasma lipids. J Cardiovasc Pharmacol. 1983;5(Suppl.):S51.

215 **Frishman WH et al.** Beta-adrenergic blockade for survivors of acute myocardial infarction. N Engl J Med. 1984;310:830.

216 **Westerlund A.** Central nervous system side effects with hydrophilic and lipophilic beta blockers. Eur J Clin Pharmacol. 1985;28(Suppl.):S73.

217 **Gengo FM et al.** The effect of beta-blockers on mental performance in older hypertensive patients. Arch Intern Med. 1988;148:779.

218 **Beller GA et al.** Double-blind, placebo-controlled trial of propranolol given once, twice and four times daily in stable angina pectoris: a multicenter study using serial exercise testing. Am J Cardiol. 1984;54:37.

219 **van den Brink et al.** One and three doses of propranolol a day in hypertension. Clin Pharm Ther. 1980;27:9.

220 **McAinsh J et al.** Pharmacokinetic and pharmacodynamic studies with long-acting propranolol. Br J Clin Pharmacol. 1978;6:115.

221 **Frohlich ED.** Hemodynamic considerations in clinical hypertension. Med Clin N Am. 1987;71:803.

222 **Gunnar RW et al.** ACC/AHS guidelines for the early management of patients with acute myocardial infarction. Circulation. 1990;82:664.

223 **Lavie CG, Gersh BJ.** Acute myocardial infarction: initial manifestations, management, and prognosis. Mayo Clin Proc. 1990;65:531.

224 **Talbert RL.** Use of beta-adrenergic blocking agents after myocardial infarction. Clin Pharm. 1983;2:68.

225 **Hayes PE, Schulz SC.** The use of beta-adrenergic blocking agents in anxiety disorders and schizophrenia. Pharmacother. 1983;2:101.

226 **Corelli R, Hart LL.** Beta-blocking agents for migraine. DICP, Ann Pharmacother. 1989;23:248.

227 **Mills GA, Horn JR.** Beta-blockers and glucose control. Drug Intell Clin Pharm. 1985;19:246.

228 **Bengtsson C et al.** Do antihypertensive drugs precipitate diabetes? Br Med J. 1984;289:1495.

229 **The Working Group on Hypertension in Diabetes.** Statement on hypertension in diabetes mellitus: final report. Arch Intern Med. 1987;147:830.

230 **Rotmensch HH et al.** Angiotensin-converting enzyme inhibitors. Med Clin North Am. 1988;72:399.

231 **Ujhelyi MR et al.** Angiotensin-converting enzyme inhibitors: mechanistic controversies. Pharmacother. 1989;9:351.

232 **Williams GH.** Converting-enzyme inhibitors in the treatment of hypertension. N Engl J Med. 1988;319:1517.

233 **Edwards CRW, Padfield PL.** Angiotensin-converting enzyme inhibitors: Past, present and bright future. Lancet. 1985;1:30.

234 **Weir MR, Wolfsthal SD.** Hypertension and the kidney. Prim Care. 1991;18:525.

235 **Working Group on Renovascular Hypertension.** Detection, evaluation, and treatment of renovascular hypertension. Arch Intern Med. 1987;147:820.

236 **Levenson DJ, Dzau VJ.** Effects of angiotensin-converting enzyme inhibition on renal hemodynamics in renal artery stenosis. Kidney Int. 1987;31 (Suppl. 20):S173.

237 **Jackson B et al.** Differential renal function during angiotensin-converting enzyme inhibition in renovascular hypertension. Hypertension. 1986;8:650.

238 **Alderman MH et al.** Antihypertensive drug therapy withdrawal in a general population. Arch Intern Med. 1986;146:1309.

239 **Cummings DM et al.** The antihypertensive response to lisinopril: the effect of age in a predominantly black population. J Clin Pharmacol. 1989;29:25.

240 **Waren SE, O'Connor DT.** Hyperkalemia resulting from captopril administration. JAMA. 1980;244:2551.

241 **Textor SC et al.** Hyperkalemia in azotemic patients during angiotensin-converting enzyme inhibition and aldosterone reduction with captopril. Am J Med. 1982;73:719.

242 **Bucca C et al.** Hyper-responsiveness of the extrathoracic airway in patients with captopril-induced cough. Chest. 1990;98:1133.

243 **Just PM.** The positive association of cough with angiotensin-converting enzyme inhibitors. Pharmacother. 1989;9:82.

244 **Tuck ML et al.** Low-dose captopril in mild to moderate geriatric hypertension. J Am Geriatr Soc. 1986;34:693.

245 **Finnerty FA.** Step-down therapy in hypertension: importance in long-term management. JAMA. 1981;246:2593.

246 **Webster J et al.** Initial dose of enalapril in hypertension. Br Med J. 1985;290:1623.

247 **Kelly JG, O'Malley K.** Clinical pharmacokinetics of the newer ACE inhibitors: a review. Clin Pharmacokinet. 1990;19:177.

248 **Leonard RG, Talbert RL.** Calcium-channel blocking agents. Clin Pharm. 1982;1:17.

249 **Bühler F et al.** Greater antihypertensive efficacy of the calcium channel inhibitor verapamil in older and low renin patients. Clin Sci. 1982;63(Suppl. 8):439s.

250 **Erne P et al.** Factors influencing the hypotensive effects of calcium channel antagonists. Hypertension. 1983;5 (Suppl. II):II-97.

251 **Zing W et al.** Calcium antagonists in elderly and black hypertensive patients: therapeutic controversies. Arch Intern Med. 1991;151:2154.

252 **Nicholson JP et al.** Hydrochlorothiazide is not additive to verapamil in treating essential hypertension. Arch Intern Med. 1989;149:125.

253 **Bauer JH, Reams GP.** Do calcium antagonists protect the human hypertensive kidney? Am J Hypertens. 1989;2:173s.

254 **Tolins JP, Raij L.** Antihypertensive therapy and the progression of chronic renal disease. Are there renoprotective drugs? Semin Nephrol. 1991;11:538.

255 **Epstein M.** Calcium antagonists and renal protection, current status and future perspectives. Arch Intern Med. 1992;152:1573.

256 **Zucchelli P et al.** Comparison of calcium channel blocker and ACE inhibitor therapy on the progression of renal insufficiency. Contrib Nephrol. 1990;81:255.

257 **Zucchelli P et al.** Calcium channel blockers: effects on progressive renal disease. Am J Kid Dis. 1991;17(Suppl. 1):94.

258 **Winniford MD et al.** Propranolol-verapamil versus propranolol-nifedipine in severe angina pectoris of effort: a randomized, double-blind, crossover study. Am J Cardiol. 1985;55:281.

259 **Parodi O et al.** Verapamil versus propranolol for angina at rest. Am J Cardiol. 1982;50:923.

260 **Frishman WH et al.** Comparison of oral propranolol and verapamil for combined systemic hypertension and angina pectoris: a placebo-controlled double-blind randomized crossover trial. Am J Cardiol. 1982;50:1164.

261 **Hoon TJ et al.** The pharmacodynamic and pharmacokinetic differences of the D- and L-isomers of verapamil: implications in the treatment of paroxysmal supraventricular tachycardia. Am Heart J. 1986;112:396.

262 **Echizen H et al.** Effects of d,L-verapamil on atrioventricular conduction in relation to its stereoselective first-pass metabolism. Clin Pharmacol Ther. 1985;38:71.

263 **Sasaki M et al.** The effects of aging and gender on the stereoselective pharmacokinetics of verapamil. Clin Pharmacol Ther. 1993;54:278.

264 **Tan ATH, Quek S.** Verapamil administered twice daily in stable angina pectoris. Chest. 1984;85:55.

265 **Snyder SH, Reynolds IJ.** Calcium-antagonists, receptor interactions that clarify therapeutic effects. N Engl J Med. 1985;313:995.

266 **Ehlert FJ et al.** The binding of [^{3}H]nitrendipine to receptors for calcium channel antagonists in the heart, cerebral cortex and ileum of rats. Life Sci. 1982;30:2191.

267 **Toyosaki N et al.** Combination therapy with diltiazem and nifedipine in patients with effort angina pectoris. Circulation. 1988;77:1370.

268 **Pucci PD et al.** Acute effects on exercise tolerance of felodipine and diltiazem, alone and in combination, in stable effort angina. Eur Heart J. 1991;12:55.

269 **Brogden RN et al.** Prazosin: a review of its pharmacological properties and therapeutic efficacy in hypertension. Drugs. 1977;14:163.

270 **Colucci WS.** New developments in alpha-adrenergic receptor pharmacology: implications for the initial treatment of hypertension. Am J Cardiol. 1983;51:639.

271 **Luther RR.** New perspectives on selective alpha₁ blockade. Am J Hypertens. 1989;2:729.

272 **Luther RR et al.** The effects of terazosin and methyclothiazide on blood pressure and serum lipids. Am Heart J. 1989;17:842.

273 **Stanazek WF et al.** Prazosin update: a review of its pharmacological and therapeutic use in hypertension and congestive heart failure. Drugs. 1983;25:339.

274 **Grimm RH.** Antihypertensive therapy: taking lipids into consideration. Am Heart J. 1991;22:910.

275 **Neusy AJ, Lowenstein J.** Effects of prazosin, atenolol, and thiazide diuretic on plasma lipids in patients with essential hypertension. Am J Med. 1986;80(Suppl. 2A):94.

276 **Frick MH et al.** Serum lipid changes in a one-year, multicenter, double-blind comparison of doxazosin and atenolol for mild to moderate essential hypertension. Am J Cardiol. 1987;59:61G.

277 **Leren P.** The cardiovascular effects of alpha-receptor blocking agents. J Hypertens. 1992;10(Suppl. 3):S11.

278 **Awan NA et al.** Efficacy of ambulatory systemic vasodilator therapy with oral prazosin in chronic refractory heart failure. Circulation. 1977;56:346.

279 **Waldo R.** Prazosin relieves Raynaud's vasospasm. JAMA. 1979;241:1037.

280 **Kirby RS et al.** Prazosin in the treatment of prostatic obstruction. A placebo-controlled study. Br J Urol. 1987;60:136.

281 **Chapple CR et al.** A 12-week placebo-controlled double-blind study of prazosin in the treatment of prostatic obstruction due to benign prostatic hyperplasia. Br J Urol. 1992;70:285.

282 **Graham RM et al.** Prazosin: the first-dose phenomenon. Br Med J. 1976;2:1293.

283 **Bouffioux CR, Penders L.** Alpha-blockers in the treatment of benign prostatic hypertrophy: physiologic basis and review of the problem. Eur Urol. 1984;10:306.

284 **Young RA, Brogden RN.** Doxazosin: a review of its pharmacodynamic and pharmacokinetic properties, and therapeutic efficacy in mild or moderate hypertension. Drugs. 1988;35:525.

285 **Sperzel WD et al.** Overall safety of terazosin as an antihypertensive agent. Am J Med. 1986;80:77.

286 **Sonders RC.** Pharmacokinetics of terazosin. Am J Med. 1986;80:20.

287 **Dauer AD.** Terazosin: an effective once-daily monotherapy for the treatment of hypertension. Am J Med. 1986;80(Suppl. 5B):29.

288 **Deger G.** Effect of terazosin on serum

289 **Fabricius PG, Hannaford JM.** Placebo-controlled study of terazosin in the treatment of benign prostatic hyperplasia with 2-year follow-up. Br J Urol. 1992;70(Suppl. 1):10.

290 **Lepor H, Laddu A.** Terazosin in the treatment of benign prostatic hyperplasia: the United States experience. Br J Urol. 1992;70(Suppl. 1):2.

291 **Carter BL.** Labetalol. Drug Intell Clin Pharm. 1983;17:704.

292 **MacCarthy EP, Bloomfield SS.** Labetalol: a review of its pharmacology, pharmacokinetics, clinical uses and adverse effects. Pharmacother. 1983;3:193.

293 **Papademetriou V et al.** Treatment of severe hypertension with intravenous labetalol. Clin Pharmacol Ther. 1982;32:431.

294 **Cumming AMM et al.** Intravenous labetalol in the treatment of severe hypertension. Br J Clin Pharmacol. 1982;13(Suppl.):93s.

295 **Pugsley DJ et al.** Controlled comparison of labetalol and propranolol in the management of severe hypertension. Br J Clin Pharmacol. 1976;3(Suppl.):777.

296 **Gerber JC, Nies AS.** Antihypertensive agents and the drug therapy of hypertension. In: Gilman et al., eds. The Pharmacological Basis of Therapeutics. 8th ed. New York: Pergamon Press; 1990:784.

297 **Hoffman BB, Lefkowitz RJ.** Adrenergic receptor antagonists. In: Gilman et al., eds. Goodman and Gilman's. The Pharmacological Basis of Therapeutics. 8th ed. New York: Pergamon Press; 1990:221.

298 **Falkner B et al.** Effectiveness of centrally acting drugs and diuretics in adolescent hypertension. Clin Pharmacol Ther. 1982;32:577.

299 **Weber MA.** Combined diuretic and sympatholytic therapy in elderly patients with predominant systolic hypertension. Chest. 1983;83:416.

300 **Davison R et al.** The effect of clonidine on the cessation of cigarette smoking. Clin Pharmacol Ther. 1988;44:265.

301 **Lee EW, D'Alonzo GE.** Cigarette smoking, nicotine addiction, and its pharmacologic treatment. Arch Intern Med. 1993;153:34.

302 **Popli S et al.** Transdermal clonidine in mild hypertension: a randomized, double-blind, placebo-controlled trial. Arch Intern Med. 1986;146:2140.

303 **Weber MA et al.** Transdermal administration of clonidine for treatment of high BP. Arch Intern Med. 1984;144:1211.

304 **Lowenthal DT et al.** Efficacy of clonidine as transdermal therapeutic system: the international clinical trial experience. Am Heart J. 1986;112:893.

305 **Stewart M, Burris JF.** Rebound hypertension during initiation of transdermal clonidine. Drug Intell Clin Pharm. 1988;22:573.

306 **Whitsett TL.** Abrupt cessation of treatment with centrally acting antihypertensive agents: a review. Chest. 1983;83:400.

307 **Hansson L et al.** Blood pressure crisis following withdrawal of clonidine (Catapres, Catapresan) with special reference to arterial and urinary catecholamine levels and suggestions for acute management. Am Heart J. 1973;85:605.

308 **Schmidt GR, Schuna AA.** Rebound hypertension after discontinuation of transdermal clonidine. Clin Pharm. 1988;7:772.

309 **Carstairs KC et al.** Incidence of a positive direct Combs' test in patients on methyldopa. Lancet. 1966;2:133.

310 **Worlledge SM et al.** Autoimmune haemolytic anaemia associated with alpha-methyldopa therapy. Lancet. 1966;2:135.

311 **Wilson MF et al.** Comparison of guanfacine versus clonidine for efficacy, safety and occurrence of withdrawal syndrome in step-2 treatment in mild to moderate essential hypertension. Am J Cardiol. 1986;57:43E.

312 **Jäättelä A.** Comparison of guanfacine and clonidine as antihypertensive agents. Br J Clin Pharmacol. 1980;10:67S.

313 **Jain AK et al.** Clonidine and guanfacine in hypertension. Clin Pharmacol Ther. 1985;37:271.

314 **Kiechel JR.** Pharmacokinetics and metabolism of guanfacine in man: a review. Br J Clin Pharmacol. 1980;10:25S.

315 **Shah RS et al.** Guanabenz effects on blood pressure and noninvasive parameters of cardiac performance in patients with hypertension. Clin Pharmacol Ther. 1976;19:732.

316 **Walker BR et al.** Long-term therapy of hypertension with guanabenz. Clin Ther. 1981;4:217.

317 **Walker BR et al.** Comparative antihypertensive effects of guanabenz and clonidine. J Int Med Res. 1982;10:6.

318 **Kluyskens Y, Snoeck J.** Comparison of guanabenz and clonidine in hypertensive patients. Curr Med Res Opin. 1980;6:638.

319 **Winer N, Carter CH.** Effects of abrupt discontinuation of guanabenz and clonidine in hypertensive patients. Clin Pharmacol Ther. 1982;31:282.

320 **Stratton MA.** Drug-induced systemic lupus erythematosus. Clin Pharm. 1985;4:657.

321 **Melander A et al.** Enhancement of hydralazine bioavailability by food. Clin Pharmacol Ther. 1977;22:104.

322 **Cameron HA, Ramsay LE.** The lupus syndrome induced by hydralazine: a common complication with low dose treatment. Br Med J. 1984;289:410.

323 **Perry HM.** Late toxicity to hydralazine resembling systemic lupus erythematosus or rheumatoid arthritis. Am J Med. 1973;54:58.

324 **Solinger AM.** Drug-related lupus: clinical and etiologic considerations. Rheum Dis Clin North Am. 1988;14:187.

325 **Ihle BU et al.** Hydralazine and lupus nephritis. Clin Nephrol. 1984;22:230.

326 **Dormois JC et al.** Minoxidil in severe hypertension: value when conventional drugs failed. Am Heart J. 1975;90:360.

327 **Pettinger WA et al.** Clonidine and the vasodilating beta blocker antihypertensive drug interaction. Clin Pharmacol Ther. 1977;2:164.

328 **Pettinger WA.** Minoxidil and the treatment of severe hypertension. N Engl J Med. 1980;303:922.

329 **Earhart RN et al.** Minoxidil-induced hypertrichosis: treatment with calcium thioglycolate depilatory. S Med J. 1977;70:442.

330 **Satinsky JD.** Chronic heart failure in the elderly: vasodilator therapy. Angiology. 1983;34:509.

331 **Hall D et al.** Serial electrocardiographic changes during long-term treatment of severe hypertension with minoxidil. J Cardiovasc Pharm. 1980;2:S200.

332 **Weinshilboum RM.** Antihypertensive drugs that alter adrenergic function. Mayo Clin Proc. 1980;55:390.

333 **Chrysant SG, Frohlich E.** Comparison of the antihypertensive effectiveness of guanadrel and guanethidine. Curr Ther Res. 1976;19:379.

334 **Bloomfield DK, Cangiano JL.** Guanadrel and guanethidine in hypertension. Clin Pharmacol Ther. 1970;11:200.

335 **Pascual AV, Julius S.** Short term effectiveness and hemodynamic actions of guanadrel, a new sympatholytic drug. Curr Ther Res. 1972;14:333.

336 **Veterans Administration Medical Centers.** Low doses vs standard dose of reserpine: a randomized, double-blind, multiclinic trial in patients taking chlorthalidone. JAMA. 1982;248:2471.

337 **Borreson RE.** The case for reserpine in hypertension. Hosp Formul. 1985;20:719.

338 **Lederle FA et al.** Reserpine and the medical marketplace. Arch Intern Med. 1993;153:705.

339 **Moser M.** Cost containment and hypertension. Ann Intern Med. 1988;108:148.

340 **Freis ED.** Mental depression in hypertensive patients treated for long periods with large doses of reserpine. N Engl J Med. 1954;251:1006.

341 **Muller JC et al.** Depression and anxiety occurring during rauwolfia therapy. JAMA. 1955;159:836.

342 **Kuetsch RM et al.** Depressive reactions in hypertensive patients. Circulation. 1959;19:366.

343 **West WO.** Perforation and hemorrhage from duodenal ulcer during the administration of rauwolfia serpentina: report of five cases. Ann Intern Med. 1958;48:1033.

344 **Materson BJ, Reda DJ.** Correction: Single-drug therapy for hypertension in men. N Engl J Med. 1994;330:1689.

345 **Brunner HR et al.** Angiotensin II blockade compared with other pharmacological methods of inhibiting the renin-angiotensin system. J Hypertens. 1993;11:553.

346 **Munafo A et al.** Drug concentration response relationships in normal volunteers after oral administration of losartan, an angiotensin II receptor antagonist. Clin Pharmacol Therap. 1992;51:513.

347 **Weber MA.** Clinical experience with angiotensin II receptor antagonist losartan. Am J Hypertens. 1992;5:2475.

348 **Burnier M et al.** The advantages of angiotensin II antagonism. J Hypertens. 1994;12:57.

349 **Foote E, Halstenson C.** New therapeutic agents in the management of hypertension: angiotensin II receptor antagonists and renin inhibitors. Ann Pharmacotherap. 1993;27:1495.

Peripheral Vascular Disorders

Bart B Lawrence
C Wayne Weart

Intermittent Claudication (IC) and Occlusive
Peripheral Vascular Disease 11-1
   Epidemiology 11-1
   Pathophysiology 11-2
   Clinical Presentation 11-4
   Treatment 11-4
      Therapeutic objectives and nonpharmacologic
        interventions 11-4
         Smoking cessation 11-4
         Diet and exercise (Also see Table 11.1) 11-5
         Arresting atherosclerosis progression 11-5
         Management of diabetes 11-5
      Vasodilators 11-6
      β-adrenergic blockers 11-6
      Pentoxifylline 11-7
         Dosing 11-7
         Monitoring 11-7
      Aspirin 11-8
      Surgery 11-8
Raynaud's Phenomenon 11-8
   Pathophysiology 11-8

   Clinical Presentation 11-9
   Treatment 11-9
      Nonpharmacologic management 11-9
      Calcium channel blockers 11-9
      Other Agents 11-9
         α_1-adrenergic antagonists 11-9
         Reserpine, guanethidine, and methyldopa 11-9
         Direct-acting vasodilators 11-9
         Serotonin receptor antagonists 11-10
         Angiotensin-converting enzyme (ACE)
           inhibitors 11-10
         Triiodothyronine (T_3) 11-10
Nocturnal Leg Muscle Cramps 11-10
   Clinical Presentation (See Table 11.3) 11-10
   Treatment 11-10
      Therapeutic objectives and nonpharmacologic
        interventions 11-10
      Quinine (See Table 11.4) 11-11
         Serum concentration 11-11
         Adverse effects 11-11
      Other drugs 11-12

Peripheral vascular and musculoskeletal diseases are common medical disorders prevalent in age groups ranging from young adults to the elderly. These disorders commonly are characterized by poor perfusion of the lower extremities due to occlusion or vasospasm of the peripheral arteries or by idiopathic contraction of the distal musculature. Occlusive vascular disorders, such as intermittent claudication (IC), have a significant effect upon the morbidity and mortality of the aging U.S. population, and generally are a further consequence of atherosclerosis. Raynaud's phenomenon is a complicated vascular disorder of unknown cause that often has an onset in early adulthood and primarily affects women. Nocturnal leg cramping is a third distinct entity which leads to considerable distress in the elderly. While the pathology of these disorders is becoming better understood, the pharmacologic treatments are less well defined.

As the elderly population continues to increase, the prevalence of these vascular diseases will rise disproportionate to the number of practitioners who specialize in their treatment. As this occurs, the management of peripheral vascular diseases will fall more into the realm of the primary care physician and the pharmacist. A basic understanding of pathophysiology and risk factors is beneficial in directing and monitoring current therapies aimed at prevention and treatment of these vascular disorders.

Intermittent Claudication (IC) and Occlusive Peripheral Vascular Disease

Intermittent claudication is a common and painful complication developing from atherosclerosis of the peripheral arteries of the legs. Some clinicians and patients have characterized claudication pain as "angina" of the legs. When one considers the risk factors and pathology of IC, the association becomes clear.

Intermittent claudication is described by those suffering from this condition as aching, cramping, tightness, or weakness of the legs which usually occurs during exertion. Relief comes to the sufferer of claudication pain with discontinuation of the physical activity. Signs and symptoms of this disorder commonly are described as a "walk-pain-rest" cycle. Numbness or continuous pain in the toes or foot may be present indicating tissue ischemia, which can lead to ulceration. It is a painful condition which can limit the patient's mobility severely and can lead to tissue necrosis or amputation of the affected limb. The development of symptoms of IC may be very gradual. Unfortunately, the patient with this distressing occlusive disease may not seek medical attention until the condition is in a far advanced stage.

Epidemiology

Intermittent claudication is a relatively common condition in the elderly and is twice as likely to be seen in men than in women.[1] The prevalence of IC in persons over 65 years of age ranges from 1.3% to 5.8% in men, and up to 1.7% in women.[1,2] IC has been shown in epidemiological studies to be nonprogressive in 75% of patients over a period of four to nine years; however, the other 25% of claudication sufferers have worsening painful ischemic episodes during this time period. Although rare, more serious complications can occur. Ischemic tissue changes, ulceration, and gangrene can accompany advanced peripheral atherosclerosis. Amputation of the affected limb may be necessary in up to 5% of patients with claudication.[4] In the Framingham study, the total mortality for men with IC was 3.9% compared with 1% of men without IC. Patients with claudication have a two- to fourfold increase in ten-year mortality, with 75% of deaths due to myocardial infarction (MI).[1,51] IC clearly reflects more generalized atherosclerosis and is associated with considerable morbidity and mortality.

The risk factors for developing occlusive peripheral vascular disease are similar to those for coronary artery disease. These risk factors include diabetes, hypertension, cigarette smoking, a low high-density lipoprotein (HDL) cholesterol, and an elevated low-density lipoprotein (LDL) cholesterol. Hypertriglyceridemia has been found to be a more common and significant risk factor for peripheral vascular disease than for coronary artery disease.[6] Claudication pain is also an important predictor of more generalized atherosclerotic vascular disease and increased cardiovascular mortality, consistent with the increase in deaths due to MI.

Long-standing diabetes is the most significant risk factor for IC, with 30% of diabetic patients affected by peripheral vascular disease.[3] Peripheral vascular disease is five times more common in diabetic patients than in nondiabetic, develops at a younger age, and progresses more rapidly. Amputations due to ischemia are four times higher among diabetics than among nondiabetics.[7] Cigarette smoking is a very important risk factor for IC with smoking having the highest correlation with the development of IC pain.[8] In patients with other cardiovascular risk factors, including hypertension or diabetes, smoking further increases the rate of claudication development. The incidence of intermittent claudication is twice as high among smokers than among nonsmokers, and the risk increases dramatically with the degree of smoking. Patients who smoke over 15 cigarettes a day are nine times more likely to develop IC than nonsmokers.[37]

Pathophysiology

Intermittent claudication is a predominant complication of occlusive peripheral vascular disease. The major cause of occlusive peripheral vascular disease is arteriosclerosis obliterans, or the development of atherosclerotic plaques in the peripheral vasculature. In patients under the age of 40, plaques tend to develop more in central vessels (e.g., in the ilioaortic artery) than in the more distal vessels, and are likely to cause pain in the buttocks and impotence in men. For older patients, 65% have femoropopliteal arterial disease and experience mostly thigh and calf pain. Similarly, occlusion of the calf arteries will produce claudication pain in the foot. The location of the plaque tends to reflect the extent of disease and predicts the sites of claudication pain. (See Figure 11.1.) Atherosclerosis of the distal abdominal aorta (ilioaortic) and the large arteries of the lower limbs (femoral, popliteal, and tibial) can lead to hemodynamic changes which reduce perfusion to the buttocks and legs. Symptoms of IC are indicative of an inadequate supply of arterial blood to these peripheral muscles. Exercise, including walking, increases metabolic demands of the muscles and can lead to claudication pain. The reductions in blood supply to the muscles are due to changes in perfusion pressures and vascular tone caused by atherosclerosis.

Atherosclerosis can impair the microcirculation of the peripheral muscles by altering the pressure gradient needed for perfusion of the capillaries. Like all organs, adequacy of blood flow to the lower limbs is a function of both perfusion pressure and the resistance to flow. There is an inverse relationship between these two factors. As perfusion pressure (e.g., systemic blood pressure) of the peripheral arteries increases, flow is enhanced; as resistance is increased (e.g., atherosclerotic plaque, stenotic lesions, vasoconstriction), perfusion pressure drops distal to the obstruction and flow is impeded (see Figure 11.2). When obstruction develops, utilization of collateral blood flow then becomes important in maintaining adequate perfusion of tissue distal to the stenotic lesion. Collateral circulation consists of new blood vessels which develop to carry blood around the occluded area.

Stenotic lesions do not appear to produce a significant decrease in blood flow until at least 75% of the artery becomes occluded,

and 90% occlusion occurs before symptoms become apparent. Even at this severe degree of occlusion the lesions usually do not reduce perfusion pressure enough to cause problems or promote claudication until exercise is performed (see Figure 11.3). Exercise increases the metabolic demand of the musculature and the accumulation of vasodilating metabolites (e.g., carbon dioxide, potassium, and adenosine), leading to precapillary vasodilation. Under normal conditions, the increase in cardiac output and vasodilation caused by exercise are beneficial to the muscle, increasing capillary blood flow. With obstructive vascular disease, the benefits of an increased cardiac output (increased blood pressure and increased perfusion pressure) are not realized distal to the stenotic plaque, and vasodilation reduces perfusion pressure. This leads to decreased capillary blood flow, and with metabolic demands not being met, ischemia and claudication pain.

An increase in vascular tone may be an important factor in the development of IC. It can lead to vasospasm around and distal to a sclerotic plaque, decreasing the volume of blood delivered to the tissues. A key component in vascular tone regulation is the endothelial lining of the blood vessels. Normal endothelium produces vasodilating substances which ''counterbalance'' other vasoconstricting substances (i.e., thromboxane A_2, serotonin, thrombin) which are produced in response to shear stress and normal endothelial tissue damage.

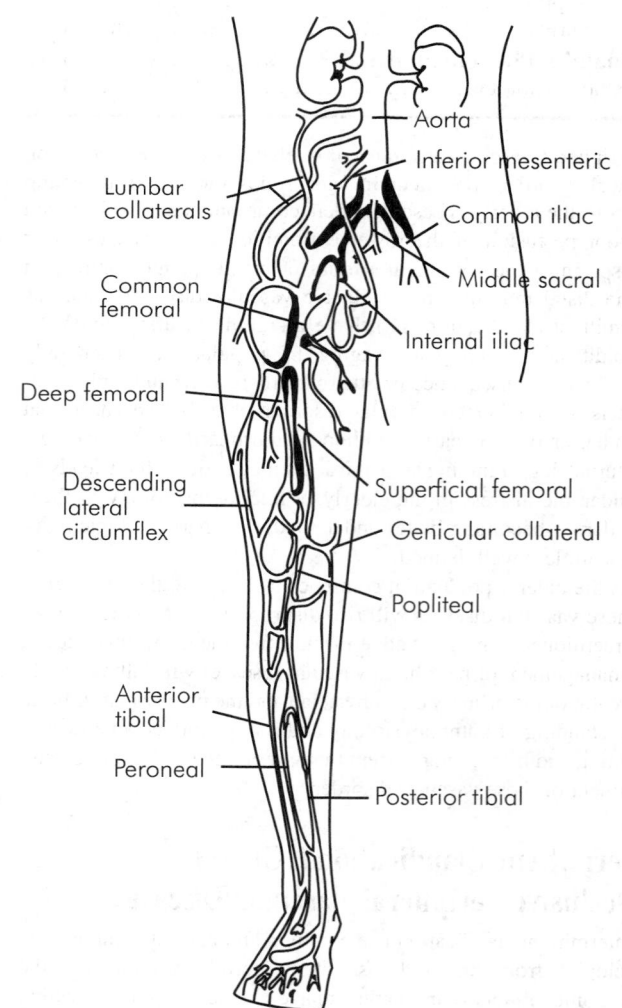

Fig 11.1 Common Sites of Atherosclerosis (Shown in Black) in the Aorta and Lower Extremities Reprinted with permission from reference 114.

LEG ARTERY

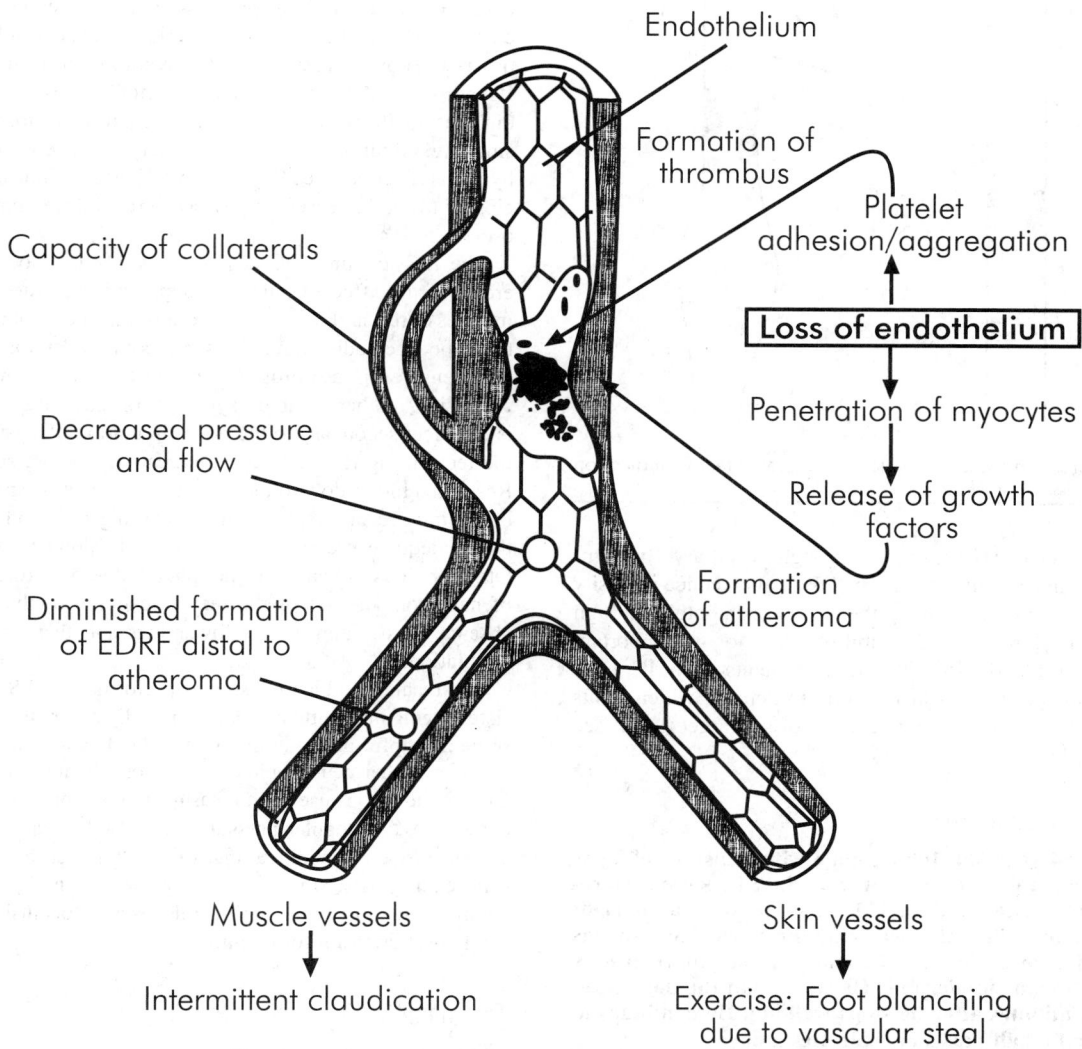

Endothelium

Formation of thrombus

Platelet adhesion/aggregation

Loss of endothelium

Penetration of myocytes

Release of growth factors

Formation of atheroma

Capacity of collaterals

Decreased pressure and flow

Diminished formation of EDRF distal to atheroma

Muscle vessels

Intermittent claudication

Skin vessels

Exercise: Foot blanching due to vascular steal

Fig 11.2   Schematic Representation of Consequences of Occlusive Atherosclerotic Disease in the Lower Limbs   Reprinted with permission from reference 114.

Endothelium-derived relaxing factor (EDRF) is a vasodilating substance which is similar to, or possibly the same as, nitric oxide and has platelet-inhibitory properties. EDRF is released naturally from the endothelium and leads to a relaxing effect upon vascular smooth muscle. Prostacyclin (PGI_2) is another vasodilating substance which has direct relaxing effects on the vascular smooth muscle, stimulates EDRF release, and is a potent inhibitor of platelet aggregation. A defect or injury to the endothelial lining can impair the production and release of these natural vasodilators, leading to an increase in vascular tone and the development of IC.

Vascular endothelial dysfunction has been detected in patients with atherosclerosis and dyslipidemia and has been shown to directly affect EDRF and prostacyclin production. Chronic atherosclerosis is associated with abnormal vasoconstriction and may be due to decreased endothelium-derived relaxing factor production or impaired diffusion of EDRF through the altered vascular wall.[105] Elevated LDL cholesterol levels decrease the production of both EDRF and PGI_2, whereas HDL cholesterol beneficially increases the production and half-life of PGI_2.[105] There is further evidence that endothelial damage or atherosclerosis affects vas-

cular tone through these mechanisms. When injected into normal arteries, acetylcholine produces vasodilation due to the presence of muscarinic receptors in the endothelial cells and the subsequent release of EDRF. However, when acetylcholine is presented to endothelium with atherosclerosis or that is mechanically injured, a paradoxical vasoconstriction occurs.[105] This vasoconstriction is associated with an impaired release of EDRF. In the case of atherosclerosis, there is evidence that HDL cholesterol not only has antiatherogenic properties, but promotes normal endothelial function. In patients with normal total cholesterol (<200 mg/dL), acetylcholine-induced vasoreactivity has been correlated positively with HDL cholesterol. A greater degree of vasoconstriction occurs with a low HDL, with more vasodilation with higher HDL cholesterol levels. There is significant evidence that hyperlipidemia and atherosclerosis are factors which contribute to an increase in vascular tone and the development of claudication.

Erythrocyte deformability has been shown *in vitro* to be an important factor in capillary perfusion and the subject of much debate in the treatment of intermittent claudication. Normal erythrocytes have the ability to deform under high shear conditions, such as

Before exercise   After exercise

Fig 11.3 Exercise-Induced Vasodilation of Intermittent Claudication
Reprinted with permission from reference 114.

when the red blood cell (RBC) passes through a capillary. By aligning themselves in a planer manner, the RBCs also reduce viscosity of the blood suspension, enabling them to pass smoothly through the capillary. Erythrocyte deformability is one of the important determinants of blood viscosity. Many patients with IC have marked decreases in this intrinsic ability to deform, which limits the RBC's ability to provide oxygenation of the target tissue (see Figure 11.4).[9–12]

Clinical Presentation

1. J.S. is a 54-year-old, 100 kg male with a history of Type II, insulin-treated diabetes mellitus; angina; hypercholesterolemia; and tobacco abuse. His chief complaint today is right upper thigh pain while walking around the block. The pain has been increasing over the past 12 months, and the pain only recently has become intolerable. He states that the pain is relieved within minutes after he stops walking. He continues to smoke one and a half packs of cigarettes a day.

J.S.'s most recent laboratory results are significant for a total cholesterol of 290 mg/dL, fasting triglyceride of 350 mg/dL, an LDL of 188 mg/dL, and an HDL of 32 mg/dL. His serum creatinine (SrCr) is 1.0 mg/dL, blood urea nitrogen (BUN) is 15 mg/dL, hemoglobin (Hgb) A1c is 10.0%, and he has a fasting glucose of 150 mg/dL. His blood pressure (BP) is 170/95 mm Hg, and his posterior tibial artery pulse is not palpable. A Doppler ultrasound study was performed, and J.S.'s ankle-to-arm pressure ratio was 0.8 (normal: >0.95).

J.S.'s medication list includes isosorbide dinitrate 20 mg TID (while awake), ASA 325 mg QD, and progressively increasing doses of insulin, of which he now takes NPH insulin 40 U in the morning and 35 U in the evening. What risk factors and elements of J.S.'s presentation are compatible with a diagnosis of IC? [SI units: total cholesterol 7.49 mmol/L; triglyceride 3.95 mmol/L; LDL 4.86 mmol/L; HDL 0.83 mmol/L; SrCr 60 mmol/L; BUN 5.3 mmol/L; Hgb A1c 0.1; glucose 8.3 mmol/L]

J.S.'s past medical history describes classic pre-existing conditions for vascular occlusion and IC, including hypercholesterolemia, hypertriglyceridemia, diabetes, hypertension, and tobacco use. In particular, his diabetes is not adequately controlled based upon an elevated hemoglobin A1c and fasting glucose. His insulin dose of 75 U/day is indicative of relative insulin resistance. The presence of angina indicates coronary artery disease secondary to his risk factors, so it is not surprising that he has peripheral vascular occlusion as well.

J.S. is an obese, hypertensive smoker who is demonstrating signs of hyperinsulinemia, insulin resistance, and glucose intolerance. His fractional lipid profile shows a decreased HDL, an increased LDL, and elevated triglycerides. This constellation of disorders is known classically as the syndrome of insulin resistance, "syndrome X," or the "deadly quartet" (obesity, hypertension, diabetes mellitus, and dyslipidemia). These factors, along with smoking, commonly are seen together and have been linked with hyperinsulinemia. (See Figure 11.5.) They also appear to be related closely to the increased risk of accelerated development of atherosclerosis.[96,97]

The classic pain of IC described by J.S. is associated with exercise of the affected muscle groups which subsides after a few minutes of rest and reperfusion. IC also may occur at rest; however, this type of claudication pain is less common and is an indication of extensive disease progression due to lower extremity atherosclerosis. Another common symptom of extensive atherosclerosis is cold feet secondary to the poor circulation. Persistent aching of the feet during rest or sleep is indicative of more severe disease. Restricted blood flow to the feet also can lead to rubor, or the foot becoming red or purple from the pooling of blood secondary to the inadequate pressure needed to push blood back up the leg. Other obvious indicators of peripheral atherosclerosis are the loss of hair from the top of the feet, thickening of the toenails, and absence of sweating of the lower legs and feet, all due to poor circulation.

The results of objective studies performed on J.S. also are consistent with intermittent claudication. Doppler ultrasound of the spine is helpful in excluding pseudoclaudication due to spinal stenosis and other neurogenic or musculoskeletal causes of leg pain. Ultrasound also is useful in measuring blood pressure of the lower extremities. A Doppler pressure ratio of 0.8 means that the ankle systolic blood pressure reading was much lower than the arm pressure reading. Also, the loss of the posterior tibial pulse is not uncommon in those with peripheral vascular occlusion and is the single best criterion for diagnosis.

Treatment

Therapeutic Objectives and Nonpharmacologic Interventions

2. What is the therapeutic objective in treating J.S.? What interventions should be initiated to prevent claudication pain and arrest progression of the disease?

The specific IC treatment goals for J.S. primarily are prevention of further claudication, arresting progression of underlying disease, avoiding vasoconstriction, and preventing ischemic ulceration. An important concept that should be stressed to J.S. when explaining these treatment goals is that all his diseases are closely interrelated, and that a beneficial intervention for one disease is beneficial for all. Interventions that can be initiated include proper dieting and weight loss, obtaining control of his diabetes, controlling his hypertension, and reducing his hyperlipidemia. However, the most important things that J.S. can do are summed up in five words: "Stop smoking and keep walking."[101]

Smoking Cessation. Smoking is the most significant risk factor for chronic obstructive peripheral artery disease, and, therefore, smoking cessation is a key to preventing IC and its associated ischemic complications.[8] It also is the intervention which will decrease J.S.'s claudication pain most rapidly. J.S. will benefit from lessened ischemic pain at rest, improved exercise tolerance, and a reduced potential need for amputation or reconstructive surgery. J.S. can double his ten-year survival rate by giving up his smoking habit.

Normal Erythrocyte Passing Through Capillary

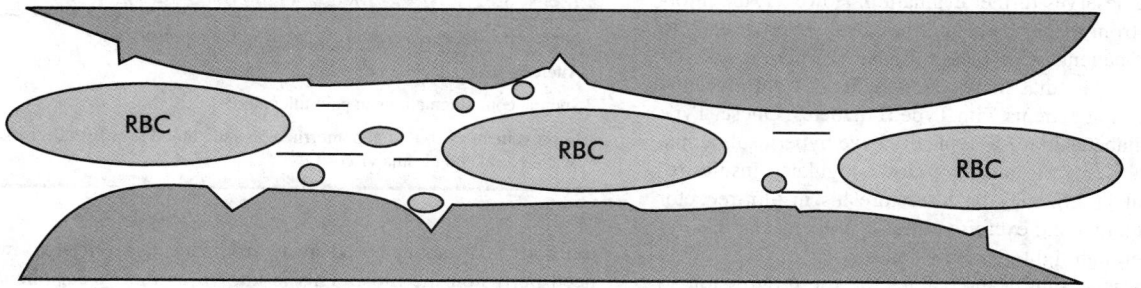

Inflexible, Rigid Erythrocyte Passing Through Abnormal Capillary

Atherosclerotic Plaque   Platelet Aggregation

Fig 11.4   Erythrocyte Inflexibility in Intermittent Claudication

Diet and Exercise. Individualized exercise and weight loss programs have been endorsed strongly for patients with IC and should be beneficial for J.S.'s other risk factors as well.[36,37] Rheologic abnormalities of increased blood viscosity, impaired RBC filterability, hyperaggregation, and polycythemia (elevated hematocrit) have been shown to return to normal in many patients who participate in a regular exercise program.[13] Participation in such a program may offset the need for pharmacological intervention. Exercise alone may increase pain-free walking distances by 25% to 30%, which may translate from a few city blocks or up to a mile in some patients.[38] The potential mechanisms in which exercise benefits the patient with IC are listed in Table 11.1.

Supervised exercise programs, including brisk walking which raises J.S.'s heart rate for at least 20 minutes duration, should be encouraged and implemented. This type of exercise program should be done at least three times a week and has been demonstrated to be beneficial in improving symptoms of intermittent claudication. At least two months of a regular exercise program should be undertaken before J.S. can be evaluated adequately for effectiveness.[99]

Arresting Atherosclerosis Progression. Since IC is a consequence of atherosclerosis, arresting the progress of J.S.'s disease is important. The initiation of a Step I American Heart Association (AHA) diet and exercise program, as well as the prescribing of cholesterol-lowering agents, will be the mainstay of attaining this goal. There are considerable data suggesting that aggressive dietary and pharmacologic management of atherosclerosis, particularly reducing total LDL cholesterol and lowering blood pressure, may lead to regression of mild to moderate atherosclerotic lesions in the coronary and carotid vasculature.[32,33,109] There also is evidence

that endothelial function in patients with coronary artery disease will improve with aggressive lowering of cholesterol.[106,107] Since the processes of atherosclerosis of the periphery are the same as those of the coronary arteries, similar benefits of therapy may be obtained. There also is limited evidence demonstrating that aggressive lipid-lowering therapy can lead to regression of femoral lesions in patients with early atherosclerosis.[34]

J.S. should begin an aggressive dietary management program (Step I and II of AHA Diet recommendations), with or without a lipid lowering agent. According to the latest guidelines on the treatment of hyperlipidemia, a goal LDL below 100 mg/dL is recommended in patients with evidence of coronary heart disease and other atherosclerotic diseases.[108] (See Chapter 9: Dislipidemias for treatment of hyperlipidemia.) J.S. has angina, along with his lower extremity atherosclerosis, which indicates a need for aggressive lipid lowering. His LDL cholesterol now is 180 mg/dL, which means a reduction of almost 50% is desired. Along with an aggressive dietary intervention, J.S. most likely will need combination drug therapy, such as an HMG-CoA reductase inhibitor plus a bile acid sequestrant, in order to reach this goal. Use of niacin may be problematic because of his diabetes.

Management of Diabetes. Patients with Type I insulin-dependent diabetes mellitus (IDDM) are able to prevent complications of their disease with aggressive early and lifetime glucose control.[35] The benefits of aggressive glucose control may include reducing the risk for, and preventing the consequences of, atherosclerosis. The Diabetes Control and Complications Trial showed that intensive therapy reduced the development of hypercholesterolemia by 34% in those with Type I diabetes. This study also showed that when all cardiovascular and vascular events were combined, intensive therapy reduced the risk of macrovascular disease by 43% and deserves further evaluation. However, the information obtained from this study cannot be extrapolated directly to the population of patients with Type II diabetes. There is no conclusive evidence to date that shows the benefits of tight glycemic control with insulin in patients with Type II diabetes. Obese, Type II patients with diabetes like J.S. typically have hyperinsulinemia, insulin insensitivity or resistance, and down-regulated insulin receptors. The goal in J.S. may be to restore his insulin-receptor sensitivity through diet and exercise rather than increasing his hyperinsulinemia through tight glycemic control.

J.S.'s diabetes is a significant risk factor for progression to further ischemic events. His progression to claudication indicates late-stage disease, and aggressive insulin therapy may not prevent further complications. Aggressive insulin therapy actually may produce further hyperinsulinemia, contributing to J.S.'s accelerated atherosclerosis.[96]

An important preventive measure that J.S. can take is proper foot care. This is important for preventing ulcerative complications of claudication, especially for patients with diabetes. He should be educated on keeping his feet warm and dry, and encouraged to wear properly fitted shoes. He also should be informed to seek medical attention immediately whenever there is minor trauma to his feet and legs.[102] These measures can reduce one of the most common causes of morbidity in these patients.

Vasodilators

3. J.S. is taking isosorbide dinitrate for his angina and also has untreated hypertension. Since IC is made worse by vasoconstrictors, should he be started on a vasodilating drug to treat both his hypertension and IC?

The use of vasodilators for J.S. at first would appear to be a logical pharmacologic intervention for the prevention of claudication pain. Vasodilators, including isosorbide dinitrate, directly or indirectly relax blood vessel walls and increase both skin and muscle blood flow as long as cardiac output is maintained. However, with obstructive arterial disease, vessels may be so sclerotic that they are unable to dilate any further. The blood vessels are likely to be dilated maximally due to vasodilating metabolites (i.e., carbon dioxide, potassium, and adenosine). With further vasodilation, blood pressure distal to the occlusion becomes lower than systemic blood pressure, decreasing perfusion pressure of the tissues.

The collateral blood vessels have become important in maintaining blood flow to the musculature for J.S. (See Figure 11.2.) However, the maintenance of collateral blood flow actually may be hindered by vasodilator therapy. Vasodilation to other areas of

Table 11.1	Mechanisms of Exercise Therapy in Intermittent Claudication

Improved oxidative metabolic capacity of the involved limb[90]

Altered walking technique[91]

Spontaneous fluctuations in pain tolerance[92]

Improvement of abnormal hemorrheology and blood flow by a decrease in whole blood and plasma viscosity[93]

the body may shunt blood away from the diseased areas which need perfusion the most. This is known as the "steal phenomenon." In addition, vasodilation may yield a net effect of increased collateral vascular resistance. This vasoconstriction of the collateral vessels may be mediated by reflex mechanisms to the overall systemic vasodilation.

Before 1980, direct-acting vasodilators (i.e., isoxsuprine, papaverine, ethaverine, cyclandelate, niacin derivatives) and centrally acting agents (i.e., reserpine, guanethidine, methyldopa, tolazoline) were accepted drugs for the treatment of IC. Papaverine, L-carnitine, ethaverine HCl, buflomedil, and nifedipine all have been shown in some small trials to have positive effects in improving walking distances.[21–25,39] Deficiencies in these poorly controlled trials, especially in study population sizes, have led to the conclusion that there are no drugs which convincingly or consistently improve exercise performance despite these earlier conclusions.[18] Vasodilators had been used for many years in peripheral vascular diseases but now generally have been discarded from the treatment of IC and related obstructive vascular disorders.[20] The use of these vasodilating agents specifically for intermittent claudication would most likely be of no benefit to J.S. and might worsen his condition. Isosorbide dinitrate, when dosed appropriately to minimize the development of tolerance, may be beneficial in controlling J.S.'s angina but may be associated with some worsening of his claudication pain.

β-Adrenergic Blockers

4. What are the risks of using β-adrenergic blockers to treat J.S.'s untreated hypertension? Are there alternative antihypertensive therapies that might be preferable for J.S.?

J.S.'s untreated hypertension likely has contributed to the development of his atherosclerosis and peripheral vascular disease. Hypertension has been associated with deficiencies in the local endothelial cell lining synthesis of vasodilating substances such as prostacyclin, bradykinin, and EDRF. Hypertension also increases concentrations of vasoconstricting substances, such as angiotensin II. As stated earlier, an increase in vascular tone can alter local hemodynamics, especially in the presence of a stenotic lesion. Hypertension also is an essential component of the "deadly quartet," along with hyperlipidemia, obesity, and diabetes. Selected antihypertensive agents may have a beneficial effect on the improvement of insulin sensitivity, particularly the use of peripheral α_1-blockers, angiotensin-converting enzyme (ACE) inhibitors, and calcium channel blockers.[98]

β-adrenergic blocking agents have been evaluated for their role in treatment of hypertension in patients with underlying IC. Although beta blockers classically are considered as contraindicated in IC, the evidence to document the degree of risk is contradictory. Hiatt et al. showed that calf blood flow and symptoms of claudication were not worsened by either metoprolol or propranolol. There was a trend with both drugs toward a lowering of blood flow during exercise which was proportional to the fall in blood pressure.[29] However, this class of drugs actually may exacerbate claudication,[26,27] possibly through attenuation of epinephrine-induced

Fig 11.5   The Insulin Resistance Syndrome and Atherosclerosis

vasodilation during exercise and the blocking of peripheral β_2-adrenergic receptors.[28] β_1-receptor blocking agents (metoprolol, atenolol) have been evaluated further because of their receptor selectivity. A six-month, placebo-controlled crossover trial of 20 patients concluded that beta blockers, including β_1 selective agents, actually do cause decreases in walking distance.[30] Roberts et al. demonstrated that atenolol (β_1 selective), labetalol (α_1 selective, beta nonselective), and pindolol (beta nonselective with ISA), but not captopril, impaired postexercise calf blood flow and treadmill pain-free walking distances. In another trial, atenolol 50 mg twice daily and nifedipine 20 mg twice daily did not show any adverse effects on claudication symptoms, while significantly lowering blood pressure; although the combination of the two medications adversely affected walking distance and foot temperature.[103] Overall, controlled studies have been inconclusive; however, a meta-analysis of placebo-controlled trials and trials with control groups concluded that beta blockers did not worsen claudication.[113]

Beta blockers should be used very cautiously in patients with peripheral vascular disease.[31] If they are used, they should be started at low doses and titrated slowly to reduce blood pressure. It should be remembered that beta blockers and diuretics are relatively contraindicated in patients with diabetes mellitus due to their effects on glucose control. The safety of calcium channel blockers in IC also is inconclusive, and they should be used with similar caution. ACE inhibitors may preserve collateral blood supply when compared to beta blockers and may be an alternative for the treatment of hypertension in claudicants.[30] An ACE inhibitor might be the most appropriate choice for J.S. because of the additional potential benefits in preserving renal function in diabetics and also may be effective in slowing the progression of renal dysfunction in patients with essential hypertension without diabetes.[110,111]

Pentoxifylline

5. J.S.'s doctor wants to start him on pentoxifylline (Trental). How does this drug benefit claudicants? Has pentoxifylline been shown to be efficacious in patients like J.S.?

Pentoxifylline, a methylxanthine derivative, is the only agent currently approved by the Food and Drug Administration (FDA) for the treatment of intermittent claudication. Its proposed mechanism of action is the improvement of abnormal erythrocyte deformability and the enhancement of the flow properties of whole blood. Pentoxifylline's mechanism for improving erythrocyte flexibility may be through intracellular increases in erythrocyte phosphoproteins and decreases in intracellular calcium. The end result may be an increase in adenosine triphosphate (ATP) content of the red blood cell, yielding a more flexible erythrocyte able to more easily deform, decrease blood viscosity, and provide better oxygenation of muscle tissue. However, this proposed mechanism of action has been questioned. A study of pentoxifylline in healthy volunteers showed no effect on RBC deformability but did show an improvement in whole blood filterability, suggesting other effects on platelets or fibrinogen.[100]

An enhanced tendency toward platelet aggregation is found in patients with IC, and one of pentoxifylline's mechanisms may be to inhibit this aggregation. Pentoxifylline also reduces plasma fibrinogen concentrations as well as increasing fibrinolytic activity. Therefore, pentoxifylline may contribute to a decrease in blood viscosity through a reduction in platelet and erythrocyte aggregating properties.[14]

Pentoxifylline is absorbed rapidly and completely and is extensively metabolized during its first pass through the liver. The 5-hydroxyhexyl metabolite has nearly the same activity as the parent compound. Renal impairment significantly increases the plasma

concentrations of both the parent and metabolite compounds, but the clinical significance of this is unknown at this time.

While the theoretical and *in vitro* data on pentoxifylline are unique and positive, the data demonstrating clinical usefulness of this agent are controversial. Subjective measures of efficacy are limited to claudication and maximum walking distance. Claudication distance is the distance the patient can walk before pain first begins, and has been judged as the most clinically significant outcome measure for pentoxifylline treatment.[37] The maximum walking distance is the furthest the patient can walk with claudication pain, and is considered a less reliable measure.

Some clinical trials of pentoxifylline have shown statistically significant improvements in these subjective measurements when compared to placebo.[15–17] In the largest study to date of pentoxifylline therapy, the Scandinavian Study Group showed a 19% improvement in claudication distance, which was statistically insignificant. The study showed a statistically significant 24% increase in the maximum walking distance.[19] When evaluating all of the double-blind, controlled trials using pentoxifylline, an inverse correlation between study sample size and a significant response to pentoxifylline therapy has been observed.[18] There tends to be a decrease in pentoxifylline efficacy as the study sample size increases. The improvements in walking distances from study to study generally are unpredictable, and the clinical importance of the increases is controversial. It must be realized that patients with a minimal walking distance (i.e., 100 to 200 meters) at baseline can have a statistically significant improvement without the change being clinically relevant. Gains in walking distance after treatment, when treadmill tests are converted to everyday walking activity, are approximately 80 to 100 meters, or a little over one city block.

The ability to target patient populations which will benefit most from pentoxifylline treatment would be helpful in directing appropriate therapy. In one study, the Scandinavian Study Group performed a subgroup analysis in an attempt to find patients who best responded to therapy. Patients with a history of claudication symptoms for greater than one year and who had a Doppler ankle-to-arm pressure ratio of ≤0.8 were most likely to benefit from pentoxifylline therapy.[19] J.S. falls within this group and may benefit from a trial of pentoxifylline treatment. All patients, whether they are a potential candidate for pentoxifylline treatment or not, should attempt risk-factor modifications and initiate a physical-training program.

6. Dosing. What dose of pentoxifylline should J.S. be given?

Pentoxifylline is available as a sustained-release tablet, with the usual dose being 400 mg three times a day. Immediate-release pentoxifylline has a shorter duration of action, is associated with increased side effects, and, therefore, is not marketed in this formulation. J.S. should be instructed to take pentoxifylline 400 mg three times a day with meals in order to avoid stomach upset, the most common side effect of therapy. Other side effects include dizziness, headache, flushing, and palpitations. If these symptoms persist, the dose may be reduced to a twice a day schedule.

7. Monitoring. How should J.S. be monitored while receiving pentoxifylline?

It is important to obtain J.S.'s baseline walking distances in order to assess the efficacy of pentoxifylline treatment. The time to pain with exertion and documented pain-free walking distances should be monitored closely and documented by J.S. during drug treatment. Clinical effects of pentoxifylline generally are not seen until the second or third week of therapy, and treatment should be continued for a full eight weeks to accurately assess efficacy. Initiating therapy in conjunction with an exercise program may cloud therapy results and make it hard to distinguish which intervention actually benefited the patient.

Aspirin

8. Is the aspirin that J.S. is taking beneficial for preventing claudication?

The interaction between endothelial damage and platelet aggregation is a component of atherosclerosis development.[43] Endothelial damage of vessels causes platelet aggregation and adhesion, promoting the formation of atherosclerosis or a mural thrombus. Platelets release the contents of their granules after aggregation, promoting smooth muscle cells to produce a connective tissue matrix and accumulate lipoproteins. These components form the early lesion of atherosclerosis. Antiplatelet drugs may protect against the development of arterial occlusion by inhibiting these mechanisms. Therefore, aspirin, dipyridamole, and ticlopidine may have a role in peripheral vascular diseases as well as coronary artery disease.

Although aspirin has been shown conclusively to be effective in secondary prevention of cardiovascular events in patients with myocardial infarction and unstable angina, there is no evidence at this time that aspirin alone, or in combination with dipyridamole, has beneficial effects in IC. There is limited evidence for improvements in claudication distances with ticlopidine, another antiplatelet agent; however, no recommendations can be made at this time concerning its use in intermittent claudication.[102] J.S. should continue to take the aspirin for its proven efficacy in preventing further complications of his angina, but, at this time, it is unknown if it will decrease the degree of claudication pain he experiences.

Surgery

9. What options are there for J.S. if nonpharmacologic and pharmacologic interventions fail?

Surgical intervention eventually may be necessary with persistent and complicated disease. Because success rates for preventing amputation and postsurgical complications vary from institution to institution, surgery should be considered only for severely ischemic limbs and should be performed in a hospital with a good history of success.[41] Arterial bypass grafting and endarterectomy, not dissimilar to cardiac bypass procedures, can be performed. Percutaneous transluminal angioplasty also can be used; guidelines for patients who should have angioplasty were published in 1994.[112] Angioplasty is beneficial in patients with localized disease, especially in the iliac or superficial femoral arteries, and should be considered in patients who truly are incapacitated by their recreational, vocational, or personal exercise limitations.[102,112] However, long-term outcome studies of angioplasty have not shown a decrease in the number of amputations.[40] The benefits and pitfalls of these skilled interventions still are unclear.

Raynaud's Phenomenon

Raynaud's disease was first described by Maurice Raynaud in 1883 and again in 1888 and remains a medical enigma to this day. This disorder is characterized by ischemia and vasospasm of the peripheral arteries which usually is limited to the skin of the hands and digits, but also can occur in the feet. Between attacks, the digits may appear cool and moist or may appear normal. This abrupt and discomforting phenomenon may be brought on by exposure to cold or emotional stress, both likely mediated through an exaggerated sympathetic response to the precipitating stimuli. While both IC and Raynaud's phenomenon are disorders of the peripheral arterial circulation, they differ significantly in that IC results primarily from atherosclerotic obstruction while Raynaud's is due to vasospasm.

This disorder can be separated into primary (idiopathic) disease or secondary phenomenon. The pathophysiology of primary Raynaud's disease still is unknown but may have a hereditary component. Primary Raynaud's disease may be diagnosed only when secondary causes have been excluded.[67,68] Common criteria for the diagnosis of primary Raynaud's disease are listed in Table 11.2. The prevalence of primary Raynaud's disease remains unknown, mainly due to difficulty in diagnosis. There are many secondary conditions which may induce Raynaud's phenomenon. Pre-existing connective tissue diseases, such as rheumatoid arthritis, scleroderma, and systemic lupus erythematosus, are associated with Raynaud's phenomenon, and smoking greatly exacerbates the disorder. β-adrenergic blocking agents are the most common drugs precipitating Raynaud's phenomenon. A number of other common medications, such as ergots, sympathomimetics, imipramine, and clonidine, also may induce vasospasm in susceptible persons. Obstructive arterial diseases, trauma to the digital areas, frequent use of the hands or utilization of heavy, vibrating machinery, and carpal tunnel syndrome are other commonly associated conditions.[69]

The disease mainly affects females between the ages of 11 and 45 years, and the number of cases in women exceeds those in men by a 4:1 ratio. When Raynaud's disease occurs in men, it is more likely to be due to a secondary cause of the disease. Many of these men have concomitant atherosclerotic disease.

Pathophysiology

The blood vessels of the digital skin have a prime role in the regulation of body temperature and are supplied with vast amounts of sympathetic vasoconstricting nerves.[67] Raynaud's disease may involve increased activity of the sympathetic nervous system leading to the exaggerated vasoconstrictive response seen, possibly through increased α_2 sensitivity in response to cold stimuli. Activation of β_2-adrenoreceptors will attenuate the vasoconstriction. An increased sensitivity to cold in the digital arteries involving α_2-adrenoreceptors also has been implicated.[69] S_2-serotonergic receptors may have a role in the pathophysiology of the disease, due to an abundance of these receptors being found in the human hand. S_2-serotonergic receptors are involved in digital vasoconstriction induced by sympathetic stimulation even in the presence of α_1- and α_2-receptor blockade. Other theories involve platelet abnormalities or increased blood viscosity.

Clinically, the patient with Raynaud's disease will present with a waxy pallor of one or more of the fingers after the sudden decrease of arterial blood flow. Cold exposure is the precipitating factor in a majority of cases, and the resultant vasospasm has been shown to decrease affected tissue blood flow by as much as 70% below normal utilizing a plethysmograph at a temperature of 22 °C.[66] Hemoglobin desaturation occurs and causes the digit to have a cyanotic appearance. The attack subsides over time, and after removal of the stimulus, the affected arteries vasodilate. As the skin temperature increases, classic "rubor," or reddening of the afflicted area, will be seen. Many patients will be observed to have pallor only during the initial attack in which the digits take on a white or yellow, sometimes patched, appearance. In most cases, the ischemia produced by the phenomena does not have important

Table 11.2	Diagnosis of Primary Raynaud's Disease[20]
1)	Vasospastic attacks induced by cold exposure
2)	Bilateral involvement of the extremities
3)	Absence of gangrene or involvement of only the skin of the fingertips
4)	No evidence of an underlying disease including the absence of antinuclear antibodies, a normal ESR,[a] and normal nail-fold capillaroscopy and esophageal motility studies

[a] ESR = Erythrocyte sedimentation rate.

consequences; however, in severe cases, atrophy of the skin, irregular nail growth, and wasting of the tissue pads may occur.[67]

Clinical Presentation

10. F.K., a 33-year-old male, presents today with a 4-day history of left hand and arm pain. He notes that the third digit of his left hand is "cold and somewhat blue," especially in the distal area. The other areas of his hand have recovered, but the distal portion of the digit remains cyanotic and numb. He has used acetaminophen (Tylenol) and warm-water soaks without success. He is a construction worker who uses his hands "quite a bit" in his work.

Upon physical examination, his extremities reveal appropriate sensation of the forearm and hand. There appear to be some blue areas on the distal portion on the third phalanx, with no other signs and symptoms. He has a history of peptic ulcer disease but has no allergies. His social history is significant for smoking one and a half packs of cigarettes a day for 15 years. His family history is negative for any arthritic or rheumatologic disease.

F.K.'s opposite hand was placed in cold water, and it was noticed that several white splotches appeared and tingling was noted in the hand. He is diagnosed as having Raynaud's phenomenon. Does F.K. present with primary or secondary Raynaud's phenomenon?

F.K. presents with a case of secondary Raynaud's phenomenon with many underlying causes. His clinical presentation is classic for Raynaud's, with vasospasm, pallor, and a cyanotic overtone. The diagnosis is confirmed by the cold-water test, which indicates that the vasospastic attack is precipitated by cold exposure. He has a significant work history consistent with trauma to the hands, and a long-standing history of smoking.

Treatment

Nonpharmacologic Management

11. What conservative measures can be taken with F.K. to prevent the vasospasm of Raynaud's disease?

A majority of patients will respond to conservative management of primary and secondary Raynaud's phenomenon. Avoidance of cold stimuli is the primary treatment. F.K. should be instructed to protect his hands and fingers from exposure by using mittens and styrofoam coasters when handling cold drinks. He should protect other parts of the body from cold exposure to prevent a sympathetic response which may trigger vasoconstriction. Avoidance of emotional situations and tobacco, along with occupational changes which prevent long periods of standing, also have been shown to be beneficial. Medications which induce Raynaud's phenomenon, particularly β-adrenergic blocking agents and ergot preparations, should be avoided if at all possible. The discontinuation of tobacco use in F.K. is especially important, as nicotine will stimulate the sympathetic nerves to initiate vasoconstriction.

Calcium Channel Blockers

12. Nifedipine 10 mg TID is ordered for F.K. What is the rationale for using a calcium channel blocker in this case? Will the response be any better than that seen in the treatment of IC with calcium channel blockers?

Drug therapy may be used in patients with primary and secondary disorders whose disease interferes with their ability to work or perform daily activities, or in whom trophic digital lesions develop. Unfortunately, most proposed treatments for Raynaud's are of variable efficacy, pose risk for significant side effects, and are expensive. The drug therapies involved in the treatment of Raynaud's disease are aimed at vasodilation of the affected areas; however, these therapies are nonspecific. Objective changes in blood flow

do not correlate well with beneficial responses, and therapy will benefit only two out of three patients treated.[69]

Calcium channel-blockers are beneficial via their ability to decrease calcium ion influx and prevent smooth muscle contraction, especially in vascular responses evoked by cold exposure and α_2-receptor-mediated activity.[69] Nifedipine, a potent peripheral vasodilating calcium channel blocker, has become the drug of choice in patients with Raynaud's disease who are uncontrolled by conservative measures. Two-thirds of patients with either primary or secondary Raynaud's disease will benefit from nifedipine treatment, although patients with primary disease may show the most improvement.[70–72] Doses of 10 to 30 mg three times daily of nifedipine have been shown to be beneficial. The sustained-release formulation has been reported to be effective, although there are no formal studies to substantiate these observations.[69]

Diltiazem, a less potent peripheral-dilating calcium channel blocker, has been shown in doses of 30 to 120 mg three times daily to benefit patients with primary and secondary Raynaud's disease. The response rates may not be as high as with nifedipine, and patients who have not responded to nifedipine probably will not gain any benefit with diltiazem. Side effects, such as headache, dizziness, or peripheral edema, may be less with diltiazem than with nifedipine. Patients responding to nifedipine but intolerant of its side effects may be given a trial of diltiazem to assess efficacy and tolerance. Verapamil, another intermediate-potency, peripheral-vasodilating calcium channel blocker, has not been studied extensively for Raynaud's, and one small study using 80 mg four times a day showed no benefit in subjective and objective findings.[73] Other vasoselective calcium channel blockers such as nicardipine, isradipine, felodipine, and amlodipine are reportedly beneficial in some patients, but small studies with these agents all are inconclusive as to their benefit.[74–79]

In summary, nifedipine appears to be the current drug of choice for both primary and secondary Raynaud's disease. Patients who do not benefit from nifedipine likely will not benefit by switching to another calcium channel blocker. However, if the patient is not tolerating the side effects of nifedipine (such as ankle edema), he might benefit by switching to another calcium channel blocker such as diltiazem.

Other Agents

13. What other drugs may be tried if F.K. is intolerant of a calcium blocker?

α_1-adrenergic antagonists have been used for Raynaud's disease, with prazosin (usually 1 mg three times a day) yielding moderate benefit in two-thirds of patients.[80,81] Side effects of prazosin are significant at maximum doses, including dizziness, edema, fatigue, and orthostasis. The investigational drug thymoxamine, a selective α_1-receptor blocking agent, is effective with potentially less side effects than prazosin. A randomized double-blind study of oral thymoxamine showed increases in the rewarming response, as well as increases in absolute digital temperatures.[82] At this time, there are no data concerning the use of the newer, longer-acting α_1-blocking agents, terazosin and doxazosin.

Reserpine, Guanethidine, and Methyldopa. These antihypertensive agents have been used for many years for the treatment of Raynaud's disease, with significant side effects including nasal congestion, postural hypotension, and fatigue. Few controlled studies have been performed with these drugs; therefore, their usefulness in patients with this condition is not well understood at this time.[69]

Direct-Acting Vasodilators. The application of nitroglycerin (NTG) ointment to the hands of Raynaud's patients has been tried since the mid1940s. High doses of NTG ointment (3.5 inches) three times a day have been applied to the hands for six weeks and resulted in fewer and less severe attacks.[83] However, side effects severely limit the use of nitroglycerin or other direct-acting vaso-dilators (e.g., nitroprusside). Niacin may or may not be beneficial, depending upon the patient's concomitant disease state. For instance, a patient who is being treated for hypercholesterolemia and Raynaud's likely will have dual benefit from the addition of the vasodilating effects of niacin. In contrast, a patient with diabetes mellitus may not benefit from niacin treatment due to the risk of losing glucose control. Patient treatment should be individualized in each case.

Serotonin Receptor Antagonists. The investigational drug ketan-serin, a serotonergic antagonist with some α_1-adrenergic-receptor blocking activity, inhibits the serotonergic-mediated vasoconstriction. One large study concluded that ketanserin, when used in patients with primary or secondary Raynaud's phenomenon, produced a significant decrease in the frequency, but not the duration of the attacks.[84] Doses used in this study were 40 mg two to three times a day, with side effects including headache, asthenia (general weakness), dizziness, sedation, edema, dry mouth, and prolongation of the QT interval.

Angiotensin Converting Enzyme (ACE) Inhibitors. The buildup of bradykinin, a potent vasodilator, by inhibition of angiotensin-con-verting enzyme has been proposed as a possible beneficial therapy in patients with Raynaud's disease. However, evidence of benefit is limited. In an open labeled trial of captopril 25 mg three times daily in 53 patients with primary Raynaud's phenomenon, a significant decrease in frequency and severity of attacks was seen.[85] These findings were supported by objective cold challenge measures. Captopril also was evaluated in a placebo-controlled trial at doses of 25 mg three times daily which failed to demonstrate a significant difference in frequency or severity of attacks, but produced a significant improvement in cutaneous blood flow.[86] A crossover study of 17 patients using enalapril at 20 mg/day showed a decrease in frequency of attacks, but objective measures were no different than placebo.[87]

Triiodothyronine (T_3). The first controlled study with triiodothy-ronine 80 µg/day demonstrated this thyroid preparation to be effective both subjectively and objectively.[88] The induction of a mild thyrotoxic state (mean total T_3: 7.9 nmol/L; normal range: 1.2 to 3.0 nmol/L) appeared to be sufficient to ameliorate the symptoms of Raynaud's disease, although no patients experienced clinical features of overt hyperthyroidism. It has been postulated that T_3 therapy enhances β_2-adrenoreceptor activity in vascular smooth muscle. Another proposed mechanism of T_3 is correction of autonomic dysfunction by increasing peripheral blood flow to ischemic peripheral nerves or by acting on the autonomic system directly.[89] T_3 should be used cautiously in patients with Raynaud's and IC, since these patients likely have concomitant coronary artery disease. Increases in oxygen demand, blood pressure, and heart rate may induce angina in these patients. Long-term side effects of a mild hyperthyroid state, such as osteoporosis and cardiac toxicities, need further evaluation.

Nocturnal Leg Muscle Cramps

Nocturnal leg muscle cramps are idiopathic, involuntary contractions occurring at rest and causing a visible and palpable knot in the affected muscle. This type of muscle cramp usually afflicts middle-aged to elderly persons and can be described by the patient as a distressing and painful condition. While the incidence of nocturnal cramps is unknown, some data indicate that it is a very common abnormality. A survey of veterans (95% men) averaging 60 years of age showed that 56% of them complained of leg

Table 11.3	Other Causes of Muscle Cramps[45,94]
Drug-Induced Cramps	**Biochemical Causes**
Alcohol	Hyponatremia
Antipsychotics (dystonia)	Dehydration
Beta agonists (e.g., albuterol, terbutaline, salbutamol)	Calcium deficiency
	Magnesium deficiency
Cimetidine	Hemodialysis
Clofibrate	
Lithium	
Narcotic analgesics	
Nicotinic acid	
Nifedipine	

cramps, with 12% having cramping nearly every night. Thirty-six percent of these veterans also were attempting some type of drug treatment.[44] Nocturnal leg cramps have been associated with lower-extremity atherosclerosis, coronary artery disease, cerebro-vascular disease, kidney disease, and hypokalemia.[44]

Clinical Presentation

14. E.A., a 62-year-old female, complains of leg cramps in her left calf beginning last night around 10:00 p.m. The cramping occurred intermittently throughout the night and has been resolving slowly since she arose this morning. She states that nighttime cramping episodes occur frequently and are very painful and describes her calf muscle as being "knotted." She denies any trauma, fever, chills, and has no other medical problems. The pain is not associated with walking and is not relieved with rest. The physical examination is unremarkable and her vital signs are stable. E.A. works at the local school and does a lot of walking up and down stairs throughout the day. Her physician associates the pain with nocturnal leg cramps. What characteristics differentiate nocturnal leg cramps from other pain syndromes?

The cramps usually occur in the early hours of sleeping, are asymmetric, and are not exclusive to, but primarily affect the calf muscle and small muscles of the foot. The nocturnal cramp occurs with the further contraction of a muscle already in its most short-ened position. For example, the weight of bed sheets on the toes may place the calf and ventral foot muscles in their most shortened and vulnerable position, predisposing these muscles to contraction.[45] The cramp will cease when the muscle is stretched. It has been hypothesized that the origin of the cramp is not in the muscle itself but rather may be due to lower motor neuron, spinal cord, or cephalad abnormality.[45] For proper diagnosis and treatment, true muscle cramps first should be distinguished from other causes of muscle cramping. (See Table 11.3.)

Treatment

Therapeutic Objectives and Nonpharmacologic Interventions

15. What are the therapeutic objectives in treating E.A.? What nonpharmacologic recommendations can be made?

First, other conditions which may mimic or induce cramps should be excluded during a physical examination. The onset of cramps at rest is characteristic of ordinary leg cramps and is the primary symptom used for diagnosis. Patients with unclear etiology of muscle spasms may be evaluated for other clinical conditions which may contribute to the cramping. Clinical signs of sodium depletion, hyper- and hypothyroidism, tetany, and lower motor neuron disease should be evaluated. Laboratory measurements such as standard electrolytes and thyroid function tests can help rule out these other conditions.

The primary goal is prevention of this uncomfortable condition. It commonly is recommended that sufferers of leg cramps attempt to stretch out the afflicted muscle or perform dorsiflexion of the feet throughout the day and before bedtime.[60] For calf cramps, dorsiflexion consists of grasping the toes and pulling them upward in the opposite direction of the cramp. As described earlier, bed sheets can place pressure on the toes, predisposing the calf muscle to cramping. Sheets on the bed should be loose-fitting to prevent cramping. If necessary, a canopy at the end of the bed can be made to keep tight blankets from pushing the toes downward. Sufferers of nocturnal cramps also can be instructed to sleep on their stomachs with their toes hanging over the edge of the bed to keep their feet extended.

Quinine

16. After evaluating E.A., her physician decides to prescribe quinine sulfate 260 mg 1 to 2 tablets Q HS for 1 week to see if E.A. achieves relief of further cramping. Has quinine been shown to be effective in preventing nocturnal leg cramps?

Quinine is the most frequently prescribed medication for nocturnal leg cramps and is available as an over-the-counter product. Quinine may exert a beneficial effect by increasing the refractory period of skeletal muscle and by decreasing the excitability of the motor endplate. Despite its frequent use, there is significant controversy over its benefit. There have been only a few controlled trials performed, with overall mixed conclusions.

Quinine has been used to treat nocturnal leg cramps since the 1940s when four patients suffering from leg cramps experienced marked improvement in symptoms after being treated with quinine.[46] When given placebo, their symptoms apparently worsened. Subsequent results of studies in patients suffering from at least two nocturnal leg cramps a week have been contradictory and nonconclusive. Prescribed doses of quinine in these studies have ranged from 200 or 300 mg at bedtime to a combination of 200 mg with dinner along with 300 mg at bedtime. There have been four double-blind, placebo-controlled trials which failed to show a significant benefit of quinine use when measuring number, duration, and severity of leg cramps.[47–50] Only three trials have concluded that quinine use is beneficial.[51–53] (See Table 11.4.)

E.A. may experience a reduction in her leg cramps with the use of quinine. With successful therapy, E.A. should see a decrease in the frequency of her cramping attacks, as well as in the duration and severity of the cramps. Quinine is available in the U.S. only

as the sulfate salt and in a number of generic doses and dosage forms. A 200 to 300 mg evening dose commonly is recommended, with an additional early evening dose taken only if needed. E.A. should be instructed to take the dose of quinine with food to minimize gastrointestinal (GI) irritation.

17. Serum Concentration. Is there a relationship between serum concentration and the effect of quinine?

Quinine is absorbed slowly from the GI tract and will not reach peak serum concentrations for one to three hours. Serum concentrations at these doses are generally in the 2 to 3 µg/mL range. Therefore, it may be beneficial for the patient to take the dose in the early evening rather than at bedtime in order to prevent leg cramping.[49,54] Differences in serum concentrations also have been noted between the sugar-coated and noncoated preparations.[49,55]

In one study, higher quinine serum concentrations were significantly correlated with beneficial effects in the treatment of nocturnal leg cramps, even though this study failed overall to show a significant difference in treatment groups.[49] Perhaps higher doses of quinine would show more clinical benefit than the traditional 300 mg dose. In another study, higher quinine doses were used (200 mg with dinner, 300 mg at bedtime) and showed a significant benefit over placebo in the number of leg cramps.[52] It also should be realized that this is the only controlled trial which showed a significant increase in side effects compared to placebo.

The design of studies involving this intervention may be made more credible with the monitoring of serum concentrations; however, routine serum concentration monitoring in patients is not necessary except in patients on long-term therapy with a risk of accumulation of the drug. It may be concluded that higher doses of quinine may be more beneficial but with an increased risk of adverse reactions, especially in the elderly.

18. Adverse Effects. E.A. has been treated with quinine for several months with a noted reduction in the number of cramps. However, she now complains of lightheadedness, dizziness, and shortness of breath. Are these side effects of quinine?

In fact, E.A. is exhibiting signs and symptoms of quinine toxicity. Cinchonism, or quininism, is characterized as ringing in the ears (tinnitus), headache, nausea, and vertigo. Symptoms may progress to deafness. Other side effects include optic atrophy, severe GI symptoms, delirium, and cardiac arrhythmias.[56] There also are a number of reported cases of thrombocytopenia and disseminated intravascular coagulation (DIC) associated with quinine use, and

Table 11.4			Studies of Quinine for Nocturnal Leg Cramps			
Drug/Study	n	Duration of Treatment (days)	Treatment Regimen[c]	Reduction in Cramp Frequency?	Reduction in Cramp Duration?	Reduction in Cramp Severity?
Jones 1983[a,b]	9	4 x 2 week periods	300 mg vs P	Yes	No	Yes
Lim 1986[b,d]	25	Assessed each a.m.	300 mg vs P	No	—	No
Smith 1985[a]	18	2 x 3 week periods	300 mg vs P	No	—	No
Wharburton 1987[a]	22	2 x 3 week periods	300 mg vs P	No	No	No
Fung 1989[a,b]	8	2 x 4 week periods	200 mg vs P	Yes	Yes	Yes
Connolly 1992[a,e,f]	27	2 x 4 week periods	500 mg vs P vs VE	Yes	—	No
Sidorov 1993[a,b]	16	4 x 2 week periods	200 mg vs P	No	No	No

[a] Crossover trial.
[b] Night cramps >2 times/week.
[c] P = Placebo; VE = Vitamin E.
[d] Inpatient.
[e] Side effects significantly greater in treatment group.
[f] Patients with >6 cramps/month.

a history of these effects with the use of quinidine would indicate a contraindication to use.[57-59] Quinine should not be used in patients with G6PD deficiency.

Only one clinical study reported significant side effects of quinine when used for cramping; however, this trial used higher-than-usual doses (500 mg/day).[52] Even so, the elderly are most likely to use quinine, and the adverse effects may be hard to differentiate from other underlying diseases and medications.[54] Alterations in quinine metabolism and drug interactions (i.e., cimetidine, acetazolamide, sodium bicarbonate) may increase the plasma concentration of quinine into the toxic range where cinchonism is more likely to occur (5 to 10 µg/mL).

Other Drugs

19. Are there other treatment options for E.A.?

Electrolyte replacement (e.g., sodium, potassium, calcium, magnesium) may be indicated if specific deficiencies are noted or if the onset of cramping is associated with a recent initiation or dosage increase of diuretic therapy. Prophylactic use with other pharmacologic agents has been attempted, but their use is mostly anecdotal. Diphenhydramine, nifedipine, fluoride, and riboflavin have been used empirically.[45] Vitamin E has been prescribed commonly; however, one controlled study with 800 IU/day of vitamin E showed no benefit.[52] Orphenadrine, an antihistamine muscle relaxant, is effective in relieving nocturnal leg cramps; however, its anticholinergic side effects may preclude its use.[61]

Verapamil has been evaluated for leg cramps and may exert its effect by limiting the rate and extent of calcium influx in response to depolarization, leading to reduced contractility and limiting ATP utilization. It also may improve muscle microcirculation secondary to vasodilation.[62] This theory is hampered by the fact that nifedipine actually may cause leg cramps as well as be used to treat them.[63,64] Verapamil has been shown in an open-labeled trial of nine elderly patients to relieve quinine resistant cramps. A dose of 120 mg of verapamil at bedtime was used, and relief was seen after six days of treatment.[65]

Update

Quinine and Nocturnal Leg Cramps

Question 14 introduced us to E.A., a 62-year-old female, who complained of leg cramps in her left calf beginning around 10:00 p.m. In Question 16, E.A.'s physician decided to prescribe quinine sulfate for her nocturnal leg cramps.

U1. E.A. read that quinine was no longer approved by the FDA for use for nocturnal leg cramps. Can E.A. still obtain quinine for her nocturnal leg cramping? What is the current status of quinine in the U.S.?

Many of the concerns discussed earlier in Questions 14 through 18 on quinine use for nocturnal leg cramps were raised by the FDA in early 1995. After re-evaluating the studies investigating quinine for nocturnal leg cramps, the FDA removed the over-the-counter status of quinine, thus eliminating self medication for this ailment.[115] The FDA went further by removing the labeled indication for nocturnal leg cramps for the prescription form of quinine, leaving quinine with an indication for malaria prophylaxis and treatment. The side effects of quinine, particularly hypersensitivity reactions, lightheadedness, dizziness, and other symptoms of cinchonism were the primary reason for this action. The side effect risks associated with quinine were determined to outweigh the questionable clinical benefit.

E.A. should once again be instructed on the nonpharmacologic options for treating nocturnal leg cramps. This includes stretching the afflicted muscle before bedtime, or ''tenting'' the end of the bed to relieve the weight of the sheets on the feet. Quinine will still be available in prescription form, but without the labeled indication for nocturnal leg cramping. Should E.A.'s physician decide to continue the use of quinine, she should be instructed to not use more than the prescribed dose, and to report any signs of cinchonism. E.A. also should be instructed to keep a record of the frequency and severity of the cramps after the initiation of quinine in order to assess the clinical benefits of this agent.

References

1   **Kannel WB et al.** Intermittent claudication: incidence in the Framingham study. Circulation. 1970;41:875–83.

2   **Crique MH et al.** The prevalence of peripheral arterial disease in a defined population. Circulation. 1985;71:510–15.

3   **Kannel WB, McGee DL.** Diabetes and cardiovascular disease: the Framingham study. JAMA. 1979;241:2035–038.

4   **McDaniel MD, Cronenwett JL.** Basic data related to the natural history of intermittent claudication. Ann Vasc Surg. 1989;3:273–77.

5   **Kallero KS.** Mortality and morbidity in patients with intermittent claudication as defined by venous occlusion plethysmography. A ten-year follow-up study. J Chronic Dis. 1981;34:455–62.

6   **Greenhalgh RM et al.** Serum lipids and lipoproteins in peripheral vascular disease. Lancet. 1971;2:947–50.

7   **Schadt DC et al.** Chronic atherosclerotic occlusion of the femoral artery. JAMA. 1961;175:937–40.

8   **Kannel WB, Shurtleff D.** The Framingham Study: cigarettes and the development of intermittent claudication. Geriatrics. 1973;28(2):61–68.

9   **Reid HL et al.** Impaired red cell deformability in peripheral vascular disease. Lancet. 1976;1:666–68.

10 **Weed RI.** The importance of erythrocyte deformability. Am J Med. 1970; 49:147–50.

11 **Braasch D.** Red cell deformability and capillary blood flow. Physiol Rev. 1971;51:679–701.

12 **Dormandy JA et al.** Clinical, hemodynamic, rheological, and biochemical findings in 126 patients with intermittent claudication. Br Med J. 1973;4: 576.

13 **Ernst E, Matrai A.** Intermittent claudication, exercise, and blood rheology. Circulation. 1987;76:1110–114.

14 **Ward A, Clissold SP.** Pentoxifylline: a review of its pharmacodynamic and pharmacokinetic properties, and its therapeutic efficacy. Drugs. 1987;34: 54–97.

15 **Accetto B.** Beneficial hemmorheologic therapy of chronic peripheral arterial disorders with pentoxifylline: results of double-blind study versus vasodilator-nylidrin. Am Heart J. 1982;103:864–69.

16 **Porter JM et al.** Pentoxifylline efficacy in the treatment of intermittent claudication: multicenter-controlled double-blind trial with objective assessment of chronic occlusive arterial disease patients. Am Heart J. 1982; 104:66–72.

17 **Rudofsky G et al.** Intravenous treatment of chronic peripheral occlusive arterial disease: a double-blind, placebo-controlled, randomized multicenter trial of pentoxifylline. Angiology. 1989;40:639–49.

18 **Cameron HA et al.** Drug treatment of intermittent claudication: a critical analysis of the methods and findings of published trials, 1965–1985. Br J Clin Pharmacol. 1988;26:569–76.

19 **Lindegarde F et al.** Conservative drug treatment in patients with moderately severe chronic occlusive peripheral arterial disease. Scandinavian Study Group. Circulation. 1989;80:1549–556.

20 **Coffman JD.** Vasodilator drugs in peripheral vascular disease. N Engl J Med. 1979;300:713–16.

21 **Seino Y et al.** Double blind study of papaverine hydrochloride on the efficacy in the treatment of intermittent claudication. Angiology. 1983;34:257–65.

22 **Trainor FS et al.** Effects of ethaverine hydrochloride on the walking tolerance of patients with intermittent claudication. Angiology. 1986;37:343–51.

23 **Trubestein G et al.** Buflomedil in arterial occlusive disease: results of a controlled multicenter study. Angiology. 1984;35:500–05.

24 **Brevetti G et al.** Increases in walking distance in patients with peripheral vascular disease treated with L-carnitine: a double-blind, crossover study. Circulation. 1988;77:767–73.

25 **Morgan RH et al.** The effects of nifedipine on blood flow in peripheral vascular disease of the lower limbs. Eur Heart J. 1987;8(Suppl. K):87–91.

26 **Fogoros R.** Exacerbation of intermittent claudication by propranolol. N Engl J Med. 1980;302:1089.

27 **Frohlich E et al.** Peripheral artery insufficiency. A complication of beta adrenergic blocking therapy. JAMA. 1969;208:2471.

28 **Houben H et al.** Effect of low dose epinephrine infusion on hemodynamics after selective and nonselective beta blockade in hypertension. Clin Pharmacol Ther. 1982;31:685.

29 **Hiatt WR et al.** Effect of beta adrenergic blockers on the peripheral circulation in patients with peripheral vascular disease. Circulation. 1985;72(6): 1226–231.

30 **Roberts DH et al.** Placebo-controlled comparison of captopril, atenolol, labetalol, and pindolol in hypertension complicated by intermittent claudication. Lancet. 1987;2(8560):650–53.

31 **Lepantalo M.** Chronic effects of metoprolol and methyldopa on calf blood flow in intermittent claudication. Br J Clin Pharmacol. 1984;18:90–3.

32 **Brown BG et al.** Regression of coronary artery disease as a result of intensive lipid lowering therapy in men with high levels of lipoprotein B. N Engl J Med. 1990;323:1289.

33 **Blankenhorn DH et al.** Beneficial effects of combined colestipol-niacin therapy on atherosclerosis and coronary venous bypass grafts. JAMA. 1987;257:3233.

34 **Barndt R Jr et al.** Regression and progression of early femoral atherosclerosis in treated hyperlipoproteinemic patients. Ann Intern Med. 1977;86: 139–46.

35 **The Diabetes Control and Complications Trial Research Group.** The effect of intensive treatment of diabetes on the development and progression of long-term complications in insulin dependent diabetes mellitus. N Engl J Med. 1993;329:977–86.

36 **Coffman JD.** New drug therapy in peripheral vascular disease. Med Clin North Am. 1988;72:259–65.

37 **Radack K, Wyderski RJ.** Conservative management of intermittent claudication of the lower limbs. Ann Intern Med. 1990;113:135–46.

38 **Ekroth R et al.** Physical training of patients with intermittent claudication. Surgery. 1978;84:640.

39 **Lewis P et al.** Nifedipine in patients with peripheral vascular disease. Eur J Vasc Surg. 1989;3:159–64.

40 **Tunis SR et al.** The use of angioplasty, bypass surgery, and amputation in the management of peripheral vascular disease. N Engl J Med. 1991;325:556–62.

41 **Coffman JD.** Intermittent claudication—be conservative. N Engl J Med. 1991;325:577–78.

42 **Young JR et al.** Peripheral Vascular Diseases. St. Louis: Mosby Yearbook; 1991.

43 **Clement DL, Shepard JT.** Vascular Diseases in the Limbs: Mechanisms and Principles of Treatment. St. Louis: Mosby Yearbook; 1993.

44 **Oboler SK et al.** Leg symptoms in outpatient veterans. West J Med. 1991; 155:256–59.

45 **McGee SR.** Muscle cramps. Arch Intern Med. 1990;150:511–18.

46 **Moss HK, Herrmann LG.** Use of quinine for relief of "night cramps" in the extremities. JAMA. 1940;115:1358–359.

47 **Sidorov J.** Quinine sulfate for leg cramps: does it work? J Am Geriatr Soc. 1993;41:498–500.

48 **Smith C et al.** Double-blind, placebo-controlled, crossover study of maintenance treatment with quinine bisulfate for night cramps. Br J Clin Pharmacol. 1986;21:108. Letter.

49 **Wharburton A et al.** A quinine a day keeps the leg cramps away. Br J Clin Pharmacol. 1987;23:459–65.

50 **Lim SH.** Randomized double-blind trial of quinine sulfate for nocturnal leg cramps. Br J Clin Pract. 1986;40:462.

51 **Fung MC, Holbrook JH.** Placebo-controlled trial of quinine therapy for nocturnal leg cramps. West J Med. 1989;151:42–4.

52 **Connolly PS et al.** Treatment of nocturnal leg cramps: a crossover trial of quinine versus vitamin E. Arch Intern Med. 1992;152:1877–880.

53 **Jones K, Castleden CM.** A double-blind comparison of quinine sulfate and placebo in muscle cramps. Age Aging. 1983;12:155–58.

54 **Peters MD, Carson DS.** Nocturnal leg cramps. Ann Pharmacother. 1990;24: 599–600.

55 **Garnham JC et al.** The bioavailability of quinine. J Trop Med Hyg. 1976;79: 264–69.

56 **Anon.** Quinine for "night cramps." Med Lett Drugs Ther. 1986;28:110.

57 **Boyd IW.** Nocturnal cramps, quinine, and thrombocytopenia. Arch Intern Med. 1991;151:1021. Letter.

58 **Frieman JP.** Fatal quinine-induced thrombocytopenia. Ann Intern Med. 1990;112:308–09.

59 **Spearing RL et al.** Quinine-induced disseminated intravascular coagulation. Lancet. 1990;336:1535–537.

60 **Daniell HW.** Simple cure for nocturnal leg cramps. N Engl J Med. 1979;301: 216.

61 **Latta D, Turner E.** An alternative to quinine in nocturnal leg cramps. Curr Ther Res. 1989;45:833–37.

62 **Lane RJM et al.** A double-blind placebo-controlled crossover study of verapamil in exertional pain. Muscle Nerve. 1986;9:635–41.

63 **Keider S et al.** Muscle cramps during treatment with nifedipine. Br Med J. 1982;285:1241–242.

64 **Peer G et al.** Relief of hemodialysis-induced muscular cramps by nifedipine. Dialysis Transplant. 1983;12:180–81.

65 **Baltadano N et al.** Verapamil vs quinine in recumbent nocturnal leg cramps in the elderly. Arch Intern Med. 1988; 148:1969–970.

66 **Peacock JH.** The effect of changes in local temperature in the blood flow of the normal hand, primary Raynaud's disease and primary acrocyanosis. Clin Sci. 1960;19:505.

67 **Shepard FJ, Shepard JT.** Primary Raynaud's disease. In: Vascular Diseases in the Limbs: Mechanisms and Principles of Treatment. St. Louis: Mosby Yearbook; 1993:153.

68 **Cohen RA, Coffman JD.** Digital vasospasm: the pathophysiology of Raynaud's phenomenon. Int Angiol. 1984; 3:47.

69 **Coffman JD.** Raynaud's phenomenon: an update. Hypertension. 1991;17:593.

70 **Smith CD, McKendry RVR.** Controlled trial of nifedipine in the treatment of Raynaud's phenomenon. Lancet. 1982;2:1299.

71 **Rodeheffer RJ et al.** Controlled double-blind trial of nifedipine in the treatment of Raynaud's phenomenon. N Engl J Med. 1983;308:880.

72 **Kiowski W et al.** Use of nifedipine in hypertension and Raynaud's phenomenon. Cardiovasc Drugs Ther. 1990; 4(Suppl. 5):935.

73 **Kinney EL et al.** The treatment of severe Raynaud's phenomenon with verapamil. J Clin Pharmacol. 1982;22:74.

74 **Ferri C et al.** Slow releasing nicardipine in the treatment of Raynaud's phenomenon without underlying diseases. Clin Rheumatol. 1992;11:76.

75 **French Cooperative Multicenter Group for Raynaud Phenomenon.** Controlled multicenter double-blind trial of nicardipine in the treatment of primary Raynaud phenomenon. Am Heart J. 1992;122:352.

76 **Wollersheim H, Thien T.** Double-blind placebo-controlled crossover study of nicardipine in the treatment of Raynaud's phenomenon. J Cardiovasc Pharmacol. 1991;18:813.

77 **Rupp PAF et al.** Nicardipine for the treatment of Raynaud's phenomenon: a double-blind crossover trial of a new calcium entry blocker. J Rheumatol. 1987;14:745.

78 **Leppert J et al.** The effect of isradipine, a new calcium channel antagonist, in patients with primary Raynaud's phenomenon: a single blind dose response study. Cardiovasc Drugs Ther. 1989;3:397.

79 **LaCivita L et al.** Amlodipine in the treatment of Raynaud's phenomenon. Br J Rheumatol. 1993;32(Suppl. 6): 524. Letter.

80 **Wollersheim H et al.** Double-blind, placebo-controlled study of prazosin in Raynaud's phenomenon. Clin Pharmacol Ther. 1986;40:219.

81 **Wollersheim H, Thien T.** Dose response study of prazosin in Raynaud's phenomenon: clinical effectiveness versus side effects. J Clin Pharmacol. 1988;28:1089.

82 **Grigg MJ et al.** The efficacy of thymoxamine in primary Raynaud's phenomenon. Eur J Vasc Surg. 1989;3: 309.

83 **Franks AG Jr.** Topical glyceryl trinitrate as adjunctive treatment in Raynaud's phenomenon. Lancet. 1982;1:76.

84 **Coffman JD et al.** International study of ketanserin in Raynaud's phenomenon. Am J Med. 1989;87:264.

85 **Tosi S et al.** Treatment of Raynaud's phenomenon with captopril. Drugs Exp Clin Res. 1987;13:37.

86 **Rustin MHA et al.** The effect of captopril on cutaneous blood flow in patients with primary Raynaud's phenomenon. Br J Dermatol. 1987;117: 751.

87 **Janini SD et al.** Enalapril in Raynaud's phenomenon. J Clin Pharm Ther. 1988; 13:145.

88 **Dessain PH et al.** Triiodothyronine treatment for Raynaud's phenomenon: a controlled trial. J Rheumatol. 1990; 17:1025.

89 **Gledhill RF et al.** Treatment of Raynaud's phenomenon with triiodothyronine corrects co-existent autonomic dysfunction: preliminary findings. Postgrad Med J. 1992;68:263.

90 **Dahllof AG et al.** Metabolic activity of skeletal muscle in patients with peripheral artery insufficiency. Eur J Clin Invest. 1974;4:9–15.

91 **Schoop W.** Mechanism of beneficial action of daily walking training of patients with intermittent claudication. Scand J Clin Lab Invest. 1973;31 (Suppl. 128):197–99.

92 **Zetterquist S.** The effect of active training on the nutritive blood flow in exercising ischemic legs. Scand J Clin Lab Invest. 1970;25:101–11.

93 **Ernst EE, Matrai A.** Intermittent claudication, exercise, and blood rheology. Circulation. 1987;76:1110–114.

94 **Eaton JM.** Is this really a muscle cramp? Postgrad Med. 1989;86:227–32.

95 **Shepard JT et al.** Endothelium dysfunction in vascular disease. In: Clement DL, Shepard JT, eds. Vascular Diseases in the Limbs. St. Louis: Mosby Yearbook; 1993.

96 **Sowers JR.** Insulin resistance, hyperinsulinemia, dyslipidemia, hypertension, and accelerated atherosclerosis. Clin Pharmacol. 1992;32:529–35.

97 **Kaplan NM.** The deadly quartet. Upper body obesity, glucose intolerance, hypertriglyceridemia, and hypertension. Arch Intern Med. 1989;149: 1514–520.

98 **Kaplan NM.** Effects of antihypertensive therapy on insulin resistance. Hypertension. 1992;19(Suppl. I):I-116–I-118.

99 **Ernst E, Fialka V.** A review of the clinical effectiveness of exercise therapy for intermittent claudication. Arch Intern Med. 1993;153:2357–360.

100 **Cummings DM et al.** Lack of effect of pentoxifylline on red blood cell deformability. J Clin Pharmacol. 1992; 32:1050–053.

101 **Housley E.** Treating claudication in five words. Br Med J. 1988;296:1483–484.

102 **Bevan EG et al.** Pharmacological approaches to the treatment of intermittent claudication. Drugs Aging. 1992; 2:125–36.

103 **Solomon SA et al.** Beta blockade and intermittent claudication: placebo-controlled trial of atenolol and nifedipine and their combination. Br Med J. 1991; 303:1100–104.

104 **Fuster V et al.** The pathogenesis of coronary artery disease and the acute coronary syndromes. N Engl J Med. 1992;326:310–18.

105 **Kuhn FE.** Cholesterol and lipoproteins: beyond atherogenesis. Clin Cardiol. 1992;15:883–90.

106 **Treasure CB et al.** Coronary endothelial responses are improved with aggressive lipid lowering therapy in patients with coronary atherosclerosis. Circulation. 1993;88:I-368. Abstract.

107 **Anderson TJ et al.** Cholesterol lowering therapy improves endothelial function in patients with coronary atherosclerosis. Circulation. 1993;88:I-368. Abstract.

108 **Expert Panel on Detection, Evaluation, and Treatment of High Blood Cholesterol in Adults.** Summary of the second report of the national cholesterol education program (NCEP) expert panel on detection, evaluation, and treatment of high blood cholesterol in adults. JAMA. 1993;269:3015–023.

109 **Blankenhorn DH et al.** Coronary angiographic changes with lovastatin therapy. The Monitored Atherosclerosis Study (MARS). Ann Intern Med. 1993;119:969–76.

110 **Lewis EJ et al.** The effect of angiotensin converting enzyme inhibition on diabetic nephropathy. N Engl J Med. 1993;329:1456.

111 **Bigazi R et al.** Long-term effects of a converting enzyme inhibitor and a calcium channel blocker on urinary albumin excretion in patients with essential

hypertension. Am J Hypertens. 1993;6:
108.

112 **Pentecost MJ et al.** Guidelines for peripheral percutaneous transluminal angioplasty of the abdominal aorta and lower extremity vessels: a statement for health professionals from a special

writing group of the Councils of Cardiovascular Radiology, Arteriosclerosis, Cardiothoracic and Vascular Surgery, Clinical Cardiology, and Epidemiology and Prevention, the American Heart Association. Circulation. 1994; 89:511.

113 **Radack K et al.** Beta adrenergic blocker therapy does not worsen intermittent claudication in subjects with peripheral arterial disease: a meta analysis of randomized controlled trials. Arch Intern Med. 1991;151:1769.

114 **Krajewski LP.** Atherosclerosis of the

aorta and lower extremity arteries. In: Peripheral Vascular Diseases. St. Louis: Mosby Yearbook; 1993.

115 **Anon.** Prescription quinine sulfate for leg cramps is new drug requiring approval. FDC Reports ("The Pink Sheet"); February 13, 1995:T&G-3.

Thrombosis

Ann K Wittkowsky

General Principles 12-1
Etiology of Thromboembolism (See Figure 12.1) 12-2
Clot Formation 12-2
   Platelet activation 12-2
   Clotting cascade (See Figure 12.2) 12-2
   Pathologic thrombi 12-2
     Arterial thrombi 12-2
     Venous thrombi 12-2
Anticoagulant Pharmacology 12-3
   Heparin (See Tables 12.1 and 12.2 and Figure
   12.3) 12-3
   Low molecular weight heparins (LMWHs)
   (See Tables 12.1 and 12.2 and Figure 12.3) 12-3
   Warfarin (See Figure 12.4 and Table 12.3) 12-4
Tests Used to Monitor Antithrombotic Therapy 12-4
   Prothrombin time (PT) (See Table 12.4) 12-4
   Activated partial thromboplastin time (aPTT) 12-5
   Thrombin time 12-6
   Bleeding time 12-6
Deep Venous Thrombosis (DVT) 12-7
Clinical Presentation 12-7
   Signs and symptoms 12-7
   Risk factors (See Figure 12.1) 12-7
   Diagnosis 12-7
Treatment 12-7
   Baseline information 12-7
   Initiation of therapy 12-7
   Heparin 12-7
     Loading dose 12-7
     Dose adjustments (See Table 12.5) 12-8
     Therapeutic monitoring 12-8
     Duration of therapy 12-8
     Adverse effects 12-8
       Thrombocytopenia 12-8
       Hemorrhage 12-9
       Osteoporosis 12-10
       Hyperkalemia 12-10
       Hypersensitivity reactions 12-10
     Adjusted Dose Subcutaneous (SQ) Administration
     (See Table 12.6) 12-10
     Overdose 12-10
Prevention (See Table 12.7) 12-10
Nonpharmacologic measures 12-11
Pharmacologic measures (See Table 12.7) 12-11
Pulmonary Embolism (PE) 12-11
Clinical Presentation 12-11
   Signs and symptoms 12-11

Diagnosis 12-11
Treatment 12-12
   Heparin initiation and dosing 12-12
   Warfarin 12-12
     Transition from heparin therapy 12-12
     Initiation therapy (See Table 12.8) 12-12
     Intensity of therapy 12-13
     Duration of therapy 12-13
     Adverse effects 12-13
       Hemorrhage 12-13
       Purple Toe syndrome 12-14
       Skin necrosis 12-14
     Patient education (See Table 12.9) 12-14
     Dietary considerations 12-15
     Alcohol ingestion 12-15
     Maintenance therapy 12-15
       Factors influencing dosing 12-15
       Dosing adjustments (See Figures 12.5 and
       12.6) 12-15
       Frequency of follow-up 12-16
     Overdose 12-16
     Effect on menstruation 12-16
     Use in pregnancy 12-16
Prevention Of Cardiogenic Thromboembolism 12-17
Atrial Fibrillation 12-17
   Anticoagulation before cardioversion 12-17
   Anticoagulation after cardioversion 12-17
   Anticoagulation for chronic atrial fibrillation 12-17
     Anticoagulation in valvular atrial fibrillation 12-17
     Anticoagulation in nonvalvular atrial fibrillation ..12-17
     Anticoagulation in lone atrial fibrillation 12-18
Cardiac Valve Replacement 12-18
   Mechanical prosthetic valves 12-18
   Bioprosthetic valves 12-18
   Combined anticoagulant/antiplatelet therapy 12-18
Left Ventricular Thrombosis 12-19
   Following myocardial infarction 12-19
   In congestive heart failure 12-19
Drug Interactions (See Table 12.10) 12-19
Disseminated Intravascular Coagulation (DIC) 12-21
Pathophysiology (See Figure 12.7) 12-21
Clinical Presentation 12-21
   Laboratory findings 12-21
   Hemorrhagic manifestations 12-21
   Thrombotic manifestations 12-21
Precipitating Events (See Table 12.11) 12-22
Treatment 12-22

General Principles

Thrombosis is the process involved in the formation of a fibrin blood clot. Both platelets and a series of coagulant proteins contribute to clot formation. An embolus is a small part of a clot that breaks off and travels to another part of the vascular system. Damage is caused when the embolus becomes trapped in a small capillary causing ischemia or infarction of the surrounding tissue. Normal clot formation maintains the integrity of the vasculature in response to injury, but pathologic clotting can occur in a variety of clinical settings. Abnormal thrombotic events include deep venous thrombosis (DVT) and its primary complication, pulmonary embolism (PE), as well as stroke and other systemic manifestations of embolization by clots that form within the heart. Anticoagulant drug therapy is aimed at preventing pathologic clot formation in patients at risk and at preventing clot extension and/or embolization in patients who have developed thrombosis. The emphasis of this chapter is on arterial and venous thromboembolic disease and the use of heparin and warfarin as anticoagulants. The reader is referred to Chapter 14: Myocardial Infarction and Chapter 53: Cerebrovascular Disorders for in-depth discussions of thrombolytic agents and antiplatelet therapy.

Etiology of Thromboembolism

Three primary factors influence the formation of pathologic clots and are described in a model referred to as Virchow's Triad.[2] (See Figure 12.1.) First, abnormalities of blood flow causing venous stasis can result in deep venous thrombosis, progressing to pulmonary embolism if embolization occurs. Intracardiac stasis also can result in clot formation, and embolization of intracardiac thrombi may lead to stroke or other systemic manifestations. Abnormalities of blood vessel walls, such as those that occur in injury or trauma to the vasculature, are a second source for thrombus formation. The presence of foreign material within the vasculature, including artificial heart valves and central venous catheters, is also thrombogenic, and, like vascular injury, represents the presence of an abnormal surface in contact with blood. Finally, hypercoagulability resulting from alterations in the availability or the integrity of blood clotting components or naturally occurring anticoagulants also represents a significant risk factor for thromboembolic disease.[3]

Clot Formation

Platelet Activation

The formation of a stable fibrin clot is the result of a complex series of events including platelet adhesion and aggregation followed by activation of the clotting cascade. Tissue injury, with release of adenosine diphosphate (ADP), thrombin, and epinephrine, or exposure of collagen and other subendothelial surfaces of a damaged vessel wall, may stimulate the initial adhesion of platelets to the site of injury. Subsequent granular release of additional ADP causes circulating platelets to adhere to those already present, resulting in platelet aggregation.

Clotting Cascade

Transformation of the relatively unstable platelet plug (i.e., the aggregated platelets) to a stable fibrin clot occurs as a result of an imbalance between other procoagulant and anticoagulant factors. As previously described, activation of the clotting cascade, secondary to tissue injury or to surface activation, initiates the clotting process (see Figure 12.2).[1] The extrinsic pathway of the clotting cascade is activated by thromboplastin (tissue factor), a protein released by injured tissues. Factor VII is activated and transformed to factor VII$_a$ which mediates the activation of factor X. The intrinsic pathway of the clotting cascade is activated by contact of blood with subendothelial components exposed during vessel injury, or by exposure of blood to foreign surfaces or platelet aggregates. The intrinsic pathways mediate factor X activation via a chain of events initiated by factor XI. The distinction between these pathways is primarily an *in vitro* phenomenon, and good evidence exists that the two pathways are activated simultaneously.[4] Once stimulated, both the extrinsic and intrinsic pathways activate the common pathway of the clotting cascade via factor X. When thrombin (factor II$_a$) is formed, it is partly consumed during the process and removed by absorption into fibrin.

Naturally occurring inhibitors of clotting factors play a role in localizing fibrin formation to the sites of injury and in maintaining the fluidity of circulating blood. Protein C, and its cofactor, protein S, inhibit the activated forms of factors II, X, XI, and XII.[5] The deposition of fibrin also is associated with activation of plasmin, which by binding with plasminogen results in lysis of the stable fibrin clot into soluble fibrin fragments (fibrin degradation products).[6] This naturally occurring process helps to prevent excessive coagulation. Thus, the process of clot formation is ongoing, involving various factors that can stimulate, inhibit, and dissolve a fibrin clot.

Pathologic Thrombi

Pathologic thrombi sometimes are classified according to location and composition.[2]

Arterial thrombi (white thrombi) are composed primarily of platelets, although they also contain fibrin and occasional leukocytes. Arterial thrombi generally occur in areas of rapid blood flow (i.e., arteries) and are formed in response to an injured or abnormal vessel wall.

Venous thrombi (red thrombi) are found primarily in the venous circulation and are composed almost entirely of fibrin and erythrocytes. Venous thrombi have a small platelet head, and generally form either in response to venous stasis or vascular injury following surgery or trauma. The areas of stasis prevent dilution of activated coagulation factors by blood flow.

The selection of an antithrombotic agent thus may be influenced by the type of thrombus to be treated. The anticoagulants, heparin and warfarin, are used to treat both arterial and venous thrombi. Drugs that alter platelet function (e.g., aspirin) have been investigated for their role in the prevention of thromboembolic disease associated with arterial thrombi, alone and in combination with

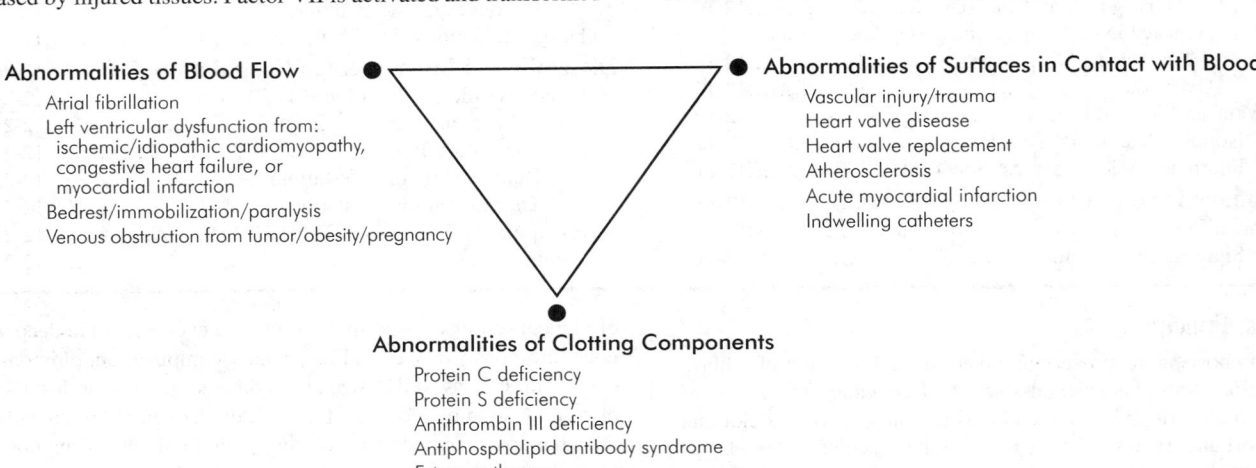

Abnormalities of Blood Flow
Atrial fibrillation
Left ventricular dysfunction from:
 ischemic/idiopathic cardiomyopathy,
 congestive heart failure, or
 myocardial infarction
Bedrest/immobilization/paralysis
Venous obstruction from tumor/obesity/pregnancy

Abnormalities of Surfaces in Contact with Blood
Vascular injury/trauma
Heart valve disease
Heart valve replacement
Atherosclerosis
Acute myocardial infarction
Indwelling catheters

Abnormalities of Clotting Components
Protein C deficiency
Protein S deficiency
Antithrombin III deficiency
Antiphospholipid antibody syndrome
Estrogen therapy
Pregnancy
Malignancy

Fig 12.1   Risk Factors for Thromboembolism

Fig 12.2 Simplified Clotting Cascade Components in boxes are influenced by heparin; components in ovals are influenced by warfarin.

anticoagulants. (See Chapters 13: Ischemic Heart Disease, 14: Myocardial Infarction, and 53: Cerebrovascular Disorders.) Fibrinolytic agents are used in various clinical settings for rapid dissolution of thromboemboli. (See Chapter 14: Myocardial Infarction.)

Anticoagulant Pharmacology

Heparin

Heparin is a rapid acting anticoagulant that is effective only when administered parenterally. Standard heparin [unfractionated heparin (UFH)] is a heterogeneous mixture of glycosaminoglycans of varying molecular weights obtained from bovine or porcine intestinal mucosa. (See Table 12.1.) The action of heparin is facilitated by its binding to the naturally circulating anticoagulant, antithrombin III (AT III), a serine protease also referred to as heparin cofactor. Binding of heparin to AT III accelerates the anticoagulant effect of antithrombin III. The heparin-antithrombin III complex attaches to and irreversibly inactivates thrombin (factor II_a) as well as activated factors IX, X, XI, and XII.[7] (See Figure 12.3.) Approximately one-third of the molecules present in unfractionated heparin bind to AT III and provide the anticoagulant properties of heparin. The remaining two-thirds of the heparin molecules bind to plasma proteins and to endothelial cells, saturable processes that contribute to the dose-dependent pharmacokinetic profile of the drug and limit its bioavailability.[8] In addition to its anticoagulant effects, heparin inhibits platelet function and increases vascular permeability; these properties contribute to the hemorrhagic effects of heparin. In cases of acute DVT or PE, the clotting cascade has been activated, generating abnormal quantities of thrombin and fibrin. In these situations, thrombin must be inactivated directly, a process that may require relatively large doses of heparin. However, when the clotting cascade is in a normal balance, it is possible to indirectly inactivate thrombin with smaller heparin doses by complexing factor X_a. Due to the multiplier effect of the clotting cascade, inactivation of relatively small amounts of factor X_a indirectly prevents the production of large quantities of thrombin. This phenomenon is the basis for low dose heparin prophylaxis following surgery or in cases of prolonged bedrest or immobilization.

Following intravenous (IV) administration, an anticoagulant effect is noted immediately. Heparin is cleared by transfer to the reticuloendothelial system with ultimate elimination controlled by the liver.[9] Heparin also is partially inactivated by "consumption" as it complexes with AT III and activated clotting factors. Thus, the more extensive the thrombotic process, the more rapid the clearance of heparin from the serum. The half-life (t½) of heparin is approximately 50 to 90 minutes in normal volunteers (see Table 12.2). A number of variables may affect the biologic half-life of heparin, the most important of which is the presence of an active coagulation process. During active thromboembolism, the high concentration of clotting factors present necessitates a higher concentration of heparin to neutralize these clotting factors. This increased dosing requirement also may be related to continuing thrombin formation on the surface of the embolus.[9,10] Once endothelialization of the clot begins and the concentration of clotting factors decreases, dosing requirements will decrease.

Heparin may be administered intravenously by continuous infusion or subcutaneously (SQ), but the intramuscular (IM) route should be avoided because of the potential for hematoma formation. The primary laboratory test for monitoring therapeutic heparinization is the activated partial thromboplastin time (aPTT) (see Tests Used to Monitor Antithrombotic Therapy).

Low Molecular Weight Heparins (LMWHs)

Using chemical or enzymatic depolymerization techniques, unfractionated heparin can be separated into fragments based on molecular weight.[11] Low molecular weight heparin (LMWH) molecules have been isolated and commercially marketed as anticoagulants. These compounds differ substantially from unfractionated heparin with respect to molecular weight, antithrombotic and pharmacokinetic properties, adverse effect profiles, and monitoring requirements (see Table 12.1).[12]

To inactivate factor X_a, only the AT III component of the heparin-AT III complex is required to bind to factor X_a (see Figure 12.3). Both the longer, high molecular weight (HMW) fragments of unfractionated heparin and the shorter, low molecular weight (LMW) fragments of LMWHs are capable of inactivating factor X_a; but to inactivate factor II_a (thrombin), both the heparin com-

Table 12.1	Comparison of Unfractionated Heparin and Low Molecular Weight Heparins[12]	
Property	UFH[a]	LMWH[a]
Molecular weight range[b]	3000–30,000	1000–10,000
Average molecular weight[b]	12,000–15,000	4000–5000
Anti-X_a:anti-II_a activity	1:1	2:1–4:1
aPTT monitoring required	Yes	No
Inactivation by platelet factor 4	Yes	No
Capable of inactivation of platelet-bound factor X_a	No	Yes
Inhibition of platelet function	++++	++
Increases vascular permeability	Yes	No
Protein binding	++++	+
Endothelial cell binding	+++	—
Dose-dependent clearance	Yes	No
Elimination half-life	50–20 min	2–5 times longer

[a] LMWH = Low molecular weight heparin; UFH = Unfractionated heparin.
[b] Measured in daltons.

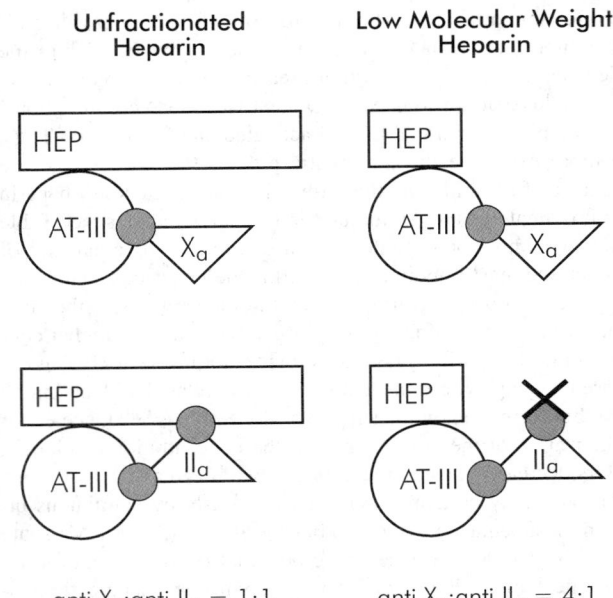

Fig 12.3 Mechanism of Action of Heparin See text for description.
AT-III = Antithrombin III; HEP = Heparin.

ponent and the AT III component of the heparin-AT III complex are required to bind to factor II_a. This binding requires heparin molecules of at least 18 saccharide units in length, which are less prevalent in low molecular weight heparins.[12,13] Therefore, the anti-X_a properties of LMWHs are more significant than their anti-II_a properties. The resultant antithrombotic effect does not prolong the aPTT, meaning that these compounds do not require laboratory monitoring to adjust therapeutic effect.

Additional advantages of low molecular weight heparins over unfractionated heparin include improved antithrombotic effects, reduced hemorrhagic complications, greater bioavailability, predictable dose response, and longer pharmacodynamic effect. In general, these compounds are administered subcutaneously every 12 to 24 hours at fixed doses. A number of LMWH products have been studied in the prevention and treatment of thromboembolic disease (see Table 12.2).[13] They differ significantly in their molecular weight distributions, methods of preparation, and anti-X_a: anti-II_a activities, as well as in their pharmacokinetic and pharmacodynamic characteristics. Several products are available commercially in Europe and Canada. In the U.S., enoxaparin (Lovenox) has been approved for deep venous thrombosis prevention in hip replacement surgery. With further study, these products may replace the use of unfractionated heparin in many clinical settings.

Warfarin

Vitamin K is essential for the conversion (carboxylation) of precursors to clotting factors II, VII, IX, and X into inactive clotting factors with increased affinity for calcium and phospholipid binding. Increased calcium and phospholipid binding affinity contributes to effective clotting. During factor conversion, vitamin K is oxidized to inactive vitamin K epoxide. (See Figure 12.4.) In the nonanticoagulated patient, vitamin K epoxide is in reversible equilibrium with vitamin K, but this equilibrium is disrupted in patients taking oral anticoagulants. Warfarin (Coumadin) interferes with the cyclic interconversion of vitamin K epoxide back to vitamin K resulting in an increased ratio of vitamin K epoxide to vitamin K in the liver.[14] The accumulation of vitamin K epoxide thus reduces the effective concentration of vitamin K and reduces its role in the synthesis of coagulation factors. Concentrations of clotting factors

II, VII, IX, and X gradually are diminished at rates commensurate with their elimination half-lives (60, 6, 24, and 40 hours, respectively).

Protein C and its cofactor protein S are vitamin K-dependent proenzymes which are activated by thrombin. Activated protein C has the ability to inhibit factors V and VII, and, therefore, demonstrates inherent anticoagulant properties. Since depression of vitamin K activity by warfarin also may depress protein C, there may be a risk of paradoxical thromboembolism at the time of warfarin initiation in patients with protein C or protein S deficiency. However, in normal patients, the antithrombotic activity of warfarin overcomes this risk.

Warfarin is completely absorbed in the upper gastrointestinal (GI) tract by passive diffusion (see Table 12.3). Peak absorption of warfarin occurs in 60 to 120 minutes. It is approximately 99% bound to serum albumin.[15] The volume of distribution (Vd) for warfarin is 12.5% of body weight. This small volume of distribution is consistent with the extensive binding of warfarin to albumin. Despite this small volume of distribution and the extent of protein binding to albumin, the actual concentration of albumin and total protein in the serum has little effect on the extent of binding. The primary laboratory test for monitoring warfarin therapy is the prothrombin time (PT). No correlation appears to exist between the prothrombin time and either the dose of warfarin, total warfarin concentration, or free warfarin concentration between individuals.

Warfarin is administered orally as a racemic mixture containing equal parts of the enantiomers R(+)-warfarin and S(−)-warfarin. The S-isomer is approximately five times more potent as an anticoagulant than the R-isomer.[16] These enantiomers are metabolized differentially in the hepatic microsomes by mixed function oxidase enzymes. Several drugs interact with warfarin by stereoselectively inhibiting the metabolism of either the R-isomer or the S-isomer. (See Drug Interactions.)

Tests Used to Monitor Antithrombotic Therapy

Before the initiation of antithrombotic therapy, an assessment of coagulation status is necessary. A baseline platelet count and hematocrit (Hct) should be obtained and the integrity of the extrinsic and intrinsic coagulation pathways should be evaluated by the prothrombin time and the activated partial thromboplastin time.[17]

Prothrombin Time (PT)

The PT is prolonged by deficiencies of clotting factors V, VII, X, and II, as well as by low levels of fibrinogen and very high levels of heparin. It reflects alterations in the extrinsic and common

Table 12.2	Selected Low Molecular Weight Heparin Products Under Investigation[13]	
Product	Manufacturer	Mean MW[a]
Ardiparin (Normiflo)	Wyeth-Ayerst	6200
Dalteparin (Fragmin)	Kabi	6370
Enoxaparin (Lovenox, Clexane)	Rhone-Poulenc-Rorer	4500
Knoll LMWH (Reviparin)	Knoll	
Nadroparin (Fraxiparine)	Choay	6370
Parnaparin (Fluxum, Opocrin)	Bristol-Myers-Squibb	6500
Sandoz LMWH (Sandoparine)	Sandoz	6300
Tinzaparin (Logiparin)	Novo	4850

[a] MW = Molecular weight (daltons).

Fig 12.4   Mechanism of Action of Warfarin

pathways of the clotting cascade, but not in the intrinsic system.[18] The prothrombin time is measured by adding calcium and tissue thromboplastin to a sample of plasma from which platelets have been removed by centrifugation. The time to clot formation is detected by automated instruments using light scattering techniques that measure optical density. The mean normal prothrombin time, obtained by averaging a number of PT results from nonanticoagulated subjects, is approximately 12 seconds for most reagents.

The thromboplastins used in PT monitoring are extracted from various tissue sources by a number of techniques and prepared for commercial use as reagents. Unfortunately, thromboplastins are not standardized among manufacturers or among batches of reagent produced by the same manufacturer, leading to significant variability in prothrombin time results for anticoagulated patients.[14] Attempts to correct this variability by expressing prothrombin time as a ratio of a patient's PT value in seconds to the mean normal PT have not been successful and have resulted in significant errors in caring for patients taking warfarin.[19] To standardize prothrombin time results, the World Health Organization developed a system by which all commercially available thromboplastins are compared to an international reference thromboplastin and then are assigned an International Sensitivity Index (ISI).[20] This value is used to mathematically convert prothrombin time to the International Normalized Ratio (INR) by exponentially multiplying the PT ratio to the power of the ISI of the thromboplastin being used in the laboratory to measure the test [INR = (PT patient/PT mean normal)^{ISI}]. The ISI of the international reference thromboplastin is 1.0.

INR is a mathematical correction of thromboplastin variability, but commercial thromboplastins still have significant inherent variability in their sensitivity to detect the clotting defect induced by warfarin. Recombinant human tissue thromboplastins with consistent sensitivity and ISI values of 1.0 may eventually replace the rabbit brain thromboplastins used currently in the U.S.[21]

Prothrombin time expressed as INR is the internationally recognized standard for monitoring warfarin therapy and has been accepted as the standard of practice in the U.S.[22] Current recommendations for intensity of oral anticoagulation therapy for accepted clinical indications are summarized in Table 12.4.[22,81] Low intensity therapy is defined as dosing warfarin to reach an INR of 2.0 to 3.0 and is appropriate for most settings that require the prevention and/or treatment of thromboembolic disease. High intensity therapy is used in mechanical valve replacement and certain situations of thromboembolic recurrence despite adequate anticoagulation, and is defined as a prolongation of the prothrombin time to an INR of 2.5 to 3.5.

Activated Partial Thromboplastin Time (aPTT)

This test reflects alterations in the intrinsic pathway of the clotting cascade and is used to monitor heparin therapy.[23] It is performed by addition of a surface activating agent (kaolin; micronized silica), a partial thromboplastin reagent (phospholipid; platelet substitute), and calcium to the plasma sample. Mean normal values vary among reagents, but typically fall between 24 and 36 seconds.

Like prothrombin time, the activated partial thromboplastin time is a highly variable test based upon differences among commercially available partial thromboplastin reagents.[24,25] However, a system equivalent to the INR has not been developed for standardization of aPTT results. Heparinization to prolong the aPTT to 1.5 to 2.5 times the mean normal value historically has been considered adequate to prevent propagation or extension of thrombus, but may not be appropriate for all reagents and testing systems. Although not suitable for routine patient monitoring, the evaluation of heparin plasma levels by protamine titration has established a range of 0.2 to 0.4 U/mL that is correlated with clinical efficacy and safety.[25] A reagent-specific therapeutic range in seconds can be determined by measuring in vitro aPTT values (in seconds) for plasma samples containing known concentrations of heparin between 0.2 U/mL and 0.4 U/mL or by using protamine titration to

Table 12.3	Clinical Pharmacokinetics and Monitoring of Anticoagulants^{a,b}	
Parameter	Heparin	Warfarin
Absorption	Parenteral only	Oral 100% (not given parenterally)
Vd	Plasma volume (≈ 0.07 L/kg)^c	$\approx 7.6–13.9$ L
Metabolism/Cl	Hepatic metabolism and uptake by reticulo-endothelial system. Also uptake (consumption) by thrombin and other clotting factors^d	Hepatic
Elimination t½	50–90 min	36–42 hr
Protein binding	Bound to antithrombin III and other serine proteases	99.4% bound to albumin
Cp (therapeutic)	0.2–0.4 U/mL	1.5 mg/L
Side effects	Bleeding,^{e} thrombocytopenia, osteoporosis	Bleeding,^{e} skin necrosis, drug interactions
Treatment of bleeding	*Mild:* Slow or stop infusion *Severe:* Protamine 1 mg/100 U of estimated heparin remaining in body	*Mild:* Hold 1–2 doses, observe and restart at lower dose *Severe:* Vitamin K or fresh frozen plasma

^{a} Reprinted with permission. Handbook of Applied Therapeutics, Vancouver: Applied Therapeutics, Inc. 1992: 13.6.
^{b} Cl = Clearance; Cp = Plasma concentration; t½ = Half-life; Vd = Volume of distribution.
^{c} Loading dose can be calculated by multiplying Vd times desired Cp. Maintenance dose can be calculated by multiplying Cl times desired Cp.
^{d} Dose requirements may be higher during active thrombosis and before endothelialization.
^{e} Monitor hemoccult of stool; observe for bleeding from injection sites, hematuria, nose bleeds, gum bleeding, increased menstrual flow, and bruising at subcutaneous sites. Monitor platelets with prolonged heparin therapy. Significant GI bleeding or hematuria may indicate an underlying lesion (e.g., ulcer or tumor).

Table 12.4	Optimal Therapeutic Range and Duration of Therapy for Oral Anticoagulation with Warfarinᵃ
Indication	**Target INR (Duration)**
Atrial Fibrillation	
In valvular/nonvalvular heart disease	2–3 (chronic)
Lone atrial fibrillation if age >60 yr	2–3 (chronic)
Precardioversion (for AF >48 hr duration)	2–3 (3 weeks)
Postcardioversion	2–3 (4 weeks)
Cardioembolic Stroke	
Large stroke	2–3 (chronic) [delayed 5–14 days]
Small stroke	2–3 (chronic) [delayed 48 hr]
Following embolic event despite anticoagulation	2.5–3.5 (chronic) [or 2–3 + antiplatelet therapy]
Left Ventricular Dysfunction	
EF <30%	2–3 (chronic)
Transient, following myocardial infarction	2–3 (1–6 mon)
Following embolic event despite anticoagulation	2.5–3.5 (chronic) [or 2–3 plus antiplatelet therapy]
Myocardial Infarction	
Following anterior MI	2–3 (chronic)
Following inferior MI with thromboembolic risk(s) (AF, left ventricular dysfunction, mural thrombus, history of thromboembolism)	2–6 (1–3 months)
Following MI with continued presence of risk(s) (AF, left ventricular dysfunction, mural thrombus)	2–3 (chronic)
Thromboembolism (DVT, PE)	
Treatment/prevention of recurrence	2–3 (3 months)
Recurrence despite anticoagulation	2.5–3.5 (chronic)
Continued presence of risk factor(s) (AT-III, protein C, protein S deficiencies; malignancy)	2–3 (chronic)
Valvular Disease	
Aortic valve disease	
With concurrent mitral valve disease	2–3 (chronic)
With associated AF	2–3 (chronic)
With history of systemic embolization	2–3 (chronic)
Mitral annular calcification	
With associated AF	2–3 (chronic)
With history of systemic embolization	2–3 (chronic)
Mitral valve prolapse	
With associated AF	2–3 (chronic)
With history of systemic embolization	2–3 (chronic)
With history of TIA despite ASA therapy	2–3 (chronic)
Following embolic event despite anticoagulation	2.5–3.5 (chronic) [or 2–3 + antiplatelet therapy]
Rheumatic mitral valve disease	
With associated AF	2–3 (chronic)
With history of systemic embolization	2–3 (chronic)
Following embolic event despite anticoagulation	2.5–3.5 (chronic) [or 2–3 + antiplatelet therapy]
Valve Replacement	
Mechanical valve prosthesis	2.5–3.5 (chronic)
Mechanical valve s/p systemic embolization	2.5–3.5 (chronic) + antiplatelet therapy
Tissue valve prosthesis	2–3 (1–3 months)
Tissue valve with history of systemic embolization	2–3 (chronic)

ᵃ AF = Atrial fibrillation; ASA = Acetylsalicylic acid; AT-III = Antithrombin III; DVT = Deep venous thrombosis; EF = Ejection fraction; MI = Myocardial infarction; PE = Pulmonary embolism, TIA = Transient ischemic attack.

measure heparin concentrations in *in vivo* samples followed by correlation of these concentrations to aPTT values.[26,27] The use of reagent-specific therapeutic ranges for monitoring heparin therapy has been successful in clinical practice and is considered a more accurate approach than relying on aPTT ratios to adjust heparin dosing.[8]

Thrombin Time

The thrombin time measures fibrinogen concentration and is useful in detecting the presence of fibrin and fibrinogen degradation products. The time required for a plasma sample to clot after the addition of thrombin is compared to that of a normal plasma control. A value of three seconds or more beyond the control value is considered abnormal. The thrombin time may be prolonged due to deficiencies of thrombin or the presence of fibrin or fibrin degradation products; therefore, it is useful in assessing fibrinolytic status.

Bleeding Time

The bleeding time is a measure of platelet aggregation and capillary contraction, but is of little value in monitoring antiplatelet or anticoagulant therapy. It is measured by making an incision in the forearm and blotting the incision every 30 seconds with filter paper until bleeding stops. The normal bleeding time ranges from two to ten minutes and is maintained in patients with simple clotting factor deficiencies, but prolonged in patients with platelet abnormalities or patients being treated with antiplatelet therapy. Clinically, an assessment of platelet count is more important than monitoring the bleeding time.

Deep Venous Thrombosis (DVT)

Clinical Presentation

Signs and Symptoms

1. D.P., a 76-year-old, obese (92 kg, 6′ tall) male, is admitted to the hospital with right calf swelling and pain of one-day's duration. On the day before admission, he noted progressive swelling and soreness of the right calf. He denies trauma to the calf, but reveals that several days before the onset of symptoms he was a passenger in an automobile for a lengthy trip, during which he sat in a fixed position for many hours. He denies shortness of breath (SOB), cough, or chest pain.

His past medical history includes coronary artery disease, myocardial infarction (MI) at ages 55 and 67, and hypercholesterolemia. His medications are diltiazem CD (Cardizem CD) 240 mg PO QD, isosorbide dinitrate (Isordil) 30 mg PO TID, atenolol (Tenormin) 50 mg PO QD, and lovastatin (Mevacor) 20 mg PO Q PM.

Initial laboratory values include Hct 36.5% (Normal: 42%–52%), PT 10.8 sec (INR 1.0), aPTT 23.6 sec (Normal: 24–36 sec), and platelet count 255,000/mm³ (Normal: 150,000–300,000).

What signs and symptoms demonstrated by D.P. are consistent with DVT? [SI Units: Hct 0.365 1 (Normal: 0.42–0.52); platelet count 255 × 10⁹/L (Normal: 150–300)]

One of the most reliable, although nonspecific, physical findings of DVT is unilateral leg swelling that frequently is accompanied by local tenderness or pain.[28] A tender, cord-like entity caused by venous obstruction sometimes can be palpated in the affected area. D.P. presented with the sudden onset of swelling along with soreness, but without evidence of a cord. Discoloration of the affected limb also may occur, including pallor from arterial spasm, cyanosis from venous obstruction, or a reddish color from perivascular inflammation. The presence or absence of a positive Homans' sign (pain behind the knee or calf upon dorsiflexion of the foot) rarely is helpful in making the diagnosis, since it is present in only about 30% of patients with deep venous thrombosis.

Risk Factors

2. What risk factors does D.P. exhibit which are associated with DVT?

The diagnosis of DVT depends not only upon the presenting signs and symptoms, but also upon the presence of a number of risk factors. A summary of risk factors for thromboembolism is presented in Figure 12.1. D.P. has presented with obesity and immobilization (i.e., prolonged sitting in an automobile), two important risk factors for thromboembolism. It is common for more than one risk factor to be present in patients developing DVT, and factors are cumulative in their effect.[29]

Diagnosis

3. How should the final diagnosis of DVT be made in D.P.?

After evaluation of the signs and symptoms of deep venous thrombosis, and consideration of risk factors for the development of thrombus, a definitive diagnosis should be made. Noninvasive testing options include ¹²⁵I-fibrinogen leg scanning (injection of radiolabelled fibrinogen followed by scanning to detect areas of

accumulation corresponding to thrombosis), impedance plethysmography (use of pneumatic cuffs to detect leg blood volume changes associated with thrombosis), and Doppler ultrasonography (use of a transducer to audibly detect venous flow changes indicative of thrombosis).[28] Each of these options differs with respect to sensitivity, specificity, and cost. Many institutions now turn to duplex scanning, combining B-mode imaging or color flow imaging with Doppler techniques to visualize veins and thrombi while investigating flow patterns.[29] Venography (radiographic visualization of the involved vessels with injection of radiocontrast material), an invasive diagnostic test, is the most sensitive and specific method for diagnosis of DVT, but exposes patients to the risks associated with contrast material.

Treatment

Baseline Information

4. What additional baseline data should be obtained before administration of anticoagulants to D.P.?

In addition to assessing the integrity of the clotting process with platelet count, Hct, PT, and aPTT, a urinalysis (UA) and a stool sample for occult blood should be obtained. Generally, it is unnecessary to type and crossmatch blood, but if this information is available, it should be recorded. Baseline values are used for comparison to parameters that will be used in monitoring both the therapeutic and adverse effects of anticoagulant therapy.

Initiation of Therapy

5. Duplex scanning was performed and revealed clot formation in D.P.'s right calf extending to the right thigh. He exhibited full and equal pulses in both legs, ruling out significant, if any, venous obstruction. He does not exhibit signs of pulmonary embolism. What is the appropriate therapy for D.P. and how should it be initiated?

On admission, D.P.'s right leg was elevated and heat was applied. Prompt and optimal anticoagulant therapy is indicated to minimize thrombus extension and its vascular complications, as well as to prevent pulmonary embolism. Heparin therapy should be initiated with a loading dose followed by a continuous infusion.

Heparin

6. Loading Dose. D.P.'s medical resident ordered a heparin bolus dose of 5000 U IV, to be followed by a continuous infusion of 1000 U/hr. Is this heparin dosing regimen appropriate?

A loading dose of heparin is required for several reasons. Based upon pharmacokinetic principles, a therapeutic serum level will be achieved more quickly; thus, pharmacodynamic and therapeutic responses to help prevent progression of clot will occur rapidly. Secondly, a relative resistance to anticoagulation exists during the active clotting process. Therefore, a larger initial dose generally is necessary to achieve a therapeutic effect.

Although many clinicians traditionally have turned to standardized doses for the initiation of heparin therapy (e.g., 5000 U loading dose; 1000 U/hour maintenance dose), this approach can result in significant delays in reaching a therapeutic intensity of anticoagulation.[30] Body weight represents the most reliable predictor of heparin dosing requirement. In a comparison to standardized dosing, weight-based dosing increased both the number of patients whose first aPTT was within the therapeutic range (32% versus 86%) and the number of patients who were within the therapeutic range within the first 24 hours of therapy (77% versus 97%).[31]

Initial heparin loading doses of 70 to 100 U/kg followed by an infusion rate of 15 to 25 U/kg/hour commonly are recommended.[32] Selection of the lower or upper dosage range is guided by severity of the patient's symptoms and his potential sensitivity to adverse effects. For this 92 kg patient, a mid-range loading dose of 7400

U (i.e., 92 kg × 80 U/kg) followed by a continuous infusion of 1700 U/hour (i.e., 92 kg × 18 U/kg/hour) is recommended. Both loading doses and maintenance infusion rates often are rounded to the nearest 100 U for convenience of administration.

Because considerable variability exists in patient responses to heparin, several pharmacokinetic approaches have been investigated to help determine heparin dosage more accurately.[33–36] The volume of distribution of heparin closely approximates blood volume. By estimating the volume of distribution based upon the patient's height, weight, and gender, and applying the basic pharmacokinetic principles of a one-compartment model, initial heparin infusion rates can be calculated.[33] However, while this technique is relatively easy to apply, many other variables may affect the response to heparin and the dosage still must be adjusted according to the results of subsequent laboratory evaluation.[36] In clinical practice, weight-based calculations of loading doses and maintenance infusion rates for heparin are recommended.[31]

7. Dose Adjustments. The orders for D.P. were rewritten by his attending physician. Based upon the data below, explain the variability in laboratory results. (At this institution, aPTT values of 60–100 sec correspond with heparin serum concentrations of 0.2–0.4 U/mL.)

Time	aPTT (sec)	Heparin Dose Order
0800	31	7400 U bolus followed by 1700 U/hr infusion
0900	130	Hold infusion for 30 min then ↓ to 1500 U/hr
1500	40	Rebolus with 2400 U then ↑ to 1700 U/hr
2100	85	Continue at 1700 U/hr; recheck aPTT Q AM

Although the aPTT drawn one hour after the initiation of the maintenance infusion (9:00 a.m.) demonstrates excessive prolongation of the aPTT (130 seconds), this value most likely is explained by inappropriate timing of the test. Activated partial thromboplastin time values drawn too soon after a heparin bolus dose, and before the maintenance infusion has achieved a steady-state concentration in serum, do not accurately reflect the level of anticoagulation in the patient and may be infinitely prolonged. To ensure accuracy, aPTT values should be obtained no sooner than six hours after a bolus dose or a change in infusion rate. Even results obtained at six hours may be excessively prolonged in some patients due to the dose-dependent pharmacokinetic characteristics of heparin.

D.P.'s heparin dose was decreased based upon this prolonged, yet inappropriately timed, value, and a repeat aPTT at 3:00 p.m. was only 40 seconds. The decrease in the dose to 1500 U/hour and the repeat aPTT of 40 seconds reflect near steady-state conditions since six hours have elapsed since the dosage change. Because the aPTT is subtherapeutic at 3:00 p.m. (40 seconds), administration of a smaller repeat bolus dose (2400 U) and an increase in the maintenance infusion to 1700 U/hour was the correct course of action. Subsequent aPTTs reflect therapeutic anticoagulation.

Dosing nomograms or protocols have been recommended for adjustment of heparin dosing based upon aPTT results.[8,31,32] A weight-based protocol, specific for a partial thromboplastin reagent with a therapeutic aPTT range of 60 to 100 seconds (and used in

the adjustment of heparin doses for D.P.), is described in Table 12.5. In settings in which reagent-specific therapeutic ranges have not been determined, heparin should be adjusted to prolong the aPTT to 1.5 to 2.5 times mean control values.

Responses to changes in infusion rates of heparin are not always linear and, to some extent, heparin doses are adjusted by trial and error. As the patient's condition improves after several days and endothelialization of the clot occurs, heparin dosing requirements may decrease.

8. Therapeutic Monitoring. How should D.P.'s heparin therapy be monitored?

Once baseline clotting parameters have been established and a loading dose of heparin has been administered, aPTT should be determined routinely to guide subsequent dosing requirements. The aPTT should be evaluated six hours after the loading dose and again six hours after any future changes in infusion rate, as noted above. If dosing is stable, aPTT should be evaluated once daily (see Table 12.5).

Additional monitoring parameters for heparin therapy include evaluation of potential adverse reactions and possible therapeutic failure. Hematocrit and platelet count should be checked every one to two days. D.P. should be examined for signs of bleeding as well as for signs and symptoms associated with thrombus extension and pulmonary embolism. Finally, the clinician caring for D.P. should consider the possible influence of solution preparation errors, infusion pump failure, infusion interruption, and administration or charting errors in the assessment of D.P.'s heparin therapy.[37]

9. Duration of Therapy. How long should heparin therapy be maintained in D.P.?

Adherence of a thrombus to the vessel wall and subsequent endothelialization or resolution usually takes between seven and ten days. As a result, heparin therapy traditionally has been administered for seven to ten days and warfarin initiated around day five. However, in a trial that compared five days of heparin with ten days of heparin in the treatment of proximal vein thrombosis, both courses were of equal efficacy with respect to successful resolution of clot and the absence of recurrent thrombosis.[38] Warfarin was initiated on day one in the short-course group and on day five in the long-course group. The incidence of rethrombosis, major bleeding, and thrombocytopenia was comparable in both groups. Minor bleeding occurred more frequently in the long-course group. Shortening the duration of heparin therapy and starting warfarin therapy on the first day of hospitalization is efficacious and can reduce both the length of hospitalization and the costs associated with DVT treatment.[39,40] Therefore, heparin therapy in D.P. can be discontinued in four to five days if a therapeutic level of oral anticoagulation has been achieved and maintained for two days. Warfarin therapy should then be continued for three months.

10. Adverse Effects. On day two of heparin therapy, the complete blood count (CBC) for D.P. reveals a platelet count of 180,000/mm^3, decreased from 255,000/mm^3 at baseline. What is a reasonable explanation for this thrombocytopenia and how should it be managed?

Thrombocytopenia induced by heparin occurs in two distinct presentations.[41] Type I heparin-induced thrombocytopenia (HIT) occurs as a direct effect of heparin on platelet function, causing transient platelet sequestration and clumping with reductions in platelet count to above 100,000/mm^3. This reversible form of thrombocytopenia occurs within the first several days of heparin therapy. Patients remain asymptomatic and platelet counts return to normal even when heparin therapy is continued. D.P.'s reduction in platelet count is somewhat modest and likely represents Type I HIT. Platelet count should be monitored daily and heparin therapy should be continued.

Table 12.5	Heparin Protocol for Acute Thromboembolic Event[a]

1) Loading Dose: 80 U/kg (rounded to nearest 100 U)

2) Maintenance Infusion: 18 U/kg/hr (rounded to nearest 100 U)

3) First aPTT Check: 6 hr after initiating therapy

4) Dosing Adjustments: Per chart below (rounded to nearest 100 U)

aPTT[b] (sec)	Heparin Bolus	Infusion Hold Time	Infusion Rate Adjustment	Next aPTT
<40	50 U/kg	0	↑ by 4 U/kg/hr	in 6 hr
40–60	25 U/kg	0	↑ by 2 U/kg/hr	in 6 hr
–60–100	0	0	None	Q AM
100–120	0	0	↓ by 1 U/kg/hr	in 6 hr
120–140	0	30 min	↓ by 2 U/kg/hr	in 6 hr
>140	0	60 min	↓ by 3 U/kg/hr	in 6 hr

[a] University of Washington Medical Center.
[b] Based upon aPTT reagent-specific therapeutic range of 60–100 sec corresponding to in vitro heparin concentrations of 0.2–0.4 U/mL.

Reductions in platelet count to below 100,000/mm^3 suggest the development of Type II heparin-induced thrombocytopenia, a more severe condition with a delay in onset of from 5 to 14 days following initiation of heparin therapy or with immediate onset in patients previously exposed to heparin. In this immune-mediated reaction, heparin binds to an IgG antibody to form a heparin-antibody complex which then binds to platelets, leading to significant platelet aggregation.[42] Laboratory analysis of the presence of the heparin-dependent platelet antibody can aid in differentiating Type II HIT from other causes of thrombocytopenia.[43]

The overall incidence of Type II HIT is less than 3% and may occur somewhat more frequently with bovine heparin than with porcine heparin.[44] Following discontinuation of heparin, platelet counts frequently return to normal within five to seven days, but recovery can be delayed. Bleeding complications are uncommon, but in approximately 0.4% of patients with Type II heparin-induced thrombocytopenia, platelet aggregation can lead to arterial thrombosis (white clot syndrome). Presenting signs of this complication include limb thrombosis, often necessitating amputation, as well as thrombotic stroke, acute myocardial infarction, skin necrosis, and thrombosis of other major arteries. Patients who develop these paradoxical signs of thrombosis while receiving heparin should have a platelet count measured on an emergency basis.

In patients who develop Type II HIT, heparin therapy should be stopped and, if anticoagulation with warfarin has been initiated, it should be continued provided that the prothrombin time is within the appropriate therapeutic range. If this is not the case, therapeutic alternatives include ancrod,[45] a snake venom extract that depletes circulating fibrinogen, and lomoparan (Org 10172; Orgaran),[46] a heparinoid compound that catalyzes the inactivation of factors X_a and II_a via AT-III, but does not contain heparin or heparin fragments and does not cross-react with heparin. Both agents are investigational and must be obtained under compassionate use protocols. Low molecular weight heparin products are contraindicated due to a high incidence of immunologic cross-reactivity with heparin. If necessary, an inferior vena cava filtration device such as the Greenfield Filter can be implanted. These devices prevent pulmonary embolization by trapping embolic material originating from areas of the vasculature distal to their placement point.[47]

Additionally, pharmacologic measures to inhibit platelet aggregation are indicated in some patients. Alternatives include aspirin therapy with or without dipyridamole; IV dextran; iloprost, a pros-

tacycline analog; and high dose intravenous immune globulin.[43] Platelet transfusions should be avoided due to the risk of worsening thrombotic complications.

11. *Hemorrhage.* **On day three of heparin therapy, D.P.'s Hct has dropped from a baseline of 36.5% to 29% and the presence of blood in his urine is noted. Describe an approach to evaluate and interpret this event.**

Bleeding is the most common adverse effect associated with heparin. A summary of eight inception cohort studies reporting heparin-associated bleeding reported the absolute frequency of fatal, major, and all (major or minor) bleeding as 0.4%, 6%, and 16%, respectively.[48] The corresponding average daily frequencies were 0.05% for fatal bleeding, 0.8% for major bleeding, and 2% for major or minor bleeding; cumulative risk increased with duration of therapy. The most common sites for heparin-associated bleeding are soft tissues, the GI and urinary tracts, the nose, and the oral pharynx.

In addition to length of therapy, a number of factors influence the risk of bleeding during heparinization, including advanced age, serious comorbid illnesses (heart disease, renal insufficiency, hepatic dysfunction, cerebrovascular disease, malignancy, and severe anemia), and concomitant aspirin therapy.[48,49] Soft tissue bleeding frequently occurs at sites of recent surgery or trauma. Previously undiagnosed lesions have been identified in a significant percentage of patients with GI or urinary tract bleeding associated with heparin therapy.[50,51]

The influence of intensity of heparinization on bleeding risk is somewhat controversial. While elevated aPTT historically has been considered a risk factor for bleeding complications,[52] several investigators have been unable to substantiate a relationship between supratherapeutic aPTT values and hemorrhagic effects.[53-56] In a comparison of high-dose to conventional-dose heparin, 85% of patients who experienced bleeding episodes had coagulation tests within the therapeutic range.[57] These conflicting results may be explained in part by the influence of additional risk factors for bleeding and by the effect of heparin on platelet function and vascular permeability. These two mechanistic factors, in addition to heparin's anticoagulant effect, influence hemorrhagic complications.

D.P. has developed hematuria despite an acceptable intensity of anticoagulation. He should be questioned and examined for the presence of nose bleeding (epistaxis), increased tendency to bruise (ecchymosis), bright red blood in the stool (hematochezia), black or tarry stool (melena), or coughing up of blood (hemoptysis). Blood pressure and pulse, both sitting and standing, should be obtained to determine whether orthostasis representing blood loss is present. A thorough evaluation of the urinary tract may reveal the presence of a previously unknown abnormality that will explain the bleeding episode.

12. What other side effects from heparin should be considered in D.P.?

Osteoporosis. Development of osteoporosis has been associated with administration of more than 20,000 U/day of heparin for six months or longer. Various mechanisms have been suggested, but the underlying pathophysiology of this rare adverse effect remains unclear.[58] Affected patients may present with bone pain and/or radiographic findings suggestive of fractures. The possibility of the development of osteoporosis should be considered in patients undergoing long-term, high-dose heparin therapy.

Hyperkalemia, although rare, has been attributed to heparin-induced inhibition of aldosterone synthesis. Hypoaldosteronism leading to hyperkalemia has been described with both high-dose and low-dose heparin therapy, may occur as quickly as within seven days after initiation of heparin therapy, and appears to be reversible following discontinuation of heparin.[59] Patients with diabetes or renal failure may be at greatest risk.

Hypersensitivity Reactions. Other rarely occurring adverse effects associated with heparin include generalized hypersensitivity reactions, such as urticaria, rash, rhinitis, conjunctivitis, asthma, and angioedema as well as a reversible temporal alopecia.[8]

13. Adjusted Dose Subcutaneous (SQ) Administration. By day four of heparinization, IV access for D.P. has become difficult. What other route of administration could be considered?

An alternative to the continuous infusion of heparin is subcutaneous administration with adjustment of dosing to maintain a therapeutic aPTT.[60–63] Typically, subcutaneous heparin is administered at 12-hour intervals and aPTT is monitored at the mid-dosing interval (i.e., six hours after a dose). A meta-analysis of trials comparing these two methods of administration has shown that adjusted dose subcutaneous heparinization is efficacious in the initial treatment of DVT and at least as safe, with respect to hemorrhagic complications, as the continuous infusion of heparin.[63]

For D.P., whose current heparin dosage is 1700 U/hour, the initial SQ heparin dose would be 20,500 U (1700 U/hour $\times$ 12 hours rounded to the nearest 500 U). Since a 20,000 U/mL preparation should be selected to prepare the dose in order to minimize the administration volume, it may be possible to simplify the dose to 20,000 U. D.P.'s aPTT should be checked six hours after the first dose with adjustment of dosing as necessary. Due to the reduced bioavailability of subcutaneous heparin in comparison to intravenous administration, increased dosing may be required.[62] A weight-based dosing nomogram, specific for a partial thromboplastin reagent with a therapeutic aPTT range of 60 to 100 seconds, is described in Table 12.6.

14. Overdose. On the fourth day of heparin therapy, V.R., a 64-year-old female with DVT, inadvertently received 25,000 U of heparin during a one-hour period due to an infusion pump malfunction. The infusion was stopped and within one-half hour, she became diaphoretic and hypotensive. Bright red blood was evident upon rectal examination and a large retroperitoneal mass was noted. How should the excessive heparin effect be reversed?

V.R. has definite signs of hemorrhage from the GI tract, a site associated with considerable mortality. Heparin should be discontinued immediately and treatment should include maintenance of fluid volume and replacement of clotting factors with whole blood,

Table 12.6	Heparin Protocol for Adjusted Dose Subcutaneous Administration[a,b]

Initial Dosage

A. Initial therapy with adjusted dose SQ heparin
  1) Give SQ heparin 240 U/kg × 1 STAT
  2) Check first aPTT 6 hr after first dose
  3) Adjust dosing per chart below

B. Conversion from continuous infusion heparin to adjusted dose SQ heparin
  1) Calculate total 24 hr heparin requirement necessary to maintain therapeutic aPTT
  2) Divide 24 hr heparin requirement by 2 to determine initial Q 12 hr SQ dosing requirement
  3) Discontinue IV heparin and administer initial Q 12 hr SQ dose within 1 hr
  4) Check first aPTT 6 hr after first dose
  5) Adjust dosing per chart below

C. Conversion from warfarin to adjusted dose SQ heparin
  1) Discontinue warfarin
  2) Give 240 U/kg SQ heparin within 24 hr
  3) Check first aPTT 6 hr after first dose
  4) Adjust dosing per chart below

Dosing Adjustments

aPTT[c] (sec)	Dosing Adjustment[d]	Next aPTT
<40	↑ by 48 U/kg Q 12 hr	6 hr after dose
40–60	↑ by 24 U/kg Q 12 hr	6 hr after dose
60–100	No change	Q AM
100–120	↓ by 12 U/kg Q 12 hr	6 hr after dose
120–140	↓ by 24 U/kg Q 12 hr	6 hr after dose
>140	↓ by 36 U/kg Q 12 hr	6 hr after dose

[a] University of Washington Medical Center.
[b] aPTT = Activated partial thromboplastin time; IV = Intravenous; SQ = subcutaneous.
[c] Based upon aPTT reagent-specific therapeutic range of 60–100 sec corresponding to *in vitro* heparin concentrations of 0.2–0.4 U/mL.
[d] Rounded to nearest 500 U.

fresh frozen plasma, or clotting factor concentrates. If hemorrhage had not been present and the only manifestation of overdose had been a prolonged aPTT, administration of heparin simply could have been discontinued permitting the effects to clear within a few hours.

Protamine has been utilized to neutralize heparin by forming an inactive protamine-heparin complex.[64] Protamine has a rapid onset of action with effects lasting for about two hours. Protamine sulfate is infused as a 1% solution in a dosage of 1 mg/100 U of heparin administered if it is given within 30 minutes of heparin administration. If protamine therapy is delayed, dosing should be based upon the estimated amount of heparin remaining, taking into consideration the elimination half-life of heparin. Response to protamine therapy can be assessed by a return of the aPTT to baseline. Adverse effects associated with protamine include systemic hypotension secondary to rapid administration; anaphylaxis characterized by edema, bronchospasm, and cardiovascular collapse; and catastrophic pulmonary vasoconstriction.[65,66]

Prevention

15. L.R., a 63-year-old obese female, is to undergo elective abdominal surgery for treatment of diverticulitis. She has a past medical history significant for mild hypertension presently controlled (BP 135/85 mm Hg), and peripheral vascular disease. What therapeutic interventions might decrease the risk of DVT or PE in L.R.?

Surgical procedures, particularly those involving the pelvis or lower extremities, represent a significant risk factor for DVT formation. Therapeutic interventions to prevent deep venous thrombosis, and thereby reduce the risk of fatal pulmonary embolism, are indicated in those settings in which vascular trauma, injury, and/or stasis may occur.

Nonpharmacologic Measures

Mechanical interventions aimed at preventing venous stasis and increasing venous return include the use of elastic compression stockings as well as leg elevation, leg exercises, and early postoperative ambulation.[67] Intermittent pneumatic compression of the leg muscles, using inflatable cuffs applied to the calf and thigh, represents another alternative for the prevention of DVT.[68]

Pharmacologic Measures

Fixed, low-dose heparin, administered as 5000 U SQ every 12 hours, is an effective pharmacologic approach to DVT prevention in the setting of venous stasis or following surgical procedures. Because low dose heparin inactivates factor X_a without a direct effect on factor II_a, the aPTT is not prolonged and, therefore, aPTT monitoring is unnecessary. Bleeding complications are minimized using this dosing regimen.

Low dose heparin is not effective in the prevention of deep venous thrombosis in elective hip replacement or hip fracture surgery.[69] These settings require adjusted-dose subcutaneous heparin therapy. Enoxaparin, a low molecular weight heparin product, has been approved for DVT prevention in hip surgery patients.[70] A summary of current recommendations for prevention of venous thromboembolism is presented in Table 12.7.[67]

L.R. is at particular risk for DVT and PE, not only because of surgery, but also because of her age, obesity, and probable postoperative immobilization. Subcutaneous heparin at 5000 U every 12 hours should be prescribed for her. The first dose should be administered several hours preoperatively, and dosing should continue postoperatively until she is fully ambulatory.

Table 12.7	Prevention of Venous Thromboembolism
Clinical Setting	Prophylaxis
General Surgery	
Low risk patients (age <40 yr; no risk factors)	Early ambulation
Moderate risk patients (age >40 yr; no risk factors)	Elastic stockings *or* Low dose heparin *or* Intermittent pneumatic compression
High risk patients (age >40 yr; other risk factors)	Low dose heparin *or* Intermittent pneumatic compression *or* Low intensity warfarin
Very high risk patients (multiple risk factors)	Low dose heparin *and* intermittent pneumatic compression *or* Low intensity warfarin
Total Hip Replacement/Hip Fracture Surgery	Adjusted dose subcutaneous heparin *or* Enoxaparin *or* Low intensity warfarin
Knee Surgery	Intermittent pneumatic compression
Intracranial Neurosurgery	Intermittent pneumatic compression
Multiple Trauma	Intermittent pneumatic compression *or* Low intensity warfarin
Prolonged Bedrest/Immobility	Elastic stockings *or* Low dose heparin *or* Intermittent pneumatic compression *or* Low intensity warfarin

Pulmonary Embolism (PE)

Clinical Presentation

16. M.S. is a 38-year-old, 90 kg male with a five-year history of ulcerative colitis. Several days ago, he developed a swollen left calf which was painful and warm. This swelling gradually increased, affecting the entire left leg to the groin, and prompting him to seek medical attention. In the emergency room (ER), he also notes the recent onset of right-sided pleuritic chest pain without SOB or hemoptysis.

His past medical history includes a gastric ulcer four years ago, treated medically without recurrence. Physical examination reveals a pleasant, obese male with an enlarged left leg and mild to moderate tenderness in the entire leg. Chest examination reveals a loud, pulmonary heart sound (P_2). Vital signs include: BP 150/85 mm Hg; pulse 100 beats/min; and respiratory rate 28 breaths/min and regular.

Laboratory data include: Hct 26.7% (Normal: 45%–52%); erythrocyte sedimentation rate 91 mm/hr (Normal: 1–13); and arterial blood gases (on room air) as follows: pO_2 72 mm Hg (Normal: 75–100), pCO_2 35 mm Hg (Normal: 35–45), pH 7.48 (Normal: 7.35–7.45). Chest x-ray and lung scan (VQ scan) are highly suggestive of PE. An angiogram was not performed. Electrocardiogram (ECG) shows sinus tachycardia. Venogram is positive for the presence of defects in the ileo-femoral artery. Coagulation tests include: PT 11.2 sec (INR 1.0); aPTT 28 sec; and a platelet count 248,000/mm³ (Normal: 150,000–350,000).

What subjective and objective evidence in M.S. is compatible with PE? [SI Units: Hct 0.267 1 (Normal 0.45–0.52; platelets 248 × 10⁹/L (Normal: 150–300)]

Signs and Symptoms

The clinical diagnosis of PE often is difficult to make because of the nonspecificity of symptoms. Experience from the Urokinase Pulmonary Embolism Trial and the Prospective Investigation of Pulmonary Embolism Diagnosis (PIOPED) study provides some helpful guidelines in utilizing the patient history and physical examination to establish the presence of acute PE in patients without pre-existing cardiac or pulmonary disease.[70,71] The most frequently observed subjective symptoms are dyspnea, pleuritic chest pain, apprehension (anxiety or a feeling of impending doom), and cough. Hemoptysis occurs infrequently. The objective signs most frequently observed are tachypnea at a rate of 20/minute or more, tachycardia of 100 beats/minute or more, accentuated pulmonary component of the second heart sound (i.e., P_2), and rales. Deep venous thrombosis precedes PE in 80% or more of patients. A combination of these signs and symptoms provides further evidence for acute pulmonary embolism. M.S. has presented with pleuritic chest pain, tachycardia, tachypnea, loud P_2, and a decrease in pO_2 and, therefore, may have developed PE.

Diagnosis

Because the clinical signs and symptoms of pulmonary embolism are difficult to distinguish from a number of other medical conditions, further evaluation may be necessary. Chest x-ray, ECG, and arterial blood gas (alveolar-arterial oxygen gradient; A-a gradient) abnormalities often are present in patients with PE but, again, are somewhat nonspecific. Lung scans and pulmonary angiograms are useful laboratory procedures in documenting the presence of pulmonary embolism. Lung scans, which incorporate an assessment of perfusion, or regional distribution of pulmonary blood flow, and ventilation are referred to as ventilation/perfusion (V/Q) scans and involve both the injection and the inhalation of radiolabelled compounds. Test results are expressed as high, intermediate, or low probability of the presence of PE. When ventilation (air movement) is normal over an area that shows abnormal perfusion (blood flow), a ventilation-perfusion mismatch exists and PE is highly probable.[72] If a matched defect is noted (i.e., abnormal ventilation over an area of abnormal perfusion), then another disease state, such as chronic obstructive airways disease, is more likely.

A positive lung scan (M.S. had one highly suggestive of pulmonary embolism) and a positive pulmonary angiogram would confirm the presence of a PE. When a diagnosis of pulmonary embolism or deep venous thrombosis of the thigh or ileo-femoral region is suspected, heparin should be initiated since it does not interfere with the measures used in diagnosis, and it helps to ensure more rapid anticoagulation if the diagnosis is confirmed.

Treatment

Heparin Initiation and Dosing

17. Heparin therapy is initiated in M.S. with a loading dose of 7200 U (80 U/kg × 90 kg) followed by continuous infusion of 1600 U/hr (18 U/kg/hr × 90 kg). The aPTT after six hours was 40 sec. The dose has subsequently been titrated upward to 2200 U/hr (25 U/kg/hr) in order to achieve an aPTT of 70 sec. What factors may influence heparin requirements in patients such as M.S.?

The presence of active thrombosis or embolism in patients often is cited as a cause of "heparin resistance."[9] Heparin requirements are higher in patients with active thromboembolism than in patients without thromboembolic disease.[10] However, whether patients with pulmonary embolism have higher dosage requirements than patients with DVT is questionable. Evidence exists to support[73–75] as well as refute[36,76,77] this.

Deficiencies of AT III also are suggested as a cause of increased heparin requirements. However, one must differentiate between the predictable decline in AT III concentrations that occurs during heparin therapy and that found in pathologic deficiencies.[78] Even in congenital AT III deficiencies, only patients with AT III activity of less than 30% exhibit significantly increased heparin dosing requirements.[79] Heparin resistance explained on the basis of AT III deficiency requires comparison to AT III at a time when the patient had no evidence of thromboembolic disease and was not on heparin. In clinical practice, such foresight simply is not a reasonable expectation because of the rarity of AT III deficiency.[80]

Warfarin

18. Transition from Heparin Therapy. When should warfarin be administered, and how should the transition be accomplished?

Heparin therapy should be continued for four to five days in the setting of pulmonary embolism and until warfarin therapy has been therapeutic for two days. As previously discussed, warfarin should be started on the first day of hospitalization and continued for three months. However, a delay in the initiation of warfarin may be acceptable in the setting of an anticipated extended hospitalization, recent or anticipated surgery or other invasive procedures, or a medical condition with the potential for uncontrolled bleeding.[81]

There are several reasons to overlap heparin and warfarin therapy. The onset of warfarin activity is dependent not only upon its inherent pharmacokinetic characteristics ($t\frac{1}{2}$ = 36 hours), but also upon the rate of elimination of circulating clotting factors. Although warfarin inhibits production of the vitamin K-dependent clotting factors, it has no influence on the rate of elimination of these clotting factors. The elimination half-lives of the four vitamin K-dependent clotting factors are approximately five hours for factor VII, 24 hours for factor IX, 40 hours for factor X, and 60 hours for factor II. Since approximately four half-lives are required for these factors to reach a new steady state after their production is inhibited, the effect of warfarin can be delayed for several days. Initial increases in prothrombin time reflect only reductions in factor VII activity, but full anticoagulation with warfarin requires adequate suppression of factors with longer elimination half-lives. By overlapping heparin with warfarin therapy, adequate anticoagulation can be continued with heparin until warfarin therapy reaches a therapeutic intensity.

In addition to suppressing the synthesis of the vitamin K-dependent clotting factors, warfarin also inhibits the formation of the naturally occurring anticoagulant protein C and its cofactor, protein S. In patients with congenital protein C or protein S deficiency, initial warfarin therapy can suppress these proteins to concentrations that may result in an unpredicted hypercoagulability and thrombus extension.[82] To avoid these complications, heparin and warfarin therapy should overlap.

Heparin therapy has been observed to prolong the PT[83] and warfarin can prolong the aPTT by several seconds.[84] Thus, interference with laboratory tests should be considered in the evaluation of intensity of anticoagulation during overlapped heparin and warfarin therapy.

19. Initiation Therapy. In an effort to discharge M.S. from the hospital as soon as possible, an initial dose of warfarin 10 mg PO Q PM for three days has been ordered. Is such a "loading dose" reasonable? What would be a more appropriate approach to initiating therapy?

The goals of initial therapy with warfarin are to reach the therapeutic PT range (expressed as INR) safely and efficiently and to predict initial maintenance dosing requirements for warfarin. A number of methods to predict maintenance dose have been described, with most relying on initiation of therapy with three 10 mg doses. A maintenance dose is then determined based upon PT response on the fourth day using linear regression models, analog computer methodology, or Baysian forecasting.[85–87] While these techniques have been moderately successful, they are based upon reaching a prothrombin time ratio of 1.5 to 2.5 rather than on reaching a therapeutic INR range and, therefore, do not account for variability in PT results due to reagent differences. Many rely on pharmacokinetic parameters derived from the population at large rather than from the individual being treated. Additionally, these techniques do not consider the *rate* of increase in the PT over the initial period of dosing. Nonindividualized dosing of the drug can lead to excessive anticoagulation with an increased risk of bleeding, especially in patients who are particularly sensitive to warfarin, including the elderly and patients with vitamin K deficiency, congestive heart failure, or hepatic dysfunction.

A flexible initiation protocol has been developed to overcome these difficulties and is presented in Table 12.8.[88] This protocol is aimed at reaching a goal INR of 2.0 to 3.0 and tapers doses based upon daily PT response expressed as INR. The dose selected on day four is the predicted maintenance dose, which then is prescribed for the first several days of maintenance therapy before prothrombin time is checked again on an outpatient basis. Flexible initiation of warfarin therapy allows for individualized dosing based upon PT response to single doses of warfarin and has been used successfully in patients with risk factors for excessive response to warfarin therapy.[88–90]

Alternatively, warfarin therapy can be initiated at average doses and adjusted as necessary. However, this empiric approach to dosing is not used to predict maintenance doses and may delay therapeutic anticoagulation as well as discharge from the hospital. The average dose to reach an INR of 2.0 to 3.0 is 4 to 5 mg in the general population. Lower doses are necessary in patients expected to be particularly sensitive to the effects of warfarin, and higher doses are required in patients with relative or acquired resistance to war-

Table 12.8	Flexible Initiation Dosing Protocol for Warfarin Therapy[88]	
Day	**a.m. PT INR**	**p.m. Warfarin Dose (mg)**
1 (baseline)	<1.4	10.0
2	<1.8	10.0
	1.8	1.0
	>1.8	0.5
3	<2.0	10.0
	2.0–2.1	5.0
	2.2–2.3	4.5
	2.4–2.5	4.0
	2.6–2.7	3.5
	2.8–2.9	3.0
	3.0–3.1	2.5
	3.2–3.3	2.0
	3.4	1.5
	3.5	1.0
	3.6–4.0	0.5
	>4.0	None
		Maintenance Dose
4	<1.4	>8.0
	1.4	8.0
	1.5	7.5
	1.6–1.7	7.0
	1.8	6.5
	1.9	6.0
	2.0–2.1	5.5
	2.2–2.3	5.0
	2.4–2.6	4.5
	2.7–3.0	4.0
	3.1–3.5	3.5
	3.6–4.0	3.0
	4.1–4.5	Omit 1 dose, then 2.0
	>4.5	Omit 2 doses, then 1.0

farin. A rare, hereditary warfarin resistance also has been described in patients requiring extremely high doses (>50 mg/day).[185]

The baseline PT obtained for M.S. on admission was 11.2 seconds, equivalent to an INR of 1.0 for the reagent being used in the laboratory where this testing occurred. Using the flexible initiation protocol presented in Table 12.8, the first dose of warfarin for M.S. should be 10 mg administered in the evening on the first day of hospitalization. Subsequent PT values obtained daily will guide dosing requirements until a therapeutic INR is reached. The order for warfarin 10 mg orally every evening for three doses should be discontinued and replaced with daily orders for warfarin and prothrombin time monitoring.

20. How high should M.S.'s PT be maintained and how long should anticoagulation be administered?

Intensity of Therapy. In patients with deep venous thrombosis or pulmonary embolism, warfarin therapy should be aimed at prolonging the PT to an INR of 2.0 to 3.0, defined as low intensity therapy.[91] This therapeutic range is recommended to maximize the antithrombotic effect of warfarin while minimizing potential bleeding complications associated with excessive anticoagulation. In patients who have developed recurrent thromboembolism despite

therapeutic anticoagulation with warfarin, high intensity therapy aimed at prolonging the PT to an INR of 2.5 to 3.5 is indicated.

Duration of Therapy. Clots, once formed, adhere to the vessel wall. Thus, the first step in resolution of a thrombus involves covering the clot with a layer of endothelial cells to prevent additional platelet aggregation at the site of vessel injury. This endothelialization process generally takes seven to ten days to be completed. Initial anticoagulant treatment is used to prevent clot extension while allowing adequate endothelialization to occur. Continued anticoagulation is directed at the prevention of further clotting.

Patients with DVT and PE should be anticoagulated with warfarin for three months.[91] A multicenter comparison of four weeks versus three months of oral anticoagulation following deep venous thrombosisor PE confirmed the appropriateness of this duration of therapy.[92] In this trial, the incidences of both treatment failure, defined as persistent signs and symptoms or new thromboembolic events during treatment, and thromboembolic recurrence during one year of follow-up were significantly lower in patients treated for three months than in patients treated for four weeks. In patients with recurrent thromboembolism or persistent risk factors, including antithrombin III deficiency, protein C or protein S deficiency, or malignancy, warfarin treatment should be continued chronically.

21. Adverse Effects. What possible adverse effects from warfarin therapy should be considered in M.S. and how should they be monitored?

Hemorrhage. Bleeding is the most common adverse effect associated with warfarin. A summary of experimental and observational inception cohort studies determined that the average annual frequency of fatal, major, and all (major or minor) bleeding in patients treated with warfarin is 0.6%, 3%, and 9.6%, respectively.[48] However, wide variation in bleeding frequencies has been reported, probably due to differences in patient characteristics, treatment protocols, and the definition and assessment of bleeding among trials.

Warfarin-associated bleeding most commonly occurs in the nose and oral pharynx and the soft tissues, followed by the GI and urinary tracts. Hemarthrosis (bleeding into joint spaces), as well as retroperitoneal and intraocular bleeding represent less common hemorrhagic complications of warfarin therapy.[48,49] Although infrequent in occurrence, intracranial bleeding resulting in hemorrhagic stroke represents the most frequent cause of fatal bleeding associated with warfarin therapy. As with heparin, GI and urinary tract bleeding associated with warfarin often is caused by previously undiagnosed lesions.[50,51]

A number of factors influence the risk of hemorrhagic complications associated with warfarin. The frequency of bleeding is higher in the first month of therapy than during subsequent months.[93] Unlike heparin, intensity of anticoagulation with warfarin directly influences risk of bleeding. In an analysis of trials comparing low intensity warfarin therapy to high intensity therapy, bleeding was approximately three times more common in patients treated with warfarin at high intensity.[48] Other patient-specific variables that influence the risk of warfarin-associated bleeding include a history of GI bleeding, serious comorbid disease including hypertension, and concomitant therapy with aspirin or nonsteroidal anti-inflammatory drugs (NSAIDs).[48,49,94]

The influence of age on bleeding risk is somewhat controversial. Elderly patients are known to require lower doses of warfarin than younger patients in order to reach a therapeutic intensity of anticoagulation.[95] This increased sensitivity to the effect of warfarin is not the result of differences in pharmacokinetic characteristics of warfarin between elderly and young patients, including protein binding and metabolism,[96,97] nor is it related to gender, weight, underlying medical conditions, or the presence of interacting drugs.[98] Inherent vitamin K deficiency or age-related differences in stereo-isomeric disposition of warfarin may explain why elderly patients are more sensitive to the effects of warfarin and, therefore, require lower doses than younger patients. Nonetheless, increased sensitivity to warfarin does not imply increased bleeding risk if elderly patients are managed appropriately.

Several epidemiologic surveys have reported age as an independent risk factor for bleeding.[93,99] However, these surveys failed to account for other factors known to increase bleeding risk and they did not control for follow-up and management of warfarin therapy, activities which may play a significant role in reducing the risk of bleeding in patients with increased sensitivity to the effects of warfarin. In two studies in which factors known to independently increase warfarin-associated bleeding risk were controlled and in which adequate monitoring and follow-up for elderly patients were provided, age was not associated with an increased risk of hemorrhagic effects associated with warfarin.[100,101]

Bleeding complications in M.S. can be minimized by careful attention to the signs and symptoms of bleeding by the patient and his caregivers, maintenance of PT expressed as INR within the therapeutic range, avoidance of therapy with concomitant drugs known to increase the risk of bleeding or to increase prothrombin time, and routine outpatient follow-up for PT monitoring and clinical assessment.

Purple Toe Syndrome. This rarely reported adverse effect typically occurs three to eight weeks after initiation of warfarin therapy and is unrelated to intensity of anticoagulation.[106] Patients initially present with painful discoloration of the toes that blanches with pressure and fades with elevation. The pathophysiology of this syndrome has been related to cholesterol microembolization from atherosclerotic plaques leading to arterial obstruction.[107] Because cholesterol microembolization has been associated with renal failure and death, warfarin therapy should be discontinued in patients who develop Purple Toe syndrome.

22. Skin Necrosis. S.G., a 34-year-old female with no significant medical history, presents to the ER with an extremely painful, erythematous lesion on her right thigh. The lesion appeared two days ago progressing in size and tenderness, and now includes a purple-black discoloration at the center. All laboratory values are within the normal range with the exception of PT, which is elevated to an INR of 4.8 and a significant reduction in protein C activity to 20% (Normal: 65%–150%). Careful questioning reveals that several days before admission, S.G. experienced pain in her right calf following a period of prolonged immobility. At that time, she began to self-administer warfarin 5 mg tablets QD that had previously been prescribed for her brother for a similar incident. According to S.G., her brother developed a blood clot in his leg and was diagnosed as a "clotter." A duplex ultrasound is positive for DVT and the additional diagnosis of warfarin-induced skin necrosis is made. What is the pathophysiology of this process?

Warfarin-induced skin necrosis is a rare, but serious adverse effect of oral anticoagulation, occurring in approximately 0.01% to 0.1% of patients treated with warfarin.[102] Patients present within three to six days of initiation of warfarin therapy with painful discoloration of the breast, buttocks, thigh, or penis. The lesions progress to frank necrosis with blackening and the presence of eschar. Skin necrosis appears to be the result of extensive microvascular thrombosis within subcutaneous fat and has been associated with hypercoagulable conditions, including protein C or protein S deficiency.[103] In these patients, rapid depletion of protein C before depletion of vitamin K-dependent clotting factors during early warfarin therapy can result in an imbalance between procoagulant and

anticoagulant activity, leading to initial hypercoagulability and thrombosis. Adequate heparinization during initiation of warfarin can prevent development of early hypercoagulability.

23. How should S.G. be managed? Is further anticoagulation with warfarin contraindicated?

Warfarin therapy should be discontinued in patients who develop skin necrosis. However, subsequent warfarin therapy is not necessarily contraindicated if it is required for treatment and/or prevention of thromboembolic disease.[103] In patients with protein C or protein S deficiency and a history of skin necrosis, warfarin therapy may be restarted at low doses as long as therapeutic heparinization has been achieved and are maintained until the PT has been within the therapeutic range for 72 hours.[104,105] Supplementation of protein C through administration of fresh frozen plasma also may be indicated.[105]

24. Patient Education. What information should be conveyed to M.S. (the patient described in Questions 16–21) by his pharmacist to assure the safety and efficacy of warfarin therapy following his discharge from the hospital?

The anticoagulant effect of warfarin is influenced by a variety of factors. Fluctuations in the intensity of the anticoagulant effect of warfarin can increase the risk of both hemorrhagic complications and recurrent thromboembolism.[108,109] Pharmacists can play a significant role in improving compliance as well as in assuring the safety and efficacy of warfarin therapy by providing appropriate education to patients treated with this agent.

Several key elements which form the basis of a thorough patient education program for warfarin therapy are listed in Table 12.9. This information may be conveyed by the provision of written teaching materials, videotaped instruction, individual or group discussion, or a combination of several of these approaches. A number of useful educational tools are available through DuPont Pharmaceuticals, the manufacturer of Coumadin.

Before he is discharged from the hospital, M.S. should participate in a warfarin education program, and convenient and timely outpatient follow-up should be arranged for him. A wallet card, medical bracelet, or alternative method of identifying him as a patient treated with warfarin should be provided. The health care provider who assumes responsibility for his outpatient warfarin therapy will need to provide continuing reinforcement of the essential elements of medication information at each follow up visit.

Table 12.9	Key Elements of Warfarin Patient Education

Identification of generic and brand names

The purpose of therapy

The expected duration of therapy

Dosing and administration

Visual recognition of drug and tablet strength

What to do in case a dose is missed

The importance of prothrombin time monitoring

Recognition of signs and symptoms of bleeding

Recognition of signs and symptoms of thromboembolism

What to do in case bleeding or thromboembolism occurs

The potential for interactions with prescription and over-the-counter medications

Dietary considerations

The significance of informing other health care providers that warfarin has been prescribed

When, where, and with whom follow-up will be provided

25. Dietary Considerations. **M.S. has read that patients taking warfarin must restrict their dietary intake of foods containing vitamin K. He is concerned that he will not be able to continue his vegetarian diet. How can his pharmacist assist him in developing a rational approach to dietary considerations during warfarin therapy?**

The two primary sources of vitamin K in humans are the biosynthesis of vitamin K_2 (menaquinone) by intestinal bacteria and dietary intake of vitamin K_1 (phytonadione). The recommended daily allowance (U.S. RDA) for vitamin K is approximately 1 gm/kg and the typical Western diet provides approximately 300 to 500 µg/day.[110] Vitamin K is found in high concentrations in certain foods, including beef and pork liver, broccoli, Brussels sprouts, cauliflower, chick peas, kale, spinach, and turnip greens, as well as in certain nutritional supplements and multiple vitamin products.[111]

Diets high in vitamin K content have been associated with acquired warfarin resistance defined as excessive warfarin dosing requirements to reach a therapeutic PT range.[112] A number of cases have been reported in which patients previously stabilized on warfarin experienced elevations in PT with or without hemorrhagic complications when dietary vitamin K sources were eliminated. Conversely, reductions in prothrombin time with or without thromboembolic complications have been reported in patients in whom dietary vitamin K sources have been added.[113]

These cases illustrate the potential clinical significance of dietary changes in patients taking warfarin. To minimize these potential effects, M.S. should be counseled to maintain a *consistent* intake of dietary vitamin K. Warfarin dosing should be based upon his typical diet. However, restriction of dietary vitamin K intake is unnecessary except in cases of significant resistance to warfarin's anticoagulant effect.[114] M.S. should be aware of the types of foods that contain large quantities of vitamin K and should be counseled to maintain a consistent diet, to avoid bingeing on foods high in vitamin K content, and to report significant dietary changes to his health care provider. Appropriate assessment and follow-up is essential in order to prevent hemorrhagic or thromboembolic complications that may result from changes in PT due to dietary alterations.

26. Alcohol Ingestion. **What counseling regarding alcohol intake should be provided for M.S.?**

Chronic alcohol ingestion has been associated with induction of the hepatic enzyme systems that metabolize warfarin. Therefore, warfarin dosing requirements are sometimes higher in alcoholic patients. Conversely, acute ingestion of large amounts of alcohol can inhibit warfarin metabolism, leading to elevations in PT and an increased risk of bleeding complications.[115] In general, however, moderate intake of alcoholic beverages is not associated with alterations in the metabolism or the therapeutic effect of warfarin as measured by the prothrombin time. In published reports, daily ingestion of 80 gm of ethanol, 592 mL of table wine, or 296 mL of fortified wine had no effect on hypoprothrombinemic response to oral anticoagulation.[116–118] M.S. does not need to abstain from drinking alcoholic beverages in moderation, but he should be counseled to avoid the sporadic ingestion of large amounts of alcohol.

27. Maintenance Therapy. **M.S.'s heparin therapy was continued for a total of five days and discontinued after his PT had been within the therapeutic INR range of 2.0–3.0 for two days. His maintenance warfarin dose was predicted based upon his response to initial therapy using a flexible initiation protocol. He was discharged from the hospital taking warfarin 5 mg PO QD and scheduled for follow-up within one week in the Anticoagulation Clinic. The following is a summary of his inpatient anticoagulation therapy:**

Date	INR	Warfarin Dose (mg)	Heparin Dose (U/hr)
10/21	1.0	10	1600
10/22	1.3	10	2200
10/23	1.6	7	2100
10/24	2.3	5	1800
10/25	2.8	5	1600
10/26	2.6	5	• Stop heparin • Discharge patient • Rx: warfarin 5 mg PO QD

A week later, M.S. is seen in the ambulatory Anticoagulation Clinic. His INR is 1.7. How should he be managed?

Outpatient management of warfarin therapy involves routine patient assessment, laboratory test interpretation, and, if necessary, warfarin dosing adjustments. Many pharmacist-managed anticoagulation clinics have developed guidelines for the appropriate management and follow-up of patients treated with warfarin and have served as models for the provision of pharmaceutical care services in the ambulatory setting.[119,120]

Factors Influencing Dosing. At each clinic visit, regardless of the PT result, patients should be evaluated for signs and symptoms of thromboembolism and hemorrhagic complications, the addition or discontinuation of any prescription or nonprescription medications (see Questions 37 to 39), and changes in diet or alcohol intake. Compliance to current warfarin dose should be verified, including tablet strength and color; missed doses should be reported. An assessment of the reliability of the laboratory result should be made and the test should be repeated if necessary.

Patients also should be questioned regarding the presence or exacerbation of various medical conditions that can influence anticoagulation status. Diarrhea-associated alterations in intestinal flora can reduce vitamin K absorption resulting in elevations in PT. Increased hypoprothrombinemic response also can occur as a result of enhanced catabolism of clotting factors due to febrile illness.[121] Congestive heart failure, hepatic congestion, and liver disease can influence warfarin metabolism leading to significant elevations in prothrombin time.

Thyroid function also can influence warfarin therapy.[121,122] Hypothyroidism decreases the catabolism of certain clotting factors, increasing their availability and producing a relative refractoriness to warfarin therapy, resulting in the need for increased dosing to reach a therapeutic PT. The addition of thyroid supplementation can cause significant reductions in warfarin dosing requirements. Conversely, hyperthyroidism increases the catabolism of clotting factors, but there is no evidence of altered warfarin metabolism associated with fluctuation in thyroid status. Thus, frequent monitoring and adjustment of warfarin therapy is necessary in patients with changing thyroid function.

Dosing Adjustments. If overanticoagulation or underanticoagulation is verified, an adjustment in warfarin dosing may be necessary. Figures 12.5 and 12.6 describe approaches to warfarin dosing adjustments for both low intensity and high intensity therapy. To improve compliance, every effort should be made to have patients take the same daily dose rather than alternating doses. Coumadin is available in a wide range of tablet strengths, allowing clinicians to make precise dosing adjustments and allowing patients to take the same dose each day.

Fig 12.5 Warfarin Maintenance Dosing Protocol for Goal INR 2.0–3.0

Frequency of Follow-Up. After a thorough assessment, it is determined that M.S. has been compliant with his prescribed dosage schedule and there is no other apparent explanation to account for the reduction in INR for M.S. Therefore, an increase in his dose to 6 mg/day is required. It will take several days for his warfarin therapy to reach a new steady state due to the long elimination of half-lives of both warfarin and the vitamin K–dependent clotting factors. His PT should be rechecked in approximately one week since a dosing adjustment has been made and, if therapeutic at that time, should be checked again in two weeks. Once a stable dose has been reached, patient assessment and PT monitoring should occur every four to six weeks. However, if M.S. should display any signs of medical instability or noncompliance, a follow-up schedule of every two to four weeks is indicated.

28. Overdose. M.J., who has been taking warfarin for 6 months with good laboratory control, noted a slight pink color to his urine. In the ER, an INR of 5.6 was reported. His Hct and Hgb were both within normal limits, as were his vital signs. A stool guaiac was negative. However, UA revealed more than 50 red blood cells per high powered field. How should this adverse effect of warfarin be treated in M.J.?

Management of overanticoagulation is dependent upon the clinical presentation of the patient. In the case of an elevated PT without bleeding complications, interruption of warfarin therapy by holding one or two doses until the prothrombin time returns to the therapeutic range usually is a sufficient intervention. Minor bleeding complications accompanied by an elevated PT also can be managed by withholding warfarin therapy for a short period of time until bleeding resolves. In either case, the patient should be questioned to determine a possible cause for overanticoagulation, including taking extra doses of warfarin, changes in diet, changes in status of underlying medical conditions, or the use of other medications. In some cases, no apparent explanation can be identified. Regardless of the cause, a reduction in maintenance dosing of warfarin may be necessary.

Alternatively, small doses of vitamin K (phytonadione) can be used to return the PT to the therapeutic range whether or not minor bleeding is present. Intravenous doses of 0.5 to 1 mg vitamin K have been used successfully. Use of these low doses reverses excessive anticoagulation within 24 hours without causing prolonged resistance to warfarin therapy, a problem that is seen frequently with larger (10 mg) doses of vitamin K.[123,124] Although alternative administration routes have not been studied, subcutaneous (1 mg) or oral (2.5 mg) dosing also may be effective, but intramuscular administration of vitamin K should be avoided due to the risk of

hematoma formation. Intravenous vitamin K should be diluted and administered by slow infusion to prevent flushing, hypotension, and cardiovascular collapse.[125] Although these symptoms resemble anaphylaxis, the mechanism of this adverse response is unclear and it is not known if it is due to phytonadione or to the vehicle in which phytonadione is formulated. If this adverse reaction should occur, administration of epinephrine may be indicated, as well as other standard measures to support blood pressure and maintain the airway.

Rapid reversal of warfarin therapy is indicated in the setting of major, life-threatening bleeding. Fresh frozen plasma or factor concentrates to replace clotting factors will decrease the PT for four to six hours and should be administered as needed with careful monitoring of volume status. Supplementation with high dose vitamin K (10 mg) also may be indicated. Oral, subcutaneous, or intravenous administration will reverse the effects of warfarin within 6 to 12 hours. However, if continued warfarin therapy is indicated, anticoagulation with heparin may be necessary for as long as 7 to 14 days until the effect of high dose vitamin K is diminished and warfarin responsiveness returns.

Hematuria may be an early sign of more serious bleeding, but in most cases, this condition is associated with minor bleeding episodes. In a reliable patient, discontinuing warfarin until the PT returns to a therapeutic level usually suffices. A more rapid return to normal can be accomplished if low dose vitamin K is administered. Since M.J. appears to be bleeding only into the urine, and is hemodynamically stable, withholding warfarin until the PT returns to the therapeutic range would be the proper treatment. He should be counseled regarding the importance of accurate compliance to therapy.

29. Effect on Menstruation. N.S., a 26-year-old female, is taking warfarin. What instructions should be provided to N.S. concerning the effect of warfarin on her menstrual flow?

Menstrual blood flow may be increased and prolonged in patients on anticoagulants.[126] This problem may be clinically significant if there is an underlying pathology resulting in abnormal vaginal bleeding. N.S. should be advised to have her PT checked at least monthly. Should unusually heavy or excessively prolonged menstrual or breakthrough bleeding occur, gynecologic evaluation should be obtained because of the risk of an ovarian hemorrhage.[127]

30. Use In Pregnancy. R.C., a 30-year-old woman, has been taking warfarin for continuing therapy of a resolved PE. She has just learned she is pregnant. What effects might warfarin have on the fetus? Is heparin a safer alternative drug in this situation?

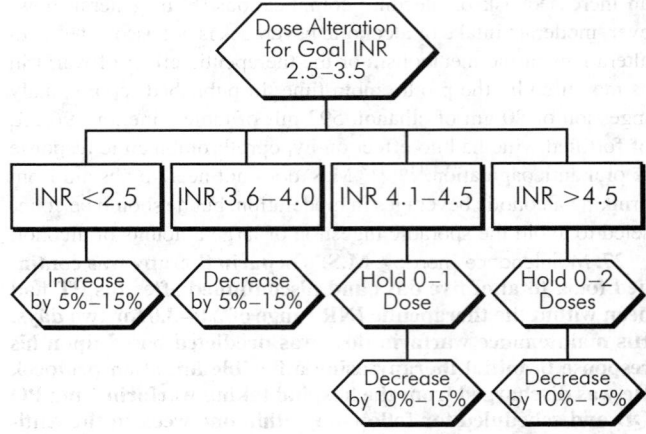

Fig 12.6 Warfarin Maintenance Dosing Protocol for Goal INR 2.5–3.5

Coumarin anticoagulants cross the placental barrier and may place the fetus at risk for hemorrhage and teratogenic effects.[128-130] Approximately one-sixth of pregnancies that involve exposure to coumarins result in abnormal liveborn infants, one-sixth in abortion or still-birth, and two-thirds in apparently normal infants. Congenital abnormalities such as stippled calcifications and nasal cartilage hypoplasia primarily occurred in infants born to mothers receiving warfarin during the first trimester of pregnancy. Other abnormalities, involving the central nervous system and eye, are more likely to occur following later exposure to warfarin.

Patients who become pregnant while receiving warfarin should be informed of the risks of continued anticoagulation to the fetus, as well as the risk to themselves of discontinuing anticoagulation. Women of child-bearing age who require anticoagulation should be counseled in some form of contraception. Since heparin does not cross the placental barrier, it is the preferred anticoagulant for use in pregnancy.[131] Heparin should be administered by the subcutaneous route with frequent (at least biweekly) monitoring of the aPTT and dosing adjustments as previously described. It should be discontinued approximately 24 hours before delivery and resumed as soon as bleeding from the delivery has been controlled.[132] Low molecular weight heparin products may offer a safe alternative and eliminate the need for frequent monitoring and dosage adjustments.[133]

Prevention of Cardiogenic Thromboembolism
Atrial Fibrillation
Anticoagulation Before Cardioversion

31. C.D., a 65-year-old female with congestive heart failure (CHF), presents in the Cardiology Clinic complaining of several days of fatigue and a "racing heart." On physical examination, her pulse is irregularly irregular and her heart rate is ≈120 beats/min. Using ECG, a diagnosis of atrial fibrillation is made and cardioversion is planned. Should C.D. be anticoagulated before cardioversion?

In atrial fibrillation, compromised atrial activity as well as atrial enlargement causes stasis of blood within the atria and the left atrial appendage, often resulting in atrial thrombus formation (mural thrombus).[134] Atrial thrombus formation increases the risk of systemic embolization; clinical manifestations include pulmonary embolism, arterial embolization of the extremities, or embolization of the splenic, renal, or abdominal arteries.[135] However, the most prevalent site of embolization is the cerebral arterial system resulting in either asymptomatic cerebral infarction or stroke with potentially devastating neurological and functional impairment.[136]

Both direct current cardioversion and pharmacologic cardioversion using antiarrhythmic drugs expose atrial fibrillation patients to an initial short-term increase in stroke risk from embolization secondary to resumption of normal atrial mechanical activity (see Chapter 16: Cardiac Arrhythmias). Data from a prospective cohort study of 437 patients noted a stroke incidence of 5.3% in atrial fibrillation patients who were cardioverted, but a significant reduction in stroke incidence to 0.8% if cardioverted patients were anticoagulated.[137] In addition to preventing the development of new atrial thrombi, anticoagulation allows any thrombus that may be present to endothelialize and adhere to the atrial wall so that thromboembolic risk is minimized. Based upon the assumed time course of thrombus development, as well as the presumed time course of clot endothelialization, it is recommended that patients who have been in atrial fibrillation for longer than 48 hours receive three weeks of anticoagulation with warfarin to an INR of 2.0 to 3.0 before cardioversion is attempted.[138]

Whether C.D. has been in atrial fibrillation for less than 48 hours is not known and, therefore, she requires a three-week course of

anticoagulation before cardioversion is attempted. If C.D. cannot tolerate her atrial fibrillation symptoms despite control of ventricular response rate, her medical team might consider immediate cardioversion without anticoagulation if transesophageal echocardiography (TEE) is used to rule out the presence of left atrial thrombi. In a series of 82 patients in whom no atrial thrombi were visualized using TEE, no embolic events occurred following immediate direct current cardioversion without precardioversion anticoagulation.[139] Transthoracic echocardiography (TTE) is not sensitive enough to visualize the left atrium and the left atrial appendage.

Anticoagulation After Cardioversion

32. After three weeks of low intensity warfarin therapy, C.D. is successfully cardioverted. Should warfarin be discontinued?

Despite normalization of atrial electrical activity, restoration of effective atrial mechanical activity following cardioversion of atrial fibrillation can be delayed for up to three weeks.[140] Additionally, a significant number of atrial fibrillation patients who initially are cardioverted successfully will revert to atrial fibrillation within one month. Both of these factors contribute to the recognized delay in stroke presentation in atrial fibrillation patients following cardioversion.[141] For these reasons, anticoagulation with warfarin should be continued following successful cardioversion until normal sinus rhythm has been maintained for four weeks.[138]

Anticoagulation for Chronic Atrial Fibrillation

33. Two weeks after successful cardioversion, C.D. presents to the ER with an exacerbation of CHF. An ECG is evaluated and atrial fibrillation is diagnosed again. What decisions regarding anticoagulation need to be made?

Anticoagulation in Valvular Atrial Fibrillation. Atrial fibrillation secondary to valvular heart disease historically has been recognized as a significant risk factor for stroke. Atrial fibrillation patients with a history of rheumatic valvular disease have a 17-fold higher incidence of stroke than in matched controls.[142] Patients with valvular atrial fibrillation require chronic, low-intensity anticoagulation with warfarin to prevent thromboembolism and stroke.[138]

Anticoagulation in Nonvalvular Atrial Fibrillation. Nonvalvular heart disease is the most common cause of atrial fibrillation and, like valvular heart disease, represents a significant risk for stroke in patients with atrial fibrillation. In comparison to matched controls, patients with atrial fibrillation associated with hypertension, CHF, or coronary artery disease have a 5.6-fold increase in the risk of stroke.[142] Additional risk factors include a history of thromboembolic disease, left atrial size greater than 2.5 cm/m^2, and left ventricular wall motion abnormalities.[143,144] Patients with paroxysmal (intermittent) atrial fibrillation have a lower risk of stroke than patients with chronic atrial fibrillation, possibly because paroxysmal atrial fibrillation often is associated with atrial fibrillation secondary to correctable, noncardiac causes. Patients with paroxysmal atrial fibrillation have a lower prevalence of CHF, a higher likelihood of recent onset atrial fibrillation, and a smaller left atrial size.[145]

A number of clinical trials have substantiated the role of warfarin in the primary prevention of systemic embolization and stroke in chronic, nonvalvular atrial fibrillation.[146-150] All five trials compared warfarin to placebo and were terminated before completion because of the substantial benefit of warfarin. In comparison to placebo, warfarin significantly reduced the risk of stroke from approximately 5% per year to approximately 2% per year in these trials. Long-term anticoagulation with warfarin aimed at prolonging the PT to an INR of 2.0 to 3.0 (i.e., high intensity) is recommended in patients with atrial fibrillation secondary to nonvalvular heart disease.[138]

Warfarin also is indicated in the secondary prevention of cardiogenic thromboembolism in patients with nonvalvular atrial fibrillation. In comparison to both aspirin 300 mg/day and placebo, warfarin substantially reduced the incidence of stroke, myocardial infarction (MI), systemic embolization, or death during 2.3 years of follow-up in patients with nonvalvular atrial fibrillation and a recent history of transient ischemic attack (TIA) or minor ischemic stroke.[151] This trial suggested that in 1000 patients, warfarin would prevent 90 vascular events, while aspirin would prevent 40 vascular events.

Anticoagulation in Lone Atrial Fibrillation. Idiopathic or lone atrial fibrillation refers to atrial fibrillation occurring in the absence of evidence for cardiac disease and without an identifiable noncardiac cause. In these patients, the risk of stroke is reduced substantially in comparison to patients with underlying heart disease. In a series of patients with lone atrial fibrillation, the cumulative incidence of stroke was 1.3% after 15 years of follow-up. No differences in stroke incidence in patients with chronic versus paroxysmal atrial fibrillation were found, but a significant age-associated risk was noted.[152] Chronic anticoagulation is recommended in lone atrial fibrillation patients older than 60 years of age, but stroke prevention is unnecessary in younger patients with lone atrial fibrillation.[138]

The decision to continue chronic anticoagulation with warfarin in C.D. should be based upon an evaluation of the likelihood that her atrial fibrillation will become chronic in nature and not amenable to cardioversion, as well as an assessment of her risk of stroke compared to her risk of warfarin-associated bleeding complications. If bleeding risk outweighs the risk of stroke, aspirin may be an alternative for stroke prevention. The Stroke Prevention in Atrial Fibrillation (SPAF) Study suggested a potential benefit of aspirin 325 mg/day in comparison to placebo in patients less than 75 years of age with nonvalvular atrial fibrillation.[147] A continuation of this trial (SPAF-II) will compare aspirin and warfarin in atrial fibrillation patients less than and older than 75 years of age and clarify the differences in incidence of stroke and bleeding complications between these two therapies and the influence of age on clinical outcomes.

Cardiac Valve Replacement

Mechanical Prosthetic Valves

34. D.L., a 56-year-old female with a history of rheumatic mitral valve disease, has undergone mitral valve replacement. A St. Jude (mechanical) valve has been implanted and heparin therapy is initiated postoperatively. Does D.L. require continued anticoagulation with warfarin?

Mechanical prosthetic valves confer a significant thromboembolic risk by providing a foreign surface in contact with blood components on which platelet aggregation and thrombus formation can occur. Valvular thrombosis can impair the integrity of valve function and can lead to embolization with systemic manifestations including stroke. The incidence of thromboembolic complications is dependent upon the type of artificial valve (e.g., ball and cage versus tilting disc) as well as the anatomic position of the replacement (mitral versus aortic).[153]

Chronic anticoagulation significantly reduces the risk of stroke and other manifestations of systemic embolization. Trials comparing different intensities of oral anticoagulation with warfarin in mechanical valve replacement have found that in comparison to the excessive anticoagulation used in historic controls or in randomized groups, a reduction in intensity protects against thromboembolic risk while reducing the incidence of hemorrhagic complications.[154,155] Patients with mechanical valve replacement

should receive chronic preventive anticoagulant therapy with warfarin to prolong the PT to an INR of 2.5 to 3.5.[153]

Bioprosthetic Valves

35. E.K., an 86-year-old female with a history of symptomatic aortic stenosis, has received a bioprosthetic aortic valve replacement. Is anticoagulant therapy required in E.K.?

Prosthetic heart valves extracted from mammalian sources (porcine or bovine xenografts; homografts) are significantly less thrombogenic than mechanical prosthetic valves. The period of greatest thromboembolic risk appears to be during the first three months after implantation. Therefore, short-term, low intensity preventive anticoagulation to prolong the PT to an INR of 2.0 to 3.0 is recommended.[153] However, therapy should be continued chronically in patients with underlying atrial fibrillation, a history of systemic embolism, or with evidence of atrial thrombus at surgery.

Combined Anticoagulant/Antiplatelet Therapy

36. W.W., a 69-year-old male, underwent mitral valve replacement six months ago with a mechanical valve prosthesis. Anticoagulation with warfarin resulted in stable INR values within the therapeutic range of 2.5–3.5. Despite adequate anticoagulation, he recently developed episodes of transient intermittent visual field and speech disturbances. Neurologic evaluation concluded that W.W. was having TIAs. Can antiplatelet therapy be added without increasing the risk of hemorrhagic complications? (Also see Chapter 53: Cerebrovascular Disorders.)

The primary approach to prevention of valvular thrombosis and systemic thromboembolism associated with mechanical prosthetic valve replacement is anticoagulation with warfarin. If evidence of thromboembolism exists despite adequate anticoagulation, the addition of antiplatelet agents is indicated. The combination of warfarin plus dipyridamole (400 mg/day) was associated with a significant reduction in the incidence of thromboembolism in one early study of 65 patients. However, the overall mortality rate between groups was not different.[156] In another study of 18 patients, the addition of dipyridamole 400 mg/day did not decrease the incidence of thromboembolism.[157] In these and other trials involving combination warfarin and dipyridamole in mechanical valve replacement, no significant differences in bleeding complications were observed between patients on warfarin alone versus patients receiving combination therapy.

High dose aspirin (500 mg/day) in combination with warfarin has been shown to help prevent systemic thromboembolism in patients with mechanical prosthetic valves, but is associated with an unacceptable risk of bleeding.[158,192] However, a trial comparing warfarin alone (adjusted to an INR of 3.0 to 4.5) and warfarin combined with low dose aspirin (100 mg/day) in 370 patients with mechanical valve replacements or with tissue valve prostheses and underlying atrial fibrillation or a history of thromboembolism, found a significant reduction in the incidence of systemic thromboembolism as well as reduced mortality in the combination therapy group.[160] Although the incidence of total bleeding was higher in patients receiving both warfarin and low dose aspirin, this difference was due entirely to differences in clinically insignificant minor bleeding. Major bleeding episodes were similar in both groups.

Because conventional anticoagulant therapy in patients with mechanical prosthetic heart valves occasionally is associated with systemic thromboembolism despite anticoagulation, the addition of an antiplatelet agent may be of benefit in W.W. Despite a favorable adverse effect profile, combined warfarin and dipyridamole is associated with mixed results with respect to preventing systemic embolization in patients with mechanical heart valves and should not be recommended. Low dose aspirin in combination with warfarin appears to offer an advantage in this setting, while minimizing the potential for clinically significant major bleeding events.

Left Ventricular Thrombosis

Following Myocardial Infarction (MI)

37. A.V., a 55-year-old female with hypercholesterolemia and a 22-pack-year smoking history, recently sustained an anterior transmural MI. She was treated with thrombolytic therapy in the ER and heparin has been initiated. Is continued anticoagulation with warfarin indicated following her discharge from the hospital?

The primary role of anticoagulation in patients with MI is the prevention of coronary artery rethrombosis and reinfarction (see Chapter 14: Myocardial Infarction). The risk of venous thromboembolism (DVT, PE) also is substantial in this patient population due to prolonged immobilization during hospitalization, and is reduced significantly by preventive anticoagulant therapy.[161] However, an additional source of thrombus formation is the infarcted myocardium. Intracardiac flow abnormalities in areas of akinesis or dyskinesis, as well as the inflammatory changes at the endocardial surface of the infarcted myocardium, represent transient, additive risk factors for the development of left ventricular, intracardiac thrombi.[162]

Approximately one-third of patients develop left ventricular thrombi following anterior myocardial infarction.[163,164] Mural thrombus formation is more common in patients with severe wall motion abnormalities associated with the left ventricle, but occurs infrequently in patients with inferior myocardial infarction.[165,166] Within 48 hours of MI, half of all left ventricular thrombi are evident by transthoracic echocardiography, and by one week, up to 100% have formed.[165]

Left ventricular thrombi represent a significant risk for systemic embolization, including stroke. Cerebral embolization occurs in up to 30% of patients with left ventricular thrombi, typically occurring within three months of MI.[166,167] The risk of embolization increases when thrombi protrude into the lumen of the left ventricle and when thrombi are freely mobile.[168]

Short-term anticoagulation with warfarin following anterior MI significantly reduces the risk of systemic embolization and stroke in patients with documented left ventricular thrombi. In two series, stroke rates were reduced by 100% in patients treated with warfarin in comparison to patients who were not anticoagulated after initial heparinization.[166,169] Based upon the high incidence of left ventricular thrombus formation in anterior myocardial infarction and the risk of stroke associated with mural thrombi, A.V. should be anticoagulated with warfarin for up to three months at a dose sufficient to prolong the PT to an INR of 2.0 to 3.0.[161] An echocardiogram before hospital discharge will document the presence of mural thrombi, as well as determine left ventricular wall motion. The absence of mural thrombus on an initial echocardiogram does not preclude preventive anticoagulation due to the possibility of delay in clot formation. However, if left ventricular thrombus or significant wall motion abnormalities are evident on follow-up echocardiography at three months, continued anticoagulation is indicated.

In Congestive Heart Failure (CHF)

38. Idiopathic cardiomyopathy has recently been diagnosed in C.A., a 39-year-old male with a left ventricular ejection fraction estimated at 18%. What is the risk of left ventricular thrombus formation in C.A. and is preventive anticoagulation indicated?

In CHF resulting from ischemic changes to the myocardium, left ventricular thrombus formation occurs as a result of transient surface and flow abnormalities, as noted above. In contrast, left ventricular thrombus formation in idiopathic dilated cardiomyopathy occurs as a result of intracavitary stasis due to systolic dysfunction.[168] The resultant reduction in blood flow, often specifically in the apex of the left ventricle, represents a risk for left ventricular thrombus formation that remains constant over time.[170]

Left ventricular thrombosis may represent a greater risk of systemic embolization in idiopathic cardiomyopathy than in ischemic cardiomyopathy, but the incidence of stroke is unclear.[171] The extent of systolic dysfunction also may increase the risk of left ventricular thrombosis and resultant embolization.[172] Two longitudinal series have noted a reduction in the incidence of systemic thromboembolic events in patients with idiopathic cardiomyopathy treated with warfarin in comparison to untreated patients.[173,174] These observations have led to the recommendation that patients with severe idiopathic cardiomyopathy, like C.A., should be chronically anticoagulated with low intensity warfarin.[161]

In chronic CHF without respect to etiology or degree of systolic dysfunction, the value of long-term anticoagulation in the prevention of systemic thromboembolism and stroke has not been substantiated, primarily due to a low frequency of observed events.[171,175] A randomized clinical trial is necessary to identify subgroups of patients with CHF who may be at increased risk for cardioembolic stroke and in whom the risk of warfarin-associated bleeding is outweighed by its antithrombotic effect.

Drug Interactions

39. J.B., a 72-year-old female, received a Bjork-Shiley tilting disc mitral valve prosthesis five years ago. She has been anticoagulated with warfarin 6 mg/day with good control. She is allergic to ampicillin and has gastric intolerance to tetracycline. Yesterday, she was seen in an acute care clinic with symptoms of an uncomplicated urinary tract infection (UTI) and prescribed one double-strength tablet of trimethoprim/sulfamethoxazole (TMP-SMX) BID. How will the combination of warfarin and TMP-SMX (Bactrim; Septra) affect J.B.'s anticoagulation control? Should her warfarin dose be adjusted or another drug substituted for TMP-SMX?

Drug interactions with warfarin occur by a number of different mechanisms and can have a significant impact on the anticoagulant effect of warfarin.[176] Elevations or reductions in PT have been observed when interacting drugs are added to or discontinued from the medication regimens of patients taking warfarin. Clinically significant hemorrhagic or thromboembolic complications can result. Careful selection of both prescription and nonprescription medications, appropriate PT monitoring, and detailed patient education regarding drug interactions are important interventions for pharmacists caring for patients treated with warfarin. A summary of drugs that interact with warfarin, including mechanisms of interaction and effect on PT, is provided in Table 12.10.

Although warfarin is highly protein bound primarily to albumin and can be displaced from protein binding sites by a number of weakly acidic drugs, these interactions typically do not result in clinically significant elevations in prothrombin time.[186] Warfarin displaced from protein binding sites is readily available for elimination by hepatic metabolism, resulting in increased clearance without a significant change in free drug concentration.[187]

Sulfamethoxazole may increase the effect of warfarin significantly by stereoselectively inhibiting the metabolism of the more potent S enantiomer of warfarin.[177,178] Potentiation of warfarin activity following inhibition of metabolism usually takes several

Table 12.10	Significant Warfarin Drug Interactions	
Drugs that Increase Prothrombin Time		
Increased Catabolism of Clotting Factors		
Androgens	Thyroid hormones	
Inhibition of Warfarin Metabolism		
Allopurinol	Amiodarone	Chloramphenicol
Cimetidine[a]	Ciprofloxacin	Disulfiram
Erythromycin	Ethanol (acute)	Fluconazole
Ketoconazole	Metronidazole[a]	Miconazole
Nalidixic acid	Norfloxacin	Phenylbutazone[a]
Propafenone	Sulfonamides (TMP-SMX)	Sulfinpyrazone[a]
Additive Anticoagulant Effect		
Cefamandole	Cefmetazole	Cefoperazone
Cefotetan	Heparin	Moxalactam
Unestablished Mechanisms		
Chloral hydrate	Clofibrate	Glucagon
Lovastatin	Phenytoin	Vitamin E
Drugs that Decrease Prothrombin Time		
Increased Synthesis of Clotting Factors		
Estrogens	Propylthiouracil	Vitamin K
Induction of Warfarin Metabolism		
Aminoglutethimide	Barbiturates	Carbamazepine
Ethanol (chronic)	Glutethimide	Griseofulvin
Nafcillin	Rifampin	
Decreased Absorption of Warfarin		
Cholestyramine	Colestipol	
Unestablished Mechanisms		
Phenytoin		
Increased Risk of Bleeding		
Aspirin (acetylated salicylates)		NSAIDs

[a] Established stereoselective interaction.
[b] Typically without effect on prothrombin time. Acceptable to take low dosed, fixed dosed aspirin for antiplatelet effect.

days and the effect may be slow to resolve once the offending agent is discontinued. Additionally, fever associated with the infection for which TMP-SMX has been prescribed may enhance the catabolism of vitamin K-dependent clotting factors, resulting in an accentuated hypoprothrombinemic response.[121] This effect will dissipate as the fever abates with antibiotic therapy.

For J.B., the best choice would be to discontinue TMP-SMX. Since ampicillin and tetracycline are contraindicated, either a first-generation cephalosporin or TMP alone may be used. Oral quinolones should be avoided because of the risk of potentiation of the anticoagulant effect of warfarin. Careful monitoring of the PT should continue since the introduction of any changes in treatment, as well as the acute illness, may alter the patient's response to warfarin therapy.

If these options are not appropriate, warfarin therapy is not an absolute contraindication to the use of TMP-SMX. If J.B. is monitored frequently and carefully, with adjustment of warfarin doses as necessary to maintain her PT within the therapeutic INR range of 2.5 to 3.5 and with attention to the potential hemorrhagic complications, TMP-SMX can be prescribed. No initial change in warfarin dose is required since it may take several days for the interaction to be apparent. If the TMP-SMX is to be taken for more than five days, J.B. should be seen in three to five days for a repeat PT.

40. D.R. is a 39-year-old female recovering from unexplained ventricular fibrillation several weeks ago with significant, but improving neurologic deficits. A defibrillator system has been implanted, with amiodarone 400 mg/day added for suppressive antiarrhythmic therapy. Due to immobility during her hospitalization, she developed a DVT and has been receiving heparin for 5 days. A full three-month course of anticoagulation is indicated. Is D.R. a candidate for warfarin therapy?

Amiodarone appears to inhibit the hepatic metabolism of warfarin, resulting in 50% to 100% increases in PT in patients previously stabilized on warfarin therapy and in whom amiodarone is added.[179–182] Elevations in prothrombin time typically occur within one week and stabilize after approximately one month of combination therapy.[181,182] These patients require frequent PT monitoring with downward adjustments in warfarin doses. Some clinicians prefer to empirically reduce warfarin doses by 25% to 50% at the time amiodarone is added (based upon the expected degree of warfarin dose reduction), but with frequent monitoring to more carefully adjust therapy over time.[182]

In the case of D.R., warfarin is to be added to pre-existing amiodarone therapy. The use of a drug known to interact with warfarin is not an absolute contraindication to the addition of warfarin. Warfarin therapy should commence according to the usual flexible initiation protocol (see Table 12.8), but with the expectation that D.R.'s INR likely will increase at a rate faster than if she were not on amiodarone, and that her maintenance dosing likely will be significantly lower than if she were not taking amiodarone concurrently. As in other settings, flexible initiation allows for daily adjustment of warfarin dosing based upon the PT response of the individual patient. Frequent monitoring will be required for D.R. in order to establish a maintenance dose.

If amiodarone therapy is discontinued while D.R. is anticoagulated, frequent monitoring also will be necessary. However, the effect of amiodarone on warfarin metabolism can continue for several months after amiodarone is discontinued based upon the long elimination half-life and large volume of distribution of amiodarone. Gradual increases in warfarin dosing requirements have been observed following discontinuation of amiodarone.[180,182]

41. M.Z., a 67-year-old male, was recently diagnosed with bursitis of the right shoulder. A course of anti-inflammatory medication is recommended by his doctor. M.Z. is presently taking warfarin 12.5 mg/day for a history of chronic atrial fibrillation. What could be prescribed for his shoulder pain that would not significantly interact with M.Z.'s warfarin?

This question illustrates one of the most difficult therapeutic dilemmas for a patient on warfarin. All NSAIDs have the potential to cause gastric irritation by inhibiting cytoprotective prostaglandins, thereby providing a focus for GI bleeding. Additionally, most NSAIDs inhibit platelet aggregation, which compromises effective clotting and can lead to bleeding complications. Some NSAIDs also may have specific pharmacokinetic interactions with warfarin which can increase the hypoprothrombinemic effect of warfarin (e.g., phenylbutazone).[183,184]

These effects can increase the risk of hemorrhagic complications significantly in patients taking warfarin who are prescribed concurrent NSAID therapy. In a retrospective cohort study of patients 65 years of age or older, the risk of hospitalization for bleeding peptic ulcer disease was approximately three times higher for patients taking concurrent warfarin and an NSAID compared to either drug alone, and almost 13 times higher than in patients taking neither warfarin nor an NSAID.[94] Warfarin therapy is considered a relative contraindication to NSAID use.

In patients who require combination therapy, clinical experience suggests that ibuprofen (Motrin) or naproxen (Naprosyn) are somewhat better tolerated than other NSAIDs with respect to additive hemorrhagic complications, particularly for short-term use. Alternative agents include the nonacetylated salicylates such as salsalate or diflunisal. However, all patients requiring combined warfarin and NSAID therapy should be followed closely, with frequent stool testing for the presence of any GI bleeding.

Disseminated Intravascular Coagulation (DIC)
Pathophysiology

42. W.K., a 63-year-old female, was admitted to the intensive care unit with respiratory failure secondary to acute pulmonary edema. She required ventilatory support until 48 hours ago when she was extubated. At that time aspiration was suspected, but no antibiotic coverage was prescribed. Within the last 24 hours, W.K. developed tachycardia (heart rate 120 beats/min), tachypnea (respiratory rate 30 breaths/min), and a fever to 39.0 °F. Sepsis was suspected, broad spectrum antibiotic coverage was started, and W.K. was reintubated. Because of the sudden appearance of bright red blood per rectum and through her nasogastric tube, a coagulation screen was ordered. Until this time, all coagulation parameters had been within normal limits. Now the results show platelets 43,000/mm³ (Normal: 150,000–350,000), PT 24 sec (Mean Normal: 12); aPTT 76 sec (Mean Normal: 34); thrombin time 48 sec (Normal: 16–27); fibrinogen 60 mg/dL (Normal: 150–400); and fibrin degradation products 580 ng/mL (Normal: <250). The diagnosis of DIC is made. How does the pathophysiology DIC explain these hematologic abnormalities? [SI Units: platelets 43 × 10⁹/L (Normal: 150–300); fibrinogen 0.6 gm/L (Normal: 1.5–4)]

Thrombosis in response to endothelial damage or the presence of an altered surface in contact with blood components is a localized phenomenon. Thrombus formation occurs at the site of injury or abnormality, where procoagulant and anticoagulant mechanisms, as well as fibrinolytic and antifibrinolytic mechanisms, are regulated. The term ''localized extravascular coagulation'' describes the site-specific nature of venous and arterial thrombosis.

In contrast, disseminated intravascular coagulation is a diffuse response to systemic activation of the coagulation system (see Figure 12.7).[188] Circulating thrombin converts fibrinogen to fibrin resulting in fibrin deposition within the microcirculation. Clinical manifestations of microvascular thrombosis are the result of tissue ischemia.

The presence of systemic circulating thrombin causes simultaneous systemic activation of the fibrinolytic system resulting in circulating plasmin within the systemic circulation. Plasmin causes systemic lysis of fibrin to fibrin degradation products and results in hemorrhagic complications.

Bleeding manifestations of DIC occur not only due to systemic fibrinolysis, but also secondary to thrombocytopenia, clotting factor deficiency, and platelet dysfunction. Circulating thrombin promotes platelet aggregation, resulting in thrombocytopenia as platelet aggregates deposit in the microcirculation. Circulating plasmin degrades clotting factors as well as fibrin, and the presence of fibrogen degradation products from fibrinolysis inhibits platelet function. Normal mechanisms of platelet and clotting factor synthesis are unable to compensate for this consumption. In essence, the patient shows paradoxical bleeding secondary to overactivation and eventual consumption of available clotting factors and platelets.

Clinical Presentation

43. What subjective and objective evidence in W.K. is consistent with the diagnosis of acute DIC?

Laboratory Findings

A number of coagulation laboratory abnormalities occur in disseminated intravascular coagulation.[189] The PT, aPTT, and thrombin time are increased due to consumption of clotting factors more quickly than they can be replenished by hepatic synthesis. Platelet count is diminished secondary to thrombin-mediated platelet ag-

gregation. Fibrinogen is reduced as a result of plasmin-mediated fibrinolysis, with an elevation in fibrogen degradation products indicative of a fibrinolytic state. W.K.'s coagulation panel findings are consistent with the laboratory abnormalities seen in acute DIC. A peripheral smear will often show thrombocytopenia and red blood cells fragmented by exposure to microcirculatory fibrin (schistocytes).

Hemorrhagic Manifestations

Hemorrhagic manifestations are the predominant clinical finding in DIC.[190] Bleeding can occur at sites of injury including surgical incisions, venopuncture sites, nasogastric tubes, or gastric ulcers. However, spontaneous bleeding also occurs from intact sites or organ systems. Spontaneous ecchymosis, petechia, epistaxis, hemoptysis, hematuria, and GI bleeding frequently are encountered. Intracranial, intraperitoneal, and pericardial bleeding also may occur.

Thrombotic Manifestations

Thrombotic manifestations of DIC result in obstruction of blood flow to multiple organ systems.[190] The resultant ischemic damage to end organs, including the skin, kidneys, brain, lungs, liver, eyes, and GI tract, can result in multiple system failure. Despite the se-

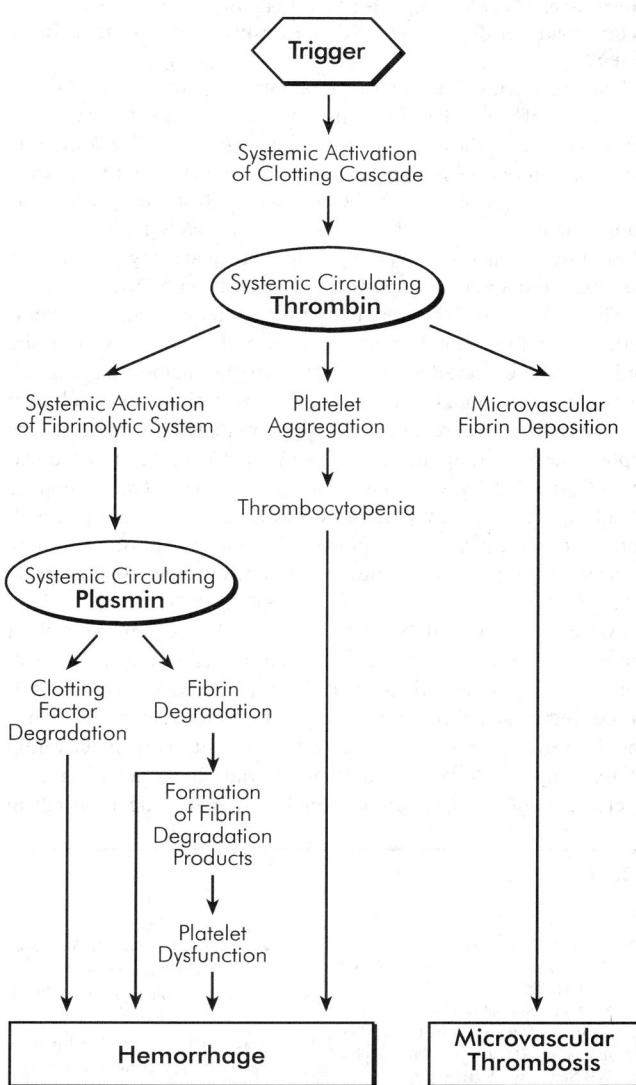

Fig 12.7   Pathophysiology of Disseminated Intravascular Coagulation (DIC)

verity of hemorrhagic complications, microvascular thrombosis represents a significant cause of morbidity and mortality in patients with acute disseminated intravascular coagulation.

Precipitating Events

44. What events may have precipitated the development of DIC in W.K.?

Disseminated intravascular coagulation is a pathologic syndrome triggered by disease states or conditions that activate coagulation systemically rather than on a local basis.[189,190] The presence of thrombin within the systemic circulation can be triggered by systemic endothelial damage (e.g., bacterial endotoxin), by systemic contact activation of the clotting cascade (e.g., cardiopulmonary bypass), or by the release of procoagulants into the systemic circulation (e.g., malignancy). Table 12.11 presents an abbreviated list of disorders associated with the development of DIC. Although the most likely stimulus for DIC in W.K. is sepsis, hypoxia and acidosis associated with respiratory compromise also may have contributed.

Treatment

45. Over the course of several hours, W.K. has developed more severe GI bleeding. Her Hct has fallen from 43% to 35%. What treatment course should be pursued? Should heparin be given?

The most critical element of treatment in patients with DIC is alleviation of the underlying cause in order to eliminate the stimulus for continued thrombosis and hemorrhage.[159,191] For W.K., this involves appropriate antibiotic therapy as well as supportive measures to correct or prevent the hemodynamic, respiratory, and metabolic manifestations of shock. Fluid replacement, maintenance of blood pressure and cardiac output, and adequate oxygenation are essential components of treatment in patients with DIC.

The selection of other therapies aimed at the correction of hemorrhagic or thrombotic manifestations of DIC are controversial and, to some extent, dependent upon whether hemorrhagic manifestations or thrombotic complications predominate in the clinical presentation. Initial treatment in patients with hemorrhage involves replacement of components of clotting that have been consumed in DIC, guided by coagulation laboratory data. Transfusion of platelets, fresh frozen plasma (containing all clotting factors), and/or cryoprecipitate (containing factor VIII and fibrinogen) may be necessary with close monitoring of platelet count and fibrinogen level.

Anticoagulation with heparin therapy in DIC is controversial. In theory, since the initial pathologic event in disseminated intravascular coagulation is activation of the clotting system with formation of intravascular thrombin, the antithrombin activity of heparin should prevent further fibrin deposition and subsequent activation of fibrinolysis. However, randomized trials have not been conducted to confirm this potential benefit. Several clinical settings in

Table 12.11	Clinical Conditions Associated with DIC[a]
Obstetric States	
Amnionic fluid embolism	Retained dead fetus
Eclampsia	Septic or saline abortion
Intravascular Hemolysis	
Hemolytic transfusion reactions	Minor hemolysis
Massive transfusions	
Tissue Injury	
Burns	Extensive surgery
Crush injuries	Multiple trauma
Infectious Diseases	
Bacterial Infections	
Gram negative sepsis	Gram positive sepsis
Viral Infections	
Cytomegalovirus	Varicella
Hepatitis	
Fungal Infections	
Aspergillosis	Histoplasmosis
Candidiasis	
Miscellaneous Infections	
Mycoplasma	Psittacosis
Mycobacteria malaria	Rocky mountain spotted fever
Miscellaneous	
Acidosis	Hepatic disease
ARDS	Hypoperfusion
Anaphylaxis	Hypovolemia
Cardiopulmonary bypass	Malignancy
Hematologic disorders	Vascular disorders
Heat stroke	Snake bites

[a] ARDS = Adult respiratory distress syndrome; DIC = Disseminated intravascular coagulation.

which full intensity heparinization may be useful have been identified based upon clinical experience and uncontrolled series.[192] These include amnionic fluid embolism, retained dead fetus, severe transfusion reactions, evidence of thrombotic manifestations of DIC, and patients who exhibit continued bleeding, thrombocytopenia, or hypofibrinogenemia despite aggressive replacement therapy.

Finally, the use of the antifibrinolytic agents tranexamic acid and aminocaproic acid to control bleeding is relatively contraindicated. These agents may worsen thrombotic complications of DIC, particularly if heparin is not used concurrently. However, antifibrinolytic therapy may be used in patients with life-threatening bleeding who fail to respond to replacement therapy or heparinization.

Acknowledgment

We gratefully acknowledge Steven R. Kayser whose work provided a foundation for this chapter.

References

1 **Brott T, Stup D.** Overview of hemostasis and thrombosis. Semin Neurol. 1991;11:305.

2 **Saitko H.** Normal hemostatic function. In: Ratnoff OD, Forbes CD, eds. Disorders of Hemostasis. Philadelphia: WB Saunders; 1991:18.

3 **Nachman RL, Silverstein R.** Hypercoagulable states. Ann Intern Med. 1993;119:819.

4 **Lammie B, Griffin JH.** Formation of the fibrin clot: the balance of procoagulant and inhibitory factors. Clin Hematol. 1985;14:281.

5 **Kwaan HC.** Protein C and protein S. Semin Thromb Hemost. 1989;15:353.

6 **Mosher DF.** Blood coagulation and fibrinolysis: an overview. Clin Cardiol. 1990;13:V15.

7 **Hirsh J.** Heparin. N Engl J Med. 1991; 324:1565.

8 **Hirsh J et al.** Heparin: mechanism of action, pharmacokinetics, dosing considerations, monitoring, efficacy and safety. Chest. 1992;102(Suppl. 4):337.

9 **Estes JW.** Clinical pharmacokinetics of heparin. Clin Pharmacokinet. 1980; 5:204.

10 **White TM et al.** Continuous heparin infusion requirements: diagnostic and therapeutic implications. JAMA. 1979; 241:2717.

11 **Hirsh J.** Low molecular weight heparins. Thromb Haemost. 1993;70:204.

12 **Hirsh J, Levine MN.** Low molecular weight heparin. Blood. 1992;79:1.

13 **Carter CA et al.** Enoxaparin: the low molecular weight heparin for prevention of post-operative thromboembolic

complications. Ann Pharmacother. 1993;27:1223.

14 Hirsh J. Oral anticoagulant drugs. N Engl J Med. 1991;324:1865.

15 Kelly JG et al. Clinical pharmacokinetics of oral anticoagulants. Clin Pharmacokinet. 1979;4:1.

16 Park BK. Warfarin: metabolism and mode of action. Biochem Pharmacol. 1989;37:19.

17 Suchman AL et al. Diagnostic uses of the activated partial thromboplastin time and the prothrombin time. Ann Intern Med. 1986;104:820.

18 Evaluation of the extrinsic pathway. In: Sirridge MS, Shannon R, eds. Laboratory Evaluation of Hemostasis and Thrombosis. Philadelphia: Lea and Febiger; 1983:151.

19 Bussey HI et al. Reliance on prothrombin time ratios causes significant errors in anticoagulation therapy. Arch Intern Med. 1992;152:278.

20 Kirkwood TBL. Calibration of reference thromboplastin and standardization of the prothrombin time ratio. Thromb Haemost. 1983;49:238.

21 Tripodi A et al. Recombinant tissue factor as substitute for conventional thromboplastin in the prothrombin time test. Thromb Haemost. 1992;67:42.

22 Hirsh J et al. Oral anticoagulants: mechanism of action, clinical effectiveness and optimal therapeutic range. Chest. 1992;102(Suppl. 4):312.

23 Evaluation of the intrinsic pathway. In: Sirridge MS, Shannon R, eds. Laboratory Evaluation of Hemostasis and Thrombosis. Philadelphia: Lea and Febiger; 1983:112.

24 Hoffman JJML, Meulendijk PN. Comparison of reagents for determining the activated partial thromboplastin time. Thromb Haemost. 1978;39:640.

25 Shojania AM et al. Variations between heparin sensitivity of different lots of activated partial thromboplastin time reagent produced by the same manufacturer. Am J Clin Pathol. 1988;89:19.

26 Zanke B, Shojania AM. Comparison of two aPTT methods of monitoring heparin therapy. Am J Clin Pathol. 1990;90:684.

27 Brill-Edwards P et al. Establishing a therapeutic range for heparin therapy. Ann Intern Med. 1993;119:104.

28 Hirsh J et al. Clinical features and diagnosis of venous thrombosis. JACC. 1986;8:114B.

29 Comerota AJ et al. Venous duplex imaging for the diagnosis of acute deep venous thrombosis. Haemostasis. 1993;23(Suppl. 1):61.

30 Wheeler AP et al. Physician practices in the treatment of pulmonary embolism and deep vein thrombosis. Arch Intern Med. 1988;148:1321.

31 Raschke RA. A weight-based heparin dosing nomogram compared with a "standard-care" nomogram: a randomized controlled trial. Ann Intern Med. 1993;119:874.

32 Carter BL. Therapy of acute thromboembolism with heparin and warfarin. Clin Pharm. 1991;10:503.

33 Chenella FC et al. Improved method for estimating initial heparin infusion rates. Am J Hosp Pharm. 1979;36:782.

34 Groce JB et al. Heparin dosage adjustment in patients with deep-vein

thrombosis using heparin concentrations rather than activated partial thromboplastin time. Clin Pharm. 1987; 6:216.

35 Saya FG et al. Pharmacist-directed heparin therapy using a standard dosing and monitoring protocol. Am J Hosp Pharm. 1985;42:1965.

36 Cipolle RJ et al. Heparin kinetics: variables related to disposition and dosage. Clin Pharmacol Ther. 1981;29:387.

37 Hattersley PG et al. Sources of error in heparin therapy. Arch Intern Med. 1980;140:1173.

38 Hull RD et al. Heparin for 5 days as compared with 10 days in the initial treatment of proximal venous thrombosis. N Engl J Med. 1990;322:1260.

39 Rooke TW. Heparin and the in-hospital management of deep vein thrombosis: cost considerations. Mayo Clin Proc. 1986;61:198.

40 Mohiuddin SM et al. Efficacy and safety of early versus late initiation of warfarin during heparin therapy in acute thromboembolism. Am Heart J. 1992;123:729.

41 Chong BH. Heparin-induced thrombocytopenia. Aust N Z J Med. 1992; 22:145.

42 Chong BH et al. Heparin-induced thrombocytopenia: mechanism of interactions of the heparin-dependent platelet antibody with platelets. Br J Haematol. 1989;73:235.

43 Warkentin TE, Kelton JG. Heparin-induced thrombocytopenia. Prog Hemost Thromb. 1991;10:1.

44 Schmitt BP, Adelman B. Heparin associated with thrombocytopenia: a critical review and pooled analysis. Am J Med Sci. 1993;305:208.

45 Demers C et al. Rapid anticoagulation using ancrod for heparin induced thrombocytopenia. Blood. 1991;78:2194.

46 Chong BH et al. Orgaran in heparin-induced thrombocytopenia. Haemostasis. 1992;22:85.

47 Becker DM et al. Inferior vena cava filter: indications, safety, effectiveness. Arch Intern Med. 1992;152:1985.

48 Landefeld CS, Beyth RJ. Anticoagulation-related bleeding: clinical epidemiology, prediction and prevention. Am J Med. 1993;85:315.

49 Levine MN et al. Hemorrhagic complications of anticoagulant treatment. Chest. 1992;102(Suppl. 4):352.

50 Schuster GA, Lewis GA. Clinical significance of hematuria in patients on anticoagulant therapy. J Urol. 1987; 137:923.

51 Jaffin BW. Significance of occult gastrointestinal bleeding during anticoagulant therapy. Am J Med. 1987;83:269.

52 Landefeld CS et al. Identification and preliminary validation of predictors of major bleeding in hospitalized patients started on anticoagulant therapy. Am J Med. 1982;82:703.

53 Hull RD et al. Optimal therapeutic level of heparin therapy in patients with venous thrombosis. Arch Intern Med. 1992;152:1589.

54 Holm HA et al. Heparin assays and bleeding complications in treatment of deep venous thrombosis with particular reference to retroperitoneal bleeding. Thromb Haemostasis. 1985;53:278.

55 Basu D et al. A prospective study of the

value of monitoring heparin treatment with the activated partial thromboplastin time. N Engl J Med. 1972;87:324.

56 Mant MJ et al. Hemorrhagic complications of heparin therapy. Lancet. 1977;1:1133.

57 Conti S et al. A comparison of high dose versus conventional dose heparin therapy for deep vein thrombosis. Surg. 1982;92:972.

58 Avioli LV. Heparin induced osteoporosis: an appraisal. Adv Exp Med Biol. 1975;52:375.

59 Lechey D et al. Heparin-induced hypoaldosteronism. JAMA. 1981;246:2189.

60 Doyle DJ et al. Adjusted subcutaneous heparin or continuous infusion heparin in patients with acute deep vein thrombosis. Ann Intern Med. 1987;107:441.

61 Andersson G et al. Subcutaneous administration of heparin: a randomized comparison with intravenous administration of heparin in patients with deep vein thrombosis. Thromb Res. 1982; 27:631.

62 Pini M et al. Subcutaneous versus intravenous administration of heparin in the treatment of deep vein thrombosis: a randomized clinical trial. Thromb Haemost. 1990;64:222.

63 Hommes DW et al. Subcutaneous heparin compared with continuous intravenous heparin administration in the initial treatment of deep vein thrombosis: a meta-analysis. Ann Intern Med. 1992;116:279.

64 Jacques LB. Protamine: antagonist to heparin. Can Med Assoc J. 1973;108: 1291.

65 Horrow JC. Protamine: a review of its toxicity. Anesth Analg. 1985;64:348.

66 Horrow JC. Protamine allergy. J Cardiothorac Anesth. 1988;2:225.

67 Clagett GP et al. Prevention of venous thromboembolism. Chest. 1992;102 (Suppl. 4):391.

68 Clagett GP. Prevention of venous thromboembolism in general surgical patients: results of meta-analysis. Ann Surg. 1988;208:227.

69 Leyvraz PF. Adjusted versus fixed dose subcutaneous heparin in the prevention of deep vein thrombosis after total hip replacement. N Engl J Med. 1983;309:954.

70 Stein PD et al. History and physical examination in acute pulmonary embolism in patients without preexisting cardiac or pulmonary disease. Am J Cardiol. 1981;47:223.

71 Stein PD et al. Clinical, laboratory, roentgenographic and electrocardiographic findings in patients with acute pulmonary embolism and pre-existing cardiac or pulmonary disease. Chest. 1991;100:598.

72 The PIOPED Investigators. Value of the ventilation/perfusion scan in acute pulmonary embolism. Results of the Prospective Investigation of Pulmonary Embolism Diagnosis (PIOPED) study. JAMA. 1990;263:2753.

73 Hirsh J et al. Heparin kinetics in venous thrombosis and pulmonary embolism. Circulation. 1976;53:691.

74 Simon TL et al. Heparin pharmacokinetics: increased requirements in pulmonary embolism. Br J Haematol. 1978;39:111.

75 Kandrotas RJ et al. Altered heparin pharmacodynamics in patients with

pulmonary embolism. Ther Drug Monit. 1992;14:360.

76 Elliott CG et al. Heparin requirements in pulmonary embolism and venous thrombosis: a prospective study. J Clin Pharmacol. 1982;22:102.

77 Tenero DM et al. Comparative dosage and toxicity of heparin sodium in the treatment of patients with pulmonary embolism versus deep vein thrombosis. Clin Pharm. 1989;8:40.

78 Marciniak E, Gockerman P. Heparin-induced decrease in circulating antithrombin III. Lancet. 1977;2:581.

79 Schulman S, Tengborn L. Treatment of venous thromboembolism in patients with congenital deficiency of antithrombin III. Thromb Haemost. 1992;68:634.

80 Hirsh J et al. Congenital antithrombin III deficiency. Incidence and clinical features. Am J Med. 1989;87(Suppl. B):3.

81 Hiatt J, Wittkowsky AK. Criteria for use of warfarin in adult inpatients and outpatients. Clin Pharm. 1993;12:307.

82 Weiss P et al. Decline of proteins C and S and factors II, VII, IX, and X during initiation of warfarin therapy. Thromb Res. 1987;45:783.

83 Schultz NJ et al. The influence of heparin on the prothrombin time. Pharmacother. 1991;11:312.

84 Hauser VM, Rozek SL. Effect of warfarin on the aPTT. Drug Intell Clin Pharm. 1986;20:964.

85 Sawyer WT et al. Multicenter evaluation of six methods for predicting warfarin maintenance dose requirements from initial response. Clin Pharm. 1985;4:440.

86 Carter BL et al. Evaluation of three dosage-prediction methods for initial in-hospital stabilization of warfarin therapy. Clin Pharm. 1987;6:37.

87 Doyle DA et al. Evaluation of a Baysian regression program for predicting warfarin response. Ther Drug Monit. 1989;11:276.

88 Fennerty A et al. Flexible induction dose regimen for warfarin and prediction of maintenance dose. Br Med J. 1984;288:1268.

89 Cosh DG et al. Prospective evaluation of a flexible protocol for starting treatment with warfarin and predicting its maintenance dose. Aust N Z J Med. 1989;19:191.

90 Doecke CJ et al. Standardized initial warfarin treatment: evaluation of initial treatment response and maintenance dose prediction by randomized trial, and risk factors for an excessive warfarin response. Aust N Z J Med. 1991; 21:319.

91 Hyers TN et al. Antithrombotic therapy for venous thromboembolic disease. Chest. 1992;102(Suppl. 4):408.

92 Research Committee of the British Thoracic Society. Optimum duration of anticoagulation for deep vein thrombosis and pulmonary embolism. Lancet. 1992;40:873.

93 Landefield CS, Goldman L. Major bleeding in outpatients treated with warfarin: incidence and prediction of factors known at the start of outpatient therapy. Am J Med. 1989;87:144.

94 Shorr RI et al. Concurrent use of nonsteroidal anti-inflammatory drugs and oral anticoagulants places elderly per-

sons at high risk for hemorrhagic peptic ulcer disease. Arch Intern Med. 1993; 153:1665.

95 Redwood M et al. The association of age with dosage requirement for warfarin. Age Aging. 1991;20:217.

96 Yacobi A et al. Serum protein binding as a determinant of warfarin body clearance and anticoagulant effect. Clin Pharmacol Ther. 1976;19:552.

97 Shepard AMM et al. Age as a determinant of sensitivity to warfarin. Br J Clin Pharmacol. 1977;4:315.

98 Gurwitz JH et al. Aging and the anticoagulant response to warfarin therapy. Ann Intern Med. 1992;116:901.

99 Launbjerg J et al. Bleeding complications to oral anticoagulant therapy: multivariate analysis of 1010 treatment years in 551 outpatients. J Intern Med. 1991;229:351.

100 Gurwitz JH et al. Age-related risks of long term anticoagulant therapy. Arch Intern Med. 1988;148:1733.

101 Fihn ST et al. Risk factors for complications of chronic anticoagulation: a multicenter study. Ann Intern Med. 1993;118:511.

102 Cole MS et al. Coumarin necrosis: a review of the literature. Surgery. 1988; 103:271.

103 Comp PC et al. Warfarin-induced skin necrosis. Semin Thromb Hemost. 1990; 16:293.

104 Anderson DR et al. Warfarin-induced skin necrosis in two patients with protein S deficiency: successful reinstatement of warfarin therapy. Haemostasis. 1992;22:124.

105 Zauber NP et al. Successful warfarin anticoagulation despite protein C deficiency and a history of warfarin necrosis. Ann Intern Med. 1986;104:659.

106 Lebsack CS, Weibert RT. Purple toes syndrome. Postgrad Med J. 1982;71:81.

107 Hyman BT et al. Warfarin-related purple toes syndrome and cholesterol microembolization. Am J Med. 1982; 82:1233.

108 Kumar S et al. Poor compliance is a major factor in unstable outpatient control of anticoagulant therapy. Thromb Haemost. 1989;62:729.

109 Roddie AMS, Pollock A. Therapeutic control of anticoagulation: how important is patient education? Clin Lab Haematol. 1988;10:109.

110 Olson JA. Recommended dietary intake of vitamin K in humans. Am J Clin Nutr. 1987;45:687.

111 Parrish D. Determination of vitamin K content in food. CRC Crit Rev Food Sci Nutr. 1980;13:337.

112 Qureshi GD et al. Acquired warfarin resistance and weight reducing diet. Arch Intern Med. 1981;141:507.

113 Chow WH et al. Anticoagulation instability with life threatening complications after dietary modifications. Postgrad Med J. 1990;66:855.

114 Kempin SJ. Warfarin resistance caused by broccoli. N Engl J Med. 1983;308:1229.

115 Hansten PD, Horn JR. Anticoagulant Drug Interactions. In: Drug Interactions and Updates Quarterly. Vancouver: Applied Therapeutics, Inc.; 1993:304.

116 Waris E. Effect of ethyl alcohol on some coagulation factors in man during anticoagulant therapy. Ann Med Exp Biol. 1963;41:45.

117 O'Reilly RA. Lack of effect of mealtime wine on the hypoprothrombinemia of oral anticoagulants. Am J Med Sci. 1979;227:189.

118 O'Reilly RA. Lack of effect of fortified wine ingested during fasting and anticoagulant therapy. Arch Intern Med. 1981;141:458.

119 Engle JP. Anticoagulation: practice focus in an ambulatory clinic. J Pharm Practice. 1990;3:349.

120 Ellis RF et al. Evaluation of a pharmacy-managed warfarin monitoring service to coordinate inpatient and outpatient therapy. Am J Hosp Pharm. 1992;49:387.

121 Loeliger EA et al. The biological disappearance rate of prothrombin and factors VII, IX and X from plasma in hypothyroidism, hyperthyroidism and during fever. Thromb Diath Haemorrh. 1963;10:267.

122 Stephens MA et al. Hypothyroidism: effect on warfarin anticoagulation. South Med J. 1989;82:1585.

123 Anderson P, Godal HC. Predictable reduction in anticoagulant activity of warfarin by small amounts of vitamin K. Acta Med Scand. 1975;198:269.

124 Shetty HGM et al. Effective reversal of warfarin-induced excessive anticoagulation with low dose vitamin K1. Thromb Haemost. 1992;67:13.

125 Lefrere JJ, Girot R. Acute cardiovascular collapse during intravenous vitamin K1 injection. Thromb Haemost. 1987;58:790.

126 van Eijkeren M et al. Measured menstrual blood loss in women with a bleeding disorder or using oral anticoagulant therapy. Am J Obstet Gynecol. 1990;162:1261.

127 Semchyshyn S et al. Ovarian hemorrhage due to anticoagulants. Am J Obstet Gynecol. 1978;131:837.

128 Hall JAG et al. Maternal and fetal sequelae of anticoagulation during pregnancy. Am J Med. 1980;68:122.

129 Iturbe-Alessio I et al. Risks of anticoagulant therapy in pregnant women with artificial heart valves. N Engl J Med. 1986;315:1390.

130 Born D et al. Pregnancy in patients with prosthetic heart valves: the effects of anticoagulation on mother, fetus, and neonate. Am Heart J. 1992;124:413.

131 Ginsberg JS, Hirsh J. Use of antithrombotic agents during pregnancy. Chest. 1992;102(Suppl. 4):385.

132 Anderson DR et al. Subcutaneous heparin therapy during pregnancy: a need for concern at the time of delivery. Thromb Haemost. 1991;65:248.

133 Gillis S et al. Use of low molecular weight heparin for prophylaxis and treatment of thromboembolism in pregnancy. Int J Gynaecol Obstet. 1992;39: 297.

134 Aronow WS. Etiology and pathogenesis of thromboembolism. Herz. 1991; 16:395.

135 Aberg H. Atrial fibrillation: a study of atrial thrombosis and systemic embolism in necroscopy material. Acta Med Scand. 1969;185:373.

136 Dunn M et al. Antithrombotic therapy in atrial fibrillation. Chest. 1989;95 (Suppl. 2):118.

137 Bjerkelund CJ et al. The efficacy of anticoagulant therapy in preventing embolism related to DC electrical conversion of atrial fibrillation. Am J Cardiol. 1969;23:208.

138 Laupacis A et al. Antithrombotic therapy in atrial fibrillation. Chest. 1992; 102(Suppl. 4):426.

139 Manning WJ et al. Cardioversion from atrial fibrillation without prolonged anticoagulation with use of transesophageal echocardiography to exclude the presence of atrial thrombi. N Engl J Med. 1993;328:750.

140 Manning WJ et al. Pulsed Doppler evaluation of atrial mechanical function after electrical cardioversion of atrial fibrillation. J Am Coll Cardiol. 1989;13:617.

141 Mancini GBJ, Goldberger AL. Cardioversion of atrial fibrillation: consideration of embolization, anticoagulation, prophylactic pacemaker and long-term success. Am Heart J. 1982;104: 617.

142 Wolf PA et al. Epidemiologic assessment of chronic atrial fibrillation and risk of stroke: the Framingham Study. Neurology. 1978;28:973.

143 The Stroke Prevention in Atrial Fibrillation Investigators. Predictors of thromboembolism in atrial fibrillation: I. Clinical features of patients at risk. Ann Intern Med. 1992;116:1.

144 The Stroke Prevention in Atrial Fibrillation Investigators. Predictors of thromboembolism in atrial fibrillation: II. Echocardiographic features of patients at risk. Ann Intern Med. 1992; 116:6.

145 Rothbart RM et al. Risk of stroke and peripheral embolism in patients with paroxysmal and constant atrial fibrillation. Circulation. 1990;92(Suppl. III): 108.

146 Peterson P et al. Placebo-controlled, randomized trial of warfarin and aspirin for prevention of thromboembolic complications in chronic atrial fibrillation: the Copenhagen AFASAK Study. Lancet. 1989;1:175.

147 Stroke Prevention in Atrial Fibrillation Investigators. Stroke Prevention in Atrial Fibrillation Study: final results. Circulation. 1991;84:527.

148 The Boston Area Anticoagulation Trial for Atrial Fibrillation Investigators. The effect of low dose warfarin on the risk of stroke in patients with nonrheumatic atrial fibrillation. N Engl J Med. 1990;323:1505.

149 Connolly SJ et al. Canadian Atrial Fibrillation Anticoagulation (CAFA) Study. J Am Coll Cardiol. 1991;18: 349.

150 Ezekowitz MD et al. Warfarin in the prevention of stroke associated with nonrheumatic atrial fibrillation. N Engl J Med. 1992;327:1406.

151 EAFT (European Atrial Fibrillation Trial) Study Group. Secondary prevention in nonrheumatic atrial fibrillation after transient ischemic attack or minor stroke. Lancet. 1993;342:1255.

152 Kopecky SL et al. The natural history of lone atrial fibrillation: a population-based study over three decades. N Engl J Med. 1987;317:669.

153 Stein PD et al. Antithrombotic therapy in patients with mechanical and biologic prosthetic heart valves. Chest. 1992;102(Suppl. 4):445.

154 Kopf GS et al. Long term performance of the St. Jude Medical valve: low incidence of thromboembolism and hemorrhagic complications with modest doses of warfarin. Circulation. 1987; 76(Suppl. III):132.

155 Saour JN et al. Trial of different intensities of anticoagulation in patients with prosthetic heart valves. N Engl J Med. 1990;322:428.

156 Sullivan JM et al. Pharmacologic control of thromboembolic complications of cardiac valve replacement. N Engl J Med. 1971;284:1393.

157 Chesebro JH et al. Trial of combined warfarin plus dipyridamole vs. aspirin therapy in prosthetic heart valve replacement: danger of aspirin compared with dipyridamole. Am J Cardiol. 1983; 51:1537.

158 Altman R et al. Aspirin and prophylaxis of thromboembolic complications in patients with substitute heart valves. J Thorac Cardiovasc Surg. 1976;72: 127.

159 Gilbert JA and Scalzi RP. Disseminated intravascular coagulation. Emerg Med Clin North Am. 1994;11:465.

160 Turpie AGG et al. A comparison of aspirin with placebo in patients treated with warfarin after heart-valve replacement. N Engl J Med. 1993;329:524.

161 Cairns JA et al. Antithrombotic therapy in coronary artery disease. Chest. 1992;102(Suppl. 4):456.

162 Fuster V, Halperin JL. Left ventricular thrombi and cerebral embolism. N Engl J Med. 1989;320:392.

163 Visser CA et al. Left ventricular thrombus following acute myocardial infarction: a prospective serial echocardiographic study of 96 patients. Eur Heart J. 1983;4:333.

164 Karen A et al. Natural history of left ventricular thrombi; their appearance and resolution in the posthospitalization period following acute myocardial infarction. J Am Coll Cardiol. 1990;15: 790.

165 Asinger RW et al. Incidence of left-ventricular thrombosis after acute myocardial infarction: serial evaluation by two-dimensional echocardiography. N Engl J Med. 1981;305:297.

166 Weinreich DJ et al. Left ventricular mural thrombi complicating acute myocardial infarction: long term follow-up with serial echocardiography. Ann Intern Med. 1984;100:789.

167 Johannson KA et al. Risk factors for embolization in patients with left ventricular thrombi and acute myocardial infarction. Br Heart J. 1988;60:104.

168 Meltzer RS et al. Intracardiac thrombi and systemic embolization. Ann Intern Med. 1986;104:689.

169 Keating EC et al. Mural thrombi in myocardial infarctions: prospective evaluation by two-dimensional echocardiography. Am J Med. 1983;74:989.

170 Maze SS et al. Flow characteristics in the dilated left ventricle with thrombus: qualitative and quantitative Doppler analysis. J Am Coll Cardiol. 1989;13: 873.

171 Katz SD et al. Low incidence of stroke in ambulatory patients with heart failure: a prospective study. Am Heart J. 1993;126:141.

172 Falk RH et al. Ventricular thrombi and thromboembolism in dilated cardiomyopathy: a prospective follow-up study. Am Heart J. 1992;123:136.

173 **Kyrle PA et al.** Prevention of arterial and pulmonary embolism by oral anticoagulants in patients with dilated cardiomyopathy. Thromb Haemost. 1985; 54:521.

174 **Fuster V et al.** The natural history of idiopathic dilated cardiomyopathy. Am J Cardiol. 1981;47:52.

175 **Dunkman WB et al.** Incidence of thromboembolic events in congestive heart failure. Circulation. 1993;87 (Suppl. VI):94.

176 **Hansten PD, Horn JR.** Anticoagulant Drug Interactions. In: Drug Interactions and Updates. Vancouver: Applied Therapeutics, Inc.; 1993:285.

177 **O'Reilly RA et al.** Racemic warfarin and trimethoprim sulfamethoxazole interaction in humans. Ann Intern Med. 1979;91:34.

178 **O'Reilly RA.** Stereoselective interaction of TMP-SMX with the separated enantiomorphs of racemic warfarin in man. N Engl J Med. 1980;302:33.

179 **O'Reilly RA et al.** Interaction of amiodarone with racemic warfarin and its separated enantiomorphs in humans. Clin Pharmacol Ther. 1987;42:290.

180 **Martinowitz U et al.** Interaction between warfarin sodium and amiodarone. N Engl J Med. 1981;304:671.

181 **Hamer A et al.** The potentiation of warfarin anticoagulation by amiodarone. Circulation. 1982;65:1025.

182 **Kerin NZ et al.** The incidence, magnitude and time course of the amiodarone-warfarin interaction. Arch Intern Med. 1988;148:1779.

183 **Aggeler PM et al.** Potentiation of anticoagulant effect of warfarin by phenylbutazone. N Engl J Med. 1967;276: 496.

184 **Schary WL et al.** Warfarin-phenylbutazone interactions in man. A longterm multiple dose study. Res Commun Chem Pathol Pharmacol. 1975;10:663.

185 **Alving BM et al.** Hereditary warfarin resistance. Arch Intern Med. 1985;145: 499.

186 **Hansten PD, Horn JR.** Principles of oral anticoagulant drug interactions. In: Drug Interactions & Updates Quarterly. Vancouver: Applied Therapeutics, Inc.; 1993;13:57.

187 **MacKichan JJ.** Pharmacokinetic consequences of drug displacement from blood and tissue proteins. Clin Pharmacokinet. 1984;9(Suppl. 1):32.

188 **Muller-Berghaus G.** Pathophysiologic and biochemical events in disseminated intravascular coagulation. Dysregulation of procoagulant and anticoagulant pathways. Semin Thromb Hemost. 1989;15:58.

189 **Bick RL.** Disseminated intravascular coagulation and related syndromes. Semin Thromb Hemost. 1988;14:299.

190 **Baker WF.** Clinical aspects of disseminated intravascular coagulation. Semin Thromb Hemost. 1989;15:1.

191 **Rubin RN, Colman RW.** Disseminated intravascular coagulation. Approach to treatment. Drugs. 1992;44: 963.

192 **Gilbert JA, Scalzi RP.** Disseminated intravascular coagulation. Emerg Med Clin North Am. 1994;11:465.

Ischemic Heart Disease: Anginal Syndromes

Cynthia L Raehl
Paul E Nolan

Definitions 13-1
Epidemiology 13-2
Coronary Anatomy (See Figure 13.1) 13-2
Pathophysiology 13-2
　Myocardial oxygen supply and demand
　　(See Figure 13.2) 13-3
　Dynamic obstruction (See Figure 13.3) 13-3
　Fixed obstruction (Also see Figure 13.4) 13-3
　Platelet aggregation and the formation
　　of thrombi 13-3
　Treatment Overview 13-4
Chronic Stable Exertional Angina 13-4
　Signs and Symptoms (See Table 13.1) 13-4
　Risk Factors 13-5
　Diagnostic Procedures 13-5
　　Exercise tolerance test 13-5
　　Myocardial imaging 13-6
　　Cardiac catheterization 13-6
　Prognosis 13-6
　Overview of Medical Management 13-6
Nitrates 13-6
　Mechanism of Action 13-7
　Short-Acting Preparations 13-7
　　Sublingual (SL) nitroglycerin (NTG) 13-7
　　　Dosing (See Table 13.2) 13-7
　　　Patient instructions 13-7
　　Nitroglycerin lingual spray 13-7
　　Adverse effects 13-7
　Long-Acting Nitrates 13-8
　　Nitrate tolerance 13-8
　　　Mechanism of action 13-9
　　　Intermittent application of transdermal NTG 13-9
　　Isosorbide dinitrate (ISDN) 13-9
　　Nitrate pharmacodynamics 13-9
　　Transdermal ointment 13-10
　　Transdermal patches (See Table 13.3) 13-10
　　Transmucosal NTG 13-11
　　Other organic nitrates 13-11
β-Adrenergic Blockers 13-11
　Mechanism of Action 13-11
　Judging Therapeutic Endpoint 13-12
　Dosing Frequency 13-12
　Beta Blocker Cardioselectivity 13-12
　　Contraindications 13-12

Adverse effects 13-12
Beta Blockers with Intrinsic Sympathomimetic
　Activity (ISA) 13-12
Central Nervous System (CNS) Side Effects 13-13
Beta Blockers in Acute Renal Failure 13-13
Abrupt Withdrawal 13-13
Withdrawal before Coronary Artery Surgery 13-13
Calcium Channel Blockers 13-13
　Classification (Also see Table 13.4) 13-13
　Pharmacology 13-14
　Indications for Use 13-14
　Nifedipine 13-15
　　Adverse effects (See Table 13.6) 13-15
　Contraindications (Also see Table 13.7) 13-15
　Diltiazem 13-16
　　Adverse effects 13-16
　Verapamil 13-16
　　Adverse effects 13-16
　　Risk/benefit assessment 13-16
　　Interaction with digoxin 13-16
　Second-Generation Dihydropyridines 13-17
　Pharmacokinetics 13-17
　Sustained-Release (SR) Calcium Channel Blockers 13-17
Combination Therapy 13-18
Bepridil 13-18
Antiplatelet Therapy 13-18
　Aspirin 13-18
Variant Angina (Coronary Artery Spasm) 13-19
　Clinical Presentation 13-19
　Ergonovine Stimulation Test 13-20
　Therapy 13-20
Microvascular Ischemia (Syndrome X) 13-20
Silent Myocardial Ischemia 13-20
　Definition 13-20
　Prognosis 13-21
　Diagnosis 13-21
　Management 13-21
**Unstable Angina and Alternatives to Medical
　Therapy** 13-21
　Management 13-21
　Percutaneous Transluminal Angioplasty (PCTA) 13-22
　Coronary Artery Bypass Graft (CABG) Surgery 13-22

Angina pectoris is a symptom of myocardial ischemia that usually is secondary to atherosclerosis of the coronary arteries [coronary heart disease (CHD)]. Other signs of coronary heart disease include myocardial infarction (MI), arrhythmias, congestive heart failure (CHF), and sudden cardiac death. Because angina is a marker for underlying heart disease, its management is of great importance.

Definitions

Angina pectoris can be defined as "a sense of discomfort arising in the myocardium as a result of myocardial ischemia in the absence of infarction."[1] Although angina usually implies severe chest pain or discomfort, its presentation is variable. At one extreme, angina may occur predictably with strenuous exercise; at the other, angina may develop unexpectedly with little or no exertion.

Patients who have a reproducible pattern of angina that is associated with a certain level of physical activity have *chronic stable angina* or exertional angina.[2] In contrast, patients with *unstable angina* are experiencing new angina or a change in their angina intensity, frequency, or duration. Both chronic stable angina and unstable angina often reflect underlying atherosclerotic narrowing of coronary arteries. Classic Prinzmetal's *variant angina*, or vasospastic angina, occurs in patients without coronary heart disease and is due to a spasm of the coronary artery that decreases myocardial blood flow.[3] When coronary vasospasm occurs at the site of a fixed atherosclerotic plaque, *mixed angina* can result.[2]

Silent myocardial ischemia, which is a transient change in myocardial perfusion, function, or electrical activity, can be detected on an electrocardiogram (ECG) in most angina patients.[4] The patient, however, does not experience chest pain or other signs of angina [e.g., jaw pain, shortness of breath (SOB)] during these episodes. Silent myocardial ischemia also can occur in patients with no angina history (see Chapter 14: Myocardial Infarction).

Epidemiology

Coronary heart disease is the leading cause of death, disease, disability, and socioeconomic loss in the U.S., and angina is the first clinical sign of this problem in about one-third of men and two-thirds of women.[5,6] The incidence of angina is difficult to assess because it often is unrecognized by patients and physicians. In one European study of factory workers aged 40 to 59 years, 4% described symptoms of chronic stable angina.[7]

The overall mortality rate from anginal syndromes is about 4%; however, mortality rates vary according to the patient's age, gender, cardiovascular risk profile, myocardial contractility, coronary anatomy, and the patient's specific anginal syndrome. The annual mortality rate increases as the number of coronary vessels with high grade atherosclerotic lesions increases. Patients with left main coronary artery disease (CAD) have an increased mortality rate compared to patients without left main coronary disease. Similarly, patients with diminished left ventricular function [ejection fraction (EF) <50%] have higher mortality rates compared to patients without impaired left ventricular function.

Coronary Anatomy

Figure 13.1 illustrates the normal distribution of the major coronary arteries, although variation among individuals is common.[8] The anterior and lateral portions of the left ventricle receive blood flow from the left coronary artery, usually the largest and shortest of all coronary arteries. From its main stem the left coronary artery divides into its two major branches, the left anterior descending coronary artery (LAD) and the circumflex. The LAD further subdivides into the first diagonal, the first septal, the right ventricular, the minor septals, the second diagonal, and the apical branches.[9] Similarly, the circumflex also may subdivide into four or five branches, the largest branch being the obtuse marginal.

The right coronary artery (RCA) usually supplies blood flow to most of the right ventricle as well as the posterior part of the left ventricle. Like the LAD, the right coronary branches into major vessels which supply blood flow to specific areas of the heart. In order of origin, the right coronary artery divides into the: conus branch, sinus node branch, right ventricular branches, atrial branch, acute marginal branch, atrioventricular (AV) node branch, posterior descending, left ventricular, and left atrial branches.[9] Because of wide variation in coronary artery distribution and the need to confirm the precise location of atherosclerotic plaques, most patients with angina will undergo coronary arteriography. There is no doubt that patients with severe left main coronary artery disease

Fig 13.1 Coronary Artery Distribution and Major Branches Reproduced with permission from reference 8.

are at higher risk since obstruction of this large coronary artery jeopardizes almost the entire left ventricle. Similarly, patients with three-vessel coronary artery disease are at higher risk than patients with single-vessel disease.

Pathophysiology

The myocardium must constantly generate a constrictive force and, unlike other muscle tissues, only can function in the presence of oxygen. Without oxygen, myocardial cells will cease energy production; and if widespread oxygen deprivation exists, the heart will deteriorate and stop pumping.

Atherosclerotic plaques that obstruct coronary blood flow, and therefore oxygen delivery, may occur as isolated lesions or throughout the coronary vasculature.[10] If the plaque size obscures less than 50% of the diameter of the vessel, coronary blood flow during exertion usually is sufficient and the patient is pain-free. In patients with chronic stable angina, most coronary artery stenoses are in the range of ≥70%; however, obstruction of greater than 50% may induce myocardial ischemia.[11] A linear decrease in coronary blood flow occurs as the plaque occupies more of the arterial lumen until high grade (≥80%) obstruction develops. At this point, the decrease in blood flow is out of proportion to plaque size. Contributing factors to impaired blood flow with high grade lesions include increased vasomotor tone, vasospasm, and thrombotic occlusion. Functionally, there is no flow with lesions of ≥95%. Atherosclerosis (coronary artery disease) generally is a progressive disease; however, regression has been demonstrated in a small number of patients.[12,13] In particular, progression may be slowed or regression induced following aggressive treatment with cholesterol-lowering drugs.[13]

Collateral blood vessels, side branches of a coronary artery which join one of the three principal arteries or connect two points along the same artery, may offer protection against myocardial ischemia.[9] The distribution and extent of the vessels is variable. They usually are very small and have no function in the normal heart;[11] however, if blood flow is obstructed the collateral vessels assume more importance and may restore some, but not all, myocardial blood flow. Unfortunately, when myocardial oxygen demand is increased excessively, collateral blood flow usually is insufficient and angina or other myocardial ischemia syndromes develop.

Myocardial Oxygen Supply and Demand. Traditionally, the pathogenesis of angina has been attributed to an imbalance of myocardial oxygen supply and demand.[14] This imbalance results from coronary artery stenosis which prevents a sufficient increase in myocardial oxygen supply to match increased demand. While this is a common mechanism of angina, it is only one of three interrelated pathophysiologic processes. Abnormalities of coronary vascular tone and platelet aggregation or thrombus formation also contribute to angina development.[14]

The *oxygen demand* of the heart is determined by its workload. The major determinants of myocardial oxygen consumption (MVO_2) include heart rate, contractility, and systolic wall force (intramyocardial wall tension) (see Figure 13.2).[15] The relative contribution of each component is difficult to distinguish, but collectively, they represent the oxygen demand placed upon the heart.[15] *Systolic wall force* or tension within the heart wall is affected primarily by changes in ventricular chamber pressures and volume. It represents the force the heart is required to develop and sustain during its contraction. Both enlargement of the ventricle (i.e., increase in volume of the chamber) or increased pressure within the ventricle will increase the systolic wall force. Increases in *contractility* and the *heart rate* will raise oxygen demand. Pharmacologic control of angina is, therefore, directed toward decreasing the myocardial oxygen demand by decreasing heart rate, myocardial contractility, or ventricular volume and pressures. Of the four factors that affect oxygen supply to the heart (see Figure 13.2), coronary blood flow and oxygen extraction are most important. Oxygen extraction by heart cells is high (about 65% to 75%) even in a resting state.[15] When extra demand is placed upon the heart, myocardial oxygen extraction increases slightly and plateaus at about 80%. The mechanisms by which oxygen extraction is increased during ischemia are not completely understood, although a release of coronary vasodilators may occur. Since the increase in oxygen extraction is minor even when the heart is heavily stressed, excessive oxygen demands must be met by increases in coronary blood flow. If coronary blood flow is limited by atherosclerotic plaques or vasospasm, myocardial ischemia and angina develop. The oxygen content of arterial blood also is important; therefore, strict attention must be paid to the hematocrit (Hct), hemoglobin (Hgb), and arterial blood gases (ABGs).

Recent evidence contradicts the traditional hypothesis that the only cause of angina is an excessive increase in oxygen demand

Dynamic Coronary Obstruction

Fig 13.3 Variation in Coronary Obstruction Due to Underlying Vasoconstrictor Tone of the Coronary Vessel Reproduced with permission from reference 18.

relative to supply in the presence of an atherosclerotic lesion.[12] About 10% of patients with angina do not have significant atherosclerosis of their coronary arteries,[12] and the severity of angina symptoms does not always correlate with the extent of coronary artery obstruction. A patient's symptoms may vary widely on a daily basis in the absence of disease progression, and angina at rest often occurs with no detectable increase in heart rate, myocardial contractility, or change in systolic wall tension.

Dynamic Obstruction. Both normal and diseased coronary arteries undergo coronary vasospasm, with vasospasm frequently superimposed on an atherosclerotic obstruction.[16,17] In dynamic obstruction (see Figure 13.3), the degree of coronary stenosis changes due to variations in smooth muscle tone.[11,18,19] The broad concept of coronary spasm ranges from frank spasm of Prinzmetal's variant angina, to subtle vasoconstriction in a diseased vessel, to spasm in the microcoronary circulation. The artery, in each case, is still responsive to vasodilating agents such as the nitrates.[18] Dynamic obstruction can be differentiated from fixed obstruction angiographically; in the latter, the decrease in lumen size is constant and due to anatomic blockage by the plaque. Dynamic obstruction due to increased coronary vasomotor tone probably is involved in most types of myocardial ischemia, including chronic stable exertional angina, variant angina, microvascular angina, and unstable angina.

Fixed Obstruction. The term "hardening of the arteries" implies that the plaques are rigid and immobile. Although some plaques are indeed fixed and calcified, stenosis morphology actually is variable. As shown in Figure 13.4, about three-fourths of plaques are eccentric, leaving a portion of the arterial wall free and able to respond to local vasodilators, whereas concentric or fixed plaques cover the entire circumference of the arterial wall.[20] Arteries with concentric plaques will not respond to vasodilators because no portion of the wall is free of plaque formation.

Platelet aggregation and the formation of thrombi are important pathophysiologic mechanisms in virtually all presentations of

O₂ Supply

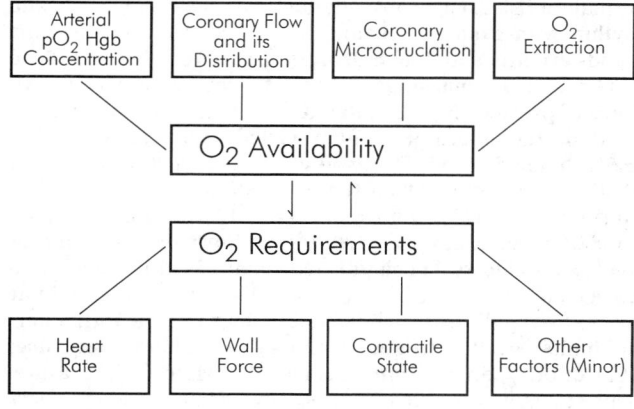

O₂ Demand

Fig 13.2 Regulation of Oxygen Supply and Demand in Heart Cells Hgb = Hemoglobin. Reproduced with permission reference 15.

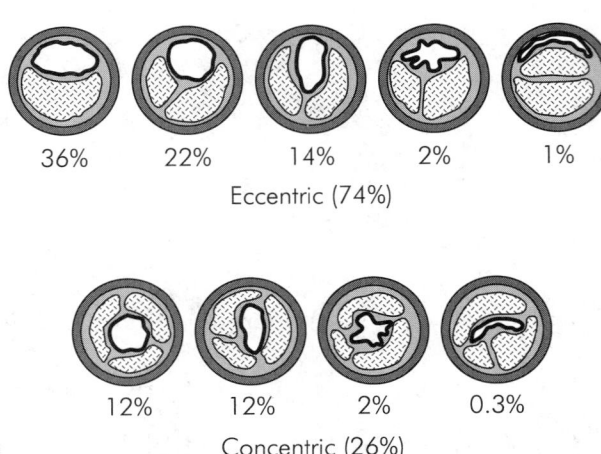

36%   22%   14%   2%   1%

Eccentric (74%)

12%   12%   2%   0.3%

Concentric (26%)

Fig 13.4 Schematic Drawing of the Plaque Variation Found in Atherosclerotic Coronary Arteries About three-fourths of lesions are eccentric and, therefore, susceptible to changes in coronary vasomotor tone. Reproduced with permission from reference 20.

ischemic heart disease including the various anginal syndromes. In response to the arterial vessel wall injury (such as an atherosclerotic lesion), platelets aggregate and release granular contents.[16,21] This causes further platelet aggregation, vasoconstriction (dynamic obstruction), and, in many cases, thrombus formation. While coronary atherosclerosis often is the underlying disease for most patients with anginal syndromes, thrombotic factors frequently play a key role in the pathogenesis of myocardial ischemia. Both blood flow turbulence and stasis can cause intermittent platelet aggregation or intermittent coronary artery thrombosis. Thus, platelet-active agents are used in the therapy of chronic stable angina; unstable angina; primary prevention of myocardial infarction; secondary prevention of myocardial ischemia; treatment of acute myocardial infarction; and before, during, and after coronary angioplasty or coronary artery bypass grafting.

Treatment Overview

The medical management of anginal syndromes is always individualized for each patient. All patients should receive extensive patient education and counseling to help them reduce the risks of coronary heart disease. Smoking cessation is absolutely essential. Dietary and drug therapy of dyslipidemias (see Chapter 9: Dyslipidemias), with attention to secondary prevention of heart disease, is a universal consideration. If present, diabetes mellitus and hypertension should be treated and any drug therapy for angina should not aggravate these commonly observed concomitant diseases. Physical conditioning is advisable; however, patients will require the input of health care providers in creating a practical and safe exercise program.

Drug therapy regimens for patients with angina syndromes must be individualized. Any one of four classes of drugs may be used, either alone or in various combinations: nitrates, beta blockers, calcium channel blockers, and aspirin. There are no simple guidelines which describe a "standard" approach to starting anti-anginals. However, most patients should have a prescription for a short-acting nitrate [either sublingual nitroglycerin (NTG) tablets or lingual spray] to relieve or prevent an acute anginal episode. Most patients also will receive prophylactic therapy to prevent recurrent anginal syndromes using a long-acting nitrate, a beta blocker, or a calcium channel blocker. The selection of the specific drug is based upon the presence of concomitant diseases and expected adverse reaction profiles. For example, a patient with both angina and mod-

erately severe heart failure may benefit from a long-acting nitrate which will relieve the congestion symptoms of heart failure and also prevent angina. The same patient may have worsening heart failure if a beta blocker is used to prevent angina.

Anginal episodes sometimes can be prevented with single drug therapy (a long-acting nitrate, a beta blocker, or a calcium channel blocker), although many patients require double or triple drug therapy. Combination drug therapy balances the patient's symptoms with the combined adverse reaction profiles of the drugs. Patients with less severe anginal syndromes may have complete prevention of angina attacks. However, patients with more severe disease will continue to have angina attacks; so the goal of drug therapy is to decrease the frequency and intensity of attacks. Aspirin therapy should be considered for all patients with coronary heart disease to slow platelet aggregation formation; however, patients with gastrointestinal (GI) bleeding, allergy, or dyspepsia may be at risk from aspirin therapy.

Chronic Stable Exertional Angina
Signs and Symptoms

1. J.P., a 62-year-old dairy farmer, is hospitalized for evaluation of chest pain. About 3 weeks before admission, he noted substernal chest pain brought on by lifting heavy objects or walking uphill. He described a crushing or vise-like pain that never occurred at rest and was not associated with meals, emotional stress, or a particular time of day. When J.P. stopped working, the pain subsided in about 5 minutes.

J.P.'s brother died of a heart attack at age 57; his father, who is alive at age 86, has survived 1 heart attack and 1 stroke. His family history is negative for diabetes mellitus. J.P. is 5'10" tall and weighs 235 pounds; he drinks 2 or 3 beers/day and does not smoke or chew tobacco.

J.P.'s other medical problems include a 10-year history of hypertension and traumatic amputation of the right hand. Until 3 weeks ago, J.P. could perform all his farm chores without difficulty, including heavy labor. He follows a no-added-salt diet, but does consume whole milk daily and about 6 eggs/week.

J.P.'s medication history reveals the following: verapamil sustained-release (SR) (Verelan) 240 mg QD and hydrochlorothiazide (HydroDIURIL) 25 mg QD. He rarely uses over-the-counter medications. Allergies include sulfa drugs.

Upon admission to the cardiac ward, J.P. appears his stated age and is in no apparent distress. Resting vital signs include: supine blood pressure (BP) 164/98 mm Hg (Normal: 120/80), regular pulse 73 beats/min (Normal: 65–75), and respiratory rate 12 breaths/min (Normal: 8–14). There is no peripheral edema or neck vein distention and lung auscultation is within normal limits. Cardiac auscultation reveals a regular rate and rhythm with a normal S_1 and S_2; no third or fourth heart sounds are heard and no murmurs are appreciated. A 12-lead ECG reveals normal sinus rhythm at a rate of 75 without evidence of previous MI. All intervals are within normal limits.

Admitting laboratory values include the following: Hct 43.5% (Normal: 45–50); white blood cell (WBC) count 5000/mm³ (Normal: 5000–10,000); sodium (Na) 140 mEq/L (Normal: 136–144); potassium (K) 4.7 mEq/L (Normal: 3.5–5.3); magnesium (Mg) 1.9 mEq/L (Normal: 1.7–2.7); random blood glucose 111 mg/dL (Normal: 65–110); blood urea nitrogen (BUN) 27 mg/dL (Normal: 10–20); serum creatinine (SrCr) 1.4 mg/dL (Normal: 0.5–1.2). Chest x-ray is within normal limits. What signs and symptoms of angina pectoris does J.P. exhibit? Can his symptoms be categorized on a measurement scale? [SI units: Hct 0.435 (Normal: 0.45–0.5); WBC count 5 × 10⁹/L (Normal: 5–10 × 10⁹/L); Na 140 mmol/L (Normal: 136–144); K 4.7 mmol/L (Normal: 3.5–5.3); Mg 0.95 mmol/L (Normal: 0.85–1.35); random blood glucose 6.16 mmol/L (Normal: 3.6–6.1), BUN 9.6 mmol/L of urea (Normal: 3.57–7.14); SrCr 124 1mol/L (Normal: 44.2–106)]

J.P.'s description of his chest pain includes several common characteristics of angina pectoris (see Table 13.1).[22] The retrosternal location is typical although some patients may describe pain radiating down the left arm or pain that is referred to the shoulder area or jaw. J.P.'s pain is crushing or vise-like in quality which also is common, although a fullness in the throat or jaw may occur simultaneously or in lieu of chest pain. Many patients will complain of shortness of breath. J.P.'s symptoms are related to exercise and exertion indicating that these precipitating factors play a key role. Most episodes of exertional angina will be relieved with rest and the duration will be several minutes. Because J.P. has never sought medical attention for his chest pain, the response to nitroglycerin cannot be assessed.

Attempts to categorize J.P.'s anginal symptoms on an objective measurement scale (e.g., Canadian Cardiovascular Society Grading Scale) are potentially misleading.[23] For example, a sedentary 65-year-old patient's class II symptoms may be tolerable, while the same symptoms will significantly disable an active 50-year-old patient. Secondly, the Canadian Scale does not consider the clinical instability of angina, such as new onset of chest pain at rest.

2. Assess J.P.'s physical examination. What signs and symptoms are relevant to the angina?

No physical findings are pathognomonic for angina pectoris, although elevated heart rate and blood pressure may be observed

Table 13.1	Characteristics of Angina Pectoris[a,b]

Quality
Sensation of pressure or heavy weight on the chest, alone or with pain
Burning sensation
Feeling of tightness
SOB with feeling of constriction about the larynx or upper trachea
Visceral quality (deep, heavy, squeezing, aching)
Gradual ↑ in intensity followed by gradual fading away (distinguish from esophageal spasm)

Location
Over the sternum or very near to it
Anywhere between epigastrium and pharynx
Occasionally limited to left shoulder and left arm
Rarely limited to right arm
Limited to lower jaw
Lower cervical or upper thoracic spine
Left inter- or suprascapular area

Duration
0.5–30 min

Precipitating Factors
Relationship to exercise
Effort which involves use of arms above the head
Cold environment
Walking against the wind
Walking after a large meal
Emotional factors involved with physical evidence
Fright, anger
Coitus

Nitroglycerin Relief
Relief of pain occurring within 45 sec–5 min of taking nitroglycerin

Radiation
Medial aspect of left arm
Left shoulder
Jaw
Occasionally, right arm

[a] Adapted from reference 22.
[b] SOB = Shortness of breath.

during an acute anginal episode. J.P.'s physical examination is typical for a man of his age with angina.[24] He is obese and hypertensive, but his cardiac examination is normal. The presence of murmurs would have required further work-up, and the absence of a third heart sound suggests that the left ventricle may be functioning normally. (See Chapter 15: Congestive Heart Failure for a description of third heart sounds.) J.P. does not have a fourth heart sound present which indicates a low probability for coronary heart disease or a complication of systemic hypertension. His chest x-ray, which is normal, was performed to detect other complications of myocardial ischemia such as an enlarged heart or congestive failure, although a physical examination should include examination for possible peripheral vascular disease or abdominal aortic aneurysm. J.P.'s eyes should have been examined for retinal arteriolar hypertensive changes. Nicotine stains on his fingers or a tobacco odor on his breath would signal a need to reappraise his smoking history. The presence of xanthomas would suggest severe hypercholesterolemia.

Risk Factors

3. What independent risk factors for CAD are present in J.P.? Which of these may be altered?

J.P. has several risk factors for coronary artery disease which he cannot alter, including middle age, male sex, and a strong family history of CAD. In a large scale, 26-year follow-up study, men aged 35 to 84 had twice the cardiovascular morbidity and mortality of women.[25] Men experiencing angina are more likely to have fatal coronary vascular events than women. J.P.'s family history for heart attack is very worrisome. In men, but not women, a positive family history of heart attack is independently predictive of death from all causes and from cardiovascular and ischemic heart disease.[26] Risk factors that can be altered include hypertension, obesity, hypercholesterolemia, smoking, and stress. J.P.'s hypertension should be controlled and a serum cholesterol test performed.[27,28] A lipid profile that includes determinations of low density lipoprotein (LDL), high density lipoprotein (HDL), and triglycerides (TG) is indicated for J.P. Dietary modification and weight reduction for J.P. are mandatory.[29] Fortunately, J.P. does not have a family history of diabetes[30] or smoke cigarettes, both of which would contribute greatly to his risk profile.[31,32] Some evidence suggests J.P.'s active lifestyle may influence his prognosis favorably.[28,33] Personality analysis may reveal Type A behavior which could be altered favorably.[34]

Diagnostic Procedures

4. Even though J.P.'s medical history and family history support the diagnosis of chronic stable angina, are there other objective diagnostic procedures which could help to confirm CHD and angina?

If J.P. should develop angina while hospitalized, a 12-lead ECG should be obtained during the anginal episode. ECG changes consistent with myocardial ischemia include nonspecific ST-T changes, T-wave inversion, or ST-segment depression; an ST-segment depression of ≥ 2 mm is considered clinically significant. A variety of arrhythmias also may be observed, but they are nonspecific. A normal ECG during chest pain would suggest a noncardiac cause for J.P.'s symptoms (e.g., esophagitis).[22]

Exercise Tolerance Test

An exercise tolerance test or treadmill test also could be performed. Under controlled circumstances, J.P. would exercise to a preset level; a positive test would be indicated by the development of angina, electrocardiographic signs of ischemia, arrhythmias, or abnormal heart rate, and blood pressure response. The product of the heart rate and systolic blood pressure (i.e., the rate-pressure or double product) correlates well with myocardial oxygen demand. The rate-pressure product normally rises progressively during exercise with the peak value best describing the cardiovascular response to stress. Normal persons usually achieve a peak rate-pressure product of 20 to 35 mm Hg $\times$ beats/minute $\times 10^{-3}$; however, patients with coronary artery disease may only achieve a rate-pressure product of 25 mm Hg $\times$ beats/minute $\times 10^{-3}$. Often, stable angina patients experience chest pain at a consistent rate-pressure product.[35]

Abnormal responses of either blood pressure or heart rate may signal coronary artery disease. A normal blood pressure response to exercise is a gradual rise in systolic pressure with the diastolic pressure remaining unchanged. A rise or fall of diastolic pressure greater than 10 mm Hg is considered abnormal. Some patients exhibit an exaggerated hypertensive response to exercise with a significant rise of both systolic and diastolic pressure. These patients generally benefit from more aggressive antihypertensive regimens. A fall in systemic blood pressure with exercise is especially ominous since this indicates that the cardiac output cannot increase enough to overcome the vasodilation in the skeletal muscle vascular bed.

During exercise, the heart rate increases steadily until it reaches a plateau rate.[35] The maximal heart rate achieved is dependent upon age, drug therapy, and training status. Some patients may exhibit an abnormal blocking of heart rate, often as the result of drugs such as propranolol (Inderal). Other patients may achieve a very high heart rate, especially if they are in poor condition or have a poorly contracting heart. In patients with a history such as J.P.'s, the exercise tolerance test helps to confirm the presence of and evaluate the severity of coronary heart disease. The adequacy of J.P.'s antihypertensive regimen also will be assessed during the stress test.

Myocardial Imaging

Stress thallium-201 myocardial perfusion imaging provides a dynamic picture of the heart. The radionuclide is injected at peak exercise, while either walking or bicycling, and an image is obtained within several minutes. A defect in myocardial uptake of the thallium indicates an area of ischemia or possible infarction. Exercise radionuclide angiography permits assessment of both ejection fraction and regional wall motion. Both radionuclide techniques are noninvasive and extremely useful in assessing a patient's prognosis once the diagnosis of coronary heart disease is established.[36] Infarct avid scintigraphy, using technetium 99m stannous pyrophosphate, can be performed within 48 to 72 hours after a suspected MI. Newer cardiac imaging techniques include cine-computed tomography (cine-CT), magnetic resonance imaging (MRI), and positron emission tomography (PET). These newer techniques may serve as suitable alternatives to cardiac catheterization.

Cardiac Catheterization

5. Should J.P. undergo cardiac catheterization? If so, how will the results of this invasive procedure influence future therapy?

The definitive diagnosis of CHD can be made only by coronary catheterization and subsequent angiography and arteriography.[37] By injecting a dye into J.P.'s coronary arteries, the cardiologist can determine the location and extent of atherosclerosis. Approximately 75% of patients with chronic stable angina such as J.P., are found to have one-, two-, or three-vessel disease by this procedure (approximately equally divided).[24] About 5% to 10% of patients have obstruction of the left anterior descending coronary artery which is handled as a medical emergency.

Prognosis

6. J.P. is found to have two-vessel CAD with lesions of 55% and 60%; the left anterior descending coronary artery is not involved. What is his prognosis?

Fortunately, J.P.'s history and physical examination suggest he does not have congestive heart failure since poor left ventricular function would be an ominous concurrent finding.[38] He also is fortunate not to have three-vessel disease or blockage of the left anterior descending artery.[39] Overall, he probably will do well with medical therapy. His life expectancy will depend upon progression of the disease and development of other complications of coronary heart disease such as heart failure, myocardial infarction, or sudden cardiac death. Medical therapy is the preferred treatment strategy for low-risk patients with chronic stable angina. Usual indications for surgical therapy include left main coronary artery disease, three-vessel disease (especially if left ventricular function is impaired), or if medical therapy is ineffective.

Overview of Medical Management

7. After consulting with a cardiac surgeon, J.P.'s cardiologist elects to control his angina medically. What are the therapeutic goals of his therapy and how can they be achieved?

The major pharmacotherapeutic goals for treating this and all patients with angina include relief of symptoms, reduction of myocardial ischemia during anginal attacks, reduction of silent ischemia, improvement in hemodynamic profile and muscle metabolism, prevention of atherosclerotic progression, and extension of life. As with any chronic disease, education of the patient and his family are important objectives with the ultimate goal of improved understanding of his disease and therapy and an improved quality of life. Every effort should be made to reverse J.P.'s modifiable risk factors which include obesity, hypertension, and a possible lipid disorder. He also could receive one or more of the following: organic nitrates, calcium channel blockers, β-adrenergic blockers, or antiplatelet drugs.[40] J.P. probably will continue verapamil therapy as it will be helpful in treating both his hypertension and angina. Even though his prescribed drug, Verelan, is only approved for hypertension, it will have added benefit in preventing angina. Reduction of precipitating factors may be difficult given J.P.'s work; however, he should be counseled to avoid sudden bursts of physical activity. Moderate exercise should be encouraged, such as a walking program. J.P.'s family members should be screened for smoking because passive (secondhand) smoke can aggravate angina.

Nitrates

Nitrates often are a cornerstone therapy for all anginal syndromes. They are effective in treating all forms of angina because they decrease venous return to the heart and therefore decrease workload on the heart. Nitrates also promote coronary vasodilation even in the presence of atherosclerosis. Nitrates generally are well tolerated and reasonably priced. However, because nitrates must be scheduled to provide a nitrate-free interval of 10 to 12 hours, they usually are used in combination with beta blockers or calcium channel blockers (e.g., verapamil, diltiazem). Nitrate monotherapy is reserved for patients with less severe angina syndromes. The individual nitrate products differ primarily in their onset and duration of action.

Mechanism of Action

8. During the first hospital day, J.P. rapidly walks up 3 flights of stairs and develops chest pain. After quickly performing a 12-lead ECG, the physician instructs J.P. to place a sublingual (SL) NTG tablet (Nitrostat) 0.4 mg under his tongue. This relieves the pain. J.P.'s physician elects to continue verapamil and add both short- and long-acting nitrates. Why should J.P. continue his verapamil therapy? What is the mechanism by which NTG relieves angina?

The mechanism of action of NTG and the other nitrate esters is not completely understood even though they have been used for over 100 years. The overall benefits of nitrates result from a reduction in myocardial oxygen demand due to venodilation and some arteriolar dilation. Nitrates produce vasodilation by at least two mechanisms: stimulation of cyclic guanosine monophosphate (GMP) production and inhibition of thromboxane synthetase. Organic nitrates are converted into nitric oxide. Nitric oxide appears to be similar to endothelium-derived relaxation factor (EDRF), an endogenous vasodilator. Nitric oxide reacts with sulfhydryl groups in the vascular smooth muscle to produce S-nitrosothiols. S-nitrosothiols subsequently activate guanylate cyclase and increase the intracellular concentration of cyclic GMP.[41,42] Cyclic GMP controls vascular smooth muscle calcium concentration by binding to calmodulin and phosphorylating myosin light chain kinase. Calcium then initiates contraction. Because cyclic GMP enhances calcium uptake into the sarcoplasmic reticulum or inhibits its cellular influx, less calcium is available; therefore, dilation occurs.

Nitrates also may alter the prostaglandin system by inhibiting thromboxane synthetase and permitting preferential formation of prostacyclin over thromboxane A_2.[43,44] Both of these short-acting vasoactive substances are formed from prostaglandin precursors. Prostacyclin is a potent vasodilator which causes smooth muscle relaxation through phosphorylation of myosin light chain kinase. This reduces its ability to be activated by calcium and calmodulin.[42] In contrast, thromboxane is a potent vasoconstrictor.[45]

The peripheral effects of sublingual NTG in J.P. will include dilation of both veins and arteries. Venous dilation probably will be more pronounced, as relaxation of arterial smooth muscle requires higher plasma NTG levels. Pronounced venodilation will reduce the preload to the heart by pooling blood in the periphery. Less blood is returned to the heart which decreases filling pressures; this, in turn, reduces myocardial oxygen demand, thereby relieving J.P.'s angina.[46–48] (See Chapter 15: Congestive Heart Failure for a more detailed discussion of preload.)

Nitrates also dilate epicardial coronary arteries.[49] Until recently, researchers assumed that arteries supplying ischemic areas already were maximally dilated and would not respond to nitrates. Angiographic studies show that coronary vessels which are not completely engulfed by the atherosclerotic lesions (eccentric lesions) will dilate further. Thus, nitrates will decrease J.P.'s coronary vasomotor tone.

J.P. will continue verapamil therapy as it both lowers blood pressure and exerts anti-anginal effects. The addition of nitrates will provide added protection against developing angina (long-acting nitrates) and will provide J.P. acute relief (short-acting NTG) when an anginal attack occurs. Both short- and long-acting nitrates have well-documented effects, low incidence of adverse reactions, and are reasonably priced. Therefore nitrates often are first-line therapy in healing chronic stable angina.

Short-Acting Preparations

Sublingual (SL) Nitroglycerin (NTG)

9. Dosing. How should J.P.'s dose of SL NTG be determined? Can NTG be used prophylactically?

Because sensitivity to nitroglycerin varies among patients, the dose should be individualized (see Table 13.2). The most common sublingual NTG dose used is 0.4 or 0.6 mg; although rare patients may tolerate only 0.15 mg. An optimal dose relieves pain and produces an objective hemodynamic response, such as a 10 mm Hg fall in systolic blood pressure or a ten beat/minute rise in heart rate; it should not, however, cause intolerable orthostatic hypotension.[50]

Five to ten minutes before J.P. is about to undergo heavy exertion, he can take an SL NTG tablet to prevent angina. This is especially helpful for angina associated with sexual intercourse.

10. Patient Instructions. What instructions should J.P. receive with regard to the use and storage of SL NTG? How rapidly will SL NTG relieve J.P.'s chest pain?

When angina occurs, J.P. should sit down immediately and place the nitroglycerin tablet under his tongue; he should not swallow it. Many patients experience dizziness and lightheadedness which is minimized by sitting. The onset of action is within one to two minutes and pain usually is relieved within three to five minutes. If he needs more than one tablet, he may take a maximum of three tablets over 15 minutes. If the pain persists for more than 30 minutes, he should seek medical aid because he may be having a myocardial infarction.

Sensations J.P. may experience include warmth, flushing, lightheadedness, faintness, tachycardia, headache, and sublingual burning or stinging. A stinging sensation on the tongue was thought to help assess tablet potency; however, reformulation of tablets in 1973 limited the burning and stinging sensation so that only 75% of patients now experience sublingual burning.[52]

The tablets should be dispensed in the original, unopened manufacturer's container and stored in the original brown bottle. Because sublingual NTG tablets are degraded by heat and light, they should be stored in a cool, dry place, but not refrigerated. The bottle should be closed tightly after each opening. Safety caps are not necessary, although patients should be cautioned to keep all medications out of the reach of children. The cotton plug sometimes is difficult to remove; therefore, it should be discarded upon initial receipt of the prescription and should not be replaced. Use of cotton other than that supplied by the manufacturer should be discouraged, since NTG tablets are volatile and are adsorbed by the cotton. This results in a significant loss in tablet effectiveness. Expiration dating should be monitored closely and tablets should be replaced immediately if they are exposed to excessive light, heat, moisture, or air. Once a container is opened, the tablets should be used only for a limited time; usually from six months to a year.

Nitroglycerin Lingual Spray

11. J.P. completes his evaluation and is maintained on SR verapamil (Verelan) 240 mg PO QD and SL NTG 0.4 mg PRN. His amputation makes use of the SL NTG tablets cumbersome. What other short-acting nitrate delivery system can be used? What are the possible side effects?

Nitroglycerin lingual spray (Nitrolingual), available in a 0.4 mg dose-metered canister, is an attractive alternative for J.P.[53–56] Each canister dispenses 200 doses and has a shelf-life of three years.[53] He should bring the canister as close to his mouth as possible and spray the nitroglycerin under or onto his tongue. The spray should not be inhaled. He should sit down and should not exceed the maximum dose recommended by his physician.

Adverse Effects

For practical purposes, side effects of all nitrates are limited to hypotension and headache.[50] Dizziness is a tolerable effect; however, syncope (passing out, fainting) mandates a dosage reduction since severe hypotension and bradycardia have caused cardiac ar-

Table 13.2			Commonly Prescribed Organic Nitrates[a,e]	
Nitrates	Dosage Form	Onset (min)	Duration	Usual Dosage
Short-Acting				
NTG[b]	SL	1–3	10–30 min	0.4–0.6 mg[c]
NTG	Translingual spray	2–4	10–30 min	0.4 mg/metered spray
NTG	IV	1–2	3–5 min[d]	Initially 5 μg/min. ↑ Q 3–5 min until pain is relieved or hypotension
Long-Acting				
NTG	Topical ointment[f]	30	4–8 hr	½"–2" Q 4–6 hr[g]
	Transdermal patch	30	4–8 hr	0.2–0.4 mg/hr
Isosorbide dinitrate[h]	SL	2–5	2–4 hr	2.5–10 mg Q 2–4 hr[g]
	PO	15–40	2–6 hr	5–60 mg Q 4–6 hr[g]
Isosorbide mononitrate	PO	30–60	7–8 hr	20 mg BID, 7 hr apart[i]
Imdur	PO	30–60	8–12 hr	60–120 mg QD

[a] Reprinted with permission. Handbook of Applied Therapeutics. Applied Therapeutics, Inc.

[b] When using sublingual or translingual spray forms of nitroglycerin, the patient should administer the dose while sitting to minimize hypotension, dizziness, headache, and flushing. The optimal dose relieves symptoms with no >10–15 mm Hg drop in systolic BP or a 10 beat/min rise in pulse. Pain relief is rapid, but up to 3 doses at 5 min intervals may be given. After this, medical assistance should be summoned.

[c] Sublingual NTG tablets are degraded rapidly by heat and light. They should be stored in a cool, dry place; do not leave the lid open or refrigerate. Tablets should be stored in the original manufacturer's container or a glass vial since the tablets volatilize and bind to many plastic vials and cotton. Previously, stinging of the tongue was an indicator of fresh tablets, but newer formulations only cause stinging in about 75% of patients. No more than three doses in 15 minutes. It is important to start with the smallest effective dose.

[d] Duration after infusion discontinued.

[e] IV = Intravenous; NTG = Nitroglycerin; PO = Oral; SL = Sublingual; SR = Sustained-release. Consider giving QD or BID to avoid tolerance.

[f] Squeeze ½"–2" of ointment onto calibrated paper enclosed in package with tube. Carefully spread the ointment on chest in a thin layer about 2" × 2" in size. Keep area covered with applicator paper. Wipe off previous dose before adding new dose or if hypotensive. If another person applies the ointment, avoid contact with fingers or eyes to prevent headache or hypotension.

[g] Dosage regimens should maintain a nitrate-free interval (e.g., bedtime). Give last dose at 7 p.m.; remove transdermal patches at 7 p.m.

[h] Longer-acting forms of nitrates are effective drugs, but one must understand their limitations to optimize effectiveness. SL ISDN tablets display an onset and duration intermediate between that of SL NTG and oral ISDN. Because of high presystemic (first-pass) metabolism of the oral forms of both NTG and ISDN, very large doses may be required compared to SL or chewable dosage forms. Small oral doses (2.5 mg NTG, 5 mg ISDN) probably are not effective; doses as large as 9 mg NTG and 60 mg ISDN are not uncommon. Despite claims for longer activity, ointments and oral forms often are only effective for 4–8 hr, even when given as SR preparations.

[i] Suggest taking first ISMO dose on awakening and second dose 7 hr later. Imdur is given once daily; the dose can be increased to 120–240 mg after beginning at initial dose of 60 mg QD.

rest in patients experiencing myocardial infarction. This probably is secondary to a nitroglycerin-induced vasovagal reaction and should be treated with leg elevation, atropine, and fluid infusion. Nitrates are converted in the body to nitrites which can oxidize the ferrous ion in hemoglobin to the ferric state, thereby producing methemoglobinemia.[57] However, this adverse effect is of clinical importance only when large intravenous (IV) NTG doses are used; it does not occur with usual doses of oral or sublingual nitrate preparations.[46]

Although headache is a common and expected side effect of the nitrates, patients usually develop a tolerance to this effect within several weeks of beginning therapy. Mild analgesics such as acetaminophen are helpful. Occasionally, patients experience continuing headaches and discontinue nitrate therapy.

Long-Acting Nitrates

12. J.P. does well over the next several months, but he is still bothered by occasional angina episodes, ranging from 1–4 times/week. The attacks usually are precipitated by strenuous work and are relieved by rest and 2 or 3 NTG sprays (0.4 mg each). The quality and location of the pain are unchanged, although the duration has increased by 1 or 2 minutes. He follows a low cholesterol, no-added-salt diet.

Physical examination is unchanged except for a 20 pound weight loss. Vital signs include the following: supine BP 118/70 mm Hg, heart rate 65 beats/min, and respiratory rate 12/min. J.P's cardiologist elected to start prophylactic nitrates as well as continuing his calcium channel blocker and diuretic ther-

apy. What therapeutic end points should be used to evaluate the efficacy of long-acting nitrates? Could a beta blocker have been used instead of the long-acting nitrate?

Long-acting nitrates occupy a key role in the prevention of angina of all types. Their mechanism of action is the same as that of short-acting NTG. The goals of therapy are to decrease the number, severity, and duration of J.P.'s anginal attacks. Although standardized bicycle ergometer or treadmill exercise tests are used for clinical studies of nitrate preparations, cost sometimes prohibits this testing use in the patient care setting.

J.P.'s doctor also could have prescribed a beta blocker instead of the nitrates since he has contraindications to this class of drugs. A beta blocker would have been a good alternative if his blood pressure had remained elevated; but for now, J.P.'s blood pressure and pulse are within a desired range. J.P.'s doctor felt that since SL nitrates were well-tolerated, a long-acting nitrate would be acceptable as well. Another prescriber could have chosen to discontinue verapamil and add a beta blocker for both angina and blood pressure control, and withhold adding the long-acting nitrate for now. This would have the advantage of using fewer drugs, but would mean discontinuing an agent (verapamil) that already has proven to be effective in controlling J.P.'s blood pressure. Ultimately, the decision is based upon the prescriber's personal choice and past experience, as well as the entire spectrum of the patient's disease complex.

Nitrate Tolerance

13. Will J.P. develop tolerance to the long-acting nitrate?

Early evidence for the development of nitrate tolerance and dependence comes from the munitions industry. Workers in this industry were constantly exposed to NTG and ethylene glycol dinitrate, components of explosives.[58] Since 1898, the "Monday Syndrome" has been recognized: workers developed mild to severe headaches late Sunday or Monday morning or during holidays. By rubbing NTG into their skin, wearing NTG impregnated headbands, or taking medicinal NTG, the workers avoided the "Monday Syndrome." Studies showed that the employees had decreased systolic blood pressures and increased pulse rates at work which normalized within 24 to 72 hours of nitrate withdrawal. Among munitions employees with coronary heart disease, the symptoms of nitrate withdrawal included chest pain and sudden cardiac death. In some workers without atherosclerosis, abrupt withdrawal from nitrates triggered coronary artery spasm.

Although tolerance to nitrate-induced headaches within several days of therapy commonly was observed, the clinical importance of this phenomenon in patients with CHD was not fully appreciated. Recent reports suggest that tolerance can be limited by maintaining a nitrate-free interval of about 10 to 12 hours daily.[59,60] Many older nitrate regimens were designed to provide 24-hour nitrate coverage against ischemia; however, this approach actually is counterproductive because it stimulates tolerance. Nitrate schedules should be arranged to permit a nitrate-free interval during which time the patient may receive angina protection from β-adrenergic blockers or calcium channel blockers. Most often, this nitrate-free interval is arranged during the night since angina is more likely to occur during the working day.[61] Patients with nocturnal angina should arrange their nitrate-free interval during the day.[60] Tolerance also is minimized by using the lowest effective nitrate dose. Because long-acting nitrates must be dosed intermittently to avoid tolerance, verapamil therapy will provide J.P. with continuous protection, even during the nitrate-free interval. Even though J.P. uses a long-acting nitrate, he still will respond favorably to sublingual nitroglycerin. There is no evidence that use of long-acting nitrates leads to resistance or tolerance to the effects of SL NTG.[62] He should clearly understand the differences between the indications for the two nitrate products.

14. Mechanism of Action. What is the mechanism of action for nitrate tolerance?

The mechanism of nitrate tolerance is not yet fully understood.[61–63] Since most evidence supports the central role of cyclic GMP stimulation in nitrate-induced vasodilation, it has been suggested that tolerance results from sulfhydryl depletion at the nitrate receptor.[61,62] Sulfhydryl depletion in turn leads to reduced S-nitrosothiol production and, therefore, a decreased production of cyclic GMP. Administration of a sulfhydryl donor, such as N-acetylcysteine, can restore vascular response to nitrates.[64,65] Torresi et al.[64] demonstrated *in vitro* development of nitrate tolerance in coronary arterial rings which was either prevented or reversed by N-acetylcysteine. A study of nitrate tolerance conducted in patients with clinically important coronary artery disease receiving an intravenous NTG infusion confirmed the development of a partial tolerance to NTG which was reversed by N-acetylcysteine.[66] Similarly, in patients with congestive heart failure, N-acetylcysteine reverses the tolerance to nitroglycerin's effect on the peripheral vasculature.[67] Despite these reports describing prevention and reversal of nitrate tolerance by N-acetylcysteine, combination therapy has not been proven beneficial and adverse reactions have not been evaluated properly. The results with sulfhydral donors do not support their coadministration; and their added cost and adverse effects further limit their usefulness.

15. Are all nitrate delivery systems capable of inducing nitrate tolerance? How can tolerance be minimized?

All organic nitrates exhibit similar hemodynamic effects through a common pharmacologic mechanism; yet, the differing pharmacokinetic profiles of the nitrate delivery systems lead to a variation in the development of tolerance.[59] Short-acting formulations such as sublingual NTG, oral NTG spray, and sublingual isosorbide dinitrate are not likely to induce tolerance given their rapid onset of action and short duration of effect. Oral nitrates, with an extended duration of action, are prone to induce tolerance; however, this may be minimized by devising a nitrate-free dosing schedule.[59] Similarly, topical nitrates, including NTG ointment and transdermal NTG patches, will induce tolerance if administered continually.[68]

Intermittent application of transdermal NTG appears to limit tolerance development in patients with both chronic stable angina and congestive heart failure. The effects of continuous (24 hours/day) and intermittent (16 hours/day) transdermal NTG (10 mg/day) were compared in 12 men with chronic stable angina who also were being treated with beta blockers or calcium channel blockers.[69] Nitrate efficacy as measured by exercise time to onset of angina, exercise duration, and development of ST segment depression was maintained with intermittent treatment and an eight-hour nitrate-free interval; however, tolerance to the anti-anginal effects occurred with continuous transdermal NTG treatment. Twelve-hour intermittent patch therapy also prevents tolerance.[70] The minimum time necessary for a nitrate-free interval is unknown.

Intravenous NTG, a cornerstone therapy in management of patients with unstable angina and severe CHF, is associated with nitrate tolerance if it is administered as a sustained infusion. The immediate hemodynamic benefits observed with NTG infusions in patients with severe chronic heart failure were greatly reduced 24 to 48 hours after continuous IV therapy.[71] This tolerance also extended to oral isosorbide dinitrate.[72,73] Both the tolerance to intravenous NTG and cross-tolerance to oral isosorbide dinitrate were prevented by infusing nitroglycerin for only 12 hours followed by a 12-hour nitrate-free interval.[71] Intermittent NTG infusions for patients with unstable angina appear reasonable, but have not been fully evaluated.

Isosorbide Dinitrate (ISDN)

16. J.P. receives a prescription for oral isosorbide dinitrate (Isordil) 30 mg PO TID. How should he be instructed to take his medication so that he is nitrate-free for 10–12 hours?

Oral isosorbide dinitrate (the immediate-release product, not the oral SR product) is the most commonly used organic nitrate. In a study of 12 patients with chronic stable angina, three times daily treatment with isosorbide dinitrate significantly improved exercise tolerance time.[60] J.P. should take his oral nitrate at 7:00 a.m., 12:00 p.m., and 5:00 p.m. since his exercise-induced angina is likely to occur during daylight hours. He may need to adjust this schedule if he arises earlier than 7:00 a.m. since early-morning angina is common. Some physicians will prescribe isosorbide dinitrate twice a day for patients with less severe anginal syndrome at 7:00 a.m. and 12 noon. Although a sustained-release oral isosorbide dinitrate is available (Dilatrate-SR), it rarely is prescribed as dosage regimen modification to avoid nitrate tolerance which has not been studied adequately.

The sustained-release verapamil could be taken in the early evening to provide anti-anginal coverage during the nitrate-free interval. However, J.P. should continue to take his diuretic in the morning.

Nitrate Pharmacodynamics

17. Is J.P.'s isosorbide dinitrate dose appropriate in light of nitrate pharmacokinetics and pharmacodynamics?

The extremely complex relationships between organic nitrate pharmacokinetics, vascular metabolism, influence of first-pass effect, and pharmacologic action are very poorly understood.[74] The most popular nitrates (NTG, isosorbide dinitrate, and isosorbide-5-mononitrate) are under intense study and some pharmacodynamic information is available; other less often used compounds such as pentaerythritol tetranitrate (Peritrate) are even less well understood. After intravenous administration in man, both NTG and isosorbide dinitrate have a high apparent volume of distribution (3 to 4 L/kg) reflecting extensive distribution in the vascular and other peripheral tissues.[74] Nitroglycerin is cleared rapidly from plasma with a venous clearance of about 50 L/minute, while isosorbide dinitrate is cleared at a rate of about 4 L/minute. Because NTG is eliminated rapidly in the plasma, plasma concentrations in the nanogram/mL range are observed. These low concentrations, along with other analytical factors, make it very difficult to conduct nitrate pharmacokinetic studies. The site of blood sampling also may influence the apparent nitrate pharmacokinetics. Furthermore even when sampled simultaneously, arterial and venous concentrations may be substantially different.

5-Isosorbide mononitrate (ISMO) is the active metabolite of isosorbide dinitrate. It has a small apparent volume of distribution (0.6 L/kg) and a low venous clearance (0.1 L/minute).[74] Thus, its elimination half-life of about 275 minutes is much longer than that of NTG ($\beta t\frac{1}{2} \approx 10$ minutes) and isosorbide dinitrate ($\beta t\frac{1}{2} \approx 65$ minutes). (Also see Question 22.) All of these nitrate pharmacokinetic parameters will be influenced profoundly by the physicochemical properties of NTG (highly lipophilic and volatile); biopharmaceutic characteristics of the product (prolongation of absorption rate and biological half-life can be achieved by using SR delivery forms); hemodynamic factors (e.g., cardiac output); disease states (especially hepatic dysfunction since both NTG and isosorbide dinitrate undergo extensive first-pass metabolism); and duration of therapy.[74]

Nitroglycerin plasma concentrations are very low and variable, making analysis extremely difficult. Recent work using a highly specific NTG assay capable of detecting two dinitrate metabolites suggests that enzyme systems in the gut, liver, skin, sublingual mucosa, and blood vessels all contribute to nitroglycerin's metabolism.[75] However, the influence of each metabolic site varies with the route of administration.

All nitrate doses must be individualized (see Table 13.2) and because larger doses contribute to nitrate tolerance, the smallest effective dose should be used. Oral isosorbide dinitrate therapy usually is initiated with a single 10 or 20 mg dose and gradually titrated upward to a maximal single dose of 40 to 60 mg. Titration also helps limit the occurrence of headaches. In many patients, maximal improvement in exercise tolerance is achieved with a single ISDN oral dose of 15 to 30 mg;[72,73] however, doses of 40 to 60 mg are common.

Transdermal Ointment

18. J.P. has a friend who uses NTG ointment. Is this a reasonable alternative for him? How should he be instructed to apply the ointment if it is prescribed?

Nitroglycerin ointment could be applied three times daily beginning in the early morning, but it should be removed around 7:00 p.m. so that a nitrate-free interval is maintained. The amount of ointment applied ranges between one-half and two inches (15 mg/inch).[47] The 2% ointment is squeezed from a tube onto a paper marked with a measuring scale. Using the paper, the ointment is spread in a thin layer over an area of about two by three inches on the skin of the anterior chest or upper limbs. Absorption can be markedly affected by administration technique.[76–78] The dose

measuring paper may be left on and held in place by a single strip of adhesive tape. Occlusive dressings should not be used. J.P. should rotate application sites to avoid skin irritation; an ointment application system which uses an adhesive unit (TSAR, Rorer Laboratories) similar to a large bandaid limits the variability and messiness of dosing. NTG ointment may be removed by first discarding the paper and then wiping off the application site with a tissue; however, the skin acts as a reservoir and NTG absorption will continue for 10 to 20 minutes after the paste is removed. Because it can be removed rather easily, some critical care physicians prefer NTG ointment over other nitrate formulations. Nurses may wish to wear gloves when removing NTG ointment to avoid NTG-induced headaches. Ambulatory patients, however, may dislike its inconvenience. Nitroglycerin ointment has a variable duration of action, but generally is effective for four to six hours. The duration may be shorter with chronic use. The therapeutic efficacy of nitroglycerin ointment is acceptable if patients do not apply the ointment continuously.

Transdermal Patches

19. J.P. likes the idea of using topical nitrates, but does not want to work with the ointment which he considers too messy. Are the transdermal patches a viable alternative? Is there any difference between products?

Transdermal NTG patches (see Table 13.3) originally were designed to provide angina protection with once-daily application. The concept of a compact, easy-to-apply transdermal NTG patch prompted pharmaceutical manufacturers to design a number of products, which the Food and Drug Administration (FDA) subsequently approved based upon plasma level data, not clinical efficacy studies. Since the FDA approval of these products, the shortcomings of plasma level data have become apparent and this has prompted numerous clinical efficacy studies.

The long-term efficacy of NTG patches is in question.[79–84] Several studies showed improvement in exercise tolerance within two to four hours after application of the last patch;[84] however, many

Table 13.3	Transdermal Nitroglycerin Systems[a]
Distributor/Product	Surface Area (cm²)
Schwarz Pharma[a]	
Deponit 0.2 mg/hr	16
Deponit 0.4 mg/hr	32
Nitrocine 0.6 mg/hr	30
Searle[a]	
Nitrodisc 0.2 mg/hr	8
Nitrodisc 0.3 mg/hr	12
Nitrodisc 0.4 mg/hr	16
Key Pharmaceuticals	
Nitro-Dur 0.1 mg/hr	5
Nitro-Dur 0.2 mg/hr	10
Nitro-Dur 0.3 mg/hr	15
Nitro-Dur 0.4 mg/hr	20
Nitro-Dur 0.6 mg/hr	30
CIBA (Summit)	
Transderm-Nitro (0.1 mg/hr)	5
Transderm-Nitro (0.2 mg/hr)	10
Transderm-Nitro (0.4 mg/hr)	20
Transderm-Nitro (0.6 mg/hr)	30
3M Pharm	
Minitran 0.1 mg/hr	3.3
Minitran 0.2 mg/hr	6.7
Minitran 0.4 mg/hr	13.3
Minitran 0.6 mg/hr	20

[a] Also generic in 0.2 mg and 0.4 mg/hr. These products differ in delivery system mechanism.

studies did not demonstrate improved exercise performance beyond six to eight hours. Repeated application of a fresh patch two or three times daily, while still retaining a nitrate-free interval, could improve the clinical efficacy of the patches and limit the development of tolerance.[70,85,86] However, each patch usually costs the patient over one dollar; therefore, this approach is unlikely to be widely accepted. Patches have fallen into disfavor and probably should not be used as monotherapy for severe angina or coronary vasospasm.[79]

Although the various patches employ different pharmaceutical delivery systems, there are no clear-cut advantages of one over another. Despite variations in surface area and NTG content, the most important common denominator of the transdermal NTG systems is the amount of drug released per hour expressed as the release rate (e.g., 0.2 mg/hour). Each product label includes this information. Since the skin is the major factor influencing NTG absorption rate, product release characteristics do not favor one system over another. The gel-like matrix system (Nitro-Dur), semipermeable membrane (Transderm-Nitro), nitroglycerin-impregnated polymer (Nitrodisc), and gradient-charged nitroglycerin film (Deponit) all produce detectable plasma nitroglycerin levels over 24 hours. Individual responses to doses are extremely variable and should be titrated. Patients may prefer one system over another based upon comfort, aesthetics, and adhesiveness.[87,88] Contact dermatitis has been reported with the transdermal patches.[89] Patient instructions are included with the patches and should be reviewed, emphasizing the appropriate time for application and removal of the patch.

Transmucosal NTG

20. Describe the transmucosal NTG tablets. How are they used and what are their advantages?

Transmucosal (buccal) nitroglycerin (Nitrogard) is a nitroglycerin impregnated methylcellulose polymer in tablet form that is placed in the buccal pouch between the upper teeth and inner lip. A gel-like seal quickly forms, releasing NTG until the tablet completely dissolves. The onset of action is within two to three minutes[90] and the duration of action averages four to five hours (the life of the tablet).[91] To minimize the development of tolerance, the last dose should be taken in the late afternoon or early evening. Removing the tablet at bedtime minimizes the risk of aspiration.

Because transmucosal nitroglycerin is ideally suited to intermittent dosing with a nitrate-free interval at night, tolerance usually is not a problem.[90,91] This dosage form also is unique because it is indicated for both acute angina and prophylaxis.[92] Typical side effects include headache and dizziness; a few patients have reported mild erythema or irritation of the buccal mucosa. Tingling and a burning sensation may develop shortly after tablet placement; however, patient acceptance of the transmucosal tablet is about 75% or more.[93] Most patients can talk, eat, and drink with the tablet in place, although some may wish to remove the tablet before eating and replace it with a fresh tablet after the meal.[93] Other patients are uncomfortable with the residues that remain after tablet dissolution.

Other Organic Nitrates

21. Do organic nitrates (other than oral ISDN or SL NTG) offer any significant advantages for J.P.?

Sublingual isosorbide dinitrate is available, but its onset of action is delayed when compared to sublingual NTG or the lingual spray; thus, it is used only for prophylaxis. Also, because the duration of action for sublingual isosorbide dinitrate is only two to three hours, it must be administered more frequently and this reduces compliance.[47] Chewable isosorbide dinitrate is prescribed

occasionally as are isosorbide dinitrate extended-release capsules and tablets; neither has undergone extensive clinical evaluation. A variety of synthetic organic nitrate derivatives [erythrityl tetranitrate (Cardilate), pentaerythritol tetranitrate (Peritrate)] also are available but not widely used in the U.S. Long-acting oral nitroglycerin capsules (e.g., Nitro-Bid) have questionable efficacy and may lead to tolerance. However, reports using higher oral NTG doses (6.5 to 9 mg) suggest clinical efficacy with physiologic effects persisting for one to six hours.[58]

22. Does isosorbide mononitrate offer any distinct advantages over other nitrate preparations for angina prophylaxis?

Isosorbide mononitrate (ISMO and Monoket) is the primary metabolite of isosorbide dinitrate; in fact, most of the clinical activity of ISDN is due to the mononitrate. Therefore, both drugs share a similar pharmacology. While ISMO is available only as a 20 mg tablet, Monoket is available as both a 10 and 20 mg tablet. Isosorbide mononitrate does not undergo first-pass metabolism and has no active metabolites. Its oral bioavailability is almost 100% and overall elimination half-life about five hours.[74] Maximum serum concentrations are observed 30 to 60 minutes after a dose. To avoid tolerance, isosorbide mononitrate should be used in a twice-daily, asymmetric dosing regimen in which the first dose is taken upon awakening and the second dose about seven hours later. Clinical trials suggested that a 10 mg dose was no better than placebo and a 40 mg dose no better than the 20 mg dose in preventing angina. Therefore, the standard recommended dose is 20 mg twice daily, seven hours apart.[94] General precautions and adverse reactions for ISMO are similar to those for the other nitrates. Potential advantages for the clinical use of ISMO are less dosage fluctuation due to the absence of presystemic clearance and an effective twice-daily dosing schedule which could perhaps lead to improved patient compliance. However, two or three times daily dosing of isosorbide dinitrate is effective clinically and likely to be much less expensive, especially if generic ISDN is dispensed.

β-Adrenergic Blockers
Mechanism of Action

23. T.I. has a 5-year history of chronic stable angina. Cardiac catheterization 3 months ago showed 2-vessel coronary disease with obstructions of 55% and 65% in the right coronary and circumflex coronary arteries, respectively. Despite appropriate use of SL NTG tablets (0.4 mg) and isosorbide dinitrate (40 mg PO at 6:00 a.m., 12:00 p.m., and 5:00 p.m.), T.I. is having 4–5 angina attacks/week. His physician writes a prescription for atenolol (Tenormin) 50 mg QD. How do β-adrenergic blockers prevent angina?

β-adrenergic blockers reduce myocardial oxygen demand by decreasing catecholamine-mediated increases in heart rate, blood pressure, and, to some extent, myocardial contractility.[95] Traditionally, beta receptors are subdivided into two classes: β_1-receptors are found only in the myocardium while β_2-receptors are distributed in the vascular and bronchial smooth muscle. Stimulation of the β_1-receptor accelerates the heart rate, while β_2-stimulation relaxes or dilates peripheral vasculature and bronchial airways.

It was once believed that no β_2-receptors were located in the heart muscle; however, recent evidence shows that β_2-receptors probably account for 10% to 40% of all beta receptors in the myocardium.[96] The functional role of myocardial β_2-receptors is not understood completely but probably involves augmentation of contractility and perhaps heart rate.[96–98]

The primary agonist of the β_1-receptor is norepinephrine, while the primary agonist of the β_2-receptor is epinephrine.[97] New theories suggest that in normal (nonstressed) situations, β_2- and β_1-

effects are additive. However, during acute stress when large amounts of epinephrine are released, increased β_2- effects result in markedly enhanced contractility and heart rate. The availability of drugs which selectively block the β_1-receptors (cardioselective) or simultaneously block the β_1- and β_2-receptors (nonselective) means that further research on the distribution and role of beta receptors will have direct implications for cardiovascular therapeutics (see Chapter 10: Essential Hypertension for a more in-depth discussion of beta blocker pharmacology and dosing, and Chapter 15: Congestive Heart Failure).

In addition to reducing myocardial oxygen demand, beta blockers may inhibit abnormally elevated platelet activity;[95] however, this effect is of questionable clinical significance. Controversial work has shown that beta blockers favorably affect myocardial metabolism, the coronary microvasculature, collateral blood flow, distribution of myocardial blood flow, and oxygen-hemoglobin affinity.[95]

Judging Therapeutic Endpoint

24. How can the efficacy of the atenolol be assessed?

All patients receiving anti-anginal drugs should be monitored for the frequency of angina attacks and NTG consumption. However this only provides an estimate of therapeutic efficacy since the patient's exercise and stress levels change from day to day. Traditionally, clinicians have monitored the reduction in resting heart rate and have progressively increased the beta blocker dose until the resting heart rate was below 55 or 60 beats/minute. Heart rates below 50 beats/minute may be acceptable provided the patient is asymptomatic and no heart block is observed. However, this approach does not take into account that while the initial beta blocker dose reduces heart rate, subsequent increases in dose may only slightly reduce the resting heart rate. Variations in resting heart rate are normal and due to the influence of the endogenous sympathetic nervous system, as well as exogenous factors such as drugs, tobacco, and caffeine-containing beverages. Beta blockers with intrinsic sympathomimetic activity will not reduce the resting heart rate as much as beta blockers void of this activity.[99]

Exercise testing probably is the best means of documenting the adequacy of beta blocker therapy.[99] During an exercise tolerance test, atenolol should substantially increase the time T.I. walks before developing angina. There also may be a reduction in ST-segment depression during exercise indicating less myocardial ischemia. The heart rate-systolic blood pressure product probably will be markedly lowered, reflecting a decrease in both heart rate and systolic wall tension.[100] Beta blocker doses needed to achieve these effects are extremely variable; therefore, therapy should be started with the lowest possible effective dose and titrated upward. Continuous assessment of T.I.'s exercise tolerance is advisable.

Dosing Frequency

25. Is once-daily dosing of atenolol sufficient to provide T.I. with 24-hour protection?

Atenolol is a good choice for once-daily dosing.[101] Because the pharmacodynamic effects of beta blockers are longer than their plasma half-lives, these drugs may be dosed once or twice a day for angina. Atenolol's half-life is about 10 hours during chronic dosing; however, clinical studies support a once-a-day dosing schedule.[101]

Propranolol has a relatively short plasma half-life of two to three hours; yet, clinicians have observed that a single dose lowers the heart rate and blood pressure for at least 12 hours. Subsequent studies have confirmed the efficacy of twice-daily dosing for propranolol in the treatment of angina.[99,102,103]

Beta Blocker Cardioselectivity

Contraindications

26. R.O. is a 65-year-old male, with a 67-pack year smoking history and a 13-year history of insulin-dependent diabetes mellitus. His walking is limited by peripheral vascular disease and claudication, as well as by exertional angina. A beta blocker is to be initiated. Is one drug preferable over another?

Although all beta blockers are equally effective in the treatment of angina, R.O.'s medical history poses several relative contraindications to the use of certain beta blockers.[104] Key factors to consider include his smoking history which may have caused chronic obstructive airways disease (COAD) with a bronchospastic component, diabetes, and peripheral vascular disease. A cardioselective beta blocker offers several advantages in R.O.[105,106] Drugs such as acebutolol (Sectral), atenolol, and metoprolol primarily inhibit β_1-receptors in the heart and produce less blockade of β_2-receptors in the bronchial and vascular smooth muscle. In patients with asthma and obstructive lung disease, β_2-receptors mediate airway responsiveness and blockade of β_2-receptors can cause severe bronchospasm and respiratory difficulty.

Cardioselective beta blockers also are less likely to inhibit β_2-mediated vasodilation in the peripheral arterioles. Therefore, they are attractive for patients with peripheral vascular disease and Raynaud's disease. Blockade of the peripheral β_2-receptor would permit unopposed alpha-mediated vasoconstriction and could decrease R.O.'s walking tolerance markedly. (See Chapter 48: Diabetes Mellitus for a discussion of the effect of beta blockers on insulin release and diabetic control.)

Adverse Effects

27. If R.O. receives a cardioselective beta blocker, could he still experience more difficulty breathing or walking?

Cardioselectivity probably is not an "all-or-none" response; instead, it is likely to be a dose-dependent phenomenon. As the dose is increased, cardioselectivity is lost. Unfortunately, the dose at which cardioselectivity will be lost in R.O. cannot be predicted; even a very low dose (e.g., metoprolol 37.5 mg) could cause wheezing.[105] Similarly, a cardioselective drug could worsen R.O.'s claudication. A better alternative for R.O. would be a calcium channel blocker either alone or with intermittent nitrate therapy.

Beta Blockers with Intrinsic Sympathomimetic Activity (ISA)

28. W.P. has a long cardiac history including 3 previous coronary artery bypass grafts, Class III CHF, and MI. He is experiencing angina that is unresponsive to maximally-tolerated doses of isosorbide dinitrate. Beta blocker therapy is being considered; however, there is concern that W.P.'s CHF and sinus bradycardia (resting heart rate 45–52 beats/min) will be worsened. Would a beta blocker with ISA be safe to use in W.P.?

Intrinsic sympathomimetic activity is a partial β-adrenergic agonist response caused by beta blockers. This dual action results from a complex drug-receptor interaction. Because the beta-blocking drugs with ISA have a chemical structure similar, but not identical, to catecholamines, they can simultaneously block the receptor and attach to a small number of stimulating sites.[107,108] Theoretically, these drugs may produce less bradycardia and heart failure, as well as less peripheral vasoconstriction and bronchial constriction, than pure β-adrenergic blockers. The clinical significance of ISA is actively debated.

Pindolol (Visken), a noncardioselective beta blocker with ISA activity, has been promoted as a vasodilating beta blocker. It may help maintain W.P.'s renal blood flow and reduce his total peripheral resistance.[107] It also may be less likely to reduce W.P.'s heart rate than a drug like propranolol.[99] The ISA activity of pindolol may offset its negative inotropic action so that left ventricular function is not significantly reduced.[109] Overall, intrinsic sympathomimetic activity appears to result in less derangement of lipid and glucose metabolism than pure beta blockers.[110] However, because clinical studies have not yet definitively demonstrated these advantages of ISA activity, pindolol should be considered only for W.P. after he has had a trial of calcium channel blockers. Other beta blockers with ISA are carteolol (Cartrol) and penbutolol (Levatol).

Central Nervous System (CNS) Side Effects

29. C.G., a 43-year-old male executive who has received metoprolol 100 mg BID at 8:00 a.m. and 8:00 p.m. for 1 month, has new complaints of awakening 5–6 times during the night, nightmares, fatigue, and diminished libido. Would switching C.G.'s therapy to atenolol alleviate these troublesome side effects?

C.G. describes some common CNS side effects of the β-adrenergic blockers: tiredness, fatigue, depression, sleep disturbances, psychomotor retardation, and sexual dysfunction.[111,112] Since patients may not associate these effects with their drug therapy, they often do not bring these complaints to their physician's attention. Therefore, all patients should be screened for these effects. Some investigators have suggested that these effects are related to the lipid solubility of the beta blockers; that is, the more lipophilic drugs can pass through the blood brain barrier more easily, thereby producing CNS disturbances.[111] On this basis, a hydrophilic drug like atenolol may be better tolerated by C.G. However, when administered in a larger single daily dose of ≥100 mg, atenolol therapy still may cause sedation.[113] (See Chapter 10: Essential Hypertension for another perspective.)

Beta Blockers in Acute Renal Failure

30. C.G. is severely injured in an automobile accident, becomes septic, and develops acute renal failure. He is to be started on hemodialysis. How will these events affect C.G.'s atenolol dose?

The beta blockers differ with regard to their pharmacokinetic profiles. The half-life of atenolol normally is about nine hours; however, because it primarily undergoes renal elimination, dosage adjustment should be considered. A dose of 12.5 or 25 mg can be used initially and titrated upward as tolerated. Since atenolol also is removed by hemodialysis, patients generally receive 25 to 50 mg after each dialysis and are monitored closely for hypotension.[104] (Also see Chapter 10: Essential Hypertension for a more thorough presentation of the comparative pharmacology of beta blockers.)

Abrupt Withdrawal

31. J.F., a 76-year-old retiree with a long history of chronic stable angina controlled with oral ISDN (generic) 40 mg TID (7:00 a.m., 12 noon, 5:00 p.m.), and propranolol 80 mg (7:00 a.m., 5:00 p.m.), stopped his propranolol abruptly 24 hours ago. He is transported to the hospital emergency room (ER) for treatment of angina unresponsive to 5 NTG tablets. How could J.F.'s situation have been avoided?

The beta blocker withdrawal syndrome, which has been well described in the medical literature, poses the highest risk to patients with severe atherosclerosis or unstable angina. Consequences may include acute myocardial infarction and sudden cardiac death. After controlling J.F.'s angina with medications and reinstituting beta blocker therapy, he should be warned not to discontinue this medication in the future. Failure to renew prescriptions and financial hardship are common reasons for abrupt discontinuation.

Mechanisms underlying this rebound phenomenon may include heightened beta receptor density and sensitivity or stimulation of sympathoadrenal activity.[114] An "overshoot" in heart rate that increases the MVO_2 and increased platelet aggregation also may contribute.[115] Withdrawal syndromes may be less severe in patients taking beta blockers with partial agonist activity.

If beta blockers are to be discontinued in the future, the following propranolol withdrawal schedule could be used for J.F.[115]

Days	Dose
1–4	40 mg BID
5–8	20 mg BID
9–12	10 mg BID
13–14	10 mg QD

J.F. should limit physical activity throughout the withdrawal period and seek prompt medical attention if angina occurs.

Withdrawal Before Coronary Artery Surgery

32. V.T., a 67-year-old male, has been taking propranolol 160 mg BID for angina and hypertension for 10 years. He is scheduled to undergo coronary artery bypass grafting and there is concern that propranolol will interact with general anesthesia to produce excessive myocardial depression. Should V.T. be tapered off propranolol before surgery? Could other drugs worsen V.T.'s angina?

No. V.T. should continue to receive propranolol because it will promote hemodynamic stability and protect V.T. from intraoperative hypertension and tachycardia. Propranolol also will protect V.T. from postoperative supraventricular tachyarrhythmias, a common complication of open heart surgery. V.T. should receive 160 mg propranolol about two hours before surgery;[115] intravenous beta blockers may be needed either during the surgery or in the immediate postoperative period. As soon as possible, oral therapy should be resumed. Although plasma propranolol levels can be measured rather easily, their clinical utility is very limited. Therefore V.T. should be monitored through use of physiologic parameters such as heart rate and blood pressure.

Most cases of drug-induced angina actually are related to withdrawal of anti-anginal drugs such as stopping propranolol abruptly. Any therapy which lowers heart rate excessively (such as beta blocker therapy or verapamil/diltiazem therapy) also could cause angina. Similarly drugs which cause tachycardia (e.g., catecholamines, theophylline) may worsen angina by increasing workload on the heart. Drugs of abuse (e.g., cocaine, nicotine, ethanol) may cause ischemia and should be avoided by patients with ischemic heart disease.

Calcium Channel Blockers

The calcium channel blockers are the most recent addition to the family of drugs used to treat angina. Their clinical applicability extends to most cardiovascular diseases, although current FDA-approved indications are limited to angina, hypertension, and supraventricular arrhythmias. One calcium channel blocker, nimodipine (Nimotop), is indicated for treatment of cerebral spasm resulting from subarachnoid hemorrhage. Ongoing research suggests calcium channel blockers may be useful in the treatment of migraines, cerebral artery spasm, Raynaud's phenomenon, cardiomyopathies, pulmonary hypertension, asthma, and GI disorders.[116,117] Calcium channel blockers will be a cornerstone of therapy for many years to come.

Classification

Calcium channel blockers are highly diverse compounds. They differ markedly in chemical structure as well as specificity for cardiac and peripheral tissue. Using these characteristics, it is possible to classify calcium antagonists into four major types (see Table 13.4).[117]

Type 1 agents may have one of two chemical structures. Verapamil and its congeners, tiapamil and gallopamil, are *diphenylalkylamines*, while diltiazem is a *benzothiazepine*. All of the Type 1 calcium antagonists exert qualitatively similar effects on myocardial and peripheral tissue. They slow conduction across the atrioventricular (AV) node and prolong its refractoriness. Ventricular refractory period is not affected; therefore, the antiarrhythmic utility of these drugs is limited to supraventricular tachyarrhythmias. Type 1 calcium channel antagonists can depress myocardial contractility. They are moderate peripheral vasodilators and potent coronary artery vasodilators. Type 1 drugs are selective calcium channel antagonists because they affect the calcium channels in the myocardium.

Type 2 calcium channel antagonists are the *dihydropyridine* derivatives of which nifedipine is the prototype compound. Amlodipine, felodipine, isradipine, and nicardipine are more-recently-approved second-generation dihydropyridines.[118–121] However, of the new agents only nicardipine and amlodipine currently are approved for the treatment of chronic stable angina pectoris. In addition, amlodipine is indicated for vasospastic angina. In contrast to the Type 1 agents, the dihydropyridines do not slow cardiac conduction and, therefore, have no antiarrhythmic action. They are, however, more potent peripheral vasodilators and this effect often is associated with a reflex increase in the heart rate. These drugs (except for nicardipine) may depress myocardial contractility, but to a lesser degree than the Type 1 agents. Type 2 compounds also can dilate coronary arteries, but vary in their potency. Like Type 1 drugs, the Type 2 dihydropyridines are selective calcium channel blockers.

Type 3 calcium antagonists include the *piperazine* derivatives cinnarazine and flunarizine.[117] They differ from both the Type 1 and Type 2 agents because they have no detectable effect on the slow calcium channels in the myocardium. They do, however, have a unique selectivity for dilating vascular beds in peripheral smooth muscle. They are likely to be used in the treatment of circulatory disorders such as migraines and peripheral vascular disease.

Type 4 calcium channel antagonists, for which bepridil serves as the prototype drug in the U.S., are pharmacologically complex compounds. Even within this group there are great differences in tissue selectivity and electrophysiologic effects.[117] Unlike other calcium channel antagonists, these drugs block the fast sodium channel in the heart as well as the calcium channel. They are, therefore, called nonselective calcium channel antagonists. They are likely to be useful in a wide range of diseases including supraventricular tachyarrhythmias, ventricular arrhythmias, and angina. The quinidine-like effect of these drugs raises concern about their deleterious arrhythmogenic effect, especially the induction of torsade de pointes. Much more information is needed before the role of the Type 4 agents in cardiovascular disease is determined.

Broad-based experience in the use of calcium channel blockers to treat angina is limited in the U.S. to selected Type 1 and Type 2 agents (see Table 13.5). During the mid-to-late 1980s, oral nifedipine, verapamil, and diltiazem emerged as key agents in treating all types of angina. With the marketing of second-generation dihydropyridines such as amlodipine and nicardipine, the clinician is faced with the difficult task of differentiating among calcium channel blockers.

Pharmacology

Calcium channel blockers can decrease myocardial oxygen demand (MVO_2) and increase myocardial blood supply.[124] By inhibiting smooth muscle contraction, the calcium channel blockers dilate blood vessels and decrease resistance to blood flow. Dilation of peripheral vessels reduces systemic vascular resistance and blood pressure, thus decreasing the workload of the heart. Coronary artery dilation improves coronary blood flow. Type 1 and 2 calcium channel blockers also decrease the myocardial contractile force (negative inotropic effect). All of these actions can reduce angina symptoms.

The overall effect of calcium channel blocker administration observed in patients will be the combined effects of vasodilator and myocardial actions with reflex-mediated adrenergic activity.[125] Potent arterial (peripheral) vasodilators, such as nifedipine, markedly reduce peripheral vascular resistance.[116] This may cause reflex stimulation of the sympathetic nervous system resulting, overall, in a slight to moderate rise in heart rate, perhaps increasing MVO_2 (see Table 13.5). The cardiodepressant effect of verapamil- and diltiazem-like drugs prevents reflex tachycardia. Verapamil and diltiazem are more likely to worsen ventricular function in patients with CHF secondary to systolic dysfunction.[126] However, even the relatively selective second-generation dihydropyridines (e.g., amlodipine, isradipine, nicardipine) should be used cautiously in patients with concomitant angina pectoris and severe systolic dysfunction.

Individualization of calcium channel blocker therapy must take into account the drug's overall pharmacologic effect and side effect profile.

Indications for Use

33. B.N., a 56-year-old male, has just undergone cardiac catheterization which showed 2-vessel CAD. He refuses to take nitrates because they cause severe headaches. His physician begins anti-anginal therapy with nifedipine (Adalat) 10 mg PO TID. Are the calcium blockers indicated for all types of angina? Is one type of calcium blocker more effective than others?

Yes, calcium channel blockers are effective in both vasospastic and classical exertional angina. Because all of the agents relieve vasospasm of the large coronary arteries, they are effective in treating Prinzmetal's variant angina. Their beneficial effect in chronic stable (effort-induced) angina is multifactorial. By vasodilating,

Table 13.4	Clinical Classification of Calcium Blocking Agents[a]

Type 1: Myocardial, Electrophysiologic, and Vascular Effects
  Diltiazem
  Gallopamil[b]
  Tiapamil[b]
  Verapamil

Type 2: Predominant Vascular Effects (Dihydropyridines)
  Amlodipine
  Felodipine
  Isradapine
  Nicardipine
  Nifedipine
  Niludipine[b]
  Nimodipine
  Nisoldipine[b]
  Nitrendipine

Type 3: Selective Vascular Effects
  Cinnarizine[b]
  Flunarizine[b]

Type 4: Complex Pharmacologic Profiles
  Bepridil
  Lidoflazine[b]
  Perhexiline[b]

[a] Adapted from reference 116.
[b] Not available in the U.S.

Table 13.5 Calcium Channel Blockers in Anginal Syndromes[c]

	Vasodilation	Decreased Contractility[a]	Decreased AV Conduction	FDA Approved[b]	Usual Dose for Chronic Stable Angina	Product Availability
Dihydropyridines						
Amlodipine (Norvasc)	Marked	None or mild	None	Hypertension Angina	2.5–10 mg QD	2.5, 5, 10 mg tab
Felodipine (Plendil)				Hypertension	5–10 mg QD	5, 10 mg ER tab
Isradipine (DynaCirc)				Hypertension	2.5–10 mg BID	2.5, 5 mg cap
Nicardipine (Cardene)	Marked	None or mild	None	Hypertension, Angina	20–40 mg TID 30–60 mg BID	20, 30 mg cap 30, 45, 60 SR cap
Nifedipine (Adalat, Procardia, generic)	Marked	None or mild	None		10–30 mg TID 30–90 mg QD 30–90 mg QD	10, 20 mg cap Adalat cc 30, 60, 90 mg ER Procardia XL 30, 60, 90, mg SR tab
Diphenylalkylamines						
Verapamil (Calan, Isoptin, Verelan, generic)	Moderate	Moderate	Mild	Hypertension, Angina	40–120 mg TID 120–240 mg BID 120–480 mg QD	40, 80, 120 mg tab Calan SR 120, 180, 240, mg SR tab Isoptin SR 120, 180, 240 mg SR tab Verelan 120, 180, 240 mg SR cap
Benzothiazepines						
Diltiazem (Cardizem, generic)	Moderate	Moderate	Mild	Hypertension, Angina	30–120 mg TID/QID 60–180 mg BID 180–360 mg QD 180–480 mg QD	30, 60, 90, 120 mg tab Cardizem SR 60, 90, 120 mg SR cap Cardizem CD 120, 180, 240, 300 mg SR cap Dilacor XR 240 mg SR cap
Bepridil (Vascor)	Moderate	None or mild	Mild	Angina	200–400 mg QD	200, 300, 400 mg tab

[a] The clinical effect of calcium blockers on myocardial contractility is variable and dependent upon the patient's degree of systolic dysfunction and underlying hemodynamic status.
[b] FDA approved indications vary among some immediate-release and sustained-release products.
[c] AV = Atrioventricular; cap = Capsules; ER = Extended-release; FDA = Food and Drug Administration; SR = Sustained-release; tab = Tablets.

they can increase myocardial oxygen supply or reduce demand. Because coronary vasospasm can occur at the site of an atherosclerotic plaque, calcium channel blockers are indicated in mixed and unstable angina. Heightened vasomotor tone in the coronary microcirculation contributes to silent myocardial ischemia, another indication for the broad-spectrum anti-anginal calcium channel blockers.[127] Therefore, B.N. may benefit from nifedipine therapy; however, some physicians elect to avoid nifedipine monotherapy because its potent peripheral vasodilation can cause reflex tachycardia and sometimes actually worsen angina.

Nifedipine

Adverse Effects

34. Two days after beginning nifedipine, B.N. calls his physician complaining of dizziness and a tripling of his angina attacks. He notices that his heart rate increases about 90 minutes after taking the nifedipine and shortly after that he develops chest pain. Could this be a side effect of nifedipine therapy?

Yes. About 10% of all patients receiving nifedipine will experience worsening of their angina.[128] B.N.'s complaints of dizziness probably are due to the powerful peripheral vasodilator effect of nifedipine that can precipitate an exaggerated reflex increase in the heart rate. Overall, the nifedipine-induced hypotension and reflex increase in heart rate can increase MVO_2.[129] In extreme cases, nifedipine can precipitate a myocardial infarction. B.N. was wise to call his physician immediately and report these symptoms. Given his history of nitrate-induced headaches, B.N. probably should have had therapy started with a less potent peripheral vaso-

dilator such as verapamil or diltiazem. These two agents are less likely to cause reflex tachycardia and precipitate angina.

Some side effects of the calcium channel blockers also reflect an extension of their hemodynamic and electrophysiologic profiles and, therefore, are predictable (see Table 13.6). Dihydropyridine-induced (nifedipine) hypotension and dizziness can occur in about 15% of patients. Patients also may complain of lightheadedness, facial flushing, headache, and nausea. Swelling of the lower legs and ankles (peripheral edema) appears to be related to the potent peripheral vasodilating effects of these agents. Overall, nifedipine-like drugs appear to have more side effects than verapamil or diltiazem.[132] Monotherapy with the dihydropyridines usually is avoided for angina patients.

35. How can B.N.'s physician modify the nifedipine regimen to avoid angina exacerbation?

Because B.N. already is receiving the lowest common daily dose, dosage reduction is not possible. B.N. could be switched to another calcium channel blocker such as verapamil or diltiazem that produces a mild resting bradycardia and a marked reduction in exercise-induced tachycardia.[130] B.N. also could receive a β-adrenergic blocker in combination with nifedipine.[131] The beta blocker would limit the reflex tachycardia induced by nifedipine and provide additional anti-anginal benefits. Monotherapy with a beta blocker also is a reasonable alternative provided B.N. has no contraindications to beta blockers.

Contraindications

36. Does B.N. have any contraindications to calcium channel blockers?

Table 13.6	Common Side Effects of Calcium Channel Blockers[a],[b]		
	Verapamil	Diltiazem	Amlodipine, Felodipine, Isradipine, Nicardipine Nifedipine
↑ Angina	R	R	F,P
Bradycardias	F,P	F,P	N
Constipation	F,P	R	N
Dyspnea	R	R	F,P
Flushing	R	R	F,P
Headache	R	R	F,P
Hypotension	R,P	R,P	F,P
Lightheadedness	R	R	F,P
Palpitations	R	R	F,P
Peripheral Edema	R	R	F,P
MI	R	R	F,P
Worsen Mild CHF	R,P	R,P	N

a Side effects generally are dose related and more frequent during the first few weeks of therapy. Actual incidence of occurrence varies widely and estimates are provided based upon authors' clinical experience and literature data.

b Some minor differences between these agents may exist. F = Frequent; P = Potential for severe effect in an individual patient; R = Rare; N = Not likely to occur; CHF = Congestive heart failure; MI = Myocardial infarction.

Contraindications to calcium channel blockers are based upon pharmacologic actions of these agents (see Table 13.7). Because B.N. has no apparent history of cardiac conduction disorders or heart failure, he is a suitable candidate for a trial of calcium blockers.

Diltiazem and Verapamil: Adverse Effects

37. Diltiazem (Cardizem CD) 180 mg/day PO is prescribed for B.N. What side effects should be anticipated with diltiazem and other calcium channel blockers?

Verapamil and diltiazem have similar side effect profiles, although some clinicians feel diltiazem is better tolerated. The lower incidence of side effects reported with diltiazem as compared to verapamil may reflect a true difference or, perhaps, less aggressive dosing regimens. Both drugs can cause sinus bradycardia and worsen already existing conduction deficits and heart blocks.[133] Neither should be used in patients with sick sinus syndrome or advanced degrees of heart block unless a functioning ventricular pacemaker is present. Patients should be monitored for signs of worsening CHF such as shortness of breath, weight gain, and peripheral edema. Verapamil-induced constipation can be particularly troublesome to the elderly. Rare instances of fecal impaction requiring surgery illustrate the need for the aggressive use of stool softening agents and, often, bulk-forming laxatives.

Generalized fatigue and nonspecific GI complaints may occur with any of the calcium channel blockers. In rare instances, elevations of hepatic enzymes and acute hepatic injury have occurred with the calcium channel blockers. Appreciation for the individual side effect profiles helps determine preference for one calcium blocker over another. B.N. is not likely to experience major side effects with verapamil or diltiazem.

38. After several weeks' therapy with Cardizem CD 180 mg QD, B.N. still is having several angina attacks weekly. He has not experienced any side effects other than an occasional headache. What is the maximum diltiazem dose that can be used?

All calcium channel blocker doses are titrated gradually upward. Most patients start diltiazem therapy with 30 or 60 mg three or

four times a day, or alternatively, an equivalent dose of a sustained-release diltiazem. The dose can be increased every one or two days as needed or tolerated. Optimal daily diltiazem doses originally were thought to be 180 or 240 mg. However, several studies demonstrated that efficacy in the treatment of angina occurred only with divided doses of ≥240 mg/day. Therefore, the usual maximum diltiazem dose is about 360 mg/day.[134] Careful monitoring for bradycardia and heart failure is imperative at this dose.

Verapamil

Risk/Benefit Assessment

39. A.E., a 65-year-old male, has newly diagnosed angina pectoris. He refused cardiac catheterization; however, his coronary risk factors include a strong family history of cardiovascular disease and hyperlipoproteinemia. He contracted rheumatic fever at age 12 and 5 years ago, his mitral valve was replaced. At that time he had 2-vessel CAD with 80% and 85% occlusion and a left ventricular EF of 30% (Normal: 55%). During this hospitalization, new-onset atrial fibrillation was observed with a ventricular response rate of 115–130/min. Current medications include: warfarin (Coumadin) 5 mg 5 days/week and 2.5 mg 2 days/week; digoxin (Lanoxin) 0.25 mg/day (serum digoxin concentration drawn 18 hours after the last dose is 1.0 ng/mL); and furosemide 40 mg/day. A.E.'s physician wishes to begin verapamil 60 mg PO QID. What is the risk versus benefit of adding verapamil to A.E.'s medical regimen?

A.E. has a complicated history. Although a repeat cardiac catheterization would help confirm the progression of atherosclerosis, it is likely that he has significant coronary artery disease. Because calcium channel blockers are effective in all forms of angina, they are especially useful in patients with mixed angina syndromes or in patients in whom the diagnosis is not firmly established. Although A.E. has mild to moderate congestive heart failure as evidenced by his depressed ejection fraction, verapamil (and diltiazem) can be used if the initial dose is titrated carefully. In A.E., verapamil or diltiazem would have the added benefit of slowing conduction through the AV node, thereby decreasing the ventricular response to his atrial fibrillation.[133] Nifedipine and related dihydropyridines which can increase the heart rate may not be a good choice for A.E., although they may cause less aggravation of his CHF. Overall, A.E. probably will benefit from verapamil. It should prevent his angina as well as control his arrhythmia.

Interaction with Digoxin

40. A.E.'s computerized medication profile highlights a drug interaction between verapamil and digoxin. Is this interaction likely to cause problems for A.E.?

Addition of verapamil can decrease the renal and nonrenal clearance of digoxin and increase the serum digoxin concentration by

Table 13.7	Contraindications to Calcium Channel Blockers[a]

Severe hypotension
Severe aortic stenosis
Extreme bradycardia
Moderate to severe heart failure
Cardiogenic shock
Sick sinus syndrome
2nd- or 3rd-degree AV block[b]
WPW syndrome with atrial fibrillation or flutter[b]

a AV = Atrioventricular; WPW = Wolf-Parkinson-White. Bepridil use requires extra precaution for potential drug-induced arrhythmias and agranulocytosis.

b Nifedipine and related dihydropyridines generally may be used safely as they do not depress sinoatrial or atrioventricular node conduction.

about 60%.[135,136] The serum digoxin concentration increases over several days until a new steady-state digoxin level is reached in about seven days. Digoxin and verapamil also have an additive effect on the heart rate.

Some patients may develop overt digoxin toxicity as a result of this interaction; however, the clinical significance varies among individuals. To evaluate the potential risk of adding verapamil to A.E.'s regimen, one should estimate his digitalization status by considering his age, weight, renal function, electrolyte status, thyroid function, and serum digoxin concentration. If he is maximally digitalized, the digoxin dose could be decreased by one-third to one-half when starting verapamil. Because A.E. has a low serum baseline digoxin concentration, the same digoxin dose could be continued; however, he should be monitored closely for signs of digoxin toxicity and frequent digoxin levels should be obtained. A.E. potentially could benefit from the additive effects of these drugs on atrioventricular conduction. Alternatively, diltiazem could be substituted for verapamil since it appears to increase digoxin levels to a lesser extent.[133] (See Chapters 15: Congestive Heart Failure and 33: Solid Organ Transplantation for further discussion of the verapamil-digoxin and calcium channel blocker-cyclosporine interactions.)

Second-Generation Dihydropyridines

41. A request has been made to add nicardipine and amlodipine to the hospital formulary. The current formulary includes verapamil, diltiazem, and nifedipine. What issues should be considered by the Pharmacy and Therapeutics (P&T) Committee?

Nicardipine and amlodipine share many similar effects with the prototype dihydropyridine, nifedipine.[118,119] Nicardipine is effective and reasonably well tolerated in the treatment of chronic stable angina pectoris.[118] It appears to be as effective as nifedipine, propranolol, and atenolol in the treatment of chronic stable angina.[118] However, nicardipine may be less effective than verapamil.[137] Nicardipine also can be combined with β-adrenergic blockers and/or nitrates.

Adverse effects attributable to nicardipine generally are related to vasodilation and include flushing, headache, dizziness, and pedal or ankle edema.[118] Up to 10% of patients may require discontinuation of nicardipine due to intolerable adverse effects. Like nifedipine, nicardipine occasionally may precipitate an episode of angina pectoris presumably secondary to reflex tachycardia or diminished coronary perfusion. However, nicardipine may impair ventricular systolic function to a lesser degree than nifedipine,[126] and it may be used safely in patients with conduction deficits as it does not depress SA or AV node functions.[118]

Amlodipine is efficacious in the treatment of both chronic stable angina and vasospastic angina.[119] In addition, it is as effective as nadolol and diltiazem in the treatment of chronic stable angina,[119] and safely can be used concomitantly with beta blockers.

Like other dihydropyridines, the majority of amlodipine's adverse effects can be attributed to its vasodilating effects.[119] Some of these, such as edema and flushing, may be dose related. Amlodipine appears to be tolerated as well as verapamil, diltiazem, and several beta blockers.

Other second generation dihydropyridines, such as felodipine and isradipine, currently are approved only for the treatment of hypertension. However, preliminary evidence suggests that these agents may be as effective as either β-adrenergic blockers or nifedipine in the management of chronic stable angina. Further clinical trials are needed to better assess the anti-anginal effects of these agents. In summary, the P&T Committee decision will be hampered by the lack of studies directly comparing the efficacy

and safety of the various dihydropyridines. However it is unlikely these drugs differ substantially in clinical effect. Therefore, the differences in acquisition cost may be a major factor in selecting agents for formulary inclusion.

Pharmacokinetics

42. Do any of the calcium channel blockers require dosage adjustment in patients with renal or hepatic disease?

Currently available calcium channel antagonists demonstrate similar pharmacokinetic properties.[118-121,138,139] With the exception of amlodipine and the sustained-release formulations, all are absorbed rapidly following oral administration and generally reach peak concentrations within one to two hours. Peak concentrations for amlodipine usually are achieved within six to nine hours after administration. Although calcium channel antagonists are well absorbed, bioavailability generally is low due largely to first-pass metabolism. In addition, calcium channel antagonists tend to have high metabolic clearances; their pharmacokinetic parameters are related to hepatic blood flow and intrinsic clearance, and they are metabolized almost exclusively by the liver. Furthermore, intra- and interindividual variations in bioavailability and total body clearance for most calcium channel antagonists are great. Therefore, dosage adjustment probably is necessary in patients with severe hepatic impairment, but not those with renal disease.

The clinical significance of the reduced plasma clearance which accompanies long-term verapamil therapy is unknown. The half-life may be prolonged from four to five hours initially to 10 to 12 hours following chronic dosing. This may reflect verapamil's effect on liver blood flow or a saturation of the hepatic removal mechanism. Future work may support the use of a twice-daily verapamil regimen for angina similar to that of propranolol.[140]

Sustained-Release (SR) Calcium Channel Blockers

43. L.M., a 45-year-old female surgeon with a 3-year history of hypertension, recently was switched to SR verapamil 240 mg BID. As a newly-diagnosed chronic stable angina patient, she wonders if studies support the use of SR calcium channel blockers in angina.

Sustained-release calcium channel blockers are attractive alternatives to immediate-release products. The sustained-release formulations of verapamil, diltiazem, and nifedipine offer promise in improving patient compliance and thereby better control of anginal episodes. L.M. uses the first sustained-release calcium channel blocker marketed in the U.S. Sustained-release verapamil is absorbed more slowly than immediate-release verapamil, thus providing more constant serum levels. The SR formulation, with a bioavailability of 0.9, extends the verapamil elimination half-life to 12 hours compared to about six hours observed with the immediate-release product.[142] While some patients experience adequate control with once-daily SR verapamil, most patients require twice-daily dosing.[142] The side effect profiles for immediate- and sustained-release verapamil are quite similar with constipation being frequent. Diltiazem SR also exhibits slowed absorption and a prolonged half-life compared to immediate-release diltiazem. Like verapamil SR, twice-daily dosing is appropriate for most patients. A newer version of sustained-release diltiazem (Cardizem CD available as 180, 240, and 300 mg capsules) may be given once daily. It is important that the Cardizem SR and Cardizem CD products are not confused. Another sustained-release diltiazem product (Dilacor SR) employs yet another delivery system; while potentially less expensive, it should not be substituted for either Cardizem SR or Cardizem CD. Both verapamil SR and diltiazem SR and CD are FDA-approved only for treatment of hypertension, although many clinicians use these drugs to treat angina. Another sustained-release verapamil product (Verlan) uses beaded capsules and can be dosed reliably once a day. Therefore verapamil SR and Verelan should not be interchanged.

Sustained-release nifedipine (Procardia XL) uses a unique drug delivery system based upon the osmotic pump principle. The GITS (gastrointestinal system) nifedipine tablet consists of a semiper-meable membrane that surrounds an active drug core. The core is composed of two layers: an active drug layer and an inert, but osmotically active push layer. Water entering the tablet from the GI tract activates the osmotic pump mechanism and pushes the active nifedipine out through a laser-drilled hole in the tablet's active layer. The inert components eventually are eliminated in the feces as a shell. The tablet should not be crushed, divided, or chewed. It should be taken at the same time each day and may be taken either with food or on an empty stomach.

The nifedipine GITS provides consistent (zero order rate), 24-hour serum nifedipine levels independent of pH or gastrointestinal motility. Although this formulation decreases the vasodilatory effects observed with immediate-release nifedipine, dose-related edema is a frequent adverse experience occurring in 10% to 30% of patients. Headache is another common adverse effect. Limited experience suggests that patients switched from immediate-release nifedipine to nifedipine GITS will experience fewer angina episodes and side effects. Another form of extended-release tablets (Adalat CC) can be administered once daily. When patients are converted to any SR calcium channel blocker, reassessment of therapeutic efficacy is necessary. Because variations in sustained-release products exist, they should not be substituted for one another. The cost of the sustained-release calcium channel blockers is similar to equivalent immediate-release doses; however, the availability of generic immediate-release alternatives should be considered.

Combination Therapy

44. E.R., a 57-year-old male with a long history of angina pectoris, has survived 1 out-of-hospital cardiac arrest and 2 MIs. He is not considered a surgical candidate for coronary artery bypass grafting because of severe COAD. His current medications include: isosorbide dinitrate 60 mg PO TID, metoprolol 50 mg PO BID, diltiazem 120 mg PO TID, theophylline 400 mg PO BID, metaproterenol inhaler 2 puffs QID, NTG spray 0.4 mg PRN chest pain, and enteric-coated aspirin 325 mg/day. Is it rational for E.R. to receive a nitrate, beta blocker, and calcium channel blocker simultaneously?

E.R. is taking near maximal doses of all his medications. Using all three classes of drugs allows E.R.'s physician to titrate doses to maximize benefits and minimize troublesome side effects. E.R. probably cannot tolerate a higher beta blocker dose because of his pulmonary disease. Disadvantages of triple drug therapy include cost[144] and the potential for additive side effects, such as the possible worsening of heart failure by a combination of metoprolol and diltiazem. Excessive vasodilation and bradycardia are common side effects of triple drug therapy, but these may be minimized by using a calcium channel blocker with less potent vasodilating properties.

The combination of verapamil (or diltiazem) plus beta blockers appears to have the greatest therapeutic efficacy, but it also poses the highest risk.[145] Patients at risk include those with clinically significant heart failure, cardiac conduction disturbances, and hypotension. Nifedipine plus a beta blocker is a safer combination, but also may be less efficacious.[146]

Simultaneous use of two calcium channel blockers is an alternative for patients who remain symptomatic despite maximal tolerated doses of single drugs and standard triple drug therapy (ni-

trate + beta blocker + calcium blocker).[147] The combination of nifedipine with diltiazem or a verapamil-like calcium channel blocker will limit dizziness and effects on cardiac conduction and contractility. Addition of the second calcium channel blocker may permit use of a lower dose of the other agent, thus minimizing the synergistic vasodilatory effects.

Bepridil

45. Could E.R. benefit from bepridil?

Bepridil (Vascor) is a calcium channel blocking agent chemically unrelated to verapamil, nifedipine, and other calcium channel blockers. It is approved for the treatment of chronic stable angina for patients who fail to respond to or who are intolerant of other anti-anginal drugs.[143] Bepridil's pharmacology is considerably different from other calcium channel blockers. It is both a calcium channel blocker and a sodium channel blocker. Therefore, it will increase the atrial and ventricular effective refractory periods and thus prolong the QT interval. About 1% of patients treated with bepridil in clinical trials developed ventricular arrhythmias. Other potentially serious adverse effects of bepridil include torsade de pointes (polymorphic ventricular tachycardia associated with a prolonged QT interval) and agranulocytosis. Even though bepridil is a once-a-day calcium channel blocker, its adverse reaction profile severely limits its role in treating chronic stable angina. Patients such as E.R. probably will be at maximally tolerated doses of a long-acting nitrate, a beta blocker, and a calcium channel blocker before being given a trial of bepridil. In addition, most patients will have prescriptions for aspirin therapy and a short-acting nitroglycerin preparation. Before trying bepridil therapy for E.R., clinicians should consider combination calcium channel blocker therapy with nifedipine and either verapamil or diltiazem. E.R. should not receive bepridil unless other anti-anginal regimens fail. If E.R. had a history of drug-induced ventricular arrhythmias or prolonged QT syndrome, he should not receive bepridil. Because electrolyte disturbances such as hypokalemia and hypomagnesemia can predispose patients to drug-induced ventricular arrhythmias, routine monitoring of serum electrolytes is advised.

Antiplatelet Therapy

Aspirin

46. E.R. is taking enteric-coated aspirin every day. He wants your advice as to why he is getting this drug and if it is safe for his stomach.

Platelet activation produces coronary occlusion either by formation of a platelet plug or through release of vasoactive compounds from the platelet. Two indices of platelet activity which have been studied intensely in patients with coronary artery disease are thromboxane A_2 and prostacyclin. The biosynthesis of thromboxane A_2, a cyclooxygenase product of arachidonic acid and a potent vasoconstrictor, was increased in patients with unstable angina, but not in patients with chronic stable angina.[148] Prostacyclin, the counterpart of thromboxane A_2, is a potent inhibitor of platelet aggregation and a vasodilator. Even though its production also is increased in unstable angina and acute myocardial infarction, it is insufficient to offset the effects of elevated thromboxane A_2 levels.

The mechanism of action for aspirin's antiplatelet effect is inhibition of cyclooxygenase. (See Chapter 12: Thrombosis.) By acetylating the active site of cyclooxygenase, aspirin blocks the formation of prostaglandin endoperoxides from arachidonic acid. This inhibits the formation of thromboxane and prostacyclin.[149] Researchers have tested various aspirin doses in hopes of finding a dose which inhibits thromboxane synthesis, but does not inhibit formation of prostacyclin. A single 100 mg aspirin dose reduces thromboxane A_2 production by 98% within one hour, while 30 mg/day virtually eliminates thromboxane A_2 synthesis.[21,148,149]

Recent research has attempted to determine the effect of aspirin doses on the thromboxane A_2/prostacyclin (prostaglandin I_2) balance. Prostacylin production can recover within hours of aspirin administration because the endothelial cell can resynthesize cyclooxygenase. In contrast, the inhibition of platelet cyclooxygenase is irreversible. Selective inhibition of platelet-generated thromboxane A_2 synthesis has been shown with 75 mg of controlled-release aspirin daily.[21] This aspirin formulation undergoes extensive first-pass metabolism forming salicylate, a weak and reversible cyclooxygenase inhibitor. Theoretically, administration of 75 mg aspirin daily in a controlled-release formulation may selectively spare vascular endothelial prostacyclin production (preserving the vasodilator activity of prostacyclin), but at the same time still inhibit platelet cyclooxygenase. Unfortunately, we do not yet have controlled clinical trials on this proposed aspirin dosage regimen. Therefore, the proposed biochemical selectivity of aspirin on platelet function versus the vascular endothelium is difficult to achieve clinically.

Two large studies have confirmed the protective effect of aspirin in patients with unstable angina. (see Question 57 for further discussion of unstable angina.) In a multicenter, double-blind, placebo-controlled trial (Veterans Administration Cooperative Study), 1266 men with unstable angina received daily aspirin (324 mg as Alka-Seltzer dissolved in water) or placebo for 12 weeks.[150] Aspirin therapy was begun within 51 hours of hospital admission. Both death and MI rates were decreased by about 50% in the aspirin group. Adverse effects including epigastric burning, decreased hemoglobin concentration, and occult blood in stool were similar in both the aspirin and placebo groups. When patients chewed a 325 mg enteric-coated aspirin tablet, thromboxane A_2 production was greatly inhibited within 15 minutes. Therefore, patients with unstable angina or evolving myocardial infarction are instructed to chew and swallow an aspirin tablet immediately on hospital arrival.

The Canadian Multicenter Trial comparing aspirin and sulfinpyrazone also supported the beneficial effect of aspirin in patients with unstable angina. Hospitalized patients with unstable angina were assigned to one of four treatment groups within eight days of admission: aspirin 325 mg four times a day, sulfinpyrazone 200 mg four times a day, both, or neither.[151] All deaths were reduced by 71%. A 51% reduction in the incidence of cardiac death and nonfatal MI was observed in the aspirin-only group. No benefit was observed with sulfinpyrazone therapy. Gastrointestinal side effects were 29% more common in the groups given aspirin than in the other groups, with potentially dangerous GI side effects occurring in 1 out of 129 placebo patients, 3 out of 139 aspirin-alone patients, 5 out of 150 sulfinpyrazone patients, and 6 of 137 aspirin plus sulfinpyrazone patients. In summary, aspirin reduces the incidence of myocardial infarction and death from cardiac causes by 50% to 70% in patients with unstable angina.

Although patients with chronic stable exertional angina have received routine aspirin therapy for many years, data to support this clinical practice first appeared in a subanalysis of the Physicians' Health Study.[21] Over 300 men with chronic stable angina received either aspirin 325 mg/day or a placebo. In these stable angina patients, daily aspirin therapy decreased the incidence of a first myocardial infarction by 87%. Even in asymptomatic men, daily aspirin therapy reduced the rate of first myocardial infarction by 44%.

Aspirin remains the most commonly prescribed antiplatelet agent, and is used in the treatment of a number of cardiovascular diseases. Further discussions of aspirin use in primary prevention of myocardial infarction, secondary prevention of MI, combined therapy with thrombolytics in the treatment of acute myocardial infarction, unstable angina, atrial fibrillation, prosthetic valves, and postoperative coronary artery bypass graft are discussed in Chapters 12: Thrombosis, 14: Myocardial Infarction, and 16: Cardiac Arrhythmias. Aspirin also is a key drug in treating cerebrovascular disease as presented in Chapter 53: Cerebrovascular Disorders.

Variant Angina (Coronary Artery Spasm)
Clinical Presentation

47. A.P., a 35-year-old female, is hospitalized for evaluation of severe chest pain which occurs almost daily at about 5:00 a.m. A.P. ranks the severity of pain as 7–8 on a 1–10 scale. It is associated with diaphoresis and is not relieved by change in position. A.P. has no cardiovascular risk factors and her hobbies include triathlon competition and rock climbing, neither of which has caused chest pain. She follows a strict vegetarian diet and takes no medications. Admission ECG reveals sinus bradycardia at 56 beats/min. Serum electrolytes, chemistry panel, and cardiac enzymes are all within normal limits.

At 6:00 a.m. the next morning, A.P. is awakened abruptly by severe chest pain. Her vital signs include: heart rate 55 beats/min, supine BP 110/64 mm Hg, and respiratory rate 12/min. A "stat" ECG shows sinus bradycardia with marked ST-segment elevation. The pain is relieved within 60 seconds by 1 NTG 0.4 mg SL tablet. During the day, she completes an exercise tolerance test without complication or evidence of CAD.

On the second day, A.P. undergoes cardiac catheterization and no coronary atherosclerosis is visualized. An ergonovine provocation test is performed during cardiac catheterization. At 3-minute intervals ergonovine maleate bolus doses are given: 0.05 mg, 0.10 mg, and 0.25 mg. At 0.25 mg A.P. develops severe chest pain associated with an ST-segment elevation of 0.3 mV. The cardiologist observes almost complete vasospasm of the right coronary artery and she immediately injects 200 µg NTG into the coronary artery along with administering 2 lingual sprays of NTG. A.P.'s chest pain resolves within 60 seconds and the ECG normalizes within 3 minutes. A.P. is diagnosed as having Prinzmetal's variant angina. Discharge medications include: SR verapamil 240 mg QD at 11:00 p.m. and NTG lingual spray 0.4 mg PRN chest pain. Is A.P.'s presentation typical for Prinzmetal's variant angina?

A.P. presents with a classical picture of variant (Prinzmetal's) angina, total occlusion of a large epicardial coronary artery as a result of severe segmental spasm.[3] Clinical manifestations include chest pain occurring at rest, often in the morning hours.[152] Like A.P., patients with Prinzmetal's variant angina generally are younger than patients with chronic stable angina and do not carry the high risk profile.[153] Other vasospastic disorders such as migraine attacks or Raynaud's phenomenon may be present; smoking and alcohol ingestion may be important contributing factors.[153,154]

The hallmark of variant angina is ST-segment elevation on the ECG, which denotes rapid and complete occlusion of the coronary artery.[155] Many patients also have asymptomatic episodes of ST-segment elevation. Transient arrhythmias and conduction disturbances may be observed during pain depending upon the severity of the myocardial ischemia. In contrast to chronic stable angina in which the heart rate-blood pressure product often is elevated with pain, no hemodynamic factors appear to contribute to Prinzmetal's variant angina.[156]

As documented by angiography, A.P. has vasospasm of the large right coronary artery. This transient, reversible narrowing probably is due to increased coronary vascular resistance. It can occur in the absence of atherosclerosis, as illustrated by A.P., or it may occur in the presence of coronary artery disease. One possible explanation for vasospasm occurring more commonly at night or during the early morning hours is increased vasomotor tone secondary to diurnal variations in catecholamines.

Ergonovine Stimulation Test

48. Why was the ergonovine test used? Was intracoronary NTG necessary to reverse the effects of ergonovine?

Because Prinzmetal's variant angina does not occur predictably, spasm must be induced under controlled circumstances. Ergonovine maleate, an ergot alkaloid that stimulates α-adrenergic and serotonergic receptors, exerts a direct vasoconstrictive effect on the vascular smooth muscle.[157] The ergonovine maleate provocation test is highly specific and sensitive, especially in patients with normal coronary arteries. The risks of the test, which often discourage some physicians from using ergonovine, include arrhythmias (heart blocks, ventricular tachycardia, ventricular fibrillation) and possible MI. Very low doses of intracoronary ergonovine (6 to 50 μg) may be safer than intravenous administration.[157]

The vasospasm induced by ergonovine should be reversed promptly. Although sublingual NTG tablets or lingual spray may relieve the episode, the coronary vasospasm may be unresponsive to these agents.[158] Direct injection of NTG into the coronary arteries immediately reverses the vasoconstrictor action of ergonovine.[157]

Therapy

49. Is one calcium channel blocker preferable to another for treatment of Prinzmetal's variant angina? Would long-acting nitrates or β-adrenergic blockers be alternatives to verapamil for A.P.?

All calcium channel blockers appear equally effective in preventing Prinzmetal's variant angina.[159] However, some patients may respond better to one agent than another.

Even though nitrates cause vasodilation by a different mechanism than calcium channel blockers, they are effective in treating Prinzmetal's variant angina.[160] To avoid tolerance, the nitrate-free interval for A.P. should be scheduled during the day so that the early morning hours are covered by NTG. For example, A.P. could apply a transdermal nitroglycerin patch at bedtime and remove it upon awakening. In patients who continue to experience pain using maximal calcium channel blocker doses, combination therapy with nitrates should be tried.[161] Aspirin therapy is indicated for A.P.

Beta blockers are likely to worsen A.P.'s angina because blockade of the β₂-receptors which mediate vasodilation may allow unopposed alpha-mediated vasoconstriction. A cardioselective beta blocker also may worsen Prinzmetal's variant angina; therefore, calcium channel blockers or nitrates are preferable.

50. Will A.P. require treatment for the remainder of her life?[150]

During the first year of therapy, up to 50% of patients experience spontaneous remission by an unknown mechanism. This occurs most frequently in patients who have had a short duration of symptoms or have normal or mildly-diseased coronary arteries.[162] If A.P. is pain-free and is not experiencing significant arrhythmias or silent ischemic episodes of Prinzmetal's angina after one year, the verapamil could be tapered and discontinued. Modification of smoking and ethanol ingestion may promote remission of Prinzmetal's angina.

51. Can variant angina lead to acute MI or death?

Variant angina, particularly in patients with multivessel coronary artery spasm, can lead to acute myocardial infarction or death. In a study of 159 consecutive patients with variant angina in Japan who required hospitalization, 76% of patients experienced a cardiac event (acute MI in 19 patients, sudden death in five patients,

and coronary artery bypass graft in 1 patient) within one month of onset of angina.[152] These patients had greatly improved outcomes if treated aggressively with calcium antagonists, nicorandil, and nitroglycerin infusion during the early stages. If variant angina persisted, revascularization of coronary arteries with underlying critical lesions was indicated.

Microvascular Ischemia (Syndrome X)

52. K.G., a 50-year-old female executive, has undergone an extensive cardiovascular work-up for exertional angina associated with a 3 mm ST-segment depression. A recent cardiac catheterization did not reveal any atherosclerosis and an ergonovine stimulation test did not produce observable coronary vasospasm. The cardiologists believe K.G. has microvascular ischemia. What drug therapy might be indicated for K.G.?

Syndrome X, increasingly known as microvascular angina, is ischemia due to increased coronary arteriolar resistance. It may be the result of either reduced responsiveness to vasodilating stimuli (e.g., endothelia relaxation factor, kinins, atrial natriuretic peptide, prostaglandin I₂) or increased sensitivity to vasoconstricting stimuli (e.g., catecholamines, vasopressin, angiotensin II, thromboxane A₂). Microvascular angina differs substantially from variant angina. While spasm-causing variant angina may be visible with coronary angiography, the microvascular intramural coronary circulation in spasm is not visible. The changes in coronary artery tone are in the distal coronary arteries and perhaps the collateral vessels. The mechanism of enhanced small vessel responsiveness in microvascular angina is unknown, but somehow involves an imbalance between vasoconstrictor responses and vasodilator responses. Some patients with microvascular ischemia have other smooth muscle disorders such as esophageal motility disorders. There is a definite link between coronary vasoconstriction and mental or psychological stress.

By symptoms alone, K.G.'s presentation is not significantly different from that of a patient with exercise-induced angina secondary to atherosclerosis. However, with a 3 mm ST depression as seen on her ECG, one would expect to find either severe coronary artery disease during catheterization or frank vasospasm during ergonovine testing. The absence of these findings in K.G. confirms the diagnosis of microvascular angina. Overall, the prognosis for patients with microvascular angina appears good; however, both subendocardial infarction and depressed left ventricular function due to repetitive ischemia may occur. Calcium antagonists, while useful, do not always relieve the prearteriolar intramural vasoconstriction of microvascular angina. Nitrates also may provide benefit. β-adrenergic blockers are much less effective in microvascular angina and may worsen the condition by permitting unopposed alpha-stimulation. However, in K.G., they may provide some benefit by blocking the catecholamine release associated with emotional stress. K.G.'s therapy probably should include a short-acting nitroglycerin for acute pain relief, a sustained-release calcium antagonist, and strict attention to avoidance of potential stimulants such as smoking, emotional stress, and perhaps early morning exercise. Although unproven, aspirin may be helpful as well.

Silent Myocardial Ischemia

Definition

53. Y.G., a 60-year-old male who has had his first complete physical examination in 12 years, is found to have Q waves on ECG indicating a previous MI. Physical findings were normal except for borderline left ventricular hypertrophy. Abnormal laboratory studies include a moderately elevated total serum cholesterol and triglycerides. His medical history is remarkable

for hypertension controlled with 1 Dyazide daily. Y.G. does not recall ever experiencing angina, nor has he ever been told he had a heart attack. What characteristic syndrome does Y.G. exhibit and how does it differ from angina pectoris?

Y.G. has suffered a silent myocardial infarction, often the first indicator of silent myocardial ischemia.[164] Silent myocardial ischemia is unrecognized by the patient because there are no symptoms of angina. It can occur in totally asymptomatic persons (Type 1), asymptomatic postinfarction patients (Type 2), and in patients with angina (Type 3).[165] The prevalence of silent myocardial ischemia is hard to estimate because it often is undetected. It is estimated that there are one to two million totally asymptomatic men with silent myocardial ischemia and that there are 50,000 new cases of postinfarction silent ischemia each year. It appears that most patients with angina also have episodes of silent ischemia, with the silent episodes occurring two to three times more frequently than the anginal episodes. The pathogenesis of silent ischemia is not fully defined. There may be an abnormality in pain threshold so that the anginal warning system is not triggered, or it may represent varying activation of coronary vasomotor tone or platelet activity.[166]

Prognosis

54. What is Y.G.'s prognosis?

Y.G.'s prognosis depends upon the extent of his underlying coronary artery disease, ventricular function, and arrhythmia status. If Y.G. has multivessel disease he is more likely to develop adverse cardiac events (reinfarction, unstable angina, sudden death) than if he has single vessel disease. Silent myocardial ischemia is especially ominous in patients with unstable angina.[165,167]

Diagnosis

55. What diagnostic tests will be used to evaluate Y.G.'s total ischemic burden both before and after therapy is started?

The total ischemic burden, the sum of painful and painless ischemic episodes that occur, is assessed with exercise testing and 24-hour ambulatory electrocardiographic (Holter) monitoring.[169] Both tests will measure ST-segment depression, the usual abnormal electrocardiographic response to ischemia. ST-segment depression greater than 2 mm at low levels of exercise or ST-depression with hypotension or arrhythmias is a strong indicator of disease.[169] Radionuclide procedures help confirm ECG responses.[170]

Management

56. What management goals and techniques are likely to apply to Y.G.?

Management of patients with silent myocardial ischemia is unresolved, but modification of risk factors is mandatory.[164,171] Y.G.'s cholesterol and hypertension should be corrected and the aim of pharmacotherapy probably will be to abolish all electrocardiographic evidence of ischemia.[172] It appears that the same drugs used to treat angina (nitrates, beta blockers, calcium channel blockers, and aspirin) also will prevent silent myocardial ischemia if used at high enough doses or in appropriate combinations.[172,173] Beta blockers may be the most effective agents in decreasing the episodes of silent ischemia. Calcium antagonists are useful; however, dihydropyridines are less efficacious than verapamil and diltiazem. Aspirin and nitrates also are key therapies in treating silent myocardial ischemia. Each patient will require careful titration to reduce both symptomatic and asymptomatic ischemic episodes. Even though many questions remain unanswered about silent myocardial ischemia, it is no longer acceptable to treat painful ischemic episodes only.

Unstable Angina and Alternatives to Medical Therapy

Management

57. F.G., a 54-year-old male, is brought to the ER by helicopter for management of severe, unrelenting chest pain of 2 hours duration. He has no history of CAD, but cardiac risk factors include a strong positive family history of CAD, a 45-pack-year smoking history, and hypertension for 5 years. He is taking propranolol 120 mg PO BID. Physical examination reveals a middle-aged male in obvious distress with the following vital signs: heart rate 110 beats/min, BP 176/108 mm Hg, respiratory rate 18 breaths/min, and temperature 37 °C. Normal lung and heart sounds are heard with the exception of an S_4 gallop. Examination of F.G.'s abdomen and extremities is unremarkable, as is the funduscopic examination. F.G. has received 10 mg morphine sulfate IV and 3 NTG SL tablets 0.4 mg and is still experiencing severe pain that is associated with ST-segment depression. He is placed on oxygen (2 L by nasal prongs) and an NTG infusion (5 µg/min). Rapid upward titration of the NTG to 60 µg/min alleviates the chest pain. His admitting diagnosis is unstable angina/MI. What general guidelines exist for the management of unstable angina?

Unstable angina (also known as preinfarction angina, crescendo angina, and angina at rest) is a medical emergency because F.G. is in danger of having an MI. Unstable angina is a syndrome falling between chronic stable angina and myocardial infarction. There are at least three distinct subgroups of unstable angina patients, each of which has a different clinical course.[174] One subgroup is comprised of patients with progressive angina of recent onset who are experiencing an increase in severity, duration, or frequency of their pain despite medical therapy; they appear to have a more benign course than the other two subgroups. F.G. exemplifies the second, higher-risk, subgroup. These patients have ST-segment depression at rest or with pain. Their chest pain is severe enough to warrant admission to a cardiac intensive care unit until acute MI is excluded as the cause. A third subgroup of unstable angina patients are those who have continuing pain after recovery from myocardial infarction. Postinfarction unstable angina patients are at high risk for reinfarction and death.

Coronary arteriographic studies of patients with unstable angina usually reveal severe atherosclerotic disease. More than 50% of unstable angina patients have silent myocardial ischemia episodes despite intensive medical therapy.[175] All patients with unstable angina are treated in a cardiac intensive care unit and most can be stabilized rapidly with aggressive pharmacologic therapy.[176] Many patients undergo cardiac catheterization. Patients may be suitable candidates for reperfusion (thrombolysis, and/or percutaneous transluminal coronary angioplasty, and/or coronary bypass surgery).[177-179] The choice of procedure depends upon the patient's coronary anatomy and the physician's experience and expertise.

The immediate challenge in the treatment of unstable angina is relief of pain and control of all ischemic episodes. Hospitalization, bedrest, diagnosis and treatment of underlying precipitating factors such as infection, anemia, hypertension, heart failure, and arrhythmias is essential. Nitrates, beta blockers, calcium channel blockers, heparin, and aspirin are all useful drugs and dosage regimens must be titrated carefully for each patient. Intravenous NTG therapy also is useful, as illustrated by F.G. The NTG infusion is begun at a rate of about 5 µg/minute and titrated upward at three- to five-minute intervals until the pain is relieved or hypotension becomes problematic.[178] Advantages of intravenous NTG include fast onset of action and rapid reversibility. Close monitoring of blood pressure is aided by insertion of an arterial line. Further studies are needed to define the clinical significance of nitrate tolerance induced by sustained (12 to 18 hours) NTG infusions. Long-acting oral or topical nitrates should be initiated after F.G. is stabilized on intravenous nitroglycerin. F.G.'s propranolol therapy should be continued, but his high resting heart rate suggests that his sympathetic system may not be adequately blocked. Addition of a calcium channel blocker to nitrate and beta blocker therapy often helps control angina. F.G. also will benefit from antiplatelet therapy (1 aspirin tablet chewed immediately and then daily)[180] and IV heparin therapy. The goal of future medical therapy should be to prevent myocardial ischemia attacks as well as recurrent angina attacks. Persistence of chest pain for more than 48 hours would be an ominous sign.[178] With the current practice of five-drug medical therapy (nitrates, calcium antagonists, beta blockers, IV heparin, and aspirin), less than 10% of patients with unstable angina are truly refractory to medical therapy.[180,181]

58. Within 12 hours, F.G.'s pain is controlled. Emergency cardiac catheterization reveals 99% occlusion of the left main coronary artery. Can F.G. be managed with intensive medical therapy alone?

Large scale studies support surgical therapy over medical therapy for patients with left main coronary disease, three-vessel disease, or two-vessel disease with proximal left anterior descending artery obstruction.[178,180] Medications are used to stabilize the patient before surgery. If possible coronary artery bypass grafting or angioplasty should be delayed until the patient becomes pain-free.

Percutaneous Transluminal Angioplasty (PCTA)

59. Would F.G. be a candidate for PCTA?

Percutaneous transluminal angioplasty is a nonsurgical method of mechanically dilating a coronary artery obstruction through arterial intimal disruption, plaque fissuring, and stretching of the arterial wall.[182] A balloon catheter is advanced through the afflicted coronary artery to the obstruction site and dilated. Balloon inflations are repeated until the plaque is compressed and coronary blood flow resumes. Because the lesion must be accessible, this procedure generally is limited to lesions present in the proximal portion of the vessel.[182] The choice between angioplasty, coronary artery bypass grafting, or medical therapy is based upon the type and distribution of atherosclerosis, vessel size, ventricular function, symptom severity, and the presence of surgical risk factors.

Angioplasty has emerged as a viable alternative in the treatment of both single- and multivessel coronary artery disease.[183] More clinical experience with angioplasty in multivessel disease suggests that the procedure is safe and effective, provides long-term relief from angina symptoms, and improves survival.[184] Acute complications of angioplasty occur in about 3% of patients and can include myocardial infarction, urgent coronary artery bypass graft surgery, and death. Repeat revascularization procedures (either repeat angioplasty or surgery) may be required in as many as 46% of first angioplasty patients. Therefore, the topic of re-stenosis following angioplasty is under intense study.

Some factors which predispose patients to re-stenosis include: angioplasty in the left anterior descending coronary artery, a large residual stenotic lesion, a large pressure gradient remaining after angioplasty, diabetes mellitus, a negative history for myocardial infarction, and persistent angina. Hypercholesterolemia, smoking, and male gender also appear to play a role in re-stenosis. A number of drugs (e.g., aspirin, dipyridamole, heparin, warfarin, nifedipine, diltiazem, corticosteroids, fish oils, prostaglandins, and platelet-derived growth factor antagonists) have been evaluated for the prevention of re-stenosis following angioplasty. None has been shown to alter the re-stenosis rate;[185] however, aspirin therapy still is rou-

tinely prescribed after angioplasty because it reduces the acute complication rate. Some clinicians routinely will prescribe calcium channel blockers to reduce presumed coronary artery spasm.

Given the failure of drugs to prevent re-stenosis, attention now is directed to testing nondrug preventative measures such as intravascular stents (mechanical supports devices) to maintain lumen patency, atherectomy, and laser angioplasty. These interventions, however, do not seem to alter the rate of re-stenosis.[185] Future drug therapy may be directed at blocking smooth muscle cell proliferation which appears to be a key mechanism for re-stenosis. Fractionated low molecular weight heparin derivatives offer some promise.[186] Even the angiotensin-converting enzyme inhibitors are undergoing study for their antiproliferative effects (see Chapter 10: Essential Hypertension).

Because traditional approaches to antiplatelet therapy have failed with agents such as aspirin, new methods are stirring excitement. Platelet adhesion results from the interaction between platelet membrane glycoproteins (glycoprotein Ia and Ib) and macromolecules in the exposed vascular subendothelium. Monoclonal antibodies to glycoproteins IIb and IIIa have protected re-stenosis in baboon models and have been tested in unstable angina patients.[186] Thrombin inhibitors such as hirudin also offer promise. Yet, the safety and efficacy of all of these strategies remain unproven.

Coronary Artery Bypass Graft (CABG) Surgery

60. F.G. is offered CABG surgery; however, he would like to know if medical therapy alone is acceptable.

Coronary artery bypass grafting is a complicated surgical procedure during which an atherosclerotic vessel is "bypassed" using either a patient's saphenous vein or internal mammary artery (MA). The "graft," the saphenous vein or IMA, then allows blood flow past the obstruction in the native vessel. F.G.'s reluctance to undergo coronary artery bypass grafting immediately is understandable. The goals of anti-anginal therapy, whether medical (pharmacologic) or revascularization, remain unchanged: 1) to prolong life, 2) to prevent MI, and 3) to improve the quality of life. Although patient enrollment was completed in 1979, the Coronary Artery Surgery Study (CASS) continues to provide valuable information. After more than ten years follow-up, CASS findings still support the original findings. Angina patient survival rates are improved after surgery compared with initial medical therapy in two groups of patients. This first subgroup is made up of patients who have three-vessel coronary artery disease and an ejection fraction less than 0.50.[186] The second subgroup includes patients with proximal left anterior descending coronary lesions of ≥70% and an ejection fraction less than 0.50. Both of these patient subgroups are more likely to live longer with surgical intervention than with medical management.

Five-year analysis of the CASS study showed that surgery patients appeared to have a better quality of life than the medically treated patients. Surgery patients have greater exercise tolerance, fewer angina episodes, and require fewer anti-anginal drugs. However, ten-year analysis of the CASS study showed that the medical and surgery groups did not differ in their quality of life.[187] The diminished benefit of surgery versus medical therapy at ten versus five years may be attributed to progression of coronary artery disease in the patient's own vessels as well as in the bypass grafts. Also, over ten years, about 35% of patients initially managed medically will require bypass surgery. The impact of newer procedures (e.g., angioplasty) and newer medications (e.g., calcium channel blockers, cholesterol-lowering agents, antiplatelet drugs) has not yet been assessed.

References

1 **Rosengren A et al.** Clinical course and symptomatology of angina pectoris in a population study. Acta Med Scand. 1986;22:117.

2 **Tofler GH, Stone PH.** Clinical patterns of angina pectoris: how pathophysiology determines therapy. Postgrad Med. 1986;80:148.

3 **Prinzmetal M et al.** Angina Pectoris 1. A variant form of angina pectoris. Am J Med. 1959;27:375.

4 **Cohn PF.** Silent myocardial ischemia: classification, prevalence, and prognosis. Am J Med. 1985;79(3A):2.

5 **Kannel WB.** Meaning of the downward trend in cardiovascular mortality. JAMA. 1982;247:887.

6 **Kannel WB et al.** Prognosis after myocardial infarction: the Framingham study. Am J Cardiol. 1979;44(1):53.

7 **Tunstall-Pedoe H.** Angina pectoris: epidemiology and risk factors. Eur Heart J. 1985;6(Suppl. F):1.

8 **Ross G.** The cardiovascular system. In: Ross G, ed. Essentials of Human Physiology. Chicago: Year Book Medical Publishers, Inc.; 1978.

9 **Gensini GC.** Coronary arteriography. In: Braunwald E, ed. Heart Disease: A Textbook of Cardiovascular Medicine. Philadelphia: WB Saunders; 1984:304.

10 **Ross R.** The pathogenesis of atherosclerosis—an update. N Engl J Med. 1986;314:488.

11 **Lichtlen PR.** Pathophysiology of coronary and myocardial function in angina pectoris: important aspects for drug treatment. Eur Heart J. 1985;6 (Suppl. F):11.

12 **Maseri A.** Pathogenetic mechanisms of angina pectoris: expanding views. Br Heart J. 1980;43:648.

13 **Malinow MR.** Atherosclerosis: progression, regression and resolution. Am Heart J. 1984;108:1523.

14 **Singh BN et al.** Newer concepts in the pathogenesis of myocardial ischemia: implications for the evaluation of antianginal therapy. Drugs. 1986;32:1.

15 **Weber RT, Janicki JS.** The metabolic demand and oxygen supply of the heart: physiologic and clinical considerations. Am J Cardiol. 1974;44:722.

16 **Freeman LJ, Nixon PGF.** Dynamic causes of angina pectoris. Am Heart J. 1985:110:1087.

17 **Ganz P et al.** Dynamic variations in resistance of coronary arterial narrowings in angina pectoris at rest. Am J Cardiol. 1987;59:66.

18 **Epstein SE et al.** Hemodynamic principles in the control of coronary blood flow. Am J Cardiol. 1985;56:4E.

19 **Epstein SE, Talbot TL.** Dynamic coronary tone in precipitation, exacerbation and relief of angina pectoris. Am J Cardiol. 1981;48:797.

20 **Brown BG.** Response of normal and diseased epicardial coronary arteries to vasoactive drugs: quantitative arteriographic studies. Am J Cardiol. 1985; 56:23E.

21 **Willard JE et al.** The use of aspirin in ischemic heart disease. N Engl J Med. 1992;327:17.

22 **Heifant RH, Banks VS.** A Clinical and Angiographic Approach to Coronary Heart Disease. Philadelphia: V.A. Davis Co.;1978:47.

23 **Cox J, Naylor CD.** The Canadian Cardiovascular Society Grading Scale for Angina Pectoris: Is it time for refinements? Ann Intern Med. 1992;117: 677.

24 **Cohn PF, Braunwald E.** Chronic ischemic heart disease. In: Braunwald E, ed. Heart Disease: A Textbook of Cardiovascular Medicine. Philadelphia: WB Saunders: 1984:1334.

25 **Lerner DJ, Kannel WB.** Patterns of coronary heart disease morbidity and mortality in the sexes: a 26-year follow-up of the Framingham population. Am Heart J. 1986;11:383.

26 **Barrett-Connor E, Khaw KT.** Family history of heart attack as an independent predictor of death due to cardiovascular disease. Circulation. 1984;69: 1065.

27 **Raichlen JS et al.** Importance of risk factors in the angiographic progression of coronary artery disease. Am J Cardiol. 1986;57:66.

28 **Crow RS et al.** Risk factors, exercise fitness and electrocardiographic response to exercise in 12,866 men at high risk of symptomatic coronary heart disease. Am J Cardiol. 1986;57: 1075.

29 **Borhani NO.** Prevention of coronary heart disease in practice. JAMA. 1985; 254:257.

30 **Fuller JH et al.** Coronary-heart-disease risk and impaired glucose tolerance. Lancet. 1980:8183.

31 **Rosenberg L et al.** The risk of myocardial infarction after quitting smoking in men under 55 years of age. N Engl J Med. 1985;313:1511.

32 **Hallstrom AP et al.** Smoking as a risk factor for recurrence of sudden cardiac arrest. N Engl J Med. 1986;314:271.

33 **Kannel WB et al.** Epidemiological assessment of the role of physical activity and fitness in development of cardiovascular disease. Am Heart J. 1985; 109:876.

34 **Friedman M et al.** Alteration of type A behavior and its effect on cardiac recurrence in post myocardial infarction patients: summary results of the recurrent coronary prevention project. Am Heart J. 1986;112:653.

35 **Sheffield LT.** Exercise stress testing. In: Braunwald E, ed. Heart Disease: A Textbook of Cardiovascular Medicine. Philadelphia: WB Saunders; 1984:258.

36 **Heifant RH et al.** Role of cardiac testing in an era of proliferating technology and cost containment. J Am Coll Cardiol. 1987;9:1194.

37 **Silverman KJ, Grossman W.** Angina pectoris: natural history and strategies for evaluation and management. N Engl J Med. 1984;310:1712.

38 **Hultgren HN, Peduzzi P.** Relation of severity of symptoms to prognosis in stable angina pectoris. Am J Cardiol. 1984;54:988.

39 **Kent KM et al.** Prognosis of asymptomatic or mildly symptomatic patients with coronary artery disease. Am J Cardiol. 1982;49:1823.

40 **Shub C et al.** Selection of optimal drug therapy for the patient with angina pectoris. Mayo Clin Proc. 1985;60:539.

41 **Winniford MD et al.** Potentiation of nitroglycerin-induced coronary dilation by N-acetylcysteine. Circulation. 1986;73:138.

42 **Zelis R.** Mechanisms of vasodilation. Am J Med. 1983;74(6B):3.

43 **Trimarco B et al.** Late phase of nitroglycerin-induced coronary vasodilatation blunted by inhibition of prostaglandin syntheses. Circulation. 1984; 71:840.

44 **Mehta J et al.** Comparative effects of nitroglycerin and nitroprusside on prostacyclin generation in adult human vessel wall. J Am Coll Cardiol. 1983; 2:625.

45 **Rehr RB et al.** Mechanism of nitroglycerin-induced coronary dilatation: lack of relation to intracoronary thromboxane concentrations. Am J Cardiol. 1984;54:971.

46 **Abrams J.** Nitrate delivery systems in perspective: a decade of progress. Am J Med. 1984;76(6A):38.

47 **Abrams J.** Pharmacology of nitroglycerin and long-acting nitrates. Am J Cardiol. 1985;56:12A.

48 **Smith ER et al.** Mechanism of action of nitrates. Am J Med. 1984;76(6A): 14.

49 **Parker JO.** Nitrate therapy in stable angina pectoris. N Engl J Med. 1987; 316:1635.

50 **Deedwania PC, Carbajal EV.** Current perspectives in treatment of angina pectoris. Postgrad Med. 1986;80:189.

51 **Reichek N.** Role of nitroglycerin in effort angina. Am J Cardiol. 1983;74(6B): 33.

52 **Hasegawa GR et al.** Subjective indices of nitroglycerin potency. N Engl J Med. 1987;316:947. Letter.

53 **Parker JO et al.** Nitroglycerin lingual spray: clinical efficacy and dose-response relation. Am J Cardiol. 1986; 57:1.

54 **Chevigne M et al.** Hemodynamic response to glyceryl trinitrate in a spray at rest and during exercise in a sitting position. Cardiology. 1982;69:84.

55 **Kimchi A et al.** Increased exercise tolerance after nitroglycerin in oral spray: a new and effective therapeutic modality in angina pectoris. Circulation. 1983;67:124.

56 **Oral nitroglycerin spray.** Med Lett Drugs Ther. 1986;28:59.

57 **Kaplan KJ et al.** Association of methemoglobinemia and intravenous nitroglycerin administration. Am J Cardiol. 1985;55:181.

58 **Abrams J.** Nitrate tolerance and dependence. Am Heart J. 1980;99:113.

59 **Abrams J.** Tolerance to organic nitrates. Circulation. 1986;74:1181.

60 **Parker JO et al.** Effect of intervals between doses on the development of tolerance to isosorbide dinitrate. N Engl J Med. 1987;316:1440.

61 **Parker JO et al.** Tolerance to isosorbide dinitrate: rate of development and reversal. Circulation. 1983;68:1074.

62 **Stewart DJ et al.** Altered spectrum of nitroglycerin action in long-term treatment: nitroglycerin-specific venous tolerance with maintenance of arterial vasodepressor potency. Circulation. 1986;74:573.

63 **Manyari DE et al.** Isosorbide dinitrate and glyceryl trinitrate: demonstration of cross tolerance in the capacitance vessels. Am J. Cardiol. 1985;55:927.

64 **Torresi J et al.** Prevention and reversal of tolerance to nitroglycerin with N-acetylcysteine. J Cardiovasc Pharmacol. 1985;7:777.

65 **Winniford MD et al.** Potentiation of nitroglycerin-induced coronary dilatation by N-acetylcysteine. Circulation. 1986;73:138.

66 **May DC et al.** *In vivo* induction and reversal of nitroglycerin tolerance in human coronary arteries. N Engl J Med. 1987;317:805.

67 **Packer M et al.** Induction of nitrate tolerance in human heart failure by continuous intravenous infusion of nitroglycerin and reversal of tolerance by N-acetylcysteine, a sulfhydryl donor. J Am Coll Cardiol. 1986;7:27A. Abstract.

68 **Roth A et al.** Early tolerance to hemodynamic effects of high dose transdermal nitroglycerin in responders with severe chronic heart failure. J Am Col Cardiol. 1987;9:858.

69 **Luke R et al.** Transdermal nitroglycerin in angina pectoris: efficacy of intermittent application. J Am Col Cardiol. 1987;10:642.

70 **Cowan et al.** Prevention of tolerance to nitroglycerin patches by overnight removal. Am J Cardiol. 1987;60:271.

71 **Packer M et al.** Prevention and reversal of nitrate tolerance in patients with congestive heart failure. N Engl J Med. 1987;317:799.

72 **Thadani U et al.** Oral isosorbide dinitrate in the treatment of angina pectoris: dose-response relationship and duration of action during acute therapy. Circulation. 1980;62:491.

73 **Thadani U et al.** Oral isosorbide dinitrate in angina pectoris: comparison of duration of action and dose-response relation during acute and sustained therapy. Am J Cardiol. 1982;49:411.

74 **Fung HL.** Pharmacokinetics and pharmacodynamics of organic nitrates. Am J Cardiol. 1987;60:411.

75 **Noonan PK, Bennet LZ.** Variable glyceryl dinitrate formation as a function of route of nitroglycerin administration. Clin Pharmacol Ther. 1987;42: 273.

76 **Kirby JA, Woods SL.** A study of variation in measurement of doses of nitroglycerin ointment. Heart Lung. 1981;10:814.

77 **Moe G, Armstrong PW.** Influence of skin site on bioavailability of nitroglycerin ointment in congestive heart failure. Am J Med. 1981;81:765.

78 **Iafrate RP et al.** Effect of dose and ointment application technique on nitroglycerin plasma concentrations. Pharmacotherapy. 1983;3:118.

79 **Frishman WH.** Pharmacology of the nitrates in angina pectoris. Am J Cardiol. 1985;56:81.

80 **Zeller FP, Klamerus FP.** Controversies in the use of transdermal nitro-

glycerin systems. Clin Pharm. 1987;6: 605.

81 **Thomas MG et al.** Antianginal efficacy of nitroglycerin patches: the jury is still out. Hosp Formul. 1986;21:918.

82 **Scheidt S.** Update on transdermal nitroglycerin: an overview. Am J Cardiol. 1985;56:31.

83 **Thadani U et al.** Transdermal nitroglycerin patches in angina pectoris. Ann Intern Med. 1986;105:485.

84 **Parker JO, Fung HL.** Transdermal nitroglycerin in angina pectoris. Am J Cardiol. 1984;54:471.

85 **Flaherty JT.** Hemodynamic attenuation and the nitrate-free interval: alternative dosing strategies for transdermal nitroglycerin. Am J Cardiol. 1985;56: 321.

86 **Abrams J.** Transdermal nitroglycerin and nitrate tolerance. Ann Intern Med. 1986;104:424.

87 **Schraeder BJ et al.** Acceptance of transcutaneous nitroglycerin patches by patients with angina pectoris. Pharmacotherapy. 1986;6:83.

88 **Cronin CM et al.** Comparative evaluation of the three commercially available transdermal nitroglycerin delivery systems. Drug Intell Clin Pharm. 1987; 21:642.

89 **Rosenfeld AS, White WB.** Allergic contact dermatitis secondary to transdermal nitroglycerin. Am Heart J. 1984;108:1061.

90 **Abrams J.** New nitrate delivery systems: buccal nitroglycerin. Am Heart J. 1983;105:848.

91 **Parker JO et al.** Comparison of buccal nitroglycerin and oral isosorbide dinitrate for tolerance in stable angina pectoris. Am J Cardiol. 1985;56:724.

92 **Nyberg G.** Onset time of action and duration up to 3 hours of nitroglycerin in buccal, sublingual and transdermal form. Eur Heart J. 1986;7:673.

93 **Parsons DG et al.** Buccal nitroglycerin in routine clinical practice: a multi-center study. Br J Clin Pract. 1983;37:295.

94 **DeBelder MA et al.** Evaluation of the efficacy and duration of action of isosorbide mononitrate in angina pectoris. Am J Cardiol. 1990;65:6J-8J.

95 **Frishman WH.** Multifactorial actions of beta-adrenergic blocking drugs in ischemic heart disease: current concepts. Circulation. 1983;67(1):11.

96 **Bristow MR, Ginsburg R.** Beta$_2$-receptors on myocardial cells in human ventricular myocardium. Am J Cardiol. 1986;57:3F.

97 **Stene-Larsen G et al.** Activation of cardiac beta$_2$-adrenoceptors in the human heart. Am J Cardiol. 1986;57:7F.

98 **Brown JE et al.** In support of cardiac chronotropic beta$_2$-adrenoceptors. Am J Cardiol. 1986;57:11F.

99 **Thadani U.** Assessment of optimal beta blockade in treating patients with angina pectoris. Acta Med Scand. 1984;694(Suppl.):178.

100 **Thadani U et al.** Comparison of the immediate effects of five beta-adrenoreceptor-blocking drugs with different ancillary properties in angina pectoris. N Engl J Med. 1979;300:750.

101 **Schwartz JB et al.** Long-term benefit of cardioselective beta blockade with once-daily atenolol therapy in angina pectoris. Am Heart J. 1981;101:380.

102 **Thadani U, Parker JO.** Propranolol in angina pectoris: comparison of therapy given two and four times daily. Am J Cardiol. 1980;46:117.

103 **Bassan MM, Weiler-Ravell D.** Effect of a twelve-hour hiatus in propranolol therapy of exercise tolerance in patients with angina pectoris. Am Heart J. 1983;105:234.

104 **Freishman WH.** Clinical differences between beta-adrenergic blocking agents: implications for therapeutic substitution. Am Heart J. 1987;113: 1190.

105 **Clue HW et al.** Influence of cardioselectivity and respiratory disease on pulmonary responsiveness to beta blockade. Eur J Clin Pharmacol. 1984;27:517.

106 **McDevitt DG.** Pharmacologic aspects of cardioselectivity in a beta-blocking drug. Am J Cardiol. 1987;59:10F.

107 **Taylor SH.** Role of cardioselectivity and intrinsic sympathomimetic activity in beta-blocking drugs in cardiovascular disease. Am J Cardiol. 1987;59: 18F.

108 **Taylor SH.** Intrinsic sympathomimetic activity: clinical fact or fiction? Am J Cardiol. 1983;52:16D.

109 **Choong CYP et al.** A comparison of the effects of beta-blockers with and without intrinsic sympathomimetic activity on hemodynamics and left ventricular function at rest and during exercise in patients with coronary artery disease. J Cardiovasc Pharmacol. 1986; 8:441.

110 **Prichard BNC.** Pharmacologic aspects of intrinsic sympathomimetic activity in beta-blocking drugs. Am J Cardiol. 1987;59:13F.

111 **Kostis JB, Rosen RC.** Central nervous system effect and beta-adrenergic-blocking drugs: the role of ancillary properties. Circulation. 1987;75:204.

112 **Friedman LM.** How do the various beta-blockers compare in type, frequency and severity of their adverse effects. Circulation. 1983;67:891.

113 **Gengo FM et al.** Lipid-soluble and water-soluble beta-blockers: comparison of the central nervous system depressant effect. Arch Intern Med. 1987; 146:39.

114 **Olsson G et al.** Rebound phenomena following gradual withdrawal of chronic metoprolol treatment in patients with ischemic heart disease. Am Heart J. 1984;108:454.

115 **Feishman WH.** Beta-adrenergic withdrawal. Am J Cardiol. 1987;59:26F.

116 **Singh BN et al.** Second-generation calcium antagonists: search for greater selectively and versatility. Am J Cardiol. 1985;55:214B.

117 **Godfraind T.** Classification of calcium antagonists. Am J Cardiol. 1987;59: 11B.

118 **Hasegawa GR.** Nicardipine, nitrendipine and bepridil: new calcium channel antagonists for cardiovascular disorders. Clin Pharm. 1988;7:97-108.

119 **Murdoch D, Heel RC.** Amlodipine. A review of its pharmacodynamic and pharmacokinetic properties, and therapeutic use in cardiovascular disease. Drugs. 1991;41:478-505.

120 **Todd PA, Faulds D.** Felodipine. A review of the pharmacology and therapeutic use of the extended release formulation in cardiovascular disorders. Drugs. 1992;44:251-77.

121 **Lopez LM, Santiago TM.** Isradipine—another calcium-channel blocker for the treatment of hypertension and angina. Ann Pharmacother. 1992;26: 789-99.

122 **Struyker-Boudier HAJ et al.** The pharmacology of calcium antagonists: a review. J Cardiovasc Pharmacol. 1990;15(Suppl. 4):S1-S10.

123 **Schwartz A.** Calcium antagonists: review and perspective on mechanism of action. Am J Cardiol. 1989;64:3I-9I.

124 **Braunwald E.** Mechanism of action of calcium-channel-blocking agents. N Engl J Med. 1982;307:1618.

125 **Soward AL et al.** The haemodynamic effect of nifedipine, verapamil and diltiazem in patients with coronary artery disease: a review. Drugs. 1986;32:66.

126 **Reicher-Reiss H, Barasch E.** Calcium antagonists in patients with heart failure. A review. Drugs. 1991;42:343-64.

127 **Cannon RO et al.** Efficacy of calcium channel blocker therapy for angina pectoris resulting from small-vessel coronary artery disease and abnormal vasodilator reserve. Am J Cardiol. 1985;56:242.

128 **Ferlinz J.** Nifedipine in myocardial ischemia, systemic hypertension, and other cardiovascular disorders. Ann Intern Med. 1986;105:714.

129 **Boden WE et al.** Nifedipine-induced hypotension and myocardial ischemia in refractory angina pectoris. JAMA. 1985;253:1131.

130 **Subramanian VB et al.** Randomized double-blind comparison of verapamil and nifedipine in chronic state angina. Am J Cardiol. 1982;50:696.

131 **Gottlieb SO et al.** Effect of the addition of propranolol to therapy with nifedipine for unstable angina pectoris: a randomized, double-blind, placebo-controlled trial. Circulation. 1986;73: 331.

132 **Dawson JR et al.** Calcium antagonist drugs in chronic stable angina: comparison of verapamil and nifedipine. Br Heart J. 1981;46:508.

133 **Kawai C et al.** Comparative effects of three calcium antagonists, diltiazem, verapamil and nifedipine, on the sino-atrial and atrioventricular nodes. Circulation. 1981;63:1035.

134 **Petru MA et al.** Long-term efficacy of high-dose diltiazem for chronic stable angina pectoris: 16-month serial studies with placebo controls. Am Heart J. 1985;109:99.

135 **Piepho RW et al.** Drug interactions with the calcium-entry blockers. Circulation. 1987;75:(II):V-181.

136 **Klein HO et al.** The influence of verapamil on serum digoxin concentration. Circulation. 1982;65:998.

137 **Rodrigues EZ et al.** Comparison of nicardipine and verapamil in the management of chronic stable angina. Int J Cardiol. 1988;18:357-69.

138 **Kelly JG, O'Malley K.** Clinical pharmacokinetics of calcium antagonists. Clin Pharmacokinet. 1992;22:416.

139 **Echizen H, Eichelbaum M.** Clinical pharmacokinetics of verapamil, nifedipine and diltiazem. Clin Pharmacokinet. 1986;11:425.

140 **McAllister RD et al.** Pharmacokinetics of calcium-entry blockers. Am J Cardiol. 1985;55:30B.

141 **Klein MD, Weiner DA.** Treatment of angina pectoris and hypertension with sustained-release calcium-channel blocking drugs. Circulation. 1987;75 (II):V-110.

142 **Davidson CL et al.** Sustained-release calcium channel blockers, Hospital Therapy. 1989 Nov; 35.

143 **Gil A et al.** Pharmacology of bepridil. Am J Cardiol. 1992;69:110.

144 **Crawford MH.** The role of triple therapy in patients with chronic stable angina pectoris. Circulation. 1987;75(II): V-122.

145 **Leon MB et al.** Combination therapy with calcium-channel blockers and beta blockers for chronic stable angina pectoris. Am J Cardiol. 1985;5:69B.

146 **Elkayam U et al.** Effects of nifedipine on hemodynamics and cardiac function in patients with normal left ventricular ejection fraction already treated with propranolol. Am J Cardiol. 1986;58: 536.

147 **Prida XE et al.** Comparison of diltiazem and nifedipine alone and in combination in patients with coronary artery spasm. J Am Coll Cardiol. 1987; 9:412.

148 **Fitzgerald DJ et al.** Platelet activation in unstable coronary disease. N Engl J Med. 1986;315:983.

149 **Kyrle PA et al.** Inhibition of prostacyclin and thromboxane A$_2$ generation by low-dose aspirin at the site of plug formation in man *in vivo*. Circulation. 1987;75:1025.

150 **Lewis HE et al.** Protective effects of aspirin against acute myocardial infarction and death in men with unstable angina. N Engl J Med. 1983;309:396.

151 **Cairns JA et al.** Aspirin, sulfinpyrazone, or both in unstable angina: results of a Canadian multicenter trial. N Engl J Med. 1985;313:1369.

152 **Waters DD et al.** Circadian variation in variant angina. Am J Cardiol. 1984; 54:61.

153 **Scholl JM et al.** Comparison of risk factors in vasospastic angina without significant fixed coronary narrowing to significant fixed coronary narrowing and no vasospastic angina. Am J Cardiol. 1986;57:199.

154 **Takizawa A et al.** Variant angina induced by alcohol ingestion. Am Heart J. 1984;107:25.

155 **Whittle JL et al.** Variability of electrocardiographic responses to repeated ergonovine provocation in variant angina patients with coronary artery spasm. Am Heart J. 1982;102:161.

156 **Friesinger GC, Robertson RM.** Vasospastic angina: a continuing search for mechanisms(s). J Am Coll Cardiol. 1986;7:30. Editorial.

157 **Hackett D et al.** Induction of coronary artery spasm by a direct local action of ergonovine. Circulation. 1987;75:577.

158 **Buxton A et al.** Refractory ergonovine-induced coronary vasospasm: importance of intracoronary nitroglycerin. Am J Cardiol. 1980;46:329.

159 **Stone PH.** Calcium antagonists for Prinzmetal's variant angina, unstable angina and silent myocardial ischemia: therapeutic tool and probe for identification of pathophysiologic mechanisms. Am J Cardiol. 1987;59:101B.

160 **Salerno JA et al.** Treatment of vasospastic angina pectoris at rest with ni-

troglycerin ointment: a short-term controlled study in the coronary care unit. Am J Cardiol. 1981;47:1128.

161 **Winniford MD et al.** Concomitant calcium antagonist plus isosorbide dinitrate therapy for markedly active variant angina. Am Heart J. 1984;108: 1269.

162 **Kishida H et al.** A new strategy for the reduction of acute myocardial infarction in variant angina. Am Heart J. 1991;122:1554.

163 **Previtali M et al.** Spontaneous remission of variant angina documented by holter monitoring and ergonovine testing in patients treated with calcium antagonists. Am J Cardiol. 1987;59:235.

164 **Grimm RH et al.** Unrecognized myocardial infarction: experience in the multiple risk factor intervention trial (MRFIT). Circulation. 1987;75:II-6.

165 **Cohn PF.** The concept and pathogenesis of active but asymptomatic coronary artery disease. Circulation. 1987; 75:II-2.

166 **Bashour TT.** Vasotonic myocardial ischemia. Am Heart J. 1991;122:1701.

167 **Nademanee K et al.** Prognostic significance of silent myocardial ischemia in patients with unstable angina. J Am Coll Cardiol. 1987;10:1.

168 **Carboni GP et al.** Ambulatory heart rate and ST-segment depression during painful and silent myocardial ischemia in chronic stable angina pectoris. Am J Cardiol. 1987;59:1029.

169 **Cohn PF.** Total ischemic burden: pathophysiology and prognosis. Am J Cardiol. 1987;59:3C.

170 **Berman DS et al.** The detection of silent myocardial ischemia: cautions and precautions. Circulation. 1987;75:101. Editorial.

171 **Nabel EG et al.** Asymptomatic ischemia in patients with coronary artery disease. JAMA. 1987;257:1923.

172 **Bleske BE et al.** Current concepts of silent myocardial ischemia. Clin Pharm. 1990;9:334.

173 **Pepine CJ, Hill JA.** Management of the total ischemic burden in angina pectoris. Am J Cardiol. 1987;59:7C.

174 **Farhi JI et al.** The broad spectrum of unstable angina pectoris and its implications for future controlled trials. Am J Cardiol. 1986;58:547. Editorial.

175 **Gottlieb SO et al.** Silent ischemia as a marker for early unfavorable outcomes in patients with unstable angina. N Engl J Med. 1986;314:1214.

176 **Lubsen J.** Medical management of unstable angina: what have we learned from the randomized trials. Circulation. 1990;82(Suppl. II);II-82–II-87.

177 **Slysh S et al.** Unstable angina and evolving myocardial infarction following coronary bypass surgery: pathogenesis and treatment with interventional catheterization. Am Heart J. 1985;109:744.

178 **Luchi RJ et al.** Comparison of medical and surgical treatment for unstable angina pectoris. Results of a Veterans Administration Cooperative Study. N Engl J Med. 1987;316:977.

179 **Bashour TT et al.** Current concepts in unstable myocardial ischemia. Am Heart J. 1988;195:850–60.

180 **Grambos DW, Topol EJ.** Effect of maximal medical therapy on refractoriness of unstable angina pectoris. Am J Cardiol. 1992;70:577.

181 **Vejar M et al.** Comparison of low-dose aspirin and coronary vasodilators in acute unstable angina. Circulation. 1990;81(Suppl. I):1–4.

182 **Reeder GS.** Vlietstra RE. Coronary angioplasty: 1986. Mod Concept Cardiovasc Dis. 1986;55:49.

183 **Subcommittee on Percutaneous Transluminal Coronary Angioplasty.** Guidelines for percutaneous transluminal coronary angioplasty: a report of the American College of Cardiology/ American Heart Association task force on assessment of diagnostic and therapeutic cardiovascular procedures. J Am Coll Cardiol. 1988;12:529–45.

184 **O'Keefe JH et al.** Multivessel coronary angioplasty from 1980 to 1989: procedural results and long-term outcome. J Am Coll Cardiol. 1990;16: 1097–102.

185 **Fanelli C, Aronoff R.** Restenosis following coronary angioplasty. Am Heart J. 1990;119:357–68.

186 **Ip JH et al.** The role of platelets, thrombin and hyperplasia in restenosis after coronary angioplasty. J Am Coll Cardiol. 1991;17:1071–078.

187 **Chaitman BR et al.** Coronary artery surgery (CASS): comparability of 10-year survival in randomized and randomizable patients. J Am Coll Cardiol. 1990;16:1071–078.

188 **Rogers WJ et al.** Ten-year follow-up of quality of life in patients randomized to receive medical therapy or coronary artery bypass graft surgery: the coronary artery surgery study (CASS). Circulation. 1990;82:1647–658.

Myocardial Infarction

Jean M Nappi
Patrick L McCollam

Epidemiology 14-1
Pathophysiology 14-1
Clinical Presentation 14-2
Diagnosis (See Tables 14.1 and 14.2 and Figures 14.1,
   14.2, and 14.3) 14-2
Complications 14-2
Overview of Drug and Nondrug Therapy 14-3
   Thrombolytics (See Tables 14.3 and 14.4) 14-3
   Antiplatelet and anticoagulant drugs 14-4
   Beta blockers 14-4
   Vasodilators 14-4
   Analgesics 14-6
   Oxygen 14-6
   Antiarrhythmics 14-6
   Stool softeners 14-6
   Nondrug therapy (See Table 14.5) 14-6
Signs and Symptoms of Acute Myocardial
  Infarction (AMI) 14-6
   Laboratory Abnormalities 14-7
   Q Wave Versus Non-Q Wave 14-9
   Anterior versus Inferior Infarction 14-9
Treatment 14-9
   Therapeutic Objectives 14-9
   Thrombolytic Therapy 14-9
     Dosage regimens 14-9
     Adjunct therapy (See Table 14.6) 14-10
     Determination of reperfusion 14-10

Time from onset of chest pain 14-11
Readministration of thrombolytics 14-12
Use in the elderly 14-12
Strokes associated with thrombolysis 14-12
Cardiopulmonary resuscitation (CPR)
  and thrombolysis 14-13
Lidocaine 14-13
  Risk of ventricular fibrillation 14-13
  Risks of using lidocaine 14-13
  Plasma concentrations 14-13
Magnesium 14-13
Beta Blockers 14-14
  Use in diabetes 14-14
  Use in hyperlipidemia 14-14
  Use in congestive heart failure (CHF) 14-14
  Use in pulmonary disease 14-14
  Use in the elderly (See Table 14.7) 14-15
Long-Term Therapy 14-15
  Angiotensin-Converting Enzyme (ACE) Inhibitors
    (See Figure 14.4) 14-15
  Calcium Channel Blockers 14-16
  Anticoagulants 14-17
Lifestyle Modifications 14-18
Postinfarction Arrhythmias 14-18
Right Ventricular Infarction 14-18
Management of AMI with Nitroglycerin (NTG) ... 14-19
Analgesic Use 14-19

Acute myocardial infarction (AMI) is a manifestation of ischemic heart disease characterized by cellular death or necrosis occurring in the setting of severe or prolonged ischemia. Acute myocardial infarction is considered to be a medical emergency requiring immediate intervention. Until the 1980s, patients with an AMI were treated symptomatically. Their pain was controlled; arrhythmic complications were treated; and the amount of oxygen required by the heart was minimized by bed rest, nitrates, and beta blockers. For almost 70 years, the role of coronary thrombosis as a cause of AMI was debated. In 1980, an angiographic study by DeWood and colleagues resolved this issue when they found total occlusion in a coronary artery in 87% of patients who were examined by angiography within the first four hours of symptoms.[1] This study renewed interest in using thrombolytics to interrupt the progression of myocardial necrosis. Thrombolytics are now considered first line therapy unless a contraindication is present.

Epidemiology

Approximately 1.5 million Americans suffer an acute myocardial infarction annually. Sixty percent of the deaths attributed to AMI occur within one hour of the event, presumably as a result of ventricular fibrillation.[2] Over the years there has been a decline in the mortality due to AMI resulting from a reduction in prevalence of coronary artery disease as well as improved medical/surgical interventions.[3] Prompt recognition and treatment of acute myocardial infarction have dramatically reduced the associated mortality

over the past two decades. Mortality associated with the acute event has been estimated to be 30%, with over half of these deaths occurring before the patient reaches the hospital. An additional 5% to 10% will die within one year following an AMI. Aggressive medical or surgical management that attempts to interrupt the process of infarction and reduce mortality is indicated.

Pathophysiology

The majority of myocardial infarctions (MIs) result from total occlusion of a coronary artery secondary to thrombus formation overlying a lipid-rich atheromatous plaque that has undergone fissuring or rupture.[3] Damage to the plaque results in blood being exposed to collagen and fatty acids which in turn activate platelets, the first step in thrombosis. Rarely, coronary artery spasm may cause an AMI in a patient with normal coronary arteries, particularly in the setting of cocaine abuse. More likely, spasm occurs either before, during, or after the AMI and further compromises blood flow in an already stenotic artery.

Most infarctions are located in a specific region of the heart and are described as such (e.g., anterior, lateral, inferior). In the past, they have been classified as transmural (full thickness) or subendocardial. Transmural and subendocardial infarcts are not synonymous with the Q wave and non-Q wave electrocardiographic descriptions that now are more commonly used to describe infarcts.[3] Patients with Q wave infarctions generally have more extensive necrosis and a higher in hospital mortality rate. However, patients with a non-Q wave infarct have a greater likelihood of experiencing postinfarction angina and early reinfarction. In addition, patients who have had an anterior wall infarction have a worse prognosis than those who have suffered an inferior or lateral wall infarction.

Clinical Presentation

It is important to make the diagnosis of acute myocardial infarction as quickly as possible so that appropriate action may be taken. The incidence of AMI is increased during the morning hours, with most infarcts occurring between 6:00 a.m. and 11:00 a.m.[4] Patients may complain of prolonged substernal chest pain or pressure, shortness of breath (SOB), diaphoresis, nausea, and vomiting. In some patients, the symptoms may be confused with indigestion or other gastrointestinal (GI) complaints. The pain may be atypical in nature as well as location. The pain might be described as stabbing or knife-like and it may occur in the arms, shoulder, neck, jaw, or back.[5] Some patients may have a fever. However, not all AMIs are symptomatic. It has been estimated that 20% of acute myocardial infarctions are ''silent'' and tend to occur in the elderly and people with diabetes and hypertension. The elderly patient may present with hypotension or cerebrovascular symptoms rather than chest pain.

The physical examination is not particularly helpful in making the diagnosis of AMI; however, the findings are important in guiding initial therapy. Signs of severe left ventricular or right ventricular dysfunction may be present. The patient may have severe hypertension or, conversely, may be hypotensive. On cardiac auscultation, a fourth heart sound may be heard, denoting an ischemia-induced decrease in left ventricular compliance.[5] New cardiac murmurs may be heard resulting from papillary muscle dysfunction. The cerebral and peripheral vasculature should be assessed. Patients with a history of cerebral vascular disease may not be eligible for thrombolytic therapy. Peripheral pulses should be examined to assess perfusion and to obtain a baseline before invasive procedures.

Diagnosis

Failure to make the appropriate diagnosis in acute myocardial infarction can lead to disastrous results. The other medical conditions that may mimic the presentation of an AMI are extensive (see Table 14.1). In addition to the patient's history and presentation, the diagnosis of AMI is based upon the electrocardiogram (ECG) and laboratory results. Usually two of the three criteria should be consistent with AMI before the diagnosis is made.

The ECG is an indispensable tool in the diagnosis of acute myocardial infarction. In an area of infarction, the heart muscle is dead and cells cannot be depolarized or repolarized. The 12-lead ECG is helpful in determining the location of an infarct. The presence of a new Q wave is consistent with an AMI. However, there are patients who may have suffered an acute myocardial infarction without developing a Q wave. These non-Q wave infarcts may occur 25% to 35% of the time.[6] Non-Q wave myocardial infarctions may occur more often in older patients, those with a previous MI, and women. About 90% of Q wave infarcts and 40% of non-Q wave infarcts also show ST segment elevation. The electrocardiographic diagnosis of an acute myocardial infarction is extremely difficult in the presence of a left bundle branch block. Figures 14.1 and 14.2 show the ECG in a patient presenting with AMI and following successful thrombolysis.

When a cardiac cell is injured, enzymes are released into the circulation. The measurement of cardiac enzymes is routine in making the diagnosis of AMI. The most sensitive enzyme for the laboratory diagnosis of AMI is creatine kinase (CK). There are

three isoenzymes of CK: the BB, MM, and MB band. BB is found predominately in the brain. MM and small amounts of MB are found in skeletal muscle. MM and large amounts of MB are found in cardiac muscle. Of these, the MB-CK isoenzyme is the most specific laboratory test available for the diagnosis of acute myocardial infarction. It can appear in the serum within three to four hours after myocardial damage and generally peaks in 12 to 24 hours.[5] Serum enzymes normally are determined at the time of admission and then repeated at six-hour intervals to determine the peak CK. The peak CK is related to the size of the infarct, but may be missed if the patient delays admission.[7] Although MB-CK enzyme is the most specific for cardiac damage, there are several conditions other than AMI where it may be elevated (see Table 14.2).[8] MB-CK may be reported as enzymatic activity or mass in either plasma or serum. Samples should be obtained every 6 to 12 hours for the routine diagnosis of AMI. Figure 14.3 graphically depicts some of the enzyme changes seen with an acute myocardial infarction.

Another laboratory change that may be seen is an increase in lactate dehydrogenase (LDH). The increase in LDH generally is seen 24 to 48 hours after the onset of chest pain and reaches its peak in three to six days.[2] Measurement of LDH may be helpful in patients who present with a history of chest pain that began several days before admission and where the CK already may have returned to normal before the patient is evaluated. Increases in LDH also are seen in patients with liver disease, hemolysis, leukemia, pulmonary embolism, myocarditis, and skeletal muscle disease. Lactate dehydrogenase is comprised of five isoenzymes. The heart muscle contains LDH_1. A ratio of LDH_1 to LDH_2 greater than one may be helpful in distinguishing acute myocardial infarction from other disorders. Other nonspecific laboratory changes that occur in the setting of AMI include hyperglycemia and increases in aspartate aminotransferase (AST) and white blood cell (WBC) count.

There are radionuclide techniques useful in diagnosing AMI. Technetium-99m pyrophosphate will accumulate in an area of infarction and may be identified as a ''hot spot'' on a nuclear scan. Some scans may become positive within a few hours; however, most are likely to be positive one to three days postinfarction and return to normal within seven to ten days.[5] Thallium-201 is distributed to the heart muscle with blood flow, so an infarcted area is shown as a ''cold spot.'' Thallium cannot distinguish an old infarct from a new infarct, so it is not used routinely in diagnosis.

Complications

The complications of acute myocardial infarction generally can be divided into three major groups: 1) pump failure, 2) arrhythmias, and 3) recurrent ischemia and reinfarction. Depression of cardiac function following an AMI is related directly to the extent of left ventricular damage. As a result of decreased cardiac output and decreased perfusion pressure associated with left ventricular dysfunction, a number of compensatory mechanisms become activated. The levels of circulating catecholamines increase in an attempt to increase contractility and restore normal perfusion pressure. In addition, the renin-angiotensin-aldosterone system is enhanced, leading to an increase in systemic vascular resistance and sodium and water retention. These compensatory mechanisms actually can worsen the imbalance between myocardial oxygen supply and consumption by increasing the myocardial oxygen demand.

Signs and symptoms of congestive heart failure (CHF) are common in patients who have abnormal wall motion affecting 20% to 25% of the left ventricle. If 40% or more of the left ventricle is

Table 14.1	Differential Diagnosis of AMI[a]
Acute cerebrovascular disease	
Aortic dissection	
Acute anxiety or panic attacks	
Esophageal rupture	
Gallbladder disease	
Pancreatitis	
Peptic ulcer disease	
Pericarditis	
Pneumothorax	
Pulmonary embolism	
Spinal or chest wall diseases	

[a] AMI = Acute myocardial infarction.

damaged, cardiogenic shock and death may occur.[2] In addition to systolic dysfunction, patients who have suffered an AMI also may have diastolic dysfunction. Scar formation following an acute myocardial infarction may lead to a decrease in ventricular compliance resulting in abnormally high left ventricular filling pressures during diastole. (See Chapter 15: Congestive Heart Failure for further discussion on systolic versus diastolic dysfunction.)

The decreased contractility and the compensatory increase in left ventricular end diastolic volume and pressure lead to increased wall stress within the left ventricle. Left ventricular enlargement is an important determinant of mortality after acute myocardial infarction. Over a period of days to months following an infarct, the infarcted area may expand as a result of dilatation and thinning of the left ventricular wall. These changes are known as ventricular remodeling. Pathophysiologic mechanisms leading to left ventricular dilatation after an AMI include early thinning and stretching of the infarcted segment which is known as infarct expansion. In addition, hypertrophy of the noninfarcted myocardium occurs. Administration of captopril and other angiotensin-converting enzyme (ACE) inhibitors may limit infarct expansion and will attenuate progressive left ventricular dilatation.[9]

During the peri-infarction period, the heart is very irritable and subject to ventricular arrhythmias. The continuous monitoring of patients in a coronary care unit has reduced the in-hospital mortality related to ventricular arrhythmias. However, the risk of sudden cardiac death (SCD) after hospital discharge has been estimated to be between 4% and 8% within the first year following a myocardial infarction, declining to 2% to 4% per year thereafter.[5] There are a number of factors that can be used to identify those patients at risk for SCD following an acute myocardial infarction. The most important predictor is an abnormal ejection fraction (EF). The lower the EF following an acute myocardial infarction, the worse the prognosis. Other factors associated with an increased risk for sudden cardiac death are: complex ventricular ectopy, frequent (>10/hour) premature ventricular complexes, and the identification of late potentials on a signal-averaged ECG.[5]

Having signs or symptoms of ischemia following an AMI adversely affects the patient's prognosis. It appears that patients who have a non-Q wave infarct (compared to patients who have a Q wave infarct) have fewer complications during the acute phase of the infarction process. However, the patients with non-Q wave infarcts tend to have higher early reinfarction rates (also called infarct extensions) as well as more reinfarctions in the months following the AMI.[6] Most patients undergo a submaximal exercise tolerance test before discharge from the hospital to help identify those patients who continue to have signs of ischemia.

Overview of Drug and Nondrug Therapy

Thrombolytics

Over the last 10 to 15 years, the emphasis on the management of the patient having an acute myocardial infarction has shifted from focusing on the prevention or management of complications like arrhythmias, pain, and blood pressure control to strategies attempting to limit the extent of myocardial necrosis and prevent reinfarction.

Since the vast majority of AMI cases result from the sudden occlusion of a coronary artery due to the formation of a thrombus, the therapeutic priority is to open the occluded artery as quickly as possible. This is accomplished by administering a thrombolytic that augments or enhances the body's own fibrinolytic system or by mechanically removing or reducing the obstruction.

There are now several very large clinical trials that have proven beyond a doubt that administration of streptokinase (SK), tissue plasminogen activator (tPA), or anistreplase reduce mortality from an acute myocardial infarction. Early mortality from AMI has been reduced by approximately one-third (from 10%–15% to 5%–10%) with the advent of thrombolytic therapy.[10]

There are four thrombolytics currently available in the U.S.: streptokinase, anistreplase, tPA, and urokinase. Streptokinase is a polypeptide derived from beta-hemolytic streptococcal cultures. It binds to plasminogen to form an active plasminogen-streptokinase complex. This complex then cleaves other molecules of plasminogen to form plasmin. Plasmin, which is an active fibrinolytic enzyme, then acts on a fibrin clot to enhance its dissolution. Anistreplase, also known as anisoylated plasminogen streptokinase activator complex (APSAC), is a combination of streptokinase and plasminogen with an anisoyl group reversibly placed within the catalytic center of the plasminogen moiety which is deacylated in the circulation at a controlled rate.[10]

Urokinase is a plasminogen activator isolated from urine or kidney cell cultures, consisting of two polypeptide chains. Urokinase directly cleaves plasminogen and converts it to its active form, plasmin. There is also a single chain urokinase type plasminogen activator (scu-PA) available in Europe which is produced by recombinant DNA technology.[10] Clinical experience with urokinase in the management of an acute myocardial infarction is limited relative to the other agents available.[11]

The fourth agent available in the U.S. is tPA. Although it is a naturally occurring enzyme, it is produced commercially by recombinant DNA technology. Tissue plasminogen activator cleaves the same plasminogen peptide bond that urokinase cleaves, but tPA has a binding site for fibrin which allows it to bind to a thrombus and preferentially lyse it over the circulating plasminogen.[10] The pharmacologic properties of these four agents are compared in Table 14.3.

The ideal thrombolytic would be thrombus-specific, rapidly acting, easily administered, highly efficacious, inexpensive, and have a low incidence of reocclusion and side effects. Unfortunately, the ideal thrombolytic does not exist. The three problems common to all the thrombolytics are: 1) the inability to open 100% of coronary artery occlusions, 2) inconsistency in the ability to maintain good blood flow in the infarct-related artery after it is successfully opened, and 3) the complication of bleeding. Good blood flow commonly is defined as Thrombolysis in Myocardial Infarct (TIMI) grade 3 flow, which is complete reperfusion of the vessel.[12]

Contraindications to the use of thrombolytics continue to be delineated as more and more patients receive the drugs. Table 14.4 outlines the conditions to be considered before administering a thrombolytic. There are relatively few absolute contraindications to thrombolytic therapy; however, each patient should be assessed carefully as to whether the potential benefit outweighs the potential risk. Because of the serious nature of intracranial hemorrhage associated with thrombolytic therapy, patients should be selected carefully before receiving these agents. Generally, the diagnosis of AMI must be assured with a history consistent with ischemic heart disease, presence of ST segment elevation in two contiguous leads, or a new left bundle branch block on the ECG. Once the diagnosis is made, the administration of the thrombolytic should commence immediately. The benefit derived from thrombolytic therapy is directly related to the time from the onset of chest pain and the time of the drug's administration. In the first Gruppo Italiano per lo studio della streptochinasi nell'infarto miocardico (GISSI) trial, the reduction in mortality due to streptokinase reached statistical significance only if given within six hours from the onset of chest pain.[13] The mortality rate was lowest in the group that received the drug within one hour from the onset of chest pain (12.9% in the streptokinase group versus 21.2% in the control group). The relationship between time and thrombolytic effectiveness has been demonstrated in subsequent trials.

Antiplatelet and Anticoagulant Drugs

When thrombolysis occurs, whether due to the administration of a thrombolytic or through activation of the body's own fibrinolytic system, the fibrin clot begins to disintegrate. As the clot dissolves, there is a paradoxical increase in local thrombin generation and enhanced platelet aggregability which may lead to rethrombosis.[10] Both aspirin and heparin have been used to minimize rethrombosis.

Other agents directed toward inhibiting thrombin and reocclusion rates are being investigated. Hirudin and hirulog are two thrombin inhibitors that bind directly to thrombin and inactivate it. Preliminary results comparing hirudin to heparin following tPA infusions are encouraging.[14]

Beta Blockers

In addition to antiplatelet and antithrombotic therapies, beta blockers are used commonly, along with thrombolytic agents, in the management of acute myocardial infarction. The usefulness of beta blockers was investigated before the widespread use of thrombolytics. Beta blockers decrease myocardial oxygen consumption, limit the amount of myocardial damage, and decrease some of the complications of myocardial infarction, specifically myocardial rupture and ventricular fibrillation. Atenolol was compared to placebo in patients with AMI in the first International Study of Infarct Survival (ISIS) trial.[15] The mortality due to vascular causes was reduced by about 15% at the end of seven days of treatment in this trial. Similar results have been found with metoprolol.[16] Retrospective analyses of trials using beta blockers in AMI estimate a reduction in mortality of about 13%.[17]

In addition to short-term benefit, there is clearly a benefit from the long-term use of beta blockers in the post-MI period. The Beta Blocker in Heart Attack Trial (BHAT) study showed benefit in using propranolol following acute myocardial infarction.[18] After 25 months of follow-up, patients receiving propranolol had a 7.2% mortality compared to 9.8% in the control group. Unless there are contraindications present, beta blockade should be considered in all patients having an acute myocardial infarction and should be continued for at least two years following an AMI.[17]

Vasodilators

Other strategies for minimizing myocardial damage include the use of vasodilators in the peri-infarction period. Progressive left ventricular dilatation occurs in some patients following an AMI. This process is known as "remodeling" and has become an important marker for prognosis. Vasodilators reduce oxygen demand and myocardial wall stress by reducing afterload and/or preload and can halt the remodeling process. Some vasodilators also may increase the blood supply to the myocardium by enhancing coronary vasodilatation.

ACE inhibitors are used frequently in the AMI setting. Enalapril was studied in the Cooperative New Scandinavian Enalapril Survival Study (CONSENSUS-II trial). In this study, over 6000 patients were randomized to either placebo or enalapril which was initiated within 24 hours from the onset of chest pain.[19] Enalaprilat was initiated by intravenous (IV) administration followed by oral enalapril administration six hours later. Patients received thrombolytics, nitrates, beta blockers, aspirin, diuretics, anticoagulants, calcium channel blockers, and analgesic agents as determined by their physician. In this trial, enalapril did not improve six-month survival; however, this may be because hypotension was more common in the enalapril-treated group. A subset of patients from the CONSENSUS-II trial were evaluated by echocardiography and

Fig 14.1 ECG Changes in AMI Admission ECG. Note extensive ST segment elevation in leads II, III, and aVF (brackets) indicating an inferior wall AMI. The patient also displays reciprocal ST segment depression in I and aVL (arrows) which are the lateral ECG leads and are opposite the inferior leads.

Fig 14.2   ECG Changes in AMI   ECG after successful thrombolysis shows no ST segment changes suggestive of ischemia, but evolution of new Q waves in leads II, III, and aVF (arrows) is apparent.

attenuation of left ventricular dilatation was found in the enalapril-treated group.[20] It would appear that intravenous administration of ACE inhibitors may result in excessive hypotension offsetting the potential benefits.

The effects of nitrates also have been evaluated in the AMI patient. The pooled effects from several small studies have shown a benefit in reducing mortality in those patients receiving nitrates. The data suggest that nitroglycerin (NTG) is more beneficial than nitroprusside in this patient population.[17] Overall, the use of vasodilators is likely to benefit patients with an AMI, although the reduction in mortality is small compared to the use of thrombolytics.

Another class of vasodilators that has been investigated in the treatment of acute myocardial infarction is the calcium channel blockers. There are several proposed mechanisms whereby a calcium channel blocker might be beneficial. As a group, they have coronary and peripheral vasodilatory actions. They potentially could alleviate some of the coronary vasospasm that may be present at the time of coronary thrombosis. Additionally, they are known to be effective anti-ischemic agents through their action in improving coronary blood supply and reducing myocardial oxygen demand. Since intracellular calcium overload has been observed in the ischemic myocardium, it was thought that calcium channel blockers would protect cardiac cells during the peri-infarction period.[21] Despite these theoretical benefits, the outcomes from clinical trials are varied depending upon the individual drug used and the timing of drug administration.

Nifedipine is not beneficial during the immediate AMI period. There have been conflicting results in trials with nifedipine regarding the drug's long-term effects on infarct size. However, in the larger clinical trials, nifedipine showed either no benefit or a trend toward increasing mortality.[21–23]

There have been two large trials with diltiazem. The first study evaluated the effect of diltiazem on reinfarction rates in patients with non-Q wave AMI. Treatment with oral diltiazem was started 24 to 72 hours after the onset of chest pain.[24] There was a 51.2%

reduction in reinfarction rate in the diltiazem group compared to placebo after 14 days of follow-up. Diltiazem also reduced the frequency of postinfarction angina.

Another trial using diltiazem for a longer period of time in patients with both Q wave and non-Q wave infarctions was published two years later.[25] In this trial, oral diltiazem was initiated 3 to 15 days after infarction and patients were followed for an average of two years. Overall, there was no difference in mortality between the two groups. However, patients assigned to diltiazem who did not have pulmonary congestion at the time of randomization had a reduced number of cardiac events when compared to placebo patients. In contrast, patients who had signs of pulmonary congestion at the time of randomization had an unfavorable response to diltiazem (i.e., more deaths from cardiac causes or nonfatal reinfarctions).

The Danish Verapamil Infarction Trial (DAVIT-II) study showed a trend toward a reduction in mortality at 18 months in patients receiving verapamil (11.1% versus 13.8% in the placebo group).[26] In patients who did not have heart failure at the time of

Table 14.2	Conditions Where CK-MB Isoenzyme May Be Elevated[5,8,a]	
AMI	Alcoholism
Cardioversion (>400 J)	Acute cholecystitis
Cardiac contusion/trauma	Carcinoma
Myocarditis	Pericarditis
Peripartum period	Reye's syndrome
Hyper/hypothyroidism	SLE
Prolonged supraventricular tachycardia	Muscular dystrophy
Skeletal muscle trauma	Polymyositis

[a] AMI = Acute myocardial infarction; CK = Creatine kinase; SLE = Systemic lupus erythematosus

randomization, verapamil showed a statistically significant benefit in reducing mortality (7.7% versus 11.8% in placebo group). In contrast to the diltiazem trial, for patients with heart failure, there was neither a demonstrable benefit nor a detrimental effect with verapamil. It has been suggested that verapamil and diltiazem be limited to those postinfarction patients who do not tolerate beta blocker therapy and who are not in heart failure.[27] (Also see Question 24.)

Analgesics

It is important to try and abolish the patient's pain as quickly as possible. The pain and accompanying anxiety associated with an acute myocardial infarction will contribute to increased myocardial oxygen demand. If the patient's pain is not relieved by administering a thrombolytic and anti-ischemic medications (like nitrates and beta blockers), then an additional analgesic may be necessary. Morphine and meperidine are the two most commonly prescribed analgesics.

Oxygen

Many patients are modestly hypoxemic during the initial hours of an AMI. Oxygen should be administered via nasal cannula to all patients suspected of having ischemic pain. Patients with severe hypoxemia or pulmonary edema may require intubation and mechanical ventilation.[28]

Antiarrhythmics

Ventricular arrhythmias, including ventricular fibrillation, are common complications associated with myocardial ischemia and acute myocardial infarction. Lidocaine is the drug of choice for the treatment of ventricular arrhythmias seen in the peri-infarction period.[28] The routine use of prophylactic lidocaine to prevent ventricular tachycardia and ventricular fibrillation is controversial. Although the routine use of lidocaine may reduce the number of episodes of ventricular fibrillation, it has been suggested that lidocaine may contribute to an increased number of episodes of asystole.[17] (Also see Chapter 16: Cardiac Arrhythmias.)

Suppression of ventricular ectopy following an AMI with the chronic use of oral antiarrhythmic agents also is controversial. Results of the Cardiac Arrhythmias Suppression Trials (CAST-I and II) demonstrated an increase in mortality in asymptomatic patients with ventricular ectopy following an acute myocardial infarction treated with flecainide, encainide, and moricizine.[29,30]

Stool Softeners

It is common to administer agents such as docusate for prevention of constipation in AMI patients since straining causes undesirable stress upon the cardiovascular system.

Nondrug Therapy

There are some patients who will present with an AMI who are not candidates for thrombolytic therapy or where thrombolytic therapy has failed to open the occluded artery. In these circumstances coronary angioplasty is an attractive alternative. The disadvantages of coronary angioplasty include the longer amount of time needed to re-establish vessel patency and its higher cost. A potential advantage of coronary angioplasty is the greater ability to achieve TIMI grade 3 flow in the affected vessel.[31] However, no studies comparing thrombolytic therapy to emergent angioplasty have shown an advantage in survival for angioplasty.[32]

Table 14.5 summarizes the common adjunctive therapy used in patients with AMI.

Signs and Symptoms of Acute Myocardial Infarction (AMI)

1. P.H., a 63-year-old, 80 kg, male admitted to the Emergency Room (ER), experienced an episode of sustained chest pain while mowing his yard (it is July and the heat index is 38.3 °C). He is transported to the ER and a physical examination reveals a diaphoretic male who appears ashen. Heart rate and rhythm are regular and no S_3 or S_4 sounds are present. His vital signs include blood pressure (BP) 180/110 mm Hg, heart rate (HR) 100 beats/min, and respiratory rate (RR) 32 breaths/min.

P.H.'s chest pain radiates to his left arm and jaw and he describes it as "crushing" and "like an elephant sitting on my chest." He rates it as a "10/10" in intensity. Thus far, his pain has not responded to 5 nitroglycerin tablets (NTG), sublingual (SL) at home or 3 more NTG SL in the ambulance. His ECG now reveals 3 mm ST segment elevation and Q waves in leads I and V_2–V_4.

Laboratory values include: Sodium (Na) 141 mEq/L (Normal: 135–145); potassium (K) 3.9 mEq/L (Normal: 3.5–5.0);

Fig 14.3 Schema of Serum Enzyme Changes Associated with AMI

Table 14.3			Pharmacological Comparison of Available Thrombolytic Agents[10,11]			
Drug	Enzymatic Efficiency for Clot Lysis	Fibrin Specificity	Potential Antigenicity	Average Dose	Dosing Administration	Cost
Streptokinase	High	Minimal	Yes	1.5 MU	1 hr IV infusion	Low
Anistreplase	High	Minimal	Yes	30 U	2–5 min IV infusion	Moderate
tPA[a]	High	Moderate	No	100 mg	15 mg IV bolus, 50 mg over 30 min, then 35 mg over 60 min[b]	Moderate
Urokinase	Low	Moderate	No	2 MU	1 MU IV bolus, 1 MU over 60 min	High

[a] tPA = Tissue plasminogen activator.
[b] Known as the accelerated or front-loaded regimen.

chloride (Cl) 100 mEq/L (Normal: 100–108); CO_2 20 mEq/L (Normal: 24–30); blood urea nitrogen (BUN) 19 mg/dL (Normal: 8–25); serum creatinine (SrCr) 1.2 mg/dL (Normal: 0.6–1.5); glucose 149 mg/dL (Normal: 70–110); magnesium (Mg) 1.3 mEq/L (Normal: 1.5–2.0); CK 1200 U/L (Normal: 60–400); cholesterol 259 mg/dL (Normal: <200), triglycerides 300 mg/dL (Normal: 40–150).

P.H.'s medical history includes a history of coronary artery disease. A previous cardiac catheterization revealed a lesion in his midleft anterior descending coronary artery (75% stenosis) and in the proximal left circumflex (30% stenosis). His ventriculogram at the time showed an EF of 58%. These lesions were deemed suitable for medical management. An echocardiogram found an EF of 52%, with no valvular or wall motion abnormalities at that time. He also has a history of recurrent bouts of bronchitis with bronchospastic disease for 10 years; P.H.'s diabetes mellitus has been controlled with insulin for 18 years, with fair control and his mild hypertension has been in fair control for 20 years.

P.H.'s father died of an MI at age 70. His mother and siblings are all alive and well.

P.H. has smoked one pack of cigarettes a day for 30 years and drinks approximately one six pack of beer a week. He has no history of IV drug use.

On admission, P.H.'s medications include: NPH insulin 15 U Q AM and 10 U Q PM; metaproterenol inhaler PRN; hydrochlorothiazide 25 mg QD; NTG patch 7.5 mg QD; NTG SL 0.4 mg PRN chest pain.

P.H. is diagnosed with an anterior infarction. The highest CK thus far is 2000 (Normal: 60–400 U/L) with a 12% MB (Normal: 0%–5%) fraction.

What signs and symptoms does P.H. have that are consistent with the diagnosis of AMI? [SI units: Na 141 mmol/L (Normal: 135–145); K 3.9 mmol/L (Normal: 3.5–5.0); Cl 100 mmol/L (Normal: 100–108); CO_2 20 mmol/L (Normal: 24–30); BUN 6.8 mmol/L (Normal: 2.9–8.9); SrCr 72 μmol/L (Normal: 36–90); glucose 8.3 mmol/L (Normal: 3.9–6.1); Mg 0.65 mmol/L (Normal: 0.75–1.0); CK 20 and 33.34 μkat/L, respectively (Normal: 1.0–6.7); cholesterol 6.7 mmol/L (Normal: <5.2); triglycerides 3.9 mmol/L (Normal: 0.45–1.7)]

P.H. has described his "pain" more as a pressure sensation. This is common with ischemic heart disease. The chest discomfort that occurs with acute myocardial infarction is described more often as pressure or as a tight band around the chest rather than pain. Although at the time the chest discomfort started P.H. was involved in physical exertion, this is not always the case. The pain associated with an AMI may begin while the patient is at rest, frequently in the early morning hours. At least 20% of patients with acute myocardial infarctions have no pain or discomfort; these are described as "silent." Patient presentations range from asymptomatic to one or more of the following: shortness of breath, hypotension, heart

failure, syncope, or ventricular arrhythmias. Silent or atypical infarctions occur more commonly in diabetics, hypertensives, and the elderly.[2,33] P.H. is diaphoretic, a common finding. Other symptoms such as nausea and anxiety are not reported by P.H. but are common findings. He also describes his pain as "10/10" in intensity, or perhaps "the worst pain I've ever experienced," which is typical of an acute myocardial infarction. The typical uncomplicated AMI patient has few useful physical findings. The diagnosis primarily lies in symptomatology and laboratory findings.

Laboratory Abnormalities

2. What laboratory abnormalities can you expect to see in P.H.?

P.H. also demonstrates the laboratory abnormalities commonly seen in acute myocardial infarction. His CK was high upon admission and continues to rise. The MB-CK of 12% (normally <5%) is indicative of myocardial necrosis. MB-CK rises acutely over the first 12 to 24 hours and returns to normal in three to four days. One would expect to see a rise in aspartate aminotransferase (AST) over the next 24 hours and a rise in LDH which will peak

Table 14.4	Risk Factors Associated with Bleeding Complications Secondary to Thrombolytic Use[a,10]
Major Thrombolytics contraindicated	Major surgery, organ biopsy, or major trauma within 6 weeks GI or GU bleeding within 6 months Intracranial tumor Previous neurosurgery Stroke within 6 months Head trauma within 1 month History of bleeding diathesis Known or suspected aortic dissection Known or suspected pericarditis
Important Relative contraindication	Uncontrolled hypertension (≥180 mm Hg systolic, ≥110 mm Hg diastolic) Remote thrombotic stroke Recent TIAs Puncture of a noncompressible vessel CPR for >10 min
Minor Increased risk of bleeding	Older age Female History of hypertension Small body size Diabetic retinopathy CPR for <10 min

[a] CPR = Cardiopulmonary resuscitation; GI = Gastrointestinal; GU = Genitourinary; TIAs = Transient ischemic attacks.

Table 14.5			Adjunctive Therapy for AMI[a]		
Drug	Indication	Dose and Duration	Therapeutic Endpoints	Precautions	Comments
Lidocaine	a) Prevention of primary VF b) Treatment of VT, VF	Variable, 1.5 mg/kg loading dose, then 1–4 mg/min. Use for <48 hr in a)	a) Absence of VF b) Cessation of arrhythmia	Bradycardia. Observe for CNS toxicity	Generalized use is controversial for a). Some data indicate increased mortality with generalized use
Morphine	a) Treatment of severe chest pain b) Venodilator	2–5 mg IV Q 3–5 min PRN	a) Decreased chest pain b) Decreased chest pain and HR	Bradycardia, right ventricular infarct	Good choice for acute pain relief along with NTG
Aspirin[b]	AMI and ischemic heart disease	160 mg chewable during AMI; then 160–325 mg/day for an indefinite period	No firm endpoint	Active bleeding, thrombocytopenia	Unless clear contraindication exists, aspirin should be given to all AMI patients
Heparin[b]	For acute anti-coagulation with or without thrombolysis	Variable; 50 U/kg loading dose, then 15 U/kg/hr. Usual duration: 24–48 hr	aPTT ratio 2–2.5 times patient's control value	Active bleeding, thrombocytopenia	Unless clear contraindication exists, heparin should be given to all AMI patients who do not receive thrombolytic therapy
Warfarin	Left ventricular thrombus	Variable; titrate to INR. Duration usually for several months	INR 2–3 times patient's control value	Usual warfarin problems such as noncompliance, bleeding diatheses	May be useful in the presence of a left ventricular thrombus to prevent embolism
Beta blockers[b]	General use in all AMI patients	Variable; titrate to HR and BP. Immediate IV therapy preferable. Used for at least 2–3 years duration at present	Titrate to resting HR ≈60 beats/min, maintain systolic BP >100 mm Hg	Usual beta blocker contraindications. Observe HR and BP closely when given IV	Unless clear contraindication exists, β_1-selective agents such as metoprolol and atenolol should be given to all AMI patients
Nitrates[b]	General use in most AMI patients	Variable; titrate to pain relief or systolic BP. 5–10 µg/min to 200 µg/min typical regimen. Usually maintain IV therapy for 24–48 hr after infarct	Titrate to pain relief or systolic BP >90 mm Hg	Use cautiously in right ventricular infarct or large inferior infarct because of effects on preload	Use acetaminophen, NSAIDs, narcotics for headache. NTG should be tapered gradually in ischemic heart disease patients
ACE inhibitors[b]	AMI with EF <40%	Usual captopril dose 12.5–50 mg TID. Duration unknown. Equivalent doses for other ACE inhibitors	Titrate to usual doses and maintain systolic BP >90–110 mm Hg	Avoid IV therapy within 48 hr of infarct	Oral therapy after AMI day 3 in patients with EF <40% beneficial
Calcium channel blockers	a) Postinfarction angina b) Non-Q wave AMI	Usual doses of calcium channel blockers are used. Duration dictated by clinical scenario	Titrate to usual doses and maintain systolic BP >90 mm Hg	Usual calcium channel blocker contraindications, avoid in patients with pulmonary congestion	a) In patients with good EF, most calcium channel blockers will exert beneficial effects; b) Some data support use of verapamil or diltiazem for non-Q wave AMI but not dihydropyridine types

[a] ACE = Angiotensin-converting enzyme; AMI = Acute myocardial infarction; aPTT = Activated partial thromboplastin time; BP = Blood pressure; EF = Ejection fraction; HR = Heart rate; INR = International normalized ratio; IV = Intravenous; NSAIDs = Nonsteroidal anti-inflammatory drugs; NTG = Nitroglycerin; VF = Ventricular fibrillation; VT = Ventricular tachycardia.

[b] Indicates specific drug therapies which are known to reduce morbidity and/or mortality.

in four to five days following an AMI. There are several other nonspecific laboratory findings to monitor in P.H. Hyperglycemia may develop because P.H. is a diabetic, but this also can occur in nondiabetic patients. In diabetic patients, ketoacidosis may occur. It also has been noted that total cholesterol and HDL cholesterol concentrations may fall dramatically within a few days following an acute myocardial infarction. Therefore, it is best to wait two months after an AMI to check serum lipid profiles.[2] Leukocytosis and an increase in the erythrocyte sedimentation rate also may be observed with acute myocardial infarction.[2,34]

Q Wave Versus Non-Q Wave

3. P.H. was noted to have "Q waves" on the ECG. What are the implications of a Q wave versus non-Q wave MI?

Perhaps the most important diagnostic test in suspected AMI is the electrocardiogram. The ECG is an important tool because it is noninvasive, can be performed rapidly, is readily available in most clinical settings, and adds valuable clues as to where the AMI is located (i.e., anterior, inferior, lateral). It also is one of the major criteria to consider for the administration of a thrombolytic. While enzyme profiles are valuable, the results often are not available for hours; therefore, enzymes allow one to confirm "retrospectively" the presence of an AMI, but do not necessarily influence the immediate therapeutic course for the patient. A thorough discussion of the ECG is beyond the scope of this chapter, but P.H. has classic ECG changes such as Q waves and ST-segment elevation. Their presence in the anterior ECG leads (V_2–V_4) indicates not only which part of the heart is affected, but also points to likely coronary arteries which are blocked (i.e., P.H.'s previous left anterior descending lesion may have had a plaque rupture and thrombosis of the vessel).

The presence of Q waves is more of an electrocardiographic finding rather than an indicator of the involved anatomy. The in hospital mortality rate usually is higher with a Q wave infarct, but one-year mortality is generally the same when compared to non-Q wave patients.[6] The Q wave infarct patient is more likely to have hypotension, ventricular tachycardia, ventricular fibrillation, and cardiac arrest. However, the data suggest that there is a higher incidence of early reinfarction (infarct extension), late reinfarction, and postinfarction angina in non-Q wave patients.[6]

Anterior Versus Inferior Infarction

4. What are the prognostic implications of an anterior versus an inferior MI?

Damage to the anterior section of the heart is more likely to be associated with increased morbidity (e.g., left ventricular dysfunction) and mortality.[35] Those patients at highest risk of death are those with an anterior AMI, left ventricular dysfunction, and complex ventricular ectopy. P.H. is at an increased risk since he has sustained an anterior AMI.

Treatment

Therapeutic Objectives

5. What are the immediate and long-term therapeutic objectives in treating P.H.?

The immediate therapeutic objectives in treating P.H. are to minimize the amount of myocardial necrosis developing, alleviate his symptoms, and prevent his death. These objectives are achieved primarily by restoring coronary blood flow (either by administering a thrombolytic or performing an angioplasty) and lowering myocardial oxygen demand. Any life-threatening ventricular arrhythmias that develop must be treated. The long-term therapeutic objectives are to prevent or minimize recurrent ischemic symptoms, reinfarction, heart failure, and sudden cardiac death. The specific therapeutic regimens are discussed in detail in the questions that follow.

Thrombolytic Therapy

6. Is P.H. a candidate for thrombolytic therapy? Is any one agent preferred?

Acute myocardial infarction is considered to be a medical emergency. The results of several major trials have shown unequivocally that if used appropriately, thrombolytics can reduce mortality associated with an AMI. Unless there are contraindications present, most patients presenting with an AMI should receive a thrombolytic. There is still controversy over which thrombolytic should be used, the amount of time from the onset of chest pain where the benefit will still outweigh the risk, the best dosing regimen of the thrombolytic, the most appropriate adjunctive therapy, and whether the risk outweighs the benefit in some subpopulations of patients (such as those with an inferior AMI).

P.H. has a history of hypertension and at presentation his blood pressure is 180/110 mm Hg. A blood pressure this high is a relative contraindication to thrombolytic therapy (because of an increased risk of developing a cerebral hemorrhage); however, P.H. has an anterior MI, and he is very likely to benefit from thrombolytic therapy. In this case, he should receive NTG IV immediately so that his blood pressure is better controlled. The onset of pressure control with nitroglycerin intravenous NTG IV is rapid, usually within a matter of minutes. Once his systolic blood pressure is less than 180 mm Hg and the diastolic is less than 110 mm Hg, a thrombolytic can be administered. The nitroglycerin also will reduce the workload on his heart and may provide pain relief.

Since P.H. has very severe pain and ECG changes consistent with an anterior AMI, he is at great risk for substantial morbidity and/or mortality. Tissue plasminogen activator (tPA) is more rapid and effective in restoring TIMI grade 3 blood flow as compared to streptokinase; however, the slight increased risk of stroke and the substantial increase in cost with tPA may outweigh the advantages. The argument for or against a specific thrombolytic is probably less important than the decision to use an agent and to deliver the medication to the patient in as short a period of time as possible.

Dosage Regimens

7. "tPA 100 mg infused over 3 hours" is ordered for P.H. Is this an appropriate dose? If streptokinase or anistreplase were ordered, what would be an appropriate regimen?

There are two dosing schedules commonly used for tPA. Many trials have infused 100 mg over three hours.[36-38] Typically, this has involved a 6 mg bolus followed by 54 mg infused over the first hour and 20 mg/hour for the next two hours. The total dose should be reduced in patients weighing less than 65 kg.[39] High doses of tPA (150 mg) have been associated with an increased risk of intracranial bleeding.[40] In an effort to enhance reperfusion, yet minimize bleeding complications, accelerated dosage regimens were investigated. Results from a small study that administered 100 mg of tPA intravenously over 90 minutes (15 mg bolus, 50 mg infusion over 30 minutes, followed by a 35 mg infusion over 60 minutes) were published.[41] The Global Utilization of Streptokinase and tPA for Occluded Arteries (GUSTO) trial also used this accelerated or front-loading regimen for administration of tPA. In this trial, tPA was compared to streptokinase and a combination of streptokinase and tPA. The results showed that tPA alone was the most effective in reducing mortality.[42] In GUSTO, the tPA regimen was also weight adjusted, such that after the 15 mg bolus dose, the infusion was 0.75 mg/kg over 30 minutes followed by 0.5 mg/kg over 60 minutes. The maximum dose received was 100 mg.

Most of the large trials with streptokinase have utilized an IV infusion of 1.5 MU administered over 60 minutes.[13,43,44] There have been some trials in which the infusion was shortened to 30 minutes; however, there have been no large studies that have compared a 30-minute infusion to a 60-minute infusion.[36,45]

Anistreplase usually is given intravenously as 30 U over two to five minutes.[46,47] This convenient dosing schedule is the major advantage for this agent. It has been suggested that prehospital administration of anistreplase by emergency services personnel would reduce the amount of time from the onset of chest pain to the administration of this life-saving drug. Unfortunately, many patients with acute myocardial infarction are not transported to the hospital by trained paramedics.[48]

In another trial, urokinase was given as a 1 MU IV bolus repeated in 60 minutes combined with heparin and compared to heparin alone in patients with AMI.[49] In this trial, there was no statistically significant difference between the two therapies. In the Thrombolysis and Angioplasty in Myocardial Infarction (TAMI-5) trial, urokinase (3 MU given over 90 minutes) was compared to tPA (100 mg over three hours) and a combination of urokinase and tPA. The combination strategy proved to be more effective in achieving early patency and was associated with a less complicated clinical course.[50] Urokinase also has been given as an IV 2 MU bolus[51] and a 1.5 MU bolus followed by 1.5 MU infusion over 90 minutes.[52]

Once P.H. has his blood pressure controlled, he should receive a thrombolytic as quickly as possible. Since he appears to be having a large anterior infarction, the added cost of tPA may be justified. Table 14.6 summarizes the major thrombolytic trials.

Adjunct Therapy

8. Orders are written for heparin 5000 U IV bolus, followed by 1000U/hr by continuous infusion. Also prescribed is aspirin 325 mg STAT. Are both these agents necessary?

The ISIS-2 trial showed that aspirin 160 mg/day alone and in combination with streptokinase reduced mortality in patients with acute myocardial infarction by 23% and 42%, respectively, when compared to a control group of patients who received neither aspirin nor streptokinase.[43] Immediate administration and daily aspirin thereafter is recommended for all patients diagnosed with AMI whether or not they receive thrombolytics.[28]

The use of heparin as adjunct therapy to prevent reocclusion also has been evaluated. The International Study Group evaluated 20,891 patients who were randomized to either streptokinase or tPA. Each group was further randomized to receive heparin given subcutaneously or no heparin.[46] No significant differences in hospital mortality rates were found between the two thrombolytics or between the heparin or no heparin groups. The heparin group did have more major bleeding complications (1% versus 0.5%) when compared to the no heparin group, but there was no difference in the incidence of stroke or reinfarction.

The ISIS-3 trial compared the three thrombolytics streptokinase, anistreplase, and duteplase (a tissue plasminogen activator), and aspirin 162 mg/day plus heparin versus aspirin alone.[44] In this trial, heparin 12,500 U was administered subcutaneously beginning four hours after randomization for seven days or until discharge. There were no statistically significant differences in mortality among the six groups of patients. Although heparin plus aspirin compared to aspirin alone had no effect on mortality measured on day 35, there was an increase in transfusions, noncerebral bleeding episodes, and definite or probable cerebral hemorrhage in the heparin and aspirin group.

The results of the International Study and ISIS-3 showed no particular benefit of adding heparin to a thrombolytic regimen; however, the difference in the route of heparin administration (IV infusion versus subcutaneous) may have played a role. The Heparin-Aspirin Reperfusion Trial evaluated 205 AMI patients with angiography 7 to 24 hours after beginning tPA and again seven days later.[37] Patients received tPA (100 mg over six hours) in addition to either aspirin 80 mg/day or IV heparin (5000 U bolus plus 1000 U/hour) adjusted to achieve a partial thromboplastin time one and one-half to two times control for seven days. The patency rates at the first angiogram were significantly higher in the heparin group (82%) as compared to the aspirin group (52%); however, there were no significant differences between the two groups at seven

days. Bleich and colleagues also found that heparin (5000 U bolus plus 1000 U/hour adjusted to achieve a partial thromboplastin time one and one-half to two times control) increased the patency of infarct-related arteries when compared to no heparin 48 to 72 hours after a tPA infusion in a small number of patients with acute myocardial infarction.[38]

The hypothesis that the efficacy of tPA is influenced by the administration regimen of heparin was tested by the GUSTO trial.[42] Over 41,000 patients suspected of having an acute myocardial infarction were randomized within six hours from the onset of chest pain. Four treatments were compared: streptokinase (SK) with subcutaneous heparin, SK with IV heparin, an accelerated tPA infusion (given over 90 minutes) with IV heparin, and a combination of SK and tPA with IV heparin. In this trial, the patients receiving accelerated tPA infusion and IV heparin had the lowest mortality rate at 30 days (6.3% versus 7.2% for streptokinase with subcutaneous heparin, 7.4% for streptokinase with IV heparin, and 7.0% for the thrombolytic combination with IV heparin). The accelerated tPA group and the combination thrombolytic group also had a significant increase in hemorrhagic stroke (0.72% and 0.94%, respectively) compared to the streptokinase with subcutaneous heparin (0.49%) and streptokinase with IV heparin (0.54%); however, the net benefit still favored the accelerated tPA group.

Overall, it appears that heparin administration offers no benefit to those patients receiving streptokinase or anistreplase. However, since P.H. will receive tPA, an IV heparin bolus followed by a continuous infusion should be started before the end of the tPA infusion. The activated partial thromboplastin time (aPTT) should be between one and one-half to two times control (generally between 60 and 85 seconds).

Based upon the ISIS-2 study and all the subsequent trials that have used aspirin as adjunctive therapy with thrombolytic, P.H. also should receive aspirin 80 to 325 mg (chewable tablet) immediately and then aspirin 160 to 325 mg/day orally indefinitely.

Determination of Reperfusion

9. How can you monitor for successful reperfusion in P.H. who has received thrombolytic therapy?

Performing coronary angiography following thrombolytic therapy will reveal if the infarcted artery is open, how vigorous the blood flow is, and the extent of residual stenosis. The TIMI-II trial compared an invasive strategy performing prophylactic percutaneous coronary angioplasty (PTCA) immediately (18 to 48 hours) following an AMI treated with thrombolysis to a more conservative approach where arteriography and PTCA were performed only in patients with ischemia.[40] There was no demonstrated benefit to the group of patients that underwent prophylactic PTCA.

There are several clinical indicators that correspond with reperfusion. One indicator of efficacy is the resolution of chest pain.[53,54] Some investigators have found the development of ''reperfusion arrhythmias'' to be associated with infarct-related artery patency. Neither of these markers is very reliable.[53,55]

Two other methods used to estimate the presence of reperfusion are ECG and laboratory changes.[56] The extent of the reduction of ST segment elevation may be related to the extent of patency. Obtaining frequent 12-lead ECGs has the advantage of being readily available, noninvasive, and inexpensive.

Early peaking of total creatine kinase and the MB-CK isoenzyme also may differentiate those patients who have achieved reperfusion from those in whom thrombolytic therapy has failed. Lewis et al. found that there was an absolute rise in CK activity of 480 U/L or a relative rise of 34% within the first hour following successful thrombolysis.[57] MB-CK activity was found to increase 48 U/L or have a relative rise of 27% during the first hour. In the

Table 14.6		Summary of Major Thrombolytic Trials			
Trial	Thrombolytics[a]	Heparin, Aspirin[a]	Number of Patients[b]	Duration of Symptoms	Results[a]
ISIS-2 1988[43]	Steptokinase 1.5 MU over 1 hr *versus* placebo	Also randomized to aspirin 160 mg/day or no aspirin. Heparin not specified	17,187	<24 hr	Streptokinase, aspirin, streptokinase + aspirin all reduced mortality compared to placebo. Most benefit from streptokinase + aspirin. Aspirin alone and in combination with streptokinase reduces mortality. Some benefit from aspirin and/or streptokinase even administered late
GISSI-2 1990[36]	tPA 100 mg over 3 hr *versus* streptokinase 1.5 MU over 1 hr	Also randomized to heparin SQ or no heparin. All patients received aspirin and atenolol unless contraindicated	20,891	<6 hr	No significant difference in hospital mortality between streptokinase and tPA. More episodes of major bleeding with streptokinase and more strokes with tPA. Results questioned due to the use of SQ heparin
ISIS-3 1992[44]	tPA (duteplase) 0.6 MU over 4 hr *versus* streptokinase 1.5 MU over 1 hr *versus* APSAC 30 U over 3 min	Also randomized to SQ heparin or no heparin. All patients received aspirin 162 mg/day	41,299	<24 hr	No significant difference in mortality between thrombolytics. More episodes of major bleeding with heparin and more strokes with tPA. Results questioned due to the use of SQ heparin
GUSTO 1993[42]	tPA 1.25 mg/kg (≤100 mg) over 90 min *versus* streptokinase 1.5 MU over 1 hr *versus* tPA 1 mg/kg + streptokinase 1 MU over 1 hr	Aspirin 160 to 325 mg/day to all patients. Heparin IV with tPA groups. Heparin IV or SQ in streptokinase groups	41,021	<6 hr	Statistically significant decrease in 30-day mortality in the tPA group (6.3%) vs. streptokinase (7.3%). More strokes in tPA groups

[a] APSAC = Anisoylated plasminogen streptokinase activator complex; SQ = Subcutaneous; tPA = Tissue plasminogen activator.
[b] No upper age limit.

absence of reperfusion, creatine kinase activity was only increased by 15 U/L or had a relative rise of 3% over the first two and one-half hour period.

Thallium-201 has been used as an imaging agent, but its usefulness is limited by the need to delay administration of the thrombolytic in order to obtain the initial baseline images. Persistently ischemic tissue also may be confused with scar tissue when using this agent.[56] Positive PPi images (technetium-99m stannous pyrophosphate) are as reliable as early peaks of CK.

Some hospitals routinely evaluate regional wall motion by using echocardiography. Unfortunately, it may take several days before improvement in wall motion is seen; therefore, it is difficult to assess the initial success of thrombolysis.

It is important to determine whether thrombolysis has been successful since the prognosis of the patient appears to be related to the presence or absence of an open infarct-related artery.[58] If thrombolytic therapy fails to open the infarct-related artery, then the patient may benefit from mechanical revascularization such as PTCA or an emergent coronary artery bypass graft (CABG) procedure.

Time from Onset of Chest Pain

10. If P.H.'s arrival at the hospital had been delayed more than six hours from the onset of his chest pain, should he still have received a thrombolytic?

Although efforts should be directed toward administering a thrombolytic as early as possible, many patients will present hours after the onset of chest pain. There are several theories why the late administration of a thrombolytic may be helpful. Some patients will present with a ''stuttering'' MI, which is chest pain that may wax and wane over a period of hours or days, presumably from recurrent or ongoing ischemia. These patients should be considered

candidates for thrombolytic therapy or angiographic evaluation.[59] The magnitude of left ventricular dilatation may be diminished by the late reperfusion of the infarct-related artery. Another potential advantage of reperfusing an infarct-related artery, even hours after a myocardial infarction, is that the reperfused artery could become a source of collateral blood flow in the future.[60] Thrombolytic therapy also is associated with a decreased occurrence of late potentials on the signal-averaged electrocardiogram (SAECG), inducible ventricular tachycardia, and sudden death. Briefly, late potentials on an SAECG relate to areas of altered refractoriness within the ventricle. In other words, areas which under the right conditions could cause or facilitate a ventricular arrhythmia.

The GISSI-1 trial enrolled patients within 12 hours from the onset of chest pain.[13] After 12 months of follow-up, the cumulative survival rate showed a statistically significant benefit from the administration of streptokinase compared to placebo. However, a subgroup analysis showed no benefit for the patients who received streptokinase after six hours from the onset of chest pain.

The ISIS-2 trial expanded their patient enrollment and included patients within 24 hours from the onset of chest pain.[43] In that trial, there was a 17% reduction in vascular death at five weeks in the streptokinase group treated 5 to 24 hours from the onset of chest pain. This is compared to a 35% reduction in the group who received streptokinase within four hours from the onset of pain. Although the benefit was reduced, a statistically and clinically significant benefit still was present.

Streptokinase had been given between 12 and 49 hours (mean: 32 hours) after the onset of symptoms.[61] Although there was no difference between the control group versus the streptokinase group in regard to deaths or reinfarction, there was a trend toward a lower incidence of angina pectoris and enhanced exercise tolerance in the streptokinase group.

Overall, there appears to be a statistically significant benefit associated with administering a thrombolytic up to 12 hours from the onset of chest pain and a trend toward benefit when given between 13 and 24 hours. Late administration may be most beneficial in those patients at highest risk for mortality. This would include the elderly, patients with large infarctions, and those with continuing pain or hypotension.[60] P.H. still may benefit from thrombolytic therapy, even if he presents beyond the six-hour time frame. If he still is having symptoms, he probably has viable myocardium at risk that may be salvaged. Streptokinase is the most cost-effective drug and the thrombolytic that has been shown to be effective in this situation.

Readministration of Thrombolytic Agents

11. This is P.H.'s first infarction. If he had a history of a previous MI that was treated with a thrombolytic would he still be eligible for thrombolysis?

The need to administer a thrombolytic for a second infarction is becoming a common occurrence. Many patients who are admitted to a hospital with AMI have a history of a previous infarction. Both streptokinase and anistreplase are associated with the formation of neutralizing antibodies within several days following administration. In a small study of 145 patients who had received streptokinase in conventional doses (1.5 MU), neutralizing antibodies were found in approximately 50% of patients four years later.[62] It is not known to what extent these antibodies could affect the efficacy of a repeat dose of streptokinase.

Another concern of repeated doses of streptokinase would be the enhancement of allergic reactions. Major allergic reactions are rare with first-time administration of streptokinase. In ISIS-2, there were no reports of anaphylactic shock and most of the allergic reactions (4.4% of individuals) consisted of shivering, pyrexia, or rashes.[36] The use of prophylactic corticosteroids did not seem to affect the incidence of allergic reactions.

If P.H. was presenting with a second infarction within a year and had received streptokinase for his first infarction, the thrombolytic of choice would be tPA. It is unclear if tPA would be the drug of choice if the second infarction were several years later.

12. P.H. was stable initially following thrombolysis, but 48 hours later he experienced recurrent chest pain and ECG changes consistent with extension of his infarct. The attending cardiologist would like to readminister tPA at this time. Is this a reasonable course of therapy?

Reocclusion of the infarct-related artery following initial successful thrombolysis is a major setback for this therapeutic strategy. If reocclusion occurs, mechanical intervention (e.g., angioplasty) often is attempted. There also have been attempts at reopening the infarct-related artery with repeat infusions of tPA. In an evaluation of 52 patients who underwent repeat thrombolysis with tPA,[63] many patients received their second thrombolytic infusion within one hour of the end of the first infusion. Forty-four of the 52 patients responded favorably with resolution of pain. Minor bleeding complications occurred in 19% of patients. Others have described experiences with repeat thrombolysis using tPA within a median of five days. One patient developed a fatal intracranial hemorrhage within six hours of the second thrombolytic infusion.[64]

In the case of P.H., a repeat infusion with tPA would probably be safe, but may not be effective. If facilities for either PTCA or surgery exist at the institution, many cardiologists would chose an invasive strategy at this point in time for P.H.

Use in the Elderly

13. B.T., a 85-year-old female, presents to the ER with a history and examination that are nearly identical to P.H.'s. Should B.T., an elderly person (i.e., >70 years old), be treated any differently with regard to thrombolytic therapy?

Some of the early trials with thrombolytic therapy excluded the elderly. Although the elderly may have a higher incidence of relative contraindications (i.e., severe hypertension, history of stroke) at the time of presentation, they also have a higher incidence of mortality following an acute myocardial infarction. The one-year cardiac mortality rate following an AMI is 17.6% in the greater than 75 years of age group compared to 12% for those between the ages of 65 and 75.[65] In a trial using streptokinase, a higher incidence of bleeding in patients over the age of 70 was reported.[66] Yet, in the ISIS-2 trial, the greatest reduction in mortality occurred in the elderly subgroup.[43] There are no controlled trials in which thrombolytic therapy has increased mortality in the elderly.

If B.T. has no contraindications to thrombolytic therapy, she should receive it. A subgroup analysis from the GUSTO trial would suggest that patients over the age of 70 receive streptokinase, since there was a higher incidence of intracranial hemorrhage in elderly patients who received tPA.[42]

Strokes Associated with Thrombolysis

14. G.M., a 45-year-old male, presents with signs and symptoms consistent with an anterolateral AMI. Upon admission, he received a front loaded regimen of tPA (100 mg over 90 min). He developed nystagmus, blurred vision, dysarthria, and paresthesias in his right hand 18 hours after the infusion. How often are stroke symptoms observed in patients with AMI? Is there a difference in the risk of stroke among the various thrombolytic agents?

Stroke is a very serious but infrequent complication of acute myocardial infarction. Before thrombolytic agents were used widely, stroke reportedly occurred in 1.7% to 3.2% of AMI patients.[67] The risk factors identified for stroke were large infarct size, anterior location, severe pump failure, atrial arrhythmias, and previous history of stroke. Most of the strokes were thought to be due to cerebral embolism.

Large anterior wall infarcts are associated with a higher risk for mural thrombi formation. An estimated one-third of patients with anterior wall infarction who do not receive a thrombolytic will develop a mural thrombus, usually within the first week of the event.[67] Many cardiologists routinely perform echocardiograms before discharge in patients who have had an anterior wall infarction to rule out the presence of a mural thrombus.

Interestingly, the overall incidence of stroke following an AMI has decreased since the use of thrombolytic agents has become widespread. This finding has occurred in both placebo- and thrombolytic-treated groups, but the reason for this decrease is unclear. In a review of six placebo-controlled trials evaluating the use of thrombolytic agents, the incidence of stroke averaged 0.86% in the patients treated with placebo. The incidence of stroke in the patients treated with thrombolytic averaged 1.06%.[67] However, these rates are only estimates since many of the strokes in these trials were unclassified and the diagnosis may have been imprecise. Mortality rates for patients who have had a stroke also are on the decline. Better measures are needed to identify patients at risk for stroke.

The risk of stroke was analyzed from the GISSI-2 and International Study trials where streptokinase was compared to tPA with and without subcutaneous heparin.[68] Of the 20,768 patients where complete records were available, 236 had a stroke while in the hospital. Thirty-one percent of the cases were intracerebral hemorrhage, 42% were ischemic stroke, and 26% were not classified. More hemorrhagic and ischemic strokes occurred in patients receiving tPA (1.33% versus 0.94% for streptokinase). Elderly patients (i.e., >70 years old) had a stroke rate of 2.6% with tPA compared to 1.6% with streptokinase. As mentioned previously, patients older than 75 years of age had a higher incidence of death and stroke compared to patients younger than age 75 in the GUSTO trial.[42] Patients over 75 years of age who were randomized to the accelerated tPA group had a higher incidence of hemorrhagic stroke (2.08%) versus those randomized to either streptokinase group (1.23%). This has prompted some to suggest that patients over the age of 75 should receive streptokinase rather than tPA.[69]

Cardiopulmonary
Resuscitation (CPR) and Thrombolysis

15. If P.H. (the patient in Questions 1 through 12) had suffered cardiac arrest before hospitalization and underwent CPR, would thrombolysis be contraindicated?

The need for CPR in the acute phase of a myocardial infarction is fairly common, with a reported incidence of cardiac arrest between 10% and 16% in some trials. Patients who have a cardiac arrest during an AMI are at a high risk for death and could potentially benefit from thrombolytic therapy. A retrospective analysis of 708 patients enrolled in the first three TAMI trials was done to answer this question.[70] Fifty-nine patients who needed less than ten minutes of CPR before receiving thrombolytic therapy or needed CPR within six hours of receiving thrombolytic therapy were assessed. The authors found that those patients who required CPR were more likely to have factors present that worsened their prognosis (i.e., anterior infarctions and lower EFs). The mortality rate was twice as high (12% versus 6%) in the CPR patient group. The deaths, however, were attributed to pump failure and there were no complications as a result of the CPR. Prolonged or traumatic CPR is listed as an absolute contraindication to thrombolytic therapy.[28] There are no firm data to suggest that thrombolytic therapy should be withheld from individuals who only require defibrillation or a brief duration of CPR. Therefore, P.H. would still be a reasonable candidate for thrombolytic therapy if the CPR was brief.

Lidocaine

Risk of Ventricular Fibrillation

16. Should P.H. receive prophylactic lidocaine?

Over one-half of the episodes of ventricular fibrillation that occur with an AMI are within one hour of the onset of symptoms. It also has been noted that patients with Q wave infarctions are more likely to have ventricular fibrillation than patients with non-Q wave infarctions. Interestingly, it has been noted that the incidence of ventricular fibrillation declines with increasing age. Patients with Q wave infarctions, less than 65 years of age, and presenting within six hours from the onset of symptoms have a lower risk of developing ventricular fibrillation if given prophylactic lidocaine.[71] It also has been suggested that patients with symptomatic arrhythmias or sustained ventricular tachycardia be given prophylactic lidocaine. Patients with ST segment elevation who do not receive a thrombolytic have a high risk for developing ventricular fibrillation and probably would benefit from receiving lidocaine.[72]

Ventricular fibrillation is a major cause of death in patients who are undergoing an acute myocardial infarction. Since ventricular fibrillation is estimated to occur in 4% to 18% of patients with AMI, prophylactic lidocaine has been used in an attempt to reduce this complication.[71] It was assumed initially that ventricular ectopy such as frequent premature ventricular complexes (PVCs) or short runs of ventricular tachycardia would precede any episodes of ventricular fibrillation. Therefore, patients with these types of "warning arrhythmias" were given lidocaine prophylactically. Subsequently, it was noted that not all patients who developed ventricular fibrillation had warning arrhythmias, so it became routine to give all patients with AMI prophylactic infusions of lidocaine.[72] Although the prophylactic use of lidocaine may decrease the incidence of ventricular fibrillation, a meta-analysis of clinical trials

concluded that it adversely affects mortality.[73] In a summary of 14 trials, lidocaine was associated with a 35% reduction of ventricular fibrillation, but it did not reduce the overall mortality. In fact, early mortality was greater in the lidocaine-treated patients. In 7 of the 14 trials, there was an excess of asystole in the lidocaine-treated patients, although this difference was not statistically significant. Since ventricular fibrillation is treated readily with defibrillation in an intensive care unit (ICU), the risk of prophylactic lidocaine in all patients may exceed the benefit. It is desirable to avoid cardioversion because it is an unpleasant experience; therefore, it is reasonable to use prophylactic lidocaine in those patients at highest risk for ventricular fibrillation. (Also see Chapter 16: Cardiac Arrhythmias.)

It would be reasonable to give P.H. lidocaine since he is less than 65 years of age and presents within six hours of symptom onset. He is at risk for ventricular fibrillation because he has a Q wave anterior infarction. However, the risk of lidocaine administration would probably outweigh the benefit in G.M. (patient in Question 14) since he already is demonstrating many of the symptoms often associated with lidocaine toxicity as a result of his stroke. These findings make the monitoring of lidocaine very difficult. Furthermore, if G.M. received lidocaine, it would complicate monitoring the symptoms of his stroke.

Risks of Using Lidocaine

17. How much lidocaine should P.H. be given and how should this therapy be monitored?

Lidocaine should be given as a loading dose and followed with a continuous infusion. Loading doses of 1 mg/kg (max: 100 mg) are used commonly. P.H. could receive an 80 mg bolus followed by a constant infusion between 20 and 50 μg/kg/min.[28] Since P.H. is not exhibiting ventricular ectopy at this time, the lidocaine therapy is prophylactic. The infusion should be stopped within 24 hours.

P.H. should be monitored for side effects of lidocaine, with the most common being those associated with central nervous system (CNS) toxicity. Patient's symptoms may include drowsiness, dizziness, tremor, paresthesias, slurred speech, seizures, and coma. Massive overdoses may cause respiratory depression. Lidocaine may suppress ventricular escape mechanisms leading to atrioventricular block or asystole. The overall incidence of side effects in studies has been approximately 15%.[71,72]

Plasma Concentrations

The likelihood of developing adverse effects from lidocaine is dose related; however, side effects frequently are reported when plasma concentrations are within the therapeutic range. The elderly and patients with congestive heart failure and hepatic dysfunction have reduced clearance of lidocaine and may be predisposed to lidocaine toxicity. Lidocaine is bound to α_1-acid glycoprotein (AAG) and albumin in the serum. AAG plasma concentrations have been shown to increase within 36 hours from the time of infarction.[74] Patients with AMI have an increased binding of lidocaine to AAG, a rise in total lidocaine plasma concentrations, but a reduced percentage of free lidocaine. This could result in a patient with a plasma lidocaine concentration that is above the "therapeutic range" without signs of toxicity. Therefore, plasma lidocaine concentrations may be difficult to interpret in the setting of acute myocardial infarction. (See Chapter 16: Cardiac Arrhythmias for a complete discussion of lidocaine dosing and toxicity.)

Magnesium

18. Will the administration of IV magnesium be beneficial for P.H.? How is magnesium administered?

There has been considerable interest in the use of magnesium in the setting of acute myocardial infarction. The potential mechanisms by which magnesium may benefit a patient include an antiarrhythmic effect, an antiplatelet effect, reversal of vasoconstriction, reduction of catecholamine secretion, and enhancement of adenosine triphosphate production.[75,76]

In a meta-analysis of seven small studies, Teo et al. found that early treatment with intravenous magnesium improved survival in the first few weeks following an AMI.[77] In LIMIT-2, a randomized, placebo controlled, double blind trial of 2316 patients with suspected AMI, intravenous magnesium was found to decrease mortality at 28 days by 24%.[78] However, this benefit was not confirmed in the much larger ISIS-4 study.[79]

At this point in time, most clinicians do not routinely administer IV magnesium to all patients because of the conflicting results of ISIS-4 and LIMIT-2. However, since P.H has a low serum magnesium concentration, he may benefit from the drug. Based upon trials using magnesium in acute myocardial infarction, P.H. should receive 8 mmol over 5 to 15 minutes followed by 65 to 72 mmol, or 8 to 9 gm, over 24 hours given as an IV infusion.[78,79]

Beta Blockers

19. The physician has written orders for IV metoprolol 5 mg Q 5 min for three doses. What are some of the benefits in administering beta blockers to P.H.? Should they be given early in his therapeutic course as IV therapy, or simply started as oral therapy a few days after the infarct?

As with thrombolytics, beta blockers offer significant benefits to the MI patient in both the acute infarct period and/or several days later as initial oral therapy. Several large trials were designed to give early intravenous beta blockers (up to 24 hours after symptom onset), followed by oral therapy; other studies used oral therapy alone beginning days after the infarct.[15-18,80] Early IV administration appears to be most beneficial, with a reduction of mortality of around 20% when the results of these trials are pooled.[17] However, late oral therapy alone, up to 21 days in the Beta-Blocker in Heart Attack Trial, also is associated with a substantial reduction in mortality in these patients (around 10%).[18]

Agents which have been studied extensively include propranolol, metoprolol, timolol, and atenolol. All have been given by early IV administration. Agents which have either not been well studied or lack good efficacy data include those drugs with intrinsic sympathomimetic activity (ISA) such as pindolol and oxprenolol. In general, if a patient has transient cardiac decompensation during the acute infarct period, early IV beta blockers are withheld. The patient's condition is then observed for a few days and if he is stabilized, oral therapy is initiated.[17,81] Since P.H. has suffered an uncomplicated myocardial infarction and is stable, he is a candidate for early IV therapy.

Use in Diabetes

20. What are the reasons for being concerned about the use of a beta blocker in P.H.? How should this therapy be monitored?

Recall that P.H. has a long-standing history of hypertension and diabetes and that his admission blood pressure was 180/110 mm Hg and heart rate was 100 beats/minute. In hypertensive patients, many clinicians would consider the presence of diabetes a relative contraindication for beta blockade due to the adverse effects on insulin release and blunting of the hypoglycemia-associated tachycardia. One must remember, however, that diabetics comprise a large portion of AMI patients and many beta blocker trials contained up to 10% diabetic AMI patients. Kjekshus et al. studied a subgroup of diabetic AMI patients and found beta blocker treatment to be beneficial in these individuals.[82] Since beta blockers have been shown to substantially decrease the morbidity and mortality in the AMI patient, these agents would have to possess major negative effects on the diabetic condition to consider them contraindicated. Diabetic patients who are given beta blockers should probably receive nonISA cardioselective agents (based upon usual practice) and be advised to monitor their blood glucose more closely for both hypo- and hyperglycemia after the beta blocker is initiated. Adjustments to insulin or oral hypoglycemic therapy may be required.

In a patient like P.H., a low dose of a $beta_1$-selective agent (i.e., metoprolol 25 mg BID) can be given and titrated to either adequate beta blockade or loss of diabetic control. At these doses the relative beta selectivity will be more likely to remain intact and less likely than some of the nonspecific beta blockers to affect his diabetes.

Use in Hyperlipidemia

P.H. has an elevated serum cholesterol (259 mg/dL) and triglyceride (300 mg/dL). His low density lipoprotein (LDL) and high density lipoprotein (HDL) cholesterol are unknown at this time. This must be taken into consideration since beta blockers have undesirable effects upon plasma lipids (i.e., decrease HDLs, increase total cholesterol and triglycerides). (See Chapter 9: Dyslipidemias.) However, similar to the reasons stated above in reference to diabetes, one must remember that beta blockers also have reduced post-MI morbidity and mortality in hyperlipidemic patients. The overall beneficial effects are clear for at least two to three years of use, so any negative effect on lipids and coronary artery disease risk is negated for at least this period of time.[2,18] Further, it is unclear how discontinuing beta blockers affects mortality. Some follow-up data show no effect or increased mortality.[2] The decision to treat P.H.'s lipid abnormalities should be based upon serum lipid determinations measured two months after his AMI.

Use in Congestive Heart Failure (CHF)

While CHF generally has been considered a contraindication to beta blockade, one must remember to differentiate the degree and type of heart failure (i.e., systolic or diastolic heart failure, an underlying ejection fraction, and severity of any concurrent ischemia). In post-MI patients with angina and EF greater than 35% or angina plus diastolic dysfunction, the use of a beta blocker, verapamil, or diltiazem may be reasonable.[83] This is of little concern in P.H. since he has no CHF symptoms and his previous ejection fraction was over 50%.

Use in Pulmonary Disease

P.H.'s acute situation is complicated by his history of intermittent pulmonary problems. In deciding whether or not to attempt use of beta blockers in patients with pulmonary disease, one must determine the nature of the pulmonary problem (i.e., reactive airways or restrictive lung disease). It also would be helpful to determine P.H.'s need for routine use of beta agonists in order to help quantify the severity of his disease. By history, P.H. does not use beta-agonist bronchodilators routinely. No history is given regarding his pulmonary function tests or degree of reversibility of his airway disease with bronchodilators. $Beta_1$-selective antagonists are the drugs of choice in these patients, but at higher doses (i.e., metoprolol doses >100 mg/day) the relative $beta_1$-selectivity may be lost.[81] Similar to the argument regarding diabetes, a patient would need to experience significant worsening of the pulmonary disease in order to justify avoiding beta blockers. A better history of P.H.'s pulmonary problems should be obtained; if they are minor, low doses of metoprolol or atenolol (started in the hospital so he may be monitored closely) should be considered.

P.H.'s physical examination reveals no evidence of acute changes in his lung function or compromised cardiac function. Weighing the risk versus benefit of beta blockers, one could make a case for cautiously administering intravenous agents to him at this time. His dose of IV metoprolol (5 mg Q 5 min for three doses) is a typical treatment plan.[17] He must have frequent monitoring of heart rate, blood pressure, and respiratory status. Therapy should be discontinued if P.H.'s heart rate drops below 60 beats/minute, systolic blood pressure falls below 100 to 110 mm Hg, or any respiratory distress is noted. Oral therapy could begin at 25 to 50 mg a few hours after his last IV dose. Substituting the ultrashort-acting agent esmolol for metoprolol is an option for P.H. since any adverse effects would be relatively short-lived. Unfortunately, there are no data to support the use of esmolol for an AMI.

Objective evidence of adequate beta blockade consists of a resting heart rate of 50 to 60 beats/minute, an exercise heart rate of less than 120 beats/minute, and/or a resting systolic blood pressure of 100 to 120 mm Hg.[84] Therefore, P.H. needs a significant reduction in heart rate and blood pressure from his admission values (100 beats/minute and 180/110 mm Hg, respectively) in order to be considered as having achieved adequate beta-blockade.

Use in the Elderly

21. If P.H. were over 70 years old, would there be a change in the decision to use beta blockers post-MI?

Unfortunately, many of the larger multicenter trials in post-MI patients excluded the elderly. Women also are underrepresented in many of these trials. A recent survey of practice patterns found the elderly (i.e., >70 years old) were significantly less likely to receive standard therapies such as thrombolytics, beta blockers, aspirin, and nitrates.[85] However, the standard of care suggests that it is reasonable and justifiable to routinely use beta blockers without regard to age. Again, we must recall the increased mortality rate secondary to AMI in the elderly. Any applicable dosage adjustments for altered clearance or pharmacologic response would still need to be made. Table 14.7 summarizes selected trials of beta blockers in AMI patients.

22. Several days later, a routine ECHO is performed on P.H. which shows the following: hypokinesis of anterior and lateral left ventricular walls, slightly enlarged left ventricle, no valvular abnormalities, EF 35%–40%, appearance of a thrombus in the left ventricle. Clinically, he has no signs or symptoms of heart failure. What are the therapeutic and prognostic implications of this ECHO?

Hypokinesis of the infarcted areas of the heart is not unusual. P.H. may have an area of "stunned" or "hibernating" myocardium which could take several weeks to recover some of the wall motion if the area is still viable.[86,87] Therefore, P.H. may recover some of the wall motion and ejection fraction over time.

The presence of a thrombus in the left ventricle is a risk factor for embolism. Several studies have shown that this may increase P.H.'s risk of experiencing a later embolic event. Other risk factors for embolism may include atrial fibrillation, CHF, a dilated left ventricle, ventricular aneurysm, and a poorly seated thrombus.[88] If P.H. is thought to be compliant with his medications, he would be a candidate for warfarin therapy [titrated to an International Normalized Ratio (INR) of two to three] for one to three months because of this thrombus. This should be enough time for the thrombus to organize and become less of an embolic threat.

Long-Term Therapy
Angiotensin-Converting Enzyme (ACE) Inhibitors

23. Even though P.H. has no signs or symptoms of heart failure, an order is written for captopril 12.5 mg TID. Is this appropriate and if so, how should his therapy be monitored?

As stated previously, after an acute myocardial infarction the heart undergoes processes which initially will compensate for the loss of contractile function. This is termed remodeling of the ventricle. The increase in the number of survivors of AMI because of thrombolytic therapy has increased the number of heart failure patients.

Ventricular remodeling consists of several steps (see Figure 14.4).[89] In the first few days after the AMI, the infarct is completed and early infarct expansion occurs. Factors which may increase the likelihood of infarct expansion include a large anterior infarct, absence of pre-existing ventricular wall hypertrophy, and increased intraventricular systolic pressure (i.e., increased afterload).[89,90] From days one to seven postinfarct, the ventricular wall thins and dilatation of the ventricle occurs; therefore, ventricular volume increases. This compensatory process can eventually lead to frank congestive heart failure in some patients. Over the next few months, the ventricle further expands resulting in volume overload and heart failure.

Gaudron et al. studied the natural history and incidence of ventricular decompensation in 70 patients.[91] During three years of follow-up, only 20% of patients developed progressive left ventricular dysfunction and an additional 26% developed limited left ventricular dysfunction. Importantly, the authors also successfully constructed a risk factor regression analysis equation to predict left ventricular dysfunction using the following data from post-MI day four: EF, infarct size, infarct location, stroke index, and TIMI grade patency of the infarct-related artery. This trial suggests that those patients who are likely to develop left ventricular dysfunction following an AMI can be identified early by evaluating these factors. P.H. would need to have stroke index and TIMI grade patency determined in order to use this model to predict his risk of heart failure. Appropriate therapy should be initiated as soon as those patients at risk for developing heart failure are identified.

An early study by Pfeffer et al. helped to establish the utility of captopril in altering the course of left ventricular dilatation after acute myocardial infarction.[92] Patients who were started on captopril therapy within 30 days after an AMI showed a significant improvement in hemodynamic measurements, such as left ventricular end-diastolic volume and pulmonary capillary wedge pressure (PCWP), versus placebo therapy. The captopril group also had an increase in exercise capacity.

In the Survival and Ventricular Enlargement Trial (SAVE), captopril (up to 50 mg TID) had a statistically significant beneficial effect on mortality when given to asymptomatic patients with an ejection fraction less than 40%, who were 3 to 16 days post-MI. This four-year follow-up study also showed significant decreases in morbidity from CHF and recurrent AMI in the captopril group. The largest risk reduction in cardiovascular death was seen in males and in patients older than 55 years.[9]

The results of two other large ACE inhibitor trials in the post-MI population are mixed. The CONSENSUS-II showed no benefit of early (within the first 24 hours) intravenous enalapril therapy on AMI patients.[19] This six-month trial did not stratify patients according to ejection fraction, however, and the protocol was altered during the study because of frequent episodes of hypotension (i.e., systolic BP <105 mm Hg).

Another large trial using ramipril, the Acute Infarction Ramipril Efficacy (AIRE) Study, enrolled post-MI patients with clinical evidence of heart failure (excluding New York Heart Association class IV).[93] Patients were randomized to ramipril (initially 2.5 mg BID) or placebo beginning between days three and ten after their infarct. During a mean follow-up of 15 months, ramipril significantly decreased all causes of mortality. Data from the ISIS-4 and GISSI-3 also have shown a benefit for captopril and lisinopril, respectively.[94,95]

Table 14.7   Selected Trials of Beta Blockers in AMI[a]

Drug[a]	Study Design[a]	Sample Size (% Male)	Average Age in Years (Age for Study Inclusion)	% with Diabetes and CHF	Treatment Duration	Endpoints Analyzed
Atenolol IV then oral[15]	R	n = 16,027 (77%)	59 (not stated)	*Diabetes:* 6% *CHF:* ?	7 days	Vascular death ↓
Metoprolol IV then oral[16]	R, DB, PC	n = 5778 (77%)	60 (<75)	*Diabetes:* 7% *CHF:* 3%	15 days	Mortality ↓
Propranolol Delayed oral[18]	R, DB, PC	n = 3837 (83%)	55 (<69)	*Diabetes:* 11% *CHF:* 9%	36 months (avg: 25 months)	Total mortality and CHD death ↓
Metoprolol IV then oral or delayed oral[46]	R	n = 1390 (85%)	55 (<76)	*Diabetes:* 10% *CHF:* 1%	42 days	Mortality not significantly ↓; Recurrent ischemia and reinfarction ↓
Propranolol Delayed oral[119]	R, DB, PC	n = 560 (85%)	58 (<70)	*Diabetes:* Excluded *CHF:* ?	12 months	Mortality and reinfarction not significantly ↓; SCD ↓
Metoprolol Delayed oral[120]	R, DB, PC	n = 301 (≈80%)	60 (<70)	*Diabetes:* 6%–10% *CHF:* ?	36 months	Mortality not significantly ↓; reinfarction and SCD ↓
Timolol Delayed oral[121]	R, DB, PC	n =1884 (78%)	? (<75)	*Diabetes:* ? *CHF:* ≈32%	12–36 months	Mortality and reinfarction ↓
Metoprolol IV then oral[122]	R, DB, PC	n = 1395 (76%)	60 (<74)	?	3 months	Mortality ↓

[a] AMI = Acute myocardial infarction; CHD = Coronary heart disease; CHF = Congestive heart failure; DB = Double blind; IV = Intravenous; PC = Placebo controlled; R = Randomized; SCD = Sudden cardiac death.

It would appear based upon these studies that oral ACE inhibitor therapy, beginning early in the post-MI period, is beneficial in patients with an ejection fraction less than 40% or clinical evidence of heart failure.[92,93] ACE inhibitors may be used either prophylactically or for treatment of heart failure in the AMI patient. The use of ''early'' IV therapy, unlike beta blockers, does not appear to be indicated at this time.[19] ACE inhibitors appear to offer most of their benefit in long-term use.

P.H. is a candidate for ACE inhibitor therapy to prevent the occurrence of heart failure symptoms. Captopril could be given on postinfarct day two or three, beginning with a test dose of 6.25 mg and then an initial maintenance dose of 12.5 to 25 mg three times daily. P.H.'s blood pressure should be monitored closely with a systolic pressure to be maintained at no less than 100 mm Hg. He also should have his renal function and serum potassium followed closely during the first few months of therapy. The studies cited above suggest he should continue ACE inhibitor therapy for at least three years and possibly indefinitely. Since P.H. is diabetic, an ACE inhibitor also may benefit his long-term renal function.[96] Once it is established that P.H. can tolerate an ACE inhibitor, he may be switched to a longer-acting agent such as lisinopril or enalapril to simplify his regimen.

Calcium Channel Blockers

24. Is there any reason to add a calcium channel blocker to P.H.'s therapeutic regimen at this time?

As reviewed by Yusuf et al., verapamil, diltiazem, and nifedipine all have been evaluated for use in the post-MI population.[97] Much less information is available regarding the newer agents (i.e., amlodipine, felodipine, isradipine). When calcium channel blockers are categorized according to agents which slow heart rate (e.g., diltiazem, verapamil) versus those agents with no effect or increase in heart rate (e.g., nifedipine and others), the data are more favorable for the former to be of benefit in some patients.

The DAVIT-II studied 1600 patients in a controlled, randomized manner using verapamil 360 mg/day or placebo.[26] Patients were enrolled during the second week after infarction, and importantly, severe heart failure or beta blocker use were exclusion criteria. When data for the entire study were analyzed by the primary endpoint of mortality, no statistically significant difference was found between verapamil and placebo at 18 months of follow-up. However, reinfarction rate was significantly lower in the verapamil group. A subgroup analysis of patients without heart failure showed a significant decrease in mortality and reinfarction.

Diltiazem is widely touted for use in the non-Q wave AMI patient. However, a frequently quoted trial only showed a reduction in reinfarction during the first two weeks after non-Q wave AMI.[24] Mortality was the same in the treatment and control groups. A separate trial that studied 2466 patients with both Q wave and non-Q wave infarcts showed no overall reduction in mortality or cardiac events.[25] However, this trial did show a trend for more frequent adverse cardiac events in patients with pulmonary congestion who received diltiazem. Positive data from either of these trials on long-term survival are limited since they were derived retrospectively using subgroup analyses. These trials demonstrate that the routine use of diltiazem or verapamil is not appropriate for all patients with AMI. In addition, their use should be limited to those patients without signs of pulmonary congestion.

The use of a calcium channel blocker is better justified in the patient who still has postinfarction angina. While the studies with diltiazem and verapamil suggest a lower rate of reinfarction, the benefit from beta blockers on mortality is more impressive. It is unknown if there is any added benefit by combining a calcium blocker with a beta blocker. Thus, while there are some supporting data for using calcium channel blockers, they are limited to only reducing non-Q wave AMI reinfarction. If a patient has left ventricular dysfunction secondary to an acute myocardial infarction and develops angina, the newer second-generation dihydropyridine calcium channel blockers might be preferable to use.[98]

P.H. does not need a calcium channel blocker at this time because he has suffered a Q wave infarct and does not demonstrate any ongoing ischemia. Consideration should be given to adding a calcium channel blocker if he develops signs or symptoms of postinfarction angina or if he is intolerant of beta blocker therapy.

Anticoagulants

25. Three days before P.H.'s anticipated discharge, the medical team is discussing the need to administer long-term anticoagulant therapy with warfarin and/or antiplatelet therapy with aspirin. Are either of these therapies indicated for P.H. at this time?

Long-term warfarin may be beneficial in some patients, but one needs to use clinical judgment to decide if the benefit is likely to exceed the risk. Kaplan reviewed data for the development of left ventricular thrombi in acute myocardial infarction and found an incidence of approximately 35% in patients who suffered an anterior infarct.[99] While anticoagulation will decrease the incidence of stroke, less than 3% of patients will develop a cerebrovascular accident following an AMI if not anticoagulated. One large trial which used empiric warfarin therapy in survivors of AMI found significant reductions in mortality, reinfarction, and total cerebrovascular accidents.[100] Warfarin was titrated to an INR of 2.5 to 4.8 (PT 1.5 to 2.0 times control) and patients were not allowed to take aspirin concomitantly.

The 1992 American College of Chest Physicians consensus conference gives a general recommendation for warfarin use in left ventricular thrombus which is not well seated (''shaggy''), concomitant atrial fibrillation, and underlying congestive heart failure.[88] However, some clinicians will use warfarin for one to three months in all patients with anterior AMI who do not have contraindications to anticoagulation.

P.H. probably is a good candidate for one to three months of warfarin therapy titrated to an INR of two to three because of his left ventricular thrombus. The use of low-dose aspirin in conjunction with warfarin in these individuals probably will not increase his risk of bleeding.[101]

In addition to its use in the AMI setting in combination with a thrombolytic, aspirin is routinely prescribed for the acute myocardial infarction patient.[17,88] The role of aspirin in primary prophylaxis of asymptomatic patients has been established by such trials as the Physicians' Health Study and in patients with chronic stable angina.[102,103]

While single-study data in the post-MI patient have not been impressive, pooled data analysis from multiple trials have shown that aspirin therapy reduces the risk of vascular death or nonfatal AMI by 14% and 31%, respectively.[17] The duration of antiplatelet therapy currently is thought to be for the remainder of the patient's life because of its effects upon secondary prevention of reinfarction.

While there appears to be no difference in efficacy over a wide range of aspirin doses (300 to 1500 mg/day), higher doses may increase the incidence of side effects.[88] A great deal of interest exists in using lower doses of aspirin for cardiovascular disease. One example of using low-dose aspirin is the Cottbus Reinfarction study.[104] This trial used aspirin 30, 60, or 1000 mg/day in AMI survivors. The cumulative mortality rate was not significantly different between the 30 and 60 mg/day groups, but fatal and nonfatal reinfarction rates after two years were significantly higher in the 60 mg/day group. Side effects (not specified) were significantly less in the 30 and 60 mg/day groups. While these low-dose data are promising, most clinicians still use dosages of 325 mg daily or every other day.[88]

Ticlopidine may be an alternative when aspirin is not tolerated or contraindicated, but it is more expensive and has a more significant side-effect profile (e.g., rash, leukopenia, thrombocytopenia). P.H. should receive aspirin 160 to 325 mg/day. (Refer to Chapters 12: Thrombosis and 53: Cerebrovascular Disorders for further discussions of anticoagulants and antiplatelet drugs.)

26. How would you summarize the long-term therapy needed by P.H. upon discharge?

In most cases of uncomplicated AMI such as P.H.'s, the patient is discharged to home on postinfarction day five. Appropriate discharge medications for P.H. consist of the following: metoprolol 25 to 50 mg twice daily, aspirin 325 mg/day, lisinopril 10 mg/day, and warfarin to achieve an INR of two to three. He also should receive a prescription for sublingual NTG to carry with him for use as needed. Some clinicians also might choose to continue his low-dose chronic nitrate therapy. All of these agents would be

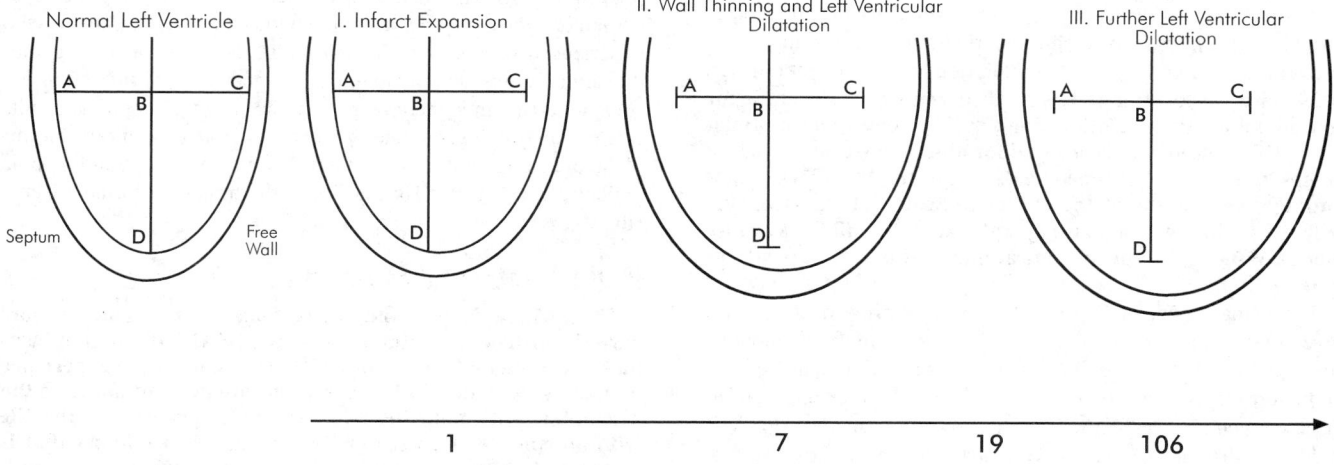

Fig 14.4 Schema of Volume Changes Occurring in the Left Ventricle During the Early and Late Postinfarction Phases The dark axis lines represent the distance from the midpoint of the left ventricle to the septum (left side in figure) and free wall (right side in figure). These distances are presented in the infarcted left ventricle over time. Reprinted with permission from reference 89.

continued long-term except for the warfarin which would be discontinued after a few months. His previous hydrochlorothiazide should be discontinued since his hypertension will be controlled with the metoprolol and lisinopril. His insulin should be continued and his blood glucose monitored closely. One would like to achieve a state of beta blockade that will allow P.H. to maintain a systolic blood pressure of greater than 100 mm Hg; therefore, one must balance the hypotensive effects of the ACE inhibitor and beta blocker. Should P.H. indeed experience postinfarction angina, then the addition of a calcium channel blocker such as diltiazem and/or chronic nitrate therapy would be indicated.

Lifestyle Modifications

27. What types of lifestyle modifications should P.H. be encouraged to pursue to reduce his risk factors?

He should be encouraged to stop smoking, perhaps the most important intervention. Rosenburg et al. showed the risk of AMI in men who quit smoking was reduced to that of nonsmokers within a few years after quitting.[105] Weight management, diabetic treatment, and serum lipid control also are important risk factors to address. (See Chapters 9: Dyslipidemias and 48: Diabetes Mellitus for further information on diet therapy and lipid-lowering drugs.)

Postinfarction Arrhythmias

28. D.T., a 45-year-old male who is recovering from an AMI (onset 12 hours ago), is noted to have sustained ventricular tachycardia on the telemetry monitor in the CCU. During the episode he was hemodynamically unstable (BP 80/40, HR >200 beats/min). The arrhythmia was terminated with a 100 J countershock. He now is in sinus rhythm and clinically stable. Would D.T. be a candidate for further work-up of the arrhythmia and if so, what test(s) are appropriate?

In the past, there has been an assumption that the presence of ventricular ectopy in the immediate post-AMI period would have negative prognostic significance especially for sudden cardiac death. Overall, ventricular arrhythmias detected with telemetry during hospitalization have not been helpful in identifying patients at high risk for SCD on long-term follow-up.[106] Since D.T.'s arrhythmia occurred within the first 48 hours after the infarct (i.e., the peri-infarct period when some residual ischemia may be occurring), he is not a candidate for any further specific arrhythmia work-up, such as electrophysiologic testing, at this time. D.T. should receive a beta blocker and aspirin during the hospitalization and after discharge to prevent reinfarction and reduce mortality.

29. Two weeks after D.T.'s AMI he returns to the clinic for routine follow-up. A Holter monitor (i.e., continuous ambulatory ECG monitoring) is ordered for him because he states that he has had several "skipped beats" since the MI (this is a new finding). The results of the Holter indicate that he is having >30 PVCs/hr (which are asymptomatic to mildly symptomatic). What is the appropriate antiarrhythmic therapy at this time?

The management of PVCs has come full circle over the past several years since the results of the Cardiac Arrhythmia Suppression Trial (CAST).[29,30] It was known for some time that frequent premature ventricular contractions in patients with organic heart disease (such as post-MI) were indicators for an increased risk of sudden cardiac death.[107] However, the CAST showed that by suppressing PVCs with flecainide, encainide, or moricizine, patient survival was significantly *worse* than in those treated with placebo. This may relate to the proarrhythmic effects of these drugs. (See Chapter 16: Cardiac Arrhythmias.) Therefore, treatment of asymptomatic or mildly symptomatic PVCs with antiarrhythmics (other

than beta blockers) in this type of post-MI patient is not recommended. A pooled-data analysis of Class I antiarrhythmic trials in these patients also supports these conclusions.[108] Preferably, therapies should be aimed at correcting the patient's underlying ischemia and/or coexisting heart failure rather than administering antiarrhythmics. D.T. should not be given any of the Class I antiarrhythmics.

There is increasing interest in using amiodarone in the post-MI patient, however. Several small pilot studies indicate that low-dose amiodarone (i.e., 200 mg daily maintenance dose) is effective in preventing sudden cardiac death in some post-MI patients.[109–111] Published in 1990, the Basel Antiarrhythmic Study of Infarct Survival (BASIS) randomized AMI survivors with complex ventricular ectopy into three groups: physician-directed individualized treatment, amiodarone, or control. At 12 months of follow-up, there was a statistically significant increase in survival among the amiodarone group. Importantly, no irreversible pulmonary toxicity was observed in this low-dose amiodarone group.[111] Long-term follow-up (mean: 72 months) showed a sustained effect of amiodarone on survival with continued separation in the survival curves between the amiodarone and control groups.[112] Ejection fraction was an important factor in predicting survival. There was a much higher (58% versus 28%) mortality rate in those patients with an EF less than 40%, regardless of treatment group, in BASIS. Larger randomized trials of amiodarone are underway to verify these effects on survival. However, at this time, D.T. probably should not receive empiric amiodarone based upon this small amount of data.

30. What are some predictors of arrhythmic mortality in the post-MI patient?

Noninvasive diagnostic tests are available to estimate a patient's mortality risk after acute myocardial infarction. The use of signal-averaged ECG, radionuclide ventriculography, Holter monitoring, and clinical variables to determine patient risk has been described.[113] Approximately two-thirds of patients in this trial had received thrombolytic therapy. When a multivariate analysis was performed to rank the variables in order of predictability, digoxin therapy at discharge (probably representing those patients with severe heart failure), abnormal signal-averaged ECG (presence of late potentials), and prior history of angina were the most powerful predictors of arrhythmic events. The presence of a poor EF (<40%) is a consistent independent predictor of mortality throughout the literature. Thus, therapy should be directed toward improving the overall function of the heart and decreasing the myocardial oxygen demand in asymptomatic patients. For patients who experienced an episode of sudden cardiac death or who have hemodynamically unstable arrhythmias beyond the peri-infarction period, antiarrhythmic therapy may be chosen based upon the results of electrophysiologic studies or repeated Holter monitors. An implantable cardiodefibrillator (ICD) may also be an option for some patients. (See Chapter 16: Cardiac Arrhythmias for further discussion.)

Right Ventricular Infarction

31. J.M., a 50-year-old black female with hypertension, chronic obstructive pulmonary disease (COPD), and noninsulin-dependent diabetes mellitus (NIDDM), begins to experience a burning sensation in her chest and attempts to alleviate the discomfort with antacids. She eventually presents to the ER with an episode of chest burning lasting several hours that is unrelieved by antacid therapy. Her BP is 110/68 mm Hg, with a heart rate of 88 beats/min. J.M.'s neck veins are elevated with jugular venous distension estimated to be at 9 cm. J.M.'s initial ECG reveals 2 mm ST segment elevation in the right precordial leads (V$_3$R, V$_4$R). A right-sided MI is suspected. Is J.M.'s presentation typical for this type of infarct?

Right ventricular infarction is associated with an obstructive lesion in the right coronary artery. Although the right coronary artery frequently is affected by atherosclerotic lesions, infarction rarely occurs, presumably because the demands of the right side of the heart are less than those of the left. Individuals with a history of pulmonary hypertension are more likely to have a right ventricular infarct. Isolated right ventricular infarctions are rare, but they frequently occur in conjunction with an inferior left ventricular infarction.[2]

Like J.M., patients with right ventricular infarctions have elevated pressures in the right side of the heart, while the pressures of the left side of the heart are near normal or slightly elevated. They also may present with unexplained systemic hypoxemia.[2]

32. What is the best treatment strategy for J.M.?

Systemic hypotension is a common problem with right ventricular infarction. It is important to recognize patients with right ventricular infarction since they frequently respond favorably to a fluid challenge. If left ventricular failure also is present, the addition of an arterial vasodilator may be helpful. Infusions of nitroglycerin or vigorous diuresis should be avoided since a reduction in filling pressure (preload) can result in a further decrease in cardiac output.[2,28] J.M. does not require a fluid challenge at this time because her blood pressure is adequate. She should be evaluated for thrombolytic therapy, aspirin, and beta blockade. Her pain may be treated with low doses of morphine or nitrates with careful monitoring of her blood pressure to avoid an excessive reduction in left ventricular filling pressure. (See Chapter 15: Congestive Heart Failure for further discussion of the relationship of left ventricular filling pressure and cardiac output.)

Management of AMI with Nitroglycerin (NTG)

33. P.J., a 75-year-old male, presents to the ER with complaints of dizziness and chest discomfort. He is a poor historian, but it appears that his symptoms have been ongoing for over 12 hours. His physician is concerned that the symptoms represent an AMI. His past medical history is significant for a GI bleed 6 weeks ago and COPD with a bronchospastic component. The ECG is consistent with new anterolateral AMI. His vital signs are: BP 150/94 mm Hg, heart rate 55 beats/min, respiratory rate 20/min. Physical examination reveals wheezing. What is the best treatment strategy for P.J.?

Because of the time delay and his history of recent GI bleeding, P.J. is not a good candidate for thrombolysis. Beta blockers also should be avoided in P.J. because of his serious pulmonary disease and current physical examination. Thus, symptomatic treatment is indicated. Nitroglycerin intravenous would be beneficial because it lowers the left ventricular filling pressure and systemic vascular resistance. By doing so, it reduces myocardial oxygen consumption and myocardial ischemia. At lower doses (<50 µg/min), NTG IV preferentially dilates the venous capacitance vessels, which leads to a decrease in left ventricular filling pressure.[114] For those patients who have signs of pulmonary congestion, nitroglycerin intravenous is of particular value.

34. How should NTG IV be administered to P.J.? How should it be monitored?

Nitroglycerin intravenous should begin with a small bolus dose of 15 µg. A constant infusion is then delivered by a controlled infusion device, starting with 5 to 10 µg/minute and increased by an additional 5 to 10 µg/minute every five to ten minutes.[28] Many cardiologists routinely give AMI patients an infusion of nitroglycerin for the first 24 to 48 hours following an acute myocardial infarction. Increasing doses may be required over this period of time to maintain the desired hemodynamic effect due to tolerance that occurs from prolonged nitrate exposure. In one study of 154 patients with AMI, hemodynamic tolerance developed progressively, although it was thought to be partial, allowing some beneficial effects to remain.[115] Overall, the frequency of tolerance was low (24% of patients), but it developed rapidly. Sixteen percent of patients had developed tolerance within ten hours. Even though tolerance developed, the patients in this subgroup still benefited from nitrate therapy as determined by the beneficial effect on infarct size. The authors also noted that 31% of patients had a problem with increased sensitivity to NTG, described as development of mean blood pressure less than 80 mm Hg. Of the patients who became hypotensive, 72% had an inferior AMI. Ferguson et al. also has noted that hypotension following nitroglycerin infusion was a common complication in patients with right ventricular infarction.[116]

P.J.'s blood pressure should be monitored closely during this infusion. Excessive doses of NTG IV can reduce left ventricular filling pressure and potentially decrease cardiac output, especially in those patients who do not have signs of heart failure like P.J. The end points for dose titration include: relief of pain or other symptoms, a 10% decrease in mean arterial pressure, or a 10% to 30% decrease in PCWP. The systolic blood pressure should always be kept at ≥90 mm Hg.[28] Nitrate tolerance can be minimized by providing a nitrate-free interval to the patient. If P.J. later receives chronic nitrate therapy with either an oral agent or a transdermal delivery system, a nitrate-free interval (e.g., withholding nighttime dose) should be used.

35. Since P.J. has an elevated BP (154/94 mm Hg), should he receive nitroprusside instead of NTG?

Nitroglycerin is preferred over nitroprusside in the setting of an AMI. Although the drugs may have similar hemodynamic effects, nitroprusside has been shown to increase ST segment elevation, whereas NTG decreases ST segment elevation.[117] Others have shown similar results and have proposed that nitroprusside may redistribute coronary blood flow away from the ischemic area, causing a worsening of the injury.[118]

Analgesic Use

36. P.J.'s chest pain becomes increasingly severe and the physician is considering use of a potent analgesic. Which analgesic would be best for P.J.?

The pain associated with AMI is due to continuing ischemia of tissue surrounding the area of infarcted tissue. The relief of pain should involve efforts to optimize the myocardial blood supply and minimize myocardial oxygen demand. Pain usually is relieved with successful thrombolysis. Other interventions can include oxygen, nitroglycerin, and beta blockers. As noted previously, P.J. is not a candidate for either thrombolysis or beta blockade. If his pain continues in the face of NTG IV, he will need an analgesic agent.

Morphine sulfate usually is the drug of choice in patients with AMI. In addition to diminishing pain and anxiety, morphine also has beneficial hemodynamic effects. By reducing pain and anxiety, the release of circulating catecholamines is diminished, possibly reducing the associated arrhythmias. Morphine also causes a peripheral venous and arterial vasodilatation, reducing preload and afterload, and consequently the myocardial oxygen demand. Morphine is administered as small (2 to 5 mg) IV doses as often as every five minutes if needed. Cumulative doses of 2 to 3 mg/kg may be required. The risks associated with morphine use include hypotension, bradycardia, and respiratory depression. P.J. already has bradycardia, so another analgesic would be preferred. In the presence of bradycardia, meperidine often is used because it has vagolytic properties.[28]

The use of thrombolytics has improved significantly the survival of patients with acute myocardial infarction. Despite the overwhelming results favoring thrombolytic therapy in all subgroups, it is believed that thrombolytics are still underused in this patient population. The major risk associated with thrombolysis is bleeding, especially within the central nervous system. Another problem associated with thrombolytic therapy is reocclusion of an artery that was initially opened. Many trials are underway to determine the best thrombolytic and optimal adjunctive therapy. Currently, aspirin should be given to all patients with AMI and, unless there

is a contraindication, beta blockers should be administered as well. The beneficial effects of ACE inhibitors have been shown in patients who also have left ventricular dysfunction (EF <40%). Nitrates also are useful, but care must be taken to maintain an adequate perfusion pressure. There are also a small number of patients who will not be eligible for thrombolysis. In that case, revascularization can be attempted using coronary angioplasty.

References

1   DeWood MA et al. Prevalence of total coronary occlusion during the early hours of transmural myocardial infarction. N Engl J Med. 1980;303:897.

2   Pasternak RC et al. Acute myocardial infarction. In: Braunwald E, ed. Heart Disease: A Textbook of Cardiovascular Medicine. Philadelphia: WB Saunders; 1992:1200.

3   Gill J. The pathophysiology and epidemiology of myocardial infarction. Drugs. 1991;42(Suppl. 2):1.

4   ISIS-2 (Second International Study of Infarct Survival) Collaborative Group. Morning peak in the incidence of myocardial infarction: experience in the ISIS-2 trial. Eur Heart J. 1992;13:594.

5   Lavie CJ, Gersh BJ. Acute myocardial infarction: initial manifestations, management, and prognosis. Mayo Clin Proc. 1990;65:531.

6   Andre-Fouet X et al. "Non-Q wave" alias "nontransmural" myocardial infarction: a specific entity. Am Heart J. 1989;117:892.

7   Adams JE et al. Biochemical markers of myocardial activity. Circulation. 1993;88:750.

8   Wallach J. Cardiovascular diseases. In: Wallach J, ed. Interpretation of Diagnostic Tests. Boston: Little, Brown and Company; 1992:113.

9   Pfeffer MA et al. Effect of captopril on mortality and morbidity in patients with left ventricular dysfunction after myocardial infarction. Results of the Survival and Ventricular Enlargement Trial. N Engl J Med. 1992;327:669.

10 Anderson HV, Willerson JT. Thrombolysis in acute myocardial infarction. N Engl J Med. 1993;329:703.

11 Alpert JS. Importance of the pharmacological profile of thrombolytic agents in clinical practice. Am J Cardiol. 1991;67(Suppl.):3E.

12 Karagounis L et al. Does thrombolysis in myocardial infarction (TIMI) perfusion grade 2 represent a mostly patent artery or a mostly occluded artery? Enzymatix and electrocardiographic evidence from the TEAM-2 study. J Am Coll Cardiol. 1992;19:1.

13 Gruppo Italiano per lo studio della streptochinasi nell'infarto miocardico (GISSI). Long-term effects of intravenous thrombolysis in acute myocardial infarction: Final report of the GISSI study. Lancet. 1987;2:871.

14 Loscalzo J et al. Comparative effects of heparin and hirudin on fibrinolytic and thrombotic activities during tissue-type plasminogen activator therapy. Circulation. 1993;88(Suppl. 2):I-200. Abstract.

15 ISIS-1 (First International Study of Infarct Survival) Collaborative Group. Randomized trial of intravenous atenolol among 16,027 cases of suspected acute myocardial infarction: ISIS-1. Lancet. 1896;2:57.

16 The MIAMI Trial Research Group. Metoprolol in acute myocardial infarction (MIAMI). A randomized placebo-controlled international trial. Eur Heart J. 1985;6:199.

17 Yusuf S et al. Routine medical management of acute myocardial infarction. Lessons from overviews of recent randomized controlled trials. Circulation. 1990;82(Suppl. II):II-117.

18 Beta-Blocker Heart Attack Trial Group. A randomized trial of propranolol in patients with acute myocardial infarction. I. Mortality Results. JAMA. 1982;247:1707.

19 Swedberg K et al. Effects of the early administration of enalapril on mortality in patients with acute myocardial infarction. N Engl J Med. 1992;327:678.

20 Bonarjee VVS et al. Attenuation of left ventricular dilatation after acute myocardial infarction by early initiation of enalapril therapy. Am J Cardiol. 1993;72:1004.

21 Babich MF, Kalin ML. Calcium-channel blockers in acute myocardial infarction. DICP. 1989;23:538.

22 Skolnick AE, Frishman WH. Calcium channel blockers in myocardial infarction. Arch Intern Med. 1989;149:1669.

23 Sirnes PA et al. Evolution of infarct size during the early use of nifedipine in patients with acute myocardial infarction: the Norwegian nifedipine multicenter trial. Circulation. 1984;70:638.

24 Gibson RS et al. Diltiazem and reinfarction in patients with non-Q wave myocardial infarction. N Engl J Med. 1986;315:423.

25 The Multicenter Diltiazem Postinfarction Trial Research Group. The effect of diltiazem on mortality and reinfarction after myocardial infarction. N Engl J Med. 1988;319:385.

26 The Danish Study Group on Verapamil in Myocardial Infarction. Effect of verapamil on mortality and major events after myocardial infarction (The Danish Verapamil Infarction Trial II-DAVIT-II). Am J Cardiol. 1990;66:779.

27 Messerli FH, Weiner DA. Are all calcium antagonists equally effective for reducing reinfarction rate? Am J Cardiol. 1993;72:818.

28 ACC/AHA Task Force Report. Guidelines for the early management of patients with acute myocardial infarction. J Am Coll Cardiol. 1990;16:249.

29 Echt DS et al. Mortality and morbidity in patients receiving encainide, flecainide or placebo. The Cardiac Arrhythmia Suppression Trial. N Engl J Med. 1991;324:781.

30 The Cardiac Arrhythmia Suppression Trial-II Investigators. Effect of the antiarrhythmic agent moricizine on survival after myocardial infarction. N Engl J Med. 1992;327:227.

31 Ribeiro EE et al. Randomized trial of direct coronary angioplasty versus intravenous streptokinase in acute myocardial infarction. J Am Coll Cardiol. 1993;32:376.

32 Muller DW, Topol EJ. Thrombolytic therapy: adjuvant mechanical intervention for acute myocardial infarction. Am J Cardiol. 1992;69(Suppl.):60A.

33 Jacoby RM, Nesto RW. Acute myocardial infarction in the diabetic patient: pathophysiology, clinical course and prognosis. J Am Coll Cardiol. 1992;20:736.

34 Wallach J. Core blood analytes-alterations by disease. In: Wallach J, ed. Interpretation of Diagnostic Tests. Boston: Little, Brown and Company; 1992:33.

35 Muller DWM, Topol EJ. Selection of patients with acute myocardial infarction for thrombolytic therapy. Ann Intern Med. 1990;113:949.

36 The International Study Group. In-hospital mortality and clinical course of 20,891 patients with suspected acute myocardial infarction randomized between alteplase and streptokinase with or without heparin. Lancet. 1990;336:71.

37 Hsia J et al. A comparison between heparin and low-dose aspirin as adjunctive therapy with tissue plasminogen activator for acute myocardial infarction. N Engl J Med. 1990;323:1433.

38 Bleich SD et al. Effect of heparin on coronary arterial patency after thrombolysis with tissue plasminogen activator in acute myocardial infarction. Am J Cardiol. 1990;66:1214.

39 Asbury WH. Guidelines for preparing and administering tissue plasminogen activator. Am J Hosp Pharm. 1988;45:2383.

40 TIMI Study Group. Comparison of invasive and conservative strategies after treatment with intravenous tissue plasminogen activator in acute myocardial infarction. N Engl J Med. 1989;320:618.

41 Neuhaus KL et al. Improved thrombolysis with a modified dose regimen of recombinant tissue type plasminogen activator. J Am Coll Cardiol. 1989;14:1566.

42 The GUSTO Investigators. An international randomized trial comparing four thrombolytic strategies for acute myocardial infarction. N Engl J Med. 1993;329:673.

43 ISIS-2 (Second International Study of Infarct Survival) Collaborative Group. Randomized trial of intravenous streptokinase, oral aspirin, both or neither among 17,187 cases of suspected acute myocardial infarction: ISIS-2. Lancet. 1988;2:349.

44 ISIS-3 (Third International Study of Infarct Survival) Collaborative Group. ISIS-3: a randomized comparison of streptokinase vs tissue plasminogen activator vs anistreplase and of aspirin plus heparin vs aspirin alone among 41,299 cases of suspected acute myocardial infarction. Lancet. 1992;339:753.

45 White HD et al. Effect of intravenous streptokinase on left ventricular function and early survival after myocardial infarction. N Engl J Med. 1987;317:850.

46 AIMS Trial Study Group. Effect of intravenous APSAC on mortality after acute myocardial infarction: preliminary report of a placebo-controlled trial. Lancet. 1988;11:1153.

47 Anderson JL et al. Multicenter reperfusion trial of intravenous anisoylated plasminogen streptokinase activator complex (APSAC) in acute myocardial infarction: controlled comparison with intracoronary streptokinase. J Am Coll Cardiol. 1988;11:1153.

48 Ornato JP. Role of emergency department in decreasing time to thrombolytic therapy in acute myocardial infarction. Clin Cardiol. 1990;13 (Suppl.):V48.

49 Rossi P et al. Comparison of intravenous urokinase plus heparin versus heparin alone in acute myocardial infarction. Am J Cardiol. 1991;68:585.

50 Califf RM et al. Evaluation of combination thrombolytic therapy and timing of cardiac catheterization in acute myocardial infarction. Results of thrombolysis and angioplasty in myocardial infarction-phase 5. Circulation. 1991;83:1543.

51 Mathey DG et al. Intravenous urokinase in acute myocardial infarction. Am J Cardiol. 1985;55:878.

52 Neuhaus KL et al. Intravenous recombinant tissue plasminogen activator (rt-PA) and urokinase in acute myocardial infarction: results of the German Activator Urokinase Study (GAUS). J Am Coll Cardiol. 1988;12:581.

53 Califf RM et al. Failure of simple clinical measurements to predict perfusion status after intravenous thrombolysis. Ann Intern Med. 1988;108:658.

54 Christian TF et al. Severity and response of chest pain during thrombolytic therapy for acute myocardial infarction: a useful indicator of myocar-

dial salvage and infarct size. J Am Coll Cardiol. 1993;22:1311.

55 Goldberger S et al. Reperfusion arrhythmia: a marker for restoration of antegrade flow during intracoronary thrombolysis for acute myocardial infarction. Am Heart J. 1983;105:26.

56 Arnold AZ, Topol EJ. Assessment of reperfusion after thrombolytic therapy for myocardial infarction. Am Heart J. 1992;124:441.

57 Lewis BS et al. Usefulness of a rapid rise of initial increase in plasma creatine kinase activity as a marker of reperfusion during thrombolytic therapy for acute myocardial infarction. Am J Cardiol. 1988;62:20.

58 Simes J et al. Mortality reduction with accelerated tissue plasminogen activator is explained by early coronary patency. Circulation. 1993;88:I-291. Abstract.

59 Tiefenbrunn AJ. Clinical benefits of thrombolytic therapy in acute myocardial infarction. Am J Cardiol. 1992; 69(Suppl.):3A.

60 White HD. Thrombolytic therapy for patients with myocardial infarction presenting after six hours. Lancet. 1992;340:221.

61 Grip L, Ryden L. Late streptokinase infusion and antithrombotic treatment in myocardial infarction reduce subsequent myocardial ischemia. Am Heart J. 1991;121:737.

62 Elliott JM et al. Neutralizing antibodies to streptokinase four years after intravenous thrombolytic therapy. Am J Cardiol. 1993;71:640.

63 Barbash GI et al. Repeat infusions of recombinant tissue-type plasminogen activator in patients with acute myocardial infarction and early recurrent myocardial ischemia. J Am Coll Cardiol. 1990;16:779.

64 White HD et al. Safety and efficacy of repeat thrombolytic treatment after acute myocardial infarction. Br Heart J. 1990;64:177.

65 Smith SC et al. Outlook after acute myocardial infarction in the very elderly compared with that in patients aged 65 to 75 years. J Am Coll Cardiol. 1990;16:784.

66 Lew AS et al. Mortality and morbidity rate of patients older and younger than 75 years with acute myocardial infarction treated with intravenous streptokinase. Am J Cardiol. 1987;59:1.

67 Sloan MA, Gore JM. Ischemic stroke and intracranial hemorrhage following thrombolytic therapy for acute myocardial infarction: a risk-benefit ratio. Am J Cardiol. 1992;69(Suppl.):21A.

68 Maggioni AP et al. The risk of stroke in patients with acute myocardial infarction after thrombolytic and antithrombotic treatment. N Engl J Med. 1992;327:1.

69 Fuster V. Coronary thrombolysis—a perspective for the practicing physician. N Engl J Med. 1993;329:723.

70 Tenaglia AN et al. Thrombolytic therapy in patients requiring cardiopulmonary resuscitation. Am J Cardiol. 1991; 68:1015.

71 Nattel S, Arenal A. Antiarrhythmic

prophylaxis after acute myocardial infarction. Drugs. 1993;45:9.

72 Jaffe AS. Prophylactic lidocaine for suspected acute myocardial infarction? Heart Disease and Stroke. 1992;1:179.

73 MacMahon S et al. Effects of prophylactic lidocaine in suspected acute myocardial infarction: an overview of results from the randomized, controlled trials. JAMA. 1988;260:1914.

74 Routledge PA et al. Increased (alpha-1-acid glycoprotein and lidocaine disposition in myocardial infarction. Ann Intern Med. 1980;93:701.

75 Shaheen BE, Cornish LA. Magnesium in the treatment of acute myocardial infarction. Clin Pharm. 1993;12:588.

76 Schechter M et al. The rationale of magnesium supplementation in acute myocardial infarction. Arch Intern Med. 1992;152:2189.

77 Teo KK et al. Intravenous magnesium for acute myocardial infarction: a meta-analysis. Br Med J. 1991;303:499.

78 Woods KL et al. Intravenous magnesium sulfate in suspected acute myocardial infarction: results of the second Leicester Intravenous Magnesium Intervention Trial (LIMIT-2). Lancet. 1992;339:1553.

79 ISIS Collaborative Group. ISIS-4: randomized study of intravenous magnesium in over 50,000 patients with suspected acute myocardial infarction. Circulation. 1993;88(Suppl. 2):I-292. Abstract.

80 The International Collaborative Study Group. Reduction of infarct size with the early use of timolol in acute myocardial infarction. N Engl J Med. 1984;310:9.

81 Yusuf S. The use of β-adrenergic blocking agents, IV nitrates and calcium channel blocking agents following acute myocardial infarction. Chest. 1988;93:(Suppl.)25S.

82 Kjekshus J et al. Diabetic patients and Beta-blockers after acute myocardial infarction. Eur Heart J. 1990;11:43.

83 Stauffer JC, Gaasch WH. Recognition and treatment of left ventricular diastolic dysfunction. Prog Cardiovasc Dis. 1990;22:319.

84 Shub C. Stable angina pectoris: part 3. Medical treatment. Mayo Clin Proc. 1990;65:256.

85 Montague TJ et al. Changes in acute myocardial infarction risk and patterns of practice for patients older and younger than 75 years, 1987–90. Can J Cardiol. 1992;8:596.

86 Conti CR. The stunned and hibernating myocardium: a brief review. Clin Cardiol. 1991;14:708.

87 Patel B et al. Postischemic myocardial "stunning": a clinically relevant phenomenon. Ann Intern Med. 1988;108:626.

88 Cairns JA et al. Antithrombotic agents in coronary artery disease. Third ACCP Consensus Conference on Antithrombotic Therapy. Chest. 1992;102 (Suppl.):457S.

89 Pfeffer JM. Progressive ventricular dilatation in experimental myocardial infarction and its attenuation by angiotensin-converting enzyme inhibition. Am J Cardiol. 1991;68(Suppl.):17D.

90 Braunwald E, Pfeffer MA. Ventricular enlargement and remodeling following acute myocardial infarction: mechanisms and management. Am J Cardiol. 1991;68(Suppl.):1D.

91 Gaudron P et al. Progressive left ventricular dysfunction and remodeling after myocardial infarction. Circulation. 1993;87:755.

92 Pfeffer MA et al. Effect of captopril on progressive ventricular dilatation after anterior myocardial infarction. N Engl J Med. 1988;319:80.

93 The Acute Infarction Ramipril Efficacy (AIRE) Study Investigators. The effect of ramipril on mortality and morbidity of survivors of acute myocardial infarction with clinical evidence of heart failure. Lancet. 1993; 342:821.

94 Collins R. Captopril, nitrates and magnesium after myocardial infarction: introduction and results-ISIS-4. Presented at the 66th Scientific Session of the American Heart Association. Atlanta, GA: 1993 Nov 8.

95 Gruppo Italiano per lo Studio della Sopravvivenza nell'Infarto Miocardico. Gissi-3: effects of lisinopril and transdermal glyceryl trinitrate singly and together on 6-week mortality and ventricular function after acute myocardial infarction. Lancet. 1994;343:1115.

96 Lewis EJ et al. The effect of angiotensin-converting-enzyme inhibition on diabetic nephropathy. N Engl J Med. 1993;329:1456.

97 Yusuf S et al. Update on effects of calcium antagonists in myocardial infarction or angina in light of the second Danish Verapamil Infarction Trial (DAVIT-II) and other recent studies. Am J Cardiol. 1991;67:1295.

98 Packer MA et al. Randomized, multicenter, double-blind, placebo-controlled evaluation of amlodipine in patients with mild-to-moderate heart failure. J Am Coll Cardiol. 1991;17 (Suppl.):274A. Abstract.

99 Kaplan K. Prophylactic anticoagulation following acute myocardial infarction. Arch Intern Med. 1986;146:593.

100 Smith P et al. The effect of warfarin on mortality and reinfarction after myocardial infarction. N Engl J Med. 1990;323:147.

101 Fuster V et al. Aspirin as a therapeutic agent in cardiovascular disease. Circulation. 1993;87:659.

102 Final report on the aspirin component of the ongoing physicians' health study. N Engl J Med. 1989;321:129.

103 Ridker PM et al. Low-dose aspirin therapy for chronic stable angina. Ann Intern Med. 1991;114:835.

104 Hoffman W, Forster W. Two year Cottbus reinfarction study with 30 mg aspirin per day. Prostaglands Leukot Essent Fatty Acids. 1991;44:159.

105 Rosenburg L et al. The risk of myocardial infarction after quitting smoking in men under 55 years of age. N Engl J Med. 1985;313:1511.

106 Rosenthal ME et al. Sudden cardiac death following acute myocardial infarction. Am Heart J. 1985;109:865.

107 Bigger JT et al. The relationships

among ventricular arrhythmias, left ventricular dysfunction, and mortality in the 2 years after myocardial infarction. Circulation. 1984;69:250.

108 Teo KK et al. Effects of prophylactic antiarrhythmic drug therapy in acute myocardial infarction. An overview of results from randomized controlled trials. JAMA. 1993;270:1589.

109 Cairns JA et al. Post-myocardial infarction mortality in patients with ventricular premature depolarizations: Canadian amiodarone myocardial infarction arrhythmia trial pilot study. Circulation. 1991;84:550.

110 Ceremuzynski L et al. Effect of amiodarone in mortality after myocardial infarction: a double-blind, placebo-controlled, pilot study. J Am Coll Cardiol. 1992;20:1056.

111 Burkart F et al. Effect of antiarrhythmic therapy on mortality in survivors of myocardial infarction with asymptomatic complex ventricular arrhythmias: Basel antiarrhythmic study of infarct survival (BASIS). J Am Coll Cardiol. 1990;16:1711.

112 Pfisterer ME et al. Long-term benefit of 1-year amiodarone treatment for persistent complex ventricular arrhythmias after myocardial infarction. Circulation. 1993;87:309.

113 McClements BM, Adgey AAJ. Value of signal-averaged electrocardiography, radionuclide ventriculography, holter monitoring and clinical variables for prediction of arrhythmic events in survivors of acute myocardial infarction in the thrombolytic era. J Am Coll Cardiol. 1993;21:1419.

114 Flaherty JT. Role of nitrates in acute myocardial infarction. Am J Cardiol. 1992;70(Suppl. 8):73B.

115 Jugdutt BI, Warnica JW. Tolerance with low dose intravenous nitroglycerin therapy in acute myocardial infarction. Am J Cardiol. 1989;64:581.

116 Ferguson JJ et al. Significance of nitroglycerin-induced hypotension with inferior wall acute myocardial infarction. Am J Cardiol. 1989;64:311.

117 Chiariello M et al. Comparison between the effects of nitroprusside and nitroglycerin on ischemic injury during acute myocardial infarction. Circulation. 1976;54:766.

118 Mann T et al. Effect of nitroprusside on regional myocardial blood flow in coronary artery disease. Circulation. 1978;57:732.

119 Hansteen V et al. One year's treatment with propranolol after myocardial infarction: preliminary report of Norwegian multicentre trial. Br Med J. 1982; 284:155.

120 Olsson G et al. Long-term treatment with metoprolol after myocardial infarction: effect on 3 year mortality and morbidity. J Am Coll Cardiol. 1985;5:1428.

121 The Norwegian Multicenter Study Group. Timolol-induced reduction in mortality and reinfarction in patients surviving acute myocardial infarction. N Engl J Med. 1981;304:801.

122 Hjalmarson A et al. Effect on mortality of metoprolol in acute myocardial infarction. Lancet. 1981;2:823.

Congestive Heart Failure

Wayne A Kradjan

Etiology 15-2
    Low versus high output failure; systolic versus
    diastolic dysfunction (See Table 15.1) 15-2
    Cardiac workload 15-3
        Preload 15-3
        Afterload 15-3
        Cardiac contractility 15-3
Pathogenesis: Frank-Starling Curve 15-3
    Cardiac 15-3
        Cardiac dilation 15-3
        Cardiac hypertrophy 15-3
    Sympathetic autonomic nervous system (SANS) ... 15-4
    Renal function and the renin-angiotensin system ... 15-4
    Hormonal; atrial natriuretic peptide (ANP) 15-4
Treatment Principles 15-4
    Bedrest 15-5
    Sodium-restricted diet 15-5
    Diuretics 15-5
    Digitalis glycosides 15-5
    Angiotensin-converting enzyme (ACE)
        inhibitors 15-5
    Vasodilators 15-5
    Other inotropic agents 15-6
Renal Function and Diuretic Pharmacology 15-6
Digitalis Therapy (See Table 15.2) 15-7
    Digoxin pharmacokinetics 15-7
    Digitoxin pharmacokinetics 15-7

Patient Evaluation 15-8
    Signs and Symptoms (See Table 15.3) 15-8
        Left heart failure 15-9
        Right heart failure 15-9
    New York Heart Association (NYHA) Classification ..15-10
    Predisposing Factors 15-10
        Age 15-10
        β-Adrenergic Blockers 15-10
    Nonsteroidal Anti-Inflammatory Drugs
        (NSAIDs) 15-10
        Diet 15-10

Etiology—Drug-Induced (See Table 51.5) 15-11
Treatment 15-11
    Therapeutic Objectives; Drug of First Choice 15-11
        Diuretics 15-11
        Digitalis 15-11
            Controversy over efficacy 15-11
        Vasodilators and ACE inhibitors; comparison
            to digoxin 15-12
    Diuretics 15-13
        Adverse effects 15-13
            Azotemia 15-13
            Hyponatremia 15-13
            Hypokalemia 15-13
            Hypochloremic alkalosis 15-13
            Hypomagnesemia 15-13
            Hyperglycemia 15-13
            Hyperuricemia 15-14
            Liver function 15-14
        Potassium supplementation 15-14
            Dosage forms 15-14

Dose requirements 15-15
Potassium-sparing diuretics 15-15
Furosemide and other loop diuretics 15-15
    Route of administration 15-15
    Dosing 15-15
    Monitoring (See Table 15.7) 15-15
    Refractory patients; combination therapy 15-15
Digitalis glycosides 15-16
    Preparation for treatment 15-16
    Loading dose 15-16
        Calculation of the loading dose 15-17
        Administration of the loading dose 15-17
    Maintenance dose 15-17
        Calculation 15-17
    Monitoring parameters 15-18
        Serum level interpretation 15-18
        Interfering substances 15-19
        Clinical evaluation 15-19
    Factors which alter response 15-19
        Patient compliance 15-19
        Digoxin bioavailability 15-19
        Malabsorption 15-19
        Altered digoxin metabolism 15-20
    Drug interactions (See Table 15.8) 15-20
        Quinidine 15-20
        Other drug interactions 15-21
    Intramuscular digoxin 15-21
    Digitalis toxicity 15-21
        Signs and symptoms 15-21
        Predisposing factors 15-23
        Treatment of 15-24
            Withhold digitalis and electrolyte
                replacement 15-24
            Antiarrhythmic agents 15-24
            Digoxin immune Fab 15-25
Pediatric dosing 15-26
Dosing in renal failure 15-26
    Loading dose 15-26
    Maintenance dose 15-27
Vasodilator Therapy (See Table 15.9) 15-27
Mechanism of action and rationale for use 15-27
Nitroprusside 15-27
Intravenous nitroglycerin (NTG) 15-28
    Dosing 15-28
Hydralazine 15-28
Oral and topical nitrates 15-29
    Sublingual NTG 15-29
    NTG ointment 15-29
    Transdermal NTG 15-29
    Isosorbide dinitrate 15-29
Hydralazine/nitrate combination 15-30
Prazosin 15-30
Angiotensin-converting enzyme (ACE)
    inhibitors 15-30
    Mechanism of action 15-30
    Captopril dosing 15-31
    Captopril side effects 15-31

(Continued)

Other ACE inhibitors: efficacy, dosing,
   and side effects 15-31
Effects on kidney function 15-32
Value of combined digoxin and vasodilators 15-32
Effect of drug therapy on mortality 15-33
Calcium channel blockers 15-34
   Choice of agent 15-34
   Interaction with digoxin 15-34
Use of Inotropic Drugs 15-34

Controversy over use of digitalis after
   myocardial infarction (MI) 15-34
Dopamine and dobutamine 15-35
Phosphodiesterase inhibitors: amrinone
   and milrinone 15-35
Other inotropes and vasodilators: enoximone,
   imazodan, xamaterol, flosequinan, vesnarinone ...15-35
Use of Beta Blockers in Diastolic and Systolic
   Heart Failure 15-36

Congestive heart failure (CHF) results when the left, right, or both ventricles fail to pump sufficient blood to meet the body's needs. It is estimated that from two to four million people in America (over 2% of the population) have CHF, accounting for 500,000 hospital admissions per year.[1–4] There is a correlation between the incidence of CHF and both gender and age; the incidence is nearly twice as high in men as in women. After the age of fifty, the prevalence doubles during each decade of life, with 0.8% of those age 50 to 59 and 9.2% of those over age 80 being afflicted.[2] As the size of the geriatric population increases, it is likely that CHF will become a more frequently encountered clinical entity. Quality of life is adversely affected by progressive fatigue, shortness of breath (SOB), and functional disability. Of greater consequence is the high mortality rate. Among those with severe symptoms, 30% to 50% will die within one year and 70% within three years.[2–4] In the Framingham study, five-year survival rates are lower in men (38%) than in women (57%).[2] Despite earlier diagnosis and aggressive medical management the prognosis is poor. Only with the advent of vasodilator and angiotensin-converting enzyme (ACE) inhibitor therapy has there been a reduction in mortality attributed to drug therapy.[5] However, even in survivors, quality of life continues to deteriorate.[6]

Etiology

Low versus High Output Failure; Systolic versus Diastolic Dysfunction

Traditionally, heart failure has been classified as either low output or high output failure (see Table 15.1). The more common of these two is *low output (congestive) failure* characterized by an inability of the heart to pump all of the blood with which it is presented. In this form of failure the *ejection fraction* (EF), defined as the percent of left ventricular volume expelled during systole, is less than 40%

and may be as low as 20%. This compares to a normal ejection fraction of 60% to 70%. As a result, the ventricles of the heart enlarge (dilate) as they become congested with retained blood. Causes of pump failure include coronary heart disease (ischemia); chronic hypertension; damage to heart muscle or valves following myocardial infarction (MI); persistent arrhythmias; poststreptococcal rheumatic heart disease; and generalized cardiomyopathy (deterioration of myocardial muscle function) secondary to chronic alcoholism, viral infections, or idiopathic causes. *High output failure*, on the other hand, occurs when the heart fails to pump enough blood to meet the metabolic needs of the tissues. This may occur in hyperthyroid patients whose metabolic demands are greater than normal or in severely anemic patients whose tissues require a greater volume of blood to supply normal metabolic needs. In high output failure, the heart itself is healthy, but it becomes exhausted from the increased workload placed upon it.

This traditional classification does not account for all patients with congestive heart failure. Consequently, low output failure is further subdivided into systolic and diastolic dysfunction or a combination of the two[7–11] (see Table 15.1). *Systolic dysfunction* is synonymous with low ejection fraction failure and is associated with a dilated, hypokinetic left ventricle as described in the previous paragraph. In contrast, *left ventricular diastolic dysfunction* is caused by impaired left ventricular filling during diastole and is characterized by a normal sized heart and a *normal ejection fraction*. Diastolic dysfunction is further characterized by left ventricular stiffness (reduced compliance) and inability of the ventricle to relax during diastole, resulting in an elevated resting pressure within the ventricle. In turn, the elevated pressure impedes ventricular filling that normally would occur by passive inflow against a low resistance pressure gradient. Cardiac muscle function (contractility) is not impaired, and although

Table 15.1		Classification and Etiology of Congestive Heart Failure[a]	
Type of Failure	Characteristics	Contributing Factors	Etiology
Low output, systolic dysfunction (dilated cardiomyopathy)	Hypofunctioning left ventricle; enlarged heart (dilated left ventricle); ↑ left ventricular end-diastolic volume; EF <40%; ↓ stroke volume; ↓ CO; S₃ heart sound present	1. ↓ contractility (cardiomyopathy) 2. ↑ afterload (elevated SVR)	1. Ischemia, MI, mitral valve stenosis or regurgitation, alcoholism, viral syndromes, nutritional deficiency, calcium and potassium defects, drug induced, idiopathic 2. Hypertension, aortic stenosis, volume overload
Low output, diastolic dysfunction	Normal contractility; normal size heart; stiff left ventricle; impaired left ventricular relaxation; impaired left ventricular filling; ↓ left ventricular end-diastolic volume; normal EF; ↓ SV; ↓ CO; exaggerated S₄ heart sound	1. Thickened left ventricle (hypertrophic cardiomyopathy) 2. Stiff left ventricle (restrictive cardiomyopathy) 3. ↑ preload	1. Ischemia, hypertension, aortic stenosis and regurgitation, pericarditis, enlarged left ventricular septum (idiopathic hypertrophic subaortic stenosis) 2. Amyloidosis, sarcoidosis 3. Sodium and water retention
High output failure	Normal or ↑ contractility; normal size heart; normal left ventricular end-diastolic volume; normal or ↑ EF; normal or increased stroke volume; ↑ CO	↑ metabolic and oxygen demands	Anemia and hyperthyroidism

[a] CO = Cardiac output; EF = Ejection fraction; MI = Myocardial infarction; SV = Stroke volume; SVR = Systemic vascular resistance.

the ejection fraction is normal, the total volume of blood pumped during systole [stroke volume (SV)] is deficient because of the low left ventricular filling volume. It is estimated that 14% to 40% of patients with CHF may have this form of disease. There are a multitude of possible etiologies for diastolic failure including coronary ischemia, hypertension, left ventricular wall scarring following myocardial infarction (MI), ventricular wall hypertrophy, hypertrophic cardiomyopathy (idiopathic hypertrophic subaortic stenosis), constrictive pericarditis, restrictive cardiomyopathy (e.g., amyloidosis and sarcoidosis), and valvular heart disease (mitral stenosis, acute aortic regurgitation, mitral regurgitation). Because hypertension, ischemia, and myocardial infarction are contributors to both systolic and diastolic failure, many patients will present with a picture of combined disease. An important therapeutic distinction between these two disorders is that digoxin and other positive inotropes may be of benefit in systolic dysfunction, but may be associated with exacerbation of symptoms in diastolic dysfunction. Conversely, negative inotropes (β-adrenergic blockers and calcium channel blockers) may improve diastolic dysfunction by slowing the heart to allow the ventricles to fill more fully, but will further compromise a heart failing because of cardiomyopathy.

Cardiac Workload

A common factor to all forms of congestive heart failure is increased cardiac workload. It is important, therefore, to define the four major determinants that contribute to left ventricular workload: preload, afterload, contractility, and heart rate.

Preload[12,13] is a term used to describe forces acting on the *venous* side of the circulation to affect myocardial wall tension. The relationship is as follows: as venous return (i.e., blood flowing into the heart) increases, the volume of blood in the left ventricle increases. This increased volume raises the pressure within the ventricle [left ventricle end-diastolic pressure (LVEDP)], which in turn increases the ''stretch,'' or wall tension, of the ventricle. Venous dilation and decreased venous volume diminish preload, while venous constriction and increased venous volume increase preload.

An elevated preload will aggravate CHF. This occurs following rapid administration of blood plasma expanders and osmotic diuretics or by administration of large amounts of sodium (Na) or sodium-retaining agents. A malfunctioning aortic valve (aortic stenosis, aortic insufficiency) which results in regurgitation of blood back into the left ventricle also can increase the volume of blood which must be pumped. A malfunctioning mitral valve (mitral regurgitation) may cause retrograde ejection of blood from the left ventricle into the left atrium with a resultant decrease in ejection fraction. In patients with systolic failure, ventricular blood is ejected less effectively because of a hypofunctioning left ventricle; the volume of blood retained in the ventricle is thus increased, and preload becomes elevated. In diastolic failure with a stiffened left ventricle, relatively small increases in end-diastolic volume from sodium and water overload may lead to exaggerated increases in end-diastolic pressure despite normal or even reduced end-diastolic volumes.[10]

Afterload[12,13] strictly defined, is the tension developed in the ventricular wall as contraction (systole) occurs. The tension developed during contraction relates to intraventricular pressure, ventricular diameter, and wall thickness. More simply, afterload is regulated by the systemic vascular resistance (SVR) or impedance against which the ventricle must pump during its ejection and is chiefly determined by arterial blood pressure (BP). Hypertension, atherosclerotic disease, or a narrow aortic valve increases arterial impedance (afterload), thereby increasing the workload on the heart. Hypertension is a major etiologic factor in the development of both systolic and diastolic CHF.[10] The Framingham group[2] found that 75% of patients who developed congestive heart failure had a prior history of hypertension. The risk of developing CHF was six times greater for hypertensive than for normotensive patients.

Cardiac Contractility. The terms contractility and inotropic state are used synonymously to describe the myocardium's (cardiac muscle) inherent ability to develop force and/or shorten independent of preload or afterload. Myocardial contractility is decreased when myocardial fibers are diminished or poorly functioning as may occur in patients with primary cardiomyopathy, valvular heart disease, coronary artery disease, or following a myocardial infarction. Defects in contractility play a major role in systolic CHF, but are not a component of pure diastolic dysfunction. Occasionally, drugs such as β-adrenergic blockers or daunomycin (Adriamycin) induce CHF by decreasing myocardial contractility. (See Questions 3 and 4 for a more complete discussion of drug-induced CHF.) As summarized in Table 15.1, the major contributors to systolic failure are decreased contractility and increased afterload, while structural abnormalities and increased preload play a greater role in diastolic failure.

Pathogenesis: Frank-Starling Curve

When the heart begins to fail, the body activates several complex compensatory mechanisms in an attempt to maintain cardiac output (CO) and oxygenation of vital organs. These include cardiac (ventricular) dilation, cardiac hypertrophy, increased sympathetic tone, and sodium and water retention. Unfortunately, the long-term consequences of these adaptive mechanisms actually may cause more harm than good (see Figure 15.1). An understanding of the potential benefits and adverse consequences of these compensatory mechanisms is essential to the understanding of the signs, symptoms, and treatment of congestive heart failure.

Cardiac

Cardiac dilation results when the ventricles fail to pump an adequate volume of blood with each contraction. If the rate at which blood is delivered (preload) remains the same, but the rate at which it is pumped to other tissues diminishes, residual blood will begin to accumulate in the ventricles. Thus, end-diastolic volume increases, myocardial fibers are stretched, and ventricle(s) become dilated.

The Frank-Starling ventricular function curve (see Figure 15.2) implies a curvilinear relationship between left ventricular myocardial muscle fiber ''stretch'' (wall tension) and myocardial work. As stretch increases, the volume of blood ejected with each systolic contraction (stroke volume) increases. In systolic CHF, the work capacity for any degree of stretch is diminished. A simple analogy may be drawn using a balloon. The more air you blow into a balloon, the more it stretches and, if released, the more it flies around a room. As the balloon gets old, it loses its elasticity and thus, has less recoil when stretched. Similarly, dilation of the ventricles initially may serve as an effective compensating mechanism in systolic failure, but it becomes inadequate as the elastic limits of the myocardial muscle fibers are reached. The downside of cardiac dilation is increased myocardial oxygen demand. Theoretically, as cardiac dilation progresses beyond a certain point, cardiac output could decrease (descending limb of the Starling Curve), but this rarely is observed clinically. Cardiac dilation is not a feature of diastolic failure since normal contractility is maintained.

Cardiac hypertrophy is a long-term adaptation to increased diastolic volume in systolic failure and represents an absolute increase in myocardial muscle mass and muscle wall thickness. Cardiac hypertrophy should not be confused with cardiac dilation. Of the two, hypertrophy provides more desirable effects, but its absolute benefit is inadequate in severe disease.

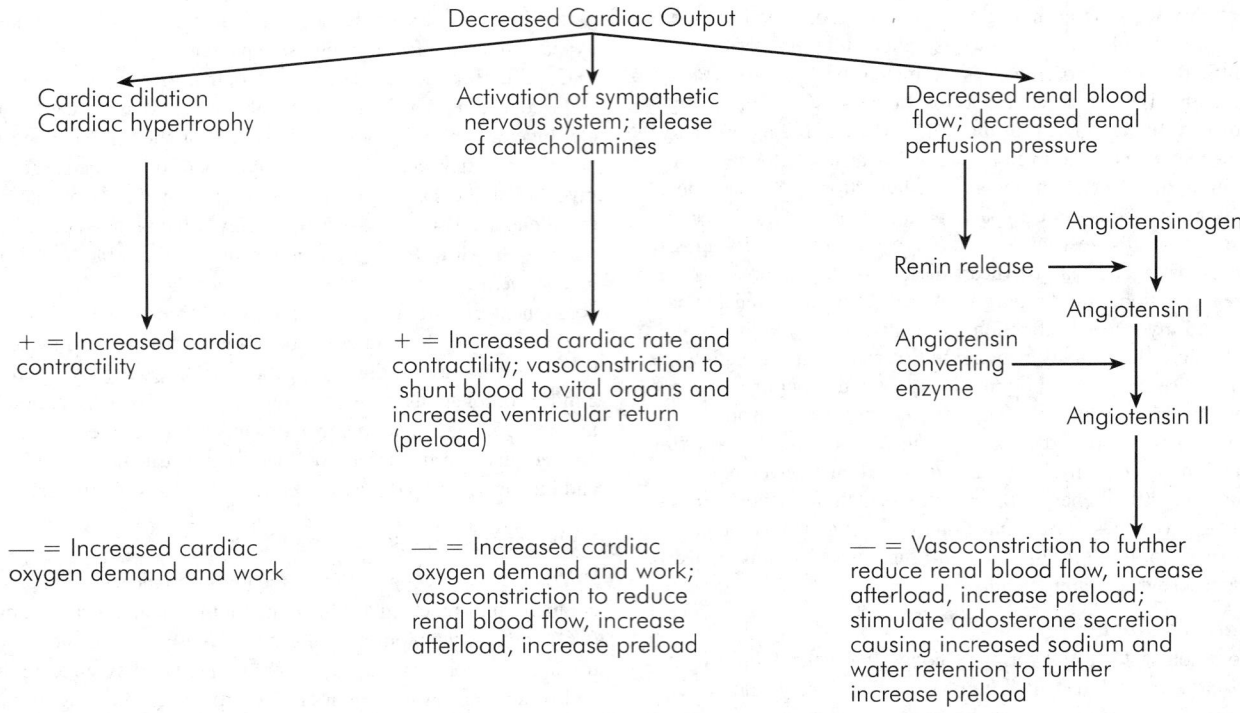

Fig 15.1   Adaptive Mechanisms in Systolic CHF. + = Beneficial results; − = Negative (detrimental) effects.

Sympathetic Autonomic Nervous System (SANS)

An important relationship to remember is that cardiac output is the product of ventricular stroke volume and heart rate (HR). A diminished stroke volume or cardiac output results in decreased tissue perfusion which in turn causes a reflex activation of the sympathetic autonomic nervous system via release of norepinephrine and other catecholamines. The inotropic (increased contractility) and chronotropic (increased HR) effects of the SANS initially may maintain near-normal cardiac output and preserve perfusion of vital organs such as the central nervous system (CNS) and myocardium. However, catecholamine-mediated vasoconstriction in the skin, gastrointestinal (GI) tract, and renal circulation decreases perfusion of these organs and ultimately increases the workload on the heart by raising systemic vascular resistance.

*Renal Function and the
Renin-Angiotensin System (see Figure 15.1)*

Both the decreased cardiac output of the CHF and vasoconstriction secondary to sympathetic tone decrease renal blood flow. This, in turn, sets off a complex chain of events leading to sodium and water retention and eventually, increased blood volume. Renal vascular resistance is increased and the glomerular filtration rate (GFR) is decreased. As the GFR decreases, more sodium is reabsorbed in the proximal tubule. Additionally, the glomerular filtrate may be preferentially shunted to nephrons with long loops of Henle, thereby increasing the surface area for sodium reabsorption. Renin is released by the kidney in response to decreased renal perfusion, leading to a corresponding increase in angiotensin formation. Angiotensin has two effects favoring sodium and water retention: its vasoconstricting effects may further decrease GFR, and it stimulates the adrenals to secrete aldosterone, a hormone which increases sodium reabsorption in the distal tubule. A diminished effective circulating plasma volume also stimulates the release of antidiuretic hormone (ADH) from the pituitary, resulting in the retention of free water in the renal collecting ducts. The net result of the kidney and angiotensin effects is detrimental. Increased sodium and water retention increase preload while angiotensin-induced vasoconstriction increases systemic vascular resistance and preload.

Hormonal; Atrial Natriuretic Peptide (ANP)

Another possible counter-regulatory mechanism in CHF is the release of atrial natriuretic peptide (ANP), also called atrial natriuretic factor (ANF), from specialized cells in atrial muscle.[14–18] This hormone-like substance is a 28 amino acid peptide released in response to stretching of atrial myocytes during periods of volume overload, such as CHF, renal failure, hypertension, and certain arrhythmias. It also may be secreted in direct response to a number of vasopressor substances, including epinephrine and vasopressin. The main pharmacologic effects of ANP are direct arterial vasodilation, increased glomerular filtration rate, and diuresis (due to vasodilation-enhanced renal blood flow).[14] It is speculated that ANP may be the primary counteractant of the plasma renin-angiotensin-aldosterone system. Cardiac output may decrease in normals due to venous dilation and reduced preload, but output increases in CHF by decreasing afterload, inducing diuresis, and counteracting angiotensin II effects. Gottlieb and colleagues found elevated ANP levels in young patients with severe cardiomyopathy that correlated with severity of symptoms.[15] A similar finding by Davis in elderly patients with CHF has led to the speculation that measurement of plasma ANP levels may have diagnostic or prognostic value in patients with suspected CHF.[16] The role of ANF in the pathogenesis of chronic CHF is unclear, but it appears that the responsiveness of the kidney becomes attenuated rather quickly. Nonetheless, investigators are actively pursuing development of new drugs that may either have ANF-like activity or will act to increase ANF levels by inhibiting its metabolism.[14,17,18]

Treatment Principles

The medical management of CHF includes correction of underlying disease states (e.g., hypertension, anemia, or hyperthyroidism), discontinuation of possible drug-induced causes, bedrest, a sodium-restricted diet, diuretics, digitalis glycosides, ACE inhibitors, vasodilators, and, in some instances, inotropic agents. The ultimate goal of therapy is to abolish disabling symptoms and improve the quality of the patient's life; none of the aforementioned measures are curative. Recently, a 16 member expert panel of physicians, consumers, nurses, and a pharmacist appointed by the Agency for Health Care Policy and Research (AHCPR) and the RAND Corporation developed a clinical algorithm for the treatment of systolic failure.[19] (See Figure 15.3.)

Bedrest

Bedrest and restricted physical activity decrease the metabolic demands of the failing heart and minimize gravitational forces contributing to the formation of edema. Renal perfusion is increased in the prone position, resulting in diuresis and eventual mobilization of edema fluid. Edema can be minimized by use of elastic hosiery which increase interstitial pressure and help mobilize fluid into vascular spaces.

Sodium-Restricted Diet

A sodium-restricted diet should be instituted to decrease blood volume and offset abnormal retention of sodium by the kidney. If the kidney's ability to excrete sodium is not severely compromised, it is possible to approach normal balance by restricting sodium intake to match excretion. Even though less than 1 gm of sodium chloride (NaCl) is required to meet physiologic needs, the average American diet contains 10 gm. A severely salt-restricted diet (<500 mg Na or 1.3 gm NaCl) is unpalatable and difficult to maintain. Dietary sodium can be reduced to 2 to 4 gm of NaCl by eliminating cooking salt. This diet is much more reasonable from the patient's point of view; it is more palatable and leads to better compliance. It is convenient to remember that 1 gm of sodium is equivalent to 2.5 gm of salt (NaCl) and that one level teaspoon of salt weighs approximately 6 gm (1 mEq Na = 23 mg; 1 gm Na = 43 mEq Na; 1 gm NaCl = 17 mEq Na).

Diuretics

Diuretics are indicated in both systolic and diastolic CHF. They usually are necessary even in the early stages of CHF when sodium restriction alone fails to control volume overload. In advanced stages of the disease, diuretic monotherapy usually is inadequate, but diuretics are continued as adjuncts to other more definitive treatments such as digitalis or ACE inhibitors.[19]

By enhancing renal excretion of sodium and water, diuretics diminish vascular volume, thus relieving ventricular and pulmonary congestion and decreasing peripheral edema. Initially, the goal of diuretic therapy is symptomatic relief of CHF by removing volume without causing intravascular depletion. Once excess volume is removed, therapy is aimed at maintaining sodium balance and preventing reaccumulation of new fluid, while at the same time avoiding dehydration. The rate at which edema fluid can be removed is limited by its rate of mobilization from the interstitial to the intravascular fluid compartment. If diuresis is too vigorous, intravascular

volume depletion, hypotension, and a paradoxical decrease in cardiac output (due to compromised venous return and inadequate ventricular filling) may result. A weight loss exceeding 1 kg/day is to be avoided except in extreme cases of acute pulmonary edema.

Digitalis Glycosides

Digitalis (digoxin, digitoxin) has two major pharmacologic actions on the heart. The first, and most important to the treatment of CHF, is to increase the force of contraction of both the normal and abnormal heart (positive inotropic effect). The second is to decrease the conduction velocity and prolong the refractory period of the atrioventricular (AV) node. This AV node blocking effect prolongs the PR interval and is the basis for use of digitalis in atrial arrhythmias. (See Chapter 16: Cardiac Arrhythmias.) Coupled with the inotropic effect of digitalis is a propensity to increase cardiac automaticity and irritability, and to decrease the refractory period of the atrial and ventricular myocardium, all of which predispose the patient to a multitude of ectopic beats and arrhythmias.

Since digitalis increases the force of contraction of the failing heart, cardiac output is increased and compensatory mechanisms are reversed. End-diastolic volume is decreased, heart size is reduced, and elevated venous pressure and pulmonary congestion are relieved. As tissue perfusion improves, sympathetic tone is lowered toward normal, resulting in diuresis and a drop in heart rate. Because it theoretically improves the primary defects of systolic CHF, digitalis traditionally has been considered a rational choice for drug therapy. Although the role of digitalis in CHF therapy has been challenged (see Question 6), the clinical guidelines for heart failure developed by the AHCPR consensus panel recommend digitalis for patients with moderate to severe CHF not responding to diuretics and ACE inhibitors.[19] (See Figure 15.3.) Digitalis is not useful in diastolic CHF and, in fact, may worsen this form of CHF.

Angiotensin-Converting Enzyme (ACE) Inhibitors

Angiotensin-converting enzyme inhibitors [e.g., captopril (Capoten), enalapril (Vasotec), and lisinopril (Prinivil, Zestril)] possess both afterload reducing properties (by blocking angiotensin-mediated vasoconstriction) and volume reducing potential (by inhibiting activation of aldosterone). These agents provide a more sustained benefit with chronic therapy than that obtained with other vasodilators. Enthusiasm for this class of drugs is increasing due to several studies that showed increased survival in patients treated with ACE inhibitors and superiority over digoxin. (See Questions 35 and 36.) According to the AHCPR guidelines, ACE inhibitors now are considered first line therapy for mild to moderate CHF and should be used before digitalis glycosides.[19] Their value in diastolic CHF still is being investigated.

Vasodilators

Hydralazine (Apresoline) is a potent arterial dilating agent that can provide symptomatic relief of CHF by decreasing arterial impedance (afterload) to left ventricular outflow. Nitrates [e.g., nitroglycerin (NTG), isosorbide] have venous dilating properties that decrease left ventricular congestion (preload). Nitroprusside and minoxidil are mixed arterial and venous dilators. Vasodilators previously were reserved for use in persons with far-advanced CHF refractory to diuretic and digitalis therapy, but now increasingly are used in mild-to-moderate CHF by those clinicians wishing to avoid the risks of digitalis therapy. The role of vasodilators in diastolic CHF is not well studied. Nifedipine (Adalat, Procardia), amlodipine (Norvasc), and nicardipine (Cardene) are examples of calcium antagonists with arterial vasodilating and antispasmodic properties. They also may be used as afterload reducing agents in CHF, but their applicability may be diminished by mild, negative inotropic effects. (See Questions 29 to 36 for a more detailed discussion of

Determinants of Preload
• Venous return
• Left ventricular end diastolic volume (LVEDV)
• Left ventricular end diastolic pressure (LVEDP)

Fig 15.2 Representation of Frank-Starling Ventricular Function Curve.

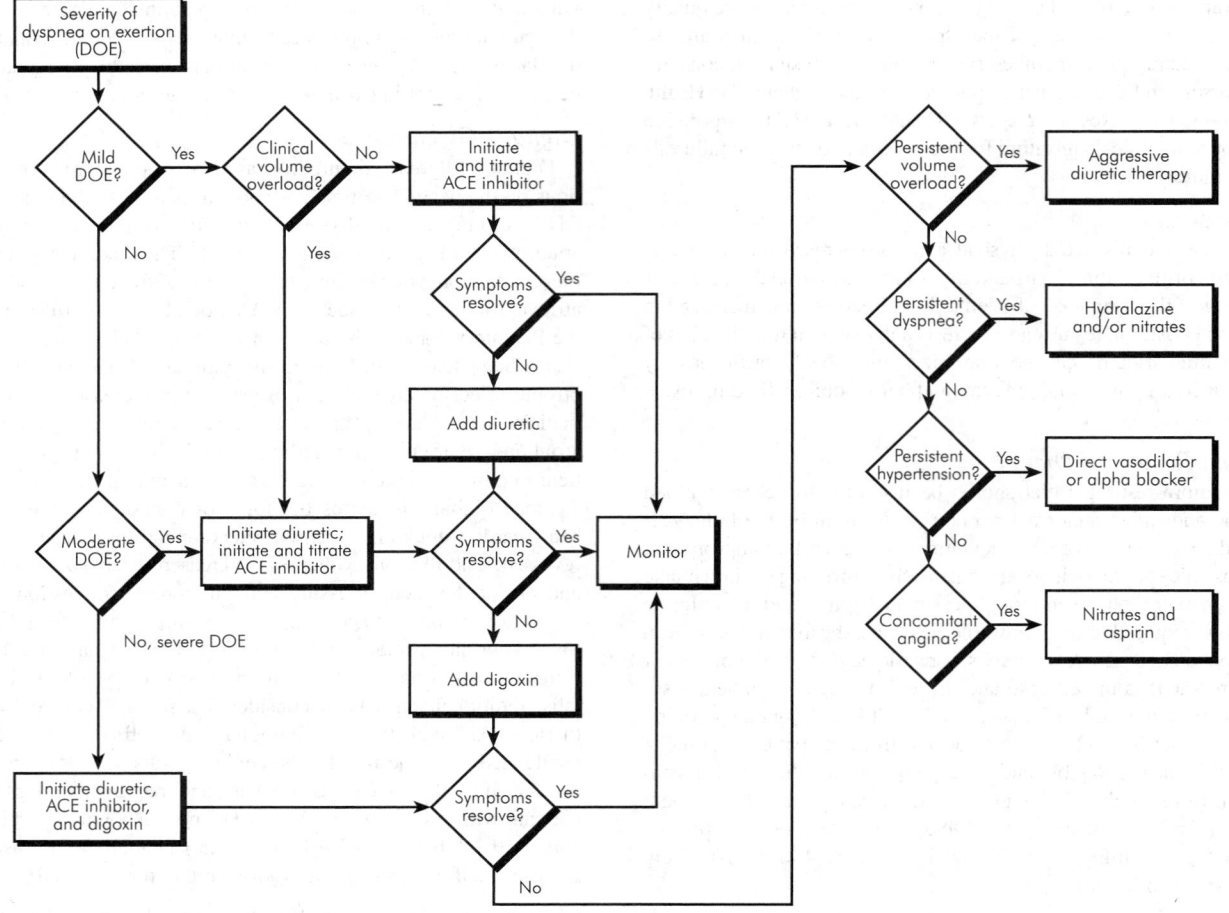

Fig 15.3   Pharmacologic Management of Patients with Heart Failure.   Reprinted with permission from reference 19.

the use of vasodilators.) On the other hand, the negative inotropic effects of some calcium antagonists, especially that of verapamil (Calan, Isoptin, Verelan), may be an indication for use in diastolic CHF.

Other Inotropic Agents

Recent doubt about the clinical effectiveness of digitalis derivatives (see Question 6) and concern over their potential for toxicity point to the need for identification of useful alternatives. Dopamine and dobutamine frequently are used in acute cardiac emergencies, but their use is limited by the need for intravenous (IV) administration. Amrinone and milrinone, nonsympathomimetic inotropes, are associated with an unacceptably high incidence of side effects when given orally, but are available in parenteral form. (See Chapter 18: Intensive Care Therapeutics for a more detailed discussion of these drugs and Question 37 for a discussion of the risks and benefits of oral inotropic therapy.) As with digitalis, these other inotropes are relatively contraindicated in diastolic CHF.

Renal Function and Diuretic Pharmacology

The reader is referred to Chapter 28: Fluid and Electrolyte Disorders for a thorough review of kidney physiology and the classification, mechanism of action, and side effects of diuretics. Only those points salient to the treatment of congestive heart failure are included in this chapter. Diuretic use also is discussed in Chapter 10: Essential Hypertension.

Diuretics provide symptomatic relief of mild to moderate CHF by reducing pulmonary congestion and mobilizing edema. However, they do nothing to counteract the underlying cause of the disease.

The effectiveness of diuretics is dependent upon the amount of sodium delivered to their site of action in the kidney and the patient's renal function. Proximal tubular reabsorption of sodium is increased in patients with severe CHF when renal blood flow is compromised, rendering thiazide diuretics (which act primarily on the distal tubule) minimally effective. Diuretics that act on the distal tubule (e.g., thiazides and potassium-sparing diuretics) increase the fractional excretion of sodium no more than 5% and lose their effectiveness when creatinine clearance (Cl_{Cr}) decreases to below 30 to 50 mL/minute. The loop diuretics (furosemide, bumetanide, and torsemide) are more potent and retain their effectiveness until the creatinine clearance is less than 5 mL/minute. Metolazone has diuretic effects intermediate to that of the thiazide and loop diuretics and may maintain activity in patients with compromised renal function. In most CHF patients, loop diuretics are preferred. Besides having activity in the ascending limb of the loop of Henle, furosemide has vasodilating properties which decrease renal vascular resistance. It also enhances sodium excretion by shifting renal blood flow from the long juxtamedullary nephrons to shorter superficial nephrons. In pulmonary edema, the initial beneficial effects of furosemide may be due more to dilation of venous capacitance vessels (decreasing preload) than to diuresis.[20]

The onset of response following an intravenous injection of the loop diuretics is five minutes, peaking within the first 30 minutes, and usually abating within two hours. Intramuscular (IM) administration results in a somewhat slower onset of action. Natriuresis usually begins 30 to 60 minutes after the oral administration of loop diuretics; it peaks within the first or second hour and lasts for six to eight hours. A 40 mg dose of furosemide is approximately equal to 1 mg of bumetanide, 10 mg of torsemide, and 50 mg of ethacrynic acid.

As discussed later in the chapter, combinations of two different classes of diuretics are used in patients refractory to high-dose loop diuretics. Because diuresis may lead to compensatory activation of the renin-angiotensin-aldosterone system, there is a theoretical basis for combining a diuretic with an ACE inhibitor.

Diuretics are indicated in diastolic CHF, but pose a difficult challenge: This form of CHF is highly volume dependent becoming markedly worse in states of fluid overload, but responding with a rapid reduction in filling pressures and resolution of dyspnea following diuresis. Conversely, chronic use of diuretic therapy runs the risk of restricting the end-diastolic volume resulting in a significant reduction of cardiac output. Thus, elevated filling pressure may be controlled at the expense of a greatly reduced stroke volume such that the symptoms of dyspnea may be traded for those of fatigue and loss of exercise tolerance.[10]

Digitalis Therapy

All of the digitalis glycosides increase cardiac output and reverse the compensatory mechanisms in CHF as described previously. However, major pharmacokinetic differences exist among the various digitalis preparations. (See Table 15.2.)

Digoxin Pharmacokinetics

Digoxin is a polar glycoside which is adequately, but incompletely absorbed. Studies from the 1970s indicated that absorption of oral tablets varied between manufacturers and from lot to lot of the same product.[21–27] In some instances, the differences were only in the *rate* of absorption, but not necessarily in the *extent* of absorption (i.e., bioavailability). At least part of the variability correlated to differences in *in vitro* dissolution. For this reason, most clinicians prefer to use the brand name product (Lanoxin), but data as to the lack of equivalence of current generic products is lacking.

Bioavailability of digoxin also is dependent upon the dosage form given. Again, the majority of the published information is from the 1970s and is subject to such limitations as differences in methodology between studies (single-dose versus multiple-dose studies) and use of nonspecific assays. The original studies appear to underestimate digoxin bioavailability.[21–27] As summarized by Reuning et al., and based upon studies using improved assay methods, the bioavailability of conventional tablets ranges from 70% to 80% (mean: 75%), while that of the commercially available elixir is slightly greater, ranging from 75% to 85%.[28] Nonetheless, considerable inter- and intrapatient variability may exist. Higher bioavailability of solutions reported in some studies may be of little clinical relevance since the solutions used were prepared extemporaneously from solutions for injection. Lanoxicaps are a liquid-filled soft gelatin capsule form of digoxin with improved bioavailability averaging 90% to 100%. However, the digoxin content of these capsules is 80% of the corresponding tablet. Thus, a 0.2 mg Lanoxicap is approximately equal to a 0.25 mg digoxin tablet. Because of high cost relative to conventional tablets, use of the capsules usually is reserved for those cases where an erratic response is achieved with the tablets.

Digoxin's rapid onset of action (30 to 60 minutes) corresponds with peak plasma levels. Maximum effects from a single dose are observed five to six hours after drug administration, a time at which drug distribution in the body is complete. Digoxin has a steady-state volume of distribution averaging 6.7 L/kg of lean body weight (range: 4 to 9 L/kg).[25,28,29] Only 23% is protein bound, but the volume of distribution may be decreased significantly in renal failure (see Question 25).[28,29] A serum level of 1 to 2 ng/mL generally is considered therapeutic (see Question 16).

Digoxin's half-life ($t\frac{1}{2}$) of 1.6 to 2 days (36 to 40 hours) is intermediate between that of ouabain and digitoxin and reflects elimination primarily by first-order pharmacokinetics.[25,27–29] In the presence of renal impairment, the half-life of digoxin is prolonged, reaching 4.4 days or more in total anuria.[28,29] The renal clearance of digoxin (1.86 mL/minute/kg) is slightly greater than creatinine clearance. Many have the erroneous impression that nonrenal excretion of digoxin is unimportant. In fact, anywhere from 20% to 40% of a given digoxin dose is excreted nonrenally, either as metabolites or in the feces,[25,27–29] corresponding to a nonrenal clearance of 40 to 60 mL/minute (0.82 mL/minute/kg). In a few individuals, up to 55% of a dose is eliminated as metabolites, primarily as inactive dihydrodigoxin.[28,30,31] Very little digoxin (6.8%) enters the enterohepatic circulation, and its metabolism has been found to be unaltered in patients with cirrhosis.

In approximately 10% of patients given digoxin, a substantial portion of the drug can be metabolized by bacteria in the gastrointestinal tract to cardio-inactive reduced metabolites.[28,30,31] In isolated cases, markedly increased requirements for digoxin dosage may be seen in patients who excrete large amounts of digoxin by this route. The resulting reduced bioavailability of digoxin is more of a problem when slowly absorbed generic tablets are used as opposed to rapidly absorbed solutions or Lanoxin brand tablets. In addition, concurrent use of oral antibiotics may alter intestinal metabolism and lead to increased digoxin toxicity.[30]

Jelliffe presents digoxin elimination in a slightly different context by describing the percent elimination in 24 hours.[32] By plotting creatinine clearance versus percent of drug eliminated per day (see Figure 15.4), he found a linear relationship between 24-hour drug excretion and renal function. As can be seen from the figure, the best fit equation of the line (y = b + mx) is:

$$\% \text{ Digoxin Eliminated/Day} = 14 + \frac{Cl_{Cr}}{5} \quad Eq\ 15.1$$

where the y intercept (b), representing nonrenal elimination, is 14% and the slope of the line (m), representing that portion of daily elimination dependent upon renal elimination, is one-fifth. At a creatinine clearance of 100 mL/minute, the percent eliminated per day is 35%, whereas at a creatinine clearance of 0 (i.e., anuria), the percent eliminated per day is 14%, all via nonrenal clearance mechanisms.

Digoxin has become the most widely used digitalis glycoside. This is because of its relatively short action compared to other digitalis products, its convenient once-daily dosage regimen, and the fact that its pharmacologic and pharmacokinetic properties are so well described. Although it is dependent in part upon the kidney for elimination, and thus requires dosage manipulation with declining renal function, many practitioners still consider it the drug of choice in uremia because a sound scientific knowledge base exists for appropriate dosage alteration.

Digitoxin Pharmacokinetics

Digitoxin is the least polar and most lipid soluble of the glycosides. It has the slowest onset of action (1 to 2 hours) and peak effect (4 to 12 hours) and the longest half-life (5 to 7 days) of all the digitalis glycosides.[27,33] Only 11.4% of the total body stores are eliminated daily. It is absorbed more completely (100%) than digoxin and undergoes enterohepatic circulation to a greater degree (26%). Digitoxin is 90% to 95% protein bound.[29,33] Its elimination occurs primarily via hepatic metabolism and renal excretion of metabolic by-products, 92% of which are inactive and 8% of which are active. Digoxin is the major active metabolite, but because the conversion half-life of digitoxin to digoxin is short in relation to the elimination half-life of digoxin, little digoxin accumulation occurs.

Table 15.2	Pharmacokinetic Summary: Digitalis Glycosides	
Parameter	Digoxin	Digitoxin
Bioavailability (F)		
Tablets	0.75 (0.5–0.9)[a]	90%–100%
Elixir	0.80 (0.65–0.9)	—
Liquid-filled Capsules	0.95 (0.8–1.0)	—
Half-Life (t½)		
Normal	1.6–2 days	7.6 (5–10) days
Renal failure	≥4.4 days	No change
Children	0.7–1.5 days	—
Volume of Distribution (Vd)[b]		
Normal	6.7 (4–9) L/kg	0.6 (0.5–0.74) L/kg
Renal failure	smaller: 4.7 (1.5–8.5) L/kg	No change
Clearance (Cl)		
Normal	$1.02\ Cl_{Cr} + 57$ mL/min or 2.7 mL/min/kg	0.02–3.7 mL/min
Severe CHF	$0.88\ Cl_{Cr} + 23$ mL/min	No change or slight
% Renally Cleared Unchanged	PO: 50%–60%	30%–49% (8% as active metabolites)
	IV: 70%–75%	
% Nonrenal Elimination	40% (20%–55%)	70%
% Eliminated/Day	$14\% + Cl_{Cr}/5$	—
% Enterohepatic Recycling	6.8%	27%
Protein binding	20%–30%	90%–95%
Therapeutic Serum Concentration[c]	1–2 ng/mL (1.2–2.6 nmol/L)	15–35 ng/mL (μg/L)
Usual Digitalizing Dose[d]	0.5–1 mg or 0.01–0.02 mg/kg	0.8–1.4 mg over 2 days
Usual maintenance Dose	0.125–0.5 mg/day	0.05–0.2 mg/day
Pediatric Dosing		
Neonate loading	0.01–0.03 mg/kg IV	—
Infant loading	0.01–0.05 mg/kg PO	—
>2-year-old load	0.05 mg/kg PO	—
Premature maintenance	0.001–0.009 mg/kg/day	—
Neonate maintenance	0.01 mg/kg/day	—
Infant maintenance	0.015–0.025 mg/kg/day	—
>2-year-old maintenance	0.01–0.015 mg/kg/day	—

[a] Mean value with range in parentheses.

[b] Volume of Distribution decreases in renal failure, possibly because of change in protein binding.

[c] There is a poor correlation between digoxin serum concentration and effect. Levels drawn <6 hr after a dose may be falsely elevated. Spironolactone and endogenous digoxin-like substances in the blood of neonates and renal failure patients may result in falsely elevated levels.

[d] In patients in acute distress, loading doses of digoxin are indicated since it takes several days (5 half-lives) to reach steady state with maintenance doses. A more specific loading dose can be calculated by multiplying the desired steady-state concentration by the volume of distribution.

[e] Higher maintenance doses may be required in patients with concurrent supraventricular arrhythmias. Dose also is adjusted in the elderly or those with renal insufficiency by first estimating Cl_{Cr} and then using the formulas for digoxin clearance. The dose is estimated by multiplying the target serum concentration times the estimated clearance.

Use of digitoxin compared to digoxin has diminished; due primarily to digitoxin's long half-life, which means that several weeks may be required before the full effects are seen if no loading dose is given. There also may be a long delay before toxicity appears, and once toxicity appears it may take a week or longer to dissipate. Some have advocated the use of digitoxin, especially in patients with renal failure, since renal excretion of the drug is minimal. Conversely, patients with hepatic disease or those who are taking drugs which affect biliary recirculation may be prone to digitoxin toxicity.

Patient Evaluation

Signs and Symptoms

1. A.J., a 58-year-old male, is admitted with a chief complaint of increasing SOB and an 8 kg weight gain. Two years before admission, he noted the onset of dyspnea on exertion (DOE) after 1 flight of stairs, orthopnea, and ankle edema. Since that time, his symptoms have progressed in spite of intermittent hydrochlorothiazide (HCTZ) therapy. Three weeks before admission, he noted the onset of episodic bouts of paroxysmal nocturnal dyspnea (PND). Since then he only has been able to sleep in a sitting position. A.J. notes a productive cough, nocturia (2–3 times/night), and mild, dependent edema.

A.J.'s other medical problems include a 4-year history of peptic ulcer disease; a 2-year history of rheumatoid arthritis, which has been managed with various nonsteroidal anti-inflammatory drugs (NSAIDs); chronic headaches; and hypertension, which has been poorly controlled with HCTZ and propranolol (Inderal). There is also a strong family history of diabetes mellitus.

Physical examination reveals a dyspneic, cyanotic, tachycardic male with the following vital signs: BP 160/100 mm Hg, pulse 100 beats/min, respiratory rate 28/min. He is 5'11" tall and weighs 78 kg. His neck veins are distended. On cardiac examination an S₃ gallop is heard; point of maximal impulse (PMI) is at the sixth intercostal space (ICS), 12 cm from the midsternal line (MSL). His liver is enlarged and tender to palpation, and a positive hepatojugular reflex (HJR) is observed. He is noted to have 3+ pitting edema of the extremities and sacral edema. Chest examination reveals inspiratory rales and rhonchi bilaterally.

The medication history reveals the following: *Present medications*: HCTZ (Hydrodiuril, Oretic) 50 mg BID; propranolol (Inderal) 80 mg TID; ibuprofen (Motrin, Rufen) 600 mg QID; ranitidine (Zantac) 150 mg HS; and Mylanta Double Strength 15 cc as needed up to QID. *Allergies*: None. He claims no dietary restrictions.

Admitting laboratory values include the following: hematocrit (Hct) 41.1% (Normal: 40–45); white blood cell (WBC) count 5300/mm^3 (Normal: 5000–10,000); Na 132 mEq/L (Normal: 136–144); potassium (K) 3.2 mEq/L (Normal: 3.5–5.3); chloride (Cl) 90 mEq/L (Normal: 96–106); bicarbonate 30 mEq/L (Normal: 22–28); magnesium (Mg) 1.2 mEq/L (Normal: 1.7–2.7); fasting blood sugar (FBS) 120 mg/dL (Normal: 65–110); uric acid 8 mg/dL (Normal: 3.5–7); blood urea nitrogen (BUN) 40 mg/dL (Normal: 10–20); serum creatinine (SrCr) 0.8 mg/dL (Normal: 0.5–1.2); alkaline phosphatase 120 U (Normal: 40–80); aspartate aminotransferase (AST) 100 U (Normal: 0–35). The chest x-ray shows bilateral pleural effusions and cardiomegaly. What signs, symptoms, and laboratory abnormalities of systolic CHF are exhibited by A.J.? Relate them to the pathogenesis of the disease and to left or right heart failure. [SI units: Hct 0.411 (Normal: 0.4–0.45); WBC count 5.3 10^9/L (Normal: 5.0–10.0); Na 132 mmol/L (Normal: 136–144); K 3.2 mmol/L (Normal: 3.5–5.3); Cl 90 mmol/L (Normal: 96–106); bicarbonate 30 mmol/L (Normal: 22–28); Mg 0.6 mmol/L (Normal: .85–1.35); FBS 6.661 mmol/L (Normal: 3.608–6.106); uric acid 475.84 μmol/L (Normal: 208.18–416.36); BUN 14.28 mmol/L UREA (Normal: 3.57–7.14); SrCr 70.72 μmol/L (Normal: 44.2–106.08); alkaline phosphatase 120 U (Normal: 40–80); AST 100 U (Normal: 0–0.58 μkat/L)]

The signs and symptoms of CHF observed in A.J. are easily visualized if one recalls that the work of the left ventricle is the major determinant of cardiac output and that blood flows from the left ventricle into the arterial system, through capillaries into the venous system, and back into the right heart. From the right heart, the blood circulates through the pulmonary tree and back into the left ventricle. Thus, left heart failure causes primarily pulmonary symptoms due to back-up of blood into the lungs, while right-sided failure causes mostly signs of systemic venous congestion. Although left ventricular failure usually develops first, most patients, including A.J., present with signs of combined left- and right-sided failure. The signs and symptoms of both left and right heart failure are summarized in Table 15.3.

Left Heart Failure

Weakness, fatigue, and cyanosis result from a decreased cardiac output and compromised tissue perfusion. If the left heart is not emptied completely, blood backs up into the pulmonary circulation. Shortness of breath, dyspnea on exertion, a productive cough, rales, pleural effusions on chest x-ray, and cyanosis all result from

Table 15.3	Signs and Symptoms of Systolic CHF^{a,c}	
	Left Ventricular Failure	Right Ventricular Failure^b
Subjective	SOB; DOE; orthopnea (2–3 pillows); PND; cough; weakness, fatigue, confusion	Peripheral edema; weakness, fatigue
Objective	LVH; EF <40%; rales, S$_3$ gallop rhythm; reflex tachycardia; ↑ BUN (poor renal perfusion)	Weight gain (fluid retention); neck vein distension; hepatomegaly; hepatojugular reflex

^{a} Adapted from Handbook of Applied Therapeutics. Vancouver: Applied Therapeutics, Inc.
^{b} Isolated right side failure occurs with long standing pulmonary disease (cor pulmonale) or after pulmonary hypertension.
^{c} BUN = Blood urea nitrogen; CHF = Congestive heart failure; DOE = Dyspnea on exertion; EF = Ejection fraction; LVH = Left ventricular hypertrophy; PND = Paroxysmal nocturnal dyspnea; SOB = Shortness of breath.

pulmonary congestion. Pulmonary symptoms are aggravated in the reclining position which minimizes the gravitational effects on excess fluids in the extremities and improves venous return to the heart and lungs. Shortness of breath in the prone position (orthopnea) often is quantified by the number of pillows the patient must lie upon to sleep comfortably. A.J., for example, could only sleep sitting upright. Paroxysmal nocturnal dyspnea (also called cardiac asthma) is characterized by severe shortness of breath which awakens the patient from sleep and is alleviated by an upright position. It results from pulmonary vascular congestion which has advanced to pulmonary edema and bronchospasm while the patient sleeps.

Left ventricular hypertrophy (LVH) and *cardiac dilation* are caused by an increased end-diastolic volume (see Pathogenesis). These effects are observed on the chest x-ray as an enlarged heart silhouette. The point of maximal impulse corresponds to the apex of the left ventricle and is visualized as an external pulsation on the left chest. It is displaced laterally and downward from its normal location at the 5th intercostal space, less than 10 cm from the midsternal line. An S$_3$ gallop rhythm denotes a third heart sound often heard in close time proximity to the second heart sound (closing of the aortic and pulmonary valves) in CHF. Rapid filling of the ventricles causes the S$_3$ sound and in an adult usually indicates decreased ventricular compliance. In patients with mitral valve regurgitation, an S$_3$ heart sound is common, and denotes the presence of systolic dysfunction and elevated filling pressure.[34] *Tachycardia* is due to compensatory increases in sympathetic tone.

Weight gain and *edema* reflect sodium and water retention resulting from decreased renal perfusion (see Pathogenesis). As renal blood flow and GFR decrease, a disproportionate amount of BUN may be retained. This phenomenon is termed *prerenal azotemia* and may be detected by an elevated BUN:serum creatinine ratio of greater than 20:1. Prerenal azotemia also may be caused by dehydration and overuse of diuretics. Frequency of urination at night (*nocturia*) is due to improved perfusion of the kidney when the patient is lying down.

Right Heart Failure

The signs and symptoms of right-sided heart failure can be related to either hypervolemia or the back-up of blood from the right ventricle into the peripheral venous circulation. The overall effect is development of *systemic venous hypertension*.

Dependent pitting edema results from increased venous and capillary hydrostatic pressure, causing a redistribution of fluid from the intravascular to interstitial spaces. Ankle and pretibial edema are common findings after prolonged standing or sitting, because

Fig 15.4 Relationship of Digoxin Elimination to Renal Function.

fluid tends to localize in the dependent portions of the body secondary to gravitational forces. Sacral edema may be present in patients at bedrest. Edema is grossly quantified on a 1+ (minimal) to 4+ (severe) scale. A.J. has 3+ pitting edema.

Hepatomegaly, hepatic tenderness, and ascites (fluid in the abdomen) arise from hepatic venous congestion and increased portal vein pressure. Metabolism of drugs highly dependent upon the liver for body elimination may be notably impaired by both the backward venous congestion of the liver from right-sided failure and the decreased arterial perfusion of the liver from left-sided failure. Congestion of the gastrointestinal tract makes the patient *anorectic*.

Neck vein distension, primarily seen as jugular venous distension (JVD), denotes the presence of an elevated jugular venous pressure (JVP). How high the neck veins are distended while the patient is lying down and how much his head has to be raised before the JVD disappears give the clinician a rough estimate of the patient's central venous pressure (CVP). Applying pressure to the liver may cause further distension of the neck veins if hepatic venous congestion is present. This phenomenon is termed the *hepatojugular reflex*.

New York Heart Association (NYHA) Classification

2. How severe is A.J.'s disability according to the NYHA functional classification of heart failure?

The NYHA classification scheme lists four categories of functional disability associated with CHF.[35] Class I patients are well compensated with no physical limitations and lack symptoms with ordinary physical activity. In Class II, ordinary physical activity results in mild enhancement of symptoms and imparts slight limitations on exercise tolerance. Class III patients are comfortable only at rest; even less than ordinary physical activity leads to symptoms. In Class IV, symptoms of CHF are present at rest and no physical activity can be undertaken without symptoms.

Upon admission, A.J. is in functional Class IV as evidenced by a need to sleep upright. Previously he had been Class II to Class III.

Predisposing Factors

3. What factors contributed to the etiology of A.J.'s heart failure?

Age. A.J.'s age of 58 puts him in a high-risk category for development of cardiovascular disease. He is especially vulnerable to heart failure because of his poorly-controlled hypertension, which places an increased afterload on his left ventricle.

β-Adrenergic Blockers. There are many drugs that potentially may precipitate or aggravate systolic CHF (also see Question 4). A.J. was receiving several agents that may have contributed to his CHF, the most significant of which was propranolol. All β-adrenergic blockers decrease myocardial contractility and slow the heart rate. Both of these factors compromise the heart's ability to empty effectively. This is a frequently encountered problem since many patients with CHF also are being treated for hypertension or angina. Beta blockers with intrinsic sympathomimetic activity [acebutolol (Sectral), pindolol (Visken), carteolol (Cartrol), penbutolol (Levatol)] have slightly less potential for inducing CHF, but still must be used with caution. Even topically applied beta blockers (e.g., timolol eye drops for glaucoma) may cause systemic toxicity in sensitive patients.[35,36] (See Questions 40 and 41 for use of beta blockers in diastolic CHF and use of newer vasodilating beta blockers in systolic CHF.)

Nonsteroidal Anti-Inflammatory Drugs (NSAIDs). Ibuprofen used for A.J.'s arthritis may contribute to sodium overload. All nonsteroidal anti-inflammatory drugs have well-documented, renally-mediated sodium-retaining properties, increasing the blood volume

by up to 50% in some individuals. (See Chapter 41: Rheumatic Disorders.) Many older formulations of antacids were high in sodium, but most popular brands (including Mylanta taken by A.J.) have been reformulated. Unless large daily quantities of antacids are consumed, they probably are of little concern to the CHF patient. An exception would be those patients using sodium bicarbonate or effervescent products such as Alka-Seltzer as an antacid. These products are exceedingly high in sodium. Table 15.4 lists selected compounds known to be high in sodium. (See reference 37 for a more complete listing.)

On admission to the hospital, both A.J.'s hypertension and CHF were poorly controlled and he had gained 8 kg. He needs increased diuresis, probably with a loop diuretic, although careful attention must be paid to his low serum potassium. Propranolol should be discontinued. An antihypertensive drug with vasodilating properties or an ACE inhibitor can be added to reduce the workload on the heart and simultaneously help control the blood pressure. The ibuprofen dose also is high. Lowering the dose may reduce sodium retention and edema.

Diet. Finally, it is possible that A.J.'s diet contains a considerable excess of sodium from foods such as canned soups and vegetables, potato chips, or overzealous use of the salt shaker at meal time. He should be placed on a low sodium (e.g., 2 gm/day) diet. If salt substitutes are used, he should be warned that they are high in potassium and may cause hyperkalemia if used concurrently with potassium supplements or potassium-sparing diuretics.

Table 15.4	Sodium Content of Medicinals: Selected Adult Medications with an Extraordinarily High Sodium Content (100 mg/dose)[a]	
Drug	Unit	mg Na+/unit[b]
Parenteral Products		
Ticarcillin	1 gm	120–150
Oral Liquids		
Cerose-DM	15 mL	157
Phenergan Expectorant	15 mL	150
(Plain/VC)	5 mL	554
Phospho-Soda	15 mL	105
Tussar	15 mL	162
Vicks Cough Syrup	15 mL	202
Vicks Formula 44 Syrup		
Oral Solid Dosage Forms		
Alka Seltzer	1 tablet	295
Alka Seltzer Pain Relief	1 tablet	551
Bisodol Powder	1 tsp	156
Bromo Seltzer	80 mg capful	760
Eno	1 tsp	818
Goody's Headache Powder	1 pack	812
Kayexalate Powder (Suspension)	15 gm (60 mL)	1500
Soda Mint	1 tablet	90
Sodium Salicylate	10 gr tablet	97
Food Supplements		
Ensure	1 L	844
Isocal	1 L	530
Meritene	1 L	880–1078
Osmolite	1 L	549
Sustacal	1 L	924–940
Vivonex	1 L	468–529
Miscellaneous		
Fleets Enema	120 mL	4439[c]

[a] Adapted from Handbook of Applied Therapeutics. Vancouver, WA: Applied Therapeutics, Inc.

[b] 23 mg Na = 1 mEq.

[c] Average absorption = 275–400 mg/enema.

Table 15.5	Drugs That May Induce CHF[a,c]
Negative Inotropic Agents	
Beta blockers[b]	May be less with agents with intrinsic sympathomimetic activity (acebutolol, carteolol, pindolol). May also be caused by use of timolol eye drops
Calcium channel blockers[b]	Verapamil has most negative inotropic and AV blocking effects; amlodipine has least
Antiarrhythmics	Most with disopyramide (Norpace). Also quinidine
Direct Cardiotoxins	
Cocaine, amphetamines	Overdoses and long-term myopathy
Anthracycline cancer chemotherapeutic drugs	Daunomycin and daunorubicin (Adriamycin). Dose related. Keep total cumulative dose <600 mg/m^2
Expansion of Plasma Volume	
NSAIDs	Prostaglandin inhibition; Na retention
Glucocorticoids, androgens, estrogens	Mineralocorticoid effect; Na retention
Licorice	Aldosterone-like effect; Na retention
Antihypertensive vasodilators (hydralazine, methyldopa, prazosin, minoxidil)	↓ renal blood flow, activation of renin-angiotensin system
Drugs high in Na$^+$	See Table 15.4

a Adapted from Handbook of Applied Therapeutics. Vancouver, WA: Applied Therapeutics, Inc.

b Beta blockers and verapamil may be beneficial in diastolic CHF.

c AV = Atrioventricular; CHF = Congestive heart failure; NA = Sodium; NSAIDs = Nonsteroidal anti-inflammatory drugs.

Etiology—Drug-Induced

4. Beta blockers, NSAIDs, and drugs high in sodium were noted as a possible cause of A.J.'s CHF. What other drugs have been implicated in the induction of CHF?

Drug-induced CHF is mediated via two basic mechanisms: inhibition of myocardial contractility (negative inotropic agents) or expansion of plasma volume (see Table 15.5). The latter category includes drugs that act primarily on the kidney (to either alter renal blood flow or increase sodium retention) or those that increase total body sodium and water due to their high sodium content.

The most recognized negative inotropic agents are the beta blockers (also see Question 3 and Chapter 10: Essential Hypertension). Other well-documented negative inotropes include the calcium channel blockers [most notably verapamil (Calan, Isoptin) (see Chapters 13: Ischemic Heart Disease and 10: Essential Hypertension)], various antiarrhythmic agents [especially disopyramide (Norpace),[38] quinidine, and the class II drugs (see Chapter 16: Cardiac Arrhythmias)], and the anthracycline cancer chemotherapeutic agents [daunomycin and doxorubicin (Adriamycin)]. The anthracyclines have a direct, dose-related cardiotoxicity which can be minimized by limiting total cumulative doses to 600 mg/m^2.[39] (For a more detailed description of anthracycline toxicity, see Chapter 91: Adverse Effects of Chemotherapy.) The final group of drugs which are gaining increased notoriety as cardiotoxins are the amphetamine-like drugs and cocaine when used chronically in large quantities or after an overdose.

Examples of drugs that induce sodium and water retention are NSAIDs (via prostaglandin inhibition), certain antihypertensive drugs, glucocorticoids, androgens, estrogens, and licorice. Antihypertensive drugs either decrease renal blood flow via direct vasodilation (e.g., hydralazine, minoxidil, diazoxide) or via inhibition of the autonomic nervous system (e.g., guanethidine, methyldopa).

Glucocorticoids and licorice (glycerrhizic acid, carbenoxolone) have an aldosterone-like action.

Treatment

Therapeutic Objectives; Drug of First Choice

5. What are the therapeutic objectives in treating A.J.?

In general terms, cure is not a feasible therapeutic objective in patients with CHF. The one exception would be the rare patient who is a candidate for cardiac transplantation. The immediate objective for A.J. is to provide symptomatic relief as assessed by a reduction in his complaints of shortness of breath and PND, an improved quality of sleep, and increased exercise tolerance. Over the next several days or weeks the goal will be to get him back to his baseline status of NYHA Class II or III CHF. Parameters used to measure success in meeting this objective might include reduced peripheral and sacral edema, weight loss, slowing of the heart rate to less than 90 beats/minute, normalization of blood pressure, reduction of the BUN back to baseline, a smaller heart size on chest X-ray, less neck vein distension, loss of the S$_3$ heart sound, and an increased ejection fraction. Long range goals are to improve A.J.'s quality of life including better tolerance of daily life activities, fewer hospitalizations in the future, avoidance of side effects of his therapy, and ultimately, an increased time of survival. How achievable these goals are will depend upon the severity of A.J.'s disease, his understanding of his disease, and his compliance to prescribed interventions.

6. Bedrest and a 1 gm sodium diet were ordered. Which is the drug of first choice for A.J., a diuretic, digoxin, or an ACE inhibitor?

Diuretics

Whichever approach to therapy one wishes to accept, all clinicians agree that excessive volume increases the workload of a compromised heart and that diuretics are an integral part of therapy. This is especially true if volume overload is symptomatic (e.g., pulmonary congestion) as in A.J. However, it is important to emphasize that vigorous diuretic therapy carries the risk of volume depletion and diminished cardiac output.

Digitalis

Correction of the underlying defect is a rational approach to the treatment of any disease. Therefore, digitalis, which traditionally has been claimed to improve cardiac contractility, cardiac output, and renal perfusion should represent the rational drug of first choice in the pharmacologic management of CHF. There is universal agreement that digitalis is a drug of choice in patients with concurrent congestive heart failure and supraventricular arrhythmias (atrial fibrillation, atrial flutter) since these rhythm disorders can make CHF worse and digitalis helps to control ventricular response (see Chapter 16: Cardiac Arrhythmias). However, the primary role of digitalis in the management of CHF in patients with normal sinus rhythm is controversial.

Controversy Over Efficacy. Cohn et al.[40] studied eight patients (four with cardiomyopathy, four with ischemic heart disease) after administration of two 0.5 mg intravenous doses of digoxin given two hours apart. There was no consistent increase in cardiac output or decrease in pulmonary arterial pressure during a four-hour observation period, suggesting minimal beneficial effect of the drug. The authors concluded that while many previous investigators consistently have demonstrated enhancement of myocardial contractility in pharmacologic tissue studies, an improvement in cardiac function in an intact heart may be less predictable. This study is limited by small sample size and use of short-term therapy. The findings cannot be extrapolated to chronic drug use or to other causes of CHF such as aortic and mitral valve defects, volume overload, or atrial arrhythmias.

Using a different methodological approach, Gheorghiade and Beller[41] found that discontinuing maintenance digoxin therapy in 24 congestive heart failure patients with normal sinus rhythm (NSR) had no adverse clinical or hemodynamic effects. Only 2 of 24 patients had an increase in heart failure score over the one month observation period after digoxin withdrawal. Similarly, Hutcheon et al.,[42] in studying 15 patients, found that treatment with vigorous diuresis was as effective as diuresis plus digitalis in controlling the symptoms of CHF.

These three studies and others engendered heated debate among the medical community and led to a division in clinicians' opinions as to the role of digitalis.[43-45] One group claims that digitalis is the drug of choice for CHF of any cause, while others claim its usefulness is limited by an unacceptably high rate of side effects. This latter group considers the effectiveness of digitalis to be minimal and reserves its use for those patients with coexisting atrial arrhythmias.

The first investigators to provide evidence that oral digoxin is of value in the long-term treatment of CHF were Arnold and his associates.[46] They studied nine patients with chronic CHF (due to idiopathic cardiomyopathy of ischemic heart disease) who were in normal sinus rhythm and had been receiving continuous oral digoxin therapy for at least two months before the study. Baseline cardiac function tests were performed while the patients were taking digoxin. Therapy was then discontinued and the patients were monitored weekly for six to seven weeks. At the end of the observation period, 1 mg of digoxin was infused and hemodynamic testing was repeated. Upon withdrawal of digoxin, pulmonary capillary wedge pressure (PCWP) increased significantly and the cardiac index decreased, suggesting a deterioration in left ventricular function. Four patients had to be hospitalized after drug withdrawal. Acute infusion of 1 mg of digoxin at the end of the study restored hemodynamic values to those observed during long-term digoxin therapy. Follow-up studies to determine if improvement was maintained with continued oral dosing were not performed.

The pendulum has now swung back toward use of digitalis in patients with normal sinus rhythm. Using multivariate analysis, Lee and associates concluded that the presence of a third heart sound (S_3 gallop rhythm), an enlarged heart, and a low ejection fraction best predicts those patients with normal sinus rhythm who will derive a beneficial response from digoxin.[47] Several other meta-analyses and critical reviews of the literature now concur that many of the original trials were designed improperly or lacked proper controls and that digoxin therapy provides a beneficial effect, especially in patients with severe symptomatic ventricular systolic dysfunction.[48,49] Smith further concludes in a subsequent editorial that digoxin helps to improve symptoms, increases exercise capacity, and reduces hospitalizations.[50] He goes on to point out, however, that the patients in most of the studies were given stable doses of diuretics.

Vasodilators and ACE inhibitors; Comparison to Digoxin

The issue of which class of drugs should be used first has become clouded by a series of trials with hydralazine, isosorbide dinitrate, and ACE inhibitors demonstrating symptomatic improvement in patients with both mild and advanced systolic CHF as well as improved survival.[5,51-53] The results of these studies have led some clinicians to begin therapy with vasodilators and ACE inhibitors much sooner than in the past. Many would argue that ACE inhibitors, in particular, should be given in preference to digoxin.[19] (See Questions 35 and 36 for a discussion of the trials showing

survival changes with vasodilator and ACE inhibitor therapy.)

Surprisingly, little data is available to directly compare digoxin to an ACE inhibitor.[54] The two most widely quoted of these studies are the Captopril-Digoxin Multicenter Research Group Study[55] and the Canadian Enalapril versus Digoxin Study Group trial.[56] Similarities between these two trials are inclusion of NYHA class II or III patients, all of whom had a reduced ejection fraction and were in normal sinus rhythm. All subjects continued to take diuretics, but other vasodilator therapy was discontinued. About half of the patients had an S_3 gallop rhythm and about 60% were taking digoxin before entry into the studies. After an appropriate run-in period during which time diuretic doses were stabilized and previous digoxin therapy was discontinued, patients were randomized to receive either digoxin or an ACE inhibitor. In the Captopril-Digoxin study, both drugs were superior to placebo as measured by symptom scores and treadmill exercise time. There was a nonsignificant trend toward a more favorable functional improvement with captopril (41% improving with captopril, 31% with digoxin, 22% with placebo.) There was a greater increase in the ejection fraction in the digoxin group. Six month mortality was unchanged with either drug compared to placebo. There were more minor side effects with captopril (44% versus 30%), but more patients had to discontinue digoxin because of side effects (4.2% versus 2.9%). In the Enalapril-Digoxin study, more patients in the enalapril group showed functional improvement at four weeks (18% versus 10%) and fewer showed functional deterioration (12.5% versus 23%). However, by the end of 14 weeks, an equal number of patients had improved with the two drugs (19%), but more patients continued to show deterioration with digoxin (30% versus 12.5%). There were no differences in the more objective measurements of exercise time, left ventricular function, blood pressure, pulse, and electrocardiographic (ECG) changes between the two groups. More patients withdrew from the digoxin arm because of side effects. Taken in the aggregate, these studies show no clear benefit of one class of drug versus the other; ACE inhibitors may be slightly more rapid in onset of effect and associated with better tolerance of side effects, but digoxin may improve ejection fraction to a greater extent. Mortality differences were undetectable in the Captopril-Digoxin study because of the relatively mild disease in the patients at the outset resulting in mortality rates of only 6% to 8% in either study group. A larger sample size and longer duration of observation would be required to detect a significant difference in mortality.

The current literature does not allow comparison of digoxin and ACE inhibitors as monotherapy in more advanced stages of CHF. As summarized by Rahimtoola,[57] monotherapy with diuretics, digitalis, or ACE inhibitors probably is equally effective in mild CHF, but none of them may be adequate when given alone for more advanced disease. The combination of a diuretic plus either digoxin or an ACE inhibitor is superior to diuretics alone, but there is no clear evidence that one combination is better than the other. The use of all three classes of drugs is indicated for severe CHF.

The final decision as to whether diuretics, digitalis, or an ACE inhibitor should be the first drug of choice must be highly individualized, based upon many patient factors and clinicians' opinions. In the case of A.J., who is in biventricular failure, a reasonable approach to management is to initiate both increased diuresis, probably with a loop diuretic, and cautious digitalization (using digoxin) since he has not responded well to diuretics in the past. He also will require a potassium supplement because he is hypokalemic and, therefore, predisposed to possible digitalis toxicity. Since he is in normal sinus rhythm, he will not require large doses of digitalis.

Diuretics

Adverse Effects

7. Examine A.J.'s laboratory values (see Question 1). Can any of the abnormal values be attributed to the HCTZ A.J. has been taking? What is the significance of these abnormalities?

More thorough discussions of diuretic-induced side effects are found in Chapters 10: Essential Hypertension and 28: Fluid and Electrolyte Disorders. Those findings pertinent to A.J.'s case are discussed below.

Azotemia. A.J. has an elevated BUN (40 mg/dL), but a normal serum creatinine (0.8 mg/dL). Normally, a BUN:creatinine ratio of 10 to 20:1 is seen. Progressive renal failure is characterized by an elevation of both BUN and creatinine. A disproportionately elevated BUN relative to creatinine is indicative of prerenal azotemia. The major causes of prerenal azotemia are dehydration (e.g., over diuresis) or poor renal perfusion (e.g., CHF). A.J.'s laboratory values reflect prerenal azotemia, but his edematous state and elevated blood pressure rule against dehydration. The most probable cause of his azotemia is decreased renal blood flow secondary to uncompensated CHF. Diuretics should not be withheld, and, in fact, judicious diuresis may improve his CHF and help to lower his BUN. Caution must be exercised since prolonged over diuresis and dehydration may cause renal ischemia, leading to true renal damage. If this happens, the serum creatinine also will begin to rise.

Hyponatremia. Another abnormality noted is a marginally low serum sodium of 132 mEq/L. It must be clearly understood that a low serum sodium is *not* necessarily a sign of overdiuresis. Serum sodium reported by the laboratory is the *concentration* of sodium in the serum. A person may be markedly overdiuresed (dehydrated) with a large body deficit of sodium, but if that sodium is lost isotonically, the serum sodium concentration will be normal. Conversely, a person such as A.J. may be volume overloaded (edema and hypertension), indicating excessive body sodium, but the serum sodium concentration may be normal or even low. Hyponatremia (low serum sodium concentration) reflects the dilutional effect of extra free water in the plasma on sodium concentration. The most frequent cause of dilutional hyponatremia is excess ADH production or excessive water drinking (i.e., electrolyte-free fluids). Persons on severely sodium-restricted diets or those who are markedly overdiuresed and who are then given salt-free fluids or who have compensatory ADH release by the body may become hyponatremic. Dilutional hyponatremia, resembling the syndrome of inappropriate antidiuretic hormone (SIADH) secretion, also has been described following treatment with thiazide and loop diuretics.[58] Patients with CHF or hepatic cirrhosis are more likely to develop this diuretic-induced dilutional hyponatremia because of pre-existing defects in free water clearance. The exact cause of hyponatremia in A.J. is unknown, but his marginally low serum sodium does not contraindicate continued diuretic therapy.

Hypokalemia. A.J. has a serum potassium of 3.2 mEq/L. Hypokalemia reflecting total body potassium depletion is a well described, but often over-stated, side effect[59–62] of thiazide and loop diuretics. Using a definition of hypokalemia as a serum potassium less than 3.5 mEq/L, the incidence is 15% to 40% of patients receiving 50 to 100 mg/day of hydrochlorothiazide.[63,64] If lower doses of diuretic are given, or if one accepts serum levels above 3.0 mEq/L as normal, the incidence is even lower. At least four groups of investigators have found little clinical or ECG evidence to suggest that a serum potassium level between 3.0 and 3.5 mEq/L is harmful.[65–68] On the other hand, Steiness,[69] Holland,[70] and Hollifield[71] all conducted studies which showed increased ectopic activity in persons with serum levels between 3.0 and 3.5 mEq/L. However, these studies have been criticized for including patients

at high risk for complications.[62] Perhaps more important than serum levels is the measurement of actual tissue and body stores of potassium. Both Kassier et al.[72] and Davidson et al.[65] found only a 3% to 7% deficit of total body potassium in a group of diuretic-treated patients. This deficit did not differ significantly from that found in a control group of subjects not taking diuretics.

One also must take into account the serum potassium concentration in patients before therapy as well as the actual degree of fall in serum potassium. The incidence of hypokalemia usually is less in patients with heart failure than in patients with hypertension because patients with heart failure have a higher serum potassium concentration before treatment.[73] A subgroup of CHF patients with poor renal blood flow and secondary hyperaldosteronism may have more hypokalemia. The opposite is true in renal failure where there is a tendency toward hyperkalemia in the absence of diuretic therapy.

It is interesting to note that the degree of hypokalemia produced by furosemide may be less than that produced by thiazides.[73,74] This seems paradoxical when one considers that furosemide blocks tubular reabsorption of sodium to a greater degree than thiazides, allowing more sodium to be presented to the distal tubule for exchange with potassium and hydrogen ions. The reason for this anomaly is not well explained. It may be that furosemide's shorter duration of activity, relative to the thiazides, allows for greater potassium recovery between doses.

A.J.'s serum potassium of 3.2 mEq/L falls in that gray area between 3.0 and 3.5 mEq/L. While the risk may be low, he will be receiving increased doses of diuretics over the next several days and will be started on digoxin. Since low serum potassium levels predispose a patient to digitalis toxicity (see Questions 22 and 23), potassium replacement is warranted for A.J. (See Potassium Supplementation.)

Hypochloremic Alkalosis. A.J.'s low serum chloride of 90 mEq/L concurrent with an elevated serum bicarbonate (total CO_2) of 30 mEq/L signify hypochloremia with a metabolic alkalosis. When sodium is lost in the urine, electroneutrality must be maintained by the concomitant loss of an anion (chloride) or the reabsorption of a cation (hydrogen). Because diuretic therapy increases sodium excretion, concomitant chloruresis is unavoidable. Moreover, diuretic programs often include salt restriction which further decreases chloride intake. (Also see Chapter 27: Acid-Base Disorders.)

The therapy of both hypochloremia and metabolic alkalosis usually is potassium chloride replacement.

Hypomagnesemia. A serum magnesium level of 1.2 mEq/L is observed in A.J. This could either be a result of magnesium diuresis induced by his diuretic therapy or malabsorption secondary to binding of magnesium ions in the intestines by his antacids. Severe hypomagnesemia can lead to somnolence, muscle spasms, a decreased seizure threshold, and cardiac arrhythmias. These effects are similar to those seen with hypocalcemia and hyperkalemia. Some investigators have claimed that many of the arrhythmias previously ascribed to diuretic-induced hypokalemia were actually due to diuretic-induced hypomagnesemia.[75] Concurrent hypokalemia and hypomagnesemia can be especially dangerous. A.J. should be given 1 gm of $MgSO_4$ intravenously and observed for changes in his magnesium level. If needed, he could be given oral supplements of magnesium.

Hyperglycemia. It can be seen that A.J. has a fasting blood sugar of 120 mg/dL. Hyperglycemia and glucose intolerance have been reported to occur during treatment with thiazide diuretics (see Chapter 48: Diabetes Mellitus). Since A.J. has a family history of diabetes, he may be at increased risk. This is only a small elevation in blood sugar over normal and in fact may be normal if the sample was not taken in the fasting state. It also may represent a stress-related diabetic reaction.

At this time A.J.'s blood sugar needs further monitoring, but no specific therapy is required.

Hyperuricemia. Increases of 1 to 2 mg/dL in uric acid levels are common during thiazide administration, although 4 to 5 mg/dL elevations have been reported. A.J. shows an increase of 1 mg/dL.

The majority of patients who develop elevated uric acid levels during treatment with diuretic agents will remain asymptomatic and need not be treated. Only those with uric acid levels persistently greater than 10 mg/dL, as well as those with a history of gout or a familial predisposition should be considered for treatment with urate-lowering agents. (Also see Chapter 40: Gout and Hyperuricemia.)

Liver Function. The elevated alkaline phosphatase and AST seen in A.J.'s laboratory values probably are not indicative of any drug-related toxicity. Although cholestatic jaundice has been reported with thiazide diuretics, the elevated liver function tests most likely are due to hepatic congestion from right-sided heart failure.

Potassium Supplementation

8. The physician gave A.J. three 20 mEq doses of potassium chloride intravenously. This raised his serum potassium to 3.9 mEq/L. Should he receive prophylactic potassium supplementation? What is the best drug and appropriate dose?

Potassium supplementation is not required in all patients receiving diuretics. Patients should be monitored frequently in the first few months of diuretic therapy to determine their potassium requirements. Prophylactic or therapeutic potassium replacement should be given only when the therapeutic gains of treatment are balanced against its risks. A fall in serum potassium concentration may be seen within hours of the first dose of a diuretic, and the maximum fall usually is reached by the end of the first week of treatment. When diuretics are stopped, it may take several weeks for serum potassium to return to normal. Therefore, we can be fairly certain that A.J.'s admitting potassium level of 3.2 mEq/L reflects the nadir of his response to hydrochlorothiazide. His initial response to potassium supplementation shows that his hypokalemia will be easily controlled. It might be argued that he should be observed for a few days and not given further supplements, but because his diuresis is to be increased and digitalis therapy begun, potassium supplementation is warranted.

Dosage Forms. Potassium replacement may consist of dietary supplementation with potassium-containing foods, pharmacologic replacement with various oral potassium salts, or use of potassium-sparing diuretics. Table 15.6 lists the potassium content of selected foods.[76] Inclusion of these foods in the patient's diet may be all that is required to maintain potassium balance, especially in the 60% to 90% of people who are not prone to hypokalemia in the first place. Unfortunately, the food products listed are expensive and many are high in sodium which makes them difficult to use in people with low salt diets. The potassium content of salt substitutes also is included in Table 15.6. Patients using these products liberally may get adequate potassium replacement; in fact, they can contribute to hyperkalemia.[77] Some patients object to the taste of salt substitutes.

If potassium replacements are prescribed, only *potassium chloride* (KCl) should be used since all potassium-wasting diuretics may cause hypochloremic alkalosis (see Question 6); if the chloride ion is not replaced, alkalosis and hypokalemia will persist, even if large quantities of potassium are given.

Slow K and Kaon-Cl are slow-release solid dosage forms of potassium chloride crystals imbedded in a wax matrix. They are equal to potassium chloride solutions in bioavailability and are associated with less gastrointestinal bleeding, ulceration, and stricture formation than enteric-coated potassium tablets. The major

Table 15.6	Potassium Content of Selected Foods and Salt Substitutes	
Food	Quantity	Potassium Content (mg, approx.)[a]
Meats		
Hamburger	3 oz	290
Beef chuck	3 oz	310
Beef round	3 oz	340
Rib roast	3 oz	290
Chicken fryer	4 oz	710
Turkey	4 oz	350
Vegetables		
Sweet Corn	1 cup	230
Lima beans	1 cup	520
Tomato	1 medium	340
Brussels sprouts	1 cup	300
Spinach	1 cup	600
Artichoke	1 medium	210
Fruits		
Banana	1 medium	630
Orange	1 medium	360
Apricot	3 medium	500
Dates	1 cup	1390
Cantaloupe	½ melon	820
Raisins	1 cup	1150
Grapefruit	1 cup	380
Watermelon	½ slice	380
Peach	1 medium	180
Juices		
Orange	8 oz	440
Grapefruit	8 oz	370
Prune	8 oz	620
Pineapple	8 oz	340
Salt Substitutes (1 tsp is ≈5 mg of salt substitute)		
Adolph's salt substitute	1 gm	333
Neocurtasal	1 gm	487
Cosalt	1 gm	476
Diasal	1 gm	442
Nusalt	1 gm	405
Morton salt substitute	1 gm	493
Morton Lite salt	1 gm	233[b]

[a] 39 mg K$^+$ = 1 mEq.
[b] Morton Lite salt also contains 550 mg of sodium per gram of product.

drawback to the use of wax matrix products is high cost and the large number of tablets needed per day. Kaon-Cl only contains 500 mg (6.7 mEq) KCl per tablet and Slow K has 600 mg (8 mEq) per tablet. Other products contain 10 mEq (K-tabs) and 12.5 mEq (Klotrix) per tablet. Slow-release potassium tablets should be avoided in patients with impaired gastrointestinal mobility, and enteric-coated potassium tablets should be avoided at all times.

A slow-release, microencapsulated form of potassium chloride has been marketed. In a series of papers comparing the effects of wax matrix slow-release tablets to the microencapsulated formulation on endoscopic changes in the gastric mucosa, McMahon found the wax matrix product produces a greater number of mucosal lesions.[78] However, two other investigators were unable to detect any difference between the two products,[79,80] and the Boston Collaborative Drug Surveillance Program could not find a positive association between wax matrix potassium use and significant upper GI bleeding.[81] Subsequently, Kendall and associates[82] postulated that the glycopyrrolate used by McMahon to slow GI transit time may have contributed to the endoscopic changes that were seen.

Another sustained-release potassium product, K-Dur, can either be swallowed whole or dissolved in water. It offers the advantage of being tasteless even when prepared as a solution. The only patient complaint is that the capsules dissolve in the mouth if not swallowed quickly.

Dose Requirements. It is difficult to predict the dose of potassium chloride that will be required to maintain proper potassium balance. Many patients do well with 20 mEq/day, but it is questionable how many of these need any supplements at all. People with well-documented hypokalemia may require anywhere from 20 to 120 mEq of KCl/day.[63,64,83] Those patients with disease states associated with high circulating aldosterone levels require doses of potassium in excess of 60 mEq/day.

Potassium-Sparing Diuretics. The potassium-sparing diuretics (amiloride, spironolactone, triamterene) may be more effective in preventing or correcting the fall in serum potassium than potassium supplements.[84] These agents reduce urinary potassium losses, minimize alkalosis, and mobilize edema. Approximate equivalent doses are spironolactone 50 mg, amiloride 20 mg, and triamterene 200 mg. At these doses, potassium replenishing capacity is similar to that observed with a 10 to 20 mEq potassium chloride supplement.[84] Dyazide and Maxzide are popular products which contain a combination of triamterene plus hydrochlorothiazide. While these products are effective in the majority of cases, their cost is warranted only in a patient with documented hypokalemia with a thiazide alone. In one study, one full strength Maxzide tablet (50 mg thiazide; 75 mg triamterene) was equivalent to 20 to 40 mEq of potassium chloride.[85] Moduretic (a combination of amiloride plus a thiazide) also may be used.

Hyperkalemia is the major toxicity from all the potassium-sparing diuretics and may occur even when they are used in combination with potassium-wasting diuretics. As a general rule, potassium-sparing diuretics should not be used together with either KCl or ACE inhibitors. However, their combined use may be warranted in those patients requiring over 50 mEq/day of KCl. Judicious monitoring is necessary, bearing in mind the slow onset of spironolactone's effects.

Furosemide and Other Loop Diuretics

9. It is decided to begin furosemide therapy for A.J. What route, dose, and dosing schedule should be used?

Route of Administration. Clinicians commonly witness erratic responses to furosemide, especially in persons with severe CHF or diminished renal function. Some patients respond promptly and vigorously to small oral doses, while others require large intravenous doses to achieve only minimal diuresis. Part of these differences can be explained by the drug's pharmacokinetics.[86,87] Compared to intravenous dosing, oral absorption is erratic and incomplete, averaging 50% to 60% in healthy subjects and 43% to 46% in those with renal failure. When taken with a meal, absorption is delayed because of slowed gastric emptying, but the total amount absorbed does not differ significantly from that in fasting states. It has been claimed that the absorption, and therefore effectiveness, of furosemide will be further diminished in patients with CHF due to edema of the bowel and decreased splanchnic blood flow. This has been partially refuted by Greither et al.[88] who showed an average bioavailability of 61% in CHF patients, the same as in normal patients. However, total absorption in patients with CHF varies widely (34% to 80%) and there is a delay in both rate of absorption and time to peak urinary excretion for both furosemide and bumetanide.[88–90]

When interpreting the bioavailability data above, another important factor must be considered. Not only are there interindividual differences in the rate and extent of absorption (as illustrated by the examples already given), but large intraindividual variability also exists.[87] Ingestion of the same brand of furosemide by the same individual on multiple occasions can show up to a threefold

difference in bioavailability. These differences are evident whether considering the innovator's brand (Lasix) or one of several generic brands.[87,91,92]

One might infer that intravenous therapy would be the preferred route, giving a better response for any given dose. Surprisingly, this is not always the case. In both normal volunteers and patients with CHF, total daily fluid and electrolyte loss after oral therapy and parenteral therapy are comparable. The major difference is in the time course of response. During the first two hours, diuresis from the intravenous dose far exceeds that from the oral therapy, but by four to six hours, the total urinary output is equivalent.[88,93,94] Therefore, considering the marked cost differential between oral and parenteral furosemide, there is little clinical advantage in using intravenous therapy. Exceptions to the rule are those patients with severe pulmonary edema who need acute symptomatic relief and those patients who have failed to respond to an adequate oral challenge.

Dosing. Another controversy exists as to whether furosemide should be given once daily or in multiple doses. The drug's short half-life of two to four hours implies the need for multiple dosing. Equivalent daily diuresis has been observed following the same dose given in single or divided doses;[95] another investigator found better effects from divided doses.[96] Since evening and nighttime doses of diuretics frequently disturb patients' sleep patterns (because of nocturnal diuresis), the total daily dose usually should be given as a single morning dose. For those patients with symptomatic nocturnal edema, two-thirds of the dose can be given in the morning and one-third in the late afternoon or, if necessary, at night. Torsemide has a slightly longer half-life and may only require once daily dosing.[97]

Since A.J. is not in acute distress, oral therapy is warranted. Typically, a patient is initiated on 20 to 40 mg of furosemide given as a single dose and monitored for responsiveness. If the desired diuresis is not obtained, the dose can be increased in 40 to 80 mg increments over the next several days to a total daily dose of 320 to 600 mg/day. For torsemide, a usual starting dose is 10 to 20 mg/day, but a ceiling effect is noted in CHF patients at a dose of 200 mg/day.[98]

10. Monitoring. A.J. is begun on 40 mg of furosemide each morning and KCl tablets 20 mEq BID. How should his therapy be monitored?

A.J. needs to be monitored for both an improvement in his CHF and for the presence of side effects (see Tables 15.3 and 15.7). Subjectively, one should monitor for decreased pulmonary distress and an increased exercise tolerance, demonstrating control of CHF. Objective monitoring parameters for disease control include weight loss (ideal: 0.5 to 1 kg/day), a decrease in edema, flattening of neck veins, and disappearance of the S_3 gallop and rales. Since A.J. has hypertension, his blood pressure also requires monitoring. Dizziness and weakness are subjective indices of volume depletion, hypotension, or potassium loss. Muscle cramps and abdominal pain may indicate rapid changes in electrolyte balance. Objectively, a lowering of blood pressure, especially upon standing, and a rising BUN (prerenal azotemia) signify overdiuresis. As discussed in Question 7, serum sodium, potassium, chloride, bicarbonate, glucose, and uric acid should be monitored routinely. Questioning the patient with regard to the onset of diuresis (relative to drug ingestion) and the duration of the diuretic effect helps to develop the most convenient schedule for the patient.

11. Refractory Patients; Combination Therapy. A 40 mg dose of furosemide provided adequate diuresis for a few days, but later, urinary output diminished and edema increased. Should the dose of furosemide be increased? Could another diuretic be added to the therapy?

Table 15.7	Monitoring Parameters with Diuretics[a,b]

↓ CHF symptoms (See Table 15.3)

1–2 pound weight loss/day until "ideal weight" achieved[c]

Signs of volume depletion
    weakness
    hypotension, dizziness
    orthostatic changes in BP[d]
    ↓ urine output
    ↑ BUN[e]

↓ Serum K+, Mg++

↑ Uric acid, glucose

[a] Reprinted with permission from Handbook of Applied Therapeutics. Vancouver, WA; Applied Therapeutics, Inc.

[b] BP = Blood pressure; BUN = Blood urea nitrogen; CHF = Congestive heart failure; K= Potassium; Mg = Magnesium.

[c] Weight loss may be greater during first few days when significant edema is present.

[d] A ↓ in systolic BP of 10–15 mm Hg or a ↓ in diastolic BP of 5–10 mm Hg.

[e] A rising BUN can be caused by either volume depletion from diuretics or poor renal flow from poorly controlled CHF. Small boluses of 0.9% saline may be given cautiously to differentiate a rising BUN from volume depletion versus poor cardiac output. If volume depletion is present, saline will cause an ↑ in urine output and a ↓ in BUN. However, if the patient has severe CHF, the saline could cause pulmonary edema.

All of the thiazide and loop diuretics must reach the tubular lumen to be effective. Since these drugs are highly bound to serum proteins, they cannot reach the tubular lumen by glomerular filtration. They must be transported into the proximal tubule by active secretion from the blood into the tubule. If this active transport is blocked, diuretics will not reach their site of action. This can lead to a diminished diuretic response in patients with either renal insufficiency or decreased renal blood flow associated with uncompensated CHF. Both the total amount of drug delivered to the tubule and the rate of delivery of the drug to the tubule determine the magnitude of diuretic response elicited.[99–101] This explains why 80 mg of furosemide yields more diuresis than a 40 mg dose and why an intravenous injection provides a more rapid and vigorous diuresis than an oral dose.

Patients with renal insufficiency or poor renal blood flow often require large doses of diuretics to achieve a desired response. This is explained partially by delayed delivery of the drug to the renal tubule. There also may be an accumulation of endogenous organic acids which avidly bind the drug and prevent its access to the site of action.[99–101] This also plays a role in diminishing the effect of diuretics in uremic individuals. Under these circumstances, thiazide diuretics are of little therapeutic benefit and doses of furosemide ranging from 80 to 1000 mg may be required. Preliminary investigations indicate that continuous infusions of furosemide (2.5 to 3.3 mg/hour) or bumetanide (1 mg/hour) may be more efficacious than intermittent bolus doses in patients with severe CHF or renal insufficiency.[102–104]

In some instances, switching from one loop diuretic to another may overcome the problem. In other cases, a combination of diuretics may be tried. The most effective regimens are those which combine drugs that work at two different parts of the tubule. For example, a loop diuretic which works on the ascending limb of the loop of Henle is added to a thiazide that further blocks sodium reabsorption in the distal tubule. Metolazone has been documented to have a synergistic effect with both furosemide and bumetanide in several poorly-controlled studies.[105] While substantiating literature is unavailable, clinical experience has shown that hydrochlorothiazide plus furosemide frequently is as effective as combination therapy with metolazone at a much lower cost. Because of the long action of metolazone, its combination with furosemide may result in a greater than predicted diuresis and electrolyte loss.

Hydrochlorothiazide with its shorter action may be a safer drug. A small dose of hydrochlorothiazide (50 mg) or metolazone (5 mg) is first added to the furosemide therapy, doubling the dose of the nonloop diuretic every 24 hours until the desired diuretic response is achieved. If the synergism desired is seen with the first dose, the dose of the loop diuretic should be decreased. Careful monitoring of weight, urine output, blood pressure, and BUN is required.

Digitalis Glycosides

Preparation for Treatment

12. A.J. is to receive digitalis. What baseline information is important to obtain before its administration? How should A.J. be managed before administration of digitalis?

Before a patient is given digitalis, it is essential to ascertain whether or not he has taken any form of the drug within the past two to three weeks. Dissipation of digitalis activity may require days to weeks depending upon the half-life of the particular preparation ingested. If a loading dose is required, it will have to be decreased if the patient already has some digitalis remaining in his body (see Questions 14, 15, and 27 for sample calculations). According to A.J.'s history, he has never taken any digitalis preparations.

Cardiac arrhythmias may be the only sign of digitalis toxicity. Therefore, a baseline ECG is essential if the clinician is to distinguish between digitalis toxicity and a cardiac arrhythmia from underlying heart disease should an arrhythmia occur. A.J. has no ECG abnormalities.

Finally, the clinician should be aware of the presence of any disease state, drugs, or physiologic disturbances which may increase the patient's susceptibility to digitalis intoxication (see Question 23). A.J.'s low serum potassium has already been corrected by intravenous potassium supplementation. Renal function (BUN and serum creatinine) also should be evaluated because many digitalis preparations depend upon the kidney for elimination. A.J. has an elevated BUN from poor renal perfusion but his serum creatinine is normal, signifying good underlying renal function. He should be at little risk for excessive digitalis accumulation, and his BUN may normalize as the CHF is controlled.

Loading Dose

13. Which digitalis glycoside should A.J. receive? Can he be started with a properly chosen maintenance dose, or is a loading (digitalizing) dose necessary?

Considering the factors discussed in the introduction and Question 6, digoxin is indicated for A.J. He is relatively young and has no renal dysfunction to impair its elimination. Relative to digitoxin, digoxin has a rapid onset and reaches a therapeutic plateau sooner whether or not a loading dose is used.

Slow initiation of therapy with maintenance doses of digoxin in lieu of a loading dose is considered the method of choice for ambulatory or nonacutely ill patients with normal renal function. Slow digitalization with maintenance doses does not require continuous monitoring of the patient and is, therefore, suitable in the outpatient setting.

The main disadvantage to foregoing a loading dose is the considerable length of time required to accumulate maximum body glycoside stores and achieve therapeutic effects. The length of time required to achieve 92% of plateau concentrations of a drug administered on a routine basis at maintenance doses is four half-lives. Thus, a patient with normal renal function ($t\frac{1}{2}$ = 1.8 days) placed on a daily dose of 0.25 mg of digoxin will reach maximum glycoside concentrations in approximately seven days. If the same patient were anephric ($t\frac{1}{2}$ = 4.4 days) it would take 17 days to reach plateau, and the maximum concentration would be approximately 2.5 times that of a normal patient receiving the same dose. If digitoxin were administered in this manner, 30 or more days would be required to reach steady state regardless of the patient's kidney function; up to 45 days would be required for patients with renal insufficiency.

When using the slow method of digitalization, the clinician should avoid increasing doses before maximum effects are observed. For example, it would be improper to increase a patient's maintenance dose after three days if no clinical improvement were observed. Slow digitalization also means that toxic signs may be delayed and go unrecognized if the patient is at home.

A.J. is in moderate-to-severe CHF. It would be possible to treat him without a loading dose, but since he is hospitalized, he can be safely given a more rapid digitalizing course. This will give him prompt relief of symptoms and allow the clinician to better assess the effects of therapy.

14. Calculation of the Loading Dose. What would be an appropriate loading dose of digoxin for A.J.?

Often, the clinician arbitrarily will choose a digoxin loading dose based upon his or her clinical experience. The usual range of empirical loading doses is 0.5 to 1.5 mg. A more appropriate method of determining a loading dose is based upon the patient's lean body weight. Jelliffe[32] notes that oral digitalizing doses ranging from 0.01 to 0.02 mg/kg produce therapeutic levels and carry minimal risk of toxicity. The lower range (0.01 mg/kg) may be used for mild CHF, while the upper range (0.02 mg/kg) may be required for control of ventricular rate in patients with atrial fibrillation. Intravenous loading doses should be lower than oral doses, taking into account the poor absorption (75%) of oral digoxin.

Since A.J. has moderate-to-severe CHF, an intermediate loading dose of 0.015 mg/kg may be used. His admitting weight is 78 kg, but we know that he has gained 8 kg since the onset of his CHF. This represents fluid weight that will be lost quickly, not lean body mass. Therefore, a more appropriate estimate of his weight is 70 kg. For obese patients, lean body mass may be estimated from tables based upon the patient's age, height, and frame size.[106]

A.J.'s oral digitalizing dose is calculated as follows: 0.015 mg/kg $\times$ 70 kg = 1.05 mg. For convenience, an oral dose of 1 mg could be given. The equivalent parenteral dose is 0.75 mg.

Alternatively, the loading dose can be calculated based upon pharmacokinetic principles.[106] It should be recalled that immediately after a rapidly administered intravenous loading dose (i.e., before any drug elimination has occurred), the total amount of drug in the body (Ab) is equal to the loading dose (LD). The amount of drug in the body is related to the volume of distribution (Vd) and plasma level (Cp) of the drug by the following relationship:

$$Ab = (Vd)(CP) \qquad Eq\ 15.2$$

Substituting the loading dose for Ab and taking into account the fraction of drug absorbed (F), the equation may be rewritten as:

$$Oral\ LD = \frac{(Vd)(Cp)}{(F)} \qquad Eq\ 15.3$$

By arbitrarily choosing a plasma (serum) level one wishes to achieve (e.g., 1.5 ng/mL) and using data from Table 15.2 for Vd, a loading dose can be calculated for A.J.:

$$Oral\ LD = \frac{(Vd)(Cp)}{(F)}$$

$$= \frac{[(6.7\ L/kg)(70\ kg)](1.5\ ng/mL)}{0.75}$$

$$= 938,000\ ng\ or\ 938\ \mu g$$

$$\approx 1.0\ mg$$

The equivalent parenteral dose is:

$$IV\ LD = (Oral\ LD)(0.75)$$

$$= (938\ \mu g)(0.75)$$

$$= 0.70\ mg$$

15. Administration of the Loading Dose. It is decided to give A.J. a 1 mg oral loading dose. How rapidly should he be digitalized?

Administration of the total loading dose of digoxin in divided doses over a 12- to 24-hour period is the method of choice for hospitalized patients. This method minimizes toxicity but allows for rapid achievement of the maximum therapeutic effect. The patient can be evaluated for toxicity and efficacy before receiving each portion of the total loading dose. If toxicity develops or the therapeutic goal is achieved before the entire loading dose is given, remaining doses can be withheld.

The usual procedure is to give 50% of the loading dose to start (e.g., 0.5 mg for A.J.); the remaining 50% is split into two equal doses (e.g., two 0.25 mg doses for A.J.) and administered at six to eight hour intervals. Separating each fraction of the digitalizing dose by six to eight hours allows for complete tissue distribution and observation of the full clinical effects of the preceding dose. Since the loading dose is administered over a 12-hour period, some drug elimination occurs between doses. Therefore, the actual amount of drug in the body is somewhat less than the desired 1 mg.

Maintenance Dose

16. Calculation. Determine the appropriate maintenance dose of digoxin for A.J.

The usual maintenance doses of digoxin range from 0.125 to 0.5 mg/day, with the most common dose being 0.25 mg/day. Equivalent doses of digitoxin are 0.05 to 0.2 mg/day (usually 0.1 mg/day). Since A.J. is of average body size and has normal kidney function, an empirical approach would be to maintain him on 0.25 mg/day of digoxin. Smaller doses of digoxin are given to patients with impaired excretion rates (e.g., those with renal failure, older patients) or small-framed individuals. At one extreme, a totally anuric patient may receive only 0.0625 mg/day, while at the other extreme, patients with atrial fibrillation may need up to 0.75 mg/day. Because of the long half-life of both digoxin and digitoxin, most patients are given a single daily dose. Twice-daily dosing occasionally is used with larger doses.

Pharmacokinetic principles can be applied to obtain more rational dosing. The principle that must be remembered is that for any drug, the maintenance dose (MD) is simply that dose which replaces the amount of drug eliminated (cleared) from the body during one dosing interval, tau (τ). For digoxin, the dosing interval usually is 24 hours.

The daily dose of digoxin may be calculated by estimating its clearance rate from the body. Clearance (Cl) is equal to the product of the elimination rate constant (Kd) and the volume of distribution (Vd):

$$Cl = (Kd)(Vd) \qquad Eq\ 15.4$$

From basic pharmacokinetic principles it is known that Kd is equal to $0.693/t\frac{1}{2}$. If it is assumed that A.J. has a normal digoxin $t\frac{1}{2}$ of 1.8 days and an average Vd of 6.7 L/kg, his clearance would be:

$$Cl = \frac{0.693\ (Vd)}{t\frac{1}{2}}$$

$$= \frac{(0.693)[(6.7\ L/kg)(70\ kg)]}{1.8\ days}$$

$$= 180.6\ L/day \qquad Eq\ 15.5$$

Another method of estimating digoxin clearance is to use equations derived by Scheiner et al.[107] from pooled data of several hundred patients:

$$Cl_{Digoxin} = 1.02\ (Cl_{Cr}) + 57\ mL/min \qquad Eq\ 15.6$$

Where 1.02 (Cl_{Cr}) represents the renal clearance of digoxin and 57 mL/minute represents the nonrenal (hepatic and biliary) clearance of digoxin for a 70 kg man. The equation must be adjusted in patients with severe CHF to account for decreased renal and hepatic perfusion. The adjusted equation is:

$$Cl_{Digoxin} = 0.88\ (Cl_{Cr}) + 23\ mL/min \qquad Eq\ 15.7$$

For A.J. who is not in severe CHF, we can use Equation 15.6:

$$Cl_{Digoxin} = 1.02\ (Cl_{Cr}) + 57\ mL/min$$
$$= 1.02\ (100\ mL/min) + 57\ mL/min$$
$$= 159\ mL/min$$
$$= 230\ L/day$$

Once clearance is determined, the maintenance dose is calculated using the general pharmacokinetic equation:

$$MD = \frac{(Cl)(Cpss\ ave)(\tau)}{F} \qquad Eq\ 15.8$$

Where Cpss ave is the average desired plasma level at steady state. Using the clearance value obtained from Equation 15.5:

$$MD = \frac{(Cl)(Cpss\ ave)(\tau)}{F}$$
$$= \frac{(180.6\ L/day)(1.5\ ng/mL)(1\ day)}{0.75}$$
$$= 361,000\ ng/day\ or\ 361\ \mu g/day$$
$$= 0.36\ mg/day$$

Using the clearance value obtained from Scheiner et al.'s method (Equation 15.6):

$$MD = \frac{(Cl)(Cpss\ ave)(\tau)}{F}$$
$$= \frac{(230\ L/day)(1.5\ ng/mL)(1\ day)}{0.75}$$
$$= 460,000\ ng/day\ or\ 460\ \mu g/day$$
$$= 0.46\ mg/day$$

Since only a limited number of digoxin tablet sizes are available (0.125, 0.25, and 0.5 mg), the maintenance dose from these methods would be given as either 0.375 or 0.5 mg/day.

As presented in the introduction, Jelliffe applies pharmacokinetic principles in a different way.[32] He first calculates the amount of drug lost from the body in a 24-hour period and then replaces this same amount as the daily dose. He estimates the percent of total body stores (drug in the body, Ab) which is lost per day by the equation:

$$\%\ Eliminated = 14 + \frac{Cl_{Cr}}{5}$$

Since A.J.'s renal function is normal, we can assume his Cl_{Cr} is 100 mL/minute, giving him a percent of drug eliminated per day of 34%.

The *amount* of drug lost per day (i.e., the desired dose) is then calculated by multiplying the maximum amount of drug you wish to achieve in the body after each dose (i.e., Ab) by the percent *lost* per day. As in calculating the loading dose (see Question 14), the

desired Ab can be estimated by multiplying the desired plasma (serum) level (e.g., 1.5 ng/mL) by the volume of distribution. Therefore, the equation defining an oral maintenance dose is:

$$Oral\ MD = \frac{(Ab)(\%\ Eliminated\ Daily)}{F} \qquad Eq\ 15.9$$

$$= \frac{(Vd)(Cp)(\%\ Eliminated\ Daily)}{F} \qquad Eq\ 15.10$$

If a loading dose already has been calculated, Equation 10 can be simplified to:

$$Oral\ MD = (Oral\ LD)(\%\ Eliminated\ Daily) \quad Eq\ 15.11$$

Note that the fraction absorbed term is not included in Equation 15.11 since it already is used to calculate the oral loading dose. If an IV loading dose is used to calculate the oral maintenance dose, then F must be included in Equation 15.11.

$$Oral\ MD = \frac{(IV\ LD)(\%\ Eliminated\ Daily)}{F} \qquad Eq\ 15.12$$

For A.J., we calculated an oral loading dose of 0.94 mg (based upon a desired serum level of 1.5 ng/mL). Using Equation 15.11, his maintenance dose would be:

$$Oral\ MD = (Oral\ LD)(\%\ Eliminated\ Daily)$$
$$= (0.94\ mg)(34\%)$$
$$= 0.32\ mg$$

Again, realizing the practical limitations of tablet size, the dose would be 0.375 mg/day.

It is apparent that there is some discrepancy in the various methods used to calculate the maintenance dose (0.36 versus 0.46 versus 0.32 mg). The principle used by Scheiner et al.[107] to calculate clearance appears to be the most valid since it eliminates the need to estimate the volume of distribution which can vary widely among patients.[28,108,109] Jelliffe's approach is limited in that it inherently assumes the volume of distribution for all subjects is constant; it now is recognized that Vd varies widely, especially in patients with renal failure. However, in general, his formula gives a reasonable first estimate in the clinical setting because his methods are derived from data garnered from CHF patients with and without renal failure rather than from healthy subjects. Based upon these pharmacokinetic methods, A.J. could be given a maintenance dose of 0.375 mg/day. It is safest to start with a low dose and assess his needs after one to two weeks of therapy.

Monitoring Parameters

17. A.J. is begun on 0.375 mg/day of digoxin. How should his digitalis therapy be monitored? How useful are digoxin serum levels in monitoring therapy?

There is no clear therapeutic endpoint for digitalis therapy. Nonspecific ECG changes (ST depression, T wave abnormalities, and shortening of the QT interval) correlate poorly with both toxic and therapeutic effects of the drug.[110] Although digoxin and digitalis serum levels are readily available from most clinical laboratories, there is no clearly defined "therapeutic level" and corresponding "toxic level."[27,28,111,112]

Serum Level Interpretation. A common goal of clinicians is to achieve a serum digoxin concentration of 0.8 to 2 ng/mL.[27,28,111,112] The corresponding goal with digitoxin therapy is a serum concentration of 15 to 25 ng/mL.[33] A small number of patients, especially if they are hypokalemic or hypomagnesemic, will manifest apparent signs of toxicity when serum digoxin concentrations are less than 1 ng/mL. At the other extreme, some patients being treated for supraventricular arrhythmias require concentrations exceeding 2 ng/mL to achieve optimum rate control, yet show no signs of overt toxicity. Such overlap between therapeutic concentrations and toxic levels limits the absolute value of serum level monitoring. Serum levels may be used as a guide in confirming suspected toxicity or in explaining a poor therapeutic response, but clinical evaluation ultimately remains the best therapeutic guide. The correlation between serum digoxin concentrations and toxicity is considered in greater detail in Questions 22 and 23.

When interpreting serum digoxin concentrations, there are several procedural problems and patient characteristics that must be taken into account. These include proper timing of sample collection, the effects of exercise, assay technique, and possible interfering substances in the patient's blood. Each of these factors is discussed below.

Following an intravenous bolus dose or a single oral dose, equilibration of digoxin between the blood and tissues is slow. Because of this slow distribution phase, digoxin levels obtained less than six to eight hours after the last dose may be falsely elevated and can lead to a misdiagnosis of toxicity. At steady state, serum digoxin concentrations obtained after 24 hours (just before the next dose) are considered most reliable.[28,106] If a sample is obtained randomly, the time of the last dose should be carefully noted.

Physical activity increases binding of digoxin to skeletal muscle; by redistributing the drug from the blood to the tissue, a lower serum digoxin concentration is observed clinically.[113,114] The more strenuous the exertion, the greater the magnitude of effect, but even everyday physical activity such as walking may decrease serum digoxin concentration by 20%.[114] About two hours of supine rest is required for digoxin levels to reach a new steady state. Clinical consequences of this effect may be to increase the digoxin dose inappropriately or failure to identify a possible toxic level in a patient who has a serum digoxin concentration drawn soon after walking briskly. Similarly, a patient's serum digoxin concentration while hospitalized may be higher than serum digoxin concentrations drawn as an outpatient even with no dose change. Obviously, a standardized approach to obtaining blood samples is key to the appropriate interpretation of results.

Interfering Substances. In addition to the poor correlation between serum digoxin concentration and clinical effect is a problem of both endogenous and exogenous substances interfering with the assay.[115–118] This is complicated further by the existence of a multitude of different assay methodologies, some of which are more susceptible to interference than others. All of the tests are based upon immunoassay methods, including several different radioimmune assays and numerous enzymatic immunoassays (e.g., ELISA, EMIT, TDx, Stratus, Advance). Among potential interfering substances are drugs and chemicals that are structurally similar to digoxin, most notably spironolactone (Aldactone) and possibly corticosteroids. Some assays also will measure accumulated digoxin metabolites. Other patient groups may have "endogenous digoxin-like substances" in their blood which impart falsely elevated measurements. This has been noted in liver and renal failure patients, pregnant women, and at two to six days postpartum in neonates. In some of these patient groups "digoxin levels" as high as 1.4 ng/mL may be measured in the absence of any drug in the body. It is essential that anyone monitoring serum digoxin levels be aware of which assay method is used in their laboratory and which substances may cause false positive reactions. Most authors have found that radioimmune assay techniques are more susceptible to interference by endogenous digoxin-like immunoreactive factors (DLIFs) than enzymatic immunoassays.[115,117,118] One theory is that excess bile acids in neonates or patients with liver or renal disease may be a source of DLIFs.[116]

Clinical Evaluation. Clinical monitoring is the key to evaluating adequacy of digitalis therapy. As A.J. begins to improve, he should become less dyspneic and complain less of orthopnea; venous distension and signs of pulmonary congestion will diminish or disappear; diuresis (monitored through urinary output and weight loss) may increase; and a lower heart rate may be observed. The response of heart rate to digitalis may be variable depending upon the patient's underlying disease. Since bradycardia and other rhythm disturbances may herald digitalis toxicity, daily monitoring of A.J.'s pulse will be needed until his condition and serum levels have reached a steady state. Ankle edema does not mobilize immediately and is a poor therapeutic endpoint.

Factors Which Alter Response

18. After 10 days on a maintenance dose of 0.375 mg, a serum digoxin level was drawn just before that day's administration. The serum level was reported as 0.7 ng/mL, and A.J. was discharged on the same dose with instruction to return to the clinic in 2 weeks. Examination in the outpatient clinic revealed that he had become progressively dyspneic and edematous since his hospital discharge. A "stat" serum digoxin level at 3:00 p.m. was 0.4 ng/mL. A.J. had taken his dose of digoxin at 8:00 a.m. What are some possible explanations for these events?

As stated in Question 17, serum levels are not an absolute guide to monitoring digitalis therapy. A partial explanation could be that A.J. was not at rest when the level was drawn. However, in this case, the low serum levels are accompanied by a deterioration in his symptoms of CHF. We can be reasonably sure of the accuracy of the serum concentration measured because it was drawn at the appropriate time (i.e., at steady state and at least 6 to 8 hours after the last dose); further, A.J.'s responses were compatible with the reported level. However, when doubt exists as to the reliability of a reported serum level, the laboratory should be asked to repeat the measurement.

Patient compliance must definitely be taken into consideration.[119] Weintraub et al.[120] determined that the mean serum digoxin concentration for noncompliant patients was 0.7 ng/mL while that for compliant patients was 1.2 ng/mL. Scheiner et al.[121] found that serum digoxin levels were lower in outpatients than inpatients. They postulate this difference may be attributable to poor compliance, but this study predated the knowledge of the effects of exercise on serum digoxin concentrations. Thirty-four percent of patients in Weintraub's study were noncompliant, but this was felt to be a conservative figure since the patient's word was taken as fact. Those patients taking two or more drugs were less likely to comply. It is possible that A.J. is a poor complier since his blood pressure was out of control on his first admission, although this could also have been related to his new onset of CHF. He should be carefully counseled on the proper use of his medications.

Digoxin bioavailability also should be considered. Since the prescription was written generically, it is possible that A.J. received a less bioavailable brand than Lanoxin the last time he filled his prescription. His dispensing records should be checked to see if he received Lanoxin brand of digoxin (see Introduction). Administration of digoxin with meals affects the rate, but not the extent of absorption.[25,28] That is, the peak concentrations are lower and delayed, but the steady-state serum concentrations are equivalent.

Malabsorption. Alteration of the absorption of digoxin following oral administration in patients with malabsorption syndromes has been studied.[26] It was found that poor and erratic absorption occurred in patients with malabsorption states such as sprue, short-bowel syndrome, and rapid intestinal transit. Mean steady-state serum levels for 0.25 mg digoxin daily were significantly less than those of controls (0.4 versus 1.2 ng/mL).[122] This difference was even more significant because the malabsorbers had a much lower mean body weight. Other investigators studied digoxin bioavailability in malabsorptive states but were unable to demonstrate large differences in serum digoxin concentrations. However, they found that use of more soluble forms, such as liquid-filled capsules, gave a better absorption than conventional tablets.[26]

Altered digoxin metabolism is rare but should be considered. Luchi et al.[123] report a patient who required 1 to 2 mg digoxin daily to control atrial fibrillation. Although her half-life for digoxin was the same as the controls, she metabolized a greater percentage of digoxin to cardioinactive products. Also, as stated in the introduction, approximately 10% of persons given digoxin demonstrate bacterially mediated metabolism of the drug in the GI tract leading to a relative decrease in total amount of drug absorbed.[31]

Concurrent metabolic abnormalities may decrease the responsiveness of digoxin. Hypocalcemia has been reported to cause a digitalis resistance,[124] as has hyperthyroidism.[28,106,125] (See Chapter 47: Thyroid Disorders.)

Drug Interactions

19. Quinidine. It was found that A.J. has been taking his digoxin only sporadically. After being counseled on the importance of good compliance, he was restarted on 0.375 mg/day. He did well for the next 6 months until he noted the onset of palpitations which were diagnosed by ECG as atrial fibrillation. A digoxin level drawn at that time was 1.6 ng/mL; but all other laboratory tests were normal. He was begun on quinidine sulfate at a dose of 200 mg QID with rapid resolution of the atrial fibrillation. Four days later, during a follow-up clinic visit, he was noted to have bradycardia with a pulse rate of 50 beats/min. He also complained of nausea, dizziness, and weakness. His digoxin level was 2.9 ng/mL. Could the quinidine be contributing to the apparent digitalis toxicity in A.J.?

Quinidine and digoxin frequently are used adjunctively in the treatment of atrial fibrillation: digoxin to control ventricular response by decreasing AV node conduction and quinidine to decrease atrial irritability. Reports show that over 90% of patients previously stabilized on digoxin who are subsequently begun on quinidine experience 2- to 2.5-fold increase in serum digoxin levels.[126–128] The actual magnitude of effect is highly variable, and may be dependent upon the dose of quinidine administered. Very little change is seen with quinidine doses of less than 500 mg/day. Serum digoxin concentrations usually begin to rise within 24 hours of starting quinidine and reach a new steady state in about five days. Conversely, when quinidine is discontinued, digoxin concentrations return to pre-quinidine levels in about five days.

At first glance, this interaction appears straightforward. However, important issues must be addressed: What is the mechanism of the interaction? Do elevated serum levels of digoxin reflect similar changes in the myocardial tissues and translate into enhanced digoxin toxicity? How should clinicians manage a patient when confronted with this interaction?

Several conflicting effects of quinidine on digoxin pharmacokinetics have been observed. The most consistent finding is a 40% to 50% decrease in total body clearance of digoxin; most of this change is accounted for by decreased renal clearance. Since neither the creatinine clearance nor GFR is altered by the addition of quinidine, the reduction in renal clearance may reflect an inhibition of tubular secretion. However, the contribution of active tubular secretion to overall digoxin clearance is variable and poorly defined.

The nonrenal clearance of digoxin also is affected by quinidine. Both Fenster[129] and Doering[130] studied patients with chronic renal failure and found that plasma levels of digoxin were doubled after the addition of quinidine. Since these patients were incapable of

excreting digoxin renally and since no changes in volume of distribution were noted, they concluded that other excretory pathways were diminished. Hedman and colleagues demonstrated simultaneous reductions in both renal and nonrenal clearance of digoxin after administration of quinidine in four healthy subjects.[131] These findings have significant potential clinical significance since up to 40% of digoxin is excreted via hepatic metabolism and/or biliary excretion in patients with normal renal function.

Because this interaction has such a rapid onset, most early reports speculated that displacement of digoxin from tissue binding sites was the primary cause. In accordance with this theory, a 10% to 40% decrease in digoxin's volume of distribution has been noted by several investigators, although others have reported no change in apparent distribution volume.[126–128] It is possible that the changes in volume of distribution and tissue binding are dose dependent and only seen at higher doses of quinidine.

Another confusing observation is the lack of consistent effect of quinidine on digoxin's half-life. Some investigators report an increased half-life and others have found no change.[128] It may be that the initial effect is a displacement from tissue binding sites followed by a more sustained impairment of renal and nonrenal clearance. The half-life does not change since the changes in distribution and clearance tend to counterbalance each other.

Digoxin is found in only small concentrations in the plasma, with the majority of the drug being distributed to lean body tissues (e.g., skeletal and cardiac muscle). Despite clear evidence that serum digoxin levels are increased in the presence of quinidine, much less is known about the importance of this interaction on the heart. If the drug is being displaced from cardiac tissue, it is possible that the increased serum concentrations actually may be accompanied by a diminished pharmacologic effect of the drug on the heart. Schenck-Gustaffson[132] documented displacement of digoxin from skeletal muscle in eight of ten patients after four days of quinidine treatment, completely accounting for the observed changes in digoxin volume of distribution. They did not, however, measure myocardial digoxin binding. Using a dog model, Doherty[132] found that the concentration of digoxin in the myocardium was 20% lower in the quinidine-digoxin group than in the digoxin group, but that brain concentrations increased by 50%. This led to the speculation that any increased cardiac effects observed during the interaction are mediated by a central nervous system effect. Warner and associates[133] were unable to confirm any alteration in cardiac to serum concentration ratios. More importantly, this same group showed myocardial inotropic activity following digoxin actually may be antagonized by quinidine.[134] They conclude that quinidine inhibits the elimination of digoxin, has no effect on myocardial digoxin concentrations, and that decreased inotropic activity may be due to quinidine itself, not to changes in digoxin activity.

Finally, clinical effects must be considered. As summarized by others,[126–128] the use of these two drugs together often is accompanied by GI intolerance (e.g., nausea, vomiting, diarrhea), AV block, and bradycardia. A disturbing report from Israel cites a nine-month study of in-hospital digitalis toxicity rates in which 50% of patients treated with the quinidine-digoxin combination had ECG evidence of digoxin toxicity compared to 5% of patients taking digoxin alone or in combination with verapamil or amiodarone.[135] Conversely, many patients tolerate the increased serum levels of digoxin with no apparent adverse consequences. A large scale retrospective analysis by the Boston Collaborative Group concluded that most gastrointestinal complaints could be explained by a simple additive effect of two drugs known to be GI irritants.[136] The bradycardia and AV blocking effects can be due to centrally-mediated toxicity (if brain tissue levels of digoxin are increased)[132] or to a direct effect of both drugs on the AV node.

Faced with the complexity of this interaction, it is difficult for the clinician to plan a course of action when using these two drugs together. It has been suggested that the dose of digoxin be reduced by 50% when adding quinidine. While this may help minimize bradycardia, ventricular tachyarrhythmias, and GI effects, it also may lead to a loss of desired positive inotropic effects. A more rational approach is to leave patients on their previous digoxin dose when adding quinidine, carefully monitoring them for undesirable side effects. A serum digoxin level can be obtained after five to seven days of concurrent therapy. If it exceeds 2.5 ng/mL, the dose can be decreased.

The effect of quinidine on digitoxin pharmacokinetics is less clear. Several investigators have shown a prolonged half-life and decreased clearance of digitoxin, while others have found no appreciable interaction.[126–128] Many of the earlier studies with digitoxin were flawed because investigators failed to wait for steady state. Kulhmann et al.[137] demonstrated no change in renal digitoxin clearance at steady state, but total digitoxin clearance and extrarenal clearance were reduced by 32% to 40.5%, respectively. Only a slight change was seen in digitoxin serum levels with an increase from 13.6 ng/mL to 19.6 ng/mL. They concluded that although there is a demonstrable interaction between digitoxin and quinidine, the underlying mechanism differs from the interaction with digoxin, and the extent of its effect is less.

Since neither procainamide (Pronestyl) or disopyramide (Norpace) interact with digoxin,[126,138] they may be used as alternatives to quinidine. A.J.'s physician decided to place him on procainamide and discontinue quinidine. This led to good control of the atrial fibrillation and a reversal of the digitalis toxicity.

20. Other Drug Interactions. Are there any other potential drug interactions with digoxin present in A.J.'s therapy? Name other drug interactions that have been reported to occur with either digoxin or digitoxin?

Three excellent, comprehensive reviews of cardiac glycoside drug interactions have been compiled.[126,138,139] The most important of these interactions involve antiarrhythmic drugs (e.g., quinidine; see Question 19) and calcium channel blockers (see Question 37). A brief summary of other interactions is found in Table 15.8. Only one of these drugs, Mylanta, is found in A.J.'s therapy. He should be counseled to avoid antacids within one or two hours before or one hour after a dose of digoxin.

Intramuscular Digoxin

21. One year later, A.J. was admitted for elective cholecystectomy. His CHF was still well controlled on digoxin 0.375 mg/day. After surgery, he was placed on a nothing by mouth (NPO) regimen and given digoxin by the IM route. On hospital day 3, he experienced severe pressing chest pain which radiated to his left arm. An ECG was performed and serial serum enzymes were ordered to rule out MI. An elevated creatine kinase (CK) was noted, but all other enzymes and the ECG were normal. Comment on the postoperative use of IM digoxin in A.J. What would you recommend?

Patients who are hospitalized and placed on an NPO regimen frequently are given medications by the parenteral route. While many drugs are well absorbed after IM injections, there is evidence for delayed or incomplete absorption of intramuscular digoxin; its availability appears intermediate between that of IV and oral digoxin.[22,25] Peak serum levels following IM injections are lower and occur later than comparable oral doses; serum-tissue equilibration requires 10 to 12 hours as opposed to the six hours required for the oral route.

Greenblatt[145] noted that IM injection of undiluted digoxin was consistently followed by intense muscular pain and fasciculations.

Pain was disabling for two hours and subsided over the next several hours; however, local tenderness and pain on motion persisted for two days.

Digoxin-induced CK elevations are of great importance in A.J. Although any intramuscular injection can cause mild elevations of serum CK, digoxin can increase control levels by 15 to 17 times eight hours after its injection.[145] A.J. has probably not had an MI, but patients have been falsely diagnosed as having an MI from creatine phosphokinase elevations due to intramuscular injections.

Based upon the above considerations, it can be concluded that there are few indications for the use of intramuscular digoxin. If IM injections must be given (for example patients on prolonged NPO regimens in whom no IV lines are established), the dose should be reduced to 80% of the previous oral dose.

The intravenous route is the preferred parenteral method of administration for A.J. The urinary recovery of digoxin is 17% higher from IV injection when compared to an IM injection of an equivalent dose. However, caution is warranted when digoxin is given intravenously. A.J.'s maintenance dose will have to be reduced by 25% to approximately 0.25 mg/day. Rapid administration may result in acute myocardial toxicity caused by a direct effect of the drug. (See Question 38.) Additionally, the commercially available preparation contains 40% propylene glycol which may cause acute myocardial depression following rapid administration. It is recommended that the commercial preparation be given at a maximum rate of 1 mL/minute, or preferably that it be diluted with 10 mL of normal saline for injection and then administered as a slow infusion.[145] A.J. should be switched back to his usual oral regimen as soon as possible.

Digitalis Toxicity

22. Signs and Symptoms. Digoxin was prescribed for Z.T., a 70-year-old male with mild CHF. The label on his prescription bottle instructed him to take 1 tablet (0.25 mg) BID for 3 days and 1 tablet daily thereafter. Ten days later Z.T. returned to clinic complaining of extreme fatigue, anorexia, nausea, and a "funny" heart beat. Close questioning and a "tablet count" disclosed that Z.T. failed to decrease his digoxin to 0.25 mg/day. An ECG revealed multiple premature ventricular contractions (PVCs) and second degree AV block. A "stat" serum digoxin level was 2.8 ng/mL. Are Z.T.'s signs and symptoms consistent with digitalis toxicity? What are some other adverse effects of digitalis?

The clinical presentation of digitalis toxicity is unpredictable. In some cases, a high serum digoxin level without any appreciable adverse effects is the only clue to possible digitalis toxicity. In other patients, such as Z.T., a multitude of symptoms may be present including both noncardiac signs (e.g., GI complaints) and rhythm disturbances (e.g., palpitation, heart block, arrhythmias).

The most important adverse effects are those relating to the heart. One must avoid the false impression that gastrointestinal or other noncardiac signs will precede cardiac toxicity. In fact, cardiac symptoms may precede noncardiac symptoms of digitalis toxicity in up to 47% of cases. Frequently (26% to 66%), nonspecific arrhythmias may be the only manifestation of toxicity with estimates that rhythm disturbances occur in 80% to 90% of all digitalis toxic patients.[110] On the other hand, the presence of rhythm disturbances in patients taking digitalis is not always related to toxicity. In one study of 100 consecutive patients with suspected digitalis-induced arrhythmias, only 24 were confirmed as being toxic as defined by resolution of cardiac irritability following drug withdrawal. In the other 76 patients, the dysrhythmia persisted long after drug removal.[146]

Most known arrhythmias can occur as a result of digoxin toxicity. Decreased conduction velocity through the AV node is man-

Table 15.8	Digitalis Glycoside Drug Interactions[a]
Drug	Effect
Digoxin Interactions[a]	
Drugs Affecting Absorption	
Antacids	↓ bioavailability via adsorption
Cancer chemotherapy	Possible ↓ bioavailability (especially combinations of cyclophosphamide and vincristine)
Cholestyramine (Questran)	↓ bioavailability via adsorption
Colestipol (Colestid)	↓ bioavailability via adsorption
Erythromycin	↑ bioavailability in persons who normally metabolize digoxin in intestinal tract
Kaolin-pectin (Kaopectate)	↓ bioavailability via adsorption
Laxatives	↓ bioavailability via hypermotility
Metoclopramide (Reglan)	↓ bioavailability via enhanced gastric emptying (slow-release digoxin only)
Neomycin	Malabsorption of digoxin
Omeprazole[140, 141]	↑ bioavailability (slight) due to altered gut metabolism
Propantheline (Pro-Banthine)	↑ bioavailability via slowed gastric emptying (slow-release digoxin only)
Psyllium hydrophilic mucilloid (Metamucil) and dietary bran fiber	Possible ↓ bioavailability
Sulfasalazine (Azulfidine)	Malabsorption of digoxin
Drugs Affecting Distribution and Excretion	
Alprazolam[142]	↑ serum digoxin levels
Amiodarone (Cordarone)	↑ serum digoxin levels
Calcium channel blockers (see Question 37)	↑ serum digoxin levels (especially verapamil)
Captopril	↑ serum digoxin levels
Quinidine (see Question 19)	↑ serum digoxin levels
Propafenone[143, 144]	↑ serum digoxin levels; dose related
Digitoxin Interactions	
Drugs Affecting Absorption	
Cholestyramine, Colestipol	Malabsorption: digitoxin affected more than digoxin due to enterohepatic recycling of digitoxin; used to treat digitoxin toxicity
Drugs Affecting Distribution and Metabolism	
Barbiturates	↓ digitoxin concentration via enzyme induction (doubtful clinical significance)
Phenylbutazone (Butazolidin)	Same as Barbiturates
Phenytoin (Dilantin)	Same as Barbiturates
Rifampin	Same as Barbiturates
Clofibrate (Atromid S)	Protein binding displacement (doubtful clinical significance)
Phenylbutazone	Same as Clofibrate
Sulfadimethoxine	Same as Clofibrate
Tolbutamide (Orinase)	Same as Clofibrate
Warfarin (Coumadin)	Same as Clofibrate

[a] References 126, 138, and 139 include a discussion of all of these interactions except where noted with additional references.

ifested as a prolonged PR interval (first-degree AV block) and is seen in many patients with therapeutic levels of digitalis. However, as exemplified in Question 19, higher concentrations of digitalis can impair conduction and result in bradycardia or a variable block (second-degree AV block). A complete AV block (third-degree AV block) results in dissociation of the atrial and ventricular rates with a very slow idioventricular rate predominating. AV block also may predispose patients to accelerated junctional rhythms. Increased automaticity of the atria can cause multifocal atrial tachycardia (MAT) with block, paroxysmal atrial tachycardia (PAT) with block, or atrial fibrillation. Ventricular arrhythmias (as seen in Z.T.) are among the most common rhythm disturbances caused by digitalis toxicity and include both unifocal and multifocal PVCs, bigeminy (every other beat is a PVC), trigeminy, ventricular tachycardia, and ventricular fibrillation. Comprehensive reviews are available on the topic of digitalis-induced arrhythmias.[110,146]

Hyperkalemia may develop as a consequence of massive digitalis poisoning.[147,148] Toxic doses of digitalis severely poison the Na^+-K^+ ATPase system, causing inhibition of the uptake of potassium by the myocardium, skeletal muscle, and liver cells. The shift of potassium from inside to outside the cell can result in sig-

nificant hyperkalemia, especially in patients with underlying renal insufficiency. These same patients also are likely to accumulate digoxin in the body because of decreased clearance of the drug. Cardiac ectopy may be potentiated by the increase in serum potassium, especially when the potassium concentration exceeds 5 mEq/L. Paradoxically, in patients with good renal function, hyperkalemia may enhance renal excretion of potassium resulting in a deficit in total body potassium despite the continued high serum concentration of potassium.

Vague gastrointestinal symptoms characteristic of digitalis toxicity may be difficult to evaluate since anorexia and nausea are also part of CHF's clinical picture. Beller et al. observed an equal frequency of anorexia and nausea in both toxic and nontoxic patients taking digoxin.[149] Over 25% of patients have GI symptoms for more than three weeks before diagnosis. Anorexia may be the earliest symptom, followed in two to three days by nausea. Nonspecific abdominal pain and bloating, due to nonocclusive mesenteric ischemia secondary to digitalis-induced vasoconstriction also has been observed.[150]

CNS symptoms of digitalis may be common, possibly associated with potassium depletion in neural tissue. Chronic digitalis intoxication resulting from misformulation was observed in 179 patients.[151] Acute extreme fatigue was a complaint in 95% of these patients. Approximately 80% experienced weakness of the arms and legs, and 65% suffered from psychic disturbances occurring in the form of nightmares, agitation, listlessness, and hallucinations. Visual disturbances were observed in 95% of these patients. Hazy vision and difficulties in both reading and red-green color perception frequently were present. Other complaints included glitterings, dark or moving spots, photophobia, and yellow-green vision. Disturbances in color vision returned to normal two or three weeks following discontinuation of digitalis.

Some prospective studies have shown a good correlation between serum digoxin levels and toxicity,[149,151,152] while other investigators have found a poor correlation.[153,154] In one study, 87% of digitalis-toxic patients had levels greater than 2 ng/mL and 90% of nontoxic patients had levels of less than 2 ng/mL. Conversely, other investigators found that nearly 50% of subjects with a serum digoxin level exceeding 3 ng/mL were clinically stable without signs of digitalis toxicity.[153] In the largest series studied to date, the average serum digoxin concentration in documented toxic patients (i.e., those with a suspected digitalis-induced arrhythmia that disappeared after drug withdrawal) was 2.9 ng/mL compared to 1.0 ng/mL in patients with suspected digitalis toxicity, but in whom the arrhythmia persisted after drug withdrawal.[146] About 38% of documented toxic patients, however, had serum digoxin concentrations of less than 2 ng/mL (false negative tests). Once levels exceed 6 ng/mL, there is a greatly increased risk of mortality.[155] Because a significant overlap between toxic and therapeutic levels exists, serum level determinations are currently most useful as an aid in confirming suspected digitalis toxicity and in individualizing dosing regimens so that toxicity may be avoided. In particular, subjects with low serum potassium concentrations may demonstrate digitalis toxicity at low serum digoxin concentrations.

Allergic reactions to digitalis are rare, as is thrombocytopenia secondary to digitoxin. Unilateral or bilateral gynecomastia often is observed during chronic digoxin administration and is reversible upon withdrawal of the drug. This latter effect may occur in addition to the gynecomastia seen with spironolactone. Even more frustrating is the fact that digitalis toxicity occasionally may present as progressive CHF.

23. Predisposing Factors. B.V., a 64-year-old alcoholic male, is admitted to the hospital with a 3-day history of epigastric pain radiating to the back and associated with nausea and vomiting. B.V. also has cirrhosis of the liver and mild CHF well controlled with furosemide 80 mg/day and digoxin 0.25 mg/day. He has a 3-year history of severe rheumatoid arthritis which is moderately relieved with NSAIDs and prednisone 15 mg/day. Since the initial impression was acute pancreatitis, B.V. was placed on a nasogastric suction and 3 L of D5 ¼ NS daily. The next evening the laboratory report disclosed the following: Na 136 mEq/L (Normal: 136–144); K 2.3 mEq/L (Normal: 3.5–5.3); Cl 90 mEq/L (Normal: 96–106); bicarbonate 32 mEq/L (Normal: 23–28); Mg 1.3 mEq/L (Normal: 1.7–2.7); creatinine 0.8 mg/dL (Normal: 0.5–1.2); AST 80 U (Normal: 40); alkaline phosphatase 130 U (Normal: 80); amylase 1200 U (Normal: 4–25); digoxin 1.8 ng/mL; Cl_{Cr} 100 mL/min (Normal: 100–125). An ECG showed a heart rate of 70 beats/min with occasional PVCs and runs of bigeminy. What factors predispose B.V. to digitalis toxicity? [SI units: Na 136 mmol/L (Normal: 134–144); K 2.3 mmol/L (Normal: 3.5–5.3); Cl 90 mmol/L (Normal: 96–106); bicarbonate 32 mmol/L (Normal: 23–28); Mg 0.65 mmol/L (Normal: 0.85–1.35); creatinine 70.72 μmol/L (Normal: 44.2–106.08); AST 80 U/L (Normal: 40); alkaline phosphatase 130 U/L (Normal: 80); amylase 1200 U/L (Normal: 4–25); Cl_{Cr} 1.67 mL/s (Normal: 1.67–2.08)]

This is an example of a subtle presentation of digitalis toxicity. The serum level is in the high end of the therapeutic range. Nev-

ertheless, B.V. shows clinical signs of digitalis toxicity (e.g., PVCs and bigeminy). His renal function is normal, so digoxin excretion should not be markedly altered. The major contribution to toxicity in B.V. is hypokalemia. The association between digitalis toxicity and hypokalemia is well recognized.[146,152,154,156,157] Jelliffe[156] has observed that twice as much digitalis is required to produce toxicity in patients with serum potassium of 5 mEq/L than in those with a serum potassium of 3 mEq/L. A small number of patients will develop signs of toxicity with serum digitalis concentrations as low as 1.5 ng/mL if hypokalemia is present. Therefore, drugs, diseases, and medical maneuvers which induce hypokalemia or reduce the serum potassium from elevated to normal levels may unmask digitalis toxicity. The mechanism of this potentiation is unclear; a low serum potassium has been observed to increase the uptake of digitalis by the myocardial tissue.[157]

B.V. is taking furosemide. All diuretics, with the exception of potassium-sparing diuretics, may cause hypokalemia through kaliuresis. In addition, prednisone in high doses may promote potassium excretion at the distal portion of the renal tubule. B.V.'s prednisone dose should be lowered or he should be switched to an equivalent dose of dexamethasone or another glucocorticoid with less mineralocorticoid effect. Similarly, diseases in which mineralocorticoid activity is high (e.g., Cushing's disease, hyperaldosteronism) also are associated with low serum potassium levels. B.V.'s history of cirrhosis may lead to development of portal hypertension and ascites, both of which are associated with hyperaldosteronism.

Other causes of hypokalemia in B.V. include vomiting and nasogastric suction. Gastrointestinal secretions contain potassium in concentrations as high as 8 to 10 mEq/L. Similarly, hypokalemia can result from diarrheal losses, including drug-induced diarrhea (e.g., ampicillin, quinidine).

While the relationship of hypokalemia to digitalis toxicity is stressed, hyperkalemia is also a risk factor.[148] A bimodal effect of potassium on the AV node has been observed whereby both hypokalemia and hyperkalemia may delay AV nodal conduction resulting in bradycardia and compensatory ventricular ectopy.

B.V. has metabolic alkalosis (HCO_3 = 32) as a result of diuretic therapy, vomiting, and nasogastric suctioning of hydrogen ion. Alkalosis results in the redistribution of potassium intracellularly and an increased renal excretion of potassium, thereby potentiating effects of hypokalemia (see Chapter 27: Acid-Base Disorders). In addition, alkalosis in and of itself has been associated with an increased incidence of digitalis toxicity. Brater et al.[157] attribute this to an intracellular depletion of potassium due to increased urinary excretion and a relative increase in the ratio of extracellular to intracellular potassium. This has the same effect on the membrane potential as digoxin.

Another metabolic problem arising in B.V. that may contribute to digitalis toxicity is hypomagnesemia. The causes are the same as for hypokalemia, including diuretic therapy, nasogastric suction losses, and chronic alcoholism. The prevalence of hypomagnesemia is higher in digitalis-toxic patients;[158,159] magnesium sulfate has been used successfully in the treatment of digitalis toxicity.[160] The long-term administration of magnesium-free fluids (e.g., hyperalimentation), diuretics, amphotericin B, and hemodialysis also has been associated with hypomagnesemia.

Although not illustrated by B.V., hypercalcemia theoretically also may predispose patients to digitalis toxicity. The electrical and contractile effects of calcium on the myocardium are similar to those of digitalis. For this reason, rapid intravenous infusions of calcium may facilitate the development of digitalis toxicity, and normal or low doses of digitalis may induce toxicity in patients with hypercalcemia (e.g., hyperparathyroidism or metastatic cancer). The clinical significance of calcium-induced digitalis toxicity is questionable, since there have been no reports of digitalis toxicity secondary to oral administration of calcium-containing products. Nonetheless, if a patient in whom digitalis toxicity is suspected should have a cardiac arrest, administration of calcium is not recommended.

Age may be an important predisposing factor in the production of digitalis toxicity in B.V. The same intravenous dose of digoxin administered to elderly and young patients produces higher serum concentrations of digoxin in the elderly. The higher levels and prolonged half-life observed in these patients are likely due to diminished renal clearance of the drug and this population's smaller body size. It is important to emphasize that although the serum creatinine of elderly patients may be within normal limits, the mean creatinine clearance is reduced.

The response to digitalis also may be altered in the very young. (See Question 26.) Lower doses are recommended in premature infants and neonates (<1 month) because of the decreased renal function normally observed in newborns.[161] Although absorption, tissue distribution, and excretion of digoxin in infants are similar to those observed in adults, infants excrete a smaller percentage of digoxin metabolites than adults.

24. Treatment. How should B.V.'s digitalis toxicity be treated?
Withhold Digitalis and Electrolyte Replacement. For many patients without life-threatening arrhythmias or major electrolyte imbalances, simple withdrawal of digitalis may be the only treatment required. Although it may take five half-lives for the drug to be totally eliminated from the body, after one to two half-lives, (2 to 3 days for digoxin and up to a week for digitoxin), the serum concentration will drop to a safe level in most individuals.

B.V. does not have markedly elevated digoxin levels, so his ectopy should disappear rapidly with drug withdrawal. His major problem is related to hypokalemia which must be corrected. As a general rule, potassium replacement should be considered in any patient with digitalis-induced ectopic beats who has low or normal serum potassium levels. Oral administration is acceptable unless the patient cannot take medication orally or has life-threatening ectopy. The following precautions should be considered when potassium is used to treat digitalis toxicity: 1) Potassium should be administered with caution in patients who have conduction disturbances characterized by second-degree or complete AV block. Potassium depresses conduction velocity in the AV node, and its use may result in an augmentation of this cardiac arrhythmia. 2) Toxic doses of digitalis inhibit the uptake of potassium by the myocardium, skeletal muscle, and liver cells. For this reason, patients occasionally may develop refractory hyperkalemia; large doses of potassium should be administered cautiously. 3) Because potassium is eliminated by the kidneys, excessive potassium loads should be avoided in patients with compromised renal function. 4) Cardiac arrhythmias have been observed following the rapid intravenous administration of concentrated potassium solutions.

If digitalis-induced arrhythmias are severe enough to warrant intravenously administered potassium, the maximum recommended rate of administration is 40 mEq/hour (preferably 10 mEq/hour) at a concentration which does not exceed 80 to 100 mEq/L. A total of several hundred mEq of potassium may be required to replete body stores. B.V. has a significant potassium deficit with potentially dangerous arrhythmias, but no contraindications to potassium therapy. He should receive 80 to 120 mEq of intravenous potassium over the next 24 hours and then be switched to an appropriate oral dose. He should be monitored for signs and symptoms of potassium toxicity with frequent ECG tracings (tall, peaked T waves; prolonged PR interval) and serum potassium determinations. (Also see Chapter 28: Fluids and Electrolytes.)

It is important to obtain a serum magnesium concentration when measuring potassium levels.[148] Patients with a low serum magnesium (<1.5 mEq/L) or who fail to respond after potassium repletion should receive a 20 mg/kg (2 gm in an adult) loading dose of magnesium sulfate administered as a 10% solution over 20 minutes, followed by a continuous infusion at a rate of 0.5 to 2 gm/hour to maintain a serum magnesium level of at least 4 to 5 mEq/L. Magnesium is relatively contraindicated in patients with renal failure, hypermagnesemia, or a high-level AV block. The infusion should be discontinued if deep tendon reflexes are diminished or serum concentrations of magnesium exceed 7 mEq/L.

Antiarrhythmic Agents. Patients with bradycardia resulting from a second or third degree AV block may respond to intravenous atropine. The usual atropine dose is 0.5 to 1 mg over one to two minutes with a repeat in 15 to 30 minutes if the patient does not respond. Doses less than 0.5 mg may paradoxically worsen the AV block. Atropine should be used with caution in patients with prostatic hypertrophy as significant urinary retention and postrenal azotemia may occur. Alternatively, a temporary pacemaker may be placed. Since B.V.'s heart rate is 70 beats/minute, atropine is not indicated.

Virtually all of the antiarrhythmic agents have been used to treat digitalis-induced arrhythmias. Intravenous lidocaine and phenytoin (Dilantin) have been used with the greatest success. Lidocaine and phenytoin have a theoretical advantage over quinidine-like agents since they do not further depress AV conduction. For B.V., potassium replacement will probably be all that is required. However, because of B.V.'s bigeminy, lidocaine could be administered for a few hours until he has been given sufficient potassium supplementation.

Although lidocaine has an elimination half-life of approximately two hours, an initial IV bolus may last only 10 to 20 minutes because of rapid tissue distribution. Generally, the drug is administered as a constant infusion (1 to 4 mg/minute) following an initial bolus dose of 50 to 100 mg (1 mg/kg). Caution should be exercised in patients with CHF since the volume of distribution and plasma clearance of lidocaine may be decreased in these patients.[106] Elimination half-life and time to reach plateau are prolonged and symptoms of lidocaine toxicity may not be evident for several hours (2 to 3 t½). (See Chapters 16: Cardiac Arrhythmias and 2: Clinical Pharmacokinetics.)

Phenytoin is particularly efficacious in the suppression of digitalis-induced tachyarrhythmias with or without first- or second-degree AV block. A loading dose of ≥1 gm (12 to 17 mg/kg in divided doses) may be required during the first 12 to 24 hours. Thereafter, the patient may be maintained at doses of 300 to 600 mg/day. The diluent for parenteral phenytoin contains 40% propylene glycol which is cardiotoxic; for this reason phenytoin should not be administered at a rate which exceeds 50 mg/minute. Phenytoin is soluble in saline but not in D₅W and can be administered by intravenous infusion only if the concentration does not exceed 1 mg/mL and the pH is greater than 10.

Intravenous propranolol is effective in abolishing digitalis-induced atrial tachycardia with AV block and premature ventricular contractions, but its use is extremely limited because it may exacerbate underlying CHF or cause significant side effects. A dose of 1 to 3 mg should be given at a rate of 1 mg/minute, with careful ECG monitoring. A similar dose may be repeated after two minutes, but further doses should be withheld for four hours. Unlike phenytoin and lidocaine, propranolol depresses conduction velocity and may worsen AV and intraventricular block. Atropine may be used to counter profound bradycardia or bronchospasm.

Procainamide and quinidine have been used less frequently because their intravenous administration is associated with hypotension and cardiotoxicity. Since conduction velocity is diminished by both of these drugs, their use should be avoided when AV or intraventricular block is present. (See Chapter 16: Cardiac Arrhythmias.)

Other agents which are used less frequently because of unpredictable or toxic effects or limited availability include EDTA (a calcium-chelating agent), magnesium, and cholestyramine. Peritoneal and hemodialysis are ineffective in removing digoxin from the body, but charcoal hemoperfusion may be used for life-threatening overdoses in patients with renal failure.[162]

25. *Digoxin Immune Fab.* **All of the treatments above are symptomatic. Is a specific antidote such as digoxin immune Fab indicated?**

Most treatment regimens for digitalis toxicity can be characterized as supportive, either by counteracting the pharmacologic effects of digitalis or by interfering with further absorption of ingested tablets. A more definitive treatment consists of administration of digoxin specific antibodies that bind either digoxin or digitoxin molecules, rendering them unavailable for binding at receptors in the heart and other parts of the body.[163–166] The antibodies bind intravascular digoxin and also diffuse into interstitial spaces to bind free digoxin. As the extracellular free digoxin concentration decreases, free intracellular digoxin diffuses into extracellular fluid and becomes available to be bound to the anti-digoxin antibodies. A concentration gradient is thus created that promotes release of digoxin from binding sites. Ultimately, the digitalis-antibody complex is excreted in the urine. The official name of this product is digoxin immune Fab, ovine (Digibind).

The fragment of antigen binding (Fab) section of an immunoglobulin allows the antibody to recognize and bind to an antigen, resulting in neutralization of that antigen. Digoxin immune Fab is smaller in size than the whole immunoglobulin and has a large volume of distribution, allowing for rapid distribution into interstitial spaces where much of the drug (digoxin) to be neutralized is located. Digoxin immune Fab provides a less immunogenic product than the whole immunoglobulin and is rapid acting and easily removed from the body by glomerular filtration.

The use of digoxin Fab products currently is restricted to potentially life-threatening intoxications (severe arrhythmias or hyperkalemia) that are either refractory to more conservative therapy or associated with extremely high serum concentrations. The major reason for this approach is the high cost of the therapy and a relative lack of experience with the product to fully appreciate possible side effects. The primary indication is for digoxin, but the product also is effective in binding of digitoxin.

Digoxin immune Fab is supplied in 40 mg vials of lyophilized powder which, after reconstitution with 4 mL of sterile water for injection, will bind approximately 0.6 mg of digoxin or digitoxin. The actual dose administered varies according to the estimated amount of digitalis glycoside in the body.[167] For digoxin, the amount of drug in the body can be estimated by the formula:

$$\text{Body Load in mg} = 5.6(\text{SDC})(\text{Weight in kg})/1000$$

where 5.6 is the volume of distribution of digoxin in L/kg. An oral absorption of approximately 80% for digoxin is assumed. From this estimate, the total number of vials required for neutralization is calculated by dividing the total body load by 0.6 mg/vial. Patients with renal failure may have a smaller volume of distribution of digoxin and thus have higher serum concentrations for any given dose. For patients toxic from digitoxin, a volume of distribution of 0.56 L/kg is substituted for the 5.6 L/kg used for digoxin. In cases of extremely large single dose ingestions where the results of digoxin or digitoxin serum concentrations are not available, an empiric dose of 400 mg (10 vials) may be given to an adult. An

additional 400 mg can be given if needed. For patients with toxicity during chronic therapy, 240 mg (6 vials) is adequate to treat most adults, while 40 mg (1 vial) is appropriate for children weighing under 20 kg. The antibody usually is administered intravenously over 30 minutes, but it can be given more rapidly if the patient is in acute distress. It is recommended that the drug be infused through a 0.22 micron filter. Efficacy and safety is the same in children as in adults.[168]

Generally, clinical improvement in the signs and symptoms of the digitalis intoxication occur within 30 minutes of antibody administration, with complete reversal of symptoms in four hours. If, after several hours, toxicity has not been adequately reversed or symptoms reappear, an additional dose may be given. In patients with renal insufficiency, the digitalis-antibody complex may be retained in the body for prolonged periods of time. If retained long enough, Fab fragments may be degraded by the reticuloendothelial system, releasing active digitalis glycosides back into the circulation and necessitating retreatment.

Immediately following treatment with digoxin-specific Fab, the active (free or unbound) digitalis concentration decreases to nearly undetectable levels, but the total (free plus antibody-bound) digoxin concentration increases. In less than one hour, the total concentration may increase by 10- to 20-fold; peaking in about ten hours at concentrations often exceeding several hundred ng/mL. The monitoring of serum digoxin and digitoxin levels following treatment with Digibind is of no value because most clinical laboratories only measure "total" serum concentrations of digitalis glycosides, a composite of both "free" and bound (to protein or Fab) drug.[167,169–171] As the antibody complexes with the digitalis glycosides, the latter become unavailable to other areas of the body and result in an extremely high total digitalis glycoside concentration in the serum. The Fab fragment-digitalis complex is then excreted via the kidneys. It may take several days before all of the complex is removed, allowing routine digitalis assays to once again become reliable.[172] In one study of patients with varying degrees of renal function, the half-life of the initial phase of total digoxin decline was 11.6 hours and the half-life of the second, or terminal, elimination phase was 118 ± 57 hours. Free digoxin levels rebound to a mean maximum free digoxin concentration of 1.7 ± 1.3 mmol/L in 77 ± 46 hours, but are delayed to a greater extent in anephric patients.[173] As long as antibodies remain in the system, further therapy with digitalis preparations is compromised because of binding of any new doses. Thus, monitoring of free concentrations is necessary.

Side effects to digoxin-specific Fab antibodies are uncommon, but several cautions must be heeded.[174] Congestive heart failure or atrial fibrillation may be precipitated by the removal of the pharmacologic effects of the digitalis glycoside. Similarly, as Na^+-K^+ ATPase enzyme activity is restored, hypokalemia may develop. Serum potassium concentrations must be monitored frequently for the first several hours after Fab administration since potassium levels can drop precipitously as potassium shifts back into cells. This may require immediate potassium supplementation.

The incidence of hypersensitivity or other allergic reactions after Fab administration is rare, but the risk after repeated ingestions is unknown.[174] Skin testing according to the directions in the digoxin immune Fab package insert[175] should be followed in high-risk individuals, especially in patients with known allergies to sheep serum or in whom digoxin-specific Fab has been administered previously. If an accelerated allergic reaction occurs, the drug infusion should be discontinued and appropriate therapy initiated, including antihistamines, corticosteroids, and airway management. Epinephrine should be used cautiously in patients with arrhythmias.

Pediatric Dosing

26. H.H., a 3-year-old female with a congenital heart defect, is displaying increased symptoms of CHF. She is awaiting surgery for repair of a ventricular septal defect and a damaged aortic valve. In the meantime, she is to be placed on digoxin therapy. All laboratory values, including renal function and electrolytes, are within normal limits. She weighs 28 pounds (12.7 kg). Should digoxin dosing for H.H. be formulated using the same guidelines as for an adult? What loading dose and maintenance dose should H.H. be given?

While many of the general principles that apply to use of digoxin in adults apply to children, certain practical considerations and changes in pharmacokinetic parameters must be considered.[161] Dosing in children is complicated by rapid changes in body size and tissue distribution, gastrointestinal motility, and maturation of the liver and kidney.

Most children are unable to swallow conventional tablets or capsules and must be given liquid dosage forms. Fortunately, digoxin is available as an elixir. Although the pediatric population does not differ significantly from adults in their ability to absorb digoxin, large individual variability is noted and one must not forget that the elixir may be more bioavailable than the tablets.

An important difference is noted between children and adults in regard to tissue uptake and volume of distribution of digoxin. As noted previously, the average adult has a steady-state digoxin Vd of 6.7 L/kg. Greater variability is seen in very young to older children with Vd reported to be 7.5, 16.3, and 16.1 L/kg in neonates, 11-month-old infants, and children, respectively.[161] Children may have slightly higher digoxin protein binding than adults, but neither group has a high enough percentage bound (i.e., <50%) to significantly affect tissue concentrations of the drug.

As in adults, clearance and half-life of digoxin in children are highly dependent upon renal function and to a lesser degree upon metabolism and biliary excretion. Elimination data in children are limited by the small number of available reports and the absence of studies in healthy pediatric subjects; nonetheless, a few generalizations can be made. Total body clearance is markedly impaired in premature and full-term neonates (with t½ ranging from 61 to 170 hours). Older children and adolescents appear to clear the drug at approximately the same rate as adults. These findings are consistent with poorly developed renal function in premature or very young newborns, but the kidney becomes highly functional by one month of life and function approaches that of an adult by one year of age.

From the above data, one can surmise that after the first year of life and through early childhood, children will need a *larger* dose on a per kilogram basis than adults. This is based upon a larger apparent volume of distribution, not altered drug clearance. While no clear consensus is available on dosing of digoxin in children, Bendayan and McKenzie offer the following guidelines:[161] premature and full-term neonates should be digitalized with 0.01 to 0.03 mg/kg intravenously; infants should be given 0.04 to 0.05 mg/kg orally. For maintenance, the premature neonate can be given 0.001 to 0.009 mg/kg/day, neonates 0.010 mg/kg/day, and infants (1 month to 2 years) 0.015 to 0.025 mg/kg/day. Above age two, the loading dose is 0.05 mg/kg orally followed by a daily maintenance dose of 0.01 to 0.015 mg/kg. As in adults, doses are adjusted based upon clinical signs, renal function, and serum levels.

For H.H., an argument can be made for starting a maintenance dose without a loading dose since she is in no acute distress. If a loading dose is required, an oral elixir could be used at 0.05 mg/kg (0.6 to 0.65 mg), split into two doses. Maintenance would be started at 0.01 mg/kg or approximately 0.125 mg/day. These doses are surprisingly large and reflect the large volume of distribution in children.

Dosing in Renal Failure

27. Loading Dose. **R.D. is an 84-year-old female admitted to the hospital in acute distress with breathlessness, markedly distended neck veins, and in atrial fibrillation. She has been an insulin-dependent diabetic for 35 years and has had progressively deteriorating renal function which has never required hemodialysis. She has no previous history of cardiovascular disease. Her only home medication is 30 units/day NPH insulin. Pertinent admitting laboratory values and physical examination reveal: Na 140 mEq/L; K 5.1 mEq/L; Cl 101 mEq/L; bicarbonate 24 mEq/L; glucose (fasting) 180 mg/dL; BUN 48 mg/dL; creatinine 3.8 mg/dL; weight 82 kg; height 5′6″; pulse 118 beats/min and irregular.**

She is given furosemide 80 mg IV and 20 mEq of potassium chloride with each dose of furosemide. Because of her distress, it is decided to give her an IV loading dose of digoxin. Calculate the loading dose for R.D. Do any alterations have to be made in the loading dose because of her decreased renal function?
[SI units: Na 140 mmol/L; Cl 101 mmol/L; bicarbonate 24 mmol/L; glucose 9.99 mmol/L; BUN 17.5 mmol UREA; creatinine 335.92 μmol/l]

Theoretically, loading doses for renally excreted drugs do not have to be altered in renal failure because a loading dose only fills up the body tissue stores and is independent of elimination. However, the volume of distribution for digoxin may vary substantially in patients with renal failure (Cl_{Cr} <25 mL/minute). Koup et al.[108] observed volumes of distribution ranging from 195 to 489 L/1.73 m² in seven renal failure patients. Reuning et al.[28] calculated volumes of distribution for renal failure patients reported in the literature and found a range of 230 to 380 L/1.78 m², 30% to 50% *less* than that observed in subjects with normal renal function. An average value for Vd of 330 L/70 kg or 4.7 L/kg in renal failure patients may be used.

As the volume of distribution decreases, the theoretical loading dose also decreases. Unfortunately, it is usually not possible to know what a given patient's volume of distribution is until the drug has already been administered and serum levels are measured. A report of 22 renal failure patients showed no toxicity using an intravenous digoxin loading dose of 0.01 mg/kg.[176]

Using the adjusted value for Vd, we can use a modification of Equation 15.3 (Question 14) for calculating a loading dose for R.D.:

$$\text{IV Loading Dose} = (Vd)(Cp) \qquad Eq\ 15.13$$

We will again assume a desired Cp of 1.5 ng/mL. In calculating Vd, we must correct R.D.'s weight to ideal body weight (IBW) since she is obese (82 kg).

$$\text{IBW (Males)} = 50\ kg + 2.3\ kg/\text{Inches Over 5 Feet} \qquad Eq\ 15.14$$

$$\text{IBW (Females)} = 45.5\ kg + 2.3\ kg/\text{Inches Over 5 Feet} \qquad Eq\ 15.15$$

For R.D.:

$$\text{IBW} = 45.5\ kg + 2.3\ kg\ (6\ Feet)$$

$$= 59.3\ kg$$

Therefore, her loading dose will be:

$$\text{IV LD} = (Vd)(Cp)$$

$$= (4.7\ L/kg)(59.3\ kg)(1.5\ ng/mL)$$

$$= 418,000\ ng\ or\ 418\ \mu g$$

$$\approx 0.4\ mg$$

This loading dose is considerably smaller than that calculated in Question 13. This is because we assumed a smaller volume of distribution and because the dose is given intravenously, not orally. She should be given 0.4 mg intravenously to start and then reassessed at six to eight hours. If at this time she is still in atrial fibrillation, an extra 0.125 mg could be given safely.

28. Maintenance Dose. Calculate a maintenance dose for R.D.

The principles for calculating a maintenance dose are the same as those used in Question 15. The major difference is that the effect of R.D.'s age and renal function on digoxin clearance must be taken into account. Both of these factors will slow drug elimination necessitating a reduced maintenance dose. Rather than repeating all of the methods described in Question 15, only the method of Scheiner (Equations 15.6 to 15.8) will be used. The reader is encouraged to apply the patient data to the method of Jelliffe (Equations 15.1, 15.10, 15.11) as well.

The first step is to make an estimate of the patient's creatinine clearance. While several methods are available, we will use the method of Cockcroft and Gault:[177]

$$Cl_{Cr} \text{ (Males)} = \frac{IBW \ (140 - Age)}{72 \ S_{Cr}}$$

$$Cl_{Cr} \text{ (Females)} = 0.85 \ Cl_{Cr} \text{ (Males)} \qquad Eq \ 15.16$$

For R.D.:

$$Cl_{Cr} = \frac{0.85 \ (59.3 \ kg)(140 - 84)}{72 \ (3.8 \ mg/dL)}$$

$$= 10.32 \ mL/min$$

As can be seen, the creatinine clearance is markedly depressed. In addition, R.D.'s CHF is poorly controlled. Therefore, digoxin clearance will be reduced substantially. Thus, the equation for digoxin clearance in severe CHF will be used:

$$Cl_{Digoxin} = 0.88 \ (Cl_{Cr}) + 23 \ mL/min$$

$$= 0.88 \ (10.3 \ mL/min) + 23 \ mL/min$$

$$= 33 \ mL/min$$

$$= 47.5 \ L/day$$

With digoxin clearance known, the maintenance dose is calculated:

$$MD = \frac{(Cl_{Digoxin})(Cpss \ ave)(\tau)}{F}$$

$$= \frac{(47.5 \ L/day)(1.5 \ ng/mL)(1 \ Day)}{0.75}$$

$$= 95,000 \ ng/day \ or \ 95 \ \mu g/day$$

$$= 0.95 \ mg/day$$

This is obviously a difficult dose to administer. It can be given in one of several ways: 0.125 mg every day or 0.125 every day for 6 days each week using tablets or 0.1 mg/day using a pediatric elixir or digoxin capsules. Capsules and elixir also may be absorbed better than the tablets.

Vasodilator Therapy

29. L.M., a 50-year-old man, was admitted with severe, progressive, and debilitating symptoms of CHF. His history was significant in that his father and two brothers succumbed to heart attacks shortly after the age of 40. L.M. had a 12-year history of CHF which was symptomatic despite treatment with full therapeutic doses of digoxin and furosemide. He had no history of hypertension, but previous studies suggested a diagnosis of cardiomyopathy. Over the previous 8 months, L.M.'s DOE became progressively worse, and for the month before admission he was confined to bed because of extreme fatigue. He awoke once or twice nightly with PND.

Physical examination revealed a dyspneic, cyanotic male in obvious distress, but with no complaints of chest pain. The blood pressure was 100/66 mm Hg and his pulse was 105 beats/min. Marked JVD, bilateral rales, hepatomegaly, and 3+ peripheral edema also were observed. Chest x-ray revealed marked cardiomegaly and pulmonary congestion. L.M. was admitted to the Cardiac Care Unit (CCU) where a Swan-Ganz catheter was passed from an antecubital vein to the pulmonary artery. Before therapy, L.M.'s PCWP was 27 mm Hg (Normal: 5–12) and his cardiac index (CI) was 1.9 L/min/m² (Normal: 2.7–4.3). IV nitroprusside was initiated at a dose of 16 µg/min and eventually increased to 200 µg/min. At this dose, L.M.'s PCWP decreased to 15 mm Hg and his CI increased to 2.5 L/min/m². He was eventually discharged on digoxin 0.375 mg/day, furosemide 80 mg BID, spironolactone 50 mg BID, hydralazine 75 mg QID, and isosorbide dinitrate 40 mg Q 6 hr. What was the importance of measuring a PCWP and CI in L.M.? What was the rationale for nitroprusside therapy?

The reader who is unfamiliar with the hemodynamic monitoring parameters presented in this question (e.g., Swan-Ganz catheterization, PCWP, and CI) should refer to Chapter 18: Intensive Care Therapeutics for a more thorough review of principles. L.M.'s PCWP is high and his cardiac index is low reflecting pulmonary vascular congestion (elevated preload) and poor cardiac output. The objective of therapy is to decrease the PCWP and increase the stroke volume or cardiac output in such patients.

Mechanism of Action and Rationale for Use

Vasodilating drugs that decrease afterload and/or preload are becoming increasingly more important in the therapy of severe CHF. (See Table 15.9.) Three general categories of vasodilators are described: those drugs that primarily dilate arterial vessels and in so doing decrease the afterload or impedance to left ventricular afterflow (e.g., hydralazine and the dihydropyridine class of calcium channel blockers); those drugs that primarily dilate venous vessels, thereby increasing venous capacity and decreasing venous return (preload) to the heart (e.g., nitrates); and those with mixed arterial and venous effects (e.g., nitroprusside and ACE inhibitors).

Vasodilators initially were used only in patients who continued to be symptomatic after maximal doses of diuretics and digitalis. They now are used frequently early in therapy, especially by those physicians who are skeptical of digoxin (see Question 6). In particular, ACE inhibitors are recommended as first line therapy in the AHCPR Guideline for CHF.[19]

The benefits gained from afterload reduction generally outweigh those from preload reduction, but combined afterload and preload reduction is often beneficial.[178,179] Decreased peripheral vascular resistance from arterial vasodilation potentially may cause hypotension and a reflex increase in heart rate. However, this is infrequently seen in patients with CHF since any decrease in blood pressure is counterbalanced by a comparable increase in cardiac output. Excessive preload reduction can cause postural hypotension from peripheral pooling of blood in the lower extremities and deficient ventricular filling. In the latter instance, less blood is available for ventricular ejection. The overall response in any given patient is determined by their baseline arterial and venous pressure, volume status, and renal function.

Nitroprusside

Nitroprusside dilates both arterial and venous vessels; therefore, it has the theoretical advantage of decreasing both afterload and preload. Its major disadvantages are: it must be given by continuous intravenous infusion; it is unstable in the presence of heat and light after reconstitution, and it occasionally causes a profound hypotension that will decrease cardiac output.

Table 15.9		Comparative Pharmacology of Unloading Agents[a],[b]
Drug	**Dose**	**Comments**
Predominantly Afterload Reduction (Arterial Dilators)		$\downarrow$ SVR; $\uparrow$ CO
Direct Vasodilators (oral)		
Hydralazine	*Start:* 12.5–25 mg *Maintenance:* 25–100 mg Q 6–8 hr	Concurrent diuretics to block Na^+ retention; less reflex tachycardia than when treating hypertension
Minoxidil	*Start:* 2.5–5 mg *Maintenance:* 5–20 mg Q 8–12 hr	Same as Hydralazine
Calcium Channel Blockers (oral)		
Amlodipine	2.5–10 mg Q 24 hr	Amlodipine, isradipine, nifedipine most vasodilating
Diltiazem[c]	30–90 mg Q 6–8 hr; 60–180 mg SR Q 12–24 hr	Concern over negative inotropic effect (V>D>N>A,F)[d]
Felodipine	5–20 mg Q 12–24 hr (*max:* 20 mg/day)	May $\uparrow$ digoxin levels (V>D>N) [d]
Nifedipine	10–40 mg Q 6–8 hr; 40–120 mg SR QD	
Verapamil[c]	40–60 mg Q 6–8 hr; 120–240 mg SR Q 12–24 hr	
Predominantly Preload Reduction (Venous Dilators)		$\downarrow$ PCWP and left ventricular filling pressure
Nitrates (NTG)		
IV[d]	5 µg/min; titrate to effect (*max:* 200 µg/min)	
SR	6.5–9 mg Q 8–12 hr PO	6–8 hr duration
Ointment	½″–2″ Q 4–8 hr	3–6 hr duration
Transdermal	5–40 mg/day (remove at night)	Concern over tolerance with SR and transdermal
Isosorbide		
SL	5–20 mg Q 3–6 hr	Short-acting (1–3 hr)
Tablets PO	10–80 mg Q 4–6 hr	4–6 hr duration
SR	20–120 mg Q 6–8 hr	6–8 hr duration
Mixed Afterload and Preload Reduction		
Nitroprusside	*Start:* 5–20 µg/min *Titrate:* 300–800 µg/min	Parenteral only
ACE Inhibitors		Mild diuretic properties also. Well documented long-term efficacy, but delayed onset
Benazepril	*Start:* 2–5 mg. *Maintenance:* 5–20 mg Q 24 hr	
Captopril	*Start:* 6.25–12.5 mg *Maintenance:* 12.5–75 mg Q 8 hr	Captopril may be fastest onset since not converted to active metabolite
Enalapril	*Start:* 2.5–5 mg *Maintenance:* 10–40 mg Q 12–24 hr	
Lisinopril	*Start:* 2.5–5 mg QD *Maintenance:* 5–40 mg	
Ramipril	*Start:* 1.25–2.5 mg Q 12 hr *Maintenance:* 2.5–10 mg Q 12 hr	

[a] See Chapter 10: Essential Hypertension and Chapter 13: Ischemic Heart Disease for side effects. On balance, the benefits of afterload reduction exceed those of preload reductions.

[b] ACE = Angiotensin-converting enzyme; CO = Cardiac output; IV = Intravenous; Na = Sodium; NTG = Nitrogen; PCWP = Pulmonary capillary wedge pressure; PO = Oral; SL = Sublingual; SR = Sustained release; SVR = Systemic vascular resistance.

[c] Diltiazem and verapamil only for patients with supraventricular arrhythmias or primarily diastolic CHF.

[d] A = Amlodipine; D = Diltiazem; F = Felodipine; N = Nifedipine; V = Verapamil.

[e] May bind to plastic IV bags and many plastic tubing sets.

Patients should be initiated on small doses of nitroprusside (6 to 20 µg/minute) which are increased slowly to a maximum of 300 to 800 µg/minute until a decrease in the PCWP or arterial pressure is observed. When stopping nitroprusside therapy, a slow taper is recommended since a rebound increase in CHF has been observed 10 to 30 minutes after drug withdrawal.[180] (For a more thorough discussion of nitroprusside use, see Chapters 17: Hypertensive Emergencies and 18: Intensive Care Therapeutics.)

30. What other parenteral vasodilators can be used to treat CHF refractory to nitroprusside?

L.M. responded well to nitroprusside and needed no other therapy. However, other parenteral products can be tried if nitroprusside fails.

Intravenous Nitroglycerin (NTG)

Nitroglycerin primarily affects the venous capacitance vessels with a slight effect on the arterial bed. The pulmonary capillary wedge pressure or left ventricular filling pressure (preload) is re-duced in patients with a PCWP greater than 18 mm Hg. However, because it may only slightly decrease or have no effect on afterload, cardiac output may remain unchanged or increase only slightly. Nitroglycerin actually may decrease cardiac output in some patients by reducing the left ventricular filling pressure to less than 15 mm Hg. Overall, nitroglycerin is most useful in those patients whose primary problem is one of pulmonary congestion with a high preload. (See Chapters 14: Myocardial Infarction and 18: Intensive Care Therapeutics for more information on dosing and side effects of intravenous nitroglycerin.)

31. Once L.M. was controlled with nitroprusside therapy, he was placed on hydralazine and isosorbide dinitrate. Why were hydralazine and isosorbide used? What other forms of nitrates can be used in place of the isosorbide? Is combination therapy rational?

Hydralazine

Hydralazine is a direct-acting smooth muscle relaxant with significant arteriolar dilating effects in the kidneys and limbs. It has essentially no effect on the venous system or hepatic blood flow. Because its predominate action is as an arteriolar dilator, hydralazine is the prototype afterload reducing agent. Decreasing aortic impedance (afterload) is of little benefit in a normal or minimally diseased heart, but it may greatly improve severely compromised left ventricular function. Systemic vascular resistance is decreased predictably and this, in turn, increases cardiac output (cardiac index).[5,6,12,13,181,182]

Fortunately, the reflex tachycardia and hypotension that frequently accompany hydralazine therapy when used in treating hypertension are minimal or absent when the drug is used to treat CHF. Increased cardiac output overrides vasodilatory effects in the latter instance. However, in patients with end-stage cardiomyopathy, significant hypotension still can occur if the heart is unable to respond appropriately. Another beneficial response to hydralazine is reduction of pulmonary vascular resistance in patients with severe pulmonary hypertension. This pulmonary arteriolar dilating effect of hydralazine is generally less beneficial than the venodilating effects of drugs such as nitrates and nitroprusside. Since hydralazine is devoid of venous dilating properties, central venous pressure and pulmonary wedge capillary pressure are unchanged.[12,13,181,182]

Several investigators have demonstrated both short-term and long-term benefit from the use of oral hydralazine in the treatment of CHF.[12,183,184] The effect of a single dose occurs in about 30 minutes and lasts up to six hours. Unfortunately, larger doses than typically used for the treatment of hypertension may be required. The average maintenance dose is 200 to 400 mg/day (50 to 100 mg Q 6 hr). L.M. required 75 mg four times a day. Comprehensive reviews by Mulrow conclude that hydralazine used as monotherapy is not associated with long-term improvement in functional status.[181,185] However, as discussed in subsequent cases, combination therapy of hydralazine with either nitrates or ACE inhibitors is highly effective.

Although tachyphylaxis generally is not thought to be a significant problem with prolonged courses of hydralazine, some patients require increased diuretic doses to counteract hydralazine-induced fluid retention.[183,184] This latter response reflects activation of the renin-angiotensin system following vasodilation of the renal vasculature. Of greater concern is a report of 11 patients whose apparent resistance to chronic hydralazine therapy was unresponsive to diuretics, but responsive to nitroprusside.[186] The investigators speculate that a defect in receptor activity to hydralazine in the vessel wall may be involved. Other side effects accompanying hydralazine include transient nausea during the first few days of therapy; headache, flushing, or tachycardia; and a lupus syndrome associated with prolonged, high doses. (See Chapter 10: Essential Hypertension for a more detailed discussion of hydralazine side effects and dosing.)

Oral and Topical Nitrates

Nitrates have complementary effects to those of hydralazine.[5,6,12,13,178,182] They primarily dilate venous capacitance vessels, with minimal effects on selected arterial beds (coronary and pulmonary arteries). Venous dilation reduces preload resulting in marked reductions in pulmonary capillary wedge pressure and right atrial pressure. The lack of significant arterial dilation accounts for the observations that systemic vascular resistance is minimally reduced and cardiac output remains unchanged. Nitrate monotherapy is indicated for CHF patients with valvular defects such as mitral or aortic regurgitation. In these patients, reduction of the ventricular filling pressure reduces left ventricular congestion.

Sublingual NTG. Various forms of nitrates have been used. Sublingual administration of NTG is limited by its brief hemodynamic effects which last for 20 to 60 minutes. Sustained-release capsular forms of nitroglycerin produce a prolonged (4 to 8 hours) response when used in the treatment of angina if the dose exceeds 6.5 mg; however, little information is available on their use in CHF.

NTG Ointment. More attention has been given to NTG ointment which also has prolonged hemodynamic effects (3 to 5 hours). Like the other nitrates, it decreases pulmonary and systemic venous pressures and the LVFP, but it has a variable effect on cardiac output. An apparent lack of response in some patients may be related to poor peripheral circulation and poor absorption of NTG from the ointment.[187] The dose may be titrated using one to four inches of 2% NTG applied to the skin of the chest, back, or thigh. Effects should be seen within 15 to 30 minutes. If a response is not observed after 30 minutes, another application can be made. The site of application should be rotated to decrease inflammatory reactions. One advantage of NTG ointment over oral forms of nitrates is that it can be wiped off if the patient becomes hypotensive (systolic BP <100 mg Hg) or develops tachycardia (HR >100 beats/minute) or severe headaches. This makes the ointment an ideal agent for use in the hospital. It is less desirable for outpatient use.

Transdermal NTG. An innovative approach to nitroglycerin administration is transdermal patch systems (Nitrodisc, Nitro-Dur, Transderm-Nitro, Minitran). Topical application of these systems is said to provide 24 hours of continuous cutaneous absorption with more convenience and less mess than NTG ointment. While the majority of published data on these dose forms are in patients with angina, there are several reports on their use in CHF. The initial enthusiasm for transdermal NTG has been tempered by the suggestion that tolerance develops quickly resulting in a benefit for much less than 24 hours following patch application.[188] Considerable debate has arisen over this topic.[189–191] Some reviewers have suggested abandoning this form of therapy, while others argue that the studies showing negative benefit were flawed. Others have suggested that removal of the patch during the night leads to restoration of response the following day. Several investigators have shown that while the antianginal effects of NTG may be attenuated with chronic therapy, the beneficial preload reducing properties for CHF are more sustained. However, large doses (20 to 40 mg/24 hours) may be required, necessitating the use of several patches per day and resulting in significant expense to the patient. (See Chapter 13: Ischemic Heart Disease for a more detailed discussion on the application and controversy surrounding NTG ointment and transdermal patches.)

Isosorbide Dinitrate. Because sublingual nitroglycerin has a short duration of response, more attention has been focused on sublingual and oral isosorbide dinitrate. Sublingual isosorbide is well absorbed and does not undergo first-pass metabolism. Its onset is rapid ($\approx$5 minutes), but its effects are relatively short (1 to 3 hours). The usual starting dose is 5 mg every four to six hours, but doses may be titrated to 20 mg or more every four to six hours. These larger doses are associated with longer beneficial effects ($\approx$3 hours), but also a high frequency of intolerable headaches and hypotension. Previous claims of a poor response to orally administered isosorbide due to a large first-pass metabolic effect have been refuted.[180–181] Large oral doses overwhelm the metabolic capacity of the liver and produce beneficial effects. Oral isosorbide has a slow onset (15 to 30 minutes), but the duration of activity is slightly longer than that associated with sublingual administration (4 to 6 hours). Oral doses of 5 mg are probably ineffective; 10 mg is the smallest effective starting dose with further titration to doses as high as 20 to 80 mg every four to six hours. The best dose for both sublingual and oral nitrates is that which provides the desired beneficial effect with the least side effects.

Hydralazine/Nitrate Combination

Clinical experience has shown that the combination of an arterial dilator with a venous dilator produces additive and complimentary effects.[12,13,178,179,182] Roth and colleagues conducted a study to differentiate the effects of hydralazine and nitroglycerin when used alone and in combination in patients with congestive heart failure secondary to mitral valve disease.[192] Hydralazine caused a more pronounced decrease in systemic vascular resistance and a greater increase in stroke volume and cardiac index than did nitroglycerin. Nitroglycerin had a superior effect on lowering pulmonary artery wedge pressure. The combination produced a positive additive benefit by lowering systemic vascular resistance and increasing cardiac index to a greater degree than with hydralazine alone and by lowering pulmonary artery wedge pressure more than with nitroglycerin alone. The additive effects were seen both at rest and during exercise.

By reducing afterload and preload simultaneously, cardiac output is increased through lowered systemic vascular resistance while ventricular congestion is relieved through decreased venous return. With combination therapy, cardiac output is greater for any given level of ventricular filling pressure. Generally, the use of the two drugs together is not accompanied by reflex tachycardia or hypotension, but one must be careful not to compromise coronary blood flow in patients with coexistent angina.

Perhaps the most compelling argument for the use of combination hydralazine/nitrate vasodilator therapy comes from the results of the two Veterans Administration Cooperative Studies (V-HeFT I and V-HeFT II).[179,182] As discussed in more detail in Questions 35 and 36, these two studies not only confirmed symptomatic relief and improved exercise tolerance with combination therapy, but they also showed improved survival.

In summary, nitrates alone may be indicated for those patients with signs and symptoms of isolated pulmonary and venous congestion (i.e., dyspnea, increased pulmonary pressure, neck vein distension, edema). Conversely, use of an arterial dilator may be more appropriate in a patient with high systemic vascular resistance, low cardiac output, and normal pulmonary capillary wedge pressure. The majority of patients, like L.M., exhibit symptoms of decreased cardiac output and elevated venous pressure, making combination therapy the most attractive option.

Prazosin

32. Rather than using combination therapy of hydralazine and a nitrate, would it not be easier to use a single drug that has both preload and afterload reducing properties? What drug would you recommend?

Prazosin, a postsynaptic, α_1-adenoreceptor blocker, was previously hailed as the ideal agent for CHF because it dilates both venous and arterial beds; therefore, it decreases LVFP (preload) as well as arterial impedance (afterload).[12,13] These properties predict that prazosin will be less likely to cause reflex tachycardia than hydralazine since α_2 presynaptic feedback receptors are left intact (see Chapter 10: Essential Hypertension). The initial enthusiasm for prazosin has been tempered by the observation of decreased response (tachyphylaxis) with chronic dosing,[193] although other clinicians have observed beneficial effects for two weeks or more.[194] In some cases, responsiveness to prazosin can be restored by adding a larger dose of diuretic, doubling the dose of prazosin, or withdrawing the drug temporarily and restarting it after several days.[195] In other cases, prazosin appears to lose its effectiveness completely. Mechanisms for tolerance include drug-induced sodium retention, accumulation of norepinephrine in the synaptic cleft which overcomes the α_1 blockade, and plasma renin accumulation leading to activation of angiotensin.[13,195,196] More sig-

nificantly, the V-HeFT I Study[179] failed to show a significant benefit on mortality reduction by prazosin as compared to placebo. For this reason, and because of the increasing popularity of ACE inhibitors (see Questions 6 and 33 to 35), the use of prazosin for CHF has been abandoned.

Angiotensin-Converting Enzyme (ACE) Inhibitors

33. A.B., a 62-year-old male, was admitted to the CCU with a 2-day history of breathlessness causing him to sleep upright in a chair and preventing him from walking to the bathroom. Physical examination showed 4+ pitting edema of the legs, scrotal and sacral edema, and markedly distended neck veins. He had a CVP of 26 mm Hg. Urine output was less than 20 mL/hr, BUN was 48 mg/dL, SrCr was 2.0 mg/dL, and serum potassium was 3.2 mEq/L. Home medications which had been faithfully administered by his wife included digoxin 0.25 mg/day, furosemide 240 mg/day, KCl 40 mEq/day, hydralazine 100 mg Q 6 hr, and isosorbide dinitrate 20 mg Q 6 hr.

A 100 mg IV bolus of furosemide in the emergency room resulted in a urine output of 600 mL over two hours, but with a subsequent rise of his BUN to 65 mg/dL. Finally, A.B. was begun on captopril 12.5 TID. Within 2 days, A.B.'s breathing improved, his CVP was down to 16 mm Hg, and he was diuresing briskly. He was discharged 1 week later with mild SOB on exertion, 2+ ankle edema, and improved renal function. Discharge medications included furosemide 120 mg/day, captopril 50 mg TID, and isosorbide dinitrate 20 mg Q 6 hr. What is the role of captopril in the treatment of CHF? Would other ACE inhibitors offer any advantages over captopril? [SI units: BUN 17.14 and 23.21, respectively; SrCr 176.9 µmol/L; K 3.2 mmol/L]

Mechanism of Action. The enzyme *renin* is released by the kidney when renal perfusion pressure is decreased. Renin acts to convert a substrate present in the blood called *angiotensinogen* into the inactive decapeptide, *angiotensin I*. Angiotensin I is further metabolized to the active decapeptide, *angiotensin II*, under the influence of circulating *angiotensin-converting enzyme*. Angiotensin II is a potent vasoconstrictor and also stimulates aldosterone release by the adrenals. It also may directly stimulate norepinephrine release. Activation of the renin-angiotensin-aldosterone system and high circulating levels of norepinephrine contribute greatly to the increase in systemic vascular resistance seen in severe cardiac failure. (See Figure 15.1.)

Captopril (Capoten) and all of the other ACE inhibitors listed in Table 15.9 inhibit the angiotensin-converting enzyme (also called kinase II), thereby reducing the activation of angiotensin II. The converting enzyme also is responsible for degradation of bradykinin and other vasodilatory substances. Thus, the beneficial effects of these drugs may be partially related to the accumulation of vasodilatory kinins or prostaglandins. Decreased circulating levels of norepinephrine and vasopressin also have been noted following captopril administration.[51-53,197] The exact mechanism of action in CHF remains to be elucidated since patients respond irrespective of their baseline plasma renin, bradykinin, or norepinephrine concentrations.

The ACE inhibitors consistently lower pulmonary capillary wedge pressure and systemic vascular resistance while at the same time increasing cardiac index. Thus, they are effective as both preload and afterload reducers. Some studies found the increase in cardiac index following captopril is less than that following hydralazine or prazosin,[197] but other investigators found the opposite result.[198,199] All investigations are consistent in finding an additive effect with combined ACE inhibitors and hydralazine therapy. Captopril's arterial vasodilatory effect is relatively selective for the renal vasculature resulting in increased renal blood flow and no adverse effects on the GFR. The beneficial effects on renal blood flow coupled with the drug's indirect inhibition of aldosterone lead to a mild diuretic response, a distinct benefit over other vasodilator compounds such as hydralazine and prazosin. Initial doses of captopril may be associated with bradycardia. If cardiac output does not increase immediately, excessive hypotension may result.

Whereas hemodynamic tolerance develops with the use of other drugs, the response to ACE inhibitors actually becomes more pronounced with time. Overall, tolerance to captopril develops in less than 20% of patients; the benefit at three months is often greater than that seen at two to four weeks.[197-200] The reasons for this delayed response may be related to the diuretic effects discussed above plus slow reversal of the vasoconstrictive effects of angiotensin, catecholamines, and vasopressin.

Captopril Dosing. Continued experience with captopril has led to a better understanding of dose-response relationships and more rational therapy. Single-dose studies suggested that large doses (25 to 150 mg) were needed for maximal improvement of CHF symptoms. Patients often were started on 25 mg every eight hours and quickly titrated to 150 to 300 mg/day. It now appears appropriate to start patients on doses as low as 6.25 to 12.5 mg every 8 to 12 hours for a few days and then titrate to the desired symptomatic and objective responses. This conservative dosing approach minimizes the bradycardia and hypotension associated with higher doses. Complete inhibition of angiotensin-converting enzyme can be achieved with 10 to 20 mg, but larger doses prolong the duration of action. It is especially important to start with low doses in persons with renal insufficiency or a very low ejection fraction. Diuretic therapy must be monitored closely to prevent volume depletion or azotemia. ACE inhibitors are relatively contraindicated in people who are volume depleted, have severe renal impairment, or suffer from severe cardiomyopathy. These drugs are more beneficial in patients with CHF secondary to valvular disease or hypertension.

Captopril Side Effects. Captopril initially was associated with significant side effects.[197,201] Ten to fifteen percent of subjects in early studies developed skin eruptions or fever. These effects are associated primarily with higher dose (average: 683 mg/day) and are less frequent when the drug is used in lower doses (<225 mg/day). Skin reactions may be edematous, urticarial, erythematous, maculopapular, or morbilliform in nature. The fact that the rashes disappear with continued therapy in some patients suggests that they may be due to potentiation of kinin-mediated skin reactions. Transient loss of taste (ageusia), reflex tachycardia, and hypotension also are common at high doses.

Perhaps the most bothersome side effect associated with captopril is a chronic dry cough that appears within the first few days to weeks of starting the drug and persists until the drug is stopped. Various reports have shown an incidence of this cough in 3% to 15% of all patients, even those taking relatively low doses.[202-204] It is now realized that this side effect occurs with all of the ACE inhibitors, but case reports indicate a possible lower incidence with fosinopril (Monopril).[205,206]

Because aldosterone is antagonized by these drugs, hyperkalemia may be observed, especially if existing potassium therapy is not altered. This is illustrated by A.B. who was taking 40 mEq of potassium chloride daily before hospitalization and had a low serum potassium. He was discharged without a potassium supplement and a normal serum potassium level, despite an increased diuretic response.

Captopril is contraindicated in pregnancy.[207] Teratogenic effects including kidney failure, skull, and facial deformities have been reported when taken during the second or third trimester of pregnancy. Risk of use during the first trimester is less clear.

Proteinuria, a transient rise in serum creatinine, agranulocytosis, and fatal pancytopenia[208] also have been attributed to captopril

therapy. The kidney and marrow toxicity are minimized by keeping total daily doses below 75 mg and avoiding the use of captopril in patients with advanced renal failure. Another study also described captopril-induced inhibition of digoxin renal clearance, resulting in increased serum digoxin levels.[209] As with other digoxin interactions (e.g., verapamil, quinidine, amiodarone), the clinical significance of this interaction remains to be defined.

Other ACE inhibitors: Efficacy, Dosing, and Side Effects. Benazepril (Lotensin), enalapril (Vasotec), lisinopril (Prinivil, Zestril), quinapril (Accupril), and ramipril (Altace) have identical hemodynamic effects as captopril and are equally effective in providing symptomatic improvement of CHF.[210-218] One study showed that lisinopril actually may increase exercise capacity and ejection fraction to a greater degree than captopril.[213] At this time, there is no published information as to the effectiveness of fosinopril (Monopril) in CHF, but there is no reason to expect it to behave any differently. Of these drugs, the greatest clinical experience is with enalapril, including several trials documenting prolonged survival and superiority to the hydralazine-isosorbide combination.[5,51-53]

Lisinopril (the lysine derivative of enalaprilat) and captopril are active as the parent compound, while the other ACE inhibitors are prodrugs that require enzymatic conversion by esterolytic enzymes to active metabolites (benazeprilat, enalaprilat, ramiprilat). There is no apparent clinical consequence of these differences other than a slightly delayed onset of effect with the first dose (2 to 6 hours for captopril, 4 to 12 hours for the others). All of them, including captopril, require several weeks to elicit their full effect. The lag period is likely due to the time needed for the body to readjust various hormonal responses rather than a pharmacokinetic or pharmacologic phenomenon. All of the newer ACE inhibitors have long half-lives compared to captopril, offering the theoretical advantage of once or twice daily dosing. On the other hand, one study comparing long-term treatment with 50 mg three times daily of captopril versus 20 mg twice a day of enalapril showed more hypotensive episodes and compromised cerebral and renal function in the enalapril treated patients.[212] From this, it was postulated that the more sustained hypotensive effect of enalapril may actually be a disadvantage. One must be cautious in interpreting the results of this study or extrapolating to other long-acting ACE inhibitors since the maximal daily dose of enalapril (40 mg) given to most patients may have been excessive relative to the maximal dose of 150 mg/day of captopril. Nonetheless, many argue that it is better to initiate therapy with a low dose of a short-acting drug like captopril to assess the patient's tolerance of side effects, especially hypotension. After an initial titration phase during which the dose is raised slowly every two to three days until symptomatic relief is achieved, the switch can be made to a longer acting drug. Bioavailability and renal clearance of ACE inhibitors may be reduced in CHF necessitating caution in establishing an appropriate dose.[219] Table 15.9 provides guidelines for dosing. More complete dosing, pharmacologic, and pharmacokinetic information regarding the ACE inhibitors is found in Chapter 10: Essential Hypertension.

Another theoretical advantage of the newer ACE inhibitors over captopril is the lack of a sulfhydryl group as part of their clinical structures. The sulfhydryl group (also found in penicillamine) is associated with a high incidence of rashes, ageusia, proteinuria, and neutropenia. The clinical significance of this difference remains to be determined, especially because captopril side effects have declined since clinicians have begun to use lower doses. Benazepril, enalapril, fosinopril, and lisinopril usually are well tolerated except for chronic cough, occasional GI upset or vasodilator-induced headache, flushing, and vertigo. Cough may be more common with enalapril than with captopril and least common with fosinopril.[202-204] Hypotension and hypokalemia occur at a rate similar to captopril. All of the newer ACE inhibitors share the teratogenic risk of captopril during the second and third trimester of pregnancy. One study comparing captopril to enalapril in the treatment of hypertension described CNS sluggishness associated with enalapril as opposed to mental alertness with captopril.[220] Rash, proteinuria, and neutropenia are rare. Other serious, but rare side effects include pharyngeal edema and worsening of renal function in patients with bilateral renal artery stenosis.

34. Effects on Kidney Function. A.B. had a BUN of 48 mg/dL and an SrCr of 2.0 mg/dL when he was started on captopril. Is not the use of ACE inhibitors contraindicated in patients with renal insufficiency? Can they be used safely with diuretics in patients with renal insufficiency?

The effects of ACE inhibitors on renal blood flow and renal function are complex. As seen in Figure 15.5, glomerular filtration is optimal when intraglomerular pressure is maintained at normal pressures. The balance between afferent flow into the glomerulus and efferent flow exiting the glomerulus determines the intraglomerular pressure. A drop in afferent flow or pressure occurring as a result of hypotension, volume loss (e.g., blood loss or overdiuresis), hypoalbuminemia, decreased cardiac output (e.g., CHF), or obstructive lesions such as renal artery stenosis all may significantly lower intraglomerular pressure and lead to a loss of renal function. Similarly, long-standing hypertension can damage glomerular basement membrane capillaries and cause renal insufficiency. In the case of low pressure or low flow states, the renin-angiotensin-aldosterone system is activated to maintain intraglomerular pressure. A key factor in preserving glomerular pressure is efferent vasoconstriction mediated by angiotensin II. Increased efferent pressure helps to maintain intraglomerular pressure by impeding blood flow out of the glomerulus. When patients with low pressure states are given ACE inhibitors, the protective mechanism of efferent vasoconstriction is inhibited and renal function may significantly and rapidly worsen. Conversely, in patients with hypertensive renal disease, glomerular function actually may improve since the ACE inhibitors lower afferent pressure and help to protect the kidney. There also is evidence that ACE inhibitors may slow the progression of diabetic nephropathy independent of their effect on blood pressure.

Patients with congestive heart failure present with a complex picture.[221] By decreasing afterload and preload, cardiac output hopefully will improve, thus preserving or even enhancing renal blood flow. This is obviously the desired effect. If, however, starting ACE inhibitors leads to a rapid decrease in systemic blood pressure that is not followed by an increase in cardiac output, worsening renal function may ensue. Since there is no way to predict which event will occur, ACE inhibitor therapy needs to be started with low doses and careful monitoring of the blood pressure and renal function as dosage is increased. Diuretics are not contraindicated, but the dosage may need to be adjusted to avoid volume depletion and hypotension. These events are illustrated in A.B. When he was first diuresed, the BUN increased. Addition of an ACE inhibitor and isosorbide in combination with a furosemide led to significant clinical benefit including improved renal function. It should be noted that nonsteroidal anti-inflammatory drugs also must be used with caution since inhibition of vasodilating renal prostaglandins in patients with low afferent flow also will cause worsening renal function.[221,222]

35. Value of Combined Digoxin and Vasodilators. A.B. is not receiving digoxin. Is there value in combining digoxin with vasodilator therapy?

As discussed in Question 6, digoxin and the ACE inhibitors offer independent beneficial effects in CHF.[55,56] Perhaps a more

↓ **afferent flow to glomerulus caused by:**

↓ cardiac output
Systemic hypotension
Blood loss
Over-diuresis, dehydration
Renal artery stenosis (obstruction)
Inhibition of PGE from NSAID

↑ **afferent flow to glomerulus caused by:**

Systemic hypertension

↑ **efferent pressure to maintain glomerular pressure if:**

↑ production of angiotensin II via activation of renin-angiotensin system

↓ **efferent pressure to protect glomerular pressure if:**

ACE inhibitors to block angiotensin II production

Fig 15.5 Factors Affecting Renal Blood Flow. Normal glomerular filtration is dependent upon maintaining normal glomerular capillary pressure by regulating the balance of afferent and efferent arteriole. NSAID = Nonsteroidal anti-inflammatory drugs; PGE = Prostaglandin E.

relevant question is the incremental benefit of digoxin when added to a regimen of diuretics plus vasodilators. The first attempt to address this issue was the RADIANCE study.[223] In this double-blind, randomized, multicenter trial, 178 subjects previously clinically stable on combined therapy with a diuretic, digoxin, and an ACE inhibitor were studied. Of note, all subjects remained in NYHA class II or III CHF before entry into the study despite the combination therapy, all had an ejection fraction of greater than 35% (denoting systolic dysfunction), and all were in normal sinus rhythm. Eighty-five of the subjects continued digoxin therapy and 93 were switched to placebo. Over the 12 week follow-up period, only four of the subjects on digoxin (4.7%) developed worsening symptoms compared to 23 (24%) of the placebo-treated patients. In addition, more of the placebo treated patients had worsening of the ejection fraction and lower quality of life scores. An interesting finding was that deterioration in symptoms after discontinuing digoxin often was delayed for several weeks, perhaps offering an explanation as to why earlier clinical trials using shorter observation periods failed to establish a benefit from digoxin. This trial establishes a beneficial effect of digoxin, even in those patients receiving concurrent ACE inhibitors. However, there are at least two factors that limit extrapolation of the RADIANCE Trial findings to all patients with CHF. First, it only measured the value of therapy indirectly by using a withdrawal design instead of the randomized initiation of therapy to patients previously untreated with digoxin. Second, the patients had advanced disease as evidenced by NYHA Class II or III symptoms despite triple drug therapy. Thus, the benefit of digoxin in early disease is still open to debate. Two studies in progress may help illuminate this issue. The Veterans Affairs Cooperative Vasodilator-Heart Failure Trial III (V-HeFT III) prospectively randomizes patients to either digoxin or amlodipine, a vasodilating calcium channel blocker.[50] In the Digoxin Investigators' Group Trial cosponsored by the National Heart, Lung, and Blood Institute and the Veterans Affairs Cooperative Studies Program, 7000 to 8000 patients with CHF and currently on diuretics and ACE inhibitors (if tolerated) will be assigned randomly to either digoxin or placebo.[224] This latter study has two additional features of note: subjects will be stratified by ejection fraction (>45% or <45%) and mortality from cardiovascular causes will be one of the endpoints measured. A.B. may be a candidate for digoxin in the future if his disease control deteriorates.

36. Effect of Drug Therapy on Mortality. Are the beneficial effects from ACE inhibitors and other vasodilators confined to symptomatic relief or is there evidence of decreased mortality? How do ACE inhibitors compare to digitalis therapy?

The documented benefits of vasodilators had been confined to decreased symptoms of CHF and increased exercise tolerance. The first evidence for decreased mortality came from the Veteran's Administration Cooperative Study (V-HeFT I) that showed combined hydralazine/isosorbide dinitrate (hydral-iso) treatment reduces mortality to a greater extent than either prazosin or placebo in patients with NYHA class III or IV CHF.[179] This study compared three groups of patients with moderate CHF, all of whom continued their previously prescribed diuretic and digitalis regimes. One group was given combination hydralazine (300 mg/day) plus isosorbide dinitrate (160 mg/day); a second group received 20 mg/day of prazosin; and a third group received matching placebos. This report confirmed previous studies finding that patients on active drug had symptomatic relief and improved exercise tolerance. More importantly, cumulative mortality over an average of 2.3 years was significantly lower in the combination therapy group (38.7%) than with either placebo (44%) or prazosin (49.7%). Left ventricular ejection fraction also was improved with combination therapy at both the eight week and one-year follow-up, but not in the placebo or prazosin group.

The Cooperative North Scandinavian Enalapril Survival (CONSENSUS) study was the first to show improved survival in CHF patients treated with an ACE inhibitor.[225-227] Two hundred and fifty-three men and women with severe heart failure (NYHA class IV) were treated with either enalapril or placebo. Digitalis, diuretics, and other vasodilators were continued. At the end of six months, 42% of patients in the enalapril group showed symptomatic improvement compared to 22% of placebo patients. More important, the mortality rate was 26% in the enalapril patients compared to 44% in the placebo group, a 40% reduction. Follow up at two years showed a sustained effect with mortality being 47% with enalapril and 74% with placebo, a 37% reduction. Almost all deaths were cardiac in origin. Interestingly, the biggest difference between the two groups was seen during the first three months of the trial with leveling off of effect between months 3 to 12.[57] The major side effect encountered in the enalapril group was hypotension, especially when starting doses of 10 mg/day were given. Accordingly, a lower starting dose of 2.5 mg/day is recommended for high-risk patients (i.e., those taking large doses of diuretics, or with pre-existing hyponatremia or renal impairment.)

Three further studies confirm these beneficial effects with enalapril[182,228] and possibly with hydral-iso[182] and captopril.[229] In addition, there is evidence that the benefit with enalapril may be greater than that with the other two treatment regimens.[182,229]

In the SOLVD study,[228] patients with NYHA class II or III CHF (EF <35%) were treated with either enalapril at a dose of 2.5 to 20 mg/day (1284 subjects) or placebo (N = 1285) in addition to conventional therapy over an average of 41.4 months. Mortality was 35.2% in the enalapril group compared to 39.7% in the placebo group, with the greatest benefit being from deaths attributed to progressive heart failure. Deaths due to arrhythmias were unchanged.

V-HeFT I compared the combination of hydral-iso to placebo.[179] In V-HeFT II[182] patients receiving diuretics and digoxin for CHF of varying degrees of severity (primarily functional class II or III) were randomized to either enalapril at a fixed dose of 20 mg/day or the hydral-iso combination at a dose of 300 mg hy-

dralazine plus 160 mg of isosorbide. Mortality was lower in the enalapril arm (18%) than with combination therapy (28%), with the greatest benefit in both groups being in patients with less severe disease (functional class I or II). Although a placebo group was not included in this trial, the survival rate with hydral-iso was the same as seen in V-HeFT I, inferring a beneficial effect with hydral-iso in V-HeFT II as well. In addition, treatment with hydral-iso was more effective than enalapril in improving body oxygen consumption during peak exercise. Ejection fraction also increased faster (but not necessarily to a greater extent) with hydral-iso than with enalapril. In both V-HeFT I and V-HeFT II, enalapril was better tolerated than hydral-iso. While not specifically studied in this trial, these trends suggest a possible benefit to using all three drugs in combination together.

The Xamaterol in Severe Heart Failure Study indirectly shows a trend toward improved survival with enalapril compared to captopril.[229] This conclusion should be interpreted cautiously since the study was not designed to directly compare these two drugs and the trial was never completed. The original intent of the study was to compare xamaterol (a positive inotrope) to placebo in patients continued on existing regimens that contained various combinations of diuretics, digitalis, and/or vasodilators (including ACE inhibitors). The study was discontinued prematurely because of excess deaths in the patients treated with xamaterol. Later analysis found that 290 subjects had been receiving captopril (average dose: 60 mg/day) and 217 had been taking enalapril (average dose: 10 mg/day) as part of their concurrent therapy. Within these subgroups, the survival was higher in the enalapril group. Beside the design flaws noted above, there is also the possibility that the doses of the two ACE inhibitors were not equivalent.

From all of these trials, plus the smaller Munich Mild Heart Failure trial,[230] it can be concluded that vasodilators combined with diuretics and digitalis improve mortality in functional class III or IV patients. Of the various regimens, ACE inhibitors appear to be better tolerated than combined hydralazine/nitrate therapy. However, there is a greater risk of renal insufficiency developing in patients treated with ACE inhibitors should they become volume depleted from excess diuresis.

Further understanding of the role of ACE inhibitors in the treatment of CHF comes from the SOLVD II prevention trial.[231] Subjects enrolled in this study were actually a subset of the original SOLVD study with one important difference: although they had an ejection fraction of less than 35% (i.e., systolic CHF), they were asymptomatic at the time of entry into the trial. Thus, it is the first study to determine if early intervention with ACE inhibitors in asymptomatic NYHA class I CHF patients can slow the progression of the disease. Patients received either placebo (2117 subjects) or enalapril titrated to a dose of 2.5 to 20 mg/day (2111 subjects). Diuretics and all other active drugs were withheld unless the patient developed overt CHF. Over the 37.4 month study period, 20% of the enalapril-treated patients developed symptoms of CHF compared to 30% in the placebo group, a 37% reduction. There were also fewer hospitalizations for anginal symptoms and myocardial infarction in the treatment group. As would be expected in this relatively low-risk population, mortality rates were low (14.9% to 15.8%) and not statistically significant between the two groups. However, the death rates became more divergent late in the study as more patients developed overt CHF. The results of this study argue for earlier initiation of treatment, but do not answer the question as to whether diuretic or digoxin therapy may have yielded similar benefit. In addition, enthusiasm over the improved mortality results in V-HeFT II must be tempered by the results of quality of life scores over an average of 2.5 years that showed progressive symptomatic deterioration in both the placebo and enalapril groups.[6] This raises an important question as to the long-term benefit on quality of life. The reader also is referred to Chapter 14: Myocardial Infarction for a related discussion on the early use of ACE inhibitors in patients following infarction (CONSENSUS II and SAVE trials).[232,233]

Calcium Channel Blockers

37. A.F., a 48-year-old male, has a 5-year history of atrial fibrillation and mild CHF stabilized on furosemide 40 mg/day and digoxin 0.25 mg/day. His previously well controlled BP is now rising; the last pressure was 160/100 mm Hg despite good compliance with his diuretic therapy. All laboratory findings are normal. The digoxin level is 1.2 mg/mL. The physician has heard that calcium channel blockers may be helpful in controlling both hypertension and CHF. Is this true and if so, what drug and dose should be used? Are there any special precautions that should be taken in A.F.?

Choice of Agent. The arterial vasodilator properties of calcium channel blockers may elicit both antihypertensive effects and afterload reduction for relief of CHF symptoms. They have no venodilating or preload reducing potential. While all available calcium channel blockers are equally effective for treating hypertension, the data for treatment of CHF are less clear cut.[234] (See Chapter 10: Essential Hypertension.) The dihydropyridine derivatives (amlodipine, felodipine, isradipine, nicardipine, nifedipine) have the most potent arterial vasodilating properties and are, therefore, the most logical agents to use in patients with CHF. Verapamil has the least vasodilatory effect and diltiazem has an intermediate effect. Limited data show nifedipine, nicardipine, and felodipine to be effective in decreasing total systemic vascular resistance and increasing the cardiac index.

Use of these drugs is limited by their negative inotropic effect resulting from inhibition of calcium influx into heart muscle cells. This may result in a paradoxical worsening of CHF.[234–236] In vitro nifedipine has potent depressant effect on contractility. In patients, however, the intrinsic negative inotropic effects are partially offset by its vasodilator properties and reflex tachycardia. Clinically, verapamil elicits the most negative inotropic effect and all of the dihydropyridine derivatives the least; diltiazem has intermediate effects. However, one should not develop a false sense of security that nifedipine and its congeners are clinically devoid of negative inotropic effects as demonstrated by Elkayami et al.[235,236] These investigators conducted a randomized crossover trial comparing intravenous hydralazine (5 to 30 mg) to oral nifedipine (20 to 50 mg) in 15 patients.[235] Both drugs were equally effective in reducing blood pressure and systemic vascular resistance (a sign of afterload reduction), but hydralazine was more effective in increasing stroke volume and cardiac index. Four of the patients taking nifedipine experienced deterioration of their CHF symptoms. The authors concluded that the vasodilatory properties of nifedipine are partially offset by its negative inotropic effect and that hydralazine is clinically superior. A follow-up study using a randomized crossover design challenged 28 patients with class II or III heart failure with nifedipine, isosorbide, and a combination of the two.[236] Twenty-four percent of patients on nifedipine and 26% on combined therapy had deterioration of symptoms and required hospitalization compared to none in the isosorbide treatment arm.

Until more evidence is available, nifedipine should not be considered as the unloading agent of first choice. However, in patients with coexistent angina and/or hypertension, its use may be considered. A usual starting dose is 10 to 20 mg every six eight hours or 30 to 60 mg every 24 hours of a sustained release preparation. Because nifedipine has no venodilatory effects, concurrent use of a nitrate or diuretic may be necessary to achieve maximal benefit. Patients with mitral or aortic regurgitation, but good myocardial

reserve may respond best while those with aortic stenosis or an underlying cardiomyopathy (EF <30%) may be at risk for CHF with nifedipine.[234]

Based upon the above discussion, nifedipine is not a good choice for A.F. Amlodipine and felodipine have been proposed as alternatives because they have fewer cardiac effects in vitro, but this has not been adequately tested in CHF patients. One might argue that verapamil should be tried. It will help lower his blood pressure and in addition help control his atrial fibrillation by virtue of its AV nodal blocking effect. However, one must again worry about the negative inotropic effect of verapamil which may be even more prominent than that of nifedipine.

Interaction with Digoxin. Another concern for A.F. is the potential interaction between calcium blockers and digoxin. A case can be made for the use of verapamil or diltiazem together with digoxin for additive benefit in the treatment of supraventricular arrhythmias; but, as with the use of digoxin and quinidine, there is a risk of increased digoxin serum levels.[126,237,238] The most reproducible interaction is with verapamil. Steady-state concentrations of digoxin are consistently increased by 44% to 70% after the addition of verapamil. In some instances, the changes are only transient in that digoxin levels return toward baseline concentrations (but not completely) after several weeks of continued combination therapy. The interaction is more pronounced in patients taking larger doses of verapamil (240 to 360 mg/day) and in patients taking quinidine as well. Verapamil's primary action is the reduction of nonrenal digoxin clearance, although reductions in both renal clearance and volume of distribution also have been reported. This mechanism is consistent with the findings of Bauer that verapamil reduces hepatic blood flow and moderately inhibits hepatic enzyme systems.[239]

An interaction with diltiazem also has been confirmed by several investigators, but the magnitude of the rise in serum digoxin concentrations (20% to 35%) is less than that seen with verapamil. One study reported a 45% increase in digoxin concentrations after nifedipine, while several other investigators were unable to detect a change in digoxin clearance. In summary, an interaction between calcium channel blockers and digoxin definitely should be considered when using verapamil; it may be of some concern with diltiazem, and is probably insignificant with nifedipine.[126,238]

Use of Inotropic Drugs

38. B.J., a 60-year-old male, is admitted to the hospital with severe, crushing substernal chest pain after a domestic quarrel at home. He has a history of occasional chest pain for the last 3 years treated with SL NTG PRN. The admitting impression is an acute myocardial infarction (AMI). Over the next 3 hours he becomes less alert, hypotensive, diaphoretic, and has a thready pulse. PCWP is elevated to 27 mm Hg, and a chest x-ray shows pulmonary edema. He is diagnosed as having cardiogenic shock. He does not have atrial fibrillation. Should B.J. be given digitalis? Are there other positive inotropic agents that can be used in place of digitalis? Is milrinone safer than amrinone? (Also see Chapter 18: Intensive Care Therapeutics.)

Controversy Over Use of Digitalis
After Myocardial Infarction (MI)

Digitalis has a well documented inotropic effect in patients who have had an MI, but its use in the immediate peri-infarction period may be deleterious. This issue is summarized best in an editorial review by Marcus.[240] Enhanced contractility may increase bulging of ischemic or infarcted segments, thereby dissipating the inotropic effect digoxin exerts on undamaged myocardium. Secondly, digitalis has a direct arteriolar vasoconstrictive effect after rapid (<10 minutes) IV injection. This increases afterload, aggravates left ventricular failure, and increases myocardial oxygen consumption.

Digitalis should not be given to patients with MI who are not in cardiac failure because it may increase infarct size. In fact, the findings of two large trials[241,242] suggest that cumulative survival following an MI may be lower in patients treated with digoxin than in those who are not treated. However, patients in the digoxin treated groups were generally much sicker initially and when the data were adjusted for factors such as atrial fibrillation and severe left ventricular failure, the differences between groups did not reach statistical significance. In patients with mild-to-moderate CHF persisting for several days after an MI, digitalis may exert a minimal but significant increase in ejection fraction without increasing the infarct size.[243] In patients with severe heart failure or cardiogenic shock, digitalis is not the initial drug of choice because of the delay in its time to peak action and its possible deleterious effect on the peri-infarction area. Nevertheless, it may have a role in the subsequent chronic treatment of CHF.

Dopamine and Dobutamine

E.J. is in cardiogenic shock and, for this reason, digitalis should be avoided. Other agents are more effective and are less likely to extend the infarct. β-adrenergic agonists such as isoproterenol have been used in cardiogenic shock, but are of limited value because they produce a high incidence of arrhythmias. Low doses of dopamine or dobutamine administered by continuous infusion increase renal blood flow, decrease afterload, and increase cardiac output.[244,245] Dopamine is more effective as an arterial dilator, especially in the kidney, while dobutamine has more potent inotropic properties. Dobutamine also has been given as long-term infusions (5–7.5 µg/kg/minute continuously for 48 to 72 hours) in patients with refractory CHF or while awaiting transplant.[245,246] The infusion is repeated as often as weekly. While the results of these trials are encouraging, there is skepticism regarding the long term safety and efficacy of inotropic therapy in general. In one study, dobutamine consistently was more effective than digoxin in increasing cardiac output.[247] It also is speculated that long-term therapy actually may be cardiotoxic, as evidenced by an acute worsening of CHF upon withdrawal of the drug. Whether this phenomenon is due to progression of the underlying heart disease, continued drug therapy, or is a true cardiotoxic effect remains unknown. The use of these drugs is discussed in detail in Chapter 18: Intensive Care Therapeutics.

Phosphodiesterase Inhibitors: Amrinone and Milrinone

The phosphodiesterase inhibitors, represented by the two bipyridine derivatives, amrinone (Inocor) and milrinone (Primacor), are alternatives to digoxin and the catecholamines for the short-term parenteral treatment of severe congestive failure.[248–254] These agents selectively inhibit phosphodiesterase F-III, the cyclic-AMP-specific cardiac phosphodiesterase. They have direct cardiac stimulating effects, but they are not sympathomimetics or inhibitors of Na^+-K^+-dependent ATP. Enzyme inhibition results in increased cyclic AMP levels in myocardial cells and thus enhances contractility. Their activity is not blocked by propranolol. Since they are phosphodiesterase inhibitors, they also act as vasodilators. It has been suggested that at low doses they act more as unloading agents rather than inotropes; others refute this viewpoint. Their overall hemodynamic effect probably is due to a combination of positive inotropic action plus preload and afterload reduction.

Amrinone initially was investigated for oral use, but it failed to gain FDA approval because of dose-dependent, reversible thrombocytopenia (up to 20% of patients), drug fever, liver function abnormalities, and possibly drug-induced ventricular arrhythmias. It has a half-life of approximately 2.5 to 3.5 hours in normal individuals; this is prolonged to 6 to 12 hours in heart failure patients.

Amrinone remains available in an intravenous form for short-term use in severe CHF. Therapy is initiated with a 0.75 mg/kg bolus over two to three minutes followed by a maintenance infusion of 5 to 10 µg/kg/minute. Higher doses occasionally have been given, but doses exceeding 18 mg/kg/day should be avoided. Lower doses may need to be given in patients with renal insufficiency since amrinone is 50% excreted unchanged in the kidney. All dilutions should be made in saline (0.45% to 0.9%) since amrinone is incompatible with dextrose-containing solutions.

With intravenous use, the major side effects to monitor are hypotension and precipitation of arrhythmias. The prevalence of thrombocytopenia is reduced to 2.4% with parenteral use. In summary, amrinone is effective in reducing systemic vascular resistance and pulmonary capillary wedge pressure and in increasing cardiac output, but it appears to be less effective than dobutamine.

Milrinone is structurally and pharmacologically similar to amrinone.[249–254] Besides inhibiting phosphodiesterase, it also may increase calcium availability to myocardial muscle. It has both inotropic and vasodilating properties. The half-life of milrinone is short (1.5 to 2.5 hours) with renal clearance accounting for approximately 80% to 90% of total body elimination. Milrinone is about 15 to 20 times more potent than amrinone on a weight basis. A typical loading dose is 50 µg/kg administered over ten minutes followed by a maintenance infusion of 0.5 µg/kg/minute. The infusion is adjusted according to hemodynamic and clinical responses and should be lowered in patients with renal insufficiency. The primary concern with the use of milrinone is inducement of ventricular arrhythmias, reported in up to 12% of patients. Supraventricular arrhythmias, hypotension, headache, and chest pain also have been reported. Thrombocytopenia is rare, a distinct advantage over amrinone.

Other Inotropes: Enoximone, Imazodan, Xamaterol, Flosequinan, Vesnarinone

39. Are there any oral inotropic agents that can be used as alternatives to digoxin?

As discussed in Question 6, controversy exists over the use of digoxin. Thus, an alternative inotrope is desirable, but the results to date have been discouraging. The first drug to be studied was amrinone. Not only was its use limited by thrombocytopenia, a possible proarrhythmic effect, and other severe side effects, it also was speculated that long-term therapy might actually be cardiotoxic, as evidenced by an acute worsening of CHF upon withdrawal of the drug. Whether this phenomenon is due to progression of the underlying heart disease that is masked by continued drug therapy or is a true cardiotoxic effect remains unknown. Milrinone initially was considered to be a safer alternative to amrinone because of a lower incidence of gastrointestinal side effects, drug fever, and thrombocytopenia. However, like amrinone, it also has been abandoned because of apparent aggravation of underlying CHF and proarrhythmic effects.

DiBianco and his colleagues[253] randomly assigned 230 patients with moderately severe heart failure and normal sinus rhythm to treatment with digoxin, milrinone, a combination of the two drugs, or placebo. Diuretics were continued, but vasodilators were not. There were more dropouts for worsening CHF in the placebo and milrinone-treated patients than in the digoxin or combination groups. While both milrinone and digoxin improved treadmill exercise times compared to placebo, the improvement was greatest with digoxin. Only digoxin and combination therapy improved left ventricular ejection fraction at rest. There were more ventricular arrhythmias in the milrinone group. Even more disturbing are the results of the Prospective Randomized Milrinone Survival Evaluation (PROMISE) Study.[254] Subjects with class III or IV CHF were treated with either 40 mg once daily of milrinone or placebo in addition to diuretics, digoxin, and ACE inhibitors. Although milrinone provided additional hemodynamic benefit, there was a 28% increase in mortality from all cases and a 34% increase in cardiovascular mortality associated with milrinone relative to placebo. Although the reasons for these deleterious effects remain speculative, it is possible that increased levels of cyclic AMP are actually injurious to the failing myocardium. In conclusion, digoxin is superior to milrinone and the combination of the two drugs offers no advantage over digoxin alone, and in fact is probably harmful.

The search for a safe and effective inotropic agent has continued with other agents representing a variety of different mechanisms. Enoximone[255] and imazodan[256] are two other phosphodiesterase inhibitors that have only minimal benefit compared to placebo in increasing exercise capacity and also may be associated with increased mortality. A third phosphodiesterase inhibitor, pimobendan, has an added mechanism of directly increasing calcium sensitivity of the cardiac myofibrils.[257–259] At doses ranging from 2.5 to 10 mg/day, this drug shows slightly greater clinical promise as demonstrated by increased exercise duration on treadmill, improved myocardial oxygen uptake, and better quality of life scores compared to placebo for up to two weeks.[257–258] A small number of subjects with advanced disease showed sustained benefit for up to 12 months using doses as high as 20 mg/day.[259]

Xamaterol[229,260] is the only direct acting, partial β-adrenergic agonist studied to date. Like amrinone and milrinone, xamaterol is no longer being considered for marketing because a major study showed increased mortality compared to placebo when it was combined with diuretics and captopril or enalapril. Ibopamine is an orally active derivative of dopamine which is metabolized to the active form, epinine.[261] It not only has catecholamine-like activity (α_1, α_2, β_1, β_2), but also dopaminergic agonist actions. Thus, it has combined vasodilating and inotropic actions. At this time, only small scale studies have been conducted with this agent so it is difficult to predict if it will have clinical promise.

Flosequinan (Manoplax), a fluoroquinolone derivative with combined venous and arterial vasodilating properties as well as a mild positive inotropic action, was marketed for a short time in the U.S.[262–264] However, it was removed from the market when excess mortality was reported in long-term studies, especially when doses of ≥ 100 mg/day were used. Vesnarinone is another investigational quinolone derivative.[265] It augments myocardial contractility with little effect on heart rate or oxygen consumption in animal models. Part of its mechanism of action may be due to a decrease in the delayed outward and inward rectifying potassium currents, an increase in intracellular sodium caused by the prolonged opening of sodium channels, an increase in the intracellular calcium current, as well as a possible phosphodiesterase inhibition. The major clinical study to date again showed more morbidity and mortality in patients taking 120 mg/day compared to placebo treated patients. However, at a lower dose of 60 mg/day, there was a 62% reduction in the risk of dying from any cause and improved symptomatology among the patients receiving vesnarinone. The principal adverse effect was a 2.5% incidence of neutropenia. Obviously, more study is needed at the lower dose to verify these results.

Taken as a whole, these results are sobering. Since the mortality in many of the trials has been greater with the study drug than with placebo, especially in those patients with far advanced disease, it is likely that the failing heart is working at its greatest potential already due to high intrinsic sympathetic activity and that stimulating it further only serves to overwork the heart and increase the risk for dangerous arrhythmias. The preliminary finding that lower doses of vesnarinone are better tolerated than higher doses will likely prompt re-evaluation of other inotropes at lower doses. This

also rekindles the argument that it may be the vasodilating properties of these drugs, not their inotropic actions, that are beneficial.

Use of Beta Blockers in Diastolic and Systolic Heart Failure

40. B.N., a 54-year-old white male, has a 5-year history CHF symptoms, including decreased exercise capacity, SOB, and distended neck veins. He has minimal peripheral edema. History is suggestive of rheumatic fever as a child, but he does not recall having any cardiac symptoms when he was younger, other than being told he had a murmur. He has no history of angina, MI, hypertension, or rhythm disturbances. He has no other medical problems and all laboratory tests are normal. Cardiac exam reveals a prominent S_4 heart sound and murmurs consistent with both significant mitral regurgitation and mild aortic regurgitation. Noninvasive echocardiography reveals a normal EF of $>50\%$. Prior treatment includes furosemide, most recently at 120 mg/day. Because of increasing symptoms, B.N.'s physician is considering adding either propranolol or verapamil to his therapy. Why might this consideration be appropriate?

This case exemplifies a patient with left ventricular diastolic dysfunction. Although he shows many of the classical signs of left-sided heart failure and some symptoms of right-sided failure, he has a near normal ejection fraction. This entity is described in detail in the introduction and pathophysiology sections of this chapter. The ideal treatment strategy for managing diastolic dysfunction has not been devised. In particular, there is no drug that selectively enhances myocardial relaxation without associated effects on left ventricular contractility or on the peripheral vasculature.[10] However, beta blockers and calcium channel blockers with negative inotropic properties (e.g., verapamil) may be efficacious by: 1) slowing the heart rate to allow more time for complete ventricular filling (via more complete left atrial emptying), particularly during exercise, 2) reducing myocardial oxygen demand, and 3) controlling blood pressure.

Left ventricular diastolic dysfunction initially is treated by slow diuresis, similar to other forms of CHF. Diuresis decreases preload, and lessens passive congestion of the ventricles. Excessive lowering of venous and ventricular filling pressures, however, can worsen cardiac output and hypotension. An important principle in treating this form of CHF is that inotropic agents such as digitalis are contraindicated. Paradoxically, beta blockers or verapamil may provide beneficial effects by allowing greater diastolic filling.[10,266–268] In addition, negative inotropic agents decrease myocardial contractility and can assist in overcoming the mechanical obstruction of the aortic and mitral valves during systole in patients with hypertrophic cardiomyopathy. Both agents also are beneficial in decreasing ischemia in patients with coronary artery disease. The relative benefits between a beta blocker and verapamil are not clear. There is more experience with beta-blocking drugs, but calcium blockers are preferred in patients with underlying pulmonary or peripheral vascular diseases.

B.N. fulfills the criteria for having diastolic dysfunction, probably on the basis of mitral and aortic regurgitation resulting from childhood rheumatic fever. Since he has no pulmonary or peripheral vascular disease and already has been on diuretics, a trial of low dose propranolol (40 to 80 mg/day) is warranted. His blood pressure should be monitored closely to avoid hypotension.

41. Under what conditions might beta blockers be indicated in the treatment of a patient with systolic CHF?

As described in greater detail in the pathophysiology section of this chapter, the body's normal physiologic response to a decreased cardiac output is a generalized activation of the adrenergic (sympathetic) nervous system as evidenced by increased circulating levels of norepinephrine. Initially, the resulting increased cardiac contractility and heart rate produce a favorable effect. However, in the long term, high levels of norepinephrine or its metabolites are potentially harmful to heart muscle causing a decreased β_1-receptor sensitivity and a reduction of β_1-receptor density on the surface of myocardial cells. This selective down regulation of β_1-receptors is accompanied by a complex phenomenon of "uncoupling of the β_1- and β_2-receptor activity" whereby there is a relative increase in the number β_2-receptors, but a subsensitivity of these receptors in eliciting a response.[269] Based upon these observations, treatment with β-adrenergic blocking agents might be protective.[269–271] Clinically, however, it is well known that the slowing of the heart rate and peripheral vasoconstriction induced by nonselective beta blockers (e.g., nadolol or propranolol) leads to exacerbation of congestive heart failure symptoms. The adverse effects of beta blockers are most evident during exercise, while improvement in left ventricular function can be demonstrated at rest.

The ideal beta blocker would be a relative β_1-receptor antagonist that allows unopposed β_2-receptor activity in both the heart and the peripheral vasculature. Of the currently available drugs in the U.S., metoprolol in very low doses (5 to 6.25 mg BID) has shown the greatest promise.[269–271] Nonetheless, up to 15% of subjects have clinical worsening, even at these low doses. Clinical trials with combined β_1/α_1-blockers (e.g., labetalol, carvedilol), beta blockers that act as β_2-partial agonists (e.g., pindolol, celiprolol, and dilevalol), and beta blockers with intrinsic sympathomimetic activity (e.g., xamaterol) have yielded mixed results. One problem is that currently available drugs with partial agonist activity (pindolol) or intrinsic sympathomimetic activity (xamaterol) are more active on peripheral β_2-receptors than they are on cardiac β_2-receptors. Also, many trials to date document only acute responses, while it appears that two months or more may be required to identify the full benefit. Paradoxically, it has been found that chronic treatment with selective beta blockers actually may increase left ventricular ejection fraction more than ACE inhibitors. Of the investigational drugs, dilevalol has been shown to have positive short-term benefit, while both carvedilol and bucindolol seem to increase cardiac output and provide symptomatic improvement with chronic dosing.

At this time, no β-adrenergic blocking drug is approved for use in CHF. It is anticipated that as newer, more selective agents are tested in larger study populations in carefully controlled trials, we will be able to better predict which type of patients respond best to which drug. While it is premature at this time to routinely recommend β-adrenergic blockers for the treatment of systolic heart failure, practitioners should be aware that some cardiologists are now attempting beta-blockade in selected patients who are refractory to more conventional therapy.

References

1 **Ghali J et al.** Trends in hospitalization rates for heart failure in the United States, 1973–1986. Arch Intern Med. 1990;150:769.

2 **Kannel WB, Belanger AJ.** Epidemiology of heart failure. Am Heart J. 1991;121:951.

3 **Smith MW.** Epidemiology of congestive heart failure. Am J Cardiol. 1985; 55:3A.

4 **Schocken DD et al.** Prevalence and mortality rate of congestive heart failure in the United States. J Am Coll Cardiol. 1992;20:301.

5 **Groden D.** Vasodilator therapy for congestive heart failure. Lessons from mortality trials. Arch Intern Med. 1993; 153:445.

6 **Rector TS et al.** Evaluation by patients with heart failure of the effects of enalapril compared with hydralazine plus isosorbide dinitrate on quality of life. V-HeFT II. Circulation. 1993;87 (Suppl. VI):V171.

7 **Stauffer JC et al.** Recognition and treatment of left ventricular diastolic dysfunction. Prog Cardiovasc Dis. 1990; 32:319.

8 **Grossman W.** Diastolic dysfunction in congestive heart failure. N Engl J Med. 1991;325:1557.

9 **Johnson J.** Diastolic dysfunction in congestive heart failure. Clin Pharm. 1991;10:850.

10 **Bonow RO, Udelson JE.** Left ventricular diastolic dysfunction as a cause of congestive heart failure. Ann Intern Med. 1992;117:502.

11 **Patterson JH, Adams KF.** Pathophysiology of heart failure. Pharmacotherapy. 1993;13(Suppl.):73S.

12 **Schwartz A, Chatterjee K.** Vasodilator therapy in chronic congestive heart failure. Drugs. 1983;26:148.

13 **Abrams J.** Vasodilator therapy for chronic heart failure. JAMA. 1985; 254:3070.

14 **Tan A et al.** Atrial natriuretic peptide. An overview of clinical pharmacology and pharmacokinetics. Clin Pharmacokinet. 1993;24:28.

15 **Gottlieb SS et al.** Prognostic importance of atrial natriuretic peptide in patients with chronic heart failure. J Am Coll Cardiol. 1989;13:1534.

16 **Davis et al.** Atrial natriuretic peptide levels in the prediction of congestive heart failure risk in frail elderly. JAMA. 1992;267:2625.

17 **Connell J et al.** Therapeutic use of atrial natriuretic factor. Br J Clin Pharmacol. 1992;34:102.

18 **Giles T et al.** Prolonged hemodynamic benefits from a high-dose bolus injection of human atrial natriuretic factor in congestive heart failure. Clin Pharmacol Ther. 1991;50:557.

19 **Agency for Health Care Policy and Research.** Heart failure: evaluation and care of patients with left-ventricular systolic dysfunction. Clinical practice guidelines, no. 11. Public Health Service, U.S. Dept. of Health and Human Services. 1994. (AHCPR Publication no. 94-0612).

20 **Dikshit K et al.** Renal and extra renal hemodynamic effects of furosemide in congestive heart failure after acute myocardial infarction. N Engl J Med. 1973;288:1087.

21 **Wagner JG.** Appraisal of digoxin bioavailability and pharmacokinetics in relation to cardiac therapy. Am Heart J. 1974;88:133.

22 **Greenblatt DJ et al.** Evaluation of digoxin bioavailability in single dose studies. N Engl J Med. 1973;289:651.

23 **Huffman DH et al.** Absorption of digoxin from different oral preparations in normal subjects during steady state. Clin Pharmacol Ther. 1974;16:310.

24 **Lindenbaum J et al.** Variation in biologic availability of digoxin from four preparations. N Engl J Med. 1971;275: 344.

25 **Aronson.** Clinical pharmacokinetics of digoxin therapy 1980. Clin Pharmacokinet. 1980;5:137.

26 **Heizer W et al.** Absorption of digoxin from tablets and capsules in subjects with malabsorption syndromes. DICP, Ann Pharmacother. 1989;23:764.

27 **Moordian A.** Digitalis: an update of clinical pharmacokinetics, therapeutic monitoring techniques and treatment recommendations. Clin Pharmacokinet. 1988;15:165.

28 **Reuning R et al.** Digoxin. In: Evans W et al., eds. Applied Pharmacokinetics. 3rd ed. Vancouver: Applied Therapeutics, Inc.; 1992:20-1.

29 **Aronson JK.** Clinical pharmacokinetics of cardiac glycosides in patients with renal dysfunction. Clin Pharmacokinet. 1983;8:155.

30 **Morton M, Cooper J.** Erythromycin-induced digoxin toxicity. DICP, Ann Pharmacother. 1989;23:668.

31 **Lindenbaum J et al.** Inactivation of digoxin by the gut flora: reversal by antibiotic therapy. N Engl J Med. 1981; 305:789.

32 **Jelliffe RW et al.** A nomogram for digoxin therapy. Am J Med. 1974;57:63.

33 **Perrier D et al.** Clinical pharmacokinetics of digitoxin. Clin Pharmacokinet. 1977;2:292.

34 **Folland E et al.** Implications of third heart sounds in patients with valvular heart disease. N Engl J Med. 1992;327: 458.

35 **The criteria committee of the New York Heart Association, Inc.** Diseases of the Heart and Blood Vessels: Nomenclature and Criteria for Diagnosis. 6th ed. Boston: Little, Brown and Co.; 1964.

35 **Linkewich J et al.** Bradycardia and congestive heart failure associated with ocular timolol maleate. Am J Hosp Pharm. 1981;38:699.

36 **Leier C et al.** Cardiovascular effects of ophthalmic timolol. Ann Intern Med. 1986;104:197.

37 **Raymond G et al.** Sodium content of commonly administered intravenous drugs. Hosp Pharm. 1982;18:560.

38 **Podrid P et al.** Congestive heart failure caused by oral disopyramide. N Engl J Med. 1980;300:614.

39 **Kantrowitz N.** Cardiotoxicity of antitumor agents. Prog Cardiovasc Dis. 1984;27:195.

40 **Cohn K et al.** Variability of hemodynamic responses to acute digitalization in chronic cardiac failure due to cardiomyopathy and coronary artery disease. Am J Cardiol. 1975;35:461.

41 **Gheorghiade M, Beller G.** Effects of discontinuing maintenance digoxin therapy in patients with ischemic heart disease and congestive heart failure in sinus rhythm. Am J Cardiol. 1983;51: 1243.

42 **Hutcheon D et al.** The role of furosemide alone and in combination with digoxin in the relief of symptoms of congestive heart failure. J Clin Pharmacol. 1980;20:59.

43 **Marcus F.** The use of digitalis for the treatment of congestive heart failure: a tale of its decline and resurrection. Cardiovasc Drugs Ther. 1989;3:473.

44 **Kimmelstiel C, Benotti J.** How effective is digitalis in the treatment of congestive heart failure? Am Heart J. 1988;116:1063.

45 **Mulrowe C et al.** Re-evaluation of digitalis efficacy. New light on an old leaf. Ann Intern Med. 1984;101:113.

46 Arnold SB et al. Long-term digitalis therapy improves left ventricular function in heart failure. N Engl J Med. 1980;303:1443.

47 Lee DCS et al. Heart failure in outpatients. N Engl J Med. 1982;306:699.

48 Jaeschke R et al. To what extent do congestive heart failure patients in normal sinus rhythm benefit from digoxin therapy? A systematic overview and meta-analysis. Am J Med. 1990;88: 279.

49 Kulick D, Rahimtoola S. Current role of digitalis therapy in patients with congestive heart failure. JAMA. 1991; 265:2995.

50 Smith T. Digoxin in heart failure. N Engl J Med. 1993;329:51.

51 Deedwania P. Angiotensin converting enzyme inhibitors in congestive heart failure. Arch Intern Med. 1990;150: 1798.

52 Pfeffler M. Angiotensin-converting enzyme inhibition in congestive heart failure: benefit and perspective. Am Heart J. 1993;126:789–93.

53 Struthers AD. The clinical pharmacology of angiotensin converting enzyme inhibitors in chronic heart failure. Pharmacol Ther. 1992;53:187.

54 Crozier I, Ikram H. Angiotensin converting enzyme inhibitors versus digoxin for the treatment of congestive heart failure. Drugs. 1992;43:637.

55 The Captopril-Digoxin Multicenter Research Group: comparative effects of therapy with captopril and digoxin in patients with mild to moderate heart failure. JAMA. 1988;259:539.

56 Davies R et al. Enalapril versus digoxin in patients with congestive heart failure: A multicenter study. J Am Coll Cardiol. 1991;18:1602.

57 Rahimtoola S. The pharmacologic treatment of congestive heart failure. Circulation. 1989;80:693.

58 Gossain VV et al. Drug-induced hyponatremia in psychogenic polydipsia. Postgrad Med J. 1976;52:720.

59 Freis E, Papademetriou V. How dangerous are diuretics? Drugs. 1985;30: 469.

60 Freis E. The cardiovascular risks of thiazide diuretics. Clin Pharmacol Ther. 1986;39:239.

61 Knochel J. Diuretic-induced hypokalemia. Am J Med. 1984;77(5A):18.

62 Freis E. Critique of the clinical importance of diuretic induced hypokalemia and elevated cholesterol level. Arch Intern Med. 1989;149:2640.

63 Kosman ME. Management of potassium problems during long-term diuretic therapy. JAMA. 1974;230:743.

64 Davidson C et al. Effect of long-term diuretic treatment on body potassium in heart disease. Lancet. 1976;2:1044.

65 Davidson S, Surawicz B. Ectopic beats and atrioventricular conduction disturbances. Arch Intern Med. 1976; 120:280.

66 Papademetriou JV. Diuretics, hypokalemia and cardiac arrhythmias: a critical analysis. Am Heart J. 1986;111: 1219.

67 Leif P et al. Diuretic induced hypokalemia does not cause ventricular ectopy in uncomplicated essential hypertension. Kidney Int. 1984;25:203.

68 Madias J et al. Non-arrhythmogenicity of diuretic hypokalemia. Arch Intern Med. 1984;144:2171.

69 Steiness E et al. Cardiac arrhythmias induced by hypokalemia and potassium loss during maintenance digoxin therapy. Br Heart J. 1976;38:167.

70 Holland OB et al. Diuretic induced ventricular ectopic activity. Am J Med. 1981;770:762.

71 Hollifield JW et al. Thiazide diuretics, hypokalemia and cardiac arrhythmias. Acta Med Scand. 1981;647:67.

72 Kassier JP et al. Diuretics and potassium metabolism: a reassessment of the need, effectiveness, and safety of potassium therapy. Kidney Int. 1977;11: 505.

73 Morgan DB, Davidson C. Hypokalemia and diuretics: analysis of publications. Br Med J (Clin Res). 1980;1:905.

74 Finnerty FA et al. Long-term effects of furosemide and hydrochlorothiazide in patients with essential hypertension. Angiology. 1977;28:125.

75 Hollifield J. Potassium and magnesium abnormalities: diuretics and arrhythmias in hypertension. Am J Med. 1987; 77(5A):28.

76 McRae MP. Foods high in potassium. Hosp Pharm. 1979;14:73.

77 Perry R. Salt substitute as potassium replacement in hypertensive patients. Clin Pharm. 1986;5:156.

78 McMahon FG et al. Effect of potassium chloride supplements on upper gastrointestinal mucosa. Clin Pharmacol Ther. 1984;38:852.

79 Patterson DJ et al. Endoscopic comparison of solid and liquid potassium chloride supplements. Lancet. 1983;2: 1077.

80 Aselton PJ, Jick H. Short term follow up study of wax matrix potassium chloride in relation to gastrointestinal bleeding. Lancet. 1983;1:184.

81 Jick H et al. A comparison of wax matrix and microencapsulated potassium chloride in relation to upper gastrointestinal illness requiring hospitalization. Pharmacother. 1989;9:204.

82 Kendall C et al. Endoscopic evaluation of slow release potassium chloride preparations. Clin Pharmacol Ther. 1985;38:20.

83 Schwartz A et al. Dosage of potassium chloride elixir to correct thiazide-induced hypokalemia. JAMA. 1974;230: 702.

84 Sklath H, Gums J. Spironolactone: a re-examination. DICP, Ann Pharmacother. 1990;24:52.

85 Schnaper H et al. Potassium restoration in hypertensive patients made hypokalemic by hydrochlorothiazide. Arch Intern Med. 1989;149:2677.

86 Cutler R, Blair A. Clinical pharmacokinetics of furosemide. Clin Pharmacokinet. 1979;4:279.

87 Hammarlund-Udenaes M, Benet L. Furosemide pharmacokinetics and pharmacodynamics in health and disease—an update. J Pharmacokinet Biopharm. 1989;17:1.

88 Greither A et al. Pharmacokinetics of furosemide in patients with congestive heart failure. Pharmacology. 1979;19: 121.

89 Brater DC et al. Bumetanide and furosemide in heart failure. Kidney Int. 1984;26:183.

90 Vasko MR et al. Furosemide absorption altered in decompensated congestive heart failure. Ann Intern Med. 1985;102:314.

91 Straughn A et al. Bioavailability of seven furosemide tablets in man. Biopharm Drug Dispos. 1986;7:113.

92 McNamara P et al. Influence of tablet dissolution on furosemide bioavailability; a bioequivalence study. Pharm Res. 1987;4:150.

93 Kelly M et al. Pharmacokinetics of orally administered furosemide. Clin Pharmacol Ther. 1979;15:1778.

94 Kelly M et al. A comparison of the diuretic response to oral and intravenous furosemide in diuretic resistant patients. Curr Ther Res. 1977;21:1.

95 Stallings S et al. Comparison of natriuretic and diuretic effects of single and divided doses of furosemide. Am J Hosp Pharm. 1979;36:68.

96 Wilson T et al. Effect of dosage regimen and natriuretic response to furosemide. Clin Pharmacol Ther. 1976;18: 165.

97 Anon. Torsemide (Demadex)—a new loop diuretic. The Medical Letter on Drugs and Therapeutics. 1994;36:73.

98 Vargo D et al. The pharmacodynamics of Torsemide in patients with congestive heart failure. Clin Pharmacol Ther. 1994;56:48.

99 Beerman B, Groschinsky-Grind M. Clinical pharmacokinetics of diuretics. Clin Pharmacokinet. 1980;5:221.

100 Barter DC. Resistance to loop diuretics. Why it happens and what to do about it. Drugs. 1985;30:427.

101 Brater DC. Resistance to diuretics. Emphasis on a pharmacologic perspective. Drugs. 1981;22:477.

102 Lahav M et al. Continuous infusion furosemide in patients with severe CHF. Chest. 1992;102:725.

103 Rudy D et al. Loop diuretics for chronic renal insufficiency: a continuous infusion is more efficacious than bolus therapy. Ann Intern Med. 1991; 115:360.

104 Van Meyd J et al. Continuous infusion of furosemide in the treatment of patients with congestive heart failure and diuretic resistance. J Intern Med. 1994; 235:329.

105 Brater DC. Mechanism of the synergistic combination of metolazone and bumetanide. J Pharmacol Exp Ther. 1985;233:70.

106 Winter M. Basic Clinical Pharmacokinetics, 3rd ed. Vancouver, WA: Applied Therapeutics, Inc.; 1994:7,147.

107 Scheiner LB et al. Estimation of population characteristics of pharmacokinetic parameters from routine clinical data. J Pharmacokinet Biopharm. 1977; 5:455.

108 Koup JR et al. Digoxin pharmacokinetics: role of renal failure in dosage regimen design. Clin Pharmacol Ther. 1975;18:9.

109 Jusko W et al. Pharmacokinetic design of digoxin dosage regimen in relation to renal function. J Clin Pharmacol. 1974;14:525.

110 Kelly R, Smith T. Recognition and management of digitalis toxicity. Am J Cardiol. 1992;69:108G.

111 Arondon J. Indication for the measurement of plasma digoxin concentrations. Drugs. 1983;26:230.

112 Dobbs RJ. Serum concentration monitoring of cardiac glycosides. How helpful is it for adjusting dosing regimens? Clin Pharmacokinet. 1991;20: 175.

113 Jogestrand T et al. Clinical value of serum digoxin assays in outpatients: improvement by standardization of blood sampling. Am Heart J. 1989;117: 1076.

114 Hall P et al. The effect of everyday exercise on steady state digoxin concentrations. J Clin Pharmacol. 1989;29: 1083.

115 Karbosk J et al. Marked digoxin-like immunoreactive factor interference with an enzyme immunoassay. Drug Intell Clin Pharm. 1988;22:703.

116 Toseland P et al. Tentative identification of the digoxin-like immunoreactive substance. Ther Drug Monit. 1988; 10:168.

117 Schrader B et al. Digoxin like immunoreactive substance in renal transplant patients. J Clin Pharmacol. 1991; 313:1126.

118 Morris R et al. Interference from digoxin like immunoreactive substances in commercial digoxin kit assay methods. Eur J Clin Pharmacol. 1990;39: 359.

119 Monane M et al. Non-compliance with congestive heart failure therapy in the elderly. Arch Intern Med. 1994; 154:433.

120 Weintraub M et al. Compliance as a determinate of serum digoxin concentration. JAMA. 1973;224:481.

121 Sheiner LB et al. Differences in serum digoxin concentrations between outpatients and inpatients: an effect of compliance? Clin Pharmacol Ther. 1974;15:239.

122 Hall WH et al. Titrated digoxin XXII. Absorption and excretion in malabsorption syndrome. Am J Med. 1974; 56:437.

123 Luchi RJ et al. Unusually large digitalis requirements: a study of altered digoxin metabolism. Am J Med. 1968; 37:263.

124 Chorpa D et al. Insensitivity to digoxin associated with hypocalcemia. N Engl J Med. 1977;197:917.

125 Shenfeld G. Influence of thyroid dysfunction on drug pharmacokinetics. Clin Pharmacokinet. 1981;6:275.

126 Hooymans P, Merkus F. Current status of cardiac glycoside drug interactions. Clin Pharm. 1985;4:404.

127 Fitchtl B, Doering W. The quinidine-digoxin interaction in perspective. Clin Pharmacokinet. 1983;8:137.

128 Bigger JT, Leahy E. Quinidine and digoxin: an important interaction. Drugs. 1982;24:229.

129 Fenster P et al. Digoxin-quinidine interaction in patients with chronic renal failure. Circulation. 1982;66:1277.

130 Doering W et al. Quinidine-digoxin interaction: evidence for involvement of an extra-renal mechanism. Eur J Clin Pharmacol. 1982;21:281.

131 Hedman A et al. Interactions in the renal and biliary elimination of digoxin. Stereoselective difference between quinine and quinidine. Clin Pharmacol Ther. 1990;47:20.

131 Schenck-Gustafsson et al. Effect of quinidine on digoxin concentrations in skeletal muscle and serum concentration in patients with atrial fibrillation. N Engl J Med. 1981;305:209.

132 Doherty JE et al. Digoxin-quinidine interaction: changes in canine tissue concentration from steady state quinidine. Am J Cardiol. 1980;45:1196.

133 **Warner N et al.** Tissue digoxin concentrations during the quinidine-digoxin interaction. Am J Cardiol. 1983; 51:1717.

134 **Warner N et al.** Tissue digoxin concentration and digoxin effect during quinidine-digoxin interaction. J Am Coll Cardiol. 1985;5:680.

135 **Mardel A et al.** Quinidine enhances digitalis toxicity at therapeutic serum digoxin levels. Clin Pharmacol Ther. 1993;53:457.

136 **Walker AM et al.** Drug toxicity in patients receiving digoxin and quinidine. Am Heart J. 1983;105:1025.

137 **Kulhmann J.** Effects of quinidine on pharmacokinetics and pharmacodynamics of digitoxin achieving steady state condition. Clin Pharmacol Ther. 1986;39:288.

138 **Rodin S, Johnson B.** Pharmacokinetic interactions with digoxin. Clin Pharmacokinet. 1988;11:227.

139 **Solomon HM et al.** Interactions between digitoxin and other drugs in man. Am Heart J. 1972;83:277.

140 **Cohen AF et al.** Effect of omeprazole on digoxin bioavailability. Br J Clin Pharmacol. 1991;31:656P. Abstract.

141 **Oosterhuis B et al.** Minor effect of multiple dose omeprazole in the pharmacokinetics of digoxin after a single oral dose. Br J Clin Pharmacol. 1991; 32:569.

142 **Guven H et al.** Age related digoxin alprazolam interaction. Clin Pharmacol Ther. 1993;54:42.

143 **Clavo M et al.** Interaction between digoxin and propafenone. Ther Drug Monit. 1989;11:10.

144 **Nolan P et al.** Effects of coadministration of propafenone on the pharmacokinetics of digoxin in healthy volunteer subjects. J Clin Pharmacol. 1989;29:46.

145 **Greenblatt DJ et al.** Pain and CPK elevation after intramuscular digoxin. N Engl J Med. 1973;288:689.

146 **Bernabei R et al.** Digoxin serum concentration measurements in patients with suspected digitalis arrhythmias. J Cardiovasc Pharmacol. 1980;2:319.

147 **Rosen M.** Cellular electrophysiology of digitalis toxicity. J Am Coll Cardiol. 1985;5:22A.

148 **Reisdorff E et al.** Acute digitalis poisoning: the role of intravenous magnesium sulfate. J Emerg Med. 1986;4: 463–69.

149 **Beller GA et al.** Digitalis intoxication. A prospective clinical study with serum level correlations. N Engl J Med. 1971; 284:989.

150 **Bhatia S.** Digitalis toxicity. Turning over a new leaf? West J Med. 1986; 145:74.

151 **Lely AH et al.** Noncardiac symptoms of digitalis intoxication. Am Heart J. 1972;83:149.

152 **Lee T, Smith T.** Serum digoxin concentration and diagnosis of digitalis toxicity. Clin Pharmacokinet. 1983;8: 279.

153 **Park G et al.** Digoxin toxicity in patients with high serum digoxin concentrations. Am J Med Sci. 1987;30:423.

154 **Shapiro W.** Correlative studies of serum digitalis levels and the arrhythmias of digitalis intoxication. Am J Cardiol. 1978;41:852.

155 **Ordog G et al.** Serum digoxin levels and mortality in 5100 patients. Ann Emerg Med. 1987;16:32.

156 **Jelliffe RW.** Factors to consider in planning digoxin therapy. J Chronic Dis. 1971;24:407.

157 **Brater C et al.** Digoxin toxicity in patients with normokalemic potassium depletion. Clin Pharmacol Ther. 1977; 22:21.

158 **Beller GA et al.** Correlation of serum magnesium levels and cardiac digitalis intoxication. Am J Cardiol. 1974;33: 225.

159 **Young IS.** Magnesium status and digoxin toxicity. Br J Clin Pharmacol. 1991;32:717.

160 **Singh RB et al.** Hypomagnesemia in relation to digoxin intoxication in children. Am Heart J. 1976;92:144.

161 **Bendayan R, McKenzie M.** Digoxin pharmacokinetics and dosage requirements in pediatric patients. Clin Pharm. 1983;2:224.

162 **Marbury T et al.** Advanced digoxin toxicity in renal failure; treatment with charcoal hemoperfusion. South Med J. 1979;72:279.

163 **Smith TW et al.** Treatment of life threatening digitalis intoxication with digoxin-specific Fab antibody fragments. N Engl J Med. 1982;307:1357.

164 **Wenger T et al.** Treatment of 63 severely digitalis toxic patients with digoxin-specific antibody fragments. J Am Coll Cardiol. 1985;5:118A.

165 **Cole P, Smith T.** Use of digoxin-specific Fab fragments in the treatment of digitalis intoxication. Drug Intell Clin Pharm. 1986;20:267–70.

166 **Antman E.** Treatment of 150 cases of life threatening digitalis toxicity. Circulation. 1990;81:1744–752.

167 **Schaumann W et al.** Kinetics of the Fab fragments of digoxin antibodies and of bound digoxin in patients with severe digoxin intoxication. Eur J Clin Pharmacol. 1986;30:527–33.

168 **Woolf A et al.** The use of digoxin-specific Fab fragments for severe digitalis intoxication in children. N Engl J Med. 1992;326:1739.

169 **Sinclair A et al.** Kinetics of digoxin and anti-digoxin antibody fragments during treatment of digoxin toxicity. Br J Clin Pharmacol. 1989;28:352–56.

170 **Hansell J.** Effects of therapeutic digoxin antibodies on digoxin assays. Arch Pathol Lab Med. 1989;113:1259–262.

171 **Ralney P.** Effect of digoxin Fab (ovine) on digoxin immunoassays. Am J Clin Pathol. 1989;92:779–86.

172 **Allen N et al.** Clinical and pharmacokinetic profiles of digoxin immune Fab in four patients with renal failure. DICP Ann Pharmacother. 1991;25:1315.

173 **Ujhelyi MR et al.** Influence of digoxin immune Fab therapy and renal dysfunction on the disposition of total and free digoxin. Ann Intern Med. 1993; 119:273.

174 **Hickey AR et al.** Digoxin immune Fab in the management of digitalis intoxication: safety and efficacy results of an observational surveillance study. J Am Coll Cardiol. 1991;17:590.

175 **Burroughs Wellcome, Co.** Digibind package insert.

176 **Gault M et al.** Loading doses of digoxin in renal failure. Br J Clin Pharmacol. 1980;9:593.

177 **Cockcroft DW, Gault MH.** Prediction of creatinine clearance from serum creatinine. Nephron. 1976;16:31.

178 **Chatterjee K et al.** Combination vasodilator therapy for severe chronic congestive heart failure. Prog Cardiovasc Dis. 1977;19:301.

179 **Cohn J et al.** Effect of vasodilator therapy on mortality in chronic congestive heart failure. N Engl J Med. 1986;314: 1547.

180 **Packer M et al.** Rebound hemodynamic events after abrupt withdrawal of nitroprusside in patients with severe congestive heart failure. N Engl J Med. 1979;301:1193.

181 **Mulrowe J, Crawford M.** Clinical pharmacokinetics and therapeutic use of hydralazine in congestive heart failure. Clin Pharmacokinet. 1989;16:86.

182 **Cohn J et al.** A comparison of enalapril with hydralazine-isosorbide dinitrate in the treatment of chronic congestive heart failure. N Engl J Med. 1991;325:303.

183 **Chatterjee K et al.** Oral hydralazine in chronic heart failure: sustained beneficial hemodynamic effects. Ann Intern Med. 1980;92:600.

184 **Magorien R et al.** Hydralazine therapy in chronic heart failure. Sustained control and regional hemodynamic responses. Am J Med. 1984;77:267.

185 **Mulrowe C et al.** Relative efficacy of vasodilator therapy in chronic congestive heart failure: implication of randomized trials. JAMA. 1988;259:3422.

186 **Packer M et al.** Hemodynamic characterization of tolerance to long term hydralazine therapy in severe chronic heart failure. N Engl J Med. 1982;306: 57.

187 **Taylor W et al.** Hemodynamic effects of nitroglycerin ointment in congestive heart failure. Am J Cardiol. 1976;38: 469.

188 **Reichek N et al.** Antianginal effects of nitroglyerin patches. Am J Cardiol. 1984;54:1.

189 **Frishman W et al.** A symposium: transdermal nitroglycerin-maximizing therapeutic efficacy. Am J Cardiol. 1985;56(Doc. 7).

190 **Scheidt S et al.** A symposium: scientific and clinical experience with transdermal nitroglycerin. Am Heart J. 1986;11(Suppl.):207–15.

191 **Raijfer S et al.** Sustained beneficial hemodynamic responses to large doses of transdermal nitroglycerin on congestive heart failure and comparison with intravenous nitroglycerin. Am J Cardiol. 1984;54:120.

192 **Roth A et al.** A randomized comparison between the hemodynamic effects of hydralazine and nitroglycerin alone and in combination at rest and during isometric exercise in patients with chronic mitral regurgitation. Am Heart J. 1993;125:155.

193 **Markham R et al.** Efficacy of prazosin in the management of chronic congestive heart failure: a six month randomized, double blind, placebo-controlled study. Am J Cardiol. 1983;51:1246.

194 **Colucci W et al.** Long-term therapy of heart failure with prazosin. Am J Cardiol. 1980;45:337.

195 **Awan NA et al.** Ambulatory prazosin treatment of chronic congestive heart failure: development of later tolerance reversible by higher dosage and interrupted substitution therapy. Am Heart J. 1981;104:541.

196 **Colucci W et al.** Mechanisms and im-

plications of vasodilator tolerance in the treatment of congestive heart failure. Am J Med. 1981;71:89.

197 **Packer M.** Converting-enzyme inhibition for severe chronic heart failure: views from a skeptic. Int J Cardiol. 1985;7:11.

198 **Schofield PM et al.** Which vasodilator drug in patients with chronic heart failure? A randomized comparison of captopril and hydralazine. Br J Clin Pharmacol. 1991;31:25.

199 **Bayliss J et al.** Captopril provides long term benefit in heart failure. Br Med J (Clin Res). 1985;290:1861.

200 **Chatterjee K.** A cooperative multicenter study of captopril in congestive heart failure: hemodynamic effects and long-term response. Am Heart J. 1985; 110:439.

201 **Davis R et al.** Treatment of chronic congestive heart failure with captopril, an oral inhibitor of angiotensin-converting enzyme. N Engl J Med. 1979; 301:117.

202 **Just P.** The positive association of cough with angiotensin converting enzyme inhibitors. Pharmacotherapy. 1989;9:82.

203 **Gibson G.** Enalapril-induced cough. Arch Intern Med. 1989;149:2701.

204 **Israili Z, Hall W.** Cough and angioneurotic edema associated with angiotensin-converting enzyme inhibitors. A review of the literature. Ann Intern Med. 1992;117:234.

205 **Punzi H.** Safety profile. Focus on cough. Am J Cardiol. 1993;72:45H.

206 **Sharif MN et al.** Cough induced by quinapril with resolution after changing to fosinopril. Ann Pharmaco Ther. 1994;28:720.

207 **Hanssens M et al.** Fetal and neonatal effects of treatment with angiotensin-converting enzyme inhibitors in pregnancy. Obstet Gynecol. 1991;78:128.

208 **Gavras I et al.** Fatal pancytopenia associated with the use of captopril. Ann Intern Med. 1981;94:58.

209 **Cleland J et al.** The effects of captopril on serum digoxin and urinary urea and digoxin clearances in patients with congestive heart failure. Am Heart J. 1986;112:130.

210 **Todd P, Heel R.** Enalapril: a review of its pharmacodynamic and pharmacokinetic properties, and therapeutic use in hypertension and congestive heart failure. Drugs. 1986;31:198.

211 **Clearly J, Taylor J.** Enalapril: a new angiotensin converting enzyme inhibitor. Drug Intell Clin Pharm. 1987;20: 177.

212 **Packer M et al.** Comparison of captopril and enalapril in patients with severe chronic heart failure. N Engl J Med. 1986;315:847.

213 **Giles T et al.** Short- and long-acting angiotensin-converting enzyme inhibitors: a randomized trial of lisinopril versus captopril in the treatment of congestive heart failure. J Am Coll Cardiol. 1989;13:1240.

214 **Zannad F et al.** Comparison of treatment with lisinopril versus enalapril for congestive heart failure. Am J Cardiol. 1992;70:78C.

215 **Colfer HT et al.** Effects of once daily benazepril therapy on exercise tolerance and manifestations of chronic congestive heart failure. Am J Cardiol. 1992;70:354.

216 **The Acute Reinfarction Ramipril Efficacy Study Investigators.** Effect of ramipril on mortality and morbidity of acute myocardial infarction with clinical evidence of heart failure. Lancet. 1993;342:821.

217 **Kholeif M et al.** A comparison of the efficacy and safety of ramipril and digoxin added to maintenance diuretic treatment in patients with chronic heart failure. J Cardiovasc Cardiol. 1991;18: S180.

218 **Pflugfelder PW et al.** Clinical consequences of angiotensin-converting enzyme inhibitor withdrawal in chronic heart failure. A double blind placebo controlled trial of quinapril. J Am Coll Cardiol. 1993;22:1557.

219 **Till A et al.** The pharmacokinetics of lisinopril in hospitalized patients with congestive heart failure. Br J Clin Pharmacol. 1989;27:199.

220 **Testa M et al.** Quality of life and antihypertensive therapy in men. A comparison of captopril with enalapril. N Engl J Med. 1993;328:907.

221 **Dietz R et al.** Angiotensin-converting enzyme inhibitors and renal function in heart failure. Am J Cardiol. 1992;70: 119C.

222 **Hall D et al.** Counteraction of the vasodilator effects of enalapril by aspirin in severe heart failure. J Am Coll Cardiol. 1992;20:1549.

223 **Packer M et al.** Withdrawal of digoxin from patients with chronic heart failure treated with angiotensin-converting-enzyme inhibitors. N Engl J Med. 1993;329:1.

224 **Yusuf S et al.** Need for a large randomized trial to evaluate the effects of digitalis on morbidity and mortality in congestive heart failure. Am J Cardiol. 1992;69:64G.

225 **The Consensus Trial Study Group.** Effects of enalapril on mortality in severe congestive heart failure: results of The Cooperative North Scandinavian Enalapril Survival Group. N Engl J Med. 1987;316:1429.

226 **Kjekshus J et al.** Effects of enalapril on long term mortality in severe congestive heart failure. Am J Cardiol. 1992;69:103.

227 **Kjekshus J et al.** Tolerability of enalapril in congestive heart failure. Am J Cardiol. 1988;62:67A.

228 **The SOLVD Investigators.** Effect of enalapril on survival in patients with reduced left ventricular ejection fractions and congestive heart failure. N Engl J Med. 1991;325:295.

229 **Pouleur H et al.** Difference in mortality between patients treated with captopril or enalapril in the xamaterol in severe heart failure study. Am J Cardiol. 1991;68:71.

230 **Kleber FX et al.** Impact of converting enzyme inhibition of progression of chronic heart failure. Results of the Munich Mild Heart Failure Trial. Br Heart J. 1992;67:289.

231 **The SOLVD Investigators.** Effect of enalapril on mortality and the development of heart failure in asymptomatic patients with reduced left ventricular ejection fractions. N Engl J Med. 1992;327:685.

232 **Swedberg K et al.** Effects of the early administration of enalapril in mortality in patients with acute myocardial infarction (CONSENSUS II). N Engl J Med. 1992;327:628.

233 **Pfeffer M et al.** Effect of captopril on mortality and morbidity in patients with left ventricular dysfunction after myocardial infarction: the Survival and Ventricular Enlargement Trial (SAVE). N Engl J Med. 1992;327:669.

234 **Reicher-Reiss H, Barasch E.** Calcium antagonists in patients with heart failure, a review. Drugs. 1991;42:343.

235 **Elkayam U et al.** Differences in hemodynamic response to vasodilators due to calcium channel antagonism with nifedipine and direct acting antagonism with hydralazine in chronic refractory congestive heart failure. Am J Cardiol. 1984;54:126.

236 **Elkayam U et al.** A prospective randomized, double blind crossover study to compare the efficacy and safety of chronic nifedipine therapy with that of isosorbide dinitrate and their combination in the treatment of chronic congestive heart failure. Circulation. 1990; 82:1954.

237 **Hedman A et al.** Digoxin verapamil interaction: reduction of biliary clearance, but not renal digoxin clearance in humans. Clin Pharmacol Ther. 1991; 49:256.

238 **DeVito J, Friedman B.** Evaluation of the pharmacodynamic interaction between calcium antagonists and digoxin. 1986;6:73.

239 **Bauer L et al.** Changes in antipyrine and indocyanine green kinetics during nifedipine, verapamil, and diltiazem therapy. Pharmacol Ther. 1986;40:239.

240 **Marcus F.** Use of digitalis in acute myocardial infarction. Circulation. 1980;62:17. Editorial.

241 **Bigger JT et al.** Effect of digitalis treatment on survival after acute myocardial infarction. Am J Cardiol. 1985; 55:263.

242 **Muller E et al.** Digoxin therapy and mortality after myocardial infarction. Experience in the MILIS study. N Engl J Med. 1986;314:265.

243 **Morrison J et al.** Digitalis and myocardial infarction in men. Circulation. 1980;62:8.

244 **Majerus T et al.** Dobutamine: ten years later. Pharmacotherapy. 1989;9:245.

245 **Thomas R.** Review of intermittent dobutamine infusions for congestive cardiomyopathy. Pharmacotherapy. 1987;7:47.

246 **Pickworth K.** Long term dobutamine therapy for refractory congestive heart failure. Clin Pharm. 1992;11:618.

247 **Goldstein R et al.** A comparison of digoxin and dobutamine in patients with acute infarction and cardiac failure. N Engl J Med. 1980;303:846.

248 **Colucci W et al.** New positive inotropic agents in the treatment of congestive heart failure. N Engl J Med. 1986; 314(2-part series):290,349.

249 **Hasegawa G.** Milrinone, a new agent for the treatment of congestive heart failure. Clin Pharm. 1986;5:201.

250 **Young R, Ward A.** Milrinone: a preliminary review of its pharmacological properties and therapeutic use. Drugs. 1988;36:158.

251 **Hillerman D, Forbes W.** Role of milrinone in the management of congestive heart failure. DICP, Ann Pharmacother. 1989;23:357.

252 **Anderson J et al.** Occurrence of ventricular arrhythmias in patients receiving acute and chronic infusion of milrinone. Am Heart J. 1986;111:466.

253 **DiBianco R et al.** A comparison of oral milrinone, digoxin and their combination in the treatment of patients with chronic heart failure. N Engl J Med. 1989;320:677.

254 **Packer M et al.** (PROMISE study research group). Effect of milrinone on mortality in severe chronic heart failure. N Engl J Med. 1991;325:1468.

255 **Uretsky BF et al.** Multicenter trial of oral enoximone in patients with moderate to moderately severe congestive heart failure: lack of benefit compared to placebo. Circulation. 1990;82:774.

256 **Goldberg AD et al.** Effectiveness of imazodan for treatment of chronic congestive heart failure. Am J Cardiol. 1991;68:631.

257 **Kubo SH et al.** Beneficial effects of pimobendan on exercise tolerance and quality of life in patients with heart failure: results of a multicenter trial. Circulation. 1992;85:942.

258 **Katz S et al.** A multicenter, randomized, double blind, placebo controlled trial of pimobendan, a new cardiotonic and vasodilator agent, in patients with severe congestive heart failure. Am Heart J. 1992;123:95.

259 **Hagemeijer F.** Intractable heart failure despite angiotensin-converting enzyme inhibitors, digoxin, and diuretics: long term effectiveness of add-on therapy with pimobendan. Am Heart J. 1991; 122:517.

260 **The Xamaterol in Severe Heart Failure Study Group.** Xamaterol in severe heart failure. Lancet. 1990;336:1.

261 **Itoh H.** Clinical pharmacology of ibopamine. Am J Med. 1991;90(Suppl. 5B):36S.

262 **Anon.** Flosequinan for heart failure. The Medical Letter on Drugs and Therapeutics. 1993;35:23–4.

263 **Packer M et al.** Double blind, placebo controlled study of the efficacy of flosequinan in patients with chronic heart failure. J Am Coll Cardiol. 1993;22:65.

264 **Marchionni N et al.** Acute and long term effects of flosequinan in patients with chronic cardiac failure. Am Heart J. 1993;126:147.

265 **Feldman A et al.** Effects of vesnarinone on morbidity and mortality in patients with heart failure. N Engl J Med. 1993;329:149.

266 **Krukemyer JA.** Use of beta adrenergic blocking agents in congestive heart failure. Clin Pharm. 1990;9:853.

267 **Gilbert EM et al.** Long term beta blocker vasodilator therapy improves cardiac function in idiopathic dilated cardiomyopathy: a double blind, randomized study of bucindolol versus placebo. Am J Med. 1990;88:223.

268 **Walsh R.** The effects of calcium entry blockade in normal and ischemic ventricular diastolic function. Circulation. 1989;80(Suppl. IV):52.

269 **Bristow M.** Pathophysiologic and pharmacologic rationales for clinical management of chronic heart failure with beta blocking agents. Am J Cardiol. 1993;71:12C.

270 **Haber H et al.** Why do patients with congestive heart failure tolerate the initiation of beta blocker therapy? Circulation. 1993;88(Pt. 1):1610.

271 **Eichhorn E.** The paradox of beta adrenergic blockade for the management of congestive heart failure. Am J Med. 1992;92:527.

Cardiac Arrhythmias

Moses SS Chow
Heather R Kertland

Electrophysiology 16-1
  Cellular Electrophysiology 16-1
  Normal Cardiac Electrophysiology 16-2
    Automaticity 16-2
    Conduction 16-2
An Approach to Reading Electrocardiograms (ECG) 16-3
  Electrocardiographic paper 16-3
  Rhythm interpretation 16-3
Pathophysiology 16-3
  Arrhythmogenesis 16-3
    Abnormal Impulse Formation 16-3
    Abnormal Impulse Conduction 16-3
      Re-entry 16-3
      Block 16-4
Classification of Arrhythmias 16-4
Antiarrhythmic Drugs 16-4
Supraventricular Arrhythmias 16-4
Atrial Fibrillation/Flutter 16-4
  Clinical manifestation and underlying causes 16-5
  Consequences of 16-5
  Treatment 16-7
    Goals of therapy 16-7
    Ventricular rate control (Also see Question 6) 16-7
      Digoxin 16-7
      β-adrenergic blocking agents 16-7
      Calcium channel blockers 16-8
      Adenosine 16-8
    Conversion to normal sinus rhythm (NSR) 16-8
      Chemical 16-8
      Electrical Conversion 16-8
    Antiarrhythmic agents 16-9
      Therapeutic monitoring 16-10
  Stroke prophylaxis 16-11
  Atrial fibrillation as a complication of
    bypass surgery 16-11
Paroxysmal Supraventricular Tachycardia (PSVT) 16-11
  Clinical presentation 16-11
  Arrhythmogenesis 16-12
  Treatment 16-12

  Nondrug treatment 16-12
  Drug therapy 16-12
Wolff-Parkinson-White (WPW) Syndrome 16-13
Conduction Blocks 16-13
Ventricular Arrhythmias 16-14
Recognition and Definition 16-14
Etiology 16-14
Evaluation of Life-Threatening Ventricular
  Arrhythmias 16-14
    Holter monitoring 16-14
    Electrophysiological studies (EPS) 16-14
Premature Ventricular Contractions (PVCs) 16-15
Nonsustained Ventricular Tachycardia (NSVT) 16-16
Sustained Ventricular Tachycardia (SuVT)
  (Also see Question 28) 16-16
    Treatment 16-16
      Lidocaine (Also see Question 24) 16-16
      Procainamide 16-16
      Sotalol 16-17
      Quinidine (See Question 28) 16-18
Torsade de Pointes 16-17
  Proarrhythmic effects of drugs and clinical
    presentation 16-17
  Treatment 16-17
Amiodarone versus Combination Therapy for
  Ventricular Tachycardia (VT) 16-18
Implantable Cardiac Defibrillators (ICDs) 16-19
Ventricular Fibrillation Prophylaxis 16-19
Cardiopulmonary Arrest 16-19
Cardiopulmonary Resuscitation (CPR) 16-19
Treatment 16-19
  Defibrillation 16-20
  Epinephrine 16-20
  Endotracheal drug administration 16-20
  Arterial blood gases (ABGs) and sodium
    bicarbonate administration 16-20
Pulseless Electrical Activity (PEA) 16-21
Asystole 16-23

The primary function of the heart is to pump blood to the rest of the body which depends upon a continuous, well-coordinated electrical activity within the heart. The generation of regular electrical activity from the sino-atrial (SA) node produces a regular rate and rhythm leading to regular cardiac contraction. Arrhythmia (dysrhythmia) results when disturbances of the rate and/or rhythm occur leading to abnormal contraction or, in the worst case, cardiac standstill. This chapter will review and discuss cardiac electrophysiology, arrhythmogenesis, common arrhythmias, and antiarrhythmic treatment.

Electrophysiology
Cellular Electrophysiology

Our understanding of the electrical activity of the heart comes from microelectrode studies of individual cells. These studies dem-

onstrate that an electrical potential exists across the cell membrane and the electrical potential changes in a cyclic manner that is related to the flux of ions across the cell membrane, principally K^+, Na^+, Ca^{2+}, Cl^-. If the change in the membrane potential is plotted against time in a given cycle of an HIS-Purkinje fiber, a typical action potential results (see Figure 16.1). The action potential can be described in five phases. Phase 0, is the rapid rate of rise which is related to depolarization resulting from rapid sodium entry into the cell. On a surface electrocardiogram (ECG), phase 0 is represented by the QRS complex for ventricular depolarization. Phase 1 is the overshoot. During phase 2, calcium enters the cell and contraction occurs. Phase 3 represents repolarization; on the surface ECG, ventricular repolarization is represented by the T wave. During phase 4, sodium moves out of the cell and potassium moves into the cell. During this phase the action potential remains flat in

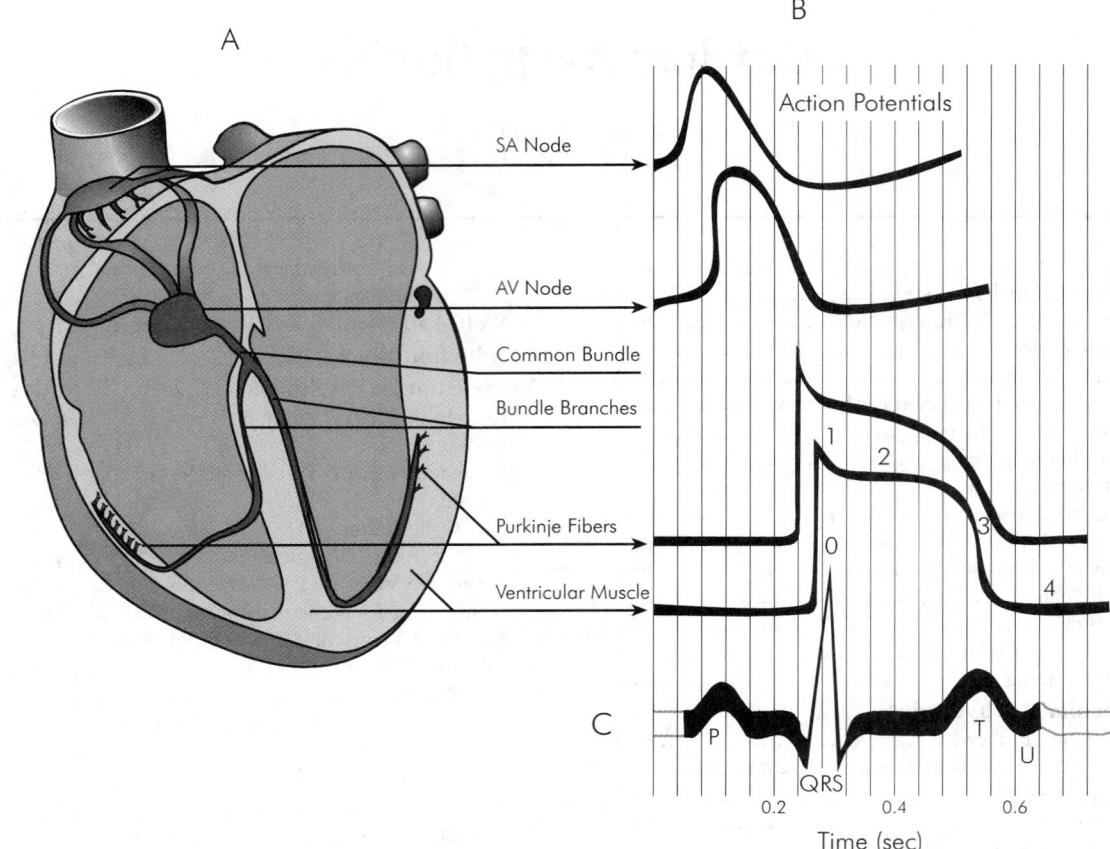

Fig 16.1   The Cardiac Conduction System   A: Cardiac conduction system anatomy; B: Action potentials of specific cardiac cells; C: Relationship of surface electrocardiogram to the action potential.

some cells (e.g., ventricular muscle) and does not change until it receives an impulse from above; while in other cells (e.g., SA node) the cell slowly depolarizes until it reaches the threshold potential, at which point it once again spontaneously depolarizes (phase 0). The shape of the action potential depends upon the location of the cell (see Figure 16.1). In both the SA and atrioventricular (AV) node, the cells are more dependent upon calcium than sodium resulting in a less negative resting membrane potential, a slow rise of phase 0, and spontaneous (automatic) phase 4 depolarization (see Figure 16.1).

The slope or rate of rise of phase 0 is referred to as Vmax and is related to the conduction velocity. The steeper the slope, the more rapid the rate of depolarization, and thus the faster the conduction velocity. Another influence on Vmax is the point at which depolarization occurs. The less negative the threshold potential, the slower Vmax will be and hence conduction velocity is slowed. Drugs can affect Vmax and conduction velocity by blocking the sodium channels or by making the resting membrane potential less negative (e.g., class I agents).

The action potential duration (APD) is the length of time from phase 0 to the end of phase 3. The effective refractory period (ERP) is the length of time that the cell is refractory and will not propagate another impulse. Both of these measurements can be obtained from intracardiac recordings of the action potential. Drugs, especially class III agents, can prolong the refractoriness of the heart.

Normal Cardiac Electrophysiology

Normal cardiac electrical activity begins with automatic impulse generation (automaticity) at the SA node and then is followed by the conduction of the impulse.

Automaticity is the ability of a cell (often referred to as a pacemaker cell) to depolarize spontaneously. These cells are located in the SA and AV nodes and the HIS-Purkinje system; the SA node is the dominant pacemaker. As the cell spontaneously depolarizes, a gradual decrease in the transmembrane potential occurs until the threshold potential is reached and an action potential (electrical impulse) is generated. At this point, the electrical impulse spreads and conducts down the conducting system of the heart. The rate of impulse generation varies at different sites, with the SA node normally depolarizing at a rate of 60 to 100 per minute. The automatic rate of the AV node is 40 to 60 per minute, while the rate of the Purkinje fibers is approximately ≤40/minute. In the healthy heart, the slower pacemaker cells of the AV node and Purkinje fibers are prevented from spontaneous depolarization (overridden) by the more frequent impulses from the SA node. If the normal conduction system is disrupted [e.g., after a myocardial infarction (MI)], the AV node or Purkinje fibers may temporarily become the dominant pacemaker.

Conduction. Under normal conditions, an impulse originates in the SA node and travels down the specialized intranodal pathways to activate the atrial muscle and the AV node. It then travels down the bundle of HIS to the right and left bundle branches and out to the ventricular myocardium via the Purkinje fibers. The ECG tracing consists of a series of complexes which correspond to electrical activity in a specific location or anatomic site. By convention, these electrical deflections have been labeled the P wave, QRS complex, and T wave. The P wave represents depolarization of the atria, while the QRS complex reflects ventricular depolarization. The T wave reflects repolarization of the ventricles. To evaluate the intact conduction system, conduction intervals at different sites can be obtained. The normal intervals as measured by ECG or intracardiac electrodes are shown in Table 16.1. Drugs and ischemia can alter the conduction and hence the ECG intervals. The effect of antiarrhythmic agents on the ECG are described in Table 16.2.

An Approach to Reading Electrocardiograms (ECG)

Electrocardiographic Paper

Calculation of the various intervals and widths is facilitated by recording the ECG waveforms on graph paper. This paper consists of large squares defined by heavier lines, which in turn are composed of smaller squares. Each small square is 1 mm in length and represents 0.04 seconds in time. The larger squares are composed of 5 small squares (5 mm in length) and represent 0.20 seconds. (See Figure 16.2.)

Rhythm Interpretation

Rhythm disturbances are approached most easily through a systematic review of the ECG tracing with particular emphasis on the following points:

1. *Rate: Is the rate fast or slow?* A simple method to rapidly determine the rate is to count the number of complexes occurring within six seconds and multiply by 10. Most ECG recording paper places vertical lines at the top of the ECG grid which are three seconds apart. Therefore, if eight complexes appear within a six second length of strip, the rate is 80 beats/minute.

2. *Are there P waves before each QRS complex and is their configuration normal? Are the P wave-to-P wave and R wave-to-R wave intervals regular or irregular?* If the rhythm is irregular, is the pattern of irregularity consistent (regularly irregular) or totally random (irregularly irregular)? P waves appearing before the QRS complex usually indicate that the impulse originated in the SA node and subsequently was conducted to the ventricle. Abnormal-appearing P waves indicate that an atrial site other than the SA node is initiating the beat. Irregular rhythms may be due to an impulse originating from a site other than the SA node before the normal pacemaker can fire (premature beat); they also may result from failure to conduct impulses from the atria.

Table 16.1		Normal Electrophysiological Intervals	
Interval	Normal Indices (msec)	Electrical Activity	Measured by[e]
PR	120–200	Atrial depolarization	Surface ECG
QRS	<140	Ventricular depolarization	Surface ECG
QT$_c$[a]	≤400	Ventricular repolarization	Surface ECG
JT[b]	—	Ventricular repolarization	Surface ECG
AH[c]	<140	—	Intracardiac lead
HV[d]	<55	—	Intracardiac lead

[a] Qt$_c$ interval is the QT interval corrected for heart rate. A common method for calculating Qt$_c$ is the QT interval/(RR interval)$^{1/2}$ (Bazette's Formula).
[b] JT interval is obtained by subtracting the QRS interval from the QT interval.
[c] AH interval is the time that it takes for an impulse to travel from the sino atrial (SA) node to the bundle of HIS.
[d] HV interval is the time that it takes for an impulse to travel from the bundle of HIS to the Purkinje fibers.
[e] ECG = Electrocardiogram.

Table 16.2		Pharmacologic Properties of Antiarrhythmics[a]			
	Surface ECG				
Type	PR Interval	QRS Interval	QT Interval	Conduction Velocity	Refractory Period
IA	0/↑	↑	↑↑	↑↓[b]	↑
IB	0	0	0	0/↓	↓
IC	↑	↑↑	↑	↓	0
II	↑↑	0	0	↓[c]	↑[c]
III	0[d]	0	↑↑	0	↑
IV	↑↑	0	0	↓[c]	↑[c]

[a] ECG = Electrocardiogram.
[b] Conduction increases at low doses; decreases at higher doses.
[c] On atrial and atrioventricular (AV) nodal tissue.
[d] May cause PR prolongation independent of Class III antiarrhythmic activity.

3. *Are the PR and QRS complexes within normal limits? Is the QRS complex normal in its configuration?* Impulses originating above the ventricles with normal conduction through the bundle branches and myocardium produce a normal-appearing, narrow QRS complex. Impulses originating in the ventricle give rise to wide, bizarre-appearing QRS complexes.

Pathophysiology

Arrhythmogenesis

Arrhythmias can occur as a result of abnormal impulse formation or abnormal impulse conduction or a combination of both. It generally is difficult to identify the specific mechanism and site of arrhythmogenesis in a given patient. However, identification of specific mechanisms is possible in some patients [see Wolff-Parkinson-White (WPW) Syndrome and Paroxysmal Supraventricular Tachycardia (PSVT)] using intracardiac recordings or "mapping." Understanding specific mechanisms by which abnormal impulses are formed and conducted allows us to understand how drugs may or may not work; these mechanisms are described below.

Abnormal impulse formation can arise from abnormal automaticity or triggered activity originating from the SA node (e.g., sinus bradycardia) or other sites (e.g., junctional or idioventricular tachycardia). Causes of abnormal automaticity include hypoxia, ischemia, or excess catecholamine activity.

Triggered activity occurs when there is an attempted depolarization before or after the cell is fully repolarized, but not by a pacemaker cell (see Figure 16.3). These after-depolarizations may occur in phase 2 or 3 (early) or phase 4 (delayed) of the action potential. Early after-depolarizations (EAD) arise from a reduced level of membrane potential and may require a bradycardic state. Torsade de Pointes, a form of polymorphic ventricular tachycardia is thought to be initiated by EAD. Delayed after-depolarizations (DAD), often seen with digoxin toxicity, are thought to be secondary to an overload of intracellular free calcium.

Abnormal Impulse Conduction: Re-Entry. The most common abnormal conduction leading to arrhythmogenesis is re-entry. A reentrant circuit is formed as normal conduction occurs down a pathway that bifurcates into two pathways (e.g., AV node or left and right bundle branches). The impulse travels along one pathway (see Figure 16.4, Pathway 1), but encounters a unidirectional antegrade block in the other pathway (see Figure 16.4, Pathway 2). The impulse which passed through the unblocked pathway propagates in a retrograde manner through the previously blocked pathway. This

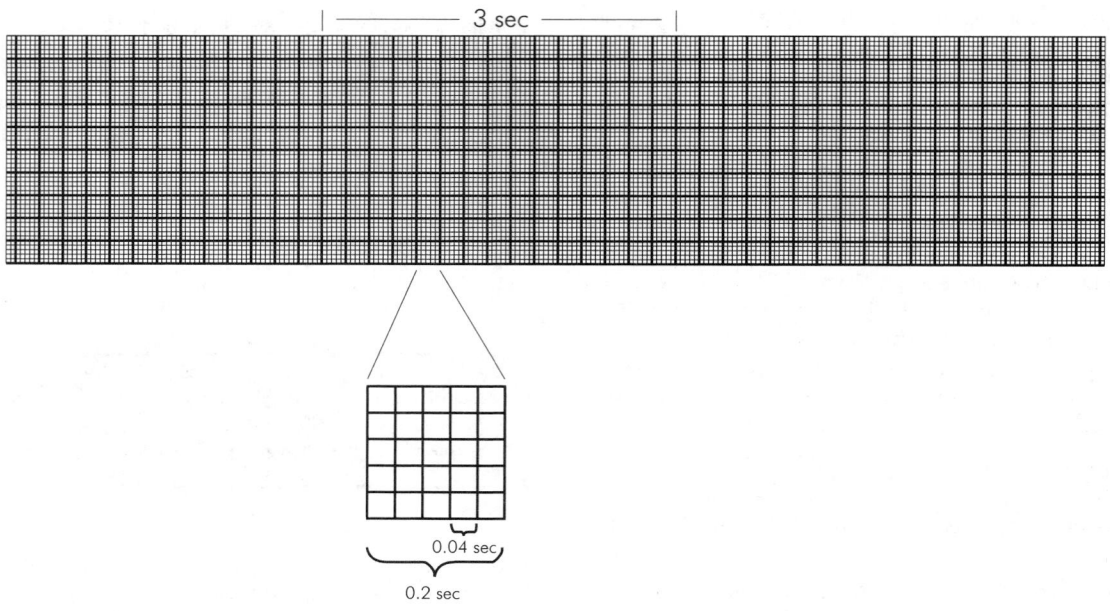

Fig 16.2   ECG Recording Paper

impulse can travel down the first pathway again when it is not refractory (see Figure 16.4). Supraventricular and monomorphic ventricular tachycardia are both examples of re-entrant arrhythmias.

Block. Another form of abnormal impulse conduction occurs when the normal conducting pathway is blocked and the impulse is forced to travel through non-pathway tissues to cause depolarization. Common examples are left and right bundle branch blocks in the ventricles. A block in one path necessitates retrograde conduction through the opposite bundle to stimulate both ventricles. Typically, the non-pathway tissue conducts the electrical impulse more slowly than conduction tissues.

Classification of Arrhythmias

One method of classifying arrhythmias is based upon their location. All arrhythmias originating above the bundle of HIS are referred to as supraventricular arrhythmias. These may include sinus bradycardia, sinus tachycardia, paroxysmal supraventricular tachycardia, atrial flutter, atrial fibrillation (AF), Wolff-Parkinson-White syndrome, and premature atrial contractions (PACs). All of these arrhythmias are characterized by normal QRS complexes (i.e., normal ventricular depolarization) unless there is a bundle branch block. Not all of these rhythm changes are necessarily a sign of pathology. For example, athletes with well-conditioned hearts and large stroke volumes commonly have slow heart rates (sinus bradycardia). Vigorous exercise commonly is accompanied by sinus tachycardia which is mediated by catecholamines that stimulate the SA node to fire more rapidly.

Arrhythmias originating below the bundle of HIS are referred to as ventricular arrhythmias. These include premature ventricular contractions (PVCs), ventricular tachycardia (VT), and ventricular fibrillation (VF). Conduction blocks often are listed separately based upon their level or location, which can be at supraventricular site (e.g., first, second, or third degree AV block) or in the ventricle (e.g., right or left bundle branch block). An alternative method of classifying arrhythmias is based upon the rate: bradyarrhythmias (those <60 beats/min) and tachyarrhythmias (those >100 beats/min).

This chapter will first address supraventricular arrhythmias, then conduction blocks, and lastly ventricular arrhythmias.

Antiarrhythmic Drugs

Based upon their electrophysiologic and pharmacologic effects, antiarrhythmic agents can be classified into four classes (Vaughn-Williams classification). Class I drugs are sodium channel blockers and are subdivided further into class IA, IB, and IC agents. These subclasses are differentiated by their effects on the sodium channel. Class II drugs are β-adrenergic blockers, Class III drugs are potassium channel blockers which invoke a significant effect on refractoriness, and Class IV drugs are calcium channel blockers. The classification, pharmacokinetics, dosages, and adverse effects of these agents are summarized in Table 16.3.

Supraventricular Arrhythmias

Supraventricular arrhythmias include all arrhythmias which originate from above the bifurcation of the bundle of HIS. The specific arrhythmias include: 1) those primarily atrial in origin such as atrial fibrillation, atrial flutter, paroxysmal sinus tachycardia, ectopic atrial tachycardia, and multifocal atrial tachycardia and 2) atrioventricular nodal re-entrant tachycardia (AVNRT) and AV re-entrant tachycardia (AVRT) involving accessory pathways that include the atria and ventricle. The last two often self-terminate and are paroxysmal (episodic) in nature; thus, they are called simply paroxysmal supraventricular tachycardias (PSVT).

The most common of these arrhythmias are atrial fibrillation, atrial flutter, and PSVT. Other arrhythmias generated at the supraventricular site such as Wolff-Parkinson-White syndrome and AV block possess unique characteristics and will be discussed separately.

Atrial Fibrillation/Flutter

Atrial fibrillation is characterized by rapid, ineffective writhing of atrial muscle with a classic "irregularly irregular" ventricular rate. The source of the arrhythmia is one or more ectopic areas (foci) that act as independent pacemakers and fire at such a rate as to suppress normal impulse generation from the SA node. On the ECG, no identifiable P waves are present (see Figure 16.5). Atrial flutter (see Figure 16.6) is characterized by typical "sawtooth" atrial waves, at a rate between 280 to 320 beats/minute and a var-

A. Early After-Depolarization

B. Delayed After-Depolarization

Time

Fig 16.3 Triggered Activity A: Early after-depolarizations; repolarization is interrupted by secondary depolarization. Such responses may excite neighboring fibers and be propagated. B: Delayed after-depolarizations; after full repolarization is achieved the cell transiently depolarizes. If the delayed after-depolarization reaches threshold, a propagating response can be seen (– – –). Reprinted with permission from reference 76.

iable ventricular rate depending upon the nature of AV block present (e.g., 2:1, 3:1, or 4:1 block). In most cases, the ventricular rate is about 150 beats/minute. Patients with atrial flutter often progress to atrial fibrillation. The underlying diseases and treatments of atrial flutter and atrial fibrillation are similar. The arrhythmogenic mechanism of atrial fibrillation may be due to multiple re-entrant wavelets, occurring in either a paroxysmal, chronic or acute pattern. The most common presentation is paroxysmal atrial fibrillation which can progress to chronic atrial fibrillation; thus, the two overlap each other. An example of paroxysmal atrial fibrillation (PAF) is presented below:

Clinical Manifestation and Underlying Causes

1. J.K., a 66-year-old male, presents with complaints of dyspnea on exertion (DOE) and palpitations for the last 2 weeks. He experienced palpitations of shorter duration 3 times in the last year, but these were not associated with DOE. His past medical history is significant for pericarditis 1 year ago, non-insulin dependent diabetes mellitus (NIDDM) for the past 5 years, and gout. There is no prior history of rheumatic heart disease, MI, congestive heart failure (CHF), pulmonary embolism, or thyroid disease. Medications include tolbutamide (Orinase) 500 mg BID, ibuprofen (Motrin) 600 mg QID, and allopurinol (Zyloprim) 300 mg/day. J.K. denies smoking and any intake of alcohol. Physical examination reveals a blood pressure (BP) of 136/84 mm Hg, pulse of 154 beats/min with an irregularly irregular pattern, respiratory rate of 16 breaths/min, and temperature of 98.2 °F. J.K.'s chest had rales at both bases. Cardiac examination revealed an irregularly irregular rhythm without murmurs, gallops, or rubs. His jugular vein was distended 4 cm, but no organomegaly was found. His extremities had 1+ pitting edema. The ECG showed AF (see Figure 16.5) and the chest x-ray was compatible with mild CHF. A cardiac echocardiogram revealed the atrial size to be <5 cm

(normal). In view of his history and previous episodes, J.K. is diagnosed to have paroxysmal atrial fibrillation. Which of J.K.'s other medical problems may predispose him to development of atrial fibrillation? What other conditions commonly are associated with AF?

Atrial fibrillation commonly is associated with or can be a common manifestation of other cardiac disease. J.K.'s previous episode of pericarditis most likely is the underlying cause of his atrial fibrillation. When treatable underlying causes are present they should be corrected since this may result in resolution of the atrial fibrillation. Other conditions commonly associated with atrial fibrillation are shown in Table 16.4.[1] In a small percentage of patients who do not have underlying heart disease, their atrial fibrillation is called "lone" atrial fibrillation which has a more benign course. J.K.'s negative alcohol history is important since both acute alcohol ingestion and cardiomyopathy associated with chronic alcoholism can trigger atrial fibrillation and other supraventricular arrhythmias.

Consequences of Atrial Fibrillation

2. What clinical findings demonstrated by J.K. typically are associated with atrial fibrillation? What are the likely consequences of his atrial fibrillation?

The most common complaint, as with J.K., is chest palpitations. This is a result of the rapid ventricular contraction rate which typically ranges from 100 to 160 beats/minute. The heart rate and RR interval (time from the R wave in one QRS complex to the R wave in the next complex) is irregularly irregular (random irregularity). During atrial fibrillation, the "atrial kick" or the atria's contribution to stroke volume, is lost. Since the "atrial kick" may account for 20% to 30% of the total stroke volume, symptoms of inadequate blood flow such as lightheadedness, dizziness, or reduced exercise tolerance may occur during atrial fibrillation. It is important to realize, however, that some patients are asymptomatic except for the palpitations. Depending upon the underlying ventricular function, the patient also may develop signs of CHF such as dyspnea on exertion and peripheral edema, as experienced by J.K. Conversely, underlying CHF may be an underlying cause of atrial fibrillation.

In patients with co-existing pre-excitation syndrome (e.g., WPW; see Question 17), dangerously rapid ventricular rates may occur as the atrial fibrillatory rate of 350 to 600 beats/minute is conducted down the accessory pathways. This predisposes patients to the development of ventricular fibrillation.

Fig 16.4 Re-Entrant Circuit of the Ventricle. A branched Purkinje fiber (PF) terminates on a strip of ventricular muscle (VM). The shaded area in branch 2 represents a depolarized area that is the site of a one-way block; thus, the sinus impulses are blocked in this area, but retrograde impulses are propagated. Retrograde conduction in branch 2 is slow enough for cells in branch 1 to recover and respond to the re-entry impulse. Reprinted with permission from reference 76.

Table 16.3	Vaughn-Williams Classification of Antiarrhythmic Agents[a]		
Drug and Classification	**Pharmacokinetics**	**Indications**	**Side Effects**
Class IA			
Quinidine sulfate (SR: Quinidex) Quinidine Gluconate (Quinaglute)	% quinidine: Sulfate = 83%, Gluconate = 62%; $t\frac{1}{2}$ = 6.2 ± 1.8 hr; Vd = 2.7 L/kg; Liver metabolism 80%; Renal clearance 20%; Cp = 2–6 µg/mL	AF, WPW, PVCs, VT	Diarrhea, hypotension, N/V, cinchonism, fever, thrombocytopenia, proarrhythmia
Procainamide (Pronestyl; SR: Pronestyl SR, Procan SR)	$t\frac{1}{2}$ = 3 ± 0.6 hr; Vd = 1.9 ± 0.3 L/kg; Liver metabolism 40%; Renal clearance 40%–60%; Active metabolite (NAPA)[b] Cp = 4–10 µg/mL	AF, WPW, PVCs, VT	Hypotension, fever, agranulocytosis, SLE, headache, proarrhythmia
Disopyramide (Norpace; SR: Norpace CR)	$t\frac{1}{2}$ = 6 ± 1 hr; Vd = 0.59 ± 0.15 L/kg; Liver metabolism 30%; Renal clearance 70%; Cp = 3–6 µg/mL	AF, WPW, PSVT, PVCs, VT	Anticholinergic (dry mouth, blurred vision, urinary retention), CHF, proarrhythmia
Class IB[c]			
Lidocaine (Xylocaine)	$t\frac{1}{2}$ = 1.8 ± 0.4 hr; Vd = 1.1 ± 0.4 L/kg; Liver metabolism 100%; Cp = 1.5–6 µg/mL	Ventricular arrhythmias only (PVCs, VT, VF)	Drowsiness, agitation, muscle twitching, seizures, paresthesias, proarrhythmia
Mexiletine (Mexitil)	$t\frac{1}{2}$ = 10.4 ± 2.8 hr; Vd = 9.5 ± 3.4 L/kg; Liver metabolism 35%–80%; Cp = 0.5–2 µg/mL	Ventricular arrhythmias only (PVCs, VT, VF)	Drowsiness, agitation, muscle twitching, seizures, paresthesias, proarrhythmia, N/V
Tocainide (Tonocard)	$t\frac{1}{2}$ = 13.5 ± 2.3 hr; Vd = 3 ± 0.2 L/kg; Liver metabolism 60%–65%; Cp = 6–15 µg/mL	Ventricular arrhythmias only (PVCs, VT, VF)	Drowsiness, agitation, muscle twitching, seizures, paresthesias, proarrhythmia, N/V, diarrhea, agranulocytosis
Class IC			
Flecainide (Tambocor)	$t\frac{1}{2}$ = 12–27 hr; Liver metabolism 75%; Renal clearance 25%; Cp = 0.4–1 µg/mL	AF, PSVT, life-threatening ventricular arrhythmias	Dizziness, tremor, lightheadedness, flushing, blurred vision, metallic taste, proarrhythmia
Propafenone (Rythmol)	$t\frac{1}{2}$ = 2 hr (extensive metabolizer); 10 hr (poor metabolizer); Vd = 2.5–4 L/kg	PAF, WPW, life-threatening ventricular arrhythmias	Dizziness, blurred vision, taste disturbances, nausea, worsening of asthma, proarrhythmia
Moricizine (Ethmozine)	$t\frac{1}{2}$ = 1.3–3.5 hr; Vd >300 L	Life-threatening ventricular arrhythmias	Nausea, dizziness, perioral numbness, euphoria
Class II			
Beta blockers Acebutalol (Sectral) Esmolol (Brevibloc) Propranolol (Inderal)	See Chapters 10: Essential Hypertension and 17: Hypertensive Emergencies	AF, A flutter, PSVT, PVCs	See Chapters 10: Essential Hypertension and 17: Hypertensive Emergencies
Class III			
Amiodarone (Cordarone)	$t\frac{1}{2}$ = 40–60 days; Vd = 60–100 L/kg; Erratic absorption; Liver metabolism 100%; Cp = 0.5–2.5 µg/mL	AF, PAF, PSVT, life-threatening ventricular arrhythmias	Blurred vision, photophobia, constipation, pulmonary fibrosis, ataxia, thyroid abnormalities, proarrhythmia (See Question 27)
Sotalol[d] (Betapace)	$t\frac{1}{2}$ = 10–20 hr; Vd = 1.2–2.4 L/kg; Renal clearance = 100%	AF, PSVT, life-threatening ventricular arrhythmias	Fatigue, dizziness, dyspnea, bradycardia, proarrhythmia
Bretylium (Bretylol)	$t\frac{1}{2}$ = 8.9 ± 1.8 hr; Vd = 5.9 ± 0.3 L/kg; Renal clearance 80%–90%	VT, VF	Hypotension, N/V, lightheadedness, dizziness, transitory hypertension, tachycardia
Class IV			
Calcium Channel Blockers Verapamil (Isoptin) Diltiazem (Cardizem)	See Chapters 13: Ischemic Heart Disease, 10: Essential Hypertension, and 17: Hypertensive Emergencies	AF, A flutter, PSVT	Hypotension, bradycardia, dizziness, headache, constipation

[a] AF = Atrial fibrillation; A flutter = Atrial flutter; CHF = Congestive heart failure; CP=Steady-state plasma concentration; N/V = Nausea and vomiting; PAF = Paroxysmal atrial fibrillation; PSVT= Paroxysmal supraventricular tachycardia; PVCs = Premature ventricular contractions; SLE = Systemic lupus erythematosus; $t\frac{1}{2}$ = Half-life; Vd = Volume of distribution; VT=Ventricular tachycardia; WPW= Wolff-Parkinson-White syndrome.
[b] N-acetylprocainamide (NAPA) is 100% renally eliminated and possesses Class III antiarrhythmic activity.
[c] Phenytoin is classified as a Class IB antiarrhythmic.
[d] Possesses both Class II and III antiarrhythmic activity.

Note undulating baseline with no discernable P waves.

Fig 16.5 Atrial Fibrillation Note the irregularly, irregular R-R intervals, undulating baseline without definitive P waves, normal width of the QRS complexes, and the ventricular rate of 140 beats/minute.

Patients with atrial fibrillation such as J.K. are at risk for a thrombotic stroke.[2,3] With the chaotic movement of the atria, normal blood flow is disrupted and atrial mural thrombi may form. The risk of stroke increases with other associated disease states or following restoration to normal sinus rhythm (NSR) which allows for more efficient cardiac contractility and expulsion of the thrombus. Patients with nonvalvular atrial fibrillation (NVAF) have a fivefold increase in the risk of stroke; this risk increases as patients have an increased number of associated risk factors. Other factors that may increase the risk of stroke are CHF, cardiomyopathy, thyrotoxicosis, congenital heart disease, and valvular heart disease.

Treatment

3. Goals of Therapy. What are the therapeutic goals and general approaches used to treat atrial fibrillation in patients like J.K.?

The primary goals of treatment are to relieve symptoms and reduce the risk of stroke. Slowing the ventricular rate during fibrillation, restoring normal sinus rhythm, and preventing recurrences are key steps to accomplishing the first goal. (See Question 4.) To accomplish the second goal, treatment with anticoagulants is needed. It is important to note, however, that in patients with long-standing asymptomatic atrial fibrillation, restoration of normal sinus rhythm often is not desired since it actually may increase the stroke risk. In these cases, control of the ventricular rate is the primary goal. Patients who remain in normal sinus rhythm following cardioversion may not require long-term treatment with anticoagulants to reduce the risk of stroke. There is no guarantee, however, that normal sinus rhythm can be maintained in each patient; thus, prolonged treatment with anticoagulation often is necessary.

4. Ventricular Rate Control. J.K. was given a 1 mg loading dose of digoxin followed by a 0.25 mg QD maintenance dose and is being started on a trial of oral quinidine sulfate 300 mg Q 6 hr. If this is not successful in 2 days, direct-current cardioversion is planned. What is the purpose of giving digoxin? What are the relative advantages and disadvantages of digoxin compared to other agents to control the ventricular rate?

Digoxin. As indicated above, the first treatment goal is to slow the ventricular response rate, thus allowing the ventricles to contract and empty more effectively. Cardioversion to normal sinus rhythm can be delayed to a later time. Because of its direct AV node-blocking effects and vagomimetic properties, digoxin prolongs the effective refractory period of atrial tissue and reduces the number of impulses conducted through the AV node.[4] Thus, it is an effective, well-tolerated, inexpensive way to control the ventricular response rate in patients with atrial fibrillation (see Table 16.5 for dosages). Another possible advantage of digoxin is its positive inotropic effect, a potential benefit in patients with CHF; however, higher doses may be needed to control the heart rate relative to those used for congestive heart failure.

There are certain disadvantages to digoxin use. First, it has a slow onset of action. Even after an intravenous (IV) dose, an effect on the heart rate may not be seen for two to six hours, with maximal effect seen at six to eight hours.[5] Second, it is less effective during exercise or stress (i.e., emotional stress) when there is a high sympathetic tone.[6] Digoxin also is unreliable in converting atrial fibrillation to normal sinus rhythm, especially in patients who do not have CHF. While it has been reported that digoxin may convert acute atrial fibrillation to normal sinus rhythm, the one trial to show this was not placebo-controlled.[7]

β-adrenergic blocking agents are another class of drugs that are used to control heart rate in patients with atrial fibrillation. Propranolol, metoprolol, and esmolol are available for IV administration (see Table 16.5 for dosages). Each rapidly controls heart rate by slowing conduction through the AV node. Heart rate is controlled both at rest and during exercise with these agents. Beta blockers should not be used in patients with congestive heart failure, although they are the first choice in high catecholamine states such as thyrotoxicosis and postcardiac surgery.

Fig 16.6 Atrial Flutter Note the "sawtooth" appearance of the rhythm strip. Reprinted with permission from reference 126.

Table 16.4	Causes of Atrial Fibrillation and Flutter[a,b]
Cardiac Causes	
ASD	Nonrheumatic heart disease
Cardiac surgery	Tachycardia-bradycardia syndrome
Cardiomyopathy	Tumors, lipomatous hypertrophy
Ischemic heart disease	WPW
Mitral valve disease	
Systemic Causes	
Alcohol ("Holiday Heart")	Pneumonia
Cerebrovascular accident	Pulmonary embolism
Chronic pulmonary disease	Sudden emotional or psychological
Defibrillation	stress
Electrolyte abnormalities	Thyrotoxicosis
Fever	Trauma
Hypothermia	
Uncommon Causes	
Acute hypovolemia	Right atrial cold-fluid injection
Hypoglycemia	Swallowing
Multiple sclerosis	Tyramine-containing foods
Pheochromocytoma	Vasovagal syncope

[a] Reproduced with permission from reference 125.
[b] ASD = Atrial septal defect; WPW = Wolff-Parkinson-White syndrome.

Calcium channel blockers are another pharmacologic class of agents which are effective in slowing ventricular rate. Both verapamil and diltiazem can be administered intravenously for a rapid (in 4 to 5 minutes) reduction in heart rate (see Table 16.5 for dosages).[8,9] They work through their effect on the slow calcium channels, which affect both the SA and AV node. Although their duration of action produced by bolus doses is short, both agents can be administered either as a continuous drip or orally. An advantage of calcium channel blockers over digoxin is their effectiveness in controlling ventricular rates both at rest and during exercise. For the long-term control of heart rate, combination therapy (digoxin and a beta blocker or calcium channel blocker) might be optimal.[10,11] This therapy can avoid large doses of any one drug that might predispose the patient to adverse effects while at the same time controlling heart rate both at rest and during exercise. However, two precautions should be noted regarding verapamil: its use is limited in patients with CHF because of its negative inotropic properties and it has been reported to inhibit the nonrenal clearance of digoxin leading to a significant increase in digoxin serum concentrations (see Chapter 15: Congestive Heart Failure).

Adenosine is another agent that effectively blocks the AV node and can be used in diagnostic maneuvers (see Table 16.5 for dosages). Because of its extremely short action it does not have a role in the long-term control of heart rate.

The goal of rate control is a resting heart rate of less than 90 beats/minute and, during exercise, less than 140 beats/minute.[12] Rates of ≤60 beats/minute indicate a possible excessive dosage.

J.K. has signs of congestive heart failure, so digoxin is the drug of choice since it will help to control his ventricular rate in addition to giving inotropic support.

5. Conversion to Normal Sinus Rhythm (NSR): Chemical Conversion. **What is the efficacy of oral quinidine for "chemical conversion" compared to other agents used for the same purpose?**

After achieving ventricular rate control, more definitive treatment can be given in an attempt to convert the patient to normal sinus rhythm. This step is more likely to be taken in a patient with an acute onset of symptoms like J.K.

Oral quinidine has well-established effectiveness for acute "chemical" cardioversion, and this is correlated to the dose and plasma concentration achieved. The conversion rate is about 82% following a rapid quinidine load (200 mg Q 2 to 3 hr for 5 to 8

doses) that produces high quinidine concentrations as advocated by Sokolow and Edgar.[13] However, rapid quinidine loading also causes frequent side effects, especially nausea, vomiting, and diarrhea. This rapid loading method, therefore, is no longer a common clinical practice. With lower does, such as that received by J.K., the efficacy is only about 60%, but the treatment is better tolerated.[14] Quinidine conversion of atrial fibrillation should occur in the hospital setting with continuous ECG monitoring.

Other class IA oral agents are likely to be effective also; however, well-controlled efficacy data are limited. Intravenous procainamide has been reported to be effective in 43% to 58% of patients treated in uncontrolled studies.[15,16] A common dosing method of procainamide is to administer repeated 100 mg IV boluses at a rate of 20 mg/minute until either the arrhythmia is controlled, toxicity is observed, or a total of 1 gm has been administered.[17] This approach should achieve a plasma procainamide concentration of about 4 to 8 µg/mL in an average adult and usually is well tolerated and effective.

6. Since quinidine can convert the patient to NSR, why is it even necessary to attempt ventricular rate control with digoxin or calcium channel blockers first?

When converting patients to a normal sinus rhythm, one needs to realize that the effects of quinidine and other type IA antiarrhythmic agents on the AV node are bimodal. At low concentrations, AV node conduction may be enhanced by the drug's antivagal properties. If this occurs before normal sinus rhythm is achieved by quinidine, the ventricular rate actually may increase. At higher concentrations, the type IA agents slow AV node conduction. Since it is difficult to predict which effect on the AV node will predominate in a given patient, it is prudent to initiate a rate-controlling agent first.

Combined digoxin-quinidine therapy can have additive depressant effects on the AV node at higher concentrations, so it is important to assess the ventricular rate continuously to be sure it remains above 60 beats/minute. The patient also should be monitored clinically for signs of dizziness or lethargy that may denote poor cardiac output. To further complicate the picture, quinidine is known to increase serum concentrations of digoxin by inhibiting its renal and nonrenal clearance. Thus, serum digoxin concentrations also should be monitored during chronic therapy (see Chapter 15: Congestive Heart Failure).

However, it is important to re-emphasize that in chronic atrial fibrillation, rate control may be all that is desired, since conversion to normal sinus rhythm may increase the risk of dislodging atrial mural thrombi. In these patients, digoxin or a calcium channel blocker becomes the main therapeutic modality.

7. *Electrical Conversion.* **J.K. remains in AF despite acute quinidine treatment. Quinidine is discontinued and J.K. is scheduled for elective cardioversion in 3 weeks. Warfarin treatment is begun and J.K's prothrombin time is maintained at an international normalized ratio (INR) of 2 to 3. What are the advantages and disadvantages of direct-current cardioversion compared to "chemical conversion?" Is it safe to cardiovert patients when they are digitalized? Why is warfarin necessary?**

Direct current (DC) cardioversion quickly and effectively restores 85% to 90% of patients with AF to normal sinus rhythm.[18] If DC conversion alone is ineffective, it can be repeated in combination with antiarrhythmic drugs. Chemical conversion generally is preferred because direct-current conversion requires general anesthesia (short-acting benzodiazepine, barbiturate, or propofol), but DC cardioversion is indicated for patients who are hemodynamically unstable. It was once thought that digoxin should be held for two to three days before direct-current cardioversion because it placed patients at an increased risk of arrhythmia. This may be

Table 16.5	Agents Used for Controlling Ventricular Rate in Supraventricular Tachycardias[a]		
Drug	Loading Dose	Usual Maintenance Dose	Comments
Digoxin (Lanoxin)	10–15 μg/kg LBW up to 1–1.5 mg IV or PO over 24 hr (e.g., 0.5 mg initially, then 0.25 mg Q 6 hr)	PO: 0.125–0.5 mg/day. Adjust for renal failure (See Chapter 15: Congestive Heart Failure)	Maximum response may take several hours; use with caution in patients with renal impairment
Esmolol (Brevibloc)	0.5 mg/kg IV over 1 min	50–300 μg/kg/min continuous infusion with bolus between increases	Hypotension common, effects additive with digoxin and calcium channel blockers
Propranolol (Inderal)	0.5–1.0 mg IV repeated Q 2 min (up to 0.1–0.15 mg/kg)	IV: 0.04 mg/kg/min PO: 10–120 mg TID	Use with caution in patients with CHF or asthma; additive effects seen with digoxin and calcium channel blockers
Metoprolol (Lopressor)	5 mg IV at 1 mg/min	PO: 25–100 mg BID	Use with caution in patients with CHF or asthma; additive effects seen with digoxin and calcium channel blockers
Verapamil (Isoptin, Calan)	5–10 mg (0.075–0.15 mg/kg) IV over 2 min; if response inadequate after 15–30 min repeat 10 mg (up to 0.15 mg/kg)	IV: 5–10 mg/hr PO: 40–120 mg TID or 120–480 mg in extended-release form daily	Hypotension with IV route; effects are additive with digoxin and beta blockers; may ↑ digoxin levels
Diltiazem (Cardizem)	0.25 mg/kg IV over 2 min; if response inadequate after 15 min, repeat 0.35 mg/kg over 2 min	IV: 5–15 mg/hr PO: 60–90 mg TID or QID or 180–360 mg in extended-release form daily	Response to IV therapy occurs in 4–5 min; hypotension; effects additive with digoxin and beta blockers
Adenosine (Adenocard)	6 mg rapid IV bolus followed by flush; if ineffective, 12 mg bolus × 2 may be administered at 5–10 min intervals	N/A	Patients may experience chest tightness or breathlessness; transient complete heart block may occur

[a] LBW = Lean body weight; CHF = Congestive heart failure; N/A = Not available.

true for patients who have toxic concentrations of digoxin, but has not been noted in patients on usual maintenance therapy.[19] If a patient shows signs of digoxin toxicity, cardioversion should be started at a low energy (10 J) and increased as needed. At the time of cardioversion, J.K. had no clinical signs of digoxin toxicity so cardioversion could proceed.

J.K. was maintained on warfarin for three weeks before cardioversion to prevent the embolization of any clots that may have formed in his atrium. Early studies in patients with atrial fibrillation showed that those who were anticoagulated before cardioversion had a lower incidence (0.8%) of emboli than those who were not anticoagulated (5.3%).[20] The shortcomings of the trial were that the patients had underlying structural heart disease and were on long-term anticoagulation therapy. Warfarin is recommended for patients who have been in atrial fibrillation for more than two days during the three-week period before cardioversion.[21] The dose should be titrated to produce an INR of 2 to 3. If cardioversion is successful, patients should remain on warfarin for four weeks since normal atrial activity/function may not return for up to three weeks and patients may be at risk of late embolization.[18] J.K. has had atrial fibrillation for a minimum of two weeks; thus, he should be maintained on warfarin for three weeks before he is scheduled for cardioversion.

8. Antiarrhythmic Agents. **After 3 weeks of anticoagulation, J.K. successfully was converted to NSR using a single 200 J electric shock. He was discharged from the hospital on digoxin and warfarin and advised to follow-up with a cardiologist 4 weeks later. Within 2 weeks, J.K. complained of several episodes of brief, but self-terminating palpitations which caused him great concern. He was seen immediately by a physician who, after obtaining an ECG, prescribed oral quinidine (Quinidex) 600 mg Q 12 hr. What type of patients are likely to remain free of AF recurrence following cardioversion and while on maintenance therapy?**

Successful conversion to and maintenance of normal sinus rhythm is determined by the duration of the arrhythmia, underlying disease processes, and left atrial size.[22] Duration of atrial fibrillation for more than one year markedly reduces the chances of maintaining a normal sinus rhythm.[23] The best responses are seen in patients with thyrotoxicosis who have a 90% response rate to quinidine. Lower response rates are observed in patients with hypertensive heart disease (80% to 87%) or mitral stenosis or regurgitation (20% to 25%). When the atrial size exceeds 5 cm, there is less than a 10% chance of maintaining normal sinus rhythm at six months.

J.K.'s chance of being maintained in NSR probably is good since duration of his atrial fibrillation is short and the echocardiogram revealed only slight enlargement of his left atrium.

9. Evaluate the use of an antiarrhythmic agent to maintain J.K. in NSR. What are the risks and benefits of the different antiarrhythmic agents used for this purpose?

Whether J.K. should be placed on an antiarrhythmic is a judgment of benefit versus risk. There is no doubt that various antiarrhythmics can prevent episodes of atrial fibrillation. However, J.K.'s need for antiarrhythmic therapy should be weighed against the potential for adverse effects. To choose the best agent for J.K., the efficacy and adverse effect profile for each agent should be reviewed.

Class IA, IC, and III antiarrhythmics (see Table 16.2 for electrophysiologic and ECG effects and Table 16.3 for dosages) effectively prevent the recurrence of atrial fibrillation. However, among these agents, only quinidine and flecainide are approved by the Food and Drug Administration (FDA) for this indication and the greatest clinical experience is with quinidine. In one meta-analysis of six controlled trials of quinidine therapy for atrial fibrillation, Coplen et al. reported that treatment with quinidine was twice as likely as placebo to maintain normal sinus rhythm at one year after conversion.[24] However, there were 12 deaths (out of 373 patients) in the quinidine group compared to only three (out of 354 patients) in the control group. These included six noncardiac and six cardiac deaths in the quinidine group as compared to one noncardiac and two cardiac deaths in the control group. The differences in the cardiac deaths are not statistically significant, but it brings attention to the pro-arrhythmic effects of quinidine and other antiarrhythmic agents. In view of the limitations inherent in meta-analysis and the possibility that an interaction between quinidine and digoxin might have contributed to the higher mortality rates, quinidine's well-established therapeutic effect outweighs its potential adverse effects, thus justifying its use as a first-line agent in a patient like J.K. who has frequent symptomatic episodes.

If quinidine is used, sustained-release (SR) formulations such as Quinidex or quinidine gluconate are preferred because they produce smaller peak-to-trough fluctuations than rapid-release products and can be administered twice daily to enhance compliance.[25] Nausea, vomiting, and diarrhea occurring early in therapy are reported in up to 30% of patients receiving quinidine, requiring 10% to discontinue therapy. Whether this effect results from a direct stimulation of the smooth muscle of the small intestine or through a central effect is unknown. It has been suggested that quinidine gluconate may cause less diarrhea than quinidine sulfate formulations, but this may be related to differences in quinidine content (62% in the quinidine gluconate versus 82% in the quinidine sulfate) as opposed to absolute difference in dosage forms. A unique symptom complex referred to as cinchonism occurs when blood levels exceed 5 μg/mL. This disorder is characterized by disturbed hearing (tinnitus, decreased auditory acuity), visual abnormalities (blurred vision, altered color perception, diplopia), and CNS alterations (headache, confusion, delirium). Rarely, quinidine can cause thrombocytopenia which may develop several weeks to months after starting quinidine therapy and results from an antibody to a quinidine-platelet complex. Congestive heart failure and digoxin alter the pharmacokinetics of quinidine and this must be considered in J.K.'s case. CHF can reduce the rate and extent of quinidine absorption and decrease its volume of distribution. The elimination half-life remains unchanged, however, suggesting that quinidine clearance also is reduced. These changes result in higher quinidine plasma concentrations in patients with CHF. Increasing age reduces total body clearance, and the half-life of quinidine is prolonged in patients over the age of 60. In addition to the quinidine-digoxin interaction, it is important to remember that quinidine is a potent inhibitor of the cytochrome P450IID6 pathway which affects the metabolism of propafenone and other similar oxidative metabolized compounds.[26]

Other class IA agents such as oral disopyramide and procainamide, although possessing electrophysiologic properties and presumed efficacy similar to quinidine, are less well studied and should be reserved for patients who cannot tolerate quinidine. Care must be taken in the dosing of procainamide in patients with renal dysfunction since approximately 40% to 60% is eliminated renally. N-acetylprocainamide (NAPA), the active metabolite which possesses class III antiarrhythmic properties, is eliminated entirely by the kidneys and quickly accumulates in renal dysfunction, causing potential toxicity. Procainamide has a short half-life, and for this reason, standard preparations must be administered every three to four hours; hence, SR preparations administered every six to eight hours are favored by many clinicians. Short-term procainamide generally is well tolerated, but following long-term therapy, systemic lupus erythematosus and agranulocytosis become more prevalent. It is thought that slow acetylators are at increased risk for these long-term adverse effects.[27]

Disopyramide is not well tolerated in the elderly due to its anticholinergic side effects; 10% to 20% of patients experience urinary retention, dry mouth (40%), constipation (30%), and blurred vision (28%). In addition, disopyramide has a significant negative inotropic effect.

Class IC agents, especially flecainide and propafenone, are effective in the treatment of atrial fibrillation.[28–32] The efficacy rate may be as high as 61% to 92% for flecainide.[33] These agents slow conduction of cardiac tissue with little effect on refractory period. Flecainide, and possibly other class IC agents, may cause arrhythmias, especially in patients with structural heart disease. Therefore, they should be avoided in such patients, but, can be considered for those with preserved ventricular function and without structural heart disease. Whether propafenone, a class IC agent with beta-blocking properties, is safer than other agents in this class is unknown, but it may be preferred in a patient who requires additional AV blockade.

Class III agents (sotalol and amiodarone) prolong refractoriness in the atria, ventricle, AV node, and accessory pathway tissue and can prevent recurrence of atrial fibrillation. In one comparison study, sotalol was about as effective as quinidine in maintaining sinus rhythm after cardioversion.[34] Because of its beta-blocking property, it can reduce ventricular rate and may be tolerated better than quinidine. However, because sotalol may be arrhythmogenic in high doses, the QT interval should be monitored carefully.

Amiodarone has been shown to be more effective than quinidine.[35] Low doses of amiodarone (200 to 400 mg/day) have a high rate of efficacy and a reduced incidence of serious adverse effects often associated with high doses of this drug.[36] In view of its unusual pharmacokinetics and potential serious adverse effects (see Table 16.3 and Question 29), amiodarone should be reserved for refractory cases, although additional prospective trials using low dose amiodarone may prove it to be a promising agent.

In summary, there are potential risks and adverse reactions associated with each antiarrhythmic agent used to treat atrial fibrillation, especially when used in patients with a history of heart failure. The risk should be weighed against benefit and the need to maintain and control atrial fibrillation. Of all class IA, IC, and II agents, quinidine is the best studied and has the greatest clinical experience. In view of J.K.'s new onset of CHF and frequent uncomfortable episodes of atrial fibrillation, quinidine is the logical first choice since disopyramide, flecainide, propafenone, and sotalol may exacerbate heart failure. J.K. was started on 600 mg every 12 hours of a sustained-release form of quinidine sulfate to help with compliance. Due to his age he may have a prolonged half-life and his symptomatic CHF may decrease his volume of distribution so a relatively small dose was used initially. J.K.'s digoxin therapy should be monitored as quinidine may increase his digoxin concentration. If quinidine fails, low dose amiodarone deserves a trial.

10. *Therapeutic Monitoring.* **How should J.K.'s antiarrhythmic therapy be evaluated to insure efficacy and safety?**

If a patient is placed on a maintenance antiarrhythmic agent, it is imperative that the efficacy of the drug be documented and drug safety be monitored carefully. For paroxysmal atrial fibrillation, spontaneous self-termination of fibrillation episodes can occur and may be misinterpreted as drug efficacy. Furthermore, maintaining a patient on a drug assumed to be effective can endanger the patient because antiarrhythmic agents can provoke serious ventricular arrhythmias. One specific tool used to document drug efficacy is the battery-operated electrocardiogram recorder (e.g., Cardiobeeper Memory monitor, Survival Technology, Bethesda, MD). These devices record the rhythm when activated by the patient in the presence of symptoms [e.g., palpitations, thumping in chest, shortness of breath (SOB), dizziness] and can be played back and transmitted via telephone to the monitoring center. The number of symptomatic episodes and rhythm disturbances associated with or without treatment of a specific antiarrhythmic agent can be documented to ascertain whether or not the drug is effective. Relative efficacy of one drug also can be compared to another.

Stroke Prophylaxis

11. Should J.K. remain on warfarin therapy? Should aspirin be added?

As mentioned previously, patients with nonvalvular atrial fibrillation have a fivefold increased risk for stroke compared to patients with no atrial fibrillation.[2,3] This risk increases to 17-fold for patients with atrial fibrillation associated with valvular disease.[2] In three large randomized trials it has been shown that patients with nonvalvular atrial fibrillation benefit from antithrombotic therapy.[38–40] In the Stroke Prevention in Atrial Fibrillation (SPAF) study, both aspirin 325 mg/day and warfarin (titrated to an INR 2 to 4.5) reduced the risk of stroke significantly with an acceptable level of hemorrhagic complications.[40] The results of SPAF II, a direct comparison of warfarin and aspirin, indicated that warfarin was more effective than aspirin in preventing stroke, but a higher incidence of bleeding complications were noted with warfarin in patients older than 75 years of age, especially those with risk factors for bleeding [previous thromboembolism, gastrointestinal (GI) or genitourinary bleeding].[41] Thus, these patients and patients under 60 years of age who have ''lone'' atrial fibrillation should be maintained on aspirin alone. All other patients should receive low intensity (INR 2 to 3) warfarin.[42]

Because J.K. has low risk of bleeding (no history of thromboembolism, GI or genitourinary bleeding, no diastolic hypertension) and an increased risk of stroke due to atrial fibrillation, he should continue to receive low intensity warfarin. He should be counseled and monitored for signs of hemorrhagic complications (also see Chapter 12: Thrombosis). If J.K. stops quinidine for any reason, his INR should be followed closely because quinidine may potentiate warfarin's effect and its withdrawal may lead to a subtherapeutic warfarin effect.

Monotherapy with warfarin is adequate for J.K. and aspirin does not need to be added. Aspirin can be used as an alternative if J.K. is unwilling to take warfarin or if he develops an intolerable side effect while on warfarin.[43]

12. Does the treatment of atrial flutter differ from the treatment of atrial fibrillation?

As mentioned previously, atrial flutter is an unstable rhythm which often reverts to sinus rhythm or progresses to atrial fibrillation. If atrial flutter is episodic, its underlying cause should be identified and treated if possible. If a patient remains in atrial flutter, the treatment goals (control of ventricular rate, return to NSR) are the same as those for atrial fibrillation. Similar agents and doses can be used to control the ventricular response. Often, atrial flutter is unresponsive to chemical conversion; thus, low energy (<50 J) direct current cardioversion is required. An alternative treatment is rapid atrial pacing. Both methods will terminate atrial flutter or convert it to atrial fibrillation.

Atrial Fibrillation as a Complication of Bypass Surgery

13. H.L., a 55-year-old female in the intensive care unit, underwent coronary artery bypass surgery 24 hours ago. Past medical history includes exercise-induced angina treated with nitrates, metoprolol, and diltiazem. The cardiac monitor indicates H.L. is in atrial fibrillation with a ventricular response of 142 beats/min and a BP of 126/75 mm Hg. Is this a typical finding following bypass surgery? How should H.L. be treated?

Atrial fibrillation occurs in 10% to 30% of patients following bypass surgery, usually within the first 24 to 48 hours.[44] The underlying mechanism is unknown, but may be related to pericarditis, atrial dilation from volume overload, manipulation of the heart during surgery, or electrolyte imbalances.[45] The arrhythmia usually is well tolerated and converts spontaneously. The decision to treat H.L.'s atrial fibrillation depends upon her heart rate and how well she tolerates the arrhythmia; antiarrhythmics are often not needed in the short-term management of this disorder. For many years, digoxin has been used to control the ventricular response; however, these patients have a high sympathetic tone following surgery and digoxin often is ineffective. Beta blockers are effective in controlling the rate and are preferred if there are no other contraindications.[46] They also are preferred postoperatively, especially if the patient was on the drug preoperatively, because withdrawal of beta blockers can increase the occurrence of postoperative atrial fibrillation.[46,47]

Since H.L. has a rapid ventricular rate, it should be controlled. Either propranolol 1 mg IV every five minutes up to 0.1 mg/kg, metoprolol 5 mg IV repeated at two-minute intervals up to a total dose of 15 mg, esmolol 0.5 mg/kg bolus followed by a continuous infusion at a rate of 50 to 300 µg/kg/minute, or verapamil 5 to 10 mg IV every one to four hours can be tried since H.L. appears to be hemodynamically stable. If this dosage is inadequate, a loading dose of digoxin can be administered intravenously.

Paroxysmal Supraventricular Tachycardia (PSVT)

Clinical Presentation

14. B.J., a 32-year-old female, presents to the emergency room (ER) complaining of fatigue and palpitations. She has had similar episodes approximately twice a year for the past 2 years but has not sought medical attention for them. Physical examination reveals a female in no apparent distress with a temperature of 98.0 °F; heart rate of 205 beats/min; BP of 95/60 mm Hg; and respiratory rate of 12 breaths/min. ECG (see Figure 16.7) shows regular rhythm with a heart rate of 185. The P waves cannot be found and the QRS complex is 110 msec (Normal: <120). The diagnosis of PSVT is made. What is the clinical presentation of PSVT and what are the consequences of this arrhythmia?

Paroxysmal supraventricular tachycardia often has a sudden onset and termination. At the time of PSVT, the heart rate is usually 180 to 200 beats/min, but may range from 150 to 250 beats/min. As illustrated by B.J., patients will experience palpitations as well as nervousness and anxiety. In those patients with a very rapid ventricular rate, dizziness and syncope (near fainting) can occur, and the rhythm may degenerate to other serious arrhythmias. Depending upon the underlying heart function, angina, CHF, or shock

Fig 16.7 Supraventricular Tachycardia Reprinted with permission from reference 7.

may be precipitated. It has not been demonstrated that patients with episodes of PSVT are at an increased risk of stroke.

Arrhythmogenesis

15. What is the arrhythmogenic mechanism of PSVT?

AV nodal re-entry probably is the most common mechanism of paroxysmal supraventricular arrhythmias (see Figure 16.4). Under certain conditions, such as following an acute myocardial infarction, atrial impulses will be blocked in one of the two AV nodal pathways in a unidirectional manner (antegrade block). After the impulse reaches the distal end of one pathway, it will conduct in a retrograde fashion through the other pathway and thus set up a circular movement causing tachycardia.

Reciprocating tachycardias occur when there is an accessory pathway. Orthodromic AV reciprocating tachycardia is a re-entry tachycardia involving antegrade conduction through the AV node and retrograde conduction through a bypass tract. Antidromic AV reciprocating tachycardia is a re-entry tachycardia involving antegrade conduction through an accessory pathway and retrograde conduction via the AV node or another accessory pathway (e.g., WPW syndrome) (see Figure 16.8). Antidromic reciprocating tachycardias manifest as wide QRS complexes resembling ventricular arrhythmias.

Treatment

16. What are the acute and chronic treatment options for B.J.?

Nondrug Treatment. If B.J. is hemodynamically unstable, she should receive synchronous direct-current cardioversion. Although her blood pressure is low at 95/60 mm Hg, she is maintaining an

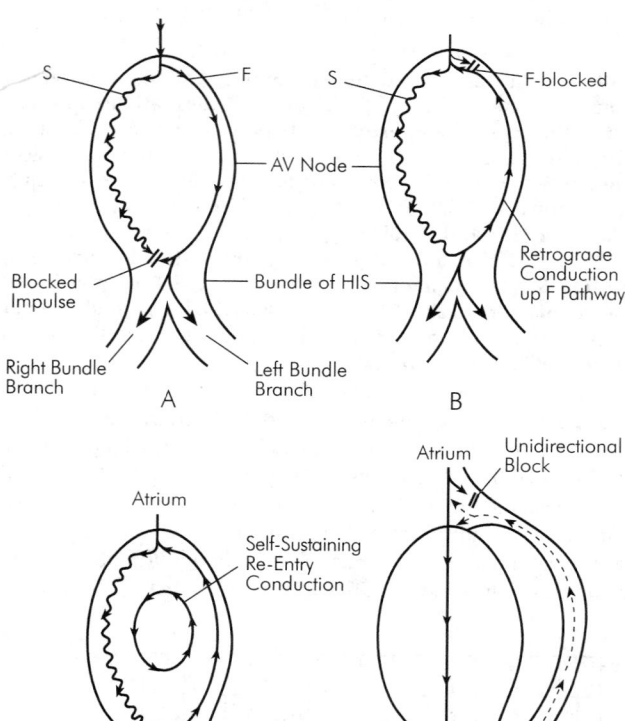

Fig 16.8 Diagramatic Representation of the AV Node in PSVT and WPW Syndrome

adequate perfusion pressure. For this reason, nondrug treatment or vagal maneuvers should be attempted first. Two common vagal techniques are pressure over the bifurcation of the internal and external carotid arteries or the Valsalva maneuver (forcible exhalation against a closed glottis; similar to bearing down to have a bowel movement). The increase in pressure induced by these maneuvers is sensed by the baroreceptors causing a reflex decrease in sympathetic tone and an increase in vagal tone. The increase in vagal tone will increase refractoriness and slow conduction in the AV node, thereby slowing the heart rate; the arrhythmia will terminate in 10% to 30% of the cases.[48]

Drug therapy involves blocking the AV node, since most PSVT rhythms involve a re-entry circuit within this area. Adenosine is considered the drug of choice for the acute treatment of PSVT because of its rapid and brief effect.[17] Adenosine is a purine nucleoside that exerts a transient negative chronotropic and dromotropic effect on cardiac pacemaker tissue.[49] An initial 6 mg IV bolus is given and if this is unsuccessful, it can be followed by one or two 12 mg IV boluses, up to a maximum of 30 mg. Because of its short half-life (9 seconds), adenosine should be administered as a rapid bolus followed by a saline flush. Patients should be warned that they may feel transient chest heaviness, flushing, or a feeling of anxiety. Shortness of breath and wheezing may be observed in patients with asthma. Theoretically, adenosine may be ineffective or higher doses may be required in patients who are receiving theophylline since this drug is an effective adenosine receptor blocker. However, theophylline did not affect the clinical effects of adenosine given to healthy volunteers during a pharmacologic stress test.[50] Conversely, concomitant use of dipyridamole may accentuate adenosine's effects because dipyridamole blocks the adenosine receptors.

Calcium channel blockers, both verapamil (2.5 to 5 mg IV given over 2 minutes, repeated at 10 to 15-minute intervals to a maximum dose of 20 mg) or diltiazem (0.25 to 0.35 mg/kg IV) have an 85% conversion rate.[51] However, verapamil should not be used in patients with wide complex tachycardia of unknown origin, since it may lead to hemodynamic compromise and, potentially, ventricular fibrillation.

Beta blockers and digoxin may be useful if calcium channel blockers or adenosine fail. Historically, pressor agents such as phenylephrine, methoxamine, and metaraminol have been used to elevate arterial pressure acutely which reflexively enhances vagal tone to cause conversion. Safer and more efficacious agents now are available obviating the need for their use.

On a long-term basis, PSVT is managed with agents such as oral verapamil, diltiazem, beta blockers, or digoxin that slow conduction and increase refractoriness in the AV node, thereby preventing a rapid ventricular response. Class IA, IC, and III agents are used occasionally to slow conduction and increase refractoriness of the fast bypass tract and prevent triggering impulses such as premature atrial and ventricular contractions. If drug therapy cannot be administered safely (e.g., in a pregnant woman), managed conveniently (e.g., in noncompliant patient), or tolerated (because of side effects), then electrophysiologic testing can be performed to determine the location of the re-entrant tract which then can be abolished by radiofrequency catheter ablation. Radiofrequency ablation uses alternating current that causes internal injury with coagulation necrosis and desiccation, interrupting the accessory pathways. This treatment approach potentially is curative and is used increasingly in medical centers under the direction of a specially-trained electrophysiologist.

Vagal maneuvers should be tried on B.J. If this fails adenosine can be tried. If she becomes hemodynamically unstable, she should receive DC cardioversion immediately. With respect to long-term therapy, B.J. and her doctor need to discuss the frequency and severity of symptoms and the need for long-term prophylactic therapy. If drug therapy is chosen, either verapamil or diltiazem would be a good initial choice.

Wolff-Parkinson-White (WPW) Syndrome

17. M.B., a 35-year-old male, presents to the ER with a chief complaint of chest palpitations for 4 hours. He relates a history of many similar self-terminating episodes since he was a teenager. He took an unknown medication 5 years ago which decreased the occurrence of the palpitations, but he stopped taking it due to side effects. M.B.'s vital signs are: BP 96/68 mm Hg; pulse 226 beats/min and irregular; respiratory rate 15/min; and temperature 98.7 °F. A rhythm strip confirms atrial fibrillation with a QRS width varying from 0.08–0.14 sec. To control the ventricular rate, 10 mg of IV verapamil is administered over 2 minutes. Within 2 minutes VF is noted on the monitor. M.B. is defibrillated successfully to NSR and a subsequent ECG demonstrates a PR interval of 100 msec (Normal: 120–200) and delta waves, compatible with WPW. What is WPW syndrome?

WPW is a pre-excitation syndrome in which there is an accessory bypass tract (known as a Kent bundle) connecting the atria to the ventricle. (See Figure 16.8.) An impulse can travel down this pathway and excite the ventricle before the expected regular impulse through the AV node; hence, the term pre-excitation. If there is antegrade conduction over the bypass tract while the patient is in normal sinus rhythm, the ECG will demonstrate a short PR interval (<100 msec), a delta wave which represents a fused complex from pre-excitation, and the regular QRS complex following AV conduction. WPW can occur in children and adults without overt cardiac disease. Paroxysmal AV reciprocating tachycardias and atrial fibrillation can occur in these patients at a higher incidence than in the general population of the same age.[52] Similar to M.B., the rapid heart rate experienced during the tachycardia may cause palpitations, lightheadedness, and fatigue. When patients with WPW develop atrial fibrillation, there is a danger that impulses will be conducted directly to the ventricle causing a rapid ventricular rate that may evolve into ventricular fibrillation.

18. Why did verapamil cause ventricular fibrillation in M.B.? What drug or drugs would be appropriate for M.B. and what drugs should be avoided?

Verapamil can block AV conduction by increasing the effective refractory period, thus allowing all impulses from atrial area to conduct down the bypass (Kent) tract. Since M.B. had atrial fibrillation, the rapid atrial impulses were conducted directly down the bypass tract to the ventricle causing ventricular fibrillation. In addition, verapamil may enhance conduction over the accessory pathway by shortening its effective refractory period and induce peripheral vasodilation causing a reflex sympathetic discharge which also may decrease the ERP of the accessory pathway.[53,54]

The most common presentation of WPW syndrome involves normal antegrade conduction down the AV node and retrograde conduction back through the accessory pathway. This will manifest

Fig 16.9 **Bundle Branch Block** Note that the QRS interval is prolonged. A 12-lead ECG is required to make the diagnosis of left bundle branch block. Reprinted with permission from reference 126.

Fig 16.10 **Second Degree AV Block Type I (Wenckeback).** The PR interval progressively prolongs until, after the third complex a QRS complex is not conducted. Reprinted with permission from reference 126.

as orthodromic reciprocating re-entrant tachycardia. Thus, drugs (e.g., verapamil, digoxin) which inhibit antegrade impulse conduction through the AV node will terminate the re-entrant tachycardia and can be suitable in the absence of atrial fibrillation. The less common variety of WPW is antegrade conduction through the accessory pathway with retrograde transmission up through the AV node resulting in an antidromic re-entrant tachycardia. Similarly, AV nodal blocking agents will terminate this type of re-entrant tachycardia. In some situations, such as experienced by M.B., rapid atrial fibrillation with an accessory pathway occurs which can lead to ventricular fibrillation and cardiac arrest.

The antiarrhythmic drugs used to treat patients with atrial fibrillation with an accessory pathway, such as M.B., include those which depress conduction and increase the ERP of the fast sodium channel-dependent tissue of the accessory pathway. This includes most class I antiarrhythmics, with the class IB agents being least effective. Of the FDA-approved drugs, procainamide is considered by many as the drug of first choice.[55] Amiodarone and possibly other class III antiarrhythmic agents also may be effective; however, clinical experience is limited.[56-58] Radiofrequency ablation of the bypass tract is used more frequently for these patients to prevent ventricular fibrillation.

Conduction Blocks

Various arrhythmias can result from blockage of impulse conduction. These can occur above the ventricle, such as first degree, second degree, and third degree (complete) AV block. Others such as right or left bundle branch block (RBBB or LBBB) and trifascicular block originate below the bifurcation of the HIS bundle. Although conduction blocks can be classified as either supraventricular or ventricular arrhythmias, they are discussed as a separate group since their mechanism of arrhythmogenesis is similar and their treatment is quite different from other arrhythmias.

19. H.T., a 63-year-old male who was admitted to the coronary care unit (CCU) 12 hours ago with an acute inferior wall MI, has remained stable. Upon admission, H.T. had the rhythm strip shown in Figure 16.9 (left bundle branch block). Twelve hours later, it has changed to the rhythm strip shown in Figure 16.10 (Wenckebach or type I, second degree AV block). Are these rhythms potentially hazardous to H.T.? How is second degree AV block different from 1st or 3rd degree AV block?

H.T.'s ECG rhythm strip revealed a diagnosis of left bundle branch block. Bundle branch block occurs when the electrical impulse cannot be conducted along the left or right fascicle of the HIS Purkinje system (see Figure 16.1). In H.T., the impulse travels down the right bundle normally, and the right ventricle contracts at the normal time. The left bundle is blocked and, therefore, the left side is depolarized from an impulse conducted from the right ventricle. This impulse must travel through atypical conduction tissues (with slower conduction) and hence the left side depolarizes

Atrial Rate = 100 (P–P)
Ventricular Rate = 40 (R–R)

P–R = 0.16   Nonconducted P Waves

Fig 16.11   Second Degree AV Block Type II (3:1 Fixed Block)

later. This is revealed on the ECG by a widened QRS complex. Bundle branch blocks, particularly in the left fascicle, are associated with coronary artery disease, systemic hypertension, aortic valve stenosis, and cardiomyopathy.[59] Typically they do not lead to clinical cardiac dysfunction on their own. Since H.T. has left bundle branch block, he can develop complete heart block (third degree block) if for any reason his right fascicle is damaged.

First degree AV block usually is asymptomatic. The ECG will denote the presence of P waves with a prolonged PR interval (>200 msec), but followed by a normal QRS complex. First degree AV block is a common finding in patients taking digoxin, verapamil, or other drugs that slow AV conduction. Second degree heart block consists of two types. Mobitz type I (Wenckebach), is characterized by progressive lengthening of the PR interval with each beat and a corresponding shortening of the RR interval until finally an impulse is not conducted; the cycle then starts over again. Mobitz Type II (see Figure 16.11) impulse conduction is blocked in a fixed, regular pattern (e.g., 3:1 block where for every 3 P waves, only 1 is conducted). Third degree heart block (complete heart block) occurs when none of the impulses from the SA node are conducted to the ventricles. During third degree block the ventricle must develop its own pacemaker (escape rhythm) which may be too slow to provide adequate cardiac output causing the patient to become symptomatic. A pacemaker is needed for treatment of third degree AV block. AV blocks can be caused by drugs, acute myocardial infarction, amyloidosis, and congenital abnormalities.[60]

20. How should H.T.'s heart block be treated?

H.T. is experiencing a Wenckebach rhythm, which often is transient following an inferior wall myocardial infarction. As long as he is hemodynamically stable he just should be monitored closely. If H.T.'s heart rate and blood pressure drop, atropine 0.5 mg IV bolus (maximum: 2 mg) can be administered to increase the heart rate. This is only a short-term therapy and if the hemodynamic compromise persists, a pacemaker must be inserted to initiate the impulse to control the heart rate.

Ventricular Arrhythmias
Recognition and Definition

Ventricular arrhythmias arise from irritable ectopic foci within the ventricular myocardium. Impulses from these ectopic foci generate wide, bizarre-looking QRS complexes leading to premature ventricular contractions (see Figure 16.12). Unifocal PVCs can arise either from the same ectopic site (unifocal), or be multifocal in origin. They can be simple (e.g., isolated or infrequent) or complex (e.g., R on T, in which the R wave of a PVC falls on top of a normal T wave). Other presentations include runs of two or more beats, bigeminal (every other beat is a PVC), or trigeminal (every third beat is a PVC). Three consecutive PVCs in a row usually are defined as ventricular tachycardia which can be nonsustained or sustained ventricular tachycardia (SuVT). Ventricular flutter, ventricular fibrillation, and Torsade de Pointes are other serious forms of ventricular arrhythmias. (See Figures 16.12 to 16.16.)

Nonsustained ventricular tachycardia (NSVT) (see Figure 16.13) commonly is defined as three or more consecutive PVCs lasting less than 30 seconds and terminating spontaneously. Sustained ventricular tachycardia is defined as consecutive PVCs lasting more than 30 seconds with a rate usually in the range of 150 to 200 beats/minute. P waves are lost in the QRS complex and are indiscernible. Sustained ventricular tachycardia (see Figure 16.16) is a serious development because it can degenerate into ventricular fibrillation. Ventricular flutter is characterized by sustained, rapid, regular ventricular beats (>250/minute) and usually degenerates into ventricular fibrillation. Ventricular fibrillation (see Figure 16.14) is characterized by irregular, disorganized, rapid beats with no identifiable P waves or QRS complexes. It is thought to be triggered by multiple re-entrant wavelets in the ventricle. There is no effective cardiac output in patients with ventricular fibrillation. Torsade de Pointes (see Figure 16.15) is a rapid, undulating or polymorphic ventricular tachycardia which easily can degenerate into ventricular fibrillation (see Question 25).

Etiology

Common factors which cause ventricular arrhythmias are ischemia, presence of organic heart disease, exercise, metabolic or electrolyte imbalance (e.g., acidosis, hypo- or hyperkalemia, hypomagnesemia), drugs (digitalis; sympathomimetic amines; antiarrhythmics; and terfenadine, especially when given with an enzyme-inhibiting drug like erythromycin or ketoconazole), vasospasm, and mental stress.[61] It is essential to identify and remove any treatable cause (e.g., metabolic or electrolyte imbalance and proarrhythmic drugs) before initiating antiarrhythmic drug therapy.

Evaluation of Life-Threatening Ventricular Arrhythmias

The occurrence of an episode of life-threatening ventricular arrhythmia (i.e., SuVT, Torsade de Pointes, ventricular fibrillation) carries a significant risk of morbidity and mortality. Adequate documentation of the arrhythmia and its suppression by either drugs or a mechanical device is essential. Patients suspected or documented to have symptoms of a life-threatening arrhythmia (e.g., syncope, out-of-hospital cardiac arrest) should be admitted to the hospital and evaluated. At present, two approaches are acceptable in clinical evaluation of the arrhythmia: ambulatory (Holter) monitoring and electrophysiology studies (EPS).

Holter Monitoring

Holter monitoring is continuous ECG monitoring, usually for 24 to 48 hours, with or without exercise (e.g., treadmill exercise). The patient wears a portable ECG monitoring device in a purse-like carrier and maintains a written log of daily activities and possible arrhythmia symptoms. The ECG is then played back in the laboratory, correlating the presence of arrhythmias with patient activity and symptoms. Monitoring should be implemented before and after drug intervention. One criterion clinically used in judging efficacy is that a drug is considered effective if it suppresses 100% of runs of ventricular tachycardia longer than 15 beats, 90% of shorter runs, 80% of paired PVCs, 70% of all PVCs, and there is an absence of exercise-induced ventricular tachycardia.[62]

Electrophysiological Studies (EPS)

Electrophysiological studies are the second approach in evaluating antiarrhythmic drug efficacy. This approach is useful especially in patients with sporadic ventricular arrhythmias that may be missed by short-term monitoring. This procedure involves right ventricular catheterization and introduction of up to three electrical stimuli at the right ventricular apex of the heart to induce baseline ventricular tachycardia.[63] If the arrhythmia is not reproducibly induced, repeated stimulation with up to three extra stimuli usually is performed at the right ventricular outflow tract. Once ventricular tachycardia is reproducibly induced at baseline, drug therapy is started. The drug is considered effective if the sustained ventricular tachycardia is rendered noninducible or occurs in runs of less than six beats. A partial response to drug therapy is obtained if the drug converts sustained ventricular tachycardia to NSVT or decreases the ventricular tachycardia rate (e.g., increase VT cycle length by 100 msec) with elimination of symptoms.[64]

Drugs which achieve satisfactory response by Holter technique or complete suppression by EPS technique have been shown to improve long-term survival in uncontrolled trials.[65-67] Similarly, a partial response by the EPS method also has been shown to improve long-term outcome.[68] In a randomized, comparative study of Holter monitoring versus EPS, Holter monitoring led to a prediction of efficacy more often than EPS, though there was no difference in the success of drug therapy as selected by either method.[67]

Premature Ventricular Contractions (PVCs)

21. A.S., a 56-year-old female, was admitted to the CCU with a diagnosis of acute anterior wall MI. On admission, her BP was 115/75 mm Hg, pulse 85 beats/min, and respiratory rate 15 breaths/min. Auscultation of the heart revealed an S₃ gallop. Her electrolytes included a potassium (K) of 3.8 mEq/L (Normal: 3.5–5.0), and magnesium (Mg) of 1.4 mEq/L (Normal: 1.6–2.4). Otherwise, her examination was within normal limits. Two days later an echocardiogram estimated her ejection fraction (EF) to be 35% (Normal: ≥50%). During A.S.'s stay in the CCU as well as the step-down unit, multiple PVCs (15/min) were noted on the bedside monitor. No antiarrhythmic agent was ordered. Should A.S.'s multiple PVCs be treated with an antiarrhythmic drug? [SI units: K 3.8 mmol/L (Normal: 3.5–5.0), Mg 0.72 mmol/L (Normal: 0.7–1.2)]

Occasional premature ventricular contractions are a benign, natural occurrence, even in a healthy heart and are not an indication for drug therapy. Similarly, asymptomatic simple forms of PVCs, even in patients with other cardiac disease, usually are not an indication for treatment. However, the presence of frequent PVCs is

Fig 16.14   Ventricular Fibrillation

a well-described risk factor for sudden cardiac death (SCD).[69] In patients with a low ejection fraction in the presence PVCs or non-sustained ventricular tachycardia, the risk for sudden cardiac death can increase 13-fold. Suppressing PVCs under these conditions may reduce the risk of sudden cardiac death. This prompted the National Institutes of Health to launch the Cardiac Arrhythmia Suppression Trial (CAST)[70,71] to assess the benefit of PVC suppression in survivors of myocardial infarction. The CAST was a prospective, randomized, placebo-controlled trial which evaluated three antiarrhythmic agents: flecainide, encainide, and moricizine (all IC agents). The choice of these three drugs was based upon results of a pilot study of 1498 patients that showed adequate suppression of arrhythmia (PVCs) in the target population.[72,73]

Ten months after initiation of the study, the CAST was discontinued because of excess total mortality and cardiac arrests in patients receiving flecainide and encainide. Forty-three of 755 patients in the flecainide/encainide group died from arrhythmia or cardiac arrest versus 16 of the 743 patients taking placebo. Furthermore, total mortality in the flecainide/encainide group was 8.3% (63 of 755) compared to 3.5% (26 of 743) in the placebo group. In the moricizine group, which was reported separately in CAST II, 16 out of 660 died in the drug group as compared to three out of 668 in the placebo group in the initial two weeks. Subsequent long-term follow-up did not show a difference between moricizine and placebo.[71]

It generally is believed that the excessive death rate in the drug-treated groups was due to the proarrhythmic effect of the drugs. Since the patients enrolled in the CAST were asymptomatic and at low risk for the development of arrhythmias, they were at greater risk for drug toxicity (relative to benefit). Although many issues have been raised concerning CAST, one conclusion is that patients

Fig 16.12   Premature Ventricular Contraction (PVC)   Every other beat is a premature ventricular (ectopic) contraction.

Fig 16.13   Nonsustained Ventricular Tachycardia   Reprinted with permission from reference 7.

R waves positively deflected

Rate ≈180 beats/min

Note the difference in QRS configuration from beat to beat

Isoelectric point at which
the electrical axis shifts

R waves after axis shift,
negatively deflected

Fig 16.15   Torsade de Pointes

with a recent MI and the presence of asymptomatic PVCs should not be treated with encainide, flecainide, or moricizine. Whether other class I antiarrhythmics will produce similar results is unknown. Thus, the decision not to treat A.S.'s premature ventricular contractions was a sound one. The proarrhythmic effects of the drug may outweigh the potential danger of PVCs. If persistent PVCs produce bothersome symptoms in A.S., treatment may be warranted. A beta blocker may be considered in this instance.

Nonsustained Ventricular Tachycardia (NSVT)

22. D.S., a 62-year-old male, was admitted recently for an inferior wall MI. Following the infarction he has been free of further pain and does not exhibit signs of CHF. An echocardiogram shows an EF of 48%, but D.S. does experience runs of ventricular tachycardia (see Figure 16.13) lasting from 3 beats to 20 seconds in length. D.S. states that he feels his heart racing during the longer episodes. Should D.S.'s ventricular tachycardia be treated, and if so, what are the treatment options?

D.S. is experiencing nonsustained ventricular tachycardia which can occur in patients with underlying heart disease, both ischemic and nonischemic (idiopathic dilated cardiomyopathy, hypertrophic cardiomyopathy). It is not clear which of these patients are at high risk for sudden cardiac death. The Multicenter Unsustained Tachycardia Trial (MUSTT) is in progress to examine if patients with NSVT following a myocardial infarction benefit from invasive studies and treatment.

The present guidelines for treatment are determined by the underlying function of the left ventricle.[74] If a patient has an ejection fraction greater than 40% and no symptoms, therapy is not indicated. If symptoms are present, (e.g., palpitations or lightheadedness) a beta blocker is preferred unless it is contraindicated by the presence of CHF or asthma/chronic obstructive airways disease (COAD). In addition to controlling symptoms, beta blockers reduce the incidence of cardiac death in post myocardial infarction patients with and without PVCs.[75] If the patient has a reduced ejection fraction (<40%), it is uncertain what the best treatment should be. Symptomatic patients can undergo EPS and serial drug testing to suppress NSVT, but this approach has yet to be shown to reduce mortality in a controlled manner. This is the population that is being studied in the MUSTT trial.

Since D.S. is symptomatic, but has preserved ventricular function, he should be started on a beta blocker. Pindolol or any beta blocker with intrinsic sympathomimetic activity should be avoided because they have not been shown to be "cardioprotective" following a myocardial infarction.

Sustained Ventricular Tachycardia (SuVT)

Treatment

23. S.L., a 64-year-old female, presents to the ER with a chief complaint of palpitations. Past medical history includes hypertension controlled with a diuretic and an inferior wall MI 6 months ago. She is pale and diaphoretic, but able to respond to commands. Her BP is 95/70 mm Hg, pulse 145 beats/min, and her respirations are 10 breaths/min. When telemetry monitoring is established, S.L. is found to be in sustained ventricular tachycardia (Figure 16.16). S.L. states she has a history of allergy to Novocain. How should S.L. be treated?

The acute treatment of patients with sustained ventricular tachycardia depends upon their hemodynamic stability. If unstable, patients should receive synchronous cardioversion which will decrease the chance of triggering ventricular fibrillation. If the patient is conscious, a short-acting benzodiazepine (e.g., midazolam) should be administered before the procedure.

Lidocaine. In patients with a stable blood pressure, intravenous agents such as lidocaine or procainamide can be used to abolish the tachycardia. The drug of choice is lidocaine administered as a 1 mg/kg bolus, no faster than 50 mg/minute. More rapid rates can cause hypotension and asystole. If the initial bolus does not "break" the tachycardia, additional boluses of 0.5 mg/kg can be administered eight to ten minutes apart until a total dose of 3 mg/kg is administered.

Procainamide is an alternative agent if lidocaine is ineffective or is not tolerated. A loading dose of 12 mg/kg can be administered at a rate of 50 mg/minute. Hypotension often is the rate-limiting factor and can be minimized by administering the drug at a slower rate (20 to 35 mg/minute). Once the patient has converted to normal sinus rhythm, a continuous infusion (dose 1 to 4 mg/minute) can be started. The infusion should be reduced in renal failure since the parent drug and the active metabolite, NAPA, can accumulate. NAPA itself has class III antiarrhythmic activity and is eliminated entirely by the kidneys.[76]

S.L. is hemodynamically stable at this time so lidocaine should be given in an attempt to abolish the tachycardia. Lidocaine can be used even though S.L. reports an allergy to procaine (Novocain). Procaine is an ester-type local anesthetic; whereas lidocaine and procainamide are amide-type local anesthetics; thus, there is no cross reactivity between the two types.

24. Once S.L. has returned to NSR, should lidocaine be continued? How should its use be monitored?

Once she has converted to normal sinus rhythm, S.L. can be maintained on a continuous lidocaine infusion at a rate based upon

---

the estimated clearance of the drug (1 to 4 mg/minute). Lidocaine clearance can be reduced by CHF, acute myocardial infarction, advanced age, and by drugs such as propranolol or cimetidine.[77,78] Under these conditions, a lower infusion rate should be started and a plasma lidocaine concentration determined in 12 to 24 hours. (See average therapeutic concentration in Table 16.3.) A lidocaine concentration also should be obtained after 24 hours if a prolonged infusion is anticipated since lidocaine clearance decreases in this situation. Phenobarbital and phenytoin may increase lidocaine clearance, thereby lowering the plasma concentration.[79]

Lidocaine toxicity typically presents as alterations in the central nervous system (CNS) such as dizziness, drowsiness, paresthesias, visual disturbances, tinnitus, slurred speech, trembling, loss of coordination, confusion, somnolence, hallucinations, unresponsiveness, seizures, and agitation. Cardiovascular toxicity (conduction disturbances, bradyarrhythmias, and hypotension) is rare and usually occurs when serum concentrations exceed 9 μg/mL. However, lidocaine possesses weak negative inotropic activity which clinically is most evident during prolonged infusions or in patients with a pre-existing depressed myocardium (e.g., acute MI).[80]

25. Sotalol. S.L.'s attending physician feels that she should undergo further testing and an electrophysiologist is consulted. It is determined that EPS testing is necessary since S.L. has a past history of SuVT. On baseline testing, SuVT at a rate of 220 beats/min was induced twice with the catheter at the right ventricular apex. Sotalol 80 mg BID is prescribed. Describe sotalol's properties and adverse effects. How effective is sotalol in this situation? Is it the right choice for S.L.?

Adverse effects associated with sotalol (e.g., fatigue, bradycardia, hypotension) mostly are a result of its class II activity. Torsade de Pointes is the most common form of arrhythmia associated with sotalol; this effect is dose related and triggered by prolongation of the QT interval.

The acute efficacy of sotalol in suppression of inducible ventricular tachycardia or fibrillation is modest; generally averaging response rates of 30% to 35% using Holter monitoring, but as high as 56% in one report.[67] On the other hand, a randomized comparative trial called the Electrophysiologic Study versus Electrocardiographic Monitoring (ESVEM) study, using both Holter monitoring and EPS, demonstrated that sotalol treatment produced a significantly lower probability of recurrence of arrhythmia, death from any cause, death from a cardiac cause, and death from arrhythmia compared to other drugs.[67] Thus the initial or acute efficacy of sotalol, though not very impressive, can lead to better long-term results than many other drugs.

Sotalol is a unique agent that possesses nonselective beta-blocking activity (class II) and prolongs repolarization (class III activity).[81] The half-life of sotalol is 8 to 18 hours. Since it is cleared by the kidneys, its clearance is reduced and half-life prolonged in patients with renal dysfunction. Like other beta blockers, sotalol is a racemic mixture. D-sotalol, which retains class III antiarrhythmic activity without significant beta-blocking activity, is being investigated for its antiarrhythmic efficacy.

Since S.L. has no contraindications and had a myocardial infarction six months ago, sotalol is a suitable initial choice. Sotalol

can be initiated at 80 mg twice daily and advanced to a maximal recommended dose of 640 mg/day. S.L.'s blood pressure, heart rate, and ECG should be monitored. If her rate-related ("corrected") QT (QT_c) interval becomes prolonged beyond 440 msec, the dose should be reduced or the drug discontinued.

Torsade de Pointes

Proarrhythmic Effects of Drugs and Clinical Presentation

26. After 3 days of sotalol 80 mg BID, S.L. complains of dizziness and then loses consciousness. The ECG monitor strip shows Torsade de Pointes. (See Figure 16.15.) What is the characteristic of this arrhythmia? Could it have been caused by antiarrhythmic drugs?

Torsade de Pointes is a form of polymorphic ventricular tachycardia that is associated with prolonged repolarization and characterized by a prolonged QT interval on ECG. Contributing factors are electrolyte imbalances (hypokalemia, hypomagnesemia) and bradycardia.[82] It has been associated with antiarrhythmic drugs (particularly class IA and III), tricyclic antidepressants, antibiotics, nonsedating antihistamines (e.g., terfenadine, astemizole), and haloperidol.[83] These drugs block potassium channels and have the potential to prolong the refractoriness of the ventricle. It also is thought that this refractoriness is not evenly distributed throughout the ventricle and that the greater the dispersion, the greater the risk of developing Torsade de Pointes.[84] Other mechanisms include early after-depolarizations.

Torsade de Pointes is one of many drug-induced arrhythmias. Proarrhythmia can be defined as a worsening of the underlying arrhythmia or provocation of a new arrhythmia; it is associated with the use of antiarrhythmic drugs in up to 13% of the population.[85] Other examples of proarrhythmia are: incessant ventricular tachycardia, faster and significantly more symptomatic ventricular tachycardia, and increases in PVC frequency. Proarrhythmic effects can be exacerbated by the presence of ischemia and electrolyte or metabolic abnormalities.[86] The incidence may be dose related, such as with sotalol, but may be idiopathic as is the case with quinidine. Typically, proarrhythmic events will occur soon after the initiation of therapy, generally within the first two weeks, but they also have been reported in patients who have been stabilized on the medication for weeks to months.[85,87] Late reactions may be due to changes in the patient's underlying cardiac disease, a new onset of electrolyte imbalances, or initiation of an interacting drug. With Torsade de Pointes, patients with a prolonged QT_c interval are at increased risk of developing this arrhythmia. Patients on agents that prolong the QT interval should be monitored and if the drug prolongs the QT ≥15% beyond baseline, the dose should be decreased or the treatment discontinued. Unfortunately, there is no way to accurately predict a proarrhythmic event in a given patient. Even with Torsade de Pointes, not everyone with a prolonged QT_c interval will develop the arrhythmia.

Treatment

27. How should Torsade de Pointes be treated?

Torsade de Pointes often is self-limiting and may revert to sinus rhythm without intervention. At the other extreme, the patient may progress into ventricular fibrillation and if this arrhythmia is sustained, the patient will require defibrillation. The arrhythmia often recurs without warning, so preventive treatment should be implemented at the first clinical sign to avoid progression to more serious events. If the offending agent is known, it should be stopped. Isoproterenol infusion or atrial or ventricular pacing will shorten the QT interval and decrease the recurrence of the arrhythmia. Intra-

Fig 16.16 Sustained Ventricular Tachycardia

venous magnesium has been shown to decrease the occurrence of early after-depolarizations associated with Torsade de Pointes as well.[88]

S.L.'s sotalol should be discontinued and she should receive magnesium sulfate 2 gm IV over 10 to 15 minutes. If additional symptomatic episodes occur after the administration of magnesium, a temporary pacemaker should be inserted.

Sustained Ventricular Tachycardia

Treatment: Quinidine

28. Sotalol was discontinued and L.S. was started on an SR quinidine sulfate preparation (Quinidex 600 mg BID). How effective is quinidine for the treatment of SuVT and what is the success rate in comparison to other agents?

As discussed earlier, quinidine and other class IA agents are effective in managing supraventricular arrhythmias. Because they are general suppressants of ectopic foci in the myocardium, they also are clinically useful in treating ventricular irritability. Quinidine's efficacy in suppressing ventricular tachycardia and ventricular fibrillation induced by EPS is about 20% to 30%, similar to other class IA and class IC agents.[63,67,89] Class IB and class II agents generally are less effective, around 10% to 20%; sotalol is slightly more effective than quinidine.[67] In patients who cannot tolerate sotalol (e.g., bradycardia, presence of CHF) or who develop proarrhythmic effects, as occurred in S.L., quinidine is a reasonable alternative. In contrast to supraventricular arrhythmias, prior digitalization is not necessary since the abnormality is arising from below the AV node.

Amiodarone versus Combination Therapy for Ventricular Tachycardia

29. After 4 days of quinidine therapy (at a serum concentration of 4 μg/mL), S.L. remained inducible and the VT cycle length was decreased only slightly compared to baseline results. S.L. has failed quinidine therapy. Should she be tried on another single drug such as amiodarone or should she be given combination drug therapy? If so, what combination is recommended?

S.L. might have responded to amiodarone; however, since she was unresponsive to quinidine, a class IA agent, which reportedly predicts a lack of response to amiodarone as well.[90] Furthermore, amiodarone's serious adverse effects (see Question 31) make this drug a last choice. Combination therapy with a IA and IB agent is a more rational approach.

Combination antiarrhythmic therapy generally is more effective than single-agent therapy for inducible arrhythmias, although most of the studies are in a small series of patients.[91–93] Of the various regimens tested, Class IA and IB combinations are the best documented. Such combinations have been shown to increase the cycle length of the ventricular tachycardia (i.e., slower VT rate), without detrimentally affecting the refractory period.[91] Among the two IB agents available, mexiletine is preferred in combination with a IA agent. Tocainide is associated with more serious adverse effects (i.e., agranulocytosis) even though mexiletine has more bothersome side effects (i.e., nausea) (see Table 16.3).

30. S.L. responded to the combination therapy based upon EPS results and is placed on long-term maintenance therapy with SR quinidine sulfate (Quinidex 600 mg BID) and mexiletine 200 mg BID. However, 3 months later she developed lethargy, tremor, and breakthrough palpitations. There is a suspicion that she has not been fully compliant with her treatment since her quinidine level is 2 μg/mL compared to 4 μg/mL previously and the mexiletine level is 0.1 μg/mL, down from 1.5 μg/mL at the time of EPS. What questions will you ask to assess

S.L.'s compliance? How frequently do patients require modification of therapy while on long-term maintenance therapy? What is the best way to ensure efficacy?

S.L. should be asked if she was taking her medications consistently and as directed. If she was not, the reasons should be determined since common adverse effects of mexiletene (e.g., nausea, dizziness, tremor, coordination difficulty, paresthesia, headache, blurred vision) may be a contributing factor. S.L. should be assessed to determine if patient education would increase her compliance.

According to one report, up to 42% of patients placed on long-term therapy (16 ± 18 months) with antiarrhythmic drugs for the treatment of inducible ventricular tachycardia require modification of the drug regimen due to either intolerance (68%) or inefficacy (32%).[94] Thus, it is important to educate and monitor these patients carefully. To ensure efficacy, maintenance of individual specific target serum drug concentrations known to prevent the induction of arrhythmias is important. In addition to noncompliance, one should consider interactions with drugs known to decrease serum antiarrhythmic concentrations (e.g., phenytoin, rifampin, phenobarbital) since this can lead to recurrence of the arrhythmia and, possibly, sudden cardiac death.[95] Use of sustained-release products may help to improve compliance and maintain specific individual target serum drug concentrations. Breakthrough arrhythmias that occur while patients are on long-term therapy with drugs known to be effective initially also may be related to progression or alteration of disease state. Thus, arrhythmia management may have to be reassessed.

31. S.L. stated that intolerable nausea and lightheadedness caused her to stop taking her medications. Since a lower dose of mexiletine may decrease side effects, but also may not be efficacious, she was deemed intolerant of the combination therapy and is to be placed on amiodarone therapy. Describe the pharmacologic properties of amiodarone. How should amiodarone be initiated and how should S.L. be monitored?

Amiodarone has unique pharmacokinetic properties. Its apparent volume of distribution is 5000 L because it is extensively bound to tissue and is lipophilic; its half-life after long-term administration is 14 to 53 days. The main metabolite of amiodarone is desethylamiodarone; while this metabolite is active, its contribution to the overall antiarrhythmic activity is not clearly delineated.

Loading doses are used to accelerate the onset of drug efficacy. One to two grams per day (200 to 500 mg QID) are given over a one-week period; after that time, a maintenance dose can be established. Typically for the treatment of ventricular arrhythmias, 300 to 400 mg/day is used for maintenance therapy, but doses may range from 100 to 800 mg/day. While a concentration-effect relationship is hard to determine for amiodarone, levels greater than 2.5 mg/L are associated with an increased incidence of adverse effects.

Amiodarone has many serious adverse effects involving a variety of organ systems, the most serious and life-threatening of which is pulmonary fibrosis. This can occur in 5% to 10% of the population and the mortality is 5% to 10% for those who develop it.[96] Pulmonary effects are not correlated with the daily dose, but may be related to the total cumulative dose. A baseline chest x-ray and pulmonary function tests (diffusion capacity in particular) are recommended. The chest x-ray should be repeated at 6- to 12-month intervals, but pulmonary function tests need be repeated only if symptoms (dyspnea, nonproductive cough, weight loss) occur.

Liver toxicity can range from an asymptomatic elevation of transaminases (2 to 4 × normal) to fulminant hepatitis. Thus, liver enzymes should be monitored at baseline and every six months.

The most common gastrointestinal complaints are nausea, anorexia, and constipation. Both hypo- and hyperthyroidism have been reported, although hypothyroidism is more common. The thyroid complications are a consequence of amiodarone's large iodine content and its ability to block the peripheral conversion of triiodothyronine (T_3) to thyroxine (T_4). Other bothersome side effects are corneal deposits (usually asymptomatic); blue-gray skin discoloration in sun-exposed areas; photosensitivity; exacerbation of congestive heart failure; and CNS effects which include ataxia, tremor, dizziness, and peripheral neuropathy. Amiodarone also possesses beta-blocking properties; thus, bradycardia and exacerbations of asthma may occur. Other than an eye examination and pulmonary function tests which should be repeated when the patient is symptomatic, all other blood tests should be repeated every six months for routine monitoring.

Implantable Cardiac Defibrillators (ICDs)

32. After 2 weeks on amiodarone, S.L. developed a run of VT lasting about 2 minutes. She was admitted for implantation of an ICD. What is an ICD and how does it work?

An implantable cardioverter/defibrillator is a device that can be surgically placed in patients who are either unresponsive or intolerant to multiple drug challenges. Electrode patches are wrapped around the right and left ventricular epicardium and serve as defibrillating paddles or a catheter with two defibrillator wire leads is advanced to the right ventricle. Electric leads placed near the heart are connected to a generator (implanted in abdomen under the skin) which will sense the rhythm and trigger defibrillation when there is an abnormal rhythm. A new-generation defibrillator [pacing cardioverter/defibrillators (PCD)] is able to pace the patient out of the arrhythmia. If that fails, a shock is delivered. Despite a rapidly increasing number of ICD implantations, patients often are prescribed antiarrhythmic drugs to decrease the number of shocks. How these devices interact with most antiarrhythmics has not been clearly determined except in a limited number of studies.[97]

Ventricular Fibrillation Prophylaxis

33. R.B., a 65-year-old, 70 kg male, presented to the ER with a chief complaint of chest pain. The ECG revealed an acute anterior wall MI and he received 100 mg of recombinant tissue plasminogen activator (r-tPA) IV. Shortly afterwards, R.B. developed multiple PVCs, several episodes of NSVT, then VF. He was cardioverted successfully, but continued to have PVCs. Then he was given a lidocaine 100 mg bolus, followed by another 75 mg in 15 minutes. Thereafter, he was maintained on a 3 mg/min infusion of lidocaine and his PVCs were eliminated successfully except for occasional beats. How effective is lidocaine in preventing ventricular fibrillation postMI? Should it be given prophylactically to prevent VT during an acute myocardial infarction?

Ventricular fibrillation occurs in 3% to 10% of patients during an acute myocardial infarction. Despite the increased use of thrombolytic agents, this incidence does not appear to be altered.[98,99] Thus, drugs which effectively prevent ventricular fibrillation in this setting would be highly desirable. Lidocaine infusions over 48 hours may suppress premature beats and decrease the incidence of ventricular fibrillation when used prophylactically.[100] A meta-analysis of several studies showed a 35% reduction in ventricular fibrillation following prophylactic lidocaine during acute MI.[101] However, there also was a trend toward increased mortality.[101,102] Based upon these results, the routine use of lidocaine prophylaxis to prevent ventricular fibrillation for the first 24 to 48 hours following an MI is controversial. In one randomized trial in patients with acute MI, a short-term (8-hour) infusion was found to have similar value (no observed VF) as a 48-hour lidocaine infusion.

However, the eight-hour infusion produced a significantly lower incidence of CHF compared to the 48-hour infusion.[80] Since 90% of primary ventricular fibrillation occurs within 12 hours of the myocardial infarction, a short-term lidocaine infusion seems to be a logical regimen for the prevention ventricular fibrillation. Since R.B. already had an episode of VF, he should be maintained on lidocaine infusion for at least eight hours. (Also see Chapter 14: Myocardial Infarction.)

Cardiopulmonary Arrest
Cardiopulmonary Resuscitation (CPR)

In any emergency situation, one first must assess the patient so that a course of action can be determined. The first step is to assess the "ABCs" of cardiopulmonary resuscitation (i.e., airway, breathing, and circulation). Upon arrival at the scene of a victim requiring assistance, one must first establish if the patient is unconscious by gently shaking the victim and shouting "are you okay?" If there is no response, call 911 and open the airway by gently pulling the jaw forward and the forehead back.

Once the airway is opened, evaluate the patient for the presence or absence of spontaneous breathing by placing one's ear over the patient's nose and mouth. Look for chest movement; listen for air moving out of the nose and mouth (and feel for air flow). If the patient is determined to be breathless, administer two breaths over 1 to 1.5 seconds each by blowing into the patient's mouth while pinching the nose closed with the thumb and index finger. In the hospital, a bag-mask device is available to deliver breaths to the patient.

Next, check for presence of a pulse (circulation) by placing two fingers into the groove between the trachea and the muscle at the side of the neck where the carotid artery lies. Continue the pulse check for at least five to ten seconds. In the absence of a pulse, begin chest compressions to provide artificial circulation. Alternate with artificial breathing at the rate of 15 compressions to two breaths if one person is present or five compressions to one breath if two rescuers are available. It is important to remember that the patient must be placed in the horizontal position on a hard surface so that external chest compression will be maximally effective. If the patient is in bed, a board should be placed under the back. This procedure is continued until equipment and personnel are available to deliver advanced life support. Upon arrival of the advanced life support team, a cuffed endotracheal tube should be inserted to protect the airway from aspiration of gastric contents and to deliver oxygen-enriched artificial ventilation by bag-valve-mask. An intravenous line should be established for administration of drugs and fluids. Electrodes should be attached for electrocardiographic diagnosis and monitoring.

In the hospital setting, defibrillation equipment and personnel capable of delivering advanced life support are available immediately; therefore, the sequence of events may be slightly different. Following a cardiac arrest, immediate countershock is the therapy of first choice if a defibrillator is readily available. The rhythm most often responsible for cardiac arrest is ventricular fibrillation or tachycardia. Under these circumstances, countershock may rapidly reverse the rhythm before excessive hypoxemia or acidosis develops.

Treatment

34. M.N., a 52-year-old male, collapsed at work and was found to be unresponsive. When the paramedics arrived, he was found to be in ventricular fibrillation (see Figure 16.14). There was no pulse or blood pressure. Should drugs be used to treat this rhythm and if so, which ones and how?

Defibrillation

Treatment of ventricular fibrillation includes electrical defibrillation, epinephrine, antiarrhythmic drugs, and possibly sodium bicarbonate.[17] If immediately available, electrical defibrillation is the treatment of choice, even before beginning CPR. Immediate defibrillation at 200 J should be administered. If there is no response and fibrillation continues, the process is repeated at a higher energy level for up to two additional shocks. A 200 J energy setting is used initially because it has been shown to be as effective as higher energy settings. Furthermore, it produces less myocardial damage and is associated with a lower incidence of bradyarrhythmias and heart blocks when the rhythm is reversed.[103] A significant percentage of patients can be converted to an organized rhythm with repeated shocks in rapid succession; however, the chance of success drops off rapidly after the third shock. Other treatments should be instituted at this point such as airway management, IV access, and chest compression. Drug therapy is indicated if defibrillation fails.

Epinephrine

Epinephrine is the initial agent of choice. Although its beta-agonist properties enhance automaticity and conduction and increase the force of ventricular contraction in the beating heart, epinephrine's α-adrenergic properties are responsible for its beneficial effects during closed chest compression.[104] Alpha receptor stimulation increases systemic vascular resistance through vasoconstriction which, in turn, elevates the aortic diastolic pressure generated during chest compression. Ultimately, coronary and cerebral blood flow are enhanced. Although alpha receptor stimulation is important, pure alpha-agonists, such as methoxamine, have not been shown to produce better effects than epinephrine.[105] Epinephrine also may convert fine ventricular fibrillation to a coarse variety which may be more amenable to defibrillation.

The conventional dose of epinephrine is 1 mg (10 mL of 1:10,000 dilution) given by IV push. The dosage can be repeated at three- to five-minute intervals if needed. The optimal dose for epinephrine has been questioned by clinicians and researchers.[106] Results of animal experiments demonstrate that higher doses of epinephrine are required to improve hemodynamics and achieve successful resuscitation.[107] Clinical case series and retrospective studies support this finding; however, randomized clinical trials in humans do not confirm a statistically significant improvement in overall rate of return of spontaneous circulation, survival to hospital admission, survival to hospital discharge, or neurologic outcome between patients treated with a standard dose of epinephrine (0.02 mg/kg or 1 mg) and those treated with high doses (0.2 mg/kg or 7 mg).[108–111] American Heart Association Advanced Cardiac Life Support guidelines state: ''Use of higher dose epinephrine is acceptable, but can be neither recommended nor discouraged.''[17]

After administration of epinephrine, electrical defibrillation should be repeated. If this fails, antiarrhythmic therapy which facilitates conversion to and maintenance of an organized rhythm is indicated. Lidocaine is recommended as the initial agent of choice because its efficacy is proven and most clinicians are familiar with the dose. Bretylium is equally effective, but it is not the first agent of choice because of its hypotensive effects.

The best route of drug administration is by the IV route due to relatively easy access. However, due to low circulation from chest compressions, the action of the drug may be delayed as indicated by the delayed peak concentration by the IV route.[112]

Endotracheal Drug Administration

35. M.N. was defibrillated immediately at 200 J without success. This was repeated at 300 J and 360 J, but M.N. remained in VF. Compressions were started and an endotracheal tube

Fig 16.17   Asystole

was inserted. Epinephrine 1 mg by IV push was ordered. However, before it could be administered, the IV line infiltrated and IV access was lost. What should be done?

Intravenous access is vitally important during a cardiopulmonary arrest and a patent line should be restored as soon as possible. Other routes of drug administration should be considered if an intravenous line is unavailable; however, intramuscular or subcutaneous administration is not appropriate during cardiac arrest because poor peripheral perfusion leads to unpredictable absorption. If an endotracheal tube is in place, many agents (epinephrine, atropine, lidocaine, naloxone, diazepam) can be delivered rapidly and safely by this route.[113–115] The patient should be horizontal rather than in the Trendelenburg position. A catheter should be passed beyond the tip of the endotracheal tube at which point chest compressions should be stopped. The drug solution should be sprayed quickly down the endotracheal tube followed by five to ten rapid ventilations with a respirator bag. Medications should be diluted in 10 mL of normal saline or distilled water. Endotracheal absorption is greater with distilled water than with normal saline, but distilled water has a more negative effect on PaO_2. In general, the total bioavailability by the endotracheal route most likely is reduced compared to the direct IV route; therefore, 2 to 2.5 times the usual dose should be given by this route.

Alternative routes for some drugs include the direct intracardiac injection or in children (≤6 years of age), the intraosseous route.[116,117]

36. Two milligrams (or 20 mL of epinephrine 1:10,000) was administered via the endotracheal tube using the suction catheter technique, followed by hyperventilation. Defibrillation was repeated at 360 J with no response. IV access was established and a lidocaine 1.5 mg/kg bolus was given. Is it necessary to start a lidocaine infusion at this time?

Past recommendations have stressed the need for multiple boluses of lidocaine coupled with an intravenous infusion to establish and maintain a therapeutic concentration. This recommendation was based upon the assumption that rapid distribution of the drug into the peripheral compartment results in low central compartment or intravascular concentrations. Although this is true under normal conditions, it may not be so during CPR. During external chest compression, the cardiac output is only 15% to 20% of normal, decreasing perfusion to the peripheral compartment. Administration of pressor agents which constrict the peripheral vasculature further decreases peripheral perfusion. Under these conditions, the serum concentration of lidocaine achieved with bolus administration may not decline as rapidly.[118] This suggests that an IV infusion is unnecessary during the period of closed chest compression.

Based upon these data and the need to simplify the number of tasks code team members must perform, only bolus therapy, repeated every three to five minutes, is recommended during an arrest. Should a perfusing rhythm be restored, however, an infusion should be instituted at a rate of 1 to 4 mg/minute.

Arterial Blood Gases (ABGs) and Sodium Bicarbonate Administration

37. Defibrillation at 360 J was repeated after the lidocaine bolus was given to M.N. After defibrillation, a brief period of

sinus rhythm was established, but degenerated immediately to VT and then to VF. CPR was resumed and the following ABGs were obtained: pH 7.15 (Normal: 7.36–7.44), pCO_2 40 mm Hg (Normal: 35–40), pO_2 110 mm Hg (Normal: 90–100), and HCO_3^- 14 mEq/L (Normal: 24–30). What do these blood values indicate? Should sodium bicarbonate be administered? [SI units: pCO_2 5.3 kPa; pO_2 14.7 kPa; HCO_3^- 14 mmol/L]

The blood gases show that M.N. has a significant metabolic acidosis. Acidosis develops rapidly during cardiopulmonary arrest secondary to hypoventilation and the accumulation of fixed acids, especially lactic acid (a product of anaerobic metabolism.)[119] Assisted ventilation and effective cardiac compression to maintain cardiac output are the major interventions used to slow the development of severe refractory acidemia during a cardiopulmonary arrest. M.N.'s blood gases indicate that ventilation is adequate (normal pCO_2), but that cardiac output is inadequate to perfuse peripheral tissues (low pH, low HCO_3^-). One should consider ineffective chest compression as a cause and check for the presence of a pulse while CPR is performed.

In the past, aggressive use of bicarbonate solutions to reverse acidosis was advocated on the theoretical basis that acidosis would alter the fibrillation threshold, impairing defibrillation and the effectiveness of exogenously-administered catecholamines. Neither of these consequences occurs in clinical trials.[120,121]

Venous acidosis is accompanied by arterial alkalosis in pigs artificially put into cardiopulmonary arrest, and this paradoxical difference in pH between the arterial and venous systems has been substantiated in humans.[122] The primary cause of venous acidemia is an increase in pCO_2 (respiratory acidosis), not a decrease in HCO_3^- (metabolic acidosis). Thus, IV bicarbonate paradoxically can aggravate intracellular acidosis because bicarbonate is a large, polarized molecule whose transport across the cell membrane can be delayed for as long as 15 minutes following its administra-

tion. During that time, the HCO_3^- combines with hydrogen, liberating CO_2 intravascularly. CO_2 is a small, nonpolar molecule which rapidly crosses the cell membrane; intracellularly, CO_2 is converted to carbonic acid which further lowers the pH. The lower intracellular pH may impair CNS tissue function leading to permanent damage. This is, however, theoretical; other animal data did not show cerebral spinal fluid acidosis from bicarbonate administration.[123] Also, CO_2 gas appears to be a more potent depressor of myocardial function than metabolic acids. In conclusion, the increased venous pCO_2 load generated by bicarbonate administration may contribute to a poor outcome in the cardiac arrest situation.

There are other negative effects of bicarbonate administration. Bicarbonate can increase serum osmolality, produce arterial alkalosis, inhibit the release of oxygen from hemoglobin, increase cerebral-vascular resistance, induce hypokalemia, and impair the effectiveness of catecholamines. Together, these effects increase myocardial irritability and mortality.[115]

Only in patients with pre-existing metabolic acidosis, hyperkalemia, or tricyclic or phenobarbital overdose is bicarbonate beneficial. After protracted arrest or long resuscitative efforts, bicarbonate may be beneficial; however, it should be considered only after the aforementioned interventions have been used. The initial dose is 1 mEq/kg, then one-half this dose every ten minutes; for practical reasons, a fixed 50 mEq dose usually is used. Blood gases should be used to guide therapy if they are available.

Pulseless Electrical Activity (PEA)

38. Following another bolus of lidocaine and defibrillation at 360 J, a rhythm was noted on the monitor, but no femoral pulse was felt. M.N. was in PEA. How should he be treated? Is calcium chloride indicated?

Table 16.6		Commonly Used Cardiopulmonary Resuscitation Drugs[a]	
Drug	Dose	Rationale/Indications	Comments
Atropine	0.5–1.0 mg IV push over 20–30 sec repeated at 3–5 min intervals up to 2 mg	Blocks parasympathetic activity due to excessive vagal activity. Useful in sinus bradycardia, heart block, asystole	Must be given rapidly to avoid paradoxical vagal activity. Contraindications: HR >60 beats/min
Bretylium	*Initial bolus:* 5–10 mg IV push. May repeat in 10 min up to total of 30 mg/kg *Continuous infusion:* 1–2 mg/min	VT and VF unresponsive to lidocaine	Questionable use in digitalis toxicity. Catecholamine release initially, followed by hypotension
Calcium	2–4 mg/kg over 2–4 min repeated PRN	Reverses the direct effects of potassium on myocardial tissue	Use only with calcium channel blocker toxicity, hyperkalemia, hypocalcemia. Avoid in digitalis toxicity. Flush lines before and after administration. Do not mix with bicarbonate
Epinephrine	0.5–1 mg IV push; may be repeated in 3–5 min	Cardiac stimulant; inotropic and chronotropic response; useful in asystole, EMD, and VF	See text regarding high dose administration and endotracheal use
Isoproterenol	2–10 µg/min by IV infusion, may begin with 100–300 µg	Inotropic and chronotropic support. Useful in bradyarrhythmias	Hypotension, tachyarrhythmias
Lidocaine	1 mg/kg IV bolus over 30–60 sec. Repeat 0.5 mg/kg if needed. Infusion: 1–4 mg/min	Suppression of ventricular arrhythmias, VF, VT, ventricular arrhythmias associated with digitalis toxicity	↓ loading dose by 50% in heart and/or liver failure. No infusion indicated during CPR
Procainamide	100 mg IV push over 5 min up to 1 gm. Infusion: 1–4 mg/min	Ventricular arrhythmias unresponsive to lidocaine, PVCs	Limit loading dose to 0.5 gm in heart failure, ↓ infusion by 50% in renal failure. May cause hypotension
Sodium bicarbonate	1 mEq/kg IV push over 30–60 sec. 0.5 mEq/kg Q 10 min of continued arrest depending upon ABGs	Reverses metabolic acidosis in shock, diabetic ketoacidosis, severe hypotension, and cardiac arrest	Generally not recommended (see text). Use cautiously in the presence of hypokalemia. Flush lines before and after use. May cause intracellular acidosis (see text)

[a] ABGs = Arterial blood gases; CPR = Cardiopulmonary resuscitation; EMD = Electromechanical dissociation; HR = Heart rate; PVCs = Premature ventricular contractions; VF = Ventricular fibrillation; VT = Ventricular tachycardia.

Fig 16.18 **Drug Use in Cardiopulmonary Arrest** Adapted from reference 17.

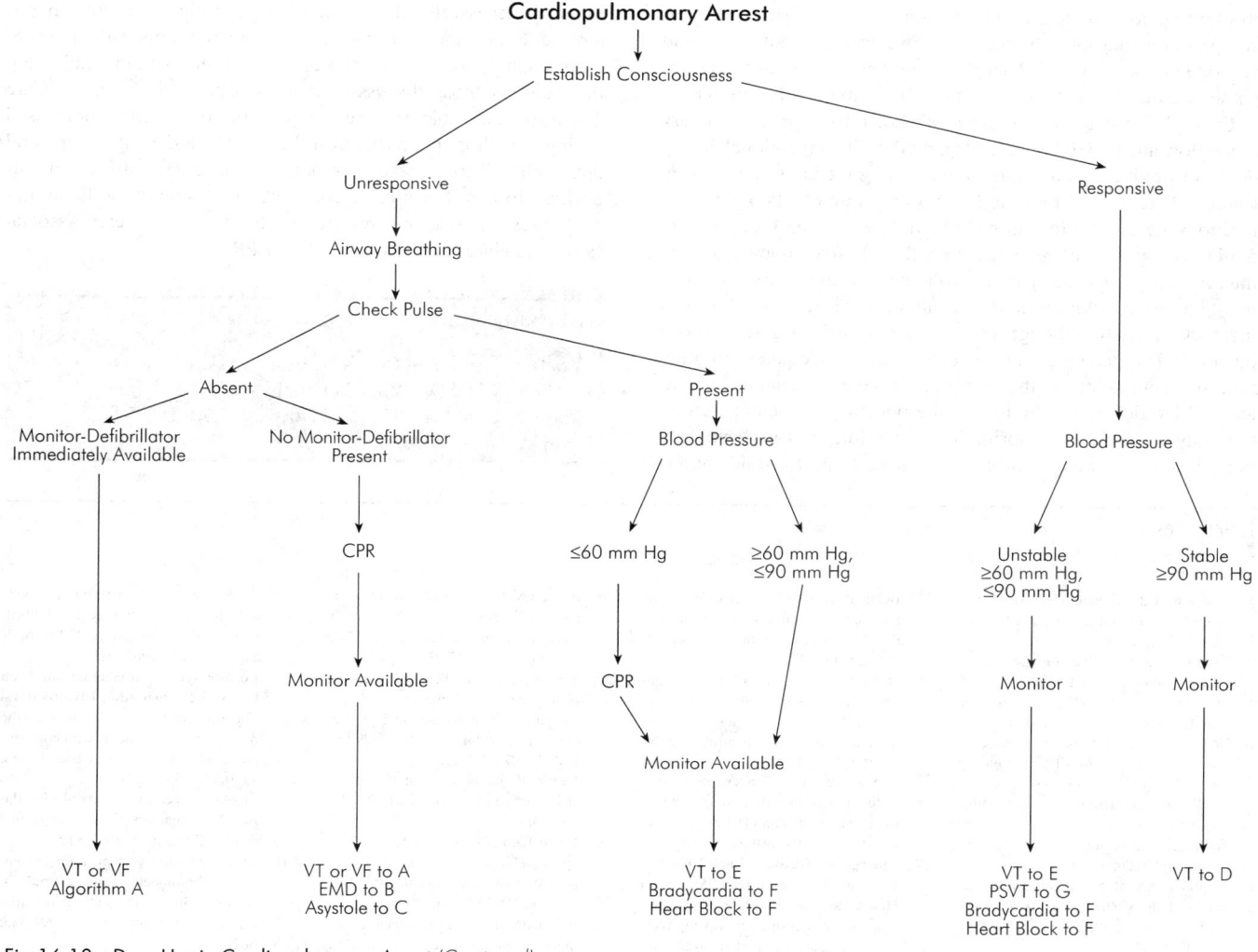

Fig 16.18   Drug Use in Cardiopulmonary Arrest *(Continued)*

The clinical situation in which there is organized electrical activity on the monitor without a palpable pulse is called pulseless electrical activity, previously known as electromechanical dissociation (EMD). Although electrical activity is present, it fails to stimulate the contractile process. Virtually all patients in true PEA succumb; however, not all patients who present with a rhythm and no pulse are in true pulseless electrical activity. Therefore, it is important to rule out treatable causes in patients who appear to be in PEA. The major entities to consider are: tension pneumothorax, cardiac tamponade, severe volume depletion, massive pulmonary emboli, hypoxia, hypothermia, hyperkalemia, and drug overdose. In establishing the diagnosis of PEA, two points should be made. First, the carotid artery is the preferred site to check for a pulse. A systolic pressure of 80 mm Hg is required to generate a radial pulse, 70 mm Hg for a femoral pulse, and 60 mm Hg for a carotid pulse. A doppler ultrasound can be used to more accurately determine if blood flow is present. Second, it may be useful to interrupt CPR and listen for heart sounds. The presence of sounds indicates that the heart valves are opening and closing and that contraction is occurring. Thus, one should intensify the search for a treatable cause. The absence of heart sounds does not confirm a lack of contraction.

Calcium, either as the chloride or gluceptate salt, has been advocated in the treatment of PEA because it plays a role in muscle contraction. The use of calcium in patients with PEA was based upon early animal data and weak anecdotal case reports; however, new insights into the role of calcium in cellular death suggest that it potentially may do more harm than good.[124] When hyperkalemia, hypocalcemia (e.g., after multiple blood transfusions), or calcium channel blocker toxicity exists the use of calcium is probably helpful; otherwise, it should not be used.

If M.N. has pulseless electrical activity, epinephrine should be administered to increase the coronary perfusion pressure during CPR and fluids should be given to provide an adequate circulating volume.

Asystole

39. M.N. has no carotid pulse and no heart tones are present. A repeat bolus of epinephrine 1 mg was administered and CPR was continued. The presence of bilateral breath sounds seemed to rule out pneumothorax and repeat ABGs to rule out pulmonary embolus show good oxygenation. A bedside echocardiogram revealed no pericardial effusion (tamponade). IV fluids were increased. Shortly thereafter, M.N. developed asystole (Figure 16.17). Is this rhythm treatable?

Lack of electrical activity or asystole, like PEA, carries a very grave prognosis. Its development usually indicates a prolonged arrest which may explain its poor response to treatment. However, a small number of patients will go directly from a sinus rhythm into asystole and may be resuscitated. Enhanced parasympathetic tone, possibly due to a vagal reaction, manipulation of the airway from intubation, suctioning or insertion of an oral airway, or chest compression may play a role in inhibiting supraventricular and ventricular pacemakers. Therefore, anticholinergic or parasympatholytic drugs which block vagal activity may be beneficial.

Epinephrine is the initial agent of choice to improve coronary blood flow and hopefully generate a rhythm. If conventional dosing does not produce results, alternative dosing methods can be used (intermediate dose: 2 to 5 mg IV Q 3 to 5 min; escalating dose: 1 to 3 to 5 mg IV Q 3 to 5 min; or high dose: 0.1 mg/kg IV Q 3 to 5 min). Atropine 1 mg repeated every three to five minutes (shorter intervals may be needed in asystolic arrest) until a total of 0.04 mg/kg has been administered. When all else fails, ventricular pacing may be tried, although this has not been shown to improve outcome. The patient should be evaluated for adequate oxygenation and ventilation or the presence of severe metabolic imbalances. Electrical defibrillation to rule out fine ventricular fibrillation may be tried, but defibrillation of asystole is of no benefit. In those instances where ventricular fibrillation and asystole are terminated successfully, it is common for the patient to become hypotensive. Fluids and inotropic and vasopressor support then are required. Guidelines for the choice of agent and administration are the same as those discussed in the Chapter 18: Intensive Care Therapeutics. Table 16.6 summarizes the drugs commonly used during a cardiopulmonary arrest. Figure 16.18 describes a general approach for drug use during a cardiac arrest situation in an algorithm format. For a more complete discussion of cardiopulmonary arrest the reader is referred to the American Heart Association's Standards and Guidelines for CPR.[17]

Acknowledgment

We are very grateful to J. Kluger, M.D., Associate Director of Cardiology and Director, Electrophysiologic Laboratory and Coronary Care Unit, Hartford Hospital, Hartford, CT for his critique and comments.

References

1 Gereats PR, Kienzie MG. Atrial fibrillation and atrial flutter. Clin Pharm. 1993;12:121.

2 Wolf PA et al. Epidemiologic assessment of chronic atrial fibrillation and the risk of stroke. The Framingham Study. Neurology. 1978;28:973.

3 Albers GW et al. Stroke prevention in non-valvular atrial fibrillation. Ann Intern Med. 1991;115:727.

4 Falk RH et al. Digoxin for converting recent onset atrial fibrillation—a randomized double blind trial. Ann Intern Med. 1987;106:503.

5 Roberts SA et al. Effectiveness and costs of digoxin treatment for atrial fibrillation and flutter. Am J Cardiol. 1993;72:567.

6 Beasley R et al. Exercise heart rates at different serum digoxin concentrations in patients with atrial fibrillation. Br Med J. 1985;290:9.

7 Weiner P et al. Clinical course of acute atrial fibrillation treated with rapid digitalization. Am Heart J. 1983;105:223.

8 Salerno DM et al. Efficacy and safety of intravenous diltiazem for treatment of atrial fibrillation and atrial flutter. The diltiazem-atrial fibrillation/flutter study group. Am J Cardiol. 1989;63:1046.

9 Waxman HL et al. Verapamil for control of ventricular rate in paroxysmal supraventricular tachycardia and atrial fibrillation or flutter: a double blind randomized cross-over study. Ann Intern Med. 1981;94:1.

10 Falk RH, Leavitt JF. Digoxin for atrial fibrillation: a drug whose time has gone? Ann Intern Med. 1991;114:573.

11 Zarowitz BJ, Gheorghiade M. Optimal heart rate control for patients with chronic atrial fibrillation: are pharmacologic choices truly changing. Am Heart J. 1992;123:1401.

12 Rawes JM. What is meant by a "controlled" ventricular rate in atrial fibrillation? Br Heart J. 1990;63:157.

13 Sokolow M, Edgar AL. Blood quinidine concentrations as a guide in the treatment of cardiac arrhythmias. Circulation. 1950;1:576.

14 Borgeat A et al. Flecainide versus quinidine for conversion of atrial fibrillation to sinus rhythm. Am J Cardiol. 1986;58:496.

15 Halpern SW et al. Efficacy of intravenous procainamide infusion in converting atrial fibrillation to sinus rhythm: relation to left atrial size. Br Heart J. 1980;44:589.

16 Fenster PE et al. Conversion of atrial fibrillation to sinus rhythm by acute intravenous procainamide infusion. Am Heart J. 1983;106:501.

17 Emergency Cardiac Care Committee and Subcommittees, American Heart Association. Guidelines for cardiopulmonary resuscitation and emergency cardiac care. Part III. Adult advanced cardiac life support. JAMA. 1992;268:2199.

18 Falk RH, Podrid PJ. Electrical cardioversion of atrial fibrillation. In: Falk RH, Podrid PJ, eds. Atrial Fibrillation: Mechanisms and Management. New York: Raven Press Ltd; 1992:181.

19 Mann DL et al. Absence of cardioversion induced ventricular arrhythmias in patients with therapeutic digoxin levels. J Am Coll Cardiol. 1988;5:882.

20 Bjerkelund CJ, Oining OM. The efficacy of anticoagulant therapy in preventing embolism related to DC electrical conversion of atrial fibrillation. Am J Cardiol. 1969;23:208.

21 Laupacis A et al. Antithrombotic therapy in atrial fibrillation. Chest. 1992; 102(Suppl.):426S.

22 Keefe DL et al. Supraventricular tachyarrhythmias: their evaluation and therapy. Am Heart J. 1986;111:1150.

23 Morris JJ et al. Electrical conversion of atrial fibrillation: immediate and long-term results. Ann Intern Med. 1966;65:216.

24 Coplen SE et al. Efficacy and safety of quinidine therapy for maintenance of sinus rhythm after cardioversion: a meta-analysis of randomized control trials. Circulation. 1990;82:1106.

25 Chow MSS. Sustained-release quinidine preparations: pharmacokinetic considerations. Hosp Formul. 1992;27(Suppl. 1):26.

26 Brosen K. Recent developments in hepatic drug oxidation. Implications for clinical pharmacokinetics. Clin Pharmacokinet. 1990;18:220.

27 Woosley RL et al. Effect of acetylator phenotype on the rate at which procainamide induced antinuclear antibodies and the lupus syndrome. N Engl J Med. 1978;298:1157.

28 Hammill SC et al. Propafenone for atrial fibrillation. Am J Cardiol. 1988; 61:473.

29 Porterfield JG, Porterfield JM. Therapeutic efficacy and safety of oral propafenone for atrial fibrillation. Am J Cardiol. 1989;63:114.

30 Pritchett EL et al. Propafenone treatment of symptomatic paroxysmal supraventricular arrhythmias: a randomized placebo-controlled, crossover trial in patients tolerating oral therapy. Ann Intern Med. 1990;114:539.

31 Pietersen A et al. Usefulness of flecainide for prevention of paroxysmal atrial fibrillation and flutter. Am J Cardiol. 1991;67:713.

32 Anderson JL et al. Prevention of symptomatic recurrences of paroxysmal atrial fibrillation in patients initially tolerating antiarrhythmic therapy. Circulation. 1989;80:1557.

33 Bolognesi R. The pharmacologic treatment of atrial fibrillation. Cardiovasc Drugs Ther. 1991;5:617.

34 Juul-Moller S et al. Sotalol vs quinidine for the maintenance of sinus rhythm after direct current conversion of atrial fibrillation. Circulation. 1990; 82:1932.

35 Vitolo E et al. Amiodarone vs quinidine in the prophylaxis of atrial fibrillation. Acta Cardiol. 1981;26:431.

36 Gosselink ATM et al. Low-dose amiodarone for maintenance of sinus rhythm after cardioversion of atrial fibrillation or flutter. JAMA. 1992;267:3289.

37 Flaker GC et al. Antiarrhythmic drug therapy and cardiac mortality in atrial fibrillation. J Am Coll Cardiol. 1992; 20:527.

38 Peterson P et al. Placebo-controlled, randomized trial of warfarin and aspirin for prevention of thromboembolic complications in chronic atrial fibrillation. The Copenhagen AFASAK Study. Lancet. 1989;1:175.

39 Boston Area Anti-coagulation Trial for Atrial Fibrillation Investigators. The effect of low-dose warfarin on the risk of stroke in patients with nonrheumatic atrial fibrillation. N Engl J Med. 1990;323:1505.

40 Stroke Prevention in Atrial Fibrillation Investigators. SPAF study: final results. Circulation. 1991;84:527.

41 Anon. Warfarin vs aspirin for prevention of thromboembolism in atrial fibrillation: Stroke Prevention in Atrial Fibrillation II Study. Lancet. 1994;343: 687.

42 Cairns JA. Stroke prevention in atrial fibrillation trial. Circulation. 1991;84: 933. Editorial.

43 American College of Physicians Guidelines for Medical Treatment for Stroke Prevention. Ann Intern Med. 1994;121:54–55.

44 Lauer MS, Eagle KA. Atrial fibrillation following cardiac surgery. In: Falk RH, Podrid PJ, eds. Atrial Fibrillation and Management. New York: Raven Press Ltd; 1992:127.

45 Lauer MS et al. Atrial fibrillation following coronary artery bypass surgery. Prog Cardiovasc Dis. 1989;31:367.

46 Rubin DA et al. Predictors, prevention and long term prognosis of atrial fibrillation after CABG operation. J Thorac Cardiovasc Surg. 1987;94:331.

47 Salazar C et al. Beta-blockade therapy for supraventricular tachyarrhythmias after coronary surgery: a propranolol withdrawal syndrome? Angiology. 1979;30:816.

48 Sager PT. Narrow complex tachycardias: differential diagnosis and management. Cardiol Clin. 1991;9:619.

49 Faulds D. Adenosine. An evaluation of its use in cardiac diagnostic procedures, and in the treatment of PSVT. Drugs. 1991;41:596.

50 Stoysich AM et al. Evaluation of pharmacodynamic interaction between adenosine and methylxanthine. Clin Pharmacol Ther. 1994;55:154. Abstract.

51 **Garrat C et al.** Comparison of adenosine and verapamil for termination of paroxysmal junctional tachycardia. Am J Cardiol. 1989;64:1310.

52 **Sung RJ et al.** Mechanism of spontaneous alternation between reciprocating tachycardia and atrial flutter/fibrillation in the Wolff-Parkinson-White syndrome. Circulation. 1977;56:409.

53 **Gulamhusein S et al.** Acceleration of the ventricular response during atrial fibrillation in the WPW syndrome after verapamil. Circulation. 1982;65:348.

54 **Falk RH.** Proarrhythmia in patients treated for atrial fibrillation or flutter. Ann Intern Med. 1992;117:141.

55 **Gaita F et al.** Wolff-Parkinson-White Syndrome; identification and management. Drugs. 1992;43:185.

56 **Mitchell LB et al.** Electropharmacology of sotalol in patients with Wolff-Parkinson-White syndrome. Circulation. 1987;76:810.

57 **Feld GK et al.** Clinical and electrophysiologic effects of amiodarone in patients with atrial fibrillation complicating the Wolff-Parkinson-White syndrome. Am Heart J. 1988;115:102.

58 **Kunze KP et al.** Sotalol in patients with Wolff-Parkinson-White syndrome. Circulation. 1987;75:1050.

59 **Goldschlager N, Goldman MJ.** Principles of Clinical Electrocardiography. Norwalk, CT: Appleton and Lange; 1989:74.

60 **Zipes DP.** Specific arrhythmias: diagnosis and treatment. In: Braunwald E, ed. Heart Disease. Philadelphia: WB Saunders; 1992:714.

61 **Lown B, Verrier RL.** Neural activity and ventricular fibrillation. N Engl J Med. 1976;294:1165.

62 **The ESVEM Investigators.** Determinants of predicted efficacy of antiarrhythmic drugs in the electrophysiologic study vs electrocardiographic monitoring trial. Circulation. 1993;87:323.

63 **Tisdale JE et al.** Efficacy of class 1C antiarrhythmic agents in patients with inducible ventricular tachycardia refractory to therapy with class 1A antiarrhythmic drugs. J Clin Pharmacol. 1993;33:623.

64 **Bleske BE et al.** Acute effects of combination of 1B and 1C antiarrhythmics for the treatment of ventricular tachycardia. J Clin Pharmacol. 1989;29:998.

65 **Graboys TB et al.** Long-term survival of patients with malignant ventricular arrhythmia treated with antiarrhythmic drugs. Am J Cardiol. 1982;50:477.

66 **Wilber DJ et al.** Out-of-hospital cardiac arrest: use of electrophysiologic testing in the prediction of long-term outcome. N Engl J Med. 1988;318:19.

67 **Mason JW et al.** A comparison of electrophysiologic testing with holter monitoring to predict antiarrhythmic-drug efficacy for ventricular tachyarrhythmias. N Engl J Med. 1993;329:445.

68 **Waller TJ.** Reduction in sudden death and total mortality by antiarrhythmic therapy evaluated by electrophysiologic drug testing: criteria of efficacy in patients with sustained ventricular tachyarrhythmia. J Am Coll Cardiol. 1987;10:83.

69 **Bigger JT et al.** The relationships among ventricular arrhythmias, left ventricular dysfunction, and mortality in the 2 years after myocardial infarction. Circulation. 1984;69:250.

70 **Echt DS et al.** Mortality and morbidity in patients receiving encainide, flecainide, or placebo. N Engl J Med. 1991;324:781.

71 **The Cardiac Arrhythmia Suppression Trial II Investigators.** Effect of the antiarrhythmic agent moricizine on survival after myocardial infarction. N Engl J Med. 1992;327:227.

72 **The Cardiac Arrhythmia Pilot Study (CAPS) Investigators.** Effects of encainide, flecainide, imipramine and moricizine on ventricular arrhythmias during the year after acute myocardial infarction: The CAPS. Am J Cardiol. 1988;61:501.

73 **Greene HL et al.** Classification of deaths after myocardial infarction as arrhythmic or nonarrhythmic (the Cardiac Arrhythmia Pilot Study). Am J Cardiol. 1989;63:1.

74 **Pires LA, Huang SKS.** Nonsustained ventricular tachycardia: identification and management of high-risk patients. Am Heart J. 1993;126:189.

75 **Friedman CM et al.** Effect of propranolol in patients with myocardial infarction and ventricular arrhythmias. J Am Coll Cardiol. 1986;7:1.

76 **Bigger JT, Hoffman BF.** Antiarrhythmic drugs. In: Gilman AG et al., eds. Goodman and Gilman's: The Pharmacological Basis of Therapeutics. New York: Pergamon Press; 1990:853.

77 **Lalka D et al.** Lidocaine pharmacokinetics and metabolism in acute myocardial infarction patients. Clin Res. 1980;28:329A.

78 **Abernathy DR et al.** Impairment of lidocaine clearance in elderly male subjects. J Cardiovasc Pharmacol. 1983;5:1093.

79 **Conrad KA et al.** Lidocaine elimination: effects of metoprolol and of propranolol. Clin Pharmacol Ther. 1983;33:133.

80 **Pharand C et al.** Prophylactic lidocaine for lethal ventricular arrhythmias following acute myocardial infarction: 8-vs 48-hour infusion. Submitted to J Am Coll Cardiol.

81 **Singh B.** Electrophysiologic basis for the antiarrhythmic actions of sotalol and comparison with other agents. Am J Cardiol. 1993;72:8A.

82 **Jackman WM et al.** The long QT syndrome: a critical review, new clinical observations and a unifying hypothesis. Prog Cardiovasc Dis. 1988;31:115.

83 **Zehender M et al.** QT interval prolonging drugs; mechanisms and clinical relevance of their arrhythmogenic hazards. Cardiovasc Drugs Ther. 1991;51:515.

84 **Surawicz B.** Electrophysiologic substrate of torsades de pointes: Dispersion of repolarization or early afterdepolarizations. J Am Coll Cardiol. 1989;14:172.

85 **Torres et al.** The arrhythmogenicity of antiarrhythmic agents. Am Heart J. 1985;109:1090.

86 **Josephson ME.** Antiarrhythmic agents and danger of proarrhythmic event. Ann Intern Med. 1989;111:101. Editorial.

87 **Arstall MA et al.** Sotalol-induced torsade de pointes: management with magnesium infusion. Postgrad Med J. 1992;68:289.

88 **Bailie DS et al.** Magnesium suppression of early afterdepolarizations and ventricular tachycardia induced by cerium in dogs. Circulation. 1988;77:1395.

89 **Colucci R et al.** Comparative effects of class IA, IB, and IC antiarrhythmic agents in patients with inducible sustained ventricular tachycardia. J Clin Pharmacol. 1988;28:929. Abstract.

90 **Pharand C et al.** Modification of inducible ventricular tachycardia by antiarrhythmics: the role of amiodarone. J Clin Pharmacol. 1992;32:742. Abstract.

91 **Greenspan AM et al.** Combination antiarrhythmic drug therapy for ventricular tachyarrhythmias. PACE Pacing Clin Electrophysiol. 1986;9:565.

92 **Levy S.** Combination therapy for cardiac arrhythmias. Am J Cardiol. 1988;61:95A.

93 **Bleske B et al.** Acute effects of combination of IB and IC antiarrhythmics for the treatment of ventricular tachycardia. J Clin Pharmacol. 1989;29:998.

94 **Ujhelyi MR et al.** Outcome of patients requiring modification of discharge antiarrhythmic therapy after electrophysiology study guide therapy. Clin Pharmacol Ther. 1991;49:188. Abstract.

95 **McCollam PL et al.** A simple method of monitoring antiarrhythmic drugs during short-and long-term therapy. Am J Cardiol. 1989;63:1273.

96 **Wilson JS, Podrid PJ.** Side effects from amiodarone. Am Heart J. 1991;121:158.

97 **Tworek DA et al.** Interference by antiarrhythmic agents with function of electrical cardiac devices. Clin Pharm. 1992;11:48.

98 **Volpi A et al.** In-hospital prognosis of patients with acute myocardial infarction complicated by primary ventricular fibrillation. N Engl J Med. 1987;317:257.

99 **Soloman SD, Antman EM.** Ventricular tachyarrhythmias in thrombolytic trials. Circulation. 1992;86:I–135. Abstract.

100 **Lie KI et al.** Lidocaine in the prevention of primary ventricular fibrillation. N Engl J Med. 1974;291:1324.

101 **MacMahon S et al.** Effects of prophylactic lidocaine in suspected acute myocardial infarction. JAMA. 1988;260:1910.

102 **Hine LK et al.** Meta-analytic evidence against prophylactic use of lidocaine in acute myocardial infarction. Arch Intern Med. 1989;149:2694.

103 **Weaver WD et al.** Ventricular defibrillation; a comparative trial using 175J and 320J shocks. N Engl J Med. 1982;207:1101.

104 **Otto CW et al.** Mechanism of action of epinephrine in resuscitation from asphyxial arrest. Crit Care Med. 1981;9:321.

105 **Bleske B et al.** Epinephrine vs methoxamine on survival post ventricular fibrillation and cardiopulmonary resuscitation in dogs. Crit Care Med. 1989;17:1310.

106 **Otto C, Yakaitis R.** The role of epinephrine in CPR, a reappraisal. Ann Emerg Med. 1987;16:743.

107 **Kosnik JW et al.** Dose related response of centrally administered epinephrine on the change in aortic diastolic pressure during closed chest massage in dogs. Ann Emerg Med. 1985;14:204.

108 **Paradis NA, Koscove EM.** Epinephrine in cardiac arrest: a critical review. Ann Emerg Med. 1990;19:1288.

109 **Gonzalez ER, Ornato JP.** The dose of epinephrine during cardiopulmonary resuscitation in humans: what should it be? DICP. 1991;25:773.

110 **Brown CG et al.** A comparison of standard-dose and high-dose epinephrine in cardiac arrest outside the hospital. The Multicenter High-Dose Epinephrine Study Group. N Engl J Med. 1992;327:1051.

111 **Stiell IG et al.** High-dose epinephrine in adult cardiac arrest. N Engl J Med. 1992;327:1045.

112 **Chow MSS et al.** Lidocaine pharmacokinetics during cardiac arrest and external cardiopulmonary resuscitation. Am Heart J. 1981;102:799.

113 **Roberts JR et al.** Blood levels following intravenous and endotracheal epinephrine administration. JACEP. 1979;8:53.

114 **Raehl CL.** Endotracheal drug therapy in cardiopulmonary resuscitation. Clin Pharm. 1986;5:572.

115 **Hasegawa EA.** The endotracheal administration of drugs. Heart Lung. 1986;15:60.

116 **Aitkenhead AR.** Drug administration during CPR: which route. Resuscitation. 1991;22:191.

117 **Haphes SA, Robertson C.** CPR-drug delivery routes and systems. A statement for the advanced life support working part of the European Resuscitation Council. Resuscitation. 1992;24:137.

118 **Chow MSS et al.** The effect of external cardiopulmonary resuscitation on lidocaine pharmacokinetics in dogs. J Pharmacol Exp Ther. 1983;224:531.

119 **Fillmore SJ et al.** Serial blood gas during cardiopulmonary resuscitation. Ann Intern Med. 1989;110:839.

120 **Telivo L et al.** Comparison of alkalizing agents in resuscitation of the heart after ventricular fibrillation. Ann Chir Gynaecol. 1968;57:221.

121 **Mimuck, Sharma GP.** Comparison of THAM and sodium bicarbonate in resuscitation of the heart after ventricular fibrillation in dogs. Anesth Analg. 1977;56:38.

122 **Weil MH et al.** Arterial blood gases fail to reflect acid-base status during cardiopulmonary resuscitation. Crit Care Med. 1985;13:884.

123 **Bleske BE et al.** Effects of different dosages and modes of sodium bicarbonate administration during cardiopulmonary resuscitation. Am J Emerg Med. 1992;10:525.

124 **Dembo DH.** Calcium in advanced life support. Crit Care Med. 1981;9:358.

125 **Podrid RJ, Falk RH.** Management of atrial fibrillation—an overview. In: Falk RH et al., eds. Atrial Fibrillation. Mechanisms and management. New York: Raven; 1992:389–411.

126 **Stein E.** Rapid analysis of arrhythmias—a self study program. Philadelphia: Lea & Febriger; 1992.

127 **Goldberger AL, Goldberger E.** Clinical Electrocardiography—a simplified approach. 4th ed. Hartford: Mosby-Year Book, Inc; 1990:196.

Hypertensive Emergencies

Robert Michocki

Definitions 17-1
   Hypertensive emergency and urgency
    (See Table 17.1) 17-1
   Malignant hypertension 17-2
   Accelerated hypertension 17-2
Signs and Symptoms 17-2
   Central nervous system (CNS) 17-2
   Other complications 17-2
Principles of Treatment 17-2
   Oral versus parenteral therapy
    (See Tables 17.2 and 17.3) 17-2
   Goals of therapy 17-3

Hypertensive Urgencies 17-3
  Patient Assessment 17-3
  Oral Drug Therapy 17-3
   Nifedipine 17-3
    Hemodynamic effects 17-3
    Administration 17-3
    Dosing, onset, and duration of action 17-4
    Contraindications 17-5
    Adverse effects 17-5
   Clonidine 17-5
    Adverse effects and precautions 17-6
   Other oral drugs 17-6
    Captopril 17-6
    Minoxidil 17-6
    Prazosin 17-6
    Labetalol 17-6
  Parenteral Therapy 17-6
   Hydralazine 17-6
    Contraindications 17-6

    Dosing and administration 17-7
  Other parenteral drugs 17-7
   Intravenous enalaprilat 17-7
   Calcium channel blockers 17-7
    Intravenous verapamil 17-7
    Intravenous diltiazem 17-7
    Intravenous nicardipine 17-7
    Intravenous urapidil 17-7
Hypertensive Emergencies 17-8
  Patient Assessment 17-8
  Treatment 17-8
   Nitroprusside 17-8
    Hemodynamic effects 17-8
    Concurrent use of diuretics 17-8
    Dosing and administration 17-8
    Therapeutic endpoint 17-9
    Cyanide toxicity 17-9
    Thiocyanate toxicity 17-10
   Labetalol 17-11
    Contraindications (Also see Question 16) 17-11
    Parenteral therapy 17-11
   Nitroglycerin 17-11
   Oral therapy 17-12
   Diazoxide 17-12
    Precautions (Also see Question 16) 17-12
    Dosing and administration 17-12
    Onset and duration of action 17-12
  Aortic Dissection 17-13
   Treatment 17-13
    Therapeutic considerations 17-13
    Trimethaphan 17-13

Definitions

Hypertensive Emergency and Urgency

The term hypertensive crisis refers to a diverse group of acute hypertensive disorders that have in common evidence of end-organ dysfunction. If these disorders are not treated promptly, a high rate of morbidity and mortality will ensue.[1] These disorders are divided into two general categories and are referred to as hypertensive emergencies and hypertensive urgencies (see Table 17.1).[2] Signs and symptoms for these disorders are nonspecific and may overlap. The distinction usually depends upon the clinical assessment of the life-threatening nature of each episode. The term hypertensive emergency describes a clinical situation in which the elevated blood pressure is immediately life threatening and requires the pressure to be lowered to a safe level within a matter of minutes to one hour. The level to which the blood pressure is elevated does not in itself represent a true emergency. A hypertensive urgency is less acute and can be accelerated or even malignant, but without severe symptoms or progressive target organ complications.[3] It is not immediately life threatening and a reduction of blood pressure to a safe level can occur more slowly over 1 to 24 hours.[4]

Hypertensive crises usually are characterized by an acute and marked elevation of arterial pressure, arteriolar spasm, necrotizing arteriolitis (necrosis in the media of the arterioles), and secondary organ damage. Hypertensive emergencies generally occur in patients with pheochromocytoma, renal vascular disease, or accelerated essential hypertension. Acute life-threatening elevations of blood pressure also can occur in previously normotensive individuals during the course of acute glomerulonephritis, head injury, severe burns, eclampsia, or in patients receiving monoamine oxidase inhibitors after ingesting foods rich in tyramine.

Rapid, severe blood pressure elevation is not always the hallmark of a hypertensive emergency. Indeed, even moderate elevations of arterial pressure in the context of a variety of disease states demand prompt treatment. Specific examples include acute left ventricular failure, intracranial hemorrhage, dissecting aortic aneurysm, and postoperative bleeding at suture sites.

Hypertensive emergencies rarely develop in previously normotensive patients. Most commonly, they complicate the accelerated phase of poorly-controlled, chronic hypertension.[5,6] In a retrospective study of patients with hypertensive emergency, a past history of hypertension was previously diagnosed in more than 90% of the patients, suggesting that hypertensive emergencies are almost entirely preventable.[7] Before effective modes of treatment for hypertension were available, it was estimated that 1% to 7% of hypertensive patients progressed to an accelerated phase. Currently, it is estimated that less than 1% of hypertensives now progress to this phase.[8–12] Even with effective therapy, the mortality for patients with a history of hypertensive crisis is 25% at one year and 50% at five years.[11] Hypertensive emergencies occur more

Table 17.1	Hypertensive Emergencies versus Urgencies[a]	
Emergencies	**Urgencies**
Diastolic >120 mm Hg. End organ damage present	Diastolic >120 mm Hg. Minimal end organ damage with no pending complications
Heart (acute aortic dissection, acute pulmonary edema, angina, myocardial insufficiency syndrome, left ventricular failure)	Accelerated and malignant hypertension
CNS (intracranial hemorrhage, thrombotic cerebrovascular accident, subarachnoid hemorrhage, hypertensive encephalopathy)	Hypertension associated with coronary disease
Eyes: grade 3 or 4 Keith-Wagener funduscopic changes, ocular hemorrhage	Postoperative or preoperative hypertension
Eclampsia	Severe hypertension in kidney transplant patients
Renal failure/insufficiency	
Pheochromocytoma crisis	

Drug-induced hypertensive crisis
        MAOI-tyramine interactions
        Overdose with phencyclidine, cocaine, LSD[b]	

Usually life threatening emergencies	Not life threatening
Requires immediate pressure reduction	Treated over several hours to days
Requires IV[b] therapy (see Table 17.2)	Oral therapy or slower-acting parenteral drugs preferred (see Table 17.4)

[a] Reprinted with permission. Young LY et al. Handbook of Applied Therapeutics. Applied Therapeutics, Inc. Vancouver: 1990.
[b] IV = Intravenous; LSD = Lysergic acid diethylamide; MAOI = Monoamine oxidase inhibitor.

frequently in blacks than whites, and it has been suggested that this could be due to late presentation or inadequate therapy.[12] Severe uncontrolled hypertension also is more likely to occur among patients with no primary care physician and among those who do not comply with their treatment regimen.[13]

Malignant Hypertension

Malignant hypertension is best described as a clinical syndrome characterized by necrotizing arteriolitis, a markedly elevated blood pressure, severe retinopathy (i.e., a Keith-Wagener Classification of III or IV), renal failure, and a rapidly deteriorating clinical course. It occurs more commonly in middle-aged hypertensive patients with a peak prevalence in the 40- to 60-year age range. If malignant hypertension occurs with no previous history of hypertension or in a patient whose age is less than 30 or greater than 60 years old, a secondary cause should be suspected.[14]

Accelerated Hypertension

Accelerated hypertension is a term used to describe a clinical picture that is similar to malignant hypertension; however, there are no papilledema or other complications and it has a less rapidly progressive course. Accelerated hypertension also has been considered a forerunner of malignant hypertension. Despite these differences, the terms accelerated and malignant often are used synonymously.[5,15] It should be remembered that although hypertensive emergencies are much less common than urgencies, it is sometimes difficult to make a clear distinction in the absence of a thorough patient history to know whether end organ dysfunction is new or has progressed.[16]

Signs and Symptoms

Symptoms associated with hypertensive crisis are highly variable and reflect the degree of damage to specific organ systems. The primary sites of damage are the central nervous system (CNS), heart, kidneys, and eyes.

Central Nervous System

CNS damage may present solely as a severe headache or may be accompanied by dizziness, nausea, vomiting, and anorexia. Mental confusion with apprehension is indicative of more severe

disease, as is nystagmus, localized weakness, or a positive Babinski sign (i.e., upward extension of the great toe and spreading of the smaller toes). CNS damage may be rapidly progressive and result in coma or death. If a cerebrovascular accident has occurred, slurred speech or motor paralysis may be present.

Other Complications

Cardiac complications of hypertensive crisis include congestive heart failure (CHF) and angina pectoris. Myocardial infarction (MI) also may be precipitated. Ocular symptoms of hypertensive crisis usually are related to changes in visual acuity. Complaints of blurred vision or loss of eyesight frequently are associated with the funduscopic findings of hemorrhages, exudates, and occasionally, papilledema. Renal complications may include hematuria, proteinuria, pyelonephritis, and an elevated serum blood urea nitrogen (BUN) and creatinine.

Principles of Treatment

Oral versus Parenteral Therapy

Accelerated hypertension, malignant hypertension, or an elevated blood pressure in the absence of life threatening signs or symptoms, are not indications for parenteral treatment. Oral antihypertensive loading regimens are more appropriate for the management of these urgent cases. In contrast, hypertensive emergencies require immediate hospitalization and administration of parenteral antihypertensive medications to reduce arterial pressure.[17] Effective therapy greatly improves the prognosis, reverses symptoms, and arrests the progression of end-organ damage. Treatment reverses the vascular changes in the eyes and slows or arrests the progressive deterioration in renal function. Treatment of malignant hypertension may transiently worsen renal function. However, after two to three months of adequate medical therapy, renal function gradually may improve to the premalignant level of renal insufficiency or to a new, slightly deteriorated level.[19,20] The time required for recovery of renal function ranges from two weeks to two years. A low serum creatinine, in the absence of marked cardiomegaly or renal shrinkage, has been associated with a good chance for recovery of renal function.[21] In patients with mild encephalopathy, neurological symptoms resolve within 24 hours following treatment.[22] Resolution of papilledema occurs in two to three weeks, while funduscopic exudates may require up to 12 weeks for complete resolution.[23] Whether treatment can completely reverse end-organ damage is related to two factors: how soon treatment is begun and the extent of damage at the initiation of therapy. Without treatment, the two-year mortality approaches 90%.[20]

There are two fundamental concepts in the management of hypertensive emergencies. First, immediate and intensive therapy is required and takes precedence over time-consuming diagnostic procedures. Secondly, the choice of drugs will depend upon how their time course of action and hemodynamic and metabolic effects meet the needs of a crisis situation. If encephalopathy, acute left ventricular failure, dissecting aortic aneurysm, or other serious conditions are present, the blood pressure should be lowered promptly with parenteral antihypertensive medications such as diazoxide (Hyperstat), diltiazem (Cardizem Injectable), enalaprilat (Vasotec IV), labetalol (Normodyne, Trandate), nicardipine (Cardene IV), nitroglycerin (Tridil, Nitrostat IV, Nitro-Bid IV), nitroprusside (Nipride), trimethaphan (Arfonad), or verapamil (Isoptin IV). (See Table 17.2.) If a slower blood pressure reduction, over several hours or days, is acceptable, parenteral hydralazine (Apresoline), methyldopa (Aldomet), oral clonidine (Catapres), nifedipine (Procardia, Adalat), captopril (Capoten), or minoxidil (Loniten) may be used (see Table 17.3).

Goals of Therapy

The rate of blood pressure lowering must be individualized. Ischemic damage to the heart and brain can be provoked by a precipitous fall in blood pressure.[24,25] Thus, antihypertensive drugs should be used cautiously in patient groups at high risk for developing hypotensive complications (e.g., elderly patients and patients with severely defective autoregulatory mechanisms, including those with autonomic dysfunction or fixed sclerotic stenosis of cerebral or neck arteries).[26] In addition, patients who have chronically elevated blood pressure are less likely to tolerate abrupt reductions in their blood pressure, and the amount of reduction appropriate for those patients is somewhat less. In patients with hypertensive encephalopathy, cerebral hypoperfusion may occur if the mean blood pressure is reduced by greater than 40%;[27] it has been suggested that the mean pressure be lowered by no more than 20% to 30%.[27,28] Although there are no absolute guidelines, a reduction of 5 mm Hg to 10 mm Hg every five to ten minutes to a diastolic pressure of 100 mm Hg or a 25% decrease in mean arterial pressure is an appropriate therapeutic endpoint for most patients.[4,29,30] Lower pressures may be indicated for patients with aortic dissection.

Hypertensive Urgencies
Patient Assessment

1. M.M. is a 48-year-old black male with a long history of mild heart failure and poorly-controlled hypertension thought to be due to noncompliance. He was referred from a community health center this morning for a more thorough evaluation of an elevated blood pressure (BP). He has not taken his digoxin (Lanoxin), nifedipine (Adalat, Procardia), or hydrochlorothiazide (Oretic) for the last 7 days. M.M. is completely asymptomatic. Physical examination reveals a BP of 220/130 mm Hg and a pulse of 92 beats/min. The funduscopic examination is pertinent for mild arteriolar narrowing. The lungs are clear and the cardiac examination is unremarkable. The electrocardiogram (ECG) indicates normal sinus rhythm (NSR) at a rate of 90 beats/min with first degree A-V block. The chest x-ray is interpreted as mild cardiomegaly. Serum electrolytes, BUN, and serum creatinine (SrCr) are within normal limits. A urinalysis (UA) is significant for 2+ proteinuria and trace hematuria.

What is the therapeutic objective in treating M.M.? How quickly should his pressure be lowered and what therapeutic options are available?

M.M. has severe hypertension with a blood pressure of 220/130 mm Hg. However, the absolute magnitude of pressure elevation does not in itself constitute a medical emergency. There is no evidence of severe headache or encephalopathy, cardiac decompensation, or rapid change in renal function. Therefore, no evidence exists to indicate a rapid deterioration in the function of target organs.

As is often the case, M.M.'s lack of blood pressure control is related to medication noncompliance. The initial goal of therapy is a lowering of his blood pressure to a diastolic pressure of 100 mm Hg over the next several hours, being careful not to induce hypotension. Since his pressure can be lowered gradually over a period of several hours, parenteral therapy is unwarranted. A number of different oral regimens using nifedipine, clonidine, captopril, labetalol, prazosin (Minipress), and minoxidil are available. Later he can be converted to a regimen designed to enhance compliance during outpatient use. Good patient counseling will be required to help M.M. better understand the severity of his disease and the need to take his medications.

Oral Drug Therapy
Nifedipine

2. How does nifedipine differ from other oral antihypertensive agents used to acutely lower blood pressure? How should nifedipine be given to M.M. and when would you expect a response?

Clonidine, labetalol, prazosin, minoxidil, and captopril have all been used to lower blood pressure acutely. However, these oral agents take several hours to adequately lower pressure and are, therefore, most useful in treating hypertensive urgencies. Oral angiotensin converting enzyme (ACE) inhibitors, other than captopril, are not useful for acutely lowering blood pressure because their onset of action is delayed. The calcium channel blockers, including diltiazem, verapamil, and nicardipine, can rapidly lower blood pressure; however, the most extensive experience is with nifedipine.[31] Nifedipine, when given orally or by the "bite and swallow" method is a rapid-acting, simple, effective, and well-tolerated alternative to parenteral therapy in the acute management of hypertension. It can therefore be used in the emergent as well as urgent cases.[32-42]

Hemodynamic Effects. Nifedipine reduces the blood pressure by decreasing the intracellular calcium ions available in vascular smooth muscle cells. This vasodilatory effect is especially pronounced in vessels with high vasoconstrictor tone;[39] therefore, the reduction in blood pressure by nifedipine directly correlates with the pretreatment pressure.[33,34,38,40] Following treatment with nifedipine, a reduction in blood pressure and systemic vascular resistance occurs. Cardiac output increases and heart rate may increase slightly as a result of baroreflex activation.[43] Tachycardia is usually more pronounced in younger patients and this is thought to be related to the presence of a more reactive baroreceptor reflex.[33,39] The potential advantages and disadvantages of nifedipine in hypertensive urgencies are summarized in Table 17.4.

Administration. Nifedipine is marketed as a soft gelatin capsule or as an extended release tablet. The extended release tablet is not suitable for rapidly lowering blood pressure. However, the soft gelatin capsule can be perforated and taken sublingually,[34,38,43] chewed,[35,40] swallowed,[33,41] or given rectally.[44] The bite and swallow approach to dosing provides the most rapid rise in plasma nifedipine concentration and produces peak levels well above those achieved with sublingual administration.[37,45] The response rate is

Table 17.2   Parenteral Drugs Commonly Used in the Treatment of Hypertensive Emergencies[3,31,96–101,106,223]

Drug	Dose/Route	Onset of Action	Duration of Action	Major Side Effects[a]	Mechanism of Action[a]	Avoid or Use Cautiously in Patients with These Conditions[a]
Diazoxide	50–150 mg IV Q 5 min or as infusion of 7.5–30 mg/min	1–5 min	4–12 hr	Hypotension, hyperglycemia, Na retention, tachycardia, painful extravasation	Vasodilator	Angina, MI, aortic dissection, pulmonary edema, intracranial hemorrhage
Diltiazem[b]	5–15 µg/kg/min IV infusion	30–60 min	Unknown	Dizziness, headache, bradycardia, atrioventricular conduction abnormalities	Vasodilator	Sick sinus, advanced degrees of heart block
Enalaprilat[b]	0.625–1.25 mg IV Q 6 hr	15 min (max: 1–4 hr)	6–12 hr	Hypotension, hyperkalemia	ACE inhibitor	Renal failure in patients with bilateral renal artery stenosis or dehydration, hyperkalemia, pregnancy
Hydralazine	IV: 10–20 mg IM: 10–50 mg	IV: 10–30 min IM: 20–40 min	2–6 hr	Tachycardia, headache, angina	Vasodilator	Angina, MI, aortic dissection
Labetalol	2 mg/min IV or 20–80 mg Q 10 min up to 300 mg total dose	≤5 min	3–6 hr	Orthostatic hypotension, abdominal pain, N/V, diarrhea	α- and β-adrenergic blocker	Asthma, bradycardia, CHF
Nicardipine[c]	IV loading dose 5 mg/hr increased by 2.5 mg/hr Q 5 min to a max 15 mg/hr followed by a maintenance infusion of 3 mg/hr	2–10 min (max: 8–12 hr)	40–60 min after discontinuing infusion	Headache, flushing, N/V, dizziness, tachycardia, local thrombophlebitis: change infusion site after 12 hr	Vasodilator	None
Nitroglycerin[d]	IV infusion pump 5–100 µg/min	2–5 min	5–10 min after discontinuing infusion	Methemoglobinemia, headache, tachycardia, N/V, flushing, tolerance with prolonged use	Vasodilator	Pericardial tamponade, constrictive pericarditis, increased intracranial pressure
Nitroprusside	IV infusion pump 0.25–8 µg/kg/min	Seconds	3–5 min after discontinuing infusion	Hypotension, cyanide toxicity, thiocyanate toxicity	Arteriolar and venous vasodilator	Renal failure, pregnancy
Trimethaphan	IV infusion pump 0.5–5 mg/min	1–5 min	10 min after discontinuing infusion	Tachyphylaxis, hypotension, ileus, constipation, urinary retention, pupillary dilation	Ganglionic blocker	Postoperative glaucoma
Verapamil[b]	5–10 mg IV; can be followed by infusion 3–25 mg/hr	1–5 min	30–60 min	Sinus arrest, N/V	Vasodilator	Atrioventricular block

[a] ACE = Angiotensin-converting enzyme; CHF = Congestive heart failure; MI = Myocardial infarction; Na = Sodium; N/V = Nausea and vomiting.
[b] Not approved by the FDA for the treatment of acute hypertension.
[c] Indicated for the short term treatment of hypertension when the oral route is not feasible or desirable.
[d] Requires special delivery system due to drug binding to PVC tubing.

85% to 95%.[34,37] Prior antihypertensive treatment does not affect response.[37] Following ingestion of intact oral capsules, nifedipine plasma concentrations may vary considerably.[46] This may be attributed to the rate of drug absorption and/or variability in the extent of first-pass hepatic extraction and metabolism. Plasma drug levels following sublingual dosing reach significantly lower peak values and occur at a later time when compared to oral capsule ingestion.[47,48] The sublingual route of administration can be used in patients who are unable to take oral medicines.

Dosing, Onset, and Duration of Action. Nifedipine reduces the mean arterial pressure by 20% to 36% in approximately 15 to 30 minutes after sublingual administration (10 mg) and one hour after oral administration (10 to 20 mg).[32–35,37] The onset of antihypertensive action occurs within five minutes following sublingual therapy compared to 10 to 20 minutes after oral treatment. The slight delay following oral administration is most likely due to the release time of the soft gelatin capsule. This delay can be avoided by biting then swallowing the capsule. The duration of action is two to five hours.

A 20 mg dose administered sublingually produces a greater decline in blood pressure than 10 mg, and a greater number of patients who initially receive 10 mg require a second dose.[37,38]

Table 17.3	Oral Drugs Commonly Used in the Treatment of Hypertensive Urgencies[3,31,98]					
Drug	Dose/Route	Onset of Action	Duration of Action	Major Side Effects[a]	Mechanism of Action[a]	Avoid or Use Cautiously in Patients with These Conditions[a]
Captopril	6.5–50 mg PO	15 min	4–6 hr	Rash, pruritus, proteinuria, loss of taste, hypotension	ACE inhibitor	Renal artery stenosis, hyperkalemia, dehydration, renal failure
Clonidine	0.2 mg PO initial then 0.1 mg/hr up to 0.8 mg total	0.5–2 hr	6–8 hr	Sedation, dry mouth, dizziness, constipation	α_2-antagonist	Altered mental status, severe carotid artery stenosis
Labetalol	200–400 mg PO Q 2–3 hr	30 min–2 hr	4 hr	Orthostatic hypotension, N/V	α- and β-adrenergic blocker	CHF, asthma, bradycardia
Minoxidil	5–20 mg PO	30–60 min (max: 2–4 hr)	12–16 hr	Tachycardia, fluid retention	Vasodilator	Angina, CHF
Nifedipine	10–20 mg PO (bite and swallow)	5–15 min	3–5 hr	Burning, paresthesia, flushing, headaches, palpitations, edema	Calcium entry blocker	Severe aortic stenosis

[a] ACE = Angiotensin-converting enzyme; CHF = Congestive heart failure; N/V = Nausea and vomiting.

M.M. should bite and swallow the contents of a 20 mg capsule of nifedipine. If the response is not adequate, another 20 mg can be given in 30 to 60 minutes. In emergency cases, nifedipine can be repeated at 15- to 20-minute intervals. The three to five hour duration allows sufficient time to initiate appropriate therapy for the stable long-term control of M.M.'s blood pressure.

3. Contraindications. Are there any contraindications to the use of nifedipine in M.M.?

Nifedipine is a simple, effective, and safe drug for the acute treatment of hypertension. It should be used cautiously in patients with cerebral artery stenosis because a rapid reduction in perfusion pressure places these individuals at risk for the development of cerebral ischemia.[39,49] However, despite the marked reduction in perfusion pressure with nifedipine, cerebral blood flow is maintained and, therefore, critical hypotensive responses are rare. Reflex cardiac stimulation and hypotension leading to a worsening of underlying ischemic heart disease has been reported with nifedipine, but appears to be an uncommon event.[16,50] Nifedipine also should be used cautiously in patients with severe aortic stenosis because the drug's slightly negative inotropic effect cannot be counterbalanced by reduced afterload.[51] For this reason, heart failure can be precipitated in such patients. M.M. has no signs or symptoms of heart failure and no carotid bruits or heart murmurs are present.

Nifedipine has been reported to increase serum digoxin concentrations by as much as 40%.[52] However, subsequent studies have failed to confirm this finding.[53,54] M.M.'s past history of digoxin use should not dissuade one from use of nifedipine. It is also unnecessary to alter the digoxin dose when the calcium antagonist is initiated.[55] (See Chapter 15: Congestive Heart Failure.)

4. Adverse Effects. M.M.'s response to a single, 20 mg oral dose of nifedipine is excellent. However, he is now complaining of a flushing sensation in his face and legs. Is this related to nifedipine?

The majority of side effects associated with nifedipine are minor and include a burning sensation in the face and legs (6%), facial flushing (5%), palpitations (4.6%), sporadic premature ventricular contractions (3.7%), ankle edema (2%), dryness of mouth (1%), postural hypotension (0.3%), and urticaria (0.3%). Most of these side effects resolve with long-term nifedipine treatment.[36] M.M.'s symptoms most likely are related to the peripheral vasodilation caused by nifedipine and should resolve with continued administration.

Clonidine

5. What is the role of clonidine in the acute treatment of hypertension? What is the correlation between the loading dose and the maintenance dose?

Clonidine is a centrally-acting, α_2-adrenergic agonist which inhibits sympathetic outflow from the CNS. Following acute administration, clonidine reduces mean arterial pressure, cardiac output, stroke volume, and cardiac rate. There is little change in the total peripheral resistance or renal plasma flow. The initial reduction in cardiac output is caused by decreased venous return to the right side of the heart secondary to venodilation and bradycardia, not to decreased contractility.[2]

The blood pressure can be lowered over several hours using oral clonidine. Usually, an oral loading dose (0.1 to 0.2 mg) is followed by a dose of 0.1 mg/hour until the desired response is achieved or until a cumulative dose of 0.5 to 0.8 mg is reached.[56–58] A significant reduction in blood pressure occurs within one hour and the mean arterial pressure decreases by 25% in most patients. Anderson et al.[57] reported a 94% response rate to an oral loading dose. Patients required a mean total dose of 0.45 mg and the maximum response occurred five to six hours after the start of therapy.

Table 17.4	Potential Advantages and Disadvantages of Nifedipine in Hypertensive Urgencies[a,31]

Advantages

The MAP is decreased proportionally to the level of pretreatment BP and SVR and averages 25%. Efficacy approaches 98%

Invasive hemodynamic monitoring is unnecessary

Tachycardia occurs, but angina and MI are rare

Decrease in left ventricular afterload

Varied nonparenteral dosage forms are available with equal efficacy (e.g., bite and chew method)

Disadvantages

Potential hypotension or normotension may reduce perfusion to vital organs and induce complications

Acute reversible renal deterioration has been reported in patients with chronic renal insufficiency

Cerebral edema and hypertensive encephalopathy may be worsened

[a] BP = Blood pressure; MAP = Mean arterial pressure; MI = Myocardial infarction; SVR = Systemic vascular resistance.

The acute response to oral clonidine loading is not predictive of the daily dose required to maintain acceptable blood pressure control. Maintenance oral therapy with clonidine is somewhat empiric. Some authors have recommended giving 80% to 100% of the cumulative loading dose per day in split doses morning and evening.[57,59] The major portion is given at bedtime to minimize daytime sedation. Guanabenz (Wytensin), is a drug which is similar to clonidine; however, documented efficacy in the acute treatment of hypertension is lacking.

6. Is there any difference in response rates between nifedipine and clonidine in the treatment of hypertensive urgency?

Nifedipine and clonidine frequently are used to acutely lower blood pressure in patients with hypertensive urgency. Houston[60] reported that clonidine and nifedipine were efficacious in 93% and 98% of the patients, respectively. Similar efficacy rates have been reported by others.[61,62] A prospective trial comparing 20 mg of nifedipine with hourly doses of 0.1 mg clonidine resulted in a prompt reduction in blood pressure (within 30 minutes) with nifedipine, whereas clonidine produced a slower, more gradual response.[61] Both drugs are considered safe and effective and either may be used as first line therapy of hypertensive urgency. However, clonidine should be avoided in patients with bradycardia, sick sinus syndrome, or cardiac conduction defects.[16,31]

7. Adverse Effects and Precautions. What precautions should be exercised when using the oral clonidine loading regimen?

Oral clonidine is relatively free of side effects. Adverse effects include orthostatic hypotension, bradycardia, sedation, dry mouth, and dizziness. Sedation is a particularly troublesome side effect and because of this, clonidine should not be used in patients where the mental status examination is an important monitoring parameter. Since clonidine can decrease cerebral blood flow by up to 28%[33,63] it should not be used in patients with severe cerebrovascular disease.[29]

Other Oral Drugs

8. What other oral agents are used to acutely lower blood pressure?

Captopril, an orally active ACE inhibitor, has been used both orally[64,65] and sublingually[66-68] to acutely lower the blood pressure. Orally, single 10 mg to 50 mg doses of captopril significantly lowered diastolic blood pressures in a small group of patients with malignant hypertension.[64] The onset of action occurred within minutes and reached a maximum between 30 and 90 minutes. Sublingually, captopril 25 mg reduces the blood pressure within 10 to 15 minutes and its effect persists for two to six hours. Captopril may be particularly useful in hypertensive crises associated with acute renal failure, progressive systemic sclerosis,[64,69,72] systemic lupus erythematosus,[73] renal vascular hypertension,[10] or renin secreting tumors.[74,75] Sublingual captopril is as effective as nifedipine in acutely reducing mean arterial pressure in both urgent and emergent conditions.[69,70] However, it should be remembered that captopril can induce severe renal failure in patients with bilateral renal artery stenosis or renal artery stenosis in a solitary kidney. Such conditions may not be easy to detect in the context of an acute hypertensive emergency. Therefore, in patients in whom these conditions can be excluded, captopril can be considered for therapy. In patients known to have these conditions, nifedipine is preferred. First-dose hypotension remains the limiting factor with the use of oral or sublingual captopril and is most likely to occur in patients who are volume depleted or in those receiving diuretics.[16,76] These same patients also may be more predisposed to captopril-induced renal function changes.

Minoxidil, a potent oral vasodilator, has also been used successfully in the treatment of severe hypertension.[77-79] Oral loading doses of 10 to 20 mg produce maximal blood pressure response in two to four hours[80] and can be followed by a dose of 5 to 20 mg every four hours if necessary. Because its use is associated with reflex tachycardia and fluid retention, beta blockers and loop diuretics generally are used concomitantly. Minoxidil should be used only in those patients who are refractory to other forms of therapy or who have previously been taking this agent.[59] Experience with this mode of therapy is needed.

Prazosin also has been used to a limited degree to treat hypertensive emergencies. An oral loading dose of 5 mg maximally reduced the blood pressure within 60 to 120 minutes.[81] However, hypotension may be a significant limiting factor and more study is required before this drug can be recommended.

Labetalol. Several studies have suggested that oral labetalol can be used acutely to treat severe hypertension.[82-85] Initial doses of 100 to 300 mg may provide a sustained response for up to four hours.[83] Labetalol, 200 mg given at hourly intervals to a maximum dose of 1200 mg, was comparable to oral clonidine in reducing mean arterial pressure.[85] An alternative regimen using 300 mg initially followed by 100 mg at two-hour intervals, up to a maximum of 500 mg, was also successful in acutely lowering blood pressure.[84] However, Wright et al.[86] were unable to achieve an adequate blood pressure response in a small series of patients using a single loading dose of 200 to 400 mg.

Oral labetalol may offer an alternative to oral nifedipine, clonidine, or captopril for the acute treatment of hypertension, but the most appropriate dosing regimen remains to be determined. Labetalol may cause profound orthostatic hypotension and, because of its beta blocking activity, it should be avoided in patients with asthma, bradycardia, or congestive heart failure.

Parenteral Therapy

Hydralazine

9. T.M., a 30-year-old male with a history of chronic glomerulonephritis and poorly controlled hypertension, came to the emergency room (ER) complaining of early morning occipital headaches that have been occurring over the last week. He has no other complaints. He has not taken any blood pressure medication in a month.

Physical examination revealed an afebrile male in no acute distress with a BP of 160/120 mm Hg without orthostasis and a regular pulse of 90 beats/min. Funduscopic examination revealed bilateral exudates without hemorrhages or papilledema. The lungs were clear. Cardiac examination was pertinent for cardiomegaly and an S_4 gallop. The remainder of the physical work-up was normal.

Laboratory results: Hct 32%; BUN 40 mg/dL; creatinine 2.5 mg/dL; and bicarbonate 18 mEq/L. UA reveals 2+ protein, 2+ hemoglobin with 4 to 10 red blood cells (RBCs) per high powered field (HPF). The ECG demonstrates NSR with left ventricular hypertrophy. The chest x-ray is unremarkable.

T.M. was given 20 mg hydralazine intramuscularly (IM), and a repeat blood pressure after 1 hour was 150/100 mm Hg.

What are the advantages and disadvantages of parenteral hydralazine, and when should it be used to acutely lower blood pressure? Are there alternatives to hydralazine for parenteral therapy of hypertensive urgencies? [SI units: Hct 0.32 1; BUN 14.28 mmol/L UREA; creatinine 221 μmol/L; bicarbonate 18 mmol/L]

Hydralazine is a direct vasodilator that reduces total peripheral resistance through relaxation of arterial smooth muscle. Hydralazine rarely is used to treat hypertensive emergencies because the antihypertensive response is less predictable than with other parenteral agents, and it is not consistently effective in controlling crises associated with essential hypertension.

Contraindications. Hydralazine should not be used in patients with coronary heart disease because the reflex tachycardia causes an increase in myocardial oxygen demand which may result in the development or worsening of ischemic symptoms. In addition, hydralazine should be avoided in patients with aortic dissection because of the reflex cardiostimulating effect. On the other hand, as is the case with T.M., hydralazine can be useful in patients with chronic renal failure since the reflex increase in cardiac output is accompanied by an increase in organ perfusion which is desirable when renal failure is present. In addition, there is considerable experience with the use of hydralazine in patients with eclampsia and these patients are less likely to have underlying coronary artery disease.

Dosing and Administration. Parenteral hydralazine should be considered as intermediate treatment between oral agents and more aggressive therapy such as diazoxide (Hyperstat) and nitroprusside (Nipride). It can be given intravenously (IV) or intramuscularly. The onset of action develops slowly over 20 to 40 minutes, thus minimizing the risk of acute hypotension. Parenteral doses are considerably lower than oral doses because of increased bioavailability.

Other Parenteral Drugs

Intravenous enalaprilat, the active metabolite of the oral prodrug enalapril (Vasotec), is approved by the Food and Drug Administration for the treatment of hypertension when oral therapy is not feasible. Although not approved for the treatment of hypertensive crisis, enalaprilat has been used to treat severe hypertension.[87–92] The initial dose is 0.625 to 1.25 mg given IV and repeated every six hours if necessary. The initial dose should not exceed 0.625 mg in those patients receiving diuretics or in those patients with clinical evidence of hypovolemia. The onset of action occurs within 15 minutes, but the maximum effect may take several hours. Concomitant diuretic therapy may enhance the response.[88] Since enalaprilat is primarily excreted by the kidney, its dosage should be adjusted in patients with renal insufficiency. Since ACE inhibitors do not impair cerebral blood flow, enalaprilat may be useful for the hypertensive patient at risk for cerebral hypoperfusion. Enalaprilat also is beneficial in patients with congestive heart failure. Precautions associated with the use of enalaprilat are similar to those of captopril (see Question 8). Because of the prolonged time required to achieve an adequate response, limited clinical experience, and variable response rates, this type of therapy cannot be recommended for the treatment of hypertensive emergencies.[93]

Calcium Channel Blockers. Parenteral verapamil,[94,95] diltiazem,[96,97] and nicardipine[98–106] are effective in the treatment of hypertensive emergencies and urgencies.

Intravenous verapamil 5 to 10 mg produces a significant reduction in blood pressure which occurs within 15 minutes and persists for six to eight hours.[94,95] However, the use of this drug in hypertensive emergencies has not been studied extensively.

Intravenous diltiazem is approved for temporary control of the ventricular rate in atrial fibrillation or atrial flutter and for rapid conversion of paroxysmal supraventricular tachycardia.[107–109] Parenteral diltiazem also has been used to control hypertension that occurs intraoperatively and postoperatively[110,111] and in patients with acute coronary artery disease.[112,113] However, published experience with the use of IV diltiazem for the treatment of severe hypertension is limited.[96,97] Onoyama et al.[96] administered a continuous infusion of diltiazem, at a dosage of 5 to 40 µg/kg/minute to a small group of patients with hypertensive crisis. A normotensive level was achieved within six hours without any signs of organ ischemia. In a follow-up study,[97] a continuous infusion of diltiazem averaging 11 µg/kg/minute resulted in a 25% reduction in both systolic and diastolic pressures within 30 minutes. The magnitude of the decrease was directly correlated with the pretreatment

blood pressure level. Atrioventricular nodal conduction abnormalities were noted in both studies and resolved when the infusion was discontinued. Patients receiving IV diltiazem require continuous monitoring by ECG and frequent blood pressure checks. This form of therapy should be avoided in patients with sick sinus syndrome or advanced degrees of heart block. Until additional information is available, caution should be exercised in using parenteral diltiazem for the acute lowering of blood pressure.

Intravenous nicardipine, a dihydropyridine calcium channel antagonist, is a potent cerebral and systemic vasodilator. Unlike other dihydropyridines, nicardipine is photoresistant, water soluble, and can be administered intravenously. Its onset of action is within one to two minutes, and its elimination half-life is 40 minutes.[114] Hemodynamic evaluations demonstrated that IV nicardipine significantly decreased mean arterial pressure and systemic vascular resistance, and significantly increased cardiac index with little or no change in heart rate.[104] Titratable intravenous nicardipine has been studied extensively for use in controlling postoperative hypertension,[100,102–105] as well as severe hypertension.[99,101,106]

In the treatment of postoperative hypertension,[102,104] IV nicardipine was administered as an infusion titrated in the following manner: 10 mg/hour × 5 minutes; 12.5 mg/hour × 5 minutes; 15 mg/hour × 15 minutes, followed by a maintenance infusion of 3 mg/hour, thereafter. The mean response time and infusion rate were 11.5 minutes and 12.8 mg/hour, respectively. Ninety-four percent of the patients responded and adverse effects included hypotension (4.5%), tachycardia (2.7%), and nausea and vomiting (4.5%).

The efficacy and safety of IV nicardipine for the treatment of severe hypertension has been documented in a recent double-blind, placebo controlled multicenter trial.[99] The patients achieved a diastolic pressure ≤95 mm Hg. Serious adverse effects were infrequent, the most common being headache which occurred in 24% of the patients. Local thrombophlebitis also may occur. This can be avoided by changing the infusion site after 12 hours. Initial therapy of IV nicardipine was begun with doses of 1 to 15 mg/hour. Adjustments were made as indicated until the therapeutic endpoint was achieved. Maintenance therapy was continued for 8 to 24 hours.[101,106] The mean dose of IV nicardipine at the end of maintenance was 7.85 mg/hour. In individual patients, the dose of nicardipine necessary for blood pressure control ranged from 3 to 15 mg/hour. Investigators noted that nicardipine blood levels in severe hypertension appeared to reach steady state at 8 to 12 hours after the onset of the infusion, although significant therapeutic effects were seen within an hour.

In summary, intravenous nicardipine is a promising drug for the treatment of both severe and postoperative hypertension. It has a rapid onset of action with sustained blood pressure control over the infusion period. It is easily titratable with a predictable response and is relatively free of severe adverse effects. It may be useful in patients with coronary artery disease, cerebral insufficiency, or peripheral vascular disease.

Intravenous urapidil is a potent alpha antagonist with a pharmacodynamic profile similar to that of prazosin.[115] Although not available in the United States, limited studies have suggested that the intravenous dosage form can be beneficial in the treatment of hypertensive emergencies.[116,117] Urapidil is administered in doses of 10 to 50 mg given intravenously over 5 minutes. Most patients require 25 to 50 mg and this often is followed by a maintenance infusion. Alternatively, therapy can be initiated as a continuous infusion at a rate of 2 mg/minute until the desired response is achieved, after which the rate of administration may be reduced. The most common adverse effects are dizziness, nausea, headache, fatigue, and palpitations.[115] Additional trials will be needed to further assess the efficacy and safety of IV urapidil in the acute treatment of hypertension.

Hypertensive Emergencies

Patient Assessment

10. M.R., a 55-year-old black male, presents to ER with a 3-day history of progressively increasing shortness of breath (SOB). Over the past two days he developed a severe headache unrelieved by aspirin, substernal chest pain, anorexia, and nausea.

His past medical history includes asthma and a 5-year history of angina which, 2 months before admission, resulted in hospitalization for an acute inferior MI. He is currently being followed in the renal clinic for chronic renal failure. He has been taking aminophylline, furosemide (Lasix), hydralazine, and methyldopa (Aldomet), but discontinued these medications on his own 3 weeks ago.

Physical examination reveals an anxious-appearing male who is alert, oriented, and in moderate respiratory distress. His vital signs include pulse rate of 125 beats/min, respiratory rate of 36/min, BP of 220/145 mm Hg without orthostasis, and a normal body temperature. Funduscopic examination shows arteriolar narrowing and AV nicking without hemorrhages, exudates, or papilledema. There is no jugular venous distension. Bilateral carotid bruits are present. Chest examination reveals decreased breath sounds with bilateral rales extending to the tip of the scapula. M.R.'s heart is displaced 2 cm left of the midclavicular line with no thrills or heaves. The rhythm is regular with an S_3 and an S_4 gallop; no murmurs are noted. The remainder of M.R.'s examination is within normal limits.

Significant laboratory values include the following: Sodium (Na) 142 mEq/L (Normal: 136–144); potassium (K) 5.5 mEq/L (Normal: 3.5–5.5); chloride (Cl) 101 mEq/L (Normal: 96–106); bicarbonate 15 mEq/L (Normal: 23–28); BUN 95 mg/dL (Normal: 10–20); creatinine 5.0 mg/dL (Normal: 0.5–1.2); Hct 33% (Normal: 40–45); Hgb 11.5 gm/dL (Normal: 14–18); white blood cell (WBC) count and differential are within normal limits. UA shows 1+ hemoglobin and 1+ protein. Microscopic examination of the urine reveals 5 to 10 RBCs/HPF and no casts. Arterial blood gases on room air reveal a pO_2 of 55, pCO_2 of 32, and a pH of 7.28.

An ECG demonstrates a sinus tachycardia and left ventricular hypertrophy. M.R.'s chest x-ray shows moderate cardiomegaly and bilateral fluffy infiltrates.

What aspects of M.R.'s history are consistent with the diagnosis of malignant hypertension? [SI units: Na 142 mmol/L (Normal: 136–144); K 5.5 mmol/L (Normal: 3.5–5.5); Cl 101 mmol/L (Normal: 96–106); bicarbonate 15 mmol/L (Normal: 23–28); BUN 33.915 mmol/L UREA (Normal: 3.57–7.14); creatinine 442 μmol/L (Normal: 44.2–106.08); Hct 0.33 (Normal: 0.40–0.45); Hgb 115 gm/L (Normal: 140–180)]

As discussed earlier, malignant hypertension occurs most frequently in blacks, males, and individuals between the ages of 40 and 60. M.R. meets all of the characteristics of this population group. Furthermore, many individuals who present with malignant hypertension have a recent history of discontinuing the use of their antihypertensives,[13] as is the case with M.R.

The recent onset of a severe headache, nausea, and vomiting are consistent with CNS signs of severe hypertension, as are the acute onset of angina (substernal pain) and congestive heart failure (shortness of breath, increased pulse and respiratory rate, cardiomegaly, S_3, and chest x-ray findings of pulmonary edema). The absence of signs of right heart failure such as jugular venous distension or hepatomegaly suggest an acute onset of congestive heart failure (CHF) caused by hypertension as opposed to a gradual worsening of chronic heart failure.

M.R. has a history of chronic renal failure, and his relatively high BUN to creatinine ratio suggests that there is also a prerenal component to his renal dysfunction which may be due to the acute rise in blood pressure as well as the CHF. M.R.'s urinary sediment is relatively unimpressive at this time, especially in light of his history and his ocular complications are minimal.

Treatment

Nitroprusside

11. Considering M.R.'s medical history, which antihypertensive agent should be used?

M.R.'s arterial pressure should be lowered with parenteral medications which have a rapid onset of action. Nitroprusside, IV nitroglycerin (NTG), and trimethaphan all decrease total peripheral resistance rapidly with minimal effect on myocardial oxygen consumption and heart rate. Of these agents, nitroprusside usually is preferred in patients with hypertension accompanied by acute left ventricular failure and in the absence of myocardial infarction. Parenteral nitroglycerin can be used to lower blood pressure in patients with ischemic heart disease (see Question 21). IV nitroglycerin is similar to nitroprusside except that it has relatively greater effect on venous circulation and less effect on arterioles. It is most useful in patients with coronary insufficiency, myocardial infarction, or in those with hypertension following coronary bypass surgery (see Question 21). Trimethaphan is not an acceptable choice since rapid tolerance develops to its hypotensive action and its use is associated with many side effects (see Question 27).

Hemodynamic Effects. Nitroprusside has many pharmacologic effects which should favor M.R.'s condition. It dilates both venous and arterial vessels. Thus, it increases venous capacitance and decreases the venous return or preload on the heart (see Chapter 15: Congestive Heart Failure). A decrease in the pulmonary capillary wedge pressure and ventricular filling pressure will ultimately improve M.R.'s pulmonary edema. Afterload also is decreased as a result of arterial dilation. This action increases cardiac output, reduces arterial pressure, and increases tissue perfusion.[118–120]

12. Concurrent Use of Diuretics. Should M.R. be given a diuretic before nitroprusside therapy is begun?

Administration of potent IV diuretics is relatively ineffective in the acute treatment of hypertension except in patients with concomitant congestive heart failure.[121,122] Many patients with hypertensive emergencies are vasoconstricted and have normal or reduced plasma volumes; therefore, diuretics have little effect and may actually aggravate renal failure or cause other adverse effects.[21,31,123] Furthermore, when diuretics are given acutely in combination with other antihypertensive agents, profound hypotension may occur.[121] In the presence of congestive heart failure, IV diuretic administration is likely to cause a reduction in blood pressure due to venodilation rather than diuresis. Venodilation decreases right-sided cardiac filling pressures, decreases pulmonary artery and wedge pressures, and increases cardiac output before diuresis occurs.[124] The presence of congestive heart failure and severely elevated blood pressure would warrant the IV administration of furosemide 40 to 80 mg or bumetanide (Bumex) 1 to 2 mg in M.R.

13. Dosing and Administration. How should nitroprusside be prepared and administered? What dose should be used initially?

Because of its extreme potency, sodium nitroprusside must be prepared in exact concentrations and administered at precisely calculated rates. Sodium nitroprusside is supplied in units of 50 mg of lyophilized powder. The powder is reconstituted with 2 to 3 mL of 5% dextrose in water which produces a red-brown solution. The contents of the vial are then added to 500 mL of 5% dextrose in water (D_5W) to produce a solution for IV administration with a drug concentration of 100 µg/mL.[118]

Nitroprusside decomposes upon exposure to light; thus, the solution should be shielded by wrapping the container with the metal foil provided in each package. It has been suggested that solutions of sodium nitroprusside be discarded four hours after reconstitution.[125,126] However, others have reported the stability, protected from light, to be 12 to 24 hours[127] or longer.[128–130] A change in the solution's color to yellow does not reduce effectiveness.[130] However, the appearance of a dark brown, green, or blue color is indicative of a loss in activity.[119,130,131] A blue color indicates almost complete degradation.[131]

Effective infusion rates range from 0.5 to 8 µg/kg/minute. For M.R., an infusion of nitroprusside should be initiated at a rate of 0.5 µg/kg/minute, using a microdrip regulator or an infusion pump. The dose should be increased slowly by 0.5 µg/kg/minute every five minutes until the desired pressure is achieved.[132] A maximum infusion rate of 10 µg/kg/minute has been recommended, but the dose must be individualized according to patient response and signs or symptoms of toxicity.

14. Therapeutic Endpoint. A nitroprusside infusion of 0.5 µg/kg/min is started. What is the goal of therapy?

M.R.'s arterial pressure should be reduced to near normal levels; however, because M.R. has renal failure and cerebral occlusive disease (carotid bruits), excessive reduction of blood pressure should be avoided. This also will favor recovery of his renal function to precrisis status. As stated earlier, even though an increase in the BUN and creatinine may occur during antihypertensive therapy, these elevations usually are transitory and reflect hemodynamic alterations rather than progressive renal disease.[133]

An excessive reduction of blood pressure in the presence of major cerebral vessel stenosis may decrease cerebral blood flow and produce strokes or other neurological complications.[25,134–136] Normal cerebral blood flow remains relatively constant over a wide range of systemic blood pressures through autoregulatory mechanisms.[31,63,137] The autoregulatory effects can prevent gross alterations in cerebral blood flow from either slow or rapid changes in systemic arterial pressures. However, there is evidence that the blood pressure required to maintain cerebral perfusion is higher in hypertensive patients than it is in normotensive individuals.[138–140] If M.R.'s blood pressure is reduced excessively, cerebral blood flow may decrease sharply. Therefore, a diastolic blood pressure of 100 to 105 mm Hg would be a reasonable initial therapeutic goal for M.R. If hypotension does occur, nitroprusside should be discontinued and M.R.'s feet should be elevated.

15. M.R. is treated with nitroprusside for 48 hours. Over the past 24 hours, the infusion has been tapered to 1 µg/kg/min and oral antihypertensive therapy has been initiated. What are the major side effects associated with nitroprusside and what indices of toxicity should be monitored? Should hydroxocobalamin or thiosulfate be given to prevent nitroprusside toxicity?

A major concern when using sodium nitroprusside is toxicity secondary to the accumulation of its metabolic by-products, cyanide and thiocyanate.

Cyanide Toxicity. Sodium nitroprusside decomposes within a few minutes after IV infusion. (See Figure 17.1.) Free cyanide, which represents 44% of nitroprusside by weight, is released in the bloodstream producing prussic acid (hydrogen cyanide) which is responsible for the acute toxicity.[141] The amount released is directly proportional to the size of the dose.[130,142] Endogenous detoxification of prussic acid occurs through a mitochondrial rhodanase system which, in the presence of a sulfur donor such as thiosulfate, converts prussic acid to thiocyanate.[141] This enzymatic detoxification of prussic acid exhibits zero-order pharmacokinetics

with the limiting factor being the low concentration of sulfur-containing substrates.[143] The rate of spontaneous detoxification of prussic acid is 1 µg/kg/minute,[130] which is considerably slower than previously reported. The previously reported rates led to false assumptions regarding toxicity of prussic acid.[141] Prussic acid can be expected to accumulate in the body when the rate of the sodium nitroprusside infusion exceeds 2 µg/kg/minute.[130,144,145] This rise can be prevented by administering sodium thiosulfate simultaneously.[130,146,147] A mixture of 0.1% sodium nitroprusside and 50 mL of 1% sodium thiosulfate is as effective as sodium nitroprusside alone, and substantially less toxic.[146] Some authors have recommended that all patients receiving nitroprusside receive concomitant thiosulfate infusions.[148] Intravenous boluses may be effective, but require frequent dosing.[130,149] Rindone and Sloane[150] noted that 10 mg of sodium thiosulfate for every 1 mg of nitroprusside should be considered in high risk patients (malnutrition) or when large doses of nitroprusside are administered (>3 µg/kg/minute). The presence of hypoalbuminemia and hepatic failure also may predispose the patient to toxicity. However, no studies that chemically determine the compatibility characteristics of nitroprusside and sodium thiosulfate are available.

Fortunately, symptomatic cyanide toxicity occurs infrequently, although several deaths have been reported following the use of sodium nitroprusside.[151–156] Two lawsuits alleged that the manufacturers of sodium nitroprusside failed to warn the medical profession of the drug's high toxicity and failed to give adequate instructions on its proper use. As a result, revised labeling warns that sodium nitroprusside administration increases the body's concentration of cyanide ion sufficient to achieve toxic, and potentially fatal, levels even when given within the range of recommended doses and that the maximum recommended dose can overwhelm the body's ability to buffer the cyanide within one hour. Cyanide toxicity occurs most commonly when high doses (total dose: 1.5 mg/kg) of nitroprusside are administered rapidly to patients undergoing a surgical procedure which requires induction of hypotension.[151,155,157,158] The concurrent use of sodium thiosulfate may reduce the risk of toxicity in these patients.

Hydroxocobalamin also has been used to reduce cyanide toxicity secondary to nitroprusside infusions.[159] The concurrent ad-

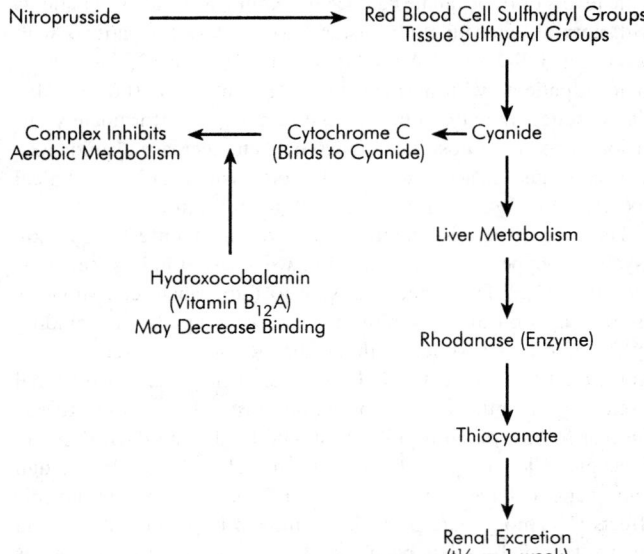

Fig 17.1 Nitroprusside Metabolism Nitroprusside is metabolized to cyanide (which may accumulate in liver disease) and to thiocyanate (which will accumulate in renal insufficiency). Reprinted with permission from reference 31.

ministration of a continuous infusion of hydroxocobalamin (25 mg/hour) lowers red blood cell and plasma cyanide concentrations.[160] Hydroxocobalamin combines with cyanide to form cyanocobalamin, which is nontoxic and excreted in the urine. It has been estimated that 2.4 gm of hydroxocobalamin would be required to neutralize the cyanide released from 100 mg of nitroprusside.[161] Its use, therefore, is limited due to poor availability and cost considerations. It should be noted that cyanocobalamin is not effective in reducing or preventing cyanide toxicity. The use of hydroxocobalamin or sodium thiosulfate is likely to be of greatest value in patients receiving high doses acutely or in patients receiving sodium nitroprusside over an extended period of time. Since cyanide toxicity occurs rarely, the empiric use of hydroxocobalamin or thiosulfate is not necessary in M.R. The duration of nitroprusside therapy has been short, and his blood pressure has been adequately maintained on relatively normal doses.

Cyanide toxicity can be detected early by monitoring M.R.'s metabolic status. Lactic acidosis is an early indicator of toxicity,[163] because the progressive inactivation of cytochrome oxidase by cyanide results in increased anaerobic glycolysis. A low plasma bicarbonate concentration and low pH, accompanied by an increase in the blood lactate or lactate-pyruvate ratio, together with an increase in the mixed venous blood oxygen tension could indicate cyanide toxicity.[142,155,163-165] Additional signs of cyanide intoxication include tachycardia, altered consciousness, coma, convulsions, and the occasional smell of almonds on the breath.[150,163] Hypoxemia due to pulmonary arterial shunting also has been reported during nitroprusside therapy.[119] Serum thiocyanate levels are of no value in detecting the onset of cyanide toxicity. If toxicity develops, the infusion should be stopped, and appropriate therapy for cyanide intoxication should be instituted.

Thiocyanate Toxicity. Sodium nitroprusside is more likely to produce thiocyanate toxicity. Although this also is rare, patients with renal failure (such as M.R.) who receive prolonged infusions are particularly susceptible. The conversion of cyanide to thiocyanate proceeds relatively slowly and thiocyanate levels rise gradually in proportion to the dose and duration of administration.[166-168] The half-life of thiocyanate is 2.7 days with normal renal function and 9 days in patients with renal failure.[169] When sodium nitroprusside is infused for several days at moderate dosages (2 to 5 µg/kg/min), toxic levels of thiocyanate can occur within 7 to 14 days in patients with normal renal function, or three to six days for patients with severe renal disease.[141] A total daily dose of up to 125 mg is nontoxic in patients with normal renal function, while 1000 mg/day may produce toxicity within 24 to 48 hours.[168] Unfortunately, infusion of sodium thiosulfate, which helps to decrease cyanide toxicity, can cause an accumulation of thiocyanate resulting in clinical toxicity,[159] especially in patients with renal failure.

Thiocyanate causes a neurotoxic syndrome manifested by toxic psychosis, hyperreflexia, confusion, weakness, tinnitus, seizures, and coma.[15,120] Prolonged exposure to thiocyanate can suppress thyroid function through inhibition of iodine uptake and binding by the thyroid.[170] Although thiocyanate toxicity is rare, it is recommended that blood levels be measured in patients with renal disease or when the duration of the nitroprusside infusion exceeds three or four days. Nitroprusside should be discontinued if serum thiocyanate levels exceed 10 to 12 mg/dL,[31,93,118,171] although some patients have tolerated levels of 20 mg/dL without adverse effects.[172] Thiocyanate is readily removed by hemodialysis, and intermittent dialysis has been used to decrease thiocyanate levels in patients receiving prolonged infusions.[173]

For M.R., the potential for thiocyanate toxicity is greater than cyanide toxicity because of his underlying renal disease. If a prolonged course of therapy had been necessary, serum thiocyanate levels would have been monitored. However, since the infusion is being tapered and the expected duration of treatment is less than 72 hours, measurement of thiocyanate levels is not indicated at this time.

Other side effects associated with nitroprusside therapy include nausea, vomiting, diaphoresis, nasal stuffiness, muscular twitching, dizziness, and weakness. These effects usually are acute and occur when nitroprusside is administered too rapidly. They can be reversed by decreasing the rate of infusion.[125]

16. Which antihypertensive agents should be specifically avoided in M.R.? Why?

Labetalol, a potent, rapidly-acting antihypertensive with both alpha- and beta-blocking activity, is very effective in the treatment of various hypertensive emergencies,[174-180] but should not be used in M.R. (See Question 17.) Hemodynamically, labetalol reduces peripheral vascular resistance (afterload), blood pressure, and heart rate with almost no change in resting cardiac output or stroke volume.[182] Labetalol does not cause the reflex tachycardia and redistribution of coronary blood flow that is noted with nitroprusside. These qualities make it ideally suited for blood pressure reduction in patients with underlying coronary artery disease, angina, acute infarction,[183] or following vascular surgical procedures.[4] In addition, labetalol may be better tolerated than nitroprusside by patients with hepatic or renal insufficiency because toxic nitroprusside metabolites accumulate in these situations.

M.R. is experiencing chest pain and he is tachycardic; these signs and symptoms are most likely due to his severely uncontrolled hypertension and the presence of acute left ventricular failure. Even though labetalol may improve M.R.'s angina, the negative inotropic action may compromise his left ventricular dysfunction. This effect outweighs the potential benefit of afterload reduction. In addition, even though labetalol may be one of the safest beta-blocking drugs when used in patients with asthma,[184] no beta blocker should be considered for the initial treatment in patients with asthma. It should be used only if alternative methods of reducing M.R.'s pressure fail.

Diazoxide, a potent, rapid-acting hypotensive agent closely related to the thiazide group of drugs, also should be avoided in M.R. for several reasons. (See Questions 23-25.) The hypotensive action is caused by a reduction in peripheral vascular resistance through direct relaxation of arterioles. As arterial pressure is lowered, baroreceptor reflexes are activated, leading to cardiac stimulation with increased heart rate, stroke volume, and cardiac output.[185] The cardiostimulating effect of diazoxide could be potentially dangerous in patients such as M.R. who have ischemic heart disease and a recent history of myocardial infarction. An early report indicated that 50% of the patients receiving diazoxide for hypertensive emergencies had significant ST and T wave changes.[186] Neurologic and cardiovascular symptoms may occur with rapid administration of diazoxide, and ischemic damage to the heart and brain have been reported.[24,187] The combination of slow infusion diazoxide preceded by a beta blocker has been recommended to prevent the reflex tachycardia.[188] However, with M.R.'s history of CHF and asthma, beta blockers should be avoided.

There are other reasons why diazoxide should be avoided or used cautiously in M.R. Although diazoxide has a thiazide-like structure, it causes significant sodium and water retention which could be deleterious in a patient such as M.R. with severe congestive heart failure and pulmonary edema.[185,189-191] The exact mechanism for this effect is unknown, but it may be through an activation of the renin system or a direct antinatriuretic effect on the renal tubules. Generally, it is recommended that a potent diuretic such as furosemide be administered before the administration of diazoxide. However, this is not necessary if diazoxide is administered by the mini-bolus or slow infusion method (see Question 24) and heart failure is absent.

M.R. also has renal failure and there is some evidence that smaller doses of diazoxide must be used in this situation. This is most likely related to decreased protein binding which produces higher levels of free or active drug and a corresponding increase in hypotensive effect.[192,193]

Even though there is no uric acid level reported, it is likely that M.R. has elevated levels associated with his chronic renal failure. Diazoxide decreases urate excretion and increases uric acid levels.[194] In patients with normal renal function this effect can be reversed with probenecid (Benemid). In M.R., allopurinol (Zyloprim) or dialysis would have to be used to lower serum uric acid levels if they become extraordinarily high.

Labetalol

17. C.M., a 52-year-old black male, is admitted to the hospital with a 3-day history of increasing exertional substernal chest pain without SOB, diaphoresis, nausea, or vomiting. His past history is significant for poorly controlled hypertension and angina pectoris. Prior medications include propranolol (Inderal), hydrochlorothiazide, and oral nitrates. Physical examination is remarkable for an anxious black male who is alert and oriented with a BP of 210/146 mm Hg, without orthostasis, and a regular pulse of 115 beats/min. Bilateral hemorrhages and exudates are present on funduscopic examination. The lungs are clear and the heart is enlarged, but there are no murmurs or gallops. Examination of the abdomen is unremarkable and there is no peripheral edema. The neurological examination is normal.

Significant laboratory values include the following: Na 140 mEq/L (Normal: 136–144); Cl 109 mEq/L (Normal: 96–106); bicarbonate 18 mEq/L (Normal: 23–28); BUN 49 mg/dL (Normal: 10–20); creatinine 2.8 mg/dL (renal function previously noted to be within normal limits). UA shows proteinuria and hematuria. The ECG demonstrates sinus tachycardia with left axis deviation, left ventricular hypertrophy, and nonspecific ST-T wave changes. The chest x-ray reveals mild cardiomegaly.

C.M. is given NTG sublingually (Nitrostat) and 1″ of NTG ointment (Nitrol Paste) is applied topically. He is started on IV labetalol. Is this choice of treatment reasonable considering C.M.'s angina and acute renal failure? [SI units: Na 140 mmol/L (Normal: 136–144); Cl 109 mmol/L (Normal: 96–106); bicarbonate 18 mmol/L (Normal: 23–28); BUN 17.493 mmol/L UREA (Normal: 3.57–7.14); creatinine 247.52 μmol/L]

The presence of chest pain, Grade III retinopathy, new onset renal disease and the magnitude of the blood pressure elevation in C.M. warrant a prompt reduction in blood pressure. The combination of sublingual and topical nitroglycerin may help in acutely lowering his blood pressure and relieving his chest pain while waiting for more definitive treatment to be implemented.[195]

Intravenous labetalol is a potent antihypertensive drug that has been used successfully in a variety of hypertensive emergencies.[173–181] Labetalol blocks both α- and β-adrenergic receptors and also may exert a direct vasodilator effect.[196,197] The beta blockade is nonselective with a beta to alpha potency of 3:1 for oral and 7:1 for IV labetalol.[198] Labetalol is particularly advantageous in C.M. because the immediate onset of action will reduce peripheral vascular resistance without causing reflex tachycardia. Myocardial oxygen demand will be reduced and coronary hemodynamics will be improved making this agent an excellent choice for patients like C.M. who have coronary artery disease or myocardial infarction.[199–201] In addition, IV labetalol does not significantly reduce cerebral blood flow; therefore, it may be useful in patients with cerebrovascular disease.[202]

Nitroprusside also could be used to treat C.M. However, high doses or a prolonged course of treatment would increase the risk of thiocyanate toxicity in C.M. with his new onset renal failure. Labetalol, on the other hand, has been used successfully in patients with renal disease without deleterious side effects.[203–205] Labetalol is eliminated by glucuronidation in the liver, with less than 5% of the dose being excreted unchanged in the urine.[206] The presence of renal disease in C.M. will not necessitate an alteration in the dose of labetalol.[205–207]

18. Contraindications. What cautions should be exercised when using labetalol in C.M.?

Labetalol's disadvantages are primarily related to its beta-blocking effects which predominate over its alpha-blocking effects. Therefore, it should not be used in patients with asthma; heart block greater than first degree; sinus bradycardia; or severe, uncontrolled heart failure[174,182,208] (see Question 16). None of these are present in C.M. Like other beta blockers, labetalol may mask the symptoms of hypoglycemia in insulin-dependent diabetics; it also should be used with caution in patients with intermittent claudication or Raynaud's syndrome.[208] Labetalol has been effective in the treatment of hypertension associated with pheochromocytoma[209,210] and excess catecholamine states.[211] However, because labetalol is primarily a beta blocker, paradoxical hypertension may occur in patients excreting high amounts of norepinephrine.[212–214] More clinical experience is required before labetalol can be recommended in patients with pheochromocytoma.[4,174]

19. Does C.M.'s age or prior use of antihypertensives affect his response to labetalol?

There appears to be a positive correlation between age and response to labetalol. Older patients will achieve a greater reduction in blood pressure and therefore will require smaller doses.[215,216] Failure to lower blood pressure has occurred with labetalol.[217–219] This phenomenon was thought to be related to single bolus administration or prior treatment with beta- and alpha-blocking drugs.[208] However, subsequent studies have confirmed labetalol's effectiveness in patients pretreated with antihypertensives, including beta blockers.[220]

20. Parenteral Therapy. How should parenteral labetalol be given to C.M.?

For acute blood pressure reduction, C.M. should be placed in the supine position. Intravenous labetalol can be given by pulse administration[174–179] or continuous infusion.[180] Small incremental bolus injections are administered beginning with 20 mg given over 2 minutes, followed by 40 to 80 mg every 10 to 15 minutes until the desired response is achieved or a cumulative dose of 300 mg is reached. The desired response usually is achieved with a mean dose of ≈200 mg in 90% of patients.[175] Following IV injection, the maximal effect occurs within five to ten minutes[178] and the antihypertensive response may persist for six hours or more.[220] Since the rate of blood pressure reduction is accelerated with an increase in infusion rate,[178] a controlled continuous infusion may provide a more gradual reduction in arterial pressure with less frequent adverse effects.[31,180,221] A solution for continuous infusion (0.5 to 2.0 mg/minute) is prepared by adding two ampules (200 mg total) to 160 mL of IV fluid to give a final concentration of 1 mg/mL. The infusion can then be started at a rate of 2 mg/minute and titrated until a satisfactory response is achieved or until a cumulative dose of 300 mg is reached.

Nitroglycerin

21. Would parenteral NTG be an acceptable alternative to labetalol for C.M.?

Severe, uncontrolled hypertension in the setting of unstable angina or myocardial infarction requires immediate blood pressure reduction. Nitroprusside has been used successfully, but IV nitroglycerin may have more favorable effects on collateral coronary flow in patients with ischemic heart disease.[222] By diminishing preload, nitroglycerin decreases left ventricular diastolic volume, pressure, and myocardial wall tension, thus reducing myocardial oxygen consumption.[223] These changes favor redistribution of coronary blood flow to the subendocardium which is more vulnerable to ischemia. At high doses, nitroglycerin dilates arteriolar smooth muscles and this reduction in afterload also decreases myocardial wall tension and oxygen consumption.[224]

Intravenous nitroglycerin has a rapid onset of action, a short duration, and is easily titratable. It is generally appropriate to begin IV nitroglycerin at doses in the range of 5 to 10 µg/minute and increase as needed to control pressure and symptoms. The usual dose is in the range of 40 to 100 µg/minute. The major limiting side effects are headache and the development of tolerance.

In general, intravenous nitroglycerin is well suited for use in patients like C.M. who have unstable angina, or in patients who have hypertension associated with myocardial infarction or coronary bypass surgery.

Oral Therapy

22. C.M. was treated with a labetalol infusion and required a cumulative dose of 180 mg to achieve a diastolic pressure of 100 mm Hg. His anginal symptoms resolved almost immediately, but 3 hours following the infusion, C.M. became faint and dizzy while ambulating. Should oral labetalol be withheld? When oral labetalol is given, what adverse effects can be expected?

Postural hypotension and dizziness are dose related and are more commonly associated with the IV route of administration.[182,208] C.M. should remain in a supine position following the intravenous administration of labetalol and his ability to tolerate an upright position should be established before permitting further ambulation. Oral labetalol can be given to C.M. when his supine diastolic BP increases by 10 mm Hg. There is no correlation between the oral maintenance dose and the total initial IV dose.[57] C.M. should be started on an empirical dose of 100 to 200 mg oral labetalol twice daily and this should be titrated as necessary. Other side effects commonly associated with labetalol include nausea, vomiting, abdominal pain, and diarrhea in up to 15% of the patients.[208] Scalp tingling is an unusual side effect that has been reported in a small number of patients after IV administration and tends to disappear with continued treatment. Other side effects include tiredness, weakness, muscle cramps, headache, ejaculation failure, and a variety of skin rashes.

Diazoxide

23. R.N., a 32-year-old black female, is admitted to the hospital with a 2-day history of nausea, blurred vision, confusion, and an intractable generalized headache. The past medical history is remarkable for asthma and diet-controlled diabetes mellitus. Physical examination reveals an alert, but disoriented black female with a BP of 220/160 mm Hg (without orthostasis) and a pulse of 110 beats/min. There is no evidence of heart failure, but the neurological examination reveals an altered mental status. Serum electrolytes, BUN, creatinine, UA, chest x-ray, and ECG are within normal limits. R.N.'s plasma glucose is 275 mg/dL. The assessment at this time is hypertensive encephalopathy. Diazoxide is ordered. Are any special precautions required in the use of diazoxide in R.N.?

Precautions. Diazoxide induces a significant rise in blood glucose. Several mechanisms have been postulated, including a direct increase in catecholamine levels, decreased peripheral glucose utilization, and direct inhibition of insulin release. However, the predominant and most important effect of diazoxide is its inhibition

of insulin secretion from pancreatic beta cells.[225] Although hyperglycemia occurs frequently, it is usually mild and does not preclude the use of the drug. In one study of 700 patients treated with diazoxide, a mild transitory elevation of serum glucose occurred in 40% of the nondiabetics, and in 75% of diabetic subjects one to four hours after treatment was initiated.[226] In another study of 41 patients who received diazoxide, the mean glucose values increased by only 6 mg/dL during the first 48 hours.[227]

Because R.N. has a history of diabetes, blood glucose levels should be monitored. If necessary, treatment with insulin or oral hypoglycemics may be required. Failure to recognize and treat significant hyperglycemia may result in ketoacidosis or hyperglycemic hyperosmolar coma. This occurs most frequently in patients with renal failure, adult onset diabetes mellitus, liver disease, and patients recovering from general anesthesia.

24. Dosing and Administration. How should diazoxide be administered to R.N. to achieve an optimal hypotensive response? Under what circumstances is diazoxide preferred over other agents?

Originally, it was recommended that diazoxide be administered as an IV bolus (5 mg/kg or 300 mg in <30 seconds).[228,229] Theoretically, this method of administration produced a higher concentration of "unbound" or "free" diazoxide which activated vasodilator receptors on the arterioles. However, it has since been found that this method results in abrupt declines in blood pressure, resulting in cerebral and cardiovascular hypoperfusion.

It is recommended that diazoxide be administered as a smaller bolus or by slow infusion. Studies confirm that diazoxide can be administered safely and effectively as a mini-bolus[230-234] (1 to 3 mg/kg every 5 to 15 minutes up to a maximum of a 150 mg in a single injection) or by slow infusion (15 to 30 mg/minute)[188,235-238] until achieving a diastolic blood pressure of 100 mm Hg. Single dose injections of greater than 150 mg should not be used. Evidence indicates that mini-bolus or slow infusion diazoxide quickly lowers blood pressure with little risk of hypoperfusion. Diazoxide also can be given by repetitive infusions according to the following schedule: loading dose of 7.5 mg/kg IV over 1.5 hours (which usually decreases mean arterial pressure by 25%) followed by 10% of the loading dose every six hours for maintenance.[239] In general, diazoxide should be used only in those patients who 1) are unable to tolerate labetalol (e.g., asthma or advanced heart block), 2) require a more gradual lowering of blood pressure than that produced by nitroprusside, and 3) require a more rapid and certain drop in blood pressure than that which can be produced by oral antihypertensive agents.[237]

25. Onset and Duration of Action. R.N. is given 150 mg of diazoxide by IV injection over 30 seconds. When will the maximum hypotensive effect occur and how long will this persist? What should be done if there is no substantial decrease in pressure?

The hypotensive effects of diazoxide begin within one minute and maximum effects occur within two to five minutes. Over the next 20 minutes, the blood pressure gradually increases because of a reflex increase in heart rate and cardiac output. The patient should remain recumbent for 15 to 30 minutes following the injection of each dose of diazoxide, and the blood pressure should be monitored every five minutes for the first 30 minutes. The duration of action is variable in that the blood pressure gradually increases to the pretreatment level in 3 to 15 hours. In a small series of patients given 105 to 150 mg of diazoxide every five minutes, 20% of the patients required a single dose while 75% needed two to three injections.[234] Only one patient required more than three injections. Diazoxide, when given by slow infusion, produces a maximum reduction in mean arterial pressure of 25% in 25 to 30 minutes which lasts up to eight hours.[234,236,237] If R.N. fails to respond to the first dose, repeated doses should be given at ten-minute intervals until a cumulative dose of 600 mg is reached. A major disadvantage of diazoxide is the occurrence of reflex tachycardia which can precipitate or worsen angina in patients with coronary artery disease. Small IV doses of propranolol (0.2 mg/kg) can be used in situations where the occurrence of tachycardia is dangerous.[237]

Aortic Dissection

Treatment

26. B.S., a 68-year-old white male with a long history of hypertension, asthma, and noncompliance, presents to the local ER complaining of the sudden onset of severe, sharp, diffuse chest pain which radiates to his back between his shoulder blades. Significant findings on physical examination include a pulse of 100 beats/min, BP of 200/120 mm Hg, grade II K-W changes, clear lungs, and an S_4 without murmurs. The laboratory data are unremarkable. The ECG results are interpreted as sinus tachycardia with left ventricular hypertrophy, but no acute changes are noted. Chest x-ray is significant for widening of the mediastinum. An emergency aortogram reveals a dissection at the arch of the aorta. What antihypertensive medication would be most appropriate for B.S. and why?

Dissection of the aorta occurs when the innermost layer of the aorta (intima) is interrupted so that blood enters and separates its layers. The ultimate treatment for dissection of the aorta depends upon its location and severity; however, the first principle of therapy is to control any existing hypertension with agents that do not increase the force of cardiac contraction.[240] This lessens the force that the cardiac impulse transmits to the dissecting aneurysm.

Therapeutic Considerations. Trimethaphan, labetalol, and sodium nitroprusside in combination with a beta blocker are the preferred drug regimens.[17] These drugs decrease blood pressure, venous return, and cardiac contractility. Initial treatment usually consists of a combination of IV sodium nitroprusside (25 to 50 μg/minute) and an IV beta-blocking drug, most commonly propranolol (0.05 to 0.15 mg/kg every four to six hours).[241] The concurrent administration of a beta-blocking agent with nitroprusside is desirable since the latter may induce reflex tachycardia in response to vasodilation.[120] Palmer et al. have documented progression of aortic dissection under combined nitroprusside-propranolol therapy and advocate a return to trimethaphan as the agent of choice.[132] Others agree that trimethaphan is the drug of choice in the hypertensive patient with aortic dissection.[15,240] Diazoxide and hydralazine should be avoided because they increase stroke volume and left ventricular ejection rate. These effects augment the

pulsatile flow and accentuate the sharpness of the pulse wave. This increases mechanical stress on the aortic wall and may lead to further dissection.

Depending upon the location of the dissection, surgical intervention may be required.[241] However, until a definitive diagnosis is made, the primary goal is to lower blood pressure and depress myocardial contractility. The ultimate objective of acute medical therapy for aortic dissection is to reduce blood pressure to the lowest level compatible with the maintenance of adequate renal, cerebral, and cardiac perfusion.[241] In aortic dissection, the systolic blood pressure should be lowered to 100 to 120 mm Hg or a mean arterial pressure below 80 mm Hg.[123]

The drug of first choice for B.S. is trimethaphan. Although labetalol[242] or a combination of nitroprusside with either propranolol or esmolol (Brevibloc)[243] have been used successfully in the antihypertensive treatment of dissecting aortic aneurysms, B.S.'s past medical history of asthma precludes the use of beta blockers.

27. Trimethaphan. How should trimethaphan be administered, and what indices of toxicity should be monitored?

Trimethaphan is a ganglionic blocking drug that inhibits sympathetic nervous effects on the arterioles, veins, and the heart. The hypotensive effect is immediate. Because minor changes in the infusion rate can produce dramatic changes in blood pressure, the rate must be carefully regulated (preferably by a constant infusion pump) and the blood pressure must be monitored continuously.

The drug usually is prepared in a concentration of 500 mg/L of 5% dextrose in water. The infusion rate is initiated at 0.5 to 1 mg/minute and is increased every three to five minutes until the desired response is obtained. The hypotensive effect is most pronounced when the patient is upright, and it is often necessary to elevate the head of the bed to achieve an optimal effect. Therapy with oral antihypertensive agents should begin simultaneously, and an attempt should be made to discontinue the ganglionic blocker within 48 hours before significant tolerance renders the patient resistant to its action.

The prolonged use of trimethaphan is limited by its important sympathoplegic side effects, as well as the rapid development of tachyphylaxis. Urinary retention often occurs with prolonged therapy, necessitating insertion of an indwelling catheter. Constipation and paralytic ileus may occur as well as paralysis of visual accommodation. Severe hypotension following administration of trimethaphan may last for 10 to 15 minutes. To correct the hypotension, the infusion should be discontinued and the patient should be placed in a Trendelenburg position where the head is kept lower than the trunk.

References

1 **Ault MJ, Ellrodt AG.** Pathophysiologic events leading to the end organ effects of acute hypertension. J Emerg Med. 1985;3(Suppl. 2):10.

2 **Anderson R, Reed WG.** Current concepts in treatment of hypertensive urgencies. Am Heart J. 1986;111:211.

3 **1993 Joint National Committee.** The fifth report of the national committee on detection, evaluation, and treatment of high blood pressure (JNC V). Arch Intern Med. 1993;153:154.

4 **Vidt DG.** Current concepts in treatment of hypertensive emergencies. Am Heart J. 1986;111:220.

5 **Koch-Weser J.** Hypertensive emergencies. N Engl J Med. 1974;290:211.

6 **Segal JL.** Hypertensive emergencies. Postgrad Med. 1980;68:107.

7 **Bennett NM, Shea S.** Hypertensive emergency: case scenarios, sociodemographic profile, and previous care of 100 cases. Am J Public Health. 1988; 78:636.

8 **Dranov J et al.** Malignant hypertension—current modes of therapy. Arch Intern Med. 1974;133:791.

9 **Gudbrandson T.** Malignant hypertension: a clinical follow up with special reference to renal and cardiovascular function and immunogenetic factors. Med Scand. 1981;650(Suppl.):1.

10 **Ledingham J.** Management of hypertensive crisis. Hypertension. 1983;5 (Suppl. III):114.

11 **Kaplan NM.** Systemic hypertension: mechanisms and diagnosis. In: Braunwald E, ed. Heart Disease. Philadelphia: WB Saunders; 1984:886.

12 **Lee TH.** Malignant hypertension. Declining mortality rate in New York City, 1958 to 1974. NY State J Med. 1978;78:1389.

13 **Shea S et al.** Predisposing factors for severe uncontrolled hypertension in an inner-city minority population. N Engl J Med. 1992;327:776.

14 **Grossman SH et al.** Recognition and treatment of hypertensive emergencies. Cardiovasc Clin. 1981;11:97.

15 **Becker CE et al.** Hypertensive emergencies. Med Clin North Am. 1979;63: 127.

16 **Ferguson RK, Vlasses PH.** Hypertensive emergencies and urgencies. JAMA. 1986;255:1607.

17 **McRae RP et al.** Hypertensive crisis. Med Clin North Am. 1986;70:749.

18 **Gonzalez DG, Ram VS.** New approaches for the treatment of hypertensive urgencies and emergencies. Chest. 1988;93:193.

19 **Woods JW et al.** Management of malignant hypertension complicated by renal insufficiency. N Engl J Med. 1967; 227:57.

20 **Mroczek WJ et al.** The value of aggressive therapy in the hypertensive patient with azotemia. Circulation. 1969; 40:893.

21 **Bakir A, Dunea G.** Accelerated and malignant hypertension: experience from a large American inner city hospital. Int J Artif Organs. 1989;12: 675.

22 **McNair A et al.** Reversibility of cerebral symptoms in severe hypertension in relation to acute antihypertensive

therapy. Acta Med Scand. 1984;6935: 107.

23 Winer N. Hypertensive crisis. Crit Care Nurs Q. 1990;13:23.

24 Henrich WL et al. Hypotensive sequelae of diazoxide and hydralazine therapy. JAMA. 237;264:1977.

25 Ledingham JG et al. Cerebral complications in the treatment of accelerated hypertension. Q J Med. 1979;48:25.

26 Bertel O et al. Effects of antihypertensive treatment on cerebral perfusion. Am J Med. 1987;82(Suppl. 3B):29.

27 Dinsdale HB. Hypertensive encephalopathy. Neurol Clin. 1983;1:3.

28 Waldman R et al. Treatment of hypertensive encephalopathy. Neurology (NY). 1983;33:118.

29 Walters B. Urgent treatment of acute hypertension. Br J Hosp Med. 1984;31: 49.

30 Anon. Drugs for hypertensive emergencies. Med Lett Drugs Ther. 1989; 31:32.

31 Houston MC. Pathophysiology, clinical aspects, and treatment of hypertensive crisis. Prog Cardiovasc Dis. 1989; 32:99.

32 Conen D et al. An oral calcium antagonist for treatment of hypertensive emergencies. J Cardiovasc Pharmacol. 1982;4:378.

33 Bertel O et al. Nifedipine in hypertensive emergencies. Br Med J (Clin Res). 1983;286:19.

34 Erbel R et al. Emergency treatment of hypertensive crisis with sublingual nifedipine. Postgrad Med J. 1983;59 (Suppl. 3):134.

35 Guazzi M et al. Nifedipine, a new antihypertensive with rapid action. Clin Pharmacol Ther. 1977;22:528.

36 Frishman W et al. Calcium entry blockers for the treatment of severe hypertension and hypertensive crisis. Am J Med. 1984;77:35.

37 Haft JI et al. Chewing nifedipine to rapidly treat hypertension. Arch Intern Med. 1984;144:2357.

38 Eccrodt AG et al. Efficacy and safety of sublingual nifedipine in hypertensive emergencies. Am J Med. 1985; 79(Suppl. 4A):19.

39 Bertel O et al. Treatment of hypertensive emergencies with the calcium channel blocker nifedipine. Am J Med. 1985;79(Suppl. 4A):31.

40 Haft JI. Use of the calcium channel blocker nifedipine in the management of hypertensive emergency. Am J Emerg Med. 1985;3(Suppl.):25.

41 Alexander T et al. Oral nifedipine in hypertensive emergencies. Pharmatherapeutica. 1985;4:335.

42 Garcia JY, Vidt DG. Current management of hypertensive emergencies. Drugs. 1987;34:263.

43 Kiowski W et al. Acute and chronic sympathetic reflex activation and antihypertensive response to nifedipine. J Am Coll Cardiol. 1986;7:344.

44 Takekoshi N et al. Treatment of severe hypertension and hypertensive emergency with nifedipine, a calcium antagonist agent. Jpn Circ J. 1981;45: 852.

45 McAllister RG. Kinetics and dynamics of nifedipine after oral and sublingual doses. Am J Med. 1986;81(Suppl. 6A):2.

46 Foster TS et al. Nifedipine kinetics and bioavailability after single intravenous and oral doses in normal subjects. J Clin Pharmacol. 1983;23:161.

47 McAllister RG. Pharmacokinetics of calcium-entry blockers. Am J Cardiol. 1985;55:30B.

48 Raemsch KD, Sommer J. Pharmacokinetics and metabolism of nifedipine. Hypertension. 1983;5(Suppl. II):II–18.

49 Pitlik S et al. Transient retinal ischaemia induced by nifedipine. Br Med J. 1983;287:1845.

50 O'Mailia J et al. Nifedipine associated myocardial ischemia or infarction in the treatment of hypertensive urgencies. Ann Intern Med. 1987;107:185.

51 Gillmer DJ et al. Pulmonary edema precipitated by nifedipine. Br Med J. 1980;280:1420.

52 Belz GG et al. Digoxin plasma concentrations and nifedipine. Lancet. 1981;1: 844.

53 Schwartz JB et al. Effect of nifedipine on serum digoxin concentration and renal digoxin clearance. Clin Pharmacol Ther. 1984;36:19.

54 Schwartz JB et al. The effect of nifedipine on serum digoxin concentrations in patients. Am Heart J. 1984;107:669.

55 De Vito JM et al. Evaluation of the pharmacodynamic and pharmacokinetic interaction between calcium antagonists and digoxin. Pharmacotherapy. 1986;6:73.

56 Cohen IM et al. Oral clonidine loading for rapid control of hypertension. Clin Pharmacol Ther. 1978;24:11.

57 Anderson RJ et al. Oral clonidine loading in hypertensive urgencies. JAMA. 1981;246:848.

58 Spitalewitz S et al. Use of oral clonidine for rapid titration of blood pressure in severe hypertension. Chest. 1983;83(Suppl. 2):404.

59 Vidt DG et al. Round table discussion. Am Heart J. 1986;111:229.

60 Houston MC. The comparative effects of clonidine hydrochloride and nifedipine in the treatment of hypertensive crisis. Am Heart J. 1988;115:152.

61 Jaker M et al. Oral nifedipine vs oral clonidine in the treatment of urgent hypertension. Arch Intern Med. 1989;149: 260.

62 Just VL et al. Evaluation of drug therapy for treatment of hypertensive urgencies in the emergency department. Am J Emerg Med. 1991;9:107.

63 Reed WG et al. Effects of rapid blood pressure reduction on cerebral blood flow. Am Heart J. 1986;111:226.

64 Case DB et al. Acute and chronic treatment of severe and malignant hypertension with the oral converting enzyme inhibitor, captopril. Circulation. 1981;64:765.

65 Biollaz J et al. Hypertensive crisis treated with orally administered captopril. Eur J Clin Pharmacol. 1982;25:145.

66 Tschollar W et al. Sublingual captopril in hypertensive crisis. Lancet. 1985; 2:34.

67 Hauger-Klevene JH. Captopril in hypertensive crisis. Lancet. 1985;2:732.

68 Hauger-Klevene JH. Comparison of sublingual captopril and nifedipine. Lancet. 1986;1:219.

69 Komsuoglu B et al. Treatment of hypertensive urgencies with oral nifedi-

pine, nicardipine, and captopril. Angiology. 1991;42:447.

70 Angeli P et al. Comparison of sublingual captopril and nifedipine in immediate treatment of hypertensive emergencies. Arch Intern Med. 1991;151:678.

71 Traub YM et al. Hypertension and renal failure (scleroderma renal crisis) in progressive systemic sclerosis. Review of 25-year experience with 68 cases. Medicine. 1983;62:335.

72 Thurm RH et al. Captopril in the treatment of scleroderma renal crisis. Arch Intern Med. 1984;144:733.

73 Herlitz H et al. Captopril treatment of hypertension and renal failure in systemic lupus erythematosus. Nephron. 1984;38:253.

74 Eddy RL et al. Renin secreting neoplasm and hypertension with hypokalemia. Ann Intern Med. 1971;75:725.

75 Genest J et al. Malignant hypotension with hypokalemia in a patient with a renin producing pulmonary carcinoma. Trans Assoc Am Physicians. 1975;88: 192.

76 Frochlich ED et al. Review of the overall experience of captopril in hypertension. Arch Intern Med. 1984;144: 1441.

77 Wood BC et al. Oral minoxidil in the treatment of hypertensive crisis. JAMA. 1979;241:163.

78 Bauer JH et al. Rapid reduction of severe hypertension with minoxidil. J Cardiovasc Pharmacol. 1980;2(Suppl. 2):S189.

79 Alpert MA, Bauer JH. Rapid control of severe hypertension with minoxidil. Arch Intern Med. 1982;142:2099.

80 Ferlinz J. Nifedipine in myocardial ischemia, systemic hypertension, and other cardiovascular disorders. Ann Intern Med. 1986;105:714.

81 Hayes JM. Prazosin in severe hypertension. Med J Aust. 1977;2(Suppl. 2): 30.

82 McDonald AJ, Yealy DM. Oral labetalol versus oral nifedipine in hypertensive urgencies. Ann Emerg Med. 1989; 18:461.

83 Gonzalez ER et al. Dose response evaluation of oral labetalol in patients presenting to the emergency department with accelerated hypertension. Ann Emerg Med. 1991;20:333.

84 Zell-Kanter M, Leikin JB. Oral labetalol in hypertensive urgencies. Am J Emerg Med. 1991;9:136.

85 Atkin S et al. Oral labetalol versus oral clonidine in the emergency treatment of severe hypertension. Am J Med Sci. 1992;303:9.

86 Wright SW et al. Ineffectiveness of oral labetalol for hypertensive urgency. Am J Emerg Med. 1990;8:472.

87 Tripathy N et al. Verapamil in hypertension. Indian Heart J. 1979;31:321.

88 Wasir HS et al. Immediate effects of intravenous verapamil in hypertension. Indian Heart J. 1979;31:326.

89 Wallin JD et al. Intravenous nicardipine for the treatment of severe hypertension. Am J Med. 1988;85:331.

90 Strauss R et al. Enalaprilat in hypertensive emergencies. Clin Pharmacol Ther. 1986;26:39.

91 Evans RR et al. The effect of intravenous enalaprilat (MK-422) administration in patients with mild to mod-

erate essential hypertension. J Clin Pharmacol. 1987;27:415.

92 Rutledge J et al. Effect of intravenous enalaprilat in moderate and severe hypertension. Am J Cardiol. 1988;62:1062.

93 DiPette DJ et al. Enalaprilat, an intravenous angiotensin-converting enzyme inhibitor, in hypertensive crises. Clin Pharmacol Ther. 1985;38:199.

94 Strauss R et al. Enalaprilat in hypertensive emergencies. J Clin Pharmacol. 1986;26:39.

95 Rutledge J et al. Effect of intravenous enalaprilat in moderate and severe systemic hypertension. Am J Cardiol. 1988; 62:1062.

96 Onoyama K et al. Effect of drug infusion or a bolus injection of intravenous diltiazem on hypertensive crisis. Curr Ther Res. 1987;42:1223.

97 Onoyama K et al. Effect of a drip infusion of diltiazem on severe systemic hypertension. Curr Ther Res. 1988;43: 361.

98 Stumpf JL. Drug therapy in hypertensive crises. Clin Pharm. 1988;7:582.

99 Wallin JD et al. Intravenous nicardipine for treatment of severe hypertension. Arch Intern Med. 1989;149:2662.

100 Bernard JM et al. Deliberate hypotension with nicardipine or nitroprusside during total hip arthroplasty. Anesth Analg. 1991;73:341.

101 Clifton GG, Wallin JD. Intravenous nicardipine: an effective new agent for the treatment of severe hypertension. Angiology. 1990;41:1005.

102 Halpern NA et al. Postoperative hypertension: a prospective, placebo controlled, randomized, double-blind trial with intravenous nicardipine hydrochloride. Angiology. 1990;41:992.

103 Halpern NA et al. Nicardipine infusion for postoperative hypertension after surgery of the head and neck. Crit Care Med. 1990;18:950.

104 IV Nicardipine Study Group. Efficacy and safety of intravenous nicardipine in the control of postoperative hypertension. Chest. 1991;99:393.

105 Kaplan JA. Clinical considerations for the use of intravenous nicardipine in the treatment of postoperative hypertension. Am Heart J. 1990;119:443.

106 Wallin JD. Intravenous nicardipine hydrochloride: treatment of patients with severe hypertension. Am Heart J. 1990;119:434.

107 Salerno DM et al. Efficacy and safety of intravenous diltiazem for treatment of atrial fibrillation and atrial flutter. Am J Cardiol. 1989;63:1046.

108 Ellenbogen KA et al. A placebo controlled trial of continuous intravenous diltiazem infusion for 24 hour heart rate control during atrial fibrillation and atrial flutter: a multicenter study. J Am Coll Cardiol. 1991;18:891.

109 Dougherty AH et al. Acute conversion of paroxysmal supraventricular tachycardia with intravenous diltiazem. Am J Cardiol. 1992;79:587.

110 Koh H et al. Clinical study of total intravenous anesthesia with droperidol, fentanyl and ketamine—control of intraoperative hypertension with diltiazem. Jap J Anesth. 1991;40:1376.

111 Boylan JF et al. A comparison of diltiazem, esmolol, nifedipine, and nitro-

prusside therapy of post-CABG hypertension. Can J Anaesth. 1990;37:S156.

112 **Jaffe AS.** Use of intravenous diltiazem in patients with acute coronary artery disease. Am J Cardiol. 1992;69:25B.

113 **Fang ZY et al.** Intravenous diltiazem versus nitroglycerin for silent and symptomatic myocardial ischemia in unstable angina pectoris. Am J Cardiol. 1991;68:42C.

114 **Cheung D et al.** Acute pharmacokinetic and hemodynamic effects of intravenous bolus dosing of nicardipine. Am Heart J. 1990;119:438.

115 **Langtry HD et al.** Urapidil: a review of its pharmacodynamic and pharmacokinetic properties, and therapeutic potential in the treatment of hypertension. Drugs. 1989;38:900.

116 **Schuster P.** Use of antihypertensive Ebrantil in hypertensive crisis. Klinikartz. 1981;10:202.

117 **Spah F et al.** Acute hemodynamic effects of urapidil and nifedipine in hypertensive urgencies and emergencies. Drugs. 1990;40(Suppl. 4):58.

118 **Palmer RF et al.** Sodium nitroprusside. N Engl J Med. 1975;292:294.

119 **Tuzel IH.** Sodium nitroprusside: a review of its clinical effectiveness as a hypotensive agent. J Clin Pharmacol. 1974;14:494.

120 **Cohn JN et al.** Nitroprusside. Ann Intern Med. 1979;91:752.

121 **Nielsen PE et al.** Emergency treatment of severe hypertension emulated in a random study: effect of rest and furosemide and a randomized evaluation of chlorpromazine, dihydralazine and diazoxide. Acta Med Scand. 1980;208:473.

122 **Burris JF.** Hypertensive emergencies. Am Fam Physician. 1985;32:97.

123 **McKinney TD.** Management of hypertensive crisis. Hosp Pract. 1992;27:133.

124 **Brater DC et al.** Prolonged hemodynamic effect of furosemide in congestive heart failure. Am Heart J. 1984;4:1031.

125 **Romankiewicz JA.** Pharmacology and clinical use of drugs used in hypertensive emergencies. Am J Hosp Pharm. 1977;34:185.

126 **Opie LH.** Vasodilator drugs. Lancet. 1980;1:966.

127 **Anon.** Sodium nitroprusside for hypertensive crisis. Med Lett Drugs Ther. 1975;17:82.

128 **Anderson RA et al.** Stability of sodium nitroprusside infusions. Aust J Pharm Sci. 1972;1:45.

129 **Schumacher GE.** Sodium nitroprusside injection. Am J Hosp Pharm. 1966;23:532.

130 **Schulz V et al.** Cyanide toxicity of sodium nitroprusside in therapeutic use with and without sodium thiosulfate. Klin Wochenschr. 1982;60:1393.

131 **Hargrave RE.** Degradation of solutions of sodium nitroprusside. J Hosp Pharm. 1974;32:188.

132 **Palmer RF et al.** Nitroprusside and aortic dissecting aneurysms. N Engl J Med. 1976;294:1403.

133 **Finnerty FA.** Malignant hypertension. Am Heart J. 1974;88:265.

134 **Hulse JA et al.** Blindness and paraplegia in severe childhood hypertension. Lancet. 1979;2:553.

135 **Pryor JS et al.** Blindness and malignant hypertension. Lancet. 1979;2:803.

136 **Graham DI.** Ischemic brain damage of cerebral perfusion failure type after treatment of severe hypertension. Br Med J. 1975;4:739.

137 **Lavin P.** Management of hypertension in patients with acute stroke. Arch Intern Med. 1986;146:66.

138 **Finnerty FA et al.** Cerebral hemodynamics during cerebral ischemia induced by acute hypertension. J Clin Invest. 1954;33:1227.

139 **Strandgaard S.** Autoregulation of cerebral blood flow in hypertensive patients: the modifying influence of prolonged antihypertensive treatment on the tolerance to acute, drug induced hypotension. Circulation. 1976;53:720.

140 **Strandgaard S et al.** Autoregulation of brain circulation in severe arterial hypertension. Br Med J. 1973;1:507.

141 **Schultz V.** Clinical pharmacokinetics of nitroprusside, cyanide, thiosulphate and thiocyanate. Clin Pharmacokinet. 1984;9:239.

142 **Vesey CJ et al.** Cyanide and thiocyanate concentrations following nitroprusside infusion in man. Br J Anaesth. 1976;48:651.

143 **Baumeister et al.** Toxicological and clinical aspects of cyanide metabolism. Arzneimittelforschung. 1975;25:1056.

144 **Aitken D et al.** Cyanide toxicity following nitroprusside induced hypotension. Can Anaesth Soc J. 1977;24:651.

145 **Lawson NW et al.** Cyanide blood levels following nitroprusside infusion for hypotensive anesthesia. Proc West Pharmacol Soc. 1982;25:281.

146 **Schultz V et al.** Hypotensive efficacy of a mixed solution of 0.1% sodium nitroprusside and 1% sodium thiosulphate. J Hyp. 1985;3:485.

147 **Pasch TH et al.** Nitroprusside-induced formation of cyanide and its detoxification with thiosulphate during deliberate hypotension. J Cardiovasc Pharmacol. 1983;5:77.

148 **Curry SC, Capell-Arnold P.** Toxic effects of drugs used in the ICU: nitroprusside, nitroglycerin, and angiotensin converting enzyme inhibitors. Crit Care Clin. 1991;7:555.

149 **Ivankovich AD et al.** Sodium thiosulfate disposition in humans: relation to sodium nitroprusside toxicity. Anesthesiology. 1983;58:11.

150 **Rindone JP, Sloane EP.** Cyanide toxicity from sodium nitroprusside: risks and management. Ann Pharmacother. 1992;26:515.

151 **Macrae WR et al.** Severe metabolic acidosis following hypertension induced with sodium nitroprusside. Br J Anaesth. 1974;46:795.

152 **Jack RD.** Toxicity of nitroprusside. Br J Anaesth. 1974;46:952.

153 **Merrifield AJ et al.** Toxicity of sodium nitroprusside. Br J Anaesth. 1974;46:324.

154 **Davies VW et al.** A sudden death associated with the use of sodium nitroprusside for induction of hypotension during anaesthesia. Can Anaesth Soc J. 1975;22:547.

155 **Rauscher LA et al.** Nitroprusside toxicity in a renal transplant patient. Anesthesiology. 1978;49:428.

156 **Montoliu J et al.** Fatal hypotension in normal dose nitroprusside therapy. Am Heart J. 1979;97:541.

157 **McDowall DG et al.** The toxicity of sodium nitroprusside. Br J Anaesth. 1974;46:327.

158 **Vesey CJ et al.** Some metabolic effects of sodium nitroprusside in man. Br Med J. 1974;2:140.

159 **Zerbe NF, Wagner BK.** Use of vitamin B_{12} in the treatment and prevention of nitroprusside induced cyanide toxicity. Crit Care Med. 1993;21:465.

160 **Cottrell JE et al.** Prevention of nitroprusside induced cyanide toxicity with hydroxocobalamin. N Engl J Med. 1978;298:809.

161 **Mushett CW et al.** Antidotal efficacy of vitamin B_{12a} (hydroxocobalamin) in experimental cyanide poisoning. Proc Soc Biol Med. 1952;81:234.

162 **Humphrey SH et al.** Lactic acidosis complicating nitroprusside therapy. Ann Intern Med. 1978;88:58.

163 **Kayser SR et al.** Hydroxocobalamin in nitroprusside-induced cyanide toxicity. Drug Intell Clin Pharm. 1986;20:365.

164 **Fahmy NR.** Consumption of Vitamin B-12 during nitroprusside administration. Anesth Analg. 1980;59:538.

165 **Anon.** Controlled intravascular sodium nitroprusside treatment. Br Med J. 1978;2:784.

166 **DuCailar J et al.** Nitroprusside, its metabolites and red cell function. Can Anaesth Soc J. 1978;25:92.

167 **Japp H et al.** Toxizitat und konzentration von thiocyanat im serum bei der therapie mit natrium-nitroprussid. Schweiz Med Wochenschr. 1978;108:1987.

168 **Schulz V et al.** Thiozyanat-vergiftung bei der antihypertensiven therapie mit natrium-nitroprussid. Klin Wochenschr. 1978;56:355.

169 **Schulz V et al.** Kinetics of elimination of thiocyanate in 7 healthy subjects and in 8 subjects with renal failure. Klin Wochenschr. 1979;57:243.

170 **Nourok DS et al.** Hypothyroidism following prolonged nitroprusside therapy. Am J Med Sci. 1964;248:129.

171 **Cole P.** The safe use of sodium nitroprusside. Anaesthesia. 1978;33:473.

172 **Lupatkin WL et al.** Prolonged use of sodium nitroprusside. J Pediatr. 1978;92:1032.

173 **Danzig LE.** Dynamics of thiocyanate dialysis. N Engl J Med. 1954;252:49.

174 **Cressman MD et al.** Intravenous labetalol in the management of severe hypertension and hypertensive emergencies. Am Heart J. 1984;107:980.

175 **Wilson DJ et al.** Intravenous labetalol in the treatment of severe hypertension and hypertensive emergencies. Am J Med. 1983;75(Suppl.):95.

176 **Cumming AM et al.** Treatment of severe hypertension by repeated bolus injections of labetalol. Br J Clin Pharmacol. 1979;8:199.

177 **Smith WB et al.** Antihypertensive effectiveness of intravenous labetalol in accelerated hypertension. Hypertension. 1983;5:579.

178 **Dal Palu C et al.** Intravenous labetalol in severe hypertension. Br J Clin Pharmacol. 1982;13(Suppl. 1):97S.

179 **Lebel M et al.** Labetalol infusion in hypertensive emergencies. Clin Pharmacol Ther. 1985;37:615.

180 **Vidt DG.** Intravenous labetalol in the emergency treatment of hypertension. J Clin Hypertens. 1985;2:179.

181 **Patel RV et al.** Labetalol: response and safety in critically ill hemorrhagic stroke patients. Ann Pharmacother. 1993;27:180.

182 **Kanto JH.** Current status of labetalol, the first alpha- and beta-blocking agent. Int J Clin Pharmacol Ther Toxicol. 1985;23:617.

183 **Timmis AD et al.** Role of labetalol in acute myocardial infarction. Br J Clin Pharmacol. 1982;13:1115.

184 **George RB et al.** Comparison of the effects of labetalol and hydrochlorothiazide on the ventilatory function of hypertensive patients with asthma and propranolol sensitivity. Chest. 1985;88:815.

185 **Koch-Weser J.** Diazoxide. N Engl J Med. 1976;249:1271.

186 **Kanada S et al.** Angina-like syndrome with diazoxide therapy for hypertensive crisis. Ann Intern Med. 1976;84:696.

187 **Kumar GK et al.** Side effects of diazoxide. JAMA. 1976;235:275.

188 **Huysmans FT et al.** Combined intravenous administration of diazoxide and beta blocking agent in acute treatment of severe hypertension or hypertensive crisis. Am Heart J. 1982;103:395.

189 **Vidt DG et al.** Safety of diazoxide administration in antihypertensive therapy: an analysis of 1,268 injections in 423 patients. Clin Pharmacol Ther. 1977;21:120. Abstract.

190 **Koch-Weser J.** Vasodilator drugs in the treatment of hypertension. Arch Intern Med. 1974;133:1017.

191 **Moser M.** Diazoxide: an effective vasodilator in accelerated hypertension. Am Heart J. 1974;87:791.

192 **O'Malley K et al.** Decreased plasma protein binding of diazoxide in uremia. Clin Pharmacol Ther. 1975;18:53.

193 **Pearson RM et al.** Renal function, protein binding and pharmacological response to diazoxide. Br J Clin Pharmacol. 1976;3:169.

194 **Thompson GR et al.** The effects of intravenous diazoxide, non-diuretic thiazide, upon blood pressure, electrolyte and uric acid secretion. Mich Med. 1966;65:17.

195 **Bussman WD et al.** Nitroglycerin im vergleich zu nifedipin bei patienten mit hypertensiver krise. Z Kardiol. 1993;82:33.

196 **Johnson GL et al.** Antihypertensive effects of labetalol. Fed Proc. 1977;36:1059.

197 **Baum T et al.** Antihypertensive and hemodynamic actions of SCH 19927. The R, R-isomer of labetalol. J Pharmacol Exp Ther. 1981;218:444.

198 **Richards DA et al.** Relationship between plasma concentrations and pharmacological effects of labetalol. Eur J Clin Pharmacol. 1977;11:85.

199 **Gagnon R et al.** Hemodynamic and coronary effects of intravenous labetalol in coronary artery disease. Am J Cardiol. 1982;49:1267.

200 **Frishman WH et al.** Labetalol therapy in patients with systemic hypertension and angina pectoris: effects of combined alpha and beta blockade. Am J Cardiol. 1981;48:917.

201 **Condorelli M et al.** Effects of combined alpha and beta blockade by labetalol in patients with coronary artery

disease. Br J Clin Pharmacol. 1982; 13(Suppl.):101.

202 **Pearson RM et al.** Comparison of effects on cerebral blood flow of rapid reduction in systemic arterial pressure by diazoxide and labetalol in hypertensive patients: preliminary findings. Cr J Clin Pharmacol. 1979;8(Suppl. 2):195S.

203 **Bailey RR.** Labetalol in the treatment of patients with hypertension and renal function impairment. Br J Clin Pharmacol. 1979;8(Suppl.):135.

204 **Thompson FD et al.** Monotherapy with labetalol for hypertensive patients with normal and impaired renal function. Br J Clin Pharmacol. 1979;8 (Suppl.):129.

205 **Walstad RA et al.** Labetalol in the treatment of hypertension in patients with normal and impaired renal function. Acta Med Scand. 1982;212 (Suppl. 665):135.

206 **Martin LE et al.** Metabolism of labetalol by animals and man. Br J Clin Pharmacol. 1976;3(Suppl. 3):695.

207 **Wood AJ et al.** Elimination kinetics of labetalol in severe renal failure. Br J Clin Pharmacol. 1982;13(Suppl.):81.

208 **MacCarthy EP et al.** Labetalol: a review of its pharmacology pharmacokinetics, clinical uses and adverse effects. Pharmacotherapy. 1983;3:193.

209 **Reach G et al.** Effect of labetalol on blood pressure and plasma catecholamine concentrations in patients with phaeochromocytoma. Br Med J (Clin Res). 1980;1:1300.

210 **Takeda TK et al.** The use of labetalol in Japan: results of multicentre clinical trials. Br J Clin Pharmacol. 1982;13 (Suppl.):49.

211 **Abrams JH et al.** Successful treatment of a monoamine oxidase inhibitor-tyramine hypertensive emergency with intravenous labetalol. N Engl J Med. 1985;313:52.

212 **Briggs RS et al.** Hypertensive response to labetalol in phaeochromocytoma. Lancet. 1978;1:1045.

213 **Navaratnarajah M et al.** Labetalol and phaeochromocytoma. Br J Anaesth. 1984;56:1179.

214 **Feek CM et al.** Hypertensive response to labetalol in phaeochromocytoma. Br Med J. 1980;281:387.

215 **Kelly JG et al.** Bioavailability of labetalol increases with age. Br J Clin Pharmacol. 1982;14:304.

216 **Eisalo A et al.** Treatment of hypertension in the elderly with labetalol. Acta Med Scand. 1982;665(Suppl.):129.

217 **McGrath BP et al.** Emergency treatment of severe hypertension with intravenous labetalol. Med J Aust. 1978;2: 410.

218 **Anderson CC et al.** Poor hypotensive response and tachyphylaxis following intravenous labetalol. Curr Med Res Opin. 1978;5:424.

219 **Yeung CK et al.** Comparison of labetalol, clonidine and diazoxide intravenously administered in severe hypertension. Med J Aust. 1979;2:499.

220 **Pearson RM et al.** Intravenous labetalol in hypertensive patients treated with B-adrenoceptor blocking drugs. Br J Clin Pharmacol. 1976;3(Suppl. 3): 795.

221 **Cumming AM et al.** Intravenous labetalol in the treatment of severe hypertension. Br J Clin Pharmacol. 1982; 13(Suppl. 1):93S.

222 **Flaherty JT et al.** Comparison of intravenous nitroglycerin and sodium nitroprusside for treatment of acute hypertension developing after coronary artery bypass surgery. Circulation. 1982; 65:1072.

223 **Chun G, Frishman WH.** Rapid-acting parenteral antihypertensive agents. J Clin Pharmacol. 1990;30:195.

224 **Francis GS.** Vasodilators in the intensive care unit. Am Heart J. 1991;121: 1875.

225 **Speight TM et al.** Diazoxide: a review of its pharmacological properties and therapeutic use in hypertensive crisis. Drugs. 1971;2:78.

226 **Finnerty F.** Hyperglycemia after diazoxide administration. N Engl J Med. 1971;285:1487.

227 **McDonald WJ et al.** Intravenous diazoxide therapy in hypertensive crisis. Am J Cardiol. 1977;40:409.

228 **Sellers EM et al.** Influence of intravenous injection rate on protein binding and vascular activity of diazoxide. Ann N Y Acad Sci. 1973;226:319.

229 **Mroczek WM et al.** The importance of the rapid administration of diazoxide in accelerated hypertension. N Engl J Med. 1971;285:603.

230 **Velasco M et al.** A new technique for safe and effective control of hypertension with intravenous diazoxide. Curr Ther Res. 1976;19:185.

231 **Wilson DJ et al.** Control of severe hypertension with pulse doses of diazoxide. J Clin Pharmacol Ther. 1978;23: 135.

232 **Ram CV et al.** Individual titration of diazoxide dosage in the treatment of severe hypertension. Am J Cardiol. 1979; 43:627.

233 **Waugh WH.** Efficacy of slow injection of diazoxide in accelerated hypertension. N C Med J. 1977;38:448.

234 **Ram VS et al.** Individual titration of diazoxide dosage in the treatment of severe hypertension. Am J Cardiol. 1979; 43:627.

235 **Johnson BF et al.** The influence of rate of injection upon the effects of diazoxide. Am J Med Sci. 1972;273:481.

236 **Thien TA et al.** Diazoxide infusion in severe hypertension and hypertensive crisis. Clin Pharmacol Ther. 1979;25: 795.

237 **Garrett BN et al.** Efficacy of slow infusion of diazoxide in the treatment of severe hypertension without organ hypoperfusion. Am Heart J. 1982;103: 390.

238 **Lee WR et al.** Nonemergency use of slow infusions of diazoxide. Clin Pharmacol Ther. 1975;18:154.

239 **Ogilvie RI et al.** Diazoxide concentration-response relation in hypertension. Hypertension. 1982;4:167.

240 **Friedman S.** The evaluation and treatment of patients with arterial aneurysms. Med Clin North Am. 1981;65: 83.

241 **DeSanctis RW et al.** Aortic dissection. N Engl J Med. 1987;317:1060.

242 **Laden N et al.** Labetalol and MRI as initial medical and diagnostic modalities in a marfanoid patient with expanding ascending aortic aneurysm. Chest. 1990;98:1290.

243 **Mohindra SK, Udeani GO.** Intravenous esmolol in an acute aortic dissection. DICP Ann Pharmacother. 1991; 25:735.

Intensive Care Therapeutics

Laura E Arrigoni
Deborah K Rogers

Shock 18-2
  Causes (Also see Table 18.1) 18-2
  Clinical Presentation 18-2
  Pathophysiology and Classic Progression of Shock 18-2
    Stage I: compensated 18-2
    Stage II: decompensated 18-2
    Stage III: irreversible 18-3
  Etiologic Classification and Common Mechanisms
    (See Table 18.1) 18-3
    Hypovolemic shock 18-3
    Cardiogenic shock 18-3
    Distributive shock 18-5
      Septic shock (See Figure 18.1) 18-5
Hemodynamic Monitoring 18-7
  Swan-Ganz Catheter (See Figures 18.2 and 18.3) 18-7
  Determinants of Cardiac Function and Hemodynamic
    Indices (See Figure 18.4 and Table 18.2) 18-7
  Measured Hemodynamic Indices 18-7
    Right atrial pressure (RAP) and central venous
      pressure (CVP) 18-7
    Pulmonary artery systolic (PAS) pressure 18-8
    Pulmonary artery diastolic (PAD) pressure 18-8
    Pulmonary capillary wedge pressure (PCWP)
      (Also see Figure 18.5) 18-8
  Derived Hemodynamic Indices 18-9
    Stroke volume (SV) 18-9
    Cardiac index (CI) 18-9
    Pulmonary vascular resistance (PVR) and
      systemic vascular resistance (SVR) 18-9
    Left ventricular stroke work index (LVSWI) 18-9
Hypovolemic Shock 18-10
  Acute Hemorrhagic Shock 18-10
  Treatment 18-10
    Choice of fluids 18-10
      Crystalloids versus colloids 18-10
    Crystalloids 18-12
      Volume requirements 18-12
    Lactated Ringer's (LD)/normal saline (NS) 18-12
    Hypertonic saline 18-13
    Blood replacement 18-13
      Hypothermia, immune hemolysis, and transfusion-
      transmitted diseases 18-13
      Acid base imbalances and electrolyte
      abnormalities 18-14
      Hemostatic abnormalities 18-14
  Postoperative Hypovolemia 18-14
    Hypovolemia versus pump failure 18-14
    Causes 18-14
    Volume replacement and ventricular function 18-14
      Left ventricular compliance 18-15
      Fluid challenge 18-15
      Albumin 18-15
      Hetastarch 18-15
Cardiogenic Shock 18-16
  Postoperative Cardiac Failure 18-16

  Assessment by hemodynamic profile 18-16
  Therapeutic interventions 18-16
    Fluid challenge (preload increase) 18-16
    Vasodilators (afterload reduction) 18-16
    Inotropic support (Also see Table 18.4) 18-17
    Dopamine 18-17
      Effect on hemodynamics 18-17
    Dobutamine 18-17
      Effects on hemodynamics 18-18
      Tapering inotropic support 18-18
  Severe Congestive Heart Failure (CHF) 18-19
  Assessment by hemodynamic profile 18-19
  Therapeutic interventions 18-19
    Furosemide 18-19
      Hemodynamic effect of diuretic therapy 18-19
    Vasodilators 18-19
    Digoxin 18-20
    Phosphodiesterase inhibitors 18-20
      Amrinone 18-20
    Initial therapy: nitroprusside 18-21
      Hemodynamic effect 18-21
      Choice of additional therapy 18-21
      Transition to oral vasodilators 18-21
  Acute Myocardial Infarction (MI) 18-22
    Immediate goals of therapy and general
      considerations 18-22
    Assessment by hemodynamic profile
      (See Table 18.5) 18-22
    Therapeutic interventions 18-23
      Fluid therapy versus inotropic support 18-23
      Combination inotropic therapy 18-23
      Norepinephrine 18-24
      Intra-aortic balloon pump 18-24
Septic Shock 18-25
  Clinical and Hemodynamic Features 18-25
  Therapeutic Approach 18-25
    Eradicating the source of infection 18-25
    Initial stabilization 18-26
    Hemodynamic management 18-26
      Fluid therapy versus inotropic support 18-26
      Inotropic agents 18-27
        Dopamine 18-27
        Dobutamine 18-27
    Vasopressors (See Table 18.6) 18-27
      Norepinephrine 18-27
      Phenylephrine 18-28
  Alternative Therapies 18-28
    Immunotherapies 18-29
    Monoclonal antibodies to endotoxin 18-29
    Monoclonal antibodies to tumor necrosis
      factor-α (TNF-α) 18-29
    Interleukin-1 (IL-1) 18-30
    Ibuprofen 18-30
    Pentoxifylline 18-30
    Naloxone 18-30
Glossary 18-31

Shock

Shock is a complex clinical syndrome which requires immediate assessment and adjustment of hemodynamic parameters to restore adequate tissue oxygenation and thus prevent cellular injury, organ dysfunction, and death. The common denominator in shock, regardless of its etiology, is a profound reduction in tissue perfusion with inadequate oxygen delivery to vital organs. If prolonged, this reduction in tissue perfusion leads to generalized cellular hypoxia and impairment of cellular function.

Causes

The most common clinical causes of shock are situations associated with a reduction in intravascular volume (hypovolemic shock), myocardial failure (cardiogenic shock), or increased vascular capacitance (distributive shock). It is important to have an understanding of the etiologic classification of shock, since recognition of the underlying pathology is essential to the management of this condition. One must realize, however, that the distinctions among subtypes of shock only apply in the relatively early stages. As the syndrome evolves and compensatory mechanisms are overwhelmed, it becomes increasingly difficult to distinguish between etiologies since the clinical and pathophysiological features of advanced shock are the same.[1-4] Table 18.1 outlines the classification of shock and precipitating events.[5-8]

Clinical Presentation

The classic findings observed with shock are:

- Systolic blood pressure (BP) of ≤90 mm Hg (or >60 mm Hg decrease from baseline in a hypertensive patient).
- Tachycardia.

Table 18.1	Classification of Shock and Precipitating Events

Hypovolemic Shock
  Hemorrhagic
    Gastrointestinal bleeding
    Trauma
    Internal bleeding: ruptured aortic aneursym, retroperitoneal bleeding
  Nonhemorrhagic
    Dehydration: vomiting, diarrhea, diabetes mellitus, diabetes insipidus, overuse of diuretics
    Sequestration: ascites, third-space accumulation
    Cutaneous: burns, nonreplaced perspiration and insensible water losses

Cardiogenic Shock
  Nonmechanical Causes
    Acute myocardial infarction
    Low cardiac output syndrome
    Right ventricular infarction
    End-stage cardiomyopathy
  Mechanical Causes
    Rupture of septum or free wall
    Mitral or aortic insufficiency
    Papillary muscle rupture or dysfunction
    Critical aortic stenosis
    Pericardial tamponade

Distributive Shock
  Septic Shock
  Anaphylaxis
  Neurogenic
    Spinal injury, cerebral damage, severe dysautonomia
  Drug-Induced
    Anesthesia, ganglionic and adrenergic blockers, and overdoses of barbiturates, narcotics
  Acute Adrenal Insufficiency

- Hyperventilation.
- Cutaneous vasoconstriction: cold, clammy, mottled skin, (not typical of distributive shock).
- Mental confusion (agitation to stupor or coma).
- Oliguria: urine output of ≤20 mL/hour.
- Metabolic acidosis (lactic acidosis secondary to anaerobic glycolysis).

The development of these symptoms varies with respect to their rapidity and sequence of onset. This depends upon the severity of the initiating event, the underlying mechanism, and the baseline condition of the patient, including medications which may alter the clinical presentation. Therefore, it is important to consider the patient's medical and pharmacologic history while closely monitoring for subtle clinical changes that may signal impending deterioration and necessitate immediate intervention.[5]

Pathophysiology and Classic Progression of Shock

The syndrome of shock progresses in stages as the body employs and exhausts various compensatory mechanisms in an effort to maintain tissue perfusion and thereby oxygen delivery to vital organs. The determinants of tissue perfusion to individual organs are systemic arterial pressure and the inherent vascular resistance of that organ. Systemic arterial pressure is a function of the product of cardiac output and systemic vascular resistance. The latter primarily is determined by vascular smooth muscle tone which is modulated by the sympathoadrenal system and by circulating humoral and local metabolic factors.

Stage I: Compensated

Reduction of either cardiac output (CO) or systemic vascular resistance (SVR) without a compensatory elevation of the other results in systemic hypotension. In hypovolemic or cardiogenic shock, a reduction in CO is responsible for the diminished perfusion, whereas in distributive shock, the SVR is significantly decreased. The initial fall in systemic arterial pressure triggers a reflex increase in the release of epinephrine and norepinephrine from the sympathoadrenal system as well as secretion of antidiuretic hormone (ADH) and activation of the renin-angiotensin-aldosterone axis. These responses mediate effective compensatory mechanisms such as increased heart rate, myocardial contractility, and arteriolar vasoconstriction; intravascular volume and venous pressure gradually increase secondary to ADH and aldosterone secretion. Cardiac output and systemic vascular resistance thereby increase, and blood flow is redistributed to the more vital organs such as the brain and heart. Consequently, arterial pressure is restored and signs and symptoms are minimal, with tachycardia, cool extremities, and anxiety as the primary clinical manifestations. Approximately 50% of intensive care unit (ICU) patients and patients undergoing cardiac surgery are in compensated shock despite normal hemodynamic parameters. Although this stage is associated with a high degree of morbidity and mortality, astute recognition and appropriate intervention at this point can potentially reverse the progression to decompensated shock.[1,2,6-9]

Stage II: Decompensated

If the shock state continues unabated, the initial mechanisms to maintain tissue perfusion to vital organs are extended beyond their capacity for effective compensation and systemic arterial pressure is decreased. Generalized vasoconstriction occurs secondary to maximal outflow of norepinephrine. This maintains intravascular perfusion pressure by redistributing vascular volume from the interstitial compartment to the central circulation. Evidence of inadequate perfusion to the brain is seen clinically as mental confusion, restlessness, and combativeness; decreased blood flow to the kidney is reflected by reduced urinary output; and patients with coronary artery disease may experience myocardial ischemia. Signs of extensive vasoconstriction are outwardly apparent as pallor, cyanosis, piloerection, and cold, clammy skin. These manifestations, primarily associated with hypovolemic and cardiogenic shock, often are referred to as "cold shock." Oxygen deprivation to tissues activates anaerobic glycolysis with subsequent lactic acidosis; and compensatory hyperventilation produces a respiratory alkalosis. At this stage, rapid, aggressive intervention to correct systemic arterial pressure and restore tissue perfusion is essential to prevent further deterioration and widespread cellular injury.

Stage III: Irreversible

Intense, prolonged vasoconstriction has now drastically reduced tissue perfusion to the extent that widespread cellular injury occurs. Severe ischemia of the kidneys leads to acute renal failure and anuria. Critical impairment of coronary perfusion, particularly in predisposed patients, decreases myocardial contractility. Hypoperfusion of the pancreas generates vasoactive and cardiac-depressant polypeptides, most notably, myocardial-depressant factor which further reduces cardiac function. Inadequate tissue oxygenation of the gastrointestinal (GI) mucosa causes translocation of bacteria and toxic bacterial products from the gut into the bloodstream and also predisposes the patient to GI bleeding. Reduced blood flow to the brain alters neurogenic regulation of arterial pressure; profound impairment of cerebral function may induce coma. On a microvascular level, local tissue hypoxia disrupts cell membrane integrity via depletion of adenosine triphosphate (ATP) and initiates the activation of numerous biochemical cascades with the resultant formation of vasoactive metabolic by-products and chemotactic factors which impair the microcirculation and directly damage capillary endothelium. These derangements contribute to the development of disseminated intravascular coagulation (DIC) in multiple organ systems, adult respiratory distress syndrome in the lungs, and ultimately, irreversible tissue destruction throughout the body.[1,2,5–10]

Etiologic Classification and Common Mechanisms

The most common clinical conditions associated with the major forms of shock are reviewed below and detailed in Table 18.1. The clinical manifestations, pathogenesis, and general management approach for each classification are briefly discussed, with further illustration in the form of specific case studies throughout the remainder of the chapter.

Hypovolemic Shock

Shock secondary to a reduction in intravascular volume generally is referred to as hypovolemic shock. Whether the primary insult is the external loss of blood, plasma, or free water or the internal sequestration of these fluids in body cavities, the overall result is reduced venous return and decreased cardiac output. The severity of hypovolemic shock is dependent upon the amount and rate of intravascular volume loss and each individual's capacity for compensation. Although responses vary, a healthy person may tolerate an acute loss of as much as 25% of their intravascular volume with minimal clinical signs and symptoms.[1,8,10] Up to this point, increases in heart rate, myocardial contractility, and systemic vascular resistance are effective compensations for this loss in volume; that is, the patient is in Stage I of shock as previously described. Losses in excess of this amount generally will overwhelm compensatory mechanisms and the patient progresses to Stages II and III if restorative measures are not taken immediately.

The most common and dramatic cause of hypovolemic shock is hemorrhagic shock in which intravascular volume depletion occurs as a result of bleeding. Trauma is responsible for most cases of acute hemorrhagic shock; other significant causes are rupture of vascular aneurysms, acute gastrointestinal bleeding, ruptured ectopic pregnancy, and postoperative bleeding. Other mechanisms for hypovolemic shock are conditions associated with either excess fluid losses from gastrointestinal or renal sources or plasma loss due to burns or sequestration (also known as "third-space" accumulation).[8,10,11]

Treatment of patients with hypovolemic shock requires replacement of intravascular volume with crystalloids, colloids, or blood products in order to optimize tissue oxygenation and meet metabolic requirements.[2,4] The choice and amount of fluid necessary to restore intravascular volume is controversial, and depends upon the etiology and severity of the hypovolemia. If cardiac output remains low despite adequate fluid replacement, and if filling pressures are elevated, the sequential addition of inotropic agents and vasopressors may be required to prevent further hemodynamic deterioration.

Cardiogenic Shock

A shock state in which abnormal cardiac function plays a major role in the establishment of the shock syndrome constitutes cardiogenic shock. The use of early revascularization techniques [i.e., thrombolytic therapy and percutaneous transluminal coronary angioplasty (PTCA)], has lowered the incidence of cardiogenic shock.[12,13] This reduction is attributed to the ability of these modalities to salvage myocardium. In the 1970s, approximately 10% to 20% of patients with acute myocardial infarction (MI) developed cardiogenic shock.[14] With thrombolytic therapy, the incidence has declined to approximately 5%.[12,13] The mortality rate of cardiogenic shock is 80% to 95% in those acute myocardial infarction patients who do not obtain reperfusion of the infarcted artery.[15–21] The in-hospital mortality rate is significantly reduced in patients who receive aggressive intervention (i.e., PTCA or surgical revascularization) to establish reperfusion.[20,22–25]

Cardiogenic shock can be separated into mechanical and nonmechanical causes (see Table 18.1).[26] Therapy and prognosis are directly related to the presence or absence of a mechanical defect.[26] The predominant cause of cardiogenic shock is extensive ventricular dysfunction secondary to acute myocardial infarction. The clinical syndrome of cardiogenic shock usually develops if necrosis exceeds 40% of the left ventricular mass. The necrosis may be the result of a single massive myocardial infarction or the cumulative effect of a number of smaller events.

The two classic manifestations of shock that enable the clinician to establish the diagnosis are hypotension and hypoperfusion. Early in the shock process laboratory tests/reports reveal:

- Arterial blood gas (ABG) measurements indicating hypoxemia secondary to pulmonary congestion with ventilation-perfusion abnormalities, and metabolic acidosis with a compensatory respiratory alkalosis.

- Elevated blood lactate levels which contributes to the acidosis.

- A complete blood count (CBC) often reveals leukocytosis and, if disseminated intravascular coagulation is present, thrombocytopenia.

- ECG may reveal infarction, left bundle branch block, sinus tachycardia, and/or dysrhythmia.

- Chest x-ray may reveal pulmonary edema or adult respiratory distress syndrome (ARDS).

- Hemodynamic monitoring usually demonstrates reduced cardiac output, arterial hypotension, an elevated pulmonary capillary wedge pressure (PCWP) and pulmonary artery pressure (PAP), and frequently, an elevation in systemic vascular resistance (SVR).[19]

Without emergency diagnostic and therapeutic interventions, the progression of cardiogenic shock may proceed rapidly over a period of hours with metabolic consequences of tissue hypoperfusion, and pulmonary congestion eventually resulting in irreversible impairment of left ventricular pump function. Before further evaluation of the cause of cardiogenic shock can proceed, stabilization of the patient must be attained. Stabilization includes: 1) establishing ventilation and oxygenation (arterial pO_2 should be >70 mm Hg); 2) restoring central arterial blood pressure with vasopressors if needed; 3) infusing fluids if hypovolemic; and 4) treating pain, arrhythmias, and acid/base abnormalities if present.[19]

Before treating patients in cardiogenic shock, the basic underlying mechanism of the shock state must be considered. Shock secondary to disorders of inadequate diastolic filling, such as tension pneumothorax or cardiac tamponade, generally is readily detectable with definitive clinical studies such as echocardiography. Most of these cases are completely reversible by measures that alleviate compression such as chest tubes and pericardiocentesis.

Shock as a result of impaired systolic performance, whether infarct- or noninfarct-induced, requires a much more aggressive diagnostic and therapeutic approach. Normalization of blood pressure and routine physical assessment are not predictive of ongoing clinical deterioration.[15] Therefore, hemodynamic monitoring is essential to accurately evaluate left and right ventricular performance and to differentiate between the various mechanical causes of cardiogenic shock such as ventricular septal defects, severe valvular incompetence, and free wall rupture.[15] If the cause is determined to be mechanical, then early operative correction is required.

Initial stabilization of the patient with impaired systolic performance involves a combination of fluid and drug therapy. Hypovolemia, as reflected by inadequate filling pressures, may occur in up to 20% of patients in cardiogenic shock. Correction of volume deficits, particularly in patients with right ventricular infarction, may effectively increase the blood pressure.[6,16] Treatment is best guided by classifying patients into one of three hemodynamic subsets:[27,28]

- Patients with elevated PCWP (>18 mm Hg), low cardiac index (CI) (<2.2 L/minute/m^2), and systolic arterial pressure less than 100 mm Hg. These patients are best managed by using a vasodilator and/or dobutamine. Dobutamine will increase cardiac output and decrease preload and afterload. Phosphodiesterase inhibitors have combined inotropic and vasodilating properties similar to dobutamine and can be used in similar situations as dobutamine.
- Patients with an elevated PCWP (>18 mm Hg), reduced CI (<2.2 L/minute/m^2), and systolic arterial pressure less than 90 mm Hg. These patients have a poor prognosis. Choice of inotropic agent is dependent upon the degree of hypotension. Dopamine may be indicated since it usually increases arterial pressure along with cardiac output. Dobutamine may be used, but the net peripheral effect is vasodilation which may reduce arterial pressure too much; therefore, it is not the drug of first choice in severely hypotensive patients. As a guideline, for systolic pressures between 70 to 90 mm Hg, dopamine should be used initially. If, however, large doses (i.e., >20 μg/kg/minute)

of dopamine are required to maintain arterial blood pressure, then norepinephrine should be considered. Mechanical assist devices (i.e., intra-aortic balloon pumps) also may be considered in this setting for hemodynamic support.

- Patients with elevated right atrial and right ventricular diastolic pressures (>10 mm Hg), reduced CI (<2.2 L/minute/m^2), and systolic arterial pressure less than 100 mm Hg. These patients have right ventricular infarction, an important factor to recognize since they are very responsive to volume expansion; therefore, diuretics should be avoided in this group. In addition to right ventricular dysfunction, there may be some left ventricular dysfunction. The right ventricular filling pressure must be increased by infusion of fluid to stabilize systemic pressure. If unsuccessful, inotropic support is required with dobutamine producing the best results.[29] Dobutamine, unlike dopamine, does not cause pulmonary vasoconstriction; therefore, it does not increase right ventricular afterload. If volume replacement and inotropic support fail, mechanical circulatory assist devices should be instituted.

Since inotropic agents and vasoconstrictors can increase myocardial oxygen consumption and potentially extend the area of necrosis in patients with infarct-induced cardiogenic shock, the careful selection and titration of agents which will best preserve myocardium while sustaining systemic arterial pressure and tissue perfusion is essential. While correction of volume deficits and early pharmacologic support may prevent the extension of myocardial damage, it must be emphasized that exclusive use of these measures does not improve survival.[15,16] Therefore, drug therapy must be considered only an interim maneuver to preserve myocardial and systemic integrity while further diagnostic and therapeutic interventions are being considered.

Nonpharmacologic treatments of cardiogenic shock consist of two forms of intervention. First is to provide circulatory support to the patient no matter what the initiating cause of circulatory failure (e.g., mechanical circulatory assist devices, cardiac transplantation). The second intervention is to correct or reverse the specific cause of the shock (e.g., PTCA, surgical correction). Nonpharmacologic interventions have had a significant positive impact on survival.[30]

Mechanical interventions [i.e., intra-aortic balloon counterpulsation (see Question 33)] can rapidly stabilize patients with cardiogenic shock, especially those with global myocardial ischemia, or infarction complicated by mechanical defects such as papillary muscle rupture or ventricular septal rupture. Intra-aortic balloon counterpulsation augments coronary arterial perfusion pressure during diastole and reduces left ventricular impedance during systole. Sometimes combined inotropic support and intra-aortic balloon counterpulsation are required to maintain an acceptable blood pressure (systolic BP >90 mm Hg) and CI (>2.2 L/minute/m^2). Recently, more advanced circulatory-assist devices (e.g., the Hemopump) have been developed. Mechanical assistance with these devices should be used only for patients with cardiogenic shock who need temporary support while awaiting definitive, corrective therapy.

Surgical intervention is the most successful in managing cardiogenic shock when mechanical defects such as acute mitral insufficiency are present.[30] Patients can be stabilized initially by mechanical circulatory assist devices with or without inotropic support. In this situation surgery should not be delayed. Cardiac transplantation is an option for a small and highly select group of individuals with cardiogenic shock.

Reperfusion strategies such as PTCA in patients who fail to respond to thrombolytic therapy are important in the early management of cardiogenic shock after acute myocardial infarction.[19,20,22,28] This should be considered in patients with persistent hypotension, evidence of ongoing ischemia, and/or clinical instability. These patients may benefit from initial stabilization with mechanical assist devices.

Distributive Shock

Shock that is precipitated by massive arteriovenous dilatation is referred to as distributive shock because the primary hemodynamic event is a redistribution of blood volume from the central compartment to the peripheral vasculature. Although a number of events may initiate distributive shock (see Figure 18.1), the majority of cases are readily reversed by supportive measures and treatment or elimination of the underlying cause.

Septic Shock. In contrast, distributive shock secondary to sepsis, or septic shock, is associated with a high mortality rate, reflecting the limited therapeutic options available at this time. The remainder of this discussion will focus on septic shock because it is the most clinically significant subclassification of distributive shock.

Septic shock develops in approximately 40% of septic patients and carries a mortality rate of 20% to 80%. With estimates of 400,000 cases of sepsis occurring annually resulting in more than 100,000 deaths, shock secondary to sepsis is the leading cause of death in intensive care units and the thirteenth most common cause of death in the U.S.[31–34]

Differing definitions of the syndrome of sepsis have led to a lack of uniformity in evaluating the true incidence of sepsis, its sequelae, and the outcome of treatment. This inconsistent approach is apparent given the wide range in mortality rates reported. To address this dilemma, a recent consensus conference recommended that the terms *sepsis*, *severe sepsis*, and *septic shock* be used to delineate increasingly severe stages of the same disease. Accordingly, *sepsis* is currently defined as a systemic response to infection as indicated by two or more of the following conditions: temperature greater than 38 °C or less than 36 °C; heart rate greater than 90 beats/minute, or $PaCO_2$ less than 32 mm Hg; and leukocyte count greater than 12,000 cells/mL^3, or less than 4000 cells/mL^3, or greater than 10% immature (band) forms. *Severe sepsis* is established when sepsis is accompanied by hypotension, and/or evidence of hypoperfusion or organ dysfunction. *Septic shock* is evident when severe sepsis persists despite adequate volume resuscitation and/or when symptoms of hypoperfusion persist despite the maintenance of arterial pressure with inotropic or vasopressor agents.[35] The term ''septic shock'' will be used throughout the remainder of the chapter since each stage of the sepsis syndrome ultimately results from the same initial pathophysiologic process. (See Figure 18.1.)

Septic shock may be initiated by systemic infection with bacterial, fungal, mycobacterial, rickettsial, protozoal, or viral microorganisms. The majority of cases are associated with aerobic or anaerobic bacteria. However, the incidence of fungal, viral, and polymicrobial infections has increased with the advent of broad-spectrum antibiotics, organ transplantation, and other conditions in which patients are immunocompromised.[31,32,36]

Gram-negative bacteremia, the most common cause of septic shock, usually is associated with nosocomial infections arising from the urinary, gastrointestinal, and respiratory tracts. The most frequently causative organisms are *Escherichia coli*, *Klebsiella*, *Enterobacter-Serratia* Species, *Proteus* species, and *Pseudomonas aeruginosa*.[33,37] In addition, gram-positive infections in patients with septic shock are becoming more prevalent, particularly with staphylococcal species in hospitalized patients secondary to in-

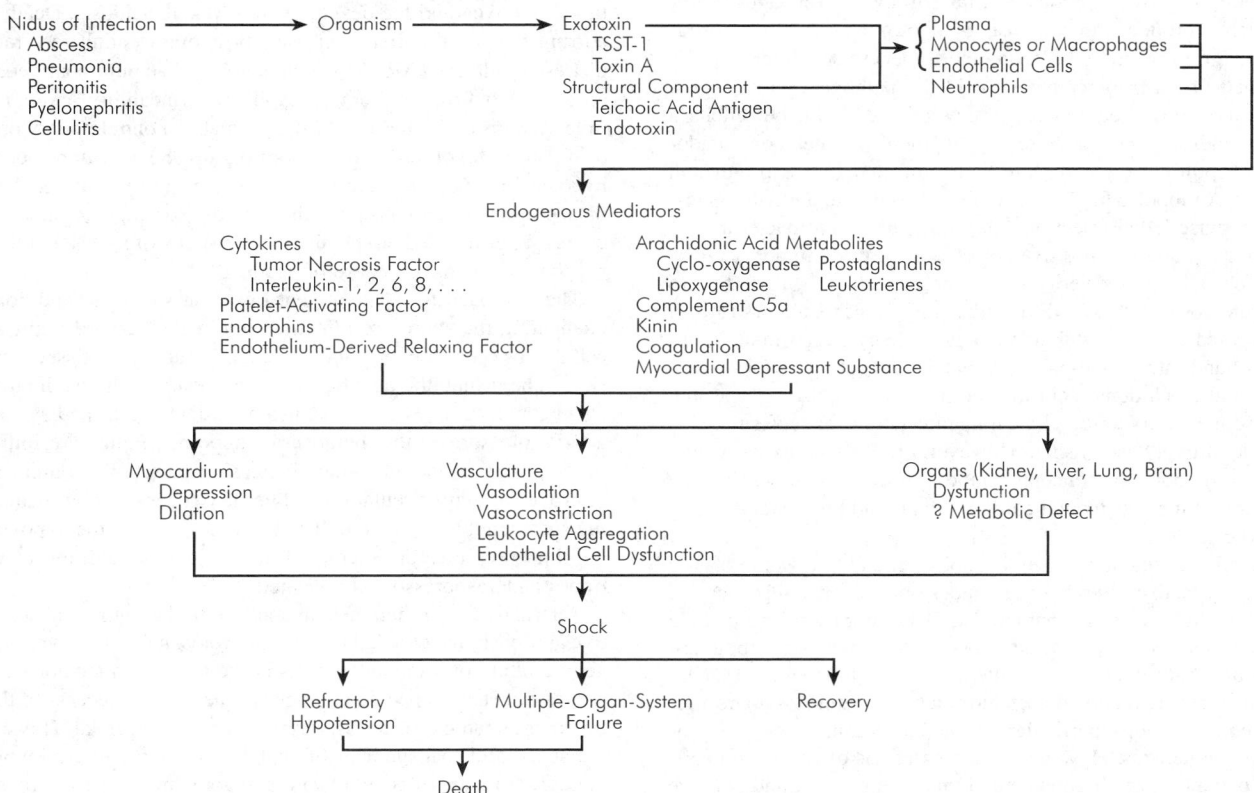

Fig 18.1   Pathogenetic Sequence of the Events in Septic Shock   TSST-1 denotes toxic shock syndrome toxin 1. Toxin A is *Pseudomonas aeruginosa* toxin A. Reprinted with permission from reference 31.

creases in invasive medical procedures.[32,38] In individuals presenting with community-acquired sepsis, infections with *Neisseria meningitidis*, *Streptococcus pneumoniae*, and *Staphylococcus aureus* are more common.[38] In any event, careful consideration of the patient's history and clinical presentation often will reveal the most likely cause, although in 30% of septic patients no bacterial source is identified.[39]

The individuals most at risk for sepsis and subsequent shock are immunocompromised or have underlying diseases or conditions which render them susceptible to bloodstream invasion. Particularly compromised are neonates, the elderly, patients with AIDS, alcoholics, those having undergone surgery or trauma, and childbearing women. Other predisposing factors include coexisting diseases such as diabetes mellitus, malignancies, chronic hepatic or renal failure, and hyposplenism; immunosuppressant drugs and cancer chemotherapy; and procedures such as insertion of urinary catheters, endotracheal tubes, and intravenous (IV) lines.[32,33,38,39]

The pathogenesis of septic shock is initiated by the proliferation of micro-organisms at a nidus of infection. The organisms may either enter the bloodstream directly, (producing positive blood cultures) or may indirectly elicit a systemic inflammatory response by locally releasing their toxins or structural components at the site of infection. These products of micro-organisms or ''initiators'' directly activate various plasma and inflammatory cells including, among others, endothelial cells, platelets, macrophage-monocytes, and neutrophils. In turn, these cells stimulate the production and release of numerous endogenous mediators, which through very complex interactions are responsible for the deleterious consequences of sepsis (see Figure 18.1).[31,32,40]

Among the numerous substances implicated in triggering this ''sepsis cascade,'' intensive research has focused on endotoxin, the lipopolysaccharide component of the gram-negative bacterial cell wall and, more recently, tumor necrosis factor (TNF-α) or cachectin, a cytokine produced primarily by macrophages. TNF-α, which is produced in response to endotoxin as well as to products of gram-positive bacteria and other micro-organisms, is thought to be a primary mediator in the pathogenesis of sepsis. TNF-α not only mediates the effects of endotoxin, but elicits a sepsis syndrome, characterized by hypotension, metabolic acidosis, and multiple organ failure when injected into experimental animals. Antibodies to TNF-α confer protection in animals against the otherwise lethal injections of endotoxin or live bacteria.[41–43] In humans, there is a positive correlation between tumor necrosis factor levels, sepsis severity score, and mortality.[44] In addition to tumor necrosis factor (TNF-α), other important mediators toward which research is being directed include the cytokines interleukin-1 (IL-1) and interleukin-6 (IL-6), platelet activating factor, endorphins, and arachidonic acid metabolites. The precise relationship of these mediators to the clinical manifestations of sepsis remains to be definitively established. However, clinical and experimental evidence supports the concept that these substances are responsible for many of the detrimental cardiovascular and pulmonary effects observed.[32,36,40,45]

The clinical features of septic shock (in addition to the classic findings typically observed with shock) are fever, chills, nausea, vomiting, and diarrhea. Characteristic laboratory findings include leukocytosis or leukopenia, thrombocytopenia with or without coagulation abnormalities, and often, hyperbilirubinemia. Usually these features are readily detectable and occur within 24 hours after bacteremia develops, particularly if the bacteremia is due to gram-negative organisms. However, in the extremes of age or in debilitated patients, hypothermia actually may be present, and positive findings may be limited to unexplained hypotension, mental confusion, and hyperventilation.[32,38,46]

The initial hemodynamic presentation of septic shock often is manifested by hypovolemia due to the release of vasodilatory mediators such as bradykinin, histamine, and endorphins. These mediators cause an increase in venous capacitance with resultant venous pooling, as well as enhanced vascular permeability with extravasation of intravascular volume. Following aggressive fluid resuscitation, the majority of patients will assume a characteristic hyperdynamic or ''warm shock'' state in which there is a marked reduction in total systemic vascular resistance and a reflex increase in cardiac output. Within 24 to 48 hours of the onset of septic shock, most patients develop myocardial dysfunction, as manifested by decreased myocardial compliance, reduced contractility, and ventricular dilatation. Although the etiology and mechanism for this abnormality are not fully understood, it is not believed to be caused by myocardial ischemia. Instead, it is thought to be due to one or more circulating myocardial depressant substances, yet to be isolated, which involve final common pathways that are independent of specific microbial types or toxins.[31,32,47] The extent of the myocardial depression and the determinants of ultimate outcome are complex, but in general they seem to correlate with the degree of peripheral vasodilation and the ability of the heart to compensate for the decrease in contractility. The survivors of septic shock are those whose hyperdynamic variables (increased CO, decreased SVR, and marked tachycardia) begin to normalize within the first 24 hours and whose ventricles dilate in response to depression of myocardial contractility.[47]

In contrast to the classic progression of shock, the majority of nonsurvivors of septic shock do not progress to a ''cold shock'' phase, but die despite a normal or elevated cardiac output. Death within the first week after the onset of sepsis occurs as a result of intractable arterial hypotension that is secondary to a markedly depressed systemic vascular resistance. This causes extensive maldistribution of blood flow in the microvasculature, with subsequent tissue hypoxia, and the development of lactic acidosis. Death occurring beyond the first week usually is due to adult respiratory distress syndrome (ARDS) which is noncardiac pulmonary edema secondary to diffuse pulmonary capillary permeability, and/or multiple systems organ failure (MSOF) which is nonpulmonary organ dysfunction involving two or more organs. Severe, unresponsive hypotension due to a decreased CO does occur in a subpopulation of septic shock patients. In other words, cardiogenic shock becomes superimposed on the distributive shock of sepsis, but this is not the most common cause of death.[31,47,48]

The approach to the treatment of septic shock, in addition to eradicating the source of infection, is directed toward improving cellular oxygen delivery and maintaining adequate tissue perfusion. The usual therapeutic regimen includes fluids, inotropic agents, and vasopressor drugs, using cardiac output and systemic arterial pressure as the therapeutic endpoints. Fluids are initially the mainstay of therapy, since increasing the cardiac output will improve capillary circulation and tissue oxygenation by maintaining sufficient blood volume. If fluids do not correct the hypoxia or if filling pressures are increased, the sequential addition of inotropes and vasopressors is indicated.[31,32,39,47]

Alternative drug therapies, in addition to the traditional supportive approach, have included corticosteroids, naloxone, cyclo-oxygenase inhibitors, and antagonists in the form of monoclonal antibodies directed at specific pathogens. The relative success of these treatment strategies often is variable and controversial. However, the successful management of septic shock most likely involves therapies that are directed toward antagonizing or preventing synthesis of the initiating mediators or of modulating the septic response through immunotherapy.[36]

Hemodynamic Monitoring

Hemodynamic monitoring is indicated when the measurement of intracardiac pressures and cardiac output is essential for the accurate assessment and management of the underlying pathological conditions. Common situations necessitating invasive monitoring, in addition to the optimization of tissue perfusion during various shock states, include the differentiation of cardiogenic versus noncardiogenic pulmonary edema or ARDS and the diagnosis of valvular or septal defects. Although the successful management of many critically ill patients often is guided by hemodynamic parameters, it is essential to incorporate these values with sound clinical judgment and realize that the prediction of hemodynamic responses to therapeutic interventions is not absolute.[49]

Swan-Ganz Catheter

The introduction of flow-directed, balloon flotation pulmonary artery (PA) catheters by Swan et al.[50] has been a major advance in bedside hemodynamic monitoring. The PA catheter enables clinicians to assess both right and left intracardiac pressures, determine cardiac output, and obtain mixed venous blood samples. These capabilities allow one to accurately evaluate volume status and ventricular performance, derive hemodynamic indices, and determine systemic oxygen consumption.[49–52]

There are several versions of the PA catheter. Some include additional lumens for intravenous infusions, temporary transvenous pacing, and continuous monitoring of mixed venous oxygen saturation. However, the essential components for hemodynamic monitoring are incorporated in the standard quadruple lumen catheter pictured in Figure 18.2. This catheter, as indicated, is comprised of four lumens, each terminating at different points along the catheter. When properly positioned, the proximal port terminates in the right atrium (RA) and is used to measure right atrium pressure, to inject fluid for cardiac output determination, and for the administration of intravenous fluids. The distal port, which terminates at the tip of the catheter, is positioned in the pulmonary artery, beyond the pulmonary valve, and is used to measure pulmonary artery and pulmonary capillary wedge pressure with balloon inflation, as well as to obtain mixed venous blood samples. Intermittent inflation of the balloon is accomplished by inserting 1.5 mL of air into the balloon inflation valve, while the thermistor contains a temperature probe and electrical leads for connection to a computer which calculates CO by the thermodilution technique.[53]

Although the pulmonary artery catheter is confined to the pulmonary vasculature, left ventricular (LV) pressures may be ascertained from the PCWP. When the balloon is inflated the PA catheter advances to a pulmonary artery branch of equal diameter and becomes lodged or ''wedged'' in this position. Since there is a cessation of forward flow beyond the wedged PA segment, a static fluid column exists between the left ventricle and PA catheter tip during diastole when the mitral valve is open. If there are no pres-

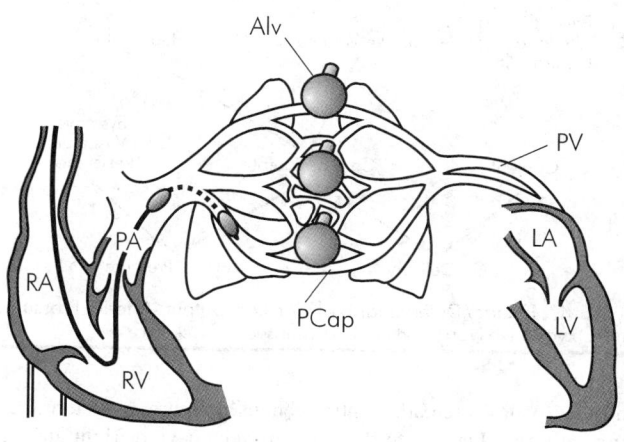

PAEDP ⟷ PCWP ⟷ PVP ⟶ LAP ⟷ LVEDP

Fig 18.3 Anatomical Position of PA Catheter in Vasculature This demonstrates the anatomical position of a pulmonary artery catheter in the pulmonary artery. The dotted line positions the inflated balloon in the ''wedged'' position. RA = Right atrium; RV = Right ventricle; PA = Pulmonary artery; ALV = Alveolus; PCAP = Pulmonary capillary; PV = Pulmonary vein; LA = Left atrium; LV = Left ventricle. The bottom is a progressive correlation of vascular pressures. Adapted with permission from reference 49.

sure gradients in the pulmonary vasculature beyond the balloon, and if mitral valve function is normal, the PCWP then equilibrates with all distal pressures and thus indirectly reflects left ventricular end-diastolic pressure (LVEDP). Figure 18.3 illustrates the anatomical position of the pulmonary artery catheter in the pulmonary artery and the progressive correlation of distal vascular pressures (i.e., the PA end-diastolic pressure, PCWP, pulmonary vein pressure, left atrial pressure, and LVEDP). It is important to recognize that under normal circumstances these pressures closely approximate each other. However, alterations in pressure or resistance within the system due to existing disease states, physiologic or anatomical derangements, or vasoactive drugs will affect these correlations and may diminish the ability of the catheter to reflect true LVEDP.[49,50,52,53]

Determinants of Cardiac Function and Hemodynamic Indices

The effective interpretation and management of hemodynamic parameters requires a thorough understanding of the physiological determinants of cardiac output and arterial pressure. Assuming oxygen content of blood is adequate, cardiac output and systemic vascular resistance are the ultimate determinants of oxygen delivery and adequate arterial pressure, and thus, the overall tissue perfusion. As outlined in Figure 18.4, CO is a function of four major factors [preload, afterload, heart rate (HR), and contractility] and may be quantified as the product of stroke volume (SV) and heart rate. The effects of these factors on hemodynamic parameters are interrelated and complex, and must be assessed carefully when selecting therapeutic interventions that will produce the desired response. A good review of the determinants of cardiac performance is found in Chapter 15: Congestive Heart Failure. Table 18.2 and the glossary provide definitions of terms and normal hemodynamic indices which are discussed in the following section.

Measured Hemodynamic Indices

Right Atrial Pressure (RAP) and Central Venous Pressure (CVP). The RAP, as measured by a PA catheter, reflects the filling pressure or end-diastolic pressure of the right ventricle (RV) and is used as

Fig 18.2   Swan Ganz Catheter

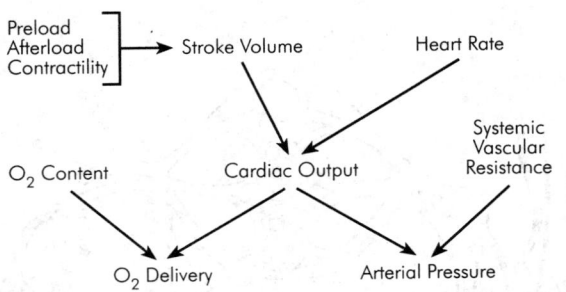

Fig 18.4   Primary Determinants of Cardiac Output, Arterial Pressure, and Oxygen Delivery   Adapted with permission from reference 49.

an index of RV preload. Central venous pressure, as determined by a catheter advanced to the superior vena cava or right atrium, is another means of measuring right ventricle filling pressure and is considered equivalent to the right atrial pressure.[52] Vascular capacitance, circulating blood volume, and myocardial contractility maintain right atrial pressure. A low right atrial pressure usually reflects hypovolemia or vasodilation. An elevated right atrial pressure may signify increased intravascular volume, right ventricle failure, tricuspid regurgitation, pulmonary embolus, pulmonary hypertension, obstructive airway disease with cor pulmonale, or pericardial tamponade. In tamponade, the left ventricle filling pressure also is elevated to the same degree as the right atrial pressure.

Right heart pressures are unreliable indicators of concurrent left ventricle function. In patients with cardiac or pulmonary disease or on mechanical ventilation, RAP or CVP measurements actually may vary inversely with the pulmonary capillary wedge pressure. Therefore, reliance on right heart pressures from CVP catheters alone is probably adequate only in the initial management of young healthy adults suffering from hypovolemic shock.[5,49]

Pulmonary artery systolic (PAS) pressure is obtained during systole, after the opening of the pulmonic valve when blood is ejected from the right ventricle into the pulmonary artery; it measures the pressure generated by the RV during contraction. Elevations in PAS pressure occur when pulmonary vascular resistance is increased. This occurs in patients with acute or chronic parenchymal pulmonary disease, pulmonary embolus, hypoxemia, acidosis, or in those receiving vasoactive drugs. A low PAS pressure usually results from a reduced circulating blood volume.

Pulmonary artery diastolic (PAD) pressure is measured during diastole after the closure of the pulmonic valve when the blood moves from the pulmonary artery into the pulmonary capillaries. As previously described with respect to the pulmonary capillary wedge pressure, the PAD pressure also may reflect left ventricular end-diastolic pressure. Under normal circumstances, the PAD pressure is approximately equal (within 1 to 3 mm Hg) to the PCWP and can be used in place of the latter as an indication of left ventricular end-diastolic pressure. However, because the catheter is more proximally located and is not in a ''wedged'' position, the PAD pressure may not correlate as well as the pulmonary capillary wedge pressure with the left ventricular end-diastolic pressure. In conditions which increase pulmonary vascular resistance, such as those mentioned for pulmonary artery systolic pressure, the pulmonary artery diastolic pressure may be substantially greater than the pulmonary capillary wedge pressure. Also, when heart rates are over 120 beats/minute, pulmonary artery diastolic pressure exceeds PCWP. This is because diastole is shortened and reduces the time necessary for equilibrium of blood flow. Therefore, in the presence of elevated pulmonary vascular resistance or significant tachycardia, one cannot assume that the pulmonary artery diastolic

pressure approximates the pulmonary capillary wedge pressure or left ventricular end-diastolic pressure.[49,51,52,54]

Pulmonary capillary wedge pressure (PCWP) is the most reliable reflection of LVEDP measured with the pulmonary artery catheter. Left ventricular end-diastolic pressure, in turn, provides the closest approximation of preload, the initial end-diastolic fiber length, which is determined clinically by left ventricular end-diastolic volume (LVEDV). Since neither LVEDV or LVEDP are readily measurable, pulmonary capillary wedge pressure is used as an indicator of preload.

Knowledge of left ventricular preload provides an objective means of evaluating LV function and optimizing cardiac output according to the length-tension relationship of cardiac muscle known as the Frank-Starling mechanism. According to this mechanism, the degree of myocardial fiber shortening, and hence cardiac output, is proportional to the initial myocardial fiber length, or ventricular volume, at the onset of contraction. As illustrated by the ventricular function curve in Figure 18.5, this proportionality of cardiac output to LVEDV is maintained within certain intrinsic limits of myocardial fiber contractility. Initially, for any given state of contractility, an increase in LVEDP or volume generates a contraction which results in a corresponding increase in cardiac output. Once an optimal preload is attained, as indicated by the flat portion of the curve, further elevations in ventricular filling pressure will not enhance cardiac output and may, in fact, result in a decline in contractility and a decrease in cardiac output. Significant increases or decreases in the level of ventricular contractility, independent of alterations in preload or afterload, result in shifts in the ventricular function curve, with corresponding changes in cardiac output. As shown in Figure 18.5, enhanced myocardial contractility due to such factors as increased sympathetic nerve activity, endogenous catecholamines, or exogenous inotropic agents, shifts the ventricular function curve upward and to the left, thus augmenting cardiac output for a given preload. Conditions which reduce contractility, such as loss of contractile mass, use of pharmacologic depressants, systemic hypoxia, local ischemia, or acidosis, shift the curve downward and to the right, thereby diminishing cardiac output.[54,55]

Although left ventricular end-diastolic pressure or pulmonary capillary wedge pressure can generally be substituted for left ventricular wedge pressure when evaluating cardiac function, the use of PCWP as a reflection of LVEDV has its limitations. In patients with mitral stenosis, pulmonary veno-occlusive disease, or high levels of positive end-expiratory pressure (PEEP) with mechanical ventilation, pulmonary capillary wedge pressure will exceed left ventricular end-diastolic volume and inaccurately reflect LVEDV.[54]

The relationship between LVEDP and LVEDV is curvilinear and is determined by compliance.[56] In conditions where ventricular compliance is abnormal, the correlation of LVEDP to LVEDV is altered, and PCWP cannot be assumed to accurately reflect preload. With increasing compliance, such as that associated with congestive myopathies, regurgitant mitral or aortic valves, and the use of vasodilators, an increase in left ventricular end-diastolic volume will not markedly affect LVEDP. In contrast, with decreased ventricular compliance, a minimal change in left ventricular end-diastolic volume may result in a substantial increase in left ventricular end-diastolic pressure. Conditions which decrease compliance include myocardial ischemia, restrictive cardiomyopathies, aortic stenosis, cardiac tamponade or effusion, hypertension, and the use of inotropic agents.[49,54] Therefore, one must be aware of the conditions or interventions that may result in potential alterations in ventricular compliance and/or PCWP and interpret measurements accordingly.

Table 18.2	Normal Hemodynamic Values and Derived Indices		
	Equation	Normal Value	Units
Directly Measured			
Blood pressure (BP) (systolic/diastolic)		120–140/80–90	mm Hg
Cardiac output (CO)	$CO = SV \times HR$	4–7	L/min
Central venous pressure (CVP)[a]		2–6	mm Hg[b]
Heart rate (HR) (pulse)		60–80	beats/min (BPM)
Mean pulmonary artery pressure (MPAP)		12–15	mm Hg
Pulmonary artery pressure (PAP) (systolic/diastolic)		20–30/8–12	mm Hg
Pulmonary capillary wedge pressure (PCWP)		5–12[c]	mm Hg
Derived Indices			
Cardiac index (CI)	$CI = \dfrac{CO}{BSA^{d}}$	2.5–4.2	L/min/m^2
Left ventricular stroke work index (LVSWI)	$LVWSI = (MAP - PCWP)(SVI)(0.0136)$	35–85	gm/m^2/beat
Mean arterial pressure (MAP)	$MAP = \dfrac{2(\text{Diastolic BP}) + \text{Systolic BP}}{3}$	80–100	mm Hg
Perfusion pressure (PP)	$PP = MAP - PCWP$	≥50	mm Hg
Pulmonary vascular resistance (PVR)	$PVR = \dfrac{(MPAP - PCWP)}{CO}(80)$	20–120	dynes · sec · cm^{-5}
Stroke volume (SV)	$SV = \dfrac{CO}{HR}$	60–130	mL/beat
Stroke volume index (SVI)	$SVI = \dfrac{SVA}{BSA}$	30–75	mL/beat/m^2
Systemic vascular resistance (SVR)[e]	$SVR = \dfrac{(MAP - CVP)}{CO}(80)$	800–1440	dyne · sec · cm^{-5}
Systemic vascular resistance index (SVRI)	$SVRI = SVR \times BSA$	1680–2580	dyne · sec · cm^{-5} · m^2

[a] CVP is essentially synonymous with RAP.
[b] 2–6 mm Hg = 3–6 cm H$_2$0 (conversion: 1 mm = 1.34 cm H$_2$0).
[c] May optimally ↑ PCWP to 16–18 mm Hg in critically ill patients.
[d] BSA = Body surface area = 1.7 m^2 (average male).
[e] SVR is synonymous with total peripheral resistance (TPR).

The pulmonary capillary wedge pressure is also a useful measure of pulmonary capillary hydrostatic pressure. The pulmonary capillary hydrostatic pressure is the major driving force for the development of pulmonary congestion. Thus, the PCWP helps to determine whether pulmonary edema is cardiogenic or noncardiogenic in origin. Pulmonary capillary wedge pressure is higher than pulmonary hydrostatic pressure in the presence of adult respiratory distress syndrome or elevated pulmonary vascular resistance.[51]

Derived Hemodynamic Indices[52,57,58]

Parameters which reflect cardiovascular function can be derived from the hemodynamic measurements obtained from the Swan-Ganz catheter (see Table 18.2 and Glossary).

Stroke volume (SV) is the amount of blood ejected by the ventricle with each systolic contraction. It is directly proportional to the contractile state of the myocardium. When cardiac output is increased by therapeutic maneuvers, it is important to know whether the increase is due to an inotropic (SV) or a chronotropic response (HR).

Cardiac index (CI) is the cardiac output adjusted for body surface area (BSA). Since cardiac output is a relative measure based upon size, it provides a more meaningful assessment of an individual's output.

Pulmonary vascular resistance (PVR) and systemic vascular resistance (SVR) are determined by dividing the change in pressure by the flow (pressure change/cardiac output = resistance). It is important to realize that therapeutic maneuvers which alter systemic vascular resistance do not indicate a change in any specific vascular bed, such as the renal or splanchnic vascular beds; changes in systemic vascular resistance reflect the overall change. The *systemic vascular resistance index (SVRI)* is a normalized SVR for body surface area.

Left ventricular stroke work index (LVSWI) is an indication of left ventricular contractility which takes into account preload, afterload, and cardiac output. The constant 0.0136 is the conversion factor which changes mm Hg/mL into gram-meters. Elevation in

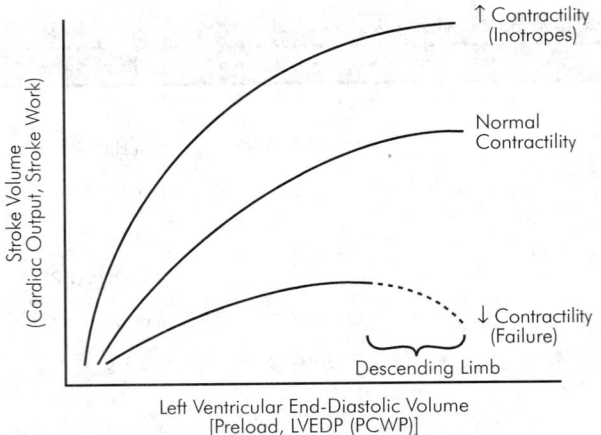

Fig 18.5 Ventricular Function Curve (General) In the normal heart, as preload (LVEDP), measured clinically by PCWP, increases, stroke volume (cardiac output, stroke work) increase, until the contractile fibers reach their capacity, at which point the curve flattens. A change in contractility causes the heart to perform on a different curve. If the contractile fibers exceed their capacity, as with severe CHF, the heart will operate on the descending limb of the curve.

left ventricular stroke work index can be achieved by changing preload, afterload, or contractility.

In summary, a single catheter in the right side of the heart provides considerable data for continuous diagnostic and therapeutic assessment. Changes in intracardiac pressures, pulmonary pressures, and cardiac output can be monitored continuously. These hemodynamic measurements can be used to calculate cardiovascular performance indices which, in turn, can be used to select specific therapeutic interventions (e.g., inotropic, vasopressor, and vasodilator agents; diuretics; and fluids).

Hypovolemic Shock
Acute Hemorrhagic Shock

1. B.J., a 32-year-old male, is brought to the emergency room (ER) with a gunshot wound to the abdomen. External blood loss and internal hemorrhage are significant, and he is anxious and disoriented to time and place. On examination, his skin is pale and cool, pulse is thready at 130 beats/min, and systolic BP is 80 mm Hg by palpation. Respirations are shallow with a rate of 36 breaths/min. What is the clinical status of B.J.? What is the primary goal in resuscitating patients with acute hemorrhagic shock?

B.J. has lost significant amounts of intravascular fluid directly from his gunshot wound and also from traumatic tissue edema. The latter results in sequestration of large amounts of fluid interstitially around the injured cells. Based upon his clinical presentation, (see Table 18.3) B.J. is in decompensated shock and has lost an estimated 30% to 40% of his blood volume.[59] Given the severity of his condition, if intravascular losses are not replaced within approximately two hours, myocardial dysfunction may ensue and lead to irreversible shock.[7,8]

The major hemodynamic abnormality in hypovolemic shock is decreased venous return (preload) to the heart secondary to a reduction in intravascular volume. When preload, as reflected by pulmonary capillary wedge pressure, is low, cardiac output is initially maintained by increases in heart rate and myocardial contractility. Blood pressure also is sustained by an increase in arteriolar vasoconstriction, thereby increasing systemic vascular resistance and reducing pulse pressure (the difference between systolic and diastolic pressure). These sympathomimetic responses successfully compensate for reductions in intravascular volumes

of up to 30% with minimal clinical signs and symptoms other than tachycardia, tachypnea, and decreased pulse pressure.[7,8,59-61]

When blood losses approach 30% to 40% ($\approx$2000 mL in an adult), compensatory mechanisms begin to fail as evidenced by marked tachycardia and tachypnea, reduced blood pressure, and signs of cerebral hypoperfusion such as anxiety and confusion. These patients almost always require transfusion. As B.J. illustrates, when intravascular volume losses exceed 40%, clinical shock becomes apparent with profound hypotension and tachycardia, shortness of breath, cold clammy skin, mental obtundation, and metabolic signs and symptoms of tissue hypoperfusion and cellular hypoxia. This degree of blood loss is extremely life-threatening and usually requires rapid transfusion and immediate surgical intervention to halt the progression to irreversible shock.[7,8,59-61] The primary goal, therefore, in resuscitating patients with hypovolemic shock, is to restore intravascular volume, thereby increasing preload and cardiac output and, hence, oxygen delivery to the tissues.

Treatment
Choice of Fluid in Hypovolemic Shock

2. What IV solution should be used initially in resuscitating B.J.?

Once an adequate airway is established and initial vital signs are obtained, the most important therapeutic intervention in hypovolemic shock is the rapid infusion of intravenous fluids. Initially, crystalloids or colloids are used to restore blood volume as blood products may not be immediately available and are frequently unnecessary to the management of mild to moderate shock (15% to 30% blood loss).[62]

Crystalloids versus Colloids. The use of crystalloid versus colloid solutions for the restoration of blood volume in hemorrhagic shock is controversial. The controversy primarily involves the ultimate distribution of these fluids in the extracellular compartment, which, in turn, depends upon their composition. Crystalloids are isotonic solutions which contain either saline [0.9% sodium chloride (normal saline)] or a saline equivalent (lactated Ringer's solution). Colloidal solutions contain large oncotically active molecules which are derived from natural products such as proteins (albumin), carbohydrates (dextrans, starches), and animal collagen (gelatin). Isotonic solutions freely distribute within the extracellular fluid compartment which is divided between the interstitial and intravascular spaces at a ratio of 3:1. This distribution is determined by the net forces of colloid oncotic pressure (COP) and hydrostatic pressure both inside and outside the capillary vascular space. Consequently, large volumes of fluid are required to expand the intravascular space during resuscitation. In contrast, colloids are relatively impermeable to intact capillary membranes, and therefore effectively expand the intravascular space with little loss into the interstitium. Comparatively smaller volumes of colloids than crystalloids are thus required for resuscitation, and since these large molecules persist intravascularly, their duration of action is longer.[11,62,63]

Proponents of colloids contend that resuscitation with these solutions more rapidly and effectively restores intravascular volume following acute hemorrhage.[64] At similar infusion volumes, colloids expand the plasma space two to four times more than crystalloids. In addition, it is argued that the large volume of crystalloids required for resuscitation dilutes the plasma protein pool, thereby promoting the development of pulmonary edema.[65-68] Proponents contend that maintenance of COP is necessary to prevent fluid extravasation into the pulmonary interstitium.[69,70] This concept is based upon Starling's law of capillary forces governing fluid movement which in the pulmonary vessel wall is determined

Table 18.3	Estimated Fluid and Blood Losses on Patient's Initial Presentation[a,c,d]			
	Class I	Class II	Class III	Class IV
Blood loss (mL)	up to 750	750–1500	1500–2000	>2000
Blood loss (% BV)	up to 15%	15%–30%	30%–40%	>40%
Pulse rate	<100	>100	>120	>140
Blood pressure	Normal	Normal	↓	↓
Pulse pressure (mm Hg)	Normal or ↑	↓	↓	↓
Respiratory rate	14–20	20–30	30–40	>35
Urine output (mL/hr)	>30	20–30	5–15	Negligible
CNS/mental status	Slightly anxious	Mildly anxious	Anxious and confused	Confused and lethargic
Fluid replacement (3:1 rule)[b]	Crystalloid	Crystalloid	Crystalloid and blood	Crystalloid and blood

[a] For a 70 kg male.

[b] These guidelines are based upon the "three-for-one" rule. This derives from the empiric observation that most patients in hemorrhagic shock require as much as 300 mL of electrolyte solution for each 100 mL of blood loss. Applied blindly, these guidelines can result in excessive or inadequate fluid administration. For example, a patient with a crush injury to the extremity may have hypotension out of proportion to his blood loss and require fluids in excess of the 3:1 guideline. In contrast, a patient whose ongoing blood loss is being replaced requires less than 3:1. The use of bolus therapy with careful monitoring of the patient's response can moderate these extremes.

[c] BV = Blood volume; CNS = Central nervous system.

[d] Reprinted with permission from reference 59.

by the COP-PCWP gradient [i.e., the net force generated by the colloid oncotic pressure minus the pulmonary hydrostatic pressure (PCWP)]. The normal colloid oncotic pressure is 25 mm Hg and an average PCWP is 12 mm Hg; thus, a net intravascular force of 13 mm Hg favors fluid retention in the vascular space. In critically ill patients, a COP-PCWP gradient of less than 6 mm Hg is thought to be associated with a higher incidence of pulmonary edema.[67]

Those favoring crystalloids believe that since the total extracellular fluid compartment is depleted in shock, by the movement of fluid from the extracellular to the intracellular space as well as third-space accumulation, these products are more appropriate as they replace both interstitial and intravascular fluid losses.[71] Studies supporting the use of crystalloids demonstrate that blood volume can be effectively restored and maintained without the use of colloids. There is no correlation between the type of fluid used and the development of pulmonary dysfunction despite significant transient reductions in serum protein and colloid oncotic pressure.[69,70–77]

The apparent discrepancies in these studies may depend more upon patient population characteristics than upon the type and amount of fluid used for resuscitation. Many of the studies associating crystalloids with pulmonary edema involved elderly patients with various forms of shock, a number of whom were chronically ill with pre-existing cardiopulmonary diseases.[65,68] This population might be expected to have low albumin reserves, and therefore be at greater risk for developing pulmonary edema. In contrast, previously healthy patients in acute hemorrhagic shock,[69,73,75] or those not in shock but undergoing major surgical operations,[71,72,76–78] were found to have no difference in the prevalence of pulmonary edema when either crystalloids or colloids were used.

Although research has suggested that certain subgroups may be at greater risk for the development of pulmonary edema, considerable variance remains due to differences in physiologic endpoints, criteria for assessing pulmonary edema, and the existence or degree of shock. Velanovich,[79] in an effort to find a consensus among these divergent clinical trials, performed a meta-analysis comparing mortality rates after resuscitation with either crystalloid or colloid solutions. For patients resuscitated from trauma, the mortality rate was 12.3% lower in those receiving crystalloids. In contrast, patients receiving colloids for nontraumatic shock had a 7.8% survival advantage. It was concluded that the administration of crystalloids may be more efficacious than colloids in the resuscitation of shock due to trauma. The explanation offered for the ineffectiveness of colloids in trauma patients was that trauma causes an increase in pulmonary capillary permeability resulting in extravasation of these fluids into the lung interstitium, a finding supported by experimental data.[60]

In a similar analysis of randomized controlled trials involving patients with varying degrees of hypovolemia, Bisonni[80] found no correlation in overall mortality and the type of fluid used. To control for underlying pathological conditions, patients were subdivided for further analysis into three groups: 1) surgical stress, 2) hypovolemia, and 3) severe pulmonary edema. To address the influence of increased capillary permeability on outcome, group 2 (hypovolemia) was subcategorized into those patients without sepsis or pulmonary failure (group 2.1) and those with serious hypovolemic shock with complications such as sepsis or pulmonary failure (group 2.2). When mortality rates were compared within subgroups again, there were no significant differences between those patients receiving crystalloids versus those given colloids, although the sample sizes within these groups were relatively small. Patients administered colloids had a trend toward higher mortality rates as compared to those given crystalloids in all groups with the exception of the surgical stress group in which mortality was 50% lower with colloids. A secondary cost-effectiveness analysis revealed that the cost of using crystalloid was $43.13 per life saved, as opposed to $1493.60 per life saved with colloid. These estimates were based upon an average per-patient intake of 6.57 L of fluid for the crystalloid group, at a cost of $5.95/L, and an average of 230 gm of albumin in the colloid group, at a cost of $5.00/gm.

Given the dramatic difference in cost and the lack of a distinct advantage between the two fluid regimens, current practice favors crystalloids for initial resuscitation from all forms of hypovolemic shock.[61,63,81–83] Colloids should be considered in patients who are still hemodynamically unstable despite initial crystalloid administration. The American College of Surgeons Advanced Trauma

Life Support course,[59] recommends the rapid infusion of isotonic crystalloids for the initial fluid resuscitation of trauma patients. (See Table 18.4.)

Crystalloids

3. A large-bore IV catheter is inserted into B.J.'s upper extremity and STAT blood samples are sent for type and cross-match, CBC, prothrombin time (PT), partial thromboplastin time (PTT), and serum chemistry (BUN, creatinine, Na, K, Cl, and bicarbonate). Two liters of warmed lactated Ringer's solution are infused rapidly and the operating room is notified. B.J.'s systolic BP has increased to 90 mm Hg, although there is no evidence that the bleeding has stopped. A Foley catheter is inserted to measure urine output. Lactated Ringer's is continued, with 250–500 cc boluses ordered to be given every 10 minutes to maintain hemodynamic stability while waiting for fully cross-matched blood. How are crystalloids used in the setting of hemorrhagic shock? Is there an advantage to using lactated Ringer's solution over normal saline? (See Update for Optimal Timing of Fluid Resuscitation.)

Volume Requirements. Since isotonic crystalloids equilibrate rapidly between the interstitial and intravascular spaces at a ratio of 3:1, for every liter of fluid infused, approximately 750 mL will pass into the interstitium, while 250 mL will remain in the plasma. Depending upon their initial clinical presentation, patients may be categorized into various classes of hemorrhage. This classification can be used to estimate fluid and blood requirements. (See Table 18.2.) Based upon estimated blood loss, the "three-to-one rule" may be applied as a general guideline; for each 1 mL of blood loss, 3 mL of crystalloid is infused.[59] Since this determination of blood loss is based solely upon clinical assessment and not on quantitative measurements, treatment is best directed by the response to initial therapy rather than the initial classification. Close observation of hemodynamic status with consideration of the patient's age, particular injury, and prehospital fluid therapy is essential to avoid inadequate or excessive fluid administration and the development of pulmonary edema.

Indications that circulation is improving include normalization of the blood pressure, pulse pressure, and heart rate. Signs that actual organ perfusion is normalizing and that fluid resuscitation is adequate include improvements in mental status, warmth and color of skin, improved acid-base balance, and increased urinary output. A urine output of approximately 50 mL/hour in an adult is a fairly reliable indicator of adequate volume replacement. Persistent metabolic acidosis in a normothermic shock patient usually indicates the need for additional fluid resuscitation; sodium bicarbonate is not recommended unless the pH is less than 7.2.[59]

A safe and effective approach for using crystalloids in the resuscitation of patients in hemorrhagic shock is to rapidly infuse 250 to 500 mL every 10 to 15 minutes. Between boluses, fluids are slowed to maintenance rates (150 to 200 mL/hour), with ongoing evaluation of the patient's physiologic response for signs of continued blood loss or inadequate perfusion which would indicate the need for additional volume replacement.

Lactated Ringer's (LR)/Normal Saline (NS)

The American College of Surgeons Committee on Trauma recommends lactated Ringer's solution as the fluid of choice for the initial resuscitation of trauma patients and normal saline as the second choice.[59] Since NS has a high chloride content (45 mEq more than LR), it may potentially cause hyperchloremic acidosis, thereby worsening the tissue acidosis that occurs in the setting of hypovolemic shock. This likelihood is increased with impaired renal function. Lactated Ringer's, in contrast, is a buffered solution designed to simulate the intravascular plasma electrolyte concentration. It contains 28 mEq/L of lactate which is metabolized to bicarbonate in patients with normal circulation and intact liver

Table 18.4		Inotropic Agents and Vasopressors							
		Receptor Specificity			Pharmacological Effect[e]				
Drug	Usual Dose (IV Infusion)	α	β₁	β₂	VD	VC	INT	CHT	Usual Infusion Concentration
Amrinone[a]	0.75 mg/kg bolus, then 5–20 µg/kg/min	—	—	—	+	—	+++	+	
Dobutamine[a]	2.5–15 µg/kg/min	+	+++	++	++	—	+++	+	1000–2000 µg/mL
Dopamine	0.5–2 µg/kg/min[b] (renal)	—	—	—	—[b]	—	—	—	800–1600 µg/mL
	2–5 µg/kg/min	—	+	—	—[b]	+	+	+	
	5–10 µg/kg/min	+	++	—	—[b]	++	++	++	
	15–20 µg/kg/min	+++	++	—	—[b]	+++	++	++	
Epinephrine[c]	0.01–0.1 µg/kg/min	+	+++	++	++	—	+++	++	4–8 µg/mL
	0.1 µg/kg/min	+++	++	++	—	+++	++	++	
Isoproterenol	0.01–0.1 µg/kg/min	—	++++	+++	+++	—	+++	+++	4–8 µg/mL
Norepinephrine	2–10 µg/min (0.5–1 µg/kg/min) Highly variable; titrate to SBP[e] 90–100 mm Hg	++++	++	—	—	++++	+[d]	+	16–32 µg/mL
Phenylephrine	20–200 µg/min Highly variable; titrate to effect	+++	—	—	—	+++	—	—	40–80 µg/mL

[a] Dobutamine and amrinone have more inotropic effect than dopamine. Amrinone onset 3–10 min, duration 1 hr.

[b] Dopamine at 0.5–2 µg/kg/min stimulates dopaminergic receptors causing vasodilation in the splanchnic and renal vasculature.

[c] Epinephrine has predominant inotropic effects; norepinephrine has predominant vasoconstrictive effect. Epinephrine may vasodilate at low dose, vasoconstrict at high doses.

[d] Cardiac output unchanged or may decline due to reflex vagal responses that slow the heart.

[e] CHT = Chronotropic; INT = Inotropic; SBP = Systolic blood pressure; VC = Peripheral vascular vasoconstriction; VD = Peripheral vascular vasodilation.

function.[62] In situations in which hepatic perfusion is reduced (≤20% of normal), or there is hepatocellular damage, lactate clearance may be significantly decreased, particularly in combination with hypoxia (O_2 saturation ≤50% of normal).[84] In patients with shock and those undergoing cardiopulmonary bypass during surgery, the half-life of lactate, normally 20 minutes, increases to four to six hours and eight hours, respectively.[85,86] Since unmetabolized lactate can be converted to lactic acid, prolonged infusion of Ringer's lactate may cause tissue acidosis in predisposed patients. In actuality, however, no differences in serum pH, electrolytes, lactate, or survival have been found in patients with hemorrhagic trauma who have received either LR or NS.[87–89] In practice, normal saline and Ringer's lactate typically are used interchangeably, since neither solution appears to be superior to the other.

Hypertonic Saline

4. What is the role of hypertonic saline in the setting of hemorrhagic shock?

The use of hypertonic saline (with and without dextran) for resuscitation in hemorrhagic shock has been studied extensively in animal models,[61,63,81] and more recently has been the focus of clinical research.[90–92] The advantage of hypertonic saline as a resuscitative fluid is the smaller volume of fluid required to expand the intravascular compartment as compared with isotonic solutions, which in the prehospital setting is significant, given the large volumes of fluids necessary to keep up with on-going blood loss.

With a high concentration of sodium, hypertonic saline exerts an osmotic effect, translocating fluid from the interstitial and cellular compartments to the intravascular space. Consequently, plasma volume is rapidly expanded to a greater extent than similar volumes of crystalloid solutions, and systemic blood pressure, cardiac output, and oxygen transport are readily increased. Hypertonic saline also has been shown to improve myocardial contractility, cause peripheral vasodilation, and redistribute blood flow preferentially to the splanchnic and renal circulation. In addition, intracranial pressure is reduced, which may be a potential advantage in trauma patients with concomitant head injury.[61,63,81,90–92]

Mattox et al.,[91] in a multicenter trial of hypotensive trauma patients, evaluated hypertonic saline-dextran [7.5% sodium chloride in 6% dextran 70 (HSD)] versus isotonic crystalloid solution for prehospital resuscitation. Patients were randomly given 250 mL of either HSD or a standard isotonic solution, after which fluids were given as necessary to achieve stabilization. There were no differences in overall survival; however, there was a significant survival advantage in the HSD group requiring surgery. Fewer complications occurred in the HSD group, including a lower incidence of adult respiratory distress syndrome, renal failure, and coagulopathy. Although serum sodium levels were significantly higher in HSD group, there were no adverse clinical symptoms of hypernatremia.

In a similar prospective, randomized trial, Younes et al.,[92] compared the effects of resuscitation with 250 mL volumes of either hypertonic saline (7.5%), hypertonic saline-dextran (HSD), or normal saline in trauma patients admitted to the emergency room in hypovolemic shock. Following the initial 250 mL bolus, normal saline and blood were given as needed until the systolic pressure was higher than 100 mg Hg. There were no significant differences in overall mortality or complication rates in the three groups. In comparison to isotonic saline, however, the hypertonic solutions significantly improved mean arterial pressure and significantly decreased the volume of fluid required to restore systolic pressure.

These clinical trials suggest that hypertonic saline may be safe and effective for the initial resuscitation of hemorrhagic shock.

Further study is needed, however, to establish a substantial benefit before these fluids may be considered for widespread clinical use.

Blood Replacement

5. B.J. has required 4 L of LR to maintain hemodynamic stability. While his BP is currently 90/72 mm Hg, it continues to decline without bolus therapy, and he remains tachycardic (114/min) and tachypneic (32/min). He is becoming more confused and combative, and a blood gas reveals a metabolic acidosis with a pH of 7.29. Urine output has been 10 cc over the last 45 minutes. A STAT CBC before fluid resuscitation revealed a hematocrit (Hct) of 24% and a hemoglobin (Hgb) of 8 gm/dL. Two units of packed red blood cells (RBCs), now available, are transfused and B.J. is transported to the operating room for surgery. What are the indications for blood transfusion in hemorrhagic shock? What potential complications should be anticipated?

The conventional approach to the transfusion of critically ill patients has been to maintain the hemoglobin above 10 gm/dL or the hematocrit above 30%. This commonly-used "transfusion trigger" is not only misleading, since in acute hemorrhage the actual degree of blood loss is not accurately reflected by these values, it also does not take into account the body's ability to compensate for the loss of oxygen-carrying capacity. A normal hematocrit (or Hgb concentration) in the setting of hemorrhagic shock does not rule out significant blood loss or indicate adequacy of transfusion. This is because it takes at least 24 hours for all fluid compartments to come to equilibrium. Only when equilibrium has been reached can these measures be used reliably to gauge blood loss. On the other hand, if cardiopulmonary function is normal and if volume status is maintained, an increase in cardiac output can compensate for a reduction in hemoglobin (O_2 content) to a certain degree.[81,83,93] (See Figure 18.4.)

Since inadequacy of tissue perfusion, and hence oxygen delivery, is the primary abnormality in shock, the need for transfusion therapy is more accurately determined by the patient's oxygen demand, rather than an arbitrary hematocrit or hemoglobin value. Various measures may be employed to determine the adequacy of oxygen supply to the tissues, including oxygen delivery (DO_2), oxygen consumption (VO_2), and mixed venous tension (PvO_2). Although these values may be calculated by use of a pulmonary artery catheter and arterial and venous blood samples, for practical purposes, the patient's response to initial fluid resuscitation and clinical signs of inadequate tissue perfusion are the primary determinants for blood transfusion.[59,81,83,93] Patients who do not respond to initial volume resuscitation or who transiently respond but remain tachycardic, tachypneic, and oliguric, clearly are underperfused and will likely require blood transfusion.[59]

Hypothermia, immune hemolysis, and transfusion-transmitted diseases are all significant complications of transfusions which the clinician should consider. Massive transfusion of refrigerated banked blood impairs metabolism, increases the affinity of hemoglobin for oxygen, causes the release of potassium from red blood cells, and may result in life-threatening ventricular arrhythmias. Therefore, warmed blood is recommended in patients requiring massive transfusions.[94,95] Massive transfusion is variously defined as the replacement of one and one-half times the circulating blood volume or 5 U of blood within one hour, or the transfusion of 100% of the patient's blood volume or 10 U of blood within 24 hours.[69] Hemolytic transfusion reactions are the most common cause of acute fatalities from blood transfusions.[96] Astute recognition of the signs and symptoms of a reaction such as anxiety, pain at infusion site, fever, hypotension, tachycardia, hemolysis, and hemoglobinuria can prevent unnecessary morbidity and mortality. With the exception of albumin and gamma globulin, all blood components can transmit infectious diseases, the most frequent and serious of which is non-A, non-B hepatitis.[83,93] (See Chapter 68: Human Immunodeficiency Virus (HIV) Infection for additional information.)

Acid-base imbalances and electrolyte abnormalities may be problematic in patients with profound liver disease or acute heart failure. In these patients, the metabolism of citrate, which has been added to stored blood to bind calcium and prevent its clotting may be impaired. This can bind the patient's calcium as well resulting in low calcium levels which may aggravate cardiac function. Citrate also lowers the pH of banked blood and may worsen the lactic acidosis present in patients with severe, unresponsive shock. Potassium concentrations in stored blood usually do not exceed 7 mEq/U. In a hypoperfused, extremely acidotic patient, rapid transfusion may result in hyperkalemia, but hypokalemia is actually more common secondary to alkalosis from the metabolism of citrate to bicarbonate. Levels of 2,3-DPG (diphosphoglycerate) in stored blood also can be depressed, impairing tissue oxygenation; however, the clinical significance of this appears to be minor.[83,93]

Hemostatic abnormalities, specifically coagulopathies and thrombocytopenia, may be transiently related to dilution from administration of large volumes of crystalloids, colloids, or banked blood, but are more likely to be due to the extent of injury and the development of disseminated intravascular coagulopathy.[97] Banked whole blood contains sufficient coagulation factors (including labile factors V and VIII) to maintain hemostasis during the life span of the unit; however, it does not contain platelets because they do not survive the temperatures required for red blood cell storage. Contrary to previous recommendations, there is no evidence to support routine prophylactic transfusions of platelets and fresh frozen plasma (FFP) to replenish clotting factors after fixed volumes of blood have been given. Rather, the presence of risk factors for bleeding (e.g., prolonged shock, large wounds, head injuries) and the results of coagulation tests and platelet counts should dictate the use of these products.[97,98] Typically, thrombocytopenia and coagulation defects are insignificant until 1.5 to 2 times the blood volume has been replaced.[98,99]

The use of whole blood as opposed to packed RBCs is controversial. Except for cases in which a coagulopathy clearly warrants the addition of plasma to red cells, there appears to be no advantage to whole blood since volume expansion is as effective with the combination of packed cells plus crystalloids or colloids.[8,81,83,93]

Packed RBCs would be an appropriate blood replacement product for B.J. His PT, PTT, platelets, electrolytes, and mixed venous blood gases, if available should be monitored frequently. These tests will enable correction of any coagulopathy or electrolyte abnormality as well as assist in the assessment of the adequacy of tissue oxygenation. This information, in addition to the aforementioned factors, can be used to gauge his response to therapy and his need for supplemental blood products such as platelets and frozen fresh plasma.

Postoperative Hypovolemia

Hypovolemia versus Pump Failure

6. J.S., a 62-year-old male, has been admitted to ICU following surgical repair of an abdominal aortic aneurysm. He is intubated and receiving 60% oxygen. He weighs 78 kg and has a BSA of 1.8 m². He has a history of hypertension (BP 140/100 mm Hg) for which he takes nadolol (Corgard) and hydrochlorothiazide. His ABGs are adequate and he is receiving 150 mL/hr of Lactated Ringer's solution intravenously. His initial and 2-hour postoperative hemodynamic profiles are as follows: BP (S/D/M) 90/50/63 mm Hg (130/78/95); pulse 88 beats/min (80); CO 4 L/min (5); RAP 3 mm Hg (6);

PCWP 8 mm Hg (12); SVR 1200 dyne·sec·cm⁻⁵ (1392); urine output 25 mL/hr (70); temperature 37 °C (34); Hct 32% (30). Based upon the hemodynamic profile, determine whether J.S. is hypovolemic or experiencing pump failure.

Most of J.S.'s hemodynamic changes are consistent with hypovolemia. These include a drop in blood pressure, cardiac output, PCWP, and urine output. The decrease in pulmonary capillary wedge pressure suggests that preload is reduced resulting in a lower cardiac output. Urine output has declined and probably reflects a compensatory drop in renal perfusion to preserve intravascular volume. The pulse pressure is narrowed suggesting blood flow has decreased. [Changes in pulse pressure correlate with changes in SV in individual patients (i.e., as pulse pressure narrows, SV decreases).] The lack of a significant increase in heart rate as well as a decrease in systemic vascular resistance are not consistent with hypovolemia. However, nadolol, a long-acting beta blocker, may have prevented a reflex increase in heart rate, and an increase in body temperature may account for the decrease in systemic vascular resistance. As the body temperature rises postoperatively, vasodilation decreases systemic vascular resistance and increases the intravascular space. If intravascular volume is inadequate and increased sympathetic tone cannot generate a sufficient cardiac output, mean blood pressure falls. The most likely explanation for the hemodynamic change in J.S. is hypovolemia, although he also should be evaluated for the occurrence of a perioperative cardiac event. Arterial blood gases should be checked to assess oxygen requirements.

Causes

7. What are the most likely causes of hypovolemia in J.S.?

Common causes of hypovolemia in surgical patients are postoperative bleeding, third-spacing, and temperature-related vasodilation. Postoperative bleeding may produce hypovolemia; however, J.S.'s initial and two-hour postoperative hematocrit of 30% and 32%, respectively, do not support bleeding as a cause.

Following major vascular or bowel surgery, it is not unusual for patients to "third space" significant amounts of intravascular volume. The bowel walls and interstitial space can sequester large amounts of fluids and this can produce a state of relative hypovolemia as is occurring with J.S. This is especially apparent for the first 12 to 24 hours following the surgical procedure. J.S. is receiving 150 mL/hour lactated Ringer's solution, but this is apparently not enough to maintain his intravascular volume.

Mild hypothermia is common during operative procedures. As patients warm up postoperatively, vasodilation occurs, expanding the intravascular space. If the amounts of intravenous fluids administered are insufficient to compensate for the increased venous capacitance, blood pressure and cardiac output will decline during the rewarming phase, which can range from one to two hours up to four to six hours. J.S. has rewarmed from 34 °C to 37 °C in two hours which is not unusual after a major operative procedure. His temperature could conceivably rise as high as 38 °C to 38.5 °C during the first 12 to 24 hours following surgery.

Other considerations include inadequate fluid administration during the operative procedure and the effects of drugs given in the operating room or in the immediate postoperative period (e.g., morphine sulfate and other narcotics which have systemic vasodilatory properties).

Volume Replacement and Ventricular Function

8. How will volume replacement improve J.S.'s CO and perfusion pressure?

Starling's mechanism indicates that the volume of blood returned to the heart is the main determinant of volume pumped by the heart. Therefore, as venous return is increased, the cardiac output also will increase within physiological limits. (See Figure 18.4.) The pulmonary capillary wedge pressure which approximates left ventricular end-diastolic volume can be used to assess venous return or preload to the left ventricle.

A ventricular function curve can be constructed by plotting a measure of cardiac pumping action (CO, SV, or LVWSI) against a measure of preload (PCWP). A change in preload will move the ventricular output upward or downward along a given curve. (See Figure 18.5.) Two hours following surgery, J.S.'s pulmonary capillary wedge pressure has fallen from 17 mm Hg to 8 mm Hg and his cardiac output has fallen from 5 L/minute to 4 L/minute. Therefore, additional volume replacement is warranted.

9. Left Ventricular Compliance. **J.S. is given a 250 mL bolus of NS over 10 minutes and this results in the following hemodynamic profile: blood pressure (S/D/M) 94/60/71 mm Hg; pulse 84 beats/min; CO 4.2 L/min; RAP 4 mm Hg; PCWP 9 mm Hg; SVR 1276 dyne·sec·cm^{-5}. Assess J.S.'s left ventricular compliance and his response to the fluid challenge.**

As previously discussed, the relationship between end-diastolic volume and end-diastolic pressure is a curvilinear function that describes compliance. In the case of J.S., since his pulmonary capillary wedge pressure did not change appreciably, it is impossible to accurately assess ventricular preload and compliance. However, for practical purposes, it can be assumed that a small change in pulmonary capillary wedge pressure in response to a volume challenge as in J.S., represents a ventricle on the flat portion of the ventricular function curve (see Figure 18.5). In contrast, a large change in pulmonary capillary wedge pressure in response to a fluid challenge represents a ventricle on the steep portion of the curve. Additional fluid therapy given to these patients may increase their risk for pulmonary edema without improving cardiac output. In J.S., the change in PCWP from 8 mm Hg to 9 mm Hg is insignificant; thus, it is reasonable to administer more fluid to enhance cardiac output.

10. Fluid Challenge. **Twenty minutes after the 250 mL NS bolus, J.S.'s hemodynamic profile has not changed significantly. ABGs are acceptable and LR solution is infusing at 200 mL/hr. J.S. is continuing to "third-space" intravascular volume. Based upon this information, develop guidelines for additional fluid challenges in J.S.**

Acceptable guidelines for the administration of additional fluid challenges to hypovolemic patients are based upon the direction and degree of changes in the various hemodynamic parameters in response to a fluid load rather than their absolute values. These include the right atrial pressure, pulmonary capillary wedge pressure, cardiac output, and blood pressure. Using the PCWP as a guide, an increase in the PCWP of ≤5 mm Hg after a 250 to 500 cc fluid challenge over ten minutes implies the left ventricle is still functioning on the flat portion of the volume-pressure curve. If the baseline pulmonary capillary wedge pressure remains below 15 mm Hg, further fluid boluses may be given as necessary until the PCWP increases by an amount ≥5 mm Hg, at which point the left ventricle may be approaching the steep portion of the curve. If the pulmonary capillary wedge pressure rises abruptly as fluid is given, with a small change in CO, the flat portion of the ventricular function curve has been reached and the intravenous infusion rate should be slowed. If signs and symptoms of inadequate tissue perfusion fail to improve or worsen and if the PCWP remains above 18 to 20 mm Hg, fluid challenges should be stopped and inotropic therapy initiated.[100] J.S. is on the lower end of the curve and needs additional normal saline fluid boluses over ten minutes every 10 to 15 minutes until the cardiac output and pulmonary capillary

wedge pressure are sufficient to maintain an acceptable blood pressure and urine output (0.5 mL/kg/hour).

Generally, most critically ill patients require a cardiac index greater than 2.5 L/minute/m^2 and a PCWP of 8 to 18 mm Hg to maintain acceptable mean arterial pressures of 65 to 75 mm Hg.[101] Ordinarily, it would be reasonable to maintain a mean arterial pressure higher than 75 mm Hg since J.S. has a history of high blood pressure; however, this is not advisable in J.S.'s case since it is important to avoid increased arterial pressures which may jeopardize the aneurysm repair.

11. J.S. has received a total of 3.5 L normal saline in boluses over the last 6 hours and remains hemodynamically unchanged. His urine output has averaged 25 cc/hr for the last 4 hours, indicating volume replacement is inadequate. Given his age and the lack of response to initial crystalloid administration, the decision is made to infuse 500 mL of 6% hetastarch over the next 30 minutes. How does hetastarch compare to human serum albumin as a volume expander for J.S.?

Albumin is the predominant protein in the plasma and accounts for approximately 75% of the colloid oncotic pressure,[62,63,102] the force which maintains fluid in the intravascular space. Human serum albumin is the colloidal agent against which all others are compared for volume-expanding properties. It is prepared commercially from pooled donor plasma which is heat-treated to eliminate the potential for disease transmission. Upon infusion, 5% albumin increases plasma volume by approximately one-half the volume infused, or 18 mL/gm,[62] with a duration of action of 24 hours.[81,103] Substantial side effects primarily involve transient clotting abnormalities[104] and the occurrence of anaphylactic reactions (0.5%),[105] both of which are rare.[63] Albumin is available as a 5% solution which is isotonic with the plasma, and a 25% solution which is hypertonic, and most useful in correcting hypoproteinemia or intravascular hypovolemia in patients with excess interstitial water.

Hetastarch, or hydroxyethyl starch (HES), is a synthetic colloid made from amylopectin which closely resembles human serum albumin but is considerably less expensive. Available as a 6% solution in normal saline, HES expands the plasma volume by an amount equal to the volume infused, with a duration of action of 24 to 48 hours.[106,107] Hetastarch generally is well tolerated with a low incidence of side effects and allergic reactions.[105] Dose-related reductions in platelet count and transient increases in prothrombin time and partial thromboplastin time have been reported with moderate infusions of HES (<1500 mL/day) and are significant with larger volumes.[108] In addition, factor VIII levels are lowered, beyond that which can be attributed to hemodilution. This places patients with Von Willebrand's disease at greater risk of bleeding.[109]

Numerous clinical studies have compared albumin and hetastarch for fluid resuscitation in shock and nonshock patients. Puri et al.,[68] reported that HES was as effective as albumin in restoring hemodynamic stability and improving oxygen delivery in patients given comparable amounts of either fluid over 24 hours. Other studies in hypovolemic patients have reported no difference in hemodynamic parameters when similar volumes of either HES or albumin were given as serial boluses to maintain cardiac output and ventricular filling pressures.[65,103,110] In postoperative cardiac surgery patients, HES and albumin were found to be equally efficacious in restoring volume status and maintaining hemodynamic stability.[106,107]

In summary, resuscitation with moderate volumes of hetastarch is safe and hemodynamically equivalent to albumin. Either 5% albumin or 6% HES would be acceptable for intravascular volume expansion in J.S.

Cardiogenic Shock

Postoperative Cardiac Failure

Assessment by Hemodynamic Profile

12. R.G., a 62-year-old male, has undergone 4-vessel coronary artery bypass graft surgery and is now in the ICU. Vital signs are stable with a mean arterial pressure of 90 mm Hg. His body weight is 74 kg and his BSA is 1.7 m². R.G. has a past medical history of two MIs 6 months and 5 years before admission; unstable angina; and hypertension. R.G.'s medications include nitroglycerin (NTG), metoprolol (Lopressor), and hydrochlorothiazide. Past surgical history includes a 3-vessel CABG 4 years before admission. One hour after admission to the ICU, R.G's blood pressure has fallen. He has the following hemodynamic profile: BP (S/D/M) 90/50/63 mm Hg; pulse 110 beats/min; CO 2.8 L/min; CI 1.65 L/min/m²; RAP 12 mm Hg; PCWP 22 mm Hg; SVR 1457 dyne·sec·cm⁻⁵; PaO_2 110 mm Hg; $PaCO_2$ 28 mm Hg; pH 7.32; HCO_3 20 mEq/L; respiratory rate (IMV) 26/min; urine output 25 mL/hr; temperature 36 °C; Hct 35% (stable). IV fluid infusion is 150 mL/hr 5% dextrose/0.45% NS. What is your assessment of R.G.'s hemodynamic profile? Is he hypovolemic or experiencing cardiac failure?

R.G.'s rapid pulse, low urine output, and low mean arterial pressure could indicate volume depletion. However, the elevated PCWP and decreased CO in the presence of a low mean arterial pressure and declining urine output suggest heart failure. The chest x-ray and breath sounds should be evaluated for signs of pulmonary edema. The low cardiac index of 1.65 L/minute/m², in the presence of a PCWP greater than 18 mm Hg, can be a poor prognostic sign.[27,113] A pulmonary capillary wedge pressure greater than 18 mm Hg is associated with pulmonary edema and a cardiac index of less than 2.2 L/minute/m² is indicative of hypoperfusion.

R.G. has a cardiac index of 1.65 L/minute/m², pulmonary capillary wedge pressure of 22 mm Hg, stroke volume of 25 mL/beat, and he is hypotensive; all of these are consistent with acute cardiac failure. R.G. has a PaO_2 of 110 mm Hg, a $PaCO_2$ of 28, and a pH of 7.32 while breathing at 26 breaths/minute. This indicates that R.G. has a metabolic acidosis with respiratory compensation. The metabolic acidosis is most likely due to his poor systemic perfusion indicated by a low CI, hypotension, and decreased urine output. Construction of a ventricular function curve with cardiac index as a measure of myocardial performance and pulmonary capillary wedge pressure as a measure of preload, shows that R.G. is on the flat portion of a depressed curve (see Figure 18.6). Whether the

elevated pulmonary capillary wedge pressure is indicative of increased ventricular volume or decreased ventricular compliance cannot be ascertained from the above data.

It appears that R.G. is in acute heart failure following cardiac surgery [coronary artery bypass graft (CABG)]. An ECG and serial blood samples for analysis of cardiac enzymes should be obtained to rule out a perioperative myocardial infarction. The hematocrit and other signs of postoperative bleeding also should be checked.

Therapeutic Interventions

13. The chest x-ray confirms the presence of mild pulmonary edema and fine rales were heard throughout the lower half of lung fields on auscultation. The ECG shows ST-T wave changes, but there is no indication of an acute MI. Cardiac enzymes are pending. Blood pressure and CO need to be improved to increase perfusion to vital organs. What therapeutic options are available to achieve this goal? How would these choices affect R.G.'s ventricular function curve?

Three therapeutic interventions are available: fluid challenge, vasodilators, and inotropic agents.

Fluid Challenge (Preload Increase). Augmentation of preload with a fluid challenge to improve cardiac output is the first option. However, R.G.'s pulmonary capillary wedge pressure is already 22 mm Hg and increasing this value above 18 to 20 mm Hg usually does not result in further benefit.[27,113] Furthermore, R.G. has signs of pulmonary edema on chest x-ray and his PaO_2 is 110 mm Hg on 60% FiO_2. Therefore, elevation of intravascular volume may increase the pulmonary vascular hydrostatic pressure and worsen his pulmonary edema. If a fluid challenge is attempted to enhance preload, no more than 100 mL normal saline should be given without repeating the hemodynamic measurements. If the pulmonary capillary wedge pressure rises, but the cardiac output does not improve, fluid challenges should be discontinued. Elevating the preload without appreciably improving cardiac output also can increase left ventricular wall tension, which is a major determinant of myocardial oxygen consumption; consequently, myocardial ischemia could develop.

Vasodilators (Afterload Reduction). A peripheral vasodilator also may be used. This will decrease pulmonary venous congestion by reducing preload (PCWP), and thus pulmonary vascular hydrostatic pressure, as well as improve cardiac output by decreasing the resistance to ventricular ejection. In the presence of myocardial ischemia, a reduction of the left ventricular filling pressure may improve subendocardial blood flow, reduce the myocardial wall tension, and reduce the left ventricular radius. The net effect is an improvement in the myocardial oxygen supply/demand ratio.[114–116] In individuals without cardiac failure, blood pressure primarily is maintained by systemic vascular tone, and the left ventricle operates on the steep ascending limb of the Starling curve. Therefore, any reduction of aortic impedance is of little importance in improving cardiac output.[54] However, in patients with left ventricular failure, arterial resistance is elevated due to a reflex increase in sympathetic tone in response to a fall in systemic arterial pressure. In left ventricular failure, cardiac output becomes increasingly dependent upon resistance to outflow from the left ventricle.[54] Lowering the systemic vascular resistance will shift the ventricular function curve up and to the left, depending upon whether an arterial, venous, or mixed vasodilator is used, thereby improving cardiac performance at a lower filling pressure (see Figure 18.6).

R.G. appears to have left ventricular failure with elevations in pulmonary capillary wedge pressure and systemic vascular resistance. These are the hemodynamic variables which usually are predictive of a beneficial response to vasodilator therapy.[114,117] However, the major risk of vasodilator therapy in R.G. is further reduction of an already low mean arterial pressure. This could re-

Fig 18.6   Ventricular Function Curve for R.G.

duce coronary pressure and thereby exacerbate or produce myocardial ischemia in addition to decreasing perfusion to other vital organ systems. Vasodilator therapy should be reserved for situations in which hemodynamic monitoring shows the patient to have left ventricular failure with elevations in PCWP, SVR and a systolic BP greater than 100.

Inotropic Support. A rapid-acting inotropic agent also can be used to increase myocardial contractility and cardiac output. This intervention shifts the ventricular function curve upward and slightly to the left (see Figure 18.6). The disadvantage of this intervention is that improved cardiac output is accompanied by an increased myocardial oxygen demand. Depending upon the agent selected, three of the determinants of myocardial oxygen consumption could be elevated: heart rate, contractility, and ventricular wall tension. Inotropic support, therefore, is directed at establishing or maintaining a reasonable arterial pressure and ensuring adequate tissue perfusion by improving the cardiac output.

In summary, the most appropriate therapeutic intervention for R.G. at this time would be inotropic support. The pulmonary capillary wedge pressure is elevated suggesting that the preload has been maximized; therefore, fluid boluses may worsen R.G.'s pulmonary edema. Although R.G.'s systemic vascular resistance is slightly elevated (1457 dyne·sec·cm^{-5}), his blood pressure is low; therefore, initial use of a peripheral vasodilator may jeopardize coronary perfusion. Thus, an acceptable initial therapeutic intervention to improve cardiac output, tissue perfusion, and renal blood flow is inotropic support. After a reasonable blood pressure has been established, addition of a peripheral vasodilator may be considered to further enhance cardiac output if needed.

14. Dopamine. Hydrochloride is prescribed for R.G. What hemodynamic changes would you anticipate?

Dopamine, a precursor of norepinephrine, has inotropic, chronotropic, and vasoactive properties, all of which are dose dependent.[28,118–123] (See Table 18.4.) At 0.5 to 2 μg/kg/minute, dopamine stimulates dopaminergic receptors in primarily the splanchnic, renal, and coronary vascular beds, producing vasodilation, improved blood flow, and natriuresis.[119,124,125] The effect on dopaminergic receptors is not blocked by beta blockers, but is antagonized by dopaminergic-blocking agents such as the butyrophenones and phenothiazines.[119,120] Depending upon the clinical state of the patient, low doses of dopamine may slightly increase myocardial contractility but usually will not alter heart rate or systemic vascular resistance significantly.

At 2 to 5 μg/kg/minute, the improved cardiac performance produced by dopamine is through direct stimulation of β_1-adrenergic receptors, and indirectly through release of norepinephrine from nerve terminals.[28,118–123] Increased β_1-adrenergic receptor stimulation increases stroke volume, heart rate, and cardiac output. This effect can be blocked by beta blockers.

At infusion rates of 5 to 10 μg/kg/minute, the α-adrenergic receptors are activated. At this dosage, the vasoactive effects on peripheral blood vessels are unpredictable and dependent upon the net effect of β_1-adrenergic stimulation, α-adrenergic stimulation, and reflex mechanisms.[28,119–123,126] Mean arterial pressure and pulmonary capillary wedge pressure usually will rise.[126,127]

At doses greater than 15 to 20 μg/kg/minute, dopamine primarily stimulates peripheral α-adrenergic receptors. Systemic vascular resistance increases, splanchnic and renal blood flow decreases, and left ventricular filling pressure is raised. Cardiac irritability is not unusual and the overall myocardial oxygen consumption is increased.[28,54,118–123,127] The increase in systemic vascular resistance limits cardiac output; thus, infusion rates should be limited to less than 10 to 15 μg/kg/minute.

15. How would you initiate a dopamine infusion in R.G.? What therapeutic goals should be accomplished and over what time period? What are the adverse effects associated with dopamine administration?

R.G. has a mean arterial pressure of 63 mm Hg, a cardiac index of 1.65 L/minute/m^2, a PCWP of 22 mm Hg, and a heart rate of 110 beats/minute. A reasonable initial infusion rate would be 3 μg/kg/minute. This dose should increase cardiac contraction and cardiac output resulting in an increase in renal blood flow. The goal of therapy is to increase the cardiac index to at least 2.5 L/minute/m^2, maintain a mean arterial pressure of at least 70 mm Hg (preferably closer to 80 mm Hg depending upon clinical signs of hypoperfusion), reduce the pulmonary capillary wedge pressure, and maintain a heart rate of less than 125 beats/minute. A urine output of at least 0.5 mL/kg/hour (37 mL/hour in R.G.) is desirable. Since the onset of action is within minutes, the patient can be reevaluated and the infusion rate can be titrated upwards by 1 to 2 μg/kg/minute every ten minutes depending upon the hemodynamic data obtained. The rate should not exceed 10 μg/kg/minute because increased left ventricular filling pressures which could exacerbate pulmonary edema can be seen at this dose.[128] The hemodynamic response to dopamine is highly variable among patients; thus, careful titration to lowest effective infusion rate is advised.

Adverse effects that can be encountered with dopamine infusion include increased heart rate, anginal pain, arrhythmias, headache, hypertension, vasoconstriction, nausea, and vomiting. Extravasation of large amounts of dopamine during infusion can cause ischemic necrosis and sloughing. At higher doses, α_1-adrenergic effects are more prominent causing peripheral arterial vasoconstriction and an increase in venous pressures which lead to increasing afterload, preload, myocardial oxygen demand, and ischemia.

16. *Effect on Hemodynamics.* Dopamine is initiated at 3 μg/kg/min in R.G. and titrated to 8 μg/kg/min over the next 2 hours. A repeat chest x-ray shows slight worsening of pulmonary edema. The following hemodynamic profile is obtained (previous values are in parentheses): BP (S/D/M) 115/62/80 mm Hg (90/50/63); pulse 140 beats/min (110); CO 3.8 L/min (2.8); CI 2.2 L/min/m^2 (1.65); RAP 10 mm Hg (12); PCWP 20 mm Hg (22); SVR 1473 dyne·sec·cm^{-5} (1457); urine output 30 mL/hr (25); temperature 37 °C (36); Hct 36% (35). Analyze the hemodynamic effects dopamine has produced in R.G.

Dopamine at 8 μg/kg/minute has established a trend in the desired direction for cardiac index; however, the heart rate has increased significantly. The systemic vascular resistance and pulmonary capillary wedge pressure have not changed appreciably, and the urine flow has increased. Further analysis reveals that the stroke volume (CO/HR) has only increased from 25 mL/beat to 27 mL/beat; thus, the major increase in cardiac output has resulted from the chronotropic rather than the inotropic effect of dopamine. The dopamine has most likely affected the myocardial oxygen supply/demand ratio adversely; however, this is difficult to assess. R.G. should be monitored closely for signs of myocardial ischemia.

17. Dobutamine. The clinician decides that a heart rate of 140 beats/min is unacceptable in R.G. who has a history of MI. Attempts to taper the dopamine to lessen the induced tachycardia without dropping the CI and perfusion pressure have been unsuccessful. Dobutamine is suggested as an alternative to dopamine. What hemodynamic changes would you expect with dobutamine in R.G.? Does dobutamine offer any advantages over dopamine? How would you initiate therapy with dobutamine? What are the adverse effects associated with dobutamine?

Dobutamine, a synthetic catecholamine, is a potent positive inotrope with predominant direct β_1-agonist effects, and weaker β_2

and α_1 effects. With greater β_2 vasodilatory than α_1 vasoconstrictive actions, dobutamine produces substantial reductions in systemic and pulmonary vascular resistances. The reduction in systemic vascular resistance also may be due to a reflex decrease in vasoconstriction secondary to enhanced cardiac output. Phenoxybenzamine blocks the α-adrenergic response and propranolol blocks the β_2 response. Unlike dopamine, dobutamine does not release endogenous norepinephrine or stimulate renal dopaminergic receptors.[28,120–123]

Several studies are available assessing the hemodynamic changes induced by dobutamine in cardiac failure patients.[127–131] The results of these studies demonstrate consistent increases in cardiac output and stroke volume, with reductions in PCWP and systemic vascular resistance. The reduction in filling pressures, as indicated by a lowered pulmonary capillary wedge pressure, results in a decrease in left ventricular wall tension and oxygen consumption. Consequently, there is improvement in coronary perfusion pressure, a major determinant of coronary blood flow, and thus, the oxygen supply to the heart (see Glossary for definition). In comparison to dopamine, dobutamine tends to induce less tachycardia. This feature, combined with the reductions in pulmonary capillary wedge pressure and systemic vascular pressure, in addition to the increased perfusion pressure, tends to reduce *overall* myocardial oxygen consumption.

Compared to dopamine, dobutamine has equal or greater inotropic action. Dobutamine lowers pulmonary capillary wedge pressure and systemic vascular resistance with increasing doses, whereas dopamine may increase pulmonary capillary wedge pressure and systemic vascular resistance with increasing doses. The effect on heart rate is variable; however, evidence suggests that dobutamine is less chronotropic than dopamine at lower infusion rates. In the clinical setting, dobutamine may be preferred in patients with depressed cardiac output, elevated pulmonary capillary wedge pressure, and increased systemic vascular resistance with mild hypotension. The increase in cardiac output may not be sufficient to raise the blood pressure in a patient who initially is moderately to severely hypotensive. Thus, dopamine may be preferred in the patient with depressed cardiac output, normal or moderately elevated pulmonary capillary wedge pressure, and moderate or severe hypotension.[19,28,120,121,123,132]

Dobutamine is a better choice than dopamine for R.G. since his initial baseline hemodynamic measurements showed a depressed cardiac index, elevated pulmonary capillary wedge pressure, and increased systemic vascular resistance. Dobutamine also may be less chronotropic, but the response is unpredictable. Although dobutamine's positive inotropic and chronotropic effects can increase myocardial oxygen consumption, the increase will not be to the same degree as with dopamine, and the decrease in pulmonary capillary wedge pressure and systemic vascular resistance ultimately will produce a more favorable effect.

Dobutamine should be started at a low dose, (i.e., 2.5 μg/kg/minute). The onset of effect is rapid and the half-life short (≈ 2 minutes) with steady state generally achieved within ten minutes of initiation of therapy. This allows for dose titration every ten minutes based upon patient tolerance. The rate of infusion required to increase cardiac output typically is between 2.5 to 10 μg/kg/minute, although higher infusion rates are sometimes required (i.e., up to 20 μg/kg/minute).[121,133]

Adverse effects that may occur during dobutamine administration are sinus tachycardia, premature ventricular contractions, nausea, anxiety, and tremors. Dobutamine also has been shown to potentiate hypokalemia.[134] In the presence of significant coronary artery disease, dobutamine-induced inotropy and increased heart rate can lead to increased oxygen demand and, therefore, precipitate myocardial ischemia.[135,136] Another limiting factor to dobutamine is tolerance to its hemodynamic effects with long-term continuous use. A statistically significant decline in cardiac output, systolic interval time, and heart rate has been seen after 72 to 96 hours of continuous infusion and is most likely due to down regulation of β_1 receptors.[137,138]

18. *Effects on Hemodynamics.* **Dobutamine is initiated and titrated up to 7.5 μg/kg/min. Concurrently, the dopamine is tapered down to 2.0 μg/kg/min resulting in the following hemodynamic profile (previous values in parentheses): BP (S/D/M) 122/60/80 mm Hg (115/62/80); pulse 115 beats/min (140); CO 4.2 L/min (3.8); CI 2.5 L/min (2.2); RAP 10 mm Hg (10); PCWP 16 mm Hg (20); SVR 1333 dyne·sec·m^{-5} (1473); PaO$_2$ 115 (110) mm Hg; PaCO$_2$ 38 (28) mm Hg; pH 7.41 (7.32); HCO$_3$ 24 mEq/L (20); urine output 60 mL/hr (30). Assess the improvement in hemodynamic change with the addition of dobutamine and decreased infusion rate of dopamine.**

The cardiac index has continued to increase and the PCWP and systemic vascular resistance have fallen. The increase in perfusion pressure in conjunction with the fall in afterload, preload, and heart rate will favorably affect the myocardial oxygen supply-demand ratio. The fall in heart rate with the increase in cardiac output indicates that the stroke volume has increased significantly from 27 mL/beat to 36 mL/beat. Other signs of improved systemic perfusion include the reversal of the acidosis observed initially and improved urine output.

The improved urine output can be attributed to the combined effects of dobutamine on the cardiac output and dopamine on the dopaminergic receptors in the renal vasculature. Davis et al.[139] studied the effects of low-dose dopamine (100 to 200 μg/minute) in 15 adult postoperative cardiac surgery patients with combined oliguria and left ventricular failure. Baseline data included a urine output of less than 0.5 mL/kg/hour and a pulmonary capillary wedge pressure greater than 12 mm Hg. Eight patients were receiving other vasoactive agents including isoproterenol, epinephrine, sodium nitroprusside, and nitroglycerin. Dopamine at 100 μg/minute improved cardiac index (2.3 ± 0.2 L/minute to 2.6 ± 0.2 L/minute) and lowered systemic vascular resistance. Urine sodium, creatinine clearance, and osmolar clearance all increased. Despite a group average increase in urine output from 22 ± 2 mL/hour to 54 ± 9 mL/hour, urine flow remained less than 0.5 mL/kg/hour in nine patients. In this subgroup of patients, an increase in dopamine to 200 μg/minute increased urine output to 50 ± 6 mL/hour and increased the cardiac index to 2.9 ± 0.2 L/minute.

Others also have shown that low-dose dopamine improves urine output either when administered alone or in conjunction with furosemide.[140–142] Whether dopamine's positive effect on renal function is due solely to an effect on the renal vasculature is difficult to conclude since most patients also demonstrated an improvement in cardiac function. The improvement in urine output produced by low-dose dopamine could result from several mechanisms. These include decreased aldosterone synthesis and release from the adrenal cortex; decreased plasma renin activity; and redistribution of intrarenal blood flow to the renal cortex.[124,125,139,143,144]

19. *Tapering Inotropic Support.* **R.G. has remained stable on dobutamine 7.5 μg/kg/min and dopamine 2.0 μg/kg/min for the past 4 hours. Urine output continues to be adequate. How would you taper the inotropic agents and what parameters would you monitor?**

An acceptable method is to taper dobutamine by 2 μg/kg/minute every 30 to 60 minutes and maintain the dopamine at 1 to 2 μg/kg/minute for its effect on renal blood flow. Dobutamine has an elimination half-life of 2.4 ± 0.7 minutes; thus, steady-state plasma levels will occur in a very short period of time. However, when tapering vasoactive agents, it is prudent to let the patient stabilize hemodynamically at new infusion rates for a time period which exceeds the time to achieve a new steady-state plasma concentration. After each reduction in the infusion rate, hemodynamic data can be assessed. Reasonable guidelines would be to keep the mean arterial pressure at 75 to 80 mm Hg, heart rate at less than 110 beats/minute, pulmonary capillary wedge pressure at 12 to 18 mm Hg, and CI at greater than 2.5 L/minute/m^2. After the dobutamine is discontinued, re-evaluation of renal function is needed to determine whether dopamine can be tapered. If urine output is greater than 0.5 mL/kg/hour and signs of pulmonary edema are minimal, the dopamine can be discontinued. R.G. should be evaluated for reinstitution of the medications he was receiving before surgery.

Severe Congestive Heart Failure (CHF)

Assessment by Hemodynamic Profile

20. B.Y., a 64-year-old female, is admitted to the ICU for treatment of severe CHF. She was brought to the ER 3 hours earlier with complaints of increasing shortness of breath (SOB), orthopnea, and increasing cough and sputum production over the past week. Vital signs included a BP of 110/68 mm Hg and a pulse of 110 beats/min. Cardiopulmonary examination revealed an S$_3$ gallop and bilateral basal rales. Chest x-ray confirmed the presence of pulmonary edema and significant cardiac enlargement. ECG showed atrial tachycardia with left ventricular strain. Urine output has been minimal over the past 12 hours. B.Y. is oriented and is mentating appropriately. She has a history of CHF and hypertension. She smokes 1 pack of cigarettes daily and admits to discontinuing her medications (furosemide, digoxin, and enalapril) 1 week before admission.

B.Y. weighs 50 kg and has a BSA of 1.6 m^2. Cardiac enzymes are pending to rule out an MI. After admission to the ICU a pulmonary artery catheter, arterial line, and Foley catheter are passed revealing the following: BP (S/D/M) 122/60/80 mm Hg; pulse 110 beats/min; CO 3 L/min; CI 1.9 L/min/m^2; RAP 20 mm Hg; PCWP 32 mm Hg; SVR 1600 dyne·sec·cm^{-5}; urine output 10 mL/hr; PaO$_2$ 70 mm Hg; PaCO$_2$ 46 mm Hg; pH 7.26; HCO$_3$ 21 mEq/L. Based upon the above data, what is your initial hemodynamic assessment of B.Y.? (Also see Chapter 15: Congestive Heart Failure.)

B.Y. is in severe congestive heart failure with evidence of pulmonary edema. The cardiac index is severely depressed (≤2.5 L/minute/m^2) and the systemic vascular resistance is significantly elevated primarily due to an increase in circulating catecholamines and an increase in sympathetic tone. Elevated angiotensin II levels also may contribute to the increase in systemic vascular resistance.

Pulmonary capillary wedge pressure, a measure of pulmonary hydrostatic pressure, is significantly elevated (32 mm Hg) which is consistent with the presence of pulmonary edema. Clinically, the onset of pulmonary congestion occurs at approximately 18 to 20 mm Hg; moderate pulmonary congestion is present at a level of 25 to 30 mm Hg; and the onset of pulmonary edema occurs at values greater than 30 mm Hg.[27] The pulmonary capillary wedge pressure is elevated because of left ventricular dysfunction resulting in excess sodium and water retention due to reflex renin release by the kidneys in response to the low cardiac output.

The heart rate is elevated as a compensatory response to the depressed cardiac output. Cardiac output is the product of heart rate and stroke volume (CO = HR × SV). As left ventricular function plateaus on the ventricular function curve, the stroke vol-

ume becomes constant; therefore, any further increase in cardiac output must be generated by an increase in heart rate.

Therapeutic Interventions

21. Furosemide. **Furosemide (Lasix) is prescribed for treatment of B.Y.'s acute pulmonary edema. What initial dose of furosemide would you recommend and how would furosemide affect B.Y.'s hemodynamic status?**

Hemodynamic Effect of Diuretic Therapy. B.Y. has not received her maintenance medications for the past week. As a consequence she has become fluid overloaded which has precipitated pulmonary edema and acute cardiac failure on top of chronic CHF. The initial dose of furosemide used to treat acute pulmonary edema is highly variable. Patients who have been taking maintenance diuretics require larger initial doses than patients who have not. In B.Y., an initial dose of 40 mg furosemide administered intravenously is reasonable. If no response is seen one hour after the first dose, a second dose of 80 mg IV can be administered. If there is still no response, dose titration of furosemide may continue at one hour intervals until a response is seen. In severe heart failure some patients exhibit diuretic resistance with an inadequate diuretic response. Combination therapy with a diuretic that exerts its action in another part of the nephron could be used when resistance to loop diuretics is seen.[260] An example of this would be a combination of a thiazide or metolazone and a loop diuretic. Significant side effects may be seen with the high doses required if resistance to loop diuretics is present (e.g., ototoxicity) or when a combination of different diuretic classes is used (e.g., electrolyte abnormalities). Another alternative for patients resistant to intermittent bolus administration of loop diuretics (i.e., furosemide, bumetanide) is continuous infusion of the same agent. Lahav et al.[261] demonstrated in patients with severe CHF that continuous IV administration of a loop diuretic leads to increased diuretic and natriuretic effects compared to intermittent bolus administration.

Furosemide is a rapid-acting diuretic and venous vasodilator. With venous capacitance increased, venous return (preload) will decrease. This combined diuresis and redistribution of intravascular fluid away from the lungs will lower the pulmonary capillary wedge pressure.[145,146] The effect of furosemide on venous capacitance often precedes the diuresis. Reduction of left ventricular filling pressure often occurs within five minutes and peaks 15 minutes after intravenous furosemide administration. The reduction in PCWP usually is unaccompanied by a change in cardiac output. The reduction in pulmonary capillary wedge pressure improves the myocardial oxygen supply:demand ratio, but does not significantly improve systemic perfusion. The major risk of using a diuretic is excessive reduction of preload and hence, cardiac output. In B.Y. with a PCWP greater than 30 mm Hg and fluid overload, diuresis with a potent loop diuretic can be safely initiated.

22. Vasodilators. **What is another therapeutic option available for treatment of B.Y.'s acute CHF and pulmonary edema?**

Vasodilators have become an accepted part of treatment for congestive heart failure. Both preload and afterload are elevated in response to a fall in cardiac output. As cardiac output falls, the sympathetic nervous system and renin-angiotensin system are activated to maintain circulatory stability.[147] Arterial pressure is maintained by the excessive increase in systemic vascular resistance. This increase in systemic vascular resistance increases the resistance to ejection of blood from the left ventricle. Venoconstriction shifts some of the blood volume from the peripheral veins to the central circulation which contributes to an elevation of right and left atrial pressures. A normal heart responds to the increase in preload and afterload by increasing contractility. In CHF, the heart's intrinsic capacity to increase contractility has been lost. As a result, the neurohormonal compensatory mechanism which is activated to maintain arterial pressure increases the workload on the heart and this leads to a further decrease in cardiac output. Patients tend to spiral down this vicious cycle until the cardiac output is lower and the systemic vascular resistance is higher than optimal for the maintenance of perfusion pressure.[148] Vasodilators disrupt the compensatory mechanisms that elevate preload and afterload and shift the ventricular function curve upward which allows for a greater cardiac output at a lower left ventricular filling pressure.

Three categories of vasodilators are available. Arterial vasodilators (e.g., hydralazine) decrease afterload thus reducing impedance to left ventricular outflow. Venous vasodilators (e.g., nitroglycerin) primarily decrease venous return (preload), thus improving ventricular compliance, subendocardial coronary perfusion, and pulmonary hydrostatic pressure. Finally, mixed arterial and venous vasodilators have balanced effects on both preload and afterload reduction (e.g., nitroprusside). The fall in systemic vascular resistance from arterial vasodilation potentially may cause hypotension and a reflex increase in heart rate; however, this is infrequently seen in patients with CHF since the decrease in systemic vascular resistance is counterbalanced by an increase in cardiac output which tends to maintain arterial pressure. Excessive preload reduction can cause deficient ventricular filling, thereby reducing the cardiac output. The overall response in any given patient depends upon their baseline hemodynamic and volume status. At this time, B.Y. has an adequate blood pressure, and should be able to tolerate a trial of a vasodilator for afterload and preload reduction.

23. Digoxin. Would reinstitution of digoxin in B.Y. be advisable at this time?

B.Y. had been taking digoxin for chronic inotropic support. Reinstitution of digoxin when chronic therapy is resumed is appropriate; however, in patients with severe heart failure, digoxin is not the initial drug of choice because its onset of action is delayed. In patients experiencing acute myocardial ischemia, the enhanced contractility seen with digoxin may increase ischemia in infarcted segments, thereby diminishing the inotropic effects that it exerts on undamaged myocardium. Until myocardial infarction has been ruled out in B.Y., digoxin probably should be withheld.

24. Phosphodiesterase inhibitors, noncatecholamine inotropic agents with vasodilator activity, are also a potential therapeutic option for treatment of B.Y.'s acute cardiac failure. Of these, amrinone was the first available in the U.S. How would you dose amrinone and what adverse effects would you expect with its administration? Does amrinone offer any advantage over catecholamine inotropic agents (e.g., dobutamine, dopamine) or nitroprusside?

The phosphodiesterase inhibitors (also referred to as inodilators) are a newer class of drugs which have the combination of inotropic and vasodilator effects.[121] All of the agents in this class have basically the same mechanism of action. They inhibit intracellular phosphodiesterase leading to an increase in the concentration of cyclic AMP. This increase in cyclic AMP causes a number of intracellular changes that could lead to increased inotropic effects. Increased cyclic AMP also causes relaxation of vascular smooth muscle and, therefore, decrease systemic vascular resistance.[121,149,150]

The hemodynamic effects seen with phosphodiesterase inhibitors include increased inotropy, reduced systemic vascular resistance, and improved left ventricular diastolic compliance.[122,149] These changes result in an increase in cardiac index and a decrease in left ventricular afterload and filling pressures. Almost all of the phosphodiesterase inhibitors have been shown to elevate cardiac

index and stroke volume index. Myocardial oxygen demand is increased by the increase in myocardial contractility and heart rate. But, on the other hand, left ventricular filling pressures and systemic vascular resistance are decreased leading to a decrease in myocardial oxygen demand. The net effect would depend upon the balance of the opposing forces. The two available injectable phosphodiesterase inhibitors in the U.S. are amrinone (Inocor) and milrinone (Primacor). Enoximone is being widely studied but is not yet available in the U.S. The studies using injectable enoximone thus far have been somewhat encouraging.[151–155]

Amrinone was the first phosphodiesterase inhibitor approved for clinical use. It is metabolized by N-acetyltransferase and eliminated by the kidneys. The elimination half-life ranges from two hours in fast acetylators to 4.4 hours in slow acetylators.[156] In patients with severe heart failure the elimination half-life ranges from 3 to 13 hours (average: 5 to 8 hours).[157,158] The onset of action occurs within minutes, and its peak effect is within 10 to 15 minutes.

The long half-life of amrinone makes a loading dose necessary before an infusion can be started. Intravenous amrinone usually is initiated with a 0.75 mg/kg loading dose administered over three minutes, followed by a maintenance infusion of 5 to 10 µg/kg/minute. Higher maintenance infusion rates have been used, although additional benefit above 20 µg/kg/minute has been questioned.[159,160] Patients with CHF or renal insufficiency will have a reduced elimination rate and require dose adjustment.[149]

Intravenous administration of amrinone in patients with severe heart failure results in a significant increase in cardiac output, while decreasing pulmonary and systemic vascular resistance.[122] Heart rate and blood pressure usually remain unaltered, although large doses have induced tachycardia and hypotension.[161,162] Theoretically, the effect of amrinone on myocardial oxygen consumption should be favorable since it does not substantially alter heart rate or blood pressure while lowering left ventricular filling pressure.[122] As with all inotropic agents, myocardial oxygen balance can be adversely affected in patients with coronary artery disease.[163] Hypotension can occur when vasodilation exceeds the increase in cardiac output and in hypovolemic patients .

Amrinone therapy has few serious side effects, the most significant being thrombocytopenia (platelet count <100,000/mm^3) which occurs in 2% to 3% of patients.[164,165] The precise mechanism of amrinone-induced thrombocytopenia has not been established but may be due to increased peripheral destruction and usually is dose related and reversible.[164,165] Hepatotoxicity, nausea, vomiting, and diarrhea are rarely seen with short term IV use of amrinone.[122] Amrinone may increase arrhythmia frequency and cause sudden death, therefore, it should not be used in patients with severe ventricular dysrhythmias.[166]

Konstam et al.[167] studied the effect of nitroprusside and amrinone in nine patients with CHF. These authors concluded that the reduction in the left ventricular end-systolic volume and improvement in cardiac index produced by amrinone exceeds that which would be expected from a pure vasodilator. This indicates that there is an inotropic contribution to amrinone's hemodynamic effects. Therefore, the advantage of amrinone over nitroprusside is that in addition to vasodilator properties it also is a positive inotropic agent. Along with this is the potential disadvantage of amrinone increasing myocardial oxygen demand.

Comparative studies of amrinone, dobutamine, and dopamine have shown that amrinone is more similar to dobutamine than to dopamine with respect to its net hemodynamic effects.[159,160] Therefore, the advantage of amrinone over dopamine would be the same as that of dobutamine over dopamine (see Question 17). In comparison to dobutamine, amrinone is a less potent inotropic agent and a more potent vasodilator. Whether amrinone offers a distinct advantage over dobutamine is questionable. The longer duration of action poses a problem if an undesirable effect occurs.

Since the inotropic mechanism of amrinone is independent of the β-receptor, it may be of value in patients who do not respond to catecholamine inotropic agents due to β-receptor blockade or to downregulation of β-receptors. In addition, since amrinone has a different mechanism of action it should have synergistic inotropic effects with catecholamines.

In summary, B.Y. will benefit from diuresis. The venous vasodilatory properties of furosemide plus the diuretic action will lessen the pulmonary edema. Institution of an IV vasodilator (i.e., nitroprusside) or an inotropic agent with vasodilator properties (i.e., dobutamine, amrinone) also may be considered. The initial choice would depend upon the patient's baseline hemodynamic status and the clinical experience of the clinician. The advantage of a vasodilator over an inotropic agent to reduce afterload and preload is that the vasodilator will not increase myocardial oxygen demand.

25. Initial Therapy: Nitroprusside. The clinician decides to begin an infusion of nitroprusside for afterload and preload reduction in B.Y. How should therapy be initiated? What are the end points of therapy? What adverse effects are associated with nitroprusside infusion?

The initial infusion rate of nitroprusside should be no greater than 0.5 μg/kg/minute. The infusion rate can be titrated upwards by 0.25 μg/kg/minute every five minutes until the mean arterial pressure falls 5 to 10 mm Hg. In B.Y., keeping the mean arterial pressure at ≥70 mm Hg is desirable. The systolic blood pressure should be kept above 100 to 110 mm Hg. The most important parameters to follow are cardiac output and arterial pressure. A cardiac index of ≥2.5 L/minute/m^2 is desirable. The "optimal" filling pressure or pulmonary capillary wedge pressure needed to maximize cardiac output via the Starling mechanism tends to be higher in patients with acute myocardial infarction and severe CHF.[115] For B.Y. or any other patient, the optimal filling pressure or pulmonary capillary wedge pressure is that pressure which maintains a cardiac output and mean arterial pressure that allows for adequate coronary and tissue perfusion without inducing pulmonary edema. For example, if at some arbitrary point in time, B.Y. has a cardiac output of 5 L/minute, a mean arterial pressure of 70 mm Hg, and a pulmonary capillary wedge pressure of 16 mm Hg, and then at a subsequent time, has a similar cardiac output and mean arterial pressure with a pulmonary capillary wedge pressure of 12 mm Hg, then this lower filling pressure (12 mm Hg) is the optimal filling pressure. Frequent analysis of hemodynamic measurements allows the clinician to construct a ventricular function curve that defines which PCWP is sufficient for maximal cardiac output.

Adverse effects associated with nitroprusside administration include excessive hypotension, reflex tachycardia, potential worsening of myocardial ischemia, thiocyanate toxicity (especially in the presence of renal dysfunction, prolonged infusions, and high infusion rates), accumulation of cyanide with subsequent cyanide toxicity, worsening arterial hypoxemia from increases in ventilation/perfusion mismatch, and, rarely, methemoglobinemia and hypothyroidism. (Also see Chapter 17: Hypertensive Emergencies for a discussion of nitroprusside.)

26. *Hemodynamic Effect.* Over the next 2 hours B.Y. received 2 doses of IV furosemide 40 mg. Nitroprusside was titrated to 1.2 μg/kg/min resulting in the following hemodynamic profile (previous values in parentheses): BP (S/D/M) 100/50/66 mm Hg (122/60/80); pulse 94 beats/min (110); CO 4.5 L/min (3); CI 2.8 L/min/m^2 (1.9); PCWP 22 mm Hg (32); SVR 906 dyne·sec·cm^{-5} (1600); urine output 50 mL/hr (10); PaO$_2$ 80 mm Hg (70); PaCO$_2$ 46 mm Hg (46); pH 7.32 (7.26); HCO$_3$ 24 mEq/L (21). Cardiopulmonary examination: S$_3$ gallop and bibasilar rales present, but diminished from previous examination. ECG: sinus rhythm. Evaluate the effect that nitroprusside and furosemide have had on B.Y.'s hemodynamic profile and clinical status.

The cardiac index has improved significantly (1.9 L/minute/m^2 to 2.8 L/minute/m^2) and the stroke volume has increased from 27 mL/beat to 48 mL/beat. The improved stroke volume has decreased endogenous catecholamine levels which, in turn, decreases the heart rate (110 beats/minute to 94 beats/minute) and systemic vascular resistance. B.Y. has improved clinically and her arterial blood gases indicate improvement of the metabolic acidosis. The increased urine output can be attributed to the combined effects of the diuretic and increased nitroprusside-induced cardiac output. Overall, B.Y. has improved substantially. Supplemental oxygen still is required, but the oxygen concentration needed to maintain an adequate arterial oxygen content has been lowered. B.Y. may have a component of chronic obstructive airways disease associated with the cigarette smoking history; therefore, a PaO$_2$ of 80 to 100 mm Hg on room air might be unattainable.

At this point, a further reduction in preload may benefit B.Y.'s respiratory function. The pulmonary capillary wedge pressure still is elevated at 22 mm Hg. However, the mean arterial pressure is slightly lower than acceptable and a further increase in the nitroprusside dose to reduce preload may lower the mean arterial pressure to a level that would compromise coronary perfusion, and perfusion to other vital organs.

27. Choice of Additional Therapy. What therapeutic interventions are available to further reduce B.Y.'s preload and improve her respiratory function?

Two options are available. The first is to continue current therapy (nitroprusside and furosemide) and wait for the diuresis to continue to reduce preload. Mean arterial pressure is slightly lower than desirable; thus, signs of inadequate systemic perfusion must be monitored closely as a guide to additional diuretic therapy. Again, the goal is to find the optimal filling pressure.

The second option is to continue the nitroprusside and add low doses of dopamine to improve renal perfusion and augment cardiac output through inotropic support. A dopamine infusion rate of 2 to 3 μg/kg/minute is reasonable. Either choice is acceptable as long as B.Y. is monitored closely.

28. Transition to Oral Vasodilators. After 48 hours of nitroprusside, intermittent furosemide, and low-dose dopamine, B.Y. has remained hemodynamically stable. The decision is made to reinstitute B.Y.'s previous medications (enalapril, digoxin, and furosemide). MI has been ruled out. How would you reinstitute the enalapril (10 mg BID) and taper the nitroprusside in B.Y.?

There are no strict guidelines for tapering short-acting vasodilators when substituting long-acting oral agents. In this case, a reasonable approach would be to give the enalapril (Vasotec) at a lower dose than B.Y. was on previously (e.g., 5 mg BID) and reduce the nitroprusside infusion rate by 25%. Obtain a cardiac output and pulmonary capillary wedge pressure every two to four hours to assess the contribution of the enalapril to the afterload and preload reduction. If the mean arterial pressure declines excessively after the addition of enalapril, the nitroprusside dose will have to be reduced further. A smooth transition from intravenous therapy to oral therapy often depends upon the skill of the nursing staff and their familiarity with the hemodynamic effects of the drugs.

Acute Myocardial Infarction (MI)

Immediate Goals of Therapy and General Considerations

29. M.J., a 57-year-old male, is brought to the ER complaining of severe chest pain and difficulty breathing. On physical examination, M.J. has a BP of 80/40 mm Hg (by cuff) with a weak pulse of 115 beats/min. His respiratory rate is 24/min and his breathing is very shallow. Heart sounds include S_3/S_4 gallops. No murmurs are heard. The jugular venous pulse is normal. He has diffuse rales over the lower lung fields with moderate wheezing. M.J. is cold and clammy to touch; however, his temperature is normal. He is restless, anxious, and confused as to time and date. ABGs on 2 L nasal prongs are: PaO_2 65 mm Hg, $PaCO_2$ 44 mm Hg, pH 7.22, and HCO_3 18 mEq/L. The ECG shows ST segment elevation in the anterior lateral leads, and 6–10 premature ventricular contractions (PVCs)/min. Serum potassium is normal. A Foley catheter is inserted to monitor urine output. Cardiac enzymes are pending. M.J. has no known prior history of cardiac disease and takes no medication. What immediate goals of therapy are necessary to stabilize M.J.?

M.J. has signs of cardiogenic shock with decreased systemic perfusion. His blood pressure is low, his heart rate is elevated, and his respiratory status is compromised. M.J. is restless, anxious, and confused indicating poor cerebral perfusion. M.J.'s arterial blood gas results indicate a component of metabolic acidosis secondary to poor systemic perfusion. The ST elevation on the ECG is consistent with an acute anterior myocardial infarction.

The goal of therapy for patients in cardiogenic shock after an acute MI is to improve ventricular performance and systemic oxygen delivery while preserving myocardium. Immediate intervention includes the determination of eligibility for thrombolytic therapy, administration of oxygen by face mask or via mechanical ventilation to maintain an arterial pO_2 greater than 70 mm Hg, optimization of systemic arterial pressure with a mean arterial blood pressure greater than 70 mm Hg, correction of metabolic acidosis,[15,19] treatment of pain and arrhythmias, and volume replacement if indicated. (See Chapter 14: Myocardial Infarction.)

Thrombolytics should be employed immediately if inclusion criteria are met and there are no contraindications to therapy (see Chapter 12: Thrombosis). Numerous trials have demonstrated a significant reduction in mortality and a decrease in the incidence of CHF and cardiogenic shock when thrombolytics are given within the first four to six hours after the onset of an infarction.[168–170] However, thrombolytic therapy has not been shown to decrease mortality in patients in whom severe left ventricular dysfunction or cardiogenic shock complicate myocardial infarction.[21,168,171] The lack of benefit from thrombolytic therapy in these patient subgroups has not been evaluated fully, but we know from Kennedy et al.[172] that in the subgroup of patients in cardiogenic shock, reperfusion occurred in only 43.2% of patients. While hospital mortality was 42% in these patients, it increased to 84% if reperfusion did not occur. This suggests that patency of the infarct-related artery, even in patients with cardiogenic shock, may have a beneficial effect on mortality.

Currently, studies are ongoing to assess the limitations of thrombolysis in patients with acute MI complicated by cardiogenic shock or severe left ventricular dysfunction. Prewitt[173] suggests the decrease in efficacy of thrombolytics may be due to systemic hypotension, impairing the delivery of the thrombolytic agent to the site of thrombosis. Becker[174] suggests efficacy is decreased because of either hemodynamic, mechanical, or metabolic factors. These factors result in coronary patency rarely being achieved in a timely manner, and if patency is achieved it typically is not maintained.

Administration of oxygen by mechanical ventilation enhances the myocardial oxygen supply and may contribute to improved ventricular performance.[175] Mechanical ventilation is indicated when arterial oxygen saturation cannot be maintained above 85% to 90% despite 100% oxygen per face mask. Once intubated, maximal sedation should be provided to alleviate anxiety and discomfort.

The arterial pressure must be increased to provide adequate coronary and systemic perfusion to meet oxygen requirements. The area of ischemia is depressed, but viable, provided myocardial oxygen supply exceeds demand. However, if the myocardial oxygen demands are not met, myocardial tissue necrosis will expand into the area of ischemia, resulting in further hemodynamic impairment and initiating a vicious positive feedback cycle which can lead to intractable pump failure and irreversible shock. To be effective, treatment of cardiogenic shock should favorably influence the balance between oxygen supply and demand in the ischemic zone.

Optimizing preload to improve cardiac output and systemic perfusion is crucial. Unfortunately, in patients with severe left ventricular impairment due to cardiogenic shock, increasing intravascular volume can worsen pulmonary congestion. M.J. currently has signs of pulmonary congestion, thus a fluid challenge must be administered cautiously, or withheld until hemodynamic monitoring can be established.

Inotropic agents or vasopressors should be used to increase systemic blood pressure and re-establish coronary perfusion in patients with cardiogenic shock and hypotension. The use of vasoactive agents, however, is not without risk as they may exacerbate ventricular arrhythmias and increase oxygen consumption in ischemic myocardium. Therefore, the minimal dose that will provide adequate perfusion pressure should be used. Achieving a mean arterial pressure of 65 to 70 mm Hg is the immediate goal of therapy. Elevation of the mean arterial pressure above 80 mm Hg is unnecessary because at this level, coronary blood flow is not significantly changed, but energy expenditure is.

Correction of metabolic acidosis is best accomplished by treating the underlying cause. Improving tissue perfusion by optimizing oxygen content and increasing cardiac output, can eventually restore aerobic metabolism and eliminate lactic acid production. The use of sodium bicarbonate to correct lactic acidosis in cardiogenic shock and other critically ill patients, is controversial. Numerous studies have demonstrated adverse effects associated with its use and lack of apparent benefit.[176–179] Some of the more significant effects include hypercapnia with the development of intracellular acidosis and associated myocardial depression; hyperosmolality, secondary to the high sodium load with aggravation of CHF; a reduction in tissue oxygen availability due to alterations in oxyhemoglobin dissociation with subsequent anaerobic metabolism; and a decrease in ionized calcium.[177–180] In addition, the purported benefits of sodium bicarbonate administration, such as improved responsiveness to catecholamines and actual reductions in mortality are unsubstantiated.[176,179] Bicarbonate therapy, therefore, warrants caution and is recommended only, if at all, when severe acidemia (pH <7.2 or HCO_3 <10 to 12 mEq/L) is present.[176]

Assessment by Hemodynamic Profile

30. M.J. has a history of cerebrovascular disease and is thus ineligible for thrombolytic therapy. Therefore, he will require surgical revascularization, in the form of balloon angioplasty or coronary artery bypass surgery to improve his chances of survival. Meanwhile, he is begun on dopamine at 5 µg/kg/min to stabilize him hemodynamically before initiation of revascularization procedures. Lidocaine (100 mg IV bolus plus a 2 mg/min infusion) also is instituted to correct the PVCs. Oxygen administration is changed to 100% via face mask. Morphine

sulfate, 2 mg IV, is given for chest pain. Intravenous NTG was initiated at 0.25 μg/kg/min for myocardial ischemia but had to be discontinued because intolerable hypotension developed. M.J. is admitted to the ICU where an arterial line and pulmonary artery line are placed revealing the following hemodynamic profile (previous values in parentheses): BP (S/D/M) 92/46/61 mm Hg (80/40 by cuff); pulse 122 beats/min (115); CO 2.8 L/min; CI 1.5 L/min/m²; RAP 16 mm Hg; PCWP 26 mm Hg; SVR 1314 dyne·sec·cm⁻⁵; PaO_2 70 mm Hg (65); $PaCO_2$ 48 mm Hg (44); pH 7.24 (7.22); HCO_3 21 mEq/L (18); urine output 10 mL/hr. (M.J. weighs 82 kg and has a BSA of 1.9 m².) The chest x-ray shows evidence of pulmonary edema. Based upon the above hemodynamic profile, assess M.J.'s response to dopamine therapy. Evaluate his clinical status on the basis of hemodynamic subsets.

M.J.'s clinical and hemodynamic parameters confirm the diagnosis of cardiogenic shock. Although his systolic blood pressure is slightly improved, his cardiac index (<1.8 L/minute/m²), PCWP (>18 mm Hg), and low urine output (<25 mL/hour), are all characteristic findings with this form of shock.[175]

Dopamine, at an infusion rate of 5 to 10 μg/kg/minute, has made M.J. more tachycardic, has not substantially enhanced cardiac output, and the mean arterial pressure is less than optimal for coronary perfusion. M.J. has signs of pulmonary edema which are consistent with the elevated pulmonary wedge pressure. The PaO_2 of 70 mm Hg is marginally acceptable considering he is on 100% oxygen per face mask.

Overall, M.J. is in severe cardiogenic shock probably secondary to acute myocardial infarction. Treatment of acute MI with pump failure can be based upon hemodynamic subsets[27,175] (see Table 18.5). Patients in subset I (SI) require little intervention except for oxygen, bed rest, sedation, morphine for chest pain, and appropriate drugs for tachycardia, bradycardia, and hypertension. Patients in subset II (SII) have an adequate cardiac index, but have evidence of pulmonary congestion (elevated PCWP) and usually are treated with diuretics. When blood pressure also is elevated, a vasodilator is helpful. Patients in subset III (SIII) are hypoperfused (CI ≤1.8 to 2.2 L/minute/m²) without pulmonary congestion and require volume expansion to raise the PCWP to 14 to 18 mm Hg. If the depressed cardiac index persists after volume expansion, an inotropic agent may be necessary to enhance contractility or increase the heart rate if the resting rate is below 50 to 70 beats/minute. Patients in subset IV (SIV) are the most difficult to manage and have the highest mortality rate. With both pulmonary congestion and hypoperfusion, therapy often includes a combination of diuretics, inotropic agents, and vasodilation.

The subset classification must be used only as a guideline because not all patients with a cardiac index of 1.8 to 2.2 L/minute/m² and a PCWP greater than 18 mm Hg will present clinically with hypoperfusion and pulmonary congestion.

Therapeutic Interventions

31. Fluid Therapy versus Inotropic Support. **The decision is made to intubate M.J. Would a fluid challenge or additional doses of dopamine improve M.J.'s status?**

In M.J. a fluid challenge could exacerbate the pulmonary edema, since after an acute myocardial infarction, ventricular compliance is decreased, and a small change in left ventricular end-diastolic volume could result in a disproportionately large increase in PCWP. Thus, in patients with an acute myocardial infarction, the benefits of a fluid challenge must be balanced against the risk of aggravating pulmonary edema. If a fluid challenge is going to be administered, no more than 100 mL of normal saline should be infused without further evaluation of hemodynamic and clinical data.

Increasing the dopamine infusion rate may improve cardiac output and perfusion pressure, but at the expense of increasing the heart rate even further. The increased heart rate, along with the elevation in PCWP, may adversely affect the myocardial oxygen supply:demand ratio. However, the increase in coronary blood flow (due to the rise in arterial pressure) and the decrease in left ventricular chamber size associated with the increase in contractility hopefully would tend to offset the increase in myocardial oxygen requirements.

Dopamine administered at an average infusion rate of 17 μg/kg/minute to eight patients with cardiogenic shock secondary to MI improved cardiac index, raised the mean arterial pressure and heart rate, and lowered the systemic vascular resistance and pulmonary capillary wedge pressure.[181] However, myocardial metabolism deteriorated in five patients as indicated by an elevated myocardial lactate production and oxygen extraction.

It is not entirely clear which patients in cardiogenic shock will respond to dopamine. Holzer et al.[182] studied 24 patients in cardiogenic shock and found that a mean infusion rate of 9.1 μg/kg/minute was required to produce beneficial effects on cardiac output, urine output, heart rate, and PCWP in survivors. Nonsurvivors had no change in mean arterial pressure, pulmonary capillary wedge pressure, or heart rate at an average infusion rate of 17.1 μg/kg/minute.

32. Combination Inotropic Therapy. **Occasionally, a patient's hemodynamic status will improve with the combined use of**

Table 18.5	Hemodynamic Subsets in Acute Myocardial Infarction[a]			
	Subset I (SI)	Subset II (SII)	Subset III (SIII)	Subset IV (SIV)
Pulmonary congestion (PCWP >18 mm Hg)	No	Yes	No	Yes
Peripheral hypoperfusion (CI = 1.8–2.2 L/min/m²)	No	No	Yes	Yes
% mortality based upon clinical signs	1	11	18	60
% mortality based upon hemodynamic signs	3	9	23	51
Therapy	Usually no specific therapy required	Diuretics, digitalis when diuretics are ineffective	Volume expansion, pacing when slow heart rate present	Vasodilators, vasopressors, inotropic agents depending upon hemodynamic measurements

[a] CI = Cardiac index; PCWP = Pulmonary capillary wedge pressure.

inotropic agents. **Would the addition of a dobutamine infusion to treat M.J.'s cardiogenic shock be beneficial?**

Richard et al.[131] studied the combination of dobutamine and dopamine in eight cardiogenic shock patients requiring mechanical ventilation. The etiology of heart failure was congestive heart failure in four patients and idiopathic cardiomyopathy in the other four patients. None of the patients had suffered an MI within the preceding seven days. Each patient received three infusions in a randomly assigned order: dopamine at 15 µg/kg/minute; dobutamine at 15 µg/kg/minute; and a combination of dopamine and dobutamine each at 7.5 µg/kg/minute. All three regimens increased cardiac index, stroke index, left ventricular stroke work index, and heart rate similarly. Mean arterial pressure increased with the dopamine and dobutamine-dopamine combination, but did not change with the dobutamine alone. Systemic vascular resistance was significantly lower with dobutamine alone compared to the other two regimens. Pulmonary capillary wedge pressure was elevated most with the dopamine infusion alone as was myocardial oxygen consumption. The combination regimen offered hemodynamic superiority over either agent alone in this group of patients.

Other studies indicate that dobutamine improves ventricular performance and hemodynamics in patients with acute myocardial infarction who are not in cardiogenic shock.[183,184] Pulmonary capillary wedge pressure was lowered, cardiac index increased, and systemic vascular resistance decreased. Mean arterial pressure remained unchanged or declined. A reduction in pulmonary capillary wedge pressure would benefit M.J.; however, no change or a reduction in mean arterial pressure would not be helpful.

In summary, further inotropic support with dopamine or the addition of dobutamine would be indicated at this time in M.J. The dopamine could be increased to 12.5 µg/kg/minute or dobutamine could be initiated at 5 µg/kg/minute; neither maneuver is without risk. The dobutamine may lower the mean arterial pressure, adversely affecting coronary perfusion pressure. The dopamine may elevate the PCWP. The addition of dobutamine or an increase in dopamine dose could increase heart rate even more. Any of these would adversely affect the myocardial oxygen supply:demand ratio and could further extend the area of ischemia or necrosis.

33. Despite the addition of dobutamine at a rate of 5 to 7.5 µg/kg/min, and initiation of ventilatory support via tracheal intubation, M.J. continues to show signs of deterioration, with progressive obtundation and loss of bowel tones. His systemic arterial pressure has continued to decline, and his dopamine is now up to 18 µg/kg/min. Preload reduction was attempted previously with NTG; however, the drop in blood pressure was intolerable. A repeat hemodynamic profile shows the following (previous values in parentheses): BP (S/D/M) 86/40/55 (92/46/61); pulse 132 beats/min (122); CO 3.0 L/min (2.8); CI 1.6 L/min/m^2 (1.5); RAP 18 mm Hg (16); PCWP 24 mm Hg (26); SVR 986 dyne·sec·cm^{-5}(1314); urine output 8 mL/hr (10); PaO$_2$ 75 mm Hg (70); PaCO$_2$ 42 mm Hg (48); pH 7.26 (7.24); HCO$_3$ 19 mEq/L (21). The ECG shows atrial tachycardia with occasional PVCs. What therapeutic alternatives can be considered at this time?

M.J. is still in severe cardiogenic shock and his tissue perfusion continues to deteriorate as evidenced by a further reduction in urine output, a loss in bowel sounds, continuing acidosis, and CNS obtundation. Since his systemic arterial pressure and tissue perfusion have declined despite the addition of dobutamine and maximal doses of dopamine, additional support with a potent vasopressor and the insertion of an intra-aortic balloon pump are indicated.[120]

Norepinephrine (Levophed) is a potent α-adrenergic agonist which vasoconstricts arterioles at all infusion rates, thereby increasing SVR and thus, systemic arterial and coronary perfusion pressures. Norepinephrine also stimulates β$_1$-adrenergic receptors

to a lesser extent, resulting in increased contractility and stroke volume. However, heart rate and cardiac output usually remain constant, or may even decrease secondary to the increased afterload and reflex baroreceptor activation. Although coronary perfusion pressure is enhanced as a result of the elevation in diastolic pressure, myocardial oxygen consumption also is increased. Consequently, myocardial ischemia and arrhythmias may be exacerbated, and left ventricular function further compromised.[16,120]

Infusions of norepinephrine are begun at 1 to 4 µg/minute, and titrated upwards to achieve a systolic blood pressure of 90 to 100 mm Hg. Administration should be through a central IV line as local subcutaneous necrosis may result from peripheral IV extravasation. Prolonged infusion of larger doses will transiently exert a beneficial effect by diverting blood flow from peripheral and splanchnic vasculature to the heart and brain; however, this ultimately may compromise capillary perfusion to the extent that end-organ failure, particularly renal failure, ensues.

To reduce the potential risk of end-organ damage, a reasonable approach would be to add norepinephrine to the infusion of dobutamine, and reduce the dopamine infusion rate to 0.5 to 2 µg/kg/minute to support renal and splanchnic perfusion. In addition, any deficits in plasma volume should be corrected as prolonged administration of norepinephrine may further decrease plasma volume secondary to fluid transudation from postcapillary venoconstriction.[16]

Adverse effects of norepinephrine are related mostly to excessive vasoconstriction and compromise of organ perfusion. Worsening of ventricular function can occur due to increased afterload. Tissue necrosis and sloughing may develop if extravasation occurs. Cardiac arrhythmias may emerge with administration, and heart rate may increase, while others may develop a slowing of heart rate secondary to baroreceptor-mediated reflex increases in vagal tone.

Again, it must be emphasized that in M.J. pharmacologic support, particularly the use of norepinephrine, is only an interim maneuver to temporarily maintain hemodynamic function while revascularization procedures are being considered. Patients who cannot be stabilized with pharmacologic intervention, and in whom systemic or myocardial perfusion is becoming compromised, may require further support via the insertion of a mechanical circulatory assist device (e.g., intra-aortic balloon pump).[30]

Intra-Aortic Balloon Pump. The intra-aortic balloon pump or intra-aortic counter pulsation (IACP) remains the most commonly used mechanical assist device with use in clinical practice for over 15 years. It is designed to improve coronary perfusion and reduce afterload, thus providing short-term reperfusion of the ischemic myocardium. A 30 to 40 mL balloon catheter is inserted into the femoral artery and advanced to just below the arch of the aorta. Balloon inflation and deflation are synchronized with the ECG to inflate during diastole (after the aortic valve closes) and deflate at the onset of systole. The inflated balloon in diastole will increase coronary perfusion by elevating the mean aortic pressure. The rapid deflation of the balloon at the onset of systole will decrease systolic blood pressure, thus reducing afterload and improving cardiac ejection.[20] The enhanced myocardial perfusion provided by IACP may reduce vasopressor requirements, thereby further decreasing myocardial oxygen consumption. Occasionally, IACP augmentation is sufficient to allow the institution of vasodilators.[15]

Intra-aortic counterpulsation, when combined with surgical revascularization, significantly decreases mortality from cardiogenic shock associated with an acute MI. The most important factor with this approach, is the finding that early surgical intervention is crucial in salvaging ischemic myocardium and thus in reducing mortality. DeWood et al.[185] reported a 17% mortality when revascularization was instituted within 5 to 16 hours after the onset of cardiogenic shock. However, if surgery was delayed beyond 18 hours, a 71% mortality rate was observed. Another study by Alcan et al.[186] revealed a 47% mortality rate when intra-aortic counterpulsation was used alone within the first 24 hours, but 94%, if intra-aortic counterpulsation was begun beyond 24 hours. Mortality was reduced to 15% in this population with the combination of intra-aortic counterpulsation and revascularization within 24 hours. Other studies employing percutaneous transluminal coronary angioplasty (PTCA) and intra-aortic counterpulsation have demonstrated similar results.[25,187,188] Whether prolonged intra-aortic balloon counterpulsation (IABP) improves survival itself still is controversial. However, Waksman et al.[189] recently report data that suggest intra-aortic balloon counterpulsation improves survival of patients with acute myocardial infarction complicated by cardiogenic shock. Although intra-aortic counterpulsation is currently the mainstay for supporting the patient in shock who cannot be stabilized with pharmacologic therapy, and may continue to be required in certain critically unstable patients, immediate PTCA may become the treatment of choice for patients in cardiogenic shock who have failed or are ineligible for thrombolytic therapy.[20,23,24]

In summary, M.J.'s condition has continued to deteriorate since arriving in the ICU. Attempts at stabilizing his hemodynamic parameters with dopamine, dobutamine, and norepinephrine have failed. This is evidenced by inadequate tissue perfusion that is reflected clinically by his continued lactic acidosis, decreased urine output, reduced bowel sounds, and CNS obtundation. M.J.'s best chance of survival is to undergo early revascularization of his ischemic myocardium with either coronary bypass surgery or percutaneous transluminal coronary angioplasty. Meanwhile, the addition of norepinephrine and intra-aortic counterpulsation can provide temporary support for M.J. before his procedure.

Septic Shock

Clinical and Hemodynamic Features

34. A.J., a 61-year-old male, was admitted 5 days ago with a chief complaint of acute abdominal pain of 3 days duration associated with bloody diarrhea, fever, tachypnea, and hypotension. A diagnosis of superior mesenteric artery occlusion with necrotic bowel was made. A.J. had surgery for removal of necrotic bowel tissue. During postoperative days 1–4, there was a slight increase in serum creatinine (SrCr) and he could not be completely weaned from ventilatory support. Vital signs were stable. Antibiotic therapy includes clindamycin and gentamicin in appropriate doses. A.J. has been receiving morphine sulfate for postoperative pain.

A.J. has a history of CHF and coronary artery disease with stable angina pectoris which have been treated with digoxin, furosemide, and NTG as needed. He had no other medical problems before admission.

On the morning of postoperative day 5, A.J. complains of chills and is noted to have a spiking fever to 39.4 °C. Physical findings include a blood pressure of 98/60 mm Hg, pulse 128 beats/min, and a respiratory rate of 28/min with an intermittent mandatory ventilation (IMV) rate of 6/min. The urine output has dropped to 25 mL/hr and bowel sounds are absent. The chest x-ray shows an enlarged heart with bilateral pulmonary infiltrates and right lower lobe atelectasis. A.J. has become confused and disoriented. ABGs on an inspiratory oxygen concentration (FiO_2) of 40% are PaO_2 76 mm Hg, PaCO_2 34 mm Hg, and pH 7.31. A.J. has had increased bronchial secretions over the past 2 days. Pertinent laboratory values are: SrCr 1.8 mg/dL, BUN 32 mg/dL, and WBC count 18,000 cells/mm³.

Urine, sputum, and blood samples are sent for culture and sensitivity. A fluid bolus of 500 mL NS is given. Arterial and pulmonary artery catheters are inserted revealing the following hemodynamic profile (A.J. weighs 70 kg and has a BSA of 1.7 m²): BP (S/D/M) 90/50/63 mm Hg; pulse 122 beats/min; CO 6 L/min; CI 3.5 L/min/m²; RAP 8 mm Hg; PCWP 12 mm Hg; SVR 733 dyne·sec·cm⁻⁵. What hemodynamic and clinical features are consistent with septic shock? [SI units: SrCr 159.12 µmol/L; BUN 11.42 mmol/L UREA; WBC count 18 × 10⁹/L]

Hemodynamic signs consistent with septic shock include hypotension, tachycardia, elevated cardiac output, and a low systemic vascular resistance and initially a low PCWP. Even though the absolute value for cardiac output is high or at the upper limits of the normal range in septic shock, it is inadequate to maintain a blood pressure that will perfuse the essential organs in the face of a decreased systemic vascular resistance.[46] A.J. has metabolic acidosis (pH 7.31 with a PaCO_2 30 mm Hg, HCO_3 15 mEq/L) indicating the presence of anaerobic metabolism and a cardiac output that is inadequate to meet the oxygen requirements of the tissues.

A.J.'s pulmonary capillary wedge pressure of 12 mm Hg is within the normal range. If A.J. did not have a history of CHF, the pulmonary capillary wedge pressure would be expected to be lower and more consistent with signs of relative hypovolemia secondary to the reduced preload from peripheral vasodilation. However, given his cardiac history, A.J.'s left ventricular compliance is most likely reduced; thus, PCWP does not accurately reflect preload or left ventricular end-diastolic volume. In patients in septic shock *without* coronary artery disease, volume resuscitation to a pulmonary capillary wedge pressure of 16 to 18 mm Hg is recommended to maximize CO and increase oxygen delivery to the tissues.[193] Patients in septic shock with coronary artery disease, may have decreased left ventricular compliance; thus, volume resuscitation to a slightly higher pulmonary capillary wedge pressure to ensure an adequate preload may be needed.[190] However, if deteriorating pulmonary function is present one should aim for the lowest possible PCWP that will produce an acceptable cardiac output and blood pressure.

Other features consistent with septic shock in A.J. include worsening pulmonary function, as indicated by arterial blood gases; declining urine output and altered sensorium, indicating decreased renal and cerebral perfusion; a rising WBC count; and a spiking fever.[31,32]

Therapeutic Approach

There are three primary areas toward which the management of septic shock is directed: 1) eradication of the source of infection; 2) hemodynamic support; and 3) inhibition or attenuation of the initiators and mediators of sepsis.[31,32]

Eradicating The Source of Infection

35. What factors should be considered in determining antimicrobial therapy in septic shock? What are the potential sources of infection in A.J.?

Eradicating the source of infection involves the early administration of antimicrobial therapy, and if indicated, surgical drainage. The use of an appropriate antibiotic regimen is associated with a significant increase in survival,[191] and in one large retrospective study reduced shock and mortality rates by 50%.[37] The selection of antibiotics should take into account the presumed site of infection; whether the infection is community- or hospital-acquired; recent invasive procedures, manipulations, or surgery; any predisposing conditions; and the likelihood of drug resistance.[33] Ideally, the primary source of the infection can be determined and therapy specifically tailored to the most likely organisms. However, if the source of infection is unclear, the early institution of broad-spectrum antibiotics generally is recommended while awaiting culture results, given a greater than 50% mortality rate due to gram-negative sepsis within the first two days of illness, and the increasing frequency of polymicrobial infections.[37] A combination of two antibiotics is suggested to provide for possible synergy, and, in addition, may reduce the emergence of resistant organisms.[192] Recommended empiric regimens typically include an aminoglycoside plus a third-generation cephalosporin or a similar broad-spectrum agent to cover for gram-positive cocci, aerobic gram-negative bacilli, and anaerobes.[20,21] (Also see Chapter 54: Principles of Infectious Diseases.)

There are several potential sources of sepsis in A.J. The first is hospital-acquired pneumonia. A.J. has been intubated for five days, infiltrates appear on chest x-ray, and sputum production has increased over the past two days. Abdominal abscess or recurrent bowel ischemia also should be considered. Bowel sounds are absent, although no complaints of abdominal tenderness have been elicited; surgical exploration may be necessary. Other potential sources for infection include the urinary tract, as A.J. has had an indwelling Foley catheter in place since admission. All IV catheters should be changed if possible.

Clindamycin is discontinued and imipenem is added to broaden A.J.'s antibiotic coverage and provide combination therapy for nosocomial gram-negative pathogens, particularly *P. aeruginosa*. Imipenem also should adequately cover *S. aureus* cocci from possible intravenous contamination, as well as abdominal anaerobic organisms.

Initial Stabilization

36. What are the immediate goals of therapy in A.J.? How can they be achieved and assessed?

The goal of treating septic shock, in addition to eradicating the precipitating infection, is to maximize tissue oxygenation by optimizing arterial oxygen content and cardiac output, thereby increasing oxygen delivery. Once anemia (if present) and hypoxemia have been corrected, the mainstay of therapy is volume expansion to enhance cardiac output. Optimal rates of survival in critically ill patients have been obtained by maintaining the cardiac index; that is, a cardiac output adjusted for body surface area that is greater than 4.5 L/minute/m^2.[193–196] If the serum albumin is greater than 2 gm/dL, crystalloids (with electrolytes to correct imbalances) should be considered to maintain a cardiac index of greater than 4.5 L/minute/m^2 as well as a mean arterial pressure of $\geq$65 mm Hg or a systolic blood pressure of $\geq$90 mm Hg. The MAP is a better reflection of systemic arterial pressure since it considers the diastolic pressure which is an essential component of blood flow. Although mean arterial pressure and blood pressure are not absolute measures of blood flow to all vital organs, these pressures are considered the therapeutic endpoints which will sustain myocardial and cerebral perfusion.[197] After optimization with fluid therapy to a PCWP of 18 mm Hg, inotropic agents are indicated if the patient remains hypotensive with a low cardiac index and signs of inadequate tissue perfusion persist.

A.J. has a cardiac index of 3.5 L/minute/m^2, a pulmonary capillary wedge pressure of 12 mm Hg, a systemic vascular resistance of 733 dynes·sec·cm^{-5}, and a mean arterial pressure of 63 mm Hg. A PaO$_2$ of 65 mm Hg is adequate for hemoglobin saturation; however, this is with a FiO$_2$ of 0.4. A further increase in cardiac output to improve oxygen delivery is necessary to minimize anaerobic metabolism and improve CNS and renal perfusion. Continued fluid challenges to increase preload in A.J. must be approached cautiously, however, for several reasons. A.J. has a history of CHF, ischemic heart disease, and ongoing evidence suggestive of pneumonia, all of which could be made worse with overly aggressive fluid boluses. In addition, patients in septic shock

are prone to the development of noncardiogenic pulmonary edema or adult respiratory distress syndrome, which can cause severe deterioration in pulmonary function. Therefore, fluid boluses of no more than 250 mL normal saline over 10 to 15 minutes should be given with ongoing monitoring to determine the PCWP at which cardiac output is maximal. This approach will avoid excessive pulmonary capillary wedge pressure's, beyond which CO is no longer increased and thereby reduce the potential for pulmonary edema formation.[197]

In summary, the immediate goal of therapy is to maximize oxygen delivery to the tissues. Fluid resuscitation is the mainstay of therapy and improves oxygen delivery by increasing cardiac output; however, inotropic agents often are required for additional cardiovascular support. A favorable response to immediate resuscitative efforts will be reflected by a reversal or halt in the progression of the metabolic acidosis, improved sensorium, and increased urine output. In A.J., surgical evaluation for an ongoing or new abdominal process and selection of appropriate antibiotics while maintaining hemodynamic support is currently the definitive therapy.

Hemodynamic Management

37. Fluid Therapy Versus Inotropic Support. A.J. is given two 250 mL fluid boluses and dopamine is begun at a rate of 5 µg/kg/min. Over the next 2 hours, he receives 3 L of fluid in boluses and the dopamine is increased to 12 µg/kg/min to maintain his blood pressure. Signs of pulmonary edema have become more prominent. A.J. has the following hemodynamic profile (previous values in parentheses: BP (S/D/M) 94/46/62 mm Hg (90/50/63); pulse 124 beats/min (122); CO 7.0 L/min (6); CI 4.1 L/min/m^2 (3.5); RAP 13 mm Hg (8); PCWP 18 mm Hg (12); SVR 560 dyne·sec·cm^{-5} (733); urine output 15 mL/hr; PaO$_2$ 62 mm Hg (76); PaCO$_2$ 38 mm Hg (34); HCO$_3$ 19 mEq/L (15); pH 7.30 (7.31); PEEP 5 cm H$_2$O). Which of the following therapeutic considerations would be reasonable for A.J. at this time: additional fluid boluses, an increase in the dopamine infusion rate, or initiation of a different inotropic agent?

A.J. continues to be hypotensive despite the fact that a pulmonary capillary wedge pressure of 18 mm Hg has been achieved with fluid therapy and a dopamine infusion rate of 12 µg/kg/minute. The goals of therapy remain the same (i.e., maximize arterial oxygen content and oxygen delivery to reverse cellular anaerobic metabolism).

A.J.'s PaO$_2$ of 62 mm Hg correlates with an oxygen-hemoglobin saturation of approximately 90%, which should provide an adequate arterial oxygen content. However, oxygen delivery still may be inadequate since the cardiac index still is less than 4.5 L/minute/m^2. In addition, decreased oxygen utilization also may contribute to the continued acidosis. Thus, further attempts to enhance cardiac index and hence, oxygen delivery are appropriate. However, A.J. has worsening signs of pulmonary edema and a history of cardiovascular disease which will influence the choice of therapeutic options.

Although fluid administration is the mainstay of therapy in septic shock, the elevation of A.J.'s pulmonary capillary wedge pressure to 18 mm Hg without a significant increase in cardiac output suggests that an optimal PCWP has been reached. Therefore, additional fluid therapy to maintain his blood pressure may worsen his pulmonary edema and further compromise his pulmonary gas exchange. A plot of cardiac output versus the PCWP (ventricular function curve) would provide a more accurate assessment of the PCWP at which CO is maximal. However, an increase in the pulmonary capillary wedge pressure above 18 mm Hg generally should be avoided. Thus, additional fluid boluses at this time should be used only to maintain the current level of intravascular volume status.

Inotropic Agents. Although the use of inotropes is well established, controlled comparative studies have not clearly determined which agent, or combination of agents, are most useful in the management of septic shock. However, since there are significant differences among the inotropic agents, selection of the most appropriate drug should be guided by careful consideration of the patient's hemodynamic status.

Dopamine is frequently the initial pharmacologic agent chosen for the treatment of septic shock. If the mean arterial pressure is low in the presence of an elevated cardiac output and a low systemic vascular resistance, dopamine is an appropriate choice since its combined α-adrenergic vasoconstrictive actions and β-adrenergic inotropic effects will increase systemic vascular resistance and cardiac output, thereby effectively raising the mean arterial pressure.[39,197–199] However, in situations where the PCWP is elevated or in patients with decreased ventricular compliance, the use of dopamine may be limited because it significantly increases venous return and ventricular filling pressure. In addition, dopamine increases shunting of pulmonary blood flow, leading to a decline in PaO_2. This effect may worsen hypoxemia in predisposed patients such as those with pneumonia or adult respiratory distress syndrome.[198,200]

Dobutamine is becoming more frequently advocated as the initial inotrope in the management of septic shock, particularly in patients with both a low mean arterial pressure and cardiac output. Dobutamine is comparable to dopamine in increasing cardiac output and is effective in raising mean arterial pressure. In contrast to dopamine, dobutamine lowers PCWP, decreases myocardial oxygen consumption, and causes less pulmonary shunting.[198–200] Since dobutamine may lower ventricular filling pressure, volume status must be monitored closely to avoid the development of hypotension and reduced MAP.[3,190] Fluids should be administered as needed to maintain the PCWP at maximum tolerated levels of 16 to 18 mm Hg. With the administration of greater amounts of fluid, cardiac output, oxygen delivery, and systemic oxygen consumption are significantly increased.

Dobutamine often is added to improve cardiac output in septic shock.[39] Dhainaut evaluated the combination of dobutamine and dopamine in septic patients with myocardial hypoxia and a low cardiac index (<3 L/minute/m^2).[201] The combination increased mean arterial pressure, systemic vascular resistance, cardiac output, and systemic oxygen consumption. In the coronary circulation, perfusion pressure increased and there was a reversal of myocardial hypoxia as indicated by decreased myocardial lactate production.

Edwards et al.[193] designed a protocol for drug administration in 29 septic patients to optimize cardiac index (>4.5 L/minute/m^2) and oxygen delivery. Following plasma volume expansion, patients were given dobutamine if the cardiac index was less than 3.5 L/minute/m^2 and norepinephrine if the systemic vascular resistance index was less than 1100 dynes·sec·cm^{-5}·m^2. Thus, patients with a high cardiac output, but an inadequate mean arterial pressure, received norepinephrine as initial therapy; dobutamine was added if the cardiac index fell. Conversely, dobutamine was infused first if cardiac output was inadequate to maintain mean arterial pressure; norepinephrine was added if the mean arterial pressure remained low and the systemic vascular resistance index had dropped below the predefined range. In addition, dopamine was added if the mean arterial pressure, cardiac index, and systemic vascular resistance index could not be maintained with norepinephrine or dobutamine. The mean cardiac index increased from 3.9 L/minute/m^2 to 5.1 L/minute/m^2 (p <0.001) and there were associated increases in oxygen delivery and consumption; the overall hospital survival rate was 52%. Unfortunately, the authors did not report mean infusion rates or the combination of agents required to achieve their ther-

apeutic endpoints. However, they did state that no relationship was found between the doses required and survival. They assert that most studies in which adrenergic agents are titrated against MAP alone report survival rates of $\leq 20\%$, despite initial reversal of hypotension. They conclude that the rational use of adrenergic agents and the achievement of appropriate therapeutic endpoints results not only in the reversal of hypotension, but also increases oxygen delivery and consumption, and may improve survival.

In summary, evidence suggests that the goal of therapy in managing patients with septic shock, or any form of shock for that matter, is not to simply normalize blood pressure, but to optimize oxygen delivery and consumption.[4,45,193,202,203] Once anemia and hypoxia have been corrected, cardiac output becomes the remaining parameter which can be adjusted to increase oxygen supply. Raising arterial blood pressure with inotropes or vasopressors before restoring adequate blood volume actually may worsen tissue perfusion. Therefore, the selection of an inotropic agent must take into consideration the patient's current hemodynamic status and the individual properties of those agents that will most effectively maintain or increase the mean arterial pressure and cardiac output. In many instances, due to individual variability and response, more than one inotrope and/or the addition of a vasopressor may be required to achieve these endpoints.

For A.J., since his mean arterial pressure remains low and his cardiac index at 4.1 L/minute/m^2 is not fully optimized, dobutamine may be used to enhance the inotropic effects of dopamine and further increase his cardiac output. In addition, dobutamine may decrease the PCWP and thereby enable further fluid administration. Dobutamine may be initiated at 2.5 µg/kg/minute and titrated upwards every five to ten minutes according to patient response, to 15 or 20 µg/kg/minute.

38. Vasopressors. Would the use of a vasopressor such as norepinephrine or phenylephrine be beneficial in A.J. at this time? Develop guidelines for the use of a vasopressor in patients with septic shock.

Norepinephrine. When fluid therapy and inotropic support fail to maintain a satisfactory mean arterial pressure, despite an elevated CO (CI), the use of a vasopressor should be considered. Norepinephrine is a predominant α-adrenergic agonist which frequently is used as an adjunct to therapy when inotropic agents alone are unsuccessful. Because there has been concern that excessive vasoconstriction may cause reflex decreases in cardiac output and hypoperfusion of vital organs, the use of norepinephrine often has been limited to end-stage shock. However, studies indicate that norepinephrine alone or in combination with inotropic agents may be beneficial in the management of septic shock.[193,204,205]

Desjars et al.[204] evaluated the effectiveness and safety of norepinephrine in septic patients with persistent hypotension despite volume expansion and therapy with dopamine at 15 µg/kg/minute. Norepinephrine, infused at a rate of 0.5 to 1 µg/kg/minute, increased the mean arterial pressure, systemic vascular resistance, and urine output while decreasing the heart rate. The cardiac index was increased or unchanged in 10 of 12 patients. They concluded that norepinephrine may restore systemic arterial pressure and urine flow in hypotensive septic patients when fluid repletion and dopamine have failed. The recommended endpoint of norepinephrine therapy was a diastolic arterial pressure that maintained a MAP of 70 mm Hg, a pressure that would sustain coronary and renal perfusion.

In a similar study,[205] norepinephrine reversed hypotension and significantly increased mean arterial pressure, systemic vascular resistance, and urine output, when previous therapy with plasma volume expansion and dopamine or dobutamine had failed. The cardiac index was increased, albeit insignificantly, in seven of ten patients, presumably due to stimulation of cardiac beta receptors. By limiting the systemic vascular resistance index to 700 dyne·sec·cm^{-5}·m^2 the investigators were able to prevent excessive vasoconstriction and promote an increased perfusion pressure to vital organs as reflected by an improved urine flow. Oxygen delivery and consumption were measured in six of ten patients with variable results. Although no patient died of refractory hypotension, four of ten patients did die of progressive hypoxia, leading the authors to conclude that regardless of the catecholamine(s) used, the ultimate goal of therapy should be to maximize oxygen delivery and consumption. These conclusions corroborate those of Edwards et al.,[193] who found that the attainment of a cardiac index greater than 4.5 L/minute/m^2 with norepinephrine, dobutamine, or a combination of both (with or without dopamine) was the best approach to ensure optimal oxygen delivery and thereby achieve a positive outcome.

Occasionally, patients may respond to epinephrine or phenylephrine when other catecholamines have failed, although neither of these agents are considered to be first-line therapy.[47,197] Epinephrine stimulates α-, β$_1$-, and β$_2$-adrenergic receptors (see Table 18.4). Cardiac output is augmented via increased contractility and heart rate, the contribution of each being highly variable. Blood vessels in the kidney, skin, and mucosa constrict in response to α-adrenergic stimulation, while vessels in the skeletal muscle vasodilate due to β$_2$ effects. A biphasic response in systemic vascular resistance is observed with increasing doses as β$_2$-receptors are activated at the lower range, while β$_1$-receptors are stimulated at higher levels. The improvement in cardiac output, therefore, may be negated by an increase in afterload at higher doses.[39]

Phenylephrine is a pure α-adrenergic agonist (see Table 18.4) and thus increases systolic, diastolic, and mean arterial pressure through vasoconstriction; reflex bradycardia may occur secondarily due to the absence of β-adrenergic effects. The increase in afterload, while increasing myocardial oxygen consumption, correspondingly increases coronary blood flow due to increased perfusion pressure and autoregulation.[206] Therefore, in patients with myocardial hypoxia, or in those experiencing atrial or ventricular arrhythmias, phenylephrine may be of benefit since it has minimal direct cardiac effects.[197] However, in situations where the cardiac output is decreased, phenylephrine may be detrimental. This is because preload is reduced from interstitial fluid losses due to increased capillary hydrostatic pressure effects. This response, in addition to the reflex bradycardia may significantly impair cardiac output.[207] (See Table 18.6 for a summary of vasopressor therapy.)

39. Given A.J.'s history of cardiovascular disease, what considerations must you account for before initiating a vasopressor agent? Outline an overall approach to maintaining adequate hemodynamic status.

A.J. has a history of coronary artery disease; therefore, a careful balance must be achieved between myocardial oxygen consumption and coronary perfusion pressure since he is more prone to myocardial ischemia. Further attempts to optimize mean arterial pressure and cardiac index with dopamine alone, could further increase myocardial oxygen consumption and precipitate ischemia. In addition, the presence of pulmonary edema and A.J.'s history of CHF limit further use of dopamine since the PCWP will increase with continued escalations in dosage. The use of a vasopressor will increase afterload and hence, myocardial oxygen consumption; however, if elevations in systemic vascular resistance are limited to produce an adequate mean arterial pressure without excessive vasoconstriction, the increase in perfusion pressure may offset the increase in myocardial oxygen consumption.

Table 18.6	Guidelines for Initiation of Vasopressor Therapy in Septic Shock[a,193,204,205]
1)	Maximize arterial oxygen content by providing supplemental oxygen with ventilatory support PRN; correct any existing anemia
2)	Expand intravascular volume with crystalloids to a PCWP of 16–18 mm Hg as tolerated. Supplement with colloids if albumin level <2 gm/dL
3)	If volume expansion fails to maintain a MAP of at least 65 mm Hg and CI >4.5 L/min/m^2, begin: a) dobutamine, if the MAP and CI are low b) norepinephrine, if MAP low, but CI adequate
4)	If MAP does not ↑, add: a) dobutamine, if CI falls below 3.5 L/min/m^2 b) norepinephrine, if SVR falls below predefined range (see #5) c) supplement with dopamine PRN to attain the desired endpoints
5)	Titrate norepinephrine to lowest effective dose which will maintain a MAP of 65 mm Hg; keep SVRI below 800–1100 dyne · sec · cm^{-5} · m^2 to avoid excessive vasoconstriction

[a] CI = Cardiac index; MAP = Mean arterial pressure; PCWP = Pulmonary capillary wedge pressure; PRN = As needed; SVR = Systemic vascular resistance; SVRI = Systemic vascular resistance index.

Based upon A.J.'s hemodynamic status, the following is a reasonable approach for further cardiovascular support. Since A.J.'s mean arterial pressure and cardiac index remain relatively low in terms of optimizing perfusion pressure and oxygen delivery, the addition of dobutamine at this point would be a logical choice. In combination with dopamine, dobutamine could further increase the cardiac index and mean arterial pressure. This would improve oxygen delivery and systemic and coronary perfusion pressures without further increasing myocardial oxygen consumption. In addition, the ventricular filling pressure (PCWP) may decrease, thereby allowing further augmentation of cardiac output with fluid administration. The dobutamine should be titrated to achieve a cardiac index of greater than 4.5 L/minute/m^2. If a mean arterial pressure ≥65 mm Hg cannot be achieved, norepinephrine should be added to increase the SVR within the aforementioned limits. Dopamine should be tapered as tolerated to 0.5 to 1 µg/kg/minute to enhance renal perfusion.

Although the above regimen is a rational approach, one should realize that the response to exogenous catecholamines in patients with septic shock is highly variable and a successful regimen in one patient may be unsuccessful in another. In addition, septic patients often require infusion rates in the moderate-to-high range.[45] Therefore, the goal is to use one or more agents at the dosages necessary to achieve the desired endpoints without unduly compromising the patient's status. The use of catecholamines, however, is only a stabilizing measure. Strict attention to all other physiologic parameters, as well as to nutritional support, antibiotic modification, and ongoing surgical intervention, cannot be overemphasized.

Alternative Therapies

Therapies directed against the initiators and mediators of sepsis are currently the focus of intense investigation. As previously discussed, and outlined in Table 18.7, numerous exogenous and endogenous substances are involved in the pathogenesis of sepsis. Strategies under development include those directed toward the initiators of sepsis (e.g., bacterial endotoxins and exotoxins), inflammatory cells (macrophage-monocytes and neutrophils), in addition to a host of inflammatory mediators (e.g., cytokines, interleukins, platelet-activating factor, kinins, endorphins). Although several experimental therapies hold considerable promise for the future, only these agents have undergone, or currently are under-going randomized, placebo-controlled clinical trials.

Immunotherapies

40. Which immunotherapies have been the primary focus of investigation in the treatment of sepsis and septic shock?

Antiendotoxin Therapies. Since endotoxin is the initiator of the inflammatory cascade of gram-negative sepsis, extensive research has been devoted to development and study of antibodies against the core lipid-A portion of endotoxin which possesses most of the biologic activity. Although the efficacy of monoclonal antibodies to endotoxin has been confirmed in animal studies,[208–210] four clinical trials have failed to demonstrate an overall survival advantage in patients with presumed gram-negative sepsis.[211–214]

Antiendotoxin antibodies were generated either from human (HA-1A) or murine (E5) splenic tissue. In initial studies,[211,212] although there were no significant differences in overall mortality rates between the treatment and the placebo groups, statistically significant differences were found within subgroups. E5 significantly improved survival and resolution of individual organ failures in patients with gram-negative sepsis who did not have shock refractory to fluid and inotropes at study entry.[211] HA-1A significantly improved survival and resolution of organ failures in a subset of patients with documented gram-negative bacteremia, with or without shock.[212] While the discordant results of these two studies could be explained by differences in methodology, such as definitions of shock and severity of illness at study entry, it was noteworthy that almost 33% of the patients in the treatment groups died despite monoclonal antibody therapy.[215]

Subsequent follow-up studies in patient subgroups, who appeared to derive benefit from antiendotoxin antibodies in the first trials, were unable to duplicate these initial results.[213,214] In a second trial of E5 in patients with suspected gram-negative sepsis, who specifically were not in refractory shock,[213] E5, in contrast to the first trial, did not improve survival in patients with documented gram-negative sepsis. Similarly, in a follow-up trial of HA-1A in patients with shock and presumptive gram-negative bacteremia, HA-1A was not effective in reducing mortality in patients with confirmed gram-negative bacteremia.[214] This trial was suspended when the first interim analysis revealed excessive mortality among patients who were treated with HA-1A who did not have gram-negative bacteremia as compared with patients in the same group who received placebo.

One explanation for the failure of antiendotoxin antibodies in clinical trials may be that the monoclonal antibodies HA-1A and E5 do not have strong binding affinity for endotoxin, and do not effectively inhibit endotoxin-mediated cytokine production.[266] Recently, a new antiendotoxin agent, *recombinant bactericidal/permeability-increasing protein (BPI)*, has demonstrated high-affinity binding for endotoxin with inhibition of endotoxin-induced cytokine release,[267] and has been shown to prevent mortality in animal models of lethal endotoxemia.[268] While these results are encouraging, further study is needed in animal models of actual sepsis before clinical trials in humans could be considered.

Monoclonal antibodies to tumor necrosis factor-a (anti-TNF-Mab), have conferred significant protection in various animal models of septic shock induced by endotoxin, gram-negative, or gram-positive bacteremia.[216,219] Numerous clinical trials have now been performed with anti-TNF-Mab in patients with presumed sepsis or sepsis syndrome,[220,221,269,270] however, none to date have achieved statistically significant benefits. Although overall mortality has not been affected, subgroups of patients have demonstrated improved survival.[220,221] In an initial study examining the safety and efficacy of anti-TNF-Mab in patients with severe sepsis or septic shock,

Table 18.7	Potential Therapies for Septic Shock

Endotoxin (Lipopolysaccharide)
Monoclonal antibodies[a]
  HA-1A, E5
Bactericidal permeability-increasing protein (BPI)[a]
Lipid-A analogues (active immunization)

Tumor Necrosis Factor (TNF)
Monoclonal Antibodies[a]
  TNF-Mab
Soluble TNF receptors[a]
Soluble TNF receptor immunoglobulin G (TNFr-IgG)

Interleukins
Interleukin-1 (IL-1)
  Receptor antagonists (IL-1ra)[a]
  Soluble IL-1 Receptors
  Monoclonal antibodies
Interleukin-6
  Monoclonal antibodies

Arachidonic Acid Metabolites
Cyclo-Oxygenase Metabolites
  Ibuprofen (cyclo-oxygenase)[a]
  Ketoconazole,[a] imidazole (thromboxane synthetase)
  Thromboxane A_2 receptor antagonists
Lipo-Oxygenate Metabolites
  Diethylcarbamazine (lipo-oxygenase)
  Leukotriene receptor antagonists
  Monoclonal antibodies
  Specific leukotriene inhibitors

Inflammatory Cells (Macrophages/Neutrophils)
Pentoxifylline
Adenosine
Amrinone
Dapsone
Antioxidants
Protease inhibitors

Platelet Activating Factor (PAF)
PAF receptor antagonists[a]

Modulators of Coagulation Disorders[b]
Antithrombin III
Protein C
Thrombomodulin
Hirudin
Plasminogen activators
Protease inhibitors

Modulation of Endothelium-Derived Factors and Adhesion Molecules
Endothelium-Derived Relaxing Factor (EDRF)/Nitric Oxide (NO)
  Diethyldithiocarbamate
  Nitricoxide Synthese Inhibitors
Adhesion Molecules
  Monoclonal antibodies

Complement
Monoclonal antibodies (fragment C5a)
MX-1 (a C5 blocker)
C1 inhibitor

Beta-Endorphin
Naloxone[a]

[a] Clinical trials in various phases (investigational agents; clinical trials evaluating efficacy of available agents.
[b] Associated clotting abnormalities include DIC, ARDS, and end-organ hypoperfusion.

there was a trend toward increased survival in patients with elevated TNF serum levels at study entry who received high-dose anti-TNF antibody treatment.[220] A larger clinical trial in patients with sepsis syndrome with or without shock, found no benefit in septic patients with organ dysfunction alone, while a 17% reduction in mortality was observed for patients in septic shock.[221] A second study is currently in progress to confirm these findings.

An alternative approach to blocking the effects of TNF involves the use of *soluble TNF receptors*, which bind to and inactivate TNF before it interacts with its cellular receptor.[270] Although effective in preclinical primate models,[270] a recently reported clinical trial examining escalating doses of soluble TNF receptor in patients with sepsis syndrome, revealed an increase in mortality in patients receiving higher doses of the receptor as compared to lower dose therapy and placebo.[271] These results, combined with the clinical observations from the anti-TNF-Mab trials to date, emphasize the complex balance of TNF levels in septic patients and the need to identify the conditions under which anti-TNF therapy is beneficial.

Interleukin-1 (IL-1) is another important mediator of septic shock. Previously known as endogenous pyrogen and leukocyte-activating factor, IL-1 is a potent proinflammatory cytokine with diverse biological effects including induction of fever, endothelial cell activation, hypotension, and shock. IL-1 also stimulates the release of other cytokines (e.g., TNF, IL-6, and platelet activating factor), and acts synergistically to cause tissue injury, particularly to the vascular endothelium.[34,36,40,213]

IL-1 receptor antagonist (IL-1ra) is a naturally occurring inhibitor of IL-1 produced by macrophages which binds avidly to the IL-1 receptor, but possesses no agonist activity.[36,213] Available in human recombinant form, IL-1ra has been shown to attenuate hemodynamic derangements and significantly improve survival in animal models of septic shock even when given two hours after the administration of endotoxin.[222–224] In an initial trial of patients with sepsis syndrome and septic shock, recombinant IL-1ra decreased mortality in a dose-dependent manner and reduced the production of IL-6, the cytokine that best correlates with mortality in septic patients.[225] In a larger, more definitive trial, to further establish the safety and efficacy of IL-1ra in the treatment of patients with sepsis syndrome, there was no significant reduction in overall mortality in patients receiving the study medication as compared with placebo.[226] Secondary and retrospective analyses of this study suggested, however, that the survival advantage with IL-1ra increased with increasing severity of illness. Patients with a predicted risk or mortality of $\geq 24\%$, and/or dysfunction of one or more organs (independent of organ system), had a statistically significant survival benefit.[226] These observations may enable prospective identification of patients who might benefit from this therapy in future trials and further define the role of IL-1ra in the management of sepsis syndrome.

41. What role do the currently available agents, ibuprofen and pentoxifylline have in the management of septic shock? What are the proposed mechanisms by which each of these agents might alter the pathogenesis of septic shock?

Ibuprofen

Arachidonic acid metabolites from both the cyclo-oxygenase and lipo-oxygenase pathways are elevated in septic shock.[227,228] The major cyclo-oxygenase metabolites implicated in the pathogenesis of septic shock are prostacyclin; thromboxane A_2 and B_2; and prostaglandins F_2, E_2, and I_2.[40,229] Inhibition of these substances results in increased survival in experimental models.[227] Studies in animals, as well as preliminary clinical trials, suggest that ibuprofen, which preferentially blocks thromboxane synthesis, may be useful in the treatment of sepsis and septic shock.[228–232] In laboratory experiments, ibuprofen, given either before or after the infusion of endotoxin or bacteria, reverses hemodynamic, metabolic, and coagulation abnormalities; blocks increases in microvascular permeability; improves mesenteric perfusion; and reduces mortality.[230,232] In addition, ibuprofen inhibits platelet aggregation, and may attenuate the effects of tumor necrosis factor and interleukin-1.[230,233] In a clinical study of patients with sepsis

syndrome or septic shock, rectally administered ibuprofen significantly decreased heart rate and temperature, improved blood pressure and respiratory function, and increased the frequency of shock reversal.[228] In contrast, a pilot study designed to evaluate the effects of combined intravenous and rectal ibuprofen in patients with severe sepsis detected no significant differences in hemodynamic or respiratory parameters or survival as compared to placebo controls.[232] The authors attributed their negative findings to a more critically ill patient population, who were thereby predisposed to poor absorption of the rectal ibuprofen. A multicenter clinical trial of ibuprofen in patients with severe sepsis currently is underway using an all-intravenous dosing regimen.

Pentoxifylline

Pentoxifylline, a methylxanthine derivative, has been found to have a variety of pharmacological effects which could be beneficial in septic shock. Pentoxifylline improves survival in experimental animal models and has been shown to increase red blood cell deformability, decrease platelet aggregation, reduce neutrophil adhesiveness to endothelium, and promote prostacyclin release.[234,236] These effects could reduce capillary occlusion and increase blood flow, thereby improving oxygen delivery to tissues with altered microcirculations.[234] In addition, pentoxifylline has been shown to inhibit tumor necrosis factor production in both animal models and in healthy human volunteers injected with endotoxin.[237,238] These data suggest a potential benefit in clinical endotoxemia and warrant further study into the mechanism of action of pentoxifylline in sepsis.

Naloxone

42. Is there any benefit to the use of naloxone or corticosteroids in the management of septic shock?

The secretion of beta-endorphin, an endogenous opiate, is elevated in septic shock. Animal studies have shown that endotoxin stimulates the release of beta-endorphin, and may contribute to the vasodilation and hypotension observed in septic shock.[239,240] Naloxone, a selective opiate antagonist, has been shown to reverse endotoxin-induced shock in various animal models.[240–243] Although initial studies and case reports in humans suggested a potential hemodynamic benefit in the treatment of septic shock,[244–246] controlled clinical trials have not shown an effect on survival or overall mortality as compared to placebo.[247,248]

The proposed rationale for the use of corticosteroids in septic shock stems primarily from their stabilizing effects on biomembranes and their potential inhibitory effects on the macrophage, which initiates many of the deleterious inflammatory responses in sepsis. *In vitro*, steroids block the synthesis of tumor necrosis factor in macrophages, inhibit phospholipase A_2 and complement-induced neutrophil aggregation, and reduce cytotoxic effects on endothelial cells.[249,251] Experimental studies in animals and an early clinical trial reported significant reductions in mortality with the use of corticosteroids and supported their initial use in the management of septic shock.[252–256] However, three prospective, placebo-controlled, clinical trials have convincingly demonstrated no survival benefit and suggest detrimental effects in selected patients.[257–259] Therefore, neither naloxone nor corticosteroids are of proven benefit in the management of patients with septic shock.

In summary, the incidence of septic shock is increasing and continues to carry a high mortality rate despite advances in antimicrobial therapy and hemodynamic support. With recent insights into the pathogenesis of sepsis and the endogenous mediators involved, immunotherapies directed toward interrupting the inflammatory cascade of sepsis are being developed. While there is conflicting evidence on the efficacy of these therapies in clinical trials, each individual agent has shown potential in subgroups of patients.[211,212,221,226] These findings illustrate the complexity of treating patients with sepsis and septic shock, and suggest that perhaps a combination of agents, given at a particular time and for a particular circumstance may provide a positive outcome. This approach of interrupting the inflammatory cascade at different levels by employing multiple inhibitors of inflammation, in addition to a therapeutic regimen that includes antibiotics and appropriate supportive care, could potentially be the most effective means for reducing the morbidity and mortality of septic shock.[31,34,40,215]

GLOSSARY

Afterload: Ventricular wall tension developed during contraction. Determined by the resistance or impedance the ventricle must overcome in order to eject end-diastolic volume. Left ventricular afterload is determined primarily by systemic vascular resistance; right ventricular afterload is determined primarily by pulmonary vascular resistance.

Arterial Pressure (BP): Pressure in the central arterial bed; determined by cardiac output and systemic vascular resistance.

Body Surface Area (BSA): Average male = 1.7 m^2.

Cardiac Index (CI): Cardiac output per square meter of body surface area (BSA).

Cardiac Output (CO): Amount of blood ejected from the left ventricle per minute; determined by stroke volume and heart rate. CO = SV × HR.

Central Venous Pressure (CVP)/Right Atrial Pressure (RAP): Measures mean pressure in right atrium and reflects right ventricular filling pressure. Primarily determined by venous return to the heart.

Compliance: Distensibility of the relaxed ventricle or stiffness of the myocardial wall.

Contractility: The inotropic state of the myocardium; affects stroke volume and cardiac output independently of preload and afterload.

Heart Rate (HR): Number of myocardial contractions per minute; regulated by autonomic nervous system. An increase or decrease alters cardiac output in same direction.

Left Ventricular Stroke Work Index (LVSWI): Amount of work the left ventricle exerts during systole; adjusted for body surface area (BSA).

Perfusion Pressure: The pressure gradient between the coronary arteries and the pressure in either the right atrium or left ventricle during diastole. A major determinant of coronary blood flow and oxygen supply to the heart.

Preload: End-diastolic fiber length before contraction; represented by ventricular volume (LVEDV); approximated by ventricular pressure (LVEDP) and pulmonary capillary wedge pressure (PCWP). Right ventricular preload reflected by central venous pressure (CVP) or right arterial pressure (RAP).

Positive End-Expiratory Pressure (PEEP): The application of positive pressure at the end of the expiratory phase of respiration to improve oxygenation.[262]

Pulmonary Artery Pressure (PAP): *Systolic (PAS):* Measures pulmonary artery pressure during systole; reflects pressure generated by the contraction of the right ventricle; *Diastolic (PAD):* Measures pulmonary artery pressure during diastole; reflects diastolic filling pressure in the left ventricle. May approximate pulmonary capillary wedge pressure (PCWP); normal gradient <5 mm Hg between PAD and PCWP.

Pulmonary Capillary Wedge Pressure (PCWP): Measures pressure distal to the pulmonary artery; reflects left ventricular filling pressures. May optimally increase to 16 to 18 mm Hg in critically ill patients. Usually lower than or within 5 mm Hg of PAD.

Pulmonary Vascular Resistance (PVR): Measure of impedance or resistance within pulmonary vasculature which right ventricle must overcome during contraction; determines right ventricular afterload.

Stroke Volume (SV): Amount of blood ejected from the ventricle with each systolic contraction. SV = CO/HR.

Stroke Volume Index (SVI): Stroke volume per square meter of body surface area (BSA).

Systemic Vascular Resistance (SVR): Measure of impedance applied by systemic vascular system to systolic effort of left ventricle; determined by autonomic nervous system and condition of vessels. Determinant of left ventricular afterload.

Systemic Vascular Resistance Index (SVRI): Systemic vascular resistance adjusted for body surface area (BSA).

Acknowledgment

We gratefully acknowledge Charles C Depew whose work provided a foundation for this chapter.

Update

Hypovolemic Shock

Timing of Fluid Resuscitation

Current management of hypotensive trauma patients with hypovolemia follows the guidelines outlined in the American College of Surgeons Advanced Trauma Life Support course.[59] Recently, however, the convention of immediately initiating fluid resuscitation before surgical correction of the hemorrhage has been challenged on the basis that aggressive administration of fluids may increase bleeding and reduce survival.[264] Postulated mechanisms for accentuated or secondary hemorrhage when fluids are given before surgical control of bleeding are: hydraulic disruption of an effective thrombus; dilution of coagulation factors; and decreased blood viscosity with subsequent reduced resistance to flow around an incomplete thrombus. In a prospective, controlled trial, Bickell et al.[264] compared immediate versus delayed fluid resuscitation in 598 hypotensive adults with penetrating torso injuries due to gunshot or stab wounds in an urban trauma care setting. The rate of survival was significantly higher in patients who did not receive fluid resuscitation until the time of operation compared with those who received traditional resuscitation before surgery (70% versus 62%). There was also a trend toward increased intraoperative blood loss and postoperative complications in the immediate-resuscitation group. Clinical findings of increased blood pressure, prolonged clotting times, and relative hemodilution in the immediate-resuscitation group were consistent with the proposed mechanisms for increased blood loss in this population. While the results of this trial challenge the volume, timing, and extent of fluid resuscitation for patients with penetrating torso injuries, further controlled trials examining additional patient variables are suggested before this practice should be adopted.[264,265] In addition, these results cannot be extrapolated to other trauma injuries or to a rural trauma care setting, in which the amount of time elapsed from the trauma scene to the operating room would be too extensive to warrant delayed resuscitation.

References

1   **Skowronski GA.** The pathophysiology of shock. Med J Aust. 1988;148:576.

2   **Shoemaker WC.** Circulatory mechanisms of shock and their mediators. Crit Care Med. 1987;15:787.

3   **Shoemaker WC.** Therapy of shock based on pathophysiology, monitoring, and outcome prediction. Crit Care Med. 1990;18:S19.

4   **Edwards DJ.** Practical application of oxygen transport principles. Crit Care Med. 1990;18:S45.

5   **Ferguson DW.** Shock. In: Wyngaarden JB, Smith LH, eds. Cecil Textbook of Medicine. Philadelphia: WB Saunders; 1992:207.

6   **Parrillo JE.** Shock. In: Wilson JD, Braunwald E, eds. Harrison's Principles of Internal Medicine. New York: McGraw-Hill; 1991:232.

7   **Effron MB, Chernow B.** Shock. In: Rubenstein E, Federman DD, eds. Scientific American Medicine: Cardiovascular Medicine. New York: Scientific American Inc; 1992:1cardIIIshock-1.

8   **Walley KR, Wood LDH.** Shock. In: Hall JB et al., eds. Principles of Critical Care. New York: McGraw-Hill; 1992:1393.

9   **Fiddian-Green RG et al.** Goals for the resuscitation of shock. Crit Care Med. 1993;21:S25.

10 **Mannix FL.** Hemorrhagic shock. In: Rosen P, ed. Emergency Medicine: Concepts and Clinical Practice. St. Louis: CV Mosby; 1988:179–202.

11 **Scheinkestel CD et al.** Fluid management of shock in critically-ill patients. Med J Aust. 1989;150:508.

12 **Simoons ML et al.** Improved survival after early thrombolysis in acute myocardial infarction. Lancet. 1985:578.

13 **Schreiber TL et al.** Management of myocardial infarction shock: current status. Am Heart J. 1989;117:435.

14 **Scheidt S et al.** Shock after myocardial infarction: a clinical and hemodynamic profile. Am J Cardiol. 1970;26:556.

15 **Chesebro JH et al.** Thrombolysis in myocardial infarction (TIMI) Trial Phase I: a comparison between intravenous tissue plasminogen activator and intravenous streptokinase: clinical findings through hospital discharge. Circulation. 1987;76:142.

16 **Ayres SM.** The prevention and treatment of shock in acute myocardial infarction. Chest. 1988;93:S17.

17 **Goldberg RJ et al.** Cardiogenic shock after acute myocardial infarction: incidence and mortality from community-wide perspective, 1975–1988. N Engl J Med. 1991;325:1117.

18 **Benapton JR et al.** Prognosis in cardiogenic shock after acute myocardial infarction in the interventional era. J Am Coll Cardiol. 1992;20:1482.

19 **Alpert JS, Becker RC.** Cardiogenic shock: elements of etiology, diagnosis, and therapy. Clin Cardiol. 1993;16:182.

20 **Lee L et al.** Multicenter registry of angioplasty therapy of cardiogenic shock: initial and long term survival. J Am Coll Cardiol. 1991;17:599.

21 **Bates ER, Topol EJ.** Limitations of thrombolytic therapy for acute myocardial infarction complicated by congestive heart failure and cardiogenic shock. J Am Coll Cardiol. 1991;18:1077.

22 **Lee L et al.** Percutaneous transluminal coronary angioplasty improves survival in acute myocardial infarction complicated by cardiogenic shock. Circulation. 1988;78:1345.

23 **Hibbard MD et al.** Percutaneous transluminal coronary angioplasty in patients with cardiogenic shock. J Am Coll Cardiol. 1992;19:639.

24 **Gacioch GM et al.** Cardiogenic shock complicating acute myocardial infarction: the use of coronary angioplasty and the integration of new support devices into patient management. J Am Coll Cardiol. 1992;19:647.

25 **Moosvi AR et al.** Early revascularization improves survival in cardiogenic shock complicating acute myocardial infarction. J Am Coll Cardiol. 1992;19:907.

26 **Farmer JA.** Cardiogenic shock. In: Civetta JM et al., eds. Critical Care. Philadelphia: JB Lippincott Co.; 1992:1129–142.

27 **Forrester JS et al.** Medical therapy of acute, myocardial infarction by application of hemodynamic subsets. N Engl J Med. 1976;295(Pt. 1,2):1356, 1404.

28 **McGhie AI, Goldstein RA.** Pathogenesis and management of acute heart failure and cardiogenic shock: role of inotropic therapy. Chest. 1992;102(5 Suppl. 2):626S.

29 **Dell'Italia LJ et al.** Comparative effects of volume-loading, dobutamine, and nitroprusside in patients with right ventricular infarction. Circulation. 1985;72:1327.

30 **Goldenberg IF.** Nonpharmacologic management of cardiac arrest and cardiogenic shock. Chest. 1992;102(5 Suppl. 2):596S.

31 **Parrillo JE.** Pathogenetic mechanisms of septic shock. N Engl J Med. 1993; 328:1471.

32 **Rackow EC et al.** Mechanisms and management of septic shock. Crit Care Clin. 1993;9:219.

33 **Bone RC.** Gram-negative sepsis: a dilemma of modern medicine. Clin Microbiol Rev. 1993;6:57.

34 **Bone RC.** The pathogenesis of sepsis. Ann Intern Med. 1991;115:457.

35 **ACCP-SCCM Consensus Conference: definitions for sepsis and organ failure and guidelines for the use of innovative therapies in sepsis.** Chest. 1992;101:1644.

36 **Giroir BP.** Mediators of septic shock: new approaches for interrupting the endogenous inflammatory cascade. Crit Care Med. 1993;21:780.

37 **Kreger BE et al.** Gram-negative bacteremia IV: re-evaluation of clinical features and treatment in 612 patients. Am J Med. 1980;68:344.

38 **Thurn JR.** Septic shock: evaluation of a life-threatening condition. Postgrad Med. 1990;87:53.

39 **Boyd JL et al.** The pharmacotherapy of septic shock. Crit Care Clin. 1989; 5:133.

40 **Casey LC et al.** Plasma cytokine and endotoxin levels correlate with survival in patients with the sepsis syndrome. Ann Intern Med. 1993;119:771.

41 **Schoeffel U et al.** The overwhelming inflammatory response and the role of endotoxin in early sepsis. Prog Clin Biol Res. 1989;308:371.

42 **Joop MH et al.** The role of tumor necrosis factor/cachectin in septic shock. Prog Clin Biol Res. 1989;308:463.

43 **Simpson SQ, Casey LC.** Role of tumor necrosis factor in sepsis and acute lung injury. Crit Care Clin. 1989;5:27.

44 **Damas P et al.** Tumor necrosis factor and interleukin-1 serum levels during severe sepsis in humans. Crit Care Med. 1989;17:975.

45 **Vincent JL, Linden P.** Septic shock: particular type of circulatory failure. Crit Care Med. 1990;18:S70.

46 **Taylor RW.** Sepsis, sepsis syndrome, and septic shock. In: Civetta JM et al., eds. Critical Care. Philadelphia: Lippincott; 1992:401.

47 **Cunnion RE, Parrillo JE.** Myocardial dysfunction in sepsis. Crit Care Clin. 1989;5:99.

48 **Ognibene FP et al.** Depressed left ventricular performance: response to volume infusion in patients with sepsis and septic shock. Chest. 1989;93:903.

49 **Vender JS.** Invasive cardiac monitoring. Crit Care Clin. 1988;4:455.

50 **Swan HJC et al.** Catheterization of the heart in man with the use of a flow-directed balloon-tipped catheter. N Engl J Med. 1970;283:447.

51 **Wiedermann HP et al.** Cardiovascular-pulmonary monitoring in the intensive care unit (Part I). Chest. 1984;85: 537.

52 **Hoffman EW.** Basics of cardiovascular hemodynamic monitoring. Drug Intell Clin Pharm. 1982;16:657.

53 **Ganz W et al.** A new technique for measurement of cardiac output by thermodilution in man. Am J Cardiol. 1971;27:392.

54 **Passmore JM, Goldstein RA.** Acute recognition and management of congestive heart failure. Crit Care Clin. 1989;5:497.

55 **Braunwald E et al.** Mechanisms of cardiac contraction and relaxation. In: Braunwald E, ed. Heart Disease: A Textbook of Cardiovascular Medicine. Philadelphia: WB Saunders; 1992:351.

56 **Lewis BS, Gotsman MS.** Current concepts of left ventricular relaxation and compliance. Am Heart J. 1980;99:101.

57 **Curley FJ.** Calculations commonly used in critical care. In: Rippe JM et al., eds. Intensive Care Medicine. Boston: Little, Brown; 1991:2001 (Appendix).

58 **Grossman W.** Clinical measurement of vascular resistance and assessment of vasodilator drugs. In: Grossman W, Baim DS, eds. Cardiac Catheterization, Angiography, and Intervention. Philadelphia: Lea and Febiger; 1991:143.

59 **Shock.** In: Advanced Trauma Life Support Program for Physicians, Student Manual. Chicago: American College of Surgeons; 1993:75.

60 **Yeston NS et al.** Transfusion Therapy. In: Civetta JM et al., eds. Critical Care. Philadelphia: JB Lippincott Co.; 1992: 427–43.

61 **Falk JL et al.** Fluid resuscitation in traumatic hemorrhagic shock. Crit Care Clin. 1992;8:323.

62 **Wagner BK et al.** Pharmacologic and clinical considerations in selecting crystalloid, colloidal, and oxygen-carrying resuscitation fluids, part 1. Clin Pharm. 1993;12:335.

63 **Imm A et al.** Fluid resuscitation in circulatory shock. Crit Care Clin. 1993;9: 313.

64 **Shoemaker WC et al.** Fluid therapy in emergency resuscitation; clinical evaluation of colloid and crystalloid regimens. Crit Care Med. 1981;9:367.

65 **Rackow EC et al.** Fluid resuscitation in circulatory shock: a comparison of the cardiorespiratory effects of albumin, hetastarch, and saline solutions in patients with hypovolemic and septic shock. Crit Care Med. 1983;11:839.

66 **Boutros A et al.** Comparison of hemodynamic pulmonary and renal effects of three types of fluids after major surgical procedures on the abdominal aorta. Crit Care Med. 1979;7:9.

67 **Brinkmeyer S et al.** Superiority of colloids over electrolyte solutions for fluid resuscitation (severe normovolemic hemodilution). Crit Care Med. 1981;9: 369.

68 **Puri VK et al.** Resuscitation in hypovolemia and shock: a prospective study of hydroxyethyl starch and albumin. Crit Care Med. 1983;11:518.

69 **Tranbaugh RF et al.** Determinants of pulmonary interstitial fluid accumulation after trauma. J Trauma. 1982;22: 820.

70 **Rackow EC et al.** The relationships of the colloid osmotic pulmonary artery wedge pressure gradient to pulmonary edema and mortality in critically ill patients. Chest. 1982;82:433.

71 **Virgillio RW et al.** Crystalloid vs colloid resuscitation: is one better than the other? Surgery. 1979;85:129.

72 **Virgillio RW et al.** Balanced electrolyte solutions: experimental and clinical studies. Crit Care Med. 1979;7:98.

73 **Moss GS et al.** Colloid or crystalloid in the resuscitation of hemorrhagic shock: a controlled clinical trial. Surgery. 1981;89:434.

74 **Peters RM, Hargens AR.** Protein vs electrolytes and all of the Starling forces. Arch Surg. 1981;116:1293.

75 **Moss GS et al.** Changes in lung ultrastructure following heterologous and hemologous serum albumin transfusion in the treatment of hemorrhagic shock. Ann Surg. 1979;189:236.

76 **Shires TG et al.** Response of extravascular lung waters to intraoperative fluids. Ann Surg. 1983;197:515.

77 **Metildi LA et al.** Crystalloid versus colloid in fluid resuscitation of patients with severe pulmonary insufficiency. Surg Gynecol Obstet. 1984;158:207.

78 **Falk JL et al.** Hemodynamic and metabolic effects of abdominal aortic cross-clamping. Am J Surg. 1981;142: 174.

79 **Velanovich V.** Crystalloids versus colloid fluid resuscitation: a meta-analysis of mortality. Surgery. 1989;105:65.

80 **Bisonni RS et al.** Colloids versus crystalloid in fluid resuscitation: an analysis

of randomized controlled trials. J Fam Pract. 1991;32:387.

81 **Gould SA et al.** Hypovolemic shock. Crit Care Clin. 1993;2:239.

82 **Wagner BK et al.** Pharmacologic and clinical considerations in selecting crystalloid, colloidal, and oxygen-carrying resuscitation fluids, part 2. Clin Pharm. 1993;12:415.

83 **Kruskall MS et al.** Transfusion therapy in emergency medicine. Ann Emerg Med. 1988;17:327.

84 **Almenoff PL et al.** Prolongation of the half-life of lactate after maximal exercise in patients with hepatic dysfunction. Crit Care Med. 1989;17:870.

85 **Canizaro PC et al.** The infusion of ringer's lactate solution during shock. Am J Surg. 1971;122:494.

86 **McKnight CK et al.** The effects of four different crystalloid bypass pump-priming fluids upon the metabolic response to cardiac operation. J Thoracic Cardiovasc Surg. 1985;90:97.

87 **Shoemaker WC.** Comparison of the relative effectiveness of whole blood transfusions and various types of fluid therapy in resuscitation. Crit Care Med. 1976;4:71.

88 **Lowery BD et al.** Electrolyte solutions in resuscitations in human hemorrhagic shock. Surg Gynecol Obstet. 1971;133:273.

89 **Cervera AL et al.** Dilutional re-expansion with crystalloid after massive hemorrhage: saline vs balanced electrolyte solutions for maintenance of normal blood volume and arterial pH. J Trauma. 1975;15:498.

90 **Holcroft JW et al.** 3% NaCl and 7.5% NaCl/dextran 70 in the resuscitation of severely injured patients. Ann Surg. 1987;206:279.

91 **Mattox KL et al.** Prehospital hypertonic saline-dextran infusion for post-traumatic hypotension. The USA multicenter trial. Ann Surg. 1991;213:482.

92 **Younes RN et al.** Hypertonic solutions in the treatment of hypovolemic shock: a prospective, randomized study in patients admitted to the emergency room. Surgery. 1992;111:380.

93 **Nacht A.** The use of blood products in shock. Crit Care Clin. 1992;8:255.

94 **Boyan CP, Howland WS.** Cardiac arrest and the temperature of banked blood. JAMA. 1963;183:58.

95 **Boyan CP.** Cold or warmed blood for massive transfusions. Ann Surg. 1964;160:282.

96 **Honig CL, Bove JR.** Transfusion-associated fatalities: review of Bureau of Biologic Reports 1976–1978. Transfusion. 1980;20:653.

97 **Hewson JR et al.** Coagulopathy related to dilution and hypotension during massive transfusion. Crit Care Med. 1985;13:387.

98 **Phillips TF et al.** Outcome of massive transfusions exceeding two blood volumes in trauma and emergency surgery. J Trauma. 1987;27:903.

99 **Counts RB et al.** Hemostasis in massively transfused trauma patients. Ann Surg. 1979;190:91.

100 **Calvin JE, Sibbald WJ.** Applied cardiovascular physiology in the critically ill with special reference to diastole and ventricular interaction. In: Shoemaker WC et al., eds. Textbook of Critical Care. Philadelphia: WB Saunders; 1989:312–26.

101 **Forrester JS et al.** Hospital treatment of congestive heart failure, management according to hemodynamic profiles. Am J Med. 1978;65:173.

102 **Tullis JL.** Albumin, background and use. JAMA. 1977;237:355, 460.

103 **Haupt MT et al.** Colloid osmotic pressure and fluid resuscitation with hetastarch, albumin, and saline solutions. Crit Care Med. 1982;10:159.

104 **Lucas CE et al.** Altered coagulation protein content after varied resuscitation regimens. J Trauma. 1982;22:1.

105 **Ring J et al.** Incidence and severity of anaphylactoid reactions to colloid volume substitutes. Lancet. 1977;1:466.

106 **Thompson WL.** Hydroxyethyl starch. Dev Biol Stand. 1980;48:259.

107 **Yacobi A et al.** Pharmacokinetics of hydroxyethyl starch in normal subjects. J Clin Pharmacol. 1982;22:206.

108 **Strauss RG.** Review of the effects of hydroxyethyl starch on the blood coagulation system. Transfusion. 1981;21:299.

109 **Strauss RG et al.** Hydroxyethyl starch accentuates Von Willebrand's disease. Transfusion. 1985;25:235.

110 **Lazrove S et al.** Hemodynamic, blood volume and oxygen transport responses to albumin and hydroxyethyl starch infusions in critically ill postoperative patients. Crit Care Med. 1980;8:302.

111 **Moggio RA et al.** Hemodynamic comparison of albumin and hydroxyethyl starch in postoperative cardiac surgery patients. Crit Care Med. 1983;11:943.

112 **Diehl JT et al.** Clinical comparison of hetastarch and albumin in postoperative cardiac patients. Surg Forum. 1981;22:260.

113 **Forrester JS et al.** Hospital treatment of congestive heart failure management according to hemodynamic profiles. Am J Med. 1978;65:173.

114 **Franciosa JA et al.** "Optimal" left ventricular filling pressure during nitroprusside infusion for congestive heart failure. Am J Med. 1983;74:457.

115 **Cohn JN et al.** Effect of short-term infusion of sodium nitroprusside on mortality rate in acute myocardial infarction complicated by left ventricular failure. Results of a Veterans Administration cooperative study. N Engl J Med. 1982;306:1129.

116 **Passamani ER.** Nitroprusside in myocardial infarction. N Engl J Med. 1982;306:1168.

117 **Cohn JN et al.** Vasodilator therapy of cardiac failure. N Engl J Med. 1977;29:254.

118 **Goldberg LI.** The role of dopamine receptors in the treatment of congestive heart failure. J Cardiovasc Pharmacol. 1989;14:S19.

119 **Murphy MB, Elliot WJ.** Dopamine and dopamine receptor agonists in cardiovascular therapy. Crit Care Med. 1990;18:S14.

120 **Lollgen H, Drexler H.** Use of inotropes in the critical care setting. Crit Care Med. 1990;18:S56.

121 **Anil OM, Hess ML.** Inotropic therapy for the failing myocardium. Clin Cardiol. 1992;16:5.

122 **Lindeborg DM, Pearl RG.** Inotropic therapy in the critically ill patient. Int Anesthesiol Clin. 1993;31:49.

123 **Kulka PJ, Tryba M.** Inotropic support of the critically ill patient: a review of agents. Drugs. 1993;45:654.

124 **Lee MR.** Dopamine and the kidney. Clin Sci. 1982;62:439.

125 **Dasta JF, Kirby MG.** Pharmacology and therapeutic use of low-dose dopamine. Pharmacotherapy. 1986;6:304.

126 **Leier CV.** Comparative systemic and regional hemodynamic effects of dopamine and dobutamine in patients with cardiomyopathic heart failure. Circulation. 1978;58:466.

127 **Chamberlain JA et al.** Dobutamine, isoprenaline, and dopamine in patients after open heart surgery. Intern Care Med. 1980;7:5.

128 **Francis GS et al.** Comparative hemodynamic effects of dopamine and dobutamine in patients with acute cardiogenic circulatory collapse. Am Heart J. 1982;103:995.

129 **Leier CV et al.** The relationship between plasma dobutamine concentrations and cardiovascular response in cardiac failure. Am J Med. 1979;66:238.

130 **Benotti JR et al.** Comparative vasoactive therapy for heart failure. Am J Cardiol. 1985;56:19B.

131 **Richard C et al.** Combined hemodynamic effects of dopamine and dobutamine in cardiogenic shock. Circulation. 1983;67:620.

132 **Carey RA, Jacob L.** The role of dopaminergic agents and the dopamine receptor in treatment for congestive heart failure. J Clin Pharmacol. 1989;29:207.

133 **Ruffolo RR.** Review: the pharmacology of dobutamine. Am J Med Sci. 1987;294:244.

134 **Goldenberg IF et al.** Effect of dobutamine on plasma potassium in congestive heart failure secondary to idiopathic or ischemic cardiomyopathy. Am J Cardiol. 1989;63:843.

135 **Meyer SL et al.** Influence of dobutamine on hemodynamics and coronary blood flow in patients with and without coronary disease. Am J Cardiol. 1976;38:103.

136 **Prozen RG et al.** Myocardial metabolic and hemodynamic effects of dobutamine in heart failure complicating coronary artery disease. Circulation. 1981;63:1279.

137 **Unverferth DV et al.** Tolerance to dobutamine after a 72-hour continuous infusion. Am J Med. 1980;69:262.

138 **Lefkowitz RJ et al.** Mechanisms of membrane receptor regulation. N Engl J Med. 1984;310:1570.

139 **Davis RF et al.** Acute oliguria after cardiopulmonary bypass: renal functional improvement with low-dose dopamine infusion. Crit Care Med. 1982;10:852.

140 **Parker S et al.** Dopamine administration in oliguria and oliguric renal failure. Crit Care Med. 1981;9:630.

141 **White DH et al.** Beneficial effects of prolonged low-dose dopamine in hospitalized patients with severe refractory heart failure. Clin Cardiol. 1979;2:135.

142 **Linder A.** Synergism of dopamine and furosemide in diuretic resistant, oliguric acute renal failure. Nephron. 1983;33:121.

143 **Van Loon GR et al.** Plasma dopamine: source, regulation, and significance. Metabolism. 1980;29:119.

144 **Whitfield L et al.** Dopaminergic control of plasma catecholamine and aldosterone response to acute stimuli in normal man. J Endocrinal Metab. 1980;51:724.

145 **Kiely J et al.** The role of furosemide in the treatment of left ventricular dysfunction associated with acute myocardial infarction. Circulation. 1973;48:581.

146 **Dikshit K et al.** Renal and extrarenal hemodynamic effects of furosemide in congestive heart failure after myocardial infarction. N Engl J Med. 1973;288:1087.

147 **Levine TB et al.** Activity of the sympathetic nervous system and renin-angiotensin system assessed by plasma hormone levels and their relationship to hemodynamic abnormalities in congestive heart failure. Am J Cardiol. 1982;49:1659.

148 **Parmley WW.** Pathophysiology of congestive heart failure. Am J Cardiol. 1985;56:7A–11A.

149 **Rocci M Jr, Wilson H.** The pharmacokinetics and pharmacodynamics of newer inotropic agents. Clin Pharmacokinet. 1987;13:91.

150 **Scholz H, Meyer W.** Phosphodiesterase inhibiting properties of newer inotropic agents. Circulation. 1986;73 (Suppl. III):III-99.

151 **Vincent JL et al.** The role of enoximone in the treatment of cardiogenic shock. Cardiol. 1990;77(Suppl. 3):21.

152 **Vincent JL et al.** Addition of phosphodiesterase inhibitors to adrenergic agents in acutely ill patients. Int J Cardiol. 1990;28:S7.

153 **Caldicott LD et al.** Intravenous enoximone or dobutamine for severe heart failure after acute myocardial infarction: a randomized double-blind trial. Eur Heart J. 1993;14:696.

154 **Iversen S et al.** Efficacy of phosphodiesterase inhibitor enoximone in management of postcardiotomy cardiogenic shock. Scand J Thor Cardiovasc Surg. 1992;26:143.

155 **Thuillez C et al.** Arterial hemodynamics and cardiac effects of enoximone, dobutamine, and their combination in severe heart failure. Am Heart J. 1993;125:799.

156 **Hamilton R et al.** Effect of the acetylator phenotype on amrinone pharmacokinetics. Clin Pharmacol Ther. 1986;40:615.

157 **Punk GB et al.** Oral bioavailability and intravenous pharmacokinetics of amrinone in humans. J Pharm Sci. 1983;72:817.

158 **Ward A et al.** Amrinone: a preliminary review of its pharmacological properties and therapeutic use. Drugs. 1983;26:468.

159 **Benetti JR et al.** Comparative inotropic therapy in heart failure patients. Circulation. 1983;68:128.

160 **Hermiller JB et al.** Amrinone in severe congestive heart failure: another look at an intriguing new cardiac drug. J Pharmacol Exp Ther. 1984;228:319.

161 **Taylor SH et al.** Intravenous amrinone in left ventricular failure complicated by acute myocardial infarction. Am J Cardiol. 1985;56:29B.

162 **Wilmshurst PT et al.** Haemodynamic effects of intravenous amrinone in patients with impaired left ventricular function. Br Heart J. 1983;49:77.

163 **Pacher M et al.** Hemodynamic and clinical limitations of long-term inotro-

pic therapy with amrinone in patients with severe chronic heart failure. Circulation. 1984;70:1038.

164 **Silverman BD et al.** Clinical effects and side effects of amrinone. Arch Intern Med. 1985;145:825.

165 **Ansell J et al.** Amrinone-induced thrombocytopenia. Arch Intern Med. 1984;144:949.

166 **Katz AM.** Potential deleterious effects of inotropic agents in the therapy of chronic heart failure. Circulation. 1986;73(Suppl. III):III-184.

167 **Konstam MA et al.** Relative contribution of inotropic and vasodilator effects to amrinone-induced hemodynamic improvement in congestive heart failure. Am J Cardiol. 1986;57:242.

168 **GISSI.** Effectiveness of thrombolytic treatment in acute myocardial infarction. Lancet. 1986;1:397.

169 **White HD et al.** Effect of intravenous streptokinase on left ventricular function and early survival after acute myocardial infarction. N Engl J Med. 1987; 371:850.

170 **Hugenholtz PG, Suryapranata H.** Thrombolytic agents in early myocardial infarction. Am J Cardiol. 1989;63: 94E.

171 **Gruppo Italiano Per Lo Studio Della Streptochinasi Nell'Infarcto Miocardico.** GISSI-2: A factorial randomized trial of Alteplase versus Streptokinase and heparin versus no heparin among 12,490 patients with acute myocardial infarction. Lancet. 1990;336:65.

172 **Kennedy JW et al.** Acute myocardial infarction treated with intracoronary streptokinase: a report of the society for cardiac angiography. Am J Cardiol. 1985;55:871.

173 **Prewitt RM.** Thrombolytic therapy in patients where hypotension or cardiogenic shock complicate acute myocardial infarction. Can J Cardiol. 1993;9: 155.

174 **Becker RC.** Hemodynamic, mechanical, and metabolic determinants of thrombolytic efficacy: a theoretic framework for assessing the limitations of thrombolysis in patients with cardiogenic shock. Am Heart J. 1993;125: 919.

175 **Mueller HS.** Management of acute myocardial infarction. In: Shoemaker WC et al., eds. Textbook of Critical Care. Philadelphia: WB Saunders; 1989;341–53.

176 **Mizock BA.** Controversies in lactic acidosis. JAMA. 1987;258:497.

177 **Iberti TJ et al.** Effects of sodium bicarbonate in canine hemorrhagic shock. Crit Care Med. 1988;16:779.

178 **Bersin RM et al.** Metabolic and hemodynamic consequences of sodium bicarbonate administration in patients with heart disease. Am J Med. 1989; 87:7.

179 **Cooper DJ et al.** Bicarbonate does not improve hemodynamics in critically ill patients who have lactic acidosis. Ann Intern Med. 1990;112:492.

180 **Stackpoole PW.** Lactic acidosis: the case against bicarbonate therapy. Ann Intern Med. 1986;105:276.

181 **Mueller HS et al.** Effect of dopamine on hemodynamic and myocardial metabolism in shock following acute myocardial infarction in man. Circulation. 1978;57:361.

182 **Holzer J et al.** Effectiveness of dopamine in patients with cardiogenic shock. Am J Cardiol. 1973;32:79.

183 **Goldsten RA et al.** A comparison of digoxin and dobutamine in patients with acute infarction and cardiac failure. N Engl J Med. 1980;303:846.

184 **Keung CH et al.** Dobutamine therapy in acute myocardial infarction. JAMA. 1981;245:144.

185 **DeWood MA et al.** Intra-aortic balloon counterpulsation with or without reperfusion for myocardial shock. Circulation. 1980;61:1105.

186 **Alcan KE et al.** Current status of intra-aortic balloon counterpulsation in critical care cardiology. Crit Care Med. 1984;12:489.

187 **Rutherford BD et al.** Direct balloon angioplasty during acute myocardial infarction in patients with severely compromised hemodynamics. Circulation. 1985;72(Suppl. 3):308.

188 **Shani J et al.** Percutaneous transluminal coronary angioplasty in cardiogenic shock. J Am Coll Cardiol. 1986; 7:149A.

189 **Waksman R et al.** Intra-aortic balloon counterpulsation improves survival in cardiogenic shock complicating acute myocardial infarction. Eur Heart J. 1993;14:71.

190 **Sibbald WJ.** Myocardial function in the critically ill: factors influencing left and right ventricular performance in patients with sepsis and trauma. Surg Clin North Am. 1985;65:867.

191 **Weinstein M et al.** The clinical significance of positive blood cultures: a comprehensive analysis of 500 episodes of bacteremia and fungemia in adults, II: clinical observations with special reference to factors influencing prognosis. Rev Infect Dis. 1983;5:54.

192 **Young LS.** Gram-negative sepsis. In: Mandell GL et al., eds. Principles and Practice of Infectious Diseases. New York: Churchill Livingstone; 1990: 611–36.

193 **Edwards JD et al.** Use of survivors' cardiorespiratory values as therapeutic goals in septic shock. Crit Care Med. 1989;17:1098.

194 **Parker MM et al.** Profound but reversible myocardial depression in patients with septic shock. Ann Intern Med. 1984;100:483.

195 **Rackow EC et al.** Hemodynamic response to fluid repletion in patients with septic shock: evidence of early depression of cardiac performance. Circ Shock. 1987;22:11.

196 **Shoemaker WC et al.** Clinical trial of survivors' cardiorespiratory patterns as therapeutic goals in critically ill postoperative patients. Crit Care Med. 1982;10:398.

197 **Parrillo JE.** Septic shock in humans: clinical evaluation, pathogenesis, and therapeutic approach. In: Shoemaker WC et al., eds. Textbook of Critical Care. Philadelphia: WB Saunders; 1989:1006–1024.

198 **De La Cal MA et al.** Dose-related hemodynamic and renal effects of dopamine in septic shock. Crit Care Med. 1984;12:22.

199 **Regnier B et al.** Comparative hemodynamic effects of dopamine and dobutamine in septic shock. Intensive Care Med. 1979;5:115.

200 **Jardin F et al.** Dobutamine: a hemodynamic evaluation in septic shock. Crit Care Med. 1981;9:329.

201 **Dhainaut JF.** Effects of the combination of dobutamine and dopamine on the hemodynamics and coronary circulation in human septic shock. Br J Clin Pract. 1986;40(Suppl. 45):59.

202 **Shoemaker WC et al.** Oxygen transport measurements to evaluate tissue perfusion and titrate therapy: dobutamine and dopamine effects. Crit Care Med. 1991;19:672.

203 **Schremmer B, Dhainaut J.** Heart failure in septic shock: effects of inotropic support. Crit Care Med. 1990;18:S49.

204 **Desjars P et al.** A reappraisal of the norepinephrine therapy in human septic shock. Crit Care Med. 1987;15:134.

205 **Meadows D et al.** Reversal of intractable septic shock with norepinephrine therapy. Crit Care Med. 1988;16:663.

206 **Weiner N.** Norepinephrine, epinephrine, and the sympathomimetic amines. In: Goodman A et al., eds. The Pharmacological Basis of Therapeutics. 7th ed. New York: Macmillian; 1985:145.

207 **Weil MH et al.** Treatment of circulatory shock: use of sympathomimetic and related vasoactive agents. JAMA. 1975;321:1280.

208 **Teng NNH et al.** Protection against gram-negative bacteremia and endotoxemia with human monoclonal IgM antibodies. Proc Natl Acad Sci USA. 1985;82:1790.

209 **Dunn DL et al.** Efficacy of type-specific and cross-reactive murine monoclonal antibodies directed against endotoxin during experimental sepsis. Surgery. 1985;98:283.

210 **Priest BP et al.** Treatment of experimental gram-negative bacterial sepsis with murine monoclonal antibodies directed against lipopolysaccharide. Surgery. 1989;106:147.

211 **Greenman RL et al.** A controlled trial of E5 murine monoclonal IgM antibody to endotoxin in the treatment of gram-negative sepsis. JAMA. 1991; 266:1097.

212 **Zeigler EJ et al.** Treatment of gram-negative bacteremia and septic shock with HA-1A human monoclonal antibody against endotoxin: a randomized, double-blind, placebo-controlled trial. N Engl J Med. 1991;324:429.

213 **St. John RC et al.** Immunologic therapy for ARDS, septic shock, and multiple-organ failure. Chest. 1993;103: 932.

214 **McCloskey RV et al.** Treatment of septic shock with human monoclonal antibody HA-1A. Ann Intern Med. 1994;121:1.

215 **Luce JM.** Introduction of new technology into critical care practice: a history of HA-1A human monoclonal antibody against endotoxin. Crit Care Med. 1993;21:1233.

216 **Silva AT et al.** Prophylactic and therapeutic effects of a monoclonal antibody to tumor necrosis factor in experimental gram-negative shock. J Infect Dis. 1990;162:421.

217 **Opal SM et al.** Efficacy of a monoclonal antibody directed against tumor necrosis factor in protecting neutropenic rats from lethal infection with *Pseudomonas aeruginosa*. J Infect Dis. 1990;161:1148.

218 **Tracey KJ et al.** Anti-cachectin/TNF monoclonal antibodies prevent septic shock during lethal bacteraemia. Nature. 1987;330:662.

219 **Hinshaw LB et al.** Survival of primates in LD100 septic shock following therapy with antibody to tumor necrosis factor (TNF). Circ Shock. 1990;30: 279.

220 **Fisher CJ et al.** Influence of an antitumor necrosis factor monoclonal antibody on cytokine levels in patients with sepsis. Crit Care Med. 1993;21: 318.

221 **Wherry J et al.** A controlled randomized double blind clinical trial of monoclonal antibody to human tumor necrosis factor (TNF-Mab) in patients with sepsis syndrome. Chest. 1993;104:53.

222 **Ohlsson K et al.** Interleukin-1 receptor antagonist reduces mortality from endotoxin shock. Nature. 1990;348:550.

223 **Dinarello CA et al.** Blocking IL-1: interleukin 1 receptor antagonist in vivo and in vitro. Immunol Today. 1991;12: 404.

224 **Arend WP.** Interleukin 1 receptor antagonist. J Clin Invest. 1991;88:1445.

225 **Opal SM et al.** The phase II interleukin-1 receptor antagonist (IL-1ra) sepsis syndrome trial: analysis of clinical, cytokine, and microbial features with outcome. Paper presented to 32nd Interscience Conference on Antimicrobial Agents and Chemotherapy. Anaheim, CA: 1992 Oct 14.

226 **Opal SM et al.** Initial findings of the interleukin-1 receptor antagonist (IL-1ra) phase III trial in patients with severe sepsis. In: Program and Abstracts of the 33rd Interscience Conference on Antimicrobial Agents and Chemotherapy. Oct 17–20, 1993, New Orleans, LA. Washington DC: American Society for Microbiology; 1993:122.

227 **Lefer A.** Significance of lipid; mediators in shock states. Circ Shock. 1989; 27:3.

228 **Bernard G et al.** Prostacyclin and thromboxane A_2 formation is increased in human sepsis syndrome. Am Rev Respir Dis. 1991;144:1095.

229 **Barron RL.** Pathophysiology of septic shock and implications for therapy. Clin Pharm. 1993;12:829.

230 **Metz CA et al.** Ibuprofen in animal models of septic shock. J Crit Care. 1990;5:206.

231 **Revhaug A et al.** Inhibitor of cyclo-oxygensase attenuates the metabolic response to endotoxin in humans. Arch Surg. 1988;123:162.

232 **Haupt MT et al.** Effect of ibuprofen in patients with severe sepsis: a randomized, double-blind, multicenter study. Crit Care Med. 1991;19:1339.

233 **Okusawa S et al.** Interleukin-1 induced a shock-like state in rabbits. J Clin Invest. 1988;21:1162.

234 **Waxman K.** Pentoxifylline in septic shock. Crit Care Med. 1990;18:243. Editorial.

235 **Bone RC.** Sepsis syndrome, new insights into its pathogenesis and treatment. Infect Dis Clin North Am.

236 **Schonharting MM, Schade UF.** The effect of pentoxifylline in septic shock—new pharmacologic aspects of an established drug. J Med. 1989;20:97.

237 **Schade UF.** Pentoxifylline increases survival in murine endotoxin shock and

decreases formation of tumor necrosis factor. Circ Shock. 1990;31:171.

238 **Zabel P et al.** Oxpentifylline in endotoxaemia. Lancet. 1989;ii:1474.

239 **Groeger JS.** Opioid antagonist in circulatory shock. Crit Care Med. 1986; 14:170.

240 **Holaday JW et al.** Naloxone reversal of endotoxin hypotension suggests role of endorphins in shock. Nature. 1978; 275:450.

241 **Faden A et al.** Naloxone treatment of endotoxin shock; stereospecificity of physiologic and pharmacologic effects in the rat. J Pharmacol Exp Ther. 1980; 212:441.

242 **Raymond RM et al.** Effects of naloxone therapy on hemodynamics and metabolism following a super lethal dose of *Escherichia coli* endotoxin in dogs. Surg Gynecol Obstet. 1981;152: 159.

243 **Reynolds DG et al.** Blockade of opiate receptors with naloxone improves survival and cardiac performance in canine endotoxic shock. Circ Shock. 1980;7:39.

244 **Peters WP et al.** Pressor effect of naloxone in septic shock. Lancet. 1981;7: 529.

245 **Hughes GS.** Naloxone and methylprednisolone enhance sympathomedullary discharge in patients with septic shock. Life Sci. 1984;3:2319.

246 **Groeger JS et al.** Naloxone in septic shock. Crit Care Med. 1983;11:650.

247 **Safani M et al.** Prospective, controlled, randomized trial of naloxone infusion in early hyperdynamic septic shock. Crit Care Med. 1989;17:1004.

248 **Demaria A et al.** Naloxone versus placebo in the treatment of septic shock. Lancet. 1985;1:1363.

249 **Hammerschmidt DE et al.** Corticosteroids inhibit complement-induced granulocyte aggregation: a possible mechanism for their efficacy in shock states. J Clin Invest. 1979;63:798.

250 **Skubitz KM et al.** Corticosteroids block binding of chemotactic peptide to its receptor on granulocytes and cause disaggregation of granulocyte aggregates *in vitro.* J Clin Invest. 1981; 68:13.

251 **Jacobs RF, Tabor DR.** Immune cellular interactions during sepsis and septic injury. Crit Care Clin. 1989;5:9.

252 **Hinshaw LB et al.** Survival of primates in LD100 septic shock following steroid/antibiotic therapy. J Surg Res. 1980;28:151.

253 **Hinshaw LB et al.** Survival of primates in lethal septic shock following delayed treatment with steroids. Circ Shock. 1981;8:291.

254 **Hinshaw LB et al.** Current management of the septic shock patient; experimental basis for treatment. Circ Shock. 1982;9:543.

255 **Hinshaw LB.** Application of animal shock models to the human. Circ Shock. 1985;17:205.

256 **Schumer W.** Steroids in the treatment of clinical septic shock. Ann Surg. 1976;184:333.

257 **Sprung CL et al.** The effects of high-dose steroids in patients with septic shock: a prospective controlled study. N Engl J Med. 1984;311:1137.

258 **Bone RE et al.** A controlled clinical trial of high-dose methylprednisolone in the treatment of severe sepsis and septic shock. N Engl J Med. 1987;317: 653.

259 **Veterans Administration Systemic Sepsis Cooperative Study Group: effect of high-dose glucocorticoid therapy on mortality in patients with clinical signs of systemic sepsis.** N Engl J Med. 1987;317:653.

260 **Kiyingi A et al.** Metolazone in treatment of severe congestive heart failure. Lancet. 1990;I:29.

261 **Lahav M et al.** Intermittent administration of furosemide vs continuous infusion preceded by a loading dose for congestive heart failure. Chest. 1992; 102:725.

262 **Steinberg KP, Pierson DJ.** Clinical approach to the patient with acute oxygenation failure. In: Pierson DJ, Kacmarek RM, eds. Foundations of Respiratory Care. New York: Churchill Livingstone; 1992:721.

263 **ASC Committee on Trauma.** ATLS Student Manual. 1993

264 **Bickell WH et al.** Immediate versus delayed fluid resuscitation for hypotensive patients with penetrating torso injuries. N Engl J Med. 1994;331:1105.

265 **Jacobs LM.** Timing of fluid resuscitation in trauma. N Engl J Med. 1994; 331:1153. Editorial.

266 **Van Dervort AL, Danner RL.** Anti-endotoxin approaches to septic shock therapy. Crit Care Med. 1994;22:539. Editorial.

267 **Marra MN et al.** Endotoxin-binding and -neutralizing properties of recombinant bactericidal/permeability-increasing protein and monoclonal antibodies HA-1A and E5. Crit Care Med. 1994; 22:559.

268 **Fisher CJ et al.** Human neutrophil bactericidal/permeability-increasing protein reduces mortality rate from endotoxin challenge: a placebo-controlled study. Crit Care Med. 1994;22: 553.

269 **Wherry JC et al.** Tumor necrosis factor and the therapeutic potential of anti-tumor necrosis factor antibodies. Crit Care Med. 1993;21:S436.

270 **Van der Pol T, Lowry SF.** Tumor necrosis factor in sepsis: mediator of multiple organ failure or essential part of host defense? Shock. 1995;3:1.

271 **Agosti JM et al.** The sTNFR Sepsis Study Group. Treatment of patients with sepsis syndrome with soluble TNF receptor (sTNFR). Proceedings of the 34th Annual ICAAC, in press.

Chapter 19

Asthma

Timothy H Self
H William Kelly

Pulmonary Function Tests 19-1
  Blood gas measurements 19-1
    Oxygen saturation
      (See Equation 19.1 and Figure 19.1) 19-2
  Spirometry (See Figures 19.2 to 19.5) 19-2
  Body plethysmography 19-3
  Obstructive versus restrictive airway disease
      (See Figure 19.4) 19-3
  Reversible airway obstruction (See Figure 19.6) 19-3
  Limitations of spirometry 19-3
  Diffusion capacity 19-3
Asthma 19-4
  Pathophysiology 19-4
  Symptoms 19-5
  Diagnosis 19-6
  Goals of Therapy 19-6
Acute Asthma 19-6
  Assessment 19-6
    Signs and symptoms 19-6
    Extent of obstruction 19-8
    Need for hospitalization 19-8
  β-Adrenergic Agonist Therapy 19-8
    Beta agonists compared to other bronchodilators ... 19-8
    Preferred routes of administration
      (See Figures 19.8 to 19.10) 19-9
    Comparison of β₂-agonists (See Table 19.1) 19-9
    Dosing (See Table 19.2) 19-10
    Cardiovascular effects 19-10
    Adverse effects 19-11
    Additive theophylline toxicity 19-13
    β-adrenergic subsensitivity 19-13
    Beta agonists in combination with theophylline 19-14
    Beta agonists in combination with
      corticosteroids 19-14
  Respiratory Failure 19-15
    Signs and symptoms 19-15
    Beta agonists 19-15
    Theophylline 19-15
      Monitoring therapy 19-15
      Loading dose (LD) (See Equations 19.2 to 19.4) ...19-15
      Maintenance dose
        (See Table 19.3 and Equations 19.5 to 19.7) 19-16

Timing of blood samples 19-17
Dosing adjustments 19-17
Response to therapy 19-17
Conversion to oral dosing 19-17
Adverse Effects of Short-Term Corticosteroid
  Therapy 19-18
Overuse of Beta Agonists 19-18
Chronic Asthma 19-19
  Goals of Therapy 19-19
  Initial Therapy (See Table 19.4) 19-19
  Cromolyn 19-19
    Mechanism of action 19-20
    Comparison to theophylline 19-20
    Dosage forms 19-20
  Seasonal Asthma 19-20
    Nedocromil, Cromolyn, Inhaled Corticosteroids ...19-20
  Corticosteroids 19-20
  Theophylline 19-22
    Dosing (See Table 19.6) 19-22
    Monitoring therapy (See Table 19.7) 19-22
    Product selection 19-22
      Bioequivalency 19-22
    In infants (See Table 19.8) 19-23
    Theophylline salts (See Table 19.9) 19-23
    Rectal theophylline 19-23
    Toxicity 19-23
    Overdose 19-24
    Drug interactions 19-24
      Inhibition of metabolism 19-24
        Erythromycin 19-24
        Cimetidine 19-24
      Induction of metabolism 19-25
  Anticholinergics 19-25
Exercise-Induced Asthma (EIA)
(See Figure 19.11) 19-25
  Treatment 19-26
Nocturnal Asthma 19-26
  Treatment 19-26
Patient Education 19-27
Drug-Induced Asthma 19-28

Pulmonary Function Tests

The principal function of the respiratory system is to exchange oxygen (O_2) and carbon dioxide (CO_2). The lungs, in conjunction with the cardiovascular system, provide adequate O_2 to the body tissues for normal cellular functions. In addition to gas exchange, the lungs filter toxic materials, metabolize compounds, and protect the body from environmental microorganisms. Disease processes can alter the mechanics of airflow to and from alveoli (ventilation), or can alter gas exchange between alveoli and the blood stream (diffusion). Thus, diseases of the respiratory system have a significant impact upon numerous bodily functions. As a result, pulmonary function tests have been developed to provide objective measurements of the integrity of the respiratory system.

Blood Gas Measurements

The best indicators of overall lung function (ventilation and diffusion) are the arterial blood gases (i.e., PaO_2, $PaCO_2$, pH). Although arterial blood gas (ABG) measurements also are dependent upon the cardiovascular status of the patient, they are indispensable in assessing both acute and chronic changes in pulmonary patients. (See Chapter 27: Acid-Base Disorders for a review of arterial blood gases.) Another means of assessing the patient's ability to oxygenate tissues adequately is to measure *oxygen saturation* which is described by Equation 19.1.

$$O_2 \text{ Saturation} = \frac{\begin{array}{c}\text{Quantity of } O_2 \\ \text{Actually Bound} \\ \text{to Hemoglobin}\end{array}}{\begin{array}{c}\text{Quantity of } O_2 \\ \text{That Can Be Bound} \\ \text{to Hemoglobin}\end{array}} \times 100\%$$

Eq 19.1

According to this equation, oxygen saturation is the *ratio* between the actual amount of oxygen bound to hemoglobin and the potential amount of oxygen that could be bound to hemoglobin at a given pressure. The denominator in the above equation is the *oxygen capacity*. The normal oxygen saturation of arterial blood at a PaO_2 of 100 mm Hg is 97.5%; that of mixed venous blood at a PO_2 of 40 mm Hg is about 75%.[1,2] Oxygen saturations can be measured continuously with transcutaneous monitors. This type of monitoring is extremely helpful in determining whether supplemental oxygen therapy is indicated in patients with various chronic respiratory diseases. At a PaO_2 of less than 60 mm Hg, O_2 saturation begins to drop precipitously. (See Figure 19.1.)

Spirometry

Lung volumes often are measured to obtain information about the size of the patient's lungs because pulmonary diseases can affect the volume of air that can be inhaled and exhaled. The classic volume displacement spirometer pictured in Figure 19.2 is used to measure lung volumes. As the patient breathes, the bell of the spirometer is displaced, and the pen deflection reflects the volume of air entering or exiting the lung. The *tidal volume* is the volume of air inspired or expired during normal breathing. The volume of air blown off after maximal inspiration to full expiration is defined as the *vital capacity (VC)*. The *residual volume (RV)* is the volume of air left in the lung after maximal expiration. The volume of air left after a normal expiration is the *functional residual capacity (FRC)*. *Total lung capacity (TLC)* is the vital capacity plus the residual volume. Patients with obstructive lung disease have difficulty with expiration; therefore, they tend to have a decreased VC, an increased RV, and a normal TLC. Classical restrictive lung diseases present with decrements in all lung volumes.[1-3] Patients also may have mixed lesion diseases, in which case the classical findings are not apparent until the disease has advanced considerably.

Fig 19.2 Spirometric Graphics During Quiet Breathing and Maximal Breathing

The spirometer also can be used to evaluate the performance of the patient's lungs, thorax, and respiratory muscles in moving air into and out of the lungs. Forced expiratory maneuvers amplify the ventilation abnormalities produced. The single most useful test for ventilatory dysfunction is the *forced expiratory volume (FEV)*. The FEV is measured by having the patient exhale into the spirometer as forcefully and completely as possible after maximal inspiration. The resulting volume curve is plotted against time (see Figure 19.3) so that flow rates can be estimated.

As a result of technological advances, the standard spirometers contain pneumotachographs in the mouthpieces that can measure air flow rates directly. A number of important measures of lung function are made from the resulting flow/volume curves (see Figure 19.4). The advantages of this technique include display of simultaneous flows at any lung volume; visual estimation of patient effort and cooperation; high reproducibility within, as well as across, individuals; and analysis of the distribution of flow limitation.[1,4]

The forced expiratory volume in the first second (FEV_1) of the FVC and the forced vital capacity (i.e., the maximum volume of air exhaled with maximally forced effort from a position of maximal inspiration) commonly are measured to determine the dynamic performance of the lung in moving air. The FEV_1 usually is expressed as a percentage of the total volume of air exhaled and is reported as the FEV_1/FVC ratio. Healthy persons generally can exhale at least 75% to 80% of their vital capacity in one second and almost all of it in three seconds. Thus the FEV_1 normally is 80% of the FVC. The patient's breathing ability is compared against ''predicted normal'' values for patients with similar physiological characteristics because lung volumes are dependent upon age, race, gender, height, and weight. For example, an average-sized young adult male may have an FVC of 4 to 5 L and a corresponding FEV_1 of 3.2 to 4 L. The FEV_1 and the FVC are the most reproducible of the pulmonary function tests.

The *peak expiratory flow rate (PEFR)* is the maximal rate of flow that can be produced during the forced expiration. The PEFR can be measured easily with various hand-held peak-flow meters (see Figure 19.5) and commonly is used in emergency rooms (ERs) and clinics to quickly and objectively assess the effectiveness of bronchodilators in the treatment of acute asthma attacks. Peak flow meters also can be used at home by asthmatics to assess chronic therapy. The changes in PEFR generally parallel those of the FEV_1; however, the PEFR is a less reproducible measure than the FEV_1.[4] A healthy average-sized young adult male typically will have a PEFR of 550 to 700 L/minute.

The forced expiratory flow ($FEF_{25\%-75\%}$) is the mean forced expiratory flow during the middle half of the FVC and is measured

Fig 19.1 The oxygen dissociation curve reveals that the percent saturation of hemoglobin increases almost linearly with increases in the arterial O_2 tension until a PaO_2 of 55 to 65 mm Hg is reached. At PaO_2 values above this, the increase in hemoglobin saturation becomes proportionately less and relatively little additional oxygen is added to the hemoglobin despite large increases in PaO_2. Reproduced with permission from reference 2.

as the slope of the line between 25% and 75% of FVC on the flow volume curve. This value formerly was called the maximal mid-expiratory flow rate (MMEF) and is expressed in L/second.[5] (See Figure 19.3.) Flows at less than 75% of FVC are limited by airway compressibility and, therefore, determined by the elastic recoil force of the lung and the resistance to flow upstream of the collapse (see Figure 19.4A). Flows at this portion of the curve (i.e., at the middle part of expiration) are said to be independent of patient expiratory effort.[1] The $FEF_{25\%-75\%}$ is a more sensitive measure of air flow resistance in the small airways (e.g., those <2 mm in diameter).[4]

Body Plethysmography

Another measure of airway mechanics that is confined principally to research laboratories is body plethysmography. The body plethysmograph measures the total volume of air in the lungs including any air trapped behind closed airways. Briefly, the patient sits in an enclosed air-tight chamber that has a known fixed volume and breathes into a pneumotachometer that measures air flow. This procedure measures *airway resistance (Raw)* and its reciprocal, *airway conductance (Gaw)*. Since the plethysmograph also simultaneously measures thoracic gas volume, airway conductance at specific gas volumes [i.e., *specific airway conductance (SGaw)*] can be measured.[1,4] Thus, with body plethysmography to calculate the patient's entire thoracic volume and the amount of air remaining in the lungs at the end of tidal expiration (i.e., the functional residual capacity). Alterations of lung volume significantly affect airway resistance; thus, measurement of SGaw which adjusts for these changes is advantageous.[4] The specific airway conductance (SGaw) frequently is measured in studies of bronchodilators; changes in SGaw generally parallel those of the FEV_1.[4]

Obstructive versus Restrictive Airway Disease

Generally, pulmonary disorders fall into two categories: those that restrict the lungs and thorax, and those that obstruct them. In simplest terms, restrictive disease limits airflow during inspiration and obstructive disease limits airflow during expiration. Restrictive disease results from a loss of elasticity (e.g., fibrosis, pneumonia) or physical deformities of the chest (e.g., kyphoscoliosis) with a consequent inability to expand the lung and a reduced total lung capacity. Therefore, a typical flow/volume curve (see Figure

19.4C) for a patient with restrictive disease shows markedly depressed volumes with increased flow rates (when corrected for the volume).

Whereas restrictive airway diseases limit lung expansion, obstructive airway diseases (e.g., bronchitis, asthma) narrow air passages, create air turbulence, and increase resistance to air flow. Disease states may produce narrowing of airways through smooth muscle constriction (bronchospasm), mucosal edema, inflammatory cell infiltration of bronchial walls and lumen, or excessive mucus secretion. In obstructive diseases, maximal expiration may begin at higher than normal lung volumes and the flow rates are depressed (see Figure 19.4B). Resistance to flow is increased at lower lung volumes giving the characteristic scooped out appearance of the obstructive flow/volume curve (see Figure 19.4B). The MMFR or FEF_{50} can detect early obstructive changes in the small airways before significant symptoms and hopefully while these objective changes are potentially reversible.

Reversible Airway Obstruction

Spirometry often is used to determine the reversibility of airways disease. Although many generally associate reversibility with bronchospasm, therapy can improve airflow by reversing any of the causative pathologic processes described in the previous paragraph. Significant clinical reversibility produced from bronchodilators is determined by the tests outlined in Figure 19.6. Due to a greater potential for variability, larger airway changes are required before the tests of small airway diseases ($FEF_{25\%-50\%}$, $FEF_{50\%}$) become significant. The FEV_1 has low variability and during acute bronchospasm shows the best correlation with clinical symptoms. Therefore, the FEV_1 is considered to be the "gold standard" test for determining reversibility of airway disease and bronchodilator efficacy. Significant clinical reversibility is defined as a 15% to 20% improvement in FEV_1 or PEFR following bronchodilator administration. An improvement of 20% in FEV_1 provides noticeable subjective relief of respiratory symptoms in most patients. For patients with a very low baseline FEV_1 (e.g., <1 L), an absolute improvement of 250 mL sometimes is considered a better indicator of therapeutic benefit than assessing percentage of change. In either case, the patient's subjective clinical impression also should be considered when using pulmonary function testing and drug challenges as predictors for future therapy.

Limitations of Spirometry

Since the FEV_1 and the PEFR are both highly effort dependent, complete patient cooperation is required for reliable results. Therefore, spirometric tests often are unobtainable in patients who are severely ill, as well as in patients who are very old or very young. The FEV_1 and PEFR also are relatively insensitive to small airway changes, and, therefore, unable to detect early mucus plugging and inflammation in small bronchioles. Although the MMFR is a more sensitive test of small airway obstruction, it is also much more variable, requiring larger changes (30% to 40%) to be clinically significant.

Diffusion Capacity

Arterial blood gases (PaO_2, $PaCO_2$, and pH) are the best laboratory tests for determining whether the lung is adequately oxygenating the blood.[2] The carbon monoxide diffusing capacity (Dco) also may be helpful if concurrent ventilation abnormalities make it difficult to determine whether the low PaO_2 is due to poor ventilation or poor diffusion. In this test, the patient inspires a gas containing a low concentration of carbon monoxide (CO) and then holds his breath for ten seconds; the CO content of the blood is then measured. Diffusing capacity is diminished in emphysema, sarcoidosis, asbestosis, pulmonary edema, and pulmonary fibrosis. It usually is normal in asthma, bronchitis, and pneumonias.

Fig 19.3

Fig 19.4 Flow/Volume Curves Resulting from a Forced Expiratory Maneuver. A Normal flow/volume curve; B typical pattern for obstructive disease; C typical pattern for restrictive disease.

Asthma

According to the National Institutes of Health (NIH) Expert Panel Report, asthma is "a lung disease with the following characteristics: 1) airway obstruction that is reversible (but not completely so in some patients) either spontaneously or with treatment; 2) airway inflammation; and 3) increased airway responsiveness to a variety of stimuli."[6] An International Consensus Report defined asthma as a "chronic inflammatory disorder of the airways in which many cells play a role, including mast cells and eosinophils. In susceptible individuals this inflammation causes symptoms which are usually associated with widespread but variable airflow obstruction that is often reversible either spontaneously or with treatment, and causes an associated increase in airway responsiveness to a variety of stimuli."[7]

At least ten million Americans have asthma. It is an underdiagnosed and undertreated condition that is estimated to have overall costs exceeding $6 billion annually in the U.S.[8] Asthma is the leading cause of lost school days in children and is a common cause of lost work days among adults.

Mortality due to asthma is rising for unknown reasons, and death rates are higher in minority populations. In response to the increased mortality from asthma noted in the 1980s and the enormous human and economic toll of this disease, the NIH published "Guidelines for the Diagnosis and Management of Asthma" (i.e., The National Asthma Education Program Expert Panel Report) in 1991.[6] A similar report was published in 1992 by a panel of international experts (including some members of the NIH Expert Panel), entitled the "International Consensus Report on Diagnosis and Management of Asthma."[7] Application of these landmark reports by clinicians and patients is considered vital to reducing asthma morbidity and mortality.

Pathophysiology

Hyperreactivity (defined as an exaggerated response of bronchial smooth muscles to trigger stimuli) of the airways to physical, chemical, immunological, and pharmacological stimuli is pathognomonic of asthma.[6,7] Examples of these stimuli include inhaled allergens, respiratory viral infection, cold air, dry air, smoke, other pollutants, and methacholine. Although patients with allergic rhinitis, chronic bronchitis, and cystic fibrosis also experience bronchial hyperreactivity, these patients do not experience bronchiolar constriction as severely as asthmatic patients.[9] The degree of bronchial hyperreactivity of asthmatics correlates with the clinical course of their disease which is characterized by periods of remissions and exacerbations. During times of remission, a more intense stimulus is required to produce bronchospasm than during times of increased symptoms. Numerous theories have been proposed to explain the bronchial hyperreactivity found in asthma, yet none fully explains the phenomenon. Inflammation appears to be the primary process in the pathogenesis of bronchial hyperreactivity; however, neurogenic imbalances in the airways also may play a significant role.[6,7,9]

The release of chemical mediators (e.g., leukotrienes) of inflammation from mast cells has been proposed as a central mechanism for the pathogenesis of asthma. Mast cell mediator release plays a role in asthma induced by allergens in atopic individuals, in some occupationally-induced asthma syndromes, and in exercise-in-

Fig 19.5 Peak Flow Meter

duced asthma.[10,11] Although attractive, this hypothesis does not explain hyperreactivity induced by ozone exposure, viral infections, sulfur dioxide, and several other triggers. Furthermore, this hypothesis does not account for the absence of asthma in many atopic individuals.

Eosinophils are a major component of asthma pathophysiology. Various mediators attract eosinophils to the airways, and these leukocytes cause airway injury via release of a range of inflammatory biochemicals. Other leukocytes also are factors in airway inflammation. For example, lymphocytes secrete cytokines which activate and prolong the life of eosinophils.[6] As a result of the inflammatory process in the airways, there are a variety of changes including epithelial damage. Inflamed airways are hyperreactive (i.e., irritable or twitchy). Hyperreactivity can be measured in the physician's office by having the patient inhale small concentrations of nebulized methacholine or histamine. The concentration of aerosolized methacholine or histamine that decreases the FEV_1 20% is referred to as the PD_{20} or the PC_{20} (provocative dose or concentration that decreases the FEV_1 20%).[6] As patients are treated with optimal anti-inflammatory therapy, the PD_{20} obviously increases because the airways become less inflamed and, therefore, less hyperreactive or twitchy.

Another concept related to inflammation is "late phase" versus "early phase" asthma. The inhalation of specific allergens in atopic asthmatics produces immediate bronchoconstriction (measured by a drop in PEFR or FEV) that spontaneously improves over an hour or is reversed easily by inhalation of a beta agonist. Although this early asthmatic response (EAR) is blocked by the preadministration of cromolyn, beta agonists, or theophylline, a second bronchoconstrictive response often occurs 4 to 12 hours later.[6,10] This late asthmatic response (LAR) often is more severe, more prolonged, and more difficult to reverse with bronchodilators than the EAR. The LAR is associated with an influx of inflammatory cells and mediators described above. Bronchodilators do not block the LAR to allergen challenge; corticosteroids block the LAR, but do not affect the EAR; cromolyn blocks both.[6,10]

Pathologic changes in asthmatics found at autopsy include: 1) marked hypertrophy and hyperplasia of the bronchial smooth muscle, 2) mucus gland hypertrophy and excessive mucus secretion, and 3) denuded epithelium and mucosal edema due to an exudative inflammatory reaction and inflammatory cell infiltration.[12] Hyperinflation of the lungs from air trapping with extensive mucus plugging is found at autopsy in patients who died from acute asthma attacks, but these also are seen at autopsy in asthmatics dying from other causes.[12] The bronchial smooth muscle hypertrophy and mucus hypersecretion are secondary to the chronic inflammatory response.

Symptoms

The heterogeneity of asthma is reflected best in its clinical presentation. Classically, asthmatic patients present with intermittent episodes of expiratory wheezing, coughing, and dyspnea. Some patients, however, experience chest tightness or a chronic cough that is not associated with wheezing. There is a wide spectrum of disease severity, from patients with occasional, mild bouts of breathlessness to patients who wheeze on a daily basis despite continuous high doses of medication. In addition, the severity of asthma may be influenced by environmental factors (e.g., specific seasonal allergens). Symptoms frequently are associated with exercise and sleep. (See Question 1.)

The frequency of symptoms is a key component of asthma classification.[6,7] *Mild* asthmatics are defined as having intermittent, brief symptoms less than one to two times a week, nocturnal asthma symptoms less than two times a month, and are asymptomatic between symptoms. *Moderate* asthmatics have exacerbations more than one to two times a week, nocturnal asthma symptoms more than two times a month, and symptoms requiring an inhaled beta agonist almost daily. *Severe* asthmatics have frequent exacerbations, continuous symptoms, frequent nocturnal asthma symptoms, and hospitalization for asthma in the previous year.[7] This classification is of major significance when selecting long-term

Parameter	Restrictive	Obstructive
FVC	↓	Normal or ↓
FEV_1	Normal or ↓	↓
FEV_1/FVC	Normal or ↑	↓
FEF_{25-75}	Normal, ↓, ↑	↓

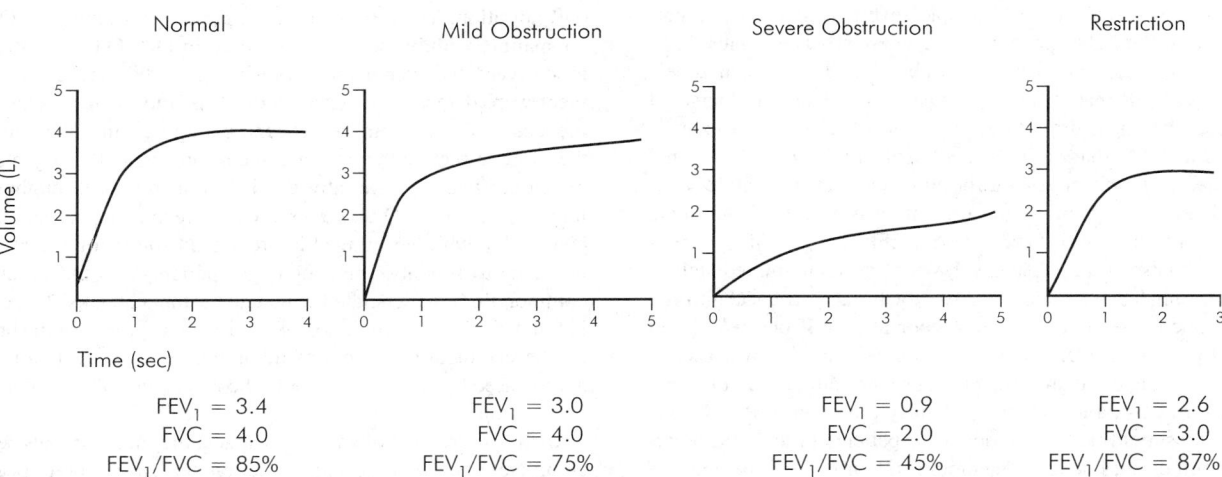

Normal	Mild Obstruction	Severe Obstruction	Restriction
FEV_1 = 3.4	FEV_1 = 3.0	FEV_1 = 0.9	FEV_1 = 2.6
FVC = 4.0	FVC = 4.0	FVC = 2.0	FVC = 3.0
FEV_1/FVC = 85%	FEV_1/FVC = 75%	FEV_1/FVC = 45%	FEV_1/FVC = 87%

Fig 19.6   Interpretation of Results of Spirometry.   The graphs depicted are for illustration only. The interpretation of flow rates may vary with the age of the patient. Reprinted with permission reference 6.

drug therapy in that inhaled anti-inflammatory agents are an essential part of management for moderate and severe asthmatics.[6,7]

Diagnosis

The diagnosis of asthma is based primarily upon a history of intermittent symptoms of reversible airway obstruction or on the demonstration of reversible airway hyperreactivity. Spirometric pulmonary function tests before, and after, the administration of a bronchodilator can be useful in assessing the reversibility of airway obstruction. If significantly depressed pulmonary function tests are not reversed by the administration of a bronchodilator acutely, a two- to three-week trial of continuous bronchodilator treatments followed by retesting might detect reversibility. If pulmonary function is normal, or near normal, at the time of spirometric assessment, the patient can be challenged by exercise or drugs that are known to produce bronchospasm in asthmatics (e.g., aerosolized histamine or methacholine). Skin testing for allergies may be useful in identifying triggering allergens, but is only of supportive value in the diagnosis of asthma.

Goals of Therapy

The NIH Expert Panel Report[6] established the following goals of therapy for asthma: 1) maintain normal activity levels, including exercise, 2) maintain (near) "normal" pulmonary function rates, 3) prevent chronic and troublesome symptoms (e.g., coughing or breathlessness in the night, in the early morning, or after exertion), 4) prevent recurrent exacerbations of asthma, and 5) avoid adverse effects from asthma medications.

In order to achieve these goals of therapy, the NIH Expert Panel also outlined some general treatment principles.[6] Asthma therapy has four components including patient education, environmental control, comprehensive pharmacologic therapy, and objective monitoring measures. Optimal long-term management requires a continuous care approach to prevent exacerbations and decrease airway inflammation. Early therapeutic interventions in managing acute exacerbations are very important in decreasing the chance of severe narrowing of the airways. Achieving the goals of asthma therapy also involves individualizing each patient's therapy. In addition, optimal care involves establishing a "partnership" between the patient, the patient's family, and the clinician.

Objective monitoring of lung function at home is an important component in attaining the goals of asthma therapy. Peak expiratory flow rate (PEFR) is dependent upon age, height, gender, and a maximal effort. Monitoring PEFR in the morning and evening should be considered in moderate and severe asthmatics.[6,7] Analogous to a traffic light, green, yellow, and red "zones" have been established to guide the patient and clinician. The "green zone" indicates a PEFR that is 80% to 100% of predicted or "personal best" (i.e., therapy is providing good control). The "yellow zone" indicates a PEFR that is 50% to 80% of predicted or "personal best" (i.e., call your physician for adjustment in preventive medication if PEFR stays in yellow zone after using 2 puffs of a beta agonist). The "red zone" indicates a PEFR that is <50% of predicted or "personal best" (i.e., call your physician immediately if use of an inhaled beta agonist does not bring you back into the yellow zone or begin a crisis management plan if one was given to you by your physician or go to an emergency room). Use of green, yellow, and red stickers, clips, or tapes directly on the peak flow meter helps patients readily identify their zones. PEFR zone values also should be written down for patients in their PEFR diaries. A full discussion of home monitoring of PEFR is beyond the scope of this chapter, and the reader is referred to more detailed sources.[6,7,14] (Also see Nocturnal Asthma.)

Since asthma consists of both bronchospasm and inflammation, therapy should be directed at both of these physiological problems. Furthermore, the treatment of asthma must not be approached with excessive timidity because the most common cause of death from asthma is undertreatment.[13] For the great majority of asthmatics, the condition can be extremely well controlled using the step care approach recommended by the International Consensus Report (see Figure 19.7). A concerted effort in patient education as an integral part of state-of-the-art long-term management has been demonstrated to improve outcomes, including quality of life in asthmatics. (See references 6, 7, 15, and 16 for additional reviews on the pathophysiology and treatment of asthma.)

Acute Asthma

Assessment

Signs and Symptoms

1. Q.C., a 5-year-old 18 kg female, presents to the ER with complaints of dyspnea and coughing that have progressively worsened over the past 2 days. These symptoms were preceded by 3 days of symptoms of a viral upper respiratory tract infection (sore throat, rhinorrhea, and coughing). She has experienced several bouts of bronchitis in the last 2 years and was hospitalized for pneumonia 3 months ago. Q.C. is not being treated with any medications at the present time. Physical examination reveals an anxious appearing young girl in moderate respiratory distress with audible expiratory wheezes, occasional coughing, a prolonged expiratory phase, a hyperinflated chest, and suprasternal, supraclavicular, and intercostal retractions. Bilateral inspiratory and expiratory wheezes with decreased breath sounds on the left side are heard on auscultation. Q.C.'s vital signs are: respiratory rate (RR) 30/min, blood pressure (BP) 110/83 mm Hg, heart rate 130 beats/min, temperature 37.8 °C, pulsus paradoxus 18 mm Hg. Q.C. is given 2.5 mg of albuterol (Ventolin) as 0.5 mL of a 0.5% solution in 2.5 mL of normal saline by a compressed air nebulizer over 10 minutes. Following the treatment, Q.C. claims some subjective improvement and appears to be more comfortable; however, wheezing on auscultation becomes louder. What signs and symptoms in Q.C. are consistent with acute bronchial obstruction?

Asthma is an obstructive lung disease; therefore, the primary limitation to airflow occurs during expiration. This outflow obstruction leads to the classical findings of dyspnea, expiratory wheezes, and a prolonged expiratory phase during the ventilatory cycle.[17] Wheezing is a whistling sound produced by turbulent airflow through a constricted opening and usually is more prominent on expiration. Thus, the audible expiratory wheezing in Q.C. is compatible with bronchial obstruction. In fact, Q.C.'s obstruction is so severe that even inspiratory wheezes and decreased air movement were detected on auscultation. It is important to realize that the classical symptom of wheezing requires turbulent airflow; therefore, effective therapy of acute asthma actually may result in increased wheezing initially as airflow increases throughout the lung. As a result, Q.C.'s increased wheezing on auscultation is compatible with her clinical improvement following the albuterol nebulizer treatments. The coughing experienced by Q.C. is another common finding associated with acute asthma attacks. The coughing may be due to stimulation of "irritant receptors" in the bronchi by the chemical mediators of inflammation (e.g., histamine) that are released from mast cells, or to the mechanics of smooth muscle contraction.

In the progression of an asthma attack, the small airways become completely occluded during expiration and air can be trapped behind the occlusion; therefore, the patient has to breathe at higher-than-normal lung volumes.[17] Consequently, the thoracic cavity be-

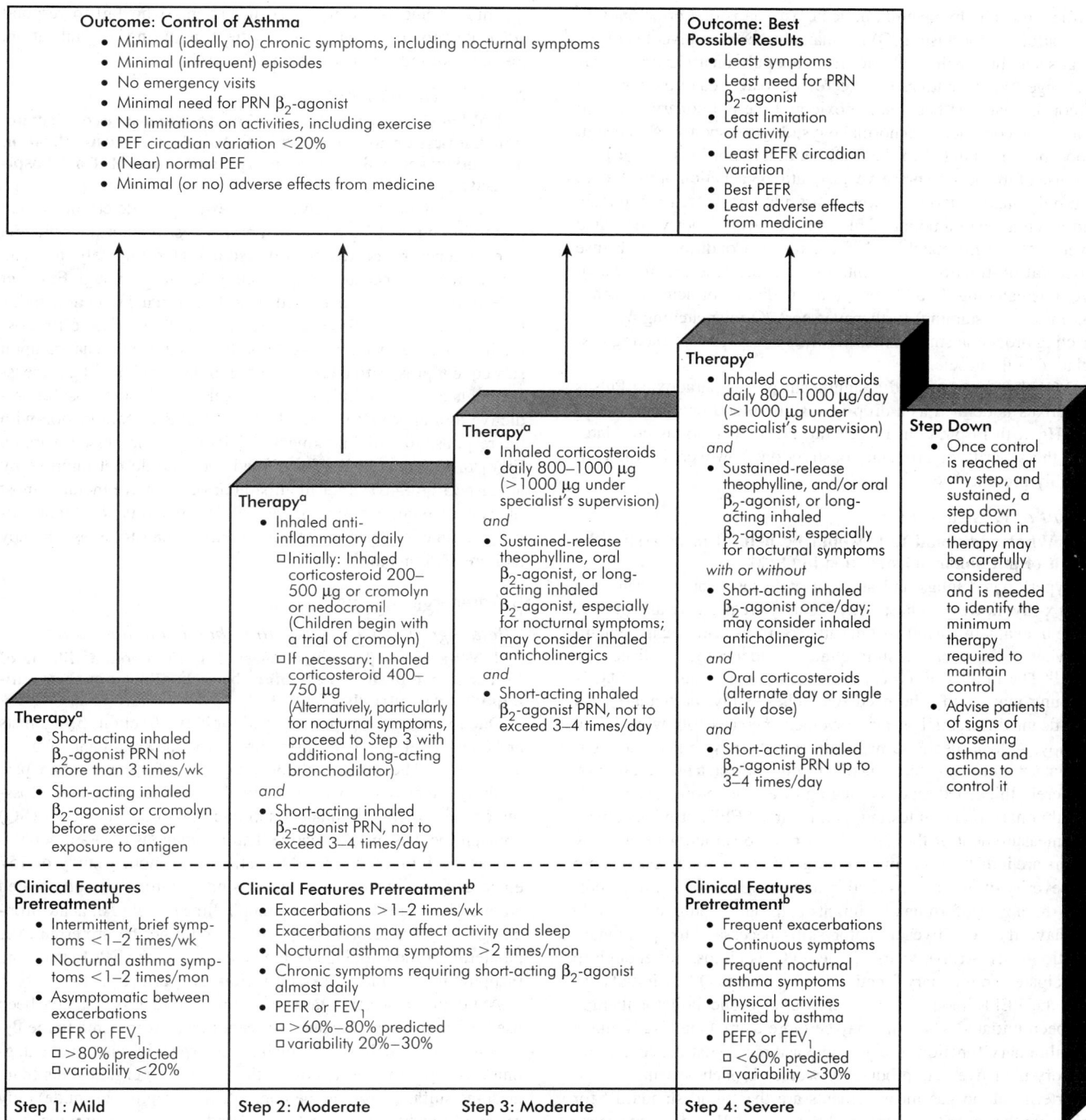

Outcome: Control of Asthma
- Minimal (ideally no) chronic symptoms, including nocturnal symptoms
- Minimal (infrequent) episodes
- No emergency visits
- Minimal need for PRN β_2-agonist
- No limitations on activities, including exercise
- PEF circadian variation <20%
- (Near) normal PEF
- Minimal (or no) adverse effects from medicine

Outcome: Best Possible Results
- Least symptoms
- Least need for PRN β_2-agonist
- Least limitation of activity
- Least PEFR circadian variation
- Best PEFR
- Least adverse effects from medicine

Therapy[a]
- Short-acting inhaled β_2-agonist PRN not more than 3 times/wk
- Short-acting inhaled β_2-agonist or cromolyn before exercise or exposure to antigen

Therapy[a]
- Inhaled anti-inflammatory daily
  - Initially: Inhaled corticosteroid 200–500 µg or cromolyn or nedocromil (Children begin with a trial of cromolyn)
  - If necessary: Inhaled corticosteroid 400–750 µg (Alternatively, particularly for nocturnal symptoms, proceed to Step 3 with additional long-acting bronchodilator)

  and
- Short-acting inhaled β_2-agonist PRN, not to exceed 3–4 times/day

Therapy[a]
- Inhaled corticosteroids daily 800–1000 µg (>1000 µg under specialist's supervision)

  and
- Sustained-release theophylline, oral β_2-agonist, or long-acting inhaled β_2-agonist, especially for nocturnal symptoms; may consider inhaled anticholinergics

  and
- Short-acting inhaled β_2-agonist PRN, not to exceed 3–4 times/day

Therapy[a]
- Inhaled corticosteroids daily 800–1000 µg/day (>1000 µg under specialist's supervision)

  and
- Sustained-release theophylline, and/or oral β_2-agonist, or long-acting inhaled β_2-agonist, especially for nocturnal symptoms

  with or without
- Short-acting inhaled β_2-agonist once/day; may consider inhaled anticholinergic

  and
- Oral corticosteroids (alternate day or single daily dose)

  and
- Short-acting inhaled β_2-agonist PRN up to 3–4 times/day

Step Down
- Once control is reached at any step, and sustained, a step down reduction in therapy may be carefully considered and is needed to identify the minimum therapy required to maintain control
- Advise patients of signs of worsening asthma and actions to control it

Clinical Features Pretreatment[b]
- Intermittent, brief symptoms <1–2 times/wk
- Nocturnal asthma symptoms <1–2 times/mon
- Asymptomatic between exacerbations
- PEFR or FEV_1
  - >80% predicted
  - variability <20%

Clinical Features Pretreatment[b]
- Exacerbations >1–2 times/wk
- Exacerbations may affect activity and sleep
- Nocturnal asthma symptoms >2 times/mon
- Chronic symptoms requiring short-acting β_2-agonist almost daily
- PEFR or FEV_1
  - >60%–80% predicted
  - variability 20%–30%

Clinical Features Pretreatment[b]
- Frequent exacerbations
- Continuous symptoms
- Frequent nocturnal asthma symptoms
- Physical activities limited by asthma
- PEFR or FEV_1
  - <60% predicted
  - variability >30%

Step 1: Mild	Step 2: Moderate	Step 3: Moderate	Step 4: Severe

Fig 19.7 Chronic Management of Asthma: Stepwise Approach to Asthma Therapy. **Step-Up:** Progression to the next higher step is indicated when control cannot be achieved at the current step and there is assurance that medication is used correctly. If PEF ≤60% predicted or personal best, consider a burst of oral corticosteroids and then proceed. **Step-Down:** Reduction in therapy is considered when the outcome for therapy has been achieved and sustained for several weeks or even months at the current step. Reduction in therapy also is needed to identify the minimum therapy required to maintain control. Reproduced with permission of reference 7.[a] All therapy must include patient education about prevention (including environmental control where appropriate) as well as control of symptoms.[b] One or more features may be present to be assigned a grade of severity; an individual usually should be assigned to the most severe grade in which any feature occurs.

comes hyperexpanded and the diaphragm is lowered. As a result, the patient must use the accessory muscles of respiration to expand the chest wall. Q.C.'s hyperinflated chest and her use of suprasternal, supraclavicular, and intercostal muscles to assist in breathing also are compatible with obstructive airway diseases. Occlusion of the small airways, airtrapping, and resorption of air distal to the obstruction can lead to atelectasis (incomplete expansion or collapse of pulmonary alveoli or of a segment of lobe of the lung).

Localized areas of atelectasis often are difficult to distinguish from infiltrates on a chest x-ray and atelectasis can be mistaken for pneumonia. Q.C.'s history of multiple bouts of "bronchitis" is significant and typical of many young asthmatics. In any patient with recurring episodes of bronchial symptoms (i.e., bronchitis, pneumonia), the possible diagnosis of asthma should be investigated.

The increased pulse, respiratory rate, and anxiety experienced by Q.C. can be attributed both to hypoxemia and the feeling of suffocation. The hypoxemia in acute asthma is due principally to ventilation (V) perfusion (Q) mismatching.[18] Each alveolus of the lung is supplied with capillaries from the pulmonary artery for gas exchange. When ventilation is decreased to an area of the lung, the alveoli in that area become hypoxic and the pulmonary artery to that region constricts as a normal physiologic response. As a result, blood flow is shunted to the well-ventilated portions of the lung because of the need to preserve adequate oxygenation of the blood. The pulmonary arteries, however, are not constricted completely and when a small amount of blood flows to the poorly ventilated alveoli, ''V/Q mismatching'' is the result. Conditions of diffuse bronchial obstruction (i.e., acute asthma) increase the amount of V/Q mismatching. In addition, some mediators of acute bronchospasm (e.g., histamine) further worsen V/Q mismatching by constricting bronchial smooth muscle while concurrently relaxing vascular smooth muscle.

Q.C. also demonstrated a significant pulsus paradoxus. Pulsus paradoxus is defined as a drop in systolic blood pressure of ≥ 10 mm Hg with inspiration. In general, pulsus paradoxus correlates with the severity of bronchial obstruction; however, it is not invariably present.[18]

Extent of Obstruction

2. What additional tests would be helpful in assessing the extent of pulmonary obstruction in Q.C.?

Hyperinflated lungs and areas of atelectasis can be seen on a chest x-ray; however, chest x-rays usually are negative and of little value in evaluating acute asthma attacks. Chest x-rays can be helpful when there is pre-existing clinical evidence of localized disease.[19] The finding of a local decrease in breath sounds in Q.C.'s left lung may justify the need for a chest x-ray, particularly if a significant differential in air movement persists following initial therapy. A local decrease in breath sounds may indicate a pneumonia, aspiration into the lung of a foreign object, a pneumothorax, or merely thickened mucus plugging of a large bronchus.

Pulmonary function testing, particularly PEFR, provides objective measurement of the degree of airway obstruction. Peak flow meters are indispensable in the emergency room for assessing both the severity of airway obstruction and the response to bronchodilator therapy. Unfortunately, infants and many young children do not have the cognitive or motor skills necessary for pulmonary function tests. At five years of age, Q.C. is almost old enough to participate in pulmonary function testing. Due to Q.C.'s initial anxiety, the PEFR should be measured after bronchodilator therapy has been initiated when she may be more calm. One disadvantage of pulmonary function tests in acute asthma is that the forced expiratory maneuver can produce or worsen bronchospasm.

Arterial blood gas measurements are the ''gold standard'' for assessing the severity of airway obstruction.[18] Blood gas measurements, however, are unnecessary if other objective measures of airway obstruction (e.g., pulmonary function tests) have been monitored.[20] In acute asthma, blood gas determinations usually indicate hypoxemia because of V/Q mismatching and hypocapnia with respiratory alkalosis because of hyperventilation.[21] The degree of hypoxemia correlates with the severity of obstruction. Severe hypoxemia ($PaO_2 < 50$ mm Hg) that is associated with an FEV_1 less than 15% of predicted, represents severe airway obstruction.[18,21] Likewise, when the FEV_1 is less than 15% of the predicted value, carbon dioxide increasingly is retained and the $PaCO_2$ begins to rise into the usual normal range.[21] Due to V/Q mismatching and the ease of correction of hypoxemia with O_2 therapy, the $PaCO_2$ is the more sensitive indicator of ventilation abnormalities in acute asthma with prolonged or chronic airway obstruction, CO_2 retention (hypercapnia) and respiratory acidosis are prominent. Blood

gas measurements are indicated in patients who fail to respond adequately to initial therapy or in patients requiring hospitalization; they are not indicated at this time for Q.C.

Need for Hospitalization

3. What signs, symptoms, or laboratory measures of obstruction can best predict whether Q.C. will require hospitalization or whether she will relapse and return to the ER if not hospitalized?

A number of studies have been designed to determine which presenting clinical signs and symptoms best predict the outcome of emergency room treatment of asthma. Unfortunately, the data are inconclusive because of poor study design. Although Fischl et al.[22] retrospectively developed a multifactorial prediction index that supposedly was 95% accurate in predicting the need for hospitalization, the index proved to be little better than chance upon subsequent prospective testing.[23,24] Initial arterial blood gas measurements also are of little predictive value.[20] The most useful predictive tool appears to be the FEV_1 or PEFR in conjunction with the response to initial treatment.[20,25] Patients who present with an FEV_1 of less than 30% of predicted and who do not improve by at least 35% to 40% after the first hour of intensive therapy, most likely will require hospitalization.[25] The inability to obtain pulmonary function tests in Q.C. makes it difficult to assess therapy and predict outcome.

β-Adrenergic Agonist Therapy

Beta Agonists Compared to Other Bronchodilators

4. Why was a β2-agonist selected as the bronchodilator of first choice in preference to other bronchodilators such as aminophylline or atropine for Q.C.?

Due to their greater potency and rapidity of action, β2-agonists are considered to be the first choice for the treatment of acute asthma.[6,7,26] The bronchodilatory properties of β2-agonists are particularly effective in reversing early phase asthma responses. Rossing et al.[27] noted that inhaled isoproterenol or subcutaneous (SQ) epinephrine was more effective than intravenous (IV) aminophylline as the initial therapy in 48 patients. In another study of 157 emergency room visits for acute asthma, parenteral and inhaled adrenergics were superior to aminophylline for relief of acute bronchospasm.[28] Therefore, theophylline would not be preferred over albuterol for the initial management of Q.C. in the ER. In addition, theophylline has more risks for serious side effects.

Anticholinergic agents are potent bronchodilators that have been used in the therapy of asthma for centuries.[29] Compared to the β2-agonists and theophylline, which are nonspecific functional antagonists of smooth muscle contraction, anticholinergic agents (e.g., atropine sulfate, atropine methonitrate, ipratropium bromide) only reverse bronchospasm due to increased parasympathetic tone. As a result, the bronchodilation from anticholinergic drugs is less consistent than that obtained with β2-agonists.[29] Several clinical trials clearly have proven that beta agonists are superior to anticholinergics as bronchodilators in asthma.[29] However, double-blind, randomized placebo-controlled trials in acute care settings using changes of PEFR or FEV_1 as end points have shown that the anticholinergic agent ipratropium given as a nebulizer solution does add clinically significant benefit to initial doses of beta agonists.[30-32] For example, one study[30] found that adult asthmatics in an emergency room albuterol-only group had a mean increase in PEFR of 31% in one hour, whereas a group with ipratropium added to albuterol had a mean rise in PEFR of 77%. The most severe asthmatics had a 93% increase in PEFR when ipratropium was added to albuterol. It is important to note that the dose of albuterol was aggressive (10 mg). Other investigators have not found such marked acute benefit of ipratropium, but have found prolonged bronchodilator responses with combination therapy.[33] If anticholinergic agents are used, quaternary ammonium compounds like ipratropium are preferred because of their excellent safety records. Atropine sulfate is a tertiary ammonium compound and can cause systemic side effects in high aerosol doses.[29,34]

While ipratropium may add benefit to the *initial* PEFR response to beta agonists, there is virtually no clinical evidence that it adds further benefit to beta agonist aerosols (and other standard therapies) after initial doses in the emergency room or during subsequent treatment in the *hospital*.[35] Although Bryant[36] reported improved response with combination therapy after 48 hours, patients were not given standard therapy with concomitant systemic corticosteroids in the hospital. Therefore, the practical value of this study is questionable (i.e., the real therapeutic value would be increased response with concurrent corticosteroids and beta agonists). Further, there is essentially no evidence to date that anticholinergic aerosols improve clinical outcomes (e.g., shorten length of stay) in acute care settings. As with most areas of therapeutics, this subject is debated. Consequently, while early addition of inhaled ipratropium in adequate doses to beta agonists may improve pulmonary function tests, Q.C.'s physician chose to use only inhaled beta agonists initially because of lack of proof of enhanced clinical outcomes with anticholinergic therapy.

Preferred Routes of Administration

5. Why was the β_2-agonist, albuterol, administered to Q.C. by nebulizer instead of by the oral or parenteral routes of administration?

Numerous trials in stable asthmatics have shown that β_2-agonists administered by the inhaled route provide as great (see Figure 19.8), or greater bronchodilation with fewer systemic side effects than either the parenteral or oral routes.[26,37] In situations of acute bronchospasm, concerns over adequate penetration of aerosols into the bronchial tree led many clinicians to believe that the parenteral route of administration would be more effective than the inhaled route of administration. In clinical trials, however, inhaled β_2-agonists were as effective as the standard treatment of subcutaneous epinephrine for emergency room treatment of acute asthma in adults and children.[27,38,39] Therefore, aerosolized β_2-agonists now are considered as effective as and safer than systemic β_2-agonists. β_2-agonists should not be administered orally to treat acute episodes of severe asthma because of the slow onset of action and erratic absorption.[37]

Fig 19.8   Time Course of Change in FEV$_1$ with Different Modes of Administration of the β_2-Selective Agonist Terbutaline. Reprinted with permission. reference 37.

6. Q.C. received albuterol by nebulization. Would intermittent positive-pressure breathing (IPPB) or metered-dose aerosol administration of the β_2-agonist have been preferred?

Aerosols are mixtures of particles (e.g., a drug-lipid mixture) suspended in a gas. A metered-dose inhaler (MDI) consists of an aerosol canister and an actuation device (valve). The drug in the canister is a suspension or solution mixed with propellant (e.g., flurochlorohydrocarbons). The valve controls the delivery of drug and allows the precise release of a premeasured amount of the product (see Figure 19.9). A second aerosol device, the air jet nebulizer, mechanically produces a mist of drug. The drug is placed in a small volume of solute (typically 5 mL of saline) and placed in a small reservoir (nebulizer) connected to an air source such as a small compressor pump, an oxygen tank, or a wall air hose. An air hose travels from the relatively large diameter tubing of the air source into a pin hole sized opening in the nebulizer. This creates a negative pressure at the site of the air entry and causes the drug solution in the bottom of the nebulizer reservoir to be sucked up through a small capillary tube where it then encounters the rapid air flow. The drug solution is forced against a small baffle that causes mechanical formation of a mist. (See Figure 19.10.) IPPB devices aerosolize drugs in a similar manner as air jet nebulizers except that the air flow that exits the nebulizer in an IPPB device is enhanced to exceed atmospheric pressure. An ultrasonic nebulizer is a type of nebulizer that uses sound waves to generate the aerosol.

Studies comparing responses to β_2-agonists administered by nebulization versus intermittent positive pressure breathing have shown no significant advantages for the IPPB method of administration.[40] Furthermore, dose-response studies that compared nebulization to IPPB and pressurized metered-dose aerosols in stable chronic asthma patients have shown no advantage among these methods of administration when equivalent doses are administered.[41,42] Each method delivers approximately 10% of the beginning dose to the patient's airways.[43] Trials comparing metered-dose aerosols of β_2-agonists to the nebulization of those same drugs in acute asthma also have shown no significant advantage for the nebulization method of administration when the metered-dose aerosolized administration was carefully supervised by experienced personnel and a spacer device was used.[44–48] However, in younger acutely ill children, it is difficult (even with supervision) to administer an effective β_2-agonist dose with a metered-dose canister. Although some studies have found in children and adults that the first dose of beta agonists delivered by MDI plus spacer device is equivalent to nebulizer, Morely et al.[49] reported that the first dose via the nebulizer was superior. Because many patients *perceive* that nebulizers provide more intensive therapy, it often is important psychologically to give at least the first dose of a beta agonist via a nebulizer. Thereafter, it is more cost effective to use the therapeutically equivalent MDI plus spacer. The dose ratio for β_2-agonists delivered by MDI plus spacer versus nebulizer has varied in the literature. In one double-blind trial in children, investigators used a dose ratio of 1:5 (i.e., albuterol MDI-spacer 1 mg: nebulized albuterol 5 mg).[48] Therefore, nebulization of albuterol with compressed air or, preferably, oxygen was the preferred method of administration for Q.C. initially.

Comparison of β_2-Agonists

7. Would another β_2-agonist have been more effective in the initial therapy of Q.C.?

Differences in the chemical structure of the various β_2-agonists produce differences in oral bioavailability, β_2-receptor selectivity, duration of action, and molar potency.[26] Table 19.1 summarizes the differences between the beta agonists. If administered in equi-

Metered Dose Inhaler (MDI)

Open Nebulizer

Closed Nebulizer

Fig 19.9

Q.C.'s breath sounds became increasingly clear and her heart rate and BP fell to 100 beats/min and 100/65 mm Hg, respectively. Were the dose and dosing interval of albuterol appropriate for Q.C.?

There is controversy regarding the optimal dose or dosing interval for aerosol sympathomimetics in acute asthma. The duration of action of aerosolized β_2-agonists depends upon the dose, physiologic state of the patient, and pharmacokinetic profile of the individual drug.[26] Patients with increased bronchiolar smooth muscle constriction will have a decreased intensity and duration of response to any given dose of a beta agonist.[26] Frequent, low doses of nebulized albuterol (i.e., 0.05 mg/kg to 1.7 mg Q 20 minutes) were superior to the standard albuterol dose (i.e., 0.15 mg/kg to 5 mg at 1 hour intervals) in alleviating bronchoconstriction in asthmatic children.[50] One apparent reason for the superiority of the frequent, low-dose regimen is that pulmonary function does not deteriorate as extensively during the interval between treatments. A follow-up study from the same center indicated that a higher dose regimen (0.15 mg/kg versus 0.05 mg/kg Q 20 minutes) produced significantly greater improvement with no greater incidence of adverse effects. Another study performed by Schuh et al.[52] demonstrated the greater efficacy of albuterol in a dose of 0.3 mg/kg (up to 10 mg) hourly over a dose of 0.15 mg/kg (up to 5 mg) hourly in children. The higher dose was tolerated as well as the 0.15 mg/kg dose. Kelly et al.[53] demonstrated the safety of high-dose terbutaline by continuous nebulization in children with acute severe asthma. Therefore, Q.C.'s albuterol regimen of 2.5 mg (0.14 mg/kg) nebulized every 20 minutes for two hours subsequent to her first dose of aerosolized albuterol was appropriate. Table 19.2 lists the recommended doses for bronchodilators.

Cardiovascular Effects

9. Q.C.'s heart rate increased from 130 beats/min at time of admission to 140 beats/min after her first dose of aerosolized albuterol, and her diastolic BP decreased from 83 to 74 mm Hg. Explain the changes in Q.C.'s heart rate and blood pressure following the initial and subsequent nebulizations of albuterol.

There are a number of possible explanations for the cardiovascular changes in Q.C. Although albuterol is a selective β_2-agonist, it can increase heart rate by directly stimulating β_2-receptors in the heart[26] and by stimulating β_2-receptors in vascular smooth muscle. The effect on cardiac β_2-receptors is only of consequence at high serum concentrations of albuterol since it has a low affinity for these receptors and because β_2-receptors are relatively low in number compared to β_1-receptors in the heart. Stimulation of vascular

---

molar potent doses, each β_2-agonist will produce the same degree of smooth muscle relaxation.[36] Therefore, in terms of intensity of bronchodilation, there is generally no major advantage of one β_2-agonist over another; however, when high dosages are required, the degree of β_2-selectivity becomes increasingly important. The β_2-agonists with intermediate durations of action (e.g., albuterol) are preferred.

Dosing

8. Because Q.C.'s symptoms were not relieved completely after the first dose of aerosolized albuterol, ABGs (on room air) were obtained with the following results: pH 7.45, PaO_2 60 mm Hg, and $PaCO_2$ 28 mm Hg. Q.C.'s heart rate was 140 beats/min; her RR was 27/min; and her BP was 110/74 mm Hg. After 20 minutes, 2.5 mg of albuterol was administered by nebulizer Q 20 min over the next 2 hours. After 3 treatments,

Fig 19.10   Air Jet Nebulizer

Table 19.1		Comparison of Selected β-Agonist Bronchodilators				
		Receptor Selectivity			
Agent	Dosages Forms[a]	β₁	β₂	β₂ Potency[b]	Duration of Action (hr)[c]
Epinephrine[d]	Inj, AS, MDI	+++	+++	2	0.5–2
Isoproterenol (Isuprel)	Inj, AS, MDI, SL	++++	++++	1	0.5–2
Isoetharine (Bronkosol)	AS, MDI	++	+++	6	0.5–2
Metaproterenol (Alupent)	AS, MDI, PO	++	++	10	3–4
Terbutaline (Brethine)	Inj, MDI, PO, AS	+	++++	4	4–8
Albuterol (Ventolin, Proventil)	AS, MDI, PO	+	++++	2	4–8
Bitolterol (Tornalate)	MDI	+	++++	4	4–8
Pirbuterol (Maxair)	MDI	+	++++	4	4–8
Formoterol	MDI	+	++++	0.24	8–12
Salmeterol (Serevent)	MDI	+	++++	0.50	12

[a] AS = Aerosol solutions; Inj = Injectable; MDI = Metered-dose inhaler (also may be termed metered-dose aerosol); PO = Oral; SL = Sublingual. Not all dosage forms are currently available in the U.S.

[b] Relative molar potency at the β₂-receptor with 1 the most potent. This gives the amount of drug to achieve the same therapeutic effect.

[c] Onset and duration data apply to aerosol therapy only. Duration of bronchodilation only applies to otherwise stable asthmatics and is not applicable to acute severe asthma or protection from significant provocation (e.g., allergen, exercise, ozone). Duration may be shorter during acute exacerbation or with chronic therapy due to down regulation of β-receptors (tolerance). Oral tablets and syrups are slower in onset, but may be slightly longer acting than aerosols (especially if using sustained-release tablets).

[d] Epinephrine also has alpha (vasoconstrictor) effects. This may help decrease edema in the airways. Found in all OTC inhalers.

β₂-receptors induces peripheral vasodilation, a decrease in diastolic blood pressure, and a reflex increase in heart rate. In addition, the administration of bronchodilators to patients like Q.C. with acute asthma initially may worsen the V/Q mismatching by producing pulmonary vasodilation or by preferentially enhancing ventilation to the already well-ventilated airways (i.e., producing greater bronchodilation in the areas of the lung that are the least obstructed due to enhanced deposition of the aerosol). These drug-induced effects often are blunted by the reversal of patient anxiety following bronchodilation.

Inhaled albuterol can lower PaO₂ and thereby increase heart rate in acute asthma.[39] Since Q.C.'s arterial blood gases were not measured before institution of therapy, the possible role of lowered PaO₂ in contributing to her tachycardia is unknown. Tachycardia induced by a low PaO₂ usually is not a consideration in this setting because all patients with severe acute asthma attacks should receive O₂ therapy. Hypoxemia also can contribute to the patient's anxiety and can worsen bronchial hyperreactivity.[54]

Despite continued administration of the β₂-adrenergic, Q.C.'s heart rate decreased to 100 beats/minute and her blood pressure returned to normal (100/65 mm Hg) when her airway obstruction was relieved. Potential cardiac stimulants (e.g., sympathomimetics, methylxanthines, anticholinergics) typically produce these physiological changes in this setting and should not be withheld in asthmatics with acute obstruction who present with tachycardia.

Adverse Effects

10. H.T., a 45-year-old, 5′8″, 91 kg male with a long history of chronic severe asthma, presents to the ER with severe dyspnea and wheezing. He is able to say only 2 or 3 words without taking a breath. He has been taking 5 mg of oral terbutaline (Brethine) TID, 4 inhalations of beclomethasone dipropionate (Beclovent) TID, and terbutaline metered-dose aerosol (Brethaire) 2 inhalations QID PRN on a chronic basis. He has been using his metered-dose aerosol of terbutaline with increasing frequency over the past week and had increased its use up to Q 3 hr on the day before admission. Due to excessive coughing, he was unable to undergo spirometry testing. Vital signs are as follows: heart rate 130 beats/min; RR 30/min; pulsus paradoxus 18 mm Hg; and BP 130/90 mm Hg. ABGs on room air were pH 7.40, PaO₂ 55 mm Hg, and PaCO₂ 40 mm Hg. Serum electrolyte concentrations were sodium (Na) 140 mEq/L; potassium (K) 4.1 mEq/L; and chloride (Cl) 105 mEq/L. Due to the severity of the obstruction, H.T. was monitored with an electrocardiogram (ECG) that showed sinus tachycardia with occasional premature ventricular contractions (PVCs). Terbutaline 0.5 mg SQ was administered with minimal improvement. H.T. then was started on O₂ at 4 L/min by nasal cannula, followed by another injection of 0.5 mg terbutaline SQ. Subsequently, H.T.'s heart rate increased to 145 beats/min, more PVCs appeared on the ECG, and he complained of palpitations and shakiness. His PEFR was 20% of predicted. Laboratory values were pH 7.39, PaO₂ 60 mm Hg, PaCO₂ 42 mm Hg, Na 138 mEq/L, and K 3.5 mEq/L. What adverse effects, experienced by H.T., are consistent with systemic β₂-agonist administration? [SI units: Na 140 mmol/L; K 4.1 mmol/L; Cl 105 mmol/L]

H.T. experienced palpitations which may have been due to the widening of his pulse pressure from vasodilation or the PVCs.[6,26] Hypoxemia also is a potent stimulus for cardiac arrhythmias and is known to potentiate the cardiotoxicity of β₂-adrenergics.[55] (See Question 9.) Therefore, H.T.'s tachycardia and PVCs may have been caused by the beta agonist, by the worsening of his airway obstruction (as reflected in the increase in PaCO₂), or by both of these variables.

The decrease in the serum potassium concentration from 4.1 mEq/L to 3.5 mEq/L could be attributed to β₂-adrenergic activation of the Na⁺-K⁺ pump and subsequent transport of potassium intracellularly.[56,57] However, at usual doses, aerosolized albuterol and terbutaline cause relatively little effect on serum potassium. The effects may be more noticeable with systemic (oral or injectable) administration or after inhaled fenoterol. The β₂-adrenergic-mediated increase in glucose and insulin secretion also can contribute to the intracellular shift of potassium.[56] What role, if any, the decrease in serum potassium has on the cardiac abnormalities associated with beta-adrenergics is unknown.[57]

The shakiness (tremors) experienced by H.T. probably can be attributed to β₂-receptor stimulation of skeletal muscle.

Table 19.2	Selected Bronchodilator Dosages			
	For Chronic Maintenance Therapy[a]		For Acute Severe Asthma	
Preparations	Pediatric	Adult	Pediatric	Adult
Albuterol (Proventil, Ventolin)				
Oral[d]				
2, 4 mg tab; 4 mg SR; 2 mg/5 mL syrup	0.1–0.2 mg/kg Q 6–8 hr	2–4 mg Q 6–8 hr 4 mg SR Q 12 hr	NR	NR
Aerosol[c]				
0.5% (5 mg/mL)	0.05–0.15 mg/kg Q 4–8 hr[c]	2.5–5 mg Q 4–8 hr[c]	0.15 mg/kg (*max:* 5 mg); then 0.05 mg/kg Q 20 min until improvement[c]	5–10 mg; then 2–5 mg Q 20 min until improvement[c]
Dry Powder Inhaler (Rotocaps)				
200 μg/cap	1 cap Q 4–8 hr	1–2 caps Q 4–8 hr	NR	NR
MDI[a]				
0.09 mg/puff, 200 puffs	1–2 puffs Q 6 hr	2–3 puffs Q 4–8 hr	2 puffs Q 20 min × 3; then 2 puffs Q 1–2 hr	3–4 puffs Q 20 min × 3; then Q 1–2 hr
Bitolterol (Tornalate)				
MDI[a]				
0.37 mg/spray	1–2 puffs Q 6 hr	2–3 puffs Q 6 hr	1–2 puffs Q 1–2 hr	3–4 puffs Q 1–2 hr
Epinephrine HCl[b]				
Injection				
1:1000 (1 mg/mL)[c]	NR	NR	0.01 mg/kg (*max:* 0.5 mg) SQ Q 20 min × 3 doses	0.3–0.5 mg SQ Q 20 min × 3 doses
Sustained Action				
Sus-Phrine 1:200 (5 mg/mL)	NR	NR	0.005–0.01 mg/kg (*max:* 0.75 mg) SQ Q 6–10 hr	0.5–0.75 mg SQ Q 6–10 hr
Fenoterol (Berotec)[b]				
Oral				
2.5, 5 mg tab	0.1–0.2 mg/kg Q 6–8 hr	2.5–5 mg Q 6–8 hr	NR	NR
Aerosol				
0.5% (5 mg/mL)	0.025–0.075 mg/kg Q 6–8 hr	2.5–5 mg Q 6–8 hr	0.075 mg/kg Q 2 hr	2.5–5 mg Q 2 hr
MDI[a]				
0.16 mg/puff	1 puff Q 6 hr	1–2 puffs Q 6 hr	2 puffs Q 20 min × 3 then Q 1–2 hr	3 puffs Q 20 min × 3 then Q 1–2 hr
Formeterol[e]				
MDI[a]				
6 μg/puff	1–2 puffs Q 12 hr	2 puffs Q 12 hr	NR	NR
Isoetharine (Bronkosol, Bronkmeter, generic)				
Aerosol 1%				
10 mg/mL	NR	NR	0.1–0.2 mg/kg Q 1–2 hr[c]	5–10 mg Q 1–2 hr[c]
MDI[a]				
0.34 gm/spray, 200–400 sprays	1–2 sprays Q 4–6	2 sprays Q 4–6 hr	1–2 sprays Q 1–2 hr	2–3 sprays Q 1–2 hr
Isoproterenol (Isuprel, generic)				
Aerosol				
1:200 (5 mg/mL)	NR	NR	0.05–0.1 mg/kg Q 2 hr	3.5–7 mg Q 2 hr
MDI[a]				
Various 45–131 μg/spray	NR	NR	NR	NR
Metaproterenol (Alupent, Metaprel)				
Oral[d]				
10, 20 mg tab; 10 mg/5 mL syrup	0.3–0.5 mg/kg Q 4–6 hr ↑ by 0.25 mg/kg as tolerated	10–20 mg Q 4–6 hr	NR	NR
Aerosol[c]				
5% (15 mg/0.3 mL) or 15 mg/2.5 mL unit dose	0.25–0.5 mg/kg (*max:* 15 mg) Q 4–6 hr[c]	15 mg Q 4 hr[c]	0.5 mg/kg Q 1–2 hr[c]	15 mg Q 1–2 hr[c]
MDI[a]				
0.65 mg/puff, 300 puffs	1–2 puffs Q 4 hr	2 puffs Q 4 hr	2 puffs Q 1–2 hr	2–4 puffs Q 1–2 hr
Pirbuterol (Maxair, Autohaler)				
MDI[a]				
0.20 mg/puff, 400 puffs	1–2 puffs Q 4–6 hr	2 puffs Q 4–6 hr	2 puffs Q 20 min × 3; then Q 1 hr	3 puffs Q 20 min × 3; then Q 1 hr

Continued

Table 19.2	Selected Bronchodilator Dosages (Continued)			
	For Chronic Maintenance Therapy[a]		For Acute Severe Asthma	
Preparations	Pediatric	Adult	Pediatric	Adult
Terbutaline (Brethine, Bricanyl)				
Injection				
1 mg/mL	NR	NR	10 µg/kg (*max:* 0.25 mg) Q 2–6 hr PRN or 10–20 µg/kg over 10 min; then 0.2–0.4 µg/kg/min; ↑ in 0.1 µg/kg steps Q 15 min as necessary	0.25–0.5 mg Q 2–6 hr PRN *or* 10 µg/kg over 1 min, then 0.1 µg/kg/min. ↑ by 0.1 µg/kg/min Q 15 min to max of 0.4 µg/kg/min
Oral[d]				
2.5, 5 mg tab	0.075–0.2 mg/kg Q 6–8 hr	2.5–5 mg Q 6–8 hr	NR	NR
Aerosol (use injection)	0.2–0.4 mg/kg Q 6 hr	5–10 mg Q 6 hr	0.3 mg/kg; then 0.2 mg/kg Q 20 min until improvement	10 mg; then 5 mg Q 20 min until improvement
MDI[a]				
0.2 mg/puff, 300 puffs	1–2 puffs Q 6 hr	2 puffs Q 6 hr	2 puffs Q 20 min × 3; then Q 1 hr	3 puffs Q 20 min × 3; then Q 1 hr
Salmeterol				
MDI				
25 µg/puff	1–2 puffs Q 12 hr	2 puffs Q 12 hr	NR	NR
Ipratropium Bromide				
Aerosol				
0.025% (0.25 mg/mL)	0.25 mg Q 6 hr	0.25–0.5 mg Q 6 hr	0.25 mg Q 4–6 hr	0.25–0.5 mg Q 4–6 hr
MDI[a]				
18 µg/puff	1–2 puffs Q 6 hr	2–3 puffs Q 6 hr	1–2 puffs Q 4 hr	2–3 puffs Q 4 hr

[a] NR = Not recommended; MDI = Metered-dose inhaler.

[b] Epinephrine also found in various OTC MDIs.

[c] All aerosol doses to be diluted to a total volume of 2.5 mL with normal saline. Note that although these doses are large compared to MDI, part will not be nebulized and part will be lost to the atmosphere. Total drug delivery to lung with MDI and aerosol at recommended doses are equivalent.

[d] Oral beta agonists have unpredictable absorption due to high first-pass metabolism. Onset is slow (30–60 min) and incidence of side effects is higher.

[e] Not available in the U.S.

Additive Theophylline Toxicity

11. Since H.T. seems unresponsive to terbutaline, the addition of theophylline is being considered. What are the risks of cardiac adverse effects if theophylline is added to a therapeutic regimen that includes β$_2$-agonists?

There has been an increasing concern about the concomitant use of β$_2$-agonists and theophylline for the treatment of asthma.[58,59] Animal studies in a variety of species show that, aminophylline in usual therapeutic doses significantly enhances beta agonist-induced cardiac arrhythmias, myocardial necrosis, and death.[58] The selective β$_2$-agonist, terbutaline, was much less likely than isoproterenol to induce these cardiac effects when used concomitantly with aminophylline.[58]

The systemic administration of β$_2$-agonists or aminophylline to stabilized chronic asthma patients with pre-existing histories of cardiac arrhythmias increases the frequency, but not the severity, of the arrhythmia.[60] Studies in outpatient asthmatics without pre-existing cardiac disease, however, have failed to demonstrate an increased risk of arrhythmias when β$_2$-adrenergic agents and theophylline are used currently in the usual therapeutic dosages.[61,62]

Studies of patients with unstable acute asthma have yielded conflicting results.[63-65] Josephson et al.[65] demonstrated increased cardiac arrhythmias (primarily ventricular and supraventricular ectopic beats) when IV aminophylline was administered subsequent to subcutaneous epinephrine therapy; however, Rossing et al.[63] did not note increased toxicity with the same combination. Both studies suffered from defects in study design.

The combination of theophylline with a β$_2$-agonist perhaps induces additive risks of cardiovascular toxicity in some patients (e.g., those with pre-existing histories of arrhythmias, unstable asthma, or acute asthma). However, a more definitive conclusion cannot be made at this time. This controversy is further complicated by the fact that ectopic beats and heart rate decrease as airway obstruction improves and hypoxia decreases.[66]

In a patient such as H.T., with severe, acute obstruction and hypoxemia, it would be prudent to decrease the potential for serious adverse cardiovascular effects by administering the beta agonist by the aerosol route and using the most β$_2$-selective agent available (see Table 19.1). The selective β$_2$-agonists clearly have less cardiostimulatory effects and are preferred.[67] (Also see Question 13 which addresses the advisability of adding theophylline to H.T.'s regimen.)

β-Adrenergic Subsensitivity

12. Why did H.T. fail to respond to the initial therapy? Could tolerance to the β$_2$-agonists have contributed?

Although tolerance to systemic effects of β$_2$-agonists is documented, tolerance to the airway response does not occur at a clinically significant level.[68] The clinical implications of β$_2$-receptor subsensitivity are minor because patients with acute asthma who have been receiving chronic β$_2$-agonists often do not respond differently than patients who have not received these agents previously.[69] Therefore, H.T.'s failure to respond to the initial therapy most likely is due to the severity of his airway obstruction. H.T.'s history of severe chronic asthma, the slow progression of this attack, and the lack of response to his inhaled β_2-agonist also are likely due in large part to a significant inflammatory component to this attack. Thus, bronchodilators would not be expected to immediately reverse the airway obstruction in H.T. It would be difficult to attribute his lack of initial response to therapy to β-adrenergic subsensitivity.

Beta Agonists in Combination with Theophylline

13. When would the addition of aminophylline to H.T.'s therapy be indicated?

Several studies on the treatment of acute asthma in the emergency room have failed to demonstrate any benefit of adding theophylline to optimal, inhaled β_2-agonist therapy.[25,28,64] Although some clinicians recommend administering aminophylline to patients presenting to the ER with acute asthma, there is no evidence that this practice improves outcome over adequate β_2-agonist therapy alone. Therefore, most clinicians would not use theophylline in H.T. Further evidence of the lack of value of theophylline in the acute care setting has emerged. Four double-blind, randomized placebo-controlled studies have demonstrated that theophylline does not add benefit to intensive inhaled beta agonists and systemic corticosteroids in hospitalized adults[70] or children who had failed aggressive emergency room therapy with β_2-agonists.[71-73] It is important to point out that the NIH Expert Panel Report recommends the use of theophylline in hospitalized asthmatics.[6] However, these studies had not been published at the time the Guidelines were drafted. Although further research is needed to establish whether theophylline may add benefit to hospitalized patients who have impending respiratory failure, *routine* use of theophylline in hospitalized asthmatics no longer seems justified.

14. Repeat measurements of PEFR and ABGs indicate continued significant bronchial obstruction. What should be the next step in H.T.'s therapy?

H.T. should be changed from systemic to an aerosolized β_2-agonist. Due to the concern for cardiac toxicity, a β_2-selective agent such as albuterol or terbutaline (see Table 19.1) should be selected. Three or four doses of albuterol, 5 mg by nebulizer administered every 20 minutes, should be started immediately with continuous monitoring of H.T.'s cardiac status. H.T.'s PEFR also should be monitored after each nebulizer treatment. (Also see Questions 5 and 6.)

Beta Agonists in Combination with Corticosteroids

15. Corticosteroids are being considered for H.T. Is it rational to add them to beta agonists? When can a response be expected? By what route should they be administered? Why would corticosteroids be useful in H.T.'s initial treatment?

Corticosteroids have potent anti-inflammatory activity and are highly effective in preventing late phase asthma responses and suppressing symptoms of severe chronic asthma (see Question 35).[6,7,74] In patients like H.T. with acute asthma, corticosteroids decrease airway obstruction,[78-81] improve oxygenation,[82] and increase the response to β_2-selective agonists.[77,83]

Corticosteroids are not smooth muscle relaxants (i.e., not direct bronchodilators); however, they can relieve bronchial obstruction by improving the responsiveness of β_2-receptors and by inhibiting numerous phases of the inflammatory response (e.g., arachidonic acid metabolism, neutrophil and eosinophil chemotaxis and migration).[6,7,74]

The anti-inflammatory activity of corticosteroids is delayed for about six to eight hours after the dose has been administered because time is needed for new protein synthesis.[74,75] Corticosteroid-induced restoration of responsiveness to endogenous catecholamines and exogenous β_2-agonists, however, occurs within one

hour of administration of the corticosteroid in severe, chronic, stable asthmatics.[76,77] Significant improvement in objective measures (e.g., pulmonary function tests) generally occurs 12 hours after administration.[80,84] Consequently, many clinicians advocate early initiation of corticosteroids in cases of acute severe asthma. Corticosteroids also hasten the recovery of acute exacerbations of asthma[85-89] and decrease the need for hospitalization if given early in the initial management of acute asthma in the emergency room.[81]

H.T. should be started on systemic corticosteroid therapy in the ER. Preferably, oral corticosteroids should have been started at home before H.T.'s exacerbation escalated to this degree of severity. Systemic corticosteroids should be continued throughout the hospital course and for several days after discharge.

16. What would be an appropriate dosing regimen of corticosteroids for H.T. in the ER? Would the dose and route be the same if he were hospitalized?

Doses of corticosteroids used to treat acute asthma are largely empiric. Studies comparing very high doses versus moderate doses have shown no advantage to very high doses.[78,89-91] Hydrocortisone and methylprednisolone appear to be the steroids of choice when given by injection. Intravenous hydrocortisone 100 to 200 mg every four to six hours (or its equivalent) appears to be an average dose for hospitalized adult patients such as H.T.[92,93] Higher corticosteroid doses have been suggested in steroid-dependent and steroid-resistant patients.[92] Methylprednisolone might be preferred over hydrocortisone in patients with heart disease, problems of fluid retention, or when high doses of corticosteroids are used; this is because it has less mineralocorticoid activity. In pediatric patients, 1 to 2 mg/kg/day of methylprednisolone (or its equivalent) in divided doses usually is used.[93] Methylprednisolone 1 mg/kg given every four to six hours has been suggested in hospitalized asthmatic children.[94]

After the hospitalized patient's condition improves (usually after 48 to 72 hours), the methylprednisolone dose usually can be tapered rapidly to 60 to 80 mg/day for adults or 1 to 2 mg/kg/day for children. Upon discharge from the hospital, prednisone 40 mg/day for less than two weeks is a common regimen and the dose is then stopped abruptly. If the patient was steroid-dependent before hospitalization, then tapering the dose to the preadmission dosage is wise. The usual oral dose of prednisone for the short-term treatment of an acute episode of asthma ranges from 20 to 80 mg/day in two to four divided doses.[85,86,92] Although it is customary initially to begin corticosteroid therapy in acute asthma by parenteral administration, there is little evidence that parenteral administration acts more rapidly than oral administration.[7,74] Harrison et al.[95] failed to demonstrate an improved effect for parenteral administration of a corticosteroid in hospitalized patients with acute severe asthma. Therefore, many clinicians prefer oral corticosteroids for initial doses. For patients who are discharged from the emergency room, seven days or less of prednisone therapy usually is sufficient.

17. H.T. was given one dose of 125 mg methylprednisolone (Solu-Medrol) IV and 3 doses of albuterol 5 mg by nebulizer Q 20 min in the ER. H.T. claimed subjective improvement after this therapy; yet, expiratory wheezes still were audible and he still was using his accessory muscles for ventilatory efforts. His PEFR only improved 35% of predicted and a repeat ABG measurement showed a PaCO$_2$ of 40 mm Hg. What should be done at this time?

H.T. still is significantly obstructed despite intensive treatments in the emergency room. As a result, he should be admitted to an intensive care unit of the hospital where he can be monitored closely.

Respiratory Failure

Signs and Symptoms

18. What would be the best method of assessing the adequacy of therapy in H.T.? What are the signs of impending respiratory failure? What measures should be taken to prevent its progression?

When patients continually must expand their chest wall with high lung volumes over a prolonged period of time, the respiratory muscles fatigue resulting in a decreased ventilatory effort. Clinical signs of impending respiratory failure include increased heart rate, decreased breath sounds, agitation from worsening hypoxia, or lethargy from increased CO_2 retention. These clinical signs and symptoms are relatively nonspecific and are affected by many variables. Thus, they should not be used to detect impending respiratory failure.

The best way to assess therapy is to monitor arterial blood gases. The PaO_2 component of an ABG determination is not very helpful because of V/Q mismatching and the administration of oxygen. The $PaCO_2$ is the best indicator of hypoventilation in acute asthma;[17,97] however, there is no single value for $PaCO_2$ that indicates impending respiratory failure since different $PaCO_2$ values are acceptable under different clinical circumstances. $PaCO_2$ values as high as 55 to 65 mm Hg may be somewhat acceptable before bronchodilator therapy; however, a $PaCO_2$ of 55 mm Hg one to two hours after intensive bronchodilator therapy, or an increase in $PaCO_2$ of 5 to 10 mm Hg/hour during aggressive therapy, is an ominous sign. The fact that H.T's $PaCO_2$ is not rising with therapy is a good sign.

The pH determination from an arterial blood gas sample is useful because severe metabolic acidosis (usually lactic acidosis) is a sign of very severe airway obstruction. Severe acidosis (pH <7.15) may produce a relative adrenergic blockade or hemodynamic dysfunction; therefore, 1 to 2 mEq/kg of intravenous $NaHCO_3$ over 20 minutes may be administered every 30 minutes until the arterial pH is greater than 7.15. However, it is unknown whether aggressive treatment with the drug alters outcome in these patients. Also, because the administration of sodium bicarbonate can result in fluid overload and hyperosmolarity, it should be done with caution. Metabolic acidosis can be exacerbated by dehydration caused by an increased rate of respiration, as well as by inadequate fluid intake during the acute phase of asthma.[96] Adequate hydration may be important to mobilize mucus secretions; however, overhydration may produce excessive fluid in the lungs and worsen the patient's condition. Patients should not receive amounts which exceed maintenance requirements after their fluid deficits are replaced.[96] H.T. does not require treatment with sodium bicarbonate because he is not in metabolic acidosis (pH = 7.39).

Beta Agonists

19. H.T. received 2 doses of terbutaline 0.5 mg SQ and 3 doses of albuterol 5 mg by nebulizer Q 20 min in ER. Why would the IV administration of a beta agonist be indicated (or not indicated) in H.T. at this time?

Although the use of intravenous beta agonists for asthmatics in the intensive care unit used to be advocated, current standards of care generally discourage use of these agents.[6,7] Intravenous isoproterenol has not been successful in preventing the need for intubation and mechanical ventilation in children with impending respiratory failure.[97] In addition, intravenous isoproterenol has caused fatal myocardial damage in children.[96] Intravenous albuterol is not superior to inhaled albuterol in severe asthma.[98] Based upon current evidence, intravenous beta agonists are not recommended. H.T.'s history of PVCs and response to inhaled albuterol also suggest that intravenous beta agonists are inappropriate at this time.

Theophylline

20. IV theophylline is being considered for H.T. Is theophylline likely to be of benefit in impending respiratory failure?

A potential benefit of theophylline in the setting of impending respiratory failure (independent of bronchodilation) is its ability to strengthen diaphragmatic contractions,[99] prevent fatigue,[100] and improve the strength of an already fatigued diaphragm.[101] In a double-blind trial of patients requiring hospitalization for acute severe asthma, Edmunds and Godfrey[98] compared IV aminophylline with both inhaled and IV albuterol. Patients receiving either the inhaled or intravenous form of albuterol had a greater improvement in PEFR than those receiving aminophylline over the first hour; however, the combination of aminophylline and the β_2-agonist produced a greater response. Also, the addition of intravenous aminophylline to either route of β_2-agonist administration in the second hour of therapy produced a further increase in peak flows. Based upon a lack of evidence in trials to date in hospitalized asthmatics,[70-73] more trials are needed to evaluate the benefit of this combination for impending respiratory failure.

21. Monitoring Therapy. It is now decided to initiate theophylline in H.T. How should his theophylline therapy be monitored?

Theophylline produces bronchodilation in a linear fashion with logarithmic increases in serum concentration.[102] Although the therapeutic range for theophylline traditionally has been claimed to be 10 to 20 µg/mL, close examination of the literature reveals that a safer range is 5 to 15 µg/mL.[103] The NIH Expert Panel Report recommends aiming for 5 to 15 µg/mL, which enhances safety while sacrificing little, if any, efficacy.[6] The incidence of theophylline side effects increases significantly when serum theophylline concentrations exceed 20 µg/mL.[104]

Since theophylline has a low therapeutic index, knowledge of its basic pharmacokinetics and of drugs or disease states that can alter its clearance is extremely important. A careful drug history should be taken to determine if theophylline has been administered within the previous 24 hours. Trying to estimate theophylline serum concentrations based upon the history of intake during the preceding day is unreliable.[105] In addition, there is significant interpatient variability in theophylline pharmacokinetics. Therefore, the most reliable method for assessing theophylline therapy is by obtaining theophylline serum concentrations. Clinical signs and symptoms of theophylline toxicity (e.g., tachycardia, headache, vomiting) also should be monitored carefully.

22. Loading Dose (LD). What would be an appropriate loading dose of aminophylline for H.T.?

A loading dose of theophylline is needed to rapidly achieve a serum concentration in the 5 to 15 µg/mL range. The loading dose can be given intravenously or orally.[25,106] A rapid release theophylline preparation (tablet or liquid) should be used if the theophylline loading dose is to be administered orally. Intravenous loading doses should be administered over 20 to 30 minutes to avoid severe cardiac arrhythmias (including cardiac arrest).[104]

The loading dose for theophylline is determined by its volume of distribution (Vd). The reported Vd for theophylline ranges from 0.3 to 0.7 L/kg and averages approximately 0.5 L/kg.[107] This Vd value remains relatively constant even in the presence of other diseases; slight differences occur in premature infants,[108] patients with hepatic cirrhosis,[109] and the elderly.[110] Theophylline is approximately 60% protein bound; however, in premature infants and newborns it is about 36% bound.[108,111] It freely crosses the placenta and serum concentrations in the mother and fetus are similar.[112]

The loading dose can be calculated as follows:

$$LD = (Cp - Cp_O)(Vd)(Weight) \qquad Eq\ 19.2$$

where LD is the calculated loading dose in mg, Cp is the desired serum theophylline concentration in µg/mL, Cp_0 is the existing serum concentration if previously taking theophylline, Vd is the volume of distribution in L/kg, and Weight is the patient's weight in kg.

Theophylline does not distribute into adipose tissue; therefore, either the ideal body weight (IBW) or real body weight if it is within 20% of the ideal weight, whichever is less, should be used to calculate the loading and maintenance doses.[113,114] Ideal body weight in kg can be calculated using the following equations:

IBW Males = 50 + (2.3)(Number of Inches Over 5 ft)   *Eq 19.3*

IBW Females = 45 + (2.3)(Number of Inches Over 5 ft)   *Eq 19.4*

For children, this weight can be obtained by using standard height and weight charts. In this 5-foot 8-inch patient, the IBW is calculated to be 68 kg [50 kg + (2.3 kg)(8)] and his real weight is 91 kg. H.T.'s IBW is less than his actual body weight and should be used in the calculation of his aminophylline loading dose.

Due to the slight interpatient variability in distribution volume, it is considered prudent to target the desired serum theophylline concentration between 10 and 15 µg/mL (or mg/L) in acutely ill patients. Many clinicians initially target 10 µg/mL. Despite the widely accepted conservative approach of targeting 10 µg/mL, the clinicians caring for H.T. choose to target 15 µg/mL because he is quite ill.

Thus, the loading dose calculation for H.T. is:

$$LD = (Cp - Cp_O)(Vd)(Weight)$$

$$= (15\ mg/L - 0\ mg/L)(0.5\ L/kg)(68\ kg)$$

$$= 510\ mg\ theophylline$$

If intravenous aminophylline is used, this loading dose is divided by 0.8 because aminophylline contains 80% anhydrous theophylline.

$$LD = \frac{510\ mg}{0.8}$$

$$= 637\ mg\ or\ 640\ mg\ Aminophylline$$

As can be seen from Equation 19.2, by assuming a distribution volume of 0.5 L/kg, every 1 mg/kg dose of theophylline will produce an approximate 2 µg/mL increase in theophylline serum concentration.

$$Cp(2\ \mu g/mL) = \frac{Dose\ (1\ mg/kg)}{Vd(0.5)(L/kg)}$$

This relationship can be used to rapidly approximate loading doses for theophylline in various situations.

23. Maintenance Dose (Continuous IV Infusion). The IV loading dose of theophylline was given over 30 minutes. How is the maintenance dose determined?

The maintenance dose is determined by the clearance of a drug according to the following relationship:

Maintenance Dose = (Cpss)(Cl)   *Eq 19.5*

where Cpss represents the steady-state plasma concentration and Cl is the clearance.

Note that this equation is used to calculate the hourly continuous IV infusion dose of theophylline. It must be increased by a factor of 20% when using aminophylline. It also can be used to estimate intermittent oral doses by multiplying the hourly dose by the desired dosing interval. (Also see Question 28.)

Theophylline is cleared primarily by hepatic metabolism mediated by the cytochrome P450 mixed-function-oxidase enzyme

system.[107] Only about 10% of a dose is excreted unchanged in the urine, except in neonates. The metabolic clearance of theophylline is affected by age, concurrent disease states, drug therapy, diet, and cigarette smoking. The mean half-life ($t\frac{1}{2}$) of elimination in premature infants ranges from 20 to 30 hours.[108] The half-life of theophylline decreases gradually during infancy (as clearance increases) to a mean half-life of three to four hours for children between 1 and 12 years old.[115] The half-life then increases in adults as clearance once again decreases to an average half-life of elimination of seven to eight hours in nonsmokers.[107] Smokers have a half-life ranging between four and five hours, (faster clearance due to enzyme induction) and this half-life increases gradually after cessation of cigarette smoking.[116,117] While there is a long-term change in theophylline half-life after smoking cessation, there also is a prompt increase in half-life one week after tobacco abstinence. Lee et al.[118] found a 35.8% increase in theophylline half-life after smoking cessation in 14 healthy men. This initial, rapid decrease in theophylline elimination could be important clinically, especially in patients whose serum concentrations are in the higher end of the therapeutic range before smoking cessation. Elderly nonsmokers have a mean half-life of about ten hours.[110]

A number of pathophysiologic conditions can alter the metabolism or clearance of theophylline. Disease states associated with a decreased theophylline clearance include hepatic cirrhosis, cor pulmonale, congestive heart failure, pulmonary edema, and prolonged fever associated with viral illnesses.[109,119–122]

Several pharmacokinetic dosing formulas and recommendations for the dosing of theophylline are available. The FDA guidelines[123] have been criticized because its recommendations for dose adjustments after the first 12 hours of infusion can cause potential problems in some patients.[124] Theophylline infusion doses that are calculated based upon mean clearance values and dosages for corresponding ages should be used only for the uncomplicated asthma patient (see Table 19.3).

In asthma patients with other complications, Chiou's[125] method or the Bayesian method of calculating doses appear to be more accurate.[126] The Chiou method is very effective for dosing theophylline using few blood samples if: 1) a constant infusion by pump is used, 2) dose (infusion rate) is constant, 3) physiologic parameters that determine theophylline clearance are not changing, 4) Volume of distribution is not changing, 5) laboratory precision to measure theophylline in the serum is excellent, and 6) the patient's elimination half-life is shorter than the time interval between blood samples.[127] Equations to use with the Chiou method are as follows:

$$Cl = \frac{2\ Ri}{C_1 + C_2} + \frac{2\ Vd\ (C_1 - C_2)}{(C_1 + C_2)(T_2 - T_1)} \qquad Eq\ 19.6$$

where Cl is clearance (L/kg/hr), Ri is infusion rate (mg/kg/hr), Vd is the volume of distribution (0.5 L/kg), C_1 is postloading dose serum concentration (mg/L), and C_2 is the second serum measurement. T_1 and T_2 are the times the samples were obtained. The blood samples should be obtained four to six hours apart for children and smokers or eight hours apart in nonsmokers. The calculated clearance is then used to calculate the new infusion rate (mg/hr) needed to achieve the desired serum theophylline concentration (Cp) according to the following equation:

$$Ri = (Cp)(Cl)(Weight) \qquad Eq\ 19.7$$

In conclusion, the general guidelines (see Table 19.3) are adequate for dosing theophylline in the uncomplicated asthma patient. If more precise determinations are desired, a more involved method such as that of Chiou should be used.

Table 19.3	Initial IV Maintenance Theophylline Infusion Rates	
Patient Population	Average t½ (hr)	Theophylline Infusion Rate (mg/kg/hr)[a]
Neonates (up to 24 days)[b,c]	20–30	0.08
Neonates (>24 days)[b,c]		0.12
Infants (6–52 wk)		0.008 (age in wk) + 0.21 mg/kg/hr
Young children (1–9 yr)[c]	3–4	0.8
Older children (9–12 yr)[c]		0.7
Adolescents (12–16 yr)		0.5
Adolescent (smoker)		0.7
Adult (>16 yr, nonsmoker)	7–8 (Range: 3–16)	0.4
Adult (smoker)	3–4	0.7[h]
Elderly (nonsmoker)[c]	10	0.3
CHF,[d] liver dysfunction, cor pulmonale, pneumonia, viral illness, high fever[e]		0.2 mg/kg/hr or ↓ above dose by 50%[e]
Cimetidine, ciprofloxacin, erythromycin, other enzyme inhibitors[f]		↓ above dose by 50%[f]
Carbamazepine, phenytoin, phenobarbital, rifampin, smoker[g]		↑ above dose by 50%[g]

[a] Doses to achieve 10 mg/L. Divide by 0.8 for aminophylline dose. Use lean body weight for obese patients.

[b] To achieve a target concentration of 7.5 mg/L for neonatal apnea.

[c] Clearance is slow in neonates due to immature hepatic function. During early childhood, clearance is most rapid. Clearance is slower in adults than in children. Clearance is further reduced with aging (>65 yr).

[d] CHF = Congestive heart failure.

[e] The influence of these variables is difficult to predict. Theophylline clearance may change several times in the same patient during fluctuations in various disease processes. Do not exceed 400 mg/day starting dose unless serum levels indicate the need for larger doses.

[f] As a general rule, enzyme inhibition effects are rapid (24–48 hr), except with erythromycin. However, the magnitude of change may be both time and dose dependent. Patients with theophylline serum concentrations >13 mg/L are at greatest risk of developing side effects with combination therapy.

[g] As a general rule, enzyme induction effects are slow (5 days–2 wk). Conversely, after stopping the drug inducer or smoking, it may take several days for the inducing effect to significantly abate.

[h] Do not exceed 900 mg/day starting dose unless indicated by serum levels.

Since H.T. had no underlying complication known to alter theophylline clearance, a constant infusion was started using 0.6 mg/kg/hour of theophylline or 50 mg/hour of aminophylline (80% theophylline). This is greater than the recommended starting dose of 0.4 mg/kg/hour from Table 19.3 because a steady-state level greater than 10 µg/mL is desired by H.T.'s clinician. H.T. must be monitored closely for indications of theophylline toxicity at this higher dosage. Higher than usual doses of theophylline should not be used if serum theophylline concentrations cannot be rapidly analyzed. Many clinicians would not choose this relatively aggressive dose initially.

24. Timing of Blood Samples. In order to use theophylline safely and optimally, serum theophylline concentrations should be monitored. When should blood samples be obtained to monitor serum concentrations?

When using the Chiou method for determining a theophylline maintenance dose, the blood samples should be obtained according to the recommendations in Question 23. When using the general guidelines in Table 19.3 for theophylline maintenance doses, an initial blood sample should be obtained 15 to 30 minutes after completion of the intravenous aminophylline loading dose. Another blood sample should be obtained four to eight hours after starting the aminophylline constant infusion to determine the serum concentration of theophylline. It should be noted, however, that obtaining a serum level at four to eight hours after starting the infusion is of little value unless there is a postloading dose concentration to use for comparison. If the aminophylline infusion dose is modified, the serum concentration of theophylline should be evaluated 12 to 24 hours after the dose change. Once the desired steady-state theophylline serum concentration has been reached (after approximately 4 to 5 estimated t½s), a blood sample should be analyzed for theophylline content whenever side effects are suspected, some factor that changes theophylline clearance is introduced, or there is a change in clinical response.

25. Dosing Adjustments. H.T.'s serum theophylline concentration 30 minutes after the theophylline loading dose was 21 µg/mL. Eight hours later, while on the constant infusion, it was 15 µg/mL. H.T.'s overall clinical condition seems to have improved; however, he is still wheezing and short of breath, and his most recent PaCO2 is 35 mm Hg. How should H.T.'s dose of theophylline be adjusted to provide additional relief of symptoms?

The initial theophylline concentration may have been high because the loading dose was excessive (possibly because H.T.'s volume of distribution is less than estimated). Also, as with most drugs metabolized by hepatic enzymes, theophylline has the potential to saturate its metabolic enzyme system. Although saturation of metabolism seldom occurs when theophylline serum concentrations are in the usual therapeutic range, a few cases have occurred when theophylline serum concentrations were less than 20 µg/mL.[128,129] When the pathway for the hepatic metabolism of theophylline is saturated, changes in the serum concentrations of theophylline are disproportionate relative to the dose, and fine tuning of the serum concentrations of this drug can be difficult. Due to the log-linear nature of the theophylline concentration response curve, an increase above 15 µg/mL would not be expected to produce further clinically significant bronchodilation. In addition, the last PaCO2 measurement indicates H.T. is improving; therefore, no dosage adjustment is necessary.

26. Response to Therapy. H.T. has continued to improve slowly over the last 72 hours. The nebulizer treatments with albuterol are now administered Q 4 hr and he is taking oral prednisone 80 mg/day in 2 divided doses. PEFR measurements taken before and after the last albuterol treatment were 65% of predicted and 90% of predicted, respectively. Is H.T.'s long duration of recovery unusual?

No. In a patient such as H.T. whose condition progressively deteriorated over a long period, one should expect a slow reversal. The prolonged deterioration most likely reflects an increasing inflammatory response in the lung. These patients require prolonged, intensive bronchodilator and anti-inflammatory therapy before maximal improvement is noted in pulmonary function tests.[96] One to two months may be required before the pulmonary function tests that reflect small airways dysfunction ($FEF_{25\%-75\%}$) return to normal baseline values. In addition, patients often will experience nonspecific bronchial hyperreactivity following a severe asthma attack. Thus, H.T. should continue to receive systemic corticosteroids for at least two weeks following such a severe acute asthma attack.

27. Conversion to Oral Dosing. Should H.T.'s IV aminophylline be switched to oral theophylline at this time?

The therapeutic response to theophylline correlates with the serum theophylline concentration rather than with a particular route of administration. If a patient is not experiencing gastrointestinal (GI) distress and can tolerate the oral administration of theophylline, there is no advantage to intravenous administration.[63,106] Oral theophylline is much more convenient and less costly than IV aminophylline. Even patients in status asthmaticus can be treated with oral theophylline if they can tolerate it.

28. The last theophylline serum concentration for H.T. (16 µg/mL) was obtained after 72 hours of treatment with IV aminophylline infused at a rate of 50 mg/hr. If theophylline therapy is to be continued, what should be the oral dose for H.T.?

The total daily dose of theophylline can be computed based upon H.T.'s daily intravenous infusion dose. This total daily dose is then divided into two, three, or four times daily dosing depending upon the type of theophylline product used. The daily dose of theophylline to achieve the same steady-state serum theophylline concentration of 16 µg/mL (or mg/L) in H.T. can be calculated as follows:

$$(50 \text{ mg/hr})(24 \text{ hr})(0.8) = 960 \text{ mg/day theophylline}$$

$$(\text{aminophylline}) = 80\% \text{ theophylline}$$

This calculation is based upon achieving a steady-state serum concentration. Since intermittent oral theophylline dosing is associated with peak and trough theophylline serum concentrations, a lower steady-state serum concentration should be chosen to avoid possible toxicity if peak theophylline serum concentrations are too high. In addition, lower concentrations are prudent because theophylline is an *adjunctive* drug in the acute and chronic care settings.[6,7] Therefore, a steady-state serum concentration of 10 µg/mL (mg/L) or less (i.e., 5–10 µg/mL) is appropriate.

$$\text{Theophylline Cl} = \frac{(50 \text{ mg/hr})(0.8)}{16 \text{ mg/L}}$$

$$= 2.5 \text{ L/hr}$$

$$\text{Dose} = (\text{Cpss})(\text{Cl})$$

$$\text{New Oral Dose} = (10 \text{ mg/L})(2.5 \text{ L/hr})(24 \text{ hr})$$

$$= 600 \text{ mg/day}$$

When the daily theophylline dose is rounded down to the nearest 50 mg, H.T. would receive 600 mg/day of theophylline. A reliable twice daily sustained-release (SR) product is preferred for most patients. Some children may require every eight hour dosing. Because a four times daily dosing interval may be needed with rapid release products, they generally are not recommended for maintenance dosing. When switching from intravenous theophylline, the oral dose should be started immediately after stopping the infusion.[130] The final dosage adjustment should be based upon theophylline serum concentration monitoring.

A *major* consideration here is that it is very likely H.T. will not need theophylline after leaving the hospital. Because of the severity of H.T.'s exacerbation, an increase in inhaled corticosteroid at home probably is needed in addition to very careful assessment of compliance and inhalation technique, as well as attention to other long-term management principles. With optimal long-term inhaled anti-inflammatory therapy, H.T. rarely, if ever, should have such a severe exacerbation again. (See Questions 55 and 56 for a complete discussion of inhalation technique.)

Adverse Effects of Short-Term Corticosteroid Therapy

29. H.T. has been on corticosteroids for a total of 6 days. Long-term corticosteroid use is associated with many adverse effects (e.g., adrenal suppression, osteoporosis, cataracts). What adverse effects are related to short-term corticosteroid usage?

Short courses of daily corticosteroids are associated with minor side effects.[85–88] Facial flushing, appetite stimulation, GI irritation, headache, and mood changes ranging from a mere sense of well-being to overt toxic psychosis are the most commonly encountered adverse effects of short-term corticosteroid therapy. Acne can be exacerbated in patients susceptible to this skin problem, and weight gain also can occur because of sodium and fluid retention. In addition, hyperglycemia, leukocytosis, and hypokalemia are possible. All of these problems are transient and will disappear over time after the steroids are discontinued. These short-term adverse effects are less common when small corticosteroid doses are used; however, corticosteroid doses must be adequate to prevent disease exacerbation. The minor risks of short-term usage are far outweighed by the marked benefits.

Overuse of Beta Agonists

30. H.T.'s history of increased use of his β₂-agonist inhaler during the early stages of this asthma attack and the cardiac irregularities noted during admission suggest improper use of this medication. What are the risks from overuse of β₂-agonists?

The contribution of medication use or misuse to asthma deaths has been disputed widely since an epidemic of asthma deaths occurred in young asthmatics (3 to 34 years of age) in England, Wales, Ireland, Australia, and New Zealand from 1959 to 1966.[96] These fatalities occurred about the time that potent isoproterenol and metaproterenol metered-dose aerosols were introduced for purchase without prescription in those countries. No increases in deaths were noted in the U.S., Canada, West Germany, or other countries in which the inhalers were not available over-the-counter (OTC) for unrestricted use.[96]

Autopsy evidence during the early epidemics failed to reveal a cardiovascular cause for the patients' deaths; however, signs of severe bronchial obstruction were evident.[13,98] Since most deaths from asthma occur outside the hospital setting before the patient can reach medical assistance,[13,96] the primary cause of death in asthma most probably is due to underestimation of the severity of the asthma attack by the patient and delay in seeking medical help.[13] The use or "overuse" of potent inhalers most likely contributed to the delay in seeking medical assistance. Indeed, in Australia, the decline in asthma deaths occurred before the decline in inhaler sales and followed an intensive campaign to educate patients and physicians on the care of asthma.[131]

Reports in the early 1990s again have raised the question of possible dangers associated with chronic overuse of inhaled beta agonists.[132,133] Patients at greatest risk of death in these controversial reports were using over two canisters per month of fenoterol, a beta agonist not used in the U.S. Many asthma experts feel that deaths in these case-control analyses were due to undertreatment of the inflammatory condition rather than to toxicity caused by the chronic use of inhaled beta agonists. In other words, patients with more severe disease were more likely to use larger doses. Thus, it is unclear if the increase in morbidity and mortality is disease or drug related.

In a related issue, Sears and associates[134,135] reported that regular use of fenoterol four times daily resulted in worse asthma control than when the same drug was used "as needed." These reports are controversial in part because the investigators claimed that this was a problem with a whole class of agents (beta agonists) even though their study involved only fenoterol. Although there is no proof that use of an inhaled β₂-agonist four times daily is harmful, many asthma experts prefer to use "as needed" rather than regularly-scheduled β₂-agonists.[6,7] By determining the frequency of "as needed" doses, the clinician has a good marker of the adequacy of inhaled anti-inflammatory therapy (e.g., if the patient needs the inhaled β_2-agonist more than two or three times a day, increase the dose of inhaled anti-inflammatory therapy).

The best way to prevent asthma deaths is "state-of-the-art" treatment and education. Patients should be instructed on the proper use of all their medications. Frequent use of bronchodilator inhalers should be a clue to instability of the airways and increasing inflammation. Appropriate measures should be taken before the need for hospitalization occurs. Setting arbitrary absolute limits to inhaler use is not useful and only leads to mutual dissatisfaction between clinician and patient. Patients should be instructed in the proper use of their inhalers during acute attacks and in recognizing when it is necessary to seek medical assistance. Nevertheless, patients can continue using their beta agonist inhalers on an as needed basis until they reach medical care. H.T. should be considered at high risk because of the severity of his latest attack and should be given oral corticosteroids to self-administer at the first sign of significant deterioration.[6,7,86,88] In addition, H.T. should have a home peak flow meter so that he can more accurately determine the severity of his attacks. Finally, the beta agonist controversy does *not* extend to use of high doses in the acute care setting. High doses are essential to the emergency room and hospital, and as previously discussed, usually are tolerated very well.

Chronic Asthma
Goals of Therapy

31. B.C., a 3-year-old, 16 kg male with a 1.5 year history of recurrent wheezing, was referred to the pulmonary clinic for difficult-to-control asthma. The following medications had been prescribed for B.C.: Slo-Phyllin Syrup (80 mg/15 mL) 1.5 tablespoonsful TID PRN wheezing, albuterol metered-dose aerosol inhalation QID, and prednisolone (Pediapred) oral liquid 1 teaspoonful BID for severe wheezing. B.C.'s mother had been administering the prednisolone whenever the child experienced respiratory difficulties; however, B.C. has been taking the prednisolone almost continuously over the past few months. The mother also relates that she seldom uses the theophylline (i.e., the Slo-Phyllin Syrup) because B.C. becomes "very hyper" when taking it. B.C. demonstrates the use of the inhaler with his mother's assistance. The mother holds the inhaler in B.C.'s mouth and actuates it at the end of a deep inhalation. What should be the immediate goal of therapy for B.C.?

The goal of therapy for B.C. is to provide maximum control of symptoms with the least amount of adverse effects. The long-term use of corticosteroids is associated with numerous adverse effects; therefore, if at all possible the prednisolone must be discontinued. The chronic use of systemic corticosteroids can lead to hypothalamic-pituitary-adrenal (HPA) axis suppression, growth retardation in children, cushingoid appearance, diabetes, hypertension, myopathy, hirsutism, osteoporosis leading to fractures, and postsubcapsular cataracts.[6,74] The degree of HPA axis suppression is both dose and duration dependent. Although B.C. has been prescribed prednisolone 5 mg BID, which is within the usual recommended dose (i.e., 0.5 to 2 mg/kg/day) for children, systemic steroids should be prescribed only for patients who are not responding adequately to other therapy and then as a single daily dose in the morning or every other day. To avoid growth retardation and the numerous other problems associated with long-term daily use of oral corticosteroids, *every* effort should be made to optimize other therapies. Subsequently, the prednisolone can be discontinued gradually as drug therapy with other asthmatic medications is optimized. B.C.'s mother must be educated about the disease, its treatment, and the appropriate use of medications (e.g., proper use of inhaler devices see Questions 55 and 56).

Initial Therapy

32. What would be a good intensive initial therapy program for B.C.?

The severity of B.C.'s asthma cannot be determined based upon his response to medications because he has not been using either his β_2-agonist inhaler or his theophylline in a manner that would prevent bronchoconstriction. Therefore, a structured medication regimen must be established for B.C. in order to properly evaluate his real need for prednisolone. The initial medication program also should be aggressive in order to establish confidence in the patient-clinician relationship. Once B.C. is stabilized on an effective drug regimen, the corticosteroid can be discontinued by gradually decreasing the dose. Subsequently, the other medications should be slowly titrated down to the minimally effective regimen.

Children less than five years of age have a difficult time coordinating the use of plain metered-dose inhalers; therefore, β_2-agonists should be administered by another mode of delivery. For example, the β_2-agonist could be administered by an air compressor nebulizer or with an inhalational aid such as InspirEase or AeroChamber which is connected to a metered-dose aerosol (see Table 19.4). Inhalation aids (also called extender devices or "spacers") significantly improve the efficiency of bronchodilators that are administered by metered-dose aerosols, particularly in very young children unable to coordinate the plain inhalers correctly.[136] Extender device-assisted delivery of aerosolized medications is as effective as nebulization in the home management of chronic severe asthma.[137] The InspirEase and AeroChamber devices contain a flow indicator whistle that sounds if the patient inhales rapidly. This whistle is particularly effective in teaching the patient the appropriate slow inhalation technique.

A selective β_2-agonist also can be administered orally to B.C. as an alternative to extender device-assisted aerosolization. The advantages of oral therapy would be ease of administration and longer duration of action; these advantages, however, are off-set by an increase in adverse effects and diminished efficacy.[37] B.C.'s history of hyperactivity on theophylline and his mother's reluctance to use theophylline would suggest that inhaled β_2-adrenergic therapy is the bronchodilator of choice. Combining an inhaled β_2-agonist with an inhaled anti-inflammatory agent (e.g., corticosteroid, cromolyn, or nedocromil) is basic therapy for virtually all moderate to severe asthmatics.[6,7]

Cromolyn

33. Should cromolyn (Intal) be added to B.C.'s β_2-agonist therapy and is it preferred over theophylline in B.C.?

Table 19.4	Examples of Inhalation Aids
ACE (Aerosol Cloud Enhancer) (DHD)	150 mL conical holding chamber with one-way valve at mouthpiece. Flow indicator whistle
AeroChamber (Monaghan Medical)	Holding chamber. Cylinder with one-way valve that releases aerosol when subject inhales. Flow indicator whistle
Brethancer (Geigy Pharmaceuticals)	Tube spacer. A 10 cm, open-ended, telescopic plastic tube
InspirEase (Schering)	Holding chamber consisting of a collapsible bag with a flow indicator whistle
Nebuhaler (A.B. Draco, Lund, Sweden)	750 mL conical holding chamber with one-way valve at mouthpiece
Optihaler (Health Scan)	Holding chamber. Cylinder. Aerosol particles are directed away from mouth initially

Mechanism of Action

The precise mechanism of action of cromolyn sodium, a furanochromone, is still unknown. Nevertheless, its mechanism of action is thought to involve stabilization of mast cell membranes and prevention of the release of chemical mediators of inflammation.[138] Mast cell mediators play an important role in the pathogenesis of bronchial hyperreactivity.[6,7,9-11] Cromolyn stabilizes mast cell membranes nonspecifically, most likely by inhibiting calcium influx.[138] Therefore, cromolyn inhibits mast cell degranulation produced by immunologic (IgE-mediated) and nonimmunologic mechanisms. Cromolyn inhibits the early and late bronchospastic responses to specific inhaled allergens in atopic asthmatics and inhibits exercise-induced bronchospasm in both atopic and nonatopic asthmatics.[138] Cromolyn also inhibits bronchoconstriction produced by inhalation of cold air, sulfur dioxide, and ultrasonically nebulized water; these effects have not been associated with mast cell mediator release.[138] Cromolyn is neither a bronchodilator nor an inhibitor of the action of any chemical mediators (e.g., histamine, leukotrienes, bradykinins) that already have been released.

Comparison to Theophylline

In studies of childhood asthma, cromolyn has effectively controlled symptoms in 60% to 80% of patients with mild to moderate chronic asthma.[138] When the six randomized, double-blind trials that compared cromolyn to theophylline for the control of chronic childhood asthma[139-144] are analyzed, neither drug seemed to offer significant advantages or disadvantages over the other. Theophylline crossover studies with cromolyn must be interpreted cautiously. When the studies are less than four weeks in duration, they are of minimal value because it may take four to six weeks to achieve optimal benefit from cromolyn.[138] Nevertheless, two follow-up four-week crossover comparisons failed to confirm an advantage for theophylline therapy over that of cromolyn.[140,144] Two crossover trials using eight-week treatment periods with two- to three-week washout periods between treatments reported no significant difference in symptom control and a greater number of adverse effects with theophylline.[141,142] Furukawa et al.[143] reported no difference in symptom control in a three-month parallel trial with a greater number of adverse effects and clinic visits in the theophylline group. School behavior problems were reported by the parents only in the theophylline group. Behavioral problems and abnormal psychological testing in children taking theophylline have improved when the theophylline was replaced by cromolyn.[144,145] Most importantly cromolyn addresses the basic problem of inflammation, is essentially devoid of serious adverse effects, and is a first choice maintenance drug in children.[6,7] In addition, B.C.'s history of hyperactivity while taking theophylline and the withholding of this drug by his mother indicate that cromolyn should be added to B.C.'s β2-agonist therapy rather than theophylline.

Dosage Forms

34. Which dosage form of cromolyn should be prescribed for B.C.?

Cromolyn is available in a 20 mg capsule that uses a special Spinhaler device to disperse the powder in the capsule for inhalation. It also is available in a 1% solution (20 mg in a 2 mL unit-dose glass ampule) for nebulization, and as a metered-dose inhaler that delivers 0.8 mg per inhalation. Although the Spinhaler does not require coordination of actuation and inhalation like the metered-dose inhaler, it requires a relatively high inspiratory flow rate to properly disperse the particles; therefore, the Spinhaler is not recommended for children less than five years of age.[150] B.C. possibly could use the metered-dose aerosol with a tube-spacer attached, but the benefits of a tube-spacer have not been investigated adequately for this product. As a result, the cromolyn nebulizer solution would be preferred for B.C. One ampule of cromolyn solution should be nebulized four times daily in B.C. in conjunction with a selective, long-acting β2-agonist such as albuterol or terbutaline. Cromolyn nebulizer solution is compatible with all of the existing β2-agonist nebulizer solutions and the two agents can be nebulized simultaneously.[150] The prophylactic nature of cromolyn and the absolute need for continuous maintenance therapy must be *emphasized* to patients and their parents. Unlike dry powder given via the Spinhaler, cromolyn nebulizer solution does not produce any significant bronchial irritation and should not be discontinued during wheezing.[150] B.C.'s family also should be instructed in the use and proper maintenance of the nebulizer as found in the manufacturer's patient package insert. After B.C.'s symptoms have been controlled on this regimen and he has been off corticosteroids for one month, the dosing frequency of cromolyn may be decreased to two to three times daily as required for control of symptoms.[155]

Seasonal Asthma

35. C.V., a 33-year-old female, presents to the clinic with a history of asthma and seasonal allergic rhinitis ("hayfever"). She describes her asthma as "mild" and intermittent. Although she has not required any ER visits for her asthma, she does relate that most mornings throughout the year she awakens with some chest tightness and cough, and on most days she requires use of her albuterol MDI (Ventolin) in the morning and at least once during the afternoon. Each springtime, these symptoms worsen, and she requires her inhaler TID or QID. During hayfever season, she takes a nonprescription antihistamine which offers some relief. How can C.V.'s management be improved?

Nedocromil, Cromolyn, Inhaled Corticosteroids

Although C.V. describes her asthma as "mild," she has daily symptoms, and by current criteria, she has moderate asthma.[6,7] Therefore, she should receive daily anti-inflammatory therapy to block the late asthmatic response,[146] and an inhaled β2-agonist for symptomatic relief.[6,7] Figure 19.7 outlines the step care approach of the International Consensus Report.[7] A relatively low dose of an inhaled corticosteroid would be an appropriate initial long-term therapy for C.V. (e.g., beclomethasone 4 puffs Q 12 hr). Alternatively, inhaled nedocromil or inhaled cromolyn also would be helpful. Inhaled nedocromil is indicated for mild to moderate adult asthma.[7] Its mechanism of action is similar to cromolyn, and like cromolyn, it is remarkably safe.[7] Finally, C.V. should receive an intranasal corticosteroid or intranasal cromolyn if antihistamines (sedating or nonsedating) do not provide optimal relief of her allergic rhinitis. Good control of rhinitis is helpful in maintaining optimal asthma control.[6] (Also see Chapter 21: Acute and Chronic Rhinitis.) Despite precautions listed in manufacturer's literature that older antihistamines should be avoided in asthma, these agents are safe in asthmatics and will help because of improved nasal systems.[6]

Corticosteroids

36. S.T., an 11-year-old female with severe chronic asthma, has been only moderately well-controlled on continuous SR theophylline, inhaled cromolyn, and inhaled albuterol (Ventolin). She has been hospitalized 4 times in the last 2 years and has required "bursts" of prednisone with increasing frequency. S.T. has missed many days of school in the past year and has withdrawn from physical education classes and her

extracurricular sports activity after school. Her parents are concerned about her increased use of prednisone now that she is approaching puberty. S.T. is just finishing a 2-week course of prednisone 20 mg/day and has a round facies appearance typical of chronic steroid use. On physical examination, S.T. has diffuse expiratory wheezes, and pulmonary function testing reveals significant reversibility. S.T. has been very compliant with all of her medications and her theophylline serum concentrations are within the therapeutic range. What are the therapeutic alternatives for S.T.?

Numerous studies have documented the efficacy of corticosteroids in asthma.[6,7,74] Since S.T. is requiring very frequent systemic corticosteroids, *all* efforts must be made to optimize other therapies and to minimize systemic corticosteroid toxicities. Long-term daily inhaled corticosteroid therapy definitely is indicated in S.T. While short "bursts" of prednisone (e.g., 40 mg/day for 3 days) are very helpful occasionally, very frequent short courses often indicate the need to optimize other therapies. Some patients require "bursts" of one to two weeks. S.T. is requiring longer frequent "bursts" and is showing signs of adverse effects.

Aerosol corticosteroids are chemically modified to maximize topical effectiveness while minimizing systemic toxicities. Aerosolized corticosteroids such as triamcinolone acetonide (Azmacort) are absorbed poorly, and others, such as beclomethasone dipropionate (Beclovent, Vanceril), are inactivated rapidly once absorbed.[147,148] Table 19.5 compares the aerosol corticosteroids. When used in the usual recommended dosages, there is little if any advantage of one product over another.[75,147] In high dosages (the equivalent of 1600 μg/day of beclomethasone dipropionate), all

will produce some degree of HPA axis suppression.[147] The clinical significance of this suppression has yet to be firmly established.

There have been few comparative studies of alternate day prednisone treatment with aerosol corticosteroids. Toogood et al.[147] compared alternate day prednisone with budesonide inhaled four times daily in a double-blind crossover study of 14 steroid-dependent asthmatics and found budesonide to be superior. Alternate day prednisone is given between 6 a.m. and 8 a.m. at two to three times the daily dose (e.g., 10 mg/day = 20 mg QOD). The lowest possible dose of corticosteroid should be used, regardless of the route of administration.

37. How would you begin S.T. on oral inhalation corticosteroids and what would be the optimal dosage regimen?

There is no single factor or constellation of factors that determines the optimal inhaled corticosteroid dosage;[147] however, current literature suggests a maximum *adult* dose of 2 mg (total daily dose for any inhaled corticosteroid) in severe asthma.[6,7] Toogood et al.[149] have outlined some general guidelines for beginning patients on aerosol corticosteroids. If the patient has been receiving daily systemic corticosteroids for long-term therapy, the corticosteroid dose should be tapered slowly; the speed by which corticosteroids are gradually discontinued depends upon the dose and duration of therapy. In S.T., most clinicians would suggest beginning with a short course (one week) of high-dose systemic steroids to maximally improve her pulmonary function. Some clinicians prefer to initiate inhaled corticosteroid therapy concomitantly with a short course of systemic corticosteroid therapy rather than waiting for one week. Patient education may have greater effectiveness because some patients will be more attentive since they have just

Table 19.5		Oral Inhalation Corticosteroid Comparison Chart[a, 74, 75, 78]				
		Dosage[b]		Relative Topical Potency[d]	Systemic Bioavailability[e]	Plasma t½
Drug	Dosage Forms	Adult	Pediatric[c]			
Beclomethasone-17, 21-dipropionate Beclovent Vanceril	Inhaled (metered dose) 42 μg/puff, 200 puffs	Inhale 2–3 puffs TID–QID[f]	Inhale 1–2 puffs TID–QID[f]	500	<5%	15 hr
Dexamethasone sodium phosphate Decadron	Inhaled (metered dose) 100 μg/puff, 170 puffs	Inhale 2 puffs TID–QID	Inhale 2 puffs TID–QID	0.8	80%	5 hr
Flunisolide AeroBid	Inhaled (metered dose) 250 μg/puff, 100 puffs	Inhale 2 puffs BID (*max: 8 puffs/day*)	Inhale 1–2 puffs BID (*max: 4 puffs/day*)	>100	20%	1.6 hr
Triamcinolone-16, 17-acetonide Azmacort	Inhaled (metered dose) 100 μg/puff, 240 puffs	Inhale 2 puffs TID–QID[f] (*max: 16 puffs/day*)	Inhale 1–2 puffs TID–QID[f] (*max: 12 puffs/day*)	100		30–60 min
Budesonide[g] Pulmicort Astra	Inhaled (metered dose) 50 μg/puff Turbuhaler 100 μg/inhalation	Inhale 400–1600 μg/day in 2–4 doses	Inhale 200–400 μg/day in 2–4 doses	1000	10%	2–2.8 hr
Fluticasone[g] Flixotide Glaxo	Inhale (diskhaler) 50 μg, 100 μg, 250 μg	100–1000 μg BID	50–100 μg BID	1000	<1%	Unknown

a Although there are differences, comparative trials to date have failed to establish any conclusive evidence that any product is clearly superior except for dexamethasone, which should not be used due to its extensive systemic effects.

b Recommended starting doses. Higher doses may be used with the realization that they will produce dose-dependent systemic effects.

c Pediatric dosing is for patients 6–12 years of age; dosages for patients <6 years have not been established.

d Topical potency based upon skin vasoconstrictive effect.

e Reflects oral bioavailability in as much as 90% of an inhaled dose is deposited in the mouth and swallowed. Most are rapidly and completely absorbed from the respiratory tract.

f BID dosing is proven efficacious for most patients and tends to improve compliance.

g Not currently available in the U.S.

experienced exacerbation and know that they need to do something differently. In some patients, the psychology of emphasizing the cornerstone of therapy on the initial encounter may be significant. Start S.T. on a high pediatric dose of aerosol corticosteroid (e.g., 600 μg/day). After S.T. is stabilized for two months, the dose hopefully can be decreased every one to two months until the optimal dose is achieved. The doses of S.T.'s other medications should not be reduced during corticosteroid therapy since they may permit use of a lower corticosteroid dose. Administration of the total daily inhaled corticosteroid dose is preferred twice daily as opposed to four times daily,[150,151] because simplified regimens tend to improve patient compliance. All inhaled corticosteroid products in the U.S. are FDA approved for twice-daily dosing. Some patients require three or four times daily dosing, but most do well on twice-daily doses of inhaled corticosteroids. Compliance is a major determinant of success or failure with aerosol corticosteroids and continued patient education and contact are essential.[147]

Theophylline

Dosing

38. K.J., an 11-year-old, 30 kg female, has a history of recurring cough and wheezing. These symptoms worsen upon vigorous running or when she has an upper respiratory infection. The symptoms seem to recur every few weeks. She has not required hospitalization for these symptoms but has missed a significant number of school days. There is a family history of asthma. A diagnosis of chronic asthma is given. How should K.J. be managed?

When asthma symptoms recur frequently, chronic prophylaxis with an inhaled anti-inflammatory agent is indicated. Cromolyn is indicated in K.J., but since multiple daily doses usually are required, compliance is a concern in children her age. After the first few weeks of therapy, some patients eventually can be maintained on two or three doses daily and do not require four times daily dosing of cromolyn. If K.J. is not controlled adequately on twice-daily cromolyn (i.e., a.m. and p.m. use at home where she does not have to be concerned about peer pressure at school), *low-dose* inhaled corticosteroid therapy twice daily is a logical alternative. A concerted effort at patient education is important at this point to explain the significance of inhaled anti-inflammatory medicine to K.J.

After a few weeks, K.J. has fewer symptoms but is not optimally controlled and because K.J. refuses to inhale cromolyn more than twice daily, her primary care clinician decides to add a low dose of theophylline twice daily as an adjunct to cromolyn. If that approach does not provide an optimal outcome, then low-dose inhaled corticosteroid will be initiated.

Table 19.6	Theophylline Dosing Guide for Chronic Use[a]

Starting dose for adults and children >1 year old:

The lesser of 400 mg/day total or 16 mg/kg/day

↑ dose if *tolerated* at 3-day intervals by ≤25% increments

Maximum dose for age

Children 1–9 yr	24 mg/kg/day
Children 9–12 yr	20 mg/kg/day
Children 12–16 yr	18 mg/kg/day
16 years and older	13 mg/kg/day or 800 mg/day total, whichever is less

Obtain peak serum theophylline concentration after no doses have been missed for at least 48 hr on the final dose tolerated

[a] Dose using IBW or actual body weight, whichever is less. These dosages do not apply if liver disease, heart failure, or other factors documented to affect theophylline clearance are present.

In the nonacute asthmatic where the theophylline dose requirement is unknown, dosages suggested for age are listed in Table 19.6.[16] Accordingly, the initial dose in K.J. would be 400 mg/day in divided doses. The dose then is increased, if tolerated, at three-day intervals by about 25% to the mean dose that usually is needed to produce a peak theophylline serum concentration between 5 and 15 μg/mL. In K.J., the maximum dose would be 600 mg/day (20 mg/kg/day) in divided doses. The final dose should be based upon response, absence of theophylline side effects, and serum theophylline concentration. Obviously, the *lowest* effective dose should be used to minimize risk.

Monitoring Therapy

39. When should serum theophylline concentrations be measured for patients who are receiving chronic oral theophylline therapy?

Peak, rather than trough, theophylline serum concentrations should be measured, especially in the pediatric population or in adults who rapidly metabolize theophylline. Both the efficacy and toxicity of theophylline correlate better with theophylline peak, rather than trough, serum concentrations particularly with the sustained-release products.

For rapid-release products, blood samples should be obtained one to two hours after a dose. For sustained-release products, peak theophylline serum concentrations should be measured four to six hours after a morning dose, depending upon the release characteristics of the product.[153] Evening serum concentrations may be less reliable due to diurnal rates of absorption (slower at night). Manufacturers of once-a-day theophylline suggest a serum sample be obtained 12 hours after a dose of THEO-24 and 8 to 12 hours after a dose of Uniphyl when determining the peak theophylline serum concentration. The final dose can be adjusted accordingly using the guidelines listed in Table 19.7. Serum theophylline concentrations should be obtained at steady state (i.e., when there have been no missed doses and no extra doses have been taken for at least 48 hours).

40. Once K.J. has been stabilized on oral theophylline, how often should her serum theophylline concentration be monitored?

Serum theophylline concentrations should be checked at least once a year in adults. In children, especially during their periods of rapid growth, serum samples should be obtained approximately every six months. If conditions that alter theophylline clearance develop (e.g., viral infections, febrile episodes, or addition of an enzyme-inhibiting drug such as erythromycin) or signs of asthma or theophylline side effects occur, more frequent serum level measurements are needed.

Product Selection

41. Would a plain tablet or SR formulation of theophylline be best for K.J.?

For treatment of chronic asthma, the sustained-release theophylline products are preferable. These products allow longer dosing intervals and minimize peak-trough serum concentration fluctuations. The rapid-release products are best suited for management of acute asthma, when short-term use is anticipated. An SR theophylline should be prescribed for K.J., particularly in light of her expected rapid theophylline clearance (see Table 19.6). The theophylline preparation should have sufficient sustained-release characteristics to provide an acceptable peak-trough fluctuation (e.g., Slo-bid, Theo-Dur) when administered every 12 hours.

42. Bioequivalency. Are various SR and rapid-release theophylline products bioequivalent and interchangeable?

Rapid-release tablets and liquids of theophylline are considered universally equivalent and interchangeable. However, the various

Table 19.7		Adjusting Doses of Theophylline Based Upon Serum Concentrations
Peak Theophylline Concentration (μg/mL)[a]	Approximate Adjustment in Daily Dose	Comment
<5.0	↑ by 25%	Recheck serum theophylline concentration
5–10	↑ by 25% if clinically indicated	Recheck serum concentration; ↑ dose only if poor response to therapy
10–12	Cautious 10% ↑ if clinically indicated	If asymptomatic, no ↑ needed. Recheck serum theophylline concentration before further dose changes
12–15	Occasional intolerance requires a 10% ↓	If asymptomatic, no dose change needed unless side effects present
16–20	↓ by 10%–25%	Even if asymptomatic and side effects absent, a dose ↓ is prudent
25–29.9	↓ by 50%	Omit next doses even if asymptomatic and side effects absent; a dose ↓ indicated. Repeat serum theophylline concentration after dose adjustment
≥30	↓ by 50%–75%	Omit next 3 doses and recheck theophylline serum concentration before restarting a reduced dose

[a] It is important that levels are obtained at steady state. If laboratory results appear questionable, suggest repeat measurements.

sustained-release theophylline products differ in their rates and extent of absorption.[153] The absorption of some slow-release theophylline products (e.g., Theo-24, Uniphyl, Theo-Dur Sprinkle) can be affected significantly by concomitant administration with food.[153] Theo-24 and Uniphyl have both increased extent and rate of absorption if taken with a large, fatty meal. Theo-Dur Sprinkle has reduced bioavailability if taken with a meal, but is unaffected by mixing the beads with a small amount of applesauce. The SR theophylline products should not be interchanged since their rates of absorption may differ significantly. Although once-daily administration of a 24-hour theophylline product would be expected to result in unacceptable serum theophylline concentration fluctuations in children, a preliminary trial demonstrated similar control of symptoms with Uniphyl once nightly and Theo-Dur twice daily.[154] Evening only dosing (e.g., Uniphyl) may have the advantage of preventing nocturnal asthma in both children and adults.[154,155]

Theophylline in Infants

43. J.D., a 6-month-old, 8 kg male, has been experiencing coughing, wheezing, and a low-grade fever for the past week due to a chest cold. A chest x-ray is normal. Family history indicates his father has asthma. This is the second episode of a respiratory problem associated with a virus during the past 6 weeks. Asthma is suspected in J.D. A trial of theophylline is to be given to J.D. to document reversibility of his airway obstruction. What pharmacokinetic differences exist in infants and how should theophylline be given?

Theophylline clearance increases rapidly during the first year of life.[156] The half-life changes from 20 to 30 hours at birth to about four hours by one year of age. This change in theophylline clearance with age makes it difficult to maintain therapeutic serum levels. Guidelines for oral theophylline dosing in infants (see Table 19.8) have been proposed by the FDA.[157] J.D. is of average weight for his age (6 months = 26 weeks) and the final theophylline dose according to the guideline is:

$$(3 \text{ mg/kg})(8 \text{ kg}) = 24 \text{ mg Q 6 hr}$$

Although theophylline liquid could be prescribed for J.D., it often is poorly accepted because the bitter taste is difficult to mask. Sustained-release, bead-filled capsules usually are preferred. Bead-filled capsules of Slo-Phyllin Gyrocaps, Slo-bid, or Somophyllin-CRT can be sprinkled on a small amount (1 teaspoonful) of food (ice cream or applesauce) immediately before administration. This amount of food will not alter the bioavailability of the beads. The beads are coated and do not have an unacceptable taste. The patient

must be observed carefully to evaluate signs and symptoms of theophylline efficacy or adverse effects because of the wide range of theophylline clearance values in infants.[156] (See Question 46.) If a liquid is prescribed, caution must be used at the time of dispensing because of the high variability in the theophylline concentration and alcohol content between products. Generally, alcohol-free preparations with the strongest concentration (thus, requiring smaller volumes of administration) are preferred. Serum theophylline levels are used to determine the final dose.

Theophylline Salts

44. How should oxtriphylline (Choledyl) or other salt forms of theophylline be dosed?

A number of theophylline "salts" or complexed forms of theophylline are available. These theophylline salts should be dosed according to their theophylline content (see Table 19.9). Some theophylline "salts" are claimed to cause fewer theophylline side effects; however, all theophylline salts are comparable to plain theophylline when prescribed in equivalent doses. Serum theophylline concentrations can be used to monitor therapy with these agents.

Dyphylline, a xanthine, is *not* a theophylline salt and serum theophylline concentrations cannot be used to monitor therapy. *In vitro* dose-response relationships for dyphylline indicate it to have one-tenth the potency of theophylline.

Rectal Theophylline

45. If a patient cannot be given theophylline PO or IV, is rectal administration advisable?

Rectal solutions of theophylline appear to be completely bioavailable; however, rectal theophylline suppositories are absorbed erratically and should not be used to treat pulmonary disease.[158] Dosing and intervals of administration for theophylline rectal solutions are similar to those for oral liquid theophylline.

Toxicity

46. A.Z., a 12-year-old girl who has been treated with Slo-bid Gyrocaps 300 mg BID, now complains of headache and difficulty in getting to sleep. Why should a theophylline serum concentration be evaluated?

Theophylline side effects can be related to excessive serum concentrations, or adverse effects can be transient and unrelated to the amount in serum. Unfortunately, it is not always possible to determine which it might be. Side effects can include headache, nausea, vomiting, irritability or hyperactivity, insomnia, and diarrhea. With higher serum theophylline levels, cardiac arrhythmias, sei-

Table 19.8	FDA Guidelines for Theophylline Dosing in Infants[a]

Preterm Infants

≤40 weeks postconception age: 1 mg/kg Q 12 hr

Term Infants (at birth or 40 weeks postconception)

≤4 weeks postnatal: 1–2 mg/kg Q 12 hr

4–8 weeks: 1–2 mg/kg Q 8 hr

>8 weeks: 1–3 mg/kg Q 6 hr

[a] Final dose determined using serum theophylline levels as a guide.

zures, and death can occur.[104] Less severe symptoms may not be present before the onset of cardiac arrhythmias or seizures, and cannot be relied upon as a forewarning of these more serious adverse theophylline effects. It is important not to ignore any symptom consistent with theophylline toxicity. The insomnia and headaches experienced by A.Z. may not be associated with excessive (i.e., out of usual therapeutic range) serum theophylline concentrations, but a reduction in dosage should be contemplated because some patients experience toxicity when serum theophylline concentrations are within the "therapeutic range." A sustained-release, oral β_2-agonist is an acceptable alternative for those patients unable to tolerate theophylline who require continuous bronchodilation.[159] A better alternative in A.Z. is a long acting inhaled β_2-agonist. In addition, her long term management should be assessed for inhaled anti-inflammatory therapy.[6,7] (See Figure 19.7)

Overdose

47. How should overdoses of theophylline be managed? What is the role of oral charcoal versus other treatments?

Initial treatment of oral theophylline overdoses should include ipecac administration or gastric lavage to remove stomach contents and tablet fragments if the patient is seen within the first few hours after ingestion of the drug. Subsequently, activated charcoal should be administered repeatedly not only to bind theophylline in the GI tract, *but also to draw out theophylline from the systemic circulation.*[160] Activated charcoal is better tolerated if administered as a plain water slurry than with sorbitol. A cathartic may be administered to prevent charcoal-induced constipation, but is not necessary to facilitate theophylline removal.[104] Monitoring of serum theophylline concentrations is imperative. Many patients with very high serum theophylline concentrations survive without after-effects; however, death or permanent brain damage is common when seizures occur.

Ventricular arrhythmias appear to respond well to propranolol (Inderal) or verapamil (Calan); however, propranolol would *not* be indicated in a patient with bronchial obstruction.[104] Patients with theophylline-induced seizures have responded to diazepam (Valium) and/or phenobarbital.[104] Some clinicians advocate the use of prophylactic phenobarbital in nonseizing patients exhibiting severe agitation. Charcoal hemoperfusion may be necessary when the serum theophylline concentration is greater than 60 μg/mL from a chronic overdose or greater than 100 μg/mL from an acute overdose.[161] Charcoal hemoperfusion probably is not warranted when the serum theophylline concentration is less than 40 μg/mL. The benefit versus risk ratio of charcoal hemoperfusion must be balanced carefully by the clinical status of the patient when serum theophylline concentrations are between 40 and 60 μg/mL. Peritoneal and hemodialysis are inadequate for management of theophylline toxicity.

Drug Interactions

48. Inhibition of Metabolism. **T.R., 55-year-old female with asthma, is reasonably well-controlled on Theo-Dur 300 mg**

BID, terbutaline inhaler 3 puffs QID PRN, and flunisolide (AeroBid) 2 puffs BID. A theophylline serum concentration obtained 3 months ago was 14 μg/mL. Six months ago, on the same dose of theophylline, her serum concentration was 15 μg/mL. She presents with an upper respiratory tract infection and erythromycin ethyl succinate 500 mg QID is prescribed. How should this potential drug interaction be followed?**

A large number of medications inhibit cytochrome P450 enzymes and are capable of inhibiting the metabolism of theophylline. Cimetidine (Tagamet), erythromycin, troleandomycin (TAO), and the quinolone antibiotics (enoxacin, perfloxacin, and ciprofloxacin) are well-documented to inhibit theophylline metabolism[162,163] Because *several* other drugs inhibit the metabolism of theophylline, all patients receiving this agent should be screened carefully for potential interactions. As with any drug interaction, mechanism, management, and clinical significance should be assessed before any interventions.

Erythromycin. The macrolide antibiotics, erythromycin and troleandomycin, substantially reduce theophylline clearance.[162] When compared to erythromycin, troleandomycin has a greater propensity to decrease theophylline clearance and should be avoided in patients taking theophylline. Although some earlier reports using short-term therapy indicated that erythromycin does not significantly decrease theophylline clearance, studies using multiple dosing provide clear evidence to support such an interaction.[162,164] This interaction is complex because of a delay in onset and wide variability in the magnitude of change seen in theophylline levels. If erythromycin is given at a time when the patient's steady-state serum theophylline concentration is ≥10 μg/mL, the theophylline dose should be decreased. If the theophylline dose is not decreased when erythromycin is added, the patient must be monitored carefully for possible signs of theophylline toxicity. The patient's serum theophylline concentration should be monitored after five days of erythromycin therapy regardless of whether toxic symptoms become apparent since serum theophylline concentrations usually do not increase until *after* five days of concurrent treatment. When patients are stabilized on theophylline, antibiotics other than TAO, erythromycin, ciprofloxacin, and enoxacin are preferred if possible.

49. *Cimetidine.* **Z.F., a 35-year-old asthmatic male, is well-controlled on Nedocromil 2 puffs QID, Theo-Dur 400 mg BID and bitolterol (Tornalate) 2–3 inhalations Q 6 hr PRN. He has been started on cimetidine 300 mg QID for treatment of a peptic ulcer. How should Z.F.'s theophylline therapy be adjusted?**

Cimetidine decreases theophylline clearance by 20% to 30%[162,164] and increases steady-state serum theophylline concen-

Table 19.9	Percentage of Anhydrous Theophylline and the Equivalent Dose of Various Theophylline Salts	
Salt	% Theophylline	Equivalent Dosage (mg)
Theophylline anhydrous	100	100
Theophylline monohydrate	91	100
Aminophylline anhydrous	86	116
Aminophylline dihydrate	79	127
Theophylline monoethanolamine	75	133
Oxtriphylline (choline theophylline)	64	156
Theophylline sodium glycinate	49	200
Theophylline calcium salicylate	48	208

tration by 40% to 60%. This drug interaction is well documented and more predictable than that with erythromycin. The theophylline dose should be reduced by 50% if cimetidine is prescribed for a patient already stabilized on theophylline. The theophylline serum concentration begins to increase immediately after the ingestion of cimetidine because of the competitive inhibition of theophylline metabolism. The magnitude of this drug interaction varies in different individuals;[164,165] subsequent adjustments in the dose of theophylline should be based upon a serum theophylline concentration obtained 72 hours after the initiation of cimetidine and the first reduction in theophylline dose. A much more logical alternative to adjusting theophylline doses would be to treat the patient with H_2-receptor antagonists such as ranitidine[165] (Zantac) or famotidine[166] (Pepcid) that do not inhibit theophylline metabolism.

50. Induction of Metabolism. N.L., a 6-year-old female asthmatic, develops a seizure disorder and is started on phenytoin (Dilantin) therapy. She had been controlled previously on Quibron T/SR 150 mg BID, terbutaline 2 inhalations TID and cromolyn MDI 2 puffs TID. How should N.L.'s theophylline dose be adjusted?

Phenobarbital, phenytoin, carbamazepine, rifampin, cigarette smoking, and intravenous isoproterenol increase theophylline clearance.[162,164] When the drugs are added to the regimen of a patient already stabilized on theophylline, periodic monitoring of theophylline serum concentrations and dose adjustments are advised. If theophylline doses were adjusted during the concurrent use of the interacting medications, potential theophylline toxicity could occur when the drugs that increased theophylline clearance are discontinued and theophylline is continued at the same dosage.

Most drugs increase theophylline clearance by stimulating hepatic cytochrome P450 enzymes that metabolize theophylline. Since enzyme induction requires the synthesis of new enzymes, a marked increase in theophylline clearance generally is delayed for several days. The degree of enzyme induction is dose dependent and most intense after the inducing agent has reached a steady-state concentration in the serum. The maximum induction of theophylline metabolism, therefore, would be expected to occur after one to two weeks of phenytoin therapy.

N.L. should have her cromolyn and terbutaline increased to four times daily until a new dosage for theophylline is established. A serum theophylline concentration should be obtained after the first and second weeks of phenytoin therapy and the doses of theophylline should be adjusted accordingly.

Finally, one might question the wisdom of using theophylline in a patient with an underlying seizure disorder as these patients may experience theophylline-induced seizures at lower theophylline concentrations,[167,168] and if status epilepticus develops, theophylline is associated with a poorer outcome in children with only mildly elevated theophylline concentrations.[169]

Anticholinergics

51. R.K. is a 24-year-old female graduate student with chronic asthma. Her asthma usually is well-controlled with Q 12 hr inhaled corticosteroid therapy and an inhaled β_2-agonist PRN. Recently she has noticed her asthma symptoms tend to worsen when she has anxiety over major examinations. What drug therapy might be helpful to R.K?

One of the myths related to asthma is that it is an emotional illness. It is true, however, that among many typical triggers (e.g., aeroallergens, exercise), emotional upset can be a precipitating factor in some asthmatics.[6] Several groups of investigators have shown that inhaled anticholinergic bronchodilators can block this response.[170] A therapeutic trial of ipratropium given by metered-dose inhaler is warranted in R.K. She probably only needs to use

ipratropium a day or so before major examinations and on the day of the examination (i.e., she is well controlled all other times).

Anticholinergic bronchodilators also are useful in patients with chronic asthma who are intolerant of the side effects of other bronchodilators and in patients who are not responding adequately to standard therapies. These agents also are helpful in some patients who have asthma and then, very unfortunately, smoke for several years and develop chronic bronchitis.

Exercise-Induced Asthma (EIA)

During sustained exercise, asthmatic patients will experience an initial improvement in pulmonary functions followed by a significant decline (see Figure 19.11). This phenomenon occurs in *at least* 80% of asthmatics and may be the only symptom of subclinical asthma.[6,171] Patients can be diagnosed by measuring the FEV_1, or PEFR before and after exercise (6 to 8 minute treadmill or bicycle exercise test). A reduction of FEV_1, by greater than 15% of the baseline value is a positive test. The presence of EIA is thought to reflect the general degree of bronchial hyperreactivity of the asthmatic, with severe asthmatics being more sensitive; however, this is not universally true.[171]

The initiating stimulus for EIA is still uncertain. Hyperventilation of cold, dry air increases the sensitivity to EIA and induces bronchospasm on its own.[171] The stimulus for exercise-induced asthma may be respiratory heat loss or water loss or both[171] since breathing heated, humidified air completely blocks EIA in many patients.[171] Masks are indicated for patients with exercise-induced asthma in the wintertime and severe asthmatics with EIA also should be encouraged to swim or engage in other exercise that does not promote EIA. However, with appropriate premedication, most exercise-induced asthma can be prevented so that virtually all asthmatics should be encouraged to exercise. The mechanism of bronchoconstriction is still incompletely understood but mast cell degranulation may play a central role.[171]

Although several drugs inhibit EIA, inhaled β_2-agonists have the highest efficacy and are the agents of choice for prophylaxis.[6,7,172] Inhaled β_2-agonists are superior to both theophylline and cromolyn.[169] Due to its lack of side effects, rapidity of onset, and convenience, cromolyn is preferred over theophylline in rare patients who may be intolerant (e.g., tremor) of inhaled β_2-agonists and require another preventive treatment. For typical periods of exercise (e.g., ≤3 hours), pretreatment with agents such as albu-

Fig 19.11 Changes in PEFR with Exercise in an Asthmatic and Normal Subject

terol or terbutaline usually provides excellent protection from EIA. Inhaled β_2-agonists, cromolyn, and theophylline have been approved for use before sanctioned competitions by the World Olympic Committee. For prolonged periods of exercise, long-acting inhaled β_2-agonists such as salmeterol provide 12 hours of protection.[173] Finally, it is important to point out that in moderate to severe asthmatics, *long-term* inhaled anti-inflammatory therapy is helpful in reducing the response to most asthma triggers, including exercise. For patients who have EIA only, use of an inhaled β_2-agonist a few minutes before exercise is all the therapy that usually is needed.

Treatment

52. T.W., a 33-year-old female, presents to the clinic with a history of severe coughing and chest tightness following exercise. She recently joined an exercise club to lose weight but is unable to keep up with others her own age and relative condition when jogging outside. She recalls having mild respiratory problems as a young child but has never taken any asthma medications. She has a positive treadmill test for EIA. How should T.W. be treated?

Due to the hyperventilation of relatively cool, dry air, jogging is a potent stimulus for exercise-induced asthma. A number of possible therapeutic interventions exist for T.W. She could be encouraged to swim since the inhalation of humidified warm air is less likely to produce EIA. However, if she wishes to continue jogging, two inhalations of a short acting β_2-agonist (e.g., albuterol, pirbuterol, terbutaline) from a metered-dose aerosol 15 minutes before exercise should provide adequate protection for two to three hours. T.W. also should be counseled to take two additional inhalations if she "breaks through" the initial protection and experiences tightness.

53. W.L., a 17-year-old male, presents to the clinic with a complaint of dyspnea and coughing that occurs during school basketball tryouts that has limited his ability to keep up with his teammates. He states that it is worse when playing outdoors unless the gym is cold, and that it seems to be worse (occurring sooner) than a month ago. On history, it is revealed that W.L. experienced several bouts of bronchitis as a young child but has not had any problems for the past 6 years. W.L.'s symptoms are consistent with EIA. How should his EIA be treated?

W.L. presents a special problem in that he is a teenager. Both for adolescents and children, peer pressure usually is extremely significant. Optimal prophylaxis is important to allow W.L. to compete at his best level. Embarrassment over not keeping up with teammates can be very hurtful now, and it has implications for setting habits of exercise into adulthood. Many asthmatic adults do not exercise because they feel they cannot do so based upon childhood experiences. Lack of exercise can have a negative impact on physiological and psychological well being. W.L. should receive preventive treatment with an inhaled β_2-agonist.

Nocturnal Asthma

Many asthmatics complain of symptoms that awaken them in the night or occur upon awakening in the morning. Morning cough with or without bronchospasm may be a clue to nocturnal asthma. Although nocturnal asthma may be appropriately viewed as simply another manifestation of airway inflammation, it is so common and troublesome among asthmatics that it deserves special note. Circadian rhythm in PEFR is exaggerated in asthmatics. The difference in PEFR in nonasthmatics averages about 8% between 4 p.m. (maximal airflow) and 4 a.m. (minimal airflow), but in patients with asthma, the average variation can be as high as about 50%.[174] Several mechanisms account for this diurnal variation in PEFR.

The following factors contribute to increased airway inflammation that usually is worst between 2 a.m. and 6 a.m.:

- Increased activity of the parasympathetic nervous system
- Lower circulating levels of epinephrine
- Lower levels of serum cortisol (lowest at about 12 a.m.)
- Increased release of inflammatory mediators[174,175]

In addition, for patients whose asthma is triggered by gastroesophageal reflux, this problem is worse at night, and is another factor to consider.

The initial approach to managing nocturnal asthma is the same as that for overall long-term therapy including adequate inhaled anti-inflammatory agents for patients who have symptoms more often than twice a week.[176] Adults should be treated with optimal doses of inhaled corticosteroids (or possibly inhaled nedocromil), and children should be initiated with oral inhalation of cromolyn. Inhaled corticosteroids frequently are effective in eliminating nocturnal asthma, including symptoms and the drop in PEFR.[177–179] After careful titration of doses and repeated observation of inhalation technique, a long-acting inhaled β_2-agonist such as salmeterol or formoterol is indicated if nocturnal symptoms persist. Also, the basic asthma treatment principle of good control of concomitant rhinitis should be considered in the nocturnal asthma patient.

Bedtime doses of traditional inhaled β_2-agonists are not long-acting enough to prevent early morning symptoms. Salmeterol has been shown to have at least a 12-hour duration of action, and it is very effective for nocturnal asthma.[180] For patients who are virtually symptom-free during the day and are receiving anti-inflammatory agents, it is logical to consider salmeterol in the evening only. On the other hand, clinical trials to date have only involved salmeterol every 12 hours, and the FDA approved "usual dose" is 2 puffs every 12 hours. For patients who frequently require a short acting inhaled β_2-agonist for "as needed" treatment, no tolerance to bronchodilator effects from every 12-hour dosing of salmeterol has been found in studies of up to one year of continuous use.[181] Therefore, dosing of salmeterol every 12 hours is appropriate in the setting of optimized inhaled anti-inflammatory therapy and frequent "rescue" short-acting inhaled beta agonists. Formoterol is another long acting β_2-agonist that has been shown to be effective in managing nocturnal asthma.[182]

Before the advent of long-acting inhaled β_2-agonists, long-acting oral agents such as sustained-release theophylline or sustained-release beta agonists often were indicated.[155,159,183] Although these agents are indeed helpful, they have more adverse effects than inhaled agents, especially causing interference with sleep and are not as efficacious.[184] Before prescribing one of these oral agents, adequate inhaled anti-inflammatory therapy should be assured and then long-acting inhaled β_2-agonists should be used. If a clinician insists on using an oral agent, then *evening only* conservative dosing of the oral agent is preferred over twice-daily dosing.[156,183] That is, serum concentrations of these drugs will be low during the day and peak at night when most needed. Relatively low doses in the evening usually provide excellent efficacy when added to basic anti-inflammatory therapy.

Treatment

54. S.T., a 41-year-old male, presents to the clinic with a history of coughing and shortness of breath (SOB) that awaken him at least 2 nights a week. The same symptoms are present virtually every morning upon awakening. He has a past medical history of asthma and currently is managed with beclomethasone 2 puffs QID via a spacer, and albuterol 2 puffs Q 6 hr PRN and before exercise. S.T.'s morning PEFR is consistently in the "yellow zone," usually at about 400 L/min (per-

sonal best: 600 L/min), whereas the evening PEFR is consistently 550–600 L/min. The clinic physician says that she is considering adding an SR theophylline product to control the nocturnal asthma. What treatment should be recommended?

Because asthma is primarily an inflammatory disease and nocturnal symptoms are due largely to airway inflammation, the first drug therapy concern in S.T. is to optimize his beclomethasone therapy. A reasonable approach would be to slightly increase the dose to six puffs every 12 hours. If 12 puffs per 24 hours is insufficient, a further gradual increase is appropriate. A careful check of S.T.'s inhalation technique with the MDI-spacer is essential, as is questioning regarding compliance (i.e., strict adherence to *regular* daily doses of inhaled corticosteroid).

As part of optimal management of nocturnal asthma, S.T. also should be asked about avoiding or minimizing exposure to his asthma triggers (e.g., if he is allergic to cats, is there a cat in the bedroom?). Once the dose of inhaled corticosteroid is optimized for S.T., the morning as well as the evening PEFR will usually stay in the ''green zone.''

While sustained-release theophylline is unquestionably helpful for nocturnal asthma, if optimal inhaled anti-inflammatory therapy is inadequate, adding a long-acting inhaled β_2-agonist such as salmeterol or formoterol is preferred because it is safer overall and has better efficacy. If theophylline is to be used because the physician insists upon it, administer a low dose in the evening only.

Several double-blind studies also have demonstrated that adding salmeterol to inhaled corticosteroids prevents the need to further increase the doses of these inhaled anti-inflammatory agents.[185,186] Adding salmeterol to beclomethasone 200 μg twice daily was as efficacious as increasing the dose of the inhaled corticosteroid to 500 μg twice daily.[185] In a similar study, over 700 patients inadequately controlled on beclomethasone 1000 μg/day were randomized to either salmeterol or to a doubling of beclomethasone to 2000 μg/day. The salmeterol group did as well as the higher dose inhaled corticosteroid group.[186]

Patient Education

If optimal long-term drug therapy of asthma is prescribed, treatment may still fail or be suboptimal if there is not adequate patient education. Asthmatics require special efforts when it comes to education because of the use of inhalation devices and peak flow meters. In addition, it often is a major challenge to have asthmatics understand the critical importance of long-term *prevention*. Of course, an important first step in educating asthmatics is to be caring and a good listener. Rather than sharing your knowledge initially, it is important to help establish a ''partnership'' with the patient by first asking the following question: ''What is bothering you the most about your asthma?'' Really listening to the patient and then addressing patient concerns is extremely important to successful education and long-term management.

Clinicians can be of invaluable assistance to the patient by repeated education on the necessity to use inhaled anti-inflammatory therapies on a regular schedule. Many patients underuse long-term preventive therapy because no health professional took the time to adequately instruct them that asthma is *preventable*. While underusing the most important medicines for long-term control, many patients overuse ''quick relievers'' (i.e., short-acting inhaled beta agonists). Health care providers must be able to detect these problems and intervene to enhance patient care.

Because a large percentage of patients have difficulty using metered-dose inhalers, teaching patients the correct use of MDIs and MDIs plus spacers is absolutely essential.[187] In one study, 89% of patients could not perform all steps correctly.[188] Competent teaching requires *observation of the patient* using the devices initially

and again on repeat visits to the clinic, hospital, or community pharmacy. Telling the patient about correct use clearly is not adequate. Health professionals must demonstrate use of the devices (live or with videotapes) for patients who cannot use the devices perfectly. Although there is more than one correct way to use an MDI, Table 19.10 summarizes two commonly accepted approaches.[6,187] Many asthma experts prefer to use spacers to help assure optimal efficacy. Spacers should be used in virtually all patients receiving inhaled corticosteroids, even those with perfect MDI technique because spacers enhance efficacy and greatly reduce the risk of oropharyngeal candidiasis.[189,190] On the other hand, spacers do not add efficacy to correct use of a beta agonist MDI.[191] Not all spacers are the same, and devices that have a flow indicator whistle when inhalation is too fast generally are preferred (e.g., AeroChamber, InspirEase). These two devices have received exhaustive clinical testing in the emergency room, hospital, and at home.[44,46,47,49,192] Some asthma experts prefer large volume over small volume spacers, especially with inhaled corticosteroids.[189] The clinical significance of differences in spacer volume is yet to be clearly demonstrated.

Studies have shown that health professionals generally are not competent in using MDIs either.[193–195] Obviously, the clinician should practice with a placebo inhaler and gain competence before teaching a patient. Among clinicians who educate asthmatics, pharmacists have been shown to be very helpful in teaching correct use of MDIs.[196,197] Unfortunately, one study showed that community pharmacists commonly are not providing such teaching.[198] In addition to teaching correct use of MDIs and spacers, clinicians can help patients via education regarding correct use of breath-activated dry powder inhalers (e.g., Rotahaler), breath-activated MDIs (e.g., Autohaler), and nebulizing machines. When using the Rotahaler, patients must clearly understand the need for a quick, rapid inhalation (not slow as with an MDI).

For patients who have several inhalers, questions regarding sequencing of the MDIs frequently are asked. First, there is no well documented evidence that outcomes are better using, for instance, a bronchodilator first or an anti-inflammatory first. A common

Table 19.10	Steps to Correct Use of Metered Dose Inhalers[a]

1. Shake the inhaler well and remove the dust cap

2. Exhale *slowly* through pursed lips[b]

3. If using the "closed mouth" technique, hold the inhaler upright and place the mouthpiece between your lips. Be careful to not block the opening with your tongue or teeth.

   If using the "open mouth" technique, open your mouth wide and hold the inhaler upright two fingerbreadths from your mouth, making sure the inhaler is properly aimed

4. Press down on the inhaler *once* as you start a *slow*, deep inhalation

5. Continue to inhale slowly and deeply through your mouth. Try to inhale over at least 5 sec

6. Hold your breath for 10 sec (use your fingers to count to 10 slowly). If 10 sec makes you feel uncomfortable, try to hold your breath for at least 4 sec

7. Exhale *slowly*[c]

8. Wait at least 1 min before inhaling the next puff of medicine

[a] If using a spacer, see manufacturer's instructions. Same basic principles of slow, deep inhalation with adequate breath hold apply. With spacers, put mouthpiece on top of your tongue to assure tongue does not block aerosol.

[b] As long as exhalation is slow, can exhale over several sec. Some experts insist on exhaling only a tidal volume, but the key is to exhale *slowly*.

[c] If patient has concomitant rhinitis, exhaling through the *nose* may be of benefit when using corticosteroids, cromolyn, or ipratropium (i.e., some medication may deposit in nose).

sense approach is that using a rapid onset bronchodilator like a beta agonist first and then an anti-inflammatory second has some appeal (i.e., quick relief and theoretically enhanced penetration of the anti-inflammatory). Unfortunately, as previously discussed, short-acting beta agonists generally are preferred for ''as needed'' use (and before exercise), and are not usually preferred as scheduled agents. Thus, if a patient is not symptomatic at the time the anti-inflammatory is scheduled, many clinicians would prefer the patient inhale only the anti-inflammatory agent. When two inhaled bronchodilators are used (e.g., a beta agonist and ipratropium), the *technically* correct answer related to sequencing is to inhale the ipratropium first and the beta agonist one hour later, which will give a greater improvement in FEV_1.[199] The obvious problem with this approach in many patients is that waiting one hour is inconvenient, and many patients may forget the dose of the second agent. Therefore, using the agents in sequence of one minute between puffs is most practical for many patients, probably using the beta agonist before ipratropium because of the quicker onset of the beta agonist. This question is much more commonly an issue in patients with chronic obstructive airways disease (COAD).

Objective monitoring of lung function at home by use of peak flow meters can be very helpful to patients and health care professionals. Instructing patients on the correct use of the devices, including use of the ''green, yellow, and red zones'' is quite important.[6]

Studies have documented the value of asthma patient education combined with aggressive ''state-of-the-art'' treatment in improving clinical outcomes.[200,201] Very recent clinical investigations have documented that pharmacists working in partnership with patients and physicians can improve outcomes. Dramatic reductions in emergency room visits and hospitalizations have resulted from pharmacist interventions, stressing application of NIH guidelines.[202-205]

55. A.B., a 26-year-old female, presents to the community pharmacy for a refill of her albuterol MDI. She has a prescription for a beclomethasone MDI, but it is past due for a refill. A.B. is a life-long asthmatic, and she complains of symptoms most days, but she has not required visits to the ER or hospitalizations. The pharmacist determines that A.B. is bothered most about daily SOB and worries that her condition may get worse. What should the pharmacist do in this situation?

A.B. needs education regarding the benefits of long-term inhaled anti-inflammatory therapy. The pharmacist should explain with enthusiasm that A.B.'s beclomethasone is an extremely effective medicine and that it is the cornerstone of her asthma management. The slow onset and safety of inhaled corticosteroids must be stressed, as well as the requirement of regular use every day. Clearly teaching A.B. the differences in ''preventers'' versus ''quick relievers'' is essential. If a spacer is not already being used, the pharmacist should assure that she receives one, and then should demonstrate its use and observe the patient's inhalation technique. A.B. needs to hear that the spacer virtually eliminates the chance for a yeast infection in her mouth, and that it enhances the efficacy of inhaled corticosteroids. Thus, it is quite cost effective. Likewise, a peak flow meter should be given to A.B. and correct use assured along with establishment of green, yellow, and red zones. A.B. needs to hear from the pharmacist that ''asthma is preventable'' and in the words of a title of an NIH booklet for patients: ''Your asthma can be controlled: Expect nothing less.'' As part of comprehensive education, such a positive message from the pharmacist can have a major impact on A.B. who has not been managing her asthma correctly.

56. A.B. tells the pharmacist that her physician insisted on her placing the MDI in front of her open mouth and spraying rather than putting the MDI in her mouth. She says she is confused because the package insert shows placement of the inhaler in the mouth.

A.B. is correct that this is a confusing issue to many patients and health professionals. Explain to her that while two studies show that the ''open mouth'' technique is better, several other studies show that the ''closed mouth'' technique is as good or better than putting the MDI in front of the open mouth.[187,206] In addition, the correctly performed ''closed mouth'' technique is as efficacious with a beta agonist as using a spacer[191] or nebulizer.[207] Thus, the ''closed mouth'' technique is perfectly acceptable as is ''open mouth'' technique. One caution with the ''open mouth'' technique is that misaiming the MDI may result in aerosol being sprayed onto the face or into the eyes. A.B. again should be encouraged always to use her spacer for her beclomethasone and preferably use it with her albuterol.

Drug-Induced Asthma

Although drug-induced asthma may present as relatively mild symptoms in some patients, fatal asthma caused by medicinal agents has been reported numerous times. Thus, it is imperative that clinicians strive to prevent this problem through education of patients and other health professionals. The most extensive literature on drug-induced asthma involves nonsteroidal anti-inflammatory drugs (NSAIDs) and beta blockers. Other drugs and drug preservatives also can induce symptoms of asthma, but because the topic is beyond the scope of this chapter, the reader is referred to other sources[208,209] and Chapter 22: Drug-Induced Pulmonary Disorders for further discussion.

The percentage of asthmatics reported to be aspirin-sensitive ranges from 5% to 20%.[6] Clinical manifestations of aspirin sensitivity include rhinorrhea, mild wheezing, or severe, life-threatening shortness of breath. Interestingly, once the reaction has occurred, there is a refractory period of two to five days.[210] If an asthmatic is aspirin-sensitive, then it is very likely that the patient also will react to most other NSAIDs. Aspirin and other NSAIDs share common mechanisms involving the arachidonic acid pathways, including inhibition of cyclo-oxygenase. A report has demonstrated the importance of the bronchoconstrictor mediators, leukotrienes, as a mechanism in that an inhibitor of 5-lipoxygenase, zileuton, was effective in blocking this response.[212] While most asthmatics do not react to aspirin and other NSAIDs, many clinicians prefer to recommend that acetaminophen be used in asthmatics for headaches and relatively minor pain. For patients who need to take aspirin (e.g., post myocardial infarction) or an NSAID (e.g., arthritis), it is possible to desensitize the patient, and daily use then prevents further reaction.

Beta blockers should be avoided strictly in asthmatics. Since even β_1-adrenergic blockers are not absolutely specific, they, as well as nonspecific blockers, should be avoided. Furthermore, ophthalmic timolol has been reported several times to cause fatal asthma, and should be absolutely avoided in patients with a history of asthma.[211] Other beta blocker eye drops (e.g., betaxolol) have been reported to have less propensity to induce asthma, but all have some risk.[208,213] Even if a patient with asthma is given a beta blocker and reports no symptoms, response to administration of a beta-agonist bronchodilator will be blocked. A more subtle risk with beta blockers involves the adult with allergic rhinitis and a family history of asthma. If this individual is given a beta blocker for hypertension, symptoms of asthma could be induced, especially if another trigger is introduced such as running in cold, dry air.

57. M.B., 32-year-old female with asthma, asks her community pharmacist for a refill of her triamcinolone oral inhaler. As the pharmacist is reviewing the purpose of the tri-

amcinolone and checking the her inhalation technique, he sees that **M.B. has placed an OTC ibuprofen product on the counter for purchase. What should the pharmacist do?**

First, the pharmacist already should have checked the computer patient profile to see if she is an aspirin-sensitive asthmatic. If there is no indication that she is, a double-check by asking her is important. Even if there is no history of problems, acetaminophen generally should be recommended in asthmatics, simply to reduce risks. The pharmacist should counsel the patient regarding the fact that aspirin-sensitive asthmatics often will react to other NSAIDs such as ibuprofen by developing an asthma attack with the first dose. This case also points out the need for health professionals to pay attention to patient use of nonprescription medications. If the pharmacist in this situation had been ''too busy'' to notice the OTC purchase, the consequences could have been disastrous to the patient; there could even be the potential for legal action being taken against the pharmacist.

References

1 **West JB.** Respiratory Physiology—The Essentials. 3rd ed. Baltimore, MD: Williams and Wilkins; 1985.

2 **Guenter CA, Welch MH.** Pulmonary Medicine. 2nd ed. Philadelphia, PA: JB Lippincott; 1982.

3 **Fishman AP.** Pulmonary Diseases and Disorders. Vol. 1 and 2. New York, NY: McGraw-Hill; 1980.

4 **Menendez R, Kelly HW.** Pulmonary-function testing in the evaluation of bronchodilator agents. Clin Pharm. 1983; 2:120.

5 **Gardner RM.** Standardization of spirometry: a summary of recommendations from the American Thoracic Society. Ann Intern Med. 1988;108:217.

6 **National Institutes of Health.** Guidelines for the Diagnosis and Management of Asthma. National Asthma Education Program Expert Panel Report, 1991; DHHS publication No. 91-3042.

7 **National Institutes of Health.** International Consensus Report on diagnosis and treatment of asthma, 1992; DHHS publication no. 92-3091.

8 **Weiss KB et al.** An economic evaluation of asthma in the United States. N Engl J Med. 1992;326:862.

9 **Kaliner MA, Barnes PJ.** The Airways: Neural Control in Health and Disease. New York, NY: Marcel Dekker; 1988.

10 **Cockcroft DW.** Mechanism of perennial allergic asthma. Lancet. 1983;2: 253.

11 **Robinson C, Holgate ST.** New perspectives on the putative role of eicosanoids in airway hyperresponsiveness. J Allergy Clin Immunol. 1985;76:140.

12 **Hogg JC.** The pathology of asthma. Chest. 1985;87:(Suppl.):152.

13 **Benatar SR.** Fatal asthma. N Engl J Med. 1986;314:423.

14 **Chrisman CR et al.** Use of peak flow meters in asthmatics. Am Pharm. 1991; NS31:340.

15 **Weiss EB et al.** Bronchial Asthma: Mechanisms and Therapeutics, 2nd ed. Boston, MA: Little, Brown and Co.; 1985.

16 **Jenne JW, Murphy SA.** Drug Therapy for Asthma: Research and Clinical Practice. New York, NY: Marcel Dekker; 1987.

17 **Hopewell PC, Miller RT.** Pathophysiology and management of severe asthma. Clin Chest Med. 1984;5:623.

18 **McFadden ER.** Clinical physiologic correlates in asthma. J Allergy Clin Immunol. 1986;77:1.

19 **Gershel JC et al.** The usefulness of chest radiographs in first asthma attacks. N Engl J Med. 1983;309:336.

20 **Nowak RM et al.** Arterial blood gases and pulmonary function testing in acute bronchial asthma: predicting patient outcomes. JAMA. 1983;249: 2043.

21 **McFadden ER, Lyons HA.** Arterial blood gas tension in asthma. N Engl J Med. 1968;278:1027.

22 **Fischl MA et al.** An index predicting relapse and need for hospitalization in patients with acute bronchial asthma. N Engl J Med. 1981;305:783.

23 **Centor RM et al.** Inability to predict relapse in acute asthma. N Engl J Med. 1984;310:577.

24 **Rose CC et al.** Performance of an index predicting the response of patients with acute bronchial asthma to intensive emergency department treatment. N Engl J Med. 1984;310:573.

25 **Fanta CH.** Emergency room treatment of asthma: relationships among therapeutic combinations, severity of obstruction and time course of response. Am J Med. 1982;72:416.

26 **Kelly HW, Murphy S.** Beta-adrenergic agonists for acute, severe asthma. Ann Pharmacotherapy. 1992;26:81.

27 **Rossing TH et al.** Emergency therapy of asthma: comparison of the acute effects of parenteral and inhaled sympathomimetics and infused aminophylline. Am Rev Respir Dis. 1980;122: 365.

28 **Fanta CH et al.** Treatment of acute asthma: is combination therapy with sympathomimetics and methylxanthines indicated? Am J Med. 1986;80:5.

29 **Kelly HW, Murphy S.** Should anticholinergics be used in acute severe asthma? DICP, Ann Pharmacother. 1990;24:409–16.

30 **O'Driscoll BR et al.** Nebulized salbutamol with and without ipratropium bromide in acute airflow obstruction. Lancet. 1989;1:1418.

31 **Reisman J et al.** Frequent administration by inhalation of salbutamol and ipratropium bromide in the initial management of severe acute asthma in children. J Allergy Clin Immunol. 1988; 81:16.

32 **Rebuck AS et al.** Nebulized anticholinergic and sympathomimetic treatment of asthma and chronic obstructive airways disease in the emergency room. Am J Med. 1987;82:59.

33 **Higgins RM et al.** Should ipratropium bromide be added to beta agonists in treatment of acute severe asthma? Chest. 1988;94:718.

34 **Kradjan WA et al.** Atropine serum concentrations after multiple inhaled doses of atropine sulfate. Clin Pharmacol Ther. 1985;38:12.

35 **Patrick DM et al.** Severe exacerbations of COPD and asthma: incremental benefit of adding ipratropium to usual therapy. Chest. 1990;98:295.

36 **Bryant DH.** Nebulized ipratropium bromide in the treatment of acute asthma. Chest. 1985;88:24.

37 **Dulfano MJ, Glass P.** The bronchodilator effects of terbutaline: route of administration and patterns of response. Ann Allergy. 1976;37:357.

38 **Ben-Zvi Z et al.** An evaluation of the initial treatment of acute asthma. Pediatrics. 1982;70:348.

39 **Becker AB et al.** Inhaled salbutamol (albuterol) vs. injected epinephrine in the treatment of acute asthma in children. J Pediatr. 1983;102:465.

40 **Fergusson RJ et al.** Nebulized salbutamol in life-threatening asthma: is IPPB necessary? Br J Dis Chest. 1983; 77:255.

41 **Shim CS, Williams MH.** Effect of bronchodilator therapy administered by canister versus jet nebulizer. J Allergy Clin Immunol. 1984;73:387.

42 **Newman SP.** Aerosol deposition considerations in inhalation therapy. Chest. 1985;88(Suppl.):152.

43 **Lewis RA, Fleming JS.** Fractional deposition from a jet nebulizer: how it differs from a metered dose inhaler. Br J Dis Chest. 1985;79:361.

44 **Turner JR et al.** Equivalence of continuous flow nebulizer and metered dose inhaler with reservoir bag for treatment of acute airflow obstruction. Chest. 1988;93:476.

45 **Morgan MDL et al.** Terbutaline aerosol given through pear spacer in acute severe asthma. Br Med J (Clin Res). 1982;285:849.

46 **Salzman GA et al.** Aerosolized metaproterenol in the treatment of asthmatics with severe airflow obstruction. Chest. 1989;95:1017.

47 **Idris AH et al.** Emergency department treatment of severe asthma: metered dose inhaler plus holding chamber is equivalent in effectiveness to nebulizer. Chest. 1993;103:665.

48 **Kerem E et al.** Efficacy of albuterol administered by nebulizer versus spacer device in children with acute asthma. J Ped. 1993;123:313.

49 **Morley TF et al.** Comparison of beta adrenergic agents delivered by nebulizer vs metered dose inhaler with InspirEase in hospitalized asthmatic patients. Chest. 1988;94:1205.

50 **Robertson CF et al.** Response to frequent low doses of nebulized salbutamol in acute asthma. J Pediatr. 1985; 106:672.

51 **Schuh S et al.** High- versus low-dose frequently administered nebulized albuterol in children with severe acute asthma. Pediatrics. 1989;83:513.

52 **Schuh S et al.** Nebulized albuterol in acute childhood asthma: comparison of two doses. Pediatrics. 1990;86:509.

53 **Kelly HW et al.** Safety of frequent high dose nebulized terbutaline in children with acute severe asthma. Ann Allergy. 1990;64:229.

54 **Ahmed T, Marchette B.** Hypoxia enhances nonspecific bronchial reactivity. Am Rev Respir Dis. 1985;132:839.

55 **Ayres SM, Grace WJ.** Inappropriate ventilation and hypoxemia as causes of cardiac arrhythmias. Am J Med. 1969; 46:495.

56 **Rohr AS et al.** Efficacy of parenteral albuterol in the treatment of asthma: comparison of its metabolic side effects with subcutaneous epinephrine. Chest. 1986;89:348.

57 **Brown MJ et al.** Hypokalemia from beta$_2$-receptor stimulation by circulating epinephrine. N Engl J Med. 1983; 309:1414.

58 **Nicklas RA et al.** Concomitant use of beta adrenergic agonists and methylxanthines. J Allergy Clin Immunol. 1984;73:20.

59 **Wilson JD et al.** Has the change to beta-agonists combined with oral theophylline increased cases of fatal asthma? Lancet. 1981;1:1235.

60 **Shenfield GM.** Combination bronchodilator therapy. Drugs. 1982;73:32.

61 **Kemp JP et al.** Concomitant bitolterol mesylate aerosol and theophylline for asthma therapy, with 24-hour electrocardiographic monitoring. J Allergy Clin Immunol. 1983;73:32.

62 **Kelly HW et al.** Lack of significant arrhythmogenicity from chronic theophylline and beta-2 adrenergic combination therapy in asthmatic subjects. Ann Allergy. 1985;54:405.

63 **Rossing TH et al.** A controlled trial of the use of single versus combined drug therapy in the treatment of acute episodes of asthma. Am Rev Respir Dis. 1981;123:190.

64 **Siegel D et al.** Aminophylline increases the toxicity but not the efficacy of an inhaled beta-adrenergic agonist in the treatment of acute exacerbation of asthma. Am Rev Respir Dis. 1985;132: 283.

65 **Josephson GW et al.** Cardiac dysrhythmias during the treatment of acute asthma. A comparison of two regimens by a double-blind protocol. Chest. 1980;78:429.

66 **Grossman J.** The occurrence of arrhythmias in hospitalized asthmatic patients. J Allergy Clin Immunol. 1976; 57:310.

67 **Tandon MD.** Cardiopulmonary effects of fenoterol and salbutamol aerosols. Chest. 1980;77:429.

68 **Lipworth BJ et al.** Tachyphylaxis to systemic but not to airway responses during prolonged therapy with high dose inhaled salbutamol in asthmatics. Am Rev Respir Dis. 1989;140:586.

69 **Rossing TH et al.** Effect of outpatient treatment of asthma with beta agonists on the response to sympathomimetics in an emergency room. Am J Med. 1983;75:781.

70 **Self TH et al.** Inhaled albuterol and oral prednisone therapy in hospitalized adult asthmatics: does aminophylline add any benefit? Chest. 1990;98:1317.

71 **Strauss RE et al.** Aminophylline therapy does not improve outcome and increases adverse effects in children hospitalized with acute asthmatic exacerbations. Pediatrics. 1994;93:205.

72 **DiGuiulio GA et al.** Hospital treatment of asthma: lack of benefit from theophylline given in addition to nebulized albuterol and intravenously administered corticosteroid. J Ped. 1993;122:464.

73 **Carter E et al.** Efficacy of intravenously administered theophylline in children hospitalized with severe asthma. J Ped. 1993;122:470.

74 **Morris HG.** Mechanisms of action and therapeutic role of corticosteroids in asthma. J Allergy Clin Immunol. 1985; 75:1.

75 **Toogood JH.** Corticosteroids. In: Jenne JW, Murphy S, eds. Drug Therapy for Asthma: Research and Clinical Practice. New York: Marcel Dekker; 1987:719.

76 **Ellul-Micallef R, Fenech FF.** Intravenous prednisolone in chronic bronchial asthma. Thorax. 1975;30:312.

77 **Ellul-Micallef R, Fenech FF.** Effect of intravenous prednisolone in asthmatics with diminished adrenergic responsiveness. Lancet. 1975;2:1269.

78 **Ellul-Micallef R.** Pharmacokinetics and pharmacodynamics of glucocorticosteroids. In: Jenne JW, Murphy S, eds. Drug Therapy for Asthma: Research and Clinical Practice. New York: Marcel Dekker; 1987:463.

79 **Shapiro G et al.** Double-blind evaluation of methylprednisolone versus placebo for acute asthma episodes. Pediatrics. 1983;71:510.

80 **Fanta CH et al.** Glucocorticoids in acute asthma. Am J Med. 1983;74:845.

81 **Littenberg B, Gluck E.** A controlled trial of methylprednisolone in the emergency treatment of acute asthma. N Engl J Med. 1986;314:150.

82 **Pierson WE et al.** A double-blind trial of corticosteroid therapy in status asthmaticus. Pediatrics. 1974;54:282.

83 **Arnaud A et al.** Treatment of acute asthma: effect of intravenous corticosteroids and β_2-adrenergic agents. Lung. 1979;156:43.

84 **Loren ML et al.** Corticosteroids in the treatment of acute exacerbations of asthma. Ann Allergy. 1980;45:67.

85 **Fiel SB et al.** Efficacy of short-term corticosteroid therapy in outpatient treatment of acute bronchial asthma. Am J Med. 1983;75:259.

86 **Harris JB et al.** Early intervention with short courses of prednisone to prevent progression of asthma in ambulatory patients incompletely responsive

to bronchodilators. J Pediatr. 1987;110: 627.

87 **Chapman KR et al.** Effect of a short course of prednisone in the prevention of early relapse after the emergency room treatment of acute asthma. N Engl J Med. 1991;324:788.

88 **Brunette MG et al.** Childhood asthma: prevention of attacks with short-term corticosteroid treatment of upper respiratory tract infection. Pediatrics. 1988;81:624.

89 **Harfi H et al.** Treatment of status asthmaticus in children with high doses and conventional doses of methylprednisolone. Pediatrics. 1978;61:829.

90 **Tanaka R et al.** Intravenous methylprednisolone in adults in status asthmaticus. Chest. 1982;4:438.

91 **Raimondi A et al.** Comparison between high and moderate doses of hydrocortisone in the treatment of status asthmaticus. Chest. 1986;89:832–35.

92 **Bernstein IL.** Asthma in adults: diagnosis and treatment. In: Middleton E Jr et al., eds. Allergy Principles and Practice. St. Louis: C.V. Mosby; 1983:863.

93 **Siegel S et al.** Asthma in infancy and childhood. In: Middleton E Jr et al., eds. Allergy Principles and Practice. St. Louis: C.V. Mosby; 1983:863.

94 **Leffert F.** The management of acute severe asthma. J Pediatr. 1980;95:1.

95 **Harrison BDW et al.** Need for intravenous hydrocortisone in addition to oral prednisolone in patients admitted to hospital with severe asthma without ventilatory failure. Lancet. 1986;1:181.

96 **Sybert A, Weiss EB.** Status asthmaticus. In: Weiss EB et al., eds. Bronchial Asthma: Mechanisms and Therapeutics. 2nd ed. Boston: Little, Brown and Co.; 1985:808.

97 **Parry WH et al.** Management of life-threatening asthma with intravenous isoproterenol infusions. Am J Dis Child. 1976;130:39.

98 **Edmunds AT, Godfrey S.** Cardiovascular response during severe acute asthma and its treatment in children. Thorax. 1981;36:534.

99 **Viires N et al.** Effects of aminophylline on diaphragmatic fatigue during acute respiratory failure. Am Rev Respir Dis. 1984;129:396.

100 **Aubier M et al.** Aminophylline improves diaphragmatic contractility. N Engl J Med. 1981;305:249.

101 **Murciano D et al.** Effects of theophylline on diaphragmatic strength and fatigue in patients with chronic obstructive pulmonary disease. N Engl J Med. 1984;311:349.

102 **Mitenko P, Ogilvie R.** Rational intravenous doses of theophylline. N Engl J Med. 1973;289:600.

103 **Self TH et al.** Reassessing therapeutic range for theophylline for laboratory report forms: the importance of 5–15 μg/mL. Pharmacotherapy. 1993;13: 590.

104 **Kelly HW.** Theophylline toxicity. In: Jenne JW, Murphy S, eds. Asthma Drugs: Theory and Practice. New York: Marcel Dekker; 1987:925.

105 **Weinberger M et al.** Intravenous aminophylline dose. Use of serum theophylline measurements for guidance. JAMA. 1976;235:2110.

106 **Carrier JA et al.** Comparison of intravenous and oral routes of theophylline

loading in acute asthma. Ann Emerg Med. 1985;14:1145.

107 **Ogilvie RI.** Clinical pharmacokinetics of theophylline. Clin Pharmacokinet. 1978;3:267.

108 **Aranda J et al.** Pharmacokinetic aspects of theophylline in premature newborns. N Engl J Med. 1976;295: 413.

109 **Piafsky K et al.** Theophylline disposition in patients with hepatic cirrhosis. N Engl J Med. 1977;296:1495.

110 **Antal E et al.** Theophylline pharmacokinetics in advanced age. Br J Clin Pharmacol. 1981;12:637.

111 **Lesko L et al.** Theophylline serum protein binding in obstructive airway disease. Clin Pharmacol Ther. 1981;29: 776.

112 **Laboritz E, Spector S.** Placental theophylline transfer in pregnant asthmatics. JAMA. 1982;247:786.

113 **Gal P et al.** Theophylline disposition in obesity. Clin Pharmacol Ther. 1987; 23:438.

114 **Zell M et al.** Volume of distribution of theophylline in acute exacerbation of reversible airway disease: effect of body weight. Chest. 1985;87:212.

115 **Loughman P et al.** Pharmacokinetic analysis of the disposition of intravenous theophylline in young children. J Pediatr. 1976;88:874.

116 **Jusko W et al.** Enhanced biotransformation of theophylline in marijuana and tobacco smokers. Clin Pharmacol Ther. 1978;24:405.

117 **Powell J et al.** The influence of cigarette smoking and sex on theophylline disposition. Am Rev Respir Dis. 1977; 116:17.

118 **Lee BL et al.** Cigarette abstinence, nicotine gum, and theophylline disposition. Ann Intern Med. 1987;106:553.

119 **Piafsky KM et al.** Theophylline kinetics in acute pulmonary edema. Clin Pharmacol Ther. 1977;21:310.

120 **Chang K et al.** Altered theophylline pharmacokinetics during acute respiratory viral illness. Lancet. 1978;1: 1132.

121 **Vicuna N et al.** Impaired theophylline clearance in patients with cor pulmonale. Br J Clin Pharmacol. 1979;7:33.

122 **Staib A et al.** Pharmacokinetics and metabolism of theophylline in patients with liver disease. Int J Clin Pharmacol Ther Toxicol. 1980;18:500.

123 **Federal Drug Administration.** IV, dosage guidelines for theophylline products. FDA Drug Bull. 1980:4.

124 **Murphy J, Ward E.** Criticism of FDA recommendations for theophylline dosages. N Engl J Med. 1980;303:760.

125 **Chiou W et al.** Method for the rapid estimation of the total body clearance and adjustment of dosage regimens in patients during constant rate intravenous infusion. J Pharmacokinet Biopharm. 1978;6:135.

126 **Rodvold K et al.** Accuracy of 11 methods for predicting theophylline dose. Clin Pharm. 1986;5:403.

127 **Johnson M, Burkle W.** Evaluation of the Chiou method for determining theophylline dosages. Clin Pharm. 1983; 3:174.

128 **Dan-Shya D et al.** Nonlinear theophylline elimination. Clin Pharmacol Ther. 1983;31:358.

129 **Weinberger M, Ginchansky E.** Dose-dependent kinetics of theophylline disposition in asthmatic children. J Pediatr. 1977;91:820.

130 **Iafrate RP et al.** Computer-simulated conversion from intravenous to sustained-release oral theophylline. Drug Intell Clin Pharm. 1982;16:19.

131 **Gandevia B.** Pressurized sympathomimetic aerosols and their lack of relationship to asthma mortality and Australia. Med J Aust. 1973;1:273.

132 **Spitzer WO et al.** The use of beta agonists and the risk of death and near death from asthma. N Engl J Med. 1992;326:501.

133 **Ernst P et al.** Is the association between inhaled beta agonist use and life-threatening asthma because of confounding by severity? Am Rev Respir Dis. 1993;148:75.

134 **Sears MR et al.** Regular inhaled beta agonist treatment in bronchial asthma. Lancet. 1990;3365:1391.

135 **Taylor DR et al.** Regular inhaled beta agonist in asthma: effects on exacerbations and lung function. Thorax. 1993;48:134.

136 **Pedersen S.** Aerosol treatment of bronchoconstriction in children with or without a tube spacer. N Engl J Med. 1983;308:1328.

137 **Prior JG et al.** High-dose inhaled terbutaline in the management of chronic severe asthma: comparison of wet nebulization and tube-spacer delivery. Thorax. 1982;37:300.

138 **Murphy S, Kelly HW.** Cromolyn sodium: a review of mechanisms and clinical use in asthma. Drug Intell Clin Pharm. 1987;21:22.

139 **Hambleton G et al.** Comparison of cromoglycate (cromolyn) and theophylline in controlling symptoms of chronic asthma. A collaborative study. Lancet. 1977;1:381.

140 **Edmunds AT et al.** Controlled trial of cromoglycate and slow-release aminophylline in perennial childhood asthma. Br Med J. 1980;281:842.

141 **Glass J et al.** Nebulized cromoglycate, theophylline, and placebo in preschool asthmatic children. Arch Dis Child. 1981;56:648.

142 **Newth CJL et al.** Comparison of nebulized sodium cromoglycate and oral theophylline in controlling symptoms of chronic asthma in pre-school children: a double-blind study. Aust N Z J Med. 1982;12:232.

143 **Furukawa CT et al.** A double-blind study comparing the effectiveness of cromolyn sodium and sustained-release theophylline in childhood asthma. Pediatrics. 1984;74:453.

144 **Springer C et al.** Clinical physiologic, and psychologic comparison of treatment by cromolyn or theophylline in childhood asthma. J Allergy Clin Immunol. 1985;5:156.

145 **Furukawa CT et al.** Cognitive and behavioral findings in children taking theophylline versus cromolyn. J Allergy Clin Immunol. 1986;77(2):186a.

146 **Larsen GL.** Late-phase reactions: observations on pathogenesis and prevention. J Allergy Clin Immunol. 1985;76: 665.

147 **Toogood JH et al.** Aerosol corticosteroids. In: Weiss EB et al., eds. Bronchial Asthma: Mechanisms and Ther-

apeutics. 2nd ed. Boston: Little, Brown and Co.; 1985:808.

148 **Brogden RN et al.** Beclomethasone dipropionate: a reappraisal of its pharmacodynamic properties and therapeutic efficacy after a decade of use in asthma and rhinitis. Drugs. 1984;28:99.

149 **Toogood JH et al.** Bioequivalent doses of inhaled vs. oral steroids for severe asthma. Chest. 1983;84:349.

150 **Nyholm E et al.** Therapeutic advantages of twice-daily over four-times-daily inhalation budesonide in the treatment of chronic asthma. Eur J Respir Dis. 1984;65:339.

151 **Meltzer EO et al.** Effect of dosing schedule on efficacy of beclomethasone dipropionate aerosol in chronic asthma. Am Rev Respir Dis. 1985;131:732.

152 **Barnes NC et al.** A comparison of fluticasone propionate, 1 mg daily, with beclomethasone dipropionate, 2 mg daily, in the treatment of severe asthma. Eur Respir J. 1993;6:877.

153 **Hendeles L et al.** A clinical and pharmacokinetic basis for the selection and use of slow-release theophylline products. Clin Pharmacokinet. 1984;9:95.

154 **Rachelefsky GS et al.** Ultra-slow release theophylline in the pediatric patient. Ped Asthma Allergy Immunol. 1988;2:109.

155 **Arkinstall WW et al.** Once-daily sustained-release theophylline reduces diurnal variation in spirometry and symptomatology in adult asthmatics. Am Rev Respir Dis. 1987;135:316.

156 **Nassif E et al.** Theophylline disposition in infancy. J Pediatr. 1981;98:158.

157 **Food and Drug Administration.** Use of theophylline in infants. FDA Drug Bull. 1985;15:17.

158 **Mason W et al.** Bioavailability of theophylline following a rectally-administered concentrated aminophylline solution. J Allergy Clin Immunol. 1980;66:119.

159 **Pierson WE et al.** Long-term, double-blind comparison of controlled-release albuterol versus sustained-release theophylline in adolescents and adults with asthma. J Allergy Clin Immunol. 1990;85:618.

160 **Radomski L et al.** Model for theophylline overdose treatment with oral-activated charcoal. Clin Pharmacol Ther. 1984;35:402.

161 **Olson KR et al.** Theophylline overdose: acute single ingestion versus chronic repeated overmedication. Am J Emerg Med. 1985;3:386.

162 **Upton RA.** Pharmacokinetic drug interactions between theophylline and other medication. Clin Pharmacokinet. 1991;20:66 and 35(Parts 1 & 2).

163 **Wijnands WJA et al.** The influence of quinolone derivatives on theophylline clearance. Br J Clin Pharmacol. 1986;22:677.

164 **Slaughter RL.** Theophylline commentary. In: Evans WE et al., eds. Applied Pharmacokinetics: Principles of Therapeutic Drug Monitoring. 3rd ed. Vancouver: Applied Therapeutics, Inc. 1992.

165 **Kelly HW et al.** Ranitidine at very large doses does not inhibit theophylline elimination. Clin Pharmacol Ther. 1986;39:577.

166 **Lin JH et al.** Famotidine does not interfere with the disposition of theophylline in man. Comparison to cimetidine. Clin Pharmacol Ther. 1985;39(2):187a.

167 **Covelli HD et al.** Predisposing factors to apparent theophylline-induced seizures. Ann Allergy. 1985;54:411.

168 **Bahls FH et al.** Theophylline-associated seizures with ''therapeutic'' or low toxic serum concentrations: risk factors for serious outcome in adults. Neurology. 1991;41:1309.

169 **Dunn DW, Parekh HU.** Theophylline and status epilepticus in children. Neuropediatrics. 1991;22:24.

170 **Neild JE, Cameron IR.** Bronchoconstriction in response to suggestion: its prevention by an inhaled anticholinergic agent. Br Med J. 1985;290:674.

171 **Anderson SD.** Exercise-induced asthma: the state of the art. Chest. 1985;87(Suppl.):191.

172 **Godfrey S, Konig P.** Suppression of exercise-induced asthma by salbutamol, theophylline, atropine, cromolyn, and placebo in a group of asthmatic children. Pediatrics. 1975;56:930.

173 **Newnham D et al.** Duration of action of inhaled salmeterol against exercise-induced asthma. Am Rev Respir Dis. 1991;143:A29. Abstract.

174 **Zoratti E, Busse WW.** Nighttime asthma symptoms: no idle threat. J Respir Dis. 1990;11:137.

175 **Barnes PJ.** Inflammatory mechanisms and nocturnal asthma. Am J Med. 1988;85(Suppl. 1B):64.

176 **Self TH et al.** Reassessment of the role of theophylline in the current therapy for nocturnal asthma. J Am Board Family Pract. 1992;5:281.

177 **Horn CR et al.** Inhaled therapy reduces morning dips in asthma. Lancet. 1984;1:1143.

178 **Lorentzson S et al.** Use of inhaled corticosteroids in patients with mild asthma. Thorax. 1990;45:733.

179 **Haahtela T et al.** Comparison of a beta$_2$ agonist, terbutaline, with an inhaled corticosteroid, budesonide, in newly detected asthma. N Engl J Med. 1991;325:388.

180 **Fitzpatrick MF et al.** Salmeterol in nocturnal asthma: a double-blind, placebo-controlled trial of a long-acting inhaled beta$_2$ agonist. Br Med J. 1990;301:1365.

181 **Britton MG et al.** A twelve-month comparison of salmeterol with salbutamol in asthmatic patients. Eur Respir J. 1992;5:1062.

182 **Maesen FP et al.** Formoterol in the treatment of nocturnal asthma. Chest. 1990;98:866.

183 **Martin RJ et al.** Circadian variations in theophylline concentrations and the treatment of nocturnal asthma. Am Rev Respir Dis. 1989;139:475.

184 **Fjellbirkeland I, Gulsvik A.** Salmeterol and theophylline sustained release: a crossover comparison in asthmatic patients. Clin Exp Allergy. 1990;20(Suppl. 1):94. Abstract.

185 **Greening AP et al.** Added salmeterol versus higher-dose corticosteroid in asthma patients with symptoms on existing inhaled corticosteroid. Lancet. 1994;344:219.

186 **Woolcock A et al.** Comparison of the effect of addition of salmeterol with doubling the inhaled steroid dose in asthmatic patients. Am J Respir Crit Care Med. 1994;149:A280. Abstract.

187 **Newman SP et al.** How should a pressurized beta-adrenergic bronchodilator be inhaled? Eur J Respir Dis. 1981;62:3.

188 **Epstein SW et al.** Survey of the clinical use of pressurized aerosol inhalers. Can Med Assoc J. 1979;120:813.

189 **Toogood JH et al.** Use of spacers to facilitate inhaled corticosteroid treatment of asthma. Am Rev Respir Dis. 1984;129:723.

190 **Salzman GA, Pyszczynski DR.** Oropharyngeal candidiasis in patients treated with beclomethasone dipropionate delivered by metered dose inhaler alone and with AeroChamber. J Allergy Clin Immunol. 1988;81:424.

191 **Rachelefsky GS et al.** Use of a tube spacer to improve the efficacy of a metered dose inhaler in asthmatic children. Am J Dis Child. 1986;140:1191.

192 **Self TH et al.** Correct use of metered dose inhalers and spacer devices. Postgrad Med. 1992;92:95.

193 **Burton AJ.** Asthma inhalation devices: what do we know? Br Med J. 1984;288:1650.

194 **Self TH et al.** Nurses' performance of inhalation technique with metered-dose inhaler plus spacer device. Ann Pharmacother. 1993;27:185.

195 **Interiano B, Guntupalli KK.** Metered-dose inhalers: do health care providers know what to teach? Arch Intern Med. 1993;153:81.

196 **Self TH et al.** The value of demonstration and role of the pharmacist in teaching the correct use of pressurized bronchodilators. Can Med Assoc J. 1983;128:129.

197 **Roberts RJ et al.** A comparison of various types of patient instruction in the proper administration of metered inhalers. Drug Intell Clin Pharm. 1982;16:53.

198 **Mickle TR et al.** Evaluation of pharmacists' practice in patient education when dispensing a metered dose inhaler. Drug Intell Clin Pharm. 1990;24:927.

199 **Bruderman I et al.** A cooperative study of various combinations of ipratropium bromide and metaproterenol in allergic asthmatic patients. Chest. 1983;83:209.

200 **Mayo PH et al.** Result of a program to reduce admissions for adult asthma. Ann Intern Med. 1990;112:864.

201 **Zeiger RS.** Facilitated referral to asthma specialist reduces relapses in asthma emergency room visits. J Allergy Clin Immunol. 1991;87:1160.

202 **Kelso T et al.** Educational and long term therapeutic intervention in the ED in adult indigent minority patients: Effect on clinical outcomes. Am Rev Respir Dis. 1993;147:A774. Abstract.

203 **Im J.** Evaluation of the effectiveness of an asthma clinic managed by an ambulatory care pharmacist. Calif J Hosp Pharm. 1993;5:5.

204 **Pauley T et al.** Results of a pharmacy managed, physician directed program to reduce ED visits in a group of inner city adult asthmatic patients. Ann Pharmacother. 1995;29:5.

205 **Self T et al.** Clinical pharmacist-initiated asthma management for adult minorities: does patient education as part of state of the art therapy affect outcomes? Patient Educ Couns. 1994;23:S32. Abstract.

206 **Self TH, Rumbak MJ.** Incorrect use of metered dose inhalers by medical personnel. Chest. 1993;103:325. Letter.

207 **Mestitz H et al.** Comparison of outpatient nebulized vs. metered dose inhaler terbutaline in chronic airflow obstruction. Chest. 1989;96:1237.

208 **Hunt LW, Rosenow EC.** Drug-induced bronchospasm. In: Weiss EB, Stein M. eds. Bronchial Asthma: Mechanisms and Therapeutics. Boston: Little, Brown and Co.; 1993:621.

209 **Meeker DP et al.** Drug-induced bronchospasm. Clinics Chest Med. 1990;11:163.

210 **Stevenson DD.** Diagnosis, prevention, and treatment of adverse to aspirin and nonsteroidal anti-inflammatory drugs. J Allergy Clin Immunol. 1984;74:617.

211 **Odeh M.** Timolol eyedrop-induced fatal bronchospasm in an asthmatic patient. J Fam Pract. 1991;32:97.

212 **Israel E et al.** The pivotal role of 5-lipoxygenase products in the reaction of aspirin-sensitive asthmatics to aspirin. Am Rev Respir Dis. 1993;148:1447–451.

213 **Dunn TL et al.** The effect of topical ophthalmic instillation of timolol and betaxolol on lung function in asthmatic subjects. Am Rev Respir Dis. 1986;133:264.

214 **Whelan AM, Hahn N.** Optimizing drug delivery from metered-dose inhalers. DICP, Ann Pharmacother. 1991;25:638.

Chronic Obstructive Airways Disease

Dennis M Williams

Risk Factors 20-1
Pathophysiology 20-1
Emphysema 20-1
Chronic Bronchitis (See Table 20.1) 20-2
Diagnosis and Patient Assessment 20-2
General Management Considerations 20-3
Clinical Assessment 20-3
Signs and Symptoms (See Table 20.2) 20-3
Risk Factors 20-3
Management 20-4
    Smoking cessation 20-4
    Immunizations 20-6
    Bronchodilators (See Figure 20.1) 20-6

Anticholinergics 20-6
    Patient education (Also see Question 12) 20-7
Beta agonists 20-7
    Patient education 20-8
Monitoring therapy: peak expiratory flow rates 20-8
Supplemental oxygen therapy 20-8
Bronchodilators and corticosteroids 20-9
Theophylline 20-9
Corticosteriods 20-9
Respiratory stimulants 20-9
Obstructive Sleep Apnea 20-10
Signs and Symptoms 20-10
Management 20-10

Chronic obstructive airways disease (COAD) refers to conditions of chronic airflow limitation. Other terms include chronic obstructive pulmonary disease (COPD) and chronic obstructive lung disease (COLD). All are characterized by a reduction in air outflow, measured as impaired expiratory flow, that does not change markedly over several months. Typically, middle-aged or elderly persons are affected. By definition, COAD includes a major component of irreversible or fixed airflow obstruction; however, some patients will exhibit varying degrees of reversible obstruction, evidenced by significant improvements in pulmonary function with bronchodilators. This may reflect reversible components of COAD or may represent the presence of asthma along with COAD.

Pulmonary diseases are a major cause of mortality in the U.S. COAD represents the fifth leading cause of death; pneumonia and influenza infections are the sixth leading cause of death.[1-4] COAD affects over 15 million people in the U.S., causing significant disability and over 99,000 deaths annually.[1] The mortality rate increased by 2% from 1990 to 1991, while other major diseases were declining.[2] Overall, the mortality rate has increased by 22% over the past decade (particularly among females) and exceeds 50% ten years after diagnosis. The indirect costs incurred as a result of COAD are substantial. Disability estimates are an average of 12 days annually for patients with chronic bronchitis and 68 days for patients with emphysema.[5] It is not uncommon to encounter COAD with other chronic illnesses, including cardiac and renal disease, presenting unique problems in the clinical management of the patient.

Chronic obstructive airways disease is a heterogenous disorder which is represented primarily by emphysema and chronic bronchitis, but also includes peripheral airways disease and asthmatic bronchitis. Many patients with COAD have characteristics of more than one of these diseases, but one typically is predominant. Despite this variability, overall approach to management is similar. In each case, there is a characteristic obstruction to expiratory airflow, which is at least partially fixed or irreversible despite therapy. The hallmark of obstructive lung disease is a decrease in the forced expiratory volume in one second (FEV_1), and the ratio of FEV_1 to the forced vital capacity (FVC) is $<75\%$. (See Chapter 19: Asthma for further discussion of pulmonary function tests.) Mild obstruction is characterized by a ratio of 60% to 75%; moderate 50% to 60%; and severe obstruction to airflow occurs when the ratio is less than 50%.[6-8] The FEV_1 is the best prognostic indicator; the five-year mortality is 50% when the FEV_1 is ≤1.0 L and the mean survival is less than two years when FEV_1 is ≤0.5 L.[8-10]

Risk Factors

The primary risk factor for COAD is cigarette smoking.[7,10,11] Up to 20% of smokers will develop significant COAD and 85% of cases of COAD are caused by cigarette smoking. Some evidence suggests that different patterns of smoke inhalation (e.g., depth of inhalation) may contribute to risk, but smoking in general should be considered the major risk factor.[12,13] Other environmental factors that may be important in COAD development include occupational exposure (grain, coal, asbestos) and air pollution.

Pathophysiology

The pathophysiology of COAD is characterized by both acute and chronic inflammation, as well as changes in cellular proliferation. This leads ultimately to tissue destruction, loss of structural ciliated columnar cells, squamous and goblet cell metaplasia, glandular and smooth muscle hypertrophy, and scarring. Patients with COAD exhibit varying degrees of bronchial hyperreactivity and reversibility of obstruction.

Three primary pathophysiologic presentations of COAD have been identified.[9,14] First, bronchial changes of enlarged mucous glands with smooth muscle hyperplasia, inflammation, and bronchial wall thickening are consistent with chronic bronchitis. Second, emphysematous changes of acinar enlargement occur following prolonged unchecked protease activity on lung tissue. Finally, inflammation, fibrosis, and narrowing of small airways contribute to increased airway resistance and obstruction.

The clinical consequences of the morphologic changes are worsened obstruction, hyperinflation of the lungs, increased sputum production, recurrent respiratory infections, and altered gas exchange. The end results include respiratory muscle fatigue, ventilatory disorders, cardiovascular compromise, and poor quality of life.

Emphysema

Emphysema results from anatomical defects of the lung characterized by abnormal permanent enlargement of the air spaces distal to the terminal bronchiole, accompanied by destruction of alveolar walls, but without obvious fibrosis.[10,15-17] Destruction of alveolar tissue results in loss of elastic recoil and structural support;

thus, obstruction and airway collapse occurs during expiration. With chronic symptoms, patients adapt and use accessory muscles of respiration and have a prolonged expiratory phase.

Emphysema sometimes is defined by areas of involvement. Centriacinar or centrilobular suggests involvement predominantly in the proximal part of the lobule. This finding is associated with a history of cigarette smoking and typically occurs after age 60. Panacinar emphysema (panlobular) is associated with α_1-antitrypsin deficiency. In this case, the entire lobule is involved. This rare form of emphysema, termed α_1-antitrypsin deficiency-associated emphysema, is caused by a genetic defect in the production of the α_1-antitrypsin enzyme which normally is protective to the alveolar lining of the lung. This genetic abnormality accounts for 2% of all reported cases of emphysema. Patients with this disease present with significant destruction much earlier in life than the typical patient with emphysema, often as early as age 20.

α_1-antitrypsin is a glycoprotein produced in the liver which functions as an antiprotease in the lung to inhibit neutrophil elastase. Normally, there is a balance of protease and antiprotease in the lungs which protects against loss of alveolar walls characteristic of emphysema. With the inherited deficiency of α_1-antitrypsin, neutrophil elastase acts unchecked to destroy alveolar walls. The most common form of deficiency is the Phenotype ZZ in which individuals exhibit circulating levels of α_1-antitrypsin which are 15% to 33% of normal.

Since emphysema is an anatomical disease, diagnosis frequently is made postmortem. This includes individuals who exhibited no significant evidence of airflow obstruction. The alveolar destruction characteristic of emphysema reduces the effective surface area available for gas exchange. The loss of elastic recoil that normally is responsible for exhalation increases the work of breathing by the patient. Typical emphysema patients are 55 to 75 years old with severe dyspnea as the primary complaint. Cough may be absent, or, if present, produces only scanty sputum. Patients often are thin, barrel-chested, and breathe through pursed lips. Carbon dioxide retention usually is not a problem and dyspnea is the most frequent complaint. Classically, emphysema patients are termed "pink-puffers" because they maintain adequate oxygenation through an increased work of breathing.

Chronic Bronchitis

Chronic bronchitis presents clinically as chronic excessive mucus production and secretion resulting in airflow obstruction secondary to inflammation and edema. Persistent productive cough is present on most days for three months or more during the year over at least two consecutive years.[10,15-17] Inflammation and edema of mucosa and mucus glands found in small and medium size airways of the bronchial tree result in copious production of thick tenacious secretions. The increased mucus is an excellent media for recurrent bronchial infections resulting in further damage. Airflow obstruction results from airway narrowing from edema of bronchial walls and occlusion by increased mucus secretion. The increase in mucus production results from hyperplasia and hypertrophy of mucous glands and goblet cells because of chronic irritation in the airway. Repeated infections result because of inability to clear the mucus and mucous plugs.

The characteristic patient with chronic bronchitis is 45 to 65 years old with a chronic productive cough, moderate dyspnea, and recurrent respiratory infections. The patient with chronic bronchitis often is obese and suffers from significant hypoxemia, cyanosis with carbon dioxide retention. Classically, this patient has been called a "blue-bloater." End-stage chronic bronchitis is complicated by polycythemia (increased red blood cell production) and

cor pulmonale [right-sided congestive heart failure (CHF) secondary to lung disease and pulmonary hypertension]. Differing characteristics of chronic bronchitis and emphysema are summarized in Table 20.1.

Diagnosis and Patient Assessment

The natural course of COAD spans 20 to 40 years. Early detection and intervention may be important in slowing progression of the disease. When patients delay seeking care until symptoms are significant, benefits of therapy are limited since changes are largely irreversible.

The diagnosis of COAD is based upon subjective and objective data. A history of tobacco use should raise strong suspicion. Physical findings often do not correlate well with early COAD. Later, objective findings include the presence of a barrel chest, rales, rhonchi, prolonged expiratory phase, and cyanosis.[10,18,19] Breath sounds upon auscultation are distant and wheezes are noted with forced exhalation. Chest roentgenograms may support the diagnosis showing nonspecific destructive changes. Increased lung markings and peribronchial thickening are characteristic of chronic bronchitis while hyperinflation, small heart size, and bullae (with loss of alveoli and wall structure) are seen with emphysema. Electrocardiographic abnormalities may be seen, including premature beats and evidence of pulmonary hypertension.

Primary laboratory data useful in the diagnosis and assessment include arterial blood gas (ABG) determinations and spirometry. In stable conditions, the pH will be normal, hypoxemia will be present in varying degrees, and hypercapnia (CO_2 retention) will be a feature in some patients. During acute exacerbation, respiratory acidosis is present. The hemoglobin (Hgb) and hematocrit (Hct) may be elevated secondary to chronic hypoxemia. Pulmonary function tests, including FEV_1 and FVC, are helpful to determine severity, prognosis, and reversibility of obstruction. Carbon dioxide retention usually develops when the FEV_1 falls to less than 0.8 L.[20-22] An α_1-antitrypsin concentration determination is indicated for patients developing COAD at less than 50 years of age, when emphysema occurs without a significant cigarette history, or if there is a family history of the genetic deficiency.

The clinical course of COAD is variable, being affected by numerous factors including genetic predisposition; continued exposure to inhaled irritants through cigarettes, workplace, or environmental pollutants; and repeated infections. The typical smoker who develops COAD remains asymptomatic for the first two decades of smoking, except for more frequent viral or bacterial upper respiratory tract infections. Clinical symptoms appear after significant irreversible lung damage occurs. After 25 to 30 years of smoking,

Table 20.1	Characteristics of Chronic Bronchitis and Emphysema	
Characteristic	Chronic Bronchitis	Emphysema
Age (onset of symptoms)	50	60
Primary symptom	Cough	Dyspnea
Sputum	Copious	Scanty
Chest x-ray changes	Peribronchial thickening	Flattened diaphragms
Hematocrit	Normal or ↑	Usually normal
Cor pulmonale	Common	Rare
Total lung capacity	Normal	↑
Weight	Frequently obese	Thin; weight loss common

mild dyspnea is noted and may be accompanied by a morning cough; however, physical examination and chest roentgenogram are normal.[14] As the disease progresses, loss of function occurs, dyspnea on exertion (DOE) develops, and sputum production and cough worsen. Ultimately, structural changes result in alveolar hypoxia and the secondary problems of pulmonary hypertension and cor pulmonale.

General Management Considerations

General management principles are directed toward educating the patient about his condition, minimizing and slowing the progression of airflow limitation, correcting any physiologic alterations, and optimizing the patient's functional abilities. Education should assure an understanding of the disease process, as well as the rationale for the various components of care. Physicians and patients should develop realistic goals of therapy in an effort to improve compliance and minimize unnecessary fear or anxiety.

Spirometry is a strong predictor of mortality and prognosis for the COAD patient.[1,18] Early detection of changes in lung function will permit initiation of efforts to retard the progression of the disease. Baseline spirometric measurements are helpful and provide information on changes in lung function over time. Lung function normally declines in adults gradually with a loss of 20 mL in FEV_1 annually in nonsmokers. Susceptible smokers may lose as much as 80 mL of function each year.[7,11] Avoidance of risk factors, including smoking cessation, can slow the rate of decline in FEV_1 to that of nonsmokers. It is unclear whether early intervention with either bronchodilators or corticosteroids is useful in slowing disease progression, but preliminary results suggest some benefit.[6,9,79]

Pulmonary rehabilitation programs involving general physical conditioning, breathing exercises, and muscle training can be beneficial for the COAD patient.[23] Exercise training usually involves walking and stair-climbing exercises. Slow diaphragmatic breathing through pursed lips relieves symptoms of dyspnea and slows the respiratory rate. Resistance devices designed to improve diaphragmatic strength and endurance can reduce respiratory failure. Adequate nutrition should be maintained since high energy requirements may be required to support the work of breathing.[24]

Reducing bronchial secretions may slow disease progression indirectly. Treatment or prevention of recurrent airway infections through vaccination (e.g., pneumococcal and influenza vaccines) or antibiotic regimens also is helpful to prevent damage to the lungs. Infectious etiologies include viruses and gram-negative and gram-positive bacteria.

Chronic obstructive airways disease patients can be taught proper coughing techniques, postural drainage, and chest percussion to mobilize thickened mucous secretions. The value of expectorants to thin airway secretions is equivocal. Although adequate fluid intake generally is considered helpful in promoting health, aggressive hydration, or nebulized humidification, is not indicated except in acutely decompensated patients. Similarly, expectorants such as guaifenesin and iodide have a limited role.[25,26] The use of postural drainage and chest percussion traditionally has been included in comprehensive care regimens, but may provide minimal benefit for many patients. Symptomatic management of dyspnea is very beneficial for selected patients.[26,30]

Medications should be selected carefully in patients with COAD. Bronchodilators can increase airflow in patients with reversible obstruction and reduce symptoms of dyspnea.[26–30] Previous practices of using single trials of inhaled bronchodilators are inadequate in predicting long-term response to bronchodilator therapy, suggesting that an adequate course should be administered before evaluating response.[31–35] Corticosteroid use also is contro-

versial. Although some patients benefit from short- and long-term therapy, it is not easy to predict which patients are candidates. The best evidence of benefit is with oral corticosteroids although the risk of this therapy is well known.[37–47] Similarly, the benefit of theophylline has been long debated. Theophylline frequently is used in COAD for its effects on diaphragm function and/or other nonbronchodilatory effects.[48–60]

Correcting the secondary physiologic changes of COAD includes attention to hypoxemia and hypercapnia and treating and managing pulmonary hypertension and cor pulmonale. The effectiveness of long-term oxygen therapy on a continuous basis is well documented in two large clinical trials.[65–68] The goal of supplemental oxygen therapy is to maintain an oxygen saturation greater than 90%. Chronic hypercapnia in COAD may be related to reduced central drive in response to respiratory muscle fatigue. Management for hypercapnia is directed at reducing the work of breathing by decreasing secretions, treating bronchoconstriction, and maintaining acid-base balance. Managing secondary complications of pulmonary hypertension and right-sided heart failure is difficult. Vasodilators are ineffective.[61] Theophylline can improve right ventricular function and exercise performance, while beta agonists show short-term beneficial effects on pulmonary vascular resistance.[20,61,69] Diuretic agents are helpful in severe volume overload by reducing airway edema.

Efforts to optimize functional ability should be directed at maintaining quality of life and addressing specific psychosocial needs. Exercise training programs can increase oxygen utilization and overall cardiopulmonary conditioning. Exercise training should be initiated carefully with an understanding of the patient's limitations. Specifically, upper extremity exercise training can improve function and reduce dyspnea. Results from respiratory muscle training have not shown significant benefit from this activity. The nutritional status of the patient should be assessed and addressed if significant nutritional deficiencies are determined. Finally, patients may benefit from biofeedback, relaxation therapy, and individual or group therapy if psychosocial stresses or other chronic diseases are interfering with their pulmonary functional capacity.

Clinical Assessment
Signs and Symptoms

1. E.H., a 52-year-old male, visits his physician for an annual physical examination. He complains of decreased exercise tolerance and has noted increasing shortness of breath (SOB) while golfing. His previous medical history is unremarkable except for mild hypertension which is controlled with sodium restriction (blood pressure today 146/88 mm Hg). He has a 60 pack year smoking history and currently smokes 1 pack/day. His mother died of a stroke at age 65, his father had COAD and died of lung cancer at age 62, and his brother is alive at age 59 with COAD. Upon physical examination, coarse breath sounds which clear after coughing are noted. Chest x-ray is normal. Spirometry shows an FEV_1 of 2.8 L (80% of predicted) and an FVC of 4.0 L (85% of predicted). What is the evidence of COAD in E.H.?

E.H. exhibits symptoms of dyspnea on exertion and decreased exercise tolerance which are early signs of COAD. His lung examination shows coarse breath sounds that clear after coughing which suggests increased mucus production. His spirometry shows an FEV_1:FVC ratio of 70%. A ratio of less than 75% is the hallmark of an obstruction to airflow.[1] The significant smoking history strongly supports a diagnosis of COAD.

Risk Factors

2. What risk factors does E.H. have for development of COAD? Based upon the information provided, can the precise type of COAD be determined?

E.H. has a significant smoking history and a family history of COAD and lung cancer. Although he only recently became symptomatic, the damage to his airways has been occurring for a number of years. The normal annual decline in FEV_1 that occurs with aging is accelerated three to four times by cigarette smoking.[7,11] Other environmental causes of COAD, including occupational exposure to various dusts, toxins, and chemicals, should be investigated.

It is not possible to differentiate chronic bronchitis from emphysema in E.H. at this point. Typically, there is significant overlap in symptoms and physical findings between both conditions. The productive cough is more consistent with chronic bronchitis at this point. α_1-antitrypsin deficiency is not a major concern based upon age of onset and the significant smoking history.

Management

Smoking Cessation

3. What interventions would be appropriate for E.H.?

The therapeutic objectives for management of a COAD patient are to slow the disease progression and maintain an acceptable quality of life. The damage that occurs in COAD is largely irreversible; thus, E.H. should be educated about the condition and what to expect. The initial management consideration in COAD patients is smoking cessation.[2,13] Benefits of smoking cessation after significant damage has occurred include an eventual return to a normal age-related rate of decline in ventilatory function and a reduction in the risk of lung cancer.

4. E.H. expresses an interest in smoking cessation but admits failure in the past. He has tried over-the-counter smoking aids, and even has stopped "cold turkey," but eventually began smoking again. He now is aware of the risks of continued exposure to tobacco smoke and is committed to making a serious effort to stop smoking. How can E.H. be assisted in his efforts to stop smoking?

Smoking is a major contributor to COAD. It is estimated that almost 20% of smokers develop COAD and that cigarette smoke is responsible for over 85% of COAD cases. The exact risk factors that determine which smokers will develop COAD are unknown, but they almost certainly are multifactorial. Thus, discontinuation of smoking is a primary intervention in the treatment of COAD. Unfortunately, smoking cessation is a tremendously complex problem with physical, psychological, and social components. Likewise, there are a variety of methods to help patients stop smoking, including both nonpharmacologic and pharmacologic interventions. Each of these types of programs has been associated with varying degrees of success. Even in programs that report high success rates initially, follow-up evaluations after one year show a return to smoking in a large number of subjects. E.H. admits to his problem and appears to have a strong desire to stop smoking. Such a recognition on the part of the patient increases his chance of success. Since E.H. has made an initial commitment to stop smoking, he should be referred to a comprehensive smoking cessation program. There he can be evaluated to determine the best treatment plan for him.

Nonpharmacologic approaches include a variety of short- and long-term behavior modification techniques including education, behavioral counseling, support groups, self-management, self-monitoring, aversive conditioning, slow withdrawal from nicotine, hypnosis, acupuncture, and relapse prevention. By themselves, education and behavior modification have relatively poor long-term success rates because they do not satiate the craving for smoking or blunt other symptoms associated with nicotine withdrawal. However, they may be effective in highly motivated patients or those who smoke only a few cigarettes a day. For further description of these techniques, the reader is referred to a comprehensive review by Haxby.[52]

The major pharmacologic intervention is nicotine replacement (substitution) therapy with either nicotine gum or transdermal patches. Clonidine and antidepressants also have been used in some treatment plans. The goal for nicotine replacement therapy is to reduce the craving to smoke and minimize the unpleasant symptoms of physical withdrawal from nicotine which include nausea, irritability, restlessness, nervousness, difficulty concentrating, insomnia, hunger, and weight gain. These symptoms usually occur within days of cessation, peak during the first week, and then subside over several weeks.

Accordingly, substitution of the nicotine from cigarettes with nicotine gum or patches usually is prescribed for four to six weeks, then tapered over one to two months to avoid acute withdrawal. Although the physical withdrawal from nicotine may have dissipated at this time, the smoker is faced with habitual pressures or cravings to smoke during certain activities previously associated with smoking. Thus, it is not surprising that pharmacologic intervention is most successful when used in conjunction with behavior modification including long-term follow-up of the patient to reinforce the need to continue to abstain from smoking. It also may become necessary to continue long-term, low-dose nicotine replacement in some patients. In any case, simply giving a patient a prescription for nicotine therapy, even when accompanied by proper counseling on the technique for using the gum or patch, is of marginal value unless the patient is committed to stopping smoking, the caregiver takes the time to educate him on the adverse health consequences of continued smoking, and the patient is provided with behavioral and emotional support.

When smoke from a cigarette is inhaled, nicotine is absorbed rapidly from the lungs delivering high concentrations of nicotine to the blood (20 to 50 ng/mL) and brain within seconds. This provides a pleasurable sensation to the patient and satisfies his craving for the drug. Chewing gums (Nicorette) contain either 2 mg or 4 mg (double strength) of nicotine polacrilex, an alkaline ion-exchange resin that allows for slow release and buccal absorption of nicotine when chewed. The actual amount of nicotine absorbed is difficult to quantitate and depends upon how vigorously the patient chews each piece and how often the gum is replaced with a new piece. Nicotine concentrations rise gradually and are more sustained at a level of approximately 8 to 12 ng/mL, thus providing a source of the drug to prevent withdrawal without causing the pleasurable consequences. The choice as to which strength of gum to start the patient on is somewhat arbitrary; the 2 mg product is used more commonly, but the 4 mg product is likely to be more effective for those with heavier smoking habits. The patient is instructed to chew the gum slowly until a peppery taste or tingling sensation is detected, then to stop chewing and "park" the gum in his cheek. When the taste dissipates, he should resume chewing slowly. This process is repeated as often as necessary, replacing the gum with a new piece when it no longer elicits the peppery taste or after about 30 minutes. Patients may chew 10 to 20 pieces a day during the first few weeks, and then taper the dosage as they see fit. Alternatively, a fixed schedule such as one piece of gum every 30 to 60 minutes can be used, followed by a gradual taper. The maximum recommended dose is 30 pieces of the 2 mg strength per day and 20 pieces of the 4 mg gum. Acidic beverages such as coffee, colas, wine, and orange juice may impair the absorption of nicotine from the buccal mucosa. Therefore, patients should be counseled to avoid eating and drinking for 15 minutes before and after chewing nicotine gum. Side effects of nausea, mouth and throat irritation, lightheadedness, and hiccups are more prominent if the patient chews the gum too rapidly or fails to discontinue chewing when the peppery taste begins. Stomach gas and belching are associated with air swallowing during gum chewing. Nicotine-containing products should be used cautiously in patients with angina or other cardiovascular diseases. If the gum is swallowed, the absorption is less because of high first-pass metabolism in the liver. Although there are concerns that long-term use of nicotine replacement may cause physical dependence on this form of nicotine, the health consequences are much less than that of smoking.

Four different brands of transdermal patch systems are marketed (see Table 20.2), each with a unique delivery mechanism and differing slightly in the number of dosage strengths available (expressed as the amount of nicotine released over a 16- to 24-hour period). However, there is no apparent difference in the efficiency of drug delivery or efficacy between products. Depending upon the dosage size of the unit applied to the skin, serum nicotine levels range from 6 to 17 ng/mL. The advantage of these systems lies in their simplicity of use since they only need to be applied once a day. Three of the products (Habitrol, Nicoderm, and ProStep) are left in place continuously for 24 hours before replacement; while Nicotrol is only left on for 16 hours followed by an eight hour drug-free period before applying a new patch. The initial onset of effect from transdermal products is delayed slightly relative to the gum, taking up to two days to reach steady state; but they provide a more continuous blood nicotine level compared to the intermittent fluctuations seen with the gum. Twenty-four-hour placement has the theoretical advantage of continuous effects throughout the night to provide coverage for early morning cravings upon awakening, while 16-hour placement may cause less sleep interference, insomnia, and vivid dreams. A typical dosage regimen is to use the 21 mg/day patch for two to eight weeks, followed by 14 mg/day for another two to four weeks, and then 7 mg/day for either two to four weeks or to complete a total of 6 to 20 weeks of treatment. Ultimately, the size of the starting dose, rate of tapering, and total duration must be individualized to the patient's body size, estimated severity of the smoking habit, development of side effects (nausea, dyspepsia, nervousness, dizziness, sweating), and the presence or absence of withdrawal symptoms or craving. Rotating the site of patch application minimizes skin irritation; nonetheless, skin reactions to the adhesive backing occur in up to 35% to 45% of patch users.

Continuing to smoke during use of gum products or while the patch is in place has been implicated in the development of angina and arrhythmia, likely due to the additive serum levels of nicotine that are achieved. Thus, patients should be strongly counseled not to smoke while using either form of nicotine replacement therapy.

A unique problem with the patches is that considerable residual nicotine remains in the patch after it has been removed. Improper disposal could lead to an infant or animal chewing on or ingesting the product and developing acute nicotine toxicity. A similar problem could occur with the gum, but the residual amount of drug in the already chewed gum is much lower.

There is no clear superiority of either patch or gum treatment. Higher initial doses (4 mg of gum or 21 mg/day patches) may produce higher quit rates than lower doses. Compliance and duration of therapy tends to be better with the patches, but if skin reactions occur, either treatment must be stopped or the gum or a different brand of transdermal system substituted for the original patch. In some cases, the two methods can be used in combination in the same patient. While combination therapy may increase the success rate, it also produces a greater incidence of side effects. Assessing overall success rates can be difficult because of variability in motivation of patients in various trials, the degree of non-pharmacologic therapy that is given along with the nicotine replacement, and the duration of follow-up. For example, quit rates with the gum have been reported to be as high as 60% at six weeks, but meta-analysis showed six-month success rates of 27% compared to 18% for placebo.[70] By one year, only 17% of subjects remain abstinent. A similar meta-analysis of 17 studies totaling 5098 patients using patch therapy reported an overall abstinence rate for active patches of 27% (versus 13% for placebo) immediately following treatment and 22% for patches compared to 9% for placebo at six months.[88] The 16- and 24-hour patches appeared equally efficacious and extending treatment beyond eight weeks did not appear to increase efficacy. While the long-term success rates seen with both therapies are disappointingly low, they exceed those of placebo treatment which only average 11% to 18% at six weeks to six months and are as low as 4% at one year.

E.H. should be counseled thoroughly on the value of stopping smoking. The pros and cons of the gum versus the patch should be presented so that he can assist in the choice of product. Before actually starting E.H. on nicotine replacement, he should be allowed to discuss his feelings about smoking and instructed to either keep a log of how many cigarettes he smokes during a week or to place all the cigarette butts from the previous week in a jar as a visual reminder of the magnitude of his habit. He also should be encouraged to prepare a written contract of his intent to quit including a stated quit date. It has been shown that these stages of preparation and contemplation enhance the response to nicotine replacement therapy. Once nicotine replacement is begun, E.H. should be given positive reinforcement at subsequent clinic visits and encouraged to join a self-help group.

5. E.H. completed a smoking cessation program and stopped smoking for 8 months. However, pressures from his job and family resulted in a return to smoking. He returns to the pulmonary physician 5 years later with complaints of a productive cough, increasing SOB, and DOE. He currently smokes 1 pack/day. His lung examination has scattered rhonchi throughout both lung fields and diffuse wheezing. His sputum is unchanged from his usual white color and a few polymorphonuclear leukocytes (PMNS) are present with gram-positive cocci and gram-negative rods. A chest x-ray shows a slightly enlarged cardiac shadow and thickened bronchial walls. Spirometry yields an FEV_1 of 1.3 L (50% of predicted) and an FVC of 2.4 L (56% of predicted). Repeat spirometry after albuterol results in an FVC of 1.4 L and FEV of 2.4 L. ABGs show a pH of 7.38, pO_2 65 mm Hg, and pCO_2 40 mm Hg. Assess the current status of E.H.'s COAD. Is the presence of either chronic bronchitis or emphysema more evident now? [SI units: pO_2 8.67 kPa; pCO_2 5.33 kPa]

Table 20.2		Nicotine Transdermal Systems	
Brand Name	Strength[a]	Total Nicotine Content (mg)	Patch Construction
Habitrol	21, 14, & 7 mg/24 hr	52.5, 35, & 17.5	Cotton pad with drug solution between 2 adhesive layers
Nicoderm	21, 14, & 7 mg/24 hr	114, 78, & 36	Drug reservoir with rate-controlling membrane
Nicotrol	15, 10, & 5 mg/16 hr	24.9, 16.6, & 8.3	—
ProStep	22 & 11 mg/24 hr	30 & 15	Nicotine gel matrix

[a] Dose absorbed in 24 hours (16 hours for Nicotrol).

E.H.'s failure in the smoking cessation program is not unusual. His subsequent return to tobacco use has resulted in continued decline in his pulmonary function and presentation with significant disease.

His complaints of cough, sputum production, shortness of breath, and decreased exercise tolerance, along with the physical examination and laboratory findings, all are consistent with chronic bronchitis. The environment of increased mucus production in the airways is an excellent media for bacterial growth. Chronic bronchitis patients typically are colonized with organisms such as *Streptococci pneumonia* and *Hemophilus influenza*. Exacerbations are characterized by an increase in these organisms or by other bacteria. E.H. has evidence of cardiac effects exhibited by an enlarged heart on chest x-ray. Persistent hypoxemia results in vasoconstriction of pulmonary vessels causing pulmonary hypertension. Subsequently, the right ventricle of the heart has to work harder to pump against this higher pressure gradient. Therefore, the chamber dilates and the heart muscle hypotrophies. The end result is cor pulmonale defined as right-sided heart failure secondary to pulmonary hypertension and lung disease. Spirometry also is consistent with chronic bronchitis since the FEV_1:FVC ratio is less than 75%. E.H.'s spirometry has declined significantly since his initial visit five years ago, suggesting disease progression. It shows no acute reversibility with albuterol ruling out an asthmatic component. It is unknown whether he would show any reversibility with an anticholinergic agent such as ipratropium. The arterial blood gases suggests hypoxemia; however, at a pO_2 of 65 mm Hg, there is adequate saturation of circulating hemoglobin.

Smoking cessation still is a major priority for E.H. to slow further deterioration of lung function and to reduce the risk for subsequent development of lung cancer.

Immunizations

6. Should E.H. receive any other preventive treatments for his lung disease?

E.H.'s immunization status should be reviewed. Specifically, he is a candidate for pneumococcal vaccine and for annual influenza vaccination. Epidemics caused by the influenza virus result in over 20,000 excess deaths annually. Individuals at greatest risk for significant morbidity and mortality from influenza pneumonia are those with chronic disease including lung disease. Protection against influenza virus, therefore, is recommended annually. Optimally, the influenza vaccine should be administered between October and January. This allows an adequate antibody response before the peak influenza season, which typically occurs within the first quarter of the year.

E.H. also is a candidate for pneumococcal vaccine (Pneumovax). Currently available pneumococcal vaccine is a 23 valent vaccine protecting against common strains of pneumococcus. Candidates for vaccination against pneumococcus include individuals who are at risk for significant morbidity and mortality if they develop a pneumococcal infection. This includes patients with chronic lung disease, as well as asplenic patients, since pneumococcus is an encapsulated organism. The benefits of pneumococcal vaccinations are less clear than those of influenza vaccination.[75] Nonetheless, since the risk:benefit ratio from pneumococcal vaccination is low, patients with chronic lung disease should receive prophylaxis. The duration of protection for the vaccine is variable. Recommendations range from a single lifetime immunization to a modification which calls for revaccination every six years. This latter recommendation is based upon findings of reducing antibody titers over a six-year period. At this point, E.H. should be immunized against pneumococcal pneumonia and the need for revaccination should be reassessed in six years. In addition, E.H.'s im-

munizations against tetanus should be determined and, if he has not had tetanus prophylaxis in the last decade, he should be administered an adult diphtheria-tetanus booster.

Bronchodilators

7. Should E.H. receive bronchodilator therapy at this time?

Bronchodilators are the primary pharmacologic therapy used in the management of COAD. Although much of the airflow obstruction is fixed, many patients exhibit some reversibility and also report subjective improvement even if objective benefit, such as changes in pulmonary function tests, is not evident. Available bronchodilator therapies include beta agonists, anticholinergics, and methylxanthines (theophylline).

Historically, decisions about the appropriateness of using bronchodilators have been based upon an improvement in the FEV_1 of at least 15% after an inhaled bronchodilator. Although this testing typically is performed with an inhaled beta agonist, reversibility following an inhaled anticholinergic agent also should be assessed. Several studies have suggested that an assessment based upon a single dose challenge with either agent is not adequate. It now is suggested that an empiric trial of inhaled bronchodilator (e.g., 2 weeks) be administered to the patient before repeating pulmonary function testing. Several studies have reported a poor correlation between pulmonary function and the COAD patient's overall quality of life, suggesting that parameters other than spirometry may be important to assess.[76]

E.H. is a candidate for initial treatment considerations for a patient with chronic bronchitis. A treatment algorithm for management of COAD is presented in Figure 20.1.[9] The key principle in this algorithm is that therapies that are initiated should be evaluated after a few months to determine their benefit. For many patients with COAD, benefits of pharmacotherapy are limited. If no objective improvement is seen after the introduction of therapy or if subjective (symptomatic) improvement is not substantial, therapy should be discontinued.

8. Anticholinergics. E.H.'s physician decides to start therapy with ipratropium bromide through a metered-dose inhaler (MDI) at a dose of 2 puffs Q 6 hr. What is the rationale for an anticholinergic agent? Is this a logical choice for E.H.?

The parasympathetic (cholinergic) nervous system plays a primary role in the control of bronchomotor tone in COAD. Not surprisingly, anticholinergic drugs are effective bronchodilators due to the inhibition of cyclic GMP in the lung. For this reason, the COAD treatment algorithm (see Figure 20.1) recommends anticholinergics as a first-line therapy.

For chronic management of COAD, bronchodilation produced by anticholinergics generally is considered to be equal or superior to that achieved by inhaled beta agonists.[72-74] This is an important distinction compared to asthma in which anticholinergics consistently are less effective than beta agonists. The benefits of combining a beta agonist with an anticholinergic have been debated. Some studies show benefit from the combination, while others suggest no additional bronchodilation.[72,77] Ultimately, each patient should be assessed individually by pulmonary function testing and subjective responses to determine which agent or combination provides the greatest benefit. For acute exacerbations of COAD, anticholinergics and beta agonists are equally effective and neither potentiates the other.

Ipratropium bromide (Atrovent) is the primary anticholinergic agent used in COAD and is an appropriate initial agent for E.H. His dose of two inhalations four times daily from a metered-dose inhaler is a typical starting dose. Based upon his response, the number of inhalations may be increased to six inhalations four times a day without significant side effects. The onset of action for

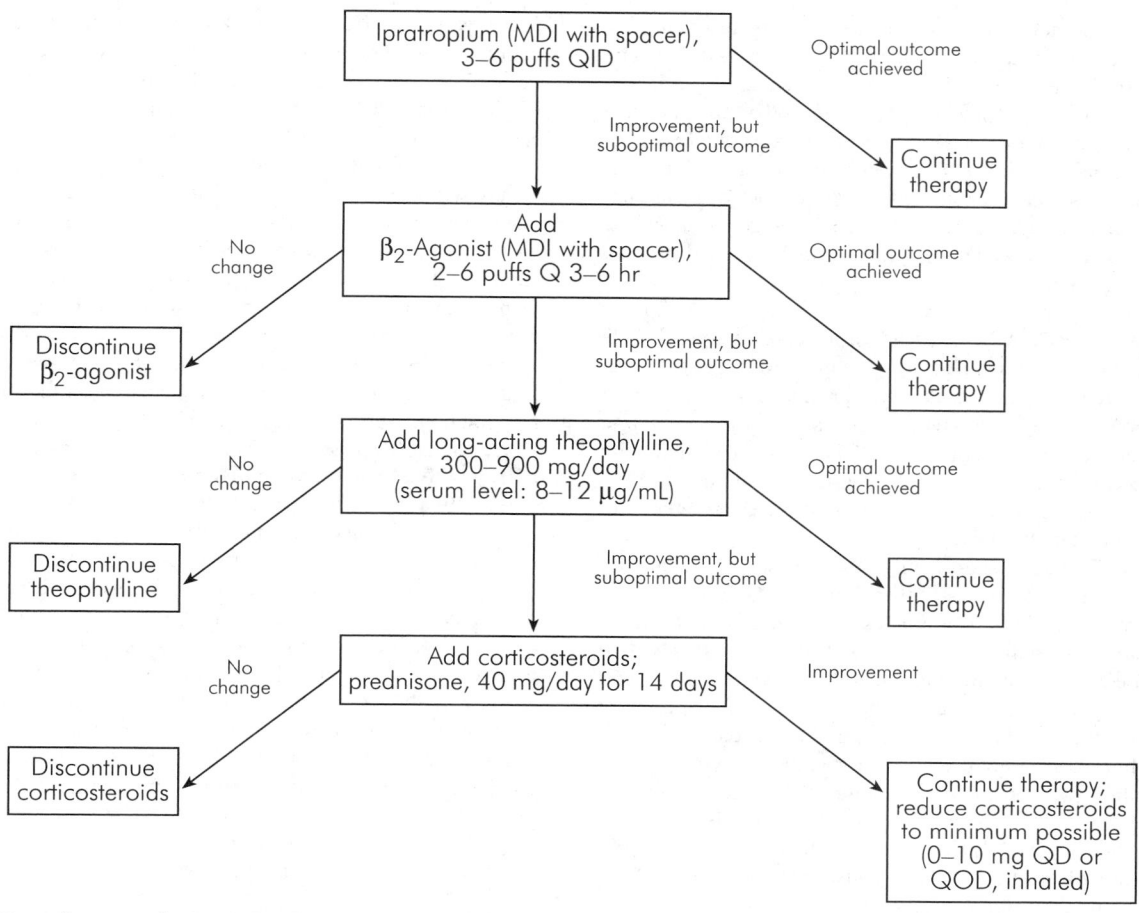

Fig 20.1 Typical Regimen for Treating COPD   Outcome was measured in terms of improvement in the FEV₁, FEV₁:FVC, and peak flow; improvement in the distance covered in a 6- or 12-minute walk; and objectively observed reduction in dyspnea, medication use, and nocturnal symptoms. MDI = Metered-dose inhaler.

ipratropium is 15 minutes with peak action in 60 minutes. The duration of action is four to six hours. Although some reports suggest a quicker onset of action, ipratropium generally is not appropriate for relief of acute symptoms. If E.H. is unable to tolerate or effectively use the metered-dose inhaler, the drug also can be administered as a nebulized solution.

Ipratropium's anticholinergic actions are localized predominately in the lungs, with an apparent specificity of action in the larger airways. Since it has minimal effects on sputum viscosity, there is little problem with drying of airway secretions. In addition, ipratropium's structure as a quaternary amine increases its polarity, thereby minimizing absorption from the lung and systemic side effects. These structural properties also reduce penetration across the blood brain barrier, reducing the incidence of confusion and other central nervous system (CNS) side effects.

Other anticholinergics that have been used clinically include atropine sulfate and glycopyrrolate. Although atropine was the first anticholinergic agent used, its benefit is limited by side effects and toxicities primarily related to its systemic absorption and, in some patients, excellent CNS penetration. Atropine can produce excessive salivary drying and, in higher doses, can cause significant CNS symptoms including hallucinations and seizures. Glycopyrrolate, like ipratropium, is a polar anticholinergic compound, but it is not approved by the Food and Drug Administration for the treatment of COAD. Its primary use is preoperatively and before diagnostic procedures to reduce secretions in the respiratory and gastrointestinal tract. The injectable form has been nebulized successfully and found to be an effective bronchodilator. Ipratropium bromide now

is available in both a metered-dose inhaler and a solution for nebulization. Because of this, glycopyrrolate may be encountered less often in a clinical setting.

9. *Patient Education.* **What advice and counseling should E.H. receive about the use of his ipratropium?**

Ipratropium is very well tolerated with primary patient complaints being dry mouth, cough, and/or nausea. Since efficacy is dependent upon drug delivery, the patient's ability to use a metered-dose inhaler should be assessed periodically. As with any anticholinergic drug, ipratropium can cause blurred vision if the medication is sprayed accidentally into the eye. Therefore, it is recommended that patients be taught to use the closed-mouth technique of MDI administration when using ipratropium. If it is necessary to improve delivery because of poor MDI technique, the patient can be instructed to use a spacer or a device such as an Aerochamber or InspirEase.

10. Beta Agonists. **Should a beta agonist be added to E.H.'s regimen?**

Inhaled beta agonists have been used for many years in the treatment of COAD, although the optimal regimens have not been determined. They are beneficial during chronic management as well as for relief of acute symptoms. Beta agonists produce bronchodilation by relaxing bronchial smooth muscle through activation of cyclic AMP. Side effects, including tachycardia and tremor, are more likely in the elderly patients; the potential for hypokalemia with aggressive therapy should be considered especially if other potassium reducing therapies are used. Generally, a β₂-selective agonist (e.g., albuterol, pirbuterol, bitolterol) should be selected.

However, the optimal way to use a beta agonist is uncertain [i.e., on a scheduled versus a PRN basis (see Question 11)]. In many cases, therapy is instituted with a fixed-dose anticholinergic and an as-needed beta agonist since most patients will require an agent for acute relief of symptoms. Other clinicians prescribe beta agonists on a scheduled basis (QID); however, there is a trend towards recommending use on an as needed basis for relief of symptoms up to four times a day. There are some advantages to using the beta agonist as needed including quantification of actual use and changes in requirements.

Beta agonists are more effective in relieving obstruction in asthma relative to COAD, based primarily upon the predictable reversible nature of asthma. However, the majority of patients with COAD will receive therapy with a beta agonist. Trials comparing anticholinergics and beta agonists suggest similar efficacy with a slight advantage for anticholinergics. The data on combination therapy are conflicting with some suggestive of additive effects, while other studies have shown no additional effect compared to optimal use of a single agent.

The onset of action of short-acting beta agonists (e.g., albuterol, pirbuterol) is significantly faster than ipratropium. Beta agonists exhibit some effect within five minutes and a maximal effect in 15 to 30 minutes. Anticholinergics work somewhat more slowly with an onset of effect within 15 minutes and the maximal effect in 60 to 90 minutes. Some data suggest that ipratropium works more quickly, but generally this is not considered to be relevant.

Anticholinergics are not useful for acute relief of symptoms associated with airway obstruction because of the delayed onset of action. In these cases, a beta agonist should be administered. Considering the above points, E.H. should remain on a regularly scheduled regimen with ipratropium and be instructed on as needed use of a short-acting inhaled beta agonist like albuterol.

11. Does chronic use of either beta agonists or anticholinergics improve pulmonary function?

The optimal method of using bronchodilator therapy to treat COAD is a subject of debate. Recent reports suggest that regular use of beta agonists in patients with asthma, as well as COAD, may be associated with a paradoxical increased rate of decline in lung function. One study compared regularly scheduled albuterol or ipratropium versus "on-demand" use of each.[76] The results showed that scheduled use of either bronchodilator drug was associated with a more rapid decline in FEV_1 versus on-demand use. However, changes in quality of life were not detected despite the spirometric decline. The authors concluded that effective bronchodilation may mask an ongoing decline in lung function of COAD, but that disease progression occurred because the inflammatory component of the disease was not treated.

In a follow-up study, the same investigators evaluated the benefits of adding inhaled corticosteroids to the therapy of patients with asthma or COAD.[78,79] In this study, patients who had experienced a significant decline in lung function over a two-year period related to continuous use of bronchodilator received 800 μg/day of beclomethasone. Greater benefit from corticosteroids was noted in patients with asthma, although there was a trend toward a slower decline in lung function in the COAD group as well.

12. *Patient Education.* **E.H. has both an ipratropium and albuterol inhaler. What additional advice should be given to supplement the counseling given in Question 9?**

It has become increasingly common for patients with airways disease to receive therapy with multiple inhalers. Since the purpose of each inhaler varies, the patient should be counseled about the purpose and action of each therapy. In particular, he should be counseled to use the ipratropium at fixed times during the day and to reserve the albuterol to provide rapid relief during periods of

acute symptoms. He should be further instructed to seek medical help if he is needing more than four doses of albuterol per day. Proper inhalation technique is required to receive benefit from any inhaled therapy. The recommended important steps in MDI therapy are described in Figure 19.2 in Chapter 19: Asthma.

When using multiple inhalers concurrently, the patient should be advised about the sequence of use. There is general agreement that when a bronchodilator is being used with a nonbronchodilator (anti-inflammatory agent), the bronchodilator should be administered first followed by the other medication. There is less agreement on the proper sequence when two bronchodilators are being used. One recommendation is to administer the fastest-acting bronchodilator first. In E.H.'s case, if he is using both medicines at the same time, he should administer the beta agonist first followed by the anticholinergic agent approximately five to ten minutes later.

13. Monitoring Therapy: Peak Expiratory Flow Rates. Should E.H. be advised to monitor his peak expiratory flow rates?

Objective monitoring by the patient, including the measurement of peak flows at home, is an integral component in the management of asthma. There is less evidence of the value of peak flow monitoring for patient with COAD. Since COAD is characterized by airflow obstruction that does not change significantly over time, the expense, inconvenience, and value of peak flow monitoring may not be warranted. It also is unclear whether periodic monitoring will allow early detection of an impending exacerbation.

Decisions about peak flow monitoring in patients with COAD should be made on an individualized basis. Patients with significant components of reversibility of airflow obstruction, for example patients with chronic bronchitis and asthma, may benefit from monitoring. Patients with largely irreversible obstruction are not good candidates for peak flow monitoring.

Supplemental Oxygen Therapy

14. A.Z., a 64-year-old female, has a 50-pack/year smoking history and a 15-year history of chronic bronchitis. She stopped smoking 5 years ago. She also has a history of mild hypertension which currently is well controlled with verapamil 180 mg/day. A.Z. has been hospitalized 2 times within the past year for acute exacerbations of her chronic bronchitis. Her medications at home are albuterol inhaler 2 puffs QID, ipratropium inhaler 3 puffs QID, and sustained-release theophylline (Theodur) 300 mg BID. Her baseline pulmonary function tests show a FEV_1 of 1.4 L and a FVC of 2.5 L, increasing to an FEV_1 of 1.6 L and an FVC of 2.9 L after albuterol. Three days ago, A.Z. began to experience increasing symptoms of SOB upon exertion, an increase in sputum production, and a change in sputum color from its normal light color to yellow. In the emergency room her peak flow is measured at 90 L/min and chest x-ray shows no signs of an infiltrate. A stat ABG assessment shows pH 7.35, pO_2 50 mm Hg, pCO_2 45 mm Hg, percent saturation is 80%, and bicarbonate 26. A theophylline concentration is 9 μg/mL. She is placed on 1 L of oxygen by nasal cannula. What are the indications for oxygen therapy in A.Z.? Will she require supplemental oxygen therapy at home?
[SI units: pO_2 6.67 kPa; pCO_2 6.0 kPa]

Oxygen therapy for COAD is used commonly in two situations: during an acute exacerbation of COAD associated with a drop in pO_2 to below 55 mm Hg and in patients who are chronically hypoxemic. The goals of supplemental oxygen therapy are to correct arterial hypoxemia and prevent secondary organ damage. As the oxyhemoglobin disassociation curve illustrates (see Figure 19.1 in Chapter 19: Asthma), a pO_2 of 55 mm HG is equivalent to an arterial O_2 saturation of approximately 90%. Based upon the slope of the curve, a pO_2 of less than 55 to 60 mm Hg results in a dramatic drop in the saturation of hemoglobin. Over a prolonged period of time, this hypoxemia results in detrimental end organ effects including declines in CNS, cardiac, and renal function. On the other hand, increasing the pO_2 above 60 is associated with small changes in the saturation of hemoglobin since the curve is relatively flat in this range.

The availability of continuous supplemental oxygen therapy at home is the most significant advance in the management of COAD in over two decades, since this therapy has been found to prolong survival. The value of home oxygen therapy for COAD patients with chronic hypoxemia (pO_2 <55 mm Hg) was documented in studies conducted over a decade ago. To obtain full benefit of home oxygen therapy, it should be used 18 to 20 hours a day. In a classic study, subjects using continuous therapy (20 hours/day) had a mortality rate half as great as patients using only nocturnal oxygen (12 hours/day).[65,66,68]

Administering supplemental oxygen to a patient with COAD is associated with some risk. Some COAD patients with poor ventilatory capacity are categorized as ''carbon dioxide retainers.'' In these cases, the patient no longer relies upon rises in the pCO_2 as the primary drive to breathe. If these patients receive too much oxygen, raising their pO_2 above their baseline, hypoventilation may occur resulting in CO_2 retention with CO_2 narcosis characterized by somnolence, lethargy, and possibly coma.

In this case, A.Z. is acutely hypoxic with a pO_2 of 50 mm Hg, but she does not appear to have a problem of chronic CO_2 retention. She has a normal pH, a slightly elevated pCO_2, and a normal serum bicarbonate calculated from the arterial blood gas. Supplemental oxygen therapy will be beneficial to her for this acute episode by increasing her pO_2 and improving oxygen delivery to tissues. She should be placed on oxygen therapy at 2 to 3 L/minute for the next 12 to 48 hours to maintain pO_2 greater than 55 mm Hg. Home oxygen therapy is not warranted unless she becomes chronically hypoxemic.

Bronchodilators and Corticosteroids

15. Theophylline. C.K., a 64-year-old female, has end-stage emphysema attributed to a 25-pack year smoking history. She is severely limited in her physical activity because of severe dyspnea even at rest. Her home life is a ''bed-to-bathroom'' existence. A home health agency visits 3 times weekly and ''Meals on Wheels'' brings her dinner. She requires home oxygen therapy at 1 L/min with baseline ABGs (on O_2) of pH 7.37, pO_2 64 mm Hg, pCO_2 45 mm Hg, and oxygen saturation 91%. Her medications include ipratropium 3 inhalations QID, albuterol 2 inhalations QID, and Theodur 200 mg Q 12 hr. A theophylline concentration 2 months ago was 9 μg/mL. One week ago, she began a course of erythromycin 500 QID for a dental infection. Today she visits her pulmonologist with the complaint of nausea and difficulty sleeping for the last 3 days. What is a possible cause of her complaints of nausea and difficulty sleeping? [SI units: pO_2 8.5 kPa; pCO_2 6.0 kPa]

Both gastrointestinal complaints such as nausea and CNS symptoms, including sleep difficulty and nervousness, are consistent with theophylline toxicity. Other adverse reactions associated with xanthines are cardiac irritability (tachycardia or arrhythmias) and seizures. All of these side effects are dose related. Gastrointestinal intolerance, nervousness, and insomnia increase in frequency when serum concentration exceeds 20 μg/mL as well.

In C.K., the addition of the enzyme inhibitor erythromycin to her regimen most likely resulted in a drug interaction causing a rise in her theophylline concentration. The interaction is dependent upon both the dose of erythromycin and the duration of erythromycin therapy, as well as the baseline serum theophylline concentration. Erythromycin-induced elevations in the theophylline concentration of 25% are typical. In C.K., a theophylline concentration should be obtained and further doses held until results are known.

In general, theophylline metabolism is associated with significant inter- and intrapatient variability. Patients should be monitored closely for early signs of toxicity, as well as for the initiation of drugs which potentially may interact. Understanding and recognizing the potential for drug interactions can allow safe and effective therapy with theophylline.

16. After holding theophylline therapy for 2 days, the physician is considering discontinuing the theophylline altogether. Is this a reasonable approach?

The role of theophylline in COAD is controversial. Theophylline provides no additional bronchodilator effect beyond that of beta agonists or anticholinergics. On the other hand, long-acting preparations may reduce overnight declines in pulmonary function and improve morning symptoms. Since much of the airway obstruction that occurs in COAD is irreversible, objective parameters such as improvements in FEV_1 may not be useful in evaluating response. However, theophylline may produce subjective improvement in patients with COAD, even in the absence of changes in FEV_1, including a lessening of dyspnea and enhanced exercise tolerance. This beneficial response may be due to the ability of theophylline to prevent diaphragmatic fatigue, stimulate mucociliary clearance, increase the central response to breathe, and reduce airway inflammation.[48,49,56,61,80] In one study, theophylline improved dyspnea, arterial blood gas findings, respiratory muscle performance, and selected pulmonary function tests over a two-month study period.[49] Thus, it may be rational to continue theophylline therapy in C.K. if she feels it is helping her. The optimal serum theophylline concentration is unclear, but keeping concentrations in the range of 5 to 15 μg/mL will minimize the incidence of side effects.

17. Corticosteroids. What is the role of corticosteroid therapy in C.K.?

As with theophylline, the benefit of corticosteroid therapy for patients with stable COAD is controversial. Although data to support clear benefit are lacking, many clinicians use oral corticosteroids when patients fail to respond to other therapies. A meta-analysis performed on studies conducted over a 38-year period suggests that only 10% of patients have clinically significant improvements in spirometry with oral corticosteroids.[37–42] Benefit versus risk should be weighed in light of this information.

Corticosteroids should be considered in the context of two clinical situations for a patient with COAD. For chronic management in stable COAD, the benefits of systemic corticosteroid therapy are minimal. It has been suggested that only 10% of patients with COAD receive significant benefit with oral corticosteroids. Patients more likely to benefit include those with a larger degree of reversibility, potentially those who have asthma. Other characteristics associated with improvement include presence of eosinophilia or eosinophils in the sputum. Since systemic corticosteroids are associated with significant toxicity, clinicians should evaluate response to therapy shortly after initiation and determine the need for continued use. A one- to two-week trial may be necessary to assess subjective or objective (pulmonary function tests) improvement.

For acute exacerbations of COAD, especially those requiring hospitalization, the role of systemic corticosteroids is stronger.[46] Steroids are useful in managing inflammation associated with acute exacerbations and in ameliorating respiratory failure. Dosing of corticosteroids in acute exacerbations of COAD is similar to that for acute asthma attacks.

Respiratory Stimulants

18. What role would respiratory stimulants play in C.K.'s therapy?

Respiratory stimulants (e.g., doxapram, progestins) generally are nonspecific CNS stimulants. Their effect is based upon stimulation of the central respiratory center in the medulla. Respiratory stimulants sometimes are useful acutely, but their utility on a long-term basis is limited.[81]

Analeptic agents, such as doxapram, are associated with unacceptable CNS effects including restlessness, agitation, sweating, mental status changes, and convulsions, as well as cardiovascular effects. Acetazolamide, a carbonic anhydrase inhibitor, produces a metabolic acidosis which can stimulate the respiratory drive. Its use acutely may be beneficial to assist in weaning a patient from the ventilator. Progestins sometimes are used as respiratory stimulants. Progesterone can cause hyperventilation and helps to lower alveolar carbon dioxide tension. Ventilatory responses to hypercapnia and hypoxia while patients are taking progestational agents are variable and not documented extensively in patients with COAD. The mechanism of action of progestins is thought to be related to stimulation of the CNS respiratory center. Onset occurs within 48 hours of administration with maximal benefits within seven days. Potential adverse effects of progesterone therapy include impotence, fluid retention, weight gain, and thromboembolism. A starting dose of a medroxyprogesterone would be 20 mg three times a day.

Obstructive Sleep Apnea

Signs and Symptoms

19. B.V., a 37-year-old morbidly obese (170 kg) male, is brought in by his family for evaluation. They state that he is extremely sleepy during the day with frequent spontaneous naps. Although he sleeps alone, his family states that he snores very loudly, sometimes disturbing the sleep of everyone else in the house. He also frequently awakens with headaches in the morning. Upon examination, he has tachycardia at a rate of 120 beats/min with regular rhythm, an enlarged heart shadow, bilateral pitting edema, and an Hct of 52% (Normal: 40–48). An arterial blood gas assessment shows pH 7.37, pO_2 50 mm Hg, pCO_2 60 mm Hg, and oxygen saturation 85%. What features of sleep apnea are present? [SI units: Hct 0.52; pO_2 6.67 kPa; pCO_2 8.0 kPa]

Sleep apnea is a breathing disorder characterized by frequent and prolonged pauses (complete cessation) in breathing that occur during sleep. Clinically important apnea periods generally last more than 15 seconds, occur repeatedly (>30 apnea episodes/night), and are associated with major reductions in arterial oxygen saturation. Three general types are described: central apnea, obstructive apnea, and mixed apnea. This syndrome is caused by disturbances of various mechanisms which maintain airway patency during sleep. Central apnea occurs because of cessation of CNS-mediated expiratory effort. There is decreased responsiveness to elevated CNS carbon dioxide concentrations (hypercapnia), although normal responses to hypoxia are retained. During central apnea episodes, both inspiration and expiration are absent. Obstructive apnea occurs because of an occlusion in the upper airway (e.g., pharyngeal collapse) preventing airflow. There is normal inspiration (CNS-mediated) with an absence of expiration. Many patients will exhibit mixed sleep apnea syndromes characterized by both obstructive and CNS components. A formal sleep study or polysomnogram is required to determine the etiology.

Typical symptoms of sleep apnea syndrome include alterations in sleep pattern (sleep fragmentation) with loud snoring, excessive daytime sleepiness, personality changes, morning headaches, erratic behavior, and severe shortness of breath with exertion. Sleepmates may describe episodes of no breathing followed by a heavy grunting snore as hypoxia finally stimulates breathing or the patient partially awakens. Obesity is a common feature. Objective signs are reduced sleep latency on electroencephalogram (EEG), pulmonary hypertension, hypoxemia, polycythemia, and hypertension.

Nearly all of the classic subjective symptoms, except for personality changes, are present in B.V. His blood gases show carbon dioxide retention and his hematocrit is elevated in an attempt to increase oxygen-carrying capacity in the blood. EEG studies have not been performed.

During apnea periods, the arterial oxygen saturation falls and leads to local vasoconstriction in the lungs due to hypoxemia. Vasoconstriction leads to pulmonary hypertension which ultimately leads to right-sided heart failure and then left-sided heart failure. This explains the enlarged heart shadow and tachycardia noted in B.V.

Management

20. How should B.V.'s sleep apnea be managed?

Management of sleep apnea involves removal of precipitating factors, continuous positive airway breathing, pharmacologic intervention, and surgery.[82–85] Simple measures should be tried first. Patient's medications should be reviewed since respiratory depressants may worsen the problem. If possible, antihistamines, sedatives, hypnotics, or alcohol should be discontinued. Other secondary causes also should be ruled out including hypothyroidism and congestive heart failure. None of these causes are apparent in B.V.

Obstructive apnea can be improved by general weight loss. Surgical procedures directed towards bypassing the obstruction or preventing collapse of the tissue at the site of obstruction have been used. For example, a tracheostomy bypasses the occlusion in the upper airway, but is not well accepted by patients because of cosmetic or psychological reasons. Tracheostomy usually is reserved for patients who fail more conservative management. Another procedure, called a uvulopalatopharyngoplasty, involves surgical excision of excessive tissue in the oropharynx. Although this procedure has been used in some patients, it is associated with some morbidity and has fallen out of favor in recent years.

For central apnea, respiratory stimulants may have some benefit, although there are limited data in this area. Medroxyprogesterone acetate (Provera) is a progestational hormone known to have respiratory stimulant properties in women during pregnancy. It may increase ventilatory response to both hypercapnia and hypoxia. It has been evaluated in a limited number of sleep apnea patients in doses of 60 to 120 mg/day in three divided doses, but most patients have shown no difference in the number of nighttime apneic episodes when comparing baseline periods before therapy to active treatment with medroxyprogesterone.[89,91] It appears that normocapneic patients do not benefit, while those with hypercapnia may be more responsive secondary to an improved respiratory drive.[83] Originally it was recommended to give this drug buccally because of concern over high first-pass metabolic clearance, but it now is recognized that standard oral therapy is satisfactory. Side effects of medroxyprogesterone include sodium retention, weight gain, impotence in men, breast enlargement or tenderness, and a possible increased risk of thromboembolism. Protriptyline (Vivactil), a partially CNS-activating tricyclic antidepressant, has shown some promise in reducing obstructive sleep apnea.[92,93] In general, patients with the fewest apneic episodes tend to respond to treatment. The major effect of protriptyline may be suppression of REM sleep resulting in fewer REM-related apneic episodes. Protriptyline may be useful in patients with mild disease when weight loss is not possible or has not proven beneficial. A starting dose of 10 mg at bedtime is recommended with upward adjustments of 5 to 10 mg every three weeks until response is seen or until adverse anticholinergic effects (e.g., dry mouth, urinary retention, tachycardia) become intolerable.[94] (Also see Question 18 for information on other CNS and respiratory stimulant drugs.)

Acetazolamide (Diamox), a carbonic anhydrase inhibitor that produces metabolic acidosis and thus induces hyperventilation, also has been used to treat central sleep apnea. When evaluated over a one- to two-week period in six subjects, acetazolamide at a dose of 250 mg four times a day was effective in substantially reducing apneic episodes.[90] However, long-term efficacy is unknown and may be limited since the body's compensatory buffering system generally corrects for the drug-induced metabolic acidosis.

Currently, the primary method of managing sleep apnea, and the one indicated for B.V., is the use of continuous positive airway pressure (CPAP). This involves having the patient sleep with a nasal cannula or a mask connected to a mechanical device that delivers air or oxygen to the patient's nose throughout the night at greater than atmospheric pressure. The elevated pressure helps to prevent airway collapse and obstruction. CPAP is relatively non-invasive and often is associated with a rapid response for the patient. Symptoms of daytime sleepiness and secondary complications, such as pulmonary hypertension, dramatically improve. Adverse effects of CPAP include feelings of suffocation, excessive nasal drying, gas due to swallowed air, and conjunctivitis. While limiting patient tolerance of the procedure, these adverse effects are not contraindications to the use of CPAP.

Update

Gastroesophageal Reflux in COAD Patients

U1. C.T. is a 62-year-old male with severe, end-stage COAD currently managed with pirbuterol inhaler, 2 puffs Q 4–6 hr, ipratropium 4 puffs Q 4 hr, Theodur 200 mg BID, and prednisone 7.5 mg/day. He also uses home oxygen therapy at 1 L/min. His baseline arterial blood gases are pH 7.36, pO_2 of 58 mm Hg (on oxygen), and pCO_2 of 50 mm Hg. His FEV_1 is 0.9 L and FVC is 1.6 L. He has complaints of gastroesophageal reflux, especially upon reclining, and worsening dyspnea for which he uses his pirbuterol Q 3–4 hr. A theophylline serum concentration is measured and reported as 11 µg/mL. What is the relationship of gastroesophageal reflux to C.T.'s COAD and his drug therapy?

C.T.'s symptoms of gastroesophageal reflux may be exacerbated by his theophylline therapy and his chronic oral corticosteroid use. Methylxanthines can decrease lower esophageal sphincter tone and worsen gastroesophageal reflux. Chronic oral steroid use may contribute to gastritis. Although his theophylline is in the therapeutic range, the risk-benefit ratio of therapy should be assessed. A trial of theophylline discontinuation may be warranted to determine if objective or subjective improvement in reflux symptoms or worsening of pulmonary function occurs. An attempt should be made to reduce the oral prednisone dose or to convert C.T. to an inhaled corticosteroid.[96,97]

The majority of patients using metered-dose inhaler therapies exhibit inadequate or improper technique.[98,99] Elderly patients are particularly susceptible to this problem due to decreased cognitive ability, or comorbid conditions (stroke, arthritis). C.T.'s inhaler technique should be assessed. Periodic observation and reinstruction about MDI technique frequently is necessary. The use of a reservoir holding chamber may be helpful if problems are detected. A breath-actuated inhaler may be preferred by some patients with COAD.[100]

Use of Salmeterol in COAD

U-2. Would C.T. benefit from the use of a long-acting inhaled beta-agonist like salmeterol?

The role of long-acting inhaled beta-agonists (salmeterol) in COAD is unclear.[101] Large, multicenter clinical trials assessing the benefit of this therapy currently are underway.[102] Based upon C.T.'s frequent use of pirbuterol, and the possibility of discontinuing theophylline therapy, a trial of salmeterol could be attempted. C.T. should be counseled that salmeterol is used on a scheduled basis, every 12 hours, but not for symptomatic relief of acute symptoms. He should continue to use pirbuterol as needed for acute exacerbations. Current recommendations are that pirbuterol use should not exceed 4 inhalations daily in this regimen.

References

1. **National Center for Health Statistics.** Monthly vital statistics report. 13 May 1994;42(12).

2. **Berwick DM.** Shifting U.S. mortality patterns. MMWR. 1993;42:891,897–900.

3. **Chronic Disease Reports.** Chronic obstructive pulmonary disease mortality–United States, 1986. MMWR. 1989;38:549–52.

4. **Anthonisen NR.** Prognosis in chronic obstructive pulmonary disease: results from multicenter clinical trials. Am Rev Respir Dis. 1989;140:S95–S99.

5. **Higgins M.** Epidemiology of COPD: state of the art. Chest. 1984;85(Suppl.):3S.

6. **Edelman NH et al.** Chronic obstructive pulmonary disease. Chest. 1992;102(3):243S–256S.

7. **Owens GR.** Public screening for lung disease: experience with the NIH lung health study. Am J Med. 1991;91(Suppl. 4A):37S–40S.

8. **Cooreman J et al.** Mortality from chronic obstructive pulmonary diseases and asthma in France, 1969–1983: comparison with the United States and Canada. Chest. 1990;97(1):213–19.

9. **Ferguson GT, Cherniack RM.** Management of chronic obstructive pulmonary disease. N Engl J Med. 1993;328:1017–022.

10. **American Thoracic Society.** Standards for the diagnosis and care of patients with chronic obstructive pulmonary disease (COPD) and asthma. Am Rev Respir Dis. 1987;136:225–43.

11. **Anthonisen NR et al.** Prognosis in chronic obstructive pulmonary disease. Am Rev Respir Dis. 1986;133:14.

12. **Medici TC et al.** Smoking pattern of smokers with and without tobacco-smoke related lung diseases. Am Rev Respir Dis. 1985;131:385.

13. **Official Statement of the American Thoracic Society, Medical Section of the American Lung Association.** Cigarette smoking and health. Am Rev Respir Dis. 1985;132:1133.

14. **Kesten S, Rebuck AS.** Management of chronic obstructive pulmonary disease. Drugs. 1989;38(1):160–74.

15. **Skorodin MS.** Pharmacotherapy for asthma and chronic obstructive pulmonary disease. Arch Intern Med. 1993;153:814–28.

16. **DeYoung GR et al.** The pharmacological treatment of ambulatory chronic obstructive pulmonary disease patients. J Pharm Practice. 1992;V(4):204–16.

17. **Weinberger SE.** Recent advances in pulmonary medicine. N Engl J Med. 1993;328(19):1389–398.

18. **Chapman KR.** Therapeutic algorithm for chronic obstructive pulmonary disease. Am J Med. 1991;91(Suppl. 4A):17S–23S.

19. **Martin JG.** Clinical intervention in chronic respiratory failure. Chest. 1990;97(3):105S–110S.

20. **Derenne JP et al.** Acute respiratory failure of chronic obstructive pulmonary disease. Am Rev Respir Dis. 1988;138:1006–033.

21. **Erbland ML et al.** Interaction of hypoxia and hypercapnia on respiratory drive in patients with COPD. Chest. 1990;97(6):1289–294.

22. **Weinberger SE et al.** Mechanisms of disease: hypercapnia. N Engl J Med. 1989;321(18):1223–231.

23. **Smith K et al.** Respiratory muscle training for chronic airflow limitation: a meta-analysis. Am Rev Respir Dis. 1992;145:533–39.

24. **Wilson DO et al.** Nutrition and chronic lung disease. Am Rev Respir Dis. 1985;132:1347–365.

25. **Irwin RS, Curley FJ.** The treatment of cough: a comprehensive review. Chest. 1991;99(6):1477–484.

26. **Tobin MJ.** Dyspnea: pathophysiologic basis, clinical presentation, and management. Arch Intern Med. 1990;150:1604–613.

27. **Pratter MR, Bartter T.** Dyspnea: time to find the facts. Chest. 1991;100(5):1187.

28. **O'Donnell DE, Webb KA.** Breathlessness in patients with severe chronic airflow limitation: physiologic correlations. Chest. 1992;102(3):824–31.

29. **Belman MJ et al.** Variability of breathlessness measurement in patients with chronic obstructive pulmonary disease. Chest. 1991;99(3):566–71.

30 **Mahler DA et al.** Sustained-release theophylline reduces dyspnea in non-reversible obstructive airway disease. Am Rev Respir Dis. 1985;131:22.

31 **Nisar M et al.** Acute bronchodilator trials in chronic obstructive pulmonary disease. Am Rev Resp Dis. 1992;146:555–59.

32 **Nisar M et al.** Assessment of reversibility of airway obstruction in patients with chronic obstructive airways disease. Thorax. 1990;45:190–94.

33 **Anthonisen NR et al.** Bronchodilator response in chronic obstructive pulmonary disease. Am Rev Respir Dis. 1986;133:184.

34 **Eliasson O, DeGraff AC Jr.** The use of criteria for reversibility and obstruction to define patient groups for bronchodilator trials. Am Rev Respir Dis. 1985;132:858.

35 **Anthonisen NR et al.** Bronchodilator response in chronic obstructive pulmonary disease. Am Rev Respir Dis. 1986;133:814–19.

36 **Petty TL.** The National Mucolytic Study: results of a double-blind, placebo-controlled study of iodinated glycerol in chronic obstructive bronchitis. Chest. 1990;97:75.

37 **Callahan CM et al.** Oral corticosteroid therapy for patients with stable chronic obstructive pulmonary disease: a meta-analysis. Ann Intern Med. 1991;114(3):216–23.

38 **Murata GH et al.** Intravenous and oral corticosteroids for the prevention of relapse after treatment of decompensated COPD: effect on patients with a history of multiple relapses. Chest. 1990;98(4):845–49.

39 **Hudson LD, Monti CM.** Rationale and use of corticosteroids in chronic obstructive pulmonary disease. Med Clin North Am. 1990;74(3):661–91.

40 **Weir DC et al.** Time course of response to oral and inhaled corticosteroids in non-asthmatic chronic airflow obstruction. Thorax. 1990;45:118–21.

41 **Gross NJ.** The influence of anticholinergic agents on treatment for bronchitis and emphysema. Am J Med. 1991;91(Suppl. 4A):11S–12S.

42 **Emerman CL et al.** A randomized controlled trial of methylprednisolone in the emergency treatment of acute exacerbations of COPD. Chest. 1989;95(3):563–67.

43 **Eliasson O et al.** Corticosteroids in COPD: a clinical trial and reassessment of the literature. Chest. 1986;89:484.

44 **Mendella LA et al.** Steroid response in stable chronic airflow limitation. Ann Intern Med. 1982;96:17.

45 **Dolce JJ et al.** Medication adherence patterns in chronic obstructive pulmonary disease. Chest. 1991;99(4):837–41.

46 **Albert RK et al.** Controlled clinical trial of methylprednisolone in patients with chronic bronchitis and acute respiratory insufficiency. Ann Intern Med. 1980;92:753.

47 **Shim C et al.** Response to corticosteroids in chronic bronchitis. J Allergy Clin Immunol. 1978;62:363–67.

48 **Murata GH et al.** Aminophylline in the outpatient management of decompensated chronic obstructive pulmonary disease. Chest. 1990;98(6):1346–349.

49 **Vaz Fragoso CA, Miller MA.** Review of the clinical efficacy of theophylline in the treatment of chronic obstructive pulmonary disease. Am Rev Respir Dis. 1993;147:540–47.

50 **Lam A, Newhouse MT.** Management of asthma and chronic airflow limitation: are methylxanthines obsolete? Chest. 1990;98(1):44–52.

51 **Nishimura K et al.** Is oral theophylline effective in combination with both inhaled anticholinergic agent and inhaled β_2-agonist in the treatment of stable COPD? Chest. 1993;104(1):179–84.

52 **Haxby D.** Treatment of nicotine dependence. Am J Health-Syst Pharm. 1995;52:265.

53 **Chetty KG et al.** Conversion of COPD patients from multiple to single dose theophylline: serum levels and symptoms comparisons. Chest. 1991;100(4):1064–067.

54 **Aubier M et al.** Aminophylline improves diaphragmatic contractility. N Engl J Med. 1981;305(5):249–52.

55 **Rice KL et al.** Aminophylline for acute exacerbations of chronic obstructive pulmonary disease. Ann Intern Med. 1987;107:305–09.

56 **Eaton ML et al.** Effects of theophylline in "irreversible" airflow obstruction. Ann Intern Med. 1980;92:758.

57 **Eaton ML et al.** Effects of theophylline on breathlessness and exercise tolerance in patients with chronic airflow obstruction. Chest. 1982;82:538.

58 **Murciano D et al.** A randomized controlled trial of theophylline in patients with severe chronic obstructive pulmonary disease. N Engl J Med. 1989;320:1521.

59 **Au WY et al.** Theophylline kinetics in chronic obstructive airway disease in the elderly. Clin Pharmacol Ther. 1985;37:472.

60 **Hill NS.** The use of theophylline in "irreversible" chronic obstructive pulmonary disease. Arch Intern Med. 1988;148:2579–584.

61 **Klinger JR, Hill NS.** Right ventricular dysfunction in chronic obstructive pulmonary disease: evaluation and management. Chest. 1991;99(3):715–23.

62 **Medical Research Council Working Party.** Long-term domiciliary oxygen therapy in chronic hypoxic cor pulmonale complicating chronic bronchitis and emphysema. Lancet. 1981;1:681.

63 **Hodgkin JE, ed.** Chronic obstructive pulmonary disease. Clin Chest Med. 1990;11:363–569.

64 **Anthonisen NR et al.** Prognosis in chronic obstructive pulmonary disease. Am Rev Respir Dis. 1986;133:14–20.

65 **Skwarski K et al.** Predictors of survival in patients with chronic obstructive pulmonary disease treated with long-term oxygen therapy. Chest. 1991;100(6):1522–527.

66 **Groves RH et al.** Long-term oxygen therapy. Chest. 1991;100:544–49.

67 **Ashutosh K et al.** Early effects of oxygen administration and prognosis in chronic obstructive pulmonary disease and cor pulmonale. Am Rev Respir Dis. 1983;127:399.

68 **Nocturnal Oxygen Therapy Trial Group.** Continuous or nocturnal oxygen therapy in hypoxemic chronic obstructive lung disease. Ann Intern Med. 1980;93:391.

69 **McFadden ER Jr.** Clinical use of β-adrenergic agonists. J Allergy Clin Immunol. 1985;76:352.

70 **Fiore MG et al.** Tobacco dependence and the nicotine patch. JAMA. 1992;268:2687–694.

71 **Gross NJ, Skorodin MS.** Role of the parasympathetic system in airway obstruction due to emphysema. N Engl J Med. 1984;311:421.

72 **Gross NJ.** Ipratropium bromide. N Engl J Med. 1988;319(8):486–94.

73 **Karpel JP et al.** A comparison of the effects of ipratropium bromide and metaproterenol sulfate in acute exacerbations of COPD. Chest. 1990;98(4):835–39.

74 **Ashutosh K, Lang H.** Comparison between long-term treatment of chronic bronchitic airway obstruction with ipratropium bromide and metaproterenol. Ann Allergy. 1984;53:401–6.

75 **Williams JH, Moser KN.** Pneumococcal vaccine and patients with chronic lung disease. Ann Intern Med. 1986;104:106–9.

76 **van Schayck CP et al.** Two-year bronchodilator treatment in patients with mild airflow obstruction: contradictory effects on lung function and quality of life. Chest. 1992;102:1384–391.

77 **Wesseling G et al.** A comparison of the effects of anticholinergic and β_2-agonist and combination therapy on respiratory impedance in COPD. Chest. 1992;101(1):166–73.

78 **Kerstjens HAM et al.** A comparison of bronchodilator therapy with or without inhaled corticosteroid therapy for obstructive airways disease. N Engl J Med. 1992;327(20):1413–419.

79 **Kerstjens HAM et al.** Variability of bronchodilator response and effects of inhaled corticosteroid treatment in obstructive airways disease. Thorax. 1993;48:722–29.

80 **Filuk RB et al.** Responses to large doses of salbutamol and theophylline in patients with chronic obstructive pulmonary disease. Am Rev Respir Dis. 1985;132:871.

81 **Galko BM, Rebuck AS.** Therapeutic use of respiratory stimulants: an overview of newer developments. Drugs. 1985;30:475–81.

82 **Hudgel DW.** Mechanisms of obstructive sleep apnea. Chest. 1992;101:541–49.

83 **Rajagopal KR et al.** Effects of medroxyprogesterone acetate in obstructive sleep apnea. Chest. 1986;90(6):815–20.

84 **Fletcher EC, Munafo DA.** Role of nocturnal oxygen therapy in obstructive sleep apnea: when should it be used? Chest. 1990;98:1497–504.

85 **Series F, Cormier Y.** Effects of protriptyline on diurnal and nocturnal oxygenation in patients with chronic obstructive pulmonary disease. Ann Intern Med. 1990;113:507–11.

86 **Stogner SW, Payne DK.** Oxygen toxicity. Ann Pharmacother. 1992;26:1554–562.

87 **National Center for Health Statistics.** Monthly vital statistics report. 24 Aug 1987;35(13).

88 **Fiore M et al.** The effectiveness of the nicotine patch for smoking cessation: a meta-analysis. JAMA. 1994;271:1940.

89 **Dolly FR, Block AJ.** Medroxyprogesterone acetate and COPD. Effect on breathing and oxygenation in sleeping and awake patients. Chest. 1983;84:394.

90 **White DP et al.** Central sleep apnea: improvement with acetazolamide therapy. Arch Intern Med. 1982;142;1816.

91 **Strohl KP et al.** Progesterone administration and progressive sleep apneas. JAMA. 1981;245:1230.

92 **Conway WA et al.** Protriptyline in the treatment of sleep apnea. Thorax. 1982;37:49.

93 **Brownell LG et al.** Protriptyline in obstructive sleep apnea: a double-blind trial. N Engl J Med. 1982;307:1037.

94 **Lombard RM Jr, Zwillich CW.** Medical therapy of obstructive sleep apnea. Med Clin North Am. 1985;69:1317.

95 **Guenter CA, Welch MH.** Pulmonary Medicine. Philadelphia, PA: JB Lippincott Co.; 1982.

96 **Weir DC, Burge PS.** Effects of high dose inhaled beclomethasone dipropionate, 750 mcg and 1500 mcg twice daily, and 40 mg per day oral prednisolone on lung function, symptoms, and bronchial hyperresponsiveness in patients with nonasthmatic chronic airflow obstruction. Thorax. 1993;48:309–16.

97 **Dompeling E et al.** Slowing the deterioration asthma and chronic obstructive pulmonary disease observed during bronchodilator therapy by adding inhaled corticosteroids. Ann Intern Med. 1993;118:770–78.

98 **Crompton GK.** The adult patient's difficulties with inhalers. Lung. 1990; Suppl 1:658–662.

99 **Goodman DE.** The influence of age, diagnosis, and gender on proper use of metered-dose inhalers. Am J Respir Crit Care Med. 1994;150:1256–61.

100 **Chapman KR et al.** A comparison of breath-actuated and conventional metered-dose inhaler inhalation techniques in elderly subjects. Chest. 1993;104:1332–37.

101 **Deltorre L et al.** Effectiveness of salmeterol in patients with emphysema. Curr Ther Res. 1992;52:888–98.

102 **Cazzola M et al.** Effect of salmeterol and formoterol in patients with chronic obstructive pulmonary disease. Pulm Pharmacol. 1994;70:103–7.

Acute and Chronic Rhinitis

Pamela A Simon

Prevalence 21-1
Applied Anatomy and Physiology of the Nose
    (See Figure 21.1) 21-1
Diagnosis and Assessment of Rhinitis 21-2
    History (See Tables 21.1 and 21.2) 21-3
    Physical examination 21-3
    Laboratory tests 21-3
Classification of Rhinitis (See Table 21.3) 21-3
Allergic Rhinitis 21-4
Pathophysiology (See Figure 21.2) 21-4
Perennial Allergic Rhinitis 21-5
    Signs and symptoms 21-5
    Diagnosis (Also see Question 4) 21-5
    Drug effects upon skin testing (See Table 21.4) 21-6
    Therapeutic objectives (See Figure 21.3) 21-7
    Nonpharmacologic therapy 21-7
        Avoidance 21-7
        Exercise 21-7
        Saline irrigation 21-7
    H_1-receptor antagonists 21-7
        Pharmacokinetics and pharmacodynamics 21-7
        Comparison of various drugs (See Table 21.6) 21-9
        Dosage titration (See Table 21.7) 21-10
        Safety in asthma 21-10
        Adverse effects 21-10
        Second-generation H_1-receptor antagonists 21-11
        Tolerance 21-11
            Cardiotoxicity and drug interactions 21-12
    Decongestants 21-10
        Dosing (See Table 21.6) 21-10
        Adverse effects 21-10
    Intranasal corticosteroids 21-12

Choice of agent (See Table 21.7) 21-13
    Patient education 21-13
    Adverse effects 21-14
Systemic corticosteroids 21-14
Immunotherapy 21-14
Seasonal Allergic Rhinitis 21-15
    Diagnosis 21-15
    Therapeutic objectives 21-16
    Intranasal cromolyn sodium 21-16
        Dosing and patient education 21-16
        Adverse reactions 21-16
        Treatment failure 21-16
Vasomotor Rhinitis 21-16
Signs and Symptoms 21-16
Treatment 21-17
    Nonpharmacologic therapy 21-17
    Pharmacotherapy 21-17
Eosinophilic Nonallergic Rhinitis 21-17
Signs and Symptoms 21-17
Pharmacotherapy 21-18
Viral Upper Respiratory Infection 21-18
Signs and Symptoms 21-18
Pharmacotherapy 21-18
    H_1-receptor antagonists 21-19
    Decongestants 21-19
    Antitussives 21-19
    Expectorants 21-19
    Analgesics and antipyretics 21-19
Drug-Induced Nasal Congestion 21-19
Clinical Presentation and Drugs Capable of Causing
    Nasal Disease (See Table 21.10) 21-19
Management 21-20

Prevalence

Rhinitis is defined as inflammation of the nasal mucous membranes and is characterized by periods of nasal discharge, sneezing, and congestion.[1] Allergic rhinitis is the fifth most prevalent chronic condition in the U.S., affecting over 24 million people, and is the most prevalent chronic condition in children and adolescents under 18 years of age.[2] The condition resulted in at least one physician visit in over 70% of patients affected and was responsible for an annual average of 30 million days of restricted activity over the three-year period of 1986 to 1988 studied in the National Health Interview Survey (NHIS).[3] Related diagnoses such as nasal polyps, deviated nasal septum, and chronic disease of the tonsils and adenoids affect an additional 5.3 million Americans.[2]

The most common cause of acute rhinitis, the common cold (viral upper respiratory infection), caused over 71 million illnesses in the U.S. in 1991. Almost 40% of these conditions were attended medically, and during that year, the common cold caused Americans to miss 25 million days of work and 22.5 million days of school.[2] Clearly, acute and chronic rhinitis greatly impact the physical, economic, and educational health of the U.S.

Applied Anatomy and Physiology of the Nose

A working knowledge of the anatomy and physiology of the nose is helpful in understanding the pathology, pathophysiology, and pharmacotherapy of rhinitis. The nose has two main functions: olfaction and preparation of air for the lower respiratory tract. Its specialized anatomical and physiologic features enable it to perform these unique functions.

The nasal cavity is divided sagittally by the nasal septum and communicates externally through the anterior nares. (See Figure 21.1.) The nasal vestibule is a slight dilation just inside each naris.[5] The internal ostium, located at the proximal end of the nasal vestibule, is the point at which the upper airway is narrowest.[6] The small size of the airway at this point creates low-velocity, high turbulent air flow.[6,7] The lateral wall of the nasal cavity has three elevations extending from the internal ostium to the nasopharynx and pharynx; these are called the inferior, middle, and superior turbinates (or concha).[4,5] The protruding turbinates increase the surface area of the nasal mucosa and contribute to air flow turbulence.[6] The orifices of the sinuses and the eustachian tubes are located near the turbinates.[5,6]

The nasal mucosa lines the entire nasal cavity, except the nasal vestibule, and is most vascular over the turbinates. The olfactory region is located on the superior turbinate and the surrounding lateral wall and septum. The cells in the olfactory region are sensory receptor cells.[5] The epithelial cells throughout the posterior two-thirds of the nasal cavity (except for the cells in the olfactory region) contain cilia.[4,6] Mucous-secreting goblet cells are interspersed among the epithelial cells.[4] Within the subepithelial tissues are seromucous glands, blood vessels, and connective tissues with associated mast cells and white blood cells (WBCs) including eosinophils, lymphocytes, macrophages, and neutrophils.[4,6]

The nasal vascular bed is made up of a unique combination of resistance and capacitance vessels.[4,6] Arterioles lie just beneath the mucosal surface,[6] and because of their proximity to the mucosal surface, contribute to the warming of inspired air. These arterioles and the underlying capillaries are fenestrated (i.e., gaps exist between the arteriolar and capillary endothelial cells) which makes these vessels very porous. Extravasation of fluid from these vessels provides the moisture necessary for humidification;[4] however, excessive fluid secretion as a result of nasal disease can be the cause of rhinorrhea (''runny nose'').[4] The arterioles also play a role in the absorption of water-soluble gases, like sulfur dioxide.[6]

An extensive system of venous sinusoids lies beneath the capillary bed. Muscular sphincters at the distal ends of the nasal vascular bed and arteriovenous shunts permit blood pooling in the venous sinusoids. In this way, nasal tissue possesses the property of erectile tissue.[4,6] Noxious stimuli will initiate blood pooling causing nasal congestion, which blocks the passage of potentially toxic materials.[7] Congestion of the nasal mucosa causes the sensation of nasal stuffiness and can occlude the orifices of the sinuses and eustachian tubes leading to secondary disease.[4] Sinusitis[8] and eustachian tube dysfunction[9] can complicate acute or chronic rhinitis. Eustachian tube dysfunction can lead to acute otitis media and otitis media with effusion in some children.[9]

The autonomic nervous system controls the structures of the nose. Parasympathetic (cholinergic) stimulation of the nasal vasculature causes vasodilation, while sympathetic (primarily α-adrenergic) stimulation causes vasoconstriction. The secretory glands are stimulated directly by parasympathetic secretomotor fibers.[4,6] Sensory innervation of the nose is through the first and second branches of cranial nerve V, the trigeminal nerve. Stimulation of the sensory receptors can produce itching and sneezing.[6]

Olfaction occurs through cranial nerve I with the impulse originating in the olfactory epithelium. Stimulation of olfactory recep-

Table 21.1	Patient History Interview

1. Is the patient experiencing the common symptoms of rhinitis: Sneezing, nasal itching, nasal congestion or obstruction, an altered sense of smell (dysosmia), and anterior or posterior rhinorrhea?

2. Is the nasal discharge watery, mucoid, or purulent?

3. What color are the secretions: clear, white, yellow, green, blood-streaked, or rusty brown?

4. When did the symptoms first appear? Did they begin in infancy, childhood, or adulthood; after a viral upper respiratory infection; after a traumatic blow to the head or face; or after a change in the patient's environment (e.g., introduction of a new pet into the home)?

5. Do the symptoms occur daily, episodically, seasonally, or constantly? Has this pattern persisted for days, weeks, months, or years?

6. To what extent have the nasal symptoms interfered with the patient's lifestyle? Are they just "annoying" or are they actually "disabling"? "Disabling" symptoms can interfere with sleep, cause incessant nose rubbing and blowing, interfere with work or school, and cause emotional disturbances.

7. Are there factors or conditions that precipitate symptoms, such as specific allergens, inhaled irritants, climatic conditions, and foods or drinks?

8. It is also important to elucidate the patient's family, environmental, and social histories. Are other members of the patient's family or household suffering from similar symptoms?

9. Are there household furnishings that could retain large amounts of dust (e.g., carpets, heavy drapes, foam or feather pillows, or stuffed toys)? What are the housecleaning habits in the household?

10. Does the patient or other members of the household smoke? Tobacco smoke will often aggravate rhinitis regardless of the etiology.

11. What is the patient's occupation and what type of leisure activities does he engage in?

tors initiates an autonomic reflex arc which causes secretion by the salivary, gastric, and pancreatic glands.[6] A decreased sense of smell (hyposmia) and, in severe cases, a total loss of smell (anosmia) are possible complications of acute or chronic rhinitis.[4]

The nose processes air for the lower airways. As previously described, the extensive and specialized nasal vasculature humidifies and warms inspired air. Foreign matter is removed through filtration, mucociliary clearance, and immunologic responses.[4,6] Filtration occurs when foreign particles are deposited on the large surface area of the turbinates, where low-velocity, turbulent air flow encourages particle deposition. Also, the thin layer of mucous covering the nasal mucosa traps virtually all particles ten micrometers and larger,[6] and approximately 80% of particles five to ten micrometers in size.[6,7] The beating cilia on the epithelial cells of the underlying nasal mucosa move the mucous layer toward the posterior nasopharynx at a rate of 8 to 10 mm/minute.[4,7] Therefore, the system is able to clear particles in 10 to 15 minutes.[4]

The tonsils and adenoids, areas dense in lymphatic tissue, are located in the oral pharynx where the particulate-laden mucous ultimately accumulates. The ability of the lymphoid tissue to produce and secrete immunoglobulins may play a role in the immunologic defenses of the upper airway, but this remains unclear.[6] The mucous of the nasal cavity is concentrated with immunoglobulins, particularly IgA.[6,10] Enzymes such as lysozyme also may play a role in inactivating or neutralizing foreign material.[4,10] There clearly exists an IgE-mediated local allergic response to inhaled allergens in sensitized patients.[7,8] The nature of this response will be discussed in detail later.

Diagnosis and Assessment of Rhinitis

Because it is difficult to measure nasal function in a completely satisfactory manner, the specific etiology of rhinitis is based upon

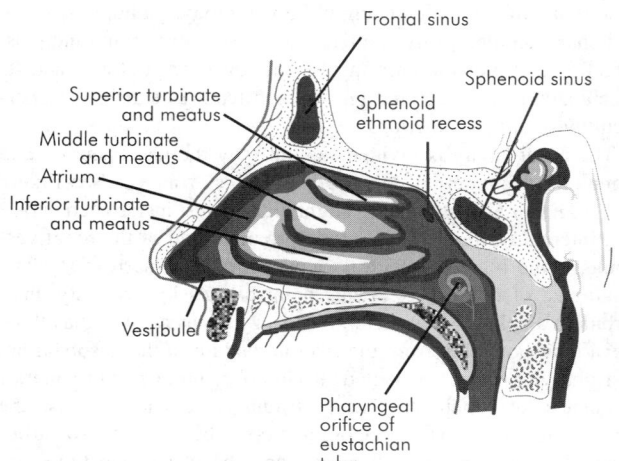

Frontal sinus

Sphenoid sinus

Superior turbinate and meatus

Sphenoid ethmoid recess

Middle turbinate and meatus

Atrium

Inferior turbinate and meatus

Vestibule

Pharyngeal orifice of eustachian tube

Fig 21.1   Sagittal View of the Nose   Reprinted with permission from reference 7.

a carefully obtained patient history, physical examination, and a limited number of relevant laboratory examinations. The pharmacist's contribution to patient evaluation is the thorough medication history.

History

The history should include the character, onset, frequency, duration, and severity of the patient's symptoms.[4,11] (See Table 21.1.) All of the questions listed in Table 21.1 may help uncover the etiology of the rhinitis and, therefore, the proper course of therapy.

Finally, data must be obtained pertaining to the patient's past medical history, current illnesses or conditions, and all past and present medications. (See Table 21.2.)

Physical Examination

The patient's nose can be inspected for nasal patency, position of the septum, appearance of the nasal mucosa (especially over the turbinates), quantity and appearance of secretions, and the presence of abnormal growths.[12] A gross measure of nasal patency and air flow can be accomplished by asking the patient to alternately occlude each nostril and breathe through the open nostril. After preliminary examination, nasal application of a topical vasoconstrictor (e.g., phenylephrine 0.25% to 1% or oxymetazoline 0.025% to 0.05%) often is necessary to permit visualization of the entire nasal passageway. The patient's facial structures are examined since chronic mouth breathing can cause recognizable facial characteristics and dental abnormalities.[13] The patient's eyes, ears (utilizing a pneumatic otoscope and possibly a tympanometer), pharynx, sinuses, and chest also are examined.[12] Gross examination of the expelled mucous for color and clarity may be helpful.

Laboratory Tests

Laboratory examination should include a cytologic analysis of a smear of nasal secretions. Nasal smears generally are considered to be a clinically useful tool in the classification of patients with rhinitis when the results are correlated with patient history and physical examination.[6,12] This test involves light microscopic examination of properly stained nasal secretions obtained by blowing the nose into waxed paper, wiping out the nose with a cotton-tipped swab, or aspirating the nose for a sample. This test is useful, particularly to qualitatively and quantitatively evaluate the extent of nasal eosinophilia which is graded from 0 (no eosinophils present) to 4+ [mean: >20 eosinophils present per ten high power fields (hpfs)].[12] Often, 50% to 100% of WBCs in nasal secretions will be eosinophils in patients with allergic rhinitis who recently have been exposed to allergens.[14] Nasal eosinophilia also can occur in patients with nasal polyps[15] and eosinophilic nonallergic rhinitis.[16]

Attempts have been made to use nasal secretion smears to quantify basophils or mast cells and correlate these numbers to clinical disease. Although more of these cell types are present in patients with allergic rhinitis than in normal subjects, there are far fewer of these cells present than eosinophils. A nasal smear, therefore, is a very specific test for detection of basophils and mast cells, but

Table 21.2	Patient History Interview: Part II

1. Does the patient have other medical conditions that can cause primary and secondary nasal symptoms (e.g., pregnancy or immunodeficiency syndrome)?

2. Is the patient taking medications that might cause or aggravate nasal symptoms? See Drug-Induced Nasal Congestion in text.

3. What prescription and nonprescription drugs have been used for the nasal symptoms in the past? Were they effective? Did the patient experience side effects?

Table 21.3	Possible Etiologies of Acute and Chronic Rhinitis	
Acute	**Chronic**	

Infectious
  viral (common cold)
  bacterial
	Allergic rhinitis
	  seasonal ("hay fever")
	  perennial	

Foreign body	Nonallergic perennial rhinitis
	  vasomotor rhinitis
	  eosinophilic nonallergic rhinitis	

Drug-induced (*rhinitis medicamentosa*)		
Hypothyroidism	Tumors	
Pregnancy	Choanal atresia	
	Nasal septal deviation	
	Nasal polyps	
	Enlarged adenoids and tonsils	
	Chronic sinusitis	
	CSF rhinorrhea	

poorly sensitive for clinically differentiating patients with disease from those without disease.[6,12]

Nasal smears also are examined for the presence of large numbers of neutrophils, bacteria, and phagocytized bacteria. The presence of such cells implies infection; however, the precise location of the infection (i.e., nasopharyngitis versus sinusitis) and whether the infectious process is primary or secondary in nature often cannot be determined.[6,12]

Other diagnostic tests may include rhinomanometry (the measurement of nasal airflow), sinus x-rays, skin testing, radioallergosorbent testing (RAST), and pulmonary function examination (spirometry).[12]

Classification of Rhinitis

Table 21.3 lists the possible etiologies of acute and chronic rhinitis. Strictly speaking, some of the items in Table 21.3 are not causes of rhinitis but disorders (e.g., nasal septal deviation, foreign body) that cause symptoms that mimic the inflammatory disorders of the nose.

The most common cause of acute rhinitis is viral upper respiratory infection or the common cold.[7] Bacterial infection can be a primary illness or may be secondary to a primary viral illness; it should be considered if acute "cold-like" symptoms persist for more than five to seven days.[4] Foreign bodies usually cause unilateral symptoms and are common in young children and institutionalized patients.[17] Hypothyroidism causes vasomotor rhinitis symptoms due to a reduction in the amount of circulating sympathomimetic thyroid hormone[18] or hypersecretion into the nasopharyngeal mucosa.[19] Vasomotor rhinitis of pregnancy is a result of direct stimulation by acetylcholine[19,20] or inhibition of acetylcholinesterase by estrogen.[21]

Atopy (an inherited tendency to develop a clinical hypersensitivity condition) is the most common cause of chronic rhinitis. Many other causes of chronic rhinitis primarily are treated surgically, not medically. These include intranasal tumors which usually are benign (e.g., papillomas, skin tumors), but can be malignant (e.g., squamous cell carcinoma, melanoma, and non-Hodgkin's lymphoma),[22] and choanal atresia, a congenital anomaly characterized by the absence of the opening from the nasal cavity into the nasopharynx on one or both sides.[23] The chronic obstructive etiologies of nasal symptoms (e.g., nasal septal deviation, tumors, choanal atresia, and some cases of nasal polyps) often present as constant unilateral symptoms rather than episodic bilateral symptoms.[12]

Chronic sinusitis or recurrent acute sinusitis may be responsible for symptoms in up to one-fourth of patients with chronic rhinitis. Chronic sinusitis can occur as a primary disease or as a secondary complication of other nasal disorders (e.g., allergic rhinitis, foreign body) or systemic disorders (e.g., hypogammaglobulinemia).[7]

Cerebrospinal fluid (CSF) rhinorrhea is caused by communication between the subarachnoid space and the nose which permits leakage of CSF. This disorder most often has a traumatic origin, usually as a result of fracture of the cribriform plate of the ethmoid bone causing a tear in the meninges. CSF rhinorrhea also can occur spontaneously. Patients with fistula formation are at risk for meningitis and all of its potential complications.[24]

Allergic Rhinitis
Pathophysiology

Allergic rhinitis is defined as nasal mucous membrane inflammation caused by a hypersensitivity response to foreign allergens mediated by IgE antibodies. Patients with allergic rhinitis have been sensitized to one or more airborne allergens and have antigen-specific IgE antibodies bound to receptors on mast cells and basophils.[8] (See Figure 21.2.) When the nasal mucosa is re-exposed to the allergens, mast cells and basophils degranulate releasing preformed chemical mediators including histamine, leukotriene C_4 (LTC_4), prostaglandin D_2 (PGD_2), and chemotactic factors.[8,25] Disruption of the mast and basophilic cell membranes generates the production and release of arachidonic acid metabolites: 5-lipoxygenase converts arachidonic acid to the leukotrienes (LTC_4,

LTD_4, LTE_4); cyclo-oxygenase produces prostaglandins, prostacyclines, and thromboxanes.[25] When histamine interacts with the H_1-receptor, it stimulates all of the clinical symptoms of allergic rhinitis: itching and sneezing (caused by stimulation of H_1-receptors on sensory nerve endings mediated by a reflex arc), rhinorrhea (due to increased vascular permeability and glandular secretion), and congestion (due to vasodilation and tissue edema).[25] The other mediators primarily cause congestion and rhinorrhea.

Histamine and the other preformed and generated mediators produce an immediate response, the *early-phase reaction* of the biphasic response to antigen challenge, in over 90% of patients with a history of allergic rhinitis and positive skin tests. The early-phase reaction starts within two to ten minutes of allergen exposure and lasts 30 to 90 minutes.[8] Four to eight hours after exposure, some of the inflammatory mediators reappear and nasal symptoms recur as a result of the *late-phase reaction* in approximately 50% of patients with seasonal allergic rhinitis.[8] Histamine alone is not able to induce the late-phase reaction[25] which is characterized by cellular infiltration, predominantly of eosinophils, basophils, neutrophils, and mononuclear cells.[8] The late-phase reaction is associated with hyperresponsiveness to inhaled irritants and allergens and has been linked to the development of chronic disease.[8] The biphasic response seen in allergic rhinitis is analogous to that seen in asthma. This similarity in pathophysiology probably explains the coexistence of allergic rhinitis and asthma in many patients. (Also see Chapter 19: Asthma.)

The drugs used to treat allergic rhinitis each act in one or more ways to inhibit the sequence of events described above.[8] H_1-re-

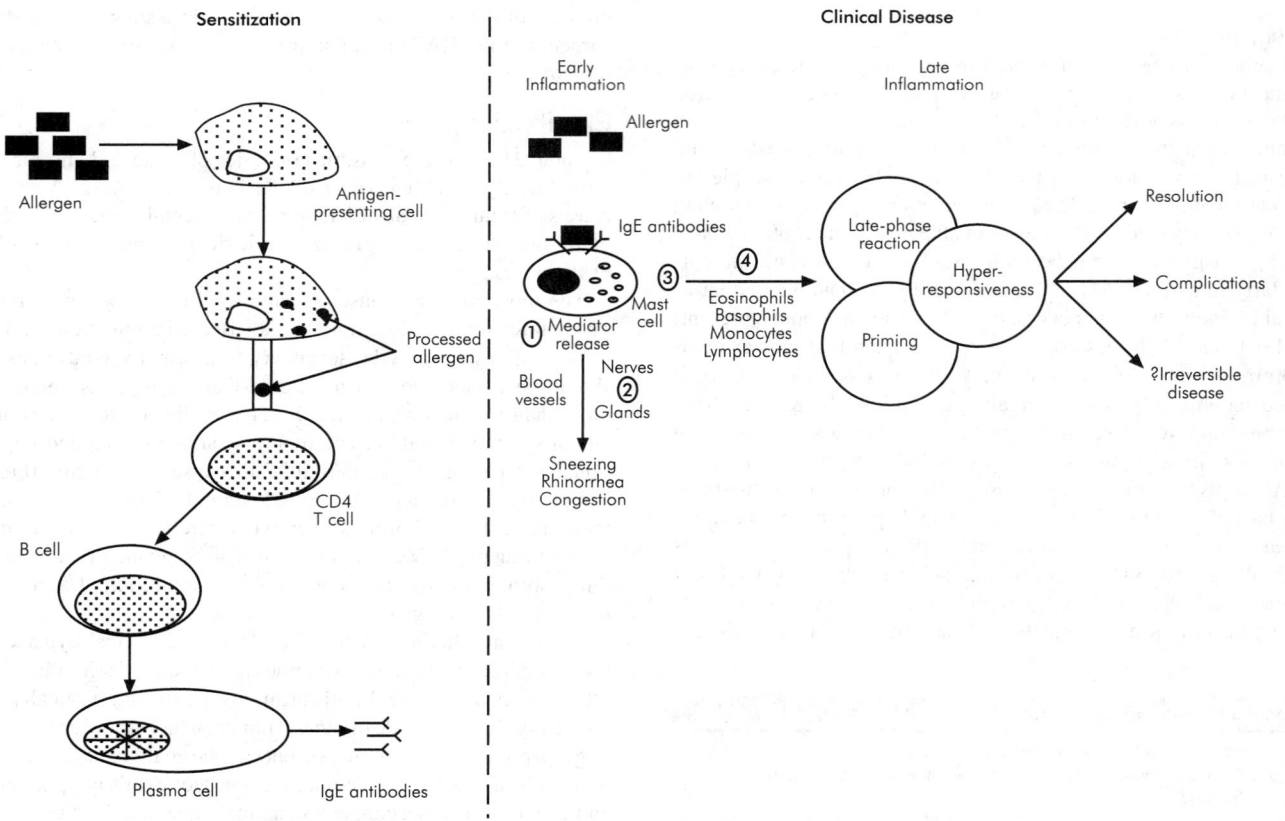

Fig 21.2 Pathophysiology of Allergic Rhinitis   1) Mediators released—Early-phase reaction. Histamine is released and is followed by itching and sneezing (caused by stimulation of H_1-receptors upon sensory nerve endings mediated by a reflex arc); rhinorrhea (due to increased vascular permeability and glandular secretion); and congestion (due to vasodilation and tissue edema). LTC_4 and PGD_2 are released, followed by rhinorrhea (due to increased vascular permeability and glandular secretion) and congestion (due to vasodilation and tissue edema). Chemotactic factors are released, which stimulate cellular infiltration of the late-phase reaction. 2) Drugs that inhibit the early-phase reaction: H_1-receptor antagonists, cromolyn sodium, topical corticosteroid, immunotherapy. 3) Mediators that induce the late-phase reaction: Chemotactic factors stimulate cellular infiltration. 4) Drugs that inhibit the late-phase reaction: Cromolyn sodium, topical corticosteroids, systemic corticosteroids, immunotherapy. Reprinted with permission from reference 8.

ceptor antagonists block the effects of histamine upon receptors after it has been released from the mast cells and, to a lesser extent, block histamine release from basophils; they interfere only with the early-phase reaction in allergic rhinitis. Cromolyn sodium, topical corticosteroids, and immunotherapy diminish both the early-phase and late-phase reactions. Systemic corticosteroids do little to affect the early-phase reaction but markedly inhibit the late-phase. An understanding of the pathophysiology of allergic rhinitis and how drugs act to alter it can aid the clinician in designing a pharmacotherapeutic plan.

Perennial Allergic Rhinitis

Signs and Symptoms

1. V.J., a 6-year-old, 22 kg female, presents to the outpatient clinic with a chief complaint of nasal itching, sneezing, rhinorrhea, and congestion for the past month (beginning in mid-August). V.J.'s mother recalls symptoms similar to these occurring last year at this time, but this year the symptoms seem to be worse. Her mother also reports that V.J. experienced these symptoms all winter last year, but she attributed them to a bad cold and flu season. The symptoms were present, but mild, throughout the spring. V.J. is constantly sneezing and rubbing her nose and the nasal secretions are clear and watery. V.J.'s teacher has complained to her mother about V.J.'s sneezing and "snorting" in the classroom. V.J. also complains of red, itchy eyes, and itching of the ears and palate.

V.J.'s mother also states that V.J. occasionally coughs and gets short of breath when she runs or plays too hard at home or on the playground at school. She states that 10 to 15 minutes of rest usually resolves these symptoms. She states that V.J. does not have these symptoms regularly at night.

V.J.'s father and two paternal aunts have a history of hay fever and had asthma as children. V.J. lives in an apartment in the city with her family; they have one window air-conditioning unit in the living room and radiator heat. Their apartment building does not allow pets, but she has no apparent symptoms when playing with her friends' pets. There are no smokers in the house.

Upon physical examination, V.J. is afebrile and in no apparent distress. She frequently rubs her nose in an upward direction, rubs her eyes, sniffs, and breathes through her mouth. There was no infraorbital discoloration. V.J. demonstrates marked nasal obstruction bilaterally. Examination of the nose reveals slight rhinorrhea with a nasal discharge that is watery and clear to slightly white in appearance. The turbinates are markedly swollen, moist, and pale. To visualize the entire nasal passageway, two drops of 0.25% phenylephrine instilled in each nostril were required. There are no abnormal growths or structural abnormalities seen. The conjunctivae are injected and the pupils are moist with slight tearing. V.J.'s tympanic membranes and oropharynx appear normal. The chest is clear to auscultation. Which factors in V.J.'s presentation indicate she is suffering from allergic rhinitis?

V.J. exhibits the classic symptoms of allergic rhinitis: nasal itching, sneezing, profuse rhinorrhea, and congestion. She also is experiencing the common sensation of itching of the palate and ears.[12] As is common in children, V.J. sniffs and snorts in response to nasal itching and discharge. These sounds frequently irritate parents and teachers. The frequent upward rubbing of the nose is known as the "allergic salute" and is caused by nasal itching. If the symptoms are long-standing, this can lead to facial abnormalities, including the formation of a nasal crease just behind the tip of the nose.[13] The concurrent conjunctivitis also supports an allergic etiology for her symptoms. Although V.J. does not demonstrate any infraorbital discoloration, this can develop from frequent rubbing of the eyes in patients with severe ocular itching and is called "allergic shiners."[13] Patients may refer to this as "black bags" under their eyes.

V.J.'s exercise-induced respiratory symptoms likely are due to asthma, and this must be investigated further with objective testing. Her family history of allergies and asthma contributes to the likelihood that V.J. has asthma and that her nasal and ocular symptoms are allergic in nature. Atopy appears to be inherited as an autosomal dominant character linked to a gene locus on chromosome 11.[26] Also, it would be typical for V.J. to have asthma and allergic rhinoconjunctivitis since multiple atopic diseases often coexist in the same patient. In one series, allergic rhinitis was present in 80% of patients with asthma and 50% of patients with atopic dermatitis or eczema.[27] Typically, patients with allergic rhinitis first present in childhood.

The physical examination findings also are consistent with allergic rhinitis. In patients with allergic rhinitis, the turbinates typically are swollen and can completely occlude the nasal airways. They also are moist (or "boggy") and discolored from their normal pale pink appearance to become erythematous or pale and, in severe cases, violaceous or bluish. The nasal discharge in allergic rhinitis typically is watery and clear, although the presence of large numbers of eosinophils can cause it to appear cloudy white or slightly yellow.[12]

The presence of symptoms throughout most of the past year indicates that V.J. suffers from perennial, as opposed to seasonal, allergic rhinitis. The signs and symptoms of perennial and seasonal allergic rhinitis are virtually identical; only the timing of symptom occurrence during the year differs. Perennial symptoms are caused by antigens that are present year-round like house-dust mites, animal and insect dander, and certain indoor molds. Commonly, patients with perennial allergic rhinitis will experience a worsening of their symptoms in the winter when they are obligated to spend more time indoors, increasing their antigen exposure. Patients also may experience seasonal worsening of their symptoms (due to seasonal antigen sensitivity) superimposed upon a history of perennial symptoms, as V.J. demonstrates. The symptom history must be correlated with objective testing for allergen sensitivity.

Diagnosis

2. What additional clinical evaluation is required to confirm that V.J. has allergic rhinitis?

A nasal smear should be performed to evaluate for the presence of nasal eosinophilia.[6,12] (See Diagnosis and Assessment of Rhinitis: Laboratory Testing for a description of this procedure.)

Skin testing using the modified prick test method or a prick-puncture method is used to confirm the diagnosis of allergic rhinitis and to determine specific allergen sensitivities.[28] Skin testing is a highly sensitive and relatively inexpensive objective measurement of allergen sensitivity. Small quantities of allergen are introduced into the skin by pricking or puncturing the skin in the immediate presence of the diluted allergen extract. Between 15 to 35 tests are placed on the upper portion of the back or the volar (palmar) surface of the forearms. A positive skin test will produce a wheal and flare at the site within 15 to 30 minutes of application. An experienced practitioner, usually an allergist, should conduct skin testing using high-quality allergen extracts and should interpret the results.

The allergens tested vary with geographic location, emphasizing the most common offending plant species which generate airborne particles.[29] Pollen, the primary particle, is produced by trees, grasses, and weeds. Each of these plant groups generally pollinate at about the same time each year: trees in the spring, grasses from early to midsummer, and weeds from late summer into fall before the first killing frost. The onset and potency of the pollen season varies with geographic location and weather, particularly with respect to temperature and moisture.[29,30] Seasonality can be misleading, however, since settled pollen particles from a previous season may be resuspended in the air following the spring snow melt or periods of heavy winds.

Mold spores also are common airborne allergens. The outdoor molds release their spores from early spring through late fall. Within this long season, spore counts will increase and decrease depending upon the presence of local flora on which these molds grow (e.g., grain and other crops, forests, orchards).[30,31] Some perennial allergens, such as house dust mites, insect and animal dander, and some indoor molds, will occur consistently across all geographic distributions.[31] In each case, skin test results must be correlated with the patient's clinical history.

V.J.'s perennial symptoms indicate a sensitivity to the common perennial allergens. Also, her history of worsening symptoms beginning in midAugust indicates a sensitivity to weed pollen. These subjective relationships observed in V.J. should be confirmed with skin testing.

An alternative to skin testing is the radioallergosorbent test, in which the patient's serum is tested for the presence of allergen-specific IgE antibodies. However, this test is less sensitive and more expensive than skin testing,[28,32] so it is indicated only in selected clinical situations: when a patient consistently reacts positively to the negative-control skin test (dermatographism); when antihistamine therapy cannot be discontinued (skin tests cannot be conducted in a patient on H_1-antagonists[33]); or when the patient suffers extensive atopic dermatitis or other skin lesions.[32] RAST testing is not indicated for V.J. at this time.

Likewise, blood eosinophil counts and serum IgE antibody measurements are neither sensitive nor specific enough to be useful in the diagnosis of allergic rhinitis.[6,12] Sinus x-rays are indicated when patient history and physical examination data create a suspicion for sinus disease or when a patient fails to respond to initial therapy.

V.J. also must have spirometry and, possibly, bronchoprovocation testing (i.e., a methacholine challenge or an exercise challenge) to evaluate her respiratory complaints thoroughly. (See Chapter 19: Asthma.)

Drug Effects upon Skin Testing

3. If V.J. had been taking antihistamines, when should they be discontinued before skin testing? What other drugs may affect skin testing?

The H_1-receptor antagonists inhibit or blunt the wheal-and-flare reaction by blocking the effects of histamine on capillaries. Different H_1-antagonists vary in the extent to which they are able to blunt wheal formation and in the duration of the inhibitory effect. (See Table 21.4.) Also, there exists considerable interpatient variability in blocking effects.[33]

Astemizole is able to block the wheal-and-flare reaction to the greatest extent and for the longest period of time.[33,34] The effect is less profound after a single 10 mg dose of astemizole than it is after a two-week course of treatment.[34] Also, a positive correlation between serum concentration and percent inhibition in histamine-induced wheal has been demonstrated with astemizole and chlorpheniramine.[35] These data indicate that the extent and duration of skin test suppression depend upon the dose and duration of treatment.[36] Inhibition with cetirizine is as extensive as with astemizole, but the duration of the effect is much shorter.[34] Of the first-generation H_1-receptor antagonists, hydroxyzine and clemastine are the most potent inhibitors of the wheal-and-flare reaction and can exert their effects for up to ten days after discontinuation of the drug.[33] For most of the other H_1-antagonists, inhibitory effects upon allergen skin tests appear to last from 12 to 72 hours.[33,35]

Other drugs also can affect allergen skin tests.[33] Tricyclic antidepressants are potent inhibitors of the wheal-and-flare reaction and their effects can last up to ten days. Phenothiazine-type antipsychotics and antiemetics (e.g., chlorpromazine, prochlorperazine) also can block skin cutaneous reactions to allergens. Most asthma medications, including inhaled beta agonists, cromolyn, theophylline, and inhaled and short-course systemic ("burst") corticosteroids have no effect upon skin tests. Oral beta agonists, long-term systemic corticosteroids, and high-potency topical/dermatologic corticosteroids (applied to the skin testing sites) may block cutaneous wheal-and-flare reactions. Beta blockers can increase skin reactivity. Depending upon the indication for drug therapy, discontinuation of these drugs before skin testing may or may not be possible.

Rational recommendations for discontinuation of H_1-antagonists before allergen skin testing are listed in Table 21.5.

4. V.J.'s nasal smear contained 4+ eosinophils. Her skin tests were positive for house dust mite (*Dermatophagoides pteronyssinus*), strongly positive for ragweed (*Ambrosia trifida, A. elatior*), and only weakly positive for outdoor molds (*Alternaria alternata, Cladosporium* sp.), grasses (timothy, orchard), and cockroach dander. Her skin tests were negative for animal dander.

Table 21.4	Effects of H_1-Receptor Antagonists upon Allergen Skin Tests[33–36]		
Drug	Extent of Suppression[a]	Half-Life[b]	Duration of Suppression (Days)
Astemizole	+ + +	13 days	5–40
Brompheniramine	+	24.9	0.5–3
Cetirizine	+ + +	7.4–11 (7)	1–3
Chlorpheniramine	+	24.4 (11)	0.5–3
Clemastine	+ +	—	1–10
Cyproheptadine	±	16	0.5–3
Diphenhydramine	±	4–9	0.5–3
Hydroxyzine	+ +	20 (7.1)	1–10
Loratadine	+/++	11–24	0.5–3
Promethazine	+	12	0.5–3
Terfenadine	+/++	4.5 (2)	1–3
Tripelennamine	±	—	0.5–3

[a] + + + = Extensive; + + = Moderate; + = Mild; ± = Minimal to none.
[b] Half-life in hours unless otherwise listed. Parenthetical numbers indicate half-life in children.

Table 21.5	Recommendations for Discontinuation of H_1-antagonists Before Allergen Skin Testing

1. Discontinue any short-acting antihistamine (i.e., those in Table 21.4 with a 0.5–3 day duration of suppression) 36 to 48 hours before skin testing. Remind the patient that, although allergic symptoms will return during the antihistamine-free period, reliable skin tests cannot be performed in a patient taking antihistamines

2. Discontinue longer-acting H_1-antagonists at an interval appropriate to their duration of effect (e.g., for astemizole 2–4 weeks before skin testing; for hydroxyzine or clemastine 5–7 days before skin testing)

3. Before applying the full battery of skin tests, apply histamine (positive) control and glycerinated diluent (negative) control tests. 1 mg/mL histamine base equivalent should yield wheal-and-flare diameters of 2–7 mm and 4.5–32.5 mm, respectively, to be considered a normal histamine reaction.[28] A normal cutaneous reaction to histamine control suggests that accurate skin testing can be performed since hydroxyzine has been shown to equally suppress reactions to histamine and allergen[37]

V.J.'s resting spirometry was normal, but exercise challenge induced a 17% drop in her FEV_1. These results confirm that V.J. has mild exercise-induced asthma. What do the skin test results indicate? Do they support the subjective information regarding V.J.'s sensitivities?

V.J.'s symptoms and skin test results are consistent with perennial allergic rhinitis due to house dust mite sensitivity with seasonal worsening due to a sensitivity to weed pollen. Although her skin tests are weakly positive for grasses and outdoor molds, she does not give a history consistent with sensitivities to those allergens at this time. Skin test results do not explain the mild symptoms that V.J. experiences in the spring (e.g., she is not sensitive to tree pollens). Her spring symptoms probably are attributable to her perennial sensitivity to house dust mites. She does not give a history of sensitivity to animal dander and, consistently, her skin tests are negative for these allergens.

Therapeutic Objectives

5. What are the therapeutic objectives in treating V.J.?

The therapeutic objectives in treating allergic rhinitis are to control symptoms while allowing all usual daily activities and to minimize adverse side effects of therapy. These objectives are achievable in almost all patients with allergic rhinitis of mild to moderate severity. Patients with severe disease may experience only a reduction in symptom severity and have to tolerate more side effects of therapy. The strategies used to achieve these therapeutic objectives are nonpharmacologic therapy (including avoidance and patient education about the disease), pharmacotherapy, and immunotherapy. (See Figure 21.3.)

Nonpharmacologic Therapy

6. What nonpharmacologic therapies may help V.J. meet these therapeutic objectives?

Avoidance. The primary nonpharmacologic treatment for allergic rhinitis is avoidance of offending allergens. This often is impractical because of the airborne nature of pollens and mold spores. It would be very difficult for V.J. to avoid weed pollen without significantly curtailing her daily activities.

However, in a patient who suffers perennial symptoms due to house dust mite sensitivity, as V.J. does, certain precautions can be taken to decrease exposure to the allergen.[8,38] The major source of exposure to house dust mites is the mattress and bedding. The patient is in close proximity to this source for six to ten hours each night. Exposure can be reduced by using an airtight plastic mattress cover; washing the pillows and bedding every month; and, for children, removing stuffed animals from the bed.[38]

Another case in which avoidance may be useful is for the patient with animal dander sensitivity. However, this situation is complicated by psychosocial issues. It may be easy for the clinician to suggest that a household pet be removed from the house, but it often is much more difficult for a family to say goodbye to a long-loved dog or cat. The animal's removal may result in a stigma that the allergic family member must bear. In each case, the severity of the patient's symptoms and the potential for good response to drug therapy must be considered before mandating a pet's removal from the household.[38]

The final beneficial form of avoidance therapy is smoking cessation. Inhaled pollutants irritate the nasal mucosa of patients with inflammation of almost any etiology. Tobacco smoke is the most ubiquitous of the inhaled irritants. Patients who smoke should be instructed and supported in a program to stop smoking. Members of the household who smoke, especially when the patient is a child, should receive similar counsel.

Exercise. Another potentially beneficial nonpharmacologic therapy is exercise.[4,12] A regular routine of vigorous exercise apparently increases sympathetic tone, causing vasoconstriction of the capacitance vessels. The recommended exercise program should be sufficient to produce perspiration for 15 to 30 minutes, once or twice a day, and patients must be otherwise healthy enough to undertake such a program. Although avoidance and nonpharmacologic therapy may be helpful, pharmacotherapy usually is necessary to adequately control symptoms for most patients. Pharmacotherapy includes systemic H_1-receptor antagonists, decongestants, intranasal cromolyn sodium, or intranasal corticosteroids. (See Figure 21.3.)

7. Saline Irrigation. Of what value is treatment with saline sprays or drops for patients with allergic rhinitis?

Normal saline irrigation can soothe irritated nasal tissues and moisturize the nasal mucosa. Commercial nasal saline sprays are useful for this purpose and should be given at a dose of two sprays in each nostril four times a day or as needed for nasal dryness. For children less than six years old, nasal saline drops may be easier to administer. The dosage is two to six drops in each nostril four times a day or as needed. Alternatively, a saline solution can be prepared by the patient using one teaspoonful of table salt in seven ounces of warm water and administered with a bulb syringe into alternating nostrils with the head held over the sink. A Water Pik also can be used to administer saline solution prepared by mixing one teaspoonful of table salt into the 800 mL reservoir of the device and, with head bent over the sink, alternately direct the pulsating flow from the device into each nostril. In each of these latter two cases, the full volume of prepared saline solution should be used and any unused portion discarded.

H_1-Receptor Antagonists

8. Are H_1-antagonists indicated in the treatment of V.J.? What criteria should be considered when choosing among the available H_1-antagonists and how should the dosage be adjusted?

The first-line treatment for both perennial and seasonal allergic rhinitis and conjunctivitis is a systemic H_1-receptor antagonist. These agents directly, but reversibly antagonize histamine at the H_1-receptor site, thereby blocking the physiologic effects of histamine.[36] It should be noted, however, that the second-generation H_1-antagonist astemizole has a very high affinity for the H_1-receptor and its effects are not reversible readily after discontinuation of the drug.[39] Additionally, terfenadine, loratadine, azatadine, and cetirizine appear to block the release of histamine and other inflammatory mediators from mast cells and basophils *in vivo*,[36,40,41] but the clinical significance of this effect is as yet unknown. Specific H_1-receptor antagonists are compared in Table 21.6.

Pharmacokinetics and Pharmacodynamics. H_1-receptor antagonists are absorbed rapidly after oral administration, achieving peak

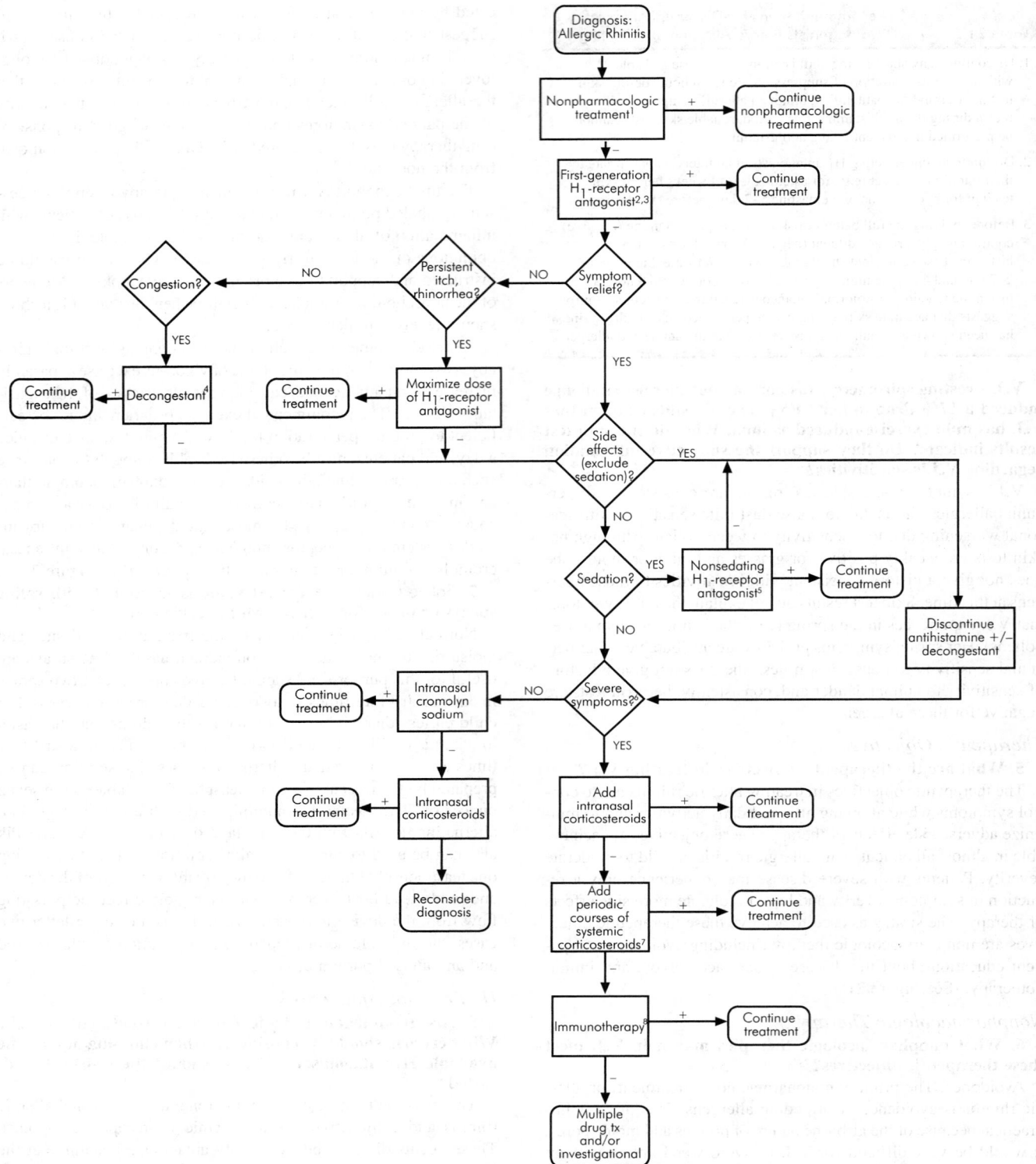

Fig 21.3 Treatment Algorithm: Allergic Rhinitis   1) Nonpharmacologic treatment includes avoidance, saline irrigation, and exercise. 2) First-generation, H₁-receptor antagonists are the first-line therapy for allergic rhinitis if there are no contraindications to their use (e.g., benign prostatic hyperplasia, narrow-angle glaucoma) and the patient agrees to therapy. 3) Must be started with a slow dosage titration. 4) Decongestant should be added to H₁-antagonist therapy for patients with nasal congestion since antihistamines do not relieve this symptom. 5) Second-generation, nonsedating, H₁-receptor antagonists are indicated if the patient experiences intolerable sedation on a first-generation H₁-antagonist despite slow dosage titration. Recommended use of a bedtime dose of a long-acting or sustained-release first-generation H₁-antagonist with or without a daytime dose of a nonsedating agent. 6) Severe symptoms defined as those that interfere with daily activities such as work or sleep. 7) Periodic or "burst" doses of oral corticosteroids are indicated for severe symptoms that are otherwise uncontrolled with maximal drug therapy. Corticosteroid bursts should be limited to fewer than four courses per year to limit systemic side effects. 8) Immunotherapy should permit dosage reduction for antiallergy medications and possibly elimination of some (but probably not all) medications. + = Positive outcome of therapy defined as relief of symptoms, no interference with daily activities, and no adverse reactions to treatment. − = Negative outcome of therapy defined as inadequate symptom relief, continued interference with daily activities, and/or adverse reactions to treatment. tx = Treatment.

serum concentrations at approximately two hours after a dose. All of the first-generation H_1-receptor antagonists and most of the second-generation agents are metabolized hepatically by the cytochrome P450 system.[36] Clearance rates and elimination half-lives vary for the specific drugs.[36,44] Serum elimination half-lives are shorter in children[45,46] and longer in the elderly.[47] In general, the volumes of distribution are large.[36]

While many of the H_1-antagonists can be used safely and effectively in children as young as one year, most are not Food and Drug Administration (FDA)-approved for young children. One agent, trimeprazine, is approved for use in children six months of age and older. Safety and efficacy have not been established for the use of cyproheptadine, promethazine, chlorpheniramine, and dexchlorpheniramine in children less than two years old; methdilazine in children less than three years old; brompheniramine, sustained-release (SR) chlorpheniramine, sustained-release dexchlorpheniramine, triprolidine, and phenindamine in children less than

six years old; and clemastine, pyrilamine, azatadine, cetirizine, terfenadine, astemizole, and loratadine in children less than 12 years old.[48]

Systemic H_1-receptor antagonists are very effective in the treatment of allergic rhinitis and conjunctivitis.[36] Because they are administered systemically, they alleviate allergic symptoms in not only the nose, but in the eyes, skin, and other sites as well. Because V.J. suffers from allergic rhinitis and conjunctivitis, a systemic H_1-receptor antagonist would be valuable in controlling all of her atopic symptoms. These agents decrease nasal itching, sneezing, rhinorrhea, conjunctival itching, and lacrimation. They do not, however, relieve nasal congestion.[36] Essentially all of the antihistamines listed in Table 21.6 are equally effective. The choice of agent is based more upon duration of action, side effect profile (especially drowsiness and anticholinergic effects), risk of drug interactions, and cost. Individual sensitivities and psychological perceptions are also possible factors. Some patients claim that one

Table 21.6	Oral Antihistamines: Classification and Dosage[12,36,42,43]		Side Effects[f]		
Drug	Adult Dose	Pediatric Dose[a]	CNS	Anticholinergic	GI
Alkylamine					
Chlorpheniramine maleate (Chlor-Trimeton)	2–4 mg Q 4–6 hr *or* 8–12 mg SR Q 12–24 hr[b]	0.35 mg/kg/day[c]	+	+ +	—
Brompheniramine maleate (Dimetane)	4–8 mg Q 4–6 hr *or* 8–12 mg SR Q 12–24 hr[b]	0.35 mg/kg/day[c]	+	+ +	—
Dexchlorpheniramine maleate (Polaramine)	2 mg Q 4–6 hr *or* 4–6 mg SR HS[c]	*6–11 years:* 1 mg Q 4–6 hr; *2–5 years:* 0.5 mg Q 4–6 hr	+	+ +	—
Triprolidine HCl (Actidil)	2.5 mg Q 4–6 hr	0.18 mg/kg/day[c]	+	+ +	—
Ethanolamine					
Diphenhydramine HCl (Benadryl)	25–50 mg Q 6–8 hr	5 mg/kg/day[c]	+ + +	+ + +	+
Carbinoxamine maleate (Clistin)	4–8 mg Q 6–8 hr	0.2–0.4 mg/kg/day[c]	+ +	+ + +	+
Clemastine fumarate (Tavist)	1.34–2.68 mg Q 8–12 hr	—[d]	+ +	+ + +	+
Ethylenediamine					
Tripelennamine HCl (PBZ)	25–50 mg Q 4–6 hr	5 mg/kg/day[c]	+ +	±	+ + +
Pyrilamine maleate (Nisaval)	25–50 mg Q 6–8 hr	—[d]	+	±	+ + +
Phenothiazine					
Promethazine HCl (Phenergan)	25 mg HS *or* 12.5 mg Q 8 hr	0.5 mg/kg/dose HS *or* 0.1 mg/kg/dose Q 6–8 hr	+ + +	+ + +	—
Trimeprazine tartrate (Temaril)	2.5 mg Q 6 hr	0.18 mg/kg/day[c]	+ +	+ + +	—
Methdilazine HCl (Tacaryl)	8 mg Q 6–12 hr	0.3 mg/kg/day[c]	+	+ + +	—
Piperidine					
Cyproheptadine HCl (Periactin)	4 mg Q 8 hr	0.25 mg/kg/day[c]	+	+ +	—
Azatadine maleate (Optimine)	1–2 mg Q 12 hr	0.05 mg/kg/day[c,d]	+ +	+ +	—
Phenindamine tartrate (Nolahist)	25 mg Q 4–6 hr	6–12 yr: 12.5 mg Q 4–6 hr	—	+ +	—
Piperazine					
Hydroxyzine HCl (Atarax)	25 mg Q 6–8 hr	2 mg/kg/day	+ +	+	—
Cetirizine (Reactine)	5–10 mg QD	—[d]	±	±	+
Other (Nonsedating)					
Terfenadine (Seldane)	60 mg Q 12 hr *or* 120 mg QD[e]	*3–6 years:* 15 mg Q 12 hr;[d] *6–12 years:* 30 mg Q 12 hr[d]	±	±	—
Astemizole (Hismanal)	10 mg QD	0.2 mg/kg/day[d]	±	±	+
Loratadine (Claritin)	10 mg QD	—[d]	±	±	+

[a] For patients ≤40 kg.
[b] SR = Sustained release. May be given as a single daily dose HS to reduce daytime sedation.
[c] To be divided into 3–4 doses/day.
[d] Not FDA-approved for use in children <12 yr old.
[e] QD dosing of terfenadine is not FDA-approved.
[f] Incidence: + + + = High; + + = Moderate; + = Low; ± = Low to none; — = None.

product is more helpful in relieving their symptoms than another, yet there is no pharmacological explanation for these observations.

H_1-receptor antagonists prevent the onset of symptoms better than they reverse symptoms that have appeared already. Also, the maximum antihistamine effects occur several hours after the drug's serum concentration peaks.[36] For maximal effect, therefore, the H_1-receptor antagonists should be administered before allergen exposure if possible. For the same reason, chronic dosing is preferred to intermittent dosing. Chronic dosing is important, particularly for V.J. since she suffers from perennial symptoms.

Dosage Titration. Initiation of H_1-receptor antagonist therapy should involve slowly titrating the dose.[51] (See Table 21.7.) A slow dosage titration allows the patient to develop tolerance to the side effects of the drug and, therefore, avoid the excessive sedation frequently experienced upon initiation of antihistamine therapy. When initiation of H_1-receptor antagonist therapy is necessary for a child during the school year, it is best to start therapy and make any dosage increases on the weekend or, if possible, during a school holiday to avoid interference with school activities.

For V.J., a first-generation H_1-receptor antagonist with minimal central nervous system (CNS) effects, like chlorpheniramine, should be chosen. Therapy is initiated with chlorpheniramine 4 mg at bedtime. Since V.J. is in school at this time, treatment should begin on Friday night and subsequent dosage adjustment should be postponed until the following weekend. In V.J.'s case, a 2 mg chlorpheniramine dose is added on the following Saturday morning. Dosing continues with chlorpheniramine 2 mg every morning and 4 mg at bedtime for one week. Then, the morning chlorpheniramine dose is increased to 4 mg the following Saturday. This is V.J.'s total chlorpheniramine dose (i.e., 8 mg/day or 0.36 mg/kg/day) and it should be continued without interruption.

9. Safety in Asthma. Should not antihistamines be avoided in V.J. since she has asthma?

The role of systemic H_1-receptor antagonists in the treatment of patients with asthma, like V.J., has been debated.[49] The theoretical concern is that the anticholinergic properties of the H_1-receptor antagonists will dry the airways and bronchial secretions which could exacerbate asthma. On the contrary, most asthmatic patients are able to take H_1-receptor antagonists without adverse pulmonary effects. In fact, some H_1-receptor antagonists have been shown to cause bronchodilation in asthmatic patients.[49,50] In the few patients who demonstrate airway obstruction after H_1-receptor antagonist administration, this effect apparently is due to bronchoconstriction, not thickening of secretions, because it is reversible with bronchodilator.[50] This is not to imply that H_1-receptor antagonists should replace bronchodilators and anti-inflammatory agents in the management of asthma, only that they are not contraindicated in most patients with asthma.[50] H_1-antagonists should not be withheld from V.J.

Table 21.7 H_1-Receptor Antagonist Titration Schedule[51]

1) Start with a small dose (e.g., chlorpheniramine 4 mg or diphenhydramine 25 mg) HS only and continue with this dose for at least 3 days or until the patient feels no residual drowsiness in the morning.

2) Add a small dose in the morning. Do not increase the dose further for at least 3 days or until the patient no longer is drowsy on this dose.

3) Continue increasing the dose in this manner, adding to the bedtime dose alternately with the morning dose, until the desired therapeutic endpoint is achieved.

4) Do not discontinue the medication once symptoms improve. It is important to take the medication continuously to prevent symptoms and to avoid unwanted sedation caused by the medication.

Decongestants

10. What role do decongestants have in the treatment of V.J.? What are the relative benefits and disadvantages of oral versus topical (nasal) therapy?

As previously noted, H_1-antagonists do little to relieve nasal congestion; therefore, many patients require a combination of an H_1-antagonist with a decongestant.[52] The combination of an H_1-antagonist and an oral decongestant is more effective than either component alone in the treatment of allergic rhinitis.[53]

All of the decongestants are sympathomimetics that directly stimulate α-adrenergic receptors, resulting in vasoconstriction. The local effects of the decongestants upon the nasal mucosa include decreased tissue hyperemia, decreased tissue edema, decreased nasal congestion, and improved nasal airway patency.[52] Normal saline irrigation is helpful in relieving nasal congestion by soothing and moisturizing irritated nasal mucosa.[4,12] (See Question 7.)

Dosing. The available decongestants are compared in Table 21.8. The oral and topical decongestants are approved for use in children two years old and older with the exception of naphazoline which is approved only for adults and children over 12 years old.[48] Phenylephrine 0.125% and 0.16% are approved for infants and children as young as six months old. Topical decongestants should never be used in infants less than six months old since they are obligate nose breathers and rebound congestion could cause obstructive apnea.

Adverse Effects. The adverse effects of the systemic decongestants include CNS stimulation (e.g., nervousness, restlessness, insomnia, tremor, dizziness, headache). These side effects can counteract the sedation caused by H_1-antagonists.[12,52] Cardiovascular stimulation (e.g., tachycardia, palpitations) also can occur.[52]

Although oral administration of these agents may result in systemic side effects, this route has the advantages of prolonged duration of action compared to topical administration of sprays or drops and carries little risk for the development of *rhinitis medicamentosa* or rebound congestion. Topical administration of decongestants generally does not cause systemic side effects. Local side effects, including nasal irritation and *rhinitis medicamentosa* with prolonged use, can be difficult to manage in the clinical setting.[54] Topical administration is not recommended for longer than three to five days, making this route an impractical choice in the chronic treatment of allergic rhinitis.[52] Occasional use of topical decongestants may be acceptable in patients with allergic rhinitis during episodes of unusually severe congestion if the patient is appropriately cautioned about the risks of prolonged use. (See Drug-Induced Nasal Congestion.)

H_1-Receptor Antagonists

11. Antihistamine therapy was initiated for V.J. with chlorpheniramine 4 mg at bedtime. This dose was increased over a period of 2 weeks to 4 mg of chlorpheniramine BID. Pseudoephedrine 30 mg TID also was started. V.J.'s symptoms improved considerably on these medications, but her mother complains that V.J. is drowsy. Her mother states that she only gives the medications to V.J. on the weekend and occasionally at bedtime.

Physical examination reveals moderate nasal congestion, moderate turbinate swelling, and moderate amounts of clear nasal discharge.

What can be done to avoid the drowsiness associated with the antihistamines? What other counselling should be given to V.J. about her antihistamine?

Adverse Effects. The traditional H_1-receptor antagonists, for all their benefits, do have many side effects. In addition to their ability to block the H_1-receptor, the H_1-antagonists also have other pharmacologic actions, including anticholinergic effects, local anes-

Table 21.8	Decongestants[42,48]
Drug	Recommended Dosage[a,b]
Phenylamine	
Pseudoephedrine HCl (Sudafed)	*Adult:* 30–60 mg Q 4–6 hr *Pediatric:* 4 mg/kg/day
Phenylpropanolamine HCl (Propagest)	*Adult:* 25 mg Q 4 hr to 50 mg Q 8 hr *Pediatric 6–12 years:* 12.5 mg Q 4 hr *2–6 years:* 6.25 mg Q 4 hr
Phenylephrine HCl (Neo-Synephrine)	*Adult (≥12 years):* 2–3 actuations/nostril Q 3–4 hr *or* 2–3 drops 0.25%–0.5% solution/nostril Q 3–4 hr *Pediatric 6–12 years:* 2–3 actuations 0.25% spray/nostril Q 3–4 hr *or* 2–3 drops 0.25% solution/nostril Q 3–4 hr. *6 months–5 years:* 1–2 drops 0.125% *or* 0.16% solution/nostril Q 3 hr
Imidazoline	
Naphazoline HCl (Privine)	*Adult (≥12 years):* 1–2 drops/nostril Q 6 hr
Oxymetazoline HCl (Afrin)	*Adult and Pediatric (≥6 years):* 2–3 actuations/nostril Q 12 hr *or* 2–3 drops 0.05% solution/nostril Q 12 hr *Pediatric (2–5 years):* 2–3 drops 0.025% solution/nostril Q 12 hr
Tetrahydrozoline HCl (Tyzine)	*Adult and Pediatric (≥6 years):* 3–4 actuations/nostril Q 4 hr *or* 2–3 drops 0.1% solution/nostril Q 3–4 hr *Pediatric (2–6 years):* 2–3 drops 0.05% solution/nostril Q 4–6 hr
Xylometazoline HCl (Otrivin)	*Adult (≥12 years):* 2–3 actuations/nostril Q 8–10 hr *or* 2–3 drops 0.1% solution/nostril Q 8–10 hr *Pediatric (2–12 years):* 2–3 drops 0.05% solution/nostril Q 8–10 hr

a Pediatric doses given for patients ≤40 kg; topical decongestants should not be used in any child <6 months old.
b Therapy with any topical decongestant should not exceed 3–5 days.

thetic effects, and α-adrenergic blocking effects.[36,44] The extent to which individual agents exert the nonH1-antagonistic effects varies, but these effects in addition to blockade of central histamine receptors cause the side effects associated with the antihistamines.[44] Some of the potential side effects include dizziness, paradoxical excitation in children and the elderly, gastrointestinal (GI) side effects (e.g., anorexia, nausea, diarrhea, abdominal pain), and anticholinergic effects (e.g., dry mouth, urinary retention, blurred vision).[55]

V.J. is sedated on the H1-receptor antagonist, chlorpheniramine. Sedation occurs because of the ability of the agents to cross the blood-brain barrier[36] and inhibit histamine-mediated pathways that control wakefulness and sleep.[56] Sedation can be a problem with any H1-antagonist, but some agents are more likely to cause it than others (see Table 21.6). Four strategies may be used to help minimize sedation with the H1-antagonists:[12,51] 1) institute antihistamine therapy with a slow dosage titration; 2) administer evening doses of long-acting or sustained-release antihistamines; 3) use the second-generation nonsedating H1-antagonists; or 4) add a decongestant.

Sedation with almost any agent often can be avoided by slowly titrating the dose[51] (see Table 21.7) and using chronic (not intermittent) dosage regimens. Patients develop tolerance to the sedative effects of the H1-antagonists, but this occurrence varies among the antihistaminic agents, individual patients, and different treatment days in the same patient.[57] The subjective feeling of drowsiness is an unreliable predictor of the degree of impairment.[58] Al-

though feelings of drowsiness significantly lessen after repeated antihistamine doses,[59,60] deteriorations in psychomotor performance only trend toward normalization[59,60] or show no evidence for the development of tolerance.[61] Further study is required to better characterize whether or not tolerance to the alterations in psychomotor tests develops after long-term antihistamine administration.

It is important to warn adult patients about the potential for sedation and impairment and the necessity to gauge the effect of the drugs before attempting to drive a car or do other tasks that require alertness and motor coordination. In addition, patients should be counseled about potential drug interactions between H1-receptor antagonists and alcohol or other CNS depressants.[62]

Second-Generation H1-Receptor Antagonists. The use of long-acting or sustained-release H1-antagonists in the early evening can provide peripheral antihistaminic effects into the daytime hours while confining most of the sedative effects caused by the drugs to the nighttime when the patient is asleep.[57] Hydroxyzine and sustained-release brompheniramine have persistent H1-receptor blocking activity which extends beyond the period of impaired performance.[63,64] In some cases, however, this strategy may not provide adequate antihistaminic coverage for the entire following day.[57] In such cases, a daytime dose of terfenadine (the least expensive and shortest-acting second-generation, "nonsedating" antihistamine) may be used. The combination of a traditional H1-antagonist in the evening with a daytime dose of terfenadine is one way to defray some of the cost of therapy with the nonsedating agents.

The second-generation, so-called "nonsedating," H1-receptor antagonists may have a role in the therapy of selected patients who are unable or unwilling to comply with chronic dosing of the traditional agents. The second-generation H1-receptor antagonists are considerably less lipophilic than the first-generation agents and, therefore, do not penetrate as extensively into the CNS. The second-generation agents also demonstrate preferential binding at peripheral rather than central histamine receptors.[36] Generally, the second-generation H1-receptor antagonists are associated with an incidence of sedation similar to that of placebo. But this placebo effect can be substantial: 14.7% for astemizole[39] and 14% for terfenadine.[65] Objective tests of psychomotor performance have demonstrated no adverse effects with the second-generation H1-receptor antagonists.[57,61,62,66] Because of their expense, these agents should be used primarily in patients who fail treatment with traditional H1-receptor antagonists due to noncompliance related to side effects. The second-generation H1-receptor antagonists do not interact with ethanol or other CNS depressants to intensify sedation or inebriation.[62,67]

V.J. was instructed to institute therapy with a slow dosage titration and she reportedly complied with these instructions. Her intermittent use of the antihistamine now is contributing to her sedation and lack of drug efficacy. She already is on a decongestant. The use of a nonsedating antihistamine for V.J. is a possibility, but this is an unlabeled use in a six year old. The best alternative for V.J. at this time is to attempt to use a long-acting or sustained-release antihistamine at bedtime only. V.J. and her mother should be counselled that continuous therapy with the H1-antagonists is important to obtain the desired effects and to avoid the side effects.

12. Tolerance. Does tolerance develop to the desired effects of the H1-receptor antagonists?

Just as tolerance to the sedative effects of the H1-receptor antagonists occurs over time, an apparent tolerance or subsensitivity to the desired antihistaminic effects has long been observed.[36,68] A reduction in the ability of chlorpheniramine[69] and hydroxyzine[70] to suppress the histamine wheal-and-flare reaction after 7 to 21 days of chronic dosing demonstrates this phenomenon. Cross-tolerance between chemical classes of H_1-receptor antagonists also has been demonstrated.[70] No tolerance of any kind ever has been demonstrated to the second-generation H_1-antagonists.[71-73] In all of the studies of tolerance, alterations in skin reactions to various provocateurs are the only indication of tolerance development. No study has attempted to correlate skin test results to loss of clinical symptom relief.[68]

At one time, this clinical problem was attributed to autoinduction of the hepatic metabolism of the drugs leading to a reduction in serum concentration. This theory was based upon animal data that since has been refuted;[74] autoinduction never has been demonstrated in humans.[36] The metabolism of chlorpheniramine does not change with long-term dosing,[69,75] but compliance with a prescribed regimen declines.[75] The latter observation may explain, at least in part, the decrease in response seen with long-term administration of the H_1-receptor antagonists,[75] although the poor compliance could follow a reduction in efficacy.[36] The occurrence of cross-tolerance would indicate a reduction in the number of histamine receptors (down-regulation) or a modulation in drug-receptor binding rather than a change in effective drug serum concentration.[69] The inability of dosage doubling to overcome the effect would support further the down-regulation theory.[69]

Other possible explanations for increasing allergic symptoms after an initial positive response to H_1-antagonist therapy are:[68] 1) intercurrent illness, such as viral or bacterial infection, or nasal polyp formation; 2) increased exposure to chemical irritants, like air pollutants or tobacco smoke; 3) increased antigen exposure or the development of new sensitivities; 4) increased hyperreactivity due to priming (a phenomenon thought to occur in response to repeated antigen challenge resulting in increased reactions to lower concentrations of provocateurs); and 5) noncompliance with chronic H_1-antagonist therapy.

The clinical management of patients with apparent development of tolerance to H_1-antagonist therapy first must involve careful questioning of the patient to rule out any of the above explanations. If it is found that noncompliance is the cause for the decline in symptom relief, the reason for the noncompliance (e.g., adverse drug reactions, lack of drug benefit, difficulty with a dosing schedule) must be sought and, if possible, corrected before concluding that H_1-antagonist therapy is ineffective. If treatment with a particular H_1-antagonist must be abandoned, there is no benefit to switching to another agent with the possible exception of changing to a second-generation, nonsedating agent. This change would be beneficial if the patient is noncompliant due to side effects (especially drowsiness) or if the patient truly is exhibiting tolerance to the H_1-antagonists (since tolerance apparently does not occur to the second-generation agents).

13. Cardiotoxicity and Drug Interactions. V.J.'s mother has heard about the newer, less sedating antihistamines. She thinks one of these drugs might be more appropriate for V.J., but she also has read in the newspaper that they have been associated with serious heart problems. What is your response?

Cardiotoxicity has been associated with overdoses of the second-generation, nonsedating H_1-antagonists astemizole and terfenadine, and also has been seen when these drugs are used in patients with impaired hepatic function or in those patients concurrently taking macrolide antibiotics or azole antifungals.[76] In a few cases, toxicity has occurred with doses as low as two times the usual prescribed dosage and in the absence of known interacting drugs. The objective findings of the cardiotoxicity include a prolonged QT interval, atrioventricular heart block, and various ventricular dysrhythmias, the most serious being ventricular tachycardia and torsades de pointes.[76,77] A common clinical presentation is unexplained dizziness, syncope, or blackout spells.

The cardiotoxicity associated with terfenadine appears to be due to the parent drug.[76] Terfenadine, but not its acid metabolite, is capable of blocking the delayed rectifier potassium current, similar and equipotent to quinidine *in vitro*.[76] Under normal circumstances, terfenadine undergoes extensive first-pass metabolism. The isoenzyme CYP3A4 (and possibly other CYP3A isoenzymes of the hepatic microsomal cytochrome P450 system) play a major role in the oxidation of terfenadine.[78] Over 99% of an absorbed dose is converted to one of two metabolites: an acid metabolite (terfenadine carboxylate), which is thought to be the active antihistamine, or a dealkylated metabolite, which is inactive.[78] Under normal metabolic conditions, terfenadine concentrations are undetectable in the plasma (i.e., <10 ng/mL),[79] but in certain situations, like hepatic dysfunction or when interacting drugs are administered concomitantly, plasma concentrations of terfenadine increase to detectable, and potentially toxic, levels.[79]

Erythromycin and clarithromycin administration have been shown to significantly alter the pharmacokinetics of terfenadine. Accumulation of the parent drug occurs in some, but not all, patients taking either antibiotic and terfenadine, and QT interval prolongation occurs in a subset of patients with terfenadine accumulation.[80,81] There are no predictive characteristics for those patients who will experience a clinically significant drug interaction between terfenadine and erythromycin or clarithromycin.[80,81] Azithromycin has no effect upon terfenadine pharmacokinetics or cardiac pharmacodynamics.[81]

One of the first case reports linking cardiotoxicity with an apparent drug interaction with terfenadine involved the azole antifungal ketoconazole.[82] Subsequently, ketoconazole has been shown to significantly alter the pharmacokinetics of terfenadine and cause accumulation of the parent drug in a much more consistent fashion than had been demonstrated previously with the macrolide antibiotics.[83] Increased levels of unmetabolized terfenadine are associated with significant QT interval prolongation.[83] Fluconazole also significantly alters the pharmacokinetics of terfenadine, but neither accumulation of the parent drug nor electrocardiogram changes have been demonstrated.[84] Two cases of cardiac arrhythmia in patients taking usual doses of terfenadine and itraconazole have been reported. Evidence of impaired terfenadine metabolism with accumulation of the unmetabolized parent drug was found in each case.[85,86] Controlled studies have not been reported to evaluate a potential interaction between terfenadine and itraconazole.

Neither cimetidine nor ranitidine affects the pharmacokinetics of terfenadine and patients taking either of these drugs together with terfenadine are at no increased cardiac risk.[87] Terfenadine does not interact with theophylline.[88]

Astemizole also has been associated with torsades de pointes in overdose situations,[77,89] but the mechanism by which this drug causes cardiotoxicity is unknown. No reports of cardiotoxicity have occurred yet with loratadine, even when very large doses have been given for an extended period of time.

In response to V.J.'s mother's question, she should be told that while there have been reports of serious heart rhythm disturbance with some of these drugs, they are very safe if prescribed doses are not exceeded. Mom also should be instructed to notify V.J.'s doctor if any new drugs are prescribed for V.J. She should also be instructed to report unusual reactions if these drugs are prescribed.

Intranasal Corticosteroids

14. V.J.'s antihistamine therapy was changed to SR brompheniramine 8 mg HS, but she continues to have allergic symptoms in spite of good compliance (confirmed by history and pharmacy refill records). Physical examination is consistent with ongoing allergic rhinitis.

What therapeutic alternatives are available to treat V.J.'s allergic symptoms?

The therapeutic alternatives for the treatment of patients like V.J. with mild to moderate perennial allergic rhinitis are intranasal corticosteroids and intranasal cromolyn sodium. Systemic corticosteroids and immunotherapy are treatment modalities reserved for patients with severe disease and probably are not necessary for V.J. at this time.

Intranasal corticosteroids are the best alternative for V.J. because they can relieve effectively all of her allergic rhinitis symptoms, including nasal congestion, with minimum potential for side effects. Although intranasal cromolyn sodium is a safe alternative, it may not be as effective for all of V.J.'s symptoms, particularly congestion.

Intranasal corticosteroids are highly effective, safe, and well tolerated in the treatment of allergic rhinitis.[90] They improve the symptoms of allergic rhinitis including itching, sneezing, rhinorrhea, and congestion.[90,91]

The precise mechanism of action of the corticosteroids is unknown. The accepted theory states that corticosteroids interact with a specific steroid receptor in the cytoplasm of a cell. The steroid-receptor complex then moves into the cell nucleus where it influences protein synthesis. Among the proteins synthesized is lipocortin, which inhibits the breakdown of phospholipids to arachidonic acid; this, in turn, inhibits the formation of prostaglandins and leukotrienes.[91] Topical corticosteroids reduce the number of eosinophils, basophils, and mast cells in the nasal mucosa and epithelium; directly inhibit the release of mediators from mast cells and basophils; reduce mucosal edema and vasodilation; stabilize the endothelium and epithelium resulting in decreased exudation; and reduce the sensitivity of irritant receptors resulting in decreased itching and sneezing.[90,91] Topical corticosteroids inhibit both the early- and late-phase reactions to antigen challenge, in contrast to systemic corticosteroids which only inhibit the late-phase reaction in allergic rhinitis.[92]

Intranasal corticosteroids primarily improve nasal symptoms associated with allergic rhinitis. Since V.J. also suffers from allergic conjunctivitis, her ocular symptoms may require separate treatment. This can be accomplished by administering systemic H₁-receptor antagonists. V.J. may require continuation of a small bedtime dose of brompheniramine. Ophthalmic antihistamine and decongestant combinations should not be recommended for prolonged use, as would be necessary to treat V.J.'s perennial allergic conjunctivitis, because rebound congestion of the blood vessels of the eye can occur in exactly the same way that it occurs in the nose leading to marked reddening of the sclera. Also, topical antihistamines can produce a local contact sensitivity reaction since the drugs are potential sensitizers.

15. Choice of Agent. What criteria should be considered when choosing among the available intranasal corticosteroids? How safe are topical corticosteroids in treating a 6-year-old like V.J.?

The corticosteroids currently available for intranasal administration are listed in Table 21.9. All of these agents have the advantages of high potency (relative to hydrocortisone) and high lipophilicity. All of the agents are absorbed from the nasal mucous membrane and from the gastrointestinal tract after incidental swallowing. However, all but dexamethasone sodium phosphate undergo extensive first-pass hepatic metabolism to less active or inactive metabolites.[91] Because dexamethasone is absorbed to a greater extent and not metabolized as efficiently, it exerts substantially greater systemic effects than the other three intranasal corticosteroid prep-

arations. For this reason, the other intranasal corticosteroids are preferable to dexamethasone for treatment of nasal disease.[93]

Efficacy trials comparing beclomethasone dipropionate and flunisolide have demonstrated no difference between them.[91] There have been no trials comparing triamcinolone acetonide with the other available preparations. Studies comparing intranasal corticosteroids to other treatment modalities for allergic rhinitis indicate that they are at least as effective as systemic H₁-receptor antagonists.[91]

All of the intranasal corticosteroids are approved for use in children six years of age and older, except triamcinolone acetonide which is not approved for children less than 12 years old.[48] A common concern regarding the use of corticosteroids in children is the risk of growth suppression. Because hypothalamic-pituitary-adrenal (HPA) axis suppression and systemic adverse effects have not been demonstrated,[90,91,93] it is very unlikely that the intranasal corticosteroids suppress growth in children. While growth suppression due to the intranasal corticosteroids has never been studied directly, one may be able to extrapolate data from the use of inhaled corticosteroids in asthma. The best designed study of growth in asthmatics treated with inhaled beclomethasone dipropionate accounted for the age of the children at the time of the study and adjusted for the age of onset of puberty. This study found no significant growth suppression in the steroid-treated patients and all patients achieved predicted adult height.[96]

Histological changes in nasal mucosa have not been demonstrated.[91,93] Intranasal candidiasis has never been documented.[91] Positive nasal and pharyngeal cultures for *Candida albicans* have been detected, but their relationship to treatment is unknown.[97,98]

A report from the National Registry of Drug-Induced Ocular Side Effects[99] linked 21 cases of bilateral posterior subcapsular cataracts to use of intranasal or inhaled corticosteroids. Nine of these patients also were treated with systemic corticosteroids. The number of these patients receiving intranasal rather than inhaled corticosteroids was not reported, but many of the patients were reported to have used the beclomethasone dipropionate for more than five years and often in doses greater than 252 μg/day. It is important for the clinician to consider the total corticosteroid load in atopic patients who may be treated with an inhaled and/or systemic preparation for asthma, intranasal preparation for rhinitis, and dermatologic preparation for eczema.[90]

16. Patient Education. V.J. is given a prescription for flunisolide, 2 sprays in each nostril BID. How should she be instructed to use this drug?

Patient education is important to ensure proper use of and response to the intranasal corticosteroids. V.J. should be instructed to blow the nose gently before instilling the nasal spray since copious nasal secretions will cause the medication to drain back out of the nose. Severe blockage of the nasal passage may prevent deposition of the drug at the site of action. If the patient is severely congested, a short course (two to three days) of topical decongestant used just before the intranasal steroid may be indicated. The patient should be instructed to direct the stream of medication onto the turbinates, not the nasal septum. This is accomplished by pointing the applicator nozzle straight and back, parallel to the septum in the sagittal plane.

Therapeutic benefit often is perceived in two to three days, but in some patients, benefit may not be realized for two to three weeks. The patient (and, in V.J.'s case, her Mother) must be informed of the possible delay in onset of action. V.J. is started on the maximum dose. If V.J.'s symptoms are well controlled on this dose, the dose may be tapered to find the lowest effective dose. For example, if V.J.'s symptoms are controlled on four sprays a day, her dose can decrease to three sprays a day, then two sprays a day, and so on until the lowest dose that controls her nasal symptoms is found. She

Table 21.9		Intranasal Corticosteroid Preparations[93–95]	
Drug	Preparations	Dose/Actuation	Recommended Dosage[a]
Beclomethasone Dipropionate (Beconase, Vancenase)	Nasal inhaler with halogenated hydrocarbon propellants	42 µg	*Adult:* 1 actuation/nostril BID–QID *Pediatric (6–12 years):* 1 actuation/nostril TID
(Beconase AQ, Vancenase AQ)	Aqueous nasal spray		
Budesonide (Rhinocort)	Nasal inhaler with halogenated hydrocarbon propellants	32 µg	*Adult and Pediatric (>6 years):* 2 actuations/nostril BID *or* 4 actuations/nostril Q AM
Dexamethasone (Decadron Phosphate Turbinaire)	Nasal inhaler with halogenated hydrocarbon propellants	84 µg	*Adult:* 2 actuations/nostril BID–TID *Pediatric (6–12 years):* 1–2 actuations/nostril BID
Flunisolide (Nasalide)	Aqueous nasal spray	25 µg	*Adult:* 2 actuations/nostril BID–TID *Pediatric (6–14 years):* 1 actuation/nostril TID *or* 2 actuations/nostril BID
Fluticasone propionate	Aqueous nasal spray	50 µg	*Adult:*[b] 2 actuations/nostril QD *or* 1 actuation/nostril BID *Adolescents:* 1 actuation/nostril QD
Triamcinolone acetonide (Nasacort)	Nasal inhaler with halogenated hydrocarbon propellants	55 µg	*Adult (>12 years):*[b] 2–4 actuations/nostril QD

[a] Dosage should be reduced to the least effective dose once symptoms have been controlled.
[b] Not FDA-approved for use in children <12 years old.

should stay on any given dosage level for at least one week. If at any point her symptoms worsen after a dosage reduction, she should be instructed to increase the dose back to the last effective dose. Since V.J. has perennial allergic rhinitis, this medication should be used chronically for an indefinite period of time.

17. Adverse Effects. V.J.'s mother telephones the clinic with the complaint that the flunisolide nasal spray is stinging so badly that she is unable to get V.J. to cooperate with drug administration. What causes this reaction? Are there ways to minimize stinging?

Adverse effects are rare and usually mild with the intranasal corticosteroids.[90,91] Local irritation manifested as stinging and burning can occur. This is more common with flunisolide (due to its propylene and polyethylene glycol vehicle and acidic pH) and beclomethasone nasal inhaler (due to its freon propellant) than with the aqueous (AQ) formulations of beclomethasone dipropionate.[93] V.J.'s therapy should be changed to beclomethasone aqueous spray. Saline irrigation before administration of the intranasal corticosteroid preparation also can help to minimize stinging.

Irritation and damage of the nasal septum can occur, presenting as hemorrhagic crusting, ulceration, and, rarely, perforation. Usually patients who incorrectly direct the stream of medication toward the septum, rather than the turbinates, suffer these complications.[90,91]

Systemic Corticosteroids

18. When, if ever, would systemic corticosteroids be indicated for V.J.?

In contrast to the minimal side effects of the topical corticosteroids, systemic administration of these drugs can cause numerous, and at times serious, adverse effects. Systemic administration, therefore, must be reserved for only short-term, adjunctive therapy in cases of severe, debilitating rhinitis. In such cases, a short course of relatively high-dose corticosteroid, so-called "burst" therapy, can be administered. Prednisone, 40 mg/day for adults or 1 to 2 mg/kg/day for children (or an equivalent dose of a comparable compound), every morning for one week will effectively relieve acute rhinitis symptoms. It should be started concurrently with the planned long-term therapy (e.g., H_1-antagonist-decongestant combination, intranasal corticosteroid, intranasal cromolyn sodium).[52]

"Burst" corticosteroid therapy rarely produces clinically important side effects.[100] An increase in appetite and mild cushingoid

effects may occur toward the end of the burst with either no[101] or only transient[102] (<10 days) HPA axis suppression. However, four or more corticosteroid "bursts" a year may place some patients at greater risk for HPA axis suppression.[103]

The use of intranasal turbinate injections of corticosteroids has been reported, but the efficacy has never been studied in a controlled manner. This practice can result in serious complications, including vision loss, and has been discouraged in favor of oral steroid therapy for those patients requiring systemic treatment.[52]

If V.J. were to have a particularly severe exacerbation of her allergic rhinitis such that it interfered with her sleep or her ability to attend school, an oral corticosteroid "burst" would be indicated. This might occur if the pollen load was particularly heavy due to an unusual weather change. Incidentally, V.J. probably also will notice a remarkable improvement in her nasal symptoms if she ever requires a corticosteroid "burst" for her asthma.

Immunotherapy

19. Two weeks ago, V.J.'s treatment was changed to intranasal beclomethasone aqueous spray, 1 actuation in each nostril TID. V.J. and her mother report a marked decrease in sneezing, nose rubbing, stuffiness, and nasal discharge. They deny drug side effects.

Physical examination reveals good air movement through the nose, absence of turbinate swelling, and only minimal clear nasal discharge.

V.J.'s mother has heard about "allergy shots" on television and asks if they would be helpful for her daughter. What are "allergy shots"? Is V.J. a candidate for this form of therapy?

"Allergy shots" or immunotherapy (also called desensitization or hyposensitization) is an alternative treatment for select patients.[104] Immunotherapy involves administration of gradually increasing concentrations of an aggravating allergen to a susceptible patient in an attempt to induce tolerance to the allergen. Increased tolerance eliminates symptoms associated with exposure to that allergen.

Immunotherapy clearly is more effective than placebo in improving allergic rhinitis.[104] It is unusual to relieve completely all allergic symptoms, but immunotherapy does significantly decrease both symptoms and medication requirements. Despite its documented effectiveness, immunotherapy is controversial because it is expensive, potentially can cause severe complications, and only partially relieves symptoms.

Immunotherapy is most beneficial and cost-effective when patients are selected carefully, using strict guidelines. Candidates for immunotherapy include patients: 1) with moderate to severe symptoms that are not controlled by allergen avoidance or maximum tolerable doses of medications; 2) who suffer severe interference with necessary activities (e.g., occupation) because of symptoms or medication side effects; 3) with life-threatening reactions to bee or wasp venoms or drugs; and 4) who are allergic to a single or very few clearly identifiable allergens.[105]

Adverse reactions to immunotherapy are common and may be quite severe.[104] The most common adverse effect is a mild local reaction consisting of induration and swelling at the injection site, although large and painful local reactions at the injection site can occur rarely. Patients may experience a worsening of their symptoms within hours after receiving the injection. Finally, anaphylaxis can occur and, for this reason, a physician must be in attendance and emergency equipment must be available when the injections are administered.

V.J. is responding well to pharmacotherapy without side effects. Since she is controlled on this relatively inexpensive and noninvasive therapeutic regimen, immunotherapy is not indicated to augment her treatment.

Seasonal Allergic Rhinitis

20. L.B. is a 57-year-old male with a history of hypertension for 10 years and seasonal allergic rhinitis since childhood. He also has a past history of childhood asthma but has not experienced any respiratory symptoms since he was 16 years old. L.B. presents to the emergency room (ER) on April 30th with complaints of acute urinary retention. He has not voided since 7:00 a.m. on April 29th and he is complaining of severe suprapubic pain.

L.B. states that he has had difficulty initiating urination and stopping the stream of urine (''dribbling'') for approximately six months. He states that he has been too busy to have this complaint evaluated by his physician.

Approximately 1 week ago, L.B. started to experience nasal stuffiness, clear rhinorrhea, and sneezing, and the symptoms have become progressively worse. These symptoms are similar to those that he suffers every year at this time. As he has in past years, L.B. decided to self-medicate his allergic rhinitis symptoms with an over-the-counter (OTC) antihistamine and decongestant: diphenhydramine (Benadryl) 50 mg TID or QID PRN and SR phenylpropanolamine 75 mg Q 12 hr. He took his first dose of both of these medications with his breakfast on April 29th.

L.B.'s other medications are hydrochlorothiazide 50 mg Q AM and diltiazem 60 mg TID. He has no previous history of adverse drug reactions or drug allergies. He does not smoke or drink alcohol.

Upon physical examination, L.B.'s blood pressure (BP) is 154/100 mm Hg and his pulse is 110/min. Other vital signs are normal. Nasal examination reveals mild obstruction bilaterally, swollen and boggy mucosa over the turbinates, and a small amount of clear nasal discharge. The chest is clear to auscultation and cardiac auscultation is normal. Digital rectal examination reveals an enlarged prostate which is smooth and mobile and without nodules.

Laboratory findings include an elevated blood urea nitrogen (BUN) to 30 mg/dL and serum creatinine (SrCr) to 1.8 mg/dL. Intravenous pyelography reveals bilateral hydronephrosis. Medical history review finds allergy skin test results showing sensitivity to tree pollen (cottonwood, oak) and cat dander. [SI units: BUN 10.7 mmol/L; SrCr 108 μmol/L]. Why could L.B.'s urinary complaints be exacerbated by treatment of his rhinitis?

L.B. is exhibiting symptoms of urinary outflow obstruction or prostatism. In addition to the hesitancy and postmicturition dribbling that L.B. is experiencing, patients also may note a need to strain to initiate voiding, slow urine stream, and bladder fullness after voiding. The most common cause of obstruction is benign prostatic hyperplasia (BPH). Because the prostate is located anatomically around the urethra, enlargement of the gland can obstruct urine flow. Long-standing BPH with a superimposed acute exacerbation has led to early postrenal or obstructive renal failure in L.B. as indicated by the elevation in plasma urea and creatinine and hydronephrosis.[106]

The bladder and urethra are made up of smooth muscle tissue and are innervated by the sympathetic and parasympathetic divisions of the autonomic nervous system. The detrusor musculature is predominantly innervated by β-adrenergic and cholinergic receptors. The bladder neck (or outlet) is innervated predominately by α-adrenergic receptors. Sympathetic stimulation causes relaxation of the detrusor muscle to allow bladder filling, closure of the urethra, and decreased bladder emptying. Cholinergic stimulation of the detrusor causes contraction of the detrusor to cause bladder emptying.[107] Initially, the detrusor musculature is able to compensate for the urethral obstruction in BPH.[106,107] Eventually, the detrusor muscle fibers hypertrophy and decompensate resulting in urinary retention and detrusor hyperreflexia manifesting as urinary frequency, urgency, urge incontinence, and nocturia.[106]

When L.B. took diphenhydramine in combination with phenylpropanolamine, he precipitated acute urinary retention by two mechanisms. First, α-adrenergic stimulation of phenylpropanolamine caused closure of the urethra and bladder neck. Second, the anticholinergic properties of diphenhydramine blocked detrusor contraction. He may be able to tolerate one of the newer agents (terfenadine, astemizole, or loratadine) since they are free of anticholinergic side effects.

21. Is L.B.'s use of phenylpropanolamine causing his elevated blood pressure and pulse?

Although the nasal decongestant agents commonly are thought to cause blood pressure elevation in both hypertensive and normotensive individuals, this concept is not well supported in the literature.[108,109] At recommended therapeutic doses, the oral decongestants rarely cause blood pressure elevation in either normotensive or hypertensive patients, although this effect may be difficult to predict.[108,110] These effects are dose dependent.[110]

In hypertensive patients with rhinitis who are experiencing marked nasal congestion such that it is interfering with their sleep, a long-acting topical decongestant (e.g., oxymetazoline) can be recommended for use at bedtime. The patient, however, should be cautioned to use the agent only as needed for severe symptoms and should be warned about the possible implications of overuse.

Considering L.B.'s clinical condition upon admission to the ER, his blood pressure and pulse elevation may be due to anxiety and pain. However, his blood pressure must be monitored and his antihypertensive therapy continued. Because of his intercurrent illness, BPH, the oral decongestants are contraindicated and should be discontinued.

22. What indicates that L.B. suffers from seasonal allergic rhinitis? How do the general treatment principles for seasonal and perennial allergic rhinitis differ?

Diagnosis

Seasonal allergic rhinitis sometimes is called ''hay fever.'' This is a misnomer, however, because seasonal allergic rhinitis neither is caused by hay nor is it associated with a fever. As previously noted, L.B.'s symptoms are the same as a those of a patient with perennial allergic rhinitis. The fact that L.B. experiences symptoms predictably at the onset of the tree pollination season, and is symptom-free during the remainder of the year, indicates that he suffers from seasonal allergic rhinitis. His gradual worsening at the beginning of the tree pollen season probably is due to rising pollen counts from the trees to which L.B. is sensitive.

Therapeutic Objectives

The therapeutic objectives for seasonal allergic rhinitis are the same as for perennial allergic rhinitis: symptom control allowing all usual daily activities with no adverse side effects of therapy. In patients with seasonal allergic rhinitis, another therapeutic objective is preventing the onset of symptoms by anticipating the patient's season of sensitivity. Given the predictability of the onset of various allergen seasons, chronic treatment should be instituted one to two weeks before the season is due to begin. In L.B.'s case, he should begin a prescribed treatment regimen in early to mid-April since the pollination season for trees in his geographic area begins in the third or fourth week of April. Treatment can be discontinued after the tree pollination season ends in the summer. This differs from the treatment plan for perennial allergic rhinitis in which treatment likewise must be perennial.

Intranasal Cromolyn Sodium

23. How should L.B.'s seasonal allergic rhinitis be treated?

L.B. appears to have mild allergic rhinitis which has not caused him to seek medical advice consistently. Nonpharmacologic treatments like saline irrigation and exercise would be beneficial for L.B. and should be instituted. Because his disease is relatively mild, cromolyn sodium would be a good alternative to antihistamines and decongestants, which are contraindicated for L.B. at this time.

Cromolyn sodium (Nasalcrom) stabilizes mast cells (possibly by calcium channel blockade); this inhibits the release of the chemical mediators from these cells.[111] Cromolyn sodium does not alter the release of mediators from basophils nor does it alter the course of histamine already released from the mast cells or basophils.[52] For this reason, treatment should be initiated *before* the onset of allergic symptoms, whenever possible.

When used correctly, intranasal cromolyn sodium is effective for the treatment of allergic rhinitis.[112,113] By inhibiting the early- and late-phase reactions to antigen stimulation,[111] cromolyn sodium relieves itching, sneezing, and rhinorrhea. However, it may not be as effective as other treatment modalities for nasal obstruction. Comparative efficacy studies indicate that cromolyn sodium generally is less effective than intranasal corticosteroids in the treatment of allergic rhinitis,[91] but it essentially is free of side effects.

Dosing and Patient Education. The initial dose for the 4% cromolyn sodium nasal spray is one spray in each nostril four to six times daily.[52] The dose eventually may be reduced to the lowest effective dose after symptoms have been controlled. Patient instruction regarding the use of intranasal cromolyn sodium is the same as for intranasal corticosteroids. If therapy is initiated after onset of symptoms, patients should be informed that relief may be delayed up to four weeks. Additional therapy, usually with a H_1-antagonist-decongestant combination, probably will be necessary until cromolyn sodium reaches full effect.[52] Once treatment is started, it should be continued chronically for the entire allergen season. Cromolyn sodium should not be used intermittently.

Adverse reactions to cromolyn sodium are rare. Local irritation occurs in less than 10% of patients, with burning, stinging and sneezing being the most common manifestations.[52]

24. Treatment Failure. L.B. returns to the clinic 3 weeks later. He complains that the cromolyn is not working. Nasal examination reveals mild obstruction bilaterally, swollen turbinates, and mild to moderate amounts of clear nasal discharge. What are the possible reasons for treatment failure with cromolyn sodium?

Possible reasons for treatment failure with cromolyn sodium include: 1) inability of the drug to prevent symptoms associated with mediator release secondary to basophil degranulation; 2) failure to start therapy before the onset of allergic symptoms; 3) inadequate exposure of the nasal mucosa to the drug due to excessive nasal congestion or improper use of the nasal spray; or 4) noncompliance with therapy due to the required frequency of administration.

L.B. did not start cromolyn sodium until after the onset of the tree pollen season, but some benefit should be apparent after three weeks of therapy. L.B. is not experiencing marked nasal obstruction, so drug disposition should not be impaired. Noncompliance is a strong possibility. The alternative to cromolyn sodium for L.B. is intranasal corticosteroids.

Vasomotor Rhinitis
Signs and Symptoms

25. M.S., a 29-year-old male, presents to the clinic with a chief complaint of profuse rhinorrhea which has been a chronic and progressively worsening problem for the past 5 years. He also experiences some nasal congestion with the rhinorrhea but denies nasal itching or sneezing. The nasal discharge is clear and watery. Although the symptoms tend to remit and exacerbate, they do not occur in any definable seasonal pattern. His symptoms are worsened by exposure to tobacco smoke, strong fumes like paint or ammonia, and dust, and often are associated with headaches. Also, the rhinorrhea is substantially worse upon exposure to cold air. M.S. has no family history for allergies. He does not smoke and drinks only occasionally. He has no other medical problems. His only medication, beclomethasone dipropionate nasal spray, 2 sprays in each nostril TID PRN, gives only partial relief of the symptoms. M.S. sniffs and blows his nose several times during the medical history. Physical examination reveals mildly erythematous nasal mucosa and a minimally edematous inferior turbinate. There is copious nasal discharge which is clear and watery and relatively good air movement through the nose. There is no sinus tenderness. The remainder of his physical examination is normal. Nasal smear demonstrates only a few neutrophils and no eosinophils. What information about M.S. supports the diagnosis of vasomotor rhinitis?

Vasomotor rhinitis is a term most often used to describe the non-eosinophilic subgroup of patients with perennial nonallergic rhinitis. The term occasionally has been used (or misused) to describe the entire group of patients with perennial nonallergic rhinitis. Vasomotor rhinitis is so named because it describes the presumed etiology of the disease: an imbalance in the autonomic nervous system in which the cholinergic parasympathetic activity exceeds the α-adrenergic activity in the nasal mucosa.[18] Theoretically, this is the reason that stimuli which normally increase parasympathetic activity in the nose, such as cold air and inhaled irritants, aggravate symptoms. Currently, however, vasomotor rhinitis is a diagnosis of exclusion encompassing those patients with idiopathic nonallergic perennial rhinitis without nasal eosinophilia.[16]

The symptoms of vasomotor rhinitis are variable. Most patients experience perennial nasal obstruction accompanied by profuse, watery nasal discharge.[18] Many patients complain of nasal obstruction as the primary symptom, while for others it is rhinorrhea. Sneezing is uncommon but can occur. Nasal itching is uncommon. Headache may occur and usually is frontal or localized over the bridge of the nose.[18] In contrast to allergic rhinitis, the onset of symptoms in patients with vasomotor rhinitis usually occurs in adulthood, but before 40 years of age.

Patients report worsening of their symptoms with exposure to nonspecific irritants including tobacco smoke, industrial pollutants, dust, strong odors, chemical fumes, changes in the environmental temperature or humidity, and ingestion of very cold or very hot beverages. Most patients have no history or evidence of atopy.[18]

The appearance of the nasal mucosa also is variable. The turbinates are usually erythematous and swollen, and during an exacerbation, considerable quantities of nasal secretions usually are present. There may be mast cells present in the nasal smear, but by definition there is no nasal eosinophilia. Skin tests are normal.[18]

M.S.'s symptoms of bothersome watery rhinorrhea, nasal congestion, and headache without itching or sneezing are typical. His complaint of worsening symptoms with exposure to noxious inhalants and cold air are supportive of the diagnosis of vasomotor rhinitis. The nasal smear notably lacking large numbers of eosinophils initially differentiates this disease from eosinophilic nonallergic rhinitis.[16]

Treatment

26. M.S. asks what causes vasomotor rhinitis and what can be done to alleviate his symptoms. What are the available treatments for vasomotor rhinitis?

Nonpharmacologic Therapy

Nasal symptoms in patients with vasomotor rhinitis have been shown to be influenced by psychic factors.[18] Some therapeutic benefit may be realized by establishing an on-going, trusting relationship between the health care provider and the patient.[18] This should include a thorough explanation of the disease state and the realistic outcomes of therapy for most patients. Psychotherapy is helpful in some cases.[18,114] In addition, patients should be instructed to avoid as many aggravating factors as possible, such as smoking, exposure to smoke or other irritants, and very cold or very hot beverages.[18] Saline irrigation is valuable as a general soothing and moisturizing treatment; exercise may be helpful particularly for patients with vasomotor rhinitis since it increases sympathetic tone.[4,12]

Pharmacotherapy

Due to their anticholinergic drying effects, *systemic H_1-receptor antagonists* may be helpful in the treatment of vasomotor rhinitis, and a therapeutic trial is worthwhile.[16,114] In general though, H_1-antagonists are less effective in the treatment of vasomotor rhinitis than of allergic rhinitis.[52] In particular, the nonsedating antihistamines have little value in vasomotor rhinitis since they also lack anticholinergic properties. *Oral decongestants* may improve nasal symptoms in some patients with vasomotor rhinitis, but objective measures of improvement such as rhinomanometry are affected variably.[53] Still, oral decongestants also warrant a therapeutic trial.[53,115] *Intranasal corticosteroids*[116] and *cromolyn sodium*[16,111] rarely are effective for vasomotor rhinitis.

Initial treatment for M.S. should include chronic administration of a systemic H_1-receptor antagonist with considerable anticholinergic action (e.g., diphenhydramine, promethazine) and an oral decongestant as needed. Intranasal beclomethasone should be discontinued.

27. M.S. returns to the outpatient clinic for follow-up. He has been taking diphenhydramine 50 mg TID for 3 months. His symptoms are improved only minimally and he is bothered by sedation from the medication. What alternative treatments are available for M.S.?

Unfortunately, M.S.'s case is typical of the often frustrating course in treating vasomotor rhinitis.[16,114] Commonly, multiple therapeutic plans fail.

In patients like M.S. who suffer rhinorrhea as their predominant symptom, *ipratropium bromide* (Atrovent), a topically active congener of atropine, may decrease nasal secretions. Because its quaternary ammonium structure makes it lipophobic, it is absorbed poorly from the nasal mucosa and GI tract and does not cross the blood-brain barrier.[117] Ipratropium bromide significantly decreases

nasal discharge after an intranasal methacholine challenge.[117] It causes a statistically significant reduction in rhinorrhea (measured by number of nose blowing episodes or daily number of tissues used), but has no effect upon sneezing or nasal obstruction.[118,119]

A representative study[118] illustrates the clinical significance of ipratropium bromide treatment for rhinorrhea. Thirty-six adults who suffered with almost daily watery rhinorrhea due to perennial nonallergic rhinitis completed the following study protocol: a two-week run-in period during which all antiallergy medications were discontinued; two three-week treatment periods in which patients received either ipratropium bromide 80 µg four times a day or placebo in a double-blind, crossover manner; and a two-week open assessment of ipratropium bromide 400 µg four times a day. Patients were monitored with daily diary cards recording the number of sneezes and nose blowing occurrences per day, and twice-daily self-assessment of nasal obstruction and treatment side effects. The average daily number of nose blowings during the run-in period was 33.6 ± 63.6 (mean ± standard deviation; range: 3.6 to 373). This value decreased to 29.4 ± 43.8 (range: 3.1 to 256) during placebo treatment and decreased further to 17.6 ± 25.2 (range: 2.4 to 139) during treatment with ipratropium bromide 80 µg four times a day (p < 0.001). No effect was demonstrated upon sneezing or nasal congestion. Overall, ipratropium bromide treatment decreased rhinorrhea, measured by nose-blowing occurrences, but there was considerable variability in the response. No predictors of response could be found. The patients on the low end of the range for nose-blowing occurrences (22% of patients included in the study) probably did not require ipratropium bromide therapy at all. Two patients (5.6%) needed the higher dose to achieve symptom control.

In most studies, ipratropium bromide was administered at a dose of 80 µg (40 µg in each nostril) four times a day or a total of 320 µg/day.[118,119] If treatment with ipratropium bromide is attempted, dosage individualization is necessary since the range of doses required for symptom relief varied from 168 µg/day[120] to 1600 µg/day.[118] Intranasal ipratropium bromide is not available in the U.S. Adaptation of oral inhalers for intranasal administration, using a baby bottle nipple with the tip cut off to direct the stream of medication, has been suggested.[51]

In general, intranasal ipratropium bromide is well tolerated. The most common side effects are nasal dryness, nasal burning, bloody nasal discharge or epistaxis, dry or sore throat, and dry mouth.[118–122] Side effects appear to be dose-related[118,120,122] and may be serious in certain patient populations with the largest doses.[118] Theoretically, elderly males with benign prostatic hyperplasia may experience difficulty in urinating, but the risk is low due to negligible systemic absorption. No significant adverse cardiovascular or blood pressure effects have been observed.[121] Rebound nasal symptoms do not occur after discontinuation of the drug.[120]

Surgical treatments have been attempted for patients in whom medical management fails. The surgical options include modification of the inferior turbinates (by turbinate displacement, electrocautery, or cryotherapy) or vidian neurectomy.[114]

Eosinophilic Nonallergic Rhinitis
Signs and Symptoms

28. P.W., a 32-year-old female, presents to the outpatient clinic with a complaint of nasal congestion, rhinorrhea (the nasal discharge is cloudy white), occasional sneezing, but no nasal itching. The symptoms have been constant for approximately 3 years and do not vary with the season. She notes a worsening of symptoms with exposure to tobacco smoke and various irritating fumes. In the past 18 months, P.W. has had

2 sinus infections which resolved after a 10-day course of amoxicillin. P.W.'s family history is negative for allergy, and she does not smoke or drink.

Upon physical examination, the nasal mucosa is pink, but the turbinates are swollen markedly. Air movement through the nose is reduced moderately. After administration of phenylephrine 0.5%, 2 drops in each nostril, polyps are visualized along the middle and superior turbinates. There are copious white, mucoid nasal secretions. There is no sinus tenderness. The remainder of her physical examination is normal. A nasal smear reveals 3+ eosinophils. Sinus x-rays demonstrate mucosal thickening to 7 mm, but there are no air-fluid levels or opacifications. What information about P.W. supports a diagnosis of eosinophilic nonallergic rhinitis?

The term eosinophilic nonallergic rhinitis has been applied to the subgroup of patients with perennial rhinitis, a negative history for seasonal or specific allergen-induced exacerbation, negative skin tests, and many eosinophils on nasal smear.[123] Others have labeled this presentation "nonallergic rhinitis with eosinophilia syndrome" (NARES),[124] but this nomenclature has been debated.[125] In adults with chronic rhinitis, 10% to 15% may have eosinophilic nonallergic rhinitis;[16] the incidence is estimated to be 1% to 5% of pediatric patients with perennial rhinitis.[126]

The symptoms of eosinophilic nonallergic rhinitis are similar to vasomotor rhinitis: profuse rhinorrhea, moderate to marked nasal obstruction, and occasional sneezing.[123] Nasal itching is less common. Anosmia may be noted.[127] Nasal examination may reveal normal mucous membranes or they may appear erythematous.[16] As illustrated by P.W., the turbinates typically are swollen. Approximately one-third of patients with eosinophilic nonallergic rhinitis have nasal polyps.[16]

Patients with eosinophilic nonallergic rhinitis are differentiated from patients with vasomotor rhinitis by demonstration of nasal eosinophilia upon nasal smear. They also have a high incidence of abnormal sinus x-rays, with or without clinical symptoms of sinusitis.[16] It has been hypothesized that eosinophilic nonallergic rhinitis is a precursor to the triad of nasal polyposis, intrinsic asthma, and aspirin intolerance.[16,127] This theory has yet to be proven.

Pharmacotherapy

29. How should P.W. be treated?

Unlike patients with vasomotor rhinitis, patients with eosinophilic nonallergic rhinitis respond well to drug therapy.[16] The majority of patients will respond to systemic H_1-receptor antagonists and oral decongestants. For those patients who cannot tolerate antihistamine therapy, intranasal corticosteroids offer an excellent therapeutic option.[16,115,126] Intranasal cromolyn sodium is ineffective.[128] P.W. should be treated with a systemic H_1-receptor antagonist and an oral decongestant. An intranasal corticosteroid preparation is an excellent alternative.

Viral Upper Respiratory Infection

Signs and Symptoms

30. C.R., a 33-year-old female, is accompanied by her 3-year-old, 15 kg daughter, F.R., and complains that they both have had runny and stuffy noses for the past 2 days. C.R. states that she also had a sore throat and a cough that kept her up all last night. C.R. attributes their symptoms to a "cold" which she claims her daughter caught at her day-care center. Neither C.R. nor F.R. have had a fever or any other symptoms including ear pain or pulling in the child. Neither patient takes medications and they have no known allergies.

Which factors in C.R.'s and F.R.'s presentations indicate that they are suffering a common cold?

Common colds are caused by six different virus families including over 200 serotypes. The two most common viruses are the rhinoviruses (30% to 50% of cases) and the coronaviruses (10% to 20% of cases). Viruses such as respiratory syncytial virus and influenza virus typically cause more severe illnesses, but occasionally can cause the common cold syndrome. Adenoviruses, parainfluenza viruses, and enteroviruses are other infrequent causes of the common cold.[129,130]

The causative virus infects the nasal epithelial cells of the host. Most serotypes of rhinovirus and coronavirus have an incubation period of two to three days. The viruses multiply in the infected epithelial cells and are shed in nasal secretions. Viral shedding peaks during the first week of infection, but viral replication may continue for two to three weeks. Symptoms typically are worst on day two or three of illness and last for about one week. In about one-fourth of cases, cold symptoms may last for two weeks or longer.[129,130]

The probable routes of viral transmission are by manual transmission and infected droplets spread by sneezing and coughing. It has been proposed that thorough hand washing with soap and water may prevent transmission.[129,130] Rhinovirus commonly is spread among children in the classroom and then to the home environment.[131]

A patient can contract a cold at any time during the year, but there are seasonal outbreaks associated with the causative viruses. Rhinoviruses are most prevalent in the fall (associated with the beginning of the school term) and in the spring. Coronaviruses are most prevalent in the midwinter through the early spring.[130,131]

Preschool children less than five years of age are the most commonly affected age group, experiencing six to ten colds a year. In contrast, adults over the age of 30 average two to four colds a year, and adults over the age of 60 average less than one cold a year. Women in the 20- to 30-year-old age group have more colds than men presumably because of their greater exposure to children.[129,132]

The symptoms of the common cold are familiar.[132] Eighty to one hundred percent of patients experience nasal discharge and obstruction. The nasal discharge initially is clear, then after one to two days secretions become turbid and more tenacious. Other typical symptoms include sneezing, sore throat, hoarseness, and cough. Less frequently, patients may have headache, malaise, myalgia, or a sensation of chills or feverishness. Fever greater than 100 °F occurs in less than 1% of patients with the common cold. In patients with the common cold, the upper respiratory complaints are the most prominent. This is in contrast to patients with influenza in whom constitutional complaints predominate and fever is present in over 95% of patients.[132]

The common cold may be complicated by secondary bacterial infection of the nasopharynx or paranasal sinuses; in children, acute otitis media can occur as a complication. Exacerbations of asthma and chronic obstructive lung disease also can occur as a result of viral upper respiratory infection.[132]

C.R. and F.R. have rhinorrhea and nasal obstruction. Additionally, C.R. has a sore throat and cough. These are all typical symptoms of the common cold. Both patients are afebrile, supporting a diagnosis of common cold and making a diagnosis of influenza or bacterial infection less likely. F.R. has no ear pain or pulling, making a diagnosis of otitis media unlikely.

Pharmacotherapy

31. C.R. asks you for a cold medication for herself and her daughter. What recommendations can you make?

The primary therapeutic goals for the common cold are to relieve the patient's symptoms, allow her to perform necessary daily activities, reduce her risk of developing complications, and inhibit spread of the infection to others.[129] Patients, with or without physician consultation, will attempt to achieve these goals with the assistance of various nonprescription cold preparations.[132] Because the predominant symptoms of the common cold are nasal, therapeutic intervention should be directed at those symptoms.

H_1-Receptor Antagonists

H_1-receptor antagonists are present in numerous nonprescription cold medications, both single agent and combination products. Any beneficial effects are thought to be due to the anticholinergic effects of these drugs and not their histamine-blocking properties.[133] These drugs have not been shown to be of any benefit for preschool age children. Symptomatic improvement has been demonstrated in children 4 to 12 years old with H_1-receptor antagonist in combination products containing at least two other ingredients, although the studies in older children did not have a placebo control.[133]

In adolescents and adults, a statistically significant improvement in symptoms has been demonstrated with chlorpheniramine, but not with diphenhydramine or triprolidine.[133] The clinical significance of the improvements is meager.[134]

Decongestants

The oral decongestants pseudoephedrine and phenylpropanolamine, and the topical decongestant oxymetazoline improve nasal patency and reduce symptoms, but can cause side effects. These agents all are effective as single agents.[133] If nasal congestion is a major symptom for an individual patient, these agents should be used alone to treat that symptom. Combination with an H_1-antagonist will cause side effects, but will add little to therapy.[134] The risk of rebound congestion with topical administration must be considered.

Antitussives

Cough due to irritation of the throat or lower airways from postnasal drip may serve a protective purpose and should not be suppressed. However, a dry cough that keeps the patient awake at night or otherwise disrupts the patient's necessary activities could be suppressed safely. Antitussives such as dextromethorphan (Vicks Formula 44) or codeine effectively suppress the cough center in the medulla. These agents can cause drowsiness which can be potentiated by other CNS depressants; dextromethorphan interacts with the monoamine oxidase inhibitors.[132] The adult dose for dextromethorphan is 60 to 120 mg/day divided every six to eight hours; the pediatric dose is 1 to 2 mg/kg/day every six to eight hours.[42] The adult antitussive dose for codeine is 10 to 20 mg/dose every four to six hours as needed (maximum: 120 mg/day); the pediatric dose is 1 to 1.5 mg/kg/day in divided doses every four to six hours as needed (maximum: 30 mg/day for children 2 to 6 years of age; 60 mg/day for children 6 to 12 years of age).[42]

Expectorants

Guaifenesin was included as the only safe and effective expectorant in the final monograph of the FDA Advisory Review Panel on OTC Cold, Cough, Allergy, Bronchodilator, and Antiasthmatic Drug Products.[135] In spite of conflicting evidence in the literature,[136] the inclusion of guaifenesin in the final monograph was based upon a single study submitted by the A.H. Robins Company which looked at the effects of guaifenesin in 40 patients with chronic bronchitis. The study demonstrated that the mean percentage of total sputum expectorated by day 7 of the 15-day study was significantly greater for the guaifenesin-treated patients compared to the placebo-treated patients (69.3% versus 53.7%, respectively; $p < 0.001$). Also, the mean number of days to expectoration of 75% of the total sputum volume was significantly lower in the guaifenesin-treated group than those in the placebo-treated

group (8.40 versus 10.65 days, respectively; $p < 0.001$), but the total sputum expectorated over the 15 study days was not significantly different between the two groups.[135] The FDA panel denied a request that guaifenesin also be given an indication as an antitussive and also classified 20 other expectorants, including potassium iodide, ammonium chloride, and tolu balsam, as nonmonograph necessitating their removal from all OTC products.[135] Concentrations of potassium iodide that must be prescribed by a physician still are labeled with an indication as an expectorant. But because of the lack of objective data to support its use for this indication,[137] its potential for toxic reactions, and harmful effects upon a developing fetus, potassium iodide probably should not be recommended. Good hydration with oral liquids and humidified air is, perhaps, the best expectorant that can be recommended.[132] In general, patients with viral upper respiratory infection seldom have thickened lower respiratory tract secretions that are difficult to expectorate[132] so guaifenesin probably is not indicated for most of these patients.

Analgesics and Antipyretics

The analgesics and antipyretics, aspirin and acetaminophen, are included in many combination cold preparations. In general, these drugs are unnecessary since neither myalgia nor fever are typical symptoms of the common cold. Additionally, aspirin may be harmful in that it has been associated with Reye's syndrome in children and may increase viral shedding in rhinovirus infection, possibly promoting spread.[132] (See Chapter 95: Pediatric Considerations.)

Specific antiviral therapy for the common cold has not been found yet. Efforts to develop such drugs have been hindered by the inability of the drugs to inhibit viruses without causing significant toxicity and by the inability to deliver adequate concentrations of the drug to the nasal epithelium where viral replication occurs.[129] Only the immunomodulator α_2 interferon has been effective in preventing rhinovirus infection. When administered intranasally, the drug has been shown to reduce the spread of the common cold in families. The cost-effectiveness of such therapy has yet to be evaluated.[129,132] This is an investigational use of α_2 interferon.

The rhinorrhea and nasal congestion that C.R. and F.R. are experiencing are bothersome. For C.R., treatment with a decongestant, like pseudoephedrine, might improve her congestion. Also, since C.R.'s cough is interfering with her sleep, a dose of dextromethorphan 30 mg at bedtime might be helpful. Unfortunately, rhinorrhea and nasal congestion have never been shown to be amenable to drug therapy in F.R.'s age group. Supportive care including rest and adequate hydration are the most helpful recommendations that can be made.[132] Since their symptoms have been present for at least two days, they have peaked already, in all likelihood.

Drug-Induced Nasal Congestion
Clinical Presentation and Drugs
Capable of Causing Nasal Disease

32. B.C., a 22-year-old female, presents to the outpatient clinic with a complaint of severe nasal obstruction. She states that these symptoms began about 6 months ago when she started taking birth control pills. The nasal congestion became so bothersome that she started using a nonprescription nasal decongestant spray to help her breathe better. Since she started using the nasal spray, the symptoms have become progressively worse. Each time she tries to stop using the nasal spray, she becomes congested so severely that she cannot breathe through her nose at all and her voice becomes extremely nasal. Within 10 minutes of using the nasal spray, her nose is clear, she is able to breathe freely, and her voice returns to normal. She is

unable to be without the nasal decongestant spray and finds that she has bottles of the medication everywhere she goes (e.g., one in her car, one at her mother's house where she frequently visits, one on her night stand in case she awakens at night with symptoms).

B.C. has no medical problems and her only medications are her oral contraceptive and topical decongestant. She has no history of rhinitis in childhood. She does not smoke but drinks alcohol socially. Upon physical examination, B.C. is obstructed completely and unable to move any air through her nose. Examination of her nose confirms that the swollen turbinates are obstructing the nasal airway completely. Application of phenylephrine 0.5%, 2 drops in each nostril, partially relieved the turbinate swelling and permitted visualization of the nasal mucosa. The mucosa was erythematous, with small patches of friable tissue and bleeding. No abnormal growths were observed. The remainder of the physical examination was normal. What is the most likely etiology of B.C.'s nasal congestion?

A number of systemic medications cause nasal congestion and other nasal disorders as a side effect.[19,54,138] (See Table 21.10.) These medications can be separated into five categories: 1) vasodilators; 2) cholinergic stimulants; 3) cocaine; 4) miscellaneous agents; and 5) topical decongestants.

Vasodilators act by a number of different mechanisms.[54,138] Antiadrenergic agents act centrally (e.g., methyldopa, clonidine) or peripherally (e.g., reserpine, prazosin) to decrease sympathetic tone resulting in vasodilation. The antipsychotic drugs thioridazine and perphenazine and the antidepressant amitriptyline all possess α-adrenergic blocking properties and, therefore, can cause vasodilation. Nonselective β-adrenergic receptor antagonists presumably cause nasal congestion by permitting unopposed cholinergic stimulation. Hydralazine directly relaxes vascular smooth muscle to cause vasodilation. In the nasal vasculature, vasodilation leads to tissue edema and nasal congestion.

Estrogens and oral contraceptives are thought to inhibit anticholinesterase, thereby increasing local acetylcholine concentrations and causing vasodilation. This is similar to the effects of endogenous estrogen during pregnancy.[19] It appears from her history that B.C.'s original complaint of nasal congestion was associated with her contraceptives. Perhaps she will tolerate a new brand containing a different estrogenic component or a lower dose.

Theoretically, rebound rhinitis could result from constant cocaine use since it is a vasoconstrictor. Also, adulterants found in cocaine available on the street, including lactose, talc, and borax, can irritate nasal mucous membranes and cause crusting and atrophic changes. These combined effects can cause ischemia of the nasal septal cartilage leading to perforation.[139]

Other drugs can cause nasal congestion by unknown mechanisms. Examples are alprazolam[138] and cromolyn sodium.[19]

Topical decongestants can cause a severe condition that usually does not occur with systemic medications called *rhinitis medicamentosa* or rebound rhinitis. The precise mechanism by which this occurs is unknown. Theories include fatigue of the constrictor muscles in the nasal vasculature; tissue hypoxemia due to prolonged vasoconstriction leading to a reactive vasodilation as the drug effects subside; and longer duration of the beta-stimulatory effects of the drugs compared to the alpha-stimulatory effects leading to secondary vasodilation.[54] Whatever the subcellular mechanism, the result is a cycle of topical vasoconstrictor use followed by a profound nasal congestion causing the patient to use the topical agent again. After only three to five days of topical decongestant use, the patient can enter this cycle of use and dependence upon the drug.

Physical examination findings in patients with *rhinitis medicamentosa* include hyperemia with erythema and edema leading to

Table 21.10	Drugs Capable of Causing Nasal Disease[19,54,138]

Antihypertensives
  Methyldopa
  Prazosin
  Reserpine
  Hydralazine
  Propranolol
  Nadolol

Psychotherapeutic Drugs
  Amitriptyline
  Thioridazine
  Perphenazine

Hormonal Products
  Oral contraceptives
  Estrogen

Rebound Vasodilation After Vasoconstriction
  Prolonged use of topical decongestants (*rhinitis medicamentosa*)

Direct Tissue Damage
  Cocaine

Miscellaneous
  Alprazolam
  Cromolyn sodium

turbinate swelling and nasal obstruction.[140] The nasal mucosa also may have areas of increased tissue friability and punctate bleeding.[54] Clear, watery rhinorrhea also may occur,[140] but usually the secretions are scanty.[54]

B.C. apparently started using the topical decongestant to relieve the nasal congestion caused by her oral contraceptive. Now, after months of continuous topical decongestant use, she has *rhinitis medicamentosa*.

Management

33. How should B.C. be managed?

The best management of *rhinitis medicamentosa* is prevention.[140] Patients must be educated about the effects and potential complications of topical decongestants whenever they are prescribed or purchased without a prescription. Topical decongestant use must be limited to three to five days.

In any case of drug-induced nasal congestion, the most important intervention is to discontinue the offending agent and, if necessary, substitute another therapy which will not cause nasal symptoms.[138] In the case of topical decongestants, discontinuation of the nasal spray can be very difficult for the patient and presents the clinician with a therapeutic challenge.[54] It also is important to appropriately treat the underlying cause of the nasal congestion that led to the use of the topical decongestant.[12]

The first step in successfully treating the patient with *rhinitis medicamentosa* is to explain carefully and completely the condition to the patient. The patient must understand why the condition has occurred and what will be necessary to successfully discontinue the topical decongestant.[54]

The second step is to discontinue the topical decongestant spray. This can be done abruptly, but is likely to cause the patient considerable discomfort for the first four to seven days after discontinuation.[54] A number of strategies can help the patient endure this initial period. Application of normal saline to the nasal mucosa can moisturize the irritated tissues and give the patient a measure of comfort; the use of a commercial saline nasal spray is appropriate.[12,54] Intranasal corticosteroids frequently are helpful in decreasing the tissue inflammation associated with *rhinitis medicamentosa* and can help patients in the immediate period after discontinuing the topical decongestant.[12,54] In refractory cases, a short course of systemic corticosteroids may be necessary.[12] If the patient has used the topical decongestant continuously for many months or years, the nasal mucosa can be damaged irreversibly, necessitating surgical intervention.[139]

An alternative to abrupt withdrawal of the topical decongestant is to have the patient slowly taper the drug over the course of several days to several weeks. This is done by having the patient decrease the amount of topical decongestant used, starting with one nostril only. When the drug is withdrawn completely from one nostril, begin decreasing the amount of drug used in the other nostril. For example, have the patient substitute normal saline nasal

spray for decongestant spray in the right nostril for every other dose. Later, use saline twice for each decongestant dose. Eventually, the decongestant is discontinued totally in the right nostril and saline is substituted. Repeat the process for the left nostril. Saline can be used as often as needed throughout this process and after the topical decongestant is completely withdrawn. This method should be combined with careful patient education, plenty of patient support, and frequent follow-up. Also, it probably should be reserved for patients with the temperament to tolerate a prolonged treatment process.

References

1 **Mygind N, Weeke B.** Allergic and nonallergic rhinitis. In: Middleton E et al., eds. Allergy: Principles and Practice. 2nd ed. St. Louis: CV Mosby; 1983:1101.

2 **Adams PF, Benson V.** Current estimates from the national health interview survey. 1991. National Center for Health Statistics Vital Health Stat 10 (184). 1991.

3 **Collins JG.** Prevalence of selected chronic conditions. United States, 1986–88. National Center for Health Statistics. Vital Health Stat 10(182). 1993.

4 **Meltzer EO et al.** Chronic rhinitis in infants and children: etiologic, diagnostic, and therapeutic considerations. Pediatr Clin North Am. 1983;30:847.

5 **Williams PL et al., eds.** Gray's Anatomy. 37th ed. Edinburgh: Churchill Livingstone; 1989:1171.

6 **Mathews KP.** Allergic and nonallergic rhinitis, nasal polyposis, and sinusitis. In: Kaplan AP. Allergy. New York: Churchill Livingstone; 1985:323.

7 **Mullarkey MF.** A clinical approach to rhinitis. Med Clin North Am. 1981;65:977.

8 **Naclerio RM.** Allergic rhinitis. N Engl J Med. 1991;325:860.

9 **Fireman P.** Otitis media and its relationship to allergy. Pediatr Clin North Am. 1988;35:1075.

10 **Raphael GD et al.** How and why the nose runs. J Allergy Clin Immunol. 1991;87:457.

11 **Booth BH.** Diagnosis of immediate hypersensitivity. In: Patterson R et al., eds. Allergic Diseases: Diagnosis and Management. Philadelphia: JB Lippencott; 1993:195.

12 **Meltzer EO et al.** Allergic and nonallergic rhinitis. In: Middleton E et al., eds. Allergy: Principles and Practice. 3rd ed. St. Louis: CV Mosby; 1988:1253.

13 **Bresolin D.** Facial characteristics of children who breathe through the mouth. Pediatrics. 1984;73:622.

14 **Pelikan Z.** The changes in the nasal secretions of eosinophils during the immediate nasal response to allergen challenge. J Allergy Clin Immunol. 1983;72:657.

15 **Kirsch JP, White JA.** Nasal polyposis. J La State Med Soc. 1990;142:11.

16 **Mullarkey MF et al.** Allergic and nonallergic rhinitis: their characterization with attention to the meaning of nasal eosinophilia. J Allergy Clin Immunol. 1980;65:122.

17 **Shapiro RS.** Foreign bodies of the nose. In: Bluestone CD, Stool SE, eds. Pediatric Otolaryngology. 2nd ed. Philadelphia: WB Saunders; 1990:752.

18 **Kimmelman CP, Ali GHA.** Vasomotor rhinitis. Otolaryngol Clin North Am. 1986;19:65.

19 **Schatz M et al.** Nasal manifestations of systemic conditions. Immunol Allergy Clin North Am. 1987;7:159.

20 **Mabry RL.** Rhinitis of pregnancy. South Med J. 1986;79:965.

21 **Principato JJ.** Chronic vasomotor rhinitis: cryogenic and other surgical modes of treatment. Laryngoscope. 1979;89:619.

22 **Komisar A.** Nasal obstruction due to benign and malignant neoplasms. Otolaryngol Clin North Am. 1989;22:351.

23 **Stahl RS, Jurkiewicz MJ.** Congenital posterior choanal atresia. Pediatrics. 1985;76:429.

24 **Brockbank MJ et al.** Cerebrospinal fluid in the rhinitis clinic. J Laryngol Otol. 1989;103:281.

25 **White MV, Kaliner MA.** Mediators of allergic rhinitis. J Allergy Clin Immunol. 1992;90:699.

26 **Cookson WOCM et al.** Linkage between immunoglobulin E responses underlying asthma and rhinitis and chromosome 11q. Lancet. 1989;1:1292.

27 **Church JA.** Allergic rhinitis: diagnosis and management. Clin Pediatr. 1980;19:655.

28 **Proceedings of the task force on guidelines for standardizing old and new technologies used for the diagnosis and treatment of allergic diseases.** J Allergy Clin Immunol. 1988; 82:487.

29 **Chang WWY.** Pollen survey of the United States. In: Patterson R et al., eds. Allergic Diseases: Diagnosis and Management. Philadelphia: JB Lippencott; 1993:159.

30 **Solomon WR, Mathews KP.** Aerobiology and inhalant allergens. In: Middleton E et al., eds. Allergy: Principles and Practice. 3rd ed. St. Louis: CV Mosby; 1988:312.

31 **Gutman AA, Bush RK.** Allergens and other factors important in atopic disease. In: Patterson R et al., eds. Allergic Diseases: Diagnosis and Management. Philadelphia: JB Lippencott; 1993:93.

32 **Nalebuff DJ.** PRIST, RAST, and beyond: diagnosis and treatment. Otolaryngol Clin North Am. 1985;18:725.

33 **Bousquet J.** In vivo methods for study

of allergy: skin tests. In: Middleton E et al., eds. Allergy: Principles and Practice. 3rd ed. St. Louis: CV Mosby; 1988:419.

34 **Simons FER, Simons KJ.** Pharmacokinetic optimization of histamine H_1-receptor antagonist therapy. Clin Pharmacokinet. 1991;21:372.

35 **Paton DM, Webster DR.** Clinical pharmacokinetics of H_1-receptor antagonists (the antihistamines). Clin Pharmacokinet. 1985;10:477.

36 **Simons FER.** H_1-receptor antagonists: clinical pharmacology and therapeutics. J Allergy Clin Immunol. 1989;84:845.

37 **Galant SP et al.** The inhibitory effect of antiallergy drugs on allergen and histamine induced wheal and flare response. J Allergy Clin Immunol. 1973;51:11.

38 **Weinberger M.** Managing Asthma. Baltimore: Williams & Wilkins; 1990:113.

39 **Richards DM et al.** Astemizole: a review of its pharmacodynamic properties and therapeutic efficacy. Drugs. 1984;28:38.

40 **Togias AG et al.** Demonstration of inhibition of mediator release from human mast cells by azatadine base: in vivo and in vitro evaluation. JAMA. 1986;255:225.

41 **Simons FER.** The antiallergic effects of antihistamines (H_1-receptor antagonists). J Allergy Clin Immunol. 1992; 90:705.

42 **Taketomo CK et al., eds.** Pediatric Dosage Handbook. 2nd ed. Hudson: Lexi-Comp; 1993.

43 **Barnes CL et al.** Cetirizine: a new, nonsedating antihistamine. Ann Pharmacother. 1993;27:464.

44 **Trzeciakowski JP et al.** Antihistamines. In: Middleton E et al., eds. Allergy: Principles and Practice. 3rd ed. St. Louis: CV Mosby; 1988:715.

45 **Simons FER et al.** Pharmacokinetics and efficacy of chlorpheniramine in children. J Allergy Clin Immunol. 1982;69:376.

46 **Simons FER et al.** Pharmacokinetics and antipruritic effects of hydroxyzine in children with atopic dermatitis. J Pediatr. 1984;104:123.

47 **Simons KJ et al.** Pharmacokinetic and pharmacodynamic studies of the H_1-receptor antagonist hydroxyzine in the elderly. Clin Pharmacol Ther. 1989;45:9.

48 **Drug Facts and Comparisons.** St. Louis: Facts and Comparisons; 1993.

49 **Meltzer EO.** To use or not to use antihistamines in patients with asthma. Ann Allergy. 1990;64:183. Editorial.

50 **Sly RM et al.** The use of antihistamines in patients with asthma. J Allergy Clin Immunol. 1988;82:481–82. Position statement.

51 **Hendeles L et al.** Medical management of noninfectious rhinitis. Am J Hosp Pharm. 1980;37:1496.

52 **Meltzer EO et al.** Pharmacotherapy of rhinitis—1987 and beyond. Immunol Allergy Clin North Am. 1987;7:57.

53 **Anggard A, Malm L.** Orally administered decongestant drugs in disorders of the upper respiratory passages: a survey of clinical results. Clin Otolaryngol. 1984;9:43.

54 **Black MJ, Remsen KA.** Rhinitis medicamentosa. Can Med Assoc J. 1980; 122:881.

55 **Schuller DE, Turkewitz D.** Adverse effects of antihistamines. Postgrad Med. 1986;79:75.

56 **Schwartz JC et al.** Histaminergic transmission in the mammalian brain. Physiol Rev. 1991;71:1.

57 **Nicholson AN.** Antihistamines and sedation. Lancet. 1983;2:211.

58 **Gengo FM, Manning C.** A review of the effects of antihistamines on mental processes related to automobile driving. J Allergy Clin Immunol. 1990; 186:1034.

59 **Seppala T et al.** Single and repeated dose comparison of three antihistamines and phenylpropanamine: psychomotor performance and subjective appraisals of sleep. Br J Clin Pharmacol. 1981;12:179.

60 **Bye CE et al.** Evidence for tolerance to the central nervous effects of the histamine antagonist, triprolidine, in man. Eur J Clin Pharmacol. 1977;12:181.

61 **Goetz DW et al.** Prolongation of simple and choice reaction times in a double-blind comparison of twice-daily hydroxyzine versus terfenadine. J Allergy Clin Immunol. 1989;84:316.

62 **Moser L et al.** Effects of terfenadine and diphenhydramine alone or in combination with diazepam or alcohol on psychomotor performance and subjective feelings. Eur J Clin Pharmacol. 1978;14:417.

63 **Nicholson AN.** Effect of the antihistamines, brompheniramine maleate and triprolidine hydrochloride, on performance in man. Br J Clin Pharmacol. 1979;8:321.

64 **Goetz DW et al.** Objective antihistamine side effects are mitigated by eve-

ning dosing of hydroxyzine. Ann Allergy. 1991;67:448.

65 **Sorkin EM, Heel RC.** Terfenadine: a review of its pharmacodynamic properties and therapeutic efficacy. Drugs. 1985;29:34.

66 **Nicholson AN, Stone BM.** Performance studies with the H₁-histamine receptor antagonists, astemizole and terfenadine. Br J Clin Pharmacol. 1982;13:199.

67 **Bateman DN et al.** Lack of effects of astemizole on ethanol dynamics or kinetics. Eur J Clin Pharmacol. 1983;25:567.

68 **Kemp JP.** Tolerance to antihistamines: is it a problem? Ann Allergy. 1989;63:621.

69 **Taylor RJ et al.** The development of subsensitivity to chlorpheniramine. J Allergy Clin Immunol. 1985;76:103.

70 **Long WF et al.** Skin test suppression by antihistamines and the development of subsensitivity. J Allergy Clin Immunol. 1985;76:113.

71 **Roman IJ et al.** Suppression of histamine-induced wheal response by loratadine (SCH 29851) over 28 days in man. Ann Allergy. 1986;57:253.

72 **Kemp JP et al.** A multicenter, open study of the non-sedating antihistamine, terfenadine (Seldane), in the maintenance therapy of seasonal allergic rhinitis. Ann Allergy. 1988;60:349.

73 **Simons FER et al.** Lack of subsensitivity to terfenadine during long-term terfenadine treatment. J Allergy Clin Immunol. 1988;82:1068.

74 **Simons KJ, Simons FER.** The effect of chronic administration of hydroxyzine on hydroxyzine pharmacokinetics in dogs. J Allergy Clin Immunol. 1987;79:928.

75 **Bantz EW et al.** Chronic chlorpheniramine therapy: subsensitivity, drug metabolism, and compliance. Ann Allergy. 1987;59:341.

76 **Woosley RL et al.** Mechanism of the cardiotoxic actions of terfenadine. JAMA. 1993;269:1532.

77 **Wiley JF et al.** Cardiotoxic effects of astemizole overdose in children. J Pediatr. 1992;120:799.

78 **Yun CH et al.** Oxidation of the antihistaminic drug terfenadine in human liver microsomes: role of cytochrome P450 3A(4) in *N*-dealkylation and C-hydroxylation. Drug Metab Dispos. 1993;21:403.

79 **Mathews DR et al.** Torsades de pointes occurring in association with terfenadine use. JAMA. 1991;266:2375.

80 **Honig PK et al.** Changes in the pharmacokinetics and electrocardiographic pharmacodynamics of terfenadine with concomitant administration of erythromycin. Clin Pharmacol Ther. 1992;52:231.

81 **Honig PK et al.** Comparison of the effect of the macrolide antibiotics erythromycin, clarithromycin and azithromycin on terfenadine steady-state pharmacokinetics and electrocardiographic parameters. Drug Invest. 1994;7:148.

82 **Monahan BP et al.** Torsades de pointes occurring in association with terfenadine use. JAMA. 1990;264:2788.

83 **Honig PK et al.** Terfenadine-ketoconazole interaction: pharmacokinetic and electrocardiographic consequences. JAMA. 1993;269:1513.

84 **Honig PK et al.** The effect of fluconazole on the steady-state pharmacokinetics and electrocardiographic pharmacodynamics of terfenadine in humans. Clin Pharmacol Ther. 1993;53:630.

85 **Pohjola-Sintonen S et al.** Itraconazole prevents terfenadine metabolism and increases risk of torsades de pointes ventricular tachycardia. Eur J Clin Pharmacol. 1993;45:191.

86 **Crane JK, Shih HT.** Syncope and cardiac arrhythmia due to an interaction between itraconazole and terfenadine. Am J Med. 1993;95:445.

87 **Honig PK et al.** Effect of concomitant administration of cimetidine and ranitidine on the pharmacokinetics and electrocardiographic effects of terfenadine. Eur J Clin Pharmacol. 1993;45:41.

88 **Luskin SS et al.** Pharmacokinetic evaluation of the terfenadine-theophylline interaction. J Allergy Clin Immunol. 1989;83:406.

89 **Tobin JR et al.** Astemizole-induced cardiac conduction disturbances in a child. JAMA. 1991;266:2737.

90 **Mygind N.** Topical steroid treatment for allergic rhinitis and allied conditions. Clin Otolaryngol. 1982;7:343.

91 **Siegel SC.** Topical intranasal corticosteroid therapy in rhinitis. J Allergy Clin Immunol. 1988;81:984.

92 **Pipkorn U et al.** Inhibition of mediator release in allergic rhinitis by pretreatment with topical glucocorticosteroids. N Engl J Med. 1987;316:1506.

93 **Dushay ME, Johnson CE.** Management of allergic rhinitis: focus on intranasal agents. Pharmacotherapy. 1989;9:338.

94 **Findlay S et al.** Efficacy of once-a-day intranasal administration of triamcinolone acetonide in patients with seasonal allergic rhinitis. Ann Allergy. 1992;68:228.

95 **Storms W et al.** Once daily triamcinolone acetonide nasal spray is effective for the treatment of perennial allergic rhinitis. Ann Allergy. 1991;66:329.

96 **Balfour-Lynn L.** Growth and childhood asthma. Arch Dis Child. 1986;61:1049.

97 **Brogden RN et al.** Beclomethasone dipropionate: a reappraisal of its pharmacodynamic properties and therapeutic efficacy after a decade of use in asthma and rhinitis. Drugs. 1984;28:99.

98 **Pakes GE et al.** Flunisolide: a review of its pharmacological properties and therapeutic efficacy in rhinitis. Drugs. 1980;19:397.

99 **Fraunfelder FT, Meyer SM.** Posterior subcapsular cataracts associated with nasal or inhalation corticosteroids. Am J Ophthalmol. 1990;109:489.

100 **Kelly HW, Murphy S.** Corticosteroids for acute, severe asthma. Ann Pharmacother. 1991;25:72.

101 **Shapiro GG et al.** Double-blind evaluation of methylprednisolone versus placebo for acute asthma episodes. Pediatrics. 1983;71:510.

102 **Zora JA et al.** Hypothalamic-pituitary-adrenal axis suppression after short-term, high dose glucocorticoid therapy in children with asthma. J Allergy Clin Immunol. 1986;77:9.

103 **Dolan LM et al.** Short-term, high-dose, systemic steroids in children with asthma: the effect on the hypothalamic-pituitary-adrenal axis. J Allergy Clin Immunol. 1987;80:81.

104 **Van Metre TE, Adkinson NF.** Immunotherapy for aeroallergen disease. In: Middleton E et al., eds. Allergy: Principles and Practice. 3rd ed. St. Louis: CV Mosby; 1988:1327.

105 **Zeiger RS, Schatz M.** Immunotherapy of atopic disorders: present state of the art and future perspectives. Med Clin North Am. 1981;65:987.

106 **Christensen MM, Bruskewitz RC.** Clinical manifestations of benign prostatic hyperplasia and indications for therapeutic intervention. Urol Clin North Am. 1990;17:509.

107 **Badlani GH, Smith AD.** Pharmacotherapy of voiding dysfunction in the elderly. Sem Urol. 1987;5:120.

108 **Radack K, Deck CC.** Are oral decongestants safe in hypertension? An evaluation of the evidence and a framework for assessing clinical trials. Ann Allergy. 1986;56:396.

109 **Puder KS, Morgan JP.** Persuading by citation: an analysis of the references of fifty-three published reports of phenylpropanolamine's clinical toxicity. Clin Pharmacol Ther. 1987;42:1.

110 **Lake CR et al.** Adverse drug effects attributed to phenylpropanolamine: a review of 142 case reports. Am J Med. 1990;89:195.

111 **Schwartz HJ.** The effect of cromolyn on nasal disease. Ear Nose Throat J. 1986;65:449.

112 **Chandra RD et al.** Double-blind, controlled, crossover trial of 4% intranasal sodium cromoglycate in patients with seasonal allergic rhinitis. Ann Allergy. 1982;49:131.

113 **Cohan RH et al.** Treatment of perennial allergic rhinitis with cromolyn sodium: double-blind study on 34 adult patients. J Allergy Clin Immunol. 1976;58:121.

114 **Mikaelian AJ.** Vasomotor rhinitis. Ear Nose Throat J. 1989;68:207.

115 **Broms P, Malm L.** Oral vasoconstrictors in perennial non-allergic rhinitis. Allergy. 1982;37:67.

116 **Small P et al.** Effects of treatment with beclomethasone dipropionate in subpopulations of perennial rhinitis patients. J Allergy Clin Immunol. 1982;70:178.

117 **Baroody FM et al.** Ipratropium bromide (atrovent nasal spray) reduces the nasal response to methacholine. J Allergy Clin Immunol. 1992;89:1065.

118 **Kirkegaard J et al.** Ordinary and high-dose ipratropium in perennial nonallergic rhinitis. J Allergy Clin Immunol. 1987;13:228.

119 **O'Dwyer TP et al.** Ipratropium bromide in the treatment of the 'rhinorrhea syndrome'. J Laryngol Otol. 1988;102:799.

120 **Druce HM et al.** Double-blind study of intranasal ipratropium bromide in nonallergic perennial rhinitis. Ann Allergy. 1992;69:53.

121 **Knight A et al.** A trial of intranasal atrovent versus placebo in the treatment of vasomotor rhinitis. Ann Allergy. 1986;57:348.

122 **Milford CA et al.** Long-term safety and efficacy study of intranasal ipratropium bromide. J Laryngol Otol. 1990;104:123.

123 **Mullarkey MF.** Eosinophilic nonallergic rhinitis. J Allergy Clin Immunol. 1988;82:941.

124 **Jacobs RL et al.** Nonallergic rhinitis with eosinophilia (NARES syndrome). J Allergy Clin Immunol. 1981;67:253.

125 **Mullarkey MF.** The classification of nasal disease: an opinion. J Allergy Clin Immunol. 1981;67:251. Editorial.

126 **Rupp GH, Friedman RA.** Eosinophilic nonallergic rhinitis in children. Pediatrics. 1982;70:437.

127 **Moneret-Vautrin DA et al.** Nonallergic rhinitis with eosinophilia syndrome a precursor of the triad: nasal polyposis, intrinsic asthma, and intolerance to aspirin. Ann Allergy. 1990;64:513.

128 **Nelson BL, Jacobs RL.** Response of the nonallergic rhinitis with eosinophilia (NARES) syndrome to 4% cromolyn sodium nasal solution. J Allergy Clin Immunol. 1982;70:125.

129 **Sperber SJ, Hayden FG.** Chemotherapy of rhinovirus colds. Antimicrob Agents Chemother. 1988;32:409.

130 **Reed SE.** The aetiology and epidemiology of common colds, and the possibilities of prevention. Clin Otolaryngol. 1981;6:379.

131 **Hendley JO, Gwaltney JM.** Mechanisms of transmission of rhinovirus infections. Epidemiol Rev. 1988;10:242.

132 **Lowenstein SR, Parrino TA.** Management of the common cold. Adv Intern Med. 1987;32:207.

133 **Smith MBH, Feldman W.** Over-the-counter cold medications: a critical review of clinical trials between 1950 and 1991. JAMA. 1993;269:2258.

134 **Hendeles L.** Efficacy and safety of antihistamines and expectorants in nonprescription cough and cold preparations. Pharmacotherapy. 1993;13:154.

135 **Cold, cough, allergy, bronchodilator, and antiasthmatic drug products for over-the-counter human use; expectorant drug products for over-the-counter human use; final monograph.** Federal Register. 1989 Feb 28;54:8495.

136 **Hirsch SR et al.** The expectorant effect of glyceryl guaiacolate in patients with chronic bronchitis: a controlled *in vitro* and *in vivo* study. Chest. 1973;63:9.

137 **Hendeles L, Weinberger M.** A time to abandon the use of iodides in the management of pulmonary diseases. J Allergy Clin Immunol. 1980;66:177.

138 **Mabry RL.** Nasal stuffiness due to systemic medications. Otolaryngol Head Neck Surg. 1983;91:93.

139 **Fairbanks DNF, Raphael GD.** Nonallergic rhinitis and infection. In: Cummings CW et al., eds. Otolaryngology—Head and Neck Surgery. St. Louis: Mosby Year Book; 1993:775.

140 **Lekas MD.** Rhinitis during pregnancy and rhinitis medicamentosa. Otolaryngol Head Neck Surg. 1992;107:845.

Drug-Induced Pulmonary Disorders

Wendy Wilkinson
Baxi Dang
H William Kelly

Drug-Induced Pulmonary Disorders
  (See Table 22.1) 22-2
    Pulmonary Eosinophilia 22-1
    Pulmonary Fibrosis 22-7

Pulmonary Complications of Intravenous (IV) Drug
  Abuse 22-8
Amiodarone-Induced Pulmonary Toxicity 22-8

Drug-induced pulmonary toxicity is almost always a diagnosis of exclusion. It is, therefore, imperative that the clinician be aware of well described clinical findings consistent with drug-induced pulmonary disorders. An understanding of the mechanism of the reaction is invaluable in selecting an alternative therapy and for avoiding or minimizing future toxicity in a given patient.

Considering the physiologic and metabolic capacity of the lung, one would expect drug-induced pulmonary disease to be encountered more commonly. The lung contains a diverse population of cells capable of various metabolic functions and is the beneficiary of the total body blood flow. Local exposure to directly acting toxins as well as their metabolites is the rule, rather than the exception. To put this into perspective, epidemiologic studies estimate that respiratory symptoms occur in only 0.5% to 1.2% of patients experiencing adverse drug reactions.[1,2] However, these reactions often are serious and require intervention. In one study, 12.3% of life-threatening adverse drug reactions,[3] and in another study 26% of drug-induced deaths were reported to be due to respiratory dysfunction.[4]

Drug-induced pulmonary disorders can be subdivided into several categories based upon the type of pathophysiologic changes that result. Table 22.1 lists the most commonly encountered pathologies, and some detail on the clinical characteristics and incidence of the reaction for drugs that have been reported most often in the literature. A number of drugs that indirectly affect the lungs through other primary mechanisms (i.e., apnea through central nervous system depression or pulmonary manifestations of drug-induced lupus syndrome) are not included. For greater detail, the reader is referred to several general reviews on this topic.[5-13] The remainder of this chapter is devoted to cases representative of clinically significant drug-induced pulmonary disorders.

Pulmonary Eosinophilia

1. C.M., a 25-year-old female, is admitted for her third episode of pneumonia this year. She complains of difficulty breathing and has a nonproductive cough. She states that previously she was treated with an oral cephalosporin with satisfactory resolution of her symptoms. Her only other significant medical problem is a history of recurrent urinary tract infections (UTIs). Physical examination shows a temperature of 39.0 °C, slight cyanosis of the extremities, and an elevated respiratory rate. Crackles are audible bilaterally on auscultation. C.M.'s blood pressure (BP) and heart rate are unremarkable. Chest x-ray reveals bilateral pulmonary infiltrates with no focal lesions. Blood and sputum are obtained and sent for culture and sensitivity (C & S) testing. C.M. is started on ceftriaxone 1 gm Q 24 hr.

Laboratory results are as follows: Gram stain of the sputum shows 3+ epithelial cells, 1+ gram positive cocci, and 1+ gram negative rods. A complete blood count with differential yields a white blood cell (WBC) count of 9000 cells/mm³ and is remarkable only for a relative eosinophilia of 6%. Blood cultures are negative. Current home medications include dextromethorphan PRN cough, a multiple vitamin, an oral contraceptive, and nitrofurantoin as needed for UTI prophylaxis. C.M. was initially diagnosed as having a possible bacterial pneumonia. What information is inconsistent with an infectious cause for her respiratory distress? [SI unit: 9000 × 10⁹ cells/L]

In an otherwise healthy individual, an infectious pneumonia would be expected to cause a significant elevation of the WBC count. C.M. has a nonproductive cough, whereas a productive cough with purulent sputum would be more likely. The sputum sample obtained is nondiagnostic, reflecting only normal flora of the oropharynx (with no predominant organism) and large numbers of epithelial cells. These findings represent either a poorly obtained sample or a noninfectious cause. More importantly, the relative eosinophilia in the differential is not associated with bacterial infection, but points to an allergic response.

2. A diagnosis of pulmonary eosinophilia is made. Which of C.M.'s medications is the most likely cause of respiratory illness mimicking community-acquired pneumonia?

More than 500 cases of adverse pulmonary reactions to nitrofurantoin have been reported, most of these being acute pneumonitis, with the remainder presenting as chronic pulmonary fibrosis. These reactions occur in less than 1% of those taking the medication, but the incidence is much greater in women, probably because women are more prone to urinary tract infections. The clinical course of the acute pneumonitis reaction is characterized by onset of fever, chills, cough, and dyspnea a few hours to seven to ten days after initiation of therapy. With the first exposure, the onset may be delayed. Repeat exposures result in rapid recurrence of symptoms. Eosinophilia occurs in about one-third of these patients. Nearly 50% will manifest an elevation in the erythrocyte sedimentation rate (ESR). Bronchospasm is rare, as is pleuritic chest pain. Pulmonary infiltrates with eosinophilia sometimes is referred to as ''Loeffler's syndrome,'' and is associated with *para*-aminosalicyclic acid, methotrexate, sulfonamides, tetracycline, chlorpropamide, phenytoin, and imipramine, in addition to nitrofurantoin. The mechanism of the acute reaction is unknown, whereas pulmonary fibrosis associated with chronic toxicity is thought to be due to an oxidant reaction.

3. What is the appropriate course of action to alleviate C.M.'s respiratory exacerbation and to prevent further recurrence?

Resolution of symptoms within 18 to 48 hours is anticipated following the discontinuation of the offending agent. Nitrofurantoin should be discontinued and not restarted. No evidence exists that adding corticosteroids will accelerate resolution, but their addition

Table 22.1	Drug-Induced Pulmonary Disorders[a]
Drugs, Frequency, Mechanism	**Clinical Remarks**

Bronchospasm

Acetaminophen[12,14,15]
Frequency: Rare
Mechanism: Same as aspirin

Acetaminophen is a very weak cyclo-oxygenase inhibitor; therefore, <6% of patients with aspirin sensitivity will react to acetaminophen. It is considered a useful antipyretic and analgesic alternative to aspirin

Angiotensin-Converting Enzyme (ACE) Inhibitors[18–21]
Frequency: Common
Mechanism: Exact mechanism unknown but may involve the ability to inhibit the degradation of bradykinin, prostaglandins, and/or substance P. These products may induce airway inflammation and bronchial hyperreactivity

Cough predominant symptom; however, wheezing and deterioration of pulmonary function have been reported in chronic asthmatics. Reported prevalence 1%–13%, with women affected more frequently than men. Most provocation studies demonstrate an ↑ cough reflex to capsaicin and ↑ bronchial reactivity to histamine, although standard spirometric studies remain unchanged. Cough is persistent; dry; nonproductive, and worse at night. A tickling sensation in the throat is a frequent complaint. Cough completely disappears upon discontinuation of the drug. Switching to an alternate ACE inhibitor not helpful. Concomitant beta blockers may ↑ risk. An NSAID or theophylline may provide relief

Aspirin[12,14–17]
Frequency: Common
Mechanism: Exact mechanism unknown, but somehow involves the inhibition of cyclo-oxygenase. Possibly diverts arachidonic acid metabolism through the lipoxygenase pathway leading to excess production of leukotrienes

Prevalence ↑ with age. Asthmatic patients >40 yr have a frequency 4x that of patients <20 yr. The classic description includes a triad of severe asthma, nasal polyps, and aspirin intolerance. Bronchospasm typically occurs min to hr following ingestion and is associated with rhinorrhea, flushing of head and neck, and conjunctivitis. The reactions often life-threatening. Therapy nonspecific and should be treated as any other acute asthma attack. Primary therapy is avoidance. Patients can be desensitized under medical supervision if alternative therapy unavailable

Beta-Adrenergic Receptor Blockers[11,12,23–26]
Frequency: Common
Mechanism: Blocks maintenance of normal airway tone by the sympathetic nervous system

Occurs only in patients with pre-existing bronchial hyperreactivity. Asthma attacks have been precipitated not only by nonselective beta blockers such as propranolol (Inderal), but also by cardioselective agents such as acebutolol (Sectral), atenolol (Tenormin), and metoprolol (Lopressor). Fatal status asthmaticus has occurred following topical administration of timolol maleate (Timoptic) ophthalmic solution. Beta blocker-induced bronchospasm can be treated with theophylline and anticholinergics and discontinuation of the beta blocker

Inhalational Agents/Aerosols[22]
Aerosolized acetylcysteine, aerosolized pentamidine (NebuPent), beclomethasone (Beclovent), cromolyn (Intal), isoetharine (Bronkosol), isoproterenol (Isuprel), racemic epinephrine

Aerosolized medications may produce cough and bronchospasm due to irritant effect of inhaled particles, propellants, and dispersants contained in MDI, and/or sulfite sensitivity from sulfite-containing nebulized solutions (isoetharine, isoproterenol, and racemic epinephrine)

Nonsteroidal Anti-Inflammatory Drugs (NSAIDs)[11,12,15–17]
Frequency: Common
Mechanism: Same as aspirin

All NSAIDs that inhibit cyclo-oxygenase cross-react in aspirin-sensitive patients. Patients exhibit a threshold dose for cyclo-oxygenase inhibition that, if exceeded, will provoke bronchospasm. Therefore, the degree of cross reactivity is dependent upon potency of cyclo-oxygenase inhibition

Sulfites[27,28]
Frequency: Uncommon
Mechanism: Exact mechanism unknown, but probably due to an inability to clear sulfites. As a result, H_2SO_3 is produced on the lung surface and the afferent parasympathetic receptors of the lung are stimulated

Occurs in <10% of asthmatics. Sulfites and metabisulfites are common antioxidants used to preserve wine and foods. They are in particularly high concentrations in open salad and vegetable bars in restaurants. Metabisulfites also occur in drugs as a preservative, including some bronchodilator aerosols, in concentrations high enough to produce bronchospasm. The bronchospasm is readily reversed by inhaled beta$_2$-agonists or anticholinergics

Tartrazine (FD&C yellow #5 dye)[11,12,14,27]
Frequency: Rare
Mechanism: Unknown

Appears to occur only in aspirin intolerant patients at a prevalence of 1%–15%

IgE-Mediated Bronchospasm and Anaphylaxis

Cephalosporins, L-asparaginase (Elspar), Penicillins, Sulfonamides
Frequency: Common

Cimetidine (Tagamet)
Frequency: Rare
Mechanism: IgE-mediated allergic response[29]

Tetracyclines
Frequency: Infrequent

Bronchospasm and anaphylaxis are the prototype disorders of the Type 1 hypersensitivity reaction. Although structurally unrelated, these drugs trigger the anaphylactic reaction by a common mechanism. Formation of IgE antibody B cells is induced by an allergen, in this case the specific drug, followed by release of vasoactive amines by basophils and mast cells upon a second exposure to the drug. Mast cell granules contain the primary mediators histamine, eosinophil chemotactic factor, neutrophil chemotactic factor, and neutral proteases. Result of their release is ↑ vascular permeability, vasodilation, bronchial smooth muscle contraction, and ↑ secretion of mucus. Principal organ affected is the lung, more specifically, the smooth musculature of pulmonary blood vessels and respiratory passages. Pulmonary obstruction accentuated by hypersecretion of mucus and laryngeal edema. This reaction is not dose related, although for some compounds desensitization protocols have been developed

Impairment of Respiratory Muscles

Hypoventilation[30]
Alcohol, narcotics, sedatives

Direct, dose dependent respiratory drive inhibition is a well-described pharmacologic effect of these drugs

Myopathy[30]
Aminocaproic acid, clofibrate, corticosteroids, diuretics, procainamide

Drug-induced necrosis (necrotizing myopathy) most commonly caused by clofibrate and aminocaproic acid. Steroid myopathy weakens respiratory muscles, as well as other striated muscles

Neuromuscular blockade[30]
Aminoglycosides, calcium channel blockers, D-penicillamine, macrolides, neuromuscular blockers, polmyxin B

Patients with myasthenia gravis and/or hepatic or renal failure at ↑ risk for drug-induced neuromuscular blockade. D-penicillamine has been reported to induce myasthenia gravis through immunologic mechanisms

Continued

Table 22.1	Drug-Induced Pulmonary Disorders[a] (Continued)
Drugs, Frequency, Mechanism	**Clinical Remarks**

Neuropathy[30]

Amiodarone, captopril, gold, isoniazid, phenytoin, vincristine, vaccines

Guillain-Barre syndrome (GBS) has been reported following vaccinations. An estimated 20%–50% of patients with GBS develop respiratory muscle paralysis. Neurotubular damage is a complication of vincristine therapy. Isoniazid neuropathy results due to the inhibition of pyridoxine metabolism; however, may be prevented by administration of pyridoxine

Pseudolymphoma

Cyclosporine (Sandimmune)[9,31–33]

Frequency: Rare

Mechanism: Inhibition of T-cell function, thus preventing a cytotoxic T-cell response to Epstein-Barr virus

Incidence 3%–5%. Lymphoproliferative disorder (or sometimes referred to as pseudolymphoma) involving the lungs occurs 2–6 months after transplantation. Strong correlation reported with primary or reactivation of Epstein-Barr virus and the development of this pulmonary disorder. Pulmonary findings appear as solitary or multiple nodules, seen mostly with heart and heart-lung transplants. Regression of the disorder occurs after reduction of cyclosporine dose

Pulmonary Edema

Chlordiazepoxide (Librium)[11]

Frequency: Rare

Mechanism: Unknown; noncardiogenic

1 case following injection of the contents of capsule has been reported. Has not been reported with the parenteral preparations

Contrast Media[11,35]

Frequency: Rare

Mechanism: Cardiogenic

Due to injection of high concentration of this highly osmotic agent into pulmonary circulation during angiocardiography

Dextran 40 (Rheomacrodex)[36]

Frequency: Rare

Mechanism: Unknown; probably ↑ capillary permeability; noncardiogenic

1 case has been reported in which symptoms occurred 4 days into therapy

Epinephrine (Adrenalin)[11]

Frequency: Rare

Mechanism: Unknown

Occurs due to accidental overdose during anesthesia

Ethchlorvynol (Placidyl)[11,37–39]

Frequency: Uncommon

Mechanism: ↑ alveolar capillary permeability; noncardiogenic

Appears to be a dose-dependent reaction which occurs more frequently with IV administration. Pulmonary edema has been reported with oral administration in fatal overdoses; however, pulmonary edema also has occurred with as little as 450 mg IV. Lung tissue levels of ethchlorvynol are much higher subsequent to IV administration. Patients present with dyspnea and dry cough within an hour following injection. X-ray picture typical of pulmonary edema. Symptoms clear rapidly. Treatment is symptomatic

Heroin[6,11,13,40,41]

Frequency: Common

Mechanism: Due to an outpouring of edema fluid into the alveoli. Mechanism of the ↑ capillary permeability unknown

Syndrome associated with a mortality rate of ≈10%. Usually occurs after IV administration, but has been reported to follow nasal administration ("snorting"). Patients usually present in coma with depressed respiration or marked respiratory distress. Dyspnea, tachypnea, hypotension, cyanosis, tachycardia, and severe hypoxemia common. Does not appear to be dose related, although it often may follow an overdose. Symptoms occur within 2 hours following administration and usually clear in 1–2 days. X-ray evidence of resolution present in 2–5 days; however, significant ↓ in pulmonary function such as FVC, dynamic compliance, and diffusing capacity take much longer to improve. Treatment consists of naloxone (Narcan), respiratory support, and oxygen therapy. Secondary bacterial and aspiration pneumonias are frequent complications

Hydrochlorothiazide (Hydrodiuril)[42,43]

Frequency: Uncommon

Mechanism: Unknown; noncardiogenic; nonimmunologic

Symptoms of pulmonary edema occur within an hour following oral administration of a single dose and rapidly subside within 24 hours. X-ray evidence of resolution present within 2–6 days. Diffusing capacity may take a month to return to normal. Most patients had a previous history of thiazide exposure with mild reactions; however, it had occurred upon 1st exposure. This pulmonary adverse effect of HCTZ has not been reported with any other thiazide diuretic

Interleukin 2 (IL-2 or Aldesleukin)[44]

Frequency: Common

Mechanism: ↑ capillary permeability

Pulmonary edema caused by a dose-related ↓ in cardiac contractility and VLS. VLS described as peripheral and pulmonary edema with concomitant intravascular depletion. >20% of patients treated with IL-2 will develop respiratory distress. Rarely, some patients may experience reversible bronchospasm. Most, if not all, patients regain full pulmonary function once IL-2 withdrawn

Intravenous fluids[11,13]

Frequency: Common

Mechanism: Cardiovascular fluid overload

Commonly occurs in shock and cardiac failure. Careful monitoring of central venous pressure will prevent this most common cause of iatrogenic pulmonary edema. Patients who develop ARDS from shock particularly susceptible. These patients should be treated with PEEP

Lidocaine (Xylocaine)[6]

Frequency: Rare

Mechanism: Unknown

Pulmonary edema developed within 5 min following nebulization of lidocaine in preparation for bronchoscopy in 1 patient

Methadone (Dolophine)[11,45,46]

Frequency: Common with overdose

Mechanism: Same as for Heroin

Occurs following oral administration as much as 6 hr after dose. Symptoms and treatment same as for heroin. May take longer to improve due to a longer duration of action relative to heroin

Muromonab CD3 (OKT-3)[7,47–49]

Frequency: Common

Mechanism: Pulmonary edema due to the release of mediators by damaged T-cells, causing left ventricular overload and pulmonary edema

Occurs with the initial doses of OKT-3. Patients with fluid overload before starting OKT-3 therapy are at highest risk for developing OKT-3 induced pulmonary edema; this has not been reported in normovolemic patients. Recommended that weight gain be limited to <3% during the week before initiating OKT-3 treatment and that a chest x-ray show no evidence of volume overload

Continued

Table 22.1	Drug-Induced Pulmonary Disorders[a] (Continued)
Drugs, Frequency, Mechanism	**Clinical Remarks**

Phenylbutazone (Butazolidin)[11]
  Frequency: Rare
  Mechanism: Cardiogenic secondary to sodium retention

Reported in elderly patients with pre-existing heart disease. Avoid in patients who should be sodium restricted

Propoxyphene (Darvon)[11,50]
  Frequency: Uncommon
  Mechanism: Same as heroin and methadone; but also may be related to postictal pulmonary edema

Chemical structure of propoxyphene similar to methadone. Propoxyphene-induced pulmonary edema has occurred exclusively following overdose situation. Treatment same as for heroin-induced edema

Salicylate[6,11,51,52]
  Frequency: Uncommon
  Mechanism: Noncardiogenic, ↑ vascular permeability to fluid and protein

Most reported cases of pulmonary edema associated with salicylate overdoses; however, also has been reported in patients at "therapeutic" anti-inflammatory serum concentrations who were being treated for acute rheumatic fever. In non-overdose situation, symptoms typically appear 2–8 days following initiation of therapy. Patients improve when salicylates discontinued

Tocolytics[8]
  Ritodrine (Yutopar), terbutaline (Brethine)
  Frequency: Infrequent
  Mechanism: Cardiovascular fluid overload

In tocolytic doses, beta-agonists are postulated to cause peripheral vasodilation that is rapidly reversed when drug discontinued. As blood vessels regain normal tone, the large intravascular volume is forced into all tissues, including the lungs

Tricyclic Antidepressants(TCAs)[7,53]
  Frequency: Uncommon
  Mechanism: ↑ capillary permeability due to degeneration of alveolar epithelium and capillary endothelium as a direct toxic effect of the TCA; ↑ levels of catecholamines caused by the TCA lead to pulmonary fat deposition or release of histamine from lung mast cells and production of bradykinin in the plasma, both of which ↑ vascular permeability

TCA-induced cases of ARDS have been reported, as well as 5 patients with noncardiogenic pulmonary edema attributed to TCA overdose. Radiographic findings revealed diffuse bilateral opacities and interstitial edema. Autopsy in 3 patients with fatal amitriptyline overdose revealed pathologic changes consistent with ARDS, as well as pulmonary fat deposition which may have interfered with gas exchange

Pulmonary Fibrosis

Amiodarone (Cordarone)[6,10,54–56]
  Frequency: Common
  Mechanism: Exact mechanism unknown, but thought to result from the amphiphilic (contains both hydrophilic and lipophilic portions) nature of the molecule. Amphiphilic compounds produce a phospholipid storage disorder with inflammation and fibrosis resulting from breakdown of phospholipid-laden macrophages

Occurs in 1%–6% of patients and appears to be dose related; clinical toxicity rarely occurs with doses <400 mg/day. Onset of symptoms usually appears after 5–6 months; symptoms have occurred as soon as 4 weeks and as late as 9 yr. No evidence for a cumulative dose effect. Clinical course variable. May be an acute onset with rapid progression into respiratory failure and death, or symptoms may begin with exertional dyspnea slowly developing over several months and improving when the drug discontinued or when the dose decreased to 200–400 mg/day. Radiographic changes nondiagnostic and consistent with a diffuse pneumonitis. Routine pulmonary function tests not predictive for identifying patients at risk

BCNU (Carmustine)[5,57–60]
  Frequency: Uncommon
  Mechanism: Unknown; but appears to be a dose-related toxicity

Pulmonary fibrosis developed after cumulative doses of 580–2100 mg/m^2 were administered over a period of 6 months to 3 years. Concomitant cyclophosphamide therapy may ↑ risk. Presents as a typical restrictive fibrosis with insidious cough, dyspnea, and hypoxemia with a diffusion defect. Steroid therapy has not been effective in altering the course of the adverse effect which often is rapidly fatal. 1 case associated with semustine, an experimental nitrosourea, also has been reported

Bleomycin (Blenoxane)[5,57,58,61,62]
  Frequency: Common; overall incidence estimated at 11%
  Mechanism: Direct cytotoxic injury to the lung epithelium probably due to free-radical generation following binding of drug to DNA

Clinical presentation characterized by nonproductive cough, dyspnea with occasional fever, dry basilar rales, and skin pigmentation. Onset 4–10 weeks after beginning therapy. The lung disease is restrictive with a severe diffusion defect. Older patients (60–70 yr) appear to be more susceptible. Toxicity potentiated by radiation given either concomitantly or sequentially, high oxygen concentrations, cyclophosphamide, and possibly adriamycin. The disease usually insidiously progressive and irreversible. Routine monitoring of pulmonary function tests has been of questionable value. Steroid therapy has been reported to be beneficial in some cases. Total cumulative dose of bleomycin should be restricted to <450 U. Bleomycin-induced pulmonary fibrosis associated with a 10% fatality rate when patients receive >550 U

Bromocriptine (Parlodel)[31,66–70]
  Frequency: Rare
  Mechanism: Potent vasoconstrictive effect, causing ischemia and resulting in pulmonary fibrosis

Pleural fibrosis affects ≈2%–3% of patients. Patients present with insidious onset of dyspnea and cough, and sometimes with fatigue and chest pain. Symptoms usually start after 18 months to 2 years of treatment; however in 1 case, symptoms occurred after only 2–3 weeks of therapy. Chest x-ray findings reveal bilateral or unilateral pleural effusions and pleural thickening. Eosinophilia and elevated ESRs and C-reactive proteins often seen. Symptoms slowly resolve with discontinuation; however, pleural thickening remains despite resolution of pleural effusions

Busulfan (Myleran)[5,10,57,58]
  Frequency: Common
  Mechanism: Exact mechanism unknown, but probably due to chemical alveolitis with proliferation of

Symptoms usually begin insidiously 3–4 yr after therapy initiated. The pulmonary fibrosis ("busulfan lung") presents as a dry hacking cough, tachypnea, cyanosis, dyspnea, and low grade fever. X-rays show diffuse interstitial and intra-alveolar infiltrates. Differential diagnosis includes opportunistic infection, leukemic infiltration, and radiation fibrosis. Pulmonary function tests are typical of restrictive lung disease with a

Continued

Table 22.1	Drug-Induced Pulmonary Disorders[a] (Continued)
Drugs, Frequency, Mechanism	**Clinical Remarks**
Busulfan (Myleran) *(Continued)* granular pneumocytes and fibrosis of alveolar walls	diffusion defect. Clinical course one of progression with no reversibility. High-dose corticosteroids have been tried with little apparent benefit

Chlorambucil (Leukeran)[5,57,58]
  Frequency: Rare
  Mechanism: Unknown; probably the same as busulfan and cyclophosphamide, which are also alkylating agents
	Typically occurs after 2 years of daily therapy. Symptoms and histology are the same as "busulfan lung"

Cyclophosphamide (Cytoxan)[5,57,58,71]
  Frequency: Rare
  Mechanism: Unknown; thought to be same as busulfan
	Clinical picture and pulmonary function same as "busulfan lung." Pulmonary fibrosis generally detected after a long period of continuous low dose therapy; it has occurred in children 4–6 yr after drug has been discontinued. Fibrosis rapidly progressive

Ganglionic Blocking Agents (Hexamethonium, Mecamylamine, Pentolinium)[6,10,11]
  Frequency: Rare
  Mechanism: Unknown
	Reaction merely of historical interest because these drugs rarely used. Patients present with classical pulmonary fibrosis a few months to a year following initiation of therapy. Hexamethonium structurally similar to busulfan

Gold (Myochrysine)[6,11,72–74]
  Frequency: Uncommon
  Mechanism: Unknown; however, does not appear to be immunologically mediated
	Clinical symptoms usually occur after 300–400 mg total dose has been given. Symptoms include dyspnea and a nonproductive cough. Radiographic studies usually compatible with diffuse interstitial fibrosis, and histologic examination is the same as for other drug-induced pulmonary fibroses. Pulmonary function tests show a restrictive pattern with a diffusion abnormality. Symptoms resolve with discontinuation of drug. Steroids have no therapeutic benefit

Melphalan (Alkeran), Uracil Mustard[5,57]
  Frequency: Rare
  Mechanism: Same as for busulfan and cyclophosphamide
	All the alkylating agents, except nitrogen mustard and thiotepa, have been associated with the syndrome. Except for busulfan, it appears to be a rare complication, but it may represent an inherent toxicity of this group of drugs. Caution should be used when these agents are given with other drugs associated with fibrosis

6-Mercaptopurine (Purinethol)[5,11]
  Frequency: Rare
  Mechanism: Unknown	

Methotrexate[5,57,58]
  Frequency: Uncommon
  Mechanism: Appears to be an allergic reaction with fibrosis; noncaseating granuloma formation with lymphocytic infiltrates
	Mean onset of toxicity occurs 12–200 days after administration. No correlation with dose and 65% of the patients will have peripheral eosinophilia. Has been reported after PO, IV, and IT use. Symptoms include dry cough, dyspnea, and cyanosis. High-dose prednisone will induce a rapid remission with radiographic evidence of resolution. Appears to be completely reversible

Methysergide (Sansert)[6,11,14]
  Frequency: Common
  Mechanism: Unknown
	Fibrosis is pleuropulmonary rather than the more common interstitial fibrosis produced by other agents. Methysergide is the only drug that will produce a chronic pleural effusion as well. Onset insidious, as well as dose and duration related. Reaction usually occurs after at least 6 months of therapy and is a component of the retroperitoneal fibrosis induced by this drug. Symptoms include acute pleuritic pain or progressive dyspnea with radiographic changes showing either unilateral or bilateral pleural fibrosis. Syndrome usually completely reversible upon discontinuation of the drug

Mitomycin (Mutamycin)[5,57,75]
  Frequency: Uncommon
  Mechanism: Unknown
	Clinical presentation like that caused by bleomycin. Mitomycin-induced pulmonary fibrosis can occur with a cumulative dose as low as 40 mg/m^2. Toxicity appears 3–6 months following initiation of treatment and may occur following the 2nd course. High oxygen tension appears to potentiate the toxicity. Postoperative patients should be ventilated with an FiO_2 of ≤30%. Corticosteroids reportedly might be of some benefit in some patients, but others have died of respiratory insufficiency in spite of steroid therapy

Nitrofurantoin (Macrodantin)[6,10,11]
  Frequency: Rare
  Mechanism: Unknown
	Chronic use of nitrofurantoin for 6 months to 6 yr has resulted in cases of pulmonary fibrosis. This pulmonary reaction is rare in comparison to the acute reaction (i.e., pulmonary infiltrates with eosinophilia) described below. Clinical pattern consists of a dry cough, exertional dyspnea, and fever. Pulmonary function testing usually consistent with a restrictive disorder; and radiological tests consistent with diffuse interstitial fibrosis and diffusion defect. Most cases have been reversible following discontinuation of the drug and institution of steroid therapy. It appears to occur most frequently in postmenopausal women

Oxygen[5,10,76–78]
  Frequency: Frequent
  Mechanism: Toxicity caused by the formation of superoxide anions (O_2^-) that are highly reactive and cytotoxic. These free radicals can oxidize sulfhydryl enzymes, inactivate DNA, and result in lipid peroxidation of cellular membranes
	Dose-dependent reaction that occurs with increasing frequency and FiO_2 >50%. Clinical pathology extensive and generally presents in 2 stages: the acute or exudative state, and the chronic proliferative stage. Acute phase consists of perivascular, peribronchiolar, interstitial, and alveolar edema, as well as alveolar hemorrhage and necrosis of the pulmonary endothelium. The 2nd or more chronic phase consists of exudate resorption, alveolar thickening, and collagen and elastin deposition in the interstitium of alveolar walls. Patient may have irreversible emphysematous and fibrotic changes. Clinical picture may be obstructive, restrictive, or mixture of the two

Paraquat (Chevron-Ortho Spot Weed and Grass Killer)[10,77,78]
  Frequency: Common, >120 deaths reported annually
  Mechanism: Attributed to O_2 toxicity by superoxide free radical production
	Oral ingestion of as little as 15–20 cc can induce pulmonary fibrosis, and the mortality rate is 33%–50%. Radiographic evidence of pulmonary edema may appear several days after ingestion and usually accompanied by complaints of progressive dyspnea. Paraquat readily inactivated by exposure to sunlight and destroyed by burning. Therefore, significant toxicity should not occur from smoking marijuana that had been sprayed with

Continued

Table 22.1	Drug-Induced Pulmonary Disorders[a] (Continued)
Drugs, Frequency, Mechanism	**Clinical Remarks**
Paraquat (*Continued*)	paraquat. All reported fatal cases have been from oral ingestion. Therapy supportive, although superoxide dismutase has been shown to improve outcome in animals by preventing formation of (O_2^-) ions. A high FiO_2 in patients requiring ventilatory support will exacerbate the problem
Penicillamine (Cuprimine)[6,11] *Frequency*: Rare *Mechanism*: Unknown	Only 15 cases of penicillamine-induced pulmonary fibrosis reported in the literature. Symptoms occurred after 18 days to 2 years of therapy. Symptoms and pulmonary function tests are consistent with an alveolitis and bronchiolitis with fibrosis. A pulmonary-renal syndrome resembling Goodpasture's also has been reported
Pindolol (Visken)[79] *Frequency*: Rare *Mechanism*: Unknown	Pindolol is a beta blocker that has a chemical structure similar to practolol. Practolol was removed from the market in the United Kingdom because of drug-induced fibrosis. This is the 1st reported case with pindolol
Radiation-Cobalt Irradiation in Hodgkin's and Breast Carcinoma[11,81] *Frequency*: Common *Mechanism*: A hypersensitivity acute reaction or a chronic dose-related toxicity when the total dose >6000 rads	Acute pulmonary reaction not dose-related; it is a hypersensitivity reaction and a fulminating process that occasionally is accompanied by effusions. Chronic dose-related pulmonary reaction usually begins insidiously with cough, dry cough, fever, rales, and occasional friction rubs generally are consistent with the chronic form of the adverse reaction. Although these symptoms occasionally respond to steroids, the steroids do not prevent the late development of pulmonary fibrosis
Tocainide (Tonocard)[6] *Frequency*: Rare; 4 case reports *Mechanism*: Unknown	Severe dyspnea with diffuse pulmonary crackles appeared 4–6 months after the initiation of therapy. Diffuse infiltrates were noted on chest x-rays, and diffusion abnormalities were detected by pulmonary function tests. All patients recovered when drug discontinued
Pulmonary Infiltrates with Eosinophilia (Loeffler's Syndrome)	
Carbamazepine (Tegretol)[6,11] *Frequency*: Rare *Mechanism*: Unknown	See Phenytoin
Cromolyn Sodium (Intal)[11,13,81] *Frequency*: Rare *Mechanism*: Allergic	Cromolyn also has been associated with a chronic allergic granulomatous disease of the lung. Cause and effect are questionable, however, because cromolyn is used in the treatment of allergic airway disease
Dantrolene (Dantrium)[31,82] *Frequency*: Rare *Mechanism*: Allergic response	Chronic pleural effusions without associated parenchymal disease have occurred in 9 patients following long-term therapy with dantrolene. After 1 month to several years of therapy, patients develop signs of an abnormally high pleural fluid eosinophilia, peripheral eosinophilia, and unilateral pleural effusion often accompanied with pleuritic chest pain and cough. Symptomatic improvement occurs within several days following discontinuation of dantrolene; however, it may take months for radiographic findings to resolve
Imipramine (Tofranil)[6,11] *Frequency*: Rare *Mechanism*: Allergy (?)	Treatment of choice is to discontinue the drug
Mephenesin (Myanesin) *Frequency*: Rare *Mechanism*: Probably allergic	See Imipramine
Minocycline (Minocin)[83–86] *Frequency*: Uncommon *Mechanism*: Allergic reaction	29 cases of minocycline-induced pneumonitis/pulmonary infiltrates and eosinophilia have been reported. Onset of pneumonitis rapid, occurring after a few days to few weeks of treatment. Symptoms described include acute chest symptoms (hacking cough, acute chest pain) and dyspnea, pulmonary infiltrates on chest x-ray, fever, hemoptysis, and eosinophilia in blood and/or bronchoalveolar lavage fluids. With continuation of minocycline, severe respiratory failure may occur. There was a definite temporal relationship between respiratory symptoms and the administration of minocycline in all cases. In addition, fever, dyspnea, and a rise in eosinophils returned upon rechallenge with the drug. This disorder carries a favorable prognosis as it quickly resolves with discontinuation of minocycline and/or administration of steroids
Nitrofurantoin[6,10,11,13] *Frequency*: Uncommon *Mechanism*: Unknown	Fever, chills, cyanosis, and dyspnea begin 2 hr to 10 days following the initiation of nitrofurantoin therapy. Clinical presentation may mimic pulmonary edema or an acute asthma attack. Diffuse alveolar infiltrates with occasional small pleural effusions can be seen on chest x-ray. Eosinophilia present in $\frac{1}{3}$ of the patients. Symptoms regress within 24–48 hr after discontinuation of drug. (Also see Pulmonary Fibrosis in Chronic Reactions)
Para-Aminosalicyclic Acid (PAS)[6,11,13] *Frequency*: Common *Mechanism*: Probably an allergic reaction	As with all the drugs known to induce Loeffler's Syndrome, PAS can induce high fever, leukocytosis, eosinophilia, cough, and dyspnea. Although eosinophils may account for as much as 26% of the leukocytes in the blood, eosinophilia not noted in the sputum. Treatment of choice is discontinuation of the PAS; rechallenge with PAS usually provokes the reaction within 2 days
Penicillin[6,11,13] *Frequency*: Rare *Mechanism*: Allergic reaction	Symptoms similar to those described for the other drugs that induce Loeffler's Syndrome
Phenytoin (Dilantin)[6,11] *Frequency*: Rare *Mechanism*: Unknown; most likely hypersensitivity	Usual symptoms of Loeffler's (e.g., cough, fever, dyspnea) develop 3–6 weeks after initiation of therapy. Maculopapular rash and lymphadenopathy usually present. Patients markedly improve within 1–2 weeks after discontinuation of drug
Procarbazine (Matulane)[57,58] *Frequency*: Rare *Mechanism*: Possibly an allergic reaction	Will improve with steroid therapy. May progress to fibrosis

Continued

| Table 22.1 | Drug-Induced Pulmonary Disorders^a (Continued) |

Drugs, Frequency, Mechanism	Clinical Remarks
Sulfonamides[6,11,13] *Frequency*: Rare *Mechanism*: Allergic reaction	Has even been reported with sulfonamide vaginal cream. Other sulfa-like drugs (e.g., sulfonylureas and sulfasalazine) will cross react and cause the syndrome
Pulmonary Hypertension **Magnesium Trisilicate (Talc)**[11,13,87] *Frequency:* Common only in drug abusers *Mechanism:* Foreign body reaction	Talc is a common inert ingredient of many oral dosage forms. When drugs that are formulated for oral use are injected intravenously by drug abusers, arteritis and angiothrombosis of the pulmonary vasculature can develop. This adverse effect was common when "blue velvet" (i.e., tripelennamine) tablets were injected intravenously. Cornstarch from dissolved tablets also has been implicated in granuloma formation and pulmonary hypertension. The reaction also has been reported after the IV use of alpha sympathomimetics from nasal inhalers

^a ARDS = Adult respiratory distress syndrome; ESRs = Erythrocyte sedimentation rates; FVC = Forced vital capacity; HCTZ = Hydrochlorothiazide; IV = Intravenous; MDI = Metered-dose inhaler; NSAID = Nonsteroid anti-inflammatory drug; PEEP = Positive end expiratory pressure; PO = Oral; VLS = Vascular leak syndrome.

is a consideration if there is no response to supportive care. Having ruled out infectious causes, ceftriaxone also can be discontinued. In many instances, it takes four or five such exacerbations before the patient or the clinician connects the medication with the reaction. A careful history elicited from C.M. might have revealed that her UTIs are associated with sexual activity; therefore, in the past year, she has used nitrofurantoin for prophylaxis only intermittently. Each time she was treated for presumed pneumonia, she discontinued taking nitrofurantoin, leading to resolution of her pneumonitis. C.M. should be followed to ensure that no other pulmonary process is occurring, and alternative arrangements should be made for prophylaxis of her recurrent urinary tract infections.

4. How do chronic reactions to nitrofurantoin differ from the acute pneumonitis described in C.M.?

The chronic reaction mimics idiopathic pulmonary fibrosis clinically, radiologically, and histologically. Chest x-ray shows a diffuse interstitial process without pleural effusion. Pulmonary function testing shows a restrictive pattern without obstructive features. Bronchoalveolar lavage (BAL) generally shows a lymphocytic predominance of the cells obtained. The only notable difference from idiopathic fibrosis is that a much better response occurs following discontinuation of the drug with resolution of the infiltrate and symptoms. The clinical picture consists of a dry cough, exertional dyspnea, and fever. The acute nitrofurantoin-induced pneumonitis and chronic fibrosis appear to be two distinct disorders. The mechanism of chronic toxicity is thought to be an oxidant reaction, although there are no reports of supplemental oxygen producing an acute worsening of disease. The acute reaction rarely is fatal, but the chronic one can progress to irreversible pulmonary fibrosis, respiratory insufficiency, and death. It is unknown how frequently patients may require a course of corticosteroids to accelerate resolution of their symptoms.[7]

Pulmonary Fibrosis

5. A.E., a 35-year-old male with recently diagnosed testicular cancer, he has completed 4 cycles of PEB (cisplatin, etoposide, and bleomycin) therapy. A residual retroperitoneal mass is identified and resection is scheduled. What is A.E.'s total lifetime dose of bleomycin and how is this information relevant to his current management?

PEB is administered every three weeks for three or four cycles in standard treatment of testicular cancer. Thirty units of bleomycin is administered weekly for 9 to 12 doses, while cisplatin and etoposide are administered at three-week intervals. Therefore, the usual lifetime dose for a patient with chemoresponsive testicular cancer is 270 U. A.E. received an additional cycle (3 doses of bleomycin) for a total of 360 U.

Pulmonary fibrosis is the dose-limiting toxicity of bleomycin. It is recommended that the cumulative lifetime dose be restricted to less than 450 U. Pulmonary toxicity is present in 10% of patients receiving bleomycin, and 10% of this group, or 1% of all patients who receive this drug, will die of pulmonary toxicity. The incidence goes up appreciably if more than 450 U are given, approaching a 10% fatality rate when patients receive cumulative doses greater than 550 U.

Furthermore, it is important to be cognizant of the total dose of bleomycin because it also will influence the anesthesiologist's management of A.E.'s FiO$_2$ during his surgical procedure. Another factor to be considered is the temporal relationship between bleomycin administration and the requirement for increased inspired oxygen. If the two are given in close succession, increased toxicity, usually pulmonary fibrosis, may occur.

6. A.E. is scheduled for surgery, during which he will receive oxygen therapy. What risk does this pose to the development of lung toxicity?

The combination of bleomycin and supplemental oxygen is thought to be synergistic for pulmonary toxicity.[64] There are a number of reports of adult respiratory distress syndrome developing in patients who have received bleomycin and subsequently have undergone general anesthesia. The onset of respiratory failure is usually three to ten days after surgery and is rapidly fatal in most reported cases. It is unknown how long after administration of bleomycin that exposure to a higher inspired oxygen may precipitate toxicity, but oxygen should be given with great caution to anyone who has received this drug at any time in his lifetime. Patients at greatest risk include those who are older than 70 years of age, recent bleomycin recipients, and those who have had prior radiation therapy. It has been conservatively recommended that patients requiring general anesthesia, such as A.E., be managed on minimal FiO$_2$ (i.e., 0.25) if at all possible while still maintaining an appropriate target PaO$_2$.[8]

7. What is the postulated mechanism for bleomycin toxicity?

Bleomycin toxicity is attributed to direct cytotoxic injury to the lung epithelium, likely due to free-radical generation following binding of the drug to DNA. Ferrous iron and oxygen are both required for bleomycin to form its active complex. Oxygen free radicals are generated in excess of the scavenging capacity of antioxidant enzymes such as superoxide dismutase, catalase, and glutathione peroxidase. Bleomycin is degraded by bleomycin hydrolase. It is postulated that the relative lack of hydrolase in the human lung may contribute to an increased tissue level of the drug in the lung. Studies in animals have confirmed that bleomycin is concentrated in the lungs and the skin.[63]

8. How can A.E. be monitored for pulmonary toxicity?

There are no pathognomonic signs or symptoms of bleomycin-related pulmonary damage. Patients usually present with dyspnea, tachypnea, and a nonproductive cough. Rales, initially at the bases and then throughout the lungs, may be present on physical examination. Signs and symptoms usually precede changes on the chest x-ray. The utility of pulmonary function tests as an indicator for the extent of the pulmonary damage produced by bleomycin is controversial. Spirometry usually shows a restrictive pattern in the presence of cytotoxic drug-induced pulmonary damage; however, such changes may not always be present in patients with subclinical bleomycin-induced pulmonary fibrosis. For this reason, pulmonary function tests are of questionable predictive value.[63]

Pulmonary Complications of Intravenous (IV) Drug Abuse

9. J.D., a 38-year-old male known to be an IV drug user, presents with a 10-day history of progressive chest pain and shortness of breath. He reports that his symptoms began 1 day after attempting several bilateral "pocket shots" of heroin. Physical examination reveals a thin, wasted man with severe dyspnea and cyanosis. His arms show evidence of scarred, sclerotic peripheral veins and large bilateral bruises are noted in the neck region. Chest radiographs show severe bilateral pneumothoraces and pneumomediastinum. All laboratory tests are within normal limits. He admits to no other prescription or nonprescription illicit drug use. What is a "pocket shot?" What drug-induced pulmonary complications are illustrated by J.D.?

A pocket shot refers to the injection of narcotics into the great vessels of the neck. IV drug users resort to alternate access sites due to sclerosis of their peripheral veins following repeated injections of contaminated substances. Commonly selected venous routes are the pocket shot (jugular, subclavian, and brachiocephalic veins) and the "groin hit" (femoral veins).[88]

J.D.'s chest radiographs show the presence of both pneumothoraces and air in his chest (pneumomediastinum). His dyspnea and cyanosis are consistent with respiratory distress and poor gas exchange associated with a collapsed lung. Pneumothorax is one of the most common complications of the pocket shot.[89,90] The IV drug user often tries to "hit" the jugular vein by himself or herself or may hire a "street doc" or "hit man" to execute the more difficult subclavian injection. Since the lung is located in direct proximity to the pocket, pneumothorax occurs when the needle deviates from the desired course and punctures the lung. Pneumomediastinum follows as air leaks into the chest. Pneumomediastinum also may occur secondary to performing the Valsalva maneuver in an attempt to distend the neck veins. The increased intra-alveolar pressure ruptures alveoli, resulting in dissection of air which can then travel and enter the mediastinum. This also has been reported with smoking crack cocaine.[65]

The IV drug user may delay seeking medical attention while waiting for the condition to resolve spontaneously; therefore, patients often present in an advanced stage with severe shortness of breath and cyanosis, as in J.D.

10. What further pulmonary complications may result from abuse of IV opiates and other drugs?

Infectious complications are a common result of intravenous drug abuse. It is seldom the narcotic itself that causes the problem, but rather the nonsterile practice of drug preparation and injection. Heroin, similar to other narcotics, is only fractionally pure, having been cut with substances such as cornstarch, talc, sawdust, and other contaminants.[91] The needle, syringe, and skin often are not asceptically prepared. Therefore, all these factors, along with the common practice of sharing needles, predispose the IV drug user to a high incidence of infection. Septic thrombophlebitis, infectious

endocarditis, and bone and soft tissue infections are common complications of nonsterile injection techniques. Once an infectious nidus is established, it can serve as a source of septic pulmonary emboli. Frequently, tricuspid valve vegetations are the source of infectious pulmonary emboli. Staphylococcal septic emboli may appear on a chest radiograph as multiple, solid nodular opacities which may stabilize during the course of the illness or may cavitate and then slowly resolve over several weeks. Aspiration (while the patient is in a drug stupor), necrotizing pneumonia, mycotic aneurysm, or traumatic pseudoaneurysm also have been reported secondary to intravenous drug abuse.[92,93]

Noncardiogenic *pulmonary edema* is a frequent complication of heroin and other opiate intoxication. Onset is usually within a few hours of narcotic use, although the development of symptoms may be delayed for as long as 24 hours. The typical patient is acutely ill on presentation with constricted pupils, depressed respiration, decreased neurological status (stupor or coma), fever, and leukocytosis. On chest x-ray, diffuse alveolar infiltrates may appear in a classic "butterfly" or "bat wing" symmetric distribution. The mechanism of pulmonary edema is thought to be increased pulmonary capillary permeability secondary to hypoxia from respiratory suppression, direct toxic effects of the drug itself, or secondary release of histamine induced by the opiate.[94]

Talcosis also may cause pulmonary complications. Talc, or magnesium trisilicate, is used commonly as a filler substance to decrease the purity of "mix" sold on the street.[88] It also is introduced into the blood following injection of methylphenidate (Ritalin) since ground-up and partially-dissolved tablets are the only available dosage form. Magnesium trisilicate forms talc granulomas in pulmonary arteries (emboli), vessel walls, and the interstitium, leading to interstitial fibrosis or pulmonary arterial hypertension. On chest radiograph, extremely tiny, round opacities appear diffusely throughout the lungs. Numerous cases of "Ritalin lung" have been reported in the literature.[95,96] In addition, massive hemoptysis with diffuse alveolar hemorrhage, resulting in respiratory failure, has been reported with smoking freebase cocaine and in chronic heroin abusers.[65]

11. What are some pharmacologic treatment options for patients such as J.D. with heroin-induced pulmonary complications?

Supportive therapy, symptomatic relief, and prevention of withdrawal are the main goals of treatment. J.D. should be supported with oxygen, mechanical ventilation if required, and narcotic antagonism with naloxone hydrochloride. However, it should be noted that naloxone has also been reported on rare occasions to cause noncardiogenic pulmonary edema, similar to heroin. Patients either respond with improving pulmonary function during the first 24 to 48 hours or rapidly proceed to death due to pulmonary edema and respiratory failure. Infectious processes should be considered, especially if patients present with fever and leukocytosis and if pulmonary edema persists after five days of therapy. Several weeks of supportive therapy may be required before complete resolution of pulmonary function with normal measurements of lung volumes, lung compliance, and diffusing capacity is achieved.

Amiodarone-Induced Pulmonary Toxicity

12. R.W., a 55-year-old man admitted with a five-day history of fatigue, exertional dyspnea, and tachypnea, reports that his symptoms have progressively worsened to the point where he can no longer walk his dog around the neighborhood without feeling "out of breath." He denies experiencing coughing or chest pain. His past medical history includes 2 episodes of

ventricular arrhythmia and a 10-year history of hypertension, controlled with nifedipine. Physical examination reveals a tachypneic, tired-looking gentleman with no signs of congestive heart failure evident on cardiac exam. Diffuse inspiratory crackles are audible on lung auscultation. His BP and temperature are unremarkable. Chest x-ray shows diffuse interstitial opacities. All laboratory tests are within normal limits, except for an elevated ESR. His medications on admission include amiodarone 400 mg QD (initiated 2 months before admission), Procardia XL 60 mg QD, and Tums 1 tablet QD. What signs and symptoms are consistent with a diagnosis of amiodarone-induced pulmonary toxicity in R.W.?

Various types of presentation have been described. The most common is an insidious progression of pulmonary symptoms, including dyspnea (especially with exertion), nonproductive cough, and fever. The chest radiograph in these cases generally reveals diffuse parenchymal infiltrates, typically in an interstitial pattern. Pleuritic chest pain, lethargy, weakness, and weight loss also may be seen. Approximately one-third of patients may present with an acute onset of symptoms associated with fever, often mimicking an infectious pneumonitis.[9] In the latter group, the chest radiograph often reveals localized opacities in a patchy acinar pattern. In addition to eliciting symptoms such as fever, tachypnea, and inspiratory crackles, a thorough physical examination is vital to exclude a diagnosis of congestive heart failure since this population is at high risk for this disorder.

Leukocytosis and an elevated ESR are also often noted in patients with amiodarone-induced pulmonary toxicity. Pulmonary function tests frequently reveal a decreased total lung capacity and diffusion capacity. A fall in the carbon monoxide diffusing capacity of the lung of 15% to 20% after starting amiodarone is consistent with pulmonary toxicity. Histologic appearance of the lungs is characterized by foamy alveolar macrophages and type II pneumocytes containing lamellar inclusions.

A bronchoalveolar lavage (BAL) is ordered and revealed the appearance of foamy alveolar macrophages and lamellated inclusion bodies, consistent with amiodarone-induced pulmonary toxicity. R.W.'s pulmonary complaints, radiographic findings, elevated ESR and BAL results are all consistent with a diagnosis of amiodarone-induced pulmonary toxicity.

13. What are some risk factors that predispose patients to developing pulmonary toxicity?

The prevalence of amiodarone-induced pulmonary toxicity is reported most frequently in the range of 4% to 6% of exposed patients.[5,97–99] The majority of patients who develop pulmonary toxicity have been taking amiodarone for more than four weeks, with symptoms developing after one to ten months of therapy.

Pulmonary toxicity appears to be dose related and is more likely to occur with doses greater than 400 mg/day.[98,100] An abnormal chest radiograph and a low carbon monoxide diffusing capacity of the lung before initiating amiodarone therapy also are significant risk factors. There is no association between the cumulative lifetime dose or serum levels of amiodarone and the development of pulmonary toxicity.

Although R.W.'s amiodarone dose does not exceed 400 mg/day, he has been exposed to the upper dose limit (400 mg/day) for approximately two months; therefore, this may have increased his risk of developing pulmonary toxicity.

14. What are the mechanisms thought to cause amiodarone-induced pulmonary toxicity? Which one is most likely in R.W.?

There is evidence for two mechanisms: a) direct chemotoxicity by the inhibition of phospholipid degradation and b) immunological mediation. Amiodarone is an amphophilic compound, containing both nonpolar and polar constituents. Its lipophilicity favors its concentration in adipose tissue and lipid-rich organs such as the lung and liver. In the lung, amiodarone diffuses into lysosomes, forming complexes with phospholipids. These complexes are resistant to enzymatic degradation by phospholipases, resulting in accumulation of abnormal phospholipids. It is thought that these accumulated phospholipids cause direct pulmonary damage. Thus, the characteristic finding of ''foamy'' alveolar macrophages and lamellar bodies is indicative of phospholipid accumulation. However, it should be noted that these findings also can occur in the lungs of patients receiving amiodarone without any clinical evidence of toxicity.[5,31,55,97–99,101]

Alternatively, it is postulated that amiodarone induces a hypersensitivity response in the lung, resulting in indirect pulmonary toxicity.[103] Supporting evidence comes from BAL results similar to those found in hypersensitivity pneumonitis.[101,103] In addition, findings of circulating immune complexes, increased numbers of inflammatory cells (polymorphonuclear leukocytes) and lymphocytes, and the observation that the damage responds to corticosteroids suggest an immune-mediated mechanism. Patients who present with an *acute* onset of pulmonary symptoms, often with fever, may represent those experiencing a ''hypersensitivity'' reaction to amiodarone, rather than those patients who present with an insidious onset of pulmonary toxicity.

R.W.'s BAL findings of foamy alveolar macrophages and lamellar bodies, as well as his insidious presentation of symptoms, suggest that the pulmonary toxicity most likely developed secondary to amiodarone's direct toxic effect on the lung from an accumulation of abnormal phospholipids.

16. What therapeutic interventions can be made?

Amiodarone pulmonary toxicity is reversible after discontinuation of the drug. Clinical symptoms may be expected to resolve within two to four weeks; however, chest radiographic findings clear slowly over three months or more.[100] An alternate antiarrhythmic agent should be prescribed. Corticosteroids have been shown to benefit some patients with amiodarone-induced pulmonary toxicity.[54,55,98,100] Typically, the patient is started on prednisone at a dose of 40 to 60 mg (or equivalent) and subsequently tapered (usually over 4 to 6 months), depending upon the severity of toxicity and the clinical response achieved.

If discontinuation of amiodarone is not feasible in R.W., the lowest effective maintenance dose should be used and corticosteroids employed, although development of irreversible pulmonary fibrosis may still occur.

References

1   Martys CR. Adverse reactions to drugs in general practice. Br Med J (Clin Res). 1979;2:1194.

2   Kramer MS et al. Adverse drug reactions in general pediatric outpatients. J Pediatr. 1985;106:305.

3   Levy M et al. Hospital admissions due to adverse drug reactions: a comparative study from Jerusalem and Berlin. Eur J Clin Pharmacol. 1980;17:25.

4   Shapiro S et al. Fatal drug reactions among medical inpatients. JAMA. 1971; 216:467.

5   Cooper JAD et al. Drug-induced pulmonary disease. Part 1: cytotoxic drugs. Am Rev Respir Dis. 1986;133:321.

6   Cooper JAD et al. Drug-induced pulmonary disease. Part 2: noncytotoxic drugs. Am Rev Respir Dis. 1986;133: 488.

7   Rosenow EC. Drug-induced pulmonary disease. Disease-a-Month. 1994; 40:255.

8   Rosenow EC et al. Drug induced pulmonary disease: an update. Chest. 1992; 102:239.

9   Aronchik JM et al. Drug-induced pulmonary disease: an update. J Thorac Imaging. 1991;6(1):19.

10 Kehrer JP, Kacew S. Systematically applied chemicals that damage lung tissue. Toxicology. 1985;35:251.

11 **Brewis RAL.** Respiratory disorders. In: Davies DM ed. Textbook of Adverse Drug Reactions. 2nd ed. New York: Oxford University Press; 1981:154.

12 **Fisher HK.** Drug-induced asthma syndromes. In: Weiss EB et al. eds. Bronchial Asthma: Mechanisms and Therapeutics. 2nd ed. Boston: Little, Brown and Co.; 1985:938.

13 **Kilbrun KH.** Pulmonary disease induced by drugs. In: Fishman AP, ed. Pulmonary Diseases and Disorders. New York: McGraw-Hill; 1980:707–24.

14 **Settipane GA.** Aspirin and allergic diseases: a review. Am J Med. 1983;74 (Suppl. 6A):102.

15 **Szczeklik A, Gryglewski FJ.** Asthma and anti-inflammatory drugs: mechanisms and clinical patterns. Drugs. 1983; 25:533–43.

16 **Stevenson DD.** Diagnosis, prevention, and treatment of adverse reactions to aspirin and nonsteroidal anti-inflammatory drugs. J Allergy Clin Immunol. 1984;74:617.

17 **Szczeklik A.** Analgesics, allergy and asthma. Br J Clin Pharmacol. 1980;10: 401.

18 **Morice AH et al.** Angiotensin-converting enzyme and the cough reflex. Lancet. 1987;ii:1116.

19 **Lindgren BR et al.** Increased bronchial reactivity and potentiated skin responses in hypertensive subjects suffering from coughs during ACE-inhibitor therapy. Chest. 1989;95:1225.

20 **Goldszer RC et al.** Prevalence of cough during angiotensin-converting-enzyme inhibitory therapy. Am J Med. 1988;85:887.

21 **Pomari C et al.** Has theophylline a role in the cure and prevention of ACE-inhibitor-related cough? Respiration. 1989;55:119.

22 **Meeker D et al.** Drug-induced bronchospasm. Clin Chest Med. 1990;11: 163.

23 **Lofdahl EG et al.** Pafenolol, a highly selective β1-adrenoceptor-antagonist in asthmatic patients: interactions with terbutaline. Clin Pharmacol Ther. 1983; 33:1.

24 **Riddell JG, Shanks RG.** Effects of betaxolol, propranolol, and atenolol on isoproterenol-induced beta-adrenoceptor responses. Clin Pharmacol Ther. 1985; 38:554.

25 **Fraunfeder FT, Barker AF.** Respiratory effects of timolol. N Engl J Med. 1984;311:1441.

26 **Dunn TL et al.** The effect of topical ophthalmic instillation of timolol and betaxolol on lung function in asthmatic subjects. Am Rev Respir Dis. 1986; 133:264.

27 **Simon RA.** Adverse reactions to drug additives. J Allergy Clin Immunol. 1984;74:623.

28 **Stevenson DD, Simon RA.** Sulfites and asthma. J Allergy Clin Immunol. 1984;74:469.

29 **Cotran RS.** Disorders of Immunity. In: Robbins SL, Kumar V, eds. Basic Pathology. 4th ed. Philadelphia: W.B. Saunders Co.; 1987:136.

30 **Aldrich T et al.** Adverse effects of drugs on the respiratory muscles. Clin Chest Med. 1990;11:177.

31 **Miller WT.** Drug-related pleural and mediastinal disorders. J Thorac Imaging. 1991;6(1):36.

32 **Harris KM et al.** Posttransplantation cyclosporine-induced lymphoproliferative disorders: clinical and radiologic manifestations. Radiology. 1987;162: 697.

33 **Starzl TE et al.** Reversibility of lymphomas and lymphoproliferative lesions developing under cyclosporine-steroid therapy. Lancet. 1984;1:583.

34 **Richman S et al.** Acute pulmonary edema associated with librium abuse. Radiology. 1972;103:57.

35 **Greenberger PA.** Contrast media reactions. J Allergy Clin Immunol. 1984; 74:600.

36 **Kaplan AL et al.** Dextran 40: another cause of drug-induced noncardiogenic pulmonary edema. Chest. 1975;68:376.

37 **Miller KS, Sahn SA.** Bilateral exudative pleural effusions following intravenous ethchlorvynol. Chest. 1989;95: 464–6.

38 **Self TH et al.** Intravenous ethchlorvynol-induced pulmonary edema. Drug Intell Clin Pharm. 1979;13:96.

39 **Glauser FL et al.** Pulmonary tissue concentration of ethchlorvynol after intravenous injection. Am Rev Respir Dis. 1977;115:83.

40 **Duberstein JL et al.** A clinical study of an epidemic of heroin intoxication and heroin-induced pulmonary edema. Am J Med. 1971;51:704.

41 **Frand UI et al.** Heroin-induced pulmonary edema: sequential studies of pulmonary function. Ann Intern Med. 1972;77:29.

42 **Anderson TJ et al.** Hydrochlorothiazide-associated pulmonary edema. Chest. 1989;96:695.

43 **Bell RT et al.** Hydrochlorothiazide-induced pulmonary edema, report of a case and review of the literature. Arch Intern Med. 1979;139:817.

44 **Siegel JP, Puri RK.** IL-2 Toxicity. J Clin Oncol. 1991;9:694.

45 **Frand UI et al.** Methadone-induced pulmonary edema. Ann Intern Med. 1972;76:975.

46 **Aronow R et al.** Childhood poisoning: an unfortunate consequence of methadone availability. JAMA. 1972;219: 321.

47 **Ortho Multicenter Transplant Study Group.** A randomized clinical trial of OKT-3 monoclonal antibody for acute rejection of cadaveric renal transplants. N Engl J Med. 1985;313:337.

48 **Kreis H et al.** A randomized trial comparing the efficacy of OKT-3 used to prevent or to treat rejection. Transplant Proc. 1989;21:1741.

49 **Cosimi AB et al.** A randomized clinical trial comparing OKT-3 and steroids for treatment of hepatic allograft rejection. Transplantation. 1987;43:91.

50 **Bogartz LJ et al.** Pulmonary edema associated with propoxyphene intoxication. JAMA. 1971;215:259.

51 **Davis PR et al.** Pulmonary edema and salicylate intoxication. Ann Intern Med. 1974;80:553.

52 **Bowers RE et al.** Salicylate pulmonary edema: the mechanism in sheep and review of the clinical literature. Am Rev Respir Dis. 1977;115:261.

53 **Varnell RM et al.** Adult respiratory distress syndrome from overdose of tricyclic antidepressants. Radiology. 1989;170:667.

54 **Rakita L et al.** Amiodarone pulmonary toxicity. Am Heart J. 1983;106: 906.

55 **Marchlinski FE et al.** Amiodarone pulmonary toxicity. Ann Intern Med. 1982;97:839.

56 **Morera J et al.** Amiodarone and pulmonary fibrosis. Eur J Clin Pharmacol. 1983;24:591.

57 **Weiss RB, Muggia FM.** Cytotoxic drug-induced pulmonary disease: update 1980. Am J Med. 1980;68:259.

58 **Batist G, Andrews JL.** Pulmonary toxicity of antineoplastic drugs. JAMA. 1981;246:1449.

59 **Durrant JR et al.** Pulmonary toxicity associated with bischloroethyl-nitrosourea (BCNU) Ann Intern Med. 1979; 90:191.

60 **Crittenden D et al.** Pulmonary fibrosis after prolonged therapy with 1,3-bis-2-chloroethyl-1-nitrosourea. Chest. 1977; 72:372.

61 **Brown WG et al.** Reversibility of severe bleomycin-induced pneumonitis. JAMA. 1978;239.

62 **Lewis BM et al.** Routine pulmonary function tests during bleomycin therapy, tests may be ineffective and potentially misleading. JAMA. 1980;243: 347.

63 **Waid-Jones MI, Coursin DB.** Perioperative considerations for patients treated with bleomycin. Chest. 1991; 99:993.

64 **Tryka AF et al.** Differences in the effects of immediate and delayed hyperoxia exposure on bleomycin-induced pulmonary injury. Cancer Treat Rep. 1984;68:759.

65 **Murray RJ et al.** Diffuse alveolar hemorrhage temporally related to cocaine smoking. Chest. 1988;93:427.

66 **McElvaney NG et al.** Pleuropulmonary disease during bromocriptine treatment of Parkinson's disease. Arch Intern Med. 1988;148:2231.

67 **Kinnunen E et al.** Pleuropulmonary involvement during bromocriptine treatment. Chest. 1988;94:1034.

68 **Rinne UK et al.** Pleuropulmonary changes during long-term bromocriptine treatment for Parkinson's disease. Lancet. 1981;1:44.

69 **Tornling G et al.** Pleuropulmonary reactions in patients on bromocriptine treatment. Eur J Respir Dis. 1986;68:35.

70 **Wiggins J et al.** Bromocriptine-induced pleuropulmonary fibrosis. Thorax. 1986;41:328.

71 **Alvarado CS et al.** Late-onset pulmonary fibrosis and chest deformity in two children treated with cyclophosphamide. J Pediatr. 1978;92:443.

72 **Winterbauer RH et al.** Diffuse pulmonary injury associated with gold treatment. N Engl J Med. 1976;294: 919.

73 **Terho EO et al.** Pulmonary damage associated with gold therapy: a report of two cases. Scand J Respir Dis. 1979; 60:345.

74 **Weaver LT et al.** Lung changes after gold salts. Br J Dis Chest. 1978;72:247.

75 **Buzdar AV et al.** Pulmonary toxicity of mitomycin. Cancer. 1980;45:236.

76 **Deneke SM, Fanburg BL.** Normobaric oxygen toxicity of the lung. N Engl J Med. 1980:303:76.

77 **Frank L, Massaro D.** Oxygen toxicity. Am J Med. 1980;69:117–26.

78 **Jackson RM.** Pulmonary oxygen toxicity. Chest. 1985;88:900.

79 **Musk AW, Pollard JA.** Pindolol and pulmonary fibrosis. Br Med J. 1979;2: 581.

80 **Stone D et al.** Fatal pulmonary insufficiency due to radiation effect upon the lung. Am J Med. 1956;21:211.

81 **Lobel H et al.** Pulmonary infiltrates with eosinophilia in an asthmatic patient treated with disodium cromoglycate. Lancet. 1972;2:1032.

82 **Sahn SA et al.** Immunologic diseases of the pleura. Clin Chest Med. 1985;6: 83.

83 **Sitbon O et al.** Minocycline pneumonitis and eosinophilia: a report on eight patients. Arch Intern Med. 1994;154: 1633.

84 **Otero M et al.** Pulmonary infiltrates and eosinophilia from minocycline. JAMA. 1983; 250:2602.

85 **Guillon JM et al.** Minocycline-induced cell-mediated hypersensitivity pneumonitis. Ann Intern Med. 1992; 117:476.

86 **Sigmann P et al.** Minocycline-induced pneumonia. Ann Intern Med. 1993; 118:749.

87 **Robertson CH.** Pulmonary hypertension and foreign body granulomas in IV drug abusers. Am J Med. 1976;61:557.

88 **McCarroll KA et al.** Lung disorders due to drug abuse. J Thorac Imaging. 1991;6(1):30.

89 **Douglass RE et al.** Pneumothorax in drug abusers. An urban epidemic? Am Surg. 1986;52:377.

90 **Lewis JW et al.** Complications of attempted central venous injections performed by drug abusers. Chest. 1980; 4:613.

91 **Gross EM et al.** Autopsy findings in drug addicts. Pathol Annu. 1978;13:35.

92 **Heffner JE et al.** Pulmonary reactions from illicit substance abuse. Clin Chest Med. 1990;11(1):151.

93 **Shetty PC et al.** Mycotic aneurysms in intravenous drug abusers. Radiology. 1985;155:319.

94 **Stern WZ et al.** Pulmonary complications of drug addiction. Semin Roentgenol. 1983;18:213.

95 **Schmidt RA et al.** Panlobular emphysema in young intravenous Ritalin abusers. Am Rev Respir Dis. 1991; 143:649.

96 **Stern EJ et al.** Panlobular emphysema caused by IV injection of methylphenidate (Ritalin): findings on chest radiographs and CT scans. Am J Roentgenol. 1994;162:555.

97 **Israil-Biet D et al.** Drug-induced lung disease: 1990 review. Eur Respir J. 1991;4:465.

98 **Kennedy JI et al.** Amiodarone pulmonary toxicity. Arch Intern Med. 1987; 147:50.

99 **Bryant DH.** Drug-induced pulmonary disease. Med J Aust. 1992;156:802.

100 **Gefter WB et al.** Lung disease caused by amiodarone, a new antiarrhythmic agent. Radiology. 1983;147:339.

101 **Sobol SM et al.** Pneumonitis and pulmonary fibrosis associated with amiodarone treatment: a possible complication of a new antiarrhythmic drug. Circulation. 1982;65:819.

102 **Martin WJ.** Mechanisms of amiodarone pulmonary toxicity. Clin Chest Med. 1990;2:131.

103 **Olson LK et al.** Pneumonitis after amiodarone therapy. Radiology. 1984; 150:327.

Upper Gastrointestinal Disorders

Candace Smith

Peptic Ulcer Disease (PUD) 23-1
  Epidemiology 23-1
    Incidence and prevalence 23-2
    Geographic variation 23-2
    Gender 23-2
    Age 23-2
    Genetic and environmental factors 23-2
    Morbidity and mortality 23-2
  Pathophysiology 23-2
  Pathogenesis 23-2
  Risk Factors 23-3
  Clinical Presentation 23-3
  Treatment (See Figure 23.1) 23-3
    Factors that influence healing 23-3
    Goals 23-4
    Options 23-4
    Histamine₂-Receptor Antagonists 23-4
      Mechanism of action 23-4
      Product selection (Also see Question 5) 23-4
        Pharmacokinetics (See Table 23.1) 23-4
        Adverse effects 23-4
        Drug interactions (See Table 23.3) 23-4
      Dosing (Also see Table 23.2 and Question 7) 23-6
      Duration of therapy 23-7
    Antacids 23-8
      Dosing 23-8
      Adverse effects (See Table 23.4) 23-8
      Product selection (See Table 23.5) 23-8
      Drug interactions (See Table 23.6) 23-9
    Sucralfate 23-9
      Mechanism of action 23-9
      Adverse effects 23-9
      Combination therapy 23-10
    Omeprazole 23-10
      Mechanism of action 23-10
      Pharmacokinetics 23-10
      Drug interactions 23-10
      Adverse effects 23-10
  Refractory Ulcers 23-10
    Treatment 23-10
  Maintenance Therapy 23-11
    Indications 23-11
    Therapy 23-11
  Helicobacter pylori 23-11
    Epidemiology 23-11
    Detection 23-12

  Therapy 23-12
    Eradication 23-13
  Drug-Induced PUD 23-13
    Etiology and clinical presentation 23-13
    Mechanism 23-13
    Risk factors 23-13
    Treatment 23-14
    Continued NSAID use 23-14
    Maintenance therapy 23-14
      Misoprostol 23-14
Zollinger-Ellison Syndrome 23-15
  Pathogenesis and Clinical Presentation 23-15
  Diagnosis 23-15
  Treatment 23-15
    H₂-receptor antagonists 23-15
    Omeprazole 23-16
      Administration 23-16
    Somatostatin 23-16
    Drug Therapy During Perioperative Period 23-16
Gastroesophageal Reflux Disorder (GERD) 23-16
  Pathogenesis 23-16
  Clinical Presentation 23-16
  Treatment 23-17
    Goals 23-17
    Life-style changes 23-17
    Drug therapy 23-17
      Antacids 23-17
      H₂-receptor antagonists 23-17
      Omeprazole 23-17
      Prokinetic agents 23-17
        Metoclopramide 23-18
        Cisapride 23-18
      Sucralfate 23-18
    Maintenance therapy 23-18
Stress Ulcers 23-18
  Epidemiology 23-18
  Pathogenesis 23-18
  Risk Factors 23-19
  Treatment 23-19
    Goals 23-19
    Drug Therapy 23-19
      Antacids 23-19
      H₂-receptor antagonists 23-19
      Sucralfate 23-19
Pearls of Wisdom (See Table 23.7) 23-20

Peptic Ulcer Disease (PUD)

Peptic ulcer disease is a heterogeneous group of disorders involving the upper gastrointestinal (GI) tract. It is a disease that results from an imbalance between aggressive forces and defensive factors. Chronic PUD is characterized by remission and recurrences, whereas acute peptic ulcers are limited to a specific patient population and clinical situation. Duodenal and gastric ulcers are the most common types of chronic peptic ulcers; however, ulcers of the esophagus and other areas of the gastrointestinal tract do occur. Zollinger-Ellison syndrome is a rare form of PUD which is caused by a gastrin-producing tumor.

Epidemiology

An estimated 10% of all Americans will develop a peptic ulcer during their lifetimes and the prevalence of active disease is probably about 1% to 2%.[1] The incidence of PUD varies with the type of ulcer, geographic location, gender, age, and environmental factors. Race, economic status, and psychologic stress do not correlate with ulcer acquisition.[2]

Incidence and Prevalence

During the beginning of this century, the incidence of peptic ulcer disease significantly increased, reaching a peak in the early 1950s.[3] Over the past two decades, there has been a decline in both outpatient episodes of duodenal ulcers and ulcers requiring hospitalization.[4] It is unclear whether this decline reflects an actual decrease in the incidence of ulcer disease or the combined influences of more effective therapy, changes in hospital diagnostic practices or criteria, and institution coding changes.[5,6] While there has been a decline in hospitalization for duodenal ulcers, hospitalization for gastric ulcers has remained stable. The reason for the lack of decline in gastric ulcers may be because these ulcers are affected by an aging of the population and the use of ulcerogenic medications.[2]

Geographic Variation

Peptic ulcer disease occurs worldwide with marked geographic variation. In Japan, the incidence of gastric ulcer is approximately five to ten times more common than duodenal ulcer,[7] whereas, in most European countries and the U.S., duodenal ulcers are approximately twice as common as gastric ulcers.[7]

Gender

In 1968 twice as many men as women had peptic ulcer disease in the U.S.[8] As of 1985, the male predominance in PUD changed. Ulcer prevalence rates for women have increased whereas rates for men have decreased primarily due to a more rapid decrease in duodenal ulcer rates.[8] Recent trends indicate that the prevalence of duodenal ulcers is similar for men and women.[9] The incidence of gastric ulcers is approximately the same for men as for women; however, hospitalizations for women with gastric ulcers have increased markedly for patients over 65 years of age.[6,8]

Age

Gastric ulcers rarely develop before age 40, and the peak incidence occurs from ages 55 to 65.[6] In contrast, the incidence of duodenal ulcer increases with age until the age of about 60 years.[1]

Genetic and Environmental Factors

Genetic and environmental factors may influence the occurrence of duodenal ulcer. Duodenal ulcers appear to be two to three times more prevalent in relatives of patients with ulcers.[2] Nonsteroidal anti-inflammatory drug (NSAID) consumption among the elderly for the treatment of chronic diseases like arthritis may be the reason for this increase.[1]

Morbidity and Mortality

The mortality of PUD has declined over the past 20 years. Less than 2% of ulcer patients receiving therapy are expected to have a complication such as bleeding, perforation, or obstruction during a one-year period.[2] Nevertheless, peptic ulcer disease remains one of the most common GI diseases that results in loss of work and high-cost medical services.[9]

Pathophysiology

The body and fundus of the stomach are made up of oxyntic glands which contain parietal and chief cells. When stimulated, the parietal cells secrete hydrochloric acid (HCl) and intrinsic factor into the gastric lumen, while the chief cells secrete pepsinogen.[9] The secretion of acid occurs against a concentration gradient and, therefore, requires a hydrogen/potassium adenosine triphosphatase (ATPase) proton pump. Under fasting conditions, acid is secreted at a low basal rate. When a physiologic event (e.g., a meal) or pathologic condition (e.g., a gastrin-producing tumor) occurs, gastric acid secretion increases due to three endogenous substances: acetylcholine, gastrin, and histamine.[10] These substances bind to specific receptors on the parietal cell and initiate a series of intracellular reactions that result in HCl secretion. The neurocrine pathway delivers acetylcholine which is released from intramural postganglionic nerve terminals.[9] Gastrin is released from antral G-cells located in the antrum and duodenum and delivered to the parietal cell via the systemic circulation (hormonal effect) and histamine is released from mucosal mast cells into the interstitial fluid via the paracrine pathway.[11,12] The effects of histamine are mediated by adenylate cyclase, whereas acetylcholine and gastrin involve cytosolic free calcium.[11] The regulation of gastric acid secretion is through a positive and negative feedback mechanism. Prostaglandin E and somatostatin are endogenous substances that inhibit acid secretion. These substances are located on the basolateral membrane of the parietal cell.[12] Pepsinogen, another substance released from the oxyntic cell, is a proenzyme that will form pepsin in an acidic environment (pH <3.5). Pepsin combines with acid to form a proteolytic complex that further aids in the digestive process.[1]

Several mechanisms protect the gastroduodenal mucosa from the digestive effects of pepsin and acid. The first level of defense is the secretion of mucus by superficial epithelial cells and mucus cells throughout the stomach. Gastric mucus is a viscous gel that acts as a mucosal lubricant and trap for micro-organisms.[6,13] It consists of water, electrolytes, glycoprotein, and nucleic acids.[14] In addition to acting as a surface lubricant, mucus also can impair the back diffusion of hydrogen ions from the mucosa.[15] There is evidence that the combination of mucus and bicarbonate, which also is secreted throughout the stomach, creates a pH gradient that neutralizes the hydrogen ions. This further protects the epithelium against injury from gastric acid.

Beneath the surface epithelium is a network of capillaries that provides another level of defense. Mucosal blood flow not only transports oxygen and substrates to the mucosa, but it removes acids that have damaged the epithelium of the stomach or duodenum.[14]

Another way in which the epithelium resists injury from acids is through rapid and continual cell renewal. In the majority of cases, disruption of the surface epithelium does not have repercussions because of the process called restitution. Restitution involves the formation of a fibrin cap over the injured area.[13]

Prostaglandins, which are produced by cells in the GI tract, play an important role in preventing injury to the gastroduodenal mucosa by inhibiting gastric acid secretion, maintaining blood flow, and stimulating mucus and bicarbonate production.[15,16]

Pathogenesis

The integrity of the upper gastrointestinal mucosa depends upon a balance between aggressive forces, mainly gastric acid and pepsin, and mucosal defensive factors.[13] Gastric acid is necessary for the formation of ulcers, but an alteration in the protective defenses plays a significant role as well. Patients with Zollinger-Ellison syndrome and the majority of duodenal ulcer patients have an increased parietal cell mass which secretes high amounts of gastric acid. On the other hand, many patients with duodenal ulcers have normal acid secretion, and patients with gastric ulcers tend to have normal or low acid production.[17] These observations support the premise that other mechanisms are involved in the pathogenesis of ulcers. Studies have focused on alteration of mucosal defenses as an etiology of ulcers. For example, prostaglandin inhibitors may render the gastric mucosa susceptible to ulceration because endogenous prostaglandins protect the GI tract.[18] Infection with a bacterium, *Helicobacter pylori*, also has been implicated in the pathogenesis of PUD, and eradication of this organism may alter the natural history of the peptic ulcer disease. As a result, many investigators have divided PUD into three etiologic groups based upon pathophysiologic abnormalities: 1) those with massive acid hypersecretion (i.e., Zollinger-Ellison syndrome); 2) those due to NSAIDs; and 3) ulcers associated with *H. pylori* infection.[19]

Risk Factors

A number of factors can predispose an individual to peptic ulcer disease. Disruption of mucosal resistance to injury appears to be one mechanism involved in the pathogenesis of ulcers. The inflammatory response associated with *H. pylori* is thought to disrupt the architecture of the gastroduodenal mucosa which then alters its natural defense mechanism. Antral gastritis associated with *H. pylori* infection has been found in 75% to 95% of patients with gastric and duodenal ulcers, respectively.[5,20–23]

Overwhelming evidence associates *nonsteroidal anti-inflammatory drugs* with PUD, particularly gastric ulcers. NSAIDs and aspirin impair ulcer healing and induce ulcer formation through prostaglandin inhibition and directly irritate the gastric and duodenal mucosa.[16,24,25]

Cigarette smoking impairs ulcer healing, promotes ulcer recurrence, and increases the likelihood of ulcer complications.[16,26,27] The mechanisms by which cigarettes cause ulcer formation are through stimulation of gastric acid secretion and bile salt reflux,[28,29] alteration in mucosal blood flow,[16] and reduction in prostaglandin synthesis.[30]

Traditionally, certain *foods* have been implicated in the development of ulcers. Although some foods and beverages increase acid secretion (e.g., caffeine-containing foods, milk, cola, beer, spicy foods) and cause dyspepsia, there are no data to support that diet imparts an increased risk for ulcer formation.[1,9] Acute *alcohol* ingestion can damage the gastric mucosal barrier, leading to acute gastric mucosal lesions and GI bleeding; however, there is no evidence to confirm it as a causative agent in the pathogenesis of peptic ulcer disease.[9]

There appears to be a *genetic predilection* towards the development of ulcers. A positive family history correlates with 20% to 50% of patients with duodenal ulcers compared to 5% to 15% of nonulcer patients.[2]

Although rigorous studies are lacking, it is believed that stressful life events can exacerbate PUD.[2]

Clinical Presentation

Patients with gastric or duodenal ulcers present with similar symptoms and cannot be differentiated upon the basis of clinical findings. An endoscopy to directly visualize the ulcer is needed for a definitive diagnosis. The most common and, in the majority of cases, the only symptom of an ulcer is epigastric pain. Overall, the pain associated with duodenal and gastric ulcers is not well localized and usually is described as annoying, burning, gnawing, and aching.[1] Pain that occurs when the stomach is empty, such as during the night or between meals, and is relieved by food and antacids is the most widely described characteristic of duodenal ulcer pain.[31] Duodenal ulcer pain is episodic in nature; symptomatic periods lasting for weeks followed by a period of no occurrence have been described by many patients. This pattern is not consistent with gastric ulcers, where the pain occurs at any time during the day but frequently occurs immediately or within one to three hours after eating a meal.[6] Pain does not always correlate with the presence or absence of an ulcer; asymptomatic patients have been diagnosed with ulcers, and patients with dyspeptic symptoms may not have active disease.[31] The lack of symptoms, despite an active

gastric lesion, is particularly common in the elderly who are on analgesic therapy and in those who have a high pain tolerance. Complications such as bleeding, obstruction, or perforation often are evident subsequent to a change in the character of a patient's pain. An increase or change in the quality of the pain, a more localized pain, or failure to respond to antacid therapy may indicate the development of an ulcer.[1,9] Other symptoms associated with both duodenal and gastric ulcers include nausea, vomiting, belching, bloating, and anorexia.

1. J.P., a 55-year-old, 70 kg male, presents to the ambulatory clinic with a chief complaint of epigastric pain. He describes the pain as gnawing; it occurs every couple of weeks, lasts for a couple of weeks, and then disappears for a while. Because the pain frequently awakens him from sleep, he finds himself "raiding the refrigerator at night." After eating, he says the pain generally subsides and allows him to go back to sleep. His past medical history is significant for asthma and arrhythmias. Medications include procainamide 1000 mg Q 6 hr, theophylline 600 mg BID, and aspirin PRN for headaches. J.P. has a difficult time remembering to take his medications, but he takes them whenever he remembers. He has a 150-pack-year smoking history and drinks 10 cups of coffee a day. In the evening he has 2 martinis before dinner and sherry after dinner. Physical examination is within normal limits.

Pertinent laboratory tests include the following: Hemoglobin (Hgb) 15 gm/dL (Normal: 13–16), hematocrit (Hct) 48% (Normal: 40%–48%), red blood cell (RBC) 4.5 × 10³/mm³ (Normal: 4.3–5.8), serum creatinine (SrCr) 2.5 mg/dL (Normal: 0.8–1.2), theophylline 5 mg/L (Normal: 10–20), procainamide 4 mg/L (Normal: 4–10 mg/L), N-acetyl procainamide (NAPA) 8 mg/L (Normal: 10–20 mg/L). An endoscopy is performed and a 0.5 cm lesion is found in the duodenum. Cultures and biopsy tests are sent for analysis. The diagnosis for J.P. is a duodenal ulcer. What signs and symptoms demonstrated by J.P. are consistent with a duodenal ulcer? [SI units: Hgb 9.31 mmol/L; RBC 4.5 × 10¹²/mm³; SrCr 190.65 μmol/L; theophylline 27.75 μmol/L; procainamide 17 μmol/L; NAPA 28.8 μmol/L]

J.P. presents with typical signs and symptoms of duodenal ulcer disease. The majority of patients initially present with epigastric pain that often is described as gnawing, burning, or hunger-like in nature. Clusters of episodic pain which can last for weeks followed by symptom-free periods of weeks to months have been described in many patients such as J.P. Duodenal ulcer pain frequently is relieved by neutralization of acid by food and provoked by fasting. Therefore, many patients typically describe nocturnal pain that usually awakens them from sleep and is relieved with food.

Treatment

Factors That Influence Healing

2. What factors may influence the healing of J.P.'s ulcer? What therapeutic measures can be taken to minimize these risk factors?

J. P. has a number of factors that put him at risk for the development of ulcers and may influence the healing of his ulcer. Because cigarette smoking may impair the healing of his ulcer, promote a recurrent ulcer, and increase the likelihood of an ulcer complication, J.P. should be counseled to cease smoking. Tylenol should be recommended to J.P. as a replacement for aspirin to treat his headaches because aspirin, a prostaglandin inhibitor, is associated with the development of ulcers. Although alcohol has not been confirmed as a causative agent in the formation of ulcers, J.P. should avoid alcohol because it is associated with GI bleeding. Coffee should be minimized and J.P. should avoid spices, particularly black and red pepper and chili powder, because they may cause dyspepsia especially during the acute ulcer healing stage.[2]

J.P. does not have to be restricted to a bland diet. Bland diets not only are distasteful, but also usually contain milk products that can cause GI discomfort and increase gastric acid secretion.[18] He should be encouraged to get adequate rest and stressful life situations should be avoided if possible.

Treatment Goals

3. What are the treatment goals for PUD?

Treatment goals of uncomplicated PUD are to relieve symptoms, promote ulcer healing, and prevent ulcer recurrence and complications. Current therapy for acute uncomplicated ulcers is directed toward reducing gastric acidity or enhancing mucosal defenses. Since the majority of duodenal ulcers are associated with increased acid secretion, it is not surprising that healing is correlated with the duration of antisecretory effect.[32] In contrast, gastric ulcers typically are associated with normal or decreased acid secretion; therefore, healing is not associated with enhanced antisecretory effect but primarily is dependent upon enhancement of mucosal resistance.[33]

Treatment Options

4. What therapeutic options are available to treat J.P.'s ulcer?

Therapeutic regimens that have been successful in the healing of peptic ulcers involve the neutralization of gastric acid, inhibition of acid secretion, and protection of the gastroduodenal mucosa. At the present time, sucralfate, antacids, H_2-receptor antagonists, and omeprazole are indicated for the treatment of peptic ulcer disease. All of these therapeutic options are equal in efficacy; therefore, the choice will depend upon patient-specific criteria. (See Figure 23.1.)

Histamine₂-Receptor Antagonists

5. J.P.'s physician wants to start him on an H_2-receptor antagonist for the treatment of his duodenal ulcer. What must be considered before selecting an appropriate drug?

The ideal therapeutic regimen should be efficacious, simple, safe, and inexpensive.[34] The decision to choose one drug over another drug for the treatment of any disease should include an evaluation of the drugs' comparative efficacies, pharmacokinetics, adverse effect profiles, and potential drug interactions.

6. Mechanism of Action. What is the mechanism by which the H_2-receptor antagonists work and is there any difference in their efficacies?

H_2-receptor antagonists are classified pharmacologically as a group of drugs that inhibits the secretion of gastric acid. Histamine, which is released primarily from mast cells, binds to H_2-receptors and activates adenylate cyclase leading to an increase in intracellular cyclic AMP. The increased levels of cyclic AMP activate the proton pump of the parietal cell to secrete hydrogen ions against a concentration gradient in exchange for potassium ions.[35] H_2-receptor antagonists competitively and selectively inhibit the action of histamine on the H_2-receptors of the parietal cells, thus reducing basal and stimulated gastric acid secretion.[36] They have no significant action on the muscarinic, nicotinic, histamine₁, or sympathetic receptors.[37] The histamine receptors on the parietal cell are of the H_2-type and, therefore, are not blocked by H_1-antihistamines such as diphenhydramine.[15]

Four H_2-receptor antagonists have been approved by the Food and Drug Administration (FDA) for the treatment of duodenal and gastric ulcer disease: cimetidine (Tagamet), ranitidine (Zantac), famotidine (Pepcid), and nizatidine (Axid). All four agents have been compared in many studies, are comparable in the healing of duodenal and gastric ulcers, and are well tolerated.[34,38-42] No one drug has demonstrated superiority over another in terms of efficacy. All four drugs provide an overall healing rate of 70% to 95% after four to eight weeks of therapy, respectively.

7. Product Selection. What pharmacokinetic differences between the H_2-receptor antagonists would be important in choosing a drug for J.P.?

Pharmacokinetics. Although these agents are similar pharmacologically, they differ pharmacokinetically (see Table 23.1). The relative antisecretory potency on a milligram-per-milligram basis of these four agents differs: famotidine has the greatest potency, followed by nizatidine, ranitidine, and lastly, cimetidine. The serum concentration that is necessary to inhibit 50% of pentagastrin-stimulated secretion of acid determines the dose and frequency of administration of each H_2-receptor antagonist. Famotidine and nizatidine are the most potent and possess the longest duration of action; however, all of the H_2-receptor antagonists can be administered once daily for treatment of acute duodenal ulcers.[43,44] This is especially beneficial for a patient like J.P. who has a compliance problem.

Oral absorption of all the H_2-receptor antagonists is rapid and peak drug concentrations usually are achieved within one to three hours after administration.[45] The bioavailability of these drugs ranges from 30% to 88% for ranitidine, cimetidine, and famotidine, and 98% for nizatidine.[35,46-48] The bioavailability is lower for cimetidine, famotidine, and ranitidine because they are absorbed incompletely and undergo first-pass hepatic metabolism. Ranitidine undergoes the most extensive first-pass metabolism which accounts for the large difference between the oral and intravenous (IV) doses of this drug. Nizatidine is the only H_2-receptor antagonist that is unavailable as an IV formulation at this time.

All four drugs are eliminated by a combination of hepatic metabolism, glomerular filtration, and renal tubular secretion.[46,49] Hepatic metabolism is the principal pathway for the elimination of cimetidine and ranitidine, while renal excretion is the major route for the elimination of famotidine and nizatidine.[46,47] For each of these agents, the half-life is increased and the total body clearance is decreased in patients with varying degrees of renal dysfunction. Therefore, alterations in the doses of these drugs are recommended for patients with moderate to severe renal insufficiency (see Table 23.2). The pharmacokinetics of the H_2-receptor antagonists appear to be unaffected by hepatic dysfunction; however, in patients with hepatic failure and renal insufficiency, the dose may need adjustment. J.P. has a calculated creatinine clearance (Cl_{Cr}) of approximately 30 mL/minute. Therefore, doses should be adjusted for any of the H_2-receptor antagonists prescribed for him.

8. *Adverse effects.* What adverse effects are associated with H_2-receptor antagonists?

These agents are remarkably safe and the frequency of severe adverse effects is low for all four drugs.[49] The most common adverse effects include GI discomfort (e.g., diarrhea, constipation), central nervous system (CNS) alterations (e.g., mental confusion, headaches, dizziness, drowsiness), and rashes.[35,50-52] Because of cimetidine's antiandrogenic effect, gynecomastia and impotence have been associated with its use. Hepatotoxicity has been observed infrequently with ranitidine. Famotidine has been associated with headaches and, therefore, may not be an ideal agent for a patient with a history of headaches. The patients who are at greatest risk for developing adverse effects are the elderly, those taking higher doses, and those with altered renal or hepatic function.[47,52] J.P.'s diminished renal capacity could predispose him to adverse effects because he is unable to eliminate the drugs as well. An appropriate H_2-receptor dose will help to minimize potential adverse effects.

9. *Drug interactions.* J.P. currently is taking a number of medications. What are potential drug interactions between these medications and the H_2-receptor antagonists?

Several drug interactions exist between other medications and H_2-receptor antagonists which can alter the clearance or absorption

Treatment of Peptic Ulcer Disease

Duodenal Ulcer	H_2R 4–8 weeks Sucralfate 4–8 weeks Omeprazole 4 weeks
Gastric Ulcer	H_2R 8–12 weeks Omeprazole 4 weeks

Unhealed Ulcer

Continue therapy for 4 more weeks

Refractory Ulcer

Omeprazole
High-dose H_2R

Helicobacter pylori therapy
Bismuth+
Metronidazole+
Tetracycline or amoxicillin

Zollinger-Ellison syndrome
High-dose omeprazole

Healed Ulcer (Prevention)

Evaluate for risk factors

Low Risk

Intermittent therapy   On-demand therapy

High Risk

Continuous maintenance therapy
Low-dose H_2R or sucralfate
Misoprostol for NSAID-associated ulcers

Relapse

Full-dose therapy   *Helicobacter pylori* therapy
H_2R Bismuth+
Omeprazole   Metronidazole+
                    Tetracycline or amoxicillin

Fig 23.1 Treatment of Peptic Ulcer Disease Adapted from references 3, 36, and 101.

Table 23.1   Pharmacokinetic Comparison of H_2-Receptor Antagonists[a]

Variable[b]	Cimetidine	Ranitidine	Nizatidine	Famotidine
Relative Potency	1	4–10	4–10	20–50
Absorption				
Bioavailability (%)[c]	30–80 (60)	30–88 (50)	75–100 (98)	37–45 (43)
Time to peak serum concentration (hr)	1–2	1–3	1–3	1–3.5
Volume of distribution (L/kg of body weight)	0.8–1.2	1.2–1.9	1.2–1.6	1.1–1.4
Elimination				
Total systemic clearance (mL/min)	450–650	568–709	667–850	417–483
Half-life in serum (hr)	1.5–2.3	1.6–2.4	1.1–1.6	2.5–4
Hepatic clearance (%)				
Oral	60	73	22	50–80
IV	25–40	30	25	25–30
Renal clearance (%)				
Oral	40	27	57–65	25–30
IV	50–80	50	75	65–80

[a] Adapted with permission from reference 35.
[b] IV = Intravenous.
[c] Average values are in parenthesis.

of other drugs. (See Table 23.3.) Cimetidine binds to the cytochrome P450 mixed-function oxidase enzyme system and has the well-known ability to inhibit the biotransformation of several drugs by the liver. It primarily affects oxidative drug metabolism while conjugation generally is not affected. The magnitude of cimetidine interaction with other drugs varies from patient to patient; however, it generally will reduce the clearance of another drug by about 20% to 30%.[53] This interaction is most clinically significant with drugs that have narrow therapeutic ranges such as phenytoin, warfarin, and theophylline.

Although ranitidine is more potent on a molar basis, it binds less intensely to the cytochrome P450 system than does cimetidine.[54] Therefore, when used in equipotent doses, there is less potential for ranitidine compared to cimetidine to interfere with the liver metabolism of other drugs.[35] In contrast, famotidine and nizatidine do not bind appreciably to the cytochrome P450 system and, therefore, have very limited ability to inhibit the metabolism of other drugs.[35,47,55] Overall, ranitidine, famotidine, and nizatidine, when used in equipotent doses, are unlikely to cause clinically-significant drug interactions when administered concurrently with other drugs eliminated by phase I oxidative metabolism by the liver. However, the introduction of cimetidine to a patient receiving a drug that requires the P450 system for metabolism may require a downward dosage adjustment of the object drug to avoid increased serum concentrations. Patients receiving drugs known to interact with H_2-receptor antagonists should be monitored to prevent or minimize the development of an adverse drug-drug interaction. J.P. currently is taking theophylline for his asthma. Since theophylline is a drug that is hepatically metabolized by the P450 enzyme system, an H_2-receptor antagonist such as cimetidine may affect its clearance. Choosing another H_2-receptor antagonist or closely monitoring theophylline levels is warranted in J.P.

Some of the H_2-receptor antagonists are eliminated via renal tubular secretion and, therefore, have the potential to compete with cationic compounds for tubular secretion.[54–56] Cimetidine and ranitidine inhibit the renal tubular secretion of procainamide and its metabolite by this mechanism.[57,58] When patients were on any one of these H_2-receptor antagonists, the areas under the concentration-time curves of procainamide and N-acetyl procainamide were increased and their renal clearance decreased. The interaction with ranitidine appears to be concentration and dose dependent; therapeutic doses of ranitidine (i.e., 300 mg/day) did not cause an in-

teraction, whereas large doses (i.e., 750 mg/day) altered the pharmacokinetics of procainamide.[59] Although famotidine is a cationic drug that is excreted via active tubular secretion, it has not been shown to inhibit the renal elimination of procainamide or its metabolite.[55] A possible reason for this discrepancy is that the serum concentrations attained by the usual therapeutic dose (i.e., 20 mg BID) of famotidine may be too low to compete with other drugs at the site of renal tubular secretion.[46] Thus, famotidine may be a more appropriate agent for J.P. since he currently is taking procainamide.

All four H_2-receptor antagonists potentially can affect the absorption and reduce the bioavailability of some drugs by altering the gastric pH.[35,51] Cimetidine, by increasing the pH of the GI tract, slows the dissolution of ketoconazole, ultimately reducing its absorption.[53] Therapeutic doses of cimetidine, ranitidine, and nizatidine, but not famotidine, enhance the absorption of ethanol following ingestion of moderate amounts of alcohol ($\approx$ 1 or 2 glasses of wine or cans of beer).[60] This interaction is thought to be a result of gastric alcohol dehydrogenase inhibition.[61] According to these findings, systemic effects of alcohol may be exacerbated and the safety of patients compromised. In a more recent study, H_2-receptor antagonists did not alter serum ethanol levels following moderate alcohol consumption.[62] Until more data are available confirming the results of the latter study, possible adverse effects associated with ethanol use should be considered when selecting an H_2-receptor antagonist for J.P. who drinks alcohol on a routine basis.

10. Dosing. When is the best time to administer an H_2-receptor antagonist?

When cimetidine was first introduced, it was administered four times a day. However, based upon clinical studies, recommendations now range anywhere from once daily to four times a day (see Table 23.2). These recommendations are based upon the pharmacokinetics of the drugs which are directly related to the drugs' potencies. The hypothesis that control of nighttime acid secretion is more effective in healing ulcers led to studies that compared nighttime dosing with multiple daily dosing regimens. Studies that have compared single, large nighttime doses of cimetidine, ranitidine, and nizatidine with multiple-dose regimens reported no significant differences in healing rates.[63–66] In addition, famotidine and ranitidine data suggest that single, large morning doses are equally effective in healing duodenal ulcers as are single doses given at nighttime.[67,68] Until more research is performed to determine the optimal time to administer the H$_2$-receptor antagonist, the FDA recommends night-time administration for single-dose therapy.

11. Duration of Therapy. What is the duration of therapy for treatment of J.P.'s ulcer?

Duodenal ulcers heal in the majority of patients after four to eight weeks of standard antiulcer therapy. Healing rates of approximately 70% to 80% generally are observed after four weeks of therapy and approximately 95% after eight weeks of therapy.[69,70] In a multicenter study, delayed healing of duodenal ulcers was associated with multiple factors, the effects of which were cumulative.[70] These risk factors included a prior history of slow-healing ulcers, large ulcers, smoking, prior complications, and multiple ulcers.[70] For patients with two or more identifiable risk factors, more than four weeks of treatment with an H$_2$-receptor antagonist probably is necessary to achieve adequate ulcer healing.[70] In general, gastric ulcers heal more slowly, are larger, and need more sustained therapy than do duodenal ulcers. Overall healing of gastric ulcers by H$_2$-receptor antagonists approaches 80%

Table 23.2					Indications and Doses for Anti-Ulcer Medications		
		Dosage					
Drug	Indications[b]	Oral	Parenteral	Renal Function Cr$_{Cl}$ (mL/min)	Dosage	Dosage Forms[b]	Strengths Available
Cimetidine (Tagamet)	Duodenal ulcer					Tab	200, 300, 400, and 800 mg
	Active	800 mg HS 400 mg BID *or* 300 mg QID	300 mg Q 6–8 hr	<30	300 mg Q 12 hr	Liq	300 mg/5 cc
	Maintenance	400 mg HS				Injectable	6 mg/mL (300 mg) in 0.9% NaCl; 150 mg/cc aqueous solution
	Gastric ulcer						
	Active	300 mg QID	300 mg Q 6–8 hr				—
	Zollinger-Ellison	300 mg QID[a]	300 mg QID[a]				
	GERD	800 mg BID *or* 400 mg QID					
Ranitidine (Zantac)	Duodenal ulcer					Tab	150 and 300 mg
	Active	150 mg BID *or* 300 mg HS	50 mg Q 6–8 hr	<50 <10	150 mg QD 150 mg QOD	Syrup Inj	15 mg/mL 0.5 mg/mL, 25 mg/mL
	Maintenance	150 mg HS					
	Gastric ulcer						
	Active	150 mg BID	50 mg Q 6–8 hr				
	Zollinger-Ellison	150 mg BID[a]	150 mg BID[a]				
	GERD	150 mg BID					
Famotidine (Pepcid)	Duodenal ulcer					Tab	20 and 40 mg
	Active	20 mg BID *or* 40 mg HS	20 mg Q 12 hr	<10	20 mg HS	Suspension Inj	40 mg/5 mL 10 mg/mL
	Maintenance	20 gm HS					
	Gastric ulcer						
	Active	40 mg HS					
	Zollinger-Ellison	20 mg BID[a]	20 mg Q 12 hr[a]				
	GERD	20 mg BID					
Nizatidine (Axid)	Duodenal ulcer		—			Cap	150 mg, 300 mg
	Active	150 mg BID *or* 300 mg HS		<50 <10	150 mg QD 150 QOD		
	Maintenance	150 HS					
	Gastric ulcer						
	Active	150 mg BID *or* 300 mg HS					
	GERD	150 mg BID					
Sucralfate (Carafate)	Duodenal ulcer		—		—	Tab	1 gm
	Active	1 gm QID		No change		Suspension	1 gm/10 cc
	Maintenance	1 gm BID 1 gm QID					
Omeprazole (Prilosec)	Duodenal ulcer		—			Tab	20 mg
	Active	20–40 mg QD		No change			
	Maintenance	10 mg QD					
	Gastric ulcer[c]	20–40 mg QD					
	Zollinger-Ellison	60 mg QD[a]					
	GERD	20 mg QD					

[a] Individualized, larger doses may be necessary.
[b] Cap = Capsules; GERD = Gastroesophageal reflux disorder; Inj = Injectable; Liq = Liquid; Tab = Tablets.
[c] Not an FDA-approved indication.

Table 23.3	Clinically Significant Drug Interactions with Cimetidine[a]		
Drug	Effect on Serum Drug Concentration	Mechanism	
Ketoconazole	↓	Absorption due to elevation of gastric pH	
Phenytoin[b]	↑	Inhibits metabolism	
Nifedipine	↑	↑ AUC[c] by 60%–90%	
Procainamide[b]	↑	Competition for renal tubular secretion	
Theophylline[b]	↑	Inhibits metabolism	
Warfarin	↑	Inhibits metabolism of R isomer	
Alcohol	↑	Gastric alcohol dehydrogenase inhibition (?)	
Benzodiazepines (diazepam, chlordiazepoxide)	↑	Inhibition of metabolism	
Carbamazepine	↑	Inhibition of metabolism	
Propranolol	↑	Inhibition of metabolism	
Quinidine	↑	Inhibition of metabolism and may ↓ renal clearance	
TCAs (imipramine, desipramine, amitriptyline)	↑	Inhibition of metabolism	
Verapamil	↑	↓ clearance by up to 35%	

[a] Adapted from reference 51.
[b] There also are less interactions with ranitidine.
[c] AUC = Area under the curve; TCAs = Tricyclic antidepressants.

after eight weeks of therapy and greater than 90% after 12 weeks.[71] Duration of therapy appears to be the most important factor for successful gastric ulcer healing.[33,63]

J.P. has been diagnosed with an uncomplicated duodenal ulcer. Since J.P. smokes cigarettes, he probably would benefit more from an eight-week, rather than a four-week course of therapy. If pain persists, another endoscopy should be performed; however, if J.P. is symptom-free, an endoscopic examination is not warranted.

Antacids

12. Dosing. Antacids "as needed" are ordered for J.P. to relieve his abdominal pain. What is the role of antacids in the treatment of duodenal ulcers?

Antacids serve two roles in the treatment of duodenal ulcers: pain relief and healing. Because one of the goals of therapy in treating PUD is elimination of symptoms, antacids can be given on an "as-needed" basis to provide relief of ulcer pain and dyspepsia. Antacids are thought to work within 5 to 15 minutes; however, the duration of relief is estimated to be only about two hours.[51] Therefore, if antacids are used for symptomatic relief, they may need to be dosed as frequently as the patient requires them.

Traditionally, antacids have been considered first-line therapy; however, the adverse effects and inconvenience of multiple daily doses have diminished their use in the management of acute duodenal ulcers (see Table 23.4). Antacids work by neutralizing gastric acid raising the intragastric pH; however, this does not appear to be the only mechanism involved in their symptomatic and healing roles.[72] Antacids also provide a protective effect and stimulate restitution of the gastric mucosa.[73,74] Since endogenous prostaglandins are important in gastric mucosal defense, their stimulation by antacids may be another mechanism by which antacids provide a cytoprotective effect on the mucosa.[73] In clinical studies using varying doses of antacids, patients with duodenal ulcers healed at a rate of 46% to 88% after four weeks of antacid therapy compared

to 24% to 45% with placebo.[72] Thus, antacids appear to provide some benefit in healing duodenal ulcers. Low to moderate doses of antacids may be as effective in healing duodenal ulcers as previously administered high doses of antacids or H₂-antagonists.[75,76] In some of the trials, duodenal healing did not increase when the total daily dose of antacid exceeded 200 mmol.[77] Therefore, the adverse effects may be kept to a minimum if high buffering doses (>200 mmol/day) are unnecessary.[72] Until further studies confirm the efficacy of low-dose antacids and demonstrate a better adverse effect profile, antacids primarily will be used for symptomatic relief of pain or in patients unable to tolerate other antiulcer therapy.

13. Product Selection. J.P. would like to take an antacid for symptomatic relief of his pain. Is one antacid better than another?

Preparations differ in terms of potency, rate of neutralization, duration of effect, and adverse effects (see Tables 23.4 and 23.5). Antacid products contain either sodium bicarbonate, aluminum hydroxide, magnesium hydroxide, calcium carbonate, aluminum phosphate, or a combination of these substances. Sodium bicarbonate is a potent, rapid-acting antacid with a short duration of dyspeptic relief.[77] It should not be used for prolonged periods of time since systemic alkalosis can result from the accumulation of the drug. Aluminum most commonly is administered as the hydroxide, but also has been given as the phosphate.[77] Aluminum hydroxide's neutralizing capacity is low compared to magnesium hydroxide and calcium carbonate. Because of its low neutralizing capacity and the undesirable constipating effect, aluminum is combined with magnesium salts. Magnesium produces diarrhea which offsets aluminum's constipating effects. Diarrhea usually predominates when high doses of aluminum/magnesium-containing antacids are used.[9] A small amount of aluminum and magnesium is absorbed after antacid administration. In patients with normal renal function, both are excreted; however, in patients with renal insufficiency, elevated aluminum or magnesium levels may result in toxicity. Regardless, aluminum can be useful in patients with chronic renal failure who have hyperphosphatemia. Aluminum hydroxide binds to and forms an insoluble salt that blocks the absorption of phosphate. In contrast, magnesium should be avoided in patients with significant renal impairment (<20 mL/min) since CNS alterations can occur. Calcium carbonate is a rapid-acting, very effective neutralizer; however, high doses of 4 to 8 gm/day can increase gastric acid production.[78] Chronic therapy with calcium-containing antacids can cause systemic complications due to high levels of calcium; this is known as the milk-alkali syndrome. Some antacid formulations contain simethicone to relieve flatulence; however, simethicone has no role in the treatment of peptic ulcer disease.

Table 23.4	Adverse Drug Reactions Associated with Antacids[a]
Drug Reaction	Adverse Effects[b]
Cation Retention	
Aluminum[c]	Encephalopathy, anemia, anorexia
Magnesium[c]	CNS depression, nausea, vomiting
Calcium[c]	Alkalosis, renal insufficiency (milk-alkali syndrome)
Sodium	Edema, CHF, hypertension
Other	
Aluminum	Constipation, phosphate depletion
Magnesium	Diarrhea

[a] Adapted permission from reference 51.
[b] CHF = Congestive heart failure; CNS = Central nervous system.
[c] Especially with renal insufficiency.

Table 23.5		Common Antacids[a]	
Agent	Acid-neutralizing capacity (mEq/mL)	Volume containing 140 mEq (mL)	Sodium content (mg/5 mL)
Antacids (Liquid)			
Aluminum hydroxide, magnesium hydroxide			
Maalox TC	4.2	33	1.2
Delcid	4.1	34	1.5
Aluminum hydroxide, magnesium hydroxide, simethicone			
Maalox Plus	2.3	61	2.5
Mylanta II	3.6	39	1.1
Gelusil	2.2	64	0.7
Gelusil II	3.0	47	1.3
Riopan Plus	1.8	78	0.7
Calcium carbonate, glycine			
Titralac	4.2	33	11.0
Antacids (Tablets)			
Aluminum hydroxide, magnesium hydroxide			
Camalox	16.7	8	1.5
Aluminum hydroxide, magnesium hydroxide, simethicone			
Maalox Plus	5.7	25	1.4
Mylanta II	11.0	39	1.1
Gelusil II	8.2	17	2.1
Riopan Plus	10.0	14	0.3
Calcium carbonate			
Tums	10.5	13	2.7
Alka-2	10.5	13	2.0
Calcium carbonate, glycine			
Titralac	9.5	15	0.3
Aluminum carbonate			
Rolaids	6.9	20	53.0
Aluminum hydroxide			
Amphojel	2.0	70	7.0

[a] Adapted from reference 78.

Because J.P. has some renal insufficiency, magnesium-containing antacids should not be used; however, aluminum hydroxide (i.e., Amphojel) can be used for short-term therapy. He should be instructed not to take antacids on an empty stomach because the duration of efficacy is only about 15 minutes. However, if taken one hour after a meal when gastric emptying is delayed, the effect of antacids can last two to three hours.[18] Although antacids are available in both liquid and tablet formulations, the liquid formulation has a more rapid acid-neutralizing action than the tablets.[77]

14. Drug Interactions. J.P. is prescribed ciprofloxacin for a urinary tract infection. What effect do antacids have on ciprofloxacin or other drugs?

Antacids potentially interfere with the absorption of many drugs through complexation or alteration in gastric pH. (See Table 23.6.) The bioavailability of ciprofloxacin is decreased by more than 50% when antacids are administered concomitantly. This interaction is due to complexation of the aluminum and magnesium to the quinolone antibiotic and can result in treatment failure. Administering the ciprofloxacin two hours before the antacid results in a greater ciprofloxacin bioavailability compared to administering the antacid first.[79] Since J.P. will be receiving ciprofloxacin to treat his urinary tract infection, he should be counseled to take the antibiotic two hours before the antacid. Another antibiotic well known to interact with antacids is tetracycline. Antacids containing metallic cations (Mg^{2+}, Ca^{2+}, Al^{3+}) have a strong affinity for tetracycline and response to the antibiotic can vary according to the extent of com-

plexation.[78] Patients taking any form of tetracycline should be counseled not to take antacids for at least two to three hours after tetracycline administration.

Frequently, antacids are ingested simultaneously with H_2-receptor antagonists. Antacids decrease the bioavailability of cimetidine by 30% to 50%, ranitidine by 30%, famotidine by 20% to 30%, and nizatidine by 10%.[46,48,80] Thus, patients receiving both antacids and H_2-antagonists should take the antacid two hours before or two hours after the H_2-receptor antagonist.

Antacids increase the intragastric pH and this can decrease the absorption of drugs requiring an acidic environment for dissolution and absorption.[78] Conversely, enteric-coated drugs may be released prematurely. Theoretically, antacids can diminish the binding of sucralfate to the gastric mucosa. They should not be given simultaneously or within 15 minutes of sucralfate administration.[78]

Other drug-antacid interactions that are of potential clinical importance include digoxin, phenytoin, quinidine, isoniazid, and ferrous sulfate.[81] Most of these antacid-drug interactions can be minimized by administering each drug two hours from the other.

Sucralfate

15. Mechanism of Action. Is sucralfate a therapeutic option for J.P.?

Sucralfate (Carafate) is a nonsystemic agent that acts primarily by protecting ulcerated tissue from aggressive factors such as pepsin, acid, and bile salts.[82] It is not an antacid. At a pH of 2.0 to 2.5, sucralfate binds to damaged and ulcerated tissue forming a physical barrier to injury from aggressive forces. Sucralfate may have other protective actions on the mucosa possibly mediated by prostaglandin and gastric bicarbonate secretion.[82] Sucralfate in doses of 1 gm four times a day is significantly more effective than placebo in healing duodenal ulcers.[83] It also appears to be as safe and effective as H_2-receptor antagonists in the treatment of acute duodenal and gastric ulcers.[84-90] Currently, sucralfate is FDA-approved for the treatment of duodenal ulcers at a dose of 1 gm four times daily. This regimen would be difficult for a patient with a compliance problem like J.P. However, studies have indicated that 2 gm twice daily are as effective as 1 gm four times daily in the short-term treatment of active duodenal ulcers.[91,92] Sucralfate has not been approved by the FDA for acute or maintenance therapy of gastric ulcers despite studies showing its efficacy.[86,87,89,90,288]

16. Adverse Effects. What adverse effects are associated with sucralfate?

Sucralfate (Carafate) is not absorbed systemically to an appreciable extent and, therefore, is a viable alternative for patients who cannot tolerate other antiulcer medications. Adverse effects are uncommon, usually transient, and seldom require discontinuation. The most common adverse side effect of sucralfate is constipation; other side effects include dry mouth, nausea, and rashes.

Because the tablet is large, some patients, particularly the elderly, may have difficulty swallowing it. Sucralfate is available both as a tablet and a suspension. In patients who have difficulty swallowing, the liquid preparation should be used.

Table 23.6	Drug Interactions Associated with Antacids (↓ Absorption)[a]
Antimicrobials	**Miscellaneous**
Tetracyclines	Warfarin
Isoniazid	Phenytoin
Ciprofloxacin	Theophylline
Cardiovascular	H_2 blockers
Digoxin	Ferrous sulfate
Quinidine	Aspirin/NSAIDs[b]

[a] Adapted from reference 51.
[b] NSAIDs = Nonsteroidal anti-inflammatory drugs.

17. Combination Therapy. Can sucralfate be combined with H$_2$-receptor antagonists?

Because sucralfate's mechanism of action is different from that of H$_2$-receptor antagonists, many clinicians combine these two drugs with the belief that they will act synergistically and achieve more rapid healing. Evidence suggests that combination therapy is not more effective, the potential for adverse effects is greater,[93] and would act to increase treatment costs.

Omeprazole

18. Mechanism of Action. What is the newest therapeutic treatment for duodenal ulcers?

The newest drug introduced for the treatment of PUD is omeprazole (Prilosec). This drug is a potent and highly specific inhibitor of gastric acid secretion and acts by irreversibly binding to H/K-ATPase, an enzyme that transports acid across the parietal cell.[69,94] A dose-dependent and sustained inhibition of basal and stimulated gastric acid secretion has been observed with omeprazole.[94] In doses of 20 to 40 mg/day, omeprazole inhibits over 90% of the 24-hour gastric acid secretion.[95] Omeprazole is effective in the treatment of active duodenal ulcers, as determined by ulcer healing and pain relief.[96] It also relieves symptoms and heals duodenal and gastric ulcers faster than H$_2$-receptor antagonists.[97–99] Higher doses (i.e., 60 mg/day) of omeprazole produce more rapid healing than do lower doses, but with continued therapy, there is no significant difference in the healing of duodenal ulcers.[100] Although omeprazole heals peptic ulcers more rapidly (i.e., 2 to 4 weeks), if given sufficient time (i.e., 4 to 8 weeks), the majority (>90%) of ulcers will heal with H$_2$-receptor antagonists.[101,103] In addition, there is some concern about the effects of prolonged achlorhydria caused by omeprazole. Therefore, it has been suggested that omeprazole therapy be reserved for patients with severe disease, a greater likelihood of complications, or refractory disease.[101]

Currently, omeprazole is approved for the short-term treatment of duodenal ulcers, reflux esophagitis, and Zollinger-Ellison syndrome but not gastric ulcers.

19. Pharmacokinetics. What is omeprazole's pharmacokinetic profile?

Omeprazole (Prilosec) is absorbed rapidly, with a time to peak of 12 to 17 minutes.[101] The bioavailability of omeprazole is low (30% to 50%) due to presystemic metabolism and dose dependent. The drug's pharmacokinetic behavior can best be described using a two-compartment model, with an apparent volume of distribution at steady state of 0.31 L/kg. The drug is highly protein bound (95%) to albumin and less extensively to α_1-acid glycoprotein. The elimination of omeprazole is almost completely by liver metabolism, with an elimination half-life of approximately one hour.[102,103] Approximately 80% of a dose is excreted as metabolites in the urine and 20% in the feces.[104] Despite omeprazole's short half-life, some antisecretory effect still is present 72 hours after a dose.[102] The long duration of action is due to the covalently linked binding of the drug to the H/K-ATPase in the parietal cell.[103] The pharmacokinetics of omeprazole are not altered in patients with impaired renal function or mild liver dysfunction.[104] Therefore, no dosage adjustment is necessary in patients with renal or mild hepatic insufficiency.

20. Drug Interactions. What are drug-drug interactions with omeprazole?

Omeprazole binds to cytochrome P450 oxidative enzymes and, therefore, has the potential to interfere with hepatic drug metabolism. Available data indicate that omeprazole has a differential affinity toward specific cytochrome P450 isoenzymes and only will affect drugs primarily metabolized by the IIC subfamily.[105,106] Therefore, not all drugs metabolized by the P450 system will be affected by omeprazole. Omeprazole does decrease the metabolism

of diazepam, phenytoin, warfarin, and tolbutamide, and serum concentrations of these drugs. The clinical condition of patients taking these drugs with omeprazole should be monitored closely for any potential adverse effects resulting from this drug-drug interaction.

21. Adverse Effects. What potential adverse effects are associated with omeprazole?

The adverse effects of omeprazole have been relatively negligible and are comparable to H$_2$-receptor antagonists. Summary data indicate that adverse effects consist primarily of GI discomforts (e.g., nausea, diarrhea, abdominal pain), CNS changes (e.g., dizziness, headache), and isolated reactions (e.g., skin rash, gynecomastia, increase in liver transaminases).[94]

Because antral G-cells release gastrin when gastric pH increases, omeprazole has the ability to cause hypergastrinemia through its profound ability to inhibit gastric secretion.[103] Chronic hypergastrinemia in humans is thought to lead to hyperplasia of enterochromaffin-like cells and carcinoid tumors of the stomach. Short-term therapy with omeprazole appears to be safe and only produces slight hypergastrinemia; however, the risk of long-term therapy has not been investigated fully.[103]

Refractory Ulcers

22. J.P. is treated for 8 weeks with famotidine, but he continues to have pain, and his therapy is continued for another 4 weeks. Now, after 12 weeks of therapy, J.P. continues to complain of pain. A repeat endoscopy shows a partially healed ulcer. What are some of the reasons why J.P.'s ulcer has not healed?

About 5% to 10% of peptic ulcers do not heal within two to three months when treated with standard doses of H$_2$-receptor antagonists and then are considered to be refractory.[94,107] When persistent ulceration is found on endoscopy, a few reasons need to be considered. Poor patient compliance with antiulcer therapy is a common cause of refractory ulcers. NSAID use, alcohol use, and smoking may be contributing factors that impair the ulcer healing process.[16] Patients with high acid output appear to be at risk for both delayed healing and peptic ulcer recurrence.[3] Since many duodenal ulcers are associated with elevated basal gastric output, some refractory ulcers may be due to inadequate acid suppression with standard doses of antiulcer therapy.[108] J.P. should be counseled on the importance of taking his medication, and he should avoid the use of aspirin and use acetaminophen (Tylenol) for any recurring headaches. The need to stop smoking should be re-emphasized to J. P. as well.

Treatment

23. What treatment options are available to treat refractory ulcers?

For healing to take place, either greater acid inhibition or stimulation of mucosal defenses is necessary.[109] Several therapeutic approaches, before considering surgery, are available for refractory ulcers. Increasing the antisecretory efficacy and duration of action likely will promote healing in the majority of patients with refractory ulcers.[16] Patients with refractory ulcers appear to do better with more aggressive therapy that uses higher-than-standard doses of H$_2$-receptor antagonists (i.e., 600 to 1200 mg/day of ranitidine).[108] Although single-dose therapy with H$_2$-receptor antagonists is effective in treating uncomplicated peptic ulcers, more frequent dosing that provides 24-hour acid suppression may be more beneficial in the case of refractory ulcers.[16,110] Based upon the hypothesis that antisecretory effectiveness and prolonged inhibition of acid is the key to refractory ulcer healing, the proton-pump inhibitor, omeprazole, should be beneficial in healing refractory ulcers. In doses of 40 mg/day, omeprazole not only is effective but may be significantly better than continued treatment with standard doses of H_2-receptor antagonists in healing these peptic ulcers.[107,111]

Maintenance Therapy

Indications

24. After J.P. is treated for 4 weeks with omeprazole 40 mg/day, endoscopy reveals a healed ulcer. J.P.'s physician decides to start him on maintenance therapy to prevent recurrent ulcers. When is it appropriate to start maintenance therapy?

Once a peptic ulcer is healed, one should consider whether or not maintenance therapy is required. The natural history of PUD is associated with ulcer recurrence. The recurrence rate within the first year after healing is approximately 50% to 90%, and maintenance therapy with H_2-receptor antagonists reduces the incidence to approximately 30%.[109,112]

Approximately 25% of duodenal ulcers are asymptomatic and about 10% eventually result in complications such as bleeding and perforation.[113] Complications are reported to develop at a rate of 2.7% a year in patients without previous complications and 5% a year in those with a prior complication.[113] Treatment strategies for the management of recurrent ulcers include intermittent full-dose therapy for symptomatic recurrences, continuous low-dose maintenance therapy, or on-demand therapy. A two-year randomized study compared the traditional approach of treating acute symptomatic recurrences with the prophylactic approach of using a long-term maintenance therapy.[112] This study demonstrated that maintenance therapy with an H_2-receptor antagonist (ranitidine) reduced the frequency of ulcer recurrence and treatment failures compared to the intermittent therapeutic approach. In this study, continuous maintenance therapy was most beneficial in patients who had two or more risk factors. Significant alcohol consumption, active smoking, early or recurrent ulcers, and duodenal scarring or erosions placed patients at greatest risk for recurrent ulcers. They benefitted the most from prophylactic therapy. Therefore, maintenance therapy is recommended for patients with three or more symptomatic recurrences per year, patients with complications such as bleeding, refractory ulcers, and patients who are candidates for surgery but refuse this intervention or are considered a high-risk surgical patient.[36,101] Patients whose overall medical conditions place them at increased risk if an ulcer occurs should be considered for maintenance therapy as well.[3]

Many patients with uncomplicated healed ulcers may have no significant associated complications and heal spontaneously. Therefore, investigators have examined on-demand therapy as an alternative treatment to continuous maintenance therapy. This approach allows patients to treat themselves with full-dose therapy when symptoms occur and to continue until ulcer symptoms resolve irrespective of ulcer healing.[114] When the efficacy of on-demand drug therapy was compared with continuous therapy, ulcer complications were not significantly different between the two groups. However, there was slower ulcer healing and a significant reduction in the cost of therapy.[114] Therefore, if a patient is young and generally healthy and has an uncomplicated ulcer with few risk factors, intermittent therapy or on-demand therapy may be reasonable.[3,109] However, for patients like J.P. who have significant health problems, refractory ulcers, and associated risk factors for recurrence, continuous maintenance therapy is warranted.

Therapy

25. What maintenance therapy is appropriate for J.P.?

Once an ulcer is healed, ulcer recurrence can be reduced by any one of numerous agents, including H_2-receptor antagonists, sucralfate, or omeprazole. Many studies have demonstrated overwhelming evidence that maintenance therapy with H_2-receptor an-

tagonists at half the healing dose can prevent ulcer recurrence in the majority of patients.[26,34,115-117] Based upon double-blind studies, no H_2-receptor antagonist clearly is superior in preventing recurrences.[117] Higher doses (e.g., ranitidine 300 mg HS) may be required in patients who smoke.[118] Sucralfate, 1 gm twice daily or 2 gm at bedtime, is as or more effective than H_2-receptor antagonists in preventing recurrences in patients with healed duodenal and gastric ulcers.[119-124] For ulcers refractory to initial therapy, a recurrent ulcer can appear more quickly than in patients with non-refractory ulcer disease.[101,112] Patients with refractory ulcers may require "healing doses" of H_2-receptor antagonists or omeprazole.[109] Intermittent low-dose omeprazole therapy has produced a lower recurrence rate compared to placebo; however, the theoretical problems associated with long-term acid suppression must be evaluated further before implementing such a preventive regimen.[93] Long-term omeprazole therapy has the potential to produce moderate hypergastrinemia and hyperplasia of antral gastrin cells which may lead to the development of gastric carcinoids.[125]

Preliminary data suggest that treating ulcers with bismuth compounds reduces the recurrence rate to a greater extent than placebos or H_2-receptor antagonists.[126-129] This may reflect bismuth's effect on *H. pylori* infection. (See Question 29.)

Maintenance therapy with an H_2-receptor antagonist or sucralfate at one-half the ulcer healing dose may be helpful in preventing ulcer recurrence in J.P. The exact length of time maintenance therapy should be continued is unclear; however, most studies show a high relapse rate if maintenance therapy is discontinued within one year.

Helicobacter pylori

Epidemiology

26. Two months later, while on maintenance therapy with ranitidine, J.P. presents with recurrent abdominal pain. Endoscopy reveals another duodenal ulcer approximately 0.6 cm in diameter. Biopsy results are positive for *H. pylori*. What is the significance of this finding?

H. pylori, formally known as *Campylobacter pylori*, is a gram-negative spiral bacterium that was isolated by Marshall and Warren in 1983 from patients with gastritis.[130] Around 1989 this bacterium's name was changed to *Helicobacter pylori* because it is significantly different from the genus *Campylobacter*.[131] *H. pylori* frequently is isolated from patients without PUD.[132] Approximately 40% to 60% of patients over 60 years of age are seropositive for *H. pylori*, whereas the prevalence in patients less than 30 years of age is only 10%.[23,133]

The mode of transmission of *H. pylori* is unknown. However, support of person-to-person transmission comes from evidence of familial clustering.[133] The organism and its associated histological changes can be found anywhere in the stomach but are found most consistently in the gastric antrum.[130] It is associated with inflammation of the gastric antrum and is the most common cause of histological gastritis.[130,134] Clearance of the organism from the gastric antrum has led to resolution of gastritis, confirming *H. pylori*'s pathogenic role in gastritis.[135,136] The exact mechanism by which *H. pylori* causes tissue injury is unknown, but possibilities include production of cytotoxin, breakdown of mucosal defenses, and adherence to epithelial cells.[132] *H. pylori* is unique in that it produces large amounts of urease, a property that may have significant pathogenic implications.[137] Urease catalyzes the hydrolysis of urea to form ammonia. The accumulation of ammonia may play a role in disrupting the integrity of gastric mucosa, rendering it susceptible to ulceration.[138,139]

H. pylori is found in approximately 90% of patients with duodenal ulcers, and 70% with gastric ulcers.[16,22,140,141] Eradication of the organism significantly decreases the recurrence rate and accelerates the ulcer healing process; therefore, *H. pylori* is implicated in the pathogenesis of peptic ulcer disease.[142-147] In contrast, *H. pylori* infection is not associated with acute perforated duodenal ulcers. This suggests that perforated duodenal ulcers have a different pathogenesis from chronic duodenal ulcer disease and that perforation is not a complication of *H. pylori* infection.[148] The frequency of PUD is much less than the prevalence of *H. pylori* infections, suggesting other factors also are involved in PUD.[22,149] It still is unclear what exact role *H. pylori* plays in the pathogenesis of peptic ulcer disease and whom it will affect adversely. However, eradication of the organism in patients with recurrent ulcers does seem to change the natural history of the disease.

Detection

27. How is *H. pylori* detected?

Methods used to identify *H. pylori* involve direct testing by culture or histologic staining or indirect testing using biochemical assays and serologic testing for the organism. Staining and culturing endoscopically obtained mucosal biopsy specimens are considered the gold standard.[23] Because the organism is distributed unevenly throughout the gastric mucosa, it is recommended that two specimens from the antrum be obtained.[150] The organism is observed histologically using the Warthin-Starry silver stain and Giemsa stain.[151] Histologic identification of *H. pylori* correlates well with culture results, with a sensitivity and specificity of 85% to 100% and 50% to 100%, respectively.[21] Factors implicated in the failure to culture the organism include ingestion of a local anesthetic or simethicone, contamination of biopsy forceps, recent antibiotic therapy, and biopsy in areas with low organism counts.[151] A more rapid endoscopic technique is the *rapid urease test*. This test is used frequently because it provides immediate results (within 2 to 3 hrs).[152] The test is used to detect the large amounts of urease produced by *H. pylori*. When urea is added to a biopsy specimen containing urease, a chemical reaction occurs resulting in the formation of ammonia and carbon dioxide. The formation of these two products raises the pH which can be detected with a pH indicator.[23,133,152]

For screening and follow-up information, noninvasive tests are preferable.[153] The *breath test* is a noninvasive test that detects urease in the stomach.[23] ^{13}C- or ^{14}C-labeled urea is administered orally. If urease is present in the stomach, presumably from *H. pylori*, the radiolabeled carbon dioxide will be expired in the breath.[23,153] This test is attractive because it is noninvasive; however, it requires an expensive mass spectrometer to detect the ^{13}C isotope and a scintillation counter to detect the ^{14}C.[153] Another noninvasive test involves the detection of antibodies via serologic studies. The enzyme-linked immunosorbent assay (ELISA) detects *IgG and IgA antibodies* to *H. pylori* in the serum. Sensitivity and specificity of the newer antibody tests are 95%. The reliability of this test has been questioned because a positive test may not reflect current infection but may represent past exposure. However, long-term serological surveillance investigations indicate that IgG and IgA anti *H. pylori* antibody values decrease rapidly and progressively after the eradication of the infection and rise with recurrence of *H. pylori* infection.[154,155] Serology is the most utilized method to determine the presence of *H. pylori* in studies because it is inexpensive and acceptable to patients.[156] Because of the potential for false positive and negative results from these five testing methods, some authors recommend using multiple diagnostic tests carried out on multiple gastric biopsies to make a definitive diagnosis of *H. pylori* infection.[157]

Therapy

28. Should J.P. be treated for the *H. pylori*?

Data at the present time are not sufficient to support treatment of asymptomatic *H. pylori*-infected individuals without ulcers.

However, current data do support the eradication of *H. pylori* in all patients with PUD. Patients infected with *H. pylori* and with a gastric or duodenal ulcer should be treated regardless of whether they are suffering from an initial presentation or recurrence of the disease.[280] J.P. currently is receiving maintenance therapy with an antisecretory agent, has a recurrent ulcer, and is positive for *H. pylori*; therefore, he should be treated for his *H. pylori* infection.

29. What is appropriate therapy for the treatment of *H. pylori* infection?

Bismuth compounds were one of the first drugs used to eradicate *H. pylori* infections because they were thought to have effective antimicrobial action against the organism.[134,158] Treatment with bismuth eradicated *H. pylori* and subsequently reduced ulcer recurrence.[139,145,159,160] Patients who remained positive for *H. pylori* had a higher recurrence rate within the first year after healing compared to patients in whom eradication of *H. pylori* was achieved. Whether the efficacy of bismuth therapy in reducing the rate of ulcer recurrence is due to its antimicrobial effect or direct protective effect is controversial. *In vitro* studies show that bismuth is moderately active against *H. pylori* with a minimum inhibitory concentration[90] of 16 µg/mL.[161] Monotherapy with bismuth has eradicated 10% to 35% of *H. pylori* infections in patients after four to six weeks, but when combined with antibiotics, eradication rates increased to 75% to 90%.[139,144,160,162] In addition, when bismuth is used alone, ulcers recur within six months after therapy; a result that is similar to placebo.[127,134,160]

H. pylori is susceptible to many antibiotics *in vitro*; however, this does not correlate well with *in vivo* situations.[161] Amoxicillin alone temporarily clears the *H. pylori* organism in patients with antral gastritis; however, it appears to be ineffective in preventing ulcer recurrences.[163] *H. pylori* is moderately sensitive to metronidazole *in vitro* and metronidazole has been used in many treatment regimens.[164,165] Unfortunately, the use of metronidazole alone has led to the development of resistance.[162,165] When combined with bismuth or another antibiotic, the incidence of resistance is decreased and eradication of *H. pylori* approaches 75%.[162,165,166]

H_2-receptor antagonists also help in the prevention of ulcer recurrence; however, approximately 30% of the patients develop a recurrent ulcer when maintenance therapy is discontinued.[112] To evaluate the differential contributions of *H. pylori* eradication and decreased acid secretion on the recurrence rate, two prospective studies compared H_2-receptor antagonists to combination antimicrobial therapy.[167,168] In these studies, combination antimicrobial therapy was superior to therapy that had no effect on *H. pylori*. The recurrence rates for both gastric and duodenal ulcers after one year were significantly lower ($\approx$10%) with antibiotic therapy than with ranitidine therapy ($\approx$85%). Therefore, effective eradication of *H. pylori* requires combination therapy, although the optimal therapeutic regimen still is being investigated. Overall, no treatment for *H. pylori* is considered best or FDA-approved. Because bismuth and antibiotic monotherapy fail to eradicate and prevent recurrence of *H. pylori* appreciably, triple therapy currently is the treatment of choice. The most widely recognized therapeutic regimen (i.e., bismuth, 2 tablets QID with meals and HS, metronidazole 500 mg QID and amoxicillin or tetracycline 500 mg QID for 14 days) results in an eradication rate of 90%.[17,23,167,169] Bismuth given on a four-times-a-day dosing schedule before meals appears to be more effective than twice-daily dosing.[166]

If a patient has an active peptic ulcer at the initiation of antimicrobial therapy, treatment with an antisecretory agent also is recommended.[280] J.P., therefore, should continue taking his ranitidine along with the prescribed antibiotics.

30. What other therapies are being investigated?

Omeprazole can decrease the colonization of *H. pylori* when used as a single agent in the treatment of refractory duodenal ulcers.[170] The drug does not eradicate the organism but does cause temporary suppression with activity returning within two to four weeks.[171,172] It is unclear whether the efficacy of omeprazole is due to a direct effect on the bacteria or to modification of the gastric mucosa.[166,173] Excellent results have been obtained with the coadministration of amoxicillin or other antibiotics and omeprazole; however, the studies are limited because of variation in duration of therapy and dose of omeprazole.[171,174–176] Amoxicillin is synergistic with omeprazole in the eradication of *H. pylori*.[177] The efficacy of this combination therapy is enhanced when omeprazole is given at least twice daily and the amoxicillin is begun at the same time.[280]

Although variable eradication rates (60% to 80%) have been reported with omeprazole and amoxicillin, this regimen may be better tolerated in some patients.[281] Until further data support omeprazole in combination with other antibiotics, J.P. should receive bismuth compounds, tetracycline, or amoxicillin and metronidazole.

Eradication

31. Should eradication of the organism be documented?

True eradication can be determined only after the patient has been off treatment for one month.[178] Ideally eradication should be documented at least four weeks after completion of therapy; however, endoscopy is expensive and uncomfortable. Currently, confirmation is patient dependent. For patients who are high risk and are candidates for long-term maintenance therapy, eradication should be documented and a second course of antimicrobial therapy considered.[179,280] For low-risk patients, documentation is optional because the return of symptoms will identify those in whom infection has not been eradicated.[6]

Drug-Induced PUD

Etiology and Clinical Presentation

32. A.C., a 65-year-old female, experienced orthostasis and diarrhea after giving a lecture. She has been in good health without any previous complaints. For the past 4 weeks she has been taking only ibuprofen 400 mg Q 4–6 hr PRN for headaches and arthritic knees. Laboratory tests are unremarkable except for an Hgb of 8 gm/dL, an Hct of 26%, and a guaiac positive stool. A.C. was admitted to the hospital for an endoscopy to rule out a GI bleed. Endoscopy revealed 2 antral ulcers (0.2 cm and 0.4 cm). What is the etiology of A.C.'s GI bleeding?
[SI units: Hgb 4.96 mmol/L, Hct 0.26]

The gastrointestinal bleeding found in A.C. probably is secondary to chronic ingestion of an NSAID. The prevalence of endoscopically confirmed gastrointestinal ulcers in NSAID users is 15% to 30%.[180–182] Although the majority of NSAID-induced ulcers are gastric ulcers (12% to 30%), duodenal ulcers (2% to 19%) often are observed as well.[183,282] Some investigators hypothesize that duodenal ulcers associated with NSAID use may represent an exacerbation, reactivation, or complication of PUD, since there is a higher incidence of duodenal ulcers unrelated to NSAID use.[16,183] There may be two distinct types of NSAID-associated ulcers: ulcers that occur in patients with normal gastric mucosa and those that occur in patients with underlying ulcer disease.[184] Symptomatic ulcers (ulcers associated with pain, bleeding, or perforation) occur in approximately 1% of patients after three to six months of NSAID use and in 2% to 4% of patients after one year of therapy.[16]

33. What symptoms are associated with NSAID-induced ulcers?

Nonsteroidal anti-inflammatory drugs-associated ulcers do not correlate well with pain[186] because the analgesic action of NSAIDs

may mask the ulcer pain.[186,187] Many patients who take NSAIDs take them for chronic pain conditions such as arthritis. Therefore, their perception of pain may be changed and they may tend to ignore ulcer symptoms. The elderly appear to be predisposed to silent ulcers; therefore, complications are likely to develop before symptoms occur. It is not unusual to find silent perforations or gastroduodenal ulcerations in asymptomatic individuals.[187,188] According to one study, the first sign of an ulcer was a life-threatening complication in 58% of patients taking NSAIDs.

Mechanism

34. How do NSAIDs cause ulcers?

The most common site for NSAID-associated ulcers is the antral portion of the stomach, although some occur in the gastric body and fundus.[184,185] NSAIDs appear to produce gastric damage by two mechanisms: a direct irritant effect and a systemic effect.[189] Therefore, both rectal and intravenous administration of NSAIDs have the potential to cause gastrointestinal damage despite the apparent absence of direct mucosal contact.[282] Agents that are more water soluble (e.g., aspirin) cause more topical injury.[190] Aspirin, in a dose-related fashion, disrupts the gastric mucosal barrier.[191] When the consumption of aspirin exceeds 22 tablets a week, the occurrence of ulcers is increased.[192] Although enteric-coated tablets are designed to minimize gastric irritation, the potential for ulceration still exists but to a lesser degree.[181] The exact mechanism by which aspirin and nonaspirin NSAIDs produce their systemic effects remains unclear and appears to be multifactorial.[184] Inhibition of mucosal prostaglandin synthesis is thought to be an important factor in the pathogenesis of aspirin- and NSAID-induced ulcers.[184,189,193] Prostaglandins protect the GI mucosa by maintaining blood flow and stimulating bicarbonate and mucus production.[184] Therefore, depletion of these protective devices would be expected to impair the gastric mucosa's ability to defend itself against aggressive factors. This hypothesis is further strengthened by a study that compared aspirin with a nonacetylated salicylate, salsalate.[194] In this study, salsalate produced less gastroduodenal mucosal damage than did aspirin presumably because salsalate does not inhibit prostaglandin synthesis. These findings suggest that ulcer induction may be a direct consequence of prostaglandin depletion.

The inhibition of prostaglandin synthesis by NSAIDs is not the only cause of mucosal damage. NSAIDs also may interfere with cellular and mitochondrial metabolism and the activity of immune and inflammatory reactions of the mucosa.[282]

Risk Factors

35. What risk factors does A.C. possess for ulcer occurrence?

Only a small proportion of NSAID users develop ulcers, suggesting that certain individuals may be predisposed. There appears to be no correlation with the incidence of NSAID-induced ulcers in patients under 55 years of age; however, in patients over 55 years of age, the odds of developing an ulcer due to an NSAID increase significantly.[185] In contrast, aspirin-induced gastric ulcers occur in all ages equally. Although characteristics that place individuals at risk of hemorrhage and perforation have not been well established, the elderly are at an increased risk.[185,195,196] Complications (i.e., perforation, bleeding) resulting from NSAID use occur more frequently in patients over 65 years of age whether or not they have gastric or duodenal ulcers.[185] Elderly females may be more likely to experience an NSAID-associated ulcer.[196,282] Other factors that may increase the risk of NSAID-induced gastrointestinal damage include previous history of PUD, corticosteroid use, dose, and recent use of NSAID.[196,282] The combined effects of corticosteroids, immunosuppressive agents, or use of multiple

NSAIDs remains uncertain.[189] However, one study suggested that the increased risk for ulcer disease among corticosteroid users was confined to patients concomitantly receiving NSAIDs.[199] Use of high doses of NSAIDs, NSAID use for less than 30 days, and NSAIDs with a long duration of action may be associated with the greatest risk of developing an ulcer.[189,196] Although the relative risk associated with patients using low-dose NSAIDs was considerable in one study, patients receiving high doses had a three times greater risk.[196] The risk also was ten times greater for patients in the first 30 days of NSAID usage.

Patients with a previous history of peptic ulcers and H. pylori infections also may be more susceptible to recurrent ulceration when NSAIDs are used.[197,198] A synergistic relationship between NSAIDs and H. pylori infection has been suggested;[196] however, another study found a correlation between duodenal ulcers and H. pylori but none with NSAIDs and H. pylori.[185] Therefore, whether H. pylori and its associated gastritis predispose an individual to NSAID-associated ulcer disease is unclear.[184] The degree of acute gastric injury caused by individual NSAIDs varies, but the propensity of one NSAID to cause ulcers over another has not been documented firmly.[184,196] Therefore, despite commercial claims that one NSAID may diminish gastrointestinal side effects, the choice of one NSAID over another should not be based upon this claim.

A.C. is an elderly female who has been taking the maximum daily dose of an NSAID for approximately one month and, therefore, is in the high-risk category for the development of an ulcer.

Treatment

36. What therapeutic steps should be taken in the treatment of A.C.'s gastric ulcer?

As a first step, the NSAID should be discontinued. For mild to moderate pain, acetaminophen can be used. If an anti-inflammatory action is required for her arthritic knee, a nonacetylated salicylate can be used. Variables that may influence the healing of NSAID-associated ulcers include continued NSAID therapy, ulcer site, ulcer size, history of PUD, and the presence of H. pylori gastritis.[184] The difference in ulcer healing rates found in a study performed by Banks et al. suggests a difference in the pathogenic mechanism between NSAID/aspirin-associated ulcers and idiopathic ulcers.[200] Therefore, withdrawal of the NSAID may allow for mucosal restitution and more rapid ulcer healing. Based upon this hypothesis, low-dose H$_2$-receptor antagonists (e.g., famotidine 20 mg HS) for eight weeks may be effective in treating NSAID-associated gastric and duodenal ulcers when the NSAID is withdrawn. However, until more data are available supporting this approach, the traditional approach is to discontinue the NSAID and use full doses of H$_2$-receptor antagonists or antacids, or a combination of both drugs, for 8 to 12 weeks.[183]

Continued NSAID Use

37. A.C. insists on continuing the use of NSAIDs to control her arthritic knee pain. What are the risks involved with continued NSAID use? Is the therapy different?

If A.C.'s pain is relieved only with NSAIDs, lower doses of a short-acting NSAID that is not apt to accumulate with continued dosing should be considered.[190] Continued NSAID therapy does not appear to prevent healing of small ulcers; however, the healing process may be delayed. Small gastric ulcers (i.e., <0.5 cm diameter) may heal within eight weeks with an H$_2$-receptor antagonist, antacids, or a combination of both.[201] H$_2$-receptor antagonists may be less effective for large gastric ulcers compared to small ulcers in which case higher doses and/or prolonged therapy may be required.[183,184,201]

The efficacy of sucralfate in the treatment of NSAID-induced ulcers is not well supported. In one study, sucralfate was effective in healing NSAID-associated ulcers despite continued NSAID therapy.[202] However, in this study duodenal ulcers predominated; therefore, no conclusion can be drawn regarding sucralfate's ability to heal NSAID-induced gastric ulcers. In another study in which there were a comparable number of NSAID-associated gastric and duodenal ulcers, mucosal healing did not differ significantly between the sucralfate and placebo-treated groups.[203] Because of the lack of data, there is no role for sucralfate in the treatment of gastric ulcers associated with continued NSAID use; however, duodenal ulcers may heal with sucralfate.[184]

Omeprazole, 40 mg/day, has been effective in treating duodenal and gastric ulcers in patients who continue to receive NSAIDs during antiulcer therapy.[204] These findings suggest that a greater reduction in acidity promotes the healing of NSAID-associated ulcers. Currently, omeprazole is FDA-approved only for the treatment of duodenal ulcers, Zollinger-Ellison syndrome, and gastroesophageal reflux disorder (GERD); however, it probably is effective for the treatment of gastric ulcers as well. More data are needed before omeprazole can be recommended for NSAID-associated ulcers.

Maintenance Therapy

38. A.C.'s ulcer is healed after 8 weeks of therapy but she requires continued ibuprofen therapy for her knee pain. Should A.C. receive continued maintenance therapy? What therapy is indicated?

Identifying risk factors for NSAID-associated ulcers is important so that preventative therapy can be initiated in patients considered to be at high risk. Prophylactic therapy should be considered in those unable to discontinue NSAID therapy; elderly, high surgical risk, debilitated patients who cannot tolerate complications; and those with a history of ulcer complications or ulcer disease.[205,206] Because A.C. is elderly, requires continued NSAID therapy, and has an ulcer history, she is a candidate for prophylactic therapy.

A few studies have examined prophylactic regimens for NSAID-associated ulcers. The H$_2$-receptor antagonist, ranitidine, significantly reduces the incidence of NSAID/aspirin-associated duodenal ulceration but not gastric ulcers.[198,207-209] Another randomized study evaluated nizatidine for the prevention of NSAID-induced ulcers.[210] The majority of patients in this study had a history of gastric/duodenal ulcers or gastric ulcers. The overall ulcer occurrence in the nizatidine group (9.7%) was not significantly different from the placebo group (13.7%). This suggests that there must be a fundamental difference between NSAID-induced gastric and duodenal ulcers. Some investigators postulate that NSAID-associated duodenal ulcers represent an exacerbation of pre-existing duodenal ulcer disease.[16,182,193] Therefore H$_2$-receptor antagonists may be useful only in the prevention of duodenal ulcer disease.

Misoprostol, a synthetic prostaglandin E$_1$ analog, has both antisecretory and cytoprotective properties and can prevent duodenal as well as gastric ulcers in the NSAID/aspirin user.[182,211,212,216] These studies used misoprostol in varying doses (100 mg QID to 200 mg BID, TID, QID) and assessed patients for three months. The 100 mg four times daily and the 200 mg twice daily regimens were inferior to those that incorporated larger doses or more frequent administration. Nevertheless, low doses were superior to placebo in preventing ulcers.[182,216] Preventative therapy exceeding three months was not addressed and needs to be. The success of both ranitidine and misoprostol in preventing NSAID-associated duodenal ulcers suggests that acid suppression is more important in preventing duodenal ulcers as opposed to gastric ulcers where protective mechanisms may be more important.[208,209,211]

Because sucralfate is an effective antiulcer agent that may enhance endogenous prostaglandins from the gastric mucosa, studies have compared the efficacy of sucralfate and misoprostol in the prevention of NSAID/aspirin-induced ulcers.[212,213] Although the data are limited, misoprostol was associated with a significantly lower frequency of gastric and duodenal ulcer formation compared to sucralfate. Of all the available drugs used in PUD, only prostaglandins appear to prevent both NSAID-associated duodenal and gastric ulcers for at least three months. Therefore, A.C. should receive misoprostol 200 mg four times daily as a preventative measure against another NSAID-induced gastric ulcer.

39. A.C. is concerned about being on a medication for a long time. What problems are associated with misoprostol therapy?

Despite the effectiveness of misoprostol in the prevention of duodenal and gastric NSAID-associated ulcers, it paradoxically causes GI symptoms such as diarrhea and abdominal pain.[214,215] Diarrhea is dose dependent and is due to stimulation of intestinal smooth muscle and fluid and electrolyte secretion. Lowering the dose to 100 mg four times daily or giving the dose less frequently (i.e., 200 mg BID) decreases the incidence of diarrhea, but also is less effective in preventing ulcers.[215,216] Prostaglandins are uterotonic and increase the frequency of uterine contractions, bleeding, and abortions.[215] Therefore, misoprostol is contraindicated in women of child-bearing age unless adequate contraceptive measures are taken.[215] Since A.C. is not of child-bearing age, teratogenicity is not a concern.

The majority of studies have looked at continuous therapy for only three months. Thus, the potential long-term consequences of misoprostol therapy cannot be addressed at this time.

Zollinger-Ellison Syndrome
Pathogenesis and Clinical Presentation

40. M.J., a 62-year-old male, was referred from his private physician for evaluation of his continuing ulcers. He has been treated for 2 to 3 years for PUD and has not experienced relief despite escalating doses of various H_2-receptor antagonists. Every year, M.J. is evaluated for a heart attack because he describes severe chest pain. He also complains of frequent diarrhea and abdominal pain. All routine laboratory tests were found to be within normal limits except a serum gastrin level which was 5243 pg/mL (Normal: 0–100). Radiographic and endoscopic studies demonstrate a distal esophageal ulceration, dilation of the duodenum and jejunum with thickened folds, and a 0.1 cm ulceration in the distal duodenum. After a secretin test, his serum gastrin level was 400 pg/mL greater than the basal level. M.J. was diagnosed with Zollinger-Ellison syndrome. What is Zollinger-Ellison syndrome? [SI unit: gastrin 5243 ng/L]

Zollinger-Ellison syndrome is characterized by a triad of clinical findings which include severe recurrent PUD, marked hypersecretion of gastric acid, and nonB-islet tumors (gastrinomas) of the pancreas.[217] Normally, gastrin G-cells in the antral mucosa secrete gastrin which stimulates the parietal cells to secrete gastric acid. In Zollinger-Ellison syndrome, an ectopic source (gastrinoma) also secretes gastrin with a subsequent stimulation of gastric acid secretion.[218] While gastrinomas are located primarily in the pancreas, they also have been found in other regions, particularly the duodenum.[219]

41. Why is M.J.'s presentation consistent with Zollinger-Ellison syndrome?

Symptoms of Zollinger-Ellison syndrome are similar to severe PUD, but may be more persistent and less responsive to standard antiulcer therapy.[218] Many patients have no endoscopically or ra-

diographically detectable GI ulcers at the time of diagnosis (18% to 25%). Some present with solitary or multiple ulcers as in M.J.'s case.[220] The majority of patients with Zollinger-Ellison syndrome have an ulcer, usually in the duodenum or jejunum.[219]

Diagnosis

Because the disease frequently presents as a routine peptic ulcer, the diagnosis of Zollinger-Ellison syndrome is not made for many years.[220] M.J. has been evaluated for many years for complaints resembling a severe peptic ulcer; Zollinger-Ellison syndrome was not considered until radiographic evidence was present. Abdominal pain and diarrhea are the most frequent symptoms at presentation and may occur in the absence of a mucosal ulcer.[219] Diarrhea occurs in approximately 30% to 50% of patients and is caused by increased amounts of gastric acid.[9] High gastric acid levels inhibit sodium and water absorption in the jejunum and damage the GI mucosa.[219] Abdominal pain remains the most common symptom of Zollinger-Ellison syndrome and is localized or diffuse in nature.[220] The pain is similar to that found in a duodenal ulcer in that food and antacids frequently relieve it.

The diagnosis of Zollinger-Ellison syndrome is based upon gastric acid hypersecretion (basal acid output >15 mmol/hour in a patient without prior gastric surgery or >5 mmol/hour in a patient with prior acid-reducing surgery) in conjunction with a fasting serum gastrin level greater than 1000 pg/mL.[9,220,221] Some healthy individuals and patients with duodenal ulcers may have marginally increased serum concentrations of gastrin.[9,220] Therefore, a provocative test is used to identify patients with Zollinger-Ellison syndrome. The secretin provocative test is the most sensitive, reliable, and simplest test for diagnosing and predicting the probability of a patient remaining disease-free.[217,220] If a patient has Zollinger-Ellison syndrome, intravenously administered secretin will cause a marked increase in serum gastrin.[220] A positive test, consistent with the diagnosis of gastrinoma, is defined as an absolute increase in serum gastrin of greater than 200 pg/mL from the basal concentration.[222]

Treatment

42. How should Zollinger-Ellison syndrome be managed in M.J.?

Due to the excessive amounts of gastric acid, patients can experience severe gastrointestinal discomfort, bleeding, and perforation of the GI mucosa. Control of gastric acid output provides excellent symptomatic relief in patients unable to undergo surgical excision of the gastrinoma.[218] The medical goal of therapy, therefore, is symptomatic pain relief and control of gastric acid secretion. An acceptable criterion for long-term control of gastric secretion is a postdrug gastric acid secretion of less than 10 mEq/hour for the last hour before the next dose of medication.[223] Successful medical management can be achieved only by titrating the drug dosage requirement for each patient individually and reassessing the patient periodically.[224]

H_2-Receptor Antagonists

Histamine₂-receptor antagonists were the first drugs successfully used to control gastric hypersecretion. They have not been totally effective in the medical management of Zollinger-Ellison syndrome, probably due to inadequate drug dosing.[224] High doses (sometimes as much as 5 to 12 gm/day) and more frequent dosing than that used to treat ordinary peptic ulcer disease generally is required.[221,225] In addition, most patients treated with H_2-receptor antagonists require an upward dosage adjustment on an annual basis as well as the addition of an anticholinergic agent.[221,226] The reason for the increased dosage requirement of H_2-receptor antagonists is unclear but may be due to decreased drug bioavailability, increased drug metabolism, parietal cell resistance, tachyphylaxis, and increased basal acid output.[224]

Omeprazole

Because many patients are resistant to treatment with H_2-receptor antagonists, omeprazole has become the treatment of choice for this condition.[227] Omeprazole has an advantage over H_2-receptor antagonists in that fewer doses are needed per day and, in some patients, it is the only drug that will resolve all symptoms. Because omeprazole selectively and irreversibly binds to H/K-ATPase, it has a long duration of action. Omeprazole resolves the acid hypersecretion in the majority of patients[227–231] with doses of 10 to 180 mg/day (median daily dose: $\approx$70 to 80 mg/day).

M.J. should be started on at least 60 mg/day of omeprazole and titrated to response.[283] Patients frequently are very ill when the initial diagnosis of Zollinger-Ellison syndrome is made, and it is important that the high gastric acid secretion be controlled.[283] Large once-daily dosing may not control acid secretion in all cases; however, administering the total daily dose in two divided doses may provide better gastric acid control.[228,229,231] The dose required appears to be related to the previous dose of H_2-receptor antagonist and not to the plasma gastrin concentration.[228,229] The need for a dosage adjustment is less common than for H_2-receptor antagonists.[228,231] Gastric carcinoid tumors remain a concern with prolonged omeprazole use. However, to date, there are few reports of carcinoma in patients with Zollinger-Ellison syndrome who have been treated with omeprazole for up to four years.[228–230,232]

Somatostatin

Somatostatin and its synthetic analogue, octreotide, are potent inhibitors of gastric acid secretion and gastrin release. Five months of therapy with high-dose octreotide have resulted in secretory improvement.[233] Clinical experience with this drug is limited; therefore, its use for the long-term management of gastric acid hypersecretion cannot be recommended. Therefore, omeprazole is the drug of choice for the treatment of Zollinger-Ellison syndrome and for M.J.

43. Omeprazole Administration. M.J. is scheduled for surgery and has a nasogastric (NG) tube. His physician wants to administer omeprazole. Can omeprazole be administered via NG tube?

Omeprazole has been formulated in a pH-sensitive gelatin capsule that releases the drug when the pH is greater than 6. Therefore, it is very similar to a sustained-release product in that it cannot be crushed or chewed. In patients with NG tubes who are unable to take medications by mouth, drugs are placed directly down the NG tube or crushed and mixed with water to make a slurry/suspension. Unfortunately, omeprazole is too large to put down an NG tube and crushing the capsule exposes the drug to acidic degradation.[234] Due to the rapid degradation at acidic pH, omeprazole should not be opened, mixed with water, chewed, or crushed.[234] Omeprazole should be administered to M.J. only as an intact capsule and swallowed whole.

Drug Therapy During the Perioperative Period

44. Can omeprazole or H_2-receptor antagonists be used for acid control during the perioperative period?

Nearly all patients with Zollinger-Ellison syndrome are likely to require some type of surgery.[235] Continuous intravenous H_2-receptor antagonists can control gastric acid hypersecretion adequately in patients with Zollinger-Ellison syndrome during surgery.[236] The mean doses required of cimetidine were about 2.9 mg/kg/hour with a wide variation (up to 6 mg/kg/hour), and ranitidine 1 mg/kg/hour (range: 0.5 to 3 mg).[283] Frequent dosage adjustments on an individual basis are required during the first three days of the postoperative period to control gastric acid output. Omeprazole administered intravenously also has been effective in controlling gastric hypersecretion, however, this use is under investigational status in the U.S.[235]

Gastroesophageal Reflux Disorder (GERD)

Pathogenesis

Gastroesophageal reflux is a disorder in which the gastric contents are refluxed into the esophagus, causing irritation and injury to the esophageal mucosa. Complications associated with this refluxing of gastric material include strictures, hemorrhage, perforation, aspiration, and the development of Barrett's esophagus.[237] The disease is associated with a disruption of the balance between defense mechanisms and aggressive factors such as acid, pepsin, and bile salts.[238] One defense is the lower esophageal sphincter (LES), a smooth muscle that helps prevent reflux of aggressive forces by maintaining a positive pressure gradient. If this positive pressure gradient is diminished or overcome, gastric material will reflux into the esophagus. Three pathophysiological mechanisms predispose a patient to reflux:[239] a spontaneous transient relaxation of the lower esophageal sphincter (e.g., during swallowing); a low resting LES pressure; and a transient increase in abdominal pressure (e.g., during deep inspiration or bending over).[240] All of these pathophysiological mechanisms can occur in normal healthy individuals but whether a patient develops esophageal damage will depend upon additional variables that may contribute to the development of esophageal damage. For example, the amount of acid and pepsin that refluxes within a 24-hour period, the length of time that acid and pepsin remain in the esophagus, and the natural sensitivity of the esophageal mucosa to damage by aggressive forces all determine the susceptibility of an individual to GERD.[49]

Clinical Presentation

45. R.L., a 37-year-old, 100 kg, 5'8" male, has been experiencing burning pain for approximately 4 to 6 weeks which is helped by Mylanta which he drinks directly from the bottle. The pain usually occurs after dinner while he is lying on the couch watching television and after his nighttime snack of chocolate just after he goes to bed. He smokes 1 to 2 packs/day of cigarettes and drinks 2 beers every evening while watching television. What symptoms does R.L. have that are consistent with GERD?

The most frequent complaint by patients with GERD is retrosternal burning, commonly referred to as heartburn or pyrosis.[237,240] It is manifested by a burning, substernal pain that travels up the esophagus toward the pharynx.[241] Aerodigestive symptoms (e.g., coughing, wheezing) may be the only symptom observed, especially in the elderly.[241] Because reflux of acid is not continuous, symptoms of GERD may come and go over long periods of time.[242] Symptoms may be aggravated by certain foods, specific body positioning, or drugs. As in R.L.'s case, certain foods with high-fat content and chocolate can lead to GERD symptoms because these foods decrease the LES pressure. Other foods such as spices, onions, citric juices, and coffee can contribute to the development of GERD by direct mucosal irritation.[237,240] Symptoms of esophageal reflux can occur in any body position at any time; however, many people, like R.L., experience symptoms primarily at night when they are supine or when bending over. GERD also can be exacerbated by concurrent drug therapy (e.g., α-adrenergic agonists, β-adrenergic agonists, calcium channel blockers, diazepam, dopamine, meperidine, progesterone, prostaglandins, theophylline).[243] The lack of symptoms does not necessarily imply the absence of esophageal damage.

Treatment

Goals

46. What are the therapeutic goals for the treatment of GERD?

The therapeutic goals for GERD are similar to those for the treatment of peptic ulcer disease: alleviate pain or symptoms, diminish the frequency and duration of esophageal reflux, promote healing, avoid complications, and prevent recurrence.[237,243]

Since GERD is an imbalance between aggressive forces and defense mechanisms, therapy is directed at enhancing body defenses and/or decreasing aggressive factors. This generally is achieved through life-style changes and drug therapy.[237]

Life-Style Changes

Initially, all patients should change their life-style to remove factors that exacerbate reflux. R.L. should be instructed to lose weight, cease smoking, avoid increasing gastroesophageal pressure by lying on the couch, and avoid foods that precipitate symptoms or decrease the LES pressure.[244] Weight loss and loose-fitting clothes are recommended because obesity and tight clothes may potentiate reflux by continuously increasing the gastroesophageal pressure gradient.[246] Cigarette smoking directly provokes acid reflux and reduces lower esophageal sphincter pressure.[245] R.L.'s symptoms appear to be the most troublesome while lying on the couch when he is watching television and at night. For patients like R.L., elevating the head with six- to eight-inch blocks while sleeping or sitting in an upright position might be helpful.[246] R.L. also should avoid foods that could make reflux worse. Foods that lower esophageal sphincter pressure include chocolate, fatty meals, carminatives (e.g., peppermint, spearmint), and alcohol.[246] Foods that irritate the gastric mucosa (e.g., spicy food, citric juices) and stimulate acid secretion (e.g., cola, beer, milk) should be avoided.[246] In patients with complicated disease, these life-style changes may not be sufficient or effective and single or combination drug therapy may be necessary.[243]

Drug Therapy

47. R.L. has lost 20 kg of weight and is avoiding his favorite foods. He cannot stop smoking and his reflux continues to be a problem for him. What drug therapy is appropriate for the treatment of GERD?

Since patients with GERD have frequent refluxes of normal amounts of acid, complete inhibition of gastric acid secretion is necessary to facilitate healing and relieve symptoms.[49] Generally, the same drugs used to treat PUD have some effect on GERD. However, the doses used for ordinary peptic ulcer disease are limited in their ability to treat GERD effectively.

Antacids are used commonly in ulcer disease because of their acid-neutralizing effect; however, because of their short duration of action, they cannot provide sustained gastric acid neutralization. Antacids may provide symptomatic relief in mild to moderate GERD but probably do not promote healing of esophagitis.[247] Consequently, antacids may be used in conjunction with other drug therapy to aid in symptomatic relief.

H_2-Receptor Antagonists are effective when used in full doses. Response to H_2-receptor antagonists appears to depend upon the severity of the disease, the dose of the drug, and the duration of therapy. There is a clear difference between healing rates in patients with mild pretreatment esophageal reflux compared to those with moderate or severe pretreatment disease.[248,249] The most important factor that negatively influences healing appears to be the extent of esophageal lesions.[250] Following eight weeks of therapy with ranitidine, endoscopic healing was observed in 65% of patients with moderate esophagitis (grade II). In contrast, endoscopic healing was observed in only 15% of patients with severe esoph-

agitis (grade III).[248] Apparently, the more severe the esophagitis was, the poorer the response to therapy. Unlike duodenal ulcers, 24-hour intragastric acidity is a predominant influence in the pathogenesis of reflux disease.[251] Sustained and prolonged acid suppression with more frequent administration of an H_2-receptor antagonist, therefore, is superior in symptom relief and ulcer healing than once-daily dosing.[248,249] Although not as important for mild esophagitis, the more frequent administration of H_2-receptor antagonists (depending upon their potency) may result in better healing rates and symptom relief for moderate or severe disease.[249] In patients with only nocturnal reflux, the H_2-receptor antagonist can be administered at night.[251] Cimetidine 800 mg every night was as effective in the treatment of grade II-III reflux esophagitis as 400 mg four times daily.[251] This dosing regimen may enhance compliance for some patients.

Esophageal ulcer healing rates appear to be directly proportional to the length of treatment.[247] Four to six weeks of therapy with H_2-receptor antagonists were not effective in the treatment of GERD. In a multicenter trial examining the healing and relapse rates associated with the use of ranitidine in esophageal reflux disease, endoscopic healing increased with the duration of therapy.[250] After six weeks of therapy, epithelial defects remained in 43% of patients (57% healed), and 70% healed after 12 weeks of therapy. In another study,[249] 45% of patients on nizatidine experienced esophageal healing after six weeks of therapy and 80% after 12 weeks. In both these studies symptom relief occurred earlier than ulcer healing, confirming the poor correlation between symptom relief and efficacy.

Omeprazole. Since prolonged suppression of gastric acid is necessary to successfully treat GERD, an agent such as omeprazole (Prilosec) which inhibits gastric acid secretion for a sustained period of time would be highly effective. In one study, omeprazole was highly effective in healing peptic esophagitis and the rate of healing was dose and severity-of-disease related.[252] After four weeks of therapy in patients with severe esophagitis (grade IV), omeprazole 20 mg and 40 mg healed reflux esophagitis in 48% and 41%, respectively. These percentages were significantly lower than those observed in patients with the mildest grade of esophagitis receiving omeprazole 20 mg (87%) or 40 mg (97%). Cigarette smoking adversely affected the healing of the esophagitis. Unfortunately, 82% of the patients relapsed within six months after therapy was stopped. The comparative efficacy of omeprazole (20 mg QD) and ranitidine (150 mg BID) was assessed later in a randomized, blinded, and controlled study.[253] The endoscopically evaluated healing occurred in 67% of patients after four weeks of omeprazole therapy compared to 31% after ranitidine therapy. After eight weeks of therapy the healing rates increased further to 50% and 85% after ranitidine and omeprazole, respectively. The higher healing rate for omeprazole also was accompanied by a faster and more substantial improvement in symptoms. Omeprazole was notably more effective than ranitidine in patients with severe esophagitis which may reflect its potency as an inhibitor of gastric secretion.[253] Another study confirms the superiority of omeprazole relative to the H_2-receptor antagonists, especially in patients with severe disease.[254] Omeprazole also is effective in esophagitis resistant to H_2-receptor antagonists. In two studies, omeprazole 20 to 40 mg was administered to patients with severe esophagitis who had unhealed esophageal ulcers after prolonged therapy with standard to high doses of H_2-receptor antagonists.[255,256] After 12 weeks of therapy, the healing rate for all patients was 80%. Thus, these studies indicate that omeprazole is effective for patients with esophagitis refractory to H_2-receptor antagonists.

Prokinetic Agents. Because delayed gastric emptying is found in a large portion of patients with esophageal reflux, prokinetic drugs such as bethanechol (Urecholine) have been used for GERD. As bethanechol is a cholinergic drug, it is poorly tolerated and interacts with many other drugs.[242]

Metoclopramide (Reglan). The dopamine antagonist, metoclopramide, is a potent prokinetic drug that selectively increases gastric emptying. The drug produces a dose-related increase in resting tone of the LES in patients with GERD.[257] It is absorbed rapidly and the effects on the gastrointestinal tract occur within one to three minutes following intravenous administration and in 30 to 60 minutes after oral administration.[257] The usual metoclopramide dose is 10 mg four times daily before meals and at bedtime.[237] The limiting factor with metoclopramide therapy is its adverse effect profile which includes GI and CNS disturbances. The most common adverse effects include restlessness, drowsiness, and fatigue. Anxiety and agitation can occur with rapid IV administration. Extrapyramidal reactions are mediated via blockade of the central dopaminergic receptors involved in motor function.[257] Gastrointestinal symptoms include diarrhea, nausea, and abdominal cramps.[237,242]

Cisapride (Propulsid) is a new drug approved for the treatment of GERD. It is a selective cholinergic agent which is devoid of antidopaminergic activity. Cisapride apparently facilitates acetylcholine release at the myenteric plexus of the gastrointestinal smooth muscle.[258] Cisapride increases LES tone through stimulation of the gastrointestinal smooth muscle, improves esophageal peristalsis, and promotes gastric emptying.

When cisapride is taken orally, peak plasma concentrations are reached within one to one and one-half hours. Due to significant first-pass metabolism, cisapride's bioavailability is only 40%. It is metabolized by the liver with a mean terminal elimination half-life of 6 to 12 hours.[259] Cisapride accumulates in patients with hepatic or renal impairment and in elderly patients; therefore, caution is recommended in these patient populations. Overall, the efficacy of cisapride, 10 mg four times daily, is superior to placebo in providing symptomatic relief and esophageal healing in patients with gastroesophageal reflux.[259] Based upon the limited studies available, cisapride appears to be a promising treatment for GERD. The most common adverse effects include diarrhea, abdominal pain, nausea, and constipation.

Sucralfate. The efficacy of sucralfate (Carafate) in the treatment of GERD is similar to H_2-receptor antagonists; however, data from large, controlled studies are not available.[260,261] Like the H_2-antagonists, sucralfate appears to be effective in mild esophagitis but not in severe disease.[261] Sucralfate must come in direct contact with the mucosa before proteinaceous binding can occur.[242] Therefore, it must be given as a suspension when used to treat GERD. Because a suspension currently is not available commercially, a suspension can be created by dropping a tablet directly into a glass of water. The sucralfate tablet will dissolve readily on its own and need not be crushed.

Maintenance Therapy

48. Is maintenance therapy recommended for GERD?

After complete healing, symptoms will recur in a large percentage of patients. When maintenance therapy with ranitidine 150 mg twice daily was given to patients with healed esophagitis, recurrences developed in 42% of patients, significant difference from the placebo group.[250] The rate of recurrence appears to be similar with the use of omeprazole.[252] At six months, 82% of patients developed ulcerative esophagitis following omeprazole use. Because of the uncertainty of long-term omeprazole use and its association with carcinoid tumors, some investigators advocate cycling omeprazole treatment for four to eight weeks with an H_2-receptor antagonist for two to four months for continued maintenance therapy.[240]

Stress Ulcers

Epidemiology

49. M.L., a 64-year-old female, is admitted to the intensive care unit (ICU) because of her deteriorating respiratory condition. She was admitted with a diagnosis of diverticulitis. She has no significant past medical history and was a healthy individual. M.L. was found in respiratory distress with a respiratory rate of 36/min, temperature of 104 °F, heart rate of 120 beats/min, and a blood pressure (BP) of 60/40 mm Hg. Relevant laboratory tests include the following: sodium (Na) 147 mEq/L, potassium (K) 5.6 mEq/L, chloride (Cl) 119 mEq/L, bicarbonate 12 mEq/L, blood urea nitrogen (BUN) 57 mg/dL, SrCr 2.7 mg/dL, and white blood cell (WBC) count 36,000 cells/mm³. Since M.L has no history of PUD, why is she at risk for stress ulcers? [SI units: Na 147 mmol/L; K 5.6 mmol/L; Cl 119 mmol/L; bicarbonate 12 mmol/L; BUN 20.3 mmol/L; WBC count 36,000 × 10⁶ cells/L]

Acute stress ulcers are distinctly different from chronic peptic ulcer disease[262] in that they are not recurring in nature and are unrelated to a previous history of ulcer disease. Stress ulcers occur in specific clinical settings such as in the critically ill patient.[263] After a major physiologic disturbance from an associated severe intercurrent illness, superficial gastroduodenal ulcers can develop rapidly.[264] Within 24 to 48 hours, the majority of critically ill patients (75% to 100%) will have endoscopically detectable mucosal lesions.[265] Unlike chronic PUD, multiple ulcer lesions usually develop in the proximal stomach along the boundaries of the acid-secreting mucosa.[262,263] Endoscopy generally shows that 50% of these lesions have signs of continuous slow bleeding.[265] Because these lesions are superficial, overt or occult bleeding will occur in only 5% to 20% of untreated patients under intensive care.[266] Patients who develop GI bleeding have a higher mortality rate (64%) than those critically ill patients who do not.[266]

During the early 1970s, stress ulcers and their complications had reached near epidemic proportions.[263] However, the occurrence of stress ulcer bleeding has decreased to less than 2% of the intensive care patient population due to widespread use of agents that prophylactically neutralize gastric acids and advanced medical care.[263,264]

Pathogenesis

50. What is the pathogenesis of stress ulceration?

Normally, the gastric and duodenal mucosa are protected from the aggressive forces of gastric acid and pepsin. Impairment of protective mechanisms can cause an imbalance between aggressive and defensive forces resulting in mucosal damage. This concept is particularly true for acute stress ulceration.[14] Aggressive factors are well defined in stress ulceration and the removal of these forces will prevent or lessen the likelihood of this disorder greatly.[267] Although hydrogen ions are necessary for the development of stress ulcers, large quantities of acid secretion are not necessary for ulcer formation.[267] In fact, traumatized patients secrete normal or decreased amounts of gastric acid after an acute event; therefore, the concentration of the luminal acid may be a more important determinant in the formation of mucosal lesions.[263]

In contrast, sepsis and central nervous system injuries frequently are associated with large amounts of gastric acid secretion.[265] Patients with small bowel resections also can have gastric acid hypersecretion.[265] Overall, it is the presence of acid, not the quantity, that is the major factor in stress ulceration.

Despite the critical role of gastric acid and other aggressive factors in the pathogenesis of stress ulceration, mucosal defenses also are important. Mucosal defenses include adequate mucosal blood flow, production of gastric mucus and bicarbonate, epithelial restitution, gastric mucosal barrier, and mucosal prostaglandins. Any deficiency in these defensive mechanisms may play a role in stress ulcer formation.

In the critically ill patient, gastric mucosal blood flow is diminished in hemorrhagic, cardiogenic, and septic shock.[267] Ischemia is probably one of the major factors leading to stress ulcers.[268] Diminution of blood flow results in a number of unfavorable events: 1) decreased nutrient and oxygen delivery; 2) inability of the mucosa to remove or neutralize gastric acids; and 3) a decrease in bicarbonate efflux into the gastric epithelium.[263,265] During stressful situations, there also is a decreased rate of proliferation and cellular turnover of the gastric mucosa.[267] Furthermore, many critically ill patients have back diffusion of bile salts from the duodenum to the stomach and urea from the blood (i.e., renal failure), and these effects can disrupt the gastric barrier and contribute to stress injury.[265,267] The lack of prostaglandin and mucus formation in the critically ill also may contribute to the development of stress-related damage.[167] As one can see, both aggressive and defensive factors are important in the development of stress ulcers.

Risk Factors

51. What associated risk factors does M.L. possess?

Numerous risk factors have been identified which include shock, burns (>35% of the body), multiple organ failure, trauma (intra-abdominal or thoracoabdominal injuries), sepsis (intraperitoneal or pulmonary infections), coagulopathy, and CNS injury.[267,268] However, in a prospective multicenter study which evaluated potential risk factors for stress ulceration in 2252 critically ill patients in the ICU, the only independent risk factors for gastrointestinal bleeding were respiratory failure and coagulopathy. If the results of this study can be further supported, prophylaxis against stress ulcers may be required only in critically ill patients that have a coagulopathy or require mechanical ventilation for greater than 48 hours.[284]

M.L. currently is in septic shock and will require mechanical ventilation; therefore, she should receive stress ulcer prophylaxis.

Treatment

Goals

52. What can be done to prevent the complications associated with stress ulceration? What are the goals of therapy?

Despite the low occurrence of serious bleeding in patients with stress ulcers, the accompanying mortality is very high. Aggressive prophylactic therapy may prevent significant complications and reduce both morbidity and mortality. Because alteration in defense mechanisms predisposes a patient to stress ulceration and bleeding; the most important approach is to treat the underlying disease state and physiologic conditions. Decreased blood flow appears to be an important factor in most patients who develop stress ulcers; therefore, correction of any shock-like state (i.e., hypotension) should be a priority in the management of M.L.[267] Other important measures should include maintaining adequate nutrition and respiratory support. Any acid-base imbalances should be corrected in patients like M.L. who have renal failure and uremia because of their propensity for injury to the gastric mucosa.

Adequate neutralization of gastric acid is of paramount importance since stress associated ulceration does not occur in the absence of acid. Maintaining an intragastric pH between 3.5 to 4 lowers the frequency of bleeding in stress patients.[262] At a pH of 4.5, pepsin is inactivated and 99.9% of acid is neutralized at a pH of 5.[267] *In vitro* observations demonstrate that when the gastric pH is less than 5 to 7, coagulation function and platelet aggregation are impaired.[262] Therefore, therapy should be directed at maintain-

ing the gastric pH between 3.5 to 4 to prevent stress-related ulcers and greater than 7 for patients with bleeding ulcers.[262,265]

Drug Therapy

53. What pharmacologic therapy can be used to prevent stress ulcers?

Antacids, H_2-receptor antagonists, and sucralfate all can prevent these ulcers.

Antacids. Aggressive antacid therapy (30 to 60 mL every hour) very effectively maintains the gastric pH above 3.5.[265,266] A randomized study compared antacids (30 mL every hour) and cimetidine (300 mg IV Q 6 hr), in preventing stress ulcers in 75 critically ill patients.[269] Cimetidine did not adequately protect these patients from gastrointestinal bleeding, whereas antacid therapy did. Although antacids are effective in preventing stress ulcers, they are associated with administration problems and adverse effects. In patients with renal failure, magnesium, aluminum, or calcium toxicity can occur depending upon which antacid is used. Diarrhea and metabolic disturbances also have been associated with antacid therapy.

H_2-Receptor Antagonists. Subsequent studies showed H_2-receptor antagonists to be effective in preventing stress ulcers. In an analysis of data from 16 prospective, randomized trials, cimetidine was as effective as antacids in preventing significant stress ulcer bleeding.[264] Another prospective, randomized trial was performed to determine the comparative efficacy of several H_2-receptor antagonists (cimetidine, famotidine, and ranitidine) and antacids in the prevention of stress ulceration.[270] Fifty-seven patients were evaluated after elective coronary artery bypass surgery. None of the patients developed a postoperative gastric hemorrhage. However, better pH control (pH >4.0) was achieved with famotidine and ranitidine compared to cimetidine or antacid therapy. In another double-blind study involving critically ill patients, famotidine was superior to cimetidine in maintaining the gastric pH at >4.0 in patients with normal and or decreased renal function.[271] In both studies, the adverse effect profile also was better with famotidine.

54. M.L. is to be started on an H_2-receptor antagonist. How should it be administered?

Because the goal is to maintain the gastric pH greater than 4.0 for the prevention of stress ulcers and greater than 7.0 for the treatment of bleeding stress ulcers, the proper administration of these agents is critical. Intermittent bolus injection always has been commonly used. However, this method of administration is labor intensive, and continuous intravenous infusion of the H_2-receptor antagonists is more effective in maintaining the gastric pH greater than 4.0.[272,273] Guidelines for administering these agents have been developed and the recommendations are as follows. If ranitidine is used, either 150 or 300 mg is administered as a 24-hour continuous infusion.[273] Some investigators recommend giving a 50 mg loading dose of ranitidine followed by a 6 to 8 mg/hour infusion.[274] A loading dose of 300 mg of cimetidine administered over 15 minutes followed by a continuous infusion of 37.5 to 50 mg/hour is more effective than 300 mg every six hours.[272,275] Famotidine is successful as a continuous infusion (1.7 mg/hour) after a 20 mg loading dose.[274] Dosages should be adjusted according to the severity of the patient's illness, renal function, and the intragastric pH. The intragastric pH can be determined with an indwelling probe or by measuring the pH of an NG aspirate. Signs of bleeding (e.g., occult blood, low blood pressure, dropping Hct and Hgb) also should be assessed constantly.

55. Sucralfate. Is there any role for sucralfate in M.L.?

In the critically ill patient receiving stress ulcer prophylaxis with acid-suppressing medications or neutralizing agents, growth of gram-negative bacteria is common.[276,277] Drugs that raise the gastric pH may promote proliferation of bacteria in the stomach,[285] and aspiration of these organisms can be important in the pathogenesis of nosocomial pneumonia.[286] Sucralfate is a drug which does not alter gastric pH significantly but is effective in preventing stress ulcers similar to the H_2-receptor antagonists and antacids.[277,278,285,287] Therefore, studies have compared various stress ulcer prophylactic regimens and the occurrence of nosocomial pneumonia in the critically ill patient.[285,286] Sucralfate in doses of 1 gm every four to six hours was associated with a lower incidence of pneumonia. However, one study suggested that only patients who received prolonged mechanical ventilation and were able to maintain a low gastric pH, will benefit from stress ulcer prophylaxis with sucralfate and these patients should be identified by monitoring gastric pH.[285]

Sucralfate currently is available as a suspension and administration through M.L.'s NG tube would be very simple. However, aluminum toxicity can occur in renally impaired patients who are receiving sucralfate. Therefore, sucralfate may not be a good therapeutic option at this time for M.L. and a continuous intravenous infusion of an H_2-receptor antagonist should be employed. The

Table 23.7	Pearls of Wisdom
Antacids	Avoid magnesium-containing products in renal failure. Space antacids 2–3 hours apart from ciprofloxacin, tetracycline, iron, and H_2-receptor antagonists
Sucralfate	May interfere with the absorption of drugs, so space them 2 hr from other drugs. Administer 30 min PC and HS. Avoid in renal failure
Omeprazole	Do not crush capsule
Misoprostol	Contraindicated in pregnant patients. Dose-dependent diarrhea, usually self-limiting with continued therapy
H_2-receptor antagonists	Dosage adjustment may be required with cimetidine and drugs that affect the P450 liver enzyme system. Dosage adjustment must be made with creatinine clearance <50 mL/min. Nizatidine is not available as an injectable or liquid formulation

dose of the H_2-receptor should be adjusted according to the M.L.'s calculated creatinine clearance (i.e., Cl_{Cr} <10 mL/minute use 0.8 mg/hour of famotidine).

References

1. **Soll A.** Duodenal ulcer and drug therapy. In: Sleisenger MH, Fordtran JS, eds. Gastrointestinal Disease: Pathophysiology Diagnosis Management. Philadelphia: WB Saunders; 1989:814.

2. **Katz J.** The course of peptic ulcer disease. Med Clin North Am. 1991;75(4):831–41.

3. **Earnest DL.** Maintenance therapy in peptic ulcer disease. Med Clin North Am. 1991;75(4):1013–027.

4. **Vogt TM, Johnson RE.** Recent changes in the incidence of duodenal and gastric ulcer. Am J Epidemiol. 1980;111:713–20.

5. **Kurata JH.** Ulcer epidemiology: an overview and proposed research framework. Gastroenterology. 1989;96:569–80.

6. **Richardson CT.** Gastric ulcer. In: Sleisenger MH, Fordtran JS, eds. Pathophysiology Diagnosis Management. Philadelphia: WB Saunders; 1989:879.

7. **Sonnenberg A.** Geographic and temporal variations in the occurrence of peptic ulcer disease. Scand J Gastroenterol. 1985;20(Suppl. 110):11–24.

8. **Kurata JH et al.** Sex differences in peptic ulcer disease. Gastroenterology. 1985;88:96–100.

9. **Berardi RR.** Peptic ulcer disease and Zollinger-Ellison syndrome. In: DiPiro JT et al., eds. Pharmacotherapy: A Pathophysiologic Approach. New York: Elsevier; 1992:511.

10. **Feldman M.** Gastric secretion in health and disease. In: Sleisenger MH, Fordtran JS, eds. Gastrointestinal Disease: Pathophysiology Diagnosis Management. Philadelphia: WB Saunders; 1989:713.

11. **Katz J.** Acid secretion and suppression. Med Clin North Am. 1991;75(4):877–87.

12. **Schubert ML, Shamburek RD.** Control of acid secretion. Gastroenterol Clin North Am. 1990;19(1):1–25.

13. **Wallace JL.** Mucosal defense—new avenues for treatment of ulcer disease? Gastroenterol Clin North Am. 1990;19(1):87–100.

14. **Schiessel R et al.** Mechanisms of stress ulceration and implications for treatment. Gastroenterol Clin North Am. 1990;19(1):101–20.

15. **Wolfe MM, Soll AH.** The physiology of gastric acid secretion. N Engl J Med. 1988;319:1707–715.

16. **Soll AH.** Pathogenesis of peptic ulcer and implications for therapy. N Engl J Med. 1990;222:909–16.

17. **Freston JW.** Overview of medical therapy of peptic ulcer disease. Gastroenterol Clin North Am. 1990;19:121–40.

18. **Rubin W.** Medical treatment of peptic ulcer disease. Med Clin North Am. 1991;75(4):981–98.

19. **Graham DY.** Treatment of peptic ulcers caused by Helicobacter pylori. N Engl J Med. 1993;328:349–50.

20. **Bartlett JG.** Campylobacter pylori: fact or fancy? Gastroenterology. 1988; 94:229–38.

21. **Ormand JE, Talley NJ.** Helicobacter pylori: controversies and an approach to management. Mayo Clin Proc. 1990; 65:414–26.

22. **Graham DY.** Campylobacter pylori and peptic ulcer disease. Gastroenterology. 1989;96:615–25.

23. **Peterson WL.** Helicobacter pylori and peptic ulcer disease. N Engl J Med. 1991;321:1043–048.

24. **Wang JY et al.** Delayed healing of acetic acid-induced gastric ulcers in rats by indomethacin. Gastroenterology. 1989;96:393–402.

25. **Soll AH et al.** Nonsteroidal anti-inflammatory drugs and peptic ulcer disease. Ann Intern Med. 1991;114:307–19.

26. **Sontag S et al.** Cimetidine, cigarette smoking and recurrence of duodenal ulcer. N Eng J Med. 1984;311:689–93.

27. **Korman MG et al.** Ranitidine in duodenal ulcer—incidence of healing and effect of smoking. Dig Dis Sci. 1982;27:712–15.

28. **Muller-Lissner A.** Bile reflux is increased in cigarette smokers. Gastroenterology. 1986;90:1205–209.

29. **Smassarrat F et al.** Increased gastric secretory capacity in smokers without gastrointestinal lesions. Gut. 1986;27 (4):433–39.

30. **Forest G et al.** Active smoking depresses prostaglandin synthesis in human gastric mucosa. Ann Intern Med. 1986;104:616–19.

31. **McColl K, Fullarton GM.** Duodenal ulcer pain—the role of acid and inflammation. Gut. 1993;34:1300–302.

32. **Burget DW et al.** Is there an optimal degree of acid suppression for healing of duodenal ulcers? Gastroenterology. 1990;99:345–51.

33. **Howden CW et al.** The treatment of gastric ulcer with antisecretory drugs. Dig Dis Sci. 1988;33(5):619–24.

34. **Hui WM et al.** Maintenance therapy for duodenal ulcer: a randomized controlled comparison of seven forms of treatment. Am J Med. 1992;92:265.

35. **Feldman M, Burton ME.** Histamine-receptor antagonists standard therapy for acid-peptic disease. N Engl J Med. 1990;323(24):1672–680.

36. **Berardi RR, Dunn-Kucharski VA.** Peptic ulcer disease: an update. Am Pharmacy. 1993;6:26.

37. **Hurwitz A, Carter CA.** The pharmacology of antiulcer drugs. Ann Pharmacother. 1989;23:S10–6.

38. **Alcala-Santaella R et al.** A multicenter, randomized, double-blind study comparing a daily bedtime administration of famotidine and ranitidine in short-term treatment of active duodenal ulcer. Digestion. 1989;42:79–85.

39. **Walt P et al.** Comparison of twice-daily ranitidine with standard cimetidine treatment of duodenal ulcer. Gut. 1981;22:319–22.

40. **Simon B et al.** Famotidine versus ranitidine for the short-term treatment of duodenal ulcer. Digestion. 1985;32 (Suppl.):32–7.

41. **Rohner G, Gugler R.** Treatment of active duodenal ulcers with famotidine a double-blind comparison with ranitidine. Am J Med. 1986;81(Suppl. 4B): 13–6.

42. **Cloud ML et al.** Healing and recurrence of active duodenal ulcer with nizatidine. Clin Pharmacol Ther. 1989; 46:310–16.

43. **Callaghan JT et al.** A pharmacokinetic profile of nizatidine in man. Scand J Gastroenterol. 1987;22(Suppl. 136): 9–17.

44. **Gitlin N et al.** A multicenter, double-blind, randomized, placebo-controlled comparison of nocturnal and twice-a-day famotidine in the treatment of active duodenal ulcer disease. Gastroenterology. 1987;92:48–53.

45. **Lin JH.** Pharmacokinetic and pharmacodynamic properties of histamine H_2-receptor antagonist. Clin Pharmacokinet. 1991;20(3):218–36.

46. **Echizen H, Ishizaki T.** Clinical pharmacokinetic of famotidine. Clin Pharmacokinet. 1991;21(3):178–94.

47. **Price AH, Brogden RN.** Nizatidine a preliminary review of its pharmacodynamic and pharmacokinetic properties, and its therapeutic use in peptic ulcer disease. Drugs. 1988;36:521–39.

48. **Knadler MP et al.** Absorption studies of the H_2 blocker nizatidine. Clin Pharmacol Ther. 1987;42:514–20.

49. **Feldman M, Burton ME.** Histamine receptor antagonists. N Engl J Med. 1990;323:1749–754.

50. **Sax MJ.** Clinically important adverse effects and drug interactions with H_2-receptor antagonists: an update. Pharmacotherapy. 1987;7(6 Pt. 2):110S–15S.

51. **Feldman M.** Pros and cons of over-the-counter availability of histamine₂ receptor antagonists. Arch Intern Med. 1993;153:2415–418.

52. **Grant SM et al.** Ranitidine. Drugs. 1989;37:801–70.

53. **Hansten PD et al.,** eds. Antifungal Drug Interactions. In: Drug Interactions and Updates Quarterly. Vancouver: Applied Therapeutics; 1993:389.

54. **Nazario M.** The hepatic and renal mechanisms of drug interactions with cimetidine. Drug Intell Clin Pharm. 1986;20:342–48.

55 **Skoutakis VA.** Comparison of the parenteral histamine$_2$ receptor antagonists. Ann Pharmacother. 1989;Vol 23:S17–22.

56 **Kosoglou T, Vlasses PH.** Drug interactions involving renal transport mechanisms: an overview. Ann Pharmacother. 1989;23:116–22.

57 **Rodvold KA et al.** Interaction of steady-state procainamide with H$_2$ receptor antagonists cimetidine and ranitidine. Ther Drug Monit. 1987;378–80.

58 **Christian C et al.** Cimetidine inhibits renal procainamide clearance. Clin Pharm Therapeut. 1984;36:221–27.

59 **Somogyi A, Bochner F.** Br J Clin Pharmacol. 1984;18:175–81.

60 **Caballeria J et al.** Effects of cimetidine on gastric alcohol dehydrogenase activity and blood ethanol levels. Gastroenterology. 1989;96:388–92.

61 **Caballeria J et al.** Effects of H$_2$-receptor antagonists on gastric alcohol dehydrogenase activity. Dig Dis Sci. 1991;Vol 36:1673–679.

62 **Raufman JP et al.** Histamine$_2$-receptor antagonists do not alter serum ethanol levels in fed, nonalcoholic men. Ann Intern Med. 1993;118:488–94.

63 **Howden CW, Hunt RH.** The relationship between suppression of acidity and gastric ulcer healing rates. Aliment Pharmacol Ther. 1990;4:25–33.

64 **Lee FI et al.** Acute treatment of duodenal ulcer: a multicentre study to compare ranitidine 150 gm twice daily with ranitidine 300 mg once at night. Gut. 1986;27:1091–095.

65 **Gitlin N et al.** A multicenter, double-blind, randomized, placebo-controlled comparison of nocturnal and twice-a-day famotidine in the treatment of active duodenal ulcer disease. Gastroenterology. 1987;92:48–54.

66 **Howden CW et al.** Nocturnal doses of H$_2$-receptor antagonists for duodenal ulcer. Lancet. 1985;647–48.

67 **De pretis G et al.** Comparison between single morning and bedtime doses of 40 mg famotidine for the treatment of duodenal ulcer. Aliment Pharmacol Ther. 1989;3:285–91.

68 **Bianchi Porro G, O Sangaletti FP.** Inhibition of nocturnal acidity is important but not essential for duodenal ulcer healing. Gut. 1990;31:397–400.

69 **Siepler JK et al.** Selecting drug therapy for patients with duodenal ulcers. Clin Pharm. 1990;9:463–67.

70 **Armstrong D et al.** Prospective multicentre study of risk factors associated with delayed healing of recurrent duodenal ulcers (RUDER). Gut. 1993;34:1319–326.

71 **Legerton CW.** Duodenal and gastric ulcer healing rates: a review. Am J Med. 1984;77(Suppl. 5B):2–7.

72 **Walt RP, Langman MJS.** Antacids and ulcer healing—a review of the evidence. Drugs. 1991;42(2):205–12.

73 **Preclik G et al.** Stimulation of mucosal prostaglandin synthesis in human stomach and duodenum by antacid treatment. Gut. 1989;30:148–51.

74 **Hollander D, Tarnawski A.** Are antacids cytoprotective? Gut. 1989;30:145–47.

75 **Zaterka S et al.** Very-low dose antacid in treatment of duodenal ulcer—comparison with cimetidine. Dig Dis Sci. 1991;36(10):1377–383.

76 **Hunter JO et al.** Double-blind randomized multicenter study comparing Maalox TC tablets and ranitidine in healing of duodenal ulcers. Dig Dis Sci. 1991;36(7):911–16.

77 **Pinson JB, Weart WC.** Antacid products. In: Covington TR et al., eds. Handbook of Nonprescription Drugs. Washington, DC: American Pharmaceutical Association; 1990:147.

78 **Van Ness MM.** Antacids. In: Van Ness MM, ed. Handbook of Gastrointestinal Drug Therapy. Boston: Little, Brown Co.; 1989:7.

79 **Nix DE et al.** Effects of aluminum and magnesium antacids and ranitidine on the absorption of ciprofloxacin. Clin Pharmacol Ther. 1989;46:700–05.

80 **Steinberg WM et al.** Antacids inhibit absorption of cimetidine. N Engl J Med. 1982;307:400–03.

81 **D'Arcy PF, McElnay JC.** Drug-antacid interactions: assessment of clinical importance. Drug Intell Clin Pharm. 1987;21:607–17.

82 **Shorrock CJ, Rees WDW.** Effect of sucralfate on human gastric bicarbonate secretion and local prostaglandin E$_2$ metabolism. Am J Med. 1989;86(Suppl. 6A):2–8.

83 **Martin F.** Sucralfate suspension 1 gm four times per day in the short-term treatment of active duodenal ulcer. Am J Med. 1989;86(Suppl. 6A):104–07.

84 **Hentschel E et al.** Controlled comparison of sucralfate and cimetidine in duodenal ulcer. Scand J Gastroenterol. 1983;18(Suppl. 83):31–5.

85 **McCarthy DM.** Sucralfate. N Engl J Med. 1991;325(14):1017–025.

86 **Martin F et al.** Short-term treatment with sucralfate or cimetidine in gastric ulcer: preliminary results of a controlled randomized trial. Scand J Gastroenterol. 1983;18(Suppl. 83):37–41.

87 **Pop P et al.** Comparison of sucralfate and cimetidine in the treatment of duodenal and gastric ulcers. A multicenter study. Scand J Gastroenterol. 1983;18(Suppl. 83): 43–7.

88 **Koelz HR, Halter F.** Sucralfate and ranitidine in the treatment of acute duodenal ulcer. Healing and relapse. Am J Med. 1989;86(Suppl. 6A):98–103.

89 **Hjortrup A et al.** Two daily doses of sucralfate or cimetidine in the healing of gastric ulcer. A comparative randomized study. Am J Med. 1989;86(Suppl. 6A):113–15.

90 **Rey JF et al.** Comparative study of sucralfate versus cimetidine in the treatment of acute gastroduodenal ulcer. Randomized trial with 667 patients. Am J Med. 1989;86(Suppl. 6A):116–20.

91 **Schubert T.** Twice-daily sucralfate dosing to heal acute duodenal ulcer. Am J Med. 1989;86(Suppl. 6A):108–12.

92 **Bandstaetter G, Kratochvil P.** Comparison of two sucralfate dosages (2 gm twice a day versus 1 gm four times a day) in duodenal ulcer healing. Am J Med. 1985;79(Suppl. 2c):36–8.

93 **Van Deventer GM et al.** Sucralfate and cimetidine as single agents and in combination for treatment of active duodenal ulcers. Am J Med. 1985;(Suppl. 2C):39–44.

94 **Massoomi F et al.** Omeprazole: a comprehensive review. Pharmacother. 1993; 13(1):46–59.

95 **Londong W et al.** Dose-response study of omeprazole on meal-stimulated gastric acid secretion and gastrin release. Gastroenterology. 1983;85:1373–378.

96 **Graham DY et al.** Omeprazole versus placebo in duodenal ulcer healing: the United States experience. Dig Dis Sci. 1990;35:66–72.

97 **Walan A et al.** Effect of omeprazole and ranitidine on ulcer healing and relapse rates in patients with benign gastric ulcer. N Engl J Med. 1989;320(2):69–75.

98 **Glise H et al.** Two and four weeks treatment for duodenal ulcer. Scand J Gastroenterol. 1991;26:137–45.

99 **Mc Farland RJ et al.** Omeprazole provides quicker symptom relief and duodenal ulcer healing than ranitidine. Gastroenterology. 1990;98:278–81.

100 **Gustavsson S et al.** Rapid healing of duodenal ulcers with omeprazole: double blind dose comparative trial. Lancet. 1983;124.

101 **Hixson LJ et al.** Current trends in the pharmacotherapy for peptic ulcer disease. Arch Intern Med. 1992;152:726–32.

102 **Regårdh CG et al.** Pharmacokinetics and metabolism of omeprazole in animals and man—an overview. Scand J Gastroenterol. 1985;20(Suppl. 108):79–94.

103 **Maton PN.** Omeprazole. N Engl J Med. 1991;324:965–75.

104 **Naesdal J et al.** Pharmacokinetics of ^{14}C omeprazole in patients with impaired renal function. Clin Pharmacol Ther. 1986;40:344–51.

105 **Andersson T.** Omeprazole drug interaction studies. Clin Pharmacokinet. 1991; 21(3):195–211.

106 **Humphries TJ.** Clinical implications of drug interactions with the cytochrome P-450 enzyme system associated with omeprazole. Dig Dis Sci. 1991;36(12):1665–669.

107 **Bardham KD et al.** Treatment of refractory peptic ulcer with omeprazole or continued H$_2$-receptor antagonists: a controlled clinical trial. Gut. 1991;32:435–38.

108 **Collen MJ et al.** Refractory duodenal ulcers (nonhealing duodenal ulcers with standard doses of antisecretory medication). Dig Dis Sci. 1989;34(2):233–37.

109 **Bardhan KD.** Personal view. Treatment of duodenal ulceration: reflections, recollections and reminiscences. Gut. 1989:1647–655.

110 **Jones DB et al.** Acid suppression in duodenal ulcer: a meta-analysis to define optimal dosing with antisecretory drugs.

111 **Guerreiro AS et al.** Omeprazole in the treatment of peptic ulcers resistant to H$_2$-receptor antagonists. Aliment Pharmacol Ther. 1990;4:309–13.

112 **Van Deventer G et al.** A randomized study of maintenance therapy with ranitidine to prevent the recurrence of duodenal ulcer. N Engl J Med. 1989;320:1113–119.

113 **Sontag SJ.** Current status of maintenance therapy in peptic ulcer disease. Am J Gastroenterol. 1988;83:607–17.

114 **Thorat VK et al.** Conventional versus on-demand therapy for duodenal ulcer: results of a controlled therapeutic trial. Am J Gastroenterol. 1990;85:243–48.

115 **Berlin RG et al.** Nocturnal therapy with famotidine for 1 year is effective in preventing relapse of gastric ulcer. Aliment Pharmacol Therap. 1991;5(2):161–71.

116 **Penston JG, Wormsley KG.** Long-term maintenance treatment of gastric ulcers with ranitidine. Aliment Pharmacol Ther. 1990;4:339–55.

117 **Freston JW.** H$_2$-receptor antagonists and duodenal ulcer recurrence: analysis of efficacy and commentary on safety, costs, and patient selection. Am J Gastroenterol. 1987;82(12):1242–249.

118 **Lee FI et al.** Maintenance treatment of duodenal ulceration: ranitidine 300 mg at night is better than 150 mg in cigarette smokers. Gut. 1991;32:151–53.

119 **Takemoto T et al.** Efficacy of sucralfate in the prevention of recurrence of peptic ulcer—double blind multicenter study with cimetidine. Scand J Gastroenterol. 1987;22(Suppl. 140):49–60.

120 **Lam SK et al.** Sucralfate versus cimetidine in duodenal ulcer—factors affecting healing and relapse. Scand J Gastroenterol. 1987;22(Suppl. 140):61.

121 **McGrath PD et al.** Prophylaxis of duodenal ulcer (DU) recurrence with sucralfate (SCR). Clin Pharmacol Ther. 1985:ID. Abstract.

122 **Tovey FI et al.** Differences in mucosal appearances and in relapse rates in duodenal ulceration treated with sucralfate or cimetidine. Am J Med. 1989;86(Suppl. 6A):141–44.

123 **Marks IN et al.** A maintenance regimen of sucralfate 2 gm at night for reduced relapse rate in duodenal ulcer disease. A one-year follow-up study. Am J Med. 1989;86(Suppl. 6A):136–40.

124 **Paakkonen M et al.** Sucralfate as maintenance treatment for the prevention of duodenal ulcer recurrence. Am J Med. 1989;86(Suppl. 6A):133–35.

125 **Lamberts R et al.** Long-term omeprazole therapy in peptic ulcer disease: gastrin, endocrine cell growth, and gastritis. Gastroenterology. 1993;104:1356–370.

126 **Tytgat GN.** Colloidal bismuth subcitrate in peptic ulcer—a review. Digestion. 1987;37(Suppl. 2):31–41.

127 **Dunk AA et al.** The safety and efficacy of tripotassium dicitrato bismuthate (De-Nol) maintenance therapy in patients with duodenal ulceration. Aliment Pharmacol Ther. 1990;4:157–62.

127 **Bardhan KO et al.** Refractory esophagitis: results of maintenance treatment with high-dose H$_2$-receptor antagonists (H2RA) or omeprazole (OM). Gastroenterology. 1990;98:A18. Abstract.

129 **Eberhardt R, Kasper G.** Effect of oral bismuth subsalicylate on *campylobacter pylori* and on healing and relapse rate of peptic ulcer. Rev Infect Dis. 1990;12(Suppl. 1):S115–S.

130 **Warren JR.** Unidentified curved bacilli on gastric epithelium in active chronic gastritis. Lancet. 1983;1273–274.

131 **Marwick C.** Helicobacter: new name, new hypothesis involving type of gastric cancer. JAMA. 1990;254:2724–725.

132 **Blaser MJ.** Epidemiology and pathophysiology of *campylobacter pylori* infections. Rev Infect Dis. 1990;12(Suppl. 1):S99–S106.

133 **Drumm B et al.** Intrafamilial clustering of *helicobacter pylori* infection. N Engl J Med. 1990;322:359–63.

134 **Ateshkadi A et al.** *Helicobacter pylori* and peptic ulcer disease. Clin Pharm. 1993;12:34–48.

135 **McNulty CM.** Bismuth subsalicylate in the treatment of gastritis due to campylobacter pylori. Rev Infect Dis. 1990; 12(Suppl. 1):S94–S98.

136 **Valle J et al.** Disappearance of gastritis after eradication of *helicobacter pylori*. A morphometric study. Scand J Gastroenterol. 1991;26:1057–065.

137 **Marshall BJ et al.** Urea protects *Helicobacter (Campylobacter) pylori* from the bactericidal effect of acid. Gastroenterology. 1990;99:697–702.

138 **Rauws EAJ.** Role of *Helicobacter pylori* in duodenal ulcer. Drugs. 1992; 44(6):921–27.

139 **Dunn BE.** Pathogenic mechanisms of *helicobacter pylori*. Gastroenterol Clin North Am. 1993;22(1):43–57.

140 **Marshall BJ.** Peptic ulcer: an infectious disease? Hosp Pract. 1987;87–96.

141 **Marshall BJ.** *Campylobacter pylori*: its link to gastritis and peptic ulcer disease. Rev Infect Dis. 1990;12(Suppl. 1):S87–S93.

142 **Marshall BJ et al.** Prospective double-blind trial of duodenal ulcer relapse after eradication of *campylobacter pylori*. Lancet. 1988:1437–441.

143 **Marshall BJ et al.** Long term healing of gastritis and low duodenal ulcer relapse after eradication of *campylobacter pyloridis*: a prospective double-blind study. Gastroenterology. 1987; 92(5, pt.2):1518.

144 **Patchett S et al.** A prospective study of helicobacter pylori eradication in duodenal ulcer. Gastroenterology. 1990; 98:A104. Abstract.

145 **Rauws EAJ, Tytgat GNJ.** Eradication of *helicobacter pylori* cures duodenal ulcer. Gastroenterology. 1990:A111. Abstract.

146 **Borody T et al.** Long-term campylobacter pylori recurrence post-eradication. Med J Aust. 1987;146:450.

147 **Graham DY et al.** Effect of triple therapy (antibiotics plus bismuth) on duodenal ulcer healing. A randomized controlled trial. Ann Intern Med. 1991; 115:266–69.

148 **Reinbach DH et al.** Acute perforated duodenal ulcer is not associated with *helicobacter pylori* infection. Gut. 1993;34:1344–347.

149 **Moss S, Calam J.** *Helicobacter pylori* and peptic ulcers: the present position. Gut. 1992;55:289–92.

150 **Brown KE, Peura DA.** Diagnosis of *helicobacter pylori* infection. Gastroenterol Clin North Am. 1993;22: 105–15.

151 **Barthel JS, Everett ED.** Diagnosis of *Campylobacter pylori* infections: the "gold standard" and the alternatives. Rev Infect Dis. 1990;12(Suppl. 1): S107–14.

152 **Fedotin MS.** *Helicobacter pylori*-associated ulcer disease: current treatment options. Hosp Formul. 1993;28: 632–40.

153 **Partipilo ML, Woster PS.** The role of helicobacter pylori in peptic ulcer disease. Pharmacotherapy. 1993;13(4): 330–39.

154 **Veenendaal RA et al.** Long term serological surveillance after treatment of Helicobacter pylori infection. Gut. 1991;32:1291–294.

155 **Morris AJ et al.** Long-term follow-up of voluntary ingestion of Helicobacter pylori. Ann Int Med. 1991;114:662–63.

156 **Megraud F.** Epidemiology of Helicobacter pylori infection. Gastroenterol Clin North Am. 1993;22:73–87.

157 **Schrader JA et al.** A role for culture in diagnosis of Helicobacter pylori-related gastric disease. Am J Gastroenterol. 1993;88:1729–733.

158 **Graham D, Borsch G.** The who's and when's of therapy for helicobacter pylori. Am J Gastroenterol. 1990;85: 1552–555.

159 **Coghlan JG et al.** *Campylobacter pylori* and recurrence of duodenal ulcers—a 12-month follow-up study. Lancet. 1987;1109–111.

160 **Rauws EAJ, Tytgat GNJ.** Cure of duodenal ulcer associated with eradication of *helicobacter pylori*. Lancet. 1990:1233–235.

161 **McNulty CA et al.** Susceptibility of clinical isolates of campylobacter pyloridis to 11 antimicrobial agents. Antimicrob Agents Chemother. 1985;28: 837–38.

162 **O'Riordan T et al.** Adjuvant antibiotic therapy in duodenal ulcers treated with colloidal bismuth subcitrate. Gut. 1990; 31:999–1002.

163 **Glupczynski Y et al.** Campylobacter pylori-associated gastritis: a double-blind placebo-controlled trial with amoxicillin. Am J Gastroenterol. 1988; 83:365–72.

164 **Glupczynski Y, Burette A.** Drug therapy for Helicobacter pylori infection: problems and pitfalls. Am J Gastroenterol. 1990;85:1545–551.

165 **Weil J et al.** Helicobacter pylori infection treated with a tripotassium dicitrato bismuthate and metronidazole combination. Aliment Pharmacol Ther. 1990;4:651–57.

166 **Tytgat GNJ et al.** Helicobacter pylori infection and duodenal ulcer disease. Gastroenterol Clin North Am. 1993;22: 127–39.

167 **Graham DY et al.** Effect of treatment of *helicobacter pylori* infection on the long-term recurrence of gastric or duodenal ulcer. A randomized, controlled study. Ann Intern Med. 1992;116:705–08.

168 **Hentschel E et al.** Effect of ranitidine and amoxicillin plus metronidazole on the eradication of *helicobacter pylori* and the recurrence of duodenal ulcer. N Engl J Med. 1993;328:308–12.

169 **Marshall BJ.** Treatment strategies for Helicobacter pylori infection. Gastroenterol Clin North Am. 1993;22: 183–97.

170 **Iwahi T et al.** Lansoprazole, a novel benzimidazole proton pump inhibitor and its related compounds have selective activity against Helicobacter pylori. Antimicrob Agents Chemother. 1991;35:490–96.

171 **Keane C, Morain C.** Omeprazole and colloidal bismuth subcitrate +/- adjuvant antibiotics in the treatment of Helicobacter pylori associated duodenal ulcer disease. Gastroenterology. 1991;100:A48.

172 **Logan RPH et al.** The urease activity of H. pylori before, during and after treatment with omeprazole. Gastroenterology. 1990;100:A112.

173 **Biasco G, Miglioli M.** Omeprazole, Helicobacter pylori, gastritis and duodenal ulcer. Lancet. 1989:1403.

174 **Labenz J et al.** Amoxicillin plus omeprazole versus triple therapy for eradication of Helicobacter pylori in duodenal ulcer disease: a prospective, randomized, and controlled study. Gut. 1993;34:1167–170.

175 **Bayerdorffer E et al.** High dose omeprazole treatment combined with amoxicillin eradicates Helicobacter pylori. Gastroenterology. 1992;102:A38.

176 **Labenz J et al.** Medium- or high-dose omeprazole plus amoxicillin eradicates Helicobacter pylori in gastric ulcer disease. Am J Gastroenterol. 1994:89: 726–30.

177 **Unge P et al.** Omeprazole and amoxicillin in patients with duodenal ulcer: Helicobacter pylori eradication and remission of ulcers and symptoms during a 6 month follow-up. A double blind comparative study. Gastroenterology. 1992:A183.

178 **Weil J et al.** Eradication of campylobacter pylori: are we being misled? Lancet. 1988:1245.

179 **Sloane R, Cohen H.** Common-sense management of Helicobacter pylori-associated gastroduodenal disease. Gastroenterol Clin North Am. 1993;22: 199–206.

180 **Griffin MR et al.** Nonsteroidal anti-inflammatory drug use and death from peptic ulcer in elderly persons. Ann Intern Med. 1988;109:359–63.

181 **Silvos GR et al.** Incidence of gastric lesions in patients with rheumatic disease on chronic aspirin therapy. Ann Intern Med. 1979;91:517–20.

182 **Graham DY et al.** Prevention of NSAID-induced gastric ulcer with misoprostol multicentre, double-blind, placebo-controlled trial. Lancet. 1988: 1277–280.

183 **McCarthy DM.** Nonsteroidal anti-inflammatory drug-induced ulcers: management by traditional therapies. Gastroenterology. 1989;196:662–74.

184 **Soll AH et al.** Nonsteroidal anti-inflammatory drugs and peptic ulcer disease. Ann Intern Med. 1991;114:307–19.

185 **Schuber TT et al.** Ulcer risk factors: interactions between Helicobacter pylori infection, nonsteroidal use and age. Am J Med. 1993;94:413–18.

186 **Pounder R.** Silent peptic ulceration: deadly silence or golden silence? Gastroenterology. 1989;96:626–31.

187 **Mellem H et al.** Symptoms in patients with peptic ulcer and hematemesis and/or melena related to the use of non-steroid anti-inflammatory drugs. Scand J Gastroenterol. 1985;20:1246–248.

188 **Armstrong CP, Blower AL.** Non-steroidal anti-inflammatory drugs and life threatening complications of peptic ulceration. Gut. 1987;28:527–32.

189 **Soll AH et al.** Ulcers, nonsteroidal anti-inflammatory drugs, and related matters. Gastroenterology. 1989;96: 561–68.

190 **Kolts B, Achem S.** Gastrointestinal side effects of nonsteroidal anti-inflammatory drug use. Hosp Formul. 1992; 27:36–46.

191 **Graham DY.** Prevention of gastroduodenal injury induced by chronic nonsteroidal anti-inflammatory drug therapy. Gastroenterology. 1989;96: 675–81.

192 **Graham DY, Smith JL.** Aspirin & the stomach. Ann Intern Med. 1986;104: 390–98.

193 **Graham DY.** The relationship between nonsteroidal anti-inflammatory drug use and peptic ulcer disease. Gastroenterol Clin North Am. 1990;19: 171–83.

194 **Cryer B et al.** Comparison of salsalate and aspirin on mucosal injury and gastroduodenal mucosal prostaglandins. Gastroenterology. 1990;99:1616–621.

195 **Collier DJ, Pain JA.** Non-steroidal anti-inflammatory drugs and peptic ulcer perforation. Gut. 1985;26:359–63.

196 **Griffin MR et al.** Non-steroidal anti-inflammatory drug use and increased risk for peptic ulcer disease in elderly persons. Ann Intern Med. 1991;114: 257–63.

197 **Taha AS, Russell RI.** Helicobacter pylori and non-steroidal anti-inflammatory drugs: uncomfortable partners in peptic ulcer disease. Gut. 1993:34; 580–83.

198 **Ehsanullah RSB et al.** Prevention of gastroduodenal damage induced by non-steroidal anti-inflammatory drugs: controlled trial of ranitidine. Br Med J. 1988;297:1017–021.

199 **Piper JM et al.** Corticosteroid use and peptic ulcer disease: role of nonsteroidal anti-inflammatory drugs. Ann Intern Med. 1991;114:735–40.

200 **Bank S et al.** Efficacy of famotidine in the healing of active benign gastric ulceration: comparison of nonsteroidal anti-inflammatory or aspirin-induced gastric ulcer and idiopathic gastric ulceration. Clin Ther. 1993;15:36–45.

201 **O'Laughlin JC et al.** Resistance to medical therapy of gastric ulcers in rheumatic disease patients taking aspirin. Dig Dis Sci. 1982;27:975–80.

202 **Manniche E et al.** Randomized study of the influence of non-steroidal anti-inflammatory drugs on the treatment of peptic ulcer in patients with rheumatic disease. Gut. 1987;28:226–29.

203 **Caldwell JR et al.** Sucralfate treatment of nonsteroidal anti-inflammatory drug-induced gastrointestinal symptoms and mucosal damage. Am J Med. 1987;83 (Suppl. 3B):74–82.

204 **Walan A, Bader JP.** Effect of omeprazole and ranitidine on ulcer healing and relapse rates in patients with benign gastric ulcer. N Engl J Med. 1989; 320:69–75.

205 **Peterson WL.** Misoprostol prevents nonsteroidal anti-inflammatory drug-induced gastric ulcers—has Pandora's box been opened? Gastroenterology. 1989;97:1053–055.

206 **Feldman M.** Can gastroduodenal ulcers in NSAID users be prevented? Ann Intern Med. 1993;119:337–38.

207 **Ehsanullah RSB et al.** NSAID-induced gastroduodenal damage; effect of ranitidine prophylaxis. Gastroenterology. 1988;A111. Abstract.

208 **Robinson MG et al.** Effect of ranitidine gastroduodenal mucosal damage induced by nonsteroidal anti-inflam-

matory drugs. Dig Dis Sci. 1989;14: 424–28.

209 **Lanza F et al.** A multi-center double-blind comparison of ranitidine vs placebo in the prophylaxis of nonsteroidal anti-inflammatory drug (NSAID)-induced lesions in gastric and duodenal mucosae. Gastroenterology. 1988;94: A250.

210 **Levine LR et al.** Nizatidine prevents peptic ulceration in high-risk patients taking nonsteroidal anti-inflammatory drugs. Arch Intern Med. 1993;153: 2449–454.

211 **Graham DY et al.** Duodenal and gastric ulcer prevention with misoprostol in arthritis patients taking NSAIDs. Ann Intern Med. 1993;119:257–62.

212 **Agrawal M et al.** Misoprostol compared with sucralfate in the prevention of nonsteroidal anti-inflammatory drug-induced gastric ulcer. Ann Intern Med. 1991;115:195–200.

213 **Lanza F et al.** Blinded endoscopic comparative study of misoprostol versus sucralfate and placebo in the prevention of aspirin-induced gastric and duodenal ulceration. Am J Gastroenterol. 1988;83:143–46.

214 **Herting RL, Nissen CH.** Overview of misoprostol clinical experience. Dig Dis Sci. 1986;31(Suppl. 2):47S–54S.

215 **Jones JB, Bailey RT.** Misoprostol: a prostaglandin E analog with antisecretory and cytoprotective properties. DICP. 1989;23:276–82.

216 **Raskin JB et al.** Efficacy and safety of misoprostol in the prevention of NSAID-induced gastric ulcers—preliminary findings. Gastroenterology. 1993:A177.

217 **Fishbeyn VA et al.** Assessment and prediction of long-term cure in patients with the Zollinger-Ellison syndrome: the best approach. Ann Intern Med. 1993;119:199–206.

218 **Vinayek R et al.** Zollinger-Ellison syndrome. Gastroenterol Clin North Am. 1990;19:197–206.

219 **Heyworth MF.** Pathophysiology of the small intestine. In: Smith LH, Thier SO, eds. Pathophysiology. Philadelphia: WB Saunders; 1985:1168.

220 **Jensen RT.** Zollinger-Ellison syndrome: current concepts and management. Ann Intern Med. 1983;98:59–75.

221 **Wolfe MM, Jensen RT.** Zollinger-Ellison syndrome. N Engl J Med. 1987; 317:1200–209.

222 **McGuigan JE, Wolfe MM.** Secretin injection test in the diagnosis of gastrinima. Gastroenterology. 1980;79:1324–331.

223 **Raufman JP, Collins SM.** Reliability of symptoms in assessing control of gastric acid secretion in patients with Zollinger-Ellison syndrome. Gastroenterology. 1983;84:108–13.

224 **Jensen RT.** Basis for failure of cimetidine in patients with Zollinger-Ellison syndrome. Dig Dis Sci. 1198;29:363–66.

225 **Vinayek R et al.** Famotidine in the therapy of gastric hypersecretory states. Am J Med. 1986;81(Suppl. 4B):49–59.

226 **Collen MJ et al.** Comparison of ranitidine and cimetidine in the treatment of gastric hypersecretion. Ann Intern Med. 1984;100:52–8.

227 **Delchier JC et al.** Effectiveness of omeprazole in seven patients with Zollinger-Ellison syndrome resistant to histamine H$_2$-receptor antagonists. Dig Dis Sci. 1986;31:693–99.

228 **Maton PN et al.** Long-term efficacy and safety of omeprazole in patients with Zollinger-Ellison syndrome: a prospective study. Gastroenterology. 1989;97:827–36.

229 **McArthur KE et al.** Omeprazole: effective, convenient therapy for Zollinger-Ellison syndrome. Gastroenterology. 1985;88:939–44.

230 **Maton P et al.** Long-term efficacy and safety of omeprazole in patients with Zollinger-Ellison syndrome. Gastroenterology. 1986;90:1537. Abstract.

231 **Frucht H, Maton PN.** Use of omeprazole in patients with Zollinger-Ellison syndrome. Dig Dis Sci. 1991;36:394–404.

232 **Maton PN et al.** The effect of Zollinger-Ellison syndrome and omeprazole therapy on gastric oxyntic endocrine cells. Gastroenterology. 1990;99:943–56.

233 **Bonfils S et al.** Prolonged treatment of Zollinger-Ellison syndrome by long-acting somatostatin. Lancet. 1986:554–55.

234 **McLean W, Ariano R.** Omeprazole nasogastric administration (Drug Consult). In: Gelman CR, Rumack BH, eds. Drugdex (R) Information System. Denver: Micromedex, Inc.; 1994 Jan.

235 **Vinayek R et al.** Intravenous omeprazole in patients with Zollinger-Ellison syndrome undergoing surgery. Gastroenterology. 1990;99:10–8.

236 **Saeed ZA et al.** Parenteral antisecretory drug therapy in patients with Zollinger-Ellison syndrome. Gastroenterology. 1989;96:1393–402.

237 **Welage LS.** Gastroesophageal reflux. In: DiPiro JT et al., eds. Pharmacotherapy: A Pathophysiologic Approach. New York: Elsevier; 1992:495.

238 **Richter JE, Casterll DO.** Gastroesophageal reflux. Ann Intern Med. 1982;97:93–103.

239 **Dodds WJ et al.** Mechanisms of gastroesophageal reflux in patients with reflux esophagitis. N Eng J Med. 1982; 307:1547–552.

240 **Gelfand MD.** Gastroesophageal reflux disease. Med Clin North Am. 1991;75: 923–40.

241 **Bozymski EM.** Pathophysiology and diagnosis of gastroesophageal reflux disease. Am J Hosp Pharm. 1993;50 (Suppl.):S4–6.

242 **Schentag JJ, Goss TF.** Pharmacokinetics and pharmacodynamics of acid-suppressive agents in patients with gastroesophageal reflux disease. Am J Hosp Pharm. 1993;50(Suppl. 1):S7–10.

243 **Garnett WR.** Efficacy, safety and cost issues in managing patients with gastroesophageal reflux disease. Am J Hosp Pharm. 1993;50(Suppl. 1):S11–8.

244 **Kozarek RA.** Complications of reflux esophagitis and their medical management. Gastroenterol Clin North Am. 1990;19:713–22.

245 **Kahrilas PJ, Gupta RR.** Mechanisms of acid reflux associated with cigarette smoking. Gut. 1990;31:4–10.

246 **Kitchin LI, Castel DO.** Rationale and efficacy of conservative therapy for gastroesophageal reflux disease. Arch

Intern Med. 1991;151:448–54.

247 **Sontag SJ.** The medical management of reflux esophagitis. Gastroenterol Clin North Am. 1990;19:683–712.

248 **Johnson NJ et al.** Acute treatment of reflux oesophagitis: a multicenter trial to compare 150 mg ranitidine BD with 300 mg ranitidine QDS. Aliment Pharmacol Ther. 1989;3:259–66.

249 **Quik RF et al.** A comparison of two doses of nizatidine versus placebo in the treatment of reflux oesophagitis. Aliment Pharmacol Ther. 1990;4:201–11.

250 **Koelz HR et al.** Healing and relapse of reflux esophagitis during treatment with ranitidine. Gastroenterology. 1986; 91:1198–205.

251 **Tytgaat GNJ et al.** Efficacy of different doses of cimetidine in the treatment of reflux esophagitis. Gastroenterology. 1990;99:629–34.

252 **Hetzel DJ et al.** Healing and relapse of severe peptic esophagitis after treatment with omeprazole. Gastroenterology. 1988;95:903–12.

253 **Sandmark S et al.** Omeprazole or ranitidine in the treatment of reflux esophagitis. Scand J Gastroenterol. 1988;23:625–32.

254 **Klinkenberg-Knol EC et al.** Double-blind multicentre comparison of omeprazole and ranitidine in the treatment of reflux oesophagitis. Lancet. 1987; 349–51.

255 **Dent J et al.** Omeprazole in the long-term management of patients with reflux oesophagitis refractory to histamine H$_2$-receptor antagonists. Scand J Gastroenterol. 1989;24(Suppl. 66):Abstract 176.

256 **Sontag S et al.** Omeprazole for esophagitis and ulcer refractory to H$_2$-blockers. Gastroenterology. 1989;94:A436.

257 **AHFS drug information 1993.** McEvoy GK, ed. Miscellaneous. Bethesda, MD: American Society of Hospital Pharmacists; 1993.

258 **Gilbert RJ et al.** Effect of cisapride, a new prokinetic agent, on esophageal motor function. Dig Dis Sci. 1987;32: 1331–336.

259 **Janssen Pharmaceuticals.** Cisapride drug monograph.

260 **Ros J et al.** Healing of erosive esophagitis with sucralfate and cimetidine: influence of pretreatment lower esophageal sphincter pressure and serum pepsingoen I levels. Am J Med. 1991; 91(Suppl. 2A):2A-107S–113S.

261 **Bremner G et al.** Reflux esophagitis therapy: sucralfate versus ranitidine in a double blind multicenter trial. Am J Med. 1991;91(Suppl. 2A):2A-119–122S.

262 **Peura DA.** Recognizing, setting therapeutic goals, and selecting therapy for the prevention and treatment of stress-related mucosal damage. Pharmacotherapy. 1987;7(6 Pt. 2):95S–103S.

263 **Levine BA.** Pathophysiology and mechanisms of stress ulcer injury. Pharmacotherapy. 1987;7(6 Pt. 2): 90S–94S.

264 **Shuman RB et al.** Prophylactic therapy for stress ulcer bleeding: a reappraisal. Ann Intern Med. 1987;106: 562–67.

265 **Pilchman J et al.** Cytoprotection and stress ulceration. Med Clin North Amer. 1991;75:853–63.

266 **Schulster DP et al.** Prospective evaluation of the risk of upper gastrointestinal bleeding after admission to a medical intensive care unit. Am J Med. 1984;76:623–29.

267 **Miller TA.** Mechanisms of stress-related mucosal damage. Am J Med. 1987;85(Suppl. 6A):8–14.

268 **Kleinman RL et al.** Stress ulcers: current understanding of pathogenesis and prophylaxis. Drug Intell Clin Pharm. 1988;22:452–60.

269 **Priebe HJ et al.** Antacid versus cimetidine in preventing acute gastrointestinal bleeding. N Engl J Med. 1980; 302:426–30.

270 **Lamothe HP et al.** Comparative efficacy of cimetidine, famotidine, ranitidine, and mylanta in postoperative stress ulcers. Gastroenterology. 1991; 100:1515–520.

271 **Schentag JJ et al.** Safety and acid-suppressant properties of histamine$_2$-receptor antagonists for the prevention of stress-related mucosal damage in critical care patients. DICP. 1989;23:S36–9.

272 **Frank W et al.** Comparison between continuous and intermittent infusion regimens of cimetidine in ulcer patients. Clin Pharmacol Ther. 1989;46: 234–39.

273 **Ballesteros MA et al.** Bolus or intravenous infusion of ranitidine: effects on gastric pH and acid secretion. Ann Intern Med. 1990;112:334–39.

274 **Siepler JK et al.** Use of continuous infusion of histamine$_2$-receptor antagonists in critically ill patients. DICP. 1989;23:S40–3.

275 **Ostro MJ et al.** Control of gastric pH with cimetidine: boluses versus primed infusions. Gastroenterology. 1985;89: 532–37.

276 **Driks MR et al.** Nosocomial pneumonia in intubated patients given sucralfate as compared with antacids or histamine type 2 blockers. N Engl J Med. 1987;317:1367–382.

277 **Tryba M.** Risk of acute stress bleeding and nosocomial pneumonia in ventilated intensive care unit patients: sucralfate versus antacids. Am J Med. 1987;83(Suppl. 3B):117–24.

278 **Bresalier RS et al.** Sucralfate suspension versus titrated antacid for the prevention of acute stress-related gastrointestinal hemorrhage in critically ill patients. Am J Med. 1987;83(Suppl. 3B):110–15.

279 **VanDeventer GM et al.** Sucralfate and cimetidine as single agents and in combination for treatment of active duodenal ulcers. Am J Med. 1985;79 (Suppl. 2C):39–44.

280 **NIH Consensus Development Panel on Helicobacter pylori in Peptic Ulcer Disease.** Helicobacter pylori in peptic ulcer disease. JAMA. 1994;272: 65–9.

281 **Fennerty MB.** Helicobacter pylori. Arch Intern Med. 1994;154:721–27.

282 **Hollander D.** Gastrointestinal complications of nonsteroidal anti-inflammatory drugs: prophylactic and therapeutic strategies. Am J Med. 1994;96: 274–81.

283 **Jensen RT, Fraker DL.** Zollinger-Ellison syndrome. JAMA. 1994;271: 1429–435.

284 **Cook DG et al.** Risk factors for gas-

trointestinal bleeding in critically ill patients. N Engl J Med. 1994;330:377–81.

285 **Prod'hom G et al.** Nosocomial pneumonia in mechanically ventilated patients receiving antacid, ranitidine or sucralfate as prophylaxis for stress ulcers. Ann Intern Med. 1994;120:653–62.

286 **Cook DJ et al.** Nosocomial pneumonia and the role of gastric pH. Chest. 1991:100(1):7–13.

287 **Tryba M.** Sucralfate versus antacids or H₂-antagonists for stress ulcer prophylaxis: a meta-analysis on efficacy and pneumonia rate. Crit Care Med. 1991;19:942–49.

288 **Blum AL et al.** Sucralfate in the treatment and prevention of gastric ulcer; multicentre double-blind placebo controlled study. Gut. 1990;31:825–30.

Inflammatory Bowel Disease

George E Dukes, Jr
Babette S Duncan

Ulcerative Colitis 24-1
  Pathophysiology and Clinical Presentation 24-1
  Remission Induction 24-3
    Corticosteroids 24-3
      Administration 24-3
        Parenteral 24-3
          Choice of agent and dosing 24-3
        Oral 24-3
        Topical 24-4
        Adverse effects 24-4
    Sulfasalazine 24-3
  Remission Maintenance 24-4
    Sulfasalazine 24-4
      Pharmacokinetics 24-5
      Mechanism of action 24-5
      Adverse effects (see Table 24.4) 24-5
      Teratogenicity 24-7
      Drug interactions 24-7
    Other agents 24-7
      Mesalamine 24-6
      Immunosuppressive agents 24-7
      Cromolyn sodium 24-8
      Cyclosporine 24-8
  Toxic Megacolon 24-8
    Signs and symptoms 24-8
    Predisposing factors 24-8

    Medical management 24-8
    Surgical intervention 24-9
  Surgical Management 24-9
    General considerations 24-9
    Indications 24-9
Crohn's Disease 24-9
  Pathophysiology and Clinical Presentation 24-9
  Remission Induction 24-10
    Corticosteroids 24-10
    Sulfasalazine 24-10
  Remission Maintenance 24-10
    Corticosteroids 24-10
    Sulfasalazine 24-11
  Chronic Symptomatic Crohn's Disease 24-11
    Corticosteroids 24-11
    Azathioprine 24-11
  Other Agents 24-11
    5-aminosalicylic acid derivatives 24-11
    Immunosuppressive agents 24-11
    Cyclosporine 24-11
    Metronidazole 24-12
    Immunomodulating agents 24-12
    Other agents 24-12
  Surgical Management 24-12
    General considerations and indications 24-12

Inflammatory bowel disease is a generic classification for a group of nonspecific, idiopathic inflammatory disorders of the gastrointestinal (GI) tract. By convention, inflammatory bowel disease is divided into two major disorders: ulcerative colitis and Crohn's disease (granulomatous enteritis). Both ulcerative colitis and Crohn's disease frequently affect a similar group of patients (see Table 24.1), run a course characterized by exacerbations and remissions, tend to be chronic in nature, have similar extra-intestinal manifestations (see Table 24.2), and may be associated with a positive family history of inflammatory bowel disease.[1,2] While there are many similarities in the natural history and clinical features of these diseases, they differ significantly in their pathophysiology, anatomic distribution, and clinical course (see Table 24.3).[1,3,4]

When considering inflammatory bowel disease therapy, one must appreciate that the etiology of the disease is unknown and, therefore, precludes definitive therapy. Additionally, specific therapy will depend upon the anatomical location of the disease. The major therapeutic goals should be to: induce remission, prevent relapse, and symptomatically control the clinical manifestations of the disease and its intestinal and extra-intestinal complications.

Ulcerative Colitis

Pathophysiology and Clinical Presentation

1. C.M., a 25-year-old female college student, has had episodic watery diarrhea and colicky abdominal pain relieved by defecation for the past 9 months. Eight weeks before admission, the diarrhea increased to 3–5 semi-formed stools daily. The frequency of the stools gradually increased to 5–10 times a day 1 week ago. At that time, C.M. noted bright red blood in the stools. Stool frequency has now increased to 10–15/day, although the volume of each stool is estimated to be only "one-half cupful." She feels a great urgency to defecate even though the volume is small. She has not traveled outside the U.S., has not been camping, and has not taken any antibiotics within the last 6 months.

C.M. complains of anorexia and a 10-pound weight loss over the past 2 months. For the past 4 months she has had intermittent swelling, warmth, and tenderness of the left knee which is unassociated with trauma. She denies any skin rashes or any difficulties with her vision. A review of other body systems and social and family history were noncontributory.

She appears to be a slightly anxious and tired young female of normal body habitus. Her temperature is 101 °F and her pulse rate is 100 beats/min and regular. Physical examination

Table 24.1	Population Characteristics of Patients at High Risk for Developing Inflammatory Bowel Disease[3–5]
No sexual predilection	
Second to fourth decades of life	
Ethnic predilection for European stock	
Urban greater than rural dwellers	
Whites greater than nonwhites	
Jews living in Europe and North America greater than non-Jews	
Occurs in familial clusters	

Table 24.2	Extraintestinal Complications of Ulcerative Colitis and Crohn's Disease[a,1,3,6,7]	
Manifestation	Ulcerative Colitis (%)	Crohn's Disease (%)
Arthritis/arthralgia	25	33
Erythema nodosum/pyoderma gangrenosum	4	5
Abnormal LFTs	50	30
Iritis/uveitis	5	4
Ankylosing spondylitis	15	10
Growth retardation	18	13

[a] LFTs = Liver function tests.

is normal except for evidence of acute arthritis of the left knee and tenderness of the left lower abdomen to palpation.

Stool examination shows a watery effluent that contains numerous red and white cells with no trophozoite. Stool cultures and an amebiasis indirect hemagglutination test are negative. Her hematocrit (Hct) is 26% with a hemoglobin (Hgb) of 8.5 gm/dL; the white blood cell (WBC) count is 15,000/mm³ with 82% PMNs; the erythrocyte sedimentation rate (ESR) is 70 mm/hr (Normal: <20); serum albumin is 2.4 gm/dL (Normal: 3.5–5.0). Other pertinent laboratory values include an alkaline phosphatase of 210 U/L (Normal: 30–110), an alanine aminotransferase (ALT) of 35 (Normal: 8–20), a serum sodium (Na) of 130 mEq/L (Normal: 135–147) and a serum potassium (K) of 3.1 mEq/L (Normal: 3.5–5.0).

Sigmoidoscopy showed evidence of granular, edematous, and friable mucosa with continuous ulcerations extending from the anus to 20 cm proximally. A barium enema shows confluent disease extending from the rectum to transverse colon. What is the most likely cause of C.M.'s diarrheal illness? What special considerations may be required for treatment of the signs and symptoms caused by this disease? [SI units: Hct 0.26; Hgb 85 gm/L; WBC count 15 × 10⁹/L; ESR 70 mm/hr (Normal: <20); albumin 24 gm/L (Normal: 35–50); alkaline phosphatase 210 U/L (Normal: 30–110); ALT 0.58 μkat/L (Normal: 0.13–0.33); Na 130 mmol/L (Normal: 135–147); K 3.1 mmol/L (Normal: 3.5–5.0)]

C.M's presentation is typical of a patient with new onset ulcerative colitis. Drug-induced (pseudomembranous colitis) and infectious (parasitic) causes of diarrhea have been ruled out by history (no travel out of the U.S., no recent camping, no antibiotic use) and stool examination. Differentiation from Crohn's disease is made by sigmoidoscopic and radiologic evidence of continuous distribution of pathology (as opposed to segmental), as well as anatomic location (confined to colon and rectum).

Ulcerative colitis is an inflammation of the mucosal layer of the colon and rectum.[3] Characteristically, the inflammation does not extend beyond the submucosa, and transmural ulcers are rare. Upon examination, the mucosa appears erythematous and is very friable. C.M. presents with the classical triad of ulcerative colitis clinical symptoms: chronic diarrhea, rectal bleeding, and abdominal pain. The diarrhea is secondary to the decreased colonic absorption of water and electrolytes and diminished colonic segmental contractions which normally serve to decrease bowel content flow. A good indication of the severity of the patient's disease is the volume of stool passed per day.[3] As the severity of the disease increases, incontinence and nocturnal diarrhea commonly occur. Diarrhea can vary in severity from three to four bowel movements daily to one to two bowel movements per hour. The stools are usually soft, mushy, formed and often contain small amounts of mucus mixed with blood, although in patients with mild, early involvement disease, blood and mucus may be totally absent.[23] In addition to the diarrhea, the malabsorption of water and electrolytes will cause dehydration, weight loss (as observed in C.M.), and electrolyte disturbances.

Treatment of the diarrhea associated with ulcerative colitis often is difficult. In patients with mild to moderate disease, antidiarrheals, such as loperamide or diphenoxylate with atropine may be helpful in minimizing chronic diarrhea. Extreme caution must be employed, however, especially in patients with severe disease due to the chance of developing toxic megacolon. For this reason, antidiarrheals are best avoided in patients with severe disease and if used, should be titrated according to the volume of stool produced. Bulk-forming agents, such as psyllium, may be helpful in patients suffering from constipation resulting from ulcerative proctitis.[314]

C.M.'s rectal bleeding is secondary to colonic mucosal erosions and occurs in most patients with ulcerative colitis.[1] Generally, bright red blood mixed in the stools indicates a colonic origin, whereas blood streaking of the stools indicates an anal or rectal origin. The anemia associated with ulcerative colitis generally is secondary to this rectal bleeding. It presents as a hemorrhagic or iron deficiency anemia depending upon the acuteness of the bleeding. Hemoglobin and hematocrit laboratory values often are decreased as in C.M's case. Iron deficiency anemias often are treated with oral iron therapy with success. If oral iron therapy is intolerable, parenteral therapy may be an option. Close monitoring of the hemoglobin and hematocrit is very important. C.M.'s hypoalbuminemia also is exacerbated by chronic colonic bleeding.[3]

C.M.'s abdominal pain and cramping are caused by spasm of the irritated and inflamed colon. This abdominal pain commonly is associated with urgency to defecate (tenesmus). As illustrated by C.M., the pain usually is relieved with defecation even though the stool volume may be small.

C.M.'s other signs and symptoms demonstrate that ulcerative colitis is a systemic disease and not just a disease of the gastrointestinal tract. Her nonspecific symptoms (i.e., anorexia, fatigue, weight loss, anxiety, and tachycardia) may become profound in

Table 24.3	Pathophysiologic Differences Between Ulcerative Colitis and Crohn's Disease[1,3,4]	
Characteristic	Ulcerative Colitis	Crohn's Disease
Incidence (per year)	6.4/100,000	5.5/100,000
Anatomical location	Colon and rectum	Mouth to anus
Distribution	Continuous, diffuse, mucosal	Segmental, focal, transmural, rigid, thick, edematous and fibrotic
Bowel wall	Shortened, loss of haustral markings, generally not thickened	—
Gross rectal bleeding	Common	Infrequent
Crypt abscesses	Common	Infrequent
Fissuring with sinus formation	Absent	Common
Noncaseating granulomas	Absent	Common
Strictures	Absent	Common
Abdominal mass	Absent	Common
Abdominal pain	Infrequent	Common
Toxic megacolon	Occasional	Rare
Bowel carcinoma	Greatly ↑	Slightly ↑

severe ulcerative colitis.[3] The arthritis and elevated liver enzymes (alkaline phosphatase and ALT) in C.M. are indicative of the extra-intestinal manifestations that occur in ulcerative colitis (see Table 24.2).[7] The fever, leukocytosis, and increased ESR are also systemic manifestations of an inflammatory disease. C.M.'s low sodium and potassium laboratory values also need to be addressed. Rehydration is important to assure fluid balance and good renal functioning. Oral potassium supplementation may be warranted in patients who have a decreased potassium level until electrolyte balance is restored. It is also important that patients maintain a well-balanced diet rich in vitamins and minerals. Close monitoring of all electrolytes should be performed frequently to decrease the risk of further complications.

Remission Induction

Corticosteroids

2. What agents can be used to induce disease remission in C.M.? What evidence is there to support your choice?

Corticosteroids are accepted widely as the most effective agents for the induction of remission of acute, severe exacerbations of ulcerative colitis.[8-11] This beneficial effect of corticosteroids was first demonstrated by Truelove and Witts in 1955.[12] In this comparative trial of cortisone and placebo, the cortisone was more effective than placebo in the induction of disease remission in all patients, but the response rate decreased with increasing severity of the disease and was greater among patients with a first attack of the disease. Subsequent controlled trials with prednisone,[13-16] prednisolone,[17,18] and hydrocortisone[13,18-22] have confirmed the beneficial effects of corticosteroid in inducing remissions in patients with this disease.

Even though corticosteroids are effective inducers of disease remission in patients with acute ulcerative colitis, they probably do not alter the underlying disease process.[10] Their beneficial effect is thought to be exerted through their nonspecific anti-inflammatory properties and is not aimed at eliminating the cause of the inflammation.

Sulfasalazine

Sulfasalazine (Azulfidine), the most frequently prescribed drug for inflammatory bowel disease therapy, has been used commonly for 50 years for the induction of disease remission in patients with mild acute exacerbations of ulcerative colitis. Initial uncontrolled observations of its efficacy indicated that 80% to 90% of patients improved with the use of this agent. The first placebo-controlled trial using objective parameters of efficacy demonstrated that 80% of the treated group improved as compared to 35% receiving placebo.[24] These data were confirmed subsequently, although improvement may not occur until after four weeks of therapy.[25] Sulfasalazine, 250 to 500 mg four times a day, often is considered the drug of choice in ulcerative colitis exacerbation due to its demonstrated efficacy and because it has less severe adverse effects than corticosteroids.[26] However, controlled trials have shown that corticosteroids may be more prompt in onset of action than sulfasalazine, alone or in combination with corticosteroid, for the treatment of severe acute ulcerative colitis. While comparative efficacy trials are lacking, the combination of sulfasalazine and prednisone does not appear to be detrimental and often has been used in combination with hopes of alleviating the patient's symptoms.[8,9,26]

3. Corticosteroid Administration. Corticosteroids are available for administration by various routes: parenteral, topical, and oral. Which route of administration should be used for C.M.'s corticosteroid therapy?

Parenteral corticosteroids and hospitalization are mandatory for patients with severe acute ulcerative colitis, such as C.M., to prevent its potentially dangerous progression.[3] The absorption and efficacy of oral corticosteroids are decreased in this type of patient.[28] Truelove and Jewell[29] defined the patient population requiring parenteral corticosteroid as those having greater than six bloody stools a day, fever greater than 99.5 °F, heart rate greater than 90 beats/minute, anemia, increased erythrocyte sedimentation rate, and abdominal tenderness. C.M. meets these criteria and should receive corticosteroid by this route.

4. *Choice of Agent and Dosing.* **What is the corticosteroid of choice for C.M.? What is the appropriate dose?**

The question of which corticosteroid is best used parenterally in ulcerative colitis has been addressed extensively. Adrenal corticotropin hormone (ACTH), which stimulates the endogenous release of corticosteroids, was advocated as the parenteral agent of choice for this disease in the past.[10] Two controlled trials comparing the efficacy of ACTH to parenteral hydrocortisone have demonstrated no overall advantage of either agent; however, hydrocortisone was superior in patients previously treated with corticosteroids.[30,31] One comparison of the two drugs indicated that ACTH was slightly superior to hydrocortisone in patients previously untreated, but was less effective in patients who had received corticosteroids before the study.[32] Because ACTH requires normal adrenal function for its effect to occur, it is a less reliable form of therapy.[33] Since both ACTH-released adrenal corticosteroid and hydrocortisone have significant mineralocorticoid effects, they may exacerbate the electrolyte imbalances already induced by ulcerative colitis. Therefore, a synthetic corticosteroid with high anti-inflammatory and low mineralocorticoid properties, such as prednisone or methylprednisolone, would be the preferred agent in this situation.[8,10]

The goal of parenteral corticosteroid therapy for C.M. should be to achieve a rapid therapeutic response as measured by decreased frequency of stools, decreased pain, and decreased fever and heart rate. This goal may be attained with a high initial dose followed by a gradual dosage reduction to minimize development of corticosteroid adverse reactions. The initial dose, as well as the rate of a subsequent dosage reduction, should be individualized based upon the severity of the patient's signs, symptoms, and disease course. Up to 75% of patients with severe ulcerative colitis will respond to corticosteroid doses equivalent to 160 mg prednisone daily (divided into two to four doses/day); the majority respond to 60 to 80 mg prednisone or its equivalent per day.[16] If the patient does not respond within 72 hours of starting high-dose corticosteroids, surgery may be indicated (see Question 19).[8] Once C.M.'s symptoms are controlled, the goal should be to switch to oral steroids and discharge her from the hospital.

5. When is the oral route of corticosteroid administration indicated in ulcerative colitis? What are the most appropriate dosages?

Oral corticosteroids are effective for the initial treatment of mild to moderate acute ulcerative colitis.[12,13] Additionally, they should be substituted for parenteral corticosteroids once a satisfactory initial response has been achieved.[9,11] As with parenteral corticosteroids, the dose should be individualized to the patient's disease course and symptomatology. In one controlled trial, 40 mg of prednisone daily was significantly more efficacious than 20 mg/day in controlling ambulatory patients with moderately severe acute ulcerative colitis.[14] Prednisone doses of 60 mg/day had no additional therapeutic value but did cause more side effects. Additionally, a single 40 mg morning dose of prednisone was as effective and more convenient than an equivalent divided dose (10 mg QID).[15] Furthermore, this dosage schedule is less toxic, and less likely to cause adrenal suppression.[15,34] Therefore, the initial dose of corticosteroid for a patient with moderately severe acute ulcerative colitis is 40 mg of prednisone or its equivalent administered once daily in the morning.

Oral corticosteroids should induce remission within two to four weeks, at which time an attempt should be made to gradually withdraw the drug.[11,14] The total corticosteroid treatment course should last only four to eight weeks.[9] If remission does not occur, the patient may require parenteral corticosteroids and hospitalization.

6. When are topical corticosteroids indicated in the management of acute ulcerative colitis? How do they exert their beneficial effect? What are the limitations for use of each topical corticosteroid dosage form in the treatment of this disease?

Topical. Topically administered corticosteroids, in the form of suppositories, foams, and retention enemas, are effective in the management of acute, mild ulcerative colitis which is limited to the distal colon and rectum.[13,17–22,36,37,40] In order to justify the use of such a difficult and socially unacceptable route of administration, a clear-cut advantage of either increased efficacy or decreased side effects over other administration routes for these agents must be demonstrated.

Theoretically, corticosteroids administered via this topical route would provide a higher concentration of drug to the diseased mucosal area, exerting a local anti-inflammatory effect while averting systemic side effects. Unfortunately, variable, but significant, systemic absorption (up to 90%) and adrenal suppression occurs from the topical administration of corticosteroid to the rectum and distal colon.[21,22,41–44] Therefore, the beneficial effects produced by topical use of these agents may accrue from systemic as well as local effects. The apparent and relatively low incidence of corticosteroid side effects associated with topical administration may be due to the low doses used and to the infrequent administration (QD to BID) needed to control mild acute ulcerative colitis. When prednisolone is given in equivalent doses orally and rectally, the incidence of side effects and therapeutic effects are similar.[9]

If corticosteroids are to be used topically for the management of mild, acute ulcerative colitis, the corticosteroid of choice would be the one with the lowest absorptive characteristics.[41] Unfortunately, there are no comparative trials of the absorption characteristics of all corticosteroids available for administration by this route. The evidence available indicates that, of the hydrocortisone salts, the acetate is the least absorbed.[21] Prednisolone metasulphobenzoate is as effective as the phosphate ester, but produces significantly lower prednisolone serum concentrations.[45,46] Betamethasone valerate causes less adrenal suppression than therapeutically equivalent doses of prednisolone-21-phosphate.[40] Additionally, rectally administered beclomethasone dipropionate appears to be equally effective as betamethasone for distal colitis while exhibiting less adrenal suppression and fewer systemic side effects.[47] Other investigational topical corticosteroids that may have fewer systemic effects include budesonide, tixocortol, and fluticasone propionate.[9,252]

Since corticosteroid topical therapy of ulcerative colitis depends in theory on drug contact with the affected mucosa, the anatomical location of the disease and the distribution characteristics of the dosage form must be considered in the selection of the proper dosage form. For instance, if the disease is limited to the distal portion of the rectum (proctitis), corticosteroid suppositories, which have a very limited area of distribution are more effective than placebo suppositories, should be used.[17] A dose of two suppositories daily for four to six weeks generally is sufficient to induce disease remission in patients with mild acute proctitis.[8]

Retention enemas of corticosteroids which will allow distribution of the drug to a much greater colonic area than the suppository dosage form can be used in patients with more extensive disease. Retention enemas can distribute corticosteroids proximal to the hepatic flexure,[48] although the extent of drug distribution varies among patients.[49] The enema volume can be individualized to the extent of the patient's disease by adding barium to the estimated enema volume needed and following its distribution by x-ray.[49]

Corticosteroid retention enemas are best used at bedtime when the patient is inactive and better able to retain the medication for a prolonged period of time.[8] Ideally, the enema should be instilled as a bolus, with the patient in the supine position. The patient should alternate positions every 30 minutes, for four periods, from supine to left decubitus to right decubitus to prone to promote maximal topical coverage.[9] If the patient cannot retain the initial volume, the rate of administration should be decreased and slowly dripped in over 20 to 30 minutes.[9] Alternatively, a foam preparation has been advocated as a dosage form that is easier for patients to retain, although the extent to which the foam distributes proximally is unknown.[36,37,50] If the patient cannot retain the enema, despite these measures, an alternate route of corticosteroid administration will have to be used.

7. *Adverse Effects.* **What particular corticosteroid adverse effects are of importance in patients with ulcerative colitis specifically, and inflammatory bowel disease in general?**

Corticosteroid side effects and precautions for use often limit the therapeutic effectiveness of these agents and should never be overlooked.[51] (See Chapters 41: Rheumatic Disorders and 42: Connective Tissue Disorders for detailed discussions of these effects.) Certain glucocorticoid side effects are of particular importance in patients with inflammatory bowel disease in that they may mimic, mask, or intensify symptoms and complications of this disease. For example, corticosteroids cause cutaneous atrophy.[52] Patients with ulcerative colitis are predisposed to intestinal wall perforation and drug-induced cutaneous atrophy will only intensify this predisposition. In addition, the symptoms of one of the major complications of intestinal perforation, peritonitis, may be masked by the use of corticosteroids. Drug-induced cutaneous atrophy and the decreased wound healing associated with corticosteroid use may contribute to operative morbidity and mortality in patients with inflammatory bowel disease,[53] although this concept has been disputed.[54] Corticosteroids have been noted to mask the clinical signs of abdominal and pelvic abscess in Crohn's disease patients resulting in septic complications.[55] Other corticosteroid side effects that may be secondary to either the drug and/or inflammatory bowel disease include retardation of growth and development in prepubertal patients; osteoporosis with secondary pathologic fractures and spinal column decompression; and hypokalemic alkalosis.[51]

Remission Maintenance

Sulfasalazine

8. C.M.'s symptoms decreased significantly after an initial course of parenteral corticosteroids. She was changed successfully to 40 mg oral prednisone QD without recurrence of her disease symptoms. What drug regimen should be used to maintain a disease remission in C.M.?

Oral sulfasalazine significantly reduces the incidence of relapse in ulcerative colitis patients who are in remission.[25,56–59] In a double-blind controlled trial, 70% of patients taking 2 gm/day of sulfasalazine by mouth maintained disease remission, whereas only 24% of those receiving placebo were symptom-free after one year.[56] The positive benefit of sulfasalazine maintenance therapy was confirmed subsequently in patients for up to three years of therapy using sigmoidoscopic and biopsy abnormalities as relapse criteria.[57] Additionally, the recurrence rate increases significantly if long-term sulfasalazine is stopped.[57,58] One investigation showed that when the dose of sulfasalazine was increased, both the prophylactic efficacy and incidence of side effects increased.[59] A 2 gm dose appeared to provide optimal balance between adverse and beneficial effects in these patients. Therefore, 2 gm is the recommended prophylactic dose, although the dose should be individualized if adverse effects appear or beneficial effects are not achieved.

Oral and topical corticosteroids are ineffective in preventing relapse of ulcerative colitis once remission has occurred. Hydrocortisone hemisuccinate 100 mg twice weekly by retention enema,[19] 50 mg oral cortisone once or twice daily,[31,60] or 15 mg oral prednisone daily[61] causes significant side effects and fails to maintain previously induced disease remission in ulcerative colitis patients.

On the basis of the above information, C.M.'s prednisone should be tapered gradually and discontinued over a one- to two-month period. If disease symptoms recur while tapering the prednisone, the dose should be increased with a subsequent slower taper schedule instituted when the patient becomes asymptomatic. Concomitantly, sulfasalazine (2 gm/day) should be initiated as prophylaxis against disease relapse. Prophylactic therapy should be continued indefinitely unless intolerable side effects develop.[9,11]

9. How will sulfasalazine cause a beneficial effect in patients with ulcerative colitis?

Pharmacokinetics. Sulfasalazine exerts an anti-inflammatory therapeutic effect through a complex series of events. Structurally, sulfasalazine is a combination of sulfonamide antibiotic, sulfapyridine, in an azo linkage with 5-aminosalicylic acid. Following oral administration, 20% to 30% of the parent compound is absorbed in the proximal small intestine.[62,63] The absorbed sulfasalazine is not metabolized *in vivo*, with the majority of the absorbed drug being excreted unchanged in the bile and the remainder by the kidneys.[63] Ultimately, 75% to 85% of the oral dose reaches the distal small intestine and colon where the diazo bond is cleaved by bacterial intracellular azoreductases to produce sulfapyridine and 5-aminosalicylic acid.[64–68] The ability to split the azo linkage is inherent in the majority of bacterial species normally found in the human intestine.[64] The liberated sulfapyridine is readily absorbed and is hepatically metabolized by acetylation, hydroxylation, and glucuronidation before it is excreted in the urine as the metabolite or free drug.[66] Since the acetylation rate of sulfapyridine is determined genetically,[69,70] its half-life of elimination is dependent upon the patient's acetylation phenotype and varies between 5 to 13 hours.[71]

The 5-aminosalicylate liberated in the colon is poorly absorbed,[72] although a small portion can be recovered in the urine in the acetylated form.[73] This is in contrast to orally administered 5-aminosalicylic acid which is well absorbed proximally in the GI tract.[9] Factors that alter the normal absorption and metabolism of sulfasalazine and therefore, increase the amount of unaltered sulfasalazine excreted in the feces and decrease the amount of liberated sulfapyridine and 5-aminosalicylic acid, include a rapid intestinal transit time,[73,74] a sterile colon,[64–68] and surgical removal of colon.[68]

Mechanism of Action. The beneficial activity of sulfasalazine probably is due to the local effects of 5-aminosalicylic acid, not the sulfapyridine component.[72,75,76] In two double-blind, controlled trials, rectally administered 5-aminosalicylic acid and sulfasalazine were significantly more effective than sulfapyridine in the treatment of patients with inflammatory bowel disease.[72,75] In another study, 5-aminosalicylate was significantly more effective than sulfapyridine or placebo in preventing disease relapses in ulcerative colitis patients.[76]

The exact mechanism by which sulfasalazine, and hence, 5-aminosalicylic acid, exerts its effect is not completely understood. It is believed that prostaglandins play a significant role in the inflammatory process of inflammatory bowel disease.[77] Patients with active, untreated ulcerative colitis have high concentrations of prostaglandins in the stool, colonic venous blood, and urine,[78–82] as well as increased prostaglandin synthetase activity in rectal mucosal biopsy specimens.[83] Sulfasalazine and 5-aminosalicylic acid, but not sulfapyridine, decrease the production of prostaglandins by inhibiting prostaglandin synthetase.[78,79,84] Since sulfasalazine and 5-aminosalicylic acid confer the beneficial effects of this drug, inhibition of prostaglandins is presumed to be their mechanism of action. This theory has been questioned with the findings that more potent prostaglandin inhibitors, indomethacin (Indocin) and flurbiprofen,[85] do not effect the clinical condition of ulcerative colitis patients.[86,87]

An alternate hypothesis to the inhibition of prostaglandins as the major mode of sulfasalazine action is decreased migration of inflammatory cells into the diseased tissues. Sulfasalazine and 5-aminosalicylate, but not sulfapyridine, inhibit neutrophilic production of chemotactic substances via inhibition of the lipo- and cyclo-oxygenase pathways.[88,89] This in turn leads to lower numbers of neutrophils, macrophages, and plasma cells in the bowel wall.[90] Other possible mechanisms include inhibition of natural killer cell activity,[253] inhibition of antibody synthesis,[253] and ability to act as a potent scavenger of oxygen radicals.[254,255]

Whatever the exact mechanism of action, sulfasalazine most likely serves as a carrier molecule which delivers the active moiety, 5-aminosalicylic acid, to the diseased colonic mucosa in relatively high concentrations. There, 5-aminosalicylic acid acts locally to suppress inflammation.

10. Adverse Effects. **C.M. was started on sulfasalazine, 1 gm QID, for ulcerative colitis maintenance therapy. Additionally, her therapeutic plan called for gradual reduction of her prednisone over a 4-week period. Three days after starting her sulfasalazine, C.M. developed anorexia, nausea, and occasional vomiting. What is the possible etiology for C.M.'s symptoms? How can they be minimized?**

C.M. appears to be suffering from adverse effects of sulfasalazine. Sulfasalazine's adverse effects occur in up to 21% of patients and can cause significant morbidity, often limiting the drug's clinical usefulness. These adverse effects appear to be of two types: dose related and idiosyncratic (see Table 24.4).

The majority of sulfasalazine's adverse reactions are dose related, tend to occur early in the course of therapy, and are more frequent when the dose is ≥4 gm/day.[27,59,91] These adverse effects correlate more specifically to serum concentrations of sulfapyridine which exceed 50 μg/mL. Since sulfapyridine is acetylated,[69,70] genetically-determined slow acetylators (60% of the population)[92] experience a higher incidence of the "dose-related" adverse effects than fast acetylators.[59,70,74,91]

Generally, sulfasalazine dose-related adverse effects occur early in the course of therapy. It is important to note that the concomitant use of corticosteroids may mask certain adverse effects of sulfasalazine (e.g., malaise, arthralgia, rash, fever) and these will become apparent once the corticosteroids are withdrawn.

Dose-related sulfasalazine adverse effects can be minimized by initiating the patient on a low dose (0.5 gm/day) and gradually increasing the amount to tolerated therapeutic levels of 2 to 4 gm/day.[10,56,59,91] If dose-related reactions do occur, the drug should be discontinued until the symptoms subside; then, sulfasalazine may be reinstituted at a lower dosage. Although enteric-coated sulfasalazine tablets are available, they are useful only for

Table 24.4	Sulfasalazine Adverse Effects

Dose-Related Reactions

General[59,91]
  Nausea, vomiting, anorexia, headache, fever, arthralgias

Hematologic
  Heinz body anemia[91,93-95]
  G6PD-deficiency hemolytic anemia[95-98]
  Reticulocytes[9,59,97]
  Leukopenia[10]
  Megaloblastic anemia[99-101]

Other
  Cyanosis[56,91]
  Male infertility (reversible)[102-106]
  Neonatal kernicterus[107-112]
  Tachycardia[113]

Idiosyncratic Reactions

Hematologic
  Agranulocytosis[114]
  Autoimmune hemolytic anemia[95,97,98,115]

Dermatologic
  Skin rash[91,116-118]
  Toxic epidermal necrolysis[119]
  Exfoliative dermatitis[9,91]

Pulmonary[120-124]
  Bronchospasm, infiltrates, eosinophilia, fibrosing alveolitis

Gastrointestinal
  Hepatotoxicity[116-118,125-128]
  Pancreatitis[129]
  Colitis exacerbation[130,131]

Other
  Lupus-like syndrome[132]
  Raynaud's phenomenon[133]
  Nephrotic syndrome[116]
  Paresthesias[134]

the occasional patient who develops dyspepsia. Because they also are more expensive, their general use is unjustified.

Idiosyncratic reactions to sulfasalazine are rare, but cause significantly higher morbidity and mortality. Since many of these reactions are similar to the sensitivity reactions associated with the sulfonamide derivatives, they are thought to be secondary to the sulfapyridine component of the parent compound.[3] The severe sequelae associated with these reactions may be minimized through vigilance for their occurrence; avoidance of the use of sulfasalazine in patients with documented sensitivity reactions to sulfonamides; prompt withdrawal of sulfasalazine at the first indication that such a reaction is occurring; and avoidance of sulfasalazine in the future. If individuals who develop idiosyncratic, sensitivity-type reactions to sulfasalazine need this form of therapy, desensitization may be effective.[135-137]

C.M.'s symptoms are probably dose-related adverse reactions to the sulfasalazine. The dose should be decreased. If tolerated, the dosage can be increased slowly as necessary.

Mesalamine

11. Despite lowering C.M.'s dose of sulfasalazine to 500 mg QID, she still complains of nausea and anorexia. What therapeutic alternatives exist that may give the same beneficial effect as sulfasalazine without the accompanying adverse effects?

5-Aminosalicylic Acid Derivatives. Since the majority of sulfasalazine adverse effects are due mainly to the sulfapyridine component, and since the active moiety of sulfasalazine is 5-aminosalicylic acid, dose formulations of 5-aminosalicylic acid have been developed. These formulations in general provide the same therapeutic effect and are better tolerated than sulfasalazine, although they tend to be more expensive. The generic name for 5-aminosalicylic acid is mesalamine in the U.S. and mesalazine in Europe. Mesalamine is available in the U.S. as a retention enema suspension (Rowasa 4 gm/60 mL), rectal suppositories (Rowasa 50 mg), and controlled-release systems (Pentasa 250 mg/capsule; Asacol 400 mg/tablet).

Administration of mesalamine by retention enemas or suppositories is significantly more effective in the treatment of active distal colitis than placebo, and at least as effective as sulfasalazine given rectally or orally.[72,75,76,147,244-247,257,258] Since radiolabeled mesalamine suppositories have been shown to release drug only to the rectum and sigmoid colon, they should be reserved for the treatment of active distal proctitis.[247] Retention mesalamine enema therapy also is significantly more effective than hydrocortisone enemas in inducing remission in patients with disease confined to the distal colon.[147,259-261] Enema-administered mesalamine is effective in patients who have been unresponsive to oral sulfasalazine.[148,149,265] Evidence is mounting that like sulfasalazine, topical formulations of mesalamine are effective as maintenance therapy in preventing relapse of distal colitis in patients whose acute disease has been treated successfully.[248,258,262-264] With the exception of anal irritation (19% to 42%)[24,265] and pruritus, (2% to 13%)[147,257] rectally administered mesalamine is well tolerated; 80% to 90% of patients intolerant to sulfasalazine can receive mesalamine without similar problems.[150,151] Other aminosalicylic acid derivatives (e.g., acetylated 5-aminosalicylate,[152] and 4-aminosalicylic acid[154]) are effective when administered rectally as an enema.

With rectal administration of these drugs, local contact is necessary for effect; thereby, limiting this therapy to patients who have disease confined to the usual enema distribution area (i.e., the distal colon).[155] In an effort to increase the area of exposure of 5-aminosalicylic acid, yet eliminate the need for linkage to sulfapyridine, a number of analogues of 5-aminosalicylate have been developed in oral dosage formulations. These include controlled-release systems of mesalamine designed to deliver the drug to the small intestine and/or the colon, as well as analogues designed along the principle of sulfasalazine: connecting 5-aminosalicylic acid to itself or an inert compound via an azolinkage.[9,11] Since these latter formulations depend upon bacterial reduction to release the 5-aminosalicylic acid, the distribution of the active moiety will be the same as orally administered sulfasalazine. Olsalazine sodium (Dipentum 250 mg), a dimer of 5-aminosalicylic acid, is not well absorbed (i.e., <2%) orally and, like sulfasalazine, most of the 5-ASA is released only after it is acted on by bacteria in the proximal colon.[266-268] Olsalazine may be as effective and could prove to be better tolerated than sulfasalazine in maintaining remission in adults with mild to moderate ulcerative colitis.[269-271] It appears to be less effective than sulfasalazine in children. In one report, 35% of adults with active ulcerative colitis who could not tolerate sulfasalazine, improved with olsalazine. Olsalazine is better than placebo[272-274] and at least as good as sulfasalazine[275-277] in providing clinical and sigmoidoscopic improvement in patients with active mild to moderate ulcerative colitis. The best results have been achieved with olsalazine doses up to 3 gm/day. The larger doses are problematic in that a high percentage of patients will not be able to tolerate olsalazine's dose-related watery diarrhea (3% to 50%)[270,272-274,278] and GI distress (6% to 18%).[266,269,273-276] These events appear to be different from those associated with the disease and are secondary to a direct effect on increasing gastrointestinal motility.[279] These effects may be minimized by initiating therapy with low doses and slowly increasing the dose.[251] The usual adult dose of olsalazine for maintenance is 500 mg orally twice a day.

Mesalamine controlled-release products are designed to deliver high concentrations of mesalamine to targeted anatomical areas of the GI tract. Asacol (400 mg mesalamine tablet) is coated with a methacrylic acid copolymer B (Eudragit S) which disintegrates at a pH greater than 7, releasing a bolus of drug in the terminal ileum or proximal colon.[280] In controlled trials, this mesalamine dosage formulation was more effective than placebo and was at least as effective as sulfasalazine in the treatment of mild to moderate ulcerative colitis and in maintaining disease remission.[281-283] Pentasa (250 mg mesalamine capsule) contains microspheres of mesalamine encapsulated in a diffusion-dependent, semipermeable ethylcellulose membrane designed to release drug slowly and continuously throughout the small and large intestine.[284] Pentasa, in doses of 2 to 4 gm/day, is more effective than placebo in the acute treatment of mild to moderate active ulcerative colitis and significantly increases quality of life.[285] Disease remission also appears to be prolonged by Pentasa.[286,288] The relatively high doses of Pentasa (4 gm/day) that appear necessary to treat ulcerative colitis are probably secondary to the release and subsequent absorption of mesalamine in the small intestine, decreasing the amount of drug which eventually is available for action in the large intestine. Both Asacol and Pentasa are effective treatments in patients who are sulfasalazine-intolerant.[287,289]

Sulfasalazine

12. Teratogenicity. **Should C.M. take sulfasalazine maintenance therapy if she becomes pregnant and plans to breast-feed her baby?**

Use of sulfasalazine during pregnancy and breast-feeding often is questioned due to the ability of sulfonamide drugs to cause congenital anomalies and neonatal hyperbilirubinemia.[138] The concentration of sulfasalazine in the fetal serum approaches 50% of maternal serum concentration, with sulfapyridine concentration being equal in both maternal and fetal serum.[5] Sulfasalazine concentrations in breast milk may reach 30% to 45% of maternal serum concentrations, while those of sulfapyridine may reach 50%.[85,86,290] Even though there is considerable theoretical basis for concern, a retrospective analysis of large numbers of cases of chronic fetal exposure to sulfasalazine has not demonstrated that the prevalence of teratogenicity or neonatal jaundice is greater than that of the general population.[109-112] Some evidence suggests that the incidence of congenital defects is more related to the severity of the disease than to the therapy.[110,139] Therefore, ulcerative colitis patients being maintained on sulfasalazine should be continued on the drug during pregnancy.

Although sulfasalazine and sulfapyridine do appear in breast milk, the actual concentrations are estimated to be low.[26] Additionally, the ability of sulfapyridine and sulfasalazine to displace bilirubin is minimal.[108] This probably explains why reports of jaundice in babies breast-feeding from mothers taking sulfasalazine are lacking in the literature. Conservatively, it is appropriate to monitor bilirubin concentrations in infants nursing from mothers taking this drug. Other agents may be used in pregnant patients with inflammatory bowel disease. In animal studies corticosteroids can cause low birth weight, cleft palate, and spontaneous abortion.[291] Human studies, in contrast, suggest that corticosteroids are well tolerated.[292] The studies of metronidazole have arrived at conflicting conclusions. Several studies, case reports, and reviews have described the use of metronidazole to be safe during pregnancy,[293,294] while others have shown possible associations with malformations.[295-298] These malformations include, but are not limited to, hydrocele (2 cases), congenital dislocated hip (1 case), metatarsus varus (1 case), mental retardation (1 case), and midline facial defects (2 cases). The long-term risks from metronidazole

exposure have not been fully elucidated. The manufacturer and the Center for Disease Control recommend that metronidazole be used only when benefit clearly outweighs risk to the fetus, especially during the first trimester.[299,300]

Immunosuppressants also are gaining popularity among patients with refractory Crohn's disease. Therapeutic advantages include decreases or elimination of steroid doses and ability to maintain remission in both diseases.[301,302] These agents cause low fetal birth weights and congenital abnormalities.[303] Seven of 103 patients had reported birth defects in renal transplant mothers taking higher doses of azathioprine than used in inflammatory bowel disease.[304] In contrast, there were no complications with the fetus when azathioprine was used throughout pregnancy.[305] Again, these agents should be used only when benefit to the mother clearly outweighs risk to the fetus.

13. Drug Interactions. **C.M. has been prescribed tetracycline by her dermatologist for acne. Is there a potential for tetracycline to interfere with her sulfasalazine therapy? What other drug-drug interactions should be of concern?**

Since bacterial cleavage of sulfasalazine's diazo bond is necessary to liberate its active moiety, 5-aminosalicylic acid, concomitant therapy with antibiotics theoretically could diminish this activity.[26] Liberated sulfapyridine itself will suppress some bacterial species in patients with inflammatory bowel disease;[140] however, a significant drug interaction does not occur because most *Escherichia coli* are resistant to this sulfonamide derivative.[141] Since the majority of intestinal bacteria have the ability to split the azo linkage of sulfasalazine,[64] the clinical significance of an antibiotic-sulfasalazine interaction is probably minimal.

The amount of liberated 5-aminosalicylic acid appears to be a function of the time period that bacterial azoreductases have to metabolize the parent compound.[66,73] Drugs or conditions that decrease intestinal transit time, thereby decreasing the bacterial contact time with sulfasalazine, may lead to decreased production of 5-aminosalicylic acid.

Therapeutic serum levels of sulfapyridine are produced following the administration of sulfasalazine;[62,64-68] therefore, drugs which interact with sulfonamides, in general, must be used cautiously in patients taking sulfasalazine. The majority of sulfapyridine interactions occur as a result of competitive protein binding with other highly bound agents (i.e., the coumarin anticoagulants,[142] oral hypoglycemic agents,[143] and bilirubin).[108]

A physical binding of sulfasalazine has been demonstrated to occur with concomitant administration of ferrous sulfate[144] or cholestyramine (Questran),[145] resulting in decreased absorption of the sulfasalazine. Although it has not been demonstrated, this chelation also should decrease the absorption of iron that often is prescribed to treat the anemia secondary to inflammatory bowel disease. This phenomenon can be minimized by maximizing the interval between the administration of the individual agents.

Other sulfasalazine drug interactions include interference with folic acid absorption[99-101] and decreased serum digoxin concentrations of up to 25%.[146] Digoxin blood concentrations should be monitored closely upon initiation of sulfasalazine.

Other Agents

14. If C.M. cannot tolerate sulfasalazine or mesalamine therapy, what alternative agents have been or are used to either induce or maintain disease remission in patients with ulcerative colitis? What is their demonstrated efficacy?

Immunosuppressive agents such as azathioprine (Imuran),[156-159] 6-mercaptopurine (Purinethol),[160,161] 6-thioguanine, busulfan (Myleran), nitrogen mustards, cyclophosphamide (Cytoxan), methotrexate, and levamisole have been used to treat ulcerative colitis patients.[162] Of these agents, only azathioprine has been studied sufficiently. Although initial clinical observations were favorable, subsequent double-blind trials indicate that these agents are ineffective in most cases of ulcerative colitis. In a controlled double-blind study, 2.5 mg/kg/day of azathioprine added to a standard corticosteroid regimen had a negligible effect on inducing remission of an acute ulcerative colitis attack.[156] These investigators continued the trial for one year to determine the effect of azathioprine on the rate of relapse of ulcerative colitis. Although not statistically significant, there was a favorable trend for azathioprine to prolong patients' remission periods. This contrasts with a trial of azathioprine versus sulfasalazine which showed no difference in efficacy in maintaining patients in disease remission, although no placebo control period was used.[157] Even though azathioprine may have no effect on the overall clinical course of ulcerative colitis, it does permit a significant reduction of the corticosteroid dose in steroid-dependent patients.[158,159] Mercaptopurine (6-MP) also eliminated or reduced the amount of steroids needed in 49 of 81 patients with recalcitrant ulcerative colitis.[306] Larger controlled trials are needed to determine methotrexate's effectiveness for maintenance remission in patients with inflammatory bowel disease. In a 21-patient open trial, 14 patients with Crohn's disease and 7 with ulcerative colitis received 25 mg of methotrexate weekly for 12 weeks and then were switched to oral tapering schedules. Eleven of 14 with Crohn's and five of seven with ulcerative colitis experienced improvements in disease activity and were able to decrease their prednisone doses.[307] Levamisole, on the other hand, currently has no place in the treatment of inflammatory bowel disease due to discouraging results from the clinical trials performed thus far.[234,235,308,309] In summary, azathioprine may have a limited effect in maintaining remission of ulcerative colitis; however, serious adverse effects (i.e., leukopenia, thrombocytopenia, alopecia, liver damage) occur in most patients, and this offsets its limited value.[163]

Cromolyn sodium (disodium cromoglycate), which inhibits the release of inflammatory substances from sensitized mast cells, has been used in attempts to alter the clinical course of ulcerative colitis.[164–171] Topically administered cromolyn sodium has been demonstrated more effective than placebo in preventing recurrent attacks of ulcerative colitis[164] and more effective than prednisolone enemas in the treatment of acute disease[165] and significantly less effective than sulfasalazine.[167–170]

IV Cyclosporine. Recently, high-dose (4 mg/kg/day) intravenous cyclosporine has been advocated for patients with severe ulcerative colitis not responsive to high-dose intravenous corticosteroids. Uncontrolled trials in a small number of subjects (32) indicated that 80% of patients responded.[310,311] Another placebo-controlled trial demonstrated that 9 of 11 of steroid resistant patients responded to cyclosporine treatment.[312] Although these results are encouraging, they should be interpreted with caution because of the small number of patients studied and the potential for the development of severe toxicity from cyclosporine.

Toxic Megacolon

15. Signs and Symptoms. **One year has passed since C.M. last had an acute attack of ulcerative colitis. She has been taking sulfasalazine 1 gm TID. Now she presents with a fever of 104 °F, a heart rate of 110 beats/min, abdominal pain, weakness, and a sudden decrease in frequency of bowel movements. Physical examination discloses abdominal distention with nonlocalized rebound tenderness, tympany, and an absence of bowel sounds. Abnormal laboratory values include a leukocytosis of 15,000 WBC/mm³ and a serum K of 3.0 mEq/L. Radiographic examination of the abdomen shows the transverse colon to be dilated to 9 cm. What is the most probable cause of C.M.'s**

symptoms? What are potential sequelae of this complication of inflammatory bowel disease? [SI units: WBC count 15 × 10⁹/L; K 0.77 μmol/L]

C.M.'s signs and symptoms are consistent with an acute dilation of the colon associated with systemic toxemia. This complication of ulcerative colitis, commonly referred to as toxic megacolon, occurs in 1% to 13% of patients at some time during their disease course.[3,177] Toxic megacolon also is a complication of Crohn's colitis and ileocolitis.[173–175]

Toxic megacolon represents the most life-threatening complication of inflammatory bowel disease and has an overall mortality rate of up to 30%.[176] It is defined as a severe attack of colitis with total or segmental colonic dilation. A patient is considered toxic if the patient has colonic dilation with two or more of the following symptoms: temperature greater than 101.5 °F, tachycardia with a pulse rate greater than 100 beats/minute, leukocytosis with a WBC count greater than 10,000 cells/mm³, or hypoalbuminemia with an albumen less than 3.0 gm/dL. Other symptoms include abdominal distention and tenderness, anemia, hypotension, and electrolyte imbalance.[313,314] Signs and symptoms present in C.M. consistent with toxic megacolon include prostration, a fever greater than 101.5 °F, tachycardia, electrolyte imbalance, abdominal pain and tenderness, leukocytosis, dilation of the colon to a diameter greater than 6 cm, and signs of diminished colonic peristalsis as evidence by decreased stool frequency and the absence of bowel sounds. Other signs consistent with this diagnosis include dehydration, anemia, and hypoalbuminemia.[3,177]

Colonic perforation followed by peritonitis and hemorrhage is the major complication of toxic megacolon. C.M.'s condition should be considered a medical emergency.

16. Predisposing Factors. **What factors does C.M. have that predispose her to toxic megacolon? What drugs ought to be avoided in C.M.?**

A contributing factor that predisposes C.M. to the development of toxic megacolon is hypokalemia which decreases bowel wall muscular tone.[176] Other factors which predispose patients with inflammatory bowel disease to toxic megacolon include the use of antispasmodics such as the opiates or anticholinergic agents;[176,178,179] irritant cathartics such as castor oil;[177] barium enemas;[177,180] and hypoproteinemia which produces bowel wall edema.[177] Additionally, consideration should be given to the fact that although corticosteroids may be necessary for the treatment of the inflammatory bowel disease, they may mask signs of peritonitis that may result in a complication of toxic megacolon.

17. Medical Management. **What medical therapeutic modalities ought to be considered for the treatment of C.M.'s toxic megacolon?**

General supportive measures are used to arrest the necrotic process taking place in the colon.[3,177] C.M.'s bowel should be put to rest. Nothing should be taken by mouth and nasogastric suction should be initiated to prevent passage of swallowed air and fluid into the colon. Fluid and electrolyte imbalances must be corrected and in C.M.'s case, the hypokalemia should be corrected as quickly as possible. She also should be given adequate nutritional support, including total parental nutrition if a prolonged course is anticipated. High doses of corticosteroids should be initiated. C.M. currently is not taking steroids, but if she were, the dose would need to be increased to prevent adrenal insufficiency. A blood sample should be sent for culture and sensitivity and C.M. should be initiated on empiric antibiotic therapy since she exhibits signs and symptoms of systemic bacteremia (e.g., leukocytosis, fever, prostration). The antibiotic regimen chosen should include an agent effective against anaerobes since these bacteria occur in large numbers in the colon. Other measures which may be appropriate in other patients with toxic megacolon would include discontinuance of any drugs (e.g., opiates, anticholinergic agents) which decrease intestinal muscle tone and might predispose the patient to this condition and blood transfusions to correct any existing anemia or hypoalbuminemia. C.M. must be monitored carefully for signs of improvement or persistent dilation, perforation, peritonitis, and hemorrhage.

18. Surgical Intervention. C.M. has been treated as described above for 3 days. Nevertheless, her abdominal radiological examination indicates no diminution in the caliber of the distended bowel, her temperature continues to spike to 103 °F with negative blood cultures, and the abdomen remains distended and silent. Fluid and electrolyte imbalances have been restored. How should C.M. be managed at this point?

Within the first 72 hours of therapy and observation, the need for corrective surgery will be determined.[3,8,177] There are three general patterns of response: improvement, status quo, or deterioration.[177]

Those who improve with medical therapy demonstrate decreased colonic distention, a return of bowel sounds, and a decreased pulse and temperature. Medical management should be continued in these patients as long as they continue to show a progressive beneficial response. Unfortunately, only 6% to 30% of toxic megacolon patients respond satisfactorily to medical therapy.[176,177]

C.M.'s course is illustrative of the majority of toxic megacolon patients who show fluctuating degrees of response to medical management. These patients may appear to respond initially with decreased tachycardia and fever, but become toxic again in two to three days. Despite signs of improvement, there is little or no change in bowel sounds or colonic size. Perforation of the colon may occur in as many as 50% of these individuals[3] unless they are managed surgically (subtotal colectomy and ileostomy).[176,177] Early surgery will reduce the overall mortality rate in patients such as C.M.[181–183]

Some patients with toxic megacolon deteriorate despite medical therapy. In these individuals, any of the following constitutes a surgical emergency:[177] perforation or peritonitis; severe, localized tenderness usually over the left quadrant; septic shock; and massive hemorrhage. Even with immediate surgery, mortality will be 50% in this group.[176]

Surgical Management

19. What factors are considered in determining whether surgery is indicated for a patient with ulcerative colitis? What are the indications for surgery in ulcerative colitis patients other than unresponsive toxic megacolon as described above?

General Considerations. Of the various therapeutic modalities available for the management of ulcerative colitis, surgery is the most definitive form of therapy in that it is curative in most instances.[3,184] Since the lesions in ulcerative colitis generally are localized and continuous, colectomy will remove the primary focus of the disease. It also will eliminate both the extra-intestinal and local complications of ulcerative colitis in most patients. Unfortunately, the operative mortality for an elective colectomy with ileostomy is at least 2%.[182] Additionally, patients may require further surgery for anastomotic leaks, intraperitoneal abscesses, adhesions, obstruction, stomal ileitis, and mechanical problems associated with the ileostomy.[3] Patient acceptability of ileostomies also is poor and major psychological adjustments are required of the patients and their families.[185,186] Patients must be given support and educated with regard to the care of their ileostomies; this includes the prevention and management of common skin problems as well as control of odor and leakage of the effluent.[186,187] There-

fore, even though ulcerative colitis can be cured by surgery, it is indicated only after all reasonable nonoperative forms of therapy have been exhausted.

Indications. Surgery is indicated in the treatment of ulcerative colitis when the patient fails to respond to medical management acutely or chronically; develops uncontrollable drug-related complications; becomes incapacitated from the disease or its drug therapy, fails to grow and develop at a normal rate, or develops carcinoma of the rectum or colon.[3,188,189] Additionally, patients who have had ulcerative colitis for more than ten years or who demonstrate premalignant changes on rectal biopsy may be managed surgically as a prophylactic measure against colonic carcinoma.[190,191]

Crohn's Disease
Pathophysiology and Clinical Presentation

20. J.P., a 30-year-old male, was entirely well until 18 months ago when he developed crampy right lower quadrant abdominal pain associated with an increased frequency of semi-formed stools (4–5/day). The pain was episodic at first, exacerbated by meals and somewhat relieved by defecation. During this period of time, J.P. experienced anorexia and a 15-pound weight loss. He denied any changes in vision, joint pains, or the appearance of skin rashes. He has not traveled out of the U.S. or taken antibiotics recently.

Physical examination was essentially normal except for a temperature of 99.5 °F and soft, loose, watery stools that were streaked with fat and guaiac positive. There was tenderness of the abdomen upon palpation of the right lower quadrant. Pertinent laboratory values included: Hct 28%, Hgb 9 gm/dL, WBC count of 14,000/mm³, and ESR 60 mm/hr (Normal: <20 mm/hr).

Sigmoidoscopy and rectal biopsy were negative. Stool cultures were negative, as was the examination for signs of trophozoites. A barium enema showed an edematous ileocecal valve and a terminal ileum which had a nodular irregularity of the mucosa. Which of J.P.'s signs, symptoms, and laboratory data are consistent with Crohn's disease? Describe the pathophysiologic basis for J.P.'s clinical presentation. [SI units: Hct 0.28; Hgb 90 gm/L; WBC count 14 × 10⁹/L; ESR 60 mm/hr]

Crohn's disease is a granulomatous inflammatory process which may involve any portion of the digestive tract from the mouth to the anus.[1,4,192,193] Unlike ulcerative colitis, the inflammation is characteristically transmural and this leads to deep ulcerations, adhesions, and fistula formation.[4,7] The inflammatory process is typically patchy with diseased bowel separated by lengths of normal bowel. The majority of patients (55%) have disease involving the colon and terminal ileum. Additionally, 14% have disease confined to the terminal ileum (terminal ileitis), 3% have involvement of other areas in the small intestine, and 15% have disease restricted to the colon.[193] The location of the disease within the GI tract is a partial determinant of the patient's clinical presentation as well as disease complications.[193,194]

J.P., like the vast majority of patients with Crohn's disease, presents with the classical symptom triad of abdominal pain, diarrhea, and weight loss.[1] He complains of the most frequent symptom, right lower quadrant abdominal pain, which is secondary to an indolent inflammatory process in the ileocecal area.[4] Diarrhea also is a characteristic symptom; however, in contrast to ulcerative colitis, the stools usually are partly formed and there is generally no gross blood visible. If the disease is limited to the colon, the diarrhea may be of the same quality and quantity as that associated with ulcerative colitis. If the disease is limited to the ileum, as it appears to be with J.P., the diarrhea generally is moderate, with four to six stools daily. Also, if there is significant ileal involvement, bile salt malabsorption will occur resulting in steatorrhea. Weight loss may be pronounced in patients with long-standing Crohn's disease;[1] this is due to anorexia and malabsorption secondary to the blind loop syndrome, bile salt malabsorption, or fistula formation which may result in large sections of small bowel being bypassed.

Another common symptom of Crohn's disease exhibited by J.P. is a low-grade fever. This fever rarely exceeds 102 °F unless disease complications (e.g., infection, intra-abdominal abscess, fistula formation) occur.[4] Fever may be the earliest and only manifestation of this disease.

Rectal bleeding occurs in patients with Crohn's disease, particularly those with colonic involvement, although it is not as common as that associated with ulcerative colitis.[193,194] Slow blood loss may occur in patients with disease limited to the small intestine and this may cause positive guaiac feces and eventually, iron-deficiency anemia, as illustrated by J.P. Massive hemorrhage usually is a late complication of Crohn's disease and generally is due to transmural ulceration and subsequent erosion into a major blood vessel.

J.P.'s leukocytosis and increased erythrocyte sedimentation rate demonstrate that, like ulcerative colitis, Crohn's disease is a systemic disease. Extra-intestinal manifestations such as arthritis, liver disease, and skin rash occur in Crohn's disease with the same frequency as ulcerative colitis (see Table 24.2).[1,7]

Most patients with Crohn's disease have recurrent, symptomatic episodes of pain and diarrhea with gradual progression of their disease to shorter and shorter asymptomatic periods.[4] Although the clinical course generally is progressive, 10% of the patients will remain essentially asymptomatic after a few acute episodes.[192] Other patients may only manifest a slight fever for years until a late complication of the disease such as fistula formation develops. Alternatively, Crohn's disease may be rapidly progressive.[193]

Remission Induction

21. What agents can be used to induce a remission of J.P.'s Crohn's disease? What evidence is there to support the use of these agents?

Since the clinical course of Crohn's disease varies so tremendously among patients,[193,194] the management of this disease must be individualized to the patient's condition.[4] The anatomical location of the disease also is an important determinant of therapy.[195–197] The majority of investigations evaluating the treatment of acute symptomatic Crohn's disease have ignored this factor, and are therefore difficult to assess or compare.

Corticosteroids are the most widely used therapeutic agents for the treatment of active, symptomatic Crohn's disease.[4] Initial uncontrolled reports of the use of these agents to induce disease remission were encouraging.[198–200] Subsequently, three large retrospective studies confirmed that 50% to 90% of patients treated with corticosteroids improved as manifested by increased appetite; decreased fever, pain, and diarrhea; increased sense of well-being; increased hematocrit; and decreased erythrocyte sedimentation rate.[201–203] These studies also demonstrated that clinical improvement does not necessarily correlate with improvement in radiographic appearance and that the beneficial effects appeared to be short term. Subsequently, the National Cooperative Crohn's Disease Study (NCCDS)[195] and the European Cooperative Crohn's Disease Study (ECCDS)[196] published the results of their independently conducted double-blind, controlled trials of corticosteroid treatment of acute symptomatic Crohn's disease. Although using different treatment regimens and different efficacy evaluative mechanisms, corticosteroids were significantly superior to placebo

for induction of disease remission for all patients as a group. When the anatomical location of the disease was considered, prednisone was significantly more effective than placebo in patients with involvement of the ileum alone or ileum and colon, but not when the disease was confined to the colon.[195] Conversely, the ECCDS demonstrated effectiveness in all anatomical locations.[196]

Sulfasalazine also is widely recommended and used in treating mild to moderately symptomatic Crohn's disease patients.[10,11,26] This use initially was based upon several uncontrolled studies until a 1974 trial concluded that sulfasalazine (3 gm/day) was significantly superior to placebo in controlling the symptoms of Crohn's disease in a subgroup of patients who had no prior surgery for their disease, although the drug was no more effective than placebo when all patients were considered.[204] Sulfasalazine is significantly superior to placebo in the induction of Crohn's disease remission.[195–197] Improvement generally occurs in the first four to six weeks of therapy.[197] Sulfasalazine's beneficial effect is confined to patients with disease involving the colon[195–197] or the colon and ileum;[195,197] is ineffective in patients who have small bowel disease exclusively;[195–197] and the effective dose is 4 to 6 gm/day.[195–197,204] The relationship between anatomical location and effect is expected since metabolism of sulfasalazine by colonic bacterial flora is necessary to release the active moiety, 5-aminosalicylic acid (see Question 8).

There are other relevant observations concerning the use of sulfasalazine and corticosteroids in inducing remission of Crohn's disease. Previously untreated patients with colonic involvement appear to respond better to sulfasalazine than to placebo or prednisone,[195] although when anatomical distribution of disease is not considered, sulfasalazine is less effective than prednisone.[195,196] The combination of prednisone and sulfasalazine is no more effective than prednisone therapy alone and the total dose of prednisone needed to control the disease symptoms is not decreased with the addition of sulfasalazine.[195,205] Additionally, extra-intestinal manifestations of Crohn's disease do not significantly improve with corticosteroid or sulfasalazine therapy.[195]

Based upon this information, the drug therapy recommendations for induction of remission of Crohn's disease patients are as follows:

- For patients with disease confined to the colon, use sulfasalazine, 3 to 4 gm/day.
- For patients with disease confined to the small bowel (such as J.P.), use prednisone in a dose which has been adjusted according to disease severity.
- Previously untreated patients with disease of the ileum and colon should receive sulfasalazine. If there is no response within one to two months, the patient should be switched to prednisone.

Remission Maintenance

22. After 4 weeks of prednisone 40 mg/day, J.P. experienced fewer symptoms of Crohn's disease; 1 to 2 well-formed stools a day, increased appetite and weight, decreased abdominal pain and tenderness, and normal body temperatures. Should the prednisone be discontinued? What agents are effective in maintaining remission of symptoms in patients with Crohn's disease?

Corticosteroids. Once prednisone has induced remission of active symptomatic Crohn's disease, attempts should be made to taper the patient off the drug.[11] The NCCDS and ECCDS have demonstrated that the incidence of relapse was the same whether corticosteroids were or were not used in patients with quiescent Crohn's disease.[195,196] These studies confirm retrospective observations.[201–203] Furthermore, continued corticosteroid therapy in several controlled trials[206–209] was ineffective in preventing relapse and may have been associated with increased mortality and increased need for surgical intervention.

Sulfasalazine. The NCCDS and the ECCDS also have demonstrated that the continued use of sulfasalazine in patients with symptomatic Crohn's disease is not significantly more effective in preventing recurrence of symptoms than placebo, irrespective of original disease location.[195,196] These findings are in agreement with earlier observations and conclusions from controlled trials.[204,207,210,211]

In summary, J.P. should not be maintained on any drugs during the remission phase since long-term prophylactic therapy with sulfasalazine or corticosteroids is ineffective in preventing relapse of active symptomatic Crohn's disease. Additionally, the problems that arise from long-term therapy with these drugs may be qualitatively and quantitatively greater than no therapy in such patients.[55,195,212]

Chronic Symptomatic Crohn's Disease

23. Five weeks after starting to taper J.P.'s prednisone dosage (currently 10 mg/day), he complains of increased diarrhea (3–4 watery stools a day), fevers of 100 °F, and increased abdominal pain. What therapeutic intervention should be undertaken to manage this apparent exacerbation of J.P's illness?

Corticosteroids. In the majority of patients who have been treated with corticosteroids to induce remission of active symptomatic Crohn's disease, reduction of the corticosteroid dosage will result in exacerbation of disease symptoms.[11] In the NCCDS, only 40% of patients receiving remission induction with prednisone could be withdrawn completely from the drug.[195] Furthermore, 30% of those patients experienced at least one flare-up of symptoms before they were withdrawn completely. The ECCDS results corroborate these findings[196] The addition of sulfasalazine does not facilitate prednisone withdrawal.[205]

A significant portion of patients with Crohn's disease experience mild symptoms chronically[4,193] and up to 50% of Crohn's disease patients will require continued low-dose corticosteroid treatment (5 to 15 mg/day prednisone) to suppress these symptoms.[9,213] Withdrawal of corticosteroid in this group of patients results in significant clinical deterioration.[195]

Azathioprine. In patients who require corticosteroid therapy to suppress symptoms of Crohn's disease, concomitant immunosuppressive therapy reduces the corticosteroid dosage requirement.[214–216] Of the immunosuppressive agents tested in this situation, azathioprine may be the agent of choice.[9] The possible steroid-sparing effect of immunosuppressive agents must be weighed against their potentially severe adverse effects (e.g., bone marrow suppression and increased incidence of malignancy).[212,217,218] In J.P.'s case, the prednisone dose should first be increased to a level that suppresses his symptoms. This should be followed by repeated attempts to withdraw the drug. If these attempts are unsuccessful, J.P. may require chronic corticosteroid suppressive therapy; the addition of azathioprine for its corticosteroid-sparing effect is also a possible consideration.

Other Agents

24. If J.P. fails prednisone therapy, what alternative therapy maybe used to either induce or maintain remission?

5-Aminosalicylic Acid Derivatives. Since sulfasalazine has a demonstrated efficacy in treating Crohn's disease located in the anatomical area where the active 5-aminosalicylic acid is liberated, sustained-release and enteric-coated dosage formulations of 5-aminosalicylic acid have been developed to deliver the drug to both the small and large intestine. These types of dosage formulations do deliver drug to both of these organs,[219,220] and may be effective in treating patients with Crohn's ileitis and ileocolitis.[221] Patients who receive 4 gm of controlled-release mesalamine daily will significantly decrease their Crohn's disease activity index, achieve quicker remission, have fewer treatment failures, and improve their general well-being more than if they received placebo, no matter the anatomical location of the disease.[315] Additionally, controlled-release mesalamine achieved remission in 42% (122/289) of patients with active Crohn's disease[316] and maintained remission for one year in 72% (31/43) of patients studied. Corticosteroid dosage in many of these patients was able to be decreased or discontinued. Doses of mesalamine less than 4 gm have not significantly altered the course of Crohn's disease.[315,317,318]

Immunosuppressive agents have been used to induce and maintain remission in patients with Crohn's disease with azathioprine being the most widely studied.[163] In three clinical trials, azathioprine was no more effective than placebo in inducing remission and the anatomical distribution of the disease was not a factor in this lack of response.[195,222,223] In contrast, Present et al. found a positive effect of 6-mercaptopurine in inducing Crohn's disease remission as compared to placebo.[216] In addition, 47% of 19 Crohn's patients showed complete or partial response to 6-MP.[1] Mercaptopurine, as all immunosuppressants, is not without its toxicities. In a retrospective review of 396 patients who received 6-MP for inflammatory bowel disease for a mean of 60.3 months,[319] pancreatitis was the most common adverse effect occurring in 3.3% of patients. This was followed by bone marrow suppression (2%), allergic reactions (2%), and drug-induced hepatitis (0.3%). All adverse effects were reversible and no deaths occurred. Mercaptopurine should be considered as an alternative in patients with refractory Crohn's disease or in those patients who cannot tolerate corticosteroid or aminosalicylates. Additionally, methotrexate has been documented to produce remission in patients with refractory disease.[249]

Thus, the use of immunosuppressives for the maintenance of remission in patients with Crohn's disease is controversial.[163] The NCCDS showed that azathioprine alone, in a dose of 1 mg/kg/day, was no more effective than placebo in preventing disease relapse.[195] This is in agreement with a trial by Watson,[224] but contradicts the conclusions of Willoughby[214] and O'Donoghue[217] who found that larger doses of azathioprine, 2 mg/kg/day, may maintain disease remission. Since the risk of toxicity from these agents is great and because an azathioprine-responsive group of patients cannot be predicted, additional investigations into immunosuppressive maintenance therapy of quiescent Crohn's disease are warranted before routine use can be justified. This form of therapy should be reserved only for those patients with disease unresponsive to other therapy.[225]

Cyclosporine, because of its potent immunosuppressive properties, has undergone investigation of its effectiveness in inducing remission in patients with otherwise resistant Crohn's disease.[10] In 1989, Brynskov and colleagues reported the results of a multicenter, placebo-controlled trial of high-dose, oral cyclosporine in 71 patients with chronic active Crohn's disease.[250] Fifty-nine percent of the patients treated with cyclosporine for three months had both clinical and laboratory improvement in their disease. This response rate was statistically greater than the 32% of placebo-treated patients. Cyclosporine-treated patients responded relatively quickly, within two weeks. As with other forms of treatment for this disease, the relapse rate after withdrawal of successful therapy was high (36%). In follow-up data, however, short course cyclosporine did not result in long-term improvement of Crohn's disease.[320] Additionally, several investigations suggest that low oral cyclosporine doses have no prophylactic or therapeutic value in Crohn's disease.[321] The potential severe cyclosporine adverse effects dictate using this agent only in patients with disease resistant to more conventional forms of therapy.

Metronidazole has been advocated for the treatment of active Crohn's disease. Use of this antimicrobial agent is based upon the theory that bacteria, particularly anaerobic bacteria, may either initiate or perpetuate the inflammatory process in individuals with a compromised bowel epithelium.[226] Some patients improved symptomatically while taking metronidazole, with the most impressive effects occurring in patients with colonic disease.[227-229] Controlled trials have demonstrated that 800 mg/day of metronidazole is at least as effective as sulfasalazine (3000 mg/day) in treating active Crohn's disease[230] and that it was more effective than placebo in patients with disease relapse.[231] In contrast to these positive reports, Ambrose et al. demonstrated in a prospective randomized trial that although metronidazole was more effective than placebo in inducing improvement after two weeks of therapy (67% versus 35%) in patients with relapse of their disease, there was no difference at the end of four weeks of therapy.[232] In another study, Crohn's disease activity index scores improved, but there were no differences in remission rates between metronidazole and placebo.[322] Additionally, concern has been raised over the potential for metronidazole to cause carcinoma in patients with Crohn's disease,[233] although the overall prevalence of adverse effects is no greater than that of sulfasalazine.[230] Until more controlled studies are conducted to accurately define metronidazole's role in the treatment of Crohn's disease, its use should be reserved as adjunctive therapy for patients with disease refractory to more proven forms of therapy.

Immunomodulating Agents. Since the immune system is thought to play a significant role in the pathogenesis of Crohn's disease,[4] various attempts to manipulate this system have been tried. Some of the immune-altering agents that have been studied in small controlled investigations are BCG vaccine,[236,237] cromolyn sodium,[171,238] transfer factor,[239] and sucralfate.[323-325] None of these studies have demonstrated promise for beneficial effects of these agents in the treatment of Crohn's disease.

Other Agents. Nonsteroidal anti-inflammatory drugs (NSAIDs), although their mechanism of action makes them attractive in the treatment of inflammatory bowel disorders, should be avoided. NSAIDs actually exacerbate the disease state instead of being efficacious.[326] Other agents which may show promise in the treatment of inflammatory bowel disease include chloroquine,[327,328] 5-lipoxygenase inhibitors,[329] clonidine,[330] and D-penicillamine.[331]

Surgical Management

General Considerations and Indications

25. After 6 years of remission, J.P. is hospitalized for an acute exacerbation of right lower quadrant pain associated with abdominal distention, lack of bowel movements, and vomiting over the last 24 hours. Radiographic studies indicate partial small bowel obstruction at the terminal ileum. Surgery revealed that the mucosa of the terminal 40 cm of the ileum was inflamed and thickened. In all, 50 cm of the terminal ileum were removed along with the ascending colon to the hepatic flexure. The remaining small bowel was anastomosed directly to the transverse colon. What factors are considered in determining whether surgery is indicated in Crohn's disease? What are the indications for surgery in Crohn's disease?

Since medical therapy of Crohn's disease often is inadequate, 78% of all patients with this disease will undergo surgery within 20 years of symptom onset.[241] In contrast to ulcerative colitis, however, surgical removal of the involved bowel in Crohn's disease is not a definitive form of therapy.[4,184] Crohn's disease can recur even after extensive resections. Various investigations have determined that cumulative recurrence rates after surgery for this disease are as high as 80%, depending upon the surgical procedure and disease location.[194,242,243] Therefore, multiple operations, and all their attendant risks, often are necessary over the life span of the Crohn's disease patient.[184] Depending upon the amount and site of the bowel removed during surgery, specific malabsorption syndromes can occur (e.g., vitamin B_{12} malabsorption with removal of the terminal ileum).[4] If an ileostomy is part of the surgical procedure, the patient will have to undergo significant psychological adjustments (see Question 18). Therefore, surgery is indicated only for specific complications which are unresponsive to alternate forms of therapy and should be postponed whenever possible.

Generally accepted indications for surgical intervention in patients with Crohn's disease include failure of medical management; incapacitation due to the disease or its drug therapy; retarded growth and development in children; intestinal obstruction, fistula formation, abscess formation; toxic megacolon; perforation and hemorrhage; and carcinoma.[4,184,188,189,193]

References

1 **Farmer RG.** Clinical features and nature history of inflammatory bowel disease. Med Clin North Am. 1980;64:1103.

2 **Lashner BA et al.** Prevalence and incidence of inflammatory bowel disease in family members. Gastroenterology. 1986;91:1396.

3 **Jewell DP.** Ulcerative colitis. In: Sleisenger MH, Fordtran JS, eds. Gastrointestinal Disease. 5th ed. Philadelphia: WB Saunders; 1993:1305.

4 **Kornbluth A et al.** Crohn's disease. In: Sleisenger MH, Fordtran JS, eds. Gastrointestinal Disease. 5th ed. Philadelphia: WB Saunders; 1993:1270.

5 **Stowe SP et al.** An epidemiologic study of inflammatory bowel disease in Rochester, New York. Gastroenterology. 1990;98:104.

6 **Rankin GB et al.** National Cooperative Crohn's Disease Study: extra in-testinal manifestations and perianal complications. Gastroenterology. 1979;77:914.

7 **Smith JN et al.** Complications and extraintestinal problems in inflammatory bowel disease. Med Clin North Am. 1980;64:1161.

8 **Sack DM et al.** Drug therapy of inflammatory bowel disease. Pharmacotherapy. 1983;3:158.

9 **Peppercorn MA.** Advances in drug therapy for inflammatory bowel disease. Ann Intern Med. 1990;112:50.

10 **Hawthorne AB et al.** Immunosuppressive drugs in inflammatory bowel disease. A review of their mechanisms of efficacy and place in therapy. Drugs. 1989;38:267.

11 **Sottile RF et al.** Medical management of inflammatory bowel disease. DICP, Ann Pharmacother. 1989;23:963.

12 **Truelove SC et al.** Cortisone in ulcerative colitis. Br Med J (Clin Res). 1955;2:1041.

13 **Lennard-Jones JE et al.** Assessment of prednisone, salazopyrin and topical hydrocortisone hemisuccinate used as out-patient treatment for ulcerative colitis. Gut. 1960;1:217.

14 **Baron JH et al.** Out-patient treatment of ulcerative colitis: comparison between three doses of oral prednisone. Br Med J (Clin Res). 1962;2:441.

15 **Powell-Tuck J et al.** A comparison of oral prednisone given as single or multiple daily doses for active proctocolitis. Scand J Gastroenterol. 1978;13:833.

16 **Kristensen M et al.** High-dose prednisone treatment in severe ulcerative colitis. Scand J Gastroenterol. 1974;9:177.

17 **Lennard-Jones JE et al.** A double-blind controlled trial of prednisolone-21-phosphate suppositories in treatment of idiopathic proctitis. Gut. 1962;3:207.

18 **Matts SGF.** Local treatment of ulcerative colitis with prednisolone-21-phosphate enemas. Lancet. 1960;1:517.

19 **Truelove SC et al.** Treatment of ulcerative colitis with local hydrocortisone hemisuccinate sodium. A report on a controlled therapeutic trial. Br Med J (Clin Res). 1958;2:1072.

20 **Watkinson G.** Treatment of ulcerative colitis with topical hydrocortisone hemisuccinate sodium. A controlled trial employing restricted sequential analysis. Br Med J (Clin Res). 1958;2:1077.

21 **Farmer RG et al.** Treatment of ulcerative colitis with hydrocortisone enemas—comparison of absorption and clinical response. Am J Gastroenterol. 1970;54:229.

22 **Farmer RG et al.** Treatment of ulcerative colitis with hydrocortisone enemas. Dis Colon Rectum. 1970;13:355.

23 **Farmer RB.** Clinical types and differential diagnosis. In: Haubrich W, Schaffner F, eds. Gastroenterology. Philadelphia: WB Saunders; 1995: 1352–356.

24 **Baron JH et al.** Sulfasalazine and salicylsulfadimidine in ulcerative colitis. Lancet. 1962;1:1094.

25 **Dick AP et al.** Controlled trial of sulfasalazine in treatment of ulcerative colitis. Gut. 1964;4:437.

26 **Peppercorn MA.** Sulfasalazine. Pharmacology, clinical use, toxicity, and related new drug development. Ann Intern Med. 1984;3:377.

27 **Truelove SC et al.** Comparison of corticosteroid and sulfasalazine therapy in ulcerative colitis. Br Med J (Clin Res). 1962;2:1708.

28 **Elliott PR et al.** Prednisone absorption in acute colitis. Gut. 1980;21:49.

29 **Truelove SC et al.** Intensive intravenous regimen for severe attacks of ulcerative colitis. Br Med J (Clin Res). 1962;1:1067.

30 **Kaplan HP et al.** A controlled evaluation of intravenous adrenocorticotropic hormone and hydrocortisone in the treatment of acute colitis. Gastroenterology. 1975;69:91.

31 **Powell-Tuck J et al.** A controlled comparison of corticotropin and hydrocortisone in the treatment of severe proctocolitis. Scand J Gastroenterol. 1977;12:971.

32 **Meyers S et al.** Corticotropin versus hydrocortisone in the intravenous treatment of ulcerative colitis: a prospective, randomized, double-blind clinical trial. Gastroenterology. 1983;85:351.

33 **Lennard-Jones JE et al.** Medical treatment of ulcerative colitis. Post Grad Med J. 1984;60:797.

34 **Myles AB et al.** Single daily dose corticosteroid treatment. Effect on adrenal function and therapeutic efficacy in various diseases. Ann Rheum Dis. 1971;30:149.

35 **HNuwe AB.** Inflammatory bowel disease revisited: newer drugs. Scand J Gastroenterol. 1990;25(Suppl. 175): 95–106.

36 **Scherl ND et al.** Adjunctive use of a steroid rectal foam in the treatment of ulcerative colitis. Dis Colon Rectum. 1973;16:149.

37 **Ruddell WSJ et al.** Treatment of distal ulcerative colitis (proctosigmoiditis) in relapse: comparison of hydrocortisone enemas and rectal hydrocortisone foam. Gut. 1980;21:885.

38 **Brynskov J et al.** Final report on a placebo-controlled, double-blind, randomized, multicentered trial of cyclosporine treatment in active chronic Crohn's disease. Scand J Gastroenterol. 1991;26:689–95.

39 **Morgan I.** Metronidazole treatment in pregnancy. Int J Gynaecol Obstet. 1978;15:501–02.

40 **Jones JH et al.** Multicenter trial. Betamethasone 17-valerate and prednisone 21-phosphate retention enemas in proctocolitis. Br Med J (Clin Res). 1971;3: 84.

41 **Powell-Tuck J.** Plasma prednisolone levels after administration of prednisolone-21-phosphate as a retention enema in colitis. Br Med J (Clin Res). 1976;1:193.

42 **Lima JJ et al.** Bioavailability of hydrocortisone retention enemas in normal subjects. Am J Gastroenterol. 1980;73:232.

43 **Lee DAH et al.** Plasma prednisolone levels and adrenocortical responsiveness after administration of prednisolone-21 phosphate as a retention enema. Gut. 1979;20:349.

44 **Halvorsen S et al.** On the absorption of prednisone and prednisolone disodium phosphate after rectal administration. Scand J Gastroenterol. 1969;4: 581.

45 **Lee DAH et al.** Rectally-administered prednisolone—evidence for a predominately local action. Gut. 1980;21:215.

46 **McIntyre PB et al.** Therapeutic benefits from a poorly absorbed prednisolone enema in distal colitis. Gut. 1985; 26:822.

47 **Kumana CR et al.** Beclomethasone dipropionate enemas for treating bowel disease without producing Cushing's syndrome or hypothalamic-pituitary suppression. Lancet. 1982;1:579.

48 **Lennard-Jones JE.** Medical management of ulcerative colitis. Can J Surg. 1974;17:420.

49 **Swarbrick ET et al.** Enema volume as an important factor in successful topical corticosteroid treatment of colitis. Proc R Soc Med. 1974;67:753.

50 **Clark ML.** A local foam aerosol in ulcerative colitis. Practitioner. 1977;219: 103.

51 **Haynes RC et al.** Adrenocorticotropic hormone: adrenocortical steroids and their synthetic analogs; inhibitors of the synthesis and actions of adrenocortical hormones. In: Gilman AG et al., eds. The Pharmacological Basis of Therapeutics. 8th ed. New York: MacMillan; 1990:1434–446.

52 **Colomb D.** Cutaneous manifestations in long-term general corticotherapy. Study of 100 cases. Presse Med. 1971; 79: 1011.

53 **Knudsen L et al.** Early complications in patients previously treated with corticosteroids. Scand J Gastroenterol. 1976;11(Suppl. 3):123.

54 **Jalon KN et al.** Influence of corticosteroids in the results of surgical treatment for ulcerative colitis. N Engl J Med. 1971;282:588.

55 **Keighley MRB et al.** Incidence and microbiology of abdominal and pelvic abscess in Crohn's disease. Gastroenterology. 1982;82:1271.

56 **Misiewicz JJ et al.** Controlled trial of sulfasalazine in maintenance therapy for ulcerative colitis. Lancet. 1965;1: 185.

57 **Dissanayake AS et al.** A controlled therapeutic trial of long-term maintenance treatment of ulcerative colitis with sulphasalazine (salazopyrin). Gut. 1973;14:923.

58 **Davies PS et al.** Maintenance of remission in ulcerative colitis with sulphasalazine or a high-fiber diet: a clinical trial. Br Med J (Clin Res). 1978;1: 1524.

59 **Azad Khan AK et al.** Optimal dose of sulphasalazine for the maintenance treatment of ulcerative colitis. Gut. 1980;21:232.

60 **Truelove SC et al.** Cortisone and corticotropin in ulcerative colitis. Br Med J (Clin Res). 1959;1:387.

61 **Lennard-Jones JE et al.** Prednisone as a maintenance treatment for ulcerative colitis in remission. Lancet. 1965; 1:188.

62 **Schroder H et al.** Absorption, metabolism, and excretion of salicylazosulfapyridine in man. Clin Pharmacol Ther. 1972;13:506.

63 **Das EM.** Small bowel absorption of sulfasalazine and its hepatic metabolism in human beings, cats, and rats. Gastroenterology. 1979;77:280.

64 **Peppercorn MA et al.** The role of bacteria in the metabolism of salicylazosulfapyridine. J Pharmacol Exp Ther. 1972;181:555.

65 **Azad Khan AK et al.** Tissue and bacterial splitting of sulphasalazine. Clin Sci. 1983;64:349.

66 **Peppercorn MA et al.** Distribution studies of salicylazosulfa-pyridine metabolites. Gastroenterology. 1973;64: 240.

67 **Schroder H et al.** Azo reduction of salicylazosulfapyridine by germ-free and conventional rats. Xenobiotica. 1973; 3:255.

68 **Das EM.** The role of the colon in the metabolism of salicylazosulfapyridine. Scand J Gastroenterol. 1973;64:240.

69 **Evans DAP et al.** Human acetylation polymorphism. J Lab Clin Med. 1964; 63:394.

70 **Clark DW.** Genetically determined variability in acetylation and oxidation. Drugs. 1985;29:342.

71 **Das KM et al.** Clinical pharmacokinetics of sulfasalazine. Clin Pharmacokinet. 1976;1:406.

72 **Klotz U et al.** Therapeutic efficacy of sulfasalazine and its metabolites in patients with ulcerative colitis and Crohn's disease. N Engl J Med. 1980; 303:1499.

73 **Van Hees PAM et al.** Influence of intestinal transit time on azo-reduction of salicylazosulfapyridine (salazopyrin). Gut. 1979;20:300.

74 **Azad Khan AK et al.** Circulating levels of sulfasalazine and its metabolites and their relation to the clinical efficacy of the drug in ulcerative colitis. Gut. 1980;21:706.

75 **Azad Khan AK et al.** An experiment to determine the active therapeutic moiety of sulphasalazine. Lancet. 1977; 2:892.

76 **Van Hees PAM et al.** Effect of sulfapyridine, 5-aminosalicylic acid and placebo in patients with idiopathic proctitis: a study to determine the active therapeutic moiety of sulphasalazine. Gut. 1980;21:632.

77 **Donowitz M.** Arachidonic acid metabolites and their role in inflammatory bowel disease. Gastroenterology. 1985; 77:580.

78 **Gould SR et al.** Production of prostaglandins in ulcerative colitis and their inhibition by sulphasalazine. Gut. 1976;17:828.

79 **Sharon P et al.** Role of prostaglandins in ulcerative colitis. Enhanced production during active disease and inhibition by sulfasalazine. Gastroenterology. 1978;75:638.

80 **Gould SR.** Increased prostaglandin production in ulcerative colitis. Lancet. 1975;2:98.

81 **Gould SR.** Assay of prostaglandin-like substances in faeces and their measurement in ulcerative colitis. Prostaglandins. 1976;11:489.

82 **Rampton DS et al.** Rectal mucosal prostaglandin E_2 release and its relation to disease activity, electrical potential difference, and treatment in ulcerative colitis. Gut. 1980;21:591.

83 **Harris DW et al.** Determination of prostaglandin synthetase activity in rectal biopsy material and its significance in colonic disease. Gut. 1978;19: 875.

84 **Butt AA et al.** Effects on prostaglandin biosynthesis of drugs affecting gastrointestinal function. Gut. 1974;15:344.

85 **Hawkey CJ et al.** Inhibition of prostaglandin synthetase in human rectal mucosa. Gut. 1983;24:213.

86 **Gilat T et al.** Prostaglandins and ulcerative colitis. Gastroenterology. 1979; 76:1083.

87 **Rampton DS et al.** Prostaglandin synthesis inhibitors in ulcerative colitis: flurbiprofen compared with conventional treatment. Prostaglandins. 1981; 21:417.

88 **Stenson WF et al.** Sulfasalazine inhibits the synthesis of chemotactic lipids by neutrophils. J Clin Invest. 1982;69: 494.

89 **Sicar JC et al.** Inhibition of soybean lipoxygenase by sulfasalazine and 5-aminosalicylic acid: a possible mode of action in ulcerative colitis. Biochem Pharmacol. 1983;32:170.

90 **Korelitz BI et al.** Responses to drug therapy in ulcerative colitis: evaluation by rectal biopsy and mucosal cell counts. Dig Dis Sci. 1976;21:441.

91 **Das KM et al.** Adverse reactions during salicylazosulfapyridine therapy and the relation with drug metabolism and acetylator phenotype. N Engl J Med. 1973;289:491.

92 **Evans DAP.** An improved and simplified method of detecting the acetylator phenotype. J Med Genet. 1969;6:405.

93 **Spriggs AI et al.** Heinz-body anaemia due to salicylazosulfa-pyridine. Lancet. 1958;1:1039.

94 **Bottiger LE et al.** The occurrence of Heinz bodies during azulfidine treatment of ulcerative colitis. Gastroenterol Basel. 1963;100–33.

95 **Gabor P.** Hemolytic anemia as adverse reaction to salicylazo-sulfapyridine. N Engl J Med. 1973;289:1372.

96 **Cohen SM.** Ulcerative coltis and erythrocyte G-6-PD deficiency. JAMA. 1968;205:116.

97 **Goodacre RL et al.** Hemolytic anemia in patients receiving sulfasalazine. Digestion. 1978;17:503.

98 **Van Hees PAM et al.** Hemolysis during salicylazosulfapyridine therapy. Am J Gastroenterol. 1979;70:503.

99 **Franklin JL et al.** Impaired folic acid absorption in inflammatory bowel disease: effects of salicylazosulfapyridine (Azulfidine). Gastroenterology. 1973; 64:517.

100 **Schneider RE et al.** Megaloblastic anemia associated with sulfasalazine treatment. Br Med J (Clin Res). 1977; 2:1638.

101 **Halsted CH et al.** Sulfasalazine inhibits the absorption of folates in ulcerative colitis. N Engl J Med. 1981;305: 1513.

102 **Levi AJ et al.** Male infertility due to sulfasalazine. Lancet. 1979;2:639.

103 **Toth A.** Reversible toxic effect of salicylazosulfapyridine on semen quality. Fertil Steril. 1979;31:538.

104 **Traub AI et al.** Male infertility due to sulfasalazine. Lancet. 1979;2:639.

105 **Toovey S et al.** Sulfasalazine and male infertility: reversibility and possible mechanism. Gut. 1981;22:445.

106 **Birnie GG et al.** Incidence of sulfasalazine-induced male infertility. Gut. 1981;22:452.

107 **Azad Khan AK et al.** Placental and mammary transfer of sulfasalazine. Br Med J (Clin Res). 1979;11:1553.

108 **Jarnerot G et al.** Sulfasalazine treatment during breast feeding. Scand J Gastroenterol. 1979;14:869.

109 **Hensleigh PA et al.** Maternal absorption and placental transfer of sulfasalazine. Am J Obstet Gynecol. 1977;127:443.

110 **Willoughby CP et al.** Ulcerative colitis and pregnancy. Gut. 1980;21:469.

111 **Gluckmann RF.** Sulfasalazine, IBD, and pregnancy. Gastroenterology. 1981;81:194.

112 **Mogadam M et al.** Pregnancy in inflammatory bowel disease: effect of sulfasalazine and corticosteroids on fetal outcome. Gastroenterology. 1981;80:72.

113 **Neeman A et al.** Salazopyrin-induced tachycardia. Biomedicine. 1980;33:1.

114 **Jamsnidi K et al.** Azulfidine agranulocytosis with bone marrow megakaryocytosis and plasmacytosis. Minn Med. 1972;55:545.

115 **Fishman FL et al.** Non-oxidative hemolysis due to salicylazo-sulfapyridine: evidence for an immune mechanism. Gastroenterology. 1973;64:A441.

116 **Chester AC et al.** Hypersensitivity to salicylazosulfapyridine: renal and hepatic toxic reactions. Arch Intern Med. 1978;138:1138.

117 **Mihas AA et al.** Sulfasalazine toxic reactions: hepatitis, fever and skin rash with hypocomplementemia and immune complexes. JAMA. 1978;239:2590.

118 **Sotolongo RP et al.** Hypersensitivity reaction to sulfasalazine with severe hepatotoxicity. Gastroenterology. 1978;75:95.

119 **Strom J.** Toxic epidermal necrolysis (Lyell's syndrome): a report on four cases with three deaths. Scand J Infect Dis. 1969;1:209.

120 **Jones GR et al.** Sulfasalazine-induced lung disease. Thorax. 1972;27:713.

121 **Davies D et al.** Fibrosing alveolitis and treatment with salicylazosulfapyridine. Gut. 1974;15:185.

122 **Tydd TF et al.** Sulfasalazine lung. Med J Aust. 1976;1:1570.

123 **Berliner S et al.** Salazopyrin-induced eosinophilic pneumonia. Respiration. 1980;39:119.

124 **Averbuch M et al.** Sulfasalazine pneumonitis. Am J Gastroenterol. 1985;80:343.

125 **Kanner RS et al.** Azulfidine-(sulfasalazine) induced hepatic injury. Am J Dig Dis. 1978;23:956.

126 **Callen JP et al.** Granulomatous hepatitis associated with salicylazosulfapyridine therapy. South Med J. 1978;71:1159.

127 **Gully RM et al.** Hepatotoxicity of salicylazosulfapyridine: a case report and review of the literature. Am J Gastroenterol. 1979;72:461.

128 **Namias A et al.** Reversible sulfasalazine-induced granulomatous hepatitis. J Clin Gastroenterol. 1981;3:193.

129 **Block MB et al.** Pancreatitis as an adverse reaction to salicylazosulfapyridine. N Engl J Med. 1970;282:380–82.

130 **Werlin SL et al.** Bloody diarrhea—a new complication of sulfasalazine. J Pediatr. 1978;92:450.

131 **Schwartz AG et al.** Sulfasalazine-induced exacerbation of ulcerative colitis. Br Med J. 1982;306:409.

132 **Griffiths ID et al.** Sulfasalazine-induced lupus syndrome in ulcerative colitis. Br Med J. 1977;4:1188.

133 **Reid J et al.** Raynaud's phenomenon induced by sulfasalazine. Postgrad Med J. 1980;56:106.

134 **Wallace IW et al.** Neurotoxicity associated with a reaction to sulfasalazine. Practitioner. 1970;204:850.

135 **Holdsworth CD.** Sulfasalazine desensitization. Br Med J (Clin Res). 1981;282:110.

136 **Korelitz BI et al.** Desensitization to sulfasalazine in allergic patients with IBD: an important therapeutic modality. Gastroenterology. 1982;82:1104.

137 **Purdy BH et al.** Desensitization for sulfasalazine skin rash. Ann Intern Med. 1984;100:512.

138 **Donaldson RM Jr.** Management of medical problems in pregnancy—inflammatory bowel disease. N Engl J Med. 1985;312:1616.

139 **Baiocco PJ et al.** The influence of inflammatory bowel disease and its treatment on pregnancy and fetal outcome. J Clin Gastroenterol. 1984;6:211.

140 **West B et al.** Effects of sulfasalazine (salazopyrin) on faecal flora in patients with inflammatory bowel disease. Gut. 1974;15:143.

141 **Cooke EM et al.** Properties of strains of *Escherichia coli* carried in different phases of ulcerative colitis. Gut. 1974;15:143.

142 **Tatro DC, Olin BR, eds.** Drug Interaction Facts. St. Louis: Facts and Comparisons; 1993:98.

143 **Hansten PD, Horn JR.** Drug Interactions and Updates Quarterly. Vancouver: Applied Therapeutics; 1993:271.

144 **Das KM et al.** Effect of iron and calcium on salicylazosulfa-pyridine metabolism. Scott Med J. 1973;18:45.

145 **Peiniaszek HJ Jr et al.** Cholestyramine-induced inhibition of salicylazosulfapyridine (sulfasalazine) metabolism by rat intestinal microflora. J Pharmacol Exp Ther. 1976;198:240.

146 **Juhl RP et al.** Effects of sulfasalazine on digoxin bioavailability. Clin Pharmacol Ther. 1976;198:240.

147 **Campieri M et al.** Treatment of ulcerative colitis with high-dose 5-aminosalicylic acid enemas. Lancet. 1981;2:270.

148 **Janssens J et al.** 5-aminosalicylic acid enemas are effective in patients with resistant ulcerative rectosigmoiditis. Gastroenterology. 1984;86:1198.

149 **Barber GB et al.** Refractory distal ulcerative colitis responsive to 5-aminosalicylate enemas. Am J Gastroenterol. 1985;80:612.

150 **Rao SS et al.** Clinical experience of tolerance of mesalazine and olsalazine in patients intolerant of sulfasalazine. Scand J Gastroenterol. 1987;22:332.

151 **Campieri M et al.** 5-aminosalicylic acid as rectal enema in ulcerative colitis. Lancet. 1984;1:403.

152 **Willoughby CP et al.** The effect of topical N-acetyl-5-aminosalicylic acid in ulcerative colitis. Scand J Gastroenterol. 1980;15:715.

153 **Bartalsky A.** Salicylazobenzoic acid in ulcerative colitis. Lancet. 1982;1:960.

154 **Campieri M et al.** A double-blind clinical trial to compare 4-aminosalicylic acid to 5-aminosalicylic acid in topical treatment of ulcerative colitis. Digestion. 1984;29:204.

155 **Kruis W et al.** Retrograde colonic spread of sulfasalazine enemas. Scand J Gastroenterol. 1982;17:933.

156 **Jewell DP et al.** Azathioprine in ulcerative colitis. Final report on a controlled clinical trial. Br Med J (Clin Res). 1974;4:627.

157 **Caprilli R et al.** A double-blind comparison of the effectiveness of azathioprine and sulfasalazine in idiopathic proctocolitis—preliminary report. Am J Dig Dis. 1973;18:317.

158 **Rosenberg JL et al.** A controlled trial of azathioprine in the management of chronic ulcerative colitis. Gastroenterology. 1975;69:96.

159 **Kirk AP et al.** Controlled trial of azathioprine in the management of chronic ulcerative colitis. Br Med J (Clin Res). 1982;284:1291.

160 **Korelitz BI et al.** Long-term immunosuppressive therapy of ulcerative colitis. Am J Dig Dis. 1973;18:317.

161 **Korelitz BI et al.** Long-term immunosuppressive observation of children with ulcerative colitis treated with an immunosuppressive drug (6-mercaptopurine). Gastroenterology. 1977;72:A60.

162 **Bean RHD.** Treatment of ulcerative colitis with antimetabolites. Br Med J (Clin Res). 1966;1:1081.

163 **Sachar AB et al.** Immunotherapy in inflammatory bowel disease. Med Clin North Am. 1978;62:173.

164 **Heatly RV et al.** Disodium cromoglycate in the treatment of chronic proctitis. Gut. 1975;16:559.

165 **Grace RH et al.** Comparative trial of sodium cromoglycate enemas with prednisolone enemas in the treatment of ulcerative colitis. Gut. 1987;28:88.

166 **Buckell NA et al.** Controlled trial of disodium cromoglycate in chronic persistent ulcerative colitis. Gut. 1978;19:1140.

167 **Langman MJS et al.** Disodium cromoglycate maintenance treatment of ulcerative colitis. Acta Allergol. 1977;13:76.

168 **Dronfield MW et al.** Comparative trial of sulfasalazine and oral sodium cromoglycate in the maintenance therapy for ulcerative colitis. Gut. 1978;19:1136.

169 **Willoughby CP et al.** Comparison of disodium cromoglycate and sulfasalazine as maintenance therapy for ulcerative colitis. Lancet. 1979;1:119.

170 **Davies PS et al.** Maintenance of remission in ulcerative colitis: effect of an orally absorbed mast cell stabilizer. Am J Gastroenterol. 1980;74:150–53.

171 **Binder SC et al.** Disodium cromoglycate in the treatment of ulcerative colitis and Crohn's disease. Gut. 1981;22:55.

172 **Jalan KN et al.** An experience of ulcerative colitis: I. Toxic dilation in 55 cases. Gastroenterology. 1969;57:68.

173 **Farmer RG et al.** Clinical patterns in Crohn's disease: a statistical study of 615 cases. Gastroenterology. 1975;6:627.

174 **Greenstein AJ et al.** Crohn's disease of the colon. III. Toxic dilatation of the colon in Crohn's colitis. Am J Gastroenterol. 1975;63:117.

175 **Grieco MB et al.** Toxic megacolon complicating Crohn's colitis. Ann Surg. 1980;191:75.

176 **Binder SC et al.** Toxic megacolon in ulcerative colitis. Gastroenterology. 1974;66:909.

177 **Fazio VW.** Toxic megacolon in ulcerative colitis and Crohn's colitis. Clin Gastroenterol. 1980;9:389.

178 **Garrett JM et al.** Colonic mortality in ulcerative colitis after opiate administration. Gastroenterology. 1967;54:43.

179 **Smith FW et al.** Fulminant ulcerative colitis with toxic dilation of the colon: medical and surgical management of eleven cases with observations regarding etiology. Gastroenterology. 1962;24:233.

180 **Goldberg H et al.** The barium enema and toxic megacolon: cause-effect relationship? Gastroenterology. 1975;68:617.

181 **Goligher JC et al.** Surgical treatment of severe attacks of ulcerative colitis, with special reference to the advantages of early operation. Br Med J (Clin Res). 1970;4:703.

182 **Ritchie JK.** Results of surgery for inflammatory bowel disease: a further survey of one hospital region. Br Med J (Clin Res). 1974;1:264.

183 **Binder SC et al.** Emergency and urgent operations for ulcerative colitis. Arch Surg. 1975;110:284.

184 **Glotzer DJ.** Operation in inflammatory bowel disease indications and type. Clin Gastroenterol. 1980;5:41.

186 **Phillips SF.** Life with an ileostomy. In: Sleisenger MH, Fordtran JS, eds. Gastrointestinal Disease. 3rd ed. Philadelphia: WB Saunders; 1983:1184.

187 **Steiner JF.** The ostomy patient: pharmaceutical aspects. US Pharm. 1980;5:53.

188 **Kirsner JB.** Current medical and surgical opinions on important therapeutic issues in inflammatory bowel disease. Am J Surg. 1980;140:391.

189 **Gryboski J et al.** Inflammatory bowel disease in children. Med Clin North Am. 1980;64:1185.

190 **Fuson JA et al.** Endoscopic surveillance for cancer in chronic ulcerative colitis. Am J Gastroenterol. 1980;73:120.

191 **Butt JH et al.** A practical approach to the risk of cancer in inflammatory bowel disease. Med Clin North Am. 1980;73:120.

192 **Hellers G.** Crohn's disease in Stockholm County, 1955 to 1974. A study of epidemiology, results of surgical treatment and long-term prognosis. Scand J Gastroenterol (Suppl.). 1979;490:1.

193 **Merkhijian HS et al.** Clinical features and natural history of Crohn's disease. Gastroenterology. 1979;77:898.

194 **Farmer RG et al.** Clinical patterns in Crohn's disease: statistical study of 615 cases. Gastroenterology. 1975;68:627.

195 **Summers RW et al.** National Cooperative Crohn's Disease Study: results of drug treatment. Gastroenterology. 1979;77:847.

196 **Malchow H et al.** European Cooperative Crohn's Disease Study: results of drug treatment. Gastroenterology. 1984;86:249.

197 **Van Hees PAM et al.** Effect of sulfasalazine in patients with active Crohn's disease: a controlled double-blind study. Gut. 1981;22:404.

198 **Gray SJ et al.** Treatment of ulcerative colitis and regional enteritis with ACTH. Arch Intern Med. 1951;87:646.

199 **Stanley MM et al.** The uses of corticotrophin (ACTH) in the treatment of chronic regional enteritis. Med Clin North Am. 1951;35:1255.

200 **Sauer WG et al.** Experiences with the use of corticotropin in regional enteritis. Gastroenterology. 1952;22:550.

201 **Jones JH et al.** Corticosteroids and corticotropin in the treatment of Crohn's disease. Gut. 1966;7:181.

202 **Sparberg N et al.** Long-term corticosteroid therapy for regional enteritis: an analysis of 58 courses in 54 patients. Am J Dig Dis. 1966;865.

203 **Cooke WT et al.** Corticosteroid or corticotropin therapy in Crohn's disease (regional enteritis). Gut. 1970;11:921.

204 **Anthonisen P at al.** The clinical effect of salazosulphapyridine (Salazopyridine) in Crohn's disease. Scand J Gastroenterol. 1974;9:549.

205 **Singleton JW et al.** A trial of sulfasalazine as adjunctive therapy in Crohn's disease. Gastroenterology. 1979;77:887.

206 **Lefton HB et al.** Ileorectal anastomosis for Crohn's disease of the colon. Gastroenterology. 1975;69:612.

207 **Bergman L et al.** Postoperative treatment with corticosteroids and salazosulphapyridine (Salazopyrine) after radical resection for Crohn's disease. Scand J Gastroenterol. 1976;11:651.

208 **Rhodes J et al.** Effect of low-dose steroids on clinical relapse in Crohn's disease. Gut. 1978;19:606.

209 **Smith RC et al.** Low-dose steroids and clinical relapse in Crohn's disease: a controlled trial. Gut. 1978;19:606.

210 **Baron JH et al.** Sulfasalazine in asymptomatic Crohn's disease: a multicentre trial. Gut. 1977;18:69.

211 **Wenckert A et al.** The long-term prophylactic effect of salazosulphapyridine (Salazopyrine) in primarily resected patients with Crohn's disease. A controlled double-blind trial. Scand J Gastroenterol. 1978;13:161.

212 **Singleton JW et al.** National Cooperative Crohn's Disease Study: adverse reaction to study drugs. Gastroenterology. 1979;77:870.

213 **Kaufman S et al.** A prospective study of the course of Crohn's disease. Dig Dis Sci. 1979;24:269.

214 **Willoughby JMT et al.** Controlled trial of azathioprine in Crohn's disease. Lancet. 1971;2:944.

215 **Rosenberg JL et al.** A controlled trial of azathioprine in Crohn's disease. Am J Dig Dis. 1975;20:721.

216 **Present DH et al.** Treatment of Crohn's disease with 6-mercaptopurine: a long-term randomized double-blind study. N Engl J Med. 1980;302: 981.

217 **O'Donoghue DP et al.** Double-blind withdrawal trial of azathioprine as maintenance treatment for Crohn's disease. Lancet. 1978;2:955.

218 **Kinlen LJ et al.** Collaborative United Kingdom—Australian study of cancer in patients treated with immunosuppressive drugs. Br Med J (Clin Res). 1979;2:1461.

219 **Rasmussen SN et al.** 5-Aminosalicylic acid in a slow-release preparation: bioavailability, plasma level, and excretion in humans. Gastroenterology. 1982;83:1062.

220 **Klotz U et al.** A new slow-release form of 5-aminosalicylic acid for the oral treatment of inflammatory bowel disease. Biopharmaceutic and clinical pharmacokinetic characteristics. Arzneimittelforschung. 1985;35:636.

221 **Rasmussen SN et al.** Treatment of Crohn's disease with peroral 5-aminosalicylic acid. Gastroenterology. 1983; 85:1350.

222 **Rhodes J et al.** Controlled trial of azathioprine in Crohn's disease. Lancet. 1971;2:1273.

223 **Klein M et al.** Treatment of Crohn's disease with azathioprine: a controlled evaluation. Gastroenterology. 1974;66: 916.

224 **Watson WC et al.** Azathioprine in the management of Crohn's disease: a randomized crossover study. Gastroenterology. 1974;66:796.

225 **Ginsberg AL.** The azathioprine controversy. Dig Dis Sci. 1981;26:364.

226 **Onderdonk JA et al.** Protective effect of metronidazole in experimental ulcerative colitis. Gastroenterology. 1974;74:521.

227 **Blichfeldt P et al.** Metronidazole for Crohn's disease: a double-blind crossover clinical trial. Scand J Gastroenterol. 1978;13:123.

228 **Bernstein LH et al.** Healing of perineal Crohn's disease with metronidazole. Gastroenterology. 1980;79: 357.

229 **Jakobovits J et al.** Metronidazole therapy for Crohn's disease and associated fistulae. Am J Gastroenterol. 1984;79: 533.

230 **Ursling B et al.** A comparative study of metronidazole and sulfasalazine for active Crohn's disease: the cooperative Crohn's disease study in Sweden. II. Results. Gastroenterology. 1982;83: 550.

231 **Keighley MRB.** Infection and the use of antibiotics in Crohn's disease. Can J Surg. 1984;27:438.

232 **Ambrose NS et al.** Antibiotic therapy for treatment in relapse of intestinal Crohn's disease. Dis Colon Rectum. 1985;28:81.

233 **Krause JR et al.** Occurrence of three cases of carcinoma in individuals with Crohn's disease treated with metronidazole. Am J Gastroenterol. 1985;80: 978.

234 **Segal AW et al.** Levamisole in the treatment of Crohn's disease. Lancet. 1977;2:382.

235 **Wesdorp E et al.** Levamisole in Crohn's disease: a double-blind controlled trial. Gut. 1977;18:A971.

236 **Burnham WR et al.** Oral BCG vaccine in Crohn's disease. Gut. 1979;20: 229.

237 **Rahban S et al.** BCG treatment of Crohn's disease. Am J Gastroenterol. 1979;71:196.

238 **Williams SE et al.** A controlled trial of disodium cromoglycate in the treatment of Crohn's disease. Digestion. 1980;20:395.

239 **Vicary FR et al.** Double-blind trial of the use of transfer factor in the treatment of Crohn's disease. Gut. 1979;20: 408.

240 **Vantrappen G et al.** Treatment of Crohn's disease with interferon: a preliminary clinical trial. Acta Clin Belg. 1980;35:4.

241 **Mekhjian HS et al.** National Cooperative Crohn's Disease Study: factors determining recurrence of Crohn's disease after surgery. Gastroenterology. 1979;77:907.

242 **de Dombal FT.** Recurrent Crohn's disease. Can J Surg. 1974;17:408.

243 **Allan R et al.** Crohn's disease involving the colon: an audit of clinical management. Gastroenterology. 1977;73: 723.

244 **Biddle WL et al.** Long-term use of mesalamine enemas to induce remission in ulcerative colitis. Gastroenterology. 1990;99:113.

245 **Sutherland LR et al.** 5-Aminosalicylic acid enemas in the treatment of distal ulcerative colitis, proctosigmoiditis, and proctitis. Gastroenterology. 1987; 92:1894.

246 **Danish 5-ASA Group.** Topical 5-aminosalicylic acid versus prednisolone in ulcerative proctosigmoiditis. A randomized, double-blind multicenter trial. Dig Dis Sci. 1987;32:598.

247 **William CN et al.** Double-blind placebo-controlled evaluation of 5-ASA suppositories in active distal proctitis and measurement of extent of spread using 99mm Tc-labelled 5-ASA suppositories. Dig Dis Sci. 1987;32:71S.

248 **Biddle WL et al.** 5-aminosalicylic acid enemas effective agent in maintaining remission in left-sided ulcerative colitis. Gastroenterology. 1988;94:1075.

249 **Korazek RA et al.** Methotrexate induces clinical and histologic remission in patients with refractory inflammatory bowel disease. Ann Intern Med. 1989;110:353.

250 **Brynskow J et al.** A placebo-controlled, double-blind randomized trial of cyclosporine therapy in active chronic Crohn's disease. N Engl J Med. 1989;321:845.

251 **Olsalazine for ulcerative colitis.** Med Lett. 1990;32:105.

252 **Carpani de Kaski M et al.** Fluticasone propionate in Crohn's disease. Gut. 1991;32:65761.

253 **Schreiber S et al.** The role of the mucosal immune system in inflammatory bowel disease. Gastroenterol Clin North Am. 1992;21(2):451–502.

254 **Harris ML et al.** Free radicals and other reactive oxygen metabolites in inflammatory bowel disease: cause, consequence or epiphenomenon. Pharmacol Ther. 1992;53:375–408.

255 **Grisham MB, Yamada T.** Neutrophils, nitrogen oxides and inflammatory bowel disease. Ann N Y Acad Sci. 1992;664:103–15.

256 **Rask-Madsen J et al.** 5-Lipoxygenase inhibitors for the treatment of inflammatory bowel disease. Agents and Actions. 1992;Spec No:C37–46.

257 **Campieri M et al.** Mesalamine (5-ASA) suppositories in the treatment of ulcerative proctitis or distal proctosigmoiditis. A randomized controlled trial. Scand J Gastroenterol. 1990;25:663–68.

258 **Biddel WL et al.** Long-term use of mesalamine enemas to induce remission in ulcerative colitis. Gastroenterology. 1990;99:113–18.

259 **Friedman LS et al.** 5-aminosalicylic acid enemas in refractory distal ulcerative colitis. A randomized, controlled trial. Am J Gastroenterol. 1986;81: 412–18.

260 **Campieri M et al.** Efficacy of 5-aminosalicylic acid enemas versus hydrocortisone enemas in ulcerative colitis. Dig Dis Sci. 1987;32(Suppl. 12):67S–70S.

261 **Mulder CJJ et al.** Comparison of 5-aminosalicylic acid (3 g) and prednisolone phosphate sodium enemas (30 mg) in the treatment of distal ulcerative colitis. A prospective, randomized, double-blind trial. Scand J Gastroenterol. 1988;23:1005–8.

262 **Campieri M et al.** 5-aminosalicylic acid suppositories in the management of ulcerative colitis. Dis Colon Rectum. 1989;32:398–99.

263 **D'Arienzo A et al.** 5-aminosalicylic acid suppositories in the maintenance of remission in idiopathic proctitis or proctosigmoiditis. A double-blind placebo-controlled clinical trial. Am J Gastroenterol. 1990;85:1079–82.

264 **Sutherland LR et al.** 5-Aminosalicylic acid enemas in the maintenance of remission in distal ulcerative colitis and proctitis. Can J Gastroenterol. 1987;1:3–6.

265 **McPhee MS et al.** Proctocolitis unresponsive to conventional therapy. Response to 5-aminosalicylic acid enemas. Dig Dis Sci. 1987;32(Suppl. 12): 76S–81S.

266 **Sanberg-Gertzen H et al.** Absorption and excretion of a single 1-g dose of azodisal sodium in subjects with ileostomy. Scand J Gastroenterol. 1983; 18:107–11.

267 **Lauritsen K et al.** Colonic azodialsaliclyate metabolism determined by in vivo dialysis in healthy volunteers and patients with ulcerative colitis. Gastroenterology. 1984;86:1496–1500.

268 **Ryde EM et al.** The pharmacokinetics of olsalazine sodium in healthy volunteers after a single i.v. dose and after oral doses with and without food. Eur J Clin Pharmacol. 1988;34:481–88.

269 **Sandbert-Gertzen H et al.** Azodisal sodium in the treatment of ulcerative colitis. A study of tolerance and relapse-prevention properties. Gastroenterology. 1986;90:1024–030.

270 **Irland A et al.** Controlled trial comparing olsalazine and sulphasalazine for the maintenance treatment of ulcerative colitis. Gut. 1988;29:835–37.

271 **Sandberg-Gertzen H et al.** Long-term treatment with olsalazine for ulcerative colitis. Safety and relapse prevention. A follow-up study. Scand J Gastroenterol. 1988;23(Suppl. 148):48–50.

272 **Selby WS et al.** Olsalazine in active ulcerative colitis. Br Med J. 1985;291: 1373–375.

273 **Hetzel DJ et al.** Olsalazine in the treatment of active ulcerative colitis. A placebo controlled clinical trial and assessment of drug disposition. Scand J Gastroenterol. 1988;23(Suppl. 48): 61–9.

274 **Feurle GE et al.** Olsalazine versus placebo in the treatment of mild to moderate ulcerative colitis. A randomized double blind trial. Gut. 1989;30:1354–361.

275 **Willoughby CP et al.** Double-blind comparison of olsalazine and sulphasalazine in active ulcerative colitis. Scand J Gastroenterol. 1988;23(Suppl. 148):40–4.

276 **Ewe K et al.** Treatment of ulcerative colitis with olsalazine and sulphasalazine. Efficacy and side-effects. Scand J Gastroenterol. 1988;23(Suppl. 148): 70–5.

277 **Rao SSC et al.** Olsalazine or sulphasalazine in first attacks of ulcerative colitis? A double blind study. Gut. 1989; 30:835–37.

278 **Jarnerot G.** Clinical tolerance of olsalazine. Scand J Gastroenterol. 1988; 23(Suppl. 148):21–3.

279 **Rao SS et al.** Influence of olsalazine and sulphasalazine on gastrointestinal time. Scand J Gastroenterol. 1988;23 (Suppl.148):96–100.

280 **Dew MJ et al.** Colonic release of 5-aminosalicylic acid from an oral preparation in active ulcerative colitis. Br J Clin Pharmacol. 1983;16:185–87.

281 **Schroeder KW et al.** Coated oral 5-aminosalicylic acid therapy for mild to moderate active ulcerative colitis. A randomized study. N Engl J Med. 1987;317:1625–629.

282 **Riley SA et al.** Comparison of delayed-release 5-aminosalicylic acid (mesalazine) and sulfasalazine as maintenance treatment for patients with ulcerative colitis. Gastroenterology. 1988;94:1383–389.

283 **Dew MJ et al.** Maintenance of remission in ulcerative colitis with 5-aminosalicylic acid in high doses by mouth. Br Med J. 1983;287:23–4.

284 **Yu DK et al.** Pharmacokinetics of pentasa capsules in man. Pharm Res. 1991; 8(Suppl. 10):S315.

285 **Hanauer S et al.** Mesalamine capsules for treatment of active ulcerative colitis. Am J Gastroenterol. 1993;88:1188.

286 **Miner P et al.** Maintenance of remission in ulcerative colitis patients with controlled-release mesalamine cap-

sules (Pentasa). Gastroenterology. 1992;102(4pt2):a666.

287 **Mulder CJJ et al.** Pentasa in lieu of sulfasalazine. Ann Intern Med. 1988; 106:911–12.

288 **Mulder CJJ et al.** Double-blind comparison of slow-release 5-aminosalicylic acid and sulfasalazine in remission maintenance in ulcerative colitis. Gastroenterology. 1983;85:1350.

289 **Habal FM et al.** Treatment of ulcerative colitis with oral 5-aminosalicylic acid including patients with adverse reactions to sulfasalazine. Am J Gastroenterol. 1988;83:15–9.

290 **Esbjorner E, Janerot G.** Sulphasalazine and sulphapyridine serum levels in children of mothers treated with sulphasalazine during pregnancy and lactation. Acta Paediatr Scand. 1987;76: 124–37.

291 **Fraser FC, Fainstat TD.** Production of congenital defects in offspring of pregnant mice treated with cortisone. Progress report. Pediatrics. 1951;8: 527–33.

292 **Bongiovanni AM, McPadden AJ.** Steroids during pregnancy and possible fetal consequences. Fertil Steril. 1960; 11:181–86.

293 **Berget A, Weber T.** Metronidazole and pregnancy. Ugeskr Laeger. 1972; 134:2085–89. In: Shepard TH. Catalog of Teratogenic Agents, 3rd ed. Baltimore: Johns Hopkins University Press; 1980:228.

294 **Scott-Gray M.** Metronidazole in obstetric practice. J Obstet Gynaecol Br Commonw. 1964;71:82–5.

295 **Beard CM et al.** Lack of evidence for cancer due to use of metronidazole. N Engl J Med. 1979;301:519–22.

296 **Heinonen OP et al.** Birth Defects and Drugs in Pregnancy. Littleton: Publishing Sciences Group; 1977:298–99, 302.

297 **Greenberg F.** Possible metronidazole teratogenicity and clefting. Am J Med Genet. 1985;22:825.

298 **Cantu JM, Garcia-Cruz D.** Midline facial defect as a teratogenic effect of metronidazole. Birth Defects. 1982;18: 85–8.

299 **Product information.** Flagyl. Searle and Company. 1990.

300 **American Hospital Formulary Service.** Drug Information 1993. Bethesda: American Society of Hospital Pharmacists. 1993:505–10.

301 **Adler DJ, Korleitz BI.** The therapeu-

tic efficacy of 6-mercaptopurine in refractory ulcerative colitis. Am J Gastroenterol. 1988;83:1042.

302 **Present DH et al.** Treatment of Crohn's disease with 6-mercaptopurine: a long term randomized, double-blind study. N Engl J Med. 1980;302: 981–87.

303 **Rosenkranz JC, Githens JH.** Azathioprine (Imuran) and pregnancy. Am J Obstet Gynecol. 1967;387–94.

304 **Davidson JM, Lindheimer MD.** Pregnancy in woman with renal allografts. Semin Nephrol. 1984;4:240–51.

305 **Alstead EM et al.** Safety of azathioprine in pregnancy in inflammatory bowel disease. Gastroenterology. 1990; 99:443–46.

306 **Adler DJ, Korelitz BI.** The therapeutic efficacy of 6-mercaptopurine in refractory ulcerative colitis. Am J Gastroenterol. 1990;85:717–21.

307 **Kozarek RA et al.** Methotrexate induces clinical and histological remission in patients with refractory inflammatory bowel disease. Ann Intern Med. 1989;321:845–50.

308 **Hermanowicz A et al.** The effect of levamisole on the maintenance of remission of ulcerative colitis. Scand J Gastroenterol. 1987;22:367–71.

309 **Sacher DB et al.** Levamisole in Crohn's disease: a randomized, double-blind, placebo-controlled trial. Am J Med. 1987;82:536–39.

310 **Lichtiger S et al.** Preliminary report: cyclosporine in treatment of severe active ulcerative colitis. Lancet. 1990; 336:16.

311 **Lichtiger S et al.** Cyclosporine therapy in inflammatory bowel disease: open label experience. Mt Sinai J Med. 1990;57:315.

312 **Lichtiger S et al.** Cyclosporine in severe ulcerative colitis refractory to steroid therapy. N Engl J Med. 1994;330: 1841.

313 **Korelitz BI.** Complications and their management. In: Haubrich W, Schaffner F, eds. Gastroenterology. Philadelphia: WB Saunders; 1995:1465–466.

314 **Myers S.** Medical management and prognosis. In: Haubrich W, Schaffner F, eds. Gastroenterology. Philadelphia: WB Saunders; 1995:1498–499.

315 **Singleton JW et al.** Mesalamine capsules for treatment of active Crohn's disease: results of a 16-week trial. Gastroenterology. 1993;104:1293–301.

316 **Hanauer SB et al.** Long-term management of Crohn's disease with mesala-

mine capsules (Pentasa). Am J Gastroenterol. 1993;88:1343–351.

317 **Rasmussen SN et al.** 5-aminosalicylic in the treatment of Crohn's disease. A 16-week, double-blind, placebo-controlled, multicenter study with Pentasa. Scand J Gastroenterol. 1987;22:877–83.

318 **Mahida YR et al.** Slow release 5-aminosalicylic acid (Pentasa) for the treatment of active Crohn's disease. Digestion. 1990;45:88–92.

319 **Present DH et al.** 6-mercaptopurine in the management of inflammatory bowel disease: short and long term toxicity. Ann Intern Med. 1989;111:641–49.

320 **Perrault J et al.** 6-mercaptopurine therapy in selected cases of corticosteroid-dependent Crohn's disease. Mayo Clin Proc. 1991;66:480–84.

321 **Feagan BG et al.** Low-dose cyclosporine for the treatment of Crohn's disease. N Engl J Med. 1994;330:1846.

322 **Sutherland L et al.** Double-blind, placebo-controlled trial of metronidazole in Crohn's disease. Gut. 1991;32: 1071–075.

323 **Carling L et al.** Sucralfate enema-effective in IBD? Endoscopy. 1986;18: 115.

324 **Campieri M et al.** 5-Aminosalicylic acid, sucralfate and placebo enemas in the treatment of distal ulcerative colitis. Gastroenterology. 1984;94:58. Abstract.

325 **Riley SA et al.** A comparison of sucralfate and prednisolone enemas in the treatment of active distal ulcerative colitis. Gastroenterology. 1988;94:377. Abstract.

326 **Rampton DS, Sladen GE.** Prostaglandin synthesis inhibitors in ulcerative colitis: flurbiprofen compared with conventional treatment. Prostaglandins. 1981;21:417–25.

327 **Doe W, Pavil P.** Antigen presentation in the gut. Can J Gastroenterol. 1990; 4:267–70.

328 **Mayer L, Sacher DM.** Efficacy of chloroquine in the treatment of inflammatory bowel disease. Gastroenterology. 1988;94:293. Abstract.

329 **Laursen LS et al.** Selective 5-lipoxygenase inhibition in ulcerative colitis. Lancet. 1990;335:683–85.

330 **Lechin F et al.** Treatment of ulcerative colitis with clonidine. J Clin Pharmacol. 1985;25:219–26.

331 **Peppercorn MA.** Advances in drug therapy for inflammatory bowel disease. Ann Intern Med. 1990;112:50–60.

Alcoholic Cirrhosis

Paula A Teichner
Joseph P Gee
Lucia K Jim

Overview 25-1
  Classification 25-1
  Pathogenesis 25-2
  Clinical Features 25-2
    Common symptoms 25-2
    Portal hypertension (See Figure 25.1) 25-2
    Laboratory findings 25-3
  Treatment 25-3
Ascites 25-3
  Dietary Implications 25-3
  Clinical Presentation 25-4
  Pathogenesis 25-4
  Goals of Therapy 25-4
  Fluid and Electrolyte Balance 25-4
    Urinary Na:K ratio 25-4
    Sodium restriction 25-4
    Water restriction 25-5
    Role of aldosterone 25-5
  Diuretic Therapy 25-5
    Choice of agent 25-5
    Monitoring 25-5
      Clinical responses 25-5
      Laboratory parameters 25-5
    Complications 25-5
      Hypokalemic-hypochloremic metabolic alkalosis
        and hyponatremia 25-5
      Prerenal azotemia 25-6
      Encephalopathy 25-6
  Paracentesis 25-6
    Albumin 25-6
    Dextran 70 25-6
  Alternative Therapy 25-6
    Albumin infusion 25-7
    Peritoneovenous shunt 25-7
    Ascites filtration and reinfusion 25-7
Esophageal Varices 25-7
  Treatment 25-7
    Goals of therapy 25-7
    General management 25-7
    Hypovolemia 25-7
    Fiberoptic esophagoscopy 25-8

Balloon tamponade 25-8
Vasopressin 25-8
Somatostatin 25-8
Sclerotherapy (Also see Question 14) 25-8
Endoscopic band ligation 25-8
Alternative treatment modalities 25-8
Vasopressin 25-8
  Route of administration 25-8
  Dosing 25-9
  Complications 25-9
Precautions to Minimize Recurrence 25-9
  Beta blockers 25-9
  Sclerotherapy 25-9
  Surgery 25-9
  Transjugular intrahepatic portal systemic shunting
    (TIPS) 25-9
  Endoscopic band ligation 25-10
Primary Prophylaxis of Variceal Bleeding 25-10
  Beta blockers 25-10
  Sclerotherapy 25-10
  Isosorbide-5-mononitrate 25-10
Patient Education 25-10
Hepatic Encephalopathy 25-10
  Pathogenesis 25-10
    Ammonia 25-10
    Amino acid balance 25-11
    Gamma aminobutyric acid (GABA) 25-11
  Clinical Presentation and Predisposing Factors
    (See Table 25.1) 25-11
  Treatment 25-12
    General management 25-12
    Lactulose 25-12
      Dosing 25-12
    Neomycin 25-12
      Comparison with lactulose 25-13
    Neomycin plus lactulose 25-13
  Alternative therapy 25-13
    Colectomy 25-13
    Branched chain amino acids 25-13
    Levodopa and bromocriptine 25-13
    Flumazenil 25-14
Hepatorenal Syndrome 25-14

Cirrhosis can be defined as a chronic disease of the liver in which widespread hepatic parenchymal cell destruction has led to the formation of connective tissue and nodular regeneration with consequent disorganization of the normal lobular architecture.[1] The liver nodules alter the anatomical location and function of the blood vessels and bile ducts, causing obstruction and resulting in portal hypertension, ascites, jaundice, and esophageal varices.

Classification

The classification of cirrhosis is still undergoing evolution: a confusing array of nomenclature and inconsistent criteria are found in current literature.[1,2] Podolsky and Isselbacher have classified cirrhosis as follows: alcoholic (Laennec's), postnecrotic, biliary, cardiac, metabolic, inherited, drug related, or miscellaneous (e.g., sarcoidosis).[3] The most prevalent type of cirrhosis in the United States and Western Europe is Laennec's cirrhosis, with alcoholism being the most common cause.[2] The incidence of cirrhosis among chronic alcoholics is reported to be 10% to 20%. Malnutrition and genetic factors might also contribute to the high incidence of alcohol-induced cirrhosis. Postnecrotic and biliary cirrhosis also are common in the United States. Worldwide, chronic hepatitis B and other forms of chronic active hepatitis significantly contribute to the development of cirrhosis.[1]

Pathogenesis

The pathogenesis of alcoholic cirrhosis is not completely understood. Alcohol, by itself, can cause fatty infiltration and ultrastructural changes in the liver of animals and humans. Although dietary supplementation does not prevent alcohol-induced lesions in humans, dietary deficiencies can potentiate the injurious effect of alcohol. The major biochemical alteration, an increase in the NADH:NAD ratio, is produced by the oxidation of alcohol and results in hyperlipidemia, fatty liver, ketosis, hypoglycemia, hyperlacticacidemia, and other abnormalities in the microsomal enzyme system. Investigators have uncovered yet another new pathway of ethanol oxidation involving P450IIE1, an ethanol-inducible enzyme in the cytochrome P450 family.[4,5] High serum concentration and chronic use of alcohol induce the microsomal enzymes (P450IIE1) which accelerate the metabolism of ethanol and other substances. The microsomal enzyme induction persists for some time after abstinence from long-term alcoholic consumption. The net result of the induced microsomal enzyme system is an increased conversion of chemical entities to their highly hepatotoxic metabolites (e.g., carbon tetrachloride, bromobenzene, halothane, isoniazid, paracetamol), and of ethanol to acetaldehyde. Confirmation of this theory may provide an explanation for the increased susceptibility of the alcoholic liver to hepatotoxic agents and the deleterious effects of acetaldehyde (see Chapter 82: Alcohol Abuse).[6,7]

Electron microscopic study of fatty liver produced experimentally by the administration of alcohol reveals changes in the mitochondria and rough endoplasmic reticulum comparable to those seen in patients with alcoholic hepatitis, suggesting that fatty liver may be a precursor of alcoholic hepatitis. Since only a few alcoholics develop hepatitis and even fewer progress to cirrhosis, other factors (e.g., genetic predisposition, exposure to hepatotoxins) in combination with alcohol probably contribute to the development of cirrhosis.[6,7] Some cases of alcoholic hepatitis do not progress to cirrhosis in spite of continued excessive drinking; others progress to cirrhosis despite documented abstinence.[8] While cirrhosis is probably the result of fibrosis secondary to hepatocyte inflammation and necrosis, the interrelationships between fatty liver, alcoholic hepatitis, and cirrhosis need clarification.

Clinical Features

Common Symptoms

Cirrhosis may be either asymptomatic for a variable length of time or actively symptomatic with alcoholic hepatitis as the primary lesion. The most common subjective complaints (anorexia, nausea, abdominal discomfort, weakness, weight loss, easy fatigability, malaise) are nonspecific for hepatocellular injuries. Hepatosplenomegaly, jaundice, ascites, and peripheral edema may be found on physical examination. Spider angiomas and palmar erythema are common signs of liver disease. Spider angiomas are fiery red vascular figures in the skin consisting of a central point from which superficial arterioles radiate, giving the total appearance of a spider's legs. When pressure is applied to that central point, the arterioles blanch and when pressure is released, the arterioles refill centrifugally. Palmar erythema involves an intense diffuse flushing of the skin over the "meaty" part of the palm opposite from the thumb (hypothenar eminence); it usually is less intense over the "meaty" part of the palm at the base of the thumb (thenar prominence).

Portal Hypertension

Many signs and symptoms of advanced liver cirrhosis are related to complications secondary to the development of portal hypertension. The portal vein collects blood from the abdominal portion of the digestive tract, pancreas, and spleen and transports the blood to the liver (see Figure 25.1). This portal blood must pass through a capillary system under high pressure (i.e., 5 to 10 mm Hg) to overcome the resistance of the hepatic sinusoids.[9] Portal venous blood also contains a high concentration of oxygen because of the relatively high blood flow through the splanchnic area. It also contains many nutrients and bacterial waste products from the digestive tract.

In advanced cirrhosis, blood flow can be blocked by regenerated endothelial and sinusoidal nodules that compress and distort the hepatic veins, thereby further increasing portal venous pressure.[10] Portal hypertension also can be caused by extrahepatic vein thrombosis, schistosomiasis, and posthepatic venous obstruction (e.g., Budd-Chiari syndrome, metastatic liver tumors).

If portal hypertension persists, it alters normal lymph and blood flow and subsequently facilitates the formation of collateral blood vessels and intrahepatic shunts.[9] The natural sites for the development of collateral circulation are the low pressure veins and venules in the submucosa of the esophagus, anterior abdominal wall, rectum, and splenic vein. Thus, portal hypertension is often accompanied by esophageal and gastric varices, abdominal collaterals, ascites, hemorrhoids, splenic enlargement, and symptoms related to the shunting of venous blood away from the liver. Ruptured esophageal varices are the most common life-threatening complications of portal hypertension. Other major complications related to advanced cirrhosis include hepatic encephalopathy and renal failure.[10,11]

While clinical presentations and laboratory evaluations may not reflect the precise nature or extent of the cirrhotic process, the triad of parenchymal necrosis, cellular regeneration, and fibrotic nodular scarring is present in all cirrhotic livers.[1] The major clinical ramifications of the pathologic changes include significant loss of functional liver cells and diversion of hepatic blood flow from the hepatic parenchyma. Resultant complications are related to the disturbance of the many synthetic, secretory, and metabolic functions of the liver.

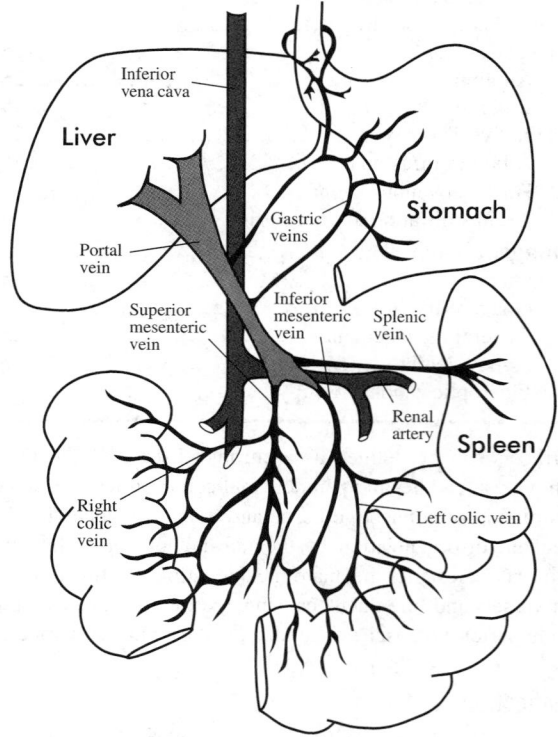

Fig 25.1 Schematic Diagram of Portal Venous System

Laboratory Findings

Conventional biochemical liver tests such as the serum aminotransferases [aspartate aminotransferase (AST formerly known as SGOT) and alanine aminotransferase (ALT formerly known as SGPT)], alkaline phosphatase, and serum bilirubin do not measure quantitatively the functional capacity of the liver; however, they do provide an approximate qualitative estimate of liver dysfunction.

The aminotransferases are released from the normal turnover of liver cells (see Chapter 4: Interpretation of Clinical Laboratory Tests). Persistently high serum concentrations of aminotransferases suggest leakage of these enzymes from injured (rather than dead) hepatocytes. Thus, the serum concentrations of AST and ALT may not be extraordinarily high when the liver dysfunction is due to hepatocellular necrosis.[12]

Since alkaline phosphatase is present in high concentrations in biliary canaliculi, an increase in the serum concentration of alkaline phosphatase to greater than three times the normal value usually suggests an obstructive (rather than a necrotic) component to the hepatotoxic process. Alkaline phosphatase serum concentrations usually increase with age and an increase of 30% to 50% above the upper limits of normal is not unusual in geriatric patients.[2] When fractionation of alkaline phosphatase demonstrates high concentrations of the hepatic isoenzyme, or when gamma glutamyl transpeptidase serum concentrations are high, hepatic toxicity is suggested.

The serum albumin concentration usually is not regarded as an indication of liver function. Although albumin is synthesized by the hepatic parenchymal cells, changes in albumin concentration are nonspecific, insensitive to liver disease, and have little value in the differential diagnosis of liver diseases. Nevertheless, a low serum albumin concentration (i.e., <3 gm/dL) that is unresponsive to therapy indicates an unfavorable prognosis.

Prolongation of prothrombin time due to chronic obstructive jaundice, celiac disease, and hypovitaminosis K usually can be improved within 24 hours after a 10 mg dose of vitamin K. This response does not occur in patients with diffuse hepatocellular disease and thus may be of some diagnostic value.[12] A prolonged prothrombin time that is unresponsive to parenteral vitamin K may indicate imminent development of fulminant hepatic failure and is a poor prognostic sign in chronic hepatocellular disease.[8,10]

A blood urea nitrogen (BUN) that is less than 5 mg/dL may be encountered in alcoholic cirrhosis, but it is uncommon in other forms of cirrhosis.[2] The low BUN is attributed to inadequate protein intake accompanied by a depressed hepatic capacity to synthesize urea. The interpretation of the BUN is difficult if the alcoholic cirrhotic patient develops renal dysfunction, manifests gastrointestinal (GI) bleeding, or is either volume depleted or volume overloaded.

Treatment

Abstinence from alcohol, rest, and nutritional supplementation are the general approaches to management of alcoholic cirrhosis. Inadequate dietary intake is common among alcoholics with liver disease.[13] Low intake of foods containing folic acid frequently results in megaloblastic anemia, which is easily reversed by 1 mg/day of folic acid for five to seven days. Thiamine (B_1), cyanocobalamin (B_{12}), riboflavin, nicotinic acid, and pyridoxine (B_6) are other vitamins that often need to be replaced in this patient population.[13] Peripheral neuropathy in alcoholics is often associated with thiamine deficiency, with a few cases related to low pyridoxine levels. Wernicke's encephalopathy is related to thiamine deficiency (see Chapter 82: Alcohol Abuse). Thiamine 100 mg/day is routinely given to patients with cirrhosis, but it need not be given for more than seven to ten days once the patient is able to eat.

Pharmacological treatment of alcoholic cirrhosis is still largely experimental. Drugs which may modify the disease process include penicillamine,[14] propylthiouracil (PTU),[15,19,22] azathioprine, and colchicine;[16] however, none appears extremely promising.

Colchicine may play a more active role in the treatment of primary biliary cirrhosis (PBC).[17,18] This progressive disease of the liver is characterized by destruction of the intrahepatic bile ducts.[55] As the damage is hypothesized to be lymphocyte-mediated, colchicine, via its anti-inflammatory activity, may be of greater benefit in PBC than in other types of cirrhosis.

There is no specific drug therapy for cirrhosis, but drugs commonly are used to treat secondary complications of cirrhosis. Therefore, this chapter will emphasize the secondary complications of cirrhosis and their management.

Ascites
Dietary Implications

1. R.W. is a 54-year-old male with a two-week history of nausea, vomiting, and lower abdominal cramps without diarrhea. Despite chronic anorexia, he has managed to eat about two meals a day and drink a fifth of vodka per day for the past two years. During this time he experienced a 30-pound weight loss. He began drinking nine years before admission when his wife became an invalid secondary to a brain tumor. His alcohol consumption increased from one pint to a fifth daily two years before this admission. Recently, he has noticed bilateral swelling of his legs, an increased tenseness and girth of his abdomen, and yellowing of his skin and the sclera of his eyes. His past medical history is noncontributory with the exception of a hospitalization for "bowel pain" two years ago. The GI work-up was negative at that time.

Physical examination revealed an afebrile, jaundiced, and cachectic male in moderate distress. Spider angiomas were found on his face and upper chest, and palmar erythema was noted. Abdominal examination revealed prominent veins on a very tense abdomen. The liver edge was percussed down to the pelvic brim and 2+ ascites was noted by shifting dullness and a fluid wave. The spleen was not palpable. On neurologic examination, R.W. was awake and oriented to time, date, and place. Cranial nerves II to XII were grossly intact, but a decrease in vibratory sensation of the lower extremities was noted bilaterally.

Admission laboratory data were as follows: sodium (Na) 132 mEq/L, chloride (Cl) 95 mEq/L, potassium (K) 3.8 mEq/L, bicarbonate 25 mEq/L, BUN 15 mg/dL, serum creatinine (SrCr) 1.4 mg/dL, glucose 136 mg/dL, hemoglobin (Hgb) 11.2 gm/dL, hematocrit (Hct) 33.4%, AST 212 IU (Normal: 5–29 IU), alkaline phosphatase 954 IU (Normal: 22–110 IU), prothrombin time (PT) was 13.5 seconds with a control of 12 seconds, bilirubin total:direct was 18.8 mg/dL:10.7 mg/dL, albumin was 2.3 gm/dL, and stool guaiac was positive. [SI units: Na 132 mmol/L; Cl 95 mmol/L; K 3.8 mmol/L; bicarbonate 25 mmol/L; BUN 5.36 mmol/L UREA; SrCr 123.76 µmol/L; glucose 7.55 mmol/L; Hgb 112 gm/L; Hct 0.334 1; AST 3.53 µkat/L (Normal: 0.08–0.48); alkaline phosphatase 15.9 µkat/L (Normal: 0.37–1.83); bilirubin 321.48:182.97 µmol/L; albumin 23 gm/L].

The impression on admission was alcoholic cirrhosis, ascites, and heme positive stools.

Why did R.W. present with cachexia and a history of weight loss despite eating two meals daily?

Deficiency in dietary protein is one of the reasons for the common history of weight loss obtained from alcoholic cirrhotic patients. In addition, chronic alcohol consumption often contributes to the depletion of liver glycogen stores and inhibition of hepatic gluconeogenesis (see Chapter 82: Alcohol Abuse).

In the cirrhotic patient, demand for glucose as a source of energy leads to mobilization of amino acid from muscles and subsequent muscle wasting. A high protein diet is unnecessary to maintain a positive nitrogen balance in the cirrhotic patient. A normal protein intake of 35 to 50 gm/day is sufficient to keep cirrhotic patients in protein equilibrium or positive nitrogen balance.[8]

Clinical Presentation

2. What subjective and objective evidence are compatible with alcoholic cirrhosis in R.W.?

R.W.'s presentation of a long history of alcohol abuse, cachexia, hypoalbuminemia, jaundice (i.e., yellowing of the skin and sclera of the eyes due to deposits of bilirubin), and his admission laboratory data are all consistent with advanced alcoholism. The finding of spider angiomas on his face and upper chest and palmar erythema also suggest significant hepatic involvement. The presence of ascites and prominent abdominal veins are suggestive of portal hypertension. His prolonged prothrombin time suggests hepatocellular dysfunction. Although a liver biopsy is usually required to confirm the presence and severity of cirrhosis, R.W.'s prolonged prothrombin time increases the risk of bleeding from a biopsy. Therefore, the risks versus benefits of a liver biopsy must be evaluated in R.W. with a modest increase in his prothrombin time. The presence of a normal BUN and an elevated direct or conjugated serum bilirubin are suggestive of some remaining hepatic parenchymal function.

The suspicion of alcoholic cirrhosis in R.W.'s case is supported primarily by his long history of alcoholism; nonspecific complaints of nausea, abdominal cramps, anorexia, and jaundice; the presence of hepatomegaly and ascites; hypoalbuminemia; and elevated liver enzymes.

The severity of cirrhosis may be assessed by noting the liver's conjugation ability (i.e., direct serum bilirubin), responsiveness of the prolonged prothrombin time to vitamin K therapy, and presence of other complications of parenchymal failure (i.e., encephalopathy, portal hypertension, esophageal varices).

The marked elevation of alkaline phosphatase and conjugated serum bilirubin in R.W.'s case suggests possible extrahepatic cholestasis, a phenomenon reported in some patients with alcoholic liver injuries.[20] More comprehensive reviews of the biochemical evaluation of liver diseases can be found elsewhere.[12]

Pathogenesis

3. What physiological mechanisms predispose R.W. to fluid accumulation in the peritoneal cavity?

Accumulation of fluid in the peritoneal cavity (i.e., ascites), is most frequently anteceded by cirrhosis. At present, four theories are postulated to explain the accumulation of ascitic fluid. The classical theory is that formation of ascites results from a combination of increased hydrostatic pressure in the portal venous system and decreased plasma oncotic pressure (i.e., low serum albumin concentration).[23] In cirrhosis, the hepatic venous outflow is blocked, eventually resulting in elevated portal vein back pressure and increased splanchnic blood volume[9] (e.g., as is evident by R.W.'s prominent abdominal veins). Exudation of fluid from the splanchnic capillary bed and the liver surface when the drainage capacity of the lymphatic system is exceeded also contributes to ascites. In addition, R.W.'s hypoalbuminemia (2.3 gm/dL), due to impaired albumin synthesis in the liver, favors the formation of ascites by decreasing the ability to hold fluid in the vascular system.

As fluid exudation continues, the arterial perfusion of vital organs is transiently reduced because of plasma volume contraction. Reduced blood flow to the kidneys and abnormal hepatic hemodynamics activate the renin-angiotensin-aldosterone system.[25] Increased aldosterone enhances the distal tubular reabsorption of sodium and water, thus expanding the total blood volume. This compensatory increase in circulating blood volume also can aggravate the portal hypertension, increase the splanchnic blood volume, and establish a vicious cycle.

A second proposed theory for the formation of ascites suggests that ascitic fluid accumulates only after the plasma volume expands from renal retention of sodium and water.[26] Excess fluid then "overflows" into the peritoneal cavity from the congested portal system.

The third explanation for the development of ascites is the "lymph imbalance" theory.[27] Visceral edema from an imbalance in lymphatic flow is suggested as the primary stimulus to retention of salt and water by the kidney. Subsequent expansion of the extracellular fluid volume further leads to increases in visceral lymph production that eventually exceeds lymph return and results in ascites.

A fourth concept describing the pathogenesis of ascites incorporates features from both the "underfilling" and "overflow" theories. This hypothesis suggests that "peripheral arterial vasodilation" is the initiating event which causes a decrease in effective blood volume and a compensatory increase in sodium and water retention by the kidney.[21,24]

The pathogenesis of ascites is multifactorial and cannot be explained by the proposed theories alone.[23] Treatment of ascites, regardless of whether the kidney initiates or secondarily contributes to ascites, is mainly directed at the removal of excess sodium and water.

Goals of Therapy

4. What are the therapeutic goals in the management of R.W.'s ascites?

The goals of therapy for R.W.'s ascites are to mobilize ascitic and edema fluid and to diminish abdominal discomfort, back pain, and difficulty in ambulation. Ultimately, treatment is aimed at preventing major complications such as hepatorenal syndrome, variceal bleeding, bacterial peritonitis, hernias, pleural effusions, and respiratory distress from compression of the diaphragm.[11,23] Treatment of ascites in R.W. should be undertaken cautiously and gradually because acid-base imbalances, hypokalemia, or intravascular volume depletion caused by overly aggressive therapy may lead to compromised renal function, hepatic encephalopathy, and death. Medical management of ascites involves bed rest, restriction of sodium and water intake, and diuretics to effect salt and water loss.[11,23,28,29,30]

Fluid and Electrolyte Balance

5. The 24-hour urinary electrolytes for R.W. were reported to be: Na 10 mEq/L and K 28 mEq/L. Why would sodium or water restriction be appropriate (or inappropriate) for R.W.?
[SI units: Na 10 mmol/L; K 28 mmol/L]

Urinary Na:K Ratio

Normally, the urine concentration of electrolytes mirrors the serum concentration of electrolytes (i.e., the sodium concentration is greater than that of potassium). A reversal of this pattern (i.e., potassium excretion exceeding sodium excretion) may indicate a relative hyperaldosteronism secondary to diminished renal blood flow and low oncotic pressure. If urine electrolyte monitoring is to be meaningful, the first sample must be obtained before initiating diuretic therapy.

Sodium Restriction

Sodium restriction of 10 to 20 mEq/day and bed rest will result in diuresis in many patients with cirrhosis and ascites; the degree of success depends upon the duration of the sodium restriction.[11,23,28,29] Patients with normal or high urine sodium concentration (i.e., >10 mEq/L) are most likely to respond to this treatment. R.W. should benefit from sodium restriction because his urine sodium concentration of 10 mEq/L suggests a borderline renal capacity to excrete free water.

Water Restriction

Although sodium restriction may be desirable for R.W., water restriction probably should be avoided as part of the initial treatment since his serum sodium concentration was within normal limits (132 mEq/L). Water restriction should be reserved for patients who have inappropriate secretion of antidiuretic hormone (ADH) which results in excessive water retention and dilutional hyponatremia (<130 mEq/L).[23,27] Patients with a low urine sodium concentration (<10 mEq/L), but normal or near normal free water clearance and normal renal function, appear to benefit from the addition of diuretics. Patients with reduced 24-hour urinary excretion of sodium, glomerular filtration rate, and free water clearance are commonly resistant to medical treatment and have a poor prognosis.

Role of Aldosterone

Successful treatment with an aldosterone-inhibiting drug such as spironolactone (Aldactone) should revert urinary electrolyte patterns back to normal after several days of treatment at pharmacologically effective doses. The value of monitoring urinary electrolytes is lost if even a single dose of a natriuretic agent such as hydrochlorothiazide (HydroDiuril) or furosemide (Lasix) is given because these drugs will cause excessive urinary sodium loss even in the presence of continued hyperaldosteronism.

Diuretic Therapy

Choice of Agent

6. R.W. was placed on 500 mg sodium restriction after initial evaluation. Spironolactone 100 mg/day was ordered to induce diuresis. Why is spironolactone a rational choice in the treatment of ascites? Can other potassium-sparing diuretics be used?

Many cirrhotic patients have high circulating levels of aldosterone because of both increased production and decreased excretion of the hormone. Fluid loss into the peritoneal cavity decreases intravascular volume, decreases renal perfusion, and subsequently activates the renin-angiotensin-aldosterone system.[21,24] Hepatic shunting also increases aldosterone production by decreasing renal blood flow. In addition, aldosterone is substantially metabolized by the liver, and hepatic dysfunction prolongs the biologic half-life and action of aldosterone.[31] Aldosterone is highly bound to albumin, and low serum albumin concentrations resulting from decreased hepatic synthesis of albumin can lead to higher "free" or active concentrations of aldosterone available to receptors. Therefore, an ideal diuretic for the treatment of ascites is one with anti-aldosterone and potassium-sparing effects. The aldosterone antagonist, spironolactone is a rational diuretic of choice for R.W. if more conservative measures fail to mobilize fluid overload.[11,23,29,30] Although the usual dose of spironolactone is 25 mg twice a day, this drug is a competitive antagonist of aldosterone and a large initial dose of 100 to 200 mg/day generally is needed to offset the high circulating levels of aldosterone present in a patient with ascites.[28,29] If the patient's response is unsatisfactory, the dose can be increased slowly (every two to four days because of the long half-life of spironolactone). Final doses of 400 mg/day are not uncommon. Triamterene (Dyrenium) and amiloride (Midamor), both potassium-sparing diuretics without anti-aldosterone activity, can be used as effective alternatives to spironolactone if

intolerable side effects (e.g., gynecomastia) occur.[23,29] Unfortunately, these diuretics often are insufficient (see subsequent questions).

Monitoring

7. Clinical Responses. What clinical responses should be monitored to ensure the therapeutic effectiveness of spironolactone therapy for R.W.?

The three primary parameters to monitor are weight loss, urine output, and abdominal girth. The usual goal is a weight loss of 0.5 to 2 kg/day; this weight loss corresponds to a net fluid volume loss of about 0.5 to 2 L. Since ascitic fluid is slow to re-equilibrate with vascular volume, any diuresis exceeding this rate of fluid loss is associated with a risk of volume depletion, hypotension, and compromised renal function.

Diuresis may be approached more aggressively if peripheral edema is present. A 2 kg/day weight loss is reasonably safe in edematous patients because the excess fluid in the peripheral tissues buffers against volume depletion by replacing vascular fluid losses.[33] Once edema has resolved, the goal of weight loss should be reduced to 0.75 kg/day to minimize the risk of renal insufficiency induced by plasma volume contraction and other diuretic-induced complications. Ideally, urine output should exceed fluid intake by about 300 to 1000 mL/day, but these measurements often are inaccurate and do not account for nonrenal fluid losses. Abdominal girth measurements with a tape measure reflect the actual change in ascitic volume, but are again subject to errors in measurement, especially if the tape measure is not placed over the same part of the abdomen with each subsequent measurement. Abdominal girth should be measured by the same person each day to minimize errors in measurement and that person should use the umbilicus as a reference point.

8. Laboratory Parameters. What laboratory parameters could be monitored to assess the therapeutic efficacy of R.W.'s spironolactone treatment?

The 24-hour urinary sodium to potassium (Na:K) ratio can be used to define the need for increasing doses of spironolactone.[34] A low baseline urinary Na:K ratio (<1.0) indicates high intrinsic mineralocorticoid (i.e., aldosterone) activity and suggests that large doses of 200 to 1000 mg/day of spironolactone may be needed.[35] Since R.W.'s urinary Na:K ratio is <1.0, the initial spironolactone dose of 100 mg/day could have been initiated with a larger dose (e.g., 150 to 200 mg/day). Generally, if there is still no response following reversal of the urinary Na:K ratio or if diuresis remains insufficient after four or more days of increasingly larger doses of spironolactone, a thiazide [e.g., hydrochlorothiazide (25 mg/day)], metolazone (5 mg/day), or furosemide (20 mg/day) can be added on a continuous or intermittent basis.[28,36] Doses of the adjunctive diuretics may be doubled after two or more days if necessary.

Complications

9. The spironolactone dose was changed to 200 mg/day. Three days later, R.W.'s urinary sodium and potassium concentrations were 48 mEq/L and 30 mEq/L, respectively. Fluid intake was 1400 mL and urinary output was 750 mL. Supplemental treatment with furosemide is being considered because of insufficient diuresis. What potential complications due to diuretic therapy might arise in R.W.? Suggest guidelines to minimize these complications. [SI units: Na 48 mmol/L; K 30 mmol/L]

The most common complications to monitor for in R.W. are potassium imbalances, hyponatremia, metabolic alkalosis, prerenal azotemia, and encephalopathy.[11,23,36]

Hypokalemic-hypochloremic metabolic alkalosis and hyponatremia occur frequently in untreated cirrhosis.[32] Many cirrhotic patients initially have a deficit in total body potassium secondary to vomiting, diarrhea, and hyperaldosteronism. Hypokalemic alkalosis generally can be corrected with adequate potassium chloride supplementation. Since R.W. has some degree of renal impairment (SrCr: 1.4 mg/dL) and is being given spironolactone, his serum potassium level should be monitored closely. Since the most frequent adverse effect of spironolactone is hyperkalemia, R.W.'s potassium chloride dosage should be adjusted when the effects of spironolactone become apparent. Hyponatremia, if present, usually can be corrected by temporary withdrawal of diuretics.

Prerenal azotemia usually results from overdiuresis with subsequent compromise of intravascular volume and decreased renal perfusion. A gradually rising BUN concentration is a warning to slow the rate of diuresis. With salt restriction alone, patients with ascites can mobilize only about 300 mL of ascitic fluid daily. Patients with both edema and ascites can mobilize up to 1440 mL of ascitic fluid per 24-hour period, but at the expense of plasma volume contraction and renal insufficiency.[33] Although diuretic agents enhance fluid mobilization, only about 930 mL/day of ascitic fluid is lost at the most as compared to about 4700 mL/day of nonascitic fluid.[33] Thus, the fluid loss during diuresis is chiefly at the expense of nonascitic fluid. The maximal daily fluid loss should be limited to less than 750 mL/day for patients with ascites alone and to less than 2 L/day for those with both ascites and edema to avoid plasma volume depletion and decreased renal perfusion.[33,37] If faster removal of ascites is required due to respiratory distress, large volume paracentesis is more effective than rapid diuresis (see Question 10).[37] Since R.W. presented with both edema and ascites, an initial fluid loss of up to 2 L/day would be reasonable. The rate of weight loss should be reduced to 0.5 to 0.75 kg/day when the edema disappears. Gradual diuresis avoids diuretic-induced depletion of extracellular fluid volume by permitting ascitic fluid to equilibrate with plasma volume. By using these guidelines, untoward effects from diuretic therapy, which may occur in as many as 75% of diuretic-treated cirrhotic patients with ascites, can be minimized.[32,37]

Encephalopathy. Disorientation and asterixis are signs of encephalopathy and demand immediate discontinuation of diuretics if present. Increases in serum creatinine (>0.5 mg/dL) or BUN (>10 mg/dL from baseline) also necessitate cessation of diuretics for a few days to allow volume expansion through fluid equilibration because of the grave prognosis of hepatorenal syndrome.[38,39]

Initiating furosemide at this time may be somewhat premature. The 200 mg spironolactone dose is well below the average requirement of 400 mg/day that is usually needed to treat ascites. Therefore, the spironolactone dose should be increased to 300 to 400 mg/day before furosemide is started. If the desired diuresis is still not achieved after three to five days, the spironolactone dose can be increased again to 600 mg/day or a low dose of furosemide could be started. Furosemide or hydrochlorothiazide can be started earlier if hyperkalemia becomes a problem with the spironolactone, or if R.W.'s condition is such that he cannot wait for the slow onset of spironolactone effect. Regardless of which diuretic is chosen (i.e., furosemide or hydrochlorothiazide), the diuresis should not exceed the previously stated goal of 0.5 to 2 kg/day weight loss.

Paracentesis

10. Over the next several days, R.W.'s spironolactone dose was increased to 600 mg/day. Subsequently, furosemide 40 mg PO BID was started and gradually increased to 160 mg BID without major improvement in diuresis. Laboratory data revealed that R.W.'s SrCr had increased to 3.2 mg/dL and BUN to 45 mg/dL. Serum electrolytes were K 3.1 mEq/L, Na 130 mEq/L, Cl 88 mEq/L, and bicarbonate 32 mEq/L. R.W. became progressively short of breath because of restricted dia-

phragmatic movement secondary to his markedly enlarged abdomen. Paracentesis was performed. Why? What are the limitations and complications of this procedure? [SI units: SrCr 282 μmol/L; BUN 16.07 mmol/L UREA; Na 3.1 mmol/L; Cl 88 mmol/L; bicarbonate 32 mmol/L]

Paracentesis is removal of ascitic fluid from the abdominal cavity with a needle or a catheter. It is usually performed for diagnostic purposes, but it is also used therapeutically in patients with ascites that is unresponsive to diuretic therapy, especially when respiratory and cardiac function are compromised (as in R.W.'s case).[11,40] Removal of as little as 1 L of fluid may provide considerable relief from the painful stretching of skin and the respiratory distress that occurs with massive ascites. The ascitic fluid usually reaccumulates rapidly after paracentesis due to transudation of fluid from the interstitial and plasma compartments into the peritoneal cavity; therefore, paracentesis usually is not considered a definitive treatment for ascites. The major complications of paracentesis that is too vigorous include hypotension, hemoconcentration, shock, oliguria, encephalopathy, and hepatorenal syndrome.[23,38] Other potential complications of paracentesis are hemorrhage, perforation of the abdominal viscera, infection, and protein depletion. Risk of spontaneous bacterial peritonitis also may be increased by large volume paracentesis.[23]

Albumin

The combination of therapeutic paracentesis with albumin infusions has been shown to be a safe and effective therapy for the treatment of ascites.[41–43] In fact, many consider this to be the initial procedure of choice in the management of cirrhotics with tense ascites.[30] In one study, 58 patients were treated with combined paracentesis (4 to 6 L/day) and intravenous albumin (40 gm after each tap). A second group of patients was treated with conventional diuretic therapy (spironolactone 200 to 400 mg/day plus furosemide 40 to 240 mg/day). Ascites was eliminated in 96.5% of the patients in the paracentesis group compared to 72.8% in the diuretic-treated group. The duration of hospitalization was decreased substantially in the group that had undergone paracentesis (11.7 ± 1.5 days) in comparison to the diuretic-treated group (31 ± 2.8 days). There was no significant worsening of hepatic, renal, or cardiovascular function with combined paracentesis and albumin infusions.[41] Even with the high cost of albumin, the decreased hospital stay makes this method of treatment cost effective. In a study comparing paracentesis with or without intravenous (IV) albumin in patients with ascites, patients who did not receive albumin had a higher frequency of renal impairment and electrolyte abnormalities.[42] Although other data suggest paracentesis without albumin infusions is safe,[203] most clinicians recommend albumin infusions be given along with large volume paracentesis. Total paracentesis plus IV albumin during a single-day hospitalization is also a safe procedure for treating tense ascites.[44]

Dextran 70

An alternative plasma expander, Dextran 70, also has been evaluated.[168,169] In one study, albumin or Dextran 70 was combined with paracentesis in patients with ascites. Both therapies were equally effective in mobilizing ascites, with Dextran 70 being a more cost-effective plasma expander.[169] However, Dextran 70 may not correct the underlying hemodynamic abnormalities induced by paracentesis.[30,168] Therefore, albumin remains the preferred plasma expander.

Alternative Therapy

11. What other modes of therapy are available for management of intractable ascites? How would these alternatives be applied in R.W.?

Albumin Infusion

Intractable ascites is uncommon, but it also is difficult to treat. Albumin infusions can promote diuresis in cirrhotic patients with ascites and edema.[11] The effects of albumin infusion are seldom long-lasting and variceal hemorrhage may be precipitated. When albumin infusions are combined with paracentesis, however, the benefits seem to be considerable (see Question 10).[11]

Peritoneovenous Shunt

In consideration of R.W.'s increasing serum creatinine concentration, rising BUN, and the grave prognosis of hepatorenal syndrome, the installation of a peritoneovenous (LeVeen) shunt might be a reasonable therapeutic alternative at this time. A LeVeen shunt consists of a surgically implanted valve in the abdominal wall, an intra-abdominal cannula, and an outflow tube tunneled subcutaneously from the valve to a vein that empties directly into the superior vena cava.[45] In this manner, ascitic fluid can be withdrawn from the abdominal cavity and be reinstilled back into the vascular space. This procedure is contraindicated in the presence of peritonitis, esophageal varices, recurrent coma, coagulopathy, significant cardiac failure, and acute alcoholic hepatitis.

Since R.W.'s prothrombin time is prolonged, extra measures must be taken before surgery (e.g., administration of vitamin K and fresh frozen plasma). Resistant ascites has been treated successfully and the usually fatal hepatorenal syndrome has been reversed by this LeVeen shunt.[46–49] However, the basic hepatic abnormalities remain unchanged, and whether the overall survival rate is improved remains to be established.[50] Pulmonary edema frequently occurs after peritoneovenous shunt from the increased volume of fluid returning to the heart. Intravenous furosemide is usually administered during the first two to three days after operation to augment diuresis.[50] Other possible complications of peritoneovenous shunt include consumption coagulopathy, fever, wound infection, septicemia, and GI bleeding.[51–54] A mortality rate as high as 25% has been noted in the first months, and shunt failure occurs in about 10% of the patients.[23]

Peritoneovenous shunting has been compared with standard medical treatment in patients with persistent or recurrent severe ascites.[170] Patients who received shunts had a shorter hospital stay and longer time interval until ascites recurred. No survival benefit was observed. When peritoneovenous shunting was compared with paracentesis plus albumin infusions, the former appeared to be more effective in the long-term management of ascites as reflected by a longer time to readmission, lower number of readmissions for ascites, and lower diuretic requirements. However, peritoneovenous shunting did not improve survival over paracentesis, and the probability of shunt occlusion was 52% after two years.[171] In summary, the lack of survival benefit and high risk of shunt occlusion suggest peritoneovenous shunting should be reserved for patients with ascites and fairly-well preserved renal and hepatic function who fail more standard therapies.

Ascites Filtration and Reinfusion

Ascites filtration and reinfusion is a new therapy undergoing evaluation for the treatment of tense ascites. This procedure involves filtering the ascitic fluid through a membrane, which separates proteins from water and solutes. The proteins are repeatedly instilled back into the abdominal cavity and passed through the filter until the ascitic fluid is sufficiently concentrated. The final concentrate is then reinfused back into the patient via the antecubital vein.[172] This procedure has the potential benefit of preserving the patient's own protein. One study comparing ascites filtration and reinfusion with total paracentesis plus albumin infusion in cirrhotic patients with tense ascites demonstrated similar efficacy, al-

though the duration of follow-up was quite short.[172] Studies investigating the long-term benefit of this procedure are warranted.

Esophageal Varices
Treatment

12. C.V., a 55-year-old, pale-looking female with known primary biliary cirrhosis, was admitted for a chief complaint of hematemesis. C.V. has a history of recurrent upper GI bleeding and documented esophageal varices, but no history of angina pectoris or myocardial infarction. On examination, blood pressure (BP) was 78/40 mm Hg, pulse rate was 110 beats/min and respiratory rate was 22 breaths/min. The skin was cold, chest and cardiac examinations were within normal limits, and abdominal examination revealed ascites and a palpable spleen. Bowel sounds were normal. Laboratory values included Hgb 7 gm/dL, Hct 22%, albumin 3.0 gm/dL, AST 160 IU (Normal: 5–29 IU), ALT 250 IU (Normal: 4–33 IU), alkaline phosphatase 40 IU (Normal: 22–110 IU), and creatinine 2.0 mg/dL. The PT was 18 seconds with a control of 12 seconds. Serum electrolytes were all within normal limits. Electrocardiogram (ECG) revealed sinus tachycardia. What treatment endeavors are of the highest priority in managing C.V.'s hematemesis?
[SI units: Hgb 70 gm/L; Hct 0.22 1; albumin 30 gm/L; AST 2.67 μkat/L (Normal: 0.08–0.48); ALT 4.17 μkat/L (Normal: 0.07–0.55); alkaline phosphatase 0.67 μkat/L (Normal: 0.37–1.83); creatinine 176.8 μmol/L]

Goals of Therapy

Massive upper GI bleeding from ruptured esophageal and gastric varices is the main complication of portal hypertension and one of the leading causes of death in patients with liver cirrhosis.[56–59] Acute variceal bleeding is a medical emergency that should be managed in a medical center with appropriate treatment facilities as soon as the bleeding has been initially controlled because subsequent management is difficult and complex. The treatment goals are: 1) stop or slow blood loss and treat hypovolemic shock if it develops; 2) prevent recurrent variceal bleeding.

General Management

Initial treatment consists of frequent saline or tap water lavage of the stomach and suction of the gastric content to avoid airway aspiration through an indwelling nasogastric tube.[9,58,97] Patients who are confused or unconscious should have endotracheal intubation to keep the airway open. Bacterial sepsis should always be considered and antibiotic therapy initiated promptly when indicated. If the prothrombin time is greater than 15 seconds, as in this case, intravenous or oral vitamin K administration is recommended. The patient should be monitored for electrolyte and metabolic abnormalities (e.g., potassium, sodium, bicarbonate), hypoxia (e.g., pO_2, pH), and decreased urinary output. Behavioral changes, mental confusion, asterixis, and other signs of hepatic encephalopathy should be closely watched for. Bowel evacuation of retained gastric blood with magnesium sulfate or lactulose is essential to prevent ammonia production and hepatic encephalopathy. Sterilization of gut flora with neomycin also is helpful.

Hypovolemia

Hypovolemic symptoms in C.V. include pallor, cold and clammy skin, rapid pulse, and a systolic blood pressure less than 80 mm Hg. These symptoms should be managed by plasma expanders (e.g., fresh frozen plasma) or by blood transfusion. Whole blood, or preferably packed red cells, can be transfused to achieve a hematocrit of approximately 30% to maintain adequate perfusion without raising the portal venous pressure.[9,97] Fresh blood is preferable because of its hemostatic properties and should constitute one-third or one-fourth of the total number of units administered if possible.[58,59]

13. Three units of whole blood and one unit of fresh frozen plasma were transfused initially. C.V.'s stomach was lavaged with saline and the gastric aspirate from the nasogastric (NG) tube continued to be strongly positive for blood. Vitamin K (Aqua-Mephyton) 20 mg was administered by slow IV push. Four hours later, her bleeding still persisted. What other therapeutic interventions can be used to control C.V.'s bleeding esophageal varices?

Fiberoptic Esophagoscopy

As soon as C.V. is stabilized, endoscopy should be performed to establish the cause of bleeding. At least 30% of patients with suspected variceal bleeding do not have varices and would require different treatment approaches.[56] Fiberoptic esophagoscopy allows direct visualization of the esophagus and location of the bleeding sites. Those with actively bleeding varices can be treated with balloon tamponade, administration of vasoconstrictive agents, sclerotherapy, or endoscopic band ligation.[9,56–59,97]

Balloon Tamponade

Balloon tamponade controls bleeding by direct compression of the varices at the bleeding site. The modified Sengstaken-Blakemore tube with four-lumens is effective in temporarily controlling variceal bleeding in more than 90% of patients.[56,58,59] However, an additional procedure generally is necessary within 6 to 24 hours to prevent rebleeding because the hemostatic effect is limited to the period that the balloons are inflated.[56,60] Aspiration (>10% incidence), pneumonitis, esophageal ulceration and rupture, chest pain, as well as asphyxia, can be complications of balloon tamponade. Aspiration should be minimized by endotracheal intubation and continued aspiration of oropharyngeal secretions.

Vasopressin

Vasopressin, a powerful vasoconstrictor that reduces blood flow in all splanchnic organs, is effective in approximately 60% of patients with variceal hemorrhage.[61,62] Due to its short half-life, vasopressin must be given as a continuous IV infusion. Terlipressin, a synthetic analog of vasopressin, is slowly metabolized *in vivo* to lysine vasopressin. Since terlipressin has a longer half-life, it can be administered as 2 mg IV boluses every six hours. Terlipressin is as effective as vasopressin and may have fewer cardiac side effects;[62–64,98] however, studies with equipotent doses of terlipressin to vasopressin have not consistently reported a difference in heart rate, blood pressure, and cardiac output.[61,63,64]

Somatostatin

Somatostatin appears comparable in efficacy to vasopressin and balloon tamponade, but seems to be associated with fewer side effects.[62,65,66,206,207] It reduces portal and collateral blood flow by constricting selective splanchnic vessels. Somastostatin usually is administered as a continuous infusion of 250 to 500 μg/hr after a bolus of 50 to 250 μg. Despite its clinical efficacy, somatostatin is expensive and its use has been questioned because of failure to lower intravariceal pressure as measured by direct variceal puncture.[67] Octreotide, a long-acting, synthetic analog of somatostatin, also is effective in the initial control of variceal bleeding.[72,74] Octreotide also is administered as an infusion of 25 to 50 μg/hr following an intravenous bolus of 50 to 100 μg.

Sclerotherapy

Sclerotherapy is considerably more effective than either vasopressin[61,62] or balloon tamponade[73] and is the treatment of choice for esophageal variceal bleeding because it controls acute variceal bleeding in 90% to 95% of patients.[68–71,73]

Sclerotherapy involves insertion of a flexible fiberoptic esophagoscope to visualize actively bleeding esophageal varices and injection of a sclerosing agent into each varix to induce immediate hemostasis. Injection of the sclerosing agent into the bleeding varix leads to an intense inflammatory response, thrombus formation, and cessation of bleeding within two to five minutes. Permanent destruction of the vessel will occur over several days. This procedure may need to be repeated several times until all of the bleeding sites have been identified. The most common complications associated with sclerotherapy include esophageal ulceration, stricture formation, retrosternal chest pain, and temporary dysphagia.[97,173,174]

Sodium tetradecyl sulfate, sodium morrhuate, or ethanolamine oleate are commonly utilized sclerosing agents.[100–107] Tetradecyl is prepared as a 1% or 1.5% solution by diluting a 3% stock solution of tetradecyl with either absolute alcohol or 50% dextrose in water. Approximately 0.5 to 2 mL of sclerosing solution is injected into each bleeding vessel at points about 2 cm apart.

Emergency sclerotherapy can be performed immediately, at the time of the first diagnostic endoscopy,[68–71] or subsequent to hemostasis that has been accomplished by either vasoconstrictive drugs (i.e., vasopressin) or balloon tamponade.

Endoscopic Band Ligation

Endoscopic band ligation is a procedure in which a "band" is placed around the mucosa and submucosa of the esophageal area containing the varix. This leads to strangulation and fibrosis of the varix, and, ideally, its obliteration.[173,174] Ligation appears to be as effective as sclerotherapy in controlling acute bleeding and is associated with fewer complications. In two studies, rebleeding occurred less frequently in patients treated by ligation compared to sclerotherapy.[174,209]

Alternative Treatment Modalities

14. Immediate intravariceal and paravariceal sclerotherapy procedures were undertaken for C.V. Although these procedures were transiently successful, variceal bleeding has developed again. What alternative treatment modalities could be utilized in lieu of a second course of sclerotherapy?

Sclerosing agents can be injected intravariceally or paravariceally. The aim of intravariceal sclerotherapy is to induce variceal thrombosis, whereas the goal of paravariceal injection is to thicken the overlying mucosa.

When initial sclerotherapy fails, bleeding first should be controlled by balloon tamponade before initiation of the second course of sclerotherapy.[56,58] Patients who do not respond to two courses of sclerotherapy generally continue to deteriorate and succumb with a mortality rate that approaches 90%. These poor responders usually require surgical correction of the underlying portal hypertension after a balloon tamponade to temporarily control the bleeding.[56,58,59,108–111]

Vasopressin

Route of Administration

15. The decision has been made to infuse vasopressin before resorting to a portacaval shunt. Should the route of administration for vasopressin be intra-arterial or intravenous?

Vasopressin (also known as antidiuretic hormone) is a potent stimulator of smooth muscle, particularly those of capillaries and arterioles. It exerts its therapeutic effects in the management of esophageal varices by vasoconstriction of the mesenteric arteriolar bed. This decreases blood flow into the portal system and results in reduction of collateral flow into the esophageal varices.[61]

Although IV bolus injections of vasopressin significantly reduce the portal pressure and control bleeding from esophageal varices,[75,76] most patients require multiple doses.[76] In an attempt to reduce its systemic adverse effects, superior mesenteric arterial

(SMA) infusion has been utilized to stop bleeding from esophageal varices.[77] Although SMA vasopressin infusion has been successful, the incidence of side effects is high.[78-81] A more sustained reduction of portal venous pressure is observed after continuous IV infusion of vasopressin than after an IV bolus.[82] The infusion also causes less abdominal cramping, substernal discomfort, and cardiac arrhythmias. When IV infusion of vasopressin was compared to SMA infusion, hemostatic control occurred in 64% of the intravenous group and 50% of the SMA group. Although these differences were not statistically significant,[83] complications were more frequent in the SMA group (i.e., catheter complications and cardiac arrhythmias).

The IV route is easier to use and does not require angiographic placement of the catheter, thus allowing prompt institution of therapy.

Dosing

16. What would be an appropriate initial infusion rate of vasopressin, and what guidelines should be followed for subsequent adjustment?

Vasopressin usually is initiated with an IV bolus dose of 20 U followed by a continuous infusion of 0.2 to 0.4 U/min, increasing to 0.9 U/min if necessary.[82-84] Larger doses (1.2 to 1.5 U/min) do not control hemorrhage in patients who are unresponsive to lower doses.[84] Intra-arterial infusions have been given at 0.1 to 0.5 U/min.[83-85] Because many of the side effects are dose related, the lowest effective dose should be used whenever possible. When the bleeding is controlled, it is customary to taper the vasopressin dose over 24 to 48 hours,[80,82,83] but there is no evidence that tapering the dose decreases the incidence of rebleeding or side effects.[86]

Complications

17. During the IV vasopressin infusion in C.V., blanching of the skin near the injection site and abdominal cramps are noted. Are these symptoms related to vasopressin therapy? What other subjective and objective data need to be monitored in C.V. to minimize the toxicities associated with vasopressin?

Skin blanching, bradycardia, and abdominal cramps are common side effects of vasopressin. Other minor complications include mild hypertension, fecal incontinence, benign arrhythmias, phlebitis, and hematoma at the infusion site.[61]

Complications from vasopressin therapy are related to its vasoconstrictive and its antidiuretic hormonal effects, as well as to the catheter placement procedure. Fatal complications have been reported.[84,87] Major complications occurred at the rate of 9% in the SMA group and 6.3% in the intravenous group in one study.[88] Minor complications occurred in 29% of the SMA group and 38% of the intravenous group. Major complications include cardiac and respiratory arrest; ventricular arrhythmias; angina and myocardial infarction; reduced cardiac output and acute cardiac failure;[84,87-89] infections (spontaneous bacterial peritonitis and sepsis);[84,88,90] vascular complications (local arterial bleeding, venous and arterial thrombosis); hepatic, gastric, intestinal, and splenic infarcts; gangrene;[82,88,91,92] and water intoxication, dilutional hyponatremia, and electrolyte imbalance.[93]

18. What drug can be utilized to enhance the efficacy and decrease the adverse effects of vasopressin?

The addition of nitroglycerin (sublingually,[94] intravenously,[95] or transdermally[96]) to vasopressin therapy enhances the reduction in portal pressure and reduces the adverse vascular and cardiac effects.[94-96] Transdermal nitroglycerin (10 mg/day) is the most convenient method of administration; however, absorption may be variable. When given by intravenous infusion, the dose is 40 to 400 μg/min.[97] The efficacy of vasopressin plus nitroglycerin in controlling variceal bleeding is about 70%.[94-96]

Precautions to Minimize Recurrence

19. C.V. subsequently recovered from her acute episode of varix bleeding. What are the long-term objectives for the management of C.V.? What interventions may help in preventing future bleeding episodes?

The long-term treatment objectives for patients with portal hypertension and esophageal varices are to either prevent the first episode of bleeding (primary prophylaxis) or to prevent recurrent bleeding (secondary prophylaxis). Although there is agreement on these two objectives, there is controversy concerning the actual long-term management of patients with esophageal varices. This controversy is fueled primarily by the lack of good therapeutic interventions other than high-risk liver transplantation. Furthermore, interpretation of the clinical outcomes observed in various studies is often difficult due to the heterogeneous patient population: different etiology of esophageal varices (e.g., schistosomiasis versus alcoholic cirrhosis), location of the flow obstruction (e.g., presinusoidal versus sinusoidal), and severity of liver disease.[56-59,167]

Beta Blockers

Propranolol (Inderal) and other beta blockers have been used after the bleeding has stopped to help reduce hepatic blood flow and portal pressure.[112-115,117,178,196,197] In one study, the incidence of rebleeding in patients receiving propranolol was 21% versus 65% in patients who received a placebo over a two-year period.[112] The propranolol-treated group of patients also experienced a lower rate of mortality. The use of beta blockers seems to be most beneficial in the patients whose cirrhosis is secondary to alcoholism, but who have less advanced disease and who stop drinking after the first bleeding episode.[114,115,178] Although beta blockers significantly reduce rebleeding from esophageal varices,[115,117] these drugs do not decrease mortality. Abrupt discontinuation of beta blockers may lead to rebleeding.[119,120] Although treatment with beta blockers seems to be effective, not all researchers have observed positive results.[113]

Sclerotherapy

Sclerotherapy (see Question 13) is another effective option for minimizing recurrent variceal bleeding and is considered the procedure of choice by most clinicians.[173-177,199,200] Data suggest sclerotherapy may be more effective than propranolol in preventing rebleeding from esophageal varices;[199] however, the lack of survival benefit and high complication rate may limit its use for long-term treatment. Although the combination of beta blockers and sclerotherapy does not offer significant benefit over monotherapy,[201] beta blockers may be a useful adjunct to sclerotherapy until variceal obliteration has occurred.[202]

Surgery

Insertion of a portacaval shunt has been shown to be effective in reducing portal pressure and in preventing recurrent bleeding. However, these shunts are associated with a high incidence of hepatic encephalopathy and may worsen the disease by the shunting of blood away from the liver. Distal splenorenal shunts also are effective in preventing variceal rebleeding and may be associated with a lower incidence of hepatic encephalopathy.[176,208]

Transjugular Intrahepatic Portal Systemic Shunting (TIPS)

Transjugular intrahepatic portal systemic shunting (TIPS) is a new technique for establishing a shunt in patients with portal hypertension. During this procedure, a needle is advanced in a catheter, via a transjugular approach, into a hepatic vein. Then, an intrahepatic branch of the portal vein is punctured to create a surgical tunnel between the two veins. Finally, an expandable metal tube (stent) is placed in the tract to decompress the portal system through the liver.[210] Although still experimental, this procedure has the advantage of being less invasive, faster, safer, and less expensive than other portal systemic shunts.[211]

Endoscopic Band Ligation

Endoscopic band ligation is effective in preventing rebleeding from esophageal varices, and appears as effective as sclerotherapy.[173,174,209] Further experience may establish this as the procedure of choice in preventing variceal bleeding.

Primary Prophylaxis of Variceal Bleeding

20. Are there any therapies that could have helped *prevent* the first episode of bleeding from C.V.'s esophageal varices?

The mortality associated with bleeding esophageal varices is quite high, ranging from 15% to 40%.[174] Therefore, the treatment goal in patients with cirrhosis and portal hypertension is to prevent the initial episode of variceal bleeding. Theoretically, minimizing the complications of portal hypertension may help improve both quality of life and survival.

Beta Blockers

Beta blockers have been evaluated for their role in preventing the first episode of bleeding from esophageal varices. Several studies have shown that propranolol and other beta blockers do prevent first bleeding from varices.[116,118,179–183,194] In these studies, beta blockers were titrated to achieve a 25% reduction in heart rate[116,179,180,182] or hepatic venous pressure gradient.[181] Mean propranolol doses ranged from 84 to 162 mg/day.[116,181,182] In one study, 22% of placebo-treated patients bled from varices compared to 4% of propranolol-treated patients, with a mean follow-up of 16.3 months and 17.1 months, respectively. Propranolol seemed to be of most benefit in alcoholic patients with large varices and a high Child Class score (a rating scale for severity of disease progression).[181] Although most studies have utilized propranolol, nadolol also has been shown to be effective.[118,183] Despite their ability to prevent first-episode variceal bleeding, beta blockers have not consistently increased survival. However, meta-analysis has suggested a reduction in mortality associated with the use of beta blocker therapy.[195–197]

Because only 25% to 40% of cirrhotic patients will bleed from esophageal varices,[184] and the survival benefit of beta blocker therapy is questionable, these drugs may not be warranted in all patients. Patients with alcoholic cirrhosis, large varices, good compliance, and no medical contraindications may derive the most benefit.

Sclerotherapy

Sclerotherapy has been evaluated for primary prophylaxis of variceal bleeding.[185,186,195,198] Although the data are conflicting, one study showed a higher mortality in sclerotherapy-treated patients with alcoholic cirrhosis.[186] Therefore, prophylactic sclerotherapy is not recommended for routine use at this time.

Isosorbide-5-Mononitrate

Isosorbide-5-mononitrate has been shown to reduce portal pressure in patients with cirrhosis. When combined with propranolol, isosorbide-5-mononitrate causes a greater reduction in the hepatic venous pressure gradient than propranolol alone.[204] One study comparing isosorbide-5-mononitrate and propranolol for the prevention of first variceal bleeding showed similar efficacy with regard to bleeding and survival.[205] However, the mean propranolol dose used in this study was lower than that used in most other clinical trials. The role of isosorbide-5-mononitrate requires further clarification.

Patient Education

21. How should C.V. be counseled about activities, alcohol, diet, and nonprescription medications before her discharge from the hospital?

Patient education should emphasize the importance of abstinence from alcohol and C.V. and her family should be referred to community resources that will help her achieve this goal. She should avoid salicylates and other medications that could irritate gastric and esophageal mucosa (e.g., aspirin, ibuprofen). To prevent worsening of portal hypertension and ascites, C.V. should adhere to a low-salt diet and avoid medications that are high in sodium content (e.g., Alka-Seltzer, Soda Mint). Avoidance of certain activities that increase the chance of bleeding must be emphasized. Heavy lifting, vomiting, coughing, sneezing, ingestion of a large meal, and stool straining due to constipation all can increase intra-abdominal pressure and should be minimized. Antacids and stool softeners which prevent mucosal irritation and constipation, respectively, can be used prophylactically.

Hepatic Encephalopathy

Hepatic coma or encephalopathy is a metabolic disorder of the central nervous system (CNS) and occurs in patients with either advanced cirrhosis or fulminant hepatic failure. It commonly is accompanied by portal-systemic shunting of blood.[10,121] The clinical features usually include altered mental state, fetor hepaticus, and asterixis.[10,121] Fetor hepaticus, a peculiar sweetish, musty, pungent odor to the breath, is believed to be due to circulating unmetabolized mercaptans.[10] Asterixis, or flapping tremor, is the most characteristic neurologic abnormality in hepatic encephalopathy. It can be demonstrated by having the patient hyperextend his wrist with the forearms outstretched and fingers separated. The tremor is characterized by bilateral, but synchronous repetitive arrhythmic motions occurring in bursts of one flap (twitch) every one to two seconds. Asterixis is not specific for hepatic encephalopathy; it also may be present in uremia, hypokalemia, heart failure, ketoacidosis, respiratory failure, and sedative overdose.

During the early phase of encephalopathy, the altered mental state may present as a slight derangement of judgment, personality, or change of mood. Drowsiness and confusion become more prominent as the encephalopathy progresses. Finally, unresponsiveness to arousal and deep coma ensue. In most cases, hepatic encephalopathy is fully reversible; therefore, it is probably a metabolic/neurophysiologic rather than an organic disorder.

Pathogenesis

There are several theories on the pathogenesis of hepatic encephalopathy. The predominant ones involve abnormal ammonia metabolism and an altered ratio of branched chain to aromatic amino acids. Other neurotransmitters such as GABA and serotonin also have been implicated as etiologic agents.[10,187,188]

Ammonia

Ammonia is a by-product of protein metabolism, and a large portion is derived from dietary ingestion of proteins or presentation of protein-rich blood into the GI tract (e.g., from bleeding esophageal varices). Bacteria present in the GI tract digest the protein into polypeptides, amino acids, and ammonia. These substances are then absorbed across the intestinal mucosa where they are either further metabolized, stored for later use, or utilized for production of new proteins. Ammonia is readily metabolized in the liver to urea (BUN) which is then renally eliminated. When blood flow and hepatic metabolism are impaired by cirrhosis, serum and CNS concentrations of ammonia are increased. The ammonia that enters the CNS combines with alpha-ketoglutarate to form gluta-mine, an aromatic amino acid. While high serum ammonia and cerebrospinal glutamine concentrations are characteristic of en-cephalopathy, they may not be the actual cause of this syndrome.

Amino Acid Balance

Body stores of both branched chain and aromatic amino acids are affected by their rate of synthesis from protein metabolism (both in the GI tract and the liver), their utilization in the resyn-thesis of new proteins within the liver, and their utilization by various tissues for energy. The normal ratio of branched chain amino acids (e.g., valine, leucine, and isoleucine) to methionine and aromatic amino acids (e.g., phenylalanine, tyrosine, and tryp-tophan) in plasma is 4.6:1. In both acute and chronic liver failure, the serum concentration of aromatic amino acids markedly in-creases while the serum concentration of branched chain amino acids either remains the same or decreases.[122–129] This results in an alteration in the ratio of the branched chain to aromatic amino acids.

The utilization of branched chain amino acids for skeletal mus-cle metabolism during liver failure is one explanation for this rel-ative or absolute deficiency in branched chain amino acids. At the same time, the blood-brain barrier appears to become more per-meable allowing increased aromatic amino acid uptake into the cerebrospinal fluid (CSF). Once in the CSF, some aromatic com-pounds are metabolized into chemicals that disrupt normal CSF neurotransmitter balance. For example, phenylalanine is converted to octopamine, and tryptophan is converted to serotonin. Both oc-topamine and serotonin can compete with norepinephrine for nor-mal CNS function.

Gamma Aminobutyric Acid (GABA)

The GABA receptor forms a supramolecular complex with both the benzodiazepine (BZ) receptor and chloride ionophore. Acti-vation of the GABA receptor results in increased chloride per-meability, hyperpolarization of the neuronal membrane, and inhi-bition of neurotransmission (see Chapter 73: Anxiety Disorders). In 1982, Schafer and Jones proposed that in liver disease, gut-de-rived GABA escapes hepatic metabolism, crosses the blood-brain barrier, binds to its postsynaptic receptor sites, and causes the neu-rologic abnormalities associated with hepatic encephalopathy.[166] Others hypothesize that endogenous benzodiazepine-like sub-stances, via their agonist properties, contribute to the pathogenesis of hepatic encephalopathy by enhancing GABA-ergic neuro-transmission.[10,187] The role of GABA and the endogenous ben-zodiazepines is not clearly defined and requires further clarification.

An altered ratio of branched chain to aromatic amino acids and increased concentrations of ammonia, GABA, mercaptans, and weak neurotransmitters have all been implicated in the pathogen-esis of hepatic encephalopathy. Nevertheless, none of these has been incriminated as the single cause in all cases. The pathogenesis of hepatic encephalopathy, therefore, must be multifactorial. Some other postulated factors include increased susceptibility to various "toxins" because of the altered permeability of the blood-brain barrier, as well as the absence of some protective substances nor-mally produced by the healthy liver.

Although the precise etiology of hepatic encephalopathy is still unknown, certain biochemical and physiologic changes help deline-ate factors that may contribute to the genesis of neuropsychiatric symptoms.[10] Portal-systemic shunting, whether a consequence of cirrhosis or surgical decompression of portal hypertension, remains the primary predisposing factor to hepatic coma. The shunted blood bypasses the liver's normal process of nitrogen detoxifica-tion, thereby predisposing the patient to hepatic encephalopathy.

Of all the toxins suspected to cause hepatic coma, ammonia and certain aromatic amino acids are the most frequently studied and are generally held responsible. Other precipitating factors (see Ta-ble 25.1) increase the serum ammonia or produce excessive som-nolence in patients with impending hepatic coma. Excess nitrogen load and metabolic or electrolyte abnormalities may increase am-monia levels.[10,13,121,130]

Clinical Presentation and Predisposing Factors

22. R.C., a 57-year-old male, was admitted to the hospital because of nausea, vomiting, and abdominal pain. He had a long history of alcohol abuse with multiple hospital admissions for alcoholic gastritis and alcohol withdrawal. Physical exam-ination revealed a cachectic male with cloudy mentation who was not responsive to questions about name and place. Tense ascites and edema were noted and the liver was percussed at 9 cm below the right costal margin. The spleen was not palpated and no active bowel sounds were heard. Laboratory results on admission included Na 132 mEq/L, K 3.7 mEq/L, Cl 98 mEq/L, bicarbonate 27 mEq/L, BUN 24 mg/dL, SrCr 1.4 mg/dL, Hgb 9.2 gm/dL, Hct 24.1%, AST 520 IU (Normal: 5–29 IU), alkaline phosphatase 218 IU (Normal: 22–110 IU), lactate dehydrogen-ase (LDH) 305 IU (Normal: 82–226 IU), and total bilirubin 3.5 mg/dL; PT was 22 seconds with a control of 12 seconds.

A 60 gm protein, 2000 kcal diet was ordered. Lasix 40 mg BID was ordered in an attempt to reduce the edema and as-cites. Morphine sulfate and prochlorperazine (Compazine) were ordered for his abdominal pain and nausea, respectively. Two days after admission, R.C. had an episode of hematemesis. He became mentally confused and at times nonresponsive to verbal command. An NG tube was inserted and produced cof-fee ground material upon continuous suctioning. Saline lavage was continued until the aspirate became clear. The next morn-ing R.C. was still in a confused mental state. He demonstrated prominent asterixis, and fetor hepaticus was noted in his breath. On the second day of his hospitalization laboratory data were as follows: Hgb 7.4 gm/dL, Hct 21.2%, K 3.1 mEq/L, SrCr 1.4 mg/dL, BUN 36 mg/dL, PT 22 seconds, and stool guaiac was 4+ positive. Impending hepatic coma and upper GI bleeding were added to the problem list.

What are the probable precipitating causes of hepatic en-cephalopathy in R.C.? [SI units: Na 132 mmol/L; K 3.7 and 3.1 mmol/L, respectively; Cl 98 mmol/L; bicarbonate 27 mmol/L; BUN 8.57 and 12.85 mmol/L UREA, respectively; SrCr 123.76 and 123.76 μmol/L, respectively; Hgb 9.2 and 7.4 gm/L, respectively; Hct 0.241 and 0.212, respectively; AST 8.67 (Normal: 0.08–0.48) μkat/L; alkaline phosphatase 3.63 (Normal: 0.37–1.83) μkat/L; LDH 5.08 (Normal: 1.37–3.77) μkat/L; total bilirubin 59.85 μmol/L]

The most apparent precipitating cause of the encephalopathy in R.C. was the sudden onset of upper GI bleeding, a frequent com-plication of advanced cirrhosis. The bacterial degradation of blood protein in the gut results in absorption of large amounts of am-monia and possibly other toxins into the portal system. Other im-portant contributory factors in this case are diuretic-induced hy-povolemia (BUN:serum creatinine >20), hypokalemia (potassium <3.1 mEq/L), azotemia (BUN >36 mg/dL), and potential for the development of systemic alkalosis (e.g., hypokalemia, continuous nasogastric suction). Overzealous diuretic therapy enhances he-patic encephalopathy by inducing prerenal azotemia, and more im-portantly, by promoting hypokalemia and metabolic alkalosis. Hy-pokalemia increases the concentration of ammonia in renal venous blood.[131] Alkalosis, frequently associated with hypokalemia, pro-motes diffusion of nonionic ammonia and other amines into the CNS. The associated intracellular acidosis "traps" the ammonia by converting it back to ammonium ion (NH_4^+).[10,130]

Sedating drugs also may be hazardous in patients with cirrhosis. Drugs that have frequently been associated with hepatic encepha-

Table 25.1	Factors That May Precipitate Hepatic Encephalopathy
Causes	Therapeutic Considerations
Excess Nitrogen Load	
Gastrointestinal Esophageal varices Hemorrhoids Peptic ulcer	Avoid gastric irritants: correct hypoprothrombinemia with vitamin K; give stool softener to prevent variceal bleeding from straining; evacuate blood in bowel with lactulose or magnesium citrate
Excess dietary protein	Limit protein intake to 1 gm/kg: avoid protein with high ammoniagenic potential
Azotemia Diuretic-induced hypovolemia Uremia of renal failure Excessive enterohepatic circulation of BUN[a]	Avoid over-diuresis; use neomycin or lactulose prophylactically to decrease gut ammonia genesis from urea
Infection: tissue catabolism	Treat infection with appropriate antibiotics
Constipation: ↑ ammonia generation due to ↓ gut transit time	Use stool softener and laxatives prophylactically
Metabolic and Electrolyte Abnormalities	
Hypokalemia Diuretic-induced Dietary deficiency Excessive diarrhea Hyperaldosteronism	Avoid over-diuresis; KCl replacement; control diarrhea; spironolactone therapy for ascites
Alkalosis Hypokalemia-induced Excessive nausea and vomiting	Correct hypokalemia and alkalosis; antiemetic therapy
Drug-Induced CNS Depression	
Sedatives	Avoid long-acting sedatives
Tranquilizers	Avoid phenothiazines because of association with hepatotoxicity
Narcotic analgesics	Avoid hypoxia from respiratory depression

[a] BUN = Blood urea nitrogen.

lopathy are: opiates (e.g., morphine, methadone, meperidine, codeine), sedatives (e.g., benzodiazepines, barbiturates, chloral hydrate, paraldehyde), and tranquilizers (e.g., phenothiazines).[132] Encephalopathy precipitated by most drugs can be explained by increased CNS sensitivity and decreased hepatic clearance with subsequent accumulation. In addition, the effects of morphine,[133] chlorpromazine,[134,135] and diazepam[136] may be increased in liver disease because of decreased plasma protein binding. Thus, the morphine and prochlorperazine that were prescribed for R.C. also may have contributed to the development of his hepatic encephalopathy.

Although not applicable to this case, excessive dietary protein, tissue catabolism from severe infections, and constipation also can contribute to excess nitrogen load and the genesis of hepatic coma (see Table 25.1).

Treatment

General Management

23. What steps should be taken to manage R.C.'s hepatic encephalopathy?

After identifying and removing precipitating causes of hepatic coma, therapeutic management is aimed primarily at reducing the amount of ammonia or nitrogenous products in the circulatory system. Protein intake should be stopped completely or markedly limited at the onset of encephalopathy. Dietary protein can then be gradually increased at 10 to 20 gm/day every two to five days depending upon the clinical response. Vegetable protein may be better tolerated than animal protein,[13,137] because vegetable protein contains less methionine and aromatic amino acids that are less ammoniagenic.[13,121]

The two agents most commonly used in the treatment of hepatic encephalopathy are lactulose and neomycin.

24. How are lactulose and neomycin used in hepatic encephalopathy? Which agent would be more appropriate for R.C.?

Lactulose

Lactulose (Cephulac) is highly efficacious in the treatment of hepatic encephalopathy.[138–140] This disaccharide is broken down by gastrointestinal bacteria to form lactic, acetic, and formic acids. The proposed mechanism of action is acidification of the colon to convert ammonia into the less readily absorbed ammonium ion. There also may be back diffusion of ammonia from the plasma into the GI tract. The net result is a lower plasma ammonia concentration. It is possible that absorption of other protein breakdown products (e.g., aromatic amino acids) also may be changed. Lactulose-induced osmotic diarrhea also decreases the intestinal transit time available for ammonia production and absorption.[121,140]

Dosing. Lactulose syrup (10 gm/15 mL) has been used successfully in both acute and chronic hepatic encephalopathy. In the acute situation, initial doses of 30 to 45 mL are given three times daily and titrated to either the resolution of symptoms or the production of three soft stools per day. When the oral route of administration is not possible, as in the treatment of comatose patients, a rectal retention enema of 300 mL of lactulose in 700 mL of tap water can be administered. The beneficial clinical effect of lactulose occurs within 12 to 48 hours.[10,141] The chronic administration of lactulose permits better dietary protein tolerance.[10,13]

Care should be taken not to induce excessive diarrhea that could lead to dehydration and hypokalemia, both of which have been associated with exacerbations of hepatic encephalopathy. Although lactulose is generally well tolerated, 20% of patients may complain of gaseous distention, flatulence, or belching.[140] The excessive sweetness of the syrup can be reduced by diluting it with fruit juice, carbonated beverages, or water.

Neomycin

Neomycin, in doses of 1 to 2 gm orally four times daily, or as a 1% solution given as a retention enema for 20 to 60 minutes four times daily, is effective in reducing plasma ammonia levels (presumably by decreasing protein-metabolizing bacteria in the GI tract). Approximately 1% to 3% of a dose of neomycin is absorbed and may cause oto- or nephrotoxicity, especially with chronic use in patients with renal failure.[142,143] Routine monitoring of the serum creatinine, the presence of protein in the urine, and creatinine clearance is advisable for patients receiving high doses for long periods. Neomycin therapy may also produce a reversible malabsorption syndrome[144] that not only suppresses the absorption of fat, nitrogen, carotene, iron, vitamin B_{12}, xylose, and glucose, but also decreases the absorption of various drugs such as digoxin, penicillin, and vitamin K.[145–147]

Comparison with Lactulose. Clinical trials comparing lactulose and neomycin reveal similar effectiveness for both agents in the treatment of hepatic encephalopathy.[138,139] Occasionally, a patient who does not respond to one will respond to the other.[140] In the treatment of an acute exacerbation, neomycin may produce a faster response than lactulose;[148] however, there does not seem to be a consensus on this matter.[149]

In view of R.C.'s decreased renal function (SrCr 1.4 mg/dL), the 1% to 3% absorption of neomycin may result in accumulation and increase the risk of toxicity. The interference of vitamin K absorption by neomycin may further impair R.C.'s already compromised coagulation status (PT 22 seconds). Therefore, lactulose may be more suitable than neomycin for R.C. To hasten the onset of response, the first doses of lactulose can be large (i.e., 30 to 40 mL every hour) until catharsis occurs. If R.C. does not have a gag reflex, lactulose should be administered by rectal enema because the oral syrup can provoke nausea.

Neomycin Plus Lactulose

25. Would the combined use of neomycin and lactulose have any additive beneficial effect for R.C.?

The combination of lactulose and neomycin may be more effective than either drug alone.[150] In a study of nine patients with hepatic encephalopathy, the combined use of lactulose and neomycin reduced fasting ammonia to half the levels achieved by the use of either agent alone.[151] Nevertheless, the concomitant use of lactulose and neomycin remains controversial. This is because sterilization of gut flora by neomycin could significantly impair the bacterial degradation of lactulose to its organic acid metabolites and prevent colonic acidification. Why the two drugs have additive effects is unclear, but the observation suggests that degradation of lactulose may not be essential for reduction of ammonia level.[121] For example, the clinical response to lactulose enema can occur within 20 to 60 minutes, a time too short for any significant bacterial degradation to take place.[141] The acidic pH (3.8) of lactulose syrup may acidify the intestine without the need for bacterial conversion of lactulose.[152] Furthermore, one study suggests that one-third to one-half of cirrhotic patients can degrade lactulose in the presence of therapeutic doses of neomycin.[153] Perhaps some strains of *Lactobacillus acidophilus* are resistant to neomycin, or perhaps neomycin therapy does not sterilize the gastrointestinal tract completely.[153,154]

Lactulose should be tried first, and if satisfactory results do not occur, neomycin alone should be given a trial.[155] If both agents fail when used singly, the two agents can then be tried together. A stool pH less than 6.0 reflects the synergistic effect of the two agents. When combination therapy fails to reduce the stool pH to less than 6.0, *Lactobacillus acidophilus* (Enpac, Bacid, Lactinex) may be given orally as a capsule or rectally as an enema to ensure lactulose is degraded in the presence of neomycin.[153] Although combined use of lactulose and neomycin is beneficial, lactulose alone may be more desirable for long-term use because it is less toxic.

Alternative Therapy

26. What alternative treatments have been tried in patients with chronic encephalopathy resistant to conventional therapy?

Colectomy

For patients with chronic encephalopathy who have become resistant to protein restriction, lactulose, and neomycin, total colectomy or colonic bypass may eliminate the source of ammonia or other nitrogenous toxins. The long-term survival rate, however, has not been affected significantly by this procedure.[121]

Branched Chain Amino Acids

Because of the increased recognition of the imbalance between aromatic amino acid (AAA) and branched chain amino acids (BCAA) in encephalopathy and the desire to maintain good nutrition in patients with cirrhosis, dietary manipulation can be an important adjunct to therapy. Protein is an essential energy source, yet excess protein may precipitate encephalopathy. Two products are marketed that provide nutrients rich in BCAA and low in aromatic amino acids.[125–129] Hepatic Aid mixed in a blender with 250 mL of water contains 15 gm of protein, 98 gm of carbohydrate, 12 gm of fat, and 560 calories. One to four packages may be given per day. Diarrhea and hyperglycemia are the major dose-limiting factors to this therapy. Hepatamine is an 8% amino acid solution designed for parenteral nutrition. The ratio of branched chain to aromatic amino acids in Hepatamine is 37:1 compared to the 5:1 ratio in standard parenteral nutrition solutions. The efficacy of these two products is controversial and their cost is high.

Eriksson and Con[156] reviewed 18 randomized clinical trials and concluded that BCAA therapy does not improve acute, chronic, or subclinical hepatoencephalopathy despite correction of plasma amino acid abnormalities.[156] Oral BCAA mixture (Hepatic Aid) was of benefit in only two of the ten trials;[13] intravenous BCAA was of benefit in improving the clinical condition of patients in hepatic encephalopathy but did not seem to affect mortality.[13] Therefore, BCAA therapy should not be used until maximal doses of lactulose and neomycin have been given and the patient has demonstrated worsening encephalopathy. If intravenous BCAA solutions are used, the patient's CSF glutamine and serum amino acid ratios should be measured before initiation of BCAA therapy to confirm the presence of excess glutamine and aromatic amino acids.

Levodopa and Bromocriptine

Levodopa and bromocriptine have been tried experimentally for the treatment of refractory chronic hepatic encephalopathy. The pharmacological basis for this treatment is the false neurotransmitter theory, believed by some to explain the pathogenesis of hepatic encephalopathy. The false neurotransmitter theory is based upon the observation that amino acid precursors such as phenylethanolamine or octopamine appear to accumulate in the CNS as the severity of hepatic encephalopathy increases.[157] These beta-hydroxylated phenylethylamines may act as false neurochemical transmitters. Normally they are metabolized by the monoamine oxidase system in the liver and excreted readily in the urine. In cirrhotic patients, with shunting of hepatic blood flow and impaired metabolic function of the hepatocytes, these false neurotransmitters accumulate and displace the active neurotransmitters, norepinephrine and dopamine. Administration of a large quantity of levodopa, a precursor of dopamine and norepinephrine, could theoretically reverse the effect of these false neurotransmitters. Indeed, early clinical trials reported striking improvement of abnormal EEG recordings and temporary improvement of sensorium in hepatic coma patients who received up to 5 gm of levodopa.[157–159] The arousal began as early as 15 minutes after levodopa was administered. Unfortunately, therapy had to be withdrawn from most patients because of concern for gastric bleeding, excessive nausea, and vomiting. In another study, levodopa was ineffective in the treatment of hepatic encephalopathy.[160]

Bromocriptine, a dopaminergic agonist, has also been studied; one study showed no beneficial effect while another reported some improvement.[161,162] Thus, the exact role of bromocriptine in hepatic coma awaits more extensive study.

Flumazenil

Based upon the theory of increased GABA-ergic neurotransmission in hepatic encephalopathy, flumazenil, a benzodiazepine antagonist, has been evaluated for its role in treatment. Several trials have demonstrated both clinical and electrophysiologic improvement in patients with acute and chronic liver disease.[99,189–192] In one study, 60% of patients were noted to have transient neurologic improvement after flumazenil administration.[190] Another study suggested a response to flumazenil may be a favorable prognostic marker, as it suggests the encephalopathy is potentially reversible.[189] Chronic hepatic encephalopathy has also been successfully treated with orally administered flumazenil (25 mg PO BID).[192] There is concern in some trials, however, that exogenous benzodiazepines and their metabolites may not have been detected in patients before treatment with flumazenil. Therefore, a positive response to flumazenil may have been attributed to reversal of the benzodiazepine effect, and not a true improvement in encephalopathy. Conversely, lack of improvement with flumazenil may be associated with other metabolic abnormalities or CNS complications such as cerebral edema or increased intracranial pressure.[190,191] Despite the potential benefit of flumazenil, additional randomized, controlled trials are needed to determine its clinical role in the treatment of hepatic encephalopathy.

Hepatorenal Syndrome

26. R.C. has remained in the hospital for 14 days, and he still has marked ascites and fluctuating mental status. He is becoming more jaundiced; his urine output is negligible, and his BP is 110/50 mm Hg. His BUN and SrCr concentration have risen to 68 mg/dL and 3.7 mg/dL, respectively. Other pertinent laboratory findings are: K 5.9 mEq/L, AST 600 IU, total bilirubin 28 mg/dL, albumin 1.8 gm/dL, and PT 22 seconds. He is presently taking spironolactone 400 mg BID, furosemide 40 mg QD, lactulose 45 mL TID, and neomycin 1 gm QID.

Hepatorenal syndrome is the most likely diagnosis at this time. How should this new problem be treated? [SI units: BUN 24.28 mmol/L UREA; SrCr 327.08 μmol/L; K 5.9 mmol/L; AST 10 μmol/L; total bilirubin 478.8 μmol/L; albumin 18 gm/L]

Acute renal insufficiency and disturbances in electrolyte metabolism occur with increased frequency in patients with hepatic failure. The concurrent impairment of kidney function and liver failure is designated as the hepatorenal syndrome. This renal failure generally occurs in the absence of other known causes of renal insufficiency, but it can be aggravated by volume depletion following vigorous diuresis, gastrointestinal bleeding, or abdominal paracentesis. Unmetabolized toxins and shock also may contribute to the renal failure, but the kidneys appear to remain anatomically and functionally intact. The development of the hepatorenal syndrome is a grave prognostic sign with mortality approaching 100% even with vigorous therapeutic intervention.[193]

R.C.'s decreasing blood pressure and urine output accompanied by increases in BUN, creatinine, and potassium indicate hypovolemia as a contributing factor to his renal insufficiency. Spironolactone also may be contributing to the worsening of the hyperkalemia. His increased AST, prolonged prothrombin time, and decreased serum albumin concentration suggest progression of liver failure despite proper management. These signs and symptoms are consistent with a diagnosis of the hepatorenal syndrome.

Spironolactone and furosemide should be discontinued and intravenous saline given to restore vascular volume. Low doses of furosemide (i.e., 20 mg) may be justified to help reduce the serum potassium concentration. Neomycin also should be discontinued because it may contribute to the renal insufficiency. If these measures fail to increase urine output or improve renal function, albumin and/or low dose dopamine infusions should be started. A typical starting dose of dopamine is 0.5 to 1 μg/kg/min by continuous intravenous infusion. The dose may be increased slowly to 2 to 4 μg/kg/min, but larger doses may be associated with unwanted vasoconstriction. If any of the dopamine crosses the blood-brain barrier, it may also help restore CSF neurotransmitter balance and improve encephalopathy. Unfortunately, the blood-brain barrier is relatively impermeable to dopamine. Lack of response to dopamine is generally followed by death within a few days. Corticosteroids, emergency portacaval shunts, or liver transplant surgery are alternatives, but these measures have not been very successful. There has been renewed interest in management of end-stage liver disease by liver transplantation;[163–165] however, the problems of postoperative viral infections, malnutrition, and acute and chronic organ rejection remain unresolved.[165]

References

1 **Conn HO.** Cirrhosis. In: Schiff L, ed. Diseases of the Liver. 7th ed. Philadelphia: JB Lippincott; 1993:875–92.

2 **Galambos JT, Smith LH Jr, eds.** Cirrhosis. Philadelphia: WB Saunders; 1979.

3 **Podolsky DK, Isselbacher KJ.** Cirrhosis of the liver. In: Braundwald E et al., eds. Harrison's Principles of Internal Medicine. 12th ed. New York: McGraw-Hill; 1991:1340.

4 **Lasker JM et al.** Purification and characterization of human liver cytochrome P-450-ALC. Biochem Biophys Res Commun. 1987;148:232–38.

5 **Nebert DW et al.** The P-450 gene super family: recommended nomenclature. DNA. 1987;6:1–11.

6 **Lieber CS, DeCarli LM.** Hepatotoxicity of ethanol. J Hepatol. 1991;12:394–401.

7 **Lieber CS.** Hepatic, metabolic and toxic effects of ethanol. Alcohol Clin Exp Res. 1991;15:573–92.

8 **Diehl AM.** Alcoholic liver disease. Med Clin North Am. 1989;73:815–30.

9 **Bosch J et al.** Portal hypertension. Med Clin North Am. 1989;73:931.

10 **Gammal SH, Jones EA.** Hepatic encephalopathy. Med Clin North Am. 1989;73:793–813.

11 **Gines P et al.** Treatment of ascites and renal failure in cirrhosis. Clin Gastroenterol. 1989;3:165–86.

12 **Farkas P, Hyde D.** The liver. In: Traub SL, ed. Basic Skills in Interpreting Laboratory Data. Bethesda: ASHP; 1992:121–38.

13 **Blendis LM.** Nutritional management of patients with chronic liver disease. 1989;3:91–109.

14 **Beukers R, Schalm SW.** Immunosuppressive therapy for primary biliary cirrhosis. J Hepatol. 1992;14:1–6.

15 **Stavinoha MW, Soloway RD.** Current therapy of chronic liver disease. Drugs. 1990;39:814–40.

16 **Kershenobich D et al.** Colchicine in the treatment of cirrhosis of the liver. N Engl J Med. 1988;318:1709–713.

17 **Zifroni A, Schaffner F.** Long-term follow-up of patients with primary biliary cirrhosis on colchicine therapy. Hepatology. 1991;14:990–93.

18 **Bodenheimer H et al.** Evaluation of colchicine therapy in primary biliary cirrhosis. Gastroenterology. 1988;95:124–29.

19 **Saunders JB.** Treatment of alcoholic liver disease. Clin Gastroenterol. 1989;3:39–65.

20 **McGill DB.** Steatosis, cholestasis, and alkaline phosphatase in alcoholic liver disease. Am J Dig Dis. 1978;23:1057.

21 **Arroyo V, Gines P.** Mechanism of sodium retention and ascites formation in cirrhosis. J Hepatol. 1993;17(Suppl. 2):S24–28.

22 **Orrego H et al.** Long-term treatment of alcoholic liver disease with propylthiouracil. N Engl J Med. 1987;317:1421.

23 **Alaniz C.** Management of cirrhotic ascites. Clin Pharm. 1989;8:645–54.

24 **Gerbes AL.** Pathophysiology of ascites formation in cirrhosis of the liver. Hepatogastroenterology. 1991;38:360–64.

25 **Bosch J et al.** Hepatic hemodynamics and the renin-angiotensin-aldosterone system in cirrhosis. Gastroenterology. 1978;78:92.

26 **Lieberman FL et al.** The relationship of plasma volume, portal hypertension, ascites, and renal sodium retention in cirrhosis. The overflow theory of ascites formation. Ann NY Acad Sci. 1970; 170:202.

27 **Witte CL et al.** Lymph imbalance in the genesis and perpetuation of the ascites syndrome in hepatic cirrhosis. Gastroenterology. 1980;78:1059.

28 **Longmire-Cook SJ.** Pathophysiologic factors and management of ascites. Surg Gynecol Obstet. 1993;176:191–202.

29 **Ginès P et al.** Pharmacotherapy of ascites associated with cirrhosis. Drugs. 1992;43:316–32.

30 **Arroyo V et al.** Treatment of ascites in cirrhosis. Gastroenterol Clin North Am. 1992;21(1):237–55.

31 **Sadee W et al.** Pharmacokinetics of spironolactone, canrenone and canrenoate-K in humans. J Pharmacol Exp Ther. 1973;185:686.

32 **Gregory PB et al.** Complications of diuresis in the alcoholic patient with ascites: a controlled trial. Gastroenterology. 1977;73:534.

33 **Pockros PJ, Reynolds TB.** Rapid diuresis in patients with ascites from chronic liver disease: the importance of peripheral edema. Gastroenterology. 1986;90:1827–833.

34 **Alexander WD et al.** The urinary sodium: potassium ratio and response to diuretics in resistant oedema. Postgrad Med J. 1977;53:117.

35 **Campra JL et al.** Effectiveness of high-dose spironolactone therapy in patients with chronic liver disease and relatively refractory ascites. Am J Dig Dis. 1978;23:1025.

36 **Hillenbrand P et al.** Use of metolazone in the treatment of ascites due to liver disease. Br Med J Psychol. 1971; 4:266.

37 **Boyer TD.** Removal of ascites: what's the rush? Gastroenterology. 1986;90: 2022. Editorials.

38 **Metz RJ et al.** The hepatorenal syndrome. Surg Gynecol Obstet. 1976; 143:297.

39 **Wong PY et al.** The hepatorenal syndrome. Gastroenterology. 1979;77:1326.

40 **Guazzi M et al.** Negative influence of ascites on the cardiac function of cirrhotic patients. Am J Med. 1975;59: 165.

41 **Gines P et al.** Comparison of paracentesis and diuretics in the treatment of cirrhotic with tense ascites. Gastroenterology. 1987;93:234.

42 **Gines P et al.** Randomized comparative study of therapeutic paracentesis with and without intravenous albumin in cirrhosis. Gastroenterology. 1988; 94:1493.

43 **Salerno F et al.** Repeated paracentesis and IV albumin infusion to treat tense ascites in cirrhotic patients. J Hepatol. 1987;5:102.

44 **Tito LI et al.** Total paracentesis plus IV albumin infusion in the treatment of cirrhotics with tense ascites. J Hepatol. 1987;5(Suppl.):S67.

45 **LeVeen HH et al.** Peritoneovenous shunting for ascites. Ann Surg. 1974; 80:580.

46 **Wapnick S et al.** LeVeen continuous peritoneal-jugular shunt: improvement of renal function in ascitic patients. JAMA. 1977;237:131.

47 **Fullen WD.** Hepatorenal syndrome: reversal by peritoneovenous shunt. Surgery. 1977;82:37.

48 **Berkowitz HD et al.** Improved renal function and inhibition of renin and aldosterone secretion following peritoneovenous (LeVeen) shunt. Surgery. 1978;84:120.

49 **Blendis LM et al.** The renal and hemodynamic effect of the peritoneovenous shunt for intractable hepatic ascites. Gastroenterology. 1979;77:250.

50 **Stanley MM.** Treatment of intractable ascites in patients with alcoholic cirrhosis by peritoneovenous shunting. (LeVeen). Med Clin North Am. 1979; 63:523.

51 **Lerner RG et al.** Disseminated intravascular coagulation complication of LeVeen peritoneovenous shunts. JAMA. 1978;240:2064.

52 **Dupas JL et al.** Superior vena cava thrombosis as a complication of peritoneovenous shunt. Gastroenterology. 1978;75:899.

53 **Markey W et al.** Hemorrhage from esophageal varices after placement of the LeVeen shunt. Gastroenterology. 1979;77:341.

54 **Greig PD et al.** Complications after peritoneovenous shunting for ascites. Am J Surg. 1980;139:125.

55 **Kaplan MM.** Primary biliary cirrhosis. In: Schiff L, ed. Diseases of the Liver. 7th ed. Philadelphia: JB Lippincott; 1993:377–99.

56 **Terblanche J et al.** Controversies in the management of bleeding esophageal varices. (First of two parts). N Engl J Med. 1989;320:1393.

57 **Terblanche J et al.** Controversies in the management of bleeding esophageal varices. (First of two parts). N Engl J Med. 1989;320:1469.

58 **Burroughs AK, McCormick PA.** Variceal bleeding: acute and long-term management. Clin Gastroenterol. 1989; 3:131.

59 **Rice TL.** Treatment of esophageal varices. Clin Pharm. 1989;8:122.

60 **Panes J et al.** Efficacy of balloon tamponade in treatment of bleeding gastric and esophageal varices: results in 151 consecutive episodes. Dig Dis Sci. 1988;33:454.

61 **Stump DL, Hardin TC.** The use of vasopressin in the treatment of upper gastrointestinal hemorrhage. Drugs. 1990; 39:38.

62 **Kravetz D et al.** A controlled comparison of continuous somatostatin and vasopressin infusions in the treatment of acute variceal hemorrhage. Hepatology. 1984;4:442.

63 **Freeman JG et al.** Controlled trial of terlipressin (glypressin) versus vasopressin in the early treatment of oesophageal varices. Lancet. 1982;2:66.

64 **Walker S et al.** Terlipressin in bleeding esophageal varices: a placebo-controlled, double-blind study. Hepatology. 1986;6:112.

65 **Saari A et al.** Comparison of somatostatin and vasopressin in bleeding esophageal varices. Am J Gastroenterol. 1990;85:804–07.

66 **Jenkins SA et al.** A prospective randomized controlled clinical trial comparing somatostatin and vasopressin in controlling acute variceal hemorrhage. Br Med J (Clin Res). 1985;290:275.

67 **Kleber G et al.** Somatostatin does not reduce oesophageal variceal pressure in liver cirrhotics. Gut. 1988;29:153.

68 **Lewis JW.** Survival and rebleed after acute and chronic injection sclerotherapy. In: Sivak MV Jr, ed. Endoscopic Sclerotherapy of Esophageal Varices. New York: Praeger; 1984;89–97.

69 **Paquet KJ et al.** Immediate endoscopic sclerosis bleeding esophageal varices: a prospective evaluation over five years. Surg Endosc. 1988;2:18.

70 **Schubert T et al.** Improved survival in variceal hemorrhage with emergent sclerotherapy. Am J Gastroenterol. 1987;82:1134.

71 **Westaby D et al.** Controlled clinical trial of injection sclerotherapy for active variceal bleeding. Hepatology. 1989;9:274.

72 **Hwang SJ et al.** A randomized controlled trial comparing octreotide and vasopressin in the control of acute esophageal variceal bleeding. J Hepatol. 1992;16:320–25.

73 **Paquet KJ, Feussner H.** Endoscopic sclerosis and esophageal balloon tamponade in acute hemorrhage from esophagogastric varices: a prospective controlled randomized trial. Hepatology. 1985;5:580.

74 **Sung JJY et al.** Octreotide infusion or emergency sclerotherapy for variceal haemorrhage. Lancet. 1993;342:637–41.

75 **Merigan T.** Effect of intravenously administered posterior pituitary extract on hemorrhage from bleeding of esophageal varices. N Engl J Med. 1962;266:134.

76 **Conn HO et al.** Multiple infusions of posterior pituitary extract in the treatment of bleeding esophageal varices. Ann Intern Med. 1962;57:804.

77 **Nusbaum M et al.** Control of portal hypertension by selective mesenteric arterial drug infusion. Arch Surg. 1968; 97:1005.

78 **Murray-Lyon IM et al.** Treatment of bleeding oesophageal varices by infusion of vasopressin into the superior mesenteric artery. Gut. 1973;14:59.

79 **Millette B et al.** Portal and systemic effect of selective infusion of vasopressin into the superior mesenteric artery in cirrhotic patients. Gastroenterology. 1975;69:6.

80 **Conn HO et al.** Intra-arterial vasopressin in the treatment of upper gastrointestinal hemorrhage: a prospective, controlled clinical trial. Gastroenterology. 1975;68:211.

81 **Sherman LM et al.** Selective intra-arterial vasopressin. Ann Surg. 1979; 189:298.

82 **Rigberg LA et al.** Continuous low dose peripheral vein Pitressin infusion in the control of variceal bleeding. Am J Gastroenterol. 1977;68:481.

83 **Johnson WC et al.** Control of bleeding varices by vasopressin. Ann Surg. 1977;186:269.

84 **Chojkier M et al.** A controlled comparison of continuous intra-arterial and intravenous infusion of vasopressin in hemorrhage from esophageal varices. Gastroenterology. 1979;77:540.

85 **Chojkier M et al.** Intra-arterial vs. intravenous vasopressin in the treatment of massive upper gastrointestinal hemorrhage. Gastroenterology. 1978;75:958.

86 **Chojkier M et al.** Reply-vasopressin infusion. Gastroenterology. 1980;78: 420.

87 **Slotnik IL et al.** Cardiac accidents following vasopressin injection (Pitressin). JAMA. 1951;146:1126.

88 **Greenfield AJ et al.** Vasopressin in control of gastrointestinal hemorrhage: complications of selective intra-arterial vs. systemic infusions. Radiology. 1979;76:1144.

89 **Alves M et al.** Gastric infarction. A complication of selective vasopressin infusion. Dig Dis Sci. 1979;24:409.

90 **Mallory A et al.** Selective intra-arterial vasopressin infusion for upper gastrointestinal tract hemorrhage. Arch Surg. 1980;115:30.

91 **Greenwald RA et al.** Local gangrene: a complication of peripheral vasopressin administration. Am J Gastroenterol. 1978;74:744.

92 **Mogan GR et al.** Infected gangrene. A serious complication of peripheral vasopressin administration. Am J Gastroenterol. 1980;73:426.

93 **McSwain GR et al.** Antidiuretic hormone effect of vasopressin therapy for gastrointestinal hemorrhage. South Med J. 1979;72:895.

94 **Tsai YT et al.** A controlled trial of vasopressin plus nitroglycerin vs vasopressin alone in the treatment of bleeding esophageal varices. Hepatology. 1986;6:406.

95 **Gimson AES et al.** A randomized trial of vasopressin and vasopressin plus nitroglycerin in the control of acute variceal hemorrhage. Hepatology. 1986;6: 410.

96 **Bosch J et al.** Association of transdermal nitroglycerin to vasopressin infusion in the treatment of variceal hemorrhage: a placebo-controlled clinical trial. Hepatology. 1989;10:962.

97 **Matloff DS.** Treatment of acute variceal bleeding. Gastroenterol Clin North Am. 1992;21(1):103–18.

98 **Walker S.** Vasoconstrictor therapy in bleeding esophageal varices. Hepatogastroenterology. 1990;37:538–43.

99 **Hoffman EJ, Warren EW.** Flumazenil: a benzodiazepine antagonist. Clin Pharm. 1993;12:641–56.

100 **Jones RS.** Sclerotherapy of bleeding esophageal varices. Gastroenterology. 1979;77:596.

101 **Cello J et al.** Management of the patient with hemorrhaging esophageal varices. JAMA. 1986;256:1480.

102 **Korula J et al.** A prospective, randomized controlled trial of chronic esophageal variceal sclerotherapy. Hepatology. 1985;5:584.

103 **Carson A et al.** Acute esophageal variceal sclerotherapy. Results of a prospective, randomized controlled trial. J Am Med Assoc. 1986;255:497.

104 **Terblanche J.** Sclerotherapy for prophylaxis of variceal bleeding. Lancet. 1986;1:961.

105 **Cello J et al.** Endoscopic sclerotherapy

vs. portacaval shunt in patients with severe cirrhosis and variceal hemorrhage. N Engl J Med. 1984;311:1589.

106 **Copenhagen esophageal varices sclerotherapy project: sclerotherapy after first variceal hemorrhage in cirrhosis.** N Engl J Med. 1984;311:1594.

107 **Potzi R et al.** Prophylactic endoscopic sclerotherapy of oesophageal varices in liver cirrhosis: a multicentre prospective controlled randomized trial in Vienna. Gut. 1989;30:873.

108 **Cello JP et al.** Endoscopic sclerotherapy versus portacaval shunt in patients with severe cirrhosis and acute variceal hemorrhage: long-term follow-up. N Engl J Med. 1987;316:11.

109 **Lacaine F et al.** Prognostic factors in survival after portasystemic shunts: multivariate analysis. Ann Surg. 1985; 202:729.

110 **Huizinga WK et al.** Esophageal transection versus injection sclerotherapy in the management of bleeding esophageal varices in patients at high risk. Surg Gynecol Obstet. 1985;160:539.

111 **Burroughs AK et al.** A comparison of sclerotherapy with staple transection of the esophagus for the emergency control of bleeding from esophageal varices. N Engl J Med. 1989;321:857.

112 **Lebrec O et al.** A randomized controlled study of propranolol for prevention of recurrent gastrointestinal bleeding in patients with cirrhosis. Hepatology. 1984;4:355.

113 **Burroughs A et al.** Controlled trial of propranolol in the prevention of recurrent gastrointestinal bleeding in patients with cirrhosis. N Engl J Med. 1983;309:1539.

114 **Poynard T et al.** Propranolol for prevention of recurrent gastrointestinal bleeding in patients with cirrhosis: a prospective study of factors associated with rebleeding. Hepatology. 1987;7: 447.

115 **Colombo M et al.** Beta-blockade prevents recurrent gastrointestinal bleeding in well-compensated patients with alcoholic cirrhosis: a multicenter randomized controlled trial. Hepatology. 1989;9:433.

116 **The Italian Multicenter Project for Propranolol in Prevention of Bleeding.** Propranolol for prophylaxis of bleeding in cirrhotic patients with large varices: a multicenter, randomized clinical trial. Hepatology. 1988;8:1.

117 **Garden OJ et al.** Propranolol in the prevention of recurrent variceal hemorrhage in cirrhotic patients. Gastroenterology. 1990;98:185.

118 **Ideo G et al.** Nadolol can prevent the first gastrointestinal bleeding in cirrhotics: a prospective, randomized study. Hepatology. 1988;8:6.

119 **Lebrec D et al.** Gastrointestinal bleeding after abrupt cessation of propranolol administration in cirrhosis. N Engl J Med. 1982;307:560.

120 **Alabaster S et al.** Propranolol withdrawal and variceal hemorrhage. J Am Med Assoc. 1983;250:3047.

121 **Marsano L, McClain C.** How to manage both acute and chronic hepatic encephalopathy. J Crit Illn. 1993;8:579–600.

122 **Fischer JE et al.** The role of plasma amino acids in hepatic encephalopathy. Surgery. 1975;78:276.

123 **Fischer JE et al.** The effect of normalization of plasma amino acids on hepatic encephalopathy in man. Surgery. 1976;80:77.

124 **Smith AR et al.** Alterations in plasma and CSF amino acids, amines and metabolites in hepatic coma. Ann Surg. 1978;187:343.

125 **Fraser C, Arieff A.** Hepatic encephalopathy. N Engl J Med. 1985;313:869.

126 **Mizok B.** Branched-chain amino acid in sepsis and hepatic failure. Arch Intern Med. 1985;145:1284.

127 **Ferenci P.** Pathophysiology of hepatic encephalopathy. Hepatogastroenterology. 1991;38:371–76.

128 **Sax H et al.** Clinical use of branched-chain amino acids in liver disease, sepsis, trauma and burns. Arch Surg. 1986; 121:358.

129 **Horst D et al.** Comparison of dietary protein with an oral branched chain-enriched amino acid supplement in chronic portal-systemic encephalopathy: a randomized controlled trial. Hepatology. 1984;4:279.

130 **Fischer JE et al.** Pathogenesis and therapy of hepatic coma. Prog Liver Dis. 1976;5:363.

131 **Shear L et al.** Potassium deficiency and endogenous ammonia overload from kidney. Am J Clin Nutr. 1970;23: 614.

132 **Breen KJ.** Hepatic coma: present concepts of pathogenesis and therapy. Prog Liver Dis. 1972;4:301.

133 **Laidlaw J et al.** Morphine tolerance with hepatic cirrhosis. Gastroenterology. 1961;40:389.

134 **Read AE et al.** Effect of chlorpromazine in patients with hepatic disease. Br Med J. 1969;3:497.

135 **Maxwell JD et al.** Plasma disappearance and cerebral effects of chlorpromazine in cirrhosis. Clin Sci. 1972;43:143.

136 **Branch RA et al.** Intravenous administration of diazepam in patients with chronic liver disease. Gut. 1976;17: 1975.

137 **Greenberger NJ et al.** Effects of vegetable and animal protein diets in chronic hepatic encephalopathy. Am J Dig Dis. 1977;22:845.

138 **Conn HO et al.** Comparison of lactulose and neomycin in the treatment of chronic portal-systemic encephalopathy. Gastroenterology. 1977;72:573.

139 **Atterbury CE et al.** Neomycin-sorbitol and lactulose in the treatment of acute portal-systemic encephalopathy. A controlled, double-blind clinical trial. Dig Dis Sci. 1978;23:389.

140 **Avery GS et al.** Lactulose. A review of its therapeutic and pharmacological properties with particular reference to ammonia metabolism and its mode of action in portal systemic encephalopathy. Drugs. 1972;4:7.

141 **Kersh ES et al.** Lactulose enemas. Ann Intern Med. 1973;78:81.

142 **Poth EJ et al.** Neomycin, a new intestinal antiseptic. Texas Rep Biol Med. 1970;8:353.

143 **Breen KJ et al.** Neomycin absorption in man: studies or oral and enema administration and effect of intestinal ulceration. Ann Intern Med. 1972;76: 211.

144 **Longstreth GF et al.** Drug-induced malabsorption. Mayo Clin Proc. 1975; 50:284.

145 **Lindenbaum J et al.** Inhibition of digoxin absorption by neomycin. Gastroenterology. 1976;71:399.

146 **Cheng SH et al.** Effect of orally-administered neomycin on the absorption of penicillin V. N Engl J Med. 1962; 267:1296.

147 **Faloon WW.** Metabolic effects of nonabsorbable antibacterial agents. Am J Clin Nutr. 1970;23:645.

148 **Simmons F et al.** Controlled clinical trial of lactulose in hepatic encephalopathy. Gastroenterology. 1970;59:827.

149 **Fessel JM et al.** Lactulose in treatment of acute hepatic encephalopathy. Am J Med Sci. 1973;266:103.

150 **Conn HO.** Interaction of lactulose and neomycin. Drugs. 1972;4:4.

151 **Pirotte J et al.** Comparative study of basal arterial ammoniemia and of orally-induced hyperammoniemia in chronic portal systemic encephalopathy, treatment with neomycin, lactulose and a combination of neomycin and lactulose. Digestion. 1974;10:435.

152 **Vince A et al.** Effect of lactulose on ammonia production in a fecal incubation system. Gastroenterology. 1978; 74:544.

153 **Read AE et al.** Lactobacilli acidophilus (Enpac) in treatment of hepatic encephalopathy. Br Med J (Clin Res). 1966;1:1267.

154 **Weinstein L et al.** Effect of paromomycin on bacterial flora of human intestine: studies of total number and specific components. JAMA. 1961;178: 891.

155 **Conn HO et al.** Lactulose and neomycin: combined therapy. In: Hepatic Coma Syndromes and Lactulose. Baltimore: Williams & Wilkins; 1979:340.

156 **Eriksson LS, Conn HO.** Branched-chain amino acids in the management of hepatic encephalopathy: an analysis of variants. Hepatology. 1989;10:728–46.

157 **Fischer JE et al.** Treatment of hepatic coma and hepatorenal syndrome. Am J Surg. 1972;123:222.

158 **Parkes JD et al.** Levodopa in hepatic coma. Lancet. 1970;2:1341.

159 **Stefanini M et al.** Levodopa in hepatic failure. JAMA. 1972;220:1247.

160 **Michel H et al.** Treatment of cirrhotic hepatic encephalopathy with L-dopa. A controlled trial. Gastroenterology. 1980; 79:207.

161 **Uribe M et al.** Treatment of chronic portal systemic encephalopathy with bromocriptine. Gastroenterology. 1979; 76:1347.

162 **Morgan MY et al.** Successful use of bromocriptine in the treatment of chronic hepatic encephalopathy. Gastroenterology. 1980;78:663.

163 **Starzl TE et al.** Liver transplantation (Part I). N Engl J Med. 1989;321: 1014–022.

164 **Starzl TE et al.** Liver transplantation (Part II). N Engl J Med. 1989;321: 1092–099.

165 **Maddrey WC, Van Thiel DH.** Liver transplantation: an overview. Hepatology. 1988;8:948–59.

166 **Schafer DF, Jones EA.** Hepatic encephalopathy and the GABA neurotransmitter system. Lancet. 1982;1:18–20.

167 **Orloff MJ et al.** Long-term results of emergency shunt for bleeding esophageal varices in unselected patients with alcoholic cirrhosis. Ann Surg. 1980; 192:325.

168 **Planas R et al.** Dextran 70 versus albumin as plasma expanders in cirrhotic patients with tense ascites treated with total paracentesis. Gastroenterology. 1990;99:1736–744.

169 **Fassio E et al.** Paracentesis with dextran 70 vs. paracentesis with albumin in cirrhosis with tense ascites. J Hepatol. 1992;14:310–16.

170 **Stanley MM et al.** Peritoneovenous shunting as compared with medical treatment in patients with alcoholic cirrhosis and massive ascites. N Engl J Med. 1989;321:1632–638.

171 **Gines P et al.** Paracentesis with intravenous infusion of albumin as compared with peritoneovenous shunting in cirrhosis with refractory ascites. N Engl J Med. 1991;325:829–35.

172 **Bruno S et al.** Comparison of spontaneous ascites filtration and reinfusion with total paracentesis with intravenous albumin infusion in cirrhotic patients with tense ascites. BMJ. 1992; 304:1655–658.

173 **Stiegmann GV et al.** Endoscopic sclerotherapy as compared with endoscopic ligation for bleeding esophageal varices. N Engl J Med. 1992;326: 1527–532.

174 **Laine L et al.** Endoscopic ligation compared with sclerotherapy for the treatment of bleeding esophageal varices. Ann Intern Med. 1993;119:1–7.

175 **Westaby D et al.** A controlled trial of oral propranolol compared with injection sclerotherapy for the long-term management of variceal bleeding. Hepatology. 1989;11:353–59.

176 **Henderson JM et al.** Endoscopic variceal sclerosis compared with distal splenorenal shunt to prevent recurrent variceal bleeding in cirrhosis. Ann Intern Med. 1990;112:262–69.

177 **Burroughs AK, McCormick PA.** Prevention of variceal rebleeding. Gastroenterol Clin North Am. 1992;21(1): 119–47.

178 **Tommasini M et al.** Beta blockers in the secondary prevention of gastrointestinal haemorrhage in well-compensated cirrhotics. Drugs. 1989;37(Suppl. 2):35–41.

179 **Poynard T et al.** Beta-adrenergic-antagonist drugs in the prevention of gastrointestinal bleeding in patients with cirrhosis and esophageal varices. N Engl J Med. 1991;324:1532–538.

180 **Andreani T et al.** Preventive therapy of first gastrointestinal bleeding in patients with cirrhosis: results of a controlled trial comparing propranolol, endoscopic sclerotherapy and placebo. Hepatology. 1990;12:1413–419.

181 **Conn HO et al.** Propranolol in the prevention of the first hemorrhage from esophagogastric varices: A multicenter, randomized clinical trial. Hepatology. 1991;13:902–12.

182 **Pascal J et al.** Propranolol in the prevention of first upper gastrointestinal tract hemorrhage in patients with cirrhosis of the liver and esophageal varices. N Engl J Med. 1987;317:856–61.

183 **Lebrec D et al.** Nadolol for prophylaxis of gastrointestinal bleeding in patients with cirrhosis. J Hepatol. 1988;7: 118–25.

184 **Grace ND.** Prevention of initial vari-

ceal hemorrhage. Gastroenterol Clin North Am. 1992;21(1):149–61.

185 **Sauerbruch T et al.** Prophylactic sclerotherapy before the first episode of variceal hemorrhage in patients with cirrhosis. N Engl J Med. 1988;319:8–15.

186 **The Veterans Affairs Cooperative Variceal Sclerotherapy Group.** Prophylactic sclerotherapy for esophageal varices in men with alcoholic liver disease. N Engl J Med. 1991;324:1779–784.

187 **Butterworth RF.** Pathogenesis and treatment of portal-systemic encephalopathy: an update. Dig Dis Sci. 1992; 37:321–27.

188 **Morgan MY.** The treatment of chronic hepatic encephalopathy. Hepatogastroenterology. 1991;38:377–87.

189 **Bansky G et al.** Effects of the benzodiazepine receptor antagonist flumazenil in hepatic encephalopathy in humans. Gastroenterology. 1989;97:744–50.

190 **Grimm G et al.** Improvement of hepatic encephalopathy treated with flumazenil. Lancet. 1988;1:1392–394.

191 **Jones EA et al.** Flumazenil: potential implications for hepatic encephalopathy. Pharmacol Ther. 1990;45:331–43.

192 **Ferenci P et al.** Successful long-term treatment of portal-systemic encephalopathy by the benzodiazepine antagonist flumazenil. Gastroenterology. 1989; 96:240–43.

193 **Gines A et al.** Incidence, predictive factors, and prognosis of the hepatorenal syndrome in cirrhosis with ascites. Gastroenterology. 1993;105:229–36.

194 **Elder C, Reynolds Restino M.** Beta-adrenergic antagonists for primary prevention of gastrointestinal hemorrhage in patients with cirrhosis and esophageal varices. Clin Pharm. 1992;11: 337–41.

195 **Pagliaro L et al.** Prevention of first bleeding in cirrhosis. A meta-analysis of randomized trials of nonsurgical treatment. Ann Intern Med. 1992;117: 59–70.

196 **Hayes PC et al.** Meta-analysis of value of propranolol in prevention of variceal hemorrhage. Lancet. 1990;336:153–56.

197 **Lewis JA et al.** Beta blockers in portal hypertension: an overview. Drugs. 1989;37(Suppl. 2):62–9.

198 **Van Ruiswyk J, Byrd JC.** Efficacy of prophylactic sclerotherapy for prevention of a first variceal hemorrhage. Gastroenterology. 1992;102:587–97.

199 **Teres J et al.** Propranolol versus sclerotherapy in preventing variceal rebleeding: a randomized controlled trial. Gastroenterology. 1993;105:1508–514.

200 **Rossi V et al.** Prevention of recurrent variceal bleeding in alcoholic cirrhotic patients: prospective controlled trial of propranolol and sclerotherapy. J Hepatol. 1991;12:283–89.

201 **Ink O et al.** Does elective sclerotherapy improve the efficacy of long-term propranolol for prevention of recurrent bleeding in patients with severe cirrhosis? A prospective multicenter, randomized trial. Hepatology. 1992;16: 912–19.

202 **Vinel J et al.** Propranolol reduces the rebleeding rate during endoscopic sclerotherapy until variceal obliteration. Gastroenterology. 1992;102:1760–763.

203 **Pinto P et al.** Large-volume paracentesis in nonedematous patients with tense ascites: its effect on intravascular volume. Hepatology. 1988;8:207–10.

204 **Garcia-Pagan JC et al.** Propranolol compared with propranolol plus isosorbide-5-mononitrate for portal hypertension in cirrhosis. Ann Intern Med. 1991;114:869–73.

205 **Angelico M et al.** Isosorbide-5-mononitrate versus propranolol in the prevention of first bleeding in cirrhosis. Gastroenterology. 1993;104:1460–465.

206 **Walker S et al.** Terlipressin vs. somatostatin in bleeding esophageal varices: a controlled, double-blind study. Hepatology. 1992;15:1023–030.

207 **Averginos A et al.** A prospective randomized trial comparing somatostatin, balloon tamponade and the combination of both methods in the management of acute variceal haemorrhage. J Hepatol. 1991;13:78–83.

208 **Spina G et al.** Distal spleno-renal shunt versus endoscopic sclerotherapy in the prevention of variceal rebleeding. A meta-analysis of 4 randomized clinical trials. J Hepatol. 1992;16:338–45.

209 **Gimson A et al.** Randomized trial of variceal banding ligation versus injection sclerotherapy for bleeding oesophageal varices. Lancet. 1993;342: 391–94.

210 **Rossle M et al.** The transjugular intrahepatic portosystemic stent-shunt procedure for variceal bleeding. N Engl J Med. 1994;330:165–71.

211 **Conn HO.** Transjugular intrahepatic portal-systemic shunts: the state of the art. Hepatology. 1993;17:148–58.

Adverse Effects of Drugs on the Liver

Lucia K Jim
Joseph P Gee

Classification of Hepatic Injury 26-1
  Acute Drug-Induced Liver Disease 26-1
    Cytotoxic, cholestatic, and mixed 26-1
    Necrosis 26-1
    Steatosis 26-1
    Cholestasis 26-2
  Chronic Drug-Induced Liver Disease 26-2
    Chronic active hepatitis (CAH) 26-2
    Chronic steatosis 26-2
    Chronic cholestasis 26-2
    Phospholipidosis (PL) 26-2
    Fibrosis and cirrhosis 26-2
    Portal hypertension without cirrhosis 26-3
    Vascular injury 26-3
    Granulomatous disease 26-3
    Hepatic tumors 26-3
Mechanisms of Hepatic Injury
(See Tables 26.1 and 26.2) 26-3
  Intrinsic Hepatotoxicity 26-3
  Idiosyncrasy 26-3
Patient Assessment 26-3
  Etiology 26-4
    Procedure to determine 26-4
    Rechallenge with offending agent 26-5
  Treatment 26-5
Drugs Reported to Cause Clinically Significant
Hepatic Dysfunction (see Table 26.3) 26-5

Over 600 drugs have been implicated in cases of hepatic injury; thus, recognizing drug-induced hepatic dysfunction is an important, but challenging task for clinicians. Drugs can produce a variety of hepatic lesions and may mimic many clinical syndromes. The liver may be the only organ involved, or there may be various concurrent extrahepatic manifestations. However, some of the tests used to assess liver function are nonspecific, and abnormalities may sometimes indicate a harmless interaction between a drug and hepatic cells or may result from effects of the drug on the other parts of the body. Problems in the interpretation of abnormal liver function tests (transferases, serum bilirubin, alkaline phosphatase, and gamma glutamyl transferase) must be kept in mind and other etiological factors must be eliminated before a drug is implicated in the pathogenesis of hepatic damage.

Drug-induced liver disease accounts for less than 5% of icteric (jaundiced) patients admitted to hospitals,[1-3] but the relative incidence might be higher in elderly patients[4] and in patients who receive psychoactive or antituberculous agents.[1,3]

The Danish Committee on Adverse Drug Reactions reported that hepatic injury accounted for 6% of all adverse drug reactions and 14.7% of lethal adverse drug reactions between 1978 and 1987. This is almost double the number reported during the previous decade.[5] The drugs most frequently suspected in hepatic injury were halothane, carbamazepine, cotrimoxazole, disulfiram, valproic acid, and nomifensine (used in Europe).

Drugs play an important role in causing hepatic necrosis and may account for 25% or more of the cases of fulminant hepatic failure.[3,6,7] Overt jaundice due to drug-related cytotoxic injury is associated with a mortality rate of 10% or more, but that of cholestatic injury is much lower.[6,8]

Classification of Hepatic Injury

Drug-induced hepatic injury can be classified according to the morphology of the injury, the presumed mechanism, or the circumstances of drug-induced damages. Hepatic injury due to the drugs can be characterized as either acute or chronic.

Acute Drug-Induced Liver Disease

Cytotoxic, Cholestatic, and Mixed

Acute hepatic injury produced by drugs can be cytotoxic (cellular destruction), cholestatic (arrested bile flow), or a mixed presentation of both. Cytotoxic hepatic injury can be due to necrosis, steatosis, or a combination thereof.

Necrosis

Drug-induced hepatocellular necrosis may primarily involve cells in a centrilobular pattern (e.g., halothane, acetaminophen), involve hepatocytes in a diffuse pattern similar to that of viral hepatitis (e.g., methyldopa), or involve significant portions of the entire liver (e.g., valproic acid). Elevated serum transferase (formerly known as transaminase) activity is the hallmark of the hepatic damage. The serum concentration of transferases in patients with hepatic necrosis often is elevated from 8 to 500 times the upper limit of normal, and values for alkaline phosphatase usually are increased modestly to no more than three times normal.[1-3,6,8]

With increasing degrees of liver cell necrosis, four clinical patterns of appearance may be observed: an increase in serum transferase levels without any clinical symptoms, anicteric hepatitis, icteric hepatitis, and fulminant hepatitis with hepatic encephalopathy and coagulopathy.

Steatosis

Drug-induced hepatic steatosis can be microvesicular, when the hepatocytes are filled with many tiny droplets that do not displace the nucleus (tetracycline, aspirin poisoning, valproate) or macrovesicular, in which the hepatocyte contains a large fat droplet that displaces the nucleus to the periphery (ethanol, methotrexate). Steatosis also can be caused by drugs such as corticosteroids resulting in lipid deposition in the liver. Although this process results in enlargement of the liver, routine liver function tests often remain normal. In contrast, fatty degeneration caused by drugs such as valproic acid may result in irreversible cell damage that is reflected by increased aspartate aminotransferase (AST) and alanine aminotransferase (ALT) serum concentrations of 100 U/mL to 500 U/mL.

The histological picture of drug-induced fatty degeneration is similar to that observed with fatty liver of pregnancy or Reye syndrome.[1,9] Certain drugs (e.g., high doses of estrogens) also can induce a form of degenerative, necrotizing liver damage known as "fatty liver hepatitis" that can eventually result in micronodular cirrhosis.[9] Fatty liver hepatitis is often asymptomatic, and the appearance of malaise, diarrhea, fever, jaundice, leukocytosis, ascites, or edema may indicate that the damage is already irreversible.

Cholestasis

Cholestasis may be due to three different mechanisms: hepatocellular cholestasis, either as the sole presentation of injury or associated with some degree of hepatic cellular damage (hepatitis); obstruction of the intrahepatic bile ducts; and extrahepatic bile duct obstruction. Cholestatic injury can be characterized as canalicular (i.e., portal inflammation) or hepatocanalicular (i.e., combined with hepatocyte injury). Canalicular cholestasis is characterized by AST and/or ALT elevations less than eightfold above normal, alkaline phosphatase less than threefold elevated, and a patient who is jaundiced or has a serum bilirubin level above 42 µmol/L. In contrast, hepatocanalicular cholestasis usually presents with AST and/or ALT levels less than eightfold elevated and alkaline phosphatase three- to tenfold above normal. Patients with AST, ALT, and alkaline phosphatase levels in the canalicular range, but with a serum bilirubin level less than 42 µmol/L, are categorized as "indeterminate type" because these values could reflect either minor hepatocellular injury or anicteric injury of the cholestatic type. Hepatocanalicular injury is typically seen in chlorpromazine jaundice, and the canalicular type usually is observed in cases due to anabolic or contraceptive steroids.[2,8–10]

Drug-induced cholestatic injury often resembles extrahepatic obstructive jaundice both clinically and biochemically.[6,8,10] Pruritus, jaundice, pale stools, and dark urine are the main manifestations. The serum bilirubin level is increased in all cases of drug-induced cholestasis, but it usually is less than 170 µmol/L (normal: 2 to 17 µmol/L); although on occasions, it can be more than 800 µmol/L.[9] The serum transferase concentrations are increased only moderately in most cases. The serum concentrations of alkaline phosphatase usually are increased more than threefold when cholestasis is caused by erythromycin estolate or chlorpromazine (hepatocanalicular), but does not increase as much when the cholestasis is not accompanied by cellular injury (e.g., anabolic and contraceptive steroids).[9,10] The mortality rate for pure cholestasis is much lower than when the cholestasis is accompanied by cytotoxic damage and is believed to be less than 1%.[1,6,10]

Mixed forms of jaundice with cytotoxic and cholestatic features can be caused by para-aminosalicylic acid, sulfonamides, and phenylbutazone.[1,2,11] The mortality rate of the mixed form seems to depend upon the extent of cytotoxic injury.

Chronic Drug-Induced Liver Disease

Chronic adverse effects of drugs on the liver can be categorized based upon the type of lesion or upon similarity to clinical syndromes. These categories include chronic active hepatitis, chronic steatosis, chronic cholestasis, phospholipidosis, pseudoalcoholic liver disease, fibrosis and cirrhosis, portal hypertension without cirrhosis, vascular injury, granulomatous disease, and hepatic tumors.[1,2,4,8]

Chronic Active Hepatitis (CAH)

Hepatic parenchymal lesions of drug-induced CAH mimic autoimmune chronic active hepatitis because they predominantly affect females and are accompanied by hyperglobulinemia, antinuclear antibodies, anti-single-strand DNA, and other serologic autoimmune markers.[1,8,12] Drugs associated with CAH include dantrolene, diclofenac, methyldopa, nitrofurantoin, oxyphenisatin, ticrynafen, and sulfonamides. Acetaminophen and isoniazid also have been incriminated in causing chronic active viral hepatitis-like disease, perhaps due to continued toxic injury rather than an autoimmune response.[8] The clinical picture of drug-induced CAH has mixed characteristics, with features of both acute and chronic hepatic injury. Patients may first present with either features of acute hepatocellular injury or clinical evidence of cirrhosis. Physical examination often reveals a firm enlarged liver, splenomegaly, and spider angiomas with or without ascites. Jaundice, anorexia, and fatigue are common. Arthralgias or "arthritis" may occur. Serum transferases are usually moderately increased; hypoalbuminemia and coagulopathy are common.[13–15] Recognition of drug-induced CAH is extremely important because withdrawal of the responsible drug may lead to marked improvement and eventually complete resolution of the injury within four weeks.

Chronic Steatosis

Ethanol, glucocorticoids, and a number of antineoplastic agents such as methotrexate and asparaginase are agents associated with chronic macrovesicular steatosis.[8,16] Glucocorticoid-induced steatosis appears to be benign, whereas methotrexate steatosis can progress to cirrhosis, and asparaginase fatty liver may be accompanied by necrosis. Valproic acid not only can induce microvesicular lipid deposits in the liver, but also causes fatty degeneration that can result in chronic liver failure with encephalopathy and a fatal outcome.[1,16] However, hepatomegaly may be the only feature in most cases of chronic steatosis.

Chronic Cholestasis

Two forms of drug-induced chronic cholestasis have been described. Most cases have features that resemble primary biliary cirrhosis. Common clinical findings are pruritus, jaundice, elevated serum bilirubin and alkaline phosphatase levels, but only moderately increased AST and ALT levels. Drugs reported to cause this syndrome include organic arsenicals, phenothiazines (chlorpromazine, prochlorperazine), haloperidol, imipramine, tolbutamide, thiabendazole, ajmaline, carbamazepine, and sulfamethoxazole-trimethoprim.[8,10] The second form, biliary sclerosis, has been observed in cases of bile duct injury produced by intrahepatic arterial infusion of floxuridine. The incidence of injury due to floxuridine appears to be high. Clinical features include upper abdominal pain, anorexia, weight loss, and jaundice.

Phospholipidosis (PL)

Phospholipidosis occurs frequently and is caused by an amphophilic drug (i.e., a drug which is both lipo- and hydrophilic) that accumulates within the lysosomes. PL is usually clinically silent or causes only mild liver dysfunction. Hepatomegaly is the predominant feature of phospholipidosis. Pseudoalcoholic hepatic lesions (steatosis, necrosis, Mallory bodies) in association with PL have been reported to cause cirrhosis in several instances after chronic administration of amiodarone and perhexiline maleate, as well as in a greater number of cases after diethylaminoethoxyhexestrol (Coralgil).[9,16]

Fibrosis and Cirrhosis

Chronic active hepatitis, alcoholic-like hepatic changes, chronic cholestatic injury, and chronic injury from methotrexate and etretinate can all lead to hepatic fibrosis and cirrhosis. Portal hypertension and its associated complications are the main characteristics in advanced cases.

Portal Hypertension Without Cirrhosis

Causes of noncirrhotic portal hypertension or hepatoportal sclerosis include chronic exposure to inorganic arsenicals, vinyl chloride, copper sulfate, and vitamin A intoxication.[17]

Vascular Injury

Vascular injury to the liver includes Budd-Chiari syndrome that can be caused by oral contraceptives, veno-occlusive disease that can be caused by azathioprine, and peliosis hepatis, a blood-filled cyst in the liver caused by anabolic steroids.[6,18]

Granulomatous Disease

Hepatic granulomas are always noncaseating and can be surrounded by eosinophils. Hepatic granulomas can be accompanied by cytotoxic or cholestatic injury as part of a hypersensitivity reaction (e.g., allopurinol, methyldopa, penicillin, phenytoin, quinidine, sulfonamides) or without any clinical evidence of hepatic injury (e.g., gold salts).[1,2,19]

Hepatic Tumors

Hepatocellular adenoma and carcinoma, although rare, are clearly associated with the use of oral contraceptives and anabolic steroids.[1,20]

In general, prognosis of drug-induced hepatotoxicity is good when the offending agent is withdrawn, but the prognosis clearly is affected by the type of liver injury, the duration of the insult, and whether the hepatic damage is irreversible.[1,6,16] The more cytotoxic the injury, the more likely is hepatic failure and death; the more cholestatic the injury, the better is the prognosis.

Mechanisms of Hepatic Injury

The two major mechanisms by which drugs induce hepatic injury are intrinsic hepatotoxicity and idiosyncrasy (see Table 26.1). Intrinsic hepatotoxins (e.g., chloroform) have the inherent property of predictably injuring the liver. Idiosyncratic or unpredictable hepatotoxins (e.g., halothane) cause hepatic damage only in a small number of uniquely susceptible individuals. The major differences between these two types of drug-induced hepatic injury are listed in Table 26.2.

Intrinsic Hepatotoxicity

Intrinsic hepatotoxins can be subdivided into direct and indirect toxins. Direct intrinsic hepatotoxins (e.g., carbon tetrachloride) destroy hepatocytes by a physicochemical attack, mostly through the toxic effects of their metabolites. There are no known direct hepatotoxins that are used as therapeutic agents.[1] Indirect hepatotoxins (e.g., antimetabolites) induce structural changes of the hepatocyte by competitive inhibition of essential metabolites or by interference with selective metabolic or secretory processes of the hepatocyte. These changes in the hepatocyte can be due to either cytotoxic or cholestatic mechanisms. Indirect intrinsic hepatotoxins that pro-

Table 26.1	Mechanisms of Drug-Induced Hepatotoxicity	
Classification	**Lesion**	**Incidence**
Intrinsic Hepatotoxicity		
Direct hepatotoxins	Necrosis and steatosis	High
Indirect hepatotoxins		
Cytotoxic	Steatosis or necrosis	High
Cholestasis	Bile casts	High
Host Idiosyncrasy		
Hypersensitivity	Cytotoxic or cholestatic	Low
Metabolic abnormality	Cytotoxic or cholestatic	Low

Table 26.2	Characteristics of Intrinsic versus Idiosyncratic Hepatotoxins	
Intrinsic	**Idiosyncratic**
A distinctive histologic pattern is observed for any given drug	Variable histologic pattern of lesions
Dose-dependent hepatotoxicity	Dose-independent hepatotoxicity
Elicited in all individuals	Only a small fraction of exposed individuals affected
Reproducible in experimental animals	Cannot be reproduced in experimental animals
Predictable appearance of lesions and usually a brief latent period following exposure	Appearance of lesions bears no temporal relationship to the institution of drug therapy
No extrahepatic manifestations of hypersensitivity	Lesions often accompanied by extrahepatic manifestations of hypersensitivity (e.g., fever, rash, eosinophilia)

duce cytotoxic changes are tetracycline, mechlorethamine, alcohol, acetaminophen, and mercaptopurine.[3,6] Indirect intrinsic cholestatic hepatotoxins produce jaundice and hepatic dysfunction by interfering with mechanisms for the excretion of bile from the liver (e.g., C-17 alkylated anabolic steroids and C-17 ethinylated contraceptive steroids).[1,8,10]

Idiosyncrasy

Hepatic injury due to host idiosyncrasy can be caused by hypersensitivity reactions or by other mechanisms (e.g., an aberrant metabolic pathway for the drug in the susceptible patient). Like intrinsic hepatic injuries, idiosyncratic injuries may be cytotoxic, cholestatic, or mixed.[3,6] The liver injury may be tentatively attributed to hypersensitivity when it develops after a "sensitization" period of one to five weeks, and is accompanied by systemic characteristics of rash, fever, and eosinophilia.[1] These hallmarks of an immunologic reaction suggest that the hepatic injury is due to drug allergy, especially when they reappear in response to a subsequent challenge dose of the drug. Examples of drugs causing allergic hepatic dysfunctions are methyldopa, phenytoin, para-aminosalicylic acid, chlorpromazine, erythromycin estolate, and sulfonamides.[1–3] Idiosyncratic hepatic injury also can be caused by toxic metabolites (e.g., isoniazid, halothane, valproate, ticrynafen, ketoconazole, methyldopa).[1,2,21,22] The idiosyncratic or unpredictable hepatic injury which results from a metabolic aberration rather than hypersensitivity usually develops after variable latent periods of 1 week to 12 months or longer, and usually is not accompanied by fever, rash, eosinophilia, or histological findings of eosinophilic or granulomatous inflammation in the liver. In addition, reproduction of the hepatic injury requires administration of the drug for a period of days or weeks, rather than for only one or two doses, presumably to allow for accumulation of toxic metabolites.

The classification of the mechanism of hepatic injury by an individual drug into either intrinsic, predictable hepatotoxicity, or unpredictable idiosyncrasy can sometimes be impossible and, in many instances, both major types of mechanisms may have a role. Thus, toxic hepatitis may occur after large overdoses of an intrinsically hepatotoxic drug or in an idiosyncratic manner after therapeutic doses. The reasons for the unique susceptibility of some patients are still poorly understood, and both genetic and acquired factors are likely to be involved.[1,2]

Patient Assessment

1. K.V., a 52-year-old woman with a 12-year history of non-insulin dependent diabetes, is admitted with a 2-week history

of nausea, anorexia, fatigue, and intense generalized pruritus. She also noted dark urine, light-colored stools, and yellow pigmentation of the skin about 10 days ago, which got progressively worse. She had no fever, rash, vomiting, abdominal pain, fatty food intolerance, alcoholism, exposure to hepatitis virus, or blood transfusion. Her past medical history includes diabetes controlled by diet and chlorpropamide, hypertension treated with hydrochlorothiazide (HCTZ) and methyldopa for the past 4 years. One month ago K.V. was started on a 10-day course of amoxicillin-clavulanic acid (Augmentin) for acute otitis media.

On admission, K.V. appears weak and icteric. Other significant findings include scratch marks and a slightly tender, but normal sized liver. Vital signs are all within normal limits. Laboratory findings show serum AST 430 U/L, serum ALT 294 U/L, alkaline phosphatase 1230 U/L, total:direct (T:D) bilirubin ratio 7.251 mg/dL:106 μmol/L (Normal: up to 0.994 mg/dL for total; up to 14 μmol/L for direct), and albumin 4.1 gm/dL. All other chemistry data are within normal limits. A complete blood count (CBC) and differential count are normal. Tests for hepatitis A and B serology are all negative. Ultrasound shows a normal biliary tract system, with no obstruction in the bile ducts, gallbladder, or near the end of the pancreas. Liver biopsy showed preserved normal liver architecture, marked centrilobular cholestasis with bile pigment in hepatocytes and canaliculi, and a mild portal inflammatory infiltrate with an excess of eosinophils.

K.V. is placed on a 1200 calorie a day with no added salt diet and lente insulin 20 U/day. All other drugs are discontinued. Cholestyramine (Questran) 4 gm PO TID is started for itching. By the fifth day of hospitalization, her laboratory values are AST 85 U/L, ALT 214 U/L, alkaline phosphatase 288 U/L, and bilirubin T:D 2.456 mg/dL:29 μmol/L. Her blood glucose is gradually controlled with increasing doses of lente insulin. Her blood pressure increased to 190/105 mm Hg and HCTZ 25 mg QD is restarted with a plan to add a calcium channel blocker if this does not adequately control her blood pressure. Her lente insulin dose has been increased to 35 U/day and a fasting blood glucose (FBG) of 190 mg/dL is noted. What signs and symptoms are suggestive of hepatitis in K.V.? [SI Units: AST 7.168 and 1.41695 μkat/L; ALT 4.90098 and 3.56738 μkat/L; alkaline phosphatase 20.5041 and 4.80096 μkat/L; T:D bilirubin ratio 124 μmol/L:106 and 42 μmol/L:29 μmol/L (Normal: up to 17 μmol/L for total; up to 14 μmol/L for direct); albumin 41 gm/L]

Routine screening of serum aminotransferases in patients taking potentially hepatotoxic drugs generally is not recommended since the changes in laboratory tests often are delayed or erratic in onset, making detection of abnormalities difficult. Elevations of less than three times normal may reflect normal variations or spurious laboratory results. On the other hand, minor elevations that continue to trend upward on repeat evaluations, or that are greater than three times normal, indicate a cause for concern.

In K.V., weakness, anorexia, dark urine, light-colored stools, icterus, pruritus, hyperbilirubinemia, and a high serum alkaline phosphatase concentration suggest cholestatic jaundice. The slightly tender liver and the high serum concentrations of AST and ALT suggest hepatocellular damage. K.V.'s clinical presentation is consistent with that of a mixed cholestatic-cytotoxic hepatic injury.

Etiology

2. How can the potential etiology of drug-induced hepatitis be determined, and what was the most likely etiology in K.V.?

Drug-induced hepatic injury should be suspected in every patient with jaundice. Negative history of fever, abdominal pain, and fatty food intolerance rule out gall bladder disease in K.V. She has no history of alcoholism, exposure to hepatitis virus, or blood transfusion. In addition, negative ultrasound studies rule out the possibility of extrahepatic obstructive jaundice.

Presence of dark urine ruled out unconjugated hyperbilirubinemia which may be associated with hemolysis. AST elevations alone may be seen in injury to cardiac and skeletal muscles, but together with increased ALT as in K.V., usually indicate hepatic origin. The presence of eosinophils in the liver biopsy, together with the rapid decline of serum aminotransferases, alkaline phosphatase, and bilirubin concentrations toward normal when all drugs are withdrawn, supports the assessment of drug-induced hepatitis in K.V.

There are four possible causes for K.V.'s drug-induced hepatitis; namely, amoxicillin-clavulanic acid, chlorpropamide, hydrochlorothiazide, and methyldopa. Hydrochlorothiazide is an unlikely candidate because allergic cholestatic jaundice is very rarely associated with thiazide diuretics, and K.V. has taken the drug for four years. Methyldopa can cause acute hepatocellular injury, chronic active hepatitis, and, rarely, cholestatic jaundice; however, most cases of methyldopa-induced hepatic injury occur within the first three months of exposure.[10] Thus, methyldopa is probably not the causative agent in K.V. Chlorpropamide, on the other hand, has been reported to cause a mixed cholestatic-cytotoxic injury. Onset of the injury is usually within two to six weeks of sulfonylurea therapy;[6,10,23] therefore it is unlikely in K.V., since she had been on chlorpropamide for four years. Amoxicillin-clavulanic acid, a semisynthetic penicillin-beta-lactamase inhibitor combination drug, has been reported to cause hepatic dysfunctions and jaundice in a number of patients.[24–28] The latent period between the initiation of the drug and onset of jaundice or hepatic dysfunctions ranged from 2 to 45 days with a mean of 27 days. In review of K.V.'s recent history of amoxicillin-clavulanic acid intake and the physical and laboratory findings, amoxicillin-clavulanic acid seems to be the most probable cause. Nevertheless, the possibility of methyldopa- or chlorpropamide-induced hepatic injury cannot be ruled out without an inadvisable rechallenge test with one or both of these drugs.

Procedure to Determine

To determine the etiology of drug-induced hepatic injury, a detailed drug history should be obtained for all patients with jaundice. Oral contraceptive use should not be overlooked. Special attention should be paid to the duration of exposure to a specific drug and its relationship to the onset of symptoms. A history of taking oral contraceptive pills, nonprescription drugs such as laxatives and vitamins, as well as illicit drug use should be sought. Predisposing factors to drug-induced hepatitis, if any, should be noted. These factors vary with the agent involved and can include nutritional status, alcoholism, pre-existent liver or kidney disease, previous history of exposure, gestation in females, gender, and age, as well as concomitant use of drugs that can induce cytochrome P450 oxidative enzymes. More than twenty P450 isoenzymes have been identified to date, which may account for the many differences in species-related, age-related, drug-related, and other susceptibility factors.

The presumptive diagnosis of drug-induced hepatic injury requires a history of exposure to a drug, awareness of the characteristic syndromes produced by various agents, and a search for supportive evidence. If the liver injury is accompanied by fever, rash, and eosinophilia, the likelihood of drug-induced disease increases. Lack of these features, however, does not exclude the possibility of drug-induced disease.[2,6] Differentiation of drug-induced hepatocellular injury from viral hepatitis involves evaluation of the epidemiologic circumstances; serologic studies to detect hepatitis A,

B, or C antigens or antibodies; and determination of whether a history of receiving blood transfusions or injection with a contaminated syringe exists. Distinction between drug-induced cholestatic jaundice and extrahepatic obstructive jaundice often requires radiographic or ultrasonic studies. If liver biopsy reveals cholestasis with an eosinophil-rich portal inflammation, drugs become a likely etiology, as in K.V.

Rechallenge with Offending Agent

3. Should K.V. be given a challenge dose of amoxicillin-clavulanic acid to confirm the etiology of her drug-induced hepatitis?

Confirmation of the etiology may be obtained by giving a rechallenge dose of the incriminated drug. Recurrence of hepatic dysfunction or hyperbilirubinemia after a test dose offers valuable support for the diagnosis. Failure to develop abnormalities, however, does not preclude drug-induced dysfunction because only 40% to 60% of patients show a recurrence of hepatic injury after a test dose.[10] Furthermore, some drugs will produce the hepatic injury only after an extended period (1 to 12 weeks) of readministration. Testing for the effect of a challenge dose can be potentially dangerous if the drug is known to cause hepatocellular injury, whereas rechallenge is considered safe if the drug usually leads to cholestasis alone. Therefore, risk must be weighed against benefit before giving a challenge dose of an incriminated drug to a patient.

Rechallenge of K.V. with amoxicillin-clavulanic acid is potentially dangerous because of her clinical picture of hepatocellular injury. Rapid occurrence of jaundice and liver enzyme abnormalities following rechallenge with amoxicillin-clavulanic acid suggests an immunoallergic type of idiosyncrasy.[25,26] Since alternative antibiotics can be used to manage K.V.'s infection, giving a test dose of the offending drug is unwarranted.

Treatment

4. How should drug-induced hepatic injuries be treated?

Once diagnosis has been made, the presumed offending drug should be withdrawn. In K.V.'s case, all medications taken before admission were discontinued. The management of drug-induced jaundice is similar to the treatment of other hepatic diseases. Treatment usually includes a diet high in carbohydrates, moderately high in protein, and adequate in calories (e.g., 2000 to 3000 calories/day). However, a lower caloric diet is prescribed for K.V. because of her diabetes. Treatment of jaundice is mainly suppor-

tive. If itching is severe, the use of cholestyramine to enhance the rate of bile acid excretion may alleviate the symptoms. If possible, the use of amoxicillin-clavulanic acid should be avoided in future therapy for K.V., and appropriate alternative drugs should be used instead.

If present, ascites, esophageal variceal bleeding, and other complications are treated accordingly. The use of large doses of glucocorticoids (e.g., 1000 mg hydrocortisone/day) in acute hepatic failure is largely empirical and may have a role in hypersensitivity related cases, but otherwise is not recommended.[6,7]

Drugs Reported to Cause Clinically Significant Hepatic Dysfunction

There are many reports of drug-related hepatitis in the literature. Most of these are reports of single cases involving one drug. Many reports of adverse drug effects on the liver are difficult to evaluate because: 1) biopsy studies are not reported or adequate descriptions and illustrations for proper morphologic classification are lacking; 2) some patients received several potentially hepatotoxic drugs concurrently; 3) certain patients had pre-existing hepatic diseases that were not drug related; and 4) very few patients had been rechallenged with the drug. Furthermore, hepatic drug effects that occurred early after exposure may differ in character from those that occurred later (e.g., chlorpromazine). In addition, certain drugs may cause various types of morphologic responses via different mechanisms (i.e., hepatotoxic versus idiosyncratic). In an attempt to summarize and facilitate discussion of the vast amount of information on this subject, only drugs that have been implicated in causing significant liver dysfunction are listed in Table 26.3. The hepatotoxicity of acetaminophen and antituberculous agents (e.g., isoniazid) are presented in other chapters (see Chapter 59: Tuberculosis). Oxyphenisatin, a laxative compound, has caused many cases of acute and chronic hepatic disease and has been banned from the U.S. since the early 1970s. For more details on oxyphenisatin-induced hepatic injury, other references may be consulted.[29–34]

The types of morphologic findings and presumed mechanisms of hepatotoxicity for each drug are presented in Table 26.3. References are listed so that more detailed information may be obtained if desired. In the column labeled "Clinical Remarks," prominent clinical features such as clinical presentation, dose and duration of therapy associated with the adverse effect, pertinent laboratory data, and prognosis are summarized.

Table 26.3	Drug-Induced Hepatotoxicity[a]
Drug I = Incidence M = Morphology Mech = Mechanism	**Clinical Remarks**
Acetaminophen	See Chapter 104: Poisonings
Alcohol	See Chapter 25: Alcoholic Cirrhosis
Allopurinol I: Occasional M: Submassive or massive necrosis cholestatic or granulomatous hepatitis Mech: Hypersensitivity[3,35–40]	Onset of symptoms varies from 7 days to 6 weeks, but mostly during the first month. Mild to moderate increases in alkaline phosphatase and AST have been reported in most cases. Hepatic granulomas are observed in about half the cases. Occurrences of fever, rash, and eosinophilia are frequent. Incidence may be increased in those on diuretics or with decreased renal function. Rarely, death may result from hepatic failure
Amiodarone I: Uncommon M: Alcoholic hepatitis-like lesions, confluent and bridging necrosis; cirrhosis Mech: Phospholipidosis[41–47]	Phospholipidosis is a frequent hallmark of amiodarone therapy. Serum transferase levels modestly increased in about 40% of patients. Liver disease frequently associated with peripheral neuropathy, corneal deposits, a bluish skin discoloration, or thyroid dysfunction. Incidence and severity of these adverse effects appear to be dose and duration related. Due to the long half-life of amiodarone, liver injury may persist for months even after the drug is discontinued. In severe hepatitis, jaundice, hepatomegaly,

Continued

Table 26.3	Drug-Induced Hepatotoxicity[a] (Continued)
Drug I = Incidence M = Morphology Mech = Mechanism	**Clinical Remarks**

Amiodarone (*Continued*)

ascites, and encephalopathy can develop. Fatal cases of amiodarone-induced hepatitis have been reported after IV loading doses. Polysorbate 80, an organic surfactant which is added to the IV solution of amiodarone, may be responsible for hepatotoxicity

Amoxicillin-clavulanic acid (Augmentin)
I: Low
M: Cholestasis; hepatocellular or mixed
Mech: Immunologic idiosyncrasy[24–28]

More than 100 cases of cholestatic jaundice have been reported with this combination. Onset of symptoms range from 2–45 days. Common clinical features include jaundice, pruritus, GI distress, and eosinophilia. Although 40% of this combination is used in pediatric patients, hepatic dysfunctions have been associated largely with adults >30 years, suggesting advancing age as a risk factor; male to female ratio was about 2:1. Since some patients had previous or later exposure to amoxicillin without complications, it has been suggested that clavulanic acid or the combination is the cause

Androgenic steroids
I: High incidence of hepatic dysfunction; cholestatic jaundice dose related
M: Cannicular cholestasis with minor or no portal inflammation; dilation of sinusoids; peliosis hepatis; adenoma and carcinoma
Mech: Indirect intrinsic hepatotoxin[8–10,18,48–59]

Anabolic steroids with an alkyl group in the C-17 position are more likely to cause hepatic dysfunction and jaundice than testosterone and 19-nortestosterone. Although hepatic enzymes can be increased by 10% to 20%, many patients may not have clinical symptoms. However, cholestatic jaundice can develop in patients taking the drug for 1–10 months. The onset of cholestatic jaundice and the severity of hepatic dysfunction are dose dependent. The larger the daily dose, the more likely is the development of jaundice. Individual susceptibility and pre-existing liver disease enhance the potential for hepatic damage. Jaundice may be preceded by nonspecific prodromal symptoms such as malaise, mild anorexia, and nausea. Pruritus may be present in about 10% of patients. Serum transferase levels usually <150 U/mL. Values for alkaline phosphatase normal or modestly increased in most patients. Serum bilirubin levels usually <170 μmol/L, but occasionally patients may reach 800 μmol/L. Recovery is prompt after cessation of the drug, but may take up to 6 months in severe cases

Anabolic-androgenic steroids have been associated with a number of cases of peliosis hepatis. Peliosis hepatis is a vascular lesion that may rupture and lead to hemoperitoneum in some patients

Hepatic adenoma and carcinoma also have been ascribed to the taking of androgens. Anabolic steroids are more likely incriminated in causing hepatic carcinoma than estrogens. The degree of risk probably relates to the type of anabolic steroid, dose, and duration of therapy. Clinically, patients with hepatocellular carcinoma may present with hepatomegaly, abdominal discomfort, pain, or jaundice. In some cases, the patients are asymptomatic with normal biochemical tests

Aspirin and other salicylates
I: 0.1%–0.5%
M: Focal necrosis; steatosis
Mech: Intrinsic hepatotoxicity[1,2,60–69]

Anicteric injury may occur in 5%–50% of patients with high salicylate blood levels (>15 mg/dL). Most patients who have developed hepatic injury have had levels >25 mg/dL, although a few instances have been noted at levels as low as 10 mg/dL. The injury is manifested by increased serum transferases (10- to 40-fold) and is reversible upon withdrawal of the drug. Fatal hepatitis is very rare. Bilirubin levels are normal or moderately elevated. Children with juvenile rheumatoid arthritis or acute rheumatic fever, and adults with active RA or SLE seem to be more vulnerable. Recently, cholestatic hepatitis during low-dose (250 mg/day) aspirin therapy has been reported. Use of salicylates in children with varicella or influenza-like illnesses is reported to be strongly associated with an increased risk of Reye's syndrome, which includes liver failure as part of the syndrome

Azathioprine
I: Rare
M: Cholestasis; minor hepatocellular injury; veno-occlusive disease
Mech: Hypersensitivity[12,70–81]

Only a few isolated instances of cholestatic jaundice have been attributed to azathioprine. Jaundice starts 3 weeks to 6 months after initiation of therapy. Generalized pruritus, widespread abdominal pain, and hypochromic greasy diarrhea may be present. While azathioprine has been used in the treatment of chronic active hepatitis, worsening of the hepatic disease also may occur

Azathioprine is the most common drug in the U.S. implicated in causing VOD. Approximately 20% of bone marrow and renal transplant patients may be affected with a mortality rate of 50%. VOD results from a nonthrombotic concentric occlusion of the lumen of small intrahepatic veins, also known as "bush tea" disease

Captopril
I: Rare
M: Mostly cholestasis; mixed hepatocellular and cholestatic injury; pure hepatocellular injury—rare
Mech: Hypersensitivity and modulation of eicosanoid metabolism by inhibition of kininase II with increased hepatic bradykinin activity[82–87]

Hepatotoxicity, usually cholestatic in nature, has been reported with captopril, enalapril, and lisinopril use. Cross-sensitivity also has been reported. Jaundice was the most common finding, followed by pruritus, nausea, other GI symptoms, fever, rash, and confusion. Onset of symptoms varied from 5 days to 12 months (mean: 14 weeks; median: 1 month). Doses employed were variable. Hepatotoxicity usually resolves in 2 weeks to 9 months after ACE inhibitors are stopped, but may progress to liver failure and death if treatment is continued

Carmustine (BCNU)
I: Dose related
M: Cytotoxic
Mech: Intrinsic hepatotoxin[88–92]

Nitrosoureas apparently act as alkylating agents and produce hepatic injury in up to 25% of patients taking therapeutic doses of BCNU. Hepatic injury produced by BCNU has ranged from reversible jaundice and abnormal levels of AST to severe hepatic necrosis

Continued

Table 26.3	Drug-Induced Hepatotoxicity[a] (Continued)
Drug I = Incidence M = Morphology Mech = Mechanism	**Clinical Remarks**
Chlorpromazine (CPZ) I: 0.1%–0.2% M: Cholestasis; scattered focal areas of necrosis Mech: Hypersensitivity; idiosyncrasy[9,16,93–101]	The effect of age, gender, race, or other predisposing factors has not been established. In approximately 80% of cases, icterus develops between 1 to 5 weeks of CPZ treatment. In rare instances, jaundice has developed after the first dose. Prodromal symptoms consist of fever, itching, abdominal pain, anorexia, and nausea. Skin rash is observed only in about 5% of reported cases. CPZ jaundice often resembles extrahepatic obstructive jaundice Severe pruritus common and may be the first evidence of hepatic injury in some patients. Serum alkaline phosphatase and cholesterol levels often markedly elevated. Serum transferase levels increased slightly to moderately in almost all patients. Eosinophilia has been noted in 25% to 50% of cases reported. The outlook for CPZ jaundice is good. Cholestatic jaundice associated with CPZ often resolves within 8 weeks but occasionally may continue for a year or longer. Some of the patients with prolonged cholestasis have developed a syndrome resembling that of primary biliary cirrhosis. The clinical syndrome is characterized by itching, xanthoma, hepatomegaly, and splenomegaly. Although it has been suggested that this syndrome is frequently benign and reversible, at least 2 cases of irreversible cirrhosis and fatality due to CPZ have been described Other phenothiazines also have been reported to cause cholestatic jaundice, but no reliable estimate of the incidence is available. Since there is a potential for cross-sensitivity between chlorpromazine and other phenothiazines, it is best to avoid using any agent in this class for patients who have had CPZ jaundice Cholestasis also has been associated with almost all other phenothiazines, and the clinical manifestations reported are similar to chlorpromazine
Chlorpropamide (and other sulfonylurea oral hypoglycemics) I: 0.1%–0.5% M: Mixed cholestatic-cytotoxic injury Mech: Hypersensitivity, hepatotoxicity[23,102–111]	Host factors that modify the susceptibility to hepatic injury unknown. Onset of jaundice usually between 2–6 weeks of chlorpropamide therapy. Initial symptoms are anorexia, nausea, and vomiting. Soon thereafter, dark urine, jaundice, and clay-colored stools appear. Pruritus and hepatomegaly common. Fever, rash, and eosinophilia occur frequently but not in all cases. Complete recovery generally occurs within 1–3 months after chlorpropamide is stopped. Patients who recover from chlorpropamide jaundice apparently do not relapse when given tolbutamide. Other sulfonylureas in clinical use (i.e., acetohexamide, tolbutamide, glibenclamide, and tolazamide) also have been reported to cause jaundice, but the incidence appears to be very low. Fatal hepatotoxicity in an elderly woman has been apparently induced by glibenclamide
Ciprofloxacin	See Fluoroquinolones
Contraceptive steroids (OCs) I: Dose related 1:10,000 in Europe and North America; 1:4000 in Chile and Scandinavia M: 1) Cholestasis[112–121]	1) Estrogens can selectively interfere with bilirubin excretion by the liver. The importance of structural specificity of the estrogen molecule in causing hepatic dysfunction has been established. The phenolic character of ring A and the addition of an alkyl group at the C-17 position of the estrogen molecule seem to be responsible for the injury. Progesterone has little or no demonstrable adverse effect on hepatic function by itself, but may enhance the hepatic injury produced by the estrogens. Hepatic dysfunction occurs much more frequently and may be as high as 40%–50% of patients taking these agents. Postmenopausal women appear to be more susceptible to hepatic dysfunction induced by estrogen than younger women. Certain ethnic groups (Swedes, Chileans) seem to be more prone to develop anicteric dysfunction than others. Susceptibility to estrogen-induced cholestasis probably is related to a genetic factor because of the strong link with recurrent cholestasis of pregnancy. The jaundice usually is noted during the first 6 months of therapy and often during the first cycle. Jaundice preceded by nonspecific symptoms including malaise, anorexia, nausea, and pruritus. Splenomegaly not seen and hepatomegaly is infrequent. Serum concentrations of bilirubin levels increased moderately in most cases (≥10 mg/dL) but values >20 mg/dL have been described. Other biochemical features resemble the jaundice produced by the C-17 alkylated anabolic steroids. Prognosis of the cholestatic jaundice good. In most individuals, the clinical syndrome resolves completely within 1 month
2) Adenoma, peliosis hepatis[122–131]	2) Hepatic adenoma was a very rare tumor before the widespread use of contraceptive steroids. Since then, the increase in incidence of adenoma seems to have paralleled the increased use of OCs. Women taking contraceptive steroids for periods >5 years appear to be at higher risk of developing an adenoma than those who have taken the drug <3 years. One-third to one-half of patients found to have adenoma remain asymptomatic. Approximately one-third may present with a painful, tender mass. The remaining one-fourth to one-third of reported patients often present with a sudden life-threatening intra-abdominal hemorrhage secondary to rupture of the adenoma. Prognosis is good if the adenoma can be resected before rupture. For patients with hemoperitoneum, the outlook is fair if the diagnosis is made promptly and the tumor resected. Otherwise, death may result from hemorrhagic shock, coagulation abnormalities, and related

Continued

Table 26.3	Drug-Induced Hepatotoxicity^a (Continued)
Drug I = Incidence M = Morphology Mech = Mechanism	**Clinical Remarks**
2) Adenoma, peliosis hepatis *(Continued)*	complications. Peliosis hepatis is a rare complication from contraceptive steroids and often occurs along with the adenoma
3) Budd-Chiari syndrome[132–134]	3) Budd-Chiari syndrome characterized by acute or subacute development of abdominal pain, hepatomegaly, portal hypertension, ascites, edema, and moderate jaundice. This syndrome is caused by thrombosis and subsequent occlusion of the hepatic veins. Although this complication is very rare, an extremely high morality rate clearly makes it an important consideration in the use of estrogens
4) Carcinoma[135–140] Mech: Indirect hepatoxin; genetic predisposition	4) Several types of malignant tumors have been associated with the use of OCs. Over 100 cases have been reported, but the incidence is low when compared to the widespread use of OCs. Hepatic carcinoma may be more likely in women who use the OCs for >8 years
Cyclosporine I: Uncommon M: Cholestasis Mech: Direct toxic effect on bile secretion[3,141–144]	Increased serum transferase and gamma-glutamyl transferase concentrations and increased serum bilirubin concentration are signs of cyclosporine hepatotoxicity. Elevated LFTs have been observed in about 4% of renal transplant, 7% of heart allograft, and 4% of liver transplant recipients, usually during the first month of cyclosporine therapy. Reduction of cyclosporine dosage usually reverses its hepatotoxic effects. Several cases of cholestasis have been reported. There was a significant increased incidence of VOD among patients who received cyclosporine and methotrexate (CYC-MTX) versus those who received cyclosporine and methylprednisolone (70% versus 18%) as prophylaxis against graft-versus-host disease for allogenic bone marrow transplantation. Incidence of early deaths due to VOD was significantly higher in the CYC-MTX group (25% versus 4.5%)
Dantrolene I: Hypertransferasemia a) Without jaundice (1.8%) b) Overt hepatic injury (0.6%) M: Severe viral hepatitis-like; submassive and massive necrosis Mech: Idiosyncrasy; toxic metabolites[145–148]	The incidence and severity of the hepatic injury appear to be related to the duration of therapy and patient age. Clinical onset of hepatic injury has been delayed for at least 45 days after starting the drug in almost all cases. In a study of 1044 patients, all fatalities have occurred in patients >30 years and after at least 2 months of therapy. Females have a higher fatality rate than males, although there appears to be no significant difference in the incidence of hepatic injury between sexes. The development and the severity of hepatic injury seem to be dose related. Doses >300 mg/day are more likely to produce hepatic injury than smaller doses, and doses of ≤200 mg/day rarely lead to liver damage. Injury is mainly hepatocellular with a pattern of either acute, subacute, or chronic hepatitis. The fatality rate of 28% is high
Diltiazem I: Rare M: Granulomatous Mech: Idiosyncrasy[149–154]	Mild to marked elevations in liver function test results have been reported in <1% of patients taking diltiazem, and drug discontinuation was not required. 6 case reports of hepatocellular injury, usually early in the therapy (1–8 weeks), have been published
Erythromycin I: 3.6/100,000 M: Cholestasis; mixed cholestatic-cytotoxic injury Mech: Hypersensitivity[2,9,155–167]	Erythromycin-associated cholestasis may be due to the estolate salt as well as the ethylsuccinate and propionate derivatives. Nevertheless, the estolate salt has been implicated most frequently. Children may be less susceptible than adults. Onset of cholestatic jaundice usually 1–3 weeks after exposure; however, patients previously exposed may exhibit symptoms within 2 days. Abdominal pain occurs in about 75% of the cases. Icterus may precede or accompany GI complaints, such as anorexia, nausea, and vomiting. Fever occurs in about 60% of patients, and rash is often absent. Eosinophilia occurs frequently (45%–80%). Serum bilirubin values are generally <100 μmol/L. Response to a challenge dose of the same erythromycin derivative is usually prompt. The hepatic injury is reversible, and jaundice often subsides within 2–5 weeks after the drug is discontinued
Fluoroquinolones I: Rare M: Cholestasis; centrilobular necrosis Mech: Idiosyncrasy?[168–172]	Elevations in aminotransferase, bilirubin, and alkaline phosphatase levels were observed in 1.8%–2.5% of patients who received fluoroquinolones. Sporadic cases of drug-induced hepatitis had appeared in the literature for ciprofloxacin, enoxacin, ofloxacin, and norfloxacin. Hepatic injury due to fluoroquinolones apparently is not dose related and generally is reversible when the drug is stopped. However, 1 fatal case of hepatic failure, apparently due to oral ciprofloxacin, was reported
Glucocorticoids I: Dose related M: Steatosis Mech: Hepatotoxicity[173–176]	Hepatic steatosis secondary to glucocorticoids usually of little clinical consequence. However, occasionally this may lead to fat embolism in the vascular bed of major organs (e.g., lung) resulting in tissue damage and fatality
Haloperidol I: Low M: Cholestasis Mech: Hypersensitivity[177,178]	Incidence has been estimated to be between 0.2%–3% of recipients. Most reported cases of jaundice appear to be cholestatic

Continued

| Table 26.3 | Drug-Induced Hepatotoxicity^a (Continued) |

Drug I = Incidence M = Morphology Mech = Mechanism	Clinical Remarks
Halothane I: 1) Mild form >25% 2) Severe 1:35,000–1:3500 M: Centrizonal necrosis; steatosis; massive necrosis Mech: Metabolic idiosyncrasy; hypersensitivity[179–196]	Halothane exposure may be followed by 2 distinct types of hepatotoxicity: Asymptomatic with abnormal laboratory values only or severe acute hepatitis with massive hepatic necrosis. The reactive metabolites of halothane, trifluoroacetyl acid chloride (TFA), and free radicals, cause mild self-limiting hepatotoxicity by binding to macromolecules, resulting in subclinical damage. The rarer form of fulminant hepatitis is believed to result from the binding of TFA to subcellular free amino groups and neoantigens, resulting in an autoimmune reaction to halothane upon repeated exposure. The incidence and severity appear to be greater in females and enhanced by obesity. Susceptibility is particularly enhanced by previous exposure to halothane, especially if the interval between the exposures is <3 months. Incidence may be increased as much as 10-fold with repeated exposure to halothane or isoflurane. Irradiation also may increase susceptibility to halothane hepatitis. Jaundice is rare in children and young adults <30 years. The clinical syndrome of halothane-induced liver disease often consists of a history of unexplained delayed fever postoperatively (>3 days) after halothane anesthesia. There is usually a latent period of 5–14 days between the anesthetic episode and the appearance of hepatic injury, but it may appear as early as 1 day after the operation in patients who have had multiple prior exposures to halothane. Fever with or without chills, aching, anorexia, nausea, and abdominal distress preceded jaundice in 75% of the patients. Once jaundice appears, other manifestations of serious hepatocellular damage often develop rapidly. Coagulation abnormalities, ascites, renal insufficiency, GI bleeding, and encephalopathy may follow Values for serum transferases are markedly elevated (≥3000 U/L) whereas alkaline phosphatase is increased only modestly. Eosinophilia has been observed in 20%–50% of reported cases. Rash uncommon. Mortality rate for halothane hepatitis ranges from 14%–67%. Serological testing for antibodies specific to halothane-altered antigens is positive in about 75% of patients and can be used as a diagnostic aid along with the drug history and clinical presentation
Isoniazid (INH)[1,2,8]	See Chapter 59: Tuberculosis. Fast and slow acetylators may be equally susceptible to the hepatotoxic effects of INH. It appears that specific P450 isoenzymes may be involved because of the enhanced hepatotoxicity by alcohol, other drugs (rifampicin), and advancing age
Ketoconazole I: 0.03%–0.1% M: Hepatocellular necrosis; mixed cholestasis-hepatocellular Mech: Metabolic idiosyncrasy[197–199]	Serum transferase concentrations can be increased in 8%–12% of patients without overt clinical symptoms. Symptomatic hepatic injury is infrequent and often presents as a mixed or cholestatic jaundice. Fulminant hepatitis also is possible. Hepatitis more common in females, especially those over 40 years, and usually occurs after 10 days to 26 weeks of therapy. Hypersensitivity manifestations usually absent
Lovastatin I: Very rare M: Mild focal hepatitis; cholestasis Mech: Hepatocellular[1,200,201]	In 613 patients who received lovastatin during controlled trials, the most common laboratory abnormalities were elevations in hepatic enzymes. Serum concentrations of ALT, AST, and CPK were increased by 7.3%, 5.9%, and 5.1%, respectively. Serum aminotransferase concentrations were increased by more than 3-fold in about 1.9% of all patients in this study. The risk of developing increases in transferase levels has been reported in patients with the homozygous form of familial hypercholesterolemia and may be dose related. Hepatitis, fatty change in the liver, cholestatic jaundice, and chronic active hepatitis have been reported rarely. Liver function tests usually are reversible after a few weeks upon discontinuation, but recovery may be delayed for up to 21 months. Rechallenge can result in elevations of aminotransferases in about 50% of patients. Lovastatin should be avoided in patients who have liver disease or a history of alcohol abuse
Mercaptopurine (6-MP) I: Dose related M: Cholestasis with fatty hepatic necrosis Mech: Indirect intrinsic hepatotoxin[202–205]	Liver injury with jaundice has been reported in 6%–40% of leukemic patients treated with 6-MP. Adults appear to be more susceptible to hepatic injury than children. Onset of overt hepatic injury is usually within 1–2 months of receiving the drug. Jaundice commonly appears as the first sign, followed by pruritus. Serum transferase values are generally <250 U/L. Alkaline phosphatase values are moderately to markedly elevated. Doses >2.5 mg/kg are more likely to cause hepatic injury. Prognosis depends on the degree of cytotoxic injury, but mortality may reach ≥10%
Methimazole I: Rare M: Cholestasis Mech: Hypersensitivity[206–209]	Onset of the syndrome is usually during the first 4 months of therapy, but may be as late as 3 months. Rash, fever, lymphadenopathy, and agranulocytosis may occur in various combinations. The cholestatic jaundice associated with methimazole is reversible. Death appears to have been the result of concomitant agranulocytosis and bone marrow depression, rather than the hepatic injury
Methoxyflurane I: Rare, but often fatal	The clinical syndrome and hepatic lesions from methoxyflurane and enflurane are very similar to those observed in halothane hepatitis, but with a lower incidence. Cross-

Continued

Table 26.3	Drug-Induced Hepatotoxicity^a (Continued)
Drug I = Incidence M = Morphology Mech = Mechanism	**Clinical Remarks**

Methoxyflurane *(Continued)*
- M: Similar findings as in halothane hepatitis
- Mech: Hypersensitivity; metabolic aberration[210–212]

sensitivity of halothane with methoxyflurane and enflurane is probable. Isoflurane, which is minimally metabolized, and nitrous oxide may be safer alternatives

Methotrexate (MTX)
- I: Dose, frequency, and duration related
- M: Macrovesicular steatosis and portal inflammation; necrosis; chronic steatosis may lead to fibrosis and cirrhosis
- Mech: Indirect intrinsic hepatotoxin[213–226]

MTX frequently causes steatosis and portal inflammation in the liver when it is used in the acute treatment of leukemia, choriocarcinoma, and other neoplastic diseases. Overt clinical symptoms occasionally accompany these lesions. Prolonged use of MTX in patients with psoriasis may lead to fibrosis and cirrhosis but apparently not in those with RA. The likelihood of hepatic injury probably is directly related to the total dose and duration of therapy; it is inversely related to the time interval between doses. Other risk factors include age, obesity, diabetes, alcoholism, and perhaps severity of psoriasis. Biochemical changes provide insensitive reflections of MTX-induced hepatic injury. Serum concentrations of AST and ALT usually are increased for 1–2 days after a single dose of MTX; however, cirrhosis can develop insidiously without increases in the liver enzyme concentrations. Serial liver biopsies at yearly intervals are recommended highly for patients with psoriasis to facilitate the discovery of cirrhosis and its complications which can progress without overt clinical symptoms. Some of these patients may progress to hepatic failure and death. Early recognition of this syndrome can decrease irreversible hepatic damage and improve long-term survival. Preventative measures include giving intermittent rather than small daily doses of MTX. Single weekly dosing regimens of <15 mg have been successful in reducing the incidence of significant hepatic injury

Methyldopa
- I: Low
- M: Cytotoxic injury; subacute or bridging necrosis; rare cholestasis; chronic active hepatitis
- Mech: Toxic metabolites; hypersensitivity[13,227–235]

Incidence of methyldopa-induced hepatic injury difficult to estimate. In some patients, serum enzyme levels have returned to normal despite continued therapy with methyldopa. Methyldopa-induced hepatitis usually hepatocellular, rarely mixed or cholestatic. The incidence of severe cytotoxic injury is estimated to be <0.1%–0.5% of recipients

Methyldopa hepatitis occurs more commonly in patients >35 years and predominantly affects females. Acute hepatic injury has appeared within 4 weeks of therapy in 50% of the patients reported and within 4–12 weeks in 25% of the cases. Others may have a latent period for several years. The syndrome of methyldopa-induced hepatic injury resembles acute viral hepatitis. There usually has been a prodromal period of fever, chills, malaise, anorexia, nausea, vomiting, occasional right upper quadrant tenderness, and pruritus. Jaundice, dark urine, and hepatomegaly usually follow in severe cases. Rash, lymphadenopathy, and arthralgia have been rare. Biochemical features resemble those of cytotoxic injury. Rechallenge usually leads to recurrence of hepatitis and can result in fatalities. The fatality rate from acute hepatic injury is estimated to be 10%. For those patients who survive, withdrawal of the drug results in rapid recovery in most cases

Chronic active hepatitis induced by methyldopa resembles "autoimmune" type CAH. Biopsy of the liver has revealed subacute hepatic necrosis with confluent areas of lobular collapse, intense inflammatory response in the portal and periportal areas, and in some cases, evidence of cirrhosis. Positive Coombs' test, LE factor, and antinuclear and antismooth muscle antibodies may be observed. Clinical presentation may be a mixture of acute and chronic hepatitis. In some patients, hepatosplenomegaly and spider angiomas may develop when the syndrome is first recognized

To prevent irreversible liver injury or death, it is advisable to monitor liver enzyme tests regularly during the first 3 months of therapy, particularly in females. Periodic checks for the first 3 years also may be indicated

Mithramycin (Plicamycin)
- I: Dose related
- M: Necrosis
- Mech: Intrinsic hepatotoxins[236–239]

Biochemical evidence of hepatic injury has been found in 25%–100% of recipients on "full" oncotherapeutic doses. Values for AST and ALT may be as high as 1000 U/L. Hepatocellular jaundice may occur. Hepatotoxicity appears to be less with the doses used to treat Paget's disease and hypercalcemia. An alternate-day regimen used to treat carcinomas also seems to have an acceptable level of hepatotoxicity

Monoamine oxidase inhibitors (MAOIs)
(iproniazid, isocarboxazid, phenelzine)
- I: ≈1%
- M: Hepatocellular damage
- Mech: Metabolic idiosyncrasy; autoimmune[240–245]

Iproniazid, the first antidepressant to produce hepatic injury, was withdrawn from the market because of many reported cases of fulminant hepatic failure. Severe hepatitis has been encountered in patients given phenelzine for periods of 18 days to 5 months. The clinical features and the histological findings in the liver are indistinguishable from those of severe viral hepatitis. The reported mortality rate is about 15%. Tranylcypromine, a nonhydrazine MAOI, rarely causes jaundice similar to that of hydrazine derivatives

Niacin (Nicotinic acid)
- I: Occasional
- M: Hepatic necrosis; cholestasis

Nicotinic acid-induced hepatitis has been associated with high-dose regimens (>3 gm/day) given for several months to years. SR formulation of niacin seems to induce hepatotoxicity at lower doses within days to weeks. Symptoms included burning

Continued

Table 26.3	Drug-Induced Hepatotoxicity[a] (Continued)
Drug I = Incidence M = Morphology Mech = Mechanism	**Clinical Remarks**

Niacin (Nicotinic acid) *(Continued)*
Mech: Unknown; dose related? direct toxicity? formulation related?[246–249]

sensation in the chest, lightheadedness, nausea, vomiting, diaphoresis, anorexia, and jaundice. Elevated hepatic enzyme levels were observed in most patients and normalized upon withdrawal. Fulminant hepatocellular failure has been attributed to the SR form more often than to the crystalline form. Rechallenge with regular formulation of niacin does not produce recurring hepatocellular damage

Nonsteroidal anti-inflammatory drugs (NSAIDs)
I: 1:100,000 recipients
M: Cholestasis, cytotoxic, or mixed
Mech: Hypersensitivity; reactive metabolites[250–261]

Hepatocellular injury, or cholestasis, has occurred in patients taking benoxaprofen and is associated with a high fatality rate. Benoxaprofen is more hepatotoxic in elderly females and in those with renal dysfunction. Benoxaprofen was, therefore, withdrawn from the market

Two-thirds of the cases of sulindac-induced hepatic injury had clinical hallmarks of hypersensitivity. Ratio of females to males was 3.5:1 with 69% of patients >50 years. Most commonly reported clinical features of sulindac-induced hepatitis were jaundice (67%), nausea (67%), fever (55%), rash (48%), pruritus (40%), and eosinophilia (35%). Other features included hepatomegaly, lymphadenopathy, splenomegaly, myalgia, pharyngitis, edema, thyroid disorders, interstitial nephritis, somnolence, and ulcerative stomatitis. Onset ranged from 1 day to 3 years, but mostly <8 weeks. Rechallenge leads to recurrence in a few days, thus suggesting an allergic mechanism. Complete recovery occurred in all patients 2–3 weeks after drug discontinuation

Severe cholestatic hepatitis, which can progress to subacute hepatic necrosis, has been reported with piroxicam. Elderly patients >60 years seem to be more prone to piroxicam-induced cholestasis. Liver enzymes may take 3–4 months to return to normal levels after piroxicam is discontinued. Other NSAIDs such as naproxen, diclofenac, ketoprofen, and ibuprofen also have been implicated

Although cases of NSAID-induced hepatitis are rare, they can be fatal. The majority of cases of hepatitis secondary to NSAIDs occur within the first few months of treatment. Therefore, laboratory tests of liver function should be monitored monthly for 6 months and quarterly thereafter

Nitrofurantoin
I: Rare
M: Mixed cholestatic-cytotoxic injury; chronic active hepatitis
Mech: Hypersensitivity; reactive metabolites[14,15,262–268]

The onset of symptoms of hepatic injury usually abrupt with fever (60%), rash (30%), and eosinophilia (70%). Approximately two-thirds of the patients have had previous exposure to nitrofurantoin. The latent period before the development of symptoms ranges from 2 days to 5 months but usually within the first 5 weeks. Cholestatic jaundice is the most common acute injury observed with nitrofurantoin. The prognosis of nitrofurantoin-induced jaundice is good. Biochemical abnormalities and jaundice are generally reversible when the drug is discontinued. CAH of the "lupoid" type is rare and may be accompanied by pulmonary lesions. Most patients have a low serum albumin concentration and a high gamma globulin serum concentration. Antinuclear and/or antismooth muscle autoantibodies are found in most patients. Few cases of cirrhosis have been reported

Oral hypoglycemics

See Chlorpropamide

Oxacillin and its derivatives
I: Low
M: Cholestasis
Mech: Hypersensitivity? Idiosyncrasy[269–278]

Oxacillin has been associated with rare cholestatic jaundice and numerous cases of anicteric hepatic dysfunction. Liver transferase levels can be as high as 1000 U/L in some cases. Alkaline phosphatase levels are only modestly elevated and serum bilirubin remains normal in most patients. Eosinophilia accompanies only about 25% of cases. Upon cessation of oxacillin, liver enzyme values generally return to normal within 2 weeks. Apparently there is no cross hepatotoxicity between oxacillin and other penicillins. Nafcillin or penicillin G often can be substituted without recurrence of liver injury. Cloxacillin and flucloxacillin also have been associated with severe cholestatic jaundice. Occasionally, the cholestatic injury may last for months to years even after the drug is stopped. Estimated incidence of flucloxacillin-induced liver dysfunction ranged from 1:11,000 to 1:30,000 prescriptions. Higher risk was dissociated with female sex, age, high daily doses, and duration of >2 weeks

Penicillin
I: Very rare
M: Necrosis; granuloma; "lupoid" hepatitis
Mech: Hypersensitivity[279–291]

Only a few cases of hepatic dysfunction have been associated with penicillin G. Almost all cases were associated with systemic hypersensitivity reactions such as urticaria, rash, anaphylactic shock, systemic granulomatous response, serum sickness, or exfoliative dermatitis. Carbenicillin, ampicillin, amoxicillin, and mezlocillin also have been associated with increased serum transferase levels

Phenindione
I: <0.5%
M: Mixed cholestatic-cytotoxic
Mech: Hypersensitivity[292–298]

Overt hepatic injury induced by phenindione always is associated with generalized allergic reactions such as rash, fever, eosinophilia, lymphocytosis, renal injury, and occasionally thrombocytopenia. Onset usually during the third or fourth week of drug administration. Hepatic injury appears to be the mixed cytotoxic and cholestatic type. Values for serum transferases usually <500 U/L. Alkaline phosphatase serum concentrations moderately to markedly increased. As a rule, hepatitis subsides following withdrawal of phenindione. The case fatality rate of patients with

Continued

Table 26.3	Drug-Induced Hepatotoxicity[a] (Continued)
Drug I = Incidence M = Morphology Mech = Mechanism	**Clinical Remarks**

Phenindione (Continued)

phenindione jaundice is estimated to be 10% and is probably the result of severe generalized hypersensitivity, rather than that of hepatic failure. Coumarin derivatives are preferred

Phenylbutazone
I: 0.25%
M: 1) Granulomatous form
    2) Severe necrosis with or without cholestasis
Mech: Hypersensitivity; intrinsic toxicity?[299–304]

Onset of illness often occurs within the first weeks of therapy, but occasionally can occur after 12 months of therapy. Hypersensitivity probably is responsible for the hepatic injury due to the accompanying fever and/or rash. Allergic symptoms, however, are found in only 50% of the cases. Since an apparent relationship between dose and toxicity was observed more frequently with large doses of phenylbutazone, the intrinsic toxicity of the drug also may play a role. Fever, rash, arthralgia, nausea, vomiting, and abdominal pain may precede or accompany the jaundice. About two-thirds experienced cytotoxic injury with or without cholestasis and steatosis. In about 30% of patients, cholestasis with little or no parenchymal injury has been observed. Granuloma also may be found in some cases with minor liver cell necrosis. A fatality rate of 12% has been reported in patients with hepatic necrosis. Patients with cholestasis and granulomatous lesion generally recover, although the lesion may take up to 4 months to resolve

Phenytoin
I: <1%
M: Submassive necrosis; lobular hepatitis; cholestatic hepatitis; granulomatous hepatitis
Mech: Hypersensitivity; idiosyncrasy; toxic metabolites[8,305–315]

Subclinical hepatic enzyme elevation is common with phenytoin but overt hepatitis is much less common. Children seem to be less vulnerable to hepatic injury from phenytoin. Almost 80% of cases involved adults >20 years. Symptoms generally occur after 1–5 weeks of therapy. Fever, rash, lymphadenopathy, and eosinophilia appear in almost all patients. Jaundice then follows. Leukocytosis with lymphocytosis and atypical lymphocytes is common. The syndrome resembles that of serum sickness or infectious mononucleosis. Biochemical features are similar to those of severe viral hepatitis. Values for AST and ALT are very high (200–4000 U/L), and the serum concentrations of alkaline phosphatase usually is only modestly increased. A case mortality rate of about 30% is due partly to accompanying severe hypersensitivity reactions (e.g., exfoliative dermatitis) and partly to resulting hepatic failure. A single case of phenytoin-induced chronic persistent hepatitis which was verified by histology and rechallenge was reported

Prochlorperazine
I: Rare
M: Cholestasis
Mech: Hypersensitivity[316,317]

See Chlorpromazine

Propylthiouracil (PTU)
I: Rare
M: Hepatocellular injury; chronic active hepatitis; cholestasis; granuloma
Mech: Hypersensitivity; toxic metabolites?[318–325]

Asymptomatic and transient elevations of liver enzymes are common in patients receiving PTU (up to 28% in 1 study). However, ALT levels decrease after dose reduction and normalize in a majority of the cases. Signs and symptoms of hepatocellular damage usually appear within 2–4 weeks after initiation of the drug and often are accompanied by rash, fever, and lymphadenopathy. CAH and cholestatic jaundice secondary to PTU have been described. Fatal cases of PTU-induced jaundice have been attributed to hepatic necrosis or accompanying granulocytosis

Quinidine
I: Rare
M: Mixed hepatocellular; granulomata
Mech: Hypersensitivity[326–330]

Mild hepatic injury induced by quinidine most commonly occurs within 6–12 days of initiation of treatment and is usually anicteric. Quinidine-induced hepatitis usually heralded by fever in association with increased AST, ALT, LDH, and alkaline phosphatase levels. Discontinuation of the drug usually results in rapid resolution of fever and laboratory abnormalities. Upon rechallenge with a single dose of quinidine, most patients have promptly developed fever and increased concentrations of serum transferases, thereby supporting hypersensitivity as a mechanism

Rifampin

See Chapter 59: Tuberculosis

Sulfamethoxazole-trimethoprim (Co-Trimoxazole)
I: Very low
M: Cholestasis; few hepatocellular
Mech: Idiosyncrasy[331–334]

12 cases of Co-Trimoxazole-induced liver injury have been reported. The cholestasis can be severe and might last for >12 months, even after the drug was stopped. 1 case of fulminant hepatic failure was fatal. Prominent features are pruritus, fever, skin rash, arthralgias, and eosinophilia

Sulfonamides
I: 0.5%–1% cholestatic jaundice
M: Mixed hepatocellular injury; subacute hepatic necrosis with cirrhosis; chronic active hepatitis; granulomatous hepatitis
Mech: Hypersensitivity; idiosyncrasy[335–344]

Clinical presentation of hepatic injury often occurs within 5–14 days, but occasionally presents as late as several months. About 25% of the patients with hepatic dysfunction have had prior exposure to sulfonamides. The reaction is characterized by fever, rash, and signs of visceral and bone marrow injury. The clinical and morphologic features of such reactions resemble those of serum sickness. Usually, the onset of symptoms is sudden, with fever, anorexia, nausea, vomiting, and sometimes rash. Jaundice appears on the third to sixth day after the onset of fever, but may be delayed for as long as 2 weeks. Dark urine and acholic stools are frequent, and hepatomegaly may be noted. Prognosis depends upon the extent of cytotoxic injury. Case fatality rate is reportedly above 10%. Patients who survive generally recover slowly over a period of several weeks to months. Fatal massive necrosis has been described with pyrimethamine-

Continued

Table 26.3	Drug-Induced Hepatotoxicity[a] (Continued)
Drug I = Incidence M = Morphology Mech = Mechanism	**Clinical Remarks**
Sulfonamides (Continued)	sulfadoxine (Fansidar). Slow acetylators are more susceptible to sulfonamide-induced hepatic injury because of a possible genetic defect in a protective mechanism against sulfonamides
Sulindac	See Nonsteroidal anti-inflammatory drugs

Tetracyclines
  I: Low
  M: Microvesicular fat droplets in hepatocytes; fatty degeneration
  Mech: Intrinsic hepatotoxicity[345–352]
	Chlortetracycline, oxytetracycline, and tetracycline have been reported to produce hepatic steatosis. The development of clinically significant fatty liver appears to depend upon the presence of high blood levels of the drug. Large doses (>1.5 gm/day) of tetracycline, especially when given IV to pregnant women or individuals with renal disease, may give rise to severe hepatic injury. Clinical manifestations usually appear 4–10 days after initiation of tetracycline therapy. Early symptoms include nausea, vomiting, abdominal pain, hematemesis, and headache. Mild jaundice then follows. Hemorrhagic complications, azotemia, hypotension, shock, and coma may develop subsequently. Tetracycline-induced massive steatosis does not differ clinically or morphologically from the spontaneous form of fatty liver of pregnancy. Mortality rate from this syndrome is ≈80%. This serious untoward reaction can be avoided by using safer alternative antibiotics whenever possible or by keeping the IV dose of tetracycline <1 gm/day

Tricyclic antidepressants (TCAs)
  (amitriptyline, imipramine, desipramine)
  I: Rare to infrequent
  M: Cholestasis; hepatic necrosis
  Mech: Hypersensitivity plus slight toxicity[2,10,353–358]
	TCAs usually cause a mixed hepatitis with either the necrotic or the cholestatic component predominating depending upon the agent. Jaundice appears within 1 week to 4 months. Hypersensitivity manifestations are seen in some patients. Severe hepatic necrosis and death are rare. Prolonged cholestasis and progressive hepatic fibrosis have been reported in a few cases

Trifluoperazine
  I: Rare
  M: Cholestasis
  Mech: Hypersensitivity[359,360]
	See Chlorpromazine

Valproic acid
  I: 0.05%–0.1%
  M: Microvesicular steatosis; focal or massive necrosis
  Mech: Toxic metabolites; idiosyncrasy[8,361–366]
	Valproate can increase the serum transferase concentration in 6%–44% of patients without overt clinical symptoms. Numerous cases of fatal and nonfatal liver disease due to valproate have been reported. Infants and young children (<2 years) are at much higher risk than adults. Lethargy, lassitude, anorexia, nausea, vomiting, edema, facial puffiness, and a frequent change in the pattern of convulsions may precede jaundice, ascites, and hemorrhage. Severe hepatic necrosis can result in coma and azotemia. Prothrombin time is prolonged, serum ammonia concentrations increased, and hypoglycemia may occur. The hepatotoxicity is thought to be related to an inherited or acquired deficiency in the beta oxidation of valproate resulting in increased formation of a toxic metabolite (4-envalproate). This toxic metabolic pathway seems to be cytochrome P450 enzyme-dependent and is inducible by other drugs such as phenobarbital and phenytoin

Vitamin A
  I: Dose related
  M: Fat-storing cell hyperplasia and hypertrophy; nonspecific hepatocellular degeneration; fibrosis; cirrhosis
  Mech: Intrinsic hepatotoxin[367–372]
	Chronic vitamin A intoxication results from intake of large amounts (25,000–1,200,000 IU/day) of the vitamin for months to years. Systemic manifestations of the syndrome include anorexia, weight loss, fatigability, mild fever, pallor, psychiatric symptoms, polyuria, polydipsia, and night sweats. Pruritus, dry skin, hair loss, as well as pain and tenderness of bone are characteristics. Hepatomegaly is associated with symptoms of portal hypertension such as splenomegaly, ascite or variceal hemorrhage in 80% of affected patients. Jaundice is rare. Laboratory studies may reveal anemia, leukopenia, increased sedimentation rate, and proteinuria. Hepatic injury may be evidenced by increased serum concentration of alkaline phosphatase and AST, hypoalbuminemia, and hypoprothrombinemia. The prognosis of patients with impaired hepatic function and hepatomegaly is usually good if the vitamin A intake is discontinued. However, once ascites and portal hypertension are present, the syndrome may persist even after cessation of the vitamin. Current restrictions in the vitamin A content of nonprescription preparations may limit the likelihood of overdose

[a] ACE = Angiotensin converting enzyme; ALT = Alanine aminotransferase; AST = Aspartate aminotransferase; CAH = Chronic active hepatitis; GI = Gastrointestinal; IV = Intravenous; LDH = Lactate dehydrogenase; LFTs = Liver function tests; OCs = Oral contraceptives; RA = Rheumatoid arthritis; SLE = Systemic lupus erythematosus; SR = Sustained release; VOD= Veno-occlusive disease.

References

1   **Lewis JH, Zimmerman HJ.** Drug-induced liver disease. Med Clin North Am. 1989;73:775.

2   **Pessayre D, Larrey D.** Acute and chronic drug-induced hepatitis. Clin Gastroenterol. 1988;2:385.

3   **Stricker BHC, Spoelstra P.** Drug-Induced Hepatic Injury. A Comprehensive Survey of the Literature on Adverse Drug Reactions up to January 1985. Amsterdam: Elsevier; 1985.

4   **Eastwood HOH.** Causes of jaundice in the elderly. A survey of diagnosis and investigation. Gerontol Clin (Basel). 1971;13:69.

5   **Friis H et al.** Drug-induced hepatic in-

jury: an analysis of 1100 cases reported to the Danish Committee on Adverse Drug Reactions between 1978 and 1987. J Intern Med. 1992;232:133.

6 Zimmerman HJ. Hepatotoxicity: Adverse Effects of Drugs and Other Chemicals on the Liver. New York, NY: Appleton Century Crofts; 1978.

7 Katelaris PH, Jones DB. Fulminant hepatic failure. Med Clin North Am. 1989;73:955.

8 Zimmerman HJ. Hepatotoxicity. Dis Mon. 1993;10:678.

9 Neuberger J. Drug-induced jaundice. Clin Gastroenterol. 1989;3:447.

10 Larrey D, Erlinger S. Drug-induced cholestasis. Clin Gastroenterol. 1988;2:422.

11 Simpson DG et al. Hypersensitivity to para-aminosalicylic acid. Am J Med. 1960;29:297.

12 Maddrey WC et al. Drug-induced chronic hepatitis and cirrhosis. Prog Liver Dis. 1979;6:595.

13 Rodman JS et al. Methyldopa hepatitis. A report of six cases and review of the literature. Am J Med. 1976;60:941.

14 Black M et al. Nitrofurantoin-induced chronic active hepatitis. Ann Intern Med. 1980;92:62.

15 Sharp JR et al. Chronic active hepatitis and severe hepatic necrosis associated with nitrofurantoin. Ann Intern Med. 1980;92:14.

16 Thaler H. Fatty change. Clin Gastroenterol. 1988;2:453.

17 Villeneuve JP et al. Idiopathic portal hypertension. Am J Med. 1976;61:459.

18 Valla D, Benhamou JP. Drug-induced vascular and sinusoidal lesions of the liver. Clin Gastroenterol. 1988;2:481.

19 Ishak KG, Zimmerman HJ. Drug-induced and toxic granulomatous hepatitis. Clin Gastroenterol. 1988;2:463.

20 Lisker-Melman M et al. Conditions associated with hepatocellular carcinoma. Med Clin North Am. 1989;73:999.

21 Mitchell JR et al. Metabolic activation. Biochemical basis for many drug-induced liver injuries. Prog Liver Dis. 1976;5:259.

22 Dybing E. Activation of methyldopa, paracetamol and furosemide by human liver microsomes. Acta Pharmacol Toxicol (Copenh). 1977;41:89.

23 Reichel J et al. Intrahepatic cholestasis following administration of chlorpropamide. Am J Med. 1960;28:654.

24 Reddy KR et al. Amoxicillin-clavulanate potassium-associated cholestasis. Gastroenterology. 1989;96:1135.

25 Dowsett JF et al. Amoxicillin/clavulanic acid (Augmentin)-induced intrahepatic cholestasis. Dig Dis Sci. 1989;34:1290.

26 Stricker BH et al. Cholestatic hepatitis due to anti-bacterial combination of amoxicillin and clavulanic acid (Augmentin). Dig Dis Sci. 1989;34:1576.

27 Silvain C et al. Granulomatous hepatitis due to combination of amoxicillin and clavulanic acid. Dig Dis Sci. 1992;37:150.

28 Hebbard GS et al. Augmentin-induced jaundice with a fatal outcome. Med J Aust. 1992;156:285.

29 Reynolds TB. Recurring jaundice associated with ingestion of a laxative "Dialose Plus." Gastroenterology. 1969;56:418.

30 McHardy G et al. Jaundice and oxyphenisatin. JAMA. 1970;211:83.

31 Reynolds TB et al. Chronic active and lupoid hepatitis caused by a laxative, oxyphenisatin. N Engl J Med. 1971;285:813.

32 Fischer MG et al. Recurrent jaundice induced by oxyphenisatin. Am J Gastroenterol. 1972;58:58.

33 Gjone R et al. Liver disease associated with a "non-constipatory" iron preparation. Lancet. 1973;1:421.

34 Dietrichson O et al. The incidence of oxyphenisatin-induced liver damage in chronic non-alcoholic liver disease. A controlled investigation. Scand J Gastroenterol. 1974;9:473.

35 Kantor G. Toxic epidermal necrolysis, azotemia and death after allopurinol therapy. JAMA. 1970;212:478.

36 Young J et al. Severe allopurinol hypersensitivity. Arch Intern Med. 1974;134:553.

37 Esperitu CR et al. Allopurinol-induced granulomatous hepatitis. Am J Dig Dis. 1976;21:804.

38 Boyer TD et al. Allopurinol hypersensitivity and liver damage. West J Med. 1977;126:143.

39 Butler RC et al. Acute massive hepatic necrosis in a patient receiving allopurinol. JAMA. 1977;237:437.

40 Favre M et al. Allopurinol-induced fulminant hepatitis. Sem Hop. 1990;66:2095.

41 McGovern B et al. Adverse reactions during treatment with amiodarone hydrochloride. Br Med J (Clin Res). 1983;287:175.

42 Babany G et al. Chronic liver disease after low daily doses of amiodarone. Report of three cases. J Hepatol. 1986;3:228.

43 Simon JB et al. Amiodarone hepatotoxicity simulating alcoholic liver disease. N Engl J Med. 1984;311:167.

44 Kalantzis N et al. Acute amiodarone-induced hepatitis. Hepatogastroenterology. 1991;38:71.

45 Jeyamalar R et al. Hepatotoxicity of amiodarone. Ann Acad Med Singapore. 1992;21:838.

46 Harrison RF et al. Amiodarone-associated cirrhosis with hepatic and lymph node granulomas. Histopathology. 1993;22:80.

47 Rhodes A et al. Early acute hepatitis with parenteral amiodarone: a toxic effect of the vehicle? Gut. 1993;34:565.

48 Schaffner F et al. Changes in bile canaliculi produced by norethandrolone. Electron microscopic study of human and rat liver. J Lab Clin Med. 1960;56:623.

49 Marquardt GH et al. Effect of anabolic steroids on liver function tests and creatine excretion. JAMA. 1961;175:851.

50 Wilder EM. Death due to liver failure following the use of methandrostenolone. Can Med Assoc J. 1962;87:768.

51 Gilbert EF et al. Intrahepatic cholestasis with fatal termination following norethandrolone therapy. JAMA. 1963;185:538.

52 deLorimier AA et al. Methyltestosterone, related steroids, and liver function. Arch Intern Med. 1965;116:289.

53 Ticktin HE et al. Effects of a synthetic anabolic agent on hepatic function. Am J Med Sci. 1966;251:674.

54 Glober GA et al. Biliary cirrhosis following the administration of methyltestosterone. JAMA. 1968;204:170.

55 Gordon GG et al. Effect of chronic alcohol use on hepatic testosterone 5-A-Ring reductase in the baboon and the human being. Gastroenterology. 1979;77:110.

56 Nadell J et al. Peliosis hepatis. Twelve cases associated with oral androgen therapy. Arch Pathol Lab Med. 1977;101:405.

57 Johnson LF et al. Association of androgenic-anabolic steroid therapy with development of hepatocellular carcinoma. Lancet. 1972;2:1273.

58 Bagheri SA et al. Peliosis hepatis associated with androgenic-anabolic steroid therapy. A severe form of hepatic injury. Ann Intern Med. 1974;81:610.

59 Karasawa T et al. Peliosis hepatis. Report of nine cases. Acta Pathol Jpn. 1979;29:457.

60 Athreya BH et al. Aspirin-induced abnormalities of liver function. Am J Dis Child. 1973;126:638.

61 Rich RR et al. Salicylate hepatoxicity in patients with juvenile rheumatoid arthritis. Arthritis Rheum. 1973;16:1.

62 Seaman WE et al. Aspirin-induced hepatotoxicity in patients with systemic lupus erythematosus. Ann Intern Med. 1974;80:1.

63 Wolfe JD et al. Aspirin hepatitis. Ann Intern Med. 1974;80:74.

64 Sillanpaa M et al. Acute liver failure and encephalopathy (Reye's Syndrome?) during salicylate therapy. Acta Paediatr Scand. 1975;64:877.

65 Barone R et al. Salicylate-induced hepatic injury. Arthritis Rheum. 1976;19:964.

66 Miller JJ et al. Correlations between transaminase concentrations and serum salicylate concentrations in juvenile rheumatoid arthritis. Arthritis Rheum. 1976;19:115.

67 Seaman WE et al. The effect of aspirin on liver tests in patients with rheumatoid arthritis or systemic lupus erythematosus and in normal volunteers. Arthritis Rheum. 1976;19:155.

68 O'Gorman T et al. Salicylate hepatitis. Gastroenterology. 1977;72:726.

69 Lopez-Morante AJ et al. Aspirin-induced cholestatic hepatitis. J Clin Gastroenterol. 1993;16:270.

70 Lemley DE et al. Azathioprine-induced hepatic veno-occlusive disease in rheumatoid arthritis. Ann Rheum Dis. 1989;48:342.

71 Davis M et al. Hypersensitivity and jaundice due to azathioprine. Postgrad Med J. 1980;56:274.

72 DePinho RA et al. Azathioprine and the liver. Evidence favoring idiosyncratic, mixed cholestatic-hepato-cellular injury in humans. Gastroenterology. 1984;86:162.

73 Sparberg M et al. Intrahepatic cholestasis due to azathioprine. Gastroenterology. 1969;57:439.

74 Zardy A et al. Irreversible liver damage after azathioprine. JAMA. 1972;222:690.

75 Briggs WA et al. Hepatitis affecting hemodialysis and transplant patients. Arch Intern Med. 1973;132:21.

76 Rashid A et al. Liver disease in kidney transplant patients receiving azathio-

77 Ware AJ et al. Spectrum of liver disease in renal transplant recipients. Gastroenterology. 1975;68:755.

78 McDonald GB et al. Veno-occlusive disease of the liver after bone marrow transplantation: diagnosis, incidence, and predisposing factors. Hepatology. 1984;4:116.

79 Read AE et al. Hepatic veno-occlusive disease associated with renal transplantation and azathioprine therapy. Ann Intern Med. 1986;104:651.

80 Perini GP et al. Azathioprine-related cholestatic jaundice in heart transplant patients. J Heart Transplant. 1990;9:577.

81 Meys E et al. Fever, hepatitis and acute interstitial nephritis in a patient with rheumatoid arthritis. Concurrent manifestations of azathioprine hypersensitivity. J Rheumatol. 1992;19:807.

82 Zimran A et al. Reversible cholestatic jaundice and hyperamylasemia associated with captopril treatment. Br Med J (Clin Res). 1983;287:1676.

83 Parker MA. Captopril-induced cholestatic jaundice. Drug Intell Clin Pharm. 1984;18:234.

84 Rahmat J et al. Captopril-associated cholestatic jaundice. Ann Intern Med. 1985;102:56.

85 Hagley MT et al. Hepatotoxicity associated with angiotensin-converting enzyme inhibitors. Ann Pharmacother. 1993;27:228.

86 Larrey D et al. Fulminant hepatitis after lisinopril administration. Gastroenterology. 1990;99:1832.

87 Hilburn RB et al. Angiotensin-converting enzyme inhibitor hepatotoxicity: further insights. Ann Pharmacother. 1993;27:1142. Letter.

88 DeVita VT et al. Clinical trials with 1,3-bis(2-chloroethyl)-1-nitrosourea, NSC-409962. Cancer Res. 1965;25:1876.

89 Moertel CG et al. Therapy of advanced gastrointestinal cancer with 1,3-bis(2-chloroethyl)-1-nitrosourea (BCNU). Clin Pharmacol Ther. 1968;9:652.

90 Thompson GR et al. The hepatotoxicity of 1,3-bis(2-chloroethyl)-1-nitrosourea (BCNU) in rats. J Pharmacol Exp Ther. 1969;166:104.

91 Walker MD et al. BCNU (1,3-bis(2-chloroethyl)-1-nitrosourea; NSC-409962) in the treatment of malignant brain tumor. Cancer Chemother Rep. 1970;54:263.

92 Lessner HE et al. Toxicity study of BCNU (NSC-409962) given orally. Cancer Chemother Rep. 1974;58:407.

93 Watson RPG et al. A proposed mechanism for chlorpromazine jaundice. J Hepatol. 1988;7:72.

94 Zelman S. Liver cell necrosis in chlorpromazine jaundice (allergic cholangitis). A serial study of 26 needle biopsy specimens in nine patients. Am J Med. 1959;27:708.

95 Herron G et al. Jaundice secondary to promazine and an analysis of possible cross sensitivities between phenothiazine derivatives. Gastroenterology. 1960;38:87.

96 Read AE et al. Chronic chlorpromazine jaundice with particular reference to its relationship to primary biliary cirrhosis. Am J Med. 1961;31:249.

97 **Walker CD et al.** Biliary cirrhosis induced by chlorpromazine. Gastroenterology. 1966;51:253.

98 **Bolton BH.** Prolonged chlorpromazine jaundice. Am J Gastroenterol. 1967;48:497.

99 **Ishak KG et al.** Hepatic injury associated with the phenothiazines. Clinicopathologic and follow-up study of 36 patients. Arch Pathol Lab Med. 1972;93:283.

100 **Russel RJ et al.** Active chronic hepatitis after chlorpromazine ingestion. Br Med J. 1973;1:655.

101 **Derby LE et al.** Liver disorders in patients receiving chlorpromazine or isoniazid. Pharmacotherapy. 1993;13:353.

102 **Knick B.** Clinical and experimental studies with chlorpropamide in diabetes mellitus, in normal individuals, and in nondiabetics with hepatic disease. Ann N Y Acad Sci. 1958–1959;74:858.

103 **Brown G et al.** Hepatic damage during chlorpropamide therapy. JAMA. 1959;170:2085.

104 **Haunz EA et al.** Liver function in chlorpropamide therapy. Five-year clinical study of 181 patients. JAMA. 1964;188:237.

105 **Goldstein MJ et al.** Jaundice in a patient receiving acetohexamide. N Engl J Med. 1966;275:97.

106 **Baird RW et al.** Cholestatic jaundice from tolbutamide. Ann Intern Med. 1960;53:194.

107 **Gregory DH et al.** Chronic cholestasis following prolonged tolbutamide administration. Arch Pathol Lab Med. 1967;84:194.

108 **Van Thiel DH et al.** Tolazamide hepatotoxicity. Gastroenterology. 1974;67:506.

109 **Rigberg LA et al.** Chlorpropamide-induced granulomas. JAMA. 1976;235:409.

110 **Wongpaitoon V et al.** Intrahepatic cholestasis and cutaneous bullae associated with glibenclamide therapy. Postgrad Med J. 1981;57:244.

111 **Van Basten JP et al.** Glyburide-induced cholestatic hepatitis and liver failure. Case-report and review of the literature. Neth J Med. 1992;40:305.

112 **Reyes H.** The enigma of intrahepatic cholestasis of pregnancy. Hepatology. 1982;2:87.

113 **Kreek MJ.** Female sex steroids and cholestasis. Semin Liver Dis. 1987;7:8.

114 **Eisalo A et al.** Hepatic impairment during the intake of contraceptive pills. Clinical trial with postmenopausal women. Br Med J. 1964;2:426.

115 **Mueller MN et al.** Estrogen pharmacology. I. The influence of estradiol and estriol on hepatic disposal of sulfobromophthalein. J Clin Invest. 1964;43:1905.

116 **Larsson-Cohn U et al.** Liver ultrastructure and function in icteric and non-icteric women using oral contraceptive agents. Acta Med Scand. 1967;181:257.

117 **Roman P et al.** The liver toxicity of oral contraceptives, a critical review of the literature. Med J Aust. 1968;2:682.

118 **Urban E et al.** Liver dysfunction with mestranol but not with norethynodrel in a patient with Enovid-induced jaundice. Ann Intern Med. 1968;68:598.

119 **Drill VA.** Benign cholestatic jaundice of pregnancy and benign cholestatic jaundice from oral contraceptives. Am J Obstet Gynecol. 1974;119:165.

120 **Kern F et al.** Effect of estrogens on the liver. Gastroenterology. 1978;75:512.

121 **Lindberg MC.** Hepatobiliary complications of oral contraceptives. J Gen Intern Med. 1992;7:199.

122 **Baker AL et al.** Liver adenoma associated with oral contraceptive pill administration. Dig Dis Sci. 1978;23:53S.

123 **Berg JW et al.** Hepatomas and oral contraceptives. Lancet. 1974;2:349.

124 **Frederick WC et al.** Spontaneous rupture of the liver in patients using contraceptive pills. Arch Surg. 1974;108:93.

125 **Ameriks JA et al.** Hepatic cell adenomas, spontaneous liver rupture, and oral contraceptives. Arch Surg. 1975;110:548.

126 **Edmondson HA et al.** Liver cell adenomas associated with the use of oral contraceptives. N Engl J Med. 1976;294:470.

127 **Klatskin G.** Hepatic tumors. Possible relationship to use of oral contraceptives. Gastroenterology. 1977;73:386.

128 **Omer FB et al.** Focal nodular hyperplasia of the liver and contraceptive steroids. Acta Hepatogastroenterol (Stuttg). 1978;25:319.

129 **Kerlin P et al.** Hepatic adenoma and focal nodular hyperplasia: clinical, pathologic and radiologic features. Gastroenterology. 1983;84:994.

130 **Marks WH et al.** Failure of hepatic adenomas (HCA) to regress after discontinuance of oral contraceptives. Ann Surg. 1988;208:190.

131 **Van Erpecum KJ et al.** Pelio hepatis and cirrhosis after long term use of oral contraceptives: case report. Am J Gastroenterol. 1988;83:572.

132 **Sterup K et al.** Budd-Chiari syndrome after taking oral contraceptives. Br Med J. 1967;4:660.

133 **Hoyumpa AM Jr et al.** Budd-Chiari syndrome in women taking oral contraceptives. Am J Med. 1971;50:137.

134 **Capron JP et al.** Portal vein thrombosis and fatal pulmonary thromboembolism associated with oral contraceptive treatment. J Clin Gastroenterol. 1981;3:295.

135 **Davis M et al.** Histological evidence of carcinoma in a hepatic tumor associated with oral contraceptives. Br Med J. 1975;4:496.

136 **Ham JM et al.** Hepatocellular carcinoma possibly induced by oral contraceptives. Dig Dis Sci. 1978;23:38S.

137 **Hoch-Ligeti C.** Angiosarcoma of the liver associated with diethylstilbestrol. JAMA. 1978;240:1510.

138 **Henderson BE et al.** Hepatocellular carcinoma and oral contraceptives. Br J Cancer. 1983;48:437.

139 **Goodman ZD, Ishak KG.** Hepatocellular carcinoma in women: probable lack of etiologic association with oral contraceptive steroids. Hepatology. 1982;2:440.

140 **Forman D et al.** Cancer of the liver and the use of oral contraceptives. Br Med J. 1986;292:1357.

141 **Klintmalm GBG et al.** Cyclosporin A hepatotoxicity in 66 renal allograft recipients. Transplantation. 1981;32:488.

142 **Schade RR et al.** Cholestasis in heart transplant recipients treated with cyclosporin. Transplant Proc. 1983;15:2757.

143 **Essell JH et al.** Marked increase in veno-occlusive disease of the liver associated with methotrexate use for graft-versus-host disease prophylaxis in patients receiving busulfan/cyclophosphamide. Blood. 1992;79:2784.

144 **Kassianides C et al.** Liver injury from cyclosporine A. Dig Dis Sci. 1990;35:693.

145 **Utili R et al.** Dantrolene-associated hepatic injury. Gastroenterology. 1977;72:610.

146 **Ogburn RM et al.** Hepatitis associated with dantrolene sodium. Ann Intern Med. 1976;84:53.

147 **Schneider R et al.** Dantrolene hepatitis. JAMA. 1976;235:1590.

148 **Donegan JH et al.** Massive hepatic necrosis associated with dantrolene therapy. Dig Dis Sci. 1978;23(Suppl.):48S.

149 **Tartalione TA et al.** Diltiazem: a review of its clinical efficacy and use. Drug Intell Clin Pharm. 1982;16:371.

150 **Pool PE et al.** Diltiazem as monotherapy for systemic hypertension: a multicenter, randomized, placebo-controlled trial. Am J Cardiol. 1986;57:212.

151 **McGraw BF et al.** Clinical experience with diltiazem in Japan. Pharmacotherapy. 1982;2:156.

152 **Sarachek NS et al.** Diltiazem and granulomatous hepatitis. Gastroenterology. 1985;88:1260.

153 **Shallcross H et al.** Fatal renal and hepatic toxicity after treatment with diltiazem. Br Med J. 1987;295:1236.

154 **Toft E et al.** Diltiazem-induced granulomatous hepatitis. Histopathology. 1991;18:474.

155 **Kohlstaedt KG.** Propionyl erythromycin ester lauryl sulfate and jaundice. JAMA. 1961;178:89.

156 **Johnson DF et al.** Allergic hepatitis caused by propionyl erythromycin ester of lauryl sulfate. N Engl J Med. 1961;265:1200.

157 **Havens WP.** Cholestatic jaundice in patients treated with erythromycin estolate. JAMA. 1962;182:30.

158 **Gilbert FJ.** Cholestatic hepatitis caused by esters of erythromycin and oleandomycin. JAMA. 1962;182:1048.

159 **Robinson MM.** Demonstration by "challenge" of hepatic dysfunction associated with propionyl erythromycin ester lauryl sulfate. Antibiot Chemother. 1962;12:147.

160 **Braun P.** Hepatotoxicity of erythromycin. J Infect Dis. 1969;119:300.

161 **Rogers RS.** Abdominal distress and erythromycin estolate. Lancet. 1972;2:1198.

162 **Oliver LE et al.** "Biliary colic" and Ilosone. Med J Aust. 1973;1:1148.

163 **Loyd-Still JD et al.** Erythromycin estolate hepatotoxicity. Am J Dis Child. 1978;132:320.

164 **Viteri AL et al.** Erythromycin ethylsuccinate-induced cholestasis. Gastroenterology. 1979;76:1007.

165 **Greenlaw CW et al.** Hepatotoxicity possibly associated with erythromycin ethylsuccinate. Drug Intell Clin Pharm. 1979;13:236.

166 **Diehl AM et al.** Cholestatic hepatitis from erythromycin ethylsuccinate. Report of two cases. Am J Med. 1984;76:931.

167 **Derby LE et al.** Erythromycin-associated cholestatic hepatitis. Med J Aust. 1993;158:600.

168 **Halkin H.** Adverse effects of the fluoroquinolones. Rev Infect Dis. 1988;10(Suppl. 1):S258.

169 **Amitrano L et al.** Enoxacin acute liver injury. J Hepatol. 1992;15:270.

170 **Blum A.** Ofloxacin-induced acute severe hepatitis. South Med J. 1991;84:1158.

171 **Grassmick BK et al.** Fulminant hepatic failure possibly related to ciprofloxacin. Ann Pharmacother. 1992;26:636.

172 **Lopez-Navidad A et al.** Norfloxacin-induced hepatotoxicity. J Hepatol. 1990;11:277.

173 **Steinberg H et al.** Hepatomegaly with fatty infiltration secondary to cortisone therapy. Case report. Gastroenterology. 1952;21:304.

174 **Hill RB Jr.** Fatal fat embolism from steroid-induced fatty liver. N Engl J Med. 1961;165:318.

175 **Jones JP et al.** Systemic fat embolism after renal homotransplantation and treatment with corticosteroids. N Engl J Med. 1965;273:1453.

176 **Wald JA et al.** Abnormal liver-function tests associated with long-term systemic corticosteroid use in subjects with asthma. J Allergy Clin Immunol. 1991;88:277.

177 **Gerle B et al.** Clinical observations of the side effects of haloperidol. Acta Psychiatr Scand. 1964;40:65.

178 **Crane GE et al.** A review of clinical literature on haloperidol. Int J Neuropsychiatry. 1967;3(Suppl.):5111.

179 **Neuberger JM.** Halothane and hepatitis. Incidence, predisposing factors and exposure guidelines. Drug Saf. 1990;5:28.

180 **Neuber J, Williams R.** Halothane anesthesia and liver damage. Br Med J. 1984;289:1135.

181 **Nomura F et al.** Effects of anticonvulsant agents on halothane-induced liver injury in human subjects and experimental animals. Hepatology. 1986;6:952.

182 **Peters RL et al.** Hepatic necrosis associated with halothane anesthesia. Am J Med. 1969;47:748.

183 **Klion FM et al.** Hepatitis after exposure to halothane. Ann Intern Med. 1969;71:467.

184 **Hughes M et al.** Recurrent hepatitis in patients receiving multiple halothane anesthetics for radium treatment of carcinoma of the cervix uteri. Gastroenterology. 1970;58:790.

185 **Carney FMT et al.** Halothane hepatitis. A critical review. Anesth Analg. 1972;51:135.

186 **Paull A et al.** Halothane hepatitis—a report of five cases. Med J Aust. 1974;1:954.

187 **Inman WHW et al.** Jaundice after repeated exposure to halothane. An analysis of reports to the Committee on Safety of Medicine. Br Med J. 1974;1:5010.

188 **Trowell J et al.** Controlled trial of repeated halothane anesthetics in patients with carcinoma of the uterine cervix treated with radium. Lancet. 1975;1:821.

189 **Moult P et al.** Halothane-related hepatitis. Q J Med. 1975;44:99.

190 **Bottinger LE et al.** Halothane-induced liver damage. An analysis of the material reported to the Swedish Adverse Drug Reaction Committee, 1966–1973. Acta Anaesthesiol Scand. 1976; 20:40.

191 **Schlipper W et al.** Recurrent hepatitis following halothane exposure. Am J Med. 1978;65:25.

192 **Kline MM.** Enflurane-associated hepatitis. Gastroenterology. 1980;79:126.

193 **Shipton EA.** Halothane hepatitis revisited. S Afr Med J. 1991;80:261.

194 **Hubbard AK et al.** Immunological basis of anesthetic-induced hepatotoxicity. Anesthesiology. 1988;69:814.

195 **Gunza JT et al.** Postoperative elevation of serum transaminases following isoflurane anesthesia. J Clin Anesth. 1992;4:336.

196 **Slayter KL et al.** Halothane hepatitis in a renal transplant patient previously exposed to isoflurane. Ann Pharmacother. 1993;27:101.

197 **Lewis JH et al.** Hepatic injury associated with ketoconazole therapy. Analysis of 33 cases. Gastroenterology. 1984;86:503.

198 **Bercoff E et al.** Ketoconazole-induced fulminant hepatitis. Gut. 1985;26:636.

199 **Stricker BH et al.** Ketoconazole-associated hepatic injury. A clinicopathological study of 55 cases. J Hepatol. 1986;3:399.

200 **Tobert JA.** New developments in lipid-lowering therapy: the role of inhibitors of hydroxymethylglutaryl coenzyme A reductase. Circulation. 1987;76:534.

201 **Raveh D et al.** Lovastatin-induced hepatitis. Isr J Med Sci. 1992;28:101.

202 **Clark PA et al.** Toxic complications of treatment with 6-mercaptopurine. Two cases with hepatic necrosis and intestinal ulceration. Br Med J. 1960;1:393.

203 **Acute leukemia group B.** Studies of sequential and combination anti-metabolite therapy in acute leukemia: 6-mercaptopurine and methotrexate. Blood. 1961;18:431.

204 **Einhorn M et al.** Hepatotoxicity of mercaptopurine. JAMA. 1964;188:802.

205 **Shorey J et al.** Hepatotoxicity of mercaptopurine. Arch Intern Med. 1968; 122:54.

206 **Schmidt G et al.** Methimazole-associated cholestatic liver injury: case report and brief literature review. Hepatogastroenterology. 1986;33:244.

207 **Rosenbaum H et al.** Agranulocytosis and toxic hepatitis from methimazole. JAMA. 1953;152:27.

208 **Martinez-Lopez JL et al.** Drug-induced hepatic injury during methimazole therapy. Gastroenterology. 1962; 43:84.

209 **Fischer MG et al.** Methimazole-induced jaundice. JAMA. 1973;223:1028.

210 **Joshi PH, Conn HO.** The syndrome of methoxyflurane-associated hepatitis. Ann Intern Med. 1974;80:395.

211 **Judson JA et al.** Possible cross-sensitivity between halothane and methoxyflurane. Anesthesiology. 1971;35:527.

212 **Lewis JH et al.** Enflurane hepatotoxicity. A clinicopathologic study of 24 cases. Ann Intern Med. 1983;98:984.

213 **Dahl MGC et al.** Liver damage due to methotrexate in patients with psoriasis. Br Med J (Clin Res). 1971;1:625.

214 **Tobias H, Auerbach R.** Hepatotoxicity of long-term methotrexate therapy for psoriasis. Arch Intern Med. 1973; 132:391.

215 **Hutter RVP et al.** Hepatic fibrosis in children with acute leukemia. A complication of therapy. Cancer. 1960;13:288.

216 **Hersh EM et al.** Hepatotoxic effects of methotrexate. Cancer. 1966;19:600.

217 **Coe RD et al.** Cirrhosis associated with methotrexate. Treatment of psoriasis. JAMA. 1968;206:1515.

218 **Muller SA et al.** Cirrhosis caused by methotrexate in the treatment of psoriasis. Arch Dermatol. 1969;100:523.

219 **McDonald CJ et al.** Parenteral methotrexate in psoriasis. A report on the efficacy and toxicity of long-term intermittent treatment. Arch Dermatol. 1969;100:655.

220 **Dubin HV et al.** Liver disease associated with methotrexate treatment of psoriatic patients. Arch Dermatol. 1970;102:498.

221 **Weinstein G.** Evaluation of possible chronic hepatotoxicity from methotrexate for psoriasis. Arch Dermatol. 1970; 102:613.

222 **Filip DJ et al.** Pulmonary and hepatic complications of methotrexate therapy of psoriasis. JAMA. 1971;216:881.

223 **Almeyda J et al.** Structural and functional abnormalities of the liver in psoriasis before and during methotrexate therapy. Br J Dermatol. 1972;87:623.

224 **Dahl MGC et al.** Methotrexate hepatotoxicity in psoriasis—comparison of different dose regimens. Br Med J (Clin Res). 1972;1:654.

225 **Lewis JH, Schiff ER.** Methotrexate-induced chronic liver injury: guidelines for detection and prevention. Am J Gastroenterol. 1988;83:1337.

226 **Bridges SL Jr et al.** Methotrexate-induced liver abnormalities in rheumatoid arthritis. J Rheumatol. 1989;16:1180.

227 **Elkington SG et al.** Hepatic injury caused by L-alpha-methyldopa. Circulation. 1969;40:589.

228 **Brouillard RP et al.** Methyldopa associated hepatitis. JAMA. 1973;224:904.

229 **Schweitzer IL et al.** Acute submassive hepatic necrosis due to methyldopa. Gastroenterology. 1974;66:1203.

230 **Toghill PH et al.** Methyldopa liver damage. Br Med J (Clin Res). 1974;3:545.

231 **Maddrey WC et al.** Severe hepatitis from methyldopa. Gastroenterology. 1975;68:351.

232 **Rehman OU et al.** Methyldopa-induced submassive hepatic necrosis. JAMA. 1973;224:1390.

233 **Goldstein GB et al.** Drug-induced active chronic hepatitis. Am J Dig Dis. 1973;18:177.

234 **Rodman JS et al.** Methyldopa hepatitis. A report of six cases and review of the literature. Am J Med. 1976;60:941.

235 **Neuberger J et al.** Antibody mediated hepatocyte injury in methyldopa-induced hepatotoxicity. Gut. 1985;26:1233.

236 **Ansfield FJ.** Clinical studies with mithramycin. Oncology. 1969;23:283.

237 **Kennedy BJ.** Mithramycin therapy in advanced testicular neoplasms. Cancer. 1970;26:755.

238 **Foley JF et al.** The treatment of metastatic testicular tumors. J Urol. 1972; 108:439.

239 **Ryan WG.** Mithramycin in Paget's disease of bone. Lancet. 1973;1:1319.

240 **Felix A et al.** Iproniazid hepatitis. Report of five cases and review of pertinent literature. Arch Intern Med. 1959; 104:72.

241 **Rosenblum LE et al.** Hepatocellular jaundice as a complication of iproniazid therapy. Arch Intern Med. 1960; 105:583.

242 **Homberg JC et al.** A new antimitochondrial antibody (anti-M6) in iproniazid-induced hepatitis. Clin Exp Immunol. 1982;47:93.

243 **Benack RT et al.** Jaundice associated with isocarboxazid therapy. N Engl J Med. 1964;264:294.

244 **Griffith GC et al.** Jaundice and hepatitis in patients who have received hydrazine-base monamine oxidase inhibitors. Am J Med Sci. 1962;244:592.

245 **Bandt C et al.** Liver injury associated with tranylcypromine therapy. JAMA. 1964;188:752.

246 **Mullin GE et al.** Fulminant hepatic failure after ingestion of sustained-release nicotinic acid. Ann Intern Med. 1989;111:253.

247 **Henkin Y et al.** Rechallenge with crystalline niacin after drug-induced hepatitis from sustained-release niacin. JAMA. 1990;264:241.

248 **Etchason JA et al.** Niacin-induced hepatitis: a potential side effect with low-dose time-release niacin. Mayo Clin Proc. 1991;66:23.

249 **Dalton TA et al.** Hepatotoxicity associated with sustained-release niacin. Am J Med. 1992;93:102.

250 **Daniele B et al.** Sulindac-induced severe hepatitis. Am J Gastroenterol. 1988;83:1429.

251 **Mitchell MR, Lietman PS.** Evidence for the role of reactive metabolites in hepatotoxicity of benoxaprofen and other non-steroidal anti-inflammatory drugs (NSAIDS). Hepatology. 1983;3:808.

252 **Wood LJ et al.** Sulindac hepatotoxicity: effects of acute and chronic exposure. Aust N Z J Med. 1985;15:397.

253 **Victorino RMM et al.** Jaundice associated with naproxen. Postgrad Med J. 1980;56:368.

254 **Jick H et al.** Liver disease associated with diclofenac, naproxen, and piroxicam. Pharmacotherapy. 1992;12:207.

255 **Australian Adverse Drug Reactions Bulletin.** NSAIDS and hepatitis. Sulindac. Nov 1990.

256 **Hepps KS et al.** Severe cholestatic jaundice associated with piroxicam. Gastroenterology. 1991;101:1737.

257 **Sherman KE et al.** Hepatotoxicity associated with piroxicam use. Gastroenterology. 1992;103:354.

258 **Ouellette GS et al.** Reversible hepatitis associated with diclofenac. J Clin Gastroenterology. 1991;13:205.

259 **Scully LJ et al.** Diclofenac induced hepatitis. Dig Dis Sci. 1993;38:744.

260 **Nores JM et al.** Acute hepatitis due to ketoprofen. Clin Rheumatol. 1991;10:215.

261 **Tarazi EM et al.** Sulindac-associated hepatic injury: analysis of 91 cases reported to the Food and Drug Administration. Gastroenterology. 1993;104:569.

262 **Jokela S.** Liver disease due to nitrofurantoin. Gastroenterology. 1967;53:306.

263 **Adverse effects of drugs commonly used in the treatment of urinary tract infection.** A report from the Australian Drug Evaluation Committee. Med J Aust. 1972;1:435.

264 **Goldstein LI et al.** Hepatic injury associated with nitrofurantoin therapy. Am J Dig Dis. 1974;19:987.

265 **Klemola H et al.** Anicteric liver damage during nitrofurantoin medication. Scand J Gastroenterol. 1975;10:501.

266 **Selroos O et al.** Lupus-like syndrome associated with pulmonary reaction to nitrofurantoin. Report of three cases. Acta Med Scand. 1975;197:125.

267 **Sharp JR et al.** Chronic active hepatitis and severe hepatic necrosis associated with nitrofurantoin. Ann Intern Med. 1980;92:14.

268 **Paiva LA et al.** Long-term hepatic memory for hypersensitivity to nitrofurantoin. Am J Gastroenterol. 1992; 87:891.

269 **Pas AT et al.** Cholestatic hepatitis following the administration of sodium oxacillin. JAMA. 1965;191:138.

270 **Dismukes WE.** Oxacillin-induced hepatic dysfunction. JAMA. 1973;226:861.

271 **Olans RN et al.** Reversible oxacillin hepatotoxicity. J Pediatr. 1976;226:861.

272 **Pollock AA et al.** Hepatitis associated with high dose oxacillin therapy. Arch Intern Med. 1978;138:915.

273 **Bruckstein AH et al.** Oxacillin hepatitis. Am J Med. 1978;64:519.

274 **Onorato IM et al.** Hepatitis from intravenous high dose oxacillin therapy. Ann Intern Med. 1978;89:497.

275 **Taylor C et al.** Oxacillin and hepatitis. Ann Intern Med. 1979;90:857.

276 **Turner IB et al.** Prolonged hepatic cholestasis after flucloxacillin therapy. Med J Aust. 1989;151:701.

277 **Olsson R et al.** Liver damage from flucloxacillin, cloxacillin and dicloxacillin. J Hepatol. 1992;15:154.

278 **Fairley CK et al.** Risk factors for development of flucloxacillin-associated jaundice. Br Med J. 1993;306:233.

279 **Waugh D.** Myocarditis, arteritis and focal hepatic, splenic and renal granulomas apparently due to penicillin sensitivity. Am J Pathol. 1952;28:437.

280 **Ross S et al.** Alpha-amino-benzyl-penicillin—new broad spectrum antibiotic. Preliminary clinical and laboratory observations. JAMA. 1962;182:238.

281 **Murphy ES et al.** Shock, liver necrosis, and death after penicillin injection. Arch Pathol Lab Med. 1962;73:13.

282 **Valdivia-Barriga V et al.** Generalized hypersensitivity with hepatitis and jaundice after the use of penicillin and streptomycin. Gastroenterology. 1963; 45:114.

283 **Girard JP et al.** Lupoid hepatitis following administration of penicillin. Helv Med Acta. 1967;34:23.

284 **Neu HC et al.** Carbenicillin. Clinical and laboratory experience with a parenterally administered penicillin for treatment of pseudomonas infections. Ann Intern Med. 1969;71:903.

285 **Bodey GP et al.** Carbenicillin therapy for pseudomonas infection. JAMA. 1971;218:62.

286 **Davies GE et al.** Drug-induced immunological effects on the liver. Br J Anaesth. 1972;44:941.

287 **Kosmidis J et al.** Amoxicillin—pharmacology, bacteriology, and clinical studies. Br J Clin Pract. 1972;26:341.

288 **Goldstein LI et al.** Hepatic injury associated with penicillin therapy. Arch Pathol Lab Med. 1974;98:114.

289 **McArthur JE et al.** Stevens-Johnson syndrome with hepatitis following therapy with ampicillin and cephalexin. N Z Med J. 1975;81:390.

290 **Wilson FM et al.** Anicteric carbenicillin hepatitis. Eight episodes in four patients. JAMA. 1975;232:818.

291 **Hargreaves JE et al.** Severe cholestatic jaundice caused by mezlocillin. Clin Infect Dis. 1992;15:179.

292 **Jones NL.** Hepatitis due to phenindione sensitivity. Br Med J (Clin Res). 1960;2:504.

293 **Brooks RH et al.** Dermatitis, hepatitis and nephritis due to phenindione (phenylindanedione). Ann Intern Med. 1960;52:706.

294 **Portal RW et al.** Phenindione hepatitis complicating anticoagulant therapy. Br Med J (Clin Res). 1961;2:1318.

295 **Perkins J.** Phenindione sensitivity. Lancet. 1962;1:127.

296 **Garnet ES et al.** A fatal case of phenindione sensitivity. Br Med J (Clin Res). 1962;2:1023.

297 **Perkins J.** Phenindione jaundice. Lancet. 1962;1:125.

298 **Mohamed SD.** Sensitivity reaction to phenindione with urticaria, hepatitis, and pancytopenia. Br Med J (Clin Res). 1965;2:1475.

299 **Benjamin SB et al.** Phenylbutazone liver injury: a clinical-pathologic survey of 23 cases and review of the literature. Hepatology. 1981;1:255.

300 **Fisher JH.** Fatal phenylbutazone hepatitis. Can Med Assoc J. 1960;83:1211.

301 **Juul J.** Acute poisoning with butazolidin (phenylbutazone). Acta Paediatr Scand. 1965;54:503.

302 **Ecker JA.** Phenylbutazone hepatitis. Am J Gastroenterol. 1965;43:23.

303 **Ishak KG et al.** Granulomas and cholestatic hepatocellular injury associated with phenylbutazone. Report of two cases. Am J Dig Dis. 1977;22:611.

304 **Fowler PD et al.** Phenylbutazone and hepatitis. Rheumatol Rehabil. 1975;14:71.

305 **Spielberg SP et al.** Predisposition to phenytoin hepatotoxicity assessed *in vitro*. N Engl J Med. 1981;305:722.

306 **Gropper AL.** Diphenylhydantoin sensitivity. Report of a fatal case with hepatitis and exfoliative dermatitis. N Engl J Med. 1956;245:522.

307 **Siegel S et al.** Diphenylhydantoin (Dilantin) hypersensitivity with infectious mononucleosis-like syndrome and jaundice. J Allergy Clin Immunol. 1961;32:447.

308 **Bajoghli M.** Generalized lymphadenopathy and hepatosplenomegaly induced by diphenylhydantoin. Pediatrics. 1961;28:943.

309 **Braverman IM et al.** Dilantin-induced serum sickness. Case report and inquiry into its mechanisms. Am J Med. 1963;35:418.

310 **Pezzimenti JF et al.** Anicteric hepatitis induced by diphenylhydantoin. Arch Intern Med. 1970;125:118.

311 **Kleckner HB et al.** Severe hypersensitivity to diphenylhydantoin with circulating antibodies to the drug. Ann Intern Med. 1975;83:522.

312 **Lee TH et al.** Diphenylhydantoin-induced hepatic necrosis. Gastroenterology. 1976;70:422.

313 **Campbell CB et al.** Cholestatic liver disease associated with diphenylhydantoin therapy. Am J Dig Dis. 1977;22:255.

314 **Parker WA et al.** Phenytoin hepatotoxicity. A case report and review. Neurology. 1979;29:175.

315 **Roy AK et al.** Phenytoin-induced chronic hepatitis. Dig Dis Sci. 1993;38:740.

316 **Mechanic RC et al.** Chlorpromazine-type cholangitis. Report of a case occurring after the administration of prochlorperazine. N Engl J Med. 1958;259:778.

317 **McFarland RB.** Fatal drug reaction associated with prochlorperazine (Compazine). Am J Clin Pathol. 1963;40:284.

318 **Amerbein JA et al.** Granulocytopenia, lupus-like syndrome, and other complications of propylthiouracil therapy. J Pediatr. 1970;74:54.

319 **Parker LN.** Hepatitis and propylthiouracil. Arch Intern Med. 1975;135:319.

320 **Fedotin MS et al.** Liver disease caused by propylthiouracil. Arch Intern Med. 1975;135:319.

321 **Eisen MJ.** Fulminant hepatitis during treatment with propylthiouracil. N Engl J Med. 1963;249:814.

322 **Mihas AA et al.** Fulminant hepatitis and lymphocyte sensitization due to propylthiouracil. Gastroenterology. 1976;70:770.

323 **Colwell AR Jr et al.** Propylthiouracil-induced agranulocytosis, toxic hepatitis, and death. JAMA. 1952;148:639.

324 **Seidman D et al.** Propylthiouracil-induced cholestatic jaundice. J Toxicol Clin Toxicol. 1986;24:353.

325 **Liaw YF et al.** Hepatic injury during propylthiouracil therapy in patients with hyperthyroidism. A cohort study. Ann Intern Med. 1993;118:424.

326 **Chajek T et al.** Quinidine-induced granulomatous hepatitis. Ann Intern Med. 1974;81:774.

327 **Handler SD et al.** Quinidine hepatitis. Arch Intern Med. 1975;135:871.

328 **Koch MJ et al.** Quinidine toxicity. A report of a case and a review of the literature. Gastroenterology. 1976;70:1136.

329 **Djur JR.** Quinidine hepatotoxicity. JAMA. 1976;235:908.

330 **Geltner D et al.** Quinidine hypersensitivity and liver involvement. A survey of 32 patients. Gastroenterology. 1976;70:650.

331 **Munoz SJ et al.** Intrahepatic cholestasis and phospholipidosis associated with the use of trimethoprim-sulfamethoxazole. Hepatology. 1990;12:342.

332 **Oliver RM et al.** Intrahepatic cholestasis associated with co-trimoxazole. Br J Clin Pract. 1987;41:975.

333 **Alberti-Flor JJ et al.** Fulminant liver failure and pancreatitis associated with the use of sulfamethoxazole-trimethoprim. Gastroenterology. 1989;84:1577.

334 **Kowdley KV et al.** Prolonged cholestasis due to trimethoprim-sulfamethoxazole. Gastroenterology. 1992;102:2148.

335 **Shear NH et al.** Differences in metabolism of sulfonamides predisposing to idiosyncratic toxicity. Ann Intern Med. 1986;105:179.

336 **Longcope WT.** Serum sickness and analogous reactions from certain drugs, particularly the sulfonamides. Medicine (Baltimore). 1943;22:251.

337 **Chaikin NW et al.** Acute hepatitis; clinical observations in 63 cases. Am J Dig Dis. 1945;12:151.

338 **Dujovne CA et al.** Sulfonamide hepatic injury. N Engl J Med. 1967;277:785.

339 **Tonder M et al.** Sulfonamide-induced chronic liver disease. Scand J Gastroenterol. 1974;9:93.

340 **Sotolongo RP et al.** Hypersensitivity reaction to sulfasalazine with severe hepatotoxicity. Gastroenterology. 1978;75:95.

341 **Abi-Mansur P et al.** Trimethoprim-sulfamethoxazole induced cholestasis. Am J Gastroenterol. 1981;76:356.

342 **Thies PW, Dull WL.** Trimethoprim-sulfamethoxazole-induced cholestatic hepatitis. Inadvertent rechallenge. Arch Intern Med. 1984;141:1691.

343 **Tanner AR.** Hepatic cholestasis induced by trimethoprim. Br Med J (Clin Res). 1986;293:1072.

344 **Zitelli BN et al.** Fatal hepatic necrosis due to pyrimethamine-sulfadoxine (Fansidar). Ann Intern Med. 1987;106:393.

345 **Peters RL et al.** Tetracycline-induced fatty liver in non-pregnant patients. Am J Surg. 1967;113:622.

346 **Schultz JC et al.** Fatal liver disease after intravenous administration of tetracycline in high dosage. N Engl J Med. 1963;269:999.

347 **Dowling HF, Lepper NH.** Hepatic reactions to tetracycline. JAMA. 1964;188:307.

348 **Whalley PJ et al.** Tetracycline toxicity in pregnancy. JAMA. 1964;189:357.

349 **Horwitz ST et al.** Fatal liver disease during pregnancy associated with tetracycline therapy. Obstet Gynecol. 1964;23:826.

350 **Kunelis CT et al.** Fatty liver of pregnancy and its relationship to tetracycline therapy. Am J Med. 1965;38:359.

351 **Davis JS et al.** Tetracycline toxicity. Am J Obstet Gynecol. 1966;95:523.

352 **Hansen CH et al.** Impaired secretion of triglycerides by the liver. A cause of tetracycline-induced fatty liver. Proc Soc Exp Biol Med. 1968;128:143.

353 **Cunningham ML.** Acute hepatic necrosis following treatment with amitriptyline and diazepam. Br J Psychiatry. 1965;111:1107.

354 **Biagi RW et al.** Intrahepatic obstructive jaundice from amitriptyline. Br J Psychiatry. 1967;113:1113.

355 **Horst DA et al.** Prolonged cholestasis and progressive hepatic fibrosis following imipramine therapy. Gastroenterology. 1980;79:550.

356 **Powell WJ et al.** Lethal hepatic necrosis after therapy with imipramine and desipramine. JAMA. 1968;206:642.

357 **Short MH et al.** Cholestatic jaundice during imipramine therapy. JAMA. 1968;206:1791.

358 **Yon J et al.** Hepatitis caused by amitriptyline therapy. JAMA. 1975;232:833.

359 **Kohn N et al.** Cholestatic hepatitis associated with trifluoperazine. N Engl J Med. 1961;264:549.

360 **Margulies AI et al.** Jaundice associated with the administration of trifluoperazine. Can Med Assoc J. 1968;98:1063.

361 **Eadie MJ et al.** Valproate-associated hepatotoxicity and its biochemical mechanisms. Med Toxicol. 1988;3:85.

362 **Zimmerman HJ, Ishak KG.** Valproate-induced hepatic injury. Analysis of 23 fatal cases. Hepatology. 1982;2:591.

363 **Donat JF et al.** Valproic acid and fatal hepatitis. Neurology. 1979;29:273.

364 **Suchy FJ et al.** Acute hepatic failure associated with the use of sodium valproate. N Engl J Med. 1979;300:962.

365 **Gerber N et al.** Reye-like syndrome associated with valproic therapy. J Pediatr. 1979;95:142.

366 **Young RSK et al.** Reye-like syndrome associated with valproic acid. Ann Neurol. 1980;7:389.

367 **Stimson WH.** Vitamin A intoxication in adults. Report of a case with a summary of the literature. N Engl J Med. 1961;265:369.

368 **Rubin E et al.** Hepatic injury in chronic hypervitaminosis A. Am J Dis Child. 1970;119:132.

369 **Muenter MD et al.** Chronic vitamin A intoxication in adults. Am J Med. 1971;50:129.

370 **Muenter MD.** Hypervitaminosis A. Ann Intern Med. 1974;80:105.

371 **Russell RM et al.** Hepatic injury from chronic hypervitaminosis A resulting in portal-hypertension and ascites. N Engl J Med. 1974;291:435.

372 **Geubel AP et al.** Liver damage caused by therapeutic vitamin A administration: estimate of dose-related toxicity in 41 cases. Gastroenterology. 1991;100:1701.

373 **Zimmerman HJ.** Drug-induced chronic hepatic disease. Med Clin North Am. 1979;63:567.

Acid-Base Disorders

Thomas G Hall
Rachel L Kleiman-Wexler

Acid-Base Physiology 27-1
   Bicarbonate-carbonic acid buffer system 27-1
Respiratory Control 27-2
Renal Control (See Figures 27.1 and 27.2) 27-2
Laboratory Assessment
   (See Tables 27.1 and 27.3) 27-3
   Arterial blood gases (ABGs) 27-3
   Total carbon dioxide content 27-3
   Anion gap (AG) 27-3
Evaluation of Acid-Base Disorders
   (See Tables 27.2 and 27.3) 27-3
Metabolic Acidosis (See Table 27.4) 27-4
   Normal Anion Gap (Hyperchloremic)
   Metabolic Acidosis 27-4
   Evaluation 27-4
   Causes 27-5
     Renal tubular acidosis (RTA) (See Figure 27.3) ...27-5
     Lead-induced 27-5
   Treatment 27-5
   Metabolic Acidosis with Elevated Anion Gap 27-6
   Evaluation and osmolal gap (See Equation 27.7) ...27-6
   Causes 27-7
     Methanol-induced 27-7
     Lactic acidosis (See Tables 27.4 and 27.5 and
       Figure 27.4) 27-7
   Treatment 27-7

Ethanol 27-7
Bicarbonate (See Equation 27.8) 27-7
Risks of bicarbonate therapy 27-7
Metabolic Alkalosis 27-8
   Evaluation 27-8
   Causes (See Table 27.6) 27-8
   Diuretic-induced 27-8
   Treatment 27-9
   Hydrochloric acid (See Equation 27.9) 27-9
   Ammonium chloride (See Equation 27.10)
     and arginine hydrochloride 27-9
Respiratory Acidosis 27-9
   Evaluation 27-10
   Causes (See Table 27.7) 27-10
   Drug-induced 27-10
   Treatment 27-10
   Doxapram 27-11
   Progesterones 27-11
Respiratory Alkalosis 27-11
   Evaluation 27-11
   Causes (See Table 27.8) 27-11
   Treatment 27-11
Mixed Acid-Base Disorders 27-11
   Evaluation 27-11
   Causes 27-12
   Treatment 27-12

A fundamental knowledge of acid-base pathophysiology is essential to all clinicians. Many diseases cause acid-base disturbances that can affect drug therapy (e.g., renal tubular acidosis). Acid-base disorders also can occur as an adverse effect of a drug or as a manifestation of drug intoxication. Finally, the clinician must understand rational treatment of acid-base disorders.

Acid-Base Physiology

Bicarbonate-Carbonic Acid Buffer System

In a normal person, the pH (i.e., the negative logarithm of the hydrogen ion concentration) of arterial blood is regulated very closely within the range of 7.36 to 7.44. Maintenance of hydrogen ion concentration within this narrow pH range is essential to normal cellular metabolism and health.[1,2] Various buffer systems assist in the maintenance of normal pH by reducing the change in pH produced by addition of acidic or basic compounds to the body. The principle extracellular buffer is the bicarbonate/carbonic acid (HCO_3^-/H_2CO_3) system:

$$HCO_3^- + H^+ \Leftrightarrow H_2CO_3 \qquad Eq\ 27.1$$

Addition of a strong acid releases hydrogen ion (H^+) that combines with bicarbonate and shifts the equilibrium of Equation 27.1 to the right. This increases the concentration of the weak acid, H_2CO_3, reduces the change in H^+ concentration, and reduces the change in pH. Components of this buffer system are measured routinely to assess acid-base status. However, other extracellular buffers (e.g., serum proteins, inorganic phosphates) and intracel-lular buffers (e.g., hemoglobin, proteins, phosphates) also contribute significant buffer activity.[3,4]

In aqueous solution, carbonic acid reversibly dehydrates to form carbon dioxide (CO_2) and water (H_2O) as follows:

$$HCO_3^- + H^+ \Leftrightarrow H_2CO_3 \overset{CA}{\Leftrightarrow} CO_2\ (dissolved) + H_2O \qquad Eq\ 27.2$$

The enzyme carbonic anhydrase (CA), present in red blood cells, renal tubular cells, and other tissues, catalyzes the interconversion of H_2CO_3 and CO_2. Some of the carbon dioxide produced by dehydration of carbonic acid remains dissolved in plasma, but most exists as a volatile gas:

$$HCO_3^- + H^+ \Leftrightarrow H_2CO_3 \overset{CA}{\Leftrightarrow} CO_2\ (dissolved) + H_2O$$
$$\uparrow\downarrow$$
$$k \times CO_2\ (gas) \qquad Eq\ 27.3$$

In Equation 27.3, k is a solubility constant which has a value of approximately 0.03 in plasma at body temperature.[3] Virtually all of the carbonic acid (H_2CO_3) in body fluids is in the form of carbon dioxide. Therefore, carbonic acid is referred to as a volatile acid. The arterial partial pressure of carbon dioxide ($PaCO_2$; CO_2 tension), a measure of carbon dioxide gas, is directly proportional to the carbonic acid in the HCO_3^-/H_2CO_3 buffer system.

Large quantities of CO_2 can be exhaled by the lungs very rapidly; as a result, acid-base balance can be maintained under very tight control. This unique property of the HCO_3^-/H_2CO_3 system contributes significantly to its importance in acid-base physiology.

The relationship between the pH and the concentrations of the acid-base pairs in buffer systems is described by the Henderson-Hasselbalch equation:

$$pH = pK + \log \frac{[base]}{[acid]} \qquad Eq\ 27.4$$

The pH is the negative logarithm of the hydrogen ion concentration, and pK is the negative logarithm of the equilibrium constant for the buffer reaction. The pK for the carbonic acid/bicarbonate buffer system is 6.1. Because most of the carbonic acid in plasma is in the form of carbon dioxide gas, the concentration of acid, [acid], can be estimated as the partial pressure of carbon dioxide ($PaCO_2$) multiplied by 0.03 (the solubility constant, k, in Equation 27.3). The concentration of base, [base], is equal to the serum bicarbonate concentration. Using these values, Equation 27.4 can be rewritten as:

$$pH = 6.1 + \log \frac{(HCO_3)}{(0.03)(PaCO_2)} \qquad Eq\ 27.5$$

As shown by Equation 27.5, the ratio of $HCO_3^-:H_2CO_3$ is approximately 20:1 when the arterial pH is normal at pH 7.40. The equivalent ratio of bicarbonate to the partial pressure of carbon dioxide is about 0.6:1. Note that it is the *ratio* of bicarbonate to the partial pressure of carbon dioxide, and not the individual values alone, that determines the arterial pH. Therefore, if the bicarbonate concentration and the partial pressure of carbon dioxide are increased or decreased proportionately, the ratio remains fixed and the pH is not affected.

The arterial bicarbonate concentration is regulated primarily by the kidneys, while the arterial partial pressure of carbon dioxide (carbon dioxide tension) is controlled by the lungs. Changes in the ratio resulting from increased or decreased HCO_3^- are metabolic acid-base disorders, while changes in the ratio caused by increased or decreased $PaCO_2$ are respiratory disorders.

Acidic substances are formed constantly during cellular metabolism. Therefore, there is a constant requirement for efficient removal of hydrogen ions from the body. Aerobic metabolism of glucose produces 15,000 to 20,000 mmol of carbon dioxide a day.[1,3] If not excreted, this carbon dioxide would shift the equilibrium of Equation 27.2 toward formation of carbonic acid. The H_2CO_3 would be free to dissociate into H^+ and HCO_3^-, and result in a lower pH. Therefore, the lungs must excrete carbon dioxide efficiently in order to maintain arterial pH within normal limits.

Nonvolatile acids that must be excreted by the kidneys also are constantly formed during normal cellular metabolism. For example, the incomplete (anaerobic) oxidation of glucose produces lactic and pyruvic acids, and the oxidation of triglycerides as an energy source produces acetoacetic acid and beta-hydroxybutyric acid. Metabolism of sulfur-containing amino acids (e.g., cysteine, methionine) and phospholipids produces sulfuric and phosphoric acids, respectively. About 1 mEq H^+/kg of body weight of these nonvolatile acids must be excreted by the kidneys each day.

Respiratory Control

The arterial partial pressure of carbon dioxide, or carbon dioxide tension, is regulated by pulmonary ventilation. Carbon dioxide diffuses easily from tissues to capillary blood and from pulmonary capillary blood into the alveoli where it is exhaled from the body.[5] Pulmonary ventilation is regulated by peripheral chemoreceptors located in the carotid arteries and the aorta and central chemoreceptors located in the medulla. The peripheral chemoreceptors are activated by arterial acidosis, hypercapnia (elevated $PaCO_2$), and hypoxia (decreased PaO_2); central chemoreceptors are activated by cerebrospinal fluid (CSF) acidosis and by elevated CO_2 tension in the CSF.[6-8] Activation of these chemoreceptors stimulates the respiratory control center in the medulla to increase the rate and depth of ventilation, which results in increased exhalation of carbon dioxide.

Renal Control

The kidneys have two important and interrelated functions in acid-base balance. First, they must reabsorb the bicarbonate that undergoes glomerular filtration and is present in the renal tubular fluid. Second, the kidneys must excrete hydrogen ions released from nonvolatile acids. Both functions are important in preventing systemic acidosis.

Bicarbonate (HCO_3^-) reabsorption in the proximal renal tubule is illustrated in Figure 27.1. Carbonic anhydrase (CA) catalyzes formation of carbonic acid from carbon dioxide and water in the renal tubular cell, and the H_2CO_3 dissociates to form H^+ and HCO_3^-. The renal tubular cell then secretes the H^+ into the lumen of the tubule in exchange for sodium ion (Na^+), and the bicarbonate from the renal tubule cell is reabsorbed into the capillary blood.

Fig 27.1   Renal Tubular Bicarbonate Reabsorption   See text for discussion.

Fig 27.2   Renal Tubular Hydrogen Ion Excretion   See text for discussion.

Inside the lumen, H_2CO_3 is reformed from secreted H^+ and filtered HCO_3^-. Carbonic anhydrase present inside the lumen (on the brush border membrane of the cell) catalyzes conversion of H_2CO_3 to CO_2 that can readily diffuse back into the blood. Thus, the net result is reabsorption of Na^+ and HCO_3^-. Although a hydrogen ion is secreted into the lumen in this process, no net excretion of acid occurs due to the reabsorption of carbon dioxide. Approximately 85% to 90% of filtered bicarbonate is reabsorbed in the proximal tubule by this process. The remaining 10% to 15% of the filtered bicarbonate usually is completely reabsorbed in the distal tubule and collecting duct; virtually no bicarbonate is lost in the urine.

Figure 27.2 illustrates H^+ excretion by the kidney, a process which occurs primarily in the distal tubule. Hydrogen ions do not remain free in solution in the urine; instead, they are buffered either by filtered phosphates or ammonia (NH_3) which is synthesized from glutamine by the kidney and secreted into the lumen. This buffering process prevents urine pH from falling below a minimum of about 4.5. Cellular carbonic anhydrase also is required for H^+ excretion. While strict Na^+/H^+ exchange does not occur in this region of the kidney, factors which increase or decrease sodium reabsorption usually will increase or decrease hydrogen ion excretion, respectively.

Laboratory Assessment

Laboratory data essential to evaluation of acid-base status are arterial pH, arterial carbon dioxide tension, and an estimate of serum bicarbonate concentration.[3,9,10] These values are obtained routinely with an arterial blood gas (ABG) determination. Estimation of the anion gap (AG) often is valuable in determining the etiology of acid-base disorders, especially metabolic acidosis. Normal values for these laboratory tests are listed in Table 27.1.

Arterial Blood Gases (ABGs)

Arterial blood gas measurements include pH, carbon dioxide tension, and oxygen tension. When the pH and carbon dioxide tension values are measured, the HCO_3^- concentration can be calculated from the Henderson-Hasselbalch equation (Equation 27.5). The arterial bicarbonate concentration in laboratory reports of arterial blood gases typically is calculated in this way rather than measured directly. Arterial pH normally is maintained in the narrow range of 7.36 to 7.44. A patient is acidemic when the pH is

less than 7.36 and alkalemic when the pH is greater than 7.44. The arterial partial pressure of oxygen and of carbon dioxide are measured to assess the adequacy of gas exchange in the lungs. Normal values for individuals breathing room air are PaO_2 of 90 to 100 mm Hg and $PaCO_2$ of 35 to 45 mm Hg.

Total Carbon Dioxide Content

The total carbon dioxide content of serum commonly is used to estimate the bicarbonate concentration, because about 95% of the total CO_2 content is bicarbonate. The CO_2 content is determined by acidifying serum to convert all of the bicarbonate to carbon dioxide and measuring the partial pressure of CO_2 gas. Because this method is more convenient than direct measurement of bicarbonate concentration, it typically is used to estimate HCO_3^- concentrations on serum electrolyte panels. The normal range of venous total CO_2 content is 24 to 30 mEq/L.

Anion Gap (AG)

The anion gap represents the concentration of unmeasured negatively charged substances (anions) in excess of the concentration of unmeasured positively charged substances (cations) in the extracellular fluid. The concentrations of total anions and cations in the body are equal because the body must remain electrically neutral. Most clinical laboratories, however, only measure a portion of these ions [i.e., sodium, chloride (Cl^-), and total carbon dioxide (an estimate of HCO_3^-)]. The concentrations of other negatively and positively charged substances such as potassium (K^+), magnesium (Mg^{++}), calcium (Ca^{++}), proteins (which usually carry net negative charges), and phosphates are less easily measured. The concentration of unmeasured anions normally exceeds the concentration of unmeasured cations by 7 to 14 mEq/L, and is calculated as follows:

$$Anion\ Gap = Na^+ - (Cl^- + HCO_3^-) \qquad Eq\ 27.6$$

An increased anion gap can provide clinicians some insight into the etiology of metabolic acidosis. Thus, cases of metabolic acidosis frequently are categorized into those with a normal anion gap and those with an increased anion gap. (See Table 27.4.)

Evaluation of Acid-Base Disorders

The four simple acid-base disorders (i.e., metabolic acidosis, metabolic alkalosis, respiratory acidosis, and respiratory alkalosis)

Table 27.1	Normal Values for Laboratory Tests
Test[a]	Normal Range
ABGs	
pH	7.36–7.44
PaO_2	90–100 mm Hg
$PaCO_2$	35–45 mm Hg
Total CO_2 content	24–30 mEq/L
AG	7–14 mEq/L

[a] ABGs = Arterial blood gases; AG = Anion gap; CO_2 = Carbon dioxide.

and the common laboratory findings of these disorders are listed in Table 27.3. In metabolic disorders, the primary abnormality is a change in serum bicarbonate concentration. Specifically, metabolic acidosis is associated with a decrease in serum HCO_3^- and metabolic alkalosis is associated with an increase in serum HCO_3^-. In respiratory disorders, the primary change is in arterial carbon dioxide tension. For example, respiratory acidosis is associated with hypoventilation and an increase in $PaCO_2$ (hypercapnia), and respiratory alkalosis is associated with hyperventilation and a decrease in $PaCO_2$ (hypocapnia).

In most cases of metabolic acidosis or alkalosis, the lungs compensate for the change in serum HCO_3^- concentration by increasing or decreasing ventilation to change $PaCO_2$ in the same direction (see Table 27.3). This respiratory compensation minimizes the change in the ratio of bicarbonate to the partial pressure of carbon dioxide and thus reduces the change in arterial pH (see Equation 27.5). Likewise, in respiratory acidosis or alkalosis, the change in $PaCO_2$ is offset partially by renal compensatory changes in serum bicarbonate concentration. These renal and pulmonary compensatory changes, however, are not sufficient to return pH completely to baseline. For normal pH to be achieved, the primary abnormality must be corrected.[11]

Normal compensatory changes for simple acid-base disorders have been identified and are outlined in Table 27.2.[1–3,11–13] For example, a patient who has metabolic acidosis with a total CO_2 content of 14 mEq/L (normal: 24 mEq/L) would be expected to have respiratory compensation resulting in a decrease in $PaCO_2$ of 10 to 14 mm Hg (normal: 40 mm Hg; new value: 26 to 30 mm Hg). This degree of respiratory compensation results in an arterial pH between 7.29 and 7.35. If no respiratory compensation had occurred, arterial pH would fall to 7.17 (see Equation 27.5). Note that renal compensation for respiratory disorders requires 36 to 72 hours to achieve maximum effect; therefore, the ability of the kidney to compensate for an acute respiratory disorder is not as great as its ability to compensate for a chronic respiratory disorder. When values for arterial carbon dioxide tension or serum bicarbonate fall outside of these normal compensatory ranges, either a mixed acid-base disorder, inadequate extent of compensation, or inadequate time for compensation should be suspected.

Metabolic Acidosis

Metabolic acidosis is characterized by loss of bicarbonate from the body, decreased acid excretion by the kidney, or increased endogenous acid production. This acid-base disorder is associated with a fall in both arterial pH and serum bicarbonate concentration. Acidosis stimulates the respiratory center to increase ventilation as a compensatory mechanism. This produces increased carbon dioxide excretion and decreased arterial CO_2 tension. As a result, the bicarbonate to carbon dioxide ratio (and therefore, arterial pH) remains more nearly normal (see Equation 27.5).

There are two categories of simple metabolic acidosis based upon the calculated anion gap (see Table 27.4). Metabolic acidosis with a normal anion gap (hyperchloremic metabolic acidosis) usually is due to loss of bicarbonate and is subdivided into hypokalemic and hyperkalemic. Elevated anion gap metabolic acidosis usually is associated with overproduction of organic acids or with decreased renal elimination of nonvolatile acids. Increased production of organic acids (e.g., formic, lactic acids) will be buffered by extracellular bicarbonate with resultant consumption of bicarbonate and appearance of an unmeasured anion (e.g., formate, lactate). The decrement in serum bicarbonate approximates the increment in the anion gap, the latter being a good estimate of the circulating anion level. In the case of renal failure, the capacity for H^+ secretion diminishes, and this results in metabolic acidosis. The accompanying increased anion gap results from decreased excretion of unmeasured anions such as sulfate and phosphate.

Normal Anion Gap
(Hyperchloremic) Metabolic Acidosis

Evaluation

1. A.B., a 27-year-old, 60 kg female, is hospitalized for evaluation of weakness. She reports ingestion of lead-containing paint from the walls of her house. A.B. has a history of depression for which she receives lithium carbonate (Eskalith) 300 mg TID. Upon admission, she appears weak and apathetic, her breath smells of paint, and she complains of anorexia. Laboratory tests reveal serum Na 143 mEq/L (Normal: 135–145); K 3.0 mEq/L (Normal: 3.5–5.0); Cl 121 mEq/L (Normal: 95–105); total CO_2 12 mEq/L (Normal: 24–30); pH 7.25 (Normal: 7.35–7.45); $PaCO_2$ 28 mm Hg (Normal: 35–45); urine pH 5.5. A.B.'s urine pH following an ammonium chloride (NH_4Cl) 0.1 gm/kg intravenous (IV) load is <5.3. A bicarbonate load of 1 mEq/kg infused IV over 1 hour induces bicarbonaturia (urinary pH: 7.0) and lowers the serum potassium to 2.0 mEq/L. Assess A.B.'s acid-base status. [SI units: Na 143 mmol/L (Normal: 135–145); K 3.0 and 2.0 mmol/L, respectively (Normal: 3.5–5.0); Cl 121 mmol/L (Normal: 95–105); total CO_2 21 mmol/L (Normal: 24–30); $PaCO_2$ 3.73 kPa (Normal: 4.7–6.0)]

A.B.'s low pH represents either metabolic or respiratory acidosis. However, the presence of low total carbon dioxide (bicarbonate) and low $PaCO_2$ suggest primary metabolic acidosis with respiratory compensation (see Table 27.3). Normal compensation for A.B.'s serum bicarbonate of 12 mEq/L would result in a decrease in the $PaCO_2$ of 12 to 17 mm Hg (see Table 27.2). Since her $PaCO_2$ has fallen by 12 mm Hg (normal: 40 mm Hg; current: 28 mm Hg), normal respiratory compensation for this degree of metabolic acidosis has occurred.

Table 27.2	Normal Compensation in Simple Acid-Base Disorders
Disorder	Compensation[a]
Metabolic acidosis	$\downarrow PaCO_2$ (mm Hg) = 1.0 – 1.4 × $\downarrow HCO_3^-$ (mEq/L)
Metabolic alkalosis	$\uparrow PaCO_2$ (mm Hg) = 0.5 – 1.0 × $\uparrow HCO_3^-$ (mEq/L)
Respiratory acidosis	
Acute	$\uparrow HCO_3^-$ (mEq/L) = 0.1 × $\uparrow PaCO_2$ (mm Hg)
Chronic	$\uparrow HCO_3^-$ (mEq/L) = 0.4 × $\uparrow PaCO_2$ (mm Hg)
Respiratory alkalosis	
Acute	$\downarrow HCO_3^-$ (mEq/L) = 0.2 × $\downarrow PaCO_2$ (mm Hg)
Chronic	$\downarrow HCO_3^-$ (mEq/L) = 0.4 – 0.5 × $\downarrow PaCO_2$ (mm Hg)

[a] Based upon change from normal $HCO_3^- = 24$ mEq/L and $PaCO_2 = 40$ mm Hg.

Table 27.3		Laboratory Values in Simple Acid-Base Disorders	
Disorder	Arterial pH	Primary Change	Compensatory Change
Metabolic acidosis	↓	↓ HCO_3^-	↓ $PaCO_2$
Respiratory acidosis	↓	↑ $PaCO_2$	↑ HCO_3^-
Metabolic alkalosis	↑	↑ HCO_3^-	↑ $PaCO_2$
Respiratory alkalosis	↑	↓ $PaCO_2$	↓ HCO_3^-

In patients with metabolic acidosis, calculation of the anion gap serves as a first step in classifying the metabolic acidosis and provides additional information about the conditions which might be responsible for the acid-base disorder. A.B.'s calculated anion gap is 10 mEq/L (see Equation 27.6). Thus, A.B. is suffering from hyperchloremic metabolic acidosis with a normal anion gap.

Causes

2. What are potential causes of metabolic acidosis in A.B.?

The common causes of metabolic acidosis are presented in Table 27.4.[2,14] A.B. reports a history of both lead ingestion and chronic use of lithium. Lead, other heavy metals (e.g., cadmium, copper, mercury), and carbonic anhydrase inhibitors (e.g., acetazolamide) are associated with proximal renal tubular acidosis (RTA). Lithium, amphotericin B, and toluene are associated with distal RTA.[15-17] Renal tubular acidosis is characterized by defective secretion of hydrogen ion in the renal tubule in the presence of essentially normal glomerular filtration rate. The recognized forms are distal (Type 1), proximal (Type 2), and Type 4 RTA. In distal RTA, the defect affects mainly the collecting duct; in the proximal type, the proximal tubule primarily is involved; and type 4 results from aldosterone deficiency or resistance. A.B.'s history of lithium and lead ingestion and the presence of hyperchloremic metabolic acidosis with a normal anion gap suggest the possibility of RTA.

3. Renal Tubular Acidosis (RTA). How do the results of NH_4Cl and sodium bicarbonate ($NaHCO_3^-$) loading help identify the type of renal tubular acidosis in A.B.?

Both proximal and distal renal tubular acidosis impair acidification of the urine.[18-22] In normal subjects, approximately 10% to 15% of the filtered HCO_3^- escapes reabsorption in the proximal tubule, but is reabsorbed in more distal segments of the nephron. Therefore, urine bicarbonate excretion is negligibly small, and urine pH is between 5.5 and 6.5 (see Figure 27.3A). Proximal RTA is associated with a decrease in proximal tubular bicarbonate reabsorption. The distal tubular cells partially compensate for this defect by increasing bicarbonate reabsorption, but urinary bicarbonate excretion still is increased (see Figure 27.3B). Like A.B., serum HCO_3^- concentration in patients with proximal RTA will stabilize around 12 mEq/L. At this point, distal HCO_3^- delivery no longer is excessive, allowing the distal nephron to acidify the urine appropriately and excrete acid in the form of titratable ammonia and phosphate (see Figures 27.3C and 27.3D). In distal RTA, there is a defect in net hydrogen ion secretion due to a back-diffusion of H^+ from the tubule lumen to the tubule cell. This defect impairs urinary acid excretion even when systemic acidosis is severe.

Evaluation of bicarbonate reabsorption during bicarbonate loading and of response to acid loading by infusion of ammonium chloride is useful in distinguishing proximal from distal RTA. A.B.'s response to the acid (NH_4Cl) load demonstrates an ability to acidify the urine (pH <5.3), which suggests that distal tubular hydrogen ion secretion is normal. This helps rule out distal RTA. During bicarbonate loading in patients with proximal RTA, serum bicarbonate concentration is increased and abnormally large amounts of bicarbonate are again delivered to the distal tubule. Its hydrogen secretory processes are overwhelmed, resulting in bicarbonaturia (see Figure 27.3B). Administration of bicarbonate to A.B. produces bicarbonaturia and an elevation in urine pH (7.0), in the presence of low blood pH. These findings indicate that the reabsorption of bicarbonate in the proximal tubule is impaired, which is characteristic of proximal RTA.

4. Lead-Induced. What is the cause of A.B.'s proximal renal tubular acidosis?

The most likely cause in A.B. is lead. The pathogenesis of lead-induced proximal RTA is not clear. Some studies suggest that carbonic anhydrase deficiency in the proximal tubule is the major factor, but these data are inconclusive.

5. Why is A.B. hypokalemic?

Bicarbonate wasting in proximal RTA also results in sodium loss, extracellular fluid reduction, and activation of the renin-angiotensin-aldosterone axis. Aldosterone increases distal tubular sodium reabsorption and greatly augments potassium and hydrogen ion secretion. This results in potassium wasting,[23] which explains A.B.'s hypokalemia. When plasma bicarbonate achieves steady state (see Figure 27.3D), less bicarbonate reaches the distal tubule, and the stimulus for aldosterone release is removed. Therefore, A.B. will experience only a mild depletion of potassium body stores. When A.B. is exposed to bicarbonate loading, the renin-angiotensin-aldosterone axis is reactivated, and hypokalemia worsens.

Treatment

6. What treatment is indicated for A.B.?

Although it is rare for patients with proximal RTA to develop severe acidosis and potassium depletion chronically, it is not uncommon in an acute situation such as this. A.B. has low serum bicarbonate; thus, she should be treated with alkali replacement, while at the same time removing her from the offending agent (lead). An initial dose of 44 mEq sodium bicarbonate and 40 mEq potassium acetate or citrate should be infused intravenously over one hour. Hourly samples of blood for electrolytes should be taken until potassium is greater than 3.5 mEq/L.

In adults like A.B., chronic treatment often is not needed because acidosis is self-limited. However, A.B. should be treated with sodium bicarbonate until proximal RTA resolves. Very large doses of bicarbonate (6 to 10 mEq/kg/day) would be required to increase serum bicarbonate to the normal range (24 to 30 mEq/L). In adults with proximal RTA, however, the goal is to increase serum bicarbonate to only 14 to 18 mEq/L. Bicarbonate can be

Table 27.4	Common Causes of Metabolic Acidosis[a]
Normal AG	Elevated AG
Hypokalemic Diarrhea	**Renal Failure**
Carbonic anhydrase inhibitors	**Lactic Acidosis** (See Table 27.5)

Renal tubular acidosis
  proximal
  distal
	Ketoacidosis
	Starvation

Hyperkalemic Hypoaldosteronism	Ethanol Diabetes mellitus
Hydrochloric acid or precursor	

Potassium-sparing diuretics
  amiloride
  spironolactone
  triamterene
	Drug Intoxications
	Ethylene glycol
	Methanol
	Salicylates

[a] AG = Anion gap.

Developmental Stages of Proximal Renal Tubular Acidosis

Fig 27.3   Evolution of Urinary pH in Stages of Proximal Renal Tubular Acidosis   See text for discussion. Reprinted with permission from reference 18.

provided as sodium bicarbonate tablets (8 mEq/600 mg tablet) or Shohl's solution. Shohl's solution, USP, contains 334 mg citric acid and 500 mg sodium citrate per 5 mL. Sodium citrate is metabolized to sodium bicarbonate in the liver. Shohl's solution provides 1 mEq of sodium and 1 mEq of bicarbonate per mL of solution. Therapy for A.B. should be initiated with 1 mEq/kg/day (either 8 $NaHCO_3^-$ tablets or 60 mL of Shohl's solution a day). A.B.'s lithium levels should be monitored while on alkali therapy. Sodium ingestion might increase renal lithium excretion and exacerbate her depressive disorder. Due to severe hypokalemia resulting from alkali administration, supplemental potassium as chloride, bicarbonate, acetate, or citrate salts also should be administered.

Metabolic Acidosis with Elevated Anion Gap

Evaluation and Osmolal Gap

7. G.D., a 34-year-old, 60 kg male, is brought to the emergency room (ER) by the police in a semicomatose state. He was found lying on the floor of his hotel room 30 minutes ago. G.D. has a long history of alcohol abuse. In the ER, supine blood pressure (BP) is 120/60 mm Hg, pulse is 100 beats/min, and respiratory rate is 50 breaths/min. G.D.'s pupils are reactive, and mild papilledema is noted. Laboratory tests reveal serum Na 140 mEq/L (Normal: 135–145); K 5.8 mEq/L (Normal: 3.5–5.0); Cl 98 mEq/L (Normal: 95–105); total CO_2 8 mEq/L (Normal: 24–30); blood urea nitrogen (BUN) 25 mg/dL (Normal: 10–26); creatinine 1.4 mg/dL (Normal: 0.7–1.4); and fasting glucose 150 mg/dL (Normal: 70–105). ABGs include pH 7.15 (Normal: 7.35–7.45); $PaCO_2$ 24 mm Hg (Normal: 35–45).

Serum osmolality is 332 mOsm/kg (Normal: 280–295). What acid-base disturbance is present in G.D., and what are possible causes of the disorder? [SI units: Na 140 mmol/L (Normal: 135–145); K 5.8 mmol/L (Normal: 3.5–5.0); Cl 98 mmol/L (Normal: 95–105); total CO_2 8 mmol/L (Normal 24–30); BUN 8.9 mmol/L (Normal: 3.57–9.28); creatinine 124 μmol/L (Normal: 61.88–123.76); fasting glucose 8.33 mmol/L (Normal: 2.8–5.82); $PaCO_2$ 3.20 kPa; osmolality (332 mmol/kg (Normal: 280–295)]

G.D. has a severe metabolic acidosis (pH 7.15) with a large anion gap (34 mEq/L), and his rapid ventilation (50 breaths/minute) explains the decrease in $PaCO_2$. Respiratory compensation for a total CO_2 of 8 mEq/L should result in a decrease in $PaCO_2$ of at least 16 mm Hg from the normal value of 40 mm Hg (see Table 27.2). Therefore, G.D.'s laboratory findings upon admission (total CO_2 8 mEq/L and $PaCO_2$ 24 mm Hg) represent metabolic acidosis with normal respiratory compensation.

An elevated anion gap metabolic acidosis often indicates lactic acidosis due to intoxications (e.g., salicylates, acetaminophen, methanol, ethylene glycol, paraldehyde) or ketoacidosis induced by diabetes mellitus, starvation, or alcohol.[24–26] Calculation of the osmolal gap may be helpful in differentiating these possible causes. Osmolal gap is defined as the difference between measured serum osmolality (SO) and calculated SO using Equation 27.7.

$$\text{Calculated SO (mOsm/kg)} = 2 \times Na^+ \text{ (mEq/L)} + \frac{\text{glucose (mg/dL)}}{18} + \frac{\text{BUN (mg/dL)}}{2.8} \quad Eq\ 27.7$$

When the difference between measured and calculated SO is greater than 10 mOsm/kg, the presence of an unmeasured osmotically active substance, such as ethanol, methanol, or ethylene glycol, should be considered.[27] G.D.'s calculated SO is 297 mOsm/kg, compared with the measured value of 332; therefore, his osmolal gap is 35 mOsm/kg. An increase in AG and osmolal gap in the absence of diabetic ketoacidosis and chronic renal failure suggests the possibility of metabolic acidosis due to a toxic ingestion.[28] On the basis of G.D.'s presentation (papilledema, history of alcohol abuse, increased osmolal gap, increased AG metabolic acidosis) methanol intoxication should be considered.

Causes

8. Methanol-Induced. How would G.D.'s methanol intake induce metabolic acidosis with an elevated anion gap?

Methanol intoxication results in formation of two organic acids, formic and lactic acid, which consume bicarbonate with production of an anion gap metabolic acidosis. Alcohol dehydrogenase in the liver metabolizes methanol to formaldehyde and then to formic acid. The formic acid contributes to the metabolic acidosis and also is responsible for the retinal edema and blindness associated with methanol intoxication.

Lactic Acidosis. Serum lactic acid concentrations also are increased in patients with methanol intoxication[29] due to disruption of mitochondrial function caused by formic acid. Methanol causes Type B lactic acidosis[30] which is associated with defective mitochondrial oxygen utilization. A wide spectrum of disorders can cause Type B lactic acidosis (see Table 27.5). Type A lactic acidosis is more common and is due to tissue underperfusion. This results in tissue hypoxia, increased lactate production via anaerobic glycolysis, and decreased lactate utilization (see Figure 27.4). Normally, lactate remains in equilibrium with pyruvate in a normal lactate:pyruvate ratio of 10:1.[31] Lactic acidosis results when there is an imbalance between lactic acid production and utilization.

Treatment

9. How should G.D.'s methanol intoxication be managed acutely?

Ethanol. Therapy is directed toward treatment of the underlying cause and may include additional supportive management. Ethanol and methanol compete for alcohol dehydrogenase binding sites. Since ethanol affinity for alcohol dehydrogenase is 100-fold greater than the affinity of methanol for this enzyme, ethanol administration reduces the metabolism of methanol to formic acid. The unmetabolized methanol then is excreted by the lungs and kidneys. G.D. should receive a loading dose of 0.6 to 0.8 gm/kg (0.75 to 1 mL/kg) of ethanol intravenously or orally followed by an infusion of ethanol at 0.1 to 0.15 gm/kg/hour (0.125 to 0.2

mL/kg/hour). The required dose of ethanol must be diluted before administration. Intravenous ethanol may be given as a 5% or 10% (v/v) solution in 5% dextrose. For example, a 60 kg patient should receive a loading dose of 60 mL of ethanol (600 mL of a 10% v/v solution) followed by 7.5 to 12 mL/hour of ethanol (75 to 120 mL/hour of a 10% v/v solution). The infusion rate is adjusted to maintain a serum ethanol level of approximately 100 mg/dL.[32,33]

If methanol blood levels are higher than 50 mg/dL, hemodialysis is indicated to rapidly reduce concentrations of methanol and its toxic metabolite. During dialysis ethanol also will be eliminated, increasing the ethanol requirement approximately twofold.[34]

Bicarbonate. Severe acidosis causes reduced myocardial contractility, impaired response to catecholamines, and impaired oxygen delivery to tissues due to 2,3-diphosphoglycerate depletion. For this reason, IV sodium bicarbonate traditionally has been administered to patients with metabolic acidosis to raise the arterial pH to 7.20 to 7.25. However, concerns about the risks of bicarbonate (see Question 10) and studies failing to demonstrate significant short-term benefits have raised questions about the appropriateness of bicarbonate therapy.[35,36] Administration of bicarbonate in metabolic acidosis is controversial.

If bicarbonate is given, the amount required to correct serum HCO_3^- and arterial pH can be estimated using Equation 27.8 as follows:

$$\begin{aligned} \text{Bicarbonate} \atop \text{Dose (mEq)} &= 0.5(\text{L/kg}) \times \text{Body Weight (kg)} \\ &\quad \times \text{Desired Increase in Serum } HCO_3^- \text{ (mEq/L)} \end{aligned}$$

Eq 27.8

Bicarbonate distributes to approximately 50% of total body weight (therefore, the factor of 0.5 L/kg in Equation 27.8). After the arterial pH is increased to 7.20 to 7.25 and the patient is hemodynamically stable, further increases in serum bicarbonate should not exceed 4 to 6 mEq/L over 6 to 12 hours to avoid the risks of overalkalinization (see Question 10). For G.D., the dose required to raise serum bicarbonate from 8 to 12 mEq/L amounts to 120 mEq of bicarbonate (0.5 L/kg × 60 kg × 4 mEq/L; Equation 27.8). The appropriate starting dose is one-third to one-half of the calculated dose. Serial measurements of arterial pH and serum bicarbonate should be performed before any additional therapy.

10. Risks of Bicarbonate Therapy. What are the risks of G.D.'s bicarbonate therapy?

Increasing attention has been focused on the potential adverse effects of bicarbonate therapy. Bicarbonate administration may result in overalkalinization and a paradoxical transient intracellular acidosis. While arterial pH can increase rapidly following bicarbonate administration, intracellular pH increases more slowly because of slow penetration of the negatively charged HCO_3^- ion across cell membranes. The bicarbonate in plasma, however, is converted rapidly to carbonic acid, and the carbon dioxide tension increases as a result (see Equation 27.2). Since CO_2 diffuses into the cells more rapidly than HCO_3^-, the intracellular HCO_3^-:CO_2 ratio decreases, resulting in a decrease in the intracellular pH. Since acid-base balance normally is restored via increased CO_2 excretion, intracellular acidosis will persist as long as bicarbonate administration exceeds the CO_2 excretion. Therefore, in patients with cardiac or pulmonary failure, CO_2 excretion via adequate tissue perfusion and ventilation must be provided.[37-39]

Overalkalinization also will cause a shift to the left in the oxygen-hemoglobin dissociation curve. This shift increases hemoglobin affinity for oxygen, decreases oxygen delivery to tissues, and potentially increases lactic acid production and accumulation. Sodium bicarbonate administration also can cause hypernatremia, hyperosmolality, and volume overload; however, the excessive

Table 27.5	Common Causes of Lactic Acidosis[a]
Type A[b]	Type B
Anemia	Diabetes mellitus
Carbon monoxide poisoning	Liver failure
CHF	Renal failure
Shock	Seizure disorder
	Leukemia
	Drugs
	biguanides
	ethanol
	isoniazid
	methanol
	salicylates

[a] CHF = Congestive heart failure.
[b] Associated with tissue hypoxia.

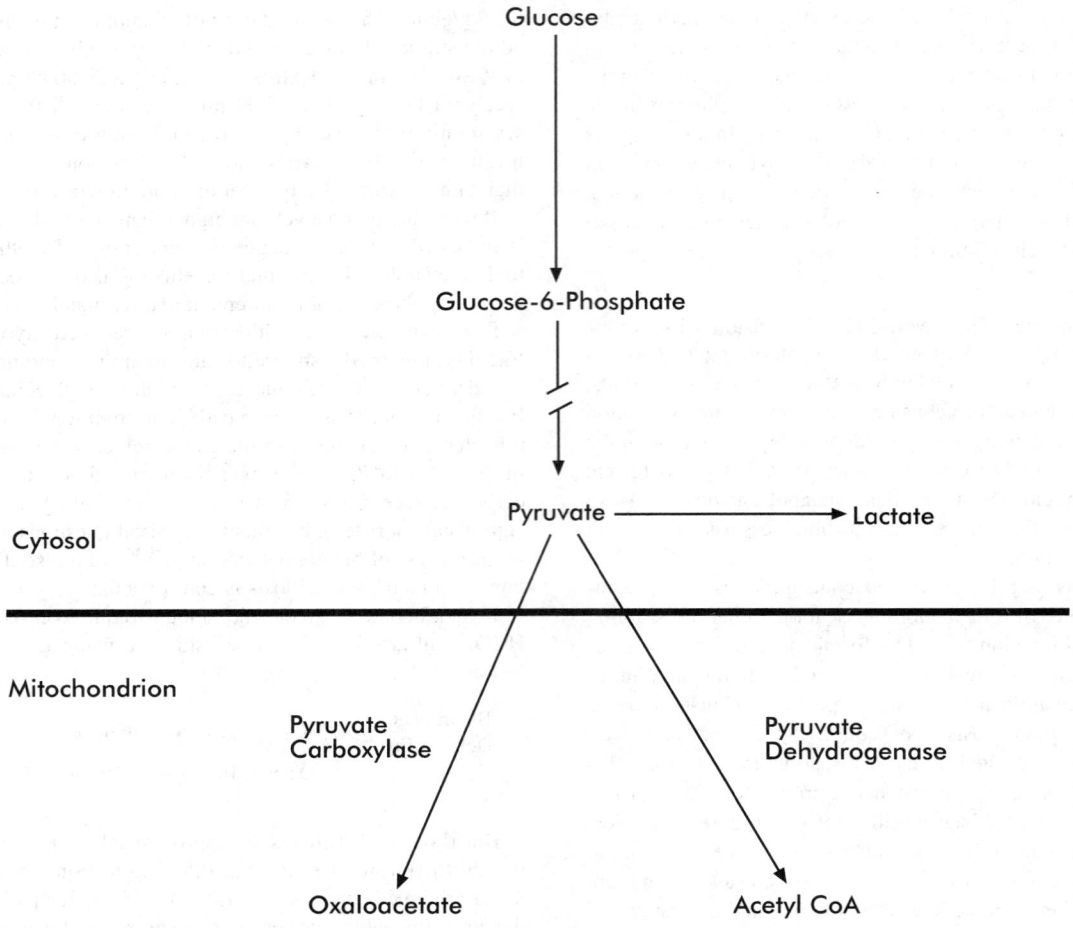

Fig 27.4   Metabolic Pathways of Lactate Production via Anaerobic Glycolysis

sodium and water retention usually can be avoided by the administration of loop diuretics. Hypokalemia is another potential adverse effect of bicarbonate therapy. Acidosis stimulates movement of potassium from intracellular to extracellular fluid in exchange for hydrogen ions. When acidosis is corrected, potassium ions move intracellularly and hypokalemia can occur. This translocation of potassium tends to reduce serum potassium levels by approximately 0.6 mEq/L for each 0.1 unit increase in pH, although wide interpatient variability in this relationship exists.[3] To prevent the risks of bicarbonate therapy, G.D.'s mental status, serum sodium and potassium levels, and arterial blood gases should be monitored.

Metabolic Alkalosis

Metabolic alkalosis is associated with an increase in serum bicarbonate concentration. There are two general classifications of metabolic alkalosis: saline-responsive and saline-unresponsive. Common causes of metabolic alkalosis are listed in Table 27.6. Respiratory compensation in patients with metabolic alkalosis occurs via a decrease in ventilation rate, leading to a compensatory hypercapnia (elevation of $PaCO_2$).

Evaluation

11. K.E., a 40-year-old obese female, is hospitalized because of hypokalemia despite administration of 120 mEq/day of KCl. She denies intake of other drugs. Physical examination reveals a 100 kg female with slight muscle weakness. K.E.'s electrocardiogram shows flattened T waves and presence of U waves.

Laboratory tests upon admission are serum Na 144 mEq/L; K 2.5 mEq/L; Cl 70 mEq/L; total CO_2 40 mEq/L; creatinine 0.9 mg/dL; BUN 25 mg/dL; pH 7.53; and $PaCO_2$ 45 mm Hg. Urine K concentration is 50 mEq/L and urine Cl concentration is 90 mEq/L. Urine drug screen reveals traces of furosemide and hydrochlorothiazide (HCTZ). K.E. then admits to taking HCTZ, furosemide, and salt tablets in an effort to lose weight. What is K.E.'s acid-base status upon admission? [SI units: Na 144 mmol/L; K 2.5 mmol/L; Cl 70 mmol/L; total CO_2 40 mmol/L; creatinine 79.6 μmol/L; BUN 8.9 mmol/L; $PaCO_2$ 6.0 kPa; urine K 50 mmol/L; urine Cl 90 mmol/L]

The elevated pH represents either respiratory alkalosis or metabolic alkalosis. However, the presence of an increased serum bicarbonate concentration, increased $PaCO_2$, low potassium, and low chloride are consistent with metabolic alkalosis with respiratory compensation. An HCO_3^- concentration of 40 mEq/L should result in an increase in $PaCO_2$ of 8 mm Hg from a normal of 40 mm Hg to approximately 48 mm Hg (see Table 27.2). K.E.'s $PaCO_2$ of 45 mm Hg suggests nearly normal respiratory compensation for metabolic alkalosis.

Causes

Diuretic-Induced

12. What is the most likely etiology for K.E.'s acid-base imbalance?

Common causes of metabolic alkalosis are listed in Table 27.6. The hypokalemic, hypochloremic, metabolic alkalosis in K.E. most likely is caused by diuretic abuse. The incidence of this adverse effect is influenced by the type, dose, and dosing regimen of the diuretic. K.E.'s diet and the condition for which therapy was initiated also will influence diuretic-induced metabolic alkalosis.

Diuretics cause metabolic alkalosis by the following mechanisms. First, they enhance excretion of sodium chloride and water, resulting in extracellular volume contraction. Volume contraction alone will cause only a modest increase in plasma bicarbonate; however, volume contraction also stimulates aldosterone release. Aldosterone increases distal tubular sodium reabsorption and induces hydrogen ion and potassium secretion, resulting in alkalosis and hypokalemia. In addition, hypokalemia induced by diuretics will stimulate intracellular movement of hydrogen ions to replace cellular potassium, producing extracellular alkalosis. Hypochloremia also is important in sustaining metabolic alkalosis. In a hypochloremic state, sodium will be reabsorbed, accompanied with bicarbonate generated by secreted hydrogen (see Figure 27.1).[40-43]

K.E. admits to chronic diuretic use. Her laboratory findings are typical of this situation: an elevated BUN:creatinine ratio consistent with volume contraction, elevated serum bicarbonate and pH, and elevated urine potassium concentration. Urine chloride concentration is elevated due to intake of salt tablets. These findings strongly suggest a diagnosis of diuretic-induced metabolic alkalosis.

Treatment

13. How should K.E.'s acid-base imbalance be corrected and monitored?

Treatment of alkalosis depends upon removing the cause; diuretic abuse in this case. K.E.'s history of diuretic abuse suggests that her alkalosis is of the saline-responsive type (see Table 27.6). The initial goal is to correct fluid deficits and replace chloride and potassium by infusing sodium and potassium chloride. As long as hypochloremia exists, renal bicarbonate excretion will not occur and the alkalosis will not be corrected.[43] The severity of alkalosis will dictate how rapidly fluid and electrolytes should be administered. In most situations, sodium and potassium chloride administration should suffice. In patients with hepatic or renal failure or congestive heart failure, infusion of large volumes of sodium and potassium salts may produce fluid overload or hyperkalemia. Thus, fluid and electrolyte replacement should proceed cautiously and these patients should be monitored closely for these complications.

Potassium chloride should be administered to correct K.E.'s hypokalemia. The amount of potassium required to replace total body stores is difficult to determine accurately since 98% of the potassium in the body is intracellular. Sterns et al. compiled the results of several studies and concluded that for each 0.27 mEq/L fall in serum potassium from a normal of 4.0 mEq/L, there is a 100 mEq decrease in the total body potassium stores.[44] K.E.'s serum potassium is 2.5 mEq/L, which correlates with a 550 mEq decrease in total body potassium stores (1.5 mEq/L × 100 mEq/0.27 mEq/L). K.E. should be treated with the chloride salt to ensure potassium retention and correction of alkalosis. Potassium replacement can be achieved over several days with supplements of 100 to 150 mEq/day given either orally in divided doses or as a constant IV infusion. K.E.'s laboratory tests for BUN, creatinine, chloride, sodium, and potassium should be monitored during sodium and potassium chloride therapy. Arterial blood gases also should be measured to monitor adequacy of replacement therapy. Hypercapnia should disappear after correction of alkalemia.

14. What other agents are available for the management of K.E.'s alkalosis if fluid and electrolyte replacement does not correct the arterial pH?

Hydrochloric Acid

In patients unresponsive to sodium and potassium chloride therapy or in those who develop complications of treatment, hydrochloric acid (HCl) or a hydrochloric acid precursor should be given. The dose of HCl required usually is estimated on the basis of chloride deficit using Equation 27.9:[45]

$$\text{Dose of HCl (mEq)} = 0.2 \times \text{Body Weight (kg)}$$
$$\times (103 - \text{Observed Chloride}) \qquad Eq\ 27.9$$

The factor, $0.2 \times$ body weight, represents the estimated chloride space. Hydrochloric acid typically is infused intravenously as a 0.1 to 0.2 N HCl solution in either 5% dextrose or normal saline.[45] The solution should be administered via central venous catheter in the superior vena cava to reduce the risk of extravasation and tissue damage. The initial rate should be 100 to 125 mL/hour (10 to 12.5 mEq/hour), with arterial blood gases monitored at least every four hours during the infusion. Most patients with severe metabolic alkalosis appear to be safely corrected over 6 to 24 hours of infusion. A parenteral preparation of hydrochloric acid is not available commercially. It usually is prepared extemporaneously by adding the appropriate amount of 1 N HCl to 5% dextrose or normal saline through a 0.22 micron filter.

Ammonium Chloride and Arginine Hydrochloride

Ammonium and arginine hydrochloride are hydrochloric acid precursors, which are metabolized to HCl and urea. The metabolism of ammonium chloride is shown in Equation 27.10.[46]

$$2\ NH_4Cl + CO_2 \Leftrightarrow CON_2H_4 + H_2O + 2HCl \qquad Eq\ 27.10$$

Ammonium chloride is available commercially as a 400 mEq/L solution for peripheral IV infusion. Ammonia intoxication with central nervous system (CNS) depression can occur with rapid infusion rates or in patients with liver disease in whom conversion of ammonia to urea is impaired. Ammonium chloride should not be infused at a rate greater than 20 gm ($\approx$400 mEq) in 24 hours. Arginine hydrochloride is another satisfactory preparation for treatment of metabolic alkalosis and is safe in patients with relative hepatic insufficiency. It is available as a 10% solution (R-Gene 10) containing 475 mEq/L of chloride. Arginine has been given at a rate of 10 gm/hour (100 mL/hour) intravenously for treatment of metabolic alkalosis. Patients with renal disease should not be treated with arginine, due to rapid intracellular potassium displacement resulting in dangerous hyperkalemia.[47] It is imperative that serum potassium concentrations be monitored during arginine administration.

Respiratory Acidosis

Respiratory acidosis occurs as a result of inadequate ventilation by the lungs. When the lungs do not excrete CO_2 effectively, the arterial partial pressure of carbon dioxide rises. This elevation in $PaCO_2$ causes a fall in pH (see Equations 27.3 and 27.5). Common causes of respiratory acidosis are listed in Table 27.7. They gen-

Table 27.6	Classification of Metabolic Alkalosis
Saline-Responsive	**Saline-Unresponsive**
Diuretic therapy	Normotensive
Extracellular volume contraction	Potassium depletion
	Hypercalcemia
Gastric acid loss	
Vomiting	
Nasogastric suction	Hypertensive
Exogenous alkali administration	Mineralocorticoids
	Hyperaldosteronism
	Hyperreninism
Blood transfusions	Licorice

Table 27.7	Common Causes of Respiratory Acidosis[a]
Airway Obstruction	**Cardiopulmonary**
Foreign body aspiration	Cardiac arrest
Asthma	Pulmonary edema or infiltration
COAD	Pulmonary embolism
Beta-adrenergic blockers	Pulmonary fibrosis
CNS Disturbances	**Neuromuscular**
Cerebral vascular accident	Amyotrophic lateral sclerosis
Sleep apnea	Guillain-Barre Syndrome
Tumor	Myasthenia gravis
CNS depressant drugs	Hypokalemia
Barbiturates	Hypophosphatemia
Benzodiazepines	Drugs
Opioids	Aminoglycosides
	Antiarrhythmics
	Lithium
	Phenytoin

[a] CNS = Central nervous system; COAD = Chronic obstructive airways disease.

erally can be categorized into conditions of airway obstruction, reduced stimulus for respiration from the central nervous system, failure of the heart or lungs, or disorders of the peripheral nerves or skeletal muscles required for ventilation.

Evaluation

15. B.B., a 56-year-old male, is admitted for treatment of exacerbation of chronic obstructive airway disease (COAD) and acute bronchitis. He complains of shortness of breath, mild headache, a flushed feeling, and drowsiness for 1 day. He has a history of COAD, hypertension, coronary artery disease, and low back pain. Current medications are metaproterenol (Alupent) inhaler 2 puffs Q 4–6 hr, propranolol (Inderal) 60 mg TID, and diazepam (Valium) 5 mg TID PRN for back pain. Vital signs include respiratory rate of 16 breaths/minute and heart rate of 90 beats/minute. Diffuse wheezes and rhonchi are heard on chest auscultation. ABGs are pH 7.34; PaO_2 56 mm Hg; $PaCO_2$ 58 mm Hg; and HCO_3^- 30 mEq/L. What signs and symptoms displayed by B.B. are consistent with the diagnosis of respiratory acidosis? [SI units: PaO_2 7.5 kPa; $PaCO_2$ 7.7 kPa; HCO_3^- 30 mmol/L]

Dyspnea (subjective shortness of breath), headache, drowsiness, and flushing are common in patients with respiratory acidosis. Respiratory acidosis also can cause more severe symptoms, including CNS effects such as disorientation, confusion, delirium, hallucinations, and coma. These CNS abnormalities probably are due in part to direct effects of carbon dioxide. Hypoxemia, which commonly accompanies respiratory acidosis, also contributes to these symptoms. Elevated arterial carbon dioxide tension causes cerebral vascular dilation, resulting in headache due to increased blood flow and increased intracranial pressure. Cardiovascular effects typically include tachycardia, arrhythmias, and peripheral vasodilation. B.B. is receiving propranolol which may mask some of these cardiovascular effects by blocking adrenergic β_1 and β_2 receptors.

16. Is the compensatory response to the respiratory acidosis present in B.B. consistent with an acute or a chronic disorder?

In respiratory acidosis, increased renal reabsorption of bicarbonate compensates for the increase in $PaCO_2$; however, at least 48 to 72 hours are needed for this compensatory mechanism to become fully established. In acute respiratory acidosis, the small increase in the serum bicarbonate concentration is due to titration of acid by other buffers (e.g., hemoglobin) that generate HCO_3^-. Acute compensation for B.B.'s $PaCO_2$ of 58 mm Hg would result in an increase in the serum concentration of bicarbonate of 1.8 mEq/L from a normal of 24 mEq/L to approximately 26 mEq/L. Chronic respiratory acidosis should be associated with a serum

bicarbonate concentration of 31 mEq/L (see Table 27.2).[1–3,12,13] Therefore, B.B. appears to have chronic respiratory acidosis.

Causes

17. What potential causes of respiratory acidosis are present in B.B.?

Respiratory acidosis frequently is caused by airway obstruction, as shown in Table 27.7.[2,3,12,14] Chronic obstructive airway disease is a common cause of both acute and chronic respiratory acidosis. Upper respiratory tract infections, such as acute bronchitis, can worsen airway obstruction and produce acute respiratory acidosis.

Drug-Induced

In addition, B.B.'s drug therapy may be contributing to respiratory insufficiency. Many drugs (see Table 27.7) decrease ventilation, but usually these drugs only significantly affect patients who are predisposed to respiratory problems because of underlying diseases. B.B. has COAD; therefore, he may be more sensitive to drugs affecting respiration. The benzodiazepines, barbiturates, and opioids minimally decrease respiration in normal subjects and most patients with COAD when given usual therapeutic doses.[48–56] However, these drugs can cause significant respiratory insufficiency when administered either in large doses or in combination with other respiratory depressant drugs. B.B.'s diazepam may be contributing to hypoventilation and respiratory acidosis and should be discontinued.

Beta-adrenergic blocking drugs, such as propranolol, may inhibit the bronchodilatory effects of catecholamines and are associated with respiratory insufficiency in patients with asthma or COAD.[57,58] Patients who are free from these diseases rarely experience significant airway obstruction with beta blockers. B.B.'s propranolol should be discontinued. If another class of antianginal and antihypertensive medicine (e.g., calcium channel blockers) cannot be substituted for the propranolol, low doses of a cardio-selective beta blocker such as metoprolol (Lopressor) or atenolol (Tenormin) would be preferable to a nonselective beta blocker such as propranolol.

Other drugs (e.g., aminoglycoside antibiotics, tetracyclines, quinidine, procainamide, beta-adrenergic blockers, penicillamine, lithium, phenytoin) may interfere with respiratory function by blocking neuromuscular transmission and weakening the muscles of respiration.[59] This adverse effect is of importance almost exclusively in patients with diseases involving neuromuscular transmission (e.g., myasthenia gravis), patients recovering from general anesthesia, or patients treated with muscle relaxants (e.g., succinylcholine) during surgery.

Treatment

18. How should B.B.'s respiratory acidosis be treated?

As with most cases of respiratory acidosis, treatment primarily involves correction of the underlying cause of respiratory insufficiency. In this case, treatment of acute bronchospasm with a beta-adrenergic agent such as inhaled metaproterenol (Alupent) and antibiotic treatment for a possible acute bacterial infection are appropriate. Administration of supplemental oxygen should be initiated. If the acidosis and associated hypoxemia progress, more severe effects such as mental status impairment, frequent cardiac arrhythmias, or seizures may be produced. If any of these occur, mechanical ventilation may be required.

Treatment with IV sodium bicarbonate is not recommended in most cases of acute respiratory acidosis, because of the risks associated with bicarbonate therapy (see Question 10) and because an absolute deficiency of bicarbonate is not present. When the excess CO_2 is excreted, arterial pH should return to normal.[60]

Doxapram

Rarely in patients with respiratory failure and acidosis, respiratory stimulants such as doxapram (Dopram) may be used to acutely lower $PaCO_2$ and lessen acidosis.[61,62] Doxapram increases the work of breathing and may cause significant adverse effects (e.g., hypertension, tachycardia, anxiety, involuntary movements). Therefore, it should be reserved for patients who are unresponsive to other measures including mechanical ventilation.

Progesterones

The respiratory stimulant effects of progesterone derivatives also have been studied in the treatment of respiratory insufficiency.[63-66] Administration of medroxyprogesterone acetate (Provera) 20 mg orally three times a day appears to be effective in improving chronic respiratory acidosis caused by CNS-mediated hypoventilation. However, in obstructive lung disease, such as COAD, progesterone derivatives are of little benefit.

Respiratory Alkalosis

Respiratory alkalosis usually is not a severe disorder. Excessive rate or depth of respiration results in increased excretion of CO_2, a fall in arterial partial pressure of carbon dioxide, and a rise in pH. Common causes of respiratory alkalosis are presented in Table 27.8. Many conditions can cause respiratory alkalosis by stimulating respiratory drive in the central nervous system. In addition, pulmonary diseases can stimulate receptors in the lung to increase ventilation, and this can cause respiratory alkalosis. Conditions which decrease oxygen delivery to tissues also can stimulate ventilation, causing respiratory alkalosis.

Evaluation

19. S.P., a 35-year-old, 60 kg female, is admitted for treatment of presumed bacterial pneumonia. She was in good health until 24 hours before presentation when she noted a fever, onset of a productive cough with thick, yellowish sputum, and chest pain on deep inspiration. She has taken aspirin 650 mg Q 4 hr since the onset of fever, with mild relief. Since arriving in the ER, she has become anxious and lightheaded and has developed tingling in her hands, feet, and lips. Vital signs are temperature 38 °C, respiratory rate 24 breaths/minute, heart rate 110 beats/minute, and BP 135/70 mm Hg. Physical examination reveals dullness to percussion, rales, and decreased breath sounds over the left lower lung field. Laboratory findings include a Gram's stain of sputum which reveals 25 white blood cells (WBCs) per high power field and many gram-positive diplococci. WBC count is 15,400 cells/mm³ (Normal: 3500–10,500) with a left shift. ABGs are pH 7.49; PaO₂ 90 mm Hg; PaCO₂ 30 mm Hg; and HCO₃⁻ 22 mEq/L. A left lower lobe infiltrate is seen on the chest radiograph. What acid-base disorder is present in S.P.? [SI units: PaO₂ 12.0 kPa; PaCO₂ 4.0 kPa; HCO₃⁻ 22 mmol/L]

Examination of the arterial pH reveals an alkalosis that could be due either to a primary respiratory disorder (with decreased $PaCO_2$) or a primary metabolic disorder (with increased HCO_3^-). S.P. has a respiratory alkalosis because her arterial carbon dioxide tension is decreased ($PaCO_2$ 30 mm Hg) and her serum bicarbonate value is not increased. According to the criteria for renal compensation in Table 27.2, S.P. has an acute respiratory alkalosis rather than chronic respiratory alkalosis. Renal compensation for hypocapnia requires 6 to 12 hours to be initiated and 36 to 48 hours to become maximal.

20. What signs and symptoms in S.P. are consistent with the diagnosis of an acute respiratory alkalosis?

Respiratory alkalosis typically produces paresthesias of the extremities and perioral region, lightheadedness, confusion, decreased mental acuity, and tachycardia.[3,12,67,68] Increased rate and depth of respiration may be evident. Simple respiratory alkalosis rarely produces life-threatening abnormalities.

Causes

21. What is the etiology of the acid-base disorder in S.P.?

Common causes of respiratory alkalosis are listed in Table 27.8.[3,12,68-70] Based upon physical examination, laboratory findings, and chest film, S.P. appears to have an acute bacterial pneumonia. Pneumonia and other pulmonary diseases can result in stimulation of ventilation and respiratory alkalosis, even in the presence of a normal PaO_2, as in this case. The anxiety S.P. is experiencing also may be contributing to respiratory alkalosis by producing the familiar anxiety-hyperventilation syndrome. Although salicylate intoxication is a potential cause of respiratory alkalosis due to the direct respiratory stimulant effect of salicylate,[71] S.P. displays few other symptoms of salicylate intoxication (e.g., nausea, vomiting, tinnitus, altered mental status, metabolic acidosis). The total aspirin dose reportedly ingested (65 mg/kg over 24 hours) is not large enough to be associated with significant risk for toxicity.[72] Therefore, salicylate intoxication is not likely to be the cause of S.P.'s respiratory alkalosis.

Treatment

22. What is the appropriate treatment for S.P.'s respiratory alkalosis?

Like respiratory acidosis, treatment of respiratory alkalosis usually involves correcting the underlying disorder. Initiation of appropriate antibiotic therapy is indicated in this case. Simple respiratory alkalosis is unlikely to cause life-threatening symptoms, although mortality for critically ill patients with this disorder can be very high.[73] The well-known remedy of rebreathing expired air from a paper bag for treatment of hyperventilation associated with anxiety appears to be effective for this cause of respiratory alkalosis and may be helpful for S.P.

Mixed Acid-Base Disorders

Evaluation

23. B.L., a 55-year-old male, was transferred from a nursing home 2 days previously with disorientation and lethargy. He was doing well until 1 week before admission, when the staff noted that he was somnolent. He progressively became more lethargic and could no longer remember the names of other persons. B.L. has a history of alcoholic cirrhosis, noninsulin-dependent diabetes mellitus, and hypertension. Medications before admission were metoprolol (Lopressor) 50 mg BID, tol-

Table 27.8	Common Causes of Respiratory Alkalosis[a]
CNS Disturbances	**Pulmonary**
Bacterial septicemia	Pneumonia
Cerebrovascular accident	Pulmonary edema
Fever	Pulmonary embolus
Hepatic cirrhosis	
Hyperventilation	**Tissue Hypoxia**
Anxiety-induced	High altitude
Voluntary	Hypotension
Meningitis	CHF
Pregnancy	
Trauma	**Other**
Drugs	Excessive mechanical ventilation
progesterone derivatives	Rapid correction of metabolic acidosis
respiratory stimulants	
salicylate overdose	

[a] CNS = Central nervous system; CHF = Congestive heart failure.

azamide (Tolinase) 250 mg BID, and spironolactone (Aldactone) 100 mg BID. Upon admission, B.L. was disoriented to person, place, and time, and difficult to arouse. Vital signs were temperature 37 °C, respirations 16 breaths/minute, heart rate 70 beats/minute, and BP 154/92 mm Hg. Physical examination revealed asterixis and ascites. Laboratory studies included Na 134 mEq/L; K 4.6 mEq/L; Cl 105 mEq/L; total CO_2 20 mEq/L; BUN 5 mg/dL; creatinine 0.7 mg/dL; and fasting glucose 150 mg/dL. ABGs were pH 7.43; $PaCO_2$ 30 mm Hg; PaO_2 90 mm Hg; and HCO_3^- 19 mEq/L. Upon admission, spironolactone was increased to 100 mg QID, and lactulose 60 mL PO QID was started for treatment of hepatic encephalopathy. Over the past 48 hours, B.L. has lost 4 kg of body weight and has developed diarrhea, his mental status has worsened, and his BP has fallen to 110/60 mm Hg. Current laboratory values are Na 136 mEq/L; K 4.8 mEq/L; Cl 110 mEq/L; total CO_2 10 mEq/L; BUN 20 mg/dL; creatinine 1.5 mg/dL; arterial pH 7.32; $PaCO_2$ 18 mm Hg; PaO_2 88 mm Hg; and HCO_3^- 9 mEq/L. Gram's stain of peritoneal fluid reveals many WBCs and gram-negative rods; the diagnosis of spontaneous bacterial peritonitis with possible septicemia is made.

Describe B.L.'s acid-base status upon admission and at the current time. [SI units: Na 134 and 136 mmol/L; K 4.6 and 4.8 mmol/L; Cl 105 and 110 mmol/L; total CO_2 20 and 10 mmol/L; BUN 1.8 and 7.1 mmol/L; creatinine 62 and 133 μmol/L; fasting glucose 8.3 mmol/L; $PaCO_2$ 4.0 and 2.5 kPa; PaO_2 12.0 and 11.7 kPa; HCO_3^- 19 and 9 mmol/L]

Although B.L.'s arterial pH was in the normal range upon admission, inspection of the $PaCO_2$ and serum bicarbonate reveals an acid-base abnormality. The direction of change of $PaCO_2$ and serum HCO_3^- is consistent with either a respiratory alkalosis with renal compensation or a metabolic acidosis with respiratory compensation. Examination of the ranges of expected compensation in Table 27.2 reveals that these values are consistent with chronic respiratory alkalosis. If this was a primary metabolic acidosis, a smaller decrease in $PaCO_2$ as compensation would be expected, and the pH would not be returned to the normal range. B.L.'s history of alcohol-induced liver disease is consistent with the diagnosis of chronic respiratory alkalosis (see Table 27.8).[74]

The second set of ABGs reflects addition of acid to the arterial blood. Because both serum bicarbonate and $PaCO_2$ have fallen, it appears that metabolic acidosis now is combined with the pre-existing respiratory alkalosis. Even if respiratory alkalosis had not been recognized previously, a fall in $PaCO_2$ of this magnitude is slightly greater than would be expected for respiratory compensation of simple metabolic acidosis (see Table 27.2).

Causes

24. What are possible etiologies for metabolic acidosis in B.L.?

The anion gap has increased from 9 to 16 (see Equation 27.6), suggesting that an elevated anion gap acidosis is present. However, the HCO_3^- has fallen by an even greater amount and the serum chloride is elevated. Therefore, more than one factor could be con-

tributing to the acidosis. Septicemia from bacterial peritonitis could cause an elevated anion gap acidosis. Intravascular volume depletion caused by the increased dose of spironolactone can produce hypotension, tissue hypoperfusion, and Type A lactic acidosis with increased anion gap. Spironolactone can cause hyperchloremic metabolic acidosis by blocking distal tubular H^+ secretion in the kidneys.[75] Hyperchloremic metabolic acidosis due to loss of bicarbonate from the gastrointestinal tract is a common acid-base disorder in patients with diarrhea. The laxative effect of lactulose used to treat B.L.'s hepatic encephalopathy also may be contributing to metabolic acidosis (see Tables 27.4 and 27.5).

Treatment

25. How should B.L.'s acid-base disorder be treated?

Antibiotic therapy for possible gram-negative sepsis should be initiated, and intravascular volume should be repleted with IV fluids. Lactulose should be discontinued until diarrhea subsides and then restarted at a lower dose. Spironolactone should be discontinued until intravascular volume is replaced. While specific therapy for metabolic acidosis with sodium bicarbonate is not needed at this time, B.L. should be monitored closely with repeated ABG determinations. Further decreases in serum bicarbonate will be associated with significant acidosis. For example, a decrease in HCO_3^- to 4 mEq/L will result in maximal respiratory compensation and a pH of approximately 7.11. If arterial pH falls below 7.20 to 7.25, or if cardiovascular or hemodynamic compromise develops, sodium bicarbonate administration should be considered (see Question 9).

26. Over the next 72 hours, B.L.'s hepatic encephalopathy and acid-base disorder are treated effectively. Despite antimicrobial treatment for peritonitis, he develops a presumed bacterial pneumonia and requires mechanical ventilation due to hypoxemia. At the time of intubation, his ABGs were pH 7.35; $PaCO_2$ 35 mm Hg; PaO_2 45 mm Hg; and HCO_3^- 24 mEq/L. Current ABGs, 12 hours later, are pH 7.60; $PaCO_2$ 25 mm Hg; PaO_2 90 mm Hg; HCO_3^- 24 mEq/L. Ventilator settings are assist-control at 16 breaths/min, tidal volume 700 mL, and inspired oxygen concentration 60%. B.L. is noted to be anxious and initiating 25 to 30 breaths/min. Describe the current acid-base status and probable etiology. [SI units: $PaCO_2$ 4.7 and 3.3 kPa; PaO_2 6.0 and 12.0 kPa; HCO_3^- 24 mmol/L]

Evaluation of the ABGs reveals an alkalemic state. The reduced $PaCO_2$ and normal bicarbonate concentration confirm an uncompensated respiratory alkalosis. In this case, respiratory alkalosis is caused by the mechanical ventilator and B.L.'s anxiety. In the assist-control mode, any inspiratory effort by B.L. results in delivery of a full assisted breath by the ventilator.[76] B.L.'s anxiety and resultant tachypnea are stimulating the ventilator to hyperventilate him, producing excessive CO_2 excretion and respiratory alkalosis. Appropriate changes in therapy include use of an anxiolytic agent, such as a benzodiazepine, changing the ventilator mode to intermittent mandatory ventilation, or both.

References

1 **Andreoli TE.** Disorders of fluid volume, electrolyte, and acid-base balance. In: Wyngarrden JB et al., eds. Cecil Textbook of Medicine. Philadelphia: WB Saunders; 1992:499.

2 **Arieff AI, DeFranzo JRA, eds.** Fluid, Electrolyte, and Acid-Base Disorders. New York: Churchill Livingstone; 1985.

3 **Cohen JJ, Kassirer JP.** Acid-Base. Boston: Little, Brown; 1982.

4 **Goodman AD et al.** Production, ex-

cretion, and net balance of fixed acid in patients with renal acidosis. J Clin Invest. 1965;44:495.

5 **Tisi GM.** Pulmonary Physiology in Clinical Medicine. Baltimore: Williams & Wilkins; 1983.

6 **Berger AJ et al.** Respiratory recovery from CO_2 breathing in intact and chemodenervated awake dogs. J Appl Physiol. 1973;35:35.

7 **Gelfand R et al.** Dynamic respiratory

response to abrupt change of inspired CO_2 at normal and high PO_2. J Appl Physiol. 1973;35:903.

8 **Berger AJ et al.** Regulation of respiration. N Engl J Med. 1977;297:92, 138,194.

9 **Gilbert R.** Spirometry and blood gases. In: Henry JB et al., eds. Clinical Diagnosis and Management by Laboratory Methods. Philadelphia: WB Saunders; 1991:103.

10 **Preuss HG et al.** Evaluation of renal function, and water, electrolyte, and acid-base balance. In: Henry JB et al., eds. Clinical Diagnosis and Management by Laboratory Methods. Philadelphia: WB Saunders; 1991:119.

11 **Shapiro JI, Kaehny WD.** Pathogenesis and management of metabolic acidosis and alkalosis. In: Schrier RW, ed. Renal and Electrolyte Disorders. Boston: Little, Brown; 1992:161.

12 **Kaehny WD.** Pathogenesis and management of respiratory and mixed acid-base disorders. In: Schrier RW, ed. Renal and Electrolyte Disorders. Boston: Little, Brown; 1992:211.

13 **Narins RG, Emmett M.** Simple and mixed acid-base disorders: a practical approach. Medicine (Baltimore). 1980; 59:161.

14 **Rose BD.** Clinical Physiology of Acid-Base and Electrolyte Disorders. New York, NY: McGraw-Hill; 1994.

15 **Emmerson B.** Metals and the kidney. In: Black D, ed. Renal Disease. Oxford: Blackwell Scientific; 1967:561.

16 **Boton R et al.** Prevalence, pathogens, and treatment of renal dysfunction associated with chronic lithium therapy. Am J Kidney Dis. 1987;10:329.

17 **Finn NT et al.** Acidifying defect induced by amphotericin B: comparison of bicarbonate and hydrogen ion permeabilities. Kidney Int. 1977;11:261.

18 **Narins RG, Goldberg M.** Renal tubular acidosis: pathophysiology, diagnosis, and treatment. Dis Mon. 1977; 13(6):1.

19 **Sebastian A et al.** Renal potassium wasting in renal tubular acidosis (RTA): its occurrence in types 1 and 2 RTA despite sustained correction of systemic acidosis. J Clin Invest. 1971;50:667.

20 **Morris RC et al.** Renal acidosis? Kidney Int. 1971;1:322.

21 **McSherry E et al.** Renal tubular acidosis in infants: the several kinds, including bicarbonate-wasting classical renal tubular acidosis. J Clin Invest. 1971;51:499.

22 **Quintanilla AP.** Renal tubular acidosis, mechanism and management. Postgrad Med. 1980;67:60.

23 **Gill JR et al.** Correction of renal sodium loss and secondary aldosteronism in renal tubular acidosis with bicarbonate loading. Clin Res. 1961;9:201.

24 **Gabow PA.** Disorders associated with an anion gap. Kidney Int. 1985;27:472.

25 **Gabow PA et al.** Diagnostic importance of an increased serum anion gap. N Engl J Med. 1980;303:854.

26 **Emmett M, Narins RG.** Clinical use of the anion gap. Medicine (Baltimore). 1977;56:38.

27 **Jacobsen D et al.** Anion and osmolal gaps in the diagnosis of methanol and ethylene glycol poisoning. Acta Med Scand. 1982;212:17.

28 **Smithline N, Garner DK.** Gaps—anionic and osmolal. JAMA. 1976;236: 1594.

29 **Smith SR et al.** Combined formate and lactic acidosis in methanol poisoning. Lancet. 1981;2:1295.

30 **Cohen RD, Woods HF.** Clinical and Biochemical Aspects of Lactic Acidosis. London: Blackwell Scientific; 1976.

31 **Madias NE.** Lactic acidosis. Kidney Int. 1986;29:752.

32 **McCoy HG et al.** Severe methanol poisoning: application of a pharmacokinetic model for ethanol therapy and hemodialysis. Am J Med. 1979;67:804.

33 **Brown CG et al.** Ethylene glycol poisoning. Ann Emerg Med. 1983;12:501.

34 **Pappas S, Silverman N.** Treatment of methanol poisoning with ethanol and hemodialysis. Can Med Assoc J. 1982; 126:1391.

35 **Cooper DJ et al.** Bicarbonate does not improve hemodynamics in critically ill patients who have lactic acidosis: a prospective, controlled clinical study. Ann Intern Med. 1990;112:492.

36 **Bersin RM et al.** Metabolic and hemodynamic consequences of sodium bicarbonate administration in patients with heart disease. Am J Med. 1989; 87:7.

37 **Hindman BJ.** Sodium bicarbonate in the treatment of subtypes of acute lactic acidosis: physiologic considerations. Anesthesiology. 1990;72:1064.

38 **Adrogue HJ et al.** Assessing acid-base status in circulatory failure: differences between arterial and central venous blood. N Engl J Med. 1989;320:1312.

39 **Von Planta M et al.** Pathophysiologic and therapeutic implications of acid-base changes during CPR. Ann Emerg Med. 1993;22:404.

40 **Hulter HN et al.** K deprivation potentiates the renal acid excretory effect of mineralocorticoids obliteration by amiloride. Am J Physiol. 1979;236:F48.

41 **Sabatine S, Kurtzman NA.** The maintenance of metabolic alkalosis: factors which decrease bicarbonate excretion. Kidney Int. 1984;25:357.

42 **Jacobson HR, Seldin DW.** On the generation, maintenance, and correction of metabolic alkalosis. Am J Physiol. 1983;245:F425.

43 **Kassirer JP et al.** The critical role of chloride in the correction of hypokalemic alkalosis in man. Am J Med. 1965;38:172.

44 **Sterns RH et al.** Internal potassium balance and the control of the plasma potassium concentration. Medicine (Baltimore). 1981;60:339.

45 **Harken AH et al.** Hydrochloric acid in the correction of metabolic alkalosis. Arch Surg. 1975;110:819.

46 **Martin WJ, Matzke GR.** Treating severe metabolic alkalosis. Clin Pharmacy. 1982;1:42.

47 **Bushinsky DA, Gennari FJ.** Life-threatening hyperkalemia induced by arginine. Ann Intern Med. 1978;89: 632.

48 **Gilman AG et al., eds.** The Pharmacological Basis of Therapeutics. New York: Macmillan; 1990.

49 **Loeschcke HH et al.** The effect of morphine and of meperidine (dolantin, demerol) upon the respiratory response of normal men to low concentrations of inspired carbon dioxide. J Pharmacol Exp Ther. 1953;108:376.

50 **Weil JV et al.** Diminished ventilatory response to hypoxia and hypercapnia after morphine in normal man. N Engl J Med. 1975;292:1103.

51 **Santiago TV et al.** Respiratory consequences of methadone: the response to added resistance to breathing. Am Rev Respir Dis. 1980;122:623.

52 **Dalen JE et al.** The hemodynamic and respiratory effects of diazepam (Valium). Anesthesiology. 1969;30:259.

53 **Lakshminarayan S et al.** Effect of diazepam on ventilatory responses. Clin Pharmacol Ther. 1976;20:178.

54 **Man GCW et al.** Effect of alprazolam on exercise and dyspnea in patients with chronic obstructive pulmonary disease. Chest. 1986;90:832.

55 **Midgren B et al.** The effects of nitrazepam and flunitrazepam on oxygen desaturation during sleep in patients with stable hypoxemic nonhypercapnic COPD. Chest. 1989;95:765.

56 **Jedeikin R et al.** Prolonged respiratory center depression after alcohol and benzodiazepines. Chest. 1985;87:262.

57 **Singh BN et al.** Effects of cardioselective beta adrenoceptor blockade on specific airways resistance in normal subjects and in patients with bronchial asthma. Clin Pharmacol Ther. 1976;19: 493.

58 **Skinner C et al.** Comparison of effects of metoprolol and propranolol on asthmatic airway obstruction. Br Med J (Clin Res). 1976;1:504.

59 **Argov Z, Mastaglia FL.** Disorders of neuromuscular transmission caused by drugs. N Engl J Med. 1979;301:409.

60 **Weinberger SE et al.** Hypercapnia. N Engl J Med. 1989;321:1223.

61 **Edwards G, Leszczynski SO.** A double-blind trial of five respiratory stimulants in patients in acute ventilatory failure. Lancet. 1976;2:226.

62 **Moser KM et al.** Respiratory stimulation with intravenous doxapram in respiratory failure: a double-blind cooperative study. N Engl J Med. 1973; 288:427.

63 **Sutton FD Jr et al.** Progesterone for outpatient treatment of pickwickian syndrome. Ann Intern Med. 1975;83: 476.

64 **Orr WC et al.** Progesterone therapy in obese patients with sleep apnea. Arch Intern Med. 1979;139:109.

65 **Skatrud JB et al.** Determinants of chronic carbon dioxide retention and its correction in humans. J Clin Invest. 1980;65:813.

66 **Dolly FR, Block AJ.** Medroxyprogesterone acetate and COPD: effect on breathing and oxygenation in sleeping and awake patients. Chest. 1983;84: 394.

67 **Saltzman HA et al.** Correlation of clinical and physiologic manifestations of sustained hyperventilation. N Engl J Med. 1963;268:1431.

68 **Laski ME, Kurtzman NA.** Acid-base disturbances in pulmonary medicine. In: Arieff AI, Defronzo RA, eds. Fluid, Electrolyte, and Acid-Base Disorders. New York: Churchill Livingstone; 1985:385.

69 **Szucs MM Jr et al.** Diagnostic sensitivity of laboratory findings in acute pulmonary embolism. Ann Intern Med. 1971;74:161.

70 **Winslow EJ et al.** Hemodynamic studies and results of therapy in 50 patients with bacteremic shock. Am J Med. 1973;54:421.

71 **Temple AR.** Pathophysiology of aspirin overdosage toxicity, with implications for management. JAMA. 1965; 193:555.

72 **Dreisbach RH, Robertson WO.** Handbook of Poisoning: Prevention, Diagnosis, and Treatment. Norwalk, CT: Appleton and Lange; 1987.

73 **Mazzara JT.** Extreme hypocapnia in the critically ill patient. Am J Med. 1974;56:450.

74 **Prytz H, Thomsen AC.** Acid-base status in liver cirrhosis: disturbances in stable, terminal, and portacaval shunted patients. Scand J Gastroenterol. 1976;11:249.

75 **Gabow PA et al.** Spironolactone-induced hyperchloremic acidosis in cirrhosis. Ann Intern Med. 1979;90:338.

76 **Barbarash RA et al.** Mechanical ventilation. DICP Ann Pharmacother. 1990;24:959.

Fluid and Electrolyte Disorders

Ignatius Tang
Alan H Lau

Basic Principles 28-1
  Body Water Compartments 28-1
  Plasma Osmolality 28-2
  Tubular Function of Nephron (Figure 28.1) ... 28-2
  Osmoregulation 28-4
  Volume Regulation 28-4
Disorders in Volume Regulation 28-4
  Sodium Depletion 28-4
  Sodium Excess 28-5
Disorders in Osmoregulation 28-6
  Hyponatremia 28-6
  Hypotonic Hyponatremia with Decreased
    Extracellular Fluid 28-6
  Hypervolemic Hypotonic Hyponatremia 28-7
  Normovolemic Hypotonic Hyponatremia 28-8
  Neurologic Manifestations 28-8
  Brain Adaptation to Hyponatremia 28-9
  Rate of Correction of Hyponatremia 28-9
  Chronic Management of the Syndrome of Inappropriate
    Antidiuretic Hormone Secretion (SIADH) 28-9
  Hypernatremia 28-10
Clinical Use of Diuretics 28-10
  Loop Diuretics 28-10
  Thiazide Diuretics 28-10
  Potassium-Sparing Diuretics 28-10
    Spironolactone 28-10
    Triamterene 28-11
    Amiloride 28-11
  Acetazolamide 28-11
  Osmotic Diuretics 28-11
  Methylxanthines 28-11
  Complications of Diuretic Therapy 28-11
    Volume depletion 28-11
    Hypokalemia 28-11
    Hyperuricemia 28-13
    Hyperlipidemia 28-13
    Hypercalcemia and calciuria 28-13
    Hypomagnesemia 28-13
    Hyponatremia 28-13
    Metabolic alkalosis and acidosis 28-13
    Hyperglycemia 28-14
  Diuretic Resistance (See Table 28.1) 28-14
    Sodium intake 28-14
    Volume depletion 28-14
    Reduced or delayed intestinal diuretic absorption ... 28-14
    Renal failure 28-14
    Nephrotic syndrome 28-15

  Hepatic cirrhosis 28-15
  Hypoalbuminemia 28-15
  Congestive heart failure (CHF) 28-15
Potassium 28-15
  Homeostasis 28-15
  Hypokalemia 28-16
    Etiology 28-16
    Clinical manifestations 28-17
    Treatment 28-17
  Hyperkalemia 28-18
    Etiology 28-18
    Clinical manifestations 28-18
    Treatment 28-18
Calcium 28-19
  Homeostasis 28-19
  Hypercalcemia 28-20
    Etiology 28-20
      Malignancy 28-20
      Hyperparathyroidism 28-20
    Clinical manifestations 28-21
    Treatment 28-21
      Hydration and diuresis 28-21
      Calcitonin 28-21
      Plicamycin 28-22
      Biphosphonates 28-22
        Etidronate 28-22
        Pamidronate 28-22
      Gallium nitrate 28-22
      Phosphate 28-23
      Corticosteroids 28-23
      Prostaglandin inhibitors 28-23
Phosphorus 28-23
  Homeostasis 28-23
  Hypophosphatemia 28-23
    Etiology 28-23
    Clinical manifestations 28-24
    Treatment (See Table 28.2) 28-24
Magnesium 28-25
  Homeostasis 28-25
  Hypomagnesemia 28-26
    Etiology 28-26
    Clinical manifestations 28-26
    Treatment 28-26
  Hypermagnesemia 28-27
    Etiology 28-27
    Clinical manifestations 28-27
    Treatment 28-27

Basic Principles

Body Water Compartments

Body water constitutes 50% to 60% of lean body weight (LBW) in men but only 45% to 55% in women because of their greater proportion of adipose tissue.[1,2] The water content per kilogram of body weight also decreases with age.[1-3] In newborns, about 75% to 85% of body weight is water.[2] After puberty, the percentage of water per kilogram of weight decreases as the amount of adipose tissue increases with age.[1,2]

Two-thirds of the total body water resides in the cells (intracellular water).[2] The extracellular water can be divided into different compartments: the interstitial fluid (12% LBW) and the plasma (5% LBW) being the two major compartments.[1,2] Other compartments of the extracellular fluid include the connective tissues and bone water, the transcellular fluids (e.g., glandular secretions), and other fluids in sequestered spaces, such as the cerebrospinal fluid.[1,2]

The electrolyte composition differs between the intracellular and extracellular compartments.[2] Potassium (K), magnesium (Mg), and phosphate (PO_4) are the major ions in the intracellular compartment while sodium (Na), chloride (Cl), and bicarbonate (HCO_3^-) are predominant in the extracellular space.[2,4] Water travels freely across cell membranes of most parts of the body.[4,5] The cell membrane, however, is only selectively permeable to solutes. The impermeant solutes are osmotically active.[4,5] They exert an osmotic pressure that dictates the distribution of water between fluid compartments. Water moves across the cell membrane from a region of low osmolality to one of high osmolality. Net water movement ceases when osmotic equilibrium occurs. Each fluid compartment contains a major osmotically active solute: potassium in the intracellular space and sodium in the extracellular fluid.[4–6] The volumes of the two compartments reflect the asymmetrically larger number of solute particles or osmoles inside the cells.

The interstitial fluid and the plasma are separated by the capillary wall.[4,5] Since sodium moves freely across the capillary wall and achieves similar concentrations in both compartments, no osmotic gradient is generated and water distribution between these two water spaces is not affected.[4,6] Plasma proteins, which are confined in the vascular space, are the osmoles that affect the distribution between the interstitium and the plasma.[4] Urea, which traverses both the capillary walls and most cell membranes, is osmotically inactive.

Plasma Osmolality

Osmolality is defined as the number of particles per kilogram of water (mOsm/kg).[6] It is determined by the number of particles in solution and not by particle size or valence. Nondissociable solutes, such as glucose and albumin, generate 1 mOsm/mmol of particles, and dissociable salts, such as sodium chloride, which liberates two ions in solution, produce 2 mOsm/mmol of salt.[6] The osmolality of body fluid is maintained between 280 and 295 mOsm/kg. Since all body fluid compartments are iso-osmotic, plasma osmolality reflects the osmolality of total body water.[4,6] Plasma osmolality can be measured by the freezing point depression method, or estimated by the following equation:

$$P_{OSM} = 2(Na)(mmol/L) + \frac{Glucose\ (mg/dL)}{18} + \frac{BUN\ (mg/dL)}{2.8}$$
Eq 28.1

This equation predicts the measured plasma osmolality within 5 to 10 mOsm/kg. Although urea contributes to the measured osmolality, it is an ineffective osmole because it readily traverses cell membranes and, therefore, does not cause significant fluid shifts within the body. Hence, the effective plasma osmolality, or tonicity, can be estimated by the following equation:

$$P_{OSM} = 2(Na)(mmol/L) + \frac{Glucose\ (mg/dL)}{18}$$
Eq 28.2

An osmolal gap exists when the measured and calculated values differ by more than 15 mOsm/kg;[7] and signifies the presence of unidentified osmoles. When the individual solute has been identified, its contribution to the measured osmolality can be estimated by dividing its concentration (mg/dL) by one-tenth of its molecular weight. Calculating the osmolal gap is useful in detecting the presence of substances such as ethanol, methanol, and ethylene glycol which have high osmolality. Occasionally, the osmolal gap also

can be due to an artificial decrease in the serum sodium resulting from severe hyperlipidemia or hyperproteinemia.

1. J.F., a 31-year-old male, is admitted to the inpatient medicine service for methanol (molecular weight = 32) intoxication. Routine laboratory analysis reveals: Na 145 mEq/L, K 3.4 mEq/L, Cl 105 mEq/L, carbon dioxide (CO_2) 20 mEq/L, blood urea nitrogen (BUN) 10 mg/dL, creatinine 1.1 mg/dL, and glucose 90 mg/dL. The blood methanol concentration was reported to be 108 mg/dL, and the measured plasma osmolality was 333 mOsm/kg. What is J.F.'s calculated osmolality? Are other unidentified osmoles present? [SI units: Na 135 mmol/L; K 3.4 mmol/L; Cl 105 mmol/L; CO_2 20 mmol/L; BUN 3.57 mmol/L; creatinine 97.4 μmol/L; glucose 5.0 mmol/L; methanol 33.7 mmol/L]

Using Equation 28.1, J.F.'s total calculated osmolality is:

$$P_{OSM} = 2(145\ mEq/L) + \frac{90\ mg/dL}{18} + \frac{10\ mg/dL}{2.8}$$

$$= 290 + 5 + 3.6$$

$$= 299\ mOsm/kg$$

$$Osmolal\ Gap = 333\ mOsm/kg - 299\ mOsm/kg$$

$$= 34\ mOsm/kg$$

In J.F., the entire osmolal gap can be accounted for by the presence of the methanol (since 108 mg/dL of methanol will provide 108/3.2 = 33.7 mOsm/kg). Therefore, it is unlikely that other unmeasured osmoles are present (e.g., ethylene glycol, isopropanol, and ethanol). The laboratory determination of osmolality measures the total number of osmotically active particles but not their permeability across cell membrane. Methanol increases plasma osmolality but not tonicity because the cell membrane is permeable to methanol. Therefore, there is no net water shift between the intracellular and extracellular compartments. Conversely, mannitol, which is confined to the extracellular space, contributes to both plasma osmolality and tonicity.

Tubular Function of Nephron

The kidney plays an important role in maintaining a constant extracellular environment by regulating the excretion of water and various electrolytes. The volume and composition of the fluid that is filtered across the glomerulus are modified as it passes through the tubule of the nephron.

The renal tubule is composed of a series of segments with heterogeneous structure and function: the proximal tubule, the medullary and cortical thick ascending limb of the loop of Henle, the distal convoluted tubule, and the cortical and medullary collecting duct[4] (see Figure 28.1). The mechanism for sodium reabsorption is different for each nephron segment, but generally is mediated by carrier proteins or channels located on the luminal membrane of the tubule cell.[4] The active reabsorption or secretion of other solutes is coupled to the sodium transport mechanism. The Na^+-K^+ adenosine triphosphatase (ATPase), situated at the basolateral side of the different tubule segments, actively pumps sodium out of the renal tubule cell in exchange for potassium in a 3:2 ratio. Hence, the intracellular sodium concentration is kept at a low level. The potassium that is pumped into the cell leaks back out through potassium channels in the basolateral membrane. The loss of potassium renders the cell interior electronegative. The low intracellular sodium concentration and a negative intracellular potential produce a favorable gradient for passive sodium entry into the cell across the luminal membrane.[4] The Na^+-K^+ ATPase also indirectly provides the energy for active sodium transport and the reabsorption and secretion of other solutes across the luminal membrane of the renal tubule. Most of the nonelectrolyte solutes in the filtrate are

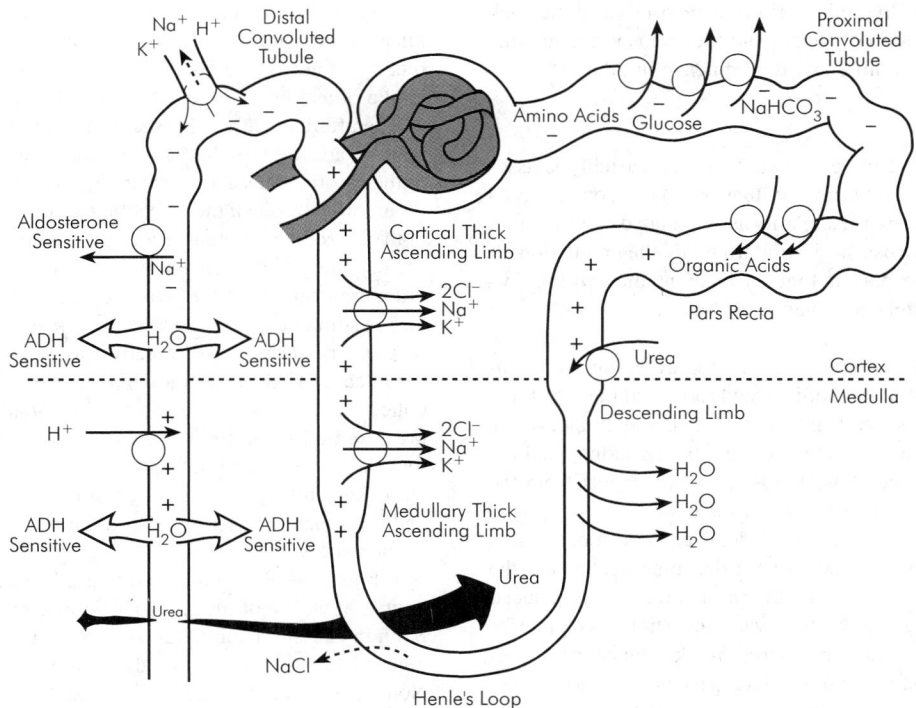

Fig 28.1 Sites of Tubule Salt and Water Absorption Sodium is reabsorbed with inorganic anions, amino acids, and glucose in the proximal tubule against an electrical gradient that is lumen-negative. In the late part of the proximal tubule (pars recta), sodium and water are reabsorbed to a lesser extent and organic acids (hippurate, urate) and urea are secreted into the urine. The electrical potential is lumen positive in the pars recta. Water, but not salt, is removed from tubule fluid in the thin descending limb of Henle's loop, but in the ascending portion salt is reabsorbed without water, rendering the tubule fluid hyposmotic with respect to the interstitium. Sodium, chloride, and potassium are reabsorbed by the medullary and cortical portions of the ascending limb; the lumen potential is positive. Sodium is reabsorbed and potassium and hydrogen ions are secreted in the distal tubule and collecting ducts. Water absorption in these segments is regulated by ADH. The electric potential is lumen negative in the cortical sections and positive in the medullary segments. Urea is concentrated in the interstitium of the medulla and assists in the generation of maximally concentrated urine. Reprinted with permission from reference 25.

reabsorbed in the proximal tubule by being coupled with sodium transport. The distal segments mainly are involved in the reabsorption of sodium and chloride ions and the secretion of hydrogen and potassium ions.

Iso-osmotic reabsorption of the glomerular filtrate occurs in the proximal tubule such that two-thirds of the sodium and water filtered and 90% of filtered bicarbonate are reabsorbed.[4,8] The Na^+-H^+ antiporter (exchanger) in the luminal membrane is instrumental in the reabsorption of sodium chloride, sodium bicarbonate, and water.[8] Most of the filtered organic and inorganic solutes such as glucose, amino acids, and phosphates are reabsorbed by being co-transported with sodium.

The thick ascending limb of the loop of Henle and the distal convoluted tubule of the nephron serve as the diluting segments of the nephron because they are impermeable to water and sodium chloride is extracted from the filtrate without water.[4,9] Sodium transport in both of these segments is flow dependent (i.e., it depends upon the amount of sodium ions delivered from the proximal segments of the nephron). Decreased sodium ions in the tubular fluid will limit sodium transport in the thick ascending limb of the loop of Henle and the distal convoluted tubule.[9]

The thick ascending limb of the loop of Henle accounts for approximately 25% of the total sodium reabsorption.[9] Active sodium transport is mediated by the Na^+-K^+-$2Cl^-$ carrier.[4,8] The leakage of reabsorbed potassium ions back into the tubular lumen, via potassium channels in the luminal membrane, makes the tubular lumen electropositive relative to the basolateral membrane.[4] This electrical gradient promotes the passive paracellular movement of cations such as sodium, calcium, and magnesium into the peritubular capillaries. In addition, by transporting sodium chloride

into the medullary interstitium and being impermeable to water, the medullary portion of the thick ascending limb of the loop of Henle plays a pivotal role in providing the osmolality required to move water from the lumen of the medullary collecting duct into the interstitium in the presence of vasopressin.[9] Therefore, the thick ascending limb of the loop of Henle is important for both urinary concentration and dilution.

The osmolality of the filtrate is reduced further as it flows through the distal convoluted tubule which accounts for 5% of sodium reabsorption.[4] Sodium entry is mediated by the Na^+-Cl^- carrier. The distal convoluted tubule also is an important site for the active regulation of calcium reabsorption.[4,10]

Sodium is transported into the principal cells of the collecting duct which is the site for sodium excretion and potassium secretion.[10] Sodium ions enter the principal cell through transport channels in the luminal membrane. Hence, the tubule lumen becomes electronegative. The luminal electronegativity promotes potassium secretion into the lumen via potassium channels.[4,10] Aldosterone enhances sodium reabsorption in the collecting duct by increasing the number of opened sodium channels.[10] Atrial natriuretic peptide (ANP) and urodilatin[12] inhibit sodium transport in the inner medullary collecting duct by generating cyclic GMP to close luminal sodium channels.[10,13]

The collecting duct usually is impermeable to water. Arginine vasopressin, also known as antidiuretic hormone (ADH), increases water permeability by increasing the number of water channels along the luminal membrane of the collecting duct.[4,10] The amount of water reabsorbed depends upon the tonicity of the medullary interstitium.[10] The latter affects water movement from tubular lumen into the medullary interstitium. The osmoles in the medullary interstitium are made of the sodium chloride reabsorbed at the thick ascending limb of the loop of Henle, and urea transported into the inner medullary interstitium under the influence of ADH.[11]

Osmoregulation

An increase in the effective plasma osmolality usually is associated with a decrease in the intracellular volume.[6] Conversely, a decreased effective plasma osmolality is associated with cellular hydration. Water homeostasis is important in the regulation of plasma osmolality. The plasma tonicity is maintained within normal limits through a delicate balance between the rates of water intake and excretion.

The average daily water intake includes the water ingested (sensible intake), the water content of ingested food, and the metabolic production of water (insensible intake).[4] To maintain homeostasis, these should be equal to the water excreted by the kidney and the gastrointestinal (GI) tract (sensible loss), and water lost from the skin and respiratory tract (insensible loss).

Changes in the plasma tonicity are detected by osmoreceptors in the hypothalamus which also houses the thirst center and the site for ADH synthesis.[14,15] When the plasma tonicity is reduced to below 280 mOsm/kg as a result of water ingestion, ADH release is inhibited.[4] Hence, no water reabsorption takes place in the collecting duct and a large volume of dilute urine is excreted. On the contrary, when the osmoreceptors in the hypothalamus sense an increased plasma osmolality, ADH is released, and water reabsorption is increased. Thus, a small volume of concentrated urine is excreted.[4,6,14] The threshold for ADH release is 280 mOsm/kg.[14] Maximal ADH secretion occurs when the plasma osmolality is 295 mOsm/kg. Thus, the kidney can vary urine osmolality from 50 mOsm/kg in the absence of ADH to 1200 mOsm/kg with maximum ADH release.[4,6] The volume of urine produced depends upon the solute load to be excreted, as well as the urine osmolality:

$$\text{Urine Volume (L)} = \left(\frac{\text{Solute Load (mOsm)}}{\text{Urine Osmolality (mOsm/kg)}}\right)\left(\frac{1}{\text{Density of Water (kg/L)}}\right)$$

$$Eq\ 28.3$$

Therefore, for a typical daily solute load of 600 mOsm:

$$\begin{array}{c}\text{Urine Volume in the}\\\text{Absence of ADH}\end{array} = \left(\frac{600\ \text{mOsm}}{50\ \text{mOsm/kg}}\right)\left(\frac{1}{1\ \text{kg/L}}\right) = 12\ \text{L}$$

$$\begin{array}{c}\text{Urine Volume with}\\\text{Maximal ADH Release}\end{array} = \left(\frac{600\ \text{mOsm}}{1200\ \text{mOsm/kg}}\right)\left(\frac{1}{1\ \text{kg/L}}\right) = 0.5\ \text{L}$$

Although the kidney has a remarkable ability to excrete free water, it is not as efficient in conserving water. ADH only minimizes further water loss but cannot correct existent water deficit. Therefore, optimal osmoregulation requires increased water intake that is mediated via thirst stimulation.

Both antidiuretic hormone and thirst can be stimulated by nonosmotic stimuli.[6,15] Volume depletion is a strong nonosmotic stimulus for ADH release.[14,15] Indeed, the response of ADH release to changes in effective arterial volume overrides the response to changes in plasma osmolality. Nausea, pain, and hypoxia also are potent stimuli for ADH secretion.[15]

Volume Regulation

Since sodium resides almost exclusively in the extracellular fluid, total body sodium determines the extracellular volume.[4,16] The daily sodium intake varies from 100 to 250 mEq. Changes in

urinary sodium according to sodium intake maintain the extracellular volume and tissue perfusion.[4,16] The ability of the kidney to retain sodium is so remarkable that one can survive with a daily intake of as low as 20 to 30 mEq.

The afferent sensors for the changes in the effective circulating volume are the intrathoracic volume receptors, the baroreceptors in the carotid sinus and aortic arch, and the afferent arteriole in the glomerulus.[16] When the effective circulating volume is decreased, both the renin-angiotensin and the sympathetic nervous systems are activated.[4,16] Angiotensin II and norepinephrine enhance sodium reabsorption at the proximal convoluted tubule. Aldosterone also is stimulated to increase sodium reabsorption at the collecting tubule. The decrease in effective arterial volume also stimulates the release of ADH, which will enhance water reabsorption at the collecting duct. Conversely, after a salt load, the increases in atrial pressure and renal perfusion pressure suppress the production of renin and, thence, angiotensin II and aldosterone. The release of atrial natriuretic peptide because of increased atrial filling pressure and intrarenal production of urodilatin increase urinary excretion of the excess sodium.[12,13]

While the kidney can excrete a 20 mL/kg water load in four hours, only 50% of the excess sodium is excreted in the first day.[4] Sodium excretion continues to increase until a new steady state is reached after three to four days when intake equals output.[4,16] Nonetheless, the extracellular volume has not returned to baseline because of the sodium retained during the first few days.

It is important to recognize that osmoregulation and volume regulation occur independently of each other.[4,6] The two homeostatic systems regulate different parameters and possess different sensors and effectors. However, both systems can be activated at the same time.

Disorders in Volume Regulation

Sodium Depletion

2. A.B., a 17-year-old female, presented to the emergency room (ER) with complaints of anorexia, nausea, vomiting, and generalized weakness for the past 3 days. She denied other medical problems. She had not used any medications. Upon examination, the supine blood pressure (BP) was 105/70 mm Hg with a pulse of 80 beats/min. Her standing BP was 85/60 mm Hg with a pulse of 100 beats/min. She complained of feeling dizzy when she stood up. Her mucous membranes were dry but the skin turgor was normal. The jugular vein was flat. Peripheral or sacral edema was not present. Laboratory blood tests showed serum Na 134 mEq/L, K 3.5 mEq/L, Cl 95 mEq/L, total CO_2 content 35 mEq/L, BUN 16 mg/dL, creatinine 0.8 mg/dL, and glucose 70 mg/dL. Random urinary Na was 40 mEq/L, K 40 mEq/L, and Cl was <15 mEq/L. The hemoglobin (Hgb) was 14 gm/dL with normal white cell and platelet counts. Why are the clinical and laboratory data in A.B. consistent with an assessment of volume depletion? [SI units: serum Na 134 mmol/L; K 3.5 mmol/L; Cl 95 mmol/L; CO_2 35 mmol/L; BUN 5.7 mmol/L; creatinine 70.72 μmol/L; glucose 3.9 mmol/L; urine Na 40 mmol/L; K 40 mmol/L; Cl <15 mmol/L; Hgb 140 gm/L]

The signs and symptoms of A.B. were consistent with volume depletion. The loss of gastric fluid due to vomiting and decreased oral intake because of anorexia had led to moderate to severe volume depletion. She was orthostatic both by blood pressure (a drop in systolic BP of 20 mm Hg) and pulse (an increase in pulse by 20 beats/min). The dry mucous membranes, the flat jugular vein, and the absence of edema all support volume depletion.[17] She also manifested symptomatic orthostasis as evidenced by her dizziness. Her hypochloremic metabolic alkalosis probably was initiated by proton loss during vomiting and maintained by volume contraction. Her decreased renal perfusion enhanced proximal tubular reabsorption of urea, resulting in her increased BUN:creatinine ratio (prerenal azotemia). When renal perfusion is decreased and the renin-angiotensin-aldosterone system is activated, the proximal reabsorption of sodium and chloride is increased; therefore, A.B.'s urinary sodium should be less than 10 mEq/L.[18] However, the poorly permeant bicarbonate ions in the tubular fluid obligate sodium loss in the urine to maintain luminal electroneutrality. Therefore, A.B.'s urinary sodium was elevated (40 mEq/L). In this situation, the urinary chloride remained low and is a better index of volume status.[18] However, one should note that both urinary sodium and chloride will be elevated in patients using diuretics, undergoing osmotic diuresis, and in those with underlying renal disease or hypoaldosteronism even in the face of volume depletion. In these situations, physical examination should be used to assess volume status. A.B.'s elevated hemoglobin concentration of 14 gm/dL probably also is a reflection of her volume depletion.

3. How should A.B.'s volume depletion be managed?

The etiology of A.B.'s vomiting should be sought and the cause removed. Normal saline should be administered intravenously to expand the extracellular space and improve tissue perfusion.[4,17] The volume deficit often is difficult to ascertain. Since A.B. was severely orthostatic, 1 or 2 L of fluid can be given over two to four hours. Subsequent rate of infusion will depend upon A.B.'s response and symptoms. One should monitor A.B.'s body weight, skin turgor, supine and upright blood pressure, jugular venous pressure, urine output, and the urine chloride concentration to assess if volume repletion is adequate. Since the goal of treatment is to achieve a positive fluid balance, the rate of infusion should be 50 or 100 mL/hour in excess of the sum of urine output, insensible losses, and other losses such as emesis and diarrhea.[4]

Sodium Excess

4. L.J., a 45-year-old male, presented to the clinic with complaints of swollen legs and puffy eyelids. He also noticed his urine been foamy recently. Upon examination, BP was 180/100 mm Hg and pulse was 80 beats/min. There were bilateral periorbital edema and 2+ bilateral pitting edema up to the thigh. Heart examination was normal. The lungs have bilateral crackles. The jugular venous pressure was elevated at 10 cm H_2O. Laboratory tests revealed serum Na 132 mEq/L, K 3.8 mEq/L, Cl 100 mEq/L, bicarbonate 26 mEq/L, BUN 40 mg/dL, creatinine 2.5 mg/dL, glucose 120 mg/dL, and albumin 2 gm/dL. The serum transaminases, alkaline phosphatase, and bilirubin were within normal limits. Serum cholesterol was 280 mg/dL and triglyceride was 300 mg/dL. Urinalysis showed specific gravity of 1.015, pH 7.0, protein >300 mg/dL, oval fat bodies, and fatty casts. A 24-hour urinary protein excretion was 6 gm with measured creatinine clearance (Cl_{Cr}) of 40 mL/min. He currently is on no medications. L.J. denies illicit drug use. Hepatitis B serology and human immunodeficiency virus (HIV) antibody were negative. The impression is anasarca (total body edema) secondary to nephrotic syndrome. What is nephrotic syndrome? What is the etiology of L.J.'s sodium excess state? [SI units: Na 132 mmol/L; K 3.8 mmol/L; Cl 100 mmol/L; bicarbonate 26 mmol/L; BUN 14.3 mmol/L; SrCr 221 μmol/L; glucose 6.7 mmol/L; albumin 20 gm/L; cholesterol 7.24 mmol/L; triglyceride 3.4 mmol/L; protein 3 gm/L; Cl_{Cr} 0.67 mL/sec]

Nephrotic syndrome is characterized by hypoalbuminemia, urine protein excretion more than 3.5 gm/day, hyperlipidemia, lipiduria, and edema.[19,20] The heavy proteinuria is a result of damage to the permselective barrier of the glomerulus. The etiologies of nephrotic syndrome are multiple and diverse.[19] The cause of nephrotic syndrome can be idiopathic (primary glomerular disease), or secondary to chronic systemic diseases (e.g., diabetes mellitus, amyloidosis, sickle cell anemia,[21] lupus), cancer (e.g., multiple myeloma, Hodgkin's disease), infections (e.g., HIV,[22] hepatitis B, syphilis, malaria), intravenous (IV) drug abuse, and medications [e.g., gold, penicillamine, captopril, nonsteroidal anti-inflammatory drugs (NSAIDs)[23]].

The heavy urinary protein loss results in various extrarenal complications.[19,20] Hypoalbuminemia leads to a reduction in plasma oncotic pressure. Thus, hepatic lipoprotein synthesis is increased. This, coupled with the decreased clearance of lipoproteins, resulted in L.J.'s hyperlipidemia.[19,24] Loss of clotting factors in the urine predisposes these patients to thromboembolism.[19] Specific therapy of nephrotic syndrome ranges from simple removal of the offending medication, treatment of the underlying infection, to the use of immunosuppressive agents in certain glomerular diseases.

The edematous state (i.e., L.J.'s anasarca) is a result of both changes in capillary hemodynamics and renal sodium and water retention.[25] His hypoalbuminemia (2 gm/dL) and heavy proteinuria (>300 mg/dL) resulted in imbalances in the Starling forces across the capillary wall, namely the hydrostatic and oncotic pressures in the capillary and interstitial compartments. Heavy proteinuria leads to hypoalbuminemia and results in the reduction of the capillary oncotic pressure. This favors the movement of fluid from the vascular space into the interstitium.[26] Contraction of the effective arterial blood volume ensues, with activation of the humoral, neural, and hemodynamic mechanisms that signal the kidney to retain sodium and water.[27-29] However, this *"underfill"* hypothesis is challenged by data which suggest that hypoalbuminemia plays a minor role in nephrotic edema.[26] For instance, in patients with minimal change disease of nephrotic syndrome successfully treated with steroids, the glomerular filtration rate and fractional excretion of sodium increased before there was any significant improvement in serum albumin concentration.[30] In addition, patients with nephrotic syndrome can have increased, normal, or decreased plasma volumes.[26]

It appears that a defect in the intrarenal sodium handling mechanism causes inappropriate sodium retention and results in nephrotic edema.[26,31] According to this *"overflow"* hypothesis, proteinuric renal disease leads to increased sodium reabsorption in the distal nephron. The mechanism is not well defined but may be related to resistance to atrial natriuretic peptide.[26] Thus, a sodium excess state occurs and edema results. It is likely that the interaction between the underfill and overflow mechanisms results in the production of nephrotic edema.[26] Patients with severe hypoalbuminemia (i.e., serum albumin level <1.5 gm/dL) who have a severe reduction in plasma oncotic pressure, are most likely to exhibit evidence of underfill.[25]

5. How should L.J.'s sodium excess state be managed?

The etiology of L.J.'s nephrotic syndrome should be searched for and specific treatment instituted. Although L.J.'s serum sodium concentration of 132 mEq/L is low, it is low because of fluid excess. The serum sodium concentration is a reflection of water balance rather than total body sodium concentration. Therefore, salt restriction is important in the control of L.J.'s generalized edema.[26] For most nephrotic patients, modest dietary sodium restriction to about 50 mEq/day may be sufficient to maintain neutral sodium balance.[25,26] However, for nephrotic patients who are very sodium-avid (urine sodium concentration <10 mEq/L), severe restriction is difficult to achieve. Slowing the rate of edema formation rather than hastening its resolution should be the goal of therapy for these patients.[26] Bedrest reduces orthostatic stimulation of the renin-angiotensin-aldosterone and sympathetic systems, thereby favoring the movement of interstitial fluid into the vascular space.[26] Thus, the central blood volume is increased and natriuresis and diuresis facilitated. However, prolonged bedrest might predispose these hypercoagulable patients to the risk of thromboembolism.[19] Similarly, use of support stockings may reduce some of the stimuli for sodium retention by redistribution of blood to the central circulation.[26,32]

Diuretics are the mainstay of therapy in the management of nephrotic edema.[4,26] A loop diuretic usually is employed. The efficacy of diuretics in nephrotic patients is influenced by the altered pharmacodynamics and pharmacokinetics in these patients.[33] In most nephrotic patients, the edema can be removed safely with rapid diuresis without compromising the systemic circulation, probably consequent to the rapid refilling of plasma volume by the interstitial fluid.[26] Nevertheless, as the edema is reduced, the rate of fluid removal and weight loss also should be decreased to avoid reduction of the effective circulating volume. The patient should be monitored for occurrence of orthostatic hypotension.

Albumin infusion to expand the plasma volume only provides a temporary relief, is expensive,[26] and should be used only in patients who have resistant edema. In patients who are resistant to the above measures, extracorporeal fluid removal, namely ultrafiltration, may be necessary.[26,35]

L.J. initially was treated with IV furosemide 60 mg twice daily and placed on a daily diet which consisted of 50 mEq sodium, 0.8 gm/kg protein of high biologic value with additional protein to match gram-per-gram of urinary protein loss, and 200 mg cholesterol with 1000 mL fluid restriction.[37] He had 5 L of diuresis in two days with resolution of respiratory symptoms and improvement of anasarca. Parenteral furosemide was discontinued on the fifth day of hospitalization and oral furosemide 120 mg twice daily was started. L.J. was discharged two days later with the above regimen of diuretic and a total weight loss of 12 kg. L.J. was instructed to adhere to the dietary restriction and diuretic regimen.

Disorders in Osmoregulation

Hyponatremia

The serum sodium concentration is the ratio of total body sodium to total body water. It is not an index of total body sodium.[38,39] Therefore, both hyponatremia and hypernatremia can occur in the presence of a low, normal, or high total body sodium.[38,39] The specific serum sodium concentration is dependent upon the volume of the total body water. Since the kidney can excrete more than 12 to 16 L/day of free water, hyponatremia does not occur unless the water intake overwhelms the kidney's ability to excrete free water (e.g., psychogenic polydipsia)[41,42] or free water excretion is impaired.[4,39]

Free water formation requires normal delivery of tubular fluid to the diluting segments, which depends upon normal glomerular filtration rate and proximal tubular reabsorption; the reabsorption of sodium chloride without water in the thick ascending limb of the loop of Henle and the distal tubule; and the excretion of a dilute urine in the absence of ADH.[39] Therefore, hyponatremia can occur in situations when the kidney's diluting ability is exceeded, or impaired because of: a) volume depletion and nonosmotic stimulation of ADH release, or b) nonhemodynamically mediated ADH production.[4,39]

Although plasma sodium is the primary determinant of plasma tonicity, hyponatremia does not always represent hypotonicity.[4,39] In patients with severe hyperlipidemia or hyperproteinemia (e.g., multiple myeloma), pseudohyponatremia may occur.[4,38,39,43] This is due to the occupation of plasma water by the lipids and proteins.[38,39] Water accounts for 93% of plasma; lipids and proteins make up the rest.[39] Sodium is distributed only in the aqueous phase. The increase in plasma lipid and protein contents expands plasma volume.[38,39] Water is displaced and the percentage of solid

in plasma is increased.[35] Therefore, the sodium content per liter of newly recomposed plasma is decreased, and the plasma sodium concentration measured by the flame photometry method is low.[38,39,43] However, the sodium concentration in plasma water remains the same. Since osmolality is a colligative property and depends upon solute concentration in plasma water, serum osmolality remains unchanged.[38] Indeed, the measured osmolality is normal. Use of an ion-selective electrode method to measure plasma sodium concentration might circumvent this problem.[39,43]

Another example of isotonic hyponatremia is found in prostate surgery during which large volumes of isotonic mannitol irrigants are used.[38,39] Absorption of these irrigation solutions has led to severe hyponatremia but a normal osmolality. In contrast, absorption of large amounts of isotonic sorbitol and isotonic, or slightly hypotonic, glycine solutions during urologic surgery may cause hypotonicity as a late complication.[38,39] Like mannitol, sorbitol and isotonic glycine initially are restricted to the extracellular space, resulting in hyponatremia without a change in osmolality.[39] Unlike mannitol, both sorbitol and glycine eventually are metabolized, leaving water behind: the result is hypotonicity. The severe hypotonic hyponatremia, in conjunction with the neurotoxic effects of glycine and its metabolites, then can cause severe neurologic symptoms.[39,44]

6. T.T., a 23-year-old male with end-stage renal disease due to diabetic nephropathy, currently is receiving chronic ambulatory peritoneal dialysis. Because of dietary noncompliance, T.T. complained of shortness of breath (SOB). His dialysis prescription was adjusted to include 6 cycles of 2.5% peritoneal dialysis solutions. Today, laboratory tests show plasma Na 128 mEq/L, K 4 mEq/L, Cl 98 mEq/L, total CO$_2$ 24 mmol/L, BUN 50 mg/dL, creatinine 6 mg/dL, and glucose 600 mg/dL. What is the etiology of T.T.'s hyponatremia? [SI units: Na 128 mmol/L; K 4 mmol/L; Cl 98 mmol/L; CO$_2$ 24 mmol/L; BUN 17.85 mmol/L; creatinine 530.4 μmol/L; glucose 33.3 mmol/L]

T.T.'s effective plasma osmolality is calculated to be 289 mOsm/L, of which 33 mOsm/L is contributed by the hyperglycemia. The slow absorption of glucose, due to the lack of insulin, causes water to move from the intracellular compartment into the plasma space, thereby lowering the plasma sodium concentration.[38,39] Despite the lowered plasma sodium concentration, the plasma osmolality is normal. Hence, no symptoms attributable to hypo-osmolality are observed. Indeed, when serum glucose is normalized, the serum sodium level increases. For each 100 mg/dL increment in serum glucose, serum sodium decreases by 1.3 to 1.6 mEq/L.[38,39] Use of hypertonic mannitol or glycine solutions in patients suffering from cerebral edema also results in a hyperosmolar hyponatremia.[38]

Hypotonic Hyponatremia with Decreased Extracellular Fluid

7. Q.B., a 30-year-old male athlete, experienced multiple bouts of diarrhea in the last several days. Q.B. has been drinking Gatorade to keep himself from getting dehydrated. Vital signs: supine BP 140/80 mm Hg and pulse 70 beats/min; standing BP was 135/70 mm Hg and pulse 80 beats/min. Respiratory rate (RR) was 12 breaths/min, and Q.B. was afebrile. Skin turgor was mildly decreased. Laboratory data revealed plasma Na 128 mEq/L, K 3 mEq/L, Cl 100 mEq/L, bicarbonate 17 mEq/L, BUN 20 mg/dL, and creatinine 1.2 mg/dL. Urinary Na and Cl were both <10 mEq/L. What is the etiology of Q.B.'s hyponatremia? [SI units: plasma Na 128 mmol/L; K 3 mmol/L; Cl 100 mmol/L; bicarbonate 17 mmol/L; BUN 7.14 mmol/L; creatinine 106.1 μmol/L; urinary Na <10 mmol/L; Cl <10 mmol/L]

Hypotonic hyponatremia in the presence of extracellular fluid depletion suggests that the total body sodium deficit is more than that of total body water.[38] The orthostasis, prerenal azotemia, and the low urinary sodium are consistent with volume depletion.[18] Determination of urinary sodium helps to distinguish between renal and nonrenal losses that result in the sodium and water deficits.[18,38,40] In the face of volume depletion, a urinary sodium less than 10 mEq/L suggests appropriate renal sodium conservation.[18] This usually is seen in patients with GI fluid loss as in vomiting, diarrhea, or profuse sweating.[38-40] Surreptitious cathartic abuse should be suspected in patients who present with hypovolemia, hyponatremia, and a low urinary sodium concentration.[39] "Third spacing" [i.e., movement of extracellular fluid into the abdominal cavity (e.g., during acute pancreatitis, ileus, or pseudomembranous colitis)] also presents with a low urinary sodium.[39,40] If urinary sodium is greater than 20 mEq/L during volume depletion, renal salt wastage should be considered.[18,39,40] The potential causes of this latter problem include diuretic use,[45-47] adrenal insufficiency,[48] and salt-wasting nephropathy[39] (e.g., chronic interstitial nephritis, medullary cystic disease, polycystic kidney disease, obstructive uropathy, and cisplatin toxicity).[49,50] In patients with renal insufficiency, neither the urinary sodium nor chloride concentration is a reliable index of volume status.[18]

Volume depletion leads to increased reabsorption of sodium and water in the proximal tubule and thus, decreased sodium delivery to the diluting segments for free water formation.[38-40] Decreased effective arterial volume also is a potent nonosmotic stimulus for ADH release.[14,15] These factors combine to dampen the ability of the kidney to form a dilute urine and result in a high urine osmolality despite a low serum sodium concentration.[38-40] Although the fluid lost in diarrhea is hypotonic, it is the replacement of fluid loss with an even more hypotonic fluid such as Gatorade or tap water that causes hyponatremia.[39,40]

Q.B.'s diarrhea probably caused loss of potassium and bicarbonate through the GI tract, leading to his hypokalemia and hyperchloremic metabolic acidosis. The potassium depletion can sensitize ADH secretion in response to hypovolemic stimuli;[39] and the hypokalemia also can lead to hyponatremia.[39] Cellular efflux of potassium results in cellular uptake of sodium and causes a further decrease in the serum sodium concentration.

8. How should Q.B.'s hyponatremia be managed?

The treatment of hypovolemic hyponatremia involves replacement of the sodium deficit. The sodium deficit can be estimated by the following formula:

$$Na\ Deficit = Vd\ of\ Na\ (Desired - Current\ Na\ Concentration)$$

Eq 28.4

$$= (0.5\ L/kg)(70\ kg)(140 - 125\ mEq/L)$$

$$= 525\ mEq$$

Roughly one-third of the deficit can be replaced over the first 12 hours at a replacement rate of less than 0.5 mEq/L/hour. The remaining amounts can be administered over the next several days.

The use of isotonic sodium chloride solution is ideal for the treatment of volume-depleted hyponatremia. As renal perfusion is restored, free water will be excreted with appropriate retention of sodium.[40] Since Q.B. only suffered from mild volume depletion, replacement fluids can be given orally. Oral solutions containing both electrolyte and glucose,[51] or rice-based solutions[52] are ideal for the management of persistent fluid loss. Glucose not only provides calories but promotes the intestinal absorption of ingested sodium.[51] Since the rice-based solution provides more glucose and amino acids, both of which promote intestinal sodium absorption, it is more effective than glucose alone.[4,51]

In patients with renal salt wasting, the ongoing daily sodium loss also should be taken into consideration when estimating the

sodium store to be replenished. Potassium should be given to correct hypokalemia and thereby improve the hyponatremia as well. One should note that the serum sodium concentration may rise faster than estimated because when the intra-arterial blood volume is replenished and tissue perfusion is restored, distal sodium delivery increases and ADH secretion is suppressed appropriately.[38-40] Hence, the ability of the kidney to generate free water is resumed. In the absence of ADH, a dilute urine is excreted. The increased free water excretion will improve the serum sodium concentration faster than estimated.

Hypervolemic Hypotonic Hyponatremia

9. T.W., a 55-year-old male with a long-standing history of alcoholic liver cirrhosis, is admitted to the hospital for worsening SOB. Past medical history includes portal hypertension and esophageal varices, and noncompliance with dietary restriction and medications. BP is 120/60 mm Hg; pulse 100 beats/min; RR 20 breaths/min, and he is afebrile. Physical examination reveals a jaundiced male in respiratory distress. His jugular vein is flat. Lung examination revealed bilateral basal rales. Abdominal examination showed tense ascites with hepatomegaly and spider angiomas (telangiectasias resembling a spider). Extremities showed 1+ pedal edema bilaterally. Laboratory data upon admission included serum Na 127 mEq/L, K 3.4 mEq/L, Cl 95 mEq/L, total CO_2 content 24 mEq/L, BUN 10 mg/dL, SrCr 1.2 mg/dL, and albumin 2.5 gm/dL. Urine Na was <10 mEq/L and osmolality was 380 mOsm/L. Identify the possible causes of hyponatremia in T.W. and discuss its pathophysiology. How should he be managed? [SI units: serum Na 127 mmol/L; K 3.4 mmol/L; Cl 95 mmol/L; CO_2 24 mmol/L; BUN 3.57 mmol/L; SrCr 106.1 μmol/L; albumin 25 gm/L; urine Na <10 mmol/L]

T.W. had no history of vomiting or diarrhea. He also had stopped using diuretics before admission. The physical findings of ascites, and bilateral edema are not consistent with volume depletion but indicate a sodium-excess state. Both sodium and water retention take place, but the disproportionate accumulation of ingested water relative to sodium leads to hyponatremia.[38-40]

Cirrhotic patients who are prone to develop hyponatremia have a decreased effective arterial blood volume.[27,39,53,54] The low urinary sodium concentration suggests that the effective arterial blood volume was decreased.[18] The high urinary osmolality in the face of hypotonic hyponatremia suggests nonosmotic stimulation of ADH release and impaired free water excretion. Peripheral vasodilation causes a decrease in systemic arterial blood pressure despite a normal to high cardiac output. These, along with splanchnic venous pooling and decreased oncotic pressure secondary to hypoalbuminemia, lead to a decrease in renal perfusion.[25,29,53] The latter activates the renin-angiotensin-aldosterone system, the sympathetic nervous system, and the release of ADH. Proximal sodium and water reabsorption is enhanced because of the consequent diminished sodium and water delivery to the distal segments of the nephron. Thus, the diluting capacity of the kidney is impaired. Increased secretion of antidiuretic hormone also promotes free water reabsorption at the collecting tubule and contributes to the hyperosmolality of urine and hyponatremia. Alternatively, a primary disturbance in renal sodium handling can reduce fluid delivery to the diluting segments of the nephron, impairing water excretion.

The hypervolemic hyponatremia seen in patients with congestive heart failure (CHF) also is mediated through a decreased effective arterial blood volume with activation of the "hypovolemic" hormones: renin, norepinephrine, and ADH.[27-29,55] Similarly, patients with nephrotic syndrome also can present with hyponatremia via the underfill mechanism.[27-29,39,40]

Chronic renal disease can be associated with hypervolemic hyponatremia when excessive water is ingested.[39,40] As the glomerular filtration rate decreases, distal delivery of sodium is reduced. Hence, the ability to generate free water is impaired. However, since the capacity to conserve sodium is impaired in these patients, their urine sodium concentration is increased.[18]

Most edematous, hyponatremic patients are asymptomatic. Indeed, the degree of hyponatremia probably reflects the severity of the underlying disease.[53–55] Unless there is an acute decrease in serum sodium, rapid therapeutic correction is not warranted.[39,40,52–54] Water restriction is the mainstay of therapy. The amount restricted depends upon the degree of hyponatremia and the severity of symptoms. Sodium restriction and judicious use of a diuretic may help to reduce the edema state. Serum BUN and creatinine concentrations should be monitored closely to detect decreased renal perfusion. Worsening prerenal azotemia may indicate overaggressive diuresis and should be avoided. In addition, diuretics can induce or worsen hyponatremia by means of volume depletion and impairment of the diluting capacity of the kidney.[45–47,54]

T.W. underwent abdominal paracentesis to relieve respiratory discomfort with no sequelae. He then was prescribed with a 1000 mg sodium diet and water restriction to 500 mL/day. Diuretics then were resumed.

Normovolemic Hypotonic Hyponatremia

10. C.C., a 50-year-old male, was diagnosed recently with small-cell lung carcinoma and is brought to the ER by his family. He has a 1-week history of progressive lethargy and stupor. Laboratory data reveal: serum Na 110 mEq/L, K 3.6 mEq/L, Cl 78 mEq/L, bicarbonate 22 mEq/L, BUN 10 mg/dL, SrCr 0.9 mg/dL, glucose 90 mg/dL, serum osmolality 230 mOsm/kg, urine osmolality 616 mOsm/kg, urine Na 60 mEq/L. An arterial blood gas (ABG) at room air showed pH 7.38, pCO_2 38 mm Hg, and pO_2 80 mm Hg. Upon physical examination, C.C. was normotensive and appeared to be euvolemic. There was no edema detected. Historical chart review showed normal adrenal and thyroid function. C.C. currently was not using medications. Upon admission to the ward, C.C. weighed 60 kg. One liter of normal saline was started to treat his hyponatremia. Repeated serum sodium afterwards was 108 mEq/L. Identify the etiology of hyponatremia in C.C. and describe its pathophysiology. [SI units: serum Na 110 mmol/L; K 3.6 mmol/L; Cl 78 mmol/L; bicarbonate 22 mmol/L; BUN 3.57 mmol/L; SrCr 79.6 μmol/L; glucose 5.0 mmol/L; serum osmolality 230 mmol/kg; urine osmolality 616 mmol/kg; urine Na 60 mmol/L; pCO_2 5.1 kPa; pO_2 853.1 mmol/L; serum Na 108 mmol/L]

In a patient with hypo-osmolar hyponatremia and apparently normal volume status, the differential diagnosis[38–40] includes hypothyroidism,[56] cortisol deficiency,[57] reset osmostat,[58] psychogenic polydipsia,[41,42] and the syndrome of inappropriate antidiuretic hormone secretion (SIADH).[59–61] The latter is a diagnosis of exclusion. The normal thyroid and adrenal function tests exclude hypothyroidism and cortisol insufficiency as the causes. The inappropriately elevated urine osmolality is inconsistent with psychogenic polydipsia or reset osmostat since free water excretion usually is not impaired in these disorders. C.C.'s presentation of apparent normovolemia and laboratory findings of: a) hypo-osmolar hyponatremia; b) an inappropriately high urine osmolality (>100 mOsm/kg); c) a urine sodium concentration greater than 40 mEq/L; d) normal renal, adrenal, and thyroid function; and e) normal acid-base and potassium balance, are consistent with SIADH.[39,60,61] In addition, SIADH is associated with a low serum uric acid concentration.[62] Although patients with cerebral salt wasting can present with very similar findings to SIADH, they are volume-depleted and exhibit renal salt wasting.[39]

In SIADH, the antidiuretic hormone secretion is considered inappropriate because of its persistence in the absence of appropriate osmotic and hemodynamic stimuli. Water ingestion is essential in

the development of hyponatremia in SIADH. Persistent ADH activity impairs water excretion, resulting in retention of ingested water, hypo-osmolar hyponatremia, and expansion of body fluids. Edema rarely is apparent because only one-third of retained water resides in the extracellular space and sodium hemostatic mechanisms are intact.[38,40] The extracellular fluid expansion activates volume receptors and leads to natriuresis. At steady state, urinary sodium excretion reflects sodium intake and usually is greater than 40 mEq/L. Nonetheless, if sodium intake is reduced severely, the urinary sodium concentration can be less than 40 mEq/L.[39]

The etiologies of SIADH are diverse and include tumors[39] (of which small-cell lung carcinoma,[63] like C.C. has, is the most common); pulmonary disorders[64] (e.g., pneumonia,[65] tuberculosis); neurologic disorders[66] (e.g., psychosis,[42] meningitis, hemorrhage); drugs[67] [e.g., desmopressin,[68] oxytocin,[69] chlorpropamide,[70,71] clofibrate,[72] carbamazepine,[73,74] tricyclic antidepressants (TCAs),[75] antipsychotics,[76] bromocriptine,[77] cyclophosphamide,[78] vincristine,[79] nicotine,[80] and NSAIDs[39,81]]; postoperative state[82] (hypoxia, nausea,[83] pain, narcotics, and hypotension being the nonosmotic stimuli[84]); and more recently, the acquired immunodeficiency syndrome.[85,86] Four different patterns of inappropriate ADH release have been identified.[39] However, there was no correlation between these patterns and the underlying causes of SIADH. Mechanisms for drug-induced SIADH include antidiuretic hormone-like action on the collecting tubule, central stimulation of ADH release, and potentiation of the ADH effect.[39,67] Small-cell lung carcinoma is most likely the cause of C.C.'s SIADH.

11. Why is C.C.'s serum Na concentration lower after the saline infusion?

Isotonic sodium chloride solution (154 mEq/L each of Na and Cl ions or 308 mOsm/L) initially will increase the plasma sodium concentration because it has a higher osmolality than C.C.'s.[87] As C.C. had a relatively fixed urine osmolality of 616 mOsm/kg due to persistent ADH activity, he would need to excrete the osmolar load of 308 mOsm in a volume of 500 mL of urine at steady state (since 308 mOsm of solute in 500 mL of water is equal to 616 mOsm/kg). Since a total of 1 L of fluid was administered with all the solutes excreted in 500 mL of urine output, 500 mL of free water are retained. Therefore, there is a reduction in serum sodium concentration.[39,87]

Neurologic Manifestations

12. Why are C.C.'s neurologic manifestations characteristic of hyponatremia?

As the plasma osmolality declines, the osmotic gradient created across the blood-brain barrier favors the movement of water into the brain and other cells.[39,40] Water movement from the cerebrospinal fluid into the cerebral interstitium results in cerebral edema. However, brain swelling is limited by the meninges and cranium, giving rise to neurologic symptoms. The degree of cerebral overhydration and the rapidity of its development appear to correlate with the severity of symptoms.[39,40]

When hyponatremia develops in less than two to three days, or the rate of decline in serum sodium exceeds 0.5 mEq/L/hour, it is regarded as acute.[39,88,89] The patient becomes symptomatic when serum sodium concentration falls to 125 mEq/L and begins to complain of nausea, vomiting, and malaise.[39,90] Severe symptoms occur more commonly when serum sodium falls below 120 mEq/L and the rate of decline is faster than 0.5 mEq/L/hour. The symptoms may include headache, tremors, incoordination, delirium, lethargy, and obtundation. As serum sodium falls below 110 to 115 mEq/L, seizure and coma can be seen.[39,90] On occasions, severe brain edema leads to transtentorial herniation and eventually death. Women, especially premenopausal women, apparently are more susceptible to develop severe neurologic symptoms and irreversible neurologic damage than men.[91,92]

In contrast, patients with chronic hyponatremia usually are asymptomatic.[39,88] Symptoms usually are vague and nonspecific and tend to occur at lower serum sodium concentrations than acute hyponatremia.[39,88,90] They include anorexia, nausea, vomiting, muscle weakness, and cramps. Irritability, hostility, confusion, and personality changes also may be seen. At extremely low sodium levels, stupor and, rarely, seizures have been reported.

Brain Adaptation to Hyponatremia

The difference in symptoms between acute and chronic hyponatremia is related to the cerebral adaptation to hypotonicity.[39,40] Two adaptive mechanisms are important in minimizing cerebral edema.[39,40,93–95] *Cerebral overhydration* increases the hydrostatic pressure in the cerebral interstitium, which results in the movement of fluid from the cerebral interstitial space to the cerebrospinal fluid. The *exodus of solutes out of the cells* results in a net reduction in cell osmolality, which affects water movement out of the cells. Sodium and potassium ions are the initial solutes extruded, followed over a period of hours to days by osmolytes such as inositol, glutamine, glutamate, and taurine.[93,94] Therefore, when the serum sodium concentration falls faster than the brain osmotic adaptation processes, serious and permanent neurologic damage may occur.[39,40,93,95] On the other hand, when hyponatremia develops over two to three days, symptoms usually are not seen unless the serum sodium concentration is reduced markedly.

It often is difficult to determine the acuity and chronicity of hyponatremia. Unless there is an obvious cause for acute hyponatremia, one should assume that the condition is chronic.[39,88,89,95] A rapid decline in serum sodium concentration usually indicates hypotonic fluid administration under conditions that overwhelm or impair renal water excretion. These include psychogenic polydipsia,[41,42] postoperative hyponatremia,[82,84,91,92] postprostatectomy syndrome,[44] and administration of thiazide diuretics,[45,46] and parenteral cyclophosphamide,[78] oxytocin,[69] arginine vasopressin or its analogues.[67] C.C.'s symptoms appeared to develop over seven days; thus, he probably had symptomatic chronic hyponatremia.

Rate of Correction of Hyponatremia

13. How should C.C.'s hyponatremia be managed?

C.C.'s water excess should be calculated to estimate the amount of water to be removed to achieve the desired sodium concentration.

$$\text{Water Excess} = \text{TBW} - \text{TBW}\left(\frac{\text{Observed Serum Na}}{\text{Desired Serum Na}}\right) \qquad Eq\ 28.5$$

$$= 30\ \text{L} - 30\ \text{L}\left(\frac{110\ \text{mEq/L}}{120\ \text{mEq/L}}\right)$$

$$= 2.4\ \text{L}$$

Where TBW = $(0.5\ \text{L/kg})(60\ \text{kg}) = 30\ \text{L}$

The treatment of hyponatremia has been controversial.[88–90,95–100] While severe hyponatremia is associated with high rates of morbidity and mortality, its treatment also is associated with morbidity.[88–90,95] The rate of correction has been implicated as the main cause of complications.[88–90,95,96,101,102]

It takes time for the brain to lose osmolytes to reduce cerebral swelling during hyponatremia; the rate of reaccumulation of these osmolytes must keep pace with the rise in serum sodium concentration lest brain dehydration and damage result.[39,40] Indeed, rapid

correction of hyponatremia has been implicated to cause a constellation of neurologic findings known as *osmotic demyelination syndrome*.[101,102] Clinical manifestations usually are delayed and occur one to several days after initiation of treatment of hyponatremia.[39,40] Neurologic findings include transient behavioral changes, seizures, akinetic mutism in mild cases, and features of a pontine disorder in severe cases (pseudobulbar palsy, quadriparesis, and coma). In some patients, the damage is irreversible. In fatal cases, central pontine myelinolysis can be documented.[101,102] Patients at greatest risk for osmotic demyelination have been those with severe hyponatremia of more than two days, and those in whom the rate of correction of hyponatremia was faster than 12 mEq/L in any 24-hour period.[39,40,95]

Retrospective reviews of large series of data suggest that acute hyponatremia can be treated promptly and rapidly with safety at a rate of 1 mEq/L/hour initially until a serum sodium concentration of 120 mEq/L is reached; thereafter, the rate of correction should be reduced to ≤0.5 mEq/L/hour, such that an increment in sodium concentration of no more than 12 mEq/L is achieved in the first 24 hours.[88,96] Slow correction is indicated for severe chronic hyponatremia.[39,40,88–90,96] No neurologic complications were seen in patients with severe hyponatremia when the average rate of correction to a serum sodium level of 120 mEq/L was less than 0.55 mEq/L/hour, or when the increase in serum sodium was less than 12 mEq/L in 24 hours or less than 18 mEq/L in 48 hours.[96]

In C.C., the serum sodium concentration should be raised to about 120 mEq/L. The rate of correction of serum sodium should be about 0.5 mEq/L/hour, using hypertonic saline and furosemide. Serum sodium concentrations should be monitored closely because the equation for calculating water excess does not take into account insensible loss which will increase the rate of sodium correction.

The use of normal saline is not useful in C.C. because he extracts salt normally. C.C.'s sodium deficit is:

$$(0.5\ \text{L/kg})(60\ \text{kg})(120 - 110\ \text{mEq/L}) = 300\ \text{mEq}$$

Since 1 L of 3% sodium chloride solution contains 513 mEq of sodium, approximately 600 mL of 3% saline solution will be required to correct the sodium deficit. This can be infused at a rate of 25 mL/hour to achieve a rate of correction less than 0.5 mEq/L/hour.

It should be noted that calculations for water excess and sodium deficits are only approximations and must be evaluated through careful monitoring of the patient's serum osmolality, serum sodium, and clinical response. Urinary losses can be replaced with 3% sodium chloride solution and appropriate amounts of potassium.

Chronic Management of the Syndrome of Inappropriate Antidiuretic Hormone Secretion (SIADH)

The syndrome of inappropriate antidiuretic hormone secretion usually is transient if the underlying cause can be removed. Chronic SIADH can occur, as evidenced in C.C. Water restriction to affect a negative water balance is the primary therapy and should be attempted first.[39,40] Since the urine osmolality is fixed, the urine output mainly is dependent upon the rate of solute excretion. Patients with a high urine osmolality will excrete the same osmotic load in a smaller volume of urine (i.e., more water retained) than those with a lower urine osmolality (i.e., less water retained). Hence, more stringent water restriction is required in patients with a high urine osmolality. Thus, providing the patient with a high-sodium, high-protein diet will enhance solute output and increase urine excretion. Alternatively, 30 to 60 gm/day of urea can be given to achieve the same effect.[103,104]

If the above measure fails, drugs to antagonize ADH action can be used.[39,40] These include a loop diuretic,[105,106] demeclocycline,[107] and lithium.[108] Furosemide, at a dose of 20 to 40 mg/day, reduces urine osmolality by blocking the concentrating ability of the kidney.[105] Demeclocycline and lithium directly impair the response to ADH at the collecting tubule, inducing nephrogenic diabetes insipidus.[39,40,107–109] Demeclocycline usually is better tolerated than lithium.[108] The dose of demeclocycline is 300 to 600 mg twice daily.[107,109] Its effect on water excretion is delayed for a few days and dissipates over a similar period of time after the drug is stopped. Nephrotoxicity has been reported with its use in cirrhotics.[110,111] V_2 (vasopressin) -receptor antagonists which directly block ADH action may be useful in the treatment of SIADH, but these drugs still are being developed.[112,113] Limited data suggest that phenytoin inhibits ADH secretion but its effectiveness is questionable.[114,115]

Hypernatremia

Hypernatremia can result in a person with: a) normal total body sodium with pure water loss; b) low total body sodium with hypotonic fluid loss; and c) high total body sodium as a result of pure salt gain.[116] Therefore, one should assess the volume status of the extracellular fluid when evaluating hypernatremia.

Pure water loss can be due to the inability of the kidney to conserve water (diabetes insipidus),[116] or to extrarenal water loss through the respiratory tract or the skin.[117] Usually, pure water loss does not cause hypernatremia unless the thirst center is damaged or the access to free water is limited.[116]

Hypotonic fluid loss can be renal as a result of osmotic diuresis, loop diuretics, postobstruction diuresis, or intrinsic renal disease. Extrarenal hypotonic fluid also can be lost by diarrhea, vomiting, burns, and excessive sweating.

Pure salt gain can result from the use of hypertonic saline during abortion, sodium bicarbonate during cardiopulmonary resuscitation, hypertonic feedings in infants, and rarely, mineralocorticoid excess.

The management of hypernatremia involves the correction of the underlying etiology of the hypertonic state, the replacement of water deficits, and adequate water administration to match ongoing losses.[116] The pure water deficit can be estimated as follows:

$$\text{Water Deficit} = \text{Normal TBW} - \text{Present TBW} \qquad Eq\ 28.6$$

$$= 0.6\left(\text{LBW}\right) - \left(\frac{\text{Normal Na Concentration}}{\text{Present Na Concentration}}\right)(0.6)(\text{LBW})$$

$$= 0.6(\text{LBW})\left[1 - \left(\frac{\text{Normal Na Concentration}}{\text{Present Na Concentration}}\right)\right]$$

The rate at which hypernatremia should be corrected depends upon the severity of symptoms and degree of hypertonicity. Too rapid correction may precipitate cerebral edema, seizures, irreversible neurologic damage, and can be fatal. For asymptomatic patients, the rate of correction probably should not exceed 0.5 mEq/L/hour. A rule of thumb is to replace half the calculated deficit with hypotonic solutions over 12 to 24 hours. The continued water loss, including insensible loss, also should be replenished with careful monitoring of the neurologic status. The rest of the deficit then can be replaced over the ensuing 24 to 48 hours. Concomitant solute deficits and ongoing solute losses also should be replaced as appropriate. If hypernatremia is caused only by pure water loss, free water can be administered as 5% dextrose in water. Half-normal or quarter-normal saline is used if sodium deficit also is present. In patients with hypotension or shock, the effective ar-

terial blood volume should be restored with normal saline or colloids before the plasma tonicity is corrected.[116]

Clinical Use of Diuretics

Diuretics reduce sodium chloride reabsorption in the kidney tubules to result in an increase in urine flow rate. The enhanced solute and fluid excretion may be initiated through osmotic diuresis or inhibition of transport in the kidney tubules. Different diuretics may be categorized according to the sites within the kidney tubules where sodium reabsorption is inhibited. (See Chapters 15: Congestive Heart Failure and 30: Chronic Renal Failure.)

Loop Diuretics

The loop diuretics, furosemide, bumetanide, torsemide, and ethacrynic acid are the most potent diuretics available. They also are known as high-ceiling diuretics since up to 20% to 25% of the filtered load of sodium may be inhibited from reabsorption. These loop diuretics act in the medullary and cortical aspects of the thick ascending limb of the loop of Henle. Sodium and chloride transport through the Na^+-K^+-$2Cl^-$ carrier in the luminal membrane is inhibited. Reabsorption of calcium and magnesium are reduced secondary to the reduction in sodium chloride transport. Torsemide also inhibits chloride conductance, which occurs from the peritubular (blood) side of the nephron; however, this effect is not significant at dosages commonly used for treatment.[118] The loop diuretics also possess a vasodilatory effect which can contribute to the diuretic action.

Thiazide Diuretics

The thiazide diuretics are a group of structurally similar compounds which share a common mechanism to induce diuresis. There are several other sulfonamide diuretics that are chemically different, such as chlorthalidone, indapamide, and metolazone, yet they have diuretic effects similar to the thiazides. The primary site of action of these diuretics is at the proximal portion of the distal tubule. Sodium reabsorption via the Na^+-Cl^- cotransporter is blocked through competition with the Cl^- site of the transporter. Some of these agents, such as chlorothiazide, also may reduce sodium transport in the proximal tubule. However, the contribution of this effect towards net diuresis is negligible since the sodium ions that are not reabsorbed in the proximal tubule subsequently will be reabsorbed in the loop of Henle. Thiazide diuretics can enhance the reabsorption of calcium ion through a direct action on the early distal tubule. These agents, therefore, are useful in patients with kidney stones to reduce calciuria. In contrast, magnesium excretion is increased by the thiazides which may result in hypomagnesemia.

Potassium-Sparing Diuretics

Spironolactone, triamterene, and amiloride are potassium-sparing diuretics that inhibit sodium reabsorption in the cortical collecting tubules through different mechanisms. Spironolactone (Aldactone) is a competitive receptor site antagonist of aldosterone in the distal segment of the renal tubule and is indicated especially for patients with hyperaldosteronism secondary to decreased renal perfusion. Patients with hyperaldosteronism can be identified by urinary electrolyte screening which shows high urine potassium excretion with concomitant diminished or absent urine sodium excretion. By serving as an aldosterone antagonist, spironolactone inhibits sodium reabsorption and decreases the excretion of potassium and hydrogen ions. Doses as high as 200 to 400 mg/day may be needed to induce natriuresis in patients with hyperaldosteronism. In contrast to spironolactone, triamterene and amiloride reduce the passage of sodium ions through the luminal membrane, independent of aldosterone activity, by directly acting on sodium and potassium transport processes in the distal renal tubular cells. Triamterene and amiloride offer the advantage of a more rapid onset of action than spironolactone.

The initial effects of spironolactone usually are delayed for two or three days and several additional days are needed to attain maximal diuretic effect. This delay is due partly to the formation of an active metabolite, canrenone, which accounts for about 70% of the antimineralocorticoid activity of spironolactone. The elimination half-life of canrenone is 13.5 to 24 hours in normal subjects, and prolonged in patients with chronic liver disease [59 hours (range: 32 to 105 hours)] or CHF [37 hours (range: 19 to 48 hours)].[414] Although the elimination half-life of canrenone is prolonged in these patients, plasma canrenone concentrations do not differ significantly from those in normal subjects because assay methods for canrenone are nonspecific and include measurement of both active and inactive metabolites.[220,415]

Triamterene (Dyrenium) is absorbed incompletely from the GI tract. The drug has a short half-life of 1.5 to 2.5 hours. Total body clearance is high because of rapid and extensive metabolism by the liver. Both the parent compound and the metabolite undergo biliary and renal excretion. As with spironolactone, the hepatic metabolism of triamterene can be altered in patients with cirrhosis.[36] The diuretic effect of triamterene (Dyrenium) begins within two to three hours of administration, and its maximum duration is 12 to 16 hours.

Amiloride (Midamor), does not undergo hepatic metabolism: about 50% of amiloride is excreted in the urine unchanged and the remainder is recovered in the stool resulting from biliary excretion or unabsorbed drug. Serum amiloride concentrations peak three hours after oral ingestion and the half-life is six hours. While commonly administered doses are in the 2.5 to 10 mg range, diuresis increases over a much greater range. The onset of action is two hours, with maximal effects at four to six hours. Duration of action is dose dependent and ranges from 10 to 24 hours. Amiloride does not undergo hepatic metabolism, and the drug can accumulate in patients with renal insufficiency.

The maximum amount of filtered sodium that can be excreted by the potassium-sparing diuretics is about 1% to 2%. The natriuretic activity is relatively limited compared with the thiazide and loop diuretics. These agents often are used in conjunction with thiazide and loop diuretics to reduce potassium loss. Spironolactone also is effective in patients with liver cirrhosis and ascites who are likely to have high levels of aldosterone.

Acetazolamide

Acetazolamide is an inhibitor of the enzyme, carbonic anhydrase, which mediates the excretion of sodium, bicarbonate, and chloride ions in the proximal tubule. Use of the drug will increase urine pH due to the increased excretion of bicarbonate ion. The net diuretic and natriuretic effects are limited, similar to those of the potassium-sparing diuretics. Due to the drug's proximal site of action, the sodium ions that are not reabsorbed will subsequently be reclaimed in the loop of Henle and the distal tubule. In addition, the metabolic acidosis associated with the use of the drug will diminish its diuretic effect.

Osmotic Diuretics

Osmotic diuretics are nonreabsorbable in the kidney tubule. They act primarily in the proximal tubule, where the osmotic pres-

sure they generate impedes the reabsorption of water and solute. Unlike other diuretics, the amount of induced water loss is more than the concurrent loss of sodium and potassium. Mannitol has been used in the early treatment of oliguric postischemic acute renal failure with the intention to convert the renal failure to a nonoliguric form. Urea, another osmotic diuretic, and mannitol are used to reduce intracranial pressure through cellular dehydration.

Methylxanthines

Of the various methylxanthines, theophylline has the most effect on the kidney. The diuretic effect of theophylline probably is due to its ability to increase renal blood flow and glomerular filtration rate. It also has a direct effect on the kidney tubules to result in enhanced sodium and chloride excretion while having little effect on urinary acidification. The methylxanthines are effective bronchodilators but rarely used as the primary agents for the treatment of edematous conditions.

Complications of Diuretic Therapy

Disturbances in fluid, electrolyte, and acid-base balance are common side effects associated with diuretic therapy. They are present as an extension of the pharmacologic properties of the diuretic agents.

Volume Depletion

Depletion of extracellular fluid volume is a common complication associated with loop diuretics and thiazides. Initial symptoms may include weakness, cramps, and dizziness. The patient also may experience orthostatic hypotension and reduced urine output. A substantial fall in blood pressure often is limited by angiotensin-induced renal vasoconstriction through a reactive increase in plasma renin activity. The decreased renal perfusion secondary to volume depletion may result in reduced glomerular filtration rate. In more serious depletion, symptoms associated with cerebral and coronary insufficiency also may be present. The patient's BUN concentration may be elevated because of increased urea reabsorption in the kidney tubule. In this situation, the rise in BUN is more than the concurrent increase in plasma creatinine concentration.[119] Urea production rate also will be increased because of increased amino acid release by the skeletal muscle and the subsequent hepatic conversion to urea. Patients who have nausea, vomiting, diarrhea, and reduced oral intake of sodium and water are more susceptible to volume depletion. However, it also may be seen in patients who have low intravascular volume despite edematous conditions.

Hypokalemia

Use of thiazide and loop diuretics commonly results in reduction of serum potassium concentration. Hypokalemia occurs in 14% to 60% of ambulatory hypertensive patients.[120,121] The extent of hypokalemia often is mild, with a mean reduction in serum potassium concentration of 0.1 to 0.6 mEq/L.[122,123] About 15% of patients receiving a daily dose of 50 mg of hydrochlorothiazide have serum potassium concentrations ≤3.5 mEq/L.[120] The extent of hypokalemia is greater in patients receiving chlorthalidone, which is a longer-acting agent.[124] In contrast, loop diuretics are less likely to cause hypokalemia than thiazides.[120]

The increased renal potassium excretion is the result of reduced sodium reabsorption which causes an increased delivery of sodium and water to the distal tubules. Sodium reabsorption at this distal site, therefore, is enhanced and is associated with increased excretion of potassium ions. The reduced extracellular fluid volume also results in an increase in aldosterone secretion. Patients with heart failure and liver cirrhosis frequently have increased aldosterone activity which enhances potassium excretion at the distal nephron.

The hypokalemia induced by diuretics is dose related and usually occurs in the first week of treatment.[125-128] The serum potassium concentrations reach a nadir within the first month of therapy and generally remain at that level afterwards. Although 98% of the total body potassium is intracellular, the clinical manifestations of potassium deficiency, such as weakness and electrocardiogram (ECG) changes, correlate better with serum concentrations than with the total body potassium store.[123] A reduction in the serum potassium concentration, therefore, may result in clinically significant events.

Several studies have evaluated the clinical significance of diuretic-induced hypokalemia in patients with hypertension. In the Oslo study of 800 men with mild hypertension, the group treated with diuretics experienced a significant reduction in stroke, aortic aneurysm, left ventricular hypertrophy, and CHF when compared with the placebo group.[129] Although there were significantly fewer nonfatal cerebrovascular events in the treatment group, a reduction in cardiovascular mortality or frequency of coronary heart disease was not observed. In 12,800 hypertensive men enrolled in the Multiple Risk Factor Intervention Trial, use of high-dose thiazide was associated with higher risk of sudden death from cardiac causes.[130] Further analysis of the data revealed that a higher mortality rate was found in a subgroup of patients who had resting electrocardiographic abnormalities at baseline. Diuretic-induced hypokalemia was postulated to be the primary reason for the increased mortality in these patients. A case-control study examined the association between thiazide treatment for hypertension and the occurrence of primary cardiac arrest.[131] One-hundred fourteen case patients were compared with 535 subjects with hypertension. Moderate-dose (50 mg) and high-dose (100 mg) hydrochlorothiazide or chlorthalidone treatment, when compared with low-dose (25 mg), were associated with moderate and large increases in risk for primary cardiac arrest, respectively. However, the risk in each group was reduced with the concurrent use of a potassium-sparing diuretic. In contrast, potassium supplements were not able to lower the risk, possibly because of poor compliance. Other trials using low doses of thiazide drugs also have shown a 20% to 25% reduction of mortality from coronary heart disease.[131]

Several mechanisms were thought to be responsible for the potential increased cardiovascular mortality associated with diuretic use. Hypokalemia increases the risk for ventricular arrhythmias.[132] The stress response associated with coronary ischemia may worsen the pre-existing hypokalemia through the release of epinephrine, which shifts plasma potassium into cells.[133] In addition, hypomagnesemia, hyperlipidemia, and hyperglycemia associated with diuretic use all may contribute to the increased cardiovascular risk, directly or through an increase of arrhythmogenic potential of other drugs, such as digoxin, class I and class III antiarrhythmic agents, and tricyclic antidepressants.[134]

Based upon these considerations, it is prudent to minimize the dose of diuretic used in treatment. Hydrochlorothiazide 12.5 mg has antihypertensive effects similar to those seen with larger doses; however, the diuretic-induced changes in plasma potassium, uric acid, and glucose concentrations are substantially smaller.[135,136]

14. What are the indications for prophylactic measures to prevent diuretic-induced hypokalemia?

Healthy, ambulatory patients with mild hypokalemia do not require treatment for the hypokalemia unless the serum potassium concentration is less than 3.5 mEq/L or the patient is symptomatic. Potassium supplementation and/or potassium-sparing diuretic therapy often are needed for patients receiving digoxin or high-dose corticosteroid therapy concomitantly and also in patients who con-

tinue to have a high dietary intake of sodium. Previous episodes of documented diuretic-induced hypokalemia, hyperaldosteronism, cirrhosis, diabetes mellitus, potassium-losing nephropathy, chronic diarrhea, surgical conditions with nitrogen loss or suction drainage, starvation or debilitation, hypokalemic familial periodic paralysis, and myocardial infarction with hypokalemia are other conditions that may necessitate potassium supplementation.

15. If potassium supplementation is needed to minimize the potential of diuretic-induced hypokalemia, what are the therapeutic options available for ambulatory patients?

Asymptomatic diuretic-induced hypokalemia can be corrected with oral potassium chloride, which is available as liquid preparations, microencapsulated tablets, and capsules. Potassium-sparing diuretics also may be used in combination with the thiazide diuretics; however, the potassium-conserving capability of these diuretics is difficult to predict quantitatively in specific patients. Although potassium-sparing diuretics may be as effective as potassium supplements in maintaining serum potassium concentrations within the normal range, they often are inadequate as sole treatment for hypokalemia.

Potassium-rich foods such as dried fruits, bananas, and orange juice are expensive, high in calories and sugar, and usually inadequate to prevent diuretic-induced hypokalemia. Diabetics and obese patients should not be encouraged to use these foods as potassium supplements without due consideration of these conditions.

Salt substitutes containing potassium salt often are recommended for hypertensive patients to minimize salt retention. Reports of hyperkalemia resulting from abuse of salt substitutes have led to concerns about the use of these products as practical dietary or therapeutic agents.[137] One teaspoonful of Morton's Salt Substitute contains 70 mEq of potassium and 0.02 mEq of sodium. Although tolerable when added modestly to soups or salads, palatability of these agents still is a common complaint. Patients with renal function impairment, heart failure, a history of electrolyte imbalance, or patients receiving potassium-sparing diuretics or potassium supplements must be cautioned about the use of salt substitutes because of the increased risk for hyperkalemia.[138]

Among the many potassium salts available, the chloride salt is the choice for replacement because in addition to hypokalemia, thiazides also can cause hypochloremia and metabolic alkalosis. Potassium salts other than potassium chloride cannot correct hypokalemic, hypochloremic, or metabolic alkalosis.

Many different oral potassium chloride preparations are available. The sustained-release formulations are preferred for replacement therapy. Enteric-coated tablets, no longer available commercially in the U.S., should not be used because they can cause small bowel ulceration accompanied by stenosis, hemorrhage, obstruction, and perforation. Fatalities have been reported from these serious adverse effects.[139] In contrast, slow-release potassium chloride tablets cause considerably fewer gastrointestinal adverse effects than the enteric-coated products and are as effective as liquid preparations. Slow release of the potassium chloride over a large segment of the intestine prevents exposure to the high, localized concentration of the potassium salt in a limited area of the bowel. The slow-release potassium chloride preparations either are sugar-coated (Slow-K, Kaon-CL) or film-coated (K-Tab, Klotrix, Klor-Con, K+10) tablets that have incorporated the salt into a wax matrix, or are gelatin capsules which contain microencapsulated potassium chloride crystals that have been coated with a water polymer (Micro-K). Both the wax-matrix and the microencapsulated potassium chloride product formulations allow slow diffusion of the salt through the gastrointestinal membrane.[140] These slow-release tablet and capsule formulations should not be chewed and should be taken with food or a large glass of water. Patients who have delayed or impaired esophageal or GI motility are susceptible to the more severe gastrointestinal adverse effects.

Hyperuricemia

Use of thiazide and loop diuretics commonly results in a dose-related hyperuricemia.[141] Urate, being a small molecule, is filtered freely into the urine. Net reabsorption and net secretion of the urate can be found in different segments of the proximal renal tubule. Net urate reabsorption is affected by sodium transport; volume contraction, as a result of diuretic use, may increase the net urate reabsorption in conjunction with the increased sodium reabsorption.[142] However, replacement of the diuretic-induced urinary salt and fluid loss will prevent such an increase in urate and sodium reabsorption.[143] Many of the diuretics are organic acids which are secreted into the urine in the proximal tubule. Such a process also may reduce the net secretion of urate which can contribute to the hyperuricemia.[144] The increased plasma concentration of uric acid often is sustained throughout the diuretic treatment and will return to pretreatment value upon diuretic discontinuation. Reducing the dose of the diuretic often normalizes the uric acid concentration; however, it might not be practical since the current diuretic effect might be needed for treatment. In most instances, diuretic-induced hyperuricemia does not require treatment and the existing dose of the diuretic may be continued. Even at plasma uric acid concentrations of 12 mg/dL, treatment is not necessary as long as the patient is asymptomatic.[145,146] A history of gout is not a contraindication to diuretic use. In patients with recurrent gout attacks, measures should be used to reduce the hyperuricemia. Probenecid is a useful uricosuric agent; it will delay the secretion of diuretic into the renal tubule without affecting its net natriuretic effect.[147] Allopurinol also may be used to reduce the plasma uric acid concentration. (See Chapter 40: Gout and Hyperuricemia.) Because of its side effect profile, allopurinol is used primarily for patients who have recurrent gouty attacks.

Hyperlipidemia

Thiazide diuretics, chlorthalidone, and furosemide can increase serum cholesterol and triglyceride concentrations.[148–152] In general, thiazide diuretics and related compounds increase total serum cholesterol concentrations by about 10 to 20 mg/dL, increase low-density lipoproteins (LDLs) by about 5 to 15 mg/dL, and increase or decrease high-density lipoproteins (HDLs) by about 1 to 3 mg/dL.[148–151] These changes in serum lipoprotein concentrations seem to be dose related and cannot be accounted for by hemoconcentration. Instead, increased hepatic lipoprotein synthesis and/or altered lipoprotein catabolism might be responsible.[148]

Since increased serum lipid levels are associated epidemiologically with coronary heart disease, the diuretic-induced alterations in serum lipids could offset the benefit gained from lowering blood pressure, especially in young patients or patients with pre-existing atherosclerotic heart disease. The reduction in mortality and morbidity rates from cardiovascular disease in patients treated with antihypertensive agents might be less than predicted because of diuretic-induced lipid abnormalities and other biochemical alterations such as hypokalemia.[130,153,154] At present, there is no evidence to substantiate an increase in mortality or morbidity secondary to the diuretic-induced lipid changes. Serum concentrations of lipids should be monitored periodically in patients with strong personal and/or family history of lipid abnormalities, premature death, or obesity. Thiazide diuretics and certain β-adrenergic blockers should be used cautiously, or not at all, in patients with moderate- to high-risk cholesterol or triglyceride concentrations. Pharmacologic interventions to lower blood lipids and dietary interventions aimed at attaining ideal body weight should be recommended vigorously. Ideally, lipids should be reduced to the 75th percentile of normal or less.

The persistence of lipid abnormalities should be documented over a period of time because this thiazide-induced effect may be transient. Lipid concentration may vary between clinic visits, and the elevations in total cholesterol, LDL-cholesterol, and triglycerides seem to return to baseline over 6 to 12 months. Patients being treated with other antihypertensive drugs, however, seem to decrease their serum lipid concentrations to below baseline values over the same period of time. The significance of these clinical observations is unknown.[155]

Hypercalcemia and Calciuria

Thiazide diuretics reduce urinary calcium excretion probably by increasing calcium reabsorption at the distal tubule and, therefore, are useful in patients with kidney stones of calcium origin.[156] Long-term use of thiazide can cause hypercalcemia; however, the small increase in serum calcium concentration is of little clinical significance and is readily reversible upon discontinuation of the diuretic.[157] In contrast, loop diuretics, such as furosemide, bumetanide, and ethacrynic acid, increase renal calcium excretion. These agents are useful for the initial treatment of hypercalcemia. Loop diuretics (instead of thiazides), therefore, should be given to patients with hypercalcemia.

Hypomagnesemia

Prolonged administration of all of the commonly used diuretics has been implicated in the pathogenesis of various cardiac arrhythmias, sudden death, and atherogenic consequences. Potassium deficiency usually is the electrolyte incriminated as the major pathogenic factor.[120] Magnesium deficiency also may be responsible for these cardiovascular events.[158] Chronic use of thiazide and loop diuretics has been reported to cause magnesium depletion which can result in cardiac arrhythmias, weakness, hypotension, and changes in sensorium.[159] Hypocalcemia also may be seen due to suppression of parathyroid hormone (PTH) secretion by magnesium depletion.[160] Patients who are alcoholic, malnourished, and chronically edematous are at risk to develop magnesium deficiency. Routine monitoring of serum magnesium concentration is not necessary for most patients except if they are at risk or are receiving large doses of the diuretic.

Hyponatremia

Thiazides induce diuresis through inhibition of sodium and water reabsorption in the kidney tubule. Since both sodium and water are lost, overdiuresis per se is not expected to cause hyponatremia. Instead, hyponatremia is a dilution of plasma sodium by excess free water. Hyponatremia is developed through an increase of ADH activity caused by volume depletion.[161,162] The enhanced ADH secretion increases free water reabsorption to result in hyponatremia. Large doses of diuretic, excessive water drinking, and severe sodium intake restriction all will accentuate the hyponatremia. Elderly patients also are prone to develop this diuretic-induced complication.

Metabolic Alkalosis and Acidosis

Metabolic alkalosis often occurs in conjunction with potassium depletion secondary to diuretic use. The diuretic-induced contraction of extracellular fluid volume results in increased secretion of aldosterone which promotes the absorption of sodium and facilitates the retention of hydrogen ions in the kidney tubule for eventual excretion. The net urinary loss of hydrogen ions results in metabolic alkalosis. Generally, reducing the dose of the diuretic will restore the acid-base balance.[163]

Acetazolamide causes metabolic acidosis because of its inhibitory effect on carbonic anhydrase which results in urinary excretion of sodium bicarbonate. Spironolactone, amiloride, and triamterene also may cause hyperchloremic metabolic acidosis because of their ability to decrease potassium and hydrogen ion secretion. Patients with renal dysfunction, receiving potassium supplements or angiotensin-converting enzyme inhibitors which reduce aldosterone secretion, are at risk to develop hyperkalemia and metabolic acidosis.

Hyperglycemia

Hyperglycemia is a common adverse effect of thiazide and loop diuretics. It has not been reported with the isolated use of potassium-sparing diuretics. Reduced insulin secretion and peripheral insulin resistance have been suggested to be the mechanisms responsible. Potassium depletion now is believed to be important in developing glucose intolerance.[164,165]

Usual therapeutic doses of thiazide and loop diuretics can worsen glucose tolerance and precipitate the onset of diabetes in patients with a history of overt or subclinical diabetes.[157,166,167] Elderly patients especially are susceptible to the diabetogenic effect of thiazides.[166] Although the thiazides can precipitate a rare nonketotic, hyperglycemic, hyperosmolar coma,[168] the hyperglycemia is of minor significance in most instances. Blood glucose concentration was found to increase by a mean of about 10 mg/dL after two years of thiazide treatment.[169] Hyperglycemia also has been associated with hypokalemia; correction of the latter has been effective in resolving the hyperglycemia in many patients. Many hypertensive patients were found to have glucose intolerance.[170] Thiazides also increased basal insulin concentration and delayed insulin response when compared with those receiving captopril.[171] These observations led to a reassessment of diuretics being a choice for first-line treatment of hypertension.[172] (See Chapter 10: Essential Hypertension.)

Diabetes is not a contraindication to the use of the thiazide and loop diuretics. Generally, diuretics have no perceptible effect on diabetes or the serum glucose concentration. If hyperglycemia develops, it can be managed by modifying the diet or increasing the dose of insulin or oral hypoglycemic agents.

Diuretic Resistance

A patient is considered resistant to diuretics if treatment with a potent diuretic in therapeutic doses fails to reduce extracellular fluid volume from an edematous state to the desired level.[173] Noncompliance to the diuretic regimen and/or sodium restriction are common reasons for diuretic resistance. Other causes are tabulated in Table 28.1.

Sodium Intake

Maintaining a low sodium intake is necessary to attain optimal response to diuretics. Net fluid loss may not be achieved despite substantial diuresis when the dietary sodium intake is excessive. Sodium chloride is reabsorbed as the diuretic action wanes.[173] Dietary sodium restriction limits the amount of sodium chloride available to compensate for the sodium loss through diuresis. Therefore, it is necessary for the patient to understand the significance of, and to comply with, a low-sodium diet. The clinician also needs to be aware of any changes in dietary habits which might affect the response to diuretic treatment. Collecting urine outflow over a 24-hour period to determine sodium excretion can be used to assess compliance of sodium restriction. Total sodium excretion of more than 100 mEq/day, when the body weight is stable, indicates the need to reduce dietary sodium intake or a higher dose of diuretic is required.[174]

Table 28.1	Causes of Resistance to Diuretics[a]

Noncompliance
  To diuretic regimen
  To sodium restriction

Volume Depletion
  ↓ GFR
  ↑ proximal tubule sodium reabsorption
  ↑ aldosterone activities

Reduced or Delayed Intestinal Diuretic Absorption
  Fluid overload
  CHF
  Hepatic cirrhosis

Reduced Diuretic Delivery to Kidney Tubule Lumen
  Renal failure
  Hypoalbuminemia

↑ **Sodium Reabsorption**
  Nephrotic syndrome
  CHF
  Nephrotic syndrome

[a] CHF = Congestive heart failure; GFR = Glomerular filtration rate.

Volume Depletion

Volume depletion is a common cause of diuretic resistance besides noncompliance of drug regimen and excessive sodium intake. Optimal response to diuretics hinges on the delivery of the diuretics to the sites of action, which often are in the loop of Henle or the distal convoluted tubule. An adequate amount of sodium ought to be present at these sites of action so that its absorption can be inhibited by the diuretics. In patients with volume depletion, the reduced glomerular filtration rate (GFR) causes a larger proportion of sodium reabsorption at the proximal tubule, leaving an insufficient amount of sodium presented to the more distal diuretic site of action. Diuresis, therefore, is impaired. Volume depletion also may reduce the amount of diuretic delivered to the luminal side of the kidney tubules, which is necessary for the diuretics to exert their effect. In addition, aldosterone secretion is increased during volume depletion. Such an increase in aldosterone increases sodium reabsorption at the distal tubule, thus impairing the net effect of the diuretics. There also is an increase in potassium excretion as sodium reabsorption is increased at the cortical collecting tubule under the influence of aldosterone.

Reduced or Delayed Intestinal Diuretic Absorption

Patients who are fluid overloaded may have reduced or delayed oral drug absorption which may compromise diuretic response. They may have intestinal mucosal edema which can delay drug absorption. In patients with advanced cardiac failure, blood flow to the intestine also is reduced. The delayed diuretic absorption in turn reduces diuretic delivery to the kidney tubules, thus limiting the renal response to the diuretic. These patients may not respond to high doses of oral furosemide but respond readily to a smaller dose if given intravenously.[175]

Renal Failure

Patients who have renal failure often demonstrate diminished response to diuretics. Thiazides generally are not effective when the GFR is less than 20 mL/minute. In contrast, loop diuretics can induce diuresis, but often at a higher dose. The primary cause for the diminished diuretic response is reduced delivery of the diuretic to the site of action. Organic acids, such as hippurate, accumulate in patients with renal failure. The anions compete with the diuretics for secretion into the kidney tubules.[176] A larger dose of loop diuretic is needed to induce an optimal response. Furosemide, at IV doses of 160 to 200 mg, attains peak diuretic responses comparable to a 40 mg dose. Doses of up to 2400 mg have been suggested for patients who are resistant. However, the risk of ototoxicity is high, especially if the dose is given as an IV bolus.

Nephrotic Syndrome

Large doses of loop diuretics are needed for patients with nephrotic syndrome even in those who have normal creatinine clearances. Delivery of furosemide to the kidney tubule is normal; however, patients with nephrotic syndrome have an abnormal amount of proteins in the urine. A larger percentage of the furosemide present in the kidney tubule is bound to the urinary proteins and rendered unavailable to interact with the receptor sites.[176] Larger doses of furosemide or more frequent administration of smaller doses are needed to overcome the binding to yield diuresis.

Hepatic Cirrhosis

Patients with hepatic cirrhosis often are resistant to loop diuretics. Delivery of the drug to the kidney tubule is not different from normal and, therefore, it is not the pharmacokinetic mechanism responsible for the resistance.[176] A limited amount of the diuretic is distributed to the ascitic fluid and also is unlikely to account for the reduced diuretic response. Patients with hepatic cirrhosis have increased aldosterone activity which is responsible for increased sodium reabsorption at the cortical collecting tubule. Sodium not reabsorbed at the loop of Henle subsequently is reabsorbed at this distal site. The diuretic action, therefore, is compromised. This is likely to account for at least some of the resistance since most cirrhotic patients respond very well to spironolactone, even though they are resistant to furosemide.[174] Other yet-to-be-identified pharmacodynamic mechanisms also may be responsible for the compromised diuretic response.[176]

Hypoalbuminemia

Patients with significant hypoalbuminemia have reduced binding of the diuretic to plasma proteins. The diuretic is freer to distribute to interstitial fluid and body tissue. A smaller amount of the drug, therefore, is available for delivery to the kidney tubules. Administration of albumin can reverse the diminished diuretic response.[177]

Congestive Heart Failure (CHF)

Patients with CHF have delayed intestinal absorption of furosemide, though the total bioavailability is not significantly different from normal subjects.[176] The diminished peak drug concentration is responsible for the diuretic resistance seen in these patients. Edema of the intestinal mucosa, reduced intestinal motility, and reduced blood perfusion are thought to be responsible for the altered drug absorption. Increasing the oral doses or the use of intravenous preparations is expected to overcome the resistance. Afterload reduction also can enhance the diuretic response through improvement in cardiovascular hemodynamics.[176] Combination therapy with metolazone also may be used.

Potassium

Homeostasis

The total potassium store is about 45 to 55 mEq/kg and varies with age and gender as well as muscle mass.[2,38] Total body potassium is decreased in the elderly, females, and persons with a low lean body mass:fat ratio.[2] Potassium is distributed unevenly between the intracellular and extracellular compartments: 98% of total body potassium resides in the intracellular compartment, predominantly the muscle, and only 2% is found in the extracellular space.[2,38,178,179] The disproportionate intracellular distribution of potassium is maintained by the Na^+-K^+ ATPase pump which transports sodium out of the cell in exchange for potassium.[178–181] The cell membrane resting potential is determined by the ratio of intracellular:extracellular potassium concentrations. As this ratio increases, hyperpolarization of the cell membrane occurs. Conversely, as it decreases, cellular depolarization results. In both situations, generation of the action potential is impaired.

The plasma potassium concentration is maintained within a narrow range, 3.5 to 5.0 mEq/L.[38,178] Although the plasma potassium concentration can be affected by the total body potassium content, one cannot accurately estimate total body potassium excess or deficit solely based upon plasma concentration. In fact, a normal plasma potassium concentration does not imply normal body potassium stores because multiple factors affect plasma potassium concentration independent of body potassium stores.[178]

Potassium homeostasis is maintained by both renal and extrarenal processes.[178,180,182] The renal process regulates total body potassium by matching potassium excretion to dietary intake (external balance).[182] The extrarenal process regulates potassium distribution across cell membrane (internal potassium balance).[178,180]

The *normal daily intake* of potassium ranges between 50 to 100 mEq.[178,182] About 90% of ingested potassium is eliminated by the kidneys and about 10% is eliminated via the GI tract.[182] Potassium is filtered freely through the glomerulus and then reabsorbed. By the time the filtrate has reached the distal convoluted tubule, over 90% of filtered potassium has been reabsorbed.[182,183] The amount of potassium excreted is determined by distal tubular potassium secretion. Potassium is secreted by the principal cells of the cortical collecting duct under the influence of aldosterone. Hyperkalemia, increased potassium load, and angiotensin II all stimulate aldosterone secretion.[178]

Factors that affect renal potassium excretion include tubular flow, sodium delivery to the distal segments of the nephron, presence of poorly absorbable anions that increase luminal electronegativity, acid-base status, and aldosterone activity.[182,183] Potassium excretion increases during hyperkalemia and decreases in times of potassium depletion. Excretion of an acute potassium load is a slow process. Only one-half of the potassium load is excreted in the first four to six hours. Lethal hyperkalemia might ensue were it not for the extrarenal process that regulates intracellular/extracellular potassium distribution.[178]

The Na^+-K^+ ATPase pump is pivotal in maintaining internal potassium balance by extruding sodium from the cell in exchange for potassium.[178,181] Different hormonal factors regulate the activity of the Na^+-K^+ ATPase pump, namely insulin, catecholamines, and aldosterone. Insulin is the most important regulator.[178–181] It enhances potassium uptake by muscle, liver, and adipose tissue by stimulating Na^+-K^+ ATPase.[185,186] Indeed, basal insulin secretion is essential for potassium homeostasis.[178] While β_2-adrenergic agonists activate the Na^+-K^+ ATPase pump via cyclic AMP and cause hypokalemia, α-adrenergic stimulation promotes hepatic potassium release and causes hyperkalemia.[187] Epinephrine, an alpha and beta agonist, causes a transient increase in plasma potassium (alpha agonism) followed by a more sustained decrease (beta agonism).[187,188] Besides its kaliuretic effect and enhanced potassium secretion in the colon, aldosterone also is important in the extrarenal regulation of potassium by stimulating Na^+-K^+ ATPase.[190]

Other factors that affect the transcellular distribution of potassium include systemic pH, plasma tonicity, and exercise.[178,181] The effect of acid-base balance on potassium distribution is not readily predictable and depends upon both the nature and the direction of the underlying disorder.[191,192] The concomitant effect of the acid-base disorder on renal potassium excretion further complicates the relationship between plasma potassium concentration and pH.[178,191] In acute inorganic acidosis, plasma potassium concentration increases by 0.2 to 1.7 mEq/L per 0.1 U decrease in pH. However, chronic inorganic metabolic acidosis usually is associated with hypokalemia because of urinary potassium loss, as seen in both proximal (type II) and distal (type I) renal tubular acidosis.[178,191] In contrast, organic acidosis usually does not affect potassium distribution.[192] However, other associated factors in the organic acidosis may affect cellular potassium distribution.[191] For example, hyperglycemia in diabetic ketoacidosis may increase serum potassium concentration because of the hypertonic effect of glucose.[193] Acute metabolic alkalosis only modestly decreases the plasma potassium concentration: 0.3 mEq/L for each 0.1 U pH increment.[178,191] Like chronic metabolic acidosis, chronic metabolic alkalosis is associated with hypokalemia and causes profound renal potassium wasting. Respiratory acid-base disorders usually are associated with less significant changes in plasma potassium concentration than metabolic acid-base disorders.[191]

Hypertonicity causes cell shrinkage and increases the intracellular to extracellular fluid potassium gradient, favoring potassium egress.[194] Exercise usually is associated with an increase in the serum potassium concentration.[195] The degree of hyperkalemia depends upon the intensity of the exercise.

Hypokalemia

Etiology

16. J.P., a 60-year-old female, was brought to the ER with complaints of malaise, generalized weakness, nausea, and vomiting for 3 days. Past medical history includes hypertension for 20 years. J.P.'s current medications include hydrochlorothiazide 25 mg/day and nifedipine XL 30 mg/day. However, she has not been able to take her medications in the past few days because of vomiting. J.P. denies recent diarrhea or use of laxatives. Her BP was 130/70 mm Hg, pulse 80 beats/min while sitting; and 120/70 mm Hg with a pulse of 95 beats/min on standing. Physical examination revealed a thin, elderly female with poor skin turgor and dry mucous membranes. The jugular vein was flat. T wave flattening was noted on ECG. Laboratory tests showed serum Na 138 mEq/L, K 2.1 mEq/L, Cl 100 mEq/L, bicarbonate 32 mEq/L, BUN 30 mg/dL, creatinine 1.2 mg/dL, and glucose 100 mg/dL. ABG showed pH of 7.50, pCO_2 45 mm Hg, and pO_2 70 mm Hg at room air. Urine electrolytes revealed Na 30 mEq/L, K 60 mEq/L, and Cl <15 mEq/L. The impression was gastroenteritis. What are the etiologies for J.P.'s hypokalemia? [SI units: serum Na 138 mmol/L; K 2.1 mmol/L; Cl 100 mmol/L; bicarbonate 32 mmol/L; BUN 10.7 mmol/L; creatinine 106.1 μmol/L; glucose 5.55 mmol/L; pCO_2 6.0 kPa; pO_2 9.33 kPa; urine Na 30 mmol/L; K 60 mmol/L; Cl <15 mmol/L]

In the evaluation of hypokalemia, one should determine whether the hypokalemia is a result of low intake, increased cellular uptake of potassium or loss of potassium via the kidneys, GI tract, or skin.[38,196] History and physical evidence of potassium depletion, medication history including use of over-the-counter medicines, as well as assessment of the patient's blood pressure, extracellular volume, and concurrent acid-base status, can provide clues to the etiologies of hypokalemia.[38,196]

As J.P. has been unable to eat in the past few days, decreased oral intake may have contributed to her hypokalemia. Since most foods are rich in potassium, inadequate intake rarely is the sole cause of potassium depletion unless there is inappropriate and continued renal or extrarenal losses, or potassium intake is severely restricted to less than 10 to 15 mEq/day.[196] The inappropriately elevated urinary potassium concentration suggests that the kidney is the source of potassium wastage.[18,38,196]

Alkalosis,[191] insulin administration,[178,186] hypertonic solution administration,[194] periodic paralysis,[197] β2-agonists,[198] barium poisoning,[199] and treatment of megaloblastic anemia with vitamin B_{12}[200] all have been associated with increased cellular potassium uptake. Although the relationship between the degree of hypokalemia and increase in blood pH varies widely,[191] J.P.'s metabolic alkalosis probably enhances the cellular uptake of potassium. However, the transcellular shift of potassium should not lead to potassium depletion.

The GI tract is important for potassium loss particularly in vomiting and diarrhea. It should be noted that the potassium content of gastric secretion (5 to 10 mEq/L) is much less than that of the intestinal secretion (up to 90 mEq/L).[196] Therefore, loss of a large volume of gastric secretion is needed to produce substantial potassium depletion. Indeed, potassium loss from vomiting is mediated by renal loss. The absence of diarrhea in J.P. also excludes the GI tract as the source of potassium loss. The potassium concentration of sweat is less than 10 mEq/L. Therefore, one needs to have profuse sweating as in vigorous exercise in a hot, humid environment or severe burns to cause substantial cutaneous potassium loss.

The inappropriately high urinary potassium concentration indicates the kidney as the source of potassium loss in J.P.[18,38,196] The urinary potassium concentration is a good marker for differentiating various hypokalemic syndromes.[38] A urinary potassium excretion of less than 20 mEq/day suggests extrarenal potassium loss. However, one cannot exclude renal potassium wastage unless the low urinary potassium excretion is accompanied by at least 100 mEq/day of sodium since a low-sodium diet can reduce renal potassium excretion.[38] In J.P., the metabolic alkalosis and the volume contraction (urinary chloride concentration <15 mEq/L) indicate renal potassium wastage.[38,196] The distal delivery of a large load of sodium bicarbonate, the increased aldosterone activity from hypovolemia to promote sodium reabsorption in the collecting duct, the increased electronegativity because of poorly absorbable bicarbonate ions, and the decreased luminal (urinary) chloride concentration all enhance potassium secretion and severely impair the kidney's ability to conserve potassium. The hydrochlorothiazide, which J.P. had been taking until three days before admission, also could induce hypokalemia and induce volume depletion, hypochloremic metabolic alkalosis, and renal potassium wastage. However, the diuretic is unlikely to be the cause for J.P.'s hypokalemia because she has stopped taking the medication. The latter is reflected by the low urinary chloride concentration.[18] Bartter's syndrome, which presents as normal blood pressure, hypokalemia, and hypochloremic metabolic alkalosis, and renal potassium wastage, also can be ruled out by the low urinary chloride concentration.[201]

Since hydrochlorothiazide can cause hypomagnesemia,[158] serum magnesium concentration should be obtained to exclude hypomagnesemia as a cause of J.P.'s hypokalemia.[202] Other causes for renal potassium wastage include renal tubular acidosis;[203] drugs such as carbonic-anhydrase inhibitors,[204] penicillins,[205] cisplatin,[206] aminoglycosides,[207] rifampin,[208] lithium[209] and L-dopa;[210] toluene;[211] and postobstructive diuresis. In a patient with hypokalemia, renal potassium wasting, and hypertension, one should consider excessive mineralocorticoid activity from hyperreninism (e.g., malignant hypertension,[212] renovascular hypertension, and renin-producing tumor); primary hyperaldosteronism[189] (e.g., adrenal adenoma, bilateral adrenal hyperplasia); increased endogenous mineralocorticoid production (e.g., Liddle's syndrome[213]); and exogenous intake (e.g., licorice or carbenoxolone use).[186,196]

Finally, in an asymptomatic hypokalemic patient with no apparent causes for potassium depletion or transcellular redistribution, pseudohypokalemia should be excluded before an intensive evaluation is pursued.[196] Spurious hypokalemia can occur in leukemic patients whose leukocyte count ranges from 100,000 to 250,000 cells/μL[214] due to the uptake of potassium by leukemic cells when the blood specimen is allowed to stand at room temperature.

Clinical Manifestations

17. What clinical manifestations of hypokalemia are evident in J.P.?

The clinical presentation of hypokalemia depends upon the severity of potassium depletion and is a result of changes in cell membrane polarization.[196] Patients usually are asymptomatic when the plasma potassium level is between 3.0 and 3.5 mEq/L although they may complain of malaise, weakness, fatigue, and myalgia. J.P.'s muscle weakness and electrocardiographic changes are the muscular and cardiac manifestations of hypokalemia, respectively.[215,216]

Potassium depletion can lead to hyperpolarization of myocardial cells and a prolonged refractory period. With serum potassium concentrations less than 3 mEq/L, T wave flattening, ST segment depression, and prominent U waves are seen on ECG.[216] Mild hypokalemia (potassium concentration between 3.0 to 3.5 mEq/L) potentially is arrhythmogenic in patients with underlying coronary artery disease. The incidence of ventricular arrhythmia increases with the degree of hypokalemia.[121,124] Patients without underlying heart disease may be prone to the effects of hypokalemia during exercise because the potassium concentration may drop below 3.0 mEq/L as a result of β_2-adrenergic receptor-mediated cellular potassium uptake, especially if the patient's pre-exercise potassium concentration is less than 3.5 mEq/L.[196] Potassium depletion also may cause elevated blood pressure,[196] and potassium supplementation can lower blood pressure.[218]

When the serum potassium concentration is less than 2.5 to 3.0 mEq/L, muscle weakness, cramps, general malaise, fatigue, restless leg syndrome, and paresthesia can occur.[196] Potassium normally allows vasodilation in skeletal muscle. Severe potassium depletion (<2.5 mEq/L) may result in elevation of serum creatine phosphokinase, aldolase, and aspartate aminotransferase levels.[196,215] Rhabdomyolysis may ensue when the serum potassium concentration falls below 2.0 mEq/L.

Chronic potassium depletion can lead to changes in renal function and structure. Decreased glomerular filtration rate, renal blood flow, disturbance in tubular sodium handling, impairment of the urinary concentrating ability with polydipsia, and ADH-resistant nephrogenic diabetes insipidus may occur.[196,219] Reversible pathologic changes include renal hypertrophy and epithelial vacuolization of the proximal convoluted tubule. However, interstitial scarring and tubular atrophy have been reported with prolonged potassium depletion.[196]

Other effects of hypokalemia and potassium depletion include decreased insulin secretion resulting in carbohydrate intolerance,[219] metabolic alkalosis, and increased renal ammoniogenesis.[221] The latter may play a role in the development of hepatic encephalopathy.

Treatment

18. How should J.P.'s hypokalemia be managed?

The etiology for J.P.'s protracted vomiting should be evaluated and corrected accordingly. Adequate fluid replacement with sodium, potassium, and chloride should be provided to replenish the volume deficit and alleviate her hypochloremic metabolic alkalosis. Hydrochlorothiazide should continue to be withheld.

The amount of potassium deficit and continued potassium loss should be determined.[196,222,223] It has been estimated that a 1 mEq/L fall in serum potassium from 4 mEq/L to 3 mEq/L represents approximately a 200 mEq deficit.[178] When the serum potassium falls below 3 mEq/L, the total body deficit increases by 200 to 400 mEq per 1 mEq/L reduction in serum concentration. More recent data suggest that greater degrees of potassium loss may occur: a deficit of 100 mEq per 0.27 mEq/L fall in serum potassium concentration.[178] It should be noted that transcellular redistribution of potassium may significantly alter the relationship between serum concentration and total body deficit.[178,196] Hence, potassium repletion should be guided by close monitoring of serum concentrations instead of using a predetermined amount. Analysis of J.P.'s urine for potassium content can help to assess the need for additional replacement.

The route of administration depends upon the acuity and severity of hypokalemia.[196,222,223] Oral supplementation usually is preferred. The parenteral route is indicated for patients who cannot tolerate high doses of potassium supplements, and those with severe or symptomatic hypokalemia.[222,223] J.P.'s potassium deficit is estimated to be between 300 to 500 mEq. Since she is only moderately symptomatic, aggressive therapy is not indicated. Potassium chloride can be added to her IV fluid in a concentration of 40 mEq/L and infused at no faster than 10 mEq/hour. For patients with life-threatening hypokalemia-induced arrhythmia, or those with potassium less than 2.0 mEq/L, a more concentrated potassium solution (60 mEq/L) can be infused at a rate not exceeding 40 mEq/hour.[222] Too concentrated a solution, or too rapid a rate of infusion, likely would cause phlebitis, and potentially cause arrhythmias, especially when administered in a central line. A concentration of 200 mEq/L administered at a rate of 20 mEq/hour has been administered safely to patients in the intensive care setting.[224] The potassium concentration should be monitored every four hours and more frequently in patients with severe potassium depletion, or when rapid infusion is given.[224] Electrocardiographic monitoring is mandatory because life-threatening hyperkalemia may ensue.[196,222-224]

Parenteral potassium can be given as chloride, acetate, or phosphate.[222-224] The chloride salt is preferred in J.P. who has concurrent hypochloremic metabolic alkalosis. The acetate preparation is useful in cases of concomitant metabolic acidosis. Potassium phosphate is in order if hypophosphatemia coexists. In the latter condition, serum calcium concentration also should be monitored because hypocalcemia may ensue. Glucose solution should be avoided as the vehicle because glucose-induced insulin secretion will promote intracellular potassium uptake.[225]

Once J.P.'s potassium levels are replenished and when she can take medicine by mouth, oral potassium chloride (13.0 mEq K$^+$/gm) can be started. Dosage can be titrated according to individual requirements. Other potassium salts that are available include gluconate (4.3 mEq K$^+$/gm), citrate (9.2 mEq K$^+$/gm), acetate (10.2 mEq K$^+$/gm), and bicarbonate (10 mEq K$^+$/gm).[224] They are available as liquids, effervescent tablets, and modified-release tablets. The liquid is absorbed rapidly but usually is not well tolerated because of its unpleasant taste and associated nausea and heartburn.[222,223] Patient compliance generally is poor. The same problem occurs with the effervescent tablets. The slow-release wax-based and the microencapsulated formulations have replaced the enteric-coated preparation because the latter has been associated with upper gastrointestinal irritation, and the hazards of small bowel ulceration, hemorrhage, perforation, and stenosis.[222]

The modified-release preparations are designed to gradually release potassium in the intestine and minimize the local, high potassium concentration that is associated with ulceration.[226,227]

Hyperkalemia

Etiology

19. A.B., a 25-year-old female with Type I diabetes and hypertension, returned to the clinic for follow-up of BP control. BP was 170/90 mm Hg with a pulse of 80 beats/min. Physical examination is remarkable for 2+ pedal edema. Laboratory tests show plasma Na 135 mEq/L, K 5.8 mEq/L, Cl 108 mEq/L, total CO_2 20 mEq/L, BUN 28 mg/dL, creatinine 2 mg/dL, and glucose 200 mg/dL. Current medications include captopril 25 mg PO TID, Dyazide 1 capsule daily, Human NPH insulin 30 U SQ Q AM. She also is using ibuprofen 200 mg PRN for arthritis. She uses salt substitute occasionally. What is the etiology of her hyperkalemia? [SI units: Na 135 mmol/L; K 5.8 mmol/L; Cl 108 mmol/L; total CO_2 20 mmol/L; BUN 10 mmol/L; creatinine 176.8 µmol/L; glucose 11.1 mmol/L]

Causes for spurious hyperkalemia always should be considered before further evaluation is pursued.[228] Spurious hyperkalemia can be caused by severe leukocytosis ($>500,000/mm^3$),[229] or thrombocytosis ($>750,000/mm^3$),[230] and hemolysis within the test tube.[231] *Pseudohyperkalemia* is a test tube phenomenon and is a result of potassium release during blood coagulation.[38] These disorders are diagnosed easily by comparing serum and plasma potassium concentrations from the same blood sample.[228] The two values should agree within 0.2 to 0.3 mEq/L. Improper tourniquet technique causing strangulation of the patient's arm before blood sampling also may result in hyperkalemia.[232]

Evaluation for the etiologies of hyperkalemia can be approached systematically by considering possible disturbances in internal and external potassium balance. The former involves transcellular flux of potassium from the intracellular to the extracellular space while the latter involves either an increased intake, including increased endogenous potassium load (e.g., rhabdomyolysis[233] and tumor lysis syndrome),[234] and decreased elimination. A thorough medication history is important in identifying drugs that are associated with hyperkalemia.[68,235,236] (Also see Chapter 30: Chronic Renal Failure for additional information on hyperkalemia.)

A dietary history should ascertain if A.B. has an increased consumption of potassium-rich foods or potassium supplements. The frequency of her use of salt substitute should be known since it predominantly is potassium chloride.[237] A.B. has mild renal insufficiency (estimated Cl_{Cr} of 40 mL/minute). Hyperkalemia usually does not occur until the glomerular filtration rate is less than 10 to 15 mL/minute, unless there is concurrent hypoaldosteronism or distal tubular potassium secretory defects.[228]

Several factors can account for A.B.'s inability to excrete potassium. Besides insulin deficiency, A.B. also exhibits a potassium secretory defect. Diabetes has a high incidence of the syndrome of hyporeninemic hypoaldosteronism which usually presents as hyperkalemia and hyperchloremic metabolic acidosis.[238] Other diseases such as obstructive uropathy, sickle cell disease, lupus nephritis, and a variety of tubulointerstitial diseases (e.g., gouty nephropathy and analgesic nephropathy) also are frequently associated with a decreased renin and aldosterone state and present with hyperkalemia.[239] Adrenal insufficiency usually presents with hyperkalemia because of mineralocorticoid deficiency.[240] It should be noted that obstructive uropathy and other tubulointerstitial diseases such as sickle cell diseases, lupus nephritis, and transplant nephropathy also can present with hyperkalemic distal renal tubular acidosis with normal aldosterone level.[241] A.B.'s poorly controlled hyperglycemia may cause movement of potassium-rich

fluid from the intracellular space to the extracellular space because of the increased tonicity.

A.B. also is using several medications that may impair her ability to excrete potassium. Captopril, by decreasing the formation of angiotensin II, indirectly decreases the secretion of aldosterone.[242,243] Similarly, ibuprofen and other NSAIDs inhibit prostaglandin production and inhibit both renin and aldosterone secretion, resulting in hyperkalemia.[244] Other drugs that cause hyperkalemia by impairment of renin and aldosterone production include β-adrenergic blockers,[245] lithium,[246] heparin,[247–249] and pentamidine.[250] Triamterene, the potassium-sparing diuretic in Dyazide, blocks sodium entry into the principal cells of the collecting duct; hence, luminal electronegativity is decreased and potassium secretion is inhibited.[251] Other drugs that inhibit tubular potassium secretion include amiloride, spironolactone, high-dose trimethoprim,[252,253] cyclosporine,[254] and digitalis preparations.[255] Digitalis inhibits Na^+-K^+ ATPase and causes decreased tubular potassium secretion as well as reduced cellular potassium uptake. Arginine,[256,257] succinylcholine,[258,259] β-adrenergic blockers, α-adrenergic agonists, and hypertonic solutions also cause hyperkalemia by impairing transcellular potassium distribution.

Clinical Manifestations

20. V.C., a 44-year-old female hemodialysis patient, returns to the outpatient unit for routine hemodialysis with complaint of severe muscle weakness. Vital signs include: BP of 120/80 mm Hg, pulse 90 beats/min, RR 20 breaths/min, and temperature 98 °F. Laboratory data include: serum K of 8.9 mEq/L, total CO_2 15 mmol/L, BUN 60 mg/dL, creatinine 9 mg/dL, and glucose 100 mg/dL. An ECG reveals increased PR interval and a widened QRS complex. What clinical manifestations of hyperkalemia are evident in V.C.? [SI units: K 8.9 mmol/L; total CO_2 15 mmol/L; BUN 21.42 mmol/L; creatinine 795.6 µmol/L; glucose 5.55 mmol/L]

Hyperkalemia decreases the intracellular:extracellular potassium ratio. Hence, the resting membrane potential becomes less negative and moves closer to the threshold excitation potential. Muscle weakness and flaccid paralysis result when the resting membrane potential approaches the threshold potential, rendering the excitable cells unable to sustain an action potential.

The cardiac toxicity of hyperkalemia is a major cause of morbidity and mortality. The electrocardiographic findings usually parallel the degree of hyperkalemia.[216] When plasma potassium exceeds 5.5 to 6.0 mEq/L, narrow, peaked T waves and a shortened QT interval are seen. As the plasma potassium concentration increases, the QRS complex widens with decreasing P wave amplitude. As the level reaches 8 mEq/L, the P wave disappears. The QRS complex continues to widen and merges with the T wave to form a sine wave pattern. If these ECG changes are not recognized and no treatment is initiated, ventricular fibrillation and asystole will ensue. Various factors can modify the cardiac effects of hyperkalemia. Hyponatremia, hypocalcemia, and hypomagnesemia all reduce the threshold potential, rendering it closer to the resting potential.[228] V.C.'s muscle weakness, ECG, chronic renal failure, and serum potassium concentration all are consistent with severe hyperkalemia.

Treatment

21. How should V.C.'s hyperkalemia be treated?

Hyperkalemia with ECG changes requires urgent treatment. Three therapeutic modalities are available: a) agents that antagonize the cardiac effects of hyperkalemia; b) agents that shift potassium from the extracellular into the intracellular space; and c) agents that enhance potassium elimination.[179,181,228,260]

Considering V.C.'s severe ECG changes, calcium should be administered at a dose of 10 to 20 mL of 10% calcium gluconate intravenously over one to three minutes.[179,181,228,260] Calcium counteracts the depolarizing effect of hyperkalemia by increasing the threshold potential, thus making it less negative and moving it away from the resting potential. The onset of action is only a few minutes, but the effect is short-lived, lasting about 15 to 60 minutes.[228,260] The dose can be repeated in five minutes if ECG changes do not resolve and repeated later as needed for recurrence of ECG changes.[228] However, if there is no response after the second dose, further administration is not beneficial. Calcium should be used cautiously in hyperkalemic patients with digitalis overdose because hypercalcemia worsens the cardiotoxicity of digoxin.[228,260]

Since calcium does not decrease serum potassium concentration, maneuvers to shift potassium from plasma into the cells should be started. Three modalities are available: insulin, β_2 agonists, and sodium bicarbonate.

Insulin rapidly shifts potassium into the cell in a dose-dependent fashion.[186,260] Maximal hypokalemic effect occurs at insulin concentrations exceeding 20 to 40 times the basal levels.[186] Endogenous insulin secretion in response to dextrose administration cannot achieve the same high concentrations as exogenous insulin does.[178] Dextrose administration may worsen hyperkalemia because of hypertonicity, particularly in diabetic patients. However, dextrose always is administered with insulin to prevent hypoglycemia.[179] Five to ten units of regular insulin can be given with 50 mL of 50% dextrose as IV boluses.[179,228] This can be followed by a continuous infusion of 10% dextrose at 50 mL/hour to prevent late hypoglycemia.[179] Twenty units of insulin can be added to 1 L of 10% dextrose and administered at a rate of 50 mL/hour to prevent fasting hyperkalemia.[261] The onset of action is 15 to 30 minutes and the effect persists for four to six hours.[228] In the hyperkalemic diabetic patient who already is hyperglycemic, insulin alone might be sufficient. In a patient with end-stage renal disease, the insulin-glucose combination is more predictable in lowering plasma potassium concentrations than epinephrine or sodium bicarbonate.[179,260,261]

β_2 agonists administered intravenously or via nebulization decrease serum potassium.[262-264] Both routes of administration can achieve a similar decrease in serum potassium concentrations, but the hypokalemic effect is evident 30 minutes after IV administration, as compared to 90 minutes after nebulization.[262] Although the IV route has a faster onset of action, nebulization is easier to set up. The duration of the hypokalemic effect is three to four hours.[262-264] The effect is additive to that of insulin.[265] Nebulized albuterol 20 mg dissolved in 4 mL of saline and inhaled over ten minutes can be given after insulin to achieve an additional effect.[265] Most patients respond favorably with minimal side effects. Tachycardia occurs with both routes of administration, but tends to be less with nebulization.[262] Caution should be exercised in patients with underlying coronary artery disease. Elderly patients may have a decreased response.[264] Epinephrine appears to be less effective, particularly in renal failure patients.[260] Interestingly, besides its additive hypokalemic effect, administration of a β_2 agonist after insulin can reduce the incidence of hypoglycemia.[265]

Although sodium bicarbonate has long been recommended for the acute treatment of hyperkalemia,[228,266] its efficacy in this setting has been questioned.[179,260] The usual dose is 44 to 50 mEq infused slowly over five minutes and can be repeated in 30 minutes when necessary.[228] Alternatively, it can be added to dextrose and saline solution to form an isotonic sodium bicarbonate infusion.[267] The effect is variable and may be delayed up to four hours. Unlike its efficacy in patients with normal renal function or mild renal insufficiency, bicarbonate has been reported to be ineffective in patients on maintenance hemodialysis. Bicarbonate therapy, therefore, is not a reliable option in the acute management of hyperkalemia. However, sodium bicarbonate may be beneficial in patients with severe metabolic acidosis (pH <7.20).[179] Volume overload and metabolic alkalosis are potential complications of sodium bicarbonate therapy.[179,228,260]

The definitive treatment of hyperkalemia is the removal of potassium from the body. Sodium polystyrene sulfonate (Kayexalate) with sorbitol is an ion-exchange resin that enhances potassium excretion in the stools.[268,269] Each gram of Kayexalate exchanges 0.5 to 1.0 mmol of potassium for an equal amount of sodium. Kayexalate can be administered orally or rectally. The latter route is preferred in the symptomatic hyperkalemic patient because intestinal potassium exchange mainly occurs in the ileum and colon.[228] A dose of 50 gm Kayexalate in sorbitol can be given as a retention enema at four- to six-hour intervals. The enema should be retained for at least 30 to 60 minutes. Alternatively, 15 to 60 gm of Kayexalate with sorbitol suspension can be given orally. The dose can be repeated as needed. The onset of action is about one to two hours after administration. The major side effects are GI intolerance, including diarrhea, and sodium overload.[179,228] Intestinal necrosis also has been reported with Kayexalate in which sorbitol appears to be the cause.[270,271]

Hemodialysis is the most efficient way of removing potassium.[179,228,260] Although peritoneal dialysis also can remove potassium, its potassium clearance is less than that of hemodialysis.[228,272] The effect is immediate as soon as hemodialysis is started and lasts for the duration of dialysis.[228,260] However, the amount of potassium removed is variable.[273] Dialysis with a glucose-free dialysate may remove 30% more potassium than one containing 200 mg/dL of glucose.[274] Although V.C. is on chronic maintenance hemodialysis, the severe cardiac effects of hyperkalemia she experienced warrant immediate institution of the measures described above while awaiting setup of the dialysis equipment.[260] Loop diuretics, which enhance kaliuresis, rarely are useful in management of severe hyperkalemia, especially in patients with renal dysfunction.[228]

After V.C.'s condition stabilized, she admitted eating a lot of fruits in the past few days. Noncompliance with dietary potassium restriction is the most common cause for acute and chronic hyperkalemia in a dialysis patient. Therefore, V.C. should be counseled on the importance of eating potassium-rich food in moderation. Medications which impair V.C.'s extrarenal potassium handling should be avoided. If V.C. remains noncompliant with dietary restriction and is chronically hyperkalemic, then Kayexalate may need to be given three to four times weekly to ameliorate hyperkalemia.[179] However, if hyperkalemia is associated with metabolic acidosis, an alkalizing agent should be added to maintain serum bicarbonate concentration of about 24 mEq/L.[179,228]

Calcium
Homeostasis

In adults, approximately 1400 gm of calcium is in the body. More than 99% of the body's calcium is stored in bone. Nonetheless, the 0.1% of the total body calcium that is in the plasma and extravascular fluid plays a critical role in many physiologic and metabolic processes. Calcium is important in maintaining nerve tissue excitability and muscle contractility. It regulates the secretory activities of exocrine and endocrine glands, serves as a cofactor for enzyme systems and the coagulation cascade. It also is an essential component of bone metabolism.

Plasma calcium concentration is maintained within a relatively narrow range: 8.5 to 10.5 mg/dL. This is accomplished through a complex interaction between parathyroid hormone, vitamin D, and calcitonin and also the effect of these hormones on calcium metabolism in bone, the GI tract, and kidneys.

Normally, about 40% of the plasma calcium is protein bound, primarily to albumin, and is nondiffusible.[276] Of the 60% that is diffusible, approximately 13% is complexed to various small ligands: phosphate, citrate, and sulfate. The remaining 47% is ionized, free, and physiologically active. Changes in serum protein concentration will alter the concentrations of both protein-bound and total calcium. Serum albumin concentration, therefore, needs to be monitored to adequately interpret the total serum calcium concentration. Each 1 gm/dL increase in serum albumin concentration is expected to increase the protein-bound calcium by 0.8 mg/dL, thus increasing the total serum calcium concentration by the same amount. The total serum calcium, therefore, can be corrected by the following equation:

$$\text{Corrected Ca} = \text{Observed Ca}$$
$$+ 0.8(\text{Normal Albumin} - \text{Observed Albumin})$$

Eq 28.7

Calcium also is bound to plasma globulins: 0.16 mg of calcium for each gram of globulin. When the total globulin concentration exceeds 6 gm/dL (normal: 2.3 to 3.5 gm/dL), a moderate hypercalcemia may be seen. Changes in pH have an effect on calcium protein binding: acidosis decreases calcium binding resulting in an increase in free calcium fraction, while an increase in pH reduces the amount of ionized calcium. Changes in serum phosphate and sulfate concentrations are expected to alter the fraction of ionized calcium due to the formation of calcium complexes with these anions. The presence of abnormal proteins in the plasma with high affinity for calcium binding, as in patients with multiple myeloma, also affects the equation presented above for serum calcium concentration correction.[277]

Serum calcium concentration is regulated by the combined effect of GI absorption and secretion, renal reabsorption, and turnover of the skeletal calcium pool. Several hormones, such as PTH, 1,25-dihydroxyvitamin D_3, and calcitonin, have significant effects on these processes. Balanced diets generally contain 600 to 1000 mg of calcium while the minimum daily requirement is 400 to 500 mg. Calcium primarily is absorbed in the duodenum and jejunum via saturable and nonsaturable processes.[278,279] The nonsaturable process is diffusive in nature and varies with luminal calcium concentration. The saturable carrier-mediated component is stimulated by 1,25-dihydroxyvitamin D_3. Absorption of calcium is enhanced when the calcium intake is low and also when the demand is increased, such as pregnancy and depletion of total body calcium. Conversely, protein deficiency can reduce intestinal calcium absorption presumably because of the reduced amount of specific calcium-binding protein.[280] Calcium also is secreted into the bowel lumen; this may be responsible for the presence of negative calcium balance when there is no oral calcium intake.[281]

The portion of plasma calcium that is not bound to protein is filtered by the glomerulus. About 97% to 99.5% of the filtered calcium is reabsorbed of which 60% is reabsorbed in the proximal tubule, 20% in the ascending limb, 10% in the distal tubule, and 3% to 10% in the collecting duct.[282,283] About 20% of the calcium in the kidney tubule is ionized while the remainder is bound to cations such as citrate, sulfate, phosphate, and gluconate. The extent of calcium resorption depends upon the presence of specific cations and also upon the urine pH which affects the fraction of calcium that is bound to cations.[281] Passive reabsorption at the proximal convoluted tubule is linked closely to sodium transport and is increased by extracellular fluid contraction and decreased by volume expansion.[284] At the proximal straight tubule, the transport process is active and dissociable from sodium and water transport.[284] Parathyroid hormone increases the calcium reabsorption at the distal tubule and also at the collecting duct independent of sodium reabsorption.[284] Acidosis also can increase renal calcium excretion by inhibiting tubule reabsorption and by increasing the ultrafilterable calcium through reduced binding of calcium to proteins. Conversely, alkalosis promotes calcium protein binding, thus reducing the amount of ultrafilterable calcium.[284] It also induces hypocalciuria with and without the effect of PTH. Phosphorus (P) administration reduces renal calcium excretion while phosphorus depletion increases urinary calcium elimination. Normally, about 50 to 300 mg of calcium is excreted by the kidneys daily; the amount may be increased to 600 mg/day.[282]

The other important factor in regulating plasma calcium concentration is bone metabolism. The rate of bone turnover and calcium resorption is influenced by parathyroid hormone, 1,25-dihydroxyvitamin D_3, and calcitonin.[284]

Hypercalcemia

Etiology

22. A.C., a 62-year-old female, is brought to the hospital by family members because she has become more lethargic and unresponsive over the past several days. Approximately 4 years ago, she underwent a radical mastectomy and node dissection followed by radiation and chemotherapy for breast carcinoma. Despite several courses of chemotherapy, she developed metastasis to the bone. About 1 week before this admission, A.C. complained of fatigue, muscle weakness, and anorexia. Since then she has spent most of her time in bed and has very limited oral intake. Medications taken before admission included hydrochlorothiazide, oral morphine sulfate, and an experimental protocol with tamoxifen.

Physical examination reveals a dehydrated, cachectic female responsive only to painful stimuli. Vital signs include BP of 100/60 mm Hg and respiratory rate of 16/min. Pertinent laboratory values are Na 138 mEq/L, K 4.5 mEq/L, Cl 99 mEq/L, CO_2 33 mEq/L, BUN 40 mg/dL, creatinine 1.2 mg/dL, Ca 19 mg/dL, P 4.5 mg/dL, and albumin 3.0 gm/dL. ECG revealed a shortened QT interval. What are the common causes of hypercalcemia? Which of these might be responsible for the hypercalcemia seen in A.C.? [SI units: Na 138 mmol/L; K 4.5 mmol/L; Cl 99 mmol/L; CO_2 33 mmol/L; BUN 14.3 mmol/L; creatinine 106.1 μmol/L; Ca 4.75 mmol/L; P 1.45 mmol/L; albumin 30 gm/L]

Malignancy and primary hyperparathyroidism are the most common etiologies for hypercalcemia.[285] Hematological malignancies, such as multiple myeloma, tend to be responsible for more hypercalcemia than patients with solid tumors. Cancer of the breast, lung, head, and neck as well as renal cell carcinoma are solid tumors commonly associated with hypercalcemia. Malignancy may cause paraneoplastic hypercalcemia secondary to bone metastasis which results in increased bone resorption. Alternatively, patients may develop hypercalcemia in the absence of bone metastasis due to the production of osteolytic humoral factors by the tumor. The mediators secreted may be PTH, parathyroid hormone-like substances, prostaglandins, cytokines, transforming growth factor alpha, and tumor necrosis factor.[286]

Hyperparathyroidism is the other common cause of hypercalcemia: the etiology of primary hyperparathyroidism is unclear. Females tend to have primary hyperparathyroidism more frequently, especially in the fourth to sixth decades of life.[287] About 75% of patients have a single adenoma while much smaller percentages of patients have multiglandular disease, hyperplasia, or carcinoma.[284] Other conditions that may result in hypercalcemia include post-kidney transplantation, immobilization, vitamin A intoxication, hyperthyroidism, Addison's disease, and pheochromocytoma.

Hypercalcemia also may occur secondary to increased intestinal calcium absorption because of vitamin D intoxication, sarcoidosis, and other granulomatous diseases. Use of thiazide diuretics, lithium, estrogens, and tamoxifen, as well as excessive calcium ingestion together with alkali, as part of the milk-alkali syndrome, also may result in hypercalcemia.

A.C.'s breast cancer bone metastasis, volume contraction, and use of hydrochlorothiazide and tamoxifen all may contribute to her hypercalcemia.

Clinical Manifestations

23. How is hypercalcemia manifested in A.C.?

The clinical presentations of hypercalcemia vary substantially among patients. The severity of the symptoms is related to the free calcium concentrations.[288] The specific clinical presentation depends upon the rate of serum calcium concentration elevation, the presence of malignancy, PTH concentration, as well as the age of the patient. Concurrent electrolyte and metabolic abnormalities and underlying diseases also will have an effect. Since calcium is an important regulator of many cellular functions, hypercalcemia, therefore, can result in abnormalities in the neurologic, cardiovascular, pulmonary, renal, GI, and musculoskeletal systems. As seen in A.C., the signs and symptoms can be nonspecific: fatigue, muscle weakness, anorexia, thirst, polyuria, dehydration, and shortened QT interval in the ECG.

The effect of hypercalcemia on the central nervous system includes lethargy, somnolence, confusion, headache, seizures, cerebellar ataxia, altered personality, acute psychosis, depression, and memory impairment.[284] The neuromuscular manifestations include weakness, myalgia, hyporeflexia or areflexia, and arthralgia.[284]

Renal function impairment may include polyuria, nocturia, and polydipsia, secondary to defective concentrating ability possibly because of resistance towards antidiuretic hormone.[289] Glomerular filtration rate may be decreased because of afferent arteriolar vasoconstriction.[284] If hypercalcemia is prolonged, nephrolithiasis, nephrocalcinosis, chronic interstitial nephritis, and renal tubular acidosis may be present.[290] Hypermagnesuria and metabolic alkalosis also may be observed.[284]

Calcium has a positive inotropic effect and reduces heart rate, similar to cardiac glycosides.[284] Electrocardiographic changes indicative of slow conduction, with prolonged PR and QRS intervals and shortened QT intervals commonly are seen.[291] In severe hypercalcemia, increased QT intervals, widened T waves, and arrhythmia may be present.

The gastrointestinal symptoms of hypercalcemia are related primarily to the depressive action of calcium on smooth muscle and nerve conduction. Constipation, anorexia, nausea, and vomiting result from reduced GI motility and delayed gastric emptying.[292] Duodenal ulcer may occur because of increased acid and gastrin secretion.[284] Pancreatitis may be present during acute hypercalcemia due to the intraductal calcium deposits causing blockade of the pancreatic ducts.[284] Proteolytic enzymes also may be activated by calcium to cause tissue damage.[284] Both ulcer disease and pancreatitis are more common in hypercalcemia associated with primary hyperparathyroidism. They are less likely to be seen in patients with malignancy-induced hypercalcemia.[291]

Treatment

24. After vigorous fluid resuscitation with IV saline, combined saline and furosemide diuresis was instituted in A.C. Her serum calcium concentration declined very slowly, prompting the use of calcitonin. Despite initial success, the serum calcium concentration rose to pretreatment values within 24 hours. Higher doses of calcitonin could have been attempted at this point; however, plicamycin was used instead. Her serum calcium concentration finally stabilized at 8 mg/dL after several days of therapy. What was the rationale for each of these regimens? What other agents are available for hypercalcemia treatment?

Several therapeutic approaches are used to lower serum calcium concentration: increasing urinary calcium excretion, inhibiting release of calcium from bone, reducing intestinal calcium absorption, and enhancing calcium complex formation with chelating agents. The underlying disease that causes the hypercalcemia also should be treated if at all possible. The specific treatment employed depends upon the serum ionized calcium concentration, presenting signs and symptoms, and also the severity and duration of hypercalcemia. Immediate therapy is needed for A.C. who had symptoms consistent with severe hypercalcemia.

Hydration and diuresis with furosemide generally are the first steps in the acute treatment of hypercalcemia. If they fail to reduce the serum calcium concentration adequately, there are several other agents available to be used in conjunction with the hydration and diuresis. Calcitonin provides a rapid onset of hypocalcemic effect; however, its duration of action is relatively short lived. One of the biphosphonates could be used to elicit a longer hypocalcemic response. Gallium nitrate is an alternative to plicamycin without such toxic effects. Other agents, such as inorganic phosphates, glucocorticoids, and prostaglandin inhibitors, also have been used to treat hypercalcemia with varying success.

Hydration and Diuresis. The first-line emergent treatment of hypercalcemia is hydration and volume expansion.[293] Most patients with hypercalcemia manifest extracellular volume depletion with accompanying polyuria, nausea, and vomiting. One to two liters of normal saline commonly are given to correct the fluid deficit. The volume expansion will increase urinary calcium excretion through an increase in GFR and inhibition of calcium reabsorption in the proximal tubule. Since both sodium and calcium are reabsorbed at the same site in the proximal tubule, saline hydration will reduce the reabsorption of both cations simultaneously.[294] A.C. was hypotensive and appeared dehydrated; therefore, saline hydration should be used initially to treat the hypercalcemia. However, in patients who have renal failure and/or CHF, saline hydration and forced diuresis should be avoided.

After adequate volume repletion has been established, IV furosemide can be administered to further augment calciuresis. Furosemide blocks the reabsorption of sodium, chloride, and calcium at the thick ascending limb of the loop of Henle. Doses of 80 to 100 mg every two to four hours can be used until a sufficient decline of the serum calcium concentration is attained.[295] However, lower doses (20 to 40 mg) commonly are given to avoid the significant loss of fluid and electrolytes caused by the more aggressive regimen. Adequate amounts of sodium, potassium, magnesium, and fluid should be used to replace any therapy-induced abnormalities. Fluid balance as well as serum and urine concentrations of these electrolytes have to be monitored closely. Urine flow has to be maintained and the renal loss of sodium chloride has to be replaced in order to preserve the calciuric effect of furosemide. In A.C., the decline of serum calcium concentration was slow, possibly because of inadequate restoration of plasma volume and/or replacement of renal sodium loss. More aggressive hydration with adequate sodium replacement will assure that the efficacy of furosemide is not compromised.[296]

Calcitonin can be used when saline hydration and furosemide diuresis fail to adequately lower serum calcium concentration or when their use is contraindicated. Calcitonin reduces serum calcium concentration by inhibiting osteoclastic bone resorption. It also may increase the renal excretion of calcium and phosphorus.[297] Salmon-derived calcitonin is more potent and longer-acting than human calcitonin.[298] The salmon calcitonin generally is the preferred preparation because of its low cost and longer duration of action. The human calcitonin usually is used for patients with resistance or allergic reactions to the salmon calcitonin.[299]

Serum calcium concentration often is reduced several hours after calcitonin is administered. The response may last for approximately six to eight hours. It is relatively nontoxic when compared with agents like plicamycin and organic phosphates. Calcitonin may be used in patients with congestive heart failure or renal failure.[296] Nausea, vomiting, diarrhea, and facial flushing are the more common side effects. Soreness and inflammation at the site of injection also may be seen.[284] Due to the potential of developing a hypersensitivity reaction to salmon calcitonin, but not the human calcitonin, the manufacturer recommends skin testing with 1 U of the salmon calcitonin before the first dose. Tolerance to the hypocalcemic effect of calcitonin can develop after 24 to 72 hours of therapy. This ''escape phenomenon,'' as seen in A.C., may be secondary to the altered responsiveness of the hormone receptors.[300] Concurrent use of corticosteroids may be effective in preventing the escape phenomenon.[301] Antibodies also may be developed in patients receiving the salmon calcitonin for long-term therapy.[299]

The dose of salmon calcitonin is 4 IU/kg given subcutaneously or intramuscularly every 12 hours. The hypocalcemic response often is limited and serum calcium concentration seldom drops to the normal range.[302] The maximum recommended dose is 8 IU/kg every six hours. The starting dose for human calcitonin usually is 0.5 mg. If used concurrently with plicamycin, the hypocalcemic effect is additive and may result in hypocalcemia.[303]

Plicamycin (Mithramycin) is an antibiotic resembling actinomycin D which was used for the treatment of refractory testicular cancer. With the advent of cisplatin-based regimens, plicamycin now is used primarily for hypercalcemia treatment. It inhibits RNA synthesis which suppresses osteoclast-mediated calcium resorption from bone.[304] The drug is effective for hypercalcemia associated with breast cancer, myelomas, lung and renal cell carcinoma, parathyroid carcinoma, and hypervitaminosis D.[287]

The recommended dose of plicamycin is 25 µg/kg infused over four to six hours. Generally, a response is seen within 24 to 48 hours and most patients attain normocalcemia after a single dose.[302] The response could last for 3 to 14 days or longer in some patients.[284,287] If adequate response is not obtained, the dose may be repeated 48 hours later.

Many potential serious adverse effects are associated with plicamycin therapy. However, the drug usually is well tolerated at the lower doses used for hypercalcemia treatment which is only one-tenth the antineoplastic dose.[302] Nausea and vomiting are common side effects which can be minimized by infusing the drug slowly and by the concurrent use of an antiemetic, such as prochlorperazine.[287] The drug is a vesicant and should be administered as a dilute solution to minimize the injury associated with extravasation. Other toxicities include impaired platelet function, proteinuria, azotemia, bone marrow suppression, and elevation of hepatic transaminases.[305] Plicamycin also may cause toxicity in the kidney and the liver. It also can result in an ''acute hemorrhagic syndrome,'' which is dose related. The drug is excreted primarily through the kidneys: renal function impairment may increase the risk for adverse effects.[284] Renal and hepatic function and platelet count, therefore, should be assessed before and during therapy.

Because of its side effect profile, plicamycin may potentiate the toxic effects of chemotherapeutic agents that frequently are used concurrently in patients with malignancy-induced hypercalcemia. Use of the agent now is limited mostly to patients who are unre-

sponsive to other antiresorptive agents. Plicamycin also is used intermittently to take advantage of its relatively long duration of action.

Biphosphonates are synthetic analogs of pyrophosphate which form stable bonds that are resistant to degradation by endogenous phosphatases during bone mineralization and resorption. The compounds adsorb to the hydroxyapatite crystals of the bone, thus inhibiting their growth and dissolution. Osteoclast-mediated bone resorption and bone mineralization are impaired. In addition, the compounds may have a direct effect on the osteoclasts. At present, etidronate and pamidronate are available in the U.S. Clodronate is available in Canada but clinical trials have been suspended in the U.S. because of concern for secondary leukemia.

Etidronate is administered in doses of 7.5 mg/kg for three consecutive days by IV infusion over at least two hours. Response may be seen after one to two days and normocalcemia is expected to be attained in most patients, with response sustained for ten days or longer.[306]

Pamidronate is more potent than etidronate as an inhibitor of bone resorption but it has negligible effect on bone mineralization. It is a newer biphosphonate approved for treatment of hypercalcemia associated with malignancies. For moderate hypercalcemia (albumin corrected serum calcium concentration of 12.0 to 13.5 mg/dL), a single dose of 60 to 90 mg of pamidronate is to be infused over a 24-hour period. For severe hypercalcemia (albumin corrected serum calcium concentration >13.5 mg/dL), the dose is 90 mg. The advantage of pamidronate is the need for only one single dose and the superior response shown in a double-blind trial comparing its single-dose effect with three doses of etidronate.[307] If the hypercalcemia recurs, the etidronate or the pamidronate regimen may be repeated after an interval of at least seven days. Etidronate also is available as an oral preparation, 20 mg/kg/day of the drug may be given to prolong the normocalcemic duration. Nausea and vomiting are common side effects associated with the oral therapy. Osteomalacia has been reported with long-term treatment because of its inhibitory effect on bone mineralization. However, the limited life expectancy of most patients may diminish the significance of this potential adverse effect.

Etidronate use has resulted in renal failure,[308] which probably is caused by the formation of biphosphonate-calcium complexes in the serum.[309] Compared with etidronate, pamidronate requires a lower molar concentration for comparable hypocalcemic effect. Pamidronate, therefore, is not as likely as etidronate to result in renal function impairment.[310] Pamidronate has been given to a limited number of patients with end-stage renal disease without any adverse consequence.[310]

Gallium nitrate is a potent inhibitor of bone resorption mediated by osteoclasts. It binds preferentially to metabolically active regions of high bone turnover. Its incorporation into the hydroxyapatite crystals increases resistance to dissolution and osteoclast-mediated resorption.[311]

Gallium nitrate is administered as a continuous IV infusion for five consecutive days at a dosage of 200 mg/m^2/day. A lower dose of 100 mg/m^2/day may be used for patients with mild hypercalcemia. Normocalcemia may be attained in 75% to 85% of the patients for approximately one week after a lag time of five to six days.[311,312] Nephrotoxicity is the primary dose-limiting toxicity when a higher dose of the drug, up to 1400 mg/m^2/day, is used as an antitumor agent. However, only isolated cases of reversible renal function impairment were reported when gallium nitrate was given at the lower doses for hypercalcemia. Adequate hydration and diuresis may minimize the risk for nephrotoxicity further.[311,313]

Phosphate. Inorganic phosphates lower serum calcium concentration by inhibiting bone resorption. They also promote the deposition of calcium salts ($CaHPO_4$) in the bone and soft tissue. If given orally, the phosphate preparation reduces intestinal calcium absorption by forming a poorly soluble complex in the bowel lumen and also by decreasing the formation of active vitamin D through enzyme inhibition.[314]

Despite its effectiveness, the main concern associated with IV phosphate administration is extensive extraskeletal calcifications. Renal failure also may develop because of nephrocalcinosis; therefore, IV phosphate is no longer the agent of choice.

Oral phosphate may be used for long-term maintenance therapy. Oral phosphate, 1 to 3 gm/day, may be given in divided doses: the optimal dose is based upon serum calcium concentrations. Serum phosphate concentration and renal function should be monitored closely during therapy. Nausea, vomiting, and diarrhea are common problems especially when the daily dose exceeds 2 gm. Soft tissue calcification also is a concern. Hyperphosphatemia and hypocalcemia may occur if the dose is not titrated appropriately. Phosphate therapy should not be given to patients with hyperphosphatemia or patients with renal failure since further deterioration of renal function may be triggered. The potassium and sodium salts in phosphate preparations also may be a therapeutic problem in certain patients.

Corticosteroids. Several possible mechanisms explain the hypocalcemic effect of corticosteroids. The corticosteroids impair the vitamin D_3-mediated intestinal calcium absorption[315] and also inhibit the action of osteoclast-activating factor, which mediates bone resorption in malignancy. In addition, corticosteroids may have a direct cytolytic effect on tumor cells and inhibit the synthesis of prostaglandins. Corticosteroids also are effective in reducing serum calcium concentrations in patients who have abnormal production of active vitamin D metabolites secondary to lymphoma.[316]

Prednisone commonly is given at 60 to 80 mg/day initially with subsequent dosage reduction. Alternately, hydrocortisone 5 mg/kg/day for two to three days may be given instead. The hypocalcemic effect will not be apparent until at least one to two days later. Patients with hematologic malignancies tend to have better response than those with solid tumors. Corticosteroids also are effective in treating hypercalcemia associated with vitamin D intoxication,[317] sarcoidosis,[318] and other granulomatous conditions. Corticosteroids generally are not used for long-term therapy because of their potential to cause serious adverse reactions.

Prostaglandin Inhibitors. Prostaglandins of the E series, especially PGE_2, may be responsible for hypercalcemia associated with some malignancies. Indomethacin is effective in lowering the serum calcium concentration in patients with renal cell carcinoma[319] but not in patients with other types of malignancy.[320] NSAIDs may be effective only in a small group of patients in whom prostaglandins play an important role in the development of their hypercalcemia. Indomethacin, 75 to 150 mg/day, may be given to selected patients unresponsive to other therapy, especially when it is used as part of a palliative treatment for cancer pain.

Phosphorus

Homeostasis

Phosphorus is found primarily in bone (85%) and soft tissue (14%), with only less than 1% of the total body store in the extracellular fluid. All the "free," nonprotein bound, phosphorus practically exists as phosphates in the plasma and it is the phosphate molecules that actually participate in various physiologic and biochemical events. However, most clinical laboratories measure and express the concentrations as elemental phosphorus contained in the phosphate molecules. One millimole of phosphate contains 1 mmol of phosphorus, while 1 mmol of phosphate is three times the weight of 1 mmol of phosphorus. It is incorrect, therefore, to equate a certain milligram weight of phosphorus as the same milligram weight of phosphate. Of the total plasma phosphorus, 70% exists as organic form and 30% as inorganic form. The organic phosphorus, found primarily as phospholipids and a small amount as esters, is bound to proteins. The inorganic form, existing as orthophosphate, is about 85% "free." The relative amounts of the two orthophosphate components: $H_2PO_4^-$ and HPO_4^{2-} vary with the pH. At pH 7.40, the ratio of the two species is 1:4, giving rise to a composite valence of 1.8 for the orthophosphate. The serum phosphate concentrations as reported in clinical laboratory tests indicate only the inorganic portion of the total plasma phosphate. To avoid confusion related to the pH effect on the valence, phosphate concentration is reported best as mg/dL or mmol/dL, rather than mEq/volume.

The normal range of serum phosphate concentration in healthy adults is 2.7 to 4.7 mg/dL. The value is higher in children possibly because of the increased amount of growth hormone and the reduced amount of gonadal hormones.[321] In postmenopausal females, the range is slightly higher, while it is lower in elderly males.[322] Serum phosphate concentration also is affected by dietary intake. Phosphate-rich foods can transiently increase the serum phosphate concentration. In contrast, glucose decreases the serum phosphate concentration because of the flux of sugar and phosphate into cells and because of the phosphorylation of glucose.[323] Similarly, insulin and epinephrine administration decreases the serum phosphate concentration because of their effects on glucose.[324] The serum concentration of phosphate is reduced in alkalosis[325] and increased during acidosis.[326]

A balanced diet contains 800 to 1500 mg/day of phosphorus. Both the organic and inorganic forms of phosphorus are present in food substances. Most of the phosphorus in milk is the organic form while the phosphorus in meat, vegetable, and other nondairy sources are organic forms bound to proteins, lipids, and sugars which usually are hydrolyzed before absorption.[327] In general, 60% to 65% of the phosphorus ingested is absorbed, mostly in the duodenum and jejunum through an energy-dependent, saturable active process.[328] Phosphorus absorption is linearly related to the dietary intake when the phosphorus intake is between 4 to 30 mg/kg/day.[329] The amount of phosphorus ingested probably is the most important factor in determining net absorption. Phosphorus absorption also is stimulated during periods of increased demand, such as active growth and pregnancy.[330] Increased intake of calcium, magnesium, and concurrent use of aluminum hydroxide antacids all may reduce phosphorus absorption due to formation of a nonabsorbable complex.[331] In addition, absorption also is affected by vitamin D, parathyroid hormone, and calcitonin.[321]

Renal phosphorus excretion depends upon the dietary phosphorus intake. Normally, over 85% of the filtered phosphate load is reabsorbed; however, the fractional urinary excretion may vary from 0.2% to 20%.[332] Renal phosphate excretion also is affected by acid-base balance, extracellular fluid volume, and calcium and glucose concentrations.[321] In addition, parathyroid hormone, thyroid hormone, thyrocalcitonin, vitamin D, insulin, glucocorticoid, and glucagon also may alter the renal phosphate excretion.[321]

Hypophosphatemia

Etiology

25. M.R., a 72-year-old female, was admitted to the hospital with a 1-week history of increasing malaise, confusion, and de-

creased activity. M.R. had a history of CHF, hypertension, Type II diabetes, and peptic ulcer disease. She was receiving hydrochlorothiazide, Maalox, sucralfate, and insulin. She was febrile and in significant respiratory distress. ABG results obtained at admission were: pH 7.5, PO_2 42 mm Hg, and PCO_2 20 mm Hg. Respiratory function continued to deteriorate requiring intubation and mechanical ventilation. Serum electrolytes were: Na 128 mEq/L, K 3.6 mEq/L, Cl 96 mEq/L, CO_2 23 mEq/L, glucose 320 mg/dL, and P 0.9 mg/dL. What may have contributed to the low serum phosphorus concentration in M.R.? [SI units: Na 128 mmol/L; K 3.6 mmol/L; Cl 96 mmol/L; CO_2 23 mmol/L; glucose 17.8 mmol/L; P 0.29 mmol/L]

Hypophosphatemia may develop as the result of a phosphorus deficiency or secondary to a net flux of phosphorus out of the plasma compartment without a total body deficit. Moderate hypophosphatemia is defined as a serum phosphorus concentration of 1.0 to 2.5 mg/dL; a concentration of less than 1.0 mg/dL, as in M.R., is considered to be severe.[333] The extent of hypophosphatemia may not be assessed accurately by a single plasma phosphorus concentration determination because of diurnal variation.[334] Patients receiving large doses of mannitol may have pseudohypophosphatemia due to the binding of mannitol with molybdate which is used in the calorimetric assay for phosphorus.[335]

Hypophosphatemia commonly is caused by conditions which impair intestinal absorption, increase renal elimination, or shift phosphorus from the extracellular to the intracellular compartments. Hypophosphatemia secondary to low dietary phosphorus is exceedingly rare because phosphorus is ubiquitous.[321] In addition, renal phosphorus excretion is reduced and intestinal phosphorus absorption will be increased to prevent a deficiency state.[332,336] Starvation in itself does not result in severe hypophosphatemia as the phosphorus content in plasma and muscles often is normal. Hypophosphatemia can develop during refeeding with a high-calorie diet deprived of phosphorus. Hyperalimentation without phosphorus supplementation, therefore, is likely to cause severe hypophosphatemia.[337]

Impaired phosphorus absorption secondary to malabsorptive conditions, prolonged nasogastric (NG) suction, and protracted vomiting also may result in hypophosphatemia. In M.R., the use of aluminum- and magnesium-containing antacids may further reduce phosphorus absorption. The antacids bind with endogenous and exogenous phosphorus in the GI tract and cause severe hypophosphatemia in patients both with or without renal failure.[338] In addition, M.R. was taking sucralfate which can bind phosphorus in the GI tract.[339] Similarly, iron preparations can bind with phosphorus.[340]

Hyperglycemia-induced osmotic diuresis and diuretic use may have increased the renal loss of phosphorus in M.R. Other conditions associated with renal phosphorus wasting include renal tubular acidosis, hyperparathyroidism, hypokalemia, hypomagnesemia, and extracellular volume expansion.[321] However, none of these situations was evident in M.R. Shifting of phosphorus into the intracellular compartment by glucose and/or insulin, and profound respiratory alkalosis, especially during alcoholic withdrawal, also may have contributed to M.R.'s hypophosphatemic state.[341,342]

26. What other conditions are commonly associated with hypophosphatemia?

Diabetic ketoacidosis, chronic alcoholism, chronic obstructive airways disease, and extensive thermal burns are other conditions commonly associated with hypophosphatemia.[343,344] They are characterized by a combination of factors which result in phosphate loss and/or intracellular phosphate use and repletion. In patients with diabetic ketoacidosis, metabolic acidosis enhances the movement of phosphate from the intracellular compartment to plasma while the concurrent osmotic diuresis secondary to hyperglycemia increases the renal elimination of extracellular phosphate.[345] The net result is a depletion of total body stores. Correction of the acidosis and administration of insulin then promote the rapid uptake of phosphorus by tissues and volume repletion dilutes the extracellular concentration. This sequence of events ultimately can lead to severe hypophosphatemia. The hypophosphatemia associated with chronic alcoholism and acute alcohol intoxication also is thought to be related to several factors including reduced intestinal phosphorus absorption due to vomiting, diarrhea, and antacid use; repeated acidosis that results in increased urinary phosphate excretion; and shift of phosphorus into cells because of respiratory alkalosis. Renal phosphorus wasting also may result from hypomagnesemia or as a direct effect of alcohol.[346]

Clinical Manifestations

27. What are the signs and symptoms associated with hypophosphatemia?

The clinical effects associated with chronic phosphorus depletion often are insidious and begin to appear gradually. In contrast, rapid decline in plasma phosphorus concentrations results in sudden and serious organ dysfunctions. Most of the effects can be attributed to impaired cellular energy stores and tissue hypoxia secondary to depletion of adenosine triphosphate (ATP) and/or erythrocyte 2,3-diphosphoglycerate (2,3-DPG).[347] Severe hypophosphatemia can result in generalized muscle weakness, confusion, paresthesias, seizures, and coma. In addition, reduced cardiac contractility, hypotension, respiratory failure, and rhabdomyolysis have been observed with acute severe hypophosphatemia.[321] Chronic phosphorus depletion has been associated with decreased mentation, muscle weakness, osteomalacia, rickets, anorexia, dysphagia, cardiomyopathy, tachypnea, reduced sensitivity to insulin, and dysfunction of red blood cells, white blood cells, and platelets. Renal function is altered as manifested by hypophosphaturia, hypercalciuria, hypermagnesuria, bicarbonaturia, and glycosuria.

Treatment

28. Outline a treatment regimen which would effectively and safely correct the phosphorus deficit in M.R. How should her therapy be monitored?

Phosphorus resides primarily in the intracellular space; the amount in the extracellular fluid is only a small percentage of the total body store. The patient's pH, blood glucose concentration, and insulin availability also may affect phosphorus distribution. Therefore, it is difficult to precisely determine the magnitude of phosphorus deficit based upon the serum concentration alone. As discussed previously, a patient may have hypophosphatemia secondary to a rapid shift of phosphorus into the intracellular space. The duration of the hypophosphatemia often is limited as it may be corrected by renal phosphorus conservation and oral intake of phosphorus-containing food substances. Aside from using serum phosphorus concentrations, determination of urinary phosphorus excretion may be used to further assess the phosphorus deficit. Typically, renal phosphorus excretion is limited severely in patients with significant deficits. A phosphorus excretion of less than 100 mg/day (fractional phosphorus excretion <10%) confirms appropriate renal phosphorus conservation when the serum phosphorus is less than 2 mg/dL. It also suggests a nonrenal etiology (e.g., impaired GI absorption) or some type of internal redistribution (e.g., respiratory alkalosis).[348]

There are several conditions that are expected to increase the risk for developing hypophosphatemia. Prophylactic phosphorus supplementation should be administered to patients who are receiving total parenteral nutrition or high doses of antacids for an extended period. Alcoholic patients and those with diabetic keto-acidosis also are at risk.

The specific treatment of hypophosphatemia depends upon the presence of signs and symptoms, as well as on the anticipated duration and severity of hypophosphatemia. In an asymptomatic patient with mild hypophosphatemia (1.5 to 2.5 mg/dL) who has no evidence of phosphorus depletion, phosphorus supplementation generally is not necessary as the condition usually is self-limited.[321] In other patients with mild and moderate hypophosphatemia who have evidence of phosphorus deficit, oral supplementation is the safest and preferred mode of replacement. Skim or low-fat milk is a convenient source of phosphorus and calcium. Whole milk, because of its high fat content, may cause diarrhea if a large amount is consumed. There are several oral phosphorus preparations that can be used in patients who are intolerant to milk products. (See Table 28.2.)

When the hypophosphatemia is severe, as in M.R., or when the patient is vomiting or unable to take oral medication, parenteral phosphorus replacement is needed. Several empiric regimens have been evaluated for treatment of hypophosphatemia. IV administration of 0.08 to 0.5 mmol of phosphorus per kilogram of body weight over 4- to 12-hour periods is safe and effective in restoring the serum phosphorus concentration.[349,350] Parenteral phosphorus replacement should be stopped once the serum phosphorus concentration attains 2.0 mg/dL. Oral supplementation then should be used subsequently. In general, no more than 32 mmol (1 gm) of phosphorus should be administered intravenously over a 24-hour period. Regardless of the regimen used, serum phosphorus and calcium concentrations should be monitored closely. IV phosphorus administration can rapidly induce hyperphosphatemia. Monitoring of urine phosphorus concentration also is helpful in determining the adequacy of therapy. In addition, the patient is at risk for hypocalcemia, metastatic soft tissue calcification, hypomagnesemia, and hypotension. Depending upon the preparation used, potassium, sodium, or volume overload may occur. This could be significant in patients such as M.R. who have a history of CHF and hypertension. Renal function and volume status, therefore, should be monitored during therapy.

Diarrhea is a common dose-related side effect associated with oral phosphorus replacement. It can be minimized by diluting the supplement and slowly titrating the dose. Large doses of the supplement also may result in metabolic acidosis.[349] Phosphorus can be administered orally in doses of 30 to 60 mmol/day using any commercially available oral supplement [e.g., Fleets or Neutra-Phos (see Table 28.2)]. Fleets Phospho-Soda, 5 mL twice daily, delivers 40 mmol/day of phosphorus. Skim milk often is the preferred agent for diluting the supplement. It contains approximately 7 mmol/cup of phosphorus and it also provides calcium and potassium concurrently.

In M.R., oral supplementation was not feasible because the patient had intermittent diarrhea and vomiting. Potassium phosphate 15 mmol (providing 22 mEq of potassium), therefore, was infused intravenously in 250 mL of 0.45% saline over a 12-hour period. The regimen was repeated once until the serum phosphorus concentration reached 2 mg/dL. Oral supplementation with Fleets Phospho-Soda then was begun by adding one teaspoonful twice daily to her enteral tube feeding.

Magnesium

Homeostasis

Magnesium is an intracellular cation that is found primarily in bone (65%) and muscle (20%).[351] Only 2% of the total body store of 21 to 28 gm (1750 to 2400 mEq) is located in the extracellular compartment. Serum magnesium concentrations, therefore, do not reflect the total magnesium body store accurately. In healthy adults, the serum magnesium concentration is 1.40 to 1.75 mEq/L. About 20% of the serum magnesium is bound to proteins.

Magnesium plays an important role in different metabolic processes, particularly in energy transfer, storage, and utilization. Deficiency of the cation can impair many ATP-mediated energy-dependent cellular processes as well as the action of phosphatases.[352] Magnesium is necessary for many enzymes involved in the metabolism of carbohydrate, fat, protein and also RNA aggregation, DNA transcription and degradation. The normal operation of many sodium, proton, and calcium pumps and the regulation of potassium and calcium channels are all dependent upon the availability of intracellular magnesium.[353,354] In addition, adequate magnesium stores are needed to maintain normal neuronal control, neuromuscular transmission, and cardiovascular tone.

The average diet in North America contains about 20 to 30 mEq of magnesium.[355] The daily requirement is about 18 to 33 mEq for young persons and 15 to 28 mEq for women.[356] Normally, 30% to 40% of the elemental magnesium is absorbed, primarily in the jejunum and ileum.[357] However, absorption may be increased to 80% in deficiency states and reduced to 25% during high magnesium intake. In patients with uremia, GI absorption of magnesium is decreased;[357] however, absorption in the jejunum can be normalized by physiologic doses of $1\alpha,25$-dihydroxyvitamin D_3.[358] In addition, parathyroid hormone also has been shown to modulate magnesium absorption.[359]

Magnesium is eliminated primarily by the kidney; only 1% to 2% of the endogenous magnesium is eliminated by the fecal route.[360] The magnitude of renal removal is determined by glomerular filtration rate and tubular reabsorption. About 20% to 30% of the tubular reabsorption takes place in the proximal tubule while the loop of Henle, primarily the thick ascending limb, is responsible for up to 65% of the total reabsorption.[361] Only about 5% to 6% of the filtered magnesium generally is eliminated in the urine. The extent of magnesium reabsorption changes in parallel with sodium reabsorption which is affected by the extracellular fluid volume. Renal threshold for urinary magnesium excretion is 1.3 to

Table 28.2	Phosphorus Replacement Preparations		
Product	Potassium (mmol)	Sodium (mmol)	Phosphorus (mmol)
K-Phos Neutral tablets	1.15	12.6	8
Uro-KP-Neutral tablets	1.27	10.9	8
Neutra-Phos			
capsules[a]	7.13	7.13	8
powder[b]	7.13	7.13	8
Neutra-Phos K			
capsules[a]	14.25	0	8
powder[b]	14.25	0	8
Fleets Phospho-soda (per mL)	0	4.8	4.1
K Phosphate IV (per mL)	4.4	0	3
Na Phosphate IV (per mL)	0	4	3
Milk			
whole (per cup)	9	5.3	7.3
skim (per cup)	9.1	5.5	7.5

[a] Phosphorus content after reconstituting 1 capsule in 75 mL water. Capsules must be reconstituted and not swallowed.
[b] Phosphorus content after reconstituting 1 packet in 75 mL water.

1.7 mEq/L, which closely resembles the normal plasma magnesium concentration. Slight changes in plasma magnesium concentration, therefore, may substantially alter the amount of magnesium excreted in the urine.[362]

Urinary magnesium reabsorption is affected by many factors, including sodium balance, extracellular fluid volume, serum concentrations of magnesium, calcium, and phosphate as well as metabolic acidosis and alkalosis.[363] Concurrent use of loop and osmotic diuretics also will modulate the reabsorption.[364,365] Hormones, such as PTH and possibly calcitonin, glucagon, and mineralocorticoids, also may affect the routine maintenance of magnesium balance.[366–368]

Hypomagnesemia

Etiology

29. R.J., a 61-year-old male, is admitted to the hospital because of trauma to his forehead after falling at home. He has a long history of conditions related to his alcohol abuse: liver disease, ascites, seizures, pancreatitis, and malabsorption. R.J. complained of abdominal pain, nausea, vomiting, and diarrhea for the past several days. At the time of admission, R.J. was confused, apprehensive, combative, and had marked tremors. He also had delirium as evidenced by hallucinations, screaming, and delusions. He also was observed to have multiple tonic-clonic seizures. His medical record revealed that R.J. was given furosemide for the last 2 months. Pertinent laboratory test results obtained at admission were: K 2.5 mEq/L, Mg 0.8 mEq/L, and creatinine 0.8 mg/dL. Phenytoin was administered for seizure control and R.J. was placed on NG suction. Fluid restriction was instituted and furosemide therapy was continued to control his ascites. What are the circumstances that have contributed to R.J.'s hypomagnesemia? [SI units: K 2.5 mmol/L; Mg 0.4 mmol/L; creatinine 70.72 μmol/L]

Magnesium body store is difficult to assess since magnesium primarily is an intracellular ion. Serum magnesium concentration does not provide an accurate indication of the total body load. In fact, cellular magnesium depletion may be present with low, normal, or even high serum magnesium concentration.[369,370] Conversely, hypomagnesemia may be seen without the net loss of body magnesium. Refeeding after starvation will result in increased trapping of magnesium by newly formed tissue resulting in hypomagnesemia. Similarly, acute pancreatitis and parathyroidectomy may cause hypomagnesemia without the net loss of the cation.[371,372]

The prevalence of hypomagnesemia in ambulatory and hospitalized patients was found to be about 6% to 12%.[373] The incidence increased to 42% in patients who were hypokalemic[374] and to 60% to 65% in those under intensive care.[375] Multiple risk factors and clinical conditions can contribute to the high rate of hypomagnesemia in critically ill patients.

Magnesium depletion and hypomagnesemia can develop due to GI, renal, and endocrinologic causes. Depletion may occur in patients whose dietary magnesium intake is severely restricted[376] and in those who have protein calorie malnutrition.[377] Also at risk are patients who receive prolonged parenteral nutrition[378] and those who undergo prolonged nasogastric suction.[379] Hypomagnesemia may be present in patients who have increased magnesium requirements, such as pregnancy and infancy.[380] Conditions associated with steatorrhea, such as nontropical sprue and short-bowel syndrome, may result in reduced GI magnesium absorption. Insoluble magnesium soaps may be formed in the GI tract due to the presence of unabsorbed fat.[381] Hypomagnesemia also may occur in patients with a bowel resection[382] and severe diarrhea.[383] A rare genetic disorder also has been reported in patients with defective GI magnesium absorption.[384] An impaired carrier-mediated magnesium transport system is believed to be responsible for the symptomatic deficiency which requires high oral magnesium intake to overcome the defect.

Renal magnesium wasting may be due to a primary defect or secondary to systemic factors. A rare form of renal magnesium wasting is congenital.[385] Various drugs can induce hypomagnesemia through increased renal loss: cisplatin,[386] aminoglycosides,[387] cyclosporine,[388] and amphotericin B.[389] Use of loop and thiazide diuretics also may result in hypomagnesemia; it can be reversed with the concurrent use of amiloride or triamterene.[390] Magnesium depletion may be associated with phosphate depletion,[391] calcium infusion,[392] and ketoacidosis.[393] Acute and chronic ingestion of alcohol will result in increased renal magnesium loss.[378,394] Various endocrinologic disorders, such as SIADH,[395] hyperthyroidism,[396] hyperaldosteronism,[397] and postparathyroidectomy,[398] also are associated with hypomagnesemia.

There are many reasons why R.J. could be hypomagnesemic. His long history of alcohol use, malnutrition, and malabsorption all may have contributed to his magnesium deficit. The vomiting and diarrhea that he experienced could have reduced GI magnesium absorption. Use of furosemide and nasogastric suction while in the hospital also can exacerbate his magnesium depletion.

Clinical Manifestations

30. What are the clinical manifestations of hypomagnesemia in R.J.?

Magnesium depletion may result in abnormal function of the neurological, neuromuscular, and cardiovascular systems. Reduced magnesium concentration will lower the threshold for nerve stimulation and result in increased irritability. Typical findings include Chvostek's and Trousseau's signs, muscle fasciculation, tremors, muscle spasticity, generalized convulsions, and possibly tetany. The patient may experience weakness, anorexia, nausea, and vomiting, as seen in R.J. Hypokalemia, hypocalcemia, and alkalosis also may be found. In moderately depleted patients, changes in ECG include widening of QRS complex and peaking of T wave.[399] In severe depletion, prolonged PR interval and diminished T wave may be seen. Ventricular arrhythmias also have been reported in some patients.[400]

Treatment

31. Outline a regimen to replenish the body store of magnesium for R.J. and develop a monitoring plan to assess efficacy and potential adverse effects.

The specific regimen for magnesium replenishment depends upon the clinical presentation of the patient. Symptomatic patients require more aggressive parenteral therapy while oral replacement may suffice for asymptomatic hypomagnesemia. Patients with life-threatening symptoms, such as seizure and arrhythmia, need immediate magnesium infusion. Since serum magnesium concentrations do not reflect the total body store, the presence of symptoms related to magnesium depletion is more important in determining the urgency and aggressiveness of therapy.

The body store of magnesium has to be replenished slowly. Serum magnesium concentration may return to the normal range within the first 24-hour period during replacement. However, total replenishment of body stores may take several days. Furthermore, about 50% of the administered IV dose of magnesium will be excreted in the urine.[401] Due to the presence of a threshold for urinary magnesium excretion, the abrupt increase in serum magnesium after an IV dose will result in increased urinary magnesium excretion despite a total body magnesium deficit. Conversely, in patients with renal insufficiency, the reduced urinary magnesium excretion will render the patient at risk for hypermagnesemia. Reduced rate of magnesium administration and frequent monitoring of serum magnesium concentration, therefore, are necessary in patients with renal dysfunction.

Oral replacement of magnesium is indicated for asymptomatic patients with mild depletion. Magnesium-containing antacids, Milk of Magnesia, or magnesium oxide are effective choices for replacement. Magnesium absorption is about 6% to 15% in a regimen consisting of 30 to 90 mL of a magnesium-containing antacid given four times daily.[402] Alternately, 5 mL of Milk of Magnesia (36 mg/mL or 3 mEq/mL of magnesium) may be given four times daily. When magnesium oxide tablets are given, most patients can tolerate doses of 250 to 500 mg (12.5 to 25 mEq of magnesium) four times daily without having diarrhea.[403] A diet high in magnesium content (cereals, nuts, meat, legumes and vegetables, fruits, fish) also will help to restore body store and prevent depletion.

For patients with symptomatic hypomagnesemia, such as R.J., parenteral magnesium replacement is indicated. The magnesium deficit in patients with chronic alcoholism is estimated to be 1 to 2 mEq/kg.[404] Since up to one-half of the IV magnesium dose will be excreted in the urine during replacement, about 2 to 4 mEq/kg will be needed to replenish his body store.[401] One milliequivalent per kilogram of magnesium, as magnesium sulfate 10% solution, should be administered intravenously in the first 24 hours. Half of this amount is to be given in the first three hours and the remaining half infused over the rest of the day. Magnesium 0.5 mEq/kg then should be replenished daily for four additional days.[401,405] Alternatively, the magnesium may be given intramuscularly as 50% solution. However, the injections are painful, potentially sclerosing, and require multiple administrations. The IV route clearly is the preferred mode of parenteral administration. For patients with seizures or life-threatening arrhythmias, 16 to 32 mEq of magnesium sulfate may be administered as a short IV infusion over two to four minutes.[401]

Careful monitoring is necessary during rapid IV administration. The patient should remain in a supine position due to the potential for developing hypotension.[401] If marked suppression of deep tendon reflexes is present, serum magnesium concentration is likely to be at 4 to 7 mEq/L. Serial serum magnesium concentration, ECG, blood pressure, and respiration should be evaluated to determine if the rate of magnesium replenishment is optimal. Facial flushing, warmth sensation, and sweatiness may result from vasodilation secondary to a rapid rate of intravenous magnesium infusion.[401] In patients with renal function impairment, the rate of magnesium replenishment should be reduced. These patients should be monitored frequently to avoid toxicities related to hypermagnesemia. IV magnesium also should be administered cautiously in patients with severe atrioventricular heart block or bifascicular blocks since magnesium possesses pharmacologic properties similar to calcium channel blockers.[401,406]

32. Over the initial 2 days of hospitalization, R.J. received 3 mEq/kg of IV magnesium sulfate. However, his serum magnesium concentration remained <1.5 mEq/L. What might have contributed to the lack of favorable response to the magnesium therapy?

The total amount of magnesium administered to R.J. over the past two days was higher than the usual recommended rate of magnesium replenishment. The total deficit should be corrected over a four- to five-day period. A substantial amount of the IV magnesium given was excreted renally due to a limit on the rate of magnesium reabsorption in the ascending limb of the loop of Henle.[407] In addition, the use of nasogastric suction and furosemide also have increased the magnesium loss during the replacement. Concurrent hypokalemia also may have reduced the effectiveness of magnesium replacement. In a patient whose serum magnesium concentration does not increase after appropriate magnesium therapy, total urine output may be collected over a 24-hour period to determine magnesium renal excretion. A low urinary magnesium concentration is consistent with magnesium depletion while high urinary magnesium excretion in the presence of hypomagnesemia suggests renal magnesium wasting.

Hypermagnesemia

Etiology

33. J.O., a 63-year-old male with renal insufficiency, was admitted to the hospital because of increasing weakness over the past several days. J.O. had experienced stomach upset about 2 weeks ago and since had used magnesium-aluminum hydroxide antacid several times daily. Physical examination revealed hypotension and depressed deep tendon reflexes. ECG revealed prolonged PR and QRS intervals. The serum Mg concentration was 6.5 mEq/dL. What is the most likely cause of hypermagnesemia in J.O.? [SI unit: Mg 3.25 mmol/L]

The kidney is the primary organ responsible for magnesium elimination from the body. In most patients, it is very unusual to have hypermagnesemia except when the renal function is impaired. (Hypermagnesemia also is presented in Chapter 30: Chronic Renal Failure.) A frequent cause of hypermagnesemia is the use of magnesium-containing medications, such as antacids and laxatives in patients with renal function impairment. When a renal failure patient, such as J.O., is given magnesium-containing medications, the serum magnesium concentration can increase substantially to result in toxicities. It is common for patients with creatinine clearance of less than 30 mL/minute to maintain serum magnesium concentrations above the normal range, with an inverse relationship observed between the serum concentrations and the creatinine clearances.[408] Hypermagnesemia also is seen in patients with acute renal failure during the oliguric phase, but not the diuretic phase.[409] Elderly patients also are at risk for developing hypermagnesemia due to their reduced renal function and frequent use of magnesium-containing medications such as laxatives and vitamins. Other potential causes of hypermagnesemia include adrenal insufficiency[352] and hypothyroidism.[410] Therapeutic use of lithium,[410] magnesium citrate as cathartic for drug overdose,[411] and parenteral magnesium for pre-eclampsia[412] all have been reported to result in hypermagnesemia.

Clinical Manifestations

34. Describe the usual clinical presentation of a patient with hypermagnesemia.

An elevated magnesium serum concentration alters the normal function of the neurological, neuromuscular, and cardiovascular systems.[412] When the serum magnesium concentration is greater than 4 mEq/L, deep tendon reflexes are depressed and usually are lost when the concentration exceeds 6 mEq/L. Flaccid quadriplegia may develop when the concentration is higher than 8 to 10 mEq/L. Respiratory paralysis, hypotension, difficulty in talking and swallowing also may be present.[413] Changes in ECG may include prolonged PR interval and widening of QRS complex. Complete heart block may be seen at concentrations of about 15 mEq/L. In mild hypomagnesemia, the patient may experience nausea and vomiting. Drowsiness, lethargy, diaphoresis, and altered consciousness may be present at higher serum magnesium concentrations.

Treatment

35. How should J.O.'s hypermagnesemia be treated?

Further exposure to magnesium-containing medications should be stopped in patients with hypermagnesemia. Serum magnesium concentration usually will return to normal range through renal elimination if the kidney function is intact. When potentially life-threatening complications are present, as seen in J.O., 5 to 10 mEq of IV calcium should be administered to antagonize the respiratory and cardiac manifestations of magnesium.[412] The dose of the calcium may be repeated as necessary since its effect is short-lived. In patients with good renal function without the life-threatening complications, IV furosemide with urine volume replaced by 0.45% sodium chloride will enhance urinary magnesium excretion while preventing volume depletion. Hemodialysis or peritoneal dialysis is indicated for patients with significant renal function impairment and possibly for those with severe hypermagnesemia.

References

1. **Fanestil DD.** Compartmentation of body water. In: Narins RG, ed. Maxwell & Kleeman's Clinical Disorders of Fluid and Electrolyte Metabolism. New York: McGraw Hill; 1994:3.

2. **Edelman IS, Liebman J.** Anatomy of body water and electrolytes. Am J Med. 1959;27:256.

3. **Lesser GT, Markofsky J.** Body water compartments with human aging using fat-free mass as the reference standard. Am J Physiol. 1979;236:R215.

4. **Rose BD.** Renal function and disorders of water and sodium balance. In: Rubenstein E, Federman DD, eds. Scientific American Medicine. New York: Scientific American Inc.; 1994;Section 10;I:1.

5. **Rose BD.** The total body water and the plasma sodium concentration. In: Rose BD, ed. Clinical Physiology of Acid-Base and Electrolyte Disorders. 4th ed. New York: McGraw Hill; 1994:219.

6. **Rose BD.** Introduction to disorder of osmolality. In: Rose BD, ed. Clinical Physiology of Acid-Base and Electrolyte Disorders. 4th ed. New York: McGraw Hill; 1994:638.

7. **Gennari FJ.** Current concepts. Serum osmolality: uses and limitations. N Engl J Med. 1984;310:102.

8. **Rose BD.** Proximal tubule. In: Rose BD, ed. Clinical Physiology of Acid-Base and Electrolyte Disorders. 4th ed. New York: McGraw Hill; 1994:66.

9. **Rose BD.** Loop of Henle and the countercurrent mechanism. In: Rose BD, ed. Clinical Physiology of Acid-Base and Electrolyte Disorders. 4th ed. New York: McGraw Hill; 1994:104.

10. **Rose BD.** Functions of the distal nephron. In: Rose BD, ed. Clinical Physiology of Acid-Base and Electrolyte Disorders. 4th ed. New York: McGraw Hill; 1994:132.

11. **Sands JM et al.** Vasopressin effects on urea and water transport in inner medullary collecting duct subsegments. Am J Physiol. 1987;253:F823.

12. **Goetz KL.** Renal natriuretic peptide (urodilatin?) and atriopeptin: evolving concepts. Am J Physiol. 1991;261:F921.

13. **Goetz K et al.** Evidence that urodilatin, rather than ANP, regulates renal sodium excretion. J Am Soc Nephrol. 1990;1:867.

14. **Gines P et al.** Vasopressin in pathophysiological states. Semin Nephrol. 1994;14:384.

15. **Zerbe RL, Robertson GL.** Osmotic and nonosmotic regulation of thirst and vasopressin secretion. In: Narins RG, ed. Maxwell & Kleeman's Clinical Disorders of Fluid and Electrolyte Metabolism. New York: McGraw Hill; 1994:81.

16. **Rose BD.** Regulation of the effective circulating volume. In: Rose BD, ed. Clinical Physiology of Acid-Base and Electrolyte Disorders. 4th ed. New York: McGraw Hill; 1994:235.

17. **Rose BD.** Hypovolemic states. In: Rose BD, ed. Clinical Physiology of Acid-Base and Electrolyte Disorders. 4th ed. New York: McGraw Hill; 1994:388.

18. **Rose BD.** Meaning and application of urine chemistries. In: Rose BD, ed. Clinical Physiology of Acid-Base and Electrolyte Disorders. 4th ed. New York: McGraw Hill; 1994:379.

19. **Kaysen GA.** Proteinuria and the nephrotic syndrome. In: Schrier RW, ed. Renal and Electrolyte Disorders. Boston: Little, Brown and Co.; 1992:681.

20. **Bernard DB.** Extrarenal complications of the nephrotic syndrome. Kidney Int. 1988;33:1184.

21. **Falk RJ et al.** Prevalence and pathologic features of sickle cell nephropathy and response to inhibition of angiotensin-converting enzyme. N Engl J Med. 1992;326:910.

22. **Korbet SM, Schwartz MM.** Human immunodeficiency virus infection and nephrotic syndrome. Am J Kidney Dis. 1992;20:97.

23. **Feinfeld DA et al.** Nephrotic syndrome associated with the use of the nonsteroidal anti-inflammatory drugs: case report and review of the literature. Nephron. 1984;37:174.

24. **Wheeler DC et al.** Hyperlipidemia in nephrotic syndrome. Am J Nephrol. 1989;9(Suppl. 1):78.

25. **Chonko AM, Grantham JJ.** Treatment of edematous states. In: Narins RG, ed. Maxwell & Kleeman's Clinical Disorders of Fluid and Electrolyte Metabolism. New York: McGraw Hill; 1994:545, 554.

26. **Humphreys MH.** Mechanisms and management of nephrotic edema. Kidney Int. 1994;45:266.

27. **Schrier RW.** Pathogenesis of sodium and water retention in high output and low output cardiac failure, nephrotic syndrome, cirrhosis and pregnancy. N Engl J Med. 1988;319:1065.

28. **Schrier RW.** Body fluid volume regulation in health and disease: a unifying hypothesis. Ann Intern Med. 1990;113:155.

29. **Schrier RW.** An odyssey into the milieu? Interieur: pondering the enigmas. J Am Soc Nephrol. 1992;2:1549.

30. **Koomans HA et al.** Renal function during recovery from minimal lesion nephrotic syndrome. Nephron. 1987;47:173.

31. **Brown EA et al.** Sodium retention in nephrotic syndrome is due to an intrarenal defect: evidence from steroid-induced remission. Nephron. 1985;39:290.

32. **Bank N.** External compression for the treatment of resistant edema. N Engl J Med. 1980;302:969.

33. **Brater DC.** Resistance to diuretics: mechanisms and clinical implications. Adv Nephrol. 1993;22:349.

34. **Davidson AM et al.** Salt-poor human albumin in the management of nephrotic syndrome. Br Med J. 1974;1:481.

35. **Fancheld P et al.** An evaluation of ultrafiltration as treatment of diuretic-resistant edema in nephrotic syndrome. Acta Med Scan. 1985;17:127.

36. **Pruitt AW et al.** Variations in the fate of triamterene. Clin Pharmacol Ther. 1977;21:610.

37. **Coggins CH, Comell BF.** Nutritional management of nephrotic syndrome. In: Mitch WE, Klahr S, eds. Nutrition and the Kidney. Boston: Little, Brown and Co.; 1988:239.

38. **Narins RG et al.** Diagnostic strategies in disorders of fluid, electrolyte and acid-base homeostasis. Am J Med. 1982;72:496.

39. **Sterns RH et al.** Hyponatremia: pathophysiology, diagnosis, and therapy. In: Narins RG, ed. Maxwell & Kleeman's Clinical Disorders of Fluid and Electrolyte Metabolism. New York: McGraw Hill; 1994:583.

40. **Faber MD et al.** Common fluid-electrolyte and acid-base problems in the intensive care unit: selected issues. Semin Nephrol. 1994;14:8.

41. **Goldman MB et al.** Mechanisms of altered water metabolism in psychotic patients with polydipsia and hyponatremia. N Engl J Med. 1988;318:397.

42. **Illowsky B, Kirch DG.** Polydipsia and hyponatremia in psychiatric patients. Am J Psychiatry. 1988;145:6.

43. **Weisberg LS.** Pseudohyponatremia: a reappraisal. Am J Med. 1989;86:315–18.

44. **Rothenberg DM et al.** Isotonic hyponatremia following transurethral prostate resection. J Clin Anesth. 1990;2:48.

45. **Ashraf N et al.** Thiazide-induced hyponatremia associated with death or neurologic damage in outpatients. Am J Med. 1981;70:1163–1168.

46. **Ashouri SD.** Severe diuretic induced hyponatremias in the elderly. Arch Intern Med. 1986;146:1355–357.

47. **Shah PJ, Greenburg WM.** Water intoxication precipitated by thiazide diuretics in polydipsic psychiatric patients. Am J Psychiatry. 1991;48:1424.

48. **Spital A.** Hyponatremia in adrenal insufficiency: review of pathogenetic mechanisms. South Med J. 1982;75:581.

49. **Hutchison FN et al.** Renal sodium wasting in patients treated with cisplatin. Ann Intern Med. 1988;108:21.

50. **Vassal G et al.** Hyponatremia and renal sodium wasting in patients receiving cisplatinum. Pediatr Hematol Oncol. 1987;4:337.

51. **Carpenter CCJ et al.** Oral rehydration therapy—the role of polymeric substrates. N Engl J Med. 1988;319:1346.

52. **Gore SM et al.** Impact of rice-based oral rehydration solution on stool output and duration of diarrhea: meta-analysis of 13 clinical trials. Br Med J. 1992;304:287.

53. **Vaamonde CA.** Renal water handling in liver disease. In: Epstein M, ed. The Kidney in Liver Disease. Baltimore: Williams & Wilkins; 1988:31.

54. **Papadakis MA et al.** Hyponatremia in patients with cirrhosis. Q J Med. 1990; 76:675.

55. **Leier CV et al.** Clinical relevance and management of the major electrolyte abnormalities in congestive heart failure: hyponatremia, hypokalemia, and hypomagnesemia. Am Heart J. 1994; 128:564.

56. **Allon M et al.** Renal sodium and water handling in hypothyroid patients: the role of renal insufficiency. J Am Soc Nephrol. 1990;1:205.

57. **Linas SL et al.** Role of vasopressin in the impaired water excretion of glucocorticoid deficiency. Kidney Int. 1980; 18:58.

58. **DeFronzo RA et al.** Normal diluting capacity in hyponatremic patients: reset osmostat or variant of SIADH. Ann Intern Med. 1975;82:811.

59. **Schwartz WB et al.** Syndrome of renal sodium loss and hyponatremia probably resulting from inappropriate secretion of antidiuretic hormone. Am J Med. 1957;23:529.

60. **Bartter FC, Schwartz WB.** The syndrome of inappropriate secretion of antidiuretic hormone. Am J Med. 1967; 42:790.

61. **Cooke RC et al.** The syndrome of inappropriate antidiuretic hormone secretion (SIADH): pathophysiologic mechanisms in solute and volume regulation. Medicine. 1979;58:240.

62. **Decaux G et al.** Mechanisms of hypouricemia in the syndrome of inappropriate secretion of antidiuretic hormone. Nephron. 1985;39:164.

63. **Lokich JJ.** The frequency and clinical biology of the ectopic hormone syndromes of small cell carcinoma. Cancer. 1982;50:2111.

64. **Rose CE et al.** Water metabolism in respiratory disorders. Semin Nephrol. 1984;4:295.

65. **Dixon BS, Anderson RJ.** Pneumonia and SIADH. Don't pour water on the fire. Am Rev Respir Dis. 1988;138:512.

66. **Shucert W.** Hyponatremia in neurosurgical patients. Clin Neurosurg. 1989; 35:93.

67. **Nanji AA.** Drug-induced electrolyte disorders. Drug Intell Clin Pharm. 1983;17:175.

68. **Brass EP, Thompson WL.** Drug-in-

duced electrolyte abnormalities. Drugs. 1982;24:207.

69 **Morgan DB et al.** Water intoxication and oxytocin infusion. Br J Obstet Gynaecol. 1977;84:6.

70 **Garcia M et al.** Chlorpropamide-induced water retention in patients with diabetes mellitus. Ann Intern Med. 1971;75:549.

71 **Hagen GA, Frawley TF.** Hyponatremia due to sulfonylurea compounds. J Clin Endocrinol Metab. 1970;31:570.

72 **Moses AM et al.** Clofibrate-induced antidiuresis. J Clin Invest. 1973;52:535.

73 **Tokihisa K et al.** Mechanism of carbamazepine-induced antidiuresis: evidence for release of antidiuretic hormone and impaired excretion of a water load. J Clin Endocrinol Metab. 1974;38:356.

74 **Lahr MB.** Hyponatremia during carbamazepine therapy. Clin Pharmacol Ther. 1985;37:693.

75 **Sandifer MG.** Hyponatremia due to psychotropic drugs. J Clin Psychiatry. 1983;44:301.

76 **Cohen BJ et al.** More cases of SIADH with fluoxetine. Am J Psychiatry. 1990;147:948.

77 **Marshal AW.** Bromocriptine-associated hyponatremia in cirrhosis. Br Med J (Clin Res). 1982;285:1534.

78 **DeFronzo RA et al.** Water intoxication in man after cyclophosphamide therapy. Time course and relation to drug activation. Ann Intern Med. 1973;78:861.

79 **Robertson GL et al.** Vincristine neurotoxicity and abnormal secretion of antidiuretic hormone. Arch Intern Med. 1973;132:717.

80 **Allon M et al.** Role of cigarette use in hyponatremia in schizophrenic patients. Am J Psychiatry. 1990;35:268.

81 **Peterson I et al.** Water intoxication associated with non-steroidal anti-inflammatory drug therapy. Acta Med Scand. 1987;221:221.

82 **Chung HM et al.** Post-operative hyponatremia. Arch Intern Med. 1986;314:1529.

83 **Coslovsky R et al.** Hypo-osmolar syndrome due to prolonged nausea. Arch Intern Med. 1984;144:191.

84 **Cochrane JPS et al.** Arginine vasopressin release following surgical operations. Br J Surg. 1981;68:209.

85 **Cusano AJ et al.** Hyponatremia in patients with acquired immunodeficiency syndrome. J Acquir Immune Defic Syndr. 1990;3:949.

86 **Hoen B et al.** Hyponatremia in AIDS: etiology and diagnosis. La Press Medicale. 1991;1028.

87 **Rose BD.** New approaches to disturbances in the plasma sodium concentration. Am J Med. 1986;81:1033.

88 **Cluitmans FHM, Meinders AE.** Management of severe hyponatremia: rapid or slow correction? Am J Med. 1990;88:161.

89 **Sterns RH.** The treatment of hyponatremia: first, do no harm. Am J Med. 1990;88:557.

90 **Sterns RH.** Severe symptomatic hyponatremia: treatment and outcome. A study of 64 cases. Ann Intern Med. 1987;107:656–64.

91 **Arieff AI.** Hyponatremia, convulsions, respiratory arrest, and permanent brain damage after elective surgery in healthy women. N Engl J Med. 1986;314:1529.

92 **Ayus JC et al.** Postoperative hyponatremic encephalopathy in menstruant women. Ann Intern Med. 1992;117:891.

93 **Lien Y et al.** Study of brain electrolytes and organic osmolytes during correction of chronic hyponatremia: implications for the pathogenesis of central pontine myelinolysis. J Clin Invest. 1991;88:303.

94 **Lundback JA et al.** Brain interstitial composition during acute hyponatremia. Acta Neurochir Suppl (Wien). 1990;51:17.

95 **Berl T.** Treating hyponatremia: damned if we do and damned if we don't. Kidney Int. 1990;37:1006.

96 **Sterns RH et al.** Neurologic sequelae after treatment of severe hyponatremia: a multicenter perspective. J Am Soc Nephrol. 1994;4:1522–530.

97 **Cheng JC et al.** Long-term neurologic outcome in psychogenic water drinkers with severe symptomatic hyponatremia: the effect of rapid correction. Am J Med. 1990;88:561.

98 **Ayus JC et al.** Rapid correction of severe hyponatremia with intravenous hypertonic saline solution. Am J Med. 1982;72:43.

99 **Worthley LG, Thomas PD.** Treatment of hyponatremic seizures with intravenous 29.2% saline. Br Med J. 1986;292:168.

100 **Hantman D et al.** Rapid correction of hyponatremia in the syndrome of inappropriate secretion of antidiuretic hormone. Ann Intern Med. 1973;78:870.

101 **Lauberg R, Karp BI.** Pontine and extrapontine myelinlysis following rapid correction of hyponatremia. Lancet. 1988;1439.

102 **Sterns RH et al.** Osmotic demyelination syndrome following correction of hyponatremia. N Engl J Med. 1986;314:1535.

103 **Decaux G et al.** Treatment of the syndrome of inappropriate secretion of antidiuretic hormone by urea. Am J Med. 1980;69:99.

104 **Decaux G et al.** Hyponatremia in the syndrome of inappropriate secretion of antidiuretic hormone. Rapid correction with urea, sodium chloride, and water restriction. JAMA. 1982;247:271.

105 **Decaux G.** Treatment of the syndrome of inappropriate secretion of antidiuretic hormone by long-loop diuretics. Nephron. 1983;35:82.

106 **Decaux G et al.** Treatment of the syndrome of inappropriate secretion of antidiuretic hormone with furosemide. N Engl J Med. 1981;304:329–30.

107 **Cherill DA et al.** Demeclocycline treatment in the syndrome of antidiuretic hormone secretion. Ann Intern Med. 1975;83:654.

108 **White MG, Fetner CD.** Treatment of the syndrome of inappropriate secretion of antidiuretic hormone with lithium carbonate. N Engl J Med. 1975;292:390.

109 **Forrest JN et al.** Superiority of demeclocycline over lithium in the treatment of chronic syndrome of inappropriate secretion of antidiuretic hormone. N Engl J Med. 1978;298:173.

110 **Carrilho F et al.** Renal failure associated with demeclocycline in cirrhosis. Ann Intern Med. 1977;87:195.

111 **Miller PD et al.** Plasma demeclocycline levels and nephrotoxicity. Correlation in hyponatremic cirrhotic patients. JAMA. 1980;243:2513.

112 **Fujisawa G et al.** Therapeutic efficacy of non-peptide ADH antagonist OPC-31260 in SIADH rats. Kidney Int. 1993;44:19.

113 **Tsuboi Y et al.** Therapeutic efficacy of the non-peptide AVP antagonist OPC-31260 in cirrhotic rats. Kidney Int. 1994;46:237.

114 **Tanay A et al.** Long-term treatment of the syndrome of inappropriate antiuretic hormone secretion with phenytoin. Ann Intern Med. 1979;90:50.

115 **Decaux G et al.** Lack of efficacy of phenytoin in the syndrome of inappropriate antidiuretic hormone secretion of neurological origin. Postgrad Med J. 1989;65:456.

116 **Morrison G, Singer I.** Hyperosmolal states. In: Narins RG, ed. Maxwell & Kleeman's Clinical Disorders of Fluid and Electrolyte Metabolism. New York: McGraw Hill; 1994:617.

117 **Snyder NA et al.** Hypernatremia in elderly patients. A heterogeneous, morbid, and iatrogenic entity. Ann Intern Med. 1987;107:309.

118 **Brater DC et al.** Clinical pharmacology of torasemide, a new loop diuretic. Clin Pharmacol Ther. 1987;42:187.

119 **Dossetor JB.** Creatininemia versus uremia: the relative significance of blood urea nitrogen and serum creatinine concentration in azotemia. Ann Intern Med. 1966;65:1287.

120 **Morgan DB, Davidson C.** Hypokalemia and diuretics: an analysis of publications. Br Med J. 1980;280:905.

121 **Holland OB et al.** Diuretic-induced ventricular ectopic activity. Am J Med. 1981;70:762.

122 **Schwartz AB, Swartz CD.** Dosage of potassium chloride elixir to correct thiazide-induced hypokalemia. JAMA. 1974;230:702.

123 **Kosman ME.** Management of potassium problems during long-term diuretic therapy. JAMA. 1974;230:743.

124 **Siegel D et al.** Diuretics, serum and intracellular electrolyte levels, and arrhythmias in hypertensive men. JAMA. 1992;267:1083.

125 **Tweeddale MG et al.** Antihypertensive and biochemical effects of chlorthalidone. Clin Pharmacol Ther. 1977;22:519.

126 **Leif PD et al.** Diuretic-induced hypokalemia does not cause ventricular ectopy in uncomplicated essential hypertension. Kidney Int. 1984;25:203.

127 **Finnerty FA.** A double-blind study of chlorthalidone and hydrochlorothiazide in an outpatient population of moderate hypertensives. Angiology. 1976;27:738.

128 **Wilson TW et al.** Effect of dosage regimen on natriuretic response to furosemide. Clin Pharmacol Ther. 1975;18:165.

129 **Helgeland A.** Treatment of mild hypertension: a five-year control drug trial. The Oslo study. Am J Med. 1980;69:725.

130 **Multiple Risk Factor Intervention Trial Research Group.** Multiple risk factor intervention trial: risk factor changes and mortality results. JAMA. 1982;248:1465.

131 **Siscovick DS et al.** Diuretic therapy for hypertension and the risk of primary cardiac arrest. N Engl J Med. 1994;330:1852.

132 **Cohen JD et al.** Diuretics, serum potassium and ventricular arrhythmias in the Multiple Risk Factor Intervention Trial. Am J Cardiol. 1987;60:548.

133 **Brown MJ et al.** Hypokalemia from beta₂-receptor stimulation by circulating epinephrine. N Engl J Med. 1983;309:1414.

134 **Bigger JT.** Diuretic therapy, hypertension and cardiac arrest. N Engl J Med. 1994;330:1899.

135 **Carlsen JE et al.** Relation between dose of bendrofluazide, antihypertensive effect, and adverse biochemical effects. Br Med J. 1990;300:975.

136 **Johnston GD et al.** Low dose cyclopenthiazide in the treatment of hypertension: a one-year community-based study. Q J Med. 1991;78:135.

137 **Haddad A et al.** Potassium substitutes. N Engl J Med. 1975;292:1082.

138 **Riddiough MA.** Preventing, detecting and managing adverse reactions to antihypertensive agents in the ambulatory patient with essential hypertension. Am J Hosp Pharm. 1977;34:465.

139 **McMahon FB et al.** Effect of potassium chloride supplements on upper gastrointestinal mucosa. Clin Pharmacol Ther. 1984;36:852.

140 **Stanaszek WF, Romankiewecz JA.** Current approaches to management of potassium deficiency. Drug Intell Clin Pharm. 1985;19:176.

141 **Kahn AM.** Effect of diuretics on the renal handling of urate. Semin Nephrol. 1988;8:305.

142 **Wienman EJ et al.** The influence of the extracellular volume on the tubular reabsorption of uric acid. J Clin Invest. 1975;55:283.

143 **Steele TH, Oppenheimer S.** Factors affecting urate excretion following diuretic administration in man. Am J Med. 1969;47:564.

144 **Chonko AM, Stewart RJ.** Pharmacologic inhibition of urate transport across perfused and nonperfused rabbit proximal straight tubules. Clin Res. 1980;28:748A.

145 **Langford HG et al.** Is thiazide-produced uric acid elevation harmful? Analysis of data from the Hypertension Detection and Follow-up Program. Arch Intern Med. 1987;147:645.

146 **Liang MH, Fries JF.** Asymptomatic hyperuricemia: the case for conservative management. Ann Intern Med. 1978;88:666.

147 **Chennavasin P et al.** Pharmacodynamic analysis of the furosemide-probenecid interaction in man. Kidney Int. 1979;16:187.

148 **Weidmann P et al.** Antihypertensive treatment and serum lipoproteins. J Hypertens. 1985;3:297.

149 **Weinberger MH.** Antihypertensive therapy and lipids: evidence, mechanisms and implications. Arch Intern Med. 1985;145:1102.

150 **Weinberger MH.** Antihypertensive therapy and lipids: paradoxical influence on cardiovascular disease risk. Am J Med. 1986;80(Suppl. 2A):64.

151 **Neusy AJ, Lowenstein J.** Effects of prazosin, atenolol and thiazide diuretic on plasma lipids in patients with essential hypertension. Am J Med. 1986; 80(Suppl. 2A):94.

152 **Freis ED.** The cardiovascular risk of diuretic-induced hypokalemia and elevated cholesterol. Ration Drug Ther. 1986;20:1.

153 **Lipid Research Clinics Program.** The lipid research clinics coronary primary prevention trial results. I. Reduction in incidence of coronary heart disease. II. The relationship of reduction in incidence of coronary heart disease to cholesterol lowering. JAMA. 1984;251: 351,365.

154 **Grimm RH, Hunninghake DB.** Lipids and hypertension: implications of new guidelines for cholesterol management in the treatment of hypertension. Am J Med. 1986;80(Suppl. 2A):56.

155 **Ames RP.** The effects of antihypertensive drugs on serum lipids and lipoproteins (I. Diuretics). Drugs. 1986;32:260.

156 **Yendt ER et al.** The use of thiazides in the prevention of renal calculi. Can Med Assoc J. 1970;102:614.

157 **Lant A.** Diuretics: clinical pharmacology and therapeutic use. Drugs. 1985; 29(Pt. 1,2):57,162.

158 **Leary WP, Reyes AJ.** Diuretic-induced magnesium losses. Drugs. 1984; 28:(Suppl. I):182.

159 **Ryan MP et al.** Effects of diuretics on the renal handling of magnesium. Drugs. 1984;28(Suppl. I):167.

160 **Rude RK et al.** PTH secretion in magnesium deficiency. J Clin Endocrinol Metab. 1978;47:800.

161 **Ashraf N et al.** Thiazide-induced hyponatremia associated with death and neurologic damage in outpatients. Am J Med. 1981;70:1163.

162 **Friedman E et al.** Thiazide-induced hyponatremia: reproducibility by single-dose challenge and an analysis of pathogenesis. Ann Intern Med. 1989; 110:24.

163 **Kassirer JP, Schwartz WB.** Correction of metabolic alkalosis in man without repair of potassium deficiency. Am J Med. 1966;40:19.

164 **Gordon P.** Glucose intolerance with hypokalemia. Failure of short-term potassium depletion in normal subjects to reproduce the glucose and insulin abnormalities of clinical hypokalemia. Diabetes. 1973;22:544.

165 **Helderman JH et al.** Prevention of the glucose intolerance of thiazide diuretics by maintenance of body potassium. Diabetes. 1983;32:106.

166 **Amery A et al.** Glucose intolerance during diuretic therapy. Results of the trial by the European working party on hypertension in the elderly. Lancet. 1978;1:681.

167 **Perez-Stable E, Caralis PV.** Thiazide-induced disturbances in carbohydrate, lipid, and potassium metabolism. Am Heart J. 1983;106:245.

168 **Rowe PA, Mather HG.** Hyperosmolar non-ketotic diabetes mellitus associated with metolazone. Br Med J (Clin Res). 1985;29:25.

169 **Veterans Administration Cooperative Study Group on Antihypertensive Agents.** Effects of treatment on morbidity in hypertension. III. Influence of age, diastolic pressure and prior cardiovascular disease. Further analysis of side effects. Circulation. 1972; 45:991.

170 **Ferannini E et al.** Insulin resistance in essential hypertension. N Engl J Med. 1987;317:350.

171 **Pollare T et al.** A comparison of the effects of hydrochlorothiazide and captopril on glucose and lipid metabolism in patients with hypertension. N Engl J Med. 1989;321:868.

172 **Chonko AM, Grantham JJ.** Treatment of edema states. In: Narins RG, ed. Maxwell & Kleeman's Clinical Disorders of Fluid and Electrolyte Metabolism. 5th ed. New York: McGraw Hill; 1994:545.

173 **Ellison DH.** The physiologic basis of diuretic synergism: its role in treating diuretic resistance. Ann Intern Med. 1991;114:886.

174 **Rose BD.** Diuretics. Kidney Int. 1991; 39:336.

175 **Odlund BOG, Freeman B.** Diuretic resistance: reduced bioavailability and effect of oral frusemide. Br Med J. 1980;280:1577.

176 **Brater DC.** Resistance to loop diuretics: why it happens and what to do about it. Drugs. 1985;30:427.

177 **Inoue M et al.** Mechanism of furosemide resistance in analbuminemic rats and hypoalbuminemic patients. Kidney Int. 1987;32:198.

178 **Sterns RH et al.** Internal potassium balance and the control of the plasma potassium concentration. Medicine. 1981;60:339.

179 **Allon M.** Treatment and prevention of hyperkalemia in end-stage renal disease. Kidney Int. 1993;43:1197.

180 **Perrone RD, Alexander EA.** Regulation of extrarenal potassium metabolism. In: Narins RG, ed. Maxwell & Kleeman's Clinical Disorders of Fluid and Electrolyte Metabolism. New York: McGraw Hill; 1994:129.

181 **Salem MM et al.** Extrarenal potassium tolerance in chronic renal failure: implications for the treatment of acute hyperkalemia. Am J Kidney Dis. 1991; 18:421.

182 **Field MJ et al.** Regulation of renal potassium metabolism. In: Narins RG, ed. Maxwell & Kleeman's Clinical Disorders of Fluid and Electrolyte Metabolism. New York: McGraw Hill; 1994: 147.

183 **Wright FS.** Renal potassium handling. Semin Nephrol. 1987;7:174.

184 **Field MJ, Giebisch GJ.** Hormonal control of renal potassium excretion. Kidney Int. 1985;276:379.

185 **Sterns RH et al.** The disposition of intravenous potassium in normal man: the role of insulin. Clin Sci. 1987;73: 557.

186 **DeFronzo RA et al.** Effect of graded doses of insulin on splanchnic and peripheral potassium metabolism in man. Am J Physiol. 1980;238:E421.

187 **Williams ME et al.** Impairment of extrarenal potassium disposal by alpha-adrenergic stimulation. N Engl J Med. 1984;311:145.

188 **Rosa RM et al.** Adrenergic modulation of extrarenal potassium disposal. N Engl J Med. 1980;302:431.

189 **White PC.** Disorders of aldosterone biosynthesis and action. N Engl J Med. 1994;331:250.

190 **Schon DA et al.** Mechanism of potassium excretion in renal insufficiency. Am J Physiol. 1974;227:325.

191 **Androgue HJ, Madias NE.** Changes in plasma potassium concentration during acute acid-base disturbances. Am J Med. 1981;71:456.

192 **Oster JR et al.** Plasma potassium response to acute metabolic acidosis induced by mineral and nonmineral acids. Miner Electrolyte Metab. 1980;4: 28.

193 **Androgue HJ et al.** Determinants of plasma potassium levels in diabetic ketoacidosis. Medicine. 1986;65:163.

194 **Makoff DI et al.** On the mechanism of hyperkalemia due to hyperosmotic expansion with saline or mannitol. Clin Sci. 1971;41:383.

195 **Hazeyama Y, Sparks HV.** A model of potassium efflux during exercise of skeletal muscle. Am J Physiol. 1979; 236:R83.

196 **Krishna GG et al.** Hypokalemic states. In: Narins RG, ed. Maxwell & Kleeman's Clinical Disorders of Fluid and Electrolyte Metabolism. New York: McGraw Hill; 1994:659.

197 **Johnsen T.** Familial periodic paralysis with hypokalemia. Dan Med Bull. 1980;28.

198 **Moravec MD, Hurlbert BJ.** Hypokalemia associated with terbutaline administration in obstetrical patients. Annesth Analg. 1980;59:917.

199 **Roza O, Bermen LB.** The pathophysiology of barium: hypokalemic and cardiovascular effects. J Pharmacol Exp Ther. 1977;177:433.

200 **Lawson OH et al.** Early mortality in the megaloblastic anemias. Q J Med. 1972;41:1.

201 **Chan JLM.** Bartter's syndrome. Nephron. 1980;26:155.

202 **Whang R et al.** Magnesium depletion as a cause of refractory potassium repletion. Arch Intern Med. 1985;145: 1686.

203 **Davidman M, Schmitz P.** Renal tubular acidosis: a pathophysiologic approach. Hosp Pract. 1988;77.

204 **Nader PC et al.** Complications of diuretic use. Semin Nephrol. 1988;8:365.

205 **Lipner HI et al.** The behavior of carbenicillin as a non-reabsorbable anion. J Lab Clin Med. 1975;86:183.

206 **Blachley JD, Hill JB.** Renal and electrolyte disturbances associated with cisplatinum. Ann Intern Med. 1981;95: 628.

207 **Bar RS et al.** Hypomagnesemic hypocalcemia secondary to renal magnesium wasting: a possible consequence of high dose gentamicin therapy. Ann Intern Med. 1975;82:646.

208 **Cheng JT et al.** Potassium wasting and other renal tubular defects with rifampin nephrotoxicity. Am J Nephrol. 1984;4:379.

209 **Habibzadeh MA, Zeller NH.** Cardiac arrhythmias and hypopotassemia in association with lithium carbonate overdose. South Med J. 1977;70:628.

210 **Graneru AK et al.** Kaliuretic effect of L-dopa treatment in parkinsonian patients. Acta Med Scand. 1977;201:291.

211 **Streicher HZ et al.** Syndromes of toluene sniffing in adults. Ann Intern Med. 1981;94:758.

212 **Holten C, Patersen VP.** Malignant hypertension with increased secretion of aldosterone and depletion of potassium. Lancet. 1956;2:918.

213 **Liddle GW et al.** A familial renal disorder simulating primary aldosteronism but with negligible aldosterone secretion. Trans Assoc Am Physicians. 1963;79:199.

214 **Adams PC et al.** Exaggerated hypokalemia in acute myeloid leukemia. Br Med J. 1981;282:1034.

215 **Knochel JP.** Neuromuscular manifestations of electrolyte disorders. Am J Med. 1982;75:521.

216 **Surawicz B.** Relationship between electrocardiogram and electrolytes. Am Heart J. 1967;73:814.

217 **Shapiro W, Taubert K.** Hypokalemia and digoxin-induced arrhythmias. Lancet. 1975;2:604.

218 **Smith SR et al.** Potassium chloride lowers blood pressure and causes natriuresis in older patients with hypertension. J Am Soc Nephrol. 1992;2: 1032.

219 **Helderman JH et al.** Prevention of the glucose intolerance of thiazide diuretics by maintenance of the body potassium. Diabetes. 1983;32:106.

220 **Merkus F.** Is canrenone the major metabolite of spironolactone? Clin Pharm. 1983;2:209.

221 **Tiaianello A et al.** Renal ammoniagenesis in humans with chronic potassium depletion. Kidney Int. 1991;40: 772.

222 **Saggar-Malik AK, Cappuccio FP.** Potassium supplements and potassium-sparing diuretics. A review and guide to appropriate use. Drugs. 1993;46: 986–1008.

223 **Stanaszek WF et al.** Current approaches to management of potassium deficiency. Drug Intell Clin Pharm. 1985;19:176.

224 **Kruse JA, Carlson RW.** Rapid correction of hypokalemia using concentrated intravenous potassium chloride infusions. Arch Intern Med. 1990;150: 613.

225 **Kunin AS et al.** Decrease in serum potassium concentration and appearance of cardiac arrhythmias during infusion of potassium with glucose in potassium-depleted patients. N Engl J Med. 1962;266:228.

226 **Lambert J, Newman A.** Ulceration and stricture of the esophagus due to oral potassium chloride (slow-release tablet) therapy. Am J Gastroenterol. 1980;73:508.

227 **McMahon F, Akdaman K.** Gastric ulceration after "slow-K." N Engl J Med. 1976;295:733.

228 **DeFronzo RA, Smith JD.** Clinical disorders of hyperkalemia. In: Narins RG, ed. Maxwell & Kleeman's Clinical Disorders of Fluid and Electrolyte Metabolism. New York: McGraw Hill; 1994:697.

229 **Bronson WR et al.** Pseudohyperkalemia due to release of potassium from white blood cells during clotting. N Engl J Med. 1966;274:369.

230 **Ingram RH Jr, Seki M.** Pseudohyperkalemia with thrombocytosis. N Engl J Med. 1962;267:895.

231 **Mather A, Mackie NR.** Effects of hemolysis on serum electrolyte values. Clin Chem. 1960;6:223.

232 **Romano AT, Young GR Jr.** Mild forearm exercise during venipuncture

and its effect on potassium determinations. Clin Chem. 1977;2:303.

233 Ward MM. Factors predictive of acute renal failure in rhabdomyolysis. Arch Intern Med. 1988;148:1553.

234 Cohen LF et al. Acute tumor lysis syndrome. Am J Med. 1980;68:486.

235 Ponce SP et al. Drug-induced hyperkalemia. Medicine. 1985;64:357.

236 Rimmer et al. Hyperkalemia as a complication of drug therapy. Arch Intern Med. 1987;147:867.

237 Sopko JA et al. Salt substitutes as a source of potassium. JAMA. 1977;238:608.

238 DeFronzo RA. Hyperkalemia and hyporeninemic hypoaldosteronism. Kidney Int. 1980;17:118.

239 Battle DC et al. Hyperkalemic hyperchloremic metabolic acidosis in sickle cell hemoglobinopathies. Am J Med. 1981;72:188.

240 Nerup J. Addison's disease–clinical studies. A report of 108 cases. Acta Endocrinol. 1974;76:127.

241 Battle DC et al. Hyperkalemic distal renal tubular acidosis associated with obstructive uropathy. N Engl J Med. 1981;30:373.

242 Textor SC et al. Hyperkalemia in azotemic patients during angiotensin-converting enzyme inhibition and aldosterone reduction with captopril. Am J Med. 1982;73:719.

243 Izzo JL et al. Hyperkalemia with enalapril in advanced renal failure. JAMA. 1986;255:2505.

244 Miller KP et al. Severe hyperkalemia during piroxicam therapy. Arch Intern Med. 1984;144:2414.

245 Carlson E et al. Beta-adrenoreceptor blockers, plasma potassium and exercise. Lancet. 1978;2:424.

246 Goggans FC. Acute hyperkalemia during lithium treatment of manic illness. Am J Psychiatry. 1980;137:860.

247 O'Kelly R et al. Routine heparin therapy inhibits adrenal aldosterone production. J Clin Endocrinol Metab. 1983;56:108.

248 Edes TE et al. Heparin-induced hyperkalemia. Arch Intern Med. 1985;145:1070.

249 Sherman RA, Ruddy MC. Suppression of aldosterone production by low dose heparin. Am J Nephrol. 1986;6:165.

250 Lachaal M, Venuto RC. Nephrotoxicity and hyperkalemia in patients with acquired immunodeficiency syndrome treated with pentamidine. Am J Med. 1989;87:260.

251 Cohen AB. Hyperkalemic effects of triamterene. Ann Intern Med. 1961;65:251.

252 Greenburg S et al. Trimethoprim-sulfamethoxazole induces reversible hyperkalemia. Ann Intern Med. 1993;119:291.

253 Velazquez H et al. Renal mechanisms of trimethoprim-induced hyperkalemia. Ann Intern Med. 1993;119:296.

254 Kamel KS et al. Studies to determine the basis for hyperkalemia in recipients of a renal transplant who are treated with cyclosporine. J Am Soc Nephrol. 1991;2:1279.

255 Bismuth C et al. Hyperkalemia in acute digitalis poisoning: prognostic significance and therapeutic implications. Clin Toxicol. 1973;6:153.

256 Hertz P et al. Arginine-induced hyperkalemia. Arch Intern Med. 1972;130:778.

257 Bushinsky DA et al. Life-threatening hyperkalemia induced by arginine. Ann Intern Med. 1978;89:632.

258 Cooperman LH. Succinylcholine-induced hyperkalemia in neuromuscular disease. JAMA. 1970;213:1867.

259 Birch AA et al. Changes in serum potassium response to succinylcholine following trauma. JAMA. 1969;210:490.

260 Blumberg A et al. Effect of various therapeutic approaches on plasma potassium and major regulating factors in terminal renal failure. Am J Med. 1988;85:507.

261 Allon M et al. Effect of insulin-plus-glucose with or without epinephrine on fasting hyperkalemia. Kidney Int. 1993;43:212.

262 Liou HH et al. Hypokalemic effects of intravenous infusion or nebulization of salbutamol in patients with chronic renal failure: comparative study. Am J Kidney Dis. 1994;23:266.

263 Montouliu J et al. Potassium lowering effect of albuterol for hyperkalemia in renal failure. Arch Intern Med. 1987;147:713.

264 Allon M et al. Nebulized albuterol for acute hyperkalemia in patients on hemodialysis. Ann Intern Med. 1989;110:426.

265 Allon M, Copkney C. Albuterol and insulin for treatment of hyperkalemia in hemodialysis patients. Kidney Int. 1990;38:869.

266 Fraley DS, Adler S. Correction of hyperkalemia by bicarbonate despite constant blood pH. Kidney Int. 1977;12:354.

267 Gutierrez R et al. Effect of hypertonic versus isotonic sodium bicarbonate on plasma potassium concentrations in patients with end-stage renal disease. Miner Electrolyte Metab. 1991;17:291.

268 Finn RB et al. Treatment of the oliguric patient with a new sodium polystyrene resin and sorbitol. A preliminary report. N Engl J Med. 1961;264:111.

269 Scherr L et al. Management of hyperkalemia with a cation-exchange resin. N Engl J Med. 1961;264:115.

270 Wootton FT et al. Colonic necrosis with kayexalate-sorbitol enemas after renal transplantation. Ann Intern Med. 1989;111:947.

271 Gestman BB et al. Intestinal necrosis associated with postoperative orally administered sodium polystyrene sulfonate in sorbitol. Am J Kidney Dis. 1992;20:159.

272 Brown ST et al. Potassium removal with peritoneal dialysis. Kidney Int. 1973;4:67.

273 Sherman RA et al. Variability in potassium removal by hemodialysis. Am J Nephrol. 1986;6:284.

274 Ward RA et al. Hemodialysate composition and intradialytic metabolic acid-base and potassium changes. Kidney Int. 1987;32:129.

275 Kethersid TL, Van Stone JC. Dialysate potassium. Semin Dial. 1991;4:46.

276 Moore EW. Ionized calcium in normal serum, ultrafiltrates and whole blood determined by ion-exchange electrode. J Clin Invest. 1970;49:318.

277 Lindgarde F, Zettervall O. Hypercalcemia and normal ionized serum calcium in a case of myelomatosis. Ann Intern Med. 1973;78:396.

278 Wills MR. Intestinal absorption of calcium. Lancet. 1973;1:820.

279 Favus MJ. Transport of calcium by intestinal mucosa. Semin Nephrol. 1981;1:306.

280 LeRoith D, Pimstone BL. Bone metabolism and composition in the protein-deprived rat. Clin Sci. 1973;44:305.

281 Popovtzer MM et al. Disorders of calcium, phosphorus, vitamin D, and parathyroid hormone activity. In: Schrier RW, ed. Renal and Electrolyte Disorders. 4th ed. Boston: Little, Brown and Co.; 1992:287.

282 Lemann J Jr et al. Urinary calcium excretion in human beings. N Engl J Med. 1979;301:535.

283 Lassiter WE et al. Micropuncture study of tubular reabsorption of calcium in normal rodents. Am J Physiol. 1963;204:771.

284 Benabe JE, Martinez-Maldonado M. Disorders of calcium metabolism. In: Narins RG, ed. Maxwell & Kleeman's Clinical Disorders of Fluid and Electrolyte Metabolism. 5th ed. New York: McGraw Hill; 1994:1009.

285 Bilezikian JP. Hypercalcemia. Dis Mon. 1988;34:739.

286 Mundy GR. Pathophysiology of cancer-associated hypercalcemia. Semin Oncol. 1990;17(Suppl. 5):10.

287 Lee DBN et al. The pathophysiology and clinical aspects of hypercalcemic disorders. West J Med. 1978;129:278.

288 Ladenson JH et al. Relationship of free and total calcium in hypercalcemic conditions. J Clin Endocrinol Metab. 1979;48:393.

289 Beck N et al. Pathogenetic role of cyclic AMP in the impairment of urinary concentrating ability in acute hypercalcemia. J Clin Invest. 1974;54:1049.

290 Ritz E, Massry SG. The kidney in disorders of calcium metabolism. Contrib Nephrol. 1977;7:114.

291 Bajorunas DR. Clinical manifestations of cancer-related hypercalcemia. Semin Oncol. 1990;17(Suppl. 5):16.

292 Eversmann JJ et al. Gastrointestinal manifestations of hyperparathyroidism. Arch Intern Med. 1967;119:605.

293 Hosking DJ et al. Rehydration in the treatment of severe hypercalcemia. Q J Med. 1981;50:473.

294 Massry SG et al. Role of serum Ca, parathyroid hormone, and NaCl infusion on renal Ca and Na clearances. Am J Physiol. 1968;214:1403.

295 Suki WN et al. Acute treatment of hypercalcemia with furosemide. N Engl J Med. 1970;283:836.

296 Mundy GR, Martin TJ. The hypercalcemia of malignancy: pathogenesis and management. Metabolism. 1982;31:1247.

297 Ardaillou R et al. Renal excretion of phosphate, calcium and sodium during and after a prolonged thyrocalcitonin infusion in man. Proc Soc Exp Biol Med. 1969;131:56.

298 Silva OL, Becker KL. Salmon calcitonin in the treatment of hypercalcemia. Arch Intern Med. 1973;132:237.

299 Singer FR et al. An evaluation of anti-bodies and clinical resistance to salmon calcitonin. J Clin Invest. 1972;51:2331.

300 Tashjian AJ Jr et al. Calcitonin binding sites in bone: relationships to biological response and escape. Recent Prog Horm Res. 1978;34:285.

301 Minstock ML, Mundy GR. Effect of calcitonin and glucocorticoids in combination on the hypercalcemia of malignancy. Ann Intern Med. 1980;93:269.

302 Ritch PS. Treatment of cancer-related hypercalcemia. Semin Oncol. 1990;17 (Suppl. 5):26.

303 Caro JF et al. Symptomatic hypocalcemia following combined calcitonin and mithramycin therapy for hypercalcemia due to malignancy. Cancer Treat Rep. 1978;62:1561.

304 Yarbro JW et al. Mithramycin inhibition of ribonucleic acid synthesis. Cancer Res. 1966;26:36.

305 Green L, Donehower RC. Hepatic toxicity of low doses of mithramycin in hypercalcemia. Cancer Treat Rep. 1884;68:1379.

306 Ryzen E et al. Intravenous etidronate in the management of malignant hypercalcemia. Arch Intern Med. 1985;145:449.

307 Gucalp R et al. Comparative study of pamidronate disodium and etidronate disodium in the treatment of cancer-related hypercalcemia. J Clin Oncol. 1992;10:134.

308 Bounameaux HM et al. Renal failure associated with intravenous diphosphonates. Lancet. 1983;1:471.

309 Francis MD, Slough CL. Acute intravenous infusions of disodium dihydrogen (1-hydroxy-ethylidene) diphosphonate: Mechanisms of cytotoxicity. J Pharm Sci. 1983;73:1097.

310 Morton AR. Biphosphonates for the hypercalcemia of malignancy in end-stage renal disease. Semin Dialysis. 1994;7:76.

311 Todd PA, Fitton A. Gallium nitrate: a review of its pharmacological properties and therapeutic potential in cancer-related hypercalcemia. Drugs. 1991;42:261.

312 Warrell RP Jr. Clinical trials of gallium nitrate in patients with cancer-related hypercalcemia. Semin Oncol. 1991;18(Suppl. 5):26.

313 Hughes TE, Hansen LA. Gallium nitrate. Ann Pharmacother. 1992;26:354.

314 Haussler MR, McCain TA. Basic and clinical concepts related to vitamin D metabolism and action. N Engl J Med. 1977;297:974.

315 Kimberg DB et al. Effect of cortisone treatment on the active transport of calcium by the small intestine. J Clin Invest. 1971;50:1309.

316 Breslau NA et al. Hypercalcemia associated with increased serum calcitriol levels in three patients with lymphoma. Ann Intern Med. 1984;100:1.

317 Streck WF et al. Glucocorticoid effects in vitamin D intoxication. Arch Intern Med. 1979;139:974.

318 Bell NH et al. On the abnormal calcium absorption in sarcoidosis. Am J Med. 1964;36:500.

319 Ito H et al. Indomethacin-responsive hypercalcemia. N Eng J Med. 1975;239:558.

320 Brenner DE et al. A study of prostaglandin E2, parahormone, and re-

sponse to indomethacin in patients with hypercalcemia of malignancy. Cancer. 1982;49:556.

321 **Lau K.** Phosphate disorders. In: Kokko JP, Tannen RL, eds. Fluids and Electrolytes. 2nd ed. Philadelphia: WB Saunders; 1990:485–595.

322 **Aitken JM et al.** The effect of long-term mestranol administration on calcium and phosphorus homeostasis in oophorectomized women. Clin Sci. 1971;41:233–36.

323 **Pollock N.** Serum and muscle phosphate changes following glucose injections. Am J Physiol. 1933;105:79.

324 **Massara F, Camanni F.** Propranolol block of adrenaline-induced hypophosphatemia in man. Clin Sci. 1970;38:245.

325 **Mostella ME, Tuttle EP Jr.** Effect of alkalosis on plasma concentration and urinary excretion of inorganic phosphate in man. J Clin Invest. 1964;43:138.

326 **Harrison HE, Harrison HC.** The effect of acidosis upon renal tubular reabsorption of phosphate. Am J Physiol. 1941;134:781.

327 **Moog F, Glazier HS.** Phosphate absorption and alkaline phosphatase activity in the small intestine of the adult mouse and of the chick embryo and hatched chick. Comp Biochem Physiol. 1972;42A:321.

328 **Fox J, Care AD.** Stimulation of duodenal and head absorption of phosphate in the chick by low-calcium and low-phosphate diets. Calcif Tissue Int. 1978;26:243–45.

329 **Wilkinson R.** Absorption of calcium, phosphorus and magnesium. In: Nordin BEC, ed. Calcium, Phosphate and Magnesium Metabolism. Edinburgh: Churchill Livingstone; 1976:36.

330 **Brommage R et al.** Vitamin D-independent intestinal calcium and phosphorus absorption during reproduction. Am J Physiol. 1990;259:G631.

331 **Sheikh MS et al.** Reduction of dietary phosphorus absorption by phosphorus binders. J Clin Invest. 1989;83:66–73.

332 **Sheldon GF, Brzyb S.** Phosphate depletion and repletion. Relation to parenteral nutrition and oxygen transport. Ann Surg. 1975;182:683–89.

333 **Levine BS, Kleeman CR.** Hypophosphatemia and hyperphosphatemia: clinical and pathologic aspects. In: Narins RG, ed. Maxwell & Kleeman's Clinical Disorders of Fluid and Electrolyte Metabolism. 5th ed. New York: McGraw Hill; 1994:1045.

334 **Portale AA et al.** Dietary intake of phosphorus modulates the circadian rhythm in serum concentration of phosphorus: implications for the renal production of 1,25-dihydroxyvitamin D. J Clin Invest. 1987;80:1147.

335 **Eisenbrey AB et al.** Mannitol interference in an automated serum phosphate assay. Clin Chem. 1987;33:2308.

336 **Lee DBN et al.** Effect of phosphorus depletion on intestinal calcium and phosphorus absorption. Am J Physiol. 1979;236:E451–57.

337 **Silvis SE, Paragas PD.** Paresthesias, weakness, seizures and hypophosphatemia in patients receiving hyperalimentation. Gastroenterology. 1972;62:513.

338 **Lotz M et al.** Evidence for phosphorus depletion syndrome in man. N Engl J Med. 1968;278:409.

339 **Roxe DM et al.** Phosphate-binding effects of sucralfate in patients with chronic renal failure. Am J Kidney Dis. 1989;13:194.

340 **Cox GJ et al.** The effects of high doses of aluminum and iron on phosphorus metabolism. J Biol Chem. 1931;92:11.

341 **Marwich TH et al.** Severe hypophosphatemia induced by glucose-insulin-potassium therapy. A case report and proposal for altered protocol. Int J Cardiol. 1988;18:327.

342 **Stein JH et al.** Hypophosphatemia in acute alcoholism. Am J Med. 1966;252:78.

343 **Fiaccadori E et al.** Hypophosphatemia in course of chronic obstructive pulmonary disease. Prevalence, mechanisms, and relationships with skeletal muscle phosphorus content. Chest. 1990;97:857.

344 **Lennquist S et al.** Hypophosphatemia in severe burns. A prospective study. Acta Chir Scand. 1979;145:1.

345 **Kebler R et al.** Dynamic changes in serum phosphorus levels in diabetic ketoacidosis. Am J Med. 1985;79:571.

346 **Massry SG.** The clinical syndrome of phosphate depletion. Adv Exp Med Biol. 1978;103:301.

347 **Lichtman MA et al.** Reduced red cell glycolysis, 1,2-diphosphoglycerate and adenosine triphosphate concentration and increased hemoglobin-oxygen affinity caused by hypophosphatemia. Ann Intern Med. 1971;74:562–68.

348 **Narins RG et al.** Diagnostic strategies in disorders of fluid, electrolyte and acid-base homeostasis. Am J Med. 1982;72:496.

349 **Lentz DR et al.** Treatment of severe hypophosphatemia. Ann Intern Med. 1978;89:941–44.

350 **Vannata JB et al.** Efficacy of intravenous phosphorus therapy in the severely hypophosphatemic patient. Arch Intern Med. 1981;141:885–87.

351 **Widdowson EM et al.** Chemical composition of human body. Clin Sci. 1951;10:113.

352 **Wacker WEC, Parisi AF.** Magnesium metabolism. N Engl J Med. 1968;278:658–62,712–17,772–76.

353 **Kurachi Y et al.** Role of intracellular Mg^{2+} in the activation of muscarinic K^+ channel in cardiac atrial cell membrane. Pflugers Arch. 1986; 407:572.

354 **White RE, Hartzell HC.** Magnesium ions in cardiac function. Regulator of ion channels and second messengers. Biochem Pharmacol. 1989;38:859.

355 **Seelig MS.** The magnesium requirement by the normal adult: summary and analysis of published data. Am J Clin Nutr. 1964;14:212.

356 **Jones JE et al.** Magnesium requirements in adults. Am J Clin Nutr. 1967; 20:632–35.

357 **Brannan PG et al.** Magnesium absorption in the human small intestine. J Clin Invest. 1976; 57:1412–418.

358 **Schmulen AC et al.** Effect of 1,25-$(OH)_2D_3$ on jejunal absorption of magnesium in patients with chronic renal disease. Am J Physiol. 1980;238:G349.

359 **Heaton FW.** The parathyroid glands and magnesium metabolism in the rat. Clin Sci. 1965;28:543.

360 **Silver L et al.** Magnesium turnover in humans studied with ^{28}Mg. J Clin Invest. 1960;39:420.

361 **Carney S et. al.** Effect of magnesium deficiency on renal magnesium and calcium transport in the rat. J Clin Invest. 1980;65:180.

362 **Massry SG et al.** Renal handling of magnesium in the dog. Am J Physiol. 1969;216:1460.

363 **Lennon EJ, Piering WFA.** A comparison of the effects of glucose ingestion and NH_4Cl acidosis on urinary calcium and magnesium excretion in man. J Clin Invest. 1970;49:1458.

364 **Quamme GA.** Effect of furosemide on calcium and magnesium transport in the rat nephron. Am J Physiol. 1981;241:F340.

365 **Wong NLM et al.** Effects of mannitol on water and electrolyte transport in the dog kidney. J Lab Clin Med. 1979;94:683.

366 **Morel F.** Sites of hormone action in the mammalian nephron. Am J Physiol. 1981;240:F159.

367 **Massry SG, Coburn JW.** The hormonal and non-hormonal control of renal excretion of calcium and magnesium. Nephron. 1973;10:66.

368 **Horton R, Biglieri EG.** Effect of aldosterone on the metabolism of magnesium. Clin Endocrinol Metab. 1962;22:1187.

369 **Lim P, Jacob E.** Tissue magnesium levels in chronic diarrhea. J Lab Clin Med. 1977;80:313.

370 **Alfrey AC et al.** Evaluation of body magnesium stores. J Lab Clin Med. 1974;84:153.

371 **Thoren L.** Magnesium metabolism. Proc Surg. 1971;9:131.

372 **Potts JT, Roberts B.** Clinical significance of magnesium deficiency and its relationship to parathyroid disease. Am J Med Sci. 1958;235:205.

373 **Jackson CE, Meier DW.** Routine serum magnesium analysis: correlation with clinical state in 5100 patients. Ann Intern Med. 1968;69:743.

374 **Rasmussen HS et al.** Intravenous magnesium in acute myocardial infarction. Lancet. 1986;1:234.

375 **Chernow B et al.** Hypomagnesemia in patients in post-operative intensive care. Chest. 1989;95:391.

376 **Shils ME.** Experimental human magnesium depletion. Medicine. 1969;118:61.

377 **Caddell JL, Goddard DR.** Studies in protein-calorie malnutrition. 1. Chemical evidence for magnesium deficiency. New Engl J Med. 1967;276:533.

378 **Flink EB et al.** Magnesium deficiency after prolonged parenteral fluid administration and after chronic alcoholism, complicated by delirium tremens. J Lab Clin Med. 1954;43:169.

379 **Baron DN.** Magnesium deficiency after gastrointestinal surgery and loss of excretions. Br J Surg. 1960;48:344.

380 **Coons CM, Blunt K.** The retention of nitrogen, calcium, phosphorus and magnesium by pregnant women. J Biol Chem. 1930;86:1.

381 **Booth CC et al.** Incidence of hypomagnesaemia in intestinal malabsorption. Br Med J. 1963;2:141.

382 **Hallberg DAG.** Magnesium problems in gastroenterology. Acta Med Scand. 1981;661:62.

383 **Thoren L.** Magnesium deficiency in gastrointestinal fluid loss. Acta Chir Scand. 1963;306(Suppl.):1.

384 **Milla PJ et al.** Studies in primary hypomagnesemia: evidence for defective carrier-mediated small intestinal transport of magnesium. Gut. 1979;20:1028.

385 **Evans RA et al.** The congenital magnesium-losing kidney: report of two patients. Q J Med. 1981;197:39.

386 **Lam M, Adelstein DJ.** Hypomagnesemia and renal magnesium wasting in patients treated with cisplatin. Am J Kidney Dis. 1986;8:164.

387 **Keating MJ et al.** Hypocalcemia with hypoparathyroidism and renal tubular dysfunction associated with aminoglycoside therapy. Cancer. 1977;39:1410.

388 **Wong NLM, Dirks JH.** Cyclosporin-induced hypomagnesaemia and renal magnesium wasting in rats. Clin Sci. 1988;75:505.

389 **Barton CH et al.** Renal magnesium wasting associated with amphotericin B therapy. Am J Med. 1984;77:471.

390 **Widman L et al.** Effect of Moduretic and Aldactone on electrolytes on skeletal muscle in patients on long-term diuretic therapy. Acta Med Scand. 1982; 661(Suppl.):33.

391 **Coburn JW, Massry SG.** Changes in serum and urinary calcium during phosphate depletion. Studies on mechanisms. J Clin Invest. 1970;49:1073.

392 **Quamme GA, Dirks JH.** Magnesium transport in the nephron. Am J Physiol. 1980;8:393.

393 **Butler AM et al.** Metabolic studies in diabetic coma. Trans Assoc Am Physicians. 1947;60:102.

394 **Kalbfleisch JM et al.** Effects of ethanol administration on urinary excretion of magnesium and other electrolytes in alcoholic and normal subjects. J Clin Invest. 1963;42:1471.

395 **Hellman ES et al.** Abnormal water and electrolyte metabolism in acute intermittent porphyria: transient inappropriate secretion of antidiuretic hormone. Am J Med. 1962;32:734.

396 **Tapley DF.** Magnesium balance in myxedematous patients treated with triiodothyronine. Johns Hopkins Med J. 1955;96:274.

397 **Horton R, Biglieri EG.** Effect of aldosterone on the metabolism of magnesium. Clin Endocrinol Metab. 1962; 22:1187.

398 **Heaton FW, Pyrah LN.** Magnesium metabolism in patients with parathyroid disorders. Clin Sci Mol Med. 1963;25:475.

399 **Seelig MS.** Magnesium deficiency and cardiac dysrhythmia. In: Seelig MS, ed. Magnesium Deficiency in Pathogenesis of Disease. New York: Plenum; 1980:219.

400 **Iseri LT.** Magnesium and cardiac arrhythmias. Magnesium. 1986;5:111.

401 **Oster JR, Epstein M.** Management of magnesium depletion. Am J Nephrol. 1988;8:349.

402 **Moore MG.** Oral therapy for hypomagnesemia. Va Med. 1978;105:232.

403 **Alfrey AC.** Normal and abnormal magnesium metabolism. In: Schrier RW, ed. Renal and Electrolyte Disorders. 4th ed. Boston: Little, Brown and Co.; 1992:371.

404 **Flink EB.** Magnesium deficiency in alcoholism. Alcoholism: clinical and experimental research. Alchol Clin Exp Res. 1986;10:590.

405 **Flink EB.** Therapy of magnesium deficiency. Ann N Y Acad Sci. 1969;162: 901.

406 **Iseri LT, French JH.** Magnesium: nature's physiologic calcium blocker. Am Heart J. 1984;108:188.

407 **Rude RK et al.** Renal tubular maximum for magnesium in normal, hyperparathyroid, and hypoparathyroid man. J Clin Endocriniol Metab. 1980;51: 1425.

408 **Coburn JW et al.** The physicochemical state and renal handling of divalent ions in chronic renal failure. Arch Intern Med. 1967;124:302.

409 **Massry SG et al.** Divalent ion metabolism in patients with acute renal failure: studies on the mechanisms of hypocalcemia. Kidney Int. 1974;5:437.

410 **Mordes JP, Wacker WEC.** Excess magnesium. Pharmacol Rev. 1978;29: 273.

411 **Jones J et al.** Cathartic-induced magnesium toxicity during overdose management. Ann Emerg Med. 1986;15: 1214.

412 **Pritchard JA.** The use of magnesium ion in the management of eclamptogenic toxemias. Surg Gynecol Obstet. 1955;100:131.

413 **Alfrey AC et al.** Hypermagnesemia after renal homotransplantation. Ann Intern Med. 1970;73:367.

414 **Beerman B, Groschinsky-Grind M.** Clinical pharmacokinetics of diuretics. Clin Pharmacokinet. 1980;5:221.

415 **Sklath H, Gums J.** Spironolactone: a re-examination. DICP. Ann Pharmacother. 1990;24:52.

Acute Renal Failure

George R Bailie

Definition 29-1
Classification 29-1
Pathogenesis (See Table 29.2) 29-2
Assessment of Renal Function 29-2
    Creatinine clearance (Cl_{Cr}) 29-2
    Blood urea nitrogen:serum creatinine (BUN:SrCr)
      ratio 29-3
    Urinalysis (UA) (See Table 29.3) 29-3
    Proteinuria 29-3
    Fractional excretion of sodium (FENa)
      (See Equation 29.9) 29-4
    Osmolality 29-4
Acute Glomerulopathies 29-4
    Rapidly Progressive Glomerulonephritis (RPGN) 29-4
    Other Acute Glomerulopathies 29-6
    Drug-Induced Acute Glomerulopathy 29-6
Tubulointerstitial Diseases 29-6
    Acute Tubular Necrosis (ATN) 29-6
      Radiocontrast media-induced ATN
        (See Table 29.4) 29-6
      Drug-Induced ATN (See Tables 29.5 and 29.6) 29-7

      Vancomycin/aminoglycoside-induced ATN
        (See Table 29.7) 29-7
      Amphotericin B-induced ATN 29-16
    Acute Interstitial Nephritis (AIN) 29-16
      Pathophysiology 29-16
      Drug-induced AIN (See Table 29.8) 29-17
**Hemodynamically-Mediated Acute Renal
  Failure (ARF)** 29-17
    Angiotensin-Converting Enzyme (ACE)
      Inhibitor-Induced ARF 29-17
    Nonsteroidal Anti-Inflammatory Drug
      (NSAID)-Induced ARF (See Table 29.9) 29-18
Postrenal Acute Renal Failure 29-19
    Nephrolithiasis 29-19
      Struvite stones 29-20
      Uric acid stones 29-20
      Cystine stones 29-20
      Calcium stones 29-20
    Other Renal Stones 29-20
    Prostate Disease 29-21
Supportive Management of Acute Renal Failure ..29-21

Renal failure remains a major cause of morbidity and mortality. While improved dialysis and transplant techniques have increased patient survival, mortality is high due to complications and other diseases associated with renal failure.

Definition

Renal failure usually is classified by the rate of decline in renal function (i.e., as acute, subacute, or chronic). There are no absolute numbers to define these rates of renal function decline, but *acute renal failure* (*ARF*) generally occurs over days to weeks, *subacute renal failure* occurs over weeks to months, and *chronic renal failure* over months to years.

The definition of acute renal failure is imprecise and simply connotes a rapid loss of renal function resulting in azotemia (i.e., an accumulation of nitrogenous waste products in blood that normally are excreted in the urine). Acute renal failure often is reversible, or less commonly, may progress to chronic renal failure. Renal failure also has been described based upon the site of renal lesions (e.g., acute tubular necrosis).[1-5]

Up to 2% to 5% of hospitalized patients will experience an episode of acute renal failure, and up to 1% of hospital admissions are due to community-acquired acute renal failure. About 70% of community-acquired acute renal failure usually results from prerenal causes (e.g., hypovolemia and diminished renal perfusion), 11% from intrinsic disease (e.g., parenchymal damage), and 17% from urinary obstruction (e.g., ureteral obstruction).[6-9] Hospital-acquired acute renal failure has been attributed to surgical causes in about 37%, medical causes in about 27%, nephrotoxic substances in about 21%, and sepsis in about 15% of cases.[2] The surgical cause of acute tubular necrosis has been associated with high mortality (>60%) and drug-induced acute tubular necrosis with a lower mortality (30% to 35%). Hospital-acquired acute renal failure increases the risk of mortality during hospitalization by 6.2-

fold, and increases the duration of hospitalization from a median of 13 days in a control group to 23 days in case subjects.[6]

When acute renal failure develops, the serum concentrations of blood urea nitrogen (BUN) and serum creatinine (SrCr) usually increase. Some clinicians have, therefore, used absolute or percentage increases in these indices to define acute renal failure (e.g., an increase in SrCr of more than 0.5 mg/dL if the baseline SrCr was <3.0 mg/dL, or an increase of more than 1.0 mg/dL if the baseline SrCr was >3.0 mg/dL). This approach is not optimal because the relationship between SrCr and glomerular filtration rate is not linear, but rather, curvilinear. An increase of BUN or SrCr by 10% to 25% over baseline is used to define acute renal failure.

Classification

Although azotemia may occur with or without a decrease in urine production, the clinical course of acute renal failure usually evolves through three phases. The first phase, frequently observed with drug-induced ARF, is the *oliguric phase*. This initial phase begins with the onset of diminished urine output of 50 to 400 mL/day. Less than 50 mL/day of urine production is defined as *anuria*. Oliguria usually occurs within one to two days of the renal insult, and may last from several days to several weeks. *Nonoliguric acute renal failure* is defined as renal failure in a setting of more than 400 mL of urine per day. Although the volume of urine is useful for defining oliguria and anuria, it is of little diagnostic value because urine volume is determined by the difference between glomerular filtration and tubular water reabsorption. Table 29.1 lists some factors which can increase BUN and SrCr in the presence of normal urine volume.[10,11]

The second, or *diuretic phase*, of acute renal failure begins with recovery from the oliguric phase, and is typified by an increased volume of urine. The diuretic phase usually lasts for several days, and patients may remain markedly azotemic in spite of their in-

Table 29.1	Common Causes of Azotemia with a Normal GFRᵃ

Drug-Induced ↑ in SrCr
  Trimethoprim
  Cimetidine
  Salicylates

Drug-Induced False Elevations in SrCr
  Flucytosine
  Methyldopa
  Cefazolin
  Cefoxitin
  Ceftizoxime

↑ Production
  Elevated BUN by high dietary protein
  Elevated SrCr by rhabdomyolysis

ᵃ BUN = Blood urea nitrogen; GFR = Glomerular filtration rate; SrCr = Serum creatinine concentration.

creased urine output. The final, or *recovery phase*, of acute renal failure begins with gradual improvement of renal function and a decline in azotemia. During the recovery phase, urine production continues and the abilities of the kidneys to concentrate and dilute urine return towards normal. The recovery phase continues over a period of weeks to months, depending upon the severity of the initial insult. While most patients resume normal activity during this time with no clinically apparent residual renal defects, complete return of the patient's renal function to preARF baseline abilities is dependent upon the severity and duration of the renal insult.

Pathogenesis

There are many causes of acute renal failure (see Table 29.2). The production of urine by normally functioning kidneys requires the delivery of blood to the glomeruli, the formation of an ultrafiltrate by the glomeruli, the processing of the ultrafiltrate by tubular activity, and the excretion of urine from the kidneys via the ureters. Any reduction in blood delivery (e.g., hypotension, acute blood loss, shock, or drug-induced renal artery vasoconstriction) might result in prerenal acute renal failure. In this situation, oliguria frequently is present, and the acute renal failure may be improved by early removal of the offending drug or correction of the causative factor.

Intrinsic acute renal failure can be caused by any factor that damages renal parenchymal tissue.[1,2] Synonyms for intrinsic acute renal failure include parenchymal acute renal failure, intrarenal acute renal failure, and acute tubular necrosis (ATN).[1,2] ATN, however, is described more accurately as a specific histopathologic finding of acute renal failure and does not occur in all cases of ARF,[12] and will be described separately in this chapter. The majority of intrinsic acute renal failure is secondary to renal ischemia resulting from hypoperfusion. The lesion may occur in glomeruli, renal tubules, or the interstitial cells. Drugs may be causative agents in any of these lesions.

Postrenal acute renal failure results from an obstruction to urine flow at any point between the renal calyces and the urinary bladder. Bilateral obstruction is necessary to stop urine flow. Common causes are prostatic disease and calculi.

Assessment of Renal Function

Creatinine Clearance (Cl$_{Cr}$)

Creatinine is a normal metabolic product of both creatine and phosphocreatine which are constituents of skeletal muscle. The daily production of creatinine is determined by an individual's muscle mass, is relatively constant for a given individual, and is matched by the daily creatine urinary excretion by healthy kidneys

(i.e., ≈15 to 20 mg/kg/24 hours for males and 10 to 15 mg/kg/24 hours for females). Therefore, individuals with healthy kidneys will have a steady-state serum concentration of creatinine. Muscle mass, however, declines with increasing age because of the aging process. After creatinine has been released from muscle into plasma, it is excreted primarily by glomerular filtration, with about 10% to 15% eliminated by active tubular secretion. As a result, creatinine clearance estimates are used as a convenient measure of the glomerular filtration rate (GFR) and as an assessment of renal function even though it does not account for the percentage of the creatinine that is secreted by the tubules. Exogenous markers, such as inulin, have been used to more accurately assess the glomerular filtration rate because inulin is not secreted by the kidney. Thus a measure of Cl$_{Cr}$ will overestimate the GFR by 10% to 20% compared to inulin clearance.

Direct measurement of a creatinine clearance using a 24-hour collection of urine is a more accurate means of assessment of the glomerular filtration rate, although an eight-hour collection may be adequate for some patient populations.[17] The Cl$_{Cr}$ can be calculated as:

$$Cl_{Cr} = \frac{(U_v)(U_{Cr})}{(SrCr)(1440)} \qquad \text{Eq 29.1}$$

This calculation provides a *midpoint serum creatinine* method, when U_v is the 24-hour urine volume in mL, U_{Cr} is the urinary creatinine concentration in mg/dL, SrCr is the serum creatinine concentration in mg/dL at the midpoint of the urine collection, and

Table 29.2	Causes of Acute Renal Failureᵃ

Prerenal
  Volume depletion (e.g., diarrhea, vomiting)
  Acute hemorrhage
  Hypotension
  Drugs
    Renal artery constriction (e.g., ACE inhibitors, NSAIDs)
    Volume depletion (e.g., diuretics)
    Heart failure (e.g., beta blockers)

Intrinsic
Glomerular
  Rapidly progressive glomerulonephritis
  Immune complex disease (e.g., postinfectious glomerulonephritis, drugs)
  Vasculitis

Tubular
  Acute tubular necrosis
    Ischemia
    Drugs
      Aminoglycosides
      Amphotericin
      Radio-contrast media
    Hemoglobin
    Myoglobin
    Tubular obstruction (e.g., uric acid)

Interstitial
  Ischemia
  Interstitial nephritis
    Cimetidine
    Ciprofloxacin
    Penicillins
  Pyelonephritis

Postrenal
  Calculi
  Uric acid crystals
  Prostatic hypertrophy
  Malignancy

ᵃ ACE = Angiotensin-converting enzyme; NSAIDs = Nonsteroidal anti-inflammatory drugs.

1440 is the number of minutes per day. The units of Cl_{Cr} are mL/minute. A 24-hour urine collection is difficult to obtain in many clinical settings unless the patient has been catherterized or has been admitted to a specialized patient care unit (e.g., intensive care unit). Furthermore, a 24-hour urine collection delays the results for at least one day. Therefore, a number of rapid bedside estimates of renal function have been devised.[14] The most accurate and precise estimates of renal function are based upon formulas or equations which incorporate those factors that can influence a serum creatinine concentration (e.g., patient's age, gender, and lean body mass). The most commonly used formula is that of Cockcroft and Gault:[15]

$$Cl_{Cr} = \frac{(140 - Age)(LBW)}{(72)(SrCr)} \qquad Eq\ 29.2$$

The LBW is an estimation of the patient's lean body weight in kilograms. Equation 29.2 must be multiplied by 0.85 for females because of the difference in lean body weight for women compared to men.

Measurements or estimates of Cl_{Cr} in patients with rapidly changing renal function are unreliable because the renal function estimate represents only one point in time and the SrCr value that is used to calculate the renal function may not reflect the present status of changing renal function. For example, the Cockcroft-Gault equation would produce a falsely high estimate of Cl_{Cr} when the glomerular filtration rate is declining rapidly (e.g., at the onset of ARF). Conversely when acute renal failure is resolving, the equation would produce a falsely low estimate of Cl_{Cr}. Thus, more precise estimates of renal function are required for patients in acute renal failure. A more precise estimate of renal function in this situation utilizes both serum and urinary creatinine concentration data as follows:

$$Cl_{Cr} = \frac{(U_V)(U_{Cr})}{0.5(SrCr_1 + SrCr_2)(Time)} \qquad Eq\ 29.3$$

This approach for estimating renal function is termed the *average serum creatinine* method, where $SrCr_1$ and $SrCr_2$ are the serum creatinine concentrations at the start and end of a timed urine collection.

If only serum creatinine data are available, the Cl_{Cr} may be estimated using the Chiou equation:

$$Cl_{Cr} = \frac{2R \times Weight\ (in\ kg)}{14.4(SrCr_1 + SrCr_2)} + \frac{2V(SrCr_1 - SrCr_2)}{(SrCr_1 + SrCr_2)(Time)} - Cl_{nr}$$
$$Eq\ 29.4$$

Where R is the serum creatinine production rate in mg/kg/day. For males, $R = 28 - (0.2 \times age)$, and for females, $R = R$ (males) $\times$ 0.8. V is an estimate of the volume of distribution of creatinine, and is calculated as $V = 600$ mL/kg $\times$ weight (kg). Cl_{nr} is non-renal clearance, determined as $8 \times 10^{-5} \times V$.

Another method of estimating Cl_{Cr} in patients with unstable renal function when only serum creatinine data are available is the Jeliffe method:

- Estimate urinary creatinine excretion rate at steady state (Ess):

  Ess (Males) = LBW (in kg)[29.3 − (0.203 × Age)]

  Ess (Females) = LBW (in kg)[25.1 − (0.175 × Age)] Eq 29.5

- Then estimate a corrected excretion rate to allow for non-renal elimination (Ess corr.):

  Ess corr = Ess × R

  where $R = 1.035 - (0.0337) \times \left(\dfrac{SrCr_1 \times SrCr_2}{2}\right)$ Eq 29.6

- Then calculate the patient's current urinary creatinine excretion rate (E):

$$E = \frac{(Ess\ corr) - [4 \times LBW(SrCr_2 - SrCr_1)]}{Time\ Between\ SrCr_2\ and\ SrCr_1} \qquad Eq\ 29.7$$

- Finally, determine the estimated Cl_{Cr}:

$$Cl_{Cr} = \frac{E}{SrCr \times 14.4} \qquad Eq\ 29.8$$

Where SrCr is the most recent serum creatinine concentration.

Because the relationship between SrCr and GFR is curvilinear, serum creatinine as a sole index of renal function provides only a coarse estimate. The shape of the curve will vary from individual to individual, and represents a steady-state phenomenon. A small change in SrCr (e.g., from 0.8 to 1.0 mg/dL in a normal individual) can represent a very large decrease in GFR. Conversely, a small change in SrCr (e.g., from 7.8 to 8.0 mg/dL in a patient with compromised renal function) represents a much smaller decline in glomerular filtration rate.

Blood Urea Nitrogen:Serum Creatinine (BUN:SrCr) Ratio

In steady-state conditions, the ratio of BUN:SrCr remains constant at about 10:1 to 15:1. During an acute or chronic decline in renal function, the ratio remains unchanged. One major exception is during prerenal acute renal failure, when tubular reabsorption of sodium and water increases to compensate for renal hypoperfusion. During this process, urea undergoes increased reabsorption, resulting in higher than normal BUN. Under these conditions the BUN:SrCr ratio may exceed 20:1.

Urinalysis (UA)

An examination of the urine (e.g., urinalysis) often identifies the cause of acute or chronic renal disease. In addition, repeat urinalyses may be used to monitor the treatment of renal failure. Urine dipstick tests can rapidly assess the presence of blood, glucose, protein, or bile in the urine, and can determine the pH and specific gravity of urine as well. Urine dipstick tests, however, are subject to many common errors and false positive results.

Diagnosis of the type of renal failure requires microscopic examination of the urinary sediment. The presence of sediment in the urine represents an abnormal finding, and may consist of cells, casts, bacteria, or crystals.[18,19] Table 29.3 lists the types of cells and casts and their likely diagnostic relevance.

Examination of the urine provides useful information about the location of renal injury. For example, the presence of high molecular weight proteins such as albumin in the urine suggests a defect in glomerular filtration. Casts, which are transparent protein envelopes, are formed in the renal tubules, especially during states of dehydration. When formed, casts trap tubular constituents that may give information about the location of renal injury. Red blood cell (RBC) casts suggest glomerular lesion, and white blood cell (WBC) casts suggest tubular or interstitial damage.[21]

Proteinuria

A loss of more than 150 mg of protein in the urine in 24 hours is abnormal for adults. Proteinuria in excess of 3.5 gm/1.75 m²/day is termed ''nephrotic-range'' proteinuria. A normal glomerulus should not permit the passage of solutes of molecular weight in excess of 50 to 70,000 daltons. Thus, the presence of excessive proteinuria indicates primarily a loss of integrity of the filtration abilities of the glomerular basement membrane. The most common protein in the urine is albumin. When other proteins and enzymes

Table 29.3	Types of Urinary Sediment and Diagnostic Relevance
Finding	**Relevance**
Cells	
RBCs	Bleeding secondary to tumor, stones; nephrotic syndrome
WBCs	Pyelonephritis (neutrophils), tubulointerstitial diseases (eosinophils)
Epithelial cells	Contamination from lower genital tract
Renal tubular cells	ATN, glomerulonephritis, nephrotic syndrome
Fat Droplets	Glomerular diseases with nephrosis
Casts	
Hyaline	No significance
Cellular	
RBCs	Glomerulonephritis, vasculitis
WBCs	Tubulointerstitial disease, nephrosis, glomerulonephritis
Epithelial	ATN, tubulointerstitial disease
Fatty	Glomerular diseases with nephrosis
Granular	Many renal diseases
Waxy	Advanced disease

ᵃ ATN = Acute tubular necrosis; RBCs = Red blood cells; WBCs = White blood cells.

are detected in the urine, some are indicative of specific abnormalities and may be used as markers.[20]

The assessment of proteinuria, for example, can distinguish between two important forms of nephrotoxicity (i.e., tubular versus glomerular disease). The low molecular weight protein, β_2-microglobulin, is filtered freely by the glomerulus and normally is reabsorbed in the proximal tubule. Therefore, excessive β_2-microglobulin proteinuria could indicate damage to tubular cells (e.g., drug-induced ATN). Tubular toxicity also can be differentiated from glomerular disease because in patients with glomerular disease, the urinary concentration of albumin rather than β_2-microglobulin, would be increased.

Fractional Excretion of Sodium (FENa)

Fractional excretion of sodium is a means of determination of the renal handling of sodium, corrected for hydration status. FENa can be calculated from the following equation:

$$FENa\ (\%) = \frac{U_{Na} \times SrCr}{Sr_{Na} \times U_{Cr}} \times 100 \qquad Eq\ 29.9$$

Where U_{Na} is the urinary sodium concentration, and Sr_{Na} is the serum sodium concentration. FENa in normal individuals is usually $\leq 1\%$, indicating that only 1% or less of the filtered load of sodium is excreted. A fractional excretion of sodium of $\leq 1\%$, however, does not exclude renal failure because in hypovolemic acute renal failure, less sodium is excreted because more is being reabsorbed. When renal tubules are damaged (e.g., ATN), sodium is less readily reabsorbed and the FENa can be in excess of 3%.

Osmolality

Urine osmolality may vary considerably, since normal renal function attempts to maintain plasma osmolality within narrow specific limits. Urine may be as dilute as less than 100 mOsm/kg or as concentrated as more than 1200 mOsm/kg. Thus, random urine osmolality measurements are of little diagnostic value unless correlated with the patient's hydration status. Since acute tubular necrosis would impair urine concentrating ability, a high urine osmolality in acute renal failure would exclude the likelihood of a diagnosis of acute tubular necrosis or other tubular damage.

Acute Glomerulopathies

Intrinsic acute renal failure may be the result of acute damage to renal parenchymal tissue such as the glomeruli. Such damage usually is referred to as being diffuse, (i.e., all glomeruli are involved to at least some extent). The three major types of diffuse, intrinsic acute renal failure are *rapidly progressive glomerulonephritis (RPGN)*, *vasculitis*, and some *immune complex diseases*.[21-26] The distinction between these types is important in clinical practice because of the differences in outcomes and response to treatment. For example, rapidly progressive glomerulonephritis may have a reasonable response to immunosuppressive agents if treatment is commenced early; certain immune complex diseases require no treatment and may be self-limiting; and the vasculitides embrace both ends of this spectrum.

Rapidly Progressive Glomerulonephritis (RPGN)

1. G.C., a 58-year-old male with no previous history of renal disease, was well until 2 weeks ago when he complained of diffuse myalgias, joint pains, and a mild fever. He had a decreased urine output and an increasing swelling in his ankles. A SrCr concentration from a routine office visit 2 years ago was 1.2 mg/dL (normal: 0.8–1.4). After 10 days of worsening symptoms, G.C. visited his family physician who referred him to a nephrologist. On examination he had peripheral edema, bilateral pulmonary rales, and pallor. UA noted the presence of non-nephrotic-range proteinuria pyuria, red cells, red cell casts, and granular casts. His SrCr concentration was 5.5 mg/dL. What type of renal disease does G.C. most likely have? What is his probable prognosis? [SI units: SrCr 106.08 and 486.20 µmol/L (Normal: 70.72–123.76), respectively]

G.C. has a nephritic sediment (i.e., hematuria, pyuria, cellular and granular casts, and varying degrees of proteinuria), but no indications of systemic allergic or vasculitic diseases. G.C. had been well up to two weeks ago until the acute onset of oliguria and the rapid increase in his serum creatinine to 5.5 mg/dL. There was no history of recent infection, systemic vasculitis, or medication involvement. A recent streptococcal infection might have suggested that G.C. had a postinfectious glomerulonephritis, while a concurrent systemic vasculitis (such as polyarteritis nodosa) would have been more suggestive of a renal vasculitic disorder. The absence of recent medication use ruled out the possibility of a drug-induced renal lesion. G.C.'s history, symptoms, and laboratory tests are suggestive of rapidly progressive glomerulonephritis.

Rapidly progressive glomerulonephritis is usually a clinical diagnosis defined as at least a 50% reduction of renal function within three months. In addition, the diagnosis of rapidly progressive glomerulonephritis is based upon pathological evidence, from renal biopsy, of glomerular inflammation and crescent formation. Rapidly progressive glomerulonephritis occurs in about 2% of all cases of glomerulonephritis.[21] G.C. has not had a biopsy, therefore, definite pathological evidence is lacking.

The majority of patients affected with rapidly progressive glomerulonephritis are men more than 40 years of age. Rapidly progressive glomerulonephritis can be a result of antiglomerular basement membrane (GBM) antibody deposition, but 40% is idiopathic. The prognosis is poor: 70% to 90% die or progress to chronic renal failure, depending upon the rapidity and severity of their disease at time of initial treatment.[27] The prognosis is worse when treatment is begun after the serum creatinine exceeds 6 mg/dL or when oliguria is present. The exact extent of the disease can be determined only on examination of a renal biopsy. In the absence of a biopsy in G.C., the presence of diminished urine output and an SrCr of 5.5 mg/dL on presentation would suggest severe disease with a poor prognosis.

2. What other diagnostic tests might be useful to confirm G.C.'s diagnosis of RPGN?

Although serum antiGBM by radioimmunoassay is positive in 60% to 85% of cases of rapidly progressive glomerulonephritis, a positive assay is not definitively diagnostic. Plasma C3 levels, antinuclear antibodies (ANA) and antineutrophil cytoplasmic antibodies (ANCA) usually are negative.[23,28] The presence of these entities usually is suggestive of a primary systemic disorder with a secondary renal involvement (e.g., systemic lupus erythematosus, amyloidosis, or Wegener's granulomatosis). An abdominal flat plate x-ray examination usually is negative, except to rule out renal stone disease, since both kidneys would be of normal size (10 to 12 cm in adults). The definitive diagnosis of RPGN is obtained by renal biopsy; however, this procedure has serious potential complications (e.g., hemorrhage). The decision to undertake a renal biopsy is, therefore, subjective. The clinician needs to compare the potential benefit of a definitive diagnosis for which a specific treatment is available and acceptable to the patient, against the risks from the procedure and the chance of missing the diagnosis of a potentially-treatable disease entity. Patients who are at higher risk of developing complications following biopsy include those with coagulopathies, those with known abnormalities in renal vasculature, or who are grossly obese. G.C. had no known contraindications to the biopsy procedure and he would benefit from a definitive diagnosis. On examination of a biopsy, the presence of cellular crescents filling Bowman's space is characteristic of RPGN. The linear disposition of IgG on immunofluorescent stain on microscopy usually is positive, but also may be seen with other glomerulopathies.[21,29]

Additional tests may be diagnostic for a variety of other renal diseases. *Ultrasonography* is noninvasive and can quantify renal size and differentiate hydronephrosis from masses and cysts. *Intravenous pyelography (IVP)* is used to assess the size and shape of the kidneys. IVPs involve the administration of intravenous radio-contrast media and the use of radiography during the excretion of the media. The resulting nephrogram can identify renal obstruction, abnormalities in cortical and parenchymal thickness, and architectural problems of papillae and calices. *Radionuclide studies*, from the administration of technetium-labeled agents can differentiate obstruction from renal scars and assist in the determination of total renal function. Contrast imaging of renal arterial and venous vasculature (e.g., *arterio-* and *venography*) is used to evaluate renal artery and renal vein stenosis, renal masses, and nephrosclerosis. *Computed tomography* (CT) can be used to further investigate abnormalities found by ultrasonography or IVP, particularly neoplasms and cysts. *Magnetic resonance imaging* (MRI) may help in the diagnosis and investigation of renal vein thrombosis and adrenal masses.

3. G.C. was given the option of a renal biopsy and he agreed to the procedure. His biopsy showed extensive glomerular crescent formation and linear IgG deposits consistent with a diagnosis of rapidly progressive glomerulonephritis. What treatment for RPGN could be initiated for G.C.?

Various immunosuppressive agents have been used in the treatment of rapidly progressive glomerulonephritis because of the involvement of the immune system in this disorder.[23] These treatments expose patients to substantial adverse effects; therefore, the risk:benefit ratio must be considered carefully for each patient. The success of treatment is dependent upon the severity of the disease and the rapidity of initiation of effective treatment. A renal biopsy is necessary to confirm the diagnosis and to differentiate rapidly progressive glomerulonephritis from other diseases which are not

controlled by immunosuppressive agents. The immunosuppressive agents reduce the production of antibodies that cause glomerular damage, and reduce the ability of leukocytes to mediate an inflammatory response. The exact immunosuppressive drug of choice, the doses, and the routes of administration are controversial. Treatment of rapidly progressive glomerulonephritis with corticosteroids alone is associated with a 70% to 80% failure rate. As a result, corticosteroids often are used in combination with other immunosuppressive drugs to increase the response to therapy. Although combination immunosuppressive therapy increases the response rate, the risk of side effects is increased significantly. Pulse corticosteroid therapy, using 1 gm boluses of intravenous methylprednisolone, followed by a course of oral prednisone at 1 mg/kg/day together with immunosuppressive agents, has improved the response (reduction of SrCr) in more than 60% of patients.[30]

In one study of 25 patients with RPGN, intravenous pulse doses of 1 gm of methylprednisolone were given on three successive days over a period of about 30 minutes.[31] The need for, and interval between, repeated pulse courses was determined by clinical and histological activity of disease, the calculated filtration fraction and the response to previous pulses. A total of between one and six pulse courses of methylprednisolone were required. Nineteen patients also received 2 mg/kg/day of cyclophosphamide and two received 2 mg/kg/day of azathioprine, for at least one year. All patients also received a low-dose oral treatment with prednisone, 20 mg/day. Seventeen patients improved after treatment, and an additional four patients experienced a temporary recovery. The mean time between pulse courses was 26 days, and the overall improvement rate was calculated as 68%.

Patients failing to respond to pulse corticosteroid therapy in combination with immunosuppressives have been treated with cyclophosphamide, azathioprine, or cyclosporine.[32–34] Cyclosporine is effective in the treatment of idiopathic nephrotic syndrome. Since nephrotic syndrome is present in 10% to 30% of patients with rapidly progressive glomerulonephritis, cyclosporine may be of some benefit in patients with rapidly progressive glomerulonephritis and concomitant nephrotic syndrome. It remains unclear whether cyclosporine should be reserved for those patients who fail to respond to conventional therapy or who have concurrent nephrotic syndrome, or if the risk of serious adverse effects can outweigh the potential benefit in all patients. Cyclosporine treatment for 12 months was successful in one patient who relapsed after corticosteroids and cyclophosphamide.[32]

The histopathology finding of crescent formation in rapidly progressive glomerulonephritis suggests fibrin deposition[33] and the use of warfarin and dipyridamole have been advocated because of their effects on fibrin clot. The value of these anticoagulants on rapidly progressive glomerulonephritis, however, has not been definitively proven. Plasmapheresis and plasma exchange are effective in removing circulating antibodies,[34] and would be expected to be effective in managing rapidly progressive glomerulonephritis. These procedures also are controversial, since they have been used in cases where there is no measurable circulating antibody. Nevertheless, renal function improved in all 12 patients in one study who underwent three to ten plasma exchanges during a long follow-up of 50 ± 31 months.[34] In these patients, the ANCA titers were significantly reduced and the serum creatinine concentration fell within four weeks from 11.7 ± 5.0 mg/dL to 2.7 ± 0.8 mg/dL. The effectiveness of plasmapheresis in these patients, however, could not be determined because all patients also were treated with methylprednisolone, cyclophosphamide, and defibrotide. The methylprednisolone initial dose of 3 to 4 mg/kg/day was gradually tapered to 0.2 to 0.3 mg/kg/day for a mean of 44 months;

the cyclophosphamide initial dose of 2 to 3 mg/kg/day was reduced to 1 to 1.5 mg/kg/day for a mean period of 32 months; and the defibrotide, an antithrombotic agent, dose of 10 mg/kg/day was given for a mean period of 30 months.

Extracorporeal immunoadsorption of IgG using staphylococcal protein A is another technique which, together with corticosteroids and cyclophosphamide, may be beneficial in rapidly progressive glomerulonephritis.[35]

Based upon the clinical picture of a rapidly declining urine output, rapid increase in his serum creatinine concentration, and severe disease from biopsy histology, G.C. could be started on a course of pulse doses of intravenous (IV) methylprednisolone 1 gm/day for three days, together with 2 mg/kg/day of oral cyclophosphamide. Oral prednisone, 20 mg/day, then could be started at the end of the three methylprednisolone pulses. The plan is to repeat the course of pulse corticosteroid with an interval dependent upon the response as measured by G.C.'s serum creatinine concentration and urine output. Follow-up biopsies should be scheduled in three and six months after the start of treatment.

Other Acute Glomerulopathies

4. How does rapidly progressive glomerular nephritis differ from the other acute-onset diffuse glomerulopathies?

Postinfectious glomerulonephritis is the most common acute-onset immune-mediated diffuse glomerulopathy. Systemic vasculitis with renal involvement usually affects small- and medium-sized arterioles. A careful medical and medication history is important to assist in the differentiation of postinfectious glomerulonephritis from systemic vasculitis and the differentiation of both of these from the nonglomerular disease, acute interstitial nephritis (see Question 16).

Streptococcal infections, such as pharyngitis or pyoderma, may produce diffuse glomerulonephritis. Five to ten percent of children with group A beta-hemolytic streptococcal throat infections or up to 25% with pyoderma may present with signs of renal insufficiency in about ten days and three weeks, respectively. These patients have classic "Coca-Cola-colored" hematuria, a low plasma C3, and raised plasma antistreptolysin-O (ASO) titer. Treatment is supportive, and immunosuppressive therapy produces little benefit. Most patients' renal function will revert to baseline within weeks to months.

Many systemic vasculitis diseases have renal involvement including polyarteritis nodosa (PAN), Wegener's granulomatosis (WG), and hypersensitivity vasculitis.[22,23,29,36-38] All are multi-system diseases and, therefore, there are various clinical presentations depending upon the affected organ system. The specific glomerulopathy can be determined by biopsy and by the results of serum complement and antibody titers. Serum antibody titers, while useful as an aid to diagnosis and monitoring of drug therapy, usually are not specific. For example, antineutrophil cytoplasmic antibodies commonly are identified with Wegener's granulomatosis, but also may be positive in idiopathic crescentic glomerulonephritis and microscopic polyarteritis. In addition, positive antinuclear antibodies are suggestive of lupus nephritis if serum C3 and C4 complements also are positive, but suggestive of a primary glomerulonephritis if the complements are negative. Treatments of polyarteritis and Wegener's granulomatosis also include variable regimens of immunosuppressive drugs.[28,29,39] The clinical course, prognosis, and outcome of renal vasculitis is, therefore, variable. (See Chapter 30: Chronic Renal Failure for further discussion.)

Drug-Induced Acute Glomerulopathy

5. What drugs can cause acute glomerulopathies?

Drugs have been implicated in causing several glomerular lesions, although the majority of these lead to chronic deterioration of renal function. Nonsteroidal anti-inflammatory drugs (NSAIDs) may cause acute renal failure (see Questions 19 to 21) which histologically is described as "minimal change glomerulonephritis."[40] Membranous glomerulonephritis has been reported after exposure to gold salts,[41] penicillamine,[42] and captopril.[43] Rare reports of glomerular lesions produced by drug-induced lupus erythematosus-like syndrome have occurred with isoniazid, procainamide, hydralazine, and methyldopa. The majority of these drug-induced glomerular lesions result in a chronic, progressive decline in renal function.

Tubulointerstitial Diseases

Tubulointerstitial diseases may involve any part of the kidney, except the glomeruli. Thus, the tubules, collecting ducts, papillae, and interstitial cells can be involved. Tubulointerstitial diseases can produce either acute or chronic renal failure, and can result from chronic lithium, cyclosporine, or heavy metal toxicity. The most common tubulointerstitial diseases leading to acute renal failure are *acute tubular necrosis* and drug-induced *acute interstitial nephritis*.[44] A true distinction between interstitial disease and tubular disease, however, is debated with some claiming that tubulointerstitial disease may be the same as interstitial nephritis. This chapter will continue to refer to acute tubular necrosis and acute interstitial nephritis to avoid further confusion.

The majority of tubulointerstitial diseases are drug-induced. Up to 15% of patients in an intensive care unit will suffer drug-induced acute renal failure[45] and up to 19% of all acute renal failure occurring in hospitals may be secondary to drugs.[6] Chemical entities, other than drugs, also may induce acute renal failure.[46] The kidneys are exquisitely sensitive to nephrotoxins for three reasons. First, renal tissue constitutes only 0.4% of total body mass; yet, it receives 20% to 25% of the cardiac output. Renal tissues, therefore, have a high exposure to circulating toxins. Second, renal excretion is a primary method of elimination of many drugs and their metabolites; and third, many agents become concentrated within interstitial tissue as a result of high concentration gradients.

Acute Tubular Necrosis (ATN)

Radiocontrast Media-Induced ATN

6. H.D. is a 72-year-old male with a 30 pack-year history of cigarette smoking, hypertension, hypercholesterolemia, and peripheral vascular disease. He was hospitalized for treatment of cardiovascular problems. Angiography was performed to visualize the vasculature of his lower legs because of progressive deterioration of touch sensation and lower extremity coldness. He was administered diatrizoate 105 mL. His relevant baseline laboratory parameters included an SrCr 1.5 mg/dL (estimated Cl$_{Cr}$ 41 mL/min) and BUN 30 mg/dL. The following day his urine output dropped from 1.5 L/day to 450 mL/day and his SrCr was 1.8 mg/dL (estimated Cl$_{Cr}$ 34 mL/min). What risk factors for contrast-associated nephropathy did H.D. exhibit before administration of the diatrizoate? [SI units: SrCr 132.6 and 159.2 μmol/L, respectively; Cl$_{Cr}$ 0.68 and 0.57 mL/s; BUN 10.71 mmol/L UREA]

Radiocontrast media are a common and well-recognized cause of acute renal failure,[47] and have been associated with a 4.9-fold increase in mortality.[6] The overall prevalence of contrast-associated nephropathy is from 1% to 30% of patients, depending upon which risk factors are involved (see Table 29.4).[47] More recent information suggests that in patients at low risk, the prevalence is 3% to 6%.[48]

H.D.'s pre-existing renal insufficiency, use of a high-osmolality contrast medium, advanced age, and hypertension increased his risk for developing acute renal failure. There is currently dispute in the literature pertaining to various other risks associated with

Table 29.4	Risk Factors Associated with the Development of ARF Secondary to the Use of Radiocontrast Media[a]	
Pre-existing renal sufficiency	Dose of radiocontrast medium	
Dehydration	PVD	
CHF	Hypertension	
Diabetes mellitus	High-osmolality contrast media	
Advanced age		

[a] ARF = Acute renal failure; CHF = Congestive heart failure; PVD = Peripheral vascular disease.

contrast media-induced acute renal failure, including the type of procedure and the site of injection, the presence of multiple myeloma, hypoalbuminemia, and elevated liver enzymes.[49-54] Such controversy probably is due to the difficulty in designing well-controlled studies. It also is unclear whether the high-osmolality agents (e.g., diatrizoate, metrizoate, iothalamate) have a higher risk than the low-osmolality agents (e.g., iohexol, iopamidol, ioversol, ioxaglate). More recent information, however, would suggest that the newer, low-osmolality media have a limited role in the prevention of nephrotoxicity.[193,194] Unless the costs of the newer agents decrease significantly, their use probably should be restricted to patients with a known contrast or iodine allergy, those who are hemodynamically unstable, or those with a baseline serum creatinine of more than 1.5 mg/dL. The high-osmolality agents are ionic and have an osmolality of 1500 to 2400 mOsm/L, about five to eight times that of plasma. The nonionic, low-osmolality contrast agents have an osmolality of 600 to 850 mOsm/L, about twice that of plasma. The cost of low-osmolality agents is about tenfold higher than high-osmolality agents and would have a substantial financial impact on the health care system because about ten million contrast injections are administered in the U.S. each year.[47]

7. What is the mechanism of radiocontrast-induced acute renal failure?

Although the type of renal injury classically is described as a direct tubular toxicity leading to acute tubular necrosis, radiocontrast dyes also can cause nephrotoxicity by ischemia resulting from reduced renal blood flow and intratubular obstruction. The change in renal blood flow is biphasic: initial renal vasodilatation resulting in an osmotic diuresis, followed by marked vasoconstriction and a significant increase in sodium reabsorption (i.e., FENa is commonly <1%). The presence of increased concentrations of β_2-microglobulin in the urine is suggestive of direct acute tubular necrosis, however, the assay of β_2-microglobulins is not widely available in most nonuniversity medical centers. The increase in intratubular cellular debris and the presence of tubular proteins results in the formation of casts, which leads to tubular obstruction.

8. What is the treatment and prognosis of acute renal failure?

Treatment of radiocontrast media-associated acute renal failure is supportive. Appropriate management reduces the risk of progression to chronic renal failure, although some patients with severe disease may require either short- or long-term hemodialysis. Hemodialysis may remove the low-osmolar, nonionic agents to a greater extent than the high-osmolar, ionic agents, although literature confirmation of this is lacking. Although the renal elimination of creatinine abruptly declines after the onset of acute renal failure, the rate of creatinine production remains essentially unchanged. Therefore, a new steady-state serum creatinine concentration will be delayed and the serum concentration of creatinine may not peak until three to seven days after the onset of acute renal failure. Thereafter, the serum creatinine concentration gradually returns toward baseline in 7 to 14 days.

9. How could the risk of radiocontrast-associated acute renal failure have been minimized in H.D.?

Careful examination of the patient's risk factors is essential before the administration of radiocontrast dyes. Although H.D.'s advanced age, history of hypertension and peripheral vascular disease, and serum creatinine of 1.5 mg/dL are not absolute contraindications to radiocontrast diagnostic evaluation, he should have been hydrated to induce a mild diuresis with normal saline (e.g., 1 to 2 L over the 6 to 12 hours) before the procedure. Alternatively, up to 750 mL of half-normal saline could have been administered during each hour of the angiography. In retrospect, H.D. probably should have received a diuretic (e.g., IV 20% mannitol 200 mL during the hour before the procedure or furosemide 40 mg IV) to induce a urine flow of about 75 mL/hour. Although calcium channel blockers also could have been administered before a radiocontrast study because the profound renal vasoconstriction produced by radiocontrast media may be mediated by calcium, these drugs are not routinely administered for this purpose.[55] In one report, a three-day treatment with nitrendipine preserved the glomerular filtration rate in 16 patients receiving nonionic low-osmolality contrast agents, whereas the glomerular filtration rate was reduced by 27% in the 19 placebo-treated control patients (p <0.01).[55] The calcium channel blocker, nifedipine, has been used to prevent cyclosporine-induced nephrotoxicity,[56] and other calcium antagonists also have been used to prevent and treat postischemic acute renal failure.[57]

Drug-Induced ATN

10. What drugs can cause ATN?

A large number of different drugs has been implicated in causing renal dysfunction (see Table 29.5) and acute tubular necrosis (see Table 29.6).[58-65] The exact incidence of drug-induced nephrotoxicity for each agent is difficult to determine. This is primarily because different criteria have been used to define renal dysfunction, patients were vulnerable to different risk factors and various concurrently administered medications, and the quality or degree of patient monitoring varied. However, the incidence of drug-induced nephrotoxicity may range from as rare as 1% to as frequent as up to 90% in at-risk patients.

11. Vancomycin/Aminoglycoside-Induced ATN. C.J., a 52-year-old 55 kg female, was being treated with broad spectrum antibiotics for a fever of unknown origin. Her fever was 100.6 °F, WBC count 28,000/mm^3 (Normal: 4000–9000) with a left shift (PMN 80%), SrCr 1.1 mg/dL, and BUN 30 mg/dL. C.J. was mildly hypotensive and adequately hydrated. Urine output was 1.4 L/day. A calculated Cl$_{Cr}$ was 52 mL/min. Cultures of urine, blood, and sputum were negative for growth with no organisms seen on Gram's stain. She was started on an initial dose of gentamicin, 120 mg IV followed by 90 mg Q 8 hr; vancomycin 1000 mg IV followed by 750 mg IV Q 12 hr; metronidazole 500 mg IV Q 6 hr; and piperacillin 3 gm IV Q 6 hr. No serum concentration data were collected until day 7 of treatment, when her gentamicin peak and trough concentrations were 6.2 and 2.8 µg/mL respectively, and her vancomycin peak (drawn 2 hours after the end of the infusion) and trough serum concentrations were 45 and 15 µg/mL, respectively. The urine showed numerous granular casts. Her SrCr concentration on day 7 was 1.3 mg/dL (calculated Cl$_{Cr}$ 44 mL/min). On day 8 the dose of vancomycin was decreased to 500 mg IV Q 12 hr, and tobramycin was substituted for gentamicin at a dose of 80 mg Q 12 hr. Thereafter, serum tobramycin, vancomycin, and creatinine concentrations were monitored daily. On day 9, peak and trough tobramycin concentrations were 6.0 and 2.7 µg/mL, respectively; peak and trough vancomycin concentra-

(*Text continues on page 14*)

Table 29.5		Chemically-Induced Renal Dysfunction[a,b]
Drug I = Incidence (Rare<Uncommon<Frequent<Invariable) M = Morphology Mech= Mechanism		**Comments**

Acetaminophen[203–210,]

I:	Rare-uncommon	Acute or chronic failure with or without hepatotoxicity described in patients taking
M:	Acute tubular necrosis	2.5–10 gm/day chronically or following acute overdose; $\uparrow$ risk if patient is a
Mech:	Prerenal	drinking alcoholic

Acetazolamide[211,212]

I:	Rare	May present with dysuria, renal colic, or hematuria. Formation of acetazolamide
M:	Tubular damage	crystals associated with acute obstructive nephropathy. Calcium phosphate stone
Mech:	Tubular obstruction	formation attributed to both acetazolamide-induced $\downarrow$ in citrate excretion and urinary
		alkalinization. Formation of calcium phosphate stones appears to be a greater
		problem with chronic therapy. Acute renal failure or tubular dysfunction due to
		hypokalemia rare

Acyclovir[213–216]

I:	Rare	ARF associated with a rapid infusion rate and concurrent administration of
M:	Interstitial inflammation without tubular necrosis	nephrotoxic agents. Needle-shaped crystals seen on UA. ARF reversible when
Mech:	Crystalluria and obstructive nephropathy	acyclovir discontinued. Rechallenge not associated with $\uparrow$ risk of recurring renal
		failure. May avoid acyclovir-induced renal failure with adequate hydration and
		infusion rates <400 mg/hr

Allopurinol

I:	Rare	Under rare conditions, excessive xanthine or oxypurinol excretion into the urine can
M:	Interstitial nephritis	result in crystal and stone formation. Several deaths have been reported with the
Mech:	Hypersensitivity reaction or obstructive nephropathy	hypersensitivity reaction. Coadministration of thiazide diuretics and pre-existing renal impairment may $\uparrow$ possibility of hypersensitivity reaction

Amikacin

See Gentamicin

Amoxicillin[220,221]

I:	Rare	See Methicillin
M:	Interstitial nephritis	
Mech:	Hypersensitivity	

Amphetamine[222]

I:	Rare	Acute renal failure. Amphetamine commonly associated with secondary ARF.
M:	Acute interstitial nephritis	However, referenced case suggests a direct nephrotoxic potential of amphetamine
Mech:	Unknown, not hypersensitivity	

Amphotericin B[223]

i) I:	Invariable	i) Azotemia, renal insufficiency, or renal failure. >80% of patients develop some
M:	Proximal and distal tubular damage; flat tubular epithelial cells; intratubular and interstitial calcification; tubular basement membrane thickening	degree of nephrotoxicity. Clinical signs of tubular dysfunction include azotemia (usually within 4 weeks), $\downarrow$ concentrating ability, polyuria, distal renal tubular acidosis, hypokalemia, hypomagnesemia, $\uparrow$ BUN and SrCr. Additive nephrotoxicity may occur with concurrent use of other nephrotoxicity agents.[224–226] NaCl loading
Mech:	Direct toxin; renal vasoconstriction contributes to renal toxicity	reported to $\downarrow$ renal toxicity associated with amphotericin.[227,228] Total doses >5 gm associated with $\uparrow$ incidence of permanent renal damage
ii) I:	Rare	ii) Medullary changes can result in diabetes insipidus
M:	Altered medullary collecting tubules[229]	
Mech:	Direct toxin; renal vasoconstriction contributes to renal toxicity	

Ampicillin[229,230]

I:	Rare	Renal insufficiency. One of the more common drugs associated with interstitial
M:	Acute tubular interstitial infiltrates and necrosis	nephritis. Clinical findings similar to methicillin-induced nephritis. If renal toxicity
Mech:	Hypersensitivity reaction	occurs, other beta-lactams may cause similar adverse effects. Renal function generally returns to normal when therapy stopped

Ascorbic Acid (Vitamin C)[146,147]

I:	Rare: Dose dependent	Therapeutic doses of vitamin C (1.5 gm/day) reported to cause acute renal failure.
M:	Tubulo-interstitial inflammation and scarring	Characterized by $\uparrow$ SrCr and urinary excretion of oxalate. Close monitoring of renal
Mech:	Direct toxic effect due to $\uparrow$ urinary excretion of oxalate, a metabolic product of ascorbic acid	function and urinary oxalate suggested

Aspirin[231–234]

I:	Rare	Renal insufficiency. May $\uparrow$ SrCr without affecting BUN. Acute renal toxicity
M:	Acute tubular necrosis, renal ischemia	reversible. Conflicting reports exist questioning the relevance of histological or
Mech:	Prerenal due to inhibition of renal prostaglandin	functional abnormalities[235,236]

Atenolol[237]

| I: | Rare | Case reported in elderly male with Leriche's syndrome following single dose |

Continued

Table 29.5		Chemically-Induced Renal Dysfunction[a,b] (Continued)
Drug **I = Incidence (Rare<Uncommon<Frequent<Invariable)** **M = Morphology** **Mech= Mechanism**		**Comments**
M: Mech:	Renal artery thrombosis Acute fall in blood pressure	
Aztreonam[238] I: M: Mech:	 Rare Unknown Probably hypersensitivity	Acute renal failure with skin rash and eosinophilia
Bacitracin[239,240] I: M: Mech:	 Frequent with parenteral therapy Proximal tubular necrosis Direct nephrotoxin	Historically, acute tubular necrosis and acute renal failure were frequent complications of parenteral bacitracin. Patients irrigated with bacitracin containing solutions have developed renal failure
Bleomycin[241–243] I: M: Mech:	 Rare; associated with cisplatin and bleomycin combination therapy Scleroderma-like endothelial injury and vasospasm Uncertain etiology may be associated with direct toxic effect and drug-induced vasospasm	Hemorrhagic cystitis. Development of hemolytic uremic syndrome in conjunction with cisplatin, bleomycin, and vincristine chemotherapy fatal in all patients >50 years with squamous cell cancers
Calcium Salts[244–246] I: M: Mech:	 Rare Tubular and interstitial calcification as well as interstitial inflammation and fibrosis Nephrocalcinosis	Renal insufficiency. Milk-alkali syndrome well-documented clinical entity
Capreomycin[247,248] I: M: Mech:	 Frequent Proximal tubular dilatation with flattening of epithelial cells Direct tubular nephrotoxin; toxicity to glomerular vasculature has also been proposed	Mild azotemia, proteinuria, hematuria, pyuria, hypokalemia, hypomagnesemia, and hypocalcemia may occur. Toxicity has not been related to dose or duration of therapy
Captopril[249–258] i) I: M: Mech:	 Rare: frequent in patients with underlying renal insufficiency Acute tubular necrosis Prerenal due to ↓ renal perfusion pressure caused by a ↓ in angiotensin effect on the efferent arteriole's regulation of glomerular hydraulic pressure	i) Renal insufficiency sometimes progressing to ARF believed to exert damage through a sulfhydryl group which binds with high affinity to glomerular structures. ACE inhibitors ↓ renal function in a kidney with renal artery stenosis, especially bilateral stenosis. (Also see Enalapril)
ii) I: M: Mech:	Rare: frequent in patinets with underlying renal insufficiency Glomerulonephritis Nephrotic syndrome	ii) Nephrotic syndrome. Glomerulonephritis and nephrotic syndrome also reported, especially with high doses[260,261]
iii) I: M: Mech:	Rare: frequent in patients with underlying renal insufficiency Interstitial nephritis Hypersensitivity reaction?	iii) Renal insufficiency sometimes progressing to ARF believed to exert damage through a sulfhydryl group which binds with high affinity to glomerular structures. ACE inhibitors ↓ renal function in a kidney with renal artery stenosis, especially bilateral stenosis. (Also see Enalapril)
Carbamazepine[262,263] I: M: Mech:	 Rare Interstitial nephritis Immunologic or direct toxin	ARF. A pediatric case presented with fever, eosinophilia, and liver dysfunction after 25 days of therapy
Cephalosporins[264] i) I: M: Mech: ii) M: iii) M: Mech:	 Rare-uncommon Acute tubular necrosis Direct nephrotoxin Glomerulonephritis Interstitial nephritis Hypersensitivity reaction	Nephrotoxicity with the cephalosporin generally mild and reversible upon drug withdrawal. All cephalosporins thought to be nephrotoxic at high doses. Pathogenesis of nephrotoxicity directly dose related. Site of renal damage most often tubule, with interstitial nephritis or hematuria occurring less frequently. Single cases of various types of renal dysfuction (primarily renal insufficiency and ↓ in renal reserve) reported with many cephalosporins including cefaclor,[265] cefazolin,[266] cefamandole,[267] cefoxitin,[268] cephalexin,[269] and cephapirin.[270] Cephaloridine, no longer available in the U.S., is most nephrotoxic cephalosporin. Toxicity due to the direct toxic effect resulting from accumulation in the proximal tubules. Tubular epithelial cell shedding frequently noted[271,272]
Cimetidine[273–278] I:	 Rare/uncommon	Reversible interstitial nephritis seen 2–6 weeks after starting therapy. Lack of cross

Continued

Table 29.5	Chemically-Induced Renal Dysfunction[a,b] (Continued)

Drug
I = Incidence (Rare<Uncommon<Frequent<Invariable)
M = Morphology
Mech= Mechanism   **Comments**

M:	Interstitial nephritis	sensitivity to ranitidine described. Cimetidine also ↑ SrCr by competing with tubular secretion of creatinine without affecting inulin clearance
Mech:	Possible delayed hypersensitivity reaction	

Ciprofloxacin[279–281]
I:	Rare	Various clinical aspects of acute interstitial nephritis reported; including fever, skin rash, peripheral eosinophilia, sterile pyuria, and hematuria. ARF nonoliguric and resolves when therapy stopped
M:	Acute tubulo-interstitial nephritis	
Mech:	Possible hypersensitivity reaction	

Cisplatin[282–285,288–290]
I:	Frequent or invariable	Use of IV hydration and osmotic diuresis substantially ↓ the incidence of ↑ BUN, SrCr, proteinuria, and hyperuricemia. Renal toxicity major dose-limiting toxicity.
M:	Acute necrosis of distal tubules and collecting ducts; proximal tubules may be affected but to lesser extent	
Mech:	Direct nephrotoxin	

Clofibrate[286,272]
I:	Rare	Patients with various chronic renal diseases have developed ARF and electrolyte abnormalities when given clofibrate. Renal function may not return to baseline after therapy stopped
M:	Acute interstitial nephritis	
Mech:	Unknown	

Colistin (Polymyxin E)[291]
I:	Uncommon or frequent	Hematuria, proteinuria, and mild azotemia occur within first 3 or 4 days of therapy. Renal dysfunction usually reversible. Doses should not exceed 5 mg/kg/day
M:	Tubular dilatation and necrosis with the tubular lumen frequently containing cellular debris	
Mech:	Direct nephrotoxin	

Co-trimoxazole[292–295]
i) I:	Rare	i) Associated with a generalized allergic reaction
M:	Interstitial nephritis	
Mech:	Possible hypersensitivity reaction	
ii) I:	Rare	ii) Readily reversible upon discontinuation of therapy. Known to interfere with creatinine secretion by the renal tubules, causing an ↑ SrCr without a change in glomerular function. ARF occurs primarily in patients with underlying renal dysfunction, including renal transplant recipients
M:	Acute tubular necrosis	
Mech:	Direct nephrotoxin	

Contrast Media[296–299]
I:	Uncommon	Renal dysfunction ranges from asymptomatic to oliguric renal failure requiring dialysis. Severe renal insufficiency occurs 12–48 hr following a radiographic procedure; milder forms occur 3–5 days after exposure. Risk factors include pre-existing renal insufficiency, diabetes mellitus, advanced age, volume depletion, dose, and multiple myeloma. Highest risk is for diabetic patients with renal insufficiency; occurs 9%. Low osmolar contrast media reduce but do not eliminate renal dysfunction
M:	Acute tubular necrosis	
Mech:	Direct tubular toxicity	
I:	Rare	
M:	Renal ischemia; intratubular obstruction	
Mech:	Urate and protein precipitation	

Cyclophosphamide[300–304]
i) I:	Rare	i) Acute renal failure, hematuria, and proteinuria
M:	Acute tubular necrosis	
Mech:	Direct nephrotoxin	
ii) I:	Frequent	ii) Hematuria, dysuria, polyuria, and hemorrhagic cystitis
M:	Mucosal ulcerations and fibrosis	
Mech:	Direct nephrotoxin	
iii) I:	Rare	iii) Antidiuretic effect similar to SIADH
M:	Unknown	
Mech:	Direct effect on the tubules	

Cyclosporine[305–309]
i) I:	Invariable; dose related	i) Functional toxicity present throughout therapy in most patients. ↑ in SrCr ≈30% due to ↓ in glomeular filtration rate and renal blood flow
M:	Selective preglomerular vasoconstriction	
Mech:	Functional toxicity	
ii) I:	Frequent	ii) Tubular toxicity seen during first few months of therapy, especially with higher doses when trough levels >1000 ng/mL (whole blood) or 200 ng/mL (serum). Characterized by greater renal impairment than seen with functional toxicity; hyperuricemia; normal N-acetyl-glucosaminidase excretion
M:	Tubular inclusion bodies (giant mitochondria); vacuolization; microcalcification	
Mech:	Tubular toxicity	
iii) I:	Common	iii) Vascular-interstitial toxicity characterized by slow, progressive deterioration of renal function and development of hypertension. Onset rare before 2nd month, usually seen after 6 months of therapy. Currently much interest in drug therapy aimed at preventing cyclosporine-induced nephrotoxicity
M:	Glomerular and arteriolar thrombi; interstitial fibrosis; tubular atrophy	
Mech:	Vascular-interstitial toxicity	

Continued

Table 29.5	Chemically-Induced Renal Dysfunction[a,b] (Continued)	
Drug I = Incidence (Rare<Uncommon<Frequent<Invariable) M = Morphology Mech= Mechanism		**Comments**

Dextran[310,311]

I:	Rare	Oliguric or anuric renal failure occurs when dextran concentrations in the urine are high and patient is dehydrated or has poor renal perfusion leading to tubular stasis
M:	Distal and proximal intratubular precipitation or swelling of the tubules	
Mech:	Obstructive nephropathy	

Diltiazem[312–314]

I:	Rare	ARF. Can be oliguric. Occurs shortly after starting therapy
M:	Unknown	
Mech:	Unknown	

Diuretics (Loop and Thiazide)[315–319]

i)	I:	Rare	i) Hypokalemic nephropathy occurs in psychiatric patients who abuse diuretics
	M:	Proximal tubule degeneration and atrophy	
	Mech:	Due to prolonged hypokalemia	
ii)	I:	Uncommon	ii) Acute oliguric renal failure, renal insufficiency displayed by ↑ in BUN, SrCr, and BUN:serum creatinine ratio (>20:1). More common with loop diuretics
	Mech:	Prerenal azotemia due to volume depletion	
iii)	I:	Rare	iii) Interstitial nephritis at times progressing to oliguric ARF
	M:	Diffuse interstitial mononuclear cell infiltrate; sometimes with interstitial edema and fibrosis	
	Mech:	Allergic reaction leading to acute tubulo-interstitial nephropathy	

Enalapril[320,321]

i)	I:	Uncommon	i) Mild renal insufficiency although marked azotemia has occurred in patients with volume and/or Na depletion. Conflicting reports exist assessing impact on renal function. Data suggest therapy may provide a renal protective effect with its control of both systemic and glomerular hypertension. Yet at low perfusion pressure states, such as renal stenosis, angiotensin II plays an important role in regulating glomerular filtration. ACE inhibition reduces renal function by this mechanism
	M:	Ischemic tubular necrosis	
	Mech:	Possibly due to a reduction in systemic BP	
ii)	I:	Rare	ii) Glomerulonephritis
	M:	Segmental or diffuse sclerosis and/or crescent formation	
	Mech:	Unknown; immunofluorescent studies have been negative	

Erythromycin[322]

I:	Rare	Although not commonly considered a cause of renal dysfunction, 1 case report of interstitial nephritis associated with therapy
M:	Lymphocyte infiltration of renal interstitium	
Mech:	Possibly immunological	

Ethambutol[323,324]

I:	Rare	Abnormal UA (hematuria, mild proteinuria, granular casts), ↑ SrCr and BUN primary observations. Eosinophilia and rash have been noted. Because of the multiple drugs used in combination with ethambutol, difficult to define its nephrotoxic potential
Mech:	Direct nephrotoxin or hypersensitivity reaction	

Fenoprofen

See NSAIDs

Foscarnet[325–328]

I:	Rare	ARF manifesting as oliguria or anuria, occurs 1–2 weeks after initiating therapy. Although hemodialysis has been required, renal function generally returns to normal within 1 month after therapy stopped
M:	Tubular necrosis and interstitial infiltration	
Mech:	Uncertain	

Furosemide

See Diuretics

Gentamicin[328–331]

I:	Frequent	Typical clinical presentation of aminoglycoside renal failure usually mild and nonoliguric, with occasional Mg++ and K++ wasting. Aminoglycoside nephrotoxicity transient, but may take up to several months to return to baseline. All aminoglycosides cause renal tubular toxicity not necessarily manifesting changes in glomerular function. Although animal data clearly demonstrate and clinical studies suggest differences in nephrotoxicity between the parenteral aminoglycosides (netilmicin < amikacin ≤ tobramycin < gentamicin ≤ kanamycin), the ability to discern the comparative incidence of renal toxicity in the clinical setting is difficult at best. Nomograms designed to predict aminoglycoside nephrotoxicity are of little value.[332–334] Choice of aminoglycoside should be based upon susceptibility tests and cost, not comparative toxicity
M:	Proximal tubular necrosis	
Mech:	Direct toxin increasing tubular debris; aminoglycosides cause damage to the renal tubular cell secondary to intracellular accumulation to concentrations substantially higher than in the plasma or other tissues	

Continued

Table 29.5	Chemically-Induced Renal Dysfunction[a,b] (Continued)	
Drug I = Incidence (Rare<Uncommon<Frequent<Invariable) M = Morphology Mech= Mechanism		**Comments**

Gold compounds[332–335]

I:	Uncommon	ARF or nephrotic syndrome. Initially noted by onset of proteinuria. Azotemia may
M:	Membranous glomerulonephritis	eventually develop. Often reversible with discontinuation of gold compound. Not
Mech:	Not typically an immune mediated reaction; however, immune-complex occurs in about 10% of gold mediated-glomerulonephritis cases	consistently related to blood levels, dose, or duration of therapy. 1 series reported that gold treatment may be continued for short periods under close supervision despite moderate proteinuria without causing permanent renal damage[336]

Hydralazine[337,338]

I:	Rare-uncommon	Hematuria, proteinuria, urinary casts, and ↑ BUN and SrCr frequent signs of
M:	Probable immune-mediated glomerulonephritis	hydralazine-induced glomerular disease
Mech:	Immune complex, autoimmune reaction; fibrotic changes also described	

Ibuprofen[339–341]

I:	Dose/duration related	Most common presentation renal insufficiency that can lead to acute or chronic renal failure. Cell-mediated nephrotic syndrome can occur. Short term use of moderate dose ibuprofen may result in ARF in patients with asymptomatic mild chronic renal failure. (Also see NSAIDs)

Ifosfamide[342]

i) I:	Rare when given with MESNA; dose-dependent occurrence invariable in high doses	Rise in the SrCr due to tubular damage, at times leading to acute tubular necrosis and renal failure
M:	Interstitial bleeding	
Mech:	Uro-epithelial direct toxicity	
ii) I:	Frequent/uncommon with high doses	
M:	Atrophy with diffuse interstitial fibrosis or tubular necrosis; glomerular damage seen less frequently	
Mech:	Tubular damage, especially after cisplatin therapy[344]	

Indomethacin

		See NSAIDs

Lithium[345]

i) I:	Frequent	i) Nephrogenic diabetes insipidus, polydipsia, and/or polyuria usually present within
M:	None	a few weeks after therapy started
Mech:	Lithium blocks activation of ADH-sensitive adenyl cyclase, resulting in ↓ ADH sensitivity	
ii) I:	Rare	ii) Lithium appears to ↓ glomerular filtration and cause varying degrees of chronic
M:	Focal and/or diffuse interstitial fibrosis, tubular atrophy, glomerulosclerosis	renal failure. Once daily slow-release lithium therapy may ↓ risk of renal failure
Mech:	Direct nephrotoxin	
iii) I:	Rare	iii) Reversible nephrotic syndrome has been reported.[346,347]
M:	Focal and/or diffuse interstitial fibrosis, tubular atrophy, glomerulosclerosis	
Mech:	Direct nephrotoxin	

Mefenamic Acid

		See NSAIDs

Methicillin[348–352]

I:	Uncommon; dose- and duration-dependent	Abnormal urinary sediment may be first sign of renal injury. Eosinophilia, rash, and
M:	Tubular damage adjacent to cellular infiltrates; acute interstitial nephritis	drug fever often occur. ARF, when it occurs, can be severe but usually is reversible when therapy stopped. Hemorrhagic cystitis has been reported[353]
Mech:	Hypersensitivity reaction	

Methotrexate[353,354]

I:	Uncommon; more common after high doses	ARF
M:	Precipitation of methotrexate or its metabolites in the renal tubules and tissue	
Mech:	Direct nephrotoxin or solubility and pH dependent obstruction of urine flow with secondary damage to tubular epithelium	

Methysergide[355]

I:	Uncommon or rare	Underlying renal lesion may lead to ureteral obstruction, hydronephrosis, and
M:	Retroperitoneal fibrosis	chronic renal failure
Mech:	Unknown	

Continued

Table 29.5	Chemically-Induced Renal Dysfunction[a,b] (Continued)
Drug I = Incidence (Rare<Uncommon<Frequent<Invariable) M = Morphology Mech = Mechanism	**Comments**

Mitomycin[356–358]

I:	Uncommon to frequent (2%–10%)
M:	Glomerular sclerosis
Mech:	Immune mediated

Azotemia, proteinuria, and ↑ SrCr at times progressing to oliguria or hypertension. Occurs in patients receiving ≤10 mg/m^2. Presents an average of 10–11 months after starting therapy. Microangiopathic hemolytic anemia with histology resembling that seen with hemolytic-uremic syndrome associated with mitomycin-induced renal failure

Nafcillin (also Oxacillin, Cloxacillin, Dicloxacillin)

I:	Rare
M:	Interstitial nephritis
Mech:	Hypersensitivity reaction

Incidence of interstitial nephritis with these agents less than that associated with methicillin[359–361]

Naproxen

See NSAIDs

Neomycin

Considered the most nephrotoxic of the aminoglycosides; therefore systemic use prohibited. Nephrotoxicity has been associated with nonsystemic therapy.[362–364] (See Gentamicin)

Netilmicin

See Gentamicin

Nonsteroidal Anti-Inflammatory Drugs (NSAIDs)[341,365–368,373,374]

i) I:	Uncommon; dose and duration related
M:	Renal papillary necrosis earliest sign of renal disease. Tubulo-interstitial abnormalities with or without granular deposits of immunoglobulin or compliment on the tubular basement membrane; interstitial nephritis; less commonly, glomerular changes
Mech:	↓ renal perfusion due to renal prostaglandin alterations. Other proposed mechanisms for the occurrence of renal lesions or dysfunction include direct nephrotoxic effect and hypersensitivity reaction. Allergic interstitial nephritis

i) All NSAIDs capable of causing renal changes. Reversible renal insufficiency most common. Other alterations include acute or chronic renal failure sometimes presenting with nephrotic syndrome. Onset of renal failure variable (i.e., hr–yr) and dose dependent. NSAIDs may cause ↓ renal perfusion, interstitial nephritis, primary glomerulopathy, and/or altered potassium homeostasis. Renal insufficiency more common in women and the elderly.[370] Documented renal changes reported with fenoprofen,[371,372,375–377] ibuprofen,[339–341] indomethacin,[387–381] mefenamic acid,[382,383] naproxen,[384] piroxicam,[385,386] sulindac,[387–389] and tolmentin[382,383]

ii) I:	Rare
M:	Unknown
Mech:	Development of severe hyponatremia[389]

ii) Nephrogenic diabetes insipidus

Oral Contraceptives[390–393]

i) I:	Rare
M:	Nonspecific structural changes at the glomeruli, afferent arterioles, and/or interlobar arteries
Mech:	Hypertensive kidney disease after prolonged exposure to estrogen containing products

i) ↑ in blood pressure due to estrogens can lead to azotemia, ARF, and end-stage renal failure. BP should be monitored. Case reports and epidemiologic studies assessing oral contraeptives' adverse effects probably irrelevant to low-dose formulations in current use

ii) M:	Membranous or ischemic glomerular changes with lesions secondary to hypertension
Mech:	Thromboemboli within a renal vein

ii) Patient may present with hematuria, proteinuria, azotemia, ARF, or nephrotic syndrome. Estrogens may cause a hypercoagulable state

Penicillamine[394–396]

I:	Uncommon or frequent
M:	Membranous glomerulonephritis
Mech:	Immune-complex mediated

Renal changes develop only after several months of therapy. Proteinuria most common clinical presentation. In severe situations, nephrotic syndrome may develop. Renal dysfunction generally resolves with withdrawal of penicillamine

Penicillin[397,398]

I:	Rare
M:	Interstitial nephritis, glomerulonephritis
Mech:	Hypersensitivity reaction

Acute renal insufficiency or ARF

Pentamidine[399–402]

I:	Frequent with IV; rare with aerosolized
M:	Proximal renal tubule necrosis
Mech:	Direct nephrotoxin

Renal insufficiency and ARF most common renal toxicities. Proteinuria and pyuria are abnormalities found on UA. Patients with AIDS have a higher incidence of renal dysfunction

Phenacetin

I:	Uncommon
M:	Chronic tubulo-interstitial toxicity with papillary necrosis
Mech:	Direct nephrotoxin

Analgesic nephropathy

Continued

Table 29.5		Chemically-Induced Renal Dysfunction[a,b] (Continued)
Drug I = Incidence (Rare<Uncommon<Frequent<Invariable) M = Morphology Mech= Mechanism		**Comments**

Phenytoin[403–405]

I:	Rare	Reversible oliguric renal failure or varying degrees of proteinuria have been reported
M:	Interstitial infiltrates, glomerulonephritis	
Mech:	Hypersensitivity reaction	

Piroxicam

	See NSAIDs

Rifampin[406–410]

I:	Uncommon	ARF or renal insufficiency associated primarily with intermittent or irregular
M:	Tubulo-interstitial nephritis	therapy. Chronic renal failure has been reported
Mech:	Hypersensitivity reaction	

Streptokinase[411,412]

I:	Uncommon	Renal insufficiency or ARF
M:	Unknown	
Mech:	Streptokinase antibody hypersensitivity reaction	

Sulfonamides[413,414]

I:	Rare	ARF reported with multisystem hypersensitivity reactions. Crystalluria has occurred
M:	Obstructive nephropathy, interstitial disease, glomerulonephritis	with the older longer half-life agents but not the newer more soluble agents such as sulfisoxazole
Mech:	Crystalluria	

Sulindac[387–389]

	The renal sparing effect probably due to the relative preservation of renal prostaglandin synthesis. (Also see NSAIDs)

Tetracyclines[415]

i) I:	Uncommon	i) Prerenal azotemia
M:	Tubular toxicity	
Mech:	Antianabolic effect	
ii) Mech:	Direct nephrotoxin occurring as a result of fatty metamorphosis of the liver	ii) Nausea, abdominal pain, lethargy, jaundice, and renal failure. More commonly seen with IV tetracycline
iii) Mech:	Direct nephrotoxin due to tetracycline degradation products	iii) More commonly seen with outdated tetracycline

Tobramycin

	See Gentamicin

Triamterene[416]

i) I:	Rare-uncommon	Variety of adverse renal effects, such as abnormalities in urinary sediment,
M:	Nephrolithiasis	nephrolithiasis, interstitial nephritis, and ARF. Renal toxicity may be exacerbated
Mech:	Formation of parent and metabolite drug renal stone	with NSAIDs
ii) M:	Acute interstitial nephritis	
Mech:	Probable hypersensitivity	

Tolmetin

	See NSAIDs

Vancomycin[417]

I:	Rare	Renal toxicity no longer considered a common complication. In an animal model for infection, vancomycin contributed to nephrotoxicity when combined with gentamicin.[231]

[a] We gratefully acknowledge the contributions of Daniel C Robinson, George S Jaresko, and Daniel E Baker who created this table for the fifth edition of Applied Therapeutics: The Clinical Use of Drugs.

[b] ACE = Angiotensin-converting enzyme; ADH = Antidiuretic hormone; AIDS = Acquired immunodeficiency syndrome; ARF = Acute renal failure; BP = Blood pressure; BUN = Blood urea nitrogen; IV = Intravenous; K = Potassium; Mg = Magnesium; Na = Sodium; NSAIDs = Nonsteroidal anti-inflammatory drugs; SIADH = Syndrome of inappropriate antidiuretic hormone secretion; SrCr = Serum creatinine; UA = Urinanalysis.

tions were 32 and 13 µg/mL, respectively; and SrCr was 1.5 mg/dL (calculated Cl$_{Cr}$ 38 mL/min). On day 10, tobramycin concentrations were 7.4 and 3.4 µg/mL, respectively; vancomycin concentrations were 51 and 28 µg/mL, respectively; and SrCr was 1.8 mg/dL (Cl$_{Cr}$ 32 mL/min). The vancomycin and tobramycin were discontinued on day 10. During this time, urine production diminished from her baseline of 1.4 L/day to about 700 mL/day (nonoliguric failure). A UA demonstrated numerous tubular epithelial cells, tubular casts, and hyaline casts. C.J.'s SrCr continued to increase, reaching 2.8 mg/dL

(Cl$_{Cr}$ 20 mL/min) on day 14. From day 14 to day 28, urine production increased slowly to a peak of about 2 L/day; thereafter, urine output and SrCr returned toward baseline. During the episode, C.J. was worked-up for possible causes of her acute renal failure. She had no severe hypotensive episodes and had no other concomitant nephrotoxic agents (apart from several IV doses of furosemide). No rashes were observed, and eosinophilia or eosinophiluria were not present. Renal blood flow was not decreased secondary to emboli or stenosis and there was no evidence of urinary tract obstruction. The pos-

Table 29.6	Drugs Associated with Acute Tubular Necrosis
Aminoglycosides	Cephalosporins
Radiocontrast dyes	Cyclosporine
Amphotericin B	Mannitol
Cisplatin	Intravenous immunoglobulin
Vancomycin	Foscarnet
Acetaminophen	Acyclovir
Pentamidine	Methoxyflurane
Tetracycline	Rifampin

sibility for infection-related renal ischemia could not be positively ruled out. What was the probable cause of C.J.'s acute renal failure? [SI units WBC 28 × 10⁹; SrCr 97.24, 114.92, 132.60, 159.12, and 247.52 μmol/L, respectively; BUN 10.71 mmol/L UREA; Cl$_{Cr}$ 0.87, 0.73, 0.63, 0.53, and 0.33 mL/s; tobramycin 12.6, 5.67, 15.54, 7.14 μmol/L, respectively]

There are many possible causes of acute renal failure. For simplicity, these can be classified as prerenal, intrinsic, or postrenal (see Table 29.2). C.J. demonstrated none of the classic reasons for prerenal acute renal failure: there was no history of volume depletion due to vomiting or diarrhea, no blood loss or significant hypotension, and no cardiogenic shock. Her workup demonstrated no urinary obstruction; therefore, a postrenal cause of acute renal failure was ruled out. A workup for interstitial disease was negative based upon the lack of eosinophils in peripheral blood or urine and other clinical signs of hypersensitivity. There was no evidence of glomerular disease in the urinalysis, although a postinfectious glomerulopathy could not be definitively excluded. The tubular cellular debris in C.J.'s urinalysis; the known potential for nephrotoxicity of aminoglycosides and vancomycin; the time-frame of the administration of the aminoglycosides and vancomycin relative to the onset of acute renal failure; and the elevation in their peak and trough serum concentrations support the diagnosis of aminoglycoside and/or vancomycin-induced acute tubular necrosis.

Aminoglycoside-induced renal failure is a well-recognized cause of morbidity that can increase the risk of death by fivefold.[6] However, there is much controversy as to whether there is a strong association between peak and trough serum concentrations of these agents and nephrotoxicity.[66] Early studies suggested an increased risk of acute renal failure when aminoglycoside peak serum concentrations exceeded 10 to 12 μg/mL (>30 μg/mL for amikacin) and 40 μg/mL for vancomycin.[67,68] Although trough concentrations often were maintained in excess of the minimum inhibitory concentration (MIC) of susceptible organisms by several fold, troughs for aminoglycosides generally were kept at less than 2 μg/mL. As a result, guidelines for optimal serum concentrations of vancomycin were 30 to 40 μg/mL for peak and 5 to 10 μg/mL for trough serum concentrations, and were 6 to 10 μg/mL for peak and <2 μg/mL for trough concentrations for gentamicin and tobramycin. However, the administration of aminoglycosides on a once-a-day basis has challenged these guidelines.[69] For example, patients receiving 4.5 to 5 mg/kg of aminoglycosides as a single daily intravenous dose may attain peak concentrations in excess of 25 μg/mL, and exhibit no greater incidence of nephrotoxicity than with conventional divided daily doses.[70] The concept of a total area-under-the-concentration-time curve is probably, therefore, a more realistic determinant of toxicity to susceptible organs.

The mean incidence of nephrotoxicity of the aminoglycosides, from a review of 400 publications, was 6.6% to 17.1%.[65] Furthermore, the combination of aminoglycosides plus vancomycin seems to be more nephrotoxic than either agent alone.[71,72]

The true incidence of vancomycin-associated nephrotoxicity is more difficult to determine. Many recommendations have been ex-

trapolated from early reports where impure vancomycin formulations were administered and where few data were reported on timing of samples with respect to the previous dose. Although the incidence of nephrotoxicity of vancomycin alone is increased from 5% to about 22% to 35% when combined with an aminoglycoside,[71,72] one prospective study noted a clinically significant deterioration in renal function (increase in SrCr of >0.3 mg/dL) occurred in 4 of 23 (17%) vancomycin-treated patients.[73]

C.J.'s serum aminoglycoside concentrations raise a number of interesting points. Her trough serum aminoglycoside and vancomycin concentrations were high (i.e., 2.8 μg/mL and 15 μg/mL, respectively) by her seventh day of therapy. Although it is difficult to determine exactly when the serum concentrations of these antibiotics started to rise in C.J., the trough concentrations of these drugs usually increase within three to seven days following a nephrotoxic insult. Therefore, more frequent monitoring of drug concentrations earlier in her treatment would have been more appropriate. As C.J.'s renal function deteriorated, the aminoglycoside and vancomycin half-lives became more prolonged (increasing from about 6 hours and 6.3 hours for gentamicin and vancomycin, respectively, on day 7, to about 10 hours and 11.5 hours for tobramycin and vancomycin, respectively, on day 10). Her serum aminoglycoside and vancomycin concentrations will, therefore, continue to increase in the face of continued deterioration in renal function and aggressive monitoring of her treatment should provide information that is needed to further adjust the doses of these antibiotics.

C.J.'s creatinine clearances calculated from simple serum creatinine estimates probably would over-estimate her actual renal function because her renal function is continuing to deteriorate and the onset of a new steady-state SrCr concentration would be delayed. It would be more appropriate to use Equations 29.3 to 29.8 for determining her renal function. Although tobramycin may be less nephrotoxic than gentamicin,[65] it is doubtful whether there was any benefit to C.J. in switching from gentamicin to tobramycin when a nephrotoxic insult was already apparent. It would have been more appropriate at this stage to review C.J.'s complete antibiotic therapy for appropriateness (i.e., need, drugs, dosing regimens, toxicity).

C.J.'s decrease in renal function was consistent with the usual time course of aminoglycoside- or vancomycin-induced nephrotoxicity. The decrease in renal function usually becomes apparent within six to ten days after initiation of therapy, and SrCr concentrations generally peak one to three weeks later depending upon when the causative agent was discontinued and the magnitude of the renal insult. Thereafter, renal function returns toward baseline values in most patients over a period of two weeks to three months.

12. What were the risk factors for aminoglycoside- and vancomycin-associated ATN in C.J.? What is the treatment when nephrotoxicity results from these drugs?

Several of the risk factors for aminoglycoside and vancomycin-induced acute tubular necrosis that are listed in Table 29.7 are applicable to C.J.'s situation. Her calculated creatinine clearance

Table 29.7	Risk Factors Associated with Aminoglycoside and Vancomycin Acute Tubular Necrosis	
Pre-existing renal insufficiency	Dehydration	
Increased age	Total dose	
Coadministration of other nephrotoxic agents	Recent exposure to aminoglycoside or vancomycin	
Sustained elevated serum concentrations	Extended duration of treatment	

of 52 mL/minute at the time of admission is suggestive of some degree of pre-existing renal insufficiency. She also received several doses of furosemide, a potent diuretic that also may have potentiated the effect of two concurrent nephrotoxic antibiotics. In addition, her trough aminoglycoside and vancomycin serum concentrations during therapy were elevated consistently.

Treatment of the acute tubular necrosis caused by these agents is supportive. The causative drug should be discontinued, if possible, and an alternative non-nephrotoxic antibiotic from a different class substituted. If it is impossible to discontinue the drug, then the lowest possible dose should be used. Aminoglycosides are readily removed by hemodialysis. Vancomycin can be significantly cleared by the newer high-flux hemodialysis, but only minimally by the cellulose and cuprophan membranes of conventional hemodialysis.[74-77]

13. Amphotericin B-Induced ATN. M.M., an elderly male, has been hospitalized for the treatment of abdominal and chest injuries following a traffic accident. Two weeks after admission he developed fever which was eventually linked to a *Candida albicans* fungemia. The decision was made to commence treatment with IV amphotericin B. How can potential amphotericin B-associated nephrotoxicity be prevented in M.M.?

Most patients undergoing treatment with amphotericin B will experience dose-dependent decreases in renal function. The incidence of nephrotoxicity increases with the total dose, and may occur in up to 80% to 90% of patients when the cumulative amphotericin dose exceeds 3 to 5 gm.[78] The mechanism of renal injury is complex, and involves both acute tubular necrosis (from renal ischemia caused by interference with the tubuloglomerular feedback mechanism) and renal tubular acidosis.

In normal circumstances, sodium is filtered freely by the glomerulus, and 100% of the filtered load reaches the proximal end of the renal tubule. As the filtrate passes down the length of the tubule, some of the filtered sodium is reabsorbed from the filtrate across the tubular epithelium back into the renal interstitium. About 40% to 60% of sodium is reabsorbed from the proximal convoluted tubule, 30% to 40% from the loop of Henle, and 10% to 20% from the distal convoluted tubule and terminal sections of the tubule. At the collecting ducts, only about 1% to 2% of the initial filtered load of sodium remains in the filtrate. The exact process of sodium reabsorption is under tight physiological control via the tubuloglomerular feedback system.

The tubuloglomerular feedback mechanism regulates the renal conservation of solutes. Under normal circumstances, if there is an increase in the filtered load of sodium or if normal mechanisms for the reabsorption of sodium are defective because of proximal tubular damage, the increased load of sodium appearing in the distal sections of the tubule can be detected by renal tubular cells. Through a complex mechanism, these cells cause constriction of the afferent renal arteriole which lies close to the distal tubule.[79] A decreased blood flow to that tubule's glomerulus will decrease the filtered load of sodium and, thereby, conserve sodium. This autoregulatory control normally maintains blood volume and fluid status. Amphotericin B can mimic the effect of filtered sodium in the renal tubule. As a result, the presence of amphotericin B in the filtrate can stimulate the tubuloglomerular feedback system and, thereby, cause inappropriate afferent renal artery constriction, decrease renal blood flow, and reduce renal function.

Salt depletion enhances the feedback system, and sodium loading in patients may prevent acute renal failure by inhibiting the tubuloglomerular feedback system.[60,80,81] The administration of 1 L of normal saline over one hour before the infusion of amphotericin B, or 500 mL of saline before and 500 mL after the amphotericin B, have been recommended to minimize the potential

for amphotericin-induced acute tubular necrosis. The exact dose of saline remains unclear, and care must be exercised in those patients for whom it may be potentially hazardous [e.g., those with congestive heart failure (CHF)]. Further, sodium loading would necessitate that the patient is not currently sodium deficient, and therefore, should be in excess of 77 mEq in addition to a normal dietary intake.[82] Urinary sodium should be monitored and should exceed 250 mEq/day.[83] Although sodium loading may have benefits in the prevention of amphotericin B-induced acute tubular necrosis, it has no effect on amphotericin B-induced renal tubular acidosis.

Acute Interstitial Nephritis (AIN)

Acute interstitial nephritis accounts for about 2% to 3% of all cases of acute renal failure in both adults and children, although this may be an underestimate.[89] A more precise estimate is difficult because the requisite renal biopsy needed for a definitive diagnosis is not commonly obtained and patients may not present with the classic pattern of signs and symptoms. Although interstitial nephritis accounts for 2% to 3% of all cases of acute renal failure, it may account for up to 15% of cases when a biopsy is performed. In adults, drugs are the most common cause of acute interstitial nephritis, while infection is the most common cause in children. The drugs that have been associated most commonly with the occurrence of interstitial nephritis are listed in Table 29.8.[84,85,90-102] Although the association of some of these drugs is based only upon isolated case reports, the NSAIDs,[103-105] rifampin,[106-109] and methicillin,[110,111] have been clearly implicated in numerous cases of drug-induced interstitial nephritis.

Pathophysiology

Acute interstitial nephritis, represents a hypersensitivity reaction that presumably involves the immune system in the pathogenesis of the disease. Nondrug causes of interstitial nephritis include inflammatory processes (e.g., systemic lupus erythematosus and sarcoidosis) or infectious diseases (e.g., acute pyelonephritis).[102] The precise pathophysiological basis for interstitial nephritis remains unclear but both humoral and cell-mediated immune processes probably are involved.[44] In nondrug acute interstitial nephritis, potential antigens include tubular basement membrane, Tamm-Horsfall mucoprotein, and other intrinsic and extrinsic proteins.

Drugs and their metabolites induce interstitial nephritis by serving as haptens that bind to a protein to make an immunogenic complex. Drug-specific antibodies (immunoglobulins) produced by B-lymphocytes then cause cell necrosis at the site of drug/protein complex formation within minutes to hours of exposure to the drug. Both IgE and IgM have been observed in renal biopsies from patients with methicillin- and rifampin-induced acute interstitial nephritis.[109,111] T-lymphocytes are involved in cell-mediated immune reactions, occurring over a longer time period of days to weeks after initial exposure. T-lymphocyte involvement has been

Table 29.8	Drugs Associated with Acute Interstitial Nephritis
Beta-lactam antibiotics	Allopurinol
Trimethoprim-sulfamethoxazole	Diazepam
Rifampin	Methyldopa
Vancomycin	Azathioprine
Fluoroquinolones	Teicoplanin
Nonsteroidal anti-inflammatory drugs	Cimetidine
Diuretics	Ranitidine
Anticonvulsants	Azithromycin
Clofibrate	

observed in cases of NSAIDs and methicillin-associated acute interstitial nephritis.[86] C3 may or may not be deposited at the affected site. Drug-induced interstitial nephritis, therefore, may occur within minutes of exposure to a drug or may not develop for several months. For example, the median time to onset of acute interstitial nephritis after administration of ciprofloxacin is six days, ten days for methicillin, three months for NSAIDs, and four to six months for rifampin.[91,92,97]

Drug-Induced AIN

14. D.R., a 40-year-old male with no significant history of disease, visited his family physician because of a fever which began 3 days ago. Ciprofloxacin PO 500 mg BID was initiated. Four days later he presented to the emergency room (ER) with a rash, malaise, hematuria, reduced urine output, and his fever was still present. The following relevant laboratory values were noted: SrCr 2.1 mg/dL, BUN 30 mg/dL, WBC 15,000/mm³ and 13% eosinophils (Normal: 0–5). The UA showed specific gravity 1.011, protein 35 mg/dL, many RBCs and WBCs per high powered field, WBC casts, eosinophiluria, and an FENa of 3%. The rash was a diffuse, macular, erythematous lesion covering his trunk and arms. D.R. was admitted for evaluation, and the ciprofloxacin discontinued. What subjective and objective data in D.R. would support a diagnosis of AIN? [SI units: SrCr 185.64 μmol/L; BUN 10.71 mmol/L UREA; WBC 15 × 10⁹]

D.R.'s malaise, rash, fever, decreased urine output, increased serum creatinine, eosinophilia, FENa >1%, and hematuria are consistent with acute interstitial nephritis. The diffuse, macular, erythematous rash over his trunk and arms along with his 13% eosinophils and eosinophiluria also are consistent with the immunological nature of drug-induced interstitial nephritis. Since his fever was present before he received the ciprofloxacin, it cannot be determined whether the fever was caused by his ciprofloxacin or from his infection. Monocytosis, elevated erythrocyte sedimentation rate, urine granular casts, glycosuria, and proteinuria were not noted in D.R., but often are present in drug-induced acute interstitial nephritis. The urine output is usually nonoliguric, but oliguria is present in those with more serious disease.

15. How should D.R.'s ciprofloxacin-induced interstitial nephritis be treated?

Continued use of the nephrotoxic agent will lead to a rapidly-worsening renal failure, and may be associated with failure of other organ systems and death in up to 20% of patients. The causative agent (i.e., ciprofloxacin) must be discontinued and D.R. provided with supportive treatment. D.R.'s fluid status must be monitored closely and short-term hemodialysis may be required.

The use of corticosteroids is controversial, but they have been used with some success in idiopathic and drug-induced interstitial nephritis.[85] Prednisone or cyclophosphamide, 1 to 2 mg/kg/day orally for one week, with a taper over the subsequent several weeks, has been recommended for the management of methicillin-induced interstitial nephritis;[112] however, few controlled studies validate this recommendation.

In a review of 43 cases of NSAID-induced interstitial nephritis with glomerulopathy, 24 episodes were treated with corticosteroids after discontinuation of the offending agent.[40] The regimens of steroids were variable, but a common regimen was prednisone 60 mg/day for four weeks, followed by a tapering dose. Some patients received prednisone 15 mg/day, others received repeated 1 gm doses of intravenous methylprednisolone, and two patients received both cyclophosphamide and corticosteroids intravenously. The data from this one study could not demonstrate that corticosteroids altered the clinical course of the renal failure and a review of the literature also found no evidence that corticosteroids reduced the duration of NSAID-induced interstitial nephritis.[93]

The lack of strong literature support for the use of corticosteroids for the management of ciprofloxacin-induced interstitial nephritis and the relatively small risk from a one-week course of prednisone leaves the clinician with the option of applying the art of medicine, rather than the science, to D.R. D.R. does not have any obvious contraindications to corticosteroids and a one-week course of prednisone 30 mg twice daily (i.e., 1 mg/kg/day) may be useful. D.R. should not be treated with future courses of ciprofloxacin because patients who have experienced drug-induced interstitial nephritis are likely to experience a similar reaction upon subsequent exposure to that drug.

Hemodynamically-Mediated Acute Renal Failure (ARF)

The afferent arterioles that supply the glomerulus and the efferent arterioles that drain the glomerulus are responsible for maintaining an intraglomerular pressure that is sufficient for ultrafiltration. Therefore, glomerular capillary hydrostatic pressure and glomerular filtration are dependent upon renal perfusion, and the tone of afferent and efferent arterioles is critical for the regulation process. In a patient with compromised renal blood flow (e.g., caused by hypovolemia), glomerular capillary perfusion would be enhanced by afferent arteriolar vasodilatation or efferent arteriolar vasoconstriction.[114,115] The tone of afferent arterioles is regulated by prostaglandins E_2 and I_2 which cause dilatation, and also possibly by nitric oxide, endothelin, and atrial natriuretic factor. Efferent arteriolar tone is regulated by the vasoconstrictor angiotensin II, endothelin, and also possibly atrial natiuretic factor. PGE_2 and PGI_2 also augment the level of activity of the renin-angiotensin system.[115–119] In a stressed kidney (one where renal blood flow has been compromised), glomerular pressure will be maintained by these compensatory processes. Any interference with these processes, such as by drugs that inhibit prostaglandin synthesis or inhibit the production of angiotensin II, may result in acute renal failure. Such effects normally would not occur in individuals who do not have compromised renal blood flow.

Angiotensin-Converting Enzyme (ACE) Inhibitor-Induced ARF

16. T.N., a 64-year-old female with Type I diabetes mellitus, had a long history of hypertension and had been treated at different times with many antihypertensive agents. She was on a low-salt diet and was taking furosemide 40 mg PO QD. After a regular visit to her family physician, therapy for her hypertension was initiated with enalapril 40 mg QD. The following day, T.N. noted a reduction in urine output and swelling of her ankles. When she appeared at an ER she was in apparent renal failure. Her BP was 100/65 mm Hg and her SrCr was 1.8 mg/dL. She was hospitalized and the enalapril and furosemide were discontinued. By day 3 she was oliguric, and her SrCr peaked on day 5 at 3.1 mg/dL. What were T.N.'s risk factors for acute renal failure? [SI units: SrCr 159.12 and 274.04 μmol/L]

Angiotensin-converting enzyme (ACE) inhibitors have been reported to cause acute renal failure and may do so in several settings.[120–127] In most cases, the ACE inhibitor precipitated renal failure is patients in whom renal efferent arterioles already had been vasoconstricted to compensate for pre-existing compromised renal blood. By inhibiting angiotensin converting enzyme, the ACE inhibitors caused the efferent arterioles to vasodilate; thereby, effectively removing the beneficial compensatory mechanism for the pre-existing compromised renal blood flow. Therefore, ACE inhibitors are contraindicated in patients with bilateral renal stenosis, or unilateral renal artery stenosis when patients have a solitary functioning kidney. ACE inhibitors must be used cautiously whenever a patient is dependent upon vasoconstricted efferent renal arterioles to maintain glomerular perfusion pressure. Although ACE inhibitors can be of significant benefit to patients with heart failure, these drugs must not be prescribed cavalierly without due concern for the removal of compensatory efferent arteriolar vasoconstriction in patients with renal hypoperfusion from severe congestive heart failure, hypovolemia from diuretic use, and possibly polycystic renal disease.[123,127]

Sodium depletion may increase the dependency of the glomeruli on an intact renin-angiotensin system.[128,129] Diuretics, therefore, can sensitize the kidneys to the adverse effects of ACE inhibitors by activating the tubuloglomerular feedback system, activating the renin-angiotensin system, and by causing hypovolemia.[122,123,128,129]

T.N. had a number of risk factors for the development of acute renal failure associated with enalapril. She was on a low-salt diet and was taking diuretics which may have compromised her fluid status and led to a degree of dehydration. She had a history of diabetes mellitus which may have led to a degree of diabetic nephropathy, which, together with long-standing hypertension, could have compromised her renal function.

17. How common is ACE inhibitor-induced ARF? Is there a similar risk from all agents in this class?

The exact incidence of acute renal failure from angiotensin-converting enzyme inhibitors is unclear. In one review of 63 patients with drug-induced renal failure, 14 (22%) had received an ACE inhibitor.[130] In another study, 40 of 146 (27%) patients with drug-induced renal failure had recently received ACE inhibitors.[131] Lisinopril (Prinivil, Zestril) and enalapril (Vasotec) may have a slightly higher potential for inducing renal failure than captopril (Capoten); therefore, initiation of treatment with shorter-acting ACE inhibitors (e.g., captopril) in patients deemed to be at risk might be preferable.

18. What renal effects can be manifested by ACE inhibitors in patients with CHF?

In patients with congestive heart failure, the effect of ACE inhibitors on renal function is inconsistent. In a stressed kidney, the inhibition of the renin-angiotensin system may result in efferent vasodilation and, therefore, a reduced glomerular filtration rate. However, in heart failure, the systemic effects of ACE inhibitor-induced vasodilation also should increase renal plasma flow.[132] ACE inhibitors both improve and exacerbate renal function in heart failure patients.[127,133,134] In one study, the most useful prognostic indicator for risk of renal failure with ACE inhibitors was an elevated filtration fraction (GFR divided by renal plasma flow), in patients taking quinapril.[127]

Rare cases of acute interstitial nephritis have been reported for captopril.[121,136–138] Although ACE inhibitors can decrease proteinuria by up to 50% in such chronic conditions as IgA nephropathy and membranous glomerulonephropathy, ACE inhibitors in high doses also might cause proteinuria.[139]

Nonsteroidal Anti-Inflammatory Drug (NSAID)-Induced ARF

19. C.S., a 56-year-old male, is hospitalized because of renal failure. C.S. has a history of CHF, which was well controlled with a thiazide diuretic. About 5 weeks before admission, he developed progressively worsening pain in the jaw, and visited his dentist. An abscess underlying his first upper molar tooth was found, and he underwent root canal surgery. C.S. was prescribed a broad-spectrum antibiotic, and advised to purchase ibuprofen and take it as necessary to provide pain relief. He suffered 2 further episodes of recurrence of the abscess, requiring further dental surgery and a single 30 mg IM dose of

ketorolac (Toradol) postsurgically each time. Throughout this time C.S. continued to self-administer ibuprofen and, occasionally, acetaminophen. On questioning, he claimed to have taken about 2400 mg of ibuprofen most days for 5 weeks, and "more than that" during his episodes of acute pain at the times of abscess recurrence. Laboratory values showed an increase in BUN which peaked at 105 mg/dL and SrCr which peaked at 7.3 mg/dL. He developed oliguria, and a UA showed 2+ hematuria. He had elevated liver enzymes: alanine aminotransferase (ALT) 140 U/L, aspartate aminotransferase (AST) 151 U/L, and lactate dehydrogenase (LDH) 542 U/L. The serum total bilirubin was 4.4 mg/dL (Normal: 0.1–1.0). Why was C.S. at risk for drug-induced renal failure? [SI units: BUN 37.49 mmol/L UREA; SrCr 645.32 μmol/L; ALT 140 U/L; AST 151 U/L; LDH 542 U/L; bilirubin 75.24 μmol/L (Normal: 1.71–17.1)]

Prostaglandin E_2 and I_2 probably maintained C.S.'s glomerular hydrostatic pressure by dilation of his renal afferent arterioles when his renal blood flow had been compromised by his diuretic and congestive heart failure.[117] In a review of 27 cases of renal failure associated with NSAIDs,[40] all the patients were more than 50 years of age and 70% were male. These patients had been taking NSAIDs for a mean of 46 days (range: 30 to 270 days) before the onset of acute renal failure. Twenty-five of the twenty-seven patients had conditions associated with poor renal perfusion before, or associated with, the onset of their episode of renal failure (see Table 29.9). Active sodium retention appears to make the renal vasculature exquisitely sensitive to NSAIDs, and conditions such as CHF, and perhaps hypertension, ascites, and cirrhosis make patients vulnerable to NSAID-induced renal failure. In these circumstances, the NSAID will oppose the afferent arteriolar compensatory mechanism, allowing unrestricted constriction with a resulting reduction in GFR. C.S. was more than 50 years of age, is a male, and had CHF which is associated with poor renal perfusion. In addition, he gave a history of self-administering large doses of ibuprofen for an extended period.

20. What features of NSAID-induced renal failure are consistent with C.S.'s clinical presentation?

The onset of acute renal failure induced by NSAIDs usually occurs several weeks to months after the initiation of chronic dosing with the NSAID. Therefore, it is noteworthy that C.S. had been taking ibuprofen (Motrin) for about five weeks before his renal failure became apparent. Although the onset for most NSAID-induced renal failure generally occurs after a delay of several weeks, ketorolac tromethamine (Toradol) can induce renal insufficiency after only a few doses and C.S. did receive an intramuscular dose of ketorolac postsurgically. In a retrospective chart review, the onset of ketorolac-associated renal insufficiency in six patients occurred in about three days and at a mean total dose of about 153 mg.[140] The mean age of these six patients was 58 years and five had underlying cardiovascular disease which presumably predis-

Table 29.9	Conditions with Poor Perfusion States Associated with Acute Renal Failure Secondary to Nonsteroidal Anti-Inflammatory Drugs[a,b]
Condition	% Patients
Diuretic use	27
Vomiting/diarrhea	27
Serum albumin <3.1 gm/dL	16
GI bleeding	11.5
CHF	9
Miscellaneous	16

[a] Adapted from reference 40.
[b] CHF = Congestive heart failure; GI = Gastrointestinal.

posed them to possible compromised renal blood flow. C.S.'s age, underlying history of congestive heart failure, and treatment with a thiazide diuretic also seem to be consistent with features noted in those patients with ketorolac-induced renal insufficiency. Significant pre-existing renal insufficiency was not a factor in any of these ketorolac-treated patients and does not seem to be an issue with C.S. The increase in the serum creatinine concentration in these six patients from 1.2 mg/dL (mean value) to a peak of 2.9 mg/dL (mean value) is somewhat lower than that experienced by C.S.; however, C.S. was taking ibuprofen for five weeks in addition to his postsurgical intramuscular doses of ketorolac. Although one patient developed acute oliguric renal failure after a single ketorolac dose and required hemodialysis, the five other patients experienced only mild renal dysfunction.

In most cases of NSAID-induced renal insufficiency, the serum creatinine and BUN concentrations rise quickly and return to about baseline levels two to three weeks after the discontinuation of the NSAID. Meanwhile the patient's urine output diminishes rapidly to oliguria, or more rarely, to anuria. C.S.'s serum creatinine peaked at 7.3 mg/dL and his BUN at 105 mg/dL, however, the rapidity of these increases cannot be determined by the presented data. C.S.'s oliguria is consistent with the typical picture of NSAID-induced renal insufficiency. Although proteinuria may not be common with NSAID-induced renal insufficiency, C.S. did present with 2+ hematuria. In one study, hematuria and proteinuria developed in 80% and granular casts were noted in 40% of patients with NSAID-induced renal failure that may have been associated with concurrent glomerulopathy.[40]

The abnormally high serum concentrations of liver enzymes in C.S. (i.e., AST 151 U/L, ALT 140 U/L, and LDH 542 U/L) also are consistent with the elevated levels of liver enzymes noted in patients with NSAID-induced renal insufficiency.

Patients with NSAID-associated renal insufficiency also can experience significant hyperkalemia which probably results from the indirect inhibition of the renin-angiotensin system combined with decreased potassium excretion from the renal dysfunction. Hyperkalemia apparently was not noted in C.S. Hyperuricemia and a fractional excretion of sodium of less than 1% also have been reported in association with NSAID-associated renal insufficiency, however, these also did not seem to occur in C.S.

21. What other renal problems associated with NSAIDs could have been experienced by D.R.'s self-administration of nonprescription ibuprofen?

Apart from hemodynamically-induced acute renal failure, NSAIDs also can cause acute interstitial nephritis with proteinuria, a syndrome of acute flank pain and acute renal failure, and a chronic interstitial nephritis with papillary necrosis. Acute interstitial nephritis probably is rare in light of the large numbers of NSAIDs in clinical use. The acute interstitial nephritis has been described, both with and without minimal changes in the glomeruli, primarily in patients taking fenoprofen (Nalfon), however, other NSAIDs have been implicated as well. A review of the literature noted 43 cases of NSAID-associated acute interstitial nephritis, about half of which were caused by fenoprofen.[93] Most patients were female and tended to be older individuals.

Glomerulopathy has been identified as a less frequent complication of NSAIDs. These patients also tend to be elderly and in one retrospective review, had been taking NSAIDs for a mean of 95 days (range: 14 to 180 days) before the onset of complications.[141] None of these patients developed oliguria, but all tended to have an immune disorder or were concomitantly taking drugs which may produce an immune-mediated glomerulopathy (e.g., allopurinol, hydralazine). Prednisolone may hasten recovery, but these findings are inconsistent.

Suprofen (Suprol) was the first NSAID to be associated with acute flank pain and acute renal failure.[142,143] The syndrome typically occurred within one to four hours after drug administration, usually following the first doses. The reaction occurred mostly in males between 20 to 40 years of age who had a history of regular physical exercise, alcohol use, and possibly a history of allergies. Since then, suprofen has been withdrawn from the U.S. Ibuprofen (Motrin) and flurbiprofen (Ansaid) also have been implicated in causing a similar acute flank pain syndrome.[144] One patient was a 14-year-old boy who ingested 100 mg of flurbiprofen every 12 hours for three doses. Another patient was a 12-year-old girl, also previously healthy, who took 200 mg ibuprofen every six hours for three days. Both patients developed acute renal failure which resolved over a period of seven to ten days. In both cases, the patients also took infrequent doses of acetaminophen, leading to the hypothesis that tubular toxicity of NSAIDs and acetaminophen is synergistic.

The exact risk of acute renal failure from NSAIDs is unclear; however, the risk appears to be small enough to permit the sale of ibuprofen as an over-the-counter (OTC) preparation. Risks generally increase when the daily dose is greater than 1.6 gm, and acute renal failure occurs almost exclusively in patients with well-defined predisposing factors.[145] A group of elderly (mean age: 69 ± 2 years), mildly hypertensive patients with mild renal impairment and hypertension controlled with hydrochlorothiazide 50 mg/day were randomized to one of three groups. These men were treated for seven days with nonprescription ibuprofen at the maximum labelled OTC (i.e., 400 mg TID), aspirin 650 mg three times a day, or acetaminophen 650 mg three times a day. No changes in either blood pressure control or in renal function (Cl_{Cr} ranged from 49 ± 3.5 to 71 ± 6 mL/minute/1.73 m^2) were noted in any of these patients. Nevertheless, isolated cases of renal failure due to small doses of OTC ibuprofen (200 mg TID for 1 week)[147] have occurred especially in patients taking triamterene concurrently.[148–150]

Postrenal Acute Renal Failure

Urinary tract obstruction at any site from the renal pelvis to the urethra can cause either a chronic progressive decline in renal function (e.g., prostatic hypertrophy, pelvic carcinoma, bilateral ureteral strictures), or an acute deterioration in renal function (e.g., obstruction caused by passage of renal stones). Although the formation of renal stones that are large enough to cause an acute obstruction may be a process occurring over months to years, the deterioration of renal function usually arises acutely.

Nephrolithiasis

Nephrolithiasis (renal stones) is relatively common, accounting for 0.7% to 1.0% of U.S. hospital admissions.[151] There are 10 to 20 cases per 10,000 of the population, and up to 20% of the U.S. population will experience nephrolithiasis at some time during their life.[152,153] About 80% of patients with nephrolithiasis are men and these men most commonly develop this problem between 20 to 30 years of age. There are four major types of renal stone: calcium salts, magnesium ammonium phosphate (struvite), uric acid, and cystine. Most calcium-containing stones are composed of calcium oxalate (60% to 80%), while calcium phosphate accounts for 5% to 10%. Uric acid and cystine stones account for about 10% and 1%, respectively. Calcium and uric acid stones primarily occur in men; struvite stones more commonly in women; and cystine stones occur in equal frequency in men and women. The diagnosis of the type of renal stone requires evaluation of patients for remediable metabolic disorders that can cause stones and chemical analyses of urine and serum. The diagnosis can be facilitated by direct assessment of any stone fragment that has been passed in the urine.

Struvite Stones

Struvite stones usually occur in the presence of a urinary tract infection caused by organisms that produce urease (e.g., *Klebsiella*, *Pseudomonas*, *Enterococci*, and especially *Proteus*).[152] Since women experience urinary tract infections much more commonly than men, struvite stones, not surprisingly, primarily occur in women. The urease degrades urea to NH_3 which subsequently hydrolyzes to form NH_4^+ and a highly alkaline urine (pH >8). The NH_4^+ precipitates phosphate and magnesium to form the $MgNH_4PO_4$ struvite stone. These stones are slow growing, and may fill the renal pelvis and produce a ''stag-horn'' like appearance. Surgical removal of the stone may be required. Long-term suppressive antibiotic therapy to prevent urinary tract infection; and urinary acidification with methenamine mandelate may be appropriate preventative measures.[171]

Uric Acid Stones

Uric acid stones can cause a rare form of acute renal failure known as acute uric acid nephropathy.[170] The most common setting for this occurrence is during chemotherapy of a malignancy (see Chapter 40: Gout and Hyperuricemia).

Cystine Stones

Cystine stones occur in patients who excrete excessive urinary cystine, and account for less than 1% of all renal stones. Excessive cystinuria results from a hereditary defect of amino acid transport. Treatment includes both a high fluid intake (>4 L/day) to reduce urinary cystine concentrations to less than 24 to 48 mg/dL, and oral d-penicillamine or tiopronin. Neither of these agents inhibit the urinary crystallization of cystine, rather they lower urinary concentrations below its solubility limit. Cystine is the disulfide of cysteine, and both d-penicillamine and tiopronin, as thiols, combine with urinary cysteine to form a soluble cysteine disulfide complex.[152] Tiopronin may have fewer dose-limiting side effects than d-penicillamine. In one study, 31% of patients discontinued tiopronin therapy because of side effects, compared to 70% of patients taking d-penicillamine.[172] The most common adverse effects were gastrointestinal, impairment of taste and smell, and a variety of dermatological complications.

Calcium Stones

22. J.B. is a 24-year-old male student who was training for a marathon. On the day of admission, he had completed an 18-mile run, with the ambient temperatures in the mid-70 °F range. On completion of the run, he felt light-headed and extremely thirsty, and for the next hour drank water freely. Several hours later, he developed severe, sudden-onset renal colic, located over the right flank. The pain was so severe he was unable to walk. The pain radiated down over the abdomen and into his groin. He experienced urgency for urination, and passed bloody urine with much pain. He called for an ambulance and was brought to the ER. His apparent diagnosis is that of renal stone disease. What factors may have predisposed J.B. to the development of a renal stone and what type of stone is most probable in this case?

Calcium oxalate and calcium phosphate stones constitute 75% to 85% of all renal stones and both of these calcium salts can coexist in the same stone. Calcium stones also are two to three times more common in men than in women and frequently become apparent in the third decade of life. Since J.B. is a male patient and 26 years of age, his renal stone is at least 75% to 85% likely to be made up of a calcium salt. Nevertheless, the composition of

his kidney stone should be determined, if possible, because treatment decisions are affected by the specific type of stone.

Kidney stones usually arise because of an imbalance between the kidney's need to conserve fluid and the need to extrude waste products of low solubility. This imbalance often is precipitated by alterations in diet, fluid intake, climate, and extent of physical activity. Since J.B.'s renal stone is temporally related to an 18-mile run when the outdoor temperature was rather warm, it is reasonable to suspect that a decrease in urine volume predisposed him to precipitation of a renal stone.

The majority of patients with calcium-containing stones excrete excessive amounts of urinary calcium (>4 mg/kg/day) and often have a urine that is a supersaturated solution of calcium and oxalate salts.[154] Calcium stone disease frequently is familial in origin. At least 20% of patients have no obvious cause for the calcium kidney stone and as much of 90% of calcium oxalate stones in particular may be idiopathic in origin. Distal renal tubular acidosis, hyperparathyroidism, hyperuricosuria, and hyperoxaluria, are the other primary causes of calcium nephrolithiasis.[152]

J.B.'s renal stone is most likely to be a calcium-containing stone rather than uric acid, struvite, or cystine in origin. J.B.'s apparent dehydrated state after a long run in warm weather potentially predisposed him to low urinary volume, supersaturation of calcium and oxalate salts, and the formation of small crystals of calcium oxalate. A more specific diagnosis of the origin of his stone can be affirmed by further chemical analyses of his urine and serum.

23. An analysis of a stone fragment in J.B.'s urine has confirmed a diagnosis of a calcium oxalate stone. How should J.B. be treated and how can further stone formation be prevented?

Acute-onset symptoms with calcium oxalate stones tend to be self-limiting, due to passage of stones in the urine. Persistent symptoms may require either surgical intervention or fragmentation using extracorporeal shock-wave lithotripsy,[155] percutaneous ultrasonic lithotripsy, or lithotripsy by endoscopic passage of an ultrasonic transducer into the ureters. Specific treatment is dependent upon the location of the stone, extent of obstruction, degree of renal dysfunction, and potential for stone passage.

The prevention of future calcium oxalate stone formation can be managed dietarily[156] and by thiazides.[157] The thiazide diuretics decrease calcium excretion in the urine by increasing fractional calcium reabsorption in the distal nephron;[158] however, the long-term usefulness of thiazides remains unclear.[159] In addition, modest sodium restriction (100 mEq/day) should be implemented because excessive sodium intake can override the hypocalciuric effect of the thiazides and hypercalciuria can be exacerbated by excess sodium in the nephron.[159,160] Fluid intake is critical: patients should drink sufficient water (i.e., 6 to 8 glasses) to produce in excess of 2 L of urine daily to decrease urinary supersaturation.[160,161] Severe dietary calcium restriction is unnecessary because only 6% of calcium appears in the urine and calcium restriction can increase intestinal oxalate production.[156] Some centers, however, advocate mild calcium restriction (<1 gm/day).[151] Dietary calcium restriction is, therefore, controversial. High intake of calcium (>1300 mg/day) also has been associated with a significant decrease in stone formation, due to a reduction in urinary oxalate excretion.[152,162] J.B. should be counseled against excessive doses of vitamin C (>1 gm/day) which becomes metabolized to oxalate.[151]

Sodium cellulose phosphate can be used to bind intra-intestinal calcium,[152] and oral phosphate (2 gm/day) also can be used to decrease intestinal calcium absorption.[163] Calcium-containing antacids should be avoided. Excessive dietary intake of animal protein should be avoided.[156,159] J.B. also needs to undertake special precautions to minimize future episodes of dehydration when training for his marathon.

J.B.'s urinalysis did not include an assessment of the citrate concentration of his urine. Nevertheless, about 19% to 63% of patients with calcium-containing renal stones will have low urinary citrate.[164,165] Since citrate binds free calcium, an increase in the urine citrate concentration would reduce the potential for formation of renal calcium oxalate stones.[166] When 80 mEq/day of potassium chloride, potassium bicarbonate, and potassium citrate were administered for two weeks to patients with hypocitraturia (mean: 2.5 mmol/day), the citrate salt doubled the mean urinary citrate concentration.[167] Effervescent calcium citrate and potassium-magnesium citrate also are effective in individuals who have calcium stones in the presence of enteric hyperoxaluria and urinary acidity. The exact influence of citrate supplementation is difficult to assess without more study and cannot be recommended for J.B. especially since the citrate concentration of his urine was not evaluated for hypocitraturia.

Endogenous inhibitors of stone formation such as nephrocalcin (glycoprotein of renal origin that inhibits calcium oxalate crystallization),[173] uropontin,[174] and uromodulin (Tamm-Horsfall muroprotein)[175] are currently under investigational study and not generally available for clinical use.

Prostate Disease

Benign prostatic hyperplasia is a common ailment among elderly men, and about two thirds of men over 65 years will show some symptoms.[176] However, it is an uncommon cause of acute renal failure. In the event of a postrenal acute renal failure, the most appropriate acute management is urethral catheterization to permit voiding of urine from the bladder. More often, benign prostatic hyperplasia leads to a progressive deterioration in renal urinary output, with progressive renal insufficiency and chronic renal failure. Evaluative procedures include a voiding cystoureterogram, measurement of uroflow indices, especially maximum urine flow rate, residual urine volume; and measurement of prostate size and symptoms. Symptomatic complaints appear to correlate poorly with the extent of bladder outflow obstruction.[177] Maximum urine flow rate correlates well with urethral cross-sectional diameter and use of magnetic resonance imaging or transrectal sonography can accurately measure prostate size during treatment.[178]

The pathogenesis and treatment of benign prostatic hyperplasia is presented in Chapter 103: Geriatric Urological Disorders.

Supportive Management of Acute Renal Failure

The outcome of acute renal failure is poor and associated with high mortality rates which are dependent upon the type of renal failure, the underlying complications, and the specific disease processes. The overall mortality ranges from about 10% (for ARF due to some drugs) to about 90% (in burn patients with complications). In one study of 250 patients in an intensive care unit, the overall survival rate for patients with all causes of renal failure was only 53%.[201] Because of this, the main thrust for care of patients at risk of renal failure should be on its prevention.

Up to 80% of cases of acute renal failure are due to prerenal failure[202] which results from decreased effective intravascular volume, decreased cardiac output, or altered intrarenal hemodynamics. Thus, preventive measures are based upon the restoration of normovolemia and renal blood flow, control of bleeding, and treatment of the underlying cardiac dysfunction. The patient at risk should have potentially nephrotoxic agents discontinued, or the dose adjusted appropriately; and urine output should be maintained or, if possible, increased to relieve any tubular obstruction.

The use of drugs to prevent acute renal failure is controversial; however, some drug nephrotoxicities may be prevented or minimized by prehydration or the use of diuretics (e.g., radiocontrast media).[55]

Plasma volume expansion with saline or mannitol can reduce renal failure in surgical patients and in those with severe burns, trauma, and shock.[181] In addition, vigorous hydration and the use of diuretics may convert oliguria to nonoliguric or polyuric failure, although it remains unclear whether this action favorably influences prognosis.[182,183] There appears to be little evidence that loop diuretics alone can prevent acute renal failure. Loop diuretics or mannitol in combination with plasma expansion may be beneficial. These agents can increase intratubular urine flow and prevent or reverse intratubular obstruction; they may improve renal blood flow and intrarenal hemodynamics; GFR may increase via inhibition of tubuloglomerular feedback; and they may act as scavengers for oxygen free radicals.[184,185] Mannitol should be administered before the development of renal failure: it may be hazardous if given in established acute renal failure due to the risk of congestive heart failure and pulmonary edema. Loop diuretics may produce a synergistic effect with dopamine in conversion of oliguric patients to nonoliguric renal failure.[186]

A variety of other drugs have been administered to patients at risk to prevent acute renal failure. These have included inotropic agents, such as low-dose (1 to 5 µg/kg/minute) dopamine, calcium antagonists, and thromboxane synthetase inhibitors, such as prostacyclin.

Once acute renal failure has been established, treatment is supportive and consists of five basic steps: 1) prompt treatment of life-threatening complications, such as hyperkalemia, pulmonary edema, and heart failure; 2) rapid correction of intravascular volume status, such as administration of packed red blood cells or plasma expanders in hypovolemic patients or removal of intravascular water in overloaded patients; 3) treatment of the precipitating condition; 4) determining the exact renal diagnosis; and 5) reversal of oliguria, if present.[187]

Water and electrolyte management requires the frequent monitoring of weight, intake and output, chest auscultations, hemodynamic monitoring, and blood chemistries. The exact fluid requirements of these patients are highly variable, and depend upon the cause of the renal failure and concomitant disease states. Oliguric patients should have a daily sodium restriction of about 30 to 40 mmol (2 to 2.5 gm NaCl). Hyperkalemia and hypokalemia must be monitored stringently and treated accordingly. The importance of nutritional and dietary management must be emphasized. The reader is referred to other chapters for full discussion of these issues.

Continuous renal replacement therapy is being used increasingly for the management of these patients, compared to intermittent dialysis. Whichever type of replacement therapy is used, there are two broad indications. Immediate initiation of renal replacement therapy is indicated when complications of uremia are present (i.e., when uremia has advanced to such an extent that is has produced deleterious effects on other organ systems). Examples of mandatory indications for renal replacement therapy include uremic bleeding, gross fluid overload, hyperkalemia, encephalopathy, and severe metabolic acidosis. Renal replacement therapy also is indicated for uremia itself. There is controversy as to exactly when the therapy should be started in uremia because the serum creatinine or blood urea nitrogen does not correlate well with the development of uremic complications. For this reason, renal replacement therapies may be initiated at different times, according to individual experiences and preferences. One recommendation

Table 29.10	Continuous Renal Replacement Therapies[a]			
Name	Blood Pump	Cl Urea (mL/min)	Ultrafiltration Rate (L/day)	Diffusion Component
CAVH	No	5–10	5–10	No
CVVH	Yes	12–20	>20	No
CAVHD	No	15–30	5–10	Yes
CVVHD	Yes	>40	>20	Yes
For comparison: Intermittent HD (4 hr)	Yes	150–200	<5	Yes

[a] CAVH = Continuous arteriovenous hemofiltration; CAVHD = Continuous arteriovenous hemodiafiltration; CL = Clearance; CVVH = Continuous venovenous hemodiafiltration; CVVHD = Continuous venovenous hemodialysis; HD = Hemodialysis.

would be to start therapy when BUN reaches 70 to 85 mg/dL and when SrCr reaches 5.5 to 8.0 mg/dL.[187]

There are four main types of continuous renal replacement therapy (see Table 29.10). The main differences are that the arteriovenous systems rely upon the patient's blood pressure gradient to provide ultrafiltration, which is therefore limited to 5 to 10 L/day, and that the venovenous systems require a blood pump which can dramatically increase ultrafiltration and clearance. Those systems which incorporate hemodialysis permit solute diffusion as well as ultrafiltration, thereby increasing performance.

The advantages of continuous over intermittent treatments include better hemodynamic stability, increased water elimination, and, possibly, less activation of complements.[188] One potential disadvantage is the necessity for continuous systemic heparinization. In one study, continuous venovenous hemodiafiltration (CVVHD) was used to treat 12 patients with oliguric acute renal failure. BUN decreased from a mean pretreatment value of 99 mg/dL to 56 mg/dL after 24 hours of treatment. Respective serum creatinine concentrations were 10.1 mg/dL and 3.4 mg/dL. The mean ultrafiltration rate was 551 mL/hour and urea clearance was 26.6 mL/minute. In this study, hemodynamic stability, control of fluid, and electrolyte balance were excellent. The technique survival was 100%, patient survival was 42%.[189] Another study compared continuous venovenous hemofiltration (CVVH) with continuous arteriovenous hemofiltration (CAVH) and continuous arteriovenous hemodiafiltration (CAVHD) in 25 critically ill patients with acute renal failure.[190] These patients were treated for a mean of 7.7 days, and patients had a mean weight loss of 7.9 kg. The mean heparin dose was 6.5 U/kg/hour and one patient had hemorrhagic complications. Twelve of a total of 111 hemofilters were changed because of clot formation, suggesting difficulties in maintaining adequate anticoagulation.

Numerous such studies exist that demonstrate the efficacy of continuous therapies. There are few adequate studies to compare continuous to intermittent therapies for ARF, and such studies probably will not be done.[209] Many centers continue to use intermittent hemodialysis in acute renal failure, and several employ peritoneal dialysis. When five patients were treated by peritoneal dialysis for a duration of 10 to 57 days for posttraumatic acute renal failure,[191] three patients survived, although three required additional intermittent hemodialysis, three developed hyperglycemia, and two developed bacterial peritonitis. In spite of these complications, peritoneal dialysis provided advantages over intermittent hemodialysis because of hemodynamic stability, no anticoagulation or vascular access, and reduced personnel requirement.

Drug dosing in continuous renal replacement therapies requires a different approach to that in intermittent dialysis.[192] To date, however, the majority of drugs have not been studied and specific guidelines are lacking.

References

1 **Agmon Y, Brezis M.** Acute renal failure: a multifactorial syndrome. Contrib Nephrol. 1993;102:23.

2 **Liano F et al.** Prognosis of acute tubular necrosis: an extended prospectively controlled study. Nephron. 1993; 63:21.

3 **Bullock ML et al.** The assessment of risk factors in 462 patients with acute renal failure. Am J Kidney Dis. 1985; 5:97.

4 **Smithies MN, Cameron JJ.** Can we predict outcome in acute renal failure? Nephron. 1989;51:297.

5 **Ronco C.** Continuous renal replacement therapies for the treatment of acute renal failure in intensive care unit patients. Clin Nephrol. 1993;40:187.

6 **Shusterman N et al.** Risk factors and outcome of hospital-acquired acute renal failure. Am J Med. 1987;83:65.

7 **Hou S et al.** Hospital-acquired renal insufficiency: a prospective study. Am J Med. 1983;74:243.

8 **Kaufman J et al.** Community-acquired acute renal failure. Am J Kidney Dis. 1991;17:191.

9 **Davidman M et al.** Iatrogenic renal disease. Arch Intern Med. 1991;151; 1809.

10 **Ducharme MP et al.** Drug-induced alterations in serum creatinine concentrations. Ann Pharmacother. 1993;27:622.

11 **Massoomi F et al.** Effect of seven fluoroquinolones on the determination of serum creatinine by the picric acid and enzymatic methods. Ann Pharmacother. 1993;27:586.

12 **Finn WF.** Diagnosis and management of acute tubular necrosis. Med Clin North Am. 1990;74:873.

13 **Lindeman RD et al.** Longitudinal studies on the rate of decline in renal function with age. J Am Geriatr Soc. 1985;33:278.

14 **Drusano GL et al.** Commonly used methods of estimating creatinine clearance are inadequate for elderly debilitated nursing home patients. J Am Geriatr Soc. 1988;36:437.

15 **Cockcroft DW, Gault MH.** Predication of creatinine clearance from serum creatinine. Nephron. 1976;16:31.

16 **Bjornsson TD.** The use of creatinine concentrations to determine renal function. Clin Pharmacokinet. 1979;4:200.

17 **O'Connell MB et al.** Accuracy of 2- and 8-hour urine collections for measuring creatinine clearance in the hospitalized elderly. Pharmacotherapy. 1993;13:135.

18 **Kohler H et al.** Acanthocyturia: a characteristic marker for glomerular bleeding. Kidney Int. 1991;40:115.

19 **Rose BD.** Clinical assessment of renal function. In: Rose BD, ed. Pathophysiology of Renal Disease. 2nd ed. New York: McGraw-Hill Inc.; 1987:1.

20 **Scherberich JE et al.** Biochemical and immunological properties of urinary angiotensinase A and dipeptidylaminopeptidase IV: their use as markers in patients with renal cell injury. Eur J Clin Chem Clin Biochem. 1992;30:663.

21 **Couser WG.** Rapidly progressive glomerulonephritis: classification, pathogenetic mechanisms and therapy. Am J Kidney Dis. 1988;11:449.

22 **Croker BP et al.** Clinical and pathologic features of polyarteritis nodosa and its renal-limited variant: primary crescentic glomerulonephritis. Hum Pathol. 1987;18:38.

23 **Jeanette JC, Falk RJ.** Diagnosis and management of glomerulonephritis and vasculitis presenting as acute renal failure. Med Clin N Am. 1990;74:893.

24 **O'Meara Y et al.** Systemic vasculitis with renal involvement. Ir J Med Sci. 1989;158:300.

25 **Balow JE.** Renal vasculitis. Kidney Int. 1985;27:954.

26 **Donadio JV, Glassock RJ.** Immunosuppressive drug therapy in lupus nephritis. Am J Kidney Dis. 1993;21:239.

27 **Johnson JP et al.** Therapy for antiglomerular basement membrane antibody disease: analysis of prognostic significance of clinical, pathologic and treatment factors. Medicine. 1985;64:219.

28 **Niles JL et al.** Antigen-specific radioimmunoassays for antineutrophil cytoplasmic antibodies in the diagnosis of rapidly progressive glomerulonephritis. J Am Soc Nephrol. 1991;2:27.

29 **Tuso P et al.** Treatment of antineutrophil cytoplasmic autoantibody-positive systemic vasculitis and glomerulonephritis with pooled intravenous gammaglobulin. Am J Kidney Dis. 1992; 20:504.

30 **Bolton WK, Sturgill BC.** Methylprednisolone therapy for acute crescentic rapidly progressive glomerulonephritis. Am J Nephrol. 1989;9:368.

31 **de Glas-Vos JW et al.** Methylprednisolone pulse therapy in rapidly progressive glomerulonephritis. Neth J Med. 1991;38:96.

32 **Maduell F et al.** Treatment of nephrotic syndrome associated with idiopathic rapidly progressive glomerulonephritis and cyclosporin A. J Clin Pharm Ther. 1993;18:59.

33 **Srivastava RN et al.** Crescentic glomerulonephritis in children: a re-

view of 43 cases. Am J Nephrol. 1992; 12:155.

34 **Frasca GM et al.** Plasma exchange treatment in rapidly progressive glomerulonephritis associated with anti-neutrophil cytoplasmic autoantibodies. Int J Artif Organs. 1992;15:181.

35 **Palmer A et al.** Treatment of rapidly progressive glomerulonephritis by extracorporeal immunoadsorption, prednisolone and cyclophosphamide. Nephrol Dial Transplant. 1991;6:536.

36 **Hoffman GS et al.** Wegener granulomatosis: an analysis of 158 patients. Ann Intern Med. 1992;116:488.

37 **Ponticelli C.** Current treatment recommendations for lupus nephritis. Drugs. 1990;40:19.

38 **Hughson MD et al.** Renal thrombotic microangiography in patients with systemic lupus erythematosus and the antiphospholipid syndrome. Am J Kidney Dis. 1992;20:150.

39 **Ludemann J et al.** Anti-neutrophil cytoplasm antibodies in Wegener's granulomatosis: immunodiagnostic value, monoclonal antibodies and characterization of the target antigen. Neth J Med. 1990;36:157.

40 **Shankel SW et al.** Acute renal failure and glomerulopathy caused by nonsteroidal anti-inflammatory drugs. Arch Intern Med. 1992;152:986.

41 **Hall CL.** The natural course of gold and penicillamine nephropathy: a long-term study in 54 patients. Adv Exp Med Biol. 1989;252:247.

42 **Banti G et al.** Extracapillary glomerulonephritis with necrotizing vasculitis in d-penicillamine-treated rheumatoid arthritis. Nephron. 1983;33:56.

43 **Sturgill BC, Shearlock KT.** Membranous glomerulopathy and nephrotic syndrome after captopril therapy. JAMA. 1983;250:2343.

44 **Jones CL, Eddy AA.** Tubulointerstitial nephritis. Pediatr Nephrol. 1992;6: 572.

45 **Corwin HL, Bonventre JV.** Factors influencing survival in acute renal failure. Semin Dial. 1989;2:220.

46 **Abuelo JG.** Renal failure caused by chemicals, foods, plants, animal venoms, and misuse of drugs. Arch Intern Med. 1990;150:505.

47 **Lawrence V et al.** Comparative safety of high-osmolality and low-osmolality radiographic contrast agents. Report of a multidisciplinary working group. Invest Radiol. 1992;27:2.

48 **Barrett BJ et al.** Contrast nephropathy in patients with impaired renal function: high versus low osmolar media. Kidney Int. 1992;41:1274.

49 **Brezis M, Epstein FH.** A closer look at radio-contrast-induced nephropathy. N Engl J Med. 1989;320:179.

50 **Wolf GL et al.** A prospective trial of ionic vs. nonionic contrast agents in routine clinical practice. Comparison of adverse effects. A J Radiol. 1989; 152:939.

51 **Parfrey PS et al.** Contrast material-induced renal failure in patients with diabetes mellitus, renal insufficiency, or both. A prospective, controlled study. N Engl J Med. 1989;320:143.

52 **Schwab SJ et al.** Contrast nephrotoxicity: a randomized controlled trial of a nonionic and an ionic radiographic

contrast agent. N Engl J Med. 1989; 320:149.

53 **Spinler SA, Goldfarb S.** Nephrotoxicity of contrast media following cardiac angiography: pathogenesis, clinical course, and preventive measures, including the role of low-osmolality contrast media. Ann Pharmacother. 1992;26:56.

54 **Hill JA et al.** Multicenter trial of ionic versus nonionic contrast media for cardiac angiography. Am J Cardiol. 1993; 72:770.

55 **Neumayer HH et al.** Prevention of radiocontrast-media-induced nephrotoxicity by the calcium channel blocker nitrendipine: a prospective, randomized clinical trial. Nephrol Dial Transplant. 1989;4:1030.

56 **Feehally J et al.** Does nifedipine ameliorate cyclosporin A nephrotoxicity? Br Med J. 1987;295:310.

57 **Russell JD, Churchill DN.** Calcium antagonists and acute renal failure. Am J Med. 1989;87:306.

58 **Dorman HR et al.** Mannitol-induced acute renal failure. Medicine. 1990;69; 153.

59 **Rabetoy GM et al.** Where the kidney is concerned, how much mannitol is too much? Ann Pharmacother. 1993; 27:25.

60 **Branch RA.** Prevention of amphotericin B-induced renal impairment: a review on the use of sodium supplementation. Arch Intern Med. 1988;148: 2389.

61 **Phillips A.** Renal failure and intravenous immunoglobulin. Clin Nephrol. 1992;37:217.

62 **Deray G et al.** Foscarnet nephrotoxicity: mechanism, incidence and prevention. Am J Nephrol. 1989;9:316.

63 **Bailie GR, Neal D.** Vancomycin ototoxicity and nephrotoxicity: a review. Med Toxicol. 1988;3:376–86.

64 **Briceland LL, Bailie GR.** Pentamidine-associated nephrotoxicity and hyperkalemia in patients with AIDS. DICP Ann Pharmacother. 1991;25: 1171–174.

65 **Kahlmeter G, Dahlager JI.** Aminoglycoside toxicity—a review of clinical studies published between 1975 and 1982. J Antimicrob Chemother. 1984; 13(Suppl. A):9–22.

66 **Freeman CD et al.** Vancomycin therapeutic drug monitoring: is it necessary? Ann Pharmacother. 1993;27:594.

67 **Waisbren BA et al.** Comparative effectiveness and toxicity of vancomycin, ristocetin and kanamycin. Arch Intern Med. 1960;106:179.

68 **McCormack JP, Jewesson PJ.** A critical reevaluation of the "therapeutic range" of aminoglycosides. Clin Infect Dis. 1992;14:320.

69 **Verpooten GA et al.** Once-daily dosing decreases renal accumulation of gentamicin and netilmicin. Clin Pharmacol Ther. 1989;45:22.

70 **Nordstrom L, Lerner SA.** Single daily dose therapy with aminoglycosides. J Hosp Infect. 1991;18(Suppl. A):117.

71 **Rybak MJ et al.** Nephrotoxicity of vancomycin, alone and with an aminoglycoside. J Antimicrob Chemother. 1990;25:679.

72 **Farber BF, Moellering RC.** Retrospective study of the toxicity of prep-

arations of vancomycin from 1974 to 1981. Antimicrob Agents Chemother. 1983;23:138.

73 **Eng RHK et al.** Effect of intravenous vancomycin on renal function. Chemotherapy. 1989;35:320.

74 **Torras J et al.** Pharmacokinetics of vancomycin in patients undergoing haemodialysis with polyacrylonitrile. Clin Nephrol. 1991;36:35.

75 **Lanese DM et al.** Markedly increased clearance of vancomycin during haemodialysis using polysulfone dialyzers. Kidney Int. 1989;35:1409.

76 **Quale JM et al.** Removal of vancomycin by high flux haemodialysis membranes. Antimicrob Agents Chemother. 1992;36:1424.

77 **DeSoi CA et al.** Vancomycin elimination during high-flux haemodialysis: kinetic model and comparison of four membranes. Am J Kidney Dis. 1992; 20:354.

78 **Gallis HA et al.** Amphotericin B: 30 years of clinical experience. Rev Infect Dis. 1990;12:308.

79 **Schnermann J.** Regulation of single nephron filtration rate by feedback: facts and theories. Clin Nephrol. 1975; 3:75.

80 **Llanos A et al.** Effect of salt supplementation on amphotericin B nephrotoxicity. Kidney Int. 1991;40:302.

81 **Gardner ML et al.** Sodium loading treatment for amphotericin B-induced nephrotoxicity. DICP. 1990;24:940.

82 **Stein RS et al.** Nephrotoxicity in leukemia patients receiving empirical amphotericin B and aminoglycosides. South Med J. 1988;81:1095.

83 **Branch RA et al.** Amphotericin B nephrotoxicity in humans decreased by sodium supplements with co-administration or ticarcillin of intravenous saline. Klin Wochenschr. 1987;65:500.

84 **Murray KM, Keane WR.** Review of drug-induced acute interstitial nephritis. Pharmacotherapy. 1992;12:462.

85 **Koselj M et al.** Acute renal failure in patients with drug-induced acute interstitial nephritis. Ren Fail. 1993;15:69.

86 **Corwin HL, Haber MH.** The clinical significance of eosinophiluria. Am J Clin Pathol. 1987;88:520.

87 **Nolan CR et al.** Eosinophiluria-a new method of detection and definition of the clinical spectrum. N Engl J Med. 1986;315:1516.

88 **Lins RL et al.** Urinary indices in acute interstitial nephritis. Clin Nephrol. 1986;26:1313.

89 **Cameron JS.** Allergic interstitial nephritis: clinical features and pathogenesis. Q J Med. 1988;250:97.

90 **Mansoor GA et al.** Azithromycin-induced acute interstitial nephritis. Ann Intern Med. 1993;119:636.

91 **Bailey JR et al.** Ciprofloxacin-induced acute interstitial nephritis. Am J Nephrol. 1992;12:271.

92 **Hatton J, Haagensen D.** Renal dysfunction associated with ciprofloxacin. Pharmacotherapy. 1990;10:337.

93 **Porile JL et al.** Acute interstitial nephritis with glomerulopathy due to nonsteroidal anti-inflammatory agents: a review of its clinical spectrum and effects of steroid therapy. J Clin Pharmacol. 1993;30:468.

94 **Eisenberg ES et al.** Vancomycin and

interstitial nephritis. Ann Intern Med. 1981;95:658.

95 **Frye RF et al.** Teicoplanin nephrotoxicity: first case report. Pharmacotherapy. 1992;12:240.

96 **Nguyen VD et al.** Acute interstitial nephritis associated with cefotetan therapy. Am J Kidney Dis. 1990;16:259.

97 **Hootkins R et al.** Acute renal failure secondary to oral ciprofloxacin: a presentation of three cases and a review of the literature. Clin Nephrol. 1989;32: 75.

98 **Magil AB et al.** Acute interstitial nephritis associated with thiazide diuretics. Am J Med. 1980;69:939.

99 **Wilkinson SP et al.** Protracted systemic illness and interstitial nephritis due to minocycline. Postgrad Med J. 1989;65:53.

100 **Gaughan WJ et al.** Ranitidine-induced acute interstitial nephritis with epithelial cell foot process fusion. Am J Kidney Dis. 1993;22:337.

101 **Neelakantappa K et al.** Ranitidine-associated interstitial nephritis and Fanconi syndrome. Am J Kidney Dis. 1993;22:333.

102 **Neilson EG.** Pathogenesis and therapy of interstitial nephritis. Kidney Int. 1989;35:1257.

103 **Whelton A, Hamilton CW.** Nonsteroidal anti-inflammatory drugs: effects on kidney function. J Clin Pharmacol. 1991;31:588.

104 **Laxer RM et al.** Naproxen-associated renal failure in a child with arthritis and inflammatory bowel disease. Pediatrics. 1987;80:904.

105 **Snyder S, Teehan SP.** Suprofen and renal failure. Ann Intern Med. 1987; 106:776.

106 **Katz MD, Lor E.** Acute interstitial nephritis associated with intermittent rifampin use. DICP Ann Pharmacother. 1986;20:789.

107 **Soffer O et al.** Light chain nephropathy and acute renal failure associated with rifampin therapy. Am J Med. 1987;82:1052.

108 **Cohn JR et al.** Rifampin-induced renal failure. Tubercle. 1985;66:289.

109 **Davis CE et al.** Rifampin-induced acute renal failure. South Med J. 1986; 79:1012.

110 **Silverstein RL et al.** Interstitial nephritis caused by methicillin; studies in a case complicating *Staphylococcus* sepsis with acute glomerulonephritis. Am J Clin Pharmacol. 1981;76:316.

111 **Border WA et al.** Antitubular basement membrane antibodies in methicillin-associated interstitial nephritis. N Engl J Med. 1974;29:381.

112 **Galprin JE et al.** Acute interstitial nephritis due to methicillin. Am J Med. 1978;65:756.

113 **Enriquez R et al.** Relapsing steroid-responsive idiopathic acute interstitial nephritis. Nephron. 1993;63:462.

114 **Tomita K et al.** Plasma endothelin leads in patients with acute renal failure. N Engl J Med. 1989;321:1127.

115 **Kon V, Badr KF.** Biological actions and pathophysiologic significance of endothelin in the kidney. Kidney Int. 1991;40:1.

116 **Scharschmidt LA et al.** Glomerular prostaglandins, angiotensin II and nonsteroidal anti-inflammatory drugs. Am J Med. 1986;81(Suppl. 2B):30.

117 **Schlondorff D.** Renal complications of nonsteroidal anti-inflammatory drugs. Kidney Int. 1993;44:643.

118 **Luscler TF et al.** Endothelium-derived relaxing and contracting factors: perspectives in nephrology. Kidney Int. 1991;39:557.

119 **Badr KF, Ichikawa I.** Prerenal failure: a deleterious shift from renal compensation to decompensation. N Engl J Med. 1988;319:623.

120 **Keane WF et al.** Angiotensin converting enzyme inhibitors and progressive renal insufficiency. Ann Intern Med. 1989;111:503.

121 **Bedogna V et al.** Effects of ACE inhibition in normotensive patients with chronic glomerular disease and normal renal function. Kidney Int. 1990;38:101.

122 **Bridoux F et al.** Acute renal failure after the use of angiotensin converting enzyme inhibitors in patients without renal artery stenosis. Nephrol Dial Transplant. 1992;7:100.

123 **Lee H-C, Pettinger WA.** Diuretics potentiate the angiotensin converting enzyme inhibitor-associated acute renal dysfunction. Clin Nephrol. 1992;38:236.

124 **Tielemans C et al.** Anaphylactoid reactions during haemodialysis on AN69 membranes in patients receiving ACE inhibitors. Kidney Int. 1990;38:982.

125 **Parnes EL, Shapiro WB.** Anaphylactoid reactions in haemodialysis patients treated with the AN69 dialyzer. J Am Soc Nephrol. 1991;2:344.

126 **Mason NA.** Angiotensin converting enzyme inhibitors and renal function. DICP Ann Pharmacother. 1990;24:496.

127 **Gottlieb SS et al.** Determinants of the renal response to ACE inhibitors in patients with congestive heart failure. Am Heart J. 1992;124:131.

128 **Hricik DE et al.** Captopril-induced functional renal insufficiency in patients with bilateral renal artery stenosis or renal artery stenosis in a solitary kidney. N Engl J Med. 1983;308:373.

129 **Packer M et al.** Hemodynamic patterns of response during long-term captopril therapy for severe chronic heart failure. Circulation. 1983;68:803.

130 **Makdassi R et al.** Aetioiogy and prognosis of iatrogenic renal failure on the basis of a 6-year experience. Nephrol Dial Transplant. 1990;5:660.

131 **Fleury D et al.** Drug-induced acute renal failure: a preventable disease linked to drug abuse. Kidney Int. 1990;38:1238. Abstract.

132 **Dzau VJ.** Renal effects of angiotensin-converting enzyme inhibition in cardiac failure. Am J Kidney Dis. 1987;10(Suppl. 1):74–80.

133 **Cleland JG et al.** Effects of enalapril in heart failure: a double-blind study of effects on exercise performance, renal function, hormones, and metabolic state. Br Heart J. 1985;54:305.

134 **Kubo S et al.** Effects of captopril on arterial and venous pressure, renal function and humoral factors in severe congestive heart failure. Clin Pharmacol Ther. 1984;36:456.

135 **Cahan DH, Ucci AA.** Acute renal failure, interstitial nephritis, and nephrotic syndrome associated with captopril. Kidney Int. 1984;25:160.

136 **Taguma Y et al.** Effect of captopril on heavy proteinuria in azotemic diabetics. N Engl J Med. 1985;313:1617.

137 **Reams GP, Bauer JH.** Effect of enalapril in subjects with hypertension associated with moderate to severe renal dysfunction. Arch Intern Med. 1986;146:2145.

138 **Abraham PA et al.** Efficacy and renal effects of enalapril therapy for hypertensive patients with chronic renal insufficiency. Arch Intern Med. 1988;148:2358.

139 **Lewis EJ.** Glomerular abnormalities in patients receiving angiotensin converting enzyme inhibitor therapy. Kidney Int. 1987;20(Suppl.):S138–42.

140 **Corelli RL, Gericke KR.** Renal insufficiency associated with intramuscular administration of ketorolac tromethamine. Ann Pharmacother. 1993;27:1055.

141 **Champion de Crespigny PJ et al.** Renal failure and nephrotic syndrome associated with sulindac. Clin Nephrol. 1988;30:52.

142 **Rossi AC et al.** Suprofen and the flank pain syndrome. JAMA. 1988;259:1203.

143 **Hart D et al.** Suprofen-related nephrotoxicity. Ann Intern Med. 1987;106:235.

144 **McIntire SC et al.** Acute flank pain and reversible renal dysfunction associated with nonsteroidal anti-inflammatory drug use. Pediatrics. 1993;92:459.

145 **Mann JFE et al.** Ibuprofen as an over-the-counter drug: is there a risk for renal injury? Clin Nephrol. 1993;39:1.

146 **Furey SA et al.** Renovascular effects of nonprescription ibuprofen in elderly hypertensive patients with mild renal impairment. Pharmacotherapy. 1993;13:143.

147 **Spierto RJ et al.** Acute renal failure associated with the use of over-the-counter ibuprofen. Ann Pharmacother. 1992;26:714.

148 **McCarthy JT et al.** Acute renal failure induced by indomethacin. Mayo Clin Proc. 1982;57:289.

149 **Favre L et al.** Reversible acute renal failure from combined Triamterene and indomethacin. Ann Intern Med. 1982;96:317.

150 **Weinberg MS et al.** Anuric renal failure precipitated by indomethacin and triamterene. Nephron. 1985;40:216.

151 **NIH Consensus Conference: prevention and treatment of kidney stones.** JAMA. 1988;260:978.

152 **Coe FL et al.** The pathogenesis and treatment of kidney stones. N Engl J Med. 1992;327:1141.

153 **Wilson DM.** Clinical and laboratory evaluation of renal stone patients. Endocrinol Metab Clin North Am. 1990;19:773.

154 **Parks JH, Coe FL.** A urinary calcium-citrate index for the evaluation of nephrolithiasis. Kidney Int. 1986;30:85.

155 **Lingeman JE et al.** The role of lithotripsy and its side effects. J Urol. 1989;141:793.

156 **Brown WW, Wolfson M.** Diet as culprit or therapy: stone disease, chronic renal failure, and nephrotic syndrome. Med Clin North Am. 1993;77:783.

157 **Urivetzky M et al.** Urinary excretion of oxalate by patients with renal hyper-

calciuric stone disease: effect of chronic treatment with hydrochlorothiazide. Urology. 1991;37:327.

158 **Coe FL et al.** Chlorthalidone promotes mineral retention in patients with idiopathic hypercalciuria. Kidney Int. 1988;33:1140.

159 **Churchill DN, Taylor DW.** Thiazides for patients with recurrent calcium stones: still an open question. J Urol. 1985;133:749.

160 **Goldfarb S.** The role of diet in the pathogenesis and therapy of nephrolithiasis. Endocrinol Metab Clin North Am. 1990;19:805.

161 **Pak CYC et al.** Evidence justifying a high fluid intake in treatment of nephrolithiasis. Ann Intern Med. 1980;93:36.

162 **Curhan GC et al.** A prospective study of dietary calcium and other nutrients and the risk of symptomatic kidney stones. N Engl J Med. 1993;328:833.

163 **Insogna KL et al.** Trichlormethiazide and oral phosphate therapy in patients with absorptive hypercalciuria. J Urol. 1989;141:269.

164 **Hosking DH et al.** Urinary citrate excretion in normal persons and patients with idiopathic calcium nephrolithiasis. J Lab Clin Med. 1985;106:682.

165 **Pak CYC.** Citrate and renal calculi. Miner Electrolyte Metab. 1987;13:257.

166 **Nicar MJ et al.** Inhibition by citrate of spontaneous precipitation of calcium oxalate, in vitro. J Bone Miner Res. 1987;2:215.

167 **Sakhee K et al.** Contrasting effects of various potassium salts on renal citrate excretion. J Clin Endocrinol Metab. 1991;72:396.

168 **Millman S et al.** Pathogenesis and clinical course of mixed calcium oxalate and uric acid nephrolithiasis. Kidney Int. 1982;22:366.

169 **Preminger GM et al.** Alkali action on the urinary crystallization of calcium salts: contrasting responses to sodium citrate and potassium citrate. J Urol. 1988;139:240.

170 **Conger JD.** Acute uric acid nephropathy. Med Clin North Am. 1990;74:859.

171 **Williams JJ et al.** A randomized double-blind study of acetohydroxamic acid in struvite nephrolithiasis. N Engl J Med. 1984;311:760.

172 **Pak CYC et al.** Management of cystine nephrolithiasis with alpha-mercaptopropionylglycine. J Urol. 1986;136:1003.

173 **Asplin J et al.** Evidence that nephrocalcin and urine inhibit nucleation of calcium oxalate monohydrate crystals. Am J Physiol. 1991;261:F824–30.

174 **Shiraga H et al.** Inhibition of calcium oxalate crystal growth *in vitro* by uropontin: another member of the aspartic acid-rich protein superfamily. Proc Natl Acad Sci U S A. 1992;89:426.

175 **Hess B et al.** Molecular abnormality of Tamm-Horsfall glycoprotein in calcium oxalate nephrolithiasis. Am J Physiol. 1991;260:F569–78.

176 **Matzkin H, Braf Z.** Endocrine treatment of benign prostatic hypertrophy: current concepts. Urology. 1991;37;1.

177 **Ball AJ et al.** The natural history of untreated prostatism. Br J Urol. 1981;53:613.

178 **Khan Z et al.** Diagnosis and grading

of outflow obstruction. Urology. 1988;32:72.

179 **Barton IK et al.** Acute renal failure treated by hemofiltration: factors affecting outcome. Q J Med. 1993;86:81.

180 **Badr KF, Ichikawa I.** Pre-renal failure: a deleterious shift from renal compensation to decompensation. N Engl J Med. 1988;319:623.

181 **Myers BD, Moran SM.** Hemodynamically-mediated acute renal failure. N Engl J Med. 1986;314:97.

182 **Risler T et al.** The efficacy of diuretics in acute and chronic renal failure. Drugs. 1991;41(Suppl. 3):69.

183 **Brown CB et al.** High dose of furosemide in acute renal failure: a controlled trial. Clin Nephrol. 1981;15:90.

184 **Boles Ponto LL, Schoenwald RD.** Furosemide: a pharmacokinetic and pharmacodynamic review (part 1). Clin Pharmacokinet. 1990;18:381.

185 **Schrier RW et al.** Protection of mitochondrial function by mannitol in ischemic acute renal failure. Am J Physiol. 1984;247:F365–69.

186 **Graziani G et al.** Dopamine and furosemide in oliguric acute renal failure. Nephron. 1984;37:39.

187 **Firth JD.** Renal replacement therapy on the intensive care unit: editorial. Q J Med. 1993;86:75.

188 **Kierdorf H.** Continuous versus intermittent treatment: clinical results in acute renal failure. In: Sieberth HG, Mann H, eds. Continuous hemofiltration. Contrib Nephrol. Basel. 1991;93:1.

189 **Bellomo R et al.** Management of acute renal failure in the critically ill with continuous venovenous hemodiafiltration. Ren Fail. 1992;14:183.

190 **Macias WL et al.** Continuous venovenous hemofiltration: an alternative to continuous arteriovenous hemofiltration and hemodiafiltration in acute renal failure. Am J Kidney Dis. 1991;18:451.

191 **Howdieshell TR et al.** Management of post-traumatic acute renal failure with peritoneal dialysis. Am Surg. 1992;58:378.

192 **Reetze-Bonorden P et al.** Drug dosage in patients during continuous renal replacement therapy. Pharmacokinetic and therapeutic considerations. Clin Pharmacokinet. 1993;24:362.

193 **Mission RT, Cutler RE.** Radiocontrast-induced renal failure. West J Med. 1985;142:657.

194 **Moore RD et al.** Increased risk of renal dysfunction due to interaction of liver disease and aminoglycosides. AM J Med. 1986;80:1093.

195 **Sawyer CL et al.** A model for predicting nephrotoxicity in patients treated with aminoglycosides. J Infect Dis. 1986;153:1062.

196 **Holloway JJ et al.** Comparative cost effectiveness of gentamicin and tobramycin. Ann Intern Med. 1984;101:764.

197 **Ambinder RF et al.** Lack of evidence for interaction between tobramycin and shock in their effect on renal function. Antimicrob Agents Chemother. 1985;27:217.

198 **Moore RD et al.** Cefotaxime vs. nafcillin and tobramycin for the treatment of serious infection. Arch Intern Med. 1986;146:1153.

199 **Smith CR et al.** Controlled compari-

son of amikacin and gentamicin. N Engl J Med. 1977;296:349.

200 **Conlon PJ.** Time to abandon nonionic contrast? J Am Soc Nephrol. 1994;5:123.

201 **Barrett BJ.** Contrast nephrotoxicity. J Am Soc Nephrol. 1994;5:125–27.

202 **Kaysen GA et al.** Combined hepatic and renal injury in alcoholics during therapeutic use of acetaminophen. Arch Intern Med. 1985;145:2019.

203 **Cobden I et al.** Paracetamol-induced acute renal failure in the absence of fulminant liver damage. Br Med J. 1982;284:21.

204 **Gabrial R et al.** Acute tubular necrosis, caused by therapeutic doses of paracetamol? Clin Nephrol. 1982;18:269.

205 **Curry RW Jr et al.** Acute renal failure after acetaminophen ingestion. JAMA. 1982;247:1012.

206 **Bjorck S et al.** Acute renal failure after analgesic drugs including paracetamol (acetaminophen). Nephron. 1988;49:45.

207 **Segasothy M et al.** Paracetamol: a cause for analgesic nephropathy and end-stage renal disease. Nephron. 1988;50:50.

208 **Keaton Mr.** Acute renal failure in an alcoholic during therapeutic acetaminophen ingestion. South Med J. 1988;81:1163.

209 **Dabbagh S, Chesney RW.** Acute renal failure related to acetaminophen (paracetamol) overdose without fulminant hepatic disease. Int J Pediatr Nephrol. 1985;6:221.

210 **Sandler DP et al.** Analgesic use and chronic renal disease. N Engl J Med. 1989;320:1238.

211 **Gordon EE et al.** The effects of acetazolamide on citrate excretion and formation of renal calculi. N Engl J. Med. 1957;256:1215.

212 **Rossert J et al.** Tamm-Horsfall protein accumulation in glomeruli during acetazolamide-induced acute renal failure. Am J Nephrol. 1989;9:106.

213 **Sawyer MH et al.** Acyclovir-induced renal failure. Am J Med. 1988;84:1067.

214 **Giustina A et al.** Low-dose acyclovir and acute renal failure. Ann Intern Med. 1988;108(2):312. Letter

215 **Spiegal DM, Lau K.** Acute renal failure and coma secondary to acyclovir therapy. JAMA. 1986;255:1882.

216 **Kumor K et al.** Renal function studies during intravenous acyclovir treatment of immune suppressed patients including renal transplantation. Am J Nephrol. 1988;8:35.

217 **Mills RM.** Severe hypersensitivity reactions associated with allopurinol. JAMA. 1971;216:799.

218 **Young JL et al.** Severe allopurinol hypersensitivity. Association with thiazides and prior renal compromise. Arch Intern Med. 1974;134:553.

219 **Handa SP.** Drug-induced acute interstitial nephritis: report of 10 cases. Can Med Assoc J. 1986;135:1278.

220 **Appel GB et al.** Acute interstitial nephritis due to amoxicillin therapy. Nephron. 1981;27:313.

221 **Walker RJ et al.** Amoxicillin-induced acute interstitial nephritis. NZ Med J. 1985;98:866. Letter.

222 **Foley RJ et al.** Amphetamine-induced acute renal failure. South Med J. 1984;77:258.

223 **Sacks P, Fellner SK.** Recurrent reversible acute renal failure from amphotericin. Arch Intern Med. 1987;147:593.

224 **Stamm Am et al.** Toxicity of amphotericin B plus flucytosine in 194 patients with Cryptococcal meningitis. Am J Med. 1987;83:236.

225 **Churchill DN, Seely J.** Nephrotoxicity associated with combined gentamicin-amphotericin B Therapy. Nephron. 1977;19:176.

226 **Fuller MA.** Use of mannitol to prevent amphotericin B nephrotoxicity. Clin Pharm. 1987;6:367.

227 **Arning M, Scharf RE.** Prevention of amphotericin-B-induced nephrotoxicity by loading with sodium chloride: a report of 1291 days of treatment with amphotericin B without renal failure. Klin Wochenschr. 1989;67:1020.

228 **Heidemann HT et al.** Amphotericin B nephrotoxicity in humans decreased by salt repletion. Am J Med. 1983;75:476.

229 **Gilbert DN et al.** Interstitial nephritis due to methicillin, penicillin and ampicillin. Ann Allergy. 1970;28:378.

230 **Ruley EJ et al.** Interstitial nephritis and renal failure due to ampicillin. J Pediatr. 1974;84:878.

231 **Ngeleka M et al.** Endoxotin increases the nephrotoxic potential of gentamicin and vancomycin plus gentamicin. J Infect Dis. 1990;161:721.

232 **Kimberly RP et al.** Elevated urinary prostaglandins and the effects of aspirin on renal function in lupus erythematosus. Ann Intern Med. 1978;89:366.

233 **Kimberly RP et al.** Apparent renal failure associated with therapeutic aspirin and ibuprofen administration. Arthritis Rheum. 1979;22:281.

234 **Muther RS et al.** Aspirin-induced depression of glomerular filtration rate in normal humans: role of sodium balance. Ann Intern Med. 1981;94:317.

235 **Emkey RD, Mills JA.** Aspirin and analgesic nephropathy. JAMA. 1982;247:55.

236 **Akyol SM et al.** Renal function after prolonged consumption of aspirin. Br Med J. 1982;284:631.

237 **Shaw AB, Gopalka SK.** Renal artery thrombosis caused by antihypertensive treatment. Br Med J (Clin Res). 1981;285:1617.

238 **Pazmino P.** Acute renal failure, skin rash and eosinophilia associated with aztreonam. Am J Nephrol. 1989;9:56.

239 **Genkins G et al.** Bacitracin nephropathy. JAMA. 1954;155:894.

240 **Kucers A, McKBennett N.** The Use of Antibiotics. 4th ed. William Heinemann Medical Books. 1987;751.

241 **Cantwell BMJ et al.** Haemorrhagic cystitis after IV bleomycin, vinblastine, cisplatin, and etoposide for testicular cancer. Cancer Treat Rep. 1986;70:548.

242 **Gardner G et al.** Hemolytic uremic syndrome following cisplatin, bleomycin, and vincristine chemotherapy: a report of a case and a review of the literature. Ren Failure. 1989;11:133.

243 **Brodsky A et al.** Stevens-Johnson syndrome, respiratory distress and acute renal failure due to synergic bleomycin-cisplatin toxicity. J Clin Pharmacol. 1989;29:821.

244 **Randall RE et al.** The milk-alkali syndrome. Arch Intern Med. 1971;107:163.

245 **Rifkind BM et al.** Chronic milk-alkali syndrome with generalized osteosclerosis after prolonged excessive intake of ''Rennie's'' tablet. Br Med J. 1960;1:317.

246 **Wenger J et al.** The milk-alkali syndrome. Hypercalcemia, alkalosis, and azotemia following calcium carbonate and milk therapy of peptic ulcer. Gastroenterology. 1957;33:745.

247 **Garfield JW et al.** The auditory vestibular and renal effects of capreomycin in humans. Ann NY Acad Sci. 1966;135:1039.

248 **Yue WY et al.** Toxic nephritis with acute renal insufficiency caused by administration of capreomycin. Dis Chest. 1966;49:549.

249 **Hricik DE et al.** Captopril-induced functional renal insufficiency in patients with bilateral renal-artery stenosis or renal-artery stenosis in a solitary kidney. N Engl J Med. 1983;308:373.

250 **Ahmad T et al.** Reversible renal failure due to the use of captopril in a renal allograft recipient treated with cyclosporin. Nephrol Dial Transplant. 1989;4:133.

251 **van der Woude FJ et al.** Effect of captopril on blood pressure and renal function in patients with transplant renal artery stenosis. Nephron. 1985;39:184.

252 **Feig PU, Rutan GH.** Angiotensin converting enzyme inhibitors: end of end-stage renal disease? Ann Intern Med. 189;111:451.

253 **Fotino S, Sporn P.** Nonoliguric acute renal failure after captopril therapy. Arch Intern Med. 1983;143:1252.

254 **Silas JH et al.** Captopril induced reversible renal failure: a marker of renal artery stenosis affecting a solitary kidney. Br Med J (Clin Res). 1983;286:1702.

255 **Packer M.** Identification of risk factors predisposing to the development of functional renal insufficiency during treatment with converting-enzyme inhibitors in chronic heart failure. Cardiology. 1989;76(Suppl. 1):50.

256 **O'Donnell D.** Renal failure due to enalapril and captopril in bilateral renal artery stenosis: greater awareness needed. Med J Aust. 1988;148:525.

257 **Smith WR et al.** Captopril-associated acute interstitial nephritis. Am J Nephrol. 1989;9:230.

258 **Steinman TI, Silva P.** Acute renal failure, skin rash and eosinophilia associated with captopril therapy. Am J Med. 1983;75:154.

259 **Burke TJ, Schrier RW.** Angiotensin converting enzyme inhibition and acute tubular necrosis. Kidney Int. 1987;31(Suppl):S143.

260 **Sturgill BC, Shearlock KT.** Membranous glomerulopathy and nephrotic syndrome after captopril therapy. JAMA. 1983;250:2343.

261 **Textor SC et al.** Membranous glomerulopathy associated with captopril therapy. Am J Med. 1983;74:705.

262 **Imai et al.** Carbamazepine-induced granulomatous necrotizing angiitis with acute renal failure. Nephron. 1989;51:405.

263 **Hogg RJ et al.** Carbamazepine-induced acute tubulointerstitial nephritis. J Pediatr. 1981;98:830.

264 **Quin JD.** The nephrotoxicity of cephalosporins. Adverse Drug React Acute Poisoning Rev. 1989;8:63.

265 **Pommer W et al.** Acute interstitial nephritis and non-oliguric renal failure after cefaclor treatment. Klin Wochenschr. 1986;64:290.

266 **Kucers A, McKBennett N.** The Use of Antibiotics. 4th ed. William Heinemann Medical Books. 1987;389.

267 **Lentnek AL et al.** Acute tubular necrosis following high-dose cefamandole therapy for Hemophilus parainfluenzae endocarditis. Am J Med Sci. 1981;281:164.

268 **Toll LL et al.** Cefoxitin-induced interstitial nephritis. South Med J. 1987;80:274.

269 **Mocan H.** Beattie TJ. Acute tubular necrosis associated with cephalexin therapy. Clin Nephrol. 1985;24;212.

270 **Lewis JA, Rindone JP.** Acute interstitial nephritis associated with cephapirin. Drug Intell Clin Pharm. 1987;21:380.

271 **Brenner EJ.** Renal damage associated with prolonged administration of ampicillin, cephaloridine and cephalothin. Antimicrob Agents Chemother. 1969;417.

272 **Murple GB et al.** The nephrotoxicity of antimicrobial agents. N Engl J Med. 1977;296:663.

273 **Dubb JW et al.** Effect of cimetidine on renal function in normal man. Clin Pharmacol Ther. 1978;24;76.

274 **Rudnick MR et al.** Cimetidine-induced acute renal failure. Ann Intern Med. 1982;96:180.

275 **Richman AV et al.** Acute interstitial nephritis and acute renal failure associated with cimetidine therapy. Am J. Med. 1981;70:1272.

276 **Kaye WA et al.** Cimetidine-induced interstitial nephritis with response to prednisone therapy. Arch Intern Med. 1983;143:811.

277 **Seidelin R.** Cimetidine and renal failure. Postgrad Med J. 1980;56:440.

278 **Potter Ph, Westby RG.** Interstitial nephritis after cimetidine but not ranitidine. JAMA. 1983;249:351.

279 **Hootkins R et al.** Acute renal failure secondary to oral ciprofloxacin therapy: a presentation of three cases and a review of the literature. Clin Nephrol. 1989;32:75.

280 **Avent CK et al.** Synergistic nephrotoxicity due to ciprofloxacin and cyclosporine. Am J Med. 1988;85:452.

281 **Rippelmeyer DJ, Synhavsky A.** Ciprofloxacin and allergic interstitial nephritis. Ann Intern Med. 1988;109:170.

282 **Sleufer D et al.** The protective potential of the combination of verapamil and cimetidine on cisplatin-induced nephrotoxicity in man. Cancer. 1987;60:2823.

283 **Goldstein RS, Mayor GH.** Minireview: the nephrotoxicity of cisplatin. Life Sci. 1983;32:685.

284 **Hutchison FN et al.** Renal salt wasting in patients treated with cisplatin. Ann Intern Med. 1988;108:21.

285 **Al-sarraf M et al.** Cisplatin hydration with and without mannitol diuresis in refractory disseminated malignant melanoma: a southwest oncology group study. Cancer Treat Rep. 1982;66:31.

286 **Cummins A.** Acute renal failure and interstitial nephritis after clofibrate treatment. Br Med J. 1980;281:1529.

287 **Dosa S et al.** Acute-on-chronic renal failure precipitated by clofibrate. Lancet. 1976;1:250.

288 **Blachley JD, Hill JB.** Renal and electrolyte disturbances associated with cisplatin. Ann Intern Med. 1981;95:628.

289 **Fillastre JP, Raguenez-Viotte G.** Cisplatin nephrotoxicity. Toxicol Lett. 1989;46:163.

290 **Finley RS et al.** Cisplatin nephrotoxicity: a summary of preventative interventions. Drug Intell Clin Pharm. 1985;19:362.

291 **Kucers A, McKBennett N.** The Use of Antibiotics. 4th ed. William Heinemann Medical Books. 1987;899.

292 **Payne FE, Giesecke TF.** Multiple system reaction to trimethoprim-sulfamethoxazole. South Med J. 1987;80:275.

293 **Smith EJ et al.** Interstitial nephritis caused by trimethoprim-sulfamethoxazole in renal transplant recipients. JAMA. 1980;244:360.

294 **Kraemer JM et al.** A generalized allergic reaction with acute interstitial nephritis following trimethoprim-sulfamethoxazole use. Ann Allergy. 1976;49:323.

295 **Berglund F et al.** Effect of trimethoprim-sulfamethoxazole on the renal excretion of creatinine in man. J Urol. 1975;114:802.

296 **Fontanarosa PB.** Radiologic contrast-induced renal failure. Emerg Med Clin North Am. 1988;6:601.

297 **Parfrey PS et al.** Contrast material-induced renal failure in patients with diabetes mellitus, renal insufficiency, or both. N Engl J Med. 1989;320:143.

298 **Vari RC et al.** Induction, prevention and mechanisms of contrast media-induced acute renal failure. Kidney Int. 1988;33:699.

299 **Berkseth RO, Kjellstrand CM.** Radiologic contract-induced nephropathy. Med Clin North Am. 1984;68:351.

300 **DeFronzo RA et al.** Water intoxication in man after cyclophosphamide therapy: time course and relation to drug activation. Ann Intern Med. 1973;78:861.

301 **Bode U et al.** Studies on the antidiuretic effect of cyclophosphamide: vasopressin release and sodium excretion. Med Pediatr Oncol. 1980;8:295.

302 **Harlow PJ et al.** A fatal case of inappropriate ADH secretion induced by cyclophosphamide therapy. Cancer. 1979;44:896.

303 **Relling MV, Schunk JE.** Drug-induced haemorrhagic cystitis. Clin Pharm. 1986;5:590.

304 **Ershler WB et al.** Adriamycin enhancement of cyclophosphamide-induced bladder injury. J Urol. 1980;123:121.

305 **Kahan BD.** Clinical summation. An algorithm for the management of patients with cyclosporine-induced renal dysfunction. Transplant Proc. 1985;17:303.

306 **Mihatsch MJ et al.** Cyclosporin A: action and side-effects. Toxicol Lett. 1989;46:125.

307 **Maiorca R et al.** Cyclosporin and renal injury. In: Amerio A et al., eds. Drugs, Systemic Diseases, and the Kidney. New York: Plenum Press; 1989:273–84.

308 **Smeesters C et al.** Prevention of acute cyclosporine. A nephrotoxicity by a thromboxane synthetase inhibitor. Transplant Proc. 1988;20(Suppl. 2):663.

309 **Luke J et al.** Prevention of cyclosporine-induced nephrotoxicity with transdermal clonidine. Clin Pharm. 1990;9:49.

310 **Chinitz JL et al.** Pathophysiology and prevention of dextran-40 induced anuria. J Lab Clin Med. 1971;77:76.

311 **Feest TG et al.** Low molecular weight dextran: a continuing cause of acute renal failure. Br Med J. 1976;2:1300.

312 **Ter Wee PM et al.** Acute renal failure due to diltiazem. Lancet. 1984;2:1338. Letter.

313 **Shallcross H et al.** Fatal renal and hepatic toxicity after treatment with diltiazem. Br Med J (Clin Res). 1987;295:1236.

314 **Achenbach V et al.** Acute renal failure due to diltiazem. Lancet. 1985;1:176. Letter.

315 **Greenblatt DJ et al.** Clinical toxicity of furosemide in hospitalized patients. Am Heart J. 1977;94:6.

316 **Naranjo et al.** Furosemide-induce adverse reactions during hospitalization. Am J Hosp Pharm. 1978;35:794.

317 **Cremer W et al.** Symptoms and course of chronic hypokalemia nephropathy in man. Clin Nephrol. 1977;8:112.

318 **Fiak MA et al.** Allergic interstitial nephritis with diuretics. Ann Intern Med. 1974;81:403.

319 **Fuller TJ et al.** Diuretic-induced interstitial nephritis. Occurrence in a patient with membranous glomerulonephritis. JAMA. 1976;235:1988.

320 **Bauer JH, Reams GP.** Renal protective effect of long-term antihypertensive therapy with enalapril. Drugs. 1988;35(Suppl. 5):62.

321 **Bailey RR, Lynn KL.** Crescentic glomerulonephritis developing in a patient taking enalapril. NZ Med J. 1986;99:958. Letter.

322 **Rosenfield J et al.** Interstitial nephritis with acute renal failure after erythromycin. Br Med J (Clin Res). 1983;286:938.

323 **Collier J et al.** Two cases of ethambutol nephrotoxicity. Br Med J. 1976;2:1105.

324 **Stone WJ et al.** Acute diffuse interstitial nephritis related to chemotherapy of tuberculosis. Antimicrob Agents Chemother. 1976;10:164.

325 **Deray G et al.** Foscarnet-induced acute renal failure and effectiveness of haemodialysis. Lancet. 1987;2:216.

326 **Nyberg G et al.** Foscarnet-induced tubulointerstitial nephritis in renal transplant patients. Transplant Proc. 1990;22:241.

327 **Cacoub P et al.** Acute renal failure induced by foscarnet: 4 cases. Clin Nephrol. 1988;29:315.

328 **Eisenberg JM et al.** What is the cost of nephrotoxicity associated with aminoglycosides? Ann Intern Med. 1987;107:900.

329 **Bennett WM.** Mechanisms of aminoglycoside nephrotoxicity. Clin Exp Pharmacol Physiol. 1989;16:1.

330 **Luft FC.** Clinical significance of renal changes engendered by aminoglyco-

sides in man. J Antimicrob Chemother. 1984;13(Suppl A):37.

331 **Kucers A, McKBennett N.** The Use of Antibiotics. 4th ed. William Heinemann Medical Books. 1987;619.

332 **Plaza JJ et al.** Membranous glomerulonephritis as a complication of oral gold therapy. Ann Intern Med. 1982;97:563.

333 **Blum M et al.** Nephrotic syndrome with reversible severe renal failure after gold therapy. Int J Clin Pharmacol Ther Toxicol. 1984;22:562.

334 **Robbins G et al.** Acute renal failure due to gold. Postgrad Med J. 1980;56:366.

335 **Hall CL.** The natural course of gold and penicillamine nephropathy: a long-term study of 54 patients. Adv Exp Med Biol. 1989;252:247.

336 **Graham JR et al.** Fibrotic disorders associated with methysergide therapy for headache. N Engl J Med. 1966;274:359.

337 **Shapiro KS et al.** Immune complex glomerulonephritis in hydralazine-induced systemic lupus erythematosus. Am J Kidney Dis. 1984;3:270.

338 **Ihle BU et al.** Hydralazine and lupus nephritis. Clin Nephrol. 1984;22:230.

339 **Whelton A et al.** Renal effects of ibuprofen, piroxicam, sulindac in patients with asymptomatic renal failure. Ann Intern Med. 1990;112:568.

340 **Marasco WA et al.** Ibuprofen-associated renal dysfunction: pathophysiologic mechanisms of acute renal failure, hyperkalemia, tubular necrosis, and proteinuria. Arch Intern Med. 1987;18:27.

341 **Poirier T.** Reversible renal failure associated with ibuprofen: case report and review of the literature. Drug Intell Clin Pharm. 1984;18:27.

342 **Willemse PHB et al.** Severe renal failure following high-dose ifosfamide and mesna. Cancer Chemother Pharmacol. 1989;23:329.

343 **Schilsky RL.** Renal and metabolic toxicities of cancer chemotherapy. Semin Oncol. 1982;9:75.

344 **Goren MP et al.** Potentiation of ifosfamide neurotoxicity, hematotoxicity and tubular toxicity by prior cis-diamminedichloroplatinum (II) therapy. Cancer Res. 1987;47:1457.

345 **Jorkasky DK et al.** Lithium-induced renal disease: a prospective study. Clin Nephrol. 1988;30:293.

346 **Moskovitz R et al.** Lithium-induced nephrotic syndrome. Am J Psychiatry. 1981;138:382.

347 **Kalina KM, Burnett GB.** Lithium and the nephrotic syndrome. J Clin Psychopharmacol. 1984;4:148.

348 **Appel GB.** A decade of penicillin related acute interstitial nephritis—more questions than answers. Clin Nephrol. 1980;13:151.

349 **Platia EV, Whelton PK.** Severe methicillin-induced renal failure treated with haemodialysis. John Hopkins Med J. 1978;142:152.

350 **Godin M et al.** Agranulocytosis, haemorrhagic cystitis and acute interstitial nephritis during methicillin therapy. J Antimicrob Chemother. 1980;6:296.

351 **Linton AL et al.** Acute interstitial nephritis due to drugs. Review of the literature with report of nine cases. Ann Intern Med. 1980;93:735.

352 **Kucers A, McKBennett N.** The Use of Antibiotics. 4th ed. William Heinemann Medical Books. 1987;90.

353 **Bracis R et al.** Methicillin haemorrhagic cystitis. Antimicrob Agents Chemother. 1977;70:1132.

354 **Pitman SW et al.** Clinical trial of high-dose methotrexate (NSC-740) and citrovorum factor (NSC-3590)—toxicologic and therapeutic observations. Cancer Chemother Rep. 1975;6:43.

355 **Stecker JF et al.** Retroperitoneal fibrosis and ergot derivatives. J Urol. 1974;112:30.

356 **Hamner RW et al.** Mitomycin-associated renal failure. Arch Intern Med. 1983;143:803.

357 **Gulati SC et al.** Microangiopathic hemolytic anemia observed after treatment of epidermoid carcinoma with mitomycin C and 5-fluorouracil. Cancer. 1980;45:2252.

358 **Price TM et al.** Renal failure with hemolytic anemia associated with mitomycin C. Cancer. 1985;55:51.

359 **Kancair LM et al.** Comparison of methicillin and nafcillin in the treatment of staphylococcal endocarditis. Clin Res. 1976;24:25.

360 **Tillman DB et al.** Oxacillin nephritis. Arch Intern Med. 1980;140:1552.

361 **Grimm PC et al.** Interstitial nephritis induced by cloxacillin. Nephron. 1989;51:285.

362 **Oriscello RG et al.** Neomycin wound irrigation: report of a case associated with massive absorption with nephro- and neurotoxicity. Am J Ther Clin Rep. 1975;1:11.

363 **Berk DP et al.** Deafness complicating antibiotic therapy of hepatic encephalopathy. Ann Intern Med. 1970;73:393.

364 **Masur H et al.** Neomycin toxicity revisited. Arch Surg. 1976;11:822.

365 **Gregg NJ et al.** Epidemiology and mechanistic basis of analgesic-associated nephropathy. Toxicol Lett. 1989;46:141.

366 **Brezin JH et al.** Reversible renal failure and nephrotic syndrome associated with nonsteroidal anti-inflammatory drugs. N Engl J Med. 1979;301:1271.

367 **Stillman MT, Schlesinger PA.** Nonsteroidal anti-inflammatory drug nephrotoxicity. Should we be concerned? Arch Intern Med. 1990;150:268.

368 **Clive DM et al.** Renal syndromes associated with nonsteroidal anti-inflammatory drugs. N Engl J Med. 1984;310:563.

369 **Peterson I et al.** Water intoxication associated with non-steroidal anti-inflammatory drug therapy. Acta Med Scand. 1987;221:221.

370 **Schwartz J et al.** Acute renal failure associated with diclofenac treatment in an elderly woman. J Am Geriatr Soc. 1988;36:482. Letter.

371 **Thomsen BS et al.** Acute renal failure possibly associated with fenoprofen therapy. Arthritis Rheum. 1983;26:234.

372 **Curt GA et al.** Reversible rapidly progressive renal failure and nephrotic syndrome due to fenoprofen calcium. Ann Intern Med. 1980;92:72.

373 **Dunn MJ, Zambraski EJ.** Renal effect of drugs that inhibit prostaglandin synthesis. Kidney Int. 1980;18:609.

374 **Blackshear JL et al.** Identification of risk for renal insufficiency from non-

steroidal anti-inflammatory drugs. Arch Intern Med. 1983;143:1130.

375 **Wenland ML.** Renal failure associated with fenoprofen. Mayo Clin Proc. 1980;55:103.

376 **Cahen R et al.** Fenoprofen-induced membranous glomerulonephritis. Nephrol Dial Transplant. 1988;3:705. Letter.

377 **Husserl FE et al.** Renal papillary necrosis and pyelonephritis accompanying fenoprofen therapy. JAMA. 1979; 242:1896.

378 **Koren JF et al.** Indomethacin-induced acute renal failure: report of a case and review of the literature. Drug Intell Clin Pharm. 1980;14:711.

379 **Mitchell H et al.** Indomethacin-induced renal papillary necrosis in juvenile chronic arthritis. Lancet. 1982;2: 558.

380 **Chan XM.** Fatal renal failure due to indomethacin. Lancet. 1987;2:340. Letter

381 **Delaney VB, Segal DP.** Indomethacin-induced renal insufficiency: recurrence on rechallenge. South Med J. 1985;78: 1390.

382 **Katz SM et al.** Tolmetin: association with reversible renal failure and acute interstitial nephritis. JAMA. 1981;37: 243.

383 **Chatterjee GP.** Nephrotic syndrome induced by tolmetin. JAMA. 1981;246: 1589.

384 **Vitting KE et al.** Naproxen and acute renal failure in a runner. Ann Intern Med. 1986;105:144. Letter.

385 **Frais MA et al.** Piroxicam-induced renal failure and hyperkalemia. Ann Intern Med. 1983;999:129.

386 **Mitnick PD, Klein WJ.** Piroxicam-induced renal disease. Arch Intern Med. 1984;144:62.

387 **Bunning RD, Werner FB.** Sulindac: a potential renal-sparing nonsteroidal anti-inflammatory drug. JAMA. 1982; 34:361.

388 **Sedor JR et al.** Effects of sulindac and indomethacin on renal prostaglandin synthesis. Clin Pharmacol Ther. 1984; 36:85.

389 **Ciabattoni G et al.** Effects of sulindac and ibuprofen in patients with chronic glomerular disease. Evidence for the dependence of renal function on prostacyclin. N Engl J Med. 1984;310:279–83.

390 **Delin K et al.** Multiple arterial occlusions and hypertension probably caused by an oral contraceptive: a patient in whom the development of renovascular hypertension has been followed. Clin Nephrol. 1976;6:453.

391 **Schoolwerth AC et al.** Nephrosclerosis postpartum in women taking oral contraceptives. Arch Intern Med. 1976; 136:178.

392 **Zachele BJ et al.** Irreversible renal failure secondary to hypertension induced by oral contraceptives. Ann Intern Med. 1972;77:83.

393 **Golbus SM et al.** Renal artery thrombosis in a young woman taking oral contraceptives. Ann Intern Med. 1979; 90:939.

394 **Bailey RR, Reddy J.** Penicillamine-induced acute renal failure. NZ Med J. 1981;93;24. Letter.

395 **Banfi G et al.** Extracapillary glomerulonephritis with necrotizing vasculitis in D-penicillamine-treated rheumatoid arthritis. Nephron. 1983;33:56.

396 **Kirby JD et al.** D-penicillamine and immune complex deposition. Ann Rheum Dis. 1979;38:344.

397 **Colvin RB et al.** Penicillin-induced interstitial nephritis. Ann Intern Med. 1974;81:404.

398 **Appel GB, Neu HC.** The nephrotoxicity of antimicrobial agents. N Engl J Med. 1977;296;663.

399 **Western KA et al.** Pentamidine isethionate in the treatment of pneumocystis carinii pneumonia. Ann Intern Med. 1970;73;695.

400 **Miller RF et al.** Acute renal failure after nebulized pentamidine. Lancet. 1989;1:1271.

401 **Lachaal M.** Venuto RC. Nephrotoxicity and hyperkalemia in patients with acquired immunodeficiency syndrome treated with pentamidine. Am J Med. 1989;87:260.

402 **Chapelon C et al.** Renal insufficiency with nebulized pentamidine. Lancet. 1989;2:1045.

403 **Yermakov VM et al.** Necrotizing vasculitis associated with diphenylhydantoin: 2 fatal cases Pathol. 1983;14:182.

404 **Hoffman EW.** Phenytoin-induced interstitial nephritis. South Med J. 1981; 74:1160.

405 **Agarwal BN et al.** Diphenylhydantoin-induced acute renal failure. Nephron. 1977;18:249.

406 **Davis CE et al.** Rifampin-induced acute renal failure. South Med J. 1986; 79;1012.

407 **Qunibi WU et al.** Toxic nephrotoxicity during continuous rifampin therapy. South Med J. 1980;73:791.

408 **Katz MD, Lor E.** Acute interstitial nephritis associated with intermittent rifampin use. Drug Intell Clin Pharm. 1986;20:789.

409 **Cochran M et al.** Permanent renal damage with rifampin. Lancet. 1975;1: 1428.

410 **Gabow PA et al.** Tubulointerstitial and glomerular nephritis associated with rifampin. JAMA. 1976;235:2317.

411 **Pick RA et al.** Acute renal failure following repeated streptokinase therapy for pulmonary embolism. West J Med. 1983;138:878.

412 **Murray N et al.** Crescentic glomerulonephritis: a possible complication of streptokinase treatment for myocardial infarction. Br Heart J. 1986;56:483.

413 **Ransohoff D, Jacobs G.** Terminal hepatic failure following a small dose of sulfamethoxazole-trimethoprim. Gastroenterology. 1981:80:816.

414 **Dorfman LF et al.** Sulfonamide crystalluria: a forgotten disease. J Urol. 1970;104:482.

415 **Kucers A, McKBennett N.** The Use of Antibiotics. 4th ed. William Heinemann Medical Books. 1987;979.

416 **Sica DA, Gehr TW.** Triamterene and the kidney. Nephron. 1989;51:454.

417 **Kucers A, McKBennett N.** The Use of Antibiotics. 4th ed. William Heinemann Medical Books. 1987;1045.

418 **Jeffery WH, Lafferty WE.** Acute renal failure after acetaminophen overdose: report of two cases. Am J Hosp Pharm. 1981;38:1355.

419 **Kher K, Makker S.** Acute renal failure due to acetaminophen ingestion without concurrent hepatotoxicity. Am J Med. 1987;82:1280. Letter.

Chapter 30

Chronic Renal Failure

Arasb Ateshkadi

Curtis A Johnson

Definitions 30-2
Epidemiology of End-Stage Renal Disease (ESRD) 30-2
   Incidence and prevalence 30-2
   Etiologies (See Table 30.1) 30-2
   Treatment methods 30-2
   Patient survival (See Table 30.2) 30-2
Pathogenesis 30-2
Evaluation of Renal Function 30-3
Preventing Progression of Chronic Renal
   Failure (CRF) 30-3
   Antihypertensives 30-3
   Dietary protein restriction 30-3
   Treatment of dyslipoproteinemia 30-3

Clinical Assessment 30-4
  Uremic Toxins 30-4
  Analgesic Nephropathy 30-4
   Management 30-5
  Lithium Nephropathy 30-5
  Sodium and Water Retention 30-5
  Potassium Imbalance 30-5
   Hyperkalemia 30-5
    Causes 30-5
    Treatment 30-6
     Calcium 30-6
     Bicarbonate 30-6
     Glucose plus insulin 30-6
     Cation exchange resins 30-6
     Dialysis 30-6
   Hypokalemia 30-6
  Metabolic Acidosis 30-7
  Other Electrolyte and Metabolic Disturbances 30-7
   Hypermagnesemia 30-7
   Hyperphosphatemia 30-7
   Hyperuricemia 30-7
  Anemia 30-7
   Characteristics and etiology 30-7
    Reduced erythrocyte production 30-7
    Inhibitors of erythropoiesis 30-7
    Reduced red blood cell (RBC) life span 30-7
    Blood loss 30-7
    Iron deficiency 30-7
    Folic acid deficiency 30-8
    Pyridoxine (vitamin B$_6$) deficiency 30-8
    Aluminum intoxication 30-8
   Treatment 30-8
    Erythropoietin therapy 30-8
    Androgens 30-8
  Hemostatic Defects 30-8
  Immune Suppression as a Result of Uremia 30-9
   Cell-mediated immunity 30-9
  Pericarditis 30-9
  Hypertension 30-10
   Diuretic therapy 30-10
   Additional therapy 30-12
  Hyperlipidemia 30-12
  Calcium and Phosphate Abnormalities 30-12
   Clinical presentation 30-12

   Treatment 30-12
    Dietary restriction 30-13
    Aluminum-containing antacids (See Table 30.5) .. 30-13
    Calcium carbonate 30-13
    Calcium acetate 30-13
    Calcium citrate 30-13
    Oral magnesium 30-13
    Sucralfate 30-14
    Vitamin D 30-14
     Oral versus intravenous calcitriol 30-14
    Parathyroidectomy 30-14
    Treatment of severe hypocalcemia 30-14
  Altered Glucose Metabolism 30-15
   Nondiabetic patients 30-15
   Diabetic patients 30-15
  Endocrine Abnormalities Caused by Uremia 30-15
  Gastrointestinal (GI) Complications 30-15
   Bleeding 30-15
    Treatment 30-15
   Treatment of peptic ulcer disease (PUD) 30-15
    Aluminum-containing antacids 30-16
     Aluminum toxicity 30-16
    Magnesium-containing antacids 30-16
    Calcium-containing antacids 30-16
  Neurological Complications 30-16
  Dermatological Complications 30-17
  Leg Cramps 30-17
  Nutritional Requirements 30-17

Diabetic Nephropathy 30-18
  Staging (See Table 30.6) 30-18
  Management 30-18
   Glycemic control 30-18
   Antihypertensive therapy 30-19
   Dietary protein restriction 30-20

Chronic Glomerulopathies 30-20
  Lupus Nephritis 30-20
   Staging (See Table 30.7) 30-20
   Treatment 30-20
    Oral corticosteroids 30-21
    Intravenous corticosteroids 30-21
    Oral cytotoxic agents 30-21
    Intravenous cytotoxic agents 30-21
    Cyclosporine 30-22
   Cyclosporine nephropathy 30-22
  Primary Systemic Amyloidosis 30-22
   Treatment 30-22
    Melphalan 30-22
    Colchicine 30-23
  Goodpasture's Disease (Antiglomerular Basement
   Membrane Antibody-Mediated Nephritis) 30-23
   Treatment 30-24
    Plasma exchange 30-24
    Pulse methylprednisolone 30-24
    Oral cyclophosphamide plus corticosteroids 30-24

(Continued)

Wegener's Granulomatosis 30-25
    Treatment 30-25
        Oral cyclophosphamide 30-25

Intravenous cyclophosphamide 30-25
    Corticosteroids 30-25
    Azathioprine 30-26

Renal failure remains a major cause of morbidity and mortality. In the U.S. during 1991, approximately 215,000 patients were treated for end-stage renal disease under the Medicare program.[1] While improved dialysis and transplant techniques have increased patient survival, mortality rates remain high due to complications and other diseases associated with renal failure.

Definitions

Chronic renal failure (CRF) usually is a progressive disease. Certain terminologies are used to describe different stages of renal dysfunction. *Renal reserve* is the difference between normal and the maximally achievable glomerular filtration rate (GFR).[2] If needed, the GFR can increase by up to 70% above baseline; however, once the glomerular filtration rate falls below 40 mL/minute, renal reserve becomes virtually negligible.[2] *Renal insufficiency* occurs when there is a mild reduction in glomerular filtration rate in the absence of overt signs and symptoms. *Azotemia* is a laboratory diagnosis in which nitrogenous wastes, such as blood urea nitrogen (BUN) and creatinine, accumulate as a result of a declining glomerular filtration rate.[3] Once renal function has been extensively diminished for a prolonged period and the prospect of recovery seems unlikely, the patient is said to have *chronic renal failure*.[4] As chronic renal failure progresses, patients usually develop *uremia*, defined as symptomatic renal failure.[5] Uremic signs and symptoms are due to accumulation of nitrogenous wastes and other toxins, which lead to a myriad of complications affecting most major organ systems (discussed later). When dialysis becomes necessary to sustain life, patients have *end-stage renal disease* (ESRD).

The decline in renal function may be either abrupt and often reversible, as in acute renal failure; or progressive, leading to end-stage disease. This chapter will examine the causes, clinical course, and therapeutic management of chronic renal failure. Acute renal failure is discussed in the preceding chapter.

Epidemiology of End-Stage Renal Disease (ESRD)

Incidence and Prevalence. Over the past decade, the number of treated end-stage renal disease patients of all age groups has increased, especially in the 65- to 74-year-old age group.[1] In 1991, over 215,000 U.S. residents received some form of end-stage renal disease treatment under the U.S. Medicare program. On December 31, 1991, the point prevalence for the Medicare End-Stage Renal Disease program was 721/million.[1] More than 92% of end-stage renal disease patients in the U.S. are enrolled in the Medicare End-Stage Renal Disease program. The ethnic breakdown of the end-stage renal disease population on Medicare is as follows: 66% white; 31% black; 2% Asian/Pacific Islanders; 1% Native American.[1] Black and Native Americans have a nearly fourfold greater rate of renal failure than whites.

In 1991, the per capita expenditure for the treatment of end-stage renal disease was $46,900, for a total of $8.59 billion from public and private sources.[1] This figure is an underestimation of the total as the cost for outpatient drugs, lost wages and salaries, lost productivity, costs associated with the Department of Veterans Administration, and Social Security payments were excluded.

Etiologies. Progressive renal insufficiency may be associated with many diseases and also occurs as a part of the normal aging process.[6] End-stage renal disease may be caused by a primary renal disease, secondarily due to a systemic disease, or by acute, irreversible damage to the kidneys. In the past, hypertensive nephrosclerosis has accounted for the majority of end-stage renal disease cases. However, diabetes mellitus now has become the most common cause of end-stage renal disease in the U.S., accounting for one-third of the cases (see Table 30.1).[1] Among Native Americans, diabetes accounts for nearly two-thirds of the end-stage renal disease cases. Hypertension still is the most common cause of end-stage renal disease among blacks, accounting for 40% of cases.[1]

While the etiologies of chronic renal failure are quite variable, the clinical and biochemical manifestations of end-stage renal disease tend to be similar.

Treatment Methods. As recently as the 1950s, end-stage renal disease was uniformly fatal. The advent of dialysis therapy and renal transplantation has dramatically reduced end-stage renal disease-related morbidity and mortality. The three major treatment modalities for chronic renal failure are renal transplantation, hemodialysis, and peritoneal dialysis. Of the end-stage renal disease patients enrolled in Medicare in 1990, 60% received in-center hemodialysis, 28% had a functioning renal transplant, and 20% were maintained on continuous ambulatory (CAPD), or continuous cycling peritoneal dialysis (CCPD).[1]

Patient Survival. The mortality rate in the end-stage renal disease population is substantially higher than the general population, and comparable to certain severe diseases. For example, a 59-year-old male with end-stage renal disease has a life expectancy comparable to a similar patient with colorectal cancer, but lower than a patient with prostate cancer.[1] The projected life expectancy of dialysis patients is one-fourth to one-sixth that for the general population through age 50; and one-third for the older age groups.

Cardiac diseases, including myocardial infarction, account for the majority of deaths in the end-stage renal disease population, followed by septicemia, and withdrawal from dialysis (see Table 30.2). Among the dialysis population, the incidence of myocardial infarction and other cardiac events is higher than the total end-stage renal disease population.[1]

Pathogenesis

The extent of renal insufficiency may be of minor significance or life-threatening. In most cases, chronic renal failure progresses until virtually no function remains. While early changes in renal function can be detected chemically, most patients remain symptom-free until function is less than 25% of normal.[7] As renal disease progresses, the patient may develop nonspecific complaints of malaise but will continue to perform daily activities quite well. However, when renal function is reduced to approximately 10%

Table 30.1	Main Causes of End-Stage Renal Disease[a]
Cause	% of ESRD Cases[b]
Diabetes	33.8
Hypertension	28.3
Glomerulonephritis	12.6
Cystic kidney disease	3.0
Interstitial nephritis	3.0
Others	19.3

[a] Data from U.S. Renal Data System 1994 Annual Data Reports.[1]
[b] ESRD = End-stage renal disease.

Table 30.2	Main Causes of Death in End-Stage Renal Disease[a,b]
Cause of Death	Per 1000 Patient Years
Cardiac disease other than pericarditis or MI	45.1
MI	19.1
Septicemia	14.8
Withdrawal from dialysis	19.5
Other	13.7
Unknown causes	11.0

[a] MI = Myocardial infarction.
[b] Data from U.S. Renal Data System 1994 Annual Data Reports.

of normal, the patient usually will develop symptoms of uremia. Appropriate medical management often will alleviate uremic symptoms until renal function is about 5% of normal, at which time dialysis or transplantation is required to sustain life.

Evaluation of Renal Function

Progression of renal failure can be assessed by the standard laboratory measurements of BUN and serum creatinine (SrCr). A more direct evaluation of the glomerular filtration rate is the measurement of the clearance of creatinine by the kidneys. Creatinine is an endogenous substance derived from the breakdown of muscle creatine phosphate. Its rate of production is constant and primarily determined by muscle mass. Because in normally functioning kidneys creatinine is excreted primarily by glomerular filtration, creatinine serves as a useful marker for renal glomerular function. However, as nephron function declines, tubular secretion of creatinine increases to the extent that a substantial portion of creatinine found in the urine is not due to glomerular filtration.[8] As a result, in patients with chronic renal failure, creatinine clearance (Cl_{Cr}) values often yield a gross underestimation of the actual progression of renal failure.[9] While a creatinine clearance measurement is used to follow the progression of renal failure, it also is essential to the proper dosing of drugs eliminated by the kidney.[10] (See Chapter 29: Acute Renal Failure for a more extensive discussion of the assessment of renal function.)

Preventing Progression of Chronic Renal Failure (CRF)

The progression of chronic renal disease occurs over months to years; however, the rate of decline of renal function tends to remain constant for individual patients. Factors that augment the progression of chronic renal failure of any cause include hypertension, a high-protein diet, and dyslipoproteinemias of renal failure. As such, intense efforts have been focused on amelioration of these factors.

Antiplatelet and anticoagulant drugs may be useful in treating progressive glomerular diseases;[11] however, this point of view has been contested.[12]

Antihypertensives. An increase in the single-nephron glomerular filtration rate is one of the many adaptive processes that develop in response to renal injury and to a decline in the population of functional glomeruli.[13] While this adaptive mechanism has been considered beneficial to maintaining homeostasis, evidence suggests that the increased perfusion of residual nephrons may have deleterious effects on the remaining nephrons, hastening their destruction.[14] Because of its association with increased single-nephron glomerular filtration rate, untreated systemic hypertension is a potent stimulus for the progression of renal disease.

Aggressive treatment of hypertension with virtually any agent, or combination of agents, is perhaps the single most important modality for slowing the rate of progression of chronic renal failure.[15-17] In addition, treatment of hypertension seems to be a major factor in reducing the risk of cardiovascular mortality in such patients.[17] Although treatment with any commonly used antihypertensive agent can reduce the progression of renal failure, preliminary data indicate that the angiotensin-converting enzyme (ACE) inhibitors, such as enalapril (Vasotec), lisinopril (Zestril), and captopril (Capoten), and the calcium channel blockers, except nifedipine, may be more effective.[18] However, long-term studies are needed to determine the superiority of one drug class over others.

Although the extent to which blood pressure must be lowered has not been defined in patients with renal impairment, the normally accepted goal of 140/90 mm Hg may not be ideal for all patients.[15] In these circumstances, the goal of treatment must be the return of blood pressure to baseline values. If this value is not attainable, efforts must be made to reduce blood pressure to 120 to 130/80 to 85 mm Hg.[15,19]

Dietary Protein Restriction. Dietary protein ingestion also has been linked to a rise in single-nephron glomerular filtration rate.[20] In a few small studies, restriction of dietary protein and phosphorous delayed the progression of chronic renal failure, although the effects of such dietary modifications may be selective, depending upon patient variables.[21-23] The Modification of Diet in Renal Disease (MDRD) study, a randomized, multi-center trial, failed to show, in patients whose glomerular filtration rates were not above 55 mL/minute/1.73 m^2, an overall beneficial effect of a low protein, low phosphate diet on the rate of progression of renal disease; however, the result may have been due to a faster initial (0 to 4 months) decline in renal function, followed by a slower subsequent decline (4 months to end).

The addition of keto acid-amino acid supplements to restricted diets also has arrested the rise in serum creatinine concentrations.[24,25]

Treatment of Dyslipoproteinemia. In a majority of patients with renal disease, lipoprotein metabolism is altered early in the course of renal disease and becomes pronounced with chronic renal failure. Up to 70% of patients with chronic renal failure have an elevated serum triglyceride concentration, although the plasma total cholesterol concentration tends to remain within the normal range. The characteristic lipid metabolism alteration in chronic renal failure patients involves the apolipoproteins rather than the lipids. This dyslipoproteinemia may serve as a risk factor for the development of cardiovascular morbidity and mortality.[26,27] The dyslipoproteinemia of renal insufficiency has been implicated in the progression of chronic renal failure;[17,28,29] however, lipoproteins appear to cause renal damage only in the presence of previous renal disease or other risk factors such as hypertension.[26,30] Although serum total cholesterol, triglycerides, and apolipoprotein B all correlate with the rate of decline in glomerular filtration rate,[31] it is not clear which is the pathogenic entity.

Unfortunately, the treatment of dyslipoproteinemia does not appear to retard the progression of chronic renal failure. However, abnormal lipid metabolism can predispose chronic renal failure patients to cardiovascular disease. Drug therapy, therefore, should be considered, especially in those with pre-existing hyperlipidemia. The choice of antihyperlipidemic drug should be based upon the patient's lipid profile. Given the characteristic lipid abnormalities of chronic renal failure, fibric-acid derivatives, such as clofibrate and gemfibrozil may be first-line agents.[32,33] The dosage of these agents must be appropriately reduced to prevent serious adverse effects, such as myositis.[34] (Also see Chapter 9: Dyslipidemias.)

Clinical Assessment

Uremic Toxins

The constellation of symptoms that develop with advanced renal dysfunction is known as the uremic syndrome. The manifestations of this syndrome will be discussed individually; however, their collective pathogenesis has been attributed in part to the accumulation of uremic toxins. The search for these uremic toxins has led to the identification of nitrogenous compounds in the serum and has given rise to the "uremic toxin" theory of uremia. Unfortunately, a cause and effect relationship between these compounds and the clinical manifestations of uremia has not been clearly established.

The analysis of uremic serum has identified several small molecular weight substances such as urea, creatinine, water, and metal ions. Other small and middle molecular weight substances that have been identified include guanidines, purine and pyridine derivatives, aliphatic and aromatic amines, indoles, and phenols.[35] Investigation of these compounds has failed to produce an etiologic explanation for the entire uremic syndrome.[5,36]

Parathyroid hormone (PTH) may play an important role as a uremic toxin. As will be discussed in Question 19, a major hormonal imbalance present in uremia is the elevated blood concentration of PTH. PTH may have adverse effects on many organ systems and may act as a catabolic agent, thus enhancing uremic toxicity.[37]

End-stage renal disease and the resulting uremic syndrome have multiple metabolic effects on the patient; these are outlined in Table 30.3 and discussed later in this chapter.

1. S.B., a 47-year-old female, has a 1-week history of nausea, vomiting, and general malaise. She has a 10-year history of lower back pain, for which she has been taking regularly a compound analgesic preparation containing 500 mg each of aspirin and acetaminophen, plus 50 mg caffeine. In addition, for the past 8 years she has been receiving lithium carbonate 300 mg TID for maintenance therapy of bipolar disorder. S.B. has been treated for peptic ulcer disease (PUD) for the past 6 months. A work-up by her local physician revealed the following

pertinent laboratory values: serum sodium (Na) 143 mEq/L (Normal: 135–144), potassium (K) 5.8 mEq/L (Normal: 3.6–4.8), chloride (Cl) 106 mEq/L (Normal: 99–108), CO_2 content 18 mEq/L (Normal: 24–33). Her SrCr was 6.0 mg/dL (Normal: 0.6–1.3) and her BUN was 75 mg/dL (Normal: 7–20). S.B. was referred to University Hospital for further evaluation. The admission physical examination revealed a blood pressure (BP) of 155/102 mm Hg, mild pulmonary congestion, and 2+ pedal edema. Additional laboratory studies showed a serum phosphate of 7.6 mg/dL (Normal: 2.6–4.4), calcium (Ca) 8.8 mg/dL (Normal: 8.8–10.4), magnesium (Mg) 2.8 mEq/L (Normal: 1.7–2.3), and uric acid 9.8 mg/dL (Normal: 2.4–6.8). Hematologic studies revealed a hematocrit (Hct) of 26% (Normal: 35–45 for females), a hemoglobin (Hgb) of 7.8 gm/dL (Normal: 11.8–15.4 for females), and a white blood cell (WBC) count of 9600/mm^3 (Normal: 3.5–10.0). Red blood cell (RBC) indices were normal. Platelet count was 175,000/mm^3 (Normal: 140–380). S.B.'s reticulocyte count was 2.0% (Normal: 0.5–2.0). Her urinalysis (UA) showed a 4+ proteinuria. What subjective and objective data in S.B. are consistent with a diagnosis of advanced renal failure? [SI units: Na 143 mmol/L (Normal: 135–144); K 5.8 mmol/L (Normal: 3.6–4.8); Cl 106 mmol/L (Normal: 99–108); CO_2 18 mmol/L (Normal: 24–33); SrCr 530.4 μmol/L (Normal: 53–114.9); BUN 26.8 mmol/L of urea (Normal: 2.5–7.1); phosphate 2.45 mmol/L (Normal: 0.84–1.42); Ca 2.2 mmol/L (Normal: 2.2–2.6); Mg 1.4 mmol/L (Normal: 0.85–1.15); uric acid 583 μmol/L (Normal: 143–404); Hct 0.26 (Normal: 0.35–0.45 for females); Hgb 78 gm/L (Normal: 118–154 for females); WBC count 9600 × 10^6/L (Normal: 3500–10,000); platelet count 175 × 10^9/L (Normal: 140–380); reticulocyte count 0.02 (Normal: 0.005–0.02)]

S.B.'s abnormal values for serum creatinine; BUN; serum potassium, magnesium, phosphate, uric acid, and CO_2 content; hemoglobin; and hematocrit are all consistent with renal failure. As the glomerular filtration rate declines, creatinine, BUN, and uric acid accumulate in the systemic circulation. As renal dysfunction reaches advanced levels, excretion of hydrogen ions, sodium, potassium, magnesium, and phosphate is severely diminished. The volume overload, due to diminished sodium and water excretion, leads to weight gain, hypertension, congestive pulmonary disease, and edema.

Metabolic acidosis results from the accumulation of hydrogen ions, while the anemia associated with chronic renal failure primarily is due to a lack of erythropoietin production by the kidneys.[38]

Analgesic Nephropathy

2. What is the cause of S.B.'s advanced renal failure?

From S.B.'s history, it appears her renal failure may be due to the compound analgesic preparation she has been using for the past ten years. Her long history of compound analgesic use, advanced renal failure, and proteinuria are all consistent with such a diagnosis.

Analgesic nephropathy is a form of tubulo-interstitial renal disease characterized by renal papillary necrosis as a primary lesion and chronic interstitial nephritis as a secondary lesion.[39] Analgesic nephropathy is part of the *analgesic syndrome*, including such non-renal complications as anemia, peptic ulcer disease, urinary tract infection, atherosclerosis, and, in 8% to 10% of the cases, uroepithelial carcinoma.[40,41] Phenacetin, an acetaminophen prodrug, was the first agent to be incriminated. Currently in the U.S., the majority of cases are caused by long-term use or misuse of compound analgesics containing acetaminophen and aspirin, usually in combination with caffeine or codeine.[42] Similar renal findings also have been observed with nonsteroidal anti-inflammatory drugs (e.g., mefenamic acid).[43–45] The cumulative amount (at least 1 to 2 kg of acetaminophen), rather than the duration of analgesic intake, is the primary risk factor for developing chronic analgesic nephropathy.[39]

Table 30.3	Metabolic Effects of Uremia
Fluid, Electrolyte, and Acid-Base Effects	**Gastrointestinal (GI)**
Fluid retention	Anorexia
Hyperkalemia	Nausea, vomiting
Hypermagnesemia	Delayed gastric emptying
Hyperphosphatemia	GI bleeding
Hypocalcemia	Ulcers
Metabolic acidosis	
	Neurological
Hematological	Lethargy
Anemia	Depressed sensorium
Hemostatic abnormalities	Tremor
Immune suppression	Asterixis
	Muscular irritability and cramps
	Seizures
Cardiovascular	Motor weakness
Hypertension	Peripheral neuropathy
Congestive heart failure	Coma
Pericarditis	
Atherosclerosis	**Dermatological**
	Altered pigmentation
	Pruritus
Endocrine	
Calcium-phosphorous imbalances	**Psychological**
Hyperparathyroidism	Depression
Metabolic bone disease	Anxiety
Altered thyroid function	Psychosis
Altered carbohydrate metabolism	
Hypophyseal-gonadal dysfunction	**Miscellaneous**
	Reduced exercise tolerance

As illustrated in S.B., analgesic nephropathy is more prevalent in females, with a female-to-male ratio of 5 to 7.1:1. The peak incidence occurs between the fourth and the fifth decade of life.[39,42] Patients usually complain of chronic pain syndromes and in over 90% of cases, psychiatric manifestations indicative of an addictive behavior are observed.[39] Upon presentation, 80% of patients have reduced glomerular filtration rate, with 14% presenting with chronic renal failure.[39] During acute necrosis, patients may suffer from flank pain, pyuria, and hematuria. As necrosis progresses, cellular debris may cause ureteral obstruction.[46] Renal dysfunction is characterized as a salt-wasting nephropathy, with a substantial reduction in urine concentrating and acidifying capabilities. The exact mechanism for renal damage is not clear. Since acetaminophen accumulates in the renal medulla, its oxidative metabolite produced by the medullary cytochrome P450 enzyme system may bind to macromolecules causing cellular necrosis. While the reduced form of glutathione in the medulla can prevent this process, agents that reduce medullary glutathione content (e.g., aspirin) may promote renal damage.[42] This mechanism may explain a lack of analgesic nephropathy associated with acetaminophen alone. Nonsteroidal anti-inflammatory drugs (NSAIDs), which attenuate prostaglandin-mediated vasodilation, may induce an ischemic state within the renal medulla, leading to papillary necrosis.[39,42]

Management

The long-term management of analgesic nephropathy primarily involves a strict abstinence from NSAIDs and combination analgesics. If possible, patients should be encouraged to maintain a high fluid intake to prevent obstruction of the tubules with necrotic debris and reduce the risk of urinary tract infection. Once patients reach end-stage renal disease, management is similar to those with renal diseases due to other causes. However, patients with analgesic nephropathy who are treated with dialysis or renal transplantation experience a higher rate of mortality compared to the rest of the end-stage renal disease population.[39]

Lithium Nephropathy

3. The following day, S.B.'s serum lithium concentration was 0.9 mEq/L (Normal: 0.7–1.2) on the same maintenance dose. A review of her medical chart revealed that her serum lithium concentrations have been mostly in the therapeutic range. Could S.B.'s CRF have been caused by chronic lithium therapy? [SI unit: lithium 0.9 mmol/L (Normal: 0.7–1.2)]

While lithium use has been associated with acute functional and histological changes in virtually all patients receiving the drug,[47] its role in the development of chronic changes (i.e., chronic interstitial nephritis) is less clear. Both renal concentrating ability and the glomerular filtration rate may decline with long-term lithium use.[48] In addition, chronic interstitial changes may develop in the kidneys of patients receiving lithium.[49] Despite these findings, however, others have failed to implicate lithium as a chronic nephrotoxic agent.[50] Nephrotoxic risk may be associated with high serum lithium concentrations.[51] Since in the past S.B.'s serum lithium concentrations have been maintained in the therapeutic range, it is unlikely that her chronic renal failure is due to long-term lithium therapy. Nonetheless, close monitoring of her serum lithium concentrations is advised. In patients undergoing chronic lithium therapy, serum creatinine measurements should be obtained annually to detect changes in renal function.[39]

Sodium and Water Retention

4. Assess S.B.'s sodium and water balance. Can serum sodium concentrations be used in the assessment of total body sodium? How should this problem be treated?

As illustrated by S.B., patients with chronic renal failure commonly retain sodium and water. This is consistent with her high blood pressure, 2+ pedal edema, and mild pulmonary congestion. Sodium and water retention also lead to weight gain. Early in the course of chronic renal failure, various glomerular and tubular adaptive processes develop, enabling patients to maintain a relatively normal sodium and water homeostasis.[52] Eventually, however, patients with advanced renal dysfunction exhibit signs of sodium and fluid retention.[53] As a result, most patients with end-stage renal disease will be placed on sodium and fluid restriction, approximately 90 mEq and 2000 mL/day, respectively. These restrictions may be altered according to the special needs of the patient. Since some patients with end-stage renal disease produce normal amounts of urine while others may produce none, fluid restrictions must be based upon the patient's urine output. Diuretic therapy, usually with loop diuretics, often is required as well. As S.B.'s normal serum sodium concentration indicates, this value is of little use in establishing the diagnosis of total body sodium and fluid excess because retention of sodium and water usually occurs in an isotonic fashion, leaving the serum sodium concentration relatively normal.[53]

Potassium Imbalance

Hyperkalemia

5. Causes. S.B. has a serum K concentration of 5.8 mEq/L. Describe the mechanisms by which potassium imbalance occurs in patients like S.B. with CRF. [SI unit: K 5.8 mmol/L]

Hyperkalemia may result from a combination of factors including diminished renal potassium excretion, redistribution of potassium into the extracellular fluid due to metabolic acidosis, and excessive potassium intake.[54] In S.B., all these mechanisms are likely to be contributing to the hyperkalemia.

Potassium normally is filtered at the glomerulus and undergoes nearly complete reabsorption throughout the renal tubule. The potassium excreted in the urine is chiefly the result of distal tubular secretion. A variety of factors affect this distal secretion of potassium including aldosterone, sodium load presented to the distal reabsorptive site, hydrogen ion secretion, the amount of nonreabsorbable anions, urinary flow-rate, diuretics, and potassium intake.[55]

Serum potassium concentrations are relatively well-maintained within normal limits in patients with chronic renal failure. With a glomerular filtration rate greater than 10 mL/minute, hyperkalemia is rare without an endogenous or exogenous load of potassium. This balance is maintained despite a decreasing nephron population and an overall drop in glomerular filtration, because the remaining nephron population undergoes adaptive changes to enhance the distal tubular secretion of potassium per nephron.[56] Increased gastrointestinal (GI) secretion and fecal losses may account for up to 50% of the daily potassium losses in patients with severe renal insufficiency.[57] S.B.'s creatinine clearance is approximately 13 mL/minute; however, given that creatinine clearance values often yield a gross overestimation of the glomerular filtration rate,[9] S.B.'s glomerular filtration rate is likely to be less than 10 mL/minute.

Episodic hyperkalemia can develop under several conditions. Excess potassium loads may result from exogenous sources such as salt substitutes, foods with high potassium content, or potassium-containing drugs, such as potassium penicillin. Endogenous sources of potassium include cellular destruction, as for example in the hemolysis of RBCs, rhabdomyolysis, and catabolic states. There is no indication of hemolysis or cellular destruction in S.B.

Metabolic or respiratory acidosis may cause a redistribution of intracellular potassium to the extracellular space. For each 0.1 unit change in blood pH, there is an average corresponding opposite change of approximately 0.6 mEq/L in the serum potassium concentration.[57]

S.B. is not taking any drugs that may contribute to hyperkalemia. However, potassium-sparing diuretics such as spironolactone (Aldactone), triamterene (Dyrenium), and amiloride (Midamor) should be avoided in the presence of renal failure since they decrease tubular secretion of potassium, and their use may cause dangerous hyperkalemia. Some diabetic patients with only mild degrees of renal failure may develop hyperkalemia from these diuretics as a result of low plasma renin activity and subsequently lowered aldosterone concentrations.[57] Angiotensin-converting enzyme inhibitors also may cause hyperkalemia in patients with renal insufficiency because they reduce aldosterone production.[58]

6. Treatment. Is treatment of S.B.'s potassium indicated? How should severe hyperkalemia be managed?

Treatment of hyperkalemia depends upon the serum concentration of potassium as well as the presence or absence of symptoms and electrocardiographic (ECG) changes. Manifestations of hyperkalemia include weakness, confusion, and muscular or respiratory paralysis. However, these symptoms may be absent, especially if hyperkalemia develops rapidly. Early ECG changes include peaked T waves, followed by a decreased R wave amplitude, widened QRS complex, and a prolonged PR interval. These changes may progress to complete heart block with absent P waves and finally, a sine wave. Ventricular arrhythmias or cardiac arrest may ensue if no effort to lower serum potassium is initiated. Hyperkalemic ECG changes are uncommon at potassium concentrations of less than 7 mEq/L but occur regularly at concentrations above 8 mEq/L.

Since S.B. has a mild potassium elevation of 5.8 mEq/L, no specific treatment is required. Generally, treatment is unnecessary if potassium concentration is less than 6.5 mEq/L and there are no ECG changes. If potassium concentrations rise above 6.5 mEq/L, especially with neuromuscular symptoms or changes in the ECG, treatment should be instituted.

Treatment of hyperkalemia consists of three modalities. The first is calcium administration to counteract the cardiac effects of excess potassium. Second, alkali therapy or glucose and insulin administration lowers serum potassium by shifting the ion from extracellular to intracellular fluid compartments. Third, exchange resins or dialysis are used to remove potassium from the body.

Calcium. In hyperkalemia-induced arrhythmias, myocardial resting membrane potential is reduced by administering 1 gm IV calcium gluconate (4.8 mEq) over one to three minutes under continuous electrocardiographic monitoring. Rhythm abnormalities usually reverse immediately. The dose of calcium gluconate may be repeated in approximately five minutes. Intravenous calcium should be used cautiously in patients receiving digitalis because of transient high plasma concentrations of calcium.[59] Calcium will have no effect on the serum potassium concentration, but will protect the myocardium until a reduction of the potassium concentration can be achieved.

Bicarbonate. An additional emergency treatment is the intravenous administration of sodium bicarbonate to encourage the movement of extracellular potassium ions back into cells, thus lowering the extracellular fluid concentration of potassium. However, the total body potassium load remains unchanged. The effect of bicarbonate on potassium concentrations may occur even in the absence of a change in blood pH. Usually, 45 mEq of sodium bicarbonate is infused intravenously over a few minutes; the effects are observed within 30 to 60 minutes. Additional doses should be administered every 10 to 15 minutes as needed. There are two po-

tential concerns regarding sodium bicarbonate administration. This drug may present some risk to patients with circulating volume overload, congestive heart failure (CHF), or pulmonary edema. By physical examination, S.B. has evidence of mild fluid retention. Therefore, sodium bicarbonate should be used cautiously should the need arise. Secondly, rapid alkalinization of the blood with bicarbonate infusions may precipitate tetany by lowering ionized serum calcium concentrations.[60]

Glucose plus Insulin. The intravenous administration of regular insulin and glucose is a second method used to shift extracellular potassium ions back into cells. Insulin stimulates potassium uptake by skeletal muscle and hepatic cells. Intravenous glucose is given concurrently to avoid the hypoglycemic effects of insulin. The usual IV dose is five to ten units of regular insulin accompanied by 25 to 50 gm glucose. Some clinicians prefer a continuous intravenous infusion of insulin in a dextrose-containing solution. The potassium-lowering effects of an IV bolus dose should be apparent within 30 minutes.

Cation Exchange Resins. Since the use of calcium, sodium bicarbonate, or insulin/glucose has no effect on reducing total body potassium, potassium stores should be reduced with the cation exchange resin, sodium polystyrene sulfonate, or dialysis. However, since these latter methods are relatively slow, previously-described emergency measures may have to be employed first.

Sodium polystyrene sulfonate (Kayexalate) exchanges sodium for potassium in the intestinal tract, primarily the colon.[61] To offset its constipating effect, the resin is mixed with sorbitol and may be given orally or, with the addition of 100 mL tap water, as a retention enema. The usual oral dose is 15 to 30 gm; the rectal dose is 30 to 60 gm. For maximal effectiveness, the enema should be retained for at least 30 minutes. Dosing should be repeated as needed. Monitoring the drug's effect will require a repeat serum potassium measurement one to two hours after dosing.

On a chronic basis, S.B. may receive oral sodium polystyrene sulfonate at a dose of 15 to 30 gm up to three to four times daily. The drug is available as a premixed suspension in sorbitol with water. The onset of action following oral administration ranges from 2 to 12 hours, somewhat longer than when given rectally. Oral administration may be preferred by some patients despite some nausea. Since this resin exchanges sodium for potassium, consideration must be given to patients with heart failure or elevated blood pressure. Although oral administration often is considered unpalatable, the drug should not be mixed with citrus juices or solutions containing high concentrations of potassium as this will render the resin ineffective.

Dialysis. Hemodialysis and, to a lesser extent, peritoneal dialysis also are effective means of lowering serum potassium; however, the results take several hours, making these methods relatively slow. Thus, they should not be used as primary treatment in emergency situations.

Hypokalemia

Hypokalemia can occur in chronic renal failure patients due to inadequate dietary intake or excessive gastrointestinal losses. These losses may result from anorexia, nausea, vomiting, and diarrhea that may occur in the uremic patient. Protracted vomiting may lead to hypokalemia through induction of a hypochloremic alkalosis and volume contraction with secondary hyperaldosteronism.[55] Other causes of hypokalemia include excessive diuretic therapy, glucocorticoid therapy, Cushing's syndrome, licorice abuse, laxative abuse, and renal tubular acidosis.[55,57] (Also see Chapters 28: Fluid and Electrolyte Disorders and 15: Congestive Heart Failure.)

Metabolic Acidosis

7. Assess S.B.'s acid base status. How should she be managed?

S.B.'s blood CO_2 content and high chloride concentration are consistent with the metabolic acidosis of chronic renal failure. Normal metabolism of ingested food adds 50 to 100 mEq of acid to the body each day. This acid must be excreted by the kidneys (primarily as ammonium ion) to maintain acid-base balance. In advanced renal failure, acid retention and possibly, renal bicarbonate wasting occur. Over time, bone carbonate stores no longer are able to serve as a source of alkali, and plasma bicarbonate concentrations stabilize below the normal range.[62] Severe acidosis usually is avoided because of compensatory hyperventilation inducing a fall in pCO_2. The stable end-stage renal disease patient often will have a mildly reduced serum bicarbonate concentration, a reduced arterial pCO_2, and a slightly reduced arterial pH.[52] No treatment of S.B.'s mild acidosis is required. However, if the acidosis becomes severe, oral or intravenous sodium bicarbonate may be required. If the patient is sodium overloaded, the administration of sodium bicarbonate may exacerbate this problem and dialysis may be required to correct extreme acidemia. Serum potassium concentrations also may rise as a result of severe acidosis necessitating the treatment of hyperkalemia. While not present in S.B., hyperchloremia occurs frequently in association with the acidosis of chronic renal failure.[63] The clinical importance of this observation is unknown.

Other Electrolyte and Metabolic Disturbances

8. What other electrolyte and metabolic disturbances consistent with CRF are exhibited by S.B.?

Hypermagnesemia. The mild degree of hypermagnesemia seen in S.B. is a common finding in chronic renal failure due to the kidney's impaired ability to excrete this ion. Serum magnesium concentrations below 5 mEq/L are rarely symptomatic. Higher concentrations may lead to nausea, vomiting, lethargy, confusion, and diminished tendon reflexes. Severe hypermagnesemia may depress cardiac conduction, requiring hemodialysis with a magnesium-free dialysate.[64] The risk of hypermagnesemia can be reduced by avoiding magnesium-containing antacids and laxatives.[65] Since peptic diseases and constipation occur frequently in patients with renal failure, the risks of using magnesium-containing over-the-counter products must be emphasized. (See Question 25.)

Hyperphosphatemia. S.B.'s decreased urinary excretion of phosphate has produced hyperphosphatemia, a disorder discussed in Question 19. Patients should be encouraged to reduce dietary phosphorous to the extent possible and to avoid the use of phosphorous-containing laxatives and enemas. Although not present in S.B., hyperphosphatemia may be associated with low serum calcium concentrations.

Hyperuricemia. S.B. also has mild hyperuricemia. Asymptomatic hyperuricemia frequently develops in renal failure due to diminished urinary excretion of uric acid. In the absence of a history of gout or urate nephropathy, asymptomatic hyperuricemia does not require treatment. (See Chapter 40: Gout and Hyperuricemia.)

Trace element abnormalities also have been observed in uremic patients; however, the clinical significance of these findings remains unclear.[66]

Anemia

Characteristics and Etiology

9. What are the characteristics and etiology of the anemia seen in S.B.?

As a result of her renal disease, S.B. has developed anemia. The RBC indices indicate her cells are of normal size, but the reticulocyte count suggests an impaired bone marrow response to the low hematocrit.

The anemia of chronic renal disease has been studied and reviewed extensively.[38,67–69] Patients with chronic renal failure inevitably develop anemia, and the occurrence of pallor and fatigue are the earliest clinical signs. The anemia worsens progressively as renal function declines.

The anemia of chronic renal failure usually will stabilize at a hematocrit of approximately 15% to 30% in the absence of other associated anemias. The anemia is characteristically normochromic and normocytic unless a concomitant iron or folate deficiency exists. Severe anemia may be an important contributor to the morbidity of chronic renal failure.[70]

Reduced Erythrocyte Production. Several factors contribute to the anemia of chronic renal failure. Reduced erythrocyte production appears to be the most significant etiologic factor. Due to progressive renal damage, the production of erythropoietin, an endocrine product of the kidney, is diminished.[38] As a result, reticulocyte formation in the marrow is reduced and anemia occurs. However, given that anephric patients can respond, though inefficiently, to hemorrhage or hypoxia with a reticulocytosis demonstrates that total hormonal control of erythropoiesis may not lie solely within the kidney.

Inhibitors of erythropoiesis also may exist in the plasma of patients with chronic renal failure. These substances may inhibit the production of erythropoietin, the bone marrow response to erythropoietin, and/or the synthesis of heme. Proposed constituents of uremic plasma that may suppress RBC production include parathyroid hormone, spermine, and low molecular weight polypeptides.[69] The existence of these substances is supported by the observation that dialyzed patients who have no increase in blood erythropoietin concentrations display improvement in erythropoiesis, although this notion has been challenged.[71]

Reduced Red Blood Cell (RBC) Life Span. The RBC life span is reduced to 30% to 60% of normal in chronic renal failure patients. The hemolysis is generally mild and is due to the abnormal chemical environment of uremia. The nature of the hemolytic factors in uremic plasma is unknown, although parathyroid hormone has been suggested as a factor.[72] Hemolysis is not uniformly reversed with dialysis. Other causes contributing to or aggravating the hemolysis are malignant hypertension, hypersplenism, and dialysis fluid that has been contaminated with copper, nitrates, or chloramine.[68] In addition, technical complications of hemodialysis can lead to acute hemolysis.[70] Yawata et al.[73] found that 50% of patients have a uremic plasma factor that inhibits the RBC hexose monophosphate shunt's ability to generate NADPH (reduced nicotinamide adenine dinucleotide phosphate), thereby reducing the RBC's ability to handle oxidative stress. Hence, cell survival is reduced.

Blood loss may be a contributing factor to the anemia of chronic renal disease.[70] Because of the impaired hemostasis of uremia, GI tract and intradermal bleeding are frequent. (See Question 12 for a further discussion of hemostatic defects.) S.B. has a peptic ulcer that can contribute to her anemia. Although a stool guaiac test was not performed in S.B., many uremic patients will have a positive guaiac reaction. In addition, hemodialysis patients may have a small obligate blood loss related to the techniques and complications inherent in dialysis. Hemodialysis patients usually are given heparin during dialysis and occasionally receive warfarin (Coumadin) or antiplatelet drugs to prevent vascular access clotting.

Iron deficiency may develop secondary to chronic blood loss and erythropoietin administration (see Question 10). While iron deficiency usually is not the primary cause of anemia in end-stage renal disease, its possible presence should be identified and treated. The diagnosis of iron deficiency anemia can be made by laboratory parameters. (Also see Chapter 88: Anemias.)

Folic acid deficiency as evidenced by low serum folate concentrations and macrocytosis is relatively uncommon in renal failure. One study noted subnormal serum folate in only 10% of chronic renal failure patients who were not on dialysis, and none had a megaloblastic anemia.[74] Folate deficiency occurs most frequently in dialyzed patients since folic acid is removed by dialysis. Therefore, the daily prophylactic administration of the water soluble vitamins, including 1 mg of folic acid is recommended. Routine use of the fat soluble vitamin A is discouraged, since hypervitaminosis A may develop and contribute to anemia.[75] Several multivitamin preparations devoid of vitamin A are available for renal failure patients (e.g., Nephrocaps).

Pyridoxine (vitamin B$_6$) deficiency may occur in both dialyzed and nondialyzed chronic renal failure patients. There are marked similarities between this deficiency and the symptoms of uremia, which include skin hyperpigmentation and peripheral neuropathy. Current multivitamin products for renal failure patients contain adequate amounts of pyridoxine to prevent deficiency.

Aluminum Intoxication. Another cause of anemia in chronic renal failure is aluminum intoxication.[76] In this type of anemia, the RBCs are typically microcytic. The major source of aluminum in patients with renal failure is gastrointestinal absorption of aluminum-containing antacids.

Treatment

10. How should S.B.'s anemia be treated?

Treatment of the anemia of chronic renal failure includes a variety of approaches. Initially, it is important to identify and correct any iron or folate deficiency. S.B.'s baseline serum folate concentration and iron indices should be determined (see below). Based upon S.B.'s history of peptic ulcer disease, both iron and folic acid replacement may be necessary. As a prophylactic measure, oral folic acid 1 mg/day may be given. If S.B. is iron-deficient, parenteral iron therapy will be required to replenish her iron stores before correcting her anemia. If she is not currently iron-deficient or iron-overloaded, oral ferrous sulfate 300 mg two or three times/day will be required to prevent iron deficiency during her anemia treatment. (See Chapter 88: Anemias.)

Although dialysis does not fully correct the anemia, regular dialysis may improve erythrokinetics. The effect of dialysis on erythropoiesis rarely restores the hematocrit to normal. Peritoneal dialysis causes a greater improvement in hematocrit than hemodialysis.[77] Recombinant human erythropoietin is now available, representing a major advance in the treatment of anemia and chronic renal failure (see Question 20).

Blood transfusions are avoided, if possible, in patients with chronic renal failure because there is a risk of viral diseases [hepatitis, human immunodeficiency virus (HIV)], iron overload, and further suppression of erythropoiesis. However, transfusions may be required in certain patients to restore oxygen carrying capacity and alleviate the symptoms of anemia. Evidence indicates that blood transfusions given to dialysis patients can increase graft survival following renal transplantation.[78]

Erythropoietin Therapy. The availability of recombinant human erythropoietin (Epogen) offers a major therapy for anemia associated with chronic renal failure, and has nearly eliminated the need for RBC transfusions. The production of recombinant human erythropoietin was made possible by the identification of the human erythropoietin gene. This gene was introduced into a mammalian host organism, a cell line of Chinese hamster ovary cells that express the recombinant erythropoietin.

Erythropoietin stimulates the proliferation and differentiation of erythroid progenitors, increases hemoglobin synthesis by red cell progenitors, and accelerates the release of reticulocytes from the bone marrow. These effects improve erythropoiesis in predialysis patients as well as those treated with dialysis.

Patients whose hematocrit value is less than 30%, such as S.B., are the best candidates for erythropoietin therapy. However, before initiating erythropoietin therapy, S.B.'s baseline iron indices should be determined. This is done by measuring the serum iron concentration, total iron-binding capacity, transferrin saturation, and serum ferritin concentrations. If S.B. is iron deficient, supplemental iron therapy should be given before or at the time of starting erythropoietin. The goal of iron supplementation is to achieve a percent transferrin saturation of greater than 20% and a serum ferritin concentration of greater than 100 ng/mL. Once her iron status is addressed, S.B. should be treated with erythropoietin (epoetin alfa), at the initial dose of 25 to 100 U/kg, intravenously or subcutaneously, three times weekly. For a given dose of erythropoietin, the subcutaneous route is more effective than the intravenous route of administration, perhaps due to a more sustained and physiologic plasma concentration-time profile as compared to intravenous administration.[77,79] Improved hematopoiesis and reticulocytosis occur over several weeks, at a dose-dependent rate. S.B.'s hematocrit should increase by 1.5% to 3.5% every two weeks, with the desired hematocrit goal of 33% to 36%. Upon reaching that goal, the dose of erythropoietin should be adjusted to maintain the target hematocrit. Maintenance dosing should be individualized for each patient. If improved erythropoiesis is not seen after eight weeks, S.B. should be evaluated for possible causes of nonresponse. These may include iron deficiency, aluminum intoxication, or underlying inflammatory processes or infection.[80] If no explanation can be found, the dose of erythropoietin should be adjusted upward.

For patients receiving erythropoietin chronically, certain monitoring guidelines are appropriate. S.B.'s hematocrit and iron status should be evaluated frequently. As hemoglobin synthesis increases, many patients will become iron deficient. With decreasing iron stores, supplemental iron therapy with oral or parenteral iron should be started. S.B.'s blood pressure also needs to be monitored carefully since approximately 25% to 30% of dialysis patients receiving erythropoietin experience an increase in blood pressure.[81] Antihypertensive therapy may be required. Other adverse effects attributed to erythropoietin therapy include a flu-like syndrome and headache. There have been no reports of allergic reactions or the development of antibodies to recombinant human erythropoietin. (Also see Chapter 88: Anemias.)

11. Androgens. Should S.B. receive androgens for the treatment of her anemia of CRF?

Androgens can increase erythropoiesis by directly or indirectly raising erythropoietin concentrations, thereby increasing red blood cell production. Various clinical trials have been conducted using a number of androgenic compounds at different dosages. However, because of a lack of consistent erythropoietic response and the frequency of adverse effects, the routine use of androgens has disappeared. Now that recombinant erythropoietin is available for clinical use, S.B. need not be considered for androgen therapy.

Hemostatic Defects

12. What factors are present in association with S.B.'s renal failure that could alter hemostasis?

Uremia frequently is complicated by excessive bleeding as evidenced by ecchymosis, purpura, low-grade GI bleeding, epistaxis, and less commonly, profuse gastrointestinal hemorrhage. Estimates of moderate to severe hemorrhage vary from 12% to 63% of patients.[82] As noted previously, blood loss may occur during hemodialysis or as a result of repeated venipuncture. More frequently, however, bleeding results from altered hemostasis secondary to renal failure. A prolonged bleeding time and increased capillary fragility have been observed in uremic patients. The underlying factors responsible for this bleeding diathesis include abnormalities in plasma coagulation factors, platelets, and vessel wall function.[83] The observed abnormalities in coagulation factors include increased amounts of fibrinogen and factor VIII, as well as impaired fibrinolysis. Qualitative platelet defects result from a deficiency in platelet factor III, reduced thromboxane synthesis, and diminished concentrations of von Willebrand factor. Defects in capillary wall function have not been studied extensively; however, prostacyclin production is increased in the vessels of uremic animals and patients. The specific factors responsible for these hemostatic defects are unknown although urea, phenols, guanidino-succinic acid, and parathyroid hormone have been implicated.[83]

Adequate dialysis and the avoidance of antiplatelet drugs[84-86] (see Table 30.4) usually reduce the risk of bleeding. Bleeding which cannot be corrected with dialysis may require other therapeutic intervention.[87] Successful hemostasis has occurred following administration of cryoprecipitate,[88] l-deamino-8-D-arginine vasopressin (DDAVP),[89,90] and conjugated estrogens.[91]

In conclusion, while S.B. has a normal platelet count, her platelets likely will function abnormally for the reasons described. S.B.'s prothrombin time and activated partial thromboplastin time are likely to be normal; however, her bleeding time measurements may be prolonged. Agents with antiplatelet activity should be avoided.

Immune Suppression as a Result of Uremia

13. Why does S.B.'s hematologic status enhance her susceptibility to infection?

Patients with chronic renal failure manifest a number of immune function abnormalities, some of which are unaffected or even worsened by hemodialysis. These relative abnormalities are part of a multifactorial process that renders the host relatively immunodeficient and predisposed to infections and neoplasms. Patients with chronic renal failure are at an increased risk of infection due to a variety of predisposing factors including malnutrition, immunosuppressive drugs, decreased immune function, and invasion of the skin for the purpose of placing dialysis catheters and performing hemodialysis. Infection is a major cause of morbidity, while ranking second as the most frequent cause of mortality in patients on hemodialysis.[92] *Staphylococcus aureus* is the most frequently isolated pathogen, usually causing infection at the vascular access site, with or without associated bacteremia.[93]

Most uremic patients have normal (as exhibited by S.B.) or modestly elevated neutrophil counts.[94-96] One plausible mechanism for the mild neutrophilia is redistribution of granulocytes among the many pools, with an increase in the freely circulating fraction.[97] Previous studies of neutrophil function in patients with chronic

renal failure have yielded inconsistent results; nonetheless, these patients may have dysfunctional neutrophils.

Transient and profound neutropenia occurs in patients within 30 minutes of initiation of hemodialysis,[98] primarily due to sequestration of neutrophils in the pulmonary capillary bed.[99] Within one to two hours of initiating hemodialysis, rebound neutrophilia occurs as a result of return to circulation and bone marrow release of neutrophils. The degree to which hemodialysis-induced neutropenia occurs depends upon the dialyzer membrane type. The cellulose membranes (cupra-ammonium cellulose, regenerated cellulose, cellulose acetate) cause the most profound neutropenia, while the noncellulose membranes (polycarbonate, polysulfone, polymethyl methacrylate, polyacrylonitrile) have the least potential for causing complement activation and subsequent neutropenia.[99] The practice of reusing dialyzer membranes reduces the severity of neutropenia.[100]

Neutrophils that remain in circulation during hemodialysis-induced neutropenia have functional defects, including diminished oxidative metabolism,[101,102] and abnormal chemotactic response.[103,104] Chronically, hemodialysis patients have consistent neutrophil defects, including decreased chemotaxis,[104,105] phagocytosis,[106] and *in vitro* killing of bacteria.[107]

The effect of peritoneal dialysis on the quantity and the quality of neutrophils is less clear. However, patients' neutrophils may have diminished chemotactic activity and radical oxygen production required for killing of fungi and bacteria.[99] These defects may have adverse clinical consequence, as a lack of intracellular killing is associated with recurrent dialysis-induced peritonitis.[108]

The mechanisms by which neutrophils from dialyzed and undialyzed chronic renal failure patients are rendered dysfunctional are complex and multifactorial. These factors include iron deficiency or iron overload,[109-111] protein-calorie malnutrition,[112] hyperparathyroidism,[113] and the presence in the uremic serum of a specific granulocyte inhibitory protein.[114]

Cell-Mediated Immunity

T_4 lymphocytes, natural killer cells, monocytes, and macrophages constitute the cell-mediated arm of the immune system. The number of total and individual subsets of lymphocytes is decreased in uremic patients.[115,116] In addition, uremia can diminish T-cell function.[117] These abnormalities may not be corrected completely with maintenance hemodialysis. Patients with chronic renal failure suffer from defects in their cell-mediated immunity as evidenced by their high incidence of tuberculosis.[117,118] Through its effect on the natural killer cells and antibody-dependent cellular cytotoxicity, chronic renal failure can reduce the effectiveness of host immune surveillance against neoplasms and microbial invasion.[118] Hemodialysis can have a similar inhibitory effect, independent of the uremic milieu.[119,120] These abnormalities may explain the increased nonselective neoplasms in hemodialysis patients.[121,122]

The daily administration of pyridoxine and zinc has restored immune competence in preliminary studies.[123,124] Additional studies are needed to confirm these observations and establish dosing requirements. H_2-receptor antagonists may have an adverse effect on T-lymphocyte function in patients with end-stage renal disease; however, others have failed to confirm this observation.[125]

Pericarditis

14. F.L., a 52-year-old male with chronic glomerulonephritis, has been receiving outpatient hemodialysis 3 times/week for 6 years. During one of his scheduled dialysis sessions, he complains of fever and the sudden onset of sharp pains in his chest. His pertinent medical history includes a history of hypertension for 8 years and a 2-year history of short-

Table 30.4	Drugs with Antiplatelet Activity
Aspirin	Indomethacin (and other NSAIDs)[a]
Carbenicillin	Penicillin G
Clofibrate	Phenylbutazone
Dextran	Prostacyclin
Dipyridamole	Sulfinpyrazone
Hydroxychloroquine	

[a] NSAIDs = Nonsteroidal anti-inflammatory drugs.

ness of breath and chest discomfort with exercise. F.L.'s current medications include metoprolol 50 mg BID, hydralazine 50 mg QID, sublingual nitroglycerin 0.4 mg PRN, aluminum hydroxide 500 mg QID, and a multivitamin with folic acid QD. Upon physical examination, F.L.'s BP (predialysis) was 165/98 mm Hg with no orthostatic change and his temperature was 37.4 °C (oral). Funduscopic examination showed grade II hypertensive changes, and chest examination revealed a pericardial friction rub. There was no evidence of cardiac tamponade. Pleural effusions were present bilaterally, but no pulmonary congestion was noted. F.L. had 1+ pedal edema. A chest x-ray revealed an enlarged cardiac silhouette, and an ECG showed ST segment elevation. The presence of a pericardial effusion was established by echocardiography. Predialysis laboratory values were as follows: normal serum electrolytes, BUN 138 mg/dL, creatinine 12.8 mg/dL, phosphate 5.2 mg/dL, Ca 8.6 mg/dL, albumin 3.2 gm/dL, cholesterol (nonfasting) 345 mg/dL, triglycerides (TG) 285 mg/dL (Normal: <190), Hct 21%, and WBC count 12,800/mm^3 with a normal differential count. Daily urine output was 100 mL. What is the most likely explanation for F.L.'s new chest pain and fever? What therapy should be employed?

Pericarditis (i.e., sterile inflammation of the pericardium) may develop in patients with renal failure. *Uremic pericarditis* occurs in previously undialyzed patients, or it may occur in patients on maintenance dialysis, in which case it is termed *dialysis-associated pericarditis*.[126] This complication may progress to a subacute or chronic phase with progressive fibrosis of the pericardium. Factors contributing to the development of pericarditis probably are multiple and include severe uremia, trauma, malnutrition, and preceding infection.[126] The complications of pericarditis include hypotension, dysrhythmias, and cardiac tamponade.

Medical management of this inflammatory process includes initiating dialysis in previously undialyzed patients or more vigorous dialysis in those already on maintenance dialysis support. This may be all that is required. While there are few clinical trials to support their use, anti-inflammatory drugs frequently are prescribed to reduce pain. Indomethacin (Indocin) (up to 200 mg/day) has been used most frequently; however, it may be no more effective than placebo.[127] The NSAIDs have antiplatelet activity, and their use may increase the risk of systemic bleeding and pericardial hemorrhage. In unresponsive patients who are uninfected, systemic corticosteroids may be of value. Fever and pain usually subside in a few days although the friction rub may persist much longer. Patients who fail to respond to medical management or who develop cardiovascular instability may require surgical treatment of the pericarditis.[128]

Hypertension

Diuretic Therapy

15. How should F.L.'s hypertension be managed? Should a diuretic be added to his therapy?

Hypertension commonly occurs with chronic renal failure and its prevalence may be influenced by the nature of the underlying renal disorder.[129] Hypertension often is the result of salt and water retention leading to volume expansion. An atrial natriuretic peptide helps to maintain volume homeostasis and blood pressure control in patients with renal failure.[130] In a minority of patients, the hypertension of chronic renal failure is mediated through diminished renal perfusion and stimulation of the renin-angiotensin-aldosterone system. Careful clinical examination and therapeutic intervention will help clarify the mechanism of hypertension in individual patients. Since successful control of blood pressure may preserve remaining renal function and improve long-term survival, F.L.'s hypertension should be treated. Diuretic therapy often is recommended because sodium and water retention are so prevalent.

Early in the course of renal failure, thiazides or thiazide-like diuretics are effective antihypertensive agents. Their pharmacologic effects result from the initial natriuresis they invoke as well as from a more sustained reduction in peripheral vascular resistance.[131] As the glomerular filtration rate is further reduced (Cl_{Cr} <30 mL/minute), the loop diuretics should be used.[132] These drugs can be effective as antihypertensives and diuretics even in advanced renal disease;[133] however, it often is necessary to give very large doses (>400 mg/day of furosemide) to achieve the desired effect. In refractory patients, the addition of a thiazide or metolazone to the loop diuretic may induce diuresis.[134] However, if diuresis is excessive, renal perfusion can be reduced; thereby, further compromising glomerular function.

16. What is the relative potency of the available diuretics? Which class of diuretics would most likely be effective for F.L.?

It is possible to predict the relative potency of diuretics and the electrolyte imbalances which are likely to result based upon the knowledge of where a diuretic exerts its major effects along the kidney tubule (see Figure 30.1). With the exception of carbonic anhydrase inhibitors, the more proximal the site of diuretic action, the more potent the diuretic effect because more sodium and water are reabsorbed at the proximal than at the distal end of the renal tubule.

All of the sodium present in the blood is filtered at the glomerulus ($\approx$25,000 mEq/24 hours) and all but a very small amount (i.e., <1%) is reabsorbed throughout the length of the renal tubule. About 60% to 70% of the filtered sodium load is reabsorbed in the proximal tubule under normal conditions. At this site, water and chloride are passively and isotonically reabsorbed along an osmotic gradient created by active sodium reabsorption. If the glomerular filtration rate is markedly reduced, the fractional sodium and water reabsorbed within the proximal tubule is increased. Thus, poor renal perfusion can lead to sodium retention. Of the currently available diuretics, only carbonic anhydrase inhibitors inhibit sodium and water reabsorption within the proximal tubule where the majority of the filtered sodium is reabsorbed. However, diuresis caused by carbonic anhydrase inhibitors is modest and self-limiting because sodium delivered out of the proximal tubule can be reabsorbed at distal sites, particularly at the loop of Henle; and the diuretic action is diminished by the formation of metabolic acidosis caused by the increased bicarbonaturia.

The remaining 30% to 40% of the sodium within the renal tubule that has not been reabsorbed arrives at the loop of Henle. In the ascending limb of the loop of Henle, about 20% to 25% of the filtered sodium load is reabsorbed. Sodium and chloride are passively reabsorbed in the thin segment of the ascending loop. In the thick portion of this segment (also called the ''cortical diluting segment'' or ''distal portion of the ascending loop''), chloride is actively reabsorbed and sodium passively follows the electrochemical gradient that has been created by the reabsorption of chloride. The loop diuretics inhibit sodium reabsorption in the proximal portion of the ascending loop of Henle by inhibiting chloride reabsorption. Since these diuretics inhibit sodium reabsorption more proximally than other diuretics, these loop diuretics are the most potent of the available diuretics. The thiazide diuretics inhibit sodium reabsorption at the distal portion of the ascending loop and are less potent.

Within the distal tubule, the remaining 5% to 10% of the filtered sodium load is actively reabsorbed in exchange for potassium and hydrogen ions. The efficiency of sodium reabsorption in the distal tubule is governed to a large extent by the mineralocorticoid, aldosterone. Amiloride, spironolactone, and triamterene exert their effects at this distal site of the renal tubule. As a result, these diuretics are the least potent of the available diuretics because 90%

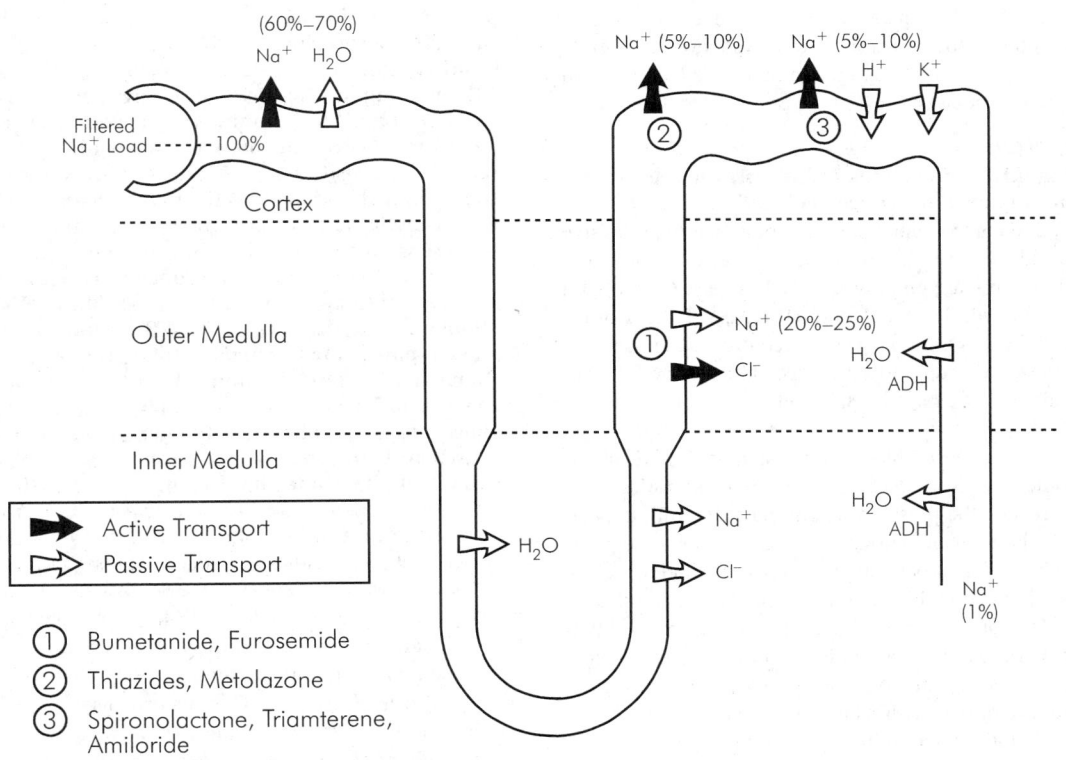

Fig 30.1 Probable Sites of Sodium Reabsorption and Diuretic Action in the Nephron

to 95% of the filtered sodium already has been reabsorbed before arriving at this distal site. Used alone, the potassium-sparing diuretics are minimally effective as diuretics. Their effects, however, are additive with other diuretics, and they often are used as adjunctive therapy to counterbalance K^+ and Mg^{++} loss from thiazide or loop diuretics. These potassium-sparing diuretics seldom should be used in patients with renal insufficiency because of their lack of effectiveness and their potential for causing significant hyperkalemia and hypermagnesemia in these patients.

The collecting duct is the final reabsorptive site through which the filtrate must pass. Antidiuretic hormone (ADH) acts within the collecting duct to increase water absorption without affecting sodium reabsorption. The susceptibility of this portion of the tubule to ADH effects is important in maintaining serum osmolality. When the serum is hyperosmolar, free water reabsorption is enhanced via ADH stimulation. Excessive ADH activity [e.g., syndrome of inappropriate antidiuretic hormone secretion (SIADH)] will result in the reabsorption of water, independent of sodium, and the serum sodium concentration is diluted as a result.

Early in the course of renal failure, thiazides or thiazide-like diuretics are effective antihypertensives. The antihypertensive effects of the thiazides result from the initial natriuresis they invoke as well as from a more sustained reduction in peripheral vascular resistance.[131] *Hydrochlorothiazide* is the least expensive of all the agents and has rapid absorption and good bioavailability, even among generic formulations. *Chlorothiazide* has a limited bioavailability from oral formulations: a 500 mg dose given as a single tablet, a 500 mg dose given as two 250 mg tablets, and a 250 mg dose given as a single tablet all deliver a similar amount of drug (about 50 mg) to the systemic circulation.[287] The only difference between the various thiazide diuretics is in the recommended doses and durations of action. The thiazide-like diuretic, *chlorthalidone* (actually a quinazoline derivative) has the longest duration of action. In some cases, chlorthalidone can be given on an intermittent

schedule (e.g., every other day or every third day) to minimize adverse effects; however, once-a-day therapy with small doses probably is a better approach because it minimizes compliance problems, especially if the patient has difficulty remembering when the last dose was taken. *Metolazone*, another long-acting quinazoline thiazide-like diuretic, also inhibits sodium reabsorption in the cortical diluting segment of the ascending limb of the loop of Henle (i.e., the early distal tubule). Metolazone also can block more proximal tubular sodium reabsorption and in large doses (up to 20 mg/day) can induce diuresis in patients with reduced glomerular filtration rates.

Since the kidney provides the only realistic route of sodium elimination, glomerular filtration and tubular reabsorption are the major determinants of sodium content in the urine. Therefore, the effectiveness of diuretics is dependent upon the amount of sodium delivered to their site of action in the renal tubule and on the patient's renal function. For example, a decrease in the GFR from 125 mL/minute to 25 mL/minute, theoretically, could result in about an 80% decrease in the amount of sodium filtered. When renal blood flow is compromised and the GFR is reduced (e.g., $Cl_{Cr} < 30$ mL/minute), the thiazide diuretics become minimally effective. The loop diuretics (i.e., *furosemide, torsemide, bumetanide, ethacrynic acid*), which work more proximally and are more potent than thiazides, need to be used in the presence of moderate-to-severe renal impairment. Besides having activity in the ascending limb of the loop of Henle, furosemide has vasodilating properties which decrease renal vascular resistance, and enhances sodium excretion by shifting renal blood flow from the long juxtamedullary nephrons to shorter superficial nephrons. In advanced renal disease, it often is necessary to give very large doses of furosemide (e.g., >400 mg/day) to achieve the desired effect. In refractory patients, the addition of a thiazide or metolazone to the loop diuretic may induce diuresis.[134] However, if diuresis is excessive, renal perfusion can be reduced and, thereby, further compromise glomerular function. In conclusion, F.L. most likely would benefit from a loop diuretic because his renal function is severely compromised as evidenced by his creatinine of 12.8 mg/dL and his thrice weekly hemodialysis.

Additional Therapy

17. Assuming F.L.'s fluid status is optimal, what additional therapy can be employed to reduce his blood pressure?

If diuretics fail to control blood pressure, other antihypertensive agents must be added. Generally, antihypertensives that minimally reduce renal blood flow are employed. F.L. has been treated with a beta blocker and hydralazine. If optimal doses of these drugs fail to produce satisfactory blood pressure control, other standard agents can be added according to F.L.'s special needs and the development of adverse effects. (See Chapter 10: Essential Hypertension.)

For patients with increased plasma renin activity, ACE inhibitors may be indicated. By reducing the efferent arteriolar tone, ACE inhibitors reduce the pressure within the glomeruli, thus attenuating glomerular damage. Dosage adjustments for these drugs are necessary when used in patients with renal insufficiency. The use of ACE inhibitors should be avoided in patients with bilateral renal artery stenoses or renal artery stenosis of a transplanted kidney because these drugs have caused an acute loss of renal function.[135] This effect may be due to blocking of intrarenal angiotensin II generation, a fall in hydrostatic filtration pressure in the stenotic kidney(s), and reduction in glomerular filtration.[136]

Hyperlipidemia

18. From the clinical history and laboratory data, what evidence exists for coronary artery disease in F.L.? Should his lipid abnormalities be treated?

F.L. has a long history of diminished exercise tolerance and chest pain typical of angina. In addition, he has elevated serum cholesterol and triglyceride concentrations. Hyperlipidemia is a common complication of renal failure and may accelerate atherogenesis. Several atherogenic factors in patients with chronic renal failure have been postulated including arterial wall injury, platelet activation and adherence, smooth muscle cell proliferation, and intra-arterial accumulation of cholesterol.[137] Hypertriglyceridemia may be a contributing factor although complex changes in lipoprotein composition and metabolism may be more important.[138]

Dietary intervention has been successful in reducing triglyceride and cholesterol concentrations.[139] Whether lowering of serum lipids will improve long-term morbidity and mortality remains to be determined. Since many β-adrenergic blocking drugs may elevate triglyceride concentrations, antihypertensive drugs with insignificant or beneficial effects on serum lipids [e.g., clonidine (Catapres), prazosin (Minipress), ACE inhibitors, calcium channel blockers] may be desirable instead. (See Chapter 10: Essential Hypertension.) Numerous drugs are available for treating lipid abnormalities in patients with end-stage renal disease. (See Chapter 9: Dyslipidemias.)

Impaired cardiac performance is a common complication of chronic renal failure and may occur early in the course of the disease.[140] Generally, adequate control of blood pressure, fluid balance, and anemia will help maintain myocardial performance.[141] Since intrinsic myocardial contractility is diminished in only a minority of uremic patients, digitalis should not be given routinely.

Calcium and Phosphate Abnormalities

Clinical Presentation

19. S.Y. is a 39-year-old female with a 25-year history of Type I diabetes mellitus with complications of diabetic ne- phropathy, retinopathy, and neuropathy. For the last 3 years she has been receiving CAPD. Her current medications include levothyroxine 0.1 mg/day, metoclopramide (Reglan) 10 mg TID, regular insulin 160 U/day (given intraperitoneally), docusate 200 mg TID, aluminum hydroxide suspension (Amphojel) 15 mL QID, and multivitamins with folic acid QD. At a recent clinic visit, her physical examination revealed a BP of 128/84 mm Hg, diabetic retinopathic changes with laser scars bilaterally, a peritoneal catheter in the abdomen, and diminished sensation bilaterally below the knees. Her laboratory values were as follows: normal serum electrolytes, a random blood glucose of 175 mg/dL (Normal: 75–110), BUN 45 mg/dL, creatinine 8.9 mg/dL, Hct 24%, WBC count 6200/mm³, Ca 7.9 mg/dL, phosphate 8.3 mg/dL, total serum protein 5.0 gm/dL (Normal: 6.3–8.0), albumin 3.1 gm/dL, uric acid 8.9 mg/dL, cholesterol 318 mg/dL (Normal: 140–270), TG 256 mg/dL. Previous x-rays revealed density changes in the bone that were consistent with renal osteodystrophy. Assess S.Y.'s bone, calcium, and phosphate abnormalities. What is their etiology? [SI units: blood glucose 9.7 mmol/L (Normal: 4.2–6.1); BUN 16.1 mmol/L; SrCr 787 µmol/L; Hct 0.24; WBC count 6200 × 10⁶/L; Ca 1.97 mmol/L; phosphate 2.68 mmol/L; total serum protein 50 gm/L (Normal: 63–80); albumin 31 gm/L; uric acid 529 µmol/L; cholesterol 8.22 mmol/L (Normal: 3.62–6.98); TG 2.89 mmol/L]

Hypocalcemia associated with hyperphosphatemia, hyperparathyroidism, and vitamin D resistance are frequent problems of chronic renal failure that may lead to the secondary complication of renal osteodystrophy. This major cause of disability refers to one or more of the following disorders associated with chronic renal failure: osteomalacia, osteitis fibrosa cystica, osteosclerosis, or osteopenia.[142]

No single mechanism is responsible for the diverse forms of bone disease observed in patients with chronic renal failure. Renal phosphate retention and secondary hyperparathyroidism play a major role in the development of osteitis fibrosa. As serum phosphate concentrations rise, ionized calcium concentrations fall, stimulating parathyroid hormone release.[143] Higher concentrations of PTH reduce the renal tubular reabsorption of phosphate and promote its excretion. Both serum phosphate and calcium concentrations then return to normal, leaving only an elevated PTH concentration. As renal failure progresses (GFR <30 mL/minute), the phosphaturic response to PTH diminishes and sustained hyperphosphatemia develops. In response to the hypocalcemia that develops because of hyperphosphatemia, calcium is mobilized from the bone; this is largely controlled by PTH. Virtually all patients with renal failure develop secondary hyperparathyroidism.

Persistent hyperphosphatemia contributes to diminished renal conversion of 25-hydroxycholecalciferol (25-HCC) to its biologically active metabolite, 1,25-dihydroxycholecalciferol (1,25-DHCC). As a result, the absorption of dietary calcium in the gut is diminished. Vitamin D deficiency also contributes to hypocalcemia and mobilization of calcium from bone. The interrelationships of phosphate, calcium, vitamin D, and PTH have been reviewed extensively.[143,144] The chronic effects of hyperparathyroidism on the skeleton lead to bone pain, fractures, and myopathy. In children these effects may be particularly severe and usually produce growth retardation.[145] The metabolic acidosis of renal failure also may contribute to a negative calcium balance in the bone; however, this hypothesis remains controversial.

Treatment

20. How should S.Y.'s renal osteodystrophy and calcium and phosphate abnormalities be managed?

The objectives of management for osteodystrophy associated with chronic renal failure are to: a) keep serum calcium and phosphorus concentrations near normal, b) suppress parathyroid hormone secretion, and c) restore normal skeletal development.

Dietary Restriction. During the early stages of renal impairment, dietary phosphorus could be reduced through restriction of meat, milk, legumes, and carbonated beverages. Significant dietary restriction of phosphate may be difficult to achieve.

Aluminum-Containing Antacids. Aluminum binds dietary phosphate present in the GI tract or enterohepatic secretions and forms an insoluble aluminum-phosphate complex that is excreted in the stool. A reduction of serum phosphate leads to a decrease in serum PTH concentrations and a normalization of serum calcium concentrations.[146] A list of aluminum-containing antacids is presented in Table 30.5.

No firm guidelines exist for dosing these antacids. A usual starting dose is 500 to 1000 mg of aluminum hydroxide with or immediately following meals and at bedtime. The dose is then titrated against the patient's serum phosphate concentration. S.Y. remains hyperphosphatemic on present therapy, so an increase in her dose to 30 mL four times a day seems warranted. Since many patients find these antacids unpalatable, experimentation with products and dosage forms may be necessary. A common adverse effect of aluminum is constipation. Therefore, the routine use of a stool softener such as docusate or laxatives such as sorbitol or bisacodyl (Dulcolax) often is recommended. If bisacodyl is used, it should not be taken with the antacid because the antacid theoretically could dissolve the enteric coating leading to gastric upset.

Since systemic aluminum toxicities include osteomalacia, encephalopathy, and microcytic anemia, other methods of decreasing serum phosphate have been sought to minimize the risk of chronic aluminum toxicity in patients with chronic renal failure.[76,147,148]

Calcium carbonate is widely recommended as an alternative, and perhaps preferred, method for phosphate binding.[149] In doses of up to 14 gm/day (5.6 gm of elemental calcium), this drug will maintain normal serum phosphate concentrations. The extent of calcium absorption is unclear; however, hypercalcemia may occur with chronic calcium carbonate administration. Before calcium therapy is initiated, the calcium-phosphate product (Ca × P) should be determined. If this value is above 70, the patient is at risk for calcium deposition in soft tissues. Under these circumstances, aluminum rather than calcium should be used initially to lower serum phosphate. Calcium carbonate then can be used to maintain a lower serum phosphate concentration. Simultaneous administration of vitamin D preparations and calcium will increase the risk of hypercalcemia, unless a low-calcium dialysate solution is used. Since S.Y.'s calcium-phosphate product is approximately 64, calcium carbonate could be instituted.

Calcium Acetate. An alternative calcium-based phosphate binder is calcium acetate.[150] Compared with calcium carbonate, calcium acetate binds approximately twice the amount of phosphorus for the same quantity of calcium absorbed,[151-154] which may be due to the increased solubility of calcium acetate in both acidic and alkaline environments.[152] However, despite the reduction in the required dose of elemental calcium, the incidence of hypercalcemia does not seem to be diminished.[150,153,154] This, in addition to its relatively higher cost, precludes the use of calcium acetate as the premier calcium-containing phosphate binder.

Calcium citrate has a phosphate-binding capacity similar to that of calcium carbonate.[151] However, its main limitation is its ability to enhance aluminum absorption from the GI tract.[155-157] Therefore, given that many chronic renal failure patients will eventually require an aluminum-containing phosphate binder, there is no role for calcium citrate as a phosphate binder.

Oral Magnesium. Magnesium-containing phosphate binders (magnesium hydroxide, magnesium carbonate) may be of some benefit in patients with renal failure.[158] In high doses required to control serum phosphate concentrations, severe diarrhea and hypermagnesemia invariably result. However, these binders can be useful in dialysis patients whose serum phosphate concentrations cannot be controlled adequately with the use of a calcium-containing phosphate binder alone. In this instance, a magnesium-containing phosphate binder may be added in conjunction with a reduction in the dialysate magnesium concentration. This strategy serves to virtually eliminate the more severe magnesium-related adverse effects, as well as obviate the need for aluminum-containing phosphate binders.[159]

Table 30.5		Selected Aluminum-Containing Antacids		
		Contents		
Product	Dosage Form	Aluminum Hydroxide	Magnesium Hydroxide	Other
AlternaGEL	Suspension	600 mg/5 mL		
Alu-Cap	Cap	475 mg/cap		
Amphojel	Tab Suspension	325 mg/tab, 650 mg/tab 320 mg/5 mL		
Basaljel	Tab Cap Suspension	Equiv. to 500 mg/tab Equiv. to 500 mg/cap Equiv. to 400 mg/5 mL		Aluminum carbonate Aluminum carbonate Aluminum carbonate
Dialume	Cap	500 mg/cap		
Nephrox	Suspension	320 mg/5 mL		Mineral oil
Gelusil[b]	Tab Suspension	200 mg/tab 200 mg/5 mL	200 mg/tab 200 mg/5 mL	Simethicone Simethicone
Maalox[b]	Suspension	225 mg/5 mL	225 mg/5 mL	
Mylanta[b]	Tab Suspension	200 mg/tab 200 mg/5 mL	200 mg/tab 200 mg/5 mL	Simethicone Simethicone
Riopan[b]	Tab Suspension			Magaldrate Magaldrate

[a] Cap = Capsule; Tab = Tablet.
[b] Chronic use should be discouraged because of magnesium content.

Sucralfate. While not approved by the Food and Drug Administration (FDA) for use as a phosphate binder, sucralfate (Carafate) is effective in reducing serum phosphate concentrations.[160] However, because it is an aluminum-containing compound, the use of sucralfate for this purpose has been associated with aluminum toxicity.[161]

Vitamin D. If the use of aluminum or calcium antacids fails to correct the serum calcium and to reduce parathyroid hormone concentrations, S.Y. may require vitamin D. Vitamin D is available as ergocalciferol (vitamin D_2), calcifediol (25-hydroxycholecalciferol), calcitriol (1,25-dihydroxycholecalciferol), and dihydrotachysterol. Since calcitriol is the final, active metabolite of vitamin D, it is preferred in patients with end-stage renal disease.[162] The response to vitamins D_2 and D_3 can vary substantially depending upon the degree of renal failure and the ability of the kidney to convert these vitamins to the biologically active 1,25-DHCC.

The potential for vitamin D intoxication and sustained hypercalcemia that may require weeks for resolution is a major hazard associated with pharmacologic doses of vitamin D. In contrast, a physiologic dose of 1,25-DHCC (0.5 to 1 µg/day) produces an initial response within days. Furthermore, because 1,25-DHCC has a short half-life, hypercalcemia can be corrected rapidly should intoxication occur.[143] Serum calcium concentrations are used to determine the dose of 1,25-DHCC. If the serum calcium does not increase by 0.5 mg/dL four to six weeks after 1,25-DHCC has been initiated, the dose should be increased by 0.25 to 0.5 µg/day. This approach may be continued until serum calcium reaches the normal range. Frequent calcium determinations are needed to detect hypercalcemia that may occur with prolonged therapy. Patients with aluminum-induced osteomalacia or severe hyperparathyroidism are at greater risk for significant hypercalcemia.[143]

Caution must be exercised to avoid hypercalcemia by administering the lowest effective dose of vitamin D and obtaining frequent serum calcium determinations. Supplemental calcium usually is unnecessary and may be dangerous if the patient is ingesting normal dietary amounts.

Oral versus Intravenous Calcitriol. With severe hyperparathyroidism, prevention of renal osteodystrophy may not be successful despite phosphate restriction, calcium supplementation, and daily administration of calcitriol. In such cases, high, intermittently administered doses of calcitriol (0.5 to 1 µg 3 times/week) are required to directly suppress PTH production and to reduce serum parathyroid hormone concentrations. The comparative efficacy of intravenous versus oral calcitriol is controversial, with some authors claiming superior efficacy with the intravenous route.[163,164] Thrice weekly administration of intravenous calcitriol is hypothetically superior, primarily because the intestinal mucosal cells are not exposed to high concentrations of calcitriol, which presumably may reduce the risk of hypercalcemia. Also, intravenous calcitriol does not undergo hepatic first-pass metabolism, thus achieving high peak concentrations in the serum and around the parathyroid gland, where calcitriol directly inhibits PTH synthesis.[144] In patients with refractory secondary hyperparathyroidism receiving daily doses of oral calcitriol, intermittent intravenous calcitriol may be effective in reducing serum PTH concentrations with a decreased risk of hypercalcemia.[164,165] This beneficial effect, however, is more likely due to the intermittent dosing than to the route of administration. Intermittent oral calcitriol suppresses serum PTH concentrations in a magnitude comparable to that of intravenous calcitriol therapy. The risk of hypercalcemia with intermittent oral calcitriol also is similar to that which occurs with intravenous therapy.[166–168] In cross-over comparisons of the two administration routes, the efficacy is comparable.[144] Regardless of the route of administration, intermittent calcitriol dosing is asso-

ciated with a reduced risk of hypercalcemia. Another added benefit is the ability to control and supervise its administration at the time of hemodialysis.

Pulse doses of calcitriol may be initiated at 0.5 to 1 µg orally or intravenously three times a week. Serum calcium and phosphorus concentrations must be monitored twice weekly during the titration period. The dose may be increased by 0.5 µg increments every two to four weeks until serum calcium is maintained between 10.5 to 11.5 mg/dL. Serum PTH should be monitored every three months. In patients with severe hyperparathyroidism, caution must be exercised in reducing the serum PTH concentration to the normal range. Such maneuvering is associated with hypercalcemia due to low bone turnover. The goals of therapy in hyperparathyroid patients are a reduction in serum PTH concentration to twice the upper limit of the normal range and avoidance of hypercalcemia.

Parathyroidectomy. The parathyroid glands enlarge as a compensatory response to disturbances of phosphate, calcium, and calcitriol metabolism in patients with end-stage renal disease. Calcitriol can reduce the secretion of PTH and inhibit the development of parathyroid hyperplasia; however, calcitriol cannot adequately reverse established hyperplasia nor suppress PTH secretion.[150,169] This observation emphasizes the importance of timely administration of calcitriol to prevent parathyroid hyperplasia. Under circumstances in which severe hyperparathyroidism cannot be controlled by dietary phosphate restriction and drug therapy, parathyroidectomy is considered. Parathyroidectomy may be subtotal, total, or total with auto-transplantation. Of these, only total parathyroidectomy has not been associated with recurrent hyperparathyroidism.[163]

One of the major complications of parathyroidectomy is the early development of postsurgical hypocalcemia. The two main determinants of the severity of hypocalcemia are the ionized serum calcium concentration and the chronicity of the disorder.[170,171] Clinical symptoms of hypocalcemia include muscle irritability, fatigue, depression, and memory loss. Two of the well-known signs of hypocalcemia are the Chvostek's and Trousseau's signs. Chvostek's sign is contraction of the facial muscle after tapping the facial nerve anterior to the ear. Trousseau's sign involves carpal spasm after induction of mild ischemia in the arm by inflating the sphygmomanometer cuff for three to five minutes.[171,172] The signs of most profound hypocalcemia involve the cardiovascular system, and include myocardial failure, arrhythmias, and hypotension unresponsive to fluid therapy.[170,171] Without immediate treatment, tetany, generalized seizures, and cardiac arrest may occur.

Treatment of Severe Hypocalcemia. All patients with signs or symptoms of hypocalcemia should be treated. Symptomatic hypocalcemia generally responds to the administration of intravenous calcium salts. The goal of acute treatment is the abatement of the most severe signs and symptoms, such as tetany, seizures, and ECG changes. Treatment is started with one or two ampules of calcium gluconate (10 mL = 93 mg elemental calcium) infused over ten minutes. Faster administration can result in cardiac arrhythmias and failure. After the first intravenous calcium dose, a continuous infusion of 15 mg/kg elemental calcium in normal saline or dextrose solution may be infused over eight to ten hours.[170] Calcium chloride contains three times the elemental calcium of the gluconate salt; however, its use is discouraged due to the associated thrombophlebitis.

In patients who have undergone subtotal parathyroidectomy, the remaining parathyroid tissues will start functioning adequately, so that the acute hypocalcemia is only transient, lasting only a few days. With total parathyroidectomy, however, hypocalcemia is permanent and necessitates long-term treatment with calcitriol and oral calcium supplements (1 to 1.5 gm of elemental calcium/day).

Altered Glucose Metabolism

21. Other than the obvious effect of S.Y.'s diabetes mellitus on blood glucose, are there any effects of renal disease itself on glucose metabolism?

Nondiabetic Patients. Uremia often is associated with glucose intolerance in nondiabetic patients.[173] Patients with chronic renal failure frequently exhibit an abnormal response to an oral glucose challenge and have sustained hyperinsulinemia. However, most patients will have a normal fasting blood glucose. The majority of patients with chronic renal failure have diminished tissue sensitivity to the action of insulin.[174] While their exact role is unclear, several uremic toxins, including urea, creatinine, guanidinosuccinic acid, and methylguanidine have been implicated as causes for insulin resistance. Elevated concentrations of growth hormone, parathyroid hormone, and glucagon also may contribute to glucose intolerance. Hemodialysis may improve glucose metabolism,[174] or have no effect.[175] Most nondiabetic patients with renal failure require no therapy for hyperglycemia.

Diabetic Patients. Patients with diabetes mellitus, like S.Y., may experience an improvement in hyperglycemia and decreased insulin requirements as renal failure progresses. Estimates are that six to eight units of insulin are degraded daily by the kidney.[174] As renal failure progresses, less insulin is cleared, and its metabolic half-life is increased. Frequently, diabetic patients require less insulin as renal insufficiency progresses. A decreased clearance of insulin by muscle tissue also may occur in patients with uremia. In the management of diabetic patients with progressive renal failure, blood glucose concentrations should be monitored to avoid hypoglycemia secondary to reduced insulin clearance. S.Y. has reached end-stage disease and is receiving her insulin in the peritoneal dialysate. Dosage adjustments should be made on the basis of repeated home blood glucose measurements and glycosylated hemoglobin determinations.

Endocrine Abnormalities Caused by Uremia

22. Does S.Y.'s hypothyroidism have any relationship to her chronic renal disease? What other endocrine abnormalities are associated with uremia?

Disturbances in thyroid function commonly are encountered in patients with end-stage renal disease because the kidney is involved in all aspects of peripheral thyroid hormone metabolism.[176] Common laboratory abnormalities include reduced serum concentrations of total thyroxine (T_4) and 3,5,3'-triiodothyronine (T_3) and a low free thyroxine index (FTI). Thyroid stimulating hormone (TSH) usually is normal. Peripheral conversion of T_4 to T_3 is reduced in uremic patients.[177] In spite of these abnormalities, clinical hypothyroidism does not occur solely as a result of renal failure, probably because the amount of free thyroid hormone in serum remains normal. Hypothyroidism in renal failure patients should be confirmed by the presence of an elevated serum TSH concentration and a low serum concentration of free T_4 as measured by equilibrium dialysis.

A high incidence of goiter has been observed in renal failure patients.[178] The factors responsible may be environmental, altered thyroid hormone metabolism, or autoimmune thyroid disease, a relatively common finding in diabetic patients.

Other endocrine abnormalities have been observed in patients with chronic renal failure. Gonadal dysfunction leading to impotence, decreased libido, and diminished testicular size has been observed in men.[179] Reduced gonadal activity also delays puberty in children with chronic renal failure.[180] Treatment with oral zinc 50 mg/day, has reversed gonadal dysfunction in some uremic men.[181] Hyperprolactinemia and altered vasoactive hormone activity are other endocrine disturbances that may occur as a result of renal failure.

Gastrointestinal (GI) Complications

23. One month before her current clinic visit, S.Y. had complaints of nausea and vomiting of partially digested food. Metoclopramide (Reglan) was begun at that time. Could S.Y.'s nausea and vomiting have been caused by her renal failure? Was the appropriate therapy selected?

Gastrointestinal abnormalities are extremely common in patients with chronic renal failure. These abnormalities include anorexia, nausea, vomiting, hiccups, abdominal pain, GI bleeding, diarrhea, and constipation.[182] Autopsy studies have shown frequent esophagitis, gastritis, duodenitis, enteritis, and colitis.[183] Although peptic ulcer disease occurs often in uremic patients, the prevalence of this problem may be no higher than in the general population. Diminished gastric motility may occur from uremia; however, this problem usually improves with adequate hemodialysis.[184] A complicating factor for S.Y. is her diabetes and diabetic neuropathy that may delay gastric emptying (diabetic gastroparesis) leading to retention of food in the upper intestinal tract. This frequently causes distention, nausea, and vomiting; metoclopramide or cisapride is recommended to relieve these symptoms.

Nausea and vomiting also occur as a result of severe azotemia and sometimes are the initial symptoms. Although antiemetics such as prochlorperazine are used, dialysis is the preferred therapy. Drug-induced nausea and vomiting always should be considered. Patients with chronic renal failure frequently take multiple drugs, and because of diminished renal function, are at risk for drug toxicity (e.g., digitalis intoxication).

Bleeding

24. During her clinic visit, S.Y. tells her physician that her bowel movements have become black and tarry in appearance. A rectal examination reveals guaiac positive stools. Is GI bleeding related to renal failure?

S.Y. should be evaluated for peptic ulcer disease as well as lower GI bleeding. As described previously, uremic patients are at risk for bleeding from mucosal surfaces such as the stomach. While gastrointestinal blood loss usually is not a major cause of anemia in chronic renal failure,[185] individual patients may develop severe bleeding episodes. Angiodysplasia of the stomach and duodenum, and erosive esophagitis are the most common sites of bleeding in patients with chronic renal failure.[186]

The relationship between peptic ulcers and renal failure remains controversial; however, elevated serum concentrations of gastrin occur in uremic patients.[187] Gastric acid production is variable and is elevated in some studies but diminished in others. Within recent years, the gram-negative bacterium *Helicobacter pylori* (formerly *Campylobacter pylori*) has been implicated as a necessary, although perhaps not sufficient, factor in the pathogenesis of peptic ulcer disease not due to nonsteroidal anti-inflammatory drugs.[188] (See Chapter 23: Upper Gastrointestinal Disorders.) However, despite a similar prevalence of *H. pylori* infection as the general population,[189,190] this bacterium does not seem to play a significant role in the ulcer diathesis in patients with chronic renal failure.[190]

Treatment of upper GI bleeding in uremic patients usually consists of intensive antacid therapy and H_2-receptor antagonists. These drugs should be given in reduced doses according to the degree of renal failure. (See Chapter 23: Upper Gastrointestinal Disorders.)

Treatment of Peptic Ulcer Disease (PUD)

25. What additional antacid therapy should be prescribed for S.Y.? What potential complications of antacids exist in patients with renal failure? How should these complications be monitored?

The treatment of peptic ulcer disease usually includes the use of aluminum hydroxide and magnesium hydroxide combinations

(Maalox, Mylanta, Gelusil). (See Chapter 23: Upper Gastrointestinal Disorders.) However, because S.Y. has renal failure, special caution must be used in selecting the appropriate antacid.

Aluminum-Containing Antacids. S.Y. has been taking aluminum hydroxide, 15 mL four times a day, as a phosphate binder. However, because of its acid neutralizing effects, aluminum hydroxide also can be used for the treatment of S.Y.'s peptic ulcer disease. Unfortunately, since aluminum hydroxide is a relatively weak acid neutralizer, large doses often are required. Therefore, increasing S.Y.'s dose of aluminum hydroxide would be indicated.

Amphojel and AlternaGEL are both antacids containing aluminum hydroxide. They contain 64 and 120 mg/mL aluminum hydroxide, respectively, and therefore, differ in their acid neutralizing capability and their phosphate binding capacity. By using AlternaGEL or increasing the dose of Amphojel, S.Y. will receive more phosphate binders. The use of aluminum-containing antacids can cause excessive *phosphate depletion* if serum phosphorus is not carefully followed. The complications resulting from hypophosphatemia include: hypercalcemia; hypercalciuria; osteomalacia and fractures; and defects in erythrocyte, leukocyte, and platelet function related to decreased adenosine triphosphate and 2,3-diphosphoglycerate (DPI). The symptoms of phosphate depletion include generalized muscle weakness, malaise, tremors, absence of deep tendon reflexes, bone pain, mental depression, convulsions, and even coma. The complications of hypophosphatemia generally are reversible upon phosphate replacement.

Aluminum Toxicity. Long-term administration of aluminum may itself cause toxicity. Aluminum antacids may be absorbed and cause aluminum accumulation, especially in patients with renal failure. Elevated serum aluminum concentrations and aluminum deposition in bone and other tissues of patients with renal failure have been associated with osteomalacia,[147] microcytic anemia,[76] and a fatal neurologic syndrome referred to as the dialysis encephalopathy syndrome.[148] Therefore, while the use of an aluminum-containing antacid is indicated for S.Y., the potential risks of this drug must be remembered.

Magnesium-Containing Antacids. Antacids containing magnesium should be used cautiously, if at all, in renal failure patients. Significant amounts of magnesium from antacids and cathartics can be absorbed from the GI tract. Since magnesium concentrations within the body are controlled by glomerular filtration and distal tubular reabsorption, a lowering of the glomerular filtration rate results in a reduced clearance of magnesium.[64] If patients with end-stage renal disease are presented with a magnesium load, *magnesium intoxication* may develop. Ingestion of magnesium-containing products can result in rapid intoxication in these patients.[65] Moderate amounts of magnesium-containing antacids can be used if a patient is on regular dialysis (e.g., hemodialysis for 3 to 4 hours, 3 times/week) and avoids ingestion of large quantities of magnesium. Periodic serum magnesium concentrations should be measured. Some clinicians recommend the use of alternating doses of aluminum hydroxide with mixtures of aluminum hydroxide-magnesium hydroxide. If a patient has advanced renal dysfunction that does not yet require dialysis, magnesium compounds should be avoided.

Treatment for hypermagnesemia consists of administration of parenteral calcium salts (5 to 10 mEq) if severe symptoms of intoxication such as respiratory depression or cardiac arrhythmias are present.[191] Unfortunately, calcium injections are not uniformly effective. If kidney function is adequate, intravenous furosemide and saline administration can be used to enhance renal magnesium excretion. Hemodialysis against a bath containing little (1.5 mEq/L) or no magnesium can substantially reduce magnesium concentrations within four to six hours.[191] In addition, all magnesium-containing preparations should be discontinued.

Calcium-Containing Antacids. Antacids containing calcium also should be used with caution because of the possibility of developing the milk-alkali syndrome, hypercalcemia, nephrocalcinosis, and/or worsening renal function.[192] Calcium carbonate also has been associated with a rebound increase in gastric acid secretion.[193] The significance of this acid rebound in patients with renal failure is not yet determined. However, this problem is of concern since calcium preparations seem to be effective acid-neutralizing agents, and patients with renal failure frequently receive calcium salts for calcium replacement therapy and as phosphate binders.

Constipation and fecal impaction also are associated with calcium and aluminum antacids. Intestinal obstruction may even result from the development of solid concretions of antacid in the intestine, especially in patients with renal failure.[194] Such obstructions may require surgical intervention and removal.

Neurological Complications

26. P.B., a 75-year-old, 85 kg male, went to his local physician because of weakness, nausea, lethargy, decreased exercise tolerance, and general malaise that developed over a several-week period. P.B. had not been seen by a physician for over 10 years. His past medical history was unremarkable except he recalls being told about 10 years ago that he had borderline hypertension. He was taking no medications. The physician's examination revealed a BP of 180/104 mm Hg and funduscopic examination showed grade III hypertensive changes. Cardiovascular examination was positive for a third heart sound (S_3) and evidence of cardiomegaly. Diffuse rales were heard in the lungs. The abdominal examination was negative but P.B. had moderate (2+) edema of both legs and the sacrum. On neurologic examination, P.B. was slightly confused, appeared somnolent, and had diminished sensation to pinprick in both lower extremities; asterixis was present. Examination of the skin showed pallor and excoriations across the abdomen, legs, and arms. Pertinent laboratory values were as follows: Hct 20%, WBC count 9100/mm³, serum Na 135 mEq/L, K 5.8 mEq/L, Cl 109 mEq/L, CO_2 content 16 mEq/L, glucose 121 mg/dL, BUN 199 mg/dL, creatinine 19.8 mg/dL, Ca 8.5 mg/dL, phosphate 11.1 mg/dL, uric acid 11.9 mg/dL (Normal: 4.0–8.0 for males), and albumin 3.0 gm/dL.

Renal ultrasonography revealed no obstruction and small kidneys bilaterally. Subsequent renal biopsy showed chronic glomerular scarring. P.B. was given the final diagnosis of CRF, perhaps due to chronic, untreated hypertension. What is the likely explanation for P.B.'s altered mental status? What treatment, if any, is indicated for his neurologic findings? [SI units: Hct 0.20; WBC 9100 × 10⁶/L; Na 135 mmol/L; K 5.8 mmol/L; Cl 109 mmol/L; CO_2 16 mmol/L; glucose 6.7 mmol/L; BUN 71.0 mmol/L of urea; creatinine 1750 µmol/L; Ca 2.12 mmol/L; phosphate 3.58 mmol/L; uric acid 708 µmol/L (Normal: 238–476 for males); albumin 30 gm/L]

Disorders of the central nervous system (CNS) that occur in patients with untreated renal failure as well as in those receiving dialysis are referred to collectively as *uremic encephalopathy*. While P.B.'s altered neurologic function most likely is due to uremia, a careful drug history should exclude the possibility of drug effects. Symptoms of uremic encephalopathy include alterations in consciousness thinking, memory, speech, psychomotor behavior, and emotion. Patients or their family members may note easy fatigability, daytime drowsiness, insomnia, diminished cognitive abilities, slurred speech, vomiting, and emotional volatility. The patient also may complain of being cold, having ''restless legs,'' or ''burning feet.'' The encephalopathy may progress to ataxia, vertigo, nystagmus, coma, and convulsions. Electroencephalograms (EEGs) of patients with chronic renal failure usually show diffuse abnormalities.

Evidence strongly supports parathyroid hormone as a major contributing factor to the altered neurologic status of patients with end-stage renal disease,[195] however, other uremic "toxins" may play a role in this disorder. PTH may enhance the entry of calcium into the brain and peripheral nerves, but also may be directly neurotoxic.[195] Brain edema and intracellular acidosis do not contribute to uremic encephalopathy. In all likelihood, P.B.'s altered mental status will improve with dialysis and correction of his hyperparathyroidism.

The peripheral nervous system also shows abnormal function in many patients with end-stage renal disease. Typically, the peripheral neuropathy will be slowly progressive, distal, and symmetrical, usually involving sensory function first. P.B. has loss of sensation in his legs. The abnormalities seen usually are indistinguishable from other types of neuropathy, especially diabetic neuropathy. Nerve conduction studies often reveal abnormalities preceding clinical symptoms. Dialysis has no effect on the neuropathy; however, successful renal transplantation may ameliorate nerve dysfunction.[196]

Abnormalities of the autonomic nervous system also have been observed in patients with advanced renal failure. In nondiabetic patients on hemodialysis, the sympathetic nervous system shows minimal dysfunction; however, altered parasympathetic activity may be present.[197] Patients with diabetes also develop parasympathetic abnormalities, but typically may show signs of altered sympathetic function as well. Hemodialysis may correct autonomic dysfunction in nondiabetic patients,[196] but not diabetic patients.[197]

Dermatological Complications

27. Why does P.B. have excoriations on his skin? What therapy would be useful?

Several dermal abnormalities have been observed in patients with chronic renal failure. These have included hyperpigmentation, abnormal perspiration, dryness, and persistent pruritus. Of these, *uremic pruritus* can be the most bothersome for the patient, and may lead to repeated scratching and skin excoriation.

Hyperparathyroidism, hypervitaminosis A, and dermal mast cell proliferation with subsequent histamine release have been suggested as causes of pruritus.[198] Pruritus often becomes more severe in patients on hemodialysis, suggesting some effect of extracorporeal circulation.

Treatment of pruritus often is a frustrating experience for the patient and clinician. While many therapies have been advocated, few have provided sustained benefit for patients. A trial and error approach is recommended. The initial treatment usually consists of oral antihistamines such as hydroxyzine. Topical emollients or topical steroids may provide benefit if antihistamine therapy is not completely successful. If pruritus is still present, other treatment options may be tried. These include ultraviolet (UVB) phototherapy and oral administration of activated charcoal.[199,200]

Leg Cramps

28. C.P. is a 70-year-old male with ESRD secondary to chronic hypertension. One week ago, his physician placed C.P. on hemodialysis. Since then, he has been dialyzed 3 times. For the past week, he has complained of severe muscle cramps in his legs, occurring especially during dialysis, but also occurring at night. His medications include prazosin 2 mg BID, aluminum hydroxide 1 gm TID, docusate 200 mg TID, and one Nephrocaps QD. C.P.'s physical examination is unremarkable except for diminished sensation in both legs. Pertinent predialysis laboratory values are as follows: Hct 23%, WBC count 7900/mm^3, serum Na 138 mEq/L, K 5.0 mEq/L, Cl 108 mEq/L, CO$_2$ content 20 mEq/L, BUN 96 mg/dL, creatinine 10.0 mg/dL, Ca 9.0 mg/dL, phosphate 5.6 mg/dL, Mg 2.6 mg/dL. Why is C.P. having leg cramps? What treatment is indicated? [SI units:

Hct 0.23; WBC 7900 × 10^6/L; Na 138 mmol/L; K 5.0 mmol/L; Cl 108 mmol/L; CO$_2$ 20 mmol/L; BUN 34.3 mmol/L of urea; creatine 884 μmol/L; Ca 2.25 mmol/L; phosphate 1.81 mmol/L; Mg 1.07 mmol/L]

Muscle cramps frequently occur in patients with chronic renal failure; however, their etiology is unknown. Most often, these muscle contractions occur in the legs, although they may be present in the abdominal wall and arms. While cramping may occur at any time, it frequently develops during the dialysis procedure. The removal of sodium chloride during dialysis, with subsequent intravascular volume contraction, may be an etiologic factor. The treatment of dialysis-related muscle cramping includes intravenous isotonic or hypertonic saline, mannitol, or hypertonic dextrose (1 mL/kg of D$_{50}$W).[201]

Interdialytic muscle cramps may be treated with stretching exercises or quinine sulfate.[202] While no well-controlled studies of quinine's effectiveness have been published on its efficacy for muscle cramps in patients with chronic renal failure, it has been studied for the treatment of nocturnal leg cramps in elderly people. In a meta-analysis of data from six randomized, controlled, cross-over studies involving 107 ambulatory elderly patients, quinine therapy (200, 300, or 500 mg) reduced the number of leg cramps by an average of 8.8 episodes per patient during a four-week period. The number of nights with leg cramps were reduced by 27.5% with quinine therapy; however, quinine did not alter the severity or duration of cramps.[288] After a review of various studies, the FDA deleted the labeled indication for the prescription use of quinine for nocturnal leg cramps and removed quinine from the over-the-counter market.[289] Although quinine is widely used for muscle cramps in patients with chronic renal failure, a trial of quinine sulfate (Quinamm) 260 to 300 mg at bedtime as needed for C.P. probably would be of minimal benefit. Although side effects from quinine are rare, serious adverse effects, including reversible leukopenia and thrombocytopenia are sufficiently important to warrant careful monitoring of patients receiving this drug.

Nutritional Requirements

29. Do stable CRF patients such as C.P. have any special nutritional needs? How would the use of peritoneal dialysis affect C.P.'s nutritional requirements?

The nutritional needs of patients with chronic renal failure are complex and critical to their care. A low serum albumin concentration, a measure of nutritional status of the patient, is a most powerful risk factor for death.[203,204] In addition, a low serum creatinine concentration, indicative of diminished muscle mass presumably due to malnutrition, also is a powerful predictor of mortality in patients with chronic renal failure.[203] These situations illustrate the importance of nutrition in maintaining visceral and somatic protein mass and metabolism.

The relationships between protein and energy requirements, vitamins, trace minerals, and divalent ion metabolism in patients with chronic renal failure have been reviewed elsewhere;[205] some general concepts will be considered here. In patients with chronic renal failure who are not yet being dialyzed, protein restriction is recommended. Diminished nitrogen ingestion, when coupled with restricted ingestion of potassium and phosphorous, reduces the load of urea, uric acid, potassium, phosphate, and acid presented to the kidney for excretion.[206] The recommended daily allowance for nondialyzed patients with renal failure is 0.6 gm/kg body weight of high biological value protein. Because amino acids are lost in the dialysate, patients on hemodialysis should have a protein intake of 1 gm/kg body weight/day. Continuous ambulatory peritoneal dialysis causes a greater dialysate loss of protein, especially in the presence of peritonitis. Therefore, patients on peritoneal dialysis should receive as much as 1.5 gm/kg body weight of protein/day.

Patients with chronic renal failure should ingest protein in the form of an essential and nonessential amino acid mixture. The value of keto acid analogues of essential amino acids remains unclear.

Patients with chronic renal failure may need as many as 50 to 55 kcal/kg of body weight/day to prevent catabolism and maintain a positive nitrogen balance.[207] Losses of 25 to 30 gm of dextrose into the dialysate may occur during hemodialysis. However, peritoneal dialysis patients receive as much as 800 kcal/day from the peritoneal absorption of glucose from the dialysis solution. As a result, chronic peritoneal dialysis may lead to substantial weight gain.

Fat requirements for renal failure patients are not different from the general population; however, lipid abnormalities frequently seen in uremic patients may necessitate dietary fat restrictions. Finally, a zinc deficiency has occurred in renal failure leading to the loss of taste acuity.[208] Daily zinc supplementation (25 mg elemental zinc) has improved taste function.[209] The effect of dialysis on folic acid requirements is discussed in Question 9.

Diabetic Nephropathy

Diabetic nephropathy is defined as a urinary albumin excretion rate of ≥ 300 mg/24 hours in a person with diabetes in the absence of other renal diseases.[210] Diabetic nephropathy is the most common cause of end-stage renal disease in the U.S.[1] With the current rate of increase, it is likely that diabetic nephropathy soon will account for nearly 50% of end-stage renal disease cases.[211] Diabetic nephropathy develops in 30% to 50% of patients with insulin-dependent diabetes mellitus (IDDM), and in 10% of white patients with noninsulin-dependent diabetes mellitus (NIDDM);[19,211] however, among certain populations, such as Native Americans, blacks, and Hispanics, the prevalence of end-stage renal disease in patients with IDDM or NIDDM is substantially higher than whites.[19,211]

The exact mechanisms leading to the development of diabetic nephropathy are not clear; however, several predictive factors exist for the development and progression of renal damage. These include a family history of, or genetic predisposition to hypertension and poor glycemic control in those predisposed to hypertension.[212,213] Although diabetic nephropathy may occur with both insulin-dependent diabetes mellitus and noninsulin-dependent diabetes mellitus, the majority of research has been focused on the pathophysiology, prevention, and treatment of IDDM, despite the fact that the majority of diabetic patients enrolled in the Medicare End-Stage Renal Disease program have NIDDM.[1] Because of the scarcity of data, it is uncertain whether many of the beneficial interventions used to prevent or slow the progression of diabetic nephropathy in insulin-dependent diabetes mellitus patients also apply to those with noninsulin-dependent diabetes mellitus. Therefore, unless otherwise stated, the primary scope of this section will be on diabetic nephropathy due to insulin-dependent diabetes mellitus.

Staging

30. T.S., a 27-year-old female with a 19-year history of Type I diabetes mellitus, presents for a routine work-up by her local physician. Pertinent laboratory values are as follows: SrCr 1.6 mg/dL, random blood glucose 220 mg/dL. Her 24-hour urine collection contained 200 mg of albumin. On physical examination, her BP was 139/90 mm Hg. At what functional stage is T.S.'s diabetic nephropathy? [SI units: SrCr 141 μmol/L; glucose 12.2 mmol/L]

The natural history of diabetic nephropathy is somewhat predictable. Diabetic nephropathy rarely develops within ten years of diagnosis of insulin-dependent diabetes mellitus. Likewise, it is rare to develop diabetic nephropathy 35 years after a diagnosis of IDDM.[19,210,211] With diabetic nephropathy, the kidneys progress through several functional stages, possibly culminating in end-stage renal disease. These functional stages are based primarily upon the glomerular filtration rate and urinary albumin excretion (see Table 30.6).[210] Normal urinary albumin excretion is less than 30 mg/24 hours; *microalbuminuria* is defined as urinary albumin excretion of 30 to 300 mg/24 hours, and *albuminuria* (*proteinuria*) is urinary albumin excretion greater than 300 mg/24 hours.[19,210] Based upon her urinary albumin excretion of 200 mg/24 hours, T.S. is classified as having Stage II (incipient) diabetic nephropathy (see Table 30.6).

31. What is the significance of T.S.'s microalbuminuria?

The magnitude of urinary albumin excretion is of great value in determining the risk of progression, as well as guiding the strategies for preventing and slowing the progression of diabetic nephropathy. Typically, the glomerular filtration rate declines once the urinary albumin excretion exceeds 100 mg/24 hours.[211] The development of microalbuminuria is highly predictive of progression within the next 15 years to clinical diabetic nephropathy.[214,215] As urinary albumin excretion increases, it serves as a predictor of mortality. Diabetic patients with daily urinary albumin excretion greater than 500 mg/24 hours have a 100-fold greater risk of mortality than the nondiabetic population, as compared to the twofold increase in diabetic patients without proteinuria.[216] The presence of albuminuria heralds irreversible renal damage, and 50% of patients progress to end-stage renal disease within seven years.[211]

Management

32. How should T.S.'s mild renal impairment be managed?

The three main risk factors for the progression of incipient diabetic nephropathy to clinical diabetic nephropathy are poor glycemic control, systemic hypertension, and high dietary protein intake (>1.5 gm/kg body weight/day). T.S.'s randomly obtained blood glucose concentration of 220 mg/dL may indicate poorly controlled diabetes, which serves as a risk factor for the advancement of her diabetic nephropathy. As such, her blood glucose concentration needs to be under stricter control.

Glycemic Control

Time from onset of diabetes to the development of clinical diabetic nephropathy is shortened by poor glycemic control.[217] With strict glycemic control, however, progression of incipient diabetic nephropathy can be arrested, both in terms of reduced urinary albumin excretion and in the slowing of glomerular filtration rate reduction.[218–220] In patients with controlled blood pressure, the urinary albumin excretion may be stabilized if the glycosylated hemoglobin (Hbg_{A1}) levels are maintained below 7.5%.[220]

The Diabetic Control and Complications Trial (DCCT) addressed how rigidly blood glucose concentrations should be controlled to reduce diabetic complication. The DCCT evaluated the effect of intensive insulin treatment of insulin-dependent diabetes mellitus on the development and progression of long-term complications, including diabetic nephropathy. As part of this study, patients with no proteinuria (urinary albumin excretion <40 mg/24 hours) or microalbuminuria (urinary albumin excretion <200 mg/24 hours) were randomized to receive either conventional (1 to 2 insulin doses/day) or intensive insulin treatment (≥ 3 insulin doses/day). The goal of the intensive regimen was to maintain fasting blood glucose concentrations between 70 and 120 mg/dL, with postprandial blood glucose concentrations less than 180 mg/dL. After a mean follow-up of 6.5 years, the intensive insulin regimen reduced the overall risk of microalbuminuria (urinary albumin ex-

Table 30.6		The Functional Stages of Diabetic Nephropathy[a]	
Stage	Onset from Diagnosis	Functional Abnormalities	Risk Factors for Progression
I: Clinically silent	Within 3 yr	↑ GFR	Hyperglycemia, intraglomerular hypertension, systemic hypertension, high protein intake
II: Incipient DN	7–15 yr	Microalbuminuria;[b] GFR starting to decline (may be normal or slightly ↑)	Hyperglycemia, systemic hypertension, high protein intake
III: Clinical DN	10–30 yr	Albuminuria;[c] GFR declining	Systemic hypertension, high protein intake
IV: ESRD	20–40 yr	GFR <10 mL/min	——

[a] DN = Diabetic nephropathy; ESRD = End-stage renal disease; GFR = Glomerular filtration rate.
[b] Microalbuminuria = Urinary albumin excretion 30–300 mg/24 hr.
[c] Albuminuria = Urinary albumin excretion >300 mg/24 hr.

cretion ≥40 mg/24 hours) by 39%, and that of albuminuria (urinary albumin excretion ≥300 mg/24 hours) by 54%.[221] Whether a reduction in the occurrence of microalbuminuria or overt albuminuria reduces the likelihood of progressing to end-stage renal disease will be clarified only by longer follow-up of DCCT cohorts.

Once overt albuminuria develops, strict glycemic control is no longer of any benefit in slowing the progression of diabetic nephropathy.[222] Likewise, in diabetic patients with no proteinuria, there is no evidence to indicate that strict glycemic control reduces the risk of clinical diabetic nephropathy. Regardless, the American Diabetes Association recommends tight glycemic control in all but those with advanced diabetic complications.[223,224]

Because T.S. has not yet developed albuminuria, she is likely to benefit from intense insulin therapy. This treatment regimen requires three or more daily doses of regular insulin by injection or an external pump. Doses are adjusted based upon the results of blood glucose tests that are monitored four times/day. T.S.'s fasting blood glucose concentration should be maintained between 70 and 120 mg/dL, with a postprandial concentration of 180 mg/dL. The Hbg$_{A1}$ should be maintained at below 7.5%. Compliance with this regimen requires the motivation of the patient, as well as the encouragement of the patient's family and health care providers. (See Chapter 48: Diabetes Mellitus for a more complete discussion of intensive insulin therapy.)

Antihypertensive Therapy

Virtually any level of untreated hypertension, either systemic or intraglomerular, can be associated with a reduction in glomerular filtration rate, regardless of the etiology of renal impairment. Upon diagnosis of insulin-dependent diabetes mellitus, most patients have elevated glomerular filtration rates, primarily due to increased intraglomerular pressure. In these patients, systemic hypertension usually occurs with the development of microalbuminuria. Diabetic nephropathy tends to occur more frequently in those with a persistently elevated glomerular filtration rate.[225] As such, the control of systemic and/or intraglomerular blood pressure is perhaps the single-most important factor for retarding the progression of renal impairment at any stage of diabetic nephropathy.[19,222] Treatment of hypertension in insulin-dependent diabetes mellitus patients with Stage I or II diabetic nephropathy can arrest the progression of renal disease. With the development of clinical diabetic nephropathy (Stage III), blood pressure reduction can only retard the progression of renal impairment.[16,19,210,211,226] Therefore, antihypertensive therapy should be initiated at the first sign of an increase from baseline blood pressure.

In patients with noninsulin-dependent diabetes mellitus, hypertension may precede any clinical renal manifestation, and is likely associated with obesity and insulin resistance.[226] Nonetheless, treatment of hypertension in noninsulin-dependent diabetes mellitus remains a useful strategy in reducing the rate of progression of diabetic nephropathy.

Diabetic patients with hypertension have elevated systemic vascular resistance and increased vasoconstriction to angiotensin II. In addition, angiotensin II plays a large role in increasing efferent arteriolar tone, leading to intraglomerular hypertension.[16,19] These angiotensin II-mediated effects are in large part responsible for the glomerular damage characteristic of diabetic nephropathy. Although the treatment of hypertension with virtually any agent can attenuate the progression of renal impairment,[16] the angiotensin converting-enzyme inhibitors, which inhibit the synthesis of angiotensin II, have become the drugs of choice for the treatment of diabetic hypertension. By reducing the efferent arteriolar tone, ACE inhibitors reduce the pressure within the glomeruli, thus attenuating glomerular damage. Clinically, ACE inhibitors slow the rate of decline in glomerular filtration rate and reduce urinary albumin excretion in a manner independent of their antihypertensive effect, and without the adverse metabolic effects seen with diuretics and β-adrenergic antagonists.[16,227,228] ACE inhibitors also can reduce glucose intolerance and diminish peripheral resistance to insulin.[228]

Captopril can slow the progression of diabetic nephropathy.[16,227] Patients with urinary albumin excretion greater than 500 mg/24 hours, with a maximum serum creatinine concentration of 2.5 mg/dL randomly received captopril 25 mg or placebo three times daily. After a median follow-up of three years, captopril showed a significant renal-protective effect in patients with a baseline serum creatinine concentration ≥1.5 mg/dL. In these patients, the risk of doubling serum creatinine concentrations (i.e., reduction of GFR by one-half) was reduced by 68%. Furthermore, there was a 61% risk reduction in the combined endpoints of death, dialysis, and renal transplantation in the captopril group. These beneficial effects were observed independent of captopril's antihypertensive effect.[227] As a result of this and other studies,[16] normotensive microalbuminuric patients such as T.S. should be treated with captopril 25 mg orally three times a day. The primary goal is to prevent the development of clinical diabetic nephropathy (urinary albumin excretion >300 mg/24 hours; see Table 30.6) and to reduce the risks of end-stage renal disease and death. Since the beneficial effects of captopril occur over months to years, T.S. must be monitored long-term for changes in kidney function and urinary albumin excretion.

Captopril is the only ACE inhibitor that has been studied in a large prospective trial to examine the progression of diabetic nephropathy. While other ACE-inhibitors may have a similar beneficial effect, their effectiveness has not yet been clearly established.

If T.S. develops a contraindication to the use of ACE inhibitors (e.g., renal artery stenosis; hyperkalemia), the calcium channel blockers (except nifedipine) are the next agents of choice, primarily due to their lack of adverse metabolic effect.[16] Diuretics should be reserved for diabetic nephropathy patients with edema. (Also see Chapters 48: Diabetes Mellitus and 10: Essential Hypertension.)

Dietary Protein Restriction

High protein consumption accelerates the progression of diabetic nephropathy, presumably due to increased glomerular hyperfiltration and intraglomerular pressure.[19,210,211] In patients with overt albuminuria, the rate of decline in glomerular filtration rate, as well as urinary albumin excretion, can be blunted by restricting protein intake to 0.6 to 0.8 gm/kg/day and maintaining an isocaloric diet.[19] There is, however, no evidence indicating a beneficial role of dietary protein restriction in diabetic patients with microalbuminuria. Nonetheless, given the risk of diabetic nephropathy progression with consumption of a high protein diet, T.S. should be advised to maintain an isocaloric diet with a protein intake of 1 gm/kg body weight/day. Since a typical Western diet is high in protein, some patients may have difficulty complying with such a low-protein diet due to its perceived unpalatability.

Chronic Glomerulopathies

Glomerulonephritis denotes inflammation of the glomerulus. In 1991, different forms of glomerulonephritis accounted for 12.6% of end-stage renal disease cases.[1] Glomerulonephritis may occur as a primary disease (Goodpasture's disease; amyloidosis; Wegener's granulomatosis), or secondarily as a manifestation of a systemic disease (lupus nephritis).[229] In humans, autoimmunity is the predominant pathogenic process leading to most forms of primary and secondary glomerulonephritis.[230] Although a number of autoantibodies are associated with glomerulonephritis, their exact role in the pathogenesis of glomerulonephritis is still unclear.[229,230] Nonetheless, analysis of autoantibodies in the clinical setting can aid in early diagnosis of glomerulonephritis.[229]

Glomerulonephritis often leads to acute renal failure. Patients with damage to greater than 50% of glomeruli in the presence of rapid loss in renal function (i.e., a 50% decline in GFR over 3 months) are classified as having *rapidly progressive glomerulonephritis*.[231] Up to 7% of biopsies from end-stage renal disease patients demonstrated rapidly progressive glomerulonephritis.[231] Rapidly progressive glomerulonephritis may be classified based upon the immunopathogenic etiology of the glomerular damage: 1) antiglomerular basement membrane antibody formation (e.g., Goodpasture's syndrome); 2) immune complex deposition (e.g., lupus nephritis); and 3) nonimmune deposit-mediated mechanism (e.g., Wegener's granulomatosis).[231] This chapter will focus on the treatment of the most common forms of chronic glomerulonephritis (i.e., lupus nephritis, amyloidosis, Wegener's granulomatosis, Goodpasture's syndrome). (See Chapter 29: Acute Renal Failure for a discussion of glomerulonephritis associated with acute renal failure.)

Lupus Nephritis

Systemic lupus erythematosus (SLE) is a multisystem autoimmune disease characterized by abnormalities in cell-mediated immunity such as B-cell hyperresponsiveness and defective T-cell-mediated suppressor activity. In certain predisposed individuals, SLE may lead to the development of lupus nephritis, a secondary form of glomerulonephritis. Lupus nephritis is the prototypical immune complex-mediated renal disease, characterized by deposition, or *in situ* formation of autoantibody-antigen complexes along the glomerular capillary network.

Lupus nephritis remains an important cause of mortality. Nearly all patients with systemic lupus erythematosus have some degree of renal involvement,[232] and up to 80% of patients develop clinical evidence of renal damage: heavy proteinuria, hematuria, decreased glomerular filtration rate, and hypertension.[233] Up to 25% of patients with SLE, without any clinical renal manifestations, may have silent lupus nephritis including its severest form, diffuse proliferative lupus nephritis.[233]

33. A.V., a 34-year-old female with a 7-year history of SLE, presents to the nephrology clinic for a follow-up of her lupus nephritis. Pertinent laboratory values are: serum Na 146 mEq/L, K 4.2 mEq/L, Cl 100 mEq/L, CO_2 content 25 mEq/L, SrCr 2.0 mg/dL, BUN 20 mg/dL, and WBC count 9600/mm³. RBC indices were normal. Platelet count was 175,000/mm³. Her 24-hour urine contained 2.3 gm of protein, and her UA contained 12 RBC/high-power field (HPF). Compared with her visit of a week ago, A.V.'s renal function and urinary indices (proteinuria, hematuria) showed substantial worsening of her nephritis. A.V. was hospitalized and a renal biopsy was performed, which showed inflammation of 40% of the glomeruli. What subjective and objective data in A.V. are consistent with a diagnosis of lupus nephritis and what is the stage of her nephritis? [SI units: Na 146 mmol/L; K 4.2 mmol/L; Cl 100 mmol/L; CO_2 25 mmol/L; SrCr 177 μmol/L; BUN 7.14 mmol/L of urea; WBC 9600 × 10⁶/L; platelet count 175 × 10⁹/L]

A.V. has clinical evidence of renal damage, as demonstrated by her proteinuria, hematuria, and increased serum creatinine concentration. The presence of RBCs in her urine indicates glomerular damage.

Staging

The World Health Organization has classified lupus nephritis based upon the patterns of glomerular disease (see Table 30.7).[234] This and other classification schemes provide a reasonable correlation among renal histopathology, renal outcome, and response to treatment (see Table 30.7).[234–237] Since A.V. has proteinuria, hematuria, and inflammation of less than 50% of her glomeruli, she is diagnosed as having class III (focal proliferative) glomerulonephritis.

Treatment

34. Should A.V.'s lupus nephritis be treated?

Lupus nephritis may present in various histological forms, and patients may transform from one form to another.[234] Unlike nonrenal manifestations of systemic lupus erythematosus, serologic markers of disease correlate poorly with lupus nephritis. Hence, elevations in serum creatinine, and worsening of proteinuria and hematuria, as seen in A.V., are used as primary markers of disease activity.[234]

There is a general consensus that patients such as A.V., who present with focal or diffuse proliferative glomerulonephritis (class III or IV), should be treated aggressively, with the primary goal of preventing irreversible renal damage.[234]

35. How should A.V.'s lupus nephritis be treated?

The treatment of lupus nephritis is somewhat empiric, but is based to some extent upon histological findings. Although appropriate treatment can improve patient outcome, vigorous attempts at suppressing systemic lupus erythematosus activity may lead to serious drug-related complications. Since the primary strategy in the treatment of lupus nephritis involves suppression of the immune system with corticosteroids and cytotoxic agents, clinicians need to be aware of the potential complications associated with therapy. Therefore, careful monitoring of patients is essential in determining the indication for treatment as well as improving prognosis.

Table 30.7	Clinical Outcome Correlation with Various Types of Lupus Nephritis[a]				
	Class				
Parameter	I: Normal Glomeruli	II: Mesangial Glomerulonephritis	III: Focal Proliferative Glomerulonephritis[b]	IV: Diffuse Proliferative Glomerulonephritis	V: Membranous Glomerulonephritis
Incidence	Quite rare	10%–30%	10%–25%	40%–60%	10%–20%
Usual clinical presentation	No urine abnormalities	Mild proteinuria and urine sediment abnormalities	Proteinuria and hematuria	Heavy proteinuria; active sediment; hypertension; renal failure	Proteinuria; often nephrotic syndrome
Renal prognosis	Excellent with treatment	Excellent without treatment	Good with aggressive treatment	Good with aggressive treatment	Renal failure in 50%; remission in 20%–30%
Transformation	To class II or IV 15%–20%; To class V 2%–5%	To class IV 20%–40%	To class V 2%–5%	To class III or V 5%–10%	—

[a] Adapted from reference 234.
[b] Focal proliferative with >50% of glomeruli involved may be included in class IV.

Toxicities associated with immunosuppressive agents depend upon both the dose and the duration of therapy. Abnormalities in hematopoiesis, such as neutropenia and thrombocytopenia, are the most common adverse effects associated with cytotoxic agents, and usually occur between 7 and 14 days after initiating therapy.[238] Immunosuppression in general increases a patient's susceptibility to a vast array of infections and to lymphocytic malignancies. In addition, the alkylating agent cyclophosphamide can cause nausea and vomiting, hemorrhagic cystitis, and alopecia. The antimetabolite azathioprine can cause pancreatitis and abnormalities in liver function.[239]

Oral Corticosteroids. Corticosteroids represent the cornerstone of therapy, especially in patients with a mild form of lupus nephritis. Low-dose prednisone should be given to patients with stable lupus nephritis. Those with a slowly progressive nephritis also may benefit from treatment with oral corticosteroids.[234] In patients with a more severe form of lupus nephritis (diffuse proliferative), prednisone 1 to 2 mg/kg/day for four to eight weeks, as a single morning dose, may be initiated. Due to the long-term complications of high-dose corticosteroid therapy, a lower starting dose of prednisone (1 mg/kg/day) may be reasonable. Gradual tapering of prednisone to a low-dose regimen of 0.2 to 0.4 mg/kg/day must be attempted once the glomerulonephritis has stabilized.

Intravenous Corticosteroids. For the treatment of acute exacerbations of lupus nephritis, as evident in A.V., high-dose pulse therapy with methylprednisolone (10 to 30 mg/kg IV, not to exceed 1 gm) for three to five days is effective in promptly reducing proteinuria and improving renal function.[240–242] Although generally well tolerated, rapid methylprednisolone injections may cause transient tremor, flushing, and altered taste sensation. Fatal arrhythmias and seizures have occurred.[243,244]

Given that A.V.'s lupus nephritis has worsened during high-dose prednisone therapy, she should receive pulse methylprednisolone until the flare-up is suppressed. Suppression of A.V.'s active lupus nephritis should be demonstrated by a reduction in proteinuria and hematuria, and an increase in her creatinine clearance. To reduce the risk of adverse effects associated with the rate of injection, A.V. should receive methylprednisolone over 30 minutes.[234] Once the flare-up is suppressed, low-dose oral prednisone (0.5 to 1 mg/kg/day) may be initiated.[232,242]

Oral Cytotoxic Agents. If A.V. fails to respond to high-dose methylprednisolone or has frequent renal flare-ups, she may require therapy with cytotoxic agents such as cyclophosphamide or azathioprine. Although controversy exists regarding the superiority of these agents as compared to oral corticosteroid monotherapy, evidence has mounted in favor of the superiority of cytotoxic agents. Compared to oral corticosteroid monotherapy, the ten-year outcome is considerably improved with cytotoxic agents (cyclophosphamide, azathioprine, or the combination).[237] Pooled analysis of eight randomized trials supports the superiority of cytotoxic agents over oral corticosteroid monotherapy, as evidenced by a reduced rate of renal deterioration, reduced incidence of end-stage renal disease, and lower mortality due to renal causes.[236] An additional benefit of cytotoxic agents is their steroid-sparing effect.[232,234] While the comparative efficacy of oral azathioprine and oral cyclophosphamide is less clear, the same pooled analysis indicates that azathioprine was better than cyclophosphamide in preserving renal function.[236] Studies at the National Institutes of Health have demonstrated azathioprine may be of most value in a specific subset of patients.[245]

The oral doses of azathioprine and cyclophosphamide should not exceed 2 mg/kg/day. Adverse effects of cytotoxic therapy include bone marrow suppression and, with chronic therapy, lymphocytic malignancies. In addition, cyclophosphamide may cause nausea, vomiting, sterile hemorrhagic cystitis, gonadal toxicity, and alopecia. Due to their low therapeutic index, oral cytotoxic agents should not be given for longer than six months.[234]

Intravenous Cytotoxic Agents. The choice between oral and intravenous cyclophosphamide for the treatment of lupus nephritis is not entirely clear. The ten-year renal outcome with intravenous cyclophosphamide is only marginally better than that of oral cytotoxic agents; however, intravenous cyclophosphamide is substantially superior to prednisone monotherapy. In addition, the risk of bladder toxicity and malignancy appears to be much lower with intravenous, as compared to oral cyclophosphamide.[237] However, the risk of toxicities such as herpes zoster and ovarian failure may be increased. Due to this unexplained difference in the adverse effect profiles of the two routes, intravenous cyclophosphamide is preferred for long-term cytotoxic therapy.

Before, and for 24 hours after initiation of intravenous cyclophosphamide, the patient must be well hydrated to prevent bladder toxicity. Therapy may be started with cyclophosphamide 0.5 to 1 gm/m^2 of body surface, infused over 30 to 60 minutes, with the lower doses reserved for patients with severe renal insufficiency.[234] This regimen may be repeated every three months for up to two years, with the dose adjusted to WBC nadir and renal function.[246] The need for a more prolonged course of therapy must be assessed on an individual basis.

36. Cyclosporine. Six months later, A.V. experiences another episode of lupus flare. This time, however, she fails to respond to the conventional immunosuppressive therapy of corticosteroids and cyclophosphamide. What should be the next step for treatment?

Although experience with cyclosporine in the treatment of lupus nephritis is preliminary,[247] patients who do not respond, such as A.V., or experience unacceptable adverse effects to conventional immunosuppressive therapy of corticosteroids or cyclophosphamide may be started on a trial of oral cyclosporine 5 mg/kg/day.[234,247] However, cyclosporine's nephrotoxicity and its effect on blood pressure may preclude its use in some patients with renal impairment or hypertension.

Cyclosporine Nephropathy

37. If A.V. requires long-term cyclosporine therapy, how should she be monitored?

Cyclosporine has been increasingly implicated in causing chronic interstitial nephritis characterized by fibrosis.[42,46] Acutely, cyclosporine causes vasoconstriction that with long-term administration, may lead to renal ischemia and damage.[46] While certain vasodilating agents such as calcium channel blockers may confer protection against cyclosporine-induced acute nephrotoxicity,[46,248] their long-term effect in reducing the risk of chronic renal failure is not known. Hence, A.V's renal function must be monitored regularly for the duration of her cyclosporine therapy. If she experiences a substantial decline in her renal function, appropriate radiologic or histologic studies will be needed to differentiate between cyclosporine nephrotoxicity and a lupus flare.

Primary Systemic Amyloidosis

Amyloid refers to substances that appear homogenous under light microscopy, but in reality consist of rigid, and linear aggregated fibrils. Amyloid is derived from plasma cells and primarily consists of immunoglobulins. These paraproteins have normal molecular structure and amino acid sequences, but have increased light chain production.[249,250] The tissue deposition of these light chains, or their fragments, leads to organ damage. *Amyloidosis* is a disorder characterized by the deposition of abnormal paraprotein fibrils in the extracellular space of multiple organs.[249,250] Amyloidosis may occur in local or systemic form, depending upon the type of abnormal protein produced by the plasma cells. Primary systemic amyloidosis, the most common form of the disease, and localized amyloidosis result from the formation and deposition of amyloid light chains (AL).[249,250] These insoluble light chains may self-aggregate and interact with other amyloid fibrils to form polymers. Structural damage leading to organ dysfunction occurs with continuous formation and accumulation of these fibril polymers.[250]

Secondary amyloidosis results from the formation and deposition of protein A. As the name implies, secondary amyloidosis develops in the presence of a coexisting condition, such as an acute or chronic infection or a chronic inflammatory process. Rheumatoid arthritis is the most common cause of secondary amyloidosis.[251] Because of its lower incidence and the general lack of effective therapy, secondary amyloidosis will not be covered in this chapter. Further information on secondary amyloidosis can be found elsewhere.[251]

Amyloidosis can involve virtually any organ, with the kidneys, heart, spleen, liver, skin, GI tract, and the nervous system being affected most often. Less frequently, the respiratory tract, and the hematopoietic and skeletal systems are affected. Although the diagnosis of amyloidosis ideally is confirmed by the demonstration of amyloid deposits on the tissues of affected organs,[249] false negative results may occur. Therefore, the diagnosis of amyloidosis

often is based upon manifestations of organ damage and the presence of paraproteins in the urine and serum.[249,252] Edema is the most common presenting symptom of amyloidosis, and is due to congestive heart failure or nephrotic syndrome.[249] Renal involvement is extremely common, with greater than 80% of patients exhibiting proteinuria. One-third of patients have proteinuria in the nephrotic range (>3.5 gm/day), while one-half may present with some degree of renal impairment. Hypertension is less common than with other forms of renal failure, occurring in nearly one-third of patients with advanced amyloidosis and renal dysfunction.[249] Renal amyloidosis may progress to CRF within a few months to years. Infrequently, progression to end-stage renal disease is rapid.

38. L.M., a 56-year-old white female, is referred by her family physician to the nephrology clinic for management of her renal insufficiency, which appears to have occurred over the past 4 months. Over the past month, she has complained of fatigue and dyspnea on exertion (DOE). Pertinent laboratory values are as follows: SrCr 2.7 mg/dL, BUN 39 mg/dL, albumin 2.8 gm/dL, total serum protein 4.9 gm/dL. The hematologic studies were normal. Her UA showed a 3+ proteinuria. Her 24-hour urine collection contained 3.3 gm of protein. Serum and urine immunoelectrophoresis confirmed the presence of λ fragment of immunoglobulin G light chain. Physical examination revealed diffuse bilateral rales in the lungs, massive hepatosplenomegaly, and a moderate (2+) edema of both legs. She has no evidence of acute or chronic infection or a chronic inflammatory process. Renal ultrasonography revealed enlarged kidneys bilaterally with no obstruction. Subsequent renal biopsy showed amyloid deposits in the mesangial area of the glomeruli extending to the basement membrane. What subjective and objective data in L.M. are consistent with a diagnosis of primary systemic amyloidosis? [SI units: SrCr 239 μmol/L; BUN 13.9 mmol/L of urea; albumin 28 gm/L; total protein 49 gm/L]

The diagnosis of amyloidosis in L.M. is confirmed due to the presence of: 1) amyloid deposits in the glomeruli; 2) multiple-organ damage; and 3) paraproteins (λ fragment of immunoglobulin G light chain) in the urine and serum. Her multiple-organ damage involves the kidneys (proteinuria, renal insufficiency, kidney enlargement), heart (fatigue, DOE, pulmonary congestion, pedal edema), liver, and spleen (hepatosplenomegaly).

Treatment

39. Should L.M.'s primary systemic amyloidosis be treated?

The prognosis of untreated primary systemic amyloidosis is poor; although, treatment often is unsatisfactory. The median survival of patients with untreated or refractory primary systemic amyloidosis is less than 15 months.[249,250,253,254] Mortality is due to cardiac causes (CHF, arrhythmias) in 40%, and to renal failure in 10% of the cases.[249,250] Patients with acute deterioration of renal function have worse survival.[250]

Given the poor prognosis of untreated primary systemic amyloidosis, treatment of L.M. is warranted. Although amyloid deposits may persist, the primary goal of treatment is resolution of all organ dysfunctions.[253]

40. How should L.M.'s primary systemic amyloidosis be treated?

Salt restriction and loop diuretics are the cornerstone of therapy for the treatment of edema due to proteinuria or heart failure. However, because of the large amount of protein that may be lost in the urine (up to 40 gm/day), urinary protein binding of diuretics may render these agents ineffective,[255] thus necessitating bilateral nephrectomy.[250] L.M. should be started on furosemide 40 mg orally twice daily. Dose adjustments must be based upon response (e.g., edema, weight loss).

Melphalan. Because primary amyloidosis involves abnormal immunoglobulin production by the plasma cells, alkylating agents such as melphalan are used to decrease both the number of these cells and their immunoglobulin production. Melphalan acts by creating DNA-protein crosslinks, thus inhibiting DNA transcription and translation.[239] The treatment of the underlying amyloidosis may involve prolonged therapy with melphalan and prednisone,[249,252–254,256–258] although the exact role of prednisone is unclear. Over the years, the use of this combination has become the standard of care in the treatment of primary systemic amyloidosis, without much scientific evidence to support this practice. Treatment of L.M. with melphalan/prednisone, given as seven-day cycles every six weeks, may be effective in prolonging survival and protecting the kidneys. In one of only two randomized trials, approximately 20% of patients responded to treatment with melphalan plus prednisone. The response rate was 40% in patients with nephrotic syndrome and normal renal function with no cardiac involvement. The median survival in patients who responded was 89.4 months, with a median five-year survival of 78%. In nonresponding patients, the median survival was less than 15 months, with a five-year survival of only 7%.[253]

L.M. should receive melphalan 0.15 mg/kg/day in two divided doses plus prednisone 0.8 mg/kg/day in four divided doses, both given for seven days every six weeks. Because of the risk of bone marrow toxicity with melphalan, a complete blood count must be obtained at least every three weeks. The platelet count may serve as the most sensitive measure of myelotoxicity.[257] The daily melphalan dose of each cycle may be increased if there is no substantial change in hematologic parameters; however, if L.M. develops leukopenia (WBC nadir 3000/mm^3) or thrombocytopenia (platelet count <100,000/mm^3), downward adjustment of the dose is warranted. Because of the prolonged time to response (median: 12 months),[253] L.M. must be treated for at least one year even if no response is observed. Despite the demonstrated benefit of this regimen,[252–254,258] up to one-fifth of patients treated for greater than 3.5 years may develop acute leukemia or other cytogenetic abnormalities.[259] Nonetheless, given the poor prognosis of untreated amyloidosis, a one-year trial with melphalan and prednisone is warranted for L.M.

Colchicine. Because of its inhibition of protein A secretion, colchicine has been effective in preventing and treating amyloidosis due to familial Mediterranean fever.[260] Based upon its ability to disrupt microtubule organization and cell function, colchicine has been tried in the treatment of primary amyloidosis. A historical-controlled study demonstrated colchicine's effectiveness in prolonging survival in patients with primary systemic amyloidosis;[261] however, there is no evidence to indicate the effectiveness of colchicine on disease regression as observed with melphalan and prednisone therapy.[252] Nonetheless, a trial of colchicine may be considered for patients in whom alkylating agents are contraindicated. In one study, eight patients who did not respond to the melphalan and prednisone combination had colchicine added to the treatment regimen; however, insufficient detail was provided on these patients to draw any conclusions regarding the benefit of such a strategy.[252] Colchicine may be administered 0.6 mg twice daily. Although the optimal length of therapy is unclear, colchicine may be continued for at least six months, and possibly longer.[252,261] Currently, colchicine is not indicated for treating L.M.

Some major questions remain unanswered in the treatment of systemic primary amyloidosis. Does addition of colchicine to the melphalan-prednisone combination improve outcome? How does melphalan monotherapy compare with the melphalan-prednisone combination? How effective is the melphalan-colchicine combination? Given the relatively low survival rate of primary amyloidosis, the pursuit of these answers is a worthy goal.

41. How should L.M.'s therapy be monitored?

Because of the prolonged time to response (median: 12 months), short-term improvements in organ function may not be observed. Hence, L.M. requires long-term monitoring for efficacy and toxicity. The toxicities of melphalan are significant, and include nausea, vomiting, myelosuppression, alopecia, and pulmonary fibrosis (with long-term therapy).[239] As with other alkylating agents, myelosuppression due to melphalan is dependent upon both the dose and the duration of therapy. Therefore, the management of myelosuppression is similar to that of cyclophosphamide and other immunosuppressive agents. Abnormalities in hematopoiesis, such as neutropenia and thrombocytopenia, are the most common adverse effects associated with cytotoxic agents, and usually occur between 7 and 14 days after initiating therapy.[239] Myelosuppression in general increases a patient's susceptibility to infections and to lymphocytic malignancies. Although the risk is small, melphalan can cause the secondary development of acute nonlymphocytic leukemia or dysmyelopoietic syndrome. In one case series,[259] the median time from first melphalan exposure to development of acute nonlymphocytic leukemia was 51 months (range: 35.5 to 89 months); the median time from the diagnosis of dysmyelopoietic syndrome was 8.1 months. Therefore, long-term monitoring of patient's blood count is essential for early detection and management of secondary leukemic or preleukemic disorders.

Goodpasture's Disease (Antiglomerular Basement Membrane Antibody-Mediated Nephritis)

Several diseases are associated with pulmonary hemorrhage and rapidly progressive glomerulonephritis. These include autoimmune, malignant, and renal disorders. Approximately one-third of these "pulmonary-renal syndromes" are associated with the presence of antiglomerular basement membrane antibodies. The majority of other cases are associated with systemic vasculitis (e.g., Wegener's granulomatosis).[262] The term Goodpasture's *syndrome* denotes the syndrome of pulmonary hemorrhage and rapidly progressive glomerulonephritis with or without antiglomerular basement membrane antibodies.[263–267] In this chapter, Goodpasture's *syndrome* will refer to the syndrome of pulmonary hemorrhage and rapidly progressive glomerulonephritis due to any cause, whereas Goodpasture's *disease* will denote the syndrome in association with antiglomerular basement membrane antibodies.[262]

In the dialysis era, most early deaths with Goodpasture's disease are due to fulminant pulmonary hemorrhage, whereas most deaths occurring later are due to secondary infections. Once significant renal disease develops, rapid progression to end-stage renal disease is possible. The etiology of Goodpasture's disease is due primarily to the development of antiglomerular basement membrane antibodies against basement membranes of the glomeruli and the pulmonary alveolar septa. The ensuing damage may lead to diffuse hemorrhage of the capillaries into the acinar portion of the lungs, and formation of crescentic necrotizing glomerulonephritis in the kidneys.[231,265,266] (Crescentic structures are the shape of the moon in its first quarter.) Antiglomerular basement membrane antibodies can cause glomerular damage; however, for alveolar damage to occur, other inciting factors need to be present to either increase capillary permeability or augment binding of the antibodies to the alveolar basement membrane.[266] Pathogens (e.g., influenza A virus), cigarette smoking, hydrocarbon inhalation, and toxic chemical exposure all have been associated with the development of antiglomerular basement membrane antibodies-induced alveolar hemorrhage.[262,265–267]

About one-half of patients have a recent history of upper respiratory infection. Alveolar hemorrhage typically precedes clinical manifestations of renal disease. Symptoms include hemoptysis, exertional dyspnea, cough, and in severe cases, acute respiratory failure. One-half of patients develop iron deficiency anemia due to sequestration of red blood cells within the alveoli.[262,265–267] The renal manifestations of Goodpasture's disease include red blood cells, red blood cell casts, and protein in the urine. In 50% of cases, patients may develop azotemia. Hypertension is an uncommon finding.[231,264,265,267]

Because of the many causes of pulmonary-renal syndrome and the nonspecific glomerular changes seen on biopsy, the diagnosis of Goodpasture's disease requires the demonstration of either circulating or tissue-fixed antiglomerular basement membrane antibodies.[266–268] However, due to the potentially rapid and fulminant progression of the disease, treatment should not await biopsy or serum antibody-titer results.

42. F.K., a 42-year-old white male, presents to the clinic with a 1-month history of anorexia, fatigue, cough, and DOE. Over the past week, he has noticed bright red blood in his phlegm, which has worsened in the past 3 days. Social history includes the following: he owns a local gasoline station and smokes 1 pack of cigarettes/day. On physical examination, he appeared pale and in mild respiratory distress. Pertinent laboratory values are as follows: serum Na 143 mEq/L, K 5.1 mEq/L, Cl 102 mEq/L, CO_2 content 24 mEq/L, SrCr 2.8 mg/dL, BUN 41 mg/dL. Hematologic studies revealed an Hct of 35%, an Hgb of 12.1 gm/dL, mean corpuscular volume (MCV) 69 μm^3 (Normal: 80–100), mean corpuscular Hgb (MCH) concentration 24% (Normal: 31–36), and reticulocyte count 1.9% (Normal: 0.5–2.0). During last year's physical check-up visit, his SrCr and BUN were within the normal range. His 24-hour urine contained 3.8 gm of protein, and revealed a Cl_{Cr} of 24 mL/min. His urine also contained many RBC casts and 16 RBC/HPF. Chest x-ray showed alveolar shadowing, spreading from the hilar region. Based upon his subjective and objective data, which of the chronic glomerulopathies is F.K. likely to have?
[SI units: Na 143 mmol/L; K 5.1 mmol/L; Cl 102 mmol/L; CO_2 24 mmol/L; SrCr 247 μmol/L; BUN 14.6 mmol/L of urea; Hct 0.35; Hgb 121 gm/L; MCV 69 fL (Normal: 80–100); MCH 0.24 (Normal: 0.31–0.36); reticulocyte count 0.019; Cl_{Cr} 0.40 mL/sec]

F.K.'s cough, hemoptysis, respiratory distress, and chest x-ray findings are suggestive of alveolar hemorrhage. He also has clinical evidence of renal damage, as demonstrated by proteinuria, hematuria, and increased serum creatinine concentration. As such, F.K. is likely to be suffering from a pulmonary-renal syndrome, presumably exacerbated by his daily exposure to hydrocarbons superimposed on his daily tobacco use. However, the definitive diagnosis of Goodpasture's disease requires the demonstration of either circulating or tissue-fixed antiglomerular basement membrane antibodies.[266–268]

Treatment

43. Should F.K.'s pulmonary-renal syndrome be treated?

Although F.K.'s pulmonary-renal syndrome has not been definitively diagnosed as Goodpasture's disease, due to the potentially rapid and fulminant progression of the disease, treatment should not await biopsy or serum antibody-titer results. Therefore, F.K. requires aggressive treatment to prevent rapid and irreversible renal damage.

44. F.K. was hospitalized and a renal biopsy was performed, which showed inflammation of 50% of the glomeruli. The results of the serum antiglomerular basement membrane antibodies titer will not be available for another week. What are the goals of therapy and how should F.K. be treated?

The goals of treatment for Goodpasture's disease are rapid control of alveolar hemorrhage and prevention of irreversible damage to the extrapulmonary organs, especially the kidneys.[266] These goals may be accomplished by removing the circulating antiglomerular basement membrane antibodies with plasma exchange (plasmapheresis), and by preventing antibody synthesis with chemotherapy. Most studies of Goodpasture's disease utilize historic controls, making the evaluation of different treatment regimens difficult.[264,265,269,270] Nonetheless, the probability of renal recovery can be predicted with reasonable certainty. Progression to end-stage renal disease may be inevitable in individuals who have one or more of the following: 1) serum creatinine concentration greater than 6 to 7 mg/dL; 2) total anuria; and 3) damage to more than 85% of the glomeruli.[231,264–268,270,271] Given the risks of immunosuppressive chemotherapy, patients with one or more of the above criteria should be treated only in the presence of pulmonary hemorrhage or in preparation for kidney transplantation. Dialysis-dependent patients who are not anuric and who do not have crescent formation in the majority of the glomeruli still may respond to aggressive treatment.[264] Since F.K. does not meet any of the above criteria, he is likely to benefit from immunosuppressive therapy.

Plasma exchange (plasmapheresis) combined with immunosuppressive therapy is the cornerstone of treatment for antiglomerular basement membrane antibody-mediated nephritis. The rationale for this approach is to rapidly remove the antibodies with plasmapheresis, while preventing their synthesis with the immunosuppressive agents. This combination can rapidly suppress the alveolar hemorrhage within 24 to 48 hours, and retard the progression of mild-to-moderate renal insufficiency.[264,272] Therefore, F.K. should receive daily plasmapheresis for 14 days, or until the circulating antiglomerular basement membrane antibodies are suppressed. To prevent fluid loss, 5% human albumin solution must be administered during plasma exchange.[262]

Pulse Methylprednisolone. High-dose (1 to 2 gm/day) intravenous methylprednisolone may be beneficial in treating alveolar hemorrhage; however, this therapy is not effective in the treatment of active renal disease.[262,268,271] Therefore, F.K. also may receive pulse doses of intravenous methylprednisolone to treat his alveolar hemorrhage.

Oral Cyclophosphamide plus Corticosteroids. Immunosuppressive therapy is essential in preventing the synthesis of antiglomerular basement membrane antibodies. Most often, patients are treated with a combination of cyclophosphamide and prednisolone or prednisone. In the absence of alveolar hemorrhage, immunosuppression alone should be tried for patients with an initial serum creatinine concentrations of less than 3 mg/dL, such as F.K., or those with less than 30% glomerular crescent formation.[268] Those with a more severe form of glomerulonephritis may benefit from concomitant plasma exchange.[231,262] F.K. should be treated with oral cyclophosphamide 3 mg/kg/day, rounded to nearest 50 mg, plus prednisolone or prednisone 1 mg/kg/day (maximum daily dose: 60 mg).[262] Patients older than 55 years may be given lower cyclophosphamide doses (2 to 2.5 mg/kg/day).[268] The dose must be reduced by one-half for patients with GFRs less than 10 mL/minute,[34] and for maintaining the WBC above 4000/mm³. F.K.'s prednisone dose may be reduced to 20 mg/day after four weeks and more slowly thereafter. Cyclophosphamide must be continued for at least eight weeks, after which withdrawal of both agents may be safely accomplished in the absence of disease activity or circulating titers of antiglomerular basement membrane antibodies.[270]

45. How should F.K.'s therapy be monitored?

Once therapy is initiated, serial antiglomerular basement membrane antibodies titer, urinalysis, and serum creatinine measurements must be obtained to monitor for disease relapse. Because relapse commonly is preceded by a viral or bacterial infection, antiglomerular basement membrane antibody titer may not rise during reactivation of Goodpasture's disease.[231,262,265] Alveolar hemorrhage may be exacerbated by cigarette smoking, circulatory volume overload, and exposure to hydrocarbons and other toxic chemicals.[231,262,265,266] Once the autoimmune activity subsides, as evidenced by a complete absence of circulating antiglomerular basement membrane antibodies, recurrence is extremely uncommon.[231,262,265,266]

Wegener's Granulomatosis

46. The result of F.K.'s cytoplasmic-staining antineutrophil cytoplasmic antibody (c-ANCA) is negative. The nephrologist has ruled out Wegener's granulomatosis. What is Wegener's granulomatosis and what is the significance of this finding?

Wegener's granulomatosis is a primary systemic vasculitis characterized by granulomatous inflammation of the upper and lower respiratory tract and secondary glomerulonephritis.[273–275] Primary systemic vasculitic syndromes, such as Wegener's granulomatosis, often cause glomerulonephritis. Although vasculitis is defined as inflammation of blood vessels of any size,[273] the small and medium size vessels are most commonly affected.[274] The etiology of Wegener's granulomatosis is unclear; however, autoimmunity is suspected mainly for two reasons. First, Wegener's granulomatosis is a systemic inflammatory disease without a known infectious etiology. Second, good treatment response can be obtained with immunosuppressive therapy.[274,276]

The clinical features of Wegener's granulomatosis include upper airway disease such as sinusitis, epistaxis, and nasopharyngitis, as well as otitis media due to blockage of the eustachian tube. Constitutional symptoms include fever, night sweats, arthralgia, anorexia, and malaise. After a few months, weakness may progress so physical activity is severely limited.[277] Although the lungs are invariably affected, most patients remain asymptomatic. However, cough and hemoptysis may be present. The laboratory signs also are nonspecific and indicate the presence of a systemic inflammatory process. They include elevated erythrocyte sedimentation rate in virtually all patients, anemia of chronic disease in more than one-half of patients, and thrombocytosis in one-third of cases.[274,276,277] Hematuria and proteinuria can be prominent features of Wegener's granulomatosis,[274,276,277] and are present upon initial presentation in 80% of patients.[278] The presence of severely diminished renal function, seen in approximately 10% of patients, is an ominous sign, with nearly one-third of these patients progressing to end-stage renal disease.[276] Patients may progress rapidly from mild to severe glomerulonephritis over weeks or even days.[276] All patients with Wegener's granulomatosis are at risk for the development of irreversible rapidly progressive glomerulonephritis. Renal histological findings are nonspecific, with the majority of patients exhibiting necrotizing crescentic glomerulonephritis.[273,276,279]

Wegener's granulomatosis is diagnosed primarily by the presenting signs and symptoms. According to the American College of Rheumatology 1990 classification, a person is diagnosed with Wegener's granulomatosis if any two of the following four criteria are present: 1) nasal or oral inflammation; 2) abnormal chest radiograph; 3) microhematuria (>5 RBCs/HPF) or red blood cell casts in the urine sediment; and 5) granulomatous inflammation on biopsy.[275] The discovery of cytoplasmic-staining antineutrophil cytoplasmic antibody and its strong association with Wegener's granulomatosis has permitted a more certain diagnosis. The specificity of the c-ANCA test is greater than 95%, while its sensitivity depends primarily upon the extent of disease activity.[280–283] Because of the substantial rise in titer that commonly precedes relapse of Wegener's granulomatosis, the c-ANCA test is best used to follow the course of disease activity and guide induction of therapy.[280,284]

Before immunosuppressive therapy, the two-year survival rate for patients with Wegener's granulomatosis was less than 10%. However, long-term treatment with cyclophosphamide and corticosteroids has achieved a greater than 90% remission induction rate, with a five-year survival rate of 80%.[276] The main predictive factors for treatment success are the extent of renal damage before therapy starts and how long therapy is delayed after symptoms develop.[274,276,279]

Treatment

Oral Cyclophosphamide. Because Wegener's granulomatosis is considered an autoimmune inflammatory disease, immunosuppressive therapy is the mainstay of treatment. The greatest experience has been with oral cyclophosphamide. Upon diagnosis of active Wegener's granulomatosis, cyclophosphamide 2 mg/kg/day, as a single morning dose, should be initiated to prevent irreversible glomerular scarring. With a more fulminant form of the disease, higher doses (4 to 5 mg/kg/day) may be used. The dose of cyclophosphamide must be titrated to keep the WBC greater than 4000/mm^3. High fluid intake (>3 L/day) reduces the risk of hemorrhagic cystitis.[273,274,276] Because of the high relapse rate, cyclophosphamide must be continued for at least one year after attainment of complete remission.[273,274,276] Then the cyclophosphamide may be tapered gradually by decreasing the daily dose by 25 mg every three months.[276]

Intravenous Cyclophosphamide. Induction treatment with pulse intravenous boluses of cyclophosphamide is not satisfactory due to high relapse rates and increased toxicity.[285] However, there are two conditions for which intravenous cyclophosphamide may be considered: 1) patients who have not responded to conventional treatment; and 2) patients who initially have developed severe renal dysfunction, including those requiring dialysis. In the former, intravenous cyclophosphamide 1 gm/m^2 in 150 mL of saline may be administered over 60 minutes. The dose must be reduced by one-half in patients with a GFR less than 30 mL/minute. This regimen may be administered monthly for six months, after which a dosage reduction may be attempted.[273,274]

In patients who initially have severe renal failure, there is less experience. Renal improvement may be obtained by administering intravenous cyclophosphamide 1 gm every 6 to 12 weeks for three doses. The dose may be reduced by 25% in patients with severe renal impairment (SrCr >5 mg/dL).

To reduce the risk of infection, the dose of cyclophosphamide must be adjusted to achieve a ten-day WBC nadir of 1500 to 3000/mm^3. To reduce bladder toxicity, mesna 200 mg every four to six hours may be administered for four doses. As with oral cyclophosphamide, high fluid intake also is necessary;[273,279] however, if the patient is oliguric, adequate urine output may be maintained by administering furosemide. Antiemetics may be administered as needed.[286]

Corticosteroids. The main role of corticosteroids is to induce remission of the disease. Upon diagnosis of active Wegener's granulomatosis, prednisone 1 mg/kg/day must be initiated along with oral cyclophosphamide and continued for two to four weeks until the immunosuppressive effect of cyclophosphamide becomes evident.[273,276] Over the next two months, the dose may be tapered to 60 mg every other day to reduce the risk of infection. Then the dose may be tapered by 5 mg/week in order to discontinue prednisone over three to six months.[273,276]

For patients with a more fulminant form of the disease, pulse methylprednisolone 1 gm/m^2/day for three doses may be administered. The dose may be repeated in one to two weeks if progression is uncontrolled.[273]

Azathioprine. Because of its poor efficacy,[276] azathioprine should not be used as a first-line agent in the treatment of active Wegener's granulomatosis. However, if remission is induced with cyclophosphamide and the patient cannot tolerate long-term treatment with that agent, azathioprine 2 mg/kg/day may be substituted.[276]

References

1 **National Institute of Diabetes and Digestive and Kidney Disease, The National Institutes of Health.** USRDS 1994 Annual Data Report, July 1994. Bethesda, MD.

2 **Rolin H, Hall PM.** Evaluation of glomerular filtration rate and renal plasma flow. In: Jacobson H et al., eds. Principles and Practice of Nephrology. Philadelphia: BC Decker; 1991:158.

3 **Cordova HR et al.** Clinical manifestations and complications of the uremic state. In: Jacobson H et al., eds. Principles and Practice of Nephrology. Philadelphia: BC Decker; 1991:690.

4 **Coe FL, Brenner BM.** Approach to the patient with diseases of the kidneys, and urinary tract. In: Wilson JD et al., eds. Harrison's Principles of Internal Medicine. New York: McGraw Hill; 1991:1134.

5 **May RC.** Pathophysiology of uremia. In: Brenner BM, Rector FCJ, eds. The Kidney. Philadelphia: WB Saunders; 1991:1997.

6 **Anderson S, Brenner BM.** Effects of aging on the renal glomerulus. Am J Med. 1986;80:435.

7 **Harrington AR, Zimmerman SW.** Chronic renal failure. In: Harrington AR, Zimmerman SW, eds. Renal Pathophysiology. New York: Wiley; 1982:167.

8 **Sjostrom PA et al.** Extensive tubular secretion and reabsorption of creatinine in humans. Scand J Urol Nephrol. 1988;22:129.

9 **Mackenzie W et al.** Creatinine measurements often yield false estimates of progression in chronic renal failure. Kidney Int. 1988;34:412.

10 **Bennett WM.** Renal function tests. In: Bennett WM, ed. Drugs and Renal Disease. New York: Churchill Livingstone; 1986:1.

11 **Kincaid-Smith P.** Anticoagulants are of value in the treatment of renal disease. Am J Kidney Dis. 1984;3:299.

12 **Border WA.** Anticoagulants are of little value in the treatment of renal disease. Am J Kidney Dis. 1984;3:308.

13 **Pullman TN, Coe FL.** Pathophysiology of chronic renal failure. Clin Symp. 1984;36:3.

14 **Hostetter TH.** Progressive glomerular injury: roles of dietary protein and compensatory hypertrophy. Pharmacol Rev. 1984;36(Suppl. 2):101.

15 **National High Blood Pressure Education Program.** National High Blood Pressure Education Program Working Group report on hypertension and chronic renal failure. Arch Intern Med. 1991;151:1280.

16 **Kasiske BL et al.** Effect of antihypertensive therapy on the kidney in patients with diabetes: a meta-regression analysis. Ann Intern Med. 1993;118:129.

17 **ter Wee PM, Donker AJ.** Clinical strategies for arresting progression of renal disease. Kidney Int Suppl. 1992; 42(Suppl. 38):S114.

18 **Salvetti A et al.** What effect does high blood pressure control have on the progression toward renal failure? Am J Kidney Dis. 1993;21(Suppl. 3):10.

19 **Tuttle KR et al.** Treatment of diabetic nephropathy: a rational approach based on its pathophysiology. Semin Nephrol. 1991;11:220.

20 **Blachley JD.** The role of dietary protein in the progression and symptomatology of chronic renal failure. Am J Med Sci. 1984;288:5.

21 **Rosman JB et al.** Prospective randomized trial of early dietary protein restriction in chronic renal failure. Lancet. 1984;2:1291.

22 **El Nahas AM et al.** Selective effect of low protein diets in chronic renal diseases. Br Med J. 1984;289:1337.

23 **Giordano C.** Early dietary protein restriction protects the failing kidney. Kidney Int. 1985;28(Suppl. 17):S66.

24 **Mitch WE et al.** The effect of a keto acid-amino acid supplement to a restricted diet on the progression of chronic renal failure. N Engl J Med. 1984;311:623.

25 **Frohling PT et al.** Influence of phosphate restriction, keto-acids and vitamin D on the progression of chronic renal failure. Proc Eur Dial Transplant Assoc. 1984;21:561.

26 **Attman PO et al.** Lipoprotein metabolism and renal failure. Am J Kidney Dis. 1993;21:573.

27 **Keane WF et al.** Is the aggressive management of hyperlipidemia in nephrotic syndrome mandatory? Kidney Int. 1992;42(Suppl. 38):S134.

28 **Jacobson HR.** Chronic renal failure: pathophysiology. Lancet. 1991;338:419.

29 **Klahr S et al.** The progression of renal disease. N Engl J Med. 1988;318:1657.

30 **Keane WF et al.** Hyperlipidemia and progressive renal disease. Kidney Int. 1991;39(Suppl. 31):S41.

31 **Mulec H et al.** Relationship between serum cholesterol and diabetic nephropathy. Lancet. 1990;1:1537.

32 **Appel G.** Lipid abnormalities in renal disease. Kidney Int. 1991;39:169.

33 **Appel GB, Appel AS.** Lipid lowering agents in proteinuric diseases. Am J Nephrol. 1990;10(Suppl. 1):110.

34 **Bennett WM.** Guide to drug dosage in renal failure. Clin Pharmacokinet. 1988;15:326.

35 **Campbell RA.** Other uremic toxins. In: Massry SG, Glassock RJ, eds. Textbook of Nephrology. Baltimore: Williams & Wilkins; 1989:1144.

36 **Schoots A et al.** Uremic toxins and the elusive middle molecules. Nephron. 1984;38:1.

37 **Massry SG.** Parathyroid hormone as a uremic toxin. In: Massry SG, Glassock RJ, eds. Textbook of Nephrology. Baltimore: Williams & Wilkins; 1989: 1126.

38 **Eschbach JW, Adamson JW.** Anemia of end-stage renal disease (ESRD). Kidney Int. 1985;28:1.

39 **Kincaid-Smith P, Nanra RS.** Lithium-induced and analgesic-induced renal disease. In: Schrier RW, Gottschalk CW, eds. Diseases of the Kidney. Boston: Little, Brown and Co.; 1993:1099.

40 **Chasko SB et al.** Urothelial neoplasia of the upper urinary tract. Pathol Annu. 1981;16(Pt. 2):127.

41 **Drukker W et al.** Analgesic nephropathy: an underestimated cause of end-stage renal disease. Int J Artif Organs. 1986;9:219.

42 **Hoitsma AJ et al.** Drug-induced nephrotoxicity: aetiology, clinical features and management. Drug Saf. 1991;6: 131.

43 **Kincaid-Smith P.** Renal toxicity of non-narcotic analgesics: at-risk patients and prescribing applications. Med Toxicol. 1986;1:14.

44 **Prescott LF.** Analgesic nephropathy: a reassessment of the role of phenacetin and other analgesics. Drugs. 1982;23: 75.

45 **Henrich WL.** Analgesic nephropathy. Am J Med Sci. 1988;295:561.

46 **Paller MS.** Drug-induced nephropathies. Med Clin North Am. 1990;74: 909.

47 **Walker RG et al.** Renal pathology associated with lithium therapy. Pathology. 1983;15:403.

48 **Walker RG et al.** Structural and functional effects of long-term lithium therapy. Kidney Int. 1982;21(Suppl. 11): S13.

49 **Hestbech J et al.** Chronic renal lesions following long-term treatment with lithium. Kidney Int. 1977;12:205.

50 **Chiu E et al.** Renal findings after 30 years on lithium. Br J Psychiatry. 1983; 143:424.

51 **Johnson GF et al.** Renal function and lithium treatment: initial and follow-up tests in manic-depressive patients. J Affect Disord. 1984;6:249.

52 **Bourgoignie JJ.** Disturbances in fluid, electrolyte and acid-base balance: patients with chronic renal failure. In: Massry SG, Glassock RJ, eds. Textbook of Nephrology. Baltimore: Williams & Wilkins; 1989:1263.

53 **Mitch WE, Wilcox CS.** Disorders of body fluids, sodium and potassium in chronic renal failure. Am J Med. 1982; 72:536.

54 **Andreucci VE et al.** Clinical diagnosis of acute renal failure. In: Andreucci VE, ed. Acute Renal Failure. Boston: Martinus Nijhoff; 1984:189.

55 **Gabow PA, Peterson LN.** Disorders of potassium metabolism. In: Schrier RW, ed. Renal and Electrolyte Disorders. Boston: Little, Brown and Co.; 1992:231.

56 **Valtin H.** Renal Function: Mechanisms Preserving Fluid and Solute Balance in Health. Boston, MA: Little, Brown and Co.; 1983:249–67.

57 **Alfrey AC, Chan L.** Chronic renal failure: manifestations and pathogenesis. In: Schrier RW, ed. Renal and Electrolyte Disorders. Boston: Little, Brown and Co.; 1992:539.

58 **Textor SC et al.** Hyperkalemia in azotemic patients during angiotensin-converting enzyme inhibition and aldosterone reduction with captopril. Am J Med. 1982;73:719.

59 **Hoffman BF, Bigger JTJ.** Digitalis and allied cardiac glycosides. In: Gillman AG et al., eds. The Pharmacologic Basis of Therapeutics. New York: Pergamon; 1990:814.

60 **Andreucci VE.** Conservative management and general care of patients with acute renal failure. In: Andreucci VE, ed. Acute Renal Failure. Boston: Martinus Nijhoff; 1984:403.

61 **Zull DN.** Disorders of potassium metabolism. Emerg Med Clin North Am. 1989;7:771.

62 **Gennari FJ.** Acid-base balance in dialysis patients. Kidney Int. 1985;28:678.

63 **Enia G et al.** Hyperchloraemia: a nonspecific finding in chronic renal failure. Nephron. 1985;41:189.

64 **Sutton RAL, Dirks JH.** Disturbances of calcium and magnesium metabolism. In: Brenner BM, Rector FCJ, eds. The Kidney. Philadelphia: WB Saunders; 1991:841.

65 **Lembcke B, Fuchs C.** Magnesium load induced by ingestion of magnesium-containing antacids. Contrib Nephrol. 1984;38:1985.

66 **Smythe WR et al.** Trace element abnormalities in chronic uremia. Ann Intern Med. 1982;96:302.

67 **McGonigle RJS et al.** Erythropoietin deficiency and inhibition of erythropoiesis in renal insufficiency. Kidney Int. 1984;25:437.

68 **Neff MS et al.** Anemia in chronic renal failure. Acta Endocrinol (Copenh). 1985;110(Suppl. 271):80.

69 **Freedman MH et al.** Anemia of chronic renal failure: inhibition of erythropoiesis by uremic serum. Nephron. 1983;35:15.

70 **Eschbach JW, Adamson JW.** Hematologic consequences of renal failure. In: Brenner BM, Rector FC, eds. The Kidney. Philadelphia: WB Saunders; 1991:2019.

71 **Mehta BR et al.** Changes in red cell mass, plasma volume and hematocrit in patients on CAPD. Trans Am Soc Artif Intern Organs. 1983;29:50.

72 **Akmal M et al.** Erythrocyte survival in chronic renal failure: role of secondary hyperparathyroidism. J Clin Invest. 1985;76:1695.

73 **Yawata Y et al.** Abnormal red cell metabolism causing hemolysis in uremia: a defect potentiated by tap water hemodialysis. Ann Intern Med. 1973;79: 362.

74 **Paine CJ et al.** Folic acid binding proteins and folate balance in uremia. Arch Intern Med. 1976;136:756.

75 **Ono K et al.** Hypervitaminosis A: a contributing factor to anemia in regular dialysis patients. Nephron. 1984;38:44.

76 **Wills MR, Savory J.** Aluminum poisoning: dialysis encephalopathy, osteomalacia, and anaemia. Lancet. 1983; 2:29.

77 **Zimmerman SW, Johnson CA.** Erythropoietin in peritoneal dialysis patients. Am J Kidney Dis. 1991; 18(Suppl. 1):38.

78 **Helderman JH, Gailiunas P.** Transplantation 1983. Am J Kidney Dis. 1983;3:194.

79 **Bommer J et al.** Subcutaneous erythropoietin. Lancet. 1988;2:406.

80 **Stivelman JC.** Resistance to recombinant human erythropoietin therapy: a real clinical entity? Semin Nephrol. 1989;9(Suppl. 2):8.

81 **Levin N.** Management of blood pressure changes during recombinant human erythropoietin therapy. Semin Nephrol. 1989;14(Suppl. 1):16.

82 **Rabiner SF.** Bleeding in uremia. Med Clin North Am. 1972;56:221.

83 **Andrassy K, Ritz E.** Uremia as a cause of bleeding. Am J Nephrol. 1985;5:313.

84 **Mustard JF et al.** Platelets, thrombosis, and drugs. Drugs. 1975;9:19.

85 **Gallus AS.** Antiplatelet drugs: clinical pharmacology and therapeutic use. Drugs. 1979;18:439.

86 **Gallus AS.** Aspirin and other platelet-aggregation inhibiting drugs. Med J Aust. 1985;142:41.

87 **Watson AJ, Whelton A.** Therapeutic manipulations in uremic bleeding. J Clin Pharmacol. 1985;25:315.

88 **Janson PA et al.** Treatment of the bleeding tendency in uremia with cryoprecipitate. N Engl J Med. 1980;303: 1318.

89 **Mannucci PM et al.** Deamino-8-D-arginine vasopressin shortens the bleeding time in uremia. N Engl J Med. 1983;308:8.

90 **Watson AJ, Keogh JAB.** L-deamino-8-D-arginine vasopressin (DDAVP): a potential new treatment for the bleeding diathesis of acute renal failure. Pharmatherapeutica. 1984;3:618.

91 **Liu Y et al.** Treatment of uraemic bleeding with conjugated estrogen. Lancet. 1984;2:887.

92 **Yu VL et al.** *Staphylococcus aureus* nasal carriage and infection in patients on hemodialysis: efficacy of antibiotic prophylaxis. N Engl J Med. 1986;315: 91.

93 **Goldblum SE et al.** Nasal and cutaneous flora among hemodialysis patients and personnel: quantitative and qualitative characterisation and pattern of staphylococcal carriage. Am J Kidney Dis. 1982;2:281.

94 **Lehrer RI.** Neutrophils and host defenses. Ann Intern Med. 1988;109:127.

95 **Gallen IR, Limarzi LR.** Blood and bone marrow studies in renal disease. Am J Clin Pathol. 1950;20:3.

96 **Vincent PC et al.** Inhibitor of in vitro granulopoiesis in plasma of patients with renal failure. Lancet. 1978;2:864.

97 **Baum J et al.** Chemotaxis and polymorphonuclear leukocyte and delayed hypersensitivity in uremia. Kidney Int. 1975;7(Suppl. 2):S147.

98 **Kaplow LS, Goffinet JA.** Profound neutropenia during the early phase of hemodialysis. JAMA. 1983;203:133.

99 **Lewis SL, Van Epps DE.** Neutrophil and monocyte alterations in chronic dialysis patients. Am J Kidney Dis. 1987; 9:381.

100 **Stronsek DF et al.** Effect of dialyzer re-use on complement activation and neutropenia in hemodialysis. J Lab Clin Med. 1984;104:304.

101 **Cohen MS et al.** A defect in the oxidative metabolism of human polymorphonuclear leukocyte that remains in circulation early in hemodialysis. Blood. 1982;60:1283.

102 **Wissow LS et al.** Altered leukocyte chemiluminescence during dialysis. J Clin Immunol. 1981;1:262.

103 **Klempner MS et al.** The effect of hemodialysis and C5a des arg on neutrophil subpopulations. Blood. 1980;55: 777.

104 **Skubitz KM, Craddock PR.** Reversal of hemodialysis granulocytopenia and pulmonary leukostasis: a clinical manifestation of selective down regulation of granulocyte responses to C5a des arg. J Clin Invest. 1981;67:1383.

105 **Spagnuolo PJ et al.** Neutrophil adhesiveness during prostacyclin and heparin hemodialysis. Blood. 1982;60: 924.

106 **Charpentier B et al.** Depressed polymorphonuclear leukocyte functions associated with normal cytotoxic functions on T and natural killer cells during chronic hemodialysis. Clin Nephrol. 1983;19:288.

107 **Waterlot Y et al.** Impaired phagocytic activity of neutrophils in patients receiving haemodialysis: the critical role of iron overload. Br Med J. 1985;291: 501.

108 **Buggy BP et al.** Intraleukocytic sequestration as a cause of persistent *Staphylococcus aureus* peritonitis in continuous ambulatory peritoneal dialysis. Am J Med. 1984;76:1035.

109 **Sherman RA, Helyar L.** Iron deficiency, immunity, and disease resistance in early life. In: Chandra RK, ed. Nutrition and Immunology. New York: Alan R Liss; 1988:169.

110 **Bhaskaram P.** Immunology of iron-deficient subjects. In: Chandra RK, ed. Nutrition and Immunology. New York: Alan R. Liss; 1988:149.

111 **Dhur A et al.** Iron status, immune capacity and resistance to infections. Comp Biochem Physiol. 1989;94:11.

112 **Toledo-Pereya LH.** Nutrition immunology. In: Pereya LH, ed. Immunology Essentials of Surgery Practice. Littleton: PSG Publishing; 1988:210.

113 **Doherty CC et al.** Effect of parathyroid hormone on random migration of human polymorphonuclear leukocytes. Am J Nephrol. 1988;8:212.

114 **Hörl WH et al.** Physicochemical characterization of a polypeptide present in uremic serum that inhibits the biological activity of polymorphonuclear cells. Proc Natl Acad Sci U S A. 1990; 87:6353.

115 **Hosking CA et al.** Immune and phagocytic functions in patients on maintenance dialysis and post-transplantation. Clin Nephrol. 1976;6:501.

116 **Hoy WE et al.** Deficiency of T and B lymphocytes in uremic subjects and partial improvement with maintenance hemodialysis. Nephron. 1978;20:182.

117 **Moran J et al.** Immunodeficiencies in chronic renal failure. Contrib Nephrol. 1990;86:91.

118 **Hammerschmidt DE et al.** Leukocyte abnormalities in renal failure and hemodialysis. Semin Nephrol. 1985;5:91.

119 **Lang I et al.** Effect of haemodialysis on the antibody-dependent and spontaneous cell-mediated cytotoxicity of patients with chronic renal failure. Immunology. 1982;5:55. Letter.

120 **Badger AM et al.** Depressed spontaneous cellular cytotoxicity associated with normal or enhanced antibody-dependent cellular cytotoxicity in patients on chronic hemodialysis. Clin Exp Immunol. 1981;45:568.

121 **Sutherland GA et al.** Increased incidence of malignancy in chronic renal failure. Nephron. 1977;18:182.

122 **Lindner A et al.** High incidence of neoplasia in uremic patients receiving long-term dialysis. Nephron. 1981;27: 292.

123 **Nelson J et al.** Host immune status in uraemia. Nephron. 1985;39:21.

124 **Waltzer WC et al.** Immunological monitoring in patients with end-stage renal disease. J Clin Immunol. 1984;4: 364.

125 **Giacchino F et al.** Cimetidine does not influence cellular immunity in patients with chronic renal insufficiency. Immunol Lett. 1983;6:303.

126 **Pabico RC.** Pericarditis. In: Massry SG, Glassock RJ, eds. Textbook of Nephrology. Baltimore: Williams & Wilkins; 1989:1171.

127 **Spector D et al.** A controlled study of the effect of indomethacin in uremic pericarditis. Kidney Int. 1983;24:663.

128 **Frame JR et al.** Surgical treatment of pericarditis in the dialysis patient. Am J Surg. 1983;146:800.

129 **Blythe WB.** Natural history of hypertension in renal parenchymal disease. Am J Kidney Dis. 1985;5:A50.

130 **Rascher W et al.** Atrial natriuretic peptide in plasma of volume-overloaded children with chronic renal failure. Lancet. 1985;2:303.

131 **Kaufman AM, Levitt MF.** The effect of diuretics on systemic and renal hemodynamics in patients with renal insufficiency. Am J Kidney Dis. 1985; 5:A71.

132 **Weidmann P.** Essential, renal and endocrine hypertension. In: Massry SG, Glassock RJ, eds. Textbook of Nephrology. Baltimore: Williams & Wilkins; 1989:1020.

133 **Dal Canton A et al.** Diuretic therapy in uremic patients. Kidney Int. 1985; 28(Suppl. 17):S154.

134 **Wollam GL et al.** Diuretic potency of combined hydrochlorothiazide and furosemide therapy in patients with azotemia. Am J Med. 1982;72:929.

135 **Curtis JJ et al.** Captopril and renal insufficiency. N Engl J Med. 1983;309: 665.

136 **Van der Woude FJ et al.** Effect of captopril on blood pressure and renal function in patients with transplant renal artery stenosis. Nephron. 1985;39: 184.

137 **Green D et al.** Putative atherogenic factors in patients with chronic renal failure. Prog Cardiovasc Dis. 1983;26: 133.

138 **Drueke T et al.** Recent advances in factors that alter lipid metabolism in chronic renal failure. Kidney Int. 1983; 24(Suppl. 16):S134.

139 **Ritz E et al.** Should hyperlipemia of renal failure be treated? Kidney Int. 1985;28(Suppl. 17):S84.

140 **Davis CL, Henrich WL.** Cardiac performance in chronic renal failure. Int J Artif Organs. 1985;8:7.

141 **Ikram H et al.** Cardiovascular changes in chronic hemodialysis patients. Kidney Int. 1983;24:371.

142 **Aurbach GD et al.** Parathyroid hormone, calcitonin and the calciferols. In: Wilson JD, Foster DW, eds. Williams, Textbook of Endocrinology. Philadelphia: WB Saunders; 1985:1137.

143 **Coburn JW, Slatopolsky E.** Vitamin D, parathyroid hormone, and renal osteodystrophies. In: Brenner BM, Rector FC, eds. The Kidney. Philadelphia: WB Saunders; 1991:2036.

144 **Ritz E et al.** Disturbed calcium metabolism in renal failure—pathogenesis and therapeutic strategies. Kidney Int. 1992;42(Suppl. 38):S37.

145 **Rizzoni G et al.** Growth retardation in children with chronic renal disease: scope of the problem. Am J Kidney Dis. 1986;7:256.

146 **Takamoto S et al.** Serum phosphate, parathyroid hormone and vitamin D metabolites in patients with chronic renal failure: effect of aluminum hydroxide administration. Nephron. 1985;40:286.

147 **Vick KE, Johnson CA.** Aluminum-related osteomalacia in renal failure patients. Clin Pharm. 1985;4:434.

148 **Alfrey AC et al.** The dialysis encephalopathy syndrome: possible aluminum intoxication. N Engl J Med. 1976;294: 184.

149 **Slatopolsky E et al.** Calcium carbonate as a phosphate binder in patients with chronic renal failure undergoing dialysis. N Engl J Med. 1986;315:157.

150 **Delmez JA, Slatopolsky E.** Hyperphosphatemia: its consequences and treatment in patients with chronic renal disease. Am J Kidney Dis. 1992;19: 303.

151 **Sheikh MS et al.** Reduction of dietary phosphorus absorption by phosphorus binders: a theoretical, in vitro, and in vivo study. J Clin Invest. 1989;83:66.

152 **Mai ML et al.** Calcium acetate, an effective phosphorus binder in patients with renal failure. Kidney Int. 1989;36: 690.

153 **Schaefer K et al.** The treatment of uraemic hyperphosphataemia with calcium acetate and calcium carbonate: a comparative study. Nephrol Dial Transplant. 1991;6:170.

154 **Fournier A et al.** Use of alkaline calcium salts as phosphate binder in uremic patients. Kidney Int. 1992; 42(Suppl. 38):S50.

155 **Nolan CR et al.** Influence of calcium acetate or calcium citrate on intestinal aluminum absorption. Kidney Int. 1990;38:937.

156 **Molitoris BA et al.** Citrate: a major factor in the toxicity of orally administered aluminum compounds. Kidney Int. 1989;36:949.

157 **Coburn JW et al.** Calcium citrate markedly enhances aluminum absorption from aluminum hydroxide. Am J Kidney Dis. 1991;17:708.

158 **O'Donovan R et al.** Substitution of aluminium salts by magnesium salts in control of dialysis hyperphosphataemia. Lancet. 1986;1:880.

159 **Moriniere P et al.** Prevention of osteitis fibrosa, aluminium bone disease and soft-tissue calcification in dialysis patients: a long-term comparison of moderate doses of oral calcium ± Mg(OH)₂ vs Al(OH)₃ ± 1 α OH vitamin D3. Nephrol Dial Transplant. 1989;4:1045.

160 **Leung ACT et al.** Aluminum hydroxide versus sucralfate as a phosphate binder in uraemia. Br Med J. 1983;286: 1379.

161 **Robertson JA et al.** Sucralfate, intestinal aluminum absorption, and aluminum toxicity in a patient on dialysis. Ann Intern Med. 1989;111:179.

162 **Dunstan CR et al.** Treatment of hemodialysis bone disease with 24,25-(OH)₂D3 and 1,25-(OH)₂D3 alone or in combination. Miner Electrolyte Metab. 1985;11:358.

163 **Sakhaee K.** Management of renal osteodystrophy. Semin Nephrol. 1992; 12:101.

164 **Malberti F et al.** Effect of chronic intravenous calcitriol on parathyroid function and set point of calcium in dialysis patients with refractory secondary hyperparathyroidism. Nephrol Dial Transplant. 1992;7:822.

165 **Andress DL et al.** Intravenous calcitriol in the treatment of refractory osteitis fibrosa of chronic renal failure. N Engl J Med. 1989;321:274.

166 **Martin KJ et al.** Pulse oral calcitriol for the treatment of hyperparathyroidism in patients on continuous ambulatory peritoneal dialysis: preliminary observations. Am J Kidney Dis. 1992; 19:540.

167 **Quarles LD et al.** Oral calcitriol and calcium: efficient therapy for uremic hyperparathyroidism. Kidney Int. 1988; 34:840.

168 **Klaus G et al.** Is intermittent oral calcitriol safe and effective in renal secondary hyperparathyroidism? Lancet. 1991;337:800.

169 **Szabo A et al.** 1,25(OH)₂ vitamin D₃ inhibits parathyroid cell proliferation in experimental uremia. Kidney Int. 1989; 35:1049.

170 **Tohme JF, Bilezikian JP.** Hypocalcemic emergencies. Endocrinol Metabol Clin North Am. 1993;22:363.

171 **Popovtzer MM et al.** Disorders of calcium, phosphorus, vitamin D, and parathyroid hormone activity. In: Schrier RW, ed. Renal and Electrolyte Disorders. Boston: Little, Brown and Co.; 1992:287.

172 **Slatopolsky E et al.** Disorders of phosphorus, calcium, and magnesium metabolism. In: Schrier RW, Gottschalk CW, eds. Diseases of the Kidney. Boston: Little, Brown and Co.; 1993:2599.

173 **Mooradian AD, Morley JE.** Endocrine dysfunction in chronic renal failure. Arch Intern Med. 1984;144:351.

174 **DeFronzo RA, Castellino P.** Glucose and insulin metabolism. In: Massry SG, Glassock RJ, eds. Textbook of Nephrology. Baltimore: Williams & Wilkins; 1989:1220.

175 **Kalhan SC et al.** Glucose turnover in chronic uremia: increased recycling with diminished oxidation of glucose. Metabolism. 1983;32:1155.

176 **Elias AN, Vaziri ND.** Thyroid dysfunction in end-stage renal disease. Int J Artif Organs. 1984;7:311.

177 **Kaptein EM, Massry SG.** Thyroid hormone metabolism. In: Massry SG, Glassock RJ, eds. Textbook of Nephrology. Baltimore: Williams & Wilkins; 1989:1248.

178 **Elias AN et al.** Pathology of endocrine organs in chronic renal failure—an autopsy analysis of 66 patients. Int J Artif Organs. 1984;7:251.

179 **Rodger RSC et al.** Prevalence and pathogenesis of impotence in one hundred uremic men. Uremia Invest. 1984–85;8:89.

180 **Oertel PJ et al.** Hypothalamo-pituitary-gonadal axis in children with chronic renal failure. Kidney Int. 1983; 24(Suppl. 15):S34.

181 **Mahajan SK et al.** Sexual dysfunction in uremic male: improvement following oral zinc supplementation. Contrib Nephrol. 1984;38:103.

182 **Sevy N, Snape WJJ.** Gastrointestinal abnormalities. In: Massry SG, Glassock RJ, eds. Textbook of Nephrology. Baltimore: Williams & Wilkins; 1989: 1210.

183 **Vaziri ND et al.** Pathology of gastrointestinal tract in chronic hemodialysis patients: an autopsy study of 78 cases. Am J Gastroenterol. 1985;80:608.

184 **McNamee PT et al.** Gastric emptying in chronic renal failure. Br Med J. 1985;291:316.

185 **Wizemann V et al.** Gastrointestinal blood loss in patients undergoing maintenance dialysis. Kidney Int. 1983; 24(Suppl. 16):S218.

186 **Zuckerman GR et al.** Upper gastrointestinal bleeding in patients with chronic renal failure. Ann Intern Med. 1985;102:588.

187 **Muto S et al.** Hypergastrinemia and achlorhydria in chronic renal failure. Nephron. 1985;40:143.

188 **Ateshkadi A et al.** *Helicobacter pylori* and peptic ulcer disease. Clin Pharm. 1993;12:34.

189 **Gladziwa U et al.** Prevalence of Helicobacter pylori in patients with chronic renal failure. Nephrol Dial Transplant. 1993;8:301.

190 **Offerhaus GJ et al.** Campylobacter pylori: prevalence and significance in patients with chronic renal failure. Clin Nephrol. 1989;32:239.

191 **Alfrey AC.** Normal and abnormal magnesium metabolism. In: Schrier RW, ed. Renal and Electrolyte Disorders. Boston: Little, Brown and Co.; 1992:371.

192 **Randall RE et al.** The milk-alkali syndrome. Arch Intern Med. 1961;107:63.

193 **Levant JA et al.** Stimulation of gastric secretion and gastrin release by single oral doses of calcium carbonate in man. N Engl J Med. 1973;289:555.

194 **Townsend CM et al.** Intestinal obstruction from medication bezoar in patients with renal failure. N Engl J Med. 1973;288:1058.

195 **Massry SG.** Neurotoxicity of parathyroid hormone in uremia. Kidney Int. 1985;28(Suppl. 17):S5.

196 **Heidbreder E et al.** Disturbances of peripheral and autonomic nervous system in chronic renal failure: effects of hemodialysis and transplantation. Clin Nephrol. 1985;23:222.

197 **Heidbreder E et al.** Autonomic neuropathy in chronic renal insufficiency. Nephron. 1985;41:50.

198 **Matsumoto M et al.** Pruritus and mast cell proliferation of the skin in endstage renal failure. Clin Nephrol. 1985;23: 285.

199 **Berne B et al.** UV treatment of uraemic pruritus reduces the vitamin A content of the skin. Eur J Clin Invest. 1984;14:203.

200 **Pederson JA et al.** Relief of idiopathic generalized pruritus in dialysis patients treated with activated oral charcoal. Ann Intern Med. 1980;93:446.

201 **Neal CR et al.** Treatment of dialysis-related muscle cramps with hypertonic dextrose. Arch Intern Med. 1981;141: 171.

202 **Anonymous.** Quinine for "night cramps." Med Lett Drugs Ther. 1986; 28:110.

203 **Lowrie EG, Lew NL.** Death risk in hemodialysis patients: the predictive value of commonly measured variables and an evaluation of death rate differences between facilities. Am J Kidney Dis. 1990;15:458.

204 **Lowrie EG et al.** Race and diabetes as death risk predictors in hemodialysis patients. Kidney Int. 1992;42(Suppl. 38):S22.

205 **Mitch WE, Walser M.** Nutritional therapy of the uremic patient. In: Brenner BM, Rector FC, eds. The Kidney. Philadelphia: WB Saunders; 1991: 1759.

206 **Walser M.** Nutrition in renal failure. Ann Rev Nutr. 1983;3:125.

207 **Mirtallo JM et al.** Nutritional support of patients with renal disease. Clin Pharm. 1984;2:253.

208 **Burge JC et al.** Taste acuity and zinc status in chronic renal disease. J Am Diet Assoc. 1984;84:1203.

209 **Mahajan SK et al.** Zinc deficiency: a reversible complication of uremia. Am J Clin Nutr. 1982;36:1177.

210 **Selby JV et al.** The natural history and epidemiology of diabetic nephropathy. JAMA. 1990;263:1954.

211 **Breyer JA.** Diabetic nephropathy in insulin-dependent patients. Am J Kidney Dis. 1992;20:533.

212 **Krolewski AS et al.** Predisposition to hypertension and susceptibility to renal disease in insulin-dependent diabetes mellitus. N Engl J Med. 1988;318:140.

213 **Viberti GC et al.** Long term correction of hyperglycaemia and progression of renal failure in insulin dependent diabetes. Br Med J. 1983;286:598.

214 **Mathiesen ER et al.** Incipient nephropathy in type I (insulin-dependent) diabetes. Diabetes. 1984;26:406.

215 **Mogensen CE.** Microalbuminuria predicts clinical proteinuria and early mortality in maturity-onset diabetes. N Engl J Med. 1984;310:356.

216 **Borch-Johnsen K et al.** The effect of proteinuria on relative mortality in type 1 (insulin-dependent) diabetes mellitus. Diabetologia. 1985;28:590.

217 **Hasslacher C, Ritz E.** Effect of control of diabetes mellitus on progression of renal failure. Kidney Int. 1987; 32(Suppl. 22):S53.

218 **Dahl-Jorgensen K et al.** Reduction of urinary albumin excretion after 4 years of continuous subcutaneous insulin infusion in insulin-dependent diabetes mellitus: The Oslo Study. Acta Endocrinol (Copenh). 1988;117:19.

219 **Feldt-Rasmussen B et al.** Effect of improved metabolic control on loss of kidney function in type 1 (insulin-dependent) diabetic patients: an update of the Steno studies. Diabetologia. 1991; 34:164.

220 **Feldt-Rasmussen B et al.** Effect of two years of strict metabolic control on progression of incipient nephropathy in insulin-dependent diabetes. Lancet. 1986;2:1300.

221 **The Diabetic Control and Complications Trial Research Group.** The effect of intensive treatment of diabetes on the development and progression of long-term complications in insulin-dependent diabetes mellitus. N Engl J Med. 1993;329:977.

222 **Bending JJ et al.** Glycaemic control in diabetic nephropathy. Br Med J. 1984; 288:1187.

223 **American Diabetes Association.** Implications of the Diabetes Control and Complications Trial. Diabetes. 1993; 42:1555.

224 **American Diabetes Association.** Clinical Practice Recommendations. 1992–1993. Diabetes Care. 1993;16(5 Suppl. 2):1.

225 **Mogensen CE, Christensen CK.** Predicting diabetic nephropathy in insulin-dependent patients. N Engl J Med. 1984;311:89.

226 **Pollare T et al.** Insulin resistance is a characteristic of primary hypertension of obesity. Metabolism. 1990;39:167.

227 **Lewis EJ et al.** The effect of angiotensin-converting-enzyme inhibition on diabetic nephropathy. N Engl J Med. 1993;329:1456.

228 **Pollare T et al.** A comparison of the effects of hydrochlorothiazide and captopril on glucose and lipid metabolism in patients with hypertension. N Engl J Med. 1989;321:868.

229 **Saxena R et al.** Autoimmunity and glomerulonephritis. Postgrad Med J. 1992;68:242.

230 **Pusey CD, Peters DK.** Immunopathology of glomerular and interstitial disease. In: Schrier RW, Gottschalk CW, eds. Diseases of the Kidney. Boston: Little, Brown and Co.; 1993:1647.

231 **Couser WG.** Rapidly progressive glomerulonephritis: classification, pathogenetic mechanisms, and therapy. Am J Kidney Dis. 1988;11:449.

232 **Glassock RJ.** The glomerulopathies. In: Schrier RW, ed. Renal and Electrolyte Disorders. Boston: Little, Brown and Co.; 1992:727.

233 **Hayslett JP, Kashgarian M.** Nephropathy of systemic lupus erythematosus. In: Schrier RW, Gottschalk CW, eds. Diseases of the Kidney. Boston: Little, Brown and Co.; 1993:2019.

234 **Ponticelli C.** Current treatment recommendations for lupus nephritis. Drugs. 1990;40:19.

235 **Balow JE et al.** Effect of treatment on the evolution of renal abnormalities in lupus nephritis. N Engl J Med. 1984; 311:491.

236 **Felson DT, Anderson J.** Evidence for the superiority of immunosuppressive drugs and prednisone alone in lupus nephritis: results of a pooled analysis. N Engl J Med. 1984;311:1528.

237 **Austin HA III et al.** Therapy of lupus nephritis: controlled trial of prednisone and cytotoxic drugs. N Engl J Med. 1986;314:614.

238 **Donadio J Jr, Glassock RJ.** Immunosuppressive drug therapy in lupus nephritis. Am J Kidney Dis. 1993;21:239.

239 **Black DJ, Livingston RB.** Antineoplastic drugs in 1990: a review (part I). Drugs. 1990;39:489.

240 **Kimberly RP et al.** High-dose intravenous pulse therapy in systemic lupus erythematosus. Am J Med. 1981;70:817.

241 **Isenberg DA et al.** Methylprednisolone pulse therapy in the treatment of systemic lupus erythematosus. Ann Rheum Dis. 1982;41:347.

242 **Ponticelli C et al.** Treatment of diffuse proliferative lupus nephritis by intravenous high-dose methylprednisolone. Q J Med. 1982;31:16.

243 **Moses RF et al.** Fatal arrhythmia after pulse methylprednisolone therapy. Ann Intern Med. 1982;95:781.

244 **Schuman AL et al.** Seizure after pulse therapy with methylprednisolone. Arthritis Rheum. 1983;26:117.

245 **Steinberg AD.** The treatment of lupus nephritis. Kidney Int. 1986;30:769.

246 **Balow JE.** Lupus nephritis: natural history, prognosis and treatment. Clin Immunol Allergy. 1986;6:353.

247 **Favre H et al.** Ciclosporin in the treatment of lupus nephritis. Am J Nephrol. 1989;9(Suppl. 1):57.

248 **Epstein M.** Calcium antagonists and the kidneys: future therapeutic perspectives. Am J Kidney Dis. 1993;21 (Suppl. 3):16.

249 **Kyle RA, Greipp PR.** Amyloidosis (AL): clinical and laboratory features in 229 cases. Mayo Clin Proc. 1983;58:665.

250 **Vaamonde CA et al.** Dysproteinemias: multiple myeloma, amyloidosis, and related disorders. In: Schrier RW, Gottschalk CW, eds. Diseases of the Kidney. Boston: Little, Brown and Co.; 1993:2189.

251 **Gertz MA, Kyle RA.** Secondary systemic amyloidosis: response and survival in 64 patients. Medicine (Baltimore). 1991;70:246.

252 **Kyle RA et al.** Primary systemic amyloidosis: comparison of melphalan/prednisone versus colchicine. Am J Med. 1985;79:708.

253 **Gertz MA et al.** Response rates and survival in primary systemic amyloidosis. Blood. 1991;77:257.

254 **Kyle RA, Greipp PR.** Primary systemic amyloidosis: comparison of melphalan and prednisone versus placebo. Blood. 1978;52:818.

255 **Rose BD.** Diuretics. Kidney Int. 1991;39:336.

256 **Kyle RA et al.** Primary systemic amyloidosis: resolution of the nephrotic syndrome with melphalan and prednisone. Arch Intern Med. 1982;142:1445.

257 **Brown MP, Walls RS.** Amyloidosis of immunoglobulin origin: useful treatment? Med J Aust. 1990;152:95.

258 **Benson MD.** Treatment of AL amyloidosis with melphalan, prednisone, and colchicine. Arthritis Rheum. 1986;29(5):683.

259 **Gertz MA, Kyle RA.** Acute leukemia and cytogenetic abnormalities complicating melphalan treatment of primary systemic amyloidosis. Arch Intern Med. 1990;150:629.

260 **Levy M et al.** Colchicine: a state-of-the-art review. Pharmacotherapy. 1991;11:196.

261 **Cohen AS et al.** Survival of patients with primary (AL) amyloidosis: colchicine-treated cases from 1976 to 1983 compared with cases seen in previous years (1961 to 1973). Am J Med. 1987;82:1182.

262 **Turner N et al.** Antiglomerular basement membrane antibody-mediated nephritis. In: Schrier RW, Gottschalk CW, eds. Diseases of the Kidney. Boston: Little, Brown and Co.; 1993:1865.

263 **Nilssen DE et al.** The many faces of Goodpasture's syndrome. Acta Med Scand. 1986;220:489.

264 **Walker RG et al.** Clinical and morphological aspects of the management of crescentic anti-glomerular basement membrane antibody (anti-GBM) nephritis/Goodpasture's syndrome. Q J Med. 1985;54:75.

265 **Holdsworth S et al.** The clinical spectrum of acute glomerulonephritis and lung haemorrhage (Goodpasture's syndrome). Q J Med. 1985;55:75.

266 **Leatherman JW et al.** Alveolar hemorrhage syndromes: diffuse microvascular lung hemorrhage in immune and idiopathic disorders. Medicine (Baltimore). 1984;63:343.

267 **Urizar RE et al.** Pulmonary-renal syndrome: its clinicopathologic approach in 1991. N Y State J Med. 1991;91:212.

268 **Johnson JP et al.** Therapy of anti-glomerular basement membrane antibody disease: analysis of prognostic significance of clinical, pathologic and treatment factors. Medicine (Baltimore). 1985;64:219.

269 **Walker JF et al.** Goodpasture's syndrome—7 years' experience of two Dublin renal units. Ir Med J. 1982;75:328.

270 **Pusey CD et al.** Plasma exchange and immunosuppressive drugs in the treatment of glomerulonephritis due to antibodies to the glomerular basement membrane. Int J Artif Organs. 1983;6(Suppl. 1):15.

271 **Bolton WK, Sturgill BC.** Methylprednisolone therapy for acute crescentic rapidly progressive glomerulonephritis. Am J Nephrol. 1989;9:368.

272 **Simpson IJ et al.** Plasma exchange in Goodpasture's syndrome. Am J Nephrol. 1982;2:301.

273 **Balow JE, Fauci AS.** Vasculitic diseases of the kidney: polyarteritis, Wegener's granulomatosis, necrotizing and crescentic granulomatosis, and other disorders. In: Schrier RW, Gottschalk CW, eds. Diseases of the Kidney. Boston: Little, Brown and Co.; 1993:2095.

274 **Specks U, DeRemee RA.** Granulomatous vasculitis: Wegener's granulomatosis and Churg-Strauss syndrome. Rheum Dis Clin North Am. 1990;16:377.

275 **Leavitt RY et al.** The American College of Rheumatology 1990 criteria for the classification of Wegener's granulomatosis. Arthritis Rheum. 1990;33:1101.

276 **Fauci AS et al.** Wegener's granulomatosis: prospective and therapeutic experience with 85 patients for 21 years. Ann Intern Med. 1983;98:76.

277 **McDonald TJ, DeRemee RA.** Wegener's granulomatosis. Laryngoscope. 1983;93:220.

278 **Appel GB et al.** Wegener's granulomatosis: clinical-pathologic correlations and long-term course. Am J Kidney Dis. 1981;1:27.

279 **Frasca GM et al.** Combined treatment in Wegener's granulomatosis with crescentic glomerulonephritis: clinical course and long term outcome. Int J Artif Organs. 1993;16:11.

280 **Cohen Tervaert JW et al.** Association between active Wegener's granulomatosis and anticytoplasmic antibodies. Arch Intern Med. 1989;149:2461.

281 **Nolle B et al.** Anticytoplasmic autoantibodies: their immunodiagnostic value in Wegener's granulomatosis. Ann Intern Med. 1989;111:28.

282 **Kallenberg CG et al.** Antineutrophil cytoplasmic antibodies: a still growing class of autoantibodies in inflammatory disorders. Am J Med. 1992;93:675.

283 **Specks U et al.** Anticytoplasmic autoantibodies in the diagnosis and follow-up of Wegener's granulomatosis. Mayo Clin Proc. 1989;64:28.

284 **Cohen Tervaert JW et al.** Prevention of relapses in Wegener's granulomatosis by treatment based on antineutrophil cytoplasmic antibody titre. Lancet. 1990;336:709.

285 **Hoffman GS et al.** Treatment of Wegener's granulomatosis with intermittent high-dose intravenous cyclophosphamide. Am J Med. 1990;89:403.

286 **Andrassy K et al.** Wegener's granulomatosis with renal involvement: patient survival and correlations between initial renal function, renal histology, therapy and renal outcome. Clin Nephrol. 1991;35(4):139.

287 **Anon.** Bioavailability problem with chlorothiazide. FDA Drug Bull. 1981;11:44.

288 **Man-Son-Hing M, Wells G.** Meta-analysis of efficacy of quinine for treatment of nocturnal leg cramps in elderly people. Br Med J. 1995;310:13–7.

289 **Anon.** Prescription quinine sulfate for leg cramps is new drug requiring approval. FDC Reports ("The Pink Sheet"); 1995 February 13: T and 63.

Renal Dialysis

Thomas J Comstock

Hemodialysis 31-1
   Principles and Transport Processes 31-1
   Dialysis Membranes 31-3
   Blood and Dialysate Flow 31-3
   Access 31-3
   Anticoagulation (Also see Question 3) 31-4
   Dialysis Prescription 31-4
   Assessment of Dialysis Adequacy 31-6
   Fluid Removal 31-6
   Complications 31-7
      Hypotension 31-7
      Cramps 31-7
      Hypersensitivity 31-7
      Dialysis disequilibrium 31-7
      Thrombosis 31-7
      Infection 31-7
      Aluminum toxicity 31-7
      Amyloidosis 31-8

      Malnutrition 31-8
Peritoneal Dialysis 31-8
   Principles and Transport Processes 31-8
   Blood and Dialysate Flow 31-8
   Fluid Removal 31-8
   Access 31-8
   Dialysis Prescription 31-9
   Assessment of Dialysis Adequacy 31-10
   Complications 31-11
      Peritonitis 31-11
      Exit-site infection 31-11
      Weight gain 31-12
Continuous Renal Replacement Therapies 31-12
   Hemofiltration: Continuous arteriovenous hemofiltration
     (CAVH), continuous venovenous hemofiltration
     (CVVH), and slow continuous ultrafiltration (SCUF) ..31-12
   Hemodialysis: Continuous arteriovenous hemodialysis
     (CAVHD) and venovenous hemodialysis (CVVHD) ...31-13

Dialysis and transplantation are the two treatments available for the management of patients with end-stage renal disease (ESRD). The prevalence of ESRD in the U.S. in 1990 was 195,000, with 45,000 new patients being enrolled per year.[1] Of these, 72% are treated with dialysis and the remainder, transplantation. The shortage of donor kidneys and cases of the patient being an unacceptable transplant recipient have continued the demand for dialysis support for patients with ESRD. Two primary modes of dialysis therapy are *hemodialysis* and *continuous ambulatory peritoneal dialysis (CAPD)*. A variation of CAPD is continuous cycling peritoneal dialysis (CCPD), which provides greater freedom for patients in the management of their disease by providing the majority of exchanges during the sleeping hours. Without dialysis, patients with ESRD soon would die from renal metabolic complications of failure. Among the more than 120,000 dialysis patients in the U.S., 86% undergo hemodialysis. The majority of these patients receive dialysis three times a week in a center designed primarily for stable, ambulatory patients. Home hemodialysis accounts for 2% of hemodialysis patients. Patients undergoing CAPD also are managed through dialysis centers for routine care, although less often than the hemodialysis patient.

Several factors are considered in the selection of the type of dialysis for each patient. Overall morbidity and mortality data generally are similar for both hemodialysis and peritoneal dialysis; however, selected subpopulations of patients sometimes benefit from one more than the other method of dialysis. Among dialysis patients, those with diabetes generally have a greater mortality rate (cardiac and infection) than patients without diabetes; and within the 45- to 64-year age range, patients with diabetes have a higher mortality with CAPD therapy than hemodialysis. Younger patients (25 to 44 years) show a slightly lower mortality with CAPD therapy.[1] Further study is needed to determine if these differences are due to the treatment or selection bias. Other factors to consider in the dialysis selection process include geographical proximity of the dialysis center, vascular or peritoneal access site suitability, patient ability to perform dialysis with a partner, and individual preference to a particular method. The patient is central to the selection of the particular dialysis method.

These demographic characteristics of the ESRD population are based primarily upon Health Care Financing Administration data, as patients with ESRD are eligible for Medicare benefits. Coverage for ESRD began in 1973 when Congress enacted the End-Stage Renal Disease Program as an amendment to Medicare. Total expenditure for the ESRD program in 1990 was approximately $7.3 billion and does not include expenses not covered by Medicare, such as most outpatient drugs and lost productivity.[1]

The rapid growth of the number of patients undergoing dialysis calls attention to the need for practitioners to be educated regarding the processes and therapies for these patients in an effort to improve patient outcome. In addition to the ambulatory population, many patients develop acute renal failure which requires temporary dialysis while hospitalized. Concomitant drug therapy and therapeutic management of complications in this setting also warrant further study of this rapidly changing field. Both of these processes for dialysis (hemodialysis and CAPD) have been developed as methods for the removal of metabolic waste products across a semipermeable membrane. Hemodialysis is an extracorporeal process whereas peritoneal dialysis utilizes the peritoneal membrane for transport. This chapter will address the fundamental clinical aspects of both hemo- and peritoneal dialysis, including principles, complications, and management.

Hemodialysis
Principles and Transport Processes

Hemodialysis is a process whereby a patient's anticoagulated blood and an electrolyte solution (dialysate) are perfused to opposite sides of a semipermeable membrane (artificial kidney). Metabolic waste products are removed from the patient's blood by diffusing down its concentration gradient into the dialysate. The blood and dialysate flow in opposite direction so that the concentration gradient for the toxin is maximized throughout its exposure to the membrane. (See Figure 31.1.) The rate of removal of toxins

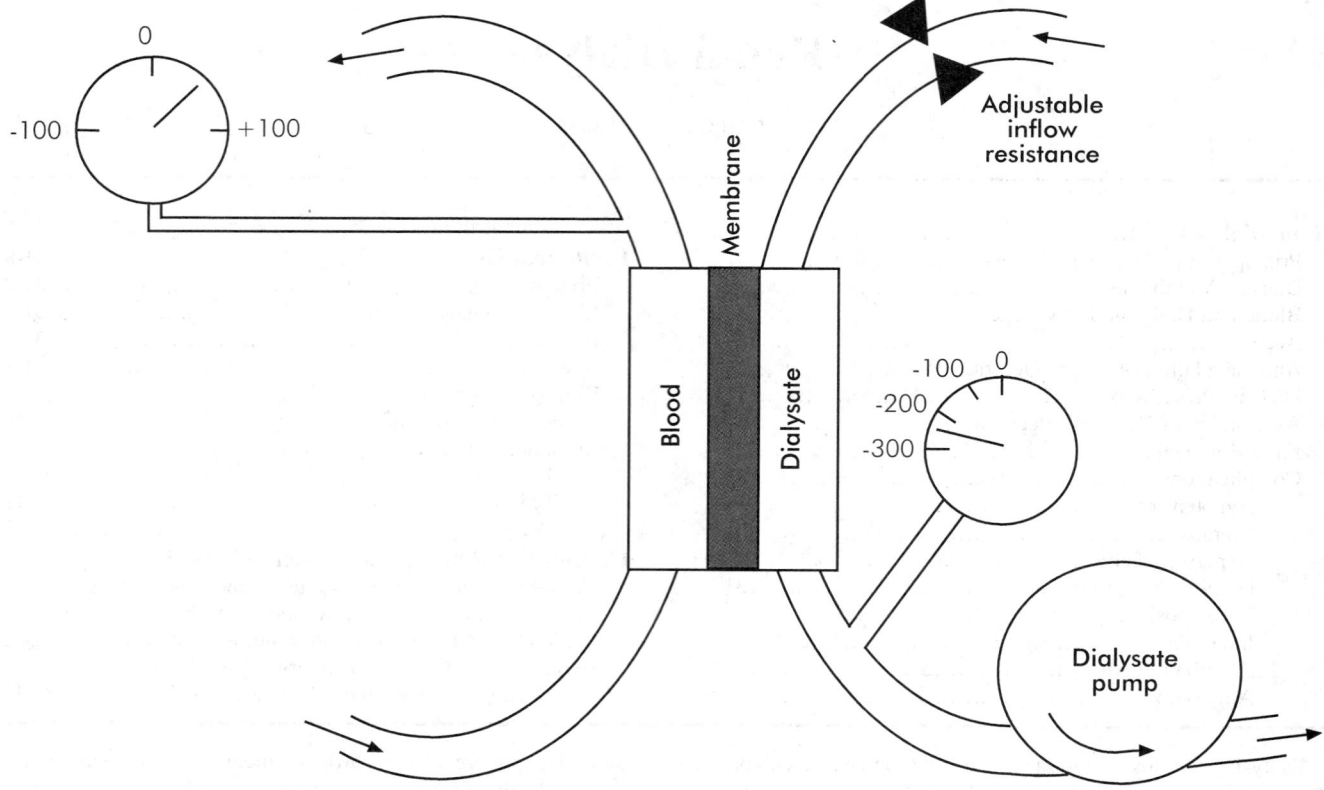

Fig 31.1   Representation of Hemodialysis with Blood Flowing in One Direction and Dialysate in the Opposite, Separated by a Semipermeable Membrane.   Note pressure monitors and dialysate pump with variable inflow resistance to create negative pressure for ultrafiltration from the blood compartment. Reproduced with permission from reference 3.

from the blood is influenced by blood and dialysate flow, membrane characteristics, and properties of the toxin being removed.

Solutes from the blood are removed through diffusion and convection. *Diffusion* is the process whereby the molecule moves down its concentration gradient by passing through pores in the dialysis membrane.[2-4] Once equilibrium is achieved, the net movement is zero, as the rate of movement from the blood to dialysate compartment is equal to the rate from the dialysate to the blood compartment. For most substances, equilibrium is not achieved, either because the blood and dialysate flow rates are too rapid or the molecule is too large to easily move through the pores. Urea (60 daltons) is a marker of small molecule transport across the dialysis membrane and serves as a measure of dialysis adequacy.[5-8] Urea distributes freely throughout body water and is cleared rapidly by hemodialysis. The rate-limiting step for the removal of urea is blood flow. A larger molecule, vitamin B_{12} (1355 daltons), also has been used as a measure of dialysis efficiency. The clearance of vitamin B_{12} is less dependent upon blood flow than urea since it is too large to easily cross the conventional dialysis membrane. The overall removal of vitamin B_{12} is dependent upon the type of membrane and the duration of dialysis. The second process for solute removal by hemodialysis is *convection*.[2-4] This occurs when plasma water is removed from the blood compartment by ultrafiltration, the result of a controlled pressure difference across the membrane which leads to water movement through the membrane pores. The water lost by ultrafiltration carries solute into the dialysate, further enhancing solute removal. Patients undergoing chronic hemodialysis typically are dialyzed for a period of three to four hours, three times a week, either Monday-Wednesday-Friday or Tuesday-Thursday-Saturday. During the interdialytic period, fluids

ingested and produced through metabolic processes are retained in the patient, and the excess fluid is removed during the subsequent dialysis session. Although patients generally are on fluid-restricted diets, accumulation of 1 to 5 kg is common between sessions and must be removed during dialysis. The removal of solutes by convection during ultrafiltration generally is small relative to their elimination through diffusion.

1. R.W., a 55-year-old male with a 25-year history of hypertension and kidney insufficiency, presents to the renal clinic for reassessment of his kidney function. His height is 70″, and weight 70 kg. Since his last visit 3 months ago, his creatinine clearance (Cl_{Cr}) has decreased from 22 mL/min to 12 mL/min and blood urea nitrogen (BUN) increased to 89 mg/dL. The serum potassium (K) is 4.5 mEq/L and HCO_3^- 17 mEq/L. He has selected hemodialysis as his form of therapy until a suitable donor kidney is available and is expected to begin dialysis within the next 1 to 3 months. When he begins dialysis, he will be dialyzed 3 times a week for 4 hours each treatment, using a Fresenius F-60 dialyzer, with blood and dialysate flows of 400 and 500 mL/min, respectively, and bicarbonate-containing dialysate. What characteristics of the Fresenius F-60 dialyzer make it a good choice for R.W.? [SI units: Cl_{Cr} 0.37 and 0.2 mL/s, respectively; BUN 31.8 mmol/L; K 4.5 mmol/L]

This dialyzer uses one of a class of membranes classified as high-flux.[9] The specific membrane is polysulfone, a synthetic membrane with larger pore sizes than conventional cellulose membranes. The F-60 has a KUf, the ultrafiltration coefficient (volume of water removed/mm Hg across the membrane/hour of dialysis), of 40 mL/mm Hg/hour indicating a high ultrafiltration capability; an *in vitro* K_0A_{urea}, the urea mass transfer area coefficient, of 760, a measure of dialyzer efficiency for urea removal; urea and vitamin B_{12} clearances of 185 and 118 mL/minute, respectively, at blood flow of 200 mL/minute; and a surface area of 1.2 m^2.[9] This information can be located in the product literature from the manufacturer or summary tables from common dialysis references. These data are used for individualization of the dialysis prescription for a patient.

Dialysis Membranes

Dialysis membranes are characterized based upon their ability to clear solutes, and hundreds exist in the market today. The two major classifications of membranes are *conventional*, consisting of cellulose and substituted cellulose, and *high-flux*, such as polysulfone, polyacrylonitrile (PAN), and polymethylmethacrylate (PMMA). The primary difference between conventional and high-flux membranes is pore size. The high-flux membranes have larger pores and, thereby, are more permeable to larger molecules (e.g., middle molecules and drugs such as vancomycin).[10] Other variations among the membranes may include surface area and thickness. A typical package insert for a dialyzer will include data regarding the clearance of various molecules such as urea, creatinine, and vitamin B_{12}. Urea clearance has become a common measure for the comparison of membranes; however, clearance also is dependent upon other factors, such as blood and dialysate flow rates.[2-4] A more standard measure for comparison is K_0A_{urea}, the mass transfer area coefficient. Based upon the urea clearance data from the package insert, K_0A_{urea} can be determined using a nomogram which accounts for blood flow differences (see Figure 31.2).[5] Once the K_0A is identified for the membrane, urea clearance can be determined for any given blood flow in order to individualize the dialysis prescription and provide a specified dose of dialysis for the patient.

Blood and Dialysate Flow

Although small molecule clearance is very dependent upon blood flow, the relationship is not strictly linear. As shown in Figure 31.3, increased blood flow yields a less than proportional response in urea clearance.[5] This likely is due to an insufficient time for equilibration to occur between the blood and dialysate compartments as well as a greater membrane resistance to diffusion from an increased stagnant layer. Typical blood flow rates for conventional and high-flux dialysis are 200 and 500 mL/minute, respectively. Dialysate flow rates generally are 500 mL/minute and

Fig 31.2 K_0A From *In Vitro* Urea Clearance Measurements. To use, find clearance on the x-axis and rise to the appropriate blood flow (Qb) line to read the K_0A from the y-axis. Dialysate flow (Qd) is constant at 500 mL/min. Clearance values >170 mL/min should not be used for 200 mL/min blood flow (---). Reproduced with permission from reference 5.

Fig 31.3 Nomogram for Estimation of *In Vivo* Urea Clearance from K_0A as a Function of Dialyzer Blood Flow. To use, rise from the dialyzer blood flow on the x-axis to the appropriate K_0A line and read the *in vivo* urea clearance. Reproduced with permission from reference 5.

may be increased to 800 mL/minute for high-flux dialysis to increase urea clearance by approximately 8%.[3]

Dialysate composition usually is standardized within certain limits of electrolyte content, yet allows for individualization as necessary. Water is obtained through the public water system, which then undergoes treatment by reverse osmosis, followed by ion exchange with activated charcoal to remove contaminants such as aluminum, copper, and chloramines, as well as bacteria and endotoxins.[11,12] The dialysate solution does not require sterilization since the dialysis membrane separates the blood and dialysate compartments. Nevertheless, pyrogen reactions may occur, possibly with a greater risk with high-flux membranes due to the increased pore size. The final dialysate solution is prepared in the dialysis machine by proportioning a dialysate concentrate with the purified water, resulting in a final product typically containing those elements listed in Table 31.1. Before delivery it is heated to 37 °C to maintain body temperature and avoid hemolysis, which can occur with excessive heating. Metabolic acidosis, associated with ESRD due to the inability to excrete the daily obligatory load of acid, is controlled through buffering by the addition of bicarbonate to the dialysate solution.[9,13] Precipitation of calcium carbonate had been a problem with bicarbonate dialysate in the past, requiring acetate to be used for the control of acidemia. Acetate enters the blood compartment by diffusion from the dialysate and is metabolized to bicarbonate *in vivo*. An undesirable effect of acetate as the buffering agent is its association with the development of hypotension and cardiac instability during hemodialysis.[13,14] Improvements in delivery systems provide for special mixing methods which prevent precipitation and the resumption of bicarbonate dialysis.

Access

2. To achieve a sufficient blood flow for dialysis, R.W. must have a vascular site for chronic access. What are the options for chronic vascular access in R.W.?

Table 31.1	Electrolyte Composition of Hemodialysis and CAPD Dialysate Solutions[a]	
Solute	Hemodialysis (mEq/L)	CAPD (mEq/L)
Sodium	135–145	132
Potassium	0–4	0
Calcium	2.5–3.5	3.5
Magnesium	0.5–1.0	1.5
Chloride	100–124	102
Bicarbonate	30–38	—
Lactate	—	35
pH	7.1–7.3	5.5

[a] CAPD = Continuous ambulatory peritoneal dialysis.

Vascular access to achieve the blood flow rates necessary for hemodialysis requires creation of an arteriovenous (AV) fistula or insertion of an AV graft, a synthetic tube made of polytetrafluoroethylene (Teflon), which connects the artery and vein. These generally are placed in the forearm of the nondominant arm, usually between the radial artery and cephalic vein, which provides for easy access to high blood flow. The fistula is preferred due to its longer survival of approximately 75% at three years, compared with 30% for the AV graft.[15] Although preferred, the fistula may not be suitable for the patient with poor vasculature, such as patients with diabetes, atherosclerosis, small vessels, or the elderly. The fistula should be created about two to three months before its intended use in order to allow for the vein to mature. The graft can be used soon after insertion, although two weeks will allow for healing to occur at the anastamosis sites and may lead to prolonged patency. If R.W. has adequate vasculature, a fistula should be created for chronic access based upon the higher long-term graft survival. Vascular access is critical for chronic hemodialysis and often has been labeled the ''Achilles' heel'' of dialysis therapy.

3. Recommend a reasonable anticoagulation regimen to begin for R.W. with the initiation of his hemodialysis.

Most patients undergoing hemodialysis will be anticoagulated with intravenous (IV) heparin during the dialysis treatment. Without evidence of bleeding disorder, recent surgery, or other risk factor to heparin anticoagulation, begin therapy with a bolus of heparin, 2000 U IV three to five minutes before initiation of dialysis, followed by an infusion of 1000 U/hour.[16] The target activated clotting time (ACT) is 40% to 80% above the average baseline for the dialysis unit. Monitor for signs of bleeding and measure the ACT at one-hour intervals during dialysis. Discontinue the heparin one hour before the end of dialysis to prevent excessive bleeding following dialysis.

Anticoagulation

Anticoagulation is necessary for the prevention of clotting of blood in the extracorporeal circuit for patients undergoing hemodialysis. Several methods have been used in an attempt to provide adequate anticoagulation without increasing the risk of bleeding. Approaches include the administration of heparin in adequate quantities to anticoagulate the patient during the dialysis procedure either by intermittent bolus injections or an initial bolus followed by a continuous infusion.[16,17] Modern hemodialysis machines have incorporated heparin infusion devices which can be programmed to provide the desired infusion rate during dialysis. Monitoring of heparin effect usually is performed using the ACT, with an end point of 200 to 250 seconds with normal values of 90 to 140 seconds.[17] Standard doses for patients without an increased risk for

bleeding are an initial bolus of 2000 U and continuous infusion of 1000 U/hour, which is discontinued during the last hour of dialysis in order to minimize postdialysis bleeding yet maintain adequate anticoagulation. The normal elimination half-life for heparin is 50 minutes for the above dose ranges and pharmacodynamic studies have shown a linear dose-response relationship for target ACTs within the above range.[16,18] Patients at increased risk of bleeding include those with recent surgery, retinopathy, gastrointestinal (GI) bleeding, and cerebrovascular bleeding. For these patients, the goal is to prevent clot formation within the dialysis circuit as well as minimize the risk of active bleeding. This may be accomplished by the use of minimal dose heparin (tight ACT control), no heparin, or regional anticoagulation. The minimal heparin approach individualizes therapy to achieve ACT values 40% above baseline following an initial bolus of 750 U.[16,19] The ACT is measured three minutes following the bolus to allow for heparin distribution. Adjustments of subsequent bolus doses are based upon a linear response, and additional heparin may be necessary to achieve the desired effect. The initial maintenance infusion rate is 600 U/hour, monitoring the ACT at 30-minute intervals to ensure an adequate response. The infusion rate should be proportionate to the bolus dose necessary to achieve the ACT at 40% above baseline. Samples collected for determination of ACT should be obtained from the arterial line, before the infusion of heparin, to reflect systemic anticoagulation effects. An alternative to heparinization for patients undergoing dialysis with high blood flow rates is a no-heparin regimen.[20,21] This approach requires pretreatment of the dialyzer with heparin in normal saline, which then is rinsed before a rapid increase of blood flow to more than 250 mL/minute. During dialysis, the dialyzer is flushed with normal saline every 15 to 30 minutes to rinse away microclots which may have formed. The incidence of clotting with this approach is approximately 5%. Regional anticoagulation of the dialysis circuit can be accomplished by the use of heparin administration into the arterial side with protamine neutralization on the venous side. This approach has fallen out of favor due to the propensity for rebound anticoagulation following dialysis as heparin dissociates from the heparin-protamine complex.

Another method to minimize systemic anticoagulation is the regional administration of trisodium citrate through the arterial line resulting in binding of free calcium which is necessary for the coagulation process. The calcium citrate complex then is removed by the dialysate and calcium chloride is administered on the venous side to replace the citrate-bound calcium. The infusion of calcium is adjusted through monitoring of plasma calcium concentrations to prevent hypo- or hypercalcemia from occurring in the patient. Some of the administered citrate is returned to the patient and is metabolized to bicarbonate, leading in some cases to metabolic alkalosis. The regional citrate anticoagulation is reserved for patients at risk for bleeding and requires additional monitoring for the dual infusions compared to the minimal or no-heparin methods.

For R.W., a recommended initial anticoagulation regimen is heparin, administered as a 2000 U bolus, followed by 1000 U/hour as a continuous infusion. The infusion generally is administered via a syringe pump as part of the hemodialyzer. R.W. will be monitored as described above, with subsequent increases or decreases in his heparin regimen.

Dialysis Prescription

Individualization of the dialysis prescription has undergone several advances during the past decade as a result of the quantification of the dose of dialysis delivered to the patient. In 1981 the report of the National Cooperative Dialysis Study (NCDS) showed a relationship between the degree of dialysis delivered to the patient and morbidity.[6,7,23] Four groups of patients were randomized to different combinations of time-averaged serum urea concentrations (50 or 100 mg/dL) and length of dialysis (2.5 to 3.5 or 4.5 to 5.0 hours). There were no differences in mortality during the one-year study; however, those patients with higher urea exposure experienced a greater withdrawal rate from the study and more hospitalizations compared to patients with lower urea concentrations. These data suggested a role for the modeling of dialysis therapy based upon urea kinetics and the concept of urea as a surrogate for adequacy of dialysis. It is well recognized that other uremic toxins contribute to the overall morbidity among these patients, and markers of their removal by dialysis have been used in an attempt to better define the relationship. These markers include creatinine (113 daltons), which is slightly larger than urea, but otherwise it distributes similarly and offers no additional benefits as a marker, and vitamin B_{12}, marker for the class of middle molecules thought to be responsible for many of the uremic complications in ESRD. Vitamin B_{12} is eliminated in a different manner than urea by dialysis, as it is larger and not cleared easily by conventional dialysis membranes. The utility of vitamin B_{12} as a surrogate for dialysis adequacy has not been established.[2]

Further analysis of the NCDS data by Gotch and Sargent[7] using a pharmacokinetic-like term, Kt/V, demonstrated a relationship between morbidity and Kt/V. The Kt/V term is based upon the pre- and postdialysis BUN values, distribution of urea, and duration of dialysis. K is the urea clearance (mL/minute), t is time (minutes), and V is distribution volume for urea (mL). (See Figure 31.4.) The unit-less term represents the quantity of dialysis delivered to the patient, or the total volume of blood cleared of urea, relative to the urea distribution volume in a given patient. Its basic relationship is dependent upon the first-order elimination of urea:

$$BUN_{post} = BUN_{pre}(e^{-Kt/V}) \qquad Eq.\ 31.1$$

$$Kt/V = -\ln\left(\frac{BUN_{post}}{BUN_{pre}}\right) \qquad Eq.\ 31.2$$

Those patients with a Kt/V less than 0.9 had a 54% failure rate, defined as death, hospitalization, or withdrawal from the study for medical reasons, whereas those greater than 0.9 had a 13% failure rate on dialysis. Based upon these data, it was recommended that patients receive a dialysis ''dose'' of Kt/V greater than 1.0 when undergoing dialysis three times weekly.

Several refinements of the Kt/V relationship have been made in order to better approximate the actual observations in hemodialysis patients. These include corrections for ultrafiltration of fluid during dialysis; access and cardiopulmonary recirculation, which result in dilution of the arterial urea concentration *in vivo*; and a two-pool (compartment) model for urea, accounting for the postdialysis rebound of urea concentration.[5] Timing of the postdialysis urea sample, which normally is recommended to occur one to two minutes after a reduction of blood flow to 50 mL/minute, is important.[24,25] Redistribution of urea may occur for 30 to 60 minutes after dialysis treatment. The effect on Kt/V is a reduction in the apparent dialysis delivered but more likely reflects the true dialysis impact and may prove to be a more appropriate measure of dialysis adequacy.

Observations subsequent to the NCDS have suggested a discrepancy between the prescribed dialysis and actual delivered dialysis, with conclusions that some patients are not receiving adequate dialysis.[26] Moreover, Collins et al. suggested higher Kt/V values are necessary in order to minimize morbidity among dialysis patients. They suggested a Kt/V ≥1.4 for patients with diabetes due to their underlying disease and higher number of comorbid conditions, and ≥1.2 for patients without diabetes.[8] Several questions remain with regard to the delivery of dialysis to patients, one of which is to determine the optimum amount of dialysis in order to improve patient outcomes. A recent consensus panel has recommended a Kt/V ≥1.2 for patients undergoing chronic hemodialysis.[27]

4. Calculate the prescribed Kt/V for R.W. Is it appropriate?

The prescribed Kt/V requires the parameters of urea clearance for specific blood and dialysate flow rates, duration of dialysis, and volume of distribution for urea. The urea clearance is estimated from the K_0A for the membrane (760) to be 220 mL/minute (see Figure 31.3). The duration of dialysis is to be 240 minutes, and the volume of distribution for urea is estimated to be 41 L. The prescribed Kt/V then is calculated to be 1.29. This is an appropriate initial dialysis prescription for a new patient. The delivered Kt/V should be evaluated at least quarterly to reassess and adjust the parameters as necessary to maintain the delivered Kt/V × 1.2.

Based upon a target Kt/V and known characteristics of the dialysis system, it is possible to develop a dialysis prescription to achieve that value.[5] The operative variables include the type and size of dialysis membrane with known urea removal characteristics, blood and dialysate flow rates, and duration of treatment. The membrane usually is determined based upon the type of dialysis delivery machine in the facility as well as economic factors. High-flux membranes are more expensive than conventional cellulose, yet with reuse systems where the filter is cleansed and sterilized,

Fig 31.4 Nomograms for the Estimation of Urea Distribution Volumes for Men and Women. Locate height on the x-axis, then rise to the appropriate weight (postdialysis) line and read the volume from the y-axis. Reproduced with permission from reference 5.

the cost per dialysis session is reduced substantially.[28,29] Both manual and automated systems are used for dialyzer reprocessing, which includes rinsing of blood and clots from the dialyzer, cleaning with agents such as dilute sodium hypochlorite (bleach), testing of dialyzer performance, and sterilization. Although there is controversy regarding reuse programs, such as the safety of disinfectants, dialyzer efficiency after processing, and contamination, more than 70% of hemodialysis patients undergo dialysis with reuse programs. The average number of times a dialyzer is reused depends upon quality control standards within the dialysis center, but generally is ten or greater. Size of the filter is determined by the size of the patient, with larger patients generally dialyzed against membranes of larger surface area. Blood flow rate is maximized based upon the type of machine and pump capability, as well as the patient and the ability of the cardiovascular system to tolerate a high blood flow. High-flux dialysis usually is carried out with blood flow of 400 to 500 mL/minute, rapid high-efficiency dialysis with blood flows of 300 to 500 mL/minute, and conventional dialysis with blood flows of 200 to 300 mL/minute.[2-4] The last variable, time, is important to consider in providing adequate dialysis therapy to the patient. Longer dialysis sessions allow for greater Kt/V values, and it is unknown whether an upper limit exists for ideal therapy. Since the introduction of high-flux membranes, dialysis duration has been decreasing in order to provide therapy to patients in a more cost-efficient manner.[30,31] The total removal of urea may be similar with shorter dialysis sessions, thereby allowing for reductions in personnel to manage the center and the ability to dialyze more patients. Reports from the United States Renal Data Systems in 1989 indicated a decrease in patient survival compared with other industrialized nations, including Japan and European countries.[32-34] Many factors likely are responsible, including an older population in the U.S., patients with more comorbid conditions being accepted to dialysis programs, and a decrease in dialysis duration resulting in decreased delivery of dialysis. Independent of high-flux membranes, the duration of dialysis appears to be very important, perhaps for the clearance of uremic toxins other than urea, as well as removal of fluid which contributes to hypertension in the dialysis population. The dialysis center with the greatest survival is located in Tassin, France, where patients are dialyzed eight hours per day, three times weekly. The mean Kt/V is 1.67 and survival is 87% at five years, 75% at 10 years, and 55% at 15 years.[34] Although these data are promising, a major dilemma in U.S. centers is insufficient funding for prolonged dialysis and unwillingness by the patient to be captive for a prolonged period of time on a chronic basis.

Calculation of the dialysis prescription for a specific patient, such as R.W., is based upon a target Kt/V, urea clearance for the membrane based upon the blood and dialysate flow rate, and solving for the duration of dialysis as:

$$Kt/V = \frac{K}{V}(t) \qquad Eq. \ 31.3$$

$$t = \frac{Kt/V}{K} \qquad Eq. \ 31.4$$

For example, consider a target Kt/V for R.W. of 1.4. The urea clearance for the Fresenius F-60 dialyzer is estimated to be 220 mL/minute at a blood flow of 400 mL/minute (see Figure 31.3), and the urea volume of distribution for R.W. is estimated to be 41 L based upon his weight of 69.1 kg (see Figure 31.4). Solving for the duration of dialysis, R.W. will need to dialyze approximately four hours and 20 minutes to achieve a Kt/V of 1.4. An alternative approach to increasing the delivered dialysis to R.W. is to choose a larger dialyzer (e.g., Fresenius F-80) with a greater membrane

surface area and/or increasing blood flow. Due to cardiovascular limitations, blood flow generally is not increased beyond 400 to 500 mL/minute.

Urea clearance is estimated based upon the *in vitro* K_0A, determined from *in vitro* urea clearance data. Further corrections for the *in vivo* urea clearance value are necessary in order to account for pump calibration, blood water content, and cardiopulmonary and access recirculation. Detailed equations and nomograms have been developed to aid in the estimation of *in vivo* urea clearance.[5,35] The volume of distribution for urea is based upon total body water content, as urea moves freely into all water compartments and can be estimated based upon patient gender, height, and weight.[5]

Assessment of Dialysis Adequacy

5. R.W. has begun dialysis therapy and the pre- and postdialysis BUN values are 88 and 31 mg/dL, respectively. Determine the delivered Kt/V if his predialysis weight was 73.4 kg and postdialysis weight 69.1 kg. Is it adequate? [SI units: BUN 31.4 and 11.1 mmol/L, respectively]

Validation of the initial prescription is performed by measurement of pre- and postdialysis BUN concentrations to determine the delivered Kt/V. Based upon the degree of ultrafiltration and postdialysis weight, the approximate Kt/V can be estimated as described above. For a typical weight loss of 3% during dialysis, the BUN ratio after dialysis ($BUN_{post}:BUN_{pre}$) should be approximately 0.30. For R.W., the weight loss was approximately 6% and his postdialysis serum urea concentration was 35% of the predialysis value. As discussed above, postdialysis blood sampling for BUN determination should be performed one to two minutes after reducing blood flow to 50 mL/minute in order to allow for dissipation of cardiopulmonary and access recirculation and to prevent false elevation of the Kt/V. Those patients with slow equilibration times for urea to redistribute to the blood compartment after dialysis may require blood sampling 30 to 60 minutes after dialysis for a more accurate determination of dialysis adequacy.[24,36,37] Conditions leading to redistribution of urea following dialysis include poor peripheral perfusion, low cardiac output, or hypotension. Once the degree of rebound has been determined, a correction factor may be used to adjust subsequent Kt/V determinations.

Several methods exist for the calculation of delivered Kt/V, and Figure 31.5 can be used as an approximation. Based upon the pre- and postdialysis weights and serum urea nitrogen values, R.W.'s Kt/V is estimated to be 1.3. This is adequate based upon current guidelines for hemodialysis therapy.[8,27]

Fluid Removal

In addition to solute removal, the artificial kidney must be used to maintain fluid balance in the patient without renal function. Most patients will become anuric once stabilized on hemodialysis, requiring control of ingested fluids between treatment sessions. Fluid removal during dialysis then is necessary to achieve the "dry weight," or weight below which the patient would become symptomatic from volume depletion. The dry weight for R.W. has been set at 69.1 kg. Below this weight, R.W. exhibited symptoms of orthostasis. Achieving the dry weight is accomplished by ultrafiltration, through adjustment of the transmembrane pressure. Negative pressure on the dialysate side of the membrane results in movement of fluid across the membrane from the blood compartment.[2-4] Dialysate membranes are characterized by their water permeability, or KUf. Most membranes have values in the range of 2.0 to 8.0 mL/mm Hg/hour, although high-flux membranes may have values as high as 60 mL/mm Hg/hour. Adjustment of the transmembrane pressure will provide the desired ultrafiltration rate, based upon the amount of fluid to be removed (predialysis weight

Fig 31.5 Estimation of Delivered Kt/V from the Postdialysis to Predialysis BUN Ratio and Fractional Fluid Loss During Dialysis. UF is fluid lost during dialysis and W is postdialysis weight, in kg. Locate the urea ratio on the x-axis, rise to the appropriate UF/W line, and read the Kt/V on the y-axis. Reproduced with permission from reference 96.

+ IV saline + ingested fluids during dialysis − dry weight). For patients undergoing dialysis three times weekly, weight gains of 1 to 5 kg are common between sessions. For membranes with KU_f values greater than 10 mL/mm Hg/hour, volumetric circuitry in newer dialysis machines should be used to avoid errors in rates of fluid removal based upon transmembrane pressure. Modern hemodialyzers have built-in functions to adjust the transmembrane pressure and remove fluid at a predetermined rate.

Complications

6. The dry weight for R.W. is 69.1 kg. During his most recent dialysis session, at 3 hours into the procedure, he complained of nausea and light-headedness. His diastolic pressure dropped from 85 mm Hg to 60 mm Hg. Ultrafiltration was discontinued. He recovered without further event and his postdialysis weight was 69.9 kg. What are possible etiologies for his hypotension?

Hypotension. Many complications may occur in patients undergoing hemodialysis. Most common is the development of hypotension resulting in a variety of clinical signs and symptoms in the patient, including nausea and vomiting, dizziness, muscle cramps, and headache. It primarily is caused by excessive fluid removal from the vascular compartment at a rate exceeding mobilization of fluid stores.[38] It may be necessary for the dry weight of the patient to be adjusted upwards if the patient is volume depleted and symptomatic following dialysis. Another cause of hypotension is related to excessive heating of the dialysate and resultant vasodilation.[39] Cooling of the dialysate to slightly below body temperature may correct this problem. The use of acetate as buffer in the dialysate also has been associated with the development of hypotension due to its direct vasodilator effects. Switching the patient to bicarbonate dialysate will correct this problem.[9,14]

Since the volume status of R.W. is associated with his weight, another consideration is a change in his lean mass. R.W. has noted an improvement in his appetite lately, and as a result, added a few extra pounds. It is important to consider ''real'' weight changes when assessing the dry weight as well as volume status. Without appropriately increasing the dry weight with ''real'' weight gain,

R.W. becomes volume depleted and hypotensive. His dry weight should be adjusted upwards to the point where he no longer is symptomatic (or to ≈70 kg).

Cramps developing during dialysis are related to excessive ultrafiltration and fluid shifts resulting in altered perfusion of the affected tissues. Several treatments have been attempted, including reduced ultrafiltration and infusion of hypertonic saline or glucose to improve circulation.[40,41] Long-term therapy may be directed at prevention with the use of quinine, 260 mg, two hours before dialysis.[42] Exercise and stretching of the affected limbs also may be beneficial.

Hypersensitivity. Reports of anaphylactic reactions to dialyzer membranes, particularly upon initial exposure, may be directly related to the membrane itself, or to ethylene oxide, commonly used to sterilize the dialyzer.[43–46] Membranes most commonly responsible for reactions are unsubstituted cellulose membranes (bioincompatible), or the high-flux polyacrylonitrile membrane when used in conjunction with angiotensin-converting enzyme (ACE) inhibitors.[46] This latter reaction is thought to be related to the additive effect of ACE inhibitors inhibiting bradykinin metabolism, resulting in an anaphylactoid reaction.

Dialysis Disequilibrium. This syndrome has been recognized since the initiation of hemodialysis more than 30 years ago. Its etiology is related to cerebral edema, and patients new to hemodialysis are at a greater risk due to the accumulation of urea.[47] Rapid removal of urea from the extracellular space lowers the plasma osmolality, thereby leading to a shift of free water into the brain. Lowering intracellular pH, as occurs with renal failure, also has been suggested as etiologic and leads to the production of organic acids intracellularly. This increases osmolality and causes water to move from the extracellular to intracellular space leading to cerebral edema. Clinical manifestations occur during or shortly after dialysis, and include central nervous system (CNS) effects such as headache, nausea, altered vision, and in some cases, seizures and coma. Treatment is aimed at prevention by the initiation of gradual dialysis using shorter treatment times in new patients at lower blood flow rates. Direct therapy can be provided in the form of IV hypertonic saline or mannitol.[47]

Some of the long-term complications associated with hemodialysis include thrombosis or infection of the access site, aluminum toxicity, and amyloidosis.

Thrombosis is the most common cause for the loss of access site. Fistula patency generally is much greater than synthetic graft patency, yet thrombosis and loss of function may occur in both.[48] The primary cause for thrombosis is venous stenosis, which may be detected by venous pressure monitoring on a regular basis or measurement of access recirculation with determination of urea kinetic modeling. The stenosis may be corrected by angioplasty or, if necessary, surgical revision of the access site. Thrombosis is managed by surgical thrombectomy or thrombolytic therapy with streptokinase or urokinase.[49–51] Thrombolytic therapy should be avoided in those patients with an increased risk of bleeding.

Infection of the access site, when it occurs, usually is caused by *Staphylococcus aureus* or *epidermidis* and is associated more often with a graft than fistula. Access infections may lead to bacteremia and sepsis with or without local signs of infection. Treatment usually is initiated with vancomycin, administered as a single 1 gm dose, repeated as necessary, depending upon the type of dialysis being used.[52] High-flux dialysis results in greater removal of vancomycin compared with conventional dialysis and, therefore, may require more than a single dose for adequate treatment.[53,54]

Aluminum Toxicity. Aluminum accumulation in patients undergoing hemodialysis had been a significant problem before the adequate treatment of water sources which removed aluminum.[11,12]

Major complications of aluminum toxicity include CNS manifestations as dementia, aluminum bone disease, and anemia.[55,56] It has been recognized that aluminum accumulation still occurs in patients treated with aluminum-containing antacids as binding agents for phosphate in the GI tract, although not to the degree associated with water supplies.[57] Aluminum toxicity is diagnosed by clinical signs and symptoms associated with the above conditions, and a serum aluminum concentration of more than 200 ng/mL or deferoxamine-stimulated serum aluminum concentration increase of more than 200 ng/mL.[58-60] Deferoxamine chelates with serum aluminum and the shift in equilibrium results in movement of aluminum from tissue storage sites. The complex can be removed by dialysis (600 daltons), and high-flux membranes are capable of removing the complexed aluminum in a single dialysis session, minimizing systemic exposure to deferoxamine and its potential adverse effects, which include mucormycosis, ocular, auditory, and neurologic toxicity.[61,62] Deferoxamine generally is continued until the stimulated aluminum concentration is less than 50 ng/mL, which may require one year of therapy.[63]

Amyloidosis. A relatively new complication of hemodialysis is amyloidosis, caused by the deposition of β_2 microglobulin-containing amyloid in joints and soft tissues over prolonged periods of time.[64] The incidence of amyloidosis is approximately 50% after 12 years of dialysis and nearly 100% after 20 years. β_2 microglobulin (11,800 daltons) normally is eliminated by filtration and metabolism in the intact nephron. Renal failure leads to reduced elimination and accumulation, even during dialysis. High-flux membranes are more effective than conventional membranes for the removal of β_2 microglobulin but have not been available long enough to evaluate its role in prevention. Carpal tunnel syndrome, manifested as weakness and soreness in the thumb from pressure on the median nerve, is the most common symptom. Bone cysts also appear along with joint deposition of amyloid resulting in impaired mobility.[65,66] The type of membrane used for dialysis also has been implicated in increasing the rate of production of β_2 microglobulin, causing more rapid deposition. Biocompatible membranes are proposed to stimulate production to a lesser degree, but prospective studies demonstrating long-term benefit have not been conducted.[67]

Malnutrition. Chronic renal failure produces a catabolic state in patients and, along with the multifactorial complications of ESRD, leads to malnutrition. Serum albumin concentrations less than 3.0 gm/dL are associated with an increased mortality rate compared to higher values. Inadequate dietary intake as well as losses of amino acids by dialysis contribute to protein malnutrition, leading to additional complications such as impaired wound healing, susceptibility to infection, and others. (See Chapter 30: Chronic Renal Failure for further discussion.)

Peritoneal Dialysis

Peritoneal dialysis is performed using several different modalities, including the most common, continuous ambulatory peritoneal dialysis, as well as continuous cycling peritoneal dialysis, intermittent peritoneal dialysis, and nocturnal intermittent peritoneal dialysis. Both CAPD and CCPD are the dominant forms of chronic peritoneal dialysis in use today and will be discussed in further detail. The number of patients undergoing treatment with CAPD/CCPD in the U.S. increased from approximately 10,000 in 1985 to 16,500 in 1990, accounting for nearly 14% of all dialysis patients.[1]

Principles and Transport Processes

Peritoneal dialysis is performed by the instillation of 1 to 3 L of sterile dialysate solution into the peritoneal cavity through a surgically placed resident catheter. The solution dwells within the cavity for a period of three to eight hours, and then is drained and replaced with a fresh solution. This process of fill, dwell, and drain is performed three to four times during the day with an overnight dwell by the patient in their normal home or work environment.[68,69] (See Figure 31.6.) Conceptually, the process is similar to hemodialysis such that uremic toxins are removed by diffusion down a concentration gradient into the dialysate solution. A primary difference is that since the dialysate solution is resident and movement primarily is by diffusion, the rate of elimination of substances decreases with time as equilibrium is approached.

Blood and Dialysate Flow

Hemodialysis maintains constant perfusion of fresh dialysate, thereby maintaining a large concentration gradient throughout the dialysis treatment. During a typical dwell period for CAPD, urea and other substances increase in the dialysate relative to free plasma concentrations. For a daytime dwell period of four hours, it can be seen that urea has achieved nearly equal concentrations with plasma; therefore, the rate of elimination has become very small. (See Figure 31.7.) Instillation of fresh dialysate solution will reestablish the diffusion gradient leading to an increased rate of urea removal. For a patient making four exchanges of 2 L each per day, assuming urea dialysate concentration equal plasma concentrations, and 1.5 L removed by ultrafiltration, the urea clearance would be approximately 6.5 mL/minute. This is substantially lower than urea clearances achieved with hemodialysis; therefore, CAPD must be performed continually throughout the week in order to achieve adequate urea removal. Clearance is dependent upon blood flow, dialysate flow, and membrane characteristics, such as size, permeability, and thickness.[68-70] Dialysate flow is the only easily adjusted variable to alter clearance and has been used effectively in acute peritoneal dialysis to achieve relatively high clearances with 30- to 60-minute dwell periods in a cycling system. CCPD employs this concept of shorter dwell periods during the sleeping hours with automatic fill, dwell, and drain periods, leaving a high dextrose dialysate in the peritoneal cavity throughout the day until the next cycling session.[71] Electrolyte concentrations in the dialysate are near physiologic concentrations to prevent substantial shifts in serum electrolyte levels. (See Table 31.1.) In addition to diffusion, substances also are removed by convection as a result of the bulk flow of water from the patient into the dialysate.

Fluid Removal

Fluid removal occurs by ultrafiltration through adjustment of the hydrostatic pressure in hemodialysis. Since hydrostatic pressure is not easily adjusted in peritoneal dialysis, fluid is removed by altering the osmotic pressure within the dialysate. This is accomplished by the addition of dextrose monohydrate (90% d-glucose) to the dialysate in varying concentrations, depending upon the degree of fluid removal necessary in the patient. Concentrations include 1.5%, 2.5%, and 4.25% dextrose with net fluid losses during a four-hour dwell period of 200 and 400 mL for the 1.5% and 2.5% solutions, respectively, and approximately 700 mL for the 4.25% solution following an overnight dwell.[72]

Acid-base balance is achieved through the absorption of lactate from the dialysate which subsequently is metabolized to bicarbonate in vivo. Bicarbonate is not compatible with the calcium and magnesium in the dialysate and would lead to precipitation.

Access

Delivery of dialysate into the peritoneal cavity is accomplished through an indwelling catheter inserted through the abdominal

Fig 31.6   Schematic Representation of CAPD Components and Techniques of Inflow and Outflow.   Reproduced with permission from reference 71.

wall. The most common design is the Tenckhoff catheter, made of silicone rubber or polyurethane and consisting of a tube, straight or curled, with many holes in the distal end for fluid inflow and outflow.[69,73] The catheter also has a single or double cuff, which serves to anchor it to the internal and external attachment sites by promoting fibrous tissue growth, which also serves as a barrier to bacterial migration. Several modifications to the original catheter have appeared on the market, mostly in an attempt to overcome problems related to outflow of dialysate. Maintaining an unobstructed outlet port is essential for successful peritoneal dialysis.

Delivery of dialysate through the catheter is accomplished in several modes. A straight transfer set uses tubing attached to the catheter at one end, and to the bag of dialysate at the other, via a spike. The transfer set usually is changed every one to two months in the dialysis clinic. For each dialysate exchange, the patient attaches a bag of fresh dialysate, warmed to body temperature, to the transfer set and infuses the solution. The tubing is clamped and rolled up with the attached bag and placed into a pouch carried on the patient. The primary purpose for maintaining the connection is avoidance of contamination and the development of peritonitis. Following the dwell period, the patient unrolls the bag and tubing, places it on the floor, unclamps the tubing and awaits drainage of the fluid, usually 5 to 15 minutes. Using aseptic technique, the patient changes the dialysate bag and infuses fresh solution to repeat the process. Another strategy for dialysate infusion employs a Y transfer set with fresh dialysate attached to the upper arm of the Y, an empty bag to the lower arm, and the common line connected to the catheter.[72] Clamping the inflow arm and opening the outflow arm allows dialysate to drain from the peritoneum into the empty bag. Reversing the clamps then permits infusion of the dialysate solution. Clamping of the catheter allows removal of the Y transfer set and bags from the patient. A disinfectant is infused into the transfer set until used again for the next exchange. Just before the exchange, the disinfectant is flushed from the lines with fresh dialysate to flush residual bacteria from the system. Use of the Y

transfer set has resulted in a reduction in episodes of peritonitis from approximately one for every 9 to 12 patient months to one for every 24 to 36 patient months.[74]

Dialysis Prescription

The initial CAPD prescription for most patients consists of three exchanges during the day with 1.5% dextrose and a fourth, overnight exchange with 4.25% dextrose. This would be expected to achieve fluid removal of approximately 1300 mL, based upon 200 mL from each daytime exchange and 700 mL overnight.[72] Based upon assessment of the patient's fluid status, it may be necessary to increase or decrease the dialysate prescription to achieve fluid balance. Fluid retention is solved by increasing the dextrose con-

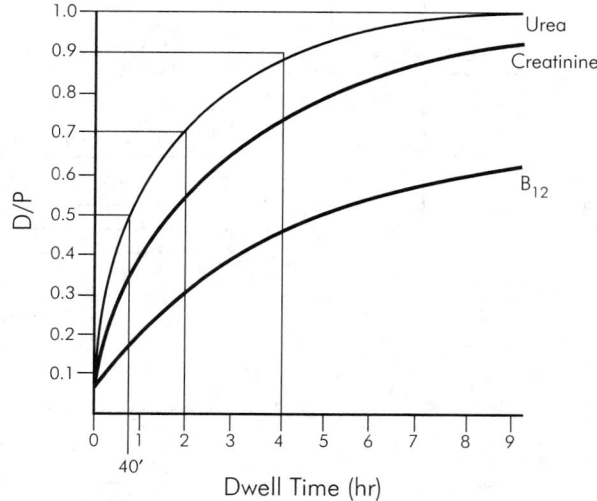

Fig 31.7   Rate of Entry into Peritoneal Dialysate of Urea, Creatinine, and Vitamin B$_{12}$.   The y-axis indicates the ratio of dialysate:plasma concentration (D:P). Reproduced with permission from reference 97.

tent of the daytime exchanges, beginning with 2.5% in place of one of the 1.5% solutions. This is expected to result in an additional removal of 200 mL, and therapy can be further adjusted as necessary. For those patients with excessive fluid removal, it may be possible to decrease the number of exchanges per day as long as adequate solute removal is present. If four exchanges are needed, the fluid intake may be liberalized to maintain adequate hydration.

7. M.J., a 27-year-old female, has a 14-year history of insulin-dependent diabetes mellitus. Her height is 5′12″, and weight 55 kg. One result of the diabetes has been development of ESRD necessitating dialysis. She has been undergoing CAPD for 1 year and until now has done well without any complications. Her dialysis prescription consists of 3 exchanges with 1.5% dextrose during the day and a 4th overnight exchange with 4.25% dextrose. She has a double-cuff Tenckhoff catheter and uses a Y transfer set for her exchanges. Her blood pressure is controlled and she shows no evidence of edema. She has no residual renal function. Her most recent serum laboratory results showed a calcium (Ca) of 10.9 mg/dL and K of 3.2 mEq/L. Calculate the prescribed amount of dialysis for M.J. [SI units: Ca 2.7 mmol/L; K 3.2 mmol/L]

Determination of the number of exchanges necessary for solute removal is based upon the clearance of urea as a surrogate for uremia. Based upon dialysate urea achieving 90% of plasma urea at the end of the dwell period, and four exchanges per day, the fluid removal would be approximately 9300 mL, or a urea clearance of 59 L/week. For M.J., body water content (urea distribution volume) is 29 L; therefore, the dialysis prescription would provide a weekly Kt/V of 2.03. Recommendations for patients undergoing CAPD are Kt/V ≥1.7, based upon total urea clearance both by dialysis and from residual renal function.[27] Larger patients may

need a larger volume for each exchange, up to 3 L, or an additional exchange per day. The increased volume is preferable due to the inconvenience of an additional exchange.

M.J. also is noted to have an elevated serum calcium concentration of 10.9 mg/dL, probably a result of her calcium carbonate requirements to serve as a binder of dietary phosphate. Dialysate preparations now are available with a low calcium concentration (2.5 mEq/L) compared with the standard concentration of 3.5 mEq/L, which can aid in the control of hypercalcemia associated with increased oral calcium intake.[72] Potassium normally is absent from the dialysate solution but may be supplemented in patients not able to maintain potassium within the normal range. M.J. has a serum potassium concentration of 3.2 mEq/L, and providing a dialysate concentration of 4 mEq/L will sustain normal concentrations and prevent hypokalemia. This is particularly important for patients receiving digitalis preparations.

Assessment of Dialysis Adequacy

8. Assess the actual dialysis provided to M.J., based upon a 24-hour collection of 9130 mL dialysate with a urea concentration of 54 mg/dL and serum urea concentration of 60 mg/dL.

Following stabilization of the patient on the new dialysis prescription, it is necessary to assess the adequacy of the delivered dialysis dose. This is accomplished by taking into account both the peritoneal and residual renal clearance of urea, and comparing with the target Kt/V, 1.7. Dialysis urea clearance is determined through the collection and measurement of the dialysate for a 24-hour period, along with the urine output for the same period of time.[72,75,76] Clearance is calculated by standard methods; rate of elimination

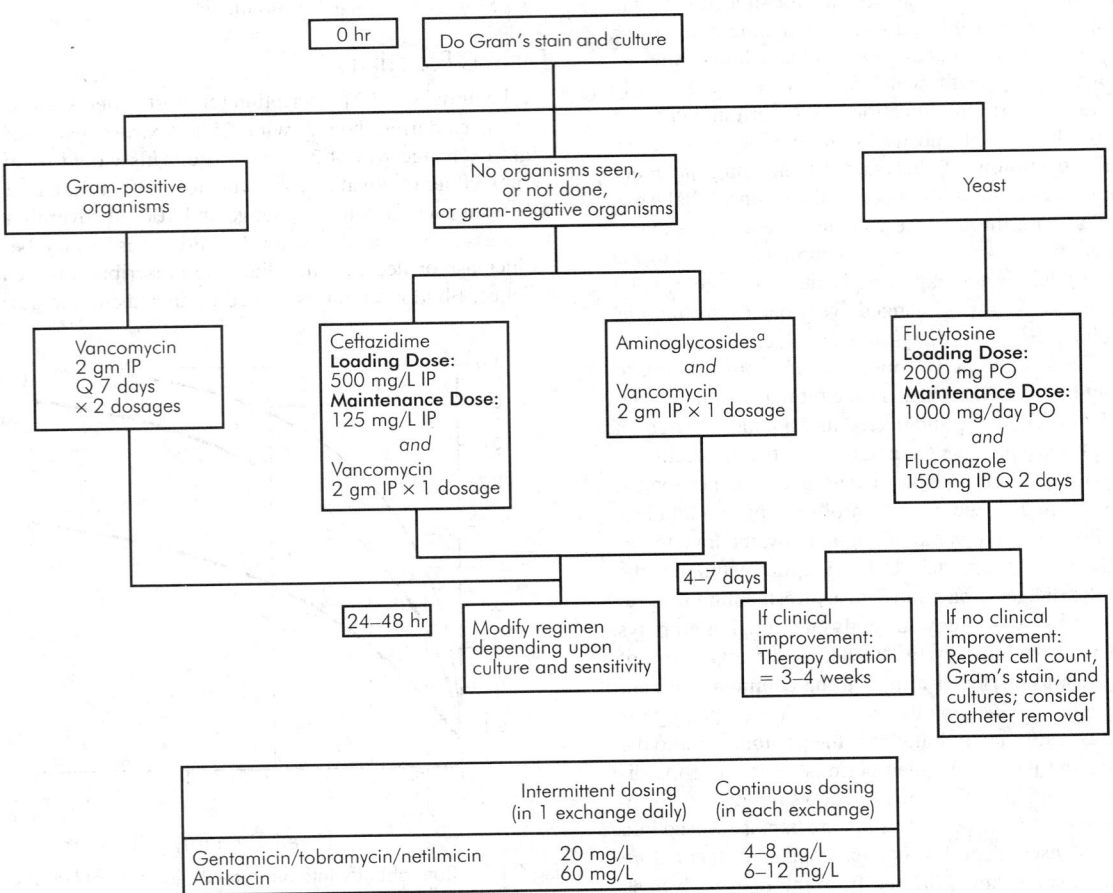

Fig 31.8   Initial Management Strategy of Peritonitis.   Reproduced with permission from reference 80.   IP = Intraperitoneally.

Fig 31.9   Management Strategy of Gram-Positive Peritonitis.   Reproduced with permission from reference 80.

divided by average plasma concentration. The sum of the two urea clearances then is multiplied by seven to determine the volume cleared per week, and then divided by the urea distribution volume, estimated from total body water content. This value then is compared to the target weekly Kt/V value of 1.7 for assessment and adjustment of the prescription. For M.J., the urea clearance was 5.7 mL/minute, or 57.5 L/week. Based upon her estimated urea distribution volume of 29 L, her weekly Kt/V is approximately 1.98, above the target of 1.7. Other measures of adequacy include BUN less than 100 mg/dL and serum creatinine less than 18 mg/dL.[76,77] These values, unlike the Kt/V, may be affected by nutritional status of the patient and be falsely low, suggesting adequate dialysis when the patient actually is underdialyzed. Other measures of effective dialysis include a weekly creatinine clearance ≥50 L/1.73m²/week.[78,79]

Complications

9. M.J. now presents to the dialysis clinic with complaints of abdominal tenderness and cloudy effluent. Examination of the dialysate revealed white blood cell (WBC) count 330 cells/µL with 62% neutrophils. Gram's stain was positive for gram-positive cocci. Her diabetes has been controlled by the addition of 10 U of regular insulin to each daytime bag and 15 U to the overnight bag. How should M.J.'s infection be treated? [SI units: WBC 330 × 10⁶ cells/L]

Peritonitis. The most significant complication among patients undergoing peritoneal dialysis is peritonitis, frequently caused by *S. epidermidis* (30%) or *aureus* (10%).[68,69] The patient usually will present with abdominal pain, nausea and vomiting, and/or fever with or without a cloudy effluent. Bacterial peritonitis generally will be accompanied by an elevated dialysate WBC count, greater than 100/mm³ with greater than 50% neutrophils. A positive Gram's stain should be followed by culture with therapy initiated

in the interim. For lower cell counts or negative Gram's stain, culture should be obtained followed by treatment for positive cultures and continued observation for negative results. Figure 31.8 illustrates a consensus algorithm for antibiotic selection in the patient with a presentation of peritonitis.[80]

Vancomycin intraperitoneally (IP) is the most effective therapy for gram-positive infections, with cefazolin or other first-generation cephalosporins as alternatives.[80,81] Without a Gram's stain, therapy should be initiated with a combination of vancomycin and aminoglycoside, both administered IP. In addition to antibiotics, heparin 1000 U/L should be added to each exchange to prevent the formation of fibrin clots which may result in catheter failure.[68] Recommendations for specific culture results are summarized in Figures 31.9, 31.10, and 31.11.[80-84]

This is M.J.'s first episode of peritonitis. The most likely pathogen, a *Staphylococcus* species, is consistent with the positive gram-stain. Her treatment should consist of 2 gm IP vancomycin, every seven days, for a total of two doses. Heparin, 1000 U/mL should be added to the dialysate to prevent fibrin clots from forming and obstructing outflow from the peritoneal cavity.[80] Her blood glucose should be monitored as a result of her infection and increased glucose and insulin absorption during the peritonitis. Inability to control the blood glucose concentration may require temporary discontinuation of the IP insulin and administration by another route.

Exit-Site Infection. Separate from peritonitis are catheter exit-site infections, most often caused by *S. aureus* and *Pseudomonas* species.[86,87] Local erythema alone can be treated with topical agents (e.g., chlorhexidine, mupirocin, or hydrogen peroxide), whereas purulent drainage indicates more significant infection and need for systemic antibiotics.[80] Gram-positive organisms are treated with first-generation oral cephalosporins or penicillinase-resistant penicillin. Rifampin may be added at 600 mg/day for nonresponding infections with positive cultures after one week of appropriate therapy. Further lack of response requires evaluation for catheter removal. Gram-negative organisms may be treated with ciprofloxacin 500 mg orally twice daily.

Weight Gain. Dextrose is present in dialysate solutions primarily to serve as an osmotic agent for the removal of fluid during each exchange. Higher concentrations are expected to result in greater fluid removal. Approximately 500 to 1000 kcal/day are absorbed as glucose from peritoneal dialysis solutions, which can lead to weight gain in patients. Some patients may require modification of oral caloric intake in order to avoid excessive weight gain. Insulin requirements generally are increased in patients with diabetes as a result of the additional calories, and when administered intraperitoneally, usually are two to three times the normal subcutaneous dose due to a bioavailability of 20% to 50%.[87,88]

Continuous Renal Replacement Therapies

Patients with acute renal failure in the acute care unit often develop cardiovascular compromise such that hemodialysis is not a treatment option. As an alternative, slow continuous therapies have developed that accomplish both fluid control as well as removal of uremic toxins.

Hemofiltration: Continuous Arteriovenous Hemofiltration (CAVH), Continuous Venovenous Hemofiltration (CVVH), and Slow Continuous Ultrafiltration (SCUF)

Hemofiltration is a process whereby blood is pumped or flows under the influence of cardiac function through a hemofilter that serves as a site for fluid removal by ultrafiltration.[89,90] Dialysate is not present, and solute removal occurs solely by convection. The ultrafiltrate (produced isosmotically) rate is equivalent to clearance

Fig 31.10 Management Strategy of Gram-Negative Peritonitis. Reproduced with permission from reference 80.

24–48 hr

Culture negative

Continue initial antimicrobial therapy

96 hr

If clinical improvement: give 2nd dose of vancomycin on day 7 and discontinue 2nd antimicrobial

If no clinical improvement

Repeat cell count, Gram's stain, and cultures

120 hr

If culture positive

If culture negative

Adjust therapy appropriately

Consider catheter removal; continue antimicrobials for 5–7 days

Duration of therapy

14 days

14 days

Fig 31.11   Management Strategy of Culture-Negative Peritonitis.   Reproduced with permission from reference 80.

for small molecules present in the unbound state. Access to the systemic circulation is either arterial (continuous arteriovenous hemofiltration) or venous (continuous venovenous hemofiltration). CAVH requires separate cannulation of the femoral artery and vein, and the patient must remain immobilized in the supine position. CVVH utilizes a double lumen catheter and access into the femoral, subclavian, or internal jugular vein. This permits patient movement during the procedure. Ultrafiltration rates with these methods are approximately 10 mL/minute, which necessitates replacement of fluids to maintain adequate hydration and perfusion.[91,92] Replacement fluids typically are lactated Ringer's and are administered either before or after the hemofilter. As for other extracorporeal procedures, anticoagulation of the blood circuit is necessary in most cases, and is accomplished with a heparin infusion administered into the arterial line, relative to the filter. A procedure similar to CVVH but without fluid replacement is slow continuous ultrafiltration.[93] This procedure is applied for fluid removal only and is not effective for sufficient solute removal in the patient with acute renal failure and uremia.

Hemodialysis: Continuous Arteriovenous Hemodialysis (CAVHD) and Venovenous Hemodialysis (CVVHD)

Continuous arteriovenous hemodialysis and venovenous hemodialysis are based upon a similar concept to CAVH and CVVH; however, sterile dialysate is added to the circuit to allow for diffusive transfer and removal of uremic toxins.[89,90] (See Figure 31.12.) The benefit of diffusion is additional removal of toxin from

Dialysate

Heparin

Collection Bag

Fig 31.12   Circuitry for Continuous Venovenous Hemodialysis (CVVHD).   A) double-lumen subclavian vein access; B) venous air trap; C) venous pressure monitor; D) air detector; E) dialyzer; x-y-z, blood and dialysate pumps. Reproduced with permission from reference 98.

the patient's blood while maintaining ultrafiltration, and cardiovascular stability through low flow rates. Blood flow rates may be 50 to 150 mL/minute, with dialysate flows of approximately 15 mL/minute.[94,95] This allows for near equilibration of the blood and dialysate compartment with respect to small molecules such as urea, and the dialysate outflow rate will approximate urea clearance. Anticoagulation is necessary for hemofiltration and is accomplished through heparin loading dose administration followed by continuous infusion.

Continuous replacement therapies may be important routes of elimination for drug therapy administered to patients in the acute care unit. Estimation of drug removal rate by filtration is determined as the product of the sieving coefficient for the drug across the filter membrane (fractional concentration of dialysate to unbound plasma drug concentration) and the dialysate outflow rate. Replacement of drug is dependent upon pharmacokinetic and pharmacodynamic characteristics of the drug, details which are presented in Chapter 32: Dosing of Drugs in Renal Failure.

References

1   **US Renal Data Systems.** USRDS 1993 annual data report. Bethesda, MD: The National Institutes of Health, Institute of Diabetes and Digestive and Kidney Diseases; March 1993.

2   **Lazarus JM, Hakim RM.** Medical aspects of hemodialysis. In: Brenner BM, Rector FC, eds. The Kidney. 4th ed. Philadelphia: WB Saunders; 1991: 2223.

3   **Van Stone JC, Daugirdas JT.** Physiologic principles. In: Daugirdas JT, Ing TS, eds. Handbook of Dialysis. 2nd ed. Boston: Little, Brown and Co.; 1994: 13.

4   **Keen ML, Gotch FA.** Dialyzers and delivery systems. In: Cogan MG, Schoenfeld P, eds. Introduction to Dialysis. 2nd ed. New York: Churchill Livingstone; 1991:1.

5   **Daugirdas JT, Depner TA.** A nomogram approach to hemodialysis urea modeling. Am J Kidney Dis. 1994;23: 33.

6   **Laird NM et al.** Modeling success or failure of dialysis therapy. The National Cooperative Dialysis Study. Kidney Int Suppl. 1983;13:S101.

7   **Gotch FA, Sargent JA.** A mechanistic analysis of the National Cooperative Dialysis Study (NCDS). Kidney Int. 1985;28:526.

8   **Collins AJ et al.** Urea index and other predictors of hemodialysis patient survival. Am J Kidney Dis. 1994;23:272.

9   **Van Stone JC.** Hemodialysis apparatus. In: Daugirdas JT, Ing TS, eds. Handbook of Dialysis. 2nd ed. Boston: Little, Brown and Co.; 1994:30.

10 **Mujais SK, Ivanovich P.** Membranes for extracorporeal therapy. In: Maher JF, ed. Replacement of Renal Function by Dialysis. 3rd ed. Boston: Kluwer Academic; 1989:181.

11 **Wathen RL et al.** Water treatment for hemodialysis. In: Cogan MG, Schoenfeld P, eds. Introduction to Dialysis. 2nd ed. New York: Churchill Livingstone; 1991:45.

12 **Keshaviah PR.** Pretreatment and preparation of city water for hemodialysis. In: Maher JF, ed. Replacement of Renal Function by Dialysis. 3rd ed. Boston: Kluwer Academic; 1989:189.

13 **Stewart W.** The composition of dialysis fluid. In: Maher JF, ed. Replacement of Renal Function by Dialysis. 3rd ed. Boston: Kluwer Academic; 1989:199.

14 **Ross EA, Nissenson.** Acid-base and electrolyte disturbances. In: Daugirdas JT, Ing TS, eds. Handbook of Dialysis. 2nd ed. Boston: Little, Brown and Co.; 1994:401.

15 **Raja RM.** Vascular access for hemodialysis. In: Daugirdas JT, Ing TS, eds. Handbook of Dialysis. 2nd ed. Boston: Little, Brown and Co.; 1994:53.

16 **Caruana RJ, Keep DM.** Anticoagulation. In: Daugirdas JT, Ing TS, eds. Handbook of Dialysis. 2nd ed. Boston: Little, Brown; 1994:121.

17 **Lindsay RM, Smith Anne.** Practical use of anticoagulants. In: Maher JF, ed. Replacement of Renal Function by Dialysis. 3rd ed. Boston: Kluwer Academic; 1989:246.

18 **Farrell PC.** Heparin modeling. In: Nissenson AR, Fine RN. Dialysis Therapy. 2nd ed. Philadelphia: Hanley and Belfus; 1993:82.

19 **Lohr JW, Schwab SJ.** Minimizing hemorrhagic complications in dialysis patients. J Am Soc Nephrol. 1991;2: 961.

20 **Sanders PW et al.** Hemodialysis without anticoagulation. Am J Kidney Dis. 1985;5:32.

21 **Schwab SJ et al.** Hemodialysis without anticoagulation. One-year prospective trial in hospitalized patients at risk for bleeding. Am J Med. 1987;83:405.

22 **Blaufox MD et al.** Rebound anticoagulation occurring after regional heparinization for hemodialysis. Trans Am Soc Artif Intern Organs. 1966;12: 207.

23 **Lowrie EG et al.** Effect of the hemodialysis prescription on patient morbidity: Report from the National Cooperative Dialysis Study. N Engl J Med. 1981;305:1176.

24 **Daugirdas JT, Schneditz.** Postdialysis urea rebound: measurement, prediction and effects of regional blood flow. Dial Transpl. 1994;23:166.

25 **Daugirdas JT.** Linear estimates of variable-volume, single pool Kt/V: an analysis of error. Am J Kidney Dis. 1993; 22:267.

26 **Delmez JA et al.** Hemodialysis prescription and delivery in a metropolitan area. The St. Louis Nephrology Study Group. Kidney Int. 1992;41:1023.

27 **Consensus Development Conference Panel.** Morbidity and mortality of renal dialysis: an NIH consensus conference statement. Ann Intern Med. 1994;121: 62–70.

28 **AAMI.** Recommended Practice for Reuse of Hemodialyzers. Arlington, VA: Association for the Advancement of Medical Instrumentation; 1993.

29 **Shusterman NH et al.** Reprocessing of hemodialyzers: a critical appraisal. Am J Kidney Dis. 1989:14:81.

30 **Held JP et al.** Mortality and duration of hemodialysis treatment. JAMA. 1991;265:871.

31 **Shaldon S.** Unanswered questions pertaining to dialysis adequacy in 1992. Kidney Int. 1993;43(Suppl. 41):S-274.

32 **US Renal Data Systems.** USRDS 1993 annual data report. Bethesda, MD: The National Institutes of Health, Institute of Diabetes and Digestive and Kidney Diseases; March 1992.

33 **Held PJ et al.** Five-year survival for end-stage renal disease patients in the United States, Europe and Japan, 1982–1987. Am J Kidney Dis. 1990; 15:451.

34 **Charra B et al.** Survival as an index of adequacy of dialysis. Kidney Int. 1992;41:1286.

35 **Barth RH.** Urea modeling and Kt/V: a critical appraisal. Kidney Int. 1993; 43(Suppl. 41):S-252.

36 **Pedrini LA et al.** Causes, kinetics and clinical implications of post-hemodialysis urea rebound. Kidney Int. 1988; 34:817.

37 **Kjellstrand C et al.** Patient related factors leading to slow urea transfer in the body during dialysis. ASAIO Trans. 1994;40:164.

38 **Daugirdas JT.** Dialysis hypotension: a hemodynamic analysis. Kidney Int. 1991;39:233.

39 **Maggiore Q et al.** Blood temperature and vascular stability during hemodialysis and hemofiltration. Trans Am Soc Artif Intern Organs. 1982;28:523.

40 **Canzanello VJ, Burkart JM.** Hemodialysis-associated muscle cramps. Semin Dial. 1992;5:299.

41 **Sherman RA.** Acute therapy of hemodialysis-related muscle cramps. Am J Kidney Dis. 1982;2:287.

42 **Kaji DM et al.** Prevention of muscle cramp in hemodialysis patients by quinine sulfate. Lancet. 1976;2:66.

43 **Tielemans C.** Immediate hypersensitivity reactions and hemodialysis. Adv Nephrol. 1993;22:401.

44 **Lemke H-D et al.** Hypersensitivity reactions during hemodialysis. Role of complement fragments and ethylene oxide antibodies. Nephrol Dial Transplant. 1990;5:264.

45 **Parnes EL, Shapiro WB.** Anaphylactoid reactions in hemodialysis patients treated with the AN69 dialyzer. Kidney Int. 1991;40:1148.

46 **Pegues DA.** Anaphylactoid reactions associated with reuse of hollow-fiber hemodialyzers and ACE inhibitors. Kidney Int. 1992;42:1232.

47 **Arieff AI.** Dialysis disequilibrium syndrome: current concepts on pathogenesis and prevention. Kidney Int. 1994; 45:629.

48 **Fan P-Y et al.** Vascular access: concepts for the 1990's. J Am Soc Nephrol. 1992;3:1.

49 **Valji K et al.** Pharmacomechanical thrombolysis and angioplasty in the management of clotted hemodialysis grafts; early and late complications. Radiology. 1991;178:243.

50 **Goldberg JP.** Intravenous streptokinase for thrombolysis of occluded arteriovenous access. Arch Intern Med. 1985;145:1405.

51 **Mangiarotti G et al.** Urokinase treatment for arteriovenous fistulae declotting in dialyzed patients. Nephron. 1984;36:60.

52 **Nghiem DD et al.** Management of the infected hemodialysis access graft. Trans Am Soc Artif Intern Organs. 1983;29:360.

53 **DeSoi CA et al.** Vancomycin elimination during high-flux hemodialysis: kinetic model and comparison of four membranes. Am J Kidney Dis. 1992; 20:354.

54 **Pollard TA et al.** Vancomycin redistribution: dosing recommendations following high-flux hemodialysis. Kidney Int. 1994;45:232.

55 **Andress DL et al.** Osteomalacia and aplastic bone disease in aluminum-related osteodystrophy. J Clin Endocrinol Metab. 1987;65:11.

56 **Rosenlof K et al.** Erythropoietin, aluminum, and anaemia in patients on hemodialysis. Lancet. 1990;335:247.

57 **DeBroe ME et al.** New insights and strategies in the diagnosis and treatment of aluminum overload in dialysis patients. Nephrol Dial Transplant. 1993;8(Suppl. 1):47.

58 **Salusky IB et al.** Aluminum accumulation during treatment with aluminum hydroxide and dialysis in children and young adults with chronic renal disease. N Engl J Med. 1991;324:527.

59 **Chazan JA et al.** Plasma aluminum levels (unstimulated and stimulated): clinical and biochemical findings in 185 patients undergoing chronic hemodialysis for 4 to 95 months. Am J Kidney Dis. 1989;13:284.

60 **McCarthy JT et al.** Clinical experience with deferoxamine in dialysis patients with aluminum toxicity. Q J Med. 1990;74:257.

61 **Boelaert JR et al.** Mucormycosis during deferoxamine therapy is a siderophore-mediated infection. In-vitro and in-vivo studies. J Clin Invest. 1993;91: 1979.

62 **Olivieri NF et al.** Visual and auditory neurotoxicity in patients receiving subcutaneous deferoxamine infusion. N Engl J Med. 1986:314:869.

Renal Dialysis

63 **Felsenfeld AJ et al.** Deferoxamine therapy in hemodialysis patients with aluminum-associated bone disease. Kidney Int. 1989;35:1371.

64 **Koch KM.** Dialysis-related amyloidosis. Kidney Int. 1992;41:1416.

65 **Charra B et al.** Chronic renal failure treatment duration and mode: their relevance to the late periarticular syndrome. Blood Purif. 1988;6:117.

66 **Kleinman KS et al.** Amyloid syndromes associated with hemodialysis. Kidney Int. 1989;35:567.

67 **Diaz RJ et al.** The effect of dialyzer reprocessing on performance and β_2 microglobulin removal using polysulfone membranes. Am J Kidney Dis. 1993;21:405.

68 **Gokal R.** Continuous ambulatory peritoneal dialysis. In: Maher JF, ed. Replacement of Renal Function by Dialysis. 3rd ed. Boston: Kluwer Academic; 1989:590.

69 **Nolph KD.** Peritoneal dialysis. In: Brenner BM, Rector FC, eds. The Kidney. 4th ed. Philadelphia: WB Saunders; 1991:2299.

70 **Mactier RA, Twardowski ZJ.** Influence of dwell time, osmolality, and volume of exchanges on solute mass transfer and ultrafiltration in peritoneal dialysis. Semin Dial. 1988;1:40.

71 **Schoenfeld P.** Care of the patient on peritoneal dialysis. In: Cogan MG, Schoenfeld P, eds. Introduction to Dialysis. 2nd ed. New York: Churchill Livingstone; 1991:181.

72 **Diaz-Buxo JA.** Chronic peritoneal dialysis prescription. In: Daugirdas JT, Ing TS, eds. Handbook of Dialysis. 2nd ed. Boston: Little, Brown and Co.; 1994:310.

73 **Ash SR.** Chronic peritoneal dialysis catheters: effects of catheter design, material, and location. Semin Dial. 1990;3:39.

74 **Port FK et al.** Risk of peritonitis and technique failure by CAPD connection technique: a national study. Kidney Int. 1992;42:967.

75 **Nolph KD.** What's new in peritoneal dialysis—an overview. Kidney Int Suppl. 1992;38:S148.

76 **Nolph KD.** Quantitating peritoneal dialysis delivery: a required standard of care. Semin Dial. 1991;4:139.

77 **Oreopoulos DG.** Criteria for adequacy of peritoneal dialysis. Perit Dial Bull. 1983;3:1.

78 **Keshaviah P.** Urea kinetic and middle molecule approaches to assessing the adequacy of hemodialysis and peritoneal dialysis. Kidney Int Suppl. 1993; 40:S28.

79 **Brandes JC et al.** Clinical outcome of continuous peritoneal dialysis predicted by urea and creatinine kinetics. J Am Soc Nephrol. 1992;2:1430.

80 **Keane WF et al.** Peritoneal dialysis-related peritonitis treatment recommendations: 1993 update. Perit Dial Int. 1993;13:14.

81 **Tranaeus A et al.** Peritonitis in continuous ambulatory peritoneal dialysis (CAPD): diagnostic findings, therapeutic outcome and complications. Perit Dial Int. 1989;9:179.

82 **Bastani B et al.** Treatment of gram-positive peritonitis with two intraperitoneal doses of vancomycin in CAPD patients. Nephron. 1987;45:283.

83 **Holley JL et al.** Polymicrobial peritonitis in patients on continuous peritoneal dialysis. Am J Kidney Dis. 1992; 19:162.

84 **Millikin SP et al.** Antimicrobial treatment of peritonitis associated with continuous ambulatory peritoneal dialysis. Perit Dial Bull. 1991;11:252.

85 **Abraham G et al.** Natural history of exit-site infection (ESI) in patients on continuous ambulatory peritoneal dialysis (CAPD). Perit Dial Int. 1988;8: 211.

86 **Kazmi HR et al.** Pseudomonas exit site infections in continuous ambulatory dialysis patients. J Am Soc Nephrol. 1992;2:1498.

87 **Amair P et al.** Continuous ambulatory peritoneal dialysis in diabetics with end-stage renal disease. New Engl J Med. 1982;303:625.

88 **Chan E, Montgomery PA.** Administration of insulin by continuous ambulatory peritoneal dialysis. Pharmacother. 1993;13:455.

89 **Ronco C.** Continuous renal replacement therapies for the treatment of acute renal failure in intensive care patients. Clin Nephrol. 1993;40:187.

90 **Golper TA.** Indications, technical considerations, and strategies for renal replacement therapy in the intensive care unit. J Intensive Care Med. 1992;7:310.

91 **Olbricht CJ.** Continuous arteriovenous hemofiltration: In vivo functional characteristics and its dependence on vascular access and filter design. Nephron. 1990;55:49.

92 **Davenport A et al.** Improved cardiovascular stability during continuous modes of renal replacement therapy in critically ill patients with acute hepatic and renal failure. Crit Care Med. 1993; 21:328.

93 **Paganini EP et al.** Slow continuous ultrafiltration in hemodialysis resistant oliguric acute renal failure patients. Trans Am Soc Artif Intern Organs. 1984;30:173.

94 **Sigler MH, Teehan B.** Solute transport in continuous hemodialysis: a new treatment for acute renal failure. Kidney Int. 1987;32:562.

95 **Van Geelan JA et al.** Continuous arteriovenous haemofiltration and haemodiafiltration in acute renal failure. Nephrol Dial Transplant. 1988;3:181.

96 **Daugirdas JT.** Second generation logarithmic estimates of single-pool variable volume Kt/V: an analysis of error. J Am Soc Nephrol. 1993;4:1205.

97 **Sorkin MI, Diax-Buxo JA.** Physiology of peritoneal dialysis. In: Daugirdas JT, Ing TS, eds. Handbook of Dialysis. 2nd ed. Boston: Little, Brown and Co.; 1994:245.

98 **Sigler MH, Teehan BP.** Slow continuous renal replacement therapies: CAVH, CVVH, CAVHD, CVVHD. In: Nissenson AR, Fine RN, eds. Dialysis Therapy. 2nd ed. Philadelphia: Hanley & Belfus; 1993:143.

Chapter 32

Dosing of Drugs in Renal Failure

Francesca T Aweeka

Basic Principles (See Figures 32.1 and 32.2) 32-1
Effect of Renal Failure on Drug Disposition 32-1
  Bioavailability 32-1
  Protein binding (See Table 32.1) 32-2
  Volume of distribution (Vd) 32-2
  Elimination 32-2
  Pharmacodynamics and renal disease 32-3
Drug Removal by Dialysis 32-3
  Drug specific properties 32-3
  High-flux hemodialysis 32-4
  Continuous ambulatory peritoneal dialysis (CAPD)
    (Also see Question 20) 32-4
  Continuous arteriovenous hemofiltration (CAVH) .. 32-4
  Hemoperfusion 32-4
Renal Failure 32-4
  Signs and Symptoms 32-4
Pharmacokinetics and Pharmacodynamics of
Specific Drugs in Renal Failure (See Table 32.2) .. 32-5
  Ceftazidime 32-5
    Dosage modification: factors to consider
      (See Equation 32.1) 32-5
  Aminoglycosides 32-5
    Alteration of dose versus dosing interval
      (See Table 32.3 and Figure 32.3) 32-5
    Determination of appropriate dose 32-11
      Patient specific methods (See Equations 32.2
        to 32.10) 32-11
      Revised parameters (See Equations 32.11 and
        32.12) 32-12
  Effect of Hemodialysis 32-12
    Conventional dialysis 32-12
      Gentamicin (See Equations 32.13 to 32.16) 32-12
      Ceftazidime 32-13

  High-flux hemodialysis 32-13
Acyclovir 32-13
  Renal clearance (See Equation 32.17) 32-13
  Effect of renal dysfunction on metabolism 32-14
Zidovudine (AZT) 32-14
  Dosage adjustment 32-14
  Hemodialysis 32-14
Penicillin 32-14
  Dosage adjustment (See Equations 32.18 and
    32.19) 32-14
  Penicillin-induced neurotoxicity 32-15
    Predisposing factors 32-15
Antipseudomonal Penicillins 32-15
  Piperacillin 32-15
Vancomycin 32-15
  Pharmacokinetic dosage calculations
    (See Equations 32.20 to 32.24) 32-15
  Hemodialysis 32-16
Amphotericin 32-16
  Dosing 32-16
  Hemodialysis 32-16
Gentamicin 32-16
Phenytoin 32-17
  Protein binding (See Figure 32.4 and Equations
    32.25 and 32.26) 32-17
Effect of Renal Failure on Metabolized Drugs 32-17
  Meperidine (See Table 32.4) 32-17
  Narcotic Analgesics 32-18
    Morphine 32-18
    Codeine 32-18
    Propoxyphene 32-19
  Procainamide (See Figure 32.5) 32-19
  Nonsteroidal Anti-Inflammatory Drugs (NSAIDs)
    (See Figure 32.6) 32-19

Basic Principles

An increasing amount of information is available on the disposition of drugs in renal disease because of the importance of designing specific therapeutic regimens for patients with renal impairment. Many of these patients are managed with multiple medications that need aggressive dosing adjustment in the presence of kidney disease. Without careful drug dosing and therapeutic monitoring, serious adverse effects associated with drugs may develop in these patients.

A number of factors associated with kidney disease may predispose patients to drug toxicity. Renal disease can affect the pharmacokinetic disposition as well as the pharmacologic effect of these drugs. This may be true for any drug regardless of whether it is primarily eliminated by the kidney. For example, the physiological changes associated with uremia can induce changes in drug absorption, protein binding, distribution, or elimination that may not be predictable. These physiological changes can alter drug concentrations within the plasma or blood and at the targeted tissue site of activity; and can affect drug efficacy and toxicity.

Little is known as to how renal disease may affect drug pharmacodynamics. Pharmacodynamics (or ''what the drug does to the body'') describes quantitatively the pharmacological or toxicolog-

ical effects of drugs and relates drug concentration to these effects. Patients with renal disease may have a different response to a given drug concentration than a patient with normal renal function.

Although data in the area of pharmacodynamics and renal disease are minimal, renal patients can be more sensitive to some drugs and can experience an increased frequency of adverse drug reactions with or without appropriate dosing modifications.

Figure 32.1 illustrates the relationship between pharmacokinetics and pharmacodynamics and the relationship of these two scientific disciplines to drug dose and concentration on one side, and drug concentration and effect on the other. Figure 32.2 illustrates how different components of drug disposition influence the ability of a drug to exert its pharmacologic effect at its site of action.

Effect of Renal Failure on Drug Disposition

Bioavailability

Although several factors can affect drug absorption in patients with kidney disease, only limited data are available that definitively document altered bioavailability. The absorption of drugs in patients with renal disorders could be inhibited by gastrointestinal (GI) disturbances present in uremia (e.g., nausea, vomiting, diarrhea), uremic gastritis, and pancreatitis. Edema of the GI tract can

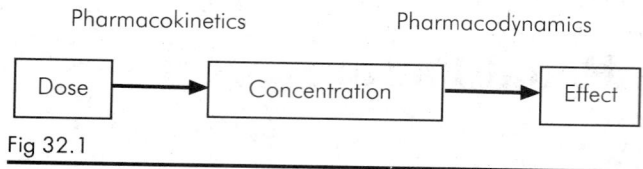

Pharmacokinetics   Pharmacodynamics

Dose ⟶ Concentration ⟶ Effect

Fig 32.1

occur in patients with nephrotic syndrome and can cause impaired absorption. Gastric and intestinal mobility as well as gastric emptying time can be altered by the neuropathy that commonly is associated with uremia. Uremia also can increase gastric ammonia leading to an increased gastric pH. Drugs such as ferrous sulfate that require an acidic medium for absorption may, therefore, be less bioavailable.[1] The aluminum and calcium containing antacids which often are required by renal failure patients for GI symptoms and hyperphosphatemia, also will neutralize the hydrochloric acid in the stomach, thereby increasing the gastric pH. These antacids also can complex with drugs, thereby decreasing their absorption.

The bioavailability of orally administered drugs also depends upon the extent to which the drug is metabolized by first-pass (presystemic) elimination. For example, the first-pass hepatic metabolism of oral propranolol is reduced in patients with renal disease leading to increased bioavailability.[2,3] Subsequent work, however, has attributed these observed increased concentrations of propranolol in renal failure to a significant increase in the blood/plasma ratio.[4] Additional drugs exhibiting increased bioavailability in renal disease include cloxacillin, propoxyphene, dihydrocodeine, encainide, and zidovudine.

Protein Binding

The extent to which a drug exerts its pharmacologic effects is related to the amount of free or unbound drug available for distribution to the target tissues. Renal disease patients often have alterations in plasma protein binding which can increase the amount of drug that is unbound.[5] Although this generally is true for acidic drugs, the binding of basic drugs usually is unchanged or possibly decreased in renal disease. Clinically this is most important for highly protein-bound drugs (>80%). Decreased binding of these drugs results in more dramatic increases in the free fraction of drug. This leads to an increase in the volume of distribution (Vd) and an increase in plasma clearance for drugs with a low extraction ratio. An increase in both the volume of distribution and clearance would result in little or no change in the half-life (t½) of these drugs. Alternatively, the volume of distribution of high extraction ratio drugs can increase without a concomitant change in clearance. In this latter situation, the drug half-life would increase.

Hypoalbuminemia is a common complication of renal failure. Since acidic rather than basic drugs are bound to albumin, their protein binding tends to be altered in renal disease patients.[6] (See Table 32.1.) Patients with uremia also accumulate acidic by-products that may displace acidic drugs from their albumin binding sites or inhibit their binding. This is supported by the observed improvement in protein binding following removal of these by-products by hemodialysis. Finally, the conformation or structural arrangement of albumin is altered in renal disease which may reduce the number or affinity of binding sites for drugs. Studies have demonstrated differences in the amino acid composition of albumin from healthy and uremic patients.[10]

The anticonvulsant, phenytoin, is an important example of a drug whose protein binding is altered in renal disease.[8,11] This will be discussed more completely below.

Volume of Distribution (Vd)

Renal disease may change the volume of distribution of various drugs. The volume of distribution or "apparent volume" is the "volume" necessary to account for the total amount of drug in the body if it were present throughout the body at the same concentration as that found in the plasma.

A decrease in the plasma protein binding of highly protein-bound drugs, such as phenytoin, leads to increases in the volume of distribution since the fraction of free drug is increased and there is more free drug to distribute into the peripheral tissue. (Also see Chapter 2: Clinical Pharmacokinetics.)

Drugs that are not highly protein bound (e.g., gentamicin, isoniazid) have little change in their distribution volume in renal disease. Digoxin is a unique exception in that its distribution volume is decreased in renal disease. This is attributed to a decrease in myocardial tissue uptake of this compound leading to a decrease in the myocardial or tissue to serum concentration ratio.[12]

Elimination

Drugs are eliminated primarily through renal excretion and hepatic metabolism and hepatic resorption. The extent to which renal disease affects the elimination of a drug depends upon the percentage of drug normally excreted unchanged in the urine and the degree of renal impairment. As kidney disease progresses and the kidney's ability to excrete uremic toxins diminishes, the ability to eliminate some drugs also decreases. If the doses of these drugs are not modified for patients with renal disease, these drugs will accumulate and increase the potential for toxicity.

The kidney primarily eliminates drugs by filtration or active secretion. Characteristics of a drug that determine its filterability include its affinity for protein and molecular weight. Drugs with low protein binding or those which are displaced from proteins in renal disease (e.g., phenytoin) are filtered more easily. Molecules of high molecular weight (e.g., those in dextran 40) cannot be filtered due to their large size.[13] The precise explanations for how renal disease selectively alters the process of glomerular filtration or tubular secretion of specific drugs, for the most part, are not known. Therefore, the renal elimination of drugs in patients with renal disease usually is estimated by measuring the ability of the kidney to eliminate substances such as creatinine [i.e., creatinine clearance (Cl$_{Cr}$)]. (See Chapter 29: Acute Renal Failure.)

Renal disease also can have an important impact on the elimination of drugs that are primarily metabolized by the liver.[13,14] Metabolic processes, such as hydroxylation and glucuronidation, often produce inactive, more polar compounds that can be eliminated readily by the kidney. The metabolites of some drugs (e.g.,

Table 32.1	Plasma Protein Binding (%) of Acidic Drugs in Renal Failure		
Drug	Normal	Renal Failure	Reference
Cefazolin	85	69	129
Cefoxitin	73	25	130
Clofibrate	97	91	128
Diazoxide	94	84	131
Furosemide	96	94	132
Pentobarbital	66	59	133
Phenytoin	88	74	103
	93	84	134
Salicylate	87	74	135
	97	84	134
Sulfamethoxazole	66	42	134
Valproic acid	92	77	136
Warfarin	99	98	137

Fig 32.2 Factors Influencing Drug Disposition and Therapeutic/Toxic Effects Following drug administration a number of factors can influence pharmacokinetic parameters such as bioavailability, volume of distribution, clearance, and target tissue binding. These factors may include first-pass metabolism, protein binding, and renal and/or liver function.

meperidine, morphine, procainamide) are pharmacologically active or toxic. In patients with renal disease, these metabolites may accumulate, leading to an increase in pharmacologic activity and/or adverse effects.[15,16] For example, the central nervous system (CNS) toxicity observed in renal disease has been attributed to accumulation of the morphine metabolite, morphine-6-glucuronide. Therefore, careful dosing modifications or avoidance of these drugs is warranted in patients with renal impairment. The kidney may play a role in the metabolism of some drugs since metabolic enzymes have been found within renal tissue.[17,18] For example, the nonrenal clearance of drugs such as acyclovir decreases in patients with renal impairment, and this is believed to be due to a decrease in ''renal'' metabolism.[19]

Pharmacodynamics and Renal Disease

Unfortunately, few studies have investigated the pharmacodynamics of drugs in renal disease. This is an exciting area of study that eventually may clarify observations that patients with renal disease are more ''sensitive'' to various drugs. For example, morphine has been associated with increased neurological depression in renal failure patients.[20-22] The ability of morphine to potentiate the CNS depressant effects of uremia may be due to an alteration in the blood-brain barrier that results in higher CNS levels of morphine accumulation of morphine-6-glucuronide.

A more quantitative example of altered drug response in uremia is that of nifedipine which, at similar unbound plasma concentrations, has an increased antihypertensive effect in patients with renal disease.[23] The mean Emax (maximal effect change in diastolic blood pressure) values in control and severe renal failure patients were 12% and 29%, respectively. Therefore, dosage adjustments of nifedipine in patients with renal disease may be required because of changes in drug effects rather than pharmacokinetic alterations.

Drug Removal By Dialysis

The effect of dialysis on the removal of a specific drug must be considered when prescribing medications for patients undergoing dialysis. Dialysis patients may need supplemental doses of a medication after a dialysis procedure or further alteration in their dosage regimen. Dialysis also can be initiated to expedite drug removal from the body in some cases of drug overdose.

When utilizing dialysis for the management of drug overdose, patients may respond clinically to factors unrelated to dialysis of the compound. For example, declining plasma concentrations may be due to concurrent drug elimination by hepatic metabolism or renal excretion which are independent of the dialysis procedure itself. Furthermore, clinical improvement may be due to removal of active metabolites by dialysis rather than the parent compound.

The ability of a drug to be dialyzed can best be determined from the primary literature. Unfortunately, the application of data from the literature to a specific clinical situation often is difficult, and data pertaining to the dialysis of a specific drug may be limited. Anecdotal case reports in the primary literature seldom provide quantitative information and the effectiveness of dialysis often is based upon a positive clinical outcome rather than upon objective measurements of drug concentrations in the blood and dialysate.

When attempting to apply information from the primary literature to a specific patient, the specifics of the dialyzer (e.g., type of machine, membrane surface area, and blood and dialysis flow rates) must be considered. Furthermore, patient specific information (e.g., time of drug ingestion, liver and renal function) from case reports in the literature also need to be evaluated appropriately. The method used for calculating dialysis clearance also should be scrutinized. In addition, be aware that clinical investigators often utilize pre- and postdialysis serum drug concentrations for estimating drug dialyzability without due consideration for the contributing effects of drug metabolism and excretion on drug elimination.

Drug Specific Properties

The physical and chemical characteristics of drugs can be used to predict the effectiveness of dialysis on drug removal.[41-43] Low molecular weight (MW) compounds are more readily dialyzed by conventional hemodialysis procedures because they can pass with greater ease across the dialysis membrane. Using standard dialysis cuprophane membranes, compounds of MW ≤500 are more likely to be significantly dialyzed than compounds of high molecular weight (e.g., vancomycin: MW = 3300). Newer high-flux procedures using polysulfone membranes are more effective at removing large chemical compounds (see High-Flux Hemodialysis). In addition, the water solubility of a compound can help predict drug dialyzability because water-soluble drugs are removed more easily than lipid-soluble compounds.

Pharmacokinetic characteristics (e.g., volume of distribution, protein binding) also can affect drug dialyzability. A drug with a large volume of distribution that distributes widely into the peripheral tissues, resides minimally in the plasma, and is, therefore, not substantially removed by dialysis. This is especially true for highly lipid-soluble drugs such as digoxin (Vd: 300 to 500 L). In addition, drugs that are highly protein bound, such as warfarin (99%) cannot be significantly removed by dialysis because the large protein-drug complex is unable to pass through the dialysis membrane.

The plasma clearance of a drug also must be compared to the dialysis clearance. Clearance terms are additive and dialysis clearance must contribute substantially to body clearance to enhance drug removal. For example, zidovudine has a large plasma clearance in patients with severe renal disease (1200 mL/minute). Therefore, despite a dialysis clearance of 63 mL/minute, the contribution of dialysis to zidovudine removal is negligible.

High-Flux Hemodialysis

High-flux hemodialysis, by utilizing higher blood and dialysate flow rates compared to conventional methods, reduces the time of a single dialysis procedure to one and a half to two hours from the three to four hours necessary for a conventional dialysis session. Owing to the enhanced efficiency of high-flux dialysis and the large pore size of the polysulfone membranes used, both small and mid-molecular weight compounds such as vancomycin (3300) can be substantially removed.

Continuous Ambulatory Peritoneal Dialysis (CAPD)

Continuous ambulatory peritoneal dialysis utilizes the patient's peritoneum as the dialysis membrane. Patients maintained on CAPD undergo infusion of a dialysate solution via a catheter inserted into the peritoneal cavity. The accumulated fluid and uremic by-products will diffuse from the blood into the dialysate solution. This solution is exchanged for new dialysate every four to eight hours on a chronic basis. (See Chapter 31: Renal Dialysis.)

Some drugs, especially antibiotics, may be administered intraperitoneally in CAPD patients. This is especially useful for patients with peritonitis that require high intraperitoneal antimicrobial concentrations. Following intraperitoneal administration of drugs such as the aminoglycosides, plasma and intraperitoneal drug concentrations eventually will reach equilibrium. Despite substantial systemic absorption of these compounds from the peritoneal fluid, peritoneal dialysis usually is inefficient at removing drugs from the plasma.[138] Therefore, CAPD contributes little to the overall elimination of most therapeutic agents and dosage modifications seldom are necessary during this procedure.

Continuous Arteriovenous Hemofiltration (CAVH)

Continuous arteriovenous hemofiltration, a form of continuous renal replacement therapy, is used in the acute renal failure patient who is unable to tolerate hemodialysis due to hemodynamic instability. As is true for hemodialysis, this procedure removes fluid, electrolytes, and low and mid-molecular weight molecules from the blood. Using a hollow fiber semipermeable membrane, water and solutes are filtered by hydrostatic pressure.

Limited data are available on the effect of CAVH on drug removal, however, the aminoglycosides, ceftazidime, ceftriaxone, vancomycin, and procainamide are easily removed by CAVH. These drugs have high sieving coefficients (i.e., the permeability of a drug through a semipermeable membrane).[139,140]

Hemoperfusion

Hemoperfusion is an additional method of dialysis that may be used to facilitate the elimination of a drug in the case of an overdose.[141] During the hemoperfusion procedure, blood is passed through a column of adsorbent material (e.g., activated charcoal, resin). Hemoperfusion can be especially useful for removal of large molecular weight compounds or highly protein-bound drugs that are not removed efficiently by hemodialysis. Large compounds are adsorbed to the high surface area resin, and drugs are removed from the drug-protein complex as blood passes through the adsorbent column.

Hemoperfusion also is advocated for removal of lipid soluble drugs not easily removed by hemodialysis. Lipid soluble drugs, however, often have large volumes of distribution, and removal by hemoperfusion is of limited value because a large percentage of these lipophilic compounds reside in peripheral tissues.

Renal Failure

1. G.G., a 31-year-old, 70 kg female with a 3-year history of systemic lupus erythematosus (SLE), presents to the emergency room (ER) with a 5-day history of fatigue, weakness, and nausea as well as worsening of her facial rash and a fever of 40 °C. Her SLE had been moderately controlled until this acute flare, and her admission laboratory work-up now reveals the following pertinent values: potassium (K) 6.0 mEq/L (Normal: 3.6–4.8), sodium (Na) 142 mEq/L (Normal: 135–144), serum creatinine (SrCr) 3.4 mg/dL (Normal: 0.6–1.3), and blood urea nitrogen (BUN) 38 mg/dL (Normal: 7–20). Complete blood count (CBC) reveals a hematocrit (Hct) of 32% [Normal: 35%–45% (females)] and a hemoglobin (Hgb) of 9.2 gm/dL [Normal: 11.8–15.4 (females)]. The platelet count was 50,000 (Normal: 140,000–300,000) and her erythrocyte sedimentation rate (ESR) was 35 mm/hr (Normal: 0–20). Physical examination was significant for a blood pressure (BP) of 136/92 mm Hg and 2+ pedal edema. She is started on prednisone at a dose of 1.5 mg/kg/day.

What is the most likely cause for G.G.'s decline in renal function? What other factors may lead to renal insufficiency?
[SI units: K 6.0 mmol/L (Normal: 3.6–4.8); Na 142 mmol/L (Normal: 135–144); SrCr 300.56 µmol/L (Normal: 53.04–114.92); BUN 13.57 mmol/L UREA (Normal: 2.5–7.14); Hct 0.32 1 (Normal: 0.35–0.45); Hgb 92 gm/L (Normal: 118–154); platelet count 50 × 10⁹/L (Normal: 140–300); ESR 35 mm/hr (Normal: 0–20)]

Systemic lupus erythematosus is the most likely cause for G.G.'s renal failure. This autoimmune disorder often leads to the development of glomerulonephritis which is a common cause of renal failure. Although G.G. presents with symptoms of acute renal failure, renal insufficiency may have developed over several days or weeks.

Acute renal failure or acute azotemia is defined as a sudden retention of body fluids and nitrogenous wastes normally excreted by the kidney. A number of factors can lead to the development of this disorder, including systemic diseases (e.g., SLE, acute post-streptococcal glomerulonephritis, malignant hypertension) or ischemic disorders (e.g., severe hemorrhage, septic shock). In addition, a large number of chemical compounds can cause nephrotoxicity such as heavy metals (e.g., lead, mercury) and organic solvents (e.g., carbon tetrachloride). Drugs such as the aminoglycosides, nonsteroidal anti-inflammatory drugs (NSAIDs), and cyclosporine also have caused an acute decline in renal function, especially when administered in high doses. Drug-induced nephrotoxicity usually is reversible when the drugs are discontinued or their doses are lowered. Acute interstitial nephritis can be caused by drugs such as the beta-lactam antibiotics (e.g., penicillins, cephalosporins) and sulfonamides. Finally, obstructive disorders such as renal artery thrombosis and bilateral renal vein thrombosis can cause acute renal dysfunction.

Signs and Symptoms

2. What are the signs and symptoms of renal failure in G.G.?
The increases in G.G.'s serum creatinine and BUN indicate that her kidneys are unable to excrete the nitrogenous waste and uremic by-products that accumulate in renal failure patients. In addition, her 2+ pedal edema and sudden increase in blood pressure indicate fluid retention which also is a sign of renal insufficiency. Initially,

symptoms can be subtle. G.G.'s generalized symptoms of fatigue and weakness are common. Gastrointestinal symptoms such as G.G.'s nausea also are reported by most patients.

Potassium normally is excreted in the urine by distal tubular secretion; therefore, hyperkalemia can be another sign of renal insufficiency. Often, in chronic renal failure this is well controlled and serum potassium levels remain normal. However, episodic hyperkalemia can occur due to possible increases in dietary potassium loads or a redistribution of intracellular potassium as a result of metabolic acidosis or hemolysis of red blood cells. (Also see Chapters 29: Acute Renal Failure and 30: Chronic Renal Failure.)

Pharmacokinetics and Pharmacodynamics of Specific Drugs in Renal Failure

Ceftazidime

Dosage Modification: Factors to Consider

3. Two weeks into her hospital course, G.G.'s condition worsens and she develops signs of sepsis. *Pseudomonas aeruginosa* is cultured from her urine. Therapy with ceftazidime (Fortaz) is initiated at a dose of 1 gm Q 8 hr, a dose commonly used for patients with good renal function. Considering that G.G.'s renal function has remained stable and that she has an estimated Cl_{Cr} of 27 mL/min, what factors should be considered before modifying her dose? What would be an appropriate dose of ceftazidime for G.G.?

Before modifying the dose of any drug, the route of elimination of the drug should be established. The elimination of most drugs that primarily are cleared renally will be decreased in the setting of renal impairment. The degree to which renal impairment affects elimination depends upon the percentage of unchanged drug that is cleared by the kidney. For many compounds that are cleared renally, relationships between some measurement of renal function (i.e., Cl_{Cr}) and some parameter of drug elimination (i.e., plasma clearance or half-life) have been established to help the clinician determine the appropriate dosing modifications in renal disease patients.

In contrast, the clearance of drugs that are eliminated primarily by nonrenal mechanisms (e.g., hepatic metabolism) is not altered significantly in patients with renal disease. Unless the metabolic products of these compounds are pharmacologically active or toxic and rely on the kidney for elimination, little dosing modification will be necessary.

Another factor important to consider is the "therapeutic window" for a given agent. The therapeutic window is the ratio between the toxic and therapeutic concentration or dose of a drug. Drug concentrations below this range usually are subtherapeutic while concentrations above this range often can lead to a greater incidence of adverse effects. For drugs with a high therapeutic window, the difference between toxic and therapeutic concentrations is large. Those that are cleared primarily by the kidney require dosing modifications in renal disease; however, these dose reductions may not need to be tightly correlated with the severity of renal impairment. This is in contrast to drugs with a narrow therapeutic window that are eliminated primarily by the kidney, such as the aminoglycosides or vancomycin. For these drugs, toxic plasma concentrations are very close to the therapeutic range, and there is little room for dosing error. Table 32.2 summarizes the pharmacokinetics and dosing guidelines for drugs commonly used in renal failure patients.

Ceftazidime is a cephalosporin that has excellent activity against most strains of *Pseudomonas* species. Like most cephalosporins, ceftazidime primarily is cleared renally with little nonrenal or hepatic elimination, and the clearance of ceftazidime is decreased in patients with renal impairment. The correlation between ceftazidime's clearance and creatinine clearance in mL/minute is represented by the following equation:[24]

$$Cl_{ceftaz} \text{ (mL/min)} = (0.95)(Cl_{Cr}) + 6.59 \qquad Eq\ 32.1$$

Using equation 32.1, the clearance of ceftazidime in G.G. is estimated to be 32 mL/minute as compared to an average normal clearance of approximately 100 mL/minute. Since her drug clearance is one-third of normal, one-third of the normal daily dose would be appropriate (i.e., 1 gm every 24 hours). Failure to reduce the dose from a normal dose (e.g., 1 gm every 8 hours) might lead to accumulation of the drug after several doses, and, theoretically, predispose G.G. to seizures and other adverse effects associated with toxic beta-lactam plasma levels.[25,26] However, as is true for the other cephalosporins, ceftazidime has a large therapeutic window,[27] in contrast to the aminoglycosides which must be dosed on highly specific pharmacokinetic calculations. Therefore, more general dosing recommendations are sufficient for ceftazidime.

Aminoglycosides

4. G.G.'s medical team decides that the addition of an aminoglycoside is now necessary to treat her infection. Considering that her renal function has to this point remained stable, how should the gentamicin be dosed in G.G.? Is it best to alter the dose or the dosing interval for this drug?

Alteration of Dose versus Dosing Interval

The aminoglycosides (e.g., tobramycin, gentamicin, amikacin, netilmicin) are effective in the treatment of serious systemic infections caused by gram-negative organisms such as *Pseudomonas*. However, unlike the cephalosporins and penicillins, the aminoglycosides have a relatively narrow therapeutic window. Utilizing pharmacokinetic calculations, doses can be designed to produce specific "peak" and "trough" serum concentrations. Peak serum concentrations $[(Cp_{peak})$ (e.g., gentamicin of 4 to 8 µg/mL)] correlate best with therapeutic efficacy while toxicity correlates best with trough levels (Cp_{trough}). To avoid toxicity, trough levels of less than 2 µg/mL should be maintained. For most patients, peak and trough levels usually are measured once steady state is achieved.[28-34]

Aminoglycosides are almost completely eliminated renally; thus, the clearance of these agents essentially is equal to the glomerular filtration rate (GFR). The pharmacokinetics of gentamicin and tobramycin are essentially the same. A close correlation exists between creatinine clearance and gentamicin total body clearance. As renal function deteriorates, aminoglycoside doses must be modified to maintain the desired peak and trough plasma concentrations. Failure to appropriately adjust the dose of aminoglycosides in renal insufficiency leads to drug accumulation and high plasma levels.

In many cases, aminoglycoside doses are modified by extending the interval of administration rather than simply reducing the dose. This permits maintenance of adequate peak plasma levels, assuring the efficacy, while allowing enough elimination between doses to produce trough levels below 2 µg/mL. The advantages and disadvantages of adjusting the dosing interval versus reducing the dose are summarized in Table 32.3.

Figure 32.3 graphically illustrates the effect of increasing the dosing interval in a patient such as G.G. with renal function that is 30% of normal. Although this is the preferred method for adjusting the dose of aminoglycosides, for many other drugs requiring dose adjustments in renal disease, dosage reduction alone while maintaining a normal interval is sufficient (see Table 32.2).

Table 32.2

Pharmacokinetics and Dosing Guidelines For Drugs Commonly Used in Renal Failure[143]

Drug	Oral Availability (%)	Protein Binding (%)	Vd (L/kg)	Metabolism and Excretion	t½ (hr)	Normal Dose ClCr >50 mL/min	Dose Change with Renal Failure ClCr (mL/min)	Effect of Dialysis
Acyclovir	15-30	15	0.7	76%-82% excreted renally; 14% hepatic	Normal: 2.1-3.2; Anephric: 20	5 mg/kg Q 8 hr	10-50: 5 mg/kg Q 12-24 hr; <10: 2.5 mg/kg Q 24 hr	Dialyzed; 80 mL/min
Allopurinol	90	0	0.6	Metabolized to active oxypurinol metabolite which is excreted renally; 6%-12% excreted unchanged renally	Normal: 1.1-1.6 Anephric: No change; 7 days oxypurinol	300 mg QD	10-50: 200 mg QD; <10: 100 mg QD	Oxypurinol; moderately dialyzed
Amikacin	Parenteral	<5	0.2-0.3	94%-99% excreted renally	Normal: 2-3; Anephric: 36-82	See section on aminoglycoside pharmacokinetics	See section on aminoglycoside pharmacokinetics	Dialyzed; 22-38 mL/min
Amphotericin B	Parenteral	90-95	4	95%-97% hepatic metabolism or inactivation in body tissue; 3.5%-5.5% excreted unchanged renally	Normal: Initial: 24-48; Terminal: 15 days Anephric: No change	0.3-1 mg/kg Q 24 hr	10-50: 100% Q 24 hr; <10: 100% Q 24-48 hr (to minimize azotemia)	Not dialyzed; large Vd
Ampicillin	32-76	29	0.3	73%-92% excreted renally; 12%-24% hepatic metabolism or biliary elimination	Normal: 0.8-1.5; Anephric: 20	1-2 gm Q 4-6 hr	10-50: 1-1.5 gm Q 6 hr; <10: 50% 1 gm Q 8-12 hr	Moderately dialyzed
Atenolol	50	<5	1.2	75% excreted renally; 10% hepatic; 10% feces	Normal: 5-6; Anephric: 42-73	50-100 mg QD	10-50: ↓50% and titrate; <10: ↓50% and titrate	Moderately dialyzed
Aztreonam	Parenteral	50-60	0.15-0.38	60%-70% excreted renally; 12% hepatic	Normal: 1.3-2.2; Anephric: 6-9	1-2 gm Q 6-8 hr	10-50: 1-2 gm Q 8-12 hr; <10: 1 gm Q 12-24 hr	Moderately dialyzed
Captopril	65	30 (↓R)	0.7	36%-42% excreted renally; 50% hepatic	Normal: 1.7-1.9; Anephric: 21-32	6.25-12.5 mg Q 8-12 hr	10-50: No change; <10: ↓25% and titrate	Moderately dialyzed; 80-120 mL/min
Cefazolin	Parenteral	84-92	0.2	>95% excreted renally; 3%-5% hepatic	Normal: 1.8-2.6; Anephric: 12-40	1-2 gm Q 8 hr	10-50: 0.5-1.5 gm Q 12 hr; <10: 0.5-1 gm Q 24 hr	Moderately dialyzed
Cefixime	50	69	0.1-1.0	20%-40% excreted renally; 50% excreted by nonrenal mechanisms	Normal: 3.5; Anephric: ?	200-400 mg Q 12-24 hr	10-50: No change; <10: 50% Q 12-24 hr	Not dialyzed
Cefoperazone	Parenteral	87-93	0.16	70%-85% excreted unchanged in bile; 15%-30% excreted renally	Normal: 1.6-2.6; Anephric: 2.5	1-2 gm Q 8-12 hr	10-50: No change; <10: ↓ with concurrent hepatic disease	Slightly dialyzed
Cefotaxime	Parenteral	38	0.22-0.36	40%-60% hepatic (desacetyl active metabolite; 25% activity of parent compound); 40%-65% excreted renally	Normal: 0.9-1.1; Anephric: 2.3-3.5, 12-20 (metabolite)	1-2 gm Q 6-12 hr	10-50: 1-2 gm Q 12 hr; <10: 0.5-1 gm Q 12 hr	Moderately dialyzed
Cefotetan	Parenteral	75-91	0.13	50%-88% excreted renally; 12% excreted in bile	Normal: 3-4.2; Anephric: 13	1-2 gm Q 12 hr	10-50: 1-2 gm Q 24 hr; <10: 0.5-1 gm Q 24 hr	Slightly/moderately dialyzed

Drug	Bioavailability (%)	Protein Binding (%)	Vd	Elimination	Half-life (Normal / Anephric)	Normal Dose	Dose Adjustment (GFR 10–50 / <10)	Dialysis
Cefoxitin	Parenteral	65–79	0.27	85% excreted renally; up to 15% biliary and/or hepatic	Normal: 0.7–0.8; Anephric: 12–24	1–2 gm Q 6–8 hr	10–50: 1–2 gm Q 12–24 hr; <10: 0.5–1 gm Q 24 hr	Moderately dialyzed
Ceftazidime	Parenteral	20–30	0.2–0.3	73%–84% excreted renally	Normal: 1.6–2; Anephric: 13–25	1–2 gm Q 8 hr	10–50: 1–2 gm Q 12–24 hr; <10: 0.5 gm Q 24 hr	Dialyzed
Ceftizoxime	Parenteral	17–25	0.2–0.4	78%–92% excreted renally	Normal: 1.4–1.7; Anephric: 19–30	1–2 gm Q 8–12 hr	10–50: 1–2 gm Q 12–24 hr; <10: 0.5 gm Q 24 hr	Moderately dialyzed
Ceftriaxone	Parenteral	83–96 (Conc. dependent)	0.1	40%–67% excreted renally; 40% excreted in bile	Normal: 6.5–8.9; Anephric: 12	1–2 gm Q 12–24 hr	10–50: 1–2 gm Q 24 hr; <10: 1–2 gm Q 24 hr	Not dialyzed
Cefuroxime	40–50 (as axetil salt)	33	0.19	90%–95% excreted renally	Normal: 1.1–1.7; Anephric: 15–17	0.75–1.5 gm Q 6–8 hr	10–50: 50%–75% Q 8–12 hr; <10: 25%–50% Q 24 hr	Moderately dialyzed
Cephapirin	Parenteral	44–62	0.13–0.5	40%–59% hepatic active desacetyl metabolite; 40%–60% excreted renally	Normal: 0.5–1.2; Anephric: 2.5	1–2 gm Q 4–6 hr	10–50: No change; <10: 1–2 gm Q 12 hr	Moderately dialyzed
Cephradine	90–100	6–20	0.25–0.33	80%–95% excreted renally; 5%–20% hepatic metabolism or biliary/fecal elimination	Normal: 0.7–0.9; Anephric: 8–15	250–500 mg Q 6 hr	10–50: 250–500 mg Q 12 hr; <10: 250–500 mg Q 24 hr	Moderately dialyzed
Cimetidine	62	20	0.9–1.1	40%–80% excreted renally; some metabolism	Normal: 1.5; Anephric: 3.3–4.6	PO: 400 mg Q 12 hr; IV: 300 mg Q 8 hr	10–50: ↓ 25%; <10: ↓ 50%	Slightly dialyzed
Ciprofloxacin	50–85	22	2.2	62% excreted renally; the rest cleared hepatically, in the bile and via intestinal mucosa	Normal: 4; Anephric: 8.5	250–750 mg Q 12 hr (PO)	10–50: 250–500 mg Q 12 hr; <10: 250–750 mg Q 24 hr	Slightly dialyzed
Clindamycin	50	94	0.6	85% hepatic to active and inactive metabolites; 10% excreted renally; 5% feces	Normal: 2–4; Anephric: 1.6–3.4	600–900 mg Q 6–8 hr	10–50: No change; <10: No change	Not dialyzed
Codeine	40–70	7	3–4	Hepatic with some active metabolites; little renal elimination (5%–17%)	Normal: 2.9–4; Anephric: 19	No change	10–50: ↓ 25% and titrate; <10: ↓ 50% and titrate	?
Cyclosporine	<5–89	>96	3.5	Extensively metabolized to active and inactive metabolites; <1% excreted renally	Normal: 6–13; Anephric: 16	No change	10–50: No change; <10: No change	Not dialyzed
Digoxin	70	25 (↓R)	5–8 (↓R)	70% excreted renally	Normal: 36–44; Anephric: 80–120	No change	10–50: ↓ 50%; <10: ↓ 75%	Not dialyzed
Enalapril[a]	36%–44%	<50	1	61% excreted renally; 33% excreted in feces	Normal: 5–11; Anephric: 36	No change	10–50: ↓ 50% and titrate; <10: ↓ 50% and titrate	Slightly/moderately dialyzed
Erythromycin	30–65 (varies with salt)	84–90	0.9	85%–95% hepatic to inactive metabolites; 5%–15% excreted renally	Normal: 1.4–2; Anephric: 4	0.25–1 gm Q 6 hr	10–50: No change; <10: No change	Slightly dialyzed
Ethambutol	75–80	<5	1.6	65%–80% excreted renally and 20% in feces; 8%–15% hepatic	Normal: 3.1; Anephric: 18–20	15 mg/kg Q 24 hr	10–50: 7.5–10 mg/kg Q 24 hr; <10: 5 mg/kg Q 24 hr	Slightly dialyzed

Continued

Table 32.2 Pharmacokinetics and Dosing Guidelines For Drugs Commonly Used in Renal Failure[143] (Continued)

Drug	Oral Availability (%)	Protein Binding (%)	Vd (L/kg)	Metabolism and Excretion	t½ (hr)	Normal Dose ClCr >50 mL/min	Dose Change with Renal Failure ClCr (mL/min)	Effect of Dialysis
Fluconazole	>85	11–12	0.8	70% excreted renally; some hepatic metabolism	*Normal:* 20–50 *Anephric:* 98	100–200 mg Q 24 hr	*10–50:* 50–200 mg Q 24 hr *<10:* 50–100 mg Q 24 hr	Moderately dialyzed
Ganciclovir	Low	?	0.5	>90% excreted renally	*Normal:* 2.5–3.6 *Anephric:* 11.5–28	*>80 mL/min:* 5 mg/kg Q 12 hr; *50–80 mL/min:* 2.5 mg/kg Q 12 hr	*10–50:* 1.25–2.5 mg/kg Q 24 hr *<10:* 1.25 mg/kg Q 24 hr	Dialyzed
Gentamicin	Parenteral	5–10	0.31	90%–97% excreted renally	*Normal:* 1.5–3 *Anephric:* 20–54	See section on aminoglycoside pharmacokinetics	See section on aminoglycoside pharmacokinetics	Dialyzed; 24–50 mL/min
Ibuprofen	>80	99	0.15	Primarily metabolized; 45%–60% excreted unchanged and as metabolites	*Normal:* 2 *Anephric:* No change	200–600 mg Q 4–6 hr	*10–50:* No change *<10:* No change	Not dialyzed
Imipenem	Parenteral	10–20	0.23–0.42	60%–75% excreted renally; 22% hepatic to inactive metabolites	*Normal:* 0.8–1.3 *Anephric:* 2.9–3.7	5–10 mg/kg Q 6–8 hr	*10–50:* 5–10 mg/kg Q 8–12 hr *<10:* 5–10 mg/kg Q 12 hr	Moderately dialyzed
Indomethacin	98	90	0.26	Hepatic metabolism to inactive metabolites; <15% excreted unchanged	*Normal:* 2.6 *Anephric:* No change	25–50 mg Q 8–12 hr	*10–50:* No change *<10:* No change	?
Ketoconazole	50–76	99	0.36	51% hepatic; 45% excreted unchanged in feces and 3% renally	*Normal:* 3–8 *Anephric:* No change	200–400 mg Q 24 hr (depends upon severity of infection)	*10–50:* No change *<10:* No change	Not dialyzed
Labetalol	20–38	50	8–10	5% excreted renally; 95% hepatic	*Normal:* 5 *Anephric:* ? prolonged	No change	*10–50:* No change *<10:* No change	Not dialyzed
Lidocaine	Parenteral	50–70	1.7 (↑H)	Hepatic metabolism to inactive and active metabolites (glycinexylidide)	*Normal:* 1.5–1.8 *Anephric:* No change	Maintenance dose: 2–4 mg/min	*10–50:* No change *<10:* No change	Not dialyzed
Lithium	100	0	0.5–0.8	95% excreted renally	*Normal:* 22–29 *Anephric:* Prolonged	Variable (titrate with ClCr to therapeutic levels of 0.4–0.8)	*10–50:* ↓ 25%–50% *<10:* ↓ 50%–75%	Moderately dialyzed/dialyzed
Meperidine	48–53	58	4.4	Hepatic hydrolysis and conjugation, active normeperidine metabolites; 10% excreted renally	*Normal:* 3–7 *Anephric:* ?	50–100 mg Q 3–4 hr (IV, IM)	*10–50:* 75%–100% Q 6 hr *<10:* 50% Q 6–8 hr (use cautiously)	?
Methotrexate	16–95 (dose dependent)	50	0.4–0.8	>90% cleared renally; 10% metabolized to 7-OH-MTX	*Normal:* α 1.5–3.5; β 8–15 *Anephric:* Prolonged	No change	*10–50:* Adjust according to serum concentration *<10:* Avoid	Not/slightly dialyzed

Drug	Bioavailability (%)	Protein binding (%)	Vd	Half-life (hr)	Excretion	Dose	10-50 / <10	Dialysis
Metoprolol	38	13	4	Normal: 3-4; Anephric: No change	90% hepatic; 10% excreted renally	50-200 mg QD	10-50: No change; <10: No change	Metabolites dialyzed
Mezlocillin	Parenteral	26-42	0.2	Normal: 0.8-1.2; Anephric: 3-6	45%-65% excreted renally; 35%-55% excreted hepatobiliary	50 mg/kg Q 4-6 hr	10-50: 100% Q 6-8 hr; <10: 50% Q 8 hr	Slightly/moderately dialyzed; 29 mL/min
Nadolol	34	20	2	Normal: 15-20; Anephric: 45	75% excreted renally; 25% hepatic	40-80 mg QD	10-50: ↓ 50% and titrate; <10: ↓ 50% and titrate	Moderately dialyzed
Nafcillin	50	85-90	0.35	Normal: 1-1.5; Anephric: 1.9	Up to 70% hepatic; 25%-30% excreted renally	1-2 gm Q 4-6 hr	10-50: No change; <10: No change	Not dialyzed
Nifedipine	45	98	0.8-1.1	Normal: 2-4; Anephric: 3.8	100% hepatic	No change	10-50: No change; <10: No change (? ↑ response in renal failure patients)	?
Penicillin G	15-30	60	0.9-2.1	Normal: 0.4-0.9; Anephric: 4-10	50% excreted renally; 19% hepatic	2-3 MU Q 4 hr	10-50: Dose (MU/D) = 3.2 + $Cl_{Cr}/7$; <10: Dose (MU/D) = 3.2 + $Cl_{Cr}/7$	Moderately dialyzed; 46 mL/min
Pentamidine	Parenteral	?	12	Normal: 6 (5-9 days, urine data); Anephric: ?	<5% eliminated renally over 24 hr	4 mg/kg/day (IV)	10-50: No change; <10: 100% QD-QOD	Probably not dialyzed
Phenobarbital	100	48-59	0.6	Normal: 100; Anephric: ?	Hepatic metabolism; renal excretion: 10%-40% unchanged and active metabolites	No change	10-50: No change; <10: Slight ↓	Moderately dialyzed/dialyzed
Phenytoin	>90%	85-95 (↓R, H)	0.5-0.7 (↑R)	Normal: 10-30; Anephric: 6-10	Hepatic metabolism; <5% excreted unchanged; 75% as inactive p-HPPH metabolites; concentration-dependent kinetics	300-400 mg QD (titrate)	10-50: No change; <10: No change (lower therapeutic level)	Not dialyzed
Piperacillin	Parenteral	16-22	0.2-0.47	Normal: 0.8-1.4; Anephric: 4-6	50%-60% excreted renally; up to 30%-40% excreted in bile	50 mg/kg Q 4-6 hr	10-50: 100% Q 6 hr; <10: 50%-75% Q 8 hr	Moderately dialyzed
Procainamide	75-95	15	1.7-2.3	Normal: 2.5-4.7 (NAPA: 6); Anephric: 11-16 (NAPA: 42)	Hepatic metabolism to active NAPA; 50%-60% excreted renally	0.5-1.5 gm Q 4-6 hr	10-50: 100% Q 6-12 hr; <10: 100% Q 12-24 hr	Moderately dialyzed
Propranolol	36-40	88-94	2.9	Normal: 3-5; Anephric: No change	Primarily hepatic; <1% excreted renally	10-40 mg Q 6 hr (PO) and titrate	10-50: No change; <10: No change	Not dialyzed
Ranitidine	52	15	0.8-1.1	Normal: 1.4-2.4; Anephric: 5-10	70% excreted renally; some hepatic	300 mg Q HS	10-50: ↓ 25%; <10: ↓ 50%	Slightly dialyzed
Sulfamethoxazole	90-100	50-70 (↓R)	0.14-0.36 (↑R)	Normal: 7-12; Anephric: 10-50	65%-80% hepatic to inactive compounds; 20%-30% excreted renally	Q 6-12 hr	10-50: Q 12-24 hr; <10: Q 24 hr	Slightly/moderately dialyzed

Continued

Table 32.2 Pharmacokinetics and Dosing Guidelines For Drugs Commonly Used in Renal Failure[143] (Continued)

Drug	Oral Availability (%)	Protein Binding (%)	Vd (L/kg)	Metabolism and Excretion	t½ (hr)	Normal Dose ClCr >50 mL/min	Dose Change with Renal Failure ClCr (mL/min)	Effect of Dialysis
Tobramycin	Parenteral	<10	0.33	90%–97% excreted renally	*Normal:* 2.5 *Anephric:* 33–70	See section on aminoglycoside pharmacokinetics	See section on aminoglycoside pharmacokinetics	Dialyzed; 50–60 mL/min
Trimethoprim	85–90	40–70	1–2	53%–80% excreted renally; 20%–35% hepatic	*Normal:* 8–16 *Anephric:* 24–62	Q 6–12 hr	*10–50:* Q 12–24 hr *<10:* Q 24 hr	Slightly/moderately dialyzed
Vancomycin	<10	10–55	0.5–0.7	80%–90% excreted renally; 10%–20% hepatic metabolism	*Normal:* 4–9 *Anephric:* 129–190	See section on vancomycin pharmacokinetics	See section on vancomycin pharmacokinetics	Conventional: not dialyzed. High flux: moderately dialyzed
Zidovudine	64	34–38	1.4	Primarily hepatic to inactive GAZT metabolite; 18% excreted renally	*Normal:* 0.8–2.9 *Anephric:* No change	100–200 mg Q 8 hr	*10–50:* No change *<10:* Possible ↓	Not dialyzed

a Pharmacokinetic values are for the active enalaprilat metabolite.

Table 32.3	Advantages and Disadvantages of General Approaches to Dosing Adjustments in Renal Disease		
Method		**Advantages**	**Disadvantages**
Variable Frequency			
Use the same dose, but ↑ the dosing interval		Same Cp_{ave}, Cp_{max}, Cp_{min} Normal dose	Levels may remain subtherapeutic for prolonged periods in patients requiring dosing intervals >24 hr
Variable Dose with Fixed Cp_{ave}			
↓ dose to maintain a target Cp_{ave}. Keep the dosing interval the same		Same Cp_{ave} Normal dosing interval	↓ peak levels which may be subtherapeutic; ↑ trough levels which may ↑ potential for toxicity

Determination of Appropriate Dose

To determine an appropriate aminoglycoside dose for patients with or without renal impairment, a number of methods have been developed and utilized.[35] For example, the "Rule of Eights" method for dose adjustment involves administering a usual maintenance dose [1 to 1.5 mg/kg ideal body weight (IBW)] at a dosing interval derived by multiplying the serum creatinine by eight.[35] The appropriate interval is established by rounding the calculation to the most convenient interval (e.g., 8 hours, 12 hours, 24 hours). In G.G., a dose of 70 mg every 24 hours would be recommended if this method were used. However, this method only estimates an approximate general regimen for G.G.

Since there is wide interpatient variability in aminoglycoside pharmacokinetic parameters and the therapeutic index for these drugs is narrow, all doses should be adjusted based upon pharmacokinetic calculations and plasma concentrations that are specific for G.G.

Patient Specific Methods. Sawchuk and Zaske developed a method to derive patient-specific estimates of volume of distribution (Vd) and clearance (Cl) based upon the patient's size and estimated creatinine clearance (Cl_{Cr}).[32] These parameters can be used in pharmacokinetic equations to derive a specific dose for G.G. that will produce the desired gentamicin peak and trough levels. If steady-state serum concentrations of gentamicin were known, these concentrations could be used to calculate more specific parameters. To initiate gentamicin therapy, pharmacokinetic parameters should first be estimated from population values.

The clearance of gentamicin (Cl_{gent}) can be calculated based upon G.G.'s Cl_{Cr}. Utilizing the Cockroft and Gault equation below,[36] the creatinine clearance (Cl_{Cr}) can be estimated as follows:

$$Cl_{Cr} \text{ (males)} = \frac{(140 - \text{age})(\text{IBW})}{(\text{SrCr})(72)} \qquad Eq\ 32.2$$

$$Cl_{Cr} \text{ (females)} = \frac{(140 - \text{age})(\text{IBW})}{(\text{SrCr})(72)} (0.85) \qquad Eq\ 32.3$$

With a measured SrCr of 3.7 mg/dL, an ideal body weight of 70 kg, and an age of 31, G.G.'s estimated Cl_{Cr} as stated earlier is 27 mL/minute.

The relationship between gentamicin clearance (Cl_{gent}) and Cl_{Cr} can be characterized by the following equation:[37]

$$Cl_{gent} \text{ In mL/min/kg} = (0.65)[Cl_{Cr} \text{ In mL/min/kg}] + 3.7 \quad Eq\ 32.4$$

However, for clinical purposes, Cl_{gent} usually is considered equal to Cl_{Cr}. Therefore, Cl_{gent} also is about 27 mL/minute or 1.6 L/hour. The Vd of gentamicin (Vd_{gent}) is approximately 0.25 L/kg in patients with normal and impaired renal function.[32,37,38]

In obese patients or those who are fluid overloaded, the Vd_{gent} will be altered and determination of this parameter will be more complex. Although G.G. does have some fluid retention, this is minimal and should not affect her Vd_{gent} significantly. Therefore, the Vd_{gent} for G.G. is:

$$Vd_{gent} = (0.25 \text{ L/kg})(\text{Body Weight}) \qquad Eq\ 32.5$$

$$= (0.25 \text{ L/kg})(70 \text{ kg})$$

$$= 17.5 \text{ L}$$

The loading dose of gentamicin can be determined using the following equation:

$$LD_{gent} = (Vd_{gent})(\text{desired } Cp_{peak}) \qquad Eq\ 32.6$$

For treatment of infections due to *Pseudomonas*, a peak level of approximately 6 to 7 μg/mL is desired:

$$\text{Gentamicin Loading Dose} = (17.5 \text{ L})(7 \text{ μg/mL})$$

$$= 122 \text{ mg or } 120 \text{ mg}$$

Using Cl_{gent} and Vd_{gent}, the elimination rate constant (Kd) and half-life for gentamicin can be estimated:

$$Kd = \frac{Cl_{gent}}{Vd_{gent}} \qquad Eq\ 32.7$$

$$= \frac{1.6 \text{ L/hr}}{17.5 \text{ L}}$$

$$= 0.091 \text{ hr}^{-1}$$

$$t^{1/2} = \frac{0.693}{0.091}$$

$$= 7.6 \text{ hr}$$

For the aminoglycosides, the dosing interval (τ) is determined by doubling the half-life since at the end of two half-lives 75% of the drug has been eliminated. This usually will lead to a desired trough level of less than 2 μg/mL. Therefore, in G.G., gentamicin should be administered at least every 16 hours. For convenience, an interval of 24 hours can be used which also will achieve the desired trough level.

Gentamicin usually is infused over 30 minutes, and serum samples are drawn 30 minutes after the infusion has been completed to measure the peak serum gentamicin concentration. Since the estimated half-life of gentamicin in G.G. is much longer than the infusion time (7.6 >>> 0.5 hours), the intravenous bolus model can be used to calculate an appropriate maintenance dose for G.G. (See Chapter 2: Clinical Pharmacokinetics.)

To achieve the peak concentration of 7 μg/mL, the following equation can be used:

$$\text{Dose} = \frac{(Cp_{peak})(1 - e^{-Kd\tau})(Vd_{gent})}{(e^{-Kd\tau})} \qquad Eq.\ 32.8$$

$$= \frac{(7 \text{ μg/mL})(1 - e^{-(0.091)(24\ hr)})(17.5 \text{ L})}{(e^{-(0.091)(1\ hr)})}$$

$$= 119.2 \text{ mg}$$

$$= 120 \text{ mg}$$

where τ usually equals 1 hour (30 minutes following a 30 minute infusion).

The expected trough level in G.G. can now be estimated by the equation:

$$Cp_{trough} = (Cp_{peak})(e^{-Kd\tau}) \qquad Eq.\ 32.9$$

$$= (7)(e^{-(0.091)(24\ hr)})$$

$$= 0.8 \text{ μg/mL}$$

Fig 32.3   Serum Concentration versus Time Profile for a Patient with Renal Function 30% of Normal in Whom the Interval of Drug Administration Has Been Extended for Dose Adjustment   *Advantages to this method are summarized in Table 32.3. Reprinted with permission from reference 145.*

Although unnecessary for G.G., patients with normal renal function may have significant elimination of gentamicin during the 30 minute infusion. In these patients the intermittent infusion model should be used for pharmacokinetic calculations to account for this loss of drug (see Chapter 2: Clinical Pharmacokinetics):

$$\text{Dose} = \frac{(Cl_{gent})(Cp_{peak})(1 - e^{-Kd\tau})(t_{in})}{(1 - e^{-Kdt_{in}})(e^{-Kdt})} \qquad Eq.\ 32.10$$

Revised Parameters

5. Following 72 hours of gentamicin therapy, G.G.'s peak and trough levels are reported from the laboratory as 7.6 and 2.6 µg/mL, respectively. Her physician attributes this to a gradual decline in renal function. (Her most recent SrCr is 4.8 mg/dL.) How would you revise G.G.'s dosing regimen based upon these levels?

A gentamicin trough level of greater than 2 µg/mL suggests that G.G.'s dosing interval is too short. Although her peak is within the normal range of 4 to 8 µg/mL, her trough level indicates that she may be predisposed to aminoglycoside toxicity. Her pharmacokinetic parameters can be revised based upon these levels and a new Kd can be estimated from the equation:

$$Kd = \frac{\ln Cp_1 - \ln Cp_2}{\Delta t} \qquad Eq.\ 32.11$$

$$= \frac{\ln 7.6 - \ln 2.6}{23\ hr}$$

$$= 0.047\ hr^{-1}$$

Since little change in G.G.'s Vd_{gent} is expected, a new Cl_{gent} (Cl_{revised}) can be estimated from her revised elimination constant:

$$Cl_{revised} = (Vd_{gent})(Kd) \qquad Eq.\ 32.12$$

$$= (17.5\ L)(0.047\ hr^{-1})$$

$$= 0.82\ L/hr$$

These revised values for Kd and Cl can now be used to calculate a revised maintenance dose to maintain the Cp_{trough} at less than 2 µg/mL utilizing Equation 32.8:

$$\text{Dose} = \frac{(7\ mg/L)(1 - e^{-(0.047\ hr^{-1})(48\ hr)})(17.5\ L)}{e^{-(0.047\ hr^{-1})(1\ hr)}}$$

$$= 115\ mg$$

$$Cp_{trough} = (7\ \mu g/mL)(e^{-(0.047\ hr^{-1})(48\ hr)})$$

$$= 0.73\ \mu g/mL$$

The revised dose is now 115 mg (or approximately 110 mg) every 48 hours.

6. What are some limitations in calculating G.G.'s Cl_{Cr} based upon her SrCr? Can this estimate safely be used to predict gentamicin clearance?

For patients with stable renal function, creatinine clearance can be estimated from serum creatinine utilizing the Cockroft and Gault equation (see Equations 32.2 and 32.3). However, in a patient such as G.G. whose renal function has diminished during the hospital course, estimation of renal function based upon her increasing SrCr becomes more difficult. Since her SrCr does not reflect a steady-state level, the above equations no longer can be used to accurately estimate her renal function. Since G.G.'s SrCr has increased rapidly from 3.7 to 4.8 over the last few days, her Cl_{Cr} is probably much lower than that estimated by the Cockroft and Gault method.

Effect of Hemodialysis

Conventional Dialysis

7. Gentamicin. G.G.'s renal function continues to deteriorate and she eventually requires maintenance hemodialysis. What additional alterations in her dosing regimen are necessary for gentamicin when she is dialyzed?

Gentamicin is a drug that is eliminated significantly by conventional hemodialysis. The molecular weight of the compound is approximately 500;[33] only 10% is bound to proteins and it has a relatively low Vd, averaging 0.25 L/kg. The dialysis clearance of gentamicin averages 45 mL/minute compared to an average plasma clearance of 5 mL/minute in patients with end-stage renal disease (ESRD).[44,45] Therefore, G.G.'s gentamicin dose must be adjusted to compensate for the amount of this drug that will be dialyzed. Since drug removal represents a combination of drug elimination by the body and dialysis:

$$Cl_t = Cl_{dial} + Cl \qquad \qquad Eq.\ 32.13$$

where Cl_t is the total clearance of the drug during dialysis, Cl_{dial} is the clearance by dialysis, and Cl is plasma clearance. If dialysis clearance is high relative to plasma clearance, drug removal will be enhanced by the dialysis procedure. The total clearance of gentamicin in a patient with normal renal function is 50 mL/minute or ten times the clearance of dialysis. Plasma clearance and dialysis clearance are related to half-life by the following equation:

$$t\tfrac{1}{2} = \frac{(0.693)(Vd)}{Cl_{dial} + Cl} \qquad \qquad Eq.\ 32.14$$

Thus, assuming a constant Vd of 17.5 L (i.e., 0.25 L/kg × 70 kg), the half-life on dialysis is approximately four hours compared to 40 hours off dialysis. In addition, the extent of drug removal can be predicted from the following equation:

$$FD = 1 - e^{-(Cl + Cl_{dial})(t/Vd)} \qquad Eq.\ 32.15$$

where t is the duration of dialysis. Therefore, the fraction of gentamicin removed (FD) during a four hour conventional dialysis procedure is approximately 50%. If specific information is not available for dialysis and plasma clearance, the following equation will predict fraction removal using half-life data alone:

$$FD = 1 - e^{-(0.693/t\frac{1}{2}\ on)(t)} \qquad Eq.\ 32.16$$

The estimated value of 50% removal is consistent with literature values reporting that 50% to 70% of a dose of gentamicin is removed during a dialysis procedure of four hours.

These data suggest that one-half of the loading dose of gentamicin should be given to G.G. following each dialysis session.

It generally is difficult to calculate an appropriate maintenance dose for patients undergoing hemodialysis that will maintain peak and trough concentrations similar to those desired in patients with normal renal function. Sustained plasma concentrations greater than 2 μg/mL can increase the incidence of toxicity, however, dosing gentamicin to achieve trough concentrations of less than 2 μg/mL may lead to prolongation of concentrations that are subtherapeutic. Therefore, doses of gentamicin in hemodialysis patients often are ordered to achieve a predialysis trough concentration of approximately 3 μg/mL. A maintenance gentamicin dose of 1 mg/kg after each dialysis session commonly is ordered for patients such as G.G. to achieve this desired concentration. (See Chapter 31: Renal Dialysis.)

8. Ceftazidime. Why does the dose of ceftazidime in G.G. have to be adjusted because of her hemodialysis when this drug has such a large "therapeutic window"?

Since only 21% of ceftazidime is protein bound and its volume of distribution is 0.2 L/kg, it should be readily dialyzable. The mean dialysis clearance of ceftazidime is 55 mL/minute with 55% of the drug eliminated during four hours of conventional hemodialysis.[46] Since the doses used in patients with end-stage renal disease are much lower than "normal" doses, a supplemental dose of ceftazidime should be given to G.G. following hemodialysis. One-half of the daily ceftazidime dose should be administered following each dialysis session.

High-Flux Hemodialysis

9. G.G.'s physician is considering changing her from a hollow fiber dialysis system to a "high-flux" system that utilizes highly efficient polysulfone membranes. How does the dialyzability of gentamicin and ceftazidime differ with high-flux hemodialysis compared to conventional hemodialysis?

"High-flux" hemodialysis more efficiently removes certain pharmacological agents (see Chapter 31: Renal Dialysis). Although very limited data are available, a greater fraction of drugs such as the aminoglycosides, ceftazidime, and vancomycin are removed by high-flux versus conventional hemodialysis.[47,48] Up to 70% of gentamicin is removed during a 2.5 hour high-flux dialysis session;[51] and data on ceftazidime also is available indicating that the dialysis clearance of ceftazidime by high-flux procedure is 75 to 240 mL/minute compared to 55 mL/minute for conventional hemodialysis.[47] Thus, further dosage adjustments for gentamicin and ceftazidime are needed for G.G. when she is converted from conventional hemodialysis.

Acyclovir

Renal Clearance

10. D.M., a 28-year-old male with acquired immunodeficiency syndrome (AIDS), presents with a severe herpetic infection requiring IV acyclovir. Due to other complications associated with his human immunodeficiency virus (HIV), D.M. has developed renal insufficiency during his hospital course. His SrCr is 4.5 mg/dL (Normal: 0.6–1.4), and his Cl_{Cr} is 20 mL/min (Normal: 80–110). What are important considerations for dosing acyclovir in D.M.? [SI units: SrCr 397.8 μmol/L (Normal: 53.04–123.76); Cl_{Cr} 0.33 mL/s (Normal: 1.33–1.83)]

Acyclovir primarily is used to treat infections caused by herpes simplex and herpes zoster viruses.[52] Acyclovir is cleared primarily by renal elimination; 70% to 80% is excreted unchanged, making dosage adjustment in renal disease necessary.[19,53,54] Since the renal clearance of acyclovir is nearly three times greater than the estimated creatinine clearance, renal tubular secretion as well as glomerular filtration plays a role in its elimination.

Acyclovir also can exacerbate D.M's renal failure by precipitating in the renal tubules, and is more likely to occur when inappropriately high doses are rapidly administered intravenously to patients with renal dysfunction.[52] In one study, increases in serum creatinine were related to peak plasma concentrations exceeding 25 μg/mL.[55] To minimize this renal toxicity, acyclovir should be administered over one hour and the patient should be adequately hydrated to maintain good urine flow, especially during the first two hours following the beginning of the infusion. Nephrotoxicity, if it occurs, usually is reversible upon discontinuation of the drug or reduction of the dose.

In renal failure patients, the clearance of acyclovir correlates closely with the creatinine clearance according to the following relationship:

$$\begin{array}{l} Cl_{acyclovir} \\ \text{in mL/min/1.73 m}^2 \end{array} = (3.4)(Cl_{Cr}\ \text{in mL/min/1.73 m}^2) + 28.7$$
$$Eq.\ 32.17$$

In patients with normal renal function, the clearance of acyclovir ranges from 210 to 330 mL/minute, while in patients with end-stage renal disease the clearance decreases to 29 to 34 mL/minute.[19,54,56] Although this change in clearance primarily is due to decreased renal clearance of the drug, nonrenal clearance of acyclovir also decreases in these patients.[19,56] Consequently, the half-life increases dramatically from approximately three hours in patients with normal kidney function to 20 hours in patients with ESRD. Therefore, doses are reduced proportionately from a normal daily dose of 15 mg/kg body weight (5 mg/kg given every eight hours) for serious herpes simplex infections, to doses as low as 2.5 mg/kg/day (given as a single daily dose) in patients with ESRD. Since D.M. has a Cl_{Cr} of 20 mL/minute with an estimated $Cl_{acyclovir}$ of 97 mL/minute (approximately one-third of normal), a single daily dose of 5 mg/kg (one-third of normal) would be appropriate to treat this infection (see Table 32.2).

Acyclovir is moderately removed by conventional hemodialysis, with plasma levels decreasing by 60% following six hours of dialysis.[57] The half-life on and off dialysis is 6 and 20 hours, respectively; and the dialysis clearance averages 80 mL/minute. Therefore, a supplemental dose of 2.5 mg/kg following dialysis is recommended in patients requiring hemodialysis. No data are available on the removal of this compound by high-flux dialysis procedures. (Also see Chapter 31: Renal Dialysis.)

Effect of Renal Dysfunction on Metabolism

11. Does D.M.'s renal dysfunction affect the metabolism of acyclovir?

Approximately 20% of acyclovir is cleared by nonrenal mechanisms.[19,56] The only significant metabolite that has been isolated is 9-carboxymethoxymethylguanine which accounts for 9% to 14% of an administered dose. Previously, it was presumed that this metabolite was a product of hepatic metabolism; however, the kidney may play an important role in the metabolism of this compound as well.[19] Whether this renal dysfunction alters hepatic metabolism or metabolic enzymes present within the kidney remains unclear. Recent studies show that renal tissue contains many of the metabolizing enzymes found in the liver. Mixed-function oxidases have been found in segments of the proximal tubule while other metabolic processes, such as glucuronidation, acetylation, and hydrolysis, also occur within the kidney.[17,18]

Several additional studies have examined the effect of renal failure on hepatic metabolic enzyme activity.[58–60] Most of these investigations were carried out in animals which were noted to have diminished microsomal, mitochondrial, and cytosolic enzyme activities. Renal dysfunction alters the nonrenal clearance of cephalosporins substantially (e.g., ceftizoxime, cefotaxime),[61–64] as well as the benzodiazepines, diazepam, and desmethyldiazepam.[65,66]

Zidovudine (AZT)

Dosage Adjustment

12. D.M. also is being treated with AZT for his HIV disease. Will his AZT doses need to be adjusted?

Zidovudine slows the progression of HIV disease in patients with AIDS and AIDS-related complex. However, it has potent bone marrow suppressive effects that often lead to severe anemia and neutropenia.[67] Doses of AZT usually are adjusted based upon the patient's clinical response and the development of toxicity.

AZT is metabolized primarily by the liver to the inactive glucuronide metabolite, GAZT, which is eliminated renally. Only 18% of unchanged AZT is eliminated renally. Therefore, little change in AZT clearance and half-life has been reported. Two studies report only slight increases in half-life (from 1.0 to 1.4 hours to 1.4 to 1.9 hours in renal failure patients),[68,69] while an additional report measured a half-life of 2.9 hours in a single patient with renal impairment.[70] Although GAZT accumulates in renal disease, this is not of clinical significance.[68]

Despite little change in AZT plasma levels, renal failure patients are predisposed to bone marrow suppression because their kidneys produce less of the hematopoietic factor, erythropoietin, and their white blood cell (WBC) counts are decreased. Therefore, AZT is used more cautiously in these patients and lower doses often are used initially. Starting doses of 100 mg every eight hours are recommended. As is true for patients with normal renal function, adjustments in doses for patients with renal impairment should be based upon clinical improvement and signs of toxicity. [See Chapter 68: Human Immunodeficiency Virus (HIV) Infection.]

Hemodialysis

13. Is AZT significantly removed by dialysis?

A number of reports describe the removal of AZT by dialysis.[68–70] Based upon the chemical characteristics of AZT, one would predict that it would be dialyzable: it has a low molecular weight of 267, a relatively small volume of distribution (1 to 2.2 L/kg), and low protein binding (34% to 38%). Nevertheless, the dialysis clearance of AZT is minimal when compared to its plasma clearance in renal failure patients. Clearance by dialysis averages 63 mL/minute compared to a plasma clearance (following oral administration) of approximately 1200 mL/minute. Little change in the AZT plasma levels during dialysis has been observed; however, the elimination of GAZT may be enhanced.[68]

Penicillin

Dosage Adjustment

14. T.H., a 57-year-old, 85 kg male with chronic renal failure secondary to poorly controlled hypertension, presents to the ER with a 24-hour history of fever (39 °C), altered mental status, nausea, and vomiting. On physical examination he was found to have nuchal rigidity and a positive Brudzinski's sign. Laboratory analysis revealed: WBC count of 22,000/mm³ with 89% neutrophils, BUN of 45 mg/dL, and SrCr of 4.4 mg/dL. A lumbar puncture revealed cerebrospinal fluid (CSF) with a WBC count of 2000/mm³ (90% polymorphonuclear neutrophils), a glucose concentration of 36 mg/dL, and a protein concentration of 280 mg/dL. Gram-positive diplococci were seen on CSF smear. A diagnosis of meningococcal meningitis was made, and potassium penicillin G was ordered. What dose should be used? [SI units: WBC count 2.2×10^9/L and 0.2×10^9/L, respectively; BUN 16.065 mmol/L UREA; SrCr 335.5 μmol/L; glucose 1.998 mmol/L; protein 2.8 gm/L]

Meningococcal meningitis can be treated with 20 to 24 MU of intravenous penicillin G in patients with normal renal function. Like many beta-lactam antibiotics, penicillin primarily is excreted unchanged in the urine with little or no evidence of hepatic metabolism. Thus, the half-life, which averages less than one hour in patients with normal kidney function, increases to four to ten hours in end-stage renal disease patients.[71–73]

Methods to modify the dose of penicillin in renal insufficiency have been developed by numerous investigators. The clearance of penicillin correlates closely to creatinine clearance according to the following equation:[73]

$$Cl_{pen} \text{ in mL/min} = 35.5 + 3.35\, Cl_{Cr} \text{ in mL/min} \qquad Eq.\ 32.18$$

This correlation is based upon data from patients with varying degrees of renal impairment. An equation to estimate the total daily dose for renal failure patients who achieve serum levels similar to those produced by large doses of penicillin (20 to 24 MU/day) in patients with normal renal function can be used for patients with an estimated Cl_{Cr} of less than 40 mL/minute. The calculated dose for T.H. should be divided equally and administered at an appropriate dosing interval (e.g., every six or eight hours):

$$Dose_{pen} \text{ in MU/day} = 3.2 + (Cl_{Cr}/7) \qquad Eq.\ 32.19$$

Using the Cockroft and Gault method, T.H.'s creatinine clearance is approximately 20 mL/minute. Therefore, his daily dose of penicillin should be 6 MU. A dose of 2 MU every eight hours would be appropriate for T.H.

As is true for many agents, these dosing recommendations are empiric and are based upon pharmacokinetic information for renal failure patients. Rarely have these recommendations been subject to carefully designed clinical trials that establish therapeutic efficacy. Therefore, other factors that can influence host response also should be considered when designing an individualized therapeutic regimen. These include the host's immune status, the presence of other disease states, microbial sensitivity patterns, and changes in pharmacokinetic disposition (e.g., concomitant liver disease, fluid overload, dehydration). If the patient's condition warrants, doses differing from published recommendations should be prescribed.

Penicillin-Induced Neurotoxicity

15. The medical intern fails to consider T.H.'s renal impairment when he prescribes penicillin and begins a dose of 4 MU Q 4 hr. Four days later T.H. is encephalopathic (confused, disoriented, and difficult to arouse) and some twitching is noted on the right side of his face. Are these toxic symptoms associated with high-dose penicillin use? What predisposing factors may contribute to this toxicity?

T.H. is experiencing signs of neurotoxicity that are consistent with high penicillin concentrations in the plasma and cerebrospinal fluid. When used appropriately, penicillin produces few serious adverse effects. However, when large doses are used in patients with renal impairment, toxic symptoms such as those exhibited by T.H. can result. Signs and symptoms of penicillin-induced CNS toxicity include myoclonus, complex or generalized seizure activity, and encephalopathy progressing to coma.[25,26]

Predisposing Factors. T.H.'s advanced age and renal dysfunction predispose him to penicillin-induced neurotoxicity. In a review of 46 cases of penicillin-associated neurotoxicity, decreased renal function was present in 35.[26] This is because penicillin accumulates if appropriate dosing adjustments are not made in patients with renal failure. Also, the binding of acidic drugs (such as penicillin) to albumin is decreased, resulting in an increased fraction of ''free'' or active drug that can pass into the CSF. An alteration in the blood-brain barrier also has been observed in uremic patients, leading to further increases in CSF drug levels.[25] High plasma concentrations of penicillin also may contribute to changes in blood-brain barrier permeability of this drug.[25] All of these factors, together with the increased sensitivity of renal failure patients to centrally-acting agents, make CNS toxicity more likely.

Antipseudomonal Penicillins

16. M.H., a 44-year-old, 70 kg woman with acute nonlymphocytic leukemia, is admitted to the Cancer Research Institute for placement of a Hickman catheter for her chemotherapy. Seven days following treatment with ARA-C and daunorubicin, she spiked a fever to 39.4 °C. Other physical findings consistent with sepsis included a BP of 109/70 mm Hg, pulse rate of 102 beats/min, and a respiratory rate of 27/min. M.H. is neutropenic with a WBC count of 1400/mm² (3% polymorphonuclear leukocytes, 70% lymphocytes, and 22% monocytes). The platelet count was 16,000/mm³. M.H. also has renal dysfunction as reflected by a SrCr and BUN of 2.7 and 38 mg/dL, respectively. Empiric therapy for sepsis is started with tobramycin, piperacillin, and vancomycin. How should piperacillin be dosed in M.H.? [SI units: platelet count 16 × 10⁹/L; SrCr 205.875 μmol/L; BUN 13.566 mmol/L UREA]

Piperacillin is an antipseudomonal penicillin that often is used in combination with the aminoglycosides to treat serious infections caused by gram-negative organisms such as *Pseudomonas aeruginosa*.[74] In patients with normal renal function, piperacillin primarily is excreted unchanged by the kidney with a clearance of 2.6 mL/minute/kg and a half-life of approximately one hour.[75,76] Doses usually are as high as 3 gm every four hours. In patients with end-stage renal disease, mean clearance and half-life values are 0.7 mL/minute/kg and 3.3 hours, respectively.[75-78] Although changes in these parameters are significant, they are less than those

expected for a drug primarily cleared by the kidneys, suggesting that some compensatory mechanism for elimination must be present. The drug partially is cleared by biliary excretion, and this route of elimination is increased in renal failure patients.[78,79] Therefore, aggressive dosage reductions in M.H. are unnecessary. An appropriate dose of piperacillin for M.H. would be 3 gm every six hours (see Table 32.2).

Vancomycin

Pharmacokinetic Dosage Calculations

17. In addition to the above regimen, vancomycin therapy is initiated at 500 mg Q 24 hr to cover the possibility of a staphylococcal infection resistant to antistaphylococcal penicillins such as nafcillin and methicillin. Is this an appropriate dosing regimen for M.H.?

Vancomycin is a bactericidal antibiotic with excellent activity against most gram-positive organisms such as nafcillin-resistant staphylococci and all streptococci including *Enterococcus faecalis*.[80] It often is used empirically in the febrile neutropenic patient since the incidence of infection secondary to resistant organisms is much higher in this patient population.

Vancomycin is poorly absorbed orally; therefore, it must be administered intravenously when used to treat systemic infections. As is true for many antimicrobials, vancomycin primarily is cleared renally.[81] In addition, significant toxicities have been associated with its use when inappropriately high doses are administered.[82,83] Therefore, careful dosing modification in renal failure is necessary.

As with the aminoglycosides, pharmacokinetic calculations usually are used to individualize a dosing regimen that is likely to produce designated peak and trough plasma levels. Unlike the aminoglycosides, however, the therapeutic range for vancomycin is less clear. Normally, doses are designed to produce peak levels of 25 to 40 μg/mL and trough levels of 10 to 15 μg/mL.[84] Unfortunately, the correlation between vancomycin toxicity (such as ototoxicity) and plasma levels is not well defined. However, some researchers have suggested that plasma levels exceeding 80 μg/mL may correlate with auditory dysfunction.

Vancomycin has an elimination half-life of three to nine hours in patients with normal renal function.[85] This increases to 129 to 189 hours in patients with ESRD.[86-88] Elaborate pharmacokinetic studies have established that the plasma clearance of vancomycin (Cl_{vanco}) is approximately 60% to 70% of Cl_{Cr}.[113] With the patient's weight and estimated creatinine clearance, estimates of plasma clearance and the volume of distribution can be made. The volume of distribution of vancomycin (Vd_{vanco}) varies from 0.4 to 1.4 L/kg, but usually averages 0.7 L/kg.[85,89,90]

To determine if a vancomycin dose of 500 mg every 24 hours is appropriate for M.H., her estimated Vd_{vanco} and Cl_{vanco} should first be calculated:

$$Cl_{Cr} = 23 \text{ mL/min (calculated from Eq. 32.2)}$$

$$Cl_{vanco} = (0.65)(Cl_{Cr}) \qquad Eq.\ 32.20$$

$$= (0.65)(23 \text{ mL/min})$$

$$= 19.5 \text{ mL/min } or \text{ 1.2 L/hr}$$

$$Vd_{vanco} = (0.7 \text{ L/kg})(\text{Body Weight}) \qquad Eq.\ 32.21$$

$$= (0.7 \text{ L/kg})(70 \text{ kg})$$

$$= 49 \text{ L}$$

Based upon estimated values for Cl_{vanco} and Vd_{vanco}, the elimination rate constant can be calculated:

$$Kd = \frac{Cl_{vanco}}{Vd_{vanco}} \qquad Eq.\ 32.22$$

$$= \frac{1.2\ L/hr}{49\ L}$$

$$= 0.024\ hr^{-1}$$

$$Cp_{peak} = \frac{\dfrac{Dose}{Vd_{vanco}}}{1 - e^{-Kd\tau}} \qquad Eq.\ 32.23$$

$$= \frac{\dfrac{500\ mg}{49\ L}}{1 - e^{-(0.024\ hr^{-1})(24\ hr)}}$$

$$= 23\ \mu g/mL$$

$$Cp_{trough} = Cp_{peak}(e^{-Kd\tau}) \qquad Eq.\ 32.24$$

$$= 13\ \mu g/mL$$

Since M.H.'s estimated peak concentration is less than 40 µg/mL and her trough falls within the range of 10 to 15 µg/mL, a starting dose of 500 mg every 24 hours is appropriate.

Although vancomycin plasma concentrations often are monitored, routine monitoring in patients with normal renal function and fluid status is controversial because the likelihood that toxicity will develop in these patients is low. However, in patients such as M.H. with renal failure, it is advisable to measure vancomycin levels three to five days after initiation of therapy to assure that they are within an acceptable range.[85,87,88,91] This especially is prudent if an extended course of therapy is anticipated. Vancomycin usually is administered over 30 to 60 minutes intravenously. Because there is a distribution phase, plasma samples should be drawn at least 30 minutes following the end of the infusion.[92]

Hemodialysis

18. Unfortunately M.H.'s renal function starts to deteriorate and she is placed on hemodialysis. How should her regimen now be altered?

Before studies evaluating vancomycin pharmacokinetics in patients with renal disease were available, it was noted that patients with ESRD continued to have measurable levels of the drug for up to three weeks following a single dose despite hemodialysis.[88] This suggested that the ability of these patients to eliminate vancomycin was minimal and that little of the drug was removed by conventional hemodialysis procedures. Further evaluation revealed that the half-life for vancomycin in these individuals averaged five to seven days, which was consistent with a measured residual vancomycin clearance in these patients of 3 to 4 mL/minute.[86-88] Only about 5% of vancomycin is metabolized hepatically in patients with normal renal function.

Conventional hemodialysis removes only 7% during a typical four-hour dialysis run.[93] The half-life on and off dialysis and plasma levels of the drug before and after hemodialysis are not significantly different. The poor dialyzability of vancomycin is attributed primarily to its large molecular weight of 3300.

Typically, patients on conventional hemodialysis are given a single 1 gm dose every seven to ten days.[85,88,91] Based upon M.H.'s estimated Vd of 49 L, this dose will produce an initial peak plasma level of approximately 22 µg/mL. If vancomycin subsequently is administered weekly, steady-state peak and trough levels of 40 and 16 µg/mL, respectively, would be predicted.

Since vancomycin is removed to a larger extent by high-flux hemodialysis than by conventional hemodialysis, more frequent dosing is necessary in patients managed by this alternative dialysis procedure. High-flux dialysis clearance of vancomycin using the Fresenius polysulfone dialyzer is 45 to 85 mL/minute and varies with membrane surface area.[48] As a result, up to 49.5% of a dose of vancomycin is removed over four hours compared to 6.9% using conventional dialysis in the same patients. A rebound phenomenon following dialysis suggests that the total amount of drug removed may be less than first reported.[49,50] In any case, the efficiency of high-flux procedures in removing vancomycin exceeds that of conventional dialysis. Therefore, plasma levels should be monitored carefully in these patients and postdialysis replacement doses as high as 500 mg may be warranted.

Amphotericin

Dosing

19. M.H. continues to be febrile despite her triple antimicrobial regimen. Amphotericin therapy is started empirically to cover a potential fungal infection. In addition, pentamidine is begun to cover *Pneumocystis carinii* pneumonia. How should amphotericin be administered in patients like M.H. with renal disease?

Amphotericin is an antifungal agent used to treat serious infections such as cryptococcal meningitis. The exact mechanism of elimination for this drug remains unclear but may involve hepatic metabolism or inactivation in body tissues. However, small amounts of amphotericin gradually are excreted in the urine for several weeks following its discontinuation.[94] This slow elimination may be due to amphotericin's extensive distribution into peripheral tissue and large volume of distribution (4 L/kg).[94,95] The drug appears to bind to cholesterol-containing cytoplasmic membranes of various tissues resulting in a very long terminal half-life of 15 days. Pharmacokinetic studies report no significant change in the disposition of this drug in patients with renal or liver disease. Therefore, no dosage adjustments are required in these patients.

Amphotericin is, however, associated with acute tubular necrosis (ATN) which is believed to be dose dependent (see Chapter 29: Acute Renal Failure).[96-98] Thus, lower doses often are administered to patients with decreased renal function to prevent exacerbation of this disorder. Administration of amphotericin every other day often is suggested for renal failure patients such as M.H.

Hemodialysis

Amphotericin is not removed significantly by hemodialysis. Amphotericin is a very large compound that distributes widely into peripheral tissues. Therefore, little drug remains in the plasma to be dialyzed. Studies report less than 5% of amphotericin is removed during a four hour conventional hemodialysis period.

Gentamicin

20. J.J., a 24-year-old male with ESRD, is maintained with CAPD. He presents to the ER with fever to 38.2 °C and complaints of severe abdominal pain. He also reports that his peritoneal dialysate has been cloudy over the last few days. All of these symptoms are consistent with peritonitis, the most common complication of CAPD. His culture results reveal *Escherichia coli*, sensitive to gentamicin. How should this drug be administered?

Management of dialysis-related peritonitis may vary from one institution to another. Antibiotics often are administered intraperitoneally with or without systemic antibiotic therapy. For less severe cases, intraperitoneal (IP) administration often is considered sufficient. With intraperitoneal administration, the goal is to administer a concentration of drug similar to the plasma concentration desired for treatment of systemic infections. Therefore, 8 mg of gentamicin into each liter of dialysate (or 16 mg into a common dialysate bag of 2 L) usually is recommended. Once equilibrium is reached and steady state achieved, the dialysate concentration will be comparable to the concentrations of gentamicin measured in plasma. Although in patients with peritonitis, more rapid transfer of drug into the plasma takes place owing to increased peritoneal membrane permeability, a substantial lag time still exists before steady state is reached. Therefore, more serious cases of peritonitis should be managed with concomitant systemic antibiotics.

21. Is gentamicin eliminated by CAPD?

Generally, drugs are not well removed via CAPD. This is especially true for drugs that are highly protein bound or drugs with a large volume of distribution. In many cases, if partially eliminated via CAPD, the clearance is too low to be clinically significant. CAPD clearance of gentamicin and other aminoglycosides has been shown to be considerably higher. Gentamicin has low protein binding, a small volume of distribution, and a very low body clearance in end-stage renal disease. Therefore, estimates of removal have ranged from 10% to 50% following intravenous administration.[142]

Phenytoin

Protein Binding

22. R.S., a 24-year-old male with ESRD secondary to rapidly progressive glomerulonephritis, is managed by hemodialysis three times weekly. He has a 7-year history of generalized tonic-clonic seizures and previously has been treated with phenytoin. He now presents to the ER after having suffered a seizure lasting about 5 minutes. His mother states that he ran out of phenytoin 4 weeks ago. Because his plasma phenytoin concentration on admission is <2.5 μg/mL, R.S. is given an IV loading dose of phenytoin: 15 mg/kg over 30 minutes. Additional admission laboratory work includes: SrCr 8.6 mg/dL (Normal: 0.6–1.4), BUN 110 mg/dL (Normal: 7–20), potassium 5.4 mEq/L, calcium 9 mg/dL, and albumin 2.9 gm/dL. Eight hours after administration of phenytoin, his level is 5 mg/dL. Is this level subtherapeutic? [SI units: phenytoin 0.99 and 19.82 μmol/L, respectively; SrCr 655.75 μmol/L (Normal: 10–40); BUN 39.27 mmol/L UREA (Normal: 3.0–6.5); potassium 5.4 mmol/L; calcium 2.24 mmol/L; albumin 29 gm/L]

R.S. has severe renal disease which affects total (bound plus free) phenytoin levels measured in plasma. The lower total phenytoin serum concentrations in these patients primarily are due to decreased plasma protein binding. Phenytoin is an acidic drug that primarily is bound to albumin. In patients with renal disease, the amount of phenytoin bound to albumin is decreased, but the fraction of unbound phenytoin is increased.[8,99–103] Thus, free or active phenytoin levels may remain the same and lower total phenytoin levels may be ''therapeutic'' in patients with renal failure. A number of mechanisms have been proposed to account for these phenomena. These include: 1) decreased albumin levels, 2) accumulation of uremic acidic by-products known to displace acidic drugs from their binding sites, and 3) alteration in the confirmation or structural arrangement of albumin in uremic patients resulting in a reduced number of binding sites or decreased affinity for drugs.

The protein binding of phenytoin in patients with normal renal function and normal albumin is approximately 90%. In patients with ESRD, the protein binding ranges from 65% to 80%.[99,102,103] Additional acidic drugs with altered protein binding in renal disease are listed in Table 32.1.

A number of changes in drug disposition may occur secondary to a decrease in protein binding. The volume of distribution may increase since there is more free unbound drug to distribute into the peripheral tissue compartments.

Furthermore, since more unbound phenytoin is available for clearance from the plasma, a normal maintenance dose will be eliminated similar to the way it is eliminated in patients with normal renal function. In other words, the steady-state plasma concentration of unbound phenytoin in patients with renal failure should not differ from those with normal renal function. However, since the total drug concentration will be lower, phenytoin levels which reflect the total drug concentration must be interpreted carefully in renal failure patients. Since the unbound fraction of phenytoin is the pharmacologically active form, lower total phenytoin levels are desired in patients with renal failure to achieve the therapeutic effect while preventing toxicity.[5] Figure 32.4 illustrates changes in phenytoin levels when uremic and nonuremic patients are given equivalent doses.[104]

The following equation should be used to correct for R.S.'s altered binding due to his renal dysfunction and hypoalbuminemia:[102]

$$Cp_{Normal\ Binding} = \frac{Cp'}{(0.48)(1-\alpha)\left(\dfrac{P'}{P_{NL}}\right) + \alpha} \qquad Eq.\ 32.25$$

Cp' is the observed plasma concentration reported by the laboratory and $Cp_{Normal\ Binding}$ is the corrected plasma concentration that would be seen if the patient had normal renal function and normal albumin. Alpha is the normal free fraction (0.1), P' is the patient's serum albumin, and P_{NL} is normal albumin (4.4 gm/dL). The factor 0.48 was derived from hemodialysis patients such as R.S. and represents the decreased affinity of phenytoin for albumin.

For R.S., 5 μg/mL is comparable to 12 μg/mL in a patient without renal failure. Since this falls within the phenytoin's therapeutic range of 10 to 20 μg/mL, his measured level is not subtherapeutic.

It should be noted that the factor 0.48 only should be used to estimate changes in protein binding for patients with end-stage renal disease. Data for patients with moderate renal disease are limited and it is unclear what changes exist in the binding of phenytoin to albumin.[102] For patients with normal or moderate renal impairment, the following equation should be used only if the serum albumin is low; the factor 0.48 should be deleted:

$$Cp_{Normal\ Binding} = \frac{Cp'}{(1-\alpha)\left(\dfrac{P'}{P_{NL}}\right) + \alpha} \qquad Eq.\ 32.26$$

Effect of Renal Failure on Metabolized Drugs

Meperidine

23. F.G., a 56-year-old female, is admitted for a cervical laminectomy. She has a history of chronic renal insufficiency (Cl$_{Cr}$ = 20 mL/min) and arrhythmias that are treated with procainamide. Her admission laboratory values are as follows: SrCr 4.4 mg/dL (Normal: 0.6–1.3); BUN 66 mg/dL (Normal: 7–20); Hct 34%; and Hgb 12.6 gm/dL.

Following surgery, she complains of severe pain and is treated with meperidine 50 to 100 mg IM Q 3–4 hr. Three days postoperatively, F.G. experiences a generalized tonic-clonic seizure. She has no seizure history. What might be responsible for this sudden occurrence? [SI units: SrCr 388.96 μmol/L (Normal: 53–114.92); BUN 23.6 mmol/L UREA (Normal: 2.5–7.14); Hct 0.34 1; Hgb 126 gm/L]

Meperidine is a narcotic analgesic commonly used to control postsurgical pain in patients undergoing orthopedic surgical procedures such as a laminectomy. This drug is metabolized hepatically via N-demethylation to normeperidine, a metabolite known to accumulate in renal insufficiency.[15] Although meperidine has both CNS excitatory and depressant properties, normeperidine is a very potent CNS stimulant that can cause seizures in renal failure patients receiving multiple doses of the parent compound.[106] In one study of 67 cancer patients treated with meperidine, 48 developed neurological adverse effects; 14 of these 48 patients had renal dysfunction defined as BUN greater than 20 mg/dL.[106] Since the renal clearance of normeperidine correlates significantly with

Fig 32.4   Plasma Phenytoin Concentrations in Uremic (○) and Nonuremic (●) Patients Following 250 mg of Phenytoin Intravenously   Reprinted with permission from reference 104.

creatinine clearance, renal dysfunction predisposes patients to normeperidine accumulation and neurological toxicity. In another study, the normeperidine:meperidine plasma concentration ratio was consistently higher in renal failure patients, averaging 2.0 compared to a mean of 0.6 for patients with good renal function.[106] Table 32.4 lists examples of additional drugs that have active or toxic metabolites that may accumulate in renal disease.

Narcotic Analgesics

24. Are the pharmacokinetics or pharmacodynamics of other narcotic analgesics altered in patients with renal insufficiency?

Morphine

The pharmacokinetic disposition of morphine does not appear to be altered in renal failure patients;[107] however, its active metabolite, morphine 6-glucuronide, does accumulate in renal disease. The half-life of morphine increases from three to four hours in normal subjects to 89 to 136 hours in renal failure subjects.[108] This metabolite penetrates the blood-brain barrier more readily, has analgesic activity that is 3.7 times greater than morphine,[109] and has a greater affinity for CNS receptors than morphine. Therefore, the accumulation of morphine 6-glucuronide may be responsible for the morphine-induced narcosis reported in several patients with severe renal disease.[20–22]

Codeine

Other analgesics that have been associated with CNS toxicity in renal failure patients include codeine, propoxyphene, and dihydrocodeine. The disposition of orally administered codeine does not appear to be altered in renal failure; however, two incidents of codeine-induced narcosis have been reported.[110,111] Even though the dose of codeine these individuals received did not exceed 120 mg/day, CNS and respiratory depression persisted for up to four days following discontinuation of codeine and required naloxone administration.

Guay et al.[112] reported a prolonged terminal elimination half-life for intravenous codeine in chronic hemodialysis patients: 18.7 ± 9 hours versus 4 ± 0.6 hours in subjects with normal renal function. Although the total body clearance was not significantly decreased, the volume of distribution for codeine was approximately twice as large in the dialysis group. The clinical significance of these alterations requires further investigation.

Table 32.4	Drugs with Active or Toxic Metabolites Excreted by the Kidney
Drug	**Metabolite**
Acetohexamide	Hydroxyhexamide
Allopurinol	Oxypurinol
Cefotaxime	Desacetylcefotaxime
Chlorpropamide	Hydroxy metabolites
Daunorubicin	Daunorubicinol
Meperidine	Normeperidine
Methyldopa	Methy-o-sulfate-α-methyldopamine
Morphine	6-glucuronide morphine
Phenylbutazone	Oxyphenbutazone
Primidone	Phenobarbital
Procainamide	N-acetylprocainamide
Propoxyphene	Norpropoxyphene
Rifampicin	Desacetylated metabolites
Sodium nitroprusside	Thiocyanate
Sulfonamides	Acetylated metabolites

Propoxyphene

Propoxyphene and its metabolite, norpropoxyphene, accumulate in renal insufficiency. Norpropoxyphene is excreted renally, and its half-life is prolonged in renal failure patients; however, the half-life of propoxyphene remains unchanged. Accumulation of propoxyphene is thought to be due to a decreased first-pass effect or systemic clearance. Similar pharmacokinetic changes have been seen in patients experiencing dihydrocodeine-associated narcosis.[113,114] The accumulation of these compounds in subjects with renal failure, especially after multiple-dose therapy, may be associated with CNS and cardiac toxicities.[107] Therefore, these drugs also should be avoided in renal failure patients.

Procainamide

25. F.G.'s procainamide level is 9 µg/mL (Normal: 4–8) and her N-acetyl procainamide (NAPA) level is 34 µg/mL (Normal: 10–20). How is the disposition of procainamide affected in patients with renal disease? [SI units: procainamide level 38.24 µmol/L (Normal: 17–34)]

The pharmacokinetics of procainamide in patients with renal insufficiency are complex. Since 50% to 70% of the parent compound is excreted unchanged in the urine, procainamide can accumulate in patients with renal disease as plasma clearance values are reduced by as much as 70%.[115,116] Procainamide also is acetylated partially to NAPA, which primarily is excreted renally.[117] Figure 32.5 summarizes the elimination of procainamide and NAPA. PA has antiarrhythmic properties similar to procainamide with some reports of equal activity when equivalent levels of the compounds are achieved.[118] However, the half-life of NAPA is longer especially in patients with renal impairment, increasing from six hours in control subjects to as long as 40 hours in patients with end-stage renal disease.[115,117] Since significant cardiac toxicity has occurred in some patients with NAPA levels greater than 30 µg/mL, plasma level monitoring of NAPA as well as procainamide is recommended in patients such as F.G., in whom accumulation is likely. In these patients, appropriate dosage reduction of procainamide may be necessary. It also is important to realize that the time required to reach steady state for NAPA in patients with renal failure may be as long as five days. Therefore, plasma levels measured early in therapy must be interpreted carefully; these concentrations may be considerably less than those which will be achieved under steady-state conditions.

Fig 32.5 Elimination of Procainamide (PCA) and N-Acetylprocainamide (NAPA) in Subjects with Normal Renal and Liver Function

Fig 32.6 Schematic Representation of Pathways of Elimination of Acyl Glucuronide Metabolites or Arylpropionic Nonsteroidal Anti-Inflammatory Drugs   Reprinted with permission from reference 144.

Nonsteroidal Anti-Inflammatory Drugs (NSAIDs)

26. After a three-week hospital stay, F.G. is discharged with a prescription for ibuprofen 400 mg Q 6 hr PRN pain. What factors should be considered when treating renal failure patients with NSAIDs?

Because the nonsteroidal anti-inflammatory drugs have been associated with nephrotoxicity, they are used cautiously in patients with renal disease.[119,120] The presenting features of renal toxicity are variable and can include acute or chronic onset with or without oliguria. Pathologic changes due to these agents also are variable and range from interstitial nephritis to acute tubular necrosis.[119–121] Possible mechanisms for NSAID-induced nephrotoxicity include inhibition of renal prostaglandins leading to altered renal blood flow and ischemic changes. Renal impairment may be more likely to occur in patients who have abnormally high plasma levels of vasoconstrictor hormones (e.g., angiotensin II, catecholamines)[121] since a compensatory increase in the synthesis of vasodilatory renal prostaglandins may be present. Blockage of this increase by an NSAID can lead to ischemic changes and acute renal failure.

A second proposed mechanism involves an autoimmune response that is triggered by changes in cell-mediated immunity.[122,123] These changes are due to similar alterations in prostaglandin synthesis by NSAIDs. Although data are limited, sulindac is an NSAID believed to have "renal-sparing" effects. Unlike other NSAIDs, studies suggest that this agent does not inhibit synthesis of renal prostaglandins.[124]

NSAIDs accumulate in renal insufficiency.[125] This is an interesting finding since renal elimination is negligible for these agents. These compounds primarily are metabolized to an acyl glucuronide metabolite that accumulates in renal failure patients. However, since this metabolite is unstable and can deconjugate, it acts as a reservoir for the parent compound, leading to increased levels of parent drug in these patients. This is represented graphically in Figure 32.6. Of additional importance is the fact that many of the NSAIDs are administered as racemates with the primary activity residing in the S enantiomer. Since the R enantiomer can convert selectively to the S enantiomer during accumulation, an even greater pharmacologic activity may be seen in patients with renal disease.[126,127] This reconversion phenomenon also has been reported for clofibric acid.[128] (See Chapter 29: Acute Renal Failure and Questions 17 to 19 of Chapter 41: Rheumatic Disorders for a further discussion of NSAIDs.)

References

1   **Gambertoglio JG.** Effects of renal disease: altered pharmacokinetics. In: Benet LZ et al., eds. Pharmacokinetic Basis for Drug Treatment. New York: Raven Press; 1984.

2   **Bianchetti GM et al.** Pharmacokinetics and effects of propranolol in terminal uremic patients and patients undergoing regular dialysis treatment. Clin Pharmacokinet. 1978;1:373.

3   **Lowenthal DT et al.** Pharmacokinetics of oral propranolol in chronic renal disease. Clin Pharmacol Ther. 1974;16:761.

4   **Wood AJJ et al.** Propranolol disposition in renal failure. Br J Clin Pharmacol. 1980;10:562–655.

5   **Reidenberg MM.** The binding of drugs to plasma proteins and the interpretation of measurements of plasma concentrations of drugs in patients with poor renal function. Am J Med. 1977; 62:466–70.

6   **Brewster D, Muir NC.** Valproate plasma protein binding in the uremic condition. Clin Pharmacol Ther. 1980; 27:76–82.

7   **Sjoholm I et al.** Protein binding of drugs in uremic and normal serum: the role of endogenous inhibitors. Biochem Pharmacol. 1976;25:1205–213.

8   **Reidenberg MM et al.** Protein binding of diphenylhydantoin and desmethylimipramine in plasma from patients with poor renal function. N Engl J Med. 1971;285:264–68.

9   **Andreasen F.** The effect of dialysis on the protein binding of drugs in the plasma of patients with acute renal failure. Acta Pharmacol Toxicol. 1974;34:284–94.

10 **Boobis SW.** Alteration of plasma albumin in relation to decreased drug binding in uremia. Clin Pharmacol Ther. 1977;22:147–53.

11 **Odar-Cederlof I.** Plasma protein binding of phenytoin and warfarin in patients undergoing renal transplantation. Clin Pharmacokinet. 1977;2:147.

12 **Jusko WJ, Weintraub M.** Myocardial distribution of digoxin and renal function. Clin Pharmacol Ther. 1977;16:448–54.

13 **Drayer DE.** Pharmacologically active metabolites of drugs and other foreign compounds. Clinical, Pharmacological, Therapeutic and Toxicological Considerations. Drugs. 1982; 24:519–42.

14 **Verbeeck RK et al.** Drug metabolites in renal failure. Clin Pharmacokinet. 1981;6:329–45.

15 **Szeto HH et al.** Accumulation of normeperidine, an active metabolite of meperidine, in patients with renal failure or cancer. Ann Intern Med. 1977; 86:738–41.

16 **Gibson TP et al.** N-acetylprocainamide levels in patients with end-stage renal disease. Clin Pharmacol Ther. 1976;19:206–12.

17 **Gibson TP.** Renal disease and drug metabolism: an overview. Am J Kidney Dis. 1986;8:7–17.

18 **Gibson TP.** The kidney and drug metabolism. Int J Artif Organs. 1985;8:237.

19 **Laskin OL et al.** Acyclovir kinetics in end-stage renal disease. Clin Pharmacol Ther. 1982;31:594–600.

20 **Don HF et al.** Narcotic analgesics in anuric patients. Anesthesiology. 1975; 42:745.

21 **Bigler D et al.** Prolonged respiratory depression caused by slow release morphine. Lancet. 1984;1:1477.

22 **Shelly MP, Park GR.** Morphine toxicity with dilated pupils. Br Med J (Clin Res). 1984;289:1071.

23 **Kleinbloesem CH et al.** Nifedipine: influence of renal function on pharmacokinetic/hemodynamic relationship. Clin Pharmacol Ther. 1985;37:563–74.

24 **Welage LS et al.** Pharmacokinetics of ceftazidime in patients with renal insufficiency. Antimicrob Agents Chemother. 1984;25:201.

25 **Nicholls PJ.** Neurotoxicity of penicillin. J Antimicrob Chemother. 1980;6:161.

26 **Fossieck B, Parker RH.** Neurotoxicity during intravenous infusion of penicillin. A review. J Clin Pharmacol. 1974;14:504.

27 **Gentry LO.** Antimicrobial activity, pharmacokinetics, therapeutic indications and adverse reactions of ceftazidime. Pharmacotherapy. 1985;5(5):254–67.

28 **Jackson GG et al.** Pseudomonas bacteremia, pharmacologic and other basis for failure of treatment with gentamicin. J Infect Dis. 1971;124(Suppl.):S185–91.

29 **Noone P et al.** Experience in monitoring gentamicin therapy during treatment of serious gram-negative sepsis. Br Med J. 1974;1:477.

30 **Dahlgre JG et al.** Gentamicin blood levels: a guide to nephrotoxicity. Antimicrob Agents Chemother. 1975;8:58.

31 **Goodman EI et al.** Prospective comparative study of variable dosage and variable frequency regimens for administration of gentamicin. Antimicrob Agents Chemother. 1975;8:434.

32 **Sawchuk RJ et al.** Kinetic model for gentamicin dosing with the use of individual patient parameters. Clin Pharmacol Ther. 1977;21:362–69.

33 **Zaske DE et al.** Gentamicin pharmacokinetics in 1,640 patients: method for control of serum concentrations. Antimicrob Agents Chemother. 1982;21:407–11.

34 **Gyselynck A et al.** Pharmacokinetics of gentamicin: distribution and plasma and renal clearance. J Infect Dis. 1971; 124(Suppl.):S70–b.

35 **McHenry MC et al.** Gentamicin dosages for renal insufficiency. Ann Intern Med. 1971;74:192–97.

36 **Cockroft DW, Gault MH.** Prediction of creatinine clearance from serum creatinine. Nephron. 1976;16:31.

37 **Matzke GR, Keane WF.** Use of antibiotics in renal failure. In: Peterson PK, Verhoef J, eds. The Antimicrobial Agents Annual. Amsterdam: Elsevier Science Publishers BV; 1986:472.

38 **Bennet WM et al.** Drug prescribing in renal failure: dosing guidelines for adults. Am J Kidney Dis. 1983;3:155.

39 **Bauer LA et al.** Influence of weight on aminoglycoside pharmacokinetics in normal weight and morbidly obese patients. Eur J Clin Pharmacol. 1983;24:643–47.

40 **Sampliner R et al.** Influence of ascites on tobramycin pharmacokinetics. J Clin Pharmacol. 1984;24(1):43.

41 **Gibson TP et al.** Artificial kidneys and clearance calculations. Clin Pharmacol Ther. 1976;20:720.

42 **Gibson TP, Nelson HA.** Drug kinetics and artificial kidneys. Clin Pharmacokinet. 1977;2:403.

43 **Gwilt PR, Perrier D.** Plasma protein binding and distribution characteristics of drugs as indices of their hemodialyzability. Clin Pharmacol Ther. 1978;24:154.

44 **Danish M et al.** Pharmacokinetics of gentamicin and kanamycin during hemodialysis. Antimicrob Agents Chemother. 1974;6:841.

45 **Halpren BA et al.** Clearance of gentamicin during hemodialysis: comparison of four artificial kidneys. J Infect Dis. 1976;133:627.

46 **Nikolaidis P, Tourkantonis A.** Effect of hemodialysis on ceftazidime pharmacokinetics. Clin Nephrol. 1985;24:142.

47 **Toffelmire EB et al.** Dialysis clearance in high flux hemodialysis with reuse using ceftazidime as the model drug. Clin Pharmacol Ther. 1989;45:160. Abstract.

48 **Lanese DM et al.** Markedly increased clearance of vancomycin during hemodialysis using polysulfone dialyzers. Kidney Int. 1989;35:1409–412.

49 **Torras J et al.** Pharmacokinetics of vancomycin in patients undergoing hemodialysis with polyacrylonitrile. Clin Nephrol. 1990;36:35–41.

50 **Quale JM et al.** Removal of vancomycin by high-flux hemodialysis membranes. Antimicrob Agents Chemother. 1992;36:1424–426.

51 **O'Hara K, Gambertoglio JG.** Removal of gentamicin using polysulfone dialyzers. Unpublished data. 1991.

52 **Richards DM et al.** Acyclovir: a review of its pharmacodynamic properties and therapeutic efficacy. Drugs. 1983;26:378.

53 **Brigden D et al.** Human pharmacokinetics of acyclovir (an antiviral agent) following rapid intravenous injection. J Antimicrob Chemother. 1981;7:399–404.

54 **Blum MR et al.** Overview of acyclovir pharmacokinetic disposition in adults and children. Am J Med Acyclovir Symposium. 1981;186–92.

55 **Bean B, Aeppli D.** Adverse effects of high-dose intravenous acyclovir in ambulatory patients with acute herpes zoster. J Infect Dis. 1985;151:362.

56 **Laskin OL et al.** Effect of renal failure on the pharmacokinetics of acyclovir. Am J Med Acyclovir Symposium. 1981;197–201.

57 **Krasney HC et al.** Influence of hemodialysis on acyclovir pharmacokinetics in patients with chronic renal failure. Am J Med Acyclovir Symposium. 1981;202–04.

58 **Patterson SE, Cohn VH.** Hepatic drug metabolism in rats with experimental chronic renal failure. Biochem Pharmacol. 1984;33:711–16.

59 **Van Peer AP, Belpaire FM.** Hepatic oxidative drug metabolism in rats with experimental renal failure. Arch Int Pharmacodyn Ther. 1977;228:180–83.

60 **Merey E et al.** Effect of uremia on rates of ethanol disappearance from the blood and on the activities of the ethanol-oxidizing enzymes. J Lab Clin Med. 1975;86:931–37.

61 **Ings RMJ et al.** The pharmacokinetics of cefotaxime and its metabolites in subjects with normal and impaired renal function. Rev Infect Dis. 1982; 4(Suppl.):S379–91.

62 **Fillastre JP et al.** Pharmacokinetics of cefotaxime in subjects with normal and impaired renal function. J Antimicrob Chemother. 1980;6(Suppl.):S103–11.

63 **Cuttler RE et al.** Pharmacokinetics of ceftizoxime. J Antimicrob Chemother. 1982;10(Suppl.):S91–7.

64 **Gibson TP et al.** Imipenem/cilastatin: pharmacokinetics profile in renal insufficiency. Am J Med. 1985;78:54–61.

65 **Ochs HR et al.** Clorazepate dipotassium and diazepam in renal insufficiency: serum concentrations and protein binding of diazepam and desmethyldiazepam. Nephron. 1984;37:100–04.

66 **Ochs HR et al.** Diazepam kinetics in patients with renal insufficiency or hyperthyroidism. Br J Clin Pharmacol. 1981;12:829–32.

67 **Richman DD et al.** The toxicity of azidothymine (AZT) in the treatment of patients with AIDS and AIDS-related complex: a double-blind, placebo-controlled trial. N Engl J Med. 1987;317:192–97.

68 **Singlas E et al.** Zidovudine disposition in patients with renal impairment: influence of hemodialysis. Clin Pharmacol Ther. 1989;46:190–97.

69 **Garraffo R et al.** Influence of hemodialysis on zidovudine (AZT) and its glucuronide (GAZT) pharmacokinetics: two case reports. Int J Clin Pharmacol Ther Toxicol. 1989;27:535–39.

70 **Tartaglione TA et al.** Zidovudine disposition during hemodialysis with acquired immunodeficiency syndrome. J Acquir Immune Defic Syndr. 1990;3:32–4.

71 **Barza M, Weinstein L.** Pharmacokinetics of the penicillins in man. Clin Pharmacokinet. 1976;1:297.

72 **Gambertoglio J et al.** Use of drugs in patients with renal failure. In: Schrrew RW, Gottschalk CW, eds. Diseases of the Kidney. 5th ed. Little Brown and Company. 1993:3211.

73 **Bryan CS, Stone WJ.** ''Comparably massive'' penicillin gm therapy in renal failure. Ann Intern Med. 1975;82:189.

74 **Reyes MP, Lerner AM.** Current problems in the treatment of infective endocarditis due to *Pseudomonas aeruginosa*. Rev Infect Dis. 1983;5:314.

75 **Aronoff GR et al.** The effect of piperacillin dose on elimination kinetics in renal impairment. Eur J Clin Pharmacol. 1983;24:453–57.

76 **Welling PG et al.** Pharmacokinetics of

piperacillin in subjects with various degrees of renal function. Antimicrob Agents Chemother. 1983;23:881–87.

77 **Heim KL et al.** The effect of dialysis on piperacillin pharmacokinetics. Drug Intell Clin Pharm. 1985;19:455.

78 **Thompson MI et al.** Piperacillin pharmacokinetics in subjects with chronic renal failure. Antimicrob Agents Chemother. 1981;19:450–53.

79 **Giron JA et al.** Biliary concentrations of piperacillin in patients undergoing cholecystectomy. Antimicrob Agents Chemother. 1981;19:309–11.

80 **Fejkety R.** Vancomycin. Med Clin North Am. 1982;284:1508–509.

81 **Moellering RC et al.** Pharmacokinetics of vancomycin in normal subjects and in patients with reduced renal function. Rev Infect Dis. 1981;3(Suppl.):S230.

82 **Banner WN Jr, Ray CG.** Vancomycin in perspective. Am J Dis Child. 1984;183:14.

83 **Farber BF, Moellering RC Jr.** Retrospective study of the toxicity of preparations of vancomycin from 1974 to 1981. Antimicrob Agents Chemother. 1983;23:138.

84 **Rotschafer JC et al.** Pharmacokinetics of vancomycin: observations in 28 patients and dosage recommendations. Antimicrob Agents Chemother. 1982;22:391.

85 **Matzke GR et al.** Clinical pharmacokinetics of vancomycin. Clin Pharmacokinet. 1986;11:257.

86 **Tan CC et al.** Pharmacokinetics of intravenous vancomycin in patients with end-stage renal failure. Ther Drug Monit. 1990;12:29–34.

87 **Golper TA et al.** Vancomycin pharmacokinetics, renal handling and nonrenal clearances in normal human subjects. Clin Pharmacol Ther. 1988;43:565–70.

88 **Cunha BA et al.** Pharmacokinetics of vancomycin in anuria. Rev Infect Dis. 1981;3(Suppl.):S269.

89 **Krogstad DJ et al.** Single-dose kinetics of intravenous vancomycin. J Clin Pharmacol. 1980;20:197.

90 **Rotschafer JC et al.** Pharmacokinetics of vancomycin: observations of 28 patients and dosage recommendations. Antimicrob Agents Chemother. 1982;22:391.

91 **Masur H et al.** Vancomycin serum levels and toxicity in chronic hemodialysis patients with staphylococcus aureus bacteremia. Clin Nephrol. 1983;20:85.

92 **Schadd UB et al.** Clinical pharmacology and efficacy of vancomycin in pediatric patients. Pediatr Pharmacol Ther. 1980;96:119.

93 **Lanese DM, Molitoris BA.** Removal of vancomycin by hemodialysis: a sig-

nificant and overlooked consideration. Seminars in Dialysis. 1989;2:73–4.

94 **Daneshmend TK, Warnock DW.** Clinical pharmacokinetics of systemic antifungal drugs. Clin Pharmacokinet. 1983;8:17–42.

95 **Starke JR et al.** Pharmacokinetics of amphotericin B in infants and children. J Infect Dis. 1987;155:766–74.

96 **Stamm AM et al.** Toxicity of amphotericin B plus flucytosine in 194 patients with Cryptococcal meningitis. Am J Med. 1987;83:236.

97 **Sacks P, Fellner SK.** Recurrent reversible acute renal failure from amphotericin. Arch Intern Med.°1987;147:593.

98 **Antoniskis D, Larsen RA.** Acute, rapidly progressive renal failure with simultaneous use of Amphotericin B and pentamidine. Antimicrob Agents Chemother. 1990;34:470–72.

99 **Tiula E et al.** Serum protein binding of phenytoin and propranolol in chronic renal disease. Intern J Pharmacol Ther Toxic. 1987;23:545–52.

100 **Allison TB, Constock TJ.** Temperature dependence of phenytoin-protein binding in serum: effects of uremia and hypoalbuminemia. Ther Drug Monit. 1988;10:376–81.

101 **Asconape JJ, Penry JK.** Use of antiepileptic drugs in the presence of liver and kidney disease: a review. Epilepsia. 1982;23(Suppl. 1):S65.

102 **Liponi DF et al.** Renal function and therapeutic concentrations of phenytoin. Neurology. 1984;34:395.

103 **Osar-Cederlof I et al.** Kinetics of diphenylhydantoin in uremic patients: consequence of decreased protein binding. Eur J Clin Pharmacol. 1974;7:31.

104 **Letteri JM et al.** Diphenylhydantoin metabolism in uremia. N Engl J Med. 1971;285:648–52.

105 **Mather LE, Meffin PJ.** Clinical pharmacokinetics of pethidine. Clin Pharmacokinet. 1978;3:352.

106 **Kaiko RE et al.** Central nervous system excitatory effects of meperidine in cancer patients. Ann Neurol. 1982;13:180.

107 **Chan GLC, Matzke GR.** The effects of renal insufficiency on the pharmacokinetics and pharmacodynamics of opioid analgesics. Drug Intell Clin Pharm. 1987;21:773–83.

108 **Osborne RJ et al.** Morphine intoxication in renal failure: the role of morphine-6-glucuronide. Br Med J (Clin Res). 1986;292:1548.

109 **Shimomura K et al.** Analgesic effects of morphine glucuronides. Tohoku J Exp Med. 1971;105:45.

110 **Levine DF.** Hypocalcemia increases the narcotic effect of codeine. Postgrad Med J. 1980:56;736.

111 **Matzke GR et al.** Codeine dosage in renal failure. Clin Pharm. 1986;5:15.

112 **Guay DRP et al.** Pharmacokinetics and pharmacodynamics of codeine in end-stage renal disease. Clin Pharmacol Ther. 1987;43:63–71.

113 **Barnes JN, Goodwin FJ.** Dihydrocodeine narcosis in renal failure. Br Med J (Clin Res). 1983;286:438.

114 **Redfern N.** Dihydrocodeine overdose treated with naloxone infusion. Br Med J (Clin Res). 1983;287:751.

115 **Gibson TP et al.** Kinetics of procainamide and NAPA in renal failure. Kidney Int. 1977;12:422–29.

116 **Lima JJ et al.** Clinical pharmacokinetics of procainamide infusions in relation to acetylator phenotype. J Pharmacokinet Biopharm. 1979;7:69–85.

117 **Stec GP et al.** N-acetylprocainamide pharmacokinetics in functionally anephric patients before and after perturbation by hemodialysis. Clin Pharmacol Ther. 1979;26:618–28.

118 **Winkle RA et al.** Clinical pharmacology and antiarrhythmic efficacy of N-acetylprocainamide. Am J Cardiol. 1981;47:123.

119 **Pirson Y, de Strihou Ypersele.** Renal side effects of nonsteroidal anti-inflammatory drugs: clinical relevance. Am J Kidney Dis. 1986;8:338–44.

120 **Garella S, Matarese RA.** Renal effects of prostaglandins and clinical adverse effects of nonsteroidal anti-inflammatory agents. Medicine (Baltimore). 1984;63:165–81.

121 **Clive DM, Stoff JS.** Renal syndromes associated with nonsteroidal anti-inflammatory drugs. N Engl J Med. 1984;310:563–71.

122 **Finkelstein A et al.** Fenoprofen nephropathy: lipid nephrosis and interstitial nephritis. Am J Med. 1982;72:81–7.

123 **Bender WL et al.** Interstitial nephritis, proteinuria and renal failure caused by nonsteroidal anti-inflammatory drugs. Am J Med. 1984;76:1006–012.

124 **Bunning RD, Barth WF.** Sulindac. A potentially renal-sparing nonsteroidal anti-inflammatory drug. JAMA. 1982;248:2864–867.

125 **Meffin et al.** Enantio-selective disposition of 2-arylpropionic acid nonsteroidal anti-inflammatory drugs. I. 2-phenylpropionic acid disposition. J Pharmacol Exp Ther. 1986;238:280–87.

126 **Lee FJD et al.** Stereoselective disposition of ibuprofen enantiomers in man. Br J Clin Pharmacol. 1985;19:669–74.

127 **Abas A, Meffin PJ.** Enantioselective disposition of 2-arylpropionic acid nonsteroidal anti-inflammatory drugs. IV. Ketoprofen disposition. J Pharmacol Exp Ther. 1987;240:637–41.

128 **Gugler R et al.** Clofibrate disposition in renal failure and acute and chronic

liver disease. Eur J Clin Pharmacol. 1979;15:341–47.

129 **Welling PG et al.** Pharmacokinetics of cefazolin in normal and uremic subjects. Clin Pharmacol Ther. 1973;15:344–53.

130 **Garcia JJ et al.** Pharmacokinetics of cefoxitin in patients with normal or impaired renal function. Eur J Clin Pharmacol. 1979;16:119–24.

131 **Pearson RM, Breckenridge AM.** Renal function, protein binding and pharmacological response to diazoxide. Br J Clin Pharmacol. 1976;3:169–75.

132 **Rane A et al.** Plasma binding and disposition of furosemide in the nephrotic syndrome and in uremia. Clin Pharmacol Ther. 1978;24:199–207.

133 **Reidenberg MM et al.** Pentobarbital elimination in patients with poor renal function. Clin Pharmacol Ther. 1976;20:67–71.

134 **Craig WA et al.** Correction of protein binding defect in uremic sera by charcoal treatment. J Lab Clin Med. 1976;87:637–47.

135 **Lowenthal DT et al.** Kinetics of salicylate elimination by anephric patients. J Clin Invest. 1974;54:1221–226.

136 **Gugler R., Mueller G.** Plasma protein binding of valproic acid in healthy subjects and in patients with renal disease. Br J Clin Pharmacol. 1978;5:441–46.

137 **Bachmann K et al.** Influence of renal dysfunction on warfarin plasma protein binding. J Clin Pharmacol. 1976;16:468–72.

138 **Keller E et al.** Drug therapy in patients undergoing continuous ambulatory peritoneal dialysis. Clinical pharmacokinetic considerations. Clin Pharmacokinet. 1990;18(2):104–17.

139 **Bickley SK.** Drug dosing during continuous arteriovenous hemofiltration. Clin Pharm. 1988;7:198–206.

140 **Golper TA et al.** Removal of therapeutic drugs by continuous arteriovenous hemofiltration. Arch Intern Med. 1985;145:1651–652.

141 **Pond S et al.** Pharmacokinetics of hemoperfusion for drug overdose. Clin Pharmacokinet. 1979;4:329.

142 **Somani P et al.** Unidirectional absorption of gentamicin from the peritoneum during continuous ambulatory peritoneal dialysis. Clin Pharmacol Ther. 1982;32:113.

143 **Schrier RW, Gambertoglio JG, eds.** Handbook of Drug Therapy in Liver and Kidney Disease. Little Brown and Company, Inc. Boston; 1990.

144 **Brater DC.** Renal Disease. In: Rational Therapeutics. Williams et al., eds. New York: Marcel Dekker, Inc.; 1990.

145 **Brater DC.** Drug Use in Renal Disease. Sydney: ADIS Health Science Press; 1983.

Solid Organ Transplantation

Robert E Dupuis

Transplant Immunology 33-3
  Major Histocompatibility Complex (MHC)
    and Human Leukocyte Antigen (HLA)
    (See Figures 33.2 and 33.3) 33-3
  Human Leukocyte Antigen Typing 33-4
Immunosuppressive Agents (See Table 33.1
  and Figures 33.4 and 33.5) 33-5
  Azathioprine 33-5
    Mechanism of action 33-5
    Pharmacokinetics 33-5
    Adverse effects (See Question 50) 33-38
  Corticosteroids 33-6
    Mechanisms of action 33-6
    Pharmacokinetics 33-6
    Adverse effects (See Question 45) 33-34
    Central nervous system (CNS) disturbances
      (See Question 37) 33-30
  Cyclosporine 33-7
    Mechanisms of action 33-7
    Absorption (See Questions 27 and 38) 33-26,31
    Drug interactions (See Question 28 and
      Tables 33.5 and 33.6) 33-26,27
    Pharmacokinetics (See Questions 37 to 40) 33-30,33
    Therapeutic drug monitoring (See Question 38) ... 33-31
  Tacrolimus 33-7
    Mechanisms of action 33-8
    Indications (See Question 46) 33-35
    Pharmacokinetics (See Question 46) 33-35
    Dosing (See Question 47) 33-36
    Adverse effects (See Question 48) 33-36
    Therapeutic drug monitoring (See Question 47) ... 33-36
  Antithymocyte Globulin 33-8
    Dosing and administration (See Question 49) 33-37
    Duration of therapy 33-37
    Adverse effects 33-37
    Monitoring 33-37
  Murine Monoclonal Antibody (OKT3) 33-8
    Mechanisms of action 33-8
    Pharmacokinetics 33-8
    Use in liver transplants (See Question 41) 33-33
    Adverse effects (See Question 42) 33-33
    Dosing (See Question 43) 33-34
  Investigational Agents 33-9
Surgical Transplantation Procedures 33-9
  Cardiac Transplantation 33-9
  Renal Transplantation 33-9
  Liver Transplantation (See Figure 33.6) 33-9
  Lung Transplantation 33-10
  Pancreas Transplantation (See Figure 33.7) 33-10
Organ Procurement, Preservation, and
  Distribution 33-10
  Donor Criteria (See Tables 33.2 and 33.3) 33-10
  Organ Preservation in Donor 33-10
  Organ Preservation Solutions 33-12
  Organ Distribution 33-12
Kidney Transplantation 33-12
  Indication and Evaluation 33-12

  Donor and Recipient Matching 33-13
  Combination Immunosuppressive Therapy
    (See Table 33.4) 33-13
  Postoperative Course and Delayed Graft Function ... 33-15
  Sequential and Induction Therapy 33-15
  Rejection 33-15
    Hyperacute rejection 33-15
    Accelerated rejection 33-16
    Acute rejection 33-16
    Vascular rejection 33-16
  Chronic Rejection 33-16
  Acute Rejection Treatment 33-16
  Kidney Rejection Versus Cyclosporine
    Nephrotoxicity 33-17
Heart Transplantation 33-18
  Indications 33-18
  Inotropic and Chronotropic Support 33-19
  Sinus Node Dysfunction 33-19
  Cardiac Denervation 33-20
  Immunosuppression 33-20
  Acute or Chronic Rejection 33-20
  Treatment of Acute Rejection 33-21
  Post-Transplant Hypertension 33-22
  Post-Transplant Hyperlipidemia 33-23
  Corticosteroid Withdrawal 33-23
Lung Transplantation 33-23
  Indications (See Table 33.7) 33-23
  Early Postoperative Complications 33-24
  Management of Complications 33-24
    Pulmonary edema 33-24
    Infection 33-24
    Acute rejection 33-25
    Bronchiolitis obliterans 33-25
    Pain 33-25
    Gastrointestinal 33-25
    Glucose 33-25
    Renal dysfunction 33-25
    Cyclosporine bioavailability (See Table 33.8) 33-26
    Cyclosporine drug interactions
      (See Tables 33.5 and 33.6) 33-26
    Secondary malignancy 33-27
      Post-transplant lymphoproliferative
        disorder (PTLD) 33-27
        Risk factors 33-27
        Clinical presentation 33-28
        Treatment and outcomes 33-28
Liver Transplantation 33-28
  Indications 33-28
  Pediatric Indications 33-29
  Pain Management 33-29
  Patient Monitoring 33-30
  Primary Graft Nonfunction 33-30
  Central Nervous System Disturbances 33-30
  Cyclosporine 33-31
    Absorption 33-31
    Therapeutic drug monitoring 33-31

(Continued)

Rejection 33-32
  Acute 33-33
  Chronic 33-33
Treatment of Rejection 33-33
OKT3 33-33
  Adverse effects (See Table 33.9) 33-33
  Dosing 33-34
    Protocol 33-34
  Antibodies to OKT3 33-34
Corticosteroid Adverse Effects 33-34
Tacrolimus (Formerly FK506) 33-35
  Indications 33-35
  Pharmacokinetics 33-36
  Dosing 33-36
  Adverse effects 33-36
  Therapeutic drug monitoring 33-36
Antilymphocyte Globulin (ALG) and
  Antithymocyte Globulin (ATG) 33-37
  Dosing and administration 33-37
  Duration of therapy 33-37
  Adverse effects 33-37
  Monitoring 33-37
Azathioprine 33-37
  Adverse effects 33-37

Complication of Leukopenia 33-38
Infection 33-38
Prophylaxis (See Table 33.10) 33-38
Cytomegalovirus (CMV) 33-39
  Etiology 33-39
  Diagnosis 33-40
  Clinical manifestations 33-40
  Treatment 33-40
    Ganciclovir 33-40
    Foscarnet 33-40
    Immune globulins 33-40
  Dosing 33-40
    Ganciclovir 33-40
    Foscarnet 33-40
    Immune globulins 33-40
  Monitoring 33-40
    Ganciclovir 33-40
    Foscarnet 33-41
    Immune globulins 33-41
  Prophylaxis 33-41
    Acyclovir 33-41
    Ganciclovir 33-41
    Immune globulins 33-41

Solid organ transplant has become the therapy of choice for patients with end-stage heart, liver, lung, and kidney disease. One-year patient survival for these major organs is about 80% to 90%, and one-year graft survival is approaching this figure as well. Pancreas or combined pancreas-kidney transplantation now is available as a treatment for diabetics with end-stage renal failure. Pediatric and elderly patients now can be transplant candidates and the pool of potential recipients has expanded as a result. Additionally, the number of small bowel transplantations continues to grow. New surgical techniques with *multiorgan* transplantation (e.g., heart with lung, liver, or kidney), pancreatic and liver *islet cell* transplantation, *living-segmental* human organ transplantation (kidney, liver, lung, pancreas), *xenotransplantation* (transplantation of an organ of animal species such as pig into human), and with *cardiomyoplasty* transplantation (autotransplant of large skeletal muscle used in place of heart) along with improvements in *mechanical assist devices* (e.g., for heart and liver transplant candidates) have made the transplantation of organs an increasingly viable treatment option.

In the 1940s, organized programs were developed to study human organ transplantation and the first successful human kidney transplantation was performed about a decade later. Drugs such as azathioprine, prednisone, and antilymphocyte serum and antilymphocyte globulin (ALG) during the 1960s made possible the success of kidney transplantation. In the late 1970s, the introduction of cyclosporine created a new era in solid organ transplantation, and in the 1980s the first monoclonal antibody approved for human use, OKT3, was introduced.[1,2]

The development and success of drugs such as cyclosporine and OKT3 has brought about the beginning of a new era in drug therapy for transplantation and other immune-related diseases. New monoclonal antibodies and drugs such as tacrolimus (formerly FK506), rapamycin, and deoxyspergualin should provide more specific and selective therapies for solid organ transplantation over the next decade.

As a result of the success in human transplantation, the number of transplants (see Figure 33.1), as well as the number of centers performing transplants, continues to grow.[3] The numbers, however, have leveled off for some organs because of the limited availability of organ donors. As a result, the waiting lists are longer. The success of organ transplant programs has led to a number of ethical and quality of life issues. Although transplantation has had a significant positive impact on the quality of life in most patients with end-stage disease, issues such as retransplantation, donation source (living-related and unrelated, neonatal organs, animal organs), and costs to individuals, insurers, and society continue to be discussed with vigor. Costs during the initial transplantation period range from $30,000 for kidney transplants up to $250,000 for heart, liver, or lung transplants. Additionally, routine follow-up monitoring and drug therapy for the first year can be $5000 to $40,000 a year.

The ultimate goal of immunosuppressive therapy is to prevent organ rejection and prolong graft and patient survival. Short-term (i.e., one- to two-year) survival after transplantation has improved dramatically, and although long-term survival also is higher, the rate per year of decline, often referred to as half-life, has been held exponentially constant.[4] The current immunosuppressive regimens have not produced a permanent state of tolerance (i.e., when the transplanted organ is seen as ''self''). Since patients now are living longer, the focus of therapy will shift towards long-term survival and management of long-term complications. Meanwhile, scientific discoveries will continue to allow more patients to experience successful transplants and the acute management of these patients will improve as well. The current drug therapies are associated with significant complications and graft loss secondary to infection, malignancy, and noncompliance: acute and chronic rejection still are significant problems. The search for safer and more effective immunosuppressive regimens continues, along with a better understanding of long-term immunosuppression. This chapter will address the immunology of transplantation and rejection, criteria for organ procurement and preservation, indications for solid organ transplantation, appropriate use of immunosuppressive agents, and the management of postoperative and long-term complications in the patient who receives a solid organ transplant. A number of these are very similar for the various types of solid organ transplants, yet at the same time there can be significant differences. This chapter will address some of these differences and similarities as they relate to kidney, liver, heart, and lung transplantation.

Fig 33.1 Solid Organ Transplant Activity in the U.S. 1981 and 1988–1993. Data obtained from reference 3. Kidney transplants = 10 × Bar value.

Transplant Immunology

The success of organ transplantation is a result of a better understanding and melding of pharmacology, microbiology, molecular and cellular biochemistry, genetics, and immunology. Suppression of the host's immune system and prevention of rejection are vital for host acceptance of the transplanted organ. The ultimate goal is to provide an environment of permanent acceptance or tolerance, where the new organ is seen as "self" by the host's immune system. The currently used immunosuppressive drugs provide a nonpermanent form of tolerance. A basic understanding of the immune system and the mechanisms of rejection is necessary to effectively use immunosuppressive drugs in organ transplantation.

Major Histocompatibility Complex (MHC) and Human Leukocyte Antigen (HLA)

The degree to which allogeneic grafting (i.e., a transplanted organ from a genetically different donor of the same species) is successful depends upon the genetic similarities or differences between the organ of the donor and the immune system of the recipient. The recipient recognizes the transplanted graft as either self or foreign. This recognition is based upon the host's reaction to alloantigens (i.e., substances that initiate an immune response which can lead to rejection of the transplanted organ). These substances also are known as histocompatibility antigens and play a very important role in organ transplantation. Another group of substances that also plays an important role is the ABO blood group system of red blood cells. The donor and recipient must be ABO-compatible otherwise immediate graft destruction occurs because of antibodies directed against the ABO antigens.[5]

Histocompatibility antigens are glycoproteins that are located on the surface of cell membranes.[6] These are encoded by the major histocompatibility complex genes located on the short arm of chromosome 6 (see Figure 33.2). In humans, the MHC is called the human leukocyte antigen. The gene products encoded on the HLA are divided into classes I, II, and III based upon their tissue distribution, antigen structure, and function. Class I antigens (HLA-A, HLA-B, and HLA-C) are present on all nucleated cell surfaces and are the primary targets for cytotoxic T-lymphocyte reactions against transplanted cells and tissues. Class I antigens are composed of a heavy polypeptide chain (alpha) that is associated noncovalently with a β_2-microglobulin (light polypeptide chain). Class II antigens occur in clusters with one or more alpha chains that are associated with one or more beta chains. The three class II antigens (HLA-DR, HLA-DQ, HLA-DP) have a more limited distribution and are found on macrophages, B-lymphocytes, monocytes, activated T-lymphocytes, dendritic cells, and some endothelial cells, all of which can act as antigen-presenting cells (APC). Individual HLA loci are extensively polymorphic. Each individual possesses two A, B, and DR antigens, one from each parent. This is called a haplotype. Recognition of this polymorphic loci by host T-lymphocytes appears to account for rejection events seen *in vivo*. Class III antigens (C4, C2, and Bf) are part of the complement system and do not play a specific role in the graft rejection process.[7,8]

Rejection of a transplanted organ is the outcome of the natural response of the immune system to a foreign substance and is a complex process in which our understanding continues to evolve. This process, in some cases, segmental and simultaneous, involves an array of interactions between foreign antigens, T-lymphocytes, macrophages, cytokines (soluble mediators secreted by lymphocytes, also called lymphokines, interleukins), adhesion molecules

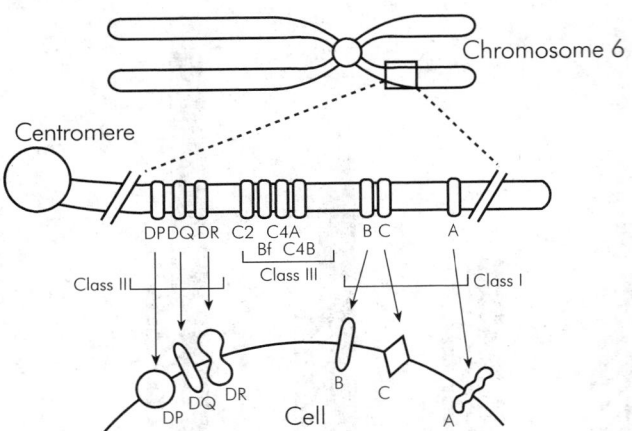

Fig 33.2   Major Histocompatibility Complex on Chromosome 6   Reproduced with permission from reference 8.

(membrane proteins expressed on a wide variety of cells which enhance binding of T-cells) and B-lymphocytes. This process of organ rejection ultimately can involve all elements of the immune response (see Figure 33.3); however, it is highly T-cell-dependent. This reaction can be divided into several steps which include antigen presentation as well as T-cell recognition, activation, proliferation, and differentiation.

In order for foreign antigen to interact with recipient T-cells and B-cells, they must be prepared for presentation by antigen-presenting cells. These APCs (see Figure 33.3) usually are recipient macrophages, although donor cells, referred to as dendritic cells or passenger leukocytes and graft endothelial cells, also can serve as APCs. This phase takes place within the blood, lymph nodes, spleen, and within the transplanted organ.

The next step involves T-cell recognition of the HLA molecules presented on the surface of the APC. The primary site for this to occur is at the CD3/T-cell receptor complex on T-lymphocytes. These T-lymphocytes also express other molecules [clusters of differentiation (CD)] on their surfaces which along with CD3 recognize and respond to different types of antigens. These T-cells are known as CD4+ cells (TH or helper/inducer T-cells) and CD8+ cells (TC or cytotoxic/suppressor T-cells). CD4+ cells interact with class II antigens. CD8+ cells interact with class I antigens. In addition, proteins known as adhesion molecules (e.g., ICAM-1, LFA-1), expressed on the surface of T-cells and APCs promote T-cell signaling and activation.[9]

Once recognition occurs, T-cell activation and proliferation are initiated. TH cells produce and secrete cytokines (e.g., interleukin-2 and interferon-γ) after interaction with class II antigens and stimulation from interleukin-1 secreted from macrophages. TH cells, along with TC cells, are stimulated to express cell surface receptors specific for interleukin-2 (IL-2R). Once the TC cells express IL-2R, they are stimulated to proliferate with the further stimulation from TH cell secreted IL-2. These committed TC cells bind directly to allogeneic cells and result in cell lysis. TH-secreted cytokines lead to the recruitment of other T-cells which results in further cytotoxicity. During this process, TH cells also produce other cytokines, such as interleukin-4, -5, -6, and tumor necrosis factor (TNF) which leads to a cascade of events involving B-cells and antibody production, complement fixation, increased macrophage infiltration, fibrin deposition, platelet activation and release, prostaglandin release, and inflammatory response at the graft site. These delayed-type hypersensitivity and humoral responses occur in conjunction with one another, and are not mutually exclusive. This results in cellular and tissue graft destruction. (See Figure 33.3.)

The antibodies produced by plasma cells, which are transformed B-cells under the influence of interleukin-4, will bind to the target antigenic cells. This will lead to local deposition of complement and result in immune-complexation and injury to the graft (complement mediated cell lysis). The newly formed antibodies will cause a series of interactions to occur with T-cells which lead to cytotoxicity (antibody-dependent, cell-mediated cytotoxicity). As a result of these cell-mediated and humoral immunologic events, organ function can be impaired significantly, and without any therapeutic intervention, complete organ graft dysfunction may occur.[7]

Under certain circumstances, which are not clear, the TC cells can actually down-regulate the immune response to alloantigen. These cells are known as suppressor T-cells and express CD8+. These cells, when present in significant quantities, appear to be associated with prolonged graft survival. With some immunosuppressive agents, these T-cells may play a role in their effectiveness.[11]

Human Leukocyte Antigen Typing

The genetic compatibility between donor and recipient can have an impact on graft survival. For example, in kidney transplantation, the closer the HLA matching is between recipient and donor, the better the outcome, particularly long-term.[12,13] In addition, the presence of preformed antibodies to donor HLA can result in immediate graft loss.[14] A number of laboratory tests, including serologic, cytometric, genetic, and cellular assessments of donor and recipient serum and lymphocytes, are needed before the transplantation of an organ. This process is referred to as tissue typing.[15]

Lymphocytes are typed for HLA-A, -B, and -DR. Typing for HLA is performed using the lymphocytotoxicity assay. Donor or recipient lymphocytes are added to antisera, obtained from multiparous women who have antibodies to known HLA types. These lymphocytes and antisera are incubated in the presence of complement. Antibodies will react with certain antigens present on lymphocytes, whereby killing of these lymphocytes occurs. Based

Fig 33.3   Activation of the Acute Rejection Response   Reproduced with permission from reference 10.

Table 33.1	Immunosuppressive Agents		
Drug	Dosage Form	Usual Dose[a]	Cost ($)[b]
Azathioprine (Imuran)	50 mg tab 100 mg injectable	1–3 mg/kg/day	84.63/100 tab 61.70/100 mg vial
Antithymocyte globulin (Atgam)	50 mg IgG/mL	10–20 mg/kg/day	209.79/5 mL
Cyclosporine (Sandimmune)	100 mg/mL oral solution 100 mg cap 25 mg cap 50 mg/mL IV solution	5–10 mg/kg/dose 5–10 mg/kg/dose 5–10 mg/kg/dose 1.5–2.5 mg/kg/dose	199.65/50 mL 119.86/30 29.99/30 17.8/5 mL
Prednisone (various)	1, 2.5, 5, 10, 20, 50 mg tab	5–20 mg/day	1.21/100 5 mg tab
Methylprednisolone sodium succinate (various)	40, 125, 500 mg 1, 2 gm injectable	10–1000 mg/dose	3.09/500 mg
Prednisolone	5 mg tab 20 mg/mL injectable	5–20 mg/day 10–1000 mg/dose	1.62/5 mg tab 27.52/5 mL
Tacrolimus	1 mg cap 5 mg cap	0.15–0.3 mg/kg/day	207.00/100 cap 1,038.64/100 cap
OKT3 (Orthoclone)	5 mg/5 mL injectable	2.5–5 mg/dose	505.00/5 mg

[a] Usual dose is highly variable and depends upon the transplanted organ and the transplant center.
[b] Acquisition cost of University of North Carolina Hospitals in 1994.

upon the percentage of killed cells, the specific HLA types for both donor and recipient can be determined. This indicates their genetic compatibility.

Blood also is crossmatched to determine the presence of preformed antibodies in the recipient's serum to the donor's lymphocytes. A positive crossmatch would indicate the presence of recipient antibodies.

In solid organ transplantation, this positive crossmatch would be considered a contraindication.[14] In liver transplantation, a positive crossmatch is not an absolute contraindication because of the urgency of the need and the liver appears to be more resistant immunologically to this type of reaction.[16] More recent data, however, suggest that liver transplantation patients can have complications post-transplantation.[17]

The panel reactive antibodies (PRA) test also is commonly used to assess organ compatibility because recipients may have HLA antibodies from previous exposure to antigenic stimuli (e.g., blood transfusions, previous transplant, pregnancy). In this test, the recipient's serum is tested against a cell panel of known HLA specificities that are representative of possible donors in the general population. The potential recipient with a high percentage of panel reactive antibodies is at higher risk for rejection.

ABO blood typing is one of the most critical of all evaluations when determining the genetic compatibility for all solid organ transplants. Transplantation of an organ with ABO incompatibility would result in hyperacute rejection and destruction of the graft.[14]

Immunosuppressive Agents

Improved and increased experience with surgical techniques, better postoperative care, and better immunosuppressive agents also have played significant roles in the success of organ transplantation. The use of these immunosuppressives, based upon a better understanding of their mechanisms of action and the mechanisms of rejection, has had the most significant impact on patient graft survival. The number of currently approved immunosuppressives is small (see Table 33.1); however; a significant number of newly developed, more selective immunosuppressives are under investigation. Sites of action of the currently used agents, along with some of the investigational agents, are represented in Figures 33.4 and 33.5.

Azathioprine

Azathioprine (Imuran) was developed in the 1950s in an attempt to prevent the metabolic degradation of 6-mercaptopurine (6-MP). Azathioprine and 6-MP are purine antagonist antimetabolites. Although azathioprine is a prodrug of 6-MP, it has a lower incidence of toxicity with equivalent *in vivo* immunosuppressive doses, and a lower dose of azathioprine produces a similar immunosuppressive effect.[18,19] Azathioprine has been a part of immunosuppressive protocols for the last 30 years; however, the introduction of cyclosporine has led to a reduction of azathioprine dosage or elimination of its use altogether in some protocols.[20]

Mechanism of Action

Azathioprine, considered a nonspecific immunosuppressive, affects both cell-mediated (i.e., T-cell) and humoral-directed (i.e., B-cell) immune responses. However, azathioprine is more specific for T-cells than B-cells.[21] It inhibits the early stages of cell differentiation and proliferation. Therefore, azathioprine is useful in the prevention of rejection and ineffective for the treatment of acute rejection.

The immunosuppressive activity of azathioprine apparently depends upon the intracellular formation of thioguanine nucleotides (TGNs), which by being incorporated into DNA and RNA, interferes with their synthesis. These active metabolites are formed when 6-MP is intracellularly converted by hypoxanthine phosphoribosyl transferase (HPRT) to thioinosinic acid and then to thioguanine nucleotides. It is postulated that 6-MP has two separate immunosuppressive effects: inhibition of cellular proliferation and cytotoxicity. A decrease in the levels of intracellular purine ribonucleotides decreases cellular proliferation, and incorporation of TGN into DNA mediates cytotoxicity.[22,23]

Pharmacokinetics

Azathioprine can be given intravenously or orally. Oral absorption is rapid but incomplete. Since the mean bioavailability of azathioprine in renal transplant patients is approximately 40% to 60%, one would expect oral (PO) doses to be twice the intravenous (IV) dose.[24,25] Nevertheless, oral doses usually are not doubled when converting from the intravenous to the oral route. The clinical significance of not taking this into consideration has not been deter-

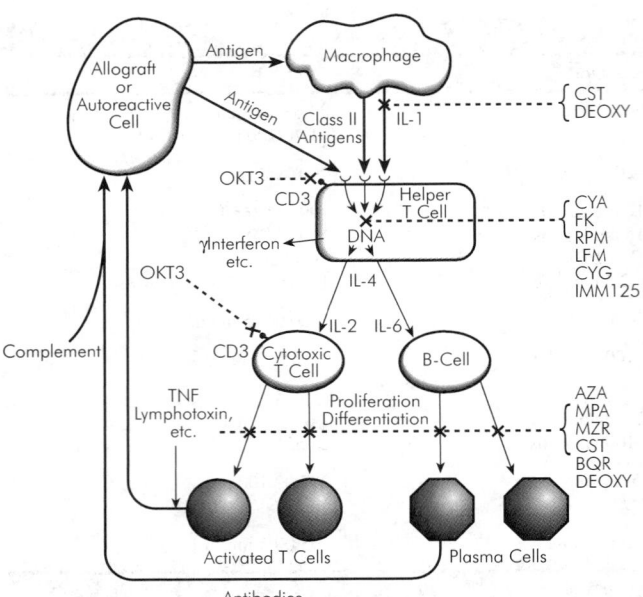

Fig 33.4 Schematic Representation Summarizing the Mechanisms of Action of Approved and Investigational Immunosuppressive Agents
Adapted from and reproduced with permission from reference 78. AZA = Azathioprine; BQR = Brequinar; CD = Cluster of differentiation; CST = Corticosteroids; CYA = Cyclosporine; CYG = Cyclosporine G; DEOXY = Deoxyspergualin; FK = Tacrolimus; IL = Interleukin; IMM125 = Sandoz IMM125; LFM = Leflunomide; MPA = Mycophenolic acid; MZR = Mizoribine; RPM = Rapamycin; TNF = Tumor necrosis factor.

mined. Renal transplants studied during the initial postoperative period after receiving oral azathioprine demonstrated a threefold to fourfold intrapatient variability in day-to-day 6-MP area under the concentration-time curve (AUC).[26]

The metabolism of azathioprine to 6-MP within 5 to 15 minutes of an azathioprine dose makes the calculation of pharmacokinetic values difficult. The half-lives for azathioprine and 6-MP are estimated to be 10 to 12 minutes and 40 to 60 minutes, respectively.[24] Major metabolic conversion of azathioprine to 6-MP is via nucleophilic attack by glutathione. The liver and red blood cells are thought to be major tissue sites for this metabolic conversion.[18] The 6-MP formed by this reaction can be metabolized further to thiopurine ribonucleosides and ribonucleotides. Azathioprine pharmacokinetics are not affected by renal dysfunction.[27] Azathioprine's immunosuppressive activity in patients with severe hepatic dysfunction, however, is absent.[28] The possible decreased biotransformation of azathioprine into active metabolites in patients with severe hepatic dysfunction could be a factor in liver transplant recipients with severe rejection or nonfunctional transplanted grafts.

Corticosteroids

Prednisone and methylprednisolone, synthetic analogues of hydrocortisone, are the primary corticosteroids used to prevent and treat rejection of transplanted organs.

Mechanisms of Action

Corticosteroids have multiple effects on most cells and tissues of the body, but it is their anti-inflammatory and immunosuppressive properties that serve as the basis for their use in organ transplant patients. These effects are exerted through specific intracellular glucocorticoid receptors. The corticosteroids bind with these receptors and interfere with the transcription of specific genes such that cell function is altered, resulting in suppression or activation of gene transcription. Corticosteroids also affect RNA translation, protein synthesis, and secretion of cytokines and proteins.[29]

The corticosteroids affect most cells and substances associated with acute allograft rejection and inflammatory reactions. They inhibit accumulation of leukocytes at sites of inflammation; inhibit macrophage functions including migration and phagocytosis; inhibit expression of Class II MHC antigens induced by interferon-γ; block release of IL-1, IL-6, and TNF;[30] inhibit the upregulation and expression of adhesion molecules and neutrophil adhesion to endothelial cells; inhibit secretion of complement protein C3; inhibit phospholipase A_2 activity; and decrease production of prostaglandins.[29]

Corticosteroids, even after a single dose, cause marked lymphocytopenia by redistribution of circulating lymphocytes to other lymphoid tissues such as the bone marrow rather than by cell lysis.[31] They inhibit a number of events associated with T-cell activation. They decrease IL-2 production and interfere with the action of IL-2 on activated T-cells[32] resulting in the inhibition of helper and suppressor T-cell function.[33] Corticosteroids also inhibit secretion of IL-3, -4, -6, and interferon-γ by activated T-cells. Moderate- to high-dose corticosteroids also inhibit cytotoxic T-cell function by inhibiting cytokine production and lysis of T-cells.[34] They can inhibit early proliferation of B-cells, but corticosteroids have a minimal effect on activated B-cells and immunoglobulin-secreting plasma cells.[35]

Pharmacokinetics

The plasma half-lives of prednisone and methylprednisolone are much shorter than their biological half-lives. Prednisone is a prodrug and rapidly converted to its active form, prednisolone. Bioavailability in transplant recipients is rapid and complete and similar to healthy subjects.[36] In transplant patients, plasma half-lives are approximately two and one-half to four hours for prednisolone[36] and methylprednisolone.[37] Prednisolone is metabolized extensively and can be converted back to prednisone. The volume of distribution and clearance of both prednisolone and methylprednisolone varies significantly. Prednisolone and methylprednisolone are 70% to 90% protein-bound. Clearance of the unbound fraction is reduced in renal and liver transplant patients.[38] Since these agents usually are given in fixed doses with little regard for pharmacokinetic differences, the relationship between pharmacokinetic parameters to efficacy and toxicity should be considered. For example, renal transplant patients who had higher prednisolone clearances had a higher prevalence of graft loss caused by acute rejection, although there was no difference in the rate of rejection when this group of patients was compared to a group of patients with lower clearances.[39] Furthermore, studies of the relationship between pharmacokinetic changes and side effects in cushingoid and noncushingoid transplant patients have shown conflicting results.[40,41] One of these studies noted that 60% of patients in the low clearance group developed severe steroid-associated complications compared to 30% in the high clearance group.[39] In another study, six black renal transplant patients had lower methylprednisolone clearances compared to six white patients.[42] Clinical applicability of these findings needs to be evaluated further.

Since the pharmacological effects of corticosteroids are unrelated to plasma half-life when given on a daily basis, other markers such as cortisol AUC or return of cortisol AUC are being explored to identify patients who are most likely to develop acute rejection or side effects from the corticosteroids.[37,43] Serum cortisol concentrations have been associated with acute rejection and infection. In one study, patients who had early morning cortisol levels greater than 4 μg/mL while on prednisolone were more likely to experience an episode of rejection than those with lower levels.[43] The corticosteroids have different *in vitro* antilymphocyte potency in renal transplant patients and the selection of a particular cortico-

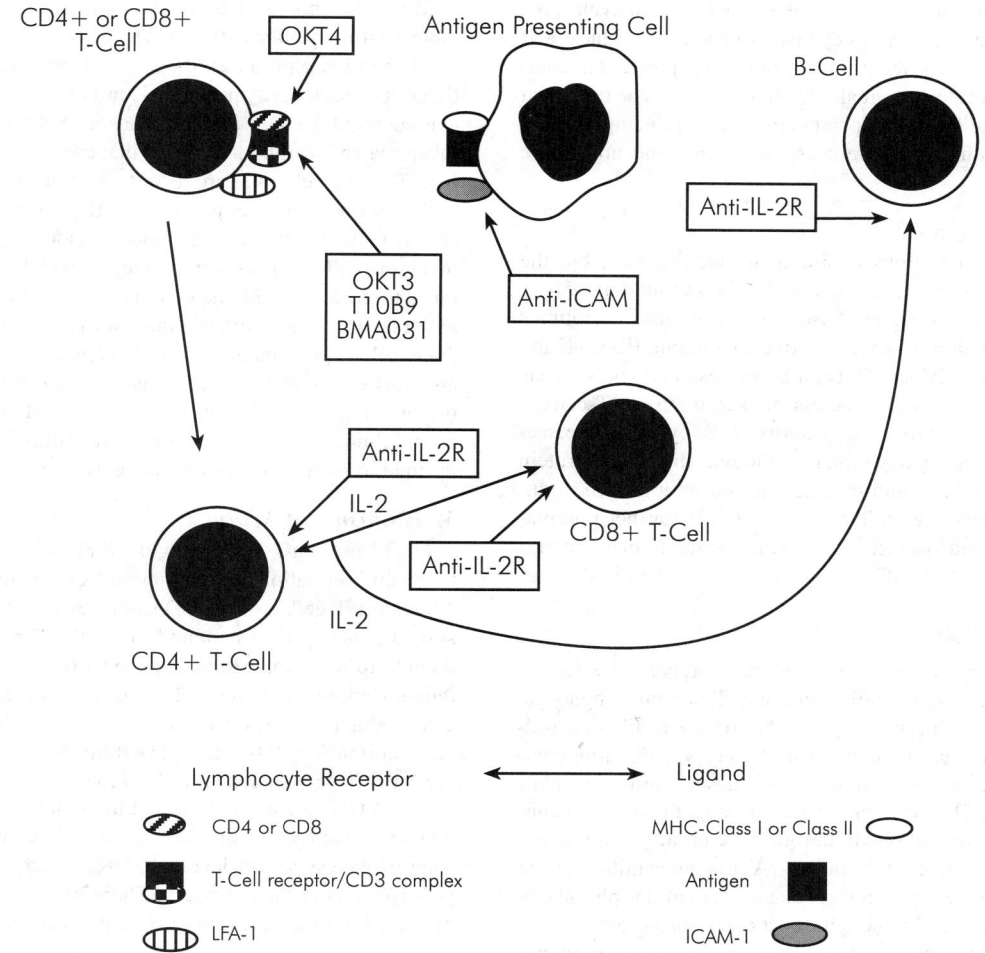

Fig 33.5   Proposed Sites of Action of Monoclonal Antibodies Under Investigation and Those Currently Used in Clinical Transplantation   Reproduced with permission from reference 67. ICAM = Intracellular adhesion molecule; IL-2 = Interleukin-2; IL-2R = Interleukin-2 receptor.

steroid potentially could be based upon this assessment.[44] These approaches, however, will require further investigation.

Cyclosporine

The introduction of cyclosporine as an immunosuppressive agent has been the single most important factor in the current success of organ transplantation. Its use has led to increased patient and graft survival, reduced morbidity associated with rejection and infection, and has extended the types and numbers of organ transplantations performed.[45] In contrast to azathioprine and corticosteroids, cyclosporine has relatively nonmyelotoxic, immunosuppressive effects. It is considered the prototype for a new group of immunosuppressives undergoing development and investigation.

Cyclosporine is an 11 amino acid undecapeptide metabolite extracted from a soil fungus, *Tolypocladium inflatum gams*. The drug is relatively insoluble in water but is highly lipid soluble. Its immunosuppressive activity is associated with amino acids in positions 1, 2, 3, 9, 10, and 11 which form a hydrophilic site on the surface of the cyclosporine molecule.[46]

Mechanisms of Action

The activity of cyclosporine is mediated through a reversible inhibition of T-cell function,[46] particularly T-helper cells. It inhibits the synthesis of interleukin-2 (IL-2) and other cytokines, including interferon-γ. These actions result in an inhibition of the early events of T-cell activation, sensitization, and proliferation.

Cyclosporine has little effect on activated mature cytotoxic T-cells; therefore, it has little utility in the treatment of acute rejection.[45,47] Its site of action is within the cytoplasm of T-cells after antigenic recognition and signaling occurs. Cyclosporine binds to an intracellular protein (immunophilin) called cyclophilin. Although binding to cyclophilin is required, it is not sufficient for immunosuppression. This cyclosporine-cyclophilin complex binds to a protein phosphatase, calcineurin. The binding of this complex to calcineurin is thought to prevent activation of nuclear factors involved in the gene transcription for IL-2 and other cytokines.[47,48] Also, cyclosporine, because of this inhibition, will indirectly impair the activity of other cells, macrophages, monocytes, and B-cells in the immune response. Cyclosporine has no effect on hematopoietic cells or neutrophils.[49] Cyclosporine is metabolized extensively in the liver to more than 25 metabolites. Two of these metabolites, AM1 (formerly M17) and AM9 (formerly M1), can elicit an *in vitro* immunosuppressive effect but have much lower activity than cyclosporine.[50] Investigations continue in assessing the role of these metabolites in the development of toxicity with cyclosporine.[51] The pharmacokinetic properties of cyclosporine are presented in Questions 37 to 40.

Tacrolimus (Formerly FK506)

Tacrolimus, a new and potent selective immunosuppressive, is isolated from a soil fungus, *Streptomyces tsukubaensis*. Tacrolimus is a macrolide with a different molecular structure than cyclosporine. Tacrolimus is as effective as cyclosporine in liver, kidney, and lung transplant patients as the primary immunosuppressant in combination with corticosteroids. It also is effective as rescue treatment in liver, kidney, and heart transplant patients experiencing acute or chronic rejection due to failure of standard immunosuppressive therapy.[52]

Mechanisms of Action

The activity of tacrolimus is similar to cyclosporine, but the concentrations of tacrolimus needed to inhibit production of IL-2 are 10 to 100 times lower than those of cyclosporine. Tacrolimus also inhibits production of other cytokines, including IL-3, -4, and interferon-γ. It has variable effects on B-cell response and also has anti-inflammatory effects. The action of tacrolimus on T-cells is more difficult to reverse than cyclosporine. Like cyclosporine, tacrolimus binds to an intracellular, although different, protein (FKBP) which interacts with calcineurin and inhibits gene transcription and interferes with T-cell activation.[52] Further pharmacological and pharmacokinetic descriptions of tacrolimus are presented in Questions 46 to 48.

Antithymocyte Globulin

Before the advent of monoclonal antibody preparations for the prevention and treatment of rejection, polyclonal antilymphocyte preparations such as antilymphocyte globulin were available. Products most commonly used today are antithymocyte globulin, commonly referred to as ATG (Atgam) and Minnesota antilymphoblast globulin (mALG). The latter product is investigational and manufactured at the University of Minnesota but currently is not available. Rabbit antithymocyte globulin (rATG) and antithymocyte serum (ATS) are investigational products with similar pharmacological effects as ATG,[53] although direct comparisons are limited. These products are used as prophylactic or induction immunosuppressive agents or as a treatment for acute graft rejection, particularly in patients who are corticosteroid-resistant.

ATG preparations made in horses, rabbits, goats, or sheep also have been synthesized for investigational study; however, the following discussion will be limited to the products produced in horses. Regardless of the species from which ATG, ATS, or ALG are formed, all have similar pharmacological effects;[53] however, potency and antibody specificity of these products vary from batch to batch.[54,55]

The production of polyclonal equine antibody begins with the injection of horses with homogenized human spleen or thymus preparations. This injection induces an immune response in the horses directed against human T-lymphocytes; serum then is collected from the horses and purified. This process results in the production of antibodies in addition to those directed against T-cells. ATG binds to all normal blood mononuclear cells in addition to T- and B-lymphocytes; and treatment with ATG depletes lymphocytes, platelets, and granulocytes from the peripheral circulation.[56] The mechanism of action of ATG is thought to be linked to lysis of peripheral lymphocytes, uptake of lymphocytes by the reticuloendothelial system, and masking of lymphocyte receptors. The clinical use of ATG is described further in Question 49.

Murine Monoclonal Antibody (OKT3)

Muromonab-CD3 (Orthoclone OKT3), the first therapeutic murine monoclonal antibody produced for use in humans, was developed as a means of suppressing T-cell mediated rejection. It is used for (prophylaxis) induction therapy or for treatment of acute graft rejection.[57]

Murine monoclonal antibodies are formed by immunizing a mouse with a specific antigen (in this case, human T-lymphocytes). After the mouse produces B-lymphocytes against the injected antigen, it is sacrificed and the spleen is removed. All the lymphocytes derived from the spleen are suspended and mixed with mouse myeloma cells, a tumor cell line that can grow indefinitely in culture. The two cell types are mixed with polyethylene glycol (PEG) which allows the cells to fuse together. This mixture of mouse spleen cells, myeloma cells, and hybridomas (fused spleen and myeloma cells) is grown in a medium which allows only hybridomas to grow. Hybridoma colonies that are producing the desired antibody are cloned, and the antibodies they produce are harvested from cell supernatants. Another method used to produce large amounts of monoclonal antibody is to inject the appropriate hybridoma into the peritoneum of a mouse. After 10 to 21 days, the ascitic fluid, which contains secreted antibodies, is harvested and purified to obtain the desired monoclonal antibody.[58]

Mechanisms of Action

OKT3 is an IgG_{2a} immunoglobulin that binds to the CD3 (cluster of differentiation 3) structure on CD3-positive T-lymphocytes. All mature T-cells express CD3 and either the CD4 or CD8 surface antigen. Once OKT3 is bound to the CD3 region of T-cells, it is thought to be opsonized and removed from the circulation by the reticuloendothelial system of the liver and the spleen. OKT3 also can modulate the antigen-recognition complex of T-cells which alters normal T-cell function. The third mechanism involves blocking killer T-cells attached to the allograft. This occurs when high levels of OKT3 are achieved and the killer T-cells are coated and rendered inactive.[57] Allograft rejection, however, has occurred in spite of excess serum levels of OKT3 and the absence of CD3 positive cells in the periphery. Therefore, a cell type not affected by OKT3 may have a role in certain rejection episodes.[59]

Pharmacokinetics

One hour after a 5 mg IV dose in adult renal transplant patients, serum OKT3 levels in one study averaged 996 ng/mL; mean levels fell to 104 ng/mL 24 hours after the dose. The decline of OKT3 serum levels of approximately 60% over the first four hours is attributed to the initial binding of OKT3 to T-cells and subsequent removal by the reticuloendothelial system. Mean trough levels of 902 ng/mL correlate well with the in vitro levels required to block T-cell killing activity. Serum levels 72 hours after the final dose of OKT3 declined to 12 ng/mL. The estimated serum half-life for OKT3 is shorter than the typical 20-day half-life observed with inert immunoglobulin in humans. This shorter half-life for OKT3 probably is the result of rapid clearance subsequent to the formation of complexes with newly formed T-lymphocytes.[60] Patients with different types of organ transplant who received OKT3 as prophylaxis or for treatment of acute rejection demonstrated trough levels greater than 800 ng/mL by day 3. This level was associated with CD3 counts less than $20/mm^3$ and an appropriate response in most patients. Patients who received a second course of OKT3 demonstrated a delay in reaching the same level, taking up to five to seven days. Several of these patients required two to three times the initial dose.[61] In a group of liver transplant recipients who received OKT3 prophylaxis, mean OKT3 trough concentrations were 576 ng/mL in the rejection group compared to 1558 ng/mL in the nonrejection group during days 6 to 9 of therapy.[62] Therefore, the use of OKT3 levels for dosage adjustment may be valuable for patients who require retreatment and for pediatric patients because of the greater need in these populations for individualized dosing.[63]

Investigational Agents

A number of agents are in various stages of development (see Figure 33.4). These include rapamycin, cyclosporine G (OG37-325), SDZ IMM125, mycophenolate mofetil (RS-61443), deoxyspergualin, brequinar, mizoribine (Bredinin), and leflunomide. These agents have more specific activity directed at T- and B-cell function.[64] Cyclosporine G and SDZ IMM125 are analogues of cyclosporine A that are inhibitors of cytokine production. Rapamycin and leflunomide are inhibitors of cytokine action. Mizoribine, mycophenolate mofetil, and brequinar are inhibitors of DNA synthesis. Deoxyspergualin inhibits cell activation and maturation.[65] In addition, a number of monoclonal antibodies have been developed and are undergoing investigation. The targets of these antibodies are antigen binding sites, adhesion molecules, and cytokines. Examples include anti-IL-2 receptor, BMA 031, anti-T12, campath-IM, anti-ICAM, T10B9, and OKT4A monoclonal antibodies.[66,67]

Surgical Transplantation Procedures

Surgical procedures used in organ transplantation are well described in other references and will not be presented in detail here. Nevertheless, a brief overview is needed because certain aspects of transplant surgical techniques affect post-transplant pharmacotherapy. Transplant operations are either heterotopic or orthotopic. In a heterotopic procedure, the donor organ or part of an organ is transplanted into a host with the original organ still in place.[68] In orthotopic procedures, the *de novo* recipient organ is removed before transplantation of the new organ. Heart, liver, and lung transplants usually involve orthotopic surgery.

Cardiac Transplantation

Cardiac transplantation involves replacement of the majority of the cardiac muscle. The donor heart is sewn to a portion of the recipient atrium and then the aorta, pulmonary artery, and pulmonary vein are joined. Once all anastomoses are formed, air is evacuated from the cardiac chambers, and the clamp is removed from the aorta. Epicardial pacing wires are placed at this time in case there is a need for chronotropic support. Spontaneous defibrillation generally occurs. One important aspect of the transplanted heart is that it is denervated; therefore, it will not feel pain or respond to drug therapy as would an innervated heart.[69]

Renal Transplantation

Renal transplantation is performed by making an incision in the lower lateral abdominal wall of the recipient. The donor renal artery is connected to the recipient internal iliac artery, and the donor renal vein is connected to the side of the external iliac vein. Drainage of urine in the recipient is accomplished by the formation of a ureteroneocystostomy in which the donor kidney is anastomosed to the recipient's bladder. In a majority of cases, the recipient's native kidneys are left intact. Kidney transplant recipients receive only one kidney.[70]

Liver Transplantation

Liver transplantation is one of the most technically difficult surgical procedures performed. The vascular anastomoses and the bile drainage are depicted in Figure 33.6. Patients with intact patent bile ducts most commonly have choledochocholedochostomy (duct-to-duct anastomosis) performed with a percutaneous T-tube drain placed at the time of bile duct reconstruction. Recipients with bile duct damage (e.g., patients with sclerosing cholangitis or children with biliary atresia) will receive a choledochojejunostomy (Roux-en-Y anastamosis). The type of surgical procedure performed can have an impact on the type of complications encountered postoperatively.[68] Drug absorption also may be variably affected by rerouting bile flow.

A

B

Fig 33.6 Commonly Employed Drainage Techniques for Orthotopic Liver Transplantation   A) Biliary tract reconstruction with choledochocholedochostomy (duct-to-duct anastomosis). A T-tube drain is placed during surgery to allow the bile to be monitored and the bile ducts to be studied radiographically after surgery. B) Biliary tract reconstruction with choledochojejunostomy using a Roux limb (Roux-en-Y anastomosis). The Roux limb is constructed by dividing the duodenum and the jejunum, closing the end of the jejunal segment, and then forming an anastomosis between the donor bile duct and the jejunal segment. Reproduced with permission from reference 68.

Lung Transplantation

Single and double lung transplantation have replaced combined heart-lung as the procedures of choice for end-stage lung disease. Heart-lung transplantation now is used for patients with primary pulmonary hypertension and Eisenmenger's syndrome. Double lung transplantation is the procedure used for septic lung disease (e.g., cystic fibrosis).

In single lung transplantation, the lung with the poorest perfusion in the recipient usually is removed before placement of the donor lung. After removal of this lung, the single lung is placed in the recipient by a left atrial anastomosis, a pulmonary artery anastomosis, and an end-to-end bronchial anastomosis. Double lung transplantation actually is two sequential single lung transplantations. While one lung is removed and replaced, the opposite lung is ventilated. Once both lungs are in place, each bronchial anastomosis is wrapped with omentum brought up from the abdomen. The omentum is used to maintain an adequate blood supply to the anastomoses, since complete revascularization is not performed with lung transplantation. Another technique used to enhance the blood supply is the telescoping bronchial anastomosis, where the smaller of the donor and recipient bronchus is placed one cartilaginous ring inside the other. Similar to heart transplantation, the transplanted lung is denervated, resulting in the loss of the cough reflex.[72]

Pancreas Transplantation

Pancreas transplantation is performed using the whole organ; however, in some cases, only the tail of the pancreas is used. Three categories of this type of transplant exist: simultaneous pancreas/kidney (SPK), pancreas after kidney (PAK), and pancreas transplant alone (PTA). One-year patient survival is no different; however, graft survival is 25% higher in the SPK group than in the PAK and PTA groups.[71] There is some controversy regarding the best way to drain the exocrine secretions of the transplanted pancreas. The exocrine function of the native pancreas is left intact along with that of the transplant pancreas which also provides endocrine function. Currently, the exocrine secretions of the pancreatic duct is managed by polymer glue injection, enteric drainage (ED), or bladder drainage (BD). Injecting the pancreatic duct with polymer eliminates exocrine function but often leads to fibrosis of the duct. Enteric drainage (i.e., exocrine secretions drained into a loop of jejunum) is more physiologic, but bacterial contamination may result. Bladder drainage (i.e., exocrine secretions drained into the bladder) is the most commonly used and the preferred technique in the U.S. (See Figure 33.7.) This technique maintains duct patency, avoids bacterial contamination, and allows for continuous monitoring of the exocrine secretions in the urine. Monitoring of these secretions (i.e., amylase) provides a way to predict pancreatic rejection episodes in combination with monitoring of renal function.[74,75]

Organ Procurement, Preservation, and Distribution

Donor Criteria

1. L.W., a 45-year-old female with a past medical history of hypertension, was found at home unresponsive and without spontaneous respirations by her husband. The Emergency Medical Service was called and resuscitated her with epinephrine and cardiopulmonary resuscitation. Upon arrival at the emergency room, she was unresponsive to verbal commands and painful stimuli. Her pupils were fixed and nonreactive to light. No gag reflex was evident. Her Glasgow Coma Scale score was 3 (scale of 3–15). Her blood pressure (BP) was 80/60 mm Hg, heart rate (HR) 86 beats/min, and temperature 36.2 °C.

An arterial blood gas (ABG) on 100% forced inspiration oxygen (FiO_2) was pH 7.35, pCO_2 27 mm Hg, pO_2 90 mm Hg. L.W. was intubated and placed on a ventilator. A head CT scan revealed a stage IV subarachnoid hemorrhage. An electroencephalogram (EEG) showed no brain wave activity. No spontaneous respirations were noted after an apnea test was performed. Based upon her family's request, she is considered for multiple organ procurement following pronouncement of brain death by the neurosurgeon. What subjective and objective data exist that make L.W. a suitable organ donor? [SI units: pCO_2 3.5 kPa; pO_2 12 kPa]

The most important requirement to qualify as an organ donor is a declaration of brain death. This must be determined and declared by a physician who is not a member of the transplant team. Criteria for the diagnosis of brain death have been established by the President's Commission for the study of Ethical Problems in Medicine and Behavioral Research.[76] These criteria are outlined in Table 33.2. These criteria have been accepted, in various forms, by all 50 United States. This diagnosis is made by determining irreversible loss of total brain function.

In L.W., subjective findings include her deep coma; unresponsiveness to auditory, ocular, or painful stimulation (low Glasgow Coma Score); lack of gag reflex; no spontaneous movements; and due to the severity of her injury, no likelihood of recovery. Objective findings include an EEG showing no brain wave activity and a failed apnea test. The apnea test is performed by providing 100% FiO_2 for ten minutes to the patient: the ventilator then is disconnected and a high flow of oxygen is provided. The patient is observed for five to ten minutes for the presence of spontaneous respirations. At that time, an ABG is drawn to document the accumulation of carbon dioxide as evidenced by a pCO_2 greater than 60 mm Hg. The absence of spontaneous respirations (apnea) also would be indicative of an irreversible loss of brain function.[77]

The criteria for determination and declaration of brain death are similar for children more than five years old. However, for younger children and infants, there is no clear consensus on these criteria, the appropriate tests, and the duration of observation necessary for the declaration of brain death.[73]

2. What other criteria are needed for L.W. to qualify as an organ donor?

Once the requirements for brain death are met, L.W.'s medical history, circumstances of death, clinical course, and organ function must be assessed carefully. L.W.'s age, blood type, body size, evidence of human immunodeficiency virus (HIV) and hepatitis, presence of active infection, malignancy, and condition of specific organs also are taken into consideration as to donor suitability. Absolute and relative contraindications to cadaveric solid organ transplantation are listed in Table 33.3; however, these can be program-specific.[79,80]

Organ Preservation in Donor

3. After admission to the intensive care unit (ICU), L.W. is started on dopamine and IV fluids to maintain an adequate BP and urine output. Over the next several hours her dopamine requirements increased from 5 to 15 µg/kg/min. Her urine output now is >400 mL/hr. Her serum potassium (K) is 2.7 mEq/L (Normal: 3.4–4.6), sodium (Na) 152 mEq/L (Normal: 135–145), CO_2 16 mEq/L (Normal: 24–30), phosphorus 7.1 mg/dL (Normal: 2.5–5.0), glucose 489 mg/dL (Normal: 65–110) and calcium (Ca) 7.6 mg/dL (Normal: 8.8–10.0). Her core temperature is 34.6 °C, BP 80/60 mm Hg, and HR 100 beats/min. What physiologic, metabolic and electrolyte abnormalities are present? What pharmacologic therapies are needed to correct them? [SI units: K 2.7 mmol/L (Normal: 3.4–4.6); Na 152 mmol/L (Normal: 135–145); CO_2 16 mmol/L (Normal: 24–30); P 2.3 mmol/L (Normal: 0.77–1.45); glucose 27.1 mmol/L (Normal: 3.9–6.1); Ca 1.91 mmol/L (Normal: 2.12–2.55)]

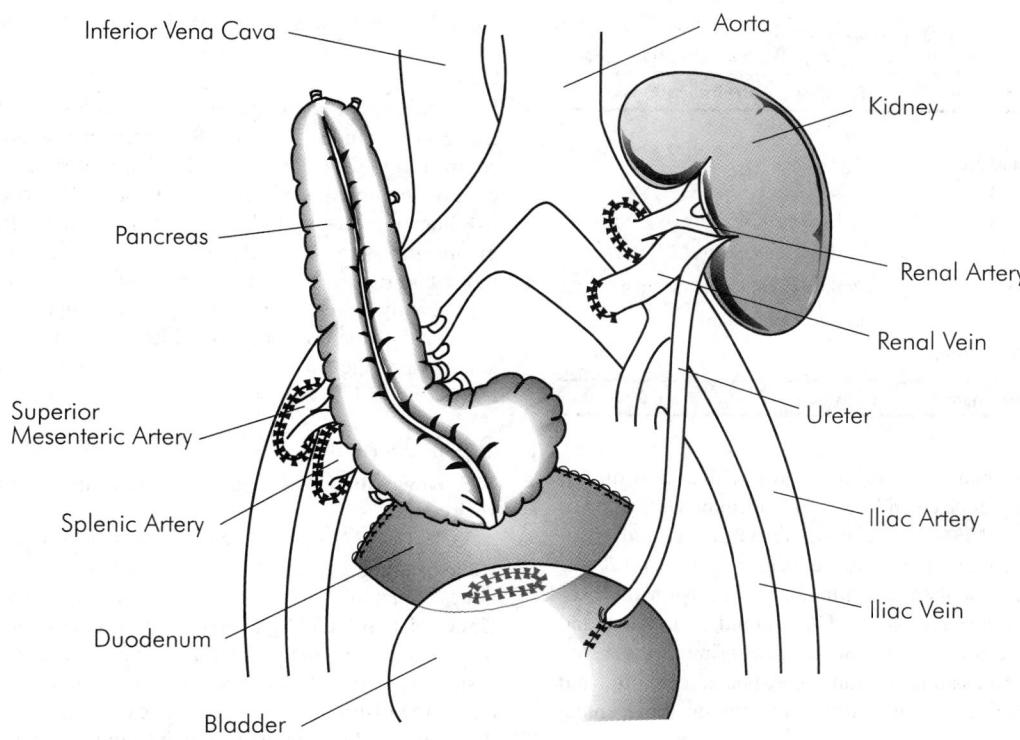

Fig 33.7 Combined Kidney-Pancreas Transplantation Employing Pancreatic Bladder Drainage Via a Duodenal Segment Adapted from reference 539.

A number of physiologic, metabolic, and electrolyte alterations are evident within a few hours to days after brain death. These alterations ultimately result in a significant deterioration in the function of all organs. Irreversible respiratory and cardiac arrest soon follow. It is imperative that all vital functions be maintained properly so that the harvested organs are in optimal condition. The major goals are to maintain oxygenation, circulation, hydration, metabolic and electrolyte homeostasis, and protection from infection.[81]

As seen in L.W., hypotension (BP 80/60 mm Hg), hypothermia (T 34.6 °C), hypernatremia (Na 152 mEq/L), hypokalemia (K 2.7 mEq/L), hyperphosphatemia (P 2.3 mEq/L), hypocalcemia (Ca 1.9 mEq/L), hyperglycemia (glucose 489 mg/dL), and diabetes insipidus commonly occur in the brain dead patient. The serum concentrations of cortisol, insulin, thyroid hormones, and catecholamines are reduced significantly after brain death; however, the serum concentrations of catecholamines initially are high.[82] The hypotension usually is managed by administering sufficient IV fluids and dopamine to maintain a systolic blood pressure greater than 90 mm Hg.

If greater than 10 µg/kg/minute of dopamine is required to manage the hypotension, dobutamine or norepinephrine infusion may be necessary; however, these should be discontinued as quickly as possible to minimize any ischemic end-organ damage from the vasoconstrictive effects of these agents.[80]

Hyperglycemia may be the result of administration of dextrose containing fluids or decreased insulin levels. The high serum concentration of glucose should be corrected to prevent dehydration, metabolic acidosis, ketosis, and osmotic diuresis that could result in further electrolyte abnormalities. A sliding-scale regular insulin administration based upon hourly blood sugar levels can be used; however, a continuous IV infusion of regular insulin at 5 U/hr often is preferred and the dose titrated to maintain a blood glucose of less than 150 mg/dL.

Electrolyte abnormalities such as altered serum concentrations of potassium, phosphorus, and calcium probably are multifactorial in origin and should be corrected with replacement therapy. The low serum concentration of bicarbonate also is the result of multiple factors and requires administration of sodium bicarbonate. One explanation for these electrolyte and other abnormalities (e.g., the high serum sodium and high urine output) in the brain dead patient is based upon the development of diabetes insipidus. In the brain dead patient, diabetes insipidus results from a deficiency of antidiuretic hormone (ADH) secondary to impairment of the hypothalamic-pituitary axis and insensitivity of the kidney to ADH. This deficiency of ADH can lead to dehydration and intravascular volume depletion. In L.W., urine output should be maintained at greater than 1 mL/kg/hr or greater than 100 mL/hr. If urine output

Table 33.2	Requirements for Establishment of Brain Death

Stem Function Evaluation
Absence of:
  Pupillary light reflex
  Corneal reflex
  Oculocephalic reflex
  Tracheobronchial reflex
  Spontaneous respiratory effort with apnea

Cerebral Function Evaluation
Absence of:
  Response to painful stimuli
  Posturing
  Seizure activity

Irreversible Condition Evaluation
Absence of:
  Intoxicating or sedating drugs
  Hypothermia
  Neuromuscular blockage
  Gross electrolyte abnormalities
  Gross endocrine disturbances

Table 33.3	Donor Contraindications to Cadaveric Solid Organ Transplantation	
Absolute Contraindications	**Relative Contraindications**	
Age >70	Age >50	
Malignancy with metastatic potential	Age <1	
Disease of primary organ	Related medical causes	
Positive HIV and HbAg[a]	Positive antihepatitis C	
Active substance abuse	Prolonged cold ischemic time	
Sepsis	Localized infection	
Prolonged warm ischemic time		

[a] HIV = Human immunodeficiency virus; HbAg = Hepatitis B antigen.

increases to greater than 4 mL/kg/hr or greater than 300 mL/hr, then urine output is replaced milliliter for milliliter with a hypotonic fluid such as 0.45% NaCl containing potassium and phosphate. If the high urine output is not reduced to 2 to 3 mL/kg/hr or to 100 to 250 mL/hr then a continuous IV infusion of vasopressin (DDAVP) at a rate of 1 to 2 U/hr should be initiated and titrated to the desired urine output. Serial monitoring of the serum concentrations of potassium, sodium, phosphate, calcium, and magnesium is required to guide further electrolyte replacement therapy.

After brain death, metabolism shifts from an aerobic to an anaerobic process, and serum concentrations of free triiodothyronine (FT_3), thyroxine (T_4) and cortisol decrease. In animals, the administration of T_3, cortisol, and insulin reversed the hemodynamic and biochemical effects associated with brain death. In humans, administration of these agents also improved hemodynamic and metabolic abnormalities and reduced dopamine requirements.[82,83] In L.W., an IV bolus of T_4, 1 μg/kg, followed by a continuous IV infusion may be given. Hydrocortisone 100 mg IV every hour for 12 hours could be administered as cortisol replacement.[79,84–86]

Organ Preservation Solutions

4. L.W. is considered a suitable multiple organ donor and is brought to the operating room (OR) where the surgical team prepares for harvesting of her heart, lungs, liver, kidneys, and pancreas. In the OR, a surgical midline line incision is made and each organ is inspected visually for trauma and undetected disease. The organs are preserved by flushing them with cold electrolyte solutions before being removed completely from L.W. They then are packed and shipped in ice-cold preservation solutions. What cold preservation solutions are available and what are the time limits for organ preservation?

The infusion of cold electrolyte solutions into L.W.'s major blood vessels rapidly cools the organs and cleanses them of blood. This use of cold solutions to induce hypothermia (cold ischemia) is the accepted approach to harvesting and preserving transplanted organs. The goal is to arrest cell metabolism, decrease energy requirements, and decrease cell membrane permeability to avoid warm ischemia and to minimize cell destruction.[87]

The two most commonly used cold solutions are Euro-Collins (EC) and University of Wisconsin (UW) solutions. These solutions contain a variety of intracellular and extracellular electrolytes as well as glucose, starches, colloids, buffers and pharmacologic agents.[87] The kidneys, pancreas, and liver usually are preserved with UW solution, and a potassium-containing cardioplegic solution often is used when harvesting the heart. The lungs usually are cooled rapidly with EC solution.[88] These cold solutions allow for

the following preservation times: kidney 24 to 36 hours, liver 8 to 24 hours, pancreas 8 to 24 hours, and heart and lung four to six hours.[89]

In one animal study, the addition of prostaglandin E_1 to either EC or UW solution extended lung preservation up to 24 hours in contrast to the current four to six hour preservation time with EC or UW solution alone.[90] A comparison of EC to UW solution in 678 human cadaveric kidney donors noted no difference in three-month graft survival. Although the cost of UW solution is 30% more than EC solution, the overall cost of using UW solution was significantly lower, as was the need for temporary dialysis in the recipients of the transplanted kidney.[91] The UW solution is marketed under the trade name of Viaspan, but most commonly is referred to as UW solution.

Organ Distribution

5. How will L.W's organs be distributed to the appropriate recipients?

In 1984 the National Organ Transplant Act was passed in the U.S., creating a national task force which examined the relevant issues concerning organ procurement and transplantation. The United Network for Organ Sharing (UNOS) coordinates the matching of donors and recipients for cadaveric solid organs. Under this system, regional Organ Procurement Organizations (OPO) coordinate the distribution of renal and extrarenal organs. The UNOS does not coordinate transplantation from living donors. Candidates awaiting cadaveric transplantation across the U.S. are placed on a central computerized waiting list. A complicated scoring system is used to find the most appropriate recipient.[92] The criteria for determining a transplant candidate's place on the waiting list will depend upon the organ to be transplanted, the time on the waiting list, clinical status (acute or nonacute), blood type, and body size.

Kidney Transplantation
Indication and Evaluation

6. G.P., a 59-year-old, 61 kg male, has end-stage renal disease (ESRD) secondary to insulin-dependent diabetes mellitus (IDDM). He has been undergoing hemodialysis 3 times a week for 4 years. Other medical problems include hypertension, anemia, hypocalcemia, and hyperphosphatemia. G.P.'s medications include verapamil 80 mg TID, enalapril 5 mg BID, calcium carbonate 1 gm TID with meals, Basaljel 30 mL TID and HS, NPH insulin 20 U BID, regular insulin 6 U BID. He has been on the kidney transplant waiting list for 8 months. He is called by the transplant coordinator and admitted for a possible cadaveric kidney transplant. He is the same blood type as the donor. His most recent panel reactive antibodies (PRA) is 10%. Crossmatch is negative and HLA typing reveals a 4-antigen match (A1, A2, B35, B62) between donor and recipient. Upon admission to the hospital, his laboratory values were as follows: Na 141 mEq/L (Normal: 135–145), K 4.7 mEq/L (Normal: 3.4–4.6), Cl 102 mEq/L (Normal: 95–105), bicarbonate (HCO_3) 23 mEq/L (Normal: 22–28), blood urea nitrogen (BUN) 44 mg/dL (Normal: 8–18), serum creatinine (SrCr) 13.9 mg/dL (Normal: 0.6–1.2), Ca 7.8 mEq/L (Normal: 8.8–10.3), phosphorus (P) 6.2 mg/dL (Normal: 2.5–5.0), glucose 225 mg/dL (Normal: 65–110), white blood cell count (WBC) 8.4 cells/mm³ (Normal: 4000–10,000), hemoglobin (Hgb) 9.3 gm/dL (Normal: 14–18), hematocrit (Hct) 24% (Normal: 39–49). His serology is negative for HIV, Hepatitis B and C, and cytomegalovirus (CMV). What are the indications and potential benefits of kidney transplantation in G.P.? [SI units: Na 141 mmol/L (Normal: 135–145); K 4.7 mmol/L (Normal: 3.4–4.6); Cl 102 mmol/L (Normal: 95–105); bicarbonate 23 mmol/L (Normal: 22–28); BUN 15.7 mmol/L (Normal: 3.0–6.5); SrCr 1228.8 μmol/L (Normal: 50–110); Ca 1.95 mmol/L (Normal:

2.20–2.58); phosphorus 2.0 mmol/L (Normal: 0.77–1.45); glucose 12.5 mmol/L (Normal: 3.9–6.1); WBC 8.4 × 10^6 cells/L (Normal: 4000 × 10^6–10,000 × 10^6); Hgb 93 gm/L (Normal: 8.45–10.65); Hct 0.24]

All patients with ESRD are potential candidates for kidney transplantation, unless contraindicated. The contraindications (absolute or relative) are determined by the individual transplant center. Absolute contraindications include current malignancy, active infection, active liver disease, HBsAg positive, HIV positive, severe or symptomatic cardiopulmonary disease, specific renal diseases with an accelerated recurrence rate, substance abuse, abnormal psychosocial and noncompliant behavior. Relative contraindications for receipt of a kidney transplant include chronic liver disease, positive for Hepatitis C, and more than 70 years of age.[93,94] The relative contraindication for the elderly with ESRD is controversial because about 40% of the ESRD population is over 65 years old and an increasing number of these patients are undergoing kidney transplantation.[95] Patients with ESRD need not wait until they are on dialysis before being considered for a kidney transplant because transplantation is associated with lower costs and a better quality of life than dialysis.[96,97] Survival rates for both dialysis and renal transplant patients appear similar; however, comorbid factors can influence survival. For example, diabetic transplant recipients have a higher survival rate than diabetic dialysis patients awaiting transplant.[98] The primary diseases leading to ESRD and transplant are IDDM, glomerulonephritis, polycystic kidneys, and arterionephrosclerosis.[99,100]

In G.P., IDDM would be the most likely etiology of his ESRD; however, hypertension also could have contributed. For G.P., a renal transplant should improve his quality of life and correct the complications of renal dysfunction such as anemia, hypocalcemia, and hyperphosphatemia.

When evaluating a patient for any organ transplant, the risk-to-benefit ratio must be considered. In general, pancreas, kidney-pancreas, and kidney transplants are performed to improve the quality of life. In other words, the disease itself may not be immediately life-threatening in patients such as G.P., but a transplant will free the patient from dialysis, insulin injections, or both. In contrast, patients who are candidates for cardiac and hepatic transplants will die if these vital organs fail. Therefore, the criteria established for organ transplantation must be evaluated carefully before organ transplantation is offered to any patient.

Donor and Recipient Matching

7. What criteria are important in determining a good match between the donor and G.P.?

G.P. underwent a series of serological tests to determine his genetic compatibility with the donor. G.P. had a negative crossmatch and low panel reactive antibodies of 10%. This would indicate that G.P.'s antibodies are not already sensitized to this donor's antigens, resulting in a more favorable post-transplant course. HLA matching also indicated a four-antigen match between G.P. and the donor. Matching of donor and recipient at the HLA-A, -B and -DR loci is associated with better graft survival and longer half-lives for both living-related and cadaveric kidney transplants.[99,100] For a group of recipients with a similar match as G.P., one might expect a projected 85% and 70% one year and three year graft survival for a first cadaveric transplant.

Combination Immunosuppressive Therapy

8. Before the transplant procedure, G.P. receives cyclosporine 120 mg IV, azathioprine 100 mg IV, and cefotaxime 2 gm IV. During the surgery, he is given IV methylprednisolone 500 mg, and furosemide 100 mg IV after the kidney has been transplanted. Cyclosporine 6 mg/hr IV is given 6 hr after the surgery and methylprednisolone 250 mg IV is to be given on the day after surgery. The methylprednisolone dose is to be decreased to 100 mg IV on the 2nd postoperative day for one dose. Prednisone 65 mg (1 mg/kg/day) PO is to be given on the subsequent day for 1 dose and tapered by 0.1 mg/kg/day to 20 mg QD by day 10 postsurgery. The cyclosporine will continue to be given intravenously and then switched to cyclosporine PO 10 mg/kg/day or 300 mg Q 12 hr. The dose of cyclosporine will be adjusted according to cyclosporine whole blood trough concentrations. Azathioprine will be continued at 100 mg IV QD and switched to oral therapy when tolerated. G.P. also is to receive cefotaxime 2 gm IV Q 12 hr for 2 doses, ranitidine 50 mg IV Q 12 hr, and sliding scale regular insulin. Why is G.P. being treated with a 3 drug immunosuppressive regimen?

The major goal of immunosuppressive therapy is to prevent rejection and infection with minimal adverse sequelae and to insure long-term patient and graft survival. About 60% to 70% of patients who undergo transplantation experience an acute allograft rejection episode. The majority of these episodes respond to acute antirejection therapy.

A consensus for the best immunosuppressive regimen has not developed and the numerous dosing regimens being used primarily depend upon the program and the specific organ to be transplanted.[101] Although a number of studies have attempted to evaluate the superiority of various regimens, comparisons are hampered by variables such as differences in donor selection, preservation and procurement, recipient's pretransplant conditions and comorbid factors, surgical procedures and individual surgical techniques, postoperative management and monitoring, and length of follow-up. The inability to conduct well-controlled studies makes it unrealistic to definitely conclude whether one immunosuppressive drug regimen is superior to another.

Immunosuppressive drug regimens for the management of solid organ transplants have included cyclosporine alone; cyclosporine with prednisone or azathioprine; azathioprine and prednisone without cyclosporine; triple therapy with cyclosporine, prednisone, and azathioprine; and quadruple therapy consisting of cyclosporine, azathioprine, prednisone, and a monoclonal or polyclonal antilymphocyte or antithymocyte preparation (see Table 33.4). The triple and quadruple therapies, all containing cyclosporine, are the most commonly used regimens.[102] When newer agents (e.g., tacrolimus which can be used as an alternative to cyclosporine and in combination with corticosteroids) are introduced, prospective randomized trials must be designed to control as many variables as possible when comparing different regimens. These trials should consider not only patient and graft survival, but also the frequency of rejection, use in high risk patients, adverse effects, health care costs, and quality of life associated with their use.

In G.P., as with other cadaveric kidney transplants, triple therapy frequently is used despite the lack of evidence demonstrating a difference between double therapy (cyclosporine and prednisone or cyclosporine and azathioprine) and triple therapy. In HLA-identical living-related kidney transplants, conventional therapy with azathioprine and prednisone gives excellent results. The use of triple and quadruple therapy is an attempt to reduce drug toxicity by using smaller doses of multiple agents rather than larger doses of any one of these agents used alone. However, these multidrug combinations can lead to increased drug costs, higher incidence of infection and malignancy, and difficulty in assessing adverse effects.[103]

After the initial transplant period, drug doses are reduced over time and either maintained at a stable dose for six months to one year, or in some cases either cyclosporine or the corticosteroid may be discontinued.[104,105] Although the discontinuation of a drug may reduce adverse effects, there is the risk of acute rejection and graft

Table 33.4	Immunosuppressive Regimens[a]					
Regimen (Transplant)	**Cyclosporine**	**Steroids**	**AZA**	**OKT3**	**ALG/ATG**	**Tacrolimus**
Single Drug						
Renal	10–14 mg/kg/day PO and adjusted to keep blood levels 150–250 ng/mL (specific monoclonal RIA)	—	—	—	—	—
Double Drug						
Renal[144]	14 mg/kg/day PO tapered to 12 mg/kg/day on day 7 and 10 mg/kg/day on day 14, adjusted to serum level 100–200 ng/mL for 1st 6 months, 50–100 ng/mL thereafter	100 mg PO on day 1, tapered to 30 mg QD by day 7	—	—	—	—
Liver[367]	6 mg/kg/day IV given BID–TID until taking PO, then 10 mg/kg BID adjusted for blood levels (polyclonal FPIA)	*Adult:* 50 mg IV Q 6 hr tapered by 40 mg QD to 20 mg/day. *Pediatric:* 25 mg IV Q 6 hr tapered by 20 mg QD to 10 mg/day	—	—	—	—
Liver	—	100 mg IV QD, switched to PO when tolerated and tapered to 7.5 mg QD at 2 months, 5 mg QD by 3 months	—	—	—	0.15 mg/kg/day IV continuous infusion on day 1, then converted to 0.15 mg/kg BID PO when tolerated
Triple Drug						
Liver	1–2 mg/kg IV BID for 1st 10–12 days then switched to PO when tolerated	50 mg Q 6 hr IV, tapered to 20 mg QD PO by 6 wk	2 mg/kg/day	—	—	—
Lung[298]	100–150 mg/24 hr IV continuous infusion until taking PO, then 300 mg BID and adjust to blood levels	—	2 mg/kg on day 1, then 1 mg/kg/day	—	10–20 mg/kg/day for 7–8 days	—
Heart[144]	2–4 mg/kg/day IV continuous infusion, then convert to oral 10 mg/kg/day (given BID), maintain serum RIA levels 200–300 ng/mL	125 mg x 3 doses IV on day 1, then oral 120 mg QD tapered to 30 mg QD by day 10	2–3 mg/kg/day	—	—	—
Renal[114]	6–12 mg/kg/day PO	1 mg/kg/day PO with taper	2.5 mg/kg/day	—	—	—
Liver[372]	3 mg/kg/day IV continuous infusion to maintain blood levels (HPLC) of 400–500 ng/mL, switched to PO when tolerated	1.5 mg/kg initially, tapered to 0.5 mg/kg/day by day 4 then to 0.3 mg/kg/day	—	—	10–20 mg/kg/day continuous IV infusion for 10–14 days	—
Quadruple Drug						
Lung[272]	3–4 mg/hr continuous IV infusion, convert to oral to maintain whole blood level of 400 ng/mL (RIA)	0.5 mg/kg/day starting day 5, taper down to 12.5–15 mg QD by 6 months, then to 12.5–15 mg QOD by end of 1st year	2 mg/kg/day	—	15 mg/kg/day IV for 5 days	—
Renal[114]	6–12 mg/kg/day PO started 3 days before last OKT3 dose	0.25–0.5 mg/kg/day with taper	2.5 mg/kg/day	5 mg IV QD for 10–14 days	—	—
Heart	3–5 mg/kg/day PO, ↑ to 7–10 mg/kg/day to maintain blood level 200–400 ng/mL (HPLC)	125 mg Q 8 hr IV x 3 doses then PO 1.5 mg/kg/day, taper to 0.2 mg/kg/day over 1 week then switch to QOD	2 mg/kg/day	5 mg IV QD for 14 days	—	—
Heart[267]	1–4 mg/kg preop; 1–5 mg/kg/day PO on day 1, to maintain blood levels (HPLC) 50–150 ng/mL for 1–2 weeks, then maintain blood levels (HPLC) 150–200 ng/mL up to 6 months then 100–150 ng/mL	500 mg IV, then 125 mg IV Q 12 hr x 3 doses, and 250 mg IV on day 15; 0.15 mg/kg/day, day 2–14; then 1.5 mg/kg on day 16 tapered to 0.5 mg/kg by 10 days then 2.5 mg/wk to discontinuation by 3 months	1.5–3 mg/kg/day	5 mg IV QD days 2–15	—	—

[a] ALG = Antilymphocyte globulin; ATG = Antithymocyte globulin; AZA = Azathioprine; FPIA = Fluorescence polarization immunoassay; HPLC = High-performance liquid chromatography; RIA = Radioimmunoassay.

loss. Approximately one-third of renal transplant patients withdrawn from cyclosporine develop acute rejection.[104,106] Patients after transplant will require lifetime immunosuppression.

Postoperative Course and Delayed Graft Function (DGF)

9. G.P. is admitted to the ICU for initial post-transplant management. His urine output during the next 3 hours has decreased from 300 mL to 40 mL/hr. He is receiving IV fluids at a rate equivalent to his urine output. He had received 3 L of fluids in the OR. His BP is 140/83 mm Hg, HR 87 beats/min, temperature 36.9 °C, with no signs of dehydration or volume overload. His BUN is 56 mg/dL (Normal: 8–18), SrCr 12.8 mg/dL (Normal: 0.6–1.2). Another dose of furosemide 100 mg IV increased his urine output to 140 mL/hr; however, his urine output returned to <40 mL/hr in a few hours. Fluids and IV furosemide were given again with similar results. Renal ultrasound indicates no urine leaks, fluid collections or ureteral obstruction. A diethylenetriamine penta-acidic acid (DTPA) renal scan indicates good perfusion, but decreased accumulation and clearance. Over the next 2 days, G.P.'s BP is 150/93 mm Hg, weight is 65 kg (4 kg higher than pretransplant), urine output has fallen to <200 mL/day, BUN 85 mg/dL, SrCr 13.2 mg/dL, K 5.8 mEq/L (Normal: 3.4–4.6). The decision is made to institute hemodialysis. What has happened to G.P.'s renal function? What is the most likely diagnosis? [SI units: BUN 20 mmol/L, 30.3 mmol/L (Normal: 3.0–6.5); SrCr 1131.5 µmol/L, 1166.9 µmol/L (Normal: 50–110); K 5.8 mmol/L (Normal: 3.4–4.6)]

The initial renal function after kidney transplantation can reflect excellent, moderate, or delayed graft function. In recipients with excellent function, a good diuresis begins immediately and continues, and the serum creatinine rapidly declines to less than 2.5 mg/dL within the first few post-transplant days. Most living-related transplants and only about 30% to 50% of cadaveric transplants generally experience this excellent graft function pattern. Kidney transplant recipients with moderate graft function usually experience a slower decline in serum creatinine which stabilizes within the first week. Recipients with delayed graft function usually experience anuria or oliguria, require dialysis in the early period, and take days to weeks to recover. Delayed graft function (DGF) is most common in cadaveric transplant recipients occurring in about 20% to 60%.

The diagnosis of delayed graft function is based upon clinical, laboratory, and diagnostic criteria that may vary from one center to another. DGF has been defined, at some centers, as simply the need for dialysis in the early transplant period, while at another center the definition of DGF may be based upon both a lack of improvement in serum creatinine and presence of anuria or oliguria after other causes of acute tubular necrosis (ATN) are ruled out. Delayed graft function is influenced by conditions affecting the donor (age, condition of organ, prolonged ischemic time), intraoperative conditions (hypotension, fluid imbalance), and recipient (prior transplantation, postoperative hypovolemia or hypotension, and nephrotoxic drugs). In G.P., poor urine output in the first hours after transplant and subsequent oliguria, the exclusion of other causes of ATN, the results of the renal scan, the lack of improvement in BUN and serum creatinine, and need for dialysis are indicative of delayed graft function.[107–109]

Sequential and Induction Therapy

10. What adjustments, if any, should be made in G.P.'s immunosuppressive drug regimen?

The impact of delayed graft function on kidney graft survival is controversial; however, it does influence a patient's early management by requiring dialysis, increasing the length of hospital stay, and increasing the costs of therapy.[110,111] It also may make the assessment of acute rejection more difficult since the patient already has impaired renal function. Cyclosporine also may contribute to the onset of DGF as well as prolong its duration.[112,113] Therefore, the cyclosporine for G.P. should be discontinued temporarily. Induction and sequential immunosuppressive protocols try to avoid use of cyclosporine, or to use only low cyclosporine doses during the initial transplant period for the first one to two weeks after a renal transplant to minimize the effect of this drug on delayed graft function. The use of ALG or OKT3 in patients with DGF have reduced the duration of DGF and the need for dialysis relative to cyclosporine and would be appropriate for G.P. at this time. Although time to first rejection appears to be increased with either ALG or OKT3,[114–116] the preferred antibody still is a matter of debate. The incidence of cytomegalovirus may be higher with ALG in high-risk patients, but the incidence of other side effects may be higher with OKT3.[117,118] Whether ALG or OKT3 prolongs organ survival is controversial; however, they both decrease DGF. Whether either should be used for patients with immediate graft function or whether they should be reserved for high-risk patients also needs to be determined because these drugs are expensive, associated with a significant number of adverse effects, and might increase the susceptibility to CMV infections in high-risk patients.[119,120]

In G.P., an antilymphocyte preparation, either ALG or OKT3, would be administered for 5 to 14 days, along with his current regimen of prednisone and azathioprine. His cyclosporine would be discontinued and reintroduced two to three days before stopping the antibody. In order to ensure that adequate cyclosporine concentrations are achieved, a cyclosporine dose of 6 to 8 mg/kg/day orally twice a day would be reasonable in G.P. when reinstituting this drug.

Rejection

11. G.P. was given ATG 900 mg (15 mg/kg) QD as a 6 hr IV infusion for 10 days along with his prednisone taper and azathioprine. Cyclosporine PO 175 mg BID (6 mg/kg/day) was initiated on day 7 of ATG therapy. During this time, G.P.'s urine output has increased gradually to ≈1600 mL/day 7 days after stopping ATG. His weight has decreased to 61 kg, BP 142/84 mm Hg, HR 82 beats/min, T 36.7 °C, BUN 23 mg/dL (Normal: 8–18), SrCr 2.4 mg/dL (Normal: 0.6–1.2), and K 4.6 mEq/L (Normal: 3.4–4.6). He is on a regular diet and taking all oral medications. His current medications include azathioprine 75 mg QD, prednisone 20 mg QD, cyclosporine 225 mg BID, ranitidine 150 mg Q HS, dioctyl sodium sulfosuccinate 100 mg BID, nystatin swish and swallow 5 mL QID, nifedipine extended release 60 mg QD, NPH insulin 28 U BID, regular insulin 10 U BID. Three days later (i.e., 10 days after stopping ATG), his weight increased to 63.6 kg, and his BP was 160/94 mm Hg, HR 98 beats/min, T 37.6 °C, BUN 30 mg/dL, SrCr 3.4 mg/dL, K 4.8 mEq/L, trough whole blood cyclosporine concentration (monoclonal TDx) was 110 ng/mL, and urine output decreased over the last 24 hours to 850 mL. He has noted feeling tired with a decreased appetite, but his fluid intake was adequate over the past day. What evidence is consistent with rejection in G.P.? [SI units: BUN 8.2 mmol/L, 10.7 mmol/L (Normal: 3.0–6.5); SrCr 212.2 µmol/L, 300.6 µmol/L (Normal: 50–110); K 4.6 mmol/L, 4.8 mmol/L (Normal: 3.4–4.6)]

Although significant improvements in graft survival have occurred over the past decade, graft rejection continues to be a major reason for graft loss in kidney transplants.[100,121] Rejection episodes in all solid organ transplants can be categorized as hyperacute, accelerated, acute, or chronic.

Hyperacute rejection occurs within minutes to hours after transplantation of the allograft, and is the result of preformed antibodies (cytotoxic antibodies) against donor specific Class I antigens. This type of rejection is associated with a poor prognosis but is rare because of ABO matching and improved HLA typing. Clinically, the patient presents with anuria, hyperkalemia, hypertension, metabolic acidosis, pulmonary edema and, in some cases, disseminated intravascular coagulopathy (DIC). Diagnostic scan of the kidney would indicate no uptake. If other causes of anuria are excluded and this diagnosis is made, then the transplanted kidney must be removed.[122]

Accelerated rejection usually occurs within two to six days after organ transplant. This is a result of prior sensitization to antigens that are similar to those of the donor and newly developed donor specific antibodies. Accelerated rejections of transplanted kidneys occur primarily in recipients who have had prior transplantation, multiple pregnancies, or blood transfusions. These patients usually maintain good renal function for a few days before developing acute renal failure. Accelerated organ rejections generally are more resistant to pharmacologic therapy.

Acute rejection is the most commonly encountered type of kidney rejection in transplant recipients. The occurrence of an acute rejection of a transplanted kidney reduces the half-life of both living and cadaveric transplants.[123,124] The half-life refers to the time it takes for one-half of the grafts that survive the first year to eventually fail. Acute rejection often occurs in the first seven to ten days after kidney transplant; however, the prophylactic use of antibody preparations may delay the onset for several weeks. The majority of transplant recipients have at least one clinically evident episode of acute rejection within the first year, most in the first 60 days after transplant.[125] The clinical presentation of patients with acute rejection of a kidney ranges from an asymptomatic patient with mild renal dysfunction to one with a flu-like illness and acute oliguric renal failure.

G.P. presents with subjective complaints of malaise or tiredness and lack of appetite. Such nonspecific complaints occur often in patients with rejection and can be accompanied by myalgias as well as pain and tenderness at the graft site. Objectively, G.P.'s fever, increased weight, hypertension, decreased urine output, and increase in serum creatinine are consistent with acute kidney rejection. In addition, the cyclosporine concentration is low and suggestive of possible inadequate immunosuppressive coverage. Acute rejection of a transplanted kidney must be distinguished from cyclosporine nephrotoxicity, and infections (e.g., pyelonephritis, cytomegalovirus) also must be ruled out. Although the clinical evidence in G.P. probably represents an acute rejection, a kidney biopsy is the gold standard in establishing the diagnosis. The results from a renal biopsy usually are available within six to eight hours. If G.P. is experiencing an acute rejection, the renal biopsy would show an interstitial infiltration of mononuclear cells with tubilitis, or intimal arteritis in more severe cases.[126] A number of laboratory tests also are being evaluated for the detection of organ rejection. For example, measurements of urinary and serum substances such as interleukins (IL-2, IL-6), interleukin receptors (IL-2R), T-cell subsets, proteins, and radioisotopes may provide additional evidence of rejection. Although these tests are reasonably sensitive, they also are expensive, time intensive, and nonspecific. Nevertheless, technological advances in the measurement of these substances may enhance the value of these tests as aids to the more rapid diagnosis of rejection.[122]

Vascular rejection is acute and humoral-mediated. It is histologically different (i.e., lacks lymphocyte infiltration on biopsy) from acute cellular rejection. It usually occurs in the first week to three months after transplant. Vascular rejection often is associated with hemodynamic compromise and is more resistant to drug therapy.[191]

Chronic Rejection

Chronic rejection is the major cause of long-term graft loss. It is a slow, insidious process that usually is manifested after about a year, although it can occur as early as three months after the transplant. The characteristic signs that commonly are associated with chronic rejection of a transplanted kidney are hypertension, proteinuria, and a progressive decline in renal function leading to renal failure. Although an immunological cause for chronic rejection is most probable, the exact cause is unknown, and nonimmunologic causes such as poor blood pressure control or lipid abnormalities may play a role. Factors that increase the likelihood of chronic rejection include previous acute rejection, inadequate immunosuppression, noncompliance to immunosuppressive therapy, and previous infection. Chronic rejection generally is irreversible and unaffected by increased immunosuppressive therapy. Therefore, therapy is symptomatic (e.g., dialysis in the case of a kidney transplant). Ultimately, retransplantation is needed. Preliminary data suggest that some patients possibly might benefit from tacrolimus.[475] The diagnosis of chronic rejection is determined by clinical signs and biopsy findings indicative of obliterative fibrosis of hollow structures and vessels within the graft. The chronic rejection of a kidney must be distinguished from chronic cyclosporine nephrotoxicity, chronic infection, and recurrence of original kidney disease.[127,128]

Acute Rejection Treatment

12. A biopsy of G.P.'s transplanted kidney shows Grade 2 moderate acute rejection. G.P. is started on methylprednisolone 500 mg QD IV for 3 doses. His oral prednisone is discontinued, but his other medications are maintained. Why is the methylprednisolone therapy of G.P.'s first acute episode of rejection appropriate?

High-dose or "pulse" methylprednisolone IV, OKT3 IV, ATG IV, or oral prednisone are several of the options for the treatment of acute rejection in all types of solid organ transplants. High-dose corticosteroids, usually IV methylprednisolone, are considered first-line therapy in treating an acute episode over the other choices. It works very quickly in decreasing lymphocyte responsiveness, is easy to administer, and reverses at least 75% of acute rejection episodes.[129] The ideal corticosteroid dose, route, and regimen are unknown, and the number of corticosteroid protocols is as varied as the number of transplant programs.[101] As one would suspect, intravenous methylprednisolone and oral prednisone are equally effective in reversal of rejection. Oral corticosteroid protocols, however, usually include a longer period of treatment and have been associated with a higher incidence of adverse effects as a result.[130,131] Although as little as 50 mg of intravenous methylprednisolone has a similar lymphocyte suppressive effect as a 1 gm IV dose of this drug,[132] most programs use methylprednisolone 250 to 1000 mg every day intravenously for three doses and adjust the prerejection oral prednisone regimen accordingly. An example of an oral prednisone regimen would be 100 to 200 mg/day and tapered over a two- to three-week period.[133,134]

For G.P., intravenous methylprednisolone is appropriate because corticosteroids are considered first-line therapy for acute rejection of a transplanted kidney, and first rejection episodes (such as G.P.'s) are very responsive to corticosteroid therapy. In addition, G.P. has received a prophylactic course of ATG recently and the potential for G.P. to develop antibodies to the ATG, and have it be rendered ineffective, can be somewhat mitigated by the methylprednisolone. Corticosteroids provide similar benefits to therapy as OKT3. Furthermore, ATG or OKT3 therapy may be associated with a higher risk of CMV infection and malignancy, is more difficult to administer, requires more intensive monitoring, is more expensive, and usually is held in reserve for cases of corticosteroid-resistant rejection.

The use of high-dose corticosteroids, however, does have its associated morbidity. For example, corticosteroids increase the risk of infection and can induce ocular, bone, and endocrine abnormalities with long-term therapy. Although this course of high dose intravenous methylprednisolone is only for three days, G.P. should be monitored for hyperglycemia and a change in insulin requirements because corticosteroids can alter glucose metabolism. Short-course methylprednisolone also can mask signs of infection (e.g., fever, changes in white blood cell counts, pain associated with inflammation) and delay the diagnosis of any infection. Insomnia, nervousness, euphoria, mood shifts, acute psychosis, and mania also can occur with short-term corticosteroid use.[135,136] If this methylprednisolone regimen is effective in reversing the acute rejection of G.P.'s transplanted kidney, his serum creatinine concentration should decline within two to three days and his urine output should improve. In addition, it would be appropriate to increase G.P.'s cyclosporine dose to 250 mg twice a day because G.P.'s cyclosporine concentration is low and there is a relationship between concentration and effect. Small changes in cyclosporine dose can lead to disproportionate increases in cyclosporine levels, and a trough cyclosporine whole blood concentration should be reevaluated in three days.

Kidney Rejection versus Cyclosporine Nephrotoxicity

13. G.P.'s acute kidney rejection has been treated successfully and his SrCr has decreased to 2.0 mg/dL within 1 week of therapy. Because of this rejection episode, G.P.'s cyclosporine dose is increased to 275 mg BID, his dose of azathioprine to 100 mg QD, and his prednisone is reinstituted at 20 mg QD. One week later in the clinic, his weight is 63.5 kg, BP is 148/94 mm Hg, HR is 83 beats/min, and he is afebrile. His SrCr is 2.3 mg/dL (Normal: 0.6–1.2), K 5.5 mEq/L (Normal: 3.5–5.0), uric acid 9.3 mg/dL (Normal: 2.0–7.0), magnesium (Mg) 1.4 mEq/L (Normal: 1.6–2.4), and his cyclosporine blood concentration is 370 ng/mL. He complains of a tingling sensation in his hands, feet, and nose; hand tremors; and peripheral edema. How would you explain these findings in G.P.? [SI units: SrCr 88.4 µmol/L, 203.3 µmol/L (Normal: 50–110); K 5.5 mmol/L (Normal: 3.5–5.0); 553.2 µmol/L (Normal: 120–420); Mg 2.8 mmol/L (Normal: 0.8–1.2)]

G.P. already has experienced an episode of acute rejection of his transplanted kidney. Some of the signs of rejection he previously demonstrated such as weight gain, increased blood pressure, edema, and an increased serum creatinine concentration are present again; however, these are not specific for rejection.[137] These findings also are consistent with cyclosporine nephrotoxicity.[138] The serum creatinine concentration usually is higher and rises more acutely during an acute rejection of a kidney; and fever and graft tenderness generally are present. With cyclosporine nephrotoxicity, the rise in the concentration of serum creatinine is more gradual and not as high as that seen with rejection. The serum concentrations of potassium, uric acid, and cyclosporine usually are increased, and the magnesium is decreased with cyclosporine nephrotoxicity.

Acute cyclosporine-induced nephrotoxicity is more likely to occur in the first months after transplant in most patients receiving therapeutic doses because cyclosporine doses and levels are highest and are being adjusted at this time.[139] Three clinical syndromes of cyclosporine-induced nephrotoxicity have been identified: 1) transient acute renal dysfunction; 2) protracted acute renal dysfunction; and 3) chronic nephropathy. *Transient acute renal dysfunction* is the most common form of renal dysfunction and is characterized by rapid reversal when the cyclosporine dose is held or reduced. This syndrome usually is not associated with histopathologic abnormalities, which suggests that it is related to severe renal vasoconstriction. Repeated episodes of transient acute renal dysfunction often result in the second syndrome, referred to as *protracted acute renal dysfunction*. Recovery of renal function after this syndrome usually is not complete, even when the cyclosporine is withdrawn. Protracted acute renal dysfunction can be associated with the development of thrombosis of glomerular arterioles or diffuse, interstitial fibrosis. Alternatively, cyclosporine may exacerbate intravascular thrombus formation or may serve as a stimulus to interstitial cell proliferation. The third syndrome is a *chronic*, usually irreversible, *nephropathy*, which often is associated with mild proteinuria and tubular dysfunction. Renal biopsies in cardiac allograft patients with chronic cyclosporine-related nephropathy showed tubulointerstitial abnormalities, sometimes with focal glomerular sclerosis.[138,139]

G.P. has evidence of cyclosporine-induced acute transient nephrotoxicity and a reduction in G.P.'s cyclosporine dose should reverse the nephrotoxicity. If the nephrotoxicity is due to cyclosporine, a decrease in the serum concentration of creatinine should be evident when the cyclosporine dose is reduced. If no such reduction occurs or if the serum concentration of creatinine continues to increase, then a renal biopsy would be needed to rule out rejection.[140]

Nephrotoxicity is one of the most common adverse effects associated with cyclosporine.[45] The pathophysiology of cyclosporine-induced transient acute renal failure is not understood completely, but primarily seems to be related to its effects on renal vessels. For example, cyclosporine can induce glomerular hypoperfusion secondary to vasoconstriction of the afferent glomerular arteriole and, thereby, reduce glomerular filtration.[141] One possible explanation for these effects is that cyclosporine alters the balance of prostacyclin and thromboxane A_2 in renal cortical tissue. Increased thromboxane A_2 results in renal vasoconstriction. Endothelin release from renal vascular cells stimulated by cyclosporine also may contribute to this acute effect through its potent vasoconstrictive properties.[142] Cyclosporine also can cause a reversible decrease in tubular function. The alterations in tubular function reduce magnesium reabsorption and decrease potassium and uric acid secretion.[141] This may be a result of direct tubular toxicity and possibly to thromboxane A_2 stimulation of platelet activation and aggregation.[143]

A chronic nephropathy, usually seen after more than six months of therapy, occurs in a small percentage of patients and is considered irreversible. In this situation, renal function progressively declines to the point whereby some patients require dialysis. Concern for chronic nephropathy led to the development of cyclosporine withdrawal or conversion protocols or protocols using low doses of cyclosporine of less than 4 mg/kg/day. More recent data indicate that renal function, followed as 1/SrCr or DTPA, declines initially when patients are treated with cyclosporine. Within six months to one year, the renal function stabilizes without a further decline.[144,145] Many cases of presumed cyclosporine-induced chronic nephropathy that involved continued deterioration of renal function probably should have been attributed to too low a dose of cyclosporine which led to late rejection and graft loss rather than to excessive cyclosporine doses.[146] A number of adjunctive therapies such as calcium channel blockers, dopamine, fish oil, pentoxifylline, prostaglandin analogues, and thromboxane synthetase inhibitors[147,148] either are being used clinically or are under investigation as a means to ameliorate the acute and chronic nephrotoxicity with cyclosporine.

Hepatotoxicity also can be a problem with cyclosporine therapy. The hepatotoxicity usually is first noted by an increase in the serum concentrations of hepatic transaminases and bilirubin and occurs most commonly when cyclosporine concentrations are high.[149] Hepatotoxicity usually is reversible when the dose is decreased.[140]

The diagnosis of cyclosporine-induced nephrotoxicity and hepatotoxicity must be differentiated from episodes of organ rejection in patients with kidney or liver transplants, respectively. The proper diagnosis often is difficult. Reduction of the cyclosporine dose during a rejection episode could worsen the rejection and lead to possible loss of the graft. Therefore, the differential diagnosis must include considerations of all possible clues. Cyclosporine toxicity often will cause characteristic effects that will help the clinician make the proper diagnosis.[140,150] Cyclosporine-induced central nervous toxicity (i.e., flushing, tingling of the extremities, tremors, confusion, cortical blindness, seizures or coma, and hypertension) has been noted concurrent but not always with nephrotoxicity or hepatotoxicity.[151-153] Other side effects associated with cyclosporine therapy include hypomagnesemia,[154] hyperuricemia and gout,[155] hypertrichosis,[156] gingival hyperplasia,[157] nausea, vomiting, diarrhea, rare hypersensitivity reactions with intravenous therapy,[140,158] and infection.[159]

G.P.'s rapid rise in serum creatinine, central nervous symptoms, and hypertension in conjunction with a high cyclosporine level suggest cyclosporine toxicity as the most likely etiology of his findings. In this case, the total cyclosporine dose should be lowered by 20% to 225 mg twice a day, and G.P. should be monitored closely for resolution of the symptoms.

Heart Transplantation
Indications

14. R.B., a 56-year-old, 65 kg, male with end-stage ischemic heart disease and functional New York Heart Association (NYHA) class IV failure, currently is in the intensive coronary care unit, where he has been for the past month, receiving continuous inotropic therapy. He is on the heart transplant waiting list (Status 1). He had an acute myocardial infarction (AMI) in 1975, coronary artery bypass graft (CABG) in 1975 and again in 1993, several admissions for exacerbation of congestive heart failure (CHF) over the past year and an episode of sudden death 1 month ago. His most recent multiple gated acquisition scan to evaluate left ventricular function reveals a left ventricular ejection fraction (LVEF) of 14%, and echocardiography shows extensive anterior, septal, lateral, and apical akinesia, and severe mitral regurgitation. Right heart catheterization shows mild pulmonary hypertension with a pulmonary vascular resistance of 2.8 Woods units. VO_2 (volume of oxygen) is 8 mL/min/kg. Past medical history also includes hypertension and hypercholesterolemia. He currently is treated with dobutamine IV infusion, enalapril 10 mg BID, warfarin 2.5 mg QD, furosemide 80 mg BID, KCl 10 mEq BID, isosorbide dinitrate 40 mg BID, and digoxin 0.25 mg QD. His vital signs are: BP 122/82 mm Hg, HR 108 beats/min, resting rate (RR) 24 breaths/min, T 36.6 °C. His laboratory values are: Na 136 mEq/L (Normal: 135–145), K 4.3 mEq/L (Normal: 3.4–4.6), Cl 94 mEq/L (Normal: 95–105), CO_2 32 mEq/L (Normal: 24–30), BUN 23 mg/dL (Normal: 8–18), SrCr 1.1 mg/dL (Normal: 0.6–1.2), total bilirubin 1.7 mg/dL (Normal: 0.1–1.0), aspartate aminotransferase (AST) 40 U/L (Normal: 0–35), alanine aminotransferase (ALT) 16 U/L (Normal: 0–35), lactate dehydrogenase (LDH) 267 U/L (Normal: 50–150), alkaline phosphatase 100 U/L (Normal: 30–120), 24-hour creatinine clearance (Cl_{Cr}) 60 mL/min (Normal: 75–125), cholesterol 225 mg/dL (Normal: <200), triglycerides 99 mg/dL (Normal: 1–249), high-density lipoproteins (HDL) 71 mg/dL (Normal: 28–71), low-density lipoproteins (LDL) 134 mg/dL (Normal:

<130). His other laboratory tests are negative for hepatitis B, HIV, and Epstein-Barr virus (EBV), but positive for CMV. What makes R.B. an appropriate candidate for heart transplantation? [SI units: Na 136 mmol/L (Normal: 135–145); K 4.3 mmol/L (3.4–4.6); Cl 94 mmol/L (Normal: 95–105); CO_2 32 mmol/L (Normal: 24–30); BUN 8.2 mmol/L (Normal: 3.0–6.5); SrCr 97.2 μmol/L (Normal: 50–110); total bilirubin 29.1 μmol/L (Normal: 2–18); AST 0.67 μkat/L (Normal: 0–0.58); ALT 0.27 μkat/L (Normal: 0–0.58); LDH 4.45 μkat/L (Normal: 0.82–2.66); alkaline phosphatase 1.67 μkat/L (Normal: 0.5–2.0); Cl_{Cr} 1.0 mL/sec (Normal: 1.24–2.08); cholesterol 5.82 mmol/L (Normal: <5.20); triglycerides 1.12 mmol/L (Normal: 0.01–2.8); HDL 1.83 mg/dL (Normal: 0.72–1.83); LDL 3.47 mmol/L (Normal: 0.26–3.34)]

The success of heart transplantation has had a significant impact on the survival of patients with end-stage heart disease (ESHD). The one- and five-year survival rates are 80% to 90% and 60% to 70%, respectively. In contrast, the one-year survival rate for patients with severe ESHD without transplant is 20% to 40%.[160]

A review of heart transplants in the U.S. from 1983 through 1992 noted that 71% were in NYHA functional class IV and 25% were in class III. About 50% of these patients already were hospitalized before the initiation of transplant surgery. Cardiomyopathy and ischemic heart disease accounted for 50% and 43%, respectively, of the indications in this group of patients. Pediatric patients (0–18 years of age) are the fastest growing segment of the population undergoing heart transplantation.[161]

The best candidates for heart transplantation are those who are least likely to survive without a transplant and who have a high likelihood of a good quality of life after transplantation. The criteria for the selection of patients for heart transplantation vary from center to center; however, general criteria for selection of appropriate candidates include a left ventricular ejection fraction less than 35%, having intolerable symptoms in spite of maximal medical and surgical management, lack of reversible factors, and a one-year life expectancy of less than 50%.[162] Secondary comorbid conditions also affect the selection of suitable patients for heart transplantation [e.g., irreversible renal, hepatic, or pulmonary disease; severe cerebrovascular or peripheral vascular disease; active infection; current malignancy; acute pulmonary embolus or pulmonary infarction; active gastrointestinal (GI) disease; IDDM with end-organ damage; coexisting illness with poor prognosis; morbid obesity; severe osteoporosis; substance abuse; acute psychological disorder]. One hemodynamic exclusion criterion specific for the heart is an elevated pulmonary vascular resistance greater than 6 Wood units or 3 Wood units after treatment with vasodilators. Patients with this characteristic are excluded as candidates for heart transplantation because they generally experience a poor outcome in the immediate post-transplant period; however, these patients could be candidates for heart-lung transplants. The age limit for recipients has increased to 65 years old and some heart transplant programs will transplant older individuals on a case-by-case evaluation.[163] Another expansion of inclusion criteria is one that allows for transplantation of diabetics without end-organ damage.[164] The lack of consistent inclusion and exclusion criteria for heart transplantation, combined with a consistent shortage of donors, has prompted the promulgation of national task force recommendations for prioritization and indications for transplant. These include a maximal VO_2 less than 10 mL/kg/minute with achievement of anaerobic metabolism; severe ischemia consistently limiting routine activity not amenable to bypass surgery or angioplasty; and recurrent symptomatic ventricular arrhythmias refractory to all accepted modalities.[160] This level of VO_2 is associated with the worst prognosis for survival without transplant.[165]

R.B. has a considerable amount of evidence indicating a progressively failing heart. For example, his increasing number of admissions for CHF, an admission for sudden death, his need for chronic intravenous inotropic support, and his poor LVEF and VO_2

provide clear indications for heart transplantation. The status of his organ function and his negative infectious serology should clear the way for placement on the waiting list for transplantation. The placement of R.B. into the appropriate status category for receipt of a transplanted heart would take into consideration his severity of illness, ABO blood type, time on waiting list, and length of the waiting list. R.B. is considered a Status I candidate according to the UNOS recipient criteria for heart transplantation. A Status I candidate refers to a patient who is in an intensive care unit and who requires inotropic support to maintain cardiac function or is requiring assistance from a total artificial heart, ventricular assist device, intra-aortic balloon pump, or ventilator, or is less than six months old.[160] Status I patients are considered priorities for transplant.

Inotropic and Chronotropic Support

15. R.B. receives azathioprine 225 mg IV, cyclosporine 400 mg PO, and cefuroxime 1.5 gm IV before surgery. During reperfusion of his new heart, methylprednisolone 500 mg IV was given and IV infusions of dopamine, nitroglycerin (NTG), dobutamine and isoproterenol were started. A temporary pacemaker was placed in the new heart. R.B. is placed in the cardiac thoracic ICU for post-transplant care. The following medications were given intravenously: cefuroxime 1.5 gm BID for 2 days, furosemide 20 mg QID, ranitidine 50 mg Q 8 hr, methylprednisolone 125 mg Q 8 hr, azathioprine 125 mg QD, OKT3 5 mg QD for 10 days, and cyclosporine 3 mg/hr. He also is maintained on continuous IV infusions of dopamine, NTG, dobutamine, and isoproterenol. Why would R.B. require vasopressor and inotropic therapy perioperatively and postoperatively?

The majority of heart transplant recipients recover rapidly from the transplant procedure, and most are extubated and off vasopressor/inotropic support within 24 to 48 hours. However, during the early postoperative period, the cardiac, respiratory, and fluid and electrolyte status of the patient must be monitored intensively. The transplanted heart becomes denervated and contractility and sinus node function temporarily are impaired to varying degrees based upon the condition of the donor heart, quality of preservation, ischemic time, surgical technique, myocardial depletion, and elevated pulmonary artery pressure (PAP). Left ventricular and right ventricular dysfunction often are present with elevated right and left heart filling pressures soon after transplantation. For the first few days after transplantation, the heart is dependent upon direct stimulation from exogenously administered catecholamines for inotropic and chronotropic support.[166,167] At this time, the heart also is especially sensitive to beta agonists such as isoproterenol because of upregulation of beta-adrenergic receptors.[168,169] During this time, inotropic and chronotropic therapy should be guided by the results from hemodynamic monitoring (see Chapter 18: Intensive Care Therapeutics).

A Swan-Ganz arterial catheter is inserted in order to monitor and guide therapy to maintain right atrial pressure 5 to 10 mm Hg (Normal: 2–6 mm Hg), pulmonary artery pressure (PAP) 25 to 30/10 to 15 mm Hg (Normal: 20–30/8–12 mm Hg), pulmonary capillary wedge pressure (PCWP) 8 to 12 mm Hg (Normal: 5–12 mm Hg), cardiac index (CI) greater than 2.5 L/minute/m^2 (Normal: 2.5–4.2 L/minute/m^2) and systemic vascular resistance (SVR) 800 to 1200 dyne·sec·cm^{-5} (Normal: 900–1400 dyne·sec·cm^{-5}). Heart rate usually is maintained at 110 to 130 beats/minute initially, then at 70 to 110 beats/minute chronically.[170]

For recipients like R.B., inotropic and chronotropic agents usually are started in the operating room at the time when the new heart is being reperfused and cardiopulmonary bypass is being discontinued. The choice of agent or combination of agents is based upon the above hemodynamic parameters, which would be monitored continuously. These agents eventually would be weaned and discontinued. Isoproterenol is the primary agent used to maintain heart rate between 110 to 130 beats/minute to maximize cardiac output. Dobutamine would be used for its inotropic effect to increase cardiac output, reduce left ventricular dysfunction, and reduce systemic vascular resistance. Dopamine, at low doses, could improve renal blood flow. Nitroglycerin or nitroprusside would reduce pulmonary arterial pressure and afterload. Temporary atrial pacing also may be used to maintain heart rate as well. In cases when elevated pulmonary artery pressures are unresponsive to these agents resulting in sustained right ventricular failure, intravenous prostaglandin E_1 and norepinephrine may be required.[171] If these interventions fail, insertion of a mechanical assist device may be effective.[172]

Sinus Node Dysfunction

16. Two days later, R.B. is extubated and hemodynamically stable. Dopamine, dobutamine, isoproterenol, and NTG are discontinued and IV medications are switched to oral formulations. On day 9 his HR has decreased to a rate of 50–60 beats/min. A continuous IV infusion of isoproterenol was restarted because his temporary pacemaker was removed 2 days earlier and the drug was successful in achieving a HR between 80–110 beats/min. TheoDur 150 mg BID will be started and the dose adjusted. Why is this appropriate therapy of R.B.'s bradycardia?

Sinus node dysfunction, seen as nodal or sinus bradycardia and episodes of sinus arrest, is common in the early postoperative period. The donor sinus node serves as the heart's pacemaker. The denervation of the transplanted heart cannot respond to cholinergic or vagal stimulation. Therefore, atropine which commonly is used for treatment of bradycardia would not be effective in a heart transplant recipient.[173] In most patients, the denervation is transient, and temporary use of isoproterenol or a pacemaker is needed. If the resistance to vagal stimuli persists (in about 5%–20%), the placement of a permanent pacemaker has been the traditional approach.[174,175] The insertion of a permanent pacemaker may increase the risk of infection and interfere with the endomyocardial biopsy (EMB) procedure which is used to assess the status of rejection. Ultimately, as many as 70% of patients with a permanent pacemaker return to normal sinus rhythm within 12 months.[176]

In one report, theophylline therapy was initiated in a group of heart transplant recipients and compared to a historical control group who did not receive theophylline for early post-transplant bradyarrhythmias in an attempt to avoid the use of a permanent pacemaker. All patients in each group had temporary atrial pacing. Theophylline was given as 150 mg every 12 hours with a goal of achieving a heart rate between 90 to 100 beats/minute. The dose of theophylline was adjusted to maintain the serum concentration of theophylline between 10 to 15 µg/mL. More than 90% of the patients who received theophylline had normal sinus rhythm restored, usually within four days of initiation of therapy. Theophylline-treated patients needed fewer days of temporary pacing, were hospitalized for fewer days, and needed a permanent pacemaker less often.[177] Theophylline may exert its effect on the transplanted heart by antagonizing the negative chronotropic and dromotropic effects of adenosine and/or causing an increase in catecholamine levels. This increase in catecholamines may stimulate the transplanted heart due to its increased sensitivity to catecholamines.[178]

Since R.B.'s temporary pacemaker was removed a few days earlier, the use of intravenous isoproterenol, followed by theophylline, would be appropriate as long as he is hemodynamically stable. Although there are no specific dosing guidelines in this situation, an aminophylline intravenous infusion at 0.5 mg/kg/hr or oral TheoDur 150 mg every 12 hours would be appropriate starting regimens. The theophylline regimen should be adjusted based upon heart rate and theophylline serum concentrations of 10 to 15 µg/mL. A benefit from theophylline should be evident within four days of starting therapy. There is no evidence that serum theophylline concentrations greater than 15 µg/mL are of any additional benefit and potentially could produce toxicity. If R.B. becomes tachycardic (i.e., heart rate >100 beats/minute), or if supraventricular tachyarrhythmias occur, the dose of theophylline should be reduced and the drug may have to be discontinued. Some patients ultimately may require a permanent pacemaker, particularly in those with unexplained syncope or near syncope.

Cardiac Denervation

17. What is the effect of denervation on the physiology of the heart and pharmacodynamic effects of cardiac medications after heart transplantation?

Although the transplanted heart usually functions very well, physiologic changes result in different responses to various stimuli in contrast to a normal innervated heart. For example, the transplanted heart has a higher resting heart rate than normal because of the loss of vagal tone. Therefore, drugs that work via the parasympathetic pathway (e.g., atropine) will be ineffective. Additionally, the transplanted heart accelerates more slowly during exercise, usually by taking several minutes to reach a maximal heart rate that is still less than the normal innervated heart during exercise. Furthermore, acute reflex changes in heart rate do not occur in response to increases or decreases in blood pressure in the denervated transplanted heart; and the ability to feel anginal pain is lost. Therefore, the clinical response to anti-anginal medications is masked. Cardiac output and blood pressure usually are normal in the nonrejecting heart.[179,180]

The adrenergic system remains intact in the transplanted denervated heart; therefore, drugs such as isoproterenol, epinephrine, norepinephrine, dopamine, phenylephrine, glucagon, and beta blockers still will exert cardiac effects. The indirect chronotropic effect of digoxin on the sinus and AV nodes will not be manifested in the denervated heart; however, the inotropic effect will be maintained.[181] The usual increase in heart rate secondary to nifedipine lowering of blood pressure usually is muted as well,[182] and responses of the denervated heart to verapamil, diltiazem, quinidine, and disopyramide also may be altered. The effect of nonprescription sympathomimetics on the transplanted heart has not been determined and should be used cautiously.[183]

Immunosuppression

18. What was the justification for using quadruple immunosuppressive therapy (i.e., methylprednisolone, azathioprine, OKT3, cyclosporine) in R.B.?

After heart transplantation, as with other solid organs, immunosuppressive therapy with three or four drugs is administered aggressively during the early transplant period because the risk of organ rejection is greater during this time. Regimens of azathioprine (AZA) with prednisone (PRED), or azathioprine with prednisone and antithymocyte globulin were associated with survival rates of 50% and 60%, respectively; and the addition of cyclosporine led to a 80% to 90% rate of organ survival.[184] When cyclosporine first was introduced, large IV or oral bolus doses of 15 to 18 mg/kg given preoperatively and in the initial postoperative period resulted in a significant degree of acute renal failure.[185] Currently, initial regimens use cyclosporine 5 to 10 mg/kg/day orally, or approximately 1.5 to 2.5 mg/kg/day, as a continuous IV

infusion. The IV infusion is used in some programs as a means of ensuring stable cyclosporine blood concentrations and avoiding the unpredictable and poor oral absorption of cyclosporine in the early postoperative period and appears to have minimal adverse effects on renal function.[186] The cyclosporine dose then is adjusted based upon targeted cyclosporine concentrations. Alternatively, preoperative and early postoperative use of cyclosporine is avoided entirely until renal function and urine output are appropriate and stable. The introduction of OKT3 and antithymocyte globulin has led to the development of induction regimens in which these agents, combined with azathioprine and prednisone, either replace cyclosporine or are used with lower doses of cyclosporine to minimize renal dysfunction in the early postoperative period as in R.B.'s case. Studies comparing ATG to OKT3 demonstrate either equivocal or superior results to one another. This therapy, in contrast to standard regimens containing only azathioprine, prednisone, and cyclosporine, is associated with a delay in the onset of the first rejection episode without differences in the frequency or severity of rejection or survival. The use of induction therapy also may allow a more rapid discontinuation of maintenance corticosteriods and reduce adverse effects.[187,188] Intravenous OKT3 5 mg every day or intravenous ATG 10 to 15 mg/kg/day every day usually is given for 10 to 14 days. A comparative study examining the difference between 10 or 14 days of OKT3 indicated that a 14-day course was of greater benefit in preventing rejection.[187] Elderly transplant recipients more than 65 years of age might experience lower rejection rates, and higher rates of infections and toxicities, although this requires further study in a larger population. An example of an immunosuppressive protocol, such as one that would be used in R.B., is listed in Table 33.4 which outlines immunosuppressive regimens for various organ transplants.[189] Since OKT3 and antithymocyte globulin seem to be equally effective, the use of OKT3, along with azathioprine, methylprednisolone, and cyclosporine, seems appropriate for R.B. Since his preoperative serum creatinine is less than 1.2 mg/dL, the early use of cyclosporine is not contraindicated. Over time, the maintenance doses of cyclosporine and prednisone will be reduced. The corticosteroid eventually might be discontinued within the first year depending upon R.B.'s clinical course.

Acute or Chronic Rejection

19. R.B. is discharged after 15 days in the hospital and returns for a routine clinic visit and scheduled endomyocardial biopsy (EMB). Current medications include cyclosporine 225 mg BID, prednisone 7.5 mg BID, azathioprine 125 mg QD, acyclovir 200 mg BID, trimethoprim-sulfamethoxazole (TMP/SMX) DS 1 tablet Monday-Wednesday-Friday, diltiazem SR 180 mg QD, nystatin 5 mL swish and swallow QID, ranitidine 150 mg Q HS, TheoDur 200 mg BID, aspirin 81 mg QD. His blood pressures, which he monitors at home, have been between 140–150 mm Hg/85–90 mm Hg. Laboratory test results are as follows: Na 134 mEq/L (Normal: 135–147), K 4.3 mEq/L (Normal: 3.5–5.0), Cl 103 mEq/L (Normal: 95–105), CO_2 26 mEq/L (Normal: 22–28), BUN 16 mg/dL (Normal: 8–18), creatinine 1.4 mg/dL (Normal: 0.6–1.2), cyclosporine trough level 233 ng/mL, theophylline level 14 µg/mL. His vital signs were: HR 110 beats/min, BP 155/84 mm Hg, T 36.8 °C. Biopsy results indicate mild Grade 1 rejection of his transplanted heart. His cyclosporine dose is increased to 250 mg BID. A repeat EMB 1 week later now shows moderate rejection. What signs and symptoms indicate that R.B. is experiencing acute rejection of his transplanted heart? [SI units: Na 134 mmol/L (Normal: 135–147); K 4.3 mmol/L (Normal: 3.5–5.0); Cl 103 mmol/L (Normal: 95–105); CO_2 26 mmol/L (Normal: 22–28); BUN 5.7 mmol/L (3.0–6.5); creatinine 173.3 µmol/L (Normal: 50–110)]

As described in the answer to Question 11, organ rejection can be classified as hyperacute, accelerated, acute, vascular, and chronic.[190]

Acute rejection of a transplanted heart accounts for approximately 20% of deaths within the first year after transplantation.[192,193] In a multicenter study, 54% of patients with a transplanted heart experienced at least one episode of rejection; about 50% of these occurred within the first six weeks and 90% in the first six months, although rejection can occur at any time.[194] These statistics for acute rejection of a transplanted heart are similar to those described for a transplanted kidney (see Question 11).[195] Risk factors for acute rejection include younger recipient age, female gender (donor and/or recipient), donor heart ischemic time, the number of HLA mismatches, and retransplant.[195]

Clinical presentation of *acute rejection* of a transplanted heart is similar to that of organs such as the kidney (e.g., nonspecific signs of fatigue, malaise, a low-grade temperature). Unlike kidney transplant patients who might experience pain at the graft site, heart patients will not experience cardiac pain due to denervation. However, when patients with a heart transplant present with significant symptoms (e.g., hypotension, increased jugular venous distention, S_3 sounds, rales), these may be indicative of advanced severe rejection. Patients experiencing an acute rejection of a transplanted heart also may present with new onset arrhythmias and congestive heart failure. The ability to detect acute rejection of organs has changed as immunosuppressive protocols have evolved. Before the introduction of cyclosporine, a major indicator of acute rejection was the electrocardiogram (ECG).[196] With the advent of cyclosporine-based regimens, the ECG no longer is a reliable index;[197] therefore, the detection of an acute rejection of a transplanted heart must be determined by an internal jugular transvenous endomyocardial biopsy. An endometrial biopsy is considered the ''gold standard'' for the diagnosis of rejection of a transplanted heart much like the renal biopsy is for detection of kidney transplant rejection. A set of histologic criteria has been developed in order to standardize the severity of rejection. A grading scale of 0 to 4 is used to describe the degree of damage to cardiac tissue. Grade 0 indicates no rejection while Grade 4 is severe acute rejection.[198]

R.B. presents without any symptoms of acute rejection. This asymptomatic finding in R.B. is consistent with the majority of patients who have biopsy-proven evidence of acute rejection, but do not present with clinical symptoms. Although patients with mild, Grade 1 rejection often are asymptomatic, 20% to 30% can go on to develop moderate, Grade 2 to 3, rejection.[199,200] Since destruction of the transplanted heart can proceed without clinical symptoms, all heart transplant recipients should undergo routine endometrial biopsy to evaluate the status of possible heart transplant rejection every week for the first six weeks, then every other week for three months, then monthly for an additional three to six months, then every three to six months thereafter. When rejection of a transplanted heart is detected, the endometrial biopsy should be repeated within one week. A number of other noninvasive electrophysiologic, echocardiographic, immunologic, radioisotopic, and biochemical methods are being investigated for their value in detecting acute rejection of a transplanted heart. Cytoimmunologic monitoring, transferrin receptors, FFT-electrocardiography, or serum prolactin concentrations may be sufficiently sensitive to be used as early predictors of impending heart rejection. These and other markers (e.g., IL-2 receptors) also can be used as possible indicators of response to therapies directed at managing the rejection episode. The limited clinical availability of these tests and their limited ability to distinguish rejection from infection or other causes of organ dysfunction[201] are major obstacles.

Chronic rejection of a transplanted heart (sometimes referred to as transplant coronary artery disease, accelerated coronary artery disease, or graft arteriosclerosis) is the leading cause of death after the first year in heart transplant recipients.[202] Despite immunosuppressive therapy, approximately 15% of patients will experience chronic rejection of a heart transplant within the first year and increasing to at least 50% within five years. The clinical presentation is insidious, nonspecific, and similar to the clinical presentation associated with acute rejection. Again, chest pain is nonexistent because of denervation. The first presentation of a patient with chronic rejection of a transplanted heart, however, may be CHF, arrhythmias, myocardial infarction, or sudden death.[203] Patients, therefore, must undergo routine coronary angiography shortly after the transplantation of the heart and every year subsequently. On angiography, chronic rejection of a transplanted heart (also known as transplant coronary artery disease) diffusely affects both arteries and veins. The pathogenesis of this condition, which results in endothelial damage and a cascade of other related events, is unknown but a number of immunologic, infectious, and nonimmunologic factors are associated with its development. Immunologic factors may be a humoral-mediated or B-cell directed event, antidonor-HLA antibody mediated, or a function of reduction in immunosuppressive therapy over time. An infectious etiology for transplant coronary artery disease seems to suggest a possible role for cytomegalovirus. Nonimmunologic factors such as hyperlipidemia, donor age, obesity, and ischemic time also may have a role in the pathogenesis of transplant coronary artery disease.[204] Pharmacologic therapy has been directed towards prevention of this condition. Antiplatelet agents, such as the aspirin used by R.B., are used routinely, but have not been shown to alter progression of the condition.[205] Anticoagulants, low molecular weight heparin,[206] and fish oils[207] are being investigated for their potential application in preventing transplant coronary artery disease. Diltiazem, which R.B. also is receiving for hypertension, has some benefit in inhibiting progressive coronary obstruction.[208] A lower prednisone dose, higher cyclosporine dose, and higher post-transplant CMV antibody titers have been correlated with a reduction in coronary artery diameter.[208] Although the above pharmacological interventions hold some promise, at this time, retransplant is the only effective therapy for chronic rejection.

Treatment of Acute Rejection

20. What approach should be taken in the treatment of R.B.'s Grade 1 acute cardiac rejection?

Acute cardiac rejection is described based upon the histological findings in the biopsy samples. It often is referred to as mild, moderate, or severe, with or without hemodynamic symptoms, usually when not being treated. This classification forms the basis for the selection of pharmacologic management. Although the individual drugs usually are given as high doses over a short period of time, the doses, routes, and regimens vary from program to program. High-dose corticosteroids are the primary agents for treatment of moderate to severe rejection, and IV methylprednisolone 1 gm every day for three days is effective in 85% of the initial episodes of acute cardiac rejection.[209]

When R.B. was asymptomatic and had a Grade 1 *mild* rejection, no treatment was the preferred approach. When mild rejection is demonstrated on biopsy without any hemodynamic changes, many of these episodes may resolve without intervention and without the morbidity associated with corticosteroid exposure.[210] An adjustment in maintenance immunosuppression is appropriate and an increase in R.B.'s cyclosporine dose certainly is reasonable especially since his blood concentration of cyclosporine was lower than desired. Nevertheless, some programs will treat mild rejection of a transplanted heart because of the concern for progression of the rejection in some patients. For example, the repeat endometrial biopsy in R.B. one week later noted a progression of his rejection from mild to moderate. In this situation, high-dose IV methylprednisolone 500 to 1000 mg or 10 mg/kg every day for three days would be given. Oral prednisone 50 mg twice a day for two to five days and tapered over 7 to 14 days to the previous maintenance is another alternative because R.B. already is on prednisone and hemodynamic compromise is not evident.[211,212] Another alternative, but less frequently used, is to increase the cyclosporine maintenance dose by 50% to 100% for seven to ten days;[213] however, this approach would significantly increase the risk of toxicity.

As done in R.B., a follow-up endomyocardial biopsy, usually within a week of the initial diagnosis, should be performed. In R.B.'s case, his Grade 1 mild acute rejection of his transplanted heart has progressed to *moderate* rejection. In this situation, methylprednisolone 500 to 1000 mg IV every day for three days would be given and his maintenance prednisone regimen reinstituted. Alternatively, a high-dose prednisone regimen with a gradual dosage reduction could be instituted after the three-day course of methylprednisolone was completed.[214] In a small, prospective, randomized study of patients with asymptomatic moderate rejection of transplanted heart, methylprednisolone 1 gm IV for three days and oral prednisone with a 7- to 14-day taper regimen resulted in greater than 90% efficacy in both groups.[215] In a retrospective study, no difference in response was noted in patients who were treated with intravenous corticosteroids at doses of 250, 500, and 1000 mg every day; however, a higher recurrence rate was associated with the 250 mg dose.[216] Therefore, R.B. probably would benefit from a course of high-dose methylprednisolone. Subsequently, he should be monitored for any hemodynamic and functional changes that might indicate further progression of rejection and an endometrial biopsy should be repeated. If R.B.'s moderate rejection has progressed to *severe* rejection, he may receive another regimen of intravenous methylprednisolone. Alternatively, therapy could be initiated with ATG or OKT3. Before starting on OKT3, an anti-OKT3 antibody titer should be obtained for R.B.

When these antilymphocyte antibodies (i.e., ATG and OKT3) are used for patients unresponsive to corticosteroids, the treatment is known as *rescue* therapy. Both ATG and OKT3 are equally advantageous in this situation.[217] A typical regimen would be ATG 10 mg/kg IV every day for seven to ten days[218] or OKT3 IV 5 mg every day for ten days.[212] As many as 90% of corticosteroid-refractory episodes of acute rejection of a transplanted heart respond to OKT3.[219]

In some patients, an acute rejection episode can be refractory to high-dose corticosteroids, ATG and OKT3. Methotrexate,[220] total body irradiation,[221] tacrolimus,[222] photochemotherapy,[223] cyclophosphamide, and plasmapheresis[224-227] can be used and have been successful in some cases.

Post-Transplant Hypertension

21. R.B.'s repeat EMB demonstrates no rejection and over the next few months he has been followed in the transplant clinic. He has been enrolled in an exercise and diet program to keep his weight, cholesterol, and BP under control. His BP is 164/95 mm Hg, HR 88 beats/min, T 36.9 °C, weight 70 kg. His BPs have been between 150–170/90–96 mm Hg. The results from his laboratory tests are as follows: Na 135 mEq/L (Normal: 135–147), K 4.4 mEq/L (Normal: 3.4–4.6), Cl 101 mEq/L (Normal: 95–105), CO$_2$ 25 mEq/L (Normal: 22–28), BUN 15 mg/dL (Normal: 8–18), creatinine 1.3 mg/dL (Normal: 0.6–1.2), uric acid 11.3 mg/dL (Normal: 2.0–7.0). His most recent lipid panel is as follows: Cholesterol 360 mg/dL (Normal: <200), HDL 81 mg/dL (Normal: >50), LDL 192 mg/dL (Normal: <130), triglycerides 250 (Normal: 1–249). His cyclosporine serum concentration is 262 ng/mL. His medications include cyclosporine 175 mg BID, prednisone 15 mg QD, azathioprine 125 mg QD, acyclovir 200 mg BID, TMP/SMX DS tablet QD on Monday-Wednesday-Friday, diltiazem SR 240 mg QD, nystatin 5 mL swish and swallow QID, ranitidine 150 mg Q HS, aspirin 81 mg QD. What would be an appropriate therapy for R.B.'s high blood pressure? [SI units: Na 135 mmol/L (135–147); K 4.4 mmol/L (Normal: 3.4–4.6); Cl 101 (Normal: 95–105); CO$_2$ 25 mmol/L (Normal: 22–28); BUN 5.35 mmol/L (Normal: 3.0–6.5); uric acid 672.1 μmol/L (Normal: 120–420); cholesterol 9.30 mmol/L (Normal: <5.2); HDL 2.1 mmol/L (Normal: 0.8–1.8); LDL 5.0 mmol/L (Normal: 1.3–4.9); triglycerides 2.8 mmol/L (Normal: <180)]

It is not surprising that R.B. has developed arterial hypertension. Hypertension commonly occurs after all types of solid organ transplantation in the majority of recipients, particularly in those treated with cyclosporine. About 40% to 90% of adult[228,229] and 40% to 60% of pediatric[230] transplant patients require therapy with antihypertensive medications. Before the introduction of cyclosporine, less than 20% of heart transplants[231] and only 40% to 50% of kidney transplants experienced problems with hypertension. Pre-existing hypertension, kidney disease, obesity, and immunosuppressive regimens consisting of corticosteroids and cyclosporine have been proposed as etiologic factors in post-transplant hypertension. Corticosteroids can cause sodium retention, increase plasma volume, and increase blood pressure independent of either of these actions. When triple (cyclosporine, azathioprine, and prednisone) immunosuppressive therapy was compared to double (cyclosporine, azathioprine) therapy in heart transplant patients, the triple therapy group required a greater number of antihypertensive medications despite comparable mean blood pressures.[232] The withdrawal of corticosteroids also has resulted in a decrease in hypertension.[233] Although corticosteroids have been implicated as a causative factor in hypertension, cyclosporine is the major factor for post-transplant hypertension. Cyclosporine-induced hypertension usually develops within the first week to six months of cyclosporine therapy.[234] Multiple etiologies have been proposed to explain the hypertensive effect of cyclosporine (e.g., volume expansion, increased sympathetic tone, increased endothelin levels, stimulation of the renin-angiotensin system, prostaglandin interference). Renal and smooth muscle vasoconstriction, which are mediated by some of the above factors, and hypomagnesemia, which results from cyclosporine's renal effect, can increase peripheral vascular resistance and induce hypertension.[235]

When the diastolic blood pressure is greater than 90 mm Hg and/or systolic blood pressure is greater than 150 mm Hg, hypertensive transplant recipients usually are treated with diet and behavior modification and aggressive combination antihypertensive medications. Calcium channel blockers are considered the drugs of choice for transplant hypertension because of their preferential effect on afferent arterioles, ability to induce renal and peripheral vasodilation, and possible renal protective properties.[236,237] Diltiazem, verapamil, and possibly nicardipine appear to inhibit the metabolism of cyclosporine, resulting in an increase in the serum concentration of cyclosporine. Nifedipine, isradipine, felodipine, and nitrendipine do not appear to interact pharmacokinetically with cyclosporine.[238-241] Diltiazem has been added intentionally to cyclosporine regimens in an effort to reduce the dose of cyclosporine and reduce the cost of therapy. In one study, the cost of cyclosporine was reduced by 38% in a group of heart transplants[242] which is consistent with recommendations that the cyclosporine dose may need to be decreased by 30% to 40% when diltiazem is administered concurrently. Angiotensin-converting enzyme (ACE) inhibitors also are effective antihypertensives with unique benefits in patients with heart failure (see Chapter 15: Congestive Heart Failure). Although ACE inhibitors must be used cautiously in patients with renal dysfunction, these agents are not contraindicated for R.B. Centrally acting alpha-agonists (e.g., clonidine), peripherally acting alpha blockers (e.g., prazosin), diuretics (e.g., furosemide, hydrochlorothiazide), and beta blockers (e.g., labetalol) all are effective antihypertensives but should not be prescribed without due concern for adverse effects (e.g., hyperlipidemia, azotemia, hyperuricemia).[155,243] The serum uric acid and lipid concentrations in R.B. already are elevated. The treatment of hypertension is presented in Chapter 10: Essential Hypertension.

Post-Transplant Hyperlipidemia

22. How should R.B.'s hyperlipidemia be managed?

Hyperlipidemia, as evidenced by increased serum concentrations of total cholesterol, low-density lipoproteins and triglycerides, occurs in 50% to 80% of patients with heart or kidney transplant[244,245] and usually develops within 6 to 18 months and persists. The association of coronary artery disease in heart transplants and the increasing number of patient deaths due to cardiovascular disease in kidney transplants make the issue of hyperlipidemia one of serious concern.[244,246] The hyperlipidemia in transplant patients seems to be associated with pretransplant ischemic heart disease, obesity, age, pretransplant hyperlipidemia, and drugs such as diuretics, beta blockers, cyclosporine, and prednisone.[247,248] Cyclosporine may have an independent as well as a synergistic effect with prednisone on lipid levels. Cyclosporine appears to interfere with conversion of cholesterol to bile acids and induce peripheral insulin resistance.[249] The strongest predictor of elevated lipid levels, however, seems to be the cumulative dose of prednisone.[247,250] Prednisone can increase the hepatic synthesis of very low-density lipoproteins, cause insulin resistance, and hyperinsulinemia. In several studies, lipid levels are reduced when the dose of prednisone either is lowered or therapy is discontinued.[245,251]

The treatment of R.B.'s hyperlipidemia should consist of weight control, dietary modification, and exercise according to the National Cholesterol Education Program guidelines (see Chapter 9: Dyslipidemias). His drug therapy should be reviewed and any drugs that may increase lipid levels should be discontinued if possible. Although R.B.'s cyclosporine dose perhaps could be reduced or the prednisone possibly discontinued, both probably need to be continued in light of his acute rejection episodes. A number of cholesterol lowering agents are available, but some of these may present problems in a transplant patient.[252] For example, cholestyramine and colestipol may adversely affect the absorption of cyclosporine[253] and potentially other drugs which these patients require. Nicotinic acid could exacerbate existing hyperuricemia, and gemfibrozil and clofibrate can cause myositis and further exacerbate myalgia. The hypolipidemic drugs of choice for transplant patients seem to be the HMCo-A reductase inhibitors (e.g., lovastatin). At one time, these were avoided due to reports of severe rhabdomyolysis and acute renal failure in transplant recipients attributed to cyclosporine-induced inhibition of lovastatin metabolism. These adverse effects occurred with high doses (>40 mg/day) of lovastatin and/or concurrent therapy with fibric acid derivatives.[254-256] Low doses of lovastatin (10–20 mg/day) are safe and effective in transplant patients[257,258] as are other drugs in this class (e.g., pravastatin,[259] simvastatin[260,261]). R.B. is a candidate for therapy with low doses of a HMCo-A reductase inhibitor. Hepatotoxicity, myalgias, muscle weakness, and other adverse effects should be monitored while he is on these agents. Corticosteroid withdrawal also should be considered in R.B.

Corticosteroid Withdrawal

23. What would be the risks and benefits of corticosteroid withdrawal in R.B.? If attempted, how would this be accomplished in R.B.?

The concept of discontinuing corticosteroids is attractive from the standpoint that their use is associated with a significant number of adverse effects[105,262,263] (e.g., hypertension and hyperlipidemia in R.B.). On the other hand, corticosteroid withdrawal could increase the risk of acute rejection, compromise long-term graft function, and possibly necessitate higher doses of the other immunosuppressives. However, in most studies, there is no adverse impact on graft survival and no need for higher doses of other immunosuppressives when corticosteroids are not included in maintenance regimens.[251,252] Furthermore, corticosteroid withdrawal has been successful in at least 50% of kidney[264,265] and heart transplant recipients[266,267] resulting in reductions in blood pressure and lipid levels.[268,269] Some protocols have withdrawn corticosteroids within the first two weeks after the initial transplant period, while others attempt to withdraw them three to six months after transplant. The rate of success has been greater when the corticosteroids were withdrawn over a period of three to six months after organ transplant because acute rejection is less likely to occur at this time.[129] The process to discontinue the corticosteroid continues unless the patient experiences at least two to three acute rejection episodes. If the corticosteroid cannot be discontinued completely, the lowest dose possible should be used; alternate day regimens may be feasible in some patients. Once withdrawal is initiated, it may take several months to eventually discontinue corticosteroids.

During this protocol, R.B. would be monitored closely for rejection (see Question 19) since acute rejection can occur, particularly if tapered too quickly. In addition, R.B. should be monitored for signs of adrenal insufficiency (e.g., lethargy, hypotension) as corticosteroids are withdrawn.

Deflazacort, an investigational corticosteroid, may have minimal adverse lipid and glucose effects.[270,271]

Lung Transplantation
Indications

24. B.U., a 33-year-old, 54 kg male with a 12-year history of cystic fibrosis, is admitted for a double lung transplant. He had been doing reasonably well until 2 years ago. Since that time he has been hospitalized 5 times for acute pulmonary exacerbations caused by *Pseudomonas aeruginosa*. In addition, he had been hospitalized twice in a 6-month period over the past year because of hemoptysis secondary to pulmonary infarcts. He now requires continuous oxygen at 3 L/min via nasal cannula for daily living. Other medical problems include diabetes mellitus, gastroesophageal reflux, pancreatic insufficiency, and sinusitis. His current medications are DNase 2.5 mL nebulizer BID, albuterol nebulizer BID, ADEKs QD, ranitidine 150 mg BID, ultralente insulin 10 U QD, Pancrease with meals and snacks. While on 3 L/min of oxygen, his oxygen saturation is 100%, forced expiratory volume in 1 second (FEV_1) 1.11 (22% predicted), forced vital capacity (FVC) 2.04 (34% predicted). His vital signs are: T 36.5 °C, BP 120/90 mm Hg, RR 20 breaths/min, HR 96 beats/min. His laboratory results are as follows: Na 137 mEq/L (Normal: 135–147), K 4.2 mEq/L (Normal: 3.5–5.0), Cl 100 mEq/L (Normal: 95–105), CO_2 28 mEq/L (Normal: 22–28), BUN 24 mg/dL (Normal: 8–18), SrCr 1.2 mg/dL (Normal: 0.6–1.2), glucose 104 mg/dL (Normal: 80–120), Ca 9.0 mg/dL (Normal: 8.8–10.3), protein 8.3 gm/dL (Normal: 6.0–8.0), albumin 3.9 gm/dL (Normal: 4.0–6.0), bilirubin 0.3 mg/dL (Normal: 0.1–1.0), AST 40 U/L (Normal: 0–35), ALT 46 U/L (Normal: 0–35), WBC 8000 (Normal: 4000–10,000), Hct 30% (Normal: 39%–49%), Hgb 9.5

mg/dL (Normal: 14.0–18.0), platelets 340,000 (Normal: 130,000–400,000), prothrombin time (PT) 11.6 sec (Normal: 9–12), partial thromboplastin time (PTT) 26.4 sec (Normal: 22–37). In the OR, he was given preoperative azathioprine 200 mg IV, tobramycin 200 mg IV, piperacillin 3 gm IV, ranitidine 50 mg IV, and metoclopramide 10 mg IV. What subjective and objective data make B.U. a likely candidate for a lung transplantation? [SI units: Na 137 mmol/L (Normal: 135–147); K 4.2 mmol/L (Normal: 3.4–4.6); Cl 100 mmol/L (Normal: 95–105); CO_2 28 mmol/L (Normal: 22–28); BUN 8.6 mmol/L (Normal: 3.0–6.5); SrCr 106.1 μmol/L (Normal: 50–110); glucose 5.8 mmol/L (Normal: 3.9–6.1); Ca 3.7 mmol/L (Normal: 2.2–2.5); protein 83 gm/L (Normal: 60–80); albumin 39 gm/L (Normal: 40–60); bilirubin 5.13 μmol/L (Normal: 2–18); AST 40 U/L (Normal: 0–35); ALT 46 U/L (Normal: 0–35); WBC 4000 × 10^6 cells/L (Normal: 4000–10,000 × 10^6); Hct 0.3 1 (Normal: 0.39–0.49); Hgb 95 gm/L (Normal: 140–180); platelets 340 × 10^9/L (Normal: 130–400 × 10^9)]

Lung transplantation has been introduced as a successful treatment of end-stage pulmonary disease. Before 1989, only about 100 patients had been transplanted; now more than 500 a year are transplanted. The one- and two-year survival rates are 60% to 70% and 55% to 65%, respectively. Some centers have reported a greater than 80% one-year survival.[272] Emphysema, idiopathic pulmonary fibrosis, and α_1-antitrypsin deficiency are the primary indications for a single lung transplant. The primary indications for a double lung transplant are cystic fibrosis, emphysema, and bronchiectasis. Double lung transplants also are referred to as bilateral single lung transplants. Heart/lung transplantation is used primarily in patients with Eisenmenger's syndrome, primary pulmonary hypertension, or congenital defects.[161]

A double lung transplant for B.U. is necessary to avoid the bacterial contamination from one lung to the other if only a single lung was transplanted. B.U.'s condition has deteriorated rapidly over the past two years, and his significantly low FEV_1 and FVC suggest that he is at a high risk of dying of respiratory failure within the next two years.[273] B.U. is a good candidate for a lung transplant because his cardiac, liver, renal (Cl_{Cr} >50 mL/minute), and hematopoietic functions are normal; he is under 60 years of age; and a nonsmoker. He also is not on a mechanical ventilator, has no active infection, and has not received corticosteroids before surgery.[274] In earlier protocols, corticosteroids were discontinued before surgery based upon animal data that their use was associated with a greater degree of airway complications after lung transplant;[275] however, lungs have been transplanted successfully in patients receiving either prednisone 10 to 20 mg/day or [276] less than 0.3 mg/kg/day of prednisolone before transplant surgery.[277] Although Pseudomonas cepacia colonization in cystic fibrosis patients is a relative contraindication in some transplant programs because it can increase the risk for a negative outcome,[278] B.U. does not seem to have this problem.

B.U.'s cystic fibrosis-associated pancreatic and gastrointestinal problems will not be corrected by a double lung transplantation; however, his pulmonary function should significantly improve. In a group of double lung transplant recipients with cystic fibrosis, mean pretransplant FEV_1 improved from 0.9 (26% predicted) to 3.3 (103% predicted) one year after the double lung transplant.[279,280] One would expect that B.U. would no longer require oxygen and that he could return to a good quality of life after a successful double lung transplant.

Early Postoperative Complications

25. B.U. underwent a 14-hour surgery for double lung transplantation. During the procedure he received 8 L of fluids and dopamine to correct hypotension. He was admitted to the ICU on a ventilator for management where he received cyclosporine 4 mg/hr IV, azathioprine 125 mg QD IV, ATG 800 mg QD IV, furosemide 10–20 mg QID, D5½NS at keep vein open, IV in- fusion dopamine 3 μg/kg/min, epidural and patient-controlled analgesia (PCA) morphine, tobramycin 200 mg QD IV, piperacillin 3 gm Q 6 hr IV, ranitidine 50 mg BID IV, albuterol nebulizer QID. What complications can occur in B.U. during the early postoperative period?

Patients like B.U. usually leave the operating room under mechanical ventilation and should be extubated within 24 to 48 hours. In the early postoperative period, the transplanted lung(s) is prone to pulmonary edema, hemorrhage, dehiscence at the anastomotic sites, airway leaks, infection, and rejection. Hemorrhage, ischemic/reperfusion injury and dehiscence have decreased due to improved donor preservation and surgical techniques. The most common serious complications are pulmonary edema, rejection, and infection. Significant incisional pain, which occurs in all patients, also can impact on how quickly B.U. will recover. Altered gastrointestinal function also is a typical problem in the initial period.

Management of Complications

26. How should the complications of pulmonary edema, infection, and rejection be managed in B.U.?

Pulmonary Edema

Pulmonary edema is thought to occur secondary to ischemia and reperfusion of the transplanted lung as well as to fluid resuscitation during the procedure. During this period, pulmonary capillary permeability increases and pulmonary compliance decreases; therefore, fluids are restricted. A considerable amount of fluids were administered to B.U. during surgery. His fluid intake should be restricted significantly, intravenous drugs should be administered in concentrated solutions, and diuretics should be administered to facilitate removal of excess fluid and proper ventilatory support. Low-dose dopamine may be useful for both pressure support and blood flow.[281]

Infection

Infection is the leading cause of death in the first 60 days after a lung transplant and contributes significantly to the number of deaths thereafter. There are several reasons for this problem. These patients usually have had several pulmonary infections before transplantation and may be colonized with organisms along the upper airways and sinuses. The donor lung may contain organisms at the time of transplant and may have ischemic damage. After lung transplantation, patients lack a cough reflex because of denervation and pulmonary secretions that can accumulate in the lungs can serve as a medium for bacterial growth. Furthermore, the transplanted lung mucociliary clearance may be impaired, alveolar macrophages may not function properly, and patients are receiving several immunosuppressives.[282,283] The majority of infections are bacterial sepsis or pneumonia associated primarily with P. aeruginosa, Enterobacter, other gram-negative organisms, and Staphylococci. In patients with cystic fibrosis, Pseudomonas, Candida, and Aspergillus infections also are common. At least 50% of lung transplant recipients develop infection despite prophylaxis.[280,283,284] Cytomegalovirus infections also occur but are more likely after the initial post-transplant period. The ideal prophylactic antibiotic regimen has not been established but usually is directed against gram-negative organisms and staphylococci and is based upon the patient's previous antimicrobial experiences before transplant. B.U. was given tobramycin and piperacillin based upon previous culture and sensitivities obtained during his past pseudomonal infections. Antibiotics also may be selected based upon the donor's previous bacterial cultures and sensitivities if available. Ceftazidime, ciprofloxacin, or imipenem often are prescribed for gram-negative coverage, and vancomycin, nafcillin, or clindamycin are given for gram-positive coverage. Antibiotics generally are administered for four to ten days. Nebulized administration of tobramycin 80 mg twice a day also has been used.[278,283,284]

Acute Rejection

Rejection, both acute and chronic, occurs in lung transplant recipients. *Acute rejection* is common in the early postoperative period, with more than 90% of patients having at least one episode within the first month in spite of aggressive immunosuppressive therapy. Nevertheless, acute rejection can occur any time. The diagnosis of acute rejection is made on clinical and histological criteria. Standardized criteria have been established for histological grading of tissue from[285] transbronchial biopsies (TBBX) which are scheduled routinely. Clinical signs of acute rejection of transplanted lung include fever, cough, dyspnea, rales, wheezes, infiltrates, and decline in FEV_1. The FEV_1 and FVC are assessed daily by the patient using a hand-held spirometer. As little as a 10% decline in pulmonary function (i.e., FEV_1, FVC) can be significant in the absence of other causes for respiratory decline, particularly infection. Treatment for acute rejection may be initiated based upon clinical signs only.[286] If clinical evidence of acute rejection is present, a TBBX is needed to firmly establish the diagnosis of rejection. The diagnosis of lung transplant rejection still can be established even in the face of a negative transbronchial biopsy if other causes are ruled out.[287]

The primary treatment for acute rejection is methylprednisolone 500 to 100 mg/day IV every day for three days. The dose of oral prednisone also can be increased to 1 mg/kg/day and tapered down to the maintenance dose over two to three weeks. More than 90% of acute rejection episodes of transplanted lungs respond to[272,286] corticosteroid therapy and OKT3 can be used for refractory cases.[288,289]

Bronchiolitis Obliterans

Chronic rejection also occurs in these patients and is referred to as bronchiolitis obliterans. It usually occurs after the first three months in at least 20% of patients with a transplanted lung and is a major cause, along with infection, of late deaths. The diagnosis of bronchiolitis obliterans is based upon clinical, physiological, and histological features.[290] Pulmonary function and exercise capacity progressively decline as a result of inflamed small airways and destruction of bronchioles. Before triple immunosuppressive therapy was instituted, the incidence of chronic rejection was greater than 50%.[291] The primary treatment of chronic rejection relies upon short courses of high-dose corticosteroids, ATG, or OKT3 to stabilize and improve the patient's condition for a short time. Shortly after a course with one of these agents, there is a high prevalence of relapse and cytomegalovirus infection. Antimicrobial prophylaxis should be considered for CMV.[286]

The current most used quadruple regimen for immunosuppression of lung transplants (see Table 33.4) is based upon experiences from other solid organ transplants.[286,272] Immunosuppressive induction usually includes ATG 15 mg/kg/day for 5 to 14 days in combination with cyclosporine and azathioprine.[272,286] Little information is available for the use of OKT3 for induction.[292] The early use of corticosteroids has been controversial and avoided in most protocols because airway dehiscence was associated with corticosteroid use for immunosuppression of transplanted lungs;[275,293] however, early, low-dose prednisone, starting on day five, now is used in some centers.[294,272] B.U.'s cyclosporine regimen would be adjusted to maintain a whole blood concentration of 350 to 450 ng/mL (monoclonal TDx) or 700 to 1000 ng/mL (polyclonal TDx). Once B.U. has an adequate oral intake, his immunosuppressive regimen will be converted to oral therapy. A prospective randomized trial of tacrolimus versus cyclosporine demonstrated similar graft survival in the first 30 days, but tacrolimus was associated with fewer episodes of acute rejection.[296] Aerosolized cyclosporine is another form of therapy that is being studied.[297]

Pain

Pain associated with lung transplant has not been studied formally, but all lung transplant recipients seem to require analgesia after surgery. Morphine or fentanyl are given either intravenously or via an epidural catheter in the first few days; however, the agent, route of administration, and regimen vary. B.U. was put on epidural morphine and a PCA pump. If the patient is sufficiently alert, a PCA pump may be used; however, epidural administration is more likely to produce a longer duration of relief. Pain relief with narcotic analgesics should not hinder ventilatory status and should allow a more successful recovery. Over several days to weeks, the patient will be placed on less potent oral analgesics (e.g., oxycodone with acetaminophen). Analgesics should be discontinued as soon as possible.

Gastrointestinal

Because of his cystic fibrosis, diabetes mellitus, and the surgical procedure, B.U. has a predisposition for postoperative ileus and gastric outlet obstruction that may be aggravated further by narcotics. B.U. also has a history of gastroesophageal reflux that may require treatment with H_2-antagonists, omeprazole, metoclopramide, or cisapride. Lactulose or polyethylene glycol-electrolyte solutions (e.g., CoLyte, GoLYTELY) can be used to increase intestinal motility and maintain bowel function. Pancreatic enzymes must be reinstituted when B.U. begins to eat because cystic fibrosis patients are susceptible to meconium ileus. Since cystic fibrosis patients often are malnourished, parenteral or enteral nutrition usually is needed until adequate solid food intake is achieved. After the initial postoperative period, B.U. should expect to see his appetite and GI function improve.[298]

Glucose

B.U. was receiving insulin to manage his diabetes before his transplant and will need continued insulin. His insulin requirements most likely will increase because he will be placed on maintenance corticosteroids, and high-dose corticosteroids will be necessary when he experiences rejection episodes. Regular insulin should be used initially and the dose adjusted based upon blood sugar concentrations. When B.U. can tolerate an oral diet, NPH insulin could be added and the doses adjusted accordingly.

Renal Dysfunction

Acute tubular necrosis also can occur in lung transplant patients. B.U. has several risk factors that potentially could produce an acute decline in renal function. He became hypotensive during surgery, which could lead to a decrease in renal blood flow. His renal perfusion potentially can be compromised because he is fluid-restricted and receiving diuretics. He also is receiving other nephrotoxins such as cyclosporine and tobramycin. Cyclosporine causes renal vasoconstriction and decreases glomerular filtration rate (GFR) by 20% to 50%,[299,300] and tobramycin is a tubular toxin. Cyclosporine also could decrease the clearance of tobramycin resulting in greater exposure of the kidneys to higher concentrations of tobramycin. The combination of these risk factors could have additive nephrotoxic effects.[301] A decrease in the serum creatinine concentration may not be evident until after the GFR has decreased significantly.[302] B.U., however, may benefit from the dopamine infusion because low doses of dopamine can enhance renal blood flow.[303] In B.U., the need for diuretics, fluid restriction, and tobramycin should be evaluated continually and should be discontinued when feasible. Antimicrobials less nephrotoxic than tobramycin should be considered based upon culture and sensitivities. If the tobramycin must be continued, evaluations of tobramycin serum concentrations probably serve as a more sensitive marker for adjustments in tobramycin dosing than the serum creatinine concentration.

Cyclosporine Bioavailability

27. B.U. now is receiving all his medications orally 3 weeks after transplant and is ready to be discharged from the hospital. He has an excellent appetite, his lung function is very good, and he has no GI complaints. His medications include cyclosporine 500 mg BID, azathioprine 100 mg QD, prednisone 15 mg BID, ranitidine 150 mg Q HS, ADEKs QD, Pancrease with meals and snacks, NPH insulin 20 U BID, regular insulin 8 U BID, acyclovir 200 mg BID, nystatin 5 mL QID (given 2 hours after cyclosporine), TMP/SMX DS on Monday-Wednesday-Friday. He experienced 1 rejection episode which was treated with high-dose pulse corticosteroids. His most significant problem at this time is his low trough cyclosporine blood concentrations which have been consistently <250 ng/mL (target range whole blood monoclonal TDx of 350–450 ng/mL) despite several increases in dosage. What are possible explanations for B.U.'s low cyclosporine concentrations?

B.U.'s maintenance immunosuppressive regimen consists of azathioprine, prednisone, and cyclosporine. His azathioprine dose of 2 mg/kg/day (100 mg) has been adjusted to maintain a WBC greater than 5000/mm³. His prednisone dose of 15 mg twice a day should be tapered over the next six months to 15 mg every other day if possible. The complete withdrawal of corticosteroids has not been studied adequately for patients with lung transplants. His oral cyclosporine regimen would have been initiated at 5 mg/kg twice a day after the IV line was discontinued, although some programs overlap IV and oral cyclosporine therapy by reducing the IV dose by 50% when oral cyclosporine is started. The target cyclosporine whole blood concentration should be the same as during the initial period and should be maintained at the same level for the first six months before reducing the targeted concentration to 250 to 350 ng/mL (monoclonal TDx) or 500 to 700 ng/mL (polyclonal TDx). These target cyclosporine concentrations should be adjusted for nephrotoxicity and other toxicities if necessary. The low cyclosporine levels could be a result of inappropriate drug administration, altered GI function, noncompliance, assay error, the poor absorption characteristics of the drug itself, drug interactions, or disease states. In this case, B.U. probably has been compliant with his medication regimen because he is hospitalized; however, his medication administration record should be examined for missing doses. Several of his cyclosporine concentrations, not just one or two, consistently are low, ruling out assay error. He has no GI complaints, such as diarrhea or constipation, that could influence the oral absorption of cyclosporine. He is not receiving any drugs (e.g., anticonvulsants, nafcillin, rifampin) that would decrease cyclosporine concentrations. He does have cystic fibrosis which is associated with malabsorption of fat-soluble substances. Since cyclosporine is a fat-soluble substance, the decreased absorption of this drug could explain B.U.'s low cyclosporine levels and his need for higher doses. Heart/lung recipients with cystic fibrosis required a mean cyclosporine dose of 16.7 mg/kg/day (± 7.2) compared to another group of heart/lung recipients without cystic fibrosis who required a mean dose of only 8.2 mg/kg/day (± 1.9).[304] The mean bioavailability in heart/lung candidates with cystic fibrosis was reported as 11%,[305] 10.5%,[306] and 21%[307] which is lower than most other populations. In B.U., the poor bioavailability of cyclosporine in cystic fibrosis patients is the most likely reason for his low cyclosporine concentrations, although an altered clearance cannot be discounted.

Cyclosporine Drug Interactions

28. What could be done to achieve the appropriate cyclosporine trough target concentrations for B.U.?

In some patients with cystic fibrosis, cyclosporine dosing requirements can range from 20 to 30 mg/kg/day which is substantially greater than the usual therapeutic doses.[305,307] One approach is to increase B.U.'s daily dose from 1000 mg/day to 1200 mg/day and decrease his dosing interval from every 12 hours to every 8 hours. Unfortunately, cyclosporine is a costly medication and a more complicated dosing regimen may reduce compliance which could result in organ rejection. One alternative would be to have B.U. take Pancrease with his cyclosporine to increase the absorption of cyclosporine; bioavailability, however, still may be less than 20%.[239,305,] A possibly more effective approach would be to administer cyclosporine with another drug that inhibits the gastrointestinal or hepatic metabolism of cyclosporine.

Ketoconazole in doses of 200 to 400 mg/day[308,309] or diltiazem[310] in variable doses have been used intentionally to decrease cyclosporine dosing requirements on average by 60% to 80% and 30%, respectively. A ketoconazole regimen of 200 mg/day appears to be as effective as 200 mg twice a day in increasing cyclosporine concentrations. As little as 100 mg/day of ketoconazole will significantly increase cyclosporine concentrations in blood. The administration of ketoconazole reduces the need for large cyclosporine doses and decreases cyclosporine drug costs without adversely affecting graft outcome.[308,311] The patient should be monitored closely for evidence of cyclosporine efficacy and toxicity and serum or blood concentrations of cyclosporine need to be evaluated carefully. Ketoconazole enhancement of cyclosporine blood concentrations begins within two days of concurrent therapy but it may take as long as two to four weeks to stabilize cyclosporine levels. Since the effects of ketoconazole on cyclosporine occur quickly, the cyclosporine dose could be decreased by 50% when ketoconazole is added. For B.U., rather than increasing his cyclosporine dose to 1200 mg/day, ketoconazole 100 to 200 mg/day could be given and his cyclosporine dose reduced to 250 mg twice a day. When ketoconazole is administered to B.U., it should not be given at the same time as his H₂-antagonist (i.e., ranitidine) because ketoconazole requires an acidic pH for absorption. The patient should be monitored for adverse effects of ketoconazole, particularly for hepatic and gastrointestinal effects.

Numerous other drugs interact with cyclosporine. Many of these are unsubstantiated single case reports which seldom provide adequate information about the clinical status of the patient, organ function, the cyclosporine assay methodology, or other concurrently administered medications. Nevertheless, clinically important pharmacokinetic and pharmacodynamic drug interactions with cyclosporine have been documented.[238,239] These drug interactions can have detrimental effects by either enhancing cyclosporine toxicity or by reducing its efficacy. The mechanism for these pharmacokinetic interactions usually involves a change in cyclosporine absorption as well as altered gastrointestinal or hepatic metabolism of cyclosporine. Cyclosporine is poorly absorbed and undergoes extensive hepatic metabolism primarily via the cytochrome P450-3A isoenzyme.[314,315] This isoenzyme, found in the intestinal tract and in the liver, is responsible for presystemic metabolism of cyclosporine and accounts in large measure for the erratic absorption of cyclosporine.[316] Therefore, induction or inhibition of these isoenzymes in both the GI tract and in the liver by other drugs can affect cyclosporine levels significantly.[317] For example, rifampin or erythromycin alter both bioavailability and hepatic metabolism.[318,319] Drugs that alter GI motility (e.g., metoclopramide) also may alter absorption of cyclosporine. The route of administration of cyclosporine also may be of significance. For example, when octreotide is given with oral cyclosporine, the absorption of cyclosporine is decreased in contrast to when cyclosporine is given intravenously. Ciprofloxacin and cimetidine have little impact on the P450-3A isoenzyme and, therefore, do not interact with cyclosporine.

Amphotericin B, aminoglycosides, and nonsteroidal anti-inflammatory drugs are associated with additive nephrotoxicity when combined with cyclosporine. TMP/SMX once was thought to enhance cyclosporine nephrotoxicity; however, it merely increases the serum creatinine concentration by blocking its tubular secretion rather than causing a direct nephrotoxicity.[320] Bromocriptine may enhance cyclosporine's effect.[321] Cyclosporine also may affect the actions of lovastatin and possibly any drug that undergoes significant renal elimination because of its effect on glomerular filtration (e.g., aminoglycosides). Cyclosporine can alter the disposition of digoxin.[322]

When drugs with the potential to interact with cyclosporine (see Tables 33.5 and 33.6) are added or discontinued, cyclosporine levels and measures of immunosuppressive response and toxicity should be monitored closely.[324]

Secondary Malignancy

29. Post-Transplant Lymphoproliferative Disorder (PTLD). *Risk Factors.* **A.L., a 17-year-old, 42 kg, female with cystic fibrosis, had a double lung transplant a year ago. She now presents with low-grade fever, malaise, pain, redness and swelling at her Port-A-Cath site, and a 1-week history of decreased appetite. She has experienced 4 episodes of rejection that were treated with 1–2 gm of methylprednisolone each time. She also received mALG, azathioprine, prednisone, and cyclosporine after transplant and has been on the latter 3 agents chronically along with ketoconazole, TMP/SMX, lactulose, and Pancrease. She has just finished the last of 2 courses of IV ganciclovir (6 weeks) for CMV infection. Donor was CMV+ and she is CMV+. Her EBV IgG-VCA titer is elevated. Upon physical examination she was noted to have mediastinal adenopathy. She denies chills, sweats, nausea, vomiting, or diarrhea. Chest CT scan revealed a mediastinal mass. Vital signs and all laboratory tests are within normal limits. Her cyclosporine level is 221 ng/mL. Seven days after admission, a biopsy of this mass shows a thoracic lymphoproliferative lesion identified as a thoracic immunoblastic lymphoma adherent to the right heart. Ten days later she developed tachy/brady syndrome and a pacemaker was implanted. Given the location of her lymphoma and symptoms, surgery and radiotherapy are not viable options and chemotherapy is started the next day. What risk factors present in A.L. are associated with the development of lymphoma?**

A.L. has developed a post-transplant lymphoproliferative disorder. PTLD is one of many types of malignancies that have been reported after solid organ transplantation. The etiology of this condition is unclear and probably multifactorial. One factor that has been strongly associated with PTLD is the presence of Epstein-Barr virus.[343,344] A.L. had an elevated positive EBV titer, indicating that she has been exposed previously to this virus which could have been reactivated as the result of her immunosuppressive therapy. The EBV also can be transmitted from the donor lung. A.L. received quadruple immunosuppression therapy initially, then triple therapy, and four courses of high-dose corticosteroids. Such extensive immunosuppression certainly could lead to an inability to suppress an active viral infection by cytotoxic T-cells. This could result in uncontrolled B-cell proliferation and polyclonal and monoclonal expansion. In addition to this T-cell defect, an imbalance or alteration in cytokine production in response to EBV, which infects B-lymphocytes, may contribute to the exaggerated B-cell expansion and transformation.[345] The majority are classified as non-Hodgkin's lymphomas primarily of B-cell origin; however, a small percent are of T-cell origin.

The incidence of post-transplant lymphoproliferative disorders has changed whenever immunosuppression therapy has been changed. For example, when cyclosporine-based regimens were compared to azathioprine- or cyclophosphamide-based regimens, lymphomas made up 26% and 11% of all cancers, respectively. The lymphomas occurred on average within 15 months in the cyclosporine group versus 48 months in the azathioprine group. One-third of these malignancies occurred in the first four months in the cyclosporine group compared to only 11% in the latter group.[346] The use of cyclosporine with other immunosuppressive agents and high cyclosporine levels also may increase the risk.

When a specific T-cell antibody (e.g., OKT3) is given as induction therapy for treatment of acute rejection or as rescue therapy, the incidence of lymphoma is increased. In one study of heart transplant patients, the incidence of PTLD was 11.4% for those who received OKT3 compared to 1.3% in the ATG group. In a group of patients who received a second course of OKT3 for a total cumulative dose greater than 75 mg, 35.7% developed PTLD compared to only 6.2% in a group that received a cumulative dose less

Table 33.6	Clinically Significant Pharmacodynamic Interactions with Cyclosporine	
Drug	Effect
Aminoglycosides[337]	Enhanced nephrotoxicity
Amphotericin B[338]	Enhanced nephrotoxicity
NSAIDs[a,339]	Enhanced nephrotoxicity
Tacrolimus[466,470]	Enhanced nephrotoxicity
Minoxidil[340]	↑ hypertrichosis
Nifedipine[341]	↑ gingival hyperplasia
Lovastatin[255]	Rhabdomyolysis
Pancuronium[342]	Prolonged paralysis

[a] NSAID = Nonsteroidal anti-inflammatory drug.

Table 33.5	Clinically Significant Pharmacokinetic Drug Interactions with Cyclosporine	
Drug	Effect on Level	Mechanism
Diltiazem[325]	↑	P450[a]
Verapamil[326]	↑	P450[a]
Nicardipine[328]	↑	P450[a]
Ketoconazole[309]	↑	P450[a]
Fluconazole[327]	↑	P450[a]
Erythromycin[319,329]	↑	P450[a]
Tacrolimus[330,331]	↑	P450[a]
Metoclopramide[332]	↑	Absorption
Octreotide[333]	↓	Absorption
Cholestyramine[253]	↓	Absorption
Rifampin[318]	↓	P450[a]
Phenytoin[334]	↓	P450[a]
Carbamazepine[335]	↓	P450[a]
Phenobarbital[336]	↓	P450[a]

[a] A mechanism also can involve alteration of gastrointestinal metabolism.

than 75 mg.[347] Some centers using OKT3 have experienced a lower prevalence of PTLD.[348,349] This difference could be related to the number of patients who were treated with a cumulative OKT3 dose greater than 75 mg. The studies finding a lower incidence of PTLD generally had fewer patients who needed larger cumulative doses of OKT3. The occurrence of post-transplant lymphoproliferative disorders also is affected by the time when OKT3 was given in relation to the activation or reactivation of EBV. The increase of EBV shedding (which is correlated with PTLD) increases in the second month post-transplant. This usually is the time a second course of OKT3 probably would be given for acute rejection.[350] ATG also has been associated with PTLD.[351] These studies indicate that PTLD is not due to any single causative agent but probably reflects the intensity of immunosuppression with multiple agents.

Factors other than immunosuppression and EBV probably are involved in the development of PTLD because most patients are treated with similar immunosuppressive agents and most have been exposed to EBV; however, only a small percentage develop PTLD. Chronic antigenic stimulation by foreign antigens, repeated infections, genetic predisposition, and indirect or direct damage to DNA are other variables that might affect the development of PTLD.[352] A.L. had two recent CMV infections which also could have contributed to this process.

Lymphomas, as a percent of all malignancies, occur more commonly in thoracic than renal transplant recipients (i.e., 42% and 11%, respectively) and are even more common in children.[353] Lymphomas seem to develop in about 1% of renal transplants, 2.3% of liver transplant recipients, and 4.6% of heart-lung transplant recipients.[354] These tumors often appear early and progress rapidly.[347]

The overall prevalence of malignancies in the transplant population averages about 6%, and the risk of cancer increases with longitudinal time after a transplant. Major organ transplant recipients are 100 times more likely to have cancer than the general population, and the number of cases of cancer, as reported by the Cincinnati Transplant Tumor Registry, has increased with the increased numbers of organ transplants.[353] The majority of cases of malignancies have occurred in renal transplants because more kidneys are transplanted than other organs; however, thoracic transplants are increasing and these are associated with a much higher risk of cancer than other organ transplants. The most common types of cancer in transplants (e.g., lymphomas, cancer of the skin and lips) are uncommon in the general population. The development of skin and lip cancers in the transplant population has been attributed partially to exposure to sunlight and sensitization of skin to sunlight by an azathioprine metabolite, methylnitrothioimidazole.[355]

30. *Clinical Presentation.* **What symptoms does A.L. have that are consistent with the clinical presentation of post-transplant lymphoproliferative disorder?**

The presentation of PTLD varies significantly. Patients can present asymptomatically, with mild mononucleosis-like symptoms, or with multiorgan failure. A.L. presents with fever, lymphadenopathy, malaise, and lack of appetite. Although these symptoms are consistent with PTLD, they also are consistent with infection and episodes of rejection. Since PTLD can involve various organ systems, patients can present with organ specific symptoms (e.g., acute abdominal pain, perforation, obstruction, and bleeding if a tumor is in the GI tract). Depending upon its location, a tumor can impinge on the function of other organs as seen in A.L.[352]

31. *Treatment and Outcomes.* **What are the therapeutic maneuvers and outcome that would be expected in A.L.?**

Treatment of a post-transplant lymphoproliferative disorder depends upon timing, presentation, symptoms, extent of involvement, histologic type, and transplant type. Early experiences with PTLD indicated that reduction or discontinuation of immunosuppression led to regression of the cancer; therefore, the first step in treating PTLD is to consider the discontinuation of all immunosuppressives. This course of action, however, is not feasible for A.L. because her transplanted lungs are essential to her life. The discontinuation of immunosuppressive therapy also is not an option for heart and liver transplants, but immunosuppressive drugs can be discontinued in kidney transplant patients because dialysis is available. A.L. will need chemotherapy for her cancer; therefore, her azathioprine probably should be discontinued to minimize the potential for severe bone marrow toxicity. If her cyclosporine levels were high, a reduction in dose could be attempted; however, her cyclosporine concentration of 221 ng/mL is on the lower end of the suggested range for this type of transplant. If her immunosuppressive drug therapy is lessened, she should be monitored very closely for rejection of her transplanted lungs.

Antiviral therapy with acyclovir has been used to inhibit EBV replication in an effort to treat post-transplant lymphoproliferative disorder. Response to this is variable and may depend upon the type and extent of PTLD. Ganciclovir is an alternative to acyclovir but its role is uncertain. A.L. already has received ganciclovir for six weeks during which time she presented with PTLD. Surgery, radiotherapy, and chemotherapy can be used to treat PTLD depending upon the situation. Interferon-α and immune globulin have been effective in a few cases that appeared unresponsive to other therapies.[356] PTLD is more likely to respond to therapy if diagnosed early and before it has metastasized. Polyclonal PTLD responds well to reduction or discontinuation of immunosuppression and high-dose acyclovir or ganciclovir therapy for several weeks to months. The role of prophylactic antivirals in prevention of PTLD is not known. Monoclonal or immunoblastic disseminated, rapidly progressive PTLD responds poorly to traditional therapy.[347] This latter type of PTLD has been associated with a mortality rate as high as 70%. Preliminary investigations with an anti-B cell antibody shows promise in treating polyclonal PTLD.[357,358] A.L. would be expected to have a poor prognosis given the type and extent of her PTLD.

Liver Transplantation
Indications

32. G.D., a 47-year-old, 57 kg female, develops temperatures of 101–104 °F associated with chills, rash, sore throat, and malaise. She is treated with tetracycline 500 mg Q 6 hr, but after 3 days of therapy her symptoms have not resolved. Her tetracycline is discontinued and therapy with amoxicillin 500 mg Q 8 hr is initiated. Her symptoms progressively worsen and she now is hospitalized. All tests for hepatitis A and B virus, EBV, CMV, bacteria, fungi, and parasites are negative. Serology for hepatitis type C is sent to a laboratory for analysis, and the results are not available yet. G.D.'s condition continues to decline. Laboratory values obtained from the initial hospitalization were AST 536 U/L (Normal: 0–35), ALT 998 U/L (Normal: 0–35), bilirubin 21 mg/dL (Normal: 0.1–1.0), PT 21 sec. A diagnosis of fulminant viral hepatitis of unknown etiology is proposed, and G.D. is transferred to a transplant center for further evaluation and possible orthotopic liver transplantation.

G.D. arrives at the transplant center on June 29 and is noted to be jaundiced, with scleral icterus, and in stage IV hepatic coma. She has a Ladd monitor placed to monitor intracranial pressure (ICP): initial readings were 26–31 mm Hg (10–20 mm Hg). At this time, orders are written to keep the head of

the bed elevated to 45°, mannitol 50 gm IV push is administered, and the ventilator is set to lower CO_2 tension to 30 torr. G.D. also is started on clindamycin 900 mg Q 8 hr and ceftazidime 1 gm IV Q 8 hr, prophylactically. ICP remains elevated despite four 50 gm boluses of mannitol and G.D. is placed in a pentobarbital coma. The pentobarbital infusion is adjusted, after the initial 10 mg/kg loading dose, to maintain the cerebral perfusion pressure (MAP-ICO) above 60 mm Hg. A CT scan notes cerebral edema with no evidence of intracranial hemorrhage. A suitable donor, matched for size and ABO blood group, is found and G.D. receives an orthotopic liver transplant on July 1, with a choledochocholedochostomy (duct-to-duct anastamosis) with T-tube bile drainage. Pertinent laboratory values are as shown in Table 33.7. CMV serology for G.D. is negative and the donor liver is positive.

After the transplant, G.D. is started on fluid maintenance with D5W; nystatin suspension 5 mL swabbed to the oral mucosa QID; cyclosporine 100 mg IV Q 12 hr; methylprednisolone, rapid taper: 50 mg IV Q 6 hr × 4 doses, 40 mg IV Q 6 hr × 4 doses, 30 mg IV Q 6 hr × 4 doses, 20 mg IV Q 6 hr × 4 doses, 20 mg IV Q 12 hr × 2 doses, then 20 mg IV QD; and famotidine 20 mg IV Q 12 hr. Cefotaxime 2 gm IV Q 8 hr was begun before transplantation and continued for 4 doses; ceftazidime and clindamycin were discontinued. An order also is written to restrict all pain medications and sedatives. G.D. returned from surgery with 3 abdominal Jackson-Pratt drains, a percutaneous T-tube bile drain, nasogastric drain, Foley catheter, and Swan-Ganz central venous catheter. What was the indication for referring G.D. for liver transplantation? [SI units: AST 536 U/L (Normal: 0–35); ALT 998 U/L (Normal: 0–35); bilirubin 359.1 mmol/L (Normal: 2–18)]

G.D. was diagnosed with fulminant hepatic failure with an unknown etiology. The most common indication for liver transplant in adults is cirrhosis from various etiologies. Each transplant center varies with respect to the most common disease states that indicate transplantation. Other indications for transplantation in adults include, but are not limited to, cholestatic liver disease (e.g., primary biliary cirrhosis); hepatocellular liver disease (e.g., chronic viral hepatitis, cryptogenic cirrhosis); vascular disease (e.g., Budd-Chiari); hepatic malignancy; inherited metabolic disorders; and

Table 33.7	Laboratory Values from G.D.'s Current Initial Hospitalization		
Tests[a]	June 30	July 1 Pretransplant	July 2 Post-Transplant
Albumin gm/dL (gm/L)	1.8 (18)	2.5 (25)	3.0 (30)
BUN mg/dL (mmol/L)	6 (2.1)	8 (2.8)	19 (6.8)
SrCr mg/dL (μmol/L)	0.7 (62)	0.7 (62)	1.1 (97)
PT/PTT sec	21.5/65	17.4/51	17.0/51
AST IU/L (μkat/L)	695 (11.58)	388 (6.47)	826 (13.77)
ALT IU/L (μkat/L)	1504 (25.07)	651 (10.85)	807 (13.45)
GGT IU/L (μkat/L)	315 (5.25)	234 (3.90)	54 (0.90)
Bilirubin total/direct mg/dL (μmol/L)	18.1/16.3 (309/108)	20/12.1 (342/207)	8.9/5.1 (152/87)

a ALT = Alanine aminotransferase; AST = Aspartate aminotransferase; BUN = Blood urea nitrogen; GGT = Gamma-glutamyl transpeptidase; PT = Prothrombin time; PTT = Partial thromboplastin time; SrCr = Serum creatinine.

fulminant hepatic failure (e.g., viral hepatitis, Wilson's disease, drug- or toxin-induced). Controversial indications include alcohol-induced disease, some types of hepatic malignancies, and hepatitis B and C.[359,360]

Age once was considered a factor in liver transplantation decisions; however, age no longer is a barrier if other organ systems are functioning properly. A number of patients over 50 years of age have been transplanted successfully with no significant difference in five-year survival compared to younger patients.[361]

Contraindications to transplantation have decreased in numbers over the past few years. Current contraindications to liver transplantation include a positive confirmed HIV, malignancy outside the liver, active infection outside the biliary system, patients with alcoholic liver disease who continue to abuse alcohol, psychosocial instability and noncompliance, severe neurological disease, and advanced cardiopulmonary disease. Patients with active infections are considered candidates after the infection has been eradicated.[359,360]

G.D. was within the age limitations for transplantation, had progressive disease (as evidenced by her hepatic transaminases), and was at risk for permanent brain damage because of increased intracranial pressure and death if she had not received a liver transplant.[362] She did not have any of the listed contraindications; therefore, a liver could be transplanted emergently.

Pediatric Indications

33. What are the indications for liver transplantation in children and when should they be referred?

Biliary atresia, a progressive obliteration of the neonatal biliary tract, is the most common indication for liver transplantation in children.[363,364] The serum concentrations of bilirubin and liver enzymes are markedly elevated in these patients. The direct bilirubin fraction is high because bilirubin is conjugated by the liver but cannot be excreted in patients with biliary atresia. These patients usually are jaundiced and have scleral icterus, hepatosplenomegaly, and ascites. Children with liver disease often fall into the normal range on height-age and weight-age charts, but these can be exaggerated by the enlarged liver and ascites. Better determinants of nutritional status are the triceps skin fold thickness and uniform muscle area tests. Nutrition is a particular problem in these patients because they often are anorectic and in a hypermetabolic state with increased caloric requirements. Significant steatorrhea also is common due to the bile acid deficiency.[365]

Many patients with biliary atresia will undergo a Kasai hepatic enterostomy procedure in an attempt to drain bile from the liver. A successful Kasai procedure may obviate the need for transplant; however, many children with successful Kasai procedures eventually develop secondary biliary cirrhosis, recurrent cholangitis, portal hypertension, or bleeding esophageal varices. Failure of this procedure usually is an indication to refer the child for transplant. Although many of these children are less than six months of age, they still should be referred because successful transplantation has been performed in children as young as two weeks old.

Other diseases often manifest with similar signs of liver failure and are an indication for referral to a transplant center. Patients with fulminant hepatic failure due to hepatitis A or drug overdose (e.g., acetaminophen) should be referred early for evaluation since their clinical course may change rapidly. Other indications for liver transplantation in children are α_1-antitrypsin deficiency, metabolic or genetic disorders, and chronic viral hepatitis.[366]

Pain Management

34. Why was no order written for pain medications or sedatives for G.D.?

Most patients who have a liver transplant have some degree of hepatic encephalopathy. Therefore, one of the early clinical indicators of a good functioning transplanted liver is the increased mental alertness of the patient. Narcotics and sedative-hypnotics decrease central nervous system (CNS) function and are avoided until the patient is awake, alert, and complaining of pain.[367] When narcotics are used, the doses should be small and administered intravenously. The IV route is preferred because of a decreased risk of complications in patients who are malnourished, have muscle wasting, decreased clotting factors, and possibly thrombocytopenia.[367] The majority of patients require no pain medication after liver transplantation because many of the dermatological nerves in the area of the incision are severed during the surgical procedure. After liver transplant, patients may take several days to achieve good liver function. Furthermore, prior disease, poor nutritional status, and surgical trauma generally result in decreased serum albumin concentrations and decreased protein binding of acidic drugs. The binding of basic drugs may be increased due to an increase in the serum concentration of α_1-acid glycoprotein. The selection of narcotics and sedatives, as well as other drugs, should include consideration of the effect of altered binding on expected pharmacodynamic effects in liver transplant recipients.[368,369] The serum creatinine may not truly reflect renal function in patients with hepatic dysfunction and the dosing of drugs that are eliminated primarily by glomerular filtration should be adjusted based upon an assessment of renal function other than the serum concentration of creatinine.

Patient Monitoring

35. How should G.D. be monitored in the initial postoperative period?

Function of the transplanted liver is essential for the survival of the patient. Therefore, extensive clinical, laboratory, and radiologic monitoring are necessary. G.D. has a percutaneous T-tube drain that must be monitored for bile production. She should be awake and alert within 12 to 24 hours after the operation. The serum concentrations of BUN, creatinine, liver function tests (LFTs), albumin, potassium, sodium, magnesium, calcium, phosphate, and glucose should be monitored every six hours on the first postoperative day. The surgical transplantation of a liver has been associated with coagulopathies and bleeding; therefore, platelets, prothrombin time, fibrinogen, factor V and VII also must be monitored and deficiencies corrected.[371]

Initial LFTs are highly variable. LFTs either can increase for the first day or two after transplantation because of ischemic damage to the allograft, or decrease because of initial dilution by high volume blood replacement. If the liver is functioning well, the LFTs, bilirubin, and prothrombin time all should begin to trend toward normal within four to five days after the operation.[367]

Magnesium, phosphate, and calcium levels may fall in the early postoperative period, and these electrolytes should be monitored closely. Ionized calcium serum concentrations are monitored rather than total calcium because most patients have low serum albumin concentrations. Hypocalcemia can occur because these patients may receive large amounts of citrate from blood transfusions and citrates lower serum calcium concentrations. Magnesium deficiency is common in patients with end-stage liver disease and may be exacerbated in the early post-transplant period by cyclosporine or diuretics. The reasons for the occurrence of hypophosphatemia are unclear; however, increased demand for phosphate for incorporation into adenosine triphosphate is a possible explanation. Electrolyte serum concentrations should be followed and electrolytes should be administered if needed[367] (see Chapter 28: Fluid and Electrolyte Disorders). Hypokalemia or hyperkalemia may oc-

cur depending upon renal function and fluid status. Hyperglycemia, which is a good indication of a properly functioning liver in this early period, may need to be controlled with insulin. In contrast, persistent hypoglycemia is an indication of a poorly functioning liver. Hypertension, which is multifactorial, also is seen during this time and usually is treated with calcium channel blockers such as nifedipine, nitroglycerin, nitroprusside, or beta blockers.

Primary Graft Nonfunction

36. In the immediate postoperative period, G.D. was noted to have no bile output from her percutaneous T-tube, increased serum concentrations of transaminases, severe coagulopathy, and acute renal failure. Furthermore, she remained unresponsive following the procedure. An ultrasound of her liver demonstrated good blood flow to the organ. G.D.'s condition deteriorated further over the next 12 hours, and she was diagnosed as having primary graft nonfunction. How should primary graft nonfunction be treated?

Primary graft nonfunction is the terminology used to describe the situation in which the transplanted liver or kidney does not function following the operation.[370] The diagnosis of primary graft nonfunction is not valid unless other causes of nonfunction (e.g., lack of blood flow) are ruled out. Hepatic nonfunction is characterized by rising serum concentrations of transaminases, renal failure, encephalopathy or failure to awaken, abnormal clotting function tests, and minimal or no bile production. Untreated, the mortality from primary liver graft nonfunction may be as high as 80%. The only definite treatment at this time is retransplantation, which is limited by donor organ availability. A potential second option for the treatment of primary nonfunction is the infusion of prostaglandin E_1. When ten patients with primary liver graft nonfunction were treated with prostaglandin E_1 by continuous infusion of 0.1 to 0.6 mg/kg/hr, 80% survived without retransplantation. The other two patients were retransplanted and one subsequently died. In comparison, the survival rate of six other patients who did not receive prostaglandin E_1 was significantly lower at 17%.[372] Controlled clinical trials are needed to define the role of prostaglandin E_1 for the treatment of primary liver graft nonfunction.

Central Nervous System Disturbances

37. Another compatible liver was found for G.D. and was transplanted successfully. G.D. was awake and alert within 24 hours after the operation. She was in the ICU for 5 days and subsequently transferred to the general surgical floor. Nurses caring for G.D. in the ICU noted that G.D. slept for only brief periods of time. The day she transferred from the ICU, G.D. was given a 1 gm dose of methylprednisolone because a minor elevation of her liver transaminases was noted. Three hours after her methylprednisolone had been administered, G.D. was delusional and combative. She was given 1 mg of haloperidol PO and EEG, CT scan, and lumbar puncture were obtained. The next morning G.D. had a clear sensorium and was cooperative. Her EEG, CT, and lumbar puncture all were normal. What is the most likely explanation for G.D.'s CNS symptoms?

G.D.'s symptoms of delusion and combative behavior coincided with the administration of a large dose of corticosteroid. Psychological effects such as insomnia, nervousness, mood shifts, acute psychosis, and mania have been associated with corticosteroid administration.[373] Therefore, the etiology of G.D.'s central nervous system symptoms most likely would be attributed to her methylprednisolone. Other variables, however, also could contribute to her altered mental status.

Solid organ transplantation is one of the most psychologically stressful procedures in modern medicine.[374,375] ICU psychosis, sleep deprivation, CNS infections, electrolyte imbalances, and other drugs such as cyclosporine also could have been responsible for G.D.'s symptoms. Many patients, such as G.D., who receive liver transplants could have experienced hepatic encephalopathy for various periods of time before the liver was transplanted. Careful screening and psychological examination before transplantation will assist in the differentiation between existing problems and new events. If a particular psychotic illness is diagnosed at the transplant evaluation, treatment is begun at that time. Organ transplant recipients who have adjustment disorders, major depression, delirium, personality disorder, or post-traumatic stress syndrome should be evaluated for all possible etiologies. If the diagnosis is established, proper treatment with counseling, neuroleptic agents, or antidepressants can be initiated. Pharmacotherapy should be based upon side effect profile, type of organ transplant, and potential interactions with other agents, particularly immunosuppressives.[376] Haloperidol and short-acting benzodiazepines have been used in the early postoperative period. Antidepressants such as trazodone, buspirone, and sertraline have been used chronically.[377] Some of these psychotropic agents can affect immunologic response by altering the neurotransmitter system.[378]

Central nervous system infections are a major concern in the immunocompromised patient and always should be investigated. Noninfectious cerebral lesions (e.g., hemorrhage, infarction) and cyclosporine-associated CNS effects should be considered as well.[379]

Cyclosporine

Absorption

38. Seven days after her second liver transplant, G.D.'s 3 Jackson-Pratt abdominal drains, Foley catheter, and nasogastric drain have been removed. Her T-tube drain currently demonstrates good bile production. Current medications include: cyclosporine 100 mg IV Q 12 hr (in glass bottles), cyclosporine 500 mg PO solution Q 12 hr, prednisone 20 mg PO TID, nystatin suspension 500,000 U to swish and swallow QID, and nifedipine XL 60 mg PO QD. Her current laboratory values include: BUN 27 mg/dL (Normal: 8–18), SrCr 0.9 mg/dL (Normal: 0.6–1.2), AST 170 U/L (Normal: 0–35), ALT 154 U/L (Normal: 0–35), gamma glutamyl transferase (GGT) 320 U/L (Normal: 0–30), total bilirubin 3.4 mg/dL (Normal: 0.1–1.0), and cyclosporine, by polyclonal whole blood TDx 973 ng/dL. What is the rationale for giving G.D. IV and oral cyclosporine at the same time? [SI units: BUN 9.6 mmol/L (Normal: 3.0–6.5); SrCr 79.6 μmol/L (Normal: 50–110); AST 170 U/L (Normal: 0–35); ALT 154 U/L (Normal: 0–35); GGT 320 U/L (Normal: 0–30); total bilirubin 58.14 μmol/L (Normal: 2–18)]

Cyclosporine is a highly lipophilic compound that must be dissolved in highly lipophilic solvents. The parenteral formulation of cyclosporine 50 mg/mL is stabilized with ethanol, 32.69% by volume, and Cremophor EL (polyoxyethylated castor oil). This formulation of cyclosporine is administered in either D5W or 0.9% NS and usually given a 24-hour expiration dating. The cyclosporine intravenous admixture should be dispensed in glass bottles because cyclosporine stored in plastic polyvinyl chloride bags can cause release of the phthalate plasticizers, which are potentially carcinogenic, from the plastic bag.[380] One milliliter of the oral solution contains 100 mg cyclosporine, 100 mg ethanol, 300 mg Labrafil (polyoxyethylated oleic glycerides), and 425 mg olive oil.[381] Cyclosporine oral capsules also are available in 25 and 100 mg strengths; these capsules are bioequivalent to the oral solution.[382,383] Oral absorption of cyclosporine can be characterized as slow, incomplete, and highly variable. The type of transplant, time after transplant, presence of food and composition of food, intestinal function (i.e., diarrhea or ileus), and presence or absence of external bile drainage all can affect the oral absorption of cyclosporine (see Table 33.8).[382,384]

Liver transplant recipients probably absorb oral cyclosporine poorly because bile production and flow are decreased in the early postoperative period. When cyclosporine is administered soon after liver transplantation, its bioavailability may be as low as 5%. The mean absorption of cyclosporine in adults with relatively normal liver function after a liver transplant is 27% and comparable to that observed in recipients of kidney (27%), heart (35%), and bone marrow (34%) transplants.[385] In pediatric liver transplant recipients, cyclosporine absorption may be less than that in adults, and cyclosporine clearance on average will be twice as high as in adults.[386] In most liver transplant recipients, cyclosporine absorption increases over time.[385] However, since G.D. is in the early postoperative phase and has external bile drainage, it is common practice to give both IV and oral cyclosporine. As the trough cyclosporine levels begin to rise, the intravenous dose is decreased gradually while the oral dose remains the same or is increased. Patients who continue to experience poor cyclosporine bioavailability may have to continue receiving cyclosporine intravenously.[382] This problem occurs commonly in pediatric patients and occasionally results in prolonged hospitalization. G.D.'s cyclosporine absorption will be expected to increase once the external bile drain is clamped.[387] Nevertheless, some patients will continue to absorb cyclosporine poorly due to the surgical procedure or the presence of chronic cholestasis.[388] In an attempt to overcome this problem of impaired cyclosporine absorption, six pediatric liver transplant recipients who required large doses of cyclosporine (29–136 mg/kg/day) were given a water-soluble vitamin E preparation along with cyclosporine. In five of the six patients, the cyclosporine dose could be reduced by 40% to 72%.[388] This beneficial effect of vitamin E was confirmed in another study of pediatric liver transplant recipients.[389] Studies in adults are not available. A new microemulsion formulation of cyclosporine (i.e., Neoral) resulted in less within day variability in cyclosporine levels in a group of kidney transplant recipients;[390] and increased cyclosporine absorption, although still poor, in one liver transplant recipient.[391]

Therapeutic Drug Monitoring

39. G.D.'s cyclosporine levels are being measured by whole blood TDx assay. How should her cyclosporine therapy be monitored and what assay methodologies are available?

Cyclosporine concentrations need to be monitored because cyclosporine therapy is associated with a number of toxicities, and patient compliance to the prescribed regimen is essential. Cyclosporine pharmacokinetic parameters (e.g., absorption, distribution, metabolism) have significant intrapatient and interpatient variability, and as a result, a poor dose response relationship.[398] The majority of institutions monitor trough cyclosporine levels because cyclosporine absorption is variable and prolonged. During the early postoperative period, G.D. should have her cyclosporine levels monitored routinely on a daily basis. Once G.D. is sent home, cyclosporine levels generally can be monitored less frequently and eventually may only need to be monitored every one to two months. The target trough therapeutic concentration of cyclospor-

Table 33.8	Factors Known to Influence Cyclosporine Absorption
Time post-transplant[392]	
Bile flow[387]	
Dietary composition[393]	
Gastrointestinal state[394]	
Liver function[395]	
Small bowel length[396]	
Vehicle[397]	

ine during the first two months would be 150 to 250 ng/mL with the monoclonal whole blood TDx assay or 700 to 1200 ng/mL with the polyclonal whole blood TDx assay. About two to six months after the liver transplant, the cyclosporine trough concentration target would be lowered to 100 to 200 ng/mL and 500 to 800 ng/mL for the monoclonal and polyclonal whole blood TDx assays, respectively. After six months, the targeted cyclosporine trough concentrations would be lowered further to 50 to 100 ng/mL and 400 to 600 ng/mL for the monoclonal and polyclonal assays, respectively. These ranges may be different at other institutions.

Cyclosporine levels can be monitored by a number of assay methodologies. Most institutions use the assay method that is most familiar to their transplant physicians. The type of cyclosporine assay used by a particular institution significantly influences interpretation of assay results, and there are significant differences between methodologies.[399] These issues have contributed to the debate on the value of monitoring cyclosporine concentrations. The pharmacological effects of cyclosporine metabolites and whether the concentrations of these metabolites should be monitored individually, or in combination with cyclosporine, also needs to be determined.[400]

Assays that are used currently include high-performance liquid chromatography (HPLC); radioimmunoassay (RIA) with polyclonal or monoclonal antibodies; enzyme immunoassay technique (EMIT), and fluorescence polarization immunoassay (FPIA).[399,401,402] Cyclosporine concentrations can be measured in either whole blood or plasma. Plasma cyclosporine levels are temperature- and concentration-dependent. Since plasma cyclosporine can differ by as much as 50% if the temperature of the plasma is 21 °C rather than the normal body temperature of 37 °C, whole blood cyclosporine concentrations are recommended.[399]

HPLC, monoclonal RIA and TDx, and EMIT cyclosporine assays are specific for the parent compound, cyclosporine. Although cyclosporine metabolites crossreact with the parent compound in these immunoassays, the crossreactivity is minor.[403] The polyclonal RIA and TDx methods measure cyclosporine metabolites as well as the parent drug. The method chosen for monitoring should be easy to perform, have a rapid turn-around time, and a high level of consistency. These criteria are met by the whole blood TDx assay. TDx assay only requires about 30 minutes to analyze 20 samples; RIA needs about two to four hours to analyze the samples; and an even longer time is needed for HPLC. In addition, the technical aspects of sample preparation and assay are less complicated for the TDx assay. TDx cyclosporine assays had the highest between-runs degree of precision when compared to other assay methodologies, and TDx cyclosporine levels correlate well with those by RIA.[404] The TDx and EMIT assays appear to be the most useful for cyclosporine monitoring. Levels obtained with the polyclonal TDx method on whole blood are approximately 15% higher than polyclonal RIA levels and three and one-half times as high as HPLC levels for the same samples.[404]

No assay appears to be superior in ability to correlate cyclosporine trough levels with clinical events. Although many studies have attempted to correlate the clinical events of acute rejection or nephrotoxicity to trough concentrations of cyclosporine in recipients of solid organ transplants, results from these studies appear to be somewhat in conflict. It may be that the ability to correlate a single blood level during the course of a day with a clinical event that takes place over a longer time period is influenced by too many other variables (e.g., other immunosuppressives, time post-transplant, dosage regimen, route, transplant type, assay method, sample matrix, donor-recipient interaction).[405] Nevertheless, the majority of transplant programs, if not all, use cyclosporine levels to guide therapy decisions.

Because of the limitations of using a single cyclosporine level, some programs use a more intensive sampling procedure (e.g., 6–10 samples collected over the course of a 24-hour period) when cyclosporine concentrations are expected to be at steady state. The area under the concentration-time curve and average steady-state concentrations are calculated and used to guide cyclosporine dosage adjustments. A more limited sampling strategy involving three samples collected over a 24-hour period also is being used.[406] Some transplant programs also monitor pre- and post-transplant clearance and bioavailability of cyclosporine, and others have developed even more complex pharmacokinetic approaches to guide cyclosporine therapy.[407] The more sophisticated pharmacokinetic monitoring programs have developed better correlations between the AUC and dose, or AUC and rejection, than correlations based upon just cyclosporine trough concentrations.[408,409] The pharmacokinetic parameters of clearance and bioavailability for cyclosporine also correlate with acute rejection. Rejection episodes and ultimate loss of transplanted kidneys have been associated with decreased cyclosporine bioavailability and higher clearance. A lower bioavailability of cyclosporine appears more commonly in blacks than in whites and blacks are more likely to experience organ rejections.[410]

As in all cases, pharmacokinetic data must be interpreted in conjunction with the patient's clinical condition. Additionally, deference always must be given to trends established by multiple cyclosporine levels over that of a single level. Single levels may be erroneous because of incorrect sampling techniques (e.g., not being obtained at the correct time, drawn from an IV catheter in which IV cyclosporine had been infused), or assay error.[399,411]

Rejection

40. G.D. was discharged from the hospital on August 12. She went to stay with her sister after 2 weeks and was followed with laboratory tests obtained 3 times a week. The following laboratory values were obtained on August 29: AST 36 U/L (Normal: 0–35), ALT 52 U/L (Normal: 0–35), GGT 65 U/L (Normal: 0–30), and bilirubin T/D 1.0/0.3 mg/dL (Normal: 0.1–1.0); and on September 4: AST 158 IU/L, ALT 322 IU/L, GGT 321 IU/L, and bilirubin T/D 3.6/3.2 mg/dL.

G.D. was readmitted to the transplant center because LFTs suggested increasing dysfunction, and a percutaneous needle liver biopsy was obtained. Upon admission, she complained of tiredness, severe headaches, and some pain over the area of the transplanted liver. She also stated that she had not felt like eating for the last 2–3 days. The pathologist interpreted the liver biopsy as moderate rejection, and G.D. was given a 1 gm IV bolus of methylprednisolone followed by rapidly tapered doses of corticosteroids. This regimen used the following IV doses of methylprednisolone: 50 mg Q 6 hr × 4 doses; 40 mg Q 6 hr × 4 doses, 30 mg Q 6 hr × 4 doses; 20 mg Q 6 hr × 4 doses; 20 mg Q 12 hr × 2 doses; and then back to the pre-tapered oral prednisone dose. Three days into the recycle, G.D.'s liver enzyme values did not reflect improvement in her condition and OKT3 therapy was initiated. Laboratory values after 14 days of OKT3 IV 5 mg/day were: AST 35 IU/L, ALT 108 IU/L, GGT 169 IU/L, and bilirubin T/D 1.0/0.6 mg/dL. Twelve-hour cyclosporine trough levels throughout the treatment course ranged from 725 ng/mL to 850 ng/mL by polyclonal whole blood TDx assay. G.D. was discharged and sent home with the following medications: cyclosporine 700 mg PO capsules BID, prednisone 20 mg PO QD, nystatin suspension 500,000 U to swish and swallow QID, prazosin 3 mg PO TID, nifedipine XL 60 mg PO QD, furosemide 20 mg PO QD, co-trimoxazole 1 tablet BID every Monday-Wednesday-Friday of each week for _Pneumocystis carinii_ pneumonia prophylaxis. What subjective and objective evidence of liver rejection is

present in G.D.? [SI units: AST 36 U/L, 158 U/L, 35 U/L (Normal: 0–35); ALT 52 U/L, 322 U/L, 108 U/L (Normal: 0–35); GGT 65 U/L, 321 U/L, 169 UL (Normal: 0–30); bilirubin 17.⅛.13 μmol/L, 61.56/54.72 μmol/L, 17.⅙.2 μmol/L (Normal: 2–18)]

Rejection episodes in liver transplant recipients can be categorized as acute or chronic. Hyperacute rejection, which may happen within minutes to hours of transplantation of other organs, rarely occurs with liver transplantation.[412] As a result, in some cases livers are transplanted despite an unfavorable donor-recipient crossmatch, unlike kidney and heart transplants. In fact, when transplanted concomitantly with other organs (e.g., skin, heart, kidneys) from the same donor, the liver appears to protect these other organs from hyperacute rejection.[415] Class I antigens with donor specificity appear in the serum of patients who receive liver transplants less than 24 hours after the procedure. These soluble antigens persist for the life of the graft and, theoretically, reduce humoral antibody titers that are observed in multiple-organ transplant recipients. A few reports of hyperacute liver rejection are beginning to raise concern, however.[413,414]

Acute

Although acute liver rejection can occur any time after the transplant, it most commonly is experienced within the first four to six weeks.[416,417] Late acute rejections often are a result of either a reduction in the dose of cyclosporine or the discontinuation of this drug. These rejection episodes, though common, rarely lead to graft loss. G.D. presents with some of the common subjective complaints of patients experiencing rejection of their transplanted liver. Commonly, patients feel poorly, and complain of anorexia, abdominal discomfort, and headache. Other symptoms such as a low-grade fever, back pain, or respiratory distress may occur. Objective evidence for rejection in G.D. includes an abrupt rise in serum concentrations of transaminases and bilirubin, and a liver biopsy that was interpreted as "moderate rejection" by the pathologist. These observations, in conjunction with the subjective signs, point to a diagnosis of rejection.[417] Acute rejection is associated with mononuclear-cell infiltration of the graft, edema, and parenchymal necrosis. Areas most commonly damaged are the bile ducts, veins, and arteries.[418]

Chronic

Chronic liver rejection, also called "ductopenic rejection," usually manifests months to years after transplant. It also can occur within the first few weeks after transplant. About 2% to 17% of liver transplant recipients may experience chronic rejection.[417] Characteristics of chronic liver rejection include occlusive arterial lesions, destruction of small intrahepatic bile ducts (often referred to as "vanishing bile duct syndrome"), intense cholestasis, accumulation of foamy macrophages within the portal sinusoids, and fibrosis which may lead to the development of cirrhosis. Chronic rejection is irreversible and unaffected by increased immunosuppressive therapy; retransplantation has been considered the only viable alternative. However, some patients with ductopenic rejection that was unresponsive to current therapy have responded to tacrolimus.[419]

Treatment of Rejection

41. Why was the treatment of G.D.'s rejection of her transplanted liver appropriate?

G.D. was receiving maintenance immunosuppression with cyclosporine and prednisone. Double therapy or triple therapy commonly is used as chronic immunosuppressive therapy of liver transplants.[420] G.D.'s cyclosporine trough whole blood concentrations were in the low normal therapeutic range of 800 to 1200 ng/dL by polyclonal whole blood TDx (normal values for therapeutic range vary with the institution). Although G.D.'s cyclosporine level ap-

peared adequate, she was treated with a bolus dose of IV methylprednisolone because of clinical evidence that supported a diagnosis of graft rejection. This treatment decision was reasonable because high-dose corticosteroids can reverse acute rejection episodes of a transplanted liver.[417,421] The decision to monitor G.D.'s response to the initial bolus steroid dose and the severity of rejection by biopsy also was appropriate before proceeding with further treatment. G.D. had experienced moderate rejection of her transplanted liver, and the subsequent initiation of another cycle of corticosteroids was reasonable because the mainstay for treatment of acute liver rejection is increased immunosuppression.[417] Adult liver transplant recipients usually are treated with 200 mg to 1000 mg/day of intravenous methylprednisolone and tapered rapidly, as described for G.D. The dose of methylprednisolone for children is 100 mg/day initially. When patients fail to respond to recycle corticosteroid therapy, two options still are available. G.D. was begun on OKT3 therapy; the other option is to use mALG or ATG. Most centers use OKT3 as a second-line agent if there is no response to high-dose corticosteroids.[421] Patients weighing more than 30 kg commonly receive 5 mg/day of OKT3; those less than 30 kg receive 2.5 mg/day. Treatment of corticosteroid resistant rejection with OKT3 has been about 70% to 80% effective in liver transplant recipients.[422,423]

OKT3

Adverse Effects

42. One hour after receiving her first 5 mg IV dose of OKT3, G.D. began to experience chills, nausea, and severe muscle and joint aches. Her temperature rose from 37.3 °C to a maximum of 39.4 °C and her BP dropped to a systolic of 100 mm Hg and diastolic of 50 mm Hg. Which of these effects are consistent with OKT3 administration?

Like the other powerful immunosuppressive drugs used for transplantation, OKT3 is not without side effects (see Table 33.9). Many of the listed adverse effects occur with higher frequency after the first and second doses of OKT3[424,425] and G.D.'s adverse reaction after her first dose of OKT3 is consistent with this finding. This complex of symptoms is referred to as the "Cytokine-Release Syndrome." The early and most common signs present as flu-like symptoms (e.g., fever, chills, myalgia, joint pains). These nonspecific signs and symptoms of this syndrome can be accompanied by less common, but more specific, symptoms that reflect the involvement of various organ systems.[426] For example, CNS symptoms such as seizures, headaches, photophobia, confusion, and hallucinations have been reported as have aseptic meningitis and encephalopathy.[430,431] Acute reversible renal dysfunction as evidenced by a rise in the serum creatinine concentration and a decrease in urine output over the first few days of therapy also have occurred. This renal dysfunction can resolve even with continued therapy.[432] Intrarenal graft thrombosis has been reported after high doses (i.e., 10 mg) of OKT3.[434] Patients with evidence of fluid overload on chest radiograph (or >3% over their base weight) should receive furosemide and some may require dialysis before the initial OKT3 dose due to the risk of possible pulmonary edema and respiratory distress that are caused by cytokine-induced increases in capillary permeability. Anaphylaxis is rare.[433]

A proposed etiology of the above adverse effects is based upon the release of cytokines, tumor necrosis factor-α, interleukin-2, and interferon-γ by T-cells after their initial binding with OKT3.[427] OKT3 stimulation of cytokine production is another proposed explanation for the etiology of these adverse effects. This effect is independent of cell lysis.[428] The serum concentration of cytokines becomes acutely elevated within one to four hours after the first and second doses of OKT3 and these high concentrations correlate

Table 33.9	Common OKT3-Induced Side Effects
Symptom	Occurrence (%)
Fever	78
Tachycardia	68
Chills	60
Headache	40
Hypertension	31
Nausea	26
Vomiting	22
Tremor	21
Diarrhea	20
Chest pains	20
Dyspnea	20
Hypotension	15
Wheezing	12

in time with the onset of the initial symptoms which usually resolve in four to six hours. These cytokines have been correlated with similar adverse effects in other patient populations.[429]

Cardiovascular effects of hypotension, hypertension, and tachycardia can occur in heart transplant patients[435] and appear as a biphasic response. The fever, hypertension, and tachycardia are followed by hypotension, hypoxemia, and decreased vascular resistance five to seven hours later.[436] The cardiopulmonary effects are secondary to a series of events involving a number of mediators including tumor necrosis factor-α, leukotrienes, prostaglandins, thromboxane A2, and arachidonic acid metabolites produced and released by endothelial cells, neutrophils, and muscle cells.[435]

Dosing

43. What special procedures should be followed in G.D. when using OKT3 therapy?

Dosing Protocol. The high incidence of side effects associated with OKT3 therapy, especially after the first two doses, has prompted strict dosing protocols in most medical institutions. If G.D. had not had a chest x-ray within the last 24 hours, one would be ordered and reviewed before initiation of OKT3 therapy. If she had evidence of pulmonary edema, a dose of IV furosemide appropriate for the patient (commonly 40 mg in an adult) is administered before the first OKT3 dose or dialysis if appropriate. G.D. should receive a dose of methylprednisolone 7 to 8 mg/kg ($\leq$500 mg) intravenously 60 minutes before the first dose of OKT3 and 4 mg/kg before the second dose to significantly reduce the amount of cytokine released after OKT3 administration.[437] Acetaminophen 650 mg orally or rectally (10 mg/kg in children) and diphenhydramine 50 mg orally or intravenously (1 mg/kg in children) also are administered before the first two doses of OKT3.[426] Indomethacin,[438] pentoxifylline,[439] and anti-tumor necrosis factor antibody[440] given before OKT3 have shown promise in minimizing some of the acute effects of OKT3.

In addition to the premedication orders, policies, and procedures for administration of OKT3 for the first two doses must be developed for all institutions treating patients with OKT3. For example, a physician is expected to give the first two doses of the drug and to remain in the patient's room for two hours after each dose, or the patient is to be admitted to the ICU for the first two doses. The emergency medication cart must be available immediately; and vital signs are to be measured every 15 minutes for the first two hours, every 30 minutes for the following two hours, and then at usual intervals when the patient is stable. Generally, OKT3 therapy

should not be initiated late in the evening because of the need for intensive monitoring of the patient.

Some transplant centers monitor peripheral T-lymphocyte populations during OKT3 therapy. IL-2-receptor levels, antimurine titers, and CMV cultures of urine, sputum, and blood are monitored for at least three weeks after discontinuation of OKT3 therapy. The effectiveness of OKT3 can be evaluated by monitoring the presence of CD3-positive cells amidst T-lymphocytes in the peripheral circulation. In some transplant centers, the number of soluble CD3-positive cells is kept to less than 10 cells/μL[441] while others are willing to accept 20 to 50 CD3-positive cells/μL.[442] Some centers also monitor OKT3 serum trough levels in conjunction with CD3-positive cells. Low OKT3 levels may provide an earlier indication that a higher dose of OKT3 is needed than an increase in the number of CD3-positive cells.[443]

Antibodies to OKT3

44. Why would doses of G.D.'s immunosuppressive drugs need to be adjusted during OKT3 administration?

When OKT3 is administered, antibodies against OKT3 can be formed. These antibodies can be anti-idiotype, anti-isotype, or in most cases both. Anti-isotype antibodies are formed against the murine proteins of OKT3, and anti-idiotype antibodies are formed against the specific CD3 region. In one study of renal transplant patients, 60% had an anti-idiotype response and 44% had an anti-isotype response. Overall, an antibody response was detected in 75% of patients. A reduction in the dose of azathioprine and prednisone or a reduction in the dose of cyclosporine while receiving OKT3 has lowered the titers of antibody against OKT3.[444,445] Anti-OKT3 antibodies have the potential to decrease the effectiveness of repeated courses of the drug; however, multiple courses of treatment with OKT3 have been successful.

When treatment of G.D.'s acute rejection is initiated with OKT3, her cyclosporine dose should be reduced by 50% and her prednisone dose should remain the same. On the tenth day of her OKT3 treatment, her cyclosporine dose should be increased to the previous dose that she was taking before the initiation of OKT3 therapy. She should be tested for an anti-OKT3 antibody titer two to four weeks after the end of OKT3 treatment. If this titer is less than 1:100, then OKT3 can be used again if necessary. Patients with low titers have been retreated successfully.[446,447]

Corticosteroid Adverse Effects

45. G.D. now weighs 64 kg as opposed to her initial weight of 57 kg. She also complains of chronic backache, increased appetite, and fluid retention. What is the most likely etiology of G.D.'s weight gain and other physical findings? What can be done to manage some of these problems?

G.D. seems to be experiencing several corticosteroid-induced side effects. Weight gain, increased appetite, and fluid and water retention as experienced by G.D. commonly are encountered by patients treated with corticosteroids. Corticosteroid administration increases lipolysis and release of free fatty acids and glycerol. The glycerol most likely is used as a substrate for increased hepatic gluconeogenesis and the free fatty acids as an alternate energy source. These effects on fat and carbohydrate metabolism result in a redistribution of fat, causing a centripetal or truncal fat deposition (i.e., "buffalo hump") with a concomitant decrease in peripheral fat stores.[29]

G.D. currently is taking furosemide, prazosin, and nifedipine to control blood pressure. High blood pressure after transplantation is a common problem and may be caused partially by the characteristic fluid and sodium retention associated with corticosteroid use.[448] Corticosteroids also can increase blood pressure independent of their ability to induce sodium and fluid retention.

G.D.'s chronic backache should be investigated since corticosteroids will predispose G.D. to osteoporosis. She is at increased risk for this side effect because her chronic liver disease may have depleted her calcium stores and she may be postmenopausal. Prolonged corticosteroid administration is associated with reduced intestinal calcium absorption, decreased activation of vitamin D in the liver, increased urinary calcium loss, secondary hyperparathyroidism, decreased bone formation, and impaired growth hormone release.[29] Osteoporosis is a growing issue as patients survive longer and a larger number of organ transplants are performed in older individuals.[449,450] Osteoporosis predisposes G.D. to spinal compression fractures which could be the source of the backache. Aseptic osteonecrosis is another severe complication seen in transplant recipients. G.D. possibly could benefit from the addition of 400 U of vitamin D and 1000 to 1500 mg of elemental calcium each day.[451] Also see postmenopausal osteoporosis in Chapter 46: Gynecological Disorders.

Other potential adverse effects of corticosteroid therapy in posttransplant patients include corticosteroid myopathy, GI distress, glucose intolerance, hypercholesterolemia, CNS disturbances (see Question 37), infections, decreased wound healing, cataracts, glaucoma, and growth retardation in children. Permanent growth retardation is uncommon because discontinuation of the corticosteroid, lowering the dose, or implementing an alternate day dosing regimen usually results in accelerated growth back to normal ranges.[452,453] Corticosteroid myopathy presents as proximal muscle weakness and wasting of the musculature. Also see Chapter 42: Connective Tissue Disorders: The Clinical Use of Corticosteroids for discussions of adverse effects to corticosteroids.

Gastrointestinal distress (e.g., nausea, vomiting, possible peptic ulceration) most likely is due to the systemic, rather than the local, effects of corticosteroids. Corticosteroid-treated patients are at increased risk for GI irritation probably because these drugs decrease the production of cytoprotective prostaglandins and usually indicates reactivation of previous condition.[454,455]

Glucose intolerance and hypercholesterolemia both are related to the metabolic effects of corticosteroids. Corticosteroid therapy can alter glucose homeostasis enough to cause manifestations of disease in previously asymptomatic diabetics. Hypercholesterolemia may lead to an increased incidence of atherosclerosis, which is of particular concern in heart and kidney transplant recipients.

All organ transplant recipients are at risk for infection because they are iatrogenically immunosuppressed. Transplant surgery patients, as a result, are at greater risk for infectious complications than general surgery patients. Although the immunosuppressive properties of corticosteroids can contribute to the risk, the other more powerful immunosuppressive agents used alone or in combination with corticosteroids have a greater potential to cause infection. Nevertheless, the anti-inflammatory effects of corticosteroids can delay diagnosis of an infection by masking characteristic signs and symptoms that commonly signal the presence of an infectious process. Specifically, tissues may not become inflamed and white blood cell counts are difficult to interpret. Within four to six hours of a corticosteroid dose, the neutrophil count increases due to an increased release of neutrophils from the bone marrow and reduced migration out of the circulation. Lymphocyte, monocyte, eosinophil, and basophil counts, in contrast, will decrease transiently.[29] In addition, corticosteroids can decrease the febrile response to infection and mislead clinicians into making incorrect assumptions as to the seriousness of an infection. For example, some asymptomatic patients with radiographic evidence of free air in the abdomen and only a low-grade fever were discovered upon surgical exploration to have peritonitis from bowel perforation. As

noted earlier, wound healing also is prolonged in corticosteroid-treated patients, and wounds are allowed to heal longer before staples and sutures are removed.[455]

As a result of the number of problems associated with chronic corticosteroid administration, several corticosteroid withdrawal protocols have been extrapolated from data in heart and kidney transplant recipients. The majority of patients experienced resolution of corticosteroid-induced adverse effects and no progression of other adverse sequelae upon discontinuation of their corticosteroids. The corticosteroids, for G.D. in particular, should be withdrawn cautiously because of her history of organ rejection. If complete withdrawal from corticosteroids is not feasible in this patient, the lowest possible dose (e.g., prednisone 5–10 mg/day or 10–20 mg every other day) may be adequate to resolve her drug-induced adverse effects without precipitating an episode of organ rejection.

Tacrolimus

46. T.P., a 4-year-old, 17 kg female, received a liver transplant for biliary atresia secondary to biliary cirrhosis. She was begun on induction therapy with ATG therapy 300 mg IV QD for 10 days, prednisolone 50 mg IV BID, azathioprine 25 mg IV QD, and continuous cyclosporine drip at 2 mg/hr and adjusted to maintain trough concentrations (by whole blood monoclonal TDx assay) between 300–400 ng/mL. A liver biopsy 11 days after transplant showed acute rejection, grade 2 which was treated with corticosteroid pulse therapy, but therapy was ineffective. T.P. ultimately developed acute rejection, grade 3, requiring OKT3 IV 2.5 mg QD for 14 days. A liver biopsy following OKT3 was worrisome for chronic rejection but upon further evaluation it was determined to be continued mild acute rejection without evidence of vanishing bile duct syndrome. Percutaneous transluminal catheterization revealed normal caliber biliary ducts with free flow into Roux-en-Y with no obstruction or stricture. However, T.P. had developed a persistent cholestatic (nonobstructive) picture. It was decided at this point that T.P. would not be a candidate for oral cyclosporine. What other drug therapy options are available for T.P. at this point?

Indications

T.P.'s cholestatic situation would make it difficult to achieve appropriate cyclosporine concentrations because of poor cyclosporine absorption. Although intravenous cyclosporine is an option for T.P., it has the potential for complications, is costly, and her continued rejection with maximal immunosuppression requires a search for another alternative. The newest approved alternative for liver transplantation is tacrolimus (Prograf). A study involving 31 pediatric liver transplant recipients was conducted to determine the safety and efficacy of conversion to tacrolimus after failing immunosuppression with cyclosporine. Indications for conversion were refractory rejection (acute or chronic); intolerable adverse effects of cyclosporine (i.e., hypertension, hirsutism); or inability to reach therapeutic cyclosporine concentrations, due primarily to malabsorption. After ten months, 87% of patients had functioning grafts after converting from cyclosporine to tacrolimus. Thirteen patients were converted to tacrolimus because of refractory rejection and 70% survived. Two-thirds of these patients experienced complete reversal of rejection within three months of conversion from cyclosporine to tacrolimus. Eight patients were converted due to the development of hypertension while on cyclosporine. Six patients experienced resolution of their hypertension within three months of conversion. Three children, converted to tacrolimus for reasons other than refractory rejection, experienced rejection after conversion. Two of these had resolution with corticosteroids or an increase in tacrolimus dose. The third child developed chronic rejection.[456] Tacrolimus is a safe and effective rescue treatment in patients who have failed or cannot tolerate cyclosporine immunosuppression.

Tacrolimus has similar efficacy as cyclosporine in liver, kidney, and lung transplant patients as the primary immunosuppressant in combination with corticosteroids.[457–459] It also is effective as a rescue treatment in liver, kidney, and heart transplant patients who experienced rejection in spite of standard immunotherapy.[460–462]

Pharmacokinetics

The absorption of oral tacrolimus is variable with bioavailability ranging from 5% to 67% (mean: 27%).[463] In contrast to cyclosporine, the bioavailability of tacrolimus does not appear to be dependent upon the presence of bile. Following oral administration of tacrolimus in dogs having bile duct ligation, the absorption of tacrolimus actually increased.[464] Therefore, cyclosporine absorption would be expected to be decreased in T.P. because of her cholestasis, but tacrolimus absorption should not be decreased. The elimination half-life ranges from 5.5 to 16.6 hours, with a mean of 8.7 hours and plasma clearance averaging 143 L/hr.[465] The time for tacrolimus to reach peak concentrations ranges from one to four hours.[465] Tacrolimus is highly lipophilic and has a large volume of distribution (5–65 L/kg).[463] It primarily is distributed within red blood cells which may contain large amounts of FK binding protein; thus, whole blood concentrations may be 10 to 30 times higher than plasma concentrations.[463] It is bound in plasma to α_1-acid glycoprotein, in contrast to cyclosporine which primarily is bound to lipoproteins.[463] The distribution of tacrolimus is affected by the hematocrit, concentration of plasma proteins, and also the temperature of the blood sample.[463] Tacrolimus is metabolized extensively in the liver with less than 1% of the dose excreted unchanged in the urine and less than 5% excreted into the bile.[463] Pediatric patients appear to have a more rapid clearance of tacrolimus, as well as a shorter half-life and larger volume of distribution, as compared to adult patients.[466]

Dosing

47. How would you initiate tacrolimus treatment in T.P.?

Tacrolimus typically is administered as a continuous infusion following transplant at an initial dose of 0.05 to 0.1 mg/kg/day.[467] It can be administered via a central or peripheral IV line, and usually is mixed in a glass bottle of D5W or 0.9NS.[468] Both bottles and tubing (nitroglycerin, glass-lined tubing) should be changed every 12 hours.[468] However, patients should be converted as soon as possible from IV to oral therapy with initial tacrolimus doses of 0.15 to 0.3 mg/kg/day divided into 12-hour intervals because adverse effects, such as headache, nausea, and vomiting, occur more commonly with intravenous administration.[460,467] Pediatric patients appear to require higher doses of tacrolimus as compared to adults. In a comparison between 16 pediatric and 33 adult liver transplant patients, the overall mean tacrolimus dose for the first year was 0.46 ± 0.4 mg/kg/day in pediatric patients versus 0.13 ± 0.01 mg/kg/day in adults to achieve similar trough concentrations.[469] When switching from cyclosporine to tacrolimus, the cyclosporine should be discontinued 24 hours before initiating tacrolimus therapy or longer if cyclosporine concentrations are elevated. The concomitant administration of cyclosporine and tacrolimus has been accompanied by increases in the serum concentrations of creatinine and urea nitrogen which declined after the discontinuation of cyclosporine.[470] Thus, combination therapy with cyclosporine and tacrolimus is not recommended due to the additive or synergistic risk of nephrotoxicity. Oral tacrolimus is available as both 1 mg and 5 mg capsules and should be administered on an empty stomach. Therefore, the cyclosporine for T.P.

should be discontinued, and oral tacrolimus therapy should be initiated 24 hours later at 0.3 mg/kg/day divided every 12 hours with subsequent doses to be adjusted based upon whole blood concentrations and clinical response.

Adverse Effects

48. What are the major adverse effects seen with tacrolimus and what clinical parameters should be monitored in T.P.?

Nephrotoxicity usually is the limiting adverse effect of tacrolimus and has been reported in greater than 50% of patients.[471] The clinical presentation of tacrolimus-induced nephrotoxicity is similar to that of cyclosporine. A reduction in tacrolimus dose usually reverses the nephrotoxicity.[471] A trial comparing nephrotoxicity of tacrolimus to cyclosporine in liver transplant patients was conducted in 37 patients.[472] Both agents resulted in significant deterioration in renal function during the first postoperative year. Actually, at one year tacrolimus-treated patients had a greater and statistically significant decline in renal dysfunction as evidenced by glomerular filtration rate (mL/minute/BSA): pre-treatment for cyclosporine group 90 ± 6 versus one year 64 ± 6 (P <0.05), pre-treatment for tacrolimus group 83 ± 8 versus one year 45 ± 4 (P <0.05). The IV administration of tacrolimus during the first week was associated with acute renal failure in 20% of patients, thus a rapid conversion to oral therapy is desired. It was proposed that liver recipients with poor graft function were unable to metabolize tacrolimus rapidly and were at a greater risk for acute renal failure. In a multicenter study involving 529 patients compared the efficacy and toxicity of tacrolimus to cyclosporine in liver transplant patients. Both agents had comparable effects on increasing serum creatinine and decreasing glomerular filtration rate.[473] Thus, T.P.'s renal function should be monitored closely, as if she were receiving cyclosporine. Major neurologic toxicities (e.g., confusion, seizures, dysarthria, persistent coma) occur in about 10% of patients.[471] Minor neurologic toxicities occur in approximately 20% to 60% of patients and include tremors, headache, and sleep disturbances.[473,474] Hypertension (40%) is another common finding in patients treated with tacrolimus;[479] however, a greater number of tacrolimus-treated patients are able to discontinue or limit their use of antihypertensives as compared to cyclosporine.[479] Other adverse effects include hyperkalemia, hemolytic anemia, increased susceptibility to infection and malignancy, and hyperglycemia [events requiring insulin vary with time (i.e., chronic administration decreases the occurrence)].[471] Hirsutism and gingival hyperplasia, in contrast to cyclosporine, do not appear to be complications of tacrolimus.[471] Effects of tacrolimus on growth in pediatric patients are unknown; however, lower doses of corticosteroids are needed for immunosuppression, than with cyclosporine.[475] This potentially is an advantage of tacrolimus over cyclosporine, especially in pediatric patients like T.P. Few drug interaction studies have been conducted, but caution should be used with drugs that induce or inhibit liver enzyme metabolism similar to cyclosporine.[479]

Therapeutic Drug Monitoring

Therapeutic drug monitoring is recommended for tacrolimus due to its narrow therapeutic range and high risk of toxicity. Recommended therapeutic trough concentrations depend upon the temperature of the plasma separation, the method of extraction, the matrix, and the specificity of the method.[476] Initially, recommended plasma trough concentrations ranged from 0.5 to 2 ng/mL whereas trough whole blood concentrations range from 5 to 20 ng/mL at 37 °C as measured by enzyme-linked immunosorbent assay (ELISA) using a monoclonal antitacrolimus mouse antibody.[477] Disadvantages of this system included potential measurement of metabolites due to crossreactivity with the antibody; required up to two days to obtain results; and large variation with the lower concentrations.[477] An IMx method for tacrolimus assays was developed which uses whole blood with the same antibody. This method appears more precise and convenient, with the major drawback being lower sensitivity with concentrations below the suggested therapeutic range.[478,480] T.P. should have tacrolimus concentrations drawn two to three times a week during the initial phase of stabilization on her maintenance regimen. Less frequent but still close monitoring will be required once her regimen is established. If adjustments in concentrations are desired, small incremental changes are recommended. There is evidence that with doses less than 10 mg/day, tacrolimus demonstrates linearity; whereas doses greater than 10 mg/day show rapid and disproportionate increases in concentration indicating nonlinear pharmacokinetic behavior.[481]

Tacrolimus is a drug therapy option in patients unable to absorb oral cyclosporine, patients unable to obtain adequate cyclosporine concentrations, patients unable to tolerate cyclosporine side effects, or patients experiencing refractory rejection. Advantages of tacrolimus over cyclosporine appear to include a decrease or discontinuation of corticosteroids; a decrease in the number or discontinuation of antihypertensive medications; and lack of hirsutism, gingival hyperplasia, or increase in cholesterol levels. Disadvantages appear to include a high incidence of neurological adverse effects, and nephrotoxicity. Thus, tacrolimus is an additional agent to add to the immunosuppressant choices for transplant patients.

Antilymphocyte Globulin (ALG) and Antithymocyte Globulin (ATG)

49. R.F. is a 35-year-old, 70 kg male, who received a combined kidney-pancreas transplant for end-stage diabetic nephropathy. He received a whole pancreas graft with the bladder drainage technique. He was begun on induction ATG therapy, 1200 mg IV over 6 hours QD, in conjunction with azathioprine 75 mg IV QD and methylprednisolone 30 mg IV Q 6 hr × 3 days. The methylprednisolone dose was tapered rapidly to 30 mg QD after the 3rd day. ATG therapy was given for 10 days, and cyclosporine was begun on the 8th postoperative day at a dose of 350 mg BID (i.e., 5 mg/kg BID) and the cyclosporine dose was adjusted to maintain trough levels (by monoclonal whole blood TDx assay) between 150 to 300 ng/mL. Blood glucose, serum and urine amylase were monitored in R.F. Q 4 hr for the first 5 days, then daily after transplant. Laboratory values were obtained daily and included electrolytes, CBC with differential count, platelets, SrCr, and BUN. How should ATG be administered and monitored in R.F.?

Dosing and Administration

Both ATG and mALG usually are administered in a dose of 10 to 20 mg/kg/day and 2.5 to 10 mg/kg/day for rATG.[482,483] These drugs can be diluted in 0.9% sodium chloride for injection and administered over four to six hours. The concentration of the mALG (or ATG) infusion ideally should not be greater than 1 mg/mL. ATG and mALG should be infused into a high-flow central vein to reduce pain, erythema, and phlebitis at the injection site.[484] Although an intradermal ATG test dose of 0.1 mL of a 1:1000 dilution has been recommended before the first full dose of ATG to test the patient for presensitization to horse serum,[485] the predictive value of this test is unclear. An epicutaneous test is safer, faster, and causes less discomfort than the intradermal test and perhaps is of better predictive value in detecting a significant allergy to horse serum.[486] The epicutaneous test uses a needle to make a small break in the epidermis under a drop of 1:10 or 1:100 ATG dilution that had been placed on the skin. Patients with pre-

vious sensitization to horse serum are at risk for anaphylactoid reactions. The prevalence of anaphylaxis has diminished with improved purification of these products.[485] Any patient with a positive pretherapy skin test should be desensitized before treatment.

Desensitization has been accomplished by giving 0.02 mL of a 5, 50, 500, and 5000 µg/mL solution intradermally at ten-minute intervals; then 0.5 mL of 50, 100, 300, 1000, 3000, and 5000 µg/mL solution subcutaneously at ten-minute intervals; then the therapeutic dose of ATG was administered by continuous infusion over a ten-day period.[486]

Duration of Therapy

Duration of therapy with ATG or mALG ranges from 7 to 21 days. The use of mALG as induction immunosuppression for longer than ten days has not resulted in better outcomes but has caused a higher incidence of infectious complications.[487] Protocols used to treat rejection commonly use a 10- to 14-day course of treatment.

Adverse Effects

A number of adverse effects have been related to the use of ATG or mALG. Local phlebitis and pain, noted in 2% of patients in one trial, usually can be avoided by administering the drug through a high-flow central vein. Chills and fever (15% to 20%), erythema (18%), pruritus (18%), and thrombocytopenia (10%) commonly are encountered.[488,489] Fever, chills, nausea, and vomiting may be due to the release of cytokines such as tumor necrosis factor from lysed lymphocytes[490] and can be decreased by concomitant administration of corticosteroids or antihistamines.[488] The rash, hives, and pruritus can be managed by slowing the infusion rate and by the administration of antihistamines and corticosteroids. Serum sickness leading to acute glomerulonephritis, hypotension, and acute respiratory distress also has been associated with ATG and mALG.[491] Serum sickness may not be evident until day 7 of therapy. Delayed side effects generally are seen as an increase in opportunistic infections of both viral and fungal origin.

Monitoring

General precautions during ATG and mALG administration include daily monitoring of WBC and platelet counts and hourly monitoring of vital signs during infusion. Patients are premedicated with acetaminophen and diphenhydramine before each dose, and 1 mg of epinephrine and 1000 mg of methylprednisolone are taped above the patient's bed in case of an anaphylactic reaction. If the patient's WBC count drops below 3000 cells/mm^3 or if the platelet count drops below 100,000 cells/mm^3, the dose of drug either is decreased by 50% or held entirely until the counts return to desired levels. The decision to decrease or hold the dose is based upon the current status of the patient's rejection and the degree of thrombocytopenia and neutropenia.

Doses also can be adjusted based upon absolute lymphocyte counts or lymphocyte subsets as a way of maximizing efficacy and minimizing infectious complications. The ATG dose can be adjusted by using a target absolute T-lymphocyte count (CD2 or T11) of between 50 cells/mm^3 to 200 cells/mm^3.[492-494] In a small study of patients with corticosteroid-resistant rejection, this latter approach resulted in a lower dose of ATG, lower costs, and lower rate of viral infection.[492]

Azathioprine

Adverse Effects

50. R.F. has finished his course of ATG and is doing well. He will be discharged from the hospital in 2 days after he has learned how to take his medications, how to monitor his BP, and the signs and symptoms of infection and rejection. His

medications at time of discharge are: cyclosporine 325 mg PO BID, prednisone 20 mg PO QD, azathioprine 100 mg PO Q HS, nystatin suspension 5 mL to swish and swallow QID, furosemide 20 mg QD, nifedipine XL 60 mg QD, and captopril 12.5 mg TID.

What azathioprine adverse effects would be expected in R.F. and what laboratory tests would be useful for monitoring these adverse effects?

The most common adverse effect of azathioprine is bone marrow suppression that presents as leukopenia or, less frequently, thrombocytopenia,[495] and megaloblastic anemia.[496] Myelosuppression is dose-dependent and typically observed after 7 to 14 days of therapy; therefore, R.S.'s hematocrit and WBC and platelet counts should be monitored.[148] Bone marrow suppression may be related to a genetic deficiency of the enzyme, thiopurine methyltransferase (TPMT) deficiency. Low activity of this enzyme is rare but does lead to greater availability of 6-mercaptopurine, elevated 6-thioguanine levels, and susceptibility to myelosuppression. Low levels of TPMT have been associated in some transplant patients with azathioprine at the time of severe myelotoxicity.[497–499]

AST, ALT, and alkaline phosphatase should be monitored periodically because hepatitis, cholestasis, and reversible and irreversible liver damage have been reported with azathioprine use.[500–502] The irreversible liver damage appears histologically compatible with central vein phlebitis and occlusion, fibrosis, lobular necrosis, and biliary stasis.[503]

R.F.'s WBC should be maintained greater than 5000/mm^3. If his WBC count decreases to 3000 to 5000/mm^3, the azathioprine dose should be reduced by 50%. If the reduction in azathioprine dose fails to keep his WBC greater than 3000/mm^3, then the medication should be discontinued and reinstituted if needed at the lower dose when the leukopenia is resolved. A similar approach should be taken if thrombocytopenia occurs. If hepatotoxicity or other serious side effects occur, azathioprine is discontinued.[148]

Pancreatitis has been associated with azathioprine administration[504] but would be difficult to discern in R.F. because of his pancreas transplant. Long-term azathioprine administration also has been associated with the occurrence of non-Hodgkin's lymphoma, squamous cell skin cancer, primary hepatic tumors,[505] fever, rigors, rash, headache, myalgia, tachycardia, hypotension, polyarthritis, and acute hypersensitivity reactions. Reports of alopecia, anorexia, nausea, and vomiting may be related to the antimitotic effect of the drug.[20]

Complication of Leukopenia

51. R.F. was discharged to home on day 12 with follow-up in clinic 3 times per week for the first month, then weekly, then every 2 weeks for the next 6 months. Laboratory parameters on day of discharge were: BUN 25 mg/dL (Normal: 8–18), SrCr 1.5 mg/dL (Normal: 0.6–1.2), blood glucose 110 mg/dL (Normal: 80–120), WBC count 7000 cells/mm^3 (Normal: 4000 –10,000) and platelets 125,000 cells/mm^3 (Normal: 130–400 × 10^3). Six months after discharge, R.F. is readmitted to the hospital with a WBC count of 1200 cells/mm^3 and the following differential: 35 segs, 3 bands, 55 lymphocytes, 4 monocytes, 3 basophils, and 0 eosinophils. He is afebrile and surveillance viral cultures for CMV and EBV obtained the previous week are negative. He is placed in modified protective isolation, and his azathioprine is discontinued. His medications upon admission are the same, except for reduced cyclosporine and prednisone doses, as those on discharge with the exception of allopurinol 300 mg QD, added by R.F.'s physician 2 weeks ago. His transplanted kidney-pancreas is functioning well. What factors are contributing to R.F.'s leukopenia? [SI units: BUN 8.9 mmol/L (Normal: 3.0–6.5); SrCr 132.6 μmol/L (Normal: 50–110); glucose 6.1

mmol/L (Normal: 4.44–6.66); WBC 700 × 10^6, 1200 × 10^6 cells/L (Normal: 4000–10,000 × 10^6); platelets 125 × 10^9/L (Normal: 130–400 × 10^9)]

Since the most common adverse effect of azathioprine is bone marrow depression, the finding of leukopenia is not surprising; however, the probability for leukopenia is enhanced in R.F. because of several contributing factors. Coadministration of captopril and azathioprine can increase the incidence of leukopenia.[506] R.F. also was started on allopurinol therapy, and there is a well-described interaction between allopurinol and azathioprine. The inhibition of xanthine oxidase by allopurinol impairs elimination of 6-MP and inhibits the metabolic formation of 6-thiouric acid. This leads to a potentiation of the pharmacologic effect of both azathioprine and 6-MP.[507] Oral doses of azathioprine should be reduced by 75% to 80% when allopurinol is administered concurrently. One or both of these drug interactions could be the cause of R.S.'s leukopenia.

Another cause of leukopenia could be a bacterial, fungal, or viral infection. Infection always should be included in the differential diagnosis of patients on immunosuppressive medications. This etiology cannot be excluded entirely, but viral cultures are negative and the patient is afebrile. If the patient has drug-induced neutropenia, the WBC count should increase after discontinuing azathioprine. If R.F.'s WBC count had fallen lower where there would be a significant risk of infection, a short course of G-CSF 5 μg/kg/day subcutaneously may be given.[508]

Infection

Despite advances in immunosuppressive regimens and improvements in surgical techniques for transplantation over the last decade, infection continues to be a major source of morbidity and mortality.[509,510] Transplant patients have the same risk of infection from the transplant surgery as any other immunocompromised patient undergoing a surgical procedure. The percentage of transplant patients who develop infections has decreased since the advent of cyclosporine;[511,512] however, infection rates were still 61% in renal, 65% in cardiac, and 79% in hepatic transplant recipients.[513]

Treatment of infection in transplant patients should be based upon principles established for other immunocompromised patients. (See Chapter 67: Infections in Immunocompromised Hosts.) One major difference between transplant patients and other immunocompromised hosts is the fact that the immunocompromised condition of transplant patients is iatrogenic. Therefore, when a transplant patient develops a life-threatening infection, the doses of immunosuppressants commonly are decreased. Once the patient has recovered from the infection, immunosuppression can be restored to preinfection levels.

Prophylaxis

Prophylactic antibiotic therapy, theoretically, can decrease the risk of surgical infections in patients undergoing transplant surgery. As with other therapies in transplantation, prophylactic and antibiotic therapy are highly institution-dependent. Kidney transplant recipients typically receive a first-generation cephalosporin such as cefazolin to cover uropathogens and staphylococci both perioperatively and for two to five days postoperatively.[513] Liver transplants are associated with the highest rate of life-threatening bacterial infection.[513] Ampicillin/sulbactam (Unasyn) commonly is used to cover *staphylococci*, *enterococci*, and *Enterobacteriaceae*.[513] Another commonly used antibiotic is cefotaxime. Heart transplant recipients routinely receive a first-generation cephalosporin such as cefazolin at anesthesia induction and for 48 hours postoperatively.[514] However, in one study, cefamandole and cefuroxime were superior to cefazolin in open-heart surgery, as far as reducing the incidence of staphylococcal infection.[514] For lung transplant candidates, common practice is to monitor the patients' sputum before transplant and individualize the prophylactic regimen to reflect the resident flora, and to include an antipseudomonal drug.[513]

Selective bowel decontamination regimens, which are nonabsorbable antibacterial agents, have been used effectively in liver transplant recipients who are susceptible to a high incidence of bacterial infections.[513] The goal of selective bowel decontamination regimens is to eradicate the aerobic gram-negative flora from the bowel while leaving the anaerobic bowel flora intact to select colonization resistance.[513] Various selective bowel decontamination regimens have been used, but typically these regimens contain polymyxin E 100 mg, gentamicin 80 mg, and nystatin 2,000,000 U/10 mL orally four times a day. Some regimens incorporate quinolones into the regimen instead of gentamicin.[515] Selective bowel decontamination can be initiated when patients are placed on the transplant list and can be continued postoperatively for three to four weeks. One study showed a 6% incidence of gram-negative infection during the first month after transplant and no fungal infection with selective bowel decontamination treatment whereas in the control group, 53% developed a gram-negative or fungal infection.[515] A low bacterial diet (excluding raw fruit, raw vegetables, cheese, and foods that are reheated or stored at room temperature for long periods) also can be instituted.

The immunosuppressives currently used are associated with a well-defined temporal sequence of infections. For example, with kidney transplant recipients, the first postoperative month is associated with infections that typically occur in any nonimmunosuppressed patient following a similar type of surgery. Patients are at greatest risk for infection between one to six months post-transplant. Opportunistic infections are common during this time as shown in Table 33.10.[513] Because the infections in Table 33.10 are so common, it is routine to provide prophylaxis for many of them (e.g., nystatin suspension 500,000 U swish and swallow four times a day for six months to reduce fungal colonization of the GI tract; acyclovir for herpes virus infection as well as for CMV; ganciclovir/immune globulins for CMV; and TMP/SMX for Pneumocystis prophylaxis).

Cytomegalovirus (CMV)

52. S.M., a 23-year-old, 50 kg male with a history of cystic fibrosis who received a double lung transplant, presents 12 weeks after transplant with new symptoms of nausea, vomiting, headache, fever, nonproductive cough, and anorexia for 3 days. He also reports weakness and increased shortness of breath (SOB). The donor lungs were positive for CMV by serology and S.M. had negative CMV serology at the time he was transplanted. His immunosuppressive regimen postoperatively included cyclosporine continuous infusion 4 mg/hr and adjusted to maintain concentrations (by whole blood monoclonal TDx assay) between 300–400 ng/mL; azathioprine 2 mg/kg IV QD; ATG 750 mg IV QD for 14 days; and ganciclovir 2.5 mg/kg Q 12 hr for 14 days. His postoperative course was complicated by a decrease in pulmonary function tests and grade 2 to 3 acute rejection. He was treated with pulse corticosteroids each time but responded poorly. His pulmonary function tests remained low despite transbronchial biopsy × 2 showing no evidence of rejection or infection. He has had normal lung perfusion scans and chest CT. Oxygen saturation on room air is 85% on presentation. Physical examination revealed: T 37.5 °C, BP 106/75 mm Hg, HR 129 beats/min, RR 28 breaths/min, decreased air movement bilaterally, diffuse inspiratory wheezes, and bilateral basilar crackles. Pertinent laboratory findings include: WBC count 14,500 cells/mm³ (Normal: 4000

Table 33.10	Common Opportunistic Infections After Transplant
Organisms[a]	Time of Onset Post-Transplant
CMV	1–4 months
HSV	2 weeks–2 months
EBV	2–6 months
VZV	2–6 months
Fungal	1–6 months
Mycobacterium	1–6 months
PCP	1–6 months
Listeria	1 month–indefinitely
Aspergillus	1–4 months
Nocardia	1–4 months
Toxoplasma	1–4 months
Cryptococcus	4 months–indefinitely

[a] CMV = Cytomegalovirus; EBV = Epstein-Barr virus; HSV = Herpes simplex virus; PCP = Pneumocystis carinii pneumonia; VZV = Varicella-zoster virus.

–10,000 cells/mm³), platelet count 301,000 cells/mm³ (Normal: 150–450 × 10³ cells/mm³), BUN 33 mg/dL (Normal: 5–22 mg/dL), SrCr 2.3 mg/dL (Normal: 0.6–1.1 mg/dL), and IgM serology for CMV is positive. Other pertinent findings include bronchoalveolar lavage (BAL) fluid showed moderate polys and large nucleated cells, total nucleated cell count 763 with 55% neutrophils; Toxo negative, serum cryptococcus negative, acid fast smear and fungal smears negative. Current medications include cyclosporine 125 mg PO BID; azathioprine 100 mg PO QD; prednisone 15 mg PO QD; ketoconazole 100 mg PO QD; TMP/SMX 80 mg BID on Monday-Wednesday-Friday; albuterol MDI 2 puffs QID; acyclovir 200 mg PO BID; multivitamins 2 tablets PO QD; ranitidine 150 mg PO Q PM; nystatin 500,000 U QID swish and swallow. What is the most likely diagnosis for S.M. at this point? [SI units: WBC 14,500 × 10⁶ cells/L (Normal: 4000–10,000 × 10⁶); platelets 301 × 10⁹/L (Normal: 150–450 × 10⁹); BUN 11.78 mmol/L (Normal: 1.8–7.9); SrCr 467.6 µmol/L (Normal: 50–110)]

Cytomegalovirus is a common infection encountered following transplantation and usually presents within 1 to 4 months.[516] It is an ubiquitous virus and belongs to the herpes virus group. In healthy immunocompetent adults, infection with the virus usually is asymptomatic; whereas, in immunocompromised patients, CMV can cause significant morbidity and mortality. CMV can potentiate the risk for other infections including *Pneumocystis*, *Nocardia*, *Listeria*, *Aspergillus*, and *Candida*.[517] CMV infection also can induce chronic injury to the transplanted organ (arteriosclerosis in the heart, obliterative bronchiolitis in the lungs, vanishing bile duct syndrome in the liver, and chronic arteriopathy in the kidneys).[517]

Etiology

Cytomegalovirus infection usually originates from a seropositive donor organ, reactivation of latent viruses due to immunosuppression, or blood products from seropositive donors.[518] Transmission of CMV from a positive donor to a negative recipient leads to an 80% to 100% infection rate and a 40% to 50% disease rate; a positive donor to a positive recipient leads to a 40% to 60% reactivation rate and a 20% to 30% disease rate; a negative donor to a negative recipient leads to a 0% to 5% infection rate.

Cytomegalovirus disease has a significant economic impact on kidney transplants as a result of extended hospitalizations (59 hospital days for the first year post-transplant for CMV cases versus 22 days for the control group).[519] Due to the morbidity, mortality, and economic impact CMV has on the transplant population, prevention, early detection, and optimal treatment of the disease are desirable. Also, the administration of ATG and/or OKT3 treatment following transplantation has resulted in an increase in CMV disease in contrast to patients not receiving these agents.[517,520] Primary infection is defined as a *de novo* infection in a previously seronegative person, which usually remains dormant for the lifetime of a healthy adult. Secondary infection is a reactivation of a latent virus or re-exposure to the virus during immunosuppression.[521] However, infection with the virus, does not necessarily mean it will progress to CMV disease.

Diagnosis

Diagnosis of CMV is based upon both clinical and laboratory findings. Serological diagnosis is based upon positive seroconversion from a previously seronegative person or a greater than, or equal to, fourfold increase in antibody titers in a previously seropositive person.[522] CMV may be detected by culturing body fluids, such as bronchoalveolar lavage, urine, and blood buffy coat, as well as, biopsy tissue.[518] CMV is contained within the host's leukocytes, which appear to have large intranuclear inclusion bodies.[521] However, identification of the virus or positive seroconversion is not diagnostic for active disease without clinical signs and symptoms. S.M. certainly has laboratory criteria for the diagnosis of primary CMV infection: previously seronegative converted to seropositive after receipt of seropositive donor lungs and large nucleated cells were noted in bronchoalveolar lavage fluid.

Clinical Manifestations

In healthy immunocompetent adults, the CMV-infected patient usually is asymptomatic but the patient may present with complaints of malaise, fever, myalgias, as well as abnormal liver enzymes and lymphocytosis. More severe reactions are rare.[521] However, CMV may be life-threatening in the immunocompromised patient. There is evidence that CMV infection can cause graft rejection and that graft rejection in the setting of immunosuppression can facilitate CMV infection.[518] It oftentimes is unclear which comes first. The actual CMV course may be limited to fever and mononucleosis or include more extensive involvement, such as pneumonia, hepatitis, gastroenteritis, colitis, disseminated infection, encephalopathy, or leukopenia.[521] S.M.'s clinical presentation meets the criteria for CMV pneumonia: decline in pulmonary function tests, increased shortness of breath, weakness, nausea, vomiting, history of fever, and nonproductive cough.[523]

Treatment

53. What are treatment options for S.M.'s diagnosed CMV pneumonia?

Ganciclovir. Historically, the method of treatment before ganciclovir was to reduce the level of immunosuppression. Reduced immunosuppression may be one of the causes for the increased prevalence of rejection after CMV infections. Graft loss in kidney or pancreas recipients is undesirable, yet it is not immediately life-threatening. However, this strategy in liver or heart transplant patients could result in patient death due to graft rejection. Treatment has been attempted in the past with acyclovir, adenine-arabinoside, and immune globulin, but these all have been unsuccessful. Presently, ganciclovir is used for the treatment of CMV disease in solid organ transplant, bone marrow transplant, and AIDS patients and has been a major advance over previous options. However, a 20% relapse rate for CMV disease has been associated with liver transplant recipients with a mean onset of 33 days after stopping ganciclovir therapy.[517] Ganciclovir, a virustatic agent, is a nucleoside analogue, which is phosphorylated in infected cells to its active form and is then incorporated into replicating viral DNA.[524] Following a solid organ transplant, patients with CMV pneumonia and treatment with ganciclovir show a 50% to 100% improvement or stabilization of the disease.[521] However, ganciclovir-resistant strains of CMV have been isolated.[524] Because ganciclovir is the drug of first choice for the treatment of CMV, S.M. should receive a course of therapy.

Foscarnet is a virustatic pyrophosphate analogue that inhibits DNA synthesis. Unlike ganciclovir, no phosphorylation is required for activation. There only is limited experience with the use of foscarnet for CMV infections other than retinitis. However, it is an option for S.M. if resistance to ganciclovir develops or if intolerable adverse effects are associated with ganciclovir therapy.[525]

Immune Globulins. The appropriate use of immunoglobulins in the management of CMV in solid organ transplant recipients is controversial. Immunoglobulins provide a means of passive immunization by potentiation of an antibody-dependent cell-mediated cytotoxic reaction; T-cell recognition of virus-infected cells is blocked.[526] Basically, the immunoglobulins modify the immunologic response that causes damage to host tissue. There has been evidence for possible synergism or additive effects with current antivirals for the treatment of CMV disease.[521] Both unselected immunoglobulins and CMV hyperimmune immunoglobulins have been studied in combination with ganciclovir. CMV hyperimmune immunoglobulin is prepared from high-titer pooled sera and has a four- to eightfold enrichment of titers as compared to unscreened immunoglobulin.[527] Most of the literature involving combination therapy for CMV disease is with bone marrow transplant recipients.[526] Initial response rates appear to favor combination therapy in this group. However, it still is unclear if this benefit will be seen with solid organ transplant recipients and which immunoglobulin is favored. Considerations for use would be for severe disease and/or no response to current treatment.

54. What dosing guidelines and monitoring parameters are appropriate for S.M.?

Dosing Ganciclovir. Ganciclovir should be used initially to treat CMV disease. The usual dose of ganciclovir in patients with normal renal function is 5 mg/kg every 12 hours or 2.5 mg/kg every eight hours for 14 to 21 days. Dosage is adjusted in patients with renal dysfunction: 2.5 mg/kg every 12 hours for creatinine clearances 50 to 79 mL/minute, 2.5 mg/kg every 24 hours for creatinine clearances 25 to 49 mL/minute, 1.25 mg/kg every 24 hours for creatinine clearances less than 25 mL/minute.[524] S.M. should receive a dose of 2.5 mg/kg (125 mg) IV twice a day for three weeks.

Foscarnet. Usual doses of foscarnet are 60 mg/kg every eight hours for 14 to 21 days in patients with normal renal function and should be altered in patients with renal dysfunction.[525]

Immune Globulins. Unselected immunoglobulin may be given as 500 mg/kg every other day for 21 days. CMV hyperimmunoglobulin may be given as 100 mg/kg every other day for 14 days or 200 to 400 mg/kg every other day for three days followed by 200 mg/kg on day 14.[521]

Monitoring Ganciclovir. The most frequent adverse effect associated with ganciclovir therapy is neutropenia, experienced in approximately 40% of patients being treated with this drug.[524] Neutropenia is defined as an absolute neutrophil count less than 1000 cells/mm^3 or 50% decrease in baseline counts.[524] The neutropenia usually resolves with a decrease in dose or discontinuation of the drug; however, colony-stimulating factors may be helpful in correcting the neutropenia.[528,529] Thrombocytopenia occurs in approximately 20% of ganciclovir recipients.[524] Patients with initial platelet counts less than 100,000/mm^3 appear to be at greater risk.[524] Other adverse effects include CNS effects, fever, rash, and abnormal liver function tests.[524] S.M.'s white blood cell and platelet counts should be assessed every three to four days during therapy and ganciclovir should be held if neutrophils fall below

$500/mm^3$ or platelets fall below $25,000/mm^3$. His CMV pneumonia also should be followed by monitoring oxygen saturation and obtaining three to four chest radiographs during his ganciclovir therapy. If S.M. becomes asymptomatic and his pneumonia resolves, further invasive studies such as bronchoscopy should not be required.

Foscarnet. The most serious adverse effect with foscarnet is nephrotoxicity found in up to 50% of patients and probably induced by acute tubular necrosis. Therefore, prehydration is suggested to help minimize or avoid the nephrotoxic potential. Other adverse effects include a decrease in hemoglobin and hematocrit, increase in liver function tests, and alteration of serum electrolyte concentrations. All of these effects appear to be reversible upon discontinuation of the drug. Serum creatinine should be monitored daily.[525]

Immune Globulins. The most common adverse effect associated with the administration of immunoglobulins include fever, chills, headache, myalgia, light-headedness, and nausea and vomiting.[526]

Prophylaxis

55. Is there any way to prevent CMV in high-risk patients such as S.M., who are seronegative at the time of solid organ transplant?

Because of the potentially fatal consequences of CMV disease, prevention in the transplant population is desirable. One way to prevent CMV in these patients is to use a seronegative donor and seronegative blood products. This practice should greatly reduce the risk of primary CMV infections in these patients. Unfortunately, this solution would be difficult if not impossible to implement because the availability of donor organs is insufficient. Currently, CMV status is not considered in the donor-matching process. Many studies have been conducted using regimens for CMV prophylaxis in organ transplant recipients. Administration of a CMV vaccine in a randomized, controlled study of renal transplant recipients noted that seronegative recipients of seropositive kidneys who were vaccinated had less severe CMV disease than control patients with same donor-recipient CMV status. There is not, however, a decreased incidence of CMV infections in any group when compared to placebo.[530]

Acyclovir is ineffective in treating established CMV disease; however, it appears beneficial in a preventive role. High-dose acyclovir (800 mg orally four times a day, dosed to renal function) given for 12 weeks after renal transplant has decreased the incidence of CMV infection and disease significantly, as well as the time required to reach these events.[531] A study in kidney transplant recipients comparing acyclovir to placebo showed there was a decrease in CMV infection (36% versus 61%) and a decrease in CMV disease (8% versus 29%).[531] This regimen appeared most effective for the prevention of primary CMV disease (seropositive donor organ to seronegative recipient).[531] Low-dose acyclovir has been compared to high-dose acyclovir with high-dose acyclovir being superior.[532] Considerations with using high-dose acyclovir include cost, compliance, and adverse effects (hematological, renal, CNS).

Ganciclovir has been studied for prophylaxis of CMV disease, as well as treatment. It was found to be beneficial in reducing the incidence of CMV disease in donor positive/recipient-positive heart transplant recipients (9% ganciclovir versus 46% placebo). However, there was no difference found with donor positive/recipient negative (35% ganciclovir versus 29% placebo). The dose of ganciclovir was 5 mg/kg every 12 hours from postoperative day 1 through day 14, then 6 mg/kg/day for five days per week on day 15 through 28.[533] Even though S.M. did receive ganciclovir prophylaxis postoperatively, he still developed CMV pneumonia. Thus, combination therapy prophylaxis might have been beneficial. Favorable results have been obtained with combination therapy for prophylaxis of CMV disease. In a trial with liver transplant recipients, high-dose acyclovir plus ganciclovir versus high-dose acyclovir alone were compared. There was an overall decrease in the incidence of CMV infection (23% versus 61%) and CMV disease (9% versus 28%). However, upon subgroup analysis, there was no difference in CMV infection when a seropositive donor organ was given to a seronegative recipient (82% versus 86%).[534] The possibility of neutropenia must be considered and monitored carefully if ganciclovir is used prophylactically.

Immune Globulins. Much controversy has existed over the appropriate use of CMV hyperimmunoglobulin versus unselected immunoglobulin. CMV hyperimmunoglobulin has been studied and found to reduce the incidence of CMV disease in comparison to placebo in both kidney and liver transplants.[535,536] In the liver transplant group, subgroup analysis revealed there was no difference in the incidence of CMV disease when seropositive donors were given to seronegative recipients.[536] The recommended dose of CMV hyperimmunoglobulin is 150 mg/kg less than 72 hours post transplant, then 100 mg/kg at weeks 2, 4, 6, 8, and 50 mg/kg at week 12 and 16.[521]

Also, the use of unselected immunoglobulins has resulted in a reduction of CMV disease in both kidney and liver transplant recipients.[521] Unfortunately, no clinical trials comparing the efficacy of CMV hyperimmunoglobulin and unselected immunoglobulin for the prophylaxis of CMV disease have been conducted.

Combination therapy with unselected immunoglobulin (0.5 gm/kg every week for 6 weeks) and acyclovir (400 mg 5 times a day, adjusted to renal function and weight, for a total of 3 months) prophylaxis was found to reduce the incidence of primary CMV disease over a control group (23.8% versus 71.4%). Thirty-three percent (5/15) of the control group that developed CMV disease experienced relapse a mean of 16 days after stopping 14 days of ganciclovir therapy. In the prophylaxis treatment group, all of the patients experiencing CMV disease were responsive to the initial 14-day course of ganciclovir.[537]

References

1 **Kahan BH.** Transplantation timeline. Transplantation. 1991;57:1–21.

2 **Murray JE.** Human organ transplantation background and consequences. Science. 1992;256:1411–416.

3 **Facts about transplantation in the United States.** UNOS Update. 1995; 11:1–48.

4 **Terasaki PI.** In: Terasaki PI, ed. Clinical Transplants. Los Angeles: UCLA Tissue Typing Laboratory; 1992:501–11.

5 **Sanfilippo F.** The influence of HLA and ABO antigens on graft rejection and survival. Clin Lab Med. 1991;11:537–50.

6 **Krensky AM et al.** T-lymphocyte antigen interaction in transplant rejection. N Engl J Med. 1990;322:510–17.

7 **Krensky AM.** T cells in autoimmunity and allograft rejection. Kidney Int 1994;44(Suppl.):S50–6.

8 **Chapel H, Haensy M.** Transplantation. In: Chapel H, Haensy M, eds. Essentials of Clinical Immunology. Oxford: Blackwell; 1993:117–30.

9 **Heeman UW et al.** Adhesion molecules and transplantation. Ann Surg. 1994;219:4–12.

10 **Hutchinson IV.** Immunological mechanisms of long-term graft acceptance. In: Paul LC, Solez K, eds. Organ Transplantation. Long Term Results. New York: Marxcel Dekker Inc; 1992: 1–31.

11 **Thomson AW, Starzl TE.** New immunosuppressive drugs: mechanistic insights and potential therapeutic advances. Immunol Rev. 1993;136:71–98.

12 **Takimoto S et al.** Survival of nationally shared, HLA-matched kidney transplant from cadaveric donors. N Engl J Med. 1992;327:834–39.

13 **Opelz G et al.** Revisiting HLA-matching for kidney transplantation. Transplant Proc. 1993;25:173–75.

14 **Cebel HM, Lebe LK.** Crossmatch pro-

cedures used in organ transplantation. Clin Lab Med. 1991;11:603–20.

15 **Scott KA.** The major histocompatibility complex. In: Concepts in Immunology and Immunotherapeutics. 2nd ed. Bethesda: ASHP; 1992:65–102.

16 **Gordon RD et al.** The antibody crossmatch in liver transplantation. Surgery. 1986;100:705–15.

17 **Takaya S et al.** The adverse impact on liver transplantation of using positive cytotoxic crossmatch donors. Transplantation. 1992;53(2):400–06

18 **Elion GB.** The George Hitchings and Gertrude Elion Lecture. The pharmacology of azathioprine. Ann N Y Acad Sci. 1993;685:400–07.

19 **Tidd DM, Paterson ARP.** Distinction between inhibition of purine nucleotide synthesis and the delayed cytotoxic reaction of 6-mercaptopurine. Cancer Res. 1974;34:733–37.

20 **Chan GLC et al.** The therapeutic use of azathioprine in renal transplantation. Pharmacotherapy. 1987;7:165–77.

21 **Fornier C et al.** Selective action of azathioprine on T cells. Transplant Proc. 1973;5:523–26.

22 **Soria-Royer C, Legendre A.** Thiopurine-methyltransferase activity to assess azathioprine myelotoxicity in renal transplant recipients. Lancet. 1993;341:1593–94.

23 **Lennard L.** The clinical pharmacology of 6-mercaptopurine. Eur J Clin Pharmacol. 1992;43:329–39.

24 **Chan GLC et al.** Azathioprine metabolism pharmacokinetics of 6-mercaptopurine, 6-thiouric acid and 6-thioguanine nucleotides in renal transplant patients. J Clin Pharmacol. 1990;30:358–63.

25 **Ding TL, Gambertoglio JG.** Azathioprine (AZA) bioavailability and pharmacokinetics in kidney transplant patients. Clin Pharmacol Ther. 1980;27:250.

26 **Bergan S et al.** Kinetics of mercaptopurine and thioguanine nucleotides in renal transplant recipients during azathioprine treatment. Ther Drug Monit. 1994;16(1):13–20.

27 **Lin SN et al.** Quantitation of plasma azathioprine and 6-mercaptopurine levels in renal transplant patients. Transplantation. 1980;29:290–94.

28 **Bach JF, Dardenne M.** Serum immunosuppressive activity of azathioprine in normal subjects and patients with liver disease. Proc R Soc Med. 1972;65:260–63.

29 **Boumpas DT et al.** Glucocorticoid therapy for immune-mediated diseases: basic and clinical correlates. Ann Intern Med. 1993;15,119(12):1198–208.

30 **Sternberg EM, Chrousos GP.** The stress response and regulation of inflammatory disease. Ann Intern Med. 1992;117:854–66.

31 **Fauci AS et al.** Glucocorticosteroid therapy: mechanisms of action and clinical considerations. Ann Intern Med. 1976;84:304–15.

32 **Paliogianni F, Ahiya SS.** Novel mechanism for inhibition of human T cells by glucocorticoids. J Immunol. 1993;151:4081–089.

33 **Boumpas DT et al.** Glucocorticosteroid action on the immune system: molecular and cellular aspects. Clin Exp Rheumatol. 1991;9(4):413–23.

34 **Almawri WY et al.** Abrogation of glucocorticoid-mediated inhibition of T cell proliferation by the synergistic action of IL-1, IL-6 and IFN-Y. J Immunol. 1991;146:3523–27.

35 **Cupps TR et al.** Effects of in vitro corticosteroids on B cell activation, proliferation, and differentiation. J Clin Invest. 1985;75:754–61.

36 **Venkataramanan R et al.** Clinical pharmacokinetics in organ transplant patients. Clin Pharmacokinet. 1989;16:134–61.

37 **Tornatore KM, Reed K.** Cortisol pharmacodynamics response to long-term methylprednisolone in renal transplant recipients. Pharmacotherapy. 1994;14:111–18.

38 **Jusko WJ, Ludwig EA.** Corticosteroids. In: Evans WE et al., eds. Applied Pharmacokinetics: Principles of Therapeutic Drug Monitoring. Vancouver: Applied Therapeutics; 1992:27-1–27-34.

39 **Ost L et al.** Clinical value of assessing prednisolone pharmacokinetics before and after renal transplantation. Eur J Clin Pharmacol. 1984;26:363–69.

40 **Gambertoglio JG et al.** Prednisolone disposition in cushingoid and noncushingoid kidney transplant patients. J Clin Endocrinol Metab. 1980;51:561–65.

41 **Frey FJ et al.** Pharmacokinetics of prednisolone and endogenous hydrocortisone levels in cushingoid and noncushingoid patients. Eur J Clin Pharmacol. 1981;21:235–42.

42 **Tornatore KM et al.** Racial differences in the pharmacokinetics of methylprednisolone in black and white renal transplant recipients. Pharmacotherapy. 1993;13:481–86.

43 **Oka K et al.** Suppression of endogenous cortisol for evaluating pharmacodynamics of prednisolone in early allograft rejection in renal transplantation. Clin Chem. 1990;36(3):481–86.

44 **Hirano T et al.** Clinical significance of glucocorticoid pharmacodynamics assessed by antilymphocyte action in kidney transplantation. Transplantation. 1994;57:1341–348.

45 **Kahan BD.** Cyclosporine. N Engl J Med. 1989;321:1725–38.

46 **Borel JF.** Pharmacology of cyclosporine (Sandimmune). IV. Pharmacological properties in vivo. Pharmacol Rev. 1989;41:259–371.

47 **Schriber SL, Crabtree GR.** The mechanism of action of cyclosporin A and FK506. Immunol Today. 1992;13(4):136–42.

48 **Lui J.** FK506 and cyclosporin, molecular probes for studying intracellular signal transduction. Immunol Today. 1993;14(6):290–95.

49 **Faulds D et al.** Cyclosporin. A review of its pharmacodynamic and pharmacokinetic properties, and therapeutic use in immunoregulatory disorders. Drugs. 1993;45(6):953–1040.

50 **Fahr A et al.** Studies on the biologic activities of Sandimmune metabolites in humans and animal models. Review and original experiments. Transplant Proc. 1993;22:1116–124.

51 **Copeland KR, Yatscoff RW.** Immunosuppressive activity and toxicity of cyclosporine metabolites characterized by mass spectrometry and nuclear magnetic resonance. Transplant Proc. 1990;22:1146–149.

52 **Petis DH et al.** Tacrolimus. A review of its pharmacology, and therapeutic potential in hepatic and renal transplantation. Drugs. 1993;46(4):746–94.

53 **Carey JA, Frist WH.** Use of polyclonal antilymphocytic preparations for prophylaxis in heart transplantation. J Heart Transplant. 1990;9(3 Pt. 2):297–300.

54 **Wakabayaski H et al.** Batch-to-batch variations in rabbit antithymocyte globulin preparations. Transplant Proc. 1991;23:1125–127.

55 **Raefsky EL et al.** Biological and immunological characterization of ATG and ALG. Blood. 1986;68(3):712–19.

56 **Greco B et al.** Antilymphocyte globulin reacts with many normal human cell types. Blood. 1983;62:1047–054.

57 **Hooks.** Murumonab-CD3. Pharmacotherapy. 1991;11:26–37.

58 **Tami JA et al.** Monoclonal antibody technology. Am J Hosp Pharm. 1986; 43:2816–822.

59 **Lazarovits AI, Shield CF.** Recurrence of acute rejection in the absence of CD3-positive lymphocytes. Clin Immunol Immunopathol. 1988;48:293–400.

60 **Goldstein G et al.** OKT₃ monoclonal antibody plasma levels during therapy and the subsequent development of host antibodies to OKT₃. Transplantation. 1986;42:507–11.

61 **Schroeder TJ et al.** Immunologic monitoring with Orthoclone OKT₃ therapy. J Heart Transplant. 1989;8(5):371–80.

62 **McDiamid TP et al.** Low serum OKT₃ levels correlate with failure to prevent rejection in orthotopic liver transplant patients. Transplant Proc. 1990;22:1774–776.

63 **Woodle ES et al.** OKT₃ therapy for hepatic allograft rejection. Transplantation. 1991;51:1207–212.

64 **Morris RE.** New small molecule immunosuppressants for transplantation: review of essential concepts. J Heart Lung Transplant. 1993;12:5275–286.

65 **Thomson AW, Starzl TE.** New immunosuppressive drugs: mechanistic insights and potential therapeutic advances. Immunol Rev. 1993;136:71–98.

66 **Schroeder TJ, First MR.** Monoclonal antibodies in organ transplantation. Am J Kidney Dis. 1994;23:138–47.

67 **Hayes JM.** The immunobiology and clinical use of current immunosuppressive therapy for renal transplantation. J Urol. 1993;149:437–48.

68 **Starzl TE et al.** Evolution of liver transplantation. Hepatology. 1982;2:614–36.

69 **Copeland JG.** Cardiac transplantation. Curr Probl Surg. 1988;25(9):607–72.

70 **Barker CR et al.** Renal transplantation. In: Sabiston DC, ed. Textbook of Surgery: The Biological Basis of Modern Surgical Practice. 14th ed. Philadelphia: WB Saunders; 1991:374–393.

71 **Sollinger HW.** Pancreas transplantation. In: Sabiston DC, ed. Textbook of Surgery: The Biological Basis of Modern Surgical Practice. 14th ed. Philadelphia: WB Saunders; 1991:433–37.

72 **Judson MA.** Clinical aspects of lung transplantation. Clin Chest Med. 1993;14(2):335–57.

73 **Brink LW, Ballew A.** Care of the pediatric organ donor. Am J Dis Child. 1992;146(9):1045–050.

74 **Bass M.** Pancreas transplantation: detecting rejection and patient care. ANNA J. 1992;19(5):476–82.

75 **Powell CS et al.** The value of urinary amylase as a marker of early pancreatic allograft rejection. Transplantation. 1987;43:921–23.

76 **President's Commission for the Study of Ethical Problems in Medicine and Biomedical and Behavioral Research.** Guidelines for determination of death. JAMA. 1981;246:2184–186.

77 **Baldwin JC et al.** Task Force 2. Donor Guidelines. J Am Coll Cardiol. 1993;22:15–20.

78 **Salazar TA, Aweeka FT.** Transplantation. In: Herfindal ET et al., eds. Clinical Pharmacy and Therapeutics. 5th ed. Baltimore: Williams and Wilkins; 1992:1528–553.

79 **Soifer B, Gelb AW.** The multiple organ donor: identification and management. Ann Intern Med. 1989;110:814–23.

80 **Detterbeck FB.** Management of the multi-organ donor. Contemp Surg. 1993;42:281–85.

81 **Robertson KM.** Logistics of donor procurement, management of the organ donor and organ preservation. In: Cook DR, Davis PJ, eds. Anesthetic Principles for Organ Transplantation. New York: Raven Press; 1994:27–43.

82 **Novitsky D et al.** Hemodynamic and metabolic responses to hormonal therapy in brain-dead potential organ donors. Transplantation. 1987;43:852–54.

83 **Novitsky D et al.** Improved cardiac allograft function following triiodothyronine therapy to both donor and recipient. Transplantation. 1990;49:311–16.

84 **Orlowski JP, Speis EK.** Eighteen month graft patient survival following liver transplantation with organs recovered from cadaveric donors managed with thyroxine: a retrospective study. J Transpl Coordin. 1991;1:144–49.

85 **Orlowski JP, Specs EK.** Improved cardiac transplant survival with thyroxine treatment of hemodynamically unstable donors. 92.5% graft survival at 6 and 30 months. Transplant Proc. 1993;25:1535–537.

86 **Novitzky D.** Heart transplantation, euthyroid sick syndrome and triiodothyronine replacement. J Heart Lung Transplant. 1992;11(Suppl. 1):5196–198.

87 **Mendler N.** The metaphysiology of organ preservation. J Heart Lung Transplant. 1992;11 (Suppl. 1):S192–S195.

88 **Wheeldon D et al.** Donor heart preservation survey. J Heart Lung Transplant. 1992;11:986–93.

89 **Toledo-Pereyra LH, Rodriguez FJ.** Scientific basis and current status of organ preservation. Transplant Proc. 1994;26:309–11.

90 **Lin PJ et al.** University of Wisconsin solution extends lung preservation after prostaglandin E infusion. Chest. 1994;105:255–61.

91 **Rutten FFH et al.** The cost-effectiveness of preservation with UW and EC solution for use in cadaveric kidney transplantation in the case of single

kidney donors. Transplantation. 1993; 56:854–58.

92 **Schaeffer MJ, Alexander DC.** US system for organ procurement and transplantation. Am J Hosp Pharm. 1992;49(7):1733–740.

93 **Figueroa JE.** Selection of patients for organ transplantation. Med Clin North Am. 1992;76:1188–195.

94 **Randall T.** Criteria for evaluating potential transplant recipients vary among centers, physicians. JAMA. 1993;269: 3091–094.

95 **Ismail N et al.** Renal replacement therapies in the elderly: Part II. Renal transplantation. Am J Kidney Dis. 1994; 23(1):1–15

96 **Evans RE et al.** The quality of life of patients with end-stage renal disease. N Engl J Med. 1985;312:553.

97 **Eggers PW.** Effect of transplantation on the Medicare end-stage renal disease program. N Engl J Med. 1988; 318:223.

98 **Port FL et al.** Comparison of survival probabilities for dialysis patients vs cadaveric renal transplant recipients. JAMA. 1993;270:1339–343.

99 **Cecka JM, Terasaki PI.** The UNOS Scientific Transplant Registry. In: Terasaki PI, Cecka JM, eds. Clinical Transplants. 8th ed. 1992:1–16.

100 **Terasaki PI, Cecka JM.** A ten-year prediction for kidney transplant survival. In: Terasaki PI, Cecka JM, eds. Clinical Transplants. 8th ed. 1992:501–12.

101 **Guide to Transplantation Protocols.** Sandoz, Inc.; 1990.

102 **Evans RW et al.** Immunosuppressive therapy as a determinant of transplantation outcomes. Transplantation. 1993; 55:1297–305.

103 **Helderman JH et al.** Chronic immunosuppression of the renal transplant patient. J Am Soc Nephrol. 1994;4(8 Suppl.):S2–9.

104 **Helderman JH, Van Buren DH.** Chronic immunosuppression of the renal transplant patient. J Am Soc Nephol. 1994;4(Suppl. 1):52–9.

105 **Hricik DE et al.** Steroid-free immunosuppression after renal transplantation. J Am Soc Nephrol. 1994;4:510–16.

106 **Kasiske BL et al.** Elective cyclosporine withdrawal after renal transplantation. JAMA. 1993;269:395–400.

107 **Shapiro R.** Kidney Transplantation. In: Makowka L, ed. Handbook of Transplantation Management. Austin: R.G. Landes Co; 1991:168–91.

108 **Hall BM et al.** Post-transplant acute renal failure in cadaver renal recipients treated with cyclosporine. Kidney Int. 1985;28:178–86.

109 **Olsen S et al.** Primary acute renal failure ("acute tubular necrosis") in the transplanted kidney: morphology and pathogenesis. Medicine. 1989;68:173–87.

110 **Almond PS et al.** Fixed-rate reimbursement fails to cover costs for patients with delayed graft function. Pharmacotherapy. 1991;11:1265–295.

111 **Sutherland DE et al.** Results of the Minnesota randomized prospective trial of cyclosporine versus azathioprine-antilymphocyte globulin for immunosuppression in renal allograft recipients. Am J Kidney Dis. 1985;5(6): 318–27.

112 **Ricart MJ et al.** Acute renal failure after renal transplantation under various immunosuppressive regimens. Transplant Proc. 1988;20(Suppl. 6):36–7.

113 **Canafax DM et al.** The effects of delayed function of recipients of cadaver renal allografts. Transplantation. 1986; 41:177–87.

114 **Norman DJ et al.** A randomized clinical trial of induction therapy with OKT$_3$ in kidney transplantation. Transplantation. 1993;55:44–50.

115 **Benvenisty AI et al.** Improved results using OKT$_3$ as induction immunosuppression in renal allograft recipients with delayed graft function. Transplantation. 1990;49:321–27.

116 **Michael HJ et al.** A comparison of the effects of cyclosporine versus antilymphocyte globulin on delayed graft function in cadaver renal transplant recipients. Transplantation. 1989;48:805–08.

117 **Hanto DW et al.** Induction immunosuppression with antilymphocyte globulin or OKT$_3$ in cadaver kidney transplantation. Transplantation. 1994;57: 377–84.

118 **Frey DJ et al.** Sequential therapy—a prospective randomized trial of MALG versus OKT$_3$ for prophylactic immunosuppression in cadaver renal allograft recipients. Transplantation. 1992; 54:50–6.

119 **Slakey DP et al.** A prospective randomized comparison of quadruple versus triple therapy for first cadaver transplants with immediate function. Transplantation. 1993;56:827–83.

120 **Mozes MF et al.** Is the routine use of induction immunosuppression with ALG or OKT$_3$ justified in cadaveric renal transplantation. Transplant Proc. 1993;25:575–76.

121 **Suthanthiran M, Strom TB.** Renal transplantation. N Engl J Med. 1994; 331:365–78.

122 **Rao KV.** Mechanism, pathophysiology, diagnosis, and management of renal transplant rejection. Med Clin North Am. 1990;74:1039–058.

123 **Matas AJ et al.** The impact of an acute rejection episode on long-term renal allograft survival (t½). Transplantation. 1994;57:857–59.

124 **Basadonna GP et al.** Early versus late acute renal allograft rejection: impact on chronic rejection. Transplantation. 1993;55:993–95.

125 **Kahan BD.** The impact of cyclosporine on the practice of renal transplantation. Transplant Proc. 1989;21:63–9.

126 **Solez K et al.** International standardization of criteria for the histologic diagnosis of renal allograft rejection: The Banff working classification of kidney transplant pathology. Kidney Int. 1993; 44:411–22.

127 **Matas AJ, Burke JF.** Chronic rejection. J Am Soc Nephrol. 1994;4(Suppl. 1):S23–S29.

128 **Tilney NL et al.** Chronic rejection—an undefined conundrum. Transplantation. 1991;52:389–98.

129 **Hricik DE et al.** Trends in the use of glucocorticoids in renal transplantation. Transplantation. 1994;57:979–89.

130 **Cray D et al.** Oral versus intravenous high-dose steroid treatment of renal allograft rejection. The big shot or not. Lancet. 1978;1:117–18.

131 **Mussche MM et al.** High intravenous doses of methylprednisolone for acute cadaveric renal allograft rejection. Nephron. 1976;16:287–91.

132 **Fan PT et al.** Effect of corticosteroids on the human immune response. Suppression of mitogen-induced lymphocyte proliferation by "pulse" methylprednisolone. Transplantation. 1978; 26:266–67.

133 **Barry JM.** Immunosuppressive drugs in renal transplantation: a review of the regimens. Drugs. 1992;44(4):554–66.

134 **Salomon DR.** The use of immunosuppressive drugs in kidney transplantation. Pharmacotherapy. 1991;11:153S–64S.

135 **Swartz SL, Dluky RG.** Corticosteroids: clinical pharmacology and therapeutic use. Drugs. 1978;16:238–55.

136 **Tczepacz PT et al.** Psychopharmacologic issue in organ transplantation. Part I: Pharmacokinetics in organ failure and psychiatric aspects of immunosuppressants and anti-infection agents. Psychosomatics 1993;34:199–207.

137 **Matas AJ et al.** Definition, diagnosis and management of rejection in the second to sixth months posttransplant—an overview. Transplant Proc. 1986;18(2 Suppl. 1):141–47.

138 **Diethelm AG.** Clinical diagnosis and management of the renal transplant recipient with cyclosporine nephrotoxicity. Transplant Proc. 1986;18(2 Suppl. 1):82–7.

139 **Myers BD.** Cyclosporine nephrotoxicity. Kidney Int. 1986;30:964–74.

140 **Kahan BD.** The impact of cyclosporine on the practice of renal transplantation. Transplant Proc. 1989;21(3 Suppl. 1):63–9.

141 **Mason J.** Pharmacology of cyclosporine (Sandimmune). VII. Pathophysiology and toxicology of cyclosporine in humans and animals. Pharmacol Rev. 1989;42:423–34.

142 **Awagu M et al.** Cyclosporine promotes glomerular endothelin binding in vivo. J Am Soc Nephrol. 1991;1: 1253–258.

143 **Kopp JB, Klotman PE.** Cellular and molecular mechanisms of cyclosporin nephrotoxicity. J Am Soc Nephrol. 1990;1:162–79.

144 **Lewis RM et al.** Impact of long-term cyclosporine immunosuppressive therapy on native kidneys versus renal allografts: serial renal function in heart and kidney transplant recipients. J Heart Lung Transplant. 1991;10(1 Pt. 1):63–70.

145 **Slomowitz LA et al.** Evaluation of kidney function in renal transplant patients receiving long-term cyclosporine. Am J Kidney Dis. 1990;15(6):530–34.

146 **Van Buren et al.** Renal function in patients receiving long-term cyclosporine therapy. J Am Soc Nephrol. 1994;4(8 Suppl.):S17–22.

147 **Finn WF.** Prevention of ischemic injury in renal transplantation. Kidney Int. 1990;37:171–82.

148 **Rossi SJ et al.** Prevention and management of the adverse effects associated with immunosuppressive therapy. Drug Saf. 1993;9:104–31.

149 **deGroen.** Cyclosporine and the liver: how one affects the other. Transplant Proc. 1990;22:1197–1202.

150 **Lorber MI et al.** Hepatobiliary complications of cyclosporine therapy following renal transplantation. Transplant Proc. 1987;24:1808–810.

151 **de Groen PC et al.** Central nervous system toxicity after liver transplantation. The role of cyclosporine and cholesterol. N Engl J Med. 1987;317:861–66.

152 **Stein DP et al.** Neurological complications following liver transplantation. Ann Neurol. 1992;31(6):644–49.

153 **Martin AB et al.** Neurologic complications of heart transplantation in children. J Heart Lung Transplant. 1992; 11:933–42.

154 **June CH et al.** Correlation of hypomagnesemia with the onset of cyclosporine-associated hypertension in marrow transplant patients. Transplantation. 1986;41:47–51.

155 **Lin HY et al.** Cyclosporine-induced hyperuricemia and gout. N Engl J Med. 1989;321:287–92.

156 **Wysocki GP, Daley TD.** Hypertrichosis in patients receiving cyclosporine therapy. Clin Exp Dermatol. 1987; 12(3):191–96.

157 **Pan WL et al.** Cyclosporine-induced gingival overgrowth. Transplant Proc. 1992;24:1393–394.

158 **Ptachinski RJ et al.** Cyclosporine. DICP. 1985;19:90–100.

159 **Fradin MS et al.** Management of patients and side effects during cyclosporine therapy for cutaneous disorders. J Am Acad Dermatol. 1990;23(6 Pt 2):1265–273.

160 **Mudge GH et al.** Task force 3: Recipient guidelines/prioritization. J Am Coll Cardiol. 1993;22:21–31.

161 **The Registry of the International Society for Heart and Lung Transplantation: Tenth official report 1993.** J Heart Lung Transplant. 1993;12:541–48.

162 **Kubo SH et al.** Trends in patient selection for heart transplantation. J Am Coll Cardiol. 1993;21:975–81.

163 **Olivari MT et al.** Heart transplantation in elderly patients. J Heart Transplant. 1988;7(4):258–64.

164 **Munoz E et al.** Long-term results in diabetic patients undergoing heart transplantation. J Heart Lung Transplant. 1992;11:943–49.

165 **Mancini DM et al.** Value of peak exercise oxygen consumption for optimal timing of cardiac transplantation in ambulatory patients with heart failure. Circulation. 1991;83(3):778–86.

166 **Bhatia SJ et al.** Time course of resolution of pulmonary hypertension and right ventricular remodeling after orthotopic cardiac transplantation. Circulation. 1987;76(4):819–26.

167 **Borow KM et al.** Left ventricular contractility and contractile reserve in humans after cardiac transplantation. Circulation. 1985;71(5):866–72.

168 **Chester MR et al.** The effect of orthotopic transplantation on total, B$_1$- and B$_2$-adrenoceptors in the human heart. Br J Clin Pharmacol. 1992;33:417–22.

169 **Yusuf S et al.** Increased sensitivity of the denervated transplanted human heart to isoprenaline both before and after beta adrenergic blockade. Circulation. 1987;75(4):696–704.

170 **Gallagher RC.** Heart Transplantation. In: Maleowkal, ed. The Handbook of Transplantation Management. Austin: RG Landes Co.; 1991:254–73.

171 **Murali S et al.** Utility of prostaglandin E in the pretransplantation evaluation of heart failure patients with significant pulmonary hypertension. J Heart Lung Transplant. 1992;11:716–23.

172 **Odom NJ et al.** Successful use of mechanical assist device for right ventricular failure after orthotopic heart transplantation. J Heart Lung Transplant. 1990;9:652–53.

173 **Leachman RD, Kokkinos DV.** Response of the transplanted denervated human heart to cardiovascular drugs. Am J. Cardiol. 1977;27:272–76.

174 **Heinz G et al.** Demographic and perioperative factors associated with initial and prolonged sinus node dysfunction after orthotopic heart transplantation. Transplantation. 1991;51:1217–232.

175 **Montero JA et al.** Pacing requirements after orthotopic heart transplantation: incidence and related factors. J Heart Lung Transplant. 1992;11:799–802.

176 **Miyamoto Y et al.** Bradyarrhythmia after heart transplantation. Incidence, time course and outcome. Circulation. 1990;82(5 Suppl.):IV313–17.

177 **Redmond JM et al.** Use of theophylline for treatment of prolonged sinus node dysfunction in human orthotopic heart transplantation. J Heart Lung Transplant. 1993;12:133–39.

178 **Gilbert EM et al.** Beta adrenergic supersensitivity of the transplanted human heart is presynaptic in origin. Circulation. 1989;79(2):344–49.

179 **Verani MS, Nishimura S.** Cardiac function after orthotopic heart transplantation: response to postural changes, exercise and beta-adrenergic blockade. J Heart Lung Transplant. 1994;13:181–93.

180 **Verani MS et al.** Systolic and diastolic ventricular performance at rest and during exercise in heart transplant recipients. J Heart Transplant. 1988;7:145–51.

181 **Goodman DJ et al.** Effect of digoxin on atrioventricular conduction: studies in patients with and without cardiac autonomic innervation. Circulation. 1975;51:251–56.

182 **Bexton RS, Cory-Pearce R.** Electrophysiological effects of nifedipine and verapamil in the transplantation of the human heart. J Heart Transplant. 1984;3:97–104.

183 **Lake KD et al.** Over the counter medications in cardiac transplant recipients: guidelines for use. Ann Pharmacother. 1992;26(12):1566–575.

184 **McGregor CG.** Evolution of heart transplantation. Cardiol Clin. 1990;8(1):3–10.

185 **Greenberg A.** Renal failure in cardiac transplantation. Cardiovasc Clin. 1990;20(2):189–98.

186 **Schroeder TJ et al.** Efficacy and safety of constant-rate intravenous cyclosporine infusion immediately after heart transplantation. J Heart Transplant. 1989;8(1):5–10.

187 **Renlund DG et al.** Feasibility of discontinuation of corticosteroid maintenance therapy in heart transplantation. J Heart Transplant. 1987;6(2):71–8.

188 **Prieto M et al.** OKT₃ induction and steroid-free maintenance immunosuppression for treatment of high-risk heart transplant recipients. J Heart Lung Transplant. 1991;10(6):901–11.

189 **McGregor CG.** Cardiac transplantation: surgical considerations and early postoperative management. Mayo Clin Proc. 1992;67(6):577–85.

190 **O'Connell JB, Renlund DG.** Diagnosis and treatment of cardiac allograft rejection. Cardiovasc Clin. 1990;20(2):147–62.

191 **Olsen SL et al.** Vascular rejection in heart transplantation: clinical correlation, treatment options, and future considerations. J Heart Lung Transplant. 1993;12(2):135–42.

192 **Kirklin JK et al.** Analysis of morbid events and risk factors for death after cardiac transplantation. J Am Coll Cardiol. 1988;11(5):917–24.

193 **Sharples LD et al.** Risk factor analysis for major hazards following heart transplantation—rejection, infection, and coronary occlusive disease. 1991;52(2):244–52.

194 **Kobashigawa JA et al.** Pretransplantation risk factors for acute rejection after heart transplantation: a multiinstitutional study. The Transplant Cardiologists Research Database group. J Heart Lung Transplant. 1993;12(3):355–66.

195 **Kirklin JK et al.** Rejection after cardiac transplantation. A time-related risk factor analysis. Circulation. 1992;86(5):II236–41.

196 **Stinson EB et al.** Cardiac transplantation in man. JAMA. 1969;207:2233–242.

197 **Keren A et al.** Heart transplant rejection monitored by signal-averaged electro cardiography in patients receiving cyclosporine. Circulation. 1984;70:I124–129.

198 **Billingham ME et al.** A working formulation for the standardization of nomenclature in the diagnosis of heart and lung rejection: Heart Rejection Study Group. The International Society for Heart Transplantation. J Heart Transplant. 1990;9(6):587–93.

199 **Yeogh TJ et al.** Clinical significance of mild rejection of the cardiac allograft. Circulation. 1992;86(Suppl. 2):II-267–II-271.

200 **Laufer G et al.** The progression of mild acute cardiac rejection evaluated by risk factor analysis. The impact of maintenance steroids and serum creatinine. Transplantation. 1991;51(1):184–89.

201 **Kemkes BM et al.** Noninvasive methods of rejection diagnosis after heart transplantation. J Heart Lung Transplant. 1992;11(4 Pt. 2):S221–31.

202 **Hosenpud JD et al.** Cardiac allograft vasculopathy: current concepts, recent developments and future directions. J Heart Lung Transplant. 1992;11(1 Pt. 1):9–23.

203 **Schroeder JS et al.** Accelerated graft coronary disease: diagnosis and prevention. J Heart Lung Transplant. 1992;11(4 Pt. 2):S258–65.

204 **Johnson MR.** Transplant coronary disease: nonimmunologic risk factors. J Heart Lung Transplant. 1992;11(3 Pt. 2):124–32.

205 **de Lorgenil M, Boissonnat P.** Low-dose aspirin and accelerated coronary disease in heart transplant recipients. J Heart Transplant. 1990;9:339–450.

206 **Aziz S et al.** A reduction in accelerated graft coronary disease and an improvement in cardiac allograft survival using low molecular weight heparin in combination with cyclosporine. J Heart Lung Transplant. 1993;12(4):634–43.

207 **Fleischhauer FJ et al.** Fish oil improves endothelium-dependent coronary vasodilation in heart transplant recipients. J Am Coll Cardiol. 1993;21(4):982–89.

208 **Schroeder JS et al.** A preliminary study of diltiazem in the prevention of coronary artery disease in heart-transplant recipients. N Engl J Med. 1993;328(3):164–70.

209 **Miller LW.** Treatment of cardiac allograft rejection with intravenous corticosteroids. J. Heart Transplant. 1990;9(3 Pt. 2):283–87.

210 **Kobashigawa JA, Stevenson LW.** Is intravenous glucocorticoid therapy better than an oral regimen for asymptomatic cardiac rejection: a randomized trial. J Am Coll Cardiol. 1993;21:1142–144.

211 **Yeogh TJ et al.** Clinical significance of mild rejection of the cardiac allograft. Circ. 1992;86(Suppl. 2):II-267–II-271.

212 **O'Connell JB, Renlund DG.** Diagnosis and treatment of cardiac allograft rejection. Cardiovasc Clin. 1990;20(2):147–62.

213 **Kobashigawa J et al.** Randomized study of high dose oral cyclosporine therapy for mild acute cardiac rejection. J Heart Transplant. 1989;8(1):53–8.

214 **Lonquist JL et al.** Reevaluation of steroid tapering after steroid pulse therapy for heart rejection. J Heart Lung Transplant. 1992;11(5):913–19.

215 **Kobashigawa JA et al.** Is intravenous glucocorticoid therapy better than an oral regimen for asymptomatic cardiac rejection? A randomized trial. J Am Coll Cardiol. 1993;21(5):1142–144.

216 **Wahlers T et al.** Treatment of rejection after heart transplantation: what dosage of pulsed steroids is necessary. J Heart Transplant. 1990;9(5):568–74.

217 **Deeb GM et al.** A randomized prospective comparison of MALG with OKT₃ for rescue therapy of acute myocardial rejection. Transplantation. 1991;51(1):180–83.

218 **Keith FM et al.** Minnesota ALG. Safe and effective immunosuppression for cardiac transplantation. Circulation. 1988;78(5 Pt. 2):III73–7.

219 **Haverty TP et al.** OKT₃ treatment of cardiac allograft rejection. J Heart Lung Transplant. 1993;12(4):591–98.

220 **Bourge RC et al.** Methotrexate pulse therapy in the treatment of recurrent acute heart rejection. J Heart Lung Transplant. 1992;11(6):1116–124.

221 **Salter MM et al.** Total lymphoid irradiation in the treatment of early or recurrent heart rejection. J Heart Lung Transplant. 1992;11(5):902–11.

222 **Armitage JM et al.** Clinical trial of FK 506 immunosuppression in adult cardiac transplantation. Ann Thorac Surg. 1992;54(2):205–10.

223 **Costanzo-Nordin MR et al.** Successful treatment of heart transplant rejection with photopheresis. Transplantation. 1992;53(4):808–15.

224 **Olsen SL, Wagonea LE.** Vascular rejection in heart transplantation: clinical correlation, treatment options and future considerations. J Heart Lung Transplant. 1993;12:S135–S142.

225 **Schuurman HJ, Jambroes G.** Acute humoral rejection in a heart transplant recipient. Transplant Proc. 1989;21:2529–530.

226 **Miller LW et al.** Task force 5: Complications. J Am Coll Cardiol. 1993;22:41–54.

227 **Costanzo-Nordin MR et al.** Task force 6: Future developments. J Am Coll Cardiol. 1993;22:54–64.

228 **Miller LW et al.** Long-term effects of cyclosporine in cardiac transplantation. Transplant Proc. 1990;22(3 Suppl. 1):15–20.

229 **Olivari MT et al.** Arterial hypertension in heart transplant recipients treated with triple-drug immunosuppressive therapy. J Heart Transplant. 1989;8(1):34–9.

230 **Broyer M et al.** Hypertension following renal transplantation in children. Pediatr Nephrol. 1987;1:16–21.

231 **Dyer PE et al.** Cyclosporin-A in cardiac allografting: a preliminary experience. Transplant Proc. 1983;15:1247–252.

232 **Keogh A et al.** Initial steroid-free versus steroid-based maintenance therapy and steroid withdrawal of the heart transplantation: two views of the steroid question. J Heart Lung Transplant. 1992;11:421–27.

233 **Ingulli E et al.** The beneficial effects of steroid withdrawal on blood pressure and lipid profile in children post-transplantation in the cyclosporine era. Transplantation. 1993;55(5):1029–033.

234 **Shapiro AP et al.** Hypertension following orthotopic cardiac transplantation. Cardiovasc Clin. 1990;20(2):179–88.

235 **First MR, Neylan JF.** Hypertension after renal transplantation. J Am Soc Nephrol. 1994;4(Suppl. 1):530–36.

236 **Neumayer HH et al.** Protective effects of calcium antagonists in human renal transplantation. Kidney Int Suppl. 1992;36:S87–93.

237 **Chitwood KK, Heim-Duthoy KL.** Immunosuppressive properties of calcium channel blockers. Pharmacotherapy. 1993;13(5):447–54.

238 **Yee GC, McGuire TR.** Pharmacokinetic drug interactions with cyclosporin (Part II). Clin Pharmacokinet. 1990;19(5):400–15.

239 **Yee GC, McGuire TR.** Pharmacokinetic drug interactions with cyclosporin (Part I). Clin Pharmacokinet. 1990;19(4):319–32.

240 **Endresen L et al.** Lack of effect of the calcium antagonist isradipine on cyclosporine pharmacokinetics in renal transplant patients. Ther Drug Monit. 1991;13(6):490–95.

241 **Sorensen SS et al.** Effect of felodipine on renal haemodynamics and tubular sodium handling in cyclosporine treated renal transplant recipients. Nephrol Dial Transplant. 1992;7(1):69–78.

242 **Valantine H et al.** Cost containment: coadministration of diltiazem with cyclosporine after heart transplantation. J Heart Lung Transplant. 1992;11(1 Pt. 1):1–7.

243 **Kahl LE et al.** Gout in the heart transplant recipient: physiologic puzzle and therapeutic challenge. Am J Med. 1989;87(3):289–94.

244 **Hricik DE.** Posttransplant hyperlipidemia: the treatment dilemma. Am J Kidney Dis. 1994;23(5):766–71.

245 **Lake KD et al.** The impact of steroid withdrawal on the development of lipid abnormalities and obesity in heart transplant recipients. J Heart Lung Transplant. 1993;12(4):580–90.

246 **Johnson MR.** Transplant coronary disease: nonimmunologic risk factors. J Heart Lung Transplant. 1992;11(3 Pt. 2):S124–32.

247 **Rudas L et al.** Serial evaluation of lipid profiles and risk factors for development of hyperlipidemia after cardiac transplantation (see comments). Am J Cardiol. 1990;66(15):1135–138.

248 **Kasiske BL, Umen AJ.** Persistent hyperlipidemia in renal transplant patients. Medicine (Baltimore). 1987; 66(4):309–16.

249 **de-Groen PC.** Cyclosporine, low-density lipoprotein, and cholesterol. Mayo Clin Proc. 1988;63(10):1012–021.

250 **Laufer G et al.** The determinants of elevated total plasma cholesterol levels in cardiac transplant recipients administered low dose cyclosporine for immunosuppression. J Thorac Cardiovasc Surg. 1992;104(2):241–47.

251 **Price GD et al.** Corticosteroid-free maintenance immunosuppression after heart transplantation: feasibility and beneficial effects. J Heart Lung Transplant. 1992;11(2 Pt. 2):403–14.

252 **Hricik DE.** Posttransplant hyperlipidemia: the treatment dilemma. Am J Kidney Dis. 1994;23(5):766–71.

253 **Keogh A et al.** The effect of food and cholestyramine on the absorption of cyclosporine in cardiac transplant recipients. Transplant Proc. 1988;20(1): 27–30.

254 **Norman DJ et al.** Myolysis and acute renal failure in a heart-transplant recipient receiving lovastatin. N Engl J Med. 1988;318(1):46–7. Letter.

255 **East C et al.** Rhabdomyolysis in patients receiving lovastatin after cardiac transplantation. N Engl J Med. 1988; 318(1):47–8. Letter.

256 **Corpier CL et al.** Rhabdomyolysis and renal injury with lovastatin use. Report of two cases in cardiac transplant recipients. JAMA. 1988;260(2): 239–41.

257 **Kuo PC et al.** Lovastatin therapy for hypercholesterolemia in cardiac transplant recipients. Am J Cardiol. 1989; 64(10):631–55.

258 **Cheung AK et al.** A prospective study on treatment of hypercholesterolemia with lovastatin in renal transplant patients receiving cyclosporine. J Am Soc Nephrol. 1993;3(12):1884–891.

259 **Yoshimura N et al.** The effects of pravastatin on hyperlipidemia in renal transplant recipients. Transplantation. 1992;53(1):94–9.

260 **Barbir M et al.** Low-dose simvastatin for the treatment of hypercholesterolaemia in recipients of cardiac transplantation. Int J Cardiol. 1991;33(2): 241–46.

261 **Castelao AM et al.** HMGCoA reductase inhibitors lovastatin and simvastatin in the treatment of hypercholesterolemia after renal transplantation. Transplant Proc. 1993;25(1 Pt. 2): 1043–046.

262 **Kirkman RL et al.** Late mortality and

morbidity in recipients of long-term renal allografts. Transplantation. 1982; 34:347–51.

263 **Davis GF.** Adverse effects of corticosteroids: II Systemic. Clin Dermatol. 1986;4(1):161–69.

264 **Hariharan S et al.** Prednisone withdrawal in HLA identical and one haplotype-matched live-related donor and cadaver renal transplant recipients. Kidney Int Suppl. 1993;43:S30–5.

265 **Hricik DE et al.** Withdrawal of steroids after renal transplantation—clinical predictors of outcome. Transplantation. 1992;53(1):41–5.

266 **Price GD et al.** Corticosteroid-free maintenance immunosuppression after heart transplantation: feasibility and beneficial effects. J Heart Lung Transplant. 1992;11(2 Pt. 2):403–14.

267 **Pritzker MR et al.** Steroid-free maintenance immunotherapy: Minneapolis Heart Institute experience. J Heart Lung Transplant. 1992;11(2 Pt. 2): 415–20.

268 **Lake KD et al.** The impact of steroid withdrawal on the development of lipid abnormalities and obesity in heart transplant recipients. J Heart Lung Transplant. 1993;12(4):580–90.

269 **Hricik DE et al.** Variable effects of steroid withdrawal on blood pressure reduction in cyclosporine-treated renal transplant recipients. Transplantation. 1992;53(6):1232–235.

270 **Arizon JM et al.** A randomized study comparing deflazacort and prednisone in heart transplant patients. J Heart Lung Transplant. 1993;12(5):864–68.

271 **Arizon JM et al.** Preliminary experience with deflazacort, a new synthetic steroid with fewer undesirable side effects, in heart transplant patients. J Heart Lung Transplant. 1993;12(3): 445–48.

272 **Cooper JD et al.** Results of single and bilateral lung transplantation in 131 consecutive recipients. Washington University Lung Transplant Group. J Thorac Cardiovasc Surg. 1994;107(2): 460–70.

273 **Kerem E et al.** Prediction of mortality in patients with cystic fibrosis. N Engl J Med. 1992;326(18):1187–191.

274 **Judson MA.** Clinical aspects of lung transplantation. Clin Chest Med. 1993; 14(2):335–57.

275 **Lima O et al.** Effects of methylprednisolone and azathioprine on bronchial healing following lung autotransplantation. J Thorac Cardiovasc Surg. 1981;82:211–15.

276 **Bryan CL et al.** Corticosteroid therapy does not potentiate bronchial anastomatic complications in a single lung transplantation. Am Rev Respir Dis. 1991;143(Suppl. 1):A460.

277 **Schafers HJ et al.** Preoperative corticosteroids: a contraindication to lung transplantation? Chest. 1992;102(5): 1522–525.

278 **Snell GI et al.** Pseudomonas cepacia in lung transplant recipients with cystic fibrosis. Chest. 1993;103(2):466–71.

279 **deHoyos AL et al.** Pulmonary transplantation. Early and late results. The Toronto Lung Transplant Group. J Thorac Cardiovasc Surg. 1992;103(2): 295–306.

280 **Ramirez JC et al.** Bilateral lung transplantation for cystic fibrosis. The To-

ronto Lung Transplant Group. J Thorac Cardiovasc Surg. 1992;103(2):287–93.

281 **Egan TM et al.** Lung transplantation. Curr Probl Surg. 1989;26(10):673–751.

282 **Paradis I et al.** Life in the allogeneic environment after lung transplantation. Lung. 1990;168(Suppl.):1172–181.

283 **Horvath J et al.** Infection in the transplanted and native lung after single lung transplantation. Chest. 1993; 104(3):681–85.

284 **Griffith BP, Bando K.** Lung transplantation at the University of Pittsburgh: 1982–1992. A decade of progress. In: Terasaki PI, Cecka JM, eds. Clinical Transplants. Los Angeles: UCLA; 1992:149–60.

285 **Yousem SA et al.** A working formulation for the standardization of nomenclature in the diagnosis of heart and lung rejection: lung rejection study group. J Heart Transplant. 1990;9: 593–601.

286 **Trulock EP.** Management of lung transplant rejection. Chest. 1993; 103(5):1566–576.

287 **Scott JP.** Noninvasive detection of lung rejection. In: Kaye, O'Connell, eds. Heart and Lung Transplantation 2000. 1993:74–7.

288 **Shennib H et al.** Successful treatment of steroid-resistant double-lung allograft rejection with Orthoclone OKT$_3$. Am Rev Respir Dis. 1991;144(1): 224–26.

289 **Shenib H, Massard G.** Efficacy of OKT$_3$ therapy for acute rejection in isolated lung transplantations. J Heart Lung Transplant. 1994;13:514–19.

290 **Cooper JD et al.** A working formulation for the standardization of nomenclature and clinical staging of chronic dysfunction in lung allografts. International Society for Heart and Lung Transplantation. J Heart Lung Transplant. 1993;12(5):713–16.

291 **Glanville AR et al.** Obliterative bronchiolitis after heart-lung transplantation: apparent arrest by augmented immunosuppression. Ann Intern Med. 1987;107(3):300–04.

292 **Waters P et al.** Experience with OKT3 and human lung transplantation. Chest. 1990;98(Suppl.):7S.

293 **Wildevuur CRH, Benfield JR.** A review of 23 human lung transplantations by 20 surgeons. Ann Thorac Surg. 1970;9:489–515.

294 **Calhoun JH et al.** Single lung transplantation. Alternative medications and technique. J Thorac Cardiovasc Surg. 1991;101:816–25.

295 **Cooper JD et al.** Results of single and bilateral lung transplantation in 131 consecutive recipients. J Thorac Cardiovasc Surg. 1994;107:460–71.

296 **Griffith BP et al.** A prospective randomized trial of FK506 versus cyclosporine after human pulmonary transplantation. Transplantation. 1994; 57(6):848–51.

297 **Dowling RD et al.** Aerosolized cyclosporine as single-agent immunotherapy in canine lung allografts. Surgery. 1990;108(2):198–204.

298 **Todd TR.** Early postoperative management following lung transplantation. Clin Chest Med. 1990;11(2): 259–67.

299 **Laskow DA et al.** Cyclosporine-induced changes in glomerular filtration rate and urea excretion. Am J Med. 1990;88(5):497–502.

300 **Myers BD et al.** Cyclosporine-associated chronic nephropathy. N Engl J Med. 1984;311:699–705.

301 **Whiting PH et al.** The toxic effects of combined administration of cyclosporine and gentamicin. Br J Exp Pathol. 1982;63:554–61.

302 **Tomlanovich S et al.** Limitations of creatinine in quantifying the severity of cyclosporine-induced chronic nephropathy. Am J Kidney Dis. 1986;8(5): 332–37.

303 **Kho TL et al.** Nephrotoxic effect of cyclosporine A can be reversed by dopamine. Transplant Proc. 1987;19(1 Pt. 2):1749–753.

304 **Tan KKC et al.** Altered pharmacokinetics of cyclosporine in heart-lung transplant recipients with cystic fibrosis. Ther Drug Monit. 1990;12:520–24.

305 **Mancel-Grosso V et al.** Pharmacokinetics of cyclosporine A in bilateral lung transplantation candidates with cystic fibrosis. Transplant Proc. 1990; 22(4):1706–707.

306 **Cooney GF et al.** Cyclosporine bioavailability in heart-lung transplant candidates with cystic fibrosis. Transplantation. 1990;49(4):821–23.

307 **Tan KK et al.** Pharmacokinetics of cyclosporine in heart and lung transplant candidates and recipients with cystic fibrosis and Eisenmenger's syndrome. Clin Pharmacol Ther. 1993;53(5):544–54.

308 **First MR et al.** Cyclosporine-ketoconazole interaction. Long-term follow-up and preliminary results of a randomized trial. Transplantation. 1993;55(5): 1000–004.

309 **Butman SM et al.** Prospective study of the safety and financial benefit of ketoconazole as adjunctive therapy to cyclosporine after heart transplantation. J Heart Lung Transplant. 1991;10(3): 351–58.

310 **Shennib H, Auger JL.** Diltiazem improves cyclosporine dosage in cystic fibrosis lung transplant recipients. J Heart Lung Transplant. 1994;13(2): 292–96.

311 **Patton PR, Brenson ME.** A preliminary report of diltiazem and ketoconazole. Their cyclosporin-sparing effect and impact on transplant outcome. Transplantation. 1994;57:889–92.

312 **Yee GC, McGuire TR.** Pharmacokinetic drug interactions with cyclosporin (Part I). Clin Pharmacokinet. 1990;19(4):310–32.

313 **Yee GC, McGuire TR.** Pharmacokinetic drug interactions with cyclosporin (Part II). Clin Pharmacokinet. 1990;19(5):400–15.

314 **Kronbach T et al.** Cyclosporine metabolism in human liver: identification of a cytochrome P-450III gene family as the major cyclosporine-metabolizing enzyme explains interactions of cyclosporine with other drugs. Clin Pharmacol Ther. 1988;43(6):630–35.

315 **Christians U, Sewing KF.** Cyclosporin metabolism in transplant patients. Pharmacol Ther. 1993;57(2-3): 291–345.

316 **Kolars JC et al.** First-pass metabolism

of cyclosporin by the gut. Lancet. 1991;338(8781):1488–490.

317 **Watkins, PB.** The role of cytochromes P-450 in cyclosporine metabolism. J Am Acad Dermatol. 1990;23(6 Pt 2):1301–311.

318 **Hebert MF et al.** Bioavailability of cyclosporine with concomitant rifampin administration is markedly less than predicted by hepatic enzyme induction. Clin Pharmacol Ther. 1992;52(5):453–57.

319 **Gupta SK et al.** Cyclosporin-erythromycin interaction in renal transplant patients. Br J Clin Pharmacol. 1989;27:475–81.

320 **Berg KJ, Gjellestad A.** Renal effects of trimethoprim in ciclosporin- and azathioprine-treated kidney-allografted patients. Nephron. 1989;53:218–22.

321 **Carrier M et al.** Bromocriptine as an adjuvant to cyclosporine immunosuppression after heart transplantation. Ann Thorac Surg. 1990;49(1):129–32.

322 **Dorian P et al.** Digoxin-cyclosporine interaction: severe digitalis toxicity after cyclosporine treatment. Clin Invest Med. 1988;11(2):108–12.

323 **Pichard L, Fabre I.** Cyclosporin A drug interactions. Screening for inducers and inhibitors of cytochrome P-450 (cyclosporin A oxidase) in primary cultures of human hepatocytes and in liver microsomes. Drug Metab Dispos Biol Fate Chem. 1990;18:595–606.

324 **Lake KD.** Management of drug interactions with cyclosporine. Pharmacotherapy. 1991;11(5):110S–18S.

325 **Brockmoller J et al.** Pharmacokinetic interaction between cyclosporin and diltiazem. Eur J Clin Pharmacol. 1990;38(3):237–42.

326 **Tortorice KL et al.** The effects of calcium channel blockers on cyclosporine and its metabolites in renal transplant recipients. Ther Drug Monit. 1990;12(4):321–28.

327 **Canafax DM et al.** Interaction between cyclosporine and fluconazole in renal allograft recipients. Transplantation. 1991;51(5):1014–018.

328 **Bourbigot B, Guisinx J.** Nicardipine increases cyclosporin blood levels. Lancet. 1986;1:1447. Letter.

329 **Gupta SK et al.** Cyclosporin-erythromycin interaction in renal transplant patients. Br J Clin Pharmacol. 1989;27(4):475–81.

330 **Jan AB et al.** Pharmacokinetics of cyclosporine and nephrotoxicity in orthotopic liver transplant patients rescued with FK506. Transplant Proc. 1991;23:2777–779.

331 **Christians U, Brann F.** Interactions of FK506 and cyclosporine metabolism. Transplant Proc. 1991;23:2794–796.

332 **Wadhwa NK et al.** The effect of oral metoclopramide on the absorption of cyclosporine. Transplant Proc. 1987;19(1 Pt. 2):1730–733.

333 **Rosenberg L et al.** Administration of somatostatin analog (SMS 201–995) in the treatment of a fistula occurring after pancreas transplantation. Interference with cyclosporine immunosuppression. Transplantation. 1987;43(5):764–66.

334 **Freeman DJ, Lanpacis A.** Evaluation of cyclosporin-phenytoin interaction with observations on cyclosporine metabolites. Br J Clin Pharm. 1984;18:887–93.

335 **Lele P et al.** Cyclosporine and tegretol. Another drug interaction. Kidney Int. 1985;27:344.

336 **Carstensen H, Jacobsen N.** Interaction between cyclosporin A and phenobarbital. Br J Clin Pharmacol. 1986;21:550–51. Letter.

337 **Termeer A et al.** Severe nephrotoxicity caused by the combined use of gentamicin and cyclosporine in renal allograft recipients. Transplantation. 1986;42(2):220–21.

338 **Kennedy MS et al.** Acute renal toxicity with combined use of amphotericin B and cyclosporine after marrow transplantation. Transplantation. 1983;35:211–15.

339 **Altman RD et al.** Interaction of cyclosporine A and nonsteroidal anti-inflammatory drugs on renal function in patients with rheumatoid arthritis. Am J Med. 1992;93(4):396–402.

340 **Bennett WM, Serra J.** Minoxidil and cyclosporine. Am J Kidney Dis. 1985;5:214.

341 **Slavin J, Taylor J.** Cyclosporin, nifedipine, and gingival hyperplasia. Lancet. 1987;26.2(8561):739. Letter.

342 **Crosby S, Robblee JA.** Cyclosporine-pancuronium interaction in a patient with a renal allograft. Can J Anaesth. 1988;35(3 Pt. 1):300–02.

343 **Hanto DW, Frizzera G.** Epstein-Barr virus, immunodeficiency, and B cell lympho proliferation. Transplantation. 1985;39:461–72.

344 **Ho M et al.** Epstein-Barr virus infections and DNA hybridization studies in posttransplantation lymphoma and lymphoproliferative lesions: the role of primary infection. J Infect Dis. 1985;152(5):876–86.

345 **Mathur A et al.** Immunoregulatory abnormalities in patients with Epstein-Barr virus-associated B cell lymphoproliferative disorders. Transplantation. 1994;57(7):1042–045.

346 **Penn I.** The changing pattern of posttransplant malignancies. Transplant Proc. 1991;23(Pt. 2):1101–103.

347 **Swinnen LJ et al.** Increased incidence of lymphoproliferative disorder after immunosuppression with the monoclonal antibody OKT3 in cardiac-transplant recipients. N Engl J Med. 1990;323(25):1723–728.

348 **Batiuk TD et al.** Incidence and type of cancer following the use of OKT3: a single center experience with 557 organ transplants. Transplant Proc. 1993;25(1 Pt. 2):1391.

349 **McAlister V et al.** Posttransplant lymphoproliferative disorders in liver recipients treated with OKT3 or ALG induction immunosuppression. Transplant Proc. 1993;25(1 Pt. 2):1400–401.

350 **Preiksaitis JK et al.** Quantitative oropharyngeal Epstein-Barr virus shedding in renal and cardiac transplant recipients: relationship to immunosuppressive therapy, serologic responses, and the risk of posttransplant lymphoproliferative disorder. J Infec Dis. 1992;166(5):986–94.

351 **Cockfield SM et al.** Post-transplant lymphoproliferative disorder in renal allograft recipients. Clinical experience and risk factor analysis in a single center. Transplantation. 1993;56(1):88–96.

352 **Penn I.** Tumors after renal and cardiac transplantation. Hematol Oncol Clin North Am. 1993;7(2):431–45.

353 **Penn I.** Incidence and treatment of neoplasia after transplantation. J Heart Lung Transplant. 1993;12(6 Pt. 2):S328–36.

354 **Nalesnik MA et al.** The diagnosis and treatment of posttransplant lymphoproliferative disorders. Curr Probl Surg. 1988;25(6):367–472.

355 **Hemmens VJ, Moore DE.** Photochemical sensitization by azathioprine and its metabolites–II. Azathioprine and nitroimidazole metabolites. Photochem Photobiol. 1986;43(3):257–62.

356 **Shapiro RS et al.** Treatment of B-cell lymphoproliferative disorders with interferon alpha and intravenous gamma globulin. N Engl J Med. 1988;318(20):1334. Letter.

357 **Benkerrou M et al.** Therapy for transplant-related lymphoproliferative diseases. Hematol Oncol Clin North Am. 1993;7(2):467–75.

358 **Armitage JM et al.** Posttransplant lymphoproliferative disease in thoracic organ transplant patients: ten years of cyclosporine-based immunosuppression. J Heart Lung Transplant. 1991;10(6):877–86.

359 **Lake JR.** Changing indications for liver transplantation. Gastroenterol Clin North Am. 1993;22(2):213–29.

360 **Zetterman RK.** Primary care management of the liver transplant patient. Am J Med. 1994;96(1A):10S–17S.

361 **Pirsch JD et al.** Orthotopic liver transplantation in patients 60 years of age and older. Transplantation. 1991;51(2):431–33.

362 **Lidofsky SD.** Liver transplantation for fulminant hepatic failure. Gastroenterol Clin North Am. 1993;22(2):257–69.

363 **Kaufman SS et al.** Preoperative evaluation, preparation, and timing of orthotopic liver transplantation in the child. Semin Liver Dis. 1989;9:176–83.

364 **Busuttil RW et al.** Liver transplantation in children. Ann Surg. 1991;213(1):48–57.

365 **Becht MB et al.** Growth and nutritional management of pediatric patients after orthotopic liver transplantation. Gastroenterol Clin North Am. 1993;22(2):367–80.

366 **Belle SH, Beringer KC.** The Pitt-UNOS transplant registry. In: Terasaki PI, Cecka JM, eds. Clinical Transplants. Los Angeles: UCLA; 1992:17–32.

367 **Shaw BW Jr et al.** Postoperative care after liver transplantation. Semin Liver Dis. 1989;9(3):202–30.

368 **Carton EG et al.** Perioperative care of the liver transplant patient: Part 2. Anesth Analg. 1994;78(2):382–99.

369 **Carton EG et al.** Perioperative care of the liver transplant patient: Part 1. Anesth Analg. 1994;78(1):120–33.

370 **Ploeg RJ et al.** Risk factors for primary dysfunction after liver transplantation-a multivariate analysis. Transplantation. 1993;55(4):807–13.

371 **Porte RJ.** Coagulation and fibrinolysis in orthotopic liver transplantation: current views and insights. Semin Thromb Hemost. 1993;19(3):191–96.

372 **Greig PD et al.** Treatment of primary liver graft nonfunction with prostaglandin E1. Transplantation. 1989;48(3):447–53.

373 **Greiner CB, Roccaforte W.** Psychiatric issues in liver transplantation. Semin Liver Dis. 1989;9(3):184–88.

374 **Surman OS.** Psychiatric aspects of liver transplantation. Psychosomatics. 1994;35(3):297–307.

375 **Levenson JL, Olrisch ME.** Psychiatric aspects of heart transplantation. Psychosomatics. 1993;34(2):114–123.

376 **Trzepacz PT et al.** Psychopharmacologic issues in organ transplantation. Part I: Pharmacologic issues in organ failure and psychiatric aspects of immunosuppressants and anti-infectious agents. Psychosomatics. 1993;34:199–207.

377 **Trzepacz PT et al.** Psychopharmacologic issues in organ transplantation. Part 2: psychopharmacologic medications. Psychosomatics. 1993;290–98.

378 **Surman OS.** Possible immunological effects of psychotropic medication. Psychosomatics. 1993;34:139–43.

379 **Singh N et al.** Central nervous system lesions in adult liver transplant recipients: clinical review with implications for management. Medicine (Baltimore). 1994;73(2):110–18.

380 **Venkataramanan R et al.** Leaching of diethylhexyl phthalate from polyvinyl chloride bags into intravenous cyclosporine solution. Am J Hosp Pharm. 1986;43:2800–802.

381 **Yee GC.** Dosage forms of cyclosporine. Pharmacotherapy. 1991;11(6):149S–52S.

382 **Venkatarmanan R et al.** Pharmacokinetics and monitoring of cyclosporine following orthotopic liver transplantation. Semin Liver Dis. 1985;5:357–68.

383 **Zehnder C et al.** Cyclosporine A capsules: bioavailability and clinical acceptance study in renal transplant patients. Transplant Proc. 1988;20(Suppl. 2):641–48.

384 **Fahr A.** Cyclosporin clinical pharmacokinetics. Clin Pharmacokinet. 1993;24(6):472–95.

385 **Lindholm A.** Factors influencing the pharmacokinetics of cyclosporine in man. Ther Drug Monit. 1991;13(6):465–77.

386 **Wandstrat TL et al.** Cyclosporine pharmacokinetics in pediatric transplant recipients. Ther Drug Monit. 1989;11(5):493–96.

387 **Mehta MU et al.** Effect of bile on cyclosporin absorption in liver transplant patients. Br J Clin Pharmacol. 1988;25(5):579–84.

388 **Sokol RJ et al.** Improvement of cyclosporin absorption in children after liver transplantation by means of water-soluble vitamin E (see comments). Lancet. 1991;338(8761):212–14.

389 **Boudreaux JP et al.** Use of water-soluble liquid vitamin E to enhance cyclosporine absorption in children after liver transplant. Transplant Proc. 1993;25(2):1875.

390 **Mueller EA et al.** Pharmacokinetics and tolerability of a microemulsion formulation of cyclosporine in renal allograft recipients—a concentration-controlled comparison with the commercial formulation. Transplantation. 1994;57(8):1178–182.

391 **Trull AK et al.** Cyclosporin absorption from microemulsion formulation in liver transplant recipient. Lancet. 1993; 341(8842):433. Letter.

392 **Tufveson G et al.** A longitudinal study of the pharmacokinetics of cyclosporine A and *in vitro* lymphocyte responses in renal transplant patients. Transplant Proc. 1986;18(6 Suppl. 5): 16–24.

393 **Gupta SK, Benet LZ.** High-fat meals increase the clearance of cyclosporine. Pharm Res. 1990;7(1):46–8.

394 **Atkinson K et al.** Detrimental effect of intestinal disease on absorption of orally administered cyclosporine. Transplant Proc. 1983;15(Suppl. 1): 2446–449.

395 **Burckant CJ et al.** Cyclosporine pharmacokinetic profiles in liver, heart and kidney transplant patients as determined by high-performance liquid chromatography. Transplant Proc. 1986;18(Suppl. 5):129–36.

396 **Whitington PF et al.** Small-bowel length and the dose of cyclosporine in children after liver transplantation. N Engl J Med. 1990;322(11):733–38.

397 **Duchame MP et al.** Trough concentrations of cyclosporine in blood following administration with grapefruit juice. Br J Clin Pharmacol. 1993;36: 457–59.

398 **Ptachcinski RJ et al.** Clinical pharmacokinetics of cyclosporine. Clin Pharmacokinet. 1986;11:107–32.

399 **Shaw LM et al.** Critical issues in cyclosporine monitoring: report of the task force on cyclosporine monitoring. Clin Chem. 1987;33:1269–288.

400 **Consensus document: Hawk's lay meeting on therapeutic drug monitoring of cyclosporine.** Transplant Proc. 1990;22:1357–361.

401 **Holt DW et al.** Quality assessment of cyclosporine measurements: comparison of current methods. Transplant Proc. 1990;22(3):1234–239.

402 **Morris RG et al.** Experiences with the enzyme-multiplied immunoassay cyclosporine specific assay in a therapeutic drug monitoring laboratory. Ther Drug Monit. 1993;15(5):410–13.

403 **Dusci LJ et al.** Comparison of cyclosporine measurement in whole blood by high-performance liquid chromatography, monoclonal fluorescence polarization immunoassay, and monoclonal enzyme-multiplied immunoassay. Ther Drug Monit. 1992;14(4):327–32.

404 **Schroeder TJ et al.** A comparison of the clinical utility of the radioimmunoassay, high-performance liquid chromatography, and TDx cyclosporine assays in outpatient renal transplant recipients. Transplantation. 1989;47(2): 262–66.

405 **Schroeder TJ et al.** Clinical correlations of cyclosporine-specific and -nonspecific assays in stable renal transplants, acute rejection, and cyclosporine nephrotoxicity. Ther Drug Monit. 1993;15(3):190–94.

406 **Grevel J.** Optimization of immunosuppressive therapy using pharmacokinetic principles. Clin Pharmacokinet. 1992;23(5):380–90.

407 **Kahan BD, Grevel J.** Optimization of cyclosporine therapy in renal transplantation by a pharmacokinetic strategy. Transplantation. 1988;46(5):631–44.

408 **Kasiske BL et al.** The relationship between cyclosporine pharmacokinetic parameters and subsequent acute rejection in renal transplant recipients. Transplantation. 1988;46(5):716–22.

409 **Grevel J.** Area-under-the-curve versus trough level monitoring of cyclosporine concentration: critical assessment of dosage adjustment practices and measurement of clinical outcome. Ther Drug Monit. 1993;15(6):488–91.

410 **Lindholm A et al.** The adverse impact of high cyclosporine. Clearance rates on the incidences of acute rejection and graft loss. Transplantation. 1993;55(5): 985–93.

411 **Busca A et al.** Monitoring of cyclosporine blood levels from central venous lines: a misleading assay? Ther Drug Monit. 1994;16(1):71–4.

412 **Starzl TE et al.** Liver transplantation (2). N Engl J Med. 1989;19.321(16): 1092–099.

413 **Ratner LE et al.** Probable antibody-mediated failure of two sequential ABO-compatible hepatic allografts in a single recipient. Transplantation. 1993; 55(4):814–19.

414 **Demetris AJ et al.** Antibody-mediated rejection of human orthotopic liver allografts: a study of liver transplantation across ABO blood group barriers. Am J Pathol. 1988;132(3):489–502.

415 **Gordon RD et al.** The antibody crossmatch in liver transplantation. Surgery. 1986;100(4):705–15.

416 **Mor E et al.** Acute cellular rejection following liver transplantation: clinical pathologic features and effect on outcome. Semin Liver Dis. 1992;12(1): 28–40.

417 **Wiesner RH et al.** Hepatic allograft rejection: new developments in terminology, diagnosis, prevention, and treatment. Mayo Clin Proc. 1993;68 (1):69–79.

418 **Williams JW et al.** Role of liver allograft biopsy in patient management. Semin Liver Dis. 1992;12(1):60–72.

419 **Winkler M et al.** Use of FK506 for treatment of chronic rejection after liver transplantation. Transplant Proc. 1991;23(6):2984–986.

420 **Lake JR et al.** Maintenance immunosuppression after liver transplantation. Semin Liver Dis. 1992;12(1):73–9.

421 **Adams DH, Neuberger JM.** Treatment of acute rejection. Semin Liver Dis. 1992;12(1):80–8.

422 **Cosimi AB et al.** A randomized clinical trial comparing OKT₃ and steroids for treatment of hepatic allograft rejection. Transplantation. 1987;43(1):91–5.

423 **Colonna JO et al.** A prospective study on the use of monoclonal anti T3 cell antibody (OKT₃) to treat steroid-resistant liver transplant rejection. Arch Surg. 1987;122(10):1120–123.

424 **Anon.** A randomized clinical trial of OKT₃ monoclonal antibody for acute rejection of cadaveric renal transplants. Ortho Multicenter Transplant Study Group. N Engl J Med. 1985;313(6): 337–42.

425 **Thistlethwaite JR Jr et al.** Complications and monitoring of OKT₃ therapy. Am J Kidney Dis. 1988;11(2): 112–19.

426 **Norman DJ et al.** Consensus statement regarding OKT₃-induced cytokine-release syndrome and human an-timouse antibodies. Transplant Proc. 1993;25(2 Suppl. 1):89–92.

427 **Abramowicz D et al.** Release of tumor necrosis factor, interleukin-2, and gamma-interferon in serum after injection of OKT₃ monoclonal antibody in kidney transplant recipients. Transplantation. 1989;47(4):606–08.

428 **Suthanthiran M et al.** OKT₃ associated adverse reactions: mechanistic basis and therapeutic options. Am J Kidney Dis. 1989;14(5 Suppl. 2):39–44.

429 **Chatenoud L et al.** In vivo cell activation following OKT₃ administration. Systemic cytokine release and modulation by corticosteroids. Transplantation. 1990;49(4):697–702.

430 **Martin MA et al.** Nosocomial aseptic meningitis associated with administration of OKT₃. JAMA. 1988;259(13): 2002–005.

431 **Shihab FS et al.** Encephalopathy following the use of OKT₃ in renal allograft transplantation. Transplant Proc. 1993;25(2 Suppl. 1):31–4.

432 **Batiuk TD et al.** Cytokine nephropathy during antilymphocyte therapy. Transplant Proc. 1993;25(2 Suppl. 1): 27–30.

433 **Abramowicz D et al.** Anaphylactic shock after retreatment with OKT₃ monoclonal antibody. N Engl J Med. 1992;3.327(10):736. Letter.

434 **Abramowicz D et al.** Induction of thromboses within renal grafts by high-dose prophylactic OKT₃ (see comments). Lancet. 1992;339(8796):777–78.

435 **Constanzo-Nordin MR.** Cardiopulmonary effects of OKT₃: determinants of hypotension, pulmonary edema, and cardiac dysfunction. Transplant Proc. 1993;25(2 Suppl. 1):21–4.

436 **Stein KL et al.** The cardiopulmonary response to OKT₃ in orthotopic cardiac transplant recipients. Chest. 1989; 95(4):817–21.

437 **Chatenoud L et al.** Corticosteroid inhibition of the OKT₃-induced cytokine–related syndrome—dosage and kinetics prerequisites. Transplantation. 1991;51(2):334–38.

438 **First MR et al.** The effect of indomethacin on the febrile response following OKT₃ therapy. Transplantation. 1992;53(1):91–4.

439 **Vincenti FG et al.** Pentoxifylline reduces first-dose reactions following OKT₃. Transplant Proc. 1993;25(2 Suppl. 1):57–9.

440 **Chatenoud L.** OKT₃-induced cytokine-release syndrome: prevention effect of anti-tumor necrosis factor monoclonal antibody. Transplant Proc. 1993;25(2 Suppl. 1):47–51.

441 **Shield CF III, Norman DJ.** Immunologic monitoring during and after OKT₃ therapy. Am J Kidney Dis. 1988; 11(2):120–24.

442 **First MR et al.** Immune monitoring during retreatment with OKT₃. Transplant Proc. 1989;2(1 Pt. 2):1753–754.

443 **McDiarmid SV et al.** Low serum OKT₃ levels correlate with failure to prevent rejection in orthotopic liver transplant patients. Transplant Proc. 1990;22(4):1774–776.

444 **Hricik DE et al.** Inhibition of anti-OKT₃ antibody generation by cyclosporine—results of a prospective ran-domized trial. Transplantation. 1990; 50(2):237–40.

445 **Schroeder TJ et al.** Antimurine antibody formation following OKT₃ therapy. Transplantation. 1990;49(1):48–51.

446 **Legendre C et al.** Prediction of successful allograft rejection retreatment with OKT₃. Transplantation. 1992;53 (1):87–90.

447 **Shield CF III.** Consequences of anti-OKT₃ antibody development: OKT₃ reuse and–long-term graft survival. Transplant Proc. 1993;25(2 Suppl. 1): 81–2.

448 **Laskow DA, Curtis JJ.** Post-transplant hypertension. Am J Hypertens. 1990;3(9):721–25.

449 **Rich GM et al.** Cyclosporine A and prednisone-associated osteoporosis in heart transplant recipients. J Heart Lung Transplant. 1992;11(5):950–58.

450 **Muchmore JS et al.** Prevention of loss of vertebral bone density in heart transplant patients. J Heart Lung Transplant. 1992;11(5):959–63.

451 **Hay JE.** Bone disease in liver transplant recipients. Gastroenterol Clin North Am. 1993;22(2):337–49.

452 **Feldhoff C et al.** A comparison of alternate day and daily steroid therapy in children following renal transplantation. Int J Pediatr Nephrol. 1984;5:11–4.

453 **Tejani A, Sullivan K.** Long-term follow-up of growth in children post transplantation. Kidney Int. 1993;44 (Suppl. 43):S56–S59.

454 **Kirkman RL et al.** Late mortality and morbidity in recipients of long-term renal allografts. Transplantation. 1982; 34:347–51.

455 **Halpert RD et al.** Abdominal complications in organ transplant recipients. Radiol Clin North Am. 1993;31(6): 1345–357.

456 **Egawa H et al.** FK506 conversion therapy in pediatric liver transplantation. Transplantation. 1994;57(8): 1169–173.

457 **Fung J et al.** A randomized trial of primary liver transplantation under immunosuppression with FK506 versus cyclosporine. Transplant Proc. 1991; 23:2977–983.

458 **Shapiro R, Jordan M.** FK506 in clinical kidney transplantation. Transplant Proc. 1991;23:3065–067.

459 **Griffith BP et al.** A prospective randomized trial of FK506 versus cyclosporine after human pulmonary transplantation. Transplantation. 1994;57 (6):848–51.

460 **Fung J et al.** Conversion from cyclosporine to FK506 in liver allograft recipients with cyclosporine related complications. Transplant Proc. 1990 (Suppl. 1):6–12.

461 **Jordan ML et al.** FK506 ''rescue'' for resistant rejection of renal allografts under primary cyclosporine immunosuppression. Transplantation. 1994; 57(6):860–65.

462 **Armitage JM et al.** The clinical trial of FK506 as primary and rescue immunosuppression in adult cardiac transplantation. Transplant Proc. 1991; 23:3054–057.

463 **Venkataramanan R et al.** Pharmacokinetics of FK506 in transplant patients. Transplant Proc. 1991;23:2736–740.

464 **Furukawa H et al.** The effect of bile duct ligation and bile diversion on FK506. Transplantation. 1992;53(4): 722–25.

465 **Venkataramanan R et al.** Pharmacokinetics of FK506: preclinical and clinical studies. Transplant Proc. 1990;22: 52–6.

466 **Jain AB et al.** Comparative study of cyclosporine and FK506 dosage requirements in adult and pediatric orthotopic liver transplant patients. Transplant Proc. 1991;23:2763–766.

467 **Prograf Product Information.** 1994.

468 **Haschak-Chicko S et al.** An overview of FK506 in transplantation and autoimmune disease. Dialysis and Transplant. 1992;21:500–04,531.

469 **McDiarmid SV et al.** Differences in oral FK506 dose requirements between adult and pediatric liver transplant patients. Transplantation. 1993;55(6): 1328–332.

470 **Jain AB et al.** Pharmacokinetics of cyclosporine and nephrotoxicity in orthotopic liver transplant patients rescued with FK506. Transplant Proc. 1991;23: 2777–779.

471 **Fung JJ et al.** Adverse effects associated with the use of FK506. Transplant Proc. 1991;23:3105–108.

472 **Porryko MK, Textons SC.** Nephrotopic effects of primary immunosuppression with FK506 and cyclosporine regimens after liver transplantation. Mayo Clin Proc. 1994;69:105–12.

473 **Klintmahn GB.** A comparison of tacrolimus (FK506) and cyclosporine for immunosuppression in liver transplantation. The U.S. Multicenter FK506 Liver Study Group. NEJM. 1994;331: 1110–115.

474 **Eidelman BH et al.** Neurologic complications of FK506. Transplant Proc. 1991;23:3175–178.

475 **Hooks MA.** Tacrolimus, a new immunosuppressant—a review of the literature. Ann Pharmacother. 1994; 28(4):501–11.

476 **Wallemacq PE, Reding R.** FK506 (tacrolimus), a novel immunosuppressant in organ transplantation: clinical, biomedical, and analytical aspects. Clin Chem. 1993;39(11 Pt. 1):2219–228.

477 **Dambrosio R et al.** Validation and quality assurance program for monitoring tacrolimus (FK506) concentrations in plasma and whole blood. Ther Drug Monit. 1993;15(5):414–26.

478 **Grenier FC, Luczkiw J.** A whole blood-FK506 assay for the IMX analyzer. Transplant Proc. 1991;23:2748–749.

479 **Peters DH et al.** A review of its pharmacology and therapeutic potential in hepatic and renal transplantation. Drugs. 1993;46(4):746–94.

480 **Winkler M, Christians U.** Comparison of different assays for the quantitation of Fk506 levels in blood or plasma. Ther Drug Monit. 1994;16: 281–86.

481 **McMichael J et al.** An intelligent and cost-effective computer dosing system for individualizing FK506 therapy in transplantation and autoimmune disorders. J Clin Pharmacol. 1993;33(7): 599–605.

482 **Carey JA, Frist WH.** Use of poly-

clonal antilymphocytic preparations for prophylaxis in heart transplantation. J Heart Transplant. 1990;9(3 Pt. 2):297–300.

483 **Fries D et al.** Optimization of antilymphocyte globulin in renal transplantation. Transplant Proc. 1990;22(4): 1793–794.

484 **Ludwin D et al.** Complications related to the route of Minnesota antilymphoblast globulin administration in renal transplant recipients. Transplant Proc. 1985;17(4):1945–946.

485 **Hardy MA.** Beneficial effects of heterologous anti-lymphoid globulins in renal transplantation: one believer's view. Am J Kidney Dis 1982;2:79–86.

486 **Bielory L et al.** Antithymocyte globulin hypersensitivity in bone marrow failure patients. JAMA. 1988;260(21): 3164–167.

487 **Stratta RJ et al.** Sequential antilymphocyte globulin/cyclosporine immunosuppression in cadaveric renal transplantation. Effect of duration of ALG therapy. Transplantation. 1989;47(1): 96–102.

488 **Cosimi AB.** The clinical value of antilymphocyte antibodies. Transpl Proc. 1981;13:462–68.

489 **Monaco AP.** Antilymphocyte globulin: a clinical transplantation research opportunity. Am J Kidney Dis. 1982;2: 67–78.

490 **Debets JM et al.** Evidence of involvement of tumor necrosis factor in adverse reactions during treatment of kidney allograft rejection with antithymocyte globulin. Transplantation. 1989;47(3):487–92.

491 **Bielory L et al.** Human serum sickness: a prospective analysis of 35 patients treated with equine anti-thymocyte globulin for bone marrow failure. Medicine (Baltimore). 1988;67(1):40–57.

492 **Clark KR et al.** Administration of ATG according to the absolute T lymphocyte count during therapy for steroid-resistant rejection. Transpl Int. 1993;6(1):18–21.

493 **Macdonald PS et al.** A prospective randomized study of prophylactic OKT₃ versus equine antithymocyte globulin after heart transplantation—increased morbidity with OKT₃. Transplantation. 1993;55(1):110–16.

494 **Clark KR et al.** Flow-cytometric monitoring of ATG therapy for steroid-resistant rejection. Transplant Proc. 1992;24(1):315.

495 **Maddocks JL et al.** Azathioprine and severe bone marrow depression. Lancet. 1986;18.1(8473):156. Letter.

496 **Lennard L, Murphy MF.** Severe megaloblastic anemia associated with abnormal azathioprine metabolism. Br J Clin Pharmacol. 1984;17:171–72.

497 **Schutz E et al.** Azathioprine-induced myelosuppression in thiopurine methyltransferase deficient heart transplant recipient. Lancet. 1993;13.341(8842): 436. Letter.

498 **Chocair PR et al.** The importance of thiopurine methyltransferase activity for the use of azathioprine in transplant recipients. Transplantation. 1992;53 (5):1051–056.

499 **Soria-Royer C et al.** Thiopurine-methyl-transferase activity to assess azathioprine myelotoxicity in renal

transplant recipients. Lancet. 1993; 19.341(8860):1593–594. Letter.

500 **DePinho RA, Goldberg CS.** Azathioprine and the liver. Gastroenterology. 1984;86:162–68.

501 **Horsmans Y et al.** Reversible cholestasis with bile duct injury following azathioprine therapy: a case report. Liver. 1991;11(2):89–93.

502 **Zardy Z, Veith FJ.** Irreversible liver damage after azathioprine. JAMA. 1972;222:690–91.

503 **Sterneck M et al.** Azathioprine hepatotoxicity after liver transplantation. Hepatology. 1991;14(5):806–10.

504 **Herskowitz LJ, Olansky S.** Acute pancreatitis associated with long-term azathioprine therapy. Arch Dermatol. 1979;115:179.

505 **Penn I.** Cancer following cyclosporine therapy. Transplantation. 1987;43: 32–8.

506 **Kirchertz EJ et al.** Successful low dose captopril rechallenge following drug-induced leukemia. Lancet. 1981; 2:1362–363.

507 **Brooks RJ, Dorr RT.** Interaction of allopurinol with 6-mercaptopurine and azathioprine. Biomed Pharmacother. 1982;36:217–22.

508 **Wang JC et al.** Use of granulocyte colony-stimulating factor (G-CSF) in leukopenic renal transplant recipients. J Am Soc Nephrol. 1992;3:887.

509 **Rubin RH.** Infection in the renal and liver transplant patient. In: Rubin RH, Young LS, eds. Clinical Approach to Infection in the Compromised Host. 2nd ed. New York: Plenum; 1988: 557–621.

510 **Coventry LO, Zeluff B.** Infection I the cardiac transplant patient. In: Rubin RA, Young LS, eds. Clinical Approach to Infection in the Compromised Host. 2nd ed. New York: Plenum; 1988: 623–48.

511 **Kusne S et al.** Infections after liver transplantation. Medicine. 1988;67: 132–43.

512 **Dumer JS et al.** Early infections in kidney, heart and liver transplant recipients on cyclosporine. Transplantation. 1983;36:259–67.

513 **Rubin RH, Talkoff-Rubin NE.** Antimicrobial strategies in the care of organ transplant recipients. Antimicrob Agents Chemother. 1993;37(4):619–24.

514 **Petri WA Jr.** Infections in heart transplant recipients. Clin Infect Dis. 1994; 18(2):141–46.

515 **Gorensek MJ et al.** Selective bowel decontamination with quinolones and nystatin reduces gram-negative and fungal infections in orthotopic liver transplant recipients. Cleve Clin J Med. 1993;60(2):139–44.

516 **Rubin RH.** Impact of cytomegalovirus infection on organ transplant recipients. Rev Infect Dis 1990;(12 Suppl. 7):S754–66.

517 **Stratta RJ.** Clinical patterns and treatment of cytomegalovirus infection after solid-organ transplantation. Transplant Proc. 1993;26(5 Suppl. 4):15–21.

518 **Ho M.** Observations from transplantation contributing to the understanding of pathogenesis of CMV infection. Transplant Proc. 1991;23:(Suppl. 3): 104–09.

519 **McCarthy JM et al.** The cost impact

of cytomegalovirus disease in renal transplant recipients. Transplantation. 1993;55(6):1277–282.

520 **Boland GJ et al.** Early detection of primary cytomegalovirus infection after heart and kidney transplantation and the influence of hyperimmune globulin prophylaxis. Transpl Int. 1993;6(1): 34–8.

521 **Levinson ML, Jacobson PA.** Treatment and prophylaxis of cytomegalovirus disease. Pharmacotherapy. 1992; 12(4):300–18.

522 **Muller GA, Muller CA.** Cytomegalovirus infection: how to manage it in the immunocompromised transplant recipient. Nephrol Dial Transplant. 1994; 9:3–4.

523 **Van son WJ, Van der Bij W.** Evidence for pulmonary dysfunction in all patients with symptomatic and asymptomatic (CMV) infection after renal transplantation. Transplant Proc. 1989; 21:2065–068.

524 **Faulds D, Heel RC.** Ganciclovir: a review of its antiviral activity, pharmacokinetic properties and therapeutic efficacy in cytomegalovirus infections. Drugs. 1990;39(4):597–638.

525 **Minor JR, Baltz JK.** Foscarnet sodium. DICP. 1991;25(1):41–7.

526 **NIH Consensus Conference.** Intravenous immunoglobulin. Prevention and treatment of disease. JAMA. 1990;264: 3189–193.

527 **Snydman DR.** Cytomegalovirus immunoglobulins in the prevention and treatment of cytomegalovirus disease. Rev Infect Dis. 1990;(12 Suppl. 7): S839–48.

528 **Kutsogiannis DJ et al.** Granulocyte macrophage colony-stimulating factor for the therapy of cytomegalovirus and ganciclovir-induced leukopenia in a renal transplant recipient. Transplantation. 1992;53(4):930–32.

529 **Sulecki M et al.** Treatment of ganciclovir-induced neutropenia with recombinant human GM-CSF. Am J Med. 1991;90(3):401–02. Letter.

530 **Brayman KL et al.** Prophylaxis of serious cytomegalovirus infection in renal transplant candidates using live human cytomegalovirus vaccine: interim results of a randomized controlled trial. Arch Surg. 1988;123(12):1502–508.

531 **Balfour HH Jr et al.** A randomized, placebo-controlled trial of oral acyclovir for the prevention of cytomegalovirus disease in recipients of renal allografts. N Engl J Med. 1989;25.320(21): 1381–387.

532 **Freise CE, Pons V.** Comparison of three regimens for cytomegalovirus prophylaxis in 147 liver transplant recipients. Transplant Proc. 1991;23: 1498–500.

533 **Merigan TC et al.** A controlled trial of ganciclovir to prevent cytomegalovirus disease after heart transplantation. N Engl J Med. 1992;30.326(18):1182–186.

534 **Martin M.** Antiviral prophylaxis for CMV infection in liver transplantation. Transplant Proc. 1993;25(5 Suppl. 4): 10–4.

535 **Snydman DR et al.** Use of cytomegalovirus immune globulin to prevent cytomegalovirus disease in renal-transplant recipients. N Engl J Med. 1987; 22.317(17):1049–054.

536 **Snydman DR et al.** Cytomegalovirus immune globulin prophylaxis in liver transplantation. A randomized, double-blind, placebo-controlled trial. The Boston Center for Liver Transplanta-tion CMVIG Study Group. Ann Intern Med. 1993;15.119(10):984–91.

537 **Stratta RJ et al.** Successful prophy-laxis of cytomegalovirus disease after primary CMV exposure in liver trans-plant recipients. Transplantation. 1991; 51(1):90–7.

538 **Yee GC, Salomon DR.** Cyclosporine. In: Evans et al., eds. Applied Pharma-cokinetics: Principles of Therapeutic Drug Monitoring. 3rd ed. Vancouver: Applied Therapeutics, Inc.; 1992:28–33.

539 **Solinger HW et al.** Experience with simultaneous pancreas-kidney trans-plantation. Ann Surg. 1988;208:475–83.

Adult Enteral Nutrition

Carol J Rollins

Patient Selection 34-1
Route of Tube Feeding (See Figure 34.1) 34-2
    Tube placement 34-2
        Nasal 34-2
        Feeding ostomies 34-2
    Site of delivery 34-3
Formula Selection 34-3
    Polymeric Formulas (See Table 34.2) 34-3
        Nutrient source 34-4
        Fiber content 34-4
        Caloric density 34-5
        Protein content 34-5
    Oligomeric Formulas (See Table 34.3) 34-5
    Specialized Formulas (See Tables 34.4 and 34.5) 34-6
        Renal failure 34-6
        Hepatic failure 34-6
        Stress/critically ill 34-6
        Pulmonary disease 34-9
        Glucose control 34-9
    Modular Components 34-12
Tube Feeding Administration Regimen 34-12
    Continuous Infusion 34-12
    Cyclic Feeding 34-12
    Intermittent or Bolus Feedings 34-12

    Initiation without transition from continuous
      infusion 34-13
        Alternative method 34-13
    Methods of Administration 34-13
Monitoring Enteral Feeding (See Table 34.6) 34-14
    Mechanical Complications 34-14
    Gastrointestinal (GI) Complications 34-14
    Metabolic Complications 34-14
Medications and Enteral Nutrition by Tube 34-17
Patient Assessment 34-18
    Evaluation of Nutritional Status 34-18
    Estimation of Nutritional Requirements 34-18
    Enteral Nutrition by Tube 34-19
    Enteral Formula Selection 34-19
    Fluid Provision 34-20
    Enteral Nutrition Administration 34-20
    Monitoring Enteral Nutrition Support 34-20
    Electrolyte Abnormalities 34-21
    Transfer to a Nursing Facility 34-22
    Evaluation of Nutritional Status 34-23
    Estimation of Nutritional Requirements 34-23
    Enteral Nutrition by Tube 34-24
    Enteral Nutrition Administration 34-24
    Tube Feeding Intolerance 34-25
    Medication Administration via Feeding Tube 34-26

Enteral nutrition refers to nutrition provided via the gastrointestinal (GI) tract. As the term commonly is used, however, enteral nutrition is synonymous with delivery of nutrients into the GI tract by tube (e.g., tube feeding). The tube allows continued use of the gastrointestinal tract when one or more steps in the normal process of obtaining nutrients from oral intake is disrupted. Although steps such as chewing or swallowing may be completely disrupted, some digestive and absorptive function must remain if tube feeding is to be a viable nutrition support option.

Patient Selection

Patients generally are considered at nutritional risk when intake is inadequate to meet nutritional requirements for seven or more days or when weight loss exceeds 10% of pre-illness weight.[1] Nutrition screening attempts to identify patients who may be at nutritional risk by evaluating a few selected parameters. In a survey of 388 dietitians, over 90% of institutional practice sites had a screening protocol, with approximately 60% screening all patients and about 25% screening patients on the basis of specific criteria.[2] Approximately 80% or more of respondents used the following screening parameters: weight, height, diagnosis, recent weight loss, and serum albumin. Availability of these parameters in the patient chart, however, sometimes is limited.[3] Two-thirds of respondents completed a nutrition assessment when patients were identified as being at nutritional risk during screening. Nutrition assessment expands the screen by including other laboratory data [hemoglobin (Hgb), hematocrit (Hct), creatinine, cholesterol, nitrogen balance, total iron-binding capacity (TIBC), prealbumin], calculation of energy requirements, dietary history, and medical history. Completion of the nutrition assessment helps identify the most appropriate route for

nutrition intervention, although the assessment itself is independent of the route selected for intervention. (See Chapter 35: Adult Parenteral Nutrition for further information on nutrition assessment.)

Routes of nutrition intervention may include modified oral diet, enteral nutrition by tube, or parenteral nutrition. Tube feeding is considered the route of choice in patients who are malnourished or are likely to become malnourished, and "will not, should not, or cannot eat," but have a functional GI tract without a contraindication to its use.[1]

The normal process of preparing nutrients for absorption includes multiple steps.[4] Table 34.1 lists the functional anatomic units of the GI tract and the major steps that occur in each unit, and provides examples of conditions and diseases that can impair the functional unit. The provision of enteral nutrition by tube may be appropriate for patients with these disorders, depending upon the extent to which normal intake, transport, digestion, and absorption of nutrients is impaired. Clinical circumstances, rather than a specific diagnosis, should be the determining factor for initiation of tube feeding. Particularly close attention must be given to the clinical condition of patients with severe pancreatitis, enterocutaneous fistulae, GI ischemia, and partial bowel obstruction because enteral feeding may be contraindicated.[1] Enteral feeding generally is contraindicated in patients with diffuse peritonitis, complete bowel obstruction, paralytic ileus, intractable vomiting, diarrhea severe enough to make metabolic management difficult, severe malabsorption, and/or early-stage short-bowel syndrome. Frequent reassessment is recommended, however, since patients may be candidates for enteral nutrition as the condition improves or resolves.

Table 34.1	Functional Units of the GI Tract[a]	
Functional Unit	Major Steps	Conditions/Diseases
Mouth and Oropharynx	Chew and lubricate food; swallow	Amylotrophic lateral sclerosis, muscular dystrophy, severe RA, CVA, end-stage Parkinson's disease, paralysis, coma, anorexia due to other disease: cardiac or cancer cachexia, renal failure and uremia, liver failure, neurologic disease
Esophagus	Transport food to the stomach	Esophageal disease: ulcer, cancer, obstruction, fistula, esophagectomy, CVA
Stomach	Hold food for mixing and grinding; add acid and enzymes; release chyme to small bowel; osmoregulation	Severe gastritis or ulceration, gastroparesis, gastric outlet obstruction, gastric cancer, severe gastroesophageal reflux
Duodenum	Osmoregulation; neutralize stomach acid	Severe duodenal ulcer, duodenal fistula, cancer: gastric, pancreatic
Small Bowel: Jejunum and Ilium	Digestion; absorption	Enterocutaneous fistula, severe enteric infection, malnutrition, malabsorption, Crohn's disease, celiac sprue, ileus and dysmotility syndrome
Pancreas	Secretion of digestive enzymes	Pancreatitis, pancreatic cancer, pancreatic injury, pancreatic fistula
Colon	Absorb fluid; ferment soluble fiber and unabsorbed carbohydrate; absorb water	Ulcerative colitis, Crohn's disease, colon cancer, colocutaneous fistula, colovaginal fistula, diverticulitis, colitis of any etiology, colon surgery

[a] CVA = Cerebral vascular accident; GI = Gastrointestinal; RA = Rheumatoid arthritis.

Route of Tube Feeding

Several options exist for the route of tube feeding. Selection of the route is determined by the anticipated duration of tube feeding, the disrupted step(s) in the normal process of obtaining nutrients, and the risk of aspiration. Figure 34.1 illustrates the two basic types of tube placement, nasal versus ostomy, and the sites available for formula delivery (e.g., gastric, duodenal, or jejunal). The name of the feeding route usually includes both the type of tube placement and the site of formula delivery. For example, nasogastric (NG) indicates nasal placement with gastric delivery of formula, while gastrostomy indicates ostomy placement with gastric delivery of formula. Exceptions are cervical pharyngostomy and esophagostomy, where the names indicate the ostomy location but not that feeding occurs into the stomach.

Tube Placement

Nasal placement of the tube is preferred for short-term tube feeding in patients expected to resume oral feeding and without obstruction of nasal, pharyngeal, or esophageal passages. Clinically evident injury from nasal intubation appears to be very low, but up to 60% of patients may suffer ulceration or mucosal bruising of the esophagus and hypopharynx.[5] Perforation of the hypopharynx, esophagus, or stomach has been reported with tube place-

ment.[5-7] Pharyngitis, sinusitis, otitis media, and incompetence of the lower esophageal sphincter also are associated with nasoenteric tubes, especially large-bore tubes.[8] Inadvertent pulmonary placement of small-bore feeding tubes has been reported in 0.3% to 5.4% of tube placements.[9-11] Complications from tracheobronchial placement generally do not occur unless the pleura is perforated or formula is infused. Perforation of the pleura can result in hemothorax, pneumothorax, pleural effusion, or development of a bronchopleural fistula.[12] Pleuritis, empyema, and sepsis can occur when formula is infused into the pleural space.[13] Formula administration into the lungs can result in dyspnea, cyanosis, sterile pneumonitis or pleuritis, and possibly bacterial superinfection.[14] Radiographic confirmation of tube placement is mandatory to rule out perforation and pulmonary intubation in unconscious patients, or if gastric contents cannot be aspirated, or if auscultation during air insufflation is uncertain in conscious and alert patients.[10,12,15-17]

Feeding ostomies (tube enterostomies) generally are reserved for long-term tube feeding. Depending upon the clinical situation and the type of tube enterostomy placed, long-term feeding may be interpreted as greater than one to three months, although nasoenteric feeding tubes occasionally are used for several months.[8,18,19] Access for enterostomies may be achieved surgically or percutaneously. Most surgical enterostomies require general anesthesia for placement, although some surgeons use local anesthesia for gastrostomy and cervical pharyngostomy or esophagostomy placement.[20] Jejunostomy tubes frequently are placed while the patient is anesthetized for laparotomy or upper gastrointestinal surgery, which allows early postoperative feeding.[1,21]

The surgical procedure used and, anticipated time the tube will be needed, determine whether an enterostomy is considered temporary or permanent. Tubes needed for more than six months generally are considered permanent. Surgical procedures that create a mucocutaneous stoma (e.g., Janeway gastrostomies, Roux-en-Y jejunostomies) denote very long-term or permanent enterostomies.[8] Procedures that place an indwelling tube with purse-string sutures and/or short seromuscular tunnels (e.g., Stamm and Witzel gastrostomies and jejunostomies and needle-catheter jejunostomies, generally are classified as temporary enterostomies. Removal of the indwelling tube generally leads to rapid closure of the stoma without surgery in these enterostomies.

Surgical placement of an enterostomy requires that the patient is stable enough to prolong the primary operation, that bacterial contamination of the primary operative site is not increased significantly, or that the patient can tolerate general anesthesia solely for enterostomy formation. The risks of surgical enterostomy frequently outweigh the benefits in patients who are poor surgical risks, have extensive GI disease, and/or have a very limited life expectancy. Relative contraindications to needle catheter jejunostomy placement include ascites, severe immunosuppression, coagulopathy at the time of surgery, and increased risk of enterocutaneous fistula formation as occurs in Crohn's disease and radiation enteritis.[22] These relative contraindications also hold for other types of surgical jejunostomies and gastrostomies.

Percutaneous endoscopic gastrostomies (PEG), gastrojejunostomies (PEGJ), and jejunostomies (PEJ) are performed under local anesthesia.[8,21] Patients requiring long-term tube feeding, but who are poor surgical risks or have no other need for surgery may be candidates for percutaneous endoscopic enterostomies. Relative contraindications to percutaneous endoscopic placement of a feeding tube include obstructions which prevent passage of the endoscope, inability to see the endoscopic light through the abdominal wall (e.g., with morbid obesity, ascites), and prior subtotal gastrectomy or laparotomy.[8,23,24]

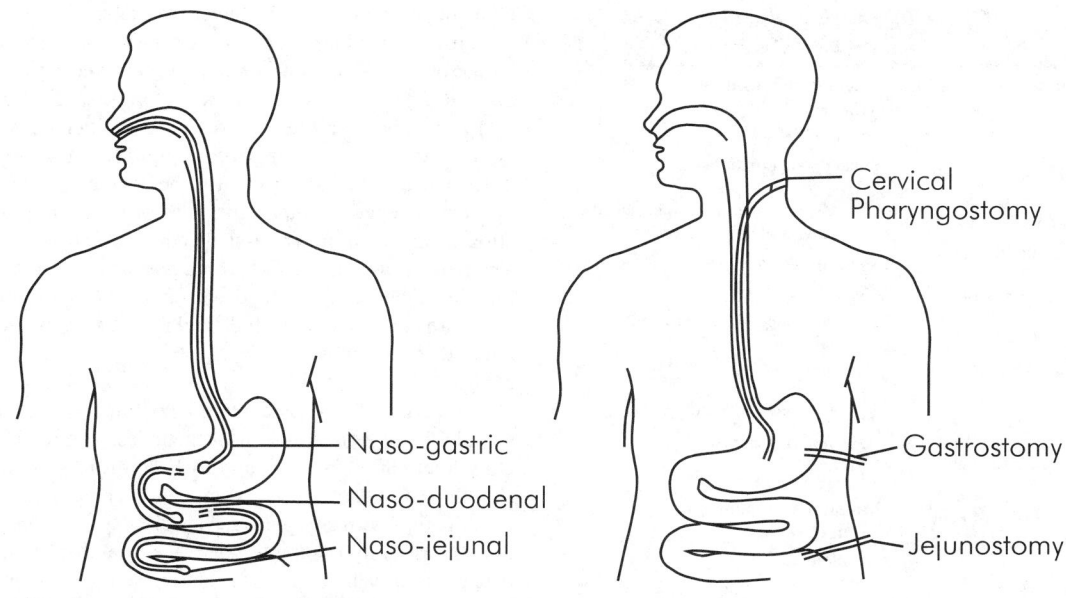

Fig 34.1 Naso-Enteric and Enterostomy Feeding Sites

The major advantages of percutaneous access versus surgical access appear to be the shorter time required for percutaneous tube placement and lower cost. Morbidity and mortality appear to be similar with percutaneous versus surgical feeding tube access.[25-27] Complication rates of about 20% in each group were found in a comparative study of PEG placement versus surgical gastrostomy in 51 patients.[27] A complication rate of 6.6% was reported for surgical gastrostomy placement in one noncomparative study, while another study reported a 6% incidence of major complications plus 10% minor complications.[28,29] Rates of complication for PEG placement vary from 0% to 9% for major complications and from 0% to 24% for minor complications.[23,30,31] Bleeding and problems with the surgical or percutaneous procedure are complications that may occur at the time of enterostomy formation. Complications after enterostomy placement include peritonitis, bowel obstruction, leakage of gastric fluids, gastric perforation, and surgical wound infection.[8,23,30]

Site of Delivery

The preferred site for enteral formula delivery is the stomach since this is the most physiologically normal feeding site. Stimulation of normal digestive processes and hormonal responses associated with eating occurs with gastric feeding. The stomach serves as a reservoir which generally allows patients to tolerate bolus, intermittent, or continuous feeding. Gastric feeding, either by nasogastric tube or gastrostomy, requires an intact gag reflex, low risk of aspiration, and adequate gastric motility to prevent accumulation of formula in the stomach. Patients with neurologic, traumatic, or degenerative diseases which impair ingestion, chewing, or swallowing may be candidates for gastric feeding. Head and neck cancer patients frequently are candidates for gastric feedings, unless the cancer has invaded the stomach or lower esophagus. Patients with gastric outlet obstruction, gastroparesis, gastric distention, gastroesophageal reflux, or poor gag reflex are not candidates for gastric feeding, but may be for duodenal or jejunal delivery of nutrients.

Transpyloric delivery of nutrients into the duodenum or jejunum may be appropriate when gastric dysfunction, obstruction, or disease is present; when the patient's risk of aspiration is high due to a need to lay flat in bed; or for early postoperative feeding when

gastric emptying may be impaired. Duodenal delivery of nutrients preserves some degree of osmoregulation, which may account for growth equivalent to gastric feeding and improved growth compared to jejunal feeding in animal studies.[32,33] Gastroesophageal reflux and aspiration are reduced with duodenal feeding compared to gastric feeding in animal studies, and with jejunal versus gastric feeding in humans.[32-34] Other studies report migration of tubes from the duodenum into the stomach and equal risk of aspiration between postpyloric and intragastric tube placement.[35,36] Patients receiving night feeding or those with gastric dysmotility appear to be at greatest risk of tube migration. Tube placement beyond the ligament of Treitz, denoting jejunal placement, may be most appropriate for patients with a high risk of tube migration and aspiration. Jejunal tube placement is necessary for patients requiring small bowel enterostomy since the duodenum is not accessible for enterostomy placement.

Formula Selection
Polymeric Formulas

Enteral formula selection is based upon total nutrient requirements, fluid restrictions, and the extent to which normal digestion and absorption of nutrients is impaired. Over 100 enteral formulas are available commercially, but most practitioners can meet the needs of their patients by being familiar with only a few products. Categorizing formulas into four ''generic'' groups and a few subgroups, as listed in Table 34.2, simplifies the formula selection process.

Polymeric formulas are the most common type of enteral formula. The use of intact or partially hydrolyzed proteins requires that patients have full digestive capability for proteins. The carbohydrate sources and fats used in polymeric formulas also require full digestive function. Osmolality is decreased and palatability increased by the use of relatively intact nutrient sources. Administration of approximately 1.5 to 2 L of most polymeric formulas provides 100% of the U.S. Recommended Dietary Allowance (RDA) for vitamins and minerals. Since 100% of the RDA is provided in a typical volume consumed daily, these formulas sometimes are called ''complete'' formulas. Polymeric formulas tend to be the least expensive enteral formulas, although prices may

Table 34.2	"Generic" Groups and Subgroups of Enteral Formulas	

Polymeric Formulas
Nutrient Source
  Blenderized
  Milk-based
  Lactose-free

Fiber Content
  Fiber-free
  Low to moderate fiber (1–8 gm/L)
  Moderate to high fiber (>8 gm/L)

Caloric Density
  Standard density (1–1.2 kcal/mL)
  Moderate density (≈1.5 kcal/mL)
  Calorically dense (2 kcal/mL)

Protein or Nitrogen Content
  Low nitrogen (≈6% of kcal)
  Standard nitrogen (11%–15% of kcal)
  High nitrogen (16%–25% of kcal)

Oligomeric Formulas
  Elemental
  Peptide-based

Specialized Formulas
Renal Failure
  Essential amino acid enriched
  Low protein and electrolytes

Hepatic Failure (BCAAs)[a]

Stress/Critically Ill
  Branched-chain enriched
  High nitrogen plus conditionally essential nutrients
  Immune modulating

Pulmonary Disease

Glucose Control

Modular Components
  Carbohydrate
  Protein
  Fats

[a] BCAAs = Branched-chain amino acids.

vary considerably based upon specific nutrient content (e.g., trace elements, fiber). Table 34.3 provides a relative cost summary for enteral formulas.

Nutrient Source

Several criteria can be used to subdivide polymeric formulas. Based upon the nutrient source, formulas can be divided into blenderized, milk-based, or lactose-free formulations. *Blenderized formulas* are designed for long-term tube feeding. Table foods are blenderized, then processed in cans to assure more consistent nutrient provision and lower risk of bacterial contamination compared to foods blenderized in the home. The high viscosity of these formulas may require a large-bore feeding tube and administration by pump. Other disadvantages include possible lactose content, higher cost than other polymeric formulas, and reluctance of some third-party payers to cover the cost of blenderized food. Compleat and Compleat Modified from Sandoz Nutrition are typical blenderized formulas. *Milk-based formulas* tend to be more palatable than other polymeric formulas for patients taking the formula by mouth. Meritene, Carnation Instant Breakfast, and Sustacal powder, but *not* ready to use Sustacal, are commonly used milk-based formulas. The greatest disadvantage of these formulas is their lactose content, which may cause bloating, flatulence, abdominal cramps, and watery diarrhea in patients with lactose intolerance. Most ethnic groups, except those from northern Europe, tend to have reduced lactase production in adulthood leading to lactose intolerance. In addition, reduced disaccharidase production during fasting, malnutrition, and many diseases of the GI tract contributes to lactose intolerance in hospitalized patients.[37] *Lactose-free formulas* are, therefore, the standard for tube-fed patients in most hospitals and nursing homes. These formulas are low residue and low viscosity unless fiber is added.

Fiber Content

Fiber content provides a second criteria for subdividing polymeric formulas. Most enteral formulas available today are *fiber-free*. The number of formulas containing fiber, however, continues to increase as the potential physiologic benefits of fiber become better documented. Physiologic responses associated with fiber in-

clude increased fecal bulk, decreased transit time in patients prone to constipation, increased transit time in patients with diarrhea, reduction of serum cholesterol, and improved glycemic control in diabetics.[38–45] *Fiber-supplemented formulas* generally contain 5 to 14 gm fiber per liter. Recommended fiber intake is 20 to 30 gm/day with an upper limit of 35 gm/day, although actual intake is estimated to be half of this for the average American.[46]

Fiber is added to enteral formulas primarily to reduce the alteration in intestinal transit associated with fiber-free formulas.[47,48] The type of fiber added to a formula is expected to affect the physiologic properties associated with fiber. Insoluble fiber is associated with changes in fecal bulk and transit time, while soluble fiber tends to be responsible for effects on cholesterol and glycemic control.[39,48]

Blenderized formulas contain a combination of soluble and insoluble fibers from fruits and vegetables. The total content of dietary fiber varies from about 4 to 10 gm/L in these formulas, with soluble and insoluble fiber being nearly equal.[49] Oat fiber, used in combination with soy polysaccharide in at least one formula (Ultracal), primarily is soluble fiber. The total dietary fiber content of oat bran is only about 20%, so relatively large amounts are required to achieve high levels of dietary fiber supplementation. Soy polysaccharide, used in the majority of fiber-containing formulas, contains approximately 75% dietary fiber, 6% of which is soluble fiber and 94% insoluble fiber.[48] Despite the low level of soluble fiber, soy polysaccharide lowers serum cholesterol levels and improves

Table 34.3	Relative Cost of Enteral Formulas[a]
Type of Formula	**Relative Cost**
Polymeric Formulas	
Blenderized	2.2
Milk-based	0.9
Lactose-free, standard caloric density, standard nitrogen content plus	
Fiber free[b]	1.0
Low to moderate fiber (1–8 gm/L)	2.3
Moderate to high fiber (>8 gm/L)	2.8
Lactose-free, standard nitrogen content, fiber-free plus	
Standard caloric density (1–1.2 kcal/mL)[b]	1.0
Moderate density (≈1.5 kcal/mL)	1.0
Calorically dense (2 kcal/mL)	0.9
Lactose-free, standard caloric density, fiber-free plus	
Low nitrogen (6% of kcal); low electrolyte	3.5
Standard nitrogen (11%–15% of kcal)[b]	1.0
High nitrogen (16%–25% of kcal)	2.2
Oligomeric Formulas	
Elemental	14.5
Peptide-based	12.7
Specialized Formulas	
Renal failure	
Essential amino acid enriched	12.6
Low protein and electrolytes	3.5
Hepatic failure (BCAAs)[c]	19.0
Stress/critically ill	
Branched-chain enriched	15.0
High nitrogen plus conditionally-essential nutrients	7.0
Immune modulating	16.0
Pulmonary disease	2.2
Glucose control	2.8

[a] Based upon average cost per 1000 calories for equivalent formulas on contract from 1991–94.
[b] Index product; given a relative value of 1.
[c] BCAAs = Branched-chain amino acids.

glycemic control.[50,51] As expected from its insoluble fiber content, soy polysaccharide increases fecal weight and water content in healthy subjects and noncritically ill patients.[40,52–55] Some studies with soy polysaccharide, however, have shown no effect on parameters of bowel function.[42,56,57] Effects of soy polysaccharide on diarrhea also are variable. No difference in stool weight and frequency in burn patients receiving fiber compared to those receiving a fiber-free liquid diet was reported, but caloric intake was improved when soy polysaccharide was included for patients with diarrhea.[58] Studies in critically ill patients have reported no difference in the incidence of diarrhea with or without soy polysaccharide added to enteral formula.[40,59–61] Given the current data, long-term stable tube feeding patients appear to be most likely to benefit from fiber-supplemented formulas.

Addition of fiber to enteral formulas creates some potential problems. Fiber tends to increase the formula viscosity, which may result in difficulty administering the formula without the use of a pump, especially with tubes less than 8 French in size. Gastrointestinal symptoms from fiber may include increased gas production and abdominal discomfort.[40,52] Gradual introduction of fiber may help reduce these symptoms. Bezoar formation also is a risk, especially if the patient has underlying GI dysfunction and/or inadequate fluid intake.[62]

Decreased mineral absorption from enteral formulas supplemented with soy fiber is a concern. Iron and copper absorption were decreased significantly in one study when 40 gm fiber was added per day, but not when 20 and 30 gm were added.[63] Decreased absorption of calcium (Ca), magnesium (Mg), zinc, potassium, and phosphorus also were noted in this study, but the decrease was not statistically significant. Another study found slightly negative copper and iron retention when 40 gm soy fiber was added daily to a fiber-free formula.[64] Decreased folate and zinc absorption also has been reported with addition of 10 to 15 gm soy polysaccharide daily to a fiber-free formula.[55] Clinical significance of reduced mineral absorption is questionable, however, since formulas generally contain minerals in excess of the RDA.[40]

Caloric Density

Caloric density is another method of subdividing polymeric enteral formulas. Total calories (kcal) are used for enteral formulas, with carbohydrates and proteins each providing 4 kcal/gm, while medium-chain triglycerides provide approximately 8.3 kcal/gm and polyunsaturated fats (e.g., corn oil, soybean oil, safflower oil, and sunflower oil) provide 9 kcal/gm. The standard caloric density is 1 to 1.2 kcal/mL. Moderate density formulas contain about 1.5 kcal/mL, while calorically dense formulas contain 2 kcal/mL. Increased caloric density reduces gastric emptying and increases formula osmolality, either of which may result in feeding intolerance.[65] Intolerance also may occur if the capacity of intestinal enzymes is overwhelmed by infusion of a calorically dense formula. The risk of dehydration is increased with increasing caloric density. Standard caloric density formulas, however, may result in fluid overload in patients with congestive heart failure or other fluid-sensitive conditions.

Protein Content

The fourth method of subdividing polymeric formulas is on the basis of protein content, either as a percentage of calories from protein or as the nonprotein calorie to nitrogen ratio. Protein calories are related directly to nitrogen content because protein is assumed to be 16% nitrogen by weight. Grams of protein times four equals protein calories, and grams of protein divided by 6.25 equals grams of nitrogen. Protein needs increase disproportionately to caloric needs during injury and critical illness. High nitrogen

enteral formulas, designed to supply this increased protein requirement, provide approximately 16% to 25% of calories from protein. Nonprotein calorie to nitrogen ratios in these formulas range from 75:1 up to 130:1. Standard protein content is 11% to 15% of calories, with nonprotein to nitrogen ratios of about 140:1 up to 200:1. Low nitrogen formulas with approximately 6% of calories from protein and a ratio of about 390:1 are available for patients requiring protein restriction.

The methods of subdividing polymeric enteral formulas overlap. A formula may be lactose-free, contain fiber, be calorically dense, and have a high nitrogen content. Several manufacturers have a standard formula which also is available with modifications in fiber content, caloric density, and nitrogen content. The base name of such formulas frequently is modified simply by adding ''with fiber,'' ''HC'' for high calorie, ''HN'' for high nitrogen, or ''HCN'' for calorically dense, high nitrogen versions of the formula.

Oligomeric Formulas

Oligomeric formulas, also called monomeric or ''chemically-defined'' formulas, require minimal digestive function and produce little residue in the colon. Pancreatic enzyme activity is required for digestion of oligosaccharides and fats. Brush border disaccharidase activity also is required. Little to no digestion is required, however, for the proteins and medium-chain triglycerides. Overall, reduced digestive function is needed to make oligomeric formulas available for absorption. These formulas frequently are used for patients with pancreatic insufficiency, reduced mucosal absorption, or reduced hydrolytic ability. Patients with prolonged parenteral nutrition support, gastrointestinal fistulae, or inflammatory bowel disease also may receive an oligomeric formula when enteral nutrition is initiated. Well-designed comparative studies establishing a difference in response between polymeric and oligomeric formulas generally are lacking, however, in these conditions.[66] Patients most likely to benefit from oligomeric formulas are those with severe pancreatic insufficiency or short bowel syndrome.[67] Pancreatic enzyme supplementation with a polymeric formula may be tried before an oligomeric formula for some patients with pancreatic insufficiency (e.g., cystic fibrosis).

There are two subgroups of oligomeric formulas based upon the protein source. True ''elemental'' formulas contain free amino acids, while ''peptide-based'' formulas contain oligopeptides plus di- and tripeptides from hydrolysis of casein, whey, and/or lactalbumin proteins. Free amino acids also may be included in the peptide-based formulas. Amino acids require no digestion, but the sodium-dependent active transport mechanism responsible for absorption appears to be somewhat slow and inefficient compared to small peptide absorption. Di- and tripeptides are absorbed by specific carriers located in small bowel mucosa. Sodium is not required for the noncompetitive transport process associated with small peptides.[68–71] Peptides longer than three amino acid units, however, require further hydrolysis within the lumen of the small bowel before they can be absorbed. Most peptide-based formulas contain a significant portion of peptides requiring hydrolysis before absorption.

Clinical studies with enteral diets high in peptides have shown reduced diarrheal output in hypoalbuminemic patients and rapid recovery of serum albumin.[70,71] Other studies question the extent of peptide absorption in critically ill patients.[72] Clinical advantages of peptide formulas for patients with diarrhea also have been questioned.[73,74] Differences in the proportion of di- and tripeptides in study formulas may account for some of the differences in clinical results. Based upon current data, it is difficult to know when a ''peptide-based'' formula should be selected rather than an ''elemental'' formula. Cost and fat content may be factors which help determine which type of oligomeric formula to select. Fat content varies from 1% to 30% of calories, with elemental formulas generally having the lowest fat content.

Elemental formulas (e.g., Tolerex, Vivonex T.E.N., and Vivonex Plus) are available only in a powdered form. Dehydration limits the browning reaction between carbohydrates and free amino acids, thus increasing the shelf-life of these formulas. Peptide-based formulas, which have a lower free amino acid concentration than elemental formulas, may be available as a ready-to-use liquid or as a powder requiring reconstitution. Accupep HPF, Alitraq, Criticare HN, Peptamen, Reabilan, Reabilan HN, Travasorb Standard, Travasorb HN, and Vital HN are examples of formulas containing peptides.

Oligomeric formulas tend to be hyperosmolar due to their partially digested nature. Osmotic diarrhea is a potential problem because of the osmolarity. Taste and cost also are disadvantages for these formulas. Although flavoring packets are available for addition to the formulas for oral use, patients commonly complain of a bitter taste. In general, it is unrealistic to expect a patient to take more than a small percentage of their daily nutritional requirements by mouth as an oligomeric formula. As shown in Table 34.3, oligomeric formulas tend to cost several times more than polymeric formulas.

Specialized Formulas

Specialized formulas are designed for specific disease states or conditions. Protein is the most frequently altered component of specialized enteral formulas, with use of free amino acids allowing manipulation of amino acid ratios. Fat to carbohydrate ratios are altered in a few formulas marketed for specific disease states. The type of fat in formulas is increasingly being altered as information regarding immune-modulating effects of fats increases.[75-77]

Specialized enteral formulas are controversial. The formulas generally have a good theoretical basis for use, but lack conclusive clinical evidence of improved efficacy compared to standard formulas. Well-designed studies showing a difference in outcome with a specialized enteral formula compared to equal nitrogenous and equal caloric provision of a standard formula are especially difficult to find. Given the high cost of most specialized formulas, it often is difficult to justify their use without evidence of improved clinical efficacy compared to standard formulas.

Renal Failure

Specialty enteral formulas designed for renal failure contain either essential amino acids plus histidine or a higher than normal concentration of essential amino acids in combination with nonessential amino acids. Recycling of urea nitrogen for nonessential amino acid synthesis, theoretically, reduces the accumulation of blood urea nitrogen (BUN).[78,79] Unfortunately, clinically significant recycling of nitrogen and incorporation into nonessential amino acids does not appear to occur.[78] Essential amino acid formulas may be appropriate for nondialyzed chronic renal failure patients with glomerular filtration rates less than 25 mL/min/1.73 m^2 who are receiving very low protein diets.[79] They are not appropriate for patients in acute renal failure or for those receiving hemo- or peritoneal dialysis. Vitamin and mineral supplementation appropriate to the patient's condition must be provided with essential amino acid formulas since the formulas themselves are incomplete. Reconstitution of these formulas with water is required before use. Travasorb Renal contains higher than normal essential amino acids in combination with nonessential amino acids, while Amin-Aid contains essential amino acid plus histidine.

Intact protein enteral formulas designed for renal failure and/or renal insufficiency have become available in the past few years. These formulas are not enriched with essential amino acids, but use a high nonprotein calorie to nitrogen ratio and lower than normal concentrations of protein, potassium, phosphorus, and magnesium. To prevent or limit problems with fluid overload, these formulas generally contain 2 kcal/mL. They are complete formulas which meet 100% of the RDA with under 2000 mL/day. Examples of intact protein renal formulas include Nepro and Suplena.

Hepatic Failure

Hepatic failure formulas contain 45% to 50% of protein as branched-chain amino acids (BCAA), compared with 15% to 20% in standard formulas. Lower than normal concentrations of aromatic amino acids (AAA), especially phenylalanine, also characterize hepatic formulas. Theoretically, hepatic encephalopathy is improved by increasing plasma BCAA and decreasing AAA, which reduces inhibitory and/or false neurotransmitter formation.[80,81] One study reported improved survival in patients with hepatic encephalopathy given BCAA plus dextrose compared to neomycin and isocaloric dextrose without protein.[82] Most other studies have not shown a clear advantage to hepatic failure formulas.[83-86] These formulas generally are incomplete, requiring supplementation with vitamins and minerals. Hepatic-Aid II is a powdered formula requiring reconstitution before use, while Nutrihep is a liquid formula.

Stress/Critically Ill

Specialized BCAA enriched formulas designed for critically ill, hypermetabolic patients frequently are referred to as "stress" formulas. A nonprotein calorie to nitrogen ratio under 100:1 (e.g., a high nitrogen content) and over 35% of protein as BCAA characterizes these formulas. Although hepatic failure and stress formulas both contain an increased concentration of BCAA, they are not therapeutically interchangeable. Stress formulas do not have a reduced concentration of aromatic amino acids and are categorized as high nitrogen formulas, compared with low to moderate protein content in hepatic failure formulas.

Enrichment of enteral and parenteral stress formulas by BCAA is based upon the theory that BCAA are preferentially utilized for energy production in skeletal muscle of critically ill patients. In addition, exogenous provision of BCAA will, at least theoretically, reduce skeletal muscle breakdown and improve protein synthesis.[87-89] Studies evaluating the effectiveness of BCAA in stressed patients primarily have involved parenterally administered BCAA. The results, as summarized in review articles, are conflicting and controversial.[90,91] Results with enteral BCAA administration also are conflicting. Encouraging results were reported with improved nitrogen balance and visceral protein status in patients receiving BCAA enriched enteral feeding.[92] Other investigators have found no difference between BCAA enriched formulas and standard high nitrogen formulas.[93] Lack of consistent, objective criteria for defining critical illness and determining entry into the studies may have contributed to the inconclusive and controversial results when these studies are viewed as a group. Improvement in clinical outcome, including morbidity, mortality, and length of stay, have not been evaluated in studies of BCAA enrichment for either parenteral or enteral nutrition.[94]

Commercially available BCAA-enriched stress formulas include Stresstein and Traum-Aid. Both formulas contain free amino acids as the protein source and require reconstitution with water before use. The formulas are complete, with 2 to 3 L providing 100% of the RDA.

Enteral formulas having a nonprotein calorie to nitrogen ratio of 100:1 or less, but without BCAA supplementation, sometimes are classified and marketed as stress or critical-care formulas. Several of these formulas, as listed in Table 34.4, also contain arginine, glutamine, or nucleic acid supplementation and/or a modified fat component, which distinguishes them from typical high nitrogen formulas. Protain XL and TraumaCal contain intact protein as calcium and sodium caseinates, plus medium-chain triglycerides (MCT) to reduce fat malabsorption. Replete contains intact protein as casein, plus canola oil and MCT. Canola oil serves as a source of essential fatty acids with a low concentration of polyunsaturated fatty acids overall, and a high concentration of monounsaturated fatty acids. Partially hydrolyzed protein (e.g., oligo- and short-peptides) plus L-arginine are used in Perative, along with MCT and canola oil. Hydrolyzed soy, lactalbumin, and whey plus free arginine and glutamine provide the protein sources, and MCT is combined with safflower oil as the fat sources for the oligomeric formula, Alitraq. Omega-3 fatty acids from menhaden oil and structured lipid provide the fat sources, while L-arginine and nucleic acid are included with sodium and calcium caseinates as the protein sources in Impact. Immun-Aid uses lactalbumin and BCAA as the protein sources, plus supplemental arginine, glutamine, and nucleic acids. Canola oil is used as the fat source in Immun-Aid. Crucial contains hydrolyzed casein with supplemental arginine, and MCT, fish oil, soy oil, and lecithin. The latter three formulas, along with Advera, also can be classified as immune-modulating formulas, a very small but growing group of formulas.

The use of arginine, glutamine, and nucleic acids in the nutritional management of critically ill patients is a more recent development; thus, studies using these components in patients are limited. Arginine is an amino acid involved in ammonia detoxification via the urea cycle. Under normal conditions, arginine is considered nonessential because it can be synthesized via the urea cycle in quantities adequate for growth and tissue repair. In metabolically stressed patients, however, endogenous arginine synthesis appears to be inadequate. The resulting decrease in plasma and serum arginine concentrations may cause reduced cellular growth and lymphocyte blastogenesis.[95] Dietary supplementation with arginine in normal volunteers has been shown to enhance wound healing and to improve response to antigens used for evaluation of immune function.[96,97] Enhanced T-lymphocyte response and increased CD4 (clusters of differentiation) counts also have been reported with arginine supplementation in cancer patients.[98] Similar results for immune response plus improved nitrogen balance were reported with postsurgery cancer patients tube fed with a formula containing supplemental arginine, nucleic acids, and omega-3 fatty acids.[99,100] Effects of arginine on nitrogen balance, however, remain inconclusive.[101] The potential for supplemental arginine to reduce the duration of hospitalization following cancer surgery also has been suggested.[102] Clearly, the potential for enhanced immune functioning is exciting, but much investigation remains to be done before definite conclusions regarding the safety and efficacy of arginine supplementation can be made. Concerns remain regarding possible metabolic effects when large doses of a specific amino acid are administered to critically ill patients. The metabolic effect from administration of the hydrochloride salt in which arginine is provided also must be evaluated carefully, especially in patients at risk of acidosis from their illness.

Nucleic acids, or nucleotides, are structural components of deoxyribonucleic acid (DNA) and ribonucleic acid (RNA), as well as components of adenosine triphosphate (ATP) and multiple coenzymes. Most parenteral and enteral nutrition formulas are lacking in nucleotides. Immune-modulating enteral formulas include nucleic acids because of their apparent necessity for maintenance of cellular immune function during hypermetabolic periods.[103] Animals fed nucleotide-free diets demonstrate reduced cellular immunity and increased susceptibility to bacterial challenges as compared to animals receiving a nucleotide-supplemented diet.[104,105] Studies to confirm these observations in humans are lacking.

Glutamine, an amino acid containing two amine moieties, functions as an intermediate in numerous metabolic pathways. It participates in gluconeogenesis and renal ammoniagenesis, and serves as a fuel source for rapidly dividing cells. Epithelial cells, actively dividing lymphocytes, and cells of the intestinal mucosa (e.g., enterocytes) appear to use glutamine as their primary fuel source.[106] Increased GI tract consumption and/or low plasma concentrations of glutamine have been associated with numerous catabolic conditions.

Supplementation of enteral formulas with glutamine is based upon the theory that glutamine will maintain intestinal mucosal integrity and prevent bacterial translocation. Studies have shown increased mucosal weight and villus height in animals receiving glutamine enriched parenteral and enteral formulas compared to standard formulas.[107–110] Human studies with glutamine supplementation have shown improved healing of radiation-induced small bowel lesions and prevention of pancreatic atrophy and fatty liver during elemental feeding.[111,112] Improved nitrogen retention also has been shown with parenteral glutamine supplementation following surgery and bone marrow transplantation.[113–115] The effect of glutamine on GI tract integrity and bacterial translocation in humans is, however, unclear based upon available data. As with arginine, the potential of glutamine is exciting, but much research remains to be done before routine use of glutamine supplementation can be recommended, especially in the high doses used in some studies.

Protein-bound glutamine is present in all enteral formulas. Only powdered formulas, however, contain supplemental free glutamine because of glutamine stability problems in ready-to-use formulas.[116] Glutamine content in enteral formulas ranges from approximately 5% to 13% of protein by weight.[116] The source of protein, processing, and protein concentration influence the glutamine content of formulas. Further research is needed to determine if physiological effects, especially effects on the GI tract, are equivalent for protein-bound and free glutamine.

Alteration in the fat component of enteral formulas can be accomplished by changing the percentage of calories from fat or by changing the source of fat. Stress or critical care and immune-modulating formulas change the source of fat to alter the type of fatty acids provided. Fat sources such as canola oil and/or fish oils are used preferentially in these formulas, while the usual polyunsaturated vegetable oils, including corn, soy, and safflower oils, are avoided or used in relatively small quantities. Polyunsaturated vegetable oils contain fatty acids from the omega-6 family, which are precursors to arachidonic acid and, therefore, to dienoic or "2" series prostaglandins, prostacyclins, and thromboxanes, and to "4" series leukotrienes. These compounds taken as a whole are potent inflammatory, vasoconstrictive, and platelet aggregating agents. In vitro studies have demonstrated immunosuppressive effects on both animal and human cells when prostaglandin E2 is present in high concentrations, but immune system stimulation with low concentrations.[117,118]

Fish oils, including menhaden oil, provide fatty acids primarily from the omega-3 family with eicosapentaenoic acid (EPA) and docosahexaenoic acid (DHA) predominating. These compounds are precursors to "3" series prostaglandins, prostacyclins, and thromboxanes, and to "5" series leukotrienes. Taken as a whole, these compounds are less inflammatory and more vasodilatory than compounds from omega-6 fatty acids. This may be beneficial in critically ill patients. Animals fed fish oils before endotoxin challenge have demonstrated increased survival time following the challenge.[75,119,120] Feeding fish oils after endotoxin challenge,

Table 34.4

High Protein Enteral Formulas with Altered Protein and/or Fat Sources[a,c]

Formula (Manufacturer)	kcal/mL (mOsm/kg)	% Free Water	Protein gm/L (% kcal)	Protein Sources[a]	ARG gm/L	GLN gm/L	Fat gm/L (% kcal)	Fat Sources[a]	MCT % fat kcal	Omega-3 Fatty Acid Source[b] (% fat kcal)	Fiber gm/L	Carnitine mg/L	Taurine mg/L
Protain XL (Sherwood)	1.0 (340)	82	55 (22)	Calcium and sodium caseinates	—	NA	30 (27)	Corn oil; MCT	NA	NA	8	—	—
TraumaCal (Mead Johnson)	1.5 (490)	78	83 (22)	Sodium and calcium caseinates	—	7.2–10.6	68 (40)	Soy oil; MCT	30	Linolenic acid (6.3)	None	—	—
Replete (Clintec)	1.0 (290)	84	62.5 (25)	Calcium-potassium caseinate	—	NA	34 (30)	Canola oil; MCT; lecithin	NA	NA	None	—	—
Replete with fiber (Clintec)	1.0 (290)	84	62.5 (25)	Calcium-potassium caseinate	—	NA	34 (30)	Canola oil; MCT; lecithin	NA	NA	14	—	—
Perative (Ross)	1.3 (385)	79	66.6 (20.5)	Partially hydrolyzed sodium caseinate; lactalbumin hydrolysate	26	NA	37.4 (25)	Canola oil; MCT; corn oil	NA	NA	None	130	130
AlitraQ (Ross)	1.0 (575)	85	52.5 (21)	Soy hydrolysate; whey; lactalbumin; free amino acids	12	14	15.5 (13)	Safflower oil; MCT	NA	Linolenic acid (<1)	None	100	200
Impact (Sandoz)	1.0 (375)	85	56 (22)	Sodium and calcium caseinates; RNA	14	3.6	28 (25)	Structured lipids with palm kernel and sunflower oils; menhaden oil	None	Menhaden oil (6.3)	None	—	—
Impact with fiber (Sandoz)	1.0 (375)	87	56 (22)	Sodium and calcium caseinates; RNA	14	3.6	28 (25)	Structured lipids with palm kernel and sunflower oils; menhaden oil	None	Menhaden oil (6.3)	10	—	—
Immun-Aid (McGaw)	1.0 (460)	82	80 (32)	Hydrolyzed lactalbumin; BCAAs; nucleic acid	15	12.5	22 (20)	Canola oil; MCT	50	Linolenic acid (5)	None	—	—
Advera (Ross)	1.28 (NA)	80	60 (18.7)	Soy protein hydrolysate; sodium caseinate	—	NA	22.8 (15.8)	Canola oil; MCT; sardine oil	20	Sardine oil (10)	8.9	127	212
Crucial (Clintec)	1.5 (490)	NA	94 (25)	Hydrolyzed casein	15	7.2	67.5 (39)	Soy oil; MCT; fish oil; lecithin	50	Fish oil (3.6)	None	150	150

a ARG = Arginine (listed values reflect added L-arginine, not the amount present in protein); BCAAs = Branched-chain amino acids; GLN = Glutamine (listed values reflect both free and protein-bound glutamine); MCT = Medium chain triglycerides; NA = Not available; RNA = Ribonucleic acid.

b Omega-3 fatty acids from linolenic acid reflect linolenic acid content of nonfish oils.

c Changes periodically occur in nutrient sources and/or content; therefore, this table should be used as a general reference only and not for specific patient care issues.

however, may not be beneficial. After endotoxin challenge, a combination of omega-6 and omega-3 fatty acids (e.g., polyunsaturated vegetable oils and fish oils) may be more appropriate.[121] Reduced wound infection and reduced mortality have been demonstrated in burn patients fed a low-fat diet containing 50% of fat as fish oil and 50% as safflower oil.[122] Further research is needed to determine the safety and efficacy of omega-3 fatty acids in various disease states. Appropriate quantities of omega-3 fatty acids and the most beneficial ratios of omega-3 and omega-6 fatty acids also must be determined before widespread supplementation with omega-3 fatty acids can be recommended.

Canola oil is another fat source used in formulas for stress and critical care. Canola oil contains about two-thirds monounsaturated fatty acids, compared to no more than one-fourth monounsaturated fatty acids in polyunsaturated vegetable oils. High-oleic safflower oil is another fat source with increased monounsaturated fatty acid content. Monounsaturated fatty acids have been popularized by reports of low cardiovascular disease in populations using olive oil, but further research is needed to determine the safety and efficacy of these fatty acids in patients requiring nutritional support. The combination of canola oil and high-oleic safflower oil also increases the content of linolenic acid, an omega-3 fatty acid.

The use of MCT in enteral formulas is intended to improve fat absorption. Absorption of medium-chain triglycerides is relatively independent of pancreatic enzymes and bile salts; thus, MCT may be absorbed in patients experiencing malabsorption of the long-chain triglycerides (LCT) found in polyunsaturated vegetable oils. Rapid, carnitine-independent metabolism occurs with medium-chain triglycerides, while long-chain triglycerides require carnitine for metabolism. Utilization of long-chain triglycerides is, therefore, compromised when carnitine deficiency occurs, but MCT utilization is unaffected. Many enteral formulas contain part of the fat calories as MCT. Formulas containing a relatively large percentage of fat calories as medium-chain triglycerides frequently are marketed for patients with malabsorption, which includes many critically ill patients. Examples of formulas containing 50% to 65% of fat calories as MCT include Accupep HPF and Attain; Entralife products; Fibersource products, Isosource products, and Stresstein; Immun-Aid; Travasorb Standard and HN. Products containing 65% to 80% of fat calories as MCT include Peptamen, Travasorb MCT, and Travasorb Renal, all from Clintec Nutrition. Lipisorb and Portagen, both from Mead Johnson, contain 86% of fat calories as MCT. Several Ross products, including Jevity, Osmolite, and Osmolite HN, have changed their fat source from 50% MCT to 20% MCT, 30% canola oil, and 50% high-oleic safflower oil.

Carnitine is an important compound in normal nutrition since it is required for transport of long-chain triglycerides into mitochondria for metabolism. The normal diet provides low but adequate levels of carnitine. Under certain conditions the requirements for carnitine may increase above the levels provided in the diet. Therefore, carnitine is considered a conditionally essential nutrient. Hypermetabolism, malnutrition, administration of carnitine-free enteral or parenteral formulas, and various other conditions may predispose patients to development of carnitine deficiency.[123,124] Improved nitrogen retention has been noted with carnitine supplementation during parenteral nutrition.[125,126] Much research remains, however, to determine which patients may benefit from carnitine supplementation, and at what dose. Carnitine currently is contained in several enteral formulas and many manufacturers are adding carnitine when reformulation is done. Alitraq, Compleat, Glucerna, Isocal HN, Jevity, Lipisorb, Peptamen, Ultracal, and Vivonex Plus are among the formulas currently including carnitine in their formulation.

Taurine is a sulfur-containing amino acid which may improve fat absorption in selected patients with malabsorption. Micelle formation may be reduced in the presence of low taurine intake since taurine is involved in the formation of bile salts.[127] Studies of taurine supplementation have shown improved fat absorption and weight gain in some patients with cystic fibrosis.[128,129] Taurine also is essential for normal retinal development in infants and children.[126] Major manufacturers of pediatric formulas, therefore, include taurine as an essential nutrient in their formulas. Taurine is considered conditionally essential for adults, being provided in low but adequate quantities in the normal diet.[124] Manufacturers of adult enteral formulas have started adding taurine to formulas marketed for populations who may be at risk of inadequate taurine intake. Alitraq, Glucerna, Isocal HN, Jevity, Lipisorb, Peptamen, Reabilan products, Ultracal, and Vivonex Plus are among the formulas currently including taurine in their formulation.

Pulmonary Disease

The percentage of calories from fat is increased to 55% in formulas marketed for patients with pulmonary disease. The rationale is that fat oxidation produces less carbon dioxide (CO_2) than carbohydrate oxidation; thereby reducing the work load of the lungs. Fats have a lower respiratory quotient (RQ) than carbohydrates. This means less CO_2 is produced per volume of oxygen consumed during fat metabolism. High carbohydrate loads have been reported to prolong or inhibit weaning from mechanical ventilation, and to result in respiratory failure in nonventilated patients.[130–133] Decreased retention of CO_2 and improvement in respiratory parameters have been demonstrated in patients with chronic obstructive airways disease (COAD) and CO_2 retention who were fed a high fat, low carbohydrate diet compared to high or moderate carbohydrate diets.[134] Reduced time on the ventilator and decreased arterial CO_2 levels also have been reported in mechanically ventilated patients receiving a high-fat, low-carbohydrate enteral formula as compared to a standard formula.[135] The respiratory status of a patient without excess CO_2 production and/or retention is unlikely to improve with the use of a high-fat formula. The slowed gastric emptying that occurs with a high-fat diet must be considered when evaluating the possible benefits and adverse effects of a high-fat enteral formula. Slow gastric emptying may lead to formula intolerance, as manifested by abdominal distention, increased gastric residuals, nausea, and vomiting. Delivery of the high-fat load, especially the long-chain triglycerides, into the small bowel may overwhelm pancreatic lipase activity in some patients, leading to fat malabsorption. Fat in Pulmocare is a blend of LCT primarily from canola oil with a small amount of high-oleic safflower oil and 20% of fat from MCT. NutriVent contains 60% LCT from a blend of canola oil and corn oil, plus 40% MCT. Respalor contains 41% of calories from canola oil and medium-chain triglycerides.

Glucose Control

Glucerna is another disease-specific formula containing an increased percentage of calories from fat. The formula is designed and marketed for patients with hyperglycemia. Fat provides 50% of calories, and carbohydrates provide about 33% of calories from glucose polymers, fiber, and fructose. Fiber, at 14 gm/L, helps minimize postprandial hyperglycemia.[39] Fructose also minimizes hyperglycemia when compared to equivalent calories from sucrose.[136] Studies have demonstrated better glucose control following feeding with a low-carbohydrate, high-fat, fiber-containing formula compared to a standard formula in diabetic patients.[137] Problems of formula intolerance secondary to slowed gastric emptying or fat malabsorption must be weighed against possible benefits of improved glucose control when evaluating Glucerna for use in patients.

Table 34.5

Enteral Formulas with Altered Fat Sources[a],[c]

Formula (Manufacturer)	kcal/mL (mOsm/kg)	% Free Water	Protein gm/L (% kcal)	Protein Sources	ARG gm/L	GLN gm/L	Fat gm/L (% kcal)	Fat Sources	MCT (% fat kcal)	Omega-3 Fatty Acid Source[b] (% fat kcal)	Fiber gm/L	Carnitine mg/L	Taurine mg/L
Accu-Pep HPF (Sherwood)	1.0 (490)	84	40 (16)	Hydrolyzed lactalbumin	—	NA	10 (8.5)	Corn oil; MCT	50	Linolenic acid (<1)	None	—	—
Attain (Sherwood)	1.0 (300)	85	40 (16)	Sodium and calcium caseinates	—	3.5–5.1	35 (30)	Corn oil; MCT	50	Linolenic acid (<1)	None	—	—
Entralife (Corpak)	1.0 (300)	NA	35 (14)	Sodium and calcium caseinates	—	NA	35 (31)	Corn oil; MCT	50	Linolenic acid (<1)	None	—	—
Entralife HN-II (Corpak)	1.25 (300)	NA	61 (20)	Sodium and calcium caseinates	—	NA	43 (31)	Corn oil; MCT	50	Linolenic acid (<1)	None	—	—
Fibersource (Sandoz)	1.2 (390)	82	43 (14)	Sodium and calcium caseinates	—	3.7–5.5	41 (30)	Canola oil; MCT	50	Linolenic acid (4.9)	10	—	—
Fibersource HN (Sandoz)	1.2 (390)	82	53 (18)	Sodium and calcium caseinates	—	4.6–6.7	41 (30)	Canola oil; MCT	50	Linolenic acid (4.9)	6.8	—	—
Isosource (Sandoz)	1.2 (360)	82	43 (14)	Sodium and calcium caseinates; soy protein isolate	—	NA	41 (30)	Canola oil; MCT	50	Linolenic acid (4.9)	None	—	—
Isosource HN (Sandoz)	1.2 (330)	82	53 (18)	Sodium and calcium caseinates; soy protein isolate	—	NA	41 (30)	Canola oil; MCT	50	Linolenic acid (4.9)	None	—	—
Stresstein (Sandoz)	1.2 (910)	NA	70 (2)	Amino acids, including branched-chain amino acids	—	NA	28 (20)	Soy oil; MCT	60	NA	None	—	—
Travasorb Standard (Clintec)	1.0 (560)	NA	30 (12)	Hydrolyzed lactalbumin	—	NA	13.5 (12)	Sunflower oil; MCT	60	NA	None	—	—
Travasorb HN (Clintec)	1.0 (560)	NA	45 (18)	Hydrolyzed lactalbumin	—	NA	13.5 (12)	Sunflower oil; MCT	60	NA	None	—	—

Continued

Product				Protein source			Fat source			ARG	GLN
Travasorb MCT (Clintec)	1.0 (312)	NA	49 (20)	Lactalbumin; sodium and potassium caseinates	—	33 (30)	Sunflower oil; MCT	80	NA	None	—	—
Travasorb Renal (Clintec)	1.35 (590)	77	23 (7)	Crystalline amino acids	NA	18 (12)	Sunflower oil; MCT	70	NA	None	—	—
Peptamen (Clintec)	1.0 (270)	NA	40 (16)	Hydrolyzed whey	1.2	39 (33)	Sunflower oil; MCT	70	NA	None	NA	NA
Peptamen VHP (Clintec)	1.0 (300)	NA	62.5 (25)	Hydrolyzed whey	1.8	39 (33)	Sunflower oil; MCT	70	NA	None	100	100
Lipisorb (Mead Johnson)	1.35 (630)	80	57 (17)	Sodium and calcium caseinates	—	57 (35)	Soy oil; MCT	86	Linolenic acid (<1)	None	NA	NA
Portagen (Mead Johnson)	1.0 (320)	NA	36 (14)	Sodium caseinate	—	48 (41)	Corn oil; MCT	86	NA	None	—	—
Jevity (Ross)	1.06 (300)	84	44 (16)	Sodium and calcium caseinates	3.8–5.7	36 (30)	High-oleic safflower oil; canola oil; MCT	20	NA	14	114	114
Osmolite (Ross)	1.06 (300)	84	37 (14)	Sodium and calcium caseinates; soy protein isolates	3.2–4.6	38 (31)	High-oleic safflower oil; canola oil; MCT	20	NA	None	80	80
Osmolite HN (Ross)	1.06 (300)	84	44 (17)	Sodium and calcium caseinates; soy protein isolates	3.8–5.5	36 (30)	High-oleic safflower oil; canola oil; MCT	20	NA	None	114	114

a ARG = Arginine (listed values reflect added L-arginine, not the amount present in protein); GLN = Glutamine (listed values reflect both free and protein-bound glutamine); MCT = Medium chain triglycerides; NA = Not available.

b Omega-3 fatty acids from linolenic acid reflect content of nonfish oils.

c Changes periodically occur in nutrient sources and/or content; therefore, this table should be used as a general reference only and not for specific patient care issues.

Modular Components

Modular components are individual nutrient substrates designed for addition to oral diets or enteral formulas. Modulars allow a single nutrient substrate to be increased in a diet or formula without changing other components. Vitamins and minerals are not included in modular components. When major changes in nutrient ratios are needed, a formula that better meets the patient's requirements should be selected, rather than attempting addition of large quantities of modular components. The potential of altering formula viscosity and texture exist when modulars are added in large quantities.

Glucose polymers are used for carbohydrate modulars. This limits the osmolality and creates a nearly tasteless product which does not alter the flavor of foods or formulas to which it is added. Powdered carbohydrate modulars contain 20 to 30 kcal per tablespoon, while liquids contain 2 kcal/mL. The protein modulars are powders containing 3 to 4 gm protein per tablespoon. Most protein modulars are intact protein. The only product marketed as a fat modular is MCT oil. Vegetable oils also can be added to formulas in small quantities as a modular component, but are not marketed as such.

Tube Feeding Administration Regimen

The route of feeding, formula selected, and anticipated duration of feeding influence the administration regimen. The location of the patient (e.g., hospital, nursing home, home) should be considered in developing an administration regimen, as should the cost. Included in the administration regimen are the schedule for formula delivery, the strength or concentration of formula for initiation and advancement of feedings, and the administration method (i.e., syringe, gravity drip, rate controller, pump). Only limited scientific data exist regarding tube feeding administration regimens. Thus, many different administration schedules are in use in various settings, all of which appear to meet the needs of the patients and personnel in the particular setting in which they are used.

Four basic schedules for formula delivery are available: continuous infusion, cyclic infusion, intermittent infusion, and bolus delivery of formula. *Continuous infusion* provides the daily volume of formula at a continuous rate over 24 hours/day. In contrast, *cyclic infusion* provides the daily volume of formula at a continuous rate for only several hours of the day. *Intermittent infusion* provides the daily volume of formula in a specified number of feedings daily. Each of three to six daily feedings is administered over 30 to 60 minutes. *Bolus delivery* basically is the same as intermittent infusion except that each feeding is administered over a few minutes.

Continuous infusion can be used for feeding by any route. Intragastric continuous infusion schedules most commonly are used for hospitalized patients.[138] Risks of gastric distention and aspiration appear to be lower with continuous infusion compared to intermittent formula delivery into the stomach.[139,140] In addition, continuous infusion may be better tolerated as judged by stool frequency and time to attain full nutritional support, especially in metabolically unstable patients.[140] One study in a neurologic intensive care unit, however, found no difference in tolerance between patients receiving gastric feedings by continuous infusion versus intermittent infusion. Tolerance was evaluated by stool consistency, number of stools daily, aspiration, and caloric intake.[141] Feeding into the duodenum or jejunum is best initiated with a continuous infusion schedule. Rapid infusion of large volumes of formula into the small bowel results in symptoms consistent with a dumping syndrome, including sweating, lightheadedness, abdominal distention, cramping, hyperperistalsis, and watery diarrhea.

With time, however, the jejunum appears to adapt to larger volumes of feeding over a shorter period of time and may tolerate an intermittent infusion schedule.[8]

Cyclic feeding most commonly is used for patients who need supplemental nutrition because of an inability to consume adequate nutrients. The infusion typically is over 10 to 15 hours at night to reduce interference with oral intake during the day. Enteral feeding into the stomach is more likely to suppress oral intake than feeding into the jejunum.[142] Patients receiving supplemental intragastric tube feedings are, therefore, more likely than jejunally fed patients to improve oral intake when "cycled." Full nutritional support occasionally is provided by cyclic enteral nutrition at night when feeding during the day interferes with normal activities such as work or school. Formula volume and osmolality may, however, limit tolerance to cyclic feedings in some patients. Full nutritional support via cyclic jejunal feedings is the most difficult to achieve. The transition from continuous infusion to cyclic infusion should be done over at least a couple days for full nutrition support into the jejunum.

Intermittent or Bolus Feedings. The reservoir capacity of the stomach allows relatively large volume feedings to be administered using an *intermittent* or *bolus schedule*. These schedules are more physiological than continuous feeding. They also are more convenient for patients in nursing homes and for ambulatory patients receiving enteral feedings at home. Patients frequently are started on continuous infusion feedings, then transitioned to intermittent infusion, and eventually to the shorter administration time of bolus feedings as tolerance permits. The majority of patients, however, need feedings over at least 30 minutes to avoid bloating, cramping, nausea, and diarrhea.[143] A rate not exceeding 30 mL/minute has been suggested to limit symptoms of GI intolerance in patients receiving bolus feedings.[144]

Various methods can be used for transitioning to intermittent or bolus feedings. One commonly used method is to give two to three times the hourly rate over 60 minutes every two or three hours for three to four feedings. The volume is then increased to the equivalent of four to five times the hourly rate every four or five hours for three to four feedings. If the patient develops abdominal distention, increased gastric residuals, or diarrhea with the increased volume, the feedings are changed back to the previously tolerated volume and time interval. Advancement to four to five times the hourly rate is attempted again in 24 to 36 hours. If the patient tolerates the larger volume of feeding without problems, the volume per feeding may be increased to six times the hourly volume every six hours. If the patient requires over 1920 mL of formula daily, it may be necessary to provide more than four feedings since 480 mL of formula per feeding (two cans) generally is not exceeded. Once the number of feedings per day has been determined, the time between feedings can be decreased to allow the daily feedings to occur over about 12 hours during the day. The time for infusing each feeding may be decreased as tolerated, after the time interval between feedings is established. The volume selected for each feeding commonly is increments of 120 mL (one-half of an 8 oz can of formula). For a patient receiving continuous infusion tube feedings at 80 mL/hour, the transition would be as follows: 240 mL over 60 minutes every three hours for three feedings, then 360 mL over 60 minutes every five hours for three feedings. If the patient demonstrated very good tolerance to 360 mL per feeding, then 480 mL over 60 minutes could be attempted every six hours. If this higher volume was not tolerated, five feedings per day would be planned, with three feedings of 400 mL each plus two feedings of 360 mL each. The time interval between the four or five daily feedings would then be decreased to about two and one-half to four hours to mimic three meals and a snack or two. For instance, feedings could be at 7 a.m., 9:30 a.m., noon, 3 p.m., and 6 p.m. The infusion time also could be decreased from 60 minutes to approximately 30 minutes, then to bolus feedings over a few minutes, as tolerated.

Initiation Without Transition from Continuous Infusion. When intermittent feedings are initiated without a transition from continuous infusion, the volume for feedings is started low. A common regimen is 50 mL of formula over 30 to 60 minutes every two hours for eight hours. The volume is then increased by 50 to 60 mL per two hours every eight hours until the goal volume per day is achieved. The next step is to double the volume of feedings and increase the interval between feedings to four hours for three to four feedings. The volume of feedings is then increased to about three times the ''per two hour'' volume, and the interval increased to every six hours. The time between feedings is then decreased to allow the four daily feedings to occur over about 12 hours during the day. For a patient requiring 1920 mL of formula daily, the initiation of feedings would be as follows: 50 mL every two hours for eight hours, then 100 mL every two hours for eight hours, then 160 mL every two hours (equivalent to 1920 mL/24 hours). After a minimum of eight hours with 160 mL every two hours, the feedings would be increased to 320 mL every four hours for three to four feedings, and then to 480 mL every six hours. If the 480 mL volume per feeding is not tolerated, five feedings daily should be attempted, with three feedings of 400 mL each plus two feedings of 360 mL each. Once the number of daily feedings is established, the time between feedings can be decreased to allow all four or five feedings within a 12-hour period during the day.

Alternative Method. An alternative method of initiating intermittent feedings is to start with 120 mL of formula (one-half of a can) over 30 to 60 minutes four times daily. The volume of each feeding is then increased by 120 mL/day until the goal volume of formula is reached. The number of feedings per day can be increased if the patient does not tolerate increases in the volume per feeding. For a patient requiring 1920 mL of formula daily, the progression of feedings would be as follows: four feedings daily of 120 mL each over 30 to 60 minutes on the first day; 240 mL each on day two; 360 mL each on day three; and 480 mL each on day four. Since feedings are given during typical meal and snack times, this method of initiating intermittent enteral feedings is easier to manage in the outpatient setting than the method starting with feedings every two hours.

The rate and strength, or concentration, of formula used for initiation of tube feeding primarily depends upon the osmolality of full-strength formula, the site of feeding, and the condition of the patient's GI tract. Diluted formula and a low infusion rate were standard for initiation of intragastric tube feedings in the past, and still are used routinely in some institutions. These ''starter regimens'' are based upon the belief that administration of full-strength formula or a large formula volume during the first few days of feeding will result in diarrhea, cramping, bloating, and/or nausea because the GI tract has not yet adapted to the formula osmolality and volume.[145] Controlled studies, however, have shown that dilution of polymeric formulas is not necessary in patients or subjects with normal GI function fed by continuous infusion into the stomach or duodenum.[146,147] Dilution to a very low osmolality delays delivery of adequate nutrients without significantly affecting the incidence of GI intolerance. Dilution of chemically defined and elemental formulas also appears to be unnecessary based upon results of intragastric and duodenal feeding in patients and subjects with Crohn's disease or normal GI function.[147–149] In addition, a slow rate for initiation of tube feeding does not appear to reduce feeding intolerance in subjects with normal GI function in some

studies. No differences in abdominal pain, bloating, passage of gas, and diarrhea were reported when normal subjects were fed polymeric and elemental formulas by nasoduodenal tube at rates equivalent to 50 kcal/hour (1 kcal/mL formula at 50 mL/hour or 2 kcal/mL formula at 25 mL/hour), 100 kcal/hour, or 150 kcal/hour.[146] This suggests that tube feedings can be started at goal rate with full-strength formula without increasing the risk of GI intolerance, at least in patients with normal GI function. Other studies, however, suggest that rapid infusion of formula increases the incidence of nausea, cramping, and abdominal discomfort. For intermittent feeding, a rate not exceeding 30 mL/minute was suggested for all feedings.[144] For patients with abnormal GI function it may be preferable to start intragastric feedings with the formula at an osmolality of about 300 mOsm and/or at a rate not exceeding 50 mL/hour, although research is limited in this area.

The most reliable method for initiating feedings into the small bowel is to use an isotonic formula at 25 to 50 mL/hour, with rate increases of 25 to 50 mL/hour each day until the goal rate is reached.[8] Rate changes of 25 to 50 mL/hour every 8 to 12 hours, however, are used routinely in some institutions to allow a quicker transition to full nutritional support. Formula strength is increased after the goal rate of infusion is achieved because the small bowel adapts to volume changes more easily than to concentration changes.[150] An increase of 0.2 to 0.5 kcal/mL/day until full strength or goal strength is reached has been suggested.[8] A general rule for enteral feedings is not to increase both strength and rate at the same time.[151] Patients with GI tract edema, as often occurs with moderate to severe hypoalbuminemia and critical illness, may benefit from dilution of the formula to half-strength or about 150 mOsm if isotonic feedings are not tolerated.[152] Transition to full support is then attempted over several days. Parenteral nutrition may be necessary during the transition period if the patient is at significant nutritional risk with several days of inadequate nutritional provision.

Methods of Administration. Methods available for administration of enteral feedings include bulb or plunger syringe, gravity drip using a drip chamber, rate controller, or pump. Use of a syringe for formula administration is the least expensive method. It is used for bolus feedings and for some relatively short intermittent infusions. Drip chambers which rely on gravity delivery are slightly more expensive than syringes for enteral formula delivery, but are easier to manage with infusions delivered over 30 minutes or more. To maintain a relatively consistent administration rate with this method, the nurse, patient, or patient caregiver must make corrections in the delivery rate as the patient's position changes from supine to sitting to standing. Rate controllers are more expensive than gravity drip, but require less attention to maintain a consistent rate. This may be an advantage in hospitalized patients when nurses are not able to make frequent adjustments in a drip rate. Tolerance to tube feedings in critically ill patients and those fed into the jejunum tends to be affected by fluctuations in administration rate. These patients and other volume-sensitive patients may benefit from tube feeding administration via rate controller or pump.[153] *Enteral pumps* are the most expensive method of providing enteral formula. Advantages associated with pumps include a consistent delivery rate, displays of delivery rate, volume delivered and/or volume remaining, and alarms to alert the nurse to improper set position, occlusion, empty delivery container, and various other problems. The alarms may prevent long, inadvertent feeding delays in a busy hospital setting, thus helping maintain adequate delivery of the formula volume ordered. Many hospitals provide all continuous infusion feedings by pump for this quality assurance reason. In some cases, pump administration of enteral formula is necessary because of viscous formula and/or a small internal diameter of the feeding tube. Gravity flow in such cases may not occur or may be too slow to provide the prescribed formula volume. Needle catheter jejunostomies routinely require administration of formula via pump due to the small diameter of the tube.

A critical issue related to enteral pumps is the selection of delivery sets used with the pump. Delivery sets that can be confused with intravenous delivery devices, including sets containing Luer-lock connectors or other distal end connectors that can be attached to IV needles should be avoided.[154] Use of connectors that are compatible with IV devices may lead to inadvertent administration of enteral formula by the IV route.

Monitoring Enteral Feeding

Appropriate monitoring of patients receiving enteral feeding via tube is essential to recognize and prevent tube feeding complications. Complications can be divided into three groups: mechanical, gastrointestinal, and metabolic (see Table 34.6).

Mechanical complications often can be avoided with good nursing technique and careful observation of feeding tolerance. Frequent assessment of tube placement by auscultation, location of markings on the tube, and/or withdrawal of gastric contents is important in preventing pulmonary aspiration of feeding formula. Tube placement should be evaluated every four to eight hours in patients receiving continuous feeding, or before each intermittent feeding.[143,155] Withdrawal of gastric contents through the feeding tube using a syringe allows both confirmation of tube placement and evaluation of volume in the stomach (gastric residual). Patients with high gastric residual are at risk of esophageal reflux and pulmonary aspiration. Residuals are evaluated every four to six hours in patients receiving intragastric feeding. A gastric residual over 100 to 200 mL, or greater than the volume infused in two hours prompts the feedings to be held temporarily.[8,21,155,156] Residuals over 200 mL appear to be important for patients with nasogastric tubes, while residuals over 100 mL are important in patients with gastrostomy tubes.[156] The residual is checked each hour until it is under 100 mL; feedings are then restarted. Soft, small-bore feeding tubes may collapse when residuals are checked, preventing accurate determination of gastric volume. Residuals are not checked through a tube placed into the small bowel because of problems with tube collapse and because the small bowel does not serve as a reservoir for residual volume. If the patient has a nasogastric tube in addition to a feeding tube in the small bowel, residuals may be checked through the nasogastric tube to assure that formula is not "backing-up" into the stomach. "Back-up" of formula also is evaluated by addition of coloring, generally methylene blue or blue food coloring, to the feeding formula. Appearance of blue coloring in tracheal or bronchial aspirates indicates formula "backing-up" into the esophagus and/or pulmonary aspiration. Tube feedings are then held until the safety of feedings can be evaluated. Post-pyloric tube placement generally is recommended if a patient has experienced aspiration.[143] Elevating the head of the bed 30° to 45° during and after feedings also is recommended to reduce the frequency and severity of aspiration.[157]

Gastrointestinal complications frequently occur with tube feeding. Diarrhea is one of the most difficult problems for nurses, patients, and caregivers to deal with. Predisposing illnesses, including diabetes, gastrointestinal infections, and malabsorption syndromes, are more likely to cause diarrhea in tube-fed patients than the enteral formula.[158] Gastrointestinal infections related to the enteral formula are a problem in tube feeding-associated diarrhea. Formulas are commercially sterile at the time of manufacture. Once the package is opened, however, contamination may occur from

water used for reconstitution or dilution, transfer to the delivery bag, formula kept in the delivery bag for a prolonged period of time, or poorly cleaned feeding bags or administration sets. Concurrent drug therapy is another major contributor to diarrhea in tube-fed patients.[158,159]

Metabolic complications of tube feedings include hyperglycemia, electrolyte abnormalities, and fluid imbalance. Hyperglycemia, hyperkalemia, hypophosphatemia, and hyponatremia have each been reported to occur in about one-third of patients.[160] Regular biochemical determinations similar to those used for parenteral nutrition are recommended to identify developing metabolic abnormalities and allow correction before severe abnormalities occur. Baseline values for serum glucose, creatinine, blood urea nitrogen, and electrolytes should be available to guide selection of the enteral formula. Every six hours fingerstick (whole blood) glucose measurements may be ordered at the start of tube feeding in patients at risk of hyperglycemia, or when hyperglycemia is noted on serum glucose in other cases. After tube feeding is initiated, serum glucose, sodium (Na), potassium (K), chloride (Cl), and bicarbonate should be determined daily for at least four to five days in hospitalized patients. The frequency of monitoring is then decreased to once or twice weekly in stable hospitalized patients, but continued daily or every other day in critically ill patients. Patients discharged to home or a nursing facility before the tube feeding goal is reached should have serum glucose and electrolytes determined two to three times during the first week of therapy, then weekly for two to three weeks in stable patients with the feeding at goal rate. Serum creatinine (SrCr) and BUN are determined daily for a few days in critically ill patients, then by the same schedule as electrolytes. These laboratory values may be needed only two to three times in the first week, then weekly in relatively stable hospitalized patients. The monitoring schedule for serum creatinine, BUN, calcium, phosphate, and magnesium in nursing facility or home patients is the same as for electrolytes. For hospitalized patients, calcium, phosphate, and magnesium are determined two to three times during the first week, then once weekly if the patient is stable on tube feeding. Nutritional monitoring also is recommended, including serum albumin and prealbumin or transferrin weekly while the patient is hospitalized. For patients receiving long-term enteral feedings, laboratory monitoring gradually is decreased from the initial monitoring schedule. Laboratory monitoring should be done at least yearly in stable patients without significant medical problems. Patients with medical problems which may affect nutrient, electrolyte, or trace element requirements or tolerances should be monitored as appropriate to the medical condition.

Weight and fluid status are important parameters to monitor throughout enteral feeding therapy. On a short-term basis in hospitalized patients, weight primarily is a reflection of fluid status. For long-term patients, however, weight is an important monitor for adequacy of caloric intake. Consistent increases or decreases from the prescribed enteral formula volume can have significant effects on weight. For instance, weight loss of about 12.5 pounds over a year is expected when daily formula intake is 120 mL less than prescribed with 1 kcal/mL formula.

Fluid status must be monitored closely in patients receiving enteral nutrition by tube, especially those with unusual losses or inability to recognize thirst and/or voluntarily adjust oral fluid intake. Enteral formula contains solutes, as well as water. Only the free water portion of a formula contributes toward meeting fluid requirements. The free water content of enteral formulas ranges from about 80% to 85% for standard caloric density formulas, and from about 65% to 70% for calorically dense formulas. Manufacturers generally list the free water content of formulas on the packages.

Table 34.6	Complications of Tube Feeding[a]	
Complication	Cause/Contributing Factor	Treatment/Prevention
Mechanical Complications		
Aspiration	Deflated tracheostomy cuff	Inflate trach cuff before feeding; keep inflated 1 hr after feeding. Consider small-bore feeding tube placed past the Ligament of Treitz (into the jejunum)
	Displaced feeding tube	Reinsert tube and check placement
		Consider hand restraints, or feeding tube bridle
	Reduced gastric emptying	Check residuals Q 4–6 hr for gastric tube. Raise head of bed at least 30°. Change formula to one with lower fat content. Try a medication to stimulate gastric emptying. Place feeding tube into small bowel
	Lack of gag reflex; coma	Place feeding tube into small bowel beyond the pylorus and Ligament of Treitz (into the jejunum)
Nasal or pharyngeal irritation or necrosis; esophageal erosion; otitis media	Large-bore, polyvinyl chloride tube for long periods of time	Reposition the tube daily and change tape. Use smaller-bore feeding tube. Position tube to avoid pressure on tissues. Moisten mouth and nose several times daily
Tube obstruction	Poorly crushed medications	Crush medications thoroughly and dissolve in water. Use liquid medications whenever possible. Check compatibility of medication with tube and formula
	Inadequate flushing after medications or thick formula	Flush tube with 50–150 mL water after medications or thick formula, and Q 8 hr with 20 mL minimum
	Poorly dissolved or mixed formula	Use a blender to mix formula (check manufacturer's guidelines for mixing). Check for formula clumping as it is poured into the container for administration
Metabolic Complications		
Hyperglycemia, glycosuria (can lead to dehydration, coma, or death)	Stress response High carbohydrate formula (e.g., elemental) Drug therapy (steroids) Diabetes mellitus	Monitor finger stick glucose Q 6 hr and have sliding scale insulin ordered Monitor in's and out's accurately
Excess CO_2 production (high RQ)[a]	High % of carbohydrate calories or excess calories from any source	↑ fat calories and/or ↓ total calories
Hyponatremia	Dilutional (fluid excess; SIADH); inadequate sodium intake; excess GI losses	Use full-strength formula or change to concentrated formula with 1.5–2.0 kcal/mL. Add salt to the tube feeding (1 tsp = 2 gm Na = 90 mEq). Use diuretics if appropriate. Replace GI losses
Hypernatremia	Inadequate free water intake	Use diluted formula or change to 1.0 kcal/mL formula. Monitor in's and out's accurately; temperature and weight daily
	Excess water losses (diabetes incipidus; osmotic diuresis from hyperglycemia; fever)	Correct hyperglycemia and the underlying cause of fever or diabetes incipidus
Hypokalemia	Medications (diuretics, antispuedomonal penicillins, amphotericin B)	Monitor serum potassium carefully; give PO or IV potassium replacement PRN
	Intra-/extracellular shifts (insulin therapy, acidosis)	Correct the underlying problem
	Excess GI losses (NG suction, small bowel fistula, diarrhea)	
Hyperkalemia	Potassium sparing medications (triamterene, amiloride, spironolactone, ACE-inhibitors); Potassium containing medications (Penicillin G potassium)	Monitor serum potassium carefully. Change to medications which do not have a potassium-sparing effect or which are not potassium salts
	Renal failure	Monitor renal function
		Change to a formula with lower potassium content
Hypercoagulability	Warfarin antagonism due to high vitamin K content of formula	Change to a formula with lower vitamin K content. Monitor coagulation status
GI Complications		
Diarrhea	Atrophy of GI microvilli; malabsorption (pancreatitis, short gut syndrome, Crohn's disease); low serum albumin	Use a peptide-based or free amino acid formula until nutritional status improves. Start with isotonic dilution and progress slowly while increasing the rate, then strength of formula. Change to a formula with lower fat content if fat malabsorption appears to be occurring
	Hypertonic formula	Dilute formula or change to an isotonic formula

Continued

Table 34.6	Complications of Tube Feeding[a] (Continued)	
Complication	Cause/Contributing Factor	Treatment/Prevention
	Formula started and/or advanced too rapidly	Reduce rate and/or strength temporarily; advance slowly once diarrhea is controlled
		Change to continuous drip if using bolus feedings
	Lactose intolerance	Use lactose-free formula
	Contaminated formula	Hang fresh formula Q 4–6 hr. Do not add new formula to remaining formula. Change feeding container and tubing every day; use clean technique. Discard open containers of formula after 24 hr. Avoid unnecessary manipulation of the feeding system. Mix formulas using aseptic technique and sterile water
	Medications	
	Magnesium-containing antacids	Alternate with, or change to, $Al(OH)_3$ or calcium carbonate
	Antibiotics	Give Lactobacillus (Lactinex) to replenish GI flora. Check for *C. difficile* and treat if present. Give an antidiarrheal agent
	Quinidine, methyldopa	Give $Al(OH)_3$ antacid; give an antidiarrheal agent
	Metoclopramide, cisapride	Reduce dose; discontinue if no longer required
	High osmolality liquid medications; irritating medications (potassium)	Dilute the medication with water before giving and/or give water through the tube before giving the medication. Use the liquid form with a lower osmolality and/or less irritating formulation if there is a choice (water base vs syrup vs alcohol/propylene glycol/sorbitol)
	Colchicine	Reduce colchicine dose; give antidiarrheal agents
	Cholinergics (bethanochol)	If diarrhea is a major problem, consider alternative medication/therapy
Nausea, vomiting, distention, cramping, hyperactive bowel sound	Too rapid administration	Slow administration rate (give bolus over longer time; ↓ continuous infusion rate)
	Intolerance to osmolality and/or volume	Reduce osmolality by diluting formula with water or by changing to an isotonic formula. Reduce volume of feeds by ↓ amount/bolus or reducing rate of continuous feeds
	Formula too cold	Bring formula to room temperature before administering
	Gastric retention; poor GI motility	Raise head of bed >30°. Check gastric residuals; hold formula if large residual. Place feeding tube past the pylorus into the small bowel. Consider medication to increase motility. Reduce dose or discontinue medications that ↓ GI motility if this will not adversely affect the patient (morphine, anticholinergics)
	Lactose intolerance	Use lactose-free formula
Dumping Syndrome (weakness, diaphoresis, palpitations)	Hyperosmolar load infused rapidly or bolused into the small bowel	↓ rate and dilute temporarily. Do not bolus into the small bowel unless the patient has a jejunostomy specially made for bolus feedings. Use an isotonic formula
	Formula strength increased too fast; formula rate too high	↓ rate and/or strength temporarily, then advance the rate or strength slowly
Constipation	Inadequate fluid/free water intake	Dilute formula if feeding continuously; give free water between or with bolus feedings
	Inadequate bulk/fiber	Use a fiber-containing/high-residue formula. Give bulk-forming laxative (Metamucil) or fruit juice
	Fecal impaction	Administer a stool softener; use daily
	Reduced gastric/GI motility	Encourage ambulation; consider medication to improve motility if more conservative measures fail
	Medications (narcotics, anticholinergics)	Use the lowest effective dose of the medication. Discontinue the medication when possible to do so without adversely affecting patient care. Change to an alternate drug if an effective one is available with less GI side effects

[a] ACE = Angiotensin-converting enzymes; $Al(OH)_3$ = Aluminum hydroxide; CO_2 = Carbon dioxide; GI = Gastrointestinal; IV = Intravenous; Na = Sodium; NG = Nasogastric; PO = Per os (orally); PRN = As needed; RQ = Respiratory quotient; SIADH = Syndrome of inappropriate secretion of antidiuretic hormone.

Water used in irrigating, or flushing, the feeding tube may contribute a significant volume of fluid daily. Tube patency is maintained by flushing the tube with fluid every four to eight hours for continuous feedings or before and after each intermittent feeding. Between 20 mL and 60 mL of water generally is used for each "flush." The tube also should be flushed before and after each administration of medication through the tube. For patients developing signs of fluid overload, the flush volume should be reduced to 20 mL or 30 mL and the number of flushes kept at a minimum. Patients requiring more daily fluid may benefit from increased flush volume and/or number of flushes.

Medications and Enteral Nutrition by Tube

Patients receiving nutrition via feeding tube generally receive medications through the same tube. Potential problems exist for both the enteral nutrition and medications when this arrangement is used. Feeding tube occlusion, adverse effects due to changes in pharmaceutical dosage forms, and alteration of medication pharmacokinetics are among the problems which may arise. There are also potential interactions related to the pharmacologic effects or physiological effects of medications or enteral nutrients.

Feeding tube occlusion has an incidence of 6% to 38%.[161,162] Pump malfunction, lack of periodic tube flushing, formula characteristics, and tube characteristics are nonmedication-related factors which may affect the incidence of tube occlusion.[163] Important tube characteristics include the inner diameter, the arrangement of formula delivery holes (ports) at the distal end, and the number of delivery ports. Large-bore nasogastric tubes which contain a large delivery port at the end appear less likely to occlude than smaller diameter tubes and/or tubes with multiple small delivery ports.[163,164] The most important formula characteristic in regard to tube occlusion appears to be the protein source. *In vitro* studies suggest that formulas containing intact protein, particularly casein or caseinates, coagulate and clump when exposed to an acidic pH.[161] Higher protein concentrations may increase the risk of protein coagulation and tube occlusion. A tendency toward greater incompatibility of intact protein formulas with acidic pharmaceutical syrups, compared to hydrolyzed protein formulas, also has been noted.[165]

Flushing protocols for feeding tubes have not been well studied. It generally is agreed that the tube should be flushed following each intermittent administration of formula or medication. The frequency and volume for tube flushes with continuous-infusion feedings varies from facility to facility. Maintenance of formula flow rate has been demonstrated with flushing 20 mL of water through the tube at eight-hour intervals in simulated gastric administration of enteral formula by pump or gravity delivery through an 8-French tube.[161] Published flushing protocols range from 50 to 150 mL of water periodically to 25 mL every four hours.[143,155] For administration of medications, 50 to 150 mL of water after instillation of medications has been recommended.[143] Another recommendation is 30 mL of warm water or saline before and after each administration of medication, although a minimum of 5 mL between multiple medications may be acceptable.[164]

Medication-related factors which may influence the incidence of feeding tube occlusion include the administration method, dosage form, pH, and viscosity. Medications admixed with enteral formula have the greatest potential for occluding feeding tubes due to alteration of the texture, viscosity, or physical form of the medication and/or formula. Therefore, medications rarely should be admixed directly with formula. Stopping the enteral formula flow, then flushing the feeding tube before and after medication administration limits the contact between medications and formula, at least within the lumen of the feeding tube, and should limit the risk of tube occlusion.

Solid dosage forms create the greatest challenge for administration by feeding tube. Whenever possible, a liquid dosage form should be selected, but these are not totally without problems. Liquids with a high viscosity may require dilution before administration. This allows easy flow through the tube and avoids a coating inside the tube which could react with enteral formula to form an occlusion. Suspensions have a tendency to coat tubes when they are thick and/or when the particles are relatively large and prone to settling. Unless the coating is washed off the tube wall and out of the ports with an adequate flush volume, occlusion will occur with repeated doses of the suspension. Pharmaceutical syrups with a pH of ≤ 4 must be used with caution since immediate clumping and tackiness of formulas mixed with the syrups have been reported.[165,166]

For medications without an available liquid form, a therapeutically equivalent medication in a liquid form should be considered. Extemporaneous preparation of a solution or suspension also may be attempted. Simple compressed tablets lend themselves to crushing, then dissolving or suspending in 10 to 30 mL of water before administration through the feeding tube. Medications in a soft gelatin capsule also are best delivered by dissolving the capsule in warm water before administration through the tube. Undissolved gelatin should not be allowed to enter the tube, as this may result in occlusion. Powders in hard gelatin capsules can be poured into water and thoroughly mixed, then administered through the feeding tube. Failure to thoroughly dissolve any of these dosage forms in water before administration via the feeding tube may result in tube occlusion. Gora et al. have listed Dyazide, ibuprofen, magnesium oxide, Metamucil, Micro-K, and Theo-Dur Sprinkles as medications most likely to clog enteral feeding tubes.[164]

Crushing a medication and dissolving or suspending the powder in water results in an altered pharmaceutical dosage form. Depending upon the design and purpose of the dosage form, changes in the form may result in adverse effects on drug efficacy or patient tolerance. Simple compressed tablets are designed to dissolve rapidly in the stomach. Crushing and dissolving these tablets in water immediately before use has little affect on efficacy or patient tolerance to the medication. Tablets and capsules designed to slowly release their medication, however, are significantly affected by crushing. Slow-release mechanisms are destroyed by crushing, resulting in the immediate release of several hours worth of the medication all at one time. An exaggerated therapeutic response may be seen initially, followed by a loss of response part way through the dosing interval. Solid dosage forms designed to release several doses of medication from one dose, therefore, should not be crushed.[167] Use of immediate-release forms of the ordered medication, with appropriate adjustment of the dose and dosing interval, therapeutically equivalent immediate-release forms, or alternate administration routes (e.g., morphine suppositories rather than slow-release morphine tablets) are possible alternatives to crushing dosage forms designed for slow release.

Enteric-coated tablets are designed to release their medication in the small bowel, because the medication is either acid labile or irritating to the stomach. Protection for the medication or stomach is lost when enteric-coated tablets are crushed and delivered via feeding tube into the stomach. The net result may be decreased efficacy of the medication or increased stomach irritation. When an irritating medication must be given by tube into the stomach, at least 60 mL of water is recommended for diluting the medication.[164] Administration of buccal or sublingual dosage forms via feeding tube may result in altered absorption and/or destruction of the medication by stomach acid. Methods to avoid crushing enteric coated tablets and buccal or sublingual dosages include using therapeutically equivalent medications (e.g., isosorbide dinitrate rather than sublingual nitroglycerine) or using an alternate route of administration (e.g., nitroglycerine ointment or transdermal system rather than sublingual nitroglycerine).

Alteration of pharmacokinetic parameters may occur when a medication is administered via feeding tube. The site of medication delivery may affect bioavailability, although few studies address this issue. Medications taken orally are delivered to the stomach where dissolution occurs for most dosage forms, and hydrolysis of some medications may occur. Delivery into the small bowel may alter these processes, thereby affecting bioavailability. For instance, recovery of digoxin from intrajejunal dosing is reported to be higher than with oral administration, primarily because of reduced intragastric hydrolysis.[168] Bioavailability of medications also may be affected by the presence of enteral formula in the GI tract. Medications affected by the presence of food are expected to be affected in a similar manner by the presence of enteral formula. For example, administration of tetracycline when formula is present in the GI tract is expected to reduce tetracycline bioavailability.[169]

Phenytoin is a particularly troublesome medication to manage in patients receiving enteral feeding. Reduced phenytoin concentrations in patients receiving enteral feedings was first reported in 1982.[170] Since then, several case reports and studies have focused on this problem. Methods suggested for management include using a meat-based formula, administering phenytoin capsules rather than suspension, and stopping enteral formula delivery for two hours before and after the phenytoin dose.[170–172] Unfortunately, none of these methods clearly has been established as preventing low phenytoin concentrations in tube-fed patients. Large-scale controlled trials are needed to determine the most appropriate method for managing the phenytoin-enteral feeding interaction.

One of the most important potential interactions related to pharmacological effects of medications or nutrients is the reversal of warfarin anticoagulation by vitamin K in enteral formulas.[173] Most enteral formulas manufactured today contain vitamin K in doses which do not interfere with anticoagulation.[174] Inability to adequately anticoagulate a tube-fed patient with oral warfarin should, however, prompt an evaluation of the enteral formula's vitamin K content. In addition, discontinuation of enteral feedings in a patient stabilized on warfarin warrants evaluation of the prothrombin time several days after the formula is stopped.

Potential problems related to physiological effects of medications center around diarrhea secondary to administration of hypertonic medications. Hypertonic medications, such as potassium chloride, cimetidine liquid, and theophylline elixir, should be diluted with 30 to 60 mL of water before administration through the feeding tube.[164,174,175] Division of the medication dose and separation of each smaller dose by a couple hours also may help reduce diarrhea secondary to some hypertonic medications. For example, 60 mEq of potassium chloride can be divided into three doses of 20 mEq each with two hours between the doses.

Patient Assessment

Evaluation of Nutritional Status

1. J.M., a 70-year-old male, was admitted to the hospital 5 days ago after a neighbor found him semiconscious in a patio chair. Physical examination on admission revealed right-sided paralysis and left-sided weakness. Confusion and disorientation were present. Mucous membranes were reported as dry. J.M. was diagnosed with mild dehydration and as having suffered a cerebral vascular accident (CVA). His condition has changed little since admission. J.M. is estimated to be 5'8" in height and weighs 130 lb (59 kg) on a bed scale. He is receiving a maintenance IV of 5% dextrose/0.45% sodium chloride with 20 mEq KCl/L at 100 mL/hr. Laboratory evaluation today shows a serum albumin of 3.2 gm/dL, down from 3.5 on the admission chemistry panel. Other biochemical data are within normal limits: glucose 97 mg/dL; creatinine 1.0 mg/dL; Na 140 mEq/L; K 4.5 mEq/L; and Cl 105 mEq/L. Assess J.M.'s nutritional status. Identify factors placing him at nutritional risk. Is nutritional support indicated at this time? [SI units: serum albumin 32 and 35 gm/L, respectively; glucose 5.384 mmol/L; creatinine 88.4 μmol/L; Na 140 mmol/L; K 4.5 mmol/L; Cl 105 mmol/L]

J.M. appears to have a mild marasmic-kwashiorkor malnutrition based upon his weight for height and serum albumin concentration. This increases his risk for more severe malnutrition during hospitalization, and possibly his risk of mortality.[176,177] The serum albumin of 3.5 gm/dL at the time of admission is falsely elevated due to dehydration; therefore, today's albumin should be used to evaluate visceral protein status. The mild visceral protein depletion may have occurred as the result of metabolic stress associated with his CVA. Weight loss to 86% of ideal body weight (IBW = 68.4 kg), however, most likely is due to chronic deficiency in total energy intake. This is consistent with marasmus.[178]

At 86% of IBW, J.M. should appear underweight. If he appears to be of normal weight, the estimated height may be wrong. A knee-height caliper could be used to obtain a more accurate height despite J.M. being in bed.[179] If the knee-height caliper is not available, a better estimate of height might be obtained by using a tape measure stretched out along J.M.'s body. Based upon the information presented, it is not clear when J.M.'s weight of 59 kg was obtained. If this weight is within the first 24 hours of admission, it is expected to be falsely low (by a few kg at most) due to J.M.'s dehydration. Records of clinic visits and hospitalizations may provide information on chronic or recent illnesses which contributed to weight loss.

Socioeconomic factors which may contribute to nutritional risk also should be considered. Home address and type of medical insurance may provide clues to his economic status. Income has been shown to have a positive correlation with nutritional status.[180] Social conditions also may influence nutrition. J.M. appears to live alone since a neighbor reported his condition rather than a family member. Elderly patients living alone, especially men, tend to skip meals more frequently and eat less than those living with others.[180]

It is reasonable to assume J.M. has been without oral intake since admission. He is unable to feed himself and is expected to have difficulty chewing and swallowing as a result of the CVA. Dextrose provided in the maintenance fluid is considered adequate nutrition for only about a week in a previously well-nourished patient with a low degree of metabolic stress. Beyond this time period more substantial support must be considered because the dextrose provided by maintenance fluids is considerably below the 3 mg/kg/minute needed to minimize protein breakdown for gluconeogenesis.[181] Patients with underlying malnutrition or a higher degree of metabolic stress generally are considered for nutritional support within one to six days, depending upon the degree of malnutrition or stress. Since J.M. has mild malnutrition and is not likely to take adequate nutrients by mouth within the next 24 hours, nutritional support is indicated.

Estimation of Nutritional Requirements

2. What are J.M.'s requirements for calories, protein, and fluid? Does he have any special nutrient requirements?

Because J.M. is below ideal body weight for his height, his actual weight should be used to estimate energy and protein requirements. Use of ideal body weight to estimate requirements for malnourished patients may result in fluid and electrolyte imbalance. Once the patient is stabilized on nutritional support, the calories can be increased, if necessary, to achieve weight gain. For patients weighing between ideal and 120% of ideal body weight, either ideal or actual weight can be used. Since the Harris-Benedict equation and several other equations used to predict caloric requirements appear to overestimate needs, it may be preferable to use IBW and adjust calories, if necessary, based upon weight changes.[182–186] An adjusted weight appears to be most appropriate for patients weighing more than 120% of ideal. Prediction equations for resting energy expenditure generally do not correlate well with measured energy expenditure for obese subjects when actual weight is used as a variable in the equation.[187,188] The adjustment accounts for the portion of excess weight which is metabolically active lean tissue and avoids providing calories for the relatively inert adipose tissue.

J.M.'s level of metabolic stress is relatively low. He has no surgical wounds to heal, no fractures or skeletal trauma, no burns, and no major infections. Caloric requirements are, therefore, only slightly higher than basal needs. Although the term ''calorie'' is used interchangeably with kilocalorie (kcal) in nutrition literature, the large ''Calorie'' or kilocalorie technically is correct. Thus, energy requirements generally are listed as kcal/day or kcal/kg body weight when specific numbers are given for a patient's requirements. Requirements can be estimated using the Harris-Benedict equations with Long's modifications, or from one of the many other guidelines for predicting energy expenditure.[182,189,190] Indirect calorimetry (metabolic cart measurements) could be used to measure energy expenditure, although this is an expensive procedure and probably is unnecessary in a mildly stressed patient. An estimation of 26 to 28 kcal/kg actual weight also can be used based upon J.M.'s low level of metabolic stress. Higher caloric intake may be needed, however, for weight gain. Protein requirements are expected to be slightly higher than the RDA of 0.8 gm/kg/day. The mild visceral protein depletion and metabolic stress experienced by J.M. are expected to increase his protein needs to approximately 1.0 to 1.2 gm/kg actual weight/day. Renal function appears adequate for J.M. to tolerate up to 1.2 gm/kg without becoming azotemic. Serum creatinine, however, may provide a poor estimate of renal function in a patient with below-normal muscle mass such as J.M. who is only 86% of ideal body weight. Fluid requirements can be estimated at 30 to 35 mL/kg body weight/day plus replacement of excess losses from hyperthermia, vomiting, or diarrhea.[180] A baseline requirement of 1500 mL for the first 20 kg of body weight plus 20 mL per each additional kg of body weight also can be used to estimate fluid requirements, although this method was developed for use in pediatric patients. Based upon caloric intake, fluid requirements can be estimated as 1 mL/kcal ingested.[191] J.M. does not appear to have any excess fluid losses at this time; therefore, calculation of baseline fluid requirements should provide adequate fluids.

J.M.'s estimated daily requirements are approximately 1535 to 1650 total calories, 59 to 71 gm protein, and 1770 to 2065 mL of fluid. These are estimated requirements that should be adjusted based upon frequent reassessment of J.M.'s response to therapy and changes in his clinical situation.

J.M.'s apparently suboptimal nutrition before hospitalization increases his risk of vitamin deficiencies. No medical, medication, or dietary histories are available to determine nutritional risks associated with specific conditions. Factors which predispose patients to vitamin deficiencies include weight loss of over 5% of usual body weight in one month or over 10% of usual body weight in six months, prolonged periods of dietary restriction, high levels of physiological stress as occurs with trauma and large areas of burn, significant alterations in biochemical tests such as serum

glucose and albumin, abnormal or protracted body fluid losses, administration of medications that alter vitamin absorption or metabolism, and diagnoses associated with alteration in vitamin absorption or requirements.[191–193] J.M.'s age and hospitalized status place him at risk of thiamine and pyridoxine deficiencies, and possibly riboflavin deficiency.[180] Given J.M.'s mild marasmic-kwashiorkor malnutrition, he is likely to have at least some subclinical vitamin deficiencies. J.M. should receive a minimum of 100% of the RDA for vitamins and minerals daily, and up to 200% of the RDA would not be unreasonable. A daily multivitamin preparation providing 100% of the RDA should be considered, in addition to vitamins and minerals from an oral diet or tube feeding. If actual deficiencies are identified J.M. will require higher, therapeutic doses of the specific vitamins which are deficient.[193]

Enteral Nutrition by Tube

3. The health-care team decides to initiate nutritional support via tube feeding. What route for tube feeding is most appropriate for J.M.?

With right-sided paralysis from the CVA it is likely that J.M. has problems with chewing and swallowing, in addition to difficulty getting food to his mouth. Otherwise, J.M.'s GI tract is expected to be functional. There is no indication that J.M. has risks associated with aspiration. Some patients have poor gag reflex following a CVA, but J.M. has no reported coughing or choking. The duration of tube feeding is uncertain since J.M. may improve with time. Use of a nasogastric tube is the least invasive until J.M.'s prognosis for recovery is better predicted. Measures to prevent J.M. from pulling the feeding tube may need to be instituted since confused and disoriented patients frequently pull tubes. In one study, 40% of patients receiving tube feeding had the tube displaced at least once.[194] Confusion was reported at least periodically in all patients experiencing tube displacement. J.M.'s right side is paralyzed, so his right hand will not be a threat for the tube. His left hand may be a threat for pulling the tube depending upon the degree of weakness. A soft mitten or restraint placed on the left wrist may be used to prevent J.M. from grabbing the feeding tube and displacing it. Patients who manage to pull the feeding tube repeatedly despite mittens or restraints may be considered for a feeding tube bridle to prevent inadvertent tube removal.[195]

Enteral Formula Selection

4. What type of enteral formula is most appropriate for J.M.?

J.M. has full digestive capability; therefore, a polymeric formula is most appropriate. Since no history is available regarding lactose tolerance, and J.M. has been ''fasting'' at least five days, a lactose-free formula is advised for initiation of tube feedings. This will avoid the possibility of bloating, cramps, and diarrhea secondary to lactose intolerance.[37] Standard caloric density of 1 to 1.2 kcal/mL should be used since J.M. has no fluid restriction and no evidence of intolerance to his maintenance IV fluid at 100 mL/hour. Using a high nitrogen formula to meet J.M.'s caloric needs will provide protein at the upper end of the estimated requirement (1.2 gm/kg/day), while a standard nitrogen formula will provide between 0.8 and 1 gm/kg/day. A high nitrogen formula may replete J.M.'s visceral protein status sooner than a standard nitrogen formula, but may not provide adequate calories for weight gain. The decision to use a high versus standard nitrogen formula will depend upon the exact nutrient composition of enteral formulas on the hospital formulary.

Fiber can be included in the selected enteral formula if desired. The benefit of fiber for short-term feeding is not clearly defined, however, so a fiber-free formula is an equally appropriate selection at this time.[44] To minimize gas and abdominal distention if a fiber-containing formula is selected initially, the formula should contain a low to moderate fiber content (5 to 7 gm/L) or be started at a low rate and advanced slowly.[40,52]

Fluid Provision

5. How much fluid must be provided daily to meet J.M.'s estimated fluid requirements?

The free water content of the selected enteral formula must be calculated to determine the volume of fluid which must be provided to J.M. in addition to the formula. Formulas with 1 to 1.2 kcal/mL generally contain 80% to 85% free water. Assuming a goal volume of 1560 mL/day (6.5 cans) of a 1 kcal/mL, 0.044 gm protein/mL formula, the free water content provided to J.M. is about 1250 to 1325 mL/day. Using 30 mL/kg/day as J.M.'s fluid requirement, he needs 1770 mL of fluid daily. Fluid needed in addition to the enteral formula is, therefore, 445 to 520 mL. This fluid can be provided with medications, irrigation of the tube (flushes), or in a diluted formula. The feeding tube should be irrigated with a minimum of 20 mL of fluid at least every eight hours, plus before and after each administration of medication through the tube.[161] Using six flushes daily with 75 mL of water each would provide 450 mL of fluid for J.M.

When large volumes of fluid are required in addition to the enteral formula, the formula may be diluted and the goal volume set for a three-fourths or half-strength formula. If a 2 kcal/mL, 0.075 gm protein/mL formula had been selected for J.M., he would need about 840 mL (3.5 cans) of formula daily to meet caloric and protein requirements. Formulas with 2 kcal/mL generally contain approximately 65% to 70% free water, meaning J.M. would receive approximately 545 to 590 mL of free water from the formula. J.M. would still need 1180 to 1225 mL of fluid to meet his fluid requirement. Rather than giving frequent, large flushes of water, use of the formula at half-strength could be considered. With 1680 mL of half-strength formula, J.M. would receive 1385 to 1430 mL of free water daily (840 mL of water plus 65% to 70% of the 840 mL of formula). The remaining 340 to 385 mL of J.M.'s fluid needs could be met by five flushes of 70 to 75 mL each.

Enteral Nutrition Administration

6. Recommend a plan for initiating and advancing J.M.'s tube feeding.

J.M. is being fed into the stomach; therefore, continuous infusion, intermittent infusion, or bolus delivery of feedings can be used. Continuous infusion most commonly is used for hospitalized patients.[138] Improved tolerance with continuous intragastric infusion versus intermittent infusion, however, has not been clearly established.[139–141]

Full-strength formula should be used to initiate tube feedings. J.M. is assumed to have full digestive capacity and is being fed into the stomach; therefore, dilution of the formula is not expected to improve tolerance to either an isotonic or hypertonic formula.[146,147] Dilution to a low osmolality is likely to delay reaching J.M.'s caloric and protein goals. Starting the feedings at a very low rate also is likely to delay reaching J.M.'s nutritional goals. Studies suggest that intragastric tube feedings can be started at goal rate in patients with normal GI function, but this is not a widely accepted practice.[146] The standard of practice in most institutions is to start continuous infusion feedings at no more than 50 mL/hour. Feedings are then advanced by 25 to 50 mL/hour every 8 to 12 hours, as tolerated, until the goal rate is achieved.

The goal volume of enteral nutrition for J.M. is 1560 mL/day of a 1 kcal/mL formula, or 65 mL/hour continuous infusion. The infusion can be started at 40 mL/hour for 8 to 12 hours, then increased to 65 mL/hour. If J.M. experiences diarrhea, abdominal distention, or large gastric residuals the feeding may be held at the initial rate for 24 hours, then increased only 10 to 15 mL/hour every 12 to 24 hours as tolerance permits. If the formula is not advanced to goal rate within 24 hours of initiating feedings, extra care must be taken to assure adequate fluid intake.

Continuous infusion enteral feedings can be administered by gravity drip using a drip chamber, rate controller, or enteral pump. To maintain a consistent flow rate with a drip chamber, frequent adjustment of the rate is necessary. This is difficult to obtain on a busy hospital ward. Rate controllers can maintain a consistent flow rate without frequent rate adjustments, but have no alarms to alert nurses to stoppage of formula flow secondary to kinked administration tubing or an empty delivery container. Thus, formula flow could stop for several hours if flow was not checked frequently. Enteral pumps provide a consistent flow rate and alarms to alert nurses to flow problems, but are more expensive than rate controllers. Pumps often are used for hospitalized patients to help maintain delivery of the prescribed volume of enteral formula. Either a rate controller or enteral pump could be used for J.M., depending upon the hospital's usual protocol for enteral feedings. If an enteral pump is used, the connector at the distal (patient) end of the delivery set should not be compatible with IV devices.[154]

Monitoring Enteral Nutrition Support

7. Recommend a plan for monitoring J.M.'s response to enteral nutrition, including clinical and biochemical parameters.

Monitoring of enteral nutrition is necessary to prevent complications and assess appropriateness of therapy. Clinical parameters to monitor include tube placement, gastric residual, GI symptoms, respiratory status, vital signs, and weight. Tube placement should be evaluated every four to eight hours by auscultation, location of markings on the tube, and/or withdrawal of gastric contents.[143,155] Displacement of the tube into the esophagus or pharynx could result in pulmonary aspiration of enteral formula.

Gastric residual is evaluated by measuring the volume of fluid withdrawn from the stomach through the feeding tube using a syringe. The fluid is then infused through the tube back into the stomach to avoid electrolyte imbalances. High residuals may increase the risk of esophageal reflux and pulmonary aspiration. The residual volume considered important for holding tube feeding in patients receiving nasogastric feeding is 200 mL.[156] For J.M., however, using about two times the hourly infusion rate of formula is more appropriate because of his low goal rate.[155] Tube feeding should be held if a residual is over 100 mL during initiation of J.M.'s feeding, or over 130 mL once the formula is infusing at the goal rate of 65 mL/hour. Residuals should be checked every four to eight hours as long as no residual is above the volume for holding feeding. If feeding is held due to a high residual, an hourly evaluation of gastric residual is recommended until the volume is below 100 mL and the feeding is restarted.

Assessment of GI symptoms is important for determining tolerance to enteral feedings. Abdominal distention and bloating should be evaluated at least every eight hours while J.M. is hospitalized. Small-bore feeding tubes may collapse during withdrawal of gastric residual, resulting in falsely low residual volume. Abdominal distention may be an indication of accumulating formula. Gas formation secondary to lactose intolerance or rapid increases in fiber intake, and poor gastric emptying secondary to a high-fat formula, medications, recent surgery, critical illness, or an underlying disease such as diabetes are among the conditions associated with distention. When considerable distention is present, the formula should be held temporarily, and the patient evaluated further to rule out a condition contraindicating continued use of the GI tract. Gastric outlet obstruction, complete or partial small bowel obstruction, or ileus would preclude restarting enteral nutrition until the condition resolved. If no contraindication to using the GI tract is found, feeding can be restarted preferably with the feeding tube placed into the small bowel, a formula with lower fat or fiber, and/or medications to increase gastric emptying, such as metoclopramide, cisapride, or erythromycin. Feeding should be restarted at a rate of 30 to 50 mL/hour and J.M. observed closely for signs of feeding intolerance. The head of the bed should be elevated 30° to 45° during feeding.[157]

Nausea, vomiting, abdominal cramping, diarrhea, and constipation are other GI symptoms which are monitored as indicators of tube feeding tolerance. Vomiting creates the most immediate concern among these symptoms since feeding tube displacement and pulmonary aspiration may occur during vomiting. Nausea and vomiting commonly occur with high gastric residuals, severe gastric distention, poor gastric emptying when feeding into the stomach, obstruction of the GI tract, and/or lack of GI tract motility. Lactose intolerance and bolus feeding into the jejunum can lead to diarrhea and abdominal cramping, as well as nausea and vomiting. Initiation of tube feeding with hypertonic formula, a rapid rate of infusion, and/or a large volume, and use of formula at refrigerator temperature are other factors often cited as causing GI symptoms.[143-145,158,159] Although controlled studies have not supported these factors as significant contributors to GI intolerance, subjective evidence suggests they are important factors.[143,146,147,159] Constipation is most likely to occur with long-term tube feeding in nonambulatory patients. Inadequate fluid intake and lack of fiber may be factors associated with constipation.[53,57]

Respiratory status should be evaluated every eight hours in hospitalized patients, to help recognize pulmonary aspiration and pulmonary edema. A stethoscope should be used for assessment at least a couple times per week, but simple observation of the patient's breathing pattern is adequate at other times unless alteration in respiration is noted. Coughing and/or respiratory distress may be indications of aspiration or other developing respiratory problems. Vital signs also may provide clues to aspiration or other developing problems, such as dehydration, fluid overload, or infection.

Weight should be monitored daily in hospitalized patients. Day-to-day changes in weight reflect fluid status. Increased weight for three to four consecutive days may be an indication that fluid intake needs to be reduced, while decreased weight may indicate a need for increased fluid. The amount of fluid provided generally can be adjusted by the number of times the feeding tube is flushed daily and/or the volume of each flush. Caloric density of the formula can be changed when alteration of flush number or volume is not adequate for fluid control. For patients with a stable fluid status, week-to-week weight change can be used as an indicator of appropriate caloric intake. A trend upward in weight (e.g., ≥3 consecutive weeks with an increase) may indicate a need for fewer calories, unless weight gain is a goal. A trend downward may indicate a need to increase caloric intake, unless weight loss is desired.

Regular monitoring of biochemical parameters is important for identifying metabolic abnormalities before they become critical problems. Serum glucose, sodium, potassium, chloride, and bicarbonate should be determined daily in J.M. for four to five days after feeding starts. Monitoring can then be decreased to once or twice weekly if J.M. has no evidence of tube feeding intolerance or metabolic abnormalities. Fingerstick glucose measurements should be ordered every six hours if hospital policy requires this for all patients started on nutritional support. If fingersticks are not required by policy, it would be reasonable to evaluate J.M.'s glucose control after tube feeding starts and then decide if fingersticks are needed. Since J.M. has a normal serum glucose (97 mg/dL) while receiving 5% dextrose in his IV fluid and is not highly stressed, hyperglycemia is not a major concern with initiation of tube feeding.

Serum creatinine, BUN, calcium, phosphate, and magnesium should be monitored a minimum of three times during the first week of tube feeding. Daily monitoring of creatinine and BUN for a few days may even be considered in J.M. because of his recent dehydration. Daily calcium, phosphate, and magnesium also may be considered for a few days in J.M. because of his low body weight. Chronic malnutrition can lead to intracellular depletion of potassium, phosphate, and magnesium, while serum concentrations are maintained. When nutrition support begins, a refeeding syndrome develops as these electrolytes move from the extracellular space into the cells, causing a decrease in serum concentrations over the first few days of feeding. Failure to monitor the patient and replace electrolytes as necessary can result in serious electrolyte abnormalities. If creatinine, BUN, calcium, phosphate, and magnesium are stable after the first four or five days, the frequency of monitoring could be reduced to once or twice weekly.

Biochemical parameters used to monitor response to protein provision, including albumin and prealbumin or transferrin should be monitored weekly. Prealbumin and transferrin are monitored as short-term indicators of visceral protein response to nutritional support, while albumin is a long-term indicator. Nitrogen balance can be used as an alternative to prealbumin or transferrin, but requires an accurate 12- to 24-hour urine collection to be useful.

Electrolyte Abnormalities

8. J.M. has been receiving tube feeding for 4 days. The feeding was started at 40 mL/hr for 8 hours, then increased to the goal rate of 65 mL/hr. The IV fluids were stopped once the tube feeding was at goal rate. J.M.'s tube feeding was stopped for about 5 hours after he pulled his tube a couple days ago, but otherwise there have been no problems. Laboratory evaluation today shows the following: K 3.1 mEq/L, decreased from 3.6 mEq/L yesterday, 3.9 mEq/L the previous day, and 4.5 mEq/L when tube feeding started; Cl 95 mEq/L; calcium 8.2 mg/dL (Normal: 9–11); Mg 2.6 mEq/L (Normal: 2.5–3.5), decreased from 3.5 mEq/L 2 days ago; phosphate 3.5 mg/dL (Normal: 3.5–4.5), decreased from 4.4 mg/dL 2 days ago; and albumin 3.0 gm/dL. Micro-K (8 mEq KCl/capsule) has been ordered as 6 capsules via feeding tube; and calcium carbonate (260 mg elemental calcium/tablet) as 2 tablets BID via feeding tube. Is the electrolyte replacement appropriate as ordered for J.M.? What changes, if any, should be considered for electrolyte replacement? [SI units: K 3.1, 3.6, 3.9, and 4.5 mmol/L, respectively; Cl 95 mmol/L; Ca 2.05 mmol/L (Normal: 2.25–2.75); Mg 1.3 and 1.75 mmol/L, respectively (Normal: 1.25–2.75); phosphate 1.13 and 1.42 mmol/L, respectively (Normal: 1.130–1.453); albumin 30 gm/L]

Calcium carbonate is a simple compressed tablet which can be crushed, suspended in 10 to 30 mL of water, and administered via the feeding tube. The risk of tube occlusion from larger pieces of tablet which are not adequately crushed may be decreased, however, by use of calcium carbonate suspension (500 mg Ca/5 mL) if this is available in the pharmacy. Administration of either the crushed and suspended tablets or the commercial suspension requires that the feeding tube be flushed with at least 30 mL of water before and after administration of medication.[164] A flush volume of 75 to 100 mL may be advisable, however, since suspensions often coat the tube and require a larger flush volume to be washed out of the tube. The need for calcium supplementation should be questioned since J.M.'s serum calcium concentration is within normal limits if corrected for his low albumin. Administration of any medication via the feeding tube presents a risk of tube occlusion. Administering an unneeded medication through the tube is an unnecessary risk.

Potassium is below normal today and has been decreasing since tube feeding began. Potassium supplementation should have been considered yesterday, rather than waiting until J.M. became hypokalemic, since a definite trend downward in serum potassium was evident. The selected potassium supplement is inappropriate for administration by tube because Micro-K is a slow-release product.[167] Crushing slow-release products destroys the slow-release mechanism. Potassium chloride powder for solution (15 mEq KCl/packet × 3 packets) or liquid (35 mL of 10% KCl, 25 mL of 15% KCl, or 15 to 20 mL of 20% KCl) should be ordered rather than the slow-release product. Dividing the potassium dose into two or three smaller doses and diluting each dose with 60 mL of water is recommended.[164] Given as a single dose, 45 to 50 mEq of potassium may cause nausea, vomiting, abdominal discomfort, and/or diarrhea. Development of these symptoms might be mistaken for intolerance to the enteral formula, resulting in the tube feeding being temporarily stopped. The larger fluid volume for administration also may help reduce the gastric irritation associated with potassium doses.

Consideration also should be given to changes occurring in other electrolytes. J.M. appears to be developing a mild refeeding syndrome. Magnesium and phosphate still are within normal range, but have decreased significantly over the past two days. Supplementation should be considered today. By starting supplementation before the electrolytes are critically low, smaller quantities of electrolytes will be needed. This may decrease the risk of diarrhea and GI upset from administration of magnesium and/or phosphate. Magnesium supplementation could be accomplished with a magnesium-oxide tablet (400 mg or 500 mg) administered two to four times daily. These are simple compressed tablets which can be crushed and suspended for administration via feeding tube. An alternative would be to use 5 mL of magnesium hydroxide suspension two to four times daily. The magnesium doses are distributed through the day to avoid the cathartic effect associated with magnesium. Phosphate supplementation could be accomplished by changing part of the potassium ordered to Neutra-Phos-K which provides 8.1 mmol phosphate and 14.2 mEq potassium per 250 mg tablet. Each tablet is designed to be dissolved in 75 mL of water for administration, so dissolution is not a concern. One Neutra-Phos-K twice a day plus KCl liquid to provide 20 mEq potassium would provide the same potassium dose as currently is ordered. The liquid KCl should be given at least two hours before or after the Neutra-Phos-K to limit GI effects. The feeding tube must be flushed adequately before and after each dose of electrolyte replacement. The flush volume before and after each dose should be a minimum of 30 mL, although 75 to 100 mL following the magnesium dose may be better to assure the electrolyte preparation is out of the tube.[164] Intermittent tube flushes can be accomplished with administration of medications to limit total fluid intake to the estimated requirement of 1770 to 2065 mL, or 445 to 815 mL in addition to that provided by a 1 kcal/mL formula.

With the current electrolyte abnormalities it is important to monitor potassium, magnesium, and phosphate for the next several days. The extent of electrolyte depletion in the body is difficult to evaluate, but one day of electrolyte replacement is not expected to replete intracellular stores of these electrolytes. It is difficult to provide large quantities of potassium, phosphate, and magnesium

via feeding tube secondary to GI intolerance. Therefore, intravenous electrolyte replacement may be necessary when intracellular depletion is extensive.

Transfer to a Nursing Facility

9. J.M. has been receiving tube feeding for 10 days. During this time he pulled his feeding tube twice despite mittens to hinder his ability to grab the tube. Feedings were off for about 5 hours each time the tube was pulled. J.M.'s electrolyte abnormalities have been corrected with 3 days of electrolyte replacement. He has tolerated his tube feeding without metabolic abnormalities or electrolyte replacement for the past 3 days. J.M. remains confused and disoriented. The prognosis for improvement in J.M.'s right-sided paralysis and, therefore, his ability to feed himself, is poor. Plans are being made to discharge J.M. in 3 to 4 days to a nursing facility. What changes in the care plan would be appropriate relative to nutritional support goals?

J.M. should be evaluated for surgical gastrostomy or percutaneous endoscopic gastrostomy (PEG) placement since he is expected to need tube feeding for a prolonged period. Gastrostomy placement also should solve the problem of repeated tube displacement in J.M., although this alone is not an appropriate reason to place a gastrostomy. Placement of a PEG can be accomplished with local anesthesia, which may be advantageous given J.M.'s age and lack of another reason for general anesthesia.[8,21] Cost also is an advantage of the PEG.[25-27] In general, cost of percutaneous endoscopic gastrostomy placement is about one-third to one-half the cost of a surgically placed gastrostomy. Rates for major complications of 0% to 9% and for minor complications of 0% to 24% have been reported for PEGs, but this is not significantly different than for surgical gastrostomies.[25-31]

If a fiber-free formula initially was selected, change to a fiber-containing formula should be evaluated. Fiber may be beneficial in preventing GI tract changes associated with prolonged use of low residue, fiber-free formulas.[40,52-55] Constipation frequently is a problem in elderly and bed-ridden patients.[180] Evaluation of fiber-supplemented versus fiber-free formula in patients receiving long-term tube feedings secondary to coma or inability to swallow demonstrated a reduction in laxative use with fiber, although fecal weight and stool frequency were not different.[57] A year long study demonstrated increased stool weight and frequency in patients with constipation who received fiber-containing formula versus fiber-free formula.[53] Starting with a low to moderate fiber content (5 to 7 gm/L) may help minimize gas and abdominal distention.[40,52] To reach the recommended fiber intake of 20 to 30 gm/day, however, a formula containing fiber at 13 or 14 gm/L will be necessary.[46] By using a combination of half J.M.'s current fiber-free formula and half a fiber-containing formula with 14 gm/L for a few days, then changing completely to the fiber-containing formula, the fiber content gradually could be increased. The fiber-free and fiber-containing formulas probably should not be mixed directly unless they are "without" and "with" fiber versions of the same product (e.g., Ensure and Ensure with fiber).

J.M. should be transitioned to an intermittent schedule before discharge. Many nursing facilities do not use enteral pumps routinely due to increased cost. Without a pump, delivery of the prescribed volume of formula at a consistent rate may not be reliable in this setting. Transitioning J.M. from 65 mL/hour continuous infusion to intermittent delivery of formula can be accomplished by various methods. Transition over approximately 48 hours can be accomplished by changing the infusion to 120 mL (one-half can of formula) every two hours for four feedings, then increasing to 240 mL (one can of formula) every four hours for three feedings, with each feeding infused over 60 minutes. The next step is to 360 mL (one and one-half cans of formula) every six hours, plus another 120 mL/day as one extra small feeding or added to one of the other feedings. If J.M. tolerates this feeding schedule, the time between feedings can be decreased further to allow three or four feedings during the 10 to 12 hours of the day when people normally take meals. Once J.M. is at the desired schedule for feedings, the infusion time for each feeding can be decreased from 60 to 30 minutes. Slower transitioning can be accomplished by extending each change in the infusion to 24 hours. With the slow method, however, J.M. will receive only 1440 mL/day for a couple days versus his goal volume of 1560 mL/day. Ideally, the transition will be completed before J.M. is discharged to the nursing facility.

The prescription for tube feeding upon discharge to the nursing facility should state clearly the desired caloric density (e.g., standard versus moderate versus calorically dense), protein content (e.g., low versus standard versus high nitrogen), fiber content (e.g., 5 to 7 gm/L versus 12 to 14 gm/L), and volume of the desired formula, or the daily calories, protein, fiber, and fluid to be provided by the formula. The brand name also may be included, but the nursing facility may not have the same brands of formula as the hospital uses. A ''generic'' formula prescription will help assure that J.M. receives the desired nutritional support. Any special considerations for the feeding schedule also should be transmitted to the nursing facility (e.g., if J.M. tolerates the extra 120 mL feeding better in the morning, or needs to have the head of the bed at 45° for at least three hours after the last daily feeding to avoid regurgitation).

Twice weekly monitoring of glucose, creatinine, and electrolytes should be recommended during the first week after discharge to the nursing facility. This may be accomplished best by ordering a chemistry panel containing the desired biochemical tests. Chemistry panels frequently are less expensive than multiple biochemical tests in the outpatient setting, but may require longer to obtain results. Careful monitoring of fluid status and tolerance to the intermittent delivery schedule also is recommended after discharge. J.M. will have been on the new schedule for only a short time before discharge, so a full evaluation of tolerance to the new regimen will not have been completed.

Evaluation of Nutritional Status

10. F.C., a 35-year-old female, was admitted to the hospital 75 days ago with necrotizing pancreatitis. Intubation has been required since shortly after admission when respiratory failure occurred. Parenteral nutrition was started the day after admission and has continued since. F.C.'s current parenteral nutrition formula is 17.5% dextrose, 5.7% amino acid, and 3.5% fat, final concentrations, at 70 mL/hr to provide 1590 nonprotein calories and 96 gm protein daily. During her hospitalization, F.C. has undergone 3 exploratory laparotomies and been treated for multiple infections, including pneumonia, sepsis, and wound infection. She also has been treated for *Clostridium difficile* diarrhea, but has not had diarrhea since therapy was completed 3 weeks ago. Lysis of adhesions, closure of an enterocutaneous fistula, and needle catheter feeding jejunostomy placement were done during the last laparotomy 2 weeks ago. Postoperative ileus prevented use of the jejunostomy until yesterday when water was started at 25 mL/hr following a dye study to confirm tube patency. Enteral feeding is to start today via the J tube. F.C. is 5′2″ and weighs 57 kg today, although her weight before surgery 2 weeks ago was 53 kg and her admission weight was 50 kg. Laboratory evaluation today shows the following: Na 133 mEq/L; Cl 97 mEq/L; glucose 198 mg/dL; BUN 30 mg/dL; creatinine 0.8 mg/dL; triglycerides 150 mg/dL; albumin 3.1 gm/dL; and prealbumin 9 mg/dL (Normal: 10–40) which was down from 12 mg/dL 4 days ago and 15 mg/dL a week ago. A urine collection ending last night shows a volume of 2500 mL/24-hr collection and a urine urea nitrogen (UUN) of 560 mg/dL. F.C. has been afebrile the past week, but remains on broad spectrum antibiotic coverage. Assess F.C.'s nutritional status and identify factors placing her at nutritional risk. [SI units: Na 133 mmol/L; Cl 97 mmol/L; glucose 10.99 mmol/L; BUN 10.71 mmol/L UREA; creatinine 61 μmol/L; triglycerides 1.694 mmol/L; albumin 31 gm/L]

F.C. is obviously at nutritional risk secondary to pancreatitis and multiple complications. Currently she appears to have a kwashiorkor-type malnutrition with her weight maintained at a relatively normal level, but visceral proteins decreased.[178] She is highly catabolic based upon large urinary nitrogen losses. This also is evident from the low prealbumin concentration despite 1.9 gm protein/kg IBW. Nutritional status should have been maintained with parenteral nutrition over the past several weeks, but it appears that visceral protein status has been declining during the past week.

F.C. is at increased risk of nutrient deficiencies because of her long-term hospitalization, antibiotic therapy, highly catabolic condition, and complications. Vitamin supplementation in parenteral nutrition generally is adequate for most patients, but highly catabolic patients such as F.C. may require increased vitamin C and perhaps thiamine.[193,196] Increased gastrointestinal losses of zinc occur with diarrhea and GI tract fistulas, both of which were problems for F.C. before the latest laparotomy.[196] It is assumed that excess losses of vitamins and trace elements that could be reasonably anticipated or measured have been managed appropriately in the parenteral nutrition formula. Thus, F.C. should not have overt deficiencies. Measurement of most vitamin and trace element concentrations is difficult in the clinical setting with metabolically unstable patients, and interpretation of values may be equally difficult. Therefore, objective measures of marginal vitamin deficiencies rarely are available. Clinical impressions must be relied upon. F.C. should receive 100% to 200% of the RDA for all vitamins and minerals.

Estimation of Nutritional Requirements

11. What are F.C.'s requirements for calories, protein, and fluid?

F.C.'s weight currently is above her ideal body weight of 50 kg by a few kg. Looking at the weight history, however, it appears that this extra weight most likely is water. F.C.'s admission weight is more reliable as an indicator of nutritional status than weights taken in the ICU. Certainly, in 75 days of hospitalization some change in actual weight could have occurred, but it would be very difficult to determine what is actual weight change versus fluid change. F.C.'s ideal body weight should be used for calculations.

The nutrition provided by parenteral nutrition gives some idea of F.C.'s requirements. Since the prealbumin has been declining despite a large protein load, the nitrogen (N) balance should be calculated to determine if current protein intake is less than protein losses. (N balance = daily N intake from all sources minus N output, including daily UUN and insensible losses.) Intake of nitrogen is calculated from grams of protein using the assumption that protein is 16% nitrogen (gm protein/6.25 = gm N). The UUN for nitrogen balance is based upon the total urine urea loss per 24 hours. The UUN reported by the lab is per 100 mL of urine; therefore, UUN loss per 24-hour urine volume must be calculated:

560 mg N/100 mL urine × 2500 mL urine/24 hr = 14,000 mg N/day

Insensible losses generally are estimated as 2 to 4 gm of nitrogen per day. Thus, the nitrogen balance for F.C. is calculated as follows:

$$N \text{ Balance} = \frac{96 \text{ gm protein from PN}}{6.25}$$

$$- (14 \text{ gm N from UUN} + 3 \text{ gm})$$

This indicates that F.C. is negative about 1.6 gm of nitrogen or 10 gm of protein. In addition, since F.C. has wounds to heal, a positive nitrogen balance of about 3 to 5 gm of nitrogen is desirable. Therefore, F.C. needs another 4.6 to 6.6 gm N/day or 29 to 41 gm protein/day above the 96 gm currently provided by parenteral nutrition.

F.C. currently is receiving 1590 nonprotein calories daily from parenteral nutrition or about 31.8 nonprotein kcal/kg. Calories have a protein-sparing effect up to a certain point. Therefore, increased calories may be beneficial for F.C.'s negative nitrogen balance if she cannot tolerate the necessary increase in protein. With F.C.'s highly catabolic state, however, maintaining the current nonprotein calorie-to-nitrogen ratio of approximately 100:1 or slightly less (e.g., down to 75:1) is advisable if F.C. can tolerate the extra protein. Indirect calorimetry (metabolic cart) measurement should be done if possible. Estimating caloric requirements in a patient such as F.C. is subject to greater error than in a patient with low metabolic stress. If a metabolic cart is not available, the total caloric intake (including protein) from parenteral nutrition plus calories from another 30 gm of protein should be calculated as a guideline for F.C.'s caloric requirement:

1590 nonprotein kcal from PN + (96 gm protein from PN

+ 30 gm for protein for positive N Balance) × 4 kcal/gm

= 2094 total kcal

Fluid requirements can be estimated at 30 to 35 mL/kg body weight/day plus replacement of excess losses from hyperthermia, vomiting, or diarrhea. Based upon this method, F.C.'s fluid requirements are 1500 to 1750 mL/day. Estimated fluid needs also may be based upon 1 mL/kcal ingested, which is more appropriate for F.C. due to her high protein requirement.[191]

Enteral Nutrition by Tube

12. Enteral feeding is to start today via the J tube. What type of enteral formula is most appropriate for F.C.?

F.C. is expected to have poor absorptive function due to her prolonged period without GI tract stimulation. Reduced digestive function also is expected secondary to severe pancreatitis. F.C. should be assumed to have lactose intolerance at this time.[37] Fat malabsorption also is likely secondary to the severe pancreatitis F.C. has experienced. An oligomeric formula is recommended for initiation of tube feeding in F.C. The selection of an elemental versus peptide-based formula should be based upon appropriate calorie, protein, and fat content since neither type of formula obviously is superior based upon available studies. If a peptide-based formula is selected, it should have a protein profile that limits pancreatic stimulation (e.g., a high di- and tripeptide percentage). To obtain the necessary nonprotein calorie-to-nitrogen ratio, a formula classified for stress or critical care may need to be selected. These formulas frequently contain arginine, glutamine, nucleic acids, and/or a modified fat component to separate them from other high nitrogen formulas. Well-designed studies of these components in critically ill patients are difficult to find since they are a relatively new development in nutritional support. Thus, a formula should be selected on the basis of appropriate calorie, protein, and fat content, and not primarily on inclusion or exclusion of these components. Exclusion of fiber may be important, however, since fiber may increase the viscosity of formula and make administration via needle catheter J tube difficult. A specialized, high BCAA stress

formula also could be considered for F.C. Results with these formulas are conflicting, however, and cost generally is high.[90,91] Improvement in morbidity, mortality, and length of hospital stay have not been evaluated for the BCAA stress formulas.[94]

Based upon formulas available on the formulary, an elemental formula providing 1 kcal/mL and protein at 45 gm/L is selected. The formula has an osmolality of about 650 mOsm/kg and contains 83% free water per the manufacturer. The goal volume of formula is 2160 mL to provide 2160 kcal, 97 gm protein, and 1793 mL fluid. The remaining fluid requirement will be met by three to four tube flushes daily and by IV antibiotics F.C. still is receiving.

This formula was selected over other high nitrogen formulas because of the very low fat content (6% of calories or 2 gm/L). The selected formula does not meet F.C.'s high protein requirement, so the formula will need to be changed to a higher protein formula at some point in the transition process or a modular protein component will need to be added to the current formula. If F.C. remains as catabolic as she is currently, 30 gm of modular protein will need to be added to the current formula. Whether the formula is changed or protein is added will depend upon F.C.'s response to enteral feeding at the time of decision. The primary issue at that time will be whether F.C. can tolerate an increase in fat or addition of intact protein.

Enteral Nutrition Administration

13. Recommend a plan for initiating and advancing F.C.'s tube feeding.

Tube feeding should be initiated slowly in F.C. since she has been without enteral intake for a prolonged period and is expected to have both impaired absorption and digestion. Formula should be provided via pump or rate controller to maintain a consistent flow rate. A pump generally is required for formula administration via needle catheter jejunostomy to obtain adequate flow. In addition to providing pressure for flow, the pump has alarms to alert nurses to a stop in flow. With these small tubes, a stop in flow can lead to occlusion, and surgery usually is required for replacement of the tube.

The protein provided by parenteral nutrition should be increased to provide adequate protein for a 3 to 5 gm positive nitrogen balance since transition to tube feeding is expected to be very slow. Considering the length of time F.C. has been on parenteral nutrition already, transitioning to enteral feeding over a couple of weeks would be acceptable. The selected formula is hypertonic; therefore, dilution of the formula to half strength ($\approx$325 mOsm/kg) should be considered. Although studies have suggested that dilution of chemically defined and elemental formulas is not required with intragastric or duodenal feeding, the studies did not include critically ill patients.[147–149] Also, the jejunum may not adapt as easily to concentration and/or volume changes as the duodenum.

Enteral feeding via J tube should be started at 25 mL/hour × 24 hours (day one) with half-strength formula. The rate should then be increased to 50 mL/hour on day two, 75 mL/hour on day three, and finally to the goal rate of 90 mL/hour on day four. Once the tube feeding is at goal rate, the strength can be increased to three-quarter strength for 24 to 48 hours, then to full strength. Each of these changes in formula strength represents an increase of 22.5 kcal/mL, which is at the lower end of the suggested increase of 0.2 to 0.5 kcal/mL/day.[8] Of course, this transition schedule assumes tolerance to the formula with each step.

A plan also must be developed to taper the parenteral nutrition off as tube feeding increases. Assume that F.C. has been changed to a parenteral nutrition formula of 14% dextrose, 6.5% amino acid, and 3% fat, final concentrations, at 85 mL/hour to provide

1583 nonprotein kcal/day (same as previous formula) or 2115 total kcal/day and 133 gm protein/day. When transitioning from parenteral nutrition to tube feeding, an attempt should be made to keep the total protein from both sources at about 125 to 137 gm since this quantity would meet F.C.'s protein requirement based upon nitrogen balance. The caloric intake may be higher than the current intake using this approach. If hyperglycemia becomes a problem, it may be necessary to give slightly less protein and keep the total caloric intake closer to that provided by parenteral nutrition and/or cover the hyperglycemia with insulin. Remember that the selected enteral formula contains a high percentage of carbohydrate calories since only 6% is from fat.

The parenteral nutrition rate should not be changed until tolerance to a given tube-feeding rate and strength has been established. That is, the parenteral nutrition rate adjustment reflects the previous enteral rate, not the increase made today. Half-strength tube feeding contains only 22.5 gm protein/L versus 65 gm/L in parenteral nutrition; therefore, each 25 mL/hour increase in tube feeding should result in a 10 mL/hour drop in the parenteral nutrition rate. On day 2 when the tube feeding is increased to 50 mL/hour of half-strength formula, the parenteral nutrition rate can be decreased to 75 mL/hour. Parenteral nutrition will be decreased to 65 mL/hour on day 3, 55 mL/hour on day 4, and 45 mL/hour on day 5. At this point the tube feeding has been at goal rate for 24 hours, and the strength of formula should increase. The following calculation demonstrates the total nutrient intake before increasing the tube-feeding (TF) strength:

$$PN \text{ at } 45 \text{ mL/hr} = 1119 \text{ total kcal} + 70 \text{ gm protein}$$
$$\underline{\text{Half-strength TF at } 90 \text{ mL/hr} = 1080 \text{ total kcal} + 49 \text{ gm protein}}$$
$$\text{Total intake (PN + TF)} = 2199 \text{ total kcal} + 119 \text{ gm protein}$$

Increasing the tube feeding to three-quarter strength increases protein by about 24 gm/day, so the parenteral nutrition rate could be decreased to 35 mL/hour after the increased strength was tolerated for 24 hours. The next step should be to stop parenteral nutrition. The current formula does not meet F.C.'s protein requirements; therefore, the parenteral nutrition could be continued at 35 mL/hour for a few days after the tube feeding is full strength at goal rate. This would allow time to document tolerance to addition of a modular protein component in the current formula or change to a higher protein formula which also would be higher in fat.

Advancement of the tube feeding rate should be held if F.C. demonstrates signs of intolerance. A rate increase can then be attempted in 24 to 48 hours if tolerance improves. F.C. is being fed into the jejunum, so residual volume will not be checked. Intolerance will be judged primarily on abdominal distention and pattern of stool output (e.g., small mucous stools as expected, no stools indicating possible ileus or obstruction, or diarrhea). Pain or cramping, if F.C. can indicate them, also can be used to judge tolerance.

Tube Feeding Intolerance

14. F.C. develops diarrhea about 18 hours after the tube feeding is increased from one-half to three-quarter strength. The parenteral nutrition is at 45 mL/hr. What is the likely cause of the diarrhea? Should the tube feeding be stopped and the parenteral nutrition increased to goal rate again?

Diarrhea in tube-fed patients is a multifactorial problem with many potential tube feeding and nontube feeding associated causes.[143,158,159] Tube feeding-related causes of diarrhea include high fat content, lactose content, and bacterial contamination. Formula temperature, caloric density, osmolality, formula strength,

lack of fiber content, and method of delivery also have been associated with diarrhea, although a cause-effect relationship for these factors is much less clear. Factors associated with diarrhea, but not related to the tube feeding include concurrent medications, especially sorbitol-containing products and antibiotics, partial small bowel obstruction or fecal impaction, bile salt malabsorption, intestinal atrophy, hypoalbuminemia, infections, and underlying conditions such as AIDS, Crohn's disease, ulcerative colitis, celiac sprue, or pancreatitis.[158,159]

F.C.'s diarrhea may be related to the change in formula strength. The jejunum adapts to concentration changes with more difficulty than to rate changes, and formula strength was increased less than 24 hours before diarrhea started.[150] Changing the formula back to half strength at 90 mL/hour should decrease stooling within 24 hours, if the strength change was responsible. If F.C. does not respond to the decrease in formula strength, the formula may be held for 24 hours to see if diarrhea decreases or stops. Diarrhea directly related to enteral formula usually is an osmotic diarrhea which stops within 24 hours of stopping the formula.[158] The parenteral nutrition rate should be increased to 85 mL/hour (goal rate) if tube feeding is stopped for more than a couple days. A more objective approach than stopping the formula would be the measurement of stool osmolality. Enteral formula induced diarrhea is associated with a large osmotic gap, while secretory diarrhea (e.g., infectious diarrhea) is associated with a low or negative osmotic gap.[158]

Potential causes of F.C.'s diarrhea other than the change in formula strength should be evaluated before stopping enteral feedings. The current formula is lactose-free and has a very low fat content, so these factors are not an issue in F.C. Preparation of the formula from a packaged powder could lead to bacterial contamination from equipment used in mixing, improper mixing technique, and/or water used for mixing. Sterile water has been suggested as the most appropriate fluid for mixing or diluting formulas.[159] The period of time the formula is in the delivery bag and methods of cleaning the delivery bag also may contribute to bacterial contamination of formula.

Medications appear to be a major contributor to diarrhea in tube-fed patients. Study results associating antibiotic therapy with diarrhea have been questioned, however, due to failure to report stool frequency and consistency, and lack of a clear definition for diarrhea in studies.[159] Treatment of antibiotic-associated diarrhea may include administration of *Lactobacillus acidophilus* preparations via the feeding tube to restore normal GI flora, changing antibiotics or stopping therapy when appropriate to do so, or administering antidiarrheal agents. When *C. difficile* is found in the stool, treatment with oral vancomycin, bacitracin, or metronidazole is indicated. Antidiarrheal agents which decrease motility should not be used when *C. difficile* is present, but adsorbents such as Kaolin-Pectin or pectin-type fibers (e.g., apple flakes or banana flakes) may be beneficial. F.C. currently is on antibiotics and has been for some time. She already has been treated for *C. difficile* once. The current diarrhea may be *C. difficile*; therefore, a stool specimen should be sent for culture and/or *C. difficile* toxin. Other medications which have been associated with diarrhea include: sorbitol-containing products, magnesium-containing antacids, oral magnesium electrolyte replacement, potassium chloride, phosphate supplements, quinidine, digitalis, aminophylline, propranolol, and H_2-receptor antagonists.[158,159] Liquid forms of medications used for administration by tube also may contribute to diarrhea because of their high osmolality.[174]

Malnutrition and hypoalbuminemia may contribute to diarrhea in tube-fed patients. F.C. is hypoalbuminemic and expected to have atrophy of the GI tract secondary to prolonged parenteral nutrition support; however, diarrhea would have been expected within 24 to 48 hours of starting feedings if this were the primary cause of F.C.'s diarrhea. F.C.'s diarrhea developed after several days on tube feeding. Continued use of the GI tract is encouraged when malabsorption and/or hypoalbuminemia are the primary cause of diarrhea in tube-fed patients.

Pancreatitis may result in diarrhea secondary to malabsorption. F.C. currently is on an elemental formula, so reduced digestive and absorptive function is needed for utilization of the formula. Some pancreatic function still is required, however, for the carbohydrates and fats. Only 6% of calories in the formula are from fats, so fat malabsorption is unlikely to account for F.C.'s diarrhea.

F.C.'s GI tract should continue to be used to the extent possible. Enteral nutrition reduces bacterial translocation, a process of enteric bacteria and/or endotoxin crossing the GI mucosa into mesenteric lymph nodes and portal circulation.[197] Bacterial translocation may increase the risk of sepsis in patients not receiving enteral stimulation of the GI tract. In addition, the GI tract serves an immune function, especially with respect to IgA secretion.[198] Respiratory tract infections (e.g., pneumonia) may increase without proper stimulation of the GI tract due to less effective protection from IgA. Compared to parenteral nutrition, enteral nutrition decreases catabolic hormone secretion in burned animals and attenuates catabolism in humans following traumatic burn.[199,200] Attenuation of catabolism also is thought to occur in other highly stressed patients, although initiation of feedings soon after the stressing event may be required to obtain this type of response. The possible benefits of improved fluid and electrolyte balance with stopping enteral nutrition due to diarrhea should be weighed against the potential benefits of reduced infections from continued use of the GI tract before a decision is made to stop enteral feedings.

Medication Administration via Feeding Tube

15. F.C. is determined to have *C. difficile* in her stool again. The tube feedings are held at 90 mL/hr with half-strength formula and the parenteral nutrition at 45 mL/hr. Kaolin-Pectin has been ordered for administration via tube feeding. Is this an appropriate order?

It generally is better to administer medication separate from the enteral formula. Interactions are more likely to occur if the medication is admixed with the formula. Many hospitals do allow addition of Kaolin-Pectin directly into the enteral formula, however, this is not advised for administration via needle catheter J tube. To the extent possible, medications should be given by a route other than the feeding tube because of the extremely small size of the tube lumen. Occlusion of the feeding tube would be more detrimental to the overall plan of transitioning F.C. to tube feedings than stopping the tube feeding for two or three days until treatment of *C. difficile* resolves the diarrhea.

References

1 **A.S.P.E.N. Board of Directors.** Guidelines for the use of parenteral and enteral nutrition in adult and pediatric patients. JPEN. 1993;17(Suppl. 4):1SA.

2 **Foltz MB et al.** Nutrition screening and assessment: current practices and dietitian's leadership role. J Am Diet Assoc. 1993;93(12):1388.

3 **Sayarath VG.** Nutrition screening for malnutrition: potential economic impact at a community hospital. J Am Diet Assoc. 1993;93(12):1440.

4 **Cashman MD.** Principles of digestive physiology for clinical nutrition. Nutr Clin Pract. 1986;1(5):241.

5 **Ghahremani GG et al.** Iatrogenic intubation injuries of the upper gastrointestinal tract in adults. Gastrointest Radiol. 1980;5:1.

6 **Iyer V, Reichel J.** Perforation of the oesophagus by a fine bore feeding tube. N Y State J Med. 1981;3:64.

7 **Keohane PP et al.** Limitations and drawbacks of fine-bore feeding tubes. Clin Nutr. 1983;2:85.

8 **Page CP et al.** Techniques in delivery of liquid diets: short-term and long-term. In: Deitel M, ed. Nutrition in Clinical Surgery. 2nd ed. Baltimore: Williams and Wilkins; 1985:60.

9 **Harris M, Huseby J.** New feeding tube insertion technique prevents inadvertent placement in the lung. Am Rev Respir Dis. 1988;137:216. Abstract.

10 **Valentine RJ, Turner WW.** Pleural complications of nasoenteric feeding tubes. JPEN. 1985;9:605.

11 **Lipman TO et al.** Nasopulmonary intubation with feeding tubes: case reports and review of the literature. JPEN. 1985;9:618.

12 **Eldar S, Mequid MM.** Pneumothorax following attempted nasogastric intubation for nutritional support. JPEN. 1984;8:450.

13 **Torrington K, Bowman M.** Fatal hydrothorax empyema complicating a malpositioned nasogastric tube. Chest. 1981;79:240.

14 **Harvey P et al.** Accidental intrapulmonary clinifeed. Anesthesia. 1981;35:518.

15 **McWey RE et al.** Complications of nasoenteric feeding tubes. Am J Surg. 1988;155:253.

16 **Scholten DJ et al.** Pneumothorax from nasoenteric feeding tube insertion. A report of five cases. Am Surg. 1986;52:381.

17 **Bohnker BK et al.** Narrow bore nasogastric feeding tube complications. Nutr Clin Pract. 1987;2:203.

18 **Rolandelli RH et al.** Critical illness and sepsis. In: Rombeau JL, Caldwell MD, eds. Clinical Nutrition. Enteral and Tube Feeding. 2nd ed. Philadelphia: WB Saunders; 1990:288.

19 **Lehmann S.** Parenteral and enteral access devices. In: Teasley-Strausburg KM et al., eds. Nutrition Support Handbook. A Compendium of Products with Guidelines for Usage. Cincinnati: Harvey Whitney Books; 1992:205.

20 **Rombeau JL, Palacio JC.** Feeding by tube enterostomy. In: Rombeau JL, Caldwell MD, eds. Clinical Nutrition. Enteral and Tube Feeding. 2nd ed. Philadelphia: WB Saunders; 1990:230.

21 **Monturo CA.** Enteral access device selection. Nutr Clin Pract. 1990;5:207.

22 **Page CP.** Needle catheter jejunostomy. Contemp Surg. 1981;19:29.

23 **Miller RE et al.** Percutaneous endoscopic gastrostomy: procedure of choice. Ann Surg. 1986;204:543.

24 **Kirby DF et al.** Percutaneous endoscopic gastrostomies: a prospective evaluation and review of the literature. JPEN. 1986;10:155.

25 **Cass OW et al.** A long-term follow-up of patients with percutaneous endoscopic gastrostomy or surgical (Stamm) gastrostomy. Gastrointest Endosc. 1986;32:147.

26 **Tanker MS et al.** A prospective randomized study comparing surgical gastrostomy and percutaneous endoscopic gastrostomy. Gastrointest Endosc. 1986;32:144.

27 **Stiegmann G et al.** Operative versus endoscopic gastrostomy: preliminary results of a prospective randomized trial. Am J Surg. 1988;155:88.

28 **Shellito PC, Malt RA.** Tube gastrostomy: techniques and complications. Ann Surg. 1985;201:180.

29 **Wasiljew BK et al.** Feeding gastrostomy: complications and mortality. Am J Surg. 1982;143:194.

30 **Stellato TA et al.** Percutaneous endoscopic gastrostomy following previous abdominal surgery. Ann Surg. 1984;200:46.

31 **Ponsky JL et al.** Percutaneous approaches to enteral alimentation. Am J Surg. 1985;149:102.

32 **Curet-Scot M, Shermeta DW.** A comparison of intragastric and intrajejunal feedings in neonatal piglets. J Pediatr Surg. 1986;21:552.

33 **Curet-Scot M et al.** Transduodenal feedings: a superior route of enteral nutrition. J Pediatr Surg. 1987;22:516.

34 **Ryan JA, Page CP.** Intrajejunal feeding: development and current status. JPEN. 1984;8:187.

35 **Methany N et al.** Monitoring patients with nasally placed feeding tubes. Heart Lung. 1985;14:285.

36 **Strong RM et al.** Equal aspiration rates from postpylorus and intragastric placed small-bore nasoenteric feeding tubes: a randomized, prospective study. JPEN. 1992;16:59.

37 **Sheehy TW, Anderson PR.** Disaccharidase activity in normal and diseased small bowel. Lancet. 1965;2(7401):1.

38 **Graham DY et al.** The effect of bran on bowel function in constipation. Am J Gastroenterol. 1982;77:599.

39 **Harold MR et al.** Effect of dietary fiber in insulin-dependent diabetics: insulin requirements and serum lipids. J Am Diet Assoc. 1985;85:1455.

40 **Heymsfield SB et al.** Fiber supplementation of enteral formulas: effects on the bioavailability of major nutrients and gastrointestinal tolerance. JPEN. 1988;12:265.

41 **Kirby RW et al.** Oat-bran intake selectively lowers serum low-density lipoprotein cholesterol concentrations of hypercholesterolemic men. Am J Clin Nutr. 1981;34:824.

42 **Raimundo AH et al.** The effect of fiber-free enteral diets and the addition of soy polysaccharide on human bowel function and short-chain fatty acid (SCFA) production. JPEN. 1992;16:29S.

43 **Schneeman BO.** Dietary fiber and gastrointestinal function. Nutr Rev. 1987;45(5):129.

44 **Silk DBA.** Progress report: fibre and enteral nutrition. Gut. 1989;30:246.

45 **Zimmaro DM et al.** Isotonic tube feeding formula induces liquid stools in normal subjects: reversal by pectin. JPEN. 1989;13:117.

46 **Cronin FJ, Shaw AM.** Summary of dietary recommendations for healthy Americans. Nutr Today. 1988;Nov/Dec:26.

47 **Jones BJM et al.** Comparison of an elemental and polymeric enteral diet in patients with normal gastrointestinal function. Gut. 1984;25:942.

48 **Slavin J.** Commercially available enteral formulas with fiber and bowel function measures. Nutr Clin Pract. 1990;5:247.

49 **Fredstrom SB et al.** Determination of the fiber content of enteral feedings. JPEN. 1991;15:450.

50 **Shorey RL et al.** Effects of soybean polysaccharide on plasma lipids. J Am Diet Assoc. 1985;85:1461.

51 **Lo GS et al.** Soy fiber improves lipid and carbohydrate metabolism in primary hyperlipidemic subjects. Atherosclerosis. 1986;622:239.

52 **Slavin JL et al.** Bowel function of healthy men consuming liquid diets with and without dietary fiber. JPEN. 1985;9:317.

53 **Liebl BH et al.** Dietary fiber and long-term large bowel response in enterally nourished nonambulatory profoundly retarded youth. JPEN. 1990;14:371.

54 **Tsai AC et al.** Effects of soy polysaccharide on gastrointestinal functions, nutrient balance, steroid excretions, glucose tolerance, serum lipids and other parameters in humans. Am J Clin Nutr. 1983;38:504.

55 **Shinnick FL et al.** Apparent nutrient absorption and upper gastrointestinal transit with fiber-containing enteral feedings. Am J Clin Nutr. 1989;49:471.

56 **Fisher M et al.** The effect of dietary fibre in a liquid diet on bowel function of mentally retarded individuals. J Ment Defic Res. 1985;29:373.

57 **Shankardass K et al.** Bowel function of long-term tube-fed patients consuming formulae with and without dietary fiber. JPEN. 1990;14:508.

58 **Heimbach DM et al.** The gastrointestinal tolerance of a fibre-supplemented tube feeding formula in burn patients. In: The Clinical Role of Fibre. Toronto: Medical Education Services; 1985:67.

59 **Frankenfield DC, Beyer PL.** Soy-polysaccharide fiber: effect on diarrhea in tube-fed, head injured patients. Am J Clin Nutr. 1989;50:533.

60 **Dobb GJ, Towler SC.** Diarrhea during enteral feeding in the critically ill: a comparison of feeds with and without fibre. Intensive Care Med. 1990;16:252.

61 **Hart GK, Dobb GJ.** Effect of a fecal bulking agent on diarrhea during enteral feeding in the critically ill. JPEN. 1988;12:465.

62 **Camuet B et al.** Fibre, diabetes and risk of bezoar. Lancet. 1980;2:862.

63 **Bowen PE et al.** Mineral absorption using fiber-augmented liquid formula diets. JPEN. 1982;6:575.

64 **Taper LJ et al.** Mineral retention in young men consuming soy-fiber-augmented liquid-formula diets. Am J Clin Nutr. 1988;48:305.

65 **Hunt JN, Stubbs DF.** The volume and energy content of meals as determinants of gastric emptying. J Physiol. 1975;245:209.

66 **Koretz RL, Meyer JH.** Elemental diets—facts and fantasies. Gastroenterology. 1980;78:393.

67 **Silk DBA.** Diet formulation and choice of enteral diet. Gut. 1986;27(Suppl. 1):40.

68 **Brinson R et al.** A reappraisal of the peptide-based enteral formulas: clinical applications. Nutr Clin Pract. 1989;4:211.

69 **Zaloga GP.** Physiologic effects of peptide-based enteral formulas. Nutr Clin Pract. 1990;5:231.

70 **Silk DBA et al.** Use of a peptide rather than a free amino acid nitrogen source in chemically defined "elemental" diets. JPEN. 1980;4:548.

71 **Meredith J et al.** Visceral protein levels in trauma patients are greater with peptide diet than with intact protein diet. J Trauma. 1980;30:825.

72 **Eimburger DC.** Peptides in clinical perspective. Nutr Clin Pract. 1990;5:225.

73 **Mowatt-Larsson CA et al.** Comparison of tolerance and nutritional outcome between a peptide and a standard enteral formula in critically-ill, hypoalbuminemic patients. JPEN. 1992;16:20.

74 **Velasco N et al.** Whole-body protein kinetics in elective surgical patients receiving peptide or amino acid solutions. Nutrition. 1991;7:28.

75 **Alexander JW et al.** The importance of lipid type in the diet after burn injury. Ann Surg. 1986;204:1.

76 **Adams S et al.** Changes in plasma erythrocyte fatty acids in patients fed enteral formulas containing different fats. JPEN. 1993;17:30.

77 **Gottschlich M et al.** Effect of a diet enriched with w-3 fatty acids on platelet lipids, platelet aggregation and transfusion requirements. JPEN. 1992;16:285.

78 **Mirtallo JM et al.** Nutritional support of patients with renal disease. Clin Pharm. 1984;3:253.

79 **Talbot JM.** Guidelines for the scientific review of enteral food products for special medical purposes. JPEN. 1991;15(Suppl.):99S.

80 **Latifi R et al.** Nutritional support in liver disease. Surg Clin North Am. 1991;3:253.

81 **Mattox TW, Brown RO.** Use of modified amino acid formulas in the enteral nutrition support of patients with portosystemic encephalopathy: a review. Nutrition. 1988;4:7.

82 **Cerra FB et al.** Disease-specific amino acid infusion (FO80) in hepatic encephalopathy: a prospective, randomized, double-blind, controlled trial. JPEN. 1985;9:288.

83 **Naylor CD et al.** Parenteral nutrition with branched-chain amino acids in hepatic encephalopathy. A meta-analysis. Gastroenterology. 1989;4:1033.

84 **Eriksson LS et al.** Branched-chain amino acids in the treatment of chronic hepatic encephalopathy. Gut. 1982;23:801.

85 **McGhee A et al.** Comparison of the effects of Hepatic-Aid and a casein modular diet on encephalopathy, plasma amino acids, and nitrogen balance in cirrhotic patients. Ann Surg. 1983;197:288.

86 **Eriksson LS, Conn HO.** Branched-chain amino acids in the management of hepatic encephalopathy: an analysis of variants. Hepatology. 1989;10:228.

87 **Cerra FB et al.** A failure of exogenous nutritional support. Ann Surg. 1980;192:570.

88 **Cynober L.** Amino acid metabolism in thermal burns. JPEN. 1989;13:196.

89 **Tweedle DE.** Metabolism of amino acids after trauma. JPEN. 1980;4:165.

90 **Teasley KM, Buss RB.** Do parenteral nutrition solutions with high concentrations of branched-chain amino acids offer significant benefits to stressed patients? DICP Ann Pharmacother. 1989;23:411.

91 **Oki JC, Cuddy PG.** Branched-chain amino acid support of stressed patients. DICP Ann Pharmacother. 1989;23:399.

92 **Cerra FB et al.** Nitrogen retention in critically ill patients is proportional to the branched chain amino acid load. Crit Care Med. 1983;11:775.

93 **Yu YM et al.** A kinetic study of leucine metabolism in severely burned patients: comparison between a conventional and branched-chain amino acid-enriched nutritional therapy. Ann Surg. 1988;207:421.

94 **Brennan MF et al.** Report of a research workshop: branched-chain amino acids in stress and injury. JPEN. 1986;10:446.

95 **Paxton J, Williamson J.** Nutrient substrates: making choices in the 1990s. J Burn Care Rehabil. 1991;12:198.

96 **Barbul A et al.** Arginine enhances wound healing and lymphocyte immune responses in humans. Surgery. 1990;108:331.

97 **Barbul A et al.** Arginine stimulates lymphocyte immune response in healthy human beings. Surgery. 1981;90:244.

98 **Daly JM et al.** Immune and metabolic effects of arginine in the surgical patient. Ann Surg. 1988;508:512.

99 **Lieberman MD et al.** Effects of nutrient substrates on immune function. Nutrition. 1990;6:88.

100 **Daly JM et al.** Enteral nutrition with supplemental arginine, RNA and omega-3 fatty acids in patients after operation: immunologic, metabolic and clinical outcome. Surgery. 1992;112:56.

101 **Sigal RK et al.** Parenteral arginine infusion in humans: nutrient substrate or pharmacologic agent? JPEN. 1992;16:423.

102 **Reynolds JV et al.** Arginine as an immunomodulator. Surg Forum. 1987;38:415.

103 **Rudolph FB.** Role of RNA as a dietary source of pyrimidines and purines in immune function. Nutrition. 1990;6(Suppl. 1):24.

104 **Kulkarni AD et al.** Effect of dietary nucleotides on response to bacterial infections. JPEN. 1986;10:169.

105 **Van Buren CT et al.** The influence of dietary nucleotides on cell-mediated immunity. Transplantation. 1983;36:350.

106 **Souba WW et al.** Glutamine metabolism by the intestinal tract. JPEN. 1985;9:608.

107 **Hwang TL et al.** Preservation of small bowel mucosa using glutamine-enriched parenteral nutrition. Surg Forum. 1986;37:56.

108 **O'Dwyer ST et al.** Maintenance of small bowel mucosa with glutamine enriched parenteral nutrition. JPEN. 1989;13:579.

109 **Fox AD et al.** Effect of glutamine-supplemented enteral diet on methotrexate-induced enterocolitis. JPEN. 1988;12:325.

110 **Salloum RM et al.** Glutamine is superior to glutamate in supporting gut metabolism, stimulating intestinal glutaminase activity, and preventing bacterial translocation. Surg Forum. 1989;40:6.

111 **Klimberg VS et al.** Oral glutamine accelerates healing of small intestine and improves outcome after whole abdominal radiation. Arch Surg. 1990;125:1040.

112 **Helton WS et al.** Glutamine prevents pancreatic atrophy and fatty liver during elemental feeding. J Surg Res. 1990;48:297.

113 **Hammarqvsit F et al.** Addition of glutamine to total parenteral nutrition after elective abdominal surgery spares free glutamine in muscle, counteracts the fall in muscle protein synthesis and improves nitrogen balance. Ann Surg. 1989;209:455.

114 **Stehle P et al.** Effect of parenteral glutamine peptide supplements on muscle glutamine loss and nitrogen balance after major surgery. Lancet. 1989;1:231.

115 **Ziegler TR et al.** Clinical and metabolic efficacy of glutamine-supplemented parenteral nutrition after bone marrow transplantation. Ann Intern Med. 1992;116:821.

116 **Swails WS et al.** Glutamine content of whole proteins: implications for enteral formulas. Nutr Clin Pract. 1992;7:77.

117 **Kinsella JE et al.** Dietary polyunsaturated fatty acids and eicosanoids: potential effects on the modulation of inflammatory and immune cells. Nutrition. 1990;6(Suppl. 1):24.

118 **Kinsella JE, Lokesh B.** Dietary lipids, eicosanoids and the immune system. Crit Care Med. 1990;18(Suppl.):S94.

119 **Murray MJ et al.** Effects of fish oil diet on pigs: cardiopulmonary response to bacteremia. JPEN. 1991;15:152.

120 **Pomposelli JJ et al.** Short-term TPN containing n-3 fatty acids ameliorate lactic acidosis induced by endotoxin in guinea pigs. Am J Clin Nutr. 1990;52:548.

121 **Peck MD et al.** Composition of fat in enteral diets can influence outcome in experimental peritonitis. Ann Surg. 1991;214:74.

122 **Alexander JW, Gottschlich MM.** Nutritional immunomodulation in burn patients. Crit Care Med. 1990;18(Suppl.):S149.

123 **Borum P.** Carnitine. Annu Rev Nutr. 1983;3:233.

124 **Rudman D, Feller A.** Evidence for deficiencies of conditionally essential nutrients during total parenteral nutrition. J Am Coll Nutr. 1986;5:101.

125 **Testasecca D.** Effects of carnitine administration to multiple injury patients receiving total parenteral nutrition. Int J Clin Pharmacol Ther Toxicol. 1987;25:56.

126 **Bohles H et al.** Improved N-retention during L-carnitine-supplemented total parenteral nutrition. JPEN. 1984;8:9.

127 **Chesney RW.** Taurine: its biological role and clinical implications. Adv Pediatr. 1985;32:1.

128 **Darling PB et al.** Effect of taurine supplements on fat absorption in cystic fibrosis. Pediatr Res. 1985;19:578.

129 **Belli DC et al.** Taurine improves the absorption of a fat meal in patients with cystic fibrosis. Pediatrics. 1987;80:517.

130 **Askanazi J et al.** Influence of total parenteral nutrition on fuel utilization in injury and sepsis. Ann Surg. 1980;191:40.

131 **Askanazi J et al.** Nutrition for the patient with respiratory failure: glucose vs. fat. Anesthesiology. 1981;54:373.

132 **Covelli HD et al.** Respiratory failure precipitated by high carbohydrate loads. Ann Intern Med. 1981;95:579.

133 **Barlett RH et al.** Metabolic studies in chest trauma. J Thorac Cardiovasc Surg. 1984;87:503.

134 **Angelillo VA et al.** Effects of low and high carbohydrate feedings in ambulatory patients with chronic obstructive pulmonary disease and chronic hypercapnia. Ann Intern Med. 1985;103:883.

135 **Al-Saady N et al.** High fat, low carbohydrate enteral feeding reduces $PaCO_2$ and the period of ventilation in ventilated patients. Chest. 1989;94 (Suppl.):49S.

136 **Crapo PA et al.** Comparison of the metabolic response to fructose and sucrose sweetened foods. Am J Clin Nutr. 1982;36:256.

137 **Peters AL et al.** Lack of glucose elevation after simulated tube feeding with a low-carbohydrate, high-fat enteral formula in patients with Type I diabetes. Am J Med. 1989;87:178.

138 **Martin D, Jastram CW.** Enteral nutrition. Part II. Nutr Supp Serv. 1987;7:8.

139 **Orr G et al.** Alternatives to total parenteral nutrition in the critically ill patient. Crit Care Med. 1980;8:29.

140 **Hiebert JM et al.** Comparison of continuous vs. intermittent tube feedings in adult burn patients. JPEN. 1981;5:73.

141 **Kocan MJ, Hickisch SM.** A comparison of continuous and intermittent enteral nutrition in NICU patients. J Neurosci Nurs. 1986;18:333.

142 **Ryan JA et al.** Early postoperative jejunal feeding of elemental diet in gastrointestinal surgery. Am Surg. 1981;47:393.

143 **Konstantinides NN, Shronts E.** Tube feeding. Managing the basics. Am J Nurs. 1983;(June):1311.

144 **Heitkemper M et al.** Rate and volume of intermittent enteral feeding. JPEN. 1981;5:125.

145 **Silk DBA.** Towards the optimization of enteral nutrition. Clin Nutr. 1987;6:61.

146 **Keohane P et al.** Relation between osmolality of diet and gastrointestinal side effects in enteral nutrition. Br Med J. 1984;288:678.

147 **Zarling EJ et al.** Effect of enteral formula infusion rate, osmolality, and chemical composition upon clinical tolerance and carbohydrate absorption in normal subjects. JPEN. 1986;10:588.

148 **Rees RGP et al.** Elemental diet administered nasogastrically without starter regimens to patients with inflammatory bowel disease. JPEN. 1986;10:258.

149 **Rees RGP et al.** Tolerance of elemental diet administered without starter regimen. Br Med J. 1985;290:1869.

150 **Chernoff R.** Nutritional support: formulas and delivery of enteral feeding. II. Delivery systems. J Am Diet Assoc. 1981;79:430.

151 **Chernoff R.** Enteral feedings. Am J Hosp Pharm. 1980;37:65.

152 **Guenter P et al.** Administration and delivery of enteral nutrition. In: Rombeau JL, Caldwell MD, eds. Clinical Nutrition. Enteral and Tube Feeding. 2nd ed. Philadelphia: WB Saunders; 1990:192.

153 **Jones BJ et al.** Indications for pump-assisted enteral feeding. Lancet. 1980;1:1057.

154 **Pipp TL.** Enteral feeding pumps. Nutr Supp Srvs. 1986;6:10.

155 **Davis PD et al.** A tube-feeding monitoring flow sheet. Nutr Supp Srvs. 1988;8:21.

156 **McClave S et al.** Use of residual volume as a marker for enteral feeding intolerance: prospective blinded comparison with physical examination and radiographic findings. JPEN. 1992;16:99.

157 **Ibanez J et al.** Gastroesophageal reflux in intubated patients receiving enteral nutrition: effect of supine and semirecumbent positions. JPEN. 1992;16:419.

158 **Eisenberg PG.** Causes of diarrhea in tube-fed patients: a comprehensive approach to diagnosis and management. Nutr Clin Pract. 1993;8:119.

159 **Kohn CL, Keithley JK.** Techniques for evaluating and managing diarrhea in the tube-fed patient. Nutr Clin Pract. 1987;2:250.

160 **Vanlandingham S et al.** Metabolic abnormalities in patients supported with enteral tube feeding. JPEN. 1981;5:322.

161 **Hofsetter J, Allen LV Jr.** Causes of non-medication-induced nasogastric tube occlusion. Am J Hosp Pharm. 1992;49:603.

162 **Nicholson LJ.** Declogging small-bore feeding tubes. JPEN. 1987;11:594.

163 **Marcuard SP.** Clogging of feeding tubes. JPEN. 1988;12:403.

164 **Gora ML et al.** Considerations of drug therapy in patients receiving enteral nutrition. Nutr Clin Pract. 1989;4:105.

165 **Fagerman KE, Ballou AE.** Drug compatibilities with enteral feeding solutions coadministered by the tube. Nutr Supp Srvs. 1988;8:31.

166 **Cutie AJ et al.** Compatibility of enteral products with commonly employed drug additives. JPEN. 1983;7:186.

167 **Mitchell JF.** Oral dosage forms that should not be crushed. Hosp Pharm. 1987;22:987.

168 **Magnusson JO.** Metabolism of digoxin after oral and intrajejunal administration. Br J Clin Pharmacol. 1983;16:741.

169 **Randle NW.** Food or nutrient effects on drug absorption: a review. Hosp Pharm. 1987;22:694.

170 **Bauer LA.** Interference of oral phenytoin absorption by continuous nasogastric feedings. Neurology. 1982;32:570.

171 **Guidry JR et al.** Phenytoin absorption in volunteers receiving selected enteral feedings. West J Med. 1989;150:659.

172 **Nishimura LY et al.** Influence of enteral feedings on phenytoin sodium absorption from capsules. Drug Intell Clin Pharm. 1988;22:130.

173 **Howard PA, Hannaman KN.** Warfarin resistance linked to enteral nutrition products. J Am Diet Assoc. 1985;85:713.

174 **Thomson C, Rollins CJ.** Enteral feeding and medication incompatibilities. Support Line. 1991;13:9.

175 **Wright B, Robinson L.** Enteral feeding tubes as drug delivery systems. Nutr Supp Srvs. 1986;6:33.

176 **Rudman D et al.** Relation of serum albumin concentration to death rate in nursing home men. JPEN. 1987;11:360.

177 **Harvey DB et al.** Biological measures for the formation of a hospital prognostic index. Am J Clin Nutr. 1981;34:2013.

178 **Waterlow JC.** Classification and definition of protein-calorie malnutrition. Br Med J. 1972;3:566.

179 **Chumlea WC.** Estimating stature from knee height for persons 60 to 90 years of age. J Am Geriatr Soc. 1985;33:116.

180 **Rollins CJ, Thomson C.** Nutrition. In: Bressler R, Katz MD, eds. Geriatric Pharmacology. New York: McGraw-Hill; 1993:9.

181 **Robert JJ et al.** Quantitative aspects of glucose production and metabolism in healthy elderly subjects. Diabetes. 1982;31:203.

182 **Harris JA, Benedict FG.** A biometric study of basal metabolism in man. Washington, DC: Carnegie Institute; 1919; Publication no. 279.

183 **Mifflin MD et al.** A new predictive equation for resting energy expenditure in healthy individuals. Am J Clin Nutr. 1990;51:241.

184 **Owen OE et al.** A reappraisal of the caloric requirements of men. Am J Clin Nutr. 1987;46:875.

185 **Owen OE et al.** A reappraisal of caloric requirements in healthy women. Am J Clin Nutr. 1986;44:1.

186 **Daly JM et al.** Human energy requirements: overestimation by widely used prediction equation. Am J Clin Nutr. 1985;42:1170.

187 **Heshka S et al.** Resting energy expenditure in the obese: a cross-validation and comparison of prediction equations. J Am Diet Assoc. 1993;93:1031.

188 **Feurer ID et al.** Resting energy expenditure in morbid obesity. Ann Surg. 1983;197:17.

189 **Long CL et al.** Metabolic response to injury and illness: estimation of energy and protein needs from indirect calorimetry and nitrogen balance. JPEN. 1979;3:452.

190 **Foster GD et al.** Caloric requirements in total parenteral nutrition. J Am Coll Nutr. 1987;6:231.

191 **Mandt JM et al.** Nutritional requirements. In: Teasley-Strausburg KM, ed. Nutrition Support Handbook: A Compendium of Products with Guidelines for Usage. Cincinnati: Harvey Whitney Books; 1992:19.

192 **Alpers DH et al.** Manual of Nutritional Therapeutics. Boston, MA: Little, Brown; 1983:185.

193 **Dickerson JWT.** Vitamin requirements in different clinical conditions. Bibl Nutr Dieta. 1985;35:44.

194 **Meer JA.** Inadvertent dislodgment of nasoenteral feeding tubes: incidence and prevention. JPEN. 1987;11:187.

195 **Barrocas A et al.** The bridle: increasing the use of nasoenteric feedings. Nutr Supp Srvs. 1982;2:8.

196 **Baumgartner TG, ed.** Clinical Guide to Parenteral Micronutrition. 2nd ed. Fujisawa, USA; 1991.

197 **Deitch EA.** Multiple organ failure. Ann Surg. 1992;216:117.

198 **Langkamp-Henken B et al.** Immunologic structure and function of the gastrointestinal tract. Nutr Clin Pract. 1992;7:100.

199 **Saito H et al.** The effect of route of nutrient administration on the nutritional state, catabolic hormone secretion, and gut mucosal integrity after burn injury. JPEN. 1987;11:1.

200 **McCardle AH et al.** Early enteral feeding of patients with major burns: prevention of catabolism. Ann Plast Surg. 1984;13:396.

Adult Parenteral Nutrition

Beverly J Holcombe

Malnutrition 35-1
Specialized Nutrition Support 35-2
Patient Assessment 35-2
   Nutritional history (See Table 35.1) 35-2
   Weight history 35-2
   Physical examination 35-3
   Anthropometrics 35-3
   Biochemical assessment 35-3
   Immunocompetence 35-3
   Classification of malnutrition 35-3
   Estimation of energy expenditure
     (See Table 35.2) 35-4
   Estimation of protein goals (See Table 35.3) 35-4
Venous Access Sites 35-4
   Peripheral 35-4
   Central 35-5
Commercially Available Nutrients (See Table 35.4) 35-5
   Carbohydrate 35-5
   Fat 35-5
   Amino acids (See Table 35.9) 35-5
   Micronutrients 35-5
Parenteral Nutrition 35-5
   Patient Assessment 35-5
   Female in no acute stress 35-5
   Goals of therapy 35-6
     Calorie and protein goals 35-6
     Access 35-7
   Formulation design 35-7
     Macro- and micronutrients 35-7
     Fluids 35-7
   Monitoring and management of complications 35-7
   Male in moderate stress 35-8
   Calorie and protein goals 35-8
   Formulation design (Also see Question 17) 35-8

Monitoring and management of complications 35-9
   Metabolic complications: essential fatty acid
     deficiency (EFAD) 35-9
     Metabolic consequences of excessive dextrose
       administration 35-9
   Total nutrient admixtures (TNAs) 35-9
     Stability 35-10
   Micronutrients: electrolytes 35-10
     Vitamins and trace elements 35-10
Monitoring and management of complications 35-10
   Metabolic complications 35-10
     Hypokalemia 35-10
     Hypophosphatemia 35-11
     Metabolic alkalosis 35-11
     Hyperglycemia 35-11
   Formulation design 35-11
     Compatibility 35-11
     Medication additives 35-12
     Monitoring parameters (See Table 35.8) 35-12
Fistulas 35-12
Short Bowel Syndrome 35-12
Home Therapy 35-13
Cyclic Therapy 35-13
   Metabolic complications: elevated liver-associated
     enzymes 35-13
Use of Parenteral Nutrition in Special
Disease States 35-13
   Hepatic Failure (Also see Table 35.9) 35-13
     Aromatic amino acids (AAA) and branched-chain
       amino acids (BCAA) 35-13
   Diabetes, Respiratory Failure, Pancreatitis,
     and Obesity 35-14
   Renal Failure 35-15
     Hemodialysis 35-15
Transitional Feedings from Parenteral
to Enteral Nutrition 35-15

Since the mid-1600s there have been many efforts to provide nutrients intravenously. Peripheral veins were cannulated and various feeding solutions including salt water, cow's milk, and glucose were administered. However, venous access through a peripheral vein necessitated the administration of large volumes (up to 5 L/day) of solutions with very low nutrient content in order to provide sufficient nutrients. This method of feeding often resulted in thrombophlebitis or fluid overload. It was not until the 1960s that Dudrick and his colleagues first used the technique of placing an intravenous (IV) catheter in the superior vena cava, a vessel with rapid blood flow and hemodilution, and were able to administer small volumes of solutions with high concentrations of nutrients.[1] This technique of intravenous feeding was then used successfully to feed an infant for more than six weeks. In turn, large series of both adults and children with abnormalities of the gastrointestinal (GI) tract were fed nutrients via a central venous catheter.[2,3] During the last three decades there have been many advances in techniques for intravenous cannulation and formulation of IV nutrient solutions. Today, the provision of intravenous nutrients, known as parenteral nutrition, is an integral part of the medical management of patients, both hospitalized and at home, who are unable to eat or ingest nutrients by the gastrointestinal tract.

Malnutrition

Adequate nutrition is important for the maintenance of optimal health. Malnutrition occurs when there is a deficiency of any nutrient resulting from abnormalities in the intake, digestion, absorption, metabolism, and/or excretion of the nutrient. A more clinically useful definition of malnutrition has been suggested as the state induced by alterations in dietary intake resulting in changes in subcellular, cellular, and/or organ function which exposes the individual to increased risks of morbidity and mortality and which can be reversed by adequate nutrition support.[4]

The incidence of malnutrition among hospitalized patients has been reported to be as high as 50%.[5-7] In the hospitalized patient, acute malnutrition occurs when there is inadequate or no nutrient intake in the face of an injury or stress such as trauma, infection, or major surgery resulting in rapid depletion of nutrient stores. An acute stress or injury increases energy needs for the repair of tissues. When this energy is not provided exogenously, the body turns to endogenous sources of energy by breaking down skeletal muscle to release amino acids for the production of glucose. This iatrogenic malnutrition can occur rapidly even in individuals who were well nourished before hospitalization. In contrast, starvation or semistarvation states, without stress or injury, allow man to slowly adapt to inadequate nutrient intake. This adaptation results in the use of endogenous fat stores for energy and a slow loss of muscle proteins. Although adaptation occurs, energy and protein stores are not unlimited. With total starvation, death occurs in normal weight individuals in about 60 days.[8] Clearly, the patient with a history of starvation or semistarvation that is faced with a stress or injury is at the greatest risk of developing malnutrition.

Protein-calorie malnutrition is the most common type of nutritional deficiency in hospitalized patients and is manifested by depletion of both tissue energy stores and body proteins. Malnourished patients are at a higher risk of developing complications during therapy. These nutrition-associated complications are the result of organ wasting and functional impairment and include weakness, decreased wound healing, altered hepatic metabolism of drugs, increased respiratory failure, decreased cardiac contractility, and infections such as pneumonia and abscesses.[9]

Specialized Nutrition Support

Hospitalized patients with inadequate intake for seven days or longer, or those with a weight loss of ≥10% of their pre-illness weight, are considered to be malnourished or at risk of developing malnutrition.[10] Nutritional intervention should be considered for these patients. Patients who cannot meet their nutritional needs by eating enough food by mouth should be considered for some type of *specialized nutrition support*. Specialized nutrition support is providing specially formulated and/or delivered parenteral or enteral nutrients.[11] For those patients unable to eat by mouth, yet who have a functional gastrointestinal tract, a method of enteral nutrition or tube-feeding should be considered. (This type of specialized nutrition support is discussed in detail in Chapter 34: Adult Enteral Nutrition.) Whenever possible, the GI tract should be used for providing nutrients. Nutrients administered enterally may be more beneficial and less expensive than those provided by the parenteral route. Stimulation of the intestine with enteral nutrients maintains mucosal barrier structure and function which is important in immunocompetence and has been associated with decreased infectious morbidity in critically ill patients as compared to those receiving nutrients parenterally.[12-15] For these reasons, parenteral nutrition is reserved only for patients whose gastrointestinal tracts should not be used or cannot be used and those patients whose GI tracts do not absorb enough nutrients to maintain adequate nutritional status.

Patient Assessment

Assessment of a patient's nutritional status allows one to analyze body composition and evaluate physiologic function. These are important in determining the presence and severity of malnutrition or the risk of developing malnutrition. Hence, the need to intervene with specialized nutrition support and direction for the goals of therapy whether that be to maintain current nutritional status or repletion of fat and lean body mass. Assessment should include evaluation of multiple factors and not reliance upon one parameter.

Nutritional History

A nutritional history is critical to assessment of nutritional status. Information can be obtained by interviewing the patient or the patient's family as well as reviewing the medical record to identify factors that may contribute to malnutrition or increase the risk of developing malnutrition. Multiple factors can contribute to the development of malnutrition. An example of a patient with multiple risk factors for malnutrition is one who lives alone on a fixed income, has a history of multiple intestinal surgeries for peptic ulcer disease (PUD), and who will receive nothing by mouth (NPO) while hospitalized for tests to evaluate a complaint of nausea and vomiting.

Medications can affect nutritional status adversely by decreasing synthesis of nutrients, decreasing intake by altering appetite and taste, producing malabsorption, altering nutrient metabolism, and increasing nutrient requirements. A nutritional history also should include evaluation of weight. The components of a nutritional history are summarized in Table 35.1.

Weight History

Weight and weight history are important in the evaluation of nutritional status. Weight loss is a sign of negative energy and protein balance and is associated with poor outcome of hospitalized patients.[16,17] A weight loss of greater than 10% is considered significant for malnutrition. If weight has been lost, it must be investigated further to determine if the loss is intentional and if the weight loss is continuing or has stabilized.

A patient's current weight often is compared to a standard such as the Metropolitan Life Insurance tables for "ideal body weight." Percentage of ideal body weight (IBW) is determined as follows.

$$\% \text{ IBW} = \frac{\text{Current Weight}}{\text{IBW}} (100) \qquad \text{Eq 35.1}$$

This method of assessing weight has its shortcomings because the patient's weight is compared to a population standard rather than using the individual patient as the reference point. For example, a patient who is significantly overweight and has lost large amounts of weight may still be greater than 100% of ideal body weight and, therefore, not considered at risk of developing malnutrition. A more patient-specific method of evaluating weight is to compare current weight to the patient's usual or pre-illness weight. This can be determined using the following equation.

$$\% \text{ Usual Body Weight} = \frac{\text{Current Weight}}{\text{Usual Body Weight}} (100) \qquad \text{Eq 35.2}$$

Using this method, the obese patient that has lost weight may be determined to be less than 90% of usual weight (weight loss of >10%) and, therefore, at risk of malnutrition. It also is important to assess over what time period the change has occurred. Weight loss is considered severe if loss exceeds 2% in one week, 5% in

Table 35.1	Components of a Nutritional History
Medical history	
Chronic illnesses	
Surgical history	
Psychosocial history	
Socioeconomic status	
History of nausea, vomiting, or diarrhea	
Diet history including weight-loss or weight-gain diets	
Food preferences and intolerances	
Medications	

Weight history
   Increase or decrease
   Intentional or unintentional
   Time period for weight change	

one month, or 10% in six months.[18] The pattern of weight loss must be evaluated. Is the loss continuing, stabilizing, or is the patient regaining some weight?

Physical Examination

Signs of nutritional deficiencies may be noted upon physical examination and require further evaluation. General evidence of muscle and fat wasting as evidenced by the presence of temporal wasting, loss of subcutaneous fat and muscle in the shoulders, and loss of subcutaneous fat in the interosseous and palmar areas of the hands are relatively easy to identify. Other physical parameters that may be less obvious are hair for color and sparseness; skin for turgor, pigmentation, and dermatitis; mouth for glossitis, gingivitis cheilosis, and color of the tongue; nails for friability and lines; and the abdomen for presence of ascites or enlarged liver.

Anthropometrics

Physical examination may include anthropometrics which measure subcutaneous fat and skeletal muscle mass. Assessment of fat stores provides information about fat loss or gain and assumes fat is gained or lost proportionally over the entire body. Measurement of triceps skinfold and subscapular skinfold thickness are examples of methods to assess subcutaneous fat and, therefore, estimate total body fat. The values obtained from the patient are compared to reference standards. Somatic protein mass or skeletal muscle mass can be estimated by measuring mid-arm circumference and then calculating arm muscle circumference. These values also are compared to standards, and the amount of muscle mass is determined. Anthropometric measurements, when used for the long-term study of large, nutritionally stable populations, reflect accurately total body fat and skeletal muscle mass. However, anthropometric measurements of hospitalized patients are of limited value. During acute illness and stress, changes in subcutaneous fat may not be proportional and the presence of peripheral edema will result in inflated values for skinfold thicknesses and midarm circumference and have no clinical application.

Biochemical Assessment

Biochemical assessment of nutritional status includes measuring concentrations of serum proteins. The visceral proteins most commonly used to assess nutritional status are albumin, transthyretin, transferrin, and retinol-binding protein. These proteins are synthesized by the liver and reflect the liver's synthetic capability. Serum concentrations decrease when intake of substrates is inadequate for synthesis of these proteins, or during stress or injury when substrates are shunted away from the synthesis of these proteins in order to synthesize other proteins, acute phase reactants. *Albumin* is the classic visceral protein used to evaluate nutritional status. Serum concentrations of <3 gm/dL correlate with poor outcome of hospitalized patients.[19,20] Albumin serves as a carrier protein for minerals and drugs and is necessary for maintaining oncotic pressure. Albumin has a large body pool of 3 to 5 gm/kg and 30% to 40% is localized to the intravascular space. The normal hepatic rate of albumin synthesis is 150 to 250 mg/kg/day. Since albumin has a half-life of 18 to 21 days, a decrease in serum albumin concentrations generally is not observed until after several weeks of inadequate nitrogen intake. Serum albumin concentrations will decrease in response to nonnutritional factors such as stress which causes albumin to shift from the intravascular to the extravascular space, burns, nephrotic syndrome, protein-losing enteropathy, overhydration, and decreased synthesis with liver disease. *Transferrin*, another visceral protein, is responsible for the transport of iron. It has a half-life (t½) of eight to ten days and, therefore, is more sensitive than albumin to acute changes in nutritional status. Normal serum concentrations for transferrin are 250 to 300 mg/dL.

Even more sensitive to changes in energy and protein intake is the visceral protein, *transthyretin*, which has a small body pool (10 mg/kg) and a half-life of two to three days. It is responsible for transporting retinol and retinol-binding protein. Normal serum transthyretin concentrations are 15 to 40 mg/dL. *Retinol-binding protein* is the visceral protein with the shortest half-life, 12 hours, and has normal serum concentrations of 2.5 to 7.5 mg/dL. Serum concentrations of retinol-binding protein, however, change so rapidly in response to alterations in nutrient intake, monitoring retinol-binding protein has limited use in clinical practice. Other proteins such as *fibronectin* and *somatomedin-C* (insulin-like growth factor-1) are being investigated as markers of nutritional status. The interpretation of serum protein concentrations in hospitalized patients may be difficult because factors more important than hepatic synthetic rate alter serum concentrations. These factors affecting serum protein concentrations may include renal, hepatic, or cardiac dysfunction, hydration status, and metabolic stress. The use of visceral proteins, as with any nutritional assessment parameter, must be used in conjunction with other parameters and requires comprehensive consideration of the patient's current clinical status.

Immunocompetence

Assessment of body fat mass, skeletal muscle mass, and visceral protein concentrations does not provide information on changes in functional capabilities secondary to changes in nutritional status. Measurement of the immune system's ability to respond provides some information on function. Immunocompetence may be assessed by determining the total lymphocyte count or by assessing delayed cutaneous hypersensitivity. The total lymphocyte count (TLC) can be calculated by multiplying the percentage of lymphocytes by the white blood cell (WBC) count.

$$TLC = \frac{\% \text{ Lymphocytes} \times WBC}{100} \qquad Eq\ 35.3$$

The normal total lymphocyte count should be greater than 1800: severe malnutrition is considered when the TLC is less than 900. Delayed cutaneous hypersensitivity can be assessed by intradermal injection of common antigens (e.g., mumps, tuberculin-purified protein derivative, *Candida*). The lack of induration response to these skin tests (i.e., anergy) has been associated with malnutrition. As with other nutritional assessment tools, many nonnutritional factors can affect cell-mediated immunity. Because of the complexity of the immune system, immunocompetence is not commonly assessed to determine nutritional status.

Classification of Malnutrition

Protein-calorie malnutrition is divided classically into three categories: marasmus, kwashiorkor and a mixed kwashiorkor-marasmus. Marasmus, which means a "dying away state," is seen in individuals who are deficient in the intake of both calories and protein over a prolonged period of time (i.e., partial starvation). Upon physical examination severe cachexia is noted by loss of both fat and muscle mass.

Kwashiorkor malnutrition results from a diet adequate in carbohydrate and fat calories, but with little to no protein. Insulin is produced to metabolize the carbohydrates and the insulin also prevents lipolysis and promotes the movement of amino acids into muscle. To meet the protein needs in kwashiorkor malnutrition, protein is mobilized from internal organs and circulating proteins such as albumin. The clinical picture is one of an individual with adequate fat and muscle mass but depleted serum proteins.

Hospitalized patients can commonly exhibit components of both marasmus and kwashiorkor malnutrition, or mixed malnutrition. This often occurs when chronic starvation is compounded by an injury or stress. With limited fat and muscle mass, and a stress causing an increased need for energy, the end result is wasting of both fat and muscle mass as well as depletion of serum proteins.

Nutritional assessment based upon determinations of body composition by using anthropometrics and biochemical parameters has many limitations. New techniques (e.g., bioelectrical impedance, isotope dilution, and neutron activation) increasingly are being used for determining body composition. Other biochemical parameters also are being investigated that relate changes in body composition to body function.

Another nutritional assessment method, Subjective Global Assessment (SGA), combines objective parameters and physiological function. This method is based upon a history of weight change, dietary intake, presence of gastrointestinal symptoms, and functional capacity, as well as physical examination to assess the loss of subcutaneous fat and muscle and the presence of edema. When using the SGA system, patients are rated as well nourished, moderately malnourished, or severely malnourished. This subjective assessment is easy to use and to diagnose malnutrition as well as objective biochemical parameters.[9,21]

Estimation of Energy Expenditure

An important aspect of patient evaluation is estimating energy expenditure. Many methods for determining energy expenditure have been described in the literature. The traditional method of assessing energy expenditure is to first calculate *basal energy expenditure* (BEE). The BEE is the amount of energy [kilocalories (kcal)] needed to support basic metabolic functions in a state of complete rest, shortly after awakening, and after a 12-hour fast. The BEE is most commonly calculated using the Harris-Benedict equations. Alternatively, basal energy expenditure can be estimated at 20 to 25 kcal/kg/day. *Resting energy expenditure* (REE) is the energy expended in the postabsorptive state (two hours after a meal) and is approximately 10% greater than the BEE. Determination of BEE or REE does not include additional energy needed for stress or activity. The Harris-Benedict equations can be modified to include stress and physical activity factors, or these variables can be estimated at 30 to 35 kcal/kg/day for moderate stress and up to 45 kcal/kg/day for severe stress. (See Table 35.2.) Energy expenditure also can be determined by indirect calorimetry which uses an analytical machine to measure the patient's breathing or respiratory gas exchange. The machine (often termed a "metabolic cart") measures the amount of oxygen consumed and the carbon dioxide produced, and through a series of equations determines the energy expenditure, including stress, for that point in time and then extrapolates it for 24 hours. As the measurement usually is conducted while the patient is at rest, activity is not included in the energy expenditure calculation. This method of determining energy expenditure has been used as a research tool for over 20 years and is gaining popularity as the technology becomes available to more clinicians for use in better predicting energy expenditure of patients.

Estimation of Protein Goals

Estimation of protein needs also must be included in nutritional assessment. Protein needs are based upon body weight, degree of stress, and disease state. The recommended daily allowance (RDA) for the U.S. is 0.8 gm/kg/day. Hospitalized patients with minimal stress who are well nourished need 1.0 to 1.2 gm/kg/day for maintenance of lean body mass. The requirement for protein intake may be as high as 2.0 gm/kg/day for a patient in a hypermetabolic, hypercatabolic state secondary to trauma. Additionally, patients with renal or hepatic dysfunction may require a decrease in protein intake as a result of altered metabolism. Guidelines for protein needs are summarized in Table 35.3.

Venous Access Sites

Once it is determined that parenteral nutrition is necessary, the type of venous access must be selected. Parenteral feeding formulations may be administered via peripheral veins or central veins. The decision to use a central or peripheral vein is dependent upon the anticipated duration of parenteral nutrition therapy.

Peripheral

Peripheral parenteral nutrition may be considered when the need for parenteral nutrition is expected to be for a period of time of less than ten days and the patient has fairly low energy and protein needs because of minimal stress. Candidates for peripheral parenteral nutrition must meet two criteria: 1) have good peripheral venous access and 2) be able to tolerate large volumes of fluids. Parenteral feeding formulations for administration via peripheral veins traditionally have been formulated with relatively low concentrations of dextrose (5% to 7.5%) and amino acids (3% to 5%) providing <1 kcal/mL. Therefore, several liters may be needed daily to meet energy and protein needs. Although dilute with nutrients, the osmolarity of these formulations is 600 to 900 mOsm/L. These hypertonic formulations are irritating to peripheral veins causing phlebitis and the need for frequent site rotations (at least every 48 to 72 hours) which may quickly exhaust venous access sites. The concurrent administration of IV lipids with dextrose/amino acid solutions, or a formulation mixing dextrose, amino acids, and lipids, provides a method to increase the caloric density without increasing the osmolarity. Additionally, the lipids may protect the vein against irritation. The ability to give peripheral parenteral feeding formulations may be improved by using midline venous access catheters, which are longer and, therefore, able to have the end of the catheter placed in a larger vein where greater blood flow can dilute the feeding formulation. These catheters also are advantageous because they are made of a material that allows them to remain in place for four to six weeks.

Table 35.2	Estimation of Energy Expenditure

Basal Energy Expenditure (BEE)

Harris-Benedict Equations[a]

$$BEE_{men} \text{ (kcal/day)} = 66.47 + 13.75\,W + 5.0\,H - 6.76\,A$$
$$BEE_{women} \text{ (kcal/day)} = 655.10 + 9.56\,W + 1.85\,H - 4.68\,A$$

OR

    20–25 kcal/kg/day

Total Energy Expenditure (TEE)

    TEE (kcal/day) = BEE × Stress Factor × Activity Factor

Stress or Injury Factors (% increase above BEE)

Major surgery	10–20
Infection	20
Fracture	20–40
Trauma	40–80
Sepsis	80
Burns	80–100

Activity Factors (% increase above BEE)

Confined to bed	20
Out of bed	30

OR

No stress	28 kcal/kg/day
Mild stress	30 kcal/kg/day
Moderate stress	35 kcal/kg/day
Severe stress	40 kcal/kg/day

[a] W = Weight in kg; H = Height in cm; A = Age in years.

Table 35.3	Estimation of Protein Requirements
US RDA[a]	0.8 gm/kg/day
Hospitalized patient, minor stress	1.0–1.2 gm/kg/day
Moderate stress	1.2–1.5 gm/kg/day
Severe stress	1.5–2.0 gm/kg/day

[a] RDA = Recommended daily allowance.

Central

Administration of parenteral feeding formulations through a central vein is preferred for patients whose GI tracts are either nonfunctional or should not be used for more than five to seven days, and for patients who have limited peripheral venous access or have energy and protein needs that cannot be met with peripheral feeding formulations. The central venous catheter should be placed in the subclavian vein and threaded through this vein so that the tip rests in the upper portion of the superior vena cava. Although the internal and external jugular veins also may be used to thread a catheter into the superior vena cava, maintaining a sterile dressing on these sites is more difficult than with the subclavian approach. The superior vena cava is an area of rapid blood flow which quickly dilutes concentrated parenteral feeding formulations and, thereby, minimizes phlebitis or thrombosis. Unlike peripheral veins, the central venous access site does not require rotation of the site every few days. In fact, some patients requiring parenteral nutrition for months to years may have permanently placed central venous catheters. Parenteral feeding formulations designed for administration through central veins can provide relatively high concentrations of dextrose (20% to 35%), amino acids (5% to 10%), and lipids giving a caloric density of >1 kcal/mL and an osmolarity of >2000 mOsm/L.

Commercially Available Nutrients

The three macronutrients required for humans, carbohydrate, fat, and protein, are available for use in parenteral feeding formulations. Each of these components is available from a variety of manufacturers.

Carbohydrate

The most common carbohydrate for intravenous use is dextrose in water. It is available commercially in concentrations ranging from 2.5% to 70%. These dextrose solutions are mixed with other components of the parenteral feeding formulation and diluted to various final concentrations. Intravenous dextrose is hydrated and provides 3.4 kcal/gm in comparison to dietary carbohydrate that has a caloric density of 4.0 kcal/gm. Glycerol also is available as a 3% mixture with 3% amino acids for administration as a peripheral parenteral feeding formulation. Glycerol has a caloric density of 4.3 kcal/gm. Other carbohydrates such as fructose, sorbitol, and invert sugar have been used investigationally in parenteral feeding formulations, but are associated with adverse effects and are not available commercially.

Fat

Fat for intravenous use is supplied as emulsions of either soybean oil or a mixture of soybean and safflower oils which provide long-chain fatty acids. The soybean oil emulsion is available in three concentrations: 10%, 20%, and 30%. Although fat has a caloric density of 9 kcal/gm, the caloric density of the IV fat emulsions is increased by the addition of glycerol and egg phospholipids. These components are added as emulsifiers and to adjust the osmolarity. Medium-chain triglycerides (MCTs) are used investi-

gationally, as well as mixtures of long-chain and medium-chain triglycerides. MCTs provide 8.3 kcal/gm.

Amino Acids

Protein for parenteral administration is available as synthetic amino acids. Amino acid concentrations of 3.5% to 15% are available commercially and vary slightly from one product to another in the specific amounts of each amino acid. Generally, the amino acid products can be divided into those that provide a balanced mix of essential, nonessential, and semiessential amino acids, "standard" amino acid mixtures, or specialty amino acid mixtures that are modified for specific disease states. For example, the specialty amino acid mixture for hepatic failure contains increased amounts of the branched-chain amino acids and decreased amounts of the aromatic amino acids. Protein formulations designed for physiologic stress are supplemented with branched-chain amino acids, but have normal amounts of the other amino acids. Finally, the renal failure amino acid products either have increased amounts of the essential amino acids or provide only essential amino acids. Protein or amino acids have a caloric density of 4 kcal/gm. These calories, however, may not always be included in the calculations of energy needs. Ideally, the protein is used for tissue repair and not oxidized for energy; however, the human body in reality cannot compartmentalize energy metabolism this way. Table 35.4 summarizes available nutrients and their caloric density.

Micronutrients

Micronutrients are considered to be the electrolytes, vitamins, and trace minerals that are needed for metabolism. These nutrients, as single entities or combinations, are available from various manufacturers. For example, the trace element zinc is available as a single trace element product or may be in a combination product with the other trace elements, copper, chromium, and manganese. It is important to be aware of the specific products used in each institution in order to avoid providing inadequate or excessive amounts of various micronutrients.

Parenteral Nutrition

Patient Assessment

1. Female in No Acute Stress. S.F., a 51-year-old cachectic female, is admitted to the hospital complaining of a 3-month history of severe abdominal pain after eating and a 30 pound weight loss. Questioning revealed that she has felt hungry, but the pain after eating is so severe she prefers to not eat. S.F.

Table 35.4	Caloric Density of Intravenous Nutrients	
Nutrient	kcal/gm	kcal/mL
Amino acids	4.0	—
Amino acids 5%	—	0.2
Amino acids 10%	—	0.4
Dextrose	3.4	—
Dextrose 10%	—	0.34
Dextrose 50%	—	1.7
Fat	9.0	—
Fat emulsion 10%	—	1.1
Fat emulsion 20%	—	2.0
Fat emulsion 30%	—	3.0
Glycerol	4.3	—
Glycerol 3%	—	0.129
Medium-chain triglycerides	8.3	

denies any nausea, vomiting, or diarrhea. Her past medical history is significant for peptic ulcer disease. Her past surgical history is significant for removal of a section of her ileum and colon for ischemia 4 months ago. Her current medication is nizatidine 150 mg PO BID. S.F.'s social history is significant for tobacco use but she quit smoking 2 years ago. Review of systems is positive only for the postprandial abdominal pain. When queried about her diet and weight loss, S.F. states that at most she eats 1 meal a day and then consumes only 25%–40% of that meal. Tolerance to food is no better if she eats liquids or solids. Furthermore, her weight loss has been continuous over the last 3 months. Physical examination reveals a very thin female with wasting of subcutaneous fat in the temporal area and very squared appearing shoulders. Her height is 5' 4"; weight 89 pounds. At the time of her colon resection, her weight was 119 pounds which is her usual weight.

Admission laboratory values are as follows: Sodium (Na) 135 mEq/L (Normal: 135–145); Potassium (K) 12.39 mg/dL (Normal: 10.84–15.48); Chloride (Cl) 100 mEq/L (Normal: 100–110); bicarbonate 25 mEq/L (Normal: 24–30); blood urea nitrogen (BUN) 4 mg/dL (Normal: 8–20); creatinine 0.6 mg/dL (Normal: 0.8–1.2); glucose 87 mg/dL (Normal: 85–110); calcium (Ca) 8.2 mg/dL (8.5–10); magnesium (Mg) 2.0 mg/dL (Normal: 1.5–2.8); phosphorus (P) 3.0 mg/dL (Normal: 2.5–4.5); total protein 6.0 gm/dL (Normal: 6.8–8.3); albumin 4 gm/dL (Normal: 3.5); and transthyretin 21 mg/dL (Normal: 15–40). WBC count 6800/mm^3 (Normal: 4000–12,000), with lymphocytes 8%.

Based upon history and physical findings, S.F.'s working diagnosis is intestinal angina also known as mesenteric ischemia. Assess S.F.'s nutritional status. [(SI units: Na 153 mmol/L (Normal: 135–145); K 4.0 mmol/L (Normal: 3.5–5.0); Cl 100 mmol/L (Normal: 100–110); bicarbonate 25 mmol/L (Normal: 24–30); BUN 1.43 mmol/L (Normal: 3–6.4), SrCr 0.01 μmol/L (Normal: 50–110); glucose 4.83 mmol/L (Normal: 3–6.1); Ca 2.04 mmol/L (Normal: 2.3–2.7); PO$_4$ 0.97 mmol/L (Normal: 0.81–1.45); albumin 40 gm/L (Normal: 35–50); WBC count 6.8 × 10^{-9}/L (Normal: 4–12)]

Assessment of nutritional status requires evaluation of multiple factors. S.F.'s nutritional history indicates that she has not been eating because of the abdominal pain, and the recent surgery on her intestine raises the question of nutrient malabsorption. Most striking about S.F.'s history is her weight loss of 30 pounds in three months or about 2.5 pounds per week. S.F. is now 75% of her usual weight (see Equation 35.2). Another way of analyzing this is that she has lost 25% of her original weight, which is a severe weight loss. S.F.'s physical findings of cachectic appearance, temporal wasting, and loss of subcutaneous fat and muscle in her shoulders are significant. No anthropometric measurements are available. S.F.'s visceral proteins (albumin and transthyretin) are within normal ranges. Although no anergy tests are available, S.F.'s absolute lymphocyte count is only 544 and, therefore, one can surmise her immune system is depressed. The combination of all of these factors leads one to the conclusion that S.F. is significantly malnourished. Her cachectic appearance with loss of subcutaneous fat and muscle, but normal visceral proteins, would be best classified as marasmus. If S.F. were to be faced with a stress or injury (e.g., major surgery, infection) necessitating use of visceral proteins for energy production, she would then exhibit characteristics of both marasmus and kwashiorkor or mixed malnutrition where fat, muscle, and visceral proteins all are depleted.

2. Why is S. F. a candidate for parenteral nutrition therapy?

S.F. is admitted to the hospital for tests to evaluate her severe postprandial abdominal pain. Many of the expected diagnostic tests will require that S.F take no food by mouth. Although S.F. appears to have a functional GI tract, her postprandial pain is so severe it is unlikely she would eat much even if given the opportunity. If the diagnosis of mesenteric ischemia is accurate, surgical correc-

tion will be required. With her malnourished state, inadequate nutrient intake for five to seven days would result in further deterioration of her nutritional status. Parenteral nutrition should be implemented.

3. Goals of Therapy. S.F. has undergone multiple tests to evaluate her abdominal pain. An arteriogram revealed occlusion of her superior mesenteric artery which supplies blood to her small and large intestines. This occlusion prevents adequate blood flow to the intestines when there is increased demand for flow, such as after eating. S.F. is to remain NPO until her surgery which is scheduled in 4 days. Parenteral nutrition is planned. What should be the goal of her nutrition therapy?

Although S.F. has lost 30 pounds, this limited time before her surgery is not adequate time to replete her fat and lean body mass. Her malnutrition occurred over several months and repletion will take equally as long. The benefits of preoperative parenteral nutrition remain unclear. Although some reports describe a trend of improved outcome with preoperative parenteral nutrition,[22–24] other studies have not demonstrated clear benefit.[25] Furthermore, preoperative parenteral nutrition should be administered for seven to ten days to be of any benefit in decreasing the complications associated with surgery in severely malnourished patients. Therefore, the goals for S.F.'s nutrition therapy at this time are to maintain her current nutritional status and prevent her from becoming more malnourished. If, however, parenteral nutrition is initiated and is to be continued after surgery, her calorie and protein goals should be adjusted for the additional stress of major surgery. Finally, once she has recovered from surgery and convalescing, a long-term goal of weight gain back to her usual weight of 119 pounds is appropriate.

4. Calorie and Protein Goals. Calculate calorie and protein goals for S.F.

S.F.'s calorie goals are to meet her current energy expenditure which is basal metabolism and activity of ambulation. The first step is to calculate a basal energy expenditure. (See Table 35.2.) For this calculation, S.F.'s actual weight of 89 pounds (40.5 kg) should be used because her metabolism and current energy expenditure reflect this decrease in body mass. Using actual weight or ideal body weight in patients who have severe weight loss will result in overfeeding.

Although S.F. certainly is not obese, overfeeding also can occur in obese patients if actual weight is used in nutrition calculations. Providing excess calories results in deposition of even more adipose tissue and metabolic complications affecting the liver and lungs. Although estimating energy expenditure in obese patients is difficult, one method is to use an adjusted weight in the calculations. Patients who are obese, defined as greater than 120% of ideal body weight, should have their weight adjusted because adipose tissue is not metabolically active. The adipose tissue does, however, have some supporting tissue which is metabolically active. This type of tissue composes approximately one-fourth of the excess or adipose tissue. Adjusted weight for obesity is calculated using the following calculation.[26]

$$\frac{\text{Adjusted}}{\text{Weight}} = (0.25)(\text{Actual Weight} - \text{IBW}) + \text{IBW} \qquad Eq\ 35.4$$

Another method to adjust for obesity is to calculate a basal energy expenditure on actual weight using a guideline of 22 to 25 kcal/kg/day for men and 18 to 22 kcal/kg/day for women.[27]

Using the Harris-Benedict equation, S.F.'s basal energy expenditure (BEE) is 1104 kcal/day. This is then modified for light hospital activity of ambulation or increased by a factor of 30%. The total estimated energy expenditure for S.F. is 1104 × 1.3 = 1435 kcal/day. (See Table 35.2.) Unlike most hospitalized patients, S.F.

does not have a factor for stress. If S.F. requires parenteral nutrition after surgery, her energy or calorie goals should be recalculated and include a stress factor. A simpler method to calculate energy expenditure is to estimate caloric requirements at 28 to 30 kcal/kg/day; or for S.F., 1134 to 1200 kcal/day. The difference in these calculations of energy expenditure demonstrates that there are many methods to estimate energy expenditure and each method gives slightly different numbers. These methods merely provide *estimates* of energy expenditure.

Protein goals are estimated based upon weight, degree of stress, and disease state. S.F. has not had surgery and, therefore, her stress is minimal. As a result, her protein goal should be based upon the desire to maintain her current protein status. Using the guidelines provided in Table 35.3, S.F.'s protein dose is 1.0 to 1.2 gm/kg/day or 41 to 49 gm/day. As with energy expenditure, calculations of protein needs only provide estimates, and the patient's clinical course should be monitored and the protein dose adjusted accordingly. The protein source for parenteral nutrition is provided as synthetic amino acids. Generally, 1 gm of protein is equivalent to 1 gm of amino acids. S.F. will need 41 to 49 gm/day of amino acids.

5. Access. S.F. does not have a central venous catheter for parenteral nutrition therapy. She does, however, have a peripheral IV and her peripheral access appears to be good. Why is she a candidate for using a peripheral parenteral nutrition formulation?

With good peripheral access, S.F. meets one of the criteria for peripheral parenteral nutrition. Furthermore, she should be able to tolerate the volume of a peripheral parenteral nutrition formulation necessary to meet her goals. Peripheral parenteral nutrition can be irritating to the veins; therefore, the addition of intravenous fat in her nutritional formulation may help preserve peripheral access.

Formulation Design

6. Macro- and Micronutrients. Design a peripheral parenteral feeding base formulation for S.F. that provides 1300 nonprotein calories and 45 gm of amino acids. The formulation should provide 60% of the nonprotein calories as fat and have maximum dextrose and amino acid concentrations of 7.5% and 3%, respectively.

S.F.'s feeding formulation is 60% fat so it will provide 780 (1300 × 0.60) calories from intravenous fat. The remaining 520 nonprotein calories will be provided by dextrose. Dextrose provides 3.4 kcal/gm and, therefore, 153 gm of dextrose are required. The volume necessary to provide 153 gm of dextrose as a 7.5% concentration is 2040 mL.

$$mL = \frac{153 \text{ gm Dextrose (1000 mL)}}{75 \text{ gm}}$$

$$= 2040 \text{ mL}$$

Similarly, the volume necessary to provide 45 gm of amino acids as a 3% concentration is calculated to be 1500 mL. To stay within the guidelines for *maximum* dextrose and amino acid concentrations, the larger volume of 2040 mL should be used. Therefore, the final dextrose and amino acid concentrations would be 7.5% and 2.2%, respectively. Next, the amount of fat to provide 780 kcal must be determined. Using 10% fat emulsion with a caloric density of 1.1 kcal/mL would require 708 mL or 390 mL of the 20% fat emulsion (2.0 kcal/mL). (See Table 35.5.) The intravenous fat can be provided in a variety of ways. One method is to infuse the lipids as a secondary infusion or "piggy-backed" into the dextrose/amino acid solution. If the 20% lipid emulsion is used, S.F.'s fluid intake from her parenteral feedings will be 2430 mL/day. Alternatively, many institutions mix the lipid with the dextrose and amino acids.

Table 35.5	Recommended Adult Daily Doses of Parenteral Vitamins	
Vitamins	**Dose**	
Fat-Soluble Vitamins		
A	3300 IU (990 retinol equivalents)	
D	200 IU (5 mg cholecalciferol)	
E	10 IU (6.7 mg dl-a-tocopherol)	
K	—	
Water-Soluble Vitamins		
Thiamine (B_1)	3.0 mg	
Riboflavin (B_2)	3.6 mg	
Pyridoxine (B_6)	4.0 mg	
Cyanocobalamin (B_{12})	5.0 µg	
Niacin	40.0 mg	
Folic acid	0.4 mg	
Pantothenic acid	15.0 mg	
Biotin	60.0 µg	
Ascorbic acid (C)	100.0 mg	

This is called total nutrient admixture (TNA), triple-mix, three-in-one, or all-in-one. Using this method the lipid could be incorporated into the 2040 mL volume.

7. Fluids. The institution uses a TNA system so that S.F.'s parenteral feeding formulation is provided in 2040 mL/day. Will this meet S.F.'s maintenance fluid requirements?

Maintenance fluid needs can be estimated using several methods. The simplest method for calculating maintenance fluid needs uses 30 to 35 mL/kg/day as the basis. Another method is to provide 1500 mL for the first 20 kg body weight plus an additional 20 mL/kg for actual weight beyond the initial 20 kg. Both of these methods provide estimates of fluid needs for basic maintenance, and additional fluid must be provided for increased losses such as vomiting, nasogastric (NG) tube output, diarrhea, or large open wounds. S.F.'s fluid needs are estimated to be:

$$mL/day = 1500 \text{ mL} + [(120 \text{ mL/kg})(40.5 \text{ kg} - 20 \text{ kg})]$$

$$= 1500 \text{ mL} + (20 \text{ mL/kg})(20.5 \text{ kg})$$

$$= 1500 \text{ mL} + 410 \text{ mL}$$

$$= 1910 \text{ mL}$$

Clearly, the peripheral parenteral feeding formulation will more than meet S.F.'s needs. In fact, with this extra fluid intake she is at risk of becoming fluid overloaded. Therefore, she should be monitored for signs of fluid overload including presence of peripheral edema, daily intake exceeding daily output, hyponatremia, and rapidly increasing weight.

Monitoring and Management of Complications

8. What additional parameters should be monitored in patients receiving peripheral parenteral nutrition?

The primary calorie source in peripheral parenteral feedings is fat. Therefore, it is important to monitor serum triglycerides to assess tolerance to this dose of IV fat. If the blood sample is obtained while the triglycerides are infusing, as with the total nutrient admixture formulation, a serum triglyceride concentration of <300 mg/dL, although elevated, is acceptable. Hypertriglyceridemia sometimes can be noted quickly by gross observation of the blood sample.

9. Forty-eight hours after S.F. begins peripheral parenteral nutrition, she begins to complain that the arm where she has the IV for the feeding is swollen, red, and painful. What is the most probable cause of these complaints?

A common complication (26% to 48%) of peripheral parenteral nutrition is phlebitis that occurs within 72 hours.[28] Phlebitis usually is attributed to the acidic pH or hyperosmolarity of the feeding formulation. The osmolarity of peripheral parenteral feedings ranges from 600 to 900 mOsm/L. Osmolarity of a dextrose/amino acid formulation can be approximated quickly by multiplying the final dextrose concentration by 50 and the final amino acid concentration by 10. Using this method, a formulation of 7.5% dextrose and 3% amino acids has an approximate osmolarity of 675 mOsm [(7.5% dextrose × 50 = 375 mOsm) + (3% dextrose × 10 = 300 mOsm)]. Although the concurrent administration of fat emulsions decreases osmolarity, buffers the pH, and improves peripheral vein tolerance, it does not prevent phlebitis.[29] Other efforts to minimize phlebitis include the addition of a combination of heparin and hydrocortisone, with or without sodium hydroxide, to the intravenous solution.[30,31] Another method to reduce the incidence of phlebitis is the use of a glycerol trinitrate patch applied near the peripheral IV site to dilate the superficial veins which constrict when there is irritation.[32]

Patient Assessment

10. Male in Moderate Stress. D.C., a 38-year-old male with a 12-year history of Crohn's disease, is admitted to the hospital after being evaluated in the clinic for a complaint of increasing abdominal pain, nausea and vomiting for 7 days, and no stool output for 5 days. Further questioning reveals that he has been drinking only liquids during the past week secondary to nausea and vomiting and his weight has decreased 8 lb during that time. D.C.'s past medical history is significant for frequent exacerbations of his disease during the last 2 years. His surgical history includes an exploratory laparotomy 6 months ago for resection of 10 cm of his small intestine. Family and social histories are noncontributory. His current medications include sulfasalazine 500 mg PO QID and prednisone 10 mg PO QD. Review of systems is positive for severe abdominal pain. Upon physical examination D.C. appears thin and his abdomen is distended. Vital signs are notable for a temperature of 38.3 °C, heart rate of 98 beats/min, and a blood pressure (BP) of 88/56 mm Hg. He is 6′ tall and weighs 60.5 kg. His medical record indicates that 1 month ago he weighed 64 kg and 6 months ago his weight was 70 kg. Abdominal radiographs are consistent with a small bowel obstruction.

Admission laboratory values are as follows: Na 131 mEq/L (Normal: 135–145); K 3.2 mEq/L (Normal: 3.5–5.0); Cl 96 mEq/L (Normal: 100–110); bicarbonate 28 mEq/L (Normal: 24–30); BUN 19 mg/dL (Normal: 8–20); Creatinine 0.9 mg/dL (Normal: 0.8–1.2); glucose 148 mg/dL (Normal: 85–110); albumin 3.4 gm/dL (Normal: 3.5–5.0); WBC count 10,900/mm³ (Normal: 4000–12,000); hematocrit (Hct) 46% (Normal: 34–50); alanine aminotransferase (ALT) 20 U/L(Normal: 2–24); aspartate aminotransferase (AST) 15 U/L (Normal: 6–17); alkaline phosphatase 45 U/L (Normal: 29–90); total bilirubin 0.9 mg/dL (Normal: 0–1.2).

D.C. is admitted with a diagnosis of a small bowel obstruction. The plan is to manage him with IV fluids, bowel rest and bowel decompression, and possible surgery. Why is D.C. a candidate for parenteral nutrition? [SI units: Na 131 mmol/L (Normal: 135–145); K 3.2 mmol/L (Normal: 3.5–5.0); Cl 96 mmol/L (Normal: 100–110); bicarbonate 28 mmol/L (Normal: 24–30); BUN 6.78 mmol/L (Normal: 2.89–7.14); SrCr 54 μmol/L (Normal: 48–110); glucose 8.2 mmol/L (Normal: 4.7–6.1 mmol/L); albumin 34 gm/L (Normal: 35–50); WBC count 10.9 × 10⁻⁹/L (Normal: 4–12); Hct 0.46 1 (Normal: 34–50); ALT 0.334 μkat/L (Normal: 0.03–0.4); AST 0.25 μkat/L (Normal: 0.1–0.28); alkaline phosphatase 0.75 μkat/L (Normal: 0.48–1.5); total bilirubin 15.39 μmol/L (Normal: 0–20)]

Parenteral nutrition should be considered when enteral intake has been inadequate for seven days or longer. D.C. has eaten very little in the last week and his 5% decrease in weight during this time is considered a severe weight loss. Furthermore, his weight has been decreasing over the last six months. D.C. is not expected to resume oral intake because his small bowel obstruction is being managed with bowel rest and decompression. Assessment of weight loss should include evaluation of hydration status, especially since D.C.'s vomiting and very minimal oral intake for the past week probably has made him dehydrated. Loss of lean body mass is probably less than that reflected by decrease in weight. Although D.C. probably is dehydrated, he also may have significant loss of muscle resulting from his chronic intake of prednisone which stimulates gluconeogenesis and muscle breakdown for amino acids. Additionally, D.C.'s admission serum albumin concentration is low at 3.4 gm/dL. His hydration status also should be taken into consideration in the evaluation of his serum albumin. His serum albumin concentration probably will decrease further after D.C. is rehydrated. One factor contributing to his low serum albumin is the loss of proteins from the gastrointestinal tract during flares of his Crohn's disease. Continued inadequate nutrient intake increases his risk of malnutrition. Some type of specialized nutrition support should be initiated and because D.C.'s GI tract is not functioning, parenteral nutrition is indicated.

11. What type of malnutrition does D.C. have?

At this point D.C. exhibits some loss of fat and muscle, as well as depletion of visceral proteins. He has components of both marasmus and kwashiorkor; therefore, he would be considered to have mixed malnutrition.

Calorie and Protein Goals

12. After hydration with IV fluids D.C.'s weight was 62.5 kg. The initiation of parenteral nutrition therapy was delayed because within 24 hours after admission, D.C.'s abdominal pain and distention was worse and he required surgery. An exploratory laparotomy was performed for perforation of his ileum and another 25 cm of his ileum was resected. His medications include hydrocortisone 100 mg IV Q 8 hr, gentamicin 90 mg IV Q 8 hr, and cefotetan 1 gm IV Q 12 hr. He has a right subclavian central venous catheter and an NG tube with high output of 2400 mL/day. Parenteral nutrition is to begin on postoperative day 1. Calculate energy and protein goals for D.C.

Using the Harris-Benedict equation for males, his current weight of 62.5 kg, height of 182.9 cm, and age of 38 years, D.C.'s BEE is 1583 (see Table 35.2). To estimate his total energy expenditure, the BEE should be modified with an activity factor for being confined to bed of 1.2 and a stress factor of 1.2 for surgery. These modifications will result in an estimated energy expenditure of 40% greater than his BEE or 2216 kcal (1583 × 1.4). Using the simpler method for moderate stress (35 kcal/kg/day) results in an estimated energy expenditure of 2188 kcal/day. Therefore, an energy goal of 2200 kcal/day is reasonable. In a similar manner, his protein goal (see Table 35.3) for moderate stress is 75 to 94 gm/day of protein (1.2 to 1.5 gm/kg/day).

Formulation Design

13. Design a parenteral feeding formulation for D.C. that provides 2200 nonprotein kcal and 90 gm of amino acids. The macronutrients available for compounding the parenteral feeding formulations are 50% dextrose, 20% fat emulsion, and 10% amino acids.

Dextrose provides 3.4 kcal/gm and, therefore, 647 gm of dextrose is required. If a 50% dextrose solution is to be used, about 1294 mL will be needed to meet this caloric goal. Since 1 gm of protein equals 1 gm of amino acids, 900 mL of the 10% amino acids product is required to provide the 90 gm of needed amino acids. The final base formulation is composed of:

$$\begin{array}{r} 1294 \text{ mL Dextrose 70\%} \\ \underline{900 \text{ mL Amino Acids 10\%}} \\ 2194 \text{ mL Total Volume} \end{array}$$

Other additives such as electrolytes, vitamins, and trace elements are included in the parenteral feeding formulation and increase slightly the final volume to 2300 mL/day. The infusion rate for this formulation can be calculated as follows:

$$\text{Hourly Infusion Rate (mL/hr)} = \frac{2300 \text{ mL/day}}{24 \text{ hr/day}}$$

$$= 96 \text{ mL/hr}$$

Clearly, D.C.'s parenteral feeding formulation of 2300 mL/day will approximate his maintenance fluid needs of 2350 mL/day. (See Question 7.) He will, however, require extra fluid to replace the fluid loss from his nasogastric tube. These additional fluids should be provided through another IV.

Many institutions utilize standard base formulations. A commonly employed base formulation is dextrose 25% and amino acids 4.25% (850 cal and 42.5 gm/L amino acids). Using this standard mixture for D.C. would require 2.6 L/day to approximate his calorie goal, but would slightly overfeed him with protein (110.5 gm/day).

Monitoring and Management of Complications

14. If the standard base formulation is used for D.C., how can D.C.'s tolerance to this excessive protein be monitored?

Most patients tolerate protein well. The most common sign of protein overload is an increasing BUN without an increase in serum creatinine (i.e., the BUN:creatinine ratio >20). Some patients receiving a high-protein feeding will develop an osmotic diuresis and subsequent dehydration from the excessive urea.[33]

15. Metabolic Complications: Essential Fatty Acid Deficiency (EFAD). **Will D.C. need any IV fat emulsions if all of his nonprotein calories are provided by dextrose?**

A small amount of lipids is necessary to prevent essential fatty acid deficiency. The essential fatty acids, linoleic, linolenic, and arachidonic, are those that cannot be synthesized by humans. Of these, linoleic acid appears to be the only one required by adults. Arachidonic acid can be synthesized from linoleic and the role of linolenic is still unclear. The continuous infusion of hypertonic dextrose is associated with high circulating concentrations of insulin. Since insulin promotes lipogenesis, rather than lipolysis, linoleic acid cannot be released from adipose tissue. Clinical symptoms of EFAD are dry, thickened, scaly skin, hair loss, poor wound healing, and diarrhea. Essential fatty acid deficiency can occur after weeks to months of fat-free parenteral feedings.[34] The requirement for essential fatty acids is 1% to 4% of total calories and can be met by the administration of 500 mL of a lipid emulsion twice weekly to patients receiving parenteral nutrition.[35] The incidence of EFAD is very low today because practitioners administer IV lipids early in the course of parenteral nutrition in order to prevent it.

An alternative approach to providing D.C.'s nutritional requirements would be to meet his protein goals with 2.2 L/day of the standard formulation which will provide 1870 carbohydrate calories each day. The remaining 330 calories can be provided as 300 mL of 10% intravenous fat emulsions or 165 mL of the 20% emulsion. This regimen would meet his calorie and protein goals and also prevent essential fatty acid deficiency.

16. Metabolic Consequences of Excessive Dextrose Administration. **What are the benefits of using a mixed-fuel system combining dextrose and fat to meet energy needs?**

Providing a portion of nonprotein calories as fat may reduce the metabolic consequences of excessive dextrose administration. The maximum rate of dextrose metabolism in humans is approximately 10 gm/kg/day. In doses in excess of 10 gm/kg/day, dextrose is used inefficiently and is converted to fat. The conversion to fat may be associated with respiratory compromise and hepatic dysfunction. Hyperglycemia also is a complication of excessive dextrose infusion, and is associated with electrolyte disturbances and altered phagocyte function. Optimal metabolism of dextrose seems to be 5.8 gm/kg/day.[36] Typically, a mixed-fuel system provides 20% to 30% of nonprotein calories as fat.

17. D.C.'s parenteral feeding formulation is changed to one providing 30% of the 2200 nonprotein calories as fat and the remaining 70% as dextrose. His protein dose remains at 90 gm/day. Design this parenteral feeding formulation using the components on the formulary: 20% fat emulsion, 70% dextrose, and 10% amino acids.

1. Fat emulsion calculation.

$$\text{Calories from Fat} = (2200 \text{ kcal})(0.3)$$

$$= 600 \text{ kcal}$$

Using the 20% fat emulsion will require 330 mL to provide 660 kcal (see Table 35.4).

$$\text{mL 20\% Fat Emulsion} = \frac{600 \text{ kcal}}{2 \text{ kcal/mL}}$$

$$= 330 \text{ mL}$$

2. Dextrose calculation.

$$\text{Calories from Dextrose} = (2200 \text{ kcal})(0.7) \text{ or } (2200 - 660)$$

$$= 1540 \text{ kcal}$$

$$\text{gm of Dextrose} = \frac{1540 \text{ kcal}}{3.4 \text{ kcal/gm}}$$

$$= 453 \text{ gm}$$

$$\text{mL 70\% Dextrose} = \frac{453 \text{ gm}}{0.7 \text{ gm/mL}}$$

$$= 647 \text{ mL}$$

3. Amino acid calculation (1 gm protein = 1 gm amino acids).

$$\text{mL 10\% Amino Acids} = \frac{90 \text{ gm}}{0.1 \text{ gm/mL}}$$

$$= 900 \text{ mL}$$

4. Calculation of final volume.

$$\begin{array}{r} 330 \text{ mL fat emulsion} \\ 647 \text{ mL dextrose} \\ \underline{900 \text{ mL amino acids}} \\ 1877 \text{ mL total volume} \end{array}$$

18. Total Nutrient Admixtures (TNAs). **What are the advantages to combining the dextrose, fat, and amino acids in one container?**

Parenteral feeding formulations which combine the entire daily nutrient requirements in a single container are called total nutrient admixtures. (See Question 6 for an alternative administration method for fat emulsions.) This system of providing one container per day offers the advantage of convenience to pharmacy staff, nursing personnel, and the patient. Pharmacy compounding is done only once per day, requires fewer supplies, and decreases inventory. Furthermore, waste of unused feeding formulations is decreased.[37,38] Nursing time to administer TNAs is decreased because only one bag is hung per day and the system avoids the need to manipulate a secondary infusion of fat emulsions, as well as additional IV tubing and an infusion pump. Finally, those patients who are ambulatory find it easier to move about with only one infusion pump.

19. *Stability*. **How stable are the TNA parenteral feeding formulations?**

TNAs are chemically stable for 10 to 28 days at 4 to 5 °C.[39–42] The commercially available fat emulsions in the U.S., however, use an anionic egg-yolk phosphatide emulsifier and the addition of any substance with cationic properties can neutralize the negative charge of the emulsifier and alter the stability of the emulsion. When the emulsion breaks down, the fat particles begin to increase in size. The destabilization of the emulsion occurs in steps beginning with creaming and ending with the coalescence of the lipid particles. A decrease in pH and the addition of divalent cations are two factors that increase fat particle size. Although dextrose decreases pH, the addition of amino acids provides an adequate buffer for this variable. Fat emulsion particles have an average size of 0.5 microns. A destabilized emulsion is not visibly apparent until the lipid particles are 40 to 50 microns. Fat particles as small as 5 microns may occlude pulmonary capillaries. Therefore, the use of a 1.2 micron filter is recommended to protect against the infusion of enlarged lipid particles.[35]

20. How does the microbial growth of TNAs compare with that of dextrose/amino acid formulations?

Dextrose/amino acid formulations are not conducive to growth of most organisms because of a high osmolarity (>2000 mOsm/L) and an acidic pH. Fat emulsions alone, however, are isotonic and have a physiologic pH providing an optimal growth medium. Combining these three substrates in a TNA provides a formulation with a growth potential somewhere between that of the fat and that of the dextrose/amino acids. The number of central venous catheter violations or manipulations also correlates with the incidence of catheter-related infections. From an infection control perspective, the use of a single daily bag TNA limits the number of manipulations of the central venous catheter to once per day, thereby minimizing touch contamination.

21. *Micronutrients: Electrolytes*. **D.C.'s current laboratory values are Na 137 mEq/L, K 4.5 mEq/L, Cl 102 mEq/L, bicarbonate 26 mEq/L, BUN 9 mg/dL, creatinine 0.8 mg/dL, glucose 188 mg/dL, Ca 8.9 mg/dL, Mg 1.9 mg/dL, P 2.8 mg/dL, and albumin 3.0 mg/dL. Which electrolytes should be included in D.C.'s parenteral feeding formulation?** [SI units: Na 137 mmol/L; K 4.5 mmol/L; Cl 102 mmol/L; bicarbonate 26 mmol/L; BUN 3.2 mmol/L; creatinine 48 μmol/L; glucose 10.44 mmol/L; Ca 2.22 mmol/L; Mg 9.5 mmol/L; P 0.9 mmol/L; albumin 30 gm/L.]

Electrolytes most commonly added are sodium, potassium, chloride, acetate, magnesium, calcium, and phosphate. Electrolytes should be added to the parenteral feeding formulation based upon the individual patient's needs. However, patients without significant fluid and electrolyte losses, hepatic or renal dysfunction, or acid-base disturbances do well with maintenance doses of electrolytes. Electrolytes may be added individually or as commercially available combination products of maintenance doses. When considering electrolyte additives to parenteral feeding formulations it is important to consider the electrolyte content of the amino acid solution. General guidelines for electrolyte requirements for parenteral feedings are included in Table 35.6.

22. *Vitamins and Trace Elements*. **What doses of multiple vitamins and trace elements should D.C. receive in his parenteral feeding formulation?**

Vitamins and trace elements are essential for normal metabolism and should be included in a patient's daily parenteral nutrition regimen. Guidelines for the 13 essential vitamins have been established by the Nutrition Advisory Group of the American Medical Association.[43] Most institutions use a multiple-vitamin product that contains 12 vitamins (Table 35.5). Vitamin K is not included in adult multivitamin formulations and usually is administered by giving 5 to 10 mg/week subcutaneously or intramuscularly. Alternatively, 1 to 2 mg can be added daily to the parenteral feeding formulation.

Guidelines for daily doses of trace elements zinc, copper, chromium, and manganese also have been developed.[44] In addition to these trace elements, many practitioners also provide selenium on a daily basis. Recommended doses of the trace elements are listed in Table 35.7. As with vitamins, trace elements are available as single entities or as combination products. Molybdenum and iodine also are available commercially.

23. D.C.'s parenteral feeding formulation of 2160 mL provides 2200 nonprotein calories (70% carbohydrate, 30% fat) and 90 gm of amino acids with the following additives per liter: 40 mEq NaCl, 40 mEq K acetate, 15 mmol phosphate as Na, 8 mEq MgSO₄, 5 mEq calcium gluconate, multivitamins 10 mL, multiple trace element product 3 mL. The infusion is initiated at an infusion rate of 40 mL/hr. Why is this infusion rate so slow?

Standard practice for administering parenteral feeding formulations containing hypertonic dextrose is to begin at a slow infusion rate and increase slowly over 24 to 48 hours. This initial period allows for assessment of tolerance of the feeding formulation components and avoids metabolic complications, primarily hyperglycemia.[45] This would be particularly important for D.C. whose glucose before beginning the parenteral feedings was 188 mg/dL. If D.C.'s glucose remains below 200 mg/dL the parenteral feeding formulation infusion rate can be increased to his goal rate.

Monitoring and Management of Complications

24. *Metabolic Complications*. **Over the next 24 hours D.C.'s infusion rate is increased to the goal rate of 75 mL/hr. A comparison of his intake and output is significant because a high volume of gastric fluid is being suctioned out from the NG tube and is placing D.C. overall in a negative fluid balance. Laboratory values at this time are Na 138 mEq/L, K 3.1 mEq/L, chloride 91 mEq/L, bicarbonate 33 mEq/L, BUN 28 mg/dL, Creatinine 0.9 mg/dL, glucose 279 mg/dL, Ca 8.1 mg/dL, Mg 1.6 mg/dL, P 1.8 mg/dL, and albumin 3.1 gm/dL. Arterial blood gas (ABG) results are pH 7.46, pO₂ 98, pCO₂ 47, bicarbonate 31. What factors contribute to these metabolic abnormalities?** [SI units: Na 130 mmol/L; K 3.1 mmol/L; Cl 91 mmol/L; bicarbonate 33 mmol/L; BUN 0.71 mmol/L; creatinine 54 μmol/L; glucose 15.5 mmol/L; Ca 2.02 mmol/L; Mg 0.8 mmol/L; P 0.58 mmol/L; albumin 31 gm/L.]

Hypokalemia is a common metabolic abnormality associated with the initiation of parenteral nutrition and usually occurs within 24 to 48 hours. Potassium moves, along with dextrose, from the extracellular to the intracellular space. Building lean body mass (i.e., anabolism) also requires potassium. D.C.'s decreased potassium is compounded by his metabolic alkalosis secondary to his loss of gastric secretions through his NG tube. With this type of metabolic alkalosis, the renal excretion of potassium is increased.

Table 35.6	Guidelines for Electrolyte Requirements Per 1000 Calories	
Electrolyte	Amount/1000 Calories
Sodium	40–50 mEq
Potassium	30–40 mEq
Chloride	40–50 mEq
Magnesium	8–12 mEq
Calcium	2–5 mEq
Phosphorus (phosphate)	15–25 mmol

Table 35.7	Recommended Daily Adult Doses of Parenteral Trace Elements
Trace Element	Dose
Zinc	2.5–4.0 mg
Copper	0.5–1.5 mg
Chromium	10–15 µg
Manganese	150–800 µg
Selenium	40–80 µg

Additional potassium should be administered and can be provided in D.C.'s parenteral feeding or through another IV.

Hypophosphatemia occurs when phosphorus moves into the cells for the synthesis of adenosine triphosphate (ATP), an important energy carrier. Phosphorus is depleted quickly with the administration of hypertonic dextrose, especially to malnourished patients. The phosphorus is used for ATP synthesis, primarily in the liver and skeletal muscle. Alkalosis also decreases phosphate stores by stimulating the phosphorylation of carbohydrates. As a component of 2,3-diphosphoglycerate (2,3-DPG), found in red blood cells, phosphorus is necessary for the regulation of the amount of oxygen delivered to cells. Clinical signs and symptoms of hypophosphatemia usually occur when serum concentrations fall below 1.0 mg/dL and include lethargy, muscle weakness, impaired white blood cell function, seizures, and hemolytic anemia. Severe, complicated hypophosphatemia can be managed by administering 0.08 to 0.32 mmol/kg of phosphate IV.[46,47] Although D.C.'s serum phosphorus is not below 1.0 mg/dL, it is low (1.8 mg/dL) and he should receive 15 to 25 mmol phosphate in the parenteral feeding formulation per 1000 calories. Additionally, supplements may be necessary to replete his phosphorus stores.

Metabolic Alkalosis. D.C. has evidence of a metabolic alkalosis based upon his arterial blood gas results, hypochloremia, and elevated bicarbonate. The continued loss of fluid and hydrochloric acid (HCl) from his nasogastric tube probably is the primary etiology of his metabolic alkalosis. Management of this type of metabolic alkalosis is to replace the fluid and chloride through another IV. Since acetate is converted to bicarbonate and further contributes to the alkalosis, the acetate salts in the parenteral feeding formulation can be changed to chloride salts. Nevertheless, it is important to remember that the parenteral feeding formulation is not the primary vehicle for adjusting and supplementing electrolytes and fluid. Generally, fluid and electrolyte balance should be adjusted with a maintenance IV.

Hyperglycemia is a very common metabolic complication of parenteral nutrition therapy, especially in stressed patients. Stress alone increases gluconeogenesis and the administration of hypertonic dextrose compounds this hyperglycemia. D.C. is at particular risk of hyperglycemia because he is recovering from surgery and also is receiving steroids which increase gluconeogenesis. Persistent hyperglycemia leads to glucosuria and an osmotic diuresis, resulting in dehydration and concomitant electrolyte abnormalities. In extreme cases, hyperglycemia progresses to hyperosmolar, nonketotic coma, a condition associated with a 40% mortality. Hyperglycemia can be prevented by gradually increasing the parenteral feeding formulation infusion rate, frequent monitoring of capillary blood glucose concentrations, checking urine for presence of glucose, and advancing therapy only when the serum glucose is less than 200 mg/dL. Insulin therapy should be administered if glucose exceeds 200 mg/dL and can be administered subcutaneously according to a "sliding scale," intravenously by continuous infusion, or by adding insulin to the parenteral feeding formulation.[48]

Parenteral nutrition therapy may be associated with multiple metabolic complications. The most common abnormalities are hypokalemia, hypophosphatemia, and hyperglycemia. The plan for parenteral nutrition therapy should include routine monitoring of these serum chemistries to identify complications early and institute methods to manage or prevent complications.

Formulation Design

25. Compatibility. In response to these serum chemistries, the electrolytes in D.C.'s parenteral feeding formulation are changed to the following per liter: 45 mEq NaCl, 60 mEq KCl, 40 mmol phosphate as K, 8 mEq MgSO₄, 15 mEq calcium gluconate. How do the doses of calcium and phosphate compare to maintenance doses? What calcium and phosphate incompatibilities should be anticipated?

The dose of calcium, as ordered for D.C., is over three times the usual maintenance dose (see Table 35.6). This amount of calcium probably is not necessary because the observed hypocalcemia merely reflects D.C.'s low serum albumin concentration and, therefore, less calcium is bound to albumin. D.C. probably is not truly hypocalcemic, because his free (or ionized) calcium, which is critical for physiologic function, has not changed. For every 1 gm/dL decrease in serum albumin concentration, there will be a 0.8 mg/dL reduction in the serum calcium concentration.[33] For D.C., a serum calcium of 8.1 mg/dL will correct to a serum concentration of 8.8 mg/dL [8.1 mg/dL + 0.72 mg/dL (4.0 gm/dL − 3.1 gm/dL albumin)].

The amount of phosphate prescribed for D.C. at this time exceeds the usual recommended dose of 15 to 25 mmol/1000 kcal (see Table 35.6). Although D.C. has a low serum phosphorus concentration and needs additional phosphate, increasing the dose in the parenteral feeding formulation to 40 mmol/L may be incompatible with the calcium content resulting in calcium phosphate precipitation. The precipitate may be visible as small "snowflakes" in a parenteral feeding formulation of dextrose and amino acids. However, in a TNA the precipitation may not be visible because the admixture is opaque. Administering a parenteral feeding formulation containing calcium phosphate crystals may occlude blood flow, especially in the lungs, and has been associated with adverse events including respiratory distress and death.[49,50] It is important to consider the factors that affect calcium phosphate solubility and to take measures to ensure that precipitates have not formed in parenteral feeding formulations. The *in vitro* precipitation of calcium phosphate is dependent upon multiple factors which include the calcium salt, concentrations of calcium and phosphate, amino acid concentration, temperature, pH of the formulation, and infusion time.[51,52] Calcium phosphate solubility can be enhanced by using calcium gluconate rather than the chloride salt. When in solution, calcium chloride dissociates more than calcium gluconate, thereby increasing the yield of free calcium available for association with phosphate. The amounts of calcium and phosphorus in the formulation are critical. Multiple investigators have varied the calcium and phosphate concentrations in parenteral feeding formulations and have developed precipitation curves to assist practitioners in determining the amounts of calcium and phosphate that can be added safely to feeding formulations. These guidelines help to predict the points where calcium phosphate precipitation is likely to occur. However, extrapolation of these data to parenteral feeding formulations that are different than those described is difficult because these are complex mixtures and numerous variables affect the interrelationship between calcium and phosphate.[52] When calculating the solubility of calcium and phosphate it should be determined based upon the volume of the formulation at the time the calcium and phosphate are mixed together, not the final volume. For example, if the electrolytes including calcium and phosphate are added to 1000 mL of a dextrose/amino acid mixture and then 300 mL of intravenous fat is added, the calcium phosphate solubility is based upon the 1000 mL, not the final 1300 mL volume. Additionally, some amino acid products contain phosphate ions and these should be considered when determining calcium phosphate solubility.[49] Lastly, calcium and phosphate should not be added in close sequence to the parenteral feeding formulation and during preparation, the parenteral feeding formulation should be agitated periodically and inspected for precipitates. Other guidelines for improving the solubility of calcium are a final amino acid concentration of greater than 2.5% and a pH below 6. Temperature is a critical variable and increased temperatures of the environment can facilitate the precipitation of calcium phosphate.

Formulations should be infused within 24 hours after compounding if stored at room temperature and if refrigerated, within 24 hours after rewarming. Furthermore, slow infusions may decrease solubility. Increasing temperature and slow infusions may result in precipitation in the intravenous catheter without occurring in the infusion container.[53] Lastly, it is recommended that a 1.2 micron air-eliminating filter be used when infusing TNA parenteral feeding formulations and a 0.22 micron air-eliminating filter for nonlipid-containing admixtures.[49]

26. Medication Additives. In addition to his parenteral feeding formulation, D.C. is receiving ranitidine 50 mg IV Q 8 hr, hydrocortisone 100 mg IV Q 8 hr, and now needs insulin. Can these medications be mixed with his parenteral feeding formulation to simplify his medication regimen?

Patients receiving parenteral nutrition therapy frequently require concomitant drug therapy. Most patients have adequate venous access or have multiple lumen central venous catheters and mixing medications with the parenteral feeding formulation is not an issue. However, for some patients with limited venous access, directly added medications or piggybacking medications via a secondary infusion must be considered. The stability of medications when mixed with parenteral feeding formulations is a complex issue. Some medications may be added directly to the parenteral feeding formulation and others are administered via a secondary infusion set (piggybacked). Many medications have been studied for physical compatibility, but few have evaluated pharmacological activity. Furthermore, the study conditions vary and different feeding formulations have been used; therefore, interpretation and application of data from a particular scientific study to a specific feeding formulation may be difficult. This area of knowledge is growing rapidly and current information regarding compatibility and stability is available in standard references such as Trissel's Handbook of Injectable Drugs.[54] Although insulin, antibiotics, chemotherapeutic agents, H₂ blockers, and heparin[52,54] have been considered for addition to parenteral feeding formulations in some specific circumstances, generally the routine addition of medications to parenteral feeding formulations is discouraged.

27. Monitoring Parameters. Design a plan to monitor the adequacy of D.C.'s specialized nutrition support and to identify and prevent adverse complications.

Routine evaluation of patients receiving nutrition support should include an assessment of nutritional and metabolic effects of therapy. Goals for nutritional therapy are estimates of a patient's needs; therefore, the adequacy of therapy to meet these needs must be evaluated. Daily monitoring parameters must include vital signs, body weight, temperature, serum chemistries, hematologic indices, nutritional intake, and fluid intake and output. Adequacy of nutritional therapy should be assessed weekly. Most important is the identification of trends that may alert one to impending com-

plications. A suggested schedule for monitoring parameters is provided in Table 35.8.

Fistulas

28. D.C. has been receiving parenteral nutrition therapy for 1 week and now has an enterocutaneous fistula with output of 2500 mL/day. How should his parenteral nutrition therapy be altered?

Management of D.C.'s enterocutaneous fistula will include nothing by mouth because food stimulates losses of fluids and electrolytes from the GI tract. The fluids secreted by the GI tract are rich in electrolytes including sodium, potassium, chloride, and bicarbonate. Measurement of the electrolyte content of the fistula output will determine those that must be replaced and in what quantities. Both fluid and electrolytes should be replaced intravenously to prevent dehydration and electrolyte and acid-base imbalances. In addition to losses of fluids and electrolytes, the trace element zinc is lost in fluid from the small intestine. Approximately 12 mg of zinc is lost in each liter of small bowel fluid and should be replaced to prevent zinc deficiency. Furthermore, zinc may play a role in wound healing.[55] Once the daily losses of these fluids and electrolytes have stabilized, they may be added to the parenteral feeding formulation. Adequate nitrogen (protein) intake is important to enhance healing and replace losses.

Short Bowel Syndrome

29. D.C.'s fistula does not heal and he requires additional surgery. The surgery entails removing large sections of the small and large intestine and D.C. now is considered to have short bowel syndrome. Will he need to receive parenteral nutrition at home after discharge?

Short bowel syndrome is characterized by malabsorption, dehydration, and both micro- and macronutrient abnormalities. Severe malnutrition will develop without optimal nutritional support. In order to maintain adequate nutritional status, D.C. will need parenteral nutrition until his intestinal tract begins to adapt to improve digestion and absorption of nutrients. This adaptive period may take several weeks to months to years. Adaptation is enhanced

Table 35.8	Routine Monitoring Parameters for Parenteral Nutrition[a]

Daily
Body weight
Vital signs (pulse, respirations, temperature)
Fluid intake
Nutritional intake
Output (urine, other losses)
Serum electrolytes (Na, K, Cl, bicarbonate, BUN, creatinine)[a]
Glucose

2–3 Times a Week
CBC
Ca
Mg
P

Weekly
Albumin
Total protein
Transthyretin
Liver-associated tests (AST, ALT, alkaline phosphatase, GGT, bilirubin)
Nitrogen balance

[a] ALT = Alanine aminotransferase; AST = Aspartate aminotransferase; BUN = Blood urea nitrogen; Ca = Calcium; Cl = Chloride; GGT = Gamma glutamyl transferase; K = Potassium; Mg = Magnesium; Na = Sodium; P = Phosphorus.

by stimulation of the enterocytes with nutrients. This stimulation can be provided by small, frequent oral meals or tube-feeding. Parenteral feeding formulations are an important part of the management of patients with short bowel syndrome.[56]

Home Therapy

30. Design a plan to transition D.C. to a home parenteral nutrition regimen.

D.C. is expected to increase his ambulation before discharge and once he's at home. To facilitate ambulation, all of D.C.'s fluids including parenteral feedings, electrolytes, vitamins, trace minerals, and water should be provided in one container per day. This requires accounting for all IV fluids and supplemental electrolytes and may be 3 to 4 L/day. Daily intake and output must be monitored and therapy adjusted based upon this information and D.C.'s clinical status. Multiple adjustments in fluids and electrolytes may be needed before a stable feeding formulation is designed.

Cyclic Therapy

31. What other measures can be undertaken to simplify D.C.'s parenteral feeding regimen and encourage ambulation?

After all of D.C.'s daily nutrient and fluid needs are consolidated and he is stable on that regimen, his parenteral feeding regimen can be cycled. Cycling is a method to infuse the parenteral feeding formulation over a period less than 24 hours to allow for some time free from this "high tech" therapy. Cycling is usually done gradually and is dependent upon the patient's ability to tolerate the changes in fluid and dextrose intake. Initially, the infusion period is decreased by two to four hours and the infusion rate is increased to compensate for the shorter infusion period. For example, a 24-hour infusion at 100 mL/hr would be changed to a 20-hour infusion at 120 mL/hour. This gradual adjustment assures that all nutrients are infused and well tolerated. With each incremental decrease in time, the infusion rate should be increased. Vital signs, fluid intake and output, and serum glucose concentrations should be monitored during this period. The serum glucose concentration should be evaluated 30 to 90 minutes after the infusion is completed to be sure that hypoglycemia does not occur as the result of the rapid cessation of the feeding formulation. If hypoglycemia occurs, the infusion rate can be tapered at the end of the infusion because a gradual decrease in glucose intake should minimize the potential for hypoglycemia. Many patients can eventually infuse the feeding formulation over 10 to 12 hours. Consequently, the feeding formulation can be infused during the night so that the patient is free during the day.

32. Metabolic Complications: Elevated Liver-Associated Enzymes. After being on home parenteral nutrition for 2 weeks, D.C.'s liver function tests (i.e., bilirubin, alkaline phosphatase, and especially AST and ALT) have increased since he was discharged from the hospital. How could his parenteral nutrition be contributing to these abnormalities?

Elevations in liver function tests are common in adults receiving parenteral nutrition. The increases in the serum concentrations of these tests may be noted as early as one to two weeks after beginning therapy, but usually do not progress to significant liver dysfunction in adults. Liver-associated enzyme elevations usually resolve when parenteral nutrition therapy is discontinued. Although parenteral nutrition-associated liver abnormalities were first noted over 20 years ago, a cause-and-effect relationship has been difficult to establish because patients have many confounding factors that also can cause liver dysfunction. For example, overfeeding with parenteral feeding formulations containing high amounts of carbohydrate, amino acid deficiencies, excess fat, essential fatty acid deficiency, carnitine deficiency, toxic effects of the amino acid

degradation products, bacterial overgrowth in the small intestine, and lack of stimulation of the GI tract all can increase the serum concentrations of liver enzymes.[57–60] The elevations in D.C.'s liver-associated enzymes should be monitored weekly for continued increases. It can be anticipated that he may not need lifelong parenteral nutrition therapy and should begin to transition to some oral food intake.

Use of Parenteral Nutrition in Special Disease States
Hepatic Failure

33. J.U., a 62-year-old male with a history of alcohol abuse, alcoholic cirrhosis, and esophageal varices, was admitted to the hospital 7 days ago with an upper GI bleed. He required gastric lavage, fluid resuscitation, and multiple transfusions of packed red blood cells and fresh frozen plasma to stabilize him hemodynamically and to stop the bleeding. Endoscopic examination showed multiple esophageal varices, gastritis, and a large bleeding gastric ulcer. He was taken to surgery and the ulcer was repaired. It is now 2 days after surgery and plans are to begin parenteral nutrition because he has not eaten in over a week, has a low serum albumin of 1.8 gm/dL (Normal: 3.0–5.0), and does not yet have return of GI function. At this time J.U. is alert, oriented, and without evidence of encephalopathy. Is J.U. a candidate for a specialty amino acid product specifically designed for use in hepatic failure? [SI unit: 18 gm/L (Normal: 30–50)]

Aromatic Amino Acids (AAA) and Branched-Chain Amino Acids (BCAA)

Patients with cirrhosis and chronic hepatic failure have increased circulating concentrations of the aromatic amino acids (AAA), phenylalanine, tyrosine, and tryptophan, and decreased concentrations of the branched-chain amino acids (BCAA), leucine, isoleucine, and valine. The AAA cross the blood-brain barrier and form false neurotransmitters which impair normal neurotransmission and brain activity.[62] These amino acids, therefore, may contribute to hepatic encephalopathy.[55] Based upon these theories, an amino acid product was designed to provide adequate protein for anabolism while also treating hepatic encephalopathy.[61] To normalize the amino acid profile in the brain, a specially designed product has increased amounts of BCAA and decreased amounts of the AAA as well as methionine (see Table 35.9). Controversy exists on the ability of this special amino acid mixture to improve encephalopathy by altering the amino acid profile of the cerebrospinal fluid.[61–65] Generally, this amino acid mixture is reserved for those patients with hepatic encephalopathy. Since J.U. is alert, oriented, and has no signs of encephalopathy, use of this product is not warranted at this time. However, should he develop signs and symptoms of hepatic encephalopathy while receiving the standard amino acids, use of the increased BCAA, decreased AAA mixture may be considered.

34. What other amino acid mixtures are enriched with BCAAs?

Branched chain amino acids have metabolic properties that are considered beneficial during physiologic stress (multiple trauma, sepsis, major surgery). The BCAAs can be used as an alternative energy source by the heart, brain, and skeletal muscle: they can increase protein synthesis in muscle and liver, decrease excessive proteolysis in muscle, and normalize abnormal plasma amino acid profiles. These unique properties led to the design of commercially available amino acid mixtures that provide about 45% of the amino acids as BCAA. In comparison, most standard amino acid mixtures contain 19% to 25% BCAA. Multiple trials have evaluated the

Table 35.9	Amino Acid Product Comparison Table		
Description	Product Name	Supplier	Available Concentrations
General Formulations Contain essential[a] and nonessential[b] amino acids, some available with electrolytes[c]	Aminosyn, Aminosyn II FreAmine III Novamine Travasol	Abbott Kendall McGaw Clintec Clintec	3.5%,[c] 5%, 7%,[c] 8.5%,[c] 10%[c] 3%, 8.5%, 10% 11.4%, 15% 3.5%,[c] 5.5%,[c] 8.5%,[c] 10%
Hepatic Failure Formulations Contain essential and nonessential amino acids with an ↑ proportion of branched-chain amino acids (leucine, isoleucine, valine)	HepatAmine	Kendall McGaw	8%
Renal Failure Formulations Contain primarily essential amino acids. RenAmin also contains a complement of nonessential amino acids	Aminess Aminosyn-RF Nephramine RenAmin	Clintec Abbott Kendall McGaw Clintec	5.2% 5.2% 5.4% 6.5%
Stress Formulations Contain ↑ percentages of leucine, isoleucine, and valine as well as all essential and nonessential amino acids	Aminosyn HBC FreAmine HBC	Abbott Kendall McGaw	7% 6.9%
Supplements Contain only branched-chain amino acids (isoleucine, leucine, valine); must be used with a general formulation	BranchAmin	Clintec	4%

[a] Essential amino acids: *isoleucine, leucine, methionine, phenylalanine, threonine, tryptophan, valine, histidine.*
[b] Nonessential amino acids: *cysteine, arginine, alanine, proline, glycine, serine, tyrosine.*
[c] These concentrations are available with or without electrolytes.

effects of BCAA-enriched amino acid formulations in critically ill patients. The majority of evidence suggests that although these formulations may improve nitrogen retention, it does not appear that they provide beneficial effects on clinical outcome.[66,67] It is important to appreciate the differences between the amino acid composition of the mixtures for hepatic failure and those designed for stress. They are not therapeutically equivalent and one should not be substituted for the other.

Diabetes, Respiratory Failure, Pancreatitis, and Obesity

35. K.L. a 59-year-old female, is admitted to the hospital complaining of increasing abdominal pain and vomiting and is diagnosed with pancreatitis. This is her third admission for pancreatitis during the last year. Her past medical history also is significant for chronic obstructive airway disease (COAD) and diabetes mellitus. An NG tube is inserted and she is placed on NPO. IV fluids are begun. Over the next 5 days K.L.'s abdominal pain subsides, her pancreatitis resolves, and she is begun on an oral diet. Two days after beginning an oral diet she complains of severe abdominal pain, is febrile, her WBC count increases to 21,000/mm³, her blood glucose concentration increases to 350 mg/dL, and she is hypotensive requiring large volumes of IV fluids. Furthermore, she develops respiratory distress and requires endotracheal intubation and mechanical ventilation. This clinical presentation is consistent with severe necrotizing pancreatitis. She is 5'7" tall and upon admission her weight was 185 pounds. After fluid resuscitation she weighs 197 pounds. Parenteral nutrition therapy is to begin because K.L. is not expected to have a functional GI tract in the near future and has had inadequate nutrient intake during her hospitalization. What special considerations should be addressed in designing a parenteral feeding formulation for K.L.? [SI units: WBC count 21/L; blood glucose concentration 19.4 mmol/L.]

First, K.L. is obese and an adjusted weight should be calculated and used in nutritional calculations. See Equation 35.4 for a description on adjusting weight for obesity. Using an adjusted weight will decrease the risk of overfeeding which has the potential to further increase adipose tissue and to compromise respiration that

is critical for patients with COAD. Overfeeding with carbohydrates is particularly detrimental because of the amount of carbon dioxide (CO_2) produced relative to the amount of oxygen (O_2) consumed. This relationship is described by the respiratory quotient (RQ) which is the ratio of the amount of CO_2 produced to the amount of O_2 consumed. The RQ differs for each substrate and is 1.0 for carbohydrate oxidation, 0.7 for fat oxidation, but 8.0 when carbohydrate is converted to fat for storage.[68] This relationship is described below:

Dextrose oxidation

$$C_6H_{12}O_6 + 6 O_2 \rightarrow 6 H_2O + 6 CO_2$$

$$RQ = 6 CO_2 / 6 O_2 = 1.0$$

Fat oxidation

$$CH_3 (CH_2CH_2)_7 COOH + 23 O_2 \rightarrow 16 CO_2 + 16 H_2O$$

$$RQ = 16 CO_2 / 23 O_2 = 0.7$$

Fat synthesis

$$4 C_6H_{12}O_6 + O_2 \rightarrow C_{16}H_{32}O_2 + 8 CO_2 + 8 H_2O$$

$$RQ = 8 CO_2 / O_2 = 8.0$$

Based upon these relationships the oxidation of soybean oil emulsions produces 7.1 mmol CO_2 per calorie oxidized and 9.0 mmol CO_2 per calorie of dextrose oxidized, a 21% reduction in carbon dioxide produced.[69,70] Lipogenesis or fat synthesis occurs when the amount of carbohydrate administered exceeds the maximum oxidative rates. Complete oxidation of carbohydrate is demonstrated at dextrose infusions of 4 to 7 mg/kg/minute.[71] Infusions above this rate increase carbon dioxide production and may cause respiratory distress. Therefore, in designing a parenteral feeding formulation for K.L. it is important to provide her with a moderate calorie dose and to limit her dextrose dose to 4 to 7 mg/kg/minute to minimize excessive carbon dioxide production.[72,73] Providing a portion of K.L.'s calories as fat also may help in the management of her diabetes mellitus. Although K.L. has diabetes mellitus, serum glucose concentrations less than 200 mg/dL can be achieved in the same manner as described in Question 24.

36. Although the use of fat to meet K.L.'s energy needs may be beneficial in managing her diabetes mellitus and COAD, is the use of fat contraindicated in patients with pancreatitis?

The oral ingestion of fats may stimulate pancreatic exocrine function and should be restricted in patients with pancreatitis. Furthermore, pancreatitis may be associated with hyperlipidemia. This has led many practitioners to avoid the use of IV fat emulsions in patients with pancreatitis. Several investigators have evaluated the effects of parenteral feeding formulations containing fat emulsions in acute pancreatitis and found no stimulation of pancreatic exocrine function.[74-76] Furthermore, the administration of intravenous lipids to patients with a history of pancreatitis did not result in abdominal pain or relapse of pancreatitis.[77] Available data indicate that IV fat emulsions should be regarded as a safe and efficacious form of calories for patients with pancreatitis.[78]

Renal Failure

37. K.L.'s pancreatitis does not improve and her clinical course is further complicated by oliguria, a rise in serum creatinine SrCr to 3.0 mg/dL, and a BUN of 65 mg/dL. Her current parenteral feeding formulation provides 1.5 gm/kg/day of protein. How should the amino acid content of her feeding formulation be altered in view of her acute renal failure? [SI units: SrCr 180 µmol/L; BUN 23.2 mmol/L.]

The protein dose in acute renal failure should be reduced to 0.6 to 1.0 gm/kg/day as K.L.'s kidneys cannot tolerate the current protein dose and nitrogenous waste.[79,80] The use of essential amino acids (EAA) orally improves uremic symptoms. Based upon this experience, parenteral amino acid mixtures containing only EAA were investigated. These studies compared parenteral feedings containing dextrose and EAA to the administration of only dextrose and found an improved rate of recovery in the group that received the EAA.[79] Subsequent studies comparing parenteral feeding formulations containing a standard mix of both EAA and nonessential amino acids to EAA alone have not noted any difference in urea appearance or nitrogen balance.[79-82] The use of EAA alone in parenteral feeding formulations for patients with acute renal failure offers no clinical advantage over those providing both EAA and nonessential AA.[83]

38. Hemodialysis. K.L.'s renal failure progresses and she requires hemodialysis. How should her nutritional therapy be altered?

Hemodialysis allows the passage of amino acids through a semipermeable membrane. Approximately 1 gm of amino acids is lost for each hour of hemodialysis with a glucose-free dialysate. This loss is reduced by 50% when a glucose-containing dialysate is used. These losses should be replaced by increasing the protein dose provided by the parenteral feeding formulation. Recommended protein dose is 1.0 to 1.2 gm/kg/day.[81,82] Additionally, hemodialysis can increase energy expenditure by increasing oxygen consumption and gluconeogenesis; therefore, energy goals should be increased to 35 kcal/kg/day.[82] Patients requiring chronic hemodialysis may need their protein doses increased to 1.2 to 1.4 gm/kg/day to maintain a positive nitrogen balance and prevent protein malnutrition. Patients requiring peritoneal dialysis have higher losses of protein through the peritoneal cavity and may need 1.2 to 1.5 gm/kg/day of protein. In contrast to patients on hemodialysis, those on peritoneal dialysis will require fewer calories provided by parenteral feedings because 600 to 800 calories/day may be absorbed through the peritoneal membrane from the glucose-containing dialysate.[82]

Transitional Feedings From Parenteral to Enteral Nutrition

39. K.L. is recovering from her pancreatitis and a small-bore NG enteral feeding tube is inserted. Tube-feeding is considered as she cannot eat by mouth secondary to the endotracheal tube and mechanical ventilation. How should she be transitioned from parenteral to enteral feedings?

Tube-feedings can begin with a full-strength isotonic enteral feeding formulation at a slow infusion rate. Concurrently, the parenteral feeding formulation should be decreased slightly to avoid fluid overload and keep the calorie and protein intake constant. It can be anticipated that K.L. can transition from parenteral to enteral feedings in 24 to 48 hours. (See Chapter 34: Adult Enteral Nutrition.)

References

1 **Dudrick SJ et al.** Long-term parenteral nutrition with growth, development and positive nitrogen balance. Surgery. 1968;64:134.

2 **Wilmore DW, Dudrick SJ.** Growth and development of an infant receiving all nutrients exclusively by vein. JAMA. 1968;203:860.

3 **Dudrick SJ et al.** Can intravenous feeding as the sole means of nutrition support growth in the child and restore weight loss in an adult? An affirmative answer. Ann Surg. 1969;169:974.

4 **Grant JP.** Nutritional assessment in clinical practice. Nutr Clin Pract. 1986;1:3.

5 **Bistrian BR et al.** Prevalence of malnutrition in general medical patients. JAMA. 1976;235:1567.

6 **Bistrian BR et al.** Protein status of general surgical patients. JAMA. 1974;230:858.

7 **Coats KG et al.** Hospital-associated malnutrition: a re-evaluation 12 years later. J Am Diet Assoc. 1989;93:27.

8 **Leiter LA, Marliss EB.** Survival during fasting may depend on fat as well as protein stores. JAMA. 1982;248:2306.

9 **Detsky AS et al.** Is patient malnourished? JAMA. 1994;271:54.

10 **A.S.P.E.N. Board of Directors.** Guidelines for the use of parenteral and enteral nutrition in adult and pediatric patients. JPEN. 1993;17(Suppl.):1SA.

11 **A.S.P.E.N. Board of Directors.** Definitions of terms used in A.S.P.E.N. guidelines and standards. Nutr Clin Pract. 1988;3:26.

12 **Lo CW, Walter WA.** Changes in the gastrointestinal tract during enteral or parenteral feeding. Nutr Rev. 1989;47:193.

13 **Moore FA et al.** TEN versus TPN following major abdominal trauma-reduced septic morbidity. J Trauma. 1989;29:916.

14 **Kudsk KA et al.** Enteral versus parenteral feeding. Ann Surg. 1992;215:503.

15 **Moore FA et al.** Early enteral feeding, compared with parenteral, reduces septic complications—the results of a meta-analysis. Ann Surg. 1992;216:172.

16 **Windsor JA, Hill G.** Weight loss with physiologic impairment: a basic indicator of surgical risk. Ann Surg. 1988;207:290.

17 **Seltzer MH et al.** Instant nutritional assessment: absolute weight loss and surgical mortality. JPEN. 1982;6:218.

18 **Blackburn GL et al.** Nutritional and metabolic assessment of the hospitalized patient. JPEN. 1977;1:11.

19 **Anderson CF, Wochos DN.** The utility of serum albumin values in nutritional assessment of hospitalized patients. Mayo Clin Proc. 1982;57:181.

20 **Rudman D et al.** Relation of serum albumin concentration to death rate in nursing home men. JPEN. 1987;11:360.

21 **Detsky AS et al.** What is subjective global assessment of nutritional status? JPEN. 1987;11:8.

22 **Muller JM et al.** Indications and effects of preoperative parenteral nutrition. World J Surg. 1986;10:56.

23 **Starker PM et al.** The influence of preoperative total parenteral nutrition upon morbidity and mortality. Surg Gynecol Obstet. 1986;162:569.

24 **The Veterans Affairs Total Parenteral Nutrition Cooperative Study Group.** Perioperative nutrition in surgical patients. N Engl J Med. 1991;325:525.

25 **Detsky AS et al.** Perioperative parenteral nutrition: a meta-analysis. Ann Intern Med. 1987;107:95.

26 **American Dietetic Association: Manual of Clinical Dietetics.** Chicago: ADA; 1988.

27 **Baxter JK, Bistrian BR.** Moderate hypocaloric parenteral nutrition in the critically ill, obese patient. Nutr Clin Pract. 1980;4:133.

28 **Bayer-Berger M et al.** Incidence of phlebitis in peripheral parenteral nutrition: effect of the different nutrient solutions. Clin Nutr. 1989;8:81.

29 **Daly JM et al.** Peripheral vein infusion of dextrose/amino acid solutions ±20% fat emulsion. JPEN. 1985;9:296.

30 **Makarewicz PA et al.** Prevention of

superficial phlebitis during peripheral parenteral nutrition. Am J Surg. 1986; 151:126.

31 **Madan M et al.** A randomized study of the effects of osmolarity and heparin with hydrocortisone on thrombophlebitis in peripheral intravenous nutrition. Clin Nutr. 1991;0:309.

32 **Wright A et al.** Use of transdermal glyceryl trinitrate to reduce failure of intravenous infusion due to phlebitis and extravasation. Lancet. 1985;289: 1148.

33 **Rose BD.** Clinical Physiology of Acid-Base and Electrolyte Disorders. 3rd ed. New York, NY: MacGraw-Hill; 1989.

34 **Goodgame JT et al.** Essential fatty acid deficiency in total parenteral nutrition: time course of development and suggestions for therapy. Surgery. 1978; 84:271.

35 **Driscoll DF.** Clinical issues regarding the use of total nutrient admixtures. DICP. 1990;24:296.

36 **Thorn DB, Tanner DJ.** Evaluation of a two-liter plastic container for parenteral nutrient solutions. Am J Hosp Pharm. 1984;41:680.

37 **Raebel MA, McDonald JB.** Twenty-four-hour-single-container for parenteral nutrient admixture. Am J Hosp Pharm. 1985;42:355.

38 **Mirtallo JM et al.** Providing 24-hour nutrient infusions to critically ill patients. Am J Hosp Pharm. 1986;43: 2205.

39 **Sayeed FA et al.** Stability of total nutrient admixtures using various intravenous fat emulsions. Am J Hosp Pharm. 1987;33:2271.

40 **Bettner FS, Stennett DJ.** Effects of pH, temperature, concentration and time on particle counts in lipid-containing total parenteral nutrition admixtures. JPEN. 1986;10:375.

41 **Barat AC et al.** Effect of amino acid solution on total nutrient admixture stability. JPEN. 1987;11:384.

42 **Parry VA et al.** Effect of various nutrient ratios on the emulsion stability of total nutrient admixtures. Am J Hosp Pharm. 1986;43:3017.

43 **Multivitamin preparations for parenteral use: a statement by the Nutrition Advisory Group.** JPEN. 1979; 3:258.

44 **Guidelines for essential trace element preparations for parenteral use: a statement by the Nutrition Advisory Group.** JPEN. 1979;3:263.

45 **Wolk R.** Metabolic complications and deficiencies of parenteral nutrition. Compr Ther. 1985;1:67.

46 **Vannatta JB et al.** High-dose intravenous phosphorus therapy for severe complicated hypophosphatemia. South Med J. 1983;76:1424.

47 **Lloyd CW, Johnson CE.** Management of hypophosphatemia. Clin Pharm. 1988;7:123.

48 **Knapke CM et al.** Management of glucose abnormalities in patients receiving total parenteral nutrition. Clin Pharm. 1989;8:136.

49 **Food and Drug Administration.** Safety alert: hazards of precipitation associated with parenteral nutrition. Am J Hosp Pharm. 1994;51:1427.

50 **Knowles JB et al.** Pulmonary deposition of calcium phosphate crystals as a complication of home parenteral nutrition. JPEN. 1989;13:209.

51 **Eggert LD et al.** Calcium and phosphorus compatibility in parenteral nutrition admixtures. Am J Hosp Pharm. 1982;39:49.

52 **Niemiec PW, Vanderveen TW.** Compatibility consideration in parenteral nutrient solution. Am J Hosp Pharm. 1984;41:893.

53 **Robinson LA, Wright BT.** Central venous catheter occlusion caused by body-heat-mediated calcium phosphate precipitation. Am J Hosp Pharm. 1982; 39:120.

54 **Trissel LA.** Handbook of Injectable Drugs. 7th ed. Bethesda, MD: American Society of Hospital Pharmacists; 1992.

55 **Baumgartner TG.** Trace elements in clinical nutrition. Nutr Clin Pract. 1993;8:251.

56 **Bernard DKH et al.** Principles of nutrition therapy for short-bowel syndrome. Nutr Clin Pract. 1993;8:153.

57 **Klein S, Nealon WH.** Hepatobiliary abnormalities associated with total parenteral nutrition. Seminars in Liver Dis. 1988;8:237.

58 **Waters B et al.** Effect of route of nutrition on recovery of hepatic organic anion clearance after fasting. Surgery. 1994;115:370.

59 **Baker AL, Rosenberg JH.** Hepatic complications of total parenteral nutrition. Am J Med. 1987;82:489.

60 **Roy CC, Belli DC.** Hepatobiliary complications associated with TPN: an enigma? J Am Coll Nutr. 1985;4:651.

61 **Hiyama DT, Fischer JE.** Nutritional support in hepatic failure. Nutr Clin Pract. 1988;3:96.

62 **Nespli A et al.** Pathogenesis of hepatic encephalopathy and hyperdynamic syndrome in cirrhosis: role of false neurotransmitters. Arch Surg. 1981; 116:1129.

63 **Rossi-Fanelli F et al.** Branched-chain amino acids vs. lactulose in the treatment of hepatic coma: a controlled study. Dig Dis Sci. 1982;27:929.

64 **Cerra FB et al.** Disease-specific amino acid infusion (F080) in hepatic encephalopathy: a prospective, randomized, double-blind, controlled trial. JPEN. 1985;9:288.

65 **Wahren JJ et al.** Is intravenous administration of branched chain amino acids effective in the treatment of hepatic encephalopathy? A multicenter study. Hepatology. 1983;4:475.

66 **Skeie B et al.** Branch-chain amino acids: their metabolism and clinical utility. Crit Care Med. 1990;18:549.

67 **Oki JC, Cuddy PG.** Branched-chain amino acid support of stressed patients. DICP. 1989;23:399.

68 **Mowatt-Larsesen, Brown RO.** Specialized nutritional support in respiratory disease. Clin Pharm. 1993;12:276.

69 **Silberman H, Silberman AW.** Parenteral nutrition biochemistry and respiratory gas exchange. JPEN. 1986;10: 151.

70 **Askanazi J et al.** Respiratory changes induced by the large glucose loads of total parenteral nutrition. JAMA. 1980; 243:1444.

71 **Wolfe RR.** Glucose metabolism in burn injury: a review. J Burn Care Rehab. 1985;6:408.

72 **Talpers SS et al.** Nutritionally associated increased carbon dioxide production. Chest. 1992;102:551.

73 **Grant JP.** Nutrition care of patients with acute and chronic respiratory failure. Nutr Clin Pract. 1994;9:11.

74 **Silberman H et al.** The safety and efficacy of a lipid-based system of parenteral nutrition in acute pancreatitis. Am J Gastroenterol. 1982;77:494.

75 **Van Gossum A et al.** Lipid associated total parenteral nutrition in patients with severe acute pancreatitis. JPEN. 1988;12:25.

76 **Raasch RH et al.** Effect of intravenous fat emulsion on experimental acute pancreatitis. JPEN. 1983;7:254.

77 **Buch A et al.** Hyperlipidemia and pancreatitis. World J Surg. 1980;4:307.

78 **Pisters PWT, Ransom JHC.** Nutritional support for acute pancreatitis. Surg Gynecol Obstet. 1992;175:275.

79 **Feinstein EI.** Total parenteral nutritional support of patients with acute renal failure. Nutr Clin Pract. 1988;3:9.

80 **Oldrizzi L et al.** Nutrition and the kidney: how to manage patients with renal failure. Nutr Clin Pract. 1994;9:3.

81 **Hak LJ, Raasch RH.** Use of amino acids in patients with acute renal failure. Nutr Clin Pract. 1988;3:19.

82 **Mirtallo JM et al.** Nutritional support of patients with renal disease. Clin Pharm. 1984;3:253.

83 **Naylor CD et al.** Does treatment with essential amino acids and hypertonic glucose improve survival in acute renal failure? A meta analysis. Ren Fail. 1987–88;10:141.

Dermatotherapy

CA Bond

Anatomy and Physiology of the Skin
(See Figure 36.1) 36-1
  Epidermis 36-1
  Dermis 36-1
  Subcutaneous Layer 36-2
Inflammatory Lesions 36-2
  Acute Lesions 36-2
  Subacute and Chronic Lesions 36-2
Dermatologic Drug Delivery Systems 36-2
  Wet Dressings (See Table 36.1) 36-2
  Baths 36-2
  Powders 36-3
  Lotions 36-3
  Emulsions (See Table 36.2) 36-4
  Gels 36-4
  Creams (See Table 36.3) 36-4
  Ointments 36-4
  Aerosols 36-4
  Other Delivery Systems 36-4
  Selection of a Delivery System 36-5
Assessing the Dermatologic Patient 36-5
Topical Corticosteroids 36-8
  General Principals of Therapy (See Table 36.5) 36-8
  Indications 36-9
  Contraindications 36-9
  Side Effects (Also see Question 8) 36-9
  Atopic Eczema 36-9
  Occlusion 36-11
  Product Selection (Also see Question 2) 36-12
    Pharmacokinetic considerations 36-12
  Side Effects (Also see Side Effects above) 36-12
    Acne 36-12

  Idiosyncratic/allergic reactions 36-12
  Systemic absorption/risk of infection 36-12
Topical Antibiotics with Corticosteroids
  (See Table 36.6) 36-13
    Side effects 36-13
Pruritus 36-13
Nondrug Recommendations for Atopic Eczema
  (See Table 36.7) 36-14
Tachyphylaxis/Specialized Corticosteroid Dosage
  Forms/Antihistamines (See Table 36.8) 36-14
Nonprescription Topical Hydrocortisone 36-15
Dry Skin (See Table 36.11) 36-15
Drug Eruptions (See Tables 36.12 and 36.13) 36-15
  Acneiform Eruptions 36-16
  Photosensitive Eruptions 36-16
  Lichen Planus-Like Eruptions 36-16
  Alopecia 36-16
  Bullous Eruptions (See Figure 36.5) 36-16
  Eczematous Eruptions 36-17
  Epidermal Necrolysis 36-17
  Erythema Multiforme 36-17
  Erythema Nodosum Eruptions 36-17
  Exfoliative Dermatitis 36-17
  Fixed Drug Eruptions 36-17
  Maculopapular Eruptions 36-17
  Purpura (See Figure 36.4) 36-17
  Stevens-Johnson Syndrome 36-17
  Urticaria 36-19
Contact Dermatitis: Poison Ivy/Oak/Sumac 36-19
  Treatment 36-20
    Systemic therapy 36-20
    Relapse 36-21
  Contact Dermatitis (See Table 36.14) 36-21

Anatomy and Physiology of the Skin

The skin is the largest single organ in the body and constitutes, on average, 17% of a person's body weight. The skin's thickness ranges from 3 to 5 mm. Figure 36.1 shows a cross-section of the anatomy of human skin. The major function of the skin is to protect underlying structures from trauma, temperature variations, harmful penetrations, moisture, humidity, radiation, and invasion of micro-organisms. There are three layers of the skin: epidermis, dermis, and subcutaneous tissue.[1-6]

Epidermis

The epidermis consists of four distinct layers: stratum corneum, stratum lucidum, stratum spinosum, and stratum germinativum. The major function of the epidermis is to serve as a barrier. This layer keeps chemicals and other substances from penetrating into the body and prevents the loss of water from the skin and under-lying tissues. The maturation of keratinocytes from the stratum germinativum to the stratum corneum is critical for this barrier function. As the keratinocytes migrate to the skin surface they change from living cells to dead, thick-walled, nonnucleated cells containing keratin, a hard fibrous protein. It normally takes 26 days

to complete the differentiation and maturation process of the ker-atinocyte, from the time it is formed until it is sloughed off. The *stratum corneum*, which is composed of the dead cells, provides the greatest resistance to the percutaneous absorption of chemicals and drugs. It behaves as a semipermeable membrane through which drugs are absorbed by passive diffusion. Factors that can affect drug absorption are hydration of the skin and damage to the stratum corneum. In general, the greater the damage to the stratum corneum, the greater is the absorption of topically applied drugs.

Dermis

The dermis, which ranges in thickness from 1 to 4 mm, is com-posed of collagen fibers, elastic fibers, and an extrafibrillar gel of mucopolysaccharides called glycosaminoglycans (formally called ground substances). The major function of the dermis is to protect the body from mechanical injury and to support the dermal ap-pendages and the epidermis. It also provides a capillary, lymphatic, and nervous supply to the skin and its appendages: apocrine and eccrine sweat glands, sebaceous glands, and hair follicles. The cap-illary network plays a major role in temperature regulation and provides nutrition to the epidermis. The nerves enable the sensa-tions of touch and pain. Finally, the dermis contains large amounts

Stratum spinosum — — Stratum lucidum
                            Stratum
                            corneum
Stratum
germinativum

Epidermis

Capillary network

Hair shaft

Sebaceous gland

Arrector pili
muscle

Dermis

Apocrine
(sweat) gland

Hair follicle

*Hypodermis
(subcutaneous
tissue)*

Blood vessel

Fig 36.1   Cross Section of the Anatomy of Human Skin

of water and serves as a water storage organ. All but the most superficial injuries to the dermis will generally result in scarring as the injury heals.

Drugs passing through the epidermis penetrate directly into the dermis and may be absorbed into the general circulation through the capillary network. Generally, only small amounts of topically applied drugs enter the dermis via the sweat glands or the pilosebaceous units.

Subcutaneous Layer

The subcutaneous layer supports the dermis and epidermis and serves as a fat storage area. This layer helps to regulate temperature, provides nutritional support, and cushions the outer skin layers.[1-6]

Inflammatory Lesions

Acute Lesions

Acute inflammatory lesions are characterized by redness, swelling, heat, itching, and oozing. Generally, the more severe the dermatitis, the milder the initial topical therapy should be. The initial treatment for acute lesions should be a wet dressing.[3,6]

Subacute and Chronic Lesions

Subacute and chronic inflammatory lesions are characterized by erythema, scaling, lichenification, dryness, and pruritus. There are no absolute rules for treating subacute or chronic lesions. If the lesion is dry, an oleaginous or occlusive base should be used. If

there are extensive, thick, or hyperkeratotic areas, a keratolytic may be incorporated into the vehicle or used separately.[3,6]

While each dermatologic delivery vehicle has specialized uses based upon the type of lesion and its location, a range of dermatologic vehicles are available for use on acute or chronic inflamed lesions.

Dermatologic Drug Delivery Systems

Dermatological formulations are available as wet dressings, baths, powders, lotions, emulsions, gels, creams, ointments, and aerosols.

Wet Dressings

Wet dressings (see Table 36.1) provide evaporative cooling which causes vasoconstriction. They soothe and cool inflamed skin, dry oozing lesions, soften crusts (see Figure 36.2), aid in cleaning wounds, and assist in the drainage of purulent wounds. If the wet dressing is ice cold, it will help relieve pruritus; however, ice cold dressings should be reserved for small lesions, since cooling large parts of the body (with a bath) can be quite uncomfortable. Wet dressings are most useful for acutely inflamed, oozing lesions; erosions; and ulcers. In most instances, wet dressings should be the sole therapy until the oozing or weeping subsides. If other topical medications are applied to oozing or weeping lesions, they will be washed away and will not provide the desired effect. The most frequently used wet dressings are normal saline and aluminum acetate 5% solution (Burow's solution) diluted 1:10 to 1:40 for use. The most important component of wet dressings is water. While many substances are added to wet dressings, the cleansing and drying effect of the water provides the major therapeutic benefit of this type of therapy. Table 36.1 lists the solutions that are useful for wet dressings. Boric acid should not be used as a topical agent because it can be absorbed through the skin, causing systemic toxicity.[7]

Depending upon the affected area and its size, a patient utilizing a wet dressing may soak the affected area directly in the solution for 15 to 30 minute periods three to six times per day. If larger areas are involved or if the affected area cannot be easily soaked (e.g., a shoulder), a clean towel or cloth soaked in the solution (lightly wrung out) may be directly applied to the lesion(s). The soaked cloth should be left in place for five to ten minutes, then resoaked in the solution and reapplied. The patient may repeat this procedure for 30 minutes to 2 hours three times daily. Wet dressings applied with a cloth should be wrapped around the lesions several times if possible. If large areas are involved, the patient may draw a bath, add appropriate amounts of medications, and soak for 15 to 30 minute periods three to six times per day.

In general, no more than one-third of the body should be soaked in this manner at any time. One should be aware that evaporation can concentrate solutions making them too irritating to use. A 1:40 concentration of Burow's solution left standing at room temperature for 30 minutes will yield a 1:10 solution. Because of this, wet dressings should always be freshly prepared, kept in closed containers, and never reused. Wet dressings are most comfortable if they are slightly cool to warm, depending upon the patient's preference. When drying the affected area after a wet dressing has been used, care must be taken not to irritate the inflamed skin by rubbing it with a towel. The proper technique for drying the skin is to pat the area gently with a soft clean towel.[7]

Baths

In addition to wet dressings, other topical therapies can be applied to large areas of the body through bathing. In using this type

Agent[a]	Strength	Preparation (H$_2$O)	Germicidal Activity	Astringent Activity	Comments
Normal Saline	0.9%	1 tsp NaCl to a pint	—	—	Inexpensive; easy to prepare
Aluminum Acetate					
Burow's Solution	5%	Dilute to 1:10–1:40 (0.5%–0.125%).	Mild	+	—
Domeboro packets/tablets	—	One packet/tablet to a pint of water yields a 1:40 solution; two yields a 1:20 solution	Mild	+	—
Potassium Permanganate	65 mg and 330 mg tablets	Dilute to 1:4000–1:16,000; 65 mg tablet to 250–1000 cc; 330 mg tablet to 1500–5000 cc	Moderate	—	Stains skin, clothing
Silver Nitrate	0.1%–0.5%	1 tsp of 50% stock solution to 1000 cc will yield a 0.25% solution	Good	+	Stains; can cause pain
Acetic Acid[b]	1%	Dilute 1:5 with standard 5% household vinegar	Good	+	Smells; can be irritating

Table 36.1   Wet Dressings[4,7]

[a] Although many substances are added to wet dressings, the cleansing and drying effect of the water is the major benefit.
[b] Used primarily for *Psuedomonas aeruginosa* infections.

of treatment the bath should be about one-half full. Soothing and antipruritic colloidal bath additives may be used to treat widespread eruptions such as lichen planus, pityriasis rosea, urticaria, and other weeping or crusting eczemas. Colloidal oatmeal [one cup of oatmeal (Aveeno) shaken with two cups of cold tap water and poured into six inches of a lukewarm bath] produces a pleasing and soothing bath. Alternatively, a starch bath utilizing two cups of hydrolyzed starch (Linit) or cornstarch mixed with four cups of tap water and added to a bath may be used. A mixture of equal parts baking soda and starch also may be used. Epsom salt baths, made by dissolving three cups of magnesium sulfate in six inches of lukewarm water in a tub, are useful in treating pyodermas, furuncles, and necrotic acne (especially when the back, shoulders, and buttocks are affected). Occasionally, potassium permanganate baths (1:10,000) may be used to treat smelly bullous or widespread ulcerating lesions, such as those seen with pemphigus or mycosis fungoides. Water-soluble coal tar preparations applied via a bath for the treatment of psoriasis may be the most acceptable way to apply this medication. Ointments or creams containing coal tar are smelly and have a tendency to stain materials on contact. A variety of bath oils are available: Alpha-Keri, Ar-Ex, Domol, Kauma, Lubath, Lubath-ML, and Lubriderm. These are most useful in preventing and treating mild cases of dry skin. With moderate to severe cases of dry skin, additional topical oleaginous products generally are required to improve the condition. Patients may make their own bath oil by adding two ounces of olive oil or Nivea oil to a cup of milk and adding it to a bath; however, patients should be cautioned to get out of the bathtub carefully because the oil will make porcelain surfaces slippery.[7]

The major problem associated with wet dressings or baths is the development of macerated skin from excessive use. Should maceration occur, this type of therapy should be temporarily discontinued. Closed wet dressings (occlusive covering over a wet dressing) rarely are used in treating dermatological conditions because of the increased risk of maceration and heat retention. They may be used rarely for abscesses or cellulitis. Additionally, irritation may occur from medicated wet dressings if they become too concentrated.

Powders

Powders are drying and cooling; they absorb moisture and create more surface area for quicker evaporation. They are used mainly in intertriginous areas to decrease friction which can cause mechanical irritation. They also are useful in the treatment of intertrigo, chafing, athlete's foot, jock itch, and diaper rash. Occasionally, powders are applied on top of ointments to protect clothing from the ointment. The liberal use of powders is helpful in prevention of bed sores or pressure sores.

Powders can be applied with a cotton puff or shaker. Care should be taken to minimize breathing the powder, since this can lead to respiratory tract irritation, particularly in infants. Powders that contain starch or cellulose should be washed off before reapplication, since continued build-up of these powders can produce mechanical irritation. Additionally, starch-containing powders should not be used if an infection is present (particularly *Candida albicans*) because starch can serve as a substrate for certain organisms. Powders should not be applied to oozing lesions since they tend to cake into hard granules, making them difficult and painful to remove. The most commonly utilized powders are talc or mixtures of talc and zinc oxide.[3,4,6,7]

Lotions

Lotions are suspensions or solutions of powder in a water vehicle. They may be lubricating, cooling, or drying depending upon the formulation. Alcohol frequently is added to lotions to provide a cooling effect; occasionally, an astringent such as aluminum is added to precipitate protein which helps to dry and seal an oozing wound. Lotions are used to treat superficial dermatoses, especially if there is slight oozing. They are useful if large or intertriginous areas are affected and are especially advantageous in the treatment of conditions characterized by significant inflammation and tenderness. In these situations, creams or ointments may cause severe pain upon application. Acute contact dermatitis, poison ivy, or poison oak are examples of conditions where this principle may apply. Generally, lotions are the least oleaginous and least occlusive of the topical vehicles; thus, they are not very useful in conditions where the skin is dry. Lotions should not be applied to hairy areas where they tend to get crumbly, or to a markedly oozing dermatitis where they tend to cake and form hard, cement-like plaques under which infections may occur.

It is not necessary to remove lotions from the skin more than once daily. Generally, lotions are applied three or four times daily with each fresh application placed over previous applications as long as possible. Since many lotions are suspensions, it is advisable to shake the lotion well before application. Six ounces of a lotion are generally adequate to cover the entire body of an average adult.[8]

Emulsions

Emulsions are solid or liquid and can be divided into two classes: *oil-in-water* and *water-in-oil*. Most creams are oil-in-water emulsions, and many ointments are water-in-oil emulsions. The indications for liquid oil-in-water emulsions are similar to those for lotions, except this dosage form provides greater occlusion and would be more useful in conditions where dry skin predominates. Liquid water-in-oil emulsions have similar indications to ointments, except they can be applied more easily than ointments. Water-in-oil emulsions are most useful in conditions where dry skin predominates; application to hairy or intertriginous areas should be avoided. As with lotions, six ounces of a liquid emulsion will cover all exposed skin on an average adult.[7]

For extemporaneously prepared emulsions, chemical compatibilities must be taken into consideration because it is important that the drug be distributed evenly throughout the base and remain distributed. Accordingly, water-soluble drugs should be dispersed in oil-in-water emulsions or other water-miscible bases and not in oils, greases, waxes, fats, or petrolatum. Lipid soluble drugs should be dispersed in oils, greases, waxes, water-in-oil emulsions, or petrolatum, and not in water-miscible bases. Insoluble medications may be incorporated in any base in which they form a stable and even mixture. Table 36.2 lists some of the commercially available oil-in-water and water-in-oil emulsions. As the amount of oil increases, the viscosity of the emulsion also will increase. Thus, emulsions containing more than 30% oil should be dispensed in wide mouth jars to aid the patient in application.

Gels

Gels are a form of ointment (semisolid emulsion). They contain propylene glycol and carboxypolymethylene and are clear, nongreasy, nonstaining, nonocclusive, and quick drying. They are thixotropic, becoming thinner with rubbing and may sting on application. Gels are most useful when applied to hairy areas or other areas such as the face where it is considered cosmetically unacceptable to have the residue of a vehicle remain on the skin.

Creams

Creams are the most commonly used vehicle in dermatology. Most are oil-in-water emulsions and are intended to be rubbed in

Table 36.2	Commercially Available Emulsion Bases
Oil-in-Water	Water-in-Oil
Acid Mantle Cream	Aquaphor
Almay Emulsion Base	C-Solve
Aquaphilic	E-Solve
Cetaphil	Eucerin (Aquaphor and Water)
Dermabase	Hydrophilic Petrolatum USP
Dermovan	Hydrosorb
Hydrophilic Ointment USP	Hydrous Lanolin
Keri Lotion	Lubriderm
Lanaphillic	Nivea Cream
Multibase	Nutraderma
Neobase	Polysorb
Unibase	Qualatum
Vanibase	Vanicream
	Velvachol

Table 36.3	Average Amounts of Cream Needed to Cover Various Parts of the Body[8]	
Single Application	Area (For Each Part Listed)	Amount Needed for 7 Days
2 gm	Both hands, head, face, genital, anal	45 gm (1.5 oz)
3 gm	One arm, front or back of trunk	60 gm (2 oz)
4 gm	One leg	90 gm (3 oz)
30–60 gm	Whole body	1–2.5 kg (2.5–5 lbs)

well until they vanish (vanishing cream). Creams generally do not provide much occlusiveness and are best suited for application on nonirritable dermatoses (nonacute). The most common mistake made by patients applying creams is that they use too much and/or do not rub them in fully. Generally, if the cream can be seen on the skin after application, the patient has made one or both of these application mistakes. Ultimately, they are wasting the preparation or are not getting the full therapeutic benefits. One gram of cream should cover 100 cm^2 of surface area. Table 36.3 lists the approximate amount of cream required for application to various parts of the body.[8]

Ointments

Ointments are made of inert bases such as petrolatum or may consist of droplets of water suspended in a continuous phase of oleaginous material. Ointments may be insoluble in water, soluble in water, or can be emulsified with water. Ointments are most useful in relieving dryness, brittleness, and treating fissures because of their occlusive properties. They often are used on chronic lesions and should not be used on acutely inflamed lesions. Because of their occlusive properties, ointments should not be applied to intertriginous or hairy areas as they tend to trap heat and sweat. Ointments are greasy and may be cosmetically unacceptable to some patients. Since ointments generally spread more easily than creams, 5% to 10% less ointment is required to cover the same surface area that a cream will cover. (See Table 36.3 for the amounts of cream required to cover various areas of the body.) Whenever the skin is damaged, occlusion should be considered (unless the lesions are wet). Protecting damaged skin from the air (by the use of a bandage or ointment) will assist in healing; probably by preventing water loss.[8]

Aerosols

Aerosols are the most expensive and inefficient way to apply dermatologicals. Their only advantage over other dosage forms is that they do not require direct mechanical contact with the skin and may be useful if mechanical application causes intolerable pain for the patient. If an aerosol is used, it should be shaken well before use, and the patient should be cautioned not to spray the product around the face where it could get into the eyes or nose or could be inhaled. Generally, aerosols should be sprayed from about six inches above the skin in bursts of one to three seconds. Aerosols also are useful for application to hairy areas if a special application nozzle is used.

Other Delivery Systems

With the addition of solvents which enhance dermal absorption, such as dimethyl sulfoxide (DMSO), many drugs potentially could be administered directly through the skin. Other skin patch delivery systems have been designed to deliver drugs directly into the bloodstream through the skin. Examples include scopolamine, nitroglycerin, clonidine, nicotine, and estrogen patches (various manufacturers). These dermatological drug delivery systems, or similar ones, offer great potential for the sustained delivery of pharmaceuticals over extended periods of time. Additional drugs will be placed in these types of delivery systems in the future.

Selection of a Delivery System

The major function of the dosage forms mentioned above is to provide a vehicle for the delivery of medication to its site of action. Drugs cross epidermal cell membranes by a process of diffusion which can be facilitated by the following factors: pH gradient, concentration gradient, increased temperature, a thin or damaged stratum corneum, increased hydration, increased dermal circulation, and epidermal injury.[7,9]

There is an old saying regarding dermatological therapy which may be particularly useful in selecting dosage forms. If a lesion is wet, dry it; if dry, wet it. Wet dressings are most useful in drying acute, inflamed lesions and ointment bases are most useful for chronic, lichenified, scaling lesions. The choice of vehicle for chronic lesions is often based upon what the patient has found to work best. Commonly, patients with chronic dermatologic conditions use several different types of vehicles concomitantly (e.g., cream bases during the day and ointment bases at night).

Assessing the Dermatologic Patient

1. C.B., a 23-year-old, 66 kg female, is complaining of a rash. What types of questions should C.B. be asked to help determine the appropriate diagnosis and treatment? What parameters are important in determining whether C.B. should be referred to a physician for evaluation and treatment?

A general approach to the patient with a dermatological complaint begins with an evaluation focused on the following.

What type of dermatologic lesions are present? Figures 36.2 through 36.9 are pictures and drawings of the basic dermatologic lesions which can be used to diagnose and treat various conditions. A patient should be referred to a physician if the patient presents with petechiae, cysts, or atrophy (see Figures 36.4, 36.6, and 36.7), unless these lesions are very small (i.e., <2 to 3 cm²) and discrete. The presence of nodules, abscesses, or ulcers (see Figures 36.6 and

36.8) dictates physician referral. Additionally, a physician should see the patient if the patient has greater than 1% of total body surface area (1% is about the size of the palm of your hand) covered by purpura, pustules, bullae, or erosions (see Figures 36.3 to 36.5). Lesions extending into the dermis should be evaluated by a physician because of the potential for scarring. Most other lesions are amenable to treatment with nonprescription medications or other remedies.

What is the size of the lesions present? In general, as the size of the area affected by dermatologic lesions increases, the greater the likelihood the patient should be referred to a physician for evaluation. As a rough rule of thumb, lesions with greater than 25% of a patient's body affected should be referred to a physician. Depending upon the type of lesions present (see above paragraph), most conditions which affect up to 24% of the body may be amenable to treatment with nonprescription, over the counter (OTC) medications.

What part of the body is affected by the lesions? All lesions involving the eyes should be evaluated by a physician. Most lesions involving the mouth, face, genitalia, nails, and rectal areas should be evaluated by a physician. Lesions in other areas of the body may be amenable to treatment with nonprescription remedies.

What is the age of the patient? In general, the younger or older the patient, the more likely the patient should be referred to a physician. In both younger (<2 years of age) and older patients (>65 years of age) new dermatological lesions may indicate systemic disease or possible allergic manifestations. The skin of younger patients is more susceptible to therapy with topical agents. Older (and/or debilitated) patients often may require prescription medications to treat a condition which in a younger patient could easily be treated with an OTC (nonprescription) medication.

Are there any systemic symptoms present? Patients with a dermatologic condition and systemic symptoms such as decreased range of motion, fever, orthostasis, ataxia, confusion, significant pain, difficulty breathing, and regional lymph node enlargement should be evaluated by a physician. Patients with a primary dermatologic problem who have these systemic symptoms generally require more effective therapy than what OTC medication can provide.

How long has the patient had this problem? There are no hard and fast rules regarding duration of a dermatologic condition and

Fig 36.2   Scales and Crusts

Macules

Fig 36.3   Macules and Papules

Purpura   Petechiae

Fig 36.4   Purpura and Petechia

Vesicles   Bullae

Fig 36.5   Vesicles and Bullae

Fig 36.6   Nodules and Cysts

Fig 36.7   Atrophy

Fig 36.8   Ulcer

Fig 36.9   Pustules

whether a clinician should treat the patient or refer him to a physician. In general, the longer a condition is present (>1 month), the more likely the patient should be referred to a physician. Recent onset of symptoms (<1 month) may be amenable to treatment if the clinician is confident of the diagnosis and has appropriate OTC medications available. The patient should be questioned further regarding whether the lesions recently have changed in size, appearance, or severity. This question is particularly important with chronic conditions as it may be the primary reason the patient is now asking for advice about his dermatologic problem (change of condition rather than new condition).

Does the patient have any allergies? This is a very important question as skin problems due to allergies to drugs and contact sensitizers are common. Most allergies can be traced to use of a new drug or product within the past one or two weeks. Drug allergies are quite common (see Drug Eruptions) and often are self-treated by the patient (usually by discontinuing the drug and the use of OTC medication). Any discontinuation of a prescription product by a patient should be discussed with the patient's physician.

What is the patient's past medical or dermatologic history? In general, pre-existing medical conditions are not contraindications for effective OTC treatment of dermatological problems. Any patient with diabetes, hepatitis, renal disease, alcoholism, malnutrition, cancer, or congestive heart failure should be referred to a physician because these conditions might be adversely affected by inappropriate or inadequate OTC therapy. Pre-existing dermatological conditions may aid in assessing the patient correctly. If the current problem is related to a pre-existing chronic dermatological condition, it increases the likelihood that the patient should be referred to a physician (to determine why a chronic condition seems to be getting worse).

How sure is the patient or the practitioner of the diagnosis? The patient and practitioner should be reasonably sure of the diagnosis before OTC treatment is even contemplated. In general, the less sure the diagnosis, the more likely the patient should be referred to a physician. Therapy with nonprescription medications only should be recommended when self-medication is based upon an accurate diagnosis.

What products/therapies have been used in the past to manage a similar episode? This is an essential question that needs to be asked before OTC therapy is recommended. A product which the

patient has used before and found to be ineffective should not be recommended because it is likely to be ineffective this time as well, and could decrease the patient's confidence in your professional abilities. The answer to this question also will provide an indication as to whether a more or less potent product is needed to treat the patient's dermatologic condition.

When should the patient expect some improvement with OTC therapy? In general most dermatologic conditions amenable to OTC therapy should improve in a few days. If no improvement is seen within a week, the patient should be instructed to notify the practitioner to determine if additional OTC therapy is needed or whether a physician referral is necessary. In general, if OTC therapy has not improved the condition within one week, most patients should be referred to their physician for evaluation.

After evaluation, it is determined that C.B. should be referred to a physician because she has an abscessed area.

Topical Corticosteroids
General Principles of Therapy

- Topical corticosteroids should be applied two to four times per day initially. Increasing the frequency of application from once daily to three times daily clearly produces superior responses. Application six times daily is no more efficacious than three times daily.[7,17,20]

- An appropriate strength preparation should be used to bring the condition under control. It should be noted that 33% to 50% of all dermatological conditions requiring topical corticosteroids can be managed with medium or low strength corticosteroid preparations.[7]

- After initial control, maintenance therapy should consist of the lowest strength formulation that will control the problem. A reduction in application frequency also should be attempted. It may be advisable to give the patient two different strength corticosteroid preparations; a mild one for routine use and a more potent one for flares or resistant lesions.[25]

- Occluded areas and certain areas of the body such as the face and flexures are more prone to the development of side effects. If corticosteroids must be used on the face or flexures, hydrocortisone should be used to reduce the probability of side effects.

- Children and patients with liver failure are at risk for systemic corticosteroid toxicities. Additionally, patients who use the highest potency preparations (see Table 36.5) for more than two weeks are susceptible to systemic toxicity.[26]
- Preparations should be rubbed in thoroughly and where possible applied while the skin is moist (e.g., after bathing) as this will enhance the effect.[7]
- With chronic conditions such as atopic eczema, it is best to discontinue therapy gradually. This will reduce chances of rebound flares of topical lesions.[17,20]

Indications

Topical corticosteroids are the drugs of first choice for treatment of atopic eczema. Generally, treatment is initiated with a potent fluorinated corticosteroid with occlusion if tolerated. After the lesions are controlled, maintenance therapy is provided by 1% hydrocortisone or a low strength fluorinated corticosteroid such as triamcinolone acetonide 0.025%.

Topical corticosteroids are also the drugs of choice for all inflammatory and pruritic eruptions. In addition, they are quite useful with hyperplastic and infiltrative disorders. The following conditions generally respond well to topical corticosteroids: allergic contact dermatitis, alopecia areata, atopic eczema, discoid lupus erythematosus, granuloma annulare, hypertrophic scars and keloids, lichen planus, lichen simplex, lichen striatus, necrobiosis lipoidica, various nail disorders, pretibial myxedema, primary irritant dermatitis, psoriasis, sarcoidosis, seborrheic dermatitis, and varicose eczema.[7,17,24]

Contraindications

The following conditions are worsened by topical corticosteroids:[27] acne vulgaris, ulcers, scabies, warts, molluscum contagiosum, fungal infections, and balanitis.

Side Effects

Side effects from topical corticosteroids are infrequent. When they occur, they are related to the potency of preparation used, frequency of application, duration of use, anatomical site of application, and individual patient factors. Any of the previously discussed factors which increase potency, such as occlusion, increase the chances of side effects.

Epidermal and dermal atrophy, telangiectasia, localized fine hair growth, bruising, hypopigmentation, and striae may result from repeated application of topical corticosteroids.[17,20,28,29] Epidermal changes consisting of a reduction in cell size may begin within several days of therapy; these changes generally are reversible after therapy is stopped.[30] Exposed areas are most vulnerable to epidermal atrophy.

Dermal atrophy generally takes several weeks to occur and is rarely irreversible, depending upon how long the patient has used the corticosteroid and individual host factors such as skin age. Inguinal, genital, and perianal areas are most vulnerable to dermal atrophy. Most cases of dermal atrophy are probably reversible within two months after stopping the corticosteroid.[31]

Telangiectasia, which occur most often on the face, neck, groin, and upper chest, may not be reversible after stopping corticosteroid therapy. Striae, which occur most commonly on the groin, axillary, and inner thigh areas, are usually permanent.[17,20,28,32] Fine hair growth may be particularly bothersome to female patients using corticosteroid preparations on the face. This problem generally is reversible after stopping therapy. Hypopigmentation, predominantly a problem of dark-skinned patients, generally is reversible after therapy is discontinued.[17,20]

Table 36.4	Common Diseases Associated with Dermatologic Lesions	
Macules and Papules		
Psoriasis	Pityriasis rosea	Eczema
Lichen planus	Diaper dermatitis	Xerosis
Tinea versicolor	Erythroderma	Actinic keratosis
Ichthyosis vulgaris	Neurodermatitis	Sarcoidosis
Drug eruptions	Lupus erythematosus	
Candidiasis	Seborrheic dermatitis	
Miliaria rubra	Dermatophyte infections	
Pityriasis rubra	Secondary syphilis	
Purpura and Petechiae Diseases		
Senile purpura	Idiopathic	Purpura fulminans
Necrotizing	thrombocytopenia	Meningococcemia
vasculitis	Coumarin or heparin	Lupus
Gonococcemia	necrosis	erythematosus
Drug eruptions	Rocky mountain spotted	Postransfusion
Disseminated	fever	purpura
intravascular	Scurvy	Lymphomas
coagulation	Leukemia	
Vesiculobullous (Blistering) Diseases		
Pemphigus vulgaris	Bullous pemphigoid	Herpes
Varicella	Contact dermatitis	Drug eruptions
Bullous impetigo	Toxic epidermal	
Staph scalded skin	neurolysis	
syndrome		
Nodular and Cystic Diseases		
Lymphoma	Sarcoidosis	Acne
Lipomas	Erythema nodosum	Vasculitis
Rheumatoid	Polyarteritis nodosum	
diseases	Xanthomas	
Scabies		
Ulcer (Skin) Diseases		
Venous stasis	Arterial insufficiency	Anesthetic ulcer
Pyoderma	Decubitus ulcer	Syphilis
gangrenosum	Lymphogranulama	Granuloma
Chancroid	venereum	inguinale
Atrophy		
Steroid use	Solar elastosis	Radiation
Striae distensae	Lichen sclerosus	dermatitis
Scales and Crusts		
Very common with many chronic and acute dermatologic diseases		
Pustules		
Acne	Acne rosacea	Folliculitis
Candidiasis	Perioral dermatitis	Miliaria rubra
Impetigo	Psoriasis	

Atopic Eczema

2. P.K., a 17-year-old male, currently is being followed in the University Dermatology Clinic for his atopic eczema. Thirty percent of his body is covered by an eczematous rash, with extensive involvement of the popliteal and antecubital fossae. His chief complaint is extreme pruritus over the involved areas, as well as cosmetic disfiguration in the antecubital fossae, around the neck, and on the forehead.

Family History (FH): P.K.'s mother and aunt have bronchial asthma; one sister (L.K.), age 15, has hay fever and atopic eczema; his father and younger brother, age 11, appear to have no atopic manifestations.

Past Medical History (PMH): An eczematous rash was first noted on P.K. one month after birth. The scalp, face, and neck were the only areas affected, and the rash continued with varying degrees of severity until age 2½ when it spontaneously resolved. P.K. developed hay fever at age six with occasional attacks of asthma (last attack: age 15). An eczematous rash appeared at age 12 and has not disappeared since that time.

Table 36.5		Topical Corticosteroid Preparations[a]	
Corticosteroid (Brand Name)		**Vehicle**	**Cost[b]**
Lowest Potency			
Dexamethasone	(Decadron) 0.1%	aerosol	+ + + +
	(Decaderm) 0.1%	gel	+ + + +
Hydrocortisone	(Cort-Dome) 0.5%–2.5%	towelettes, spray	+ + + +
	(Cortef) 0.5%–2.5%	aerosol	+ + + +
	(Penecort) 0.5%–2.5%	cream	+
	(Penecort) 0.5%–2.5%	gel, ointment	+ + +
	(Synacort) 0.5%–2.5%	cream	+ + +
	(Hytone) 0.5%–2.5%	lotion	+ + +
Methylprednisolone acetate	(Medrol) 0.25%	ointment	+ + + +
	(Medrol) 1.0%	ointment	+ + + +
Low Potency			
Betamethasone valerate	(Valisone, Decreased Strength) 0.01%	cream	+ + +
Clocortolone	(Cloderm) 0.1%	cream	+ + + +
Desonide	(Desowen) 0.05%	cream	+ + +
	(Tridesilon) 0.05%	cream, ointment	+ + +
Fluocinolone acetonide	(generic) 0.01%	cream	+
	(Synalar) 0.01%	cream	+ + +
Flurandrenolide	(Cordran, Cordran SP) 0.025%	cream, ointment, solution	+ + +
Triamcinolone acetonide	(generic) 0.025%	cream, ointment	+
	(Aristocort) 0.025%	cream, lotion, aerosol	+ + +
	(Aristocort A) 0.025%	cream	+ + +
	(Kenalog) 0.025%	cream, ointment, lotion	+ + + +
Immediate Potency			
Betamethasone benzoate	(Benisone) 0.025%	cream, gel, lotion	+ + +
	(Uticort) 0.025%	cream, gel, ointment, lotion	+ + +
Betamethasone valerate	(generic) 0.1%	cream, gel, lotion	+ + +
	(Valisone) 0.1%	cream, ointment	+ + + +
Desoximetasone	(Topicort) 0.05%	cream, ointment, gel	+ + +
Fluocinolone acetonide	(generic) 0.025%	cream, ointment	+
	(Fluonid) 0.025%	cream, ointment	+ + +
Flurandrenolide	(generic)	lotion	+
	(Cordran, Cordran SP)	tape, solution, cream, ointment	+ + + +
Fluticasone propionate	(Cutivate) 0.005% and 0.05%	cream, ointment	+ + + +
Halcinonide	(Halog) 0.025%	cream	+ + + +
Hydrocortisone valerate	(Westcort) 0.2%	cream, ointment	+ + +
Mometasone furoate	(Elocon) 0.1%	cream, lotion	+ + + +
Triamcinolone acetonide	(generic) 0.1%	cream, ointment, lotion	+
	(Aristocort) 0.1%	cream, ointment	+ + +
	(Aristocort A) 0.1%	cream, ointment	+ + + +
	(Kenalog) 0.1%	cream, ointment, lotion	+ + +, + + + +
High Potency			
Amcinonide	(Cyclocort) 0.1%	cream, ointment, lotion	+ + + +
Betamethasone dipropionate	(generic) 0.05%	cream, ointment, lotion	+ + +
	(Alphatrex) 0.05%	cream, ointment, lotion	+ + +
	(Diprosone) 0.05%	cream, ointment	+ + + +
Desoximetasone	(Topicort) 0.25%	cream, ointment, gel	+ + +

Continued

Table 36.5	Topical Corticosteroid Preparations[a] (Continued)		
Corticosteroid (Brand Name)		Vehicle	Cost[b]
Diflorasone diacetate	(Florone) 0.05%	cream, ointment	+ + + +
	(Maxiflor) 0.05%	cream, ointment	+ + + +
Fluocinolone	(Synalar HP) 0.2%	cream	+ + + +
Fluocinonide	(Lidex, Lidex-E) 0.05%	cream, gel, ointment, solution	+ + + +
Halcinonide	(Halog, Halog-E) 0.1%	cream, ointment, solution	+ + + +
Triamcinolone acetonide	(generic) 0.5%	cream, ointment	+ + +
	(Aristocort A) 0.5%	cream	+ + + +
	(Aristocort) 0.5%	cream, ointment	+ + + +
	(Kenalog) 0.5%	cream, ointment	+ + + +
Highest Potency			
Betamethasone dipropionate	(Diprolene) 0.05%	cream, ointment, aerosol	+ + + +
Clobetasol propionate	(Temovate) 0.05%	cream, ointment	+ + + +
Diflorasone diacetate	(Psorcon) 0.05%	ointment	+ + + +
Halobetasol propionate	(Ultravate) 0.05%	cream, ointment	+ + + +

[a] Adapted from The Medical Letter. 1991;33:109.
[b] + = <$2; + + = $2–$5; + + + = $5–$10; + + + + = >$10.

His skin has followed a variable course; clearing in the summer and during periods of little stress and worsening during the winter and periods of stress.

Physical Examination (PE): P.K. presented as a well-nourished, well-developed male with no physical abnormalities noted except for his skin. Skin: oozing, crusted, erythematous, hyperkeratotic, hyperpigmented, maculopapular, and fine vesicular eruptions on face, neck, dorsal aspects of both arms and legs, hands, and chest. There is some evidence of secondary bacterial infection in both antecubital fossae and on portions of the left leg.

What are the relevant biopharmaceutical considerations for selecting a topical corticosteroid for P.K.?

A human bioassay procedure based upon the intensity of blanching of the skin is useful in predicting the bioavailability and clinical effectiveness of various corticosteroid topical preparations.[10–12] Clinical response also is evaluated by applying the agents to areas of experimentally produced irritation.[9,13,14]

The various proprietary formulations of topical corticosteroids have a wide range of potencies (see Table 36.5).[15] The relative potency assigned to a topical corticosteroid is determined by the ability of the preparation to penetrate the skin after release from the vehicle, the intrinsic activity of the corticosteroid at the receptor, and the rate of clearance from the receptor. It is believed that topical corticosteroids penetrate into the stratum corneum by passive diffusion which varies considerably depending upon the part of the body to which the preparation is applied. When a standard hydrocortisone preparation was applied to various parts of the body, absorption was found to be 0.14% on the plantar surface of the foot, 1% on the forearm, 4% on the scalp, 7% on the forehead, 13% on the cheeks, and 36% on the scrotum. Because penetration is high in the groin, axillae, and face, lower potency topical preparations (hydrocortisone 0.5% to 1%) should be used on these areas.[7,9,16] In areas where penetration is poor, such as the elbows, knees, palms, or soles, higher strength preparations should be used. (See Table 36.5.)

For P.K., a 1% hydrocortisone cream should be used on his face and other areas of high penetrability to reduce the possibility of complications.[17] Since P.K. appears to be in considerable distress, a high potency cream (intermediate or higher potency classification from Table 36.5) should be used initially on acutely inflamed areas or where high penetration is not a problem. This will "cool down" these lesions quickly.

If equal amounts of a corticosteroid are incorporated into ointments, gels, creams, and lotion bases, the gel and ointment bases generally are more active.[5,16,18] The addition of certain substances will enhance penetration and potency. For example, adding urea doubles the potency of hydrocortisone.[19] Increasing the concentration of a corticosteroid in a preparation will also increase its potency, but not in a linear fashion. Increasing the concentration of hydrocortisone tenfold only increases its potency by a factor of four, resulting in considerable wastage.[20] Since P.K. has a fine vesicular eruption, a cream should be used initially. However, patients often express a preference (e.g., cream, gel, ointment), and this should be considered.

Occlusion

3. Since it has been some time since P.K. has been aggressively treated for his atopic eczema and he has many hot, inflamed lesions, should occlusion be used? What complications could develop from occlusion? How would you occlude the lesions on P.K.'s chest?

Occlusion increases the hydration of the skin and also will increase the penetration and potency of a corticosteroid preparation. As a general rule, occlusion will enhance the potency of a corticosteroid by at least a factor of ten.[19] Occlusion may be accomplished by selecting an ointment-based corticosteroid; applying a nonmedicated ointment base over another corticosteroid preparation (gel, cream, lotion, or aerosol); wrapping the medicated area with plastic (e.g., Saran Wrap); or by wearing a plastic suit (space suit) over the affected area.[7,20] Several hours of occlusion are all that is necessary to increase potency; thus, relatively short periods of occlusion are clinically useful. Occlusion can be uncomfortable and can lead to sweat retention and an increased risk of bacterial and Candida infections. To reduce these problems and the chances of systemic side effects, occlusion should not be maintained for more than 12 hours in a 24-hour period. For P.K., occlusions could be used only on the "hottest" lesions; when these are brought under control, occlusion should be discontinued. However, most patients with atopic eczema may not tolerate occlusion because their itch threshold is low and pruritus is increased by heat, sweat retention, and maceration. Therefore, while occlusion is quite useful for "cooling off" hot, inflamed areas, the long-term benefit in a patient with atopic eczema is reduced by the increased pruritus which often leads to noncompliance.[21,22] For other chronic dermatologic conditions (e.g., psoriasis) that are not associated with severe pruritus, occlusion could be used for prolonged periods of time if necessary. Increasing the hydration of the skin (after a shower or bath) also increases the effects of medications immediately applied after the bath or shower. This would be an appropriate recommendation for P.K.

When using occlusion in patients with atopic eczema, care should be taken not to occlude unaffected skin (because of the low itch threshold). Of the methods described above, the best approach would be to apply a corticosteroid cream, rub it in thoroughly, and apply an occlusive ointment base over the cream. The most severe lesions on P.K.'s chest could be treated in this manner.

Product Selection

Pharmacokinetic Considerations

4. P.K. was given a prescription for halcinonide (Halog) 0.1% cream, 3 ounces, apply once at bedtime, and refill five times. Why, based upon biopharmaceutical considerations, is this prescription inappropriate?

Corticosteroids tend to penetrate human skin very slowly, leading to a reservoir effect. With low potency preparations, this reservoir effect will persist for several days, and with the most potent preparations under occlusion, the effects may persist for up to 14 days.[7,16,18,20,23,24] The clinical implication of this reservoir effect on chronic conditions is a cumulative effect with repeated application of topical corticosteroids. As a result, the number of applications per day can be reduced and less potent preparations can be used after the acute inflammatory process has been brought under control. P.K.'s present regimen is inappropriate because multiple daily applications will be needed initially to control inflamed lesions. Once control is achieved, a less potent preparation can be used and the number of applications can be reduced.

Many of the newer, more potent corticosteroids have been placed in specially formulated bases which maximize their release and potency. Mixing these preparations with other bases or vehicles may markedly reduce the potency far beyond that which would normally be expected from the dilution. It is recommended that the manufacturer be consulted before mixing commercially available products with other bases or vehicles to determine if an incompatibility exists.[7,20]

Side Effects

Acne

8. P.K. has acne lesions on his face as well as the atopic eczema. What problems could this present with use of topical corticosteroid therapy on the face?

The face is particularly vulnerable to corticosteroid side effects because of enhanced penetration.[17,20,32] Acne, rosacea, and perioral dermatitis can be seen on the face secondary to corticosteroid application. It may take several weeks to months for these problems to develop. They can be distinguished from naturally occurring disorders because the corticosteroid-induced lesions are generally at the same level of development, and they occur in areas where a history of corticosteroid application can be elicited. Generally, steroid acne, rosacea, and perioral dermatitis resolve after discontinuing the drug. Application of corticosteroid preparations (particularly the potent ones) to areas around the eye can lead to

increased intraocular pressure, glaucoma, cataracts, increased risk of ocular mycotic infections, and exacerbation of pre-existing herpes simplex infections.[24]

P.K.'s acne lesions may get worse secondary to the application of topical corticosteroids. He should be warned to apply the corticosteroid preparation only to the atopic eczema and avoid areas where acne exists. If the atopic eczema and acne lesions are in the same area and his acne gets worse after using the topical corticosteroid, P.K. must make a decision as to which of these two dermatologic conditions bothers him more (probably the atopic eczema) and treat the condition which is most disturbing. Some improvement in corticosteroid-exacerbated acne may be seen by decreasing the strength of the topical product applied to the face and/or reducing the frequency of application. An alternative to this approach, if P.K.'s acne is severe, would be to continue topical corticosteroid therapy but treat the acne systemically.[6,7] (See Chapter 37: Acne, for a more extensive discussion of acne.)

Idiosyncratic/Allergic Reactions

9. P.K. states that L.K. (his sister), who also has atopic eczema, started using a new topical corticosteroid preparation (halcinonide) 10 days ago. She complained of a burning sensation lasting for 1 hour after every application of this product. The burning has occurred after each application since the first day of therapy, and she stopped using the product 2 days ago because of this. He wonders if she may be allergic to the product. Why is it logical (or illogical) for an individual such as L.K. to become allergic to a corticosteroid-containing medication?

Cortisol is endogenously secreted by the adrenal gland and is essential to life. As a result, allergic reactions to topical corticosteroid preparations are rare. When allergic symptoms do occur, they generally are not due to the corticosteroid but to preservatives (e.g., parabens) or other ingredients in the formulation or the base (e.g., lanolin). Allergic sensitization may be seen within two weeks of therapy and may be difficult to diagnose because the corticosteroid may modify the allergic reaction.[17,20,33] One should suspect an allergic reaction if lesions change appearance after starting therapy, healing does not occur within the expected period of time, or the condition improves and then abruptly gets worse. Most case reports of allergic reactions to topical corticosteroids have been in patients with atopic eczema.[33,34] It should be noted that in a clinical trial of over 2000 patients, problems associated with the use of topical corticosteroids (e.g., dryness, itching, burning, or irritations) were no greater than when the base was used alone.[35]

Because of the time course of the burning sensation in L.K. (starting the first day and lasting only one hour), it is doubtful that she actually is allergic to this product. However, atopic eczema patients often have "sensitive" skin and may have idiosyncratic reactions to a variety of topical preparations.[3,21,22] To remedy this situation, L.K. should be given another topical corticosteroid preparation which has a different formulation (base and preservatives). If the reaction continues with a new product, an allergy work-up may be necessary and patch testing may be considered.

Systemic Absorption/Risk of Infection

10. P.K. also states that L.K. was given hydrocortisone injections several months ago when she was hospitalized for knee surgery. He wonders if he will require such injections if he has to have an operation or if he should wear a Medi-Alert tag. P.K. also states that L.K. received a lot of antibiotics and wonders if he is at risk for developing skin infections. Why would P.K. need (or not need) systemic corticosteroid administration during a surgical procedure?

Systemic adrenal axis suppression from topically applied corticosteroids appears to be more of a theoretical risk than a clinical entity in adults, except when the highest potency preparations are used. (See Table 36.5.) While suppression has been reported with lower potency agents, these cases can be attributed to excessive use by the patient or to application of corticosteroids over large areas of the body for prolonged periods under occlusion. Whatever suppression that may occur with mild to moderate potency topical corticosteroid preparations usually stops within two to four weeks after application is stopped. Patients using ≥ 200 gm/week of a high potency corticosteroid (see Table 36.5) are at risk for adrenal axis suppression.[36]

Because young children absorb corticosteroids to a greater extent, they have a greater risk of developing adrenal axis suppression and other systemic side effects.[29] To reduce this risk, hydrocortisone topical preparations should be used in children and their use should be limited to short periods of time. Additionally, patients with impaired corticosteroid clearance (e.g., liver failure) also should use hydrocortisone and be monitored closely for signs of systemic toxicity. Use of the highest potency preparations in Table 36.5 is associated with a significant risk of systemic adrenal axis suppression.[37–40] Therefore, the use of preparations such as clobetasol (Temovate) should be limited to no more than 50 gm/week for no more than two weeks. Additionally, these preparations should not be used under occlusion and should be reserved for dermatoses which are unresponsive to less potent preparations.[40]

Infections secondary to topically administered corticosteroids are also a theoretical risk which occurs uncommonly. While anecdotal reports of secondary bacterial infections appear in the literature, there is scant evidence to suggest they occur frequently. Topical corticosteroids do not alter normal skin flora.[41]

Although the risk of developing an addisonian crisis in surgery secondary to topical steroids is extremely low, patients who have used potent topical corticosteroids over large areas of their bodies (>30%) or those who have used occlusion are at greater risk (see above) and are often given systemic hydrocortisone prophylactically before surgery. Because P.K. is not likely to require such supplementation, a Medi-Alert tag is unnecessary.

Topical Antibiotics with Corticosteroids

11. Since P.K. appears to have a bacterial infection associated with his atopic eczema, can a corticosteroid and an antibiotic preparation be used together? What are the risks associated with topical antibiotics?

Evidence suggests that combination therapy with a corticosteroid-antibiotic preparation is more efficacious than either agent alone in treating impetiginized eczema.[42–44] Presumably, the corticosteroid suppresses the clinical signs of infection and helps to re-establish the normal skin barrier function. This allows the skin's normal defense mechanisms to ward off the infection. Otitis externa, certain intertriginous eruptions, and possibly seborrheic eczema also respond favorably to this combination.[24]

The rationale for combining several antibiotics is to cover a wide spectrum of potential infecting organisms; therefore, a combination of at least two antibiotics is required. Dermatologic infections frequently are mixed, with cultures showing two or more organisms present in sufficient quantities to be responsible for the infection. Bacitracin commonly is combined with neomycin and/or Polymyxin B to treat superficial dermatologic infections. All three of these bactericidal agents are synergistic, resulting in increased efficacy and perhaps a broader spectrum of activity.[7] Topically applied gentamicin should be avoided if possible because other agents generally are equally effective and there is a risk of developing gentamicin-resistant organisms.

Since P.K.'s secondarily infected lesions probably harbor a variety of organisms, a product containing bacitracin and/or neo-

Table 36.6	Spectrum of Activity of Antibiotics Available for Topical Use

Bacitracin

Effective against all anaerobic cocci, most strains of streptococci, staphylococci, and pneumococci. Not effective against most gram-negative organisms

Gentamicin

Effective against most gram-negative organisms (similar to neomycin) including *Pseudomonas* and many strains of *S. aureus*[a]

Mupirocin

Very effective against *S. aureus*[a] and does not interfere with wound healing. Currently, the only topical antibiotic that has been proven to be more effective than the vehicle based upon FDA guidelines

Gramicidin

Effective against most gram-positive organisms; not effective against most gram-negative organisms

Neomycin

Effective against most gram-negative organisms (except *Pseudomonas*) and some gram-positive organisms. Group A streptococci are resistant

Polymyxin B

Effective against most gram-negative organisms (including *Pseudomonas*). Most strains of Proteus, Serratia, and gram-positive organisms are resistant

[a] *S. aureus = Staphylococcus aureus.*

mycin and/or polymyxin B should be used. Topical antibiotics should only be used to treat superficial infections; systemic antibiotics should be employed for deep infections because of greater efficacy.

Side Effects

There have been many reports of contact dermatitis caused by topical antimicrobials. *Neomycin sensitivity* has been reported in 50% of patients with allergic eczematous contact dermatitis,[45] 6% of patients patch tested with common allergens,[46,47] and 8% of randomly selected subjects tested with both patch and intradermal methods.[48] In a study of 1158 patients, the incidence of sensitization to neomycin was 1.1%.[47] This report is interesting because the population studied had no pre-existing dermatologic problems, and it probably represents the true incidence of allergic sensitization to neomycin in the general population. Also, a high incidence of sensitization was reported when preparations containing neomycin were used in the long-term treatment of leg ulcers.[49] The corticosteroid contained in many neomycin preparations does not prevent these allergic reactions, although it may decrease the severity of the reaction. Additionally, ointment vehicles containing neomycin may have a higher rate of sensitization than creams.

Hypersensitivity reactions, usually manifested by a rash, have followed the topical use of nitrofurazone (Furacin). Because the overall incidence of sensitization is relatively high, nitrofurazone is not recommended for the treatment of bacterial infections complicating serious burns.

Ethylenediamine, employed as a stabilizer in ointment preparations such as Mycolog (neomycin, nystatin, gramicidin, and triamcinolone acetonide), has been associated with contact dermatitis.[6,7] Tetracycline and oxyquinoline (e.g., Vioform) topical preparations also can cause sensitivity reactions.[45,46]

If the skin infection is severe, deep, or associated with fever or other systemic manifestations, systemic antibiotics should be used. If a topical antibiotic preparation is indicated, it should be employed with full awareness of its sensitizing properties.

Pruritus

12. As stated in Question 2, P.K.'s chief complaint is pruritus. What could P.K. do for relief of pruritus?

Pruritus is the most common cutaneous symptom. It has many different causes and has been associated with many systemic diseases. Among these are: obstructive biliary disease, uremia, iron deficiency anemia, hypertension, gout, breast carcinoma, gastric carcinoma, lung carcinoma, multiple myeloma, lymphoma, polycythemia vera, mycosis fungoides, Hodgkin's disease, carcinoid syndrome, thyroid disease (both hyper- and hypothyroid), diabetes mellitus, multiple sclerosis, brain abscess, central nervous system infarct, and pregnancy (usually the first trimester).[50,51] In the absence of a cutaneous dermatitis, a careful history and physical examination should be performed to rule out one of the systemic causes of pruritus. Additionally, a chest x-ray, stool examination for occult blood, complete blood count (CBC) with differential, thyroid panel, blood urea nitrogen (BUN), creatinine, liver function panel, glucose, and urinalysis (UA) should be performed to help screen for the above systemic diseases.[51,52]

Although often detrimental, scratching, which probably damages or fatigues receptor nerve endings, is the most common method of relieving pruritus. One would therefore expect topically applied *local anesthetics* or *antihistamines* to be effective in dulling the sensation. However, this approach is often disappointing, probably because the salt forms of these drugs are poorly absorbed by the intact epidermis. Also, low concentrations are used in many OTC preparations. If adequate concentrations of local anesthetics are employed (benzocaine 20% or lidocaine 3% to 4%), pruritus or pain may be reduced for up to 45 minutes. These agents are most useful for relieving pruritus or pain for short periods of time when the patient requires most relief (e.g., when trying to go to sleep at night).[53] A drawback to the use of these agents is their ability to cause allergic contact dermatitis (benzocaine: 0.17% incidence; lidocaine: extremely rare).[47,53] Topical antihistamine preparations provide only a mild topical anesthetic effect when compared to benzocaine 20% or lidocaine 3% to 4%, and it is doubtful they exert a true antihistaminic effect when administered topically.

P.K. could also try cold water or ice cubes which are effective in the relief of pruritus, as are products containing aluminum acetate (Burow's solution), tannic acid, or calamine. A cool bath may be useful for relief of pruritus from dermatological lesions if they are widespread.

Moisturizing mixtures such as Keri Lotion, Lubriderm, or simply mineral or baby oil are useful in the treatment of pruritus caused by dry skin. This problem often is encountered in the elderly and others during the winter months. Bathing should be restricted to avoid the drying effect of water, the irritant effect of alkaline soaps, and the trauma of toweling.[7]

Topical corticosteroid applications can be very effective. They reduce inflammation and often are contained in a cream base which helps to soothe the affected area.

Systemic antihistamines evoke a favorable response for many patients suffering from pruritus, although their major beneficial effect may be due to sedation. There is disagreement over which antihistamine or antiserotonin agent is more effective in the treatment of pruritus.[54,55] There is evidence, based upon clinical trials and the relative amounts of histamine required to produce itching, that hydroxyzine may be more effective than diphenhydramine (Benadryl) or cyproheptadine (Periactin).[56,57] Many practitioners now consider hydroxyzine to be the antihistamine of choice for the treatment of pruritus; doses of 10 to 25 mg three to four times a day are commonly employed. There is little evidence that antihis-

tamines are effective in treating non-histamine mediated pruritus, except that their inherent sedative effect may be somewhat beneficial in all pruritic conditions.[3,6,7]

Nondrug Recommendations for Atopic Eczema

13. P.K. is prescribed the following: hydroxyzine 25 mg TID PRN, #90, refill × 6; triamcinolone acetonide cream 0.1%, apply TID, 2 lb, refill × 6; betamethasone valerate ointment 0.1%, 30 gm, apply PRN flare, refill × 3; triple antibiotic ointment, apply QID to infected areas, 1 oz, nonrefillable. P.K. has a return appointment in the Dermatology Clinic in 3 weeks. What nondrug interventions might be suggested to P.K. at this time?

The general goals of therapy for atopic eczema are to decrease pruritus, suppress inflammation, lubricate the skin, and reduce anxiety. Additionally, the recommendations shown in Table 36.7 are useful for patients such as P.K. with atopic eczema or any other irritant dermatitis.

P.K. should be warned to avoid people with active herpes simplex infections since severe disseminated infections can occur.[4,7,8,22,27]

Tachyphylaxis/Specialized Corticosteroid Dosage Forms/Antihistamines

14. P.K. continued to do well and returns to the outpatient clinic pharmacy 3 months later to request refills of his topical corticosteroid prescriptions. He states that the infected areas have cleared except he is still having problems with his fingers. He has applied the betamethasone valerate ointment to his hands 5 to 6 times/day for the last 3 weeks without any noticeable improvement. He used the triamcinolone cream according to directions on other areas of his body. P.K. followed other recommendations faithfully and wonders if anything else could be done for his hands. He is occasionally bothered by sedation from the hydroxyzine. Why is P.K. seemingly not responding to therapy, and how should his excessive sedation be managed?

First, P.K. is over-using the topical corticosteroids, and tachyphylaxis is probably occurring. Tachyphylaxis can occur within one week of therapy, but generally takes several weeks to a month to occur.[58–61] To treat this problem, P.K. should stop applying the betamethasone valerate ointment for four to seven days and then restart therapy, applying the medication in the proper manner. It has been suggested that limited courses of treatment separated by short rest periods might be more effective than continuous treatment. However, documentation for this type of therapy is lacking.

Table 36.7	Recommendations for Patients with Atopic Eczema or Other Irritant Dermatitis

1) Clothing should be soft and light. Cotton or corduroy is preferred. Wools and coarse, heavy synthetics should be avoided

2) Heat should be avoided because it often makes the eczema worse. The environment should be well ventilated, cool, and low in humidity (30% to 50%). Rapid changes in ambient temperature should be avoided

3) Bathing should be kept to a minimum (no longer than five minutes) and the patient should use a nonirritating soap (e.g., Basis soap). A colloid bath or the use of appropriate amounts of bath oil may be useful

4) The skin should be kept moist with frequent applications of emollients (e.g., Keri, Lubriderm, Nivea, Aquaphor, Eucerin, or petrolatum)

5) Primary irritants such as paints, cleansers, solvents, and chemical sprays should be avoided

Table 36.8	Ways to Minimize Sedation from Hydroxyzine

1) Reduce the strength of hydroxyzine to 10 mg tablets

2) Have the patient take the hydroxyzine on a scheduled basis since some tolerance to the sedative properties probably will develop

3) Switch to a less sedating antihistamine. However, part of the benefit derived from antihistamines is related to their sedative action; this property helps the patient sleep and decreases the anxiety which is common with persistent pruritus

4) If the above three measures have been tried and sedation is still a problem, the patient must decide which is worse, the sedation or the pruritus, and make a decision whether or not to use the antihistamine

5) A trial of one of the newer nonsedating antihistamines (e.g., terfenadine) may be employed if the above measures fail

Flurandrenolide 4 $\mu g/cm^2$ tape (Cordran) may be useful after P.K. stops the corticosteroids for four to seven days. While this product is expensive, it is very useful for small areas because the tape serves as a protectant and provides occlusion. It is very useful on the hands, particularly the fingers, where P.K. is having problems, because other vehicles are often quite messy when applied to the hands. When using Cordran tape, the general principles previously outlined for occlusion should be followed.[7,17,20]

Sedation from hydroxyzine is fairly common. See Table 36.8 for ways to minimize or reduce the sedation.

Nonprescription Topical Hydrocortisone

15. M.P., a 29-year-old housewife, requests Rhulicort Cream (hydrocortisone 1%) for her hands, which are irritated from dishwater. Why is this use of hydrocortisone cream a reasonable indication for the management of this condition?

A 0.5% to 1% hydrocortisone preparation is indicated for temporary relief of minor skin irritations; itching and rash due to eczema, dermatitis, insect bites, poison ivy, poison oak, poison sumac, soaps, detergents, cosmetics, and jewelry; and itchy genital and anal areas. These preparations should not be used in children under two years of age without approval of the child's physician.[53] At present, it is difficult to evaluate whether higher strength corticosteroid preparations are more effective for these conditions than 0.5% to 1% hydrocortisone. The minimum concentration of hydrocortisone considered to be effective is 0.5%, although 0.25% concentrations have been found effective for certain dermatoses in some studies.[53,60]

Before recommending a 0.5% to 1% OTC hydrocortisone product for M.P., an assessment should be made as to whether or not the use of such a preparation is warranted (see Table 36.9).

16. T.C., a 26-year-old, 60 kg female, requests one of the topical, nonprescription hydrocortisone preparations for a rash on her face. T.C. states that the rash is on her cheeks and gets worse when she goes out into the sun. She also complains of feeling tired and would like a vitamin product. Additionally, she requests a bottle of 1000 five-grain aspirin for her sore joints. The rash appears erythematous and covers both cheeks in a butterfly configuration. T.C. admits to using no other medications. Should a hydrocortisone preparation be recommended?

The symptoms that T.C. describes are consistent with systemic lupus erythematosus and she should be referred to her physician for an appropriate diagnostic work up. (See Chapter 42: Connective Tissue Disorders: The Clinical Use of Corticosteroids.) See Table 36.9 for things to consider when assessing the need for 0.5% to 1% hydrocortisone in patients like M.P. and T.C.

If after assessment, it is determined that 0.5% to 1% hydrocortisone is indicated, Table 36.10 should be considered in selecting a product and monitoring the patient's response.

Dry Skin

17. C.R., a 54-year-old female, requests something for dry skin on her arms and back. She has had this problem for a number of years and it gets better in the summer and worse in the winter. She has no other medical problems and only takes an occasional aspirin for her "arthritis." What recommendations would you provide C.R. on her management of this condition?

C.R.'s case represents a simple case of dry skin. Before recommending therapy, the following differentials should be considered: ichthyosis vulgaris (familial history usually present), atopic eczema, psoriasis, contact dermatitis, and hypothyroidism. Usually, simple questioning can rule out these conditions. Most cases of dry skin are caused by dehydration of the stratum corneum.[3,4,6]

Table 36.11 gives general recommendations for the treatment of dry skin.[3-7,27,62]

Drug Eruptions

Clinically recognizable adverse drug reactions are manifested more often on the skin than any other organ or organ system.[63-65] It has been estimated that between 1% and 5% of hospitalized patients develop a drug eruption.[27,63,66] Outpatient statistics are much more difficult to obtain but probably are within the same range. There is no correlation between age, diagnosis, or severity of illness and the likelihood of developing a drug eruption.[5] Women appear to be twice as likely to develop a drug eruption as men.

Table 36.9	Factors to Consider When Assessing the Need for 0.5% to 1% Hydrocortisone

1) Does the patient have constitutional symptoms such as: fever, joint pains, muscle pains, headache, difficulty moving the affected area, or excessive swelling of the affected area?

2) Does the patient have a history of severe chronic disease process such as: anemia, malnutrition, lung disease, kidney disease, heart disease, diabetes mellitus, cancer, alcoholism, or a systemic infection? Is the patient being treated by a physician for a dermatological condition?

3) Does the patient's drug history indicate a possible drug allergy (See Question 18)?

4) Is the patient taking any medication which may impair the immune system? This may include: systemically-administered corticosteroid preparations, antimetabolites or other cancer chemotherapeutic agents, and radiation therapy

5) Does the area appear macerated, eroded, or infected? Is bleeding present? If infected, the area generally will appear red and swollen, and pus or drainage may be present

6) Does the affected area involve the eye or mucous membranes?

7) For the patient with poison ivy/oak/sumac, is there a possibility that the patient may have inhaled the smoke from the burning of one of these plants?

8) For patients with renal complaints, check for bleeding, hemorrhoids, or venereal disease

9) For patients with genital complaints, check for venereal disease, lice, or scabies

10) Has the patient's problem worsened after using a 0.5% to 1% hydrocortisone preparation or has the condition remained unchanged after one week of therapy?

11) Did the patient's problem return after appearing to clear up with the use of a 0.5% to 1% hydrocortisone preparation?

Table 36.10	Considerations for Selecting a Hydrocortisone Product and Monitoring Patient Response

1) Determine which product(s) the patient already may have used to treat this problem and if the treatment was effective

2) The patient should note some improvement in two to three days. If this does not occur, the patient should see a physician

3) The preparation should be applied to the affected area three to four times a day and rubbed in thoroughly. This is very important if the patient is to receive the full anti-inflammatory benefits

4) Occlusion will enhance the effects of 0.5% to 1% hydrocortisone preparations (See Question 3 for further instructions.)

5) If pain is present, consider recommending aspirin or acetaminophen 650 mg four times a day

6) If itching is severe, consider recommending an OTC sleep aid. Generally, itching bothers people most when they are trying to go to sleep. If the area that itches is small, an ice cube or cold compress applied to the affected area will bring relief. If there are numerous scratch marks around the affected area, consider recommending that the patient wear cotton gloves at night to protect the area and reduce the chances of infection

7) If the patient has a contact dermatitis due to soaps, detergents, cosmetics, or jewelry, the condition generally will persist until the patient stops contact with the offending agent. Many times, the patient's skin problem may be traced to recent use of a new cosmetic or cleaning agent, or to new clothes. Some detective work may be necessary to discover the cause of the problem. If the hands are affected (a common occurrence), recommend that the patient purchase rubber gloves and wear them while using the offending agent or other irritating substances which will aggravate the underlying problem. Recommend applying the 0.5% to 1% hydrocortisone preparation before wearing the gloves as this will enhance the anti-inflammatory effect

The most common type of eruption encountered in clinical practice, and probably the one most often overlooked, is the exanthematic eruption. This type of reaction comprises both morbilliform (measles-like) and scarlatiniform (scarlet fever-like) eruptions.[5,65] Since drug eruptions often mimic other types of dermatitis, it is necessary to have a good understanding of the mimicked disease state to make the proper diagnosis. Medications commonly associated with drug eruptions are listed in Table 36.12.

Acneiform Eruptions

Acneiform eruptions appear very much like common acne. They may be differentiated from acne by their sudden occurrence, the absence of comedones in affected areas, and the fact that they may occur on any part of the body. Cysts and scarring are rare with drug-induced acne. Eruptions also can occur during any period of the patient's life; thus, acne that appears in age brackets where it normally does not appear may be suspected of being caused by drugs. For someone who already has acne, existing lesions may be worsened by drugs such as corticosteroids, bromides, iodides, and lithium (also see Chapter 37: Acne).

Photosensitive Eruptions

These eruptions require the presence of both drug and light source to occur. Photosensitive eruptions are divided into two subtypes based upon different mechanisms of action. The first type is called *photoallergic* and requires the presence of light (UVA) to alter the drug so that it becomes an antigen or acts as a hapten. Photoallergic eruptions require previous contact with the offending drug, are not dose related, exhibit cross-sensitivity with chemically related compounds, and may appear as a variety of lesions includ-

ing urticaria, bulla, and sunburn. These lesions usually are secondary to the use of topical agents. The second type of photosensitive eruption is known as *phototoxic* reaction in which the light source alters the drug to a toxic form, resulting in tissue damage independent of allergic response. This eruption may occur on first exposure to a drug, is dose related, usually has no cross-sensitivity, and almost always appears as an exaggerated sunburn. In some instances, a drug may produce both photoallergic and phototoxic reactions. Most phototoxic and photoallergic reactions occur fairly soon after exposure to light (also see Chapter 39: Photosensitivity and Burns).

Lichen Planus-Like Eruptions

These lesions appear as flat-topped papules which have a distinctive sheen. Pruritus usually is quite pronounced and any part of the body may be affected (most commonly the arms and legs), including the mucous membranes. The lesions sometimes are confused with fixed eruptions but easily can be differentiated histologically.

Alopecia

Although alopecia is not a true drug eruption, hair may occasionally be lost when such reactions occur. Eruptions that may lead to alopecia are exfoliative dermatitis and erythema multiforme. Hair loss may be attributed to a toxic action of a drug, such as an antimetabolite, or to an interference with the normal growth phases of hair (e.g., warfarin).

Bullous Eruptions

Bullous lesions (see Figure 36.5) may occur in combination with other drug eruptions, such as erythema multiforme or toxic epidermal necrolysis, or by themselves. The lesions may be round or irregular in shape and contain a clear, serous fluid. The fluid-filled sacs may be either tense or flaccid and can occur on mucous membranes as well as the skin. These lesions are very similar to what

Table 36.11	General Recommendations for the Treatment of Dry Skin

1) Use room humidifiers

2) Keep room temperature as low as comfortable to prevent sweating and water loss from the skin

3) Keep bathing to a minimum (every one to two days) with warm but not hot water. After bathing, the patient should immediately apply an emollient (see Table 88.2). When the skin is soaked for five to ten minutes the stratum corneum can absorb as much as six times its weight in water. Application of an emollient immediately after bathing will trap the water in the skin and reduce dryness

4) Eliminate exposure to solvents, drying chemicals, harsh soaps, and cleaners. These substances remove oils from the skin and reduce its barrier function. As the barrier function is lost, water loss from the skin is increased up to 75 times above normal. Exposure to cold, dry winds also will enhance water loss

5) Apply emollients (see Table 88.2) three to six times a day. Many patients find the use of a urea-containing product to be effective and more cosmetically acceptable because it does not leave a greasy residue on the skin after application.

6) If scaling is a problem, keratolytic (Keralyt Gel) or a higher strength urea-containing preparation (20%) may be useful

7) If inflammation is present, a mild to moderately potent topical corticosteroid may be very useful (see Table 88.5). An ointment vehicle is more effective than others

is seen with pemphigus and pemphigoid reactions. Lesions usually resolve after discontinuing the drug but occasionally become chronic.

Eczematous Eruptions

Eczematous lesions are seen more often with contact sensitizers than with internally administered compounds. A description of these types of lesions is provided in Question 2.

Epidermal Necrolysis

This type of eruption was first described by Lyell in 1956 and may be preceded by a prodrome characterized by malaise, lethargy, fever, and occasionally throat or mucous membrane soreness. Epidermal changes follow, and consist of erythema and massive bullae formations which easily rupture and peel. The skin appears to be scalded. Hairy parts of the body usually are not affected, but mucous membrane involvement is common. Approximately 30% of the patients with toxic epidermal necrolysis succumb, often within eight days after bullae appear. The usual cause of death is infection complicated by massive fluid and electrolyte loss. Epidermal necrolysis is the most severe type of drug eruption. Even though the skin takes on a very grave appearance, healing occurs within two weeks in about 70% of patients, usually with no scarring. In addition to drugs, certain bacterial infections and foods are believed to cause this type of eruption. Most causes of toxic epidermal necrolysis in children are due to infection: *Staphylococcus aureus* has been implicated. There appears to be a higher incidence of this type of drug eruption in HIV-positive patients.

Erythema Multiforme

As the name implies, erythema multiforme eruptions take on a variety of morphological forms. The lesions are discrete and sharply circumscribed, and usually are arranged symmetrically. They appear as acute, polymorphous, bright or dark red maculae, papules, vesicles, or bullae; however, only one type of lesion usually predominates in a given patient. Erythema multiforme is more common in children and young adults. Sometimes malaise, a low-grade fever, and itching or burning may be seen with this type of eruption. Etiological factors associated with erythema multiforme include drugs, *mycoplasma* and herpes infections, deep x-ray therapy, foods, and sometimes neoplasms. Sulfonamides, phenothiazines, thiazides, and phenytoin are the drugs most often implicated in erythema multiforme eruptions.

Erythema Nodosum Eruptions

These lesions appear as red, tender nodules usually located around the shins, but they can occur elsewhere. Occasionally, these lesions may be accompanied by mild constitutional symptoms, but there is usually no mucous membrane involvement. Etiological factors associated with the development of erythema nodosum include drugs, female gender, rheumatic fever, sarcoidosis, leprosy, certain bacterial infections (e.g., tuberculosis), and systemic fungal infections. Usually the lesions heal slowly over several weeks after the offending agent is removed. Oral contraceptives are the most frequently implicated drug with this type of eruption.

Exfoliative Dermatitis

Exfoliative dermatitis, as the name would imply, is characterized by large areas of skin becoming scaly and erythematous and then sloughing off. Hair and nails are sometimes lost. In most patients, a generalized systemic toxicity also accompanies the eruption. Secondary bacterial infections may occur and most fatalities are due to infections. Exfoliative dermatitis also may follow other drug eruptions; thus, a less severe eruption may culminate with an exfoliative dermatitis. This type of eruption may take weeks or months to resolve, even after withdrawal of the offending agent.

Fixed Drug Eruptions

This eruption, unlike the others mentioned, is caused exclusively by drugs. The lesions are erythematous, sharply bordered, and have a tendency to be darker than the surrounding, unaffected skin. They also may be eczematous, urticarial, vesicular, bullous, or nodular. Because these lesions have a marked propensity to recur at the same location, the word ''fixed'' is applied. The face and genitalia are more common sites for this type of drug eruption. Although the eruptions heal after withdrawal of the causative drug, there usually is a marked hyperpigmentation of the area which may take months to resolve. The mechanism by which fixed drug eruptions occur has not been elucidated but is believed to be allergic in nature. It can be described figuratively as islands of hypersensitivity; one area of the skin having the ability to evoke an allergic response and other areas lacking this ability.

Maculopapular Eruptions

Maculopapular eruptions are subdivided into two groups: scarlatiniform and morbilliform. Most drug eruptions fall within one of these two groups. *Scarlatiniform* eruptions are erythematous and usually involve extensive areas. They are differentiated from scarlet fever by the lack of other diagnostic signs and laboratory studies. *Morbilliform* eruptions usually begin as discrete, reddish brown maculae which may coalesce to form a diffusion rash. Likewise, morbilliform eruptions are differentiated from measles by the lack of other diagnostic signs and laboratory studies. In either type of exanthematic eruption, pruritus may or may not be present. Generally, this type of eruption will appear within one week after the causative drug (with penicillins two or more weeks) has been started and will completely clear within 7 to 14 days after stopping it. Morbilliform eruptions commonly are caused by ampicillin, amoxicillin, and allopurinol.

Purpura

Purpuric lesions (see Figure 36.4) are characterized as hemorrhages into the skin. They are purplish, sharply bordered, and have a tendency to become brownish as they get older. These lesions may or may not be associated with thrombocytopenia. Etiological factors other than drugs that are associated with purpura are: vitamin C deficiency, snake bites, and infections. The mechanism by which these lesions are produced is not known, but they have a tendency to recur with re-exposure to the causative agent. Sometimes purpura may develop from other types of eruptions, such as erythema multiforme.

Stevens-Johnson Syndrome

The Stevens-Johnson syndrome is probably the most common type of severe drug eruption. It is classified as a serious variant of bullous erythema multiforme. In addition to what has been described earlier, the Stevens-Johnson syndrome usually involves the mucous membranes and includes constitutional symptoms of fever and malaise. The skin can become hemorrhagic and pneumonia and joint pains may occur. Serious ocular involvement is common and can culminate in partial or complete blindness. Besides drugs, this syndrome has been associated with infections, pregnancy, foods, deep x-ray therapy, and neoplasms. Mortality is estimated to be in the range of 5% to 18%. The duration of the syndrome is usually four to six weeks. The long-acting sulfonamides are most often implicated.

Table 36.12	Medications Commonly Associated with Drug Eruptions[3,4,6,63–66,73,75–86,88–101]

Acneiform[a]
ACTH[c]
Actinomycin D
Amoxicillin
Ampicillin
Androgens
Barbiturates
Carbamazepine
Cephalosporins
Chloral hydrate
Chloramphenicol
Contraceptives, oral[b]
Corticosteroids[b]
Ethambutol
Ethionamide
Iodides/bromides[b]
Isoniazid[b]
Lithium[b]
Naproxen
Phenytoin
Quinidine
Scopolamine
Streptomycin
Trimethadione

Alopecia[a]
Allopurinol
Anticoagulants[b]
Antimetabolites[b]
Bromocriptine
Captopril
Carbamazepine
Cimetidine
Clofibrate
Colchicine
Contraceptives, oral
Ethionamide
Gold
Indomethacin
Levodopa
Lithium
Propranolol
Quinacrine
Thallium
Trimethadione
Valproate sodium
Vitamin A (High Doses)

Bullous[a]
Aminosalicylic acid
Ampicillin
Barbiturates[b]
Chloral hydrate
Clonidine
Coumarins
Gold
Iodides/bromides[b]
Mesantoin
Nalidixic acid
NSAIDs[b,c]
Penicillins
Phenothiazines
Phenytoin
Promethazine
Sulfonamides
Tetracycline

Eczematous[a]
Aminophylline
Antimetabolites
Chloral hydrate
Chlorpropamide

Chlorothiazide
Cephalosporins[b]
Codeine
Disulfiram
Gentamicin[b]
Gold
Iodides
Kanamycin
Meprobamate
Neomycin
Nitrofurantoin
Penicillins[b]
Procaine
Promethazine
Quinacrine
Streptomycin
Sulfonamides
Thiamine
Tolbutamide

Epidermal Necrolysis[a]
Ampicillin
Allopurinol[b]
Barbiturates
Carbamazepine[b]
Chlorpropamide
Hydantoin derivatives
Ibuprofen
Indomethacin
NSAIDs
Penicillins[b]
Pentamidine[b]
Phenylbutazone[b]
Phenytoin
Quinine
Sulfonamides[b]
Sulindac
Tolmetin

Erythema Multiforme[a]
Acetazolamide
Acetylsalicylic acid
Ampicillin
Barbiturates[b]
Bromides
Carbamazepine
Chloral hydrate
Chlorpropamide
Diflunisal
Griseofulvin[b]
Gold
Hydantoins[b]
Ibuprofen
Minoxidil
NSAIDs
Penicillins[b]
Phenolphthalein
Phenothiazines
Phenylbutazone
Procaine
Propranolol
Quinine
Rifampin
Salicylates
Sulfapyridine
Sulfonamides
Sulfonylureas
Sulindac
Thiazides

Erythema Nodosum[a]
Aminosalicylic acid

Codeine[b]
Contraceptives, oral[b]
Iodides/Bromides[b]
Penicillins[b]
Phenacetin
Salicylates
Sulfonamides

Exfoliative Dermatitis[a]
Actinomycin D
Allopurinol
Aminosalicylic acid
Barbiturates[b]
Bismuth
Captopril
Carbamazepine[b]
Chloroquine
Chlorpropamide
Cimetidine
Diltiazem
Gold
Griseofulvin
Hydantoins[a]
Iodides
Isoniazid
Lithium
Mesantoin
Nitrofurantoin
Penicillamine
Penicillins
Phenothiazines
Phenylbutazone
Phenytoin
Quinidine
Stilbestrol
Streptomycin
Sulfonamides
Sulfonylureas
Tetracycline
Thiouracil
Vitamin A

Fixed Drug[a]
Acetaminophen
Acetylsalicylic acid
Amphetamines
Anticoagulants
Barbiturates[b]
Belladonna
Bismuth
Chloral hydrate
Chlordiazepoxide
Chloroquine
Codeine
Contraceptives, oral[b]
Dapsone
Digitalis
Diphenhydramine
Disulfiram
Epinephrine
Ergot
Ethchlorvynol
Griseofulvin
Gold
Hydralazine
Hydroxyurea
Ibuprofen
Iodides/bromides
Ipecac
Meprobamate
Methenamine
Metronidazole

Morphine
Penicillins
Phenacetin
Phenophthalein
Phenothiazines
Phenylbutazone
Quinidine
Reserpine
Saccharin
Salicylates
Stilbestrol
Streptomycin
Sulfonamides
Sulindac
Tetracyclines
Trimethoprim
Vermouth

Maculopapular[a]
Aminosalicylic acid
Ampicillin[b]
Allopurinol[b]
Antimetabolites[b]
Atropine
Barbiturates[b]
Benzodiazepines
Busulfan
Carbamazepine
Cephalosporins[b]
Chloramphenicol
Chlordiazepoxide[b]
Chloroquine
Chlorothiazide
Chlorpromazine
Contraceptives, oral
Diazepam[b]
Erythromycin[b]
Ethionamide
Gentamicin[b]
Griseofulvin
Gold[b]
Hydantoin derivatives
Ibuprofen
Indomethacin[b]
Isoniazid[b]
Insulin
Lithium[b]
Meprobamate
Morphine
Naproxen
Nitrofurantoin[b]
NSAIDs[b]
Penicillamine[b]
Penicillins[b]
Phenothiazines
Phenylbutazone
Piroxicam
Promethazine
Quinacrine
Rifampin
Streptomycin
Sulfonamides
Sulfonylureas
Sulindac
Thiazides
Thiouracil
Tetracyclines
Tolmetin

Photosensitive[a]
Amiodarone[b]
Ampicillin

Continued

Table 36.12   Medications Commonly Associated with Drug Eruptions[3,4,63–66,73,75–86,88–101] (Continued)

Barbiturates	Sulindac	Chlorpropamide	Fluorides
Carbamazepine	Tetracyclines[b]	Fansidar	Griseofulvin
Chlordiazepoxide	Thiazides[b]	Lithium	Gold
Chlorothiazide	Tolbutamide	Meprobamate	Hydralazine
Chlorpropamide	Vinblastine	Penicillins	Heparin
Cimetidine		Phenacetin	Ibuprofen
Contraceptives, oral	**Purpura[a]**	Phenytoin	Indomethacin
Dacarbazine	ACTH	Sulfonamides	Insulin
Diazepam	Allopurinol	Trimethadione	Iodides/bromides
Furosemide	Barbiturates		Lithium
Griseofulvin[b]	Chlorothiazide		Morphine
Gold	Corticosteroids	**Urticarial[a]**	Naproxen
Ketoprofen	Coumarins[b]	ACTH	Nitrofurantoin[b]
Methoxsalen[b]	Ephedrine	Ampicillin[b]	NSAIDs[b]
Methyldopa	Gold[b]	Allopurinol	Penicillins[b]
Nalidixic acid[b]	Hydrochlorothiazide	Anticoagulants	Phenacetin
Naproxen	Indomethacin	Aspirin	Phenylbutazone
Phenothiazines[b]	Iodides/bromides	Barbiturates	Pilocarpine
Phenylbutazone	Meprobamate	Cephalosporins	Promethazine
Piroxicam	Penicillins	Chloral hydrate	Quinidine
Promethazine	Quinidine	Chlordiazepoxide	Quinine
Proptriptyline[b]	Sulfonamides	Chlorpromazine	Reserpine
Quinidine		Codeine[b]	Saccharin
Reserpine	**Stevens-Johnson Syndrome[a]**	Contraceptives, oral	Sulfonamides
Sulfonamides	Barbiturates[b]	Dextrans	Sulindac
Sulfonylureas	Chloroquine	Diazepam	Thiouracil
		Erythromycin	Tolmetin

Urticaria

Urticarial eruptions are immediate hypersensitivity reactions and usually appear as sharply circumscribed, edematous and erythematous plaques with an abrupt onset. In most cases, the lesions disappear within a few hours, rarely last more than 24 hours, and are associated with an intense itching, stinging, or prickling sensation. Urticarial eruptions commonly are called "hives" and frequently are associated with certain drugs, foods, psychic upsets, and serum sickness. Rarely, parasites or neoplasms may precipitate hives. Angioneurotic edema, a variation of urticaria, can be explained best as a more severe form where giant hives predominate. The most frequently implicated drugs with this type of reaction are aspirin, penicillin, and blood products.[3,4,6,63,64]

18. D.Z., a 42-year-old male, is currently taking penicillin V 250 mg QID, carbamazepine 200 mg TID, diazepam 5 mg TID PRN, and Maalox 30 mL PRN. He now complains of a red maculopapular rash that recently has appeared on his arms and chest. He has been taking the penicillin V for 8 days and the other medications for more than a year. What is the typical time of onset for drug-induced dermatological reactions? How should the drug eruption in D.Z. be managed?

In assessing drug eruptions a number of factors are important. Most drug eruptions occur within one to two weeks after starting therapy. Penicillins sometimes can be the exception to this rule by having a slightly more prolonged onset of up to several weeks. Since D.Z. has been taking diazepam and carbamazepine for more than a year and has only been taking penicillin for eight days, the time of onset of this drug eruption would lead to the conclusion that the penicillin is the cause of his drug eruption.

Penicillins are the most frequently implicated class of drugs causing eruptions. In a ten-year study of drug eruptions, antibiotics caused 53% of drug eruptions and penicillins accounted for over one-half of the antibiotic-induced eruptions.[64] Frequently implicated drugs and the percentage of people given the drug who actually develop an eruption are listed in Table 36.13.

For D.Z., a different antibiotic should be substituted for the penicillin, and the lesion should begin to clear in a day or two (if the penicillin is the cause of the drug eruption). If the rash does not begin to clear in a couple of days, another cause should be investigated.

Generally, all that is needed to treat a drug eruption is withdrawal of the offending agent. The lesions should clear completely within 7 to 14 days. Treatment is primarily supportive and if the reaction is severe, a one to two week course of prednisone, 40 to 60 mg/day, will control most symptoms within 48 hours.[7] For less severe reactions, topical corticosteroids and systemic antihistamines (if pruritus is present) can be used.

Contact Dermatitis: Poison Ivy/Oak/Sumac

Poison Ivy (Rhus) dermatitis is the major cause of allergic contact dermatitis in the United States, exceeding all other causes combined. It is estimated that 50% to 95% of the population is sensitive to the plant to some degree. The severity of the condition varies from mild discomfort to an extremely painful, debilitating condition. Rhus dermatitis is caused by sensitization to an allergic substance in the leaves, stems, and roots of poison ivy, poison oak, and poison sumac plants. All three plants contain the same sensitizing oleoresin, urushiol oil, which contains pentadecacatechol, the actual sensitizing agent. Therefore, the dermatitis caused by the three different plants is identical.

Direct contact with the plant is unnecessary for the rash to occur. Highly sensitive individuals may develop severe dermatitis merely from exposure to Rhus oleoresin carried by pollen or by smoke from burning leaves. The oleoresin may remain active for months on clothing, shoes, tools, and sporting equipment. Once the toxic substance comes in contact with the skin, it can be spread by the hands to other areas of the body (e.g., genitals or eyes) or to people who may come into close contact with the exposed person. Although washing with soap and water will not prevent the dermatitis

Table 36.13	Frequently Implicated Drugs[63-65]
Drug	Incidence (%)[a]
Amoxicillin	5.1
Trimethoprim/sulfamethoxazole	3.4
Ampicillin	3.3
Corticotropin	2.8
Erythromycin	2.3
Cephalosporins	2.1
Semisynthetic penicillin	2.1
Cyanocobalamin	1.8
Sulfisoxazole	1.7
Gentamicin	1.6
Penicillin G	1.6
Atropine sulfate	1.6
Cimetidine	1.3
Quinidine	1.3

[a] Percentage of patients receiving medication who actually develop an eruption.

unless this is done within 15 minutes of exposure, it will prevent spread of the oleoresin to other parts of the body.[5,27,67-74]

Rhus dermatitis can be contracted throughout the year, including the winter, when it can result from exposure to the roots of the plant. The virulence of the leaf sap varies little during the foliage period. The incidence of poison ivy is higher during the spring because the leaves are tender and bruise easily and the call to the outdoors is stronger. Sensitive individuals should be instructed to avoid contact with the offending plant. If contact is inevitable, every effort should be made to shield exposed areas of the skin with appropriate clothing. Exposed individuals should bathe or shower as soon as they come in from outdoors and should wash their clothes.

After an initial incubation period of 5 to 21 days, a patient would be expected to react to the oleoresin in 12 to 48 hours following re-exposure. A mild exposure to these plants in a sensitized person results in a typical erythematous, vesicular, and sometimes oozing rash after two to three days; complete clearing occurs in one to three weeks. If a large area is exposed, lesions will appear within 6 to 12 hours and may appear blistered and eroded; in some cases, ulcers may appear. Healing will occur more slowly, often requiring two to three weeks for complete resolution. Factors which contribute to the development of poison ivy/oak/sumac are: the concentration of the oleoresin to which the skin is exposed, area of exposure, duration of exposure, site of exposure, genetic factors, and immune tolerance. It is important to determine the areas of the body that are affected. If the eyes, genital areas, mouth, respiratory tract, or more than 15% of the body is affected, the patient should receive a course of systemic corticosteroids.

Since different sites of the body differ in their sensitivity to the oleoresin and because patients spread the Rhus oleoresin to different parts of their bodies over a period of time, lesions will often erupt over a period of several days. A common misconception many people have is that the fluid from the Rhus-induced vesicles will spread the disease to unaffected areas.

Treatment

19. K.P., a 27-year-old female, has recently returned from an outing in the woods. She now has vesicular eruptions which appear in a linear pattern on one arm and hand. She believes she has poison oak and requests therapy. What should be recommended at this point? What should be recommended if the condition becomes more severe?

Weeping lesions should be treated with wet dressings as outlined in the beginning of this chapter. Lesions which are not wet or weeping should be treated with calamine lotion applied two to four times daily. Alternatively, a topical 1% hydrocortisone preparation could be used. More effective treatment would require prescription of a potent topical corticosteroid preparation. If K.P.'s poison oak becomes much more severe, additional treatment with prednisone 60 mg/day for at least two or three weeks will be required; such therapy should be withdrawn slowly (over one to two weeks) to prevent recurrence of the lesions.[67-72]

Systemic Therapy

20. Z.T., a 19-year-old male, has just returned from a fishing trip and now has an erythematous, linear, dry eruption on his leg and arm and a generalized eruption on his hands and face. He has been in areas that have dense poison ivy and may have burned some in the campfire. Z.T. has washed himself and his clothes thoroughly. How should he be treated?

The fact that Z.T.'s facial rash is not linear (as one would expect if he had just contacted the plant) suggests that he may have contacted the smoke of a burning poison ivy plant. This can be quite serious since the oleoresin can be carried in smoke and, if inhaled, can cause severe respiratory problems. Z.T. should be observed for signs of respiratory difficulties and should be treated with a course of systemic corticosteroids.[6,7]

Relapse

21. Z.T.'s physician prescribed prednisone. He was instructed to take 80 mg/day for 14 days and to decrease the dose by 5 mg/day each day thereafter. Calamine lotion (TID to affected areas) also was prescribed. After 12 days, Z.T. complains that the lesions seem to be getting worse. The lesions cleared after 8 days of treatment and he began rapidly tapering the prednisone at this time. Why is he experiencing a relapse?

Table 36.14	Frequent Contact Sensitizers
Substance	Found In
Ammonia	Soaps, chemicals, hair dyes
Balsam of Peru	Cosmetics
Benzyl alcohol	Medications, cosmetics
Caine anesthetics	Medications
Carba	Rubber
Chromium	Jewelry
Epoxy resin	Glue
Ethylenediamine	Stabilizer in many topical products
Formaldehyde	Shoes, clothing, soaps, insulations
Mercaptobenzothiazol	Rubber
Naphthyl	Rubber
Neomycin	Topical medications
Nickel sulfate	Jewelry, fasteners
Parabens	Preservative in many topical products
Paraphenylenediamine	Hair dyes, leather
Potassium dichromate	Shoes, leather
Thiomersal	Preservatives, contact lens products
Thiram	Rubber products
Turpentine	Paint products
Wool alcohols	Lanolin containing products, clothes

Two weeks is the absolute minimum course of treatment when systemic corticosteroids are used for severe cases of poison ivy/oak/sumac. The oleoresin remains fixed in the skin, and if the systemic corticosteroid is withdrawn too soon, the lesions will return. This is probably the most common reason for treatment failure with systemic corticosteroids.[7]

Contact Dermatitis

22. Z.T.'s corticosteroid therapy was reinstated. After several weeks, most of the lesions had disappeared and the prednisone therapy was discontinued. However, he continued to complain of a rash on his hands. Further questioning revealed that he was continuing to apply Caladryl lotion, which he had substituted for calamine lotion. What is a likely cause of this persistent rash?

Caladryl contains diphenhydramine in addition to the usual constituents of calamine lotion. Topical application of this and other antihistamines may cause an allergic contact-sensitivity reaction. Z.T. should stop using this product to see if his rash clears. A list of common contact sensitizers is found in Table 36.14.

The treatment for sensitivity reactions is basically the same as that outlined for poison ivy/oak/sumac.[3,4,7]

References

1 **Sauer GC.** Manual of Skin Diseases. 5th ed. Philadelphia: J.B. Lippincott Co.; 1991.

2 **Hood AF et al.** Primer of Dermatopathology. 2nd ed. Boston: Little, Brown, and Co.; 1993.

3 **Arnold HL et al.** Andrew's Diseases of the Skin. 8th ed. Philadelphia: WB Saunders; 1990.

4 **Rook A et al.** Textbook of Dermatology. 5th ed. Philadelphia: FA Davis; 1992.

5 **Fitzpatrick TB et al.** Dermatology in General Medicine. 4th ed. New York: McGraw Hill; 1993.

6 **Moschella SL, Hurley HJ.** Dermatology. 2nd ed. Philadelphia: WB Saunders; 1992.

7 **Arndt KA.** Manual of Dermatologic Therapies. 4th ed. Boston: Little, Brown, and Co.; 1991.

8 **Schlagel C et al.** The weights of topical preparations required for total and partial body coverage. J Invest Dermatol. 1964;42:253.

9 **Maibach HI, Wester RC.** Issues in measuring percutaneous absorption of topical corticosteroids. Int J Dermatol. 1992;(Suppl.):21.

10 **Cornell RC, Stoughton RB.** Correlation of vasoconstrictor assay and clinical activity in psoriasis. Arch Dermatol. 1985;121:63.

11 **Pershing LK.** New approaches to assess topical corticosteroid bioequivalence: pharmacokinetic evaluation. Int J Dermatol. 1992;(Suppl.):14.

12 **Gibson JR.** Correlation of the vasoconstrictor assay and clinical activity in psoriasis. Arch Dermatol. 1985;121:1105.

13 **Stoughton RB.** The vasoconstrictor assay in bioequivalence testing: practical concerns and recent developments. Int J Dermatol. 1992;(Suppl.):26.

14 **Cornell RC.** Clinical trials of topical corticosteroids in psoriasis: correlations with the vasoconstrictor assay. Int J Dermatol. 1992;(Suppl.):38.

15 **Anon.** Topical corticosteroids. Med Lett Drugs Ther. 1991;33:108.

16 **Barry BW et al.** Comparative bioavailability of proprietary topical corticosteroid preparations: vasoconstrictor assays on thirty creams and gels. Br J Dermatol. 1974;91:323.

17 **Giannotti B et al.** Symposium on topical corticosteroids. Auckland: Adis Press; 1988.

18 **Barry BW et al.** Comparative bioavailability and activity of proprietary topical corticosteroid preparations: vasoconstrictor assays on thirty-one ointments. Br J Dermatol. 1975;93:563.

19 **Maibach HI.** *In vivo* percutaneous penetration of corticosteroids in man and unresolved problems in the efficacy. Dermatologica. 1976;162(Suppl. 1):11.

20 **Giannotti B and Pimpinelli N.** Topical corticosteroids—which drug and when. Drugs. 1992;44:65–71.

21 **Hanifin JM.** Atopic dermatitis. J Am Acad Dermatol. 1982;6:1.

22 **Roth HL.** Atopic dermatitis revisited. Int J Dermatol. 1987;26:139.

23 **Lane AT et al.** Once daily treatment of psoriasis with topical glucocorticosteroid ointments. J Am Acad Dermatol. 1987;8:523.

24 **Miller JA et al.** Topical corticosteroids—clinical pharmacology and therapeutic use. Drugs. 1980;19:119.

25 **Takeda K et al.** Side effects of topical corticosteroids and their prevention. Drugs. 1988;36(Suppl. 5):15.

26 **Harper J.** Topical corticosteroids for skin disorders in infants and children. Drugs. 1988;36(Suppl. 5):34.

27 **Robertson DB, Maibach HI.** Topical corticosteroids. Semin Dermatol. 1986; 2:238.

28 **Smith J et al.** Corticosteroid-induced atrophy and telangiectasia. Arch Dermatol. 1976;112:115.

29 **Turpeinen M.** Influence of age and severity of dermatitis on the percutaneous absorption of hydrocortisone in children. Br J Dermatol. 1988;26:517.

30 **Delforno C et al.** Corticosteroid effect on epidermal cell size. Br J Dermatol. 1978;98:619.

31 **Lavker R et al.** Effects of topical corticosteroids on human dermis. Br J Dermatol. 1986;115(Suppl. 31):101.

32 **Kligman A et al.** Steroid addiction. Int J Dermatol. 1980;18:23.

33 **Guin JD.** Contact sensitivity to topical corticosteroids. J Am Acad Dermatol. 1984;10:773.

34 **Retamo S et al.** Delayed hypersensitivity to topical corticosteroids. J Am Acad Dermatol. 1986;14:582.

35 **Akers WA.** Risks of unoccluded topical steroids in clinical trials. Arch Dermatol. 1980;116:786.

36 **Goa K.** Clinical pharmacology and pharmacokinetic properties of topically applied corticosteroids. Drugs. 1988; 36(Suppl.):51.

37 **Aso M.** Effects of potent topical corticosteroids on adrenocortical function. J Dermatol. 1983;10:145.

38 **Lawlor F, Ramabala K.** Iatrogenic Cushing's syndrome—a cautionary tale. Clin Exp Dermatol. 1984;2:286.

39 **Miyachi Y.** Adrenal axis suppression caused by a small dose of potent topical corticosteroid. Arch Dermatol. 1982; 118:451.

40 **Stoughton RB, Cornell RC.** Review of super-potent topical corticosteroids. Semin Dermatol. 1987;6:72.

41 **Chan HL et al.** Effect of topical corticosteroid on microbial flora of human skin. J Am Acad Dermatol. 1982;7:346.

42 **Leyden JJ et al.** The case for steroid-antibiotic combinations. Br J Dermatol. 1977;91:179.

43 **Wachs GW et al.** Cooperative double blind trial of antibiotic corticoid combination in impetiginized atopic dermatitis. Br J Dermatol. 1976;95:323.

44 **Ortonne J.** Clinical potential of topical corticosteroids. Drugs. 1988;36(Suppl. 5):38.

45 **Epstein E.** Allergy to dermatologic agents. JAMA. 1966;198:517.

46 **Rudner ES et al.** Epidemiology of contact dermatitis in North America. Arch Dermatol. 1972;108:537.

47 **Prystowsky SD.** Allergic contact hypersensitivity to nickel, neomycin, ethylenediamine, and benzocaine. Arch Dermatol. 1979;115:959.

48 **Patrick J et al.** Neomycin sensitivity in the normal (nonatopic) individual. Arch Dermatol. 1970;102:532.

49 **Kirton V et al.** Contact dermatitis from neomycin and framycin. Lancet. 1965; 1:138.

50 **Martin J.** Pruritus. Int J Dermatol. 1985;24:634.

51 **Denman ST.** A review of pruritus. J Am Acad Dermatol. 1986;14:375.

52 **Gilchrest BA.** Pruritus. Arch Intern Med. 1982;142:101.

53 **FDA.** Report on topical analgesics. Federal Register. 1979;44:234.

54 **Davies MG, Greaves MW.** The current status of histamine receptors in human skin: therapeutic implications. Br J Dermatol. 1981;104:601.

55 **Fisher AA.** The antihistamines. J Am Acad Dermatol. 1980;3:303.

56 **Flowers FP et al.** Antihistamines. Int J Dermatol. 1986;25:224.

57 **Simons F et al.** H_1 receptor antagonists: clinical pharmacology and use in allergic disease. Pediatr Clin North Am. 1983;30:899.

58 **Senter TP.** Topical fluocinonide and tachyphylaxis. Arch Derm. 1983;119: 363.

59 **Duvivier A et al.** Acute tolerance to effects of topical glucocorticosteroids. Br J Dermatol. 1976;94(Suppl. 12):25.

60 **Anon.** OTC topical hydrocortisone. Med Lett Drugs Ther. 1980;22:37.

61 **de Vivier A.** Tachyphylaxis to topically applied steroids. Arch Dermatol. 1976;112:1245.

62 **Rand RE, Baden HP.** The ichthyoses: a review. J Am Acad Dermatol. 1983; 8:285.

63 **Arndt K et al.** Rates of cutaneous reactions to drugs. JAMA. 1976;235: 918.

64 **Kauppinen K, Stubb S.** Drug eruptions: causative agents and clinical types. Acta Derm Venereol (Stockh). 1984;64:320.

65 **Wintroub BU, Stern R.** Cutaneous drug reactions: pathogenesis and clinical classification. J Am Acad Dermatol. 1985;13:167.

66 **Bigby M et al.** Drug-induced cutaneous reactions—a report from the Boston Collaborative Drug Surveillance program on 15,438 consecutive patients, 1975–1982. JAMA. 1986;256: 3358.

67 **Epstein W.** Poison oak hyposensitization. Arch Dermatol. 1974;109:356.

68 **Adams RM.** Occupational Contact Dermatitis. Philadelphia: Lippincott; 1962.

69 **Fisher A.** Contact Dermatitis. 3rd ed. Philadelphia: Lea and Febiger; 1986.

70 **Rodner EJ et al.** The frequency of contact sensitivity in North America, 1972–1974. Contact Dermatitis. 1975; 1:277.

71 **Orchard SM et al.** Poison ivy/oak. Arch Dermatol. 1986;122:783.

72 **Marderosian AHD.** Poison ivy and related dermatitis. Drug Ther. 1977;112: 57.

73 **Hutchinson TA, Lane DA.** Assessing methods for causality assessment of suspected adverse drug reactions. J Clin Epidemiol. 1989;42:5.

74 **Epstein E.** Hand dermatitis: practical management and current concepts. J Am Acad Dermatol. 1984;10:395.

75 **Bronner AK, Hood AF.** Cutaneous complications of chemotherapeutic agents. J Am Acad Dermatol. 1983;9: 645.

76 **Bruinsma WA.** A guide to drug eruptions. Oosthuizen: De Zwaluw; 1990.

77 **Alanko K et al.** Cutaneous drug reactions: clinical types and causative

agents. Acta Derm Venereol. 1989;69:223.

78 **Torok H.** Dermatitis medicamentosa: a ten year study. Derm Int. 1969;6:57.

79 **Bigby M, Stern R.** Cutaneous reactions to nonsteroidal antiinflammatory drugs. J Am Acad Dermatol. 1985;12:866.

80 **Korkij W, Soltani K.** Fixed drug eruption. Arch Dermatol. 1984;120:520.

81 **Anon.** Drugs that cause photosensitivity. Med Lett. 1986;28:51.

82 **Shapiro S et al.** Drug rash with ampicillin and other penicillins. Lancet. 1969;2:969.

83 **Weary P et al.** Acneiform eruptions resulting from antibiotic administration. Arch Dermatol. 1969;100:179.

84 **Rostenberg A et al.** Life-threatening drug eruptions. JAMA. 1965;194:660.

85 **Jelinek JE.** Cutaneous side effects of oral contraceptives. Arch Dermatol. 1970;101:181.

86 **Brodin MB.** Drug related alopecia. Dermatol Clin. 1987;5:571.

87 **Adams RM, Maibach HI.** A five year study of cosmetic reactions. J Am Acad Dermatol. 1985;13:1062.

88 **Davies DM.** Textbook of adverse reactions. 4th ed. Oxford: Oxford University Press; 1991.

89 **Dahl MV.** A guide to the guises of drug-induced skin eruptions. Mod Med. 1982;50:104.

90 **Jick H.** Adverse drug reactions: The magnitude of the problem. J Allergy Clin Immunol. 1984;74:555.

91 **Revuz J et al.** Toxic epidermal necrolysis: Clinical findings and prognosis factors in 87 patients. Arch Dermatol. 1987;123:1160.

92 **Kramer MS et al.** An algorithm for the operational assessment of adverse drug reactions. JAMA. 1979;242:623.

93 **Adkinson NF.** Risk factors for drug allergy. J Allergy Clin Immunol. 1984;74:567.

94 **Emmett EA.** Phototoxicity from exogenous agents. Photochem Photobiol. 1979;30:429.

95 **Waitzer S et al.** Cutaneous ultrastructural changes and photosensitivity associated with amiodarone therapy. J Am Acad Dermatol. 1987;16:779.

96 **Horn JR et al.** Warfarin-induced skin necrosis: report of four cases. Am J Hosp Pharm. 1981; 38:1763.

97 **Gordin FM et al.** Adverse reactions to trimethoprim-sulfamethoxazole in patients with the acquired immunodeficiency syndrome. Ann Intern Med. 1989;100:495.

98 **West AJ et al.** A comparative histopathologic study of photodistributed and nonphotodistributed lichenoid drug eruptions. J Am Acad Dermatol. 1990; 23:689.

99 **Pisani M, Ruocco V.** Drug-induced pemphigus. Clin Dermatol. 1986;4:118.

100 **Hodak E et al.** Bullous pemphigoid: an adverse effect of ampicillin. Clin Exp Dermatol. 1983;15:50.

101 **Weiss ME, Adkinson NF.** Immediate hypersensitivity reactions to penicillin and related antibiotics. Clin Allergy. 1988;18:515.

102 **The Medical Letter.** 1991;33:100.

Acne

Terry L Seaton

Overview 37-1
  Definition, Clinical Signs and Symptoms 37-1
  Incidence and Prevalence 37-1
  Etiology 37-1
  Pathogenesis 37-1
  Therapy 37-2
    Nondrug Therapy 37-2
    Drug Therapy 37-2
      Benzoyl peroxide 37-2
      Retinoids 37-2
      Antibiotics 37-3
      Miscellaneous topical agents 37-4
      Zinc salts 37-4

    Antiandrogens and hormones 37-4
    Corticosteroids 37-4
Clinical Assessment 37-4
Treatment and Monitoring Plans 37-4
  Benzoyl Peroxide 37-4
  Antibiotics 37-5
  Tretinoin 37-5
  Isotretinoin 37-5
    Monitoring parameters 37-6
      Lipids 37-6
      Liver function 37-6
      Others 37-6
    Adverse effects 37-6

Definition, Clinical Signs, and Symptoms

Acne vulgaris is a common self-limiting skin disease involving the pilosebaceous units of the skin (see Figure 36.1 in Chapter 36: Dermatotherapy). The earliest lesions generally appear on the face, but the chest, back, or upper arms may be affected as well. The acne lesions can be inflammatory or noninflammatory and of varying severity. The noninflammatory lesions are described as closed comedones (''whiteheads'') or open comedones (''blackheads''). The dark pigmentation in open comedones is caused by oxidation of sebaceous material rather than by the public misperception that it is caused by dirt. The inflammatory lesions usually are described as papules, pustules, cysts, or nodules that are typically erythematous. Although most cases are mild, the severity of these lesions can be assessed by standardized clinical grading scales that can be helpful in the determination of treatment options.[1,2]

The major long-term complication of acne is the scarring of tissue that can present as ''ice pick'' pitting or as major disfigurement. The scarring can be exacerbated by tissue excoriation related to picking at or squeezing lesions.[3] These complications of acne can be accompanied by significant psychological distress, low self esteem, and other psychosocial effects, especially in affected adolescents, that must be addressed.[4] Fortunately, most cases of acne are mild and do not lead to scarring or other complications.

Acne afflicts patients at various ages, from neonates to patients in their eighth or ninth decade of life; however, it primarily afflicts teenagers and young adults.[5,6] Acne may also be associated with systemic diseases such as SAPHO (synovitis, acne, pustulosis, hyperostosis, osteitis) and Apert's (acrocephalosyndactyly) syndromes.[7-9] The differential diagnosis of acneiform eruptions includes acne rosacea, gram-negative folliculitis, mechanical folliculitis, chloracne, steroid acne, and perioral dermatitis.[10] Severe variants of acne such as pyoderma faciale (rosacea fulminans), acne conglobata, and acne fulminans are not presented in this chapter which focuses solely on acne vulgaris.

Incidence and Prevalence

Acne vulgaris affects about 90% of all adolescents and is the cause for more physician visits than for any other dermatologic disorder.[3,11] Although no gender preference exists, females typically develop acne earlier, but have milder cases than males.[10] Acne can occur in children as young as eight years of age; how-

ever, the majority of the cases occur in young people between 14 and 19 years of age.[10] Mild forms of acne may persist longer in females and may, in rare cases, persist in some throughout their lives.[12] Asians and blacks have a slightly lower incidence of acne.[13] Females treated with antiepileptic drugs such as phenytoin and phenobarbital experience acne more commonly than age-matched controls (80% versus 30%);[15] and cases of severe acne may be more common in some families.[14]

Etiology

The development of acne is related to increased sebum production, abnormal keratinization within the pilosebaceous canal (i.e., hypercornification), bacterial colonization, and an immune-mediated inflammatory reaction.[16] Multiple exogenous and endogenous factors can affect the development of acne vulgaris. Despite rare individual exceptions, diet, psychological stress, cleanliness, and sexual activity are generally *not* thought to contribute to severity or exacerbations of acne.[14] Premenstrual exacerbations of acne are very common. Sex hormone imbalance (relative androgen excess), certain cosmetics, pomades, and moisturizers also affect the development of acne.[14] Hot and humid conditions that stimulate sweating often worsen acne. Dry and sunny conditions often improve acne.

Occupational or environmental exposure to halogenated compounds, ultraviolet light, animal fats, dioxin, or petroleum derivatives may cause ''chloracne'' and other acneiform lesions.[13,17] It is important to identify drug-induced acne (see Table 36.12 in Chapter 36: Dermatotherapy) because treatment outcomes likely depend upon drug therapy modification. Mechanical skin irritation, caused by headbands, hats, chin straps, backpacks, or shoulder pads, also may precipitate acne flare-ups (acne mechanica).

Pathogenesis

The earliest stage in the development of acne lesions involves abnormal shedding and accumulation of the unusually ''sticky'' horny cells that line the sebaceous follicle in the pilary (hair) canal. These horny cells continue to accumulate and eventually plug the sebaceous follicle. As sebum accumulates in the plugged sebaceous follicle, a clinically undetectable microcomedone is formed.[18] As this process continues, the microcomedone enlarges and a closed comedone becomes the first clinically visible lesion. With increas-

Table 37.1	Pertinent Historical Components to be Obtained From a Patient With Acne[a]

- Duration, including onset and peak severity
- Location and distribution
- Seasonal variation
- For *females*, relation to menstrual periods, pregnancy status, scalp hair thinning, contraceptive method if used
- Present and past treatments, topical and systemic, prescription and OTC
- Family history, including severity
- Other skin disorders or medical problems
- Medications and drug allergies
- Occupational exposure to chemicals or oils
- Use of cosmetics, moisturizers, hairstyling products (pomades)
- Areas of skin friction or irritation

[a] OTC = Over-the-counter.

ing keratinization, an open comedone is formed. An inflammatory reaction occurs if the follicular wall ruptures from pressure caused by accumulated sebum or from mechanical pressure. Lymphocytes, monocytes, macrophages, and cytokines such as interleukins and tumor necrosis factor in the disrupted follicular wall then mediate inflammation.[10,20] Both the classical and alternative complement pathways may be activated.[21]

Androgen-induced increased sebocyte activity and bacterial colonization significantly increase comedone formation.[3] Testosterone, of testicular origin in males or ovarian and adrenal origin in females, is metabolized in the skin by 5-α-reductase to dihydrotestosterone (DHT). DHT has a high affinity for sebocyte receptors. The DHT-receptor complex then is translocated within the cytoplasm to the nucleus where sebum biosynthesis is stimulated. The microaerophilic gram-positive diphtheroid *Propionibacterium acnes* produces proteases, hyaluronidases, and lipases which then release free-fatty acids from sebum to stimulate local inflammation.[19] Other skin bacteria such as staphylococci, do not contribute to comedone or pustule formation; but a lipophilic yeast (*Pityrosporum orbiculare*) which resides on skin surfaces may play a role.[74]

Therapy

There is no known cure of acne, but treatment can reduce its severity. In most cases, particularly in severe forms, treatment is more of an ''art'' than a science and therapy must be individualized. The goal of treatment is to relieve discomfort, improve skin appearance, prevent pitting or scarring, and prevent psychological distress or social rejection.

Treatment is largely preventive since little can be done for existing lesions. Slow improvement, often over several weeks to months, is the rule for *all* treatments.[23] Therefore, treatment regimens, should not be modified more frequently than every two months. Patient counseling should include a basic discussion of the chronicity and natural history of acne, proper drug administration or application technique, potential adverse effects, and actions to be undertaken if adverse reactions are experienced. General treatment guidelines by the American Academy of Dermatology[24] serve as the current standards of practice.[16,25] These guidelines need to be used with patient specific data (see Table 37.1).

Nondrug Therapy

The primary nondrug approach to the management of acne is based upon good skin hygiene. Twice daily washing with warm water and a *mild*, nonmoisturizing soap is sufficient to remove excess sebum and improve skin appearance. Aggressive skin washing does not alter the course of acne and antibacterial or abrasive cleansers are not recommended.[22] Manipulation (e.g., squeezing or picking) of acne lesions should be discouraged strongly. Drugs, cosmetics, or other known precipitants also should be avoided. Trial and error may be necessary to find cosmetics that will not exacerbate acne.[26] Dermatologists may use one of several physical modalities in the treatment of acne, especially in severe cases. These include surgical comedone extraction, dermabrasion, and cryotherapy.[3] Ultraviolet light and x-ray therapy rarely are necessary. Acne scarring often is treated with dermabrasion.

Drug Therapy

Although many drugs and drug combinations ultimately may be used, all therapies are based upon treating one or more of the primary pathogenic factors.[16] Effective drugs work by: 1) normalizing follicular keratinization (e.g., retinoids); 2) decreasing sebum production (e.g., isotretinoin, hormone manipulation); 3) suppressing bacterial (*P. acnes*) flora (e.g., antibiotics, benzoyl peroxide); and 4) preventing inflammation (e.g., antibiotics, retinoids). Topical therapy generally is preferable for mild to moderate acne (see Table 37.2).

Benzoyl Peroxide. One of the most effective treatments available is topical benzoyl peroxide. Benzoyl peroxide causes mild desquamation and comedolysis by increasing epithelial cell turnover and unblocking pores, but its main effects are due to its antibacterial property.[27] Bacterial proteins are oxidized by the oxygen free radicals which are released by the metabolism of benzoyl peroxide on the skin. Bacterial resistance does not develop to benzoyl peroxide.[18] Benzoyl peroxide minimally reduces sebum production, but significantly lowers free fatty acid concentrations.[28] The irritant effects from benzoyl peroxide also vasodilate and increase blood flow which may hasten resolution of inflammatory lesions.[22] Benzoyl peroxide improves both inflamed and noninflamed lesions,[29] and is similar to topically applied retinoids in improving comedonal acne. Treatment is associated with a 50% to 75% reduction in inflammatory lesions in 8 to 12 weeks.[27] Its efficacy is enhanced when combined with other systemic or topical agents.[30] Benzoyl peroxide is available over-the-counter (OTC) and by prescription in a variety of dosage forms (cleansers, lotions, creams, and gels) and concentrations (2.5% to 10%).

The topical application of benzoyl peroxide may cause transient warmth or stinging, significant drying, or skin irritation. Patients should decrease the frequency of application if excessive skin dryness or peeling occurs. A lower strength or less drying formulation also may need to be used. Allergic contact dermatitis due to benzoyl peroxide, is characterized by inflammation and pruritus, and occurs in less than 1% of patients. Patients who develop benzoyl peroxide-contact dermatitis should discontinue use of the drug. Benzoyl peroxide has been associated with tumors in mice; but data on long-term use associated with skin cancer are inconclusive.[31]

Retinoids. Tretinoin (Retin-A), also called all-*trans*-retinoic acid, is the naturally occurring form of vitamin A acid and is available for topical application as a cream (0.025%, 0.05%, 0.1%), gel

Table 37.2	Choice of Topical versus Oral Acne Therapy	
Clinical Characteristics	Topical Therapy	Oral Therapy
Lesion type	Noninflammatory	Inflammatory
Severity	Mild to moderate	Moderate to severe
Location	Face	Back, chest, arms
Treatment resistant	Not indicated	Indicated
Likelihood of scarring	Not indicated	Indicated

(0.025%, 0.01%), and liquid (0.05%). Isotretinoin (Accutane), a synthetic 13-*cis*-isomer of tretinoin, has greater biologic activity and orally is administered as 10, 20, or 40 mg capsules. Vitamin A and its analogues have been used to treat acne for over 50 years.[32]

Unlike benzoyl peroxide, retinoids have no *in vitro* antibacterial properties. Isotretinoin reduces *P. acnes* colonization indirectly by reducing sebum production[33] because *P. acnes* requires a sebum-rich environment for survival. Retinoids also normalize keratinization by decreasing horny cell cohesiveness and by stimulating epidermal cell turnover. These actions combine to unplug follicles and prevent microcomedone formation.[34] In addition to decreasing sebum and *P. acnes* colonization, the retinoids reduce inflammation by directly inhibiting neutrophil and monocyte chemotaxis.[35,36] Because retinoids affect each of the four known pathogenic factors (previously described), they are very effective agents. Tretinoin (Retin A) often is applied topically in patients with mild to moderate comedonal acne who become resistant to, or cannot tolerate, benzoyl peroxide or antibiotics. Retin A also may be used in combination with antibiotics or benzoyl peroxide for management of severe inflammatory acne, and to treat fine acne scarring.[37,38] Systemic isotretinoin (Accutane) is the only effective agent for severe cystic acne, and can induce remissions for months to years after one or two courses of therapy (3 to 5 months/ course).[39,40] The high cost, risk of serious adverse effects, and potential overuse have resulted in guidelines for rational retinoid use (see Table 37.3).[41,42] The use of isotretinoin in severe acne is cost effective.[43]

Adverse effects with retinoids are common and occur to some extent in nearly all patients. Topical tretinoin (Retin A) causes local skin irritation, characterized by dryness, redness, and peeling. Predisposing factors are similar to those for benzoyl peroxide but true hypersensitivity is very rare. Sun exposure significantly intensifies skin irritation. Therapy should begin with single bedtime applications of the 0.01% formulation and a more concentrated formulation can be used if necessary after four to eight weeks. Topical tretinoin may darken skin in blacks and other patients with dark skin. Adverse effects associated with systemic isotretinoin are listed in Table 37.4. Although related to vitamin A, systemic effects which resemble hypervitaminosis A syndrome are uncommon.[44] Chronic use of systemic retinoids for up to 15 years has failed to reveal long-term adverse effects, but more data are needed.[45] Retinoids should be avoided during pregnancy because of their well-established teratogenic effects. Contraception should be used during therapy and continued for at least one month after drug discontinuation.

Table 37.3	Guidelines for Isotretinoin Use in Acne[a]
Patient Selection	
Severe cystic acne	
Moderate acne, but resistant to conventional therapy	
Unusually severe acne variants (conglobata, fulminans)	
Dosage	
0.5 to 1 mg/kg/day	
Use higher dose in: Young patients, males, severe acne, acne involving the trunk	
Duration of Therapy	
Usually 4 months	
15% require longer therapy	
Relapse Rate	
31% at 9 years	
Retreatment is safe and effective	
Some patients may require 3–5 courses	

[a] Adapted from reference 41.

Table 37.4	Adverse Effects of Systemic Retinoids[a]	
Body System	**Adverse Effect**	**Management**
Common, Pharmacologic		
Skin	Dryness, peeling, pruritus Photosensitivity	Moisturizing creams or ointments Sunscreens, protective clothes
Hair, nails	Alopecia, nail fragility	None, discontinue drug if severe
Mucous membranes	Cheilitis Dry mouth, nose, eyes Blepharoconjunctivitis	Lip balms Sugarless gum/candy, saline nasal spray, artificial tears or ophthalmic ointment ↓ dosage if severe or bothersome
Uncommon, Toxic		
Liver	↑ transaminases; hepatitis	Monitor if mild elevation. Avoid in patients with previous liver dysfunction. Discontinue drug if hepatitis
Bones	Pain, hyperostoses	Monitor at 6–12 month intervals in chronic therapy
Muscle, ligaments	Pain, calcifications	Avoid strenuous exercise
Eyes	↓ night vision	Patients should use caution
Metabolic	↑ triglycerides ↑ cholesterol ↑ VLDL, LDL	Reduce/eliminate alcohol; low fat diet; consider dosage reduction, or drug discontinuation

[a] LDL = Low-density lipoprotein; VLDL = Very low-density lipoprotein.

Antibiotics. Acne is not an "infectious" disease and certainly is not contagious. Rather, *P. acnes* helps transform comedones to inflammatory pustules or papules. Antibiotics do not affect existing lesions, but prevent future lesions by decreasing sebaceous fatty acid metabolic byproducts (a known inflammatory stimuli) by decreasing *P. acnes* colonization. In addition, antibiotics themselves seem to suppress neutrophil chemotaxis, even at subliminal inhibitory concentrations.[46,47] Development of antibiotic resistance has been correlated with treatment failure and guidelines for rational antibiotic use have been suggested.[48] Tetracyclines, erythromycin, clindamycin, trimethoprim/sulfamethoxazole, and metronidazole are effective.[49–51] No data exist to suggest single agent superiority, but tetracycline is studied most extensively and is relatively inexpensive. Drug choice should be based upon cost, adverse effects, pregnancy status, and age.

Topically-applied antibiotics are effective for mild to moderate acne.[52] Topical erythromycin and clindamycin are used most commonly. The entire susceptible area, not just the lesions, should be treated for optimal results. Twice daily application is most effective and patient compliance is important. Skin discoloration, especially with the tetracyclines, can occur in addition to tingling and stinging.[53] Combination products containing benzoyl peroxide and erythromycin are available for moderate to severe acne and are easier for patients to use. Although case reports exist, systemic adverse effects, including antibiotic-associated colitis, are very rare.[54] Oral antibiotics should be used in patients with moderate to severe acne, patients intolerant or unresponsive to topical agents, and patients with acne on the trunk, back, or shoulders.[18] Twice daily dosing of all agents improves compliance and is usually as effective as more frequent dosing. Less frequent dosing may be used chronically. Long-term use of antibiotics usually is safe and effective.

Miscellaneous Topical Agents.[58] Three unique topical preparations also are available for treatment of mild to moderate acne. Salicylic acid, sulfur, and resorcinol have been used for many years, but with varying degrees of success. Topical salicylic acid, a concentration dependent keratolytic, is more effective than placebo but probably less effective than topical benzoyl peroxide or tretinoin.[20,55,56] It may augment the effectiveness of other agents when used in combination.[2] Chronic use over large body surfaces should be avoided to prevent systemic toxicity. Sulfur preparations have both antibacterial and comedolytic properties. Disadvantages of sulfur include a displeasing odor, skin discoloration, and limited effectiveness. Sulfur also has been shown to be comedogenic.[10] Resorcinol alone is not effective and is available only in combination with sulfur preparations.[57]

Zinc Salts. The role of zinc salts in the treatment of acne is controversial. A reduction in granulocyte zinc concentration and associated inhibition of chemotaxis appears to produce anti-inflammatory effects.[59] Zinc also blocks the formation of DHT from testosterone by inhibiting 5-α-reductase.[60] However, more supporting clinical data are necessary before zinc supplementation can be recommended routinely.

Antiandrogens and Hormones. The critical role of androgens in the pathogenesis of acne has stimulated great interest in the use of antiandrogens. Cyproterone (Androcur) is the only agent available in the U.S. and is listed as an orphan drug for treatment of severe hirsutism. Cyproterone and spironolactone (Aldactone), which also have antiandrogenic effects, are used in Europe for treatment of acne.[61,62] Safety and effectiveness data are lacking. Antiandrogens should not be used in males due to the likely development of gynecomastia. In females, the drugs usually are given with estrogens to prevent menstrual irregularities.[63] High dose estrogens, usually ethinyl estradiol in the form of cycled combination oral contraceptives, may improve acne in females via antiandrogenic effects.[64]

Corticosteroids. While corticosteroids have been implicated as causing acne, they also can be used to treat severe acne. Intralesional injections of triamcinolone (usually diluted with normal saline to concentration of 1.25 to 5 mg/mL) markedly improve severe inflammatory acne.[11,65] Systemic corticosteroids have been used for both short- and long-term treatment of severe cystic acne. A seven-day course of high-dose (e.g., 20 mg/day) prednisone can be used for "prom acne," to quickly and dramatically improve acne for important events such as a prom or wedding. Low dose prednisone (e.g., ≤5 mg/day) also may have antiandrogenic effects.[66] Topical application of corticosteroids is not effective.[67]

Clinical Assessment

1. T.N., a white, 15-year-old freshman cheerleader, presents to her physician complaining of worsening "zits." Since several of her classmates are taking antibiotics for acne, she wants a "strong medicine" to make them go away. T.N. began having acne at age 13 when her lesions infrequently appeared on her chin and forehead. Her acne seemed to progressively worsen, especially in the summer, and now she consistently has 4 to 8 lesions at a time. In fact, her lesions have spread to her cheeks and nose. Other than having common childhood infections, T.N. is healthy and her immunizations are up to date. Menarche occurred at age 12. Her only surgery was an appendectomy

at age 11. She has 2 older brothers, 1 with mild and 1 with severe acne. Her father and mother are well. T.N. denies alcohol, tobacco, or illicit drug use. She has a boyfriend but denies sexual intercourse. She works part-time at a fast food restaurant, plays doubles on the varsity tennis team, and enjoys playing the violin. She takes no chronic prescription medications, but uses Stri-Dex pads as needed when her acne "gets really bad." She has used a "medicated" soap in the past, but stopped because of excessively dry skin. She wears a headband while playing tennis. She commonly uses a hair styling mousse. On physical exam, T.N. appears healthy and well nourished. She has 5 pustules and 2 closed comedones on her forehead and 6 excoriated lesions, covered with make-up, on her cheeks and chin. There are 2 well-healing areas on her nose and no open comedones. Her back is clear, except for 2 pustules, as are her chest and arms. She has no facial hair and her voice is normal in pitch. What were the key components in the clinical assessment of T.N.'s acne?

The clinical assessment of T.N.'s acne included all of the following steps:

- Evaluation of distribution of lesions as to body sites such as the face, scalp, neck, shoulders, back, or arms.
- Evaluation of provocative factors such as family history, work-related exposure, systemic or topical medications, or mechanical pressure on the skin.
- Evaluation of hormonal factors such as absence of signs of virilization or atypical menstrual cycles.
- Evaluation of whether the acne lesions are inflammatory or noninflammatory.

A detailed medical history is critical to acne evaluation and clinicians must take time with the patient to assess the above factors and further document the time course, lesion type, location, severity, and the likelihood of scarring. The potential contribution of exogenous factors (e.g., drugs, headbands) and the effectiveness of current or past treatments should not be underestimated. Treatment plans then can be developed from this information (see Table 37.2) after acne has been diagnosed clinically.

2. What subjective and objective data support a diagnosis of acne in T.N.?

T.N.'s age and the relationship of her age to the significant hormonal changes that are taking place in her at this time predispose her to the development of acne vulgaris. Additionally, her social environment augments her perception of the disease severity. The facial distribution of lesions, while sparing most other areas, further supports acne as does a strong positive family history. Activities, such as tennis, because of sweating and mechanical irritation from wearing a headband, and violin playing, which also may aggravate lesions on the chin, likely contribute to her acne severity. Other environmental factors include the use of make-up and styling mousse and possible exposure to cooking oils at the fast-food restaurant.

Treatment and Monitoring Plans
Benzoyl Peroxide

3. Assess T.N.'s current management of her acne and select a more reasonable initial treatment regimen for T.N.'s acne.

T.N.'s current use of acne medication is probably suboptimal and could explain the progressive worsening of her acne. While appropriate use of Stri-Dex (i.e., routine use on entire susceptible areas) initially might treat mild acne, topical benzoyl peroxide would be a better initial choice for T.N. because she has predominantly inflamed lesions. Since topical tretinoin (Retin A) primarily is effective for the treatment of the noninflamed lesions of acne, it would not be a good choice for her present condition. Although systemic isotretinoin would likely be very effective, it is expensive, has significant side effects, requires close monitoring, and is not warranted at this time.

The initial benzoyl peroxide dosage form and potency should be selected with the intent of minimizing skin irritation while still achieving the desired therapeutic efficacy. Factors that worsen skin irritation include increased benzoyl peroxide concentration and contact time, gel and lipophilic vehicles, thin and sensitive skin, low environmental humidity, use of irritating adjunctive therapies, and increased application frequency.[27] Benzoyl peroxide lotions provide shorter contact time on skin than creams, and creams are shorter-acting than gels. Therefore, benzoyl peroxide gels are more irritating to skin than creams and creams more than lotions. In order to minimize skin irritation, T.N. should begin therapy by applying a thin film of a 5% lotion, to the entire susceptible area, once daily at bedtime. She should not use medicated cleansers. She could increase her once daily application of benzoyl peroxide to twice daily if needed. If the desired therapeutic effects have not been achieved after four weeks, the more potent benzoyl peroxide cream (5% or 10%) can be used if tolerated. The inflamed lesions usually resolve slowly and progressively. She eventually may need a prescription for a gel formulation, which is more effective but potentially more irritating.

Antibiotics

4. After 2 months of therapy, T.N.'s acne has slightly improved but skin irritation from the benzoyl peroxide has limited the treatment. She continues to predominantly have pustulopapules on the face. What would be an alternative second-line approach to therapy?

T.N. continues to have mainly inflammatory pustulopapular lesions; therefore, antibiotics are the next most logical choice based upon the pathophysiology of acne. Since the patient is not taking drugs that can interact with antibiotics (e.g., oral contraceptives), either topical or systemic antibiotics can be prescribed safely. Topical antibiotics are associated with less severe side effects than systemic antibiotics and are preferred. The systemic antibiotics should be reserved for acne that fails to respond to topical antibiotics. Topical erythromycin or clindamycin, therefore, should be given an eight-week trial in T.N. especially because her lesions are relatively localized. Both erythromycin and clindamycin are equally effective and relatively inexpensive. If greater clinical improvement is desired after two months of twice daily application of either topical antibiotic, oral antibiotics can be considered. Similarly, systemic antibiotics would be preferred if lesions are distributed over various parts of the body since topical administration would be difficult.

5. T.N.'s acne is eventually well-controlled with tetracycline 500 mg BID. She only occasionally has outbreaks and the number and severity of lesions are decreased dramatically. Outline a long-term treatment and monitoring plan for T.N.

Although acne is both a *chronic* and a self-limiting skin disease, systemic antibiotics may be necessary for long periods of time. The lowest effective antibiotic dose should be used to minimize the risk of adverse effects. Now that T.N.'s acne is controlled, the tetracycline dose can be reduced to 250 mg twice a day or 500 mg once a day. If she remains well controlled for another one to three months, the tetracycline dose should be reduced further to a single daily 250 mg dose. Although low-dose tetracycline therapy can be continued for several years without long-term adverse effects, discontinuation of the antibiotic should be attempted periodically. The single daily doses of tetracycline should be taken on an empty stomach without dairy products to maximize drug absorption. The dose of tetracycline can be increased to 1 gm/day for four to eight weeks for acute "flare-ups" of acne, but the dose should again be decreased when feasible. Because acne severity fluctuates, well-educated patients may be given some latitude in making these decisions.

Potential for systemic adverse effects, mainly diarrhea, rash, photosensitivity, and vulvovaginal candidiasis, is greater with oral antibiotics than topical. T.N. should be counseled to contact her physician if these adverse effects occur. Routine laboratory monitoring is not necessary for most young, healthy patients receiving long-term oral tetracyclines or erythromycin because the incidence of serious adverse effects is low.[69]

Tretinoin

6. F.R., an 18-year-old male, is a construction worker. Since being diagnosed 2 years ago with moderate to severe comedonal acne, primarily located on the face, chest, and back, he has tried topical benzoyl peroxide and systemic erythromycin with limited success. He has found that his acne is fairly well controlled when he borrows his sister's Retin-A cream for his face. He takes ibuprofen 800 mg TID for a rotator cuff injury and an antacid for "heart burn." He does not smoke, but frequently binges on alcohol on the weekends. His favorite hobbies are hiking and waterskiing. At a health maintenance visit to his doctor a month ago, blood work (i.e., blood chemistry) was normal, except for mildly elevated serum concentrations of GGT and total cholesterol. Physical examination confirms the presence of moderate noninflammatory lesions, with predominantly closed comedones. At this visit, he received a prescription for topical tretinoin (Retin-A) 0.05% cream. What adverse effect associated with the use of tretinoin would be most likely to be experienced by F.R.?

Since F.R. spends most of his time in the sun, he would be at high risk for developing a photosensitivity reaction to his topical tretinoin therapy. Severe sunburn can occur in any patient using tretinoin. The use of protective clothing should be recommended but may not be realistic expectation for F.R. given his occupation and choice of physical activities. A sunscreen, with a sun protection factor of at least 15, should be recommended for F.R. along with special instructions on the need for reapplication of the sunscreen at periodic intervals. These measures are important because the photosensitivity reactions to tretinoin can be debilitating. (See Chapter 39: Photosensitivity and Burns for a more detailed discussion of sunscreens.) Tretinoin also might accelerate the tumorigenic effect of ultraviolet light based upon evidence in mice, but not humans.

Isotretinoin

7. F.R.'s acne has progressively worsened over the last year. On physical examination, a large number of open and closed comedones still are present on his face and shoulders, along with many new inflammatory papules and pustules. There are also 4 cystic lesions on F.R.'s face and 2 on his back. What treatment regimen is indicated now?

F.R. has failed most therapies and now has potentially the most severe form of acne. Because cystic acne is associated with a significant amount of scarring, F.R. should be started on systemic isotretinoin. This is the only drug which is effective for all forms of acne, including cysts. An initial dose of at least 1 mg/kg/day of isotretinoin (Accutane) is recommended because smaller doses are associated with a higher relapse rate. The decision to use isotretinoin is somewhat difficult because of F.R.'s history of hyperlipidemia and elevated liver enzymes. Although these laboratory test elevations are only modestly abnormal and perhaps related to increased alcohol consumption, both hyperlipidemia and hepatotoxicity are adverse effects associated with isotretinoin. For this reason, the 1 mg/kg/day dose of isotretinoin is preferred over the 2 mg/kg/day dose initially.

Monitoring Parameters

8. What baseline and periodic monitoring parameters should be followed in F.R.?

Lipids. A baseline, fasting, fractionated-lipid panel should be ordered for F.R. because of the association of isotretinoin (Accutane) with hyperlipidemia. His blood sample should be collected at least 36 hours after alcohol consumption. The panel should be repeated periodically, but there is no consensus on the frequency. Maximal lipid changes usually occur within four to eight weeks in about 30% of patients after beginning isotretinoin therapy. Mild triglyceride elevations (≤400 mg/dL) should be treated with diet and reduction of alcohol intake. Serum triglycerides greater than 800 mg/dL may cause acute pancreatitis and isotretinoin dosage reduction or drug discontinuation should be considered. These lipid abnormalities usually resolve within several weeks after the dose of isotretinoin is reduced. High-density lipoprotein (HDL) concentrations may decrease slightly and total cholesterol concentrations may increase.

Liver Function. A baseline liver panel that includes serum transaminases and bilirubin should be obtained from F.R. because of the association of hepatotoxicity with systemic isotretinoin therapy. The tests must be repeated in patients with clinical symptoms of hepatitis. Mild elevations in the serum concentrations of aminotransferases (less than twice the upper limit of normal) occur in about 15% to 25% of patients. Isotretinoin dosage reduction or drug discontinuation should be considered in asymptomatic patients with persistent enzyme elevations. Hepatitis occurs in less than 1% of patients taking isotretinoin but requires drug discontinuation if suspected.

Others. Although other laboratory abnormalities may be encountered during isotretinoin therapy, no guidelines have been established for the need to routinely monitor the serum concentrations of glucose and electrolytes, urinalysis, red or white blood cell counts, creatine kinase, or the erythrocyte sedimentation rate. Obtaining at least baseline values seems prudent. Because F.R. is a male, teratogenic effects are less of a concern; however, *all* females of child bearing potential *must* have a negative pregnancy test before beginning therapy. Some clinicians recommend monthly pregnancy tests in sexually active fertile females, regardless of contraceptive method used. Bone scintigraphy and ophthalmologic examinations are optional, but are recommended for long-term therapy.

Adverse Effects

9. F.R. complains of dry eyes and cracks with bleeding in the corners of his mouth after 4 weeks of therapy. How might these bothersome mucocutaneous side effects be managed?

While other causes of these symptoms are possible, mucocutaneous dryness is the most common adverse effect occurring in almost all patients receiving systemic isotretinoin therapy. Frequent application of a lip balm or emollient, particularly one with a sunscreen, is recommended to treat F.R.'s cheilitis. Daytime artificial tear instillation should relieve the discomfort of F.R.'s dry eyes. Bedtime application of a lubricating ophthalmic ointment also may be helpful. If the symptoms become intolerable, a small reduction in the dose of isotretinoin usually decreases the intensity of skin and mucous membrane reactions. Drug discontinuation is rarely necessary.[44]

Application of normal saline spray (e.g., Ocean) to the nasal mucosa also should be recommended because about 60% of isotretinoin-treated patients experience dry nasal mucosa and bloody noses. About 95% of patients receiving isotretinoin also develop dry skin that should be treated with appropriate lotions, creams, or ointments (see Chapter 36: Dermatotherapy).

References

1 **Burke BM, Cunliffe WJ.** The assessment of acne vulgaris—the Leeds technique. Br J Dermatol. 1984;111:83.

2 **Billow JA.** Acne Products. In: Covington TR, ed. Handbook of Nonprescription Drugs. Washington: American Pharmaceutical Association. 10th ed. 1993:511.

3 **Arnold HL Jr.** Acne. In: Arnold HL Jr et al., eds. Andrews' Diseases of the skin. Philadelphia: WB Saunders; 1990:250.

4 **Krowchuk DP et al.** The psychosocial effects of acne on adolescents. Pediatr Dermatol. 1991;8:332.

5 **Kligman AM.** Postmenopausal acne. Cutis. 1991;47:425.

6 **Aizawa H, Niimura M.** Adrenal androgen abnormalities in women with late onset and persistent acne. Arch Dermatol Res. 1993;284:451.

7 **Falcini F et al.** Musculoskeletal syndromes associated with acne. J Rheumatol. 1991;18:1770. Letter.

8 **Krafchik B.** Acne in Apert syndrome. Clin Plast Surg. 1991;18:407.

9 **Kahn MF, Chamot AM.** SAPHO syndrome. Rheum Dis Clin North Am. 1992;225.

10 **Ebling FJG, Cunliffe WJ.** Disorders of the sebaceous glands. In: Champion RH et al., eds. Textbook of Dermatology. Boston: Blackwell Scientific Publications; 1992:1699.

11 **Goldstein BG, Goldstein AO.** Acne and related disorders. In: Goldstein BG, Goldstein AO, eds. Practical Dermatology. St. Louis: Mosby Yearbook; 1992:45.

12 **Sauer GC.** Acne. In: Sauer GC, ed. Manual of Skin Diseases. Philadelphia: JB Lippincott Company; 1991:123.

13 **Fitzpatrick TB.** Disorders of sebaceous and apocrine glands. In: Fitzpatrick TB et al., eds. Color Atlas and Synopsis of Clinical Dermatology. New York: McGraw-Hill; 1992:2.

14 **Reeves JRT, Maibach H.** Acne. In: Reeves JRT, Maibach H, eds. Clinical Dermatology Illustrated: A Regional Approach. Philadelphia: FA Davis; 1991:40.

15 **Swart E et al.,** eds. Skin conditions in epileptics. Clin Exp Dermatol. 1992; 17:169.

16 **Gollnick HPM et al.** Pathogenesis and pathogenesis related treatment of acne. J Dermatol. 1991;18:489.

17 **Kokelj F.** Occupational acne. Clin Dermatol. 1992;10:213.

18 **Winston MH, Shalita AR.** Acne vulgaris: Pathogenesis and treatment. Pediatr Clin North Am. 1991;38:889.

19 **Strauss JS.** Biology of the sebaceous gland and the pathophysiology of acne vulgaris. In: Soter NA, Baden HP, eds. Pathophysiology of Dermatologic Diseases. New York: McGraw-Hill; 1991: 195.

20 **Pochi PE.** The pathogenesis and treatment of acne. Annu Rev Med. 1990; 41:187.

21 **Webster GF, Leyden JJ.** Characterization of serum-independent polymorphonuclear leukocyte chemotactic factors produced by *Propionibacterium acnes*. Inflammation. 1980;4:261.

22 **Wilson BB.** Acne vulgaris. Prim Care. 1989;16:695.

23 **Lever L, Marks R.** Current views on the aetiology, pathogenesis and treatment of acne vulgaris. Drugs. 1990;39: 681.

24 **Drake LA et al.** Guidelines of care for acne vulgaris. J Am Acad Dermatol. 1990;22:676.

25 **Kumasaka BH, Odland PB.** Acne vulgaris: Topical and systemic therapies. Postgrad Med. 1992;92:181.

26 **Strauss JS, Jackson EM.** American Academy of Dermatology Invitational Symposium on comedogenicity. J Am Acad Dermatol. 1989;20:272.

27 **Ives TJ.** Benzoyl peroxide. Am Pharm. 1992;NS32:33.

28 **Shalita AR.** Topical acne therapy. Dermatol Clin. 1983;1:399.

29 **Hughes BR et al.** A double-blind evaluation of topical isotretinoin 0.05%, benzoyl peroxide gel 5% and placebo in patients with acne. Clin Exp Dermatol. 1992;17:165.

30 **Cunliffe WJ.** Evolution of a strategy for the treatment of acne. J Am Acad Dermatol. 1987;16:591.

31 **Zbinden G.** Scientific opinion on the carcinogenic risk due to topical administration of benzoyl peroxide for the treatment of acne vulgaris. Pharmacol Toxicol. 1988;63:307.

32 **Straumfjord JV.** Vitamin A—its effects in acne vulgaris. Northwest Med. 1949;42:219.

33 **Gilchrest BA.** Retinoid pharmacology and skin. In: Mukhtar H, ed. Pharmacology of the skin. Ann Arbor: CRC Press; 1992:167.

34 **Lavker RM et al.** An ultrastructural study of the effects of topical tretinoin on microcomedones. Clin Ther. 1992; 14:773.

35 **Falcon RH et al.** In vitro effect of isotretinoin on monocyte chemotaxis. J Invest Dermatol. 1986;86:550.

36 **Pigatto PD et al.** Effects of isotretinoin on the neutrophil chemotaxis in cystic acne. Dermatologica. 1983;167:16.

37 **Bondi EE.** Topical tretinoin therapy. Am Fam Physician. 1989;39:269.

38 **Harris DWS et al.** Topical retinoic acid in the treatment of fine acne scarring. Br J Dermatol 1991;125:81. Letter.

39 **Farnes SW, Setness PA.** Retinoid therapy for aging skin and acne. Postgrad Med. 1992;92:191.

40 **Lehucher-Ceyrac D, Weber-Buisset MJ.** Isotretinoin and acne in practice: a prospective analysis of 188 cases over 9 years. Dermatology. 1993;186: 123.

41 **Layton AM, Cunliffe WJ.** Guidelines for optimal use of isotretinoin in acne. J Am Acad Dermatol. 1992;27:S2.

42 **Kauffman RE et al.** Retinoid therapy for severe dermatological disorders. Pediatrics. 1992;90:119.

43 **Lee ML, Cooper A.** Isotretinoin: Cost-benefit study. Australas J Dermatol. 1991;32:17.

44 **Saurat JH.** Side effects of systemic retinoids and their clinical management. J Am Acad Dermatol. 1992;27:S23.

45 **Vahlquist A.** Long-term safety of retinoid therapy. J Am Acad Dermatol. 1992;27:S29.

46 **Akamatsu H et al.** Inhibition of neutrophil chemotactic factor production in comedonal bacteria by subminimal inhibitory concentrations of erythromycin. Dermatology. 1992;185:41.

47 **Akamatsu H et al.** Effects of subminimal inhibitory concentrations of minocycline on neutrophil chemotactic factor production in comedonal bacteria, neutrophil phagocytosis and oxygen metabolism. Arch Dermatol Res. 1991;283:524.

48 **Eady EA et al.** Antibiotic resistant propionibacteria in acne: need for policies to modify antibiotic usage. Br Med J. 1993;306:555.

49 **Nielsen PG.** Topical metronidazole gel: use in acne vulgaris. Int J Dermatol. 1991;30:662.

50 **Hughes BR et al.** Strategy of acne therapy with long-term antibiotics. Br J Dermatol. 1989;121:623.

51 **Freeman K.** Minocycline in the treatment of acne. Br J Clin Pharmacol. 1989;43:112.

52 **Eady EA et al.** Topical antibiotics for the treatment of acne vulgaris: a critical evaluation of the literature and their clinical benefit and comparative efficacy. J Dermatol Treatment. 1990;1:215.

53 **Burton J.** A placebo-controlled study to evaluate the efficacy of topical tetracycline and oral tetracycline in the treatment of mild to moderate acne. J Int Med Res. 1990;18:94.

54 **Facklam DP et al.** An epidemiologic postmarketing surveillance study of prescription acne medications. Am J Public Health. 1990;80:50.

55 **Shalita AR.** Comparison of a salicylic acid cleanser and a benzoyl peroxide wash in the treatment of acne vulgaris. Clin Ther. 1989;11:264.

56 **Zander E, Weisman S.** Treatment of acne vulgaris with salicylic acid pads. Clin Ther. 1992;14:247.

57 **Mills OH, Kligman AM.** Drugs that are ineffective in the treatment of acne vulgaris. Br J Dermatol. 1983;108:371.

58 **Food and Drug Administration.** Topical acne products for over-the-counter human use-final monograph. Fed Regist. 1991;56:41008.

59 **Dreno B et al.** Zinc salts effects on granulocyte zinc concentration and chemotaxis in acne patients. Acta Derm Venereol (Stockh). 1992;72:250.

60 **Stamatiadis D et al.** Inhibition of 5α-reductase by zinc and azelaic acid. Br J Dermatol. 1988;119:627.

61 **Sawaya ME, Hordinsky MK.** The antiandrogens—when and how they should be used. Dermatol Clin. 1993;11:65.

62 **Shaw JC.** Spironolactone in dermatologic therapy. J Am Acad Dermatol. 1991;24:236.

63 **Jurzyk RS et al.** Antiandrogens in the treatment of acne and hirsutism. Am Fam Physician. 1992;45:1803.

64 **Wishart JM.** An open study of Triphasil and Diane 50 in the treatment of acne. Australas J Dermatol. 1991;32:51.

65 **Matsuoka LY.** Acne and related disorders. Clin Plastic Surg. 1993;20:35.

66 **Eichenfield LF, Leyden JL.** Acne: current concepts of pathogenesis and approach to rational treatment. Pediatrician. 1991;18:218.

67 **Macdonald Hull S, Cunliffe WJ.** The use of a corticosteroid cream for immediate reduction in the clinical signs of acne vulgaris. Acta Derm Venereol (Stockh). 1989;69:452.

68 **Hughes BR, Cunliffe WJ.** Interactions between the oral contraceptive pill and antibiotics. Br J Dermatol. 1990;122:717.

69 **Fleischer AB, Resnick SD.** The effect of antibiotics on the efficacy of oral contraceptives: a controversy revisited. Arch Dermatol. 1989;125:1562.

70 **Szoka PR, Edgren RA.** Drug interactions with oral contraceptives: compilation and analysis of an adverse experience report database. Fertil Steril. 1988;49(Suppl.):31S.

71 **Ellsworth AE, Leversee JH.** Oral contraceptives. Primary Care. 1990;17:603.

72 **Driscoll MS et al.** Long-term oral antibiotics for acne: is laboratory monitoring necessary. J Am Acad Dermatol. 1993;28:595.

73 **Ortho Dermatological.** Retin—A package insert. Raritan, NJ: 1992 November.

74 **Swerlick RA, Lawley TJ.** Eczema, psoriasis, cutaneous infections, acne and other common skin disorders. In: Isselbacher KJ et al., eds. Harrison's Principles of Internal Medicine. 13th ed. New York: McGraw-Hill; 1994:278.

Psoriasis

Allan Ellsworth

Epidemiology 38-1
Pathogenesis 38-1
Signs and Symptoms 38-1
Prognosis 38-1
Topical Drug Therapy 38-1
Topical Steroids 38-1
Coal Tar 38-2
Anthralin 38-2
Calcipotriene 38-2
Phototherapy 38-3
Ultraviolet-B (UVB) 38-3
Photochemotherapy 38-3

Systemic Therapy 38-3
Etretinate 38-3
Methotrexate (MTX) 38-3
Mild to Moderate (≤20% Body) Psoriasis 38-4
Classic Presentation 38-4
Psoriasis as Adverse Drug Effect 38-5
Topical Steroids 38-5
Alternative Topical Steroids 38-5
Severe (>20% Body) Psoriasis 38-6
Psoralens and Ultraviolet-A Light (PUVA) 38-6
Psoriatic Arthritis 38-6
Methotrexate 38-6

Epidemiology

Psoriasis, a chronic, proliferative skin disease characterized by sharply defined erythematous patches covered with a distinctive silvery scale, occurs in 1% to 3% of the population world-wide. Typical age at onset is the third decade, however, the disease can occur at any time. Men and women are affected equally. A family history of psoriasis is found in 30% of patients.[1] Persons with the histocompatibility antigen HLA-Cw6 are 9 to 15 times more likely to develop psoriasis than are others, and the coexistence of HLA-B17 or B27 portends more severe skin disease or associated psoriatic arthritis.[1]

Pathogenesis

The pathogenesis of psoriasis remains unclear, despite the demonstration of several biochemical abnormalities.[2] Separating the primary defect from changes secondary to the disease itself has proven difficult. Time required for psoriatic epidermal cells to travel to the surface and be cast off (3 to 4 days versus 26 to 28 days) is reduced markedly.[3] This six- to nine-fold transit time decrease does not allow the normal events of cell maturation and keratinization to take place, reflected clinically as diffuse scaling.

Signs and Symptoms

Most psoriatic lesions are asymptomatic. Pruritus is highly variable (noted in 20% of patients). The primary lesion is a relapsing eruption of scaling papules that rapidly coalesce or enlarge to form circumscribed, erythematous, scaly, plaques. The scale is adherent, silvery white, and reveals bleeding points when removed (called Auspitz's sign). Scale may become extremely dense on the scalp or macerated and dispersed in intertriginous areas.

Lesions of active psoriasis can develop at the site of epidermal trauma (called Köbner's phenomenon). Scratch marks, sunburn, or surgical wounds may heal leaving psoriatic lesions in their place. Elbows, knees, scalp, gluteal cleft, fingernails, and toenails are favored areas of involvement. Extensor surfaces are affected more than the flexor surfaces and the disease usually spares the palms, soles, and face. Nails may show punctate pitting or profuse collections of keratotic material. A yellow-brown subungual discoloration ("oil spot") is characteristic.

Most patients have chronic localized disease, but there are several other presentations. *Erythrodermic psoriasis* describes a con-

dition of acute inflammatory erythema and scales that involve greater than 90% of the body surface area. *Pustular psoriasis* generally is localized to the palms and soles, but there is also a generalized pustular version. *Guttate psoriasis* describes small, scaly, erythematous spots of psoriasis, (classically following beta-hemolytic streptococcal pharyngitis). *Flexural psoriasis* lacks scales and appears like intertrigo.

Prognosis

The disease is lifelong and characterized by chronic recurrent exacerbations and remissions that are generally more emotionally than physically disabling ("the heartbreak of psoriasis").[4] Therefore, even when a patient has only a few asymptomatic chronic plaques, the disease is more serious than it appears.[5] It is important to emphasize that psoriasis is a treatable disease. Optimism and encouragement are justified and make it easier for the patient to conscientiously apply sometimes awkward and messy topical treatments. The goal of therapy should be to achieve complete clearing of psoriatic lesions, particularly during emotionally critical times, such as the commencement of school, puberty, and the summer months.

Topical Drug Therapy

Many topical and systemic agents are available, varying from simple emollients to highly potent, potentially dangerous therapies for more recalcitrant conditions. Patients with limited disease can be managed with topical therapy (see Table 38.1). Patients with psoriasis covering more than 20% of the body often need the more specialized systemic treatment programs (see Table 38.2).

Topical Steroids

Topical steroids are effective in the treatment of psoriasis because of their anti-inflammatory, antimitotic, and antipruritic properties. These properties are explained by the reduction of phospholipase A_2, DNA synthesis and epidermal mitotic activity, as well as the vasoconstrictive actions of steroids.[6] Although they provide prompt relief and patients find them convenient and acceptable, though expensive, tachyphylaxis can occur and long-term use leads to side effects (atrophy and telangiectasia). Topical steroids are best used in an adjunctive role.[6] Psoriasis is generally a steroid-resistant disease, thus the more potent corticosteroids are necessary, often with plastic occlusion, for best results. Less potent agents are more ap-

Table 38.1	Psoriatic Therapeutic Options Mild–Moderate Psoriasis[a]	
Treatment	Advantages	Disadvantages
Topical steroids	Rapid response; controls inflammation and itching; best for intertriginous areas and face; convenient, not messy	Temporary relief (tachyphylaxis occurs); less effective with continued use; atrophy and telangiectasia occur with continued use; expensive
Anthralin	Effective for scalp; new preparations "pleasant"	Only moderately effective when combined with UVB (Goeckerman regimen)
Tar	Convenient; short programs preferred; long remissions	Purple-brown staining; irritating; careful application required
Calcipotriene	Convenient; well-tolerated	Expensive; potential effects on bone metabolism
UVB and lubricating agents or tar	Insurance reimburses; effective as maintenance; no need for topical steroids	Expensive, office-based therapy

[a] <20% body involvement.

propriate in intertriginous areas, on the face, and for maintenance. Intermittent dosing or "pulse therapy" seems to yield the best long-term results and minimizes tachyphylaxis and adverse effects. Topical steroids occasionally can cause a reversible suppression of the hypothalamic-pituitary-adrenal (HPA) axis, as indicated by a decrease in the morning plasma cortisol level.[7] Continuous application for more than three weeks should be discouraged in patients with psoriasis.[6] During a flare, steroids will help reduce inflammation, redness, and irritation and prepare the involved area for initiation of other potentially irritating, but more appropriate maintenance topical treatments such as coal tar or anthralin.

Coal Tar

Crude coal tar is a complex mixture of thousands of hydrocarbon compounds.[8] It affects psoriasis by enzyme inhibition and anti-mitotic action. The combination of tar and ultraviolet-B light (Goeckerman regimen) led to tar's increased popularity in the 1920s. Tar preparations of 2% to 10% are processed as creams, ointments, lotions, gels, oils, shampoos, and as coal tar solution (liquor carbonis detergens). Tar may be helpful for patients with mild to moderate disease. Overall the potential severity of side effects from tars is less than that from anthralin and much less than that from topical steroids. However, because tar, in every form, is messy, stains the skin, and has an odor, it has been relegated to second-line therapy for most patients.[9]

Tar creams and ointments generally are used once or twice daily. Tar creams are useful in psoriasis of the scalp and often are used overnight. The combination of ultraviolet-B (UVB) therapy with tar may be no more effective than either agent alone.[10]

Patients should be warned about the staining properties on clothing and bedding. Other side effects include photosensitivity, acneform eruptions, folliculitis, and irritation dermatitis. Because of its irritative properties, care should be taken to avoid use of tar on the face, flexures, and genitalia and with inflammatory psoriasis.

There is a theoretical increased risk of skin cancer and internal malignancies with the topical use of tars. Large numbers of poly-aromatic hydrocarbons are contained in coal tar. These compounds may be metabolized to active carcinogens by epidermal microsomal enzymes. An increased incidence of hyperkeratotic lesions, including squamous-cell carcinomas, is well reported after pro-

longed industrial exposure to tar.[10] However, extensive reviews of patients who have used tar in psoriasis have failed to demonstrate an increased risk of carcinoma.[11]

Anthralin

Anthralin, an anthrone derivative, inhibits DNA synthesis yielding an antiproliferative effect. It is effective for treatment of widespread, discrete psoriatic plaques. The primary disadvantages of anthralin are its irritant and staining properties to skin and clothing, in addition it can be difficult to apply.

Most commercial products also contain 2% to 3% salicylic acid, which acts as an antioxidant. The salicylic acid retards the inactivation of anthralin and enhances the therapeutic effect.[12] Tar may be combined with anthralin, or applied before the anthralin, because tar reduces the irritant effect of anthralin without reducing its efficacy.[13] The standard regimen involves liberal application of gradually increasing anthralin concentrations (0.1% to 0.2% up to 1%) for 8 to 12 hours (often overnight), depending upon irritancy and the clinical response. Removal is facilitated with a bath or mineral oil in the morning. A steroid cream may be used during the day.

Alternative, shorter contact (10 to 60 minutes BID) regimens generally are used as they deliver more anthralin through diseased skin than normal skin and time to clearing of psoriasis is the same as with continuous application methods.[14–16] Higher concentrations of anthralin are used in the shorter contact regimens. Irritancy is more of a problem, though staining is reduced. Many patients prefer short-contact anthralin to its continuous application. Both methods are used daily for clearing of psoriasis, then once or twice weekly for maintenance therapy.

Calcipotriene

Calcipotriene ointment is a topical vitamin D_3 analog that, *in vitro*, regulates cell differentiation and proliferation and suppresses lymphocyte activities.[17] These actions are very similar to those of the natural hormone $1,25-(OH)_2-D_3$. In contrast, the systemic effects on calcium and bone metabolism are at least 100 to 200 times less than those of the natural hormone.[18] Because of this unique pharmacological profile, calcipotriol, is effective and safe for both short- and long-term treatment of psoriasis. The ointment is applied twice daily in amounts up to 100 gm/week. By following these guidelines, the drug does not affect calcium or bone metabolism. If comparisons with tars and anthralin continue to be favorable, calcipotriol may become a first-line drug for plaque-type psoriasis.

Table 38.2	Psoriatic Therapeutic Options Severe Disease[a,b]	
Treatment	Advantages	Disadvantages
UVB and lubricating agents or tar	Insurance reimburses; effective as maintenance; no need for topical steroids	Expensive, office-based therapy
PUVA	80% efficacy; "sun tan" cosmetically desirable	Time consuming; expensive, office-based therapy; dermal changes; restrictive
MTX	"Gold standard" for efficacy; helps arthritis	Hepatotoxicity; liver biopsy periodically required
Etretinate	Alternative to PUVA or MTX; arthritis efficacy	Hematopoietic toxicity; flu-like syndrome; vitamin A toxicity; teratogen

[a] >20% body involvement.
[b] MTX = Methotrexate; PUVA = Psoralens and ultraviolet-A light.

Phototherapy
Ultraviolet-B (UVB)

Ultraviolet-B light is effective in managing psoriasis by reducing DNA synthesis of epidermal cells.[19] In contrast, ultraviolet-A (UVA) light without psoralens is ineffective. Heat and humidity from sunlight provide additional positive effects. Aggressive UVB phototherapy may be the most rapid and effective single-agent regimen for clearing psoriasis. Ultraviolet light treatment can produce long-lasting remissions. UVB therapy is pleasant to use and relatively nontoxic.

Regimens combining UVB with anthralin (Ingram's regimen) or tar (Goeckerman regimen) have been used for years, theoretically, taking advantage of the photosensitizing properties of tar and anthralin. The Goeckerman regimen involves daily application of coal tar and exposure to ultraviolet light. The Ingram regimen combines daily application of anthralin plus tar baths with exposure to ultraviolet light. Both these regimens can clear widespread psoriasis in three to four weeks and effect remissions that last for weeks to months. Ordinary lubricants (i.e., petrolatum, mineral and "baby" oil, Eucerin) applied before UV exposure also provide relief. The emollient or vehicle decreases the reflectance characteristics of the psoriatic scale, thereby increasing light transmission into psoriatic skin. Reportedly, treatment with UVB and lubricating agents is just as effective as UVB and topical steroids.[20,21] It is possible that costly topical steroids and messy tars can be avoided in the future during light therapy, with proper use of emollients.

Photochemotherapy

Photochemotherapy combines the systemic psoralens and ultraviolet-A light spectrum (PUVA). The psoralens (methoxsalen, 5-methoxypsoralen, and trioxsalen) are a group of photoactive compounds that upon absorption of ultraviolet light, are excited into an unstable energy state. Absorbed energy is dissipated by the formation of complexes with DNA which interfere with the replication of cells and may have immunosuppressive properties. Psoralens are not active without UVA. This form of therapy is used to control severe, recalcitrant, disabling plaque psoriasis. Over 80% of patients experience clearing of symptoms after 10 to 20 treatments over four to eight weeks, that can be maintained with periodic (twice monthly) treatments.[22] Because UVA penetrates the skin more deeply than UVB, it may have marked effects on the dermis. PUVA requires careful consideration because of the necessity of photoprotective measures that can affect lifestyle significantly. Patients unwilling to use PUVA may prefer UVB treatment, as it is much less restrictive.

Acute phototoxic side effects, such as erythema and blistering, are dose related and, therefore, controllable. Topical steroid therapy should be continued until the psoriasis is brought under control. If topical steroids are discontinued at the start of PUVA, an exacerbation of psoriasis usually occurs. Patients should wear protective clothing (with long sleeves and high necklines), use sunscreens that filter out both UVA and UVB, and wear sunglasses that block UVA after PUVA. (See Chapter 39: Photosensitivity and Burns.) Since methoxsalen has a short half-life and 80% is eliminated within six to eight hours, physical barriers are most important during the eight hours immediately following PUVA therapy. Of greater concern, are the potential long-term side effects: mutagenicity, carcinogenicity, and cataract formation.[23] Long-term maintenance and high cumulative dosages should be avoided. Shielding the face and genitalia during treatment and performing annual examinations to detect skin cancer at an early stage may lessen the risk of long-term adverse effects of photochemotherapy. (See Table 38.3.)

Topical psoralens are extremely photosensitizing, hence difficult to administer. However, application of methoxsalen 0.1% followed by lower UVA doses ($\approx$20% of the level of usual doses for oral PUVA) has been used to treat localized areas, and to avoid gastrointestinal side effects.[24] It is very difficult to calibrate therapy with topical methoxsalen.

Systemic Therapy
Etretinate

Etretinate is a vitamin A analogue that is effective for treatment of severe recalcitrant disease, especially for generalized pustular, erythrodermic, and palmoplantar pustular variants, but less effective for plaque-type psoriasis.[25] However, in combination with PUVA (Re-PUVA) or UVB phototherapy, etretinate may be useful as a short-term adjunctive treatment for treating chronic plaque psoriasis and reducing the amount of ultraviolet light and the number of treatments required to produce clearing of psoriasis.[26] Etretinate may work through its anti-inflammatory actions and its regulation of epidermal differentiation and proliferation; the drug also may alleviate the arthritis that accompanies psoriasis.[26] Etretinate should be considered initial treatment for moderate to severe pustular or erythrodermic psoriasis and for plaque-type psoriasis in the following situations: 1) for patients who have received extensive radiation with PUVA;[27] 2) as a one to three week pretreatment for PUVA to accelerate the response rate; 3) for patients who fail to respond to UVB with anthralin or tar; or 4) for patients who are not candidates for methotrexate. Liver biopsy is not a routine part of etretinate therapy. Most patients require maintenance or intermittent therapy to prevent relapses.[28]

There are numerous side effects associated with etretinate use including hypervitaminosis A syndrome; skin thinning and fragility; thin, soft nails; reversible hair loss; retinoid rash; extraspinal tendon and ligament calcification; bone changes in children; hyperlipidemia with elevated levels of serum triglycerides and cholesterol; and liver enzyme alteration and hepatitis.[28] Patients should be monitored closely (see Table 38.4).[29] Many patients find the side effects intolerable and stop treatment. Topical steroids can reduce some of the cutaneous side effects. Etretinate is a teratogen. With continued therapy, the drug accumulates in adipose tissue and the liver and may be detectable in serum for two years and longer after discontinuation. Pregnancy should be avoided following treatment with etretinate.[28] Etretinate's major metabolic derivative, etretin, which is as effective but has a far shorter half-life (2 days versus 100 days) and is 50 times less lipophilic, is expected to replace etretinate when available.[28]

Methotrexate (MTX)

Methotrexate is a folic acid analogue that inhibits dihydrofolate reductase, needed for the synthesis of thymidine and purines and subsequently DNA synthesis. Thus, MTX therapy induces a

Table 38.3	Measures to Reduce the Toxicity of Photochemotherapy

- Avoid long-term maintenance treatment and high cumulative dosages of radiation (200 treatments or a total UVA dose of 1200 J/cm^2) appears to be the threshold for development of skin cancer
- Shield the face and male genitalia (which are at a particular risk of skin cancer) during treatment
- Perform thorough annual examinations to detect skin cancer at an early age
- Use sunscreens, protective clothing, and sunglasses

Table 38.4	Etretinate Therapy: Patient Monitoring[a,b]
Type of Evaluation	Comments
Clinical evaluation	Performed twice in 1st month, monthly for 6 months, and Q 3 months thereafter
Laboratory testing CBC, UA, fasting glucose, renal function tests, calcium	Performed at each visit during 1st year and twice yearly thereafter
Liver function tests	Performed at each visit
Fasting lipids	Performed at each visit in 1st 4 months and every 2–3 months thereafter; stop etretinate if serum triglycerides >800 mg/mL to reduce risk of pancreatitis
Pregnancy test	Performed before, monthly during, and for at least 1 year after therapy
Radiographs	*Adults:* no routine radiographs if patient >40 yr *Children:* radiographic monitoring for long-term (>0.5 yr) treatment

[a] Adapted from reference 29.
[b] CBC = Complete blood count; UA = Urinalysis.

marked suppressive effect on rapidly proliferating cells, including those in psoriatic skin.[30] Unlike other cytotoxic drugs, it produces effects in doses that are much lower than those used in cancer chemotherapy.[31]

Methotrexate induces remissions in the majority of patients treated and maintains remissions for long periods with continued therapy. MTX is relatively safe and well tolerated, but the need for periodic liver biopsies discourages many patients and physicians from using it. Hepatotoxicity, resulting in fibrosis and cirrhosis, is a concern following long-term therapy.[32] Alcohol and methotrexate are a particularly potent hepatotoxic combination. Therefore, if there is any suspicion of active alcohol abuse, methotrexate should not be used. Other conditions associated with an increased risk of methotrexate hepatotoxicity include obesity and diabetes mellitus.[32]

Although in part related to the cumulative dose, hepatotoxicity as a result of MTX therapy is related especially to a constant blood level. Therefore, daily administration of MTX has been replaced by weekly dosage schedules. Normal results of liver function tests can occur in the presence of methotrexate-induced liver disease. Therefore, guidelines (see Table 38.5) call for a liver biopsy in all patients after a cumulative dose of 1.5 to 2.0 gm of MTX.[31,32]

Other side effects include bone marrow depletion, nausea, diarrhea, and stomatitis. Teratogenesis and miscarriage have occurred and MTX may cause reversible oligospermia. Pneumonitis may occur early in the course of treatment, particularly when MTX is given in doses similar to those used in cancer chemotherapy regimens. Certain drugs enhance the toxicity of methotrexate by reducing tubular secretion (e.g., salicylates, sulfonamides, probenecid, and penicillin) or by displacing MTX from the sites at which it binds to plasma proteins (e.g., salicylates, probenecid, barbiturates, and phenytoin). Many of the nonsteroidal anti-inflammatory drugs (NSAIDs) and trimethoprim-sulfamethoxazole enhance methotrexate toxicity.[31] Contraindications include decreased renal function, pregnancy or breast-feeding, hepatic fibrosis, cirrhosis, hepatitis, anemia, leukopenia, thrombocytopenia, active peptic ulcer disease, active infectious disease, alcohol abuse, and patient unreliability.[31]

Mild to Moderate (≤20% Body) Psoriasis

Classic Presentation

1. M.M., a 35-year-old male, presents with a worsening of psoriasis. Approximately 1 year before presentation, he was given triamcinolone 0.025% cream to apply to several thick, well-defined, erythematous plaques, covered with silvery scales, on his elbows and knees. He recently returned from a trip to the Dominican Republic where he noted gradual worsening of redness and scaling despite adherence to a twice daily triamcinolone regimen. He is quite emotionally distraught because of this "flare" which had prevented him from enjoying his vacation in the "sun." On examination, besides erythematous, scale-covered plaques on his elbows and knees, there are several scattered, circumscribed, erythematous, scaly plaques on the flexural surfaces of both arms and legs. A dense scale was evident on his scalp (forehead). These and other areas, demonstrating typical psoriatic involvement, including the gluteal fold and fingernails, now totaled approximately 20% of his body area. Past medical history is noncontributory. His only medication besides the topical corticosteroid is a recently completed course of chloroquine for malaria prophylaxis during his recent travel. Characterize the classic psoriatic lesions demonstrated by M.M.

The classic plaques of psoriasis appear symmetrically on the extensor surfaces of the elbows and knees as distinctive, chronic, erythematous patches that are covered with silvery scales. Removal of scales reveals small, punctate areas of bleeding (Auspitz's sign). Although Auspitz's sign was not noted in M.M., he did present with "several thick, well-defined, erythematous plaques covered with silvery scales." Patients can present a broad clinical spectrum from scalp only involvement, to scattered plaques on the trunk and extremities to, in the most serious cases, a generalized erythroderma accompanied by a rheumatoid factor-negative symmetric arthritis. Additionally, the finding of very small pits in the nail plates of the hands and feet ("oil spots"), the presence of gluteal "pinking" (erythema and slight scaling of the intergluteal cleft), and the occurrence of lesions conforming to specific sites of skin trauma (Köebner phenomenon) help characterize psoriatic plaques from seborrheic dermatitis and eczema. Most psoriatic lesions are asymptomatic, but pruritus is noted in 20% of patients.

2. What part does emotional support play in the total management of M.M.'s psoriasis?

Psoriasis is often more emotionally or psychologically disturbing than often is recognized, and may cause a reluctance to partic-

Table 38.5	Methotrexate Therapy: Patient Monitoring[a]
Type of Evaluation	Comments
Clinical evaluation	Performed twice in 1st month, monthly for 6 months; then Q 3 months thereafter
Laboratory testing CBC, UA, serum albumin, renal function tests, LFTs	Performed at each visit during 1st year; then Q 3 months
Liver biopsy	Baseline; then Q 2–3 yr (or 1–1.5 gm cumulative dose). Alternatively, if LFTs within normal limits at baseline, postpone biopsy 2–4 months until efficacy and lack of toxicity established, then biopsy (before 1.5 gm cumulative dose)

[a] CBC = Complete blood count; LFTs = Liver function tests; UA = Urinalysis.

ipate in swimming and other sports. Even though exposure to sunlight helps most psoriatics, there is an unwillingness to sunbathe if the lesions can be seen. Furthermore, if the psoriatic lesions become pruritic and are scratched, there is further deterioration because of the Köebner phenomenon (i.e., the appearance of lesions of psoriasis at the site of an injury). More patients than we realize alter their lifestyles or consult nontraditional medicine (perhaps quacks) in desperation. This is unfortunate as there is so much that can be done to control psoriasis.

Emotional support should begin with explanation of the psoriatic condition. M.M. needs to be reassured that many other people suffer from the same affliction, that the disorder is not contagious or fatal, and that it can be controlled even though we have as yet no cure. Patients usually are glad to know that there is a wide range of treatments available. Optimism and encouragement are justified and make it easier for the patient to conscientiously apply sometimes awkward and messy topical treatments. Realistic goals might include complete clearing during emotionally critical times, such as vacation or summer months.

3. What are the potential causes of M.M.'s psoriatic exacerbation? List other factors that can precipitate or aggravate psoriasis.

A thorough medical history may reveal a cause for exacerbations of psoriatic lesions. Most patients report that hot weather, sunlight, and humidity help clear psoriasis, whereas cold weather has an adverse effect on its course. Anxiety or psychologic stress is believed to contribute adversely. Viral or bacterial infections, especially streptococcal pharyngitis may precipitate the onset or flare-up of psoriasis. Trauma to the uninvolved skin can cause a lesion to appear at the exact site of injury (Köebner response). Cuts, burns, abrasions, injections, and other trauma can elicit this reaction. Any drug that causes a skin eruption to develop may exacerbate psoriasis via this response.

Psoriasis as Adverse Drug Effect

Antimalarial agents such as chloroquine, usually have an adverse effect on the course of psoriasis and can cause exfoliative erythroderma.[33,34] Hydroxychloroquine, however, does not share this association and induces a beneficial response in 75% of patients with psoriatic arthritis.[33,34] Hydroxychloroquine, therefore, would be preferred over chloroquine in psoriasis patients who need prophylactic treatment for malaria when both are effective against the particular plasmodium species in the area (see Chapter 71: Parasitic Infections).[35]

Lithium also can precipitate psoriasis and contribute to resistance to treatment through its effects on cell kinetics (increase in circulating neutrophils; accelerated neutrophil turnover; increased epidermal cell proliferation).[36,37] Psoriasis, however, is not a general contraindication to lithium therapy. More intensive psoriasis treatment can be used if these reactions occur and lithium must be continued.[37]

Beta blockers[38] and some nonsteroidal anti-inflammatory drugs[39] also can precipitate a psoriasiform state. Since both lithium and propranolol inhibit cyclic AMP, cyclic nucleosides may play a role in the onset and clinical course of psoriasis.[38] Chemotactic substances, including 12-HETE and leukotrienes, may accumulate in the epidermis of some patients taking indomethacin and, thereby, precipitate psoriasis. Indomethacin, when compared to other NSAIDs, may selectively inhibit cyclo-oxygenase more than lipo-oxygenase pathways of arachidonic acid metabolism.[40] As a result, indomethacin may have a more significant adverse psoriatic effect than other NSAIDs, as some have been reported to ameliorate psoriasis.[41]

Finally, flares of pustular psoriasis may be precipitated by withdrawal from systemic steroids or withdrawal from high-potency topical steroids that are applied under occlusion to large areas.[42] Systemic steroids virtually have been abandoned as a routine treatment for psoriasis because of this problem and the deaths that resulted from systemic corticosteroid use and withdrawal.

Chloroquine prophylaxis, a Caribbean sunburn, and triamcinolone tachyphylaxis probably all contributed to the exacerbation of M.M.'s psoriasis.[33,42]

Topical Steroids

4. Are additional potent topical steroids appropriate for M.M.'s psoriasis? Outline the place of steroids in the pharmacotherapy of psoriasis.

For isolated hyperkeratotic plaques, potent topical steroids are probably the most widely used for the initial treatment of psoriasis. They give fast relief especially for reducing inflammation and controlling itching. Patients find them convenient and acceptable. However, their relief is temporary as they become less effective with continued use (tachyphylaxis).[42] Additionally, psoriasis is a relatively steroid-resistant disease which responds only to potent or superpotent agents.[43] Long-term use of potent agents also leads to side effects (atrophy and telangiectasia) and they are quite expensive. For these reasons, topical steroids are best used in an adjunctive role for anything but mild disease for short periods of time. Continuous application of topical steroids for more than three weeks should be discouraged. An interval of several weeks between successive courses of therapy is recommended. High potency steroids produce better clinical results than low potency steroids, but the potential for side effects is greater. Potent topical steroids can suppress the HPA axis.[7] Intermittent maintenance therapy should use the lowest potency topical steroid possible.

A short course of potent topical steroid is appropriate for this "flare" of erythema. With plastic occlusion, topical steroids will help reduce inflammation, redness, and irritation before initiation of more appropriate chronic topical treatments such as coal tar or anthralin with UVB, which are potentially irritating. Topical steroids also may continue to be useful on the face and flexures-sites where these alternative topical agents are tolerated poorly. Potent fluorinated steroid preparations only should be used for short periods on the face and flexures, if at all. Scalp psoriasis may be treated with steroid preparations in gels, lotions, or aerosol sprays, but a coal tar shampoo lathered into the scalp for five to ten minutes then rinsed out generally is more effective for scaling and pruritus.

Topical steroids two or three times a day have been recommended,[45–47] however, the response to once and twice daily application is as effective or better than that observed with more frequent regimens (steroid reservoir effect). Patients should apply steroids after a bath, at bedtime with occlusion, and possibly again, during the day without occlusion. As the lesions subside, occlusion should be decreased or omitted, emollient use should increase and steroid potency decreased. After lesions have flattened, steroids can be continued intermittently [e.g., 1 to 2 weeks on, 1 to 2 weeks off or on alternative days (e.g., 1, 3, 5, 7 etc.)].

Alternative Topical Steroids

5. Assuming that a short course of potent topical steroid is effective in reducing the acute flare, what alternative topical therapeutic regimens are available for patients like M.M. with localized disease (involving <20% of the body)?

Two effective alternative topical therapies are crude coal tar and anthralin. Though both agents have irritating properties, generally stain clothing and skin, and are inconvenient to apply, tachyphylaxis does not occur with chronic use. Once corticosteroids have flattened acute psoriatic lesions and diminished erythema significantly, daily application of these alternative agents can be used until the lesions are totally clear.

Coal tar, though effective, is of low potency when compared with anthralin. Tars such as Estar or T/Derm which are colorless, or 1% to 5% crude coal tar ointment (messy but more effective), commonly are used on the body at night. There is no advantage to short contact therapy, unlike anthralin. Tar is useful in psoriasis of the scalp. A number of tar shampoos and bath additives are available. The combination of tar with salicylic acid (2% to 6%) is useful in reducing scaling.

Anthralin clears lesions in some patients within two to three weeks. Although overnight regimens are well known, short contact therapy, which is more appealing, starts with 0.1% anthralin applied for 20 to 30 minutes and then washed off.[15,16] Irritation should be checked for at 48 hours. According to tolerance, the potency can be increased (up to 1%) and the contact time shortened, or for resistant plaques, increased. This regimen is used daily for clearing, then once or twice weekly for maintenance therapy.

Phototherapy also is an option. Ultraviolet light can be used as an outpatient modality, produces comparatively long-lasting remissions, is pleasant to use, and is relatively nontoxic. Different protocols call for daily or multiple times per week exposure for varied lengths of time depending upon patient variables. The optimal effect of UVB on psoriasis is a dose which produces minimal erythema at 24 hours. The usual time to induce clearing of psoriasis is approximately four to six weeks.

Both tar (Goeckerman regimen) and anthralin (Ingram's regimen) have been used in combination with UVB, however, there are a number of recent studies that conclude that there is no benefit in adding these agents to UVB.[20,21]

Severe (>20% Body) Psoriasis
Psoralens and Ultraviolet-A Light (PUVA)

6. G.L., a 35-year-old male with a several year history of psoriasis (generally fairly localized) presents with diffuse, erythematous plaque-like lesions now extending over 80% of his body surface area. The areas have become inflamed and application of his maintenance topical medication (anthralin) causes pain and irritation. He expresses a real frustration with the messiness of the current topical regimen. He has reinitiated topical steroids, which helped the redness and itching, but are too expensive to use for long. He is free of cardiovascular, renal, or hepatic disease and takes no systemic medications. He is self-employed as a business consultant. Which "systemic" therapy would be most appropriate for G.L. at this point?

Systemic therapies for psoriasis include PUVA, etretinate, and methotrexate. The risk-to-benefit ratio of using etretinate or methotrexate is not as favorable as PUVA since the patient has no arthritic symptoms. Psoralens and ultraviolet-A irradiation is effective in over 80% of patients.[22] The regimen is time-consuming (UV radiation treatments are required at least 3 times a week), but G.L. has some flexibility in his schedule. There are adverse effects (premature photoaging, dyskaryotic or precancerous dermal changes, nonmelanomatous skin cancer, immunological changes, and cataracts), which can be minimized with patient selection and monitoring. Generally, 8-methoxypsoralen is administered then followed by UVA, one hour later when peak blood levels occur. The erythema that is induced by PUVA takes longer to appear than with UVB therapy, reaching a peak by 48 hours. Consequently, treatment is not administered more frequently than every second day. The time to produce clearing with PUVA is longer than with UVB therapy (average 10 weeks compared with ≈3 weeks for UVB).[22] Treatment must be decreased slowly once clearing of

plaques has been achieved (frequency of treatment is reduced over a 2 to 3 month period) or psoriasis will reoccur rapidly. In contrast, UVB therapy may be ceased abruptly. Taking time off from work three times weekly for photochemotherapy is disrupting to some patients' work schedule. Absolute contraindications to treatment with PUVA include a history of photosensitivity diseases (i.e., lupus erythematosus, porphyria), idiosyncratic or allergic reactions to psoralens, arsenic intake, exposure to ionizing radiation, skin cancer (relative), pregnancy, and lactation. Measures that may lessen the risk of long-term adverse effects of photochemotherapy are listed in Table 38.3. Other photosensitizing drugs should be avoided in patients receiving PUVA. Examples of these drugs include nalidixic acid, fluoroquinolones, phenothiazines, sulfonamides, sulfonylureas, tetracyclines, and thiazides.

Psoriatic Arthritis

7. R.T., a 38-year-old male, is an aerospace machinist with psoriasis and increasing joint complaints. He describes a "flare-up" over the last month or so involving predominantly the middle finger of the right hand. He also has had arthralgias of the shoulders, knees, and the rest of his hands. Concomitantly, his skin disease has once again become active, despite nightly betamethasone dipropionate (Diprolene). He has a history of chronic depression and alcoholism, although he is currently sober and off all antidepressant medication. Physical examination reveals a significant amount of tenderness of the right third metacarpophalangeal joint without a great deal of active synovitis. He also has a moderate effusion of his right knee, but the rest of the joint examination was otherwise benign. There are active psoriatic lesions on his feet, knees, elbows, and he has characteristic psoriatic nail changes. An erythrocyte sedimentation rate is mildly elevated. Which systemic therapy would be most appropriate for both R.T.'s skin and joint complaints at this point?

Psoriatic arthritis is a distinct form of arthritis in which the rheumatoid factor usually is negative. The incidence in the psoriatic population is about 20% but up to 40% of psoriatic patients suffer from arthralgias. The prevalence of psoriatic arthritis is higher among patients with more severe cutaneous disease. Nail involvement occurs in over 80% of patients with psoriatic arthritis, as compared with 30% of patients with uncomplicated psoriasis.[48]

Nonsteroidal anti-inflammatory drugs suppress symptoms but do not induce remissions, and may exacerbate cutaneous symptoms.[37] Systemic steroids are avoided because of possible rebound of the skin disease during withdrawal.[42] Some patients treated with photochemotherapy (PUVA) experience improvement in joint symptoms as well as psoriatic lesion clearing.

Methotrexate

Methotrexate is the "gold standard" systemic agent for patients with advanced joint and skin disease. It is very effective, produces prompt results, and, in the doses that are used, is relatively nontoxic. Methotrexate is best given in a single weekly oral dose of 10 to 20 mg or in three 2.5 to 7.5 mg doses at 12 hour intervals during a 24-hour period (e.g., 8:00 a.m., 8:00 p.m., and again at 8:00 a.m.). A pretreatment aspiration needle biopsy of the liver should be performed when medically feasible to assess baseline status of liver function. More practically, if there are no risk factors for hepatotoxicity, the liver biopsy may be postponed for two to four months until the drug's efficacy and lack of toxicity have been established for the patient and long-term therapy is about to be initiated. Delaying the biopsy for this period would not pose a risk, because liver disease from MTX therapy usually does not occur until after a 1.5 gm cumulative dose of the drug has been administered.[31,32] Unfortunately, hepatotoxicity may not be apparent on routine laboratory evaluation. Liver biopsy is recommended when the cumulative dosage level reaches 1.5 gm and after each subsequent 1.0 to 1.5 gm increase in the cumulative dose. Risk factors for hepatotoxicity include daily methotrexate administration, heavy alcohol intake, diabetes, obesity, intravenous drug abuse, previous exposure to hepatotoxic drugs, and pretreatment liver dysfunction. Liver function abnormalities may improve after cessation of MTX therapy for six months or more.[49]

8. During a follow-up visit to his family doctor several months later, several somatic complaints lead to a diagnosis of recurrent depression. Subsequent history reveals that R.T. also has resumed his use of alcohol. He tends to drink 4 to 5 beers a night on weekends and when he is feeling low, although he does admit that sometimes the level of use is higher. His skin disease is relatively well controlled but joint complaints have persisted. What additional options now exist for R.T.?

Methotrexate should be discontinued as risks probably now exceed benefits, particularly since rheumatic complaints have not been controlled. Nonsteroidal anti-inflammatory agents can be given symptomatically. Hydroxychloroquine may be beneficial for joint symptoms despite the historical concerns about exacerbation of skin lesions. Though etretinate has many other effects and some hepatic enzyme abnormalities are encountered in 10% of patients, the drug does not show significant liver toxicity. This might be an alternative maintenance agent.

References

1 **Watson W.** Psoriasis: epidemiology and genetics. Dermatol Clin. 1984;2:363.

2 **Voorhees JJ.** Cyclic adenosine monophosphate regulation of normal and psoriatic epidermis. Arch Dermatol. 1982;118:869.

3 **Weintein GD et al.** Cell kinetic basis for pathophysiology of psoriasis. J Invest Dermatol. 1985;85:579.

4 **Updike J.** Personal history: at war with my skin. New Yorker. 2 Sept 1985.

5 **Rotstein H, Baker C.** The treatment of psoriasis. Med J Aust. 1990;152:153.

6 **Liden S.** Optimal efficacy of topical corticoids in psoriasis. Semin Dermatol. 1992;11:275.

7 **Katz HI et al.** Superpotent topical steroid treatment of psoriasis vulgaris—clinical efficacy and adrenal function. J Am Acad Dermatol. 1987;16:804.

8 **Lowe NJ et al.** The pharmacological variability of crude coal tar. Br J Dermatol. 1982;107:475.

9 **Dodd WA.** Tars—their role in the treatment of psoriasis. Dermatol Clin. 1993;11:131.

10 **Lin AN, Moses K.** Tar revisited. Int J Dermatol. 1985;24:216.

11 **Jones SK et al.** Further evidence of the safety of tar in the management of psoriasis. Br J Dermatol. 1985;113:97.

12 **Whitefield M.** Pharmaceutical formulation of anthralin. Br J Dermatol. 1981;105(Suppl. 20):28.

13 **Schulze H et al.** Combined tar-anthralin versus anthralin treatment lowers irritancy with unchanged antipsoriatic effect. J Am Acad Dermatol. 1987;14:19.

14 **Schaefer H et al.** Limited application period for dithranol in psoriasis. Preliminary report on penetration and clinical efficacy. Br J Dermatol. 1980;102:571.

15 **Marsden JR et al.** Measurement of the response of psoriasis to short-term application of anthralin. Br J Dermatol. 1983;108:209.

16 **Statham BN et al.** Short—contact dithranol therapy—a comparison with the Ingram regimen. Br J Dermatol. 1984;110:703.

17 **Krabgalle K et al.** Calcipotriol—a new topical antipsoriatic. Dermatol Clin. 1993;1:137.

18 **Binderup L, Bramm E.** Effects of a novel vitamin D analogue MC 903 on cell proliferation and differentiation in vitro and on calcium metabolism in vivo. Biochem Pharmacol. 1988;37:889.

19 **Parrish JA, Jaenicke KF.** Action spectrum for phototherapy of psoriasis. J Invest Dermatol. 1981;76:359.

20 **Stern RS et al.** Contribution of topical tar oil to ultraviolet B phototherapy for psoriasis. J Am Acad Dermatol. 1986;14:742.

21 **Lowe NJ, Stern RS.** Contribution of topical tar oil to ultraviolet B phototherapy for psoriasis. J Am Acad Dermatol. 1986;15:1053.

22 **Sander HM et al.** The annual cost of psoriasis. J Am Acad Dermatol. 1993;28:422.

23 **Abel EA.** Clinical and histological changes in PUVA-treated skin. In: Callen JP et al., eds. Current Issues in Dermatology. Vol 2. Boston: GK Hall; 1984:163.

24 **Abel EA et al.** Treatment of palmoplantar psoriasis with topical methoxsalen plus long-wave ultraviolet light. Arch Dermatol. 1980;116:1257.

25 **Wolska H et al.** Etretinate in severe psoriasis: results of a double-blind study and maintenance therapy in pustular psoriasis. J Am Acad Dermatol. 1983;9:883.

26 **Kaplan RP et al.** Etretinate therapy for psoriasis: clinical responses, remission times, epidermal DNA and polyamine responses. J Am Acad Dermatol. 1983;8:85.

27 **Logan RA.** Efficacy of etretinate for the PUVA-dependent psoriatic. Clin Exp Dermatol. 1987;12:98.

28 **Geiger JM, Saurat JH.** Acitretin and etretinate—how and when they should be used. Dermatol Clin. 1993;11:117.

29 **Ellis CN, Voorhees JJ.** Etretinate therapy. J Am Acad Dermatol. 1987;16:267.

30 **Bleyer WA.** The clinical pharmacology of methotrexate. Cancer. 1978;41:36.

31 **Roenigk HH et al.** Methotrexate in psoriasis: revised guidelines. J Am Acad Dermatol. 1988;196:145.

32 **Ashton RE et al.** Complications in methotrexate treatment of psoriasis with particular reference to liver fibrosis. J Invest Dermatol. 1982;79:229.

33 **Slagel GA, James WD.** Plaquenil-induced erythroderma. J Am Acad Dermatol. 1985;12:857.

34 **Abel EA et al.** Drugs in exacerbation of psoriasis. J Am Acad Dermatol. 1986;15:1007.

35 **Schur PH et al.** Clinical, immunologic and genetic study of 100 patients with psoriatic arthritis. Arthritis Rheum. 1979;22:656.

36 **Lowe NJ, Ridgway HB.** Generalized pustular psoriasis precipitated by lithium carbonate. Arch Dermatol. 1978;114:1788.

37 **Skoven I, Thormann J.** Lithium compound treatment and psoriasis. Arch Dermatol. 1979;115:1185.

38 **Gold MH et al.** Beta-blocking drugs and psoriasis. J Am Acad Dermatol. 1988;19:837.

39 **Katayama H, Kawada A.** Exacerbation of psoriasis induced by indomethacin. J Dermatol. 1981;8:233.

40 **Voorhees JJ.** Cyclic adenosine monophosphate regulation of normal and psoriatic epidermis. Arch Dermatol. 118:869.

41 **Winthrop GJ.** Does meclofenamate help psoriasis and arthritis. N Engl J Med. 1982;307:1528. Letter.

42 **Degreef H, Dooms-Goossens A.** The new corticosteroids: are they effective and safe? Dermatol Clin. 1993;11:155.

43 **Liden S.** Optimal efficacy of topical corticoids in psoriasis. Semin Dermatol. 1992;11:275.

44 **Lowe NJ.** Therapy of scalp psoriasis. Dermatol Clin. 1984;2:471.

45 **Chuang T, Samson CR.** 0.05 percent betamethasone dipropionate in optimized cream vehicle for psoriasis. Cutis. 1989;43:178.

46 **Ellis CN et al.** A controlled clinical trial of a new formulation of betamethasone dipropionate cream in once-daily treatment of psoriasis. Clin Ther. 1989;11:768.

47 **Bickers D et al.** Clobetasol propionate ointment once daily versus fluocinonide ointment three times daily in psoriasis. Clin Trials. 1988;27:54.

48 **Elmets LA.** Drug-induced photo allergy. Dermatol Clin. 1986;4:231,332.

49 **Stern RS.** The epidemiology of joint complaints in patients with psoriasis. J Rheumatol. 1985;12:315.

50 **Newman M et al.** The role of liver biopsies in psoriatic patients receiving long-term methotrexate treatment: improvement in liver abnormalities after cessation of treatment. Arch Dermatol. 1989;125:1218.

Photosensitivity and Burns

Allan T Mailloux

Photosensitivity 39-1
  Effects of Ultraviolet Radiation 39-1
    Ultraviolet radiation (UVR) spectrum
      (See Figure 39.1) 39-2
    Environmental Effects on UVR 39-2
      Ozone and chlorofluorocarbons (CFCs) 39-2
      Solar flare 39-2
      Time of day, cloud cover, and surface
        reflection 39-2
    Erythema, sunburn, and tanning 39-2
      Erythema, oxygen free radicals, and
        antioxidants 39-2
      Histology of sunburn 39-2
      Immediate pigment darkening 39-2
      Delayed tanning 39-2
      Skin types (See Table 39.1) 39-3
    Photocarcinogenesis 39-3
      Risk factors 39-3
      Squamous cell (SCC) and basal cell carcinoma
        (BCC) 39-4
      Cutaneous malignant melanoma (CMM) 39-4
      The mechanisms of carcinogenesis 39-4
      Tanning booths 39-4
    Photoaging 39-5
      Normal aging and histology of photodamaged
        skin 39-5
      Topical tretinoin 39-5
        Patient selection 39-5
        Patient counseling 39-5
    Phototoxicity and photoallergy 39-6
      Patient history 39-6
      Photosensitizers and symptoms of
        phototoxicity 39-6
      Photosensitizers and symptoms of
        photoallergy 39-7
      Treatment 39-7
  Photoprotection 39-7
    Broad-spectrum products (See Table 39.2) 39-7
    Evaluation of sunscreens 39-7
      Sun protection factor (SPF) 39-7
      Substantivity (See Table 39.3) 39-7
      Sunburn preventative and suntanning agents 39-9
    Chemical sunscreens 39-9
      Molar absorptivity and absorbance spectrum 39-9
      Para-aminobenzoic acid (PABA) and esters 39-9

      Cinnamates 39-9
      Salicylates 39-9
      Benzophenones 39-9
      Anthranilates 39-9
      Dibenzoylmethanes 39-9
    Physical sunscreens 39-10
    Product selection 39-10
      Cross-sensitivity 39-10
      Application 39-10
    Photoprotection for children 39-11
      Age-related recommendations and other
        protective behavior 39-11
      Product selection 39-11
    Photoeffects on the eye 39-11
      Cataract formation 39-11
      Protective eyewear 39-11
    Treatment of sunburn 39-11
Minor Burns 39-11
  Epidemiology 39-12
  Pathophysiology 39-12
    Structure and function of the skin 39-12
    Zones of injury 39-12
    Complications of burn wounds 39-12
      Fluid loss 39-12
      Infection 39-12
      Inhalation injury 39-12
  Extent of injury 39-13
    ''Rule of nines'' 39-13
    Classification of wounds 39-13
      First-degree burns 39-13
      Second-degree burns 39-13
      Third-degree burns 39-13
      Fourth-degree burns 39-13
  Triage 39-13
    American Burn Association treatment
      categories 39-13
    Age-related recommendations 39-13
    Disease-related recommendations 39-13
    Etiology of burn 39-14
  Treatment 39-14
    Goals of treatment and immediate care 39-14
    Synthetic dressings 39-14
    Topical antimicrobials 39-14
    Oral analgesics and topical protectants 39-14
    Tetanus immunization 39-14

Photosensitivity

Effects of Ultraviolet Radiation

Over the last several decades, human exposure to sunlight has increased considerably because of changing life-styles: more outdoor recreational activities, more emphasis on tanning, people living longer, and population shifts to the sunbelt. Public attitudes towards tanning and sun exposure have not changed even though epidemiologic evidence clearly implicates sunlight as a causative factor in many skin diseases. Squamous cell carcinoma (SCC) and basal cell carcinoma (BCC), which together account for more than half of all malignancies in the U.S., are linked closely to exposure to ultraviolet radiation (UVR).[1] Malignant melanoma, incidence of which has increased more than 100% in the last decade, most likely is linked to UVR exposure.[2] Sunburn, photoaging, immunologic changes in the skin, cataracts, photodermatoses, phototoxicity, and photoallergy are other commonly encountered photosensitivity reactions. Photoprotective agents, or sunscreens and sunblocks, are effective at protecting the skin against these adverse effects of UVR. Patient education and the use of sunscreens or other protective behaviors can help reduce the incidence of the adverse effects of UVR.

Ultraviolet Radiation (UVR) Spectrum

The spectrum of electromagnetic radiation that reaches the earth's surface represents a continuum of wavelengths from radio waves to UVR.[3] Within this continuum of wavelengths, UVR is the primary inducer of photosensitivity reactions in humans. UVR is divided into ranges according to the biological effects of the different wavelengths: UVA, UVB, and UVC (see Figure 39.1). *UVA* with wavelength of 320 to 400 nm is closest in wavelength to visible light.[3] UVA can cause erythema, but is about 1000 times less potent than a comparable dose of UVB to cause the same effect.[4-6] Unlike UVB, UVA penetrates to the dermis of human skin and may cause additional deleterious effects not caused by UVB.[7,8] UVA is attenuated only slightly by the earth's stratospheric ozone layer and reaches the earth's surface in 10 to 100 times the amount of UVB. Consequently, it may contribute up to 15% of the erythemal response at midday.[4,6,8] UVA has been divided further according to the biological effects on the skin. UVA I ranges in wavelength from 340 to 400 nm and is less erythrogenic and melanogenic than UVA II or UVB. UVA II ranges in wavelength from 320 to 340 nm and is similar in effect to UVB.[9] UVR of wavelengths greater than 340 nm have little erythrogenic potential. *UVB* ranges in wavelength from 290 to 320 nm and is the most erythrogenic and melanogenic of the three UVR bands.[3,4,7] Ninety percent of UVB is blocked by the earth's stratospheric ozone layer and it is absorbed completely by the epidermal layer of the skin.[8,10] Small amounts of UVB are required for the homeostasis of vitamin D in the body, which is the only known beneficial effect of UVR in humans.[8] UVC ranges in wavelength from 200 to 290 nm and is absorbed completely by the earth's stratospheric ozone layer. Artificial sources of UVC have found applications in laboratories and hospital operating rooms as germicidal lamps and may cause erythema or cataracts if mishandled.[4,7]

Environmental Effects on UVR

Ozone and Chlorofluorocarbons (CFCs). The amount of UVR that reaches the earth's surface is influenced by many factors. Recent concern has been focused on the implications of the possible depletion of the ozone layer.[6,10,11] Since detected in 1983, ozone levels above the Antarctic have fallen to 50% of normal during the Antarctic spring.[12] Estimates from the Environmental Protection Agency (EPA) predict a 40% depletion of ozone would occur by the year 2075 if controls on chlorofluorocarbons (CFCs) are not enacted. The EPA also concluded that for every 1% decrease in ozone, UVB radiation reaching the earth's surface would increase by 2% per year, possibly resulting in a 1% to 3% increase per year in nonmelanoma skin cancer.[10,13] These losses in the ozone layer are thought to be caused by man-made pollutants such as nitrous oxides from stratospheric aviation and CFCs from propellants and refrigerants.

Solar flare activity, which follows an 11-year cycle, also influences the amount of ozone in the stratosphere.[10] With increased solar flare activity, more UVR from the sun is available to split doublet oxygen molecules, which then recombine with another doublet oxygen molecule to form the ozone molecule, or oxygen triplet molecule. The equilibrium of ozone is shifted towards higher concentrations of ozone, which absorbs more UVB. Since UVA is only slightly filtered by the ozone layer, any decrease in the ozone layer would result in a disproportionate increase in UVB reaching the earth.

Time of Day, Cloud Cover, and Surface Reflection. Time of day also influences the amount of UVR reaching the earth's surface; 20% to 30% of the total daily UVR is received from 11 a.m. to 1 p.m. and 75% between 9 a.m. and 3 p.m. Cloud cover can decrease UV intensity by 10% to 80% but decreases infrared radiation to an even greater extent. This greater attenuation of infrared radiation by cloud cover may lead to an increased risk of UVR overexposure because less infrared radiation will be absorbed by the body and transformed into heat resulting in less warning of overexposure to UVR. Reflection of UVR by substances (e.g., sand, water) also may be important in certain situations. Sand reflects about 25% of incident UVB radiation; therefore, sitting under an umbrella at the beach may not offer adequate protection. Fresh snow may reflect 50% to 95% of incident sunlight. Water probably reflects only about 5% of erythemal UVR, whereas 75% of the radiation is transmitted through 2 m of water, offering swimmers little protection.[3,5] Seasonal changes, geographic latitude, and altitude also influence the amount of UVR reaching the earth's surface.

Erythema, Sunburn, and Tanning

Erythema, Oxygen Free Radicals, and Antioxidants. Excessive exposure of the epidermal and dermal layers of the skin to UVR can result in an inflammatory erythematous reaction. Both UVA and UVB can cause release of vasodilatory mediators (e.g., histamine, prostaglandins, cytokines) resulting in increased blood flow, erythema, tissue exudates, swelling, and increased sensation of warmth.[4,7,8,14] These neurochemical mediators, therefore, cause the characteristic burning and itching associated with sunburn.[7] Severe exposure to UVR may result in blister formation, desquamation, fever, chills, weakness, and shock.[15] The epidermis is affected most by UVB. Erythema caused by UVB begins within three to five hours after exposure, is maximal after 12 to 24 hours, and disappears over the ensuing three days.[7,9] Erythema caused by UVA begins immediately, plateaus between 6 and 12 hours, and remains for 24 hours.[9] UVA changes in the dermis are characterized by greater damage to the vasculature and dense cellular infiltrates that penetrate to deeper levels of the skin.[8] Dermal layers also may be damaged when endogenous components of the skin absorb UVR energy and subsequently interact with oxygen to form tissue-damaging oxygen free radicals.[9] These concepts serve as the basis of the rationale for the treatment of UVR-induced skin damage with topically applied and orally ingested antioxidants such as vitamins A, C, and E, and beta-carotene.[16,17]

Histology of Sunburn. The skin also undergoes adaptive changes in response to exposure to UVR. Keratinocytes in the epidermis are damaged and lose their typical organization, resulting in hyperkeratosis, or thickening of the epidermis and stratum corneum.[6,8] Hyperkeratosis then serves as a more effective barrier to UVR, particularly to UVB. These damaged keratinocytes are called sunburn cells. The skin's normal immune response is altered with exposure to UVR. Langerhans' cells, antigen-presenting cells found in the skin, are decreased in number and function even after small doses of UVB.[6,18] These cells abnormally activate suppressor T-lymphocytes and lose their ability to activate normal effector pathways of the immune system.[6,19,20] UVR also inhibits contact hypersensitivity in exposed skin.[21]

Immediate Pigment Darkening and Delayed Tanning. Tanning is an adaptive mechanism of the skin to UVR. Tanning occurs by two different mechanisms: immediate pigment darkening and delayed tanning. The primary cell involved in tanning is the melanocyte, which produces the radiation-absorbing chemical, melanin.[3,4,6] Immediate pigment darkening begins during exposure to UVA and certain bands of visible light,[4,6] and is the result of oxidation of existing melanin in the skin which transiently turns the skin grayish, brown. The degree of immediate pigment darkening is dependent upon the duration and intensity of exposure, the extent of previous tanning (or amount of pre-existing melanin), and the skin type of the individual.[4] Immediate pigment darkening is not

Fig 39.1   Ultraviolet Radiation Spectrum   *Erythrogenic and melanogenic bands of UVR.

protective against UVB erythema.[6] Delayed tanning is caused by either UVA or UVB and occurs 48 to 72 hours after exposure. It then peaks at seven to ten days and may last for weeks to months.[4] Delayed tanning is the result of increased production of melanin, an increase in the size and dendricity of the melanocyte, and the rate of transfer of melanosomes (particulate bodies of melanin) to keratinocytes.[4,6] The keratinocyte, now pigmented with melanosomes, migrates to the epidermis, producing the characteristic suntan. Delayed tanning caused by UVA is less protective against sunburn than delayed tanning caused by UVB probably because thickening of the epidermis is not caused by UVA.[4]

1. Skin Types. L.M., a 26-year-old female, and G.M., a 28-year-old male, are a recently married couple going on a 2-week cruise to the Caribbean and are inquiring about sunscreens for their trip. L.M. is of fair complexion with blond hair and blue eyes and G.M. is of light-brown complexion with brown hair and brown eyes. Upon summer's first sun exposure to about an hour of intense sunlight, L.M. almost always develops a deep red, painful sunburn with only minimal subsequent tanning. She freckles easily when exposed to sunlight and remembers being severely sunburned on several occasions as a child. G.M., upon first significant sun exposure of the summer, usually only develops mild redness followed by moderate tanning. He does not remember ever being severely sunburned as a child but does recall becoming moderately tanned each summer as a child and adolescent. L.M. is employed as a receptionist for an accounting firm and G.M. works outdoors for a construction company. Both spend considerable amounts of time participating in outdoor activities. What data in this history would influence your recommendation of a sunscreen product for G.M. and L.M.?

One of the most important pieces of information to include in the patient history is the patient's skin type.[9,22] Patients can be classified into six sun-reactive skin types based upon their skin color, tendency to sunburn, ability to tan, and personal history of sunburn (see Table 39.1). L.M.'s fair complexion, propensity to sunburn, and minimal tanning would classify her as skin type II. G.M.'s light-brown complexion, minimal sunburn reaction, and moderate tanning would classify him as skin type IV. *Hair and eye color* also give an indication as to skin-reactiveness to sunlight. Individuals who have blond, red, or light-brown hair, or who have blue or green eyes, tend to have greater skin-reactivity to sunlight than do individuals with darker colored hair or eyes. *History of severe sunburn* also may be associated with skin reactivity to sunlight, although self-reported patient histories of sunburn (as well as tanning) may be unreliable.[23] L.M.'s propensity to freckle and her history of severe sunburns as a child may give an indication as to her skin sun-reactiveness. Other important information to consider in the patient history includes a medication history, history of sun-reactive dermatoses, history of allergies (particularly contact hypersensitivities to cosmetics or other topical agents), and intended activities while using the sunscreens.

Photocarcinogenesis

2. Risk Factors. What subjective and objective evidence do L.M. and G.M. exhibit that place them at risk for the long-term adverse effects of UVR? What are the risk factors for these long-term adverse effects of UVR?

The long-term effects of UVR include photocarcinogenesis and photoaging (premature aging of the skin). Risks for these long-term effects are related directly to the congenital pigmentation of

Table 39.1	Patient Skin Types for Sunburn Potential and Suggested Product SPF[a-c]		
Complexion Description	Skin Type	Patient Skin Characteristics	Suggested Product SPF
Very fair	I	Always burns easily; never tans	≥15
Fair	II	Always burns easily; tans minimally	≥15
Light	III	Burns moderately; tans gradually	10–15
Medium	IV	Burns minimally; always tans well	6–10
Dark	V	Rarely burns; tans profusely	4–6
Very dark	VI	Never burns; deeply pigmented	None necessary

[a] Reprinted with permission from reference 22.
[b] Based upon first 45–60 min of sun exposure after winter season (no sun exposure).
[c] SPF = Sun protection factor.

an individual (which includes skin type and hair and eye color) and intensity, duration, and frequency of exposure to UVR.[24] L.M., who is of skin type II, is at high risk for carcinogenesis and photoaging, whereas G.M., who is of skin type IV, is considered to have relatively low risk.[9] Excessive sun exposure, especially during childhood, increases the risk of nonmelanoma and melanoma skin cancers. During the first 18 years of life, the average child receives three times the dose of UVB of the average adult; consequently, the majority of sun exposure occurs during childhood.[25] A history of frequent sunburn, or intermittent high-intensity exposures to UVR, may be associated with the occurrence of malignant melanoma, whereas large cumulative doses of UVR over a lifetime seem to contribute to the incidence of nonmelanoma skin cancers.[25,26] L.M.'s history of several severe sunburns as a child may more than double her risk of cutaneous malignant melanoma (CMM).[24] Cumulative doses of UVR received unintentionally from working outdoors or from participating in outdoor recreational activities also can contribute significantly to the risk photocarcinogenesis and photoaging.[5,21,25] A large number of moles, congenital moles greater than 1.5 cm in diameter, and abnormal moles also appear to be a risk factor for malignant melanoma.[27,28]

Squamous Cell (SCC) and Basal Cell Carcinoma (BCC). Evidence linking skin cancer in humans and UVR exposure are mostly clinical and epidemiological in nature. Nonmelanoma skin cancers, squamous cell carcinoma and basal cell carcinoma, occur most commonly on areas exposed to sunlight: the head, neck, arms, and hands.[4,19] Their incidence is inversely related to geographic distance from the equator and to the melanin content of the skin.[19] Persons of skin types most sensitive to sunlight, as well as those persons working outdoors, have higher incidences of skin cancers.[4] Albinism, a genetic disease characterized by partial or total absence of pigment in the skin, hair, and eyes, is associated with increased and premature development of skin cancers.[4,19] SCC is linked more strongly to UVR than BCC.[4,19,21] Laboratory animal models clearly demonstrate the relationship of skin cancer to UVR exposure.[4,6,19,21]

Cutaneous malignant melanoma (CMM) also may be linked to UVR exposure, although the evidence is not as clear as for squamous and basal cell carcinoma. Cutaneous malignant melanoma, like nonmelanoma skin cancers, demonstrates an inverse relation-

ship to geographic distance from the equator and melanin content of the skin.[4] A history of sunburn is common in individuals with CMM[4] and exposure early in life may be important.[21] Unlike nonmelanoma skin cancers, however, cutaneous malignant melanoma does not demonstrate a clear relationship to the cumulative dose of UVR, nor does it occur on areas of the body most frequently exposed to sunlight.[6] In addition, it occurs most commonly in the middle-aged and individuals who work indoors.[4]

The mechanisms of carcinogenesis may include damage to DNA and alterations in immunologic status. Epidermal and dermal DNA can absorb UVR, which can result in the abnormal formation of pyrimidine dimers. In normal circumstances, these pyrimidine dimers are excised and repaired. If left uncorrected, these DNA lesions can lead to interruption of transcription and possibly mutagenesis and malignancy.[9,29] An example of this process is the genetic disease *xeroderma pigmentosa*. Individuals with xeroderma pigmentosa are unable to repair pyrimidine dimers and are extremely susceptible to sun-induced skin cancers.[21] Pyrimidine dimer formation can be caused by both UVB and UVA, with UVB of shorter wavelengths being more efficient.[4,29,30]

Altered immunologic function of the skin also may be a mechanism in carcinogenesis. As mentioned above, Langerhans' cells are decreased in number and function, resulting in possible failure of the immune system to recognize tumor antigens. In addition, UVR-induced changes in Langerhans' cells may abnormally activate suppressor T-lymphocytes. This may promote tumor growth by causing the emergence of ''tumor-specific suppressor T-cells'' that prevent the immune system from destroying the cancer cells.[19] Additional evidence for the role of the immune system in carcinogenesis comes from patients receiving immunosuppressant drugs. Immunosuppressed renal transplant patients experience a higher incidence of sun-induced skin cancers.[21,29]

3. Tanning Booths. **N.B., a 20-year-old female, is preparing for her trip to Florida. She is seeking advice about the use of a tanning booth to stimulate melanin for the prevention of sunburn while on her trip. N.B. has skin type III with light brown hair and green eyes. She recently heard, however, that suntans produced by artificial sunlight may not protect against sunburn and may even cause skin cancer. What advice will you offer N.B.? What precautions would you recommend if she decides to frequent a tanning booth?**

Tanning booths and salons use an artificial light source which emits about 95% UVA and 1% to 5% UVB.[17] Even though UVA is much less likely to produce photoaging and photocarcinogenic changes of the skin than UVB, the high doses of UVA received during a tanning session and increasing cumulative doses of UVA over time, coupled with increased exposure to sunlight in general, raise great concern over the long-term effects of UVA. UVA causes many of the same effects on the skin as UVB including: immunologic, degenerative, and neoplastic changes, as well as damage to DNA and the formation of oxygen-reactive species. UVA also causes cataract formation and activates herpetic lesions.[17,31] In addition, UVA may augment the photocarcinogenic effect of UVB.[2]

Being of skin type III, N.B. may be able to gradually achieve a moderate tan with minimal burning, which may provide some protection from UVR due to increased melanization of the skin. This UVA-induced tan, however, may not be as protective as a tan achieved under normal sunlight conditions because thickening of the stratum corneum is not caused by UVA.[31] There is no evidence that an artificially produced tan plus subsequent sun exposure provides any net reduction in long-term damage to the skin when compared to the same amount of tan obtained by sunbathing alone.[1] For these reasons, N.B. should not use the tanning booth to obtain a protective tan for her trip. She should, however, use appropriate photoprotective measures while on her trip.

If N.B. decides to artificially tan despite your recommendation, it is important that she follow some guidelines. Since she is skin type III, she should limit her exposure to ≤30 to 50 half-hour sessions a year and keep a total record of joules of exposure that she has received over time.[4] N.B. always should wear protective eye wear that absorbs all UVA, UVB, and visible light up to 500 nm; simply closing her eyes or wearing regular sunglasses does not protect against eye damage. The tanning device should be calibrated properly with an accurate timer and staffed by an attendant in case of an emergency.[4]

Photoaging

Normal Aging and Histology of Photodamaged Skin. Photoaging, or premature aging of the skin, involves skin changes that are different from those associated with normal chronological aging.[32,33] Normal aging of the skin involves fine wrinkling of the skin, atrophy of the dermis, and a decrease in the amount of subcutaneous adipose tissue, all of which lead to a state of hypocellularity of the skin.[32] Photoaging involves a chronic inflammatory state induced by long-term exposure to sunlight, leading to a hypermetabolic state of the skin.[14,34] Photodamaged skin is characterized histologically by excessive quantities of thickened, tangled elastic fibers. This accumulation of degenerated connective tissue is called elastosis.[4,14,21,32] In normal skin, type I collagen predominates, but in photodamaged skin, there is about a fourfold increase in type III collagen with a slight decrease in type I collagen.[34] Photodamaged skin, therefore, contains a decreased amount of mature collagen matrix. These degenerative changes in connective tissue may be caused by hyperactive fibroblasts or by enzymatic degradation via cellular infiltrates in inflamed skin.[4,34] The elastotic (degenerated connective tissue) material then replaces the collagen in upper parts of the dermis.[32] The ground substance, composed of proteoglycans and glycosaminoglycans, also is increased greatly in photoaged skin.[4,34] Capillaries in the dermis become dilated and tortuous resulting in telangiectasias, ecchymosis, and purpura.[4,32,34] The epidermis becomes thickened and epidermal cells become hyperplastic, and possibly neoplastic.[34] Actinic keratosis is a premalignant lesion found mostly in the older population, where a small percentage of these lesions transform into squamous cell carcinoma.[4] UVB is strongly implicated as the cause of these changes in photoaged skin.[4,21,33,34] Large cumulative doses of UVA, and even infrared radiation, over a lifetime may play a significant role in its genesis as well.[21,34]

Clinically, photodamaged skin is characterized by wrinkled, yellowed, and sagging skin. Mildly affected skin becomes irregularly pigmented, rough and dry with mild wrinkles.[14] Moderately affected skin becomes deeply wrinkled, sagging, thickened, and leathery, with vascular lesions.[14] Deep furrows formed behind the neck commonly may be seen and are called cutis rhomboidalis nuchae. Severely affected skin may become deeply furrowed, permanently (and irregularly) pigmented, and may manifest premalignant and malignant lesions.[14] The areas of the body most frequently affected are the face, back of the neck, back of the arms and hands, the ''V''-line of the neck of women, and the bald head of men.[4] These changes are largely irreversible.

4. Topical Tretinoin. P.B., a 38-year-old female who has enjoyed many outdoor activities over the years, lives in a moderate climate with hot, sunny summers and cold winters. She feels that she appears older than women her age due to wrinkling and color changes of her skin. She has noticed that her facial color has become somewhat yellowish in appearance and that the fine wrinkles at the corners of her eyes and mouth have become more obvious. She has noticed the formation of small brown spots mottling parts of her face, hands, and forearms. P.B. has skin type III, a clear complexion, and skin that is sensitive to soaps, heavy cosmetics, and perfumes. She presently is not sexually active. Is topical tretinoin (Retin-A) therapy effective for the treatment of skin changes associated with photoaging? Would P.B. be an appropriate candidate for therapy with topical tretinoin cream?

Tretinoin (all-trans-retinoic acid) in the form of a cream (0.05% and 0.1%) and an emollient cream (0.001%, 0.01%, and 0.05%) is effective in partially reversing some of the clinical and histological changes of photoaging.[35–42] In a double-blind, controlled study of 30 patients treated with tretinoin 0.1% cream, all tretinoin-treated forearms and 93% of tretinoin-treated faces were improved clinically and histologically after 16 weeks of treatment.[43] No patients in the placebo vehicle-treated groups showed improvement. Statistically significant clinical improvements included lessening of fine and coarse wrinkling and increased pinkness and smoothness of the skin. Statistically significant histological improvements included increased epidermal thickness, decreased dysplasia of the stratum corneum, and decreased melanocyte activity. During the study, 92% of subjects experienced dermatitis characterized by erythema, scaling, peeling, itching, and burning or tingling. In a subsequent open-label trial, these same patients, along with 480 clinic patients, continued to experience improvements in fine and coarse wrinkling for more than two years, despite reductions in dose or frequency of tretinoin application.[44] Substantial improvements were achieved in most patients between 9 and 16 months of treatment.[44,45] In a large multicenter, double-blind, vehicle-controlled study, tretinoin 0.01% and 0.05% emollient cream were administered for six months to 251 patients 29 to 50 years of age who had mild to moderate photoaging.[42] Subjects treated with the 0.05% strength experienced reductions in fine wrinkling, mottled hyperpigmentation, and roughness compared to pretreatment scores. These improvements were significantly better than those observed with the 0.01% tretinoin or the control-vehicle. Histologic changes included significant increases in epidermal thickness and granular layer thickness after six months of 0.05% or 0.01% tretinoin and decreased melanin content in subjects who applied 0.05% tretinoin. Side effects, which included erythema, peeling, burning, and stinging, were more common in the 0.05% tretinoin group than in the 0.01% tretinoin or vehicle groups. The side effects, as well as the clinical and histological improvements, appear to be dose dependent. These reactions were reported as mild to moderate and were noted to decrease gradually after the second week of therapy. Other investigations have demonstrated similar clinical and histological results. Additional benefits of tretinoin therapy include the formation of new dermal collagen and vessels, reduction in the number and melanization of freckles, resorption of elastotic masses, and treatment of premalignant and malignant skin lesions.[45,46]

Patient Selection. Topical tretinoin therapy is most effective for patients 50 to 70 years of age with moderate to severe photoaging and for prophylactic use in patients undergoing the initial changes of photoaging.[46] P.B. recently has noticed some of the skin changes consistent with early photoaging and would be a good candidate for prophylactic therapy with topical tretinoin. Treatment may improve her sallow skin color and lessen the mottling on her face and forearms and fine wrinkles at the corners of her eyes and mouth, as well as prevent worsening of the photoaging process that she is experiencing.

5. *Patient Counseling.* **Recommend appropriate therapy and provide patient counseling for P.B.**

Since both the beneficial and adverse effects of topical tretinoin are dose dependent, the underlying goal for topical tretinoin therapy is to provide the maximal benefit by using the highest strength of tretinoin that causes minimal skin irritation. Considering P.B.'s skin sensitivity to soaps, cosmetics, and perfumes, her skin is likely to be irritated easily by tretinoin; therefore, it would be best to initiate therapy with the lowest strength, tretinoin 0.025% cream. The tretinoin usually is applied every night at bedtime, but in some instances it is applied on an every-other-night basis. Tretinoin is available in a 0.05% and 0.1% cream, a 0.05% solution, and a 0.01% and 0.025% gel. The likelihood of irritation depends upon the type of vehicle more than on the strength of tretinoin.[46] The cream causes the least skin irritation of the three formulations and would be preferred for initiating therapy for P.B. The solution tends to be quite drying and irritating and is preferred for patients with persistent acne or in patients with focal actinic lesions. The gel vehicle can evaporate resulting in the potentiation of the effects of tretinoin. Younger patients often prefer the gel because it leaves no residue and is compatible with most cosmetics. Both the solution and gel may be better tolerated in older patients with oily, thick, pigmented skin.[46]

Before applying the cream to her face at bedtime, P.B. should wash her face gently using her fingertips and mild soap, then pat her skin dry with a towel. If gentle washing with her fingers does not remove the dry, peeling skin, a washcloth can be used gently on the face. The tretinoin-treated stratum corneum is fragile, and erosions may occur if P.B. is not careful when washing. After waiting about 15 minutes, she should apply a pea-sized amount of cream to her forehead and spread the cream evenly over her entire face. Care should be exercised while applying the cream to the areas adjacent to the eyes and mouth, since it can cause irritation and burning of mucous membranes. Skin irritation can be expected to start in the first days of therapy and hopefully will subside in one to three months. If P.B. experiences excessive irritation, she can apply the cream on an every-other-night or every-third-night basis to reduce skin irritation, or apply a topical steroid such as hydrocortisone 1% cream. As she begins to tolerate the therapy, her frequency of applications and strength of cream should be titrated to cause mild scaling with only occasional mild erythema. A thicker film of cream can be applied to photodamaged areas. After 9 to 12 months of therapy, she can begin maintenance therapy, which consists of application two or three nights a week indefinitely.[45,46]

P.B. should be counseled about a few other issues as well. Since tretinoin therapy dries the skin, daytime application of moisturizers will help to decrease the dryness and irritability of the skin. Nighttime application of moisturizers should be discouraged because the moisturizers can cause a pH incompatibility with the tretinoin cream and perhaps dilute the concentration of tretinoin. Since tretinoin causes thinning of the stratum corneum, P.B.'s skin may be more susceptible to the effects of UVR. For this reason, as well as to prevent further actinic damage, P.B. should begin prophylactic daytime application of a sunscreen. Considering her skin type (III) and early photoaging changes, a sunscreen with a sun protection factor (SPF) of ≥15 would be appropriate. P.B. should be counseled to not become discouraged by any apparent lack of response; her skin damage is mild, her response to therapy will be gradual, and part of the goal of therapy is to prevent further damage. Actually, her wrinkles may appear to worsen early in therapy due to an initial buildup of the stratum corneum. P.B. should avoid facial saunas and irritating soaps and cosmetics. Even though topical tretinoin is not well absorbed systemically and has not been associated with teratogenic effects of oral retinoids, P.B. should be counseled to discontinue tretinoin therapy if she desires to become pregnant.

Phototoxicity and Photoallergy

6. Patient History. **D.L., a 16-year-old, blond-haired, blue-eyed male of skin type II, presents to your clinic with the chief complaint of severe sunburn. He states that this sunburn, which occurred during the first day of his summer job (2 days ago), is worse than he normally gets for the amount of sun that he received. What nonprescription remedies might you recommend for D.L. at this time?**

Treatment recommendations for D.L.'s sunburn are inappropriate without first obtaining additional data (e.g., a history and brief visual examination of the condition). Information that may be important in the history of the condition include the temporal relationship between sun exposure and onset of symptoms, the nature and duration of symptoms, recent ingestion or topical application of medications, possible exposure to photosensitizers, chemical irritants, or plants that may cause allergic contact dermatitis (e.g., poison ivy), and the potential for arthropod bites. Information that may be important from the physical examination include the distribution and morphology of the reaction, as well as areas of the body spared of the reaction.

7. Photosensitizers and Symptoms of Phototoxicity. **Upon further questioning, you discover that D.L. first experienced painful erythema of the extensor surface of his hands and forearms, the anterior aspect of his neck, and parts of his face within hours of starting his new job at an outdoor garden and greenhouse. Besides painful erythema, the symptoms also included an immediate prickling and burning sensation. The symptoms continued to worsen until the following morning, about 24 hours after initial exposure to the sun. D.L. does not recall orally ingesting or topically applying any medication or other preparation to his skin, nor does he recall exposure to any chemical irritants or poison ivy or oak. The morphology of the skin lesions is that of an exaggerated sunburn. The skin lesions are patchy in distribution with greater density on his forearms and hands than on his neck and face. The posterior aspect of his neck and covered areas of his body were spared completely. What are some possible causes of his exaggerated sunburn reaction?**

The most likely explanation for D.L.'s exaggerated sunburn reaction is *phototoxicity* secondary to contact with psoralen-like chemicals from the plants at his job at the outdoor garden and greenhouse. Phototoxicity occurs when a UVA-absorbing compound reaches sufficient concentrations in or on the skin and when the skin is exposed simultaneously to an offending wavelength of light.[47] Polycyclic compounds are the main photosensitizers.[14] These compounds include many drugs (see Table 36.14 in Chapter 36: Dermatotherapy) and furocoumarin (psoralen-like) compounds. Furocoumarin compounds are found in many plants (e.g., citrus peels, parsley, celery, dandelions, sunflowers, Bishop's weed, and figs).[1] When the photosensitizing compound is deposited on the skin surface, the photosensitizer absorbs the radiologic energy and transfers the energy to surrounding molecules, which then become destructive to the surrounding tissue.[4,48] Clinically, phototoxicity is characterized by rapid onset of erythema, pain, prickling, or burning sensation of only the areas exposed to the sun, with peak symptoms occurring 24 to 48 hours after initial exposure. Blistering, desquamation, and subsequent hyperpigmentation may occur in severe cases.[1,48] Because phototoxicity reactions do not involve the immune system, prior exposure to the photosensitizer is not necessary for this reaction to occur.

D.L.'s contact with furocoumarin-containing plants and simultaneous exposure to sunlight, the unusual distribution of lesions on his hands, forearms, neck, and face, the lack of lesions on areas not contacted by the plants or sunlight, and the temporal relationship between the exposure and onset of symptoms make phototoxicity a likely diagnosis.

Photosensitizers and Symptoms of Photoallergy. Another possible diagnosis includes photoallergy. Photoallergy is much less common than phototoxicity and requires prior or prolonged exposure to the photosensitizing compound. Photoallergy results from a similar mechanism to phototoxicity except the immune system is involved. It is caused most commonly by polycyclic photosensitizers which react with UVA to form antigenic macromolecules evoking a delayed hypersensitivity response.[1,14,48] Clinically, photoallergy differs from phototoxicity in that it is an intensely pruritic, eczematous dermatitis (a severe rash).[14,48] The rash is preceded by pruritus and may subside within one hour.[4] In about 5% to 10% of cases, persistent hypersensitivity to light occurs, even when the offending chemical is eliminated.[48]

D.L. is unlikely to have a photoallergic reaction due to the lack of a delayed temporal relationship between the onset of symptoms and combined exposure to the plant furocoumarins and sunlight. Since photoallergy is a delayed hypersensitivity reaction, several days are needed before an immune response is mounted against the antigenic macromolecules. Also, unlike phototoxicity reactions, photoallergic reactions can spread to areas that have not been exposed to sunlight. Since D.L.'s lesions were limited to areas of skin exposed to sunlight, photoallergy is unlikely for this reason as well.

8. Treatment. What treatment recommendations should you give D.L.?

General treatment recommendations for phototoxicity and photoallergy reactions are to eliminate exposure to the photosensitizer, reduce exposure to the sun, and counsel patients not to receive any drugs, orally or topically, that can cause these reactions. In effort to eliminate exposure to the plant photosensitizers, D.L. should try wearing long-sleeve shirts, pants, and gloves when working. He also may try applying a broad-spectrum sunscreen to protect his skin from UVB and UVA radiation. If these measures do not prevent further photosensitivity reactions, D.L. should look for a different summer job. (See Question 13 for a discussion of treatment of acute sunburn.)

Photoprotection

Broad-Spectrum Products

Sunscreens are used to prevent sunburn and reduce the incidence of premature aging and carcinogenesis. Original formulations were developed to protect against the effects of UVB radiation because the potential adverse effects of UVA were not yet recognized. Since it is now recognized that UVA plays a significant role in many of the adverse effects of UVR, sunscreens with absorption spectra in the UVA range have been developed. Absorbers of UVA are used in combination with absorbers of UVB, resulting in broad-spectrum sunscreen products. These broad-spectrum products can provide additional benefit for patients with photosensitivity reactions caused by wavelengths not covered by single-ingredient sunscreens.

Sunscreens originally were considered in the U.S. to be cosmetics. In 1978 the Food and Drug Administration (FDA) Over-the-Counter (OTC) Review Panel on sunscreens reclassified sunscreens as drugs intended to protect "the structure and function of the human integument against actinic damage."[16,49] Table 39.2 lists the available sunscreens that are judged to be both safe and effective.

Evaluation of Sunscreens

Sun Protection Factor (SPF). The effectiveness of a sunscreen formulation is based upon its sun protection factor and its substan-

Table 39.2	Sunscreens and UVR Absorbances[a,b]
Suncreen	**Absorbances (nm)**
Anthranilate	
Methyl anthranilate[c]	260–380[f]
Benzophenones	
Oxybenzone[c]	270–350[f]
Dioxybenzone[c]	250–390[f]
Sulisobenzone[c]	260–375[f]
Cinnamates	
Ethyl hexyl p-methoxycinnamate[c]	290–320
Diethanolamine p-methoxycinnamate[c]	280–310
Octocrylene (Octyl-cyano-phenyl cinnamate)[c]	250–360[f]
Dibenzoylmethane	
Butyl methoxydibenzoylmethane (Parsol 1789)[d]	320–400
PABA and PABA Esters	
PABA[c]	260–313
Padimate O[c]	290–315
Glyceryl PABA[c]	264–315
Salicylates	
Ethylhexyl salicylate[c]	280–320
Homosalate[c]	295–315
Triethanolamine salicylate[c]	260–320
Others	
Phenylbenzimidazole sulphonic acid[c]	290–340[f]
Red petrolatum	290–365[e]

[a] Adapted with permission from reference 22.
[b] FDA = Food and Drug Administration; PABA = Para-aminobenzoic acid; UVR = Ultraviolet rays.
[c] Recommended by FDA Review Panel (1978) as safe and effective.
[d] FDA approved as a new drug (UVA absorber).
[e] Absorbs rays in the UVB range; at 334 nm transmits 16% of radiation and at 365 nm transmits 58% radiation; also is a physical blocker.
[f] Several of the Review Panel's recommended sunscreens have UVA and UVB absorbances, as seen above; 250 to >320 nm.

tivity.[1] The SPF is defined as the ratio of the minimal dose of UVR required to produce an erythemal response in sunscreen-protected skin compared to unprotected skin.[9,22] SPFs are based upon tests of volunteers with skin types I through III using either natural sunlight or a solar simulator that generates both UVB and UVA.[9,16] Since the SPF can be influenced by the composition, chemical properties, emollient properties, and pH of the vehicle, sunscreen formulations must be evaluated on an individual basis.[1] The SPF also is influenced by the amount applied to the skin and by environmental factors; therefore, the SPF achieved during actual use can be significantly less than indicated on the label.[50]

Substantivity also is a measure of the sunscreen formulation's effectiveness. The substantivity of a sunscreen formulation is its ability to adhere to the skin while swimming or perspiring. Labeling of a product as waterproof or water-resistant indicates that the SPF of the product was maintained after 80 minutes of moderate activity or 40 minutes while swimming, respectively. Labeling of the product as sweat-resistant indicates that the SPF of the product was maintained after 30 minutes of profuse sweating.[9,50–52] Testing normally is performed in indoor conditions, so the effects of the environment and evaporation of the vehicle may reduce the effectiveness of the sunscreen considerably.[24] The substantivity of a product is dependent upon the active ingredient and the vehicle (see Table 39.3).[50] Sunscreens which are lipophilic and vehicles such as ointments and water-in-oil emulsions tend to be of greater

Table 39.3	Common Commercially Available Sunscreen Products[a]			
Brand Name	Formulation	SPF	Substantivity[b]	Active Ingredients[b]
Hawaiian Tropic Baby Faces Sunblock	Lotion	50	Waterproof	Titanium dioxide, octocrylene, octyl
Hawaiian Tropic Sunblock	Lotion	45+		methoxycinnamate, octyl salicylate, benzophenone, octyl methoxycinnamate
PreSun 46 Moisturizing Sunscreen	Lotion	46	NA	Octyl dimethyl PABA, oxybenzone
PreSun 15 Moisturizing Sunscreen	Lotion	15		
PreSun Facial	Cream	15		
PreSun 8 Moisturizing	Lotion	8		
Water Babies Sunblock	Lotion	45	Waterproof	Ethylhexyl p-methoxycinnamate,
Shade Sunblock	Lotion	45		2-ethylhexyl salicylate, octocrylene, oxybenzone
PreSun Active 30	Gel	30	Waterproof	Oxybenzone, octyl salicylate, octyl
PreSun 29 Sensitive Skin Sunscreen	Cream	29		methoxycinnamate
PreSun 25 Moisturizing Sunscreen	Lotion	25		
PreSun 23	Spray Mist	23		
PreSun 15 Sensitive Skin Sunscreen	Cream	15		
PreSun Active 15	Gel	15		
Shade Sunblock	Stick, Lotion	30	Waterproof	Ethylhexyl p-methoxycinnamate, oxybenzone,
Water Babies Sunblock	Lotion	30		2-ethylhexyl salicylate, homosalate
Hawaiian Tropic Sunblock	Lotion	30+	Waterproof	Homosalate, octyl salicylate, octyl methoxycinnamate, menthyl anthranilate, benzophenone
Hawaiian Tropic Baby Faces Sunblock	Lotion	25	Waterproof	Ethylhexyl p-methoxycinnamate, oxybenzone, octyl salicylate, methyl anthranilate
Coppertone 25 All Day Protection	Lotion	25	Waterproof	Ethylhexyl p-methoxycinnamate
Shade Sunblock	Gel	25	NA	Ethylhexyl p-methoxycinnamate, octyl salicylate, homosalate, oxybenzone
Hawaiian Tropic Water Sport 20	Lotion	20	Waterproof	Octyl methoxycinnamate, titanium dioxide, benzophenone
Hawaiian Tropic Land Sport 20	Lotion	20	Waterproof	Octyl methoxycinnamate, octyl salicylate, benzophenone
Hawaiian Tropic Baby Faces	Lotion	20	Waterproof	Octyl methoxycinnamate, menthyl anthranilate, octocrylene, benzophenone
Hawaiian Tropic 15 Plus Sunblock	Lotion	15+	Waterproof	Octyl methoxycinnamate, menthyl anthranilate,
Hawaiian Tropic 10 Plus Sunblock	Lotion	10+		benzophenone
Hawaiian Tropic 8 Plus Sunblock	Lotion	8+		
InZinc	Stick	20	Water resistant	Zinc oxide
Sunsparkle	Stick	18	Water resistant	Ethylhexyl p-methoxycinnamate, benzophenone-3, titanium dioxide
TI-Screen Natural	Lotion	16	Waterproof	Titanium dioxide
Hawaiian Tropic 15 Plus	Gel	15+	Waterproof	Octyl methoxycinnamate, menthyl anthranilate, benzophenone, octocrylene
Shade Sunblock	Gel	15	Waterproof	Ethylhexyl p-methoxycinnamate, oxybenzone
Coppertone 15	Lotion	15		
Water Babies Sunblock	Lotion	15		
Coppertone 8 All Day Protection	Lotion	8		
Coppertone 6	Lotion	6		
Coppertone 4	Lotion	4		
Photoplex Broad Spectrum Sunscreen	Lotion	15+	Water resistant	Padimate O, avobenzone, butyl methoxydibenzoylmethane
Total Eclipse Oily and Acne Prone Skin Sunscreen	Lotion	15	NA	Padimate O, oxybenzone, glyceryl PABA
Shade UVAguard	Lotion	15	Water resistant	Octyl methoxycinnamate, avobenzone, oxybenzone
Hawaiian Tropic Protective Tanning Dry Oil	Oil	6	Waterproof	Ethylhexyl p-methoxycinnamate homosalate, menthyl anthranilate
Coppertone 2	Oil	2	Waterproof	Homosalate

[a] Adapted with permission from reference 88.
[b] NA = Not available; PABA = Para-aminobenzoic acid.

substantivity. The addition of a film-forming polymer to the formulation, such as polyacrylamide, can add to the substantivity of a product.[9,53]

Sunburn Preventative and Suntanning Agents. The FDA has designated sunscreens according to their therapeutic use in sunscreen or sunburn products.[49] Sunburn preventative agents are those active ingredients that absorb ≥95% of UVB radiation and have the potential to prevent sunburn. Suntanning agents are those with active ingredients that absorb between 85% and 95% of UVB radiation; thereby allowing suntanning without significant sunburn in the average individual. Chemical sunscreens include both of the above designations. Opaque sunblocks, or physical sunscreens, are those active ingredients that reflect or scatter all UVA, UVB, and visible light; thereby preventing or minimizing sunburn and suntanning.[49]

Chemical Sunscreens

When electromagnetic energy encounters human skin, it is either reflected by the stratum corneum, absorbed by different constituents in the skin (e.g., melanin), or transmitted to deeper levels of the dermis.[50] Chemical sunscreens generally are aromatic compounds capable of absorbing UV energy at selective wavelengths. When applied to the skin, chemical sunscreens serve as exogenous filters of UVR, thereby protecting the skin structures from the adverse effects of the wavelengths absorbed.[22,50] These aromatic compounds then convert the high UVR energy into harmless longer-wave radiation, which may or may not be perceived as warmth.[50] Chemical sunscreens usually are nonopaque, because they do not absorb the wavelengths of visible light.[1]

Molar Absorptivity and Absorbance Spectrum. The effectiveness of an individual chemical sunscreen agent is determined by its molar absorptivity and absorption spectrum, which are determined mostly by the chemical structure of the sunscreen. The molar absorptivity is a measure of the amount of UVR absorbed by a particular sunscreen[50] and depends upon the concentration of the sunscreen in the product and the amount applied to the skin.[54] Sunscreens with an absorbance spectrum in the UVB range, and specifically a maximal absorbance around 310 to 320 nm, are the most effective at preventing sunburn.[54] Chemical sunscreens with absorption spectra in the UVB range are para-aminobenzoic acid (PABA) and its esters, cinnamates, and the salicylates. Those sunscreens with absorption spectra which extend into the UVA range are the anthranilates and benzophenones. The newer drug, butyl methoxydibenzoylmethane (Parsol 1789), has an absorption spectrum of 320 to 400 nm, or the entire UVA range.[55,56]

Para-Aminobenzoic Acid (PABA) and Esters. PABA, as an active ingredient in sunscreens, found widespread use in the 1950s and 1960s. Its absorption spectrum is in the UVB range from 260 to 313 nm[56] with maximal absorbance around 290 nm. Its molar absorptivity is considered to be high.[50] PABA readily penetrates and binds to the stratum corneum and, after several days of application, may remain in the skin and provide prolonged protection even after swimming, perspiring, and bathing.[50,56] It usually is formulated as an alcoholic mixture, which may cause stinging, dryness, or tightness, particularly when applied to the face.[57]

The major disadvantage of PABA is its ability to cause contact and photocontact dermatitis.[64,65] PABA is responsible for more sensitivity reactions than any other sunscreen.[50,56] It also may cause cross-sensitivity reactions with benzocaine, thiazides, sulfonamides, paraphenylenediamine (an ingredient of hair dyes), and other PABA derivatives.[57] The use of PABA in commercial sunscreens has decreased to the point where products are marketed as PABA-free formulations.[50,58] PABA also can cause discoloration of clothes and fiberglass.[52]

The esters of PABA include octyl dimethyl PABA (Padimate O), amyl PABA (Padimate A), and glyceryl PABA. These esters are incorporated easily into formulations, demonstrate good substantivity, and do not cause discoloration of clothing or fiberglass.[57] Their absorption spectra are similar to that of PABA (see Table 39.2). Padimate O has found widespread use among sunscreens in the U.S. It has a maximal absorbance of 311 nm and is the least likely of PABA and its esters to cause cross-sensitivity reactions or contact and photocontact dermatitis.[50] Padimate A can cause photocontact dermatitis and no longer is used in the U.S.[22,58,59] Glyceryl PABA causes contact dermatitis and cross-sensitivities, both of which may be due to benzocaine impurities in the commercial products.[57,58]

Cinnamates have been used widely in Europe for their UVB-absorbing qualities. Ethylhexyl para-methoxycinnamate (Parsol MCX), which has high molar absorptivity and a maximal absorbance of 305 nm, is the most commonly used cinnamate.[50,60] Cinnamates are related chemically to balsam of Peru, balsam of Tolu, coca leaves, cinnamic acid, cinnamic aldehyde, cinnamic oil—ingredients used in perfumes, topical medications, cosmetics, and flavorings.[52,58] Cross-sensitivity with these compounds is possible. The major disadvantage of cinnamates is that they do not bind well to the stratum corneum and, therefore, have poor substantivity.[1,52] Sunscreens containing cinnamates tend to be comedogenic because the vehicle may contain ingredients to improve their substantivity.[56] Cinnamates commonly are used in combination with benzophenones, appear to be nonstaining, and rarely cause contact dermatitis.[52,60] However, ethoxyethyl para-methoxycinnamate (cinoxate), which no longer is available, can cause contact and photocontact dermatitis.[58]

Salicylates are weak UVB absorbers often found in PABA-free products. Topical salicylates are considered to be among the safest sunscreens, even though they are used in high concentrations.[61] Salicylates have low molar absorptivities because the molecules are disubstituted in the ortho-positions of the aromatic ring, which causes stearic strain within the molecule. They are incorporated easily into formulations and are used to boost the SPF of combination products.[56] Sensitization to the salicylates is rare.[52,61] The three salicylates used in the U.S. are listed in Table 39.2.

Benzophenones are UVB-absorbing sunscreens which have absorbance spectra extending into the UVA range. Oxybenzone and dioxybenzone have been used in many sunscreen products in the last 15 years because of their UVA-absorbing quality.[52] The maximal absorbance for each is about 290 nm.[62] Their limitations are poor substantivity and sensitization. There have been many reports of photocontact dermatitis with oxybenzone and contact dermatitis with dioxybenzone, with the latter usually occurring as a contact urticaria.[52] Benzophenones also are found in shampoos, soaps, hair sprays, and dyes, paints, varnishes, and lacquers.[62]

Anthranilates. Methyl anthranilate is a weak UVB-absorbing sunscreen with an absorbance spectrum extending into the UVA range. Like the salicylates, it is an ortho-disubstituted PABA derivative with low molar absorptivity. Its maximal absorbance is about 336 nm.[50] Because methyl anthranilate rarely causes sensitization and has a desirable absorbance spectrum, it commonly is used in combination with other sunscreens to give broad-spectrum protection.[50,61]

Dibenzoylmethanes. Butyl methoxydibenzoylmethane (also known as avobenzone) and isopropyl dibenzoylmethane (Eusolex 8020) are sunscreens with high molar absorptivity and absorption spectra exclusively in the UVA range. Both derivatives have maximal absorbance around 360 nm. Eusolex 8020 has not been approved by the FDA because it is associated with a high incidence of contact and photocontact dermatitis.[56,58] Avobenzone, thus far, has not been associated with a high incidence of sensitization[52] and has been formulated in combination with Padimate O (Photoplex) and with oxybenzone and octyl methoxycinnamate (Shade UVAGuard).[55] These products each have an SPF of 15. Even though these products provide protection through the UVA and UVB ranges, it is not known if they will offer enough protection for highly UVA-sensitive patients.[55,63] Avobenzone loses about 35% of its absorbance capacity 15 minutes after exposure to UVR probably because of instability of the compound.[2]

Physical Sunscreens

Physical sunscreens are opaque formulations made of particulate insoluble compounds, incorporated into a vehicle. The skin is shielded from sunlight due to reflection and scattering of both UV and visible radiation; both size of the particles and thickness of the film determine the amount of protection.[9,61] The most effective and commonly used physical sunscreens are titanium dioxide and zinc oxide, which also absorb UVR as well as reflect and scatter.[9] Other physical sunscreens include magnesium oxide, red veterinarian petrolatum, iron oxides, kaolin, ichthammol, and talc.[50,51,56] These compounds are used in conjunction with chemical sunscreens to formulate products of higher SPF[9] and as single-ingredient sunblocks in an ointment base designed specifically for vulnerable parts of the body, such as the nose, cheeks, lips, ears, and shoulders.[9,56,61] Physical sunscreens also are particularly helpful for persons with vitiligo, a skin condition with amelanotic lesions surrounded by areas of normally pigmented skin. Appropriately colored formulations can be used to camouflage and protect the vulnerable amelanotic lesions.[61] Products using physical sunscreens also are of particular value for persons who need absolute UVR and visible light protection, which include young children, persons with skin types I through IV who receive constant exposure, and persons with drug photosensitivity reactions, xeroderma pigmentosa, lupus erythematosus, and other photosensitive skin reactions.[9,56] Physical sunscreens are not widely accepted because they tend to be visible, messy, and occlusive when applied to the skin. They are highly substantive but may melt in the heat of the sun, limiting their protection to a few hours. Physical sunscreen products tend to be so occlusive that they may cause acne and sweat gland obstruction (miliaria).[61]

Product Selection

9. C.S. and her husband, J.S., are parents of 2 females, a 6-month-old, D.S., and an 18-month-old, M.S. They are attending a week-long family reunion on the coast of South Carolina in early summer. They are looking forward to lots of activities with family members on the beach as well as on the tennis court. C.S. is 28 years old and has skin type V. She has brown hair and brown eyes and has no previous history of photosensitivity reactions or allergies to medications. She does recall developing contact dermatitis on her scalp and around her hairline on several occasions after dying her hair and using certain shampoos. J.S. is 31 years old and has skin type II with blond hair and blue eyes. As a teenager, he suffered from frequent sinus infections and often was treated with trimethoprim-sulfamethoxazole [TMP-SMX (Bactrim)], because of an allergy to penicillin. He remembers developing a severe sunburn after minimal exposure to the sun while taking the sulfa antibiotic. He recently has been started on hydrochlorothiazide for hypertension. What considerations are important in recommending sunscreens for C.S. and J.S.? Recommend an appropriate sunscreen for each with appropriate directions for application while on vacation.

Cross-Sensitivity. The first consideration for recommending an appropriate sunscreen for C.S. and J.S. is their skin type. C.S. has

skin type V, suggesting that a sunscreen with an SPF of 4 to 6 would provide adequate protection for her (see Table 39.1). J.S.'s skin type II suggests that a sunscreen with an SPF of ≥15 would be required to provide adequate protection for him. The contact dermatitis and photosensitivity reaction exhibited by each provide important information for the recommendation of a sunscreen. The contact dermatitis that C.S. experienced from hair dyes and shampoos may have been caused by paraphenylenediamine, an ingredient of hair dyes,[57] or a benzophenone, which sometimes is included in products like hair dyes and shampoos.[62] Since cross-reactivity between paraphenylenediamine and PABA or its derivatives is possible, it is important to recommend a sunscreen for C.S. that does not contain PABA or a benzophenone. A PABA-free sunscreen containing a salicylate [e.g., Hawaiian Tropic Protective Tanning Dry Oil (SPF 6)] may be ideal for C.S. since salicylates rarely cause contact dermatitis. Even though salicylates are weak UVB absorbers, it would most likely provide the level of protection C.S. needs.

The photosensitivity reaction that J.S. experienced while taking TMP-SMX would indicate that J.S. may be susceptible to a cross-sensitivity reaction with PABA or its derivatives. This reaction to TMP-SMX also indicates that J.S. may be susceptible to a photosensitivity reaction with hydrochlorothiazide. If a photosensitivity reaction is likely, it is advisable to recommend an SPF up to 30.[17,22] Since drug-induced photosensitivity reactions are caused by UVA,[64] a PABA-free broad-spectrum sunscreen that absorbs UVA as well as UVB would be necessary to provide J.S. adequate protection. Broad-spectrum sunscreens commonly contain a benzophenone and Padimate O. Since Padimate O is the least likely of the PABA derivatives to cause photocontact dermatitis,[57] a broad-spectrum product containing Padimate O [e.g., Photoplex Broad Spectrum Sunscreen (SPF 15+)] may be recommended for J.S. A broad-spectrum sunscreen containing avobenzone, oxybenzone, and octyl methoxycinnamate would be an alternative to a broad-spectrum product with Padimate O. If the photosensitivity reaction is caused by visible light, it would be necessary to recommend a physical sunscreen to block all sunlight or complete avoidance.[50] With these issues considered, it may be preferable to recommend an antihypertensive medication for J.S. that would not place him at risk for a photosensitivity reaction.

Application. Since C.S. and J.S. are planning to be active on the beach, sunscreens that are water-resistant or water-proof are recommended (see Table 39.3). For protection in the beach environment, an average-size adult should apply and rub in 2 to 2.5 ounces evenly to all exposed skin surfaces 15 to 30 minutes before exposure.[9] It is best to reapply the sunscreen every two hours or after sweating, swimming, or toweling off. Photoprotection of the face, neck, and arms is all that is necessary for casual exposure to sunlight.

10. How long might J.S. expect to be protected with the sunscreen properly applied? Do products with SPF >15 provide any additional benefit?

If J.S. (skin type II) normally burns after 30 minutes of exposure to the sun, a sunscreen with SPF of 15 may provide up to 7.5 hours (0.5 hours × 15) of photoprotection from UVB, but may provide only partial protection against UVA and little or no protection from infrared radiation.[9] Therefore, sunbathing should be limited to 90 to 120 minutes for each outing. It also should be remembered that environmental factors and inadequate application may reduce photoprotection by as much as half.[50]

Sunscreen formulations with SPFs as great as 50 can be made using combinations of chemical and physical sunscreen agents.[4] Individuals who are extremely sensitive to the sun may benefit from formulations of higher SPFs, but the average fair-skinned person gains adequate protection for sunbathing or for average daily exposure from a product with an SPF of 15.[17]

Photoprotection for Children

11. What photoprotective measures should C.S. and J.S. provide for D.S. and M.S.? What nonsunscreen protection could C.S. and J.S. provide for D.S. and M.S.? What sunscreen products are appropriate for use on children?

Age-Related Recommendations and Other Protective Behavior. Sun protection during childhood is very important considering that most of one's lifetime of sun exposure occurs in childhood and that the harmful effects of UVR are cumulative.[24,26] The FDA has recommended that sunscreen agents not be used for children less than six months of age due to the possibility that the agents might be absorbed through the skin and children of this age probably do not have the ability to metabolize the drug if it is absorbed.[65] D.S. needs to be kept out of direct sunlight and, when outside, must be protected with proper clothing and shading.[9] The FDA has recommended that children under the age of two should not be treated with an SPF less than 4 because this SPF range provides inadequate protection.[65] M.S. should be protected with a PABA-free sunscreen with an SPF of ≥15. Regular use of a sunscreen with an SPF of at least 15 for the first 18 years of life can reduce the lifetime incidence of nonmelanoma skin cancers by about three-fourths.[66] Avoidance of sunlight between 10 a.m. and 3 p.m. also significantly reduces the potential danger of sunlight exposure.[17] If M.S. is in the sun during these five hours of the day, or otherwise for an extended time period, she should wear protective clothing covering as much of her body as possible.[9] Tightly knit clothing protects the skin from almost all UVR, whereas loosely knit clothing or wet T-shirts may allow up to 30% of UVR to pass through to the skin. Broad-rimmed hats also may provide protection for the ears, nose, and cheeks.[1,9]

Product Selection. Two types of sunscreens would be appropriate for use in children. A milky lotion is preferred for total body application versus an alcoholic lotion or gel because alcoholic preparations can cause stinging, burning, and irritation of the skin and eyes. Physical sunscreens are available in bright colors and are recommended for selected body areas, such as the nose, cheeks, and shoulders. PABA and its derivatives are considered to be potentially harmful to children's tender skin. For adolescents with acne, an oil-free, noncomedogenic sunscreen formulation is appropriate.[17,24]

Photoeffects on the Eye

12. Why should C.S. and J.S. be concerned about photoeffects on their eyes? Recommend appropriate protective eyewear for them while on vacation.

Cataract Formation. Age-related opacification of the ocular lens, or senescent cataracts, has been attributed to a lifetime of exposure to sunlight. The incidence of cataracts increases steadily after age 50, reaching nearly 50% of individuals over the age of 75.[67] UVB is absorbed by the cornea and lens, which slowly results in protein oxidation and precipitation within the lens. UVA penetrates the ocular lens and can cause cumulative damage to deeper structures of the eye. Decreased transmittance and increased scattering of light by the opacified lens eventually results in blurred vision, rings or halos around lights, changes in color perception, and blindness.[68,69] When the cataract is advanced, the only therapy is surgery.

High exposure of the eye to UVR, which can range from a few seconds' exposure to arc welding, a few minutes' exposure to a UVC-emitting germicidal lamp, commercial tanning, or UVR reflection by snow or sand, can cause painful inflammation of the cornea (photokeratitis) or conjunctivitis. Photokeratitis usually begins 30 minutes to 24 hours after the exposure and time to onset depends upon the intensity of the exposure.[54] Conjunctivitis commonly accompanies photokeratitis and is characterized by the sensation of a foreign body or grit in the eyes. Varying degrees of photophobia, lacrimation, and blepharospasm also may accompany photokeratitis.[54] Since corneal epithelium is highly regenerative, photokeratitis tends to be transient and abates in 24 to 48 hours; treatment consists of cool, wet compresses and mild pain relievers.

Protective Eyewear. C.S. and J.S. should wear sunglasses when outdoors to decrease their life-long exposure to solar radiation and while at the beach to prevent high exposure of UVR and possible photokeratitis or conjunctivitis. Many manufacturers of sunglasses label their products according to three categories: cosmetic, general purpose, and special purpose. Cosmetic sunglasses block at least 70% of UVB, at least 20% of UVA, and less than 60% of visible light and are appropriate for casual wear when high exposure to UVR is unlikely. General purpose sunglasses block at least 95% of UVB, at least 60% of UVA, and 60% to 92% of visible light and are appropriate for most activities in sunny environments. Special purpose sunglasses block at least 99% of UVB, at least 60% of UVA, and at least 97% of visible light and are appropriate for very bright environments such as ski slopes or tropical beaches.[15] General or special purpose sunglasses would be appropriate recommendations for C.S. and J.S. to wear while on vacation.

Treatment of Sunburn

13. G.B., a 31-year-old male with skin type IV, has returned a few hours ago from an afternoon of activity in the sun. His shoulders, back, neck, and arms are bright red and are beginning to feel hot, stretched, and painful. G.B. has been otherwise healthy, has no significant past medical history, and has no known allergies to medications. What treatment recommendations would you give G.B. for his sunburn?

Sunburn usually is self-limiting and treatment is directed at alleviating symptoms. The most effective treatments that G.B. can try for his first-degree burn are oral analgesics, cooling compresses applied to the skin, or cool baths. Treatment by a physician usually is not required unless the sunburn is extensive with constitutional symptoms, involves second-degree burns on the eyes or genitalia, or becomes infected. Aspirin and ibuprofen have the theoretical advantage over acetaminophen because they may block the prostaglandin-mediated sunburn process and are anti-inflammatory at high doses, although evidence substantiating this theory is lacking at this time.[70] Topical anesthetics, such as benzocaine or lidocaine, are effective at relieving pain for 15 to 45 minutes, but should not be used in large quantities; applied more than three or four times a day; or used on raw, blistered, or damaged skin. Benzocaine has minimal systemic toxicities but is associated with contact sensitization, whereas lidocaine is associated with a low incidence of contact sensitization, but has the potential to cause significant systemic toxicities if adequate serum concentrations are reached.[71] If G.B. desires to try one of these agents, application is recommended when the pain is particularly bothersome, such as at bedtime. Topical hydrocortisone, when applied to mild to moderate sunburn, may provide some additional benefit.[72] If G.B. experiences fever, chills, nausea, vomiting, and prostration, he should be referred to his physician. These symptoms generally respond to oral prednisone 20 mg/day for three days. Antihistamines may help control itching associated with sunburn, as well as aid with sleep, if taken at bedtime.[72]

Minor Burns

Burn injuries rank second only to motor vehicle accidents as the leading cause of death in children between one and four years of age and rank third after motor vehicle accidents and drowning as leading cause of injury and death in persons between 0 and 19 years of age.[73] Of the 2.5 million Americans who seek medical attention for burns each year, 100,000 require hospitalization and 12,000 die as a result of their burn injury.[74] The estimated cost for treatment of all fire- and burn-related injuries is estimated to be 3.8 billion dollars annually.[75] Severe burns often require hospitalization or burn center referral due to complications such as fluid and electrolyte imbalances, metabolic derangements, respiratory failure, sepsis, scarring, and functional impairment. Most burns, however, are minor and can be managed adequately in an outpatient setting, provided the burned patient is evaluated carefully, the severity of the burn is assessed accurately, and proper follow-up care is ensured.

Epidemiology

Burn injuries range from relatively minor, superficial injuries to severe, extensive skin loss resulting from contact with hot solids and liquids, steam, chemical agents, electricity, or other physical agents such as UVR or infrared radiation. House fires, which commonly are caused by cigarettes or malfunctioning heating or electrical equipment, are responsible for 84% of fire- and burn-related deaths.[73] These house-fire deaths occur most commonly in the southeast U.S., at night during the winter months, and usually are caused by asphyxia and inhalation injury rather than by burn injury.[76] The peak incidence of burn injuries occurs in preschool-aged children. These children most commonly are scalded by hot liquids.[77,88] School-aged children and adolescents often are injured when experimenting with matches or gasoline, or in association with cars, motorcycles, fireworks, or flammables.[78] Teenagers and adults between 17 and 30 years of age most commonly are involved in accidents with flammable liquids.[77] The death rate from clothing ignition has dropped 40% since the introduction of flame-retardant clothing in 1974, but clothing ignition still remains a significant cause of death caused by burns in the elderly.[75] Persons at increased risk for burn injuries are the very young or elderly, the male gender, blacks, the economically disadvantaged, handicapped children, and children with previous history of burn.[78,79] Child abuse, which can cross all socioeconomic classes, involves burns in 10% of cases, where scalding by immersion is the most common type of burn.[78] Alcohol consumption is implicated in 50% of all burn-related deaths.[75]

With the development of multidisciplinary burn centers and a better understanding of the pathophysiology of the burn wound, survival of patients with second- and third-degree burns has improved greatly over the last three decades. In 1964 the mortality of patients 10 to 30 years of age with burns encompassing 50% of the total body surface area (BSA) was about 50%. In 1974 the mortality in similar patients was 30%. In 1984 burn centers have reported mortality rates of about 10% in patients with these types of injuries.[77] Techniques of improved burn wound management include topical antimicrobial therapy, early excision of devitalized tissue, and skin grafting.

Pathophysiology

Structure and Function of the Skin

The skin constitutes about 15% of the average person's body weight, making it the largest organ of the body. It is composed of an outer protective layer of epidermis; the dermis, which contains nerves, glands, hair follicles, and blood vessels; and the subcutaneous tissue, which contains adipose tissue and connective tissue (see Figure 36.1 in Chapter 36: Dermatotherapy). The skin functions as a protective barrier of the underlying organ systems from trauma, temperature variations, harmful penetrations, moisture, humidity, radiation, and invasion by micro-organisms. It also is involved with carbohydrate, protein, fat and vitamin D metabolism; produces secretions which lubricate the skin; is involved with the immune response; and provides the body with the sense of touch.

Zones of Injury

The burn wound caused by thermal injury can be described by varying zones of injury.[80–82] The central-most area, or the *zone of coagulation*, is characterized by thrombosed vessels and necrosed tissue. This area absorbs the most thermal energy, resulting in the greatest tissue damage. The next area of injury, extending from the zone of coagulation, is the *zone of stasis*. This area involves ischemic, damaged tissue with blood vessels only partially thrombosed. The damaged endothelial linings of blood vessels within this zone of injury may trigger further thrombosis, resulting in further ischemia and cell death and deepening of the burn wound. This process of further injury occurs 24 to 48 hours postinjury. Drying of the burn wound or infection also may cause deepening of the burn wound by preventing re-establishment of circulation to injured tissue. The most peripheral area of injury is the *zone of hyperemia*. The tissue in this area is characterized by inflammatory changes with minimal damage to tissue. Minor burns may involve only the most peripheral zones of injury, whereas severe burns encompass all three zones of injury.

Complications of Burn Wounds

Fluid Loss. In severe burns, release of vasoactive mediators and capillary injury cause sequestration of large amounts of body fluid, plasma, and electrolytes in extravascular compartments resulting in edema both locally and throughout the whole body. This redistribution of fluid is compounded by the loss of large amounts of fluid, electrolytes, and protein into the open wound, all of which can lead to a marked decrease in blood volume, a fall in cardiac output, and decreased tissue and organ perfusion. During the first 24 to 48 hours after a severe burn injury, adequate fluid must be given to replace fluid lost from the vascular space to prevent shock and, possibly, multiple organ failure and death.[83,84]

Infection. The most important threat to survival of the fully resuscitated patient is infection, with burn wound sepsis and pneumonia being the leading causes of death.[77,84] The local mechanical defenses of the skin and respiratory tract frequently are damaged in burn victims, making these common foci for fatal infections. Loss of circulation to the burn wound margins disallows proper functioning of cellular and humoral defense mechanisms, which also increases susceptibility to infection. Devitalized tissue and tissue exudates provide an ideal environment for the proliferation of bacteria. Colonization of gram-positive bacteria occurs if topical antimicrobial therapy is not initiated promptly and gram-negative bacteria may predominate by the fifth day postinjury.[72] Systemic antibiotics are of limited benefit in full-thickness burns and are used only to treat infections documented by wound biopsy, revealing $\geq 10^5$ bacteria/gm of burn tissue.[84] Topical antimicrobials, local wound care, and strict infection control practices are the mainstays of controlling burn wound infections.[77] Devitalized tissue initiates and perpetuates a sepsis-like state in the absence of an identifiable focus of infection.[84] For this reason, as well as for infection control, early excision of devitalized tissue and closure of the burn wound by skin grafting has been adopted by many burn centers.

Inhalation Injury. Burn injuries complicated by inhalation injury are associated with greatly increased mortality rates. Injury to the tracheobronchial mucosa is caused by inhalation of smoke or flames and may result in bronchospasm, ulceration of the mucous membranes, damage to cell membranes, edema, and impairment of bacterial ciliary clearance. Even patients with minor burns may have inhalation injury and require hospital admission. The early symptoms of pulmonary injury (hoarseness, dyspnea, tachypnea, and wheezing) may not be evident for 24 to 48 hours, so patients with suspected inhalation injury (i.e., facial burns or entrapment in a closed space) must be examined carefully. Singed nasal hair, soot-coated tongue or oropharynx, and mucosal edema are indications of inhalation injury. The diagnosis is established by bronchoscopy and management may include endotracheal intubation and mechanical ventilation. Corticosteroids can increase morbidity and mortality associated with burns and inhalation injury by increasing the risk of infection.[72,77,83,84]

Extent of Injury

"Rule of Nines"

The severity of a burn is proportional to the percent of body surface area involvement and the depth of the wound. The percent of BSA for adults can be estimated by using the "rule of nines," where each arm constitutes 9% of the BSA, the head 9%, each leg 18%, and each the front and back of the torso 18%. For children under 10 years, the determination of the percent BSA must be adjusted because their bodies have different proportions. At birth, the infant's head constitutes about 19% of the BSA. For each additional year of age, the head decreases by about 1% and the BSA of the legs increases by about 1% of the patient's total BSA, so a quick estimation of the percent BSA of a burn can be made.[76]

Classification of Wounds

Burn wounds also are classified according to the depth of tissue damage. Determining the depth of the burn wound can be difficult during the first 24 to 48 hours because of the presence of edema and continued tissue ischemia and/or infection, both of which may cause deepening of the wound. In addition, the depth of destruction may vary within the same burn and skin surface characteristics may not match underlying tissue damage, also making assessment of the burn wound difficult.[72,83]

First-degree burns result from injury to the superficial cells of the epidermis. The burned skin does not form blisters, but it does become erythematous and mildly painful. This partial-thickness burn heals within three to four days without scarring.[72]

Second-degree burns may be superficial or deep, depending upon the depth of dermal involvement. Superficial second-degree burns involve the epidermis and the upper layer of the dermis. The burn surface often is erythematous, blistered, weeping, painful, and very sensitive to stimuli. The erythema blanches with pressure and the hair follicles, sweat, and sebaceous glands are spared. Superficial second-degree burns heal spontaneously within three weeks with little, if any, scarring. Deep second-degree burns involve the deeper elements of the dermis and may be difficult to distinguish from third-degree burns. The burn surface is pale, feels indurated or boggy, and does not blanch with pressure. This wound is less painful than more superficial wounds; some areas may be insensitive to stimuli. Healing occurs slowly over about 35 days with eschar formation and possible severe scarring and permanent loss of hair follicles and sweat and sebaceous glands.[72,83]

Third-degree burns entail complete destruction of the full thickness of the skin including all skin elements. The wound may appear pearly white, gray, or brown and is dry and inelastic. Pain is sensed only when deep pressure is applied. If the wound is small, healing over several months can occur by epithelial migration from the margins of the injury, with scar and contracture formation. For the most part, third-degree burns must be repaired by excision and grafting of the wound to prevent contractures of the skin.[81,83]

Fourth-degree burns are similar to third-degree burns except that devitalized tissue extends into the subcutaneous tissue, fascia, and bone. These burns are blackened in appearance, are dry and generally painless, and confer great risk for infection.

Triage

14. T.B., a 17-year-old, nonobese male, has just burned the calf of his right leg on the muffler of his motorcycle. Immediately after being burned, T.B. was able to rinse his leg with cool water from a garden hose. The burn on his leg is about twice the size of the palm of his hand and appears erythematous and weeping. He sustained no other injury, but now he is in considerable pain. T.B. has no significant past medical history. Should T.B. be referred to a physician or can he safely self-treat his burn? What patient information is necessary to consider in making this decision?

Before recommending treatment for a patient with a minor burn, it is important to accurately assess the patient to determine if he can self-treat safely or if physician referral or hospitalization is necessary. The location and severity of the burn, the patient's age and state of health, and etiology of the burn injury all must be considered.

American Burn Association Treatment Categories

Three different treatment categories for burn injuries have been recommended by the American Burn Association: major burn injuries; moderate, uncomplicated burn injuries; and minor burn injuries.[81] *Major burn injuries* are considered to be second-degree burns with greater than 25% BSA involvement in adults (20% in children); all third-degree burns with ≥10% BSA involvement; all burns involving the hands, face, eyes, ears, feet, and perineum that may result in functional or cosmetic impairment; high-voltage electrical injury; and burns complicated by inhalation injury, major trauma, or poor-risk patients (elderly patients and those with debilitating disease). *Moderate, uncomplicated burns* are considered to be second-degree burns with 15% to 25% BSA involvement in adults (10% to 20% in children); third-degree burns with 2% to 10% BSA involvement; and burns not involving risk to areas of specialized function such as the eyes, ears, face, hands, feet, or perineum. Hospital admission is advised for patients with *major or moderate, uncomplicated burns* and admission and surgical referral is recommended for patients of all ages who have deep second- or third-degree burns covering ≥3% of the total body surface area.[72] *Minor burn injuries* include second-degree burns with less than 15% BSA involvement in adults (10% in children); third-degree burns with less than 2% BSA; and burns not involving functional or cosmetic risk to areas of specialized function. Patients with burns of this category may be treated by a physician on an outpatient basis if no other trauma is present; circumferential burns of the neck, trunk, arms, or legs are not present; and if the patient is able to comply with therapy. Patients may self-treat a second- or third-degree burn only if less than 1% BSA is involved.

Age-Related Recommendations

Children less than two years of age and elderly patients with a burn injury should be referred to a physician because these patients may not tolerate well the trauma from the burn. Children with burns that result from suspected child abuse should be hospitalized for legal and social reasons. Burns in varying stages of healing, demarcated patterns of burns (e.g., stocking or glove distribution), or more than two burn sites may be clues in identifying an abused child.[85]

Disease-Related Recommendations

Burn patients with any condition which may compromise wound healing, such as diabetes, cardiovascular disease, immunodeficiency disorders, renal disease, obesity, or alcoholism, should be referred to a physician. These patients may be more susceptible to complications from the burn and may not tolerate the burn trauma well.

Etiology of Burn

Attention also needs to be given to the etiology of the burn. Electrical burns may appear to be superficial because external injury may occur at only the entrance and exit sites of the current. These burns, however, may cause extensive damage to underlying nervous and muscle tissue that is not initially evident. Except for very minor electrical burns, these patients should be referred to a physician. Burns caused by low concentrations of hydrofluoric acid initially are painless but may cause severe tissue necrosis several days later. Hospitalization of these patients often is required.[72]

T.B. has sustained a superficial second-degree burn over about 2% of his BSA. Even though the burn wound on his leg was caused by thermal injury and is relatively minor, T.B. should be referred to a physician for treatment.

Treatment

15. How should T.B.'s burn be treated? What treatment alternatives may be used for T.B.? What immunization should T.B. be questioned about?

Goals of Treatment and Immediate Care

Treatment goals for first- and second-degree burns are to relieve pain associated with the burn, prevent desiccation and deepening of the wound, prevent infection, and provide a protective environment for healing. Immediate care of the wound should be application of cold, wet compresses or immersion in cool water.[86] T.B. may have prevented extension of the burn to deeper layers of tissue and alleviated some of his pain from the burn by immediately irrigating the wound with cool water. The area then should be cleansed with a mild soap and water and a sterile, nonadherent, fine-mesh gauze dressing that is impregnated with hydrophilic petrolatum (Xeroflo, Adaptic) should be placed over the wound. This type of gauze dressing prevents the gauze from adhering to the wound and allows the burn exudate to flow freely through the dressing, thus preventing maceration. A second layer of absorbent gauze should be placed over the petrolatum gauze and a supportive layer of rolled gauze can be used to keep the dressing in place.[81] The outer layer must not be too constricting, and the dressing should be replaced every 48 hours after recleansing the area and inspecting for signs of infection. If T.B.'s wound continues to weep, it may be beneficial to soak his wound or apply a towel saturated with water, normal saline, or Burrow's solution (diluted 1:20 or 1:40) for 15 to 30 minutes several times daily. (See Chapter 36: Dermatotherapy.) The use of butter, grease, or similar home remedies should be avoided in the treatment of burns.

Synthetic Dressings

Alternatives in treating T.B.'s burn are the use of synthetic dressings and topical antimicrobials. Synthetic dressings (Duo-derm, Opsite) serve as skin substitutes which are applied to fresh, clean, and moist burns. They are trimmed to about the size of the burn and left in place until the burn essentially is healed or the dressing separates from the wound spontaneously. The synthetic dressings keep the wound warm and moist, require absorbent dressings that must be changed daily, and are indicated for superficial second-degree burns. The chief advantage over gauze dressings is that synthetic dressings prevent mechanical injury from daily cleansing and dressing changes.[81]

Topical Antimicrobials

Topical antimicrobials typically used in the hospital setting to treat or prevent severe burn wound infections include silver sulfadiazine, povidone iodine, mafenide acetate, and silver nitrate solution.[83,87] *Silver sulfadiazine* usually is the agent of choice because it has broad-spectrum gram-positive and gram-negative antibacterial activity, provides reasonable eschar penetration, and is easy and painless to apply and wash off. Silver sulfadiazine may cause leukopenia and should not be used around the eyes or mouth, in patients with hypersensitivity to sulfonamides, or in pregnant or nursing women.[86] *Povidone iodine* provides good eschar penetration, but causes pain upon application and dries and hardens the eschar. *Mafenide acetate* provides excellent eschar penetration and antibacterial activity, but is a potent carbonic anhydrase inhibitor that may cause bicarbonate wasting and acid/base imbalances. *Silver nitrate solution* causes hyponatremia, hypokalemia, hypochloremia, and hypocalcemia and, along with mafenide acetate, should not be used on an outpatient basis.[87] In T.B.'s case, *silver sulfadiazine cream* could be chosen to treat his burn on an outpatient basis if it is felt that he is at particular risk for infection. The cream would be applied in a thin layer over the wound and covered with absorbent gauze and wrapped with rolled gauze. The dressing must be changed twice daily to maintain an application of cream that is biologically active. Topical bacitracin and the combination of polymyxin B, bacitracin, and neomycin are transparent formulations that also may be used, but because of limited efficacy, may be desirable for use only on small, second-degree burns on the face.[83]

Oral Analgesics and Topical Protectants

T.B.'s burn pain can be treated with the oral analgesics, aspirin, acetaminophen, or ibuprofen. If these analgesics do not provide adequate relief, acetaminophen with codeine may be of additional benefit. Topical protectants, such as allantoin, calamine, white petrolatum, or zinc oxide, have been recommended by the FDA OTC Review Panel as safe and effective in treating first- and minor second-degree burns. These agents protect the burn from mechanical irritation caused by friction and rubbing and prevent drying of the stratum corneum.[71]

Tetanus Immunization

Since burns are prone to tetanus infection, T.B. should receive a tetanus toxoid booster if he has not been immunized within the previous ten years.

References

1 **Taylor CR et al.** Photoaging/photodamage and photoprotection. J Am Acad Dermatol. 1990;22:1–15.

2 **Dobak J, Liu F.** Sunscreens, UVA, and cutaneous malignancy: adding fuel to the fire. Int J Dermatol. 1992;31:544–48.

3 **Kochevar IE et al.** Photophysics, photochemistry, and photobiology. In: Fitzpatrick TB et al., eds. Dermatology in General Medicine. 4th ed. New York: McGraw-Hill; 1993:1627–638.

4 **Council on Scientific Affairs.** Harmful effects of ultraviolet radiation. JAMA. 1989;262:380–84.

5 **Diffey BL.** Human exposure to ultraviolet radiation. Semin Dermatol. 1990;9:2–10.

6 **National Institutes of Health Consensus Development Panel.** National Institutes of Health summary of the consensus development conference on sunlight, ultraviolet radiation, and the

skin. J Am Acad Dermatol. 1991;24:608–12.

7 **Soter NA.** Acute effects of ultraviolet radiation on the skin. Semin Dermatol. 1990;9:11–15.

8 **Norris PG et al.** Acute effects of ultraviolet radiation on the skin. In: Fitzpatrick TB et al., eds. Dermatology in

General Medicine. 4th ed. New York: McGraw-Hill; 1993:1651–658.

9   **Pathak MA.** Prevention of sunburn, dermatoheliosis, and skin cancer with sunprotective agents. In: Fitzpatrick TB et al., eds. Dermatology in General Medicine. 4th ed. New York: McGraw-Hill; 1993:1689–717.

10 **Coldiron BM.** Thinning of the ozone layer: facts and consequences. J Am Acad Dermatol. 1992;27:653–62.

11 **Thrush B.** Causes of ozone depletion. Nature. 1988;332:784–811.

12 **McCally M, Cassel CK.** Medical responsibility and global environmental change. Ann Intern Med. 1990;113:467–73.

13 **Environmental Protection Agency.** Regulatory impact analysis: protection of stratospheric ozone. Washington, DC: US Environmental Protection Agency, US Government Printing Office; 1988.

14 **Prawer SE.** Sun-related skin diseases. Postgrad Med. 1991;89:51–66.

15 **DeSimone EM II.** Sunscreen and suntan products. In: Feldmann EG, Blockstein WL, eds. Handbook of Nonprescription Drugs. 9th ed. Washington, DC: American Pharmaceutical Association; 1990:909–29.

16 **Pathak MA.** Sunscreens: topical and systemic approaches for protection of human skin against harmful effects of solar radiation. J Am Acad Dermatol 1982;7:285–312.

17 **Pathak MA.** Sunscreens and their use in the preventive treatment of sunlight-induced skin damage. J Dermatol Surg Oncol. 1987;13:739–50.

18 **Cooper KD et al.** UV exposure reduces immunization rates and promotes tolerance to epicutaneous antigens in humans: relationship to dose, CD1a-DR+ epidermal macrophage induction, and Langerhans' cell depletion. Proc Natl Acad Sci. USA 1992;89:8497–501.

19 **Cruz PD, Bergstresser PR.** Ultraviolet radiation, Langerhans' cells, and skin cancer: conspiracy and failure. Arch Dermatol. 1989;125:975–79.

20 **Alcalay J et al.** Variations in the number and morphology of Langerhans' cells in the epidermal component of squamous cell carcinomas. Arch Dermatol. 1989;125:917–20.

21 **Young AR.** Cumulative effects of ultraviolet radiation on the skin: cancer and photoaging. Semin Dermatol. 1990; 9:25–31.

22 **Zanowiak P.** Protecting the skin from solar radiation. U.S. Pharmacist. 1993; 18(Suppl.):14–29.

23 **Rampen FHJ et al.** Unreliability of self-reported burning tendency and tanning ability. Arch Dermatol. 1989;124:885–88.

24 **Truhan AP.** Sun protection in childhood. Clin Pediatr. 1991;30:676–81.

25 **Hurwitz S.** The sun and sunscreen protection: recommendations for children.

J Dermatol Surg Oncol. 1988;14:657–60.

26 **Mallory SB, Watts JC.** Sunburn, sun reactions, and sun protection. Pediatr Ann. 1987;16:17–84.

27 **Williams ML, Sagebiel RW.** Sunburns, melanoma, and the pediatrician. Pediatrics. 1989;84:381–82.

28 **Gallagher RP et al.** Suntan, sunburn, and pigmentation factors and the frequency of acquired melanocytic nevi in children. Arch Dermatol. 1990;126:770–76.

29 **Granstein RD.** Photoimmunology. Semin Dermatol. 1990;9:16–24.

30 **Granstein RD.** Photoimmunology. In: Fitzpatrick TB et al. eds. Dermatology in General Medicine. 4th ed. New York: McGraw-Hill; 1993:1638–650.

31 **Morrison WL et al.** Photobiology. J Am Acad Dermatol. 1991;25:327–29.

32 **Uitto J et al.** Molecular mechanisms of cutaneous aging: age-associated connective tissue alterations in the dermis. J Am Acad Dermatol. 1989;21:614–22.

33 **Gilchrest BA.** Skin aging and photoaging: an overview. J Am Acad Dermatol. 1989;21:610–13.

34 **Kligman LH.** Photoaging: manifestations, prevention, and treatment. Clin Geriatr Med. 1989;5:235–51.

35 **Kligman AM et al.** Topical tretinoin for photoaged skin. J Am Acad Dermatol. 1986;15:836–59.

36 **Leyden JJ et al.** Treatment of photodamaged facial skin with topical tretinoin. J Am Acad Dermatol. 1989;21:638–44.

37 **Grove GL et al.** Optical profilometry: objective methodology for quantification of facial wrinkles. J Am Acad Dermatol. 1989;21:631–70.

38 **Olsen EA et al.** Tretinoin emollient cream: a new therapy for photodamaged skin. J Am Acad Dermatol. 1992; 26:215–24.

39 **Andreano JM et al.** Tretinoin emollient cream 0.01% for the treatment of photoaged skin. Cleve Clin J Med. 1993;60:49–55.

40 **Marks R, Lever L.** Studies on the effects of topical retinoic acid on photoageing. Br J Dermatol. 1990;122 (Suppl. 35):93–5.

41 **Goldfarb MT et al.** Topical tretinoin: its use in daily practice to reverse photoageing. Brit J Dermatol. 1990;122 (Suppl. 35):87–91.

42 **Weinstein GD et al.** Topical tretinoin for the treatment of photodamaged skin: a multicenter study. Arch Dermatol. 1991;127:659–65.

43 **Weiss JS et al.** Topical tretinoin improves photoaged skin: a double-blind vehicle-controlled study. JAMA. 1988; 259:527–32.

44 **Ellis CN et al.** Sustained improvement with prolonged topical tretinoin (retinoic acid) for photoaged skin. J Am Acad Dermatol. 1990;23:629–37.

45 **Goldfarb MT et al.** Topical tretinoin

therapy: its use in photoaged skin. J Am Acad Dermatol. 1989;21:645–50.

46 **Kligman AM.** Guidelines for the use of topical tretinoin (Retin A) for photoaged skin. J Am Acad Dermatol. 1989;21:650–54.

47 **Johnson BE, Ferguson J.** Drug and chemical photosensitivity. Semin Dermatol. 1990;9:39–46.

48 **Bickers DR.** Photosensitivity and other reactions to light. In: Isselbacher KJ et al., eds. Harrison's Principles of Internal Medicine. 13th ed. New York: McGraw-Hill; 1994:307-312.

49 **Anon.** Federal Register. 1978;43:38209–8213.

50 **Sterling GB.** Sunscreens: a review. Cutis. 1992;59:221–24.

51 **Stiller MJ et al.** A concise guide to topical sunscreens: state of the art. Int J Dermatol. 1992;31:540–43.

52 **O'Donoghue MN.** Sunscreen: one weapon against melanoma. Dermatol Clin. 1991;9:789–93.

53 **Lowe NJ.** Photoprotection. Semin Dermatol. 1990;9:78–83.

54 **Anon.** Sunscreen agents. In: McEvoy GK et al., eds. American Hospital Formulary Service Drug Information. Bethesda, MD: American Society of Hospital Pharmacists; 1993:2272–274.

55 **Anon.** Shade UVAGuard—a second broad-spectrum sunscreen. Med Lett Drugs Ther. 1993;35:53–4.

56 **O'Donoghue MN.** Sunscreen: the ultimate cosmetic. Dermatol Clin. 1991; 9:99–104.

57 **Fisher AA.** Sunscreen dermatitis: para-aminobenzoic acid and its derivatives. Cutis. 1992;50:190–92.

58 **Dromgoole SH, Maibach HI.** Sunscreening agent intolerance: contact and photocontact sensitization and contact urticaria. J Am Acad Dermatol. 1990;22:1068–078.

59 **Lowe NJ.** Photoprotection. Semin Dermatol. 1990;9:78–83.

60 **Fisher AA.** Sunscreen dermatitis: Part II—the cinnamates. Cutis. 1992;50:253–54.

61 **Fisher AA.** Sunscreen dermatitis: Part IV—the salicylates, the anthranilates, and physical agents. Cutis. 1992;50:397–98.

62 **Fisher AA.** Sunscreen dermatitis: Part III—the benzophenones. Cutis. 1992;50:331–32.

63 **Lener ME.** Photoplex. Am Pharm. 1991;NS31:39–43.

64 **Johnson BE, Ferguson J.** Drug and chemical photosensitivity. Semin Dermatol. 1990;9:39–46.

65 **Anon.** Federal Register. 1978;43:38217.

66 **Stern RS et al.** Risk reduction for nonmelanoma skin cancer with childhood sunscreen use. Arch Dermatol. 1986;122:537–45.

67 **Schachat AP.** Common problems associated with impaired vision: cataracts and age-related macular degeneration. In: Barker LR et al., eds. Principles of

Ambulatory Medicine. 3rd ed. Baltimore: Williams and Wilkins; 1990:1322–329.

68 **Honigsmann H.** Phototherapy and photochemotherapy. Semin Dermatol. 1990;9:84–90.

69 **Hu H.** Effects of ultraviolet radiation. Med Clin N Am. 1990;74:509–14.

70 **Stern RS, Dodson TB.** Ibuprofen in the treatment of UV-B-induced inflammation. Arch Dermatol. 1985;121:508–12.

71 **Moore RH III.** Burn and sunburn products. In: Covington TR, eds. Handbook of nonprescription drugs. 10th ed. Washington, DC: American Pharmaceutical Association; 1993:563-575.

72 **Peate WF.** Outpatient management of burns. Am Fam Physician. 1992;45:1321–332.

73 **McLoughlin E, McGuire A.** The causes, cost, and prevention of childhood burn injuries. Am J Dis Child. 1990;144:607–13.

74 **Department of Health, Education and Welfare reports of the epidemiology and surveillance of injuries.** Atlanta: Centers for Disease Control, 1979: DHEW publication no. HSM 73-10001.

75 **Baker SP et al.** The injury fact book. 2nd ed. New York: Oxford University Press; 1992:161.

76 **Schonfeld N.** Outpatient management of burns in children. Pediatr Emerg Care. 1990;6:249–53.

77 **Demling RH.** Burns. N Engl J Med. 1985;313:1389–398.

78 **Finkelstein JL et al.** Pediatric burns: an overview. Pediatr Clin North Am. 1992;39:1145–163.

79 **Herndon DN et al.** Management of the pediatric patient with burns. J Burn Care Rehabil. 1993;14:3–8.

80 **Wong L, Munster AM.** New techniques in burn wound management. Surg Clin North Am. 1993;73:363–71.

81 **Griglak MJ.** Thermal injury. Emerg Med Clin North Am. 1992;10:369–83.

82 **Dziewulski P.** Burn wound healing: James Ellsworth Laing memorial essay for 1991. Burns. 1992;18:466–78.

83 **Bruke JF, Bondoc CC.** Burns: the management and evaluation of the thermally injured patient. In: Fitzpatrick TB et al., eds. Dermatology in General Medicine. 4th ed. New York: McGraw-Hill; 1993:1592–598.

84 **Deitch EA.** The management of burns. N Engl J Med. 1990;323:1249–253.

85 **Hobbs CJ.** Burns and scalds. Br Med J. 1989;298:1302–305.

86 **Phillips LG et al.** Treating minor burns. Postgrad Med. 1989;89:219–31.

87 **Monafo WW, West MA.** Current treatment recommendations for topical burn therapy. Drugs. 1990;40:364–73.

88 **Olin B, ed.** Drug Facts and Comparisons. 48th ed. St. Louis: Facts and Comparisons; 1994:2447–459.

Chapter 40

Gout and Hyperuricemia

Lloyd Y Young
Keith D Campagna

Pathophysiology 40-1
  Definition 40-1
  Uric Acid Disposition 40-1
    Overproduction 40-1
    Underexcretion 40-2
Acute Gout 40-2
  Clinical Features 40-2
    Epidemiology 40-2
    Number of joints 40-2
    Podagra 40-3
    Physical stress 40-3
    Nocturnal occurrence 40-3
    Pain 40-3
  Laboratory Data 40-3
    Baseline tests 40-3
    Infectious component 40-3
  Diagnosis 40-3
    Differential diagnosis: pseudogout 40-4
      Calcium pyrophosphate dihydrate deposition
        disease 40-4
      Calcium hydroxyapatite deposition disease 40-4
      Calcium oxalate deposition disease 40-4
  Treatment of Acute Gout 40-4
    Goals of therapy 40-4
    Drug therapy overview 40-4
      Indomethacin 40-5
      Nonsteroidal anti-inflammatory drugs (NSAIDs) .. 40-5
      Colchicine 40-5
      Corticosteroids 40-5
      Phenylbutazone 40-5
    Choice of agent 40-5
    Delay of hypouricemic therapy 40-6
    Nonsteroidal anti-inflammatory drugs (NSAIDs) ... 40-6
    Corticosteroids 40-6
    Colchicine 40-7
      Intravenous (IV) use 40-7

Onset of effects 40-7
  Guidelines for use 40-8
  Concomitant use of opiate analgesics 40-8
  Dosing interval 40-8
  Limiting doses 40-8
  Adverse effects 40-8
Uric Acid Urine Quantification 40-8
Hyperuricemia 40-9
  Choice of Allopurinol versus Uricosurics 40-9
  Allopurinol 40-9
    Initiation of therapy: dose 40-9
    Onset of effects 40-9
    Once daily dosing 40-9
    Adverse effects 40-10
      Hypersensitivity reactions 40-10
    Drug interactions (See Table 40.2) 40-10
    Indications 40-11
  Probenecid 40-11
    Initiation of therapy 40-11
    Onset of effects 40-11
    Contraindications 40-11
    Salicylate interaction 40-12
  Asymptomatic Hyperuricemia 40-12
    Clinical significance 40-12
    Laboratory tests of uric acid 40-12
    Drug-induced hyperuricemia (See Table 40.3) 40-12
    Treatment 40-12
  Special Situations 40-13
    Urate nephropathy 40-13
    Urine alkalinization (See Table 40.4) 40-13
    Hemodialysis 40-13
    Renal transplants and cyclosporine 40-13
      Mechanism 40-14
      Treatment 40-14
      Risks 40-15

Pathophysiology

Definition

The disease of gout is due to a disorder of uric acid metabolism. It is manifested by acute or chronic recurrent arthritis and deposits of monosodium urates, and is associated most often with hyperuricemia. However, attacks of acute gouty arthritis have been documented in the presence of persistently normal serum urate levels and, as will be discussed later, many individuals who are hyperuricemic may never experience an attack of gouty arthritis.[148] Hence, gout should be considered as a clinical diagnosis, and *hyperuricemia* as a biochemical one. These two terms are not synonymous and are not interchangeable.

Uric Acid Disposition

Uric acid serves no biological function; it is merely the end-product of purine metabolism. Unlike other animals, humans lack the enzyme uricase, which degrades uric acid into more soluble products for excretion. As a consequence, uric acid is not metabolized in humans and must be excreted renally. Therefore, increased serum uric acid concentrations can result from an increase in the production of uric acid, a decrease in the renal excretion, or a combination of these two mechanisms.[1]

Overproduction of uric acid can result from excessive *de novo* purine synthesis, excessive dietary purines, or excessive nucleoprotein turnover. Excessive *de novo* purine synthesis is associated primarily with rare enzyme mutation defects. For example, a deficiency of hypoxanthine-guanine phosphoribosyltransferase (HGPRTase) is associated not only with hyperuricemia and gout, but also with mental retardation, choreoathetosis, and self-mutilation by biting (i.e., Lesch-Nyhan syndrome).[2] Likewise, excessive purine biosynthesis leading to hyperuricemia and gout have been associated with Type 1 glycogen-storage disease (von Gierke's) because of the deficiency of the glucose phosphatase enzyme. Excessive dietary ingestion of yeast or liver tablets, which are high in purines, has caused hyperuricemia. Generally, however, diet plays only a very minor role in the development of hyperuricemia and dietary restrictions (with the exception of alcohol) cannot be advocated in the management of hyperuricemia. Excessive nucleoprotein turnover from neoplastic diseases such as multiple myeloma, leukemias, lymphomas, and Hodgkin's disease, as well as from myeloproliferative disorders such as myeloid metaplasia or polycythemia vera, have all been associated with gout and hyperuricemia.[1,3]

Underexcretion of uric acid results from a defect in renal excretion. Uric acid is filtered in the renal glomerulus and is almost completely (i.e., >99%) reabsorbed in the proximal tubule by a high-capacity system. The uric acid then is secreted distal to the proximal tubular reabsorption site and, subsequently, about 75% of the secreted urate is reabsorbed again.[4] Therefore, urinary uric acid excretion is almost entirely attributable to the tubular secretory process.

When large urate loads are filtered during hyperuricemia, urate reabsorption increases to avoid the dumping of large amounts of poorly soluble urate into the urinary tract. Tubular urate secretion, however, does not appear to be influenced by serum urate concentrations, and impaired tubular secretion of urate is the probable explanation for hyperuricemia.[4]

Acute Gout
Clinical Features

1. W.S., a 46-year-old male professor, is seen by his physician because of a chief complaint of severe pain at the base of his left great toe and around the forward portion of his arch. This pain was first noted ≈2 days ago, a few hours after an uneventful 4 mile run. While asleep that evening, W.S. experienced pain severe enough to awaken him. The pain was more constant the next morning, and for the remainder of the day he walked with a significant limp. He was still unconcerned as he attributed the pain to a sprain from his jogging. Last night, while asleep, W.S. was awakened several times with episodes of pain around the base of his left great toe and around the instep of his left foot. The pain, which was at first moderate, became more intense. The pain was not sharp or knife-like; rather, it was a constant gnawing pain which did not abate with time. His foot felt like it was being tightened slowly in a vise and the pain was more of a constant squeezing pressure sensation than an acute transient phenomenon. By this morning, his foot was so exquisitely painful that he could not tolerate even the weight of the bedcovers.

Pertinent past medical history includes left foot trauma during a motorcycle accident ≈10 years ago and essential hypertension of ≈5 years duration. His systolic blood pressure (BP) is generally about 140 to 145 mm Hg and diastolic pressure about 90 to 95 mm Hg during treatment. W.S. currently is receiving hydrochlorothiazide 50 mg/day and metoprolol (Lopressor) 100 mg/day. This happily married patient's social history is noncontributory except for a nightly bedtime glass of wine.

On physical examination the first metatarsophalangeal joint is warm and tender to touch. The entire periarticular area is erythematous and swollen to such an extent that it is difficult to determine which joint is the focus of the inflammation. What subjective or objective data in W.S.'s history are compatible with the clinical features of gout?

Epidemiology. The risk of gouty arthritis is about the same for both men and women at any given serum uric acid concentration; however, many more men are hyperuricemic. For example, men are six times more likely than women to have serum uric acid concentrations greater than 7 mg/dL. Overall, only about 5% of gouty arthritis cases occur in women and these are most likely to occur in postmenopausal women.

The onset of gout is rare in prepubertal children and is uncommon before the age of 30. The onset is classically during middle age: in one study, the average individual age at the time of the first attack was 48 years.[5] The appearance of gout in a man less than 30 years of age or in a premenopausal woman is unusual and should alert clinicians to the possibility of a renal parenchymal disease that decreases urate clearance or to an enzymatic defect that is associated with increased purine production.

A controversial epidemiological association of gout with coronary heart disease (CHD) has gained increased credibility from the Framingham study group finding that "gout is a marker for susceptibility to coronary heart disease."[6] Gout may be an independent risk factor for CHD or it may serve simply as a clinical marker for increased risk of CHD without being causally related to coronary heart disease. A biological explanation for the association of gout with CHD might be related to the activation of platelets by monosodium urate crystals and subsequent release of chemical mediators such as serotonin and adenosine diphosphate (ADP) which have been implicated in the endothelial damage of atherosclerosis. Other epidemiological correlations with race, intelligence, geographical locale, or genetic disposition probably contribute more confusion than clarity. There is, however, a strong association between the risk of gout and lead exposure through diet (e.g., moonshine whiskey) or occupation (e.g., painters, plumbers, shipbuilders).[7,111] Lead exposure does not appear to be a factor in W.S.

Epidemiologically, the age and gender of W.S. are compatible with the typical profile of a gouty patient; and W.S. has a history of hypertension. The most important epidemiological relationship of gouty arthritis for W.S., and indeed for all patients, is the association of gout and hyperuricemia (see Questions 31 and 32).

Number of Joints. Acute gout attacks usually affect a single joint and the initial attack in 75% to 90% of patients involves a joint of the lower extremity (especially the first metatarsophalangeal joint).[3,8] Although initial gout attacks are primarily monoarticular, as many as 39% of the patients in one study experienced polyarticular involvement as their first manifestation of gout.[9] In another study, 8 of 30 patients with gout had crystal-proven polyarticular onset and 60% subsequently experienced polyarticular symptoms.[10] In a prospective investigation of 106 patients with crystal-documented gouty arthritis, 42 (40%) had articular inflammation at two or more sites.[11] In addition, radionuclide imaging has demonstrated that multiple joints can be undergoing asymptomatic, low-grade inflammatory reactions despite the presence of only one symptomatic joint.[12] Gout attacks, therefore, usually are monoarticular, but polyarticular gout also is common. When the first attack of gout involves multiple joints, only two to three joints usually are affected.

Generally, recurrent attacks are of longer duration than first attacks and are more likely to be polyarticular.[8] Patients with polyarticular recurrent gout tend to experience attacks of a more smoldering onset, and these attacks are of longer duration. The polyarticular joint involvement tends to occur in an ascending and asymmetrical fashion (i.e., the joints in the upper extremities usually become involved only after several attacks involving joints in the lower extremities).[11]

W.S. seems to be experiencing polyarticular gout, as both his great toe and instep appear to be afflicted. This clinical presentation is compatible with cases of gouty arthritis that have presented as polyarticular disease.[9-13] Nevertheless, it is difficult to determine whether W.S.'s gout truly is polyarticular because the area around the base of his left great toe is too inflamed to attribute the inflammatory process to one or multiple contiguous joints.

Podagra. An acute attack of the great toe (podagra) is the most frequent manifestation of acute gouty arthritis in Western societies. Approximately 50% of patients with gout have the initial attack in either great toe and about 84% will have at least one attack of podagra sometime during the course of this disease.[5] If the great toe is not affected, the acute attacks almost always affect other peripheral joints in the feet and ankles. The small joints in the hands usually are affected next, then the knees and elbows. While acute gouty arthritis can occur in other joints such as the shoulder, hips, and vertebrae, occurrence in these sites is extremely rare except in patients with established severe disease. The involvement of W.S.'s great toe is typical of the usual acute attack of gout.

An explanation for the predilection of the great toe to acute gouty arthritic attacks is based upon the premise of a transient local increase in the concentration of monosodium urate in this joint.[14] Since urate diffuses more slowly across a synovial membrane than water,[15,16] resorption of synovial effusion from traumatic joints when the patient is in a recumbent position increases the urate concentration within a joint. Synovial effusions are increased in the great toe during the day because of degenerative changes in that joint: the first metatarsophalangeal joint is the most common and often the only joint affected in degenerative joint disease of the foot. According to radiographic surveys and surgical dissections, the frequency of degenerative joint disease at the base of the great toe far exceeds that in any other weight-bearing joint.[14] Although this concept explains why the great toe is most commonly affected by gout attacks, additional studies are needed to explain why all hyperuricemic individuals with presumably similar degenerative joint changes do not experience acute gouty arthritis.

It probably is not coincidental that the left foot of W.S. is afflicted because it was this foot that was traumatized in the motorcycle accident ten years ago.

Most acute attacks have no obvious precipitating event, but trauma,[14] excessive alcohol intake (presumably due to increased serum concentrations of lactic acid),[17] or initiation of hypouricemic therapy (presumably because of mobilization of urate stores) may contribute to the development of an acute attack. In older patients, attacks often follow surgical procedures or a medical illness such as stroke, pneumonia, myocardial infarction, or urinary tract infection.[18] The precipitation of acute gouty attacks in hyperuricemic individuals most likely involves a multitude of factors.[19]

Physical Stress. Gouty attacks also seem to be more common during episodes of increased physical exercise. Long walks, hikes, golf games, or tight new shoes historically have been associated with the subsequent onset of podagra.[14] Thus, this painful episode of foot pain experienced by W.S. after a four-mile run also is compatible with these clinical observations.

Nocturnal Occurrence. Acute gouty arthritis commonly begins at night. Even Thomas Sydenham's 18th century classic description of an acute gouty attack begins: ''The victim goes to bed and sleeps in good health. About two o'clock in the morning he is awakened by a severe pain in the great toe; more rarely in the heel, ankle, or instep.'' According to the Simkin hypothesis,[14] small amounts of effusion fluid gravitationally enter into degenerative joints of the feet during the day when most people are busily walking about and are reabsorbed during the night when the lower extremities are elevated. Thus, the onset of foot pain in W.S. during the night also is typical of gout.

Pain. Thomas Sydenham continues his classical description of an acute gouty attack as follows: ''This pain is like that of a dislocation. The pain, which was at first moderate, becomes more intense. After a time this comes to a height. Now it is a violent stretching and tearing of the ligaments—now it is a gnawing pain and now a pressure and tightening. So exquisite and lively meanwhile is the feeling of the part affected, that it cannot bear the weight of bedclothes nor the jar of a person walking in the room. The night is spent in torture, sleeplessness, turning of the part affected, and perpetual change of posture.'' This description of the affected part is remarkably similar to the description presented by W.S.

Laboratory Data

2. What laboratory data should be obtained at this time if the clinical assessment is gout?

Baseline Tests. The cardiovascular and renal systems of all patients with gout should be examined because hypertension or impaired renal function is common in many gouty patients. It would be especially prudent to monitor W.S.'s blood pressure because of his history of hypertension. Preliminary laboratory investigations should include a complete blood count (CBC), urinalysis (UA), blood urea nitrogen (BUN) or serum creatinine (SrCr), and a serum uric acid.[20]

Infectious Component. The sudden appearance of acute swelling and tenderness of a joint without a background of arthritis, such as in W.S., can be attributed not only to gout, but also to septic arthritis. If the patient is a young single man, the possibility of an infectious etiology for the acute inflammation would be more seriously considered because of the lack of a history of chronicity.[1] Furthermore, the infectious organism may be presumed to be gonococcus unless another organism is suspected.[21] Although febrile reactions, leukocytosis, and elevation of the erythrocyte sedimentation rate generally can be attributed to infectious disease, such symptoms also are common to acute gouty arthritis.[10] Systemic signs are most likely to occur in patients with polyarticular attacks.[11,22] In view of W.S.'s age, social history, and classic clinical features, acute gouty arthritis would be the most likely cause of his pain.

Diagnosis

3. What objective data would confirm the diagnosis of gout in W.S.?

Although hyperuricemia is a precursor of gout, hyperuricemia is not a disease and, by itself, is not diagnostic of gout. Many hyperuricemic individuals never develop symptomatic gout, and acute gout may be present in some patients with normal serum uric acid concentrations.

Radiographic findings during the early phase of gout are nonspecific and generally characterized by asymmetric soft tissue swelling overlying the involved joint; bone mineralization and joint spaces are well preserved.[17] However, when gout has been long-standing, bony changes can be noticed, and repeated attacks can lead to calcium deposition with a resultant increase in density in the areas of soft tissue swelling.[17]

The diagnosis of acute gouty arthritis is confirmed only when large numbers of polymorphonuclear leukocytes and monosodium urate crystals are demonstrated in synovial fluid aspirated from the inflamed joint.[1,3,23] Acute inflamed joints will have intracellular urate crystals in 85% of patients with gout, and this finding is specific for gout.[7,24]

Monosodium urate crystals when viewed through a microscope with normal illumination are long and needle-shaped in appearance. However, a polarizing microscope with a first-order red compensator usually is needed to demonstrate the presence of these negatively birefringent urate crystals.[25] In selected cases, electron microscopic examination of synovial fluid may be needed for the initial documentation of urate crystal-induced synovitis when po-larizing microscopy has failed to identify these crystals.[26]

In an occasional patient with acute gout, urate crystals cannot be found in fluid aspirated from the inflamed joint.[27–29] Therefore, a diagnosis of acute gouty arthritis cannot be ruled out entirely when urate crystals are not present in the initial synovial aspirate. Repeated search of other involved joints,[28] or even of the same joint a few hours later,[27,29] may demonstrate the diagnostic urate crystals. When synovial fluid was aspirated from the knees of 50 patients with asymptomatic, nontophaceous gout (synovial fluid monosodium urate crystals had been previously documented in the knees or other joints of these patients), urate crystals were found in 58% of these asymptomatic patients.[30]

W.S. should have his first metatarsophalangeal joint aspirated to confirm the clinical assessment of gout. Although his instep might be the primary focus of his acute attack, the first metatar-sophalangeal joint is by far the most commonly affected. Aspira-tion of this joint, even if asymptomatic and even if never previously involved clinically, can be recommended as an aid in establishing a definitive diagnosis of gout.[31,32]

Since examination of joints is difficult in some clinical situa-tions, and almost impossible in large-scale epidemiological studies, investigators have relied on patients' descriptions of previous gouty attacks. As a result, gout has been defined by focusing on the oligoarticular nature of the attack, its finite duration, complete relief of pain after the attack, a positive response to colchicine, and the criteria described in Question 1. Nonetheless, two reports by Wolfe indicate an overdiagnosis of gout by a factor of three, and misdiagnosis by community physicians of 164 patients later seen in a rheumatology clinic.[149,150] The most common misdiagnoses were in patients with psoriatic arthritis and pseudogout. The Amer-ican College of Rheumatology, however, has set forth the criteria needed to establish a diagnosis of gout for epidemiological studies. When 6 of the 11 criteria listed in Table 40.1 are present, the diagnosis of gout can be distinguished from pseudogout with a specificity of 92.7% and an overall sensitivity of 84.8%.[7] These criteria are useful not only for epidemiological studies, but for clinical use when the aspiration of a joint is not viable.

Differential Diagnosis: Pseudogout

4. W.S. refused to have his affected joints aspirated. Al-though he meets many of the criteria commonly attributed to gout, what other crystal-induced arthritides should be consid-ered in the differential diagnosis of W.S.?

Deposition of microcrystals such as calcium pyrophosphate, cal-cium oxalate, and calcium hydroxyapatite into joints can cause acute or chronic arthritis in a manner similar to that caused by monosodium urate deposition.[3] The role of these microcrystals in causing acute synovitis has been greater than previously expected

Table 40.1	Criteria for Epidemiological Diagnosis of Gout[7]
>1 acute attack of arthritis	
Exquisite pain involving joint	
Joint inflammation maximal within 1 day	
Oligoarthritis	
Erythema over involved joints	
Podagra (1st metatarsophalangeal joint)	
Unilateral podagra	
Tophi	
Hyperuricemia	
Asymmetric swelling within a joint on a radiological examination	
Complete termination of acute attack	

because new crystallographic technology (e.g., electron micros-copy, x-ray diffraction) can differentiate these diagnoses from that of acute gout.

Crystal-induced diseases tend to occur in older patients because prior joint disease, especially osteoarthritis (which is generally a disease of the elderly), predisposes them to crystal deposition and acute episodes of joint inflammation. The elderly also are more prone to microcrystal-induced arthritis because these crystals gen-erally accumulate over a long period of time and must attain a sufficient concentration and size before they precipitate into the synovial fluid and begin causing inflammation.[33]

Calcium Pyrophosphate Dihydrate Deposition Disease. Acute calcium pyrophosphate dihydrate deposition disease also has been referred to in the literature as "pyrophosphate gout" and pyro-phosphate arthropathy. Although these terms connote specificity, the term "pseudogout" will no doubt remain in common use to describe the acute intermittent arthritis induced by calcium pyro-phosphate dihydrate crystals. Although other crystals may mimic gouty arthritis, pseudogout is but one of a number of common syndrome names that need not be threatened by a taxonomic re-classification of the underlying deposition processes.[34] The ar-thropathy may be acute or chronic, or cause acute synovitis super-imposed upon chronically involved joints. The initial episode of pseudogout, or calcium pyrophosphate dihydrate deposition dis-ease, usually occurs between ages 65 and 75 and most frequently affects the knee.

Calcium hydroxyapatite deposition disease, or apatite gout, oc-curs far less commonly than gout or pseudogout. It usually occurs in younger persons, however, people of all ages can be affected. Calcium hydroxyapatite is the primary mineral of bone and teeth.[33]

Calcium oxalate deposition disease, or oxalate gout, is a rela-tively new complication of end-stage renal disease. It was not until 1982 that calcium oxalate crystal deposition was noted to produce gout-like acute arthritis, usually in patients with chronic renal fail-ure undergoing long-term hemodialysis.[3] Many of these patients have a history of taking pharmacologic doses of ascorbic acid which is metabolized to oxalate.

The diagnosis of these nonurate microcrystal-induced arthridi-ties can be made based upon light microscopy demonstration of these crystals in synovial fluid.

Treatment of Acute Gout

Goals of Therapy

5. What is the primary goal in the treatment of this acute gout attack in W.S.?

The immediate goal in the treatment of an acute attack of gout is to relieve pain and inflammation. The immediate goal of therapy should not be aimed at decreasing the serum uric acid concentra-tion with hypouricemic agents such as allopurinol (Zyloprim) or probenecid (Benemid). Patients most likely have been hyperuri-cemic for several months or years and it is not necessary to treat the hyperuricemia immediately. Furthermore, a decrease in the se-rum urate concentration at this time might mobilize urate stores and precipitate yet another acute gouty attack.

Drug Therapy Overview

6. W.S.'s serum uric acid concentration. was found to be 10.5 mg/dL. His other laboratory tests [i.e., CBC, hemoglobin (Hgb), hematocrit (Hct), SrCr concentration, serum electro-lytes, and UA] were within normal limits. W.S. could not be convinced of the necessity for aspiration of his first metatar-sophalangeal joint and just wanted treatment for his excruci-ating pain. What medications are effective in the treatment of acute gout? [SI unit: Serum uric acid 624 μmol/L]

Acute gouty arthritis can be effectively treated in most instances by indomethacin; a nonsteroidal anti-inflammatory drug (NSAID) such as ibuprofen (Motrin), naproxen (Naprosyn), fenoprofen (Nalfon), or piroxicam (Feldene); various corticosteroids; colchicine; or phenylbutazone.

Indomethacin (Indocin), a "first-generation" NSAID, is commonly prescribed for the treatment of acute attacks of gouty arthritis, and many consider it to be the drug of choice.[140] Doses of 50 mg three to four times daily should be given until there is significant relief of symptoms (usually within 2 to 3 days). This dose then should be decreased to 25 mg three to four times daily until there is total resolution of the attack.[53] Adverse effects [e.g., gastrointestinal (GI) disturbances, mental changes, headaches, rash, leukopenia] are minimized when indomethacin is used in this manner. At one time, indomethacin was associated with a high incidence of adverse effects because large doses of 100 to 200 mg four times daily were prescribed unnecessarily.

Nonsteroidal anti-inflammatory drugs (NSAIDs) such as ibuprofen, naproxen, and piroxicam are widely used in the management of numerous inflammatory disorders because they are highly effective and have minimal toxicities. As a result, these agents have largely replaced colchicine in the treatment of acute gout. In a multicenter study, naproxen (Naprosyn) 750 mg as a single dose followed by 250 mg three times a day was highly effective;[36] and in another study, a similar dosing regimen consisting of an initial 750 mg dose of naproxen followed by 500 mg eight hours later and 250 mg every eight hours for the next two to three days had better results than a regimen that did not utilize large initial doses.[37] Alternatively, success also can be achieved with naproxen 500 mg for the first two doses followed by 250 mg three times a day. Ibuprofen (Motrin) 2400 mg/day in one patient[38] and in ten other patients[39] resulted in rapid improvement and complete resolution of gouty arthritis within 72 hours. Fenoprofen (Nalfon) in various doses up to 3.2 gm/day (800 mg three to four times daily) was effective in 27 patients affected with acute gouty arthritis.[40] When fenoprofen was compared in a double-blind study with phenylbutazone, both drugs were equally successful in relieving acute gouty arthritis.[41] Other NSAIDs such as piroxicam (Feldene) 40 mg/day,[42,43] flurbiprofen (Ansaid) 100 mg four times a day for one day followed by 50 mg four times a day,[44] ketoprofen (Orudis) 50 mg four times a day,[45] tolmetin (Tolectin) 400 mg three to four times a day,[46] meclofenamate (Meclomen) 100 mg three to four times a day,[47] and sulindac (Clinoril) 200 mg twice a day[48,49] have all been proven effective in the treatment of acute gouty arthritis. NSAIDs such as isoxicam,[50] carprofen,[51] and indoprofen[52] that are not yet available in the U.S. have been used successfully to treat acute gout. Adverse effects of NSAIDs have been modest. (See Chapter 41: Rheumatic Disorders for a further discussion of NSAIDs.)

Colchicine, at one time, was the agent of choice for the treatment of an acute attack of gout. This drug not only provided symptomatic relief to greater than 95% of patients when administered early in the course of an attack of gout, but it also provided diagnostic confirmation because of its relative specificity for relieving only the symptoms of acute gout. For the fully developed acute attack, the traditional dose of colchicine has been one or two 0.5 to 0.6 mg tablets initially, followed by 0.5 to 0.6 mg hourly, or every other hour until joint pain was relieved or gastrointestinal side effects (e.g., diarrhea, nausea, vomiting) intervened.[140]

Corticosteroids probably are the most potent anti-inflammatory drugs presently available, and one would expect these drugs to be highly useful in the management of an acute gouty attack. Their use, however, has been dismissed by most major textbooks[1,3] and review articles[22,53] because of the alleged potential for rebound flares of arthritis when therapy was discontinued. Corticosteroids, however, in doses of 20 to 30 mg/day of oral prednisone, or its equivalent, are clearly effective in the treatment of acute gouty attacks. The dose of the corticosteroid should be decreased gradually over the ensuing ten days.[54] Presumably, the beneficial effects of adrenocorticotropic hormone (ACTH) are due to its stimulation of cortisol release. ACTH can be given by slow intravenous (IV) infusion of 20 U or by intramuscular (IM) injection of 40 to 80 U every 6 to 12 hours for one to three days.[53] When 100 patients with acute gouty arthritis were randomly assigned to receive a single IM injection of 40 U of ACTH or indomethacin 50 mg four times a day, patients who received the ACTH within 24 hours of the onset of pain experienced pain relief sooner and with fewer adverse effects than those who received indomethacin.[55] Corticosteroids probably would be more widely used in the treatment of acute gout attacks if NSAIDs and indomethacin were not so highly effective.

Phenylbutazone (Butazolidin), another "first-generation" NSAID, at a dose of 200 mg four times a day for the first day, followed by 200 mg three times a day for two additional days, can control 85% to 95% of acute attacks of gout within 24 to 36 hours.[56] The potential hematological toxicities of phenylbutazone are well documented, but are rare with short-term therapy. Although thrombocytopenia[57] and acute gastrointestinal hemorrhages[58] have occurred after a single day of phenylbutazone therapy, rare individual reports of toxicity to any drug are possible.

Choice of Agent

7. What therapeutic intervention would be the most appropriate for W.S. at this time?

As presented above, many drugs can effectively manage an acute attack of gout. Indomethacin, more recent NSAIDs, colchicine, corticosteroids, and phenylbutazone are all highly effective. The pharmacodynamic differences between these agents are relatively minor when treating acute gout because these drugs are used for only a few days at a time. Therefore, the selection of the most appropriate drug for an acute attack of gout depends primarily upon coexistent conditions (e.g., renal dysfunction) and physician or patient preferences.

Potent prostaglandin inhibitors such as indomethacin can inhibit diuretic-induced increases in renal sodium excretion[59-62] and decrease the hypotensive effect of diuretics and other antihypertensive drugs (e.g., beta blockers).[63,133] Although it seems doubtful that hypertensive patients will experience problems with indomethacin when it is to be used only for a few days, three patients reportedly have experienced hyperkalemia and renal insufficiency subsequent to the use of indomethacin for treatment of gouty arthritis.[64]

The newer NSAIDs also have the potential of reversing the effects of antihypertensive drugs; however, the potential for such a drug interaction is not as great as that with indomethacin and is not likely to be highly significant when the duration of therapy is to be less than one week. The hematological toxicities associated with phenylbutazone are more daunting despite its short-term use for the treatment of an acute gouty attack. Furthermore, the sodium and fluid retention properties of phenylbutazone would be undesirable in W.S., and its mild uricosuric properties may complicate the scheduling of urinary uric acid excretion studies that might be ordered. Therefore, one of the NSAIDs such as naproxen should be prescribed for this acute attack of gout in W.S.; and it would be prudent to monitor his blood pressure as well.

Some clinicians with long-standing experience with colchicine might select it over an NSAID for W.S. if there was concern for reversal of his blood pressure control. Many young clinicians, however, have not had much experience with colchicine or its potential for adverse effects when used inappropriately.[65] Although colchicine, historically, has been the classic drug chosen to treat patients with acute gouty arthritis, growing awareness of its potential for fatal complications has limited the selection of this drug. When the risks and benefits of colchicine for treatment of acute gout were rigorously studied, colchicine was deemed to have ''the smallest benefit to toxicity ratio of drugs that are effective for acute gout.''[65] The predictable diarrhea that accompanies colchicine use is especially disturbing to patients with podagra who must hobble to the bathroom on a painful joint and provides further explanation for the increasing disfavor of colchicine use.

Thus, an NSAID would seem to be a reasonable choice for W.S. because it has both analgesic and anti-inflammatory effects and minimal adverse effects.

Delay of Hypouricemic Therapy

8. W.S. experienced dramatic relief of pain from his oral naproxen therapy. In fact, his response was much better than expected. After receiving 750 mg of naproxen, W.S. could feel that the pain at the base of his great toe was no longer accelerating in intensity, and after his second dose of 500 mg, the pain began to lessen somewhat. Within 72 hours of initiating therapy, his metatarsophalangeal joint was no longer inflamed. Neither a synovial aspirate of the inflamed joint, nor a 24-hour urine sample for uric acid quantification was obtained. Other laboratory tests were within normal limits and W.S. was instructed to monitor his BP daily. Why should (or should not) W.S. receive hypouricemic therapy at this time?

After the initial attack of acute gout, the interval between subsequent attacks varies from a few days to several years. Some patients may never again experience another acute attack of gout; however, more than 60% will have a second attack of gouty arthritis within one to two years of the initial presentation.[3,137] No specific therapy is required during this interval, although it often is tempting to initiate hypouricemic therapy because of the clear association of hyperuricemia with gout. Antihyperuricemic drugs, however, should not be prescribed indiscriminately. Once started, such therapy usually is continued indefinitely. Hypouricemic therapy should be initiated only when gouty patients have frequent acute attacks, urate tophi, or evidence of urate nephropathy (e.g., uric acid stones or renal damage). If these indications are absent, hypouricemic drug therapy should await the natural course of events because nothing is lost by waiting. The acute attack always can be treated when it appears and it usually is resolved within days.

Long-term hypouricemic medications should not be started for W.S. at this time because the above criteria for therapy are not met and, more importantly, the diagnosis of gout has not been firmly established by demonstration of urate crystals in the synovial fluid of an inflamed joint. In today's era of routine laboratory tests, there is the tendency to overdiagnose gout in hyperuricemic individuals. It is not uncommon to find a hyperuricemic patient with a musculoskeletal problem inappropriately treated with urate lowering drugs. Therefore, W.S. should not be treated with hypouricemic drugs at this time.

Finally, antihyperuricemic drugs may not be needed in W.S. because his hyperuricemia and presumed acute gouty attack may have been the result of the hydrochlorothiazide therapy. Hyperuricemia is a commonly encountered adverse effect of thiazide and other diuretics including furosemide, ethacrynic acid, chlorthalidone, and acetazolamide.[66,67] These diuretics indirectly increase serum urate concentrations during extracellular fluid volume contraction. The volume depletion may enhance urate retention because of altered renal blood flow or changes in intrarenally generated angiotensin.[68] The volume contraction also could cause

hyperuricemia by inducing a generalized reabsorption of all solutes.[69] Replacement of urinary salt and water losses prevents diuretic-induced hyperuricemia.[67] Therefore, discontinuation of hydrochlorothiazide, although it would require reformulating his antihypertensive therapy, may be all that is needed to lower W.S.'s serum urate concentration. Initiation of hypouricemic medications such as allopurinol or probenecid at this time would be premature. In any case, probenecid should not be initiated until uric acid overproduction is ruled out by urine uric acid analysis.

Nonsteroidal Anti-Inflammatory Drugs (NSAIDs)

9. After being relatively symptom-free since his first acute gouty attack 8 months ago, W.S. now complains of pain around the base of his left great toe similar to that experienced in the past along with some pain in several joints in his left foot including his left ankle. This apparent gouty attack began last night after a late evening lecture. He was awakened by acute pain and took 3 nonprescription ibuprofen (Advil) tablets (200 mg/tablet) which seemed to be beneficial. Upon physical examination, the first metatarsophalangeal joint of his left foot is markedly inflamed, tender, and brightly erythematous in appearance. His entire left foot appears somewhat inflamed and is tender to touch. Other findings are unremarkable and his BP of 135/85 mm Hg continues to be well controlled on metoprolol 100 mg/day.

About 3 months before this episode he had taken two 600 mg doses of ibuprofen because of some vague pain in the same region; and ≈1 month ago, similar vague discomfort responded to several doses consisting of three to four 200 mg tablets of nonprescription ibuprofen. Why would it be reasonable (or unreasonable) to initiate therapy for acute gout with an NSAID at this time?

In W.S.'s case, there is presumptive evidence for a diagnosis of gout; however, in other cases, patients have been treated with NSAIDs for nonspecific joint pains without due consideration for gout as the primary cause of the treated disorder. In one report, the escape from detection of chronic polyarticular gout resulted in a needless dependence upon NSAIDs, failure to correct the metabolic problem, and, in some cases, progression of joint destruction. Although acute inflammation was modified in these patients, the basic pathogenic mechanisms remained unresolved and the joint disease continued.[70] The indiscriminate use of NSAIDs may, by promoting misdiagnosis, prevent the effective control of gout which is perhaps the most correctable rheumatic disorder. The spontaneous resolution of symptoms within three to ten days[33] in most patients with mono- or oligoarthritic disease further complicates management if the diagnosis of gout is not confirmed.

Since the diagnosis of gout has not been confirmed in W.S., it would be prudent to obtain an aspirate of his inflamed joint before initiating further NSAID therapy. W.S. responded well to naproxen and appears to have gained relief from his pain and inflammation by utilization of nonprescription ibuprofen tablets. It also would be reasonable to obtain further laboratory data (e.g., SrCr) to rule out possible underlying adverse effects from using nonprescription ibuprofen in large doses.

Corticosteroids

10. The synovial fluid obtained from W.S.'s first metatarsophalangeal joint contained numerous polymorphonuclear leukocytes and the diagnostic monosodium urate crystals. A review of his laboratory results noted a SrCr of 2.5 mg/dL and a low Hgb count that was consistent with W.S.'s complaint of considerable GI pains within the last month. Pending further evaluation of W.S.'s renal and GI system, what medication should be prescribed for this particular acute gouty attack? [SI unit: SrCr 221 µmol/L]

W.S.'s hemoglobin count was normal at the time of his last medical visit but his history of GI distress with concurrent use of ibuprofen suggests the possibility of peptic ulcer disease. Likewise, the serum creatinine concentration of 2.5 mg/dL could suggest NSAID-induced renal insufficiency. Since contraindications to NSAID therapy include renal insufficiency, anticoagulation, GI intolerance, or prior NSAID toxicity such as rash or wheezing, it would be prudent to treat this acute attack of gout in W.S. with a medication other than an NSAID until the status of his renal and GI systems are known.

The Textbook of Rheumatology states "rebound attacks may occur as steroids are withdrawn unless other prophylactic measures can be used."[1] Wallace states that "at least one third of patients treated with ACTH or oral corticosteroids develop rebound flares of arthritis when the therapy is stopped."[53] Although statements such as these are commonly encountered in the literature, scientific documentation has not accompanied them. To the contrary, evidence refutes "rebound flare-ups" or relapses following corticosteroid discontinuance.

Groff and associates[54] treated 13 consecutive patients and 15 episodes of acute gout with systemic corticosteroids and concluded that the unsatisfactory results from corticosteroids that were previously reported could be attributed primarily to under-dosage or premature discontinuation of the corticosteroid. Their finding that adequate doses given for a sufficiently long period of time resulted in successful outcomes affirmed the clinical experiences of others. When initial doses of prednisone of 20 to 50 mg/day (mean: 37 mg) were decreased gradually over a mean of 11 days, 10 of 13 episodes of acute gout completely resolved within seven days. Patients with gout involving more than five joints and patients with prolonged duration of symptoms before the initiation of therapy required longer courses of corticosteroid therapy. All patients improved within 12 to 48 hours. One patient required treatment with a higher dose of prednisone for 20 days because a "rebound gouty inflammation" was noted when the prednisone was tapered over a shorter period of time. No other patients experienced any episodes that could be construed to represent a possible rebound effect. In another study,[55] 8 of 144 gouty episodes (5.6%) needed to be retreated because symptoms recurred in patients who received a single intramuscular dose of ACTH; in comparison, the incidence of relapse was higher in patients treated with 50 mg of indomethacin four times a day. Further evidence is provided by a more recent study in which 27 patients were treated with either indomethacin 50 mg three times daily or triamcinolone acetonide 60 mg IM, that demonstrated comparable efficacy and produced no episodes of rebound gout attacks when triamcinolone acetate therapy was completed.[158] The potential for relapse of gouty arthritis when corticosteroids are prescribed, therefore, does not seem to be higher when compared to therapy with other anti-inflammatory drugs.

Corticosteroid adverse effects such as osteoporosis, myopathy, peptic ulcer disease, central nervous system effects, hypertension, and predisposition to infections are not expected with short courses of therapy and seldom appear unless continued for a long period of time. Glucose intolerance, however, can occur with short-term therapy.

Since colchicine, indomethacin, and NSAIDs are associated with increased risks in patients with renal and gastrointestinal disorders, this acute attack of gout in W.S. probably would be best treated with systemic corticosteroid therapy. A prednisone dose of 40 mg orally, followed by a 20 mg dose six to eight hours later should be a reasonable approach to the management of this particular episode of gout. Subsequently, a prednisone dose of 10 mg twice a day can be decreased gradually over the next five to ten days in response to symptoms. Although intra-articular corticosteroid injections can provide quick relief when only one or two joints are involved, W.S. seems to have polyarticular involvement at this time. Parenteral ACTH also could be used; however, most patients most likely would prefer the less costly oral prednisone therapy over the more painful IV or IM injections.

Colchicine

11. The repeat laboratory SrCr measurement in W.S. was normal and the previous elevated value was attributed to laboratory error. Why might colchicine be considered as an alternative to the corticosteroids in W.S.?

Colchicine, unlike general anti-inflammatory drugs, is relatively specific for relieving the symptoms of acute gout.[71] A positive therapeutic response to colchicine, in a hyperuricemic patient with monoarticular arthritis, is considered supportive evidence for the diagnosis of gout. Support for the diagnosis of gout is of value when synovial fluid cannot be obtained from small joints for inspection of urate crystals. Joints are not always aspirated for various reasons and occasionally when aspirated, even well-qualified clinicians may fail to find urate crystals in as many of 15% of acute gouty effusions.[27-29] As a result, colchicine was preferred by some clinicians for the first acute attack of gout because it not only provided symptomatic relief to greater than 95% of patients when administered early in the course of an attack, but it also was a useful diagnostic tool.[71] Nevertheless, the response to colchicine must be interpreted with some caution. The arthritis that accompanies psoriasis and sarcoidosis sometimes responds to colchicine.[71] Likewise, colchicine also can prevent acute attacks of familial Mediterranean fever[73,74] and perhaps even alleviate amyloidosis.[75] As a diagnostic test, colchicine is neither so specific nor so sensitive as to be completely diagnostic. The preferred treatment of acute gout in most cases is NSAIDs.

12. Intravenous (IV) Use. Although a corticosteroid might have been preferred for W.S., his family physician has considerable experience using colchicine in this setting and has decided to treat this attack of gout with IV colchicine. What is the role for IV colchicine in the management of acute gout?

Intravenous colchicine commonly was prescribed for treatment of acute gout after clinical trials in the 1960s clearly established its efficacy. This route of administration was preferred over the oral route because it was considered to be associated with a lower incidence of gastrointestinal adverse effects. Although IV colchicine had been used commonly for the treatment of acute gout, it is no longer frequently prescribed. According to one estimate, probably less than 1% of the patients with gout received parenteral colchicine in the U.S. in 1984 and IV colchicine is no longer licensed for clinical use in Britain.[65] Since intravenous colchicine is used infrequently, the risks of toxicity with this drug very likely outweigh its benefits when prescribed by clinicians who are inexperienced in its use. In exceptional cases where IV colchicine is the only suitable alternative, one can expect rapid relief of gouty arthritis symptoms following its administration.

13. Onset of Effects. When should the therapeutic effects of colchicine begin to become apparent?

When given parenterally, colchicine is one of the quicker acting drugs in the treatment of gout. IV colchicine provides relief from acute gout in 6 to 12 hours in most patients and in less than six hours in some patients. The onset of effectiveness of colchicine can be delayed if treatment is not initiated early.[53] Generally, the pain, redness, and swelling are resolved completely within 48 to 72 hours after the initiation of colchicine therapy. Nevertheless, there is considerable interpatient variation to this time frame for response.

14. Guidelines for Use. **Since IV colchicine was prescribed for W.S., what guidelines should be followed to optimize the safe IV use of this drug?**

When intravenous colchicine is used infrequently in hospitals, supervision of its use would be appropriate. Automatic review of IV colchicine orders by the pharmacy department can prevent the use of excessive doses.[65] It would be advantageous to monitor the IV doses of colchicine when it is prescribed for elderly patients. As with most medications, the elderly seem to be more sensitive to therapeutic and toxic effects even when renal or hepatic function seems to be normal. Elderly patients should not receive more than 2 mg of colchicine intravenously per attack, nor should they receive another dose until at least a three week interval has elapsed. In young patients, no further colchicine should be administered for one or two weeks following IV colchicine.[151] In all patients before IV use renal and hepatic dysfunction must be ruled out, and the drug should be avoided in patients where function is impaired.

The entire 2 to 3 mg dose of colchicine should be diluted with normal saline to 30 mL and administered slowly over a period of five minutes. One additional IV dose may be repeated in six to eight hours if needed, but the total intravenous dose of colchicine should not exceed 4 mg for a given attack of gouty arthritis. The dose of IV colchicine should be restricted to no more than 1 or 2 mg (not 4 mg) if the patient has been receiving long-term oral colchicine therapy.[146] Furthermore, intravenous colchicine should not be substituted mg for mg for oral colchicine.[65]

These dosing guidelines are underscored by the death of a 70-year-old man with apparently normal renal and hepatic function who developed marrow aplasia and pancytopenia after receiving 10 mg of IV colchicine over a period of five days for acute gouty arthritis.[76] Other anecdotal reports of serious toxicities have resulted when established dosing guidelines were significantly modified.[65]

Intravenous colchicine solutions are extremely irritating, and care also must be taken to prevent extravasation during administration. The needle which is used to aspirate the colchicine solution into the syringe should be discarded, and a new needle used for the actual venipuncture to diminish potential phlebitis.

15. Concomitant Use of Opiate Analgesics. **W.S. is in excruciating pain and requests an analgesic to supplement his antigout medication. Why might a narcotic analgesic be appropriate?**

A dose or two of a narcotic analgesic may be a reasonable adjunct to blunt the pain of acute gouty arthritis while awaiting the apparent benefits of colchicine action. Additionally, the narcotic analgesics have the added advantage of decreasing the troublesome diarrhea that accompanies colchicine use. Gastrointestinal side effects such as hyperperistalsis, nausea, abdominal cramping pain, or watery diarrhea occur in about 80% of patients given full therapeutic courses of colchicine.[53]

16. Dosing Interval. **W.S. responded well to the IV colchicine and was discharged. His physician intends to treat his future gout attacks with NSAIDs unless contraindications are still present. If another gout attack developed over the next several days, W.S. was instructed to call his physician immediately and to take two 0.5 mg tablets of colchicine initially, followed by 1 tablet every other hour until he experienced relief of joint pain or the onset of GI adverse effects. Why is this colchicine dosing interval selected?**

Colchicine is administered hourly to minimize gastrointestinal toxicity because patients vary considerably with respect to the amount of colchicine they can tolerate. Even with hourly colchicine, however, titration of dose to a maximal therapeutic response with gastrointestinal toxicity is difficult. Therefore, a longer dosing interval of 0.5 mg every other hour following the initial 1 mg dose could decrease GI problems and still not compromise the therapeutic response.[77,78]

If, through past experience, the approximate therapeutic or toxic dose of colchicine is known for a particular patient, one-half to two-thirds of this dose can be administered at once with the remainder given as 0.5 to 0.6 mg every other hour. This method of administration saves the patient much suffering since delays in treatment may result in greater failure rates as well as increased severity and duration of attacks.

17. Limiting Doses. **Why should all orders for colchicine limit the number of doses or tablets for a particular acute gouty attack?**

The colchicine prescription for W.S. should have stated the maximum number of doses that he was to receive over the course of his next acute attack of gout. A maximum of 10 to 15 tablets generally is recommended because an occasional patient may not develop florid GI distress or simply may not have gout. Although colchicine is relatively safe, serious toxicities and fatalities have resulted from doses as small as 5 to 7 mg.[65,78] It also is crucial to ensure that all patients who receive colchicine have normal hepatic and renal functions. Even when the serum creatinine concentration is within normal limits, the reduced renal function that commonly accompanies aging will increase the potential for colchicine toxicity when the dose is not decreased in the elderly.

18. Adverse Effects. **What toxicities might be expected from an overdose of colchicine?**

Adverse effects from colchicine usually are reversible and consist most commonly of nausea, diarrhea, abdominal pain, and vomiting. More severe toxic effects from therapeutic doses of colchicine affect the hepatic, hematopoietic, and nervous systems, but occur primarily in elderly patients[78] or those with prior cardiac, hepatic, or renal disease.[79] Reports of a toxic effect of colchicine on sperm production are contradictory.[80,81]

Large overdoses or acute poisonings with colchicine can cause life-threatening multiple system disturbances. *Neurological* dysfunctions have been manifested as persistent mental confusion, loss of deep tendon reflexes, ascending paralysis, and respiratory failure. *Gastrointestinal* toxicities result in abdominal pain, vomiting, severe watery diarrhea, and a hemorrhagic gastritis that has led to dehydration and shock. Hepatotoxicity and pancreatitis also may be associated with colchicine's effects on the GI system. *Musculoskeletal* problems such as myopathy, myoglobinuria, and large increases in muscle enzymes have been reported. Myopathy and neuropathy[35] may be a common, unrecognized disorder in patients with renal dysfunction who take customary doses for gout. The myopathy usually presents with proximal weakness and always presents with elevation of the serum concentration of creatine kinase; both features remit within three to four weeks after the drug is discontinued. This neuromuscular toxicity has been largely unrecognized until the report of 12 cases by Kuncl and associates.[35] *Hematological* abnormalities include severe leukopenia followed by recovery leukocytosis and complete bone marrow aplasia. *Renal* complications present as reversible azotemia with urinalysis showing proteinuria, myoglobinuria, hematuria, and many hyaline casts. *Respiratory* problems may be the result of neurological failure as well as of chest wall weakening or pulmonary edema with hypoxemia.[79]

Uric Acid Urine Quantification

19. **W.S. revisited his physician ≈6 months after his last gout attack. At that time, the clinical laboratory noted that his serum uric acid concentration was 10.4 mg/dL, and he was provided with instructions for a 24-hour urine collection. Why is it important to assess the 24-hour urine for uric acid? [SI unit: serum uric acid 619 µmol/L]**

Some believe that urine concentrations of uric acid should be measured in every hyperuricemic patient,[82] while most practitioners are unconvinced as to the benefit of such studies. Urinary uric acid excretion studies are of diagnostic benefit in defining the cause of hyperuricemia and could be useful in determining the choice of the most appropriate hypouricemic agent.

Urinary uric acid excretion usually is measured in a 24-hour collection to ascertain whether the patient overproduces or underexcretes uric acid. Patients excreting less than 750 mg/day of uric acid into the urine generally are considered underexcretors, and those excreting more than 800 mg/day are categorized as overproducers. A few overproducers of uric acid suffer from genetic defects in enzymes such as hypoxanthine-guanine phosphoribosyltransferase (HGPRTase), or from disorders such as leukemias which are associated with increased turnover of cells. Moreover, overproducers are probably best treated with the hypouricemic drug allopurinol, which inhibits the formation of uric acid, as opposed to a hypouricemic agent such as probenecid, which increases urate excretion.

Predictions of urinary uric acid overproducers by use of uric acid:creatinine [or creatinine clearance (Cl_{Cr})] ratios based upon spot midmorning serum and urine samples[82] have been advocated because of the inherent difficulties in 24-hour excretion predictions based upon spot urine samples.[83]

Hyperuricemia
Choice of Allopurinol versus Uricosurics

20. W.S. apparently has experienced at least 2, and perhaps 4, attacks of gout within the past 8 months. His thiazide diuretic was discontinued at the time of his first attack; however, he is still hyperuricemic with a serum uric acid concentration of 9.4 mg/dL. The uric acid excretion study noted that 690 mg of uric acid was excreted over the course of the 24-hour collection. What hypouricemic medication should W.S. receive? [SI unit: serum uric acid 559 μmol/L]

Two types of hypouricemic drugs have withstood the test of time and are commonly used in the management of symptomatic hyperuricemia. Uricosuric drugs reduce the serum urate concentration by increasing the renal excretion of uric acid; and xanthine-oxidase inhibitors decrease serum uric acid by inhibiting uric acid synthesis. The uricosuric drugs, probenecid (Benemid) and sulfinpyrazone (Anturane), are the most logical hypouricemic agents for the management of patients who are underexcretors of uric acid; and the uric acid synthesis inhibitor, allopurinol (Zyloprim), is the most logical agent for the overproducers of uric acid. Although this strategy for managing hyperuricemia certainly seems attractive, an inhibitor of uric acid synthesis should be effective in both underexcretors and overproducers. Consequently, allopurinol is prescribed most commonly for the management of hyperuricemia because it is an effective hypouricemic in all patients and because comparisons of the relative propensity for adverse effects of uricosurics and allopurinol are not definitive.

Although a 24-hour urine uric acid excretion of 690 mg would numerically label W.S. as an underexcretor, this test result actually is inconclusive. Patients excreting less than 750 mg/day of uric acid generally are considered to be underexcretors; however, 24-hour urine collections are notoriously difficult[84] and to conclude that W.S., who excretes 690 mg/day, is an underexcretor is too categorical. W.S. does not have corroborating evidence of myeloproliferative disease, tophaceous deposits, or renal insufficiency and neither allopurinol nor the uricosuric drug probenecid is better than the other in this situation. Likewise, neither probenecid nor allopurinol is effective for the acute gouty attack, and both are effective only in the long-term management of hyperuricemia.

Allopurinol
Initiation of Therapy: Dose

21. W.S.'s hyperuricemia is to be treated with allopurinol. What would be an appropriate dose of this drug to initiate therapy?

The ability of allopurinol to lower serum uric acid is a dose-related phenomenon. The higher the dose of allopurinol, the greater is the decrease in uric acid serum concentration. Generally, the dose required to normalize hyperuricemia in patients with mild disease is 200 to 300 mg/day, 400 to 600 mg/day in those with moderate or severe disease.[85] Allopurinol doses of 300 mg/day in one study reduced the serum urate concentration to less than 7 mg/dL and halved the urinary uric acid excretion in about 70% of patients. The remaining patients needed 400 to 600 mg/day, although 200 mg/day sufficed in some.[86] Therefore, it would be reasonable to expect that 300 mg/day of allopurinol would be appropriate for W.S. In patients with normal renal function, the initial allopurinol dose should not exceed 300 mg every 24 hours.[87] The serum urate concentration can be used as an excellent guide for subsequent allopurinol doses when managing the hyperuricemia of gout.[88]

Symptoms of acute gout may be slightly exacerbated during the first six weeks of allopurinol therapy because of uric acid mobilization from tissues. Although this claim is not well documented, allopurinol therapy should be initiated slowly simply because nothing is lost by so doing. Patients generally have been hyperuricemic for a good many years and the extra week or two required to reach usual therapeutic doses is inconsequential. Therefore, W.S. should receive 100 mg/day of allopurinol for the first two weeks of therapy. Thereafter, the dose should be increased to whatever is needed to reduce the urate serum concentration to less than 6.5 mg/dL. This gradual approach to initiating allopurinol in this situation is admittedly conservative and perhaps unnecessary.

Onset of Effects

22. When should the hypouricemic effect from allopurinol become apparent?

Serum uric acid levels usually begin to fall within one to two days after initiation of allopurinol therapy; maximal uric acid suppression to a given dose usually requires seven to ten days.[85,86] Serum concentrations of oxypurinol (the active metabolite of allopurinol) comparable to those achieved at steady state, however, may be achieved within minutes after IV administration of 300 to 400 mg of allopurinol or within one to three hours of an oral dose. Therapeutic blood levels for prevention of uric acid nephropathy may, therefore, be achieved quite rapidly in patients with neoplastic disease who must suddenly undergo neoplastic treatment.[88] Clinically observable improvement takes longer. After approximately six months, one should observe a gradual decrease in size of established urate tophi and the absence of new tophaceous deposits if these were present in W.S.

Once Daily Dosing

23. If the half-life of allopurinol is <2 hours why is this drug commonly administered QD?

Approximately 80% of an oral dose of allopurinol is rapidly absorbed when administered by the oral route. Once absorbed (30 minutes to 2 hours), allopurinol is rapidly cleared from plasma with a probable plasma half-life of less than two hours.[88,89] A small portion of allopurinol is excreted in the urine unchanged; the remainder is rapidly oxidized to alloxanthine (oxypurinol). Oxypurinol is eliminated slowly from the blood by renal excretion, and has a serum half-life of 13 to 18 hours and perhaps as much as 30 hours in man.[88,90,145] Oxypurinol thus may accumulate in patients with renal impairment.

Oxypurinol and allopurinol are not bound to plasma proteins and are filtered at the glomerulus. Therefore, factors that decrease glomerular filtration rate would be expected to decrease the clearance of oxypurinol as well. For example, a decrease in the dietary intake of protein decreases creatinine clearance, renal blood flow, and the clearance of oxypurinol by 64%. During a low protein diet (e.g., patients receiving prolonged IV dextrose infusions without amino acid or protein supplements), the plasma oxypurinol half-life increased almost threefold in one study from 17.3 hours to 49.9 hours.[145]

After glomerular filtration, oxypurinol, unlike allopurinol, undergoes proximal tubular reabsorption.[92] As with urate tubular reabsorption, the tubular reabsorption of oxypurinol is significantly enhanced by volume contraction.[87] For example, thiazide diuretics can inhibit the excretion of oxypurinol as they do that of uric acid.[92]

Oxypurinol also is a potent inhibitor of xanthine oxidase and most of allopurinol's xanthine oxidase inhibitory effects are attributable to that of oxypurinol. Due to oxypurinol's long half-life and its acknowledged xanthine-oxidase inhibitory effects, allopurinol can be administered on a once-daily basis. In fact, dosing with allopurinol on any dosing schedule results in the same steady-state effect within a few days.[92] The daily administration of a single 300 mg tablet of allopurinol gives results identical in all parameters to 100 mg three times a day.[90,93]

Adverse Effects

24. What adverse effects are encountered with allopurinol therapy and which one adverse effect is the most clinically significant?

Allopurinol generally is well-tolerated with few significant adverse effects. Occasionally, GI intolerance, bone marrow suppression, renal or hepatic toxicities, or mild skin rash are reported. Hyperuricemic patients receiving allopurinol might be more susceptible to ''ampicillin rash'';[91] and to some interactions with other drugs (see Table 40.2).

Whether allopurinol causes cataracts is controversial. In one study, allopurinol use for more than two years was associated with the formation of cataracts.[145] This adverse reaction has been attributed to above-average exposure to sunlight that enhances the photobinding of allopurinol in the lens resulting in the formation of cataracts.[95] This report disputes the finding of the Boston Collaborative Drug Surveillance Program that any association between the use of allopurinol and the development of cataracts was merely coincidental.[145] However, a subsequent study by Clair et al. found no evidence to confirm a higher risk of cataract formation in allopurinol users than in nonusers.[152]

Hypersensitivity Reactions. Of the adverse drug reactions that sometimes are encountered with allopurinol, hypersensitivity-type reactions have been the most notorious. These generally present as mildly erythematous, dusky red purpuric, or scaly maculopapular skin eruptions. When allopurinol is discontinued promptly, these hypersensitivity reactions subside without sequelae.

The continued administration of allopurinol to hypersensitive individuals, however, has resulted in progression of these symptoms and several fatalities.[96–105] The cutaneous reactions often progressed to include necrosis of the skin and mucous membranes, exfoliative dermatitis, Stevens-Johnson syndrome, or toxic epidermal necrolysis. Hepatomegaly, jaundice, hepatic necrosis, and renal impairment often accompanied these reactions.[144] The hepatic and renal changes usually were reversible when the drug was discontinued and these organ failures were not correlated with any one cutaneous reaction pattern. Patients with renal insufficiency, those receiving thiazide diuretics, and those with chronic alcoholism or severe liver disease have been the most commonly afflicted with this syndrome.

Table 40.2	Allopurinol Drug Interactions[a,b]

Major Documentation

Azathioprine (Imuran). Metabolized to 6-mercaptopurine and then to inactive metabolites by xanthine oxidase. Allopurinol-inhibition of xanthine oxidase ↑ the serum concentration of 6-mercaptopurine and the risk of bone marrow depression. When a patient is stabilized on azathioprine (or 6-mercaptopurine), the azathioprine dose should be ↓ to ¼ of the recommended dose when allopurinol is added[133]

Mercaptopurine (Purinethol). See as Azathioprine

Moderate Documentation

ACE Inhibitors. May predispose patients to severe allopurinol-hypersensitivity reactions (e.g., Stevens-Johnson syndrome). Concurrent and subclinical renal impairment may be important variables

Anticoagulants. Occasional patients on oral anticoagulants and allopurinol will develop enhanced anticoagulant effects; however, this interaction is unpredictable and primarily based upon isolated case reports

Cyclophosphamide. Allopurinol ↑ cyclophosphamide-bone marrow depression based upon epidemiological data and also possibly may inhibit cyclophosphamide clearance

Anecdotal Documentation

Ampicillin. Dermatological reactions occurred in 22.4% of 67 patients receiving concomitant allopurinol and ampicillin, as compared to 7.5% receiving only ampicillin, and 2.1% receiving only allopurinol.[94] The observations from this 1 epidemiological report in 1972 have not been noted subsequently

Antacids. Aluminum hydroxide inhibited the GI absorption of allopurinol in 3 patients on hemodialysis; however, the interaction can be avoided by administration of allopurinol ≥3 hr before aluminum hydroxide

Chlorpropamide. Allopurinol or its metabolites might compete with chlorpropamide for renal tubular secretion and can result in an ↑ chlorpropamide effect in an occasional patient

Phenytoin. Allopurinol inhibits the hepatic metabolism of some drugs and seemed to inhibit the metabolism of phenytoin in 1 patient

Probenecid. Allopurinol can inhibit the metabolism of probenecid and probenecid can enhance the renal elimination of the active oxypurinol

Theophylline. Allopurinol in high doses (300 mg Q 12 hr for 14 days) can ↑ mean theophylline AUC by ≈27% and t½ by 25%; clearance can be ↓ ≈21%. An active metabolite (1-ethylxanthine) also can accumulate[134–136]

Vidarabine. An active metabolite of vidarabine is metabolized by xanthine oxidase and accumulation of this metabolite can ↑ neurotoxicity

---

[a] Adapted from reference 133.
[b] ACE = Angiotensin-converting enzyme; AUC = Area-under-the-concentration-time curve; GI = Gastrointestinal.

The toxic syndrome generally appeared within the first five weeks of therapy; however, it has appeared as part of a delayed hypersensitivity reaction as late as 25 months after the initiation of therapy.[105] The mechanism by which this toxicity syndrome occurs is unknown. The cutaneous reaction and renal failure have been consistent with a diffuse systemic vasculitis and the nonfatal cases did not improve until large steroid doses were instituted despite the discontinuation of the allopurinol. Biopsy specimens from patients provide support for the premise that the vasculitis results from an immune hypersensitivity reaction to allopurinol.[96,99,102,144] Although a specific mechanism or causative agent producing this toxicity has not been identified, the accumulation of allopurinol or a metabolite is postulated to be a primary factor, especially since 80% of patients with this syndrome had significantly impaired renal function before the initiation of allopurinol.[138] In one particular incident, allopurinol serum concentrations were 50 times normal values.[105] Therefore, maintenance doses of allopurinol should be adjusted based upon individual creatinine clearance measurements.[87,102]

25. If a patient has recovered from an allopurinol hypersensitivity syndrome but continues to need this drug because of cytotoxic therapy for malignancy, can a smaller dose of allopurinol be prescribed?

Patients who have recovered from an allopurinol hypersensitivity syndrome should avoid the future use of this drug because most probably will experience a similar reaction upon re-exposure. A few hypersensitive individuals, however, may tolerate low 50 to 100 mg/day doses. If there is no reaction after a few days, the allopurinol dose can be increased gradually. Nevertheless, severe toxic reactions have been produced by doses of allopurinol as low as 1 mg. Some hypersensitive patients have been "desensitized" with daily doses as small as 0.05 mg that were increased gradually over a period of 30 days. One report describes a protocol for intravenous desensitization which was successful in a patient in whom oral desensitization failed.[153] The safety and success rates of these procedures need clarification.[92] Whenever desensitization is planned, the patient must be advised to henceforth take the allopurinol continually. The unreliable patient who may stop and then restart her/his allopurinol is at high risk of precipitating a severe hypersensitivity episode and should not undergo desensitization.

Indications

26. Since allopurinol hypersensitivity syndrome has the potential for significant sequelae, what are reasonable indications for the use of allopurinol?

The indications for the use of allopurinol are now more conservative than in earlier years and include the following:[103]

- tophaceous gout;
- substantial uric acid overexcretors (>900 mg/24 hours);
- frequent gout attacks unresponsive to periodic prophylactic colchicine, when uricosuric agents cannot be used due to intolerance, lack of efficacy, renal insufficiency, or poor patient compliance;
- recurrent uric acid renal calculi;
- recurrent calcium oxalate renal calculi when associated with hyperuricosuria;
- prevention of acute urate nephropathy in patients receiving cytotoxic therapy for malignancies; or
- protection of tissues from reperfusion injury following ischemia.[106]

There is increasing use of allopurinol for patients with myocardial ischemia based upon numerous experimental studies that demonstrate improved function in ischemic hearts pretreated with allopurinol. Apparently, the process of ischemia converts xanthine dehydrogenase to xanthine oxidase, and hypoxanthine accumulates in the cell. Cytotoxic free radicals are formed when xanthine oxidase acts on oxygen and hypoxanthine. Allopurinol works by metabolically preventing the formation of these radicals by inhibiting xanthine oxidase. As a result, some practitioners now administer allopurinol to all patients who are undergoing bypass surgery unless it is specifically contraindicated.[106]

Probenecid

Initiation of Therapy

27. W.S. has not experienced any gouty attacks since the initiation of allopurinol ≈10 months ago. During a routine yearly physical examination, aspartate aminotransferase (AST) was noted to be slightly increased to 90 U/L. All other liver function tests were within normal limits. W.S. stated that he did develop a localized rash that later subsided despite continuation of his medications. Although these findings probably do not represent allopurinol hypersensitivity, the allopurinol is to be discontinued as a precautionary measure and probenecid started. **How should uricosuric therapy be initiated?** [SI unit: AST 90 U/L]

Probenecid (Benemid) is well absorbed orally, and peak plasma concentrations occur within two to four hours. Its biological half-life is 6 to 12 hours and its active metabolites help prolong the uricosuria. The dose of probenecid should be 250 mg twice daily for the first week of therapy; thereafter 500 mg may be given twice a day. If necessary, the dose may be increased to 2 gm/day. Initiation of uricosuric therapy must begin slowly because excretion of large amounts of uric acid increases the risk of urate stone formation in the kidney. This risk can be minimized by starting with small doses of uricosurics so that the kidney is not overwhelmed with a flood of uric acid. Maintenance of a high fluid intake to maintain urine flow of at least 2 L/day also minimizes renal stone formation. This gradual approach to the initiation of hypouricemic therapy also decreases the likelihood of precipitating an acute attack of gout.

Since the initiation of uricosuric therapy has been associated on occasion with acute attacks of gouty arthritis, prophylactic colchicine often is prescribed concurrently. The combination product ColBenemid (colchicine and probenecid) has been formulated to facilitate the administration of these two products.[141] Although it might be reasonable to administer prophylactic colchicine initially opinions on whether to use colchicine in small, prophylactic doses for an indefinite duration are divided. Those who consider it unreasonable to use colchicine for prolonged periods of time cite myopathy which may occur in patients with gout who take customary doses of the drug but who have elevated plasma drug levels because of altered renal function (see Question 17). Their position is strengthened by the case report of the long-term administration of colchicine which led to colchicine toxicity and death in one individual.[107] Nonetheless, prophylactic colchicine still is recommended by those who cite its high efficacy and minimal toxicity when patients with renal and/or hepatic dysfunction are identified and either colchicine avoided completely, or used with great caution in these patients.[154,155] Wallace advocates extreme caution in using colchicine doses of ≥0.6 mg twice daily in patients whose serum creatinine is ≥1.6 mg/dL, or when creatinine clearance is less than 50 mL/minute.[156]

Sulfinpyrazone (Anturane) is a phenylbutazone analogue that is also a very effective uricosuric agent. Like all uricosurics, it inhibits tubular secretion of uric acid at low doses; but at normal therapeutic doses, it inhibits the tubular reabsorption of uric acid. As with probenecid, therapy should be initiated slowly and doses increased gradually.

Onset of Effects

28. How long after the initiation of probenecid would it take for the decrease in the serum uric acid concentration to become noticeable?

When therapy is begun, plasma urate concentrations promptly decrease. After the first day or two, the urinary uric acid excess disappears in normal man; but in hyperuricemic individuals, the excess uric acid is continually mobilized until the body pool of urate is reduced to normal levels.[147] In W.S., probably no change in the serum uric acid concentration will be noted because he has been receiving allopurinol.

Contraindications

29. Does W.S. have any contraindications to the use of probenecid uricosuric therapy?

The fact that uricosuric drugs do not affect the production of uric acid, but merely increase its excretion, places limitations on their use. Probenecid should not be used in patients with a creatinine clearance of less than 20 to 30 mL/minute or a BUN greater than 40 mg/dL. Patients with a history of frequent renal stones and patients who are gross overexcretors (>1000 mg/day) of uric acid should not be treated with uricosurics. Additionally, these agents should not be used in patients suffering an acute attack of gout. None of these contraindications are applicable to W.S., and probenecid can be safely prescribed for him.

Salicylate Interaction

30. W.S. is a health-conscious person who realizes that he has 2 risk factors for ischemic heart disease: hypertension and hyperuricemia. Therefore, to reduce the chance of a coronary event he self-medicates with a dose of aspirin 1 tablet/day. Is there a problem with aspirin use in W.S.?

Two tablets of aspirin 300 mg every six hours can completely antagonize the uricosuric effects of 2 gm of probenecid. This drug interaction probably involves several mechanisms including competition for renal tubular transport.[108] Doses of salicylate that do not produce serum salicylate levels of at least 5 mg/dL do not significantly affect probenecid uricosuria.[133] Therefore, a single daily aspirin probably will not interfere with the probenecid he is taking, but W.S. should be warned not to exceed one aspirin per day. Monitoring of his serum uric acid, however, should take into account the possible effect of even this low dose of aspirin. Interestingly, salicylates do not affect the ability of probenecid to inhibit the tubular secretion of penicillin, and when used in high doses (e.g., 1.3 gm QID) aspirin exhibits a degree of uricosuric activity of its own. Acetaminophen (Tylenol) and the NSAIDs do not interfere with probenecid and are reliable alternatives for antipyresis and mild analgesia in patients taking uricosuric agents.

Asymptomatic Hyperuricemia

Clinical Significance

31. L.M., a 50-year-old man, is seen by his physician for a routine evaluation. His physical examination is unremarkable and his laboratory evaluations are all within normal limits except for a serum uric acid concentration of 9.5 mg/dL which was noted on an SMA-12 panel. What is the clinical significance of this hyperuricemia? [SI unit: serum uric acid 565 μmol/L]

Hyperuricemia is common, is associated with many medications (most commonly the thiazide diuretics), and can be affected by laboratory methods of analysis for uric acid. Some common medications associated with hyperuricemia are listed in Table 40.3.

Laboratory Tests of Uric Acid

There are several methods for the analysis of uric acid and each method and laboratory has different standard normal values for the same sample. The phosphotungstate or colorimetric method, commonly utilized in automated laboratory screening panels, is not as specific as the uricase method of uric acid analysis and generally provides readings that are about 1 mg/dL higher, for the same sample.

In normal subjects, plasma becomes saturated with sodium urate at a concentration of 7 mg/dL. Supersaturated solutions of monosodium urate, however, form readily and serum urate concentrations as high as 40 to 60 mg/dL are not uncommon in untreated, nongouty patients with myeloproliferative disorders.[109] It is unclear how uric acid can remain in a supersaturated solution and then, suddenly, under certain conditions, begin to precipitate out. Nevertheless, it is known that plasma urate-binding protein deficiency, urate affinity for chondroitin sulfate, local pH changes, cold, trauma, and stress can cause seeding of urate crystals.

Table 40.3	Drugs Commonly Associated with Hyperuricemia
Cyclosporine	
Dideoxyinosine	
Diuretics: acetazolamide, chlorthalidone, ethacrynic acid, furosemide, indapamide, mercurials, spironolactone, thiazides	
Ethambutol	
Ethanol	
Glucocorticoids	
Granulocyte macrophage colony stimulating factor	
Ketoconazole	
Levodopa	
Methyldopa	
Niacin	
Pancreatin	
Pancrelipase	
Pyrazinamide	
Salicylates (low dose)	
Theophylline	

When maximum serum uric acid concentrations from the Framingham Heart Study[5] were analyzed, gouty arthritis was noted to occur in 1.8% of those patients with serum uric acid concentrations between 6 to 6.9 mg/dL and in 11.8% of those with levels between 7 to 7.9 mg/dL. Nevertheless, 15% of the men who actually had developed gouty arthritis did not have a serum uric acid value above 6.9 mg/dL and 81% of subjects with serum uric acid values of greater than 7 mg/dL did not develop gouty arthritis. The higher the serum concentration of uric acid, the greater was the risk of developing gouty arthritis, but a high serum uric acid concentration was not a guarantee for the development of gout.

Treatment

32. Should asymptomatic hyperuricemia, such as that noted in L.M., be treated?

Individuals with high serum uric acid levels are more likely to develop acute gouty arthritis than normouricemic individuals, and the magnitude of the risk increases with increasing degrees of hyperuricemia. Nevertheless, it would be excessive to treat all hyperuricemic individuals with uric acid lowering medications for a lifetime solely for the prevention of acute attacks of gouty arthritis. A large percentage of hyperuricemic patients may never experience an acute attack of gout.[115] If an attack should occur, it can be treated easily within 48 to 72 hours, and after the acute episode has subsided, uric acid lowering medications can then be considered.

The key issue in the treatment of hyperuricemia concerns the effect of uric acid on renal function. Renal disease commonly was associated with gout, and renal failure was thought to be the eventual cause of death in as many as 25% of gouty patients. Thus, treatment of asymptomatic hyperuricemia is justifiable if renal disease is prevented. This renal damage, however, was noted to occur in a setting that included either hypertension, diabetes, renal vascular disease, glomerulonephritis, pyelonephritis, renal calculi, or some other cause of primary nephropathy independent of gout.[110] In fact, the coexistence of gout and renal insufficiency without hypertension is so rare that its presence should raise the suspicion of chronic lead toxicity.[111,112] Therefore, the consensus now seems to be that hyperuricemia by itself has no deleterious effect on renal function.[113,114] Considering the financial costs, risks of adverse drug reactions, and practical considerations such as patient compliance, drug treatment of asymptomatic hyperuricemia is difficult to justify.[115]

The relationship of hyperuricemia to hypertension in individuals who have not had gout was studied prospectively in 124 hyperuricemic subjects. None of these patients had evidence of gout, hypertension, or cardiovascular, renal, or other diseases. After ten years, 22.5% of these individuals with ''asymptomatic hyperuricemia'' had developed hypertension and 5.4% had developed atherosclerotic heart disease. The incidences of hypertension and atherosclerotic heart disease in the control group were 2.1% and 0.5%, respectively.[116] Atherosclerosis and hypertension apparently were more serious problems in this population than renal disease. Although hyperuricemia may represent an important risk factor for the development of cardiovascular disease,[6] the evidence is not sufficiently compelling to justify the treatment of asymptomatic hyperuricemia at this time.

Special Situations

Urate Nephropathy

33. Q.A., a 54-year-old male with a history of congestive heart failure (CHF), is hospitalized with a diagnosis of acute myelogenous leukemia. On admission, BUN was 49 mg/dL; SrCr was 2.1 mg/dL; and serum uric acid was 16.2 mg/dL. On the following hospital day, chemotherapy was begun. His white blood cell (WBC) count decreased within a week from 90,000 cells/mm^3 on admission to 7500 cells/mm^3 as a result of the cytotoxic treatment. On the seventh day he complained of nausea, and his urine volume decreased to 35 mL/24 hr. At this time, BUN increased to 115 mg/dL, SrCr increased to 10.6 mg/dL, serum potassium (K) was 5.9 mEq/L, and serum uric acid increased to 22.6 mg/dL. IV furosemide and urine alkalinization had no effect on Q.A.'s clinical condition, and hemodialysis was started because of continued clinical deterioration. During the ensuing 2 days, the urine output increased and then gradually returned to normal. Q.A.'s renal function continued to improve, and 16 days after hemodialysis was initiated, SrCr was again 2.1 mg/dL. What was the probable cause for the increased serum uric acid concentration that was noted upon Q.A.'s admission? [SI units: BUN 17.5 41 mmol/L of urea, respectively; SrCr 186 and 937 μmol/L, respectively; serum uric acid 964 and 1344 μmol/L, respectively; WBC 90 × 10^9/L; serum K 5.9 mmol/L]

Upon superficial review, it would appear that the hyperuricemia in Q.A. is a result of both overproduction and underexcretion of uric acid. The major cause of hyperuricemia in this case, however, is most likely due to the overproduction of nucleic acids secondary to the leukemia and subsequent tumor lysis syndrome accompanying chemotherapy. Mild to moderate renal failure is not usually a cause of hyperuricemia as long as the creatinine clearance is greater than 15 mL/minute. Renal urate secretory mechanisms remain functional and do not become defective until the creatinine clearance falls to less than 10 mL/minute. At this level of renal function, the defective secretory mechanism is unable to compensate entirely for the decrease in urate reabsorption, and hyperuricemia occurs.[119,143]

Urine Alkalinization

34. Why was urine alkalinization tried in Q.A.?

Urine alkalinization was instituted because the serum uric acid was 22.6 mg/dL in the presence of oliguria. Uric acid is poorly soluble in water, but a pKa of 5.75 allows for greater solubility of the ionized form in alkaline environments. At a urine pH of 5, only 6 to 8 mg of uric acid are soluble per deciliter of urine. When urine is alkalinized to pH 7, the solubility of uric acid increases 20-fold to 120 to 160 mg/dL. Although asymptomatic hyperuricemia is not associated with renal impairment, unusually high serum uric acid concentrations in the presence of oliguria and undue acidity may result in the intrarenal and urinary precipitation of urate.[114] Thus, the desire to alkalinize the urine can be appreciated.

Urine can be alkalinized using sodium or potassium bicarbonate in an initial oral dose of 4 gm followed by 1 to 2 gm every four

hours. Intravenous sodium bicarbonate also can be used, as it was in Q.A. The urine pH should be tested (e.g., nitrazine paper) at intervals throughout the day and the dose of bicarbonate should be adjusted accordingly. Potassium or sodium citrate also can be used in doses of 1 gm three to six times daily or Shohl's solution 10 to 30 mL four times daily. The citrates have the same urine alkalinizing properties of sodium bicarbonate and neither neutralize gastric secretions nor promote a dumping syndrome. The bicarbonate and citrate doses should be divided evenly throughout the day and night. During the night, the urine becomes the most concentrated and acidic; thus, it may be necessary to add an intravenous dose to the IV solution during the night in hospitalized patients. Acetazolamide (Diamox) also is capable of alkalinizing urine, but it can produce a mild metabolic acidosis which is undesirable in a patient with renal decompensation.

Although an alkaline urine theoretically is desirable to increase the solubility of uric acid, it often is difficult to achieve clinically without affecting other organ systems. In Q.A. with his CHF, sodium intake is a problem and the benefits from alkalinization probably are not worth the effort. In patients with hematologic malignancies a primary goal is to prevent the hyperuricemia that developed in Q.A. Every effort should be made to identify patients at risk of tumor lysis syndrome, and pretreat with hydration, allopurinol, and urine alkalinization during the first one to two days of chemotherapy. The ability of the kidneys to excrete potassium also may be of critical importance. The cation content of various alkalinizing agents is listed in Table 40.4.

Hemodialysis

35. Hemodialysis was initiated in Q.A. How well is uric acid dialyzed and would prophylaxis against an acute attack be needed?

Uric acid is readily dialyzable despite the finding that it is bound to plasma proteins.[118] Apparently, this urate-albumin bond is weak and influenced by many factors. In fact, hemodialysis is so efficient in removing uric acid that each six-hour dialysis can reduce the uric acid level by 50%. In 16 patients with hyperuricemia and renal failure, each six-hour dialysis removed 1.5 to 13.4 gm of uric acid. Although 3.4 to 4.8 gm of uric acid can be removed by peritoneal dialysis, hemodialysis is estimated to be between 10 to 20 times more efficient in eliminating uric acid.[119] Disequilibrium does not occur even with rapid hemodialysis and prophylaxis against an acute gouty attack is unnecessary.

Renal Transplants and Cyclosporine

36. T.M., a 42-year-old renal transplant patient, developed an acute attack of gout localized to the great toe of the left foot while being treated with prednisone, cyclosporine, and azathioprine for maintenance immunosuppression. His cyclosporine dose of 14 mg/kg/day during the first posttransplant week subsequently was reduced based upon SrCr concentrations (<2 mg/dL) and trough cyclosporine blood levels (between 100–200 ng/mL). The prednisone dose of 2 mg/kg/day (50 mg BID) was gradually tapered to 20 mg QD 3 months after transplant and to 10 mg/day subsequently. The azathioprine dose of 1.5 to 2.5 mg/kg/day was adjusted to maintain a WBC count

Table 40.4	Cation Content of Alkalinizing Agents
Product	mEq/gm
Na HCO$_3$	11.9
Na Citrate • 2H$_2$O	8.4
K HCO$_3$	9.9
K Citrate • H$_2$O	9.3

of >3000 cells/mm^3. **The serum urate concentration at time of presentation was 11.8 mg/dL. Which of T.M.'s medications is most likely to cause his hyperuricemia and attack of gout?** [SI units: SrCr <177 µmol/L; WBC >3000 × 10^9; serum urate 702 µmol/L]

The incidence of hyperuricemia in renal allograft recipients receiving azathioprine, prednisone, and antilymphocyte globulin is similar to that of the general population; however, hyperuricemia is common in cyclosporine-treated renal allograft recipients[120] and heart transplant patients.[121]

The hyperuricemia occurs independently of cyclosporine-induced nephrotoxicity and occurs in about 30% to 80% of patients depending upon the definition of hyperuricemia.[122] The University of Minnesota renal transplant team noted that 105 of 131 patients (80%) who were treated with both cyclosporine and prednisone experienced hyperuricemia (serum uric acid >8 mg/dL) and 13 of 131 (10%) were severely hyperuricemic (serum uric acid >14 mg/dL).[120] Lin et al. at the University of Michigan reported that among the patients with stable allograft function and serum creatinine concentrations less than 3 mg/dL, hyperuricemia occurred in 84% of the cyclosporine-treated group versus 30% of the azathioprine group.[122] Despite the frequent occurrence of hyperuricemia, gout occurred in only about 5% to 10% of these patients.

A longitudinal study of a subgroup of the cyclosporine-treated patients revealed that hyperuricemia usually developed within three months after renal transplantation and the mean length of time from transplantation to the first attack of gout was 24 months.[122] The prevalence of gout and the onset of gout may be higher in heart transplant patients because of the larger doses of cyclosporine.

37. Mechanism. What is the mechanism of cyclosporine-induced hyperuricemia?

Whenever the serum concentration of any substance is noted to be at a greater concentration than expected, the question that must always be asked is whether the high concentration should be attributed to increased input (e.g., overproduction), decreased clearance, or a combination of decreased clearance and increased production. This principle holds true for all substances regardless of whether the problem is a high serum concentration of potassium, glucose, or uric acid. Since uric acid is produced primarily as a by-product of purine metabolism and is excreted renally, cyclosporine-induced hyperuricemia must be evaluated both as to increased production and decreased clearance.

The urate metabolism of 13 patients (6 adults with stable, functioning transplanted kidneys who were receiving cyclosporine therapy, 4 normal adults, 1 renal-transplant donor, and 2 renal-transplant recipients who were being treated with azathioprine and prednisone) was studied.[122] At least seven days before the study, all subjects discontinued medications that were known to affect uric acid clearance and were placed on a purine-free diet. Urine samples were collected every eight hours on the first day, every 12 hours on the second day, and then every 24 hours for the ensuing five days. The purine-enzyme activities of erythrocytes and the plasma concentrations of adenosine, inosine, hypoxanthine, and xanthine were measured. The rates of urate turnover were similar in all 13 patients, and there was no change in purine-metabolite levels or in the activity of enzymes involved in purine metabolism. As a result, hyperuricemia was deemed to occur as a consequence of decreased urate clearance rather than as a consequence of the overproduction of urate.[122]

Acute cyclosporine-prerenal nephrotoxicity is associated with intrarenal vasoconstriction and diminished glomerular filtration rate (GFR); and chronic renal insufficiency caused by cyclosporine is associated with renal parenchymal injury.[123] Renal tubular, glomerular, renovascular, and interstitial lesions all have been associated with cyclosporine. Since the clearance of urate in the kidney occurs by glomerular filtration, proximal tubular reabsorption, proximal tubular secretion, and postsecretory reabsorption, cyclosporine-induced renal insufficiency could modify urate clearance by affecting one or all of these processes. Serum creatinine concentrations, however, did not change significantly in the 13 patients enrolled in the University of Michigan study and no direct correlation was noted with trough cyclosporine concentrations.[122] Nevertheless, cyclosporine-induced hyperuricemia is deemed to be the result of decreased renal urate clearance. Serum creatinine values do not adequately reflect renal function in cyclosporine-treated patients because cyclosporine enhances creatinine clearance relative to glomerular filtration rate resulting in spuriously low serum creatinine concentrations despite marked reductions in GFR.[124,125]

Cyclosporine also may have an independent effect on urate transport within the tubules.[126]

38. Treatment. What drug-specific factors influence the selection of the most effective agent for treating acute gout in T.M.?

The drug therapy of uncomplicated acute gout with NSAIDs and corticosteroids is relatively straight forward because all of the drugs in these categories are effective and relatively nontoxic when used for only a few days. Even colchicine, when appropriate precautions are taken, is relatively safe to use. The management of acute gout in transplant patients, however, poses several special problems. Colchicine is to be used with caution in patients with decreased renal function because of the increased potential for neuromuscular toxicity and bone marrow dysplasia (see Question 17). The NSAIDs can reduce renal prostaglandin synthesis and can cause serious nephrotoxicity especially in heart transplant patients who are receiving cyclosporine and perhaps diuretics as well.[121] The concurrent use of corticosteroids and cyclosporine has the potential to increase the plasma concentrations of both drugs and, possibly, to be associated with increased seizure activity based upon preliminary anecdotal reports.[127-130]

Since all of these drugs seem to be associated with increased potential for toxicity, the clinical experience of others, although anecdotal, is worthy of review. Kahl et al.[121] describe four patients with acute gout who experienced a prompt increase in serum creatinine concentrations of 0.7 mg/dL to 1.7 mg/dL after only a few doses of an NSAID. Two of these cases involved the use of sulindac (Clinoril), the NSAID with the least adverse effects on renal prostaglandins (see Chapter 41: Rheumatic Disorders). Although these patients experienced difficulty with the NSAIDs, their gout responded to modest doses of colchicine. In three patients, however, the use of colchicine was limited by diarrhea, and it was withheld in two patients who were experiencing azathioprine-leukopenia because of the possible additive bone marrow suppressing effects of colchicine.[121] The acute attacks of gout in six renal transplant patients were controlled with colchicine.[120] Experience with large corticosteroid doses for the treatment of acute gout in transplant patients is limited, but perhaps will increase because of the newer trials in nontransplant patients.[54,55]

Treating acute gout in the transplant patient presents a serious therapeutic dilemma. All drugs carry hazards, yet patients like T.M. require relief from the pain and inflammatory discomfort of the attack. Furthermore, cyclosporine-induced gout appears to be particularly aggressive in some patients even though clinical symptoms probably are ameliorated by the concomitant immunosuppressive and anti-inflammatory drugs being administered.[157] Since the acute attack compels treatment, the apparent option is to select an agent from among the NSAIDs, corticosteroids, or colchicine that potentially appears to be the least damaging, then to dose it cautiously, closely monitor key parameters, and discontinue it as soon as possible. Pre-existing hyperurecemia prior to transplantation should be treated aggressively in the pretransplant waiting period. In T.M.'s case since there is monoarticular involvement, an intra-articular injection of corticosteroid, which provides minimal systemic effects, might be a reasonable choice when supplemented with a few doses of opiate analgesic, if needed.

39. Risks. Is hypouricemic treatment feasible in T.M.? If so, what adverse effects must be guarded against?

The management of hyperuricemia in the transplant patient is a therapeutic dilemma because uricosuric drugs and xanthine-oxidase inhibitors are relatively contraindicated. Alternative hypouricemic drugs are unavailable in America, although uricase, an enzyme that metabolizes uric acid, is under study[131] and urate oxidase has been used in Europe.[132]

The uricosuric drugs sulfinpyrazone (Anturane) and probenecid (Benemid) are ineffective in patients with decreased renal function (i.e., Cl_{Cr} <30 mL/minute or BUN >40 mg/dL). These drugs, therefore, would be ineffective in many renal transplant patients and would increase the risk of intrarenal urate precipitation.

The xanthine-oxidase inhibitor, allopurinol, is associated with a greater potential for significant adverse effects in patients with decreased renal or hepatic function.[100,102] (Also see Question 24.) Furthermore, allopurinol interacts in a clinically significant manner with azathioprine, an immunosuppressive agent commonly used in combination with cyclosporine and prednisone for the prevention of organ rejection in transplant recipients.

Azathioprine is first metabolized to 6-mercaptopurine and then to inactive metabolites via a metabolic pathway controlled by xanthine oxidase. The inhibition of xanthine oxidase by allopurinol, therefore, impairs the conversion of 6-mercaptopurine. Since the principal toxic effect of mercaptopurine is bone marrow depression, the increased blood concentrations of 6-mercaptopurine can exert profound toxic effects on the bone marrow and other tissues. Allopurinol and azathioprine should never be given together without meticulous attention to adjusting the dosage of the azathioprine. When allopurinol is prescribed for a patient stabilized on either azathioprine or 6-mercaptopurine, the azathioprine dose should be reduced to one-fourth of the recommended dose.[133] Since pre-existing renal dysfunction predisposes patients to this drug interaction, the use of allopurinol in renal transplant recipients, who already are stabilized on azathioprine, is especially hazardous.

The dose of allopurinol also should be adjusted in patients with renal impairment. The plasma half-life of oxypurinol, an active metabolite of allopurinol, is 18 to 30 hours in patients with normal renal function and increases in proportion to the reduction of glomerular filtration in patients with renal impairment.[78,88] The high serum concentrations of allopurinol and oxypurinol purportedly increase the intrinsic hepatotoxicity of allopurinol.[105]

References

1 **Kelley WN, Schumacher HR Jr.** Gout. In: Kelley WN et al., eds. Textbook of Rheumatology. Philadelphia: WB Saunders; 1993.

2 **Lesch M et al.** Familial disorder of uric acid metabolism and central nervous system function. Am J Med. 1964;36:561.

3 **Wortman RL.** Gout and other disorders of purines metabolism. In: Isselbacher KJ et al., eds. Harrison's Principles of Internal Medicine. 13th ed. New York: McGraw-Hill; 1994.

4 **Puig JG et al.** Renal handling of uric acid in gout: impaired tubular transport of urate not dependent on serum urate levels. Metabolism. 1986;35:1147.

5 **Hall AP et al.** Epidemiology of gout and hyperuricemia: a long-term population study. Am J Med. 1967;42:27.

6 **Abbott RD et al.** Gout and coronary artery disease: the Framingham study. J Clin Epidemiol. 1988;41:237.

7 **Roubenoff R.** Gout and hyperuricemia. Rheum Dis Clin North Am. 1990;16:539.

8 **Hermann G, Bloch C.** Gout. In: Taveras JM, Ferrucci JT, eds. Radiology: Diagnosis, Imaging, Intervention. Philadelphia: JB Lippincott; 1988;1–11.

9 **Hadler NM et al.** Acute polyarticular gout. Am J Med. 1974;56:715.

10 **Baraf HSB et al.** Acute arthritis: prevalence of chronic synovitis, polyarticular attacks, and positive serological test for rheumatoid factor. Arthritis Rheum. 1978;21:544.

11 **Lawry GV et al.** Polyarticular versus monoarticular gout: a prospective comparative analysis of clinical features. Medicine (Baltimore). 1988;67:335.

12 **Rosenthall L et al.** Radionuclide joint imaging in the diagnosis of synovial disease. Semin Arthritis Rheum. 1977;7:49.

13 **Lipsmeier EA.** Acute gouty arthritis presenting as polyarticular disease. South Med J. 1982;75:82.

14 **Simkin PA.** The pathogenesis of podagra. Ann Intern Med. 1977;86:230.

15 **Simkin PA et al.** Transsynovial exchange of small molecules in normal human subjects. J Appl Physiol. 1974;36:581.

16 **Simkin PA.** Synovial permeability in rheumatoid arthritis. Arthritis Rheum. 1979;22:689.

17 **Cardenosa G, Deluca SA.** Radiographic features of gout. Am Fam Physician. 1990;4:539.

18 **Campbell SM.** Gout: how presentation, diagnosis, and treatment differ in the elderly. Geriatrics. 1988;43:71.

19 **McCarty DJ.** The gouty toe—a multifactorial condition. Ann Intern Med. 1977;86:234.

20 **Scott JT.** Long-term management of gout and hyperuricemia. Br Med J. 1980;281:1164.

21 **Fessel WJ.** Distinguishing gout from other types of arthritis. Postgrad Med. 1978;63:134.

22 **German DC, Holmes EW.** Hyperuricemia and gout. Med Clin North Am. 1986;70:419.

23 **McCarty DJ et al.** Identification of urate crystals in gouty synovial fluid. Ann Intern Med. 1961;54:452.

24 **Wallace SL et al.** Preliminary criteria for the classification of the acute arthritis of primary gout. Arthritis Rheum. 1977;20:895.

25 **Becker MA.** Clinical aspects of monosodium urate crystal deposition disease (gout). Rheum Dis Clin North Am. 1988;14:377.

26 **Honig S et al.** Crystal deposition disease. Diagnosis by electron microscopy. Am J Med. 1977;63:161.

27 **Schumacher HR et al.** Acute gouty arthritis without urate crystals identified on initial examination of synovial fluid. Arthritis Rheum. 1975;18:603.

28 **Abeles M et al.** Acute gouty arthritis. The diagnostic importance of aspirating more than one involved joint. JAMA. 1977;238:2526.

29 **Romanoff NR et al.** Gout without crystals on initial synovial fluid analysis. Postgrad Med J. 1978;54:95.

30 **Bomalski JS et al.** Monosodium urate crystals in the knee joints of patients with asymptomatic nontophaceous gout. Arthritis Rheum. 1986;29:1480.

31 **Agudelo CA et al.** Definitive diagnosis of gout by identification of urate crystals in asymptomatic metatarsophalangeal joints. Arthritis Rheum. 1979;22:559.

32 **Weinberger A et al.** Urate crystals in asymptomatic metatarsophalangeal joints. Ann Intern Med. 1979;91:56.

33 **Finch W.** Acute crystal-induced arthritis. Postgrad Med. 189;85:273.

34 **Simkin PA.** Articular oxalate crystals and the taxonomy of gout. JAMA. 1988;260:1285.

35 **Kuncl RW et al.** Colchicine myopathy and neuropathy. N Engl J Med. 1987;316:1562.

36 **Sturge RA et al.** Multicenter trial of naproxen and phenylbutazone in acute gout. Ann Rheum Dis. 1977;36:80.

37 **Wilkens RF et al.** The treatment of acute gout with naproxen. J Clin Pharmacol. 1975;15:363.

38 **Franck WA et al.** Ibuprofen in acute polyarticular gout. Arthritis Rheum. 1976;19:269.

39 **Schweitz MC et al.** Ibuprofen in the treatment of acute gouty arthritis. JAMA. 1978;239:34.

40 **Wanasukaput S et al.** Effect of fenoprofen calcium on acute gouty arthritis. JAMA. 1978;239:34.

41 **Weiner GI et al.** Double-blind study of fenoprofen versus phenylbutazone in acute gouty arthritis. Arthritis Rheum. 1979;22:425.

42 **Widmark PH.** Piroxicam: its safety and efficacy in the treatment of acute gout. Am J Med. (Suppl. 16 Feb 1982):63–5.

43 **Bluestone RH.** Safety and efficacy of piroxicam in the treatment of gout. Am J Med. (Suppl. 1 Feb 1982):66–9.

44 **Lomen PL.** Flurbiprofen in the treatment of acute gout. Am J Med. 1986;80(Suppl. 3A):134.

45 **Tamisier JN.** Ketoprofen. Clin Rheum Dis. 1979;5:381.

46 **Petera P et al.** Treatment of acute gout attacks with tolmetin. Wien Med Wochenschr. 1982;132:43.

47 **Eberl R, Dunky A.** Meclofenamate sodium in the treatment of acute gout. Arzneimittelforschung. 1983;33:641.

48 **Karachalios GN, Donas G.** Sulindac in the treatment of acute gout arthritis. Int J Tiss React. 1982;4:297.

49 **Calabro JJ et al.** Clinoril in acute gout. Acta Rheum Report. 1974;8:163.

50 **Fletcher MA, Wade AG.** Clinical experience with isoxicam in patients with acute gout. Br J Clin Pract. 1985;39:108.

51 **Hutzel H.** Treatment of acute gouty attack and gout prophylaxis with carprofen. Eur J Rheumatol Inflamm. 1982;5:514.

52 **Marcolongo R et al.** Intravenous indoprofen for prompt relief of acute

gout: a regimen-finding study. J Int Med Res. 1980;8:326.

53   Wallace SL, Singer JZ. Therapy in gout. Rheum Dis Clin North Am. 1988; 14:441.

54   Groff GD et al. Systemic steroid therapy for acute gout: a clinical trial and review of the literature. Semin Arthritis Rheum. 1990;19:329.

55   Axelrod D, Preston S. Comparison of parenteral adrenocorticotropic hormone with indomethacin in the treatment of acute gout. Arthritis Rheum. 1988;31:803.

56   Gutman AB. Treatment of primary gout: the present status. Arthritis Rheum. 1965;8:911

57   Seegmiller JE. The acute attack of gouty arthritis. Arthritis Rheum. 1965; 8:714.

58   Meyler L et al. Side Effects of Drugs. Baltimore, MD: Williams and Wilkins; 1968:116,449,500.

59   Patak RV et al. Antagonism of the effects of furosemide by indomethacin in normal and hypertensive man. Prostaglandins. 1975;10:649.

60   Frolich JC et al. Suppression of plasma renin activity by indomethacin in man. Circ Res. 1976;39:447.

61   Smith DE et al. Attenuation of furosemide's diuretic effect by indomethacin: pharmacokinetic evaluation. J Pharmacokinet Biopharm. 1974;7:265.

62   Brater DC. Analysis of the effect of indomethacin on the response to furosemide in man: effect of dose of furosemide. J Pharmacol Exp Ther. 1979; 210:386.

63   Durao V et al. Modification of antihypertensive effect of beta-adrenoreceptor blocking agents by inhibition of endogenous prostaglandin synthesis. Lancet. 1977;2:1005.

64   Findling JW et al. Indomethacin-induced hyperkalemia in three patients with gouty arthritis. JAMA. 1980;244:1127.

65   Roberts WN et al. Colchicine in acute gout: reassessment of risks and benefits. JAMA. 1987;257:1920.

66   Demartini FE. Hyperuricemia induced by drugs. Arthritis Rheum. 1965;8:823.

67   Steele TH et al. Factors affecting urate excretion following diuretic administration in man. Am J Med. 1969;47:564.

68   Manuel MA et al. Changes in urate handling after prolonged thiazide treatment. Am J Med. 1974;57:741.

69   Wyngaarden JB. Diuretics and hyperuricemia. N Engl J Med. 1970;283:1170.

70   Scopelitis E, McGrath H Jr. NSAID-masked gout. South Med J. 1987;80;1464.

71   Wallace SL et al. Diagnostic value of the colchicine therapeutic trial. JAMA. 1967;199:525.

72   Talbott JH. Gouty arthritis: a disease for all ages. Geriatrics. 1980;35:71.

73   Dinarello CA et al. Colchicine therapy for familial Mediterranean fever. N Engl J Med. 1974;294:934.

74   Zemer D et al. A controlled trial of colchicine in preventing attacks of familial Mediterranean fever. N Engl J Med. 1974;294:932.

75   Rubinow A et al. Amyloidosis secondary to polyarticular gout. Arthritis Rheum. 1981;24:1425.

76   Liu YK et al. Marrow aplasia induced by colchicine: a case report. Arthritis Rheum. 1978;21:731.

77   Yu TF. Milestones in the treatment of gout. Am J Med. 1974;56:676.

78   Insel PA. Analgesics-antipyretics and anti-inflammatory agents: drugs employed in the treatment of gout. In: Gilman AG et al., eds. The Pharmacological Basis of Therapeutics. 8th ed. New York: McMillan; 1990:638–81.

79   Naidus RM et al. Colchicine toxicity. Arch Intern Med. 1977;137:394.

80   Merlin HE. Azoospermia caused by colchicine: a case report. Fertil Steril. 1972;23:180.

81   Bremmer WF et al. Colchicine and testicular function in man. N Engl J Med. 1976;294:1384.

82   Simkin PA et al. Uric acid excretion: quantitative assessment from spot, midmorning serum and urine samples. Ann Intern Med. 1979;91:44.

83   Wortmann RL et al. Limited value of uric acid to creatinine ratios in estimating uric acid excretion. Ann Intern Med. 1980;93:822.

84   Turner WJ et al. Vicissitudes in research: the twenty-four hour urine collection. Clin Pharmacol Ther. 1971;12:163.

85   Rundles RW et al. Allopurinol in the treatment of gout. Ann Intern Med. 1966;64:229.

86   Yu TF et al. Effect of allopurinol [4 hydroxypyrazolo-3(4-d) pyrimidine] on serum and urinary uric acid in primary and secondary gout. Am J Med. 1964;37:885.

87   Cameron JS, Simmonds HA. Use and abuse of allopurinol. Br Med J. (Clin Res). 1987;294:1504.

88   Hande K et al. Allopurinol kinetics. Clin Pharmacol Ther. 1978;23:598.

89   Elion GB. Enzymatic and metabolic studies with allopurinol. Ann Rheum Dis. 1966;25:608.

90   Elion GB et al. Renal clearance of oxypurinol, the chief metabolite of allopurinol. Am J Med. 1968;45:69.

91   Boston Collaborative Drug Surveillance Program. Excess of ampicillin rashes associated with allopurinol or hyperuricemia. N Engl J Med. 1972;286:505.

92   Rundles RW. The development of allopurinol. Arch Intern Med. 1985;145:1492.

93   Rodman GP et al. Allopurinol and gouty hyperuricemia. JAMA. 1975;231:1143.

94   Berlinger WG et al. The effect of dietary protein on the clearance of allopurinol and oxypurinol. N Engl J Med. 1985;313:771.

95   Fraunfelder F, Lerman S. Allopurinol therapy. Am J Ophthalmol. 1985;99:215. Letter.

96   Kantor GL. Toxic epidermal necrolysis, azotemia, and death after allopurinol therapy. JAMA. 1970;212:478.

97   Mills RM. Severe hypersensitivity reaction associated with allopurinol. JAMA. 1971;216:799.

98   Young JL Jr et al. Severe allopurinol hypersensitivity. Arch Intern Med. 1974;134:553.

99   Boyer TD et al. Allopurinol-hypersensitivity vasculitis and liver damage. West J Med. 1977;126:143.

100 Al-Kawas FH et al. Allopurinol hepatotoxicity: report of two cases and review of the literature. Ann Intern Med. 1981;95:588.

101 Lang PG. Severe hypersensitivity reactions to allopurinol. South Med J. 1979;72:1361.

102 Hande KR et al. Severe allopurinol toxicity: description and guidelines for prevention in patients with renal insufficiency. Am J Med. 1984;76:47.

103 Singer JZ, Wallace SL. The allopurinol hypersensitivity syndrome: unnecessary morbidity and mortality. Arthritis Rheum. 1986;29:82.

104 Rundles RW et al. Metabolic effects of allopurinol and alloxanthine. Ann Rheum Dis. 1966;25:615.

105 Tam S, Carroll W. Allopurinol hepatotoxicity. Am J Med. 1989;86:357.

106 Johnson WD et al. A randomized controlled trial of allopurinol in coronary bypass surgery. Am Heart J. 1991;121:20.

107 Neuss MN et al. Long-term colchicine administration leading to colchicine toxicity and death. Arthritis Rheum. 1986;29:448.

108 Yu TF et al. Mutual suppression of the uricosuric effects of sulfinpyrazone and salicylate: a study of interactions between drugs. J Clin Invest. 1963;42:1330.

109 Smyth CJ. Disorders associated with hyperuricemia. Arthritis Rheum. 1975;18(Suppl.):713.

110 Berger L et al. Renal function in gout. Am J Med. 1975;59:605.

111 Batuman V et al. The role of lead in gout nephropathy. N Engl J Med. 1981;304:520.

112 Reif MC et al. Chronic gouty nephropathy: a vanishing syndrome? N Engl J Med. 1981;304:535.

113 Yu TF et al. Renal function in gout. Factors influencing the renal hemodynamics. Am J Med. 1979;67(Pt. V):766.

114 Yu TF et al. Impaired renal function in gout. Its association with hypertensive vascular disease and intrinsic renal disease. Am J Med. 1982;72:95.

115 Liang MH et al. Asymptomatic hyperuricemia: the case for conservative management. Ann Intern Med. 1978;88:666.

116 Fessel WJ et al. Correlates and consequences of asymptomatic hyperuricemia. Arch Intern Med. 1973;132:44.

117 Rastegar A et al. The physiologic approach to hyperuricemia. N Engl J Med. 1972;286:470.

118 Campoin DS et al. Binding of urate by serum proteins. Arthritis Rheum. 1975;18(Suppl.):747.

119 Kjelstrand CM et al. Hyperuricemia and acute renal failure. Arch Intern Med. 1974;133:349.

120 Gores PF et al. Hyperuricemia after renal transplantation. Am J Surg. 1988;156:397.

121 Kahl LE et al. Gout in the heart transplant recipient: physiologic puzzle and therapeutic challenge. Am J Med. 1989;87:289.

122 Lin HY et al. Cyclosporine-induced hyperuricemia and gout. N Engl J Med. 1989;321:287.

123 Myers BD et al. Cyclosporine-associated chronic nephropathy. N Engl J Med. 1984;311:699.

124 Tomlanovich S et al. Limitations of creatinine in quantifying the severity of cyclosporine-induced chronic nephrotoxicity. Am J Kidney Dis. 1986;8:332.

125 Ross EA et al. The plasma creatinine concentration is not an accurate reflection of the glomerular filtration rate in stable renal transplant patients receiving cyclosporine. Am J Kidney Dis. 1987;10:113.

126 Noordzij TC et al. Cyclosporine-induced hyperuricemia and gout. N Engl J Med. 1990;322:334. Letter.

127 Durrant S et al. Cyclosporin A, methylprednisolone, and convulsions. Lancet. 1982;2:829. Letter.

128 Boogaerts MA et al. Cyclosporin, methylprednisolone, and convulsions. Lancet. 1982;2:1216. Letter.

129 Ost L. Effects of cyclosporin on prednisolone metabolism. Lancet. 1984;1:451.

130 Klintmalm G et al. High-dose methylprednisolone increases plasma cyclosporin levels in renal transplant recipients. Lancet. 1984;1:731.

131 Chua CC et al. Use of polyethylene glycol-modified uricase to treat hyperuricemia in a patient with non-Hodgkin's lymphoma. Ann Intern Med. 1988;109:114.

132 Farge D et al. Hyperuricemia and gouty arthritis in heart transplant recipients. Am J Med. 1990;88:553. Letter.

133 Hansten PD, Horn JR. Drug Interactions & Updates Quarterly. Vancouver, WA: Applied Therapeutics; 1995.

134 Manfredi RL, Vesell ES. Inhibition of theophylline metabolism by long-term allopurinol administration. Clin Pharmacol Ther. 1981;29:224.

135 Van Gennip AH et al. Urinary excretion of methylated purines in man and in the rat after the administration of theophylline. J Chromatogr. 1979;21:351.

136 Grygiel JJ et al. Effects of allopurinol on theophylline metabolism and clearance. Clin Pharmacol Ther. 1979;26:660.

137 Grahame R et al. Clinical survey of 354 patients with gout. Ann Rheum Dis. 1970;29:461.

138 Arellano F, Sacristan JA. Allopurinol hypersensitivity syndrome: a review. DICP, Ann Pharmacother. 1993;27:337.

139 Malawista SE. Discussion of a case report. Arthritis Rheum. 1978;21:735.

140 Gutman AB. The past four decades of progress in the knowledge of gout, with an assessment of the present status. Arthritis Rheum. 1973;16:431.

141 Yu TF. Efficacy of colchicine prophylaxis in gout. Ann Intern Med. 1961;55:179.

142 Steele TH. Control of uric acid excretion. N Engl J Med. 1971;284:1193.

143 Steele TH. Renal excretion of uric acid. Arthritis Rheum. 1975;18 (Suppl.):793.

144 Jarobski J et al. Vasculitis with allopurinol therapy. Am Heart J. 1970;79:116.

145 Jick H, Brandt D. Allopurinol and cataracts. Am J Ophthalmol. 1984;98:355.

146 Freeman DL. Frequent doses of intravenous colchicine can be lethal. N Engl J Med. 1983;304:310.

147 Gutman AB. Uricosuric drugs with special reference to probenecid and sul-

finpyrazone. Adv Pharmacol Chemother. 1966;4:91.

148 **McCarty DJ.** Gout without hyperuricemia. JAMA. 1994;271:302.

149 **Wolfe F.** Gout and hyperuricemia. Am Fam Physician. 1991;43:2141.

150 **Wolfe F, Cathey MA.** The misdiagnosis of gout and hyperuricemia. J Rheumatol. 1991;18:1232.

151 **Putterman C et al.** Colchicine intoxication: clinical pharmacology, risk factors, features and management. Semin Arthritis Rheum. 1991;21:143.

152 **Clair WK et al.** Allopurinol use and the risk of cataract formation. Br J Ophthalmol. 1989;73:173.

153 **Walz-LeBlanc BAE et al.** Allopurinol sensitivity in a patient with chronic tophaceous gout: success of intravenous desensitization after failure of oral desensitization. Arthritis Rheum. 1991; 34:1329.

154 **Diamond HS.** Control of crystal-induced arthropathies. Rheum Dis Clin North Am. 1989;15:557.

155 **Yu TF.** The efficacy of colchicine prophylaxis in articular gout—a reappraisal after 20 years. Semin Arthritis Rheum. 1982;12:256.

156 **Wallace SL et al.** Renal function predicts colchicine toxicity: guidelines for the prophylactic use of colchicine in gout. J Rheumatol. 1991;18:264.

157 **Burack DA et al.** Hyperuricemia and gout among heart transplant recipients receiving cyclosporine. Am J Med. 1992;92:141.

158 **Alloway JA et al.** Comparison of triamcinolone acetonide with indomethacin in the treatment of gouty arthritis. J Rheumatol. 1993;20:111.

Rheumatic Disorders

Stephen L Dahl

Rheumatoid Arthritis (RA) 41-1
  Overview 41-1
    Epidemiology (See Tables 41.1 and 41.2) 41-1
    Treatment 41-2
      Nonsteroidal anti-inflammatory drugs (NSAIDs) .. 41-2
      Second-line agents 41-2
      Corticosteroids 41-3
      Alkylating cytotoxic agents 41-3
      Treatment limitations 41-3
  Early Rheumatoid Arthritis
    (See Questions 1 to 19) 41-4–41-9
  Progressive Rheumatoid Arthritis
    (See Questions 20 to 46) 41-9–41-20
  Signs and Symptoms (See Table 41.3) 41-3
  Treatment of Rheumatoid Arthritis 41-4
    Nondrug treatment 41-4
      Rest 41-4
      Exercise and heat 41-4
      Emotional support 41-4
    NSAIDs 41-5
      Aspirin 41-5
        Dosing (See Figure 41.1) 41-5
        Dose adjustment 41-5
        Alteration of salicylate excretion 41-5
        Patient instructions 41-5
        Alternative formulations 41-6
        Aspirin allergy 41-6
        Prolongation of bleeding time 41-6
        Use in pregnancy 41-7
      Nonaspirin NSAIDs 41-7
        Combination with aspirin 41-7
        Choice of agent (See Table 41.4) 41-7
        Adverse effects 41-8
        Use in renal disease 41-9
    Second-line agents (See Table 41.5) 41-9
      Gold 41-10
        Preparations 41-10
        Dosing 41-10
        Adverse reactions (Also see Question 24) 41-11
          Monitoring for 41-11
          Blood count 41-11
        Duration of therapy 41-11
        Poor response to therapy 41-11

      Auranofin 41-11
    Antimalarials 41-12
      Dosing 41-12
      Risk of retinopathy 41-12
    Sulfasalazine 41-12
    Methotrexate 41-13
      Dosing 41-13
      Adverse effects (See Table 41.6) 41-13
    Penicillamine 41-14
      Previous gold therapy 41-14
      Dosing 41-14
      Adverse effects 41-14
        Proteinuria 41-15
        Rashes 41-15
        Hematological toxicities 41-15
        Nausea, vomiting, abnormalities of taste,
          and anorexia 41-15
        Immunologic/autoimmune disorders 41-15
    Combination therapy (See Tables 41.7 to 41.9
      and Figures 41.2 to 41.4) 41-15
  Corticosteroids 41-19
    Indications 41-19
    Dosing 41-19
    Osteoporosis 41-20
    Pulse therapy 41-20
Juvenile Rheumatoid Arthritis (JRA) 41-20
  Signs and Symptoms 41-20
  Patterns of Onset 41-20
  Treatment 41-21
    Diagnosis of systemic-onset JRA 41-21
    Aspirin 41-21
      Dosing 41-21
      Hepatotoxicity 41-21
      Reye's syndrome 41-21
    Nonaspirin NSAIDs 41-21
    Second-line agents 41-21
    Uveitis 41-22
Osteoarthritis (OA) 41-22
  Signs and Symptoms 41-22
  Treatment 41-23
    Acetaminophen 41-23
    Corticosteroids 41-23
    NSAIDs 41-23

Rheumatoid Arthritis (RA)

Epidemiology

Rheumatoid arthritis is a chronic systemic inflammatory disorder characterized by potentially deforming polyarthritis and a wide spectrum of extra-articular manifestations. Since no single chemical or laboratory finding is specific for this disease, the diagnosis of RA is based primarily upon clinical criteria (see Table 41.1).[1] The prevalence of RA is estimated from epidemiologic studies to range from 0.3% to 1.5% reflecting, in part, differences in the interpretation of criteria for RA and perhaps some regional differences in prevalence due to population constituency.[2] Overall, rheumatoid arthritis afflicts approximately 2 to 4 million individuals in

the U.S. RA is two to three times more frequent in females than in males, and the prevalence of the disease increases with advancing age up to the seventh decade.[2]

Although the etiology of RA remains unknown, this disease probably results from an interaction between an initiating agent (or agents) and a genetically susceptible host. Support for the concept of genetically controlled susceptibility comes from studies demonstrating an association between RA and class II gene products of the major histocompatibility complex. For example, in one study the presence of the B lymphocyte alloantigen HLA-DR4 conferred a four- to fivefold higher relative risk for the development of RA.[3]

Rheumatoid arthritis is a chronic, debilitating disease for most who are afflicted. The development and application of standardized

Table 41.1	Criteria for Diagnosis of RA[a,c]

1) Morning stiffness in and around joints lasting at least 1 hr before maximal involvement[b]

2) Soft tissue swelling (arthritis) of three or more joint areas observed by a physician[b]

3) Swelling (arthritis) of the proximal interphalangeal, metacarpophalangeal, or wrist joints[b]

4) Symmetric arthritis[b]

5) Subcutaneous nodules

6) Positive test for RF

7) Radiographic erosions or periarticular osteopenia in hand or wrist joints

[a] RA = Rheumatoid arthritis; RF = Rheumatoid factor.
[b] Criteria 1–4 must be present for at least 6 weeks; 4 or more criteria must be present.
[c] Adapted from reference 1.

criteria of remission (see Table 41.2)[4] in a cross-sectional evaluation of rheumatology clinic patients revealed a remission rate of about 1%.[5] Over two and one-half years in another clinic, 18% of patients were in remission at sometime, including slightly over 10% of patients not receiving second-line drugs.[6] However, remissions were temporary, with less than 4% experiencing a remission lasting up to two years and only 1.2% of patients experiencing a remission lasting up to three years.

The economic impact of RA is significant. Evaluation of non-treatment-related costs of RA reported from a university center revealed that patients with advanced RA lost 61% of their premorbid income.[7] Fifty percent of those employed stopped work within a decade. Estimates of direct total annual costs of treatment in 1981 dollars were $2532 per patient.[8] Medication formed the largest single category of costs (16%). Over 15% of patients were hospitalized during the one-year period at a mean cost of $7845;[9] 54% of the hospitalizations involved orthopedic surgery. These studies reveal not only the significant economic impact of RA but also provide additional evidence of the progressive nature of the disease. Perhaps most significantly, the natural history of rheumatoid arthritis includes a shortening of life span by 8 to 15 years,[10] with the five-year survival rate for some patients being less than 50%.[11]

The course of RA is variable.[2] Approximately one-third of patients will initially experience mild intermittent symptoms which resolve over the course of several weeks to months. The patient may be symptom-free for several weeks to months and then experience symptoms which may be more severe than those experienced during the initial onset. Another group of patients experience a rather sudden onset of symptoms followed by a prolonged clinical remission of disease activity. A third group experience progressive uninterrupted disease which ultimately results in characteristic disabling joint deformities. The rate of disease progression in this group may be rapid or slow, but the outcome remains the same: destructive, disabling disease. Patients within this group may be divided further into a subgroup that responds to ''aggressive'' therapy and a subgroup that does not.

Treatment

The treatment of rheumatoid arthritis involves a combination of interventions including rest, exercise (physical therapy), emotional support, occupational therapy, and drugs. Specific treatment is individualized and based upon such factors as joint function, degree of disease activity, patient age, gender, occupation, family responsibilities, and response to previous therapy.[2] The overall goals of therapy are to minimize symptoms, maintain the patient's lifestyle, maintain joint function, and, to the extent possible, prevent disease progression.

Anti-inflammatory drugs are an important component in the treatment of RA. Nonsteroidal anti-inflammatory drugs (NSAIDs) are the traditional cornerstone of drug therapy. Second-line drugs [i.e., gold, D-penicillamine (DPEN), hydroxychloroquine (HCQ), sulfasalazine (SSA), methotrexate (MTX), or azathioprine (AZA)] are added frequently when NSAIDs alone do not sufficiently suppress joint inflammation. Due to the potential for serious toxicity, corticosteroids and alkylating cytotoxic drugs generally are reserved for active disease uncontrolled by NSAIDs and second-line agents. Nevertheless, these drugs play an important role in suppressing both articular and extra-articular manifestations of rheumatoid arthritis.

Nonsteroidal Anti-Inflammatory Drugs (NSAIDs). Because of its efficacy and low cost, aspirin remains a useful NSAID for those who tolerate it and the standard by which all other NSAIDs are measured.[2] A number of nonaspirin NSAIDs also are available. Although NSAIDs differ in chemical structure, they have similar pharmacologic properties (e.g., antipyresis, analgesia, anti-inflammatory activity, inhibition of prostaglandin synthesis), adverse effects [e.g., gastrointestinal (GI) intolerance and nephrotoxicity], and pharmacokinetic properties (e.g., highly protein-bound and extensively metabolized to inactive metabolites that are excreted renally).[12] Although nonaspirin NSAIDs are more similar to aspirin than different, they often are better tolerated. Since individual patients may respond to or tolerate one agent better than another, therapeutic trials with several nonaspirin NSAIDs may be necessary to determine the best agent for a given patient.

Second-Line Agents. Patients who do not respond sufficiently to a regimen of rest, physical exercise, and NSAIDs usually are treated with one of the second-line agents. These drugs have the potential to cause serious toxicity. Nevertheless, they also have the potential to substantially reduce joint inflammation and approximately two-thirds of patients who tolerate a second-line drug experience additional benefit. The onset of action of most of these agents is slow [they are sometimes referred to as slow-acting antirheumatic drugs (SAARDs)]. Except for methotrexate (MTX), three or more months of therapy frequently are required before objective benefits are apparent to the patient.[13] The agent of choice is determined primarily by physician and patient preference. Few

Table 41.2	Criteria for Complete Clinical Remission in RA[a,c]

A minimum of 5 of the following requirements must be fulfilled for at least 2 consecutive months in a patient with RA:[b]

1) Morning stiffness not >15 minutes

2) No fatigue

3) No joint pain

4) No joint tenderness or pain on motion

5) No soft tissue swelling in joints or tendon sheaths

6) ESR (Westergren's) <30 mm/hr (females) or 20 mm/hr (males)

[a] RA = Rheumatoid arthritis; ESR = Erythrocyte sedimentation rate.
[b] Exclusions: manifestations of active vasculitis, pericarditis, pleuritis, myositis, or unexplained recent weight loss or fever secondary to RA prohibit designation of complete clinical remission.
[c] Adapted from reference 4.

comparative trials are available to provide objective comparisons among these agents.[14–16] A meta-analysis of second-line drug therapy revealed that the most effective second-line drugs appeared to be parenteral gold, methotrexate, sulfasalazine, and penicillamine. Auranofin (AUR) appeared the least effective. Parenteral gold appeared to be most toxic while auranofin and antimalarials were best tolerated.

Corticosteroids. These potent anti-inflammatory agents play an important role in the treatment of many patients with RA; however, corticosteroids have no effect on the factors initiating or perpetuating the disease. Disease progression is similar in patients treated for two to five years with aspirin alone compared to patients treated with corticosteroids.[18] The long-term use of daily doses of corticosteroids inevitably leads to side effects. Hypothalamic-pituitary-adrenal axis suppression, osteoporosis, proximal muscle weakening, and impaired wound healing particularly are worrisome.[19] Consequently, systemic corticosteroid therapy is reserved for patients unresponsive to conservative measures. Since initiation of steroid therapy frequently results in a life-long commitment, treatment is initiated reluctantly.

Alkylating Cytotoxic Agents. Cyclophosphamide and chlorambucil are effective in the treatment of severe progressive cases of RA, but they also carry the risk of potentially serious toxicity.[20–22] Thus, use of these drugs usually is limited to patients with progressive RA unresponsive to more conservative management or, in some cases, potentially life-threatening complications of RA.

Treatment Limitations. Numerous studies document the short-term efficacy of gold, penicillamine, antimalarials, azathioprine, sulfasalazine, and methotrexate in attenuating clinical and laboratory manifestations of rheumatoid arthritis.[17] For example, a meta-analysis of the four published placebo-controlled trials that employed strict research methodologies supports parenteral gold as an effective intervention.[23] Using a stringent definition of improvement, 27% of patients treated with gold achieved 50% reduction in active joint count compared to 11% of placebo-treated patients within six months.[24] Yet long-term, positive therapeutic outcomes have not been realized for these drugs. Sustained treatment with any of these therapies is uncommon. Fewer than 20% of individuals started on parenteral gold, penicillamine, or antimalarials remain on initial therapy for up to five years.[25] Many discontinue therapy for loss of responsiveness and still more discontinue due to toxicity. Furthermore, over a 20-year period, function may improve during the first ten years, but decline considerably during the following ten years, resulting in severe disability.

These observations have been confirmed repeatedly. In a retrospective survey of 154 patients involving 251 second-line drug-patient exposures randomly selected from a pool of 2320 RA patients, 57% improved after a delay of one to seven months.[26] Of those withdrawn after less than two months of therapy, 25% subsequently improved without further second-line therapy. For those continuing second-line therapy, the probability of uninterrupted therapy 8 months, 24 months, and 36 months after the start of treatment was 50%, 25%, and 10%, respectively. The majority of withdrawals were for drug toxicity.

In another series reported over a 14-year observation period in 671 patients receiving 1017 courses of second-line antirheumatic drugs, the median time to discontinuation for intramuscular gold, auranofin, hydroxychloroquine, or penicillamine was ≤2 years.[27] Again, adverse reactions were the most common reason for withdrawal.

In a prospective study, long-term use was evaluated by survival analysis in 245 patients with recently diagnosed RA receiving 432 courses of second-line therapy: hydroxychloroquine, sulfasalazine, gold, and penicillamine.[28] When indexed for side effects, 40% of

gold regimens were discontinued at two years, 12% of hydroxychloroquine, 19% of sulfasalazine, and 13% of penicillamine. Indexed for lack of efficacy, 61% of hydroxychloroquine patients had discontinued by two years; sulfasalazine 46%; gold 43%; and penicillamine 43%. These studies reveal the limited effectiveness of second-line drug therapy in RA and provide important insight regarding the inability of relatively short-term efficacy studies to fully characterize therapeutic outcomes achievable for chronic diseases. Long-term experience with sulfasalazine and methotrexate is more limited. Some long-term follow-up studies suggest a greater potential for patients receiving methotrexate to be maintained long-term,[29] but others are conflicting.[30]

Signs and Symptoms

1. T.W., a previously healthy 42-year-old, 60 kg female, has been suffering from morning stiffness that persists for several hours, anorexia, fatigue, and generalized muscle and joint pain during the past 4 months. In addition, she has noticed that her eyes seem red most of the time and are unusually dry. Her symptoms have been much worse during the past month and a half, and she has been forced to limit her physical activities. She also notes that she no longer is able to wear her wedding ring due to swelling of her hand. Physical examination revealed bilaterally symmetrical swelling, tenderness, and warmth of the metacarpophalangeal and proximal interphalangeal joints of the hands and the metatarsophalangeal joints of the feet. A subcutaneous nodule was evident on the extensor surface of the left forearm. Pertinent laboratory findings included: erythrocyte sedimentation rate (ESR) by the Westergren method 52 mm/hr; hemoglobin (Hgb) 10.6 gm/dL (Normal: 12–16); hematocrit (Hct) 33% (Normal: 36%–47%); platelets 480,000 (Normal: 140,000–400,000); albumin 3.8 gm/dL (Normal: 4.3–5.6); serum uric acid 3.0 mg/dL (Normal: 2–8); serum iron 40 mg/dL (Normal: 60–180); total iron binding capacity (TIBC) 275 mg/dL (Normal: 200–400); and positive rheumatoid factor (RF) performed by latex fixation method in a dilution of 1:320. Tests for antinuclear antibodies (ANA) and tuberculin sensitivity were negative. X-ray films of the hands and feet showed soft tissue swelling with no evidence of tophi or calcification. Other routine laboratory data and physical findings were normal. What signs and symptoms of RA are manifested by T.W.?

The presentation of rheumatoid arthritis at onset can be variable but characteristically, 50% to 70% of cases have a rather insidious onset of disease over weeks to months.[2] Early nonspecific symptoms such as fatigue, malaise, diffuse musculoskeletal pain, and morning stiffness may precede more specific symptoms. Prominent features of rheumatoid arthritis in T.W. include fatigue and morning stiffness. About one-half of the patients with RA initially experience fatigue which later in the disease serves as a useful index of disease activity. Patients usually experience prolonged morning stiffness upon awakening. This stiffness usually lasts 30 minutes to an hour, but may be present all day with decreasing intensity after arising. Duration of morning stiffness also may be a useful index of disease activity. Over time, nonspecific musculoskeletal pain localizes to the joints bilaterally. Bilaterally symmetrical joint swelling and pain, involving the metacarpophalangeal (MCP) and proximal interphalangeal (PIP) joints of the hands and metatarsophalangeal (MTP) joints of the feet, as illustrated by T.W., are characteristic of RA. The peripheral joints of the hands, wrists, and feet usually are involved first. Although MCP and PIP joints of the hands often are affected, the distal interphalangeal (DIP) joints usually are spared. Ultimately, any or all of the diarthrodial joints may be involved including the elbows, knees, shoulders, ankles, hips, temporomandibular joints, sternoclavicular joints, and glenohumeral joints.

Joint involvement is characterized by soft tissue swelling and warmth, decreased range of motion, and, sometimes, muscle atrophy around affected joints. Progressive disease is characterized by irreversible joint deformities such as ulnar deviation of the fingers, boutonniere deformities (hyperextension of the DIP joint and flexion of the PIP joint), or swan neck deformities (hyperextension of the PIP joint and flexion of the DIP joint). Similar irreversible deformities also may involve the feet.

Rheumatoid arthritis is a systemic disease which is reflected by the extra-articular manifestations that may accompany joint involvement. *Subcutaneous nodules* are found in up to 35% of individuals with RA.[2] As in the case of T.W., these nodules usually develop along extensor surfaces such as the olecranon process and the proximal ulna but occasionally may be found in the hands, sacral areas, eyes, lungs, and heart. In addition, they may occur on the soles of the feet and along the Achilles tendon. Patients who develop rheumatoid nodules almost always are rheumatoid factor positive.

Organ system involvement may be extensive. *Pleuropulmonary manifestations* (e.g., pleuritis, development of pulmonary nodules, interstitial fibrosis, pneumonitis and, very rarely, arteritis of the pulmonary vasculature) also may accompany the articular involvement of RA.[2] *Cardiac involvement* may present as pericarditis or myocarditis. Additionally, rheumatoid nodules can produce conduction defects or valve defects.

Some extra-articular manifestations occur as syndromes. *Sjögren's syndrome* includes dry eyes (keratoconjunctivitis sicca) and dry mouth (xerostomia) in addition to the presence of connective tissue disease.[31] T.W.'s eye complaints may be an extra-articular manifestation of her rheumatoid arthritis. *Felty's syndrome* is characterized by chronic arthritis, splenomegaly, and neutropenia; thrombocytopenia, anemia, and lymphadenopathy also may be present.[32]

Vasculitis is another extra-articular manifestation of RA which can involve any organ system and may vary in seriousness from mild to potentially life-threatening (see Chapter 42: Connective Tissue Disorders: The Clinical Use of Corticosteroids).

2. What abnormal laboratory values in T.W. could be used to monitor the efficacy of drug therapy or disease progression?

The laboratory findings in RA are characteristic of a chronic systemic inflammatory disease. There is no specific test for rheumatoid arthritis. T.W.'s elevated ESR is a nonspecific indication of inflammation. Her hematological findings are consistent with a mild anemia of chronic inflammation. Although her serum iron concentration is decreased, her normal iron-binding capacity makes a diagnosis of iron-deficiency anemia unlikely. Her anemia probably results from a failure of iron release from the reticuloendothelial tissues and would not be expected to respond to iron therapy. The mild thrombocytosis is additional evidence of a systemic inflammatory response.

The serum albumin concentration may be low in RA patients such as T.W. A low serum albumin concentration theoretically could result in decreased protein binding of salicylates and other highly protein-bound drugs and yield higher free drug serum concentrations.[33]

Rheumatoid factor, an autoantibody (usually IgM or IgG) which reacts with the Fc portion of antigenic IgG to form an immune complex *in vitro*, is found in the serum of up to 80% of patients with RA.[2] Rheumatoid factor is not found in some patients with RA and may be present in healthy individuals as well as in patients with diseases other than rheumatoid arthritis; therefore, it does not establish the diagnosis of RA. Although rheumatoid factor titers do not parallel disease activity, high titers early in the disease course are associated with more severe and progressive disease.[2]

The test for antinuclear antibodies ruled out systemic lupus erythematosus in T.W. However, ANA may be positive in some patients with rheumatoid arthritis.[2]

The laboratory manifestations of inflammation should improve with effective drug therapy and along with many of the clinical features of RA, are useful parameters for monitoring disease activity and response to therapy (see Table 41.3).

Treatment of Rheumatoid Arthritis

Nondrug Treatment

3. What nondrug therapy should be included in the management of T.W.'s RA?

Treatment objectives in rheumatoid arthritis are reduction of joint pain and inflammation, preservation of joint function, and prevention of deformity, if possible. A conservative approach combining rest and physical therapy in conjunction with drug treatment is the safest means of achieving these objectives.[34]

Rest. Systemic and articular rest (achieved by splinting the affected joints) may reduce inflammation markedly.[35] In a comparison of complete bed confinement versus ad lib activity in hospitalized patients, most patients benefited from rest without complete confinement. The benefits probably were due to reduction of physical and emotional stresses and to the provision of regular physical therapy in addition to salicylates.[36] Therefore, a liberal rest program should be prescribed for T.W. If an adequate rest program cannot be carried out at home, hospitalization may be considered.

Exercise and Heat. Passive exercise (e.g., range of motion exercises) should be prescribed for T.W. until the acute inflammation subsides. Passive exercise will minimize muscle atrophy and flexion contractures, and maintain joint function without increasing inflammation. The external application of heat, by soaking her hands and feet in warm water, hot baths, or hot paraffin treatments, may reduce joint stiffness and allow greater benefit from passive exercise programs.[35]

Emotional Support. Finally, emotional support should be provided to all patients such as T.W. A patient's reaction to this disease may be affected by age, personality, and work and home environments. As with all chronic debilitating diseases, the potential loss of independence and self-esteem, altered interpersonal relationships with friends and family, and potential loss of employment may be encountered.[37] Therefore, time must be spent with the patient and her family to ensure that the treatment will have an optimal effect.

Table 41.3	Parameters Used to Assess Disease Activity and Drug Response in RA[a]
Duration and intensity of morning stiffness	
Number of painful or tender joints	
Number of swollen joints; severity of joint swelling	
Range of joint motion	
Time to onset of fatigue	
ESR or CRP	
Radiographic changes: osteopenia, joint space narrowing, bony erosions	
Hgb/Hct	
Presence of subcutaneous nodules, pleuritis, pneumonitis, myocarditis, vasculitis	
AIMS	
HAQ	

[a] AIMS = Arthritis impact measure scale; CRP = C-reactive protein; ESR = Erythrocyte sedimentation rate; HAQ = Health assessment questionnaire; Hct = Hematocrit; Hgb = Hemoglobin; RA = Rheumatoid arthritis.

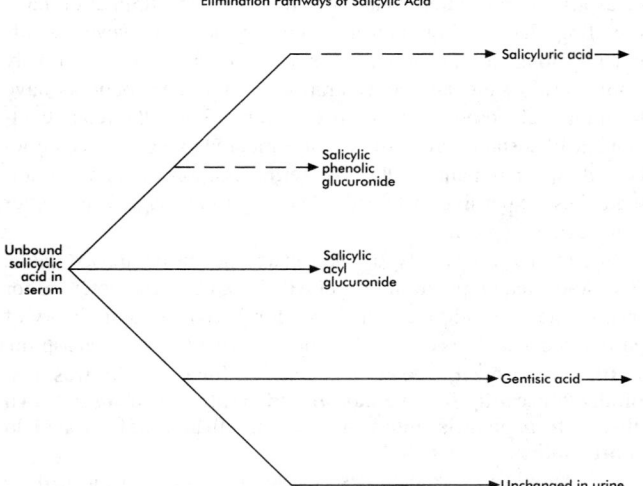

Fig 41.1   Elimination Pathways of Salicylic Acid   The dotted lines indicate saturable pathways. With anti-inflammatory doses, elimination via the nonsaturate metabolic pathways and urinary excretion become relatively more important as routes of elimination.

NSAIDs

4. Aspirin: Dosing. **T.W. is to begin taking aspirin, 975 mg QID (3.9 gm/day) in conjunction with an appropriate program of physical therapy and rest. Why is this an appropriate dose of aspirin?**

For many clinicians, aspirin remains an important first-line treatment for patients who tolerate it. To be effective, it must be prescribed in doses sufficient to provide serum salicylate concentrations ranging from 15 to 30 mg/dL.[33] The dose required to achieve optimal anti-inflammatory responses varies widely due to interindividual variation in metabolism. For example, following administration of 65 mg/kg/day of aspirin (the dose that has been prescribed for T.W.) plasma salicylate concentrations ranging from 5 to 28 mg/dL were observed among nine patients with RA after three days of therapy.[38] Similarly, a range of 12 to 35 mg/dL was observed among 13 pair of twins receiving a fixed dose of aspirin.[39] When a group of patients with backache or RA were given this dosage, concentrations ranging from 13 to 29 mg/dL were reported.[40]

Because it is not possible to predict the optimal anti-inflammatory aspirin dosage for T.W., therapy usually is initiated at 2.6 to 3.9 gm/day (45 to 60 mg/kg) in divided doses (15 to 20 mg/kg Q 8 hr or 10 to 15 mg/kg Q 6 hr) and slowly adjusted to optimize the therapeutic response.[41]

5. *Dose Adjustment*. **Five days later, T.W.'s serum salicylate level was 17 mg/dL and her symptoms were improved marginally. How rapidly can her aspirin dose be increased?** [SI unit: salicylate level 1.23 mmol/L]

After intestinal absorption, aspirin is hydrolyzed rapidly to salicylate. Salicylate (or salicylic acid) subsequently is metabolized via multiple pathways (see Figure 41.1). Metabolism to salicyluric acid and salicyl phenolic glucuronide is capacity limited.[41] With small analgesic doses of aspirin, the elimination half-life of salicylate is about 2.5 hours. However, when aspirin is taken in large daily doses for anti-inflammatory effects, the two capacity-limited pathways of salicylate elimination become saturated, prolonging elimination half-life to about 18 to 20 hours.[42] Salicylate pharmacokinetics, therefore, are complex, following both first order and Michaelis-Menten elimination processes. In anti-inflammatory doses, several days of therapy are needed before steady-state serum concentrations of salicylate are attained. Since T.W. has been tak-

ing aspirin for five days, her serum salicylate concentration should be near steady state. If her daily aspirin dose is increased, a new steady-state plateau will not be reached for at least another five to seven days. Consequently, T.W.'s aspirin dose should be changed no more frequently than at five-day intervals.

6. Could tinnitus, rather than serum concentrations, be used as an endpoint for salicylate dosing for T.W.? What are the relative merits of each approach?

Gradually increasing the daily doses of aspirin to the point of tinnitus (i.e., a ringing or high-pitched buzzing sensation in the head) and then reducing the dose by a couple of tablets a day is a time-honored technique which clinically results in anti-inflammatory activity.[33] Tinnitus may be a useful therapeutic endpoint in patients with normal hearing as it usually occurs when the salicylate concentration exceeds 20 mg/dL and at average serum concentrations of about 30 mg/dL.[43] Thus, when tinnitus occurs, serum salicylate concentrations usually are within the therapeutic range. However, patients with pre-existing hearing loss may not experience tinnitus despite potentially toxic concentrations.[44] Therefore, patients with known pre-existing hearing loss and older subjects who may have undetected hearing loss should be monitored by serum salicylate concentrations rather than by the occurrence of tinnitus. If T.W. experiences tinnitus at therapeutic serum concentrations, this can be used as a therapeutic endpoint. Otherwise, monitoring serum salicylate concentrations is preferable.

7. *Alteration of Salicylate Excretion*. **After several weeks of treatment with excellent results, T.W. experienced tinnitus on the day of a scheduled clinic visit. A serum salicylate was ordered and reported as 32 mg/dL. Previously, her serum salicylate concentrations were about 25 mg/dL. The only change in her treatment was recent discontinuation of the antacid (Maalox) she was taking with each aspirin dose. Explain this increase in her serum salicylate. How can this problem be avoided in the future?** [SI units: salicylate concentration 2.3 and 1.81 mmol/L, respectively]

When aspirin is used in anti-inflammatory doses, renal excretion of unchanged salicylate becomes an important elimination pathway (see Question 5). Renal excretion of salicylate is highly pH dependent. Both sodium bicarbonate and the "nonsystemic" antacids are capable of increasing salicylate excretion. Regular therapeutic doses of magnesium and aluminum hydroxides (e.g., Maalox) increased urinary pH and decreased serum salicylate concentrations from 30% to 70% in a group of pediatric patients.[45] Daily administration of Maalox, 15 mL four times daily, increased average urinary pH approximately 0.7 U after several days of therapy; an equivalent fall in urinary pH was noted two days after discontinuation of the antacid.[46,47] A decrease in urinary pH from 6.5 to 5.5 in a patient whose serum salicylate concentration is within the therapeutic range of 20 to 30 mg/dL could double the serum salicylate concentration.[33] Thus, T.W.'s discontinuation of Maalox may have resulted in a more acidic urine, elevated serum salicylate concentrations, and tinnitus.

If T.W. is able to tolerate aspirin without an antacid, the aspirin dosage can be decreased. She should be encouraged to take her aspirin with meals to prevent epigastric discomfort.

8. *Patient Instructions*. **What instructions should accompany T.W.'s aspirin prescription?**

First, T.W. should appreciate the important role that large, regularly taken doses of aspirin play in the treatment of RA. The daily ingestion of large amounts of aspirin commonly is approached with considerable skepticism unless the patient receives some explanation and encouragement. The patient should be aware that, in addition to providing substantial analgesia, large doses of aspirin are anti-inflammatory. When anti-inflammatory doses of aspirin are replaced with large oral doses of meperidine, codeine, or propoxyphene, patients experience a marked increase in symptoms. Fatigue and stiffness become severe, finger joint size is increased, range of motion is decreased, and grip strength is decreased.[48]

Patients should be instructed to keep the aspirin container tightly closed and to avoid storing aspirin in moist environments (e.g., the bathroom) because aspirin is hydrolyzed to salicylic acid and acetic acid in the presence of moisture. Childproof safety closures are required on aspirin containers, but many arthritic patients are unable to cope with these safety closures due to diminished grip strength and hand deformities. If aspirin is dispensed in a conventional closure container, it is necessary to explain the hazards of accidental ingestion by children and, as required by law in most states, obtain a signed release form.

9. *Alternative Formulations.* **P.D., a male with an alleged aspirin allergy, avoids aspirin because it has upset his stomach in the past. However, he is able to take large doses of an enteric-coated aspirin (Ecotrin) without experiencing GI intolerance. Is this a rational alternative to regular aspirin? What are appropriate alternatives for patients who do not tolerate therapeutic doses of aspirin?**

Aspirin therapy is effective, frequently well tolerated, and inexpensive for initial management of rheumatoid arthritis. Epigastric distress is the major limitation to the successful use of large doses of aspirin. In addition, acute gastric mucosal injury results in loss of small amounts of blood (microbleeding) with each aspirin dose.[49] Chronic aspirin therapy may cause iron-deficiency anemia secondary to significant blood loss in some patients, but major GI bleeding from aspirin appears to be a rare occurrence.[50] Although microbleeding caused by aspirin can be minimized by concurrent ingestion of therapeutic doses of antacids or H_2-receptor antagonists,[51,52] the significance of microbleeding remains unknown and prophylactic use of either H_2-receptor antagonists or antacids have not reduced chronic complications such as gastric ulcers or gastrointestinal hemorrhage (see Question 16). If repeated therapeutic doses of antacids are used, their effects on urinary pH and serum salicylate concentrations must be considered (see Question 7). Ingesting aspirin with generous quantities of liquids at mealtimes is advocated to minimize gastric intolerance.

Aspirin formulations that contain buffering agents (e.g., Alka-Seltzer, Ascriptin, Bufferin) are used frequently by patients who complain of gastrointestinal side effects. Although the antacid content in Alka-Seltzer may be sufficient to reduce acute GI microbleeding and symptoms, Alka-Seltzer contains more than a gram of sodium for each 650 mg of aspirin, making it undesirable for chronic use. Ascriptin and Bufferin probably contain too little antacid to appreciably reduce gastrointestinal microbleeding,[53] but occasionally are better tolerated than regular aspirin. All of these formulations are more expensive than regular aspirin.

Enteric-coated aspirin is associated with fewer GI complaints than uncoated aspirin.[53] Although enteric coating increases the likelihood of incomplete absorption,[33] Enseals and Ecotrin were absorbed reliably in one study involving small numbers of patients,[54] and other newer enteric-coated aspirin preparations may be absorbed reliably as well. Thus, enteric-coated aspirin may be a useful alternative to regular aspirin in some patients. Easprin enteric-coated tablets contain 975 mg of aspirin per tablet and, therefore, are available only by prescription. It provides the convenience of taking fewer tablets each day, but small adjustments in dose are not possible.

Sustained-release (SR) aspirin (e.g., ZORprin, Measurin) is intended to provide more stable salicylate concentrations with less frequent administration. Twice-daily dosing of Measurin produces average serum salicylate concentrations comparable to equal doses of aspirin administered four times daily.[55] The elimination half-life of regular aspirin in anti-inflammatory doses, however, is sufficiently long that twice-daily dosing also would yield relatively stable serum salicylate concentrations[56] and some patients have been maintained on a once-daily regimen.[57] Thus, the relative advantage of sustained-release aspirin compared to regular or enteric-coated aspirin remains unclear. Nevertheless, some patients do tolerate these expensive sustained-release aspirin dosage forms better than regular aspirin.

In summary, a variety of aspirin dosage forms are available. Enteric-coated preparations, despite their expense and potential for incomplete absorption, are preferred for patients with a history of gastroduodenal ulcers or who develop ulcers while on regular aspirin.

10. *Aspirin Allergy.* **Aspirin is ordered for C.S. who was hospitalized recently for evaluation and treatment of his RA. An allergy to aspirin is noted in C.S.'s medical chart. Is aspirin contraindicated for C.S.?**

C.S. should be asked to describe his reaction to aspirin. If he describes symptoms consistent with a hypersensitivity reaction, aspirin is contraindicated. Most patients who claim to be allergic to aspirin merely experience GI distress. In these patients, aspirin may be tolerated if administered with food or if the formulation is switched to an enteric-coated preparation.

Aspirin intolerance (hypersensitivity) in association with asthma is cause for serious concern. Challenge with aspirin in these patients can precipitate an acute, life-threatening, bronchospastic reaction.[58] Approximately 2% to 4% of asthmatics have a history of aspirin-induced bronchospasm;[59] a somewhat smaller percentage of patients with recurrent rhinitis also suffer from this problem.[60] The frequency of aspirin intolerance in patients with nasal polyps is as high as 22%, and 70% of these patients have asthma.[59] All of these patients experience a high degree of cross-reactivity to other chemicals, including indomethacin (Indocin), naproxen (Naprosyn), ibuprofen (Motrin), fenoprofen (Nalfon), mefenamic acid (Ponstel), sodium benzoate (a widely used preservative), and tartrazine dye (FD&C Yellow No. 5), which is used in foods and some drugs.[64–68] These substances are structurally dissimilar, but most are inhibitors of prostaglandin synthesis. Therefore, this reaction may result from an abnormal response to a common pharmacologic effect. Weak prostaglandin synthesis inhibitors such as sodium and choline salicylate have been administered cautiously to such aspirin-intolerant patients without untoward reactions.

Some patients with chronic urticaria as well as rhinitis patients with aspirin allergy may be at increased risk to develop urticaria or angioedema upon exposure to aspirin.[58] The pathogenic mechanism for this urticarial form of aspirin intolerance is unknown. For patients requiring aspirin therapy, desensitization procedures have been used successfully to allow long-term treatment.[58]

11. *Prolongation of Bleeding Time.* **T.W. (the patient in Questions 1–8) is scheduled to have an impacted wisdom tooth removed. How will her aspirin therapy affect this procedure?**

Aspirin alters hemostasis and, if possible, should be discontinued before any type of surgery. Several mechanisms may be responsible for altered hemostasis. First and most important, low doses of aspirin irreversibly impair platelet aggregation and, thereby, prolong bleeding time.[61] Since new platelets must be released into the circulation before the bleeding time will normalize, the bleeding time may be prolonged for several days following the ingestion of aspirin.[62] Secondly, salicylates appear to enhance blood fibrinolytic activity.[63] Finally, near toxic doses of salicylates may induce a hypoprothrombinemia which is reversible by vitamin K.[41] Salicylate-induced hypoprothrombinemia usually is not clinically significant, but it can be the cause of bleeding when associated with severe liver dysfunction or malnutrition.[64]

Bleeding times normalize within three to six days following discontinuation of aspirin.[62] Therefore, aspirin should be discontinued about seven days before surgery, when possible. Nonaspirin nonsteroidal anti-inflammatory drugs also may prolong bleeding times via inhibition of platelet aggregation, but the inhibition is reversible.[12] Nonacetylated salicylates have minimal effects on platelet function.[41] Thus, a nonacetylated salicylate or a nonaspirin NSAID with a short elimination half-life may be considered for presurgical patients if an analgesic such as acetaminophen does not provide sufficient symptomatic benefit after aspirin is discontinued.

12. *Use in Pregnancy.* **K.H., a 28-year-old pregnant female with RA, is concerned about the possible effects of aspirin on her baby. What are the risks to the fetus with uninterrupted consumption of aspirin?**

In a prospective study of more than 50,000 pregnancies, malformation rates among children whose mothers had been moderately or heavily exposed to aspirin were similar to those whose mothers had not been exposed to aspirin during the first four months of pregnancy.[65] In another study, teratogenic effects were not evident in the infants of 144 mothers who had ingested large doses of salicylates regularly throughout pregnancy.[66] In contrast, an association between aspirin use during pregnancy and increased risk of congenital heart deformities was noted in a more recent study.[67]

Although the teratogenic potential of aspirin is unclear, the potential for adverse effects on the mother, as well as perinatal morbidity and mortality secondary to aspirin ingestion, appear to be real. Adverse effects on the mother include anemia, prolonged gestation, prolonged labor, and antepartum and postpartum hemorrhage.[68,69] Perinatal complications include an increased number of complicated deliveries and stillbirths.[69,70]

The pharmacodynamic effects of aspirin on hemostasis (see Question 11) appear to contribute to perinatal complications. The rate of intracranial hemorrhage in premature infants whose mothers ingested aspirin within the last week of pregnancy was higher compared to a control population of premature infants.[70] Hemostatic abnormalities were more common in infants of mothers who ingested aspirin within five days of delivery compared to controls; excess intrapartum and postpartum blood loss was noted in the mothers.[69]

Pharmacokinetic studies of salicylates during the intrapartum and postpartum periods reveal neonatal salicylate concentrations about 1.5 times higher than those of the mother because of greater protein binding[82,83] and reduced clearance in newborns.[71,72]

13. How should the arthritis symptoms be managed during the course of K.H.'s pregnancy?

About 75% of women with RA will experience a temporary remission of arthritis symptoms during the first trimester of pregnancy which persists for more than one month into the postpartum period.[73] Consequently, aspirin therapy may be discontinued successfully in many women during pregnancy. Aspirin therapy, however, may be continued if necessary during the first and second trimesters, since the benefits in patients with RA probably outweigh the potential risks (see Question 12). Aspirin should be avoided, if possible, during the final stages of pregnancy. The effects of other NSAIDs on the fetus are unknown. If anti-inflammatory therapy is required and aspirin cannot be used, low-dose corticosteroid therapy is an acceptable alternative. Although corticosteroids cross the placenta, clinically significant hypothalamic-pituitary-adrenal suppression in the neonate is unlikely and evidence that the incidence of congenital defects is increased in humans is lacking.[74,75]

14. Nonaspirin Nonsteroidal Anti-Inflammatory Drugs: Combination with Aspirin. **Is adding another NSAID to aspirin rather than starting a second-line agent effective?**

The addition of another NSAID to aspirin therapy has been used to achieve a greater anti-inflammatory response, but efficacy has not been substantiated by controlled studies. In an eight-week, double-blind, crossover study involving 36 patients with rheumatoid arthritis, aspirin plus placebo was compared to aspirin plus naproxen.[76] Overall, the aspirin-naproxen combination was more effective and as well tolerated as aspirin alone; however, those receiving optimal aspirin doses were less likely to benefit from addition of naproxen. No differences in safety or efficacy between treatments were noted in a trial comparing full-dose choline magnesium salicylate plus naproxen to single-drug treatment.[77] Thus, the benefit of adding another NSAID to optimal doses of aspirin remains unproven as does the practice of combining two nonaspirin NSAIDs. If additional benefits are anticipated, additive toxicities also should be expected.

The potential for drug interactions also needs to be considered when combining aspirin with other NSAIDs. Some investigators have found that aspirin impairs absorption of indomethacin,[78,79] although others have been unable to confirm this effect.[80–82] All of the NSAIDs are highly protein bound and drug displacement by aspirin may account for the observation that concomitant aspirin administration lowers serum concentration of ibuprofen, naproxen, and most dramatically, fenoprofen.[81,83]

Despite lack of proof of efficacy, addition of another NSAID to suboptimal anti-inflammatory doses of aspirin may be justified where optimal anti-inflammatory aspirin doses are not tolerated. For example, if tinnitus prevents use of optimal anti-inflammatory aspirin doses, addition of a bedtime dose of a long-acting NSAID (e.g., piroxicam 10 mg, SR indomethacin 75 mg, naproxen 750 mg) to mealtime doses of aspirin may allow for continued aspirin use.[84]

15. *Choice of Agent.* **M.F., a female with RA, has been placed on an aspirin regimen of 3 tablets (325 mg/tablet) QID. After 3 days of therapy, M.F. discontinued her treatment because of severe abdominal pain. Which NSAID would be the best alternative to aspirin for M.F.?**

The choice of NSAID is based upon a number of considerations including relative efficacy, toxicity, concomitant drugs, concurrent disease states, patient age, renal function, dosing frequency, and cost. Because of cost considerations, aspirin has been the mainstay of NSAID therapy when tolerated. However, a number of nonaspirin NSAIDs are available as alternatives to aspirin (see Table 41.4). Included among these alternatives are salicylic acid derivatives. These products may be better tolerated than aspirin. In studies involving small numbers of patients, the anti-inflammatory efficacy of a nonacetylated salicylate was comparable to aspirin or indomethacin.[41] Aspirin irreversibly inactivates an enzyme, cyclo-oxygenase, via acetylation of the enzyme. Nonacetylated salicylates, except diflunisal (Dolobid), are weak inhibitors of cyclo-oxygenase *in vitro*. Cyclo-oxygenase inhibition may be relatively more important to antipyresis and analgesia than to suppressing inflammation.[85] Considering the favorable toxicity profile of non-acetylated salicylates, a large-scale controlled trial seems justified to clarify the relative efficacy and toxicity of these compounds in the treatment of chronic inflammatory disorders. Of the nonacetylated salicylates, sodium salicylate is the least expensive. Salsalate (a salicylate prodrug) may be activated erratically, resulting in variable salicylate concentrations.[86] Nonacetylated salicylates may be useful alternatives when the antiplatelet effects of aspirin are to be avoided (see Question 11).

Other nonaspirin NSAIDs also are available as alternatives to aspirin. Individuals vary both in their response and ability to tolerate these drugs.[87] Therefore, other factors being equal, cost and convenience of administration become important considerations in

Table 41.4		Nonsteroidal Anti-Inflammatory Drugs[a]		
NSAID	Half-life (hr)	Maximum Daily Dose (mg)	Cost Index[a,d]	Comments
Salicylate				
Aspirin	0.25–0.33	6000[b]	1.0	—
Choline salicylate (Anthropan)	3–20[c]	4800[b]	12.0	Available as 870 mg/57 mL liquid formulation
Diflunisal (Dolobid)	8–12[c]	1500	10.9	—
Magnesium choline salicylate (Trilisate)	3–20[c]	4800[b]	18.3	Available as 650 mg/5 mL solution
Magnesium salicylate (Magan, Mobidin)	3–20[c]	4800[b]	9.9	500 mg salicylate/tablet
Salsalate (Disalcid)	3–20[c]	4800[b]	4.4	Absorption/activation may be erratic
Sodium salicylate	3–20[c]	4800[b]	0.9	—
Propionic Acid				
Carprofen (Rimadyl)	—	—	—	Approved as 2nd-line NSAID but not marketed
Fenoprofen (Nalfon)	2.5	3200	18.7	
Flurbiprofen (Ansaid)	3–4	300	20.0	—
Ibuprofen (Motrin, Rufen, Advil)	1–3	3200	5.2	100 mg/5 mL suspension approved for JRA
Ketoprofen (Orudis)	3–5	300	26.6	—
Naproxen (Naprosyn)	13	1500	18.4	125 mg/15 mL suspension approved for JRA
Naproxen sodium (Anaprox)	13	1375	20.9	
Oxaprozin (Daypro)	56	1800	21.1	—
Acetic Acid				
Diclofenac (Voltaren)	25–33	200	19.9	Enteric-coated
Etodolac (Lodine)	7	1200	31.6	FDA-approved for OA only
Indomethacin (Indocin, Indocin SR)	2–5	200 SR: 1500	3.6 19.9	Also available as 25 mg/5 mL suspension
Ketorolac (Toradol)	6	40	30.9	Not FDA-approved for RA or OA
Nabumetone (Relafen)	24	200	22.2	Prodrug: Active metabolite 6-MNA
Sulindac (Clinoril)	18	400	12.6	Prodrug: Active metabolite sulindac sulfide
Tolmetin (Tolectin)	1	2000	16.2	Approved for JRA. False positive urinary protein by sulfocalicylic acid reagent assay
Anthranilic Acid				
Meclofenamate sodium (Meclomen)	2	400	5.8	Loose stools/diarrhea dose related
Mefenamic acid (Ponstel)	2	1000	32.8	Not indicated for chronic therapy
Oxicam				
Piroxicam (Feldene)	38–45	20	9.9	—
Pyrazolone				
Oxyphenbutazone		400	6.5	Not indicated for chronic therapy
Phenylbutazone (Butazolidin, Azolid)		400	11.1	Oxyphenbutazone is also an active metabolite

[a] FDA = Food and Drug Administration; JRA = Juvenile rheumatoid arthritis; NSAIDs = Nonsteroidal anti-inflammatory drugs; OA = Osteoarthritis; RA = Rheumatoid arthritis.
[b] Highly variable; anti-inflammatory doses associated with serum concentrations of 15–30 mg/dL.
[c] Half-life refers to metabolism to salicylic acid which is dose-dependent.
[d] Source for cost data: Physicians GenRx. Data Pharmaceutica Inc., 1994.

the selection of a nonaspirin NSAID (see Table 41.4). Because of their relative potential for serious toxicity, phenylbutazone, oxyphenbutazone, and mefenamic acid should be avoided, especially when chronic treatment is indicated. The incidence of central nervous system side effects frequently precludes the use of optimal anti-inflammatory doses of indomethacin, particularly in the elderly.[88] Loose stools or diarrhea may be dose limiting for some patients receiving meclofenamate.[88]

In M.F., ibuprofen is an inexpensive alternative to aspirin. If convenience of administration is a more important consideration,

longer-acting agents such as naproxen, sulindac, piroxicam, or nabumetone may be tried. If the first agent is ineffective or not well tolerated, trials of several alternatives may be necessary to identify the optimal NSAID for M.F.

16. *Adverse Effects*. Should M.F. be placed on misoprostol or other antiulcer therapy for prophylaxis against GI complications of NSAID therapy?

Up to 60% of patients taking NSAIDs for extended periods experience nausea, dyspepsia, heartburn, and/or epigastric pain.[89] These symptoms may be associated with gastrointestinal lesions ranging from erythema, edema, and various forms of mucosal hemorrhage and erosions to ulcers.[90] Ulcers may be acute or chronic. Conversely, GI ulcers may be silent in up to 20% of patients taking NSAIDs and the elderly may be at increased risk for painless ulcer complications.[89,91] Simple measures, such as taking the NSAID with meals or a large glass of water, may minimize symptoms but are of unproven benefit for preventing gastrointestinal ulcers and associated complications. Fries et al. estimated NSAID use in patients with RA leads to approximately 20,000 hospitalizations and 2600 deaths annually from GI complications.[92] Although these figures are concerning, Langman, after reviewing published studies, estimated that serious GI complications occur in about 1 in 5500 patient-months of NSAID therapy.[93] Thus, a minority of patients on chronic therapy experience gastrointestinal ulcers and a smaller percentage experience more serious complications such as major bleeding or ulcer perforation. Consequently, routine prophylactic therapy may not be cost effective and is not warranted yet.[89] Currently identified risk factors associated with hospitalization or death from GI complications of NSAID therapy include previous peptic ulcer disease, age greater than 60 years, concomitant use of corticosteroids, prior discontinuation of NSAIDs for GI side effects, total daily NSAID dosage, and significant disability.[94] Knowledge of these risk factors is helpful in identifying patients who are most likely to benefit from antiulcer prophylaxis.

Currently, misoprostol, 100 to 200 µg four times daily, is the only agent proven effective in preventing gastric and duodenal ulcers in chronic NSAID users.[95] H_2-receptor antagonists appear to decrease the incidence of duodenal lesions but have failed to significantly prevent gastric ulcers.[96] Sucralfate and antacids are of unproven benefit as well.

Antacids and H_2-antagonists appear to heal gastroduodenal ulcers in chronic NSAID users although gastric ulcer healing may require prolonged therapy. Sucralfate appears to be useful only for duodenal ulcers.[97] Continuous NSAID therapy does not prevent or delay healing of duodenal or small (<3 mm) gastric ulcers.[98] In the absence of history of previous peptic ulcer disease or the presence of additional risk factors, M.F. need not be placed on misoprostil if she tolerates the NSAID without GI complaints.

17. Use in Renal Disease. T.Z., a patient with congestive heart failure previously well controlled on furosemide 40 mg/day, digoxin 0.125 mg/day, and potassium chloride 60 mEq/day, returns for a prescription refill of ibuprofen 600 mg TID which he takes for his RA. He has noticed increased leg swelling over the past 2 weeks associated with a weight gain of several pounds, increasing shortness of breath (SOB), and easy fatigability. What information should be provided about potential ibuprofen side effects to T.Z.?

Nonsteroidal anti-inflammatory drug therapy should be monitored carefully in patients with congestive heart failure, liver disease with associated ascites, compromised renal function, or when diuretics are administered concomitantly. In these situations, renal function is highly dependent upon local production of prostaglandin E_2 within the kidney to offset the vasoconstrictor effects of high concentrations of angiotensin, vasopressin, and catecholamines.[99] Inhibition of cyclo-oxygenase by NSAIDs within the kidney leads to reduced prostaglandin concentrations and unopposed vasoconstriction. Consequently, urine output declines, serum blood urea nitrogen begins to rise, serum creatinine eventually increases, and fluid is retained. This phenomenon is a potential complication associated with all of the currently marketed NSAIDs.[100] T.Z. should be informed that his leg swelling, weight gain, shortness of breath, and fatigability may be due to ibuprofen.

18. How should this drug-related problem be managed?

Initially, ibuprofen (Motrin) should be discontinued until renal function normalizes. A number of studies suggest that this com-

plication may be less likely to occur when sulindac (Clinoril) is used.[101–104] The reason(s) for this are unclear but one explanation is that the active sulfide metabolite undergoes renal metabolism and, therefore, may not achieve tissue concentrations within the kidney sufficient to reduce prostaglandin production.[105] Unfortunately, patients do not seem to benefit from sulindac as well as from other NSAIDs. Alternatively, a nonacetylated salicylate might be considered. In either case, close monitoring of renal function continues to be warranted.

19. What other renal syndromes are associated with NSAID therapy?

In addition to acute renal failure described above, NSAIDs may produce a variety of renally mediated complications including nephrotic syndrome, interstitial nephritis, hyponatremia, abnormalities of water metabolism, and hyperkalemia.[106] Nephrotic syndrome, unlike NSAID-induced acute renal failure, may occur anytime (i.e., from days to years) after starting therapy; resolution following discontinuation of the NSAID also may follow a prolonged course (as short as a month or as long as a year). The presence of hematuria, pyuria, and proteinuria in the absence of prior renal disease differentiates nephrotic syndrome from other NSAID-induced renal problems. Histologically, nephrotic syndrome is characterized by interstitial lymphocytic infiltrates, vacuolar degeneration of proximal and distal tubules, and fusion of epithelial foot processes of glomeruli.

Prostaglandin-mediated inhibition of active chloride transport, regulation of medullary blood flow within the kidney, and antagonism of antidiuretic hormone can be suppressed by NSAIDs. As a result, urine is maximally concentrated, free water clearance is limited, and water retention that is disproportionate to sodium retention can occur. The resulting hyponatremia can be severe and might be potentiated by thiazide diuretics.[106]

Local prostaglandin synthesis also may stimulate renin production within the kidney. NSAID therapy may critically attenuate this regulatory mechanism in some situations, resulting in reduced aldosterone-mediated potassium excretion and hyperkalemia.

Second-Line Agents

20. T.W. (the patient from Questions 1–8 and 11) returns to clinic 3 months after beginning a conservative program of rest, physical therapy, and anti-inflammatory doses of aspirin. Despite good compliance to this regimen, her disease has continued to progress, as evidenced by more extensive joint involvement and worsening of her fatigability and morning stiffness. Increased ankle pain and swelling have forced her to consider seeking employment that would require less time on her feet. Inflammation and tenderness in her hands are approaching the same degree of severity that existed before therapy. X-ray examination of the hands revealed soft tissue swelling, localized osteopenia about the MCP and PIP joints bilaterally, narrowing of joint spaces, and marginal erosions of the second and third MCPs bilaterally. Laboratory data included a Westergren ESR of 65 mm/hr and a serum salicylate concentration of 22 mg/dL. What therapeutic alternatives to aspirin or NSAIDs are available for patients like T.W. who fail to respond to these first-line drugs? What should the next step in therapy be for T.W.? [SI unit: salicylate concentration 1.6 mmol/L]

The symptoms of rheumatoid arthritis often can be controlled in the majority of patients by conservative management. Nevertheless, the disease may progress in many patients and more aggressive therapy often is needed to manage the disease. The decision to treat with second-line drugs is a major step and universally accepted criteria to guide the clinician are unavailable as current measures of disease progression are imprecise. Factors other than disease severity also must be considered. Table 41.5 summarizes criteria frequently used to assist in identifying acceptable candidates for such treatment. Any second-line agent may provide substantial relief of arthritis symptoms when added to aspirin or other NSAIDs; however, these drugs are associated with potentially serious side effects. Fortunately, most of the adverse reactions are reversible and seldom lead to serious complications if the patient is monitored appropriately.

Ideally, the initial choice of therapy for progressive RA is determined by objectively assessing the relative risk:benefit ratio of the treatment alternatives and then individualizing treatment based upon patient-specific considerations.[84] In reality, the order in which second-line drugs are used is empiric and remains the subject of much debate. Whether second-line drugs should be used individually or in combination also is debated (see Question 42). Parenteral gold therapy has a long tradition of early use in this disorder.[107] However, many practitioners are using methotrexate early in the disease and it now is regarded as the drug of first choice by many rheumatologists.[108] Antimalarials and auranofin are used initially for ''milder'' progressive rheumatoid arthritis by some clinicians. Sulfasalazine is the initial second-line drug for other clinicians, particularly those practicing in Europe. Because methotrexate currently is approved in the U.S. for severe, active RA unresponsive to full-dose NSAIDs and usually at least one second-line antirheumatic drug, many rheumatologists still use parenteral gold as first-line therapy. It is recommended that T.W. begin a course of parenteral gold therapy.

21. Gold: Preparations. Which gold preparation should be used in T.W.?

Two parenteral gold preparations are in wide use: gold sodium thiomalate (Myochrysine), an aqueous solution, and aurothioglucose (Solganol), an oil suspension. In addition, an oral gold formulation, auranofin (Ridaura), is approved for treatment of progressive RA uncontrolled by more conservative therapy. The parenteral formulations, containing approximately 50% gold by weight expressed as mg of complex, generally are considered to be equally effective.[109] Aurothioglucose must be shaken thoroughly before withdrawal from its vial and a large bore needle is necessary to draw up this very viscous suspension. Lumps at the intramuscular (IM) injection site sometimes can be troublesome to the patient.[110]

Table 41.5	Suggested Criteria for Second-Line Antirheumatic Drugs in RA[a,b]

1) Correct diagnosis and presence of one or more of the following:

  a) Persistently active disease despite NSAIDs reflected by:
    i) elevated ESR or CRP
    ii) falling Hgb
    iii) thrombocytosis
    iv) synovitis remains active or ↑ in intensity

  b) High titers of IgM RF

  c) Radiographic evidence of osteopenia, joint space narrowing, or new bony erosions

  d) Glucocorticoid dependency ≥7.5 mg/day prednisone or equivalent

  e) Presence or development of extra-articular disease
    i) subcutaneous nodules
    ii) pleuritis/pneumonitis
    iii) myocarditis
    iv) uveitis
    v) vasculitis

2) Absence of contraindications

3) Informed, cooperative patient

[a] CRP = C-reactive protein; ESR = Erythrocyte sedimentation rate; Hgb = Hemoglobin; RA = Rheumatoid arthritis; RF = Rheumatoid factor.
[b] Adapted from reference 13.

The toxicity profiles of the parenteral gold preparations differ. A vasomotor reaction (also termed nitritoid reaction), which manifests as nausea, weakness, flushing, tachycardia, and/or syncope, may occur in up to 5% of patients receiving gold sodium thiomalate. These reactions generally are mild, transient, and frequently can be alleviated by having the patient lie down. Rarely, severe myocardial ischemia or infarction may result.[111] The etiology of this reaction is unknown but may be related to the vehicle or preservative in the thiomalate preparation. It has not been reported with aurothioglucose. Patients with concomitant cardiovascular disease or patients who experience a nitritoid reaction following an injection of gold sodium thiomalate, therefore, can be managed safely with aurothioglucose. Nonvasomotor reactions, consisting of transient stiffness, Oarthralgias, and myalgias, developed in 15% of patients following initiation of gold sodium thiomalate therapy in one retrospective study.[112] Substituting aurothioglucose resulted in decreased severity in 40% of the patients. In another series, a higher incidence of skin eruptions, stomatitis, and albuminuria developed in patients who received the aqueous gold sodium thiomalate preparation compared to patients who received the oil suspension of aurothioglucose.[113]

Auranofin capsules, containing 3 mg of gold, are 25% bioavailable.[114] The recommended auranofin daily dose of 6 mg can be given either as single or divided doses. Auranofin is better tolerated than parenteral gold formulations, but it also may be less effective. For example, in a carefully conducted parallel placebo-controlled trial involving 193 eligible patients, several outcome measures suggested gold sodium thiomalate was more effective than auranofin, but these differences were not large enough to be statistically significant.[24] In a randomized open study, 82% of patients receiving gold sodium thiomalate were in ''remission'' after two years compared to 56% of those receiving auranofin.[115] Conclusions from this latter study are limited because patients did not appear to have similar disease activity upon entering the study. Like parenteral chrysotherapy, benefit may occur as early as six to eight weeks after starting auranofin, but objective benefits may not be apparent for several months. Overall, auranofin has a slower onset of action when compared to gold sodium thiomalate.[116] Auranofin must be monitored in a manner similar to parenteral therapy. Proteinuria and bone marrow suppression occur with auranofin, but the incidence is low.[117] The incidence of rashes necessitating auranofin withdrawal is lower compared to parenteral gold therapy, but loose stools and diarrhea are encountered more commonly.

None of the gold formulations are ideal. Gold sodium thiomalate is easier to administer, but is associated with more frequent side effects compared to aurothioglucose. Auranofin is the best tolerated gold preparation, but probably is the least effective. In T.W., therapy can be initiated with any of the preparations.

22. Dosing. What would be appropriate initial doses of gold for T.W. and should her serum gold levels be monitored?

The optimal dosing schedule for parenteral gold is unknown. The standard treatment schedule consists of an initial intramuscular test dose of 10 mg followed by a 25 mg IM dose one week later. The third and subsequent weekly intramuscular injections of 25 to 50 mg should be continued until the cumulative dose reaches 1 gm, toxicity occurs, or major benefit is derived.[109,110] If a satisfactory response is achieved, maintenance doses of 25 to 50 mg every other week are recommended. If the disease remains stable, doses may be administered every third and subsequently every fourth week for an indefinite period.[110]

Alternative parenteral gold regimens have been evaluated. Higher weekly doses are no more effective and toxicity is greater.[118-120] Conversely, smaller doses administered weekly may be effective. A preliminary double-blind trial comparing 10 and 50 mg weekly doses suggested similar outcomes between treatments.[121] A subsequent trial comparing 10 and 50 mg weekly also found similar response rates in both treatment groups; however, a significant decline in ESR occurred only in the group treated with 50 mg weekly.[122] A study comparing 25 mg weekly to approximately 50 mg weekly found no difference between the treatments.[123]

Attempts to correlate serum gold concentrations to clinical outcomes generally have been unsuccessful. Although some clinicians believe that clinical response is related to optimal serum gold concentrations,[124–126] this has not been confirmed by retrospective and prospective studies.[127,128] Furthermore, toxicity has not been correlated with serum gold concentrations.[127]

The standard treatment schedule described above should be used for T.W. Serum gold concentrations should not be monitored.

23. *Adverse Reactions: Monitoring For.* **What subjective or objective patient data should be monitored to detect gold adverse reactions?**

Patients receiving gold injections should have their urine tested for the presence of protein, and complete blood counts, including platelet count, evaluated before each injection. In addition, patients should be asked about the occurrence of pruritus, skin eruptions, purpura, sore throat, and stomatitis before each dose of gold is administered. Cutaneous reactions (e.g., pruritus, erythema, a fine morbilliform rash on the neck or extremities) may develop after the first few injections of gold. Cutaneous reactions are common, usually subside within several days, and do not seem to be affected by subsequent injections. Although a highly pruritic localized eruption resembling pityriasis rosea is common, gold dermatitis may assume many different forms, including exfoliative dermatitis.[109] Therapy should be discontinued if a pruritic dermatitis develops. Mild dermal reactions may be managed with topical corticosteroids.[109] If discontinued, gold can be reintroduced in a reduced dosage following resolution of rashes (see Question 24).

Mild and transient proteinuria during gold treatment does not mandate a discontinuation of therapy unless protein excretion exceeds 1000 mg/24 hours.[107] Proteinuria is reversible when gold therapy is stopped.[109]

Blood Count. Gold treatments should be discontinued if white blood cells (WBCs) decline to less than 3500 cells/mm³, platelets to less than 100,000 cells/mm³, or if the hemoglobin concentration falls rapidly.[109] Although eosinophilia may be associated with toxic reactions, it is not a reliable predictor of gold toxicity and is not an indication to discontinue gold therapy.[129]

Thrombocytopenia may be life-threatening and sometimes is difficult to treat because of the long half-life of gold.[110] Most cases respond to cessation of gold therapy although administration of steroids also has been tried with apparent success in selected cases.[109] Platelet transfusion is indicated if hemorrhage occurs.

Other unusual but potentially serious complications of gold therapy include colitis, pneumonitis, and cholestatic hepatitis.[130–133] Corneal chrysiasis also may occur but does not lead to ocular complications.[134]

Chelating agents such as dimercaprol and penicillamine are of unproven benefit in the treatment of gold toxicity.[135,136] Substantial removal of gold by peritoneal dialysis has been reported, but more study of this technique is needed.[137]

24. After 10 weeks of treatment with aurothioglucose (total: 435 mg), T.W. developed pruritus and a rash on her abdomen. Gold was withheld and she was given a prescription for triamcinolone cream. Should T.W.'s gold therapy be discontinued?

Dermatological reactions to gold occur in 15% to 30% of patients.[108] Due to fears of subsequent exfoliative dermatitis and the belief that dermatological reactions recur upon rechallenge, there is a natural reluctance to continue gold treatment after the appearance of dermatitis or stomatitis. However, in one series of patients, gold treatments were reinstituted successfully in 28 of 30 patients who developed dermatological reactions.[138] One of these patients who presented initially with severe exfoliative dermatitis was treated successfully with gold several years later. Gold therapy was reinstituted in these patients as follows: After waiting at least six weeks after the lesions had healed completely, a 1 mg test dose of gold was administered intramuscularly. Subsequent doses were increased to 2 mg, then to 5 mg, and then to 10 mg at two- to four-week intervals. Thereafter, 5 mg increments were added until a dose of 50 mg weekly was attained. Dermatologic reactions did not develop in any of these patients subsequently. Gold therapy, therefore, need not be abandoned in T.W.

25. *Duration of Therapy.* **T.W. responded well to gold therapy and now, 1 year later, her RA is in remission. She currently is receiving monthly gold shots. How long should treatment be continued?**

Gold treatments should be continued indefinitely to sustain the remission. In one study, 73% of patients who continued chrysotherapy for three years continued to experience excellent responses.[139] In the Empire Rheumatism Council Study, patients evaluated one year after completing a 20-week course of chrysotherapy remained significantly improved compared to a placebo-treated control group;[140] the improvement in the gold-treated group was no longer apparent after two years when compared to the placebo-control group.[141] In contrast, other patients have been maintained under good control for many years with continuous gold injections.[142]

26. *Poor Response to Therapy.* **B.R., a 60-year-old male with RA of 3 years' duration, has been receiving weekly gold injections for 23 weeks with neither toxicity nor therapeutic benefit despite a cumulative dose of 1 gm. Should B.R.'s gold therapy be discontinued?**

Continuing gold therapy in patients who fail to improve during a standard course will result in benefit for only a few. Some clinicians continue therapy several additional weeks, increasing the dose of gold by increments of 10 mg every one to four weeks (not to exceed 100 mg in a single injection).[110] In the presence of active disease unresponsive to a standard course of gold, the clinician must weigh the risk:benefit of continuing gold versus switching to an alternative second-line treatment.

27. *Auranofin.* **J.M., a patient receiving gold sodium thiomalate for 1 year and responding well on a maintenance regimen of 50 mg IM Q 4 wk asks about switching to auranofin. Will switching to auranofin from parenteral gold maintain J.M.'s RA under good control? Can patients who have discontinued parenteral therapy due to adverse effects be treated with auranofin?**

Some patients originally started on parenteral therapy can be switched to auranofin and remain well controlled.[143,144] This experience is not universal, however, and it is not possible to predict which patients can be switched successfully to oral therapy.

When parenteral gold is injected weekly, the relative cost of parenteral gold therapy (including office visits and monitoring) is more than the costs associated with daily auranofin therapy. When gold injections are given every two to three weeks, the cost of parenteral and oral therapy is similar depending upon local laboratory and medical costs. When injections are given monthly, the cost of parenteral therapy usually is less than for oral therapy. Since this patient is well controlled, there is little to be gained by switching from parenteral therapy to auranofin, either from an economic or therapeutic standpoint.

Data are limited on the use of auranofin in patients who experienced adverse effects from parenteral gold. Because rashes usually are mild and proteinuria is reversible if the patient is properly monitored, a trial of auranofin in patients withdrawn from parenteral gold for these reasons may be justified.[145] It is inadvisable, however, to initiate auranofin in patients who were withdrawn from parenteral gold due to bone marrow suppression.

28. Antimalarials: Dosing. S.R., a middle-aged, 75 kg female who had been treated with aspirin for approximately 3 years, is to receive hydroxychloroquine treatment for her RA. What doses would be appropriate and when should patient improvement be expected?

Chloroquine and hydroxychloroquine are useful second-line drugs in the treatment of rheumatoid arthritis. Although both drugs probably are equally effective, hydroxychloroquine has become the primary agent of this class of compounds for the treatment of rheumatic disorders.[146] Recommended doses for hydroxychloroquine range from 2 to 6.5 mg/kg/day,[107,146] although the manufacturer's literature recommends an initial adult dose of 400 to 600 mg/day (310 to 465 mg of base). If the patient responds well, the manufacturer recommends that the maintenance dose be reduced by 50% and the medication be continued at a dose of 200 to 400 mg/day (155 to 310 mg of base). Doses of chloroquine not exceeding 4.0 mg/kg/day are claimed to be equivalent to hydroxychloroquine (6.5 mg/kg) in efficacy and safety;[146] however, this claim is somewhat arbitrary.[147] Approximately two-thirds of patients who tolerate hydroxychloroquine will respond favorably. A minimum of 6 to 12 weeks usually elapse before objective benefit becomes apparent and up to six months of therapy may be necessary.

29. *Risk of Retinopathy.* **How great is the risk of retinopathy from antimalarials when used for the treatment of RA? What monitoring parameters are appropriate?**

All of the 4-amino-quinolines can cause permanent and sometimes progressive loss of vision from retinopathy.[148] Although some studies suggest hydroxychloroquine may be less toxic compared to chloroquine, it is uncertain whether equivalent anti-inflammatory doses were compared.[149]

The risk of retinopathy appears to be dose related. Retinal lesions are noted more frequently when daily doses exceed 250 mg of chloroquine or 650 mg of hydroxychloroquine.[146,148] The issue of whether duration of therapy and cumulative dose are risk factors for retinopathy remains unclear. Cumulative doses exceeding 200 gm have been reported to increase the risk of retinopathy, but Tobin et al. observed no toxicity in patients taking as much as 1255 gm.[150] Mackenzie found no retinopathy in 84 patients who had taken more than 1 kg of antimalarials in a low daily dose whereas a second group of patients with retinopathy had taken lower cumulative doses and higher daily doses.[151]

Symptoms of antimalarial retinopathy are blurred vision, night blindness, missing or blanched out areas in the central or peripheral fields, light flashes and streaks, and photophobia.[152] The fully developed lesion of antimalarial retinopathy is seen on ophthalmoscopy as a pigmentary disturbance with a characteristic "bulls eye" appearance in the macular region. Because 4-amino-quinolines bind to melanin, they concentrate in the uveal tract and retinal pigment epithelium. They are retained for years in the retina, and retinopathy may be progressive even after stopping the drug. In two instances, visual disturbances from chloroquine retinopathy did not occur until several years after the drug had been discontinued.[153]

Currently, eye examinations at three-month intervals are recommended by the manufacturer of hydroxychloroquine. However, many rheumatologists consider examinations at six-month inter-

vals to be sufficient to detect a "pre-maculopathy" stage which is reversible when the drug is discontinued.[146,152] Baseline patient studies should include an ophthalmologic examination and testing of paracentral visual fields to red test objects.

Benign corneal deposits of antimalarial drug may occur during therapy. Although this adverse effect may be symptomatic, it is harmless, reversible when the antimalarial drug is discontinued, and not related to the more serious and less frequent retinopathy.[152]

The risk of drug-induced retinopathy must be weighed against the satisfactory, although unspectacular, benefits achievable with antimalarials. Regular ophthalmologic examinations and conservative dosing can minimize this risk.

30. Sulfasalazine. Could sulfasalazine be used to treat S.R. rather than an antimalarial?

Sulfasalazine was synthesized in the late 1930s in an attempt to treat "rheumatic polyarthritis." Initial reports of benefit were not confirmed by others, but sulfasalazine was noted to be useful for colitis in patients receiving it for arthritis.[155] World War II prevented widespread use of sulfasalazine in the U.S. until the 1950s. By this time, the discovery of hydrocortisone temporarily preempted further interest in new antirheumatic drugs and sulfasalazine's use in inflammatory bowel disease had become established. In the 1970s, sulfasalazine was tried once again in the management of rheumatoid arthritis. The sulfapyridine moiety in sulfasalazine resembles dapsone, a drug used in inflammatory disease, and sulfasalazine is effective in ulcerative colitis and dermatitis herpetiformis, two disorders characterized by immunological abnormalities.[155] Early uncontrolled reports of benefit were followed by controlled trials demonstrating efficacy when compared to placebo and other second-line agents.[156-158] The active moiety appears to be sulfapyridine.[159] Like other second-line agents, onset of effect is delayed, requiring several weeks to months for objective symptomatic improvement. Compared to other second-line drugs, adverse effects associated with sulfasalazine are relatively mild, consisting of nausea, abdominal discomfort, heartburn, dizziness, headaches, skin rashes, and rarely hematological effects such as neutropenia or thrombocytopenia.[160] To minimize GI-related adverse effects, sulfasalazine is initiated at 500 mg or 1 gm daily and the dosage is increased at weekly intervals by 500 mg until 2 gm/day is attained. In S.R., sulfasalazine is an acceptable alternative to antimalarial therapy.

31. How does acetylator phenotype status affect the likelihood of deriving benefit or experiencing adverse effects to sulfasalazine when used to treat RA?

Sulfasalazine consists of two chemical entities, 5-amino salicylic acid (mesalamine) and sulfapyridine, conjugated chemically to form a single compound. In rheumatoid arthritis, sulfapyridine has been established as the active moiety. Sulfapyridine undergoes acetylation, a metabolic process whose rate is bimodally distributed among whites.

The disposition of sulfasalazine and its metabolites was studied in eight young and 12 elderly patients with active RA.[161] The elimination half-life of sulfasalazine was greater in the elderly patients. Of the many disposition parameters of sulfapyridine, increased steady-state serum concentrations in the slow acetylators were of greatest significance. Age did not seem to affect sulfapyridine disposition, but the steady-state serum concentrations of N-acetyl-5-acetylsalicylic acid were greater in the elderly than in young patients. Thus, age is a determinant of the steady-state concentrations of salicylate moieties, but acetylator phenotype plays a greater role in determining the serum concentration of sulfapyridine.

In a group of 54 patients with RA treated with sulfasalazine 3 gm/day for 24 weeks, the efficacy of the drug was similar for fast (n = 31) and slow (n = 33) acetylators.[162] In a second study, 40 fast acetylators were allocated to 3 gm/day and 20 slow acetylators to 1.5 gm/day. At 24 weeks, the fast acetylators given the high dose markedly improved in contrast to the slow acetylators given low dose. The toxicity of sulfasalazine in a total of 149 patients (83 fast, 66 slow acetylators) also was studied. Significantly more slow acetylators stopped treatment because of nausea or vomiting, or both, but serious toxicity was not confined to either group.

In an attempt to establish a relationship between dose (in mg/kg body weight) and outcome, metabolism of sulfasalazine was assessed in 79 patients with response defined as good (n = 43) or none (n = 36).[163] The dose of sulfasalazine in relationship to body weight was similar in the two treatment outcome groups. Slow acetylators tended to be distributed more frequently in the group of good responders to treatment.

Acetylator phenotype, therefore, may be important in determining the incidence of nausea and/or vomiting associated with sulfasalazine therapy in patients with RA but has no effect on either potentially serious toxicity or efficacy. Therefore, prior measurement of acetylator phenotype in patients with RA confers little practical benefit in predicting response to sulfasalazine.

32. Methotrexate: Dosing. D.C., a female with RA, developed proteinuria in excess of 2 gm/24 hours on gold sodium thiomalate. Following the discontinuation of the drug, her symptoms resolved. However, her RA has become increasingly active despite optimal aspirin therapy and the addition of prednisone 7.5 mg/day to her treatment regimen. Methotrexate is to be started. How should methotrexate be administered when it is used in the treatment of RA?

Methotrexate may be administered either parenterally or orally. Approximately 67% of low oral doses of methotrexate is absorbed.[164] The optimal dosing regimen for methotrexate has not been established. Current dosing regimens are based upon regimens used to treat psoriatic arthritis where the pulse approach was used in an attempt to synchronize cell division in this disorder and, thereby, enhance efficacy.[165] The rationale for pulsing methotrexate doses in RA is unclear; however, it is effective and may be associated with reduced hepatotoxicity.[166] One frequently used treatment regimen consists of initiating methotrexate 2.5 mg orally every 12 hours for a total of three doses administered weekly. If no objective response is obtained by six weeks, the dosage is increased to 5.0 mg orally every 12 hours for three doses weekly. This is continued for a minimum of an additional 12 weeks.[167] If no response is seen at this time, some rheumatologists increase the dosage further, others may treat with the same dose for a longer period, and some discontinue the drug. Some patients with RA may respond particularly well to methotrexate.[167] These patients usually respond early to a weekly regimen of 7.5 mg. Although some researchers suggest that a good response may be associated with human lymphocyte antigen (HLA) DR haplotype,[168] others have been unable to corroborate these findings.[170]

33. Adverse Effects. How should MTX therapy be monitored?

The most frequent side effects associated with low-dose methotrexate therapy include nausea, malaise, and dizziness. These side effects usually are limited to the days on which methotrexate is taken and usually do not necessitate discontinuation of therapy. Other, more serious side effects include leukopenia, alopecia, mouth or GI tract ulcerations, and dermatitis.[165] These generally are reversible upon discontinuation or dosage reduction. Patients should have a complete blood count performed at regular intervals. Of greatest concern with chronic methotrexate therapy is the potential for hepatic fibrosis. To date, this complication has been reported rarely and may reflect careful patient selection.

Routine liver function test monitoring should be performed in all patients receiving methotrexate. Studies should be obtained just before each scheduled round of methotrexate as mild increases in

liver enzymes are seen commonly for one to two days after administration.[171] Methotrexate is withheld if liver enzymes rise to three times baseline or remain elevated for sustained periods during therapy.[172] Uncertainty exists regarding the ability of liver function test monitoring to predict risk for serious hepatotoxicity. In psoriatic patients receiving methotrexate, liver enzyme elevations do not predict risk of serious hepatotoxicity.[173] It is noteworthy that in these studies liver function tests were performed only on the day of biopsy rather than at regular intervals before biopsy. Abnormal elevations of liver enzymes, particularly aspartate aminotransferase (AST) elevation, seem to correlate with overall hepatic histological change over time (when monitored every 6 weeks throughout therapy) during methotrexate treatment of RA.[174]

34. Should a baseline liver biopsy be performed before starting methotrexate?

A dilemma pertaining to methotrexate therapy is the issue of whether liver biopsies are necessary before initiating methotrexate and at regular intervals throughout therapy. The hepatotoxic potential of methotrexate was documented first in patients with psoriasis. Cirrhosis was reported in up to 26% of patients.[175] Risk factors include excessive alcohol intake, obesity, diabetes mellitus, impaired renal function, significant abnormal premethotrexate liver biopsy, and total cumulative dose greater than 1.5 gm.[176] With the exception of total cumulative dose, many clinicians consider the presence of one or more of these risk factors as relative contraindications to methotrexate therapy for RA.

In 1987 the Health and Public Policy Committee of the American College of Physicians recommended pretreatment biopsies only if the patient has pre-existing liver disease; otherwise, biopsies should be considered every two to three years (or every 1.5 gm cumulative dose).[172]

The American College of Gastroenterology offers a stronger recommendation. Liver biopsies should be performed regularly in all individuals, even if liver enzymes are normal and no liver injury is suspected.[177] In its judgment, insufficient data are available to rule out the possibility that serious liver injury will develop over a longer period of time (higher cumulative dose).

Kremer has proposed an alternative set of guidelines in patients receiving methotrexate for RA (see Table 41.6), strongly emphasizing the importance of avoiding ethanol completely.[178] The American College of Rheumatology currently is developing guidelines regarding the use of liver biopsies to monitor methotrexate therapy.[263]

35. Should either supplemental folate or folinic acid be administered along with methotrexate to reduce risk of drug-related toxicity?

Both folic acid and folinic acid (leucovorin) supplementation have been advocated to reduce toxicity associated with methotrexate therapy. Experience using folinic acid has been confusing. Tishler et al. administered 45 mg *folinic acid* weekly immediately after methotrexate (MTX) in RA patients.[179] Although nausea related to MTX improved, joint disease showed significant deterioration. Buckley et al. administered a weekly dose of folinic acid equal to the weekly dose of methotrexate, four hours after the methotrexate.[180] Methotrexate efficacy was not impaired and the frequency of stomatitis and GI toxicity was lower during folinic acid treatment. In an eight-week double-blind, crossover study, 20 mg of folinic acid given two days before IM methotrexate[181] did not affect disease control adversely, and *leucovorin* was no more useful than placebo in reducing drug-induced nausea. The Canadian Leucovorin Study Group reported on the use of 2.5 or 5 mg/week of supplemental leucovorin during low-dose methotrexate therapy.[182] After 52 weeks, side effects were decreased without loss of methotrexate efficacy. In an eight-week, double-blind, placebo-controlled study of leucovorin (1 mg) in 16 patients with RA receiving chronic methotrexate, clinical variables of arthritis activ-

Table 41.6	Proposed Criteria for Liver Biopsies during MTX Therapy[a,b]

Baseline liver biopsy if patient has

1) History of significant regular ethanol consumption, arbitrarily
    defined as ≥3 drinks/day
2) History of hepatitis, jaundice, or liver disease

Liver biopsy during therapy if

1) 6 of 12 monthly determinations of AST are elevated into the
    abnormal range
2) Baseline normal serum albumin falls to ≤3.3 gm/dL
3) 3–5 of 12 monthly elevations of AST are in the abnormal range for
    3 consecutive years

Liver biopsy results

Biopsy showing Roenigk class I, II or IIIA (minimal fibrosis) would be
grouped as a "benign" hepatic outcome and a repeat biopsy would be
performed only if serum albumin falls to <3.3 gm/dL. Roenigk Class
IIIB (significant hepatic fibrosis) or IV (cirrhosis) would be cause to
permanently discontinue MTX

---

[a] AST = Aspartate aminotransferase; MTX = Methotrexate.
[b] Adapted from reference 178.

ity did not change in the leucovorin-treated population.[183] Low weekly doses of folinic acid, therefore, may alleviate some mild toxicities associated with methotrexate therapy without increasing RA activity.

In one study, 32 patients with RA were evaluated in a 24-week, placebo-controlled, double-blind trial of *folic acid* supplementation during low-dose methotrexate therapy.[184] Administration of daily folate significantly lowered toxicity scores without affecting efficacy, as measured by joint counts, joint indices, and patient and physician evaluation of disease activity. Fifteen patients experienced some sort of toxicity; 67% were in the placebo group. Four patients in the placebo group had toxicity serious enough to require discontinuation of methotrexate, while no patients in the folic acid supplement group discontinued methotrexate because of toxicity. Low-normal initial plasma and red blood cell folate levels were predictive of future toxicity with methotrexate therapy. In a second study, the incidence of adverse effects in 198 patients receiving folic acid in conjunction with methotrexate was compared to a historical control group.[185] A significant reduction in adverse affects was reported for the following gastrointestinal complications: nausea/vomiting, diarrhea, and stomatitis. The decrease of liver function abnormalities in this study was remarkable, suggesting some folate depletion occurs in methotrexate liver toxicity.

Retrospective analysis of 23 rheumatoid arthritis patients receiving low-dose methotrexate demonstrated an association between the mean cell volume (MCV) and hematologic toxicity.[186] All six patients who developed hematologic toxicity were folate deficient, and four of six had marked macrocytosis. Furthermore, the mean MCV of the patients who developed toxicity was significantly higher than that of the controls without toxicity. This difference in MCV was associated with an increased probability of developing toxicity with time. These results suggest that sustained elevation in the MCV may be a predictor of impending hematologic toxicity due to folate depletion.

Thus, folic acid or folinic acid supplementation may reduce the likelihood of mild GI side effects related to methotrexate; however, the risk of more serious side effects remains unaffected. Whether supplementation with folic acid is superior to simply reducing the methotrexate dose if mild adverse effects develop remains to be determined.

36. D.C. is started on methotrexate, 2.5 mg PO Q 12 hr for three doses weekly. Nine weeks later she returns to the clinic with subjective and objective improvement in morning stiffness, fatigability, and joint tenderness and swelling. However, she has noticed increased SOB and dyspnea over the past week. How can this be related to methotrexate?

A rare but important complication of methotrexate therapy is a pulmonary reaction characterized by a nonproductive cough, malaise, and fever, progressing to severe dyspnea.[187] Recognition of this unusual reaction is important to ensure that methotrexate is discontinued before progression to respiratory failure occurs. After discontinuation of methotrexate, pulmonary function improves. Corticosteroids have been used to accelerate improvement in pulmonary symptoms. D.C.'s dyspnea and shortness of breath may be related to methotrexate. If appropriate tests rule out other causes for her pulmonary complaints, methotrexate-induced pulmonary toxicity should be considered and treatment discontinued.

37. Penicillamine. M.M., a 55-year-old male, has progressive RA which has not been responsive to gold. Salicylates and other NSAIDs do not provide adequate control of his arthritis. Why would penicillamine therapy be indicated for M.M.? How should it be dosed and when is a response expected?

Previous Gold Therapy. Penicillamine is a second-line agent that is effective for the treatment of progressive RA and often is used in patients who do not respond to or tolerate gold therapy.[84] Failure to respond to gold therapy does not appear to lessen the likelihood of a response to penicillamine.[188] Conversely, previous gold therapy has been suggested as a risk factor for toxicity to penicillamine therapy in some studies.[189] An association between HLA-DR3 and nephrotoxicity to both gold and penicillamine suggests that patients discontinued from gold because of nephrotoxicity may be at risk for nephropathy from penicillamine.[190] Otherwise, penicillamine is an appropriate alternative for M.M.

Dosing. Penicillamine at doses of 1.5 gm/day is effective, but adverse reactions occur in 40% of patients.[191] Consequently, smaller doses have been used successfully with fewer side effects.[192] Currently, a "go low, go slow" approach is recommended.[193] Most practitioners initiate penicillamine at 250 mg/day and increase the dose to 500 mg/day after four to eight weeks. If therapeutic benefits are not observed after an additional four to eight weeks, the dose is increased to 750 mg daily, then occasionally to 1000 mg. As with gold and the antimalarials, up to six months of therapy may be necessary before therapeutic benefits become apparent.

38. *Adverse Effects.* M.M. is allergic to penicillin. Can he still receive D-penicillamine for treating symptoms of RA?

Metabolites of penicillin, rather than penicillin itself, are responsible for allergic reactions. The penicilloyl group is recognized as the major haptenic determinant, but other metabolites such as penicillinate, penicillate, panamaldoyl, and penicillamine groups are considered important. Penicillamine is an end product of metabolic processes starting with penicilloyl or penicillinic groups. The recommendation that penicillamine be given with caution, if at all, to penicillin-allergic patients is based upon *in vitro* studies demonstrating cross-sensitivity to penicillamine in 44% to 65% of penicillin-allergic patients.[194] However, none of these patients received an oral penicillamine challenge. In a study of 40 patients giving histories of penicillin allergy, confirmed by positive skin tests in 80%, none experienced an immediate or delayed reaction following an oral dose of 250 mg of penicillamine.[195] Three patients who had positive penicillin skin test reactions also had RA. All three subsequently received penicillamine without experiencing hypersensitivity reactions during therapy. Penicillamine, therefore, does not have to be withheld in patients with a history of penicillin allergy. The potential for cross-reactivity, although real, appears to be small.

39. *Proteinuria.* **M.M. has been receiving penicillamine for 3 months and currently is taking 750 mg/day. A routine urinalysis reveals 4+ proteinuria and a 24-hour quantitative urine collection contains 2.3 gm protein. Why should future treatment with penicillamine be abandoned?**

Proteinuria occurs in 7% to 20% of patients receiving penicillamine, usually between the sixth and twelfth month of therapy.[196,197] It appears to be related both to the duration of therapy and to the rate at which the penicillamine dosage is increased. Increasing the dosage slowly during initiation of therapy, or decreasing the daily dosage may reverse mild proteinuria.[193] In M.M., however, the appearance of more than 2 gm of protein in the urine is ominous and a clear indication to discontinue penicillamine immediately.[107,193] Although penicillamine-induced proteinuria is reversible, resolution may be slow.[198]

Reintroduction of penicillamine in patients who previously developed proteinuria usually is followed by a return of proteinuria at about the same time and about the same cumulative dose as on the first occasion. Nevertheless, penicillamine has been restarted successfully in patients when reintroduced at 50 mg/day and increased by 50 mg at monthly intervals until a maintenance dose of 150 mg/day was achieved. After four months, incremental 50 mg doses may be added at three-month intervals if necessary.[199] Thus, rechallenging M.M. with penicillamine is likely to result in recurrent proteinuria unless it is restarted in very low doses over a prolonged period of time. Most clinicians prefer another antirheumatic drug in this situation in order to achieve more rapid disease control.

40. What other side effects should be monitored during therapy with penicillamine?

Rashes. A number of adverse effects are associated with penicillamine therapy. Rashes are the most frequent complication and may present early in therapy as maculopapular eruptions, urticarial or eczematous rashes, or pruritus without rash.[200] These may be transitory and resolve during continued therapy, upon drug discontinuation, with antihistamines, or with dosage reduction.[193] "Late" rashes, occurring after six months of therapy, generally are intensely pruritic, discrete, appear as scaly macules with reddish edges, and may progress to bullous pemphigus if therapy is not discontinued.[200]

Hematological toxicities include leukopenia, agranulocytosis, aplastic anemia, and thrombocytopenia.[193] Thrombocytopenia is most common and dose related. It rarely may precede aplastic anemia.

Nausea, vomiting, abnormalities of taste, and anorexia also occur early in the course of therapy. Abnormalities of taste usually resolve despite continued therapy.[196] A rare adverse effect is obliterative bronchiolitis, which is irreversible in some cases.[196]

41. *Immunologic/Autoimmune Disorders.* **After 1 year of successful therapy with penicillamine, 750 mg/day, G.R. complains of increasing weakness that is worse in the afternoon than in the morning. In addition, several of his friends have observed that his eyelids are drooping. Why are these symptoms related to this therapy?**

A number of immunologic or autoimmune disorders have been reported during long-term penicillamine therapy including myasthenia gravis, lupus erythematosus, Goodpasture's syndrome, dermatomyositis, pemphigus vulgaris, and pemphigus foliaceous.[201-205] G.R.'s complaints are consistent with penicillamine-induced myasthenia gravis, and therapy should be withheld until this possibility has been evaluated.

42. *Combination Therapy.* **Would earlier use or combining second-line drug therapies in RA improve treatment outcomes?**

Theoretically, initiating second-line therapies earlier and using them in combination may improve patient outcomes beyond that obtained by more traditional methods. The rationale for combination therapy is similar to that of combination cancer chemotherapy or antimicrobial therapy. Combining drugs may yield additive or synergistic interactions by working at different sites or through different mechanisms. Combining drugs also may allow for use of lower doses of individual drugs, thereby reducing the risk of toxicity while maintaining or increasing efficacy. Early in the disease process, the response potential also may be greater. However, earlier use and combination therapy also may expose the patient to unnecessary drug toxicity. Although the concept of a therapeutic "window of opportunity" in which the entire process may be totally reversible is an appealing concept, there remains an almost complete lack of knowledge about the clinical course and pathophysiology of "early RA." Moreover, there is no reason to assume that more aggressive therapy with second-line agents, either alone or in combination, will improve outcomes or that they will be acceptably safe. A major problem in RA is the tremendous gap between clinical desire to treat the disease and the body of scientific knowledge on which to base the treatment.[206]

Despite these uncertainties, combination second-line therapy is becoming widespread. In a survey of 92 Canadian and 77 Australian rheumatologists, the combination of an antimalarial drug and gold was prescribed by 45% of Canadian rheumatologists and 31% of Australian rheumatologists.[207] An antimalarial and penicillamine were used by 31% of Canadian rheumatologists and 18% of Australian rheumatologists.

In the U.S., the use of "remission-inducing" agents, either alone or in combination, early in therapy is advocated based upon the premise that the rate of joint damage is greatest in the first two years.[208] Many approaches have been described. Several of these are reviewed below.

Fries et al. hypothesized that after an initial response to a second-line treatment, disease progression accelerates (even on therapy), explaining the apparent paradox of short-term improvement but failure to alter long-term outcomes in RA (see Figure 41.2).[209] Second-line treatment, therefore, makes progression to disability irregular, like the tooth of a saw. To improve disease outcome and at the same time to keep overall drug toxicity near traditional levels, they proposed initiating second-line drugs as soon as possible, before substantial damage to the joints occurs. One or multiple second-line drugs are used continually, throughout the entire disease course, while monitoring for evidence of disease progression. A ceiling is set in terms of progression, which triggers treatment changes. Second-line therapy is changed serially, alone or in combination, at each decision point. Analgesics and NSAIDs are used only as adjunctive therapy for symptomatic relief as required.

A more aggressive approach, the "Step Down Bridge" paradigm, proposes initiating a combination of second-line medications early in the disease course to induce remission.[210] Bridging to a simplified program then is attempted by withdrawing drugs sequentially (see Figure 41.3).

Yet another, more conservative approach is the "Graduated Step" paradigm. Disease severity and activity are matched to "appropriate" initial and long-term therapy (see Figure 41.4).[211] Goals of this strategy include increasing objectivity of therapeutic decision-making throughout the course of disease treatment and exposing only those patients with sufficiently active disease to the risks of combination second-line therapy. Patients are re-evaluated at three months and disease activity is scored quantitatively (see Tables 41.7 and 41.8). Patients with disease activity index values of 0 to 3 are designated as responders with inactive disease. Values between 6 to 8 are active, unresponsive disease; treatment should be escalated. Values of 4 to 5 are subacute; decisions regarding

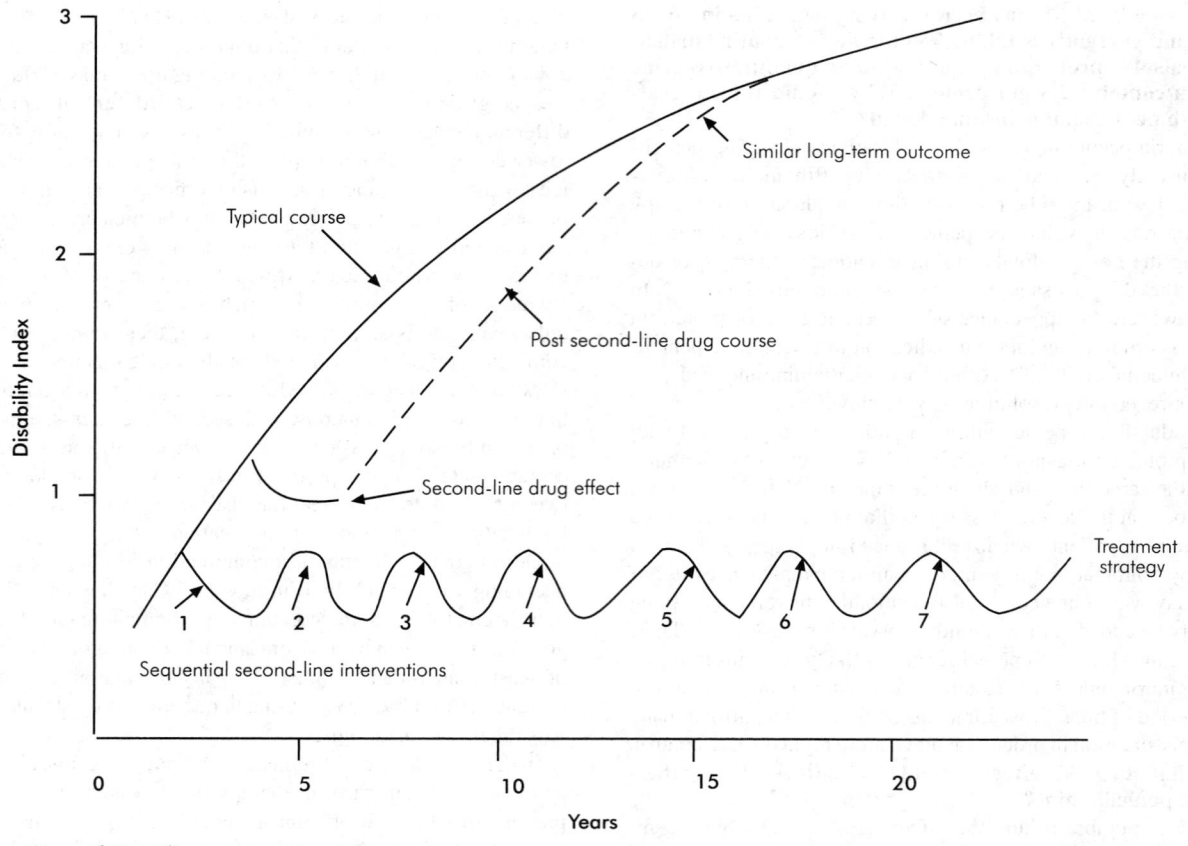

Fig 41.2   Sawtooth Paradigm   Adapted from reference 209.

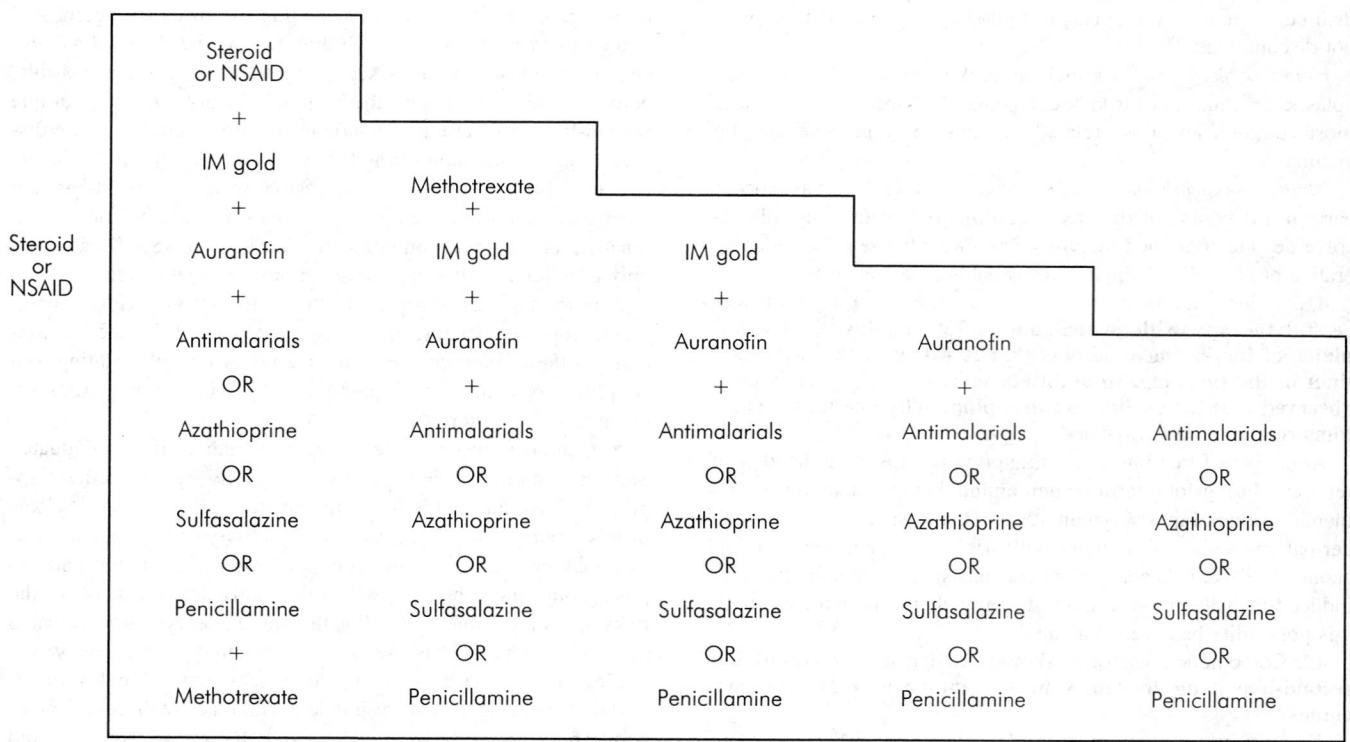

Fig 41.3   "Step-Down Bridge" Paradigm   Adapted from reference 210.

Fig 41.4 Stepped Care Paradigm Adapted from reference 211. NSAIDs = Nonsteroidal anti-inflammatory drugs; PT = Physical therapy; OT = Occupational therapy; Pt Ed = Patient Education.

these patients will be based upon additional information beyond disease activity criteria, including time of onset of afternoon fatigue, change in grip strength, change in hemoglobin concentration, or the onset or worsening of extra-articular disease manifestations.

Alternative proposals include a *pathophysiologic staging paradigm* for characterizing disease progression and optimizing second-line drug therapy as well as a *prognostic staging paradigm*.[34,212]

Although each strategy differs in specifics, they share the concepts of starting second-line therapy earlier and a willingness to combine second-line drugs to achieve improved short-term as well as long-term outcomes. Early uncontrolled observations suggested that combination second-line therapy may achieve therapeutic outcomes not possible with second-line drugs used alone.[213] However, controlled studies generally have failed to support these initial impressions and combination therapy is not without potential serious toxicity (see Table 41.9).[214]

The earliest controlled trial compared penicillamine and hydroxychloroquine, either alone or in combination, in 56 patients with progressive RA.[215] In this two-year, parallel, double-blind trial, the group receiving penicillamine alone improved most. At six months, 43% of patients receiving penicillamine were classified as markedly improved compared to 7% of the combination group and 17% of the hydroxychloroquine group. By 12 months, 33% of patients receiving penicillamine still were markedly improved, compared with 7% in the combination group. By two years, differences in improvement were no longer significant among groups because of a decline in efficacy for penicillamine during the second year.

Table 41.7							Scoring Criteria for "Stepped Care" Paradigm[a]	
	Inactive		Subacute		Active			
Disease Activity	Marked Response	Score	Partial Response	Score	Poor Response	Score	Prognostic Factors	Score
Pain	None	0	Intermittent	1	Constant	2	Deteriorating function capacity	1
a.m. stiffness	<15	0	15–30	1	>30	2	Sustained (≥6 months) elevated ESR	1
Swollen/tender joints	0–2	0	3–5	1	>5	2	RF titer ≥1:640	1
ESR or CRP	<30 <2.0	0	30–45 2.0–2.6	1	>45 >2.6	2	Extra-articular manifestation	1
							Radiologic joint damage	1
Total points		0		4		8		5

[a] CRP = C-reactive protein; ESR = Erythrocyte sedimentation rate; RF = Rheumatoid factor.

A second study also assessed the relative efficacy of combined penicillamine and antimalarials in 72 patients with early, progressive RA.[216] In this single-blinded, parallel randomized trial, clinical response to combination therapy was similar to monotherapy.

Sulfasalazine was compared to the combination of sulfasalazine plus penicillamine in an open-label study involving 32 patients with active RA.[217] Significant improvement compared to baseline occurred in each group at six months. Nine (56%) of the patients receiving combination therapy were judged responders compared to six (38%) in the sulfasalazine group. Three patients (19%) were withdrawn from the sulfasalazine treatment group compared to seven (44%) in the combination group.

The combination of parenteral gold and hydroxychloroquine was compared to parenteral gold plus placebo in a 12-month prospective, randomized, controlled trial involving 101 patients with active RA.[218] Forty-two patients were withdrawn before study completion; 25 taking combination therapy and 17 taking gold alone. Analyzing only patients completing the study, clinical improvement in the combination group was 20% to 25% greater than the patients treated with only gold. At six months, the change in disease activity was similar in both groups. Between months 9 and 12, however, the disease activity index worsened in the gold group, whereas it remained relatively unchanged in the combination therapy group. Each of these studies is limited by one or more methodologic deficiencies: insufficient statistical power, unblinded study design, or failure to provide appropriate control groups for comparison.

Two subsequent studies overcame these limitations in evaluating methotrexate combined with either azathioprine or auranofin. In the first, 212 patients with active RA participated in a 24-week, prospective, controlled, double-blind, multicenter trial comparing methotrexate, azathioprine, and combination therapy.[219] One hundred fifty-eight patients completed the study. No remissions were observed. Using intent to treat analysis, outcome with combination

therapy was not significantly different than with methotrexate alone, but both were superior to azathioprine. Fifty-eight percent met criteria for improvement on a combination regimen compared to 57% receiving methotrexate and 41% receiving azathioprine. When analyzed using only patients completing 24 weeks, mean improvement was greater for azathioprine compared to methotrexate; combination therapy was the most active.

In the second study involving methotrexate, 335 patients with active RA were enrolled into a 48-week, prospective, controlled, double-blinded, multicenter trial and randomly assigned to methotrexate, auranofin, or methotrexate/auranofin.[220] Two hundred eleven completed the trial. No remissions were observed. Similar percentages of patients entering the study achieved "important improvement" among the three treatment groups, although patients taking auranofin had a slower onset of response. When only patients completing the study were evaluated, no statistically significant differences in clinical endpoints emerged. Using laboratory criteria, the median decline in platelet count (acute phase reactant during inflammation) was significantly greater for combination therapy (43,000) compared to either auranofin (15,000) or methotrexate (28,500). The median decline in ESR for combination therapy (15 mm/hour) was not significantly different than for auranofin (10 mm/hour) or methotrexate (8 mm/hour), however. Withdrawals for lack of response were more common in single-drug groups and withdrawals due to adverse reactions were slightly more common for combination therapy.

These two studies represent the largest controlled experiences to date with combination second-line therapy. Neither study demonstrates compelling advantages for combined therapy in the short-term treatment of RA. However, even studies of these magnitude may not provide sufficient power to significantly differentiate among treatments. Whether small differences, if they exist, would be clinically meaningful is debatable. Whether important differences would emerge with longer term therapy remains speculative, as does using combinations earlier in the disease course. Fewer patients tolerated combination therapy compared to methotrexate alone, abrogating one of the purported advantages of methotrexate compared to other second-line drugs. Porter et al. added hydroxychloroquine or placebo to IM gold in suboptimal responders.[221] After six months of combination therapy or continued IM gold, no significant clinical differences were noted.

In summary, earlier intervention with second-line antirheumatic drugs and combining second-line treatments are being imple-

Table 41.8	Disease Severity Classification
Score	Classification
0–4	Mild
5–7	Moderate
8–13	Severe

Table 41.9					Controlled Trials of Combination Second-Line Therapy in RA[a]
Year	Investigator	Combination	No. of Patients	Duration (months)	Results
1984	Bunch et al.[69]	HCQ + DPEN	56	24	At 6 and 12 months, "markedly improved" significantly higher on DPEN compared to combination. By 24 months, differences no longer significant, due to deterioration in DPEN group. 62% continued DPEN for 24 months compared to 41% for combination. Subset of HCQ patients derived prolonged benefit
1987	Gibson et al.[70]	Chloroquine + DPEN	72	12	At 12 months, no significant differences among groups. ESR declined to greater degree for DPEN and combination; grip strength improved to greater extent for DPEN. Withdrawals due to adverse reactions: DPEN 2; chloroquine 1; combination 6
1987	Taggart et al.[71]	SSA + DPEN	32	6	Unblinded study comparing SSA and SSA + DPEN. Improvement compared to baseline observed in both groups. More combination patients judged to have "responded" but at end of 24 weeks, disease activity between groups not significantly different by any measured parameter. Withdrawals for adverse reactions: SSA 3; combination 5
1989	Scott et al.[72]	HCQ + IM gold	101	12	Combination compared to gold + placebo. 27/52 combination and 32/49 gold completed study. For those completing, overall improvements similar. Only CRP decline significantly greater for combination. A derived "disease activity index" significantly lower for combination at 12 months but at no other period during the study. Withdrawals for adverse reactions: combination 18; gold 10
1992	Willkens et al.[35]	AZA + MTX	212	6	157 completed study. "Responders" in intent to treat analysis: combination 58%; MTX 57%; AZA 41%. Combination and MTX significantly superior to AZA. Withdrawals for adverse effects: combination 16; MTX 3; AZA 22. For those completing study, 30% improvement for combination compared to 22% for AZA and 20% for MTX by physician global assessment (differences not statistically significant)
1992	Williams et al.[33]	AUR + MTX	335	12	211 completed study. "Important improvement" in joint swelling by intent to treat analysis: AUR 34%; MTX 43%; combination 36%. No significant differences among groups. AUR group experienced slower response onset. For those completing study, no significant differences among groups. Withdrawals for adverse reactions: AUR 16; MTX 17; combination 22
1993	Porter et al.[73]	HCQ + IM gold	142	6	HCQ 400 mg/day or placebo added in suboptimal responders to gold. At 6 months no differences in efficacy or toxicity
1993	Haar et al.[77]	HCQ + Dapsone	80	6	63 completed study. For those completing no differences among 3 groups in most variables. Combination improved significantly compared to baseline in all clinical and laboratory variables. Withdrawals for adverse effects: combination 4 for hemolytic anemia; Dapsone 0

[a]AUR = Auranofin; AZA = Azathioprine; CRP = C-reactive protein; DAP = Dapsone; DPEN = D-penicillamine; ESR = Erythrocyte sedimentation rate; HCQ = Hydroxychloroquine; MTX = Methotrexate; RA = Rheumatoid arthritis; SSA = Sulfasalazine.

mented more frequently. These experimental treatment regimens remain unproven and should be initiated only with appropriate patient consent.

Corticosteroids

43. Indications. At the time M.M. (the patient in Question 37) was started on D-penicillamine, would it also have been appropriate to initiate corticosteroids?

Despite the potential for serious adverse effects with long-term therapy, the judicious use of low-dose corticosteroids represents an important component of treatment during the course of unremitting disease. Although it is hoped that M.M. will respond well to penicillamine, his RA is sufficiently active that it is compromising his ability to earn an income. Thus, beginning an intermediate-acting corticosteroid such as prednisone in a daily or divided dose of 5 to 10 mg is justified.[19] The onset of action of corticosteroids is relatively rapid and their immediate benefits will allow M.M. to maintain his current employment and continue taking care of home responsibilities. The corticosteroid dose can be decreased gradually and eventually discontinued as M.M. begins to respond to penicillamine therapy. The goal is to provide "bridge therapy" until the second-line therapy becomes effective.[84] Un-

fortunately, this goal is not always realized. In some cases, patients do not respond to one second-line agent and then must be started on another. In some instances, patients fail to experience sufficient benefit from any second-line agent, and discontinuation of the corticosteroid is never realized.

44. Dosing. Why are corticosteroids sometimes administered in divided daily doses rather than as single daily doses or on an every-other-day regimen when used to treat RA?

Administering intermediate- or short-acting corticosteroids as a single daily dose each morning most closely mimics the early morning physiologic secretion of cortisol, and thereby minimizes hypothalamic-pituitary-adrenal (HPA) axis suppression. Administering corticosteroids on alternate mornings further reduces the risk of HPA axis suppression by allowing the adrenal glands to respond to hypothalamic and pituitary mediators during the "off" day.[222] Once-a-day and alternate-day steroid therapies are most advantageous when used to prevent reactivation of diseases such as asthma, ulcerative colitis, chronic active hepatitis, and sarcoidosis.[75] In contrast, when corticosteroids are used to provide symptomatic relief in RA during periods of active, ongoing inflammation, switching patients to single daily doses or every-other-day regimens frequently results in increased symptoms during the latter part of each day and during the ''off'' day. If larger average daily doses of corticosteroids are necessary for alternate-day therapy than those needed for divided daily dose administration, some of the advantages of less frequent drug administration may be negated.[223]

45. Osteoporosis. What therapeutic interventions can prevent steroid-induced osteoporosis?

Chronic corticosteroid therapy induces osteoporosis by inhibiting bone formation and enhancing bone resorption. Steroids impair bone formation by inhibiting the production of bone-forming osteoblasts and enhance bone resorption by reducing gastrointestinal calcium absorption and increasing the renal excretion of calcium.[224] Trabecular bone of the spine and ribs seems to be affected primarily by corticosteroid therapy.

Although the effects of long-term supraphysiologic corticosteroid therapy on bone mineralization are well recognized, drug treatment to prevent or reverse these complications remains of unproven benefit. Pharmacologic doses of vitamin D_3 or 25-dihydroxycholecalciferol and calcium supplements can correct the decreased GI absorption of calcium in patients treated with corticosteroids.[224] Thiazide diuretics reduce urinary calcium excretion and maintain bone mineral content.[225] Thus, vitamin D_3 50,000 U two or three times weekly, calcium 1 to 1.5 gm/day, and a thiazide diuretic if hypercalciuria is present theoretically could correct the metabolic abnormalities induced by high-dose corticosteroids.[226] In patients with rheumatic, immunologic, or respiratory diseases started on corticosteroids, calcitriol, with or without calcitonin, was superior to calcium supplementation alone in preventing bone loss from the lumbar spine.[227] Bone loss at the femoral neck and distal radius was not affected by any treatment, however. Intermittent etidronate therapy given for six months with prednisone to postmenopausal women with temporal arteritis prevented vertebral bone loss in another study.[228] Deflazacort, an investigational corticosteroid, is purported to impair calcium absorption to a lesser degree than prednisone at comparable anti-inflammatory doses.[229]

For established osteoporosis, the use of sodium fluoride 50 mg/day, vitamin D 50,000 U twice weekly, and calcium 1 gm/day has been advocated.[230] Calcitonin in combination with calcium increased lumbar, femoral, and radial bone density as compared with untreated patients in a randomized controlled study.[231]

In summary, the risk for corticosteroid-induced osteopenia in patients receiving suraphysiologic doses of corticosteroids chronically is real. However, other than ensuring that such patients are receiving adequate calcium intake (1.0 to 1.5 gm/day of elemental calcium), and replacement estrogens if postmenopausal, measures designed to enhance calcium absorption, reduce calcium reabsorption from bone, reduce renal excretion of calcium, or enhance bone mineralization still need to be validated by controlled clinical studies.

46. Pulse Therapy. What is the role of ''pulse steroid'' therapy in the treatment of RA?

''Pulse steroid'' treatment in rheumatic disorders consists of giving very large parenteral doses of corticosteroids for one to three days followed by small daily doses of an oral corticosteroid that are decreased gradually and ultimately discontinued.[231] Subsequent ''pulses'' of steroids may be administered at 4- to 12-week intervals. One ''pulse steroid'' regimen consisting of intravenous methylprednisolone 1 gm once a month was associated with modest improvement in patients after six months of treatment.[232]

The efficacy and toxicity of pulse steroid regimens compared to standard low-dose oral steroid therapy in the treatment of refractory rheumatoid arthritis is not clear. Therefore, ''pulse steroid'' therapy should be considered experimental until proven to have a superior benefit to toxicity ratio than traditional corticosteroid treatment.[234] Serious side effects, including sudden death, have been reported in patients receiving pulse steroid therapy.[235,236]

Juvenile Rheumatoid Arthritis (JRA)

Arthritis is the most common pediatric connective tissue disease. In the past, all arthritis of childhood has been referred to as juvenile rheumatoid arthritis. Because of increasing efforts to subclassify this disease, the term ''chronic arthritis of childhood'' is used more frequently to encompass the many forms of childhood arthritis. JRA affects all races and afflicts an estimated 60,000 to 200,000 children in the U.S.[237] By definition, JRA begins before the age of 16. The onset of disease is rare before six months of age and the peak age of onset ranges from one to three years. However, new cases are seen throughout childhood.

Signs and Symptoms

Morning stiffness and joint pain probably occur in JRA as frequently as in RA; however, children should be observed carefully for symptoms because they often are unable to articulate complaints. The morning stiffness and joint pain may manifest as increased irritability, guarding of involved joints, or refusal to walk. Fatigue and low-grade fever, anorexia, weight loss, and failure to grow are other manifestations. JRA may be divided into a number of subsets based upon characteristic signs and symptoms during the first four to six months of disease. In one classification, patients are categorized according to one of three distinct subsets of symptoms: polyarthritis, oligoarthritis, and systemic disease.[237]

Patterns of Onset

When the disease involves five or more joints with few or no systemic manifestations of disease, patients are classified as ''polyarthritis onset.'' Although the onset of disease in this category may be acute, it more commonly is insidious. Generally, the large, fast-growing joints such as the knees, wrists, elbows, and ankles are affected, but the small joints of the hands and feet also may be involved. Although the joints at onset usually are symmetrically involved, asymmetrical patterns also may be seen. Temporomandibular joint involvement is relatively common and may lead to limitation of bite and micrognathia. Systemic manifestations of disease in children with ''polyarthritis onset'' are rare and include low-grade fever, slight hepatosplenomegaly, lymphadenopathy, pericarditis, and chronic uveitis. Subcutaneous nodules are seen most typically in children with ''polyarthritis onset'' JRA. When present, nodules are associated with positive rheumatoid factor in greater than 75% of patients. Approximately 40% to 50% of JRA will present as polyarthritis.

''Oligoarthritis'' involving four or fewer joints accounts for approximately 40% of children with JRA. Joint involvement in these children most commonly includes the knees, ankles, or wrists. When only one joint is involved, the knee most commonly is the joint affected. Extra-articular manifestations are rare in children with ''oligoarthritis''; however, inflammation of the iris and ciliary body (i.e., iridocyclitis) is especially prone to occur in young females with ''oligoarthritis onset'' JRA. Furthermore, these patients usually are seropositive for antinuclear antibody.

A smaller percentage (10% to 20%) of children experience severe systemic involvement associated with or preceding the onset of arthritis. The hallmarks of the ''systemic-onset'' category of JRA are a high spiking fever and a rheumatoid rash. Once or twice daily, the body temperature may increase. The temperature increase may be accompanied by a rash consisting of small, discrete erythematous morbilliform macules that are seen most commonly on the trunk and proximal extremities. The lesions tend to be migratory and of short duration in any one location. Other manifestations of ''systemic-onset'' JRA are hepatosplenomegaly, lymphadenopathy, and pericarditis.

Overall, 70% to 90% of children with JRA experience no long-term disability. Preservation of joint function is least favorable in children with unremitting ''polyarthritis.'' Children with ''oligoarthritis'' experience the least joint disease and the worst uveitis. Children with ''systemic-onset'' are most prone to develop life-threatening or fatal complications.

Treatment

Diagnosis of Systemic-Onset JRA

47. J.R., a 4-year-old female, was hospitalized for high fever and arthritis. Several weeks before admission, J.R. developed a daily fever ranging from 103 to 106 °F. One week before admission, her knees became painful and swollen. Upon physical examination, J.R. was listless and irritable. The rectal temperature was 102.4 °F. She refused to walk. The right hip was tender and the right wrist and both knees were warm, red, and swollen. Minimal generalized lymphadenopathy and splenomegaly were present. The Westergren ESR was 82 mm/hr, the WBC count 37,000 cells/mm³ with a mild left shift , and Hct 33%. Cultures of the throat, urine, stool, and blood were negative. An intermediate-strength purified protein derivative, antistreptolysin-O titer, ANA titer, and RF titer all were normal. X-rays of the chest and involved joints all were normal. An electrocardiogram revealed only tachycardia. After hospitalization and withholding aspirin, an evanescent rash became apparent in conjunction with fever spikes. What signs and symptoms of JRA are manifested by J.R.?

The signs and symptoms (i.e., the spiking fever episodes, evanescent rash, arthritis) that were experienced by J.R. are characteristic of ''systemic-onset'' JRA. These children also may have a normocytic, hypochromic anemia, elevated ESR, thrombocytosis, and leukocytosis. Leukocytosis is common and a WBC count of 30,000 to 50,000 cells/mm³ is seen occasionally. A positive RF titer is uncommon in JRA and is present in only 20% of all cases.[237] The ANA titer more frequently is positive and is most prevalent in young females, and children with oligoarthritis and uveitis.[237]

Aspirin

48. Dosing. What is the initial drug therapy for treatment of JRA?

Aspirin is the drug of choice for treating the joint manifestations as well as the febrile episodes in systemic-onset JRA. Aspirin is initiated in divided doses totaling 60 to 80 mg/kg/day.[237] The dosage should be increased slowly to 130 mg/kg/day to achieve anti-inflammatory serum salicylate concentrations ranging from 20 to 30 mg/dL. One authority recommended initiating therapy with 1800 to 2500 mg/m² for children weighing over 25 kg to reduce the risk of toxicity.[238] Salicylate therapy in children is monitored in a manner similar to adults. Satisfactory treatment can be achieved in approximately 70% of children with aspirin alone and may be continued for up to two years after all manifestations of disease activity have been suppressed.[237]

49. Hepatotoxicity. J.R. is started on aspirin and 4 weeks later is symptomatically improved. A serum salicylate concentration at that time is 25 mg/dL, and serum concentrations of AST and alanine aminotransferase (ALT) were 102 and 87, respectively. How are these related to J.R.'s aspirin therapy and should the aspirin be discontinued?

Although serum aminotransferase concentrations are elevated in the setting of untreated JRA, increased concentrations of these enzymes also are noted in more than 50% of children receiving high dose salicylate therapy.[239] Hypertransaminasemia also has been

associated with salicylate therapy of systemic lupus erythematosus, RA, and otherwise normal individuals.[240,241] Salicylate-induced transaminitis (as opposed to hepatotoxicity) is dose and serum concentration-dependent and, therefore, frequently resolves following a reduction in dose. The transaminitis even may resolve without a reduction in the aspirin dose.[242]

50. Reye's Syndrome. Should aspirin be discontinued in a JRA patient who experiences chickenpox due to the potential for causing Reye's syndrome?

Unrelated to the mild, reversible, dose-related transaminitis, Reye's syndrome occurs in association with the use of aspirin as an antipyretic in children during the prodromal phase of viral illnesses such as influenza and chickenpox. Reye's syndrome is characterized by fatty vacuolization of the liver producing hepatic injury, vomiting, hypoglycemia, and progressive encephalopathy. The suggestion that aspirin might be a factor in the development of Reye's syndrome first was proposed in the early 1960s.[243] Subsequently, retrospective case-controlled studies revealed a statistically significant difference in the prevalence of salicylate use in patients with Reye's syndrome compared to controls.[244-246] Virtually all cases of Reye's syndrome were exposed to salicylates during an antecedent illness. In the control population, salicylate use varied from approximately 40% to 70%. Based upon these findings, the Committee of Infectious Diseases of the American Academy of Pediatrics issued a statement that aspirin should not be given to febrile children who are at risk for Reye's syndrome by virtue of possible infection with either influenza virus or chickenpox.[247] The risk of Reye's syndrome in children receiving salicylate therapy for JRA is unknown. However, in a retrospective study, 6 of 176 patients with biopsy-confirmed Reye's syndrome were treated with salicylates for connective tissue disease.[248] Three of these children experienced a preceding upper respiratory tract infection; the other three experienced no apparent prodromal illness. Therefore, patients with JRA also should avoid salicylate ingestion during febrile illnesses which represent possible infection with either influenza or chickenpox.

Nonaspirin NSAIDs

51. If J.R. does not tolerate anti-inflammatory doses of aspirin, can other NSAIDs be used to treat her JRA?

Six NSAIDs have been tested by the Pediatric Rheumatology Collaborative Study Group.[237] To date, tolmetin, naproxen, and ibuprofen have been approved by the FDA for treatment of JRA. Tolmetin 15 mg/kg/day in divided doses generally is used to initiate therapy when indicated and doses up to 30 mg/kg/day (max: 1800 mg) can be used for maintenance therapy.[249] Naproxen 10 to 15 mg/kg/day (max: 750 mg) in two daily divided doses may be advantageous in school-age children.[238] Ibuprofen doses should not exceed 40 to 50 mg/kg/day. Suspensions of naproxen and ibuprofen are available for use in children. Sulindac requires additional study in children but recommended doses are approximately 6 mg/kg/day (max: 400 mg). Indomethacin has been implicated in the deaths of three children and its use remains controversial, although the relationship of indomethacin to these deaths is unclear.[250]

Second-Line Agents

52. Are second-line agents ever used in JRA? Are they of benefit? If so, how should they be used?

The heterogeneity of JRA is an important consideration in approaching treatment. Fortunately, most children with JRA improve significantly with NSAID treatment, particularly those with pauciarticular disease. Only a small number of these patients are considered for second-line treatment, usually because of the evolution of their condition into the polyarticular type. Patients with polyarticular, RF-positive disease and patients with early-onset polyarthritis in association with systemic-onset disease both have poor prognosis in terms of ultimate joint function, and should receive early consideration for second-line treatment. Injectable gold is the drug of choice for the former patients, if an initial trial of NSAIDs has failed.[237,238] Brewer reported that the "polyarthritis onset" category of JRA patients may respond best.[251] Traditionally, a test dose of 5 mg is administered and weekly doses are increased gradually to 0.75 mg/kg not to exceed 50 mg. If satisfactory response is obtained after 20 weeks and a cumulative dose of approximately 15 mg/kg, maintenance therapy is instituted similarly to the maintenance regimen for adults.

Children with polyarticular-onset, RF-negative disease generally have a better prognosis than patients with polyarticular involvement. One may wait considerably longer before introducing a second-line agent for these patients. An antimalarial agent may be a reasonable choice for these patients, especially those with limited polyarticular involvement (5 to 10 active joints). This latter principle also may be applied to patients who evolve from pauciarticular to polyarticular involvement. When used in JRA, hydroxychloroquine is initiated in doses of 5 to 7 mg/kg. After six to eight weeks of therapy, the daily hydroxychloroquine dose should be reduced. Some clinicians recommend that initial therapy not exceed one to two years. As in adults, regular ophthalmologic examinations are a necessity. Penicillamine also may be considered but is almost never used as first choice. The maximum daily dosage is 10 mg/kg.[237] Penicillamine is initiated at approximately one-third of this dosage and increased at 12-week intervals to the maximum daily dosage if necessary. The importance of carefully considering the risks before initiating treatment is emphasized by failure of either therapy to prove superior to placebo in a large, multicenter-controlled study.[252]

For a young child, the difficulty with injecting gold and the hazards of antimalarial agents may limit the use of these treatments. In situations such as this, auranofin or sulfasalazine may be considered. Auranofin has been used in doses of 0.1 to 0.2 mg/kg/day but is not yet approved for JRA.[253]

Methotrexate also has been evaluated in JRA. In patients with resistant disease, nearly two-thirds of those receiving six months of therapy with 10 mg/m^2 weekly improved compared to approximately one-third of children receiving weekly doses of 5 mg/m^2 or placebo.[254] Methotrexate was well tolerated during this study. Response may vary by type of disease onset. In one study, the systemic form seemed less responsive than the ANA-positive form with a polyarticular course or polyarticular onset. Initiating therapy early in disease, before development of major erosions, may improve response potential. However, many rheumatologists reserve cytotoxic/antimetabolite therapy for those children who have continued to have active disease despite full courses of two slow-acting antirheumatic drugs or for those who have been unable to take SAARDs because of their side effects.

Uveitis

53. J.R. is scheduled to be seen by an ophthalmologist every 6 months to screen for uveitis. How should her uveitis be managed?

Uveitis associated with JRA is a nongranulomatous inflammation involving the iris and ciliary body. This type of uveitis sometimes is referred to as iridocyclitis. The posterior uveal tract, or choroid, rarely is affected.[237] Chronic uveitis can progress to blindness and, therefore, careful screening is necessary for early detection. Uveitis occurs most often in young females of early-age onset with limited joint disease and who are ANA-positive serologically. Treatment must be supervised by an ophthalmologist and initially

consists of a topically administered corticosteroid and a short-acting mydriatic drug (e.g., tropicamide or cyclopentolate) to dilate the eye and prevent adhesion of the iris to the lens or cornea. In up to 30% to 50% of children, the response is incomplete and oral corticosteroid therapy may be necessary.[237]

Osteoarthritis (OA)

Osteoarthritis or degenerative joint disease (DJD) is the most common form of arthritis in humans and also is probably the most common human disease. It is the single most common cause of rheumatic symptoms and results in the most loss of time from work. Radiologic studies suggest that more than 80% of people over age 65 have OA.[255] Men and women generally are affected equally, although women are more likely to present with distal interphalangeal joint involvement.

Signs and Symptoms

The clinical presentation of osteoarthritis is variable and dependent upon which joints are involved. Unlike RA, which is characterized by synovial proliferation within joints and systemic disease, the symptoms of OA are limited to the involved joints in which progressive degeneration of cartilage with secondary reactive bone changes (osteophyte formation) occurs. Occasionally, secondary synovial inflammation may contribute to symptoms. The primary symptom is a deep aching pain localized to the involved joint or joints. The joints most commonly involved are the distal interphalangeal, proximal interphalangeal, first carpometacarpal, knees, hips, cervical and lumbar spine, and the first metatarsophalangeal joints.[255] Associated with joint pain is the presence of morning stiffness and stiffness after rest during the day lasting less than 30 minutes and limited to involved joints. Joint motion limitation may be present secondary to loss of integrity of the joint surfaces, development of osteophytes, intra-articular loose bodies, and protective muscle spasm. Crepitus, a sense of grating or crackling, may be associated with both passive and active motion in involved joints.

54. G.R., a 190-pound, 60-year-old school teacher, developed painful, tender swelling in the right knee ≈1 year ago. Since then she has experienced intermittent pain in the right knee and hip. She now has moderate morning stiffness in the hip and knee and some joint stiffness after inactivity. Her pain is increased significantly by ambulation. Examination of her joints revealed the presence of Heberden's nodes in both hands, limitation of flexion of the right hip to 90°, no synovial thickening, patellar crepitus, and some tenderness at the joint margin of the right knee. Laboratory studies were all normal and an RF was negative. What signs and symptoms of OA are manifested in G.R.?

Symptoms of osteoarthritis usually are referable to the particular joint or joints involved. Common complaints include joint pain, particularly on motion and for weight-bearing joints, stiffness after periods of rest, and aching at times of inclement weather. Crepitation on joint motion, limitation of motion, and changes in the shape of the joint may be detected upon physical examination. The joint(s) may be tender to palpitation, but signs of inflammation are relatively uncommon, except for effusion, which may be noted following trauma or vigorous use of the involved joint. The Heberden's nodes observed in C.R.'s hands are bony protuberances (osteophytes) at the margins on the dorsal surfaces of the distal interphalangeal joints. These nodes are more common in women, tend to occur in families, and often are associated with other joint involvement. Degenerative disease of the hip generally progresses and eventually range of motion is lost. Degenerative disease of the knee is observed frequently in older women and is associated with crepitus, loss of motion, and flexion deformities. In addition to the above characteristics, most of which were observed in G.R., other manifestations frequently observed are vertebral column involvement and the presence of Bouchard's nodes (osteophytes on the proximal interphalangeal joints).

Results of laboratory studies usually are normal unless an underlying disease coexists. Rheumatoid factor is negative.

Treatment

Acetaminophen

55. How should G.R. be treated?

Because the etiology and much of the pathophysiology pertaining to OA remain unexplained, drug therapy is empiric and directed toward providing symptomatic relief. Salicylates or acetaminophen usually are initiated to provide analgesia. Sometimes an opioid is used concomitantly for more severe pain symptoms.[256] In a four-week study of patients with symptomatic osteoarthritis of the knee,[257] acetaminophen 1 gm four times daily was comparable to an analgesic regimen of ibuprofen (1.2 gm/day) as well as an anti-inflammatory regimen (2.4 gm/day). Although an NSAID traditionally has been considered the drug of choice if signs of inflammation such as swelling, warmth, or effusion in the afflicted joints are present,[257] synovitis did not predict a better response to the anti-inflammatory dose of ibuprofen in this study. In a multicenter, randomized, double-blind, two-year trial in which naproxen 750 mg/day was compared with acetaminophen 2.6 gm/day, no significant differences were noted between treatments except for improvement in knee flexion and walking time in the naproxen group.[259] Most significant was the high overall dropout rate of 65%, suggesting that neither treatment provides long-term benefit. Whether higher daily acetaminophen doses would prove more effective in the long term is unclear.

The results of these studies argue that a trial of acetaminophen should be prescribed initially, in doses as high as 4 gm/day, for patients with osteoarthritis. Only if joint symptoms persist after a reasonable period should an NSAID be considered. Once therapy is initiated, the need for continuation of that treatment requires ongoing reassessment. In many cases it is possible to reduce the daily NSAID dose or use the agent intermittently during times of disease exacerbation.

Corticosteroids

56. G.R. is started on a regimen of acetaminophen 1 gm QID and returns to clinic 4 weeks later. At that time she states that she is improved symptomatically and is functioning much better. Her only problem now is that her right knee really has not responded. In her estimation, it is more bothersome to her now than 1 month ago. At this point, are corticosteroids indicated for management of G.R.'s arthritis?

Systemic corticosteroids are rarely, if ever, justified in the management of OA. The well-known, potentially serious side effects associated with chronic corticosteroid therapy warrant against their use in a disorder which is not life-threatening or associated with serious morbidity not treatable by other means. However, intra-articular injections of corticosteroids, when used judiciously, can be justified.[256] Symptomatic improvement may last only a few days but may persist for a month or longer. Initial relief of pain may permit more effective use of physical therapy and appropriate balance of rest and exercise, thus attenuating the need for repeated injections. The dilemma, of course, is that symptomatic improvement may lead to overuse of the joint and potentially accelerate the degenerative process. Moreover, corticosteroids may have direct effects on articular cartilage. Repeated weekly joint injections for up to nine weeks in animals resulted in histologic evidence of cartilage degeneration and depressed collagen and proteoglycan synthesis.[260] In weight-bearing joints, these changes were associated with degenerative changes in the cartilage. Following termination of corticosteroid injections, recovery and normalization of the biochemical indices occurred over a several-month period. Other potential, but rare, complications of intra-articular injections include tendon rupture, microcrystalline corticosteroid deposition in the synovial fluid, and joint capsule calcification.[261] Thus, frequent injections into the same joint, particularly weight-bearing joints, should be avoided. In G.R., increased severity of her knee pain most likely is the result of increased activity secondary to symptomatic improvement since starting acetaminophen therapy. Starting G.R. on an activity regimen that temporarily reduces her weight-bearing activities should be attempted before resorting to intra-articular steroid injections.

NSAIDs

57. Will treatment with NSAIDs alter the course of osteoarthritis?

Drug therapy of OA is symptomatic, directed primarily toward relief of pain and secondary inflammation. However, symptomatic improvement is not associated with suppression of the underlying pathophysiologic process that results in cartilage degeneration and bony proliferation of joint margins. Theoretically, reduced symptomatology may allow the patient to increase activities that enhance the rate of joint degeneration and, in this sense, NSAIDs may enhance the progression of joint disease.

Some NSAIDs, when added to culture media containing osteoarthritic cartilage, inhibit proteoglycan synthesis. Salicylate, fenoprofen, and ibuprofen inhibited proteoglycan synthesis in a dose-dependent fashion.[262] Other NSAIDs, such as sulindac and indomethacin, did not. Thus, certain NSAIDs ultimately may prove to be preferable in the treatment of OA. However, it remains to be determined whether any of the NSAIDs have detrimental effects on cartilage metabolism *in vivo* despite, paradoxically, providing symptomatic improvement.

In summary, treatment of OA using currently employed NSAID regimens does not deter the progression of OA. Evidence suggesting that some NSAIDs may enhance the rate of disease progression is limited and awaits additional study in the clinical setting.

References

1 **Arnett FC et al.** The American Rheumatism Association 1987 revised criteria for the classification of rheumatoid arthritis. Arthritis Rheum. 1988; 31:315.

2 **Harris ED Jr.** Clinical features of rheumatoid arthritis. In: Kelley WN et al., eds. Textbook of Rheumatology. 4th ed. Philadelphia: WB Saunders; 1993:874.

3 **Stastny P.** Association of the B-cell alloantigen DRw4 with rheumatoid arthritis. N Engl J Med. 1978;298:869.

4 **Pinals RS et al.** Preliminary criteria for clinical remission in rheumatoid arthritis. Arthritis Rheum. 1981;24:1308.

5 **Alarcón GS et al.** Evaluation of the American Rheumatism Association preliminary criteria for remission in rheumatoid arthritis: a prospective study. J Rheumatol. 1987;14:93.

6 **Wolfe F, Hawley DJ.** Remission in rheumatoid arthritis. J Rheumatol. 1985;12:245.

7 **Meenan RF et al.** The costs of rheumatoid arthritis. A patient-oriented study of chronic disease costs. Arthritis Rheum. 1978;21:827.

8 **Yelin E et al.** The work dynamics of the person with rheumatoid arthritis. Arthritis Rheum. 1987;30:507.

9 **Wolfe F et al.** A multicenter study of hospitalization in rheumatoid arthritis. Frequency, medical-surgical admissions, and charges. Arthritis Rheum. 1986;29:614.

10 **Pincus T, Callahan LF.** Remodeling

the pyramid or remodeling the paradigms concerning rheumatoid arthritis—lessons from Hodgkin's disease and coronary artery disease. J Rheumatol. 1990;17:1582.

11 **Pincus T et al.** Questionnaire, walking time and button test measures of functional capacity as predictive markers for mortality in rheumatoid arthritis. J Rheumatol. 1987;14:240.

12 **Schlegel SI.** General characteristics of nonsteroidal anti-inflammatory drugs. In: Paulus HE et al., eds. Drugs for Rheumatic Disease. 1st ed. New York: Churchill Livingstone; 1987:203.

13 **Ward JR.** Role of disease-modifying antirheumatic drugs versus cytotoxic agents in the therapy of rheumatoid arthritis. Am J Med. 1988 Oct 14;84 (Suppl. 4A):39.

14 **Hochberg MC.** Auranofin or D-penicillamine in the treatment of rheumatoid arthritis. Ann Intern Med. 1986; 105:528.

15 **Paulus HE et al.** Azathioprine versus D-penicillamine in rheumatoid arthritis patients who have been treated unsuccessfully with gold. Arthritis Rheum. 1984;27:721.

16 **Rau R et al.** A double blind randomized parallel trial of intramuscular methotrexate and gold sodium thiomalate in early erosive rheumatoid arthritis. J Rheumatol. 1991;18:328.

17 **Felson DT et al.** The comparative efficacy and toxicity of second-line drugs in rheumatoid arthritis. Arthritis Rheum. 1990;33:1449.

18 **Bernstein CA et al.** Rheumatoid patients after five or more years of corticosteroid treatment: a comparative analysis of 1983 cases. Ann Intern Med. 1961;54:938.

19 **Nelson AM, Conn DL.** Glucocorticoids in rheumatic disease. Mayo Clin Proc. 1980;55:758.

20 **Cooperating Clinics Committee of the ARA.** A controlled trial of cyclophosphamide in rheumatoid arthritis. N Engl J Med. 1970;283:883.

21 **Williams HJ et al.** Comparison of high- and low-dose cyclophosphamide therapy in rheumatoid arthritis. Arthritis Rheum. 1980;23:521.

22 **Cannon GW et al.** Chlorambucil therapy in rheumatoid arthritis: clinical experience in 28 patients and literature review. Semin Arthritis Rheum. 1985;15: 106.

23 **Clark P et al.** Meta-analysis of injectable gold in rheumatoid arthritis. J Rheumatol. 1989;16:442.

24 **Ward JR et al.** Comparison of auranofin, gold sodium thiomalate, and placebo in the treatment of rheumatoid arthritis. Arthritis Rheum. 1983;26:1303.

25 **Scott DL et al.** Long-term outcome of treating rheumatoid arthritis: results after 20 years. Lancet. 1987:1108.

26 **Thompson PW et al.** Practical results of treatment with disease-modifying antirheumatoid drugs. Br J Rheumatol. 1985;24:167.

27 **Wolfe FE et al.** Termination of slow acting antirheumatic therapy in rheumatoid arthritis: a 14-year prospective evaluation of 1017 consecutive starts. J Rheumatol. 1990;17:994.

28 **Wijnands MJH et al.** Long-term second-line treatment: a prospective drug survival study. Br J Rheumatol. 1992; 31:253.

29 **Weinblatt ME, Maier AL.** Longterm experience with low dose weekly methotrexate in rheumatoid arthritis. J Rheumatol. 1990;17(Suppl. 22):33.

30 **Scully CJ et al.** Long-term methotrexate therapy for rheumatoid arthritis. Semin Arthritis Rheum. 1991;1991: 317.

31 **Fox RI, Kang Ho-I.** Sjögren's syndrome. In: Kelley WN et al., eds. Textbook of Rheumatology. 4th ed. Philadelphia: WB Saunders; 1993:931.

32 **Pinals RS.** Felty's syndrome. In: Kelley WN et al., eds. Textbook of Rheumatology. 4th ed. Philadelphia: WB Saunders; 1993:924.

33 **Dromgoole SH et al.** Rational approaches to the use of salicylates in the treatment of rheumatoid arthritis. Semin Arthritis Rheum. 1981;11:257.

34 **Harris ED Jr.** Rheumatoid arthritis: pathophysiology and implications for therapy. N Engl J Med. 1990;322: 1277.

35 **Anon.** Conservative management of rheumatoid arthritis—Medical Staff Conference—University of California, San Francisco. West J Med. 1978;129: 121.

36 **Mills JA et al.** Value of bedrest in patients with rheumatoid arthritis. N Engl J Med. 1971;284:453.

37 **Rogers MP et al.** Psychological care of adults with rheumatoid arthritis. Ann Intern Med. 1982;96:344.

38 **Paulus HE et al.** Variations of serum concentrations and half-life of salicylate in patients with rheumatoid arthritis. Arthritis Rheum. 1971;14:527.

39 **Furst DE et al.** Salicylate metabolism in twins: evidence suggesting a genetic influence and induction of salicylurate formation. J Clin Invest. 1977;60:32.

40 **Gibson T et al.** Kinetics of salicylate metabolism. Br J Clin Pharmacol. 1975;2:233.

41 **Dromgoole SH, Furst DE.** Salicylates. In: Evans WE et al., eds. Applied Pharmacokinetics: Principles of Therapeutic Drug Monitoring. 3rd ed. Vancouver: Applied Therapeutics; 1992:32.

42 **Day RO et al.** The clinical pharmacology of aspirin and the salicylates. In: Paulus HE et al., eds. Drugs for Rheumatic Disease. New York: Churchill Livingstone; 1987:227.

43 **Mongan E et al.** Tinnitus as an indication of therapeutic serum salicylate levels. JAMA. 1973;226:142.

44 **Anderson RJ et al.** Unrecognized adult salicylate intoxication. Ann Intern Med. 1976;85:745.

45 **Levy G et al.** Decreased serum salicylate concentrations in children with rheumatic fever treated with antacid. N Engl J Med. 1975;293:323.

46 **Gibaldi M et al.** Effect of antacids on pH of urine. Clin Pharmacol Ther. 1974;16:520.

47 **Gibaldi M et al.** Time course and dose dependence of antacid effect on urine pH. J Pharm Sci. 1975;64:2003.

48 **Fremont-Smith K et al.** Salicylate therapy in rheumatoid arthritis. JAMA. 1965;192:1133.

49 **Graham DY, Smith JL.** Aspirin and the stomach. Ann Intern Med. 1986; 104:390.

50 **Levy M.** Aspirin use in patients with major gastrointestinal bleeding and peptic ulcer disease. A report from the Boston Collaborative Drug Surveillance Program, Boston University Medical Center. N Engl J Med. 1974;290: 1158.

51 **Bowen BK et al.** Effect of sodium bicarbonate on aspirin-induced damage and potential difference changes in human gastric mucosa. Br Med J. 1977; 2:1052.

52 **MacKercher PA et al.** Protective effect of cimetidine on aspirin-induced gastric mucosal damage. Ann Intern Med. 1977;87:676.

53 **Lanza FL et al.** Endoscopic evaluation of the effects of aspirin, buffered aspirin, and enteric-coated aspirin on the gastric and duodenal mucosa. N Engl J Med. 1980;303:136.

54 **Orozco-Alcala JJ, Baum J.** Regular and enteric coated aspirin: a reevaluation. Arthritis Rheum. 1979;22:1034.

55 **Karahalios WJ et al.** Comparative bioavailability of sustained-release and uncoated aspirin tablets. Am J Hosp Pharm. 1981;38:1754.

56 **Cassell S et al.** Steady-state serum salicylate levels in hospitalized patients with rheumatoid arthritis. Arthritis Rheum. 1979;22:384.

57 **Mann CC, Boyer JT.** Once-daily treatment of rheumatoid arthritis with choline magnesium trisalicylate. Clin Ther. 1984;6:170.

58 **Szczeklik A.** Aspirin-induced asthma. In: Vane JR, Botting RM, eds. Aspirin and Other Salicylates. London: Chapman & Hall Medical; 1993:548.

59 **Settipane GA.** Aspirin and allergic diseases: a review. Am J Med. 1983; 74(6A):102.

60 **Slepian IK et al.** Aspirin-sensitive asthma. Chest. 1985;87:386.

61 **Sutor AYH et al.** Effect of aspirin, sodium salicylate, and acetaminophen on bleeding. Mayo Clin Proc. 1971;46: 178.

62 **Stuart MJ et al.** Platelet function in recipients of platelets from donors ingesting aspirin. N Engl J Med. 1972; 287:1105.

63 **Moroz LA.** Increased fibrinolytic activity after aspirin ingestion. N Engl J Med. 1977;296:525.

64 **Goldsweig HG et al.** Bleeding, salicylates, and prolonged prothrombin time: three case reports and a review of the literature. J Rheumatol. 1976;3:37.

65 **Slone D et al.** Aspirin and congenital malformations. Lancet. 1976;1:1373.

66 **Turner G, Collins E.** Fetal effects of regular aspirin ingestion in pregnancy. Lancet. 1975;2:338.

67 **Zierler S, Rothman KJ.** Congenital heart disease in relation to maternal use of Bendectin and other drugs in early pregnancy. N Engl J Med. 1985;313: 347.

68 **Rudolph AM.** Effects of aspirin and acetaminophen in pregnancy and the newborn. Arch Intern Med. 1981;141: 358.

69 **Stuart MJ et al.** Effects of acetylsalicylic-acid ingestion on maternal and neonatal hemostasis. N Engl J Med. 1982;307:909.

70 **Rumack CM et al.** Neonatal intracranial hemorrhage and maternal use of aspirin. Obstet Gynecol. 1981;58 (Suppl.): 52S.

71 **Garrettson LK et al.** Fetal acquisition and neonatal elimination of a large amount of salicylate. Study of a neonate whose mother regularly took therapeutic doses of aspirin during pregnancy. Clin Pharmacol Ther. 1975;17: 98.

72 **Levy G et al.** Distribution of salicylate between neonatal and maternal serum at diffusion equilibrium. Clin Pharmacol Ther. 1975;18:210.

73 **Persellin RH.** The effect of pregnancy on rheumatoid arthritis. Bull Rheum Dis. 1977;27:922.

74 **Bulmash JM.** Rheumatoid arthritis and pregnancy. Obstet Gynecol Annu. 1979;8:223.

75 **Axelrod L.** Glucocorticoids. In: Kelley WN et al., eds. Textbook of Rheumatology. 4th ed. Philadelphia: WB Saunders; 1993:779.

76 **Willkens RF, Segre EJ.** Combination therapy with naproxen and aspirin in rheumatoid arthritis. Arthritis Rheum. 1976;19:677.

77 **Furst DE et al.** A controlled study of concurrent therapy with a nonacetylated salicylate and naproxen in rheumatoid arthritis. Arthritis Rheum. 1987; 30:146.

78 **Jeremy R, Towson J.** Interaction between aspirin and indomethacin in the treatment of rheumatoid arthritis. Med J Aust. 1970;2:127.

79 **Rubin A et al.** Interactions of aspirin with nonsteroidal antiinflammatory drugs in man. Arthritis Rheum. 1973; 16:635.

80 **Brooks PM et al.** Indomethacin-aspirin interaction: a clinical appraisal. Br Med J. 1975;3:69.

81 **Champion GD et al.** The effect of aspirin on serum indomethacin. Clin Pharmacol Ther. 1972;13:239.

82 **Kaldestad E et al.** Interactions of indomethacin and acetylsalicylic acid as shown by the serum concentrations of indomethacin and salicylate. Eur J Clin Pharmacol. 1975;9:199.

83 **Grennan DM et al.** The aspirin-ibuprofen interaction in rheumatoid arthritis. Br J Clin Pharmacol. 1970;8:423.

84 **Harris ED Jr.** Treatment of rheumatoid arthritis. In: Kelley WN et al., eds. Textbook of Rheumatology. 4th ed. Philadelphia: WB Saunders; 1993:912.

85 **Abramson SB, Weissmann G.** The mechanisms of action of nonsteroidal antiinflammatory drugs. Arthritis Rheum. 1989;32:1.

86 **Dromgoole SH et al.** Availability of salicylate from salsalate and aspirin. Clin Pharmacol Ther. 1983;34:539.

87 **Clements PJ, Paulus HE.** Nonsteroidal anti-inflammatory drugs (NSAIDs). In: Kelley WN et al., eds. Textbook of Rheumatology. 4th ed. Philadelphia: WB Saunders; 1993:700.

88 **Brooks PM, Day RO.** Nonsteroidal antiinflammatory drugs—differences and similarities. N Engl J Med. 1991; 324:1716.

89 **Barrier CH, Hirschowitz BI.** Controversies in the detection and management of nonsteroidal antiinflammatory drug-induced side effects of the upper gastrointestinal tract. Arthritis Rheum. 1989;32:926.

90 **Semble EL, Wu WC.** Antiinflammatory drugs and gastric mucosal damage. Semin Arthritis Rheum. 1987;16:271.

91 **Griffin MR et al.** Nonsteroidal anti-inflammatory drug use and death from

peptic ulcer in elderly persons. Ann Intern Med. 1988;109:359.

92 **Fries JF et al.** Toward an epidemiology of gastropathy associated with nonsteroidal antiinflammatory drug use. Gastroenterology. 1989;96:647.

93 **Langman MJ.** Epidemiologic evidence on the association between peptic ulceration and antiinflammatory drug use. Gastroenterology. 1989;96:640.

94 **Gabriel SE et al.** Risk of serious gastrointestinal complications related to use of nonsteroidal anti-inflammatory drugs: a meta analysis. Ann Intern Med. 1991;115:787.

95 **Walt RP.** Drug therapy: misoprostol for the treatment of peptic ulcer and antiinflammatory-drug-induced gastroduodenal ulceration. N Engl J Med. 1992;327:1575.

96 **Robinson MG et al.** Effect of ranitidine on gastroduodenal mucosal damage induced by nonsteroidal antiinflammatory drugs. Dig Dis Sci. 1989;134:424.

97 **Caldwell JR et al.** Sucralfate treatment of nonsteroidal anti-inflammatory drug-induced gastrointestinal symptoms and mucosal damage. Am J Med. 1987;83(Suppl. 3B):74.

98 **O'Laughlin JC et al.** Resistance to medical therapy of gastric ulcers in rheumatic disease patients taking aspirin. A double-blind study with cimetidine and follow-up. Dig Dis Sci. 1982;27:976.

99 **Dunn MJ et al.** Nonsteroidal anti-inflammatory drugs and renal function. J Clin Pharmacol. 1988;28:524.

100 **Patrono C, Dunn MJ.** The clinical significance of inhibition of renal prostaglandin synthesis. Kidney Int. 1987;32:1.

101 **Ciabottoni G et al.** Effects of sulindac and ibuprofen in patients with chronic glomerular disease. N Engl J Med. 1984;310:279.

102 **Swainson CP, Griffiths P.** Acute and chronic effects of sulindac on renal function in chronic renal disease. Clin Pharmacol Ther. 1985;37:298.

103 **Berg KJ, Talseth T.** Acute renal effects of sulindac and indomethacin in chronic renal failure. Clin Pharmacol Ther. 1985;37:447.

104 **Sedor JR et al.** Effects of sulindac and indomethacin on renal prostaglandin synthesis. Clin Pharmacol Ther. 1984;36:85.

105 **Miller MJS et al.** Renal metabolism of sulindac: functional hypothesis. J Clin Pharmacol Exp Ther. 1984;231:449.

106 **Clive DM, Stoff JS.** Renal syndromes associated with nonsteroidal antiinflammatory drugs. N Engl J Med. 1984;310:563.

107 **Bunch TW, O'Duffy JD.** Disease-modifying drugs for progressive rheumatoid arthritis. Mayo Clin Proc. 1980;55:161.

108 **Cash JM, O'Duffy JD.** Disease-modifying drugs for progressive rheumatoid arthritis. Mayo Clin Proc. 1980;55:161.

109 **Blocka K, Paulus HE.** The clinical pharmacology of gold compounds. In: Paulus HE et al., eds. Drugs for Rheumatic Disease. New York: Churchill Livingstone; 1987:49.

110 **Gordon DA.** Gold compounds in the rheumatic diseases. In: Kelley WN et al., eds. Textbook of Rheumatology. 4th ed. Philadelphia: WB Saunders; 1993:743.

111 **Gottlieb NL, Brown HEJ.** Acute myocardial infarction following gold sodium thiomalate induced vasomotor (nitritoid) reaction. Arthritis Rheum. 1977;20:1026.

112 **Halla JT et al.** Postinjection nonvasomotor reactions during chrysotherapy. Constitutional and rheumatic symptoms following injection of gold salts. Arthritis Rheum. 1977;20:1188.

113 **Lawrence JS.** Comparative toxicity of gold preparations in treatment of rheumatoid arthritis. Ann Rheum Dis. 1976;35:171.

114 **Gottlieb NL.** Comparative pharmacokinetics of parenteral and oral gold compounds. J Rheumatol. 1982;9(Suppl. 8):99.

115 **Lewis D, Capell HA.** Oral gold: a comparison with placebo and with intramuscular sodium aurothiomalate. Clin Rheum. 1984;3(Suppl. 1):83.

116 **Ward JR et al.** Comparison of auranofin, gold sodium thiomalate and placebo in the treatment of active rheumatoid arthritis: response by treatment duration. In: Capell HA et al., eds. Auranofin: Proceedings of a Smith Kline & French International Symposium. Amsterdam: Excerpta Medica; 1982:115.

117 **Morris RW et al.** Worldwide clinical experience with auranofin. Clin Rheumatol. 1984;3(Suppl. 1):105.

118 **Rothermich NO et al.** Chrysotherapy: a prospective study. Arthritis Rheum. 1976;19:1321.

119 **Cats A.** A multi-center controlled trial of the effects of different dosages of gold therapy, followed by a maintenance dosage. Agents Actions. 1976;6:355.

120 **Furst DE et al.** A double-blind trial of high versus conventional dosages of gold salts for rheumatoid arthritis. Arthritis Rheum. 1978;20:1473.

121 **McKenzie JM.** An initial report on a double-blind trial comparing small and large doses of gold in the treatment of rheumatoid arthritis. Rheumatol Rehabil. 1977;16:78.

122 **Griffin AJ et al.** A comparison of conventional and low dose sodium aurothiomalate treatment in rheumatoid arthritis. Br J Rheumatol. 1983;22:82.

123 **Sharp JT et al.** Comparison of two dosage schedules of gold salts in the treatment of rheumatoid arthritis. Arthritis Rheum. 1977;20:1179.

124 **Lorber A et al.** Monitoring serum gold values to improve chrysotherapy in rheumatoid arthritis. Ann Rheum Dis. 1973;32:133.

125 **Jessop JD, Johns RG.** Serum gold determinations in patients with rheumatoid arthritis receiving sodium aurothiomalate. Ann Rheum Dis. 1973;32:228.

126 **Gerber RC et al.** Clinical response and serum gold levels in chrysotherapy: lack of correlation. Ann Rheum Dis. 1972;31:308.

127 **Gottlieb NL.** Serum gold levels. Arthritis Rheum. 1975;18:626.

128 **Dahl SL et al.** Lack of correlation between gold concentrations and clinical response in patients with definite or classical rheumatoid arthritis receiving auranofin or gold sodium thiomalate. Arthritis Rheum. 1985;28:1211.

129 **Edelman J et al.** Prevalence of eosinophilia during gold therapy for rheumatoid arthritis. J Rheumatol. 1983;10:121.

130 **Podell TE et al.** Pulmonary toxicity with gold therapy. Arthritis Rheum. 1980;23:347.

131 **Smith W, Ball GV.** Lung injury due to gold treatment. Arthritis Rheum. 1980;23:351.

132 **Stein HB, Urowitz MB.** Gold-induced enterocolitis: case report and literature review. J Rheumatol. 1976;3:21.

133 **Favreau M et al.** Hepatic toxicity associated with gold therapy. Ann Intern Med. 1977;87:717.

134 **Gottlieb NL, Major JC.** Ocular chrysiasis correlated with gold concentrations in the crystalline lens during chrysotherapy. Arthritis Rheum. 1978;21:704.

135 **England JM, Smith DS.** Gold-induced thrombocytopenia and response to dimercaprol. Br Med J. 1972;2:748.

136 **Davis P, Barraclough D.** Interaction of D-penicillamine with gold salts: *in vivo* studies on gold chelation and *in vitro* studies on protein binding. Arthritis Rheum. 1977;20:1413.

137 **Combs RJ et al.** Gold toxicity and peritoneal dialysis. Arthritis Rheum. 1976;19:936.

138 **Klinefelter HF.** Reinstitution of gold therapy in rheumatoid arthritis after mucocutaneous reactions. J Rheumatol. 1975;2:21.

139 **Srinivasan R et al.** Long-term chrysotherapy in rheumatoid arthritis. Arthritis Rheum. 1979;22:105.

140 **Empire Rheumatism Council.** Gold therapy in rheumatoid arthritis. Report of a multicentre controlled trial. Ann Rheum Dis. 1960;19:95.

141 **Empire Rheumatism Council.** Gold therapy in rheumatoid arthritis. Final report of a multi-centre controlled trial. Ann Rheum Dis. 1961;20:315.

142 **Kean WF, Anastassiades TP.** Long-term chrysotherapy: incidence of toxicity and efficacy during sequential time periods. Arthritis Rheum. 1979;22:495.

143 **Hull RG et al.** A double-blind study comparing sodium aurothiomalate and auranofin in patients with rheumatoid arthritis previously stabilized on sodium aurothiomalate. Int J Clin Pharmacol Res. 1984;4:395.

144 **Wenger ME et al.** Therapy of rheumatoid arthritis. Transferring treatment from injectable gold to auranofin. In: Capell HA et al., eds. Auranofin: Proceedings of a Smith Kline & French International Symposium. Amsterdam: Excerpta Medica; 1982:201.

145 **Tosi S et al.** Injectable gold dermatitis and proteinuria: retreatment with auranofin. Int J Clin Pharmacol Res. 1985;5:265.

146 **Rynes RI.** Antimalarial drugs. In: Kelley WN et al., eds. Textbook of Rheumatology. 4th ed. Philadelphia: WB Saunders; 1993:731.

147 **Adams EM et al.** Hydroxychloroquine in the treatment of rheumatoid arthritis. Am J Med. 1983;75:321.

148 **Mackenzie AH.** Dose refinements in long-term therapy of rheumatoid arthritis with antimalarials. Am J Med. 1983;75(1A):40.

149 **Rynes RI.** Antimalarial treatment of rheumatoid arthritis: 1985 status. J Rheumatol. 1985;12:657.

150 **Tobin DR et al.** Hydroxychloroquine. Seven-year experience. Arch Ophthalmol. 1982;100:81.

151 **MacKenzie AH.** Ocular safety of huge cumulative antimalarial dosage. Arthritis Rheum. 1981;24(Suppl.):S70. Abstract.

152 **Bernstein HN.** Ophthalmologic considerations and testing in patients receiving long-term antimalarial therapy. Am J Med. 1983;75(1A):25.

153 **Burns RP.** Delayed onset of chloroquine retinopathy. N Engl J Med. 1966;275:693.

154 **Watkinson G.** Sulphasalazine: a review of 40 year's experience. Drugs. 1986;32(Suppl. 1):1.

155 **McConkey B.** History of the development of sulphasalazine in rheumatology. Drugs. 1986;32(Suppl. 1):12.

156 **McConkey B et al.** Sulphasalazine in rheumatoid arthritis. Br Med J. 1980;280:442.

157 **Williams HJ et al.** A controlled trial comparing sulfasalazine, gold sodium thiomalate, and placebo in rheumatoid arthritis. Arthritis Rheum. 1988;31:702.

158 **Pinals RS et al.** Sulfasalazine in rheumatoid arthritis. A double-blind, placebo-controlled trial. Arthritis Rheum. 1986;29:1427.

159 **Taggart AJ et al.** 5-aminosalicylic acid or sulfapyridine. Which is the active moiety of sulphasalazine in rheumatoid arthritis? Drugs. 1986;32(Suppl. 1):27.

160 **Farr M et al.** Side effects profile of 200 patients with inflammatory arthritides treated with sulphasalazine. Drugs. 1986;32:49.

161 **Taggart AJ et al.** The effect of age and acetylator phenotype on the pharmacokinetics of sulfasalazine in patients with rheumatoid arthritis. Clin Pharmacokinet. 1992;23:311.

162 **Pullar T et al.** Effect of acetylator phenotype on efficacy and toxicity of sulphasalazine in rheumatoid arthritis. Ann Rheum Dis. 1985;44:831.

163 **Bax DE et al.** Sulphasalazine for rheumatoid arthritis: relationship between dose, acetylator phenotype and response to treatment. Br J Rheumatol. 1986;25:282.

164 **Furst DE.** Clinical pharmacology of very low dose methotrexate for use in rheumatoid arthritis. J Rheumatol. 1985;12(Suppl. 12):11.

165 **Groff GD et al.** Low dose oral methotrexate in rheumatoid arthritis: an uncontrolled trial and review of the literature. Semin Arthritis Rheum. 1983;12:333.

166 **Dahl MG et al.** Methotrexate hepatotoxicity in psoriasis—comparison of different dose regimens. Br Med J. 1972;1:654.

167 **Williams HJ.** Comparison of low-dose oral pulse methotrexate and placebo in the treatment of rheumatoid arthritis. Arthritis Rheum. 1985;28:721.

168 **Williams HJ et al.** Methotrexate and placebo therapy in rheumatoid arthritis. Rheumatology. 1986;9:174.

169 **Weinblatt ME et al.** Efficacy of low-

dose methotrexate in rheumatoid arthritis. N Engl J Med. 1985;312:818.

170 **Alarcón GS et al.** Lack of association between HLA-DR2 and clinical response to methotrexate in patients with rheumatoid arthritis. Arthritis Rheum. 1987;30:218.

171 **Weinblatt ME.** Methotrexate. In: Kelley WN et al., eds. Textbook of Rheumatology. 4th ed. Philadelphia: WB Saunders; 1993:767.

172 **Health and Public Policy Committee AC of P.** Methotrexate in rheumatoid arthritis. Ann Intern Med. 1987;107:418.

173 **Tobias H, Auerbach R.** Hepatotoxicity of long-term methotrexate therapy for psoriasis. Arch Intern Med. 1973;132:391.

174 **Kremer JM, Koff R.** A debate: should patients with rheumatoid arthritis on methotrexate undergo liver biopsies? Semin Arthritis Rheum. 1992;21:376.

175 **Zachariae H et al.** Methotrexate induced liver cirrhosis. Studies including serial liver biopsies during continued treatment. Br J Dermatol. 1980;102:407.

176 **Weinstein GD et al.** Psoriasis-liver methotrexate interactions. Arch Dermatol. 1973;108:36.

177 **Lewis JH, Schiff E.** Methotrexate-induced chronic liver injury: guidelines for detection and prevention. Am J Gastroenterol. 1988;88:1337.

178 **Kremer JM.** Liver biopsies in patients with rheumatoid arthritis receiving methotrexate: where are we going? J Rheumatol. 1992;19:189.

179 **Tischler M et al.** The effects of leucovorin (folinic acid) on methotrexate therapy in rheumatoid arthritis. J Rheumatol. 1988;31:906.

180 **Buckley LM et al.** Administration of folinic acid after low dose methotrexate in patients with RA. J Rheumatol. 1990;17:1158.

181 **Hanrahan PS, Russell AS.** Concurrent use of folinic acid and methotrexate in RA. J Rheumatol. 1988;15:1078.

182 **Shiroky JB et al.** Low dose methotrexate with leucovorin (folinic acid) rescue in the management of rheumatoid arthritis. Results of a multicenter randomized, double-blind, placebo-controlled trial. Arthritis Rheum. 1993;36:795.

183 **Weinblatt ME et al.** Low dose leucovorin does not interfere with the efficacy of methotrexate in rheumatoid arthritis: an 8 week randomized placebo controlled trial. J Rheumatol. 1993;20:950.

184 **Morgan SL et al.** The effect of folic acid supplementation on the toxicity of low-dose methotrexate in patients with rheumatoid arthritis. Arthritis Rheum. 1990;33:9.

185 **Stewart KA et al.** Folate supplementation in methotrexate-treated rheumatoid arthritis patients. Semin Arthritis Rheum. 1991;20:332.

186 **Weinblatt ME, Fraser P.** Elevated mean corpuscular volume as a predictor of hematologic toxicity due to methotrexate therapy. Arthritis Rheum. 1989;32:1592.

187 **Carson CW et al.** Pulmonary disease during the treatment of rheumatoid arthritis with low dose pulse methotrexate. Semin Arthritis Rheum. 1987;16:186.

188 **Halla JT et al.** Sequential gold and penicillamine therapy in rheumatoid arthritis: comparative study of effectiveness and toxicity and review of the literature. Am J Med. 1982;72:423.

189 **Webley M, Coomes EN.** An assessment of penicillamine therapy in rheumatoid arthritis and the influence of previous gold therapy. J Rheumatol. 1979;6:20.

190 **Wooley PH et al.** HLA-DR antigens and toxic reaction to sodium aurothiomalate and D-penicillamine in patients with rheumatoid arthritis. N Engl J Med. 1980;303:300.

191 **Multicentre Trial Group.** Controlled trial of D(-)penicillamine in severe rheumatoid arthritis. Lancet. 1973;1:275.

192 **Dixon AJ et al.** Synthetic D(-)penicillamine in rheumatoid arthritis. Double-blind controlled study of a high and low dosage regimen. Ann Rheum Dis. 1975;34:416.

193 **Jaffe IA.** Penicillamine. In: Kelley WN et al., eds. The Textbook of Rheumatology. 4th ed. Philadelphia: WB Saunders; 1993:760.

194 **Assem ESK, Vickers MR.** Immunological response to penicillamine in penicillin-allergic patients and in normal subjects. Postgrad Med J. 1974;50(Suppl. 2):65.

195 **Bell C, Graziano F.** The safety of administration of penicillamine to penicillin-sensitive individuals. Arthritis Rheum. 1983;26:801.

196 **Stein HB et al.** Adverse effects of D-penicillamine in rheumatoid arthritis. Ann Intern Med. 1980;92:24.

197 **O'Brien WM.** Toxicity of D-penicillamine in rheumatoid arthritis. Ann Intern Med. 1980;92:120.

198 **Hall CL et al.** Natural course of penicillamine nephropathy: a long-term study of 33 patients. Br Med J. 1988;296:1083.

199 **Hill H et al.** Resumption of treatment with penicillamine after proteinuria. Ann Rheum Dis. 1979;38:229.

200 **Day RO, Paulus HE.** D-Penicillamine. In: Paulus HE et al., eds. Drugs for Rheumatic Disease. London: Churchill Livingstone; 1987:85.

201 **Atcheson SG, Ward JR.** Ptosis and weakness after start of D-penicillamine therapy. Ann Intern Med. 1978;89:939.

202 **Gordon RA, Burnside JW.** D-penicillamine-induced myasthenia gravis in rheumatoid arthritis. Ann Intern Med. 1977;87:578.

203 **Sternlieb I et al.** D-penicillamine-induced Goodpasture's syndrome in Wilson's disease. Ann Intern Med. 1975;82:673.

204 **Chalmers A et al.** Systemic lupus erythematosus during penicillamine therapy for rheumatoid arthritis. Ann Intern Med. 1982;97:659.

205 **Halla JT et al.** Penicillamine-induced myositis. Observations and unique features in two patients and review of the literature. Am J Med. 1984;77:719.

206 **Klippel JH.** Winning the battle, losing the war? Another editorial about rheumatoid arthritis. J Rheumatol. 1990;17:1118.

207 **Paulus HE.** The use of combinations of disease-modifying antirheumatic agents in rheumatoid arthritis. Arthritis Rheum. 1990;33:113.

208 **McCarty DJ.** Suppress rheumatoid inflammation early and leave the pyramid to the Egyptians. J Rheumatol. 1990;17:1115.

209 **Fries JF.** Reevaluating the therapeutic approach to rheumatoid arthritis: the "sawtooth" strategy. J Rheumatol. 1990;17(Suppl. 22):12.

210 **Wilske KR, Healey LA.** Challenging the therapeutic pyramid: a new look at treatment strategies for rheumatoid arthritis. J Rheumatol. 1990;17(Suppl. 25):4.

211 **Wilke WS, Clough JD.** Therapy for rheumatoid arthritis: combinations of disease-modifying drugs and new paradigms of treatment. Semin Arthritis Rheum. 1991;21(Suppl. 1):21.

212 **Willkens RF.** Prognostic staging for therapy of rheumatoid arthritis. Semin Arthritis Rheum. 1991;21(Suppl. 1):40.

213 **McCarty DJ, Carrera GF.** Intractable rheumatoid arthritis: treatment with combined cyclophosphamide, azathioprine, and hydroxychloroquine. JAMA. 1982;248:1718.

214 **Csuka M et al.** Treatment of intractable rheumatoid arthritis with combined cyclophosphamide, azathioprine, and hydroxychloroquine. JAMA. 1986;255:2315.

215 **Bunch TW et al.** Controlled trial of hydroxychloroquine and D-penicillamine singly and in combination in the treatment of rheumatoid arthritis. Arthritis Rheum. 1984;27:267.

216 **Gibson T et al.** Combined D-penicillamine and chloroquine treatment of rheumatoid arthritis—a comparative study. Br J Rheumatol. 1987;26:279.

217 **Taggart AJ et al.** Sulphasalazine alone or in combination with D-penicillamine in rheumatoid arthritis. Br J Rheumatol. 1987;26:32.

218 **Scott DL et al.** Combination therapy with gold and hydroxychloroquine in rheumatoid arthritis: a prospective, randomized, placebo-controlled study. Br J Rheumatol. 1989;28:128.

219 **Willkens RF et al.** Comparison of azathioprine, methotrexate, and the combination of both in the treatment of rheumatoid arthritis: a controlled clinical trial. Arthritis Rheum. 1992;35:849.

220 **Williams HJ et al.** Comparison of auranofin, methotrexate, and the combination of both in the treatment of rheumatoid arthritis. Arthritis Rheum. 1992;35:259.

221 **Porter DR et al.** Combination therapy in rheumatoid arthritis—no benefit of addition of hydroxychloroquine to patients with a suboptimal response to intramuscular gold therapy. J Rheumatol. 1993;20:645.

222 **Myles AB et al.** Single daily dose of corticosteroid treatment. Ann Rheum Dis. 1976;35:73.

223 **Nugent CA et al.** Glucocorticoid toxicity: single contrasted with divided daily doses of prednisolone. J Chronic Dis. 1965;18:323.

224 **Hahn TJ.** Metabolic bone disease. In: Kelley WN et al., eds. Textbook of Rheumatology. 4th ed. Philadelphia: WB Saunders; 1993:1593.

225 **Wasnich RD et al.** Thiazide effect on mineral content of bone. N Engl J Med. 1983;309:344.

226 **Baylink DJ.** Glucocorticoid-induced osteoporosis. N Engl J Med. 1983;309:306.

227 **Sambrook P et al.** Prevention of corticosteroid osteoporosis—a comparison of calcium, calcitriol, and calcitonin. N Engl J Med. 1993;328:1747.

228 **Meunier PJ.** Is steroid-induced osteoporosis preventable? N Engl J Med. 1993;328:1781.

229 **Aicardi G et al.** Dose-dependent effects of deflazacort and prednisone on growth and skeletal maturation. Br J Rheumatol. 1993;32(Suppl. 2):39.

230 **Jowsey J et al.** Effect of combined therapy with sodium fluoride, vitamin D and calcium in osteoporosis. Am J Med. 1972;53:43.

231 **Scott JC, Hochberg MC.** Prevention of osteoporosis. Bull Rheum Dis. 1993;42(5):4.

232 **Fan PT et al.** Effect of corticosteroids on the human immune response: comparison of one and three daily 1 gm intravenous pulses of methylprednisolone. J Lab Clin Med. 1978;91:625.

233 **Liebling MR et al.** Pulse methylprednisolone in rheumatoid arthritis. Ann Intern Med. 1981;94:21.

234 **Hess EV, Kammen PL.** Pulse therapy in rheumatoid arthritis. Ann Intern Med. 1981;94:128.

235 **Garrett R et al.** Complications of intravenous methylprednisolone pulse therapy. Arthritis Rheum. 1980;26:677.

236 **Bocanegra TS et al.** Sudden death after methylprednisolone pulse therapy. Ann Intern Med. 1981;95:122.

237 **Cassidy JT.** Juvenile rheumatoid arthritis. In: Kelley WN et al., eds. Textbook of Rheumatology. 4th ed. Philadelphia: WB Saunders; 1993:1189.

238 **Fink CW.** Treatment of juvenile rheumatoid arthritis. Bull Rheum Dis. 1982;32:21.

239 **Rich RR, Johnson JS.** Salicylate hepatotoxicity in patients with juvenile rheumatoid arthritis. Arthritis Rheum. 1973;16:1.

240 **Seaman WE et al.** Aspirin-induced hepatotoxicity in patients with systemic lupus erythematosus. Ann Intern Med. 1974;80:1.

241 **Seaman WE, Plotz PH.** Effect of aspirin on liver tests in patients with RA or SLE and in normal volunteers. Arthritis Rheum. 1976;19:155.

242 **Baum J.** Aspirin in the treatment of juvenile arthritis. Am J Med. 1983;74(Suppl. 6A):10.

243 **Mortimer EA et al.** Varicella with hypoglycemia possibly due to salicylates. Am J Dis Child. 1962;103:583.

244 **Starko KM et al.** Reye's syndrome and salicylate use. Pediatrics. 1980;66:859.

245 **Waldman RJ et al.** Aspirin as a risk factor in Reye's syndrome. JAMA. 1982;247:3089.

246 **Halpin TJ et al.** Reye's syndrome and medication use. JAMA. 1982;248:687.

247 **Committee on Infectious Diseases AA of P.** Aspirin and Reye syndrome. Pediatrics. 1982;69:810.

248 **Rennebohm RM et al.** Reye syndrome in children receiving salicylate therapy for connective tissue disease. J Pediatr. 1985;107:877.

249 **Levinson JE et al.** Comparison of tolmetin sodium and aspirin in the treatment of juvenile rheumatoid arthritis. J Pediatr. 1977;91:799.

250 **Jacobs JC.** Sudden death in arthritic children receiving large doses of indomethacin. JAMA. 1967;199:932.

251 **Brewer EJJ et al.** Gold therapy in the management of juvenile rheumatoid arthritis. Arthritis Rheum. 1980;23:404.

252 **Brewer EJ et al.** Penicillamine and hydroxychloroquine in the treatment of severe juvenile rheumatoid arthritis. Results of the U.S.A.-U.S.S.R. double-blind placebo-controlled trial. N Engl J Med. 1986;314:1269.

253 **Giannini EH et al.** Auranofin in the treatment of juvenile rheumatoid arthritis. J Pediatr. 1983;102:138.

254 **Giannini EH et al.** Methotrexate in resistant juvenile rheumatoid arthritis: results of the U.S.A.-U.S.S.R. double-blind, placebo-controlled trial. N Engl J Med. 1992;326:1043.

255 **Mankin HJ.** Clinical features of osteoarthritis. In: Kelley WN et al., eds. Textbook of Rheumatology. 4th ed. Philadelphia: WB Saunders; 1993: 1374.

256 **Brandt KD.** Management of osteoarthritis. In: Kelley WN et al., eds. Textbook of Rheumatology. 4th ed. Philadelphia: WB Saunders; 1993: 1385.

257 **Bradley JD et al.** Comparison of an antiinflammatory dose of ibuprofen, an analgesic dose of ibuprofen, and acetaminophen in the treatment of patients with osteoarthritis of the knee. N Engl J Med. 1991;325:87.

258 **Bollet AJ.** Analgesic and anti-inflammatory drugs in the therapy of osteoarthritis. Semin Arthritis Rheum. 1980; 11:130.

259 **Williams HJ et al.** Comparison of naproxen and acetaminophen in a two-year study of treatment of osteoarthritis of the knee. Arthritis Rheum. 1993;36: 1196.

260 **Behrens F et al.** Metabolic recovery of articular cartilage after intra-articular injections of glucocorticoids. J Bone Joint Surgery. 1976;58:1157.

261 **Gray RG et al.** Local corticosteroid injection treatment in rheumatic disorders. Semin Arthritis Rheum. 1981;10: 231.

262 **Palmoski MJ, Brandt KD.** Effects of some nonsteroidal antiinflammatory drugs on proteoglycan metabolism and organization in canine articular cartilage. Arthritis Rheum. 1980;23:1010.

263 **Kremer JM et al.** Methotrexate for rheumatoid arthritis. Suggested guidelines for monitoring liver toxicity. American College of Rheumatology. Arthritis Rheum. 1994;37;(3 Mar):316–28.

Connective Tissue Disorders:
The Clinical Use of Corticosteroids

Ralph E Small
Laurie J Cooksey

Overview 42-1
   General signs and symptoms 42-1
   Treatment: nonpharmacologic and pharmacologic ... 42-1
Selected Rheumatic Diseases 42-2
   Lupus erythematosus: discoid and systemic 42-2
     Epidemiology 42-2
     Prognosis 42-2
     Clinical presentation (Also see Question 3) 42-2
     Treatment 42-2
   Drug-induced lupus 42-2
   Scleroderma 42-2
   Polymyalgia rheumatica (PMR) and giant cell
     arteritis (GCA) 42-3
   Reiter's disease 42-3
   Polymyositis and dermatomyositis 42-3
Clinical Use of Corticosteroids 42-4
   Predictable Pharmacological Effects Relative to
     Chemical Structure 42-4

Active Corticosteroid Compounds 42-4
Mechanism of Action 42-6
Dosage Forms and Dosing Regimens
   (See Tables 42.4 to 42.6) 42-6
     Once daily dosing 42-7
Hypothalamic-Pituitary-Adrenocortical (HPA)
   Axis Suppression 42-7
     Adrenal function testing 42-8
Dosing During Stressful Events 42-8
Leukocytosis 42-8
Alternate Day Therapy 42-9
   Conversion to 42-9
Discontinuation of Therapy 42-9
Adverse Effects (See Table 42.7) 42-9
   Osteoporosis 42-9
   Gastrointestinal 42-10
   Hyperglycemia 42-10
   Ecchymosis 42-10

Rheumatism currently is defined as a general term for acute and chronic conditions characterized by inflammation, soreness and stiffness of muscles, and pain in joints and associated structures.[1,2] *Rheumatic* or *rheumatoid disorders* include arthritis (infectious, rheumatoid, gouty), arthritis due to rheumatic fever or trauma, degenerative joint disease, neurogenic arthropathy, hydroarthrosis, myositis, bursitis, fibromyositis, and many other conditions.

Connective tissue disease is a group of diseases of the tissue that supports and connects other tissues and tissues and body parts. Connective tissue includes cartilage and bone, therefore, diseases currently included in this category are: cutaneous and systemic lupus erythematosus (SLE), scleroderma, polymyositis and dermatomyositis, and polyarteritis.

Arthralgias refers to pain in a joint while arthritis refers to the inflammation of a joint, usually accompanied by pain, swelling, and, frequently, changes in structure. Gout, juvenile rheumatoid arthritis (RA), rheumatoid arthritis, and osteoarthritis are other forms of arthritis that are presented in other chapters. An inflammation of an artery is known as arteritis and can occur in association with rheumatoid arthritis or rheumatic fever.

General Signs and Symptoms

The patient with a rheumatic illness may give a chief complaint of joint pain or systemic problems. Inflammatory disease is suggested by morning stiffness of greater than one hour (a similar problem occurs with sitting or resting), swelling, fever, weakness, and systemic fatigue. In some patients activities of daily living and function may be excellent despite pain and deformity; in others, because of psychologic and systemic disease, there may be poor function with minimum articular involvement. Other psychosocial aspects of their life, including sexuality, may be affected by many of the inflammatory disorders.

Some dermatological changes are more often associated with a particular rheumatic disease. Examples include alopecia with sys-temic lupus erythematosus, onycholysis and keratoderma blenorrhagica with Reiter's syndrome, buccal or genital ulcers with SLE or Reiter's syndrome, Raynaud's phenomenon with SLE or systemic sclerosis, calcinosis and rash over the knuckle's (Gottron's papule) with dermatomyositis, and sun sensitivity malar rash with SLE.

The presence of nodules, tophi, telangiectasia, or vasculitic changes also may be detected, helping to differentiate which inflammatory disease is present and what management is necessary.

The rheumatologic diseases commonly are associated with musculoskeletal changes. Joints may display warmth, redness and effusion, synovial thickening, deformities, decreased range of motion, pain on motion, tenderness on palpation, and decreased function. Often a patient's hand and arm function, as well as, gait may be altered.

In addition to the signs and symptoms used to differentiate various rheumatic diseases, laboratory evaluation of patients with rheumatic complaints can often define the extent of disease or detect other organ systems that may be involved.[3]

Treatment: Nonpharmacologic and Pharmacologic

The aim of present therapy is to provide pain relief, decrease joint inflammation, and, more importantly, maintain or restore joint function and prevent bone and cartilage destruction. The current approach to treatment is to interrupt the complex inflammatory process.

The general treatment program consists of patient education, balance between rest and exercise, physical and occupational therapy, adequate nutrition, local heat, the use of supportive or rehabilitative devices, and orthopedic surgery.

Depending upon the disorder being treated, various drugs may be used from the classes of salicylates or other nonsteroidal antiinflammatory drugs (NSAIDs), slow-acting antirheumatic drugs (SAARDs) or disease-modifying antirheumatic drugs (DMARDs), and corticosteroids. All drugs other than corticosteroids have been reviewed extensively in other chapters.

The agents used in the treatment of systemic rheumatic disorders may have systemic toxicity as well. Such involvement can be deduced by appropriate laboratory testing, such as renal or liver function tests, blood counts, muscle enzyme levels, or urinalysis (UA). For some patients, more elaborate testing may be indicated.

Functional evaluation and health status outcome measurements are ultimately the most important measurement tools in evaluating treatment. Psychological function typically is assessed in terms of affective domains such as depression and anxiety, while social function usually is measured in terms of social interactions and social support.

Selected Rheumatic Diseases

The following pages contain a synopsis of some selected rheumatic diseases that often are treated with the use of corticosteroids.

Lupus Erythematosus: Discoid and Systemic

SLE is a prototypic autoimmune disease characterized by the production of antibodies to components of the cell nucleus in association with a diverse array of clinical manifestations.[4] Discoid lesions are chronic cutaneous lesions, which may occur in the absence of any systemic manifestations.

Epidemiology. SLE is primarily a disease of young women. Its peak incidence occurs between the ages of 15 and 40, with a female to male ratio of approximately 5:1. Overall, the female to male ratio approximates 2:1. In a general outpatient population, SLE affects approximately 1 in 2000 individuals, being more prevalent in the black and hispanic population.[5] Systemic lupus erythematosus shows a strong familial aggregation with a much higher frequency among first-degree relatives of patients.[6]

Prognosis. Most patients with lupus will live nearly normal lives; the ten-year survival rate exceeds 80%. Deaths are usually the result of renal failure, gastrointestinal (GI) hemorrhage, central nervous system (CNS) disease, or infections.[7]

Clinical Presentation. The frequencies of various clinical manifestations at presentation or any time during the course of disease are in Table 42.1. Arthralgias and arthritis constitute the most common presenting manifestations of SLE.

The presence of malaise, overwhelming fatigue, fever, and weight loss are nonspecific manifestations that affect most patients at some time in their disease. The most recognized skin manifestation is the "butterfly" rash, commonly precipitated by exposure to sunlight. The majority of patients with SLE demonstrate photosensitivity. Alopecia is a common feature of systemic lupus erythematosus.

The Diagnostic and Therapeutic Criteria Committee of the American College of Rheumatology listed 11 characteristic signs, symptoms, and laboratory values most often associated with a positive diagnosis of SLE (see Table 42.2). The presence of four or more of these criteria, either serially or simultaneously, during any period of observation, confers greater than 95% sensitivity and specificity for the diagnosis of lupus.

Treatment. Therapy can be divided into preventive disease management that applies to the chronic disease course or drug interventions aimed at exacerbations of the disease. Decisions regarding SLE management are guided by the concepts of disease activity and severity. Activity refers to the contribution of inflammation to the clinical setting, while severity could indicate those in whom active lupus nephritis or central nervous system lupus is evident.[7]

Many SLE patients are highly photosensitive and must be reminded of the importance of avoiding intense sun exposure and photosensitizing drugs, particularly antibiotics. Infections are common and must be evaluated promptly. Antibiotic prophylaxis should be used for all dental and genitourinary procedures.

Drug management of SLE patients includes the use of NSAIDs, antimalarials for cutaneous features, immunosuppressives, cyclophosphamide, investigational agents, and corticosteroids. Some investigational therapies employed include cyclosporine, immune globulin, plasma exchange, and total lymphoid irradiation.

Drug-Induced Lupus

The clinical presentation of drug-induced lupus is similar to idiopathic SLE but with milder visceral involvement.[10] Renal, lymph, gastrointestinal, and CNS involvement are notably rare, while fever, rash, anemia, and cardiac problems occur slightly less frequently than with spontaneous lupus. Although the lupus erythematosus (LE) cell and antinuclear antibody (ANA) titer can be positive, antibodies to native or double-stranded DNA are not found. Drug-induced lupus generally occurs in patients taking large doses of the offending drug for longer than six months (e.g., hydralazine); however, drug-induced lupus has occurred when small doses were used for only a short period of time. Hydralazine-induced lupus is more common in phenotypically slow acetylators of drugs, and a genetic predisposition to drug-induced lupus is suspected.[10] Although many drugs have been associated with drug-induced lupus procainamide, hydralazine, and the anticonvulsants have been implicated most commonly.[10-18] According to one estimate, a lupus-like reaction can be noted in about 10% of patients taking large doses of hydralazine.[10]

Lupus likely will subside upon discontinuation of the causative drug, although treatment may be required until symptoms have abated.

Scleroderma

The specific types of scleroderma identified are:

1) Localized
   a) Morphea
   b) Linear

2) Systemic sclerosis
   a) Diffuse scleroderma
   b) CREST syndrome with its manifestations of calcinosis, Raynaud's, esophageal dysfunction, sclerodactyly, and telangiectasia.

3) Chemical or drug-induced

The development of calcinosis with scleroderma was described before the concomitant features of Raynaud's phenomenon, esophageal dysfunction, and telangiectasias were noted. The combination of these symptoms was later named the CREST Syndrome.

Scleroderma is a chronic disease of unknown etiology that occurs four times as frequently in women as in men. It causes sclerosis of the skin and certain organs including the GI tract, lungs, heart, and kidneys. The skin is taut, firm, and edematous and is firmly bound to subcutaneous tissue; it feels tough and leathery, may itch, and later becomes hyperpigmented. The skin changes usually, but not always, precede the development of signs of visceral involvement. For a limited period the only findings may be the CREST syndrome.[19]

The prognosis is variable and unpredictable. Progress is worse in white males and black females. When the onset of the disease is later in life, the prognosis is poor.

There is no specific therapy so general supportive therapy is indicated. Corticosteroids, vasodilators, d-penicillamine, and im-

Table 42.1	Frequency of Lupus Manifestations at Onset and at Any Time During the Course of Lupus	
Manifestations	Onset (108)[a]	Anytime (605)[a]
Constitutional	73%	84%
Arthritis	56%	63%
Arthralgia	77%	85%
Skin	57%	81%
Mucus membranes	18%	54%
Pleurisy	23%	37%
Lung	9%	17%
Pericarditis	20%	29%
Myocarditis	1%	4%
Raynaud's	33%	58%
Thrombophlebitis	2%	8%
Vasculitis	10%	37%
Renal	44%	77%
Nephrotic syndrome	5%	11%
Azotemia	3%	8%
Central nervous system	24%	54%
Cytoid bodies	5%	5%
Gastrointestinal	22%	47%
Pancreatitis	1%	4%
Lymphadenopathy	25%	32%
Myositis	7%	5%

[a] University of Toronto. Frequency at onset based upon 108 patients diagnosed at Lupus clinic, and frequency at anytime for 605 patients registered before December 1990.

munosuppressive agents have been tried. Their proposed mechanism of action is depicted in Figure 42.1.

Alteration of immune cell activation and function, prevention of endothelial cell injury and activation, and other mechanisms may interfere with the over production of collagen by fibroblasts.

Polymyalgia Rheumatica (PMR) and Giant Cell Arteritis (GCA)

Polymyalgia rheumatica almost always is found in patients over 50 years of age and four times more frequently in women. It is characterized by pain in the muscles of the shoulder and pelvic girdle, marked elevation of Westergren erythrocyte sedimentation rate (ESR), absence of inflammatory arthritis, and absence of muscle disease signs such as atrophy, weakness, or fibrillation.[20] Patients will display a dramatic response to a starting dose of 10 to 20 mg/day of prednisone which is tapered to 5 to 7.7 mg/day. Symptoms will disappear and the sedimentation rate approach normal within a week. Approximately one-third of patients require prolonged treatment to control inflammation.[21]

Giant cell or temporal arteritis may be associated with polymyalgia rheumatica.[20] GCA is a chronic inflammation of large arteries, accompanied by the presence of giant cells. It causes thickening of intima with narrowing and eventual occlusion of the lumen.[22] GCA occurs primarily in females over 50 years of age. The local manifestations of giant cell arteritis depend upon the location of the involved artery; temporal headaches, blindness (15% of patients), scalp necrosis, tongue gangrene, and jaw claudication are some of the features that may be encountered. The Westergren ESR may increase to 80 to 100 mm/hour in many cases. Corticosteroids are the most effective therapy for GCA. Prednisone (1 mg/kg/day) will reduce symptoms within one to two days and often eliminate symptoms within a week. After one month of treatment or return of the Westergren ESR to normal, the dose of prednisone can be tapered.

Reiter's Disease

The recurrence of arthritis and/or ocular inflammation (conjunctivitis) with urethritis, is known as Reiter's disease. Urethritis usually appears first in this syndrome which occurs mainly in young men.[23]

There is no specific therapy. Broad-spectrum antibiotics are used for the urethritis and no treatment is necessary for the conjunctivitis. The arthritis is treated symptomatically with NSAIDs as discussed previously. Aggressive and unremitting Reiter's syndrome may benefit from immunosuppressive drugs.

Polymyositis and Dermatomyositis

Both dermatomyositis and polymyositis may be associated with malignancy in 20% of all patients. Fifty percent of these patients are men over 40 years of age. If either of these disorders are present in childhood, they may be associated with vasculopathy.

Both of these diseases are characterized by edema, inflammation, and degeneration of muscles. The proximal muscles of the arms and legs are primarily affected with symmetric involvement. Patients with dermatomyositis may display fever, malaise, general weakness, weakness of the pelvic and shoulder girdle muscles, and skin and mucosal lesions. About 33% of patients will have dysphagia.[24]

Management of these patients is accomplished with bed rest, physiotherapy, salicylates, and glucocorticoids. Warm baths and moist heat applications are helpful in the relief of stiffness. Mouth lesions may be irrigated with warm saline solution as needed.[25]

Table 42.2	Revised Criteria for Classification of Systemic Lupus Erythematosus[8]
Criteria	Explanation[a,b]
1) Malar rash	Classic red butterfly rash over bridge of nose and cheeks
2) Discoid rash	Disc-shaped, red, thick, scaly patches found anywhere on the body. Occurs in ≈15% of SLE patients.
3) Photosensitivity	Skin rash resulting from an unusual reaction to sunlight
4) Oral ulcers	Painless oral or nasopharyngeal ulcers
5) Arthritis	Nonerosive arthritis involving ≥2 peripheral joints; characterized by tenderness, swelling, or effusion
6) Serositis	Evidence of inflammation of either the pleura or pericardium
7) Renal disorder	As manifested by persistent proteinuria (>0.5 gm/day or >3+) or cellular casts
8) Neurologic disorder	Seizures or psychosis occurring without any other explanation
9) Hematologic disorder	Leukopenia (<4000/mm^3), hemolytic anemia, lymphopenia (<1500/mm^3), or thrombocytopenia (<100,000/mm^3)
10) Immunologic disorder	Positive LE cell test, presence of anti-(native) ds DNA antibody, anti-Sm antibody, or false positive serologic test for syphilis (confirmed by FTA-Abs)
11) Antinuclear antibody[9]	An abnormal ANA titer in the absence of drugs known to be associated with drug-induced lupus

[a] The diagnosis of systemic lupus erythematosus is made when ≥4 of the 11 criteria are present, serially or simultaneously, during an interval of observation.
[b] ANA = Antinuclear antibody; anti-Sm = anti-Smith; ds = double-stranded; FTA-Abs = Fluorescent treponemal antibody absorption; SLE = Systemic lupus erythematosus.

Fig 42.1 Pathogenetic Events in Systemic Sclerosis and Location of Possible Sites Where Drugs Might Be Useful for Therapeutic Intervention

Clinical Use of Corticosteroids

Corticosteroids play an important role in the treatment of a wide variety of disease states. In the last 30 years much has been learned about the class of compounds called corticosteroids, however, the exact mechanism by which corticosteroids exert their anti-inflammatory and immunosuppressive effects remains unknown.[26-28] Corticosteroids may be used for the treatment of many rheumatologic disorders including ankylosing spondylitis, bursitis, tenosynovitis, acute gouty arthritis, rheumatoid arthritis, osteoarthritis, dermatomyositis, polymyalgia rheumatica, acute rheumatic carditis, systemic lupus erythematosus, mixed connective tissue disease, polymyositis, and vasculitis.[37,38]

Predictable Pharmacological Effects Relative to Chemical Structure

1. A.H., a 62-year-old male with a 1 year history of scleroderma, originally was treated with prednisone 60 mg/day and azathioprine 50 mg/day. Recently he enrolled in an investigational drug trial testing a new steroid, datisone. The chemical structure of this compound is:

Datisone

His vital signs and laboratory test results are as follows: weight 292 pounds; blood pressure (BP) 180/102 mm Hg; pulse 62 beats/min and regular; and fasting blood sugar (FBS) 110 mg/dL. A.H. is without complaints except for occasional headaches, a "swollen face," and a modest weight gain since the initiation of datisone. Based upon the structure of the experimental corticosteroid, are any of the symptoms voiced by A.H. related to his drug therapy? [SI unit: FBS 6.11 mmol/L]

The new corticosteroid, datisone, is structurally most similar to hydrocortisone (see Figure 42.2) and would be expected to have similar high sodium-retaining properties. The addition of a 16 α-hydroxyl group (triamcinolone) or 16 α-methyl group (dexamethasone) results in corticosteroids with virtually no mineralocorticoid (i.e., sodium-retaining) properties. The 1, 2 double bond (prednisone, dexamethasone) within the A-ring of the structure enhances anti-inflammatory potency relative to sodium-retaining properties. Since datisone has neither of these features, A.H.'s modest weight gain possibly might be attributed to sodium and water retention as a consequence of the high-dose steroid therapy.[42] A.H.'s weight gain cannot be attributed solely to the predicted mineralocorticoid effects of datisone because of the myriad of other possible causes (e.g., corticosteroid-induced appetite stimulation, alterations in physical activity or dietary habits). His "swollen face" could represent a cushingoid feature resulting from long-term corticosteroid use. Hypercortisolism alters normal body fat distribution, resulting in moon facies, buffalo hump, truncal obesity, and other localized fatty deposits. A.H.'s complaint of headache could be related to his increased blood pressure (BP: 180/102 mm Hg) as a consequence of fluid retention resulting from his corticosteroid; however, hypertension usually is asymptomatic (see Chapter 10: Essential Hypertension). Although corticosteroids with the greatest mineralocorticoid activity are more likely to produce fluid retention and increase blood pressure, even those without mineralocorticoid action (see Table 42.3) can increase blood pressure.[31] A history of high blood pressure and advanced age can predispose individuals to corticosteroid-induced increases in blood pressure. Whether hypertension is related to dose or duration of corticosteroid therapy is unknown; it rarely occurs in patients receiving alternate-day therapy. The hypertension usually resolves after discontinuation of the steroid. In A.H., however, the hypertension also can be attributed to other possible etiologies (e.g., scleroderma).

The equivalent potency, sodium-retaining potency, plasma half-life, and biologic half-life of several synthetic analogues of cortisol are listed in Table 42.3. Cortisone and hydrocortisone have the highest sodium-retaining potency and, therefore, are seldom prescribed for long-term anti-inflammatory therapy.[26] All of the corticosteroids are 21-carbon steroid molecules. The chemical structures of the corticosteroids have been modified resulting in large differences in duration of action, potency, and mineralocorticoid activity.[29] Corticosteroids are synthesized in the body through a series of reactions. Cholesterol is converted to pregnenolone which in turn is converted to progesterone. This is then converted to cortisol, the major corticosteroid in man.[26]

Active Corticosteroid Compounds

2. M.H. is a 43-year-old female with RA awaiting a liver transplant. Her total bilirubin is 3.1 mg/dL, aspartate aminotransferase (AST) 93 U/L, and alanine aminotransferase (ALT) 65 U/L. She has been well maintained on prednisone for her arthritis until recently when her arthritis failed to respond despite escalating doses of prednisone. Why has her prednisone seemed to have stopped being effective? What factors need to be considered when selecting an alternative corticosteroid for M.H.? [SI units: bilirubin 53.01 μmol/L; AST 93 U/L; ALT 65 U/L]

Fig 42.2   Commonly Used Corticosteroids   The arrows indicate the structural differences between cortisol and each of the other corticosteroids.

Although orally administered corticosteroids are well absorbed, exogenously administered corticosteroids which are 11-keto compounds are devoid of corticosteroid activity until converted *in vivo* into active 11-betahydroxyl compounds.[33] Cortisone and prednisone must be converted respectively to the active compounds, cortisol and prednisolone, in the liver.[27] M.H. has very little hepatic capacity and, therefore, might not have been converting the prednisone to its active prednisolone metabolite. To circumvent this problem, M.H. should be given prednisolone or perhaps a different corticosteroid (e.g., methylprednisolone).

Approximately 95% of cortisol is bound to alpha-globulin transcortin[1] and the remaining 5% is bound to albumin after this carrier is saturated. However, the bond between cortisol and albumin is weak, and about 25% of the steroid disassociates from albumin and is free to circulate in the plasma. Although the dosing of corticosteroids is not a very precise science, it is important to consider adjusting doses for patients who have decreased serum albumin concentrations. In these patients a greater amount of free hormone will result in increased side effects. Since albumin is synthesized by the liver, M.H. is likely to have decreased serum albumin concentrations and could be more susceptible to the pharmacologic effects of corticosteroids when given an active corticosteroid moiety.

When selecting an alternative corticosteroid to replace M.H.'s prednisone, the dosing interval of the replacement corticosteroid should not be based strictly upon the plasma half-lives shown in Table 42.3. Corticosteroids have biological half-lives that are 2 to 36 times longer than their plasma half-lives. In addition, the onset of biological effects lags behind peak plasma levels.[34] Practitioners must always be mindful that the serum or plasma half-life of a drug might not be synonymous with the biological half-life. For example, prednisone with a plasma half-life of only about one hour can be dosed on alternate days for some disorders.

3. Clinical Presentation of SLE. L.D., a 33-year-old black female with recently diagnosed lupus erythematosus, has experienced a recent weight loss of 15 pounds (down to 130 pounds), joint pain, fatigue, and a worsening of her facial rash. She has a temperature of 105 °F, serum creatinine (SrCr) of 2.8 mg/dL, Westergren ESR of 50 mm/hr, ANA titer of 1:320, and positive anti-dsDNA and anti-Sm tests. UA reveals 3+ proteinuria and a modest amount of casts. What subjective and objective data are consistent with SLE and would therapy be likely to reflect resolution of these signs and symptoms? [SI unit: SrCr 247.52 μmol/L]

According to some of the objective data (fever, increased Westergren ESR, proteinuria, weight loss, high ANA titer, increased serum creatinine, positive anti-dsDNA and anti-Sm tests) and subjective data (fatigue, joint pain, worsening facial rash), L.D. is

Table 42.3	Comparison of Corticosteroid Preparations[32]			
Compound	Equiv. Potency (mg)	Na Retaining Potency (Mineral-corticoid Activity)	Plasma t½ (min)	Biological t½ (hr)
Short Acting				
Cortisone	25	2+	30	8–12
Hydrocortisone (Cortisol)	20	2+	90	8–12
Prednisone	5	1+	60	12–36
Prednisolone	5	1+	200	12–36
Methyl-prednisolone	4	0	180	12–36
Triamcinolone	4	0	300	12–36
Long Acting				
Dexamethasone	0.75	0	200	36–54
Betamethasone	0.6	0	300+	36–54

Table 42.4	The Multiple Uses of Corticosteroids in SLE[a]
Indication	**Corticosteroid Regimen**
Cutaneous manifestations	Topical or intralesional corticosteroids
Minor disease activity	Prednisone (or equivalent) at a dose of <0.5 mg/kg in a single or divided daily dose
Major disease activity	*Oral:* Prednisone (or equivalent) at a dose of 1 mg/kg in a single or divided daily dose; duration should not exceed 4 weeks *IV bolus:* Methylprednisolone (1 gm or 15 mg/kg) over 30 min; dose often repeated for 3 consecutive days

[a] SLE = Systemic lupus erythematosus.

experiencing a flare of her SLE (major disease activity shown on Table 42.4). This disease tends to wax and wane and the aggressiveness of therapy should be adjusted to accommodate these changes.

Mechanism of Action

4. Why might corticosteroids be effective in managing these signs and symptoms of SLE in L.D.?

The exact mechanisms by which corticosteroids exert their anti-inflammatory and immunosuppressive effects are not completely understood. They may interrupt the inflammatory and immune cascade at several levels including: 1) impairment of antigen opsonization; 2) interference with inflammatory cell adhesion and migration through vascular endothelium; 3) interruption of cell-cell communication by alteration of the release of cytokines; 4) impairment of leukotriene and prostaglandin synthesis; and 5) inhibition of neutrophil superoxide production.[1] After administration of corticosteroids, there is an increase in the number of neutrophils which are prevented from leaving the circulation.[1,26] This results in a decrease of neutrophils at the site of inflammation. Conversely, the lymphocyte count in the circulation, especially T cells, is di-

minished. The lymphocytes leave the circulation and travel to the bone marrow and other sites. The greatest decrease of lymphocytes occurs about four to eight hours after administration, but the number of lymphocytes will return to normal after approximately 24 hours. Leukocyte migration to the site of inflammation is the proposed mechanism by which these agents produce their anti-inflammatory and immunosuppressive actions. It also is hypothesized that corticosteroids interfere with the action of the available leukocytes at the inflammation site.[27,35,36]

L.D.'s fever, joint pain, fatigue, and worsening facial rash all reflect an inflammatory response to her systemic lupus erythematosus. These subjective symptoms along with the objective measurements of her disease activity (e.g., increased ESR, ANA, and serum creatinine) are mediated by leukotrienes, prostaglandins, lymphocytes, and the other inflammatory responses described above. Therefore, corticosteroids are indicated for the treatment of L.D.

Dosage Forms and Dosing Regimens

5. What would be a reasonable corticosteroid dose for L.D.?

Because of the great variety of clinical applications and the wide variety of corticosteroid compounds and dosages, the selection of the most appropriate dose of a corticosteroid is as much an art as it is a science. Generally, the higher the dose and the shorter the dosing interval of the corticosteroid translates into an increased anti-inflammatory effect and increased side effects.[36] Therefore, the need to modify disease activity must be balanced against the need to minimize toxicities.

There are multiple dosage forms and uses of corticosteroids in SLE, including topical preparations for inflammatory rashes, intralesional injections for discoid lupus, low-dose oral therapy for mild active disease, and high-dose oral or bolus intravenous (IV) infusions for acute, severe manifestations. These indications and the corresponding dose of corticosteroid are listed in Table 42.4.

A review of L.D.'s subjective and objective data would suggest that her disease activity probably represents a major flare-up of her systemic lupus erythematosus. Therefore, a short course of a high-

Table 42.5		Corticosteroid Dosing Regimens[d,e]		
			Relative	
Regimen	**Indication**	**Rationale**	**Efficacy[a]**	**Side Effects[a]**
Oral, QD low dose (≤10 mg prednisone)	Maintenance therapy	"Physiologic" dose, suppress symptoms	+	+
Alternate day moderate dose (>10 mg prednisone)	Nonsymptomatic manifestations of mild to moderate disease; maintenance therapy	Some adverse reactions less often; less adrenal suppression	++	+
QD moderate[b] to high dose	Control of active disease	Effective in many rheumatic diseases; less adverse reactions than split dose	++	++
Split daily dose	Rapid control of active disease	↑ efficacy over equivalent single dose	+++	+++
"Mini-pulse"[c]	Rapid control of severe disease	More rapid control; possibly allows lower maintenance dose	+++	++
Parenteral IM depo-steroids	Limited use as rescue (targeted injections preferred)	Temporary disease control	++	++
IV pulse	Severe/emergent life- or organ-threatening disease	Rapid control of severe disease; possibly ↓ maintenance dose	++++	++++

[a] Efficacy and side effects vary with the dose given.
[b] Given in morning to minimize adrenal suppression.
[c] E.g., 100–200 mg/day prednisone for 2–5 days.
[d] IM = Intramuscular; IV = Intravenous.
[e] Reprinted with permission from reference 69.

dose corticosteroid regimen probably would be a reasonable treatment for this episode of SLE in L.D.

A short course of steroids or even a single treatment with a high-dose corticosteroid typically can result in prompt and complete resolution of most manifestations of lupus erythematosus. Pulse therapy with methylprednisolone 1000 mg IV daily for one to three days has proven effective for SLE, vasculitis, and rheumatoid arthritis.[36,39,40] Additional or more frequent toxicities occur with high-dose steroid pulses and this must be considered on an individualized basis.[41] Alternatively, the use of mini-pulses of oral prednisone (100 to 200 mg/day) for several days also may help in disease control. Table 42.5 provides a summary of different steroid regimens which may be used and the rationale for intravenous pulse therapy seems applicable to L.D.

6. After finishing her bolus "pulse" therapy of methylprednisolone (1 gm/day IV for 3 days), L.D.'s lupus has responded well to therapy. Her joint pain is decreased and her temperature decreased to normal. The current laboratory test results are: Westergren ESR 22 mm/hr; SrCr 2.5 mg/dL; ANA titer of 1:80; and positive anti-dsDNA. L.D. wishes to go home to finish her recovery. What dose of oral corticosteroid would be reasonable to prescribe for L.D. upon her discharge from the hospital?

Along with adjustments of the other medications that she may be taking (such as NSAIDs or other immunosuppressive agents), L.D. needs to have her methylprednisolone converted to an oral formulation (see Table 42.6), and consideration given to reducing the steroid dose. Because the steroid dose L.D. received is considered massive supraphysiologic or suprapharmacologic, the corticosteroid effects on lymphocyte function can be prolonged. Therefore, the residual benefits from the suprapharmacological doses of methylprednisolone will be additive to the effect of the oral steroid that will be prescribed for her upon departure from the hospital. Due to this fact, L.D. does not require an oral corticosteroid dose that is equivalent to the intravenous dose and a lower oral daily dose can be prescribed because she responded well to her IV doses. In some patients with presumably modest disease activity, alternate-day dosing of corticosteroids may be adequate to maintain disease suppression,[42] however, more study is needed to better determine the role of alternate-day dosing of corticosteroids after patients have successfully completed a pulse-course of high-dose corticosteroids.

In the U.S., prednisone is the most commonly prescribed corticosteroid for oral use in the treatment of connective tissue diseases. Prednisone is rapidly and substantially absorbed following oral administration, has an intermediate duration of action (12 to 36 hours), is available in a variety of dosage forms and strengths, and is relatively inexpensive.[36] The recommended dose of prednisone for the majority of connective tissue diseases is 1 mg/kg/day in three to four divided doses. Administration of daily corticosteroids in a split dose given two to four times per day yields a more rapid onset and a greater degree of anti-inflammatory effect. Considering the severity of L.D.'s lupus flare this dosing would be appropriate. The dosing of oral corticosteroids is a balancing act to minimize toxicity but avoid flare-up of disease activity.[30] For L.D. who weighs approximately 59 kg, a maintenance regimen of prednisone 20 mg three times a day (for a total of 60 mg/day) or an equivalent dose of another corticosteroid should be prescribed. L.D. also might need an immunosuppressive agent, such as azathioprine or cyclophosphamide, because of her increased serum creatinine and possibility of lupus nephritis. These latter drugs would not be initiated in L.D. because she seems to be responding to her methylprednisolone without adverse sequelae thus far. The addition of immunosuppressives may have a "steroid sparing" effect and could allow for steroid dosage reduction.

Table 42.6	Routes of Administration of Various Corticosteroids
Corticosteroid	**Route of Administration**[a]
Betamethasone	PO, IM, intra-articular, intrasynovial, intradermal, soft tissue injection
Cortisone	PO, IM
Dexamethasone	PO, IM, IV, intra-articular, intradermal, soft tissue injection
Hydrocortisone	IM, IV
Methylprednisolone	PO, IM, IV
Prednisolone	PO, IM, IV, intra-articular, intradermal, soft tissue injection
Prednisone	PO
Triamcinolone	PO, IM, intra-articular, intrasynovial, intradermal, soft tissue injection

[a] IM = Intramuscularly; IV = Intravenously; PO = Oral.

Once Daily Dosing

7. L.D. was discharged from the hospital taking ibuprofen 600 mg QID with food and prednisone 20 mg TID. After 3 weeks, her flare has subsided and her symptoms are now at the baseline that was present before her recent flare of SLE. Why should a change in her medication be considered?

Once the patient's lupus flare is under control and has responded to steroids, the divided daily doses of a steroid can be consolidated into a single daily dose, usually administered in the morning.[36] Endogenous cortisol levels are normally highest at about 7:00 to 8:00 a.m. and decline to their lowest at midnight. Thus, a once-a-day morning corticosteroid dose coincides in time with high endogenous plasma cortisol. Since this is the time that the patient's tissues would normally be exposed to the highest levels of endogenous cortisol, suppression of the hypothalamic-pituitary-adrenocortical (HPA)-axis is minimized somewhat. If the divided dose regimen has been used for less than two weeks, the dose can be combined into a single daily dose immediately; however, if the divided dose regimen has been used for more than two weeks, the dose should be converted over a two-week period to a single daily dose.[42] Since L.D. received her dosage for three weeks, the daily dose should be converted to 60 mg each morning over a two-week period.

Hypothalamic-Pituitary-Adrenocortical (HPA) Axis Suppression

8. R.S., a 48-year-old, 135 pound, 5′ 5″ male, is recently diagnosed with polyarteritis. After a recent hospitalization, R.S. was discharged taking 15 mg of prednisone QID. He has been on this regimen for approximately 1 month and his symptoms are well controlled. R.S. now is scheduled for major surgery. His laboratory test evaluation revealed: SrCr 1.4 mg/dL; blood urea nitrogen (BUN) 17 mg/dL; white blood cell (WBC) count 11,200 cells/mm³, and Westergren ESR 29 mm/hr. Why should R.S.'s corticosteroid regimen be adjusted? [SI units: SrCr 123.76 μmol/L; BUN 6.07 mmol/L UREA; WBC 11.2 × 10⁹; ESR 29 mm/hr]

The HPA axis regulates the amount of circulating cortisol.[27,43,44] Corticotropin-releasing factor, a hormone secreted by the hypothalamus, stimulates the release of adrenocorticotropin (ACTH) for the anterior pituitary. ACTH, in turn, stimulates the adrenal cortex to secrete cortisol.[43] As serum cortisol levels rise, a negative-feedback mechanism inhibits corticotropin-releasing factor and ACTH secretion, resulting in decreased secretion of cortisol (see Figure 42.3). Under normal conditions about 12 to 30 mg/day of cortisol is secreted by the adrenal cortex.[27] This amount increases about tenfold under conditions of stress.[37]

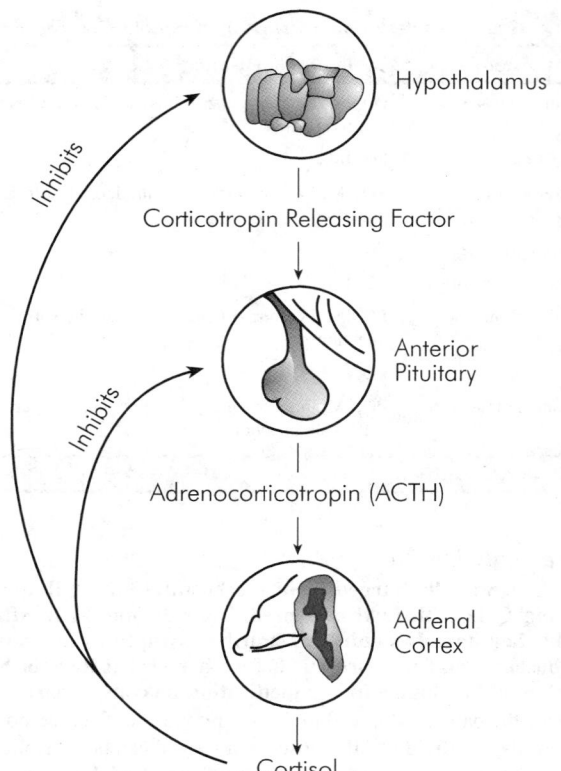

Fig 42.3   Hypothalamic-Pituitary-Adrenocortical Axis Regulation

Corticosteroid doses can be classified as physiologic (e.g., replacement) or pharmacologic (e.g., supraphysiologic).[43,45] A physiologic dose of a corticosteroid is equal to the amount of corticosteroid usually secreted by the adrenal cortex each day and is equal to about 5 mg/day of prednisone. A dose of prednisone of 0.1 to 0.25 mg/kg/day is low supraphysiologic dose; 0.5 mg/kg/day of prednisone is supraphysiologic; 1 to 3 mg/kg/day is a high supraphysiologic dose; and 15 to 30 mg/kg/day is a massive supraphysiologic dose.

Shortly after cortisone and ACTH were accepted into clinical practice,[29] adrenocortical insufficiency and subsequent adrenal atrophy were noted in patients who received doses of exogenous corticosteroids that exceeded the normal amount needed for hormone replacement.[29,43] When corticosteroids are discontinued abruptly in the patients who had been treated with supraphysiological doses of corticosteroids for a prolonged period, the HPA axis cannot respond to situations where there is a need for increased cortisol (such as illness, stress, or surgery).[46] The minimum dose, dose interval, and therapy duration required to suppress the HPA axis are difficult to assess. Following long-term therapy, this suppression can last up to one full year. The duration of adrenal suppression following a short course of corticosteroid therapy is unknown. Since R.S. is receiving prednisone 1 mg/kg/day, he is receiving a massive supraphysiologic dose that is capable of suppressing endogenous cortisol secretion. Surgery is a stressful event and supplemental doses of a corticosteroid with mineralocorticoid effects probably are warranted for R.S. because he most likely has some degree of HPA axis suppression. Although corticosteroids can decrease wound healing, this is a minor consideration relative to HPA axis suppression.

Adrenal Function Testing

9. How can the degree of adrenal suppression in R.S. be assessed?

The clinician has two options when HPA axis suppression is suspected. The first option is to treat the suspected patient as though adrenocortical insufficiency is present. The second is to try to quantify the adrenocortical reserves of the pituitary and hypothalamus. In today's environment of cost containment, the former approach usually is taken. Tests currently available for assessment include: insulin-induced hypoglycemia, metyrapone, lysine-vasopressin, and ACTH stimulation.[27] Although the first three methods are more sensitive, they also are more involved, expensive, and not used routinely. The ACTH (cosyntropin) test correlates best with adrenocortical response to clinical stress. Glucocorticoid therapy is first withheld for 12 to 24 hours to determine a baseline plasma cortisol level at 8:00 a.m. After this is completed, a parenteral dose of 250 µg of cosyntropin is administered. A serum cortisol level is then obtained 30 minutes to one hour later. A subnormal cortisol concentration (<20 µg/dL) increase indicates adrenal insufficiency.

Dosing During Stressful Events

10. R.S. has a cosyntropin test performed and it demonstrates an increase of 80 mmol/L to a level of 190 mmol/L. In the consideration of this laboratory report, what doses of corticosteroid should be ordered to prevent an addisonian crisis during R.S.'s surgery?

A normal response includes an increase in plasma cortisol of greater than 170 mmol/L (6 µg/dL) from baseline to a level of more than 550 mmol/L (20 µg/dL). R.S. apparently has adrenal insufficiency and needs supplementation during periods of stress.[27,37,43] A recommended corticosteroid replacement regimen for patients with suppressed HPA axis who are undergoing surgery is 100 mg of hydrocortisone every six hours on the day of operation. Since the adrenal gland can secrete as much as 300 mg/day during acute stress, 150 mg of hydrocortisone every six hours certainly would be a reasonable regimen for R.S. on the day of his surgery.

Leukocytosis

11. R.S. was doing fine until 3 days after surgery when his temperature spiked to 103 °F. R.S. has been back on his original prednisone dose. Urine, blood, and sputum cultures were ordered as well as a stat complete blood count (CBC), drawn at 4:00 p.m. His CBC revealed an increase in WBCs with a differential showing an increase in segmented neutrophils (granulocytes 16,000/mm³, from 11,000 at baseline) along with decreases in both total lymphocyte and monocyte count from baseline. No "left shift" was noted. What could be causing these results?

At first, it would be reasonable to assume there may be an infectious process present. The effects of prednisone on peripheral or circulating WBC count are well documented and predictable (e.g., granulocytosis along with lymphopenia and monocytopenia). T-cell lymphocytes are decreased more than B-cell lymphocytes. The occurrence of a "left shift" (e.g., an increase in immature leukocytes, such as bands) is variable, and only slight if present. The increase in granulocytes (PMNs) and decrease in lymphocytes and monocytes is most significant four to six hours after a prednisone dose; these values return to normal in 24 hours. The decrease in monocyte accumulation at tissue-sites of inflammation may persist for several days.

Prednisone increases granulocytes by an average of 4000/mm³ with a range of 1700 to 7500/mm³. The increase in granulocytes results primarily from release of cells from bone marrow and secondarily from the shift of cells from the marginal or noncirculating cell pool to the circulating or peripheral pool.[65,66] The temporal relationship of white blood cell changes in patients taking multiple doses of corticosteroids is less predictable due to the constant flux in steroid effect.

The results from R.S.'s most recent CBC should be compared to his baseline complete blood count. The temporal relationship to his prednisone dose also should be determined. Because a "stat" CBC, at the time of a temperature spike, was obtained only seven hours after his prednisone dose was administered, the CBC changes (leukocytosis, monocytopenia, and lymphocytopenia) are difficult to interpret. An additional complete blood count, 24 hours after his dose, was ordered to differentiate the cause of his CBC abnormalities. This complete blood count was normal, indicating that the abnormalities on the first CBC were probably steroid induced.

Alternate Day Therapy

12. One month later, R.S. states he feels much better. He has recovered from his surgery, and his polyarteritis is now asymptomatic; his WBC count, BUN, SrCr, and Westergren ESR are returning toward the normal range. Why should R.S.'s prednisone dose be adjusted at this time?

Once a stable clinical response is attained with a single daily dose of a corticosteroid, an attempt should be made to decrease R.S.'s corticosteroid dose to the lowest effective dose and, if possible, to taper the steroid to an alternate day regimen.[36,42] If used appropriately, alternate day corticosteroid therapy can help minimize HPA axis suppression and undesirable side effects, while allowing effective treatment of the disease process. A corticosteroid with a short or intermediate duration of action should be chosen for alternate day therapy to minimize accumulation from subsequent doses which would negate the benefits of every other day dosing. If the dosing interval is substantially longer than the biological half-life (e.g., giving prednisone Q 48 hr), nearly normal hypophyseal-pituitary-adrenal function can be maintained. This can minimize the risks of daily therapy. Alternate-day steroid dosing can be used to maintain disease suppression in chronic therapy, but to achieve control of the active disease process more intensive dosage schedules usually are required.

Conversion to Alternate Day Therapy

13. How would you convert R.S. to alternate-day therapy from his current 60 mg/day dose?

Before converting a patient to alternate-day therapy, the minimum effective daily dose must be determined. Generally, the optimum every-other-day dose is two and one-half to three times the minimal daily dose.[36,42] The dose on the "off" day should be tapered gradually by the equivalent of 2.5 to 5 mg of prednisone or its equivalent per week until the patient is on the steroid every other day.[46] Tapering of the alternate-day dose can continue until the minimum dose sufficient to control the underlying disorder is achieved.[47] For R.S., one approach would be to decrease the dose of prednisone by 5 mg/week until the minimum daily dose is reached that controls his polyarteritis. For illustrative purposes, assume this dose is 30 mg/day. The 30 mg dose is multiplied by 2.5 so R.S. would take 75 mg on one day alternating with 30 mg of prednisone the next. The 30 mg dose would then be tapered each week by 5 mg/week until discontinued. R.S. would then be taking 75 mg of prednisone every other day. Should R.S. be asymptomatic at this dosage, a taper of the 75 mg could then be attempted. Tapering should be 2.5 mg/week until the lowest possible dose is achieved which will control his disease.

Discontinuation of Therapy

14. R.S. has now received prednisone 60 mg QOD for 5 months and his polyarteritis is well controlled. What would be a reasonable dosing schedule for implementing the gradual discontinuation of R.S.'s corticosteroid?

Many methods of tapering steroid dosages have been tried.[36,43,46,47] Some suggest decreasing the corticosteroid dosage by the equivalent of 2.5 to 5 mg of prednisone every three to seven days until the physiologic dose is reached. Others suggest decreasing the dose by 2.5 mg of prednisone (or the equivalent of another corticosteroid) every one to two weeks if on daily therapy, or by 5 mg of prednisone every one to two weeks if on alternate-day therapy, until it can be discontinued. Some clinicians follow this procedure until a physiologic dose is reached, and at that time will convert the patient to hydrocortisone 20 mg/day. After two to four weeks, this dose can be decreased by 2.5 mg every week until 10 mg/day is achieved. At this time, the patient should have a plasma cortisol concentration measured. If this is normal, the hydrocortisone can be discontinued.[42,47]

During the tapering process, disease flare-up is a definite possibility; therefore, the patient must be monitored closely. Also, if the patient is stressed during this period, exogenous corticosteroid supplementation may be necessary. Abrupt withdrawal of steroids following long-term, high-dose therapy should be avoided since this may produce a steroid withdrawal syndrome manifested by the presence of nausea, vomiting, anorexia, headache, joint pain, fever, lethargy, myalgia, hypotension, and weight loss. These symptoms are thought to occur as a consequence of rapidly falling serum corticosteroid concentrations rather than the presence of low concentrations.

R.S.'s prednisone dose of 60 mg every other day can now be decreased by 5 mg at one to two week intervals until he is receiving 5 mg on alternate days. R.S. can then be converted to hydrocortisone 20 mg/day for two to four weeks. Weekly reductions of the hydrocortisone by 2.5 mg could be undertaken until the daily dose of 10 mg is reached. At this point, R.S.'s morning dose should be held and a cortisol level taken. If the serum cortisol concentration is normal (>10 µg/dL), the hydrocortisone can be discontinued. This is but one of the many possible approaches.[47] All approaches to discontinuing corticosteroids must be modified based upon factors such as dose, duration of therapy, disease status, patient condition, and existence of adverse effects.

Adverse Effects

Besides suppression of the HPA axis, corticosteroid therapy produces inevitable side effects.[48-52] A compilation of documented complications is listed in Table 42.7.

Osteoporosis

15. D.L., a 28-year-old, 5'4", 105 pound female, is diagnosed with SLE. After an acute episode of lupus nephritis, D.L. has been maintained on high-dose prednisone, currently at a level of 15 mg/day. Her lupus seems well controlled but she comes in today with complaints of back pain. A physical examination reveals no apparent joint involvement typical of a lupus flare. What are possible explanations for her back pain and what additional data are needed to assist in the differential diagnosis?

It is important to look at some physical and laboratory indicators to first rule out the possibility that D.L. is having arthralgias due to her SLE. It also is important to remember that corticosteroids can cause osteoporosis. Bone loss leading to fractures at sites such as the spine, hip, and ribs are well-recognized complications of corticosteroid therapy.[33] Corticosteroids can directly inhibit osteoblastic activity necessary for new bone formation. They also increase bone resorption and decrease intestinal calcium absorption, which results in a compensatory increase in parathyroid hormone

Table 42.7	Adverse Effects of Systemic Corticosteroids[a,53]
Short-Term, High-Dose	**Long-Term Use**
Cerebral edema	Amenorrhea
Diabetes mellitus	Aseptic necrosis of bone
GI bleed	Cataracts
Glaucoma	Centripetal obesity
Hypertension	Growth failure
Hypokalemic alkalosis	HPA suppression
↑ BUN	Hyperlipidemia
Mood disorders	Hypertension
Pancreatitis	Immunosuppression
Proximal myopathy	Mood disorders
Sodium/water retention	Muscle weakness
	Osteoporosis
	Seizures

[a] BUN = Blood urea nitrogen; GI = Gastrointestinal; HPA = Hypothalamic-pituitary-adrenocortical axis.

secretion.[54,55] Parathyroid hormone further increases calcium resorption from bone in an effort to maintain normal calcium homeostasis. Trabecular (spine and rib) bone primarily seems to be affected.[56] Osteoporosis in postmenopausal women with rheumatoid arthritis is more evident at the hip than the spine, and the most important determinants of bone loss are disability and cumulative corticosteroid dose.[57] The degree of bone loss correlates to the dose of the corticosteroid, as well as to the duration of treatment; however, the absolute amount and/or duration of corticosteroid therapy has not been determined. When high doses are used, vertebral bone loss can be rapid, with compression fractures occurring weeks to months after therapy initiation.[36]

Because D.L. has multiple risk factors for osteoporosis (young, female, and small stature), a vertebral x-ray should be taken to look for a compression fracture. Prophylactic calcium and calcitriol, with or without calcitonin, should be started on any patient with multiple risk factors who possibly will be maintained on corticosteroid therapy.[58] Reversal of existing bone loss in D.L. will be difficult. Osteoporosis can be minimized in patients by prescribing 1000 mg/day of elemental calcium along with calcitriol 0.5 to 1.0 μg/day. Periodic radiographic comparisons to baseline can be used to determine if additional therapy is warranted.

Gastrointestinal

16. **C.W., a 66-year-old, 5′6″, 68 kg female, is newly diagnosed with PMR. She is an occasional drinker and smoker (1–2 packs/week). She was started on prednisone 15 mg/day and naproxen 500 mg Q 12 hours PRN one week ago and has shown dramatic improvement in the muscle pain of her shoulder and pelvic girdle. She comes in today to begin a taper of her prednisone and comments she's been having some ''stomach'' problems. Why do the predisposing factors for peptic ulcer disease in C.W. warrant prophylactic therapy?**

Whether or not corticosteroids lead to peptic ulcer disease is controversial despite early observations of a probable correlation.[59] A 1976 retrospective analysis of 42 prospective, controlled investigations involving 5331 patients randomly selected to receive steroid therapy or placebo showed no association between corticosteroid use and ulcers (relative risk: 1.4; 95% CI, 0.7 to 2.6).[60] Nevertheless, the controversy continues.

The prevalence of peptic ulcer disease is increased with the combined use of nonsteroidal anti-inflammatory drugs and corticoster-

oids.[59,61] Corticosteroids and NSAIDs commonly are prescribed concomitantly because many patients with connective tissue disorders have symptoms such as arthralgias, inflammation, and pain. Corticosteroids have the ability to induce tissue atrophy and probably enhance the ulcerogenic potential of environmental factors and other drugs.[27] The risk also depends upon the underlying disease and the dose and duration of the steroid therapy.[62,63]

In C.W.'s case, it is unclear whether her gastrointestinal problems are due to gastric irritation from the medication (which can be decreased if taken with food) or if they are symptoms of peptic ulcer disease (see Chapter 23: Upper Gastrointestinal Disorders). In many cases, common risk factors for ulcers also must be considered. C.W. is at increased risk due to her gender, advanced age, and her smoking and drinking history. Because of her concomitant use of NSAIDs and steroids and her risk factors, prophylactic therapy against ulceration would be reasonable.

Hyperglycemia

17. **G.P., a 58-year-old male, has a past medical history of dermatomyositis, adult onset diabetes mellitus (× 5 years), hypercholesterolemia, and obesity. G.P.'s current medications are prednisone 80 mg/day (started 2 months ago), lovastatin 20 mg Q HS, and glyburide 5 mg Q AM. He came into clinic this morning with the following physical findings: weight 285 pounds; BP 140/90 mm Hg; pulse 50 beats/min and regular; and FBS 290 mg/dL. G.P.'s diabetes has been controlled for 3 years; what are likely explanations for his hyperglycemia?** [SI unit: FBS 16.1 mmol/L]

The hyperglycemia in G.P. can be attributed to corticosteroid-stimulation of gluconeogenesis or impairment of peripheral glucose utilization; however, other etiologies (e.g., missed glyburide dose) also should be considered. Corticosteroids can promote pancreatic glucagon secretion with resultant glycogenolysis and formation of sugar from breakdown of amino acids and lactate produced during glycogenolysis. This process is not generally ketosis producing. Corticosteroids also decrease peripheral glucose utilization by decreasing glucose cell entry and cell membrane insulin receptors.[64] Increases in blood glucose are usually mild, with doses of prednisone as low as 15 mg/day reported to cause this effect. Alternate day therapy does not prevent this adverse effect.[42] Hyperglycemia peaks two to four hours after administration of the corticosteroid and can last from 12 to 24 hours, depending upon the size of the dose.

Because G.P. has been well controlled in the past, no immediate medication changes are warranted. He should assess his capillary blood glucose twice daily and report the results on the next clinic visit. Urine sugar determinations also may be helpful to detect glycosuria especially if his blood sugar is consistently elevated. It is important to note that hyperglycemia can occur in nondiabetic patients as well. Blood sugars in many nondiabetic patients will return to normal as the patient adjusts to the excess glucose concentration. If glycosuria persists and G.P.'s blood sugar results remain elevated, increasing the oral hypoglycemic dose or even changing to insulin may be necessary.

Ecchymosis

18. **Several weeks after discharge, R.D. began noticing large purple blotches on her arms that did not blanch upon application of local pressure. Also, these ''bruises'' did not seem to disappear very rapidly. Why is this dermatological effect probably prednisone induced?**

Ecchymosis, easy bruisability, is a common side effect of prolonged corticosteroid use; it occurs most often in the elderly and is dose related. Steroids destroy the collagen support of small blood vessels, resulting in leakage of blood into surrounding tissue. The anti-inflammatory effects of steroids reduce the normal resorption of blood-leakage into tissue, making the "bruise" last longer.[67,68] A reduction in the dose of prednisone or the use of an alternate-day prednisone dosing regimen should lessen the purpura. Unfortunately, patients such as R.D. often are already receiving the lowest dose of corticosteroid that is compatible with keeping the clinical condition under control.

References

1 **Schumacher HR et al.** Primer on the Rheumatic Diseases. 10th ed. Arthritis Foundation: Atlanta, GA; 1993.

2 **Anon.** Taber's Cyclopedic Medical Dictionary. 17th ed. FA Davis Company: Philadelphia, PA; 1993.

3 **Crofford LJ et al.** Corticotropin-releasing hormone in synovial fluids and tissues of patients with rheumatoid arthritis and osteoarthritis. J Immunol. 1993;151:1587–596.

4 **Mills JA.** Systemic lupus erythematosus. N Engl J Med. 1994;330:1871–879.

5 **Fessel WJ.** Systemic lupus erythematosus in the community. Arch Intern Med. 1974;134:1027.

6 **Arnett FC, Shulman LE.** Studies in familial systemic lupus erythematosus. Medicine. 1976;55:313.

7 **Feinglass EJ et al.** Neuropsychiatric manifestations of systemic lupus erythematosus: diagnosis, clinical spectrum and relationship to other features of the disease. Medicine. 1976;55:323.

8 **Tan CM et al.** The 1982 revised criteria for the classification of SLE. Arthritis Rheum. 1982;25:1271–277.

9 **Tan EM.** Autoantibodies to nuclear antigens (ANA): their immunobiology and medicine. Adv Immunol. 1982;33:176–240.

10 **Greenberg JH, Lutcher CL.** Drug-induced systemic lupus erythematosus. JAMA. 1972;222:191.

11 **Innes A et al.** Drug-induced lupus caused by very low-dose hydralazine. Br J Rheumatol. 1986;25:225. Letter.

12 **Blomgren SE et al.** Procainamide-induced lupus erythematosus—clinical and laboratory observations. Am J Med. 1972;52:338.

13 **Dubois EL et al.** Chlorpromazine-induced systemic lupus erythematosus. JAMA. 1972;221:595.

14 **Presley AP et al.** Antinuclear antibodies in patients taking lithium carbonate. Br Med J. 1976;2:280.

15 **Harrington TM, Davis DE.** Systemic lupus-like syndrome induced by methyldopa therapy. Chest. 1981;79:696.

16 **Chalmers A et al.** Systemic lupus erythematosus during penicillamine therapy for rheumatoid arthritis. Ann Intern Med. 1982;97:659.

17 **Bar-El Y et al.** Quinidine-induced lupus erythematosus. Am Heart J. 1986;111:1209.

18 **Griffiths ID, Kane SP.** Sulfasalazine-induced lupus syndrome in ulcerative colitis. Br Med J. 1977;2:1188.

19 **McGee BA et al.** Current options for the treatment of systemic scleroderma. Clin Pharm. 1991;10:14–25.

20 **Chuang T et al.** Polymyalgia rheumatica: a ten-year epidemiologic and clinical study. Ann Intern Med. 1982;97:672.

21 **Lestico MR et al.** Polymyalgia rheumatica. Clin Pharm. 1993;12:571–80.

22 **Bengtsson B, Malmvall B.** The epidemiology of giant cell arteritis including temporal arteritis and polymyalgia rheumatica. Arthritis Rheum. 1981;24:899.

23 **Keat A, Rowe I.** Reiter's syndrome and associated arthritides. Rheum Dis Clin North Am. 1991;17:25–42.

24 **Medsger TA et al.** The epidemiology of polymyositis. Am J Med. 1970;48:715.

25 **Hochberg MC et al.** Adult onset polymyositis/dermatomyositis: an analysis of clinical and laboratory features and survival in 76 patients with a review of the literature. Semin Arthritis Rheum. 1986;15:168.

26 **Kehrl JH, Fauci AS.** The clinical use of glucocorticoids. Ann Allergy. 1983;50(1):2–8.

27 **Holland EG, Taylor AT.** Glucocorticoids in clinical practice. J Fam Pract. 1991;32:512–19.

28 **Kimberly RP.** Glucocorticoid therapy for rheumatic diseases. Curr Opin Rheumatol. 1992;4:325–31.

29 **Axelrod L.** Glucocorticoid therapy. Medicine. 1976;55:39–59.

30 **Gallant C et al.** Oral glucocorticoids and their complications. J Am Acad Dermatol. 1986;14:161.

31 **Anon.** Corticosteroids general statement. American Hospital Formulary Service. Drug Information 1995. ASHP: Bethesda, MD; 1995;2094–102.

32 **Fauci AS.** Corticosteroids in autoimmune disease. Hosp Pract. 1983;18:99.

33 **Swartz SL, Dluhy RG.** Corticosteroids: clinical pharmacology and therapeutic use. Drugs. 1978;16:238.

34 **Jamieson T.** Corticosteroids for rheumatic disease. Postgrad Med. 1986;79:239.

35 **Fauci AS.** Glucocorticoid therapy: mechanism of action and clinical considerations. Ann Intern Med. 1976;84:304–15.

36 **Kimberly RP.** Mechanism of action, dosage schedules, and side effects of steroid therapy. Curr Opin Rheumatol. 1991;3:373–79.

37 **Iannuzzi LP.** Oral steroids in rheumatoid arthritis. Postgrad Med. 1987;82:295–301.

38 **Rodnan GP.** Treatment of gout and other forms of crystal-induced arthritis. Bull Rheum Dis. 1982;32:77–81.

39 **Kimberly RP et al.** High-dose intravenous methylprednisolone pulse therapy in systemic lupus erythematosus. Am J Med. 1981;70:817.

40 **Fan PT et al.** Effect of corticosteroids on the human immune response: comparison of one and three daily 1 gram intravenous pulses of methylprednisolone. J Lab Clin Med. 1979;91:625.

41 **Tornatore KM et al.** Racial differences in the pharmacokinetics of methylprednisolone in black and white renal transplant patients. Pharmacotherapy. 1993;13(5):481–86.

42 **Walton J et al.** Alternate-day vs. short-interval steroid administration. Arch Intern Med. 1970;126:601.

43 **Helfer EL, Rose LI.** Corticosteroids and adrenal suppression: characterizing and avoiding the problem. Drugs. 1989;38(5):838–45.

44 **LaRochelle GE et al.** Recovery of the hypothalamic-pituitary-adrenal (HPA) axis in patients with rheumatic diseases receiving low-dose prednisone. Am J Med. 1993;95:258–64.

45 **Laan R et al.** Low-dose prednisone in patients with rheumatic arthritis. Ann Intern Med. 1993;119:963–68.

46 **Koch-Weser J.** Withdrawal from glucocorticoid therapy. N Engl J Med. 1976;295:30–2.

47 **Kountz DS.** An algorithm for corticosteroid withdrawal. Clin Pharm. 1989;39:250–54.

48 **Davis GF.** Adverse effects of corticosteroids: II. Systemic. Clin Dermatol. 1986;4:161–69.

49 **Truhan AP, Ahmed AR.** Corticosteroids: a review with emphasis on complications of prolonged systemic therapy. Ann Allergy. 1989;62:375–91.

50 **The Boston Collaborative Drug Surveillance Program: acute adverse reactions to prednisone in relation to dosage.** Clin Pharmacol Ther. 1972;13:694.

51 **Kershner P, Wang-Cheng R.** Psychiatric side effects of steroid therapy. Psychosomatics. 1989;30:135–39.

52 **Sharfstein SS et al.** Relationship between alternate-day corticosteroid therapy and behavioral abnormalities. JAMA. 1982;248:2987–989.

53 **Skorodin MS.** Pharmacotherapy for asthma and chronic obstructive pulmonary disease. Arch Intern Med. 1993;153:814–28.

54 **Baylink DJ.** Glucocorticoid-induced osteoporosis. N Engl J Med. 1983;309:306–8.

55 **Seale JP, Compton MR.** Side effects of corticosteroid agents. Med J Aust. 1986;144:139–42.

56 **Hahn TJ.** Corticosteroid-induced osteopenia. Arch Intern Med. 1978;138:882–85.

57 **Hall GM et al.** The effect of rheumatoid arthritis and steroid therapy on bone density in postmenopausal women. Arthritis Rheum. 1993;36(11):1510–516.

58 **Sambrook P et al.** Prevention of corticosteroid osteoporosis. N Engl J Med. 1993;328:1747–752.

59 **Piper JM et al.** Corticosteroid use and peptic ulcer disease: role of nonsteroidal anti-inflammatory drugs. Ann Intern Med. 1991;114:735–40.

60 **Conn HO, Blitzer BL.** Nonassociation of adrenocorticosteroid therapy and peptic ulcer. N Eng J Med. 1976;294:473–79.

61 **Messer J et al.** Association of adrenocorticosteroid therapy and peptic ulcer disease. N Eng J Med. 1983;309:21–4.

62 **Guslandi M, Tittobello A.** Steroid ulcers: a myth revisited. Br Med J. 1982;304(6828):655,656.

63 **Spiro H.** Is the steroid ulcer a myth? N Eng J Med. 1983;309:405–7.

64 **Letsky JM, Kimmerling G.** Effects of glucocorticoids on carbohydrate metabolism. Am J Med Sci. 1976;271:203.

65 **Bishop CR et al.** A non-steady state kinetic evaluation of the mechanism of cortisone-induced granulocytosis. J Clin Invest. 1968;47:249–60.

66 **Dale DC et al.** Alternate-day prednisone. N Engl J Med. 1974;291:1154–158.

67 **Scarborough H, Shuster S.** Corticosteroid purpura. Lancet. 1960;1:93.

68 **Shuster E, et al.** Skin collagen in rheumatoid arthritis, and the effect of corticosteroids. Lancet. 1967;1:525.

69 **Paulus HE, Bulpitt KJ.** Nonsteroidal Anti-Inflammatory Agents and Corticosteroids. Primer on The Rheumatic Diseases. 10th ed. Arthritis Foundation; Atlanta, GA; 1993:302.

Contraception

Ronald J Ruggiero

Menstrual Cycle Physiology
(See Figures 43.1 and 43.2) 43-2
    Follicular phase 43-2
    Ovulatory phase 43-2
    Luteal or secretory phase 43-2
Comparison of Contraceptive Method Effectiveness
(See Table 43.1) 43-4
Hormonal Contraception Pharmacology 43-4
Four Generations of Combination Oral
Contraceptives (COCs) (See Table 43.2) 43-4
Progestin-Only Minipills 43-4
Synthetic Estrogens as Contraceptives 43-4
Synthetic Progestins as Contraceptives
(See Table 43.3) 43-4
Estrogenic, Progestational, and Androgenic Side
Effects of Combination Oral Contraceptives
(See Table 43.4) 43-6
Use of Hormonal Contraceptives 43-6
Patient Qualifications 43-6
    Baseline information (See Table 43.5)
    and contraindications to COC use
    (See Tables 43.6 and 43.7) 43-6
Combination Oral Contraceptives (COCs) 43-6
    Choice (Also see Table 43.8) 43-6
    Patient instructions (Also see Table 43.9) 43-8
        When to start COCs 43-8
        Need for backup method of contraception 43-8
        Choice of 21-day versus 28-day cycle 43-8
        Optimal time to take COC 43-8
        Avoid chloasma 43-8
        Anticipate drug interactions with COCs 43-8
        Importance of checkups 43-8
        What to do if pills are missed 43-8
Clinical Use of Progestin-Only Minipills 43-9
    Minipill versus COCs in breast-feeding 43-9
    Advantages 43-9
    Disadvantages (See Table 43.10) 43-10
    Patient instructions 43-10
Managing Patients' Problems 43-10
    Drug interactions 43-10
        Antibacterials (See Table 43.12) 43-10
        Liver enzyme induction (See Table 43.13) 43-11
        Breakthrough bleeding, spotting, and
        amenorrhea 43-12
        Biphasic and triphasic COCs 43-12
Major COC risks 43-13
    Cervical dysplasia and cervical cancer 43-13
    Breast cancer 43-13
    Cardiovascular disease 43-13

Thromboembolic events 43-14
Hypertension and subarachnoid
    hemorrhage (SAH) 43-14
Diabetes 43-15
Gallbladder disease 43-15
Liver tumors 43-15
"Postpill" amenorrhea and galactorrhea 43-15
Teratogenicity 43-16
Headache 43-16
Depression 43-16
Benefits of COCs 43-16
    Pelvic inflammatory disease and ectopic
    pregnancy 43-16
    Ovarian cancer and functional ovarian cysts 43-17
    Endometrial cancer 43-17
    Benign breast disease 43-17
    Dysmenorrhea 43-17
    Premenstrual syndrome (PMS) 43-17
    Iron deficiency anemia 43-17
    Acne and hirsutism 43-17
Postcoital (morning-after) pills
(See Table 43.14) 43-17
    High-dose estrogens 43-17
    Ovral 43-18
Long-acting progestin injections: Depo-Provera
(DMPA) (See Tables 43.15 and 43.16) 43-18
Other Birth Control Methods 43-19
Subdermal Levonorgestrel Implants (Norplant)
(See Tables 43.17 to 43.19) 43-19
Intrauterine Devices (IUDs) (See Tables 43.20
and 43.21) 43-19
    Risks and mechanisms of action 43-19
    Complications 43-20
Diaphragms 43-20
    Mechanism of action 43-20
    Types 43-20
        Flat spring rim 43-20
        Coil spring rim 43-20
        Arcing spring rim 43-20
        Wide seal 43-21
    Fitting 43-21
    Patient instructions 43-21
Cervical Caps 43-22
Condoms 43-22
Vaginal Spermicides 43-22
Investigatory Contraceptive Agents 43-22
    Male contraceptive methods 43-22
    Luteinizing hormone releasing hormone (LHRH)
    downregulators for women 43-23

The population of the world is 5.6 billion and growing by more than 89 million each year. By 2025 there may be 50% more humans on the earth than there are today, or 8.4 billion, the largest population growth ever seen in so short a time. Birth control policies established and implemented in this decade, therefore, could determine whether world population stops growing at less than 9 billion or surpasses 19 billion by the year 2100.[1]

There are approximately 250 million people in the U.S. and the U.S. population is growing at 0.7% per year. The estimated world population in mid 1994 of 5.59 billion has been increasing at a rate of 1.7% a year. This rate of growth results in the addition of 245,480 people every day, or 10,228 people every hour.[2]

Without contraceptive intervention, approximately 80% of women age 35 to 39 would become pregnant during a five-year

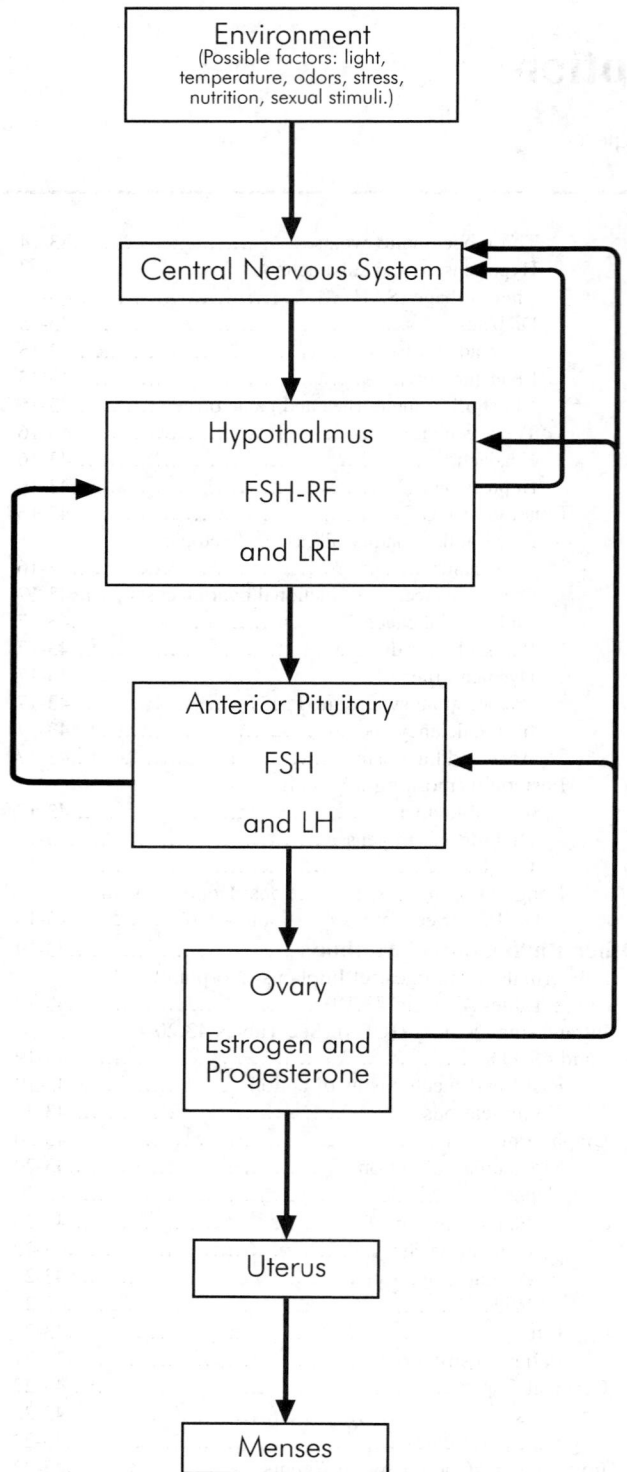

Fig 43.1 Interrelationships and Feedback Mechanisms Relating to the Human Menstrual Cycle The two gonadotropin releasing factors, FSH-RF and LRF, may be the same. FSH-RF = Follicle-stimulating hormone releasing factor; LRF = Luteinizing hormone releasing factor; FSH = Follicle-stimulating hormone; LH = Luteinizing hormone.

interval, compared with 91% of women age 20 to 24.[3,4] On the average, a woman conceives for the first time after seven months of unprotected intercourse. In the U.S. and the U.K., only 25% to 30% of women desiring pregnancy become pregnant during the first month of intercourse without contraception. By 12 months, 80% to 90% have become pregnant.[5,6] One out of ten women aged

15 to 19 in the U.S. will become pregnant each year, according to a comprehensive publication that has summarized the tragic epidemic of teenage pregnancies.[7]

Menstrual Cycle Physiology

Feedback biological mechanisms involving the hypothalamus, pituitary gland, ovaries, and endometrial lining of the uterus control the average 28-day menstrual cycle. Using the ovary as a reference point, the menstrual cycle can be divided into three phases: the follicular or preovulatory phase, the ovulatory phase, and the luteal or postovulatory phase. When the uterus is used as a reference point, the menstrual cycle also can be divided into three phases: the menstrual, proliferative, and secretory phases. The menstrual and proliferative phases coincide with the follicular phase, and the secretory phase coincides with the luteal phase of the ovary. (See Figures 43.1 and 43.2.)[8]

Follicular Phase

As can be seen in Figure 43.2, this phase, dominated by estrogen, begins at the onset of menstruation (menstrual phase) and lasts approximately 14 days. At the beginning of this phase, estrogen levels are low and no longer able to inhibit the production of follicle-stimulating hormone-releasing factor (FSH-RF) by the hypothalamus (see Figure 43.1). FSH-RF stimulates the anterior pituitary to secrete follicle-stimulating hormone (FSH) and a small amount of luteinizing hormone (LH). FSH stimulates the development of several primordial follicles within the ovary. The small amount of LH initiates estrogen secretion by the new follicles. Increasing levels of estrogen stimulate the production of luteinizing hormone releasing factor (LRF), which may be the same as FSH-RF, from the hypothalamus. Subsequently, more LH is produced in the anterior pituitary while FSH production is inhibited. Most of the developing follicles atrophy, while the dominant follicles develop further. As the follicles mature, they produce estrogen in increasing amounts. Estrogen is responsible for endometrial growth, an increase in the size and tortuosity of the uterine glands, and for the increased thickness and hyperemia of the uterine mucosa (proliferative phase).

Ovulatory Phase

Estradiol levels greater than 200 pg are necessary for at least 50 hours in order to stimulate the pituitary to release a surge of LH. This LH surge is responsible for final stage growth and maturation of the follicle, ovulation, and the formation of the corpus luteum. This LH surge represents the most dramatic rise and fall in serum of any pituitary or ovarian hormone and is a major point of reference in endocrinologic studies of the menstrual cycle.[8] Ovulation takes place at days 14 or 15 in an ideal 28-day cycle.

Luteal or Secretory Phase

In 90% of women, this phase is 13 to 15 days in duration and is the least variable part of the human reproductive cycle. During this progesterone-dominant phase, the corpus luteum produces progesterone and estrogen. Progesterone thickens the endometrium, increases the tortuosity of the uterine glands, and stimulates these glands to secrete a thick fluid in preparation for implantation of a fertilized ovum. A single luteal phase serum progesterone level of ≥3 ng/mL is presumptive evidence of ovulation.[9] If implantation does not occur by the 23rd to 25th day of the cycle, corpus luteum regression decreases the levels of estrogen and progesterone. When these hormone levels decrease, the endometrium cannot be maintained and is sloughed off (menstrual phase).

If fertilization and implantation occur, the trophoblast of the developing placenta produces the luteotropic hormone of preg-

Fig 43.2 The Menstrual Cycle FSH = Follicle-stimulating hormone; LH = Luteinizing hormone; HCG = Human chorionic gonadotropin.

nancy, human chorionic gonadotropin (HCG), within a week of conception. HCG takes the place of LH in maintaining the secretory capacity of the corpus luteum. HCG is the hormone measured by various pregnancy tests, the best of which can detect HCG as early as six to eight days postconception. Pregnancy can be maintained without a corpus luteum by the sixth to eighth week of gestation because the placenta is secreting sufficient amounts of progesterone and estrogen at this time.

Comparison of Contraceptive Method Effectiveness

The effectiveness of any contraceptive method depends upon its mechanism of action, availability (taking into account cost), and acceptability (taking into account religious and social beliefs, side effects, and ease of use). Any or all of these reasons can account for the discrepancy between the lowest observed failure rate and the actual failure rate in typical users. Table 43.1 compares the first-year failure rates of various birth control methods.

Hormonal Contraception Pharmacology

Four Generations of Combination Oral Contraceptives (COCs)

Manipulations of normal physiologic feedback mechanisms of the menstrual cycle by varying amounts of estrogen and/or progestin have proven to be a very effective method of contraception. Although today the contraceptive estrogens and progestins are

Table 43.1	First Year Failure Rates of Birth Control Methods[8]	
	Lowest Observed Failure Rate[a] (%)	Failure Rate in Typical Users[b] (%)
Subdermal progestin implant (Norplant6)	0.0	0.04
Tubal sterilization	0.0	0.4
Vasectomy	0.0	0.15
Injectable progestin	0.0	0.3
Combined birth-control pills	0.0	3
Progestin-only pill	1.1	3
IUD[c]	0.5	3
Condom	4.2	12
Diaphragm (with spermicide)	2.1	18
Sponge (with spermicide)	13.9 Nullips 27.7 Parous	18 Nullips 28 Parous
Cervical cap	8	18
Foams, creams, jellies, and vaginal suppositories	0–3	21
Coitus interruptus	6.7	18
Fertility awareness techniques (basal body temperature, mucous method, calendar, and "rhythm")	2–14.4	20
Douche	—	40
Chance (no method of birth control)	43.1	85

[a] Designed to complete the sentence: "In 100 users who start out the year using a given method and who use it correctly, and consistently, the lowest observed failure rate has been ____."
[b] Designed to complete the sentence: "In 100 typical users who start out the year using a given method, the number of pregnancies by the end of the year will be ____."
[c] IUD = Intrauterine device.

among the most studied drugs in history, in 1960 this was not the case. In that year, the Food and Drug Administration (FDA) released Enovid 10, the first combination oral contraceptive. This contraceptive exposed the patient to 200 mg of the progestin, norethynodrel (NOR), and 3000 μg of the estrogen, mestranol (ME), in one cycle; the resulting side effects prompted the search for better COC products. Biphasic and triphasic COCs are the most recent solutions, allowing great reductions in estrogen and progestin content. (See Table 43.2.)

There have been four generations of COCs available in the U.S. The "first-generation" COCs contained 50 to 100 μg of estrogen and 1 to 10 mg of progestin. The second generation of COCs included the sequential oral contraceptives (Oracon, C-Quens). These sequentials were highly estrogen dominant and were withdrawn from the marketplace in 1970 because of lower efficacy and associations with endometrial carcinoma.[10] The third generation of COCs contain <50 μg of estrogen and ≤1.5 mg of progestin and are designated "low-dose" COCs. The fourth-generation COCs, the biphasics and triphasics, attempt to mimic the hormonal fluctuations in a normal menstrual cycle more closely and reduce progestin metabolic effects.[11] (See Table 43.2.)

Progestin-Only Minipills

The progestin-only minipills were developed to avoid the liabilities of estrogen. (See Table 43.2.) Besides avoiding unwanted effects on lactation and possibly the nursing infant, the minipill has the added advantage of being devoid of the other undesirable effects of estrogen contained in COCs (e.g., nausea, fluid retention, breast tenderness, leukorrhea, hypermenorrhea, headaches, chloasma, hypertension, corneal edema, changes in the quality of tears that lead to visual refraction changes).[15]

Synthetic Estrogens as Contraceptives

In the U.S., COCs contain one of two synthetic estrogens, ethinyl estradiol or mestranol. Since 1970, only ethinyl estradiol has been used because mestranol is inactive and must be converted within the body to ethinyl estradiol. Mestranol 50 μg has approximately the same activity as ethinyl estradiol (EE) 35 μg.[15] In 1988 the FDA halted the production of any COC containing more than 50 μg of either estrogen since there was no increase in efficacy and a greater risk of side effects and complications.

Estrogens inhibit ovulation by suppressing hypothalamic release of FSH-RF and LRF and the subsequent pituitary release of FSH and LH (see Figure 43.1). Ovulation may be suppressed in only 95% to 98% of cycles when COCs contain ≤50 μg of estrogen. Estrogens also inhibit ovum implantation because large postcoital doses of estrogen have antiprogestational effects on the uterus. This alters secretory development resulting in areas of marked edema alternating with areas of dense cellularity.[8] In addition, large postcoital doses of estrogen can accelerate ovum transport, thereby decreasing the time available for fertilization in the fallopian tubes. Large doses of estrogen also break down the corpus luteum (i.e., luteolysis), thereby preventing implantation and placental attachment of the fertilized ovum.

Synthetic Progestins as Contraceptives

In the U.S., combination oral contraceptives contain one of the following progestins: the estranes, ethynodiol diacetate (ED), norethindrone (NE), and norethindrone acetate (NEAC); the gonanes, a mixture of equal parts of dextronorgestrel (DNG) and levonorgestrel (LNG), desogestrel (DSG), levonorgestrel and norgestimate (NGM). Dextronorgestrel appears to be progestationally inert compared to levonorgestrel.[14] As a result, dextronorgestrel was deleted

Table 43.2		Oral Contraceptives		
Product	Manufacturer	Progestin[a]		Estrogen[b]
Low-Dose COCs[c]				
Brevicon (*Blue, orange*[g])	Syntex	0.5 mg NE		35 µg
Demulen (*White, pink*[g])	Searle	1.0 mg ED		50 µg
Demulen 1/35 (*White, blue*[g])	Searle	1.0 mg ED		35 µg
Desogen (*White, green*[g])	Organon	0.15 mg DSG		30 µg
Genora 0.5/35 (*White, peach*[g])	Rugby	0.5 mg NE		35 µg
Genora 1/35 (*Pale blue, peach*[g])	Rugby	1.0 mg NE		35 µg
Genora 1/50 (*White, peach*[g])	Rugby	1.0 mg NE		50 µg[d]
Levlen (*Light orange, pink*[g])	Berlex	0.15 mg LNG		30 µg
Levora (*White, peach*[g])	Hamilton	0.15 mg LNG		30 µg
Loestrin 1/20[e] (*White*)	Parke-Davis	1.0 mg NEAC		20 µg
Loestrin 1.5/30[e] (*Green*)	Parke-Davis	1.5 mg NEAC		30 µg
Loestrin FE 1/20 (*White, brown*[g])	Parke-Davis	1.0 mg NEAC		20 µg
Loestrin FE 1.5/30 (*Green, brown*[g])	Parke-Davis	1.5 mg NEAC		30 µg
Lo/Ovral (*White, pink*[g])	Wyeth-Ayerst	0.3 mg DLNG		30 µg
Modicon (*White, green*[g])	Ortho	0.5 mg NE		35 µg
N.E.E. 1/35 (*Yellow, peach*[g])	Lexis	1.0 mg NE		35 µg
Nelova 0.5/35E (*Light yellow, white*[g])	Warner Chilcott	0.5 mg NE		35 µg
Nelova 1/35E (*Dark yellow, white*[g])	Warner Chilcott	1.0 mg NE		35 µg
Nelova 1/50M (*Light blue, white*[g])	Warner Chilcott	1.0 mg NE		50 µg[d]
Nordette (*Light orange, pink*[g])	Wyeth-Ayerst	0.15 mg LNG		30 µg
Norethin 1/35E (*White, blue*[g])	Roberts	1.0 mg NE		35 µg
Norethin 1/50 M (*White, blue*[g])	Roberts	1.0 mg NE		50 µg[d]
Norinyl 1 + 35 (*Orange, green*[g])	Syntex	1.0 mg NE		35 µg
Norinyl 1 + 50 (*White, orange*[g])	Syntex	1.0 mg NE		50 µg[d]
Ortho-Cept (*Orange, green*[g])	Ortho	0.15 mg DSG		30 µg
Ortho-Cyclen (*Blue, green*[g])	Ortho	0.25 mg NE		35 µg
Ortho-Novum 1/35 (*Peach, green*[g])	Ortho	1.0 mg NE		35 µg
Ortho-Novum 1/50 (*Yellow, green*[g])	Ortho	1.0 mg NE		50 µg[d]
Ovcon-35 (*Peach, green*[g])	Mead Johnson	0.4 mg NE		35 µg
Ovcon-50 (*Yellow, green*[g])	Mead Johnson	1.0 mg NE		50 µg
Ovral (*White, pink*[g])	Wyeth-Ayerst	0.5 mg DLNG		50 µg
Biphasic COCs				
Jenest (*White*)	Organon	0.5 mg NE (days 1–7)		35 µg
Jenest (*Peach, green*[g])	Organon	1.0 mg NE (days 8–21)		35 µg
Jenest 28 (*White, peach, green*[g])	Organon	0.5 mg NE (days 1–7) 1.0 mg NE (days 14–21)		35 µg (first 21 days)
N.E.E. 1/35 (*Yellow, peach*[g])	Lexis	1.0 mg NE		35 µg
Nelova 10/11 (*Light yellow*)	Warner Chilcott	0.5 mg NE (days 1–10)		35 µg
Nelova 10/11 (*Dark yellow, white*[g])	Warner Chilcott	1.0 mg NE (days 11–21)		35 µg
Nelova 10/11 (*Lt. yellow, dk. yellow, white*[g])	Watson	0.5 mg NE (days 1–10) 1.0 mg NE (days 11–21)		35 µg (first 21 days)
Nelova 1/50 (*Light blue, white*[g])	Watson	1.0 mg NE		50 µg[d]
Ortho Novum 10/11 (*White*)	Ortho	0.5 mg NE (days 1–10)		35 µg
Ortho Novum 10/11 (*Peach, green*[g])	Ortho	1.0 mg NE (days 11–21)		35 µg
Triphasic COCs				
Ortho Novum 7-7-7[f] (*White*) (*Light peach*) (*Peach, green*[g])	Ortho	0.5 mg NE (days 1–7) 0.75 mg NE (days 8–14) 1.0 mg NE (days 15–21)		35 µg (first 21 days)
Ortho Tri-Cyclen (*White*) (*Light blue*) (*Blue, green*[g])	Ortho	0.18 mg NGM (days 1–7) 0.215 mg NGM (days 8–14) 0.25 mg NGM (days 15–21)		35 µg 35 µg 35 µg
Tri-Levlen (*Brown*) (*White*) (*Light yellow, light green*[g])	Berlex	0.05 mg LNG (days 1–6) 0.075 mg LNG (days 7–11) 0.125 mg LNG (days 12–21)		30 µg 40 µg 30 µg
Tri-Norinyl[f] (*Blue*) (*Yellow-green*) (*Blue, orange*[g])	Syntex	0.5 mg NE (days 1–7) 1.0 mg NE (days 8–16) 0.5 mg NE (days 17–21)		35 µg (first 21 days)
Triphasil[f] (*Brown*) (*White*) (*Light yellow, light green*[g])	Wyeth-Ayerst	0.05 mg LNG (days 1–6) 0.075 mg LNG (days 7–11) 0.125 mg LNG (days 12–21)		30 µg 40 µg 30 µg

Continued

Table 43.2		Oral Contraceptives (Continued)	
Product	Manufacturer	Progestin[a]	Estrogen[b]
Minipill (Progestin-Only)			
Micronor (*Lime*)	Ortho	0.35 mg NE	
Nor-Q.D. (*Yellow*)	Syntex	0.35 mg NE	
Ovrette (*Yellow*)	Wyeth-Ayerst	0.075 mg DLNG	

[a] DLNG = dl-norgestrel; DSG = Desogestrel; ED = Ethynodiol diacetate; LNG = Levonorgestrel; NE = Norethindrone; NEAC = Norethindrone acetate.
[b] Estrogen (ethinyl estradiol) in μg.
[c] COC = Combination oral contraceptive.
[d] Estrogen (Mestranol) in mg.
[e] Also available with 75 mg ferrous fumarate; pills are brown when they contain iron.
[f] These triphasics mimic the follicular, ovulatory, and luteal phases of the menstrual cycle. Hormonal side effects due to insufficient progestin (e.g., late-cycle bleeding) are sometimes a problem. The estrogen dominance may be partly responsible for the minimal effects on lipids and the reduced prevalence of acne. Women with cardiovascular or metabolic abnormalities may benefit more from the triphasics because of reduced progestin content and the low estrogen content.
[g] Placebo for 28-day cycles.

from Lo/Ovral to create the newer COCs: Levlen, Levora, and Nordette (see Table 43.2). Norgestrel is the 13-ethyl analog of norethindrone and is shown by the Clauberg's test (which is based upon endometrial changes in immature rabbits pretreated with estrogen) to be 100 times as progestational as norethindrone. These progestins not only differ significantly in progestational potency, but also in the extent of their metabolism to estrogenic substances. Thus, progestins have both estrogenic and antiestrogenic effects. Since the progestins have a chemical structure similar to that of testosterone, they also have varying degrees of androgenic activity. (See Table 43.3).[15] Minor structural changes in all of the progestins may lead to significant changes in their progestational, estrogenic, antiestrogenic, and androgenic activities which may vary widely in effect from patient to patient. (See Table 43.4.)

Progestins hamper the transport of sperm through the cervical canal by thickening cervical mucus and disturbing the critical time sequence required for fertilization in the fallopian tube by slowing ovum transport. The increased incidence of ectopic (tubal) implantations in women using certain progestin-only contraceptives has been attributed to this latter progestational effect. Progestins also inhibit the activation of the hydrolytic spermatic enzymes required for fertilization and inhibit implantation by altering FSH and LH peaks so that progestin production by the corpus luteum is decreased. Furthermore, progestins inhibit ovulation by disturbing hypothalamic-pituitary-ovarian function and by modifying the midcycle surge of FSH and LH. The progestin-only minipills, levonorgestrel implants (Norplant), and depo-medroxyprogesterone acetate [(DMPA) (Depo-Provera Contraceptive Injection)] rely solely upon these mechanisms for their contraceptive efficacy.

Use Of Hormonal Contraceptives

Patient Qualifications

Baseline Information and Contraindications to COC Use

1. M.F., a 23-year-old, healthy nonsmoking female, wants to know if she is a good candidate for the safe use of COCs. What baseline information is needed before beginning M.F. on COCs and what contraindications to oral contraceptive therapy must be considered?

The baseline information as shown in Table 43.5 should be obtained before starting any patient on combination oral contraceptives. Contraindications to COCs are listed in Table 43.6 and Table 43.7 lists specific medical conditions of women who cannot safely use estrogens but may use progestin-only minipills, DMPA, IUDs, or barrier methods. Without this baseline information and basic

screening, management of patient problems is very difficult and serious; avoidable consequences may occur.

Combination Oral Contraceptives (COCs)

Choice

2. You determine that M.F. is a healthy, uncomplicated female. Her family and social histories are negative for major COC concerns and her health is perfect. Which COC should be selected for M.F.?

Confusion abounds in the selection of combination oral contraceptives. This arises from the multitude of COCs on the market and the lack of studies comparing one product to others. The following thought process may be helpful in simplifying the choice of a COC.

As discussed previously, it is first desirable to use a COC with ≤35 μg ethinyl estradiol. All COCs with low-dose estrogen then are evaluated based upon their progestin content. Norethindrone acetate and ethynodiol diacetate are about equally potent per unit weight with regard to progestational activity, endometrial support, and lipid metabolic effects. Since these progestins are metabolized to norethindrone,[165] they offer no significant advantages over norethindrone and all COCs containing these progestins can be deleted from the initial selection. This leaves only the estrane, norethindrone, and the gonanes, d,1-norgestrel, desogestrel, levonorgestrel, and norgestimate containing COCs, from which to choose. The d,1-norgestrel-containing COC, Ovral, is excessively potent both progestationally and estrogenically. Lo/Ovral, the only other COC containing d,1-norgestrel, contains less progestin and estrogen than Ovral; however, it has been replaced by levonorgestrel-containing products, Levlen, Levora, and Nordette, because d-norgestrel has little pharmacological activity. Ovral now is used clinically as the morning-after pill. Therefore, only COCs that contain the progestins norethindrone, desogestrel, levonorgestrel, or norgestimate usually need be considered. COCs containing desogestrel are preferred over those containing norgestimate because desogestrel is more estrogen dominant. This increases high-density lipoprotein (HDL), decreases low-density lipoprotein (LDL), and increases sex hormone binding globulin (SHBG) leading to decreased acne.[128] Norgestimate has a more complex metabolic pathway than desogestrel and is preferred clinically by many practitioners, although it appears unlikely that clinical differences between the two levonorgestrel analogs are of any significance.

In current clinical practice, most health care providers choose a COC that has either ≤1 mg of norethindrone, ≤0.15 mg of desogestrel or levonorgestrel, or ≤0.25 mg of norgestimate. It also

Table 43.3	Progestin Pharmacology and Contraceptive Pill Activity Listed According to Estrogen Content and Endometrial Potency[j]					
Drug[a]	Endometrial Activity: % spotting and bleeding in 3rd cycle of use[b]	Estrogenic Activity: μg ethinyl estradiol equivalents/day[c]	Progestational Activity: mg norethindrone equivalents/day[d]	Androgenic Activity: mg methyl testosterone equivalents/28 days[e]	Estrogenic Effect of Progestin[f]	Anti-Estrogenic Effect of Progestin[g]
50 μg Estrogen						
Ovral (DLNG)	4.5	42	1.3	0.80	0.00	18.5
Genora 1/50 Norethin 1/50 M Norinyl 1 + 50 Ortho-Novum 1/50 (NE)	10.6	32	1	0.34	1.00	2.5
Ovcon 50 (NE)	11.9	50[h]	1	0.34	1.00	2.5
Demulen 50 (ED)	13.9	26	1.4	0.21	3.44	1.0
<50 μg Estrogen Monophasic						
Desogen/Ortho-Cept (DSG)	9.9	30	1.5	0.17	——	Weak
Lo-Ovral (DLNG)	9.6	25	0.8	0.46	0.00	18.5
Ovcon 35 (NE)	11.0	40[h]	0.4	0.15	1.00	2.5
Levlen/Levora/Nordette (LNG)	14.0	25	0.8	0.46	0.00	18.5
Ortho-Cyclen (NGM)	14.3	35	0.3	0.18	——	Weak
Brevicon/Modicon/Nelova 0.5/35E (NE)	14.6	42	0.5	0.17	1.00	2.5
Genora 1/35 Nelova 1/35E Norinyl 1 + 35 Ortho-Novum 1/35 (NE)	14.7	38	1.0	0.34	1.00	2.5
Loestrin 1.5/30 (NEAC)	25.2	14	1.7	0.8	1.52	25.0
Loestrin 1/20 (NEAC)	29.7	13	1.2	0.53	1.52	25.0
Demulen 1/35 (ED)	37.4	19	1.4	0.21	3.44	1.0
<50 μg Estrogen Multiphasic						
Jenest 7/14 NE	14.1	39	0.8	0.28	1.00	2.5
Nelova/Ortho-Novum 10/11 (NE)	19.6	40	0.8	0.25	1.00	2.5
Ortho-Novum 7-7-7 (NE)	12.2	48[h]	0.8	0.26	1.00	2.5
Ortho Tri-Cyclen (NGM)	17.5	35	0.3	0.15	——	Weak
Triphasil Tri-Levlen (LNG)	15.1[i]	28[h]	0.5	0.29	0.00	18.5
Tri-Norinyl (NE)	14.7	40[h]	0.7	0.24	1.00	2.5
Progestin Only						
Ovrette (DLNG)	34.9	0	0.08	0.12	0.00	18.5
Micronor/Nor Q.D.	42.3	1	0.12	0.12	1.00	2.5

[a] DLNG = dl-norgestrel; NE = Norethindrone; ED= Ethynodiol diacetate; DSG = Desogestrel; LNG = Levonorgestrel; NGM = Norgestimate; NEAC = Norethindrone-acetate.

[b] Information submitted to the U.S. FDA by the manufacturer. These rates are derived from separate studies conducted by different investigators in several population groups, and therefore, a precise comparison cannot be made.

[c] Estrogenic activity of entire tablet—mouse uterine assay.[15,209,210]

[d] Induction of glycogen vacuoles in human endometrium.[15,211,213]

[e] Rat ventral prostate assay.[15,213]

[f] Relative estrogen potencies of progestins on rat vaginal histology.[8,214]

[g] Relative anti-estrogenic potencies of progestins.[8,148]

[h] Estimated.

[i] Information submitted to the Health Protection Branch of Canada.

[j] Adapted from reference 15.

is desirable to choose a COC that contains ≤35 μg of ethinyl estradiol. Therefore, one of the following COCs could be selected for most patients (listed in order of increasing progestational activity): Ovcon-35, Brevicon/Genora/Modicon/Nelova 0.5/35E, Tri-Norinyl, Ortho-Novum 7/7/7, Tri-Levlen/Triphasil, Ortho-Tri-Cyclen, Genora/Nelova/Norethin/Norinyl 1 + 35 or Ortho-Novum 1 + 35, Levlen/Levora/Nordette, Desogen/Ortho-Cept, or Ortho-Cyclen.

The COCs listed first have less progestational activity and presumably fewer side effects of progestational excess. For patients with significant risks for cardiovascular or carbohydrate metabolic abnormalities, norethindrone- or desogestrel-containing products are preferable because they have little effect on carbohydrate metabolism[76,78] or the cardiovascular system. The effects of other progestins are unknown.

Many refinements on the above COC list and selection criteria are found in three major clinical management texts.[8,9,15]

Table 43.8 may be used to select an initial contraceptive pill for most patients and to change pills when side effects necessitate an alternative choice. According to section B of the guide, any pill containing less than 50 μg of ethinyl estradiol can be used for M.F. since she is a healthy, uncomplicated female.

Table 43.4	Estrogenic, Progestational, and Androgenic Side Effects of COCs[a,209]
Estrogenic Side Effects	
Nausea	↑ breast ductal and fatty tissue
Breast neoplasia	Fluid retention
Cyclic weight gain from fluid	Leukorrhea
Cervical erosion or ectopia	Thromboembolic complications
Pulmonary emboli	Cerebrovascular accidents
Hepatocellular adenomas	Hepatocellular cancer
↑ in bile cholesterol	Leiomyomata growth
Telangiectasia	Hypertension
Progestational and Androgenic Side Effects of Progestins	
↑ appetite	Weight gain
Depression, fatigue, lethargy	↓ libido
↑ breast alveolar tissue	Breast tenderness
Acne, oily skin	Diabetogenic effect
Hirsutism	Sebaceous cysts
Pruritus	↑ LDL and ↓ HDL cholesterol
Headaches	Hypertension

[a] COC = Combination oral contraceptive; HDL = High-density lipoprotein; LDL = Low-density lipoprotein.

Patient Instructions

3. What instructions should be given to M.F. about her COC?

When to Start COCs. M.F. should start the first cycle of COCs according to the manufacturers' package instructions or according to one of the two following recommendations:

1. Take the first tablet in the COC packet on the first day of menses; this avoids the risk of early ovulation and the need to use alternative methods of contraception (e.g., condoms, foam) concurrently.

2. Take the first tablet in the COC packet on the first Sunday after the beginning of menstruation and use an alternative method of contraception for the first seven COC days (according to various manufacturers).

Need For A Backup Method. Some clinicians recommend an alternative method of contraception for the entire first cycle.[8] Others claim that alternative methods of birth control are unnecessary if the COC is started on or before the sixth menstrual day.[15]

Choice of 21-Day versus 28-Day Cycle. Many clinicians prefer the use of 28-day cycle COCs to minimize confusion. After taking the last tablet of a 28-day pack of COCs, patients should be instructed to begin a new pack the next day. However, when continuous ovarian suppression is indicated to treat estrogen-dependent disorders such as endometriosis, the 21-day-cycle COCs are preferred to facilitate taking active tablets only. Alternatively, the dispensing pharmacist could remove the placebo tablets from 28-day cycle packets.

Optimal Time To Take COC. M.F. should take the COC tablets at the exact (i.e., hour and minute) same time each day, preferably in the evening before bedtime to optimize contraceptive efficacy and minimize side effects such as nausea, breast tenderness, or chloasma (i.e., a skin pigmentary change that is exacerbated by exposure to sunlight when serum concentrations of estrogens are high).

Avoid Chloasma. When sunbathing, M.F. should use a sunscreen with a sun protection factor (SPF) of 15 to help prevent chloasma.[15] In general, she should avoid sunbathing and wear protective wide-rim hats when sun exposure cannot be avoided.

Anticipate Drug Interactions with COCs. Before taking a new prescription medication, M.F. should ask her physician or pharmacist whether it could interfere or interact with her COC.

Importance of Checkups. M.F. should maintain scheduled clinic or physician appointments and return for a checkup three months after beginning a new COC. Her breasts should be examined professionally once yearly.

What To Do If Pills Are Missed. If M.F. forgets to take one pill, she must take it as soon as she remembers and then take the next pill at the regular time that day; alternative methods of birth control are unnecessary.

If she misses two tablets in a row in week one or two of her pack, she must take two pills on the day she remembers and two pills the next day. She should use an alternative method of contraception for seven days after missing the pills.

If M.F. misses two tablets in a row in the third week, (for day 1 starters) she must discard the rest of the pack, start a new pack on that same day, and use an alternative method of contraception for seven days after she missed the pills, or (for Sunday starters) keep taking one pill every day until Sunday, start a new pack on Sunday, and use an alternative method of contraception for seven days after missing the pills. She may not have her period this month but this is expected.

If M.F. misses three or more pills in a row during the first three weeks, (for day 1 starters), she must discard the rest of her pack and start a new pack that same day, or (for Sunday starters) keep taking one pill every day until Sunday, start a new pack on Sunday, and use an alternative method of contraception for seven days after missing the pills. She may not have a period this month.

If she becomes sick and has severe diarrhea or vomiting for several days, she should use another method of contraception until her next period.[8]

Table 43.5	Patient Data to Be Considered Before Treatment with COCs[a]
Menstrual History	
Age of menarche	
Date of LMP	
Duration of average menses	
Regularity of menses or cycle length from month to month	
Incidence of spotting (droplets of blood) and BTB in the time interval between periods	
Incidence of premenstrual tension symptoms: breast tenderness and enlargement, nausea, fluid retention and bloating, weight gain, headaches, depression, anxiety, tension, irritability, or inability to concentrate	
Contraceptive History	
Use, response, side effects, and compliance	
Routine Physical Examination Including	
BP	
Breast examination (teach patient to do self-breast examination)	
Pelvic examination	
Pap smear	
Liver function evaluation	
Family history	
Social history	

[a] BP = Blood pressure; BTB = Breakthrough bleeding; COCs = Combination oral contraceptives; LMP = Last menstrual period.

Table 43.6 — Contraindications to COCs[a,e]

Absolute Contraindications[b]
Thromboembolic disorder[b]
Cerebrovascular accident[b]
Coronary artery disease[b]
Known or suspected carcinoma of the breast[b]
Known or suspected estrogen-dependent neoplasia[b]
Benign or malignant liver tumor[b]
Pregnancy
Known impaired liver function at present time

Strong Relative Contraindications
Severe headaches
Hypertension with resting diastolic BP >90 or resting BP >140 on ≥3 separate visits
Diabetes
Active gallbladder disease
Mononucleosis
SS disease or SC disease
Elective major surgery planned in next 4 weeks or major surgery requiring immobilization
Long-leg cast or major injury to lower leg
>40 years of age; accompanied by a second risk factor for the development of cardiovascular disease
>35 years of age and currently a heavy smoker (>15 cigarettes/day)[c]

Other Possible Relative Contraindications
Prediabetes or a strong family history of diabetes
Previous cholestasis during pregnancy, congenital hyperbilirubenemia (Gilbert's disease)
Undiagnosed, abnormal vaginal bleeding
≥45 years of age[c]
Impaired liver function within past year
Completion of term pregnancy within past 10–14 days[c]
Weight gain of ≥10 lb while on COCs[c]
Failure to have established regular menstrual cycles[d]
Cardiac or renal disease[b,c]
Conditions likely to make patient unreliable (mental retardation)
Lactation[c]
Use of rifampin unless the woman is willing to use a backup contraceptive

May Initiate COCs for Women with these Problems and Observe Carefully for Worsening or Improvement of the Problem
Family history of death of a parent or sibling due to MI before age 50. MI in a mother or sister is especially significant and indicates a "coronary risk"
Family history of hyperlipidemia (check 14-hour fasting lipids first)
Depression[c]
Chloasma or hair loss related to pregnancy[b, c]
Asthma[c]
Epilepsy[c]
Varicose veins[c]

[a] BP = Blood pressure; COC = Combination oral contraceptive; MI = Myocardial infarction; SC = Sickle c; SS = Sickle cell.
[b] History of this condition also is considered a contraindication, relative contraindication, or caution.
[c] Refers to contraindication to COCs which may not be a contraindication to progestin-only mini-pills.
[d] There is no convincing evidence to suggest COC use increases a woman's difficulty of becoming pregnant once COC use is discontinued than if a COC had never been used.
[e] Adapted from reference 8.

M.F. should examine her breasts for lumps or other changes once each month when she starts a new pill pack and be aware of Early Danger Signs (see Table 43.9).

Clinical Use of Progestin-Only Minipills

Minipill versus COCs in Breast-Feeding

4. P.K., a 39-year-old, black, female, plans to breast-feed her newborn infant and undertake some type of contraception following her discharge from the maternity ward. Her past experience with condoms and concurrent spermicidal foams or gels resulted in itching and burning, and IUDs caused severe cramping and bleeding. She has a strong family history of cardiac disease and smokes 2 packs of cigarettes a day. What are the advantages of the minipill as a contraceptive for P.K.? Are there any alternative methods of contraception for P.K.?

Progestins, unlike estrogens, do not inhibit the binding of prolactin to its receptors; therefore, they do not interfere with the quantity of milk produced by a nursing mother.[160] Thus, an oral contraceptive containing only progestin is preferred for a patient who plans to breast-feed her infant. Progesterone, however, may decrease the protein quality of the nursing mother's milk.[161] Depo-Provera and Norplant are viable alternatives (see Questions 34 and 35).

For patients without contraindications to COCs, the American Academy of Pediatrics considers COCs to be compatible with breast-feeding[212] and, clinically, the majority of patients can successfully breast-feed while taking COCs. Nevertheless, many clinicians do not recommend the use of COCs in nursing mothers because the infant will be exposed to the estrogen component. When using a COC containing 50 µg of ethinyl estradiol, 600 mL of breast milk contains 3 to 6 µg of estrogen in nonovulating women and 6 to 12 µg in ovulating women. Withdrawal vaginal bleeding in female infants and cases of infant gynecomastia that resolved upon discontinuation of the COC have been reported with the high-dose COCs. Most of these reports were anecdotal and have not been corroborated in women using low-dose COCs.[8] Progesterone, which usually is not present in the milk of oral contraceptive users, is metabolized easily by the infant.[162] If one accepts the remote risk that the small amounts of estrogen and progestin from COCs could have some effect on infants, the progestin-only minipill (e.g., Micronor, Nor-Q.D.) would be the most desirable oral contraceptive for nursing mothers.

The minipill is devoid of the nuisance side effects caused by COC estrogen (e.g., nausea, fluid retention, breast tenderness, hypermenorrhea, headaches, chloasma, corneal edema, and changes in the quality of tears that may lead to visual refraction changes). More importantly, estrogen-mediated hypertension and clotting factor changes will be avoided in this smoker who has a strong family history of cardiovascular disease.

Advantages

5. A clinician asks if the progestin-only minipill is less likely to produce problems with progestational excess than the COCs. What is your reply?

The progestin content of the minipill is less than the amount commonly found in COCs. The minipill, Ovrette, contains 0.075 mg of d,1-norgestrel. This small amount of progestin in Ovrette is only 20% of the progestin content in the COC, Ovral; approximately equivalent to 33% of the progestin (levonorgestrel) in Nordette; and about 55% of the progestin a patient taking Triphasil would ingest in 28 days. The Nor-Q.D. and Micronor minipills

Table 43.7 — Women Who Cannot Take Estrogens Safely[a,b,209]

History of cerebrovascular accident	Ischemic heart disease
Uncontrolled hypertension	IDDM with vascular disease
Classic migraine worsened by estrogen	Breast cancer history
Estrogen-dependent neoplasia	Impaired liver function
DVT	Smokers >35 years old

[a] Consider progestin-only minipills, DMPA, Norplant, IUDs, or barrier methods of contraception for these patients.
[b] DVT = Deep vein thrombosis; IDDM = Insulin-dependent diabetes mellitus.

Table 43.8	Guide for Choosing an Oral Contraceptive[a,209]

Choose Progestin-Only Minipill if the Patient Has/Is:[b]

History of CVA	Current liver impairment
Ischemic heart disease	Current liver tumor
Uncontrolled hypertension	Current DVT
IDDM with vascular disease	Smoker >35 years old
Migraine worsened by ethinyl estradiol	Breast-feeding

Most Women Can Use Any BCP with <50 μg Ethinyl Estradiol BCP[c] Safely, However

Prescribe Loestrin 1/20 if patient is
    40–50 years old and need to minimize the risk of thrombosis
    Poorly controlled diabetic
    Heavy smoker
    Perimenopausal

Prescribe Levlen/Levlor/Nordette, Lo-Ovral to avoid

Nausea	Hypermenorrhea
Breast tenderness	Chloasma
Vascular headaches	Hypertension
Leukorrhea	Visual changes

Prescribe Levlen/Levora/Nordette, Lo-Ovral, Desogen/Ortho-Cept, Ortho-Cyclen to avoid

Spotting	Dysmenorrhea
Break through bleeding	

Prescribe Desogen/Ortho-Cept, Ortho-Cyclen, Ortho Tri-Cyclen, Desogen/Ortho-Cept, Ovcon-35, Brevicon/Modicon to avoid the side effects of

Acne	Sebaceous cysts
Hirsutism	Weight gain
Oily skin	

Prescribe Desogen/Ortho-Cept, Ortho-Cyclen, Ortho Tri-Cyclen, Desogen/Ortho-Cept, Ovcon-35, Brevicon/Modicon
    If family history of atherosclerotic cardiovascular disease
    For most favorable lipid profile

---

[a] BCP = Birth-control pill; CVA = Cerebrovascular accident; DVT = Deep venous thrombosis; IDDM = Insulin-dependent diabetes mellitus.

[b] Norplant, Depo-Provera, IUDs, etc. also may be used.

[c] i.e., Norinyl 1 + 35/Ortho-Novum 1/35, Ortho-Novum 7/7/7, Levlen/Levora/Nordette, Tri-Levlen/Triphasil.

contain 0.35 mg of norethindrone which is 47% of the progestin contained in either Norinyl 1 + 35 or Ortho-Novum 1 + 35; 62% of the progestin in Ortho-Novum 7/7/7; and 65% of the progestin a patient taking Tri-Norinyl would ingest in 28 days.

The minipill user must take one pharmacologically active tablet at exactly the same time daily compared to 21 active tablets per cycle with the COCs. The common symptoms of progestational excess (e.g., tiredness, fatigue, depression, alopecia, acne, appetite increase, early cycle spotting or breakthrough bleeding, moniliasis, oligomenorrhea, amenorrhea, hirsutism) should be less because of the reduced dose of progestin in the minipills. Signs of progestin deficiency (e.g., late cycle spotting or breakthrough bleeding, dysmenorrhea, amenorrhea), however, may occur with the minipill. Just how much safer minipills are to use than COCs has not been established.[8] Nevertheless, absence of estrogen liability and greatly reduced progestin content suggest a substantial reduction in possible side effects as well as oral contraceptive contraindications.

6. Why is the progestin-only minipill a good oral contraceptive choice for P.K.?

Spermicidal agents and intrauterine devices are unacceptable for P.K. because of her history of adverse reactions with these contraceptive methods. The COCs also would be somewhat undesirable in this older, black, smoker with a significant family history of cardiovascular disease. Since the minipills do not contain estrogens and contain only small amounts of progestin, they should not expose P.K. to the cardiovascular risks attributed to the estrogen component in COCs.

Furthermore, P.K. meets many of the characteristics that generally are considered to be ideal for patients who benefit the most from progestin-only minipills.[8] She wants to use oral contraceptives, is more than 30 years old, smokes more than 14 cigarettes/day, is at greater risk for cardiovascular disease because of her family history, prefers oral contraceptive medication immediately postpartum (patients usually must wait 10 to 14 days postpartum before COCs are initiated), and is nursing her baby. Although P.K. does not have a problem with headaches, hypertension, or varicose veins, other patients with these problems would be better candidates for the minipill than for COCs.

Disadvantages

7. What disadvantages of the minipill should you discuss with P.K.?

The minipills, with a failure rate of 1.1% to 3.0%, are less effective than the COCs which have a failure rate of 0.0% to 3.0%. (See Table 43.1.) When these progestin-only minipills are compared, Ovrette seems to have one-half the pregnancy rate associated with Micronor or Nor-Q.D. minipills after two years of use.[163] Approximately 40% of women on minipills consistently have ovulatory cycles and 20% shift back and forth between ovulatory and anovulatory cycles.

Irregular menses, decreased duration and amount of menstrual flow, spotting, and amenorrhea occur frequently in women treated with the minipill. Patients often are concerned that they may be pregnant. Some women may have as few as two menstrual periods annually; if no period occurs within 45 days or more, patients should have a pregnancy test.[8]

The high incidence of irregular menses associated with the minipill may mask underlying pathology.[8] Minipills should be avoided if there is a history of gestational diabetes, mononucleosis, or ectopic pregnancy.[164] (See Table 43.10.)

Patient Instructions

8. What instructions should P.K. receive regarding the use of a minipill?

P.K. should be instructed to begin using the minipill as detailed in Table 43.11.

Managing Patients' Problems

Drug Interactions

9. Antibacterials. M.H. is a 26-year-old female whose last menstrual period (LMP) was 7 weeks ago. She has a history of regular menstrual cycles both before and during the use of COCs. Six weeks ago she developed an *Escherichia coli* urinary tract infection which was treated with ampicillin in 500 mg QID for 7 days. This coincided with the first 7 tablets of her COC cycle. She has been taking Norinyl/Ortho-Novum 1 + 35 for 3 years and tetracycline 250 mg QD for acne. What is the clinical significance of the potential drug interactions in M.H.?

Table 43.9	Pill Early Danger Signs (ACHES)
5 Signals	**Possible Problem**
Abdominal pain (severe)	Gallbladder disease, hepatic adenoma, blood clot, pancreatitis
Chest pain (severe), shortness of breath, or coughing up blood	Blood clot in lungs or myocardial infarction
Headaches (severe)	Stroke, hypertension, or migraine headache
Eye problems: blurred vision, flashing lights, or blindness	Stroke, hypertension, or temporary vascular problem
Severe leg pain (calf or thigh)	Blood clot in legs

Table 43.10	Disadvantages of Minipill (Progestin Only)

Less effective than COCs[a]

High incidence of irregular menses

Amenorrhea

↓ menstrual flow and amount

Spotting

Concern about becoming pregnant

[a] COCs = Combination oral contraceptives.

Ethinyl estradiol is conjugated in the liver, excreted in the bile, hydrolyzed by intestinal bacteria, and reabsorbed as active drug. Antibiotics, by reducing the population of intestinal bacteria, interrupt the enterohepatic circulation of the estrogen resulting in a decreased concentration of circulating estrogen. The significance of similar antibiotic interactions with contraceptive progestins is less clear. Although this proposed mechanism for the drug interaction is not firmly established, a variety of antibiotics have been reported to decrease oral contraceptive efficacy.[130–140,213]

Ampicillin has long been known to affect plasma and urinary estrogen concentrations in women[141–143] and more than 25 cases of unintended pregnancies have been reported in women taking concurrent oral contraceptives and ampicillin. This drug interaction of ampicillin with oral contraceptives has not always been evident in controlled clinical studies. Hansten's analysis of these studies, however, concludes that the disparate results are not necessarily contradictory.[141] For example, if ampicillin-induced contraceptive failure occurs only occasionally, clinical studies involving 10 to 15 patients might not involve a large enough study population to detect the interaction. If the ampicillin effect is transient (as noted in one study),[141] the serum sample may have been obtained too late to detect changes in serum hormone concentrations. Hansten further notes that evidence was present for this drug interaction even in those clinical studies that failed to prove the interaction. For example, in one of the studies that could not document the drug interaction, 2 of 11 women receiving oral contraceptives developed breakthrough bleeding while on ampicillin, and none of the subjects developed menstrual irregularities when placebo was substituted for the ampicillin.[144]

Whether ampicillin inhibits oral contraceptive efficacy is not certain; however, all clinical data are consistent with the premise that ampicillin occasionally impairs oral contraceptive efficacy. It would be prudent to use supplemental methods of contraception during cycles in which ampicillin is used. In this particular case, M.H. should discontinue her COC until the results of a reliable monoclonal antibody pregnancy test or serum pregnancy test are available. If she is pregnant, harm to the fetus from the COC or antibiotics is unlikely (see Question 22).

Theoretically, other antimicrobials with significant effects on intestinal bacterial flora also could affect contraceptive efficacy by interfering with the enterohepatic recycling of exogenous estrogen and possibly progestin. Several cases of unintended pregnancies and menstrual irregularities have been reported following the use of tetracyclines during treatment with oral contraceptives.[136,144,145] Likewise, unintended pregnancies have been reported in women taking COCs following the use of cephalosporins, chloramphenicol (Chloromycetin), dapsone, erythromycin, isoniazid (INH), nitrofurantoin (Furadantin), phenoxymethylpenicillin, sulfonamides, and trimethoprim-sulfamethoxazole (Bactrim).[132–135,144,145]

A practical approach to managing COC patients taking antibiotics would be to educate patients as shown in Table 43.12.[213]

The probability of a clinically significant drug interaction between COCs and antimicrobials depends upon numerous factors:

the hormonal content of the oral contraceptive relative to the requirements of the patient; the dose and duration of use of the interacting drug; variation in patient response to bacterial flora alteration; and fertility of the couple involved.[141] The number and complexity of these variables make prediction of outcome in a specific patient exceedingly difficult. Even if a drug produces a several-fold increase in unwanted pregnancies in women taking oral contraceptives, the likelihood of pregnancy in a given patient still will be very low. For these reasons, reports of interactions between nitrofurantoin and oral contraceptives could be anecdotal and unfounded.[146] Long-term, low-dose tetracycline use for M.H.'s acne is unlikely to interfere with her contraceptive efficacy, but data to support this supposition are unavailable. Topical antibiotics often can control acne and are viable alternatives to oral tetracycline.[140]

10. Liver Enzyme Induction. **S.R., a 22-year-old female, is taking phenytoin (Dilantin) 300 mg/day, phenobarbital 120 mg/day, and carbamazepine (Tegretol) 200 mg TID. Her serum concentrations of these drugs have been consistently in the therapeutic range for at least 2 years, and she has not experienced seizures for 18 months. Is S.R. a good candidate for COCs?**

In patients with seizure disorders, COCs may increase the incidence of seizures, perhaps by increasing fluid retention.[149] Therefore, patients with poor seizure control might not be good candidates for COCs. There also is one report that COCs might increase serum phenytoin concentrations substantially.[143]

The efficacy of COCs was not decreased significantly by other drugs in earlier years because of their large hormonal content. Because the estrogen and progestin concentrations of COCs have gradually been decreasing, and as a result, reports of menstrual irregularities (e.g., spotting, breakthrough bleeding) and unintended pregnancies due to drug interactions have been increasing.[147,148]

Besides carbamazepine and phenytoin, other anticonvulsants such as butabarbital, ethosuximide, phenobarbital, and primidone (notably, not felbamate, gabapentin or valproic acid),[142,147,149] and the anti-infectives griseofulvin[133,150] and rifampin[133,151] also may significantly induce liver enzymes that may result in reduced contraceptive estrogen and, possibly, contraceptive progestin levels. This will present clinically as spotting or breakthrough bleeding and sometimes pregnancy. (See Table 43.13.)

S.R. should be started on Ovcon-50 and monitored carefully for spotting or breakthrough bleeding and seizures. COCs should be discontinued if seizures occur or bleeding irregularities continue

Table 43.11	Minipill Patient Instructions

1) Begin the minipill on the first day of menstrual bleeding

2) Take one pill every day at exactly the same time

3) Use a secondary method of contraception for the first two months

4) Use a secondary means of contraception at midcycle every month (i.e., about 4 days before and 4 days after possible ovulation) to improve effectiveness

5) Take a pill as soon as she remembers that she missed 1 and take the next pill at her regular time; use a secondary means of contraception until her next period. If she misses 2 pills, take 2 when she remembers, 2 the next day, and use another method of contraception until her next period

6) Use a back-up method of contraception for 2 days if she is more than 3 hours late taking a minipill

7) Examine her breasts for lumps or other changes once each month when she starts a new pill pack

8) Be aware of the Pill Early Danger Signs, "ACHES,"[8] and immediately notify her practitioner if any are noted (See Table 43.9)

| Table 43.12 | Managing COC Patients Taking Antibiotics[a] |

Category A: Likely to Reduce COC Effectiveness
  Rifampin
Category B: Associated with COC Failure in ≥3 Case Reports
  Ampicillin, amoxicillin, metronidazole, tetracycline
Category C: Associated with COC Failure in at Least 1 Case Report
  Cephalexin, clindamycin, dapsone, erythromycin, griseofulvin, isoniazid, phenoxymethylpenicillin, trimethoprim

[a] COCs = Combination oral contraceptives.

for more than three months. Unlike many drug classes which are carefully dosed to maintain a therapeutic range of monitored blood levels, contraceptive estrogen and progestin blood levels are obtained only in clinical drug studies. Therefore, patients are managed by monitoring side effects and especially menstrual pattern changes. It is no wonder, therefore, that the drug interaction literature is less than satisfactory and that patient management is at best haphazard. Because of this uncertainty, the estrogen and/or progestin content of the oral contraceptive is increased which usually necessitates a product change which leads to patient confusion, doubt about the efficacy of the method, and often, more side effects. In the case of systemic antibiotics at therapeutic doses, a backup method of contraception is recommended by many practitioners until menses occurs.

11. Breakthrough Bleeding, Spotting, and Amenorrhea. V.S. returns to the family planning clinic after taking Ovcon-35 for 2 months. She had been started on Ovcon-35 to help with her acne, since this preparation has only 0.4 mg of norethindrone which results in an estrogen dominant COC. Her only complaints are spotting and occasional breakthrough bleeding at various times during her last 2 menstrual cycles. What action should be taken to correct V.S.'s bleeding pattern?

Generally, most clinicians will continue with the same COC for at least three months if irregular bleeding is the only complaint. Intermenstrual bleeding that requires a pad or tampon is designated breakthrough bleeding, while a lesser amount of intermenstrual bleeding is called spotting. Intermenstrual bleeding is the most frequent explanation for the discontinuation of oral contraception.

Early-cycle intermenstrual bleeding that usually starts before the fourteenth day of the menstrual cycle (or never ceases completely after menses) usually is due to insufficient estrogen. Late-cycle intermenstrual bleeding, occurring after day 14, is thought to be due to insufficient progestational support of the endometrium. Intermenstrual bleeding episodes gradually decrease until a plateau is reached in the second, third, or fourth cycle of COC use. Other causes of intermenstrual bleeding can be the result of progressive endometrial atrophy over many months of COC use or secondary to drug interactions (see Question 9).[15]

The balance between estrogen and progestin components in a COC will determine its endometrial activity and, therefore, its liability to cause intermenstrual bleeding problems. (See Table 43.3.) For V.S., if her intermenstrual bleeding irregularities continue late in her cycle after three months, another COC with the same estrogen dose and a larger amount of norethindrone should be prescribed. A desogestrel-, levonorgestrel-, or norgestimate-containing COC that has more progestational activity on the endometrium is another alternative.[15] Desogen/Ortho-Cept would be a good choice since progestational activity would be increased and estrogenic activity would be maintained with minimal androgenic liability.

If a patient develops intermenstrual bleeding early in the cycle after many months of use, giving seven days of ethinyl estradiol

20 µg along with the first seven days of one COC cycle usually is enough to alleviate this problem.[69] If she develops amenorrhea after several COC cycles, pregnancy should be ruled out. Subsequently, ethinyl estradiol 20 µg can be added to her COC for three months to build up her endometrium.[69]

12. Biphasic and Triphasic COCs. Why is Desogen/Ortho-Cept a better choice for V.S. than a biphasic or triphasic COC? How do the biphasic COCs differ from the triphasics? What are the advantages and disadvantages of the triphasic COCs relative to other oral contraceptives?

Due to metabolic and physiologic effects related to the progestin component of COCs, the biphasic and triphasic products were formulated to contain less progestin overall. These products attempt to provide adequate endometrial support while also providing adequate contraception.[11]

Currently, Nelova 10/11, Ortho-Novum 10/11, and Jenest 28 are the only *biphasic COCs* marketed in the U.S. The "10/11" biphasic product contains a 10-day regimen of Modicon followed by an 11-day regimen of Ortho-Novum 1 + 35. Unfortunately, the biphasic 10/11 results in more "periovulatory" (days 11 to 17 of a normal 28-day cycle) and intermenstrual bleeding than either Modicon or Ortho-Novum 1 + 35 because it does not provide adequate endometrial support.[11,15] Jenest 28 is a "7/14" product with the equivalent of 7 days of Modicon followed by 14 days of Ortho-Novum 1/35; it also may fail to provide endometrial support.

The *triphasic COCs* (i.e., Tri-Norinyl, Ortho-Novum 7/7/7, Tri-Levlen, Triphasil, Ortho Tri-Cyclen) mimic the follicular, ovula-

Table 43.13	Oral Contraceptive Drug Interactions[a]
Interacting Drug	**Net Effect**

Drugs Which May Reduce COC Enterohepatic Circulation

Interacting Drug	Net Effect
Ampicillin[130–133,141,142,146,148]	Spotting, BTB, pregnancy
Cephalosporins[142,145]	Spotting, BTB, pregnancy
Chloramphenicol[137]	Spotting, BTB, pregnancy
Dapsone[142]	Spotting, BTB, pregnancy
Erythromycin[134,142]	Spotting, BTB, pregnancy
Isoniazid[134,137,138,152]	Spotting, BTB, pregnancy
Phenoxymethyl penicillin[134,142]	Spotting, BTB, pregnancy
Sulfonamides[142,206]	Spotting, BTB, pregnancy
Tetracyclines[136,142,145]	Spotting, BTB, pregnancy
TMP-SMX[132–135,142,145]	Spotting, BTB, pregnancy

Drugs Which May Induce COC Liver Enzymatic Metabolism

Interacting Drug	Net Effect
Butabarbital[142,147,149]	Spotting, BTB, pregnancy
Carbamazepine[142,147,149]	Spotting, BTB, pregnancy
Ethosuximide[142,147,149]	Spotting, BTB, pregnancy
Griseofulvin[133,150]	Spotting, BTB, pregnancy
Mephobarbital[142,147,149]	Spotting, BTB, pregnancy
Phenobarbital or primidone[142,147,149]	Spotting, BTB, pregnancy
Phenytoin[142,147,149]	Spotting, BTB, pregnancy
Rifampin[133–140,147,149,151]	Spotting, BTB, pregnancy

Miscellaneous Drug Interactions with COCs

Interacting Drug	Net Effect
Anticoagulants[153,154]	↓ anticoagulation
Benzodiazepines[155,156]	Enhanced benzodiazepine effect
Phenytoin[149]	↑ serum phenytoin
Prednisolone[157]	50% reduction in prednisolone clearance
Theophylline[158]	33% reduction in theophylline clearance
Insulin[159]	19% require ↑ insulin dosage

[a] BTB = Breakthrough bleeding; COC = Combination oral contraceptives; TMP-SMX = Trimethoprim-sulfamethoxazole.

tory, and luteal phases of the menstrual cycle fairly well and all appear to support the endometrium more consistently than the biphasic COCs (see Table 43.3).[15] There are no studies, however, that show a relative superiority of one triphasic over another. The identically formulated triphasics, Triphasil and Tri-Levlen, have been evaluated more extensively (77 studies involving 2931 women) than the other triphasics.[11] The triphasic, Ortho Tri-Cyclen, has been evaluated extensively and is less androgenic than the other triphasics.[128]

The progestin content of the triphasics, as well as that of the biphasics, is substantially less than that of other COCs. Although the reduced progestin content is desirable, hormonal side effects due to insufficient progestin sometimes are a factor in women receiving triphasic COCs. Women, such as V.S., with side effects related to progestin deficiency (e.g., late-cycle bleeding) or conditions necessitating progestin dominance (e.g., benign breast disease) may do better with monophasic COCs.[27] Women with cardiovascular or metabolic abnormalities, however, may benefit more from the triphasics due to the reduced progestin content.[27]

The estrogen dominance of the triphasics may be partly responsible for their minimal effects on lipids,[38,77] and for the reduced prevalence of acne associated with their use.[127] (See Question 32.) Among the liabilities of estrogen dominance are breast tenderness and headaches that diminish with continued use.[38,126] Menstrual bleeding during triphasic use is variable; it seems to be excessive[38] in some and diminished in others.[11]

Probably the largest drawback associated with triphasic COC use is the confusion caused by the lack of a uniform set of patient instructions for the different triphasic COCs. Ortho Tri-Cyclen, Tri-Levlen, and Triphasil instruct patients to take the first tablet in the packet on the first day of menstrual flow, whereas the other triphasic products instruct patients to start on Sunday if menstrual flow begins on Sunday, or on the following Sunday if menstrual flow begins Monday through Saturday (also see Question 3). Substitution of one triphasic COC for another is further complicated by the different colored tablets in each of the three different phases and differences in packaging.

Drug interactions (see Question 9) with the triphasics may lead more easily to spotting, breakthrough bleeding, ovulation, and pregnancy than with other COCs due to the lower hormonal content of the triphasics. Patients should be instructed to compulsively take their triphasics at the same time each day and always question the possible interaction of any other medicine with their triphasic COCs.

Major COC Risks

13. Cervical Dysplasia and Cervical Cancer. M.F., the uncomplicated patient described in Question 2, has an older sister who had cervical dysplasia that progressed to carcinoma *in situ*. Her sister never took COCs. What can you tell M.F. about cervical dysplasia and cancer risks associated with COCs?

Cervical dysplasia may progress to carcinoma *in situ* in about 12 to 43 months depending upon the initial severity. The risk for both dysplasia and carcinoma *in situ* of the cervix increases after more than one year of COC use. The risk for invasive cervical cancer increases after five years of use and doubles after ten years.[16] Because other risks such as multiple partners, age at first intercourse, exposure to human papilloma virus, and smoking must be considered as well, a causal relationship between COCs and cervical cancer has not been established. Five of thirteen epidemiologic studies noted a significantly increased risk of cervical neoplasia; however, seven did not find a statistically increased risk. Epidemiological comparisons of the prevalence of cervical cancers in COC users versus nonusers often are difficult to interpret because yearly medical examinations (e.g., Pap smears) of COC users

result in early detection and treatment of precancerous dysplastic lesions.[8] Furthermore, epidemiological data based upon the use of earlier generations of higher potency COCs may not be applicable to the lower potency COCs currently being used. A recent case-control study concluded that there is minimal risk for invasive squamous cell carcinoma [relative risk (RR) = 1.1], but there is a significantly increased risk for invasive adenocarcinoma (RR = 2.4).[17] Some experts believe it is reasonable to perform Pap smears every six months in women using oral contraceptives for five or more years and who are also at higher risk because of multiple partners or a history of sexually transmitted diseases (STDs).[18]

Currently, 12 of 13 leaders in the fields of family planning and reproductive endocrinology would prescribe COCs even to a woman who is a DES daughter (exposed *in utero* to diethylstilbestrol or other nonsteroidal estrogens)[13] despite the propensity of those individuals to develop vaginal adenosis, cervical erosion, and very rarely (<150 cases in the U.S. since 1940), adenocarcinoma of the vagina or cervix.

14. Breast Cancer. The medical history and physical examination of M.F. are negative for breast disease except for a history of breast cancer in her maternal grandmother. How will the use of COCs affect M.F.'s risk of breast cancer?

Some studies have suggested an increased risk of breast cancer in young, nulliparous women using COCs with high progestin activity.[19,20] In addition, the Royal College of General Practitioners' Oral Contraceptive Study in 1981 reported a significant increase in risk for breast cancer in women 30 to 34 years of age that use COCs.[21] In contrast, both the Oxford/Family Planning Association Contraceptive Study in 1977[22] and the Walnut Creek Contraceptive Drug Study in 1981[23] found no association between breast cancer and COC use in any age group.[24] The Centers for Disease Control Cancer and Steroid Hormone Study in 1983 reported there was a relative risk of 0.9 for COC users compared with never-users, despite the presence of other risk factors for breast cancer such as early menarche, later age at first birth and menopause, family history of breast cancer, or benign breast disease. Although these other strong risk factors make it difficult to evaluate the relationship between COCs and breast cancer,[25] COCs would not be expected to increase the risk of breast cancer in M.F.

COC users tend to have a greater awareness of breast cancer, examine their breasts more frequently, and be examined by clinicians more frequently than nonusers. Thus, early detection of breast abnormalities can preclude the progression of these abnormalities into cancerous lesions.[26,27]

15. Cardiovascular Disease. M.F.'s fiancé has been reading about the cardiovascular risks of COCs in the lay press. He is so concerned that he has contacted M.F.'s practitioner. What is the effect of COCs on M.F.'s risk of morbidity and mortality from cardiovascular disease?

Both the Royal College of General Practitioners,[28] and the Oxford/Family Planning Association[29] COC studies showed that women under the age of 35, regardless of smoking status, taking the new low-dose COCs did not have a significantly increased mortality risk from cardiovascular disease.[30] The increase in mortality is concentrated in smokers over the age of 35.

Several studies have focused on the effect of COCs on serum lipoprotein concentrations due to the association of lipoproteins with atherosclerotic cardiovascular disease. Total cholesterol, triglyceride, LDL cholesterol, and very low-density lipoprotein (VLDL) cholesterol serum concentrations are associated with the risk of developing atherosclerotic circulatory diseases, whereas HDL cholesterol has an inverse relationship.[31]

An early study of 4800 women[32] suggested that estrogen tended to increase serum concentrations of HDL, while decreases in HDL were linked to progestin dose and potency. Decreases in HDL also were associated with increasing age, weight, and cigarette smoking. In 1983 a report on 1600 women over a five-year period confirmed that progestin-dominant COCs increased LDL and decreased HDL levels.[33] When COCs containing 1 mg of norethindrone and 50 μg mestranol (Genora 1/50, Norethin 1/50M, Norinyl 1 + 50, Ortho-Novum 1/50) were compared with COCs containing either norethindrone 1 mg and 35 μg ethinyl estradiol (Genora 1/35, N.E.E. 1/35, Nelova 1/35E, Norethin 1/35, Norinyl 1 + 35, Ortho-Novum 1/35) or norethindrone 0.5 mg and ethinyl estradiol 35 μg (Brevicon, Genora 0.5/35, Modicon, Nelova 0.5/35E), high density lipoprotein, low density lipoprotein, and total serum cholesterol concentrations did not change significantly during the first four cycles with any of these three COCs. Triglycerides, however, were increased significantly with the lowest dose product.[34] The monophasic levonorgestrel COC (Levlen, Levora, or Nordette) may increase LDL cholesterol and apoprotein B and decrease HDL cholesterol and apoprotein A. In contrast, the triphasic version (Tri-Levlen or Triphasil) does not significantly alter HDL cholesterol, LDL cholesterol, or apoprotein B levels and produces no change or an increase in apoprotein A.[35] The monophasic desogestrel COC (Desogen or Ortho-Cept) produces a favorable lipoprotein profile, while the triphasic gestodene COC (Tri-Minulet, not marketed in the U.S.) produces slight beneficial changes in the HDL:LDL and apoprotein B:apoprotein A ratios.[36,37] The manufacturers of two triphasic COCs containing ethinyl estradiol and norethindrone (Ortho-Novum 7/7/7, Tri-Norinyl) claim that total cholesterol, LDL, and HDL serum concentrations should not be altered based upon their studies of COCs containing 0.5 mg to 1 mg of norethindrone in combination with 35 μg of ethinyl estradiol.[38]

Since increased serum triglyceride concentrations are related to the estrogen content of the COC as well as to the antiestrogenic effect of progestin component,[39] levonorgestrel-containing COCs should have the least effect on triglycerides.

A very extensive critique of the major epidemiological studies of COC-induced cardiovascular risks concluded that study bias prevented meaningful conclusions about the causal relationship between COCs and cardiovascular diseases.[40] Nevertheless, low-dose COCs should be safer on a theoretical basis.

Progestins can modify the composition of total HDL by changing the relative amounts of HDL_2 and HDL_3.[41,42] HDL_2 is protective against cardiovascular disease, unlike HDL_3.[43] Unfortunately, few laboratories fractionate HDL into its HDL_2 and HDL_3 components, and most COC studies do not break HDL data into HDL_2 and HDL_3 subfractions.

16. Thromboembolic Events. B.C., a 21-year-old woman, came to the emergency room (ER) with a tender, swollen left calf. While waiting to be evaluated medically, she developed shortness of breath and a slight fever. Her family and personal history are negative for cardiovascular disease. She smokes 2 packs of cigarettes a day and has blood Type A. Her only medication has been Demulen for 2 years. She was hospitalized with a diagnosis of deep vein thrombosis (DVT) and secondary pulmonary embolism. How could the COC have contributed to these events and which component of the COC was responsible?

Progestins can cause venous stasis through venous dilation and estrogens increase coagulability and the possibility of clot formation in dilated veins. Estrogens can increase the serum concentrations of some clotting factors and decrease the prothrombin time after one to three cycles of use.[44,45] Factors VII, X, and XII are increased in all users, and Factors I, II, V, VIII, and IX are increased in most users. Estrogens also may reduce antithrombin III activity and decrease the inhibitory activity of activated Factor X.[45–58] Long-term COC use is associated with an increased platelet count and increased platelet aggregation.[46] Finally, the progestin component (e.g., norethindrone acetate) has been linked to an increased risk of subclinical thrombosis.[49–51] Thus, both the estrogenic and progestinic components of COCs contribute to the formation of deep venous thrombi.

Women using COCs have a two to four times greater risk than nonusers of developing superficial or deep venous thrombosis and pulmonary embolism.[46,52–54] Patients requiring emergency major surgery while on COCs are more prone to thromboembolism than nonusers.[55] The risk of DVT does not seem to be associated with duration of COC use,[56] past COC use,[49] mild obesity, or cigarette smoking.[56,57] The risk of DVT is less with smaller estrogen doses (i.e., <50 μg ethinyl estradiol or 80 μg of mestranol).[49,50]

White females with Type O blood have one-third the risk of developing DVT[58] while receiving COCs as compared with females with blood Type A. Patients with thromboembolic disease in this latter group[59,60] exhibit a greater ''hypercoagulability'' while on COCs,[61] and have slightly lower levels of antithrombin III.[61] Black women are less likely to get thromboembolic disease while on COCs than white women.[59]

17. Hypertension and Subarachnoid Hemorrhage (SAH). A.M., a 26-year-old obese black female, became hypertensive during all of her pregnancies. She restarted her Ovral after her last pregnancy and continues to smoke cigarettes, 1 pack/day. Her average blood pressure (BP) over the last 3 clinic visits (145/95 mm Hg) is higher than her average value (126/76 mm Hg) before treatment with COCs. Explain to A.M.'s physician how COCs can be safely used by A.M. in spite of her history of hypertension during pregnancy. What is the mechanism of COC-induced hypertension?

Surprisingly, women with a history of hypertension or preeclampsia during pregnancy are not predisposed to the hypertensive effects of COCs.[62] Furthermore, no consistent pattern of clinical hypertension secondary to COC use has been found in black women.[63] COC-induced hypertension, however, clearly is an entity in white women and is most likely related to both the estrogen and progestin components. This difference between black and white women simply might reflect the difference in study design; all hypertensive women receiving combination oral contraceptives should be evaluated for possible COC-induced hypertension.

The underlying mechanisms for COC-induced hypertension may be sodium and water retention and increased renin activity.[49,62] Data on older and more potent oral contraceptives (e.g., Ovral) show a two to three times higher incidence of hypertension (BP >140/90 mm Hg) in COC users than nonusers.[64–66] In one prospective study,[66] the incidence of hypertension was 4% for women using COCs compared to 1.5% for nonusers. Although the 4 mm Hg systolic rise and the 1 mm Hg diastolic rise in this study are not clinically significant, substantial increases in blood pressure are encountered occasionally.[67]

Hypertension secondary to COCs may develop slowly over a period of 3 to 36 months and may not decline for three to six months after COC discontinuation.[68] Hypertension is encountered infrequently with the third- and fourth-generation COCs (e.g., those with low progestin content and <50 μg of estrogen) even in women with a past history of elevated blood pressure.[69,70] A.M.'s highly potent COC, Ovral, should be discontinued. Instead, she deserves a short trial using a COC with small amounts of estrogen and progestin (e.g., Ovcon-35, Brevicon, Genora 0.5/35, Nelova 0.5/35, N.E.E. 0.5/35, Modicon, or one of the triphasics). The effect of this change in medication on A.M.'s blood pressure should be monitored to determine if continued use is warranted.

The possibility of subarachnoid hemorrhage in a hypertensive patient receiving a COC also must be considered. There is an increased risk of SAH coinciding with duration of COC use and this persists after discontinuation.[53] Cigarette smoking and hypertension increase the risk of SAH, which has a higher incidence of fatalities than thrombotic stroke. Therefore, A.M. also should be advised to discontinue her cigarette smoking and lose weight.

18. Diabetes. R.D., a 33-year-old female, experienced glucose intolerance during pregnancy which resolved after delivery. She has a father and sister with diabetes. Why would a low-dose COC (Levlen, Levora, Nordette) be inappropriate for R.D.?

Women with a history of gestational diabetes and those with a strong family history of diabetes in parents or siblings are at greater risk for oral contraceptive-induced glucose intolerance.[15,71,72] COCs have complex effects on carbohydrate metabolism. Progestins decrease, and estrogens increase, the number of insulin receptors on the cell membrane.[15] Progestins also may alter insulin receptor affinity. The different progestins in COCs have different propensities to induce glucose intolerance (e.g., norgestrel, ethynodiol diacetate, norethindrone, desogestrel, or norgestimate).[15,73–75]

For R.D., Levlen, Levora, and Nordette (0.15 mg levonorgestrel with 30 µg ethinyl estradiol) would be poor choices because they are known to cause glucose intolerance in patients with previous gestational diabetes.[76] Interestingly, the triphasic levonorgestrel product, containing 39% less progestin than the monophasic product, did not alter glucose tolerance.[77] Although norgestrel-induced hyperglycemia may be dose related, and perhaps avoidable with the low progestin triphasic levonorgestrel COC, it seems prudent to put R.D. on a norethindrone-containing triphasic because norethindrone is the progestin that is least likely to alter glucose tolerance.

Lowering the estrogen content of a COC without changing progestin content also has improved glucose tolerance and increased insulin secretion.[71] Generally, COCs with ≤35 µg of ethinyl estradiol have not altered glucose tolerance.[78] Results of a one controlled, randomized, prospective study showed no adverse effect on carbohydrate or lipid metabolism in women with a history of gestational diabetes after 6 to 13 months of low-dose oral contraceptive use. Both the oral contraceptive and the nonoral contraceptive groups showed a significant and similar deterioration in glucose tolerance with an overall prevalence of 14% impaired glucose tolerance and 17% diabetes mellitus. The authors concluded that low-dose oral contraceptives could be prescribed safely and that serum lipids and glucose tolerance should be monitored closely, regardless of contraceptive choice.[79]

19. Gallbladder Disease. T.A., a 26-year-old female, presents to the ER with acute epigastric pain accompanied by nausea, vomiting, and diarrhea. She has been taking Demulen (1 mg ethynodiol diacetate with 50 µg ethinyl estradiol) for 1 year. A number of gallstones are apparent on the cholecystogram. What is the association between gallbladder disease and COC therapy? What would be an appropriate COC for T.A.?

The incidence of cholelithiasis reportedly doubles, especially in the first year of COC use.[80] Estrogens and progestins contribute to bile stasis and cholelithiasis because they reduce cholesterol clearance and alter bile acid composition.[81] During the first years of COC use, the incidence of gallbladder disease increases, but then declines steadily to a rate lower than that of controls.[82] In another large study, long-term COC users experienced slightly lower rates of gallbladder disease than nonusers.[83] The newer third- and fourth-generation COCs with lower progestin and estrogen concentrations should have little effect, if any, on gallstone formation in normal patients. In T.A., COCs should be discontinued because of her gallbladder disease. Demulen is another antiquated COC that, in general, should not be used because of its excessive potency. After this problem has resolved, a fourth-generation COC could be considered for T.A.

20. Liver Tumors. T.A.'s physician is concerned about the possibility of hepatic tumors. What is the risk of hepatomas in patients using COCs?

Approximately 300 cases of benign liver tumors have been reported since 1973 in COC users; the actual incidence probably is higher.[84] The two most common hepatic tumors in this population of women are focal nodular hyperplasia and liver cell adenomas. The latter is more ominous because the risk of potential hemorrhage is much greater.[84,85]

The incidence rate of benign liver tumors for women using low-dose COCs for two years or more is 3.4 per 100,000 users per year compared to 0.1 per 100,000 in nonusers or short-term users.[43] Although the tumors generally are benign, death can result from intrahepatic or extrahepatic tumor rupture and hemorrhagic shock. Since animal studies suggest both estrogen and progestin may accelerate abnormal liver cell proliferation,[87] the lowest effective dose of COCs should be used in all patients. Although hepatomas are rare, the clinician still should palpate the liver each year.[69]

Cholestatic jaundice also has been associated with COC use. This disorder usually presents as malaise, nausea, anorexia, and pruritus. These symptoms usually appear four weeks after the initiation of COC use. Discontinuation of the COC results in complete clinical remission within a few weeks to a month.[88]

21. "Postpill" Amenorrhea and Galactorrhea. G.T., a 23-year-old female, has taken Demulen 1/50 (1 mg ethynodiol diacetate with 50 µg ethinyl estradiol) for 2 years. This COC was discontinued 1 year ago. Since then, she has experienced occasional nipple discharge and no menstrual flow except when induced by medroxyprogesterone 10 mg/day for 5 days. G.T.'s provider is concerned about her future fertility. How prevalent is "postpill" amenorrhea and how should it be managed?

Most women resume regular menstrual cycles soon after discontinuing COCs, and G.T. should have as well. A retrospective study of over 10,000 births noted that former long-term COC users experienced a markedly lower conception rate compared to former short-term users only in the first month after COC discontinuation. Conception rates among both long-term and short-term users were similar by the second or third months.[89] Although 0.5% to 2.6% of former COC users experienced amenorrhea lasting six months or more,[90–92] irregular and/or scanty menses were experienced by 24% to 53% of "postpill" amenorrhea patients before COCs were initiated. Therefore, COCs may mask fertility problems because they produce artificially regular menses.[93,94] Birth delivery rates of former COC users and former diaphragm users also are comparable.[94] Overall, "postpill" amenorrhea really is quite rare. Other causes of amenorrhea also should be considered (e.g., polycystic ovaries, pregnancy, ovarian failure, physiological factors such as starvation or excessive exercise, anorexia, growth hormone producing pituitary adenomas).[95]

As illustrated by G.T., postpill amenorrhea can be accompanied by galactorrhea in 20% of patients. Hypothalamic deficiency, hyperplasia of lactotroph cells, a prolactin or growth-hormone-secreting pituitary adenoma, psychotropic drugs, or increased thyroid stimulating-hormone, however, are other causes of galactorrhea.[95] It is the estrogen component of COCs that probably induces increased prolactin production and galactorrhea. Prolactin prevents ovulation and subsequent menses by inhibiting gonadotropin-releasing-hormone production by the hypothalamus and by blocking the ovarian response to luteinizing hormone. Interestingly, intramuscular (IM) injections of progestins for contraception increase the amount of milk production.[15,95]

For G.T., serum prolactin levels should be obtained to rule out pituitary microadenoma. Other causes of amenorrhea should be considered and G.T.'s menstrual history before COC use should be reviewed.

22. Teratogenicity. P.S., a 25-year-old female, was started on Norinyl 1 + 35 (1 mg norethindrone with 35 µg ethinyl estradiol) 4 months ago because of a history of abnormal menstrual periods. Unknowingly, she was pregnant at that time and continued her COC for the first 9 gestational weeks. What can you tell the parents about the possible effects of COC use on their unborn child?

The acronym VACTERL (vertebral, anal, cardiac, tracheal, esophageal, renal or radial, and limb) appears in early literature to describe the fetal malformations produced by COCs.[96,97] Although cardiac anomalies were two to three times more common among offspring of women who took COCs during pregnancy in two studies, this finding was not statistically significant.[98,99] In one study, significantly greater risks of congenital limb defects were noted if COCs were taken early in pregnancy.[100] Nevertheless, almost all studies report that malformations are not greater in fetuses exposed to COCs.[101] Simpson summarized all available data on contraceptive steroid exposure during pregnancy and concluded that such exposures did not substantially increase the risk of anomalies over that expected in other uneventful pregnancies.[102] Since P.S. was using a low-dose COC during the first nine weeks of gestation, the risk to the fetus should be minimal.

Oral contraception was once thought to be a risk factor for pregnancy-induced hypertension (PIH), preeclampsia-eclampsia which may lead to miscarriage, perinatal deaths, and maternal mortality. Fortunately, a retrospective controlled review of 341 patients showed no increased risk of PIH in women who unintentionally took COCs during pregnancy.[103]

23. Headache. G.R., a 32-year-old female, comes to the clinic complaining of persistent depression and headaches which predominantly occur midcycle or during the 7-day placebo phase of her 28-day cycle of Nordette. The throbbing headaches are preceded by blurred vision, nausea, and vomiting. Aspirin and acetaminophen, which normally relieve her tension headaches, are ineffective. Lying down in a dark room provides some headache relief. Her family history is pertinent because her mother and maternal grandmother suffer from migraine headaches. Are these headaches a relative contraindication for the continued use of COCs?

There is an increased incidence of vascular headaches in women who use COCs.[167] Of those women who develop headaches with COCs, approximately one-half report pre-existing migrainous attacks; the other half develop migrainous attacks *de novo*.[168] Headaches usually develop within the first months of COC use, but occasionally may not occur until after several years have elapsed.[167] Upon discontinuation of the COC, 30% to 40% of women who develop headaches on COCs improve.[169] For the others, it is not clear whether COCs set in motion a mechanism that was to be unstable for years or whether migraine developed coincidentally during COC use.[170]

Clinical experience indicates that those women who show increasing migraine attacks with COCs are not likely to improve with a change to a COC that has a different hormone balance.[171,172] Since G.R.'s symptoms are typical of migraine headache and since she has a family history of migraine headaches, she may need to discontinue COCs and use another method of birth control. Subsequent to a thorough medical evaluation of her headaches, she should be monitored carefully if COCs are to be continued. Although headaches may improve in a small number of women who take COCs,[174] the risk of cerebral infarction may be increased in some COC users who suffer from migraine headaches due to hyperplasia of the intima lining of cerebral arteries.[169]

24. Depression. In consideration of G.R.'s persistent depression, would a COC with high or low estrogen or progestin balance be preferred?

COC-related depression has been attributed to estrogen excess, progestin excess, estrogen deficiency, and pyridoxine (vitamin B_6) deficiency in approximately 5% to 6% of COC users.[173] A low-dose estrogen and progestin COC such as Ovcon-35 or the minipill (Micronor or Nor-Q.D.) should be prescribed in hopes of alleviating depression that might be due to either estrogen or progestin excess. Since the gonanes (i.e., desogestrel, d,1-norgestrel, levonorgestrel, norgestimate) seem to be more potent progestins than the estrane, norethindrone, Desogen/Ortho-Cept, Ovral, Ovrette, Levlen/Levlor/Nordette, Tri-Levlen/Triphasil, Ortho-Cyclen and Ortho Tri-Cyclen could be avoided. Some clinicians have treated COC-induced depression with vitamin B_6, 25 to 50 mg/day, based upon the theory that B_6 deficiency in these women results in abnormal tryptophan metabolism that can cause depression.[175]

Benefits of COCs

Although significant noncontraceptive benefits of COCs have been known for many years, they generally have been disregarded, even by the FDA which finally added noncontraceptive benefits to the package inserts in mid 1988.[9]

25. Pelvic Inflammatory Disease (PID) and Ectopic Pregnancy. C.P., a 20-year-old female with several sexual partners, presents to the ER with a fever of 38.2 °C and lower abdominal cramping. Pelvic examination is compatible with the diagnosis of PID. Her white blood cell (WBC) count is 13,000/mm³ and the differential shows a shift to the left. She has been wearing a Paragard T380A IUD for 2 years. Why might COCs be a more suitable contraceptive for C.P.? [SI unit: WBC 13 × 10⁹/L.]

Many clinicians preferentially prescribe COCs over other forms of contraception for sexually active young women with multiple sexual partners because PID has been found to be less prevalent with this form of contraception.[104] In one study, COC users were one-half as likely to develop PID as nonusers.[105] Although early studies failed to distinguish between gonococcal and nongonococcal pelvic inflammatory disease, the PID protective effects of COCs may be organism dependent. A Swedish study found that COCs protect against both gonococcal and chlamydial PID.[106] In contrast, one report suggests that COCs may promote chlamydial PID;[107] and another concluded that COC users were neither more or less likely to get pelvic inflammatory disease.[108] A 1990 case control study has shown protection against symptomatic PID among women infected with chlamydia but not among those infected with gonococcus.[109] Despite the contradictory data, it is logical that the thickening of cervical mucus caused by COCs prevents the ascension of bacteria into the uterus and fallopian tubes. Finally, it is estimated that the COCs use in the U.S. prevents 51,000 hospitalizations and averts 100 deaths stemming from pelvic inflammatory disease annually, and prevents 9900 hospitalizations and averts 10 deaths stemming from ectopic pregnancies annually.[110]

About 3% to 4% of pregnancies in IUD users are ectopic compared to 0.8% in nonusers.[111] IUD users have higher rates of PID than nonusers and the risk of ectopic pregnancy is greater for women who have had pelvic inflammatory disease.[112] A recent study looking at 22,908 IUD insertions and 51,399 woman-years of follow-up showed an overall PID rate of 1.6/1000 woman-years of use. The PID risk was more than six times higher during the 20 days after insertion than during later times.[113] COC users may be one-tenth as likely to develop ectopic pregnancies as nonusers due to decreased PID incidence.[114] In view of these data, C.P.'s IUD should be removed, her pelvic inflammatory disease treated, and COCs should be initiated if no contraindications are present. Patients and clinicians should be alert for the symptoms of cervicitis or salpingitis in women on COCs who are at high risk for sexually transmitted diseases. Lower genital tract infections caused by chlamydia are on the rise in the U.S.[69]

26. Ovarian Cancer and Functional Ovarian Cysts. After resolution of her PID, C.P. is found to have ovarian cysts. What is the probability of COC-induced ovarian cancer?

There is a decreased risk of developing functional ovarian cysts, more rapid resolution of pre-existing cysts, and reduced surgery rates for ovarian masses in women on COCs.[115] The risk of ovarian cancer is reduced 33% to 60% by COCs, and this protection continues for 10 to 15 years after discontinuation of the COCs.[116,117] It is estimated that COCs prevent 1700 hospitalizations and avert 1000 deaths annually in the U.S. from ovarian cancer.[110]

27. Endometrial Cancer. C.P. is hesitant to take COCs since her grandmother, who had been on estrogen replacement therapy (ERT) for 5 years, died of endometrial cancer in 1970. What is the relationship between COCs and endometrial cancer?

Clinical data suggest that cyclic COCs contain enough progestin to prevent endometrial hyperplasia and to reduce the risk of endometrial cancer by 50% to 66%. The protection is directly related to duration of use and may persist for five years after discontinuation of the COCs.[110,117] C.P.'s grandmother may have been the victim of unopposed ERT. It is estimated that COC usage in the U.S. prevents 2000 cases of endometrial cancer and averts 100 deaths annually.[110]

28. Benign Breast Disease. What influence do COCs have on fibrocystic breast disease?

There appears to be a 50% to 75% reduction in the risk of fibroadenomas, chronic cystic breast disease, and unbiopsied breast lumps in COC users. Protection seems directly related to length of use. Since the progestin component may be primarily responsible for this protection, progestin-dominant COCs that contain a less estrogenic progestin such as levonorgestrel are preferred.[118] The progestin-only minipill could be of use here except that its contraceptive effect is not as good as the COCs. In addition, it does not provide endometrial stability and other benefits of COCs such as decreased dysmenorrhea, iron deficiency anemia, acne, and hirsutism.

29. Dysmenorrhea. C.P. relates that her IUD has worsened menstrual cramping. What effect might she expect from COCs?

With prolonged use, the endometrium of a COC user becomes progressively thinner; therefore, prostaglandin formation may be lower at the time of menses. Studies have shown a 40% to 67% decrease in complaints of menstrual pain subsequent to COC therapy.[119,120]

30. Premenstrual Syndrome (PMS). C.P. also has a history of PMS. What is the effect of COCs on PMS?

Premenstrual tension has been reported to be reduced 29% in COC users[120] and other premenstrual symptoms seem to improve as well.[121] Nevertheless, the effect of COCs on PMS symptoms is inconsistent and unpredictable probably because PMS symptoms are neither consistent nor predictable.[122] The possible augmentation of depression and mood swings by the progestational component of the COC should be monitored closely. (See Chapter 46: Gynecological Disorders for further discussion of dysmenorrhea and PMS.)

31. Iron Deficiency Anemia. C.P. is noted to have a hematocrit (Hct) of 31% and a hemoglobin (Hgb) of 10.1 gm/dL. Her anemia may be due to heavy menses secondary to her past IUD use. What will be the effect of COC use on her iron deficiency anemia? [SI unit: Hct 0.31; Hgb 6.27 mmol/L.]

The total amount of menstrual blood flow in established COC users may be decreased by 50%.[115,119,123] This may reflect the progressive thinning of the endometrium of COC users and the lack of dysfunctional bleeding.[124]

32. Acne and Hirsutism. D.S., a 20-year-old female, has had severe acne since menarche at age 13. Upon physical examination it is noted that she has more than the usual amount of facial hair. Her serum androgen profile is checked and found to be normal. She is on no current medications but wants to begin birth control pills. What effect, if any, would oral contraceptives have on her acne condition? Which COCs would you recommend for D.S.?

Depending upon whether the COC is estrogen or progestin dominant, acne may appear, disappear, or markedly improve.[125] Progestins that are strongly androgenic (e.g., norgestrel) stimulate sebaceous glands to produce more sebum while estrogens suppress the activity of sebaceous glands. Estrogens also decrease the production of androgens by the ovaries and by the adrenal glands through inhibition of pituitary function. Furthermore, estrogens increase the synthesis of sex hormone binding globulin which binds androgens and, thereby, diminishes their effects.[126] The triphasic COCs are modestly estrogen-dominant, and these lower dose contraceptives still markedly reduce the overall incidence of acne.[127] Both desogestrel and norgestimate containing COCs are less androgenic, thereby increasing SHBG levels and decreasing acne.[128]

Since the serum androgen profile is normal in D.S., her acne and hirsutism, which are both androgen-mediated conditions, should improve with a triphasic COC, a desogestrel or norgestimate monophasic product, or perhaps Ovcon-35 with 0.4 mg of norethindrone, or a 0.5 mg containing norethindrone product.

D.S. should be warned that postcontraceptive acne flares have been reported commonly in women who have been using COCs for at least one year and that it occurs three to four months after the COC has been discontinued. The self-limiting acne subsides in 6 to 12 months without treatment and also is responsive to conventional forms of acne therapy.[129]

Postcoital (Morning-After) Pills

33. B.P., a 24-year-old female, has just returned home from a vacation in Europe. Her luggage containing her COCs was stolen 2 weeks ago and she had unprotected midcycle intercourse 34 hours ago. What can be done to prevent an unwanted pregnancy at this time?

Postcoital contraception is a controversial issue since some people view it as abortifacient, while others consider it a means to reduce planned abortions.[176] Many healthcare providers may not prescribe this method of contraception because of the moral issues, lack of FDA approval, and the risks associated with the use of morning-after pills.

Unprotected intercourse three days before, one day before, and on the day of ovulation results in pregnancy roughly 20%, 25%, and 15% of the time, respectively. The probability of pregnancy approaches zero when more than two days have passed after ovulation.[177] Several postcoital regimens have been used successfully when initiated within 72 hours of the unprotected intercourse. (See Table 43.14 for typical regimens.)

High-dose Estrogens may have a direct effect on the endometrial lining or may decrease progesterone production by the corpus luteum, the net effect of which is probably prevention of blastocyst implantation in the endometrium.[8] Unfortunately, postcoital contraception does not seem to interfere with ectopic pregnancies; approximately one out of ten morning-after pill failures results in an ectopic pregnancy. The total number of ectopic pregnancies, however, is approximately equal to that which would be expected if no contraception had been used. Failure rates of 0.0% to 2.4% have been reported with high-dose estrogens.[178] Side effects are limited mainly to nausea in 70% and vomiting in 33% of all women treated.[179] Doses lost to emesis should be repeated.

Table 43.14	Postcoital Contraception

High-Dose Estrogens

Diethylstilbestrol	25 mg BID x 5 days
Ethinyl estradiol	2.5 mg BID x 5 days
Esterified estrogens	10 mg BID x 5 days
Conjugated estrogens	10 mg BID x 5 days
Estrone	5 mg x 5 days

Ovral[a]
2 tablets immediately followed by 2 tablets 12 hours later

Lo/Ovral, Levlen/Levlor/Nordette
4 tablets immediately followed by 4 tablets 12 hours later[b]

Tri-Levlen/Triphasil (Yellow Pills Only)
4 tablets immediately followed by 4 tablets 12 hours later[b]

[a] Seems to be preferred because of low failure rate (0.16%–1.7%) and low incidence of nausea and vomiting.
[b] Research on emergency contraception has only been reported for norgestrel products.

The teratogenicity of all morning-after pills may be significant; therefore, abortion should be considered if high-dose estrogen postcoital contraception is unsuccessful. Informed consent should be obtained and written instructions should be provided. Patients should be evaluated one week after completing the high-dose estrogen regimen and re-evaluated five weeks later to detect complications of therapy and to provide an opportunity for discussion and institution of more appropriate contraceptive methods.[180] Finally, B.P. should be taught the warning signs of "ACHES" (see Table 43.9).

Ovral appears to be the morning-after pill of choice because of its low failure rate (0.16% to 1.6%)[177,180,181] and its low potential for causing nausea and vomiting. Four active tablets of Lo/Ovral, or Levlen/Levlor/Nordette, or the yellow tablets in Tri-Levlen/Triphasil may be used instead of two active Ovral tablets for each dose.[211] There is no correlation between oral contraceptive exposure during pregnancy and still-births, perinatal mortality, or fetal malformations (see Question 22). Informed consent, written instructions, evaluation of the patient one and six weeks after therapy, and "ACHES" education are similar to the recommendations for high-dose estrogen postcoital therapy.

Long-Acting Progestin Injections:
Depo-Provera (DMPA)

34. A.K., a lactating 35-year-old female, returns to the gynecology clinic for her second injection of DMPA. She was given her first injection 3 months ago immediately postpartum and is a smoker with a history of thromboembolism. She is experiencing prolonged intermenstrual bleeding and a 2 pound weight gain. What are the benefits and risks of DMPA? How are the side effects managed?

Since its development in the early 1960s, DMPA has become the most commonly used injectable contraceptive approved for use in 90 countries and has been used by 30 million women worldwide,[182] finally gaining FDA approval in 1992. DMPA almost completely inhibits ovulation, thickens cervical mucus, and suppresses endometrial growth, making it a very effective contraceptive. (See Table 43.15 for a discussion on ideal candidates for DMPA and Table 4.16 for instructions on DMPA administration.)

Depo-Provera is a good contraceptive choice for A.K. since she is 35 years old, smokes, is lactating, and has a history of thromboembolism. Among its benefits are a low failure rate of 0.3% (see Table 43.1), lack of estrogen side effects, and a reduced risk of endometrial cancer.[183] Other noncontraceptive benefits may include inhibition of intravascular sickling and increased hemoglobin

and red cell survival in patients with sickle-cell disease, an increase in the quantity and protein content in breast milk for A.K., less PID, fewer ectopic pregnancies, less endometriosis, and a 30% reduction in seizure frequency in seizure patients. Furthermore, contraceptive efficacy is not reduced by the concurrent use of anticonvulsants as seen with the COCs.[184]

Some experts disagree with the Depo-Provera Contraceptive Injection U.S. package insert which lists a history of prior thromboembolism as a contraindication, since clotting factors have not been shown to be clinically affected by DMPA. Some clinicians also begin DMPA immediately postpartum rather than waiting six weeks postpartum as directed by the package insert. Patients started earlier are more likely to report frequent episodes of bleeding or spotting, however.[184]

Patients should be told that the risks of DMPA use may include breast cancer and decreased bone density. The overall relative risk of breast cancer is 1.2 (95% CI: 1.0 to 1.5). The risk is elevated in short-term users as well as women under age 35 and is highest in women who use DMPA for three months or less. Overall, the risk of breast cancer is no greater than the risk associated with COC use.[184] After at least five years of DMPA use, bone density of the lumbar spine was 7.5% lower than premenopausal controls and 6.5% lower at the femoral neck. This is probably due to estrogen suppression and is reversible upon discontinuation of DMPA.[185] However, there is a need for a well-controlled, prospective study to clarify this issue since 40% of the DMPA users were smokers compared to only 10% of the premenopausal controls. In addition, DMPA users had greater lumbar spine bone density than did postmenopausal controls.

A.K. must understand that DMPA side effects include irregular bleeding and spotting for up to seven days during the first few months of DMPA use and a 57% incidence of amenorrhea following one year of use and 68% after two years. The latter effect leads to discontinuation of DMPA in 13% of patients.[182] In an uncontrolled study, the mean weight gain after one year of therapy with DMPA was about five pounds. This increased to about 15 to 16 pounds by the third year and then remained constant. A weight gain of 2.2 to 6.6 pounds is common.[182] Following a 150 mg DMPA injection, the mean interval before ovulation resumes is four and one-half months, although conception may be delayed approximately nine months after the last injection.[182]

All patients beginning Depo-Provera should be informed that during the first year of use they may have one or more of the following menstrual changes: 1) irregular or unpredictable bleeding or spotting for up to seven days; 2) an increase or decrease in menstrual flow; and 3) amenorrhea. If unusually heavy or continuous bleeding occurs, it should be checked immediately. A.K. should be counseled and reassured that her intermenstrual bleeding probably will resolve in the next few months. If she insists on something to reduce the bleeding, a 10- to 21-day course of oral estrogen (e.g., conjugated estrogen 1.25 to 2.5 mg/day) will min-

Table 43.15	Depo-Provera Candidates

Candidates are Patients in Whom:

Contraception of at least 1 year's duration is desired
Estrogen should be avoided
Compliance problems exist with other contraceptive methods
Intrauterine devices should be avoided
Barrier methods are undesirable
Breast-feeding is desirable
There is a seizure history
Amenorrhea is desirable

Table 43.16	DMPA Administration[a]

150 mg DMPA deep IM injection in the deltoid or gluteal site using a 1½", 21–23-gauge needle[b]

First injection during day 1–5 of cycle or after ruling out pregnancy

Reinjections given Q 12 weeks ± 14-day "grace period"

[a] DMPA = Depo-medroxyprogesterone acetate; IM = Intramuscular
[b] Do not massage site after injection to avoid reduction of the depot.

imize or eliminate the bleeding. However, the bleeding frequently recurs after discontinuation of the estrogen.[184] There is no need for the patient to be checked more frequently for menstrual changes than when she comes in every three months for an injection, unless she has heavy or continuous bleeding. Even if amenorrhea occurs, it is unlikely that she would be pregnant unless she missed one of her injections by more than the two-week "grace period" of DMPA protection. She should be counseled that DMPA's effect on weight gain is individual and unpredictable. The merits of caloric restriction and exercise should be discussed along with the offer of assistance in quitting smoking.

Other Birth Control Methods

Subdermal Levonorgestrel Implants (Norplant)

35. A.K. returns to the gynecology clinic on the first day of her flow after missing 3 consecutive DMPA injections because she "just cannot remember to come in for her shots and did not like the weight gain (she now weighs 163 pounds) and prolonged intermenstrual bleeding that occurred for 6 months." Her periods have been normal and regular for the last 6 months. She now is 36 years old, continues to smoke, and has just stopped breast-feeding. Would the long-acting levonorgestrel-containing product that is implanted under the skin be effective and safe for A.K.? What information should be given to her?

The Norplant System brand of subdermal levonorgestrel implants, approved by the FDA in 1990, consists of a set of six Silastic capsules 2.4 mm in diameter and 34 mm in length that are implanted under the skin of the medial aspect of the upper arm. The set contains a total of 36 mg of levonorgestrel that is released at a constant rate of only 20 to 30 μg/day over five years, after which time they are replaced. See Table 43.17 for a discussion of ideal candidates for subdermal implants.

Fertility returns within 24 hours after removal of these subdermal implants. Intermenstrual bleeding episodes are encountered, but tend to diminish after the first three to six months. The pregnancy rate of 0.0 to 0.04 pregnancies per 100 women-years is similar to that achieved with tubal sterilization.[186] (See Table 43.1.)

Unlike DMPA users, women using Norplant who weigh ≥154 pounds experience an increased pregnancy rate beginning in the second year of use as the daily release of levonorgestrel diminishes. The cumulative failure rate is 3.9 per 100 over five years of use according to combined data from the original "hard" and second-generation "soft" tubing. The "soft" tubing allows a more complete release of levonorgestrel, and, in a current study, this has led to a failure rate of only 1.1 per 100 over four years of use.[215] This is good news for A.K. Norplant users ovulate in about 50% of their cycles and only 7% of the patients experience amenorrhea.[188] DMPA causes amenorrhea more frequently apparently because more drug is released than in the Norplant System. Unlike DMPA, contraception with Norplant is not reliable in patients taking anticonvulsants other than valproic acid or gabapentin.[189] The average pregnancy rate is 0.0 to 0.4 pregnancies per 100 women-years

which is similar to that achieved with tubal sterilization. (See Table 43.1.) Finally, there is virtually no delay in conception after Norplant is discontinued.

A.K. should be told that, as with DMPA, the Norplant System causes irregular bleeding in approximately 60% of patients in the first year of use and this is responsible for 9.1% of patients opting for its removal.

Three drugs have been used to control prolonged vaginal bleeding in Norplant users:[143] ethinyl estradiol 0.05 mg/day for 20 days, ibuprofen 800 mg orally three times a day for five days, and levonorgestrel 0.03 mg (equivalent to Ovrette) twice a day for 20 days. The use of ethinyl estradiol produced the greatest reduction in bleeding while ethinyl estradiol and ibuprofen shortened the duration of the longest bleeding runs. Although there was an overall improvement of bleeding beyond the treatment intervals, the results of this study need to be confirmed to ascertain the effect of these drugs on the safety and efficacy of the Norplant System. Many practitioners use a combination of ethinyl estradiol and ibuprofen.

As with DMPA, most practitioners feel that the only contraindications to the use of the Norplant System are active thrombophlebitis, undiagnosed abnormal genital bleeding, acute liver disease, known or suspected carcinoma of the breast or other progestin dependent neoplasia, and pregnancy. Therefore, Norplant often is inserted immediately postpartum in lactating mothers even if they have a history of thrombophlebitis, since there is no clinical evidence that levonorgestrel causes coagulation abnormalities. See Tables 43.18 and 43.19 for patient information on Norplant insertion and removal, respectively.

Surprisingly, most patients are not overly concerned with the insertion and removal procedures or the cosmetic effect of Norplant placement because the advantages relative to other contraceptive choices are great. DMPA requires intramuscular injections every three months and other oral contraceptive methods require a high level of daily compliance. In contrast, the use of Norplant is carefree for five years.

Intrauterine Devices (IUDs)

Risks and Mechanisms of Action

36. R.P., a 23-year-old G₀P₀ female with hydrocephalus, is brought to the gynecology clinic by her mother, S.P., to determine the best method of contraception for her mentally impaired daughter. R.P. is in a monogamous relationship with a mentally impaired partner. According to S.P., R.P. wishes to put off pregnancy for many years and any method of contraception that necessitates compliance is a virtual impossibility for the couple. DMPA and Norplant have been considered, but are unacceptable due to the possibility of menstrual irregularities which would upset R.P. Discuss your evaluation of IUDs

Table 43.17	Norplant Candidates

Candidates are Patients in Whom

Long-term (≈5 years) contraception is desired

Estrogen should be avoided

There are compliance problems with other contraceptive methods

IUDs[a] are not indicated

Barrier methods are undesirable

There are seizures controlled by valproic acid or gabapentin

Amenorrhea is undesirable

There is a need for prompt return of fertility upon discontinuation

[a] IUDs = Intrauterine devices.

Table 43.18	Patient Information on Norplant Insertion

It is a minor surgical procedure under local anesthesia lasting 5–10 min

There is little discomfort, usually related to injection of local anesthesia. After adequate anesthesia, a pressure sensation is felt

It is placed in the nondominant upper arm between days 1 and 7 of the cycle or after pregnancy is ruled out

Bruising or tenderness at the site with touch or motion is common during the first 7–10 days after insertion. The use of an ice pack applied over the bandage for 20 min on the day of insertion and the application of warm moist heat will decrease symptoms

Complications are rare but include expulsion and infection

with S.P. who has expressed serious reservations about the risks of IUD use. What are the mechanisms of action of the IUDs?

Because the Dalkon Shield increased PID susceptibility with subsequent tubal scarring and infertility, only one IUD (Progestasert) remained on the market in the U.S. in 1986. The Progestasert IUD contains 38 mg of progesterone with a release rate of 65 µg/day for one year. The Dalkon IUD created a major liability problem for its manufacturer and forced the reorganization of the A.H. Robins Company.

In 1988 the ParaGard IUD, model T380A was introduced in the U.S. Its polyethylene body is wound with copper wire. Unlike the Progestasert which must be replaced each year, the ParaGard may be left in place for eight years. In an effort to reduce liability, the manufacturer insists that each patient read, understand, and sign a copy of the "Patient Information for an Informed Decision" brochure.

The failure rate of IUDs is 0.5 to 3.0 pregnancies per 100 women-years compared to 0.0 to 3.0 with COCs. Interuterine device users have been reported to have about 3% to 4% chance of ectopic pregnancy compared to 0.8% in nonusers,[111] and a tenfold greater likelihood of ectopic pregnancies compared to COC users because of an increased incidence of PID.[114] However, women with only one sexual partner, like R.P., have had little increase in PID risk associated with IUD use and therefore little increase in the risk of ectopic pregnancy. For all patients, the greatest risk of PID occurs shortly after insertion.[190] (See Question 25.)

Possible mechanisms of action for IUDs include local foreign body inflammatory response causing lysis of the blastocyst and sperm and prevention of implantation, increased local production of prostaglandins that inhibit implantation, disruption of the implanted blastocyst from the endometrium, increased motility of the ovum through the fallopian tube, immobilization of sperm in the uterine cavity, endometrial suppression and impairment of implantation, and progestin-induced thick cervical mucus for the Progestasert IUD.[191]

Complications

37. S.P. asks for the early signs or symptoms that might suggest a possible IUD complication.

Progestasert IUDs must be replaced yearly and ParaGard IUDs every eight years, provided contraindications to IUD use as listed in Table 43.20 are not present. Patients using the IUDs should be instructed to watch out for the early IUD danger signs, "PAINS." (See Table 43.21.)

38. What are some of the major complications of IUDs?

Approximately 10% to 15% of IUDs must be removed because of excessive uterine bleeding, spotting, or pain. The removal of an IUD can be quite difficult at times. Another 5% to 20% of women spontaneously expel their IUD within the first year.

There is about a 50% chance of spontaneous abortion if an IUD is left in place during pregnancy compared to a 25% chance if it is not. Furthermore, the risk of tubal infertility (secondary to tubal damage during PID episodes preventing conception) is doubled. Dalkon Shield users seem to be the most prone to tubal infertility, and copper-laden IUDs[192] seem to be the least likely to induce this problem. Although as many as 77 million women, most of them in China, use IUDs, IUD use in the U.S. today is tenuous, at best.[193]

Diaphragms

Mechanism of Action

39. R.C., a 16-year-old G₁P₁ female who is currently breast feeding her 6-week-old child, will consider only a barrier method of contraception. She asks you how diaphragms prevent pregnancies.

The diaphragm is a soft latex, silicone rubber, or gum rubber cap with a metal spring reinforcing the rim. The device is inserted vaginally and placed over the cervical os to mechanically block access of sperm to the cervix. It is held in place by the spring tension of the rim, vaginal muscle tone, and the pubic bone. Since the diaphragm does not fit tightly enough to be a complete barrier to sperm, spermicidal cream or jelly ($\approx$1 tablespoon in the dome and around the rim) must be used so that the diaphragm acts as a holder to keep the spermicide in place as well as a mechanical barrier.[8] The first-year failure rate with diaphragms according to Table 43.1 is 2.1 to 18 pregnancies per 100 women-years. Since some estrogen and progestin from COCs passes into breast milk, many practitioners recommend diaphragms for breast-feeding mothers. (See Question 4.)

Types

40. What types of diaphragms are available?

Diaphragms must be properly fitted to be effective. They are available in different sizes and in four different styles of construction of the circular rim.

Flat Spring Rim. Ortho-White Diaphragm, sized 55 to 95 mm, latex, folds flat; it may be used with a diaphragm introducer. The Ortho-White Diaphragm is indicated for women with firm vaginal muscle tone (nulliparous) or for those women who wish a thin delicate rim with a gentle spring strength for more comfort.[8]

Coil Spring Rim. The Koromex Diaphragm and the Ortho Diaphragm are made of latex and are available in 50 to 90 mm sizes. Ramses Flexible Cushioned Diaphragms also are available in the same sizes, but are made of gum rubber rather than latex. The coil spring rim diaphragms fold flat and may be used with a diaphragm introducer. These diaphragms are indicated for women with average vaginal muscle tone and for women who can tolerate the sturdy rim and firm spring strength.[8]

Arcing Spring Rim. The Koro-Flex Diaphragm and the All-Flex Diaphragm (Ortho) are latex constructed and available in 60 to 95 mm and 55 to 95 mm sizes, respectively. The Ramses Bendex Diaphragm is of gum rubber construction and available in 65 to

Table 43.19	Patient Information on Norplant Removal

Ease of removal depends upon skill of clinician and proper insertion[a]

It is performed under local anesthesia lasting 20–60 min

Discomfort is minimal. Burning sensation with administration of local anesthetic, then pressure sensation

Complications include fracture of implant; rarely, infections

Levonorgestrel is metabolized rapidly after removal so initiate another method of contraception on the day of removal

[a] Difficult removal is secondary to deep insertion or adhesions.

Table 43.20	Contraindications to IUD Insertion[a,d]

Absolute Contraindications

Active pelvic infection (acute or subacute), including known or suspected gonorrhea or chlamydia

Known or suspected pregnancy

Strong Relative Contraindications

Multiple sexual partners or strong likelihood of multiple sexual partners while the IUD is in place

Multiple sexual partners by partner of IUD user

Emergency treatment difficult to obtain should complications occur; primarily a problem in very rural areas

Recent or recurrent pelvic infection, postpartum endometritis, or infected abortion within the past 3 months

Acute or purulent cervicitis

Bleeding disorders not yet definitively diagnosed

History of ectopic pregnancy or predisposing conditions

Single episode of pelvic infection if patient desires subsequent pregnancy

Impaired response to infection (e.g., diabetes, steroid treatment)

Blood coagulation disorders

Other Conditions That May Contraindicate IUD Use

Valvular heart disease[b]

Endometrial or cervical malignancy

Severe cervical stenosis

Small uterus

Endometriosis

Leiomyomata

Endometrial polyps

Congenital uterine abnormalities or fibroids that prevent proper placement

Severe dysmenorrhea[c]

Heavy menstrual flow or irregular menses or spotting

Allergy to copper (known or suspected) or diagnosed Wilson's disease (a rare, inherited copper disorder) if copper containing IUD

Anemia

Impaired ability to check for danger signals

Inability to check IUD string

History of gonorrhea, chlamydia, syphilis, or herpes

History of severe vasovagal reactivity or fainting

Concern for future fertility

Blood type incompatible with partner's (e.g., Rh neg)

Diabetes

Vaginal discharge or infection

Previous pelvic surgery

[a] IUD = Intrauterine device.
[b] Valvular heart disease potentially makes patient susceptible to subacute bacterial endocarditis; some clinicians recommend prophylactic antibiotics in this situation.
[c] Progestasert IUD may be therapeutic as may be the levonorgestrel implants.
[d] Adapted from reference 8.

95 mm sizes. The Allflex folds at any point along its rim and is slightly less rigid than the Koro-Flex or Ramses Bendex diaphragms which have a hinge or bow-bend construction. The latter of the two arcing spring rim diaphragms fold at two points only and are preferred by many women because the two stiff halves of the ''arc'' can be held in the folded position close to either end of the arc for ease of insertion. In contrast, the Allflex must be held in the middle for insertion. Most women, even those with lax vaginal muscle tone, can tolerate the firm spring strength of these arcing spring rim diaphragms.[8]

Wide-Seal. The Milex Wide-Seal Arcing Diaphragm and the Mile Wide-Seal Omniflex Coil Spring Diaphragm have a silicone rubber construction and are available in 60 to 85 mm sizes. A flexible flange about 1.5 cm wide is designed to hold spermicide in place inside these diaphragms and to create a better seal between the diaphragm and vaginal wall.[8] According to Mile, patients with latex allergies will be able to use their silicone rubber diaphragm. The silicone rubber will withstand indefinite sterilizations by autoclaving or boiling which is an advantage when fitting patients in the clinical setting because of the concerns of human immunodeficiency virus (HIV) transmission. Twenty minutes soaking of diaphragms in one part sodium hypochlorite 5% solution to seven parts of water for 20 minutes also will rid HIV from diaphragms of any type material.

Fitting

41. How is a diaphragm size selected?

The goal of fitting a diaphragm is to select the largest rim size that is comfortable for the patient. A common error in diaphragm fitting is choosing a size that is too small because the patient may be tense during the diaphragm fitting procedure. Women usually are more relaxed when they insert the diaphragm themselves. A diaphragm that is too small may become dislodged during intercourse because vaginal depth increases 3.5 cm (in nulliparous women) during sexual arousal. Conversely, a diaphragm that is too large may cause vaginal pressure, abdominal pain or cramping, vaginal ulceration, or recurrent urinary tract infections.[8]

Patient Instructions

42. What instructions should be provided to R.C. concerning the use of a diaphragm?

The diaphragm should not remain in the vagina for more than 24 hours, nor should it remain in place during menses. Toxic shock syndrome (TSS) has been associated with diaphragm use and women should be alert to its symptoms which include fever (temperature: ≥101 °F), diarrhea, vomiting, muscle aches, and a sunburn-like rash. Allergic reactions to the latex, gum rubber, or spermicides also have been reported.[8,193]

In one case-control study, the risk of nonmenstrual TSS attributed to sponge or diaphragm use was 2.40 cases per 100,000 users per year: approximately 40 excess cases of nonmenstrual TSS in contraceptive sponge users and 54 cases in diaphragm users. Since the mortality rate for nonmenstrual TSS is 8%, eight deaths would be expected per year, or 0.18 deaths per 100,000 users.[193] In response to this article, Ortho Pharmaceutical Corporation revised its labeling for its Ortho Diaphragm products to include a new Physician Information Leaflet that warns ''patients who ever had, or suspect they have had, TSS are advised not to use a diaphragm and to consult with their physician or healthcare provider regarding the selection of another method of birth control.'' Additionally, the revised patient information booklets accompanying diaphragms warns patients to leave their diaphragms in place for at least six hours after intercourse for contraceptive effectiveness; however, they should be removed as soon as possible thereafter.

The diaphragm always should be inserted before intercourse if contraception is to be maximized, and it can be inserted as long as six hours before intercourse if necessary. The diaphragm should not be removed for at least six hours after intercourse, and some clinicians suggest a second vaginal application of spermicide after

Table 43.21	IUD Early Danger Signs (PAINS)ᵃ
Period late (pregnancy) or abnormal spotting or intermenstrual bleeding	
Abdominal pain or pain with intercourse	
Infection exposure (e.g., gonorrhea) or abnormal vaginal discharge	
Not feeling well, fever, chills	
String missing, shorter, or longer	

ᵃ IUD = Intrauterine device.

two hours. If intercourse is repeated within a six-hour period, a new application of spermicide should be inserted vaginally without removal of the diaphragm. While the diaphragm is in place, douching is contraindicated because this can dilute or remove the spermicide.

When the diaphragm is removed, it should be washed with mild soap and water, rinsed and dried with a towel, and stored in its plastic container. Do not use talcum or perfumed powder on the diaphragm because these may damage the diaphragm or harm the vagina or cervix. Petroleum products also may decompose the diaphragm and should not be used with the diaphragm. Contraceptive jelly, however, may be used if vaginal lubrication is needed. If the patient gains or loses 10 to 20 pounds, her diaphragm fitting should be checked.

Cervical Caps

43. R.C.'s obstetrician asks how effective cervical caps are in the prevention of pregnancy.

The Prentif Cavity-Rim Cervical Cap has been made in England since 1930 and was approved by the FDA in 1988. It is a small, flexible, cup-like device made out of natural rubber and designed to fit closely around the base of the cervix; it is available in 22 mm, 25 mm, 28 mm, and 31 mm internal rim diameter sizes. The cap was 82.6% effective overall compared to 83.3% for the diaphragm.[196] Table 43.1 shows a failure rate of 8 to 18 per 100 women-years.

44. How long should cervical caps remain in place?

The patient fills the cap about one-third full with spermicide cream or jelly and suction holds it in place. It should be left in place at least eight hours after intercourse, but no longer than 48 hours according to the manufacturer. According to most experts, the cap should remain in place only 24 hours because of problems with strong vaginal odor at 36 to 48 hours and the theoretical risk of TSS.[8]

45. How well are cervical caps accepted by women?

Women generally prefer other methods of contraception over cervical caps. In one study, 50% of women discontinued the use of cervical caps after six months, and 50% were pregnant after two years of use.[197]

Adverse effects associated with cervical caps include acute pelvic infections, acute cervicitis, and development of abnormal Pap smears.[8]

Condoms

46. How effective are condoms in the prevention of pregnancy?

Condoms are yet another method of birth control and are reasonably effective when utilized properly. According to Table 43.1, the failure rate with condoms is 4.2 to 12 per 100 women-years use of condoms. All condoms in the U.S. are equally effective and differ only in their shapes, the presence or absence of lubricants, and the presence or absence of a spermicide on the inside and outside of the condom.

Ramses Extra brand of condoms has 0.5 gm of the spermicide nonoxynol-9 on the inner and outer surfaces of the condom. The percentage of motile sperm in these condoms is 10.3% at 30 seconds, 4.3% at 60 seconds, and 1.5% at 120 seconds compared to 55.9% at 30 seconds, 52.3% at 60 seconds, and 50.2% at 120 seconds with other types of condoms. The effectiveness of the spermicides on the outside of the condom, should a condom break, has not been evaluated.[198] Since the pre-ejaculatory secretions may contain sperm, the condom should be applied before vaginal contact. Most practitioners recommend lubricated condoms with reservoir ends to collect the ejaculate and prevent breakage.[8]

For men or women allergic to the rubber or spermicide in condoms, lambskin condoms may be useful. The chief noncontraceptive benefit of condoms is the prevention of sexually transmitted diseases. Condoms also prevent the development of or cause the regression of intraepithelial neoplasia.[199]

Vaginal Spermicides

47. What are the preferred dosage forms of vaginal spermicide?

Vaginal spermicides currently are available in creams, jellies, gels, suppositories, vaginal tablets, foams, condoms, and sponges. The majority of these products utilize a nonionic surfactant, nonoxynol-9, as the spermicide; the balance use octoxynol-9. The *in vitro* spermicidal potencies of various preparations are highest with foam, followed by cream, jelly, and gel, respectively.[200] The least effective is Encare Oval.[201] First-year failure rates with these dosage forms range from 0.0 to 21 failures per 100 women-years of use.

Clinically, it has become apparent that the least desirable vaginal spermicidal products on the market today are Encare Oval and the Today Vaginal Contraceptive Sponge. Both are associated with high pregnancy rates (i.e., 18 to 28 failures or more per 100 women-years of use rather than the manufacturer's claims of less than one-half).[201,202] Furthermore, the vaginal sponge is associated with a high risk of TSS (≈10 per 100,000 compared to the 5 to 10 per 100,000 with the vaginal tampon).[193]

A study linking spermicides to major congenital anomalies in the fetus[203] has been discounted by a panel of experts at the Atlanta Center for Disease Control because of severe study design flaws.[8]

Contraceptive foam or one of the creams or jellies with the higher concentration of spermicide which are designed to be used without an additional contraceptive barrier can be recommended. Nevertheless, the best over-the-counter barrier method of contraception is the combined use of contraceptive vaginal foams and condoms.

48. When should vaginal spermicide be applied to be most effective?

The spermicide should be inserted vaginally not more than 30 to 60 minutes before intercourse and should be repeated before additional acts of intercourse. Douching, in general, is not recommended and should never be done within eight hours of intercourse. Women and men who are sensitive to detergents may have allergic reactions to spermicides.[8] Finally, spermicides may kill *in vitro* some organisms responsible for sexually transmitted diseases (e.g., gonorrhea, trichomonas, herpes, chlamydia,[204] and possibly HTLV III).

Investigatory Contraceptive Agents

Male Contraceptive Methods

49. What male contraceptive methods appear to be the most promising?

At this time, there are no commercially available or FDA-approved male contraceptives other than condoms. There are, however, several methods currently under investigation.

Gossypol, a cottonseed derivative developed in China, alters sperm structure and motility, and decreases sperm production. The recommended dose is 12 to 20 µg/day for two and one-half months or until an infertile state is reached, then 12.5 µg twice weekly. Fertility returns several months after discontinuation. The major side effects include a slight decrease in serum potassium and gastrointestinal complaints.[7,205]

A testosterone plus estradiol salve that is rubbed on the stomach has been formulated to decrease sperm production. However, it is extremely difficult to control dosages with a salve and extensive human testing must be undertaken.[206]

Phenoxybenzamine (Dibenzyline), an orally active adrenergic blocking agent, can be an effective male contraceptive, but probably will be unacceptable. At oral doses up to 20 mg/day in two to three days, it blocks ejaculation via paralysis of the vas deferens, the ampulla, and the ejaculatory ducts. Cessation of the drug brings back ejaculatory function. Men complaining of premature ejaculation reported marked improvement in their sexual performance. The blood pressure of normotensive men was unchanged.[207]

A biodegradable testosterone microcapsule formulation that provides uniform eugonadal levels of testosterone for 10 to 11 weeks is promising.[214]

Luteinizing hormone releasing hormone (LHRH) agonists (LHRH-Ag) and antagonists (LHRH-An) have been promising in the reversible suppression of spermatogenesis in men. These agents, however, depress testosterone synthesis, and cause loss of libido unless androgen supplements also are administered. They exert their activity on the pituitary by binding to membrane receptors on the gonadotrophs, and since they have greater affinity to LHRH receptors and a greater resistance to enzymatic degradation, their activity is prolonged. Normally, pulsatile release of LHRH every 60 to 90 minutes is necessary for the release of follicle-stimulating hormone and luteinizing hormone. Constant LHRH receptor stimulation by nasally administered LHRH-Ag or LHRH-An downregulates follicle-stimulating hormone and luteinizing hormone production leading to suppression of spermatogenesis that normally depends upon pulsatile release of endogenous LHRH from the hypothalamus.

Luteinizing Hormone Releasing Hormone (LHRH) Downregulators for Women

50. What is the role of LHRH downregulators or progesterone antagonists for women?

Successful clinical studies have been conducted in women with an intranasally administered, long-acting, potent luteinizing hormone releasing hormone agonist to block ovulation. Normal pulsatile LHRH release is needed for follicle-stimulating hormone and luteinizing hormone release from the anterior pituitary. Constant stimulation of the LHRH receptors in the pituitary leads to desensitization. LHRH antagonists also may inhibit the action of LHRH on the pituitary and block ovulation. Though no significant side effects have been observed, concern has been voiced about the possibility of unopposed estrogen actions in some women leading to endometrial hyperplasia. Estrogen deficiency in others could lead to hot flashes and osteoporosis.[208] Adjustments in dosage amount and frequency should limit the need for estrogen supplementation in future clinical trials.

Since progesterone supports endometrial implantation of the fertilized ovum, a progesterone antagonist theoretically should block this process and could thus have contraceptive potential. RU-486 (Mifepristone), a competitive progesterone antagonist, when given as a single oral dose of 10 mg/kg of body weight in the midluteal phase, consistently induced menses within 72 hours in women with normal cycles and no risk of pregnancy without inducing adverse side effects. When RU-486 was given to rhesus females on day 25 of the cycle (5 mg/kg IM) the 28% pregnancy rate of control animals in these monkeys was totally eliminated.[209] These preliminary studies suggest that RU-486 and other progesterone antagonists hold promise as safe and effective forms of fertility control that can be administered once a month.

RU-486 also appears to be an efficient and safe abortifacient with a success rate of 85% if used to terminate gestations no longer than five weeks. It is administered in a total oral dosage of 400 to 800 mg over two to four days. However, the occurrence of failed abortions and prolonged uterine bleeding in some subjects mandates that this drug be used only under close medical supervision when used as an abortifacient.[210]

References

1 **Haub C, Yanagishita M.** World Population Data Sheet. Washington: Population Reference Bureau; 1994.

2 **Anon.** The environment and population growth: decade for action. Popul Rep. 1992;20(2):1.

3 **Bongaarts J.** Infertility after age 30: a false alarm. Fam Plann Perspect. 1982; 14:75.

4 **Bongaarts J.** Involuntary childlessness with increasing age. Res Reprod. 1982; 14:1.

5 **Tietze C et al.** Time required for conception in 1727 planned pregnancies. Fertil Steril. 1950;1:338.

6 **Vessey MP et al.** Fertility after stopping different methods of contraception. Br Med J. 1978;1:265.

7 **Jones L et al.** Teenage Pregnancy in Developed Countries. New York: Alan Guttmacher Institute; 1985.

8 **Hatcher RA et al.** Contraceptive Technology 1990–1992. 15th ed. New York: Irvington Publishers; 1990.

9 **Goldzieher JW.** Hormonal Contraception: Pills, Injections, and Implants. 1st ed. Dallas, TX: Essential Medical Information Systems; 1989.

10 **DeLia J, Emery M.** Clinical pharmacology and common minor side effects of oral contraceptives. Clin Obstet Gynecol. 1981;24:879.

11 **Upton GW.** The phasic approach to oral contraception: the triphasic concept and its clinical application. Int J Fertil. 1983;28:121.

12 **Goldzieher JW et al.** Comparative studies of the ethinyl estrogens used in oral contraception: II antiovulatory potency. Am J Obstet Gynecol. 1975;122:619.

13 **Anon.** Experts reveal OC preferences in eight clinical situations 1985. Contraceptive Technology Update. 1985; 6:13.

14 **Briggs MH.** Choosing contraceptive steroids and doses. J Reprod Med. 1983;28(Suppl. 1):57.

15 **Dickey RP.** Managing Contraceptive Pill Patients. 8th ed. Durant, OK: Essential Medical Information Systems; 1994.

16 **Brinton LA.** Oral contraceptives and cervical neoplasia. Contraception. 1991;581:43.

17 **Brinton LA et al.** Oral contraceptive use and risk of invasive cervical cancer. Int J Epidemiol. 1990;19:4.

18 **Speroff L, Darney P.** A Clinical Guide for Contraception. Baltimore, MD: Williams & Wilkins; 1992:55.

19 **McPherson K et al.** Oral contraception and breast cancer. Lancet. 1983;2: 144. Letter.

20 **Pike MC et al.** Breast cancer in young women and use of oral contraceptives: possible modifying effect of formulation and age of use. Lancet. 1983;2: 926.

21 **Royal College of General Practitioners' Oral Contraception Study.** Breast cancer and oral contraceptives: findings in Royal College of General Practitioners' Study. Br Med J. 1981; 282:2088.

22 **Vessey MP et al.** Mortality among women participating in the Oxford/Family Planning Association Contraceptive Study. Br Med J. 1977;282: 731.

23 **Ramcharan S et al.** General summary of findings: general conclusions; implications. In: Ramcharan S et al., eds. The Walnut Creek Contraceptive Drug Study: A Prospective Study of the Side Effects of Oral Contraceptives. Vol. 3. An interim report—a comparison of disease occurrence leading to hospitalization or death in users and nonusers of oral contraceptives. Bethesda, MD: Center for Population Research; 1981:1.

24 **Vessey MP et al.** Breast cancer and oral contraceptives: findings in Oxford-Family Planning Association Contraceptive Study. Br Med J. 1981;282: 2093.

25 **The Centers for Disease Control Cancer and Steroid Hormone Study.** Oral contraceptive use and the risk of breast cancer. JAMA. 1983;249:1591.

26 **Matthews PN et al.** Breast cancer in women who have taken contraceptive steroids. Br Med J. 1981;282:774.

27 **Smith MA, Youngkin EQ.** Current perspectives on combination oral contraceptives. Clin Pharm. 1984;3:485.

28 **Royal College of General Practitioners' Oral Contraceptive Study.** Incidence of arterial disease among oral contraceptive users. J R Coll Gen Pract. 1983;33:75.

29 **Vessey MP et al.** Mortality in oral con-

traceptive users. Lancet. 1981;1:549.

30 **Vessey MP et al.** Mortality among oral contraceptive users: 20 year follow up of women in a cohort study. Br Med J. 1989;299:1487.

31 **Gorton T et al.** High density lipoprotein as a protective factor against coronary heart disease: the Framingham study. Am J Med. 1977;62:707.

32 **Bradley DD et al.** Serum high density lipoprotein cholesterol in women using oral contraceptives, estrogens, and progestins. N Engl J Med. 1978;299:17.

33 **Wahl P et al.** Effect of estrogen/progestin potency on lipid/lipoprotein cholesterol. N Engl J Med. 1983;308:862.

34 **Pasquale SA et al.** Results of a study to determine the effects of three oral contraceptives on serum lipoprotein levels. Fertil Steril. 1982;38:559.

35 **Burkman RT et al.** Lipid and lipoprotein changes associated with oral contraceptive use: randomized clinical trial. Obstet Gynecol. 1989;161:1396.

36 **Gevers Leuven JA et al.** Estrogenic effects of gestodene-desogestrel-containing oral contraceptives on lipoprotein metabolism. Am J Obstet Gynecol. 1990;163:358.

37 **Kloosterboer HJ, Rekers H.** Effects of three combined oral contraceptive preparations containing desogestrel plus ethinyl estradiol on lipid metabolism in comparison with two levonorgestrel preparations. Am J Obstet Gynecol. 1990;163:370.

38 **Pasquale SA et al.** Rationale for a triphasic oral contraceptive. J Reprod Med. 1984;29(Suppl.):560.

39 **Stokes T, Wynn V.** Serum lipids in women on oral contraceptives. Lancet. 1971;2:677.

40 **Realini TP, Goldzieher JW.** Oral contraceptives and cardiovascular disease: a critique of the epidemiologic studies. Am J Obstet Gynecol. 1985;152:729.

41 **Tikkanen MJ et al.** High density lipoprotein-2 and hepatic lipase: reciprocal changes produced by estrogen and norgestrel. J Clin Endocrinol Metab. 1982; 54:1113.

42 **Tikkanen MH et al.** Reduction of plasma high density lipoprotein-2 cholesterol and increase of post-heparin plasma hepatic lipase activity during progestin treatment. Clin Chim Acta. 1981;115:63.

43 **Miller NE et al.** Relation of angiographically defined coronary artery disease to plasma lipoprotein subfractions and apolipoprotein. Br Med J. 1981; 282:1741.

44 **Dugdale M et al.** Hormonal contraception and thromboembolic disease, effects of oral contraceptives on hemostatic mechanisms. J Chronic Dis. 1971;23:775.

45 **Wessler S et al.** Estrogen containing oral contraceptive agents: a basis for their thrombogenicity. JAMA. 1976; 236:2179.

46 **Stadel BV.** Oral contraceptives and cardiovascular disease. N Engl J Med. 1981;305(Pt. 1):612–18.

47 **Petersen C et al.** Antithrombin III: comparison of functional and immunologic assays. Am J Clin Pathol. 1978;69:500.

48 **von Kaulla E et al.** Antithrombin III depression and thrombin generation acceleration in women taking oral contra-

ceptives. Am J Obstet Gynecol. 1971; 109:868.

49 **Royal College of General Practitioners' Oral Contraception Study.** Oral contraceptives, venous thrombosis, and varicose veins: Royal College of General Practitioners' Oral Contraceptive Study. J R Coll Gen Pract. 1978;28: 393.

50 **Inman WHW et al.** Thromboembolic disease and steroidal content of oral contraceptives: a report to the Committee on Safety of Drugs. Br Med J. 1970;2:203–09.

51 **Lawson DH et al.** Oral contraceptive use and venous thromboembolism: absence of an effect of smoking. Br Med J. 1977;2:729.

52 **Layde PM et al.** Further analysis of mortality in oral contraceptive users. Lancet. 1981;1:541.

53 **Petitti DB et al.** Risk of vascular disease in women. Smoking, oral contraceptives, noncontraceptive estrogens, and other factors. JAMA. 1979;242: 1150.

54 **Vessey MP.** Female hormones and vascular disease: an epidemiological overview. Br J Fam Plan. 1980;(Suppl. 3):1.

55 **DeStefano F et al.** Oral contraceptives and post-operative venous thrombosis. Am J Obstet Gynecol. 1982;143:227.

56 **Sartwell PE et al.** Thromboembolism and oral contraceptives: an epidemiological case-control study. Am J Epidemiol. 1969;90:365.

57 **Lawson DH et al.** Oral contraceptive use and venous thromboembolism: absence of an effect of smoking. Br Med J. 1977;2:729.

58 **Jick H et al.** Venous thromboembolic disease and ABO blood type. Lancet. 1969;1:539.

59 **Jick H et al.** Venous thromboembolic disease and "A", "B", "O" blood type. Lancet. 1972;2:123.

60 **Mourant AE et al.** Blood groups and blood clotting. Lancet. 1971;1:223.

61 **Fagerhol MK et al.** Antithrombin III concentration and ABO blood groups. Lancet. 1971;2:664.

62 **Tapla HR et al.** Effect of oral contraceptive therapy on the renin angiotensin system in normotensive and hypertensive women. Obstet Gynecol. 1973; 41:643.

63 **Blumenstein BA et al.** Blood pressure changes and oral contraceptive use: a study of 2676 black women in the southeastern United States. Am J Epidemiol. 1980;112:539.

64 **Fisch TR et al.** Oral contraceptives and blood pressure. JAMA. 1977;237: 2499.

65 **Fisch TR et al.** Oral contraceptives, pregnancy and blood pressure. In: Ramcharan S, ed. The Walnut Creek Contraceptive Drug Study: A Prospective Study of the Side Effects of Oral Contraceptives. Vol. 1. Washington, DC: Government Printing Office, 1974; 105. DHEW publication no. (NIH)74-562.

66 **Ramcharan S et al.** The occurrence and course of hypertensive disease in users and nonusers of oral contraceptive drugs. In: Ramcharan S, ed. The Walnut Creek Contraceptive Drug Study: A Prospective Study of the Side Effects of Oral Contraceptives. Vol. 2.

Washington, DC: Government Printing Office, 1976; 1. DHEW publication no. (NIH)74-562.

67 **Weir RJ et al.** Contraceptive steroids and hypertension. J Steroid Biochem. 1975;6:961.

68 **Rinehart W et al.** COCs—update on usage, safety, and side effects. Popul Reports, Series A, Number 5. Population Information Program. Baltimore: The Johns Hopkins University; 1979.

69 **Speroff L (Moderator).** Symposium: prescribing OCs for safety. Contemp Obstet Gynecol. 1986;27:128.

70 **Tsai CC et al.** Low-dose oral contraception and blood pressure in women with a past history of elevated blood pressure. Am J Obstet Gynecol. 1985; 151:28–32.

71 **Briggs MH et al.** Randomized prospective studies on metabolic effects of oral contraceptives. Acta Obstet Gynecol Scand. 1982;105(Suppl.):25.

72 **Wynn V.** Effect of duration of low-dose oral contraceptives administration on carbohydrate metabolism. Am J Obstet Gynecol. 1982;142:739.

73 **Spellacy WN.** Carbohydrate metabolism during treatment with estrogen, progestin, and low-dose oral contraceptives. Am J Obstet Gynecol. 1982; 142:732.

74 **Spellacy WN et al.** Effects of norethindrone on carbohydrate and lipid metabolism. Obstet Gynecol. 1975;46: 560.

75 **Spellacy WN et al.** Carbohydrate metabolism prospectively studied in women using a low-estrogen oral contraceptive for six months. Contraception. 1979;20:137.

76 **Skouby SO.** Low dosage oral contraception in women with previous gestational diabetes. Obstet Gynecol. 1982; 59:325.

77 **Skouby SO et al.** Triphasic oral contraception: metabolic effects in normal women and those with previous gestational diabetes. Am J Obstet Gynecol. 1985;153:495.

78 **Spellacy WN et al.** Carbohydrate metabolism with three months of low-estrogen contraceptive use. Am J Obstet Gynecol. 1980;138:151.

79 **Kjos SL et al.** Effect of low-dose oral contraceptives on carbohydrate and lipid metabolism in women with recent gestational diabetes: results of a controlled, randomized, prospective study. Am J Obstet Gynecol. 1990;163:1822.

80 **Boston Collaborative Drug Surveillance Programme: Oral contraceptives and venous thromboembolic disease, surgically confirmed gallbladder disease, and breast tumors.** Lancet. 1973;1:1399.

81 **Bennion LJ et al.** Effects of oral contraceptives on the gallbladder bile of normal women. N Engl J Med. 1976; 294:189.

82 **Royal College of General Practitioners' Oral Contraception Study.** Oral contraceptives and gallbladder disease. Lancet. 1982;2:957.

83 **Ramcharan S et al.** The Walnut Creek Contraceptive Drug Study: A Prospective Study of the Side Effects of Oral Contraceptives. Vol. 3. An interim report—a comparison of disease occurrence leading to hospitalization or death in users and nonusers of oral con-

traceptives. Bethesda, MD: Center for Population Research, 1981; NIH publication no. 81564: 349.

84 **Sturtevant FM.** Oral contraceptives and liver tumors. In: Moghissi SK, ed. Controversies in Contraception. Baltimore, MD: Williams and Wilkins; 1979:93.

85 **Edmondson HA, Henderson BB.** Liver cell adenomas associated with the use of oral contraceptives. N Engl J Med. 1976;294:470.

86 **Rooks JB et al.** Epidemiology of hepatocellular adenoma: the role of oral contraceptive use. JAMA. 1979;242: 644.

87 **Desser-Wiest L.** Promotion of liver tumors by steroid hormones. J Toxicol Environ Health. 1979;5:203.

88 **Ockner R et al.** Hepatic effects of oral contraceptives. N Engl J Med. 1967; 276:331.

89 **Harlap S, Davies AM.** The pill and births; the Jerusalem study. Part 1, Text, Final Report. Rockville, MD: National Institute of Child Health and Development, 1978; (Contract No. NO1-HD-4-2853):116.

90 **Evrard JR et al.** Amenorrhea following oral contraception. Am J Obstet Gynecol. 1976;124:88.

91 **Rice-Wray E et al.** Return of ovulation after discontinuation of oral contraceptives. Fertil Steril. 1967;18:212.

92 **Furuhjelm M, Carstrom K.** Amenorrhea following use of combined oral contraceptives. Obstet Gynecol Scand. 1973;52:373.

93 **March CM et al.** Amenorrhea, galactorrhea, and pituitary tumors: post-pill and non-pill. Fertil Steril. 1977;28:346.

94 **Vessey MP et al.** Fertility after stopping different methods of contraception. Br Med J. 1978;1:265.

95 **Dickey RP.** Treatment of post-pill amenorrhea. Int J Gynecol Obstet. 1977;15:125.

96 **Wilson JG, Brent RL.** Are female sex hormones teratogenic? Am J Obstet Gynecol. 1989;141:567.

97 **Corcoran R, Entwistle GC.** VACTERL congenital malformations and the male fetus. Lancet. 1975;2:981.

98 **Heinonen OP et al.** Cardiovascular birth defects and antenatal exposure to female sex hormones. N Engl J Med. 1977;296:67.

99 **Janerich DT et al.** Congenital heart disease and prenatal exposure to exogenous sex hormones. Br Med J. 1977; 1:1058.

100 **McCredie J et al.** Congenital limb defects and the pill. Lancet. 1983;2:623.

101 **Ferencz C et al.** Maternal hormone therapy and congenital heart disease. Teratology. 1980;21:225.

102 **Simpson JL.** Relationship between congenital anomalies and contraception. Adv Contracept. 1985;1:3.

103 **Bracken MB, Srisuphan W.** Oral contraception as a risk factor for preeclampsia. Am J Obstet Gynecol. 1982;142:191.

104 **Sherris JD, Fox G.** Infertility and sexually transmitted disease: a public health challenge. Popul Rep [L]. 1983; 11:113.

105 **Rubin GL et al.** Oral contraceptives and pelvic inflammatory disease. Am J Obstet Gynecol. 1982;140:630–35.

106 **Wolner-Hanssen P et al.** Laparo-

scopic findings and contraceptive use in women with signs and symptoms suggestive of acute salpingitis. Obstet Gynecol. 1985;66:233.

107 **Washington AE et al.** Oral contraceptives, chlamydia trachomatous infection, and pelvic inflammatory disease. JAMA. 1985;253:2246.

108 **Cramer DW et al.** Tubal infertility and the intrauterine device. N Engl J Med. 1985;312:941.

109 **Wolner-Hanssen P et al.** Decreased risk of symptomatic chlamydial pelvic inflammatory disease associated with oral contraceptive use. JAMA. 1990; 263(1):54.

110 **Ory HW.** The noncontraceptive health benefits from oral contraceptive use. Fam Plann Perspect. 1982;14:182.

111 **Perlmutter JF.** Pregnancy and the IUD. J Reprod Med. 1978;20:133.

112 **Rubin GL et al.** Ectopic pregnancy in the United States, 1970–1978. JAMA. 1983;249:1725.

113 **Farley TMM et al.** Intrauterine devices and pelvic inflammatory disease: an international perspective. Lancet. 1992;339:785.

114 **Ory HW and Women's Health Study.** Ectopic pregnancy and intrauterine contraceptive devices: new perspectives. Obstet Gynecol. 1981;57:137.

115 **Darney PD.** Evaluating the pill's long-term effects. Contemp Obstet Gynecol. 1982;20:57.

116 **Rosenberg L et al.** Epithelial ovarian cancer and the combination oral contraceptives. JAMA. 1982;247:3210.

117 **The Center for Disease Control Cancer and Steroid Hormone Study.** Oral contraceptive use and the risk of ovarian cancer. JAMA. 1983;249:1596.

118 **Brinton LA et al.** Risk factors for benign breast disease. Am J Epidemiol. 1981;113:203.

119 **Barber HRK.** The pill: noncontraceptive benefits. Female Patient. 1982;7:12.

120 **Royal College of General Practitioners.** Oral contraceptives and health: an interim report from the oral contraception study of the Royal College of General Practitioners. Pitman, NY: Royal College of General Practitioners; 1974.

121 **Speroff L.** PMS: looking for new answers to an old problem. Contemp Obstet Gynecol. 1983;21:102.

122 **True BL et al.** Review of the etiology and treatment of premenstrual syndrome. Drug Intell Clin Pharm. 1985; 19:714.

123 **Halbert DR.** Noncontraceptive uses of the pill. Clin Obstet Gynecol. 1981;24:987.

124 **Grace E et al.** Clinical and laboratory observations: hematologic abnormalities in adolescents who take the oral contraceptive pills. J Pediatr. 1982; 101:771.

125 **Barranco VP, Jones DD.** Effects of oral contraceptives on acne. South Med J. 1974;67:703.

126 **Cunliffe WJ.** Acne, hormones and treatment. Br Med J. 1982;285:912.

127 **Allen HH et al.** A Canadian multicenter clinical trial of a triphasic oral contraceptive. In: Elstein M, ed. Update on Triphasic Oral Contraception. Princeton. Amsterdam: Excerpta Medica; 1983:82.

128 **Speroff L et al.** Evaluation of a new

generation of oral contraceptives. Obstet Gynecol. 1993;81:1034.

129 **Kligman AM.** Pimples following the pill. Arch Dermatol. 1972;105:298.

130 **Joshi JV et al.** A study of interaction of low-dose combination oral contraceptive with ampicillin and metronidazole. Contraception. 1980;22:643.

131 **Back DJ et al.** The interaction between ampicillin and oral contraceptive steroids in women. Br J Clin Pharmacol. 1982;13:280.

132 **Robertson YR, Johnson ES.** Interactions between oral contraceptives and other drugs: a review. Curr Med Res Opin. 1976;3:647.

133 **D'Arcy PF.** Drug interactions with oral contraceptives. Drug Intell Clin Pharm. 1986;20:353.

134 **Back DJ et al.** Interindividual variation and drug interactions with hormonal steroid contraceptives. Drugs. 1981;21:46.

135 **Grimmer SFM et al.** The effect of cotrimoxazole on oral contraceptive steroids in women. Contraception. 1983; 28:53.

136 **Bacon JF, Shenfield GM.** Pregnancy attributable to interaction between tetracycline and oral contraceptives. Br Med J. 1980;280:293.

137 **Back DJ et al.** Drug interactions with oral contraceptives. Int Planned Parenthood Federation Med Bull. 1978; 12:4.

138 **Hempel E et al.** Drug stimulated biotransformation of hormonal steroid contraceptives: clinical implications. Drugs. 1976;12:442.

139 **Back DJ et al.** The effect of antibiotics on enterohepatic circulation of ethinylestradiol and norethisterone in the rat. J Steroid Biochem. 1978;9:527.

140 **Hudson P.** The tetracycline-oral contraceptive controversy. J Am Acad Dermatol. 1982;7:269.

141 **Hansten PD, Horn JR.** Inhibition of oral contraceptive efficacy. Drug Interactions Newsletter. 1985;5:7.

142 **Orme MLE.** The clinical pharmacology of oral contraceptive steroids. Br J Clin Pharmacol. 1982;14:31.

143 **William K, Pulkkinen MO.** Reduced maternal plasma and urinary estriol during ampicillin treatment. Am J Obstet Gynecol. 1971;109:893.

144 **DeSano EA, Hurley SC.** Possible interactions of antihistamines and antibiotics with oral contraceptive effectiveness. Fertil Steril. 1982;37:853.

145 **Friedman CI et al.** The effect of ampicillin on oral contraceptive effectiveness. Obstet Gynecol. 1980;55:33.

146 **D'Arcy PF.** Drug Interactions Update: Nitrofurantoin. Drug Intell Clin Pharm. 1985;19:540.

147 **Coulam CB, Annegers JF.** Do anticonvulsants reduce the efficacy of oral contraceptives? Epilepsia. 1979;2:519.

148 **Dickey RP.** Medical approaches to reproductive regulation: the pill. ACOG. Semin Fam Plan. 1974;Table IX:32.

149 **McArthur J.** Oral contraceptives and epilepsy. Br Med J. 1967;3:162.

150 **Van Dijke CPH, Weber JCP.** Interaction between oral contraceptives and griseofulvin. Br Med J. 1984;288:1125.

151 **Joshi JV et al.** A study of interaction of a low-dose combination oral contraceptive with antitubercular drugs. Contraception. 1980;21:617–29.

152 **Adlercreutz H et al.** Effect of ampicillin administration on plasma conjugated and unconjugated estrogen and progesterone levels in pregnancy. Am J Obstet Gynecol. 1977;128:266.

153 **Schroggie JJ et al.** Effect of oral contraceptives on vitamin K-dependent clotting activity. Clin Pharmacol Ther. 1967;8:670.

154 **de Teresa E et al.** Interaction between anticoagulants and contraceptives: an unsuspected finding. Br Med J. 1979; 2:1260.

155 **Abernethy DR et al.** Impairment of diazepam metabolism by low-dose estrogen-containing oral contraceptive steroids. N Engl J Med. 1982;306:791.

156 **Stoehr GP et al.** The effect of low-dose estrogen-containing oral contraceptives on the pharmacokinetics of triazolam, alprazolam, temazepam, and lorazepam. Drug Intell Clin Pharm. 1984;18:495. Abstract.

157 **Boekenoogen SJ et al.** Prednisone disposition and protein binding in oral contraceptive users. J Clin Endocrinol Metab. 1983;56:702.

158 **Tornatore KM et al.** Effect of chronic contraceptive steroids on theophylline disposition. Eur J Clin Pharmacol. 1982;23:129.

159 **Steele JM, Duncan LJP.** Effect of oral contraceptives on insulin requirements in diabetics. J Fam Plan Doctors. 1978; 3:77.

160 **Smith RD et al.** Prolactin binding to mammary gland, 7,12-dimethylbenz(a) anthracene-induced mammary tumors, and liver in rats. Cancer Res. 1976;36:3726.

161 **Turkington RW, Hill RL.** Lactose synthetase: progesterone inhibition of the induction of alpha-lactalbumin. Science. 1969;163:1458.

162 **Jewell ME.** Breast feeding. Am Fam Pract. 1984;30:167.

163 **Sheth A et al.** A randomized double-blind study of two combined and two progestin-only oral contraceptives. Contraception. 1982;25:243.

164 **Anon.** The minipill—a limited alternative for certain women. Popul Rep A, Number 3. Population Information Program. Baltimore: The Johns Hopkins University; 1979.

165 **Dorflinger LI.** Relative potency of progestins used in oral contraceptives. Contraception. 1985;31:557.

166 **Loudon NB et al.** Instructions for starting the use of oral contraceptives. N Engl J Med. 1984;311:1634.

167 **Carey HM.** Principles of oral contraception. 2. Side effects of oral contraceptives. Med J Aust. 1971;2:1242.

168 **Kudrow L.** The relationship of headache frequency to hormone use in migraine. Headache. 1975;15:36.

169 **Dennerstein L et al.** Headache and sex hormone therapy. Headache. 1978;18:146.

170 **Raskin NH, Appenzeller O.** Headache Vol. 19 in the series. Major Problems in Internal Medicine. Philadelphia: WB Saunders; 1980.

171 **Desrosiers HH.** Headaches related to contraceptive therapy and their control. Headache. 1973;13:117.

172 **Dalton K.** Migraine and oral contraceptives. Headaches. 1976;15:247.

173 **Leeton J.** Depression induced by oral contraception and the role of vitamin

B6 in its management. Aust N Z J Psychiatry. 1974;8:85.

174 **Ryan RE.** A controlled study of the effect of oral contraceptives on migraine. Headache. 1978;17:250.

175 **Adams PW et al.** Effects of pyridoxine HCl (vitamin B6) upon depression associated with oral contraception. Lancet. 1973;1:897.

176 **Anon.** Postcoital contraception: a delicate issue. Contraceptive Technol Update. 1984;5:41.

177 **Yuzpe AA.** Postcoital hormonal contraception: uses, risks, and abuses. Int J Gynecol Obstet. 1977;15:133.

178 **Notelovitz M.** Estrogens and postcoital contraception. Female Patient. 1981;6:36.

179 **Anon.** Ovral as a "morning-after" contraceptive. Med Lett Drugs Ther. 1989; 31(Issue 803):93.

180 **Yuzpe AA et al.** A multi-center clinical investigation employing ethinyl estradiol combined with DL norgestrel as a postcoital contraceptive. Fertil Steril. 1982;37:508.

181 **Yuzpe AA, Lancee WJ.** Ethinyl estradiol and d1 norgestrel as a postcoital contraceptive. Fertil Steril. 1977;9:932.

182 **Kaunitz AM.** Injectable contraception. Clin Obstet Gynecol. 1989;32:356.

183 **WHO Collaborative Study of Neoplasia and Steroid Contraceptives.** Depot medroxyprogesterone acetate (DMPA) and risk of endometrial cancer. Int J Cancer. 1991;49:186.

184 **Kaunitz AM, Rosenfield A.** Injectable contraception with depot medroxyprogesterone acetate. Current status. Drugs. 1993;45(6):857.

185 **Cundy T et al.** Bone density in women receiving depot medroxyprogesterone acetate for contraception. Br Med J. 1991;303:13.

186 **Darney PD et al.** Sustained release contraceptives. Curr Prob Obstet Gynecol Fertil. 1990;13(3):90.

187 **Diaz S et al.** Clinical assessment of treatments of prolonged bleeding in users of Norplant users. Contraception. 1990;42(1):97.

188 **Shoupe D et al.** The significance of bleeding patterns in Norplant implant users. Obstet Gynecol. 1991;77(2):256.

189 **Haukkamaa M.** Contraception by Norplant subdermal capsules not reliable in epileptic patients on anticonvulsant treatment. Contraception. 1986; 33(6):559.

190 **Lee NC et al.** The intrauterine device and pelvic inflammatory disease revisited: new results from the women's health study. Obstet Gynecol. 1988;72:1.

191 **Ortiz ME, Croxatto HB.** The mode of action of IUDs. Contraception. 1987; 36:37.

192 **Cramer DW et al.** Tubal infertility and the intrauterine device. N Engl J Med. 1985;312:941.

193 **Tatum HJ, Connell EB.** A decade of intrauterine contraception: 1976–1986. Fertil Steril. 1986;46:173.

194 **Centers for Disease Control.** Toxic shock syndrome and the vaginal contraceptive sponge. MMWR. 1984;33:43.

195 **Schwartz B et al.** Nonmenstrual toxic shock syndrome associated with barrier contraceptives: report of a case control study. Rev Infect Dis. 1989;2(Suppl. 1):s43.

196 **Anon.** The cervical cap. Med Lett Drugs Ther. 1988;30(Issue 776):93.

197 **Smith GG, Lee RJ.** The use of cervical caps at the University of California, Berkeley: a survey. Contraception. 1984;30:115.

198 **Dale E.** A laboratory investigation of the anti-spermatozoa action of condoms treated with a spermicidal preparation. Schmid Products Company; 1982.

199 **Richardson AC, Lyon JB.** The effect of condom use on squamous cell cervical intraepithelial neoplasia. Am J Obstet Gynecol. 1981;140:909.

200 **Homm RE et al.** A comparison of the *in vivo* contraceptive potencies of a variety of marked vaginal contraceptive dosage forms. Curr Ther Res. 1977;22:588.

201 **Anon.** Encare Oval overpromoted. FDA Drug Bull. 1978;8:20.

202 **Anon.** A vaginal contraceptive sponge. Med Lett Drugs Ther. 1983;25:78.

203 **Jick H et al.** Vaginal spermicides and congenital disorders. JAMA. 1981; 245:1329.

204 **Cutler JC et al.** Vaginal contraceptives as prophylaxis against gonorrhea and other sexually transmissible disease. Adv Plann Parenthood. 1977;12:45.

205 **National Coordinating Group on Male Antifertility Agents.** Gossypol—a new antifertility agent for males. Chin Med J (Engl). 1978;4:417.

206 **Steinberg S.** Male contraceptive in stomach salve. Science News. 1983; 124:117.

207 **Homonnai ZT et al.** Phenoxybenzamine—an effective male contraceptive pill. Contraception. 1984;29:479.

208 **Thau RB.** Luteinizing hormone-Releasing Hormone (LHRH) and its analogs for contraception in women: a review. Contraception. 1984;29:143.

209 **Nieman LK et al.** The progesterone antagonist RU-486. A potential new contraceptive agent. N Engl J Med. 1987;316:187.

210 **Couzinet B et al.** Termination of early pregnancy by the progesterone antagonist RU-486 (Mifepristone). N Engl J Med. 1986;315:1565.

211 **Hatcher RA et al.** Contraceptive Technology. 16th ed. New York: Irvington Publishers; 1994.

212 **Committee on Drugs, American Academy of Pediatrics.** The transfer of drugs and other chemicals into human milk. Pediatrics. 1994;93:137.

213 **Miller DM et al.** A practical approach to antibiotic treatment in women taking oral contraceptives. J Am Acad Dermatol. 1994;30:1008.

214 **Bhasin S et al.** A biodegradable testosterone microcapsule formulation provides uniform eugonadal levels of testosterone for 10–11 weeks. J Clin Endocrinol Metab. 1992;74:75.

215 **Klaisle C.** Personal communication. RN, MSN. OB Gyn Nurse Practitioner. Family Planning Research. San Francisco General Hospital. San Francisco, CA: 1994 Aug.

Obstetrics

Rosalie Sagraves
Nancy A Letassy
Terri L Barton

Pregnancy 44-2
  Fertilization and Implantation (See Figure 44.1) 44-2
  Development of the Placenta 44-2
    Fetal and maternal components 44-3
    Placental hormones 44-3
      Human chorionic gonadotropin (hCG) 44-3
      Estrogens and progesterone 44-3
      Human placental lactogen (hPL) 44-3
      Relaxin 44-4
  Embryonic Membranes 44-4
  Definitions 44-4
    Parity and gravida 44-4
    Trimesters of pregnancy 44-4
    Delivery terms 44-4
  Diagnosis of Pregnancy (See Table 44.1) 44-4
    Presumptive evidence 44-4
    Probable evidence 44-5
    Positive evidence 44-5
  Prenatal Care 44-5
    Goals of care (See Table 44.2) 44-5
    Initial visit 44-5
    Follow-up visits 44-5
  Determination of Gestational Age 44-6
  Nutrition 44-6
    Weight gain (See Table 44.3) 44-6
    Energy requirements 44-7
    Protein requirements 44-7
    Iron requirements 44-7
    Folate requirements 44-7
      Women with a History of Neural Tube
        Defects (NTDs) 44-7
    Calcium requirements 44-8
  Common Complaints of Pregnancy 44-8
    Morning sickness 44-8
      Management 44-8
        Antiemetics 44-8
    Constipation 44-9
    Hemorrhoids 44-9
    Reflux esophagitis 44-9
Diabetes Mellitus in Pregnancy (See Table 44.4) ... 44-9
  Pre-Existent Diabetes 44-10
    Infants of diabetic mothers (IDM) 44-10
      Mortality 44-10
      Risk of congenital anomalies 44-10
      Macrosomia 44-10
    Maternal risks 44-10
      Common complications and contraindications 44-10
      Prepregnancy assessment 44-10
    Prepregnancy management 44-10
    Pregnancy management 44-11
      Insulin regimens 44-11
      Blood glucose monitoring, HbA$_{lc}$, and urine
        ketone determinations 44-11
  Gestational Diabetes Mellitus (GMD) 44-11
    Diagnostic criteria (See Table 44.5) 44-11

  Management 44-11
    Treatment goals 44-11
    Dietary management 44-12
    Insulin therapy 44-12
  Risk of developing diabetes mellitus 44-12
Seizure Disorders In Pregnancy 44-12
  Epilepsy-Associated Complications 44-12
  Effects of pregnancy on seizure disorders 44-12
  Effects of seizure disorders on pregnancy 44-12
  Phenytoin Use 44-13
    Fetal hydantoin syndrome (FHS)
      (See Table 44.6) 44-13
    Congenital defects and the effects of
      folic acid 44-13
    Hemorrhagic disease 44-13
    Fetal tumors 44-13
    Pharmacokinetics during pregnancy 44-13
  Other Anticonvulsants 44-14
    Carbamazepine 44-14
    Other agents 44-14
  Counseling 44-14
Hypertension During Pregnancy 44-14
  Classification and Definitions 44-14
  Signs, Symptoms, and Evaluation
    (See Table 44.7) 44-15
  Etiology 44-15
    Increased vasoconstrictor tone 44-15
    Prostaglandin imbalance 44-15
    Response to low-dose aspirin 44-15
  Treatment 44-16
    Mild preeclampsia 44-16
      Controversy regarding hospitalization 44-16
      Ambulatory management (See Table 44.8) 44-16
      Controversy regarding antihypertensive therapy ..44-16
    Moderate preeclampsia 44-16
      Methyldopa 44-17
      β-adrenergic blockers 44-17
      Other antihypertensive agents 44-18
        Calcium channel blockers 44-18
        Angiotensin-converting enzyme (ACE)
          inhibitors 44-18
        Diuretics 44-18
    Severe preclampsia 44-18
      Signs and symptoms 44-18
      Complications 44-18
      Magnesium sulfate 44-18
      Hydralazine 44-19
      Labetalol 44-19
      Diazoxide 44-19
    Ketanserin 44-20
**Isoimmunization and Hemolytic Disease
  of the Newborn (HDN)** 44-20
  Prevention 44-20

(Continued)

Rh$_o$(D) immune globulin (human)
(See Tables 44.9 and 44.10) 44-20
Management during pregnancy 44-21
Therapy For Preterm Labor 44-21
Etiology (See Table 44.11) 44-21
Mechanisms Initiating Preterm Labor 44-22
Clinical Presentation and Evaluation 44-22
Tocolytic Therapy 44-23
Betamimetics 44-23
Mechanism of action 44-23
Agents 44-23
Ritodrine 44-23
Contraindications 44-23
Dosing 44-24
Other agents 44-24
Cost effectiveness 44-24
Adverse maternal effects of 44-24
Cardiovascular 44-24
Pulmonary edema 44-25
Hyperglycemia 44-25
Hypokalemia 44-25
Others 44-25
Adverse fetal effects of 44-25
Fetal lung maturity 44-25
Other tocolytics 44-25
Magnesium sulfate 44-25
Prostaglandin synthetase inhibitors 44-25
Calcium channel blockers 44-25
Oxytocin antagonists 44-26
Labor Induction 44-26

Prostaglandin E$_2$ (PGE$_2$) 44-26
Indications and contraindications
(See Table 44.12) 44-26
Role in labor induction 44-26
Dosing 44-26
Adverse effects 44-26
Intravaginal administration 44-26
Oxytocin 44-26
Mechanism of action 44-26
Indications and contraindications 44-27
Dosing 44-27
Adverse effects 44-27
Other Methods 44-28
Amniotomy 44-28
Breast stimulation 44-28
Postpartum Hemorrhage 44-28
Oxytocin 44-28
Ergot Alkaloids 44-28
Carboprost Tromethamine 44-28
Lactation 44-29
Stimulation 44-29
Nonpharmaceutical measures 44-29
Oxytocin 44-29
Other drugs 44-29
Suppression 44-29
Nonpharmaceutical measures 44-29
Bromocriptine 44-29
High-dose pyridoxine 44-30
Estradiol valerate 44-30

Pregnancy

During pregnancy, a woman's body undergoes physiologic changes to provide for the growth and development of a fetus while maintaining homeostasis.[1] Before this century, routine prenatal care was nonexistent. Midwives assisted in the birthing process calling on a physician only when complications occurred. Prenatal care did not become a standard of practice until the early 1900s. Good prenatal care now is available to women regardless of socioeconomic status.

The majority of live births are delivered by women 20 to 40 years of age. Unfortunately, the U.S. has one of the highest rates of adolescent (11 to 20 years old) pregnancy in the world. Of the approximate three million births in this country every year, adolescent pregnancy accounts for 20%; 43% of these occur in young women less than 15 years old. Teenage pregnancy prevention is important for several reasons: the social and psychological ramifications of early pregnancy, pregnant adolescents have twice the risk of complications compared to women in their 20s, and infants born to teenagers have a higher morbidity and mortality than infants born to older women.[2]

Fertilization and Implantation

The female reproductive tract is composed of the external genitalia and the internal organs located in and protected by the pelvic cavity. The external genitalia include the mons pubis, labia majora, labia minora, and the vestibule of the vagina; the internal reproductive organs include the ovaries, fallopian tubes, uterus, cervix, and vagina. (See Figure 44.1.)

Women begin life with a fixed number of primary oocytes that undergo maturation or atresia during the reproductive years.[3] At puberty, gonadotropic stimulation begins and the ovaries release one or more ova per month in response to luteinizing hormone

(LH) and follicle-stimulating hormone (FSH). At ovulation, the ovum enters the ampulla of the fallopian tube where it may encounter sperm, but only one spermatozoa penetrates the ovum. After penetration, a change occurs in the membranes surrounding the fertilized ovum preventing other sperm from entering.

Fertilization occurs around day 14 of the menstrual cycle. The fertilized ovum takes four to five days to reach the uterus and another one to two days before it implants in the endometrium. The time between fertilization and implantation corresponds to days 14 through 21 of the menstrual cycle. During this time, the endometrium is being prepared for implantation by the estrogen and progesterone. Implantation occurs on approximately day 20 or 21 of the menstrual cycle.[4]

During the first 72 hours after fertilization, mitotic divisions cleave the fertilized egg into blastomeres. As cell division continues, the mass of cells organize to form a hollow fluid-filled sphere, the blastocyst. The external blastomeres of the blastocyst form a single layer of cells referred to as the trophoblast, while the internal blastomeres give rise to the embryo.[5] Six to seven days after fertilization, the blastocyst implants in the uterine wall and is covered by surface epithelium. After implantation, the trophoblast secretes human chorionic gonadotropin (hCG), which maintains the corpus luteum so that menstruation is prevented.[6] (See Chapter 43: Contraception for a detailed discussion of the menstrual cycle.)

Development of the Placenta

The trophoblast has two functional layers: the inner cytotrophoblast which develops into the chorion and the outer syncytiotrophoblast.[7] Soon after implantation, the trophoblast secretes proteolytic and cytolytic enzymes which allow the syncytiotrophoblast to invade the endometrium. (*Note:* During pregnancy, the endometrium is referred to as the decidua.) The advancing trophoblast creates lacunae which fill with maternal blood. The cytotrophoblast sends projections (chorionic villi) into these cavities in the maternal tissue. This contact with the maternal blood allows hCG to enter the maternal circulation by 11 days gestation where it can be measured to aid in the diagnosis of pregnancy. The fetal blood in the villi is separated from the maternal blood by thin layers of tissue. Maternal arterioles terminate in the intervillous spaces and direct blood toward the chorionic villi. These spaces are drained by decidual veins. The circulation of blood in the intervillous spaces is dependent upon maternal blood pressure (BP) and uterine contractions.[8]

By four weeks gestation, the placenta can function as an organ which exchanges nutrients and gases between the fetal and maternal circulations. The maternal blood carries oxygen and nutrients which pass into the fetal circulation. Carbon dioxide and waste products from the fetal circulation diffuse into the intervillous spaces and are carried away by the maternal blood flow.[7] The placenta continues to grow in size until 20 weeks gestation. From this time until term, the placenta thickens so that at birth it weighs 400 to 600 gm.[9]

Fetal and Maternal Components

The placenta has two components: fetal and maternal. The fetal components are the chorionic villi and its circulation. The maternal portion is the decidua basalis and its circulation. The fetus and placenta regulate the course of pregnancy, and this functional relationship is referred to as the fetoplacental unit. In addition to its respiratory, nutritional, and excretory functions, this unit also is an endocrine system. It produces a number of hormones including chorionic gonadotropin, estrogens, progesterone, and placental lactogen that maintain and regulate pregnancy. The placenta also produces many other hormones, enzymes, proteins, and releasing factors, the physiologic functions of which are unknown.[10]

Placental Hormones

Human chorionic gonadotropin (hCG) produced by the syncytiotrophoblast appears in the maternal circulation eight to nine days after fertilization; it maintains the corpus luteum's ability to produce estradiol and progesterone which is essential for the establishment and maintenance of pregnancy. If corpus luteum function is interrupted before seven weeks gestation, the pregnancy is aborted. Thereafter, the placenta can secrete sufficient quantities of steroid hormones to sustain pregnancy.[10]

Human chorionic gonadotropin is composed of an alpha and a beta subunit. The alpha subunit is identical to the alpha subunit of other pituitary hormones FSH, LH, and thyroid-stimulating hormone; however, the beta subunit is specific to the hormone. Pregnancy tests that are specific for this beta subunit are useful diagnostic tests for confirming pregnancy. Human chorionic gonadotropin serum concentrations increase rapidly, doubling every 1.7 to 2 days. By 14 days gestation, serum concentrations reach 100 mIU/mL. Peak serum concentrations occur at approximately nine to ten weeks gestation with levels averaging 40,000 to 60,000 mIU/mL. Thereafter, hCG concentrations decline to 10,000 mIU/mL and remain low for the duration of pregnancy[10] (1 mg/mL = 9 to 11 mIU/mL).

Estrogens and Progesterone. The placenta differs from the ovaries in the production of gonadal steroids because it lacks some enzymes necessary for steroidogenesis. The fetoplacental unit depends upon maternal and fetal steroid precursors to produce large quantities of estrogens (estrone, estradiol, and estriol) and progesterone during pregnancy.[10] Estrone and estradiol production depend upon both fetal and maternal precursors, while estriol is synthesized by the placenta from precursors produced by the fetal adrenal glands.[8] Measurement of estriol in the serum or urine has been used to monitor fetal well-being in high-risk pregnancies complicated by diabetes mellitus, prolonged gestation, or intrauterine growth retardation (IUGR). During pregnancy, estrogens increase blood flow to the uterus, increase hepatic protein synthesis, increase angiotensin and aldosterone production, and suppress FSH and LH production. Placental synthesis of progesterone relies on maternal cholesterol and is independent of fetal precursors. Progesterone decreases uterine sensitivity to oxytocin and helps to maintain pregnancy by preventing propagation of uterine contractions. Progesterone also may prevent maternal immunologic rejection of the trophoblast by blocking the immune response to this foreign antigen.[10]

Human Placental Lactogen (hPL). Another hormone produced by the placenta is human placental lactogen, also called chorionic growth hormone prolactin and human chorionic somatomammotropin. The majority of hPL is secreted into the maternal compartment where it antagonizes the effects of insulin. This results in the mobilization of free fatty acids and a glucose-sparing effect which ensures an uninterrupted flow of nutrients to the fetus.[10,11]

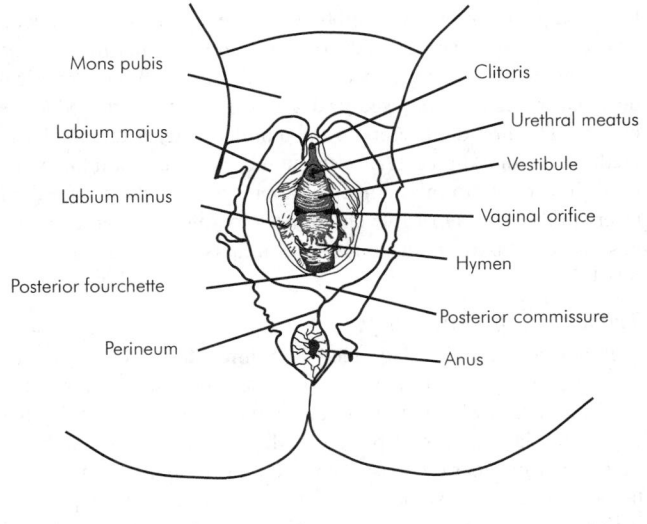

Fig 44.1   The Female Reproductive Glands

Relaxin, a hormone produced by the corpus luteum throughout pregnancy, also plays a role in the early maintenance of pregnancy. It works synergistically with progesterone and prostacyclin (PGI_2) to decrease spontaneous uterine activity. Relaxin also increases the distensibility of the cervix.[11]

Embryonic Membranes

Two embryonic membranes, the chorion and the amnion, begin developing at 10 to 14 days of gestation to support and protect the developing embryo. The chorion, the outermost membrane, develops from the trophoblast and the inner membrane; the amnion develops from the ectodermal cells. The fluid-filled space between the amnion and the embryo is the amniotic cavity. The membranes surround the developing baby and function to contain the amniotic fluid and assist in its formation. This fluid provides a mechanically buffered, stable environment in which the infant develops. The amniotic fluid has maternal and fetal sources. The maternal source is plasma filtrate and, as pregnancy advances, the fetal contributions are from urine and excretion of lung fluids. The volume of amniotic fluid ranges from 30 mL at ten weeks gestation, to about 1 L at 40 weeks gestation.[8] The hourly turnover rate later in pregnancy can vary from 300 to 600 mL/hour.[3] The composition of the amniotic fluid includes water, cells, hormones, lecithin, sphingomyelin, albumin, glucose, lipids, proteins, enzymes, creatinine, urea, and bilirubin.[8] Some of these substances are monitored to determine fetal well-being in some high-risk pregnant women.

Definitions

Parity and Gravida

Parity and gravida are terms used to describe a pregnant woman. Parity is the number of deliveries after 20 weeks gestation; it is independent of the number of fetuses delivered stillborn or live, or the method of delivery.[12] The term ''nullipara'' describes a woman who has never delivered a fetus after 20 weeks gestation regardless of whether or not she has aborted previously; a ''primipara'' describes a woman who has delivered a fetus or fetuses beyond 20 weeks gestation; and ''multipara'' describes a woman who has had two or more deliveries past 20 weeks of pregnancy.[13] Gravida refers to the number of pregnancies a woman has had regardless of the outcome (abortion, ectopic, normal pregnancy, hydatiform mole). A nulligravida woman has never been pregnant, a primigravida woman has been pregnant once, and a multigravida woman has been pregnant two or more times. For example, a woman who has had two spontaneous abortions and three normal intrauterine pregnancies may be described as gravida 5 para 3. A numerical designation also can be used to describe a woman's reproductive history. The first digit refers to the number of term infants delivered, the second digit refers to the number of preterm infants, the third digit refers to the number of abortions, and the fourth digit refers to the number of live children. For example, a woman who has had one abortion and three term infants can be described as 3-0-1-3.[12]

Trimesters of Pregnancy

Pregnancy usually is divided into three trimesters, approximately 13 weeks each; however, it is more precise to refer to the weeks gestation which refers to the number of weeks since the first day of the last menstrual period (LMP).[12,13] Pregnancy also can be divided into periods based upon the developmental processes taking place. The development of the baby *in utero* is the prenatal period which is approximately 40 weeks in duration. This period can be divided into three parts: the embryonic period is the first eight weeks gestation, during which the germ layers form and early

organogenesis occurs; during weeks 9 through 26, the fetal period, organs become functional; finally, the perinatal period begins at week 27 and continues until delivery.[5]

Delivery Terms

Depending upon the weeks gestation of a pregnancy, the delivery of a baby may be referred to as an abortion, preterm, term, or postterm birth. An abortion is a delivery before 20 weeks gestation. A term infant is a fetus delivered after the completion of 37 weeks gestation and before 43 weeks gestation. A preterm birth is one which occurs between 20 and 37 weeks gestation, and a postterm (postmaturity) birth occurs after the beginning of 43 weeks gestation.[12]

Diagnosis of Pregnancy

1. S.C., a 29-year-old, primigravida (1-0-0-1) female, presents to her family physician to confirm a suspected pregnancy. Her LMP was 6 weeks ago and this menstrual period is 16 days overdue. She has begun to experience waves of nausea early in the morning for the past week with several episodes of vomiting. She bought an over-the-counter pregnancy test 2 days ago and the result was positive.

Her past medical history is noncontributory except for her obstetrical history which is significant for an uncomplicated delivery of a normal, full-term infant 3 years ago. The significant findings upon pelvic examination are an enlarged uterus and a softening of the uterine isthmus. The rest of the physical examination is normal. The following laboratory results are within normal limits: urinalysis (UA), complete blood count (CBC), and Pap smear. She also has a positive serum pregnancy test, negative Venereal Disease Research Laboratory test, and a negative endocervical culture for gonorrhea. What signs and symptoms is S.C. experiencing that are consistent with pregnancy? What other tests can be used to confirm this diagnosis?

All signs and symptoms in S.C. are consistent with a pregnancy of approximately six weeks gestation. (Also see Question 2.)

Presumptive Evidence

A diagnosis of pregnancy is based upon the symptoms, physical changes, and biochemical test results consistent with pregnancy. The signs and symptoms of pregnancy can be divided into three groups: presumptive, probable, and positive evidence of pregnancy (see Table 44.1). The presumptive evidence of pregnancy includes

Table 44.1	Diagnosis of Pregnancy[14]

Presumptive Evidence
Absence of an expected menstrual period
Breast changes (tenderness and enlargement)
Discoloration of vaginal mucous (Chadwick's sign)
Nausea and/or vomiting ("morning sickness")
↑ in urinary frequency
Perception of fetal movement
Fatigue
Changes in skin pigmentation

Probable Evidence
Enlargement of abdomen
Changes in the size, shape, and consistency of the uterus (Hegar's sign)
Cervical changes
Braxton-Hicks contractions
Palpation of the fetus
Endocrine tests

Positive Evidence
Identification of fetal heart sounds
Perception of active fetal movements by examiner
Recognition of the embryo or fetus by sonography or roentgenography

the physical signs and symptoms a woman can identify. The absence of an expected menstrual period described by S.C. usually is the first sign of pregnancy for most women but this sign cannot be used in women with oligomenorrhea. S.C. also complains of nausea, which occurs in the first 3 to 12 weeks along with fatigue, mastodynia (painful breasts), and urinary frequency. She did not note any ''quickening'' or the maternal perception of fetal movement which usually appears at 16 weeks gestation but may occur earlier in multigravidas. Because most of these symptoms are subjective and may be due to other causes, pregnancy should be confirmed with other tests.[13,14]

Probable Evidence

The physical changes in S.C.'s uterus and cervix and the presence of hCG (as indicated by the positive pregnancy test) are the probable signs of pregnancy. Softening of the uterine isthmus (Hegar's sign) occurs at six weeks gestation; very few conditions besides pregnancy cause this change. At the same time, the examiner can detect a softening and bluish discoloration of the cervix. After 12 to 16 weeks gestation, S.C.'s uterus will enlarge from a pelvic to an abdominal organ that can be palpated above the symphysis pubis. By the end of the first trimester, she may experience Braxton-Hicks contractions (intermittent, irregular, painless uterine contractions), which can continue throughout pregnancy. Neither the presumptive nor probable evidence of pregnancy can differentiate between an ectopic and uterine pregnancy.[13,14]

Endocrine tests for pregnancy rely upon the presence of hCG in the serum or urine. The most accurate tests are specific for the beta subunit of hCG. Radioimmunoassays and monoclonal assays are highly sensitive and can provide accurate results one week after ovulation. A variety of home pregnancy tests are available without prescription and one was used by S.C. to confirm her suspected pregnancy. These tests are easy to interpret and can be performed privately. The results can be obtained in two hours or less and are accurate if the test results are positive. However, these tests are expensive and complicated instructions must be followed precisely to achieve accurate results. False negative results may delay the initiation of prenatal care. Many home pregnancy tests include a second test to be performed one week after a negative test result but some women may not repeat the test, thereby missing an ongoing pregnancy.[13]

Positive Evidence

None of the following were noted in S.C. who is only in her sixth gestational week. The positive evidence of pregnancy includes visualization of the fetus and detection of fetal movement and heart sounds. Cardiac motion can be detected as early as five weeks gestation by echocardiography and by seven weeks gestation using real-time sonography. However, the fetoscope and the ultrasonic Doppler unit are used more commonly. The fetoscope can detect fetal heart sound at 17 to 20 weeks gestation and the ultrasonic Doppler instrument can demonstrate fetal cardiac activity at 10 to 12 weeks gestation. The fetal heart rate, 120 to 160 beats/minute, must be distinguished from the maternal heart rate for diagnosis.[13,14]

Fetal movement usually can be detected by the examiner after 20 weeks gestation. Even though the mother may recognize fetal movement earlier in the pregnancy, it is only a diagnostic finding when the examiner substantiates these movements. Pregnancy can be confirmed as early as five to eight weeks gestation by sonographic demonstration of a gestational sac. By 11 weeks gestation, the gestational sac no longer can be identified but, at this time, fetal cardiac activity can be demonstrated using real-time sonography. The fetal head and thorax can be identified by sonography by 14

weeks gestation. Sonography can be used to estimate gestational age, assess fetal growth and development, and detect fetal anomalies.[13,14]

Radiographic visualization of the fetus is unreliable until 16 weeks gestation; however, unnecessary radiation of the fetus should be avoided. Sonography provides the same information as radiographic visualization but without the dangers associated with radiation. Sonography has not been reported to cause adverse effects on the embryo or the fetus.[16]

Prenatal Care

2. What are the goals of prenatal care? What should be accomplished on this initial visit? When should follow-up visits be scheduled?

Goals of Care

The goal of prenatal care is to promote a safe and successful pregnancy and delivery of a healthy infant. This goal is accomplished through education and by monitoring the health of the mother and fetus. S.C. should be educated about proper nutrition, general hygiene, and the danger signals of pregnancy (see Table 44.2). Prenatal care should begin as early as possible after pregnancy is confirmed, so that women at risk for complicated pregnancies can be identified and potential problems can be monitored and treated.

Initial Visit

During the initial prenatal visit, a medical history and examination will be performed to determine the health status of the mother and fetus, gestational age will be determined, and a plan set up for prenatal care. The pregnancy should be confirmed as discussed previously. The medical history should include menstrual, obstetrical, medical, and medication history and the physical examination should include a general and a pelvic examination. As illustrated by S.C.'s visit, the pelvic examination should include a Pap smear, culture for gonococci, and inspection for genital herpes, venereal warts, trichomonas, or candidal infection. A CBC, blood type and Rh factor, serologic test for syphilis, rubella antibody titer, and a urinalysis to screen for glucosuria, proteinuria, and bacteriuria should be ordered.[14] Risk assessment should be performed during the initial visit. High-risk pregnancies include patients with certain pre-existing medical illnesses or conditions, a history of poor obstetrical performance, or evidence of malnutrition.[12] Women should be educated about diet during pregnancy; the use of medications, caffeine, alcohol, and tobacco; general hygiene; exercise; the danger signals of pregnancy (see Table 44.2); and the importance of follow-up appointments.[14]

Follow-Up Visits

The frequency of return visits depends upon the health status of the mother and fetus. Traditionally, visits are scheduled every four weeks for seven months, then every two weeks until the last month, then weekly until delivery. On every return visit S.C. should be weighed; blood pressure, fundal height, and urinalysis for protein and glucose should be monitored and recorded. She also should be evaluated for danger signals of pregnancy. The fetus should be

Table 44.2	Danger Signs of Pregnancy[13,14]
Vaginal spotting or bleeding	Oliguria
Leakage of fluid from vagina	Persistent vomiting
Abdominal pain or cramping	Chills or fever
Severe or continuous headaches	Dysuria
Change in vision	Marked changes in the intensity or
Swelling of the fingers or face	frequency of fetal movement

evaluated for fetal heart rate, growth, position, activity, and amount of amniotic fluid. In high-risk pregnancies, it may be necessary to order genetic tests and monitor the fetus for the development of complications.[13,14]

Determination of Gestational Age

3. How is gestational age determined? What is the importance of determining gestational age?

One very important objective of prenatal care is an accurate determination of gestational age. This assessment is important to determine the expected date of confinement (EDC), schedule a cesarean section, or determine when it is safe to end a pregnancy prematurely. Errors in estimating the gestational age may result in delivery of a child with respiratory distress syndrome (RDS).[16] Gestational age also is used to interpret some laboratory tests used to monitor fetal well-being such as maternal serum α-fetoprotein.[16] Gestational age can be determined by several methods: date of LMP, pelvic examination, uterine size, and measurement of fetal parameters using ultrasound. Date of last menstrual period, which was six weeks ago for S.C., has been used to estimate the gestational age of the fetus.

The average duration of pregnancy from conception to term is 266 days; however, the day of conception rarely is known so it is more practical to measure the duration of pregnancy from the first day of the last normal menstrual period. When measured from this time, the average duration of pregnancy is 279 to 282 days.[16] The EDC also can be determined by adding seven days to the first day of LMP, counting back three months and adding one year (Nägele's rule). This method assumes that ovulation occurs on day 14 of a 28-day menstrual cycle. The problem with this method is that only 20% to 40% of pregnant women know the date of their last menstrual period and it is inaccurate in women with irregular or prolonged menstrual cycles. Even when the LMP is known with certainty, this method can predict the EDC only within three weeks with 90% confidence.[16]

During the first trimester, changes in the uterus and cervix observed upon pelvic examination can be used to determine gestational age. In a woman with an anteverted uterus, gestational age can be determined within ±2 weeks; however, in a woman with a retroverted uterus (occurring in 30% of women) the accuracy falls to ±4 weeks.[16] Progressive uterine enlargement during pregnancy also can be used to estimate gestational age. The uterus usually can be palpated above the pubic symphysis 12 weeks after the LMP; at 16 weeks, it is midway between the pubic symphysis and the umbilicus; at 20 weeks, it reaches the umbilicus; and by 26 weeks, it reaches the xiphoid process where it remains until the onset of labor.[14] McDonald's rule attempts to relate the uterine fundal height to the gestational age. This method states that the distance in centimeters from the uterine fundus to the pubic symphysis arc divided by 3.5 approximately equals the lunar month (lunar month = 28 days) of pregnancy after the sixth month.[14] The uterine fundal height should be measured and recorded at each prenatal visit. This information can be used to confirm other methods of estimating gestational age. Discrepancies in estimations of gestational age should alert the physician to problems such as large fetal size, multiple pregnancies, oligohydramnios (a reduction in the amount of amniotic fluid), or intrauterine growth retardation.[16] Currently, ultrasound is the most accurate method for determining gestational age when performed in the first half of pregnancy. Gestational age is determined by measuring fetal parameters such as the presence of a gestational sac (6 to 8 weeks), crown to rump length (8 to 14 weeks), biparietal diameter (15 to 26 weeks), and femur length (14 to 26 weeks).[16] When using these parameters,

estimation of gestational age is accurate within one week in greater than 90% of pregnancies.[17,18]

Nutrition

4. What nutritional advice should be given? How much weight should S.C. expect to gain throughout the pregnancy?

Pregnancy increases the requirements of all nutrients. Poor nutrition before conception and inadequate nutritional intake during pregnancy can affect the mother and fetus adversely. Therefore, assessing the nutritional status of a pregnant woman and nutritional counseling are critical early in prenatal care.

A nutritional history should be obtained, including the birth weight and length of all infants (noting any low-birth-weight infants) and the development of all children. A prior history of eclampsia, anemia, or hyperemesis and the patient's weight, age, and diet history should be noted. A medication history which screens for alcohol, nicotine, and drugs that may alter nutrient absorption or utilization should be taken.[19]

Some women are at risk for nutritional problems during pregnancy. Adolescents still are developing and growing themselves and often have inadequate diets.[19] Therefore, requirements for calories, protein, and calcium are higher in pregnant adolescents than in pregnant adults. Women who have had multiple pregnancies over a short period of time have additional nutritional requirements as do women from lower socioeconomic groups, those who ingest unusual diets, and alcoholics.[12] Women with chronic systemic diseases such as diabetes mellitus or malabsorption problems also have special nutritional needs.

Women with nutritional deficiencies before conception and those whose deficiencies are not corrected during pregnancy may deliver low-birth-weight infants. A low prepregnant weight, inadequate protein and caloric intake, and inadequate weight gain during pregnancy all are associated with delivery of low-birth-weight infants. Low-birth-weight infants are at increased risk for neurological impairment, retarded growth, and increased perinatal mortality. To ensure normal fetal development and maintain maternal health, nutrition during pregnancy should stress a diet that provides an intake of protein, calories, and nutrients that allows for adequate weight gain during pregnancy.[19]

Weight Gain

The recommendations of the Food and Nutrition Board's Subcommittee on Nutritional Status and Weight Gain during Pregnancy for healthy women in the U.S. are listed in Table 44.3. These recommendations for weight gain use body mass index (BMI), defined as weight/height^2 (kg/m^2), instead of weight only. BMI is used as an indicator of nutritional status, assuming that thin women have low tissue reserves while obese women have excessive ones. There is a wide variation in maternal weight gain (16 to 40 pounds, corresponding to the 15th and 85th percentiles, respectively) in women of normal weight before pregnancy who delivered term infants weighing 3 to 4 kg.[21] Therefore, the weight gain recom-

Table 44.3	Recommended Weight Gain During Pregnancy[20]
Prepregnancy Weight For Height (BMI)[a]	Total Weight Gain Recommendations (lb)
Low: <19.8	28–40
Normal: 19.8–26	25–35
High: 26.1–29	15–25
Obese: >29	≥15
[a] BMI = weight/ht (kg/m^2); kg = 2.2 lb; m = 39.37 in.	

mendations should be used as a guide only. Low gestational weight gain is associated with intrauterine growth retardation and increased perinatal mortality. Excessive maternal weight gain may result in a high-birth-weight baby (>9 pounds), increasing the risk of difficult delivery (prolonged labor, forceps or cesarean delivery) and infant morbidity and mortality (shoulder dystocia, birth trauma, or asphyxia).[22] The weight gain recommendations are for singleton pregnancies. A 35- to 45-pound weight gain has been associated with a favorable pregnancy outcome in women carrying twins.[23]

S.C. should be weighed at every prenatal visit. The pattern of weight gain during a normal singleton pregnancy can be characterized as minimal during the first trimester (2 to 4 pounds) and an average of one pound weekly during the last two trimesters.[25] Weight gains of less than one to two pounds per month or greater than six pounds in the same time period should be evaluated and a cause determined. A weekly weight gain of 1.5 pounds is the goal during the last two trimesters of a twin pregnancy.[23] The weight gain of pregnancy can be attributed to an increase in maternal blood volume, uterine size, and breast enlargement during the first trimester; deposition of maternal fat stores during the second trimester; and fetal and placental growth, as well as amniotic and interstitial fluid accumulation, during the third trimester.

Energy Requirements

To ensure an adequate maternal weight gain and to provide energy required to build tissue for the developing fetus, there is an increase in the requirements for caloric intake during pregnancy. The total energy cost of pregnancy is estimated to be 55,000 kcal.[25] This cost is due to increased requirements during the second and third trimesters, translating into an increase of 200 to 300 kcal/day over prepregnancy need. Obese women and those who continue to be physically active may require a greater energy intake.

Protein Requirements

Daily protein requirements increase by about 10 gm/day during pregnancy to support fetal and placental growth, increased maternal tissues (uterus and breasts) and blood volume, and amniotic fluid formation. The National Research Council recommends that pregnant women consume at least 60 gm/day of protein through a balanced diet that includes milk, cheese, legumes, meats, and grains.[26]

5. Will S.C. require additional vitamin and mineral supplementation? If so, what would you recommend and at what point in the pregnancy should she begin taking these products?

S.C.'s diet should be evaluated for adequate intake of iron, folic acid, and calcium.

Iron Requirements

A singleton pregnancy requires approximately 1000 mg of iron.[27] This estimate is based upon calculated iron needs of the fetus, placenta, maternal blood volume expansion, basal blood losses, and loss of blood during delivery.[28] The fetus and placenta require approximately 350 mg of iron. A 20% to 30% increase in maternal red blood cells (RBCs) consumes another 450 mg of iron. Basal blood loss and loss at time of delivery account for another 500 mg of iron. These iron requirements total 1200 to 1300 mg of iron but the decline in RBC mass after a vaginal delivery reduces the permanent iron loss to approximately 1000 mg.

Because the average diet of women in the U.S. will not meet these requirements and because some women may have inadequate body stores of iron, the Food and Nutrition Board of the National Research Council recommends a daily elemental iron supplementation of 30 mg beginning the second trimester of pregnancy.[29] Factors which increase the risk of iron deficiency include menor-

rhagia, multiple gestation, frequent pregnancies closely spaced, diets low in meat and ascorbic acid, chronic use of aspirin or non-steroidal anti-inflammatory drugs, and donating blood more than three times per year.[28] These women may require 60 to 100 mg/day of elemental iron during the last two trimesters of pregnancy.

Iron supplementation during pregnancy eliminates the development of iron deficiency anemia, a complication which increases the risk for a poor pregnancy outcome. Anemic women are more likely to suffer adverse effects from blood loss during delivery or hemorrhage secondary to other causes.[30] Women should be advised of the potential gastrointestinal (GI) side effects of iron which include heartburn, nausea, abdominal discomfort, constipation or diarrhea, and discoloration of stools. Iron absorption can be enhanced by taking the supplements between meals with ascorbic acid-containing foods and by avoiding the concurrent ingestion of milk, tea, coffee, or antacids.

Folate Requirements

The 1989 recommended dietary allowance (RDA) for folic acid during pregnancy is 400 μg/day as compared to the 3 μg/kg of body weight for the nonpregnant female.[31] The National Academy of Sciences subcommittee on nutritional supplements during pregnancy recommends that folate requirements be met through a diet rich in folate-containing foods instead of through vitamin supplements except for women who smoke, abuse alcohol, or are unable to comply with dietary recommendations.[32] Other women who also may be included in this at-risk group are adolescents and women with multiple gestations. For all these women, the committee recommends a daily supplement of 300 μg. Fortified cereals, green vegetables, legumes, citrus fruits, and liver are good sources of folate.[33] It is estimated that the average woman in the U.S. consumes about 200 μg of folate daily.[34]

Women with a History of Neural Tube Defects (NTDs). Evidence that folic acid supplementation during pregnancy could reduce the incidence of NTDs, such as spina bifida, anencephaly, and encephalocele, led the Centers for Disease Control (CDC) to publish recommendations for folate supplementation in 1991.[35] For women with previous NTD-affected pregnancies who plan another pregnancy, the CDC recommends 4 mg/day of folic acid at least one month before conception and through the first three months of pregnancy. Folic acid should be prescribed separately and not as prenatal vitamins which usually contain 400 to 800 μg of folic acid. This is because the use of several prenatal tablets to meet the folic acid requirements could produce toxic doses of vitamins A and D. These recommendations should be considered interim until studies showing the efficacy of lower doses of folic acid in preventing NTD have been conducted. These high doses of folic acid are based upon the results of the Medical Research Council (MRC) Vitamin Study. Women with a previous NTD pregnancy were randomized into one of four groups who received either 4 mg/day of folic acid, a multivitamin, both, or neither. Of the 1195 women with a known pregnancy outcome, 27 infants were born with an NTD: six in the folic acid groups and 21 in the groups who did not receive folic acid. These results translated into a 72% reduction in the risk of an NTD in the folic acid treatment groups. The folic acid dose used in this trial was ten times the RDA for folic acid in pregnancy and was chosen to avoid a negative effect based upon an insufficient dose. Critics of this study point out that the effects of high-dose folic acid on the fetus and the mother have not been delineated. No untoward effects were reported in the MRC study.

Approximately 4000 infants are born in the U.S. each year with an NTD.[37] While women who have had an NTD-affected pregnancy are at high risk of another such outcome, the majority of NTD pregnancies occur in women without a previous history. Several observational studies in the U.S. investigating the effects of 400 to 800 µg/day of folic acid before and during the first trimester of pregnancy documented a significant reduction (60% to 72%) in the occurrence of NTD-affected pregnancies.[38-40] In Hungary, Czeizel and Dudas conducted a randomized, controlled, intervention study to evaluate the efficacy of 800 µg/day of folic acid versus a trace element supplement in the prevention of NTD in women without a history of NTD-affected pregnancies.[41] The supplements were given at least one month before conception and continued for at least two months afterwards. There were six NTD-affected pregnancies in the 2052 women who received trace element supplementation without folic acid, while none occurred in the 2104 women who received folic acid.

Neural tube closure occurs during the fourth week of gestation (≈10 to 14 days after the last menstrual period was due) when a woman may or may not be aware that she is pregnant. If a woman is planning a pregnancy, then folic acid supplementation can begin before conception and be continued through the first trimester; however, it is estimated that more than 50% of pregnancies in the U.S. are unplanned.[42] In 1992 the U.S. Public Health Service recommended that all women with child-bearing potential should consume 400 µg/day of folic acid to reduce the risk of an NTD-affected pregnancy.[43] It estimated that if this practice were implemented in the U.S., the incidence of NTD would be reduced by 50%. It also is recommended that the daily intake of folate be less than 1 mg unless directed by a physician to avoid masking a vitamin B_{12} deficiency.

S.C. already is past the critical point of neural tube closure. Her diet should be evaluated for adequate folic acid intake. If it is inadequate and she is unwilling or unable to eat folate-rich foods then a folic acid supplement providing 400 µg/day should be prescribed.

Calcium Requirements

Calcium is needed during pregnancy for adequate mineralization of the fetal skeleton and teeth. In contrast to iron and folic acid, maternal stores of calcium greatly exceed the calcium requirement of pregnancy. The total calcium requirement of pregnancy is 30 gm which represents approximately 2.5% of total maternal stores (1200 gm). Most of the fetal calcium needs occur during the third trimester when the fetus takes up 250 to 300 mg/day of calcium. The RDA for calcium is 1200 mg for pregnant women, the amount contained in a quart of milk.[44] Other foods rich in calcium such as cheese and yogurt should be used to meet the calcium RDA instead of supplements; however, women who do not consume dairy products may require calcium supplementation during pregnancy.

Common Complaints of Pregnancy

Morning Sickness

6. What is the incidence and cause of S.C.'s nausea and vomiting?

The nausea and vomiting associated with pregnancy commonly is referred to as ''morning sickness'' which occurs in 70% of pregnancies. Approximately half of these women have mild nausea and vomiting and the other half experience moderate nausea and vomiting that requires treatment.[45] Severe nausea and vomiting requiring hospitalization and nutritional support is referred to as hyperemesis gravidarum and occurs in 1 out of 250 to 1 out of 350 pregnancies. Hyperemesis gravidarum can lead to metabolic acidosis, ketosis, hypovolemia, electrolyte disturbances, and weight loss.[45] Morning sickness usually appears by four to eight weeks gestation and disappears by 14 to 16 weeks gestation. The nausea and/or vomiting usually are self-limiting.[46] The etiology is unknown, although hCG has been implicated because of the temporal

relationship between increasing hCG concentrations and the incidence of nausea and vomiting. However, some investigators have found no relationship between hCG and the prevalence of nausea and vomiting.[47] Neural and endocrine changes that occur during pregnancy may change the threshold for vomiting. Progesterone-induced relaxation of the stomach smooth muscle and a delay in gastric emptying also may play a role.[48]

7. Management. How should S.C.'s nausea and vomiting be managed?

Most mild forms of morning sickness can be managed with psychological support and diet. The patient should be assured that the nausea and vomiting rarely continue past the fourth month of pregnancy. A light snack can be recommended upon rising for women with morning sickness symptoms. Women should avoid cooking or smelling foods that precipitate symptoms. Eating smaller, frequent meals rich in carbohydrates and sipping small quantities of fluids may help to decrease nausea and vomiting as well. It may be helpful to avoid highly seasoned, spicy foods and dairy products until morning sickness passes which usually is by the end of the first trimester.[45] If calcium needs cannot be met by diet then supplementation may be necessary (see Question 5).

8. When are antiemetics indicated for the treatment of morning sickness? What agents may be used safely?

Antiemetics are indicated for the treatment of moderate nausea and vomiting that fails to respond to nonpharmacologic interventions. These agents also are necessary when the nausea and/or vomiting threatens the metabolic and nutritional status of the mother. Unfortunately, nausea and vomiting most commonly occur during the first trimester when the developing embryo is most susceptible to the teratogenic effects of drugs.[49] Antiemetics that have been used to treat nausea and vomiting associated with pregnancy are: Bendectin (doxylamine and pyridoxine), meclizine, dimenhydrinate, pyridoxine, metoclopramide, and various phenothiazines.

Bendectin was used widely in the U.S. between 1956 and 1983 when the manufacturer voluntarily removed the drug from the market. During this time, 10% to 25% of pregnant women were prescribed this agent during the first trimester. The incidence of malformations reported in the babies of women who took Bendectin was very low considering the large number of women who received the drug. In large epidemiologic studies, no association was found between Bendectin use and the occurrence of birth defects.[50-56]

Meclizine (Antivert), used in doses of 25 to 50 mg/day, has been suggested as the agent of choice because of its low teratogenic risk.[49] The incidence of fetal malformations was no higher in women who used this drug during pregnancy than those pregnant women who were not exposed to this agent.[57-60] *Dimenhydrinate* (Dramamine), in oral doses of 50 to 100 mg every four hours or parenteral doses of 50 mg every three to four hours, has been used to treat nausea and vomiting and appears to have a low potential for producing teratogenic effects.[49] Another agent advocated for nausea and vomiting, *pyridoxine*, has not been shown to be more effective than placebo.[61] *Metoclopramide* (Reglan), in doses of 5 to 10 mg three times a day or 5 to 20 mg intravenously (IV) or intramuscularly (IM) three times a day, has been used to control vomiting and gastric reflux associated with pregnancy.[49] Although no malformations have been reported in infants born to mothers given this drug, it has been used in a relatively small number of women.[49,62] More studies are needed to determine the teratogenic potential of this agent.

Contradictory results regarding the teratogenicity of various phenothiazines in treating nausea and vomiting associated with pregnancy have been reported. Several studies have not produced evidence to support the teratogenicity of phenothiazines.[57,58,63,64]

Other studies have found an increased rate of malformations in infants whose mothers took these drugs during the first trimester.[64,65] Agents that have been used to treat pregnancy-related nausea and vomiting are *promethazine* (Phenergan) 12.5 to 25 mg orally (PO) or IM two to four times a day, *thiethylperazine* (Torecan) 10 to 20 mg PO or IM one to three times a day, and *prochlorperazine* (Compazine) 5 to 10 mg PO or IM three to four times a day.[49] Because evidence of the teratogenic potential is inconclusive, phenothiazines should be reserved for women with persistent nausea and vomiting that is uncontrolled by other methods and threaten the nutritional status of the mother and fetus.

9. During her third trimester, S.C. returns for a follow-up visit complaining of constipation and heartburn. What GI complaints are associated with pregnancy? How should these complaints be treated?

Constipation

Constipation commonly occurs during pregnancy secondary to progesterone-induced relaxation of the muscles of the intestines and compression of the intestines by the enlarging uterus.[13] Iron supplementation also can contribute to this problem. Women should be instructed to maintain bowel function by drinking plenty of water; exercising; and increasing bulk in the diet with vegetables, fruits, high fiber cereals, whole grains, and legumes. If these nonpharmacologic interventions do not work, stool softeners (docusate 100 to 200 mg/day), mild laxatives (e.g., milk of magnesia 30 cc QD to BID), or bulk-producing products (e.g., Metamucil 1 teaspoonful QD to TID) can be used. Strong cathartics and enemas should be avoided.

Hemorrhoids

Hemorrhoids occur during pregnancy because the enlarging uterus exerts pressure on the middle and inferior hemorrhoidal vessels. Hemorrhoids produce itching, burning, swelling, pain, and, occasionally, bleeding. Maintaining normal bowel function and preventing constipation can prevent or relieve the discomfort of hemorrhoids. Treatment of hemorrhoids includes anal hygiene, external hemorrhoidal products, and stool softeners. The anorectal area should be cleansed with soap and water after each bowel movement. Sitz baths two to three times daily also can be used to decrease hemorrhoidal symptoms.[66]

Reflux Esophagitis

Reflux esophagitis or heartburn occurs in approximately 25% of pregnant women, usually in the third trimester.[46] The enlarging uterus increases intra-abdominal pressure and progesterone relaxes the esophageal sphincter. These two factors cause the reflux of stomach acid into the lower esophagus, producing symptoms of substernal burning worsened by eating, lying down, bending over, or lifting heavy objects. Treatment includes eating smaller, more frequent meals; avoiding meals close to bedtime; and avoidance of products containing salicylates, caffeine, alcohol, and nicotine. Elevation of the head of the bed by four to six inches may be helpful. Aluminum-magnesium antacids may be used after meals and at bedtime, but H_2-receptor antagonists and metoclopramide are not approved for use during pregnancy.[46]

Diabetes Mellitus In Pregnancy

Approximately 3% to 4% of all pregnancies in the U.S. will be complicated by maternal diabetes mellitus.[67] Women with pre-existing diabetes are classified as either insulin-dependent (Type I) or noninsulin-dependent diabetics (Type II); those developing carbohydrate intolerance during pregnancy (usually during the third trimester) are classified as having gestational diabetes mellitus (GDM). Classification systems most commonly used to describe pregnant diabetic patients are the White Classification[68] (see Table 44.4), which has been modified at various times during the last few decades, and the newer National Diabetes Data Group nomenclature.[69] Although the White Classification is older and relies upon age at onset, length of diabetes, and complications for patient classification rather than the current status of diabetic control, it still is advocated by many diabetologists when comparing treatment and pregnancy outcomes for women with pre-existing diabetes mellitus.[70,71]

Approximately 0.3% of all pregnancies in the U.S. occur in women with Type I diabetes mellitus.[67] The majority of these women will be insulin-dependent patients who developed their diabetes during childhood, adolescence, or young adulthood. Many will have histories of poor diabetic control, especially after leaving the care and close supervision of their families. For those patients who had good diabetic control before pregnancy, the first signs of pregnancy may be diabetes "suddenly out of control" with ketonuria, hyperglycemia followed by hypoglycemia, and a time period when many insulin dosage changes must be made to retain carbohydrate control.[72] Their infants will be at an increased risk for mortality, congenital defects, macrosomia (large for gestational age), dystocia (difficult parturition due to abnormal size or position), and prematurity. The latter often is complicated by respiratory distress syndrome, hypoglycemia, hypocalcemia, and hyperbilirubinemia.[67]

A smaller number of women will have Type II diabetes. These women typically are older, obese, and treated with diet alone or diet combined with oral hypoglycemic agents. If hyperglycemia in Type II patients cannot be controlled by diet alone during pregnancy, insulin should be initiated since oral hypoglycemic agents may be teratogenic or can result in fetal hyperinsulinemia and neonatal hypoglycemia.[72] Infants of Type II diabetic mothers may exhibit the same complications observed in the infants of Type I mothers.

Women with established diabetes before pregnancy (especially those with Type I disease) are at an increased risk for ketoacidosis; hypertension during pregnancy; exacerbation of microvascular, ocular, neurologic, and renal complications; urinary tract infections and hydramnios.[67,70]

Table 44.4	White's Classification of Diabetes During Pregnancy[a,68,77]
Class	**Criteria**
A	Abnormal oral GTT Normal FBG Diet controlled
B	Insulin-dependent Onset >20 yr duration <10 yr Absence of vascular disease or retinopathy
C	Insulin-dependent Onset between ages 10–20 yr Duration between 10–20 yr Background retinopathy observed
D	Insulin-dependent Onset before age 10 yr Duration >20 yr Background retinopathy observed
F	Presence of diabetic nephropathy
H	Presence of cardiac disease
R	Presence of proliferative retinopathy

[a] FBG = Fasting blood glucose; GTT = Glucose tolerance test.

Approximately 90,000 women (2% to 3% of all pregnancies in the U.S.) who give birth annually develop GDM during pregnancy; it is estimated that an equal number go undetected.[67] Complications noted in the offspring of these women include increased mortality, macrosomia, dystocia, birth trauma, hypocalcemia, and hyperbilirubinemia.[73] Approximately 35% to 50% of women with GDM develop carbohydrate intolerance or diabetes mellitus within 15 years of delivery. Some women diagnosed with GDM really may have Type II diabetes that previously was undiagnosed.[67,74,75]

Pre-Existent Diabetes

Infants of Diabetic Mothers (IDM)

10. P.S., a 25-year-old, 60 kg, female known to have insulin-dependent diabetes since age 12, has married recently and wishes to have children. She is concerned about the effects of pregnancy on her health and the effect of her diabetes on the health of a child she might conceive. P.S. has been conscientious in her diabetic care and self-monitors her blood glucose concentrations with a glucose reflectance meter. Over the past month, her fasting blood glucose (FBG) concentrations have ranged from 90–140 mg/dL. today, her FBG and HbA$_{1c}$ laboratory results are 134 mg/dL (Normal: 70–110) and 7.8% (Normal: 4.5–6.5), respectively. She rarely has detectable ketonuria, but it was noted when she had a urinary tract infection 6 months ago. Her current human insulin regimen consists of a combination of 16 units of isophane insulin (NPH) and 8 units of Regular 30 min before breakfast, and 8 units of NPH and 4 units of Regular 30 min before supper. She wants to know what her chances are for having a normal infant. [SI unit: glucose 7.4 mmol/L (Normal: 3.9–6.1); HbA$_{1c}$ 0.078 (Normal 0.045–0.065)]

Mortality. P.S. should be informed that perinatal mortality for the infants of diabetic mothers declined dramatically with the introduction of insulin. In the last few years some medical centers have reported perinatal morality rates of 1.6% to 2% which approach those for infants of nondiabetic mothers.[70] Gabbe et al. have reported higher mortality rates of 3.8% for IDM.[76] These rates are not reported universally and vary with the level of diabetic control before conception and the quality of prenatal care.

Risk of Congenital Anomalies. Perinatal morbidity and mortality of IDM are associated primarily with the increased incidence of spontaneous abortions and congenital anomalies. The rate of spontaneous abortions is estimated to be 30%, approximately twice the rate of the general population.[78] The incidence of major congenital anomalies is 6% to 12% as compared to a 2% to 3% incidence in the general population.[79,80] The commonly occurring congenital anomalies include caudal regression, neural tube defects, cardiac defects such as transposition of the great vessels, and ventricular and atrial septal defects, anal/rectal atresia, renal agenesis, cystic kidney, and ureter duplex.[81]

Many of these congenital anomalies occur before the seventh week of gestation, a time when organogenesis is occurring. Thus, several studies have shown that the risk of giving birth to an infant with a major congenital anomaly correlates with the degree of glycemic control during the time just before and the two months after conception.[82–84] Women with higher HbA$_{1c}$ values during this time period had a significantly higher incidence of infants with anomalies as compared to women with HbA$_{1c}$ closer to the normal range. Normalization of the blood glucose before conception and during the period of organogenesis has been demonstrated to reduce the risk of miscarriage and congenital anomalies in IDM.[82,85–87]

Macrosomia. Infants of diabetic mothers are at increased risk for problems during delivery and the neonatal period. Macrosomia, an infant greater than 4 kg or in the greater than 90th percentile of weight for gestational age, occurs more commonly in women with glucose intolerance.[88] These infants are at greater risk for trauma during delivery because of their size. Trauma to the head, clavicle, abdominal organs, or brachial plexus is common. IDM also are at increased risk for respiratory distress syndrome, hypoglycemia, hypocalcemia, hypomagnesemia, and hyperbilirubinemia during the neonatal period.[88]

P.S. should be informed that her chances of having a normal infant will be increased if she normalizes her glucose control and HbA$_{1c}$ before conception and especially during the first eight weeks postconception. She should be encouraged to inform her physician that she desires to have a baby so that she can be educated before pregnancy about the healthy practices she can institute now to improve a successful pregnancy outcome.

Maternal Risks

11. P.S. wants to know what health risks she might incur from becoming pregnant and what could be done to minimize these risks?

Common Complications and Contraindications. The common complications that occur in pregnant women with diabetes are changes in blood glucose control which may result in hypoglycemia or ketoacidosis, hypertension, infections including pyelonephritis, polyhydraminos, preterm labor and deterioration of retinopathy, nephropathy, cardiac disease, or neuropathy.[81] Prepregnancy assessment of a woman by her obstetrician and endocrinologist or primary care provider can decrease the effect of pregnancy on her diabetes by establishing optimal glycemic control, treating pre-existing hypertension, ruling out the presence of ischemic heart disease, treating proliferative retinopathy, assessing renal status, and determining if gynecologic abnormalities are present.[81] Potential contraindications to pregnancy for women with diabetes are ischemic heart disease, untreated proliferative retinopathy, renal insufficiency characterized by a creatinine clearance less than 50 mL/minute or proteinuria greater than 2 gm/24 hours, or the presence of severe gastroenteropathy.[81]

Prepregnancy Assessment. P.S. should undergo a prepregnancy assessment of her general health so that her physician can advise her of the specific risks of pregnancy to her. Since she has had her diabetes for more than ten years, she should undergo the appropriate cardiac testing to rule out ischemic heart disease; a high rate of maternal mortality is associated with this complication during pregnancy.[81] P.S.'s eyes should be examined by an ophthalmologist because retinopathy is known to progress in some pregnant women with diabetes.[81] If proliferative retinopathy is found, it should be treated and stabilized before conception. If renal disease is present, P.S. should be advised of the increased risk of perinatal morbidity and mortality associated with this complication.[89] Gastroenteropathy also should be ruled out because the more severe form of this complication makes it increasingly difficult to maintain good metabolic control and nutrition for the fetus and mother.[81] P.S.'s blood pressure should be measured and normalized if necessary with agents that have low teratogenic potential. (See Questions 25 to 27.)

Prepregnancy Management

12. After undergoing a prepregnancy assessment by her primary care provider, P.S. is advised that she safely may plan for a pregnancy. How should she be managed before conception?

P.S. should be instructed on diet, glycemic control, monitoring glucose through multiple daily determinations, and monthly monitoring of HbA$_{1c}$. If she is not doing so already, she should practice a healthy life-style by exercising, not smoking, and avoiding alcohol and medications.

Her insulin therapy should be titrated to reduce her preprandial glucose concentrations to 70 to 100 mg/dL and two-hour postprandial glucose concentrations to below 150 mg/dL.[81] P.S.'s current regimen (a combination of a short- and intermediate-acting insulin, two-thirds administered before breakfast and one-third before supper) is unlikely to achieve euglycemia. This regimen is not as flexible as three- and four-injection regimens which allow for finer adjustment of the insulin dose based upon blood glucose determinations and the NPH before dinner may produce nocturnal hypoglycemia. Alternative regimens may include a short-acting insulin before each meal with an intermediate- or long-acting insulin twice daily or a combination of an intermediate- plus short-acting insulin in the morning, short-acting before supper and an intermediate-acting insulin before bedtime. (See Chapter 48: Diabetes Mellitus.) Self-monitoring of blood glucose should be performed at least four to eight times daily to optimize her insulin regimens. Preprandial and two-hour postprandial determinations should be made as well as at bedtime and during the middle of the night.[90] Although P.S. already is using a glucometer, her ability to demonstrate appropriate technique should be verified. A monthly HbA$_{1c}$ should be performed to confirm normalization of blood glucose concentrations; these values should be within the normal range before attempting conception. Because there is an increased risk of hypoglycemia associated with these glycemic control goals, P.S. and her husband should be instructed on the signs, symptoms, and treatment of hypoglycemia. (See Chapter 48: Diabetes Mellitus.)

Pregnancy Management

13. How will pregnancy alter P.S.'s glycemic control and insulin requirements?

Insulin Regimens. During the first trimester of pregnancy, glucose and gluconeogenic substances in the blood are taken up by the fetus which can lead to a decrease in insulin requirements (usually 10% to 20%) and an increasing occurrence of nocturnal hypoglycemia. If the woman experiences nausea and vomiting during this time, blood glucose control may be more unstable and should be monitored closely. In the second trimester of pregnancy, insulin doses begin to increase, requiring a readjustment every five to ten days. These needs continue to increase during the third trimester to as much as twice the prepregnancy dose, and are due, in part, to the placental hormones, lactogen, prolactin, estrogen, and progesterone which antagonize the action of insulin. At 36 weeks gestation, the insulin requirements level out and change very little until delivery.[91] An insulin regimen described in Question 12, using human insulin since it is the least immunogenic, should be administered to maintain the same glycemic goals established for P.S. before pregnancy.

Blood Glucose Monitoring, HbA$_{1c}$, and Urine Ketone Determinations. In addition to daily blood glucose concentrations and monthly HbA$_{1c}$ determinations, urine ketone testing is vital to a successful pregnancy outcome for a woman with diabetes.[92–96] With regard to self-monitoring of blood glucose, periodic evaluation of the P.S.'s technique is essential to ensure that the most accurate data are used to adjust the insulin regimen and to assess glycemic control throughout the pregnancy. Four to eight determinations daily are necessary. P.S. should measure her glucose before and after meals, at bedtime, and occasionally at 3:00 a.m. to rule out nocturnal hypoglycemia. This is especially important for women administering an intermediate-acting insulin before supper. The increased fuel demands of pregnancy increase the risk for ketone production. Thus, daily urine ketone testing should be performed on the first morning urine because ketones are most likely to occur after the overnight fast. Ketone testing also is important during illness, when meals are missed, or when glucose

concentrations exceed 200 mg/dL.[90] Early intervention to treat or prevent ketosis from occurring may avoid the development of ketoacidosis which carries a high infant mortality rate.[97]

Gestational Diabetes Mellitus (GDM)

14. G.G., a 22-year-old, 5′2″, 75 kg (prepregnancy weight, BMI = 30) female in the 26th week of her first pregnancy, sees her obstetrician for a regular prenatal visit. An oral glucose screening test for GDM is recommended. G.G. has no family history of diabetes and has had normal blood glucose concentrations and no glucosuria during pregnancy. What is GDM? Is G.G. at risk for GDM? Is this test necessary?

Gestational diabetes mellitus, which affects approximately 2% to 3% of pregnancies, is defined as the onset of glucose intolerance during pregnancy.[69,75,98] This definition applies without reference to the severity of the glucose intolerance or the type of treatment required. Women who are at greatest risk for GDM are those who are obese, have glucosuria or a first-degree relative with diabetes, have given birth to an infant greater than 4 kg, a history of a stillbirth, or a diagnosis of GDM in a prior pregnancy.[99,100] G.G. is obese and is at some risk for developing GDM. The test is necessary because 40% to 50% of women who meet the diagnostic criteria for GDM have no risk factors.[100,101] The diagnosis of GDM is important to the mother and the fetus because of the increased risks described in Questions 10 and 11.[102,103]

Diagnostic Criteria

15. What are the diagnostic criteria for GDM?

The screening and diagnostic criteria for GDM recommended by the Third International Workshop-Conference on Gestational Diabetes Mellitus are listed in Table 44.5. It is appropriate for G.G. to be screened at this time for GDM according to the guidelines.

Management

16. How should GDM be managed?

Treatment Goals. The overall goals of treatment are to reduce the maternal and fetal morbidity and mortality associated with GDM. Treatment of GDM includes dietary management, appropriate maternal weight gain, insulin therapy to normalize glycemic control, and exercise if possible.

Table 44.5	Screening and Diagnostic Criteria for GDM[a,b]

Screening

By glucose measurement in plasma

50 gm oral glucose load administered between the 24th and 28th week and without regard to the time of day or time of last meal to all pregnant women who have not been identified as having glucose intolerance before the 24th week

Venous plasma glucose measured 1 hour later

A value of ≥140 mg/dL in venous plasma indicates the need for a full diagnostic GTT

Diagnosis

100 gm oral glucose load administered in the morning after overnight fast for at least 8 hr but not >14 hr and after at least 3 days of unrestricted diet (≥150 gm carbohydrate) and physical activity

Venous plasma glucose is measured fasting and at 1, 2, and 3 hr; subject should remain seated and not smoke throughout the test

≥2 of the following venous plasma concentrations must be met or exceeded for positive diagnosis:

Fasting	105 mg/dL
1 hr	190 mg/dL
2 hr	165 mg/dL
3 hr	145 mg/dL

[a] Reprinted with permission from reference 98.
[b] GDM = Gestational diabetes mellitus; GTT = Glucose tolerance test.

Dietary Management. Dietary management is the cornerstone of therapy for GDM. The goals are to ensure fetal growth and development, appropriate weight gain for the mother, and to normalize glucose concentrations. A diet that meets the RDA for nutrient intake during pregnancy[104] is advised by The Third International Workshop-Conference on Gestational Diabetes Mellitus.[98] Concerning maternal weight gain, they also recommend following the guidelines of the Food and Nutrition Board's Subcommittee on Nutritional Status and Weight Gain during Pregnancy.[20] (See Table 44.3.) The use of calorie-restricted diets (1200 to 1800 kcal) to treat GDM has decreased the incidence of macrosomia in mothers with GDM.[105] However, these findings should be considered preliminary until more studies evaluating the long-term effects of these diets on the infant are available.[98] Hypocaloric diets versus insulin therapy for mild GDM need to be evaluated as well.

Insulin Therapy. Insulin is recommended to treat GDM if dietary management fails to maintain fasting blood glucose concentrations below 105 mg/dL or two-hour postprandial plasma glucose concentrations below 120 mg/dL.[98] Insulin reduces the average birth weight and incidence of macrosomia in infants of mothers with GDM. Self-monitoring of blood glucose should be encouraged to allow optimal insulin therapy and glycemic control by the mother.

Risk of Developing Diabetes Mellitus

17. Are women with GDM at risk for glucose intolerance after delivery?

There is sufficient evidence that GDM is associated with an increased risk for the development of diabetes mellitus.[98] There is a wide range in the reported incidence of diabetes mellitus in women with GDM (6% to 62%) which can be attributed to the use of different diagnostic criteria for GDM and the follow-up period of the studies.[106] For most women, glucose tolerance normalizes after delivery; however, some women will go on to develop impaired glucose tolerance or overt diabetes mellitus within several years. The Third International Workshop-Conference on Gestational Diabetes Mellitus recommends that at the six-week postpartum visit, a 75 gm oral glucose tolerance test be performed in women with GDM.[98] If the test results are normal, she is classified as "previous abnormality of glucose tolerance (GDM)." If the response to the oral glucose tolerance test is abnormal then the diagnosis will be determined by the current definitions of impaired glucose tolerance or diabetes mellitus.[69]

Seizure Disorders In Pregnancy

Pregnant women with seizure disorders may be divided into the following groups: those with known seizure disorders before pregnancy and those who experience their first noneclamptic seizure during pregnancy. Approximately 25% of this latter group will seize only during pregnancy and may be classified as having "gestational epilepsy."[107,108] Gestational epilepsy usually presents as focal seizures that occur late in pregnancy.[107,109] Women with a history of gestational epilepsy may not develop seizures during subsequent pregnancies. Seizure recurrence rates in patients with gestational epilepsy have not been reported.

Epilepsy-Associated Complications

18. T.R., a 24-year-old female, has a history of idiopathic tonic-clonic seizures since age 6. Currently, she is well controlled on phenytoin (Dilantin Kapseals) 300 mg/day PO. Her phenytoin serum concentrations have ranged between 12 and 16 μg/mL during the past 2 years, and she has had only 2 tonic-clonic seizures in the past 3 years. T.R. has married recently, and both she and her husband desire children. The only other history of seizures in either family is a maternal aunt who had

febrile seizures as a child. Before considering pregnancy, T.R. wants to know if epilepsy could affect her or her unborn infant.

Epilepsy-associated complications that could occur in T.R. or her infant during pregnancy may be divided into the effects of pregnancy on epilepsy and the effects of epilepsy on pregnancy.

Effects of Pregnancy on Seizure Disorders

Although the incidence of seizures is more likely to increase during pregnancy, some investigators have found that seizure frequency is unpredictable; others have reported that women with more severe epilepsy will experience increased seizure frequency.[107,108] Dalessio, in his review of the literature, reported that seizure activity typically increased in 40% of pregnant epileptics, decreased in 10%, and did not change in 50%.[108] Schmidt et al. studied the relationship between medication compliance and seizure control during pregnancy. They found increased seizure activity in 50 of 136 pregnant women. Of these, 34 (68%) were noncompliant with anticonvulsant therapy.[110] Other factors which may be associated with increased seizure frequency during pregnancy include duration and severity of epilepsy and maternal age, sex of the child, and anticonvulsant compliance.[107–110] Additionally, seizure frequency may depend upon increased sodium and water retention or estrogen concentrations during pregnancy.[109] More studies are needed to verify whether these factors affect seizure occurrence in pregnancy.

Although status epilepticus is uncommon during pregnancy, it may result in an average maternal mortality of 33% and a fetal mortality of 50%.[109] If it occurs, the primary therapeutic aim is to control the seizures; if this cannot be accomplished, pregnancy may have to be terminated to resolve maternal seizures.

Effects of Seizure Disorders on Pregnancy

The risk of hyperemesis gravidarum, abruptio placentae, and eclampsia appears similar in women with or without epilepsy.[108,109] Epileptic women may experience increased bleeding during delivery which may result from anticonvulsant-related (phenytoin, phenobarbital) vitamin K deficiency or thrombocytopenia.[108]

Although conducted from 1959 to 1966 when anticonvulsant serum drug monitoring was not performed frequently, The Collaborative Perinatal Project of the National Institute of Neurological and Communicative Disorders and Stroke enrolled and followed approximately 45,000 women, including 982 women who had at least one seizure before or during pregnancy (2.1%). Women and their offspring were followed from the first prenatal visit until the children reached seven years of age.[111] Of the women enrolled in the study, 4.4 out of 1000 had a noneclamptic seizure during pregnancy. Although 80% of the women who had a seizure disorder delivered infants without problems, the risk of any unfavorable outcome in the offspring of the women with seizures was twice that observed for women who had never had seizures. Unfavorable outcomes reported with a statistically significant difference ($p < 0.05$ to $p < 0.01$ level) were stillbirth, nonfebrile seizures, and mental retardation (IQ <70) when seizures occurred during pregnancy. Additionally, microcephaly was statistically increased in women who had seizures anytime. There were no statistical differences between offspring of women with and without seizures when comparing the incidences of low birth weight, neonatal seizures, and death during the first year of life.[111]

T.R. should be informed of the complications that may occur in the pregnant epileptic patient, but it should be emphasized that her risk for complications may be low because of the infrequency of her seizures, her good medication compliance, and her use of a single anticonvulsant.

Obstetrics
44-13

Phenytoin Use

19. Will T.R. be at increased risk for delivering a child with birth defects or other drug-related problems if she continues treatment with phenytoin?

Yes. Phenytoin is classified as a category D drug for fetal risk by Briggs et al.[112] This classification, based upon a definition set forth by the Food and Drug Administration (FDA), means that there is evidence for fetal risk when the medication is used during pregnancy, but the risk:benefit ratio may be acceptable if the drug is needed for a serious disease when safer drugs cannot be used. (See Chapter 45: Teratogenicity and Drugs in Breast Milk.)

Fetal Hydantoin Syndrome (FHS)

Malformations most frequently associated with phenytoin exposure in utero include cleft lip, cleft palate, and cardiac anomalies.[108] A pattern of congenital anomalies, usually consisting of craniofacial and limb defects, has been associated with in utero phenytoin exposure; these, with or without the presence of growth retardation (prenatal and postnatal) and decreased mental ability, may be called the fetal hydantoin syndrome.[113,114] Whether growth and mental retardation should be included in a comprehensive definition of FHS has been debated.[113]

Limb and craniofacial anomalies consistently have been the best markers of FHS.[113] (See Table 44.6 for many of these abnormalities and Figure 45.4 in Chapter 45: Teratogenicity and Drugs in Breast Milk.)[112,113,115–117] Other anomalies associated with in utero hydantoin exposure include cardiovascular anomalies, various types of hernias, and genitourinary anomalies.[113,114] Between 5% and 10% of infants exposed to phenytoin in utero will have FHS, whereas another approximately 30% may exhibit some features.[113,114]

Phenytoin crosses the placenta. Concentrations in umbilical cord plasma of fetuses 12 to 15 weeks gestation have been reported to be 50% of maternal plasma concentrations, while phenytoin concentrations in term infants were reported to be equal to or slightly lower than maternal concentrations.[118] Phenytoin primarily distributes to the fetal kidney, adrenal glands, liver, and heart. Rane et al.[119] reported the presence of the phenytoin metabolite p-HPPH in a neonate's serum whose mother received phenytoin during pregnancy. This raises the issue as to whether p-HPPH crosses the placenta or whether phenytoin is metabolized by the placenta or the fetal liver. Thus, it appears that the fetus is exposed to varying concentrations of phenytoin and its metabolites throughout pregnancy and such exposure may result in various fetal anomalies. Buehler[114] suggests that the teratogenic effects of anticonvulsants may be mediated by oxidative metabolites. If so, fetuses at risk for

FHS may be those with insufficient concentrations of epoxide hydrolase, the enzyme that detoxifies reactive epoxides to inactive metabolites. Epoxide hydrolase activity appears to be regulated genetically by a single gene with two alleles; fetuses homozygous for the dominant allele should have 75% or more enzymatic activity to metabolize intermediary compounds, whereas fetuses homozygous for the recessive alleles would have 30% or less activity. Those determined to be heterozygotes would have intermediate activity. These observations ultimately may lead to diagnostic methods that can be used to identify fetuses at risk for FHS.

Congenital Defects and the Effects of Folic Acid

Congenital defects may be associated with low maternal and/or fetal folic acid concentrations during pregnancy.[120] Biale and Lewenthal studied the effects of folic acid on fetal malformations in epileptic women receiving anticonvulsant therapy in both a retrospective and prospective manner.[121] In the retrospective part of the study, 10 out of 66 infants born to mothers receiving phenytoin and a variety of other anticonvulsants who also had low erythrocyte folate concentrations, had congenital malformations. In the prospective part of the study, 33 pregnant women taking phenytoin and other anticonvulsants began taking folic acid before conception or within the first six weeks of pregnancy; none of the infants had birth defects and none of the mothers had increased seizure frequency during pregnancy. Other studies have shown no association between maternal folic acid serum concentrations or folic acid supplementation and fetal malformation.[122,123]

Hemorrhagic Disease

Phenytoin and phenobarbital have been associated with hemorrhagic disease of the newborn (HDN) which usually occurs within 24 hours of birth. The exact mechanism for this bleeding is unknown, but it probably is secondary to drug suppression of vitamin K-dependent clotting factor production by the fetus in the presence of normal maternal vitamin K concentrations.[108] Drug-induced bleeding usually occurs earlier than physiologic HDN and usually is more life-threatening. Therefore, infants born to mothers taking phenytoin should receive 1 mg of vitamin K_1 (phytonadione) IM after birth and should be observed for signs of bleeding over the next 24 to 48 hours. Additional vitamin K_1 or fresh frozen plasma should be administered if indicated by prolonged prothrombin times or bleeding.[107]

Fetal Tumors

Case reports of tumor occurrence in infants exposed in utero to phenytoin raised the possibility that phenytoin may be a transplacental carcinogen.[113]

Pharmacokinetics During Pregnancy

20. Are there any physiologic changes during pregnancy that would alter phenytoin pharmacokinetics?

Phenytoin serum concentrations during pregnancy generally are lower when compared to prepregnancy concentrations.[118,124,125] Decreased absorption, altered metabolism, or increased clearance all have been implicated as the cause for lower phenytoin serum concentrations. In a case study by Ramsay et al., approximately 50% of a phenytoin dose was eliminated unchanged in stool and only 33% of the dose was eliminated renally as the p-HPPH metabolite ($\approx$50% of a dose is eliminated as this metabolite in nonpregnant women).[126] Kochenour et al. also reported differences in the percentage of p-HPPH renally eliminated during pregnancy.[127] They observed that 40% of a dose was eliminated as p-HPPH during the third trimester of pregnancy while 60% was eliminated as this metabolite after pregnancy. These results may be due to decreased absorption, altered metabolism, or both.

Table 44.6	Some Clinical Features Associated with FHS[a,112,113,115–117]
Craniofacial Features	**Limb Abnormalities**
Cleft lip/cleft palate	Altered palmar crease
Open fontanel	Absent or small nails
Microcephaly	Hypoplastic distal phalanges
Low hairline	
Coarse scalp hair	
Digital thumb	
Broad alveolar ridge	
Broad nasal ridge	
Short neck	
Low-set or abnormal ears	
Epicanthal folds	
Ptosis of eyelids	
Ocular hypertelorism	

[a] FHS = Fetal hydantoin syndrome.

Decreased protein binding of phenytoin in pregnant women also has been reported. This decreased binding may result from low albumin concentrations or competition with circulating endogenous substances at binding sites.[118,128] This change in binding may help explain why free phenytoin concentrations are unchanged even though total phenytoin concentrations are decreased. Therefore, low total phenytoin serum concentrations (usual therapeutic range: 10 to 20 μg/mL) may not result in decreased seizure control in pregnant women.

More studies are needed to define phenytoin pharmacokinetics during pregnancy and determine whether the current therapeutic range for total phenytoin serum concentrations is appropriate for monitoring pregnant women needing this medication. Presently, it would appear prudent to clinically monitor T.R. and closely follow her serum phenytoin concentrations. If possible, both free and total phenytoin concentrations should be monitored because of pregnancy-associated albumin binding changes.

Other Anticonvulsants

21. Is there another anticonvulsant which could be used to treat T.R. that is less likely to produce birth defects?

Carbamazepine (Tegretol) has been considered the anticonvulsant of choice for women with tonic-clonic seizures who wish to become pregnant because few major fetal anomalies have been associated with its use during pregnancy. Jones et al.[129] reported a pattern of malformations that consisted of minor craniofacial defects, fingernail hypoplasia, and development delays in infants identified as being exposed to carbamazepine *in utero*. Of the 35 women in the study who received only carbamazepine during pregnancy, 36% delivered infants with fingernail hypoplasia; and 20% had offspring who were classified as developmentally delayed. The investigators speculated that the teratogen responsible for the fetal abnormalities might be an epoxide intermediate rather than the parent compound. Rosa[130] reported a 1% incidence of neural tube defects in fetuses exposed *in utero* to carbamazepine. Other anomalies associated with maternal carbamazepine use include the absence of a gallbladder and thyroid gland, polydactyly, congenital heart defect, anal atresia, meningomyelocele, ambiguous genitalia, hip dislocation, and inguinal hernia.[112]

Other Agents. Valproic acid has been reported to cause neural tube defects in approximately 1% to 2% of exposed fetuses.[131] Other defects involve the heart, face, and limbs.[112] This agent is best avoided during pregnancy. There are insufficient data to evaluate any of the newer anticonvulsants (e.g., felbamate, gabapentin) in pregnancy.

Counseling

22. If it is decided to maintain phenytoin therapy, how should T.R. be counseled?

T.R. should be informed that infants born to epileptic women needing anticonvulsant therapy are at risk for birth defects, but approximately 60% will be born without malformations and another 30% will have minor malformations.[113,114] She also must be reminded that the risk of possible drug-related congenital defects must be weighed against the consequence of *in utero* fetal hypoxia secondary to maternal seizures. If her obstetrician wishes to change her seizure medication, it should be done before the pregnancy is planned so that her seizure incidence may be monitored and her anticonvulsant dose stabilized. T.R. should be informed that other anticonvulsant medications also may have teratogenic risk (see Chapters 45: Teratogenicity and Drugs in Breast Milk and 52: Seizure Disorders).

T.R. should be counseled on the importance of medication compliance during pregnancy to help maintain her phenytoin serum concentrations in the therapeutic range. She also should be advised to take prenatal vitamins with folic acid to maintain an adequate folate intake. Even though a relationship between maternal epilepsy, low maternal folic acid serum concentrations, and fetal malformations has not been definitely established, pregnant epileptic women should take supplemental folic acid.

Hypertension During Pregnancy

Classification and Definitions

Hypertension occurring during pregnancy is one of the major causes of maternal and fetal morbidity and mortality in the western world and occurs in up to 10% of all pregnancies.[132] Of these women, many are teenagers or primigravids older than 35 years. Approximately 1% to 5% of all pregnancies occur in women with chronic hypertension.[132] Also, 20% to 40% of women who have chronic hypertension secondary to chronic renal or vascular disease before pregnancy will experience an increase in the severity of their hypertension during pregnancy or have preeclampsia or eclampsia superimposed on their chronic hypertension.[132,133] Hypertension occurring before conception or before the 20th week of gestation or that last six weeks or more postpartum may be classified as chronic hypertension.[132] This may be due to essential hypertension or other conditions such as diabetes mellitus or chronic renal failure. Hypertension noted after the 20th week of pregnancy may be difficult to classify, particularly if a woman has had inadequate prenatal care without appropriate blood pressure monitoring.

Systolic and diastolic blood pressure decline during the initial two trimesters of a normal pregnancy; a nadir of 15 to 20 mm Hg in systolic blood pressure below prepregnancy levels may occur in the second trimester.[132] Only during the third trimester does blood pressure return to or exceed prepregnancy levels. The American Obstetrical Committee recommends that 130/80 mm Hg be considered the upper limit for normal blood pressure anytime during pregnancy. Hypertension during pregnancy may be defined as an increase in the systolic blood pressure of 30 mm Hg or an increase in the diastolic blood pressure of 15 mm Hg (above the prepregnancy baseline measurement) any time during pregnancy. A blood pressure of ≥140/90 mm Hg during the latter half of pregnancy meets the definition of hypertension.[132,133] Elevations in blood pressure must be confirmed by repeat measurements at least six hours apart on two separate occasions. Positioning of the patient during blood pressure measurements must be considered because a blood pressure obtained while the patient is sitting may be 10 to 15 mm Hg higher than when the patient is lying in the left lateral decubitus position.[134]

Various systems have been used to classify hypertensive disorders that occur during pregnancy, but some have not adequately differentiated pre-existing hypertension from that which occurs only during pregnancy. The National High Blood Pressure Education Program Working Group in their Report on High Blood Pressure in Pregnancy reviewed various classification systems and decided to endorse (with modification) the one originally proposed by the American College of Gynecologists in 1972 that divides women with increased blood pressure during pregnancy into the following groups:[132]

- Chronic hypertension
- Preeclampsia-eclampsia
- Preeclampsia superimposed on chronic hypertension
- Transient hypertension

This classification system helps to differentiate women with chronic hypertension from those with pregnancy-induced or pregnancy-specific hypertension (i.e., preeclampsia or eclampsia). Women with chronic hypertension before pregnancy have elevated blood pressure as the "cardinal pathophysiologic feature" of their disease, while those with the latter problem have an increased blood pressure "as a sign of the underlying disorder." In addition, some women have hypertension that is transient.[132]

Chronic hypertension already has been defined in the first paragraph of this section on hypertension during pregnancy. *Preeclampsia* is the presence of hypertension with proteinuria, edema, or both that occurs after week 20 of pregnancy.[132] Proteinuria may be defined as having 30 mg/dL of protein in a random urine specimen (i.e., 1+ protein on dipstick) or ≥300 mg of protein in a 24-hour urine collection.[132] If preeclampsia occurs in a woman with chronic hypertension, it may be termed *preeclampsia superimposed on chronic hypertension.* Hypertension that precedes pregnancy or persists postpartum but did not worsen during pregnancy and was not accompanied by signs or symptoms of preeclampsia may be termed *coincidental hypertension.*

Preeclampsia ranges in severity from mild to severe. Table 44.7 lists signs and symptoms that may mirror a severe form of preclampsia. Preeclampsia can lead to a preeclampsia variant, HELLP, in which a woman exhibits hemolytic anemia, elevated liver enzymes, and has a decreased platelet count or to *eclampsia* which may be defined as convulsions or seizures that occur in a patient with preeclampsia. Both are considered medical emergencies, as is severe preeclampsia; all require immediate hospitalization, antihypertensive therapy, possible anticonvulsant therapy, and delivery of the fetus depending upon the status of the mother and fetus. Although patients may progress from mild preeclampsia to eclampsia, some will have eclampsia before being diagnosed as having preeclampsia.[132,133] Therefore, pregnant women should be monitored closely for hypertension and for other symptoms associated with preeclampsia.

Transient hypertension is the development of an increased blood pressure during pregnancy or in the first 24 hours postpartum without signs or symptoms of preeclampsia in a woman who did not have pre-existing hypertension.[132] The diagnosis of transient hypertension often is made retrospectively.

Signs, Symptoms, and Evaluation

23. T.D., a 19-year-old, primigravid female, is 30 weeks pregnant and has a BP of 140/90 mm Hg on a routine prenatal visit. Two BP values measured 6 hours apart were 140/95 and 135/95 mm Hg. T.D.'s BP was normal before conception and was 115/70 mm Hg 1 month ago. T.D. denies headaches, visual disturbances, or abdominal pain. She has mild ankle, hand, and facial edema but her weight gain since her last prenatal visit is appropriate. T.D.'s urine was positive for a 1+ protein by dipstick. She, therefore, is hospitalized for further evalua-

Table 44.7	Ominous Signs and Symptoms Associated with Preeclampsia[a,132]
BP ≥110 mm Hg diastolic or ≥160 mm Hg systolic	
Proteinuria ≥2 gm in 24 hr (2+ or 3+ upon qualitative examination)	
SrCr >1.2 mg/dL (unless previously elevated)	
Elevated liver enzyme tests	
Platelet count <100,000/mm^3	
Headache or other visual or cerebral disturbances	
Epigastric pain	
Retinal hemorrhage, exudate, or papilledema	
Pulmonary edema	

^{a} BP = Blood pressure; SrCr = Serum creatinine.

tion, bedrest, and BP monitoring for 48 hours. If possible, T.D. then will be followed in the ambulatory setting. How should T.D. be evaluated?

T.D. has a blood pressure consistent with mild preeclampsia symptoms. Because she did not have a history of hypertension before pregnancy, preeclampsia superimposed on chronic hypertension is unlikely. T.D. denies headaches, visual disturbances, and abdominal pain which usually are present in women with severe preeclampsia. To definitely exclude a more severe form of preeclampsia, urine output should be determined, and serum creatinine (SrCr), serum bilirubin, liver function tests (LFTs), and a platelet count should be obtained. A 24-hour urine collection for protein also should be considered. Ultrasonography should be performed serially to determine fetal age and follow fetal development because fetal growth retardation is consistent with severe preeclampsia.

Etiology

24. What is the cause of preeclampsia?

The etiology of preeclampsia currently is debated, but it may be associated with increased maternal vasoconstrictor tone, prostaglandin imbalance, and/or an immunologic problem during pregnancy.

Increased Vasoconstrictor Tone

Women with preeclampsia appear to have markedly increased vasoconstrictor tone and are extremely sensitive to intravenously administered pressor agents such as angiotensin II when compared to pregnant women without preeclampsia.[132,135,136] This increased responsiveness to angiotensin II may be detected before the clinical development of preeclampsia; thus, preeclampsia may be a chronic problem during pregnancy that persists until the fetus is delivered. It has been speculated that the placenta may be the source of vasoactive agents which play a role in the development of preeclampsia.[132] The role of angiotensin II in preeclampsia development currently is under debate.

Prostaglandin Imbalance

The development of preeclampsia may reflect a deficiency of certain prostaglandins that can occur as a result of prostaglandin precursor deficiency, defective prostaglandin activity, or lowered prostaglandin synthetase action.[132,136] (See Figure 46.2 in Chapter 46: Gynecological Disorders for the arachidonic cascade.) There is speculation that a disruption in the conversion of endoperoxides to prostaglandins E_2 and $F_{2\alpha}$, prostacyclin (PGI_2), and thromboxane occurs in women with preeclampsia. These women have reduced concentrations of PGE_2, a vasodilator, and exhibit a decreased response to angiotensin II when they receive exogenously administered PGE_2.

Prostacyclin and thromboxane A_2 are classified as prostanoids and have opposing effects on vascular tone and platelet aggregation in both pregnant and nonpregnant women.[133] Prostacyclin is a potent vasodilator (more potent than PGE_2) which also inhibits platelet aggregation, while thromboxane A_2 is a powerful vasoconstrictor which promotes platelet aggregation.[133] Low prostacyclin generation has been reported in women with preeclampsia,[137,138] but this phenomenon may be even more profound in the fetus resulting in significant impairment of fetal-placental blood flow.[138] The consequence of an apparent prostacyclin and thromboxane A_2 imbalance (resulting from low prostacyclin generation) may be vasoconstriction, hypertension, and platelet aggregation, all of which have been observed in women with preeclampsia.

Response to Low-Dose Aspirin

Based upon the premise that low-dose aspirin can normalize prostacyclin to thromboxane A_2 ratios,[139] Wallenburg et al.[140] conducted a placebo-controlled, double-blind study to evaluate the incidence of hypertension and preeclampsia in pregnant women who received 60 mg/day of aspirin or placebo. All women selected for the study (23 in each group) were normotensive, 28 weeks pregnant, and responded to IV angiotensin II with an increased blood pressure. Two women in the aspirin group developed mild hypertension. In the placebo group, four developed hypertension; seven, preeclampsia; and one, eclampsia. Imperiale and Petrulis performed a meta-analysis and reported that aspirin in varying doses for different durations of therapy decreased the incidence of hypertension during pregnancy.[141]

The results of a large, multicenter investigation to study the effect of low-dose aspirin versus placebo on the development of preeclampsia in healthy, nulliparous pregnant women were published.[142] Investigators enrolled 3135 women, of whom 2985 were followed throughout pregnancy and the immediate puerperium period. Of the original women enrolled, 1570 received aspirin 60 mg/day, while 1565 received placebo. The incidence of preeclampsia was lower in the aspirin group [69 of 1485 (4.6%)] versus the placebo group [94 of 1500 (6.3%)] (relative risk: 0.7; 95% confidence interval: 0.6 to 1; p = 0.05), while gestational hypertension was noted in 6.7% and 5.9%, respectively. Although aspirin decreased the incidence of preeclampsia, it did not appear to decrease perinatal morbidity. Aspirin therapy did appear to have a beneficial effect on women whose initial systolic blood pressures were elevated. There was an increased incidence of abruptio placentae among those enrolled in the aspirin group. Therefore, it was concluded that low-dose aspirin should not be used routinely to prevent preeclampsia, except for women in high-risk groups (e.g., those who previously had preeclampsia, multiple gestations, or those with chronic hypertension or diabetes mellitus).[142]

Treatment

Mild Preeclampsia

25. Is the treatment plan for T.D.'s mild preeclampsia appropriate? Are antihypertensive medications indicated?

Yes. The treatment plan prescribed for T.D. is appropriate. T.D. should benefit from bedrest which will help reduce her blood pressure by decreasing vasoconstriction and improving renal perfusion.[134] She should experience diuresis, weight loss, and a lowered blood pressure. Approximately 80% of hypertensive pregnant women become normotensive with bedrest alone and this decreases the risk of premature labor.[133,134] T.D. also may benefit from reassurance, relaxation, and isotonic exercise. She should receive a regular diet without sodium restriction because salt intake appears to have no effect on the development of preeclampsia.

Controversy Regarding Hospitalization. Whether T.D. should be hospitalized for mild preeclampsia is debated. Investigators at Parkland Hospital in Dallas have reported a decreased fetal mortality rate when nulliparous women with mild to moderate hypertension were hospitalized (fetal mortality rate: 9 out of 1000) when compared to those who left the hospital against medical advice (fetal mortality rate: 129 out of 1000). Fetal outcome also was improved in that 75% of the hospitalized patients delivered infants weighing more than 2.5 kg; the cost of prenatal care was lower than the cost of caring for premature infants after birth.[143] Others recommend home bedrest for women who become normotensive within 48 hours after hospitalization if they have someone to care for them and monitor their blood pressures.[133,144,145] (See Table 44.8 for the ambulatory management of women with mild preeclampsia.)

Controversy Regarding Antihypertensive Therapy. It is controversial whether antihypertensive therapy should be instituted in patients with mild preeclampsia, especially if the patient is approaching her delivery date and the fetus is mature enough to survive without major complications. T.D. is only 30 weeks pregnant; her fetus should not be delivered at this time unless T.D. develops severe preeclampsia, HELLP, or eclampsia; or fetal distress ensues. When mild to moderate hypertension occurs in a previously normotensive woman, maternal morbidity does not appear to be increased significantly.[144,145] Antihypertensive therapy does not confer any benefit when maternal blood pressure is between 140 to 169/90 to 109 mm Hg.[144] Although uteroplacental perfusion is decreased, vascular resistance is increased and uterine blood flow is decreased in preeclamptic women; uteroplacental perfusion appears to be normal or even increased in patients with mild to moderate hypertension, such as T.D., and there generally are no signs of fetal distress. Therefore, there appears to be little indication for antihypertensive therapy.

26. If T.D. had a history of hypertension before pregnancy, would antihypertensives be indicated now to prevent progression to preeclampsia?

There currently are no data to support or refute the use of antihypertensive agents early in pregnancy to prevent superimposed preeclampsia in women with chronic hypertension.[132] Many women with chronic hypertension do not require antihypertensive therapy until the third trimester, because blood pressure generally decreases during the first half of pregnancy. When the maternal diastolic blood pressure is greater than 90 mm Hg, nonpharmaceutical measures should be instituted; antihypertensives should be used when diastolic pressures reach 100 mm Hg to prevent maternal vascular damage. The goal of therapy for women with hypertension during pregnancy is to minimize the short-term risk to the mother during pregnancy while making sure that placental perfusion and fetal well-being are not compromised.[132]

Fetal outcomes in pregnancies in which hypertension developed in the second half of pregnancy without accompanying preeclampsia are similar to those observed for normal pregnancies.[144,145] Mortality rates for infants born to women whose blood pressures were ≥140/90 mm Hg have decreased from 30% in the 1940s to less than 2% today. This decrease cannot be associated with any specific change in therapy, but may reflect early detection of high blood pressure and advances in maternal, fetal, and neonatal care.[134]

Moderate Preeclampsia

27. T.D.'s BP increased from 120/85 mm Hg to 135/90 mm Hg. Because she lived alone and had no family support, it was decided that she should be hospitalized. T.D.'s BP was <90 mm Hg diastolic for the next 3 weeks; but thereafter, her BP at bedrest began to increase (145/90 mm Hg to 160/110 mm Hg). Her weight gain and urine output remained within normal limits and she was asymptomatic except for mild edema. Laboratory results were: sodium (Na) 135 mEq/L (Normal: 135–145),

Table 44.8	Ambulatory Management of Mild Preeclampsia[a,145]

- Bedrest
- Relaxation techniques, limitation of activity, and reassurance
- Home BP monitoring and urine dipstick measurements for proteinuria
- Recording of fetal activity
- Report CNS problems or epigastric pain
- Have prenatal visits at least 2 times a week
- Platelet counts and LFTs 2 times a week

[a] BP = Blood pressure; CNS = Central nervous system; LFTs = Liver function tests.

potassium (K) 3.5 mEq/L (Normal: 3.5–5), chloride (Cl) 100 mEq/L (Normal: 100–106), bicarbonate 25 mEq/L (Normal: 24–28), SrCr 1 mg/dL (Normal: 0.6–1.5), total bilirubin 0.8 mg/dL (Normal: 0.2–1), aspartate aminotransferase (AST) 35 units/mL (Normal: 10–40), platelets 230 × 10^3/mm^3 (Normal: 200–400), hematocrit (Hct) 38% (Normal: 37–48), Hgb 12 gm/dL (Normal: 12–16); UA reveals 1 white blood cell (WBC)/HPF (Normal: up to 1–2), 1+ to 2+ protein (Normal: 0), and pH 5.5 (Normal: 4.6–8). Recent ultrasonography showed a normal growing fetus of ≈33 weeks gestation. T.D.'s only medication is a prenatal vitamin with iron which she takes daily. A decision is made to continue bedrest and monitor T.D. closely for the next 48 hours to see if her BP normalizes. Over the following 48 hours her BP ranged from 140/85 to 160/110 mm Hg. Oral methyldopa (Aldomet) 250 mg TID was initiated and, within 24 hours, T.D.'s BP ranged from 135/85 to 145/100 mm Hg. After 1 week of therapy, she remained normotensive and her only complaint was increased tiredness. Was it appropriate to begin antihypertensive therapy? If so, was methyldopa the appropriate drug for preeclampsia? [SI units: Na 135 mmol/L (Normal: 135–145); K 3.5 mmol/L (Normal 3.5–5); Cl 100 mmol/L (Normal: 100–106); bicarbonate 25 mmol/L (Normal: 24–28); SrCr 88.4 μmol/L (Normal: 53–132); total bilirubin 13.68 μmol/L (Normal: 3.42–17.1); AST 0.58 μkat/L (Normal: 0.17–0.67); platelets 230 10^9/L (Normal: 200–400) ; Hct 0.38 (Normal: 0.37–0.48); Hgb 120 gm/L (Normal: 120–160)]

T.D. appears to have moderate hypertension. Even though some blood pressure readings approach those associated with severe preeclampsia, she has no clinical signs or laboratory test abnormalities consistent with severe preeclampsia. Since T.D.'s hypertension no longer is controlled by nonpharmaceutical measures alone, she may be considered a candidate for antihypertensive therapy. Drugs used most frequently include methyldopa, labetalol, and various β-adrenergic blockers.

Methyldopa (Aldomet) is a centrally acting β$_2$-agonist which decreases sympathetic outflow to decrease blood pressure. It is the most commonly used antihypertensive for hypertension during pregnancy in the U.S. because it has had a long history of use, is effective, and there have been relatively few problems reported in the offspring of pregnant women taking it. Although studies to evaluate methyldopa use during pregnancy enrolled small numbers of patients or did not have adequate study design, no teratogenicity was reported and there were few adverse effects in neonates resulting from maternal exposure.[146–150] One study reported a 4 to 5 mm Hg decrease in systolic blood pressures lasting two days after delivery in 24 full-term infants.[151] In a seven-year follow-up of neonates who were exposed *in utero* to methyldopa, there was a significant decrease in the head circumferences without changes in intelligence for boys when compared to matched controls; this association was not noted in female offspring. The mothers of the children in the methyldopa group began therapy between the 16th to 20th week of gestation.[152]

The problem of decreased head size was not noted in a study by Sibai et al. in which 87 of 334 chronic hypertensive pregnant women were randomized into the methyldopa group early in pregnancy.[153] Methyldopa is classified as a category C drug by Briggs et al. based upon its potential risk to the fetus when used during pregnancy (category C drugs are those for which one of the following is true: animal studies show fetal teratogenic effects, there are no controlled studies in women, or studies in women and animals are not available).[112]

The effectiveness of methyldopa for the treatment of hypertension during pregnancy depends upon the criteria used in a particular study. In some studies, outcomes included the drug's effect on blood pressure and other criteria (e.g., a decrease in proteinuria), while in others, an improvement in perinatal outcome was explored as well.

As illustrated by T.D., lethargy, drowsiness, and somnolence are common adverse effects of methyldopa described by pregnant women. In addition, pregnant women may experience loss of energy and even mild dizziness. Most adverse effects occur early in therapy and usually subside, but some recur.[144] Because of these adverse effects and the potential for depression, many clinicians do not like prescribing methyldopa.

T.D.'s methyldopa dose is appropriate. The usual starting dose is 750 mg/day to 1 gm/day in three to four divided doses. This can be increased to 2 or 3 gm/day if needed. (Also see Chapter 10: Essential Hypertension.)

β-Adrenergic Blockers. Labetalol (Normodyne, Trandate) is an antihypertensive agent that might have been considered for T.D. Labetalol antagonizes β$_1$-, β$_2$-, and α$_1$-receptors (α:β antagonism ratio of 1:4 when administered orally). It reduces total peripheral resistance and reduces cardiac output with little or no reduction in heart rate. Additional benefits of the drug for the pregnant hypertensive patient include: maintenance of an adequate uteroplacental blood flow despite a drop in maternal blood pressure, increased fetal lung maturation resulting from increased surfactant production, and decreased platelet consumption in women with preeclampsia.[144,154–156] This effect on platelets was not confirmed in another study.[157]

Michael reported a 6.4% perinatal mortality rate for infants (n = 95) whose mothers (n = 85) took labetalol (≤1200 mg/day) to control blood pressures of greater than 160/100 mm Hg.[156,158] He also reported intrauterine fetal growth retardation in 24 out of 89 births. Lardoux et al. reported no difference in blood pressure control of 56 pregnant hypertensive patients who received either atenolol or labetalol, but infants whose mothers were in the labetalol group had significantly higher birth weights.[159] Lamming et al. reported a significantly greater lowering of mean arterial blood pressure in 14 women who received labetalol 400 to 850 mg/day compared to the blood pressure reduction in 12 women who received methyldopa 750 to 1500 mg/day orally.[160] The results from another study report that labetalol may decrease the incidence of preterm delivery, but the number of patients enrolled was small.[157]

Labetalol crosses the placenta and concentrations in cord blood average 40% to 80% of peak maternal concentrations.[112] Fetal malformations have not been associated with labetalol therapy, but there are no reports of its use during the first trimester. Drug-associated adverse effects reported in infants exposed *in utero* to labetalol include bradycardia and hypotension. It has been classified as a category C drug.[112] Maternal adverse effects include tremulousness, headache, postural hypotension, and scalp tingling.[144] (Also see Chapter 10: Essential Hypertension.)

The β-adrenergic blockers atenolol (Tenormin), metoprolol (Lopressor), pindolol (Visken), and propranolol (Inderal) have been used to treat hypertension during pregnancy. This class of drugs does not appear to be associated with fetal malformations, although the effects of first-trimester exposure have not been extensively studied for many of these agents.[112] Atenolol and metoprolol readily cross the placenta, achieving fetal serum concentrations approximately equivalent to maternal serum concentrations. Fetal serum concentrations are approximately 37% to 67% of maternal concentrations for pindolol, and 19% to 127% for propranolol.[112]

More fetal and neonatal adverse effects have been reported for propranolol during pregnancy than for other beta blockers, but this may reflect its more extensive use. After analyzing 23 studies and case reports of 167 infants exposed *in utero* to propranolol, Briggs et al.[112] reported the following incidences of adverse effects: intrauterine growth retardation 14%, hypoglycemia 10%, bradycardia 7%, hyperbilirubinemia 4%, respiratory depression at delivery 4%, and polycythemia 1%. Most of the adverse effects reported occurred in mothers taking more than 160 mg/day of propranolol. Other medications and diseases also may have contributed to these effects.

Fetal and neonatal adverse effects reported for atenolol include lower birth weight in infants exposed *in utero* to atenolol or when compared to infants exposed to pindolol or labetalol, although this was not seen in a placebo-controlled study.[159,161–163] Additional studies with larger populations are needed to determine the true effects of beta blockers on infant weight. Rare cases of bradycardia also have been reported in neonates exposed *in utero* to atenolol.[112] Currently, few fetal and/or neonatal adverse effects have been attributed to maternal use of metoprolol or pindolol. Nevertheless, infants exposed *in utero* to any agent in this class of drugs should be monitored closely during delivery and for the first few days of life for possible signs of beta blockade.

Other Antihypertensive Agents. Clonidine is a centrally acting α-adrenergic inhibitor that has been used in pregnancy, but experience with this drug in this population is limited. Clonidine has been classified by Briggs et al. as a category C drug.[112]

Calcium Channel Blockers. Information about the use of calcium channel blockers during pregnancy is limited. The administration of calcium channel blockers to pregnant animals has been shown to decrease maternal mean arterial blood pressure and uterine blood flow that resulted in fetal hypoxia and acidosis.[112] There are few studies that address the use of these agents as antihypertensives during pregnancy, although nifedipine has been used as a tocolytic (can decrease or stop uterine contractions); it is classified as a category C drug.[112] Lindow et al. compared the effects of nifedipine sublingually in nine hypertensive women who were in the third trimester of pregnancy to nine hypertensive women who received placebo.[164] They noted that nifedipine significantly lowered maternal blood pressure and uterine artery perfusion pressure but did not appear to reduce uteroplacental blood flow. In another study, no adverse fetal effects including decreased heart rate were observed with maternal nifedipine use.[165] The resolution of thrombocytopenia has been noted in women treated with nifedipine.[144] Neuromuscular blockade and significant falls in maternal blood pressure have occurred in pregnant women who received nifedipine and magnesium sulfate.[112] Adverse maternal effects include flushing, headache, and reflex tachycardia.[144] In summary, controlled clinical trials are needed to determine the safety and efficacy of nifedipine and other calcium channel blockers during pregnancy.

Angiotensin-Converting Enzyme (ACE) Inhibitors. Animal and human data are not sufficient to demonstrate that these drugs are teratogens. There are sufficient animal data and human case reports, though, to show that drug use during pregnancy may result in fetal renal effects (e.g., oligohydramnios, anuria, renal impairment) as well as pulmonary hypoplasia and possible growth retardation.[144] For these reasons, ACE inhibitors are not recommended for use during pregnancy.[132]

Diuretics. Because the maternal intravascular volume may be constricted in patients with preeclampsia, especially those with severe preeclampsia or eclampsia, diuretics could decrease this volume further, leading to decreased uteroplacental perfusion and, ultimately, fetal compromise. Therefore, diuretics are not recommended for the control of preeclampsia. Possibly a woman with chronic hypertension who used diuretic therapy before pregnancy may be continued on the diuretic. Diuretics are used to treat maternal pulmonary edema or congestive heart failure.

Severe Preeclampsia

28. For approximately 3 weeks T.D. remained normotensive on methyldopa therapy which had been increased to 2 gm/day in divided doses. Thereafter, her BP began to increase and ranged from 160/110 mm Hg to 190/115 mm Hg while she was at bedrest. She now complains of headaches, dizziness, and visual disturbances and has signs of significant edema in her face, hands, legs, and ankles. Her urine output has decreased to 350 mL over the last 24 hours despite adequate hydration. Laboratory results include: Na, K, Cl, glucose, and bicarbonate within the normal range; blood urea nitrogen (BUN) 30 mg/dL; SrCr 2 mg/dL; total bilirubin 2.5 mg/dL; AST 155 units/L; platelets $100 \times 10^3/mm^3$; Hct 39%; Hgb 12 gm/dL; UA reveals O WBC/HPF with 3+ protein and pH 5.5. A chest x-ray reveals pulmonary edema bilaterally. Recent ultrasonography shows a fetus of ≈36 weeks gestation. A decision is made to monitor T.D. and her fetus, prevent seizure activity with magnesium sulfate, reduce T.D.'s BP gradually with hydralazine, and deliver her infant as soon as she is stable. T.D. is started on 4 gm of magnesium sulfate IV administered at a rate not to exceed 1 gm/min to be followed by 5 gm of 50% magnesium sulfate in each buttock by deep IM injection. One milliliter of lidocaine 2% was added to decrease the pain of the injections. Hydralazine 5 mg was administered IV Q 15 to 20 min for a diastolic BP >110 mm Hg. What is T.D.'s current problem? [SI units: BUN 10.7 mmol/L; SrCr 176.8 μmol/L; AST 2.58 μkat/L; platelets 100 10^9/L; Hct 0.39; Hgb 120 gm/L]

Signs and Symptoms. T.D. has developed severe preeclampsia. Her systolic and diastolic blood pressures at bedrest have been above 160 and 110 mm Hg, respectively. She has greater than 3+ protein in her urine, a urine output of less than 400 mL/24 hours, and an elevated serum creatinine. She complains of headaches and visual disturbances and has pulmonary edema, thrombocytopenia, and abnormal liver function tests. All of the above are consistent with severe preeclampsia. Currently, she is not having seizures, but she should be monitored closely for pending eclampsia.

Complications. In addition to hypertension, women such as T.D. who develop severe preeclampsia may experience cardiac failure, pulmonary edema, cerebral complications, and hepatic dysfunction. They also are prone to various coagulopathies; the most common form is microangiopathic thrombocytopenia and overt thrombocytopenia associated with severe disease.

In women with preeclampsia, cerebral vascular resistance is increased approximately 50%, but hypertension overcomes the resistance and maintains a fairly normal blood flow to the brain. If the hypertension becomes overwhelming, the patient may develop a cerebral hemorrhage, one of the most common causes of death in women with PIH.[133,143] This complication can be decreased by controlling the patient's blood pressure. A patient such as T.D. could experience other central nervous system (CNS) problems including cerebral edema and seizures. If seizures occurred, T.D. would be classified as having eclampsia. Symptoms of cerebral edema include altered consciousness, scotoma, headache, and blurred vision, some of which T.D. has experienced.

Not only is severe preeclampsia dangerous to T.D., but it also is dangerous to her fetus because uteroplacental perfusion is compromised. The placenta can become infarcted and, with time, the fetus can exhibit growth retardation secondary to decreased placental perfusion. Although it is important to reduce the maternal blood pressure, it must be accomplished gradually while the fetus is *in utero* because a large and sudden drop in maternal blood pressure could result in an even greater reduction in uteroplacental perfusion.

29. Was T.D.'s drug treatment appropriate? How should she be monitored?

Magnesium Sulfate. The use of magnesium sulfate for T.D. is appropriate. Parenterally administered magnesium sulfate prevents the occurrence of seizures in a preeclamptic patient such as T.D. and alleviates seizures in women with eclampsia. Because it does not cause maternal sedation or fetal depression, magnesium sulfate may be preferred over parenterally administered barbiturates and benzodiazepines. The drug may be administered intravenously or intramuscularly, but IM therapy should be preceded by an IV loading dose if the patient has eclampsia or symptoms associated with cerebral edema (i.e., headaches, visual disturbances, scotoma, altered consciousness). Because T.D. was exhibiting symptoms associated with cerebral edema, she received a 4 gm IV loading dose of magnesium sulfate so that a therapeutic magnesium serum concentration could be achieved more rapidly. If she had not had symptoms associated with cerebral edema, she should have received magnesium sulfate 10 gm IM as her initial dose. Thereafter, 5 gm should be administered intramuscularly every four hours in alternating buttocks.[166]

Before magnesium sulfate maintenance administration, T.D. should be evaluated for signs of magnesium toxicity (see below). Additionally, magnesium serum concentrations should be obtained to assess therapeutic effectiveness and possible toxicity. Magnesium serum concentrations normally are 1.5 to 2 mEq/L, while magnesium serum concentrations needed for anticonvulsant activity range from 4 to 7 mEq/L.[166]

Magnesium sulfate also can be administered as a continuous IV infusion using an infusion pump. Maintenance doses of 1 to 3 gm/hour have been recommended following an initial loading dose of 4 gm intravenously.[167,168] However, IV maintenance doses of 1 gm/hour inadequately controlled preeclamptic patients since 98% of the women (n = 98) had serum concentrations below the therapeutic range.[167,168] Of the women who received maintenance doses of 2 gm/hour IV (n = 25), 50% had serum concentrations below the therapeutic range; all patients receiving 3 gm/hour (n = 12) had serum concentrations in the therapeutic range. To determine the appropriate IV dosing, serum magnesium concentrations must be followed.

To prevent magnesium toxicity, it is important to monitor magnesium serum concentrations and evaluate patients before each dose is administered. A patellar reflex should be elicited (this response usually disappears at serum concentrations of 8 to 10 mEq/L), the respiratory rate should be normal (respiratory depression and/or respiratory arrest may occur at serum concentrations of $\geq$12 mEq/L), and the urine output should be at least 100 mL/hour (magnesium can accumulate with decreased renal function because the drug is eliminated by glomerular filtration).[166] Hypocalcemia and hypocalcemic tetany also can occur secondary to hypermagnesemia. Calcium can be administered for a magnesium overdose or for magnesium serum concentrations in the toxic range.

Neuromuscular depression can occur in infants whose mothers received magnesium sulfate. Neonatal toxicity usually is associated with maternal renal dysfunction and/or prolonged IV administration before delivery. Although respiratory depression and hyporeflexia have been reported in infants whose mothers received various doses of magnesium sulfate IV over extended time periods, these toxic effects were not observed when the drug was administered intramuscularly following a protocol similar to that used for T.D.[166] Why the difference in neonatal outcome occurred is not well understood. Maternal magnesium serum concentrations should be obtained before delivery; rarely is neonatal toxicity observed in infants whose mothers have magnesium serum concentrations in the normal therapeutic range.

Hydralazine. Although magnesium sulfate has a mild antihypertensive effect, it usually is transient. Therefore, an antihypertensive agent is needed to control blood pressure elevations. Hydralazine (Apresoline), a vasodilator which has a greater effect on arteries than on veins, is the most commonly used antihypertensive to control severe preeclampsia. The primary reason that it remains popular in the U.S. is its long history of use in pregnant women.

Hydralazine may be administered intramuscularly or intravenously. The onset of its antihypertensive effect occurs 20 to 30 minutes after IV administration or 30 to 40 minutes after an IM dose.[144] Commonly, an initial hydralazine dose of 5 mg is given slowly intravenously followed by 5 to 10 mg every 20 to 30 minutes to achieve a diastolic blood pressure of 90 to 100 mm Hg.[132,166] This usually is accomplished after a total dose of 5 to 50 mg has been administered.[133] Thereafter, additional doses of hydralazine are administered for a diastolic pressure greater than 110 mm Hg. If doses are administered too frequently, the patient may develop hypotension. Lowering the maternal blood pressure excessively may decrease uteroplacental perfusion and compromise the fetus. Therefore, as repeated doses are administered, the blood pressure must be monitored closely.

Common adverse effects noted in patients receiving hydralazine for preeclampsia include nausea, vomiting, tachycardia, flushing, headache, and tremors. Some of these may mimic symptoms associated with preeclampsia and eclampsia, making it difficult for a clinician to differentiate between drug-associated and disease-related problems. This could result in early termination of pregnancy. The use of hydralazine is contraindicated in pregnant women with pre-existing coronary disease.

Fetal hydralazine serum concentrations reportedly are about the same as or higher than maternal serum concentrations, but no drug-associated fetal abnormalities have been reported.[112]

Therefore, it appears that T.D. was started on appropriate hydralazine and magnesium sulfate therapy. She should receive additional hydralazine therapy based upon her blood pressure, and her magnesium sulfate therapy should be continued until she delivers and even 24 hours postdelivery. After she is stabilized, her infant should be delivered because her fetus is approaching term and is sufficiently mature for delivery.

30. What alternative antihypertensive drugs might have been initiated in T.D.?

Antihypertensives most commonly used instead of hydralazine for severe preeclampsia are labetalol, diazoxide (Hyperstat), or a calcium channel blocker. These agents could be used if a patient does not respond adequately to hydralazine.

Labetalol can be administered as an initial IV dose of 0.25 mg/kg up to 20 mg followed by 40 to 80 mg every ten minutes up to a total of 300 mg or until the blood pressure is controlled.[170] Others recommend repeated doses at 20- to 30-minute intervals.[144] An IV infusion of 1 to 2 mg/minute also has been recommended with a rate reduction as the diastolic blood pressure is lowered. Studies have shown that labetalol is as effective as hydralazine in lowering blood pressure in patients with hypertension during pregnancy but has fewer reported adverse effects.[144] Furthermore, labetalol does not appear to decrease uteroplacental blood flow even with a decrease in maternal blood pressure.[144]

Diazoxide is an arterial vasodilator with a rapid onset of action. When administered as an IV bolus, its peak antihypertensive action may be observed in two to five minutes.[144] It has never achieved wide use for blood pressure control during pregnancy because precipitous falls in maternal blood pressure have resulted in maternal hypotension, cerebral ischemia, and death. Fetal distress and neonatal hyperglycemia also have been reported.[132,144] Women with decreased intravascular volumes appear more prone to these adverse effects. Diazoxide also is a uterine smooth muscle relaxant, and if administered during labor, can inhibit uterine contractility. This phenomenon may be dose dependent.[112]

The administration of diazoxide as 30 mg mini-boluses every one to two minutes produces a smooth drop in the blood pressure to desired levels. When diazoxide is administered as intermittent boluses, a total dose of less than 150 mg is required.[171]

Calcium channel blockers have been used with success in some cases. Nifedipine's effect on blood pressure after oral administration has been observed within 10 to 20 minutes; this effect may occur more rapidly if the capsule is punctured before swallowing or if it is chewed.[132]

Women with severe preeclampsia such as T.D. should be monitored closely for hypotension, nausea, vomiting, respiratory problems, sodium and fluid retention, cardiac dysrhythmias, CNS toxicity, and hyperglycemia. The patient should remain supine after drug administration until blood pressure stabilizes. (Also see Chapter 17: Hypertensive Emergencies.)

Ketanserin

31. Are there any drugs on the horizon to control hypertension associated with preeclampsia?

Ketanserin, a serotonin receptor antagonist, has been used to reduce both the systolic and diastolic blood pressure in patients with severe preclampsia.[172] It reportedly has controlled blood pressure and decreased the frequency of uterine contractions from 3.6 to 4.2 per ten-minute period (p <0.005); adverse effects include maternal dizziness and drowsiness and fetal tachycardia.[172]

The antihypertensive effect of ketanserin is mediated by its competitive inhibition of serotonin at 5-HT$_2$ receptor sites found on platelets and vascular smooth muscle. Elevated concentrations of serotonin, which cause hypertension, vasospasm, and oliguria in experimental animals, have been found in the plasma and placentas of pre-eclamptic women.

Isoimmunization and Hemolytic Disease of the Newborn (HDN)

32. G.G., a 24-year-old primigravida female, has her ABO blood group and Rh status determined during her initial prenatal visit. She is determined to be type O, Rh-negative. Her husband is known to be type O, Rh-positive. What are the risks associated with Rh incompatibility? Is it the only type of blood group incompatibility that could affect G.G.'s unborn infant?

There are at least 100 different blood group antigens of which the ABO and Rh systems are only two. Of these, about one-third can induce isoimmunization in a pregnant woman. This process occurs when a woman, exposed during pregnancy or immediately postpartum to a fetal antigen she does not possess, produces antibodies to that antigen. If sufficient antibody production occurs and the antibody produced is immunoglobulin G (IgG), then the placental transfer of the antibody may result in hemolytic disease of the fetus or newborn infant. Only maternal IgG production will result in HDN, because IgG is the only immunoglobulin that usually is capable of placental transfer.[173,175]

ABO incompatibility occurs in 20% to 25% of all pregnancies, but HDN is clinically present in approximately 10% of fetuses. Fetal erythrocyte destruction occurs when maternal antibodies interact with antigens on fetal erythrocytes causing the destruction of fetal red blood cells. This ABO incompatibility occurs almost exclusively when a type O mother is carrying a type A (specifically A$_1$) or B fetus. Type O mothers produce antiA and antiB antibodies which are predominantly IgG, while antibodies produced by individuals who are type A or B are predominately immunoglobulin M (IgM).[175]

ABO incompatibility in the newborn is manifested clinically in the first 24 hours after birth as jaundice, hyperbilirubinemia, and hemolytic anemia. The problem usually is managed by following serial bilirubin serum concentrations and using phototherapy when necessary. Occasionally, exchange transfusion may be required.[175]

An ABO incompatibility should not be a problem for G.G.'s unborn child because both she and her husband are type O. The Rh blood group also is classified as the CDE blood group.

Although Rh incompatibility is second only to ABO incompatibility in causing HDN, the HDN that occurs generally is more severe. An Rh-negative woman will have a 10% chance of delivering an Rh-positive infant if she is white, 5% if she is black, and 1% if she is Asian.[173] The probability that an Rh-negative woman who delivers an Rh-positive, ABO-compatible infant will become Rh isoimmunized is approximately 16%. Of these, 1.5% to 2% will be Rh isoimmunized by the time of delivery, 7% within six months of delivery, and 7% will mount a secondary immune response at the time of their next Rh-positive pregnancy.[176] If the mother and infant are ABO incompatible, a protective effect is seen and only 1.5% to 2% of these Rh-negative women will become isoimmunized within six months of delivery.[176] Since both G.G. and her husband are type O, an ABO incompatibility is unlikely to occur; therefore, there is little chance that a protective effect on the potential Rh incompatibility will be present. Whether an Rh-positive father is homozygous or heterozygous for the D antigen (an antigen strongly associated with Rh-positivity) determines the likelihood of having an Rh-positive offspring. If the father is homozygous for the D antigen, all of his offspring will be D positive (Rh-positive). If he is only heterozygous for the D antigen, then 50% will be Rh-positive.

Individuals who are Rh-positive may be designated Rh$_o$(D)-positive or Rh$_o$(Du)-positive because the D antigen is not homogenous and variations in its expression are term "Du variants."[175] Most Rh$_o$(Du)-positive individuals genetically are Rh-positive, but the expression of the D antigen is weak; such individuals should be considered Rh-positive.[175,176]

The severity of Rh-associated HDN or erythroblastosis fetalis depends upon the concentration of antibodies that the fetus is exposed to *in utero*. Mild disease may result only in hemolysis, but the placental transfer of significant amounts of antibody may cause substantial RBC destruction. This initially results in anemia and hyperbilirubinemia with compensatory erythropoietic hyperplasia. If the hematopoietic system cannot compensate, the fetus may develop hepatosplenomegaly, portal hypertension, edema, ascites, hepatic failure, and cardiac failure. The clinical presentation of profound anemia, anasarca, hepatosplenomegaly, cardiac failure, and circulatory collapse has been termed hydrops fetalis.[173,175,177]

While *in utero*, the fetus may be protected from high bilirubin concentrations because of maternal and placental metabolism. After birth, the neonate may become jaundiced rapidly as bilirubin concentrations exceed the infant's ability to bind bilirubin to albumin. Once this occurs, the infant becomes clinically jaundiced and will develop kernicterus if bilirubin is deposited in the basal ganglia, cerebellum, and hippocampus of the CNS.[173,175,177]

The severity of Rh-associated HDN also may increase with each pregnancy in the isoimmunized mother. Thus, it is important to discuss the consequences of isoimmunization with any woman who is known to be isoimmunized and wishes to have more children in the future.

Prevention

Rh$_o$(D) Immune Globulin (Human)

33. Can anything be done to prevent HDN from occurring in G.G.'s fetus or in any future children she and her husband may wish to have?

Maternal isoimmunization may be prevented by the administration of human Rh$_o$(D) immune globulin (RhoGAM, Gamulin Rh, HypRho-D, Resonativ) before or shortly after she has been exposed to fetal Rh-positive RBCs. The mechanism by which Rh$_o$(D) immune globulin suppresses sensitization is unknown but there are many theories which are discussed in detail elsewhere.[175]

A standard single-dose vial or prefilled syringe of $Rh_o(D)$ immune globulin contains approximately 300 µg of $antiRh_o(D)$. This amount can suppress the immune response to 15 mL of Rh-positive packed RBCs or 30 mL of whole blood. $Rh_o(D)$ immune globulin approaches 100% effectiveness if administered intramuscularly to an Rh-negative woman as soon as possible following exposure to Rh-positive cells. A dose greater than 300 µg may be indicated if a large transplacental bleed (>15 mL of packed RBCs or 30 mL of whole blood) occurs at the time of delivery (0.4% of cases). To confirm this, tests are available to detect fetal RBCs in the maternal circulation. Once the amount of fetal RBCs in the maternal circulation is determined, an appropriate $Rh_o(D)$ immune globulin dose can be administered. For each 15 mL of fetal RBCs present, 300 µg should be administered.[173]

Viruses (including HIV) are inactivated by the manufacturing process used to produce $Rh_o(D)$ immune globulin.[175] Adverse reactions associated with the use of $Rh_o(D)$ immune globulin are rare. Discomfort at the injection site and fever are the most commonly reported adverse effects. $Rh_o(D)$ immune globulin must be administered intramuscularly (never IV) to the mother; the product should never be administered to the neonate.[178]

The Rh-negative [$Rh_o(D)$-negative] mother should be monitored closely during pregnancy. Her ABO and Rh status should be determined and an Rh antibody screen (indirect Coombs' test) should be performed as early in pregnancy as possible. An initial antibody screen should be performed at the beginning of each pregnancy and follow-up screens should be done at 28 weeks, 35 weeks, and postpartum; some recommend monthly screens.[175,176,178] (See Table 44.9.)

The transfer of fetal RBCs across the placenta during pregnancy results in a 1% to 2% incidence of isoimmunization in $Rh_o(D)$-negative women who deliver either an $Rh_o(D)$-positive or $Rh_o(Du)$-positive infant. $Rh_o(D)$ immune globulin administered at 28 to 32 weeks gestation decreases the sensitization rate to 0.1%.[178] Controversy about the cost:benefit ratio of antepartum prophylaxis [administration of $Rh_o(D)$ immune globulin at 26 to 28 weeks gestation] in addition to the originally recommended postpartum prophylaxis has been reported in the literature. Many investigators[175,176,179] believe that antepartum administration is necessary to reduce the incidence of maternal isoimmunization and that the cost of $Rh_o(D)$ immune globulin has been reduced sufficiently so that its use should no longer be controversial on a cost basis.

Other antepartum indications for the administration of a standard 300 µg dose of $Rh_o(D)$ immune globulin to an Rh-negative female impregnated by a male who is Rh-positive or whose Rh status is unknown are listed in Table 44.10. If $Rh_o(D)$ immune globulin is administered during weeks 13 to 18 of gestation (e.g., following amniocentesis or trauma), additional standard doses of $Rh_o(D)$ immune globulin should be administered at 26 to 28 weeks of pregnancy and again within 72 hours after delivery if the infant is Rh-positive. The half-life of $Rh_o(D)$ immune globulin is 23 to 26 days.[175,178]

Commercially available 50 µg doses of $Rh_o(D)$ immune globulin (MICRhoGAM, Mini-Gamulin Rh, HypRho-D Mini-Dose) may be used to prevent maternal isoimmunization following an abortion or termination of a tubal pregnancy up to and including 12 weeks gestation.[175,176] The risk of maternal isoimmunization associated with abortion during the initial trimester of pregnancy is 3% to 5.5%.[175]

Thus, G.G. should be told that with the proper institution of $Rh_o(D)$ immune globulin, there is little chance for a $Rh_o(D)$-neg-ative woman like her to become isoimmunized. She need not worry about her present pregnancy or future pregnancies.

Management of Isoimmunization During Pregnancy

34. If an Rh-negative mother is isoimmunized or becomes isoimmunized during her current pregnancy, how should the pregnancy be managed?

The primary goal is to determine how severely the fetus is affected and when the fetus should be delivered. A fetus with mild HDN may remain *in utero* and be delivered when the lungs have matured, while a moderately affected fetus may have to be delivered before pulmonary maturity. Fetuses that are severely affected will need *in utero* therapy if they are not sufficiently mature to survive in a neonatal intensive care unit. Presently, the earliest age at which delivery is considered, if necessary, is about 32 weeks gestation; this age will change as survival rates for low-birth-weight infants increase because of improved neonatal care.[173,175]

Both maternal antiD antibody titers and amniotic fluid ΔOD450 values are used to evaluate the condition of the fetus. (ΔOD450 values refer to the peak spectrophotometric absorption of indirect bilirubin which occurs at a wavelength of 450 nm). AntiD antibody titers may be valuable to determine when amniocentesis should be performed, but serial ΔOD450 values should be used to assess fetal status.[175] Standardized nomograms use ΔOD450 values plotted versus fetal gestational age to determine the severity of fetal involvement.

Serial ultrasonography should be performed to determine gestational age and monitor for signs of erythroblastosis fetalis (e.g., ascites, edema). If an infant must be delivered before term, amniotic fluid should be obtained for a lecithin:sphingomyelin (L:S) ratio and a phosphatidylglycerol spot test to assess the degree of fetal lung maturation. If the fetal lungs are immature, maternal glucocorticoid therapy (e.g., betamethasone, dexamethasone) may be instituted to stimulate fetal lung maturation.[175,180] Surfactant also may be needed by the infant after birth. (Also see Chapter 96: Neonatal Therapy.)

A severely affected fetus that is too immature for delivery may require intrauterine transfusions. Currently, intrauterine transfusions may be performed as early as 20 weeks gestation. Their use has resulted in perinatal survival rates of 80% to 92% depending upon the time of intervention, severity of the erythroblastosis fetalis at initial intervention, and the technique used for intrauterine transfusion.[175] If intrauterine transfusions are unsuccessful and severe signs of erythroblastosis fetalis are observed upon ultrasonography, delivery may be considered as early as gestational age 30 weeks.[175] Thus, to assure the best outcome for the fetus, modern technology must be employed to determine the level of fetal severity and the optimal time for delivery.

Therapy For Preterm Labor

Preterm labor, labor that begins before 37 weeks of gestation, occurs in approximately 5% to 15% of pregnancies in western nations and is the most common complication that occurs during the third trimester. Nine percent of all live births in the U.S. involve the delivery of a preterm infant.[181] (See Chapter 96: Neonatal Therapy.)

Etiology

The exact etiology of preterm labor may be multifactorial, but approximately one-third of women experiencing preterm labor also have premature rupture of the membranes (PROM).[181] Although it is unclear whether PROM results in preterm labor or vice versa, it appears that a bacterial infection of the chorionic membranes may be an etiology for both. Such an infection may initiate labor

Table 44.9	Guidelines for the Administration of Rh$_O$ Immune Globulin to an Rh-Negative Female[174,175,177]

Antepartum[a]
Maternal Antibody Screen Negative Weeks 1–28

Father is Rh Positive
or
Paternal status unknown
↓
Rh$_O$(D) immune globulin 300 µg should be administered at 28–32 weeks;
↓ incidence of isoimmunization from 1%–2% to 0.1%[175,176,178]

Father is Rh-negative
↓
Rh$_O$(D) immune globulin not indicated

Maternal Antibody Status: Positive Anytime During Pregnancy
Manage as if Rh sensitized

Postpartum
Maternal and Cord Blood Antibody Screen Negative

Infant status known:

Infant Rh-positive or Du-positive
↓
Give mother 300 µg Rh$_O$(D) immune globulin within 72 hours of delivery;[177] isoimmunization may be prevented if administered within 28 days after exposure[175]

Infant's Rh status unknown within 72 hours postpartum and:

Father is Rh-negative or Du-negative
↓
No Rh$_O$(D) immune globulin

Father is Rh-positive Du-positive, or status unknown
↓
Give mother 300 µg Rh$_O$(D) immune globulin

[a] Also see Table 44.10.

indirectly by producing an endotoxin that stimulates decidual cells to produce prostaglandins and cytokines that are known inducers of labor.[182] Cytokines, including interleukin-1, tumor necrosis factor, and interleukin-6, have been found in amniotic fluid, but it is not known if these substances initiate labor or their presence merely is the result of preterm labor.[182] Other etiologies for preterm labor are listed in Table 44.11. Factors which predispose patients to premature delivery are discussed in detail elsewhere.[182]

Mechanisms Initiating Preterm Labor

Mechanisms underlying the initiation of preterm labor are not understood clearly. Huszar and Naftolin state that the coordination of myometrial activity and cervical maturation are important in the initiation of both normal and preterm labor.[183] These may be regulated by complex biochemical events. The critical reaction for muscle contraction is a phosphorylation of the myosin light-chain

Table 44.10	Recommendations for Prophylactic Administration of 300 µg of Rh$_O$(D) Immune Globulin[a,174,175,177]

Threatened abortion at any stage of gestation when the pregnancy is continued

Abortion or termination of ectopic pregnancy beyond the 1st trimester[b]

Amniocentesis

Percutaneous umbilical blood sampling

Chorionic villus sampling

Abdominal trauma during the 2nd or 3rd trimesters

Antepartum prophylaxis (weeks 26–28)[d]

Postpartum prophylaxis (if newborn is Rh-positive)[d]

[a] Recommendations apply to Rh-negative females who have been impregnated by an Rh-positive male or a male whose Rh status is unknown.
[b] If abortion or termination of an ectopic pregnancy occurs up to and including 12 weeks gestation, a 50 µg dose of Rh$_O$(D) immune globulin may be used.
[c] If antepartum prophylaxis is indicated, the mother also should receive a postpartum dose if the infant is Rh-positive.
[d] Also see Table 44.9.

kinases which leads to the actin-myosin interaction. This process is mediated through the release of myometrial calcium. It is believed that prostaglandins, especially $F_{2\alpha}$ and E_2, directly stimulate uterine contractility by modulating myometrial calcium.[183,184] During pregnancy, there is a progesterone dominance or a low estrogen:progesterone ratio. Before labor, elevated estrogen concentrations or estrogen:progesterone ratios may be important for myometrial contractility and cervical ripening.

Some women at risk for preterm labor (e.g., those with a history of prior preterm births or cervical dilatation after midpregnancy) have increased uterine activity several weeks before labor begins. Some also may experience a bloody or watery vaginal discharge, pelvic pressure, or lower back pain. These women may be candidates for ambulatory tocodynamometry which enables one to monitor uterine activity and intervene if needed for preterm labor.[182]

Myometrial smooth muscle contractions may result in labor before or at term. When a woman develops painful uterine contractions, cramps, low back pain, vaginal spotting, increased vaginal discharge, and/or pelvic pressure before the completion of 37 weeks gestation, then preterm labor should be suspected. A woman also may present with PROM. Many times, preterm labor is hard to diagnose because uterine contractions associated with labor must be differentiated from Braxton Hicks contractions (irregular contractions that occur with or without pain). But if a woman has regular uterine contractions that occur at least every ten minutes and last for at least 30 seconds each, she may be experiencing labor. This uncertainty in evaluating contractions has resulted in using other criteria besides contractions alone to diagnose preterm labor, and has made it difficult to evaluate the effectiveness of therapy to stop preterm labor. Herron et al. recommend that preterm labor be based upon the presence of regular uterine contractions every five to eight minutes as well as the presence of cervical changes that are progressive, dilatation ≥2 cm has occurred, or effacement is ≥80%.[185]

Clinical Presentation and Evaluation

35. B.B., a 19-year-old primigravid female, ≈31 weeks pregnant, is admitted to the obstetrical unit with complaints of backache, cramps, and uterine contractions. Her contractions vary in intensity, last 30 seconds, and occur ≈8–10 minutes

apart. B.B. denies fluid leakage that might be associated with PROM. Her pregnancy had been uncomplicated until this admission and she has no major medical problems. A vaginal examination reveals 2 cm cervical dilation and 80% effacement without signs of PROM. Maternal vital signs (temperature, pulse, respirations, BP), uterine contractions, and fetal heart tones are to be monitored. UA, cervical-vaginal culture, CBC with differential, serum electrolytes, and blood glucose are ordered. Ultrasonography is to be performed to estimate gestational age and fetal size. What evidence exists that B.B. is in preterm labor? How should she be managed?

B.B. meets many of the criteria for preterm labor discussed earlier. She has contractions of approximately 30 seconds in duration which are occurring at least every ten minutes, and her cervix is dilated (2 cm) and effaced (80%). She also is experiencing a backache and cramps which may be associated with labor, but she does not have PROM.

Once it has been established that B.B. meets the criteria for preterm labor, one should determine if there is an underlying cause. If an initiating event (such as a urinary tract infection) is diagnosed and treated appropriately, preterm labor may resolve spontaneously. It also is important at this time to determine if the cause for preterm labor is preterm rupture of the membranes (i.e., rupture of the membranes before 38 weeks gestation). The gestational age and fetal lung maturation also should be evaluated to determine if delaying delivery will benefit the fetus. If PROM has occurred, management can be either expectant (i.e., no intervention and waiting for spontaneous labor) or active intervention. The latter can include the administration of corticosteroids for fetal lung maturation and tocolytic agents to stop labor or to prolong labor long enough to administer and achieve effect from the corticosteroids.[182] In any case, the pregnant woman and fetus should be monitored for signs of infection or other complications.

There are few prospective, randomized studies that compare management methods. Garite et al. studied 160 pregnant women who were assigned to an expectant management or active intervention group. The active intervention group received corticosteroids and tocolysis (i.e., IV magnesium sulfate or IV ethanol).[186] There was no improvement in the perinatal outcome of those whose mothers were in the active management group; in fact, the mothers in that group had more complications such as infection. Two other comparison studies have affirmed the findings of Garite et al.[187,188] However, a prospective, randomized study[189] demonstrated that infants whose mothers were randomized into an ampicillin-plus-corticosteroids group had less respiratory problems than those whose mothers were randomized into other treatment groups: expectant-management-only group, corticosteroids-only-for-fetal-lung-maturation group, or an ampicillin-only group. The gestational age at the time of delivery and neonatal survival were not affected.

Table 44.11	Etiologies for Preterm Labor[a,180,181]
• PROM	• Fetal death
• Infection of amniotic fluid	• Cervical incompetency
• Previous preterm delivery or late abortion	• Uterine anomalies
	• Maternal disease
• Faulty placentation (e.g., abruptio placentae and placenta previa)	• Retained IUD
	• Elective induction of labor too early in gestation
• Overdistended uterus (e.g., hydramnios)	• Unknown causes
• Multifetal gestation	

a IUD = Intrauterine device; PROM = Premature rupture of the membranes.

If there are signs of chorioamnionitis (infection of the chorioamnionic membranes) such as fever ≥ 38 °C and possibly an increased white blood cell count with the presence of preterm rupture of the membranes, then delivery usually is undertaken as soon as possible. Morales et al.[190] reported that 13% of 700 women they followed between 26 and 34 weeks gestation were diagnosed as having chorioamnionitis. The infants born to women with chorioamnionitis were three times more likely to have respiratory problems, intraventricular hemorrhage, and/or sepsis, and they were at greater risk for mortality.

B.B. does not have ruptured membranes, however, and her uterine contractions are accompanied by cervical dilation and effacement as noted in the case. Had these two symptoms not been present, she may have responded to conservative, nondrug measures such as bedrest[182,191] although there is no controlled study that shows the efficacy of bedrest alone. Studies such as one by Valenzuela et al.[192] showed that bedrest, hydration, and mild sedation decreased contractions in approximately 55% of women who met the investigators criteria for preterm labor. However, women responding to these therapeutic modalities might have "threatened" preterm labor rather than true preterm labor. If a patient does not respond to bedrest, other modalities that might be initiated include tocolytic therapy and corticosteroids. Tocolytic therapy may be used to prolong gestation as long as possible or to delay delivery for 48 to 72 hours, while maternally administered corticosteroids help the fetal lungs mature.[191] If any signs of infection are present, the patient should receive appropriate antibiotic therapy.

Since B.B.'s effacement is $\geq 80\%$ and her cervical dilation is greater than 1 cm, agents that inhibit labor (tocolytics) should be considered.

Tocolytic Therapy

Betamimetics

36. Tocolytic therapy is being considered for B.B. Betamimetics commonly are used for tocolysis. What is their mechanism of action and which agents are approved for this purpose?

Mechanism of Action. Tocolytics are therapeutic agents that decrease or inhibit uterine contractions. Betamimetics with β_2 selectivity appear to be useful pharmacologic agents for the inhibition of preterm labor although they may have adverse effects that require careful monitoring of the mother and fetus. These agents selectively bind to beta receptors in uterine smooth muscle and activate adenylate cyclase which mediates the conversion of adenosine triphosphate (ATP) to cyclic AMP (cAMP). Increased intracellular cAMP concentrations may reduce myometrial contractility by modulating myosin light chain kinase phosphorylation and increasing cellular calcium sequestration. The latter is necessary for myosin phosphorylation and actin-myosin interaction.[183,184]

Agents. Ritodrine HCl (Yutopar) and terbutaline sulfate (Brethine, Bricanyl) are the betamimetics most frequently used for tocolysis in the U.S. Ritodrine is the agent most extensively studied and currently is the only betamimetic approved for use as a tocolytic in the U.S. Other betamimetics that have been used to treat preterm labor include isoxsuprine (Vasodilan), albuterol (Proventil, Ventolin), metaproterenol (Alupent, Metaprel), nylidrin (Arlidin), and fenoterol.

37. *Ritodrine: Contraindications.* **What maternal and fetal conditions would preclude the use of ritodrine?**

Maternal factors that preclude the initiation of ritodrine therapy include severe cardiac or renal disease, uncontrolled hypertension, severe preeclampsia, eclampsia, uncontrolled diabetes mellitus, hyperthyroidism, chorioamnionitis, vaginal bleeding, and abruptio placentae. Maternal conditions that may be affected adversely by the use of betamimetic agents include hypovolemia, cardiac dysrhythmias, pheochromocytoma, and a known hypersensitivity to this class of drugs. Fetal factors precluding the use of ritodrine include fetal distress, growth retardation, an anomaly incompatible with life, and intrauterine death.[181,193–195]

Tocolysis usually is unsuccessful if the pregnant woman has an incompetent cervix, PROM, a urinary tract infection, or is in advanced labor (cervix dilated >5 cm). B.B. has no contraindications to the use of tocolytics and does not exhibit any of the characteristics that could make her unresponsive to these agents.

38. *Dosing.* **A decision is made to use ritodrine in an effort to arrest B.B.'s preterm labor. What doses should be used?**

Ritodrine can be administered intravenously or orally. When used orally, the drug undergoes a first-pass effect which reduces its bioavailability to 30%.[196] Ritodrine should be initiated at a dose of 50 to 100 µg/minute by continuous IV infusion. This dose can be increased by 50 µg every 10 to 20 minutes until contractions cease, adverse effects develop, or a maximum dose of 350 µg/minute is reached. Once a therapeutic dose is determined, the infusion should be continued for at least 12 hours after contractions cease.[181,195] As an alternative, once contractions cease, the tocolytic is maintained at the rate that stopped the contractions for one hour and then it can be decreased slowly by 50 µg/minute every one-half hour until the lowest dose is achieved that abates uterine activity. Intravenous doses are continued for 12 hours.[196] If contractions begin again, tocolysis should be restarted. If oral ritodrine is to be initiated, B.B. should receive 10 mg orally before the infusion is discontinued followed by 10 mg of ritodrine every two hours for one day. The usual maintenance dose thereafter is 10 to 20 mg every four to six hours, not to exceed 120 mg/day. If labor recurs, it may be necessary to restart IV therapy.[181,195]

39. *Other Agents.* **Are any of the other betamimetic agents likely to be more effective than ritodrine?**

No. However, it is extremely difficult to compare the effectiveness of tocolytic agents because clinical trials use different patient selection criteria, doses, study durations, and therapeutic endpoints. Even studies evaluating the same drug may be difficult to compare.

Isoxsuprine, a nonspecific β-adrenergic agonist, was used with some success in the past; however, a high incidence of maternal tachycardia and hypertension has limited its use as a tocolytic agent.[174]

The effectiveness of betamimetics in preventing or delaying preterm labor (tocolytic effect) and their risk:benefit ratio is under debate. Success rates for ritodrine range from 38% to 100% in placebo-controlled studies.[197–199] It is superior to placebo and as effective as terbutaline, albuterol, and fenoterol.[197–204] In a prospective, randomized, double-blind study that compared the effectiveness of IV ritodrine and terbutaline for tocolysis,[204] there were no statistically significant differences in the success rates (69% versus 45%) or length of time that gestation was prolonged (43 versus 55 days). However, the incidence of adverse effects in those who received ritodrine (38%) was significantly lower than in those who received terbutaline (60%). However, the adverse effects associated with terbutaline might have been dose related because the investigators used higher initial doses (20 µg/minute IV) than those used by others. Caritis et al.[201] also found no differences in success rates between IV terbutaline and IV ritodrine, but oral terbutaline (30 mg/day) was significantly more successful than oral ritodrine (120 mg/day) in preventing recurrent labor during a five-day period of drug administration. Although betamimetics appear to *inhibit* preterm labor, none effectively *prevent* preterm labor.

The effects of betamimetics on perinatal outcome are not clear. A study by Leveno et al. showed no difference in perinatal outcome between mothers who received ritodrine and those who received no tocolytics for preterm labor.[205] Similar results were noted in the Canadian Preterm Labor Investigators Group.[206] Tocolytic failure may be explained by a desensitization of β-adrenergic receptors to betamimetics.[182]

40. Cost Effectiveness. **How cost effective are betamimetics in arresting labor and increasing infant survival?**

To determine if there are gestational limits for administering a tocolytic agent based upon cost considerations and pregnancy outcomes, Korenbrot et al.[207] retrospectively compared the cost of neonatal and maternal care in 229 pregnant women who received tocolysis (i.e., IV isoxsuprine or terbutaline) to those who delivered early without tocolytic therapy (n = 136). The results indicate that tocolysis for the mothers who were 20 to 25 weeks pregnant saved $39,000 per birth in 1981, but for women whose fetuses were between 26 to 33 weeks gestation, the savings were $11,240 per birth. There was no difference in cost between the group that received tocolysis (n = 43) and the group that did not (n = 10) after 33 weeks gestation.

In women 20 to 25 weeks pregnant at the onset of labor (n = 22), tocolytic therapy prolonged gestation by a mean of 14.1 weeks with a fetal survival rate of 80%. This compared favorably to a survival rate of 14% for neonates of the same gestational age whose mothers did not receive tocolysis (n = 3). For women 26 to 33 weeks pregnant at the start of tocolytic therapy (n = 164), labor was arrested in 55% and gestation was extended by 4.3 to 6 weeks. Infant survival rates for the group ranged from a mean of 89% to 97% and increased as the gestational age at the onset of therapy increased. Women whose fetuses were the same gestational age but did not receive tocolysis (n = 32) had infant survival rates ranging from 75% to 95%. The success rate for arresting labor in women who received tocolytic therapy during weeks 34 to 37 was 68%, but fetal survival rates were not statistically different between the tocolytic and nontocolytic groups (98% versus 97%). In summary, although the numbers of those enrolled in various gestational groups were not divided equally and the overall numbers of those enrolled were small, it appears that the use of tocolytics may not be cost-justified when fetal age exceeds 33 weeks.

Gonik and Creasy[208] advocate the initiation of tocolytic therapy until 36 weeks gestation and continuing it through 37 to 38 weeks gestation to decrease neonatal respiratory problems, patent ductus arteriosus, and intensive care admission. Cost analyses of various home care programs for high-risk pregnant women have found that it is cost beneficial to monitor and treat these women through week 37 of pregnancy.[191] Because the gestational age of B.B.'s fetus is 31 weeks, tocolytic therapy is likely to be cost effective.

41. Maternal and Fetal Adverse Effects of Betamimetics. **What adverse effects have been associated with ritodrine or other betamimetics when used for tocolysis? What are the mechanisms and predisposing factors for these adverse effects? How should B.B. and her fetus be monitored?**

Most adverse effects associated with betamimetic therapy are extensions of the pharmacologic effects of these drugs and usually can be controlled by dose reduction. The effects on other tissues besides the uterus occur because $β_2$-receptors also are found in the bronchi, heart, and other sites.

Cardiovascular. The most frequently encountered adverse effects associated with IV ritodrine include dose-related fetal and maternal tachyarrhythmias and maternal hypotension.[207] Katz et al. reported a 5% incidence of cardiovascular problems associated with IV terbutaline administration.[209] During pregnancy, cardiac output increases and the administration of betamimetics can further increase cardiac output by 40% to 60%. Therefore, betamimetics should not be used in women with underlying cardiac problems. Supraventricular tachycardia is the most common dysrhythmia noted with betamimetic therapy, but others have been reported.[210] Many of the cardiovascular complications associated with betamimetics appear to be associated with the following factors: cardiac abnormalities, sustained maternal heart rate of ≥140 beats/minute, betamimetic infusions of longer than 24 to 48 hours, fluid overload, hyperkalemia, betamimetic infusion in saline, multiple gestations, gestational age of 28 to 32 weeks, and concurrent corticosteroid administration to enhance fetal lung maturation.[193,200] Other cardiovascular effects of concern include a number of cases of myocardial ischemia.[210] For these reasons, vital signs, electrocardiograms, fluid intake and output, and serum electrolytes must be monitored before and during therapy. Fetal heart tones also should be followed externally to assure that fetal distress does not occur.

Pulmonary edema associated with betamimetic therapy has become widespread with over 80 cases and 14 maternal deaths reported.[182,210] This may be due to infection, increased cardiac demands resulting from pregnancy, pre-existing cardiac disease, or fluid overload.[182] Alternatively, pulmonary edema may be due to the increased pulmonary capillary hydrostatic pressure and decreased osmotic pressure observed in pregnant women.[182] Patients receiving corticosteroids, expecting multiple births, or those who have preeclampsia or polyhydramnios appear to be at increased risk.[181,182,184] Thus, women on betamimetic therapy must be observed closely for signs and symptoms of pulmonary edema. Therapy can include oxygen, decreasing the dose or discontinuing betamimetic therapy, fluid restriction, and possibly diuretics.[181]

Hyperglycemia can result from increased gluconeogenesis and glycogenolysis and commonly occurs during the first 24 to 48 hours of betamimetic therapy. It usually resolves even if drug therapy is continued. However, patients with insulin-dependent diabetes may experience hyperglycemia, ketoacidosis, and occasionally, lactic acidosis necessitating an increase in insulin requirements or continuous IV insulin infusion therapy. Serial plasma glucose and urine ketones must be monitored carefully.[210] Elevated free fatty acids also have been reported.[210]

Hypokalemia may develop within a few hours after IV betamimetic therapy is initiated due to rapid shifts in serum potassium, but serum potassium concentrations return to preinfusion levels usually within 10 to 20 hours despite continued betamimetic infusion.[210] B.B. should be monitored for hypokalemia, but since the total body potassium is normal, potassium supplements should not be needed unless serum concentrations drop significantly, a cardiac dysrhythmia is noted, or a diuretic is needed.[210] If potassium is administered in such situations, it should be done with caution and adequate monitoring.[210]

Others. Other frequent maternal adverse effects include tremors, nausea, vomiting, erythema, and headaches (10% to 15%). Occasional adverse effects include restlessness, nervousness, anxiety, hallucinations, and malaise.[181,182,195,196,210]

Fetal Adverse Effects of Betamimetics. The most commonly reported fetal or neonatal adverse effects associated with betamimetic therapy include tachycardia, hypotension, hypoglycemia, and hypocalcemia.[210] To date, no congenital anomalies have been associated with the use of ritodrine; however, the use of this drug before the 20th week of pregnancy has not been studied,[112] and the manufacturer does not recommend its use before this time period.[195] A group of infants exposed *in utero* to ritodrine were followed for two years and had no growth, maturation, or developmental abnormalities.[204]

Fetal Lung Maturity

External fetal monitoring should be performed as needed. Amniocentesis may be used to rule out chorioamnionitis[181] and assess fetal lung maturation. The latter may be accomplished by determining the lecithin:sphingomyelin (L:S) ratio. If this test determines the fetal lungs are mature, tocolysis may be stopped. If the opposite is true, glucocorticoid therapy (e.g., betamethasone, dexamethasone) may be initiated to stimulate lung maturation.

Other Tocolytics

42. What other drugs are used as tocolytics? Should any of these agents be used as a therapeutic modality for B.B.?

Other agents that have been used to inhibit preterm labor include ethanol (no longer used), magnesium sulfate, calcium channel blockers, prostaglandin synthetase inhibitors, and progestational steroids.

Magnesium sulfate effectively relaxes uterine smooth muscle and decreases myometrial contractility.[181,182] The mechanism by which it exerts this effect is not understood clearly, but it may decrease calcium influx into uterine smooth muscle, interfere with the neuronal release of acetylcholine, or alter acetylcholine sensitivity at the motor endplate.[181,183,193] Magnesium also may replace calcium in nerve impulse conduction by blocking or decreasing nerve transmission.

The effectiveness of magnesium sulfate as a tocolytic varies with positive results being shown in some studies while in others little effect is noted. Magnesium sulfate also has been used with ritodrine to control preterm labor unresponsive to ritodrine alone or to decrease ritodrine dose requirements. An increased incidence of adverse cardiovascular effects from the combination was reported by one group of investigators while other investigators reported an increase in clinical effectiveness without increased adverse effects.[211,212] (Also see Question 29.)

Prostaglandin Synthetase Inhibitors. Because prostaglandins (primarily $F_{2\alpha}$ and E_2) are important regulators of myometrial contractility and cervical ripening, prostaglandin synthetase inhibitors have been used for tocolysis. Although aspirin, naproxen (Anaprox, Naprosyn), and flufenamic acid (not currently available in the U.S.) have been used, indomethacin (Indocin) has been studied most thoroughly as an inhibitor of preterm labor. (Also see Chapter 46: Gynecologic Disorders.) Indomethacin appears to be an effective tocolytic agent,[213-215] but it may inhibit fetal prostaglandin synthesis and cause premature closure of the ductus arteriosus.[216] A retrospective examination of the hospital records of infants exposed to indomethacin before 30 weeks gestation because of maternal preterm labor found that these infants had a higher incidence of increased serum creatinines at birth, necrotizing enterocolitis, grade II to IV intracranial hemorrhage, and patent ductus arteriosis.[217] Despite these adverse reports, the use of indomethacin should be considered on an individual basis with its benefits as well as its risks being evaluated. The use of prostaglandin synthetase inhibitors for preterm labor prevention may increase once the length and timing of therapy, dosage, route, and safety issues are clarified. (Also see Chapter 96: Neonatal Therapy.)

Calcium channel blockers appear to inhibit preterm labor by decreasing calcium influx into uterine smooth muscle and inhibiting myometrial contractions. Studies have evaluated the tocolytic effects of nifedipine with success rates of 80% to 100% (success was defined as delaying delivery for ≥3 days).[218,219] Two newer studies also have shown nifedipine to be an effective tocolytic.[220,221]

Orally administered nifedipine has been shown more effective in the treatment of preterm labor before 36 weeks gestation than either no pharmacologic therapy or intravenously administered ritodrine. Less problematic adverse effects were reported for those receiving nifedipine.[222]

Maternal adverse effects associated with nifedipine use include transient tachycardia, facial flushing, and headaches. Adverse effects have been noted in the offspring of various species of animals that have received calcium channel blockers. These effects included acidosis, hypoxemia, and hypercapnia.[182] Calcium channel blockers appear promising as tocolytic agents, but additional studies are needed.

Oxytocin Antagonists. Research is beginning in the development of a synthetic receptor antagonist to inhibit oxytocin. This may be helpful in the future to decrease preterm labor.[182]

In conclusion, ritodrine is an appropriate choice of therapy for B.B. If she was not a candidate for betamimetic therapy or if her labor was unresponsive to maximum ritodrine doses, magnesium sulfate could be used as an alternative agent or added to betamimetic therapy. Indomethacin or nifedipine also may be considered for B.B. if she does not respond to other therapy.

Labor Induction

Prostaglandin E₂ (PGE₂)

43. J.T., a 22-year-old primigravida female, is admitted to the obstetrical unit for labor induction. Her obstetrician has determined that she is 42 weeks gestation and recommends induction of labor for a postdate pregnancy. She has a normal obstetrical examination; however, her cervix is unfavorable for induction of labor with oxytocin. She is admitted to the hospital and is given 0.5 mg of PGE₂ gel intracervically. What is the role of PGE₂ in the induction of labor?

Indications and Contraindications. Table 44.12 lists the common indications for labor induction. A postterm pregnancy (>42 weeks gestation) is the most frequent reason for induction of labor.[223] When maternal or fetal indications for induction of labor are present and the cervix is not yet ripe, the use of PGE₂ is appropriate if no contraindications to use exist. Contraindications to the use of PGE₂ for cervical ripening include previous uterine surgery including cesarean section delivery, ruptured membranes, significant cephalopelvic disproportion, fetal malpresentation, fetal distress, grand multiparity (≥6), history of difficult or traumatic delivery, presence of uterine contractions, asthma, glaucoma, or liver disease in the mother, undiagnosed vaginal bleeding, or known hypersensitivity to prostaglandins.[224]

Role in Labor Induction. Knowledge that the myometrium and fetal membranes produce prostaglandins PGE₂ and PGF₂ₐ, which play a role in cervical ripening and uterine contractions, lead to the pharmacological application of PGE₂ to soften and ripen the cervix before the induction of labor with oxytocin. Prepidil Gel (0.5 mg dinoprostone in 2.5 mL of triacetin gel) is a commercially available preparation of PGE₂ for intracervical administration which deposits the drug directly into the cervical canal. In clinical trials evaluating the efficacy of Prepidil Gel there was significant improvement in cervical ripening during the 12 hours following application.[226–229] Approximately 50% of women who received the PGE₂ went into labor during this time period as compared to 10% of women in the control group. Twenty-five percent of women in the PGE₂ group delivered without requiring oxytocin as compared to 5% of women in the control group; however, this information was not available for all women entered in the study. Two favorable trends that did not reach statistical significance were a decrease in the time from induction to delivery and a lower cesarean section rate in the PGE₂ group compared to the control group.

Dosing. The effective dosage range of intracervical PGE₂ is 0.25 to 1.0 mg with the most commonly administered dose being 0.5 mg.[226,230–232] The dose can be given at any time but usually is given in the evening with the anticipation of inducing labor in the morning. The time interval between the application of PGE₂ and the initiation of oxytocin ranges from 4 to 24 hours with the average being 12 hours.[231,233–235] After administration, the patient should remain recumbent for one to two hours and be monitored for the onset of uterine contractions; the fetal heart rate should be monitored as well.[223] The cervix should be assessed every six hours for softening and dilatation.[224] Some studies have reported success with up to three applications every six hours; however, most women require only one application.[236,237]

44. Adverse Effects. What adverse effects can be anticipated in the mother and baby after the PGE₂ gel is applied?

Adverse effects associated with PGE₂ include nausea, vomiting, fever, pyrexia, and shivering which reportedly occur in 0.2% of women.[234,235,238,239] Severe vulvular edema also has been reported.[240] The most serious side effect associated with PGE₂ administration is uterine hyperstimulation which is associated most frequently with intravaginal administration.[238,239,241] The rate of occurrence is reported to be 0.6% to 6.0%, similar to the rate associated with oxytocin. Effects on the fetus such as heart rate abnormalities are rare in the absence of uterine hyperstimulation.[238] There have been no reports of adverse sequelae associated with the administration of PGE₂ gel in babies born to mothers who received this agent.

45. Intravaginal Administration. Can PGE₂ be administered intravaginally?

Yes, PGE₂ can be administered intravaginally by applying the drug to the posterior vaginal fornix. This is the route preferred by many clinicians because it is easier to administer and intracervical administration does not appear to increase myometrial activity to the same extent as intravaginal administration.[235,240] Currently, there is no commercial intravaginal PGE₂ product available in the U.S., so it must be prepared extemporaneously by a pharmacist using dinoprostone (Prostin E₂).[242,243] While the practice of using extemporaneously prepared PGE₂ for intravaginal administration appears to be widespread, the preparation of this product has not been standardized with regard to composition, potency, or purity nor have its efficacy and safety been demonstrated in large-scale, well-designed studies.[244] Neither have the questions of the sterility and stability of this dosage form been answered. Until this dosage form is approved by the FDA, the clinician should treat the preparation of this product as any other investigational agent.

Oxytocin

46. Mechanism of Action. Twelve hours after the administration of PGE₂ gel, J.T.'s cervix has responded and her Bishop score now is 9, but she has not developed a consistent pattern of uterine contractions. A decision is made to initiate an oxytocin (Pitocin) drip at 1 million units/min using an IV infusion pump. What are the pharmacologic effects of oxytocin on the myometrium? How does it induce labor?

Exogenously administered oxytocin stimulates uterine smooth muscle to contract; myometrial excitability and the velocity, fre-

Table 44.12	Indications for Labor Induction[a,223–225]
Maternal	Fetal
Pregnancy-associated hypertensive diseases	IUGR
	Macrosomia
Diabetes mellitus	Rh immunization
Renal disease	Chorioamnionitis
PROM	Oligohydraminos
COAD	Fetal death
Logistical problems (i.e., distance from hospital, risk of rapid labor)	

[a] COAD = Chronic obstructive airways disease; IUGR = Interuterine growth retardation; PROM = Premature rupture of the membranes.

quency, and strength of myometrial contractility are increased. The uterine response to oxytocin increases throughout pregnancy but becomes significant after week 30 of pregnancy.[245]

Concentrations of naturally occurring oxytocin gradually increase throughout pregnancy and peak during the second stage of labor. At that time, oxytocin also may be produced by the fetus. It has been postulated that increased oxytocin concentrations also are needed to trigger prostaglandin production necessary to maintain orderly and effective myometrial contractions and enhance cervical ripening.[246,247]

47. Indications and Contraindications. When should the induction of labor be considered? Is labor induction appropriate in J.T.?

Table 44.12 lists clinical conditions for which labor induction may be considered. If labor is induced before 32 weeks of pregnancy, the benefits of early delivery must outweigh the risks to the mother and her unborn child. Not only must criteria be established for the induction of labor, criteria also must be established for the use of oxytocin to stimulate or augment labor. A physical and obstetrical examination, in addition to constant maternal and fetal monitoring, must be undertaken to establish that the infant is sufficiently mature and has a weight appropriate for vaginal delivery. Some obstetricians consider multiple gestation, major vaginal bleeding, disproportional pelvis, unfavorable fetal presentation, and uterine infection contraindications to the use of oxytocin.[245,248] Other contraindications include fetal distress and severe maternal preeclampsia or eclampsia. Oxytocin should be discontinued when adequate uterine concentrations do not result in satisfactory progress.[249] The success of labor induction depends upon cervical ripeness which may be assessed by pelvic scoring methods, such as the Bishop[250] or Lange[251] methods. Using the Bishop method, scores are assigned based upon the station of the fetal head, and the extent of cervical dilation, effacement (thinness of the cervix), consistency, and position. Bishop scores of nine or more are associated with 100% inducibility while scores of five to nine are associated with 95% inducibility.[252] The Lange method assesses the station of the fetal head, length of the cervix, and the extent of cervical dilation. Scores of eight or higher are associated with nearly 100% inducibility while scores of five to seven are associated with a rate of at least 75%.[251]

J.T. is to be induced because she has had a prolonged pregnancy (42 weeks). Since there are no contraindications to the use of oxytocin, she is an appropriate candidate for induction.

48. Dosing. Is J.T. receiving an appropriate oxytocin dose?

Oxytocin injection is a commercially available, synthetic preparation that contains 10 units/mL. For the induction of labor, oxytocin should be administered by continuous IV infusion using an infusion pump for accuracy. The solution for administration may be prepared by adding 10 units of oxytocin injection to 1 L of IV solution (10 million units/mL).[253] The goal of oxytocin administration is to induce uterine contractions that dilate the cervix and aid in the descent of the fetus while avoiding uterine hyperstimulation and fetal distress.[254]

Many protocols for oxytocin administration have been published and they differ with regard to the initial dose, dosing increment, dose increment interval, and maximum dose. The initial dose used varies widely from 0.5 million units/minute to 6.0 million units/minute. The American College of Obstetricians and Gynecologists (ACOG) recommends an initial oxytocin infusion of 0.5 to 1.0 million units/minute to be increased by 1.0 to 2.0 million units/minute every 40 to 60 minutes until a pattern of five contractions in a ten-minute period is achieved and cervical dilation is 5 to 6 cm.[255] In a study evaluating three different starting doses of 0.7, 1.7, and 3.3 million units/minute with dosing increments of 1.3, 3.3, and 6.7

million units/minute every 30 minutes titrated to uterine response, there was no difference in induction time to delivery, the cesarean section rate, or perinatal outcome between the groups.[256] However, the total dose administered was significantly less for the low-dose group versus the intermediate- or high-dose groups. Since the adverse effects of oxytocin (uterine hyperstimulation, water intoxication and neonatal hyperbilirubinemia) are dose related, the minimally effective dose should be employed.[257,258]

The dose increment interval for most oxytocin protocols ranges from 15 to 60 minutes. Studies that have evaluated shorter intervals (15 to 20 minutes) versus longer intervals ($\geq$30 minutes) have found no difference in time to delivery, cesarean delivery rate, or neonatal outcome.[259-261] Protocols using shorter adjustment intervals usually result in a significantly higher dose of oxytocin administered compared to those using longer dosing intervals. The interval recommendation of the ACOG is based upon the time to steady-state concentrations of oxytocin which is approximately 40 minutes.[262]

Oxytocin administration to augment labor (labor that has arrested or is considered to be progressing too slowly) usually requires lower oxytocin doses than those used to induce labor.[263] Seitchik and Castillo reported that infusion rates of 2 to 8 million units/minute effectively produced cervical dilatation at the rate of 1 cm/hour.[264]

There have been several reports comparing pulsatile oxytocin administration to a continuous infusion for either labor induction or augmentation.[265-267] The rationale behind the pulsatile administration of oxytocin is to mimic the endogenous release of oxytocin during labor. The pulsatile protocols used a ten-second pulse of oxytocin initiated at 1.0 million units every eight minutes. The dose is increased every 24 minutes based upon uterine response up to 32 million units; then, the dose is increased each pulse until the desired uterine contraction pattern is achieved. Compared to a continuous infusion of oxytocin, there were no differences in time to delivery, cesarean section rate, neonatal outcome, or the incidence of uterine hyperstimulation. Pulsatile administration of oxytocin resulted in a significantly lower dose of oxytocin required for response. These data involve small numbers of women and experience is limited, but further investigation is warranted to demonstrate if this method of administration should replace the standard continuous infusion of oxytocin.

J.T. is receiving an appropriate starting dose of oxytocin. How she responds to the oxytocin infusion will determine whether she will need an increased dose. J.T.'s contraction pattern and cervical dilatation should be assessed at least every 30 to 60 minutes. The goal is to establish a pattern of one uterine contraction every two minutes and cervical dilatation of 5 to 6 cm. If the response is inadequate, then the oxytocin drip can be increased by 1 to 2 million units/minute. This titration may continue every 30 to 60 minutes until the goals for uterine contraction and cervical dilatation have been met or side effects occur. Additionally, it is important that J.T. be monitored for blood pressure, heart rate, uterine contraction pattern, and uterine tonus in order to recognize uterine hyperstimulation early. Uterine hyperstimulation is characterized by uterine contractions more frequent than two minutes, contractions lasting longer than 90 seconds, or a baseline uterine tonus greater than 15 to 20 mm Hg.[268] Continuous fetal monitoring of fetal heart rate also should be maintained throughout the infusion to detect fetal distress.

49. Adverse Effects. What maternal or fetal problems have been associated with oxytocin administration when used to induce labor?

Uterine hypercontractility, usually associated with excessive maternal dosing or sensitivity to oxytocin effects, may result in maternal hemorrhage, uterine rupture, vaginal and cervical lacerations, and abruptio placentae. Increased uterine contractions can result in fetal trauma and/or decreased uterine blood flow which may cause fetal distress (e.g., fetal hypoxia, deceleration of fetal heart rate, cardiac dysrhythmias). Brain damage and death secondary to asphyxia have been reported.[269]

Maternal hypotension, tachycardia, and even cardiac dysrhythmias can result when high doses of oxytocin are administered. Additionally, because maternal hypotension has been associated with IV bolus administration, bolus or the rapid administration of oxytocin is not recommended.[270] Oxytocin has antidiuretic properties; water intoxication, seizures, coma, and death have been reported with prolonged use.[269] Finally, iatrogenic prematurity can occur if the gestational age of the fetus is determined incorrectly before labor is induced.

Other Methods

50. Are there any other methods of labor induction that might have been considered for J.T.?

Amniotomy, artificial rupture of amniotic membranes, has been used to induce labor with success reported in 70% to 80% of women.[271] Amniotomy initiates uterine contractions and dilatation of the cervix by increasing prostaglandin production.[272] Amniotomy also is used to accelerate labor and decrease the risk of dystocia. In the Canadian Early Amniotomy Study, Fraser et al. compared the effects of early amniotomy (as soon as possible after entry into the study) to conservative management. Early amniotomy decreased the frequency of dystocia and the median length of the first stage of labor by 136 minutes compared to the conservative management group. The subjects were nulliparous women in labor whose cervixes were dilated to ≥3 cm at the time of the amniotomy.[273] There were no significant differences in cesarean section rates nor were there any differences in outcomes between infants delivered to the two groups.

The risks associated with amniotomy include umbilical cord prolapse, intrauterine infection, fetal heart rate decelerations, and bleeding.[274] Before amniotomy is performed, the station of the fetal head should be determined as well as the cord presentation. Fetal heart rate should be monitored before and immediately after the procedure to diagnose fetal distress.[292]

Breast Stimulation. Because breast stimulation results in endogenous oxytocin release, investigators currently are evaluating this method for labor induction.[275,276] If proven effective, it will provide a natural, nonpharmacologic method for labor induction.

Postpartum Hemorrhage

Oxytocin

51. Are there other uses for oxytocin in a pregnant patient such as J.T.?

Another use for oxytocin is the reduction of postpartum hemorrhage that most commonly occurs secondary to uterine atony. Treatment for this obstetric problem includes manipulative procedures (manual massage or bimanual compression), medical management (administration of pharmacologic agents and the resolution of blood volume), and surgery when needed.[277-279] Oxytocin is the drug of choice. It has been infused intravenously at rates of 20 to 40 million units/minute to control hemorrhaging following delivery of the infant and placenta. Alternatively, 10 units intramuscularly can be administered after the placenta has been delivered.[245,249]

Oxytocin also can be used to decrease the time required for placental separation. For this purpose, oxytocin is administered after the delivery of the anterior shoulder. The advantages for this use of oxytocin are debated.[245]

Ergot Alkaloids

52. If postpartum hemorrhage does not respond to oxytocin, are there other medical management alternatives?

If hemorrhaging does not respond to oxytocin administration, ergot alkaloids may be used to decrease the bleeding. Ergonovine maleate (Ergotrate Maleate) and its semisynthetic derivative, methylergonovine maleate (Methergine), are the ergot alkaloids of choice for this purpose because they have potent effects on the atonic uterus. They are available as tablets and parenteral products. If the parenteral route is needed, IM is the preferred route unless there is an emergency such as severe uterine hemorrhaging; the IV route is associated more frequently with adverse effects.[280,281] Adverse effects associated with ergonovine maleate administration include nausea, vomiting, and hypertension. Injury and death due to hyperstimulation of the uterus as well as myocardial infarction (MI) have been reported. Overdose has resulted in the previous mentioned adverse effects as well as hypotension and hypertension, numbness in the extremities, gangrene of fingers and toes, chest pain, mental confusion, delirium, excitation, hallucinations, seizures, coma, and coagulability states.[280] Adverse effects associated with methylergonovine maleate administration include nausea, vomiting, hypertension, headache, chest pain, dizziness, tinnitus, and diaphoresis. Overdoses have resulted in symptoms including the previously mentioned adverse effects as well as numbness and tingling in extremities, respiratory depression, hypothermia, seizures, and coma.[281]

The dose of either drug when administered intravenously is 0.2 mg; the intramuscular dose also is 0.2 mg and this may be repeated at two- to four-hour intervals if needed. Oral doses of ergonovine maleate (0.2 to 0.4 mg BID or QID) or methylergonovine maleate (0.2 mg TID or QID) may be administered to promote involution of the uterus; ergonovine maleate tablets may be administered sublingually.[280,281]

Carboprost Tromethamine

When bleeding due to uterine atony does not respond to medical therapies that have been discussed previously, a prostaglandin such as (15S)-15-methyl prostaglandin $F_{2\alpha}$-tromethamine salt (Hemabate, carboprost tromethamine equivalent to 250 µg carboprost and 83 µg tromethamine/mL) may be used.[277-279] Carboprost tromethamine, like naturally occurring prostaglandins, stimulates uterine contraction and decreases postpartum hemorrhage; it is more potent and has a longer duration of effect than its parent compound, prostaglandin $F_{2\alpha}$. Prostaglandin E_2 also may be useful in treating severe postpartum hemorrhage.[279]

Carboprost tromethamine is approved for intramuscular use but also has been administered intramyometrially.[277-279,282-284] Initial doses of 0.25 mg may be administered deep intramuscularly using a tuberculin syringe. As an alternative to the 0.25 mg dose, a 0.1 mg test dose may be administered. Subsequent doses of 0.25 mg may be given at 1.5- to 3.5-hour intervals with the exact time between doses dependent upon uterine response. If a patient does not respond to several 0.25 mg IM doses of carboprost tromethamine, doses of 0.5 mg should be given. The manufacturer recommends against a total dose exceeding 12 mg or a duration of therapy longer than two days.[284] Carboprost tromethamine is effective in 60% to 95% of patients; the majority of those failing therapy had chorioamnionitis rather than uterine atony as the cause of uterine hemorrhage.[278-280,282-283] Improvement in bleeding typically occurs 15 to 45 minutes after the IM injection and may occur rapidly (within 4 minutes) following intramyometrial administration.

A number of adverse effects associated with carboprost tromethamine administration have been reported; those frequently reported include nausea, vomiting, diarrhea, headaches, flushing, chills, coughing, hiccoughs, a mild temperature increase ($<2°F$), pain (e.g., muscle, back, eye), and breast tenderness.[284] Many of the adverse effects are related to the drug's contractile effect on smooth muscle. Most adverse effects are transient and some adverse effects may be reduced by pretreating with antiemetic and antidiarrheal agents.[284] Hypertension, although rare, typically occurs in women who have been diagnosed as having pre-existing hypertension or preeclampsia. Because prostaglandin use has been reported to cause uterine rupture, pulmonary, and/or cardiac problems, its administration is contraindicated in women with pulmonary, cardiac, renal, or hepatic disease as well as those with hypersensitivity to the product.[279,284] Carboprost also is contraindicated in women with acute pelvic inflammatory disease.[284]

Lactation

Approximately 60% of women in the U.S. choose to breast-feed at the time of hospital discharge.[285,286] This declines to 27% by the time infants reach the age of five to six months. Public health officials had hoped that by 1990 75% of all infants born in the U.S. would be breast-fed, but this goal has been achieved only on the West Coast.[287]

Lactation is controlled primarily by prolactin (PRL), but the entire process is under the intricate control of several hormones. Breast growth and the development of the lobuloalveolar system require estrogen, progesterone, PRL, growth hormone, and cortisol, all of which are increased at various times during pregnancy. Prolactin, insulin, and cortisol regulate and facilitate the synthesis of human milk protein and fat. PRL concentrations gradually increase during pregnancy and reach concentrations of around 200 ng/mL at the time of delivery, but during pregnancy high estrogen concentrations inhibit milk secretion by blocking PRL's effect on the breast epithelium.[11,288,289]

After delivery, estrogen and progesterone dramatically decrease and milk production increases during the first three days following delivery. Infant suckling at the breast then is necessary to maintain an adequate milk supply. With nipple stimulation, sensory impulses are transmitted to the hypothalamus which mediates PRL release from the anterior pituitary. Prolactin stimulates the production and secretion of breast milk. This process is under the control of hypothalamic PRL-inhibitory factors (e.g., dopamine) and PRL-releasing factors (thyrotropin-releasing hormone, estrogen, serotonin, gamma-aminobutyric acid).[11,288,289]

Hypothalamic stimulation also is necessary for oxytocin synthesis and transport to the posterior pituitary from which it is released into the circulation. Oxytocin stimulates the contraction of the myoepithelial cells in the breast alveoli and ducts so that milk can be ejected from the breast ("the let-down reflex").[11,288]

Stimulation

53. C.C., a 22-year-old female, vaginally delivered her first child, a healthy full-term infant. C.C. plans to breast-feed and was educated about breast-feeding during obstetrical visits and prenatal classes. After giving birth, C.C. tried to breast-feed in the delivery room with great difficulty. Afterwards, she became extremely apprehensive and continued to have trouble breast-feeding. What can be done to encourage C.C. and help her with lactation?

Nonpharmaceutical Measures. The most effective stimulus for lactation is suckling. Many women nurse in the delivery room after uncomplicated vaginal deliveries because nursing increases maternal-infant bonding and helps establish good milk production. If a mother does not nurse immediately after delivery, she should be encouraged to do so as soon as she is physically able. C.C. did try

to nurse after delivery but had problems which may have been related to her emotional or physical state or to the physical state of her infant. It is of utmost importance that the nursing staff offer encouragement and emotional support to C.C. They should help her relax, be comfortable, and relieve her anxiety about breast-feeding since the "let-down reflex" occurs more readily when a woman is relaxed and confident. Nursing personnel also should emphasize appropriate feeding techniques and proper positioning for breast-feeding. Arrangements which allow the child to sleep in the mother's room rather than a nursery also help mothers to develop a nursing routine.

Most new mothers who have difficulty breast-feeding initially respond to the emotional and educational support of a good obstetrics nursing staff. Few will require pharmaceutical intervention.

Synthetic oxytocin (Syntocinon) nasal spray has been used with some success by women who may have an adequate milk supply but have difficulty with the "let-down reflex" due to anxiety, stress, or other problems. It also has been used to relieve breast engorgement. Oxytocin is not useful when inadequate milk production is the problem.

The commercially available oxytocin preparation contains 40 units/mL and the usual dose of oxytocin to stimulate lactation is one spray in one or both nostrils two to three minutes before breast-feeding.[284] The onset of action occurs within minutes and lasts about 20 minutes. Oxytocin has a short plasma half-life (3 to 5 minutes) and is eliminated hepatically and renally.[269]

Other Drugs. Although not approved for use in lactation induction or the re-establishment of lactation, chlorpromazine and metoclopramide have been used experimentally for these purposes. Metoclopramide, taken orally in doses of 20 to 30 mg/day in divided doses for six to ten days, increased milk volume in five women who wished to prolong breast-feeding when their milk volume decreased.[285,286] Chlorpromazine has been administered orally in doses of 25 to 100 mg three times daily for seven to ten days.[286]

C.C. should respond to support from obstetrical personnel and probably will not need drug therapy. If a drug is needed, oxytocin would be the treatment of choice.

Suppression

54. After delivery, J.G. informs her obstetrician that she does not wish to breast-feed. What methods are available to suppress lactation?

Suppression of lactation is indicated for women who do not want to breast-feed, women who have delivered a stillborn infant, and those who have had an abortion. Both drugs and nonpharmaceutical methods have been used.

Nonpharmaceutical measures include avoidance of breast stimulation, the use of tight breast binders, and fluid restriction (with or without accompanying diuretic therapy). If breast stimulation is avoided (with or without the use of a breast binder), breast milk production will continue, leading to engorgement and distension of breast alveoli. This leads to the termination of lactation after several days. Approximately 40% of women using this method experience breast discomfort and pain; 30% experience milk leakage from their nipples.[287] Ice packs may be applied to the breasts for comfort and a mild analgesic used if necessary. Fluid restriction (with or without accompanying diuretics) has little effect on breast milk production.[287] In other countries, the expression of milk is used to relieve pain and even the topical application of jasmine flowers to the breasts has been used.[288]

Bromocriptine. Drugs used to suppress lactation can be divided into nonhormonal (pyridoxine) and hormonal agents (estrogens). Bromocriptine (Parlodel) no longer is indicated for lactation suppression. This medication was removed voluntarily by the company because of the number of reported adverse effects. Although most adverse effects associated with bromocriptine usually were mild (e.g., nausea, vomiting, headaches, dizziness, fatigue, abdominal cramps, diarrhea),[289–291] they occasionally were severe. Hypotension occurred in some women started on bromocriptine postpartum (especially those who had experienced hypertension during pregnancy, preeclampsia, or eclampsia). Seizures (with or without accompanying hypertension), strokes, and MIs have been reported in women using bromocriptine for lactation suppression.[297–299,301] Many patients who suffered from bromocriptine-associated seizures and strokes reported headaches and visual disturbances be-

fore these occurred. Case reports of postpartum psychosis also have been linked to its use.[300,302,303]

55. How effective are pyridoxine (vitamin B$_6$) and estradiol valerate (Delestrogen) for the suppression of lactation?

High-dose pyridoxine has been reported to increase CNS concentrations of dopamine. This theoretically could decrease PRL secretion resulting in lactation suppression; however, double-blind studies have shown that pyridoxine is no more effective than placebo in suppressing puerperal lactation.[304–306]

Estradiol valerate may be administered as a single 10 to 25 mg dose at the end of the first stage of labor to suppress postpartum breast engorgement.[307]

References

1   **Pitkin RM.** Nutrition in obstetrics and gynecology. In: Danforth DN, Scott JR, eds. Obstetrics and Gynecology. Philadelphia: JB Lippincott; 1986:181.

2   **Marrs RP.** Oocytes: from development to fertilization. In: Mishell DR, Davajan V, eds. Infertility, Contraception and Reproductive Endocrinology. Oradell: Medical Economics Books; 1986:105.

3   **Carroll C.** Pregnancy in the adolescent. In: Rivlin ME et al., eds. Manual of Clinical Problems in Obstetrics and Gynecology. Boston: Little, Brown and Co.; 1986:79.

4   **Fertilization, pregnancy, birth and lactation.** In: Avers CJ, ed. Biology of Sex. New York: John Wiley and Sons; 1974:122.

5   **Jirasek JE.** External form of the embryo and developmental stages. In: Atlas of Human Prenatal Morphogenesis. Boston: Martinus Nijhoff Publishers; 1983:3.

6   **Reproduction.** In: Fox SI, ed. Human Physiology. Dubuque: William C Brown; 1984:626.

7   **Carrington ER.** Fertilization, development, physiology and disorders of the placenta-fetal development. In: Wilson JR et al., eds. Obstetrics and Gynecology. St. Louis: CV Mosby; 1983:125.

8   **Cell biology, embryology and the placenta.** In: Chard T, Lilford R, eds. Basic Sciences for Obstetrics and Gynecology. New York: Springer-Verlag; 1983:1.

9   **Conception and fetal development.** In: Olds SB et al., eds. Obstetrical Nursing. Menlo Park: Addison-Wesley Publishing Co.; 1980:66.

10 **Goebelsmann U.** Endocrinology of pregnancy. In: Mishell DR, Davajan V, eds. Infertility, Contraception, and Reproductive Endocrinology. Oradell: Medical Economics Books; 1986:113.

11 **Yen SSC.** Endocrine physiology of pregnancy. In: Danforth DN, Scott JR, eds. Obstetrics and Gynecology. Philadelphia: JB Lippincott; 1986:340.

12 **Danforth DN.** Conduct of normal labor. In: Danforth DN, Scott JR, eds. Obstetrics and Gynecology. Philadelphia: JB Lippincott; 1986:647.

13 **Prenatal Care.** In: Pritchard JA, MacDonald NF, eds. Williams Obstetrics. Norwalk: Appleton-Century-Crofts; 1985:245.

14 **Kochenour NK.** Course and conduct of normal pregnancy. In: Danforth DN, Scott JR, eds. Obstetrics and Gynecology. Philadelphia: JB Lippincott; 1986:365.

15 **Pregnancy Testing.** In: Williams NB, ed. Contraceptive Technology 1986–1987. New York: Irvington Publishers; 1986:257.

16 **Sabbagha RE.** Ultrasound in obstetrics and gynecology. In: Danforth DN, Scott JR, eds. Obstetrics and Gynecology. Philadelphia: JB Lippincott; 1986:259.

17 **Persson PH, Kullander S.** Long-term experience in general ultrasound screening in pregnancy. Am J Obstet Gynecol. 1983;146:942.

18 **Sabbagha RE et al.** The use of ultrasound in obstetrics. Clin Obstet Gynecol. 1982;25:735.

19 **Pregnancy.** In: Alpers DH et al., eds. Manual of Nutritional Therapeutics. Boston: Little, Brown and Co.; 1983:401.

20 **Institute of Medicine.** Summary. In: Nutrition During Pregnancy. Washington, DC: National Academy Press; 1990:10.

21 **Taffel SM.** National Center for Health Statistics, Public Health Service, U.S. Department of Health and Human Services. Maternal weight gain and the outcome of pregnancy, United States 1980. Hyattsville, MD: National Center for Health Statistics, 1986:25. (Vital and health statistics; series 21; no. 44).

22 **Institute of Medicine.** Effects of gestational weight gain on outcome in singleton pregnancies. In: Nutrition During Pregnancy. Washington, DC: National Academy Press; 1990:176.

23 **Institute of Medicine.** Weight gain in twin pregnancies. In: Nutrition During Pregnancy. Washington, DC: National Academy Press; 1990:212.

24 **Institute of Medicine.** Total amount and pattern of weight gain: physiologic and maternal determinants. In: Nutrition During Pregnancy. Washington, DC: National Academy Press; 1990:96.

25 **Institute of Medicine.** Energy requirements, energy intake, and associated weight gain during pregnancy. In: Nutrition During Pregnancy. Washington, DC: National Academy Press; 1990:137.

26 **National Research Council.** Protein and amino acids. In: Recommended Dietary Allowances. Washington, DC: National Academy Press; 1989:52.

27 **Hallberg L.** Iron balance in pregnancy. In: Berger H, ed. Vitamins and Minerals in Pregnancy and Lactation. New York: Raven Press; 1988:115.

28 **Institute of Medicine.** Iron nutrition during pregnancy. In: Nutrition During Pregnancy. Washington, DC: National Academy Press; 1990:272.

29 **National Research Council.** Trace elements. In: Recommended Dietary Allowances. Washington, DC: National Academy Press; 1989:195.

30 **Kochenour NK.** Normal pregnancy and prenatal care. In: Scott JR et al., eds. Danforth's Obstetrics and Gynecology. Philadelphia: JB Lippincott; 1990:123.

31 **National Research Council.** Water-soluble vitamins. In: Recommended Dietary Allowances. Washington, DC: National Academy Press; 1989:115.

32 **Institute of Medicine.** Water-soluble vitamins. In: Nutrition During Pregnancy. Washington, DC: National Academy of Sciences; 1990:351.

33 **Human Nutrition Information Service.** Good Sources of Nutrients. Washington, DC: US Dept of Agriculture, 1989; Report no. 371:23.

34 **Human Nutrition Information Service.** Nationwide food consumption survey. Continuing survey of food intakes by individuals. Women 19–50 years and their children 1–5 years, 1 day, 1986. Hyattsville, MD: U.S. Department of Agriculture, 1987; Report No. 86-1.

35 **Use of folic acid for prevention of spina bifida and other neural tube defects—1983–1991.** MMWR. 1991; 40:513.

36 **MRC Vitamin Study Research Group.** Prevention of neural tube defects: results of the Medical Research Council Vitamin Study. Lancet. 1991; 338:131.

37 **Economic burden of spina bifida USA—1980–1990.** MMWR. 1989;38:264.

38 **Mulinare J et al.** Periconceptional use of multivitamins and the occurrence of neural tube defects. JAMA. 1988;260:3141.

39 **Milunsky A et al.** Multivitamin/folic acid supplementation in early pregnancy reduces the prevalence of neural tube defects. JAMA. 1989;262:2847.

40 **Werler MM et al.** Periconceptional folic acid exposure and risk of occurrence neural tube defects. JAMA. 1993;269:125.

41 **Czeizel AE, Dudas I.** Prevention of the first occurrence of neural-tube defects by periconceptional vitamin supplementation. N Engl J Med. 1992;327:1832.

42 **Grimes DA.** Unplanned pregnancies in the U.S. Obstet Gynecol. 1986;67:438.

43 **Recommendations for the use of folic acid to reduce the number of cases of spina bifida and other neural tube defects.** MMWR. 1992;41:RR-14.

44 **National Research Council.** Minerals. In: Recommended Dietary Allowances. Washington, DC: National Academy Press; 1989:174.

45 **Nausea and vomiting of pregnancy and hypergravidarum.** In: Bernstine RL, Molby C, eds. Obstetrics and Gynecology: Problem Oriented Approach. New York: Elsevier Science Publishing Co.; 1986:197.

46 **Medical and surgical complications of pregnancy.** In: Danforth DN, Scott JR, eds. Obstetrics and Gynecology. Philadelphia: JB Lippincott; 1986:492.

47 **Soules MR et al.** Nausea and vomiting of pregnancy: role of human chorionic gonadotropin and 17-hydroxyprogesterone. Obstet Gynecol. 1980;55:696.

48 **Key TC, Resnik R.** Maternal changes in pregnancy. In: Danforth DN, Scott JR, eds. Obstetrics and Gynecology. Philadelphia: JB Lippincott; 1986:327.

49 **Leatham AM.** Safety and efficacy of antiemetics used to treat nausea and vomiting in pregnancy. Clin Pharm. 1986;5:660.

50 **Mitchel AA et al.** Birth defects in relation to Bendectin use in pregnancy. II. Pyloric stenosis. Am J Obstet Gynecol. 1983;147:737.

51 **Eskenazi B, Bracken MB.** Bendectin as a risk factor for pyloric stenosis. Am J Obstet Gynecol. 1982;144:919.

52 **Aselton P et al.** Pyloric stenosis and maternal Bendectin exposure. Am J Epidemiol. 1984;120:251.

53 **Shapiro S et al.** Antenatal exposure to doxylamine succinate and dicyclomine hydrochloride (Bendectin) in relation to congenital malformations, perinatal mortality rate, birth weight and intelligence quotient score. Am J Obstet Gynecol. 1977;128:480.

54 **Smithello RW, Sheppard SL.** Teratogenicity testing in humans: a method demonstrating safety of Bendectin. Teratology. 1978;17:31.

55 **Fleming DM et al.** Debendox in early pregnancy and fetal malformations. Br Med J (Clin Res). 1981;283:99.

56 **Mitchell AA et al.** Birth defects related to Bendectin use in pregnancy. JAMA. 1981;245:2311.

57 **Milkovich L, Van den Berg BJ.** An evaluation of the teratogenicity of certain antinauseant drugs. Am J Obstet Gynecol. 1976;125:244.

58 **Greenberg G et al.** Maternal drug histories and congenital abnormalities. Br Med J. 1977;2:853.

59 **Shapiro S et al.** Meclizine in pregnancy in relation to congenital malformations. Br Med J. 1978;1:483.

60 **Michaelis J et al.** Prospective study of suspected associations between certain drugs administered during early pregnancy and congenital malformations. Teratology. 1983;27:57.

61 **Hesseltine HC.** Pyridoxine failure in nausea and vomiting of pregnancy. Am J Obstet Gynecol. 1946;51:86.

62 **Harrington RA et al.** Metoclopramide: an updated review of its pharmacological properties and clinical use. Drugs. 1983;25:451.

63 **Slone D et al.** Antenatal exposure to the phenothiazines in relation to congenital malformations, perinatal mortality rate, birth weight, and intelligence quotient score. Am J Obstet Gynecol. 1977;128:486.

64 **Nelson MM, Forfar JO.** Associations between drugs administered during pregnancy and congenital abnormalities of the fetus. Br Med J. 1971;1:523.

65 **Rumeau-Rouquette C et al.** Possible teratogenic effect of phenothiazines in human beings. Teratology. 1977;15:57.

66 **Hodes B.** Hemorrhoidal products. In: Handbook of Nonprescription Drugs. Washington, DC: American Pharmaceutical Association; 1993:469.

67 **Division of Diabetes Control, Center for Prevention, Centers for Disease Control.** Public health guidelines for enhancing diabetes control through maternal- and child-health programs. MMWR. 1986;35:201.

68 **White P.** Classification of obstetric diabetes. Am J Obstet Gynecol. 1978; 130:228.

69 **National Diabetes Data Group.** Classification and diagnosis of diabetes mellitus and other categories of glucose intolerance. Diabetes. 1979;28:1039.

70 **Freinkel N et al.** Care of the pregnant woman with insulin-dependent diabetes mellitus. N Engl J Med. 1985;313:96.

71 **Buchanan TA et al.** The medical management of diabetes in pregnancy. Clin Perinatol. 1985;12:625.

72 **Hollingsworth DR.** Pregnancy, diabetes and birth: a management guide. Baltimore: Williams and Wilkins; 1984.

73 **Landon MB, Gabbe SG.** Antepartum fetal surveillance in gestational diabetes mellitus. Diabetes. 1985;34(Suppl. 2):50.

74 **Gabbe SG.** Diabetes mellitus. In: Danforth DN, Scott JR, eds. Obstetrics and gynecology. Philadelphia: JB Lippincott; 1986:546.

75 **Chairmen, The Second International Workshop-Conference on Gestational Diabetes Mellitus.** Summary and recommendations. Diabetes. 1985; 34:123.

76 **Gabbe SG et al.** Current patterns of neonatal morbidity and mortality in infants of diabetic mothers. Diabetes Care. 1978;1:335.

77 **Gabbe SG.** Diabetes mellitus. In: Queenan JT, ed. Management of High-Risk Pregnancies. Oradell, NJ: Medical Economics Books; 1980:341.

78 **Miodovnik M et al.** Spontaneous abortion among insulin-dependent diabetic women. Am J Obstet Gynecol. 1984; 150:372.

79 **Kitzmiller JL et al.** Diabetic pregnancy and perinatal outcome. Am J Obstet Gynecol. 1978;131:560.

80 **Reece EA et al.** The prevention of diabetes associated birth defects. Semin Perinatol. 1988;12:292.

81 **Prepregnancy counseling and management of women with preexisting diabetes or previous gestational diabetes.** In: Medical Management of Pregnancy Complicated by Diabetes. Alexandria: American Diabetes Association; 1993:1.

82 **Greene MF et al.** First-trimester hemoglobin A_1 and risk for major malformation and spontaneous abortion in diabetic pregnancy. Teratology. 1989;39:225.

83 **Miller E et al.** Elevated maternal hemoglobin A_{1c} in early pregnancy and major congenital anomalies in infants of diabetic mothers. N Engl J Med. 1981;304:1331.

84 **Ylinen K et al.** Risk of minor and major fetal malformations in diabetics with high hemoglobin$_{A1c}$ values in early pregnancy. Br Med J. 1984;289:345.

85 **Fuhrmann K et al.** The effect of intensified conventional insulin therapy before and during pregnancy on the malformation rate in offspring of diabetic mothers. Exp Clin Endocrinol. 1984;83:173.

86 **Johnstone FO et al.** Can prepregnancy care of diabetic women reduce the risk of abnormal babies? Br Med J. 1990; 301:1070.

87 **Kitzmiller JL et al.** Preconception care of diabetes: glycemic control prevents congenital anomalies. JAMA. 1991;265:731.

88 **Neonatal care of infants of diabetic mothers.** In: Medical Management of Pregnancy Complicated by Diabetes. Alexandria: American Diabetes Association; 1993:91.

89 **Hare JW, White P.** Pregnancy in diabetes complicated by vascular disease. Diabetes. 1977;26:953.

90 **Monitoring.** In: Medical Management of Pregnancy Complicated by Diabetes. Alexandria: American Diabetes Association; 1993:31.

91 **Use of insulin during pregnancy in preexisting diabetes.** In: Medical Management of Pregnancy Complicated by Diabetes. Alexandria: American Diabetes Association; 1993:57.

92 **Karlsson K, Kjellmer I.** The outcome of diabetic pregnancies in relation to mother's blood sugar level. Am J Obstet Gynecol. 1972;112:213.

93 **Jovanovic L et al.** Effect of euglycemia on the outcome of pregnancy in insulin-dependent women as compared with normal control subjects. Am J Med. 1981;71:921.

94 **Jovanovic L et al.** Feasibility of maintaining normal glucose profiles in insulin-dependent pregnant diabetic women. Am J Med. 1980;68:105.

95 **Coustan DR et al.** Tight metabolic control of overt diabetes in pregnancy. Am J Med. 1980;68:845.

96 **Jovanovic L, Peterson CM.** Management of the pregnant insulin-dependent diabetic woman. Diabetes Care. 1980; 3:63.

97 **Reece EA, Quintero R.** Management of pregnant diabetic patients. In: Lebovitz HE, ed. Therapy for Diabetes Mellitus and Related Disorders. Alexandria: American Diabetes Association; 1991:16.

98 **Summary and recommendations of the Third International Workshop-Conference on Gestational Diabetes Mellitus.** Diabetes. 1991;40(Suppl. 2): 197.

99 **Gabbe SG et al.** Management and outcome of class A diabetic mellitus. Am J Obstet Gynecol. 1977;127:465.

100 **O'Sullivan JB et al.** Screening criteria for high-risk gestational diabetic patients. Am J Obstet Gynecol. 1973;116: 895.

101 **Carpenter MW, Coustan DR.** Criteria for screening tests for gestational diabetes. Am J Obstet Gynecol. 1982; 144:768.

102 **O'Sullivan JB et al.** Gestational diabetes and perinatal mortality rate. Am J Obstet Gynecol. 1973;116:901.

103 **Mestman JH.** Outcome of diabetes screening in pregnancy and perinatal morbidity in infants of mothers with mild impairment in glucose tolerance. Diabetes Care. 1980;3:447.

104 **National Research Council.** Summary Table. In: Recommended Dietary Allowances. Washington, DC: National Academy Press; 1989:284.

105 **Dornhorst A et al.** Calorie restriction for the treatment of gestational diabetes. Diabetes. 1991;40(Suppl. 2):161.

106 **O'Sullivan JB.** Diabetes mellitus after GDM. Diabetes. 1991;40(Suppl. 2): 131.

107 **Knight AH, Rhind EG.** Epilepsy and pregnancy: a study of 153 pregnancies in 59 patients. Epilepsia. 1975;16:99.

108 **Dalessio DJ.** Seizure disorders and pregnancy. N Engl J Med. 1985;312: 559.

109 **Philbert A, Dam M.** The epileptic mother and her child. Epilepsia. 1982; 23:85.

110 **Schmidt D et al.** Changes in seizure frequency in pregnant epileptic women. J Neurol Neurosurg Psychiatry. 1983;46:751.

111 **Nelson KB, Ellenberg JH.** Maternal seizure disorder, outcome of pregnancy, and neurologic abnormalities in the children. Neurology. 1982;32: 1247.

112 **Briggs CG et al.** Drugs in Pregnancy and Lactation. 4th edition Baltimore: Williams and Wilkins; 1994.

113 **Hanson JW.** Teratogen update: fetal hydantoin effects. Teratology. 1986; 33:349.

114 **Buehler BA.** Prenatal prediction of risk of the fetal hydantoin syndrome. N Engl J Med. 1990;322:1567.

115 **Hanson JW et al.** Risks to the offspring of women treated with hydantoin anticonvulsants, with emphasis on the fetal hydantoin syndrome. J Pediatr. 1976;89:662.

116 **Monson RR et al.** Diphenylhydantoin and selected congenital malformations. N Engl J Med. 1973;289:1049.

117 **Meadow SR.** Anticonvulsant drugs and congenital abnormalities. Lancet. 1968;2:1296.

118 **Nau H et al.** Anticonvulsants during pregnancy and lactation: transplacental, maternal and neonatal pharmacokinetics. Clin Pharmacokinet. 1982;7: 508.

119 **Rane A et al.** Kinetics of placentally-transferred phenytoin and its p-hydroxylated metabolites in newborn infants. Br J Clin Pharmacol. 1979;8:465.

120 **Ogawa Y et al.** Serum folic acid levels in epileptic mothers and their relationship to congenital malformations. Epilepsy Res. 1991;8:75–8.

121 **Biale Y, Lewenthal H.** Effect of folic acid supplementation on congenital malformations due to anticonvulsive drugs. Eur J Obstet Gynecol Reprod Biol. 1984;18:211.

122 **Hiilesmaa VK et al.** Serum folate concentrations during pregnancy in women with epilepsy: relation to antiepileptic drug concentrations, number of seizures, and fetal outcome. Br Med J (Clin Res). 1983;287:577.

123 **Pritchard JA et al.** Maternal folate deficiency and pregnancy wastage. IV. Effects of folic acid supplements, anticonvulsants, and oral contraceptives. Am J Obstet Gynecol. 1971;109:341.

124 **Dam M et al.** Antiepileptic drugs: metabolism in pregnancy. Clin Pharmacokinet. 1979;4:53.

125 **Eadie MJ et al.** Plasma drug level monitoring in pregnancy. Clin Pharmacokinet. 1977;2:427.

126 **Ramsay RE et al.** Status epilepticus in pregnancy: effect of phenytoin malabsorption on seizure control. Neurology. 1978;28:85.

127 **Kochenour NK et al.** Phenytoin metabolism in pregnancy. Obstet Gynecol. 1980;56:577.

128 **Dean M et al.** Serum protein binding of drugs during and after pregnancy in humans. Clin Pharmacol Ther. 1980; 28:253.

129 **Jones KL et al.** Pattern of malformations in the children of women treated with carbamazepine during pregnancy. N Engl J Med. 1989;320:1661.

130 **Rosa FW.** Spina bifida in infants of women treated with carbamazepine during pregnancy. N Engl J Med. 1991; 324:674.

131 **Robert E, Guibaud P.** Maternal valproic acid and congenital neural tube defects. Lancet. 1982;2:937.

132 **National High Blood Pressure Education Program Working Group report on high blood pressure in pregnancy.** Am J Obstet Gynecol. 1990; 163:1689.

133 **Scott JR, Worley RJ.** Hypertensive disorders of pregnancy. In: Scott JR et al., eds. Danforth's Obstetrics and Gynecology. Philadelphia: JB Lippincott; 1990:411.

134 **King K.** Hypertension in pregnant women. Med J Aust. 1985;143:23.

135 **Worley RJ.** Pathophysiology of pregnancy-induced hypertension. Clin Obstet Gynecol. 1984;27:821.

136 **Gant NF et al.** A study of angiotensin II pressor response throughout primigravid pregnancy. J Clin Invest. 1973; 52:2682.

137 **Goodman RP et al.** Prostacylin production during pregnancy: comparison

of production during normal pregnancy and pregnancy complicated by hypertension. Am J Obstet Gynecol. 1982; 142:817.

138 **Remuzzi G et al.** Reduced umbilical and placental vascular prostacyclin in severe preeclampsia. Prostaglandins. 1980;20:105.

139 **Hanley SP et al.** Differential inhibition by low-dose aspirin of human venous prostacyclin synthesis and platelet thromboxane synthesis. Lancet. 1981; 1:969.

140 **Wallenburg HCS et al.** Low-dose aspirin prevents pregnancy-induced hypertension and pre-eclampsia in angiotensin-sensitive primigravidae. Lancet. 1986;1:2.

141 **Imperiale TF, Petrulis AS.** A meta-analysis of low-dose aspirin for the prevention of pregnancy-induced hypertensive disease. JAMA. 1991;266:260.

142 **Sibai BM et al.** Prevention of preeclampsia with low-dose aspirin in healthy, nulliparous pregnant women. N Engl J Med. 1993;329:1213.

143 **Cunningham FG, Pritchard JA.** How should hypertension during pregnancy be managed? Experience at Parkland Memorial Hospital. Med Clin North Am. 1984;68:505.

144 **Kyle PM, Redman WG.** Comparative risk-benefit assessment of drugs used in the management of hypertension in pregnancy. Drug Saf. 1992;7:222.

145 **Sibai BM.** Hypertension in pregnancy. Obstet Gynecol Clin North Am. 1992; 19:615.

146 **Redman CWG et al.** Fetal outcome in trial of antihypertensive treatment in pregnancy. Lancet. 1976;2:753.

147 **Gallery EDM et al.** Randomized comparison of methyldopa and oxyprenolol for treatment of hypertension in pregnancy. Br Med J. 1979;1:1591.

148 **Kincaid-Smith P et al.** Prolonged use of methyldopa in severe hypertension in pregnancy. Br Med J. 1966;1:274.

149 **Redman CWG et al.** Treatment of hypertension in pregnancy with methyldopa: blood pressure control and side effects. Br J Obstet Gynecol. 1977;84: 419.

150 **Fidler J et al.** Randomized controlled comparative study of methyldopa and oxprenolol in treatment of hypertension in pregnancy. Br Med J (Clin Res). 1983;286:1927.

151 **Whiteclaw A.** Maternal methyldopa treatment and neonatal blood pressure. Br Med J (Clin Res). 1981;283:471.

152 **Cockburn J et al.** Final report of study on hypertension during pregnancy: the effects of specific treatment on the growth and development of the children. Lancet. 1982;1:647.

153 **Sibai BM et al.** A comparison of no medication versus methyldopa or labetalol in chronic hypertension during pregnancy. Am J Obstet Gynecol. 1990;162:960.

154 **Lunell N et al.** Circulatory and metabolic effects of a combined alpha and beta adrenoreceptor blocker (labetalol) in hypertension of pregnancy. Br J Clin Pharmacol. 1981;12:345.

155 **Lunell N et al.** Acute effect of an antihypertensive drug, labetalol, on uteroplacental blood flow. Br J Obstet Gynecol. 1982;89:640.

156 **Michael CA.** Use of labetalol in the treatment of severe hypertension during pregnancy. Br J Clin Pharmacol. 1979;8(Suppl. 2):211S.

157 **Sibai BM et al.** A comparison of labetalol plus hospitalization versus hospitalization alone in the management of preeclampsia remote from term. Obstet Gynecol. 1987;70:323.

158 **Michael CA.** The evaluation of labetalol in the treatment of hypertension complicating pregnancy. Br J Clin Pharmacol. 1982;13(Suppl. 1):127S.

159 **Lardoux H et al.** Hypertension in pregnancy: evaluation of two beta blockers atenolol and labetalol. Eur Heart J. 1983;4(Suppl. G):35.

160 **Lamming GD et al.** Comparison of the alpha and beta blocking drug, labetalol, and methyldopa in the treatment of moderate and severe pregnancy-induced hypertension. Clin Exp Hypertens. 1980;2:865.

161 **Rubin PC et al.** Placebo-controlled trial of atenolol in treatment of pregnancy-associated hypertension. Lancet. 1983;1:431.

162 **Dubois D et al.** Treatment of hypertension in pregnancy with beta-adrenoreceptor antagonists. Br J Clin Pharmacol. 1982;13(Suppl.):375S.

163 **Butters L et al.** Atenolol in essential hypertension during pregnancy. Br Med J. 1990;301:587.

164 **Lindow SW et al.** The effect of sublingual nifedipine on uteroplacental blood flow in hypertensive pregnancy. Br J Obstet Gynaecol. 1988;95:1276.

165 **Walters BNJ, Redman CWG.** Treatment of severe pregnancy-associated hypertension with calcium antagonist nifedipine. Br J Obstet Gynaecol. 1984; 91:330.

166 **Hypertensive disorders during pregnancy.** In: Cunningham FG et al., eds. Williams Obstetrics. Norwalk, CT: Appleton & Lange; 1993:763.

167 **Sibai BM et al.** Reassessment of intravenous MgSO4 therapy in preeclampsia-eclampsia. Obstet Gynecol. 1981; 57:199.

168 **Sibai BM et al.** A comparison of intravenous and intramuscular magnesium sulfate regimens in preeclampsia. Am J Obstet Gynecol. 1984;150:728.

169 **Lipitz PJ, English IC.** Hypermagnesemia in the newborn infant. Pediatrics. 1967;40:856.

170 **Labetalol.** In: Olin B, ed. Facts and Comparisons. St. Louis: Facts and Comparisons; 1989:159d.

171 **Dudley DKL.** Minibolus diazoxide in the management of severe hypertension in pregnancy. Am J Obstet Gynecol. 1985;151:196.

172 **Hulme VA, Odendaal HJ.** Intrapartum treatment of preeclampsia hypertension by ketanserin. Am J Obstet Gynecol. 1986;155:260.

173 **Meeks GR.** Rh isoimmunization. In: Rivlin ME et al., eds. Manual of Clinical Problems in Obstetrics and Gynecology. Boston: Little, Brown and Co.; 1990:90.

174 **Schenken R et al.** Treatment of premature labor with beta-sympathomimetics: results with isoxsuprine. Am J Obstet Gynecol. 1980;137:773.

175 **Scott JR.** Immunologic disorders in pregnancy. In: Scott JR et al., eds. Danforth's Obstetrics and Gynecology. Philadelphia: JB Lippincott; 1990:461.

176 **Bowman JM.** Controversies in Rh prophylaxis: who needs Rh immune globulin and when should it be given? Am J Obstet Gynecol. 1985;151:289.

177 **Kliegman RM, Behrman RE.** The fetus and the neonatal infant: hemolytic disease of the newborn. In: Behrman RE et al., eds. Nelson Textbook of Pediatrics. Philadelphia: WB Saunders; 1987:411.

178 **Rho Gam.** Physicians' Desk Reference. Montvale, NJ: Medical Economics Data Publishing Co.; 1990:1097.

179 **Baskett TF, Parsons ML.** Prevention of Rh(D) alloimmunization: a cost-benefit analysis. Can Med Assoc J. 1990;142:337.

180 **Kwong MS, Egan FA.** Reduced incidence of hyaline membrane disease in extremely premature infants following delay of delivery in mother with preterm labor: use of ritodrine and betamethasone. Pediatrics. 1986;78:767.

181 **Andersen HF, Merkatx IR.** Preterm labor. In: Scott JR et al., eds. Danforth's Obstetrics and Gynecology. Philadelphia: JB Lippincott; 1990:335.

182 **Preterm and postterm pregnancy and fetal growth retardation.** In: Cunningham FG et al., eds. Williams Obstetrics. Norwalk, CT: Appleton & Lange. 1993;853.

183 **Huszar G, Naftolin F.** The myometrium and uterine cervix in normal and preterm labor. N Engl J Med. 1984; 311:571.

184 **Nuwayhid B, Rajabi M.** Beta-sympathomimetic agents: use in perinatal obstetrics. Clin Perinatol. 1987;14:757.

185 **Herron MA et al.** Evaluation of preterm birth prevention program: preliminary report. Obstet Gynecol. 1982;59: 452.

186 **Garite TJ et al.** Prospective randomized study of corticosteroids in the management of premature rupture of the membranes and the preterm gestation. Am J Obstet Gynecol. 1981;141:508.

187 **Garite et al.** A randomized trial of ritodrine tocolysis versus expectant management in patients with premature rupture of membranes at 24 and 30 weeks gestation. Am J Obstet Gynecol. 1987;157:388.

188 **Nelson LH et al.** Premature rupture of membranes: a prospective, randomized evaluation of steroids, latent phase, and expectant management. Obstet Gynecol. 1985;66:55.

189 **Morales WJ et al.** Use of ampicillin and corticosteroids in premature rupture of membranes: a randomized study. Obstet Gynecol. 1989;73:721.

190 **Morales WJ et al.** The effect of chorioamnionitis on the developmental outcome of preterm infants at one year. Obstet Gynecol. 1987;70:183.

191 **Gjerdingen DK.** Preterm labor, part II: management. J Am Board Fam Pract. 1992;5:601.

192 **Valenzuela G et al.** Follow-up of hydration and sedation in the pretherapy of premature labor. Am J Obstet Gynecol. 1983;147:396.

193 **Swigart SA, Clayton BD.** When should drugs be tried in preterm labor? US pharmacist. 1986 July:H1.

194 **Lipshitz J.** Preterm labor. In: Rivlin ME et al., eds. Manual of Clinical Problems in Obstetrics and Gynecol-

ogy. Boston: Little, Brown and Co.; 1990:102.

195 **Yutopar.** Physicians' Desk Reference. Montvale, NJ; Medical Economics Data Publishing Co.; 1990:647.

196 **Travis BE, McCullough JM.** Pharmacotherapy of preterm labor. Pharmacotherapy. 1993;13:28.

197 **Wesselius-de Casparis A et al.** Results of a double-blind, multicenter study with ritodrine in premature labour. Br Med J. 1971;3:144.

198 **Spellacy WN et al.** Treatment of premature labor with ritodrine: a randomized controlled study. Obstet Gynecol. 1979;54:220.

199 **Christensen KK et al.** Effect of ritodrine on labor after premature rupture of the membranes. Obstet Gynecol. 1980;55:187.

200 **Souney PF et al.** Pharmacotherapy of preterm labor. Clin Pharm. 1983;2:29.

201 **Caritis SN et al.** A double-blind study comparing ritodrine and terbutaline in the treatment of preterm labor. Am J Obstet Gynecol. 1984;150:7.

202 **Hastwell G, Lambert BE.** A comparison of salbutamol and ritodrine when used to inhibit premature labour complicated by ante-partum haemorrhage. Curr Med Res Opin. 1979;5:785.

203 **Richter R, Hinselmann MJ.** The treatment of threatened premature labor by betamimetic drugs: a comparison of fenoterol and ritodrine. Obstet Gynecol. 1979;53:81.

204 **Beall MH et al.** A comparison of ritodrine, terbutaline, and magnesium sulfate for the suppression of preterm labor. Am J Obstet Gynecol. 1985;153: 854.

205 **Leveno KJ et al.** Single-centre randomized trial of ritodrine hydrochloride for preterm labour. Lancet. 1986; 1:1293.

206 **Canadian Preterm Labor Investigators Group.** Treatment of preterm labor with the beta-adrenergic agonist ritodrine. N Engl J Med. 1992;327:308.

207 **Korenbrot CC et al.** The cost effectiveness of stopping preterm labor with beta-adrenergic treatment. N Engl J Med. 1984;310:691.

208 **Gonick B, Creasy RK.** Preterm labor: its diagnosis and management. Am J Obstet Gynecol. 1986;154:3.

209 **Katz M et al.** Cardiovascular complications associated with terbutaline treatment for premature labor. Am J Obstet Gynecol. 1981;139:605.

210 **Besinger RE, Niebyl JR.** The safety and efficacy of tocolytic agents for the treatment of preterm labor. Obstet Gynecol Survey. 1990;45:415.

211 **Ferguson JE et al.** Adjunctive use of magnesium sulfate with ritodrine for preterm labor tocolysis. Am J Obstet Gynecol. 1984;148:166.

212 **Hatjis CG et al.** Addition of magnesium sulfate improves effectiveness of ritodrine in preventing premature delivery. Am J Obstet Gynecol. 1984; 150:142.

213 **Zuckerman H et al.** Further study of the inhibition of premature labor by indomethacin. Parts I and II. J Perinat Med. 1984;12:19.

214 **Niebyl JR et al.** The inhibition of premature labor with indomethacin. Am J Obstet Gynecol. 1980;136:1014.

215 **Besinger RE et al.** Randomized com-

parative trial of indomethacin and ritodrine for the long-term treatment of preterm labor. Am J Obstet Gynecol. 1991;164:981.

216 **Eronen M et al.** The effects of indomethacin and a β-sympathomimetic agent on the fetal ductus arteriosus during treatment of preterm labor: a randomized double-blind study. Am J Obstet Gynecol. 1991;169:141.

217 **Norton ME et al.** Neonatal complications after the administration of indomethacin for preterm labor. N Engl J Med. 1993;329:1602.

218 **Ulmsten U et al.** Treatment of premature labor with the calcium antagonist nifedipine. Arch Gynecol. 1980;229:1.

219 **Ulmsten U.** Treatment of normotensive and hypertensive patients with preterm labor using oral nifedipine, a calcium antagonist. Arch Gynecol. 1984;236:69.

220 **Ferguson JE et al.** A comparison of tocolysis with nifedipine or ritodrine: analysis of efficacy and maternal, fetal, and neonatal outcome. Am J Obstet Gynecol. 1990;163:105.

221 **Murray C et al.** Nifedipine for treatment of preterm labor: a historic prospective study. Am J Obstet Gynecol. 1992;167:52.

222 **Read MD, Wellby DE.** The use of a calcium antagonist (nifedipine) to suppress preterm labor. Br J Obstet Gynaecol. 1986;93:933.

223 **Rayburn WF.** Prostaglandin E$_2$ gel for cervical ripening and induction of labor: a critical analysis. Am J Obstet Gynecol. 1989;160:529.

224 **Bernstein EP.** Therapeutic considerations for preinduction cervical ripening with intracervical prostaglandin E$_2$ gel. J Reprod Med. 1993;38(Suppl.):73.

225 **Husslein P.** Use of prostaglandins for induction of labor. Semin Perinatol. 1991;15:173.

226 **Trofatter KF et al.** Preinduction cervical ripening with prostaglandin E$_2$ (Prepidil) gel. Am J Obstet Gynecol. 1985;153:268.

227 **Yonekura ML et al.** Preinduction cervical priming with PGE$_2$ intracervical gel. Am J Perinatol. 1985;2:305.

228 **Nager CW et al.** Cervical ripening and labor outcome with preinduction intracervical prostaglandin E$_2$ (Prepidil) gel. J Perinatol. 1987;7:189.

229 **Bernstein P.** Prostaglandin E$_2$ gel for cervical ripening and labour induction: a multicentre placebo-controlled trial. Can Med Assoc J. 1991;145:1249.

230 **Bernstein P et al.** Cervical ripening and labor induction with prostaglandin E$_2$ gel: a placebo-controlled study. Am J Obstet Gynecol. 1987;156:336.

231 **Laube DW et al.** Preinduction cervical ripening with prostaglandin E$_2$ intracervical gel. Obstet Gynecol. 1986;68:54.

232 **Nimrod C et al.** Cervical ripening and labor induction with intracervical triacetin base prostaglandin E$_2$ gel: a placebo controlled study. Obstet Gynecol. 1984;64:476.

233 **O'Herlihy C, MacDonald HN.** Influence of preinduction prostaglandin E$_2$ vaginal gel on cervical ripening and labor. Obstet Gynecol. 1979;54:708.

234 **Dyson DC et al.** Management of prolonged pregnancy: induction of labor versus antepartum fetal testing. Am J Obstet Gynecol. 1987;156:928.

235 **Ekman G et al.** Intravaginal versus intracervical application of prostaglandin E$_2$ in viscous gel for cervical priming and induction of labor at term in patients with an unfavorable cervical state. Am J Obstet Gynecol. 1983;147:657.

236 **Mainprize T et al.** Clinical utility of multiple-dose administration of prostaglandin E$_2$ gel. Am J Obstet Gynecol. 1987;156:341.

237 **Hannah ME et al.** Induction of labor as compared with serial antenatal monitoring in post-term pregnancy. N Engl J Med. 1992;326:1587.

238 **Ulmsten U et al.** Local application of prostaglandin E$_2$ for cervical ripening or induction of term labor. Clin Obstet Gynecol. 1983;26:95.

239 **Mackenzie I, Embrey M.** The influence of pre-induction vaginal prostaglandin E$_2$ gel upon subsequent labour. Br J Obstet Gynaecol. 1987;85:657.

240 **Graves GR et al.** The effect of vaginal administration of various doses of prostaglandin E$_2$ gel on cervical ripening and induction of labor. Am J Obstet Gynecol. 1985;151:178.

241 **Noah M et al.** Preinduction cervical softening with endocervical E$_2$ gel. Acta Obstet Gynecol Scand. 1987;66:3.

242 **Gauger LJ.** Extemporaneous preparation of a dinoprostone gel for cervical ripening. Am J Hosp Pharm. 1983;40:2195.

243 **Gauger LJ.** Hydroxyethyl cellulose gel as a dinoprostone vehicle. Am J Hosp Pharm. 1984;41:1761.

244 **Nishioka FY.** Prostaglandin E$_2$ preparations for preinduction cervical ripening. Pharmacy considerations. J Reprod Med. 1993;38(Suppl.):83.

245 **Kruse J.** Oxytocin: pharmacology and clinical application. J Fam Pract. 1986;23:473.

246 **Husslein P et al.** Oxytocin and the initiation of human parturition: I. Prostaglandin release during induction of labor by oxytocin. Am J Obstet Gynecol. 1981;141:688.

247 **Fuchs AR et al.** Oxytocin and the initiation of human parturition: II. Stimulation of prostaglandin production in human decidua by oxytocin. Am J Obstet Gynecol. 1981;141:694.

248 **Petrie RH.** The pharmacology and use of oxytocin. Clin Perinatol. 1981;8:35.

249 **Oxytocin.** In: Olin B, ed. Facts and Comparisons. St. Louis: Facts and Comparisons; 1990:117h.

250 **Bishop EH.** Pelvic scoring for elective induction. Obstet Gynecol. 1964;24:266.

251 **Lange AP et al.** Prelabor evaluation of inducibility. Obstet Gynecol. 1982;60:137.

252 **Friedman EA et al.** Relation of prelabor evaluation to inducibility and the course of labor. Obstet Gynecol. 1966;28:495.

253 **Oxytocin.** In: Olin B, ed. Facts and Comparisons. St. Louis: Facts and Comparisons; 1994:117h.

254 **ACOG issues report on induction and augmentation of labor.** AFP. 1991;44:1045.

255 **American College of Obstetricians and Gynecologists.** Induction and augmentation of labor. Technical bulletin 157. Washington, DC: American College of Obstetricians and Gynecologists; 1991.

256 **Wein P.** Efficacy of different starting doses of oxytocin for induction of labor. Obstet Gynecol. 1989;74:863.

257 **Pittman GC.** Water intoxication due to oxytocin. N Engl J Med. 1963;268:481.

258 **D-Souza SW et al.** The effect of oxytocin in induced labor on neonatal jaundice. Br J Obstet Gynaecol. 1979;86:133.

259 **Foster TC-S et al.** Oxytocin augmentation of labor: a comparison of 15- and 30-minute dose increment intervals. Obstet Gynecol. 1988;71:147.

260 **Blakemore KJ et al.** A prospective comparison of hourly and quarter-hourly oxytocin dose increase intervals for the induction of labor at term. Obstet Gynecol. 1990;75:757.

261 **Mercer B et al.** Labor induction with continuous low-dose oxytocin infusion: a randomized trial. Obstet Gynecol. 1991;77:659.

262 **Seitchik J, Castillo M.** Oxytocin augmentation of dysfunctional labor. II. Uterine activity data. Am J Obstet Gynecol. 1983;145:526.

263 **Hauth JC et al.** Uterine contraction pressures with oxytocin induction/augmentation. Obstet Gynecol. 1986;68:305.

264 **Seitchik J, Castillo M.** Oxytocin augmentation of dysfunctional labor. I. Clinical data. Am J Obstet Gynecol. 1982;144:899.

265 **Cummiskey KC et al.** Pulsatile administration of oxytocin for augmentation of labor. Obstet Gynecol. 1989;74:869.

266 **Cummiskey KC, Dawood MY.** Induction of labor with pulsatile oxytocin. Am J Obstet Gynecol. 1990;163:1868.

267 **Odem RR et al.** Pulsatile oxytocin for induction of labor: a randomized prospective controlled study. J Perinat Med. 1988;16:31.

268 **Brodsky PL, Pelzar EM.** Rationale for the revision of oxytocin administration protocols. JOGN Nurs. 1991;20:440.

269 **Oxytocin.** In: McEvoy GK, ed. American Hospital Formulary Service Drug Information 91. Bethesda, MD: American Society of Hospital Pharmacists; 1991:1963.

270 **Hendricks CH, Brenner WE.** Cardiovascular effects of oxytoxic drugs used postpartum. Am J Obstet Gynecol. 1970;108:751.

271 **Sellers SM et al.** Release of prostaglandins after amniotomy is not mediated by oxytocin. Br J Obstet Gynaecol. 1980;87:43.

272 **Greer IA.** Prostaglandins: a key factor in human labor. Acta Obstet Gynecol Scand. 1990;69:371.

273 **Fraser WD et al.** Effect of early amniotomy on the risk of dystocia in nulliparous women. N Engl J Med. 1993;328:1145.

274 **El-Torkey M, Grant JM.** Sweeping of the membranes is an effective method of induction of labour in prolonged pregnancy: a report of a randomized trial. Br J Obstet Gynaecol. 1992;99:455.

275 **Chayen B et al.** Induction of labor using an electric breast pump. J Reprod Med. 1986;31:116.

276 **Mashini IS et al.** Comparison of uterine activity induced by nipple stimulation and oxytocin. Obstet Gynecol. 1987;69:74.

277 **Herbert WNP, Cefalo RC.** Management of postpartum hemorrhage. Clin Obstet Gynecol. 1984;27:139.

278 **Diagnosis and management of postpartum hemorrhage.** ACOG Technical Bulletin. 1990;143.

279 **Reed BD.** Postpartum hemorrhage. AFP. 1988;111.

280 **Ergonovine maleate.** In: Olin B, ed. Facts and Comparisons. St. Louis: Facts and Comparisons; 1988:118d.

281 **Methylergonovine maleate.** In: Olin B, ed. Facts and Comparisons. St. Louis: Facts and Comparisons; 1988:118b.

282 **Hayashi RH.** The role of prostaglandins in the treatment of postpartum hemorrhage. J Obstet Gynecol. 1990;10(Suppl. 2):S21.

283 **Oleen MKA, Mariano JP.** Controlling refractory atonic postpartum hemorrhage with Hemabate sterile solution. Am J Obstet Gynecol. 1990;162:205.

284 **Upjohn Company.** Hemabate package insert. Kalamazoo, MI: 1989 Nov.

285 **Martinez GA, Kriegar FW.** 1984 milk-feeding patterns in the United States. Pediatrics. 1985;76:1004.

286 **Formon SJ.** Reflections on infant feeding in the 1970s and 1980s. Am J Clin Nutr. 1987;46:171.

287 **Lawrence RA.** Breastfeeding and medical disease. Med Clin North America. 1989;73:583.

288 **Barbieri RL, Ryan KJ.** Bromocriptine: endocrine pharmacology and therapeutic applications. Fertil Steril. 1983;39:727.

289 **Easterling WE Jr, Herbert WNP.** The puerperium. In: Danforth DN, Scott JR, eds. Obstetrics and Gynecology. Philadelphia: JB Lippincott; 1986:755.

290 **Oxytocin, synthetic, nasal.** In: Olin B, ed. Facts and Comparisons. St. Louis: Facts and Comparisons; 1990:118a.

291 **Sousa PLR et al.** Re-establishment of lactation with metoclopramide. J Trop Pediatr. 1975;21:214.

292 **Anon.** ACOG issues report on induction and augmentation of labor. AFP. 1991;44:1045.

293 **Kochenour NK.** Lactation suppression. Clin Obstet Gynecol. 1980;23:1045.

294 **Eaton J.** Suppressing lactation. Nurs Times. 1991;87:27.

295 **Shapiro AG, Thomas L.** Efficacy of bromocriptine versus breast binders as inhibitors of postpartum lactation. South Med J. 1984;77:719.

296 **Kinch RA.** The use of bromocriptine in obstetrics and gynecology. Fertil Steril. 1980;33:463.

297 **Sandoz Pharmaceuticals Corp.** Parlodel package insert. East Hanover, NJ: 1991 April.

298 **Iffy L et al.** Acute myocardial infarction in the puerperium in patients receiving bromocriptine. Am J Obstet Gynecol. 1986;155:371.

299 **Watson DL.** Bromocriptine mesylate for lactation suppression: a risk for postpartum hypertension? Obstet Gynecol. 1989;74:573.

300 **Kemperman JF, Zwanikken GJ.** Psychiatric side effects of bromocriptine therapy for postpartum galactorrhea. J R Soc Med. 1987;80:389.

301 **Ruch A, Duhring JL.** Postpartum myocardial infarction in a patient receiving bromocriptine. Obstet Gynecol. 1989;74:448.

302 **Taneli B et al.** Bromocriptine-induced schizophrenic syndrome. Am J Psychiatry. 1986;143:7.

303 **Randolph J et al.** Postpartum psychosis induced by bromocriptine. South Med J. 1987;80:1463.

304 **Pepperell RJ.** Suppression of lactation. Med J Aust. 1986;144:37.

305 **Canales ES et al.** The influence of pyridoxine on prolactin secretion and milk production in women. Br J Obstet Gynaecol. 1976;83:387.

306 **MacDonald HN et al.** The failure of pyridoxine in suppression of puerperal lactation. Br J Obstet Gynaecol. 1976; 83:54.

307 **Estradiol valerate.** In: Olin B, ed. Facts and Comparisons. St. Louis: Facts and Comparisons. 1993:99.

Teratogenicity and Drugs in Breast Milk

Gerald G Briggs

Drugs in Pregnancy 45-2
  Terminology 45-2
  Prevalence of Congenital Malformations 45-2
  Drug Consumption During Pregnancy 45-2
  Placental Transfer 45-2
    Placental layers 45-2
    Mechanisms of substance transfer 45-3
    Factors influencing rate of chemical transfer 45-3
  Fetal Development and Drug Effects
    (See Table 45.1) 45-3
  Etiology of Malformations 45-3
    Classification 45-3
    Proven human teratogens (See Table 45.3) 45-5
      Fetal alcohol syndrome (see Table 45.2
        and Figure 45.1) 45-5
    Food and Drug Administration (FDA) risk factors
      (See Table 45.4) 45-5
    Fetal and neonatal effects of drugs
      (See Table 45.5) 45-7–20

Drug Excretion in Human Milk 45-5
  Drug Excretion 45-6
    Pharmacokinetics (See Figure 45.2) 45-6
    Mechanisms of transfer from blood to milk 45-6
    Factors affecting excretion in breast milk 45-6
    Contraindicated drugs (See Table 45.7) 45-22
    Drugs and breast-feeding (See Table 45.8) 45-22–29

Therapeutic Dilemmas in Pregnant and
Lactating Women 45-21
  Anticoagulation 45-21
    Warfarin 45-21

  Fetal warfarin syndrome (FWS) (See Figure 45.3
    and Tables 45.9 and 45.10) 45-21
    In the second and third trimesters 45-22
  Heparin 45-21
    Breast-feeding 45-29
Anticonvulsants 45-29
  Fetal hydantoin syndrome (FHS) (See Table 45.11
    and Figures 45.4 and 45.5) 45-30
  Carcinogenic potential of phenytoin 45-30
  Hemorrhagic disease of the newborn (HDN) 45-30
  Reducing fetal risks 45-30
    Supplemental folic acid 45-31
  Teratogenicity of nonhydantoin anticonvulsants ...45-31
    Phenobarbital 45-31
    Carbamazepine 45-32
    Clonazepam 45-32
    Valproic acid 45-32
    Trimethadione (See Table 45.12) 45-32
  Phenytoin in breast milk 45-32
Isotretinoin 45-32
Tretinoin 45-33
Enalapril and Hydrochlorothiazide (HCTZ) 45-33
  Skull defect 45-33
  Renal defect 45-33
  Other toxicity 45-33
Indomethacin 45-33
  Premature labor 45-33
  Polyhydramnios 45-34
  Interaction with beta blockers 45-34
Beta Blockers and Breast-Feeding 45-34
Methylene blue and indigo carmine 45-34

Glossary 45-34

Two subjects that generate considerable discussion in the health sciences and the lay public are covered briefly in this chapter: drug effects on the developing fetus and drug excretion in human breast milk and the effect of this excretion on the nursing infant. A comparison of the volume of published literature on these two topics shows a marked predominance for drug effects on the fetus. This, of course, reflects the serious nature of drug-induced fetal changes which usually are permanent and accompanied with a high incidence of morbidity and mortality. In contrast, the biosystem of the nursing infant is much better able to defend itself and, hence, is not as vulnerable to drug-induced toxicity. Drug exposure for an infant also takes place in the open, not in a closed and hidden environment, and changes in behavior or function can be recognized more readily than when these changes take place *in utero*. It should be apparent then that the reported adverse effects of drug exposure via breast milk are fewer in number than those occurring during gestation. Although this distinction and the probable clinical significance between these topics are important, the reader should bear in mind that the long-term effects of drug exposure from breast milk, especially those effects that are subtle or covert, have rarely been studied, a situation that warrants change.

Much of the human data available for study in teratology is anecdotal which frequently makes interpretation difficult. The safe use of a drug in a single pregnancy or even in a large number of pregnancies does not assure that the drug is safe in all pregnancies. Very few medicinal agents can be declared "safe in pregnancy." While the bulk of maternal chemical exposures (i.e., fetal exposures) do not result in noticeable birth defects, our present state of knowledge does not allow us to predict, with any degree of certainty, when a particular drug will prove teratogenic to a particular fetus. We can describe only relative risks for a specific population, not specific risks for specific patients. In addition, animal studies, while beneficial in determining the relative toxicity of an agent, usually cannot be extrapolated directly to humans. These two points, the lack of certainty in extrapolation of data within the species and from species to species, always must be considered when applying this knowledge to individual patients.

In the sections that follow, a broad overview of teratology is presented including discussions of terminology, incidence, drug consumption during pregnancy, placental transfer, fetal development, and causes of malformations. An understanding of these topics is necessary to place the problem of drug-induced fetal toxicity in its proper perspective. Table 45.5 lists the effects of common drugs on the fetus while Table 45.2 and Tables 45.10 to 45.13 describe specific drug-induced fetal syndromes.

Drug excretion in milk is a less complex topic, although little or nothing is known about the presence of many drugs in human milk. The physiochemical properties of individual drugs allow a prediction, with a fair degree of accuracy, of whether or not the drug will be excreted in human milk in measurable quantities. Other parameters, as shown in Table 45.6, determine the amount of drug excretion into breast milk and the dose consumed by the nursing infant. The problem then becomes one of predicting the effects in the infant from consuming the drug. This prediction is the major problem because the majority of drugs available today have not been studied in infants, especially during the neonatal period. In this chapter, factors affecting the excretion of drugs in breast milk and recommendations to limit toxicity in the nursing infant are presented after the section on teratology. Tables 45.7 to 45.9 list drugs which are compatible or incompatible with breast-feeding.

The final part of this chapter covers a few therapeutic dilemmas that the author has encountered in pregnant and lactating women.

Drugs in Pregnancy

Terminology

The term "congenital malformations" is defined as ". . . structural abnormalities of prenatal origin that are present at birth and that seriously interfere with viability or physical well-being."[1] While this definition is widely accepted among clinicians, some drug-induced defects relate to changes in functions or conditions that are not structural abnormalities [e.g., mental or physical growth retardation, central nervous system (CNS) depression, deafness, tumors, or biochemical changes]. The broader term, "congenital anomalies" (i.e., birth defects), includes these toxicities as well as structural changes.[2] Except for the sections on prevalence and causes of malformations, the latter term will be used throughout this chapter.

Prevalence of Congenital Malformations

The prevalence of major congenital malformations discovered at or shortly after birth in the general population is approximately 3%.[1,3,4] This number has been derived from large epidemiological studies completed over the past several decades and is dependent upon the definition of terms (e.g., major versus minor congenital malformations), the thoroughness with which the infant is examined, and how long the exposed persons are followed after birth.[1,5] Although the collection of data on the occurrence of malformations would seem to be straight-forward, it is in fact a very complicated task subject to numerous errors and biases. Several problems cited in various studies were noted by Thelander.[6] Chief among these was the lack of consistency in reports on congenital malformations. Some studies examined only "significant anomalies," others "major malformations," while still others reported only "live births" or "single births" or "birth weights over 500 gm." Stillbirths and spontaneous abortions, both often associated with congenital malformations, frequently were excluded from epidemiological data. Hospital records in some countries are biased due to the large number of home deliveries with only high-risk pregnancies being hospitalized. Also, hospitals conducting studies on congenital malformations are more likely to record these problems and, hence, usually report higher rates. Other inconsistencies identified involved diagnostic criteria, the lack of follow-up studies, and inadequate maternal histories.

The prevalence of defects varies widely depending upon the population studied. The World Health Organization (WHO) study, completed between 1961 and 1964, included 16 countries and 421,781 pregnancies.[7] The frequency of all malformations varied between 3.1 to 22.5 per 1000 births with a mean of 12.7 per 1000. By five years of age, these figures were expected to increase by one and one half- to twofold. Other epidemiological reports in-

volving very large numbers of patients noted variations in the prevalence from 0.27% to 9.41%.[6] Down's syndrome (mongolism) and neural tube defects were cited in the WHO study as the two most common congenital malformations, but their prevalence varied greatly depending upon the race and location of the population studied. The frequency of consanguineous marriages in a population also influenced the prevalence of defects.[6] Consanguinity is known to increase the incidence of malformations, a situation that has been studied extensively in Japan and elsewhere.

Although the 3% prevalence rate is widely accepted for major malformations recognized at birth, a similar rate of prevalence is discovered in the months or years following birth.[1] Anomalies of internal organs, such as the heart, kidneys, reproductive system, and the gastrointestinal (GI) tract, may go unrecognized for years or be discovered only at autopsy.[4] Minor malformations are not included in this 3% rate of prevalence. Some examples of minor malformations are umbilical and inguinal hernias, single umbilical artery, phimosis, slight malformations of the external ear, slight epispadias and hypospadias, cryptorchidism, hydrocele, abnormal dermatoglyphics, small nevus, and angioma (see Glossary).[2] In effect, malformations that are of little medical significance usually are not included in incidence data even if the emotional impact is significant as with cosmetic defects.

Another measure of the magnitude of the problem of congenital malformations is provided by examining years of potential life lost before age 65 (YPLL). In the U.S. in 1986, congenital malformations were the fifth leading cause of YPLL with cardiovascular defects, accounting for about 45% of the total number.[8] These figures understate the problem, however, since infant deaths may not be attributed to congenital malformations and the data examine only live births, not stillbirths or spontaneous abortions.

In summary, one can estimate that approximately six newborn infants in every 100 will be born with a major malformation, but only three of these will be identified at birth or in the neonatal period. To these numbers, one can add an unknown number of infants with mental and physical growth retardation and those that have minor structural anomalies. Thus, the exact magnitude of the problem is not known with precision, but a large number of births are affected to one degree or another, resulting in significant morbidity and mortality.

Drug Consumption During Pregnancy

Pregnancy is a symptom-producing condition. As a result, a large number of drugs regularly are consumed during gestation, including some which are potential teratogens. A number of epidemiological studies conducted in the past 20 years have identified these drug exposure patterns during pregnancy.[9-19] Virtually all categories of drugs were consumed in these studies; analgesics, especially aspirin, led the list of consumed drugs. The mean number of medications consumed per woman in three studies was five to nine, the majority of these taken without medical supervision.[17-19] The hidden nature of maternal drug use was demonstrated in two studies in which the medical chart identified less than a fourth of the drugs actually consumed by the patient.[18,19] In all of the surveys, exposure to known potential teratogens, including x-radiation, was commonplace.

Placental Transfer

Placental Layers

At one time, the placenta was thought to present a barrier to the passage of drugs and noxious chemicals to the fetus. It is now known, however, that most medications cross the placenta to the fetus and, in general, what the mother consumes also is consumed by the fetus. Although the placenta acts like a biological membrane, it initially is composed of four layers effectively separating two distinct individuals.[2] These layers are: 1) the endothelial lining of fetal vessels, 2) the connective tissue in the core of the villus, 3) the cytotrophoblastic layer, and 4) the covering syncytium.[2] During gestation, the surface area of the placenta increases while placental thickness decreases from approximately 25 microns during the first trimester to two to six microns at term. Both processes tend to favor the transfer of chemicals to the fetus.

Mechanisms of Substance Transfer

Drugs, nutrients, and other substances cross the placenta by five mechanisms: 1) simple diffusion (e.g., most drugs); 2) facilitated diffusion (e.g., glucose); 3) active transport (e.g., some vitamins, amino acids); 4) pinocytosis (e.g., immune antibodies); and 5) breaks between cells (e.g., erythrocytes).[2,20] The latter two mechanisms are of no practical importance in the transfer of drugs.

Factors Influencing Rate of Chemical Transfer

Several factors influence the rate of drug transfer across the placenta including molecular weight, lipid solubility, ionization, protein binding, uterine and umbilical blood flow, and maternal diseases.[2] Drugs with molecular weights (MW) less than 600 cross easily, while those greater than 1000 (e.g., heparin) cross with difficulty or not at all. Since most drugs have molecular weights less than 600, it is safe to assume that most drugs reaching the mother's circulatory system also will reach the fetus. Like other biological membranes, lipid-soluble substances are transferred rapidly with the rate of entry primarily governed by the lipid solubility of the nonionized molecule. Conversely, those molecules that are ionized at physiologic pH (e.g., the cholinergic quaternary amines) cross slowly, while weak acids and bases with pKa values between 4.3 and 8.5 are transferred rapidly to the fetus.[20] The penetration of highly protein-bound drugs also is inhibited; only the free, unbound drugs cross the placenta. Uterine blood flow, a major factor in determining the rate of drug transfer, increases throughout gestation. A number of variables can affect uterine blood flow and the rate of drug transfer including maternal blood pressure, cord compression, and drug therapy. Maternal hypotension reduces uterine blood flow and the rate at which substances are delivered to the membrane. Cord compression reduces the blood flow on the fetal side of the membrane. The use of drugs such as α-adrenergic stimulants may constrict uterine vessels and thereby reduce blood flow because these vessels normally are maximally dilated and contain α-adrenergic receptors.[21] Maternal diseases such as pregnancy-induced hypertension, erythroblastosis, and diabetes change the permeability of the placenta and may reduce or increase transfer.[20]

Fetal Development and Drug Effects

Little is known about the effects of drugs on human development before the period of organogenesis (14 to 56 days after conception). The mature maternal oocyte seems to be relatively resistant to drug-induced damage or change. Limited animal work has shown that exposure of the male to certain chemical agents, such as caffeine and tobacco, can affect sperm quality and ultimately affect litter size, sex ratio, and intrauterine growth.[22] At present, no evidence for these effects has been found in humans.

Very early in the embryonic period (conception to 56 days), during the preimplantation and presomite stages (0 to 14 days), exposure to a teratogenic agent usually produces an "all or none" effect on the ovum.[4] The ovum either dies from exposure to a lethal dose of a teratogenic drug or it regenerates completely after exposure to a sublethal dose. However, some animal studies have suggested that exposure to some drugs during the preimplantation stage can halt growth and development before implantation.[23] Al-

though the damage can be repaired, intrauterine growth may be retarded in the offspring. During organogenesis, insult with the same teratogen may produce major morphological changes. The stages and the time frames for the stages of human development are shown in Table 45.1.

These stages of development differ markedly from other species and knowledge of these stages is essential for the interpretation of the relationship between congenital malformations and drugs. For example, if a specific drug exposure occurs after the time of organ development, then a structural defect in that organ could not be due to the specific drug. The fetal period (57 days to term) includes most of the stages of histogenesis and functional maturation although the latter continues for some time after birth.[4] Minor structural changes are still possible during histogenesis, but anomalies are more likely to involve growth and functional aspects such as mental development and reproduction.

Etiology of Malformations

Classification

The current understanding of the causes of congenital malformations has been reviewed.[1,24] Basically, malformations can be classified into one of five categories: 1) monogenic origin; 2) chromosomal abnormalities; 3) interaction between hereditary tendencies and nongenetic, environmental factors; 4) environmental factors; and 5) unknown.[1]

The first two categories are pure genetic defects.[1,2,24] Together, they account for approximately 12.5% to 26% of all congenital malformations in live-born infants (monogenetic: 7.5% to 20% and chromosomal: 5% to 6%), a figure that is changed only slightly by the inclusion of stillbirths.[1] Down's syndrome, resulting from a chromosomal abnormality, is the single most prevalent malformation observed from pure genetic causes.

Interactions between hereditary tendencies and nongenetic environmental factors make up the largest percentage of malformations with a known cause, accounting for approximately 20% of all defects.[1,5,24] The etiology of these defects is multifactorial, involving polygenic genetic predisposition and usually multiple, unknown environmental factors.[25] Congenital dislocation of the hip is an example of a defect in this category where the depth of the acetabular socket and joint laxity are genetically determined and a frank breech malposition is one of the environmental factors.[25] In most cases, however, the environmental factors are unknown.

The fourth category, environmental factors, includes maternal infections and other diseases, deformations, chemicals, and drugs.[1,5,24,26] This group, as a whole, accounts for approximately 8% to 9% of all congenital defects. Only two viruses and a protozoan have been proven to induce congenital malformations.[1,24,27] Bacteria tend to release toxins which cause extensive tissue damage and fetal death rather than structural anomalies.[27] Probably the most well known of the teratogenic viruses is rubella and the resulting fetal rubella syndrome consisting of cataracts, heart disease, and deafness.[28] Cytomegalovirus (CMV) infection also commonly is found, infecting 0.5% to 1.5% of newborn children in the U.S. and resulting in deafness and mental retardation in 5% to 10% of these infants.[1] Characteristics of cytomegalic inclusion disease, the syndrome produced by CMV, include intrauterine growth retardation and microcephaly, and at times, chorioretinitis, seizures, blindness, and optic atrophy.[29] The protozoan generally accepted as a teratogen is *Toxoplasma gondii*.[1] Most infants infected with *T. gondii* show no symptoms and develop normally. When toxicity does occur, the anomalies may consist of hepatosplenomegaly, icterus, maculopapular rash, chorioretinitis, cerebral calcifications, and hydrocephalus or microcephalous.[29] Other infectious agents

Table 45.1		Stages of Human Development[a,2,29]	

Blastula	4–6 days	**Excretory System**	
Implantation	6–7 days	Mesonephric (Wolffian) duct	4
Primitive streak	16–18 days	Wolffian duct reaches cloaca	4.5
Total gestational time	267 days	Ureteric bud	5
		Paramesonephric (Müllerian) duct	6
Central Nervous System		Müllerian duct reaches urogenital sinus	9
Neural groove	3		
Neural crest	3.5	**Integumentary System**	
Three brain vesicles	3.5	Milk hillocks	6
Closure anterior neuropore	3.5	Earliest hair follicles	10
Closure posterior neuropore	4		
Cerebral hemisphere	4.5	**Musculoskeletal System**	
Cerebellum	5	Anterior upper limb bud	4.33
Cessation cell proliferation	6–8 months postnatally	Myotomes	4.5
		Epiphysis	4.5
Circulatory System		Posterior lower limb bud	4.67
Fused tubular heart	3	End of somite formation	5
Heart first beats	3	Digits upper limb	6
Aortic arches (I–VI)	3–4.5	Chondrification centers	6
Interatrial septum	4	Digits lower limb	6.5
Interventricular septum	4	First indication ossification	7
Spleen	5.5		
Atrioventricular valves	5.5	**Respiratory System**	
Aortic-pulmonary septum	6	Paired lung buds	4
Closure interventricular septum	6.5	Closure cervical sinus	5.5
		Occlusion lower larynx	6
Digestive System		Completion diaphragm	7
Rupture oral membrane	4		
Liver diverticulum	4	**Reproductive System**	
Cloacal membrane	4	Gonadal fold	5
Dorsal pancreas	4.5	Gonadal sex differentiation	6.5
Laryngotracheal groove	5	Differentiation external genitalia	9
Ventral pancreas	5	Regression heterologous genital duct	10
Tongue	5.5	Vagina opens	5 months
Fusion pancreas	6	Descent testis	7 months
Palatine shelf	6		
Beginning umbilical hernia	6	**Sense Organs**	
Salivary glands	6	Optic vesicle	3.5
Dental lamina	6.5	Optic placode	3.5
Upper lip	6.5	Optic cup	4
Hepatopancreatic duct	7	Olfactory placode	4.5
Rupture anal membrane	7	Closure optic cup	4.5
Withdrawal umbilical hernia	9	Lens placode	4.5
Completion of palate	10	Closure lens vesicle	5.5
Eruption incisor	7 months postnatally	Pigment layer retina	5.5
		Utriculus and sacculus	5.5
Endocrine System		Cochlea	5.5
Thyroid	4	Olfactory pit	5.5
Rathke's pouch	4.5	Disappearance lens cavity	6.5
Neurohypophysis	4.5	Semicircular canals	6.5
Thymus	5	External auditory meatus	6.5
Adrenal cortex	5	Pinna	6.5
Parathyroids	5.5	Eyelids	6.5
Adrenal medulla	5	Nasolacrimal duct	7
Interstitial cells in testis	17	Corti's organ	7.5
Primary ovarian follicles	30	Closure eyelids	8
		Opening external naris	24
		Reopening eye lids	7–8 months

[a] Postconceptional time in weeks unless otherwise indicated.

Table 45.2	Fetal Alcohol Syndrome[a]

Craniofacial

Eyes	Short palpebral fissures, ptosis, strabismus, epicanthal folds, myopia, microphthalmia, blepharophimosis
Ears	Poorly formed conchae, posterior rotation
Nose	Short, upturned hypoplastic philtrum
Mouth	Prominent lateral palatine ridges, thinned upper vermilion border, retrognathia in infancy, micrognathia or relative prognathia in adolescence, cleft lip or palate, small teeth with faulty enamel
Maxilla	Hypoplastic

Central Nervous System (CNS)

Mild to moderate retardation, microcephaly, poor coordination, hypotonia, irritability in infancy and hyperactivity in childhood (both mental and motor development are delayed)

Growth

Prenatal (affecting body length more than weight) and postnatal deficiency

Cardiac

Murmurs, atrial septal defect, ventricular septal defect, great vessel abnormalities, tetralogy of Fallot

Renogenital

Labial hypoplasia, hypospadias, renal defects

Cutaneous

Hemangiomas, hirsutism in infancy

Skeletal

Abnormal palmar creases, pectus excavatum, restriction of joint movement, nail hypoplasia, radioulnar synostosis, pectus carinatum, bifid xiphoid, Klippel-Feil anomaly, scoliosis

Muscular

Hernias of diaphragm, umbilicus or groin, diastasis recti

Other Problems Associated with Heavy Alcohol Consumption in Pregnancy

Intrauterine growth retardation (IUGR), increased risk of spontaneous abortions, neonatal withdrawal

[a] Adapted from reference 30.

such as herpes simplex virus Type 2, Group B coxsackievirus, Venezuelan equine encephalitis virus, varicella, and *Treponema pallidum* (syphilis) are not proven teratogens although some studies have associated them with malformations. Maternal infections account for approximately 2% of major congenital malformations.[1]

Maternal diseases, other than infections, contribute about 1.5% to the total of malformations.[1,5,24] Over 90% of this is accounted for by maternal diabetes mellitus existing before conception. An average of 9% (range: 6.6% to 13.0%) of infants of diabetic mothers develop major congenital defects that primarily consist of cardio-vascular, neural tube, and skeletal malformations. Phenylketonuria, virilizing tumors, and perhaps maternal hyperthermia (e.g., fever) compose a very small percentage of disease-induced malformations. Fetal deformations (i.e., mechanical factors), such as abnormal cord constrictions and disparity between uterine size and contents, are thought to contribute 1% to 2% to the total number of anomalies.[24]

Proven Human Teratogens

A long list of environmental chemicals suspected of inducing congenital malformations is presented by Kalter and Warkany but they consider only organic mercury a proven teratogen.[1] Their list includes chemicals classified as contaminants and additives, natural substances, personal habits, and occupational exposures. However, heavy alcohol (ethanol) consumption is considered by many to produce a recognizable pattern of defects (see Table 45.2 and Figure 45.1).[30]

Numerous drugs have been associated with congenital anomalies (see Table 45.5) but only in a few cases has a consensus been reached that a specific agent is teratogenic. Table 45.3 lists those agents generally considered to be proven human teratogens. Taken in total, environmental chemicals and drugs may cause up to 6% of all congenital malformations.[1,5,24]

Food and Drug Administration (FDA) Risk Factors

The FDA has prepared a list of risk factors that are assigned to all new drugs to provide some measure of the risk the drug presents to the fetus (see Table 45.4). At least one reference source has used these definitions to assign risk factors to old drugs as well.[30] Table 45.5 summarizes the reported effects of common drugs on the fetus.

The final category, those defects of unknown etiology, makes up the greatest percentage of congenital malformations, accounting for about 60% to 65% of the total.[1,5,24] This area, therefore, offers the greatest hope for the future reduction of the physically and emotionally debilitating problem of congenital defects.

Drug Excretion in Human Milk

A large number of women choose to breast feed their infants, a situation with many positive benefits for both the mother and the infant.[137] Unfortunately, a majority of these women also consume medications and, hence, inadvertently expose their nursing children to a variety of pharmacologic agents. The passage of drugs into human breast milk has been a major concern of the health

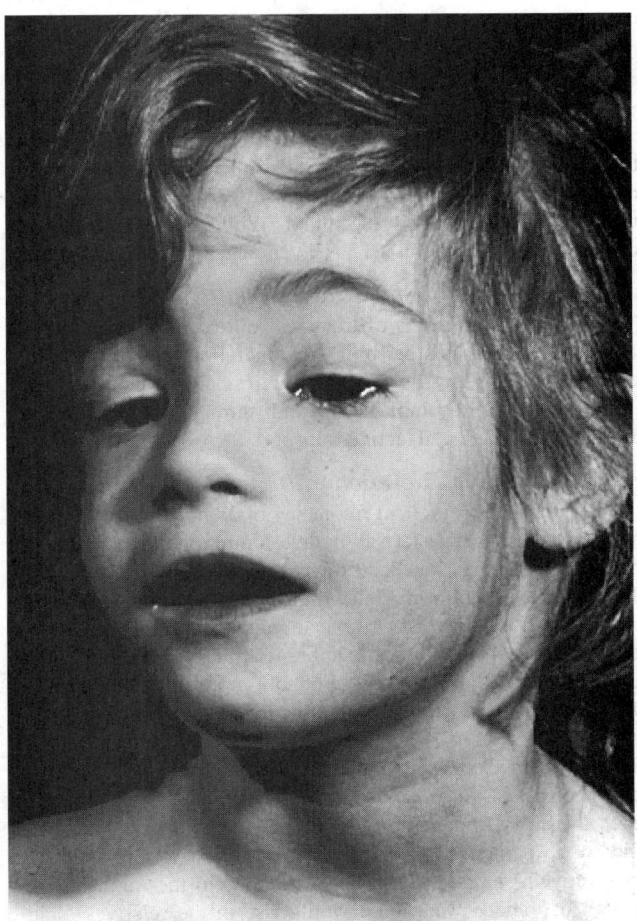

Fig 45.1 Fetal Alcohol Syndrome Note strabismus, short palpebral fissures, ptosis, long smooth philtrum, and thinned upper vermilion border. Photo courtesy of K. L. Jones, M.D., UC San Diego.

Table 45.3	Drugs Considered to Be Proven Human Teratogens[a]
Aminopterin/methotrexate	Isotretinoin
Androgens	Lithium
ACE inhibitors	Methyl mercury (organic)
Busulfan	Paramethadione/trimethadione
Carbamazepine	Phenytoin
Cocaine (abuse)	Polychlorinated biphenyls (PCBs)
Coumarin derivatives	Tetracycline
Cyclophosphamide	Thalidomide
Diethylstilbestrol	Valproic acid
Ethanol (high dose)	Vitamin A (>18,000 international
Etretinate	units/day)

[a] ACE = Angiotensin-converting enzyme.

sciences and the lay public for decades, but it is only in the past few years that the basic physiochemical principles of drug excretion have been proposed. Although an understanding of these principles allows general predictions, insufficient quantitative data for most of the factors outlined in Table 45.6 prevent accurate and clinically useful predictability for individual drugs. Thus, the great majority of the information cited in the literature is derived from actual measurements of drug concentrations in milk or clinical observations in breast-feeding infants. Even with these limitations, however, some understanding of the physiochemical processes is essential for health practitioners.

Drug Excretion

Pharmacokinetics

The pharmacokinetics of drug excretion in milk have been postulated to resemble a deep compartment model shown diagrammatically in Figure 45.2. The amount of drug in the deep compartment is modulated by the infant. While the proposed model may be of research interest, it has no clinical application at present.

Mechanisms of Transfer From Blood to Milk

The basic mechanisms of transfer from blood to milk are the same as those across other biological membranes: 1) diffusion of low molecular weight substances through small, water-filled pores; 2) diffusion of lipid soluble compounds through lipid membranes; and 3) carrier-mediated, active transport.[138]

Factors Affecting Excretion in Breast Milk

The drug dose, route and frequency of administration, and metabolism are important factors in determining the amount of drug that will be available for excretion into milk. Since diffusion occurs along a concentration gradient, high maternal serum levels may produce high milk levels. Drug metabolites are usually polar, ionized substances which cross membranes poorly. Milk pH and the pKa of the drug, however, are probably more important determinants of drug transfer. Human milk has an average pH of 7.1 (range: 6.35 to 7.65), making it slightly more acidic than the plasma.[139] Since only the unionized portion of free drug can transfer, the pKa will, for the most part, determine how much drug can reach the milk. In general, the milk:plasma (M:P) ratio for weak acids (e.g., penicillin) is less than one and for weak bases (e.g., erythromycin) is greater than one.[140] Once in the milk, the proportion of ionized weak base would rise in the relatively acidic solution and, thus, drug "trapping" would occur. Drug reabsorption has been found for some agents, and the prevention of passage back into the plasma by "trapping" may be clinically important. Lipid solubility also is determined to a large extent by the degree

of ionization since drugs with relatively high lipid solubility exist in the unionized form. Diffusion through lipid membranes is probably the most important pathway for drug transfer. However, some drugs (e.g., urea), are 100% unionized and still have low lipid solubility and, consequently, slow transfer across lipid membranes.[140] Although pH, pKa, and lipid solubility are important elements, other factors may markedly modify predictions based solely upon these chemical characteristics. Two of these other factors are protein binding and molecular weight.

Heparin, with a molecular weight of around 15,000, is too large of a molecule to cross a lipid barrier and, hence, is not excreted in milk.[141] Warfarin (Coumadin), on the other hand, is a weakly acidic drug (pKa 5.05), highly ionized (>99%) at physiologic plasma pH, and also is 97% bound to serum albumin.[141] This high degree of ionization and plasma binding effectively prevents the passage of warfarin into milk in amounts that could pharmacologically affect the infant.

The yield of milk is related to blood flow and prolactin secretion.[139] Lactation is associated with a high blood flow to the breasts, but little is known about this flow during or between feedings. The milk yield (volume) differs slightly depending upon the duration of lactation and the time of day. A diurnal pattern has been observed with highest yields at 6:00 a.m. and lowest yields at 6:00 p.m. or 10:00 p.m. The mean composition of human milk is 88.1% water, 0.9% protein, 3.8% fat, 7.0% lactose, and 0.2% ash.[139] The proportions of these components may vary widely from individual to individual and even within the same individual. For example, hind milk contains four- to fivefold the fat content of fore milk while colostrum contains little fat. Fat content also has exhibited a diurnal variation.

After a drug reaches the milk it will equilibrate between the aqueous and lipid phases and the nature of this equilibration can

(Text continues on page 45-21)

Table 45.4	FDA Categories: Teratogenic Risks of Drugs[a]
Category	Risk Factors
A	Controlled studies in women fail to demonstrate a risk to the fetus in the first trimester (and there is no evidence of a risk in later trimesters), and the possibility of fetal harm appears remote
B	Either animal reproduction studies have not demonstrated a fetal risk, but there are no controlled studies in pregnant women *or* animal reproduction studies have shown an adverse effect (other than a decrease in fertility) that was not confirmed in controlled studies in women in the first trimester (and there is no evidence of a risk in later trimesters)
C	Either studies in animals have revealed adverse effects on the fetus (teratogenic, embryocidal, or other) and there are no controlled studies in women *or* studies in women and animals are not available. Drugs should be given only if the potential benefit justifies the potential risk to the fetus
D	There is positive evidence of human fetal risk, but the benefits from use in pregnant women may be acceptable despite the risk (e.g., if the drug is needed in a life-threatening situation or for a serious disease for which safer drugs cannot be used or are ineffective)
X	Studies in animals or human beings have demonstrated fetal abnormalities or there is evidence of fetal risk based upon human experience or both, and the risk of the drug in pregnant women clearly outweighs any possible benefit. The drug is contraindicated in women who are or may become pregnant

[a] Adapted from reference 143.

Table 45.5	Fetal and Neonatal Effects of Drugs[a]

Any tabular listing of drug effects on the fetus and newborn is necessarily incomplete because space limitations do not allow a full narration of the published data. For example, in this table, reference 31 is a prospective study that reported many associations between drugs and various defects. However, the authors of this study cautioned that their data could not be evaluated statistically and independent confirmation was required to determine the actual risk. For the reader requiring detailed information, or specific references, and for those who will be counseling patients, the author recommends they have access to reference 30. This latter source has summarized the published experience with individual drugs in human pregnancy. The risk factors in this table are defined in Table 45.4 and a glossary is provided at the end of this chapter.

Drug (Risk Factor)	Fetal/Neonatal Effects
Acebutolol (C)	No evidence of teratogenicity but 1st trimester experience is limited. Reduced birth weight may result from use of some beta blockers in 2nd and 3rd trimesters but effect also may be due to severe maternal disease. Use near term of acebutolol, atenolol, and nadolol has caused beta-blockade in newborns[30]
Acetaminophen (B)	Considered safe in therapeutic doses at any stage of gestation.[30] Continuous high daily dosage in 1 case may have resulted in fatal kidney disease in newborn. Theoretically, fetal liver toxicity may occur if mother consumed toxic amounts but in 2 such cases, both treated promptly with acetylcysteine, fetal or newborn toxicity was not observed.[30] An infant with craniofacial and digital anomalies was exposed *in utero* to large daily doses of propoxyphene and acetaminophen; the authors speculated that the combination may have been teratogenic[32]
Acetohexamide (D)	Animal teratogen but apparently not in humans. Use near term may result in prolonged neonatal hypoglycemia. Not recommended in pregnancy since it will not provide better control than diet alone[30]
Acetophenazine (C)	See Chlorpromazine
Acyclovir (C)	Estimated that 7500 live births annually in the U.S. are exposed to acyclovir during various stages of gestation by both PO and IV routes. No adverse effects attributable to the drug have been reported[30,33]
Adenosine (C)	Limited human experience but apparently safe[30]
Albuterol (C)	See Epinephrine and Ritodrine
Alfentanil (C)	Apparently safe[30]
Allopurinol (C)	Limited human experience but apparently safe[30]
Alphaprodine (C)	See Meperidine
Alprazolam (D)	Isolated reports of adverse fetal outcomes reported, including single cases of pyloric stenosis, umbilical hernia and ankle inversion, stillbirth with multiple anomalies, and an infant with cat's eye with Pierre Robin syndrome. Relationship between defects and drug unknown. Neonatal withdrawal after *in utero* exposure reported[34,35]
Amantadine (C)	Only 1 case of pregnancy exposure known; mother took 100 mg/day during 1st trimester and delivered infant with single ventricle and pulmonary atresia.[36] Drug is embryotoxic and teratogenic in animals[30]
Amikacin (C)	See Gentamicin
Amiloride (B)	A patient treated during 1st trimester with amiloride, propranolol, and captopril aborted a fetus with limb and skull defects, but effect attributed to captopril[37]
Aminoglutethimide (D)	May cause virilization due to inhibition of adrenocortical function when used in 3rd trimester[30]
Aminophylline (C)	See Theophylline
Aminopterin (X)	Structurally similar to MTX. Human teratogen when used as unsuccessful abortifacient in 1st trimester: meningoencephalocele, cranial anomalies, cleft lip/palate, low-set ears, abnormal positioning of extremities, hypoplasia of thumb and fibula, short forearms, brachycephaly, hydrocephaly, anencephaly, talipes, incomplete skull ossification, hypognathia, and retrognathia[30]
Amiodarone (C)	Goiter observed in 1 infant. No toxicity observed in 10 other infants exposed during pregnancy. Since the drug contains 75 mg iodine/200 mg dose, newborn thyroid status should be closely monitored[30,38]
Amitriptyline (D)	Limb reduction defects reported, but analysis of 86 1st trimester exposures did not confirm association. Other defects observed in 3 infants: micrognathia, anomalous right mandible, left talipes equinovarus (1 case), swelling of hands/feet (1 case), hypospadias (1 case). Urinary retention in 1 newborn after nortriptyline use[30]
Amlodipine (C)	No reports of use in human pregnancy;[30] see Nifedipine for representative agent in this class
Amobarbital (D)	A study reported possible association after 298 1st trimester exposures resulting in: cardiovascular defects, polydactyly in blacks, GU tract defects, inguinal hernia, and clubfoot. A 2nd study found association between all barbiturates and following defects: anencephaly, heart defects, limb defects, cleft lip/palate, intersex, papilloma of forehead, hydrocele, congenital dislocated hip, soft tissue deformity of neck, hypospadias, accessory auricle, polydactyly, and nevus. HDN and neonatal withdrawal possible[10,30,31]
Amphetamines (C)	Medical use of amphetamines does not present significant risk to fetus and newborn, but mild neonatal withdrawal may occur. Agents in this class do not appear to be human teratogens, although anomalies have been observed after their use, including cardiac defects, bifid exencephaly, biliary atresia, and multiple eye and CNS defects. Illicit maternal use associated with IUGR, premature birth, and increased fetal and newborn morbidity[30]
Amphotericin B (B)	Apparently safe[30]
Amyl nitrite (C)	15 pregnancies treated in 1st trimester resulted in 4 malformed children; 7/15 treated with amyl nitrite or NTG but study did not identify which vasodilators were used. NTG has been used at term to control severe maternal hypertension without fetal or newborn toxicity[30,31]

Continued

Table 45.5	Fetal and Neonatal Effects of Drugs[a] (Continued)
Drug (Risk Factor)	Fetal/Neonatal Effects
Asparaginase (C)	Used in 2nd and 3rd trimesters in combination with other agents; no adverse fetal effects observed but exposure in 1st trimester has not been reported[30]
Aspartame (B)	Apparently safe in pregnancy. Since drug is a minor source of phenylalanine, women with phenylketonuria should include this in their dietary planning[30]
Aspirin (C)	Commonly used in pregnancy either as single agent or in combination products. Most studies do not indicate association with congenital malformations, but prolonged use of high doses may be teratogenic.[30] Use in early pregnancy in 1 study associated with 2-fold increase over nonexposed controls for congenital heart disease (defects in septation of truncus arteriosus).[39] Has been used alone or in combination with β-mimetics to treat premature labor. Low dose (e.g., 40–150 mg/day) has been used to prevent pregnancy-induced hypertension, pre-eclampsia, and eclampsia. Use near term of full-dose aspirin may prolong gestation and labor; may adversely affect clotting ability of newborn by reducing collagen-induced platelet aggregation, and may increase risk in premature or low-birth weight infants for intracranial hemorrhage[30]
Atenolol (C)	See Acebutolol
Atropine (C)	May induce fetal tachycardia.[30] Based upon 2323 exposures, possible association between the total anticholinergic group and minor malformations may exist[31]
Azathioprine (D)	Most reports have found safe in pregnancy. Immunosuppression may occur characterized by lymphopenia, ↓ survival of lymphocytes, absence of IgM, reduced amounts of IgG, leukopenia, thrombocytopenia, and pancytopenia. Reducing dose in 3rd trimester may lessen immunosuppression. Congenital defects reported in a few infants but not thought to be related to azathioprine[30]
Baclofen (C)	Skeletal defects in some rodent species only with large doses; no human exposures reported[30]
BCG Vaccine (C)	Live, attenuated virus vaccine; fetal risk unknown, but not recommended during pregnancy[30]
Beclomethasone (C)	Animal teratogen but apparently safe in humans[30]
Belladonna (C)	Possible association with congenital defects based upon 554 1st trimester cases.[31] (Also see Atropine)
Benazepril (D)	See Captopril
Bendroflumethiazide (D)	See Chlorothiazide
Benzthiazide (D)	See Chlorothiazide
Benztropine (C)	Paralytic ileus in 2 newborns exposed at term; chlorpromazine and other anticholinergics may have contributed.[30,40] (Also see Atropine)
Bepridil (C)	No reports of use in human pregnancy;[30] see Nifedipine for representative agent in this class
Betamethasone (C)	No congenital defects reported. Used primarily at 26–34 weeks gestation to stimulate fetal lung maturity. Increased risk of neonatal sepsis if maternal membranes rupture before use. Use in asthmatic mothers does not increase risk of fetal morbidity[30]
Betaxolol (C)	No reports of use in human pregnancy;[30] see Acebutolol for representative agent in this class
Bismuth subsalicylate (C)	Hydrolyzed in GI tract to bismuth salts and sodium salicylate; absorption of bismuth salts negligible but chronic exposure to salicylates may present fetal risk (see Aspirin); restrict use to 1st half of pregnancy and do not exceed recommended doses[30]
Bisoprolol (C)	No reports of use in human pregnancy;[30] see Acebutolol for representative agent in this class
Bleomycin (D)	2 cases of 2nd and 3rd trimester use without apparent fetal toxicity. In a 3rd case, mother was treated with bleomycin and 2 other agents 1 week before delivery at 27 weeks' gestation. Baby developed profound leukopenia with neutropenia, alopecia, and deafness. None of the toxicities were thought to be due to bleomycin[30,41]
Brompheniramine (C)	10 malformations after 65 1st trimester exposures in 1 study.[31] Use of antihistamines during last 2 weeks of pregnancy has been associated with an increased risk of retrolental fibroplasia in premature infants[42]
Buclizine (C)	Animal teratogen but apparently safe in humans[30]
Bumetanide (D)	See Furosemide
Bupropion (B)	No reports of human pregnancy exposure[30]
Busulfan (D)	Used in 38 pregnancies, 22 in 1st trimester resulting in 6 infants with defects: unspecified malformations (aborted at 20 weeks); anomalous deviation left lobe liver, bilobular spleen, and pulmonary atelectasis; pyloric stenosis; cleft palate, microphthalmia, cytomegaly, hypoplasia of ovaries and thyroid gland, corneal opacity, and IUGR; myeloschisis, aborted at 6 weeks; IUGR, left hydronephrosis and hydroureter, absent right kidney and ureter, and hepatic subcapsular calcifications[30]
Butalbital (C)	Neonatal withdrawal in 1 infant after 150 mg/day during last 2 months of pregnancy. Also see Amobarbital[30]
Butoconazole (C)	Topical agent; no 1st trimester experience reported but recommended for 2nd/3rd trimester treatment of vulvovaginal mycotic infections[30,43]
Butorphanol (B)	See Meperidine

Continued

Table 45.5	Fetal and Neonatal Effects of Drugs[a] (Continued)
Drug (Risk Factor)	**Fetal/Neonatal Effects**
Caffeine (B)	Most studies have not found evidence of congenital abnormalities or other adverse fetal outcome[30]
Captopril (D)	ACE inhibitors should be avoided in 2nd and 3rd trimesters because of severe fetal and neonatal toxicity (oligohydramnios, pulmonary hypoplasia, renal failure, anuria, death); severe, persistent, neonatal hypotension may occur. Structural defects after exposure in 2nd or 3rd trimesters include fetal calvarial hypoplasia and, possibly, renal anomalies[30,44–46]
Carbamazepine (C)	May produce malformations similar to those seen with phenytoin (see Table 45.11).[30] ↓ head circumference observed in some infants. In 1 stillborn infant, multiple defects (closely set eyes, flat nose with single nasopharynx, polydactyl, atrial septal defect, patent ductus arteriosus, absent gallbladder and thyroid gland, and collapsed fontanel) were observed.[47] A 1989 study concluded that carbamazepine exposure in the 1st trimester is associated with a pattern of malformations whose main features are minor craniofacial defects, fingernail hypoplasia, developmental delay, and ↑ risk for neural tube defects[48–50]
Carbarsone (D)	No association with congenital defects but drug contains 29% arsenic. Not recommended for use in pregnancy[30]
Carbimazole (D)	See Methimazole
Carteolol (C)	No reports of use in human pregnancy;[30] see Acebutolol for representative agent in this class
Casanthranol (C)	Considered safe in human pregnancy[30]
Cascara sagrada (C)	See Docusate salts
Cephalosporins (B)	Apparently safe; moxalactam is category C[30]
Chenodiol (X)	Contraindicated due to potential for hepatotoxicity[30]
Chlorambucil (D)	Infants with defects after 1st trimester: unilateral agenesis of left kidney and ureter (2 cases), multiple cardiovascular anomalies (1 case)[30]
Chloramphenicol (C)	Use with caution at term. Unconfirmed report of cardiovascular collapse (gray syndrome) in newborns exposed in final stage of pregnancy[30,51]
Chlordiazepoxide (D)	Use in 172 women during 1st 42 days of gestation associated with 4-fold ↑ in severe congenital defects: mental deficiency, spastic diplegia and deafness, microcephaly and retardation, duodenal atresia, Meckel's diverticulum, and ↑ fetal death rate. In 1 report, 390 infants with congenital heart disease had higher incidence of exposure to drugs, including chlordiazepoxide, than controls. In contrast, another study reported 257 1st trimester exposures without evidence of association with congenital defects. Severe neonatal depression and withdrawal have been observed when used close to delivery[30,31]
Chloroquine (C)	Drug of choice for sensitive malaria species during pregnancy. Defects in 3 infants from 1 mother: Wilms' tumor at age 4 years, left-sided hemihypertrophy (1 case), and cochleovestibular paresis (2 cases)[30,52,53]
Chlorothiazide (D)	Many experts consider diuretics contraindicated in pregnancy except for patients with heart disease, since they do not prevent or alter course of toxemia and may ↓ placental perfusion. No evidence of teratogenicity. Neonatal thrombocytopenia in 11 newborns (with 2 deaths) following use near term of chlorothiazide, hydrochlorothiazide, and methyclothiazide. Hemolytic anemia in 2 newborns after chlorothiazide and bendroflumethiazide. Fetal electrolyte disturbances observed in a few cases when used during 3rd trimester[30]
Chlorotrianisene (X)	See Estradiol
Chlorpheniramine (C)	Based upon 3931 pregnancy exposures, possible associations with congenital malformations found in 57 infants: eye/ear defects (7 cases), polydactyly in blacks (7 cases), GI defects (13 cases), hydrocephaly (8 cases), dislocated hip (16 cases), and female genitalia defects (6 cases)[31]
Chlorpromazine (C)	Most studies indicate the phenothiazines are nonteratogenic but there are reports of defects in infants exposed to these drugs during the 1st trimester. 1 study found no evidence for an association with defects, perinatal mortality, birth weight, or IQ scores at 4 years of age. Another found a correlation between propylamino derivatives (e.g., chlorpromazine) and defects, but not with other phenothiazine groups. Toxic effects observed after high doses near term include: hypotonia, lethargy, depressed reflexes, paralytic ileus, jaundice, and persistent extrapyramidal syndrome[30,31]
Chlorpropamide (D)	See Acetohexamide
Chlorthalidone (D)	See Chlorothiazide
Chlorzoxazone (C)	Apparently safe in pregnancy based upon limited human experience[30]
Cholera vaccine (C)	Killed bacteria vaccine; fetal risk unknown. Recommended to meet international travel requirements[30]
Cholestyramine (C)	Used in pregnancy without fetal effects. Potential for deficiency of fat-soluble vitamins after long-term use[30]
Cimetidine (B)	Apparently safe in pregnancy[30]
Ciprofloxacin (C)	Avoid during pregnancy because of potential for arthropathy in newborn[30]
Clavulanic acid (B)	Apparently safe during pregnancy when combined with penicillins[30,54]
Clemastine (C)	Apparently safe[30]
Clindamycin (B)	Apparently safe[30]

Continued

Table 45.5	Fetal and Neonatal Effects of Drugs[a] (Continued)
Drug (Risk Factor)	Fetal/Neonatal Effects
Clofazimine (C)	Apparently safe in pregnancy based upon limited number of exposures[30]
Clomiphene (X)	Used to induce ovulation. Several reports of neural tube defects and miscellaneous anomalies after ovulation stimulation, but most studies indicate no association with malformations. Multiple features may occur after ovulation stimulation. Inadvertent use in early pregnancy may have resulted in 1 infant with a ruptured lumbosacral meningomyelocele, and 1 infant with esophageal atresia with fistula, congenital heart defect, hypospadias, and absent left kidney[30]
Clomipramine (D)	Use in 3 women resulted in newborn lethargy, hypotonia, cyanosis, jitteriness, irregular respirations with respiratory acidosis, and hypothermia.[30] Neonatal convulsions in 2 infants exposed to high maternal doses[55]
Clonazepam (C)	No reports of teratogenicity.[30] 1 case of prolonged toxicity in newborn at 6 hours of age that consisted of apnea, cyanosis, lethargy, and hypotonia; infant exhibited normal neurologic development at 5 months[56]
Clonidine (C)	Limited experience in pregnancy but no fetal toxicity reported[30]
Clorazepate (D)	1 newborn with multiple anomalies after 1st trimester exposure; expired at 24 hours of age[30,57]
Clotrimazole (B)	Apparently safe[30]
Cocaine (C)	Maternal cocaine abuse associated with in utero cerebrovascular accidents, bowel atresias, and congenital defects of the GU tract, heart, limbs, and face. Other fetal and newborn consequences of maternal abuse are fetal growth retardation, and ↑ morbidity and mortality, including a possible association with SIDS. Maternal complications include shorter gestations, premature delivery, spontaneous abortions, abruptio placentae, and death[30]
Codeine (C)	Normally combined with non-narcotic analgesics or other drugs. 1st trimester use in 563 cases associated with: respiratory malformations (8 cases), GU tract defects other than hypospadias (7 cases), Down's syndrome (1 case), tumors (4 cases), umbilical hernia (3 cases), inguinal hernia (12 cases).[31] After 2522 exposures to codeine anytime in pregnancy, the following were noted: hydrocephaly (7 cases), pyloric stenosis (8 cases), umbilical hernia (7 cases), inguinal hernia (51 cases).[31] In 4 retrospective studies, inguinal hernias, cardiac and circulatory system defects, cleft lip/palate, dislocated hip, musculoskeletal defects, and alimentary tract defects were associated with maternal consumption of codeine[30,58]
Colchicine (D)	Use with caution due to very limited human experience and teratogenicity observed in animals[30]
Cyclizine (B)	See Buclizine
Cyclobenzaprine (B)	Apparently safe[30]
Cyclopenthiazide (D)	See Chlorothiazide
Cyclophosphamide (D)	8 malformed infants after 1st trimester exposure: unspecified anomalies (3 cases); flattened nasal bridge, palate defect, skin tag, 4 toes on each foot, hypoplastic middle phalanx 5th finger, and bilateral inguinal hernia sacs (1 case); absent toes and single coronary artery (1 case); hemangioma and umbilical hernia (1 case); imperforate anus, rectovaginal fistula, and growth retardation (1 case); multiple craniofacial and defects anomalies (1 case). No defects observed when used in the 2nd trimester or later[30]
Cyclothiazide (D)	See Chlorothiazide
Cyproheptadine (B)	No apparent fetal toxicity in limited number of 1st trimester exposures[30]
Cytarabine (D)	2 infants with malformations after 1st trimester exposure: bilateral microtia/atresia external auditory canals, lobster claw hand with 3 digits, bilateral lower limb defects (1 case); 2 medial digits both feet missing, distal phalanges both thumbs missing with hypoplastic remnant right thumb (1 case)[30]
Dactinomycin (C)	6 reports of 2nd or 3rd trimester use without apparent fetal harm[30]
Danazol (X)	Use after the 8th week of gestation (the onset of androgen receptor sensitivity) may result in masculinization of the female fetus (i.e., pseudohermaphroditism); male fetuses usually not affected but 1 male had multiple anomalies after 1st trimester exposure[30,59]
Danthron (C)	See Docusate salts
Dantrolene (C)	No reports of use in 1st and 2nd trimesters; no toxicity observed after limited use near term[30]
Daunorubicin (D)	29 exposed fetuses, 4 in 1st trimester. Outcomes of these exposures included 4 stillbirths, but no congenital abnormalities[30]
Deferoxamine (C)	Only 7 women known to have received drug during pregnancy. No toxicity was observed except low serum iron in 1 infant[30]
Desipramine (C)	Neonatal withdrawal has been observed[30]
Dexamethasone (C)	See Betamethasone
Diatrizoate (D)	Agents in this class contain high concentrations of organically bound iodide; although they have been used safely for amniography, they may cause fetal thyroid gland suppression[30]
Diazepam (D)	Use during 1st trimester has been associated with cleft lip/palate, inguinal hernia, cardiac defects, and pyloric stenosis. Several studies also have reported no association with defects. Diazepam and cigarette smoking in 1 study increased risk of delivering infant with defects 3.7-fold over smoking alone. A single dose of 580 mg on

Continued

Table 45.5	Fetal and Neonatal Effects of Drugs[a] (Continued)
Drug (Risk Factor)	Fetal/Neonatal Effects
Diazepam (Continued)	43rd day of gestation was thought to have resulted in an infant with cleft lip/palate, craniofacial asymmetry, ocular hypertelorism, and bilateral periauricular tags. Other defects attributed to diazepam: absence of thumbs, spina bifida, absence of left forearm and syndactyly. Severe neonatal depression ("floppy infant syndrome") and withdrawal observed when diazepam was used close to delivery[30,60]
Diazoxide (C)	A potent relaxant of uterine smooth muscle, may inhibit labor. Newborn hyperglycemia (glucose: 500–700 mg/dL) may persist up to 3 days. In an infant exposed during 3rd trimester, alopecia, hypertrichosis lanuginosa, and $\downarrow$ ossification of the wrist were observed[30]
Dicyclomine (B)	Apparently safe[30]
Dienestrol (X)	See Estradiol
Diethylstilbestrol (DES) (X)	Contraindicated in pregnancy. An estimated 6 million pregnant women were exposed to DES from 1940–1971 to treat obstetric problems. Exposure resulted in reproductive system defects in both female and male offspring:[30] *Female:* Lower Müllerian tract: vaginal adenosis; vaginal and cervical clear cell adenocarcinoma (>400 cases); cervical/vaginal fornix defects; cockscomb, collar, pseudopolyp, and hypoplastic cervix; vaginal defects exclusive of fornix; incomplete transverse and/or longitudinal septum. Upper Müllerian tract: uterine structural defects; fallopian tube structural defects *Male:* Altered semen ($\downarrow$ count, concentration, motility, morphology); epididymal cysts; hypotrophic testis; microphallus; varicocele; capsular induration DES exposure has not been related to defects other than those found in the reproductive system
Diflunisal (C)	See Ibuprofen
Digoxin (C)	Digitalis derivatives are not teratogenic. Routinely used for both maternal and fetal indications[30]
Diltiazem (C)	No adverse fetal effects in 1 case; also see Nifedipine[30]
Dimenhydrinate (B)	Apparently safe in pregnancy. IV use at term may produce oxytocic effects[30]
Diphenhydramine (C)	Based upon 2948 pregnancy exposures, possible associations with congenital malformations found in 40 infants: GU defects (5 cases), hypospadias (3 cases), eye/ear defects (3 cases), syndromes (other than Down's) (3 cases), inguinal hernia (13 cases), clubfoot (5 cases), any ventricular septal defect (5 cases), and defects of diaphragm (3 cases).[31] A 2nd study found possible association with cleft palate.[58] Neonatal withdrawal reported in 1 newborn[30]
Diphenoxylate (C)	Limited use in pregnancy has not resulted in fetal toxicity. Potential for fetal addiction from prolonged use of paregoric[30]
Dipyridamole (C)	No defects or fetal/newborn toxicity attributed to its use in gestation. Most experience involves 2nd and 3rd trimester use in studies designed to prevent toxemia[30]
Disopyramide (C)	Has been used during all stages of gestation without fetal or newborn toxicity; in 1 case, drug may have induced uterine contractions[30,61]
Docusate salts (C)	Considered safe in human pregnancy. Prolonged use of docusate sodium may have cause hypomagnesemia in a mother and newborn[30]
Dopamine (C)	Limited use in 2nd and 3rd trimesters without apparent fetal/neonatal toxicity.[30] (Also see Epinephrine)
Doxepin (C)	Combination with chlorpromazine may have caused paralytic ileus in newborn[30]
Doxorubicin (D)	Several reports of use during gestation, but only 3 during 1st trimester: 2 infants were normal and 1 had imperforate anus, rectovaginal fistula, and impaired neonatal growth (1 case).[30] 1 report of fetal death 36 hours after exposure[62]
Doxylamine (B)	Formerly combined with pyridoxine as Bendectin but combination product no longer available. Over 160 case reports of infants with congenital defects associated with drug combination but most well-controlled studies did not find a relationship between Bendectin and anomalies.[30] 3 studies found an association between Bendectin and pyloric stenosis,[63–65] but FDA and others concluded that a definite causal relationship could not be established[64–66]
Droperidol (C)	Apparently safe in human pregnancy[30]
Dyphylline (C)	See Theophylline
Edrophonium (C)	Apparently safe in pregnancy[30]
Enalapril (D)	See Captopril
Ephedrine (C)	No evidence of teratogenicity based upon 873 exposures; $\uparrow$ in fetal heart rate and beat-to-beat variability have been observed.[30,31] (Also see Epinephrine)
Epinephrine (C)	Statistically significant association found between 189 1st trimester exposures and major or minor anomalies in 1 study. Association also found between use anytime in pregnancy and inguinal hernia. Data may reflect serious maternal conditions requiring use of drug. After 9719 exposures, adrenergics as a group were associated with minor anomalies, inguinal hernia, and clubfoot.[31] Adrenergics, including epinephrine, are teratogenic in some animal species[30]

Continued

Table 45.5	Fetal and Neonatal Effects of Drugs[a] (Continued)
Drug (Risk Factor)	**Fetal/Neonatal Effects**
Epoetin alfa (C)	Apparently safe based upon very limited human experience; maternal hypertension and/or renal disease may be worsened; maternal thrombosis is a potentially serious complication[30]
Ergotamine (D)	Small, infrequent doses probably safe; large doses or frequent use may cause teratogenicity due to disruption of fetal blood supply; oxytocic properties of drug may cause dysfunctional labor marked by prolonged contractions resulting in fetal hypoxia[30]
Erythromycin (B)	Apparently safe[30]
Estradiol (X)	Contraindicated in pregnancy. A study found an association between estrogen exposure and cardiovascular defects, eye and ear anomalies, and Down's syndrome. Further analysis of these data failed to support the association with cardiac malformations. Other studies also have failed in finding association with congenital defects[30,31,67]
Estrogens, conjugated (X)	See Estradiol
Estrone (X)	See Estradiol
Ethacrynic acid (D)	Ototoxicity in mother and newborn treated with diuretic and kanamycin in 3rd trimester[30]
Ethambutol (B)	Apparently safe[30]
Ethanol (X)	Heavy consumption during pregnancy associated with IUGR and a pattern of anomalies known as the "fetal alcohol syndrome" (see Table 45.2). No known safe levels in pregnancy. Potent fetal brain toxin[30]
Ethinyl estradiol (X)	See Estradiol
Ethiodized oil (D)	See Diatrizoate
Ethisterone (D)	See Progesterone
Ethosuximide (C)	Succinimide anticonvulsants considered drugs of choice for treatment of petit mal epilepsy in 1st trimester (phensuximide not recommended due to high incidence of toxicity). Defects observed after 1st trimester use of these drugs: ambiguous genitalia, inguinal hernia, pyloric stenosis (3 cases with phensuximide); none (5 cases with methsuximide); cleft lip/palate, hydrocephalus, mongoloid facies with short neck, altered palmar crease and accessory nipple, patent ductus arteriosus (10 cases with ethosuximide)[30]
Ethotoin (D)	See Table 45.11[30]
Ethynodiol (D)	See Progesterone
Evan's blue (C)	Used safely for plasma volume determinations during pregnancy and intra-amniotically for diagnosis of ruptured membranes. May cause temporary staining of fetus' skin when injected into amniotic fluid[30]
Famotidine (B)	No reports of human pregnancy exposure; also see Cimetidine[30]
Fenoprofen (B)	See Ibuprofen
Fenoterol (B)	See Epinephrine and Ritodrine
Fentanyl (B)	See Meperidine
Fluconazole (C)	1 case report described grossly dysmorphic features in a newborn exposed throughout gestation; features were consistent with a known autosomal recessive genetic disorder but also similar to those described in fetal rats exposed to the antifungal[30,68]
Flucytosine (C)	Embryotoxic and teratogenic in some animal species. 1st trimester human use has not been reported. Only 3 women treated in 2nd or 3rd trimesters; no fetal harm reported[30]
Fluorouracil (D)	Multiple defects observed in 1 aborted fetus with 1st trimester exposure.[69] After 3rd trimester exposure, neonatal cyanosis and jerking movements were observed in 1 newborn[30]
Fluoxetine (B)	No adverse fetal effects observed in 17 cases[30,70]
Fluphenazine (C)	See Chlorpromazine
Flurazepam (X)	Fetal risk is considered low[71] but manufacturer classifies as contraindicated in pregnancy. (Also see Diazepam)[30]
Folic Acid (A)	Evidence indicates that folic acid deficiency (either drug or nondrug induced), or abnormal folic acid metabolism, very early in gestation, may cause congenital malformations, especially neural tube defects;[30] FDA, CDC, and NIH recommended that all women of childbearing age receive 0.4 mg/day; women who already have had a fetus or infant affected by an NTD should take 4 mg/day 1 month before conception and continued through the 12th week of gestation[30,72,73]
Fosinopril (D)	See Captopril
Furosemide (C)	During pregnancy, indicated only for severe cardiovascular disease (e.g., pulmonary edema, severe hypertension, CHF). No fetal toxicity reported, but 1st trimester use limited[30]
Gadopentetate dimeglumine (C)	1 report of exposure shortly after conception; no adverse effects in infant[30,74]

Continued

Table 45.5	Fetal and Neonatal Effects of Drugs[a] (Continued)
Drug (Risk Factor)	Fetal/Neonatal Effects
Gentamicin (C)	Potential for VIII cranial nerve toxicity with high doses. Prolonged therapy with kanamycin produced VIII cranial nerve damage; 9/391 (2.3%) of infants had hearing loss.[2,30] Short-term therapy with streptomycin (1 gm/day for 4.5 days) combined with ethacrynic acid resulted in complete hearing loss in both mother and infant[30]
Glyburide (D)	See Acetohexamide
Gold sodium thiomalate (C)	Used in a limited number of pregnancies to treat maternal RA and other conditions. In 119 mothers treated during 1st trimester, 1 had a dislocated hip, and the other had flattened acetabulum. The relationship of these skeletal defects to gold is unknown. Drug concentrates in the fetal liver and kidneys[30]
Griseofulvin (C)	Embryotoxic and teratogenic in some animal species. Possible association with conjoined twins after 1st trimester use in human pregnancy, but confirmation needed[30,75]
Guanfacine (B)	No fetal adverse effects observed after small number of exposures, primarily in late pregnancy[30]
Haloperidol (C)	Limb reduction anomalies reported. 1 infant with ectromelia, another with multiple upper and lower limb defects, aortic valve defect, and death. No adverse effects seen in 98 women treated during 1st trimester for hyperemesis gravidarum[30]
Heparin (C)	Does not cross placenta to fetus; considered safe in pregnancy.[30] Long-term use (>25 weeks) may be related to development of maternal osteopenia. Supplemental calcitriol recommended[48]
Hepatitis B vaccine (C)	Fetal risk unknown to killed virus (surface antigen HBsAg) vaccine. Recommended for pre-exposure prophylaxis[30]
Hydralazine (C)	No reports of defects. 3 cases of neonatal thrombocytopenia and bleeding after 3rd trimester exposure; may have been related to severe maternal disease[30,76]
Hydrochlorothiazide (D)	See Chlorothiazide
Hydrocodone (B)	See Meperidine
Hydrocortisone (C)	See Prednisone
Hydroflumethiazide (D)	See Chlorothiazide
Hydroiodic acid (D)	See Potassium Iodide
Hydromorphone (B)	See Meperidine
Hydroxychloroquine (C)	Apparently safe for antimalarial prophylaxis.[30] Use for RA or SLE during pregnancy should be avoided[30,77]
Hydroxyprogesterone (D)	See Progesterone
Ibuprofen (B)	No evidence of teratogenicity with 1st trimester use, but experience limited. Use after 34–35 weeks' gestation may cause premature closure of ductus arteriosus resulting in PPHN. Naproxen use at 30 weeks associated with PPHN in 3 infants[30]
Idoxuridine (C)	Teratogenic in animals, not studied in humans[30]
Imipramine (D)	Bilateral amelia observed in 1 infant, but analysis of 161 1st trimester exposures did not confirm association with limb reduction defects. Other defects reported in 7 infants: defective abdominal muscles (1 case), diaphragmatic hernia (2 cases), exencephaly, cleft palate, adrenal hypoplasia (1 case), cleft palate (2 cases), and renal cystic degeneration (1 case). Neonatal withdrawal has been observed[30]
Indapamide (D)	See Chlorothiazide
Indigo carmine (B)	Intra-amniotic injection apparently safe[30]
Indomethacin (B)	Used to treat premature labor; oliguric renal failure, hemorrhage, and intestinal perforation have been reported in some premature infants exposed just before delivery. Reduced fetal urine output may be therapeutic in cases of polyhydramnios. May cause constriction of the fetal ductus arteriosus, with or without tricuspid regurgitation[30,78]
Influenza vaccine (C)	Inactivated virus vaccine to be used only in pregnant women with serious underlying diseases. Consult public health officials for current recommendations. Fetal risk unknown[30]
Insulin (B)	Drug of choice for diabetes occurring in pregnancy.[30] Infants of diabetic mothers have 2- to 4-fold increase in incidence of congenital defects compared to controls. Toxicity probably related to high maternal serum glucose levels, but other factors may be operating. Most common defects: vertebrae and limb defects, cardiovascular defects (transposition of great vessels, ventricular septal defects, coarctation of aorta), and neural tube defects. Less common anomalies: GU tract defects, GI defects (tracheoesophageal fistula, bowel atresias, imperforate anus, narrowed colon).[30] Macrosomia may occur when blood glucose levels are >130 mg/dL[80]
Iocetamic acid (D)	See Diatrizoate
Iodamide (D)	See Diatrizoate
Iodinated glycerol (X)	See Potassium iodide
Iodipamide (D)	See Diatrizoate

Continued

Table 45.5	Fetal and Neonatal Effects of Drugs[a] (Continued)
Drug (Risk Factor)	**Fetal/Neonatal Effects**
Iodoxamate (D)	See Diatrizoate
Iopanoic acid (D)	See Diatrizoate
Iothalamate (D)	See Diatrizoate
Ipodate (D)	See Diatrizoate
Isoniazid (C)	10 malformed infants after 85 exposures.[31] Other reports have observed retarded psychomotor activity, psychic retardation, convulsions, myoclonia, myelomeningocele with spina bifida and talipes, and hypospadias. Additional studies/reviews did not observe an increased rate of malformations. Single case of malignant mesothelioma in 9-year-old. No carcinogenic effects observed in 660 children exposed during gestation. HDN suspected in 2 infants; prophylactic vitamin K recommended[30,81,82]
Isotretinoin (X)	Documented animal and human teratogen. Critical period of exposure is 4–7 weeks. Multiple defects involve the CNS, cranium and face, cardiovascular system, thymus gland, and miscellaneous other structures[30,83]
Isoxsuprine (C)	See Epinephrine and Ritodrine
Kanamycin (D)	See Gentamicin
Kaolin/pectin (C)	Apparently safe in pregnancy[30]
Ketoconazole (C)	Teratogenic in some animal species; recommended for symptomatic vaginal candidiasis in women with AIDS;[84] because doses >400 mg/day inhibit testosterone and cortisol synthesis, drug was used in 1 pregnancy for treatment of mother's Cushing's syndrome; normal infant was delivered[30]
Labetalol (C)	See Acebutolol
Leuprolide (X)	Teratogenic in animals; no adverse fetal effects in over 100 cases of human exposure; spontaneous abortions and IUGR may occur because drug suppresses endometrial proliferation[30]
Levothyroxine (A)	Safe in pregnancy. Levothyroxine (T_4) and liothyronine (T_3) do not cross placenta to fetus[30]
Lincomycin (B)	Apparently safe[30]
Lindane (B)	No reports of adverse effects, but use with caution since small amounts absorbed through skin. Potential for neurotoxicity, convulsions, and aplastic anemia[30]
Liothyronine (A)	See Levothyroxine
Liotrix (A)	See Levothyroxine
Lisinopril (D)	See Captopril
Lithium (D)	Congenital defects have been reported in 22 infants, 17 (77%) involving cardiovascular system; 5/17 had rare Ebstein's anomaly (tricuspid valve malformation). Transient lithium toxicity in newborn has been reported frequently: cyanosis, hypotonia, bradycardia, thyroid suppression with goiter, atrial flutter, hepatomegaly, ECG anomalies (T wave inversion), cardiomegaly, GI bleeding, diabetes insipidus, and shock[30]
Loperamide (B)	See Diphenoxylate
Lovastatin (X)	1 case of 1st trimester exposure with subsequent birth of an infant with constellation of malformations termed the VATER association (vertebral anomalies, anal atresia, tracheoesophageal fistula with esophageal atresia, and renal and radial dysplasias)[30,85]
Lynestrenol (D)	See Progesterone
Lysergic acid diethylamide (LSD) (C)	Pure chemical does not cause chromosomal abnormalities, spontaneous abortions, or congenital anomalies. Reported adverse fetal effects in maternal abusers probably due to multiple factors, including reporting bias[30]
Marijuana (C)	Maternal use may be associated with fetal growth retardation, but other factors such as multiple drug use, lifestyles, diseases, socioeconomic status, and nutrition may play significant role. 1 report has associated *in utero* exposure to marijuana to the development of acute nonlymphoblastic leukemia in childhood[30,86]
Measles vaccine (X)	Most live, attenuated virus vaccines are contraindicated during pregnancy because fetal infection potentially may occur. Vaccination with smallpox in 1st and 2nd trimesters has resulted in fetal death[30]
Mechlorethamine (D)	Most gestational exposures have not caused fetal damage. 2 malformed infants after 1st trimester exposure: 1 case of oligodactyly of both feet with webbing of 3rd and 4th toes, 4 metatarsals on left, 3 on right, bowing of right tibia, cerebral hemorrhage; and 1 case with markedly reduced size and malpositioned kidneys[30]
Meclizine (B)	See Buclizine
Meclofenamate (B)	See Ibuprofen
Medroxyprogesterone (D)	See Progesterone
Mefloquine (C)	Apparently safe[30]
Menadiol (X)	See Menadione

Continued

Table 45.5	Fetal and Neonatal Effects of Drugs[a] (Continued)
Drug (Risk Factor)	Fetal/Neonatal Effects
Menadione (X)	Use near term or close to delivery has resulted in marked hyperbilirubinemia and kernicterus in newborn. If vitamin K needed during pregnancy, use phytonadione (K_1)[30]
Meningococcus vaccine (C)	Fetal risk to killed bacteria vaccines unknown. Use only if risk of maternal infection is high or in high-risk patients[30]
Meperidine (B)	No associations with congenital malformations; prolonged use causes fetal/newborn addiction. Use at term may cause neonatal respiratory depression. Sinusoidal fetal heart rate patterns may occur when used during labor. Neonatal respiratory depression after use of meperidine in labor; the respiratory depression markedly increases if delivery occurs ≥60 min after injection and reaches a peak effect at 2–3 hr[30]
Mephenytoin (C)	No defects observed after 12 1st trimester exposures[30]
Mephobarbital (D)	See Phenobarbital
Mepindolol (C)	See Acebutolol
Mercaptopurine (D)	34 fetuses were exposed in 1st trimester and 45 in 2nd or 3rd trimesters. When abortions or stillbirths were excluded, defects or toxicity found in 4 cases: cleft palate, microphthalmia, hypoplasia of ovaries and thyroid, corneal opacity, cytomegaly, and intrauterine growth retardation (1 case); neonatal pancytopenia (fetus exposed to 6 antineoplastic agents in 3rd trimester) (1 case); microangiopathic hemolytic anemia (1 case); and transient severe bone marrow hypoplasia (1 case)[30]
Mesalamine (B)	Apparently safe[30]
Mesoridazine (C)	See Chlorpromazine
Mestranol (X)	See Estradiol
Methadone (B)	See Meperidine
Methimazole (D)	9 cases of aplasia cutis in infants exposed *in utero* to carbimazole or methimazole. Transposition of great arteries, umbilical defects, imperforate anus, bilateral cataracts, partial adactyly of foot, and nonspecified malformations also have been reported. When used close to term, may rarely produce small, nonobstructing goiters in the newborn[30,87]
Methocarbamol (C)	Apparently safe[30]
Methotrexate (D)	Data available for 26 pregnancy exposures involving 10 1st trimester cases. 3 of the latter exposures had congenital defects: unspecified anomalies (1 case); absence of lambdoid and coronal sutures, oxycephaly, absence of frontal bone, low-set ears, ocular hypertelorism, dextroposition of heart, absence of digits on feet, growth retardation, very wide posterior fontanel, hypoplastic mandible, and multiple anomalous ribs (1 case); oxycephaly due to absent coronal sutures, large anterior fontanel, depressed/wide nasal bridge, low-set ears, long webbed fingers, and wide-set eyes (1 case).[30] Use before pregnancy with retention in maternal tissues may have resulted in desquamating fibrosing alveolitis in 1 newborn[88]
Methsuximide (C)	See Ethosuximide
Methyclothiazide (D)	See Chlorothiazide
Methyldopa (C)	No known association with congenital defects. Frequently used for treatment of pregnancy-induced hypertension.[30] A decrease in intracranial volume after 1st trimester use has been reported but no relationship between small head size and retarded mental development at 4 years of age[89–91]
Methylene blue (D)	Intra-amniotic injection has caused hemolytic anemia, hyperbilirubinemia, methemoglobinemia, and possibly small bowel obstructions[30]
Methyl mercury (X)	Organic mercury poisoning has occurred primarily in Japan and Iraq. Known as Minamata disease in Japan. Nonspecific neurological symptoms after 3rd trimester exposure were observed in about 72 known cases[1]
Metoclopramide (C)	Limited use during all stages of pregnancy has not demonstrated fetal toxicity. Has been used for hyperemesis gravidarum[30]
Metolazone (D)	See Chlorothiazide
Metoprolol (C)	See Acebutolol
Metrizamide (D)	See Diatrizoate
Metronidazole (C)	No confirmed evidence of teratogenicity, but agent is mutagenic in bacteria and carcinogenic in rodents. No evidence of human cancer. FDA data indicate an estimated relative risk for birth defects after exposure to metronidazole to be 0.92. 2 women exposed during 5th–7th weeks of gestation delivered infants with midline facial defects (holotelencephaly and unilateral cleft lip/palate). Excessive fetotoxicity and teratogenicity noted in mice when combined with alcohol[30,92–96]
Mexiletine (C)	Apparently safe based upon very limited human data[30]
Midazolam (D)	Only 3rd trimester exposures have been reported; neonatal neurobehavioral and respiratory depression have been observed.[30] (Also see Diazepam)

Continued

Table 45.5	Fetal and Neonatal Effects of Drugs[a] (Continued)
Drug (Risk Factor)	**Fetal/Neonatal Effects**
Mifepristone (X)	RU 486; antiprogesterone agent used to induce abortion; also used for cervical ripening before abortion and for induction of labor at term; data are too limited to determine if it is a human teratogen[30]
Mineral oil (C)	Considered safe in human pregnancy but prolonged use could result in deficiency of fat-soluble vitamins[30]
Minoxidil (C)	5 cases of pregnancy exposure; multiple drugs, including minoxidil, used for severe maternal hypertension throughout gestation in each case. Results of these pregnancies were: normal infant (1 case), normal infant with transient (2–3 months) hypertrichosis (1 case), multiple anomalies including hypertrichosis (1 case), and fatal congenital heart disease (1 case)[30,97–99]
Misoprostol (X)	Antisecretory prostaglandin has been combined with RU 486 to induce abortions; also has been used alone as abortifacient; conflicting data on its teratogenicity in humans[30]
Morphine (B)	See Meperidine
Mumps vaccine (X)	See Measles vaccine
Nadolol (C)	See Acebutolol
Nalbuphine (B)	See Meperidine
Naproxen (B)	See Ibuprofen
Neomycin (C)	See Gentamicin
Neostigmine (C)	Apparently safe in pregnancy[30]
Nicardipine (C)	40 women treated for hypertension in 3rd trimester; no fetal adverse effects observed[30]
Nicotinyl alcohol (C)	See Amyl nitrite
Nifedipine (C)	Limited use in 2nd and 3rd trimesters not associated with fetal toxicity but severe maternal hypotension may occur. Has been used for treatment of premature labor.[30] May potentiate neuromuscular blocking action of magnesium resulting in pronounced maternal muscle weakness and hypotension; of 3 fetuses, 1 was stillborn[100–104]
Nitrofurantoin (B)	Apparently safe but use with caution at term due to theoretical potential for hemolytic anemia in newborn[30]
Nitroglycerin (NTG) (C)	See Amyl nitrite
Nitroprusside (C)	Limited use in pregnancy; no known fetal toxicity[30]
Nizatidine (C)	See Cimetidine
Nonoxynol-9/Octoxynol-9 (C)	No evidence that these vaginal spermicides affect the fetus. FDA states these agents do not cause birth defects[30,105]
Norethindrone (D)	See Progesterone
Norethynodrel (D)	See Progesterone
Norgestrel (D)	See Progesterone
Nortriptyline (D)	See Amitriptyline
Nylidrin (C)	See Epinephrine and Ritodrine
Omeprazole (C)	20 women treated before cesarean section; no adverse fetal effects observed[30]
Ondansetron (B)	2 reports of use for hyperemesis gravidarum; no adverse fetal effects observed[30,106,107]
Opium (B)	See Meperidine
Oral contraceptives (X)	See Estradiol
Oxprenolol (C)	See Acebutolol
Oxtriphylline (C)	See Theophylline
Oxycodone (B)	See Meperidine
Oxymetazoline (C)	Apparently safe at recommended dosage; overdose has been associated with fetal hypoxia[30,108]
Oxymorphone (B)	See Meperidine
Oxyphenbutazone (D)	See Ibuprofen
Paramethadione (D)	Fetal effects similar to trimethadione[30]
Paregoric (B)	See Diphenoxylate
Penicillamine (D)	In <100 pregnancies, 5 infants with connective tissue anomalies were observed after use of drug: cutis laxa (1 case); cutis laxa, hypotonia, hyperflexion of hips and shoulders, pyloric stenosis, vein fragility, varicosities, impaired wound healing, and death (1 case); cutis laxa, IUGR, inguinal hernia, simian crease, perforated bowel,

Continued

Table 45.5	Fetal and Neonatal Effects of Drugs[a] (Continued)
Drug (Risk Factor)	Fetal/Neonatal Effects
Penicillamine (Continued)	and death (1 case); cutis laxa, mild micrognathia, low-set ears, and inguinal hernia (1 case); cutis laxa, and inguinal hernia (1 case). Miscellaneous defects observed in 4 other infants may have not been due to drug. Some clinicians suggest keeping daily dose <500 mg/day to lessen incidence of toxicity; others recommend avoiding drug during pregnancy[30,109]
Penicillins (B)	Apparently safe[30]
Pentaerythritol (C)	See Amyl nitrite
Pentazocine (B)	See Meperidine
Pentobarbital (D)	One study found no evidence of teratogenicity after 250 pentobarbital and 378 secobarbital 1st trimester exposures. HDN and neonatal withdrawal possible.[30] (Also see Amobarbital)
Perphenazine (C)	See Chlorpromazine
Phencyclidine (X)	Persistent irritability, jitteriness, hypertonicity, and poor feeding reported in newborns[30]
Phenelzine (C)	See Tranylcypromine
Phenobarbital (D)	May produce malformations similar to those seen with phenytoin when used in epileptic patients (see Table 45.11). May cause early HDN. Also may cause fetal/newborn addiction[30]
Phenolphthalein (C)	Apparently safe[30]
Phenoxybenzamine (C)	Indicated for treatment of maternal hypertension due to pheochromocytoma; no exposures during 1st trimester reported[30]
Phensuximide (D)	See Ethosuximide
Phentolamine (C)	Apparently safe but may cause marked decrease in maternal blood pressure with resulting fetal hypoxia; most common use involves treatment of maternal pheochromocytoma[30]
Phenylbutazone (D)	See Ibuprofen
Phenylephrine (C)	Use in treatment of maternal hypotension could result in fetal hypoxia due to constriction of normally maximally dilated α-adrenergic receptors in uterus. Severe persistent maternal hypertension with possible rupture of a cerebral vessel may occur if used with oxytocics or ergot derivatives. Based upon 1249 1st trimester exposures, a possible association was found with malformations including: eye/ear defects, syndactyly, preauricular skin tag, and clubfoot. After 4194 exposures during anytime of pregnancy, possible associations were found with congenital dislocation of hip, other musculoskeletal defects, and umbilical hernia.[30,31] (Also see Epinephrine)
Phenylpropanolamine (C)	See phenylephrine for potential problem with fetal hypoxia. Based upon 726 1st trimester exposures, a possible association was found with malformations including: hypospadias, eye and ear defects, polydactyly, cataracts, and pectus excavatum. After 2489 exposures during anytime of pregnancy, 12 infants had congenital dislocation of the hip.[30,31] (Also see Epinephrine)
Phenytoin (D)	See Table 45.11[30]
Physostigmine (C)	Apparently safe in pregnancy[30]
Pindolol (B)	See Acebutolol
Piroxicam (B)	See Ibuprofen
Plague vaccine (C)	See Meningococcus vaccine
Pneumococcal, polyvalent vaccine (C)	See Meningococcus vaccine
Poliovirus, inactivated vaccine (C)	Fetal risk unknown. Use only if increased risk of exposure. Use oral vaccine (Poliovirus Live) if immediate protection required[30]
Poliovirus, live vaccine (C)	Fetal risk unknown. Use only if immediate protection required[30]
Polythiazide (D)	See Chlorothiazide
Potassium iodide (D)	Iodine is active ingredient. Prolonged use or ingestion close to term may cause suppression of fetal thyroid resulting in goiter in fetus and newborn; tracheal compression may cause newborn death. AAP considers iodides used as expectorants contraindicated during pregnancy[30,110]
Prazosin (C)	Limited experience in pregnancy; no fetal/newborn adverse effects observed[30]
Prednisolone (B)	See Prednisone
Prednisone (B)	Apparently safe in human pregnancy; 1 case of newborn infant with cataracts after exposure throughout gestation. Multiple defects reported with hydrocortisone but association doubtful; Collaborative Perinatal Project found no association after 34 1st trimester exposures[30,31]
Primaquine (C)	Apparently safe[30]
Primidone (D)	May produce malformations similar to those seen with phenytoin (see Table 45.11)
Procainamide (C)	Apparently safe in pregnancy[30]

Continued

Table 45.5	Fetal and Neonatal Effects of Drugs[a] (Continued)
Drug (Risk Factor)	Fetal/Neonatal Effects
Procarbazine (D)	7 pregnancy exposures, 5 during 1st trimester, 1 of which electively aborted and 4 others which resulted in malformed infants: multiple hemangiomas (1 case); same as described with mechlorethamine (2 cases); and small secundum atrial septal defect, and IUGR (1 case). Accidental 2nd trimester exposure in 1 case apparently caused no damage[30]
Prochlorperazine (C)	See Chlorpromazine
Progesterone (D)	In 1977 FDA restricted use in pregnancy based upon reports of cardiac malformations, CNS defects, masculinization of female fetuses, and limb defects. Re-evaluation of some of these data and new, well-designed studies have failed to show an association between these defects and progesterones. Progesterone is used frequently to prevent imminent abortion during the 1st trimester. Use of hydroxyprogesterone or medroxyprogesterone during early pregnancy may have been associated with esophageal atresia but the absolute risk was very low (about 6/10,000 exposed lived births)[30,111]
Promazine (C)	See Chlorpromazine
Promethazine (C)	No association with congenital defects. When used during labor, marked impairment of platelet aggregation in newborn, but clinical significance unknown[30]
Propofol (B)	Apparently safe when used near term; no reports of exposure in 1st or 2nd trimesters[30]
Propoxyphene (C)	Association suggested in 4 malformed infants but other drugs used in each case: Pierre Robin syndrome, arthrogryposis, severe mental and growth retardation;[112] absence of left forearm and radial 2 digits, syndactyly of ulnar 3 digits and left 4th/5th toes, hypoplastic left femur;[113] omphalocele, defective anterior left wall, diaphragmatic defect, congenital heart disease with partial ectopic cordis due to sternal cleft, dysplastic hips;[113] micrognathia, widely spaced sutures, beaked nose, bifid uvula, defects of toes, withdrawal seizures.[32] In study examining 2914 exposures during pregnancy, possible associations with: microcephaly (6 cases); ductus arteriosus persistens (5 cases); cataract (5 cases); benign tumors (12 cases); clubfoot (18 cases).[31] Heavy maternal ingestion resulted in neonatal withdrawal in 5 infants[30]
Propranolol (C)	See Acebutolol
Propylthiouracil (PTU) (D)	Drug of choice for treatment of hyperthyroidism during pregnancy; anomalies reported in 7 infants after *in utero* exposure, but no association between PTU and defects suggested. May produce mild hypothyroidism in fetus when used close to term, evident as a goiter and elevated levels of neonatal TSH. Goiters in 2 infants sufficiently massive to cause death in 1 infant and respiratory distress in the other[30]
Protirelin (C)	Apparently safe[30]
Pyrethrins with piperonyl butoxide (C)	No reports of pregnancy use. Topical absorption poor; it is considered drug of choice for lice infestations[30]
Pyridostigmine (C)	Apparently safe in pregnancy[30]
Pyrilamine (C)	Based upon 121 pregnancy exposures, possible associations with congenital malformations found in 12 infants (6 had benign tumors)[31]
Pyrimethamine (C)	Apparently safe; give supplemental folic acid to prevent folate deficiency[30]
Quinacrine (C)	A report of newborn with renal agenesis, hydronephrosis, spina bifida, megacolon, and hydrocephalus; not an animal teratogen[30,114]
Quinapril (D)	See Captopril
Quinethazone (D)	See Chlorothiazide
Quinidine (C)	No evidence of teratogenicity. Neonatal thrombocytopenia has been observed after pregnancy exposure. Considered by some as drug of 2nd choice after digoxin for fetal tachyarrhythmias[30]
Quinine (D)	Apparently not teratogenic at therapeutic doses. High doses (used as unsuccessful abortifacient) produced numerous defects, primarily of CNS and limbs. Thrombocytopenic purpura and hemolysis in G6PD deficient newborns has occurred[2,30]
Rabies, human vaccine (C)	Fetal risk unknown to killed virus vaccine. Use for postexposure prophylaxis[30]
Ramipril (D)	See Captopril
Ranitidine (B)	See Cimetidine
Reserpine (D)	After 48 1st trimester exposures, 4 infants with defects. Infants (25) with anomalies after 475 exposures anytime during pregnancy: microcephaly (7 cases), hydronephrosis (3 cases), hydroureter (3 cases), and inguinal hernia (12 cases).[31] Use near term resulted in nasal discharge, retraction, lethargy, and anorexia in 1 newborn[30]
Ribavirin (X)	Teratogenic and/or embryolethal in nearly all animal species tested. Only 1 report of human fetal exposure. Mother treated at 33 weeks gestation for severe influenza pneumonia. Delivery occurred, for maternal indication, shortly after treatment had begun. Infant is alive and well at 1 year of age.[115] CDC considers the use of ribavirin during pregnancy contraindicated and recommends alternate job responsibilities for women who are pregnant, or who may become pregnant, if their functions place them in direct contact with patients receiving ribavirin via oxygen tent or mist mask[116]
Rifampin (C)	Although not proven teratogen, 1 report observed 9 defects in 204 pregnancies: anencephaly (1 case),

Continued

Table 45.5	Fetal and Neonatal Effects of Drugs[a] (Continued)
Drug (Risk Factor)	**Fetal/Neonatal Effects**
Rifampin (Continued)	hydrocephalus (2 cases), limb malformations (4 cases), renal tract defect (1 case), and congenital hip dislocation (1 case).[117] HDN observed in 3 infants; prophylactic vitamin K recommended[30]
Ritodrine (B)	Used to treat premature labor; no congenital defects observed but 1st trimester experience lacking. Fetal tachycardia may occur. Fetal hyperglycemia followed by increased serum insulin levels may produce newborn hypoglycemia if birth occurs before effects have terminated (usually 48–72 hr), especially pronounced in diabetic patients[30]
Rubella vaccine (X)	See Measles vaccine
Saccharin (C)	No evidence that agent is harmful to fetus but conflicting recommendations have been published on its safety[30,118–121]
Scopolamine (C)	Tachycardia, decreased heart rate variability, and decreased heart rate deceleration observed in fetus when used at term. A mother given 1.8 mg during labor resulted in severe toxicity in newborn: fever, tachycardia, lethargy, and "barrel chested" appearance without respiratory depression.[30] (Also see Atropine)
Secobarbital (D)	See Pentobarbital
Simethicone (C)	Apparently safe but limited data in pregnancy[30]
Smallpox vaccine (X)	See Measles vaccine
Sodium iodide (D)	See Potassium iodide
Sodium iodide (X) (I^{125}) and (I^{131})	Administration at 12 weeks gestation or later will cause partial or complete destruction of fetal thyroid gland; effect is dose dependent with toxic doses ranging from 10 mCi and above[30]
Sotalol (B)	Apparently safe.[30] (Also see Acebutolol)
Spectinomycin (B)	Apparently safe[30]
Spiramycin (C)	Apparently safe[30]
Streptomycin (D)	See Gentamicin
Sucralfate (B)	Apparently safe[30]
Sulfasalazine (B)	Most reports indicate drug is safe in pregnancy. Use near term has not been associated with newborn kernicterus or severe neonatal jaundice[30]
Sulfonamides (B)	Most reports indicate drug safe in pregnancy. Jaundice and hemolytic anemia may occur if used close to term. Premature infants especially at risk; kernicterus is theoretical problem.[30] Based upon 5689 pregnancy exposures, possible associations with congenital malformations found in 54 infants: ductus arteriosus persistens (8 cases), coloboma (4 cases), limb hypoplasia (7 cases), miscellaneous foot defects (4 cases), urethral obstruction (13 cases), hypoplasia/atrophy of adrenal glands (6 cases), and benign tumors (12 cases)[31]
Sulindac (B)	See Ibuprofen
Teniposide (D)	Used in 2nd and 3rd trimesters in 1 case with normal outcome[30,122]
Terbutaline (B)	See Epinephrine and Ritodrine
Terconazole (C)	Apparently safe[30]
Terfenadine (C)	Possible association with polydactyly found in 1 unpublished study[30]
Tetracyclines (D)	Use after 5th month of gestation will result in permanent yellow-brown staining of teeth. Inhibition of fibula growth may occur in premature infants.[30] Based upon 1944 pregnancy exposures, possible associations with congenital anomalies found in 61 infants: hypospadias (5 cases), inguinal hernia (47 cases), limb hypoplasia (6 cases), and clubfoot (3 cases)[31]
Tetranitrate (C)	See Amyl nitrite
Theophylline (C)	Nonteratogenic. May cause toxicity in newborn when used near term consisting of tachycardia, irritability, and vomiting. Toxic effects most likely when maternal levels in high therapeutic range or above. Theophylline withdrawal reported in 1 newborn characterized by apnea spells[30,123]
Thioguanine (D)	26 pregnancy exposures, 4 during 1st trimester resulting in 1 infant with malformations: 2 medial digits of both feet missing, distal phalanges of both thumbs missing with a hypoplastic remnant of the right thumb (also exposed to cytarabine)[30]
Thioridazine (C)	See Chlorpromazine
Thiotepa (D)	1 report of 2nd and 3rd trimester use without fetal harm[124]
Thyroglobulin (A)	See Levothyroxine
Thyroid (A)	See Levothyroxine
Thyrotropin (C)	See Levothyroxine
Timolol (C)	See Acebutolol

Continued

Table 45.5	Fetal and Neonatal Effects of Drugs[a] (Continued)
Drug (Risk Factor)	**Fetal/Neonatal Effects**
Tobramycin (C)	See Gentamicin
Tolazamide (D)	See Acetohexamide
Tolazoline (C)	See Amyl nitrite
Tolbutamide (D)	See Acetohexamide
Tolmetin (B)	See Ibuprofen
Tranylcypromine (C)	1 study reported 21 1st trimester exposures to MAGIs; possible association with malformations found[31]
Triazolam (X)	Manufacturer has reports of anomalies in newborns exposed to drug, but published information is lacking to support a cause-and-effect relationship;[30] 2 reviews concluded that the fetal risk is low[34,71]
Trichlormethiazide (D)	See Chlorothiazide
Trientine (C)	Teratogenic in animals but no defects observed in 11 pregnancies except for 1 infant with an isochromosome X (both parents had normal X chromosomes)[30,125]
Trifluoperazine (C)	See Chlorpromazine
Triflupromazine (C)	See Chlorpromazine
Trimeprazine (C)	Based upon 140 pregnancy exposures, possible associations with congenital malformations found in 5 infants[31]
Trimethadione (D)	Phenotype exists for fetal trimethadione syndrome (see Table 45.12). Use in 9 families (36 pregnancies) resulted in 25 infants with wide spectrum of defects. Not recommended in pregnancy[30]
Trimethobenzamide (C)	Apparently safe in human pregnancy[30]
Trimethoprim (C)	Most reports indicate use is safe in pregnancy even though drug is a folate antagonist.[30] Single case report of Niikawa-Kuroki syndrome (mental and physical growth retardation and craniofacial anomalies) in non-Japanese girl[126]
Tularemia vaccine (C)	Fetal risk to live, attenuated bacteria vaccine unknown. Use for pre-exposure prophylaxis in high-risk patients[30]
Typhoid vaccine (C)	Fetal risk to killed bacteria vaccine unknown. Recommended in close, continued exposure or travel to endemic areas[30]
Tyropanoate (D)	See Diatrizoate
Ursodiol (B)	Normal infants after 4 cases of 1st trimester exposure[30]
Valproic acid (D)	Risk for NTDs is $\approx$1%–2% (exposure must occur between the 17th and 30th day after fertilization).[127] A valproic acid syndrome has been suggested to consist of anomalies involving the following: NTDs, craniofacial, digits, and urogenital. Retarded psychomotor development and low birth weight also have been observed[30,128–130]
Verapamil (C)	Limited use in 2nd and 3rd trimesters; has not been associated with fetal toxicity. Has been used for treatment of premature labor[30]
Vidarabine (C)	Animal teratogen after topical and IM administration. Human pregnancy experience limited to 4 cases, all in the 2nd or 3rd trimester. No fetal or newborn adverse effects attributable to the drug were observed[30,131–134]
Vinblastine (D)	Use in all trimesters has resulted in normal infants. 2 infants with defects observed after exposure to multiple antineoplastic agents: 1 infant same as 1st case described with mechlorethamine; and 1 infant same as 4th case described with procarbazine[30]
Vincristine (D)	34 pregnancy exposures, 8 during 1st trimester resulting in 2 malformed infants: 1 infant same as 4th case described with procarbazine; and 1 infant same as 2nd case described with mechlorethamine. Fetal toxicity after exposure to vincristine and other agents has included intrauterine death and severe bone marrow hypoplasia[30]
Vitamin A (high doses) (X)	Both deficiency and excess are thought to be teratogenic. Prolonged high doses (>25,000 international units/day) associated with: microtia, craniofacial and CNS anomalies, facial palsy, micro/anophthalmia, facial clefts, cardiac defects, limb reductions, GI atresia, and urinary tract defects[30,135,136]
Warfarin (D)	Teratogenic; see Table 45.10[30]
Yellow Fever vaccine (D)	Fetal risk to live, attenuated virus vaccine unknown. Contraindicated in pregnancy except if exposure is unavoidable[30]
Zidovudine (C)	No evidence of fetal adverse effects but experience limited[30]

[a] AAP = American Academy of Pediatrics; CDC = Centers for Disease Control; CHF = Congestive heart failure; CNS = Central nervous system; ECG = Electrocardiogram; FDA = Food and Drug Administration; GI = Gastrointestinal; GU = Genitourinary; HDN = Hemorrhagic disease of newborn; IV = Intravenous; IUGR = Intrauterine growth retardation; MAOIs = Monoamine oxidase inhibitors; MTX = Methotrexate; NIH = National Institutes of Health; NTDs = Neural tubal defects; NTG = Nitroglycerin; PO = Oral; PPHN = Persistent pulmonary hypertension of the newborn; RA = Rheumatoid arthritis; SIDS = Sudden infant death syndrome; TSH = Thyroid stimulating hormone.

Table 45.6	Factors Affecting Excretion of a Drug in Breast Milk and Dose Consumed by Infant[a]

Maternal Pharmacology	**Infant**
Drug dose, frequency, and route	Suckling behavior, including equal time on each breast
Clearance rate	Amount consumed per feeding
Plasma protein binding	Feeding intervals (regular or irregular)
Metabolite profile	Time of feeding in relation to maternal dosing
Breast	**Drug**
Blood flow and pH	pKa (ionization at plasma and milk pH)
Yield capacity	
Ion and other transport mechanisms	Solubility characteristics in fat and water
Drug metabolism (and reabsorption?)	Protein binding characteristics
	Molecular weight
Milk	
Composition (fat, protein, water)	
pH	

[a] Reprinted with permission from reference 144.

modify how much drug actually reaches the infant. Infant feeding patterns differ markedly from one nursling to another. The time spent sucking at each breast and the volume of milk taken in also will determine the amount of drug ingested, especially if the drug has partitioned into one phase more so than the other. Once ingested by the infant, an entirely new set of problems arises. The gut absorption of the drug, its metabolic fate in the systemic circulation, its rate of elimination, and its pharmacologic effect on the infant all are governed by processes dependent upon the age of the infant and whether the infant is premature or full-term.

The above discussion provides some indication of the multiple parameters affecting the excretion of drugs in milk. While it is possible at present to predict in general terms how much of a drug will appear in milk and the possible effect upon the infant, it is possible to formulate some guidelines to lessen the potential occurrence of an adverse reaction.[142] Chief among these is to consider if the drug can be safely given directly to the infant. Drugs in this category might be some antibiotics (e.g., penicillin) or phenobarbital. Consideration must be given to the amount of drug the infant could ingest via the milk, but in most cases this will be a very small dose. Nevertheless, even small doses of some drugs (e.g., antineoplastics) may be potentially toxic. In the case of phenobarbital, the mother should be warned to watch for changes in her infant that might be due to excessive accumulation of the drug. In this regard, long-term drug usage is more of a problem than short-term usage. Another consideration is whether exposure to the small amounts in milk could cause sensitization of the infant. The pencillins are examples of this concern. Antibiotics also can modify the infant's bowel flora and interfere with the interpretation of culture results if a febrile illness needs to be evaluated. Other means of minimizing the effect of maternal medication upon the breast-feeding infant are: 1) administration of the drug immediately after a breast-feeding; 2) observation of the infant for unusual signs or symptoms (e.g., sedation, irritation, rash, decreased appetite, failure to thrive); and 3) if possible, use of drugs with the lowest predicted M:P ratio.[142]

Table 45.7 lists the very few drugs considered contraindicated during breast feeding and Table 45.8 lists when breast-feeding should be halted temporarily to allow clearance of the drug from the milk.

Table 45.8 summarizes the reported adverse effects of drug exposure via breast milk in nursing infants and indicates those agents normally considered compa[...]verse effects are relatively [...] seen, adof available pharmacologic [...] e number ber of toxic agents in Tab [...] ned number. consider that a large num [...] ne should during lactation. Manufac [...] n studied obligation to investigate the passage of their p[...] into milk, and from an economic and often ethical standpoint, it is much cheaper and easier to state that the drug should not be used during breast-feeding.

Therapeutic Dilemmas in Pregnant and Lactating Women

Anticoagulation

Warfarin

1. Fetal Warfarin Syndrome (FWS). H.P. is a 25-year-old female with a 5-week intrauterine pregnancy. She had a mitral valve commissurotomy approximately 5 years ago, followed by a mitral valve replacement 2 years ago, both for rheumatic heart disease. Her current medications are warfarin 5 mg/day, penicillin VK 500 mg/day, and digoxin 0.25 mg/day. Do these drugs present a therapeutic problem to the fetus, and, if so, what changes should be made?

Neither penicillin VK (Pen-Vee K) nor digoxin (Lanoxin) present a known fetal risk. Both drugs have been used extensively in pregnancy, including the first trimester, without causing an increase in the expected rate of fetal loss or congenital malformations (see Table 45.5). Serum digoxin concentrations should be monitored at frequent intervals due to the increased drug elimination rate that normally occurs during pregnancy.

Use of warfarin (Coumadin) in the first trimester has been associated with a characteristic pattern of defects collectively known as the Fetal Warfarin syndrome.[251] The susceptible period seems to be between the sixth and ninth weeks of gestation. Nasal hypoplasia and a depressed nasal bridge (see Table 45.9 and Figure 45.3) are common to all known cases of FWS. The nares and air passages may be constricted to such a degree as to cause neonatal respiratory distress. As seen roentgenographically, stippling in uncalcified epiphyseal regions occurs in most newborns inflicted with the FWS, but may not be evident after the first year of life.[251] The axial skeleton, proximal femurs, and the calcanei are the sites primarily involved in FWS and this pattern of distribution distinguishes it from other syndromes and genetic disorders.[251] Less common features (see Table 45.9) are reduced birth weight, eye and ear defects, hypoplasia of extremities, development retardation, congenital heart disease, laryngeal calcification, and death.

Based upon data from the literature, the incidence of adverse fetal outcome following first trimester exposure to warfarin is about 37% (96/263) (see Table 45.10) with the FWS accounting for about 28% (27/96) of this number. Spontaneous abortions, stillbirths, neonatal deaths, and central nervous system and other defects make up the remainder of the adverse outcome. Since the predicted risk is unacceptably high, another anticoagulant should be substituted for warfarin. Heparin is the drug of choice for pregnant women and should be administered to H.P.

Heparin

2. Heparin therapy (10,000 units SQ BID) was initiated and warfarin was discontinued. What considerations are required for heparin therapy in H.P.?

Heparin is a large molecule (MW: 15,000) and does not cross the placenta to the fetus. Other than the risk of maternal hemorrhage or thrombocytopenia, it does not pose a direct risk to the fetus. Although not teratogenic, the use of heparin does not guar-

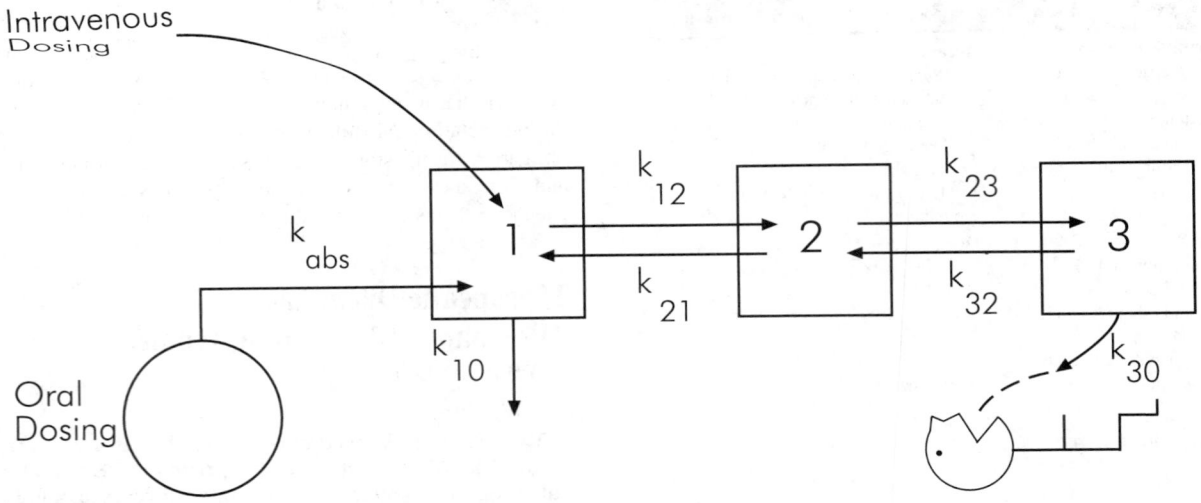

Fig 45.2   An Infant-Modulated 3-Compartment Open Model for Drug Excretion in Breast Milk   Compartments: 1 = Central; 2 = Interstitial, intracellular; 3 = Breast milk. Rate constants: K_{10} = Rate constant for elimination from plasma; K_{30} = Rate constant for excretion with milk. Reproduced with permission from reference 140.

antee a favorable outcome. In cases where heparin was used without other anticoagulants, 22% (30/135) of cases resulted in complications.[251] The complications included stillbirths, neonatal deaths, and spontaneous abortions. This incidence was not much better than the data summarized for warfarin where 27% (129/471) of the pregnancies ended unfavorably.[30] Another analysis of the same heparin data, however, arrived at a different conclusion[252] when 15 adverse outcomes were eliminated from the total group of 135 patients for the following reasons:

- heparin therapy inappropriate—all with pregnancy-induced hypertension (four neonatal deaths);
- severe maternal disease making successful pregnancy outcome unlikely (one neonatal death);
- maternal death due to pulmonary embolism (mistakenly listed as a spontaneous abortion);
- heparin therapy not indicated (seven stillbirths); and
- heparin and warfarin used (two stillbirths).

The percentage of remaining adverse outcomes, 13% (15/120), appears to be significantly better than the 22% originally reported, and probably reflects severe maternal disease rather than any direct or indirect effect of heparin on the fetoplacental unit.

Table 45.7	Drugs Contraindicated During Breast-Feeding[a,30,145]
Contraindicated	
Amphetamine[b]	Heroin[b]
Bromocriptine	Lithium
Cocaine[b]	Marijuana[b]
Cyclophosphamide	Methotrexate
Cyclosporine	Nicotine (smoking)[b]
Doxorubicin	Phencyclidine (PCP)[b]
Ergotamine	Phenindione
Requiring Temporary Cessation of Breast-Feeding	
Metronidazole (after single-dose therapy)	
Radiopharmaceuticals	

[a] See Table 45.8 for specific details.
[b] Drugs of abuse considered to be contraindicated during breast feeding by the American Academy of Pediatrics.[145]

Long-term use of heparin may result in maternal osteopenia.[48] Doses greater than 10,000 units/day for more than 25 weeks carry the greatest risk for severe bone demineralization, but lower doses (e.g., 10,000 units/day) also have been associated with this adverse effect. Exposure to heparin in previous pregnancies also increases the risk.[30] Since demineralization is dose related, it is important to keep the dose as low as possible to prevent clinical signs of osteoporosis.[253] Although a slight maternal risk, similar problems in the fetus and newborn have not been reported. The mechanism behind this effect is thought to be heparin inhibition of the renal activation of calcifediol (25-hydroxyvitamin D_3, a major transport form of vitamin D), to calcitriol, one of the active forms of vitamin D_3.[48] Supplemental calcitriol (Rocaltrol) should be added to H.P.'s regimen if heparin therapy is to be continued to term.

3. Warfarin in the Second and Third Trimesters. H.P. presents again at 14 weeks gestation with fever and multiple peripheral emboli. An allergic reaction to heparin is diagnosed after a trial with preservative-free heparin does not reverse the symptoms. A decision is made to restart warfarin. What is the expected fetal risk from second and third trimester use of warfarin?

Warfarin exposure after the first trimester (more specifically, after the ninth week) poses the risk of CNS malformations (see Table 45.9). These malformations appear to be a result of abnormal growth arising from an earlier fetal hemorrhage and subsequent scarring.[251] Two distinct patterns of CNS damage may occur: 1) dorsal midline dysplasia characterized by agenesis of corpus callosum, Dandy-Walker malformation, midline cerebellar atrophy, and encephaloceles in some; and 2) ventral mid-line dysplasia characterized by optic atrophy. The effects of CNS abnormalities include mental retardation (ranging from mild to severe in all affected children), blindness (≈50%), hydrocephalus, deafness, spasticity, seizures, scoliosis and growth failure, and death. Long-term sequelae in children with CNS defects are more serious and debilitating than those from the FWS.

The predicted adverse fetal outcome after second and third trimester warfarin exposure is approximately 16% (33/208).[30] The incidence of CNS and other defects in this population was 5% (10/208) with spontaneous abortions (2%) and stillbirths/neonatal deaths (9%) composing the balance. Although the risk of CNS anomalies and other fetal adverse effects are high, the risk to the

(Text continues on page 45-29)

Table 45.8	Drugs and Breast-Feeding

The majority of drugs either have not been studied during lactation (thus it is unknown if they are excreted in breast milk) or are known to be excreted in milk, but exposure of the nursing infant has not been studied. Many of the drugs listed below belong to this latter category. If adverse effects in the nursing infant have not been observed with drugs known to pass into milk, they are listed either as such or "compatible" (i.e., compatible with breast-feeding), a designation used by the American Academy of Pediatrics (AAP).[145] Even drugs that have been observed to cause toxicity may be listed as "compatible," because toxicity may be rare or limited only to certain types of patients. Drugs shown as "contraindicated" during breast-feeding are so listed either by the AAP[145] or by another reference source.[30] For the reader requiring detailed information, specific references, or counseling patients, the author recommends they have access to reference 30.

Drugs	Effects on Nursing Infant
Acebutolol	Compatible; observe exposed infants for signs of beta blockade (hypotension, bradycardia, and other symptoms). Atenolol, metoprolol, and nadolol are concentrated in milk; oxprenolol has lowest reported M:P ratio; beta blockade evidenced by hypotension, bradycardia, cyanosis, hypothermia, or tachypnea observed in infants exposed to acebutolol or atenolol in breast milk[30,145–147]
Acetaminophen	Compatible. Maculopapular rash on upper trunk and face of a nursing infant has been reported[145,148]
Acetazolamide	Excreted in milk; no effects reported;[30,149] compatible[145]
Acyclovir	Concentrated in milk; compatible[145,150,151]
Alfentanil	Excreted in milk; probably compatible[30]
Allopurinol	Excreted in milk; no effects reported.[30] Compatible[145]
Alprazolam	Apparent drug withdrawal after 9-month exposure via milk in 1 infant. Use of other agents in class during breast-feeding considered cause for concern by AAP[30,35,145]
Amantadine	Excreted in milk; no effects reported[30]
Amikacin	Excreted in milk; no effects reported[30]
Aminophylline	Irritability in 1 infant after use of rapidly absorbed oral solution[152]
p-Aminosalicylic acid	Excreted in milk; no effects reported[30]
Amiodarone	Excreted in milk; not recommended due to long elimination half-life and high proportion of iodine contained in each dose[30,153,154]
Amitriptyline	No adverse effects reported, but AAP considers use as cause for concern[145]
Amoxapine	See Amitriptyline
Amphetamines	Amphetamines accumulate in breast milk and may cause irritability and poor sleep patterns. Contraindicated if maternal amphetamine abuse[30,145,155]
Aspartame	Excreted in milk; use with caution if infant has phenylketonuria[30,145]
Aspirin	1 case severe salicylate intoxication (metabolic acidosis); potential for platelet dysfunction and rash; AAP recommends using with caution[30,145,156]
Atenolol	See Acebutolol
Atropine	Excretion in milk not documented. Compatible[30,145]
Baclofen	Compatible[30,145]
Benazepril	See Captopril
Bendroflumethiazide	See Thiazide diuretics
Benzthiazide	See Thiazide diuretics
Bethanechol	Abdominal pain and diarrhea in 1 infant[30]
Bismuth subsalicylate	Significant amounts of bismuth in milk not expected due to poor oral absorption;[30] salicylate portion excreted in milk (see Aspirin) and because of this, some advise that the drug should not be used during nursing[157]
Bromides	Drowsiness and rash observed in several infants;[30] AAP considers compatible[145]
Bromocriptine	Contraindicated; suppresses lactation[30,145]
Brompheniramine	Symptoms observed in 1 infant exposed to brompheniramine and d-isoephedrine: irritability, excessive crying, and disturbed sleeping patterns. Compatible[30,145,158]
Bupropion	Accumulates in milk; use with caution during breast-feeding[30,159]
Butorphanol	Compatible[145]
Caffeine	Accumulation may occur when mother is moderate to heavy consumer; irritability and poor sleeping habits observed. Compatible in usual amounts[30,145]
Captopril	Excreted in milk; compatible[145,160,161]
Carbamazepine	Compatible[145]
Carbimazole	See Methimazole

Continued

Table 45.8	Drugs and Breast-Feeding (Continued)
Drugs	Effects on Nursing Infant
Casanthranol	Compatible. May produce diarrhea in nursing infant[30,145]
Cascara sagrada	See Casanthranol
Cephalosporins	Excreted in milk; no effects reported. Compatible[30,145]
Chloral hydrate	Excreted in milk; drowsiness in 1 infant. Compatible[30,145]
Chloramphenicol	Excreted in milk. Potential bone marrow depression exists; AAP recommends using with caution[30,145]
Chloroform	Compatible[145]
Chloroquine	Excreted in milk. Compatible[145,162,163]
Chlorothiazide	See Thiazide diuretics
Chlorotrianisene	See Estradiol
Chlorpromazine	Excreted into milk; drowsiness and lethargy observed in 1 infant; AAP considers use a cause for concern due to these effects and potential for galactorrhea[30,145,164]
Chlorpropamide	Excreted in milk; no effects reported[30]
Chlorprothixene	Excreted in milk; no effects reported. Use classified by AAP as cause for concern[145,165]
Chlorthalidone	See Thiazide diuretics
Cimetidine	Compatible. May accumulate in milk. Theoretical potential for suppression of gastric acidity, inhibition of drug metabolism, and CNS stimulation[30,145,166]
Ciprofloxacin	Excreted in milk; use with caution due to the potential for arthropathies in the infant;[30,167–169] waiting 48 hr after last dose before resuming breast-feeding will decrease infant exposure[30]
Cisplatin	Excreted in milk. Contraindicated[30,170]
Clemastine	Drowsiness, irritability, refusal to feed, neck stiffness, and high-pitched cry in 1 infant. AAP recommends using with caution[30,145,171]
Clindamycin	Grossly bloody stools in infant whose mother received clindamycin and gentamicin. Considered compatible by AAP[30,145]
Clofazimine	Excreted in milk; slowly reversible pigmentation of the infant's skin may result[30,172]
Clomipramine	Excreted in milk;[173] no adverse effects reported but use with caution.[30] (Also see Amitriptyline)
Clonazepam	Persistent apnea in 1 infant; monitor for CNS depression[30]
Clonidine	Excreted in milk; no effects reported[174]
Clorazepate	Probably excreted in milk. (Also see Diazepam)[30]
Cocaine	Excreted in milk; contraindicated due to CNS stimulation and intoxication[30,145,175,176]
Codeine	Compatible[145]
Colchicine	Excreted in milk; no adverse effects reported.[30,177] Compatible[145]
Colistimethate	Excreted in milk; no effects reported[30]
Cyclopenthiazide	See Thiazide diuretics
Cyclophosphamide	Excreted in milk; contraindicated due to potential for immune suppression, carcinogenesis, neutropenia, and unknown effect on growth[30,145]
Cyclosporine	Contraindicated. Excreted in milk; potential for immune suppression and neutropenia, unknown effect on growth, and carcinogenic effects[145,178–181]
Cyclothiazide	See Thiazide diuretics
Danthron	See Casanthranol
Desipramine	See Amitriptyline
Diazepam	Lethargy and weight loss reported with diazepam; watch for accumulation in infant; considered cause for concern by AAP[30,145]
Dicumarol	Compatible[145]
Dicyclomine	Excreted in milk; 1 case report of apnea in a breast-fed 12-day-old infant whose mother was receiving the drug; similar reactions have been observed when given directly to infants. Contraindicated[30]
Dienestrol	See Estradiol
Diethylstilbestrol	See Estradiol
Diflunisal	Excreted in milk[30]

Continued

Table 45.8	Drugs and Breast-Feeding (Continued)
Drugs	Effects on Nursing Infant
Digoxin	Excreted in milk. Compatible[30,145]
Diltiazem	Excreted in milk. Compatible[30,145]
Diphenhydramine	Excreted in milk; no effects reported[30]
Diphenoxylate with atropine	Excreted in milk; no effects reported[30]
Dipyridamole	Excreted in milk; no effects reported[30]
Disopyramide	Excreted in milk. Compatible[30,145,182–185]
Docusate sodium	See Casanthranol
Dothiepin	See Amitriptyline
Doxepin	Metabolites accumulate in infant serum; 1 infant found pale, limp, and near respiratory arrest. AAP recommends using with caution[145,186,187]
Doxorubicin	See Cyclophosphamide
Dyphylline	Compatible; accumulates in milk[145]
Enalapril	See Captopril
Encainide	Excreted in milk; no effects reported[30]
Enoxacin	See Ciprofloxacin
Ephedrine	See Brompheniramine
Ergotamine	Contraindicated; vomiting, diarrhea, and convulsions reported from doses used in migraine medications;[30,145] may inhibit breast milk production[30]
Erythromycin	Excreted in milk. Compatible[30,145]
Esmolol	See Acebutolol
Estradiol	Estrogens are excreted in milk. Potential for ↓ milk volume and ↓ nitrogen and protein content; chlorotrianisene and estradiol used to suppress postpartum breast engorgement in nonbreast-feeding women. Withdrawal vaginal bleeding observed. Use of oral contraceptives associated with shortened duration of lactation, ↓ infant weight gain, ↓ milk production, and ↓ milk content of nitrogen and protein; report of breast tenderness and hypertrophy in 1 infant exposed to large doses of oral contraceptives. Compatible once breast-feeding has started[30,145]
Estrogens, conjugated	See Estradiol
Estrone	See Estradiol
Ethambutol	Excreted in milk. Compatible[145,188]
Ethanol	Passes freely into milk; high maternal intake may cause, in nursing infants, sedation, diaphoresis, deep sleep, weakness, ↓ in linear growth, and abnormal weight gain. Chronic exposure also may be related to retarded psychomotor development. ↓ in milk ejection reflex may occur. Infants of alcoholic mothers may be at risk for potentiation of severe hypoprothrombic bleeding and pseudo-Cushing's syndrome. AAP classifies as compatible, but should be considered contraindicated.[30,145,189] 1 review suggested waiting 1–2 hr/drink before breast-feeding[157]
Ethinyl estradiol	See Estradiol
Ethosuximide	Compatible[145]
Ethyl biscoumacetate	Bleeding in 5 of 64 exposed infants[30]
Famotidine	Accumulates in milk but to lesser degree than either cimetidine or ranitidine;[190] may be preferred over the latter 2 drugs during breast-feeding.[30,157] Compatible[145]
Fenoprofen	Excreted in milk; no effects reported[30]
Fluconazole	Not known if excreted in milk but no adverse effects were observed when given in therapeutic doses to newborns and is probably safe to use during breast feeding[30]
Flunitrazepam	Excreted in milk; no effects reported[191,192]
Fluoxetine	Excreted in milk; no adverse effects reported but use with caution.[30,193] (Also see Amitriptyline)
Flupenthixol	Excreted in milk; no effects reported.
Flurazepam	Excretion in milk has not been reported, but see Diazepam[30]
Fosinopril	See Captopril
Furosemide	Excreted in milk; no effects reported[30]
Gadopentetate dimeglumine	Excreted in milk of lactating rats but no human studies; pumping the breast after 6 hr and discarding milk should markedly decrease infant exposure[30]

Continued

Table 45.8	Drugs and Breast-Feeding (Continued)
Drugs	Effects on Nursing Infant
Gentamicin	See Amikacin. (Also see Clindamycin)
Glyburide	Milk excretion has not been studied but probably similar to chlorpropamide[30]
Gold salts	Compatible. Excreted in milk; some investigators recommend avoiding nursing because of the prolonged maternal elimination time and the potential for toxicity in infant[30,145,196]
Guanfacine	Excreted in milk of animals; reduces serum prolactin concentrations in some patients and may inhibit milk secretion[30]
Haloperidol	Excreted in milk; no effects reported. Use classified by AAP as cause for concern[145,197,198]
Heroin	Sufficient quantities present in milk to cause addiction in infant; contraindicated[30,145]
Hexachlorophene	Excreted in milk after use as a nipple wash between nursings; no adverse effects in the infant reported[30]
Hydralazine	Compatible[145]
Hydrochlorothiazide	See Thiazide diuretics
Hydroflumethiazide	See Thiazide diuretics
Hydroxychloroquine	Accumulates in milk with slow elimination from the infant; milk concentrations too low to provide antimalarial protection for infant;[30] compatible[145]
Hydroxyurea	Excreted in milk. Contraindicated[30,199]
Ibuprofen	Compatible. Small amounts excreted in milk[30,145,200–202]
Imipramine	See Amitriptyline
Indomethacin	Compatible. Possible seizure due to drug in 1 infant[30,145]
Iodine/iodides	Concentrated in milk; after maternal use of povidone-iodine vaginal gel for several days, nursing infant had strong odor of iodine on skin and grossly elevated serum and urine iodide levels. AAP considers compatible[30,145,203,204]
Iopanoic acid (and related agents)	Compatible. Excreted in milk; use with caution since many diagnostic agents contain large amounts of iodine. (Also see Iodine/iodides)[30,145]
Isoniazid	Compatible. Excreted in milk; potential for hepatotoxicity and peripheral neuritis[30,145]
Kanamycin	See Amikacin
Labetalol	See Acebutolol
Levothyroxine (T_4)	Excreted in milk. Levels too low to protect hypothyroid infant completely from effects of hypothyroidism[30]
Lincomycin	Excreted in milk; no effects reported[30]
Lindane	Excreted in milk; no effects reported[30]
Liothyronine (T_3)	See Levothyroxine
Liotrix	See Levothyroxine
Lisinopril	See Captopril
Lithium	Milk and serum concentrations average 40% of maternal serum levels causing potential for toxic reactions. Contraindicated[30,145]
Lomefloxacin	See Ciprofloxacin
Lorazepam	See Diazepam
Lovastatin	Excreted in milk of rats but no human studies; use with caution during lactation due to potential for adverse effects in infant[30]
Lysergic acid diethylamide (LSD)	Probably excreted in milk; contraindicated[30]
Magnesium sulfate	Compatible[145]
Mandelic acid	Excreted in milk; no effects reported[30]
Maprotiline	Excreted in milk; no effects reported[30]
Marijuana	Excreted in milk; contraindicated[30,145,205–208]
Mebendazole	Possible inhibition of milk production[209]
Medroxyprogesterone	Compatible[30,145]
Mefenamic acid	Compatible[145]
Mefloquine	Excreted in milk;[210] no adverse effects have been reported in infants; milk concentrations too low to provide antimalarial protection for infant[30,211]
Meperidine	Excreted in milk; no effects reported[30]

Continued

Table 45.8	Drugs and Breast-Feeding (Continued)
Drugs	Effects on Nursing Infant
Mepindolol	See Acebutolol
Meprobamate	Excreted in milk; no effects reported[30]
Mesalamine	Excreted in milk;[30] diarrhea observed in 1 infant whose mother was treated with 500 mg BID mesalamine rectal suppositories
Mesoridazine	No effects reported, but use classified by AAP as cause for concern[30,145]
Mestranol	See Estradiol
Methadone	Compatible; no toxic effects if mother receiving <20 mg/day. 1 report of infant death from methadone obtained via milk[30,145]
Metharbital	Excreted in milk; no effects reported[30]
Methenamine	Excreted in milk; no effects reported[30]
Methimazole	May cause thyroid dysfunction (goiter) in nursing infant; small doses (≤10–15 mg/day) may be safe in thyroid function of infant monitored. Use propylthiouracil if antithyroid agent required; AAP considers compatible[30,145]
Methocarbamol	Compatible[30,145]
Methotrexate	See Cyclophosphamide
Methyclothiazide	See Thiazide diuretics
Methyldopa	Compatible[145]
Methyprylon	Compatible but drowsiness may occur[145]
Metoclopramide	Stimulates milk production. Mild intestinal upset observed. AAP considers use as a cause for concern due to potential potent CNS effects[30,145,213–215]
Metolazone	See Thiazide diuretics
Metoprolol	See Acebutolol
Metrizamide	Excreted in milk. Compatible[145,216]
Metronidazole	Excreted in milk; diarrhea and secondary lactose intolerance in 1 infant; mutagenic and carcinogenic in some species; AAP recommends halting breast-feeding for 12–24 hr to allow clearance of drug from the milk if single-dose therapy administered[145,217,218]
Mexiletine	Concentrated in milk; no adverse effects observed in nursing infants; compatible[30,145]
Mifepristone	Milk excretion has not been studied but contraindicated during lactation due to potent antiprogestogen effect[30]
Minoxidil	Compatible[145]
Misoprostol	Excretion in milk has not been studied but contraindicated due to potential for severe diarrhea in infant[30]
Morphine	Compatible[145]
Nadolol	See Acebutolol
Nalidixic acid	Hemolytic anemia in infant with G6PD deficiency. Considered compatible by AAP[30,145]
Naproxen	Small amounts excreted in milk; no effects reported.[30,219,220] Compatible[145]
Nicotine (excess)	Shock, vomiting, diarrhea, rapid heart rate, and restlessness; ↓ milk production. Contraindicated[145]
Nifedipine	Excreted in milk; no effects reported.[221] Compatible[145]
Nitrofurantoin	Excreted in milk; compatible. Hemolytic anemia in infants with G6PD deficiency possible[30,145]
Nizatidine	Excreted in milk; probably compatible[30,222]
Norethindrone	Compatible. Dose-related suppression of lactation may occur.[30,145] (Also see Estrogens)
Norethynodrel	See Norethindrone
Norfloxacin	See Ciprofloxacin
Norgestrel	See Norethindrone
Nortriptyline	Excreted in milk; no effects reported[30]
Novobiocin	Excreted in milk; no effects reported[30]
Ofloxacin	See Ciprofloxacin
Oral contraceptives	See Estradiol and Norethindrone
Oxazepam	See Diazepam

Continued

Table 45.8	Drugs and Breast-Feeding (Continued)
Drugs	**Effects on Nursing Infant**
Oxprenolol	See Acebutolol
Oxycodone	Excreted in milk; no effects reported[30]
Paregoric	See Morphine
Penicillins	Excreted in milk; candidiasis and diarrhea after ampicillin in 1 infant. Compatible[30]
Pentobarbital	Excreted in milk; no effects reported[30]
Pentoxifylline	Excreted in milk; no effects reported[223]
Phenacetin	Excreted in milk; no effects reported[30]
Phencyclidine	Excreted in milk; no effects reported. Contraindicated due to potent hallucinogenic properties[30,145,224]
Phenindione	Massive scrotal hematoma and wound oozing after herniotomy in 1 infant; contraindicated[30,145]
Phenobarbital	May accumulate in infant due to slow elimination. Infant levels may exceed maternal levels; sedation has been observed. Monitor infant serum levels. AAP recommends using with caution[30,145]
Phenolphthalein	Metabolized drug excreted in milk; no adverse effects reported[30]
Phenylbutazone	Small amounts excreted in milk. Compatible[30,145]
Phenytoin	Methemoglobinemia, drowsiness, and ↓ sucking activity in 1 infant; considered compatible by AAP[30,145]
Pindolol	See Acebutolol
Piroxicam	Excreted in milk, compatible[30,145]
Polythiazide	See Thiazide diuretics
Prazepam	See Diazepam
Prednisolone	Excreted in milk. Compatible[145,225–227]
Prednisone	See Prednisolone
Primidone	May cause sedation and feeding problems. AAP recommends using with caution[145]
Procainamide	Accumulates in milk; compatible[145,228]
Propofol	Excreted in milk; no adverse effects reported[30]
Propoxyphene	Compatible[145]
Propranolol	See Acebutolol
Propylthiouracil (PTU)	Excreted in milk. Compatible[145,230,231]
Pseudoephedrine	Excreted in milk. Compatible[145,232]
Pyrazinamide	Excreted in milk; no effects reported[223]
Pyridostigmine	Excreted in milk. Compatible[145,234]
Pyrimethamine	Excreted in milk. Compatible[145,163,235]
Quazepam	See Diazepam
Quinapril	See Captopril
Quinethazone	See Thiazide diuretics
Quinidine	Excreted in milk. Compatible[145,236]
Quinine	Excreted in milk. Compatible[30,145]
Radiopharmaceuticals	Halt breast-feeding temporarily to allow clearance of radioactivity from milk; suggested times for individual agents are:[145] Gallium-67 (Ga^{67}) 2 wk; Indium-111 (In^{111}) 20 hr; Iodine-125 (I^{125}) 12 days; Iodine-131 (I^{131}) 2–4 days; Radioactive Sodium 96 hr; Technetium-99m (Tc^{99m}) 15 hr–3 days; ($^{99m}TcO_4$) (Tc^{99m} macroaggregates) 15 hr–3 days
Ramipril	See Captopril
Ranitidine	Concentrated in milk; no effects reported[30,237]
Reserpine	Excreted in milk; no effects reported[30]
Rifampin	Excreted in milk. Compatible[30,145]
Saccharin	Accumulates in milk, but probably safe[30]
Scopolamine	See Atropine
Secobarbital	Compatible. Excreted in milk[145]

Continued

Table 45.8	Drugs and Breast-Feeding (Continued)
Drugs	Effects on Nursing Infant
Senna	Compatible; not excreted in milk[30,145]
Sotalol	Concentrated in milk; no adverse effects observed in nursing infants[30,238–240] Compatible.[145] (Also see Acebutolol)
Spiramycin	Bacteriostatic concentrations in milk[30]
Spironolactone	Metabolite excreted in milk. Compatible[30,145]
Streptomycin	See Amikacin
Sucralfate	Safe during breast-feeding[30]
Sulfonamides	Excreted in milk; use caution in infants with jaundice, G6PD deficiency, or if premature. 1 case of bloody diarrhea observed with sulfasalazine. AAP advises using sulfasalazine with caution[30,145]
Terbutaline	Excreted in milk. Compatible[145,241,242]
Tetracyclines	Compatible; although excreted in milk, absorption by infant negligible[30,145]
Theophylline	Compatible. Excreted in milk; use slowly absorbed preparations to avoid toxic levels in sensitive infants[30,145,152,243,244]
Thiazide diuretics	May suppress lactation, but compatible[30,145]
Thiouracil	Compatible; not used in U.S.[145]
Thyroid	See Levothyroxine
Timolol	See Acebutolol
Tobramycin	See Amikacin
Tolbutamide	Compatible, but jaundice possible complication[30,145]
Tolmetin	Excreted in milk; compatible[145,245]
Trazodone	Excreted in milk;[30,246] use with caution.[145] (See Amitriptyline)
Triazolam	Probably excreted. (See Diazepam)
Trichlormethiazide	See Thiazide diuretics
Trimeprazine	Excreted in milk; no effects reported[30]
Trimethoprim	Excreted in milk. Compatible[30,145]
Triprolidine	Compatible[145]
Valproic acid	Compatible[145]
Vancomycin	Excreted in milk; no effects reported: Systemic absorption by infant poor[30,247]
Verapamil	Excreted in milk. Compatible[145,248,249]
Vitamins	All vitamins are excreted in milk and classified as compatible. Maternal ingestion of pharmacologic doses of Vitamin D may cause hypercalcemia in the nursing infant; monitor infant's serum calcium levels[30,145]
Warfarin	Compatible[145]
Zuclopenthixol	Excreted in milk; no effects reported[30,195,250]

mother in this case is greater. The mother should be fully informed of the risks to herself and to her fetus if the pregnancy is continued and, if she concurs, warfarin therapy restarted. Oral anticoagulant therapy should be stopped three to five days before scheduled delivery to allow clearance of the drug from the mother and fetus. Low-dose heparin should be reinstituted at this time with appropriate measures taken to treat any symptoms of heparin allergy. Approximately 12 hours before delivery, heparin therapy should be stopped to prevent severe maternal hemorrhage during and after delivery.

Breast-Feeding

4. Following vaginal delivery, H.P. is restarted on low-dose heparin and then changed to warfarin on day 5. H.P. also is breast-feeding. Do either of these drugs present a risk to the nursing infant?

Heparin does not cross into breast milk (see Drug Excretion in Human Milk) because of the high molecular weight ($\approx$15,000).

Therefore, risk from this anticoagulant is nil. Warfarin is both highly ionized and protein bound in the maternal serum. These factors, working together, prevent excretion into milk of amounts that could affect the infant's coagulability state. The mother should observe the infant for bruising or other signs of hemorrhage, even though the apparent risk is very low.

Anticonvulsants

5. L.F., a 30-year-old epileptic, wants to become pregnant. She suffers from generalized tonic-clonic seizures which have been well controlled with oral phenytoin 100 mg QID. L.F. has had no seizures for the past year. What are the risks of phenytoin to the fetus?

Children of epileptic mothers are at an increased risk for congenital malformations over the general population. Epidemiologic studies have suggested that this increased incidence is due to anticonvulsant drug therapy; however, other contributing factors,

Table 45.9	Fetal Warfarin Syndrome[a]

Exposure 6th–9th Weeks

Common Features
Nasal hypoplasia
Depressed bridge of nose
Stippling in uncalcified epiphyseal regions (axial skeleton, proximal femurs, and calcanei)

Less Common Features
Birth weight <10th percentile for gestational age
Development retardation
Congenital heart disease
Deafness/hearing loss
Death
Laryngeal calcification
Scoliosis
Seizures
Eye anomalies (blindness, optic atrophy, and microphthalmia)
Hypoplasia of extremities ranging from severe rhizomelic dwarfing to dystrophic nails and shortened fingers

Exposure in 2nd and 3rd Trimesters

CNS Anomalies
Dorsal midline dysplasia characterized by agenesis of corpus callosum, Dandy-Walker malformation, and midline cerebellar atrophy; encephaloceles
Ventral mid-line dysplasia characterized by optic atrophy

Effects of CNS Anomalies
Blindness
Deafness
Death
Growth failure
Hydrocephalus
Mental retardation
Scoliosis
Seizures
Spasticity

[a] Adapted from reference 251.

such as the underlying seizure disorder or genetics, cannot be eliminated entirely. Animal and biochemical studies, however, seem to indicate that drug therapy itself is the primary factor.[254]

A study published in 1990 demonstrated a relationship between levels of activity of the enzyme, epoxide hydrolase, and the risk of fetal hydantoin syndrome (FHS).[255] Toxic oxidative metabolites of phenytoin normally are removed by the epoxide hydroxylase which appears to be regulated by a single gene with two allelic forms. Furthermore, only fetuses with low activity of this enzyme appear to be at risk from phenytoin. If further studies confirm these findings, this would be an example of an interaction between the mother's genetic makeup and her environment (i.e., in this case, a drug).

Fetal Hydantoin Syndrome (FHS)

Infants of treated mothers, especially those treated with phenytoin (Dilantin), have a recognizable pattern of malformations in 7% to 11% of cases. This pattern is known as the fetal hydantoin syndrome and may occur in infants exposed *in utero* to nonhydantoin anticonvulsants.[256] The incidence of all congenital anomalies from treated mothers ranges from 2.2% to 26.1%, compared to 0% to 15.2% from untreated epileptics.[254] Some of the studies involved small numbers of patients, but the accepted relative risk estimate for treated versus untreated epileptics is two to three and is statistically significant in most series. Most of the malformations and developmental disabilities in children of untreated mothers are nonspecific, as are some of the defects observed in offspring of treated women.[254]

The FHS consists of variable degrees of hypoplasia and ossification of the distal phalanges and craniofacial malformations.[30] Mental and physical growth retardation and congenital heart disease often are present. Table 45.11 lists the characteristic defects

observed in this syndrome. Figures 45.4 and 45.5 show some of these defects in a newborn. Nonspecific malformations are highly variable, prompting one reviewer to conclude that nearly all possible types of malformations have been observed in the progeny of epileptic parents.[256]

Carcinogenic Potential of Phenytoin

Phenytoin may be a human transplacental carcinogen as several tumors have been observed in children exposed to this drug during gestation.[30] The reported tumors and number of cases are: neuroblastoma (5), ganglioneuroblastoma (1), melanotic neuroectodermal tumor (1), extrarenal Wilms' tumor (1), mesenchymoma (1), lymphangioma (1), and ependymoblastoma (1). Exposed children must be evaluated closely for several years since tumors may take that long before appearing.

Hemorrhagic Disease of the Newborn (HDN)

Use of phenytoin and other anticonvulsants during the third trimester increases the risk of hemorrhagic disease of the newborn.[30] Both early HDN (onset: 0 to 24 hours) and classic HDN (onset: 2 to 5 days) may occur in gestationally exposed infants. The hemorrhage is frequently life threatening, with intracranial bleeding common, and it is thought to result from phenytoin induction of fetal liver microsomal enzymes that further deplete the already low reserves of fetal vitamin K. Suppression of the vitamin K-dependent clotting factors, II, VII, IX, and X results from the hypovitaminosis. Phenytoin-induced thrombocytopenia also may play a role in the bleeding. Prophylactic vitamin K_1 (phytonadione), 0.5 to 1.0 mg, must be given to the newborn to prevent this condition.

Reducing Fetal Risks

6. If L.F. chooses to become pregnant, what steps should her physician implement to lessen the risks of anticonvulsant toxicity to her fetus?

Fig 45.3   Fetal Warfarin Syndrome   Note depressed nasal bridge and nasal hypoplasia. Photo courtesy of K. L. Jones, M.D., UC San Diego.

Table 45.10	Incidence of Fetal Warfarin Syndrome (FWS)[a,b]	
1st Trimester		
Normal	167	(64%)
Spontaneous abortions	41	(16%)
Stillborn/neonatal death	17	(6%)
FWS	27	(10%)
CNS/other defects	11	(4%)
2nd/3rd Trimesters		
Normal	175	(84%)
Spontaneous abortions	4	(2%)
Stillborn/neonatal death	19	(9%)
CNS/other defects	10	(5%)
Total Number of Exposed Infants	471	(100%)
Normal	342	(73%)
Spontaneous abortions	45	(10%)
Stillborn/neonatal death	36	(8%)
FWS/CNS/other defects	48	(10%)

[a] Adapted from reference 30.
[b] CNS = Central nervous system; FWS = Fetal warfarin syndrome.

Although a predictable dose response has not been observed, the lowest possible dose to control L.F.'s seizures should be used. In some cases, it may be possible to discontinue the drug completely, but if this cannot be done, the lowest effective dose should be given before pregnancy. Since L.F. has had no seizure activity for the past year, a careful reduction of her dose may be possible. Close monitoring of phenytoin serum levels will be required during pregnancy to assure that therapeutic levels are maintained and to help prevent seizures, which may increase the risk of fetal malformations. Consideration also should be given to changing L.F.'s drug therapy to another anticonvulsant (see Question 7).

Supplemental Folic Acid. The addition of folic acid to L.F.'s drug regimen also should be considered. Although animal and biochemical studies indicate that more than one mechanism for anticonvulsant teratogenicity may exist, the use of folic acid was successful in one study in preventing phenytoin-induced malformations.[257] In this study, a group of 24 women treated with phenytoin and other anticonvulsants produced 66 infants, ten (15%) with major congenital malformations. A second group of 22 women taking similar anticonvulsants then were given folic acid, 2.5 to 5.0 mg/day, starting before conception in 26 pregnancies and within the first 40 days in six. This second group produced 33 newborns (one set of twins), none of whom had defects, a significant difference from the first group. None of the women taking folic acid suffered loss of seizure control, a problem known to occur due to folic acid lowering of phenytoin serum levels. (See Chapter 52: Seizure Disorders.) In a similar study, women were supplemented with folic acid (0.1 to 1.0 mg/day; average: 0.5 mg) from the sixth to sixteenth week of gestation.[258] From the 133 women taking anticonvulsants, 20 infants (15%) had defects, a number that seems to indicate that supplementation had little or no effect on the fetal toxicity of these drugs. The major differences between these two studies are the timing of folic acid supplementation and the dosage used. More studies in this area certainly are needed to determine if either of these differences are significant. Anticonvulsants, such as phenytoin and phenobarbital, induce maternal folic acid deficiency either by impairing gastrointestinal absorption or by increasing hepatic metabolism of the vitamin.[30] However, the fetus is very efficient at drawing upon available maternal stores of the vitamin and, thus, it is unknown if folic acid deficiency also is induced in the fetus.[30] Based upon the above considerations, it seems prudent to recommend that L.F. be given folic acid supple-

mentation before conception in a dose range of 2.5 to 5.0 mg/day. Phenytoin levels also should be determined at frequent intervals.

Teratogenicity of Nonhydantoin Anticonvulsants

7. Do other anticonvulsants offer an advantage over phenytoin in pregnancy?

For patients with generalized tonic-clonic seizures, the drugs that offer the most effective therapy are phenytoin, carbamazepine (Tegretol), and valproic acid (Depakene). Primidone (Mysoline), phenobarbital, and possibly clonazepam (Klonopin) may be effective, while ethosuximide (Zarontin) and trimethadione (Tridione) are of little value. Some of these anticonvulsants may offer advantages over phenytoin if seizure control can be maintained. If L.F. already was pregnant, however, it would probably be best to continue her present therapy at the lowest effective dose.

Phenobarbital often is used in combination with phenytoin, although it is used much less frequently as a single agent for the treatment of the type of seizures inflicting L.F. While a recognizable pattern of malformations, such as FHS, does not occur in epileptic women treated only with phenobarbital, some of the minor anomalies composing FHS are observed.[30] In three cases, women treated during the first trimester with only primidone, a structural analog of phenobarbital, produced infants with malformations similar to those in FHS. Mephobarbital (Mebaral), which is partially demethylated by the liver to phenobarbital, has very limited first trimester use which does not allow conclusions as to its safety.[30] All of the above agents may induce maternal folic acid deficiency, a situation identical to that observed with phenytoin, but the clinical significance of this is currently unknown. Hemorrhagic disease of the newborn has been reported after phenobarbital and primidone and should be expected after mephobarbital. The mechanism of this effect and its treatment are the same as that described for phenytoin. In addition, barbiturate withdrawal has been observed in newborns exposed to phenobarbital during gestation. The average onset of symptoms was six days (range: 3 to 14 days) after birth and has been reported with daily doses as low as 64 mg.[30] Summarizing the available information on phenobarbital and related anticonvulsants, the fetus is at risk for minor congenital malformations, hemorrhagic disease of the newborn, and neonatal withdrawal. If L.F.'s disease could be controlled with

Table 45.11	Fetal Effects of Hydantoins[a,b]
Fetal Hydantoin Syndrome	
Craniofacial	Broad nasal bridge, wide fontanel, low-set hairline, ocular hypertelorism, cleft lip/palate, epicanthal folds, coloboma, broad alveolar ridge, metopic ridging, short neck, microcephaly, abnormal or low-set ears, ptosis of eyelids, coarse scalp hair
Limbs	Small or absent nails, altered palmar crease, dislocated hip, hypoplasia of distal phalanges, digital thumb
Other	Impaired growth (physical and mental), congenital heart defects
Other Birth Defects/Toxicities Associated with Phenytoin	
Multiple malformations	Nearly all possible types have been reported
Tumors	Neuroblastoma, ganglioneuroblastoma, melanotic neuroectodermal, extrarenal Wilms', mesenchymoma, lymphangioma, ependymoblastoma
HDN	Involves various organ systems

[a] Adapted from reference 30.
[b] HDN = Hemorrhagic disease of the newborn.

Fig 45.4 Fetal Hydantoin Syndrome   Note broad nasal bridge, short nose, and nail hypoplasia. Photo courtesy of K. L. Jones, M.D., UC San Diego.

phenobarbital alone, or another similar agent, this therapy may offer an advantage over phenytoin.

Carbamazepine, an anticonvulsant structurally related to the tricyclic antidepressants, has been used frequently in pregnancy.[30] However, several case reports have described infants with congenital malformations after first trimester exposure. As with phenytoin, multiple nonspecific defects have been observed, including many of the minor malformations making up FHS. One review found no statistical relationship between carbamazepine and congenital malformations.[259] Another review concluded that carbamazepine is the drug of choice in women at risk for pregnancy who require anticonvulsant therapy for the first time.[260] Until 1989, the teratogenicity of this anticonvulsant was open to question, but carbamazepine now also is considered to be a teratogen. In a prospective study of 72 epileptic women treated in early pregnancy, carbamazepine use was associated with a pattern of malformations, the main features of which were minor craniofacial defects, fingernail hypoplasia, and developmental delay.[49] Since these defects were similar to those of FHS, and because both carbamazepine and phenytoin are metabolized through the arene oxide pathway, the teratogenic mechanism presumably involved the epoxide intermediates rather than the specific drugs. Additional data were presented later in 1989 indicating that carbamazepine may be related to a ninefold increase in the incidence of neural tube defects.[50]

Clonazepam. The benzodiazepine anticonvulsant, clonazepam, has very limited experience in human pregnancy. One infant exposed in utero and delivered prematurely at 36 weeks gestation developed apnea, cyanosis, lethargy, and hypotonia at six hours of age.[56] Although there was no evidence of congenital malformations, the toxic symptoms persisted for several days. Clonazepam usually is given in combination with other anticonvulsants; hence, an increased rate of malformation due to the agent would be dif-

ficult to detect. Thus, too little information is available to recommend this drug.

Valproic Acid. The use of valproic acid during gestation carries with it an approximate 1% to 2% risk of producing a child with a neural tube defect (includes entire spectrum from spina bifida to meningomyelocele).[30] Other major adverse fetal effects that have been observed with this drug include craniofacial, cardiac, digital, skeletal and limb, urogenital, skin and muscle, and miscellaneous anomalies.[30] Nonteratogenic fetal toxicity appears to be dose related. In one series, 50% of the cases (7/14) had fetal distress (i.e., late decelerations, silent or accelerated beat-to-beat variations) during labor requiring cesarean section in four of them.[130] Low Apgar scores also were observed in four of the newborns. The authors concluded that a high serum concentration of the free fraction of valproic acid during labor and at birth was responsible for the fetal/newborn toxicity. Due to the high incidence of toxicity, valproic acid does not offer any advantage over phenytoin in L.F.

The fetal effects of ethosuximide are shown in Table 45.5 while those of trimethadione are shown in Table 45.12. As stated above, neither drug would be effective for L.F.'s seizures.

Phenytoin in Breast Milk

8. If L.F. decides to breast-feed her newborn, would the use of phenytoin be expected to cause any problems?

Although phenytoin is excreted in milk with an M:P ratio of 0.18 to 0.54, there is little risk of toxicity in the nursing infant (see Table 45.8).[30]

Isotretinoin

9. P.J. is a 19-year-old female with severe cystic acne for which she has been taking isotretinoin. After several months of therapy, P.J. suspects she is pregnant. What is the risk to P.J.'s fetus from isotretinoin exposure in early pregnancy?

Fig 45.5 Fetal Hydantoin Syndrome   Note nail hypoplasia on far left finger. Photo courtesy of K. L. Jones, M.D., UC San Diego.

Table 45.12		Fetal Trimethadione Syndrome[a]
Cardiac	Septal defects	Patent ductus arteriosus
Limb	Simian crease, hand defects	Clubfoot
Craniofacial	Low-set, cupped/abnormal ears; high arched or cleft lip and/or palate; microcephaly; irregular teeth	Epicanthic folds, broad nasal bridge, strabismus, low hairline, facial hemangiomata
Growth/Performance	Prenatal/postnatal deficiency, speech disorder	Mental retardation, myopia, impaired hearing
Genitourinary	Kidney/ureter defects, hypospadias, clitoral hypertrophy	Inguinal hernias, ambiguous genitalia, imperforate anus
Other	Tracheoesophageal fistula	Esophageal atresia

[a] Adapted from reference 30.

Isotretinoin (Accutane), an isomer of vitamin A, was introduced in 1982 as a treatment for severe recalcitrant cystic acne. The drug is a major human teratogen.[30] The critical period of exposure appears to be four to seven weeks following the onset of the last menstrual period. Isotretinoin exposure in 69 pregnant women resulted in 24 spontaneous abortions, 24 apparently normal children, and 21 infants with major congenital malformations.[30] Of further concern, the normal infants had not been examined for a year or more at the time of the above reports so there is a possibility that additional malformations will be found. Therefore, P.J. has a significant chance of spontaneously aborting her pregnancy, and if her pregnancy continues to term, of producing an infant with a major congenital malformation (see Table 45.5).

Tretinoin

10. If P.J. had been treated with topical retinoic acid (tretinoin), another vitamin A derivative used for acne vulgaris, would this have placed her fetus at risk?

Tretinoin, like other retinoids, is a potent teratogen when taken systemically. However, topical use makes the risk very minimal because, at the most, only about one-third of a topical dose is absorbed.[30] Assuming a 1 gm/day application of a 0.1% preparation, this would amount to about one-seventh of the vitamin A activity received from a typical prenatal vitamin supplement. P.J.'s fetus would not have been at risk from this degree of exposure.

Enalapril and Hydrochlorothiazide (HCTZ)

11. A.R. is a 34-year-old woman with severe chronic (essential) hypertension that is well controlled on enalapril 20 mg/day and HCTZ 50 mg/day. She is currently in the first month of pregnancy. Her internist wants to know if either of these agents may be harmful to her developing fetus and, if so, what changes should be made.

Diuretics, such as hydrochlorothiazide, usually are contraindicated in pregnancy because they may decrease placental perfusion and prevent the normal plasma volume expansion that occurs in pregnancy.[30] There is no strong evidence that they are human teratogens.

Enalapril, a competitive inhibitor of angiotensin-converting enzyme (ACE) inhibitors, exerts its teratogenic effects in the second and third trimesters, rather than in the first trimester, unlike most drugs. The toxicities associated with ACE inhibitors include oligohydramnios, pulmonary hypoplasia, fetal and neonatal renal failure, and fetal and neonatal death. These agents also produce structural defects, such as fetal calvarial hypoplasia and, possibly, renal anomalies.[30]

Skull Defect

The mechanism of the fetal calvarial hypoplasia is thought to be related to the drug-induced oligohydramnios that allows the uterine musculature to exert direct pressure on the top of the head. This mechanical insult, combined with drug-induced fetal hypotension, inhibits peripheral perfusion and ossification of the calvaria.[46]

Renal Defect

A 1990 report described the following kidney abnormalities in a newborn who had been exposed throughout gestation to enalapril 20 mg/day, propranolol 40 mg/day, and hydrochlorothiazide 50 mg/day: irregular corticomedullary junctions; glomerular maldevelopment with a decreased number of lobulations in many of the glomeruli, and some congested glomeruli; a reduced number of tubules in the upper portion of the medulla with increased mesenchymal tissue; and tubular distension in the cortex and medulla.[44] Since renal anomalies had not been reported previously, either with diuretics or beta blockers, the investigators concluded that the defects were either a result of reduced renal blood flow secondary to enalapril, or a direct teratogenic effect of the drug.

Other Toxicity

Fetal and neonatal renal failure has been reported frequently following *in utero* exposure to ACE inhibitors.[30] Fetal renal toxicity is characterized by oligohydramnios with the resulting risk of pulmonary hypoplasia and fetal skull defects (see Skull Defects). Newborn infants may present with anuria and severe hypotension that is resistant to volume expansion and pressor agents. Dialysis may be required, but may not achieve a return to normal renal function. The mechanism for the fetal kidney failure may be due to the low renal blood flow and perfusion pressure that occurs normally during gestation.[261] High concentrations of angiotensin II, the formation of which is blocked by enalapril, may be physiologically necessary to maintain fetal renal blood flow at low perfusion pressures.

Based upon the above data, enalapril and hydrochlorothiazide should be deleted from A.R.'s antihypertensive regimen. Other therapy, such as atenolol or labetalol, may be tried to control her elevated blood pressure. Methyldopa and hydralazine also could be considered based upon extensive experience during pregnancy.

Indomethacin

Premature Labor

12. J.B. is 30 weeks pregnant when premature labor is diagnosed. IV magnesium sulfate is administered to stop her uterine contractions and progressive cervical changes. Several attempts to wean her from the IV therapy onto oral terbutaline have failed. Indomethacin, 50 mg one time, then 25 mg Q 6 hr, is started as the magnesium is tapered again. No contractions or cervical changes are noted on this therapy, and the IV magnesium is discontinued. What are the risks to the fetus from indomethacin?

The use of indomethacin for tocolysis has become more common in obstetrics as experience is gained with the therapy. Nonsteroidal anti-inflammatory agents (NSAIDs) and indomethacin have been associated with premature closure of the ductus arteriosus and subsequent primary pulmonary hypertension of the newborn.[30] In severe cases, this can be a fatal complication. Based upon fetal echocardiography, ductal constriction occurred within hours of the first dose and was not correlated with either gestational age or maternal indomethacin serum levels.[78] In some fetuses, tricuspid regurgitation also was observed. Tricuspid regurgitation was attributed to increased pressure in the right ventricular outflow tract caused by ductal constriction and resulted in mild endocardial ischemia with papillary muscle dysfunction. However, all of the cases evaluated by echocardiography returned to normal physiology within 24 to 40 hours of stopping indomethacin. Reduced fetal urine output with subsequent oligohydramnios has been encountered when indomethacin was used as a tocolytic agent. In premature infants exposed to the drug immediately before delivery, anuria, hemorrhage, and intestinal perforation have developed.[30] Infants exposed *in utero* to indomethacin and who are delivered at, or before, 30 weeks gestation have a significantly increased risk for necrotizing enterocolitis, intracranial hemorrhage grade II to IV, and patent ductus arteriosus that may require surgical correction.[262] Exposed infants also can have lower urine output and higher serum creatinine concentrations during the first three days of life.[262] In most cases, however, short-term therapy (24 to 48 hours) has not been associated with toxicity in the newborn if allowance is made for at least 24 hours or more between the last dose and delivery. This often is adequate time to change the patient to oral betamimetic therapy (e.g., ritodrine or terbutaline), or to allow the patient to be controlled as an outpatient with the investigational use of pump-administered subcutaneous terbutaline.

Polyhydramnios

13. M.M. is in her 26th week of gestation when polyhydramnios and premature uterine contractions are diagnosed. How might the use of indomethacin differ in M.M.'s from J.B.'s case?

One of the effects of indomethacin on the fetus is reduced renal output. In most cases, this drug effect would be considered detrimental to the fetus. In M.M., however, reduced fetal urine output is therapeutic because fetal urine is the major component of amniotic fluid. Decompression (i.e., mechanical removal of excess amniotic fluid) can be attempted, but often the condition quickly recurs. In a limited number of both published and unpublished cases, long-term therapy (2 to 11 weeks) with indomethacin has resolved the condition without producing fetal or newborn toxicity.[30] Fetal echocardiography has been used in conjunction with the therapy to ensure that the ductus arteriosus remained patent.

Interaction with Beta Blockers

14. T.V., a patient, similar to M.M., also was being treated with atenolol for hypertension. How would this complication have changed the planned therapy with indomethacin?

An interaction between indomethacin and beta blockers resulted in severe maternal hypertension in two women.[263] In both cases, a marked rise in blood pressure, to 240/140 mm Hg in the mother treated with propranolol and to 230/130 mm Hg in the patient treated with pindolol, occurred on the fourth and fifth days of combined treatment, respectively. The mechanism of the interaction is unknown, but one reference source has described several other cases of this interaction.[264] Since fetal distress occurred in both of the above cases, presumably due to reduced placental blood flow, long-term therapy with indomethacin should not be attempted in patients receiving beta blockers.

Beta Blockers and Breast-Feeding

15. B.B., a 38-year-old woman, developed hypertension in the postpartum period. She is nursing her newborn infant. B.B.'s internist plans to start acebutolol for her hypertension. Is this beta blocker a good antihypertensive for a nursing patient?

Acebutolol (Sectral) accumulates in milk to a greater degree than other beta blockers.[30] The M:P ratios of acebutolol and its metabolite, N-acetylacebutolol, are 7.1:1 and 12.2:1, respectively. Other available beta blockers that also accumulate in milk are atenolol (Tenormin), metoprolol (Lopressor), and nadolol (Corgard).

Pindolol (Visken) is probably excreted in milk but an M:P ratio has not been determined. Timolol (Blocadren) and propranolol (Inderal) have M:P ratios of 0.8 and 0.2 to 1.5, respectively, while oxprenolol, which has been approved for the treatment of hypertension but is not marketed in the U.S., has M:P ratios of 0.14 to 0.43. In a report involving seven breast-feeding women receiving chronic acebutolol therapy, one neonate had symptoms of beta-blockade including hypotension, bradycardia, and tachypnea.[146] Because of this, acebutolol probably should not be used for the treatment of B.B.'s hypertension. Beta-blockade in a nursing infant also has been described with atenolol.[147] Based entirely upon milk levels, either timolol or propranolol would be better choices to treat the hypertension. However, other factors such as cost, maternal side effects, convenience, efficacy, and predicted compliance also must be considered. B.B.'s infant should be monitored closely for hypotension, bradycardia, and other signs or symptoms of beta-blockade.

Methylene Blue and Indigo Carmine

16. Methylene blue has been ordered for B.D., a woman at 35 weeks gestation. The dye is to be injected into the amniotic fluid to assist in the diagnosis of premature rupture of the membranes. What are the fetal risks from this use and would indigo carmine be a better choice?

The dark blue dye, methylene blue, has been injected intra-amniotically to help visualize the leakage of amniotic fluid into the vagina, an indication that rupture of the membranes has occurred. This use has been associated with hemolytic anemia, hyperbilirubinemia, and methemoglobinemia in the newborn.[30] Moreover, if delivery occurs shortly after injection, the newborn will be stained a deep blue that will impair the clinical assessment of hypoxia.[265] The staining is reversible, but may require several weeks to dissipate. Use of methylene blue in the second trimester by injection into one of the amniotic sacs of twin pregnancies has been associated with multiple ileal occlusions and jejunal atresia.[266-268] In contrast, none of the toxicities described for methylene blue have been observed after the use of indigo carmine. This diagnostic dye, therefore, is a better choice.

Glossary

Adactyly: A developmental anomaly characterized by the absence of digits on the hand or foot.

Alopecia: Baldness; absence of hair from skin areas where it normally is present.

Amelia: Congenital absence of a limb or limbs.

Anencephaly: Congenital absence of the cranial vault, with cerebral hemispheres completely missing or reduced to small masses attached to the base of the skull.

Aneuploidy: Any deviation from an exact multiple of the haploid number of chromosomes, whether few or more; individuals exhibiting aneuploidy are usually abnormal physiologically and morphologically.

Angioma: A tumor whose cells tend to form in blood or lymph vessels.

Aplasia Cutis: Localized failure of development of skin, most commonly of the scalp, less frequently of the trunk and limbs; the defects are usually covered by a thin translucent membrane or scar tissue, or may be raw, ulcerated, or covered by granulation tissue.

Arthrogryposis: Persistent flexure or contracture of a joint.

Bifid Xiphoid: Cleft of the xiphoid process into two parts.

Blastula: The usually spherical structure produced by cleavage of a fertilized ovum, consisting of a single layer of cells (blastoderm) surrounding a fluid-filled cavity (blastocoele).

Blepharophimosis: Abnormal narrowness of the palpebral fissure in the horizontal direction, caused by lateral displacement of the inner canthi.

Brachycephaly: The fact or quality of having a short head, with a cephalic index of 81.0 to 85.4.

Calvaria Hypoplasia: Failure of the domelike superior portion of the cranium to form.

Choanal Atresia: Congenital bony or membranous occlusion of one or both choanae, due to failure of the embryonic bucconasal membrane to rupture.

Coloboma: An apparent absence or defect of some ocular tissue, usually resulting from a failure of a part of the fetal fissure to close.

Chorioretinitis: Inflammation of the choroid and retina.

Coronal: Pertaining to the crown of the head.

Corpus Callosum: An arched mass of white matter found in the depths of the longitudinal fissure, composed of transverse fibers connecting the cerebral hemispheres.

Cryptorchidism: A developmental defect characterized by failure of the testes to descend into the scrotum.

Cutis Laxa: A congenital hereditary disorder in which the skin and subcutaneous tissues hypertrophy, the skin hanging in folds as a result.

Dandy-Walker Malformation: Congenital hydrocephalus due to obstruction of the foramina of Magendie and Luschka.

Dermatoglyphics: The study of the patterns of ridges of the skin of the fingers, palms, toes, and soles; may be a clinical and genetic indicator, particularly of chromosomal abnormalities.

Diastasis Recti: Separation of the rectus muscles of the abdominal wall.

Diplegia: Paralysis affecting like parts on both sides of the body; bilateral paralysis.

Ebstein's Anomaly: A malfunction of the tricuspid valve, the septal and posterior leaflets being attached to the wall of the right ventricle to a varying degree, and the anterior leaflet being normally attached to the anulus fibrosis.

Ectromelia: Gross hypoplasia or aplasia of one or more long bones of one or more limbs; the term includes amelia, hemimelia, and phocomelia.

Encephalocele: Hernia of the brain, manifested by protrusion of brain substance through a congenital or traumatic opening of the skull.

Epicanthal Folds: See Epicanthus.

Epicanthus: A vertical fold of skin on either side of the nose, sometimes covering the inner canthus; it is present as a normal characteristic in persons of certain races and sometimes occurs as a congenital anomaly in others.

Epididymal Cyst: A cyst of the elongated cordlike structure along the posterior border of the testis, in the ducts of which the spermatozoa are stored.

Epispadias: A congenital defect in which the urethra opens on the dorsum of the penis.

Exencephaly: A developmental anomaly characterized by an imperfect cranium, the brain lying outside of the skull.

Hamartoblastoma: A tumor developing from a hamartoma.

Hamartoma: A benign tumor-like nodule composed of an overgrowth of mature cells and tissues that normally occur in the affected part, but often with one element predominating.

Hemangioma: A benign tumor made up of new-formed blood vessels.

Hydrocele: A collection of fluid in the tunica vaginalis of the testicle or along the spermatic cord.

Hydrocephalus: A condition characterized by abnormal accumulation of fluid in the cranial vault, accompanied by enlargement of the head, prominence of the forehead, atrophy of the brain, mental deterioration, and convulsions.

Hydronephrosis: Distention of the pelvis and calices of the kidney with urine, as a result of obstruction of the ureter, with accompanying atrophy of the parenchyma of the organ.

Hydrops Fetalis: The abnormal accumulation of serous fluid in the entire body of the newborn infant.

Hydroureter: Abnormal distention of the ureter with urine or with a watery fluid.

Hypertrichosis Lanuginosa: Excessive growth of hair on the body of the fetus.

Hypognathia: Having a protruding lower jaw.

Hypospadias: A developmental anomaly in the male in which the urethra opens on the under side of the penis or on the perineum.

Imperforate Anus: Abnormally closed anus.

IUGR: Intrauterine growth retardation.

Klippel-Feil Anomaly: A condition characterized by shortness of the neck resulting from reduction in the number of cervical vertebrae or the fusion of multiple hemivertebrae into one osseous mass; the hairline is low and motion of the neck is limited.

Macrosomia: Greatly increased body size.

Meckel's Diverticulum: An occasional socculation or appendage of the ileum, derived from an unobliterated yolk stalk.

Megacolon: Abnormally large or dilated colon.

Meningoencephalocele: Hernial protrusion of the meninges and brain substance through a defect in the skull.

Meningomyelocele: Hernial protrusion of a part of the meninges and substance of the spinal cord through a defect in the vertebral column.

Microcephaly: Abnormal smallness of the head, usually associated with mental retardation.

Micrognathia: Unusual or undue smallness of the jaws.

Microphallus: Abnormal smallness of the penis.

Microphthalmia: Abnormal smallness of the eyes.

Microtia: Gross hypoplasia or aplasia of the pinna of the ear, with a blind or absent external auditory meatus.

Müllerian Duct: Ductus paramesonephricus; either of the paired embryonic ducts arising as a peritoneal pocket, extending caudally to join the urogenital sinus, and developing into uterine tubes and uterus.

Myelomeningocele: Hernial protrusion of the spinal cord and its meninges through a defect in the vertebral canal.

Myeloschisis: A developmental anomaly characterized by a cleft spinal cord, owing to failure of the neural plate to form a complete tube.

Myoclonia: Any disorder characterized by myoclonus.

Myoclonus: Shock-like contractions of a muscle.

Myotomes: The muscle plate or portion of a somite that develops into voluntary muscle.

Neuropore: The open anterior end or the posterior end of the neural tube of the early embryo; openings gradually close as the tube develops.

Nevus: A circumscribed stable malformation of the skin and occasionally of the oral mucosa, which is not due to external causes; excess (or deficiency) of tissue may involve epidermal, connective tissue, adnexal, nervous, or bascular elements.

Ocular Hypertelorism: Abnormal increase in the interorbital distance.

Oligodactyly: A developmental anomaly characterized by a smaller-than-usual number of fingers or toes.

Oligohydramnios: The presence of <300 mL of amniotic fluid at term.

Omphalocele: Protrusion, at birth, of part of the intestine through a large defect in the abdominal wall at the umbilicus, the protruding bowel being covered only by a thin transparent membrane composed of amnion and peritoneum.

Oxycephaly: A condition in which the top of the head is pointed.

Palpebral Fissures: The longitudinal opening between the eyelids.

Pectus Carinatum: Undue prominence of the sternum; also called chicken or pigeon breast.

Pectus Excavatum: Undue depression of the sternum; also called funnel breast or chest.

Philtrum: The vertical groove in the median portion of the upper lip, a part of the prolabium.

Phimosis: Tightness of the foreskin, so that it cannot be drawn back from over the glans; also the analogous condition in the clitoris.

Phocomelia: A developmental anomaly characterized by absence of the proximal portion of a limb or limbs, the hands or feet being attached to the trunk of the body by a single small, irregularly shaped bone.

Pierre Robin Syndrome: Micrognathia in association with cleft palate and glossoptosis, and with absent gag reflex.

Placode: A plate-like structure, especially a thickened plate of ectoderm in the early embryo, from which a sense organ develops.

Polydactyly: A developmental anomaly characterized by the presence of supernumerary digits (fingers or toes) on the hands or feet.

Polyhydramnios: An excess of amniotic fluid, called also hydramnios.

Potter Facies: A facial condition resembling that seen in Potter syndrome (oligohydramnios due to renal agenesis) and caused by a lack of amniotic fluid and resulting fetal compression.

Prognathia: Having projecting jaws.

Rathke's Pouch: A diverticulum from the embryonic buccal cavity, from which the anterior lobe of the pituitary gland is developed.

Retrognathia: Position of the jaws back of the frontal plane of the forehead.

Rhizomelic Dwarfing: A dwarfing pertaining to or involving the hip joint and shoulder joint.

Sacculus: The smaller of the two divisions of the membranous labyrinth of the vestibule, which communicates with the cochlear duct by way of the ductus reuniens.

Scoliosis: An appreciable lateral deviation in the normally straight vertical line of the spine.

Simian Crease: A single transverse palmar crease formed by fusion of the proximal and distal palmar creases.

Somite: One of the paired, block-like masses of mesoderm, arranged segmentally alongside the neural tube of the embryo, forming the vertebral column and segmented musculature.

Spina Bifida: A developmental anomaly characterized by defective closure of the bony encasement of the spinal cord through which the cord and meninges may or may not protrude.

Syndactyly: The most common congenital anomaly of the hand, marked by persistence of the webbing between adjacent digits, so they are more or less completely attached.

Synostosis: A union between adjacent bones or parts of a single bone formed by osseous material, such as ossified connecting cartilage or fibrous tissue.

Talipes: A congenital deformity of the foot, which is twisted out shape or position; also called clubfoot.

Talipes Equinovarus: A deformity of the foot in which the heel is turned inward from the midline of the leg and the foot is plantar flexed.

Tetralogy of Fallot: A combination of congenital cardiac defects consisting of pulmonary stenosis; interventricular septal defect; dextroposition of the aorta so that it overrides the interventricular septum and receives venous as well as arterial blood; and right ventricular hypertrophy.

Utriculus: The larger of the two divisions of the membranous labyrinth, located in the posterosuperior region of the vestibule; the major organ of the vestibular system.

Varicocele: A varicose condition of the veins of the pampiniform plexus, forming a swelling that feels like a ''bag of worms,'' appearing bluish through the skin of the scrotum, and accompanied by a constant pulling, dragging, or dull pain in the scrotum.

Vermilion Border: The exposed red portion of the upper or lower lip.

Wolffian Duct: Ductus mesonephricus; mesonephric duct, an embryonic duct initiated in association with rudiments of the pronephric kidney, taken over as excretory duct by the mesonephros, developed into various ducts of the reproductive system in the male and into vestigial structures in the female.

References

1 Kalter H, Warkany J. Congenital malformations. Etiologic factors and their role in prevention. Part I. N Engl J Med. 1983;308:424.

2 Nishimura H, Tanimura T. Clinical Aspects of the Teratogenicity of Drugs. New York, NY: American Elsevier; 1976.

3 Shepard TH. Teratogenicity from drugs—an increasing problem. Dis Mon. 1984 June.

4 Shepard TH. Teratogenicity of therapeutic agents. Curr Prob Pediatr. 1979; 10(#2).

5 Oakley GP Jr. Frequency of human congenital malformations. Clin Perinatol. 1986;13:545.

6 Thelander HE. Interference with organogenesis and fetal development. Tex Rep Biol Med. 1973;31:4.

7 Stevenson AC et al. Congenital malformations. A report of a series of consecutive births in 24 centres. WHO Bull. 1966;34(Suppl.):9.

8 Centers for Disease Control. Premature mortality due to congenital anomalies—United States. MMWR. 1988; 37:505.

9 Nora JJ et al. Maternal exposure to potential teratogens. JAMA. 1967;202: 91.

10 Nelson MM, Forfar JO. Associations between drugs administered during pregnancy and congenital abnormalities of the fetus. Br Med J. 1971;1:523.

11 Hill RM. Drugs ingested by pregnant women. Clin Pharmacol Ther. 1973; 14:654.

12 Kullander S et al. Exposure to drugs and other possible harmful factors during the first trimester of pregnancy. Comparison of two prospective studies performed in Sweden 10 years apart. Acta Obstet Gynecol Scand. 1976;55: 395.

13 Degenhardt KH et al. Drug usage and fetal development: preliminary evaluations of a prospective investigation. Adv Exp Med Biol. 1972;27:467.

14 Richards IDG. A retrospective enquiry into possible teratogenic effects of drugs in pregnancy. Adv Exp Med Biol. 1972;27:441.

15 Medalie JH et al. The use of medicines before and during pregnancy—preliminary results from an epidemiological study of congenital defects. Adv Exp Med Biol. 1972;27:481.

16 Forfar JO, Nelson MM. Epidemiology of drugs taken by pregnant women: drugs that may affect the fetus adversely. Clin Pharmacol Ther. 1973;14: 632.

17 Doering PL, Stewart RB. The extent and character of drug consumption during pregnancy. JAMA. 1978;239:843.

18 Bleyer WA et al. Studies on the detection of adverse drug reactions in the newborn. I. Fetal exposure to maternal medication. JAMA. 1970;213:2046.

19 Bodendorfer TW et al. Obtaining drug exposure histories during pregnancy. Am J Obstet Gynecol. 1979; 135:490.

20 Moya F, Thorndike V. Passage of drugs across the placenta. Am J Obstet Gynecol. 1962;84:1778.

21 Smith NT, Corbascio AN. The use and misuse of pressor agents. Anesthesiology. 1970;33:58.

22 Hill LM. Effects of drugs and chemicals on the fetus and newborn. Part I. Mayo Clin Proc. 1984;59:707.

23 Fabro S et al. Chemical exposure of embryos during the preimplantation stages of pregnancy: mortality rate and intrauterine development. Am J Obstet Gynecol. 1984;148:929.

24 Beckman DA, Brent RL. Mechanism of known environmental teratogens: drugs and chemicals. Clinics Perinatol. 1986;13:649–97.

25 Carter CO. Genetics of common single malformations. Br Med Bull. 1976; 32:21.

26 Kalter H, Warkany J. Congenital malformations. Part II. N Engl J Med. 1983;308:491.

27 Mims C. Comparative aspects of infective malformations. Br Med Bull. 1976;32:84.

28 Dudgeon JA. Infective causes of human malformations. Br Med Bull. 1976;32:77.

29 **Shepard TH.** Catalog of Teratogenic Agents. 7th ed. Baltimore, MD: Johns Hopkins University Press; 1992.

30 **Briggs GG et al.** Drugs in Pregnancy and Lactation. A Reference Guide to Fetal and Neonatal Risk. 4th ed. Baltimore, MD: Williams & Wilkins; 1994.

31 **Heinonen OP et al.** Birth Defects and Drugs in Pregnancy. Littleton: Publishing Sciences Group; 1977.

32 **Golden NL et al.** Propoxyphene and acetaminophen: possible effects on the fetus. Clin Pediatr. 1982;21:752.

33 **Key TC et al.** Successful pregnancy after cardiac transplantation. Am J Obstet Gynecol. 1989;160:367.

34 **Barry WS, St Clair SM.** Exposure to benzodiazepines in utero. Lancet. 1987; 1:1436.

35 **Anderson PO, McGuire GG.** Neonatal alprazolam withdrawal—possible effects of breast feeding. DICP Ann Pharmacother. 1989;23:614.

36 **Nora JJ et al.** Cardiovascular maldevelopment associated with maternal exposure to amantadine. Lancet. 1975; 2:607.

37 **Duminy PC et al.** Fetal abnormality associated with the use of captopril during pregnancy. S Afr Med J. 1981; 60:805.

38 **Laurent M et al.** Neonatal hypothyroidism after treatment by amiodarone during pregnancy. Am J Cardiol. 1987; 60:942.

39 **Zierler S, Rothman KJ.** Congenital heart disease in relation to maternal use of Bendectin and other drugs in early pregnancy. N Engl J Med. 1985;313: 347.

40 **Falterman CG, Richardson CJ.** Small left colon syndrome associated with maternal ingestion of psychotropic drugs. J Pediatr. 1980;97:308.

41 **Raffles A et al.** Transplacental effects of maternal cancer chemotherapy: case report. Br J Obstet Gynaecol. 1989;96: 1099.

42 **Zierler S, Purohit D.** Prenatal antihistamine exposure and retrolental fibroplasia. Am J Epidemiol. 1986;123:192.

43 **Weisberg M.** Treatment of vaginal candidiasis in pregnant women. Clin Ther. 1986;8:563.

44 **Cunniff C et al.** Oligohydramnios sequence and renal tubular malformation associated with maternal enalapril use. Am J Obstet Gynecol. 1990;162:187.

45 **Rosa FW et al.** Neonatal anuria with maternal angiotensin-converting enzyme inhibition. Obstet Gynecol. 1989; 74:371.

46 **Brent RL, Beckman DA.** Angiotensin-converting enzyme inhibitors, an embryopathic class of drugs with unique properties: information for clinical teratology counselors. Teratology. 1991;43:543.

47 **Niebly JR et al.** Carbamazepine levels in pregnancy and lactation. Obstet Gynecol. 1979;53:139.

48 **Pitkin RM.** Calcium metabolism in pregnancy and the perinatal period: a review. Am J Obstet Gynecol. 1985; 151:99.

49 **Jones KL et al.** Pattern of malformations in the children of women treated with carbamazepine during pregnancy. N Engl J Med. 1989;320:1661.

50 **Jones KL et al.** Teratogenic effects of carbamazepine. N Engl J Med. 1989; 321:1481.

51 **Oberheuser F.** Praktische erfahrungen mit medikamenten in der schwangerschaft. Therapiewoche. 1971;31:2200. As reported in Manten A. Antibiotic drugs. In: Dukes MNG, ed. Meyler's Side Effects of Drugs, Vol VIII. New York: American Elsevier; 1975:604.

52 **Anon.** Malaria in pregnancy. Lancet. 1983;2:84.

53 **Strang A et al.** Malaria in pregnancy with fatal complications: case report. Br J Obstet Gynaecol. 1984;91:399.

54 **Pedler SJ, Bint AJ.** Comparative study of amoxicillin-clavulanic acid and cephalexin in the treatment of bacteriuria during pregnancy. Antimicrob Agents Chemother. 1985;27:508.

55 **Cowe L et al.** Neonatal convulsions caused by withdrawal from maternal clomipramine. Br Med J. 1982;284: 1837.

56 **Fisher JB et al.** Neonatal apnea associated with maternal clonazepam therapy: a case report. Obstet Gynecol. 1985;66(Suppl.):34S.

57 **Patel DA, Patel AR.** Clorazepate and congenital malformations. JAMA. 1980; 244:135.

58 **Saxen I.** Cleft palate and maternal diphenhydramine intake. Lancet. 1974;1: 407.

59 **Rosa FW.** Virilization of the female fetus with maternal danazol exposure. Am J Obstet Gynecol. 1984;149:99.

60 **Rivas F et al.** Acentric craniofacial cleft in a newborn female prenatally exposed to a high dose of diazepam. Teratology. 1984;30:179.

61 **Leonard RF et al.** Initiation of uterine contractions by disopyramide during pregnancy. N Engl J Med. 1978;299:84.

62 **Karp GI et al.** Doxorubicin in pregnancy: possible transplacental passage. Cancer Treat Rep. 1983;67:773.

63 **Eskenazi B, Bracken MB.** Bendectin (Debendox) as a risk factor for pyloric stenosis. Am J Obstet Gynecol. 1982; 144:919.

64 **Anon.** Bendectin and pyloric stenosis. FDA Drug Bull. 1983;13:14.

65 **Aselton P et al.** First-trimester drug use and congenital disorders. Obstet Gynecol. 1985;65:451.

66 **Mitchell AA et al.** Birth defects in relation to Bendectin use in pregnancy. II. Pyloric stenosis. Am J Obstet Gynecol. 1983;147:737.

67 **Wiseman RA, Dodds-Smith IC.** Cardiovascular birth defects and antenatal exposure to female sex hormones: a reevaluation of some base data. Teratology. 1984;30:359.

68 **Lee BE et al.** Congenital malformations in an infant born to a woman treated with fluconazole. Pediatr Infect Dis J. 1992;11:1062.

69 **Stephens JD et al.** Multiple congenital anomalies in a fetus exposed to 5-fluorouracil during the first trimester. Am J Obstet Gynecol. 1980;137:747.

70 **Cooper GL.** The safety of fluoxetine—an update. Br J Psychiatry. 1988; 153(Suppl. 3):77.

71 **Friedman JM et al.** Potential human teratogenicity of frequently prescribed drugs. Obstet Gynecol. 1990;75:594.

72 **CDC.** Use of folic acid for prevention of spina bifida and other neural tube defects—1983–1991. MMWR. 1991; 40:513.

73 **CDC.** Recommendations for the use of folic acid to reduce the number of cases of spina bifida and other neural tube defects. MMWR. 1992;41:1.

74 **Barkhof F et al.** Inadvertent IV administration of gadopentetate dimeglumine during early pregnancy. AJR. 1992;158:1171.

75 **Rosa FW et al.** Griseofulvin teratology, including two thoracopagus conjoined twins. Lancet. 1987;1:171.

76 **Widerlov E et al.** Hydralazine-induced neonatal thrombocytopenia. N Engl J Med. 1980;303:1235.

77 **Roubenoff R et al.** Effects of antiinflammatory and immunosuppressive drugs on pregnancy and fertility. Semin Arthritis Rheum. 1988;18:88.

78 **Moise KJ Jr et al.** Indomethacin in the treatment of premature labor: effects on the fetal ductus arteriosus. N Engl J Med. 1988;319:327.

79 **Dignan PSJ.** Teratogenic risk and counseling in diabetes. Clin Obstet Gynecol. 1981;24:149.

80 **Willman SP et al.** Glucose threshold for macrosomia in pregnancy complicated by diabetes. Am J Obstet Gynecol. 1986;154:470.

81 **American Thoracic Society.** Treatment of tuberculosis and tuberculosis infection in adults and children. Am Rev Respir Dis. 1986;134:355.

82 **Medchill MT, Gillum M.** Diagnosis and management of tuberculosis during pregnancy. Obstet Gynecol Surv. 1989; 44:81.

83 **Lammer EJ et al.** Retinoic acid embryopathy. N Engl J Med. 1985;313: 837.

84 **Minkoff HL.** Care of pregnant women infected with human immunodeficiency virus. JAMA. 1987;258:2714.

85 **Ghidini A et al.** Congenital abnormalities (VATER) in baby born to mother using lovastatin. Lancet. 1992;339: 1416.

86 **Robinson LL et al.** Maternal drug use and risk of childhood nonlymphoblastic leukemia among offspring: an epidemiologic investigation implicating marijuana (a report from the Childrens Cancer Study Group). Cancer. 1989; 63:1904.

87 **Milham S Jr.** Scalp defects in infants of mothers treated for hyperthyroidism with methimazole or carbimazole during pregnancy. Teratology. 1985;32: 321.

88 **Walden PAM, Bagshawe KD.** Pregnancies after chemotherapy for gestational trophoblastic tumours. Lancet. 1979;2:1241.

89 **Myerscough PR.** Infant growth and development after treatment of maternal hypertension. Lancet. 1980;1:883.

90 **Moar VA et al.** Neonatal head circumference and the treatment of maternal hypertension. Br J Obstet Gynaecol. 1978;85:933.

91 **Dunsted M et al.** Infant growth and development following treatment of maternal hypertension. Lancet. 1980;1: 705.

92 **Finegold SM.** Metronidazole. Ann Intern Med. 1980;93:585.

93 **Beard CM et al.** Lack of evidence for cancer due to use of metronidazole. N Engl J Med. 1979;301:519.

94 **Rosa FW et al.** Pregnancy outcomes after first-trimester vaginitis drug therapy. Obstet Gynecol. 1987;69:751.

95 **Cantu JM, Garcia-Cruz D.** Midline facial defect as a teratogenic effect of metronidazole. Birth Defects. 1982;18: 85.

96 **Giknis MLA, Damjanov I.** The transplacental effects of ethanol and metronidazole in Swiss-Webster mice. Toxicol Lett. 1983;19:37.

97 **Valdivieso A et al.** Minoxidil in breast milk. Ann Intern Med. 1985;102:135.

98 **Kaler SG et al.** Hypertrichosis and congenital anomalies associated with maternal use of minoxidil. Pediatrics. 1987;79:434.

99 **Rosa FW et al.** Fetal minoxidil exposure. Pediatrics. 1987;79:434.

100 **Lindow SW et al.** The effect of sublingual nifedipine on uteroplacental blood flow in hypertensive pregnancy. Br J Obstet Gynaecol. 1988;95:1276.

101 **Walters BNJ, Redman CWG.** Treatment of severe pregnancy-associated hypertension with the calcium antagonist nifedipine. Br J Obstet Gynaecol. 1984;91:330.

102 **Constantine G et al.** Nifedipine as a second line antihypertensive drug in pregnancy. Br J Obstet Gynaecol. 1987;94:1136.

103 **Snyder SW, Cardwell MS.** Neuromuscular blockade with magnesium sulfate and nifedipine. Am J Obstet Gynecol. 1989;161:35.

104 **Waisman GD et al.** Magnesium plus nifedipine: potentiation of hypotensive effect in preeclampsia? Am J Obstet Gynecol. 1988;159:308.

105 **Anon.** Data do not support association between spermicides, birth defects. FDA Drug Bull. 1986;16:21.

106 **Guikontes E et al.** Ondansetron and hyperemesis gravidarum. Lancet. 1992; 340:1223.

107 **World MJ.** Ondansetron and hyperemesis gravidarum. Lancet. 1993;341: 185.

108 **Baxi LV et al.** Fetal heart rate changes following maternal administration of a nasal decongestant. Am J Obstet Gynecol. 1985;153:799.

109 **Ostensen M, Husby G.** Antirheumatic drug treatment during pregnancy and lactation. Scand J Rheumatol. 1985; 14:1.

110 **Committee on Drugs, American Academy of Pediatrics.** Adverse reactions to iodide therapy of asthma and other pulmonary diseases. Pediatrics. 1976;57:272.

111 **Lammer EJ, Cordero JF.** Exogenous sex hormone exposure and the risk for major malformations. JAMA. 1986; 255:3128.

112 **Barrow MV, Souder DE.** Propoxyphene and congenital malformations. JAMA. 1971;217:1551.

113 **Ringrose CAD.** The hazard of neurotrophic drugs in the fertile years. Can Med Assoc J. 1972;106:1058.

114 **Vevera J, Zatlovkal F.** Pripad uruzenych malformact zpusobenych pravdepodobne atebrinem-ym uranen tehotenstui. In: Nishmura H, Tanimura T, eds. Clinical Aspects of the Teratogenicity of Drugs. New York: American Elsevier; 1976:145.

115 **Kirshon B et al.** Favorable outcome after treatment with amantadine and ribavirin in a pregnancy complicated by influenza pneumonia: a case report. J Reprod Med. 1988;33:399.

116 **Centers for Disease Control.** Assessing exposures of health-care personnel to aerosols of ribavirin—California. MMWR. 1988;37:560.

117 **Steen JSM, Stainton-Ellis DM.** Rifampicin in pregnancy. Lancet. 1977;2:604.

118 **Nabors LO.** Letter to the editors. J Reprod Med. 1988;33:102.

119 **London RS.** Saccharin and aspartame: are they safe to consume during pregnancy? J Reprod Med. 1988;33:17.

120 **Council on Scientific Affairs, American Medical Association.** Saccharin: review of safety issues. JAMA. 1985;254:2622.

121 **London RS.** Letter to the editors. J Reprod Med. 1988;33:102.

122 **Lowenthal RM et al.** Normal infant after combination chemotherapy including teniposide for Burkitt's lymphoma in pregnancy. Med Pediatr Oncol. 1982;10:165.

123 **Horowitz DA et al.** Apnea associated with theophylline withdrawal in a term neonate. Am J Dis Child. 1982;136:73.

124 **Gililland J, Weinstein L.** The effects of cancer chemotherapeutic agents on the developing fetus. Obstet Gynecol Surv. 1983;38:6.

125 **Walshe JM.** The management of pregnancy in Wilson's disease treated with trientine. Q J Med. 1986;58:81.

126 **Koutras A, Fisher S.** Niikawa-Kuroki syndrome: a new malformation syndrome of postnatal dwarfism, mental retardation, unusual face, and protruding ears. J Pediatr. 1982;101:417.

127 **Lammer EJ et al.** Teratogen update: valproic acid. Teratology. 1987;35:465.

128 **DiLiberti JH et al.** The fetal valproate syndrome. Am J Med Genet. 1984;19:473.

129 **Ardinger HH et al.** Verification of the fetal valproate syndrome phenotype. Am J Med Genet. 1988;29:171.

130 **Jager-Roman E et al.** Fetal growth, major malformations, and minor anomalies in infants born to women receiving valproic acid. J Pediatr. 1986;108:997.

131 **Hillard P et al.** Disseminated herpes simplex in pregnancy: two cases and a review. Obstet Gynecol Surv. 1982;37:449.

132 **Peacock JE Jr, Sarubbi FA.** Disseminated herpes simplex virus infection during pregnancy. Obstet Gynecol. 1983;61(Suppl.):13S.

133 **Berger SA et al.** Herpes encephalitis during pregnancy: failure of acyclovir and adenine arabinoside to prevent neonatal herpes. Isr J Med Sci. 1986;22:41.

134 **Landsberger EJ et al.** Successful management of varicella pneumonia complicating pregnancy: a report of three cases. J Reprod Med. 1986;31:311.

135 **Rosa FW et al.** Teratogen update: vitamin A congeners. Teratology. 1986;33:355.

136 **Centers for Disease Control.** Use of supplements containing high-dose vitamin A—New York state, 1983–1984. MMWR. 1987;36:80.

137 **Wilson JT.** Prevalence and advantages of breast feeding. In: Wilson JT, ed. Drugs in Breast Milk. Sydney: ADIS Press; 1981:3.

138 **Berglund F et al.** Drug use during pregnancy and breast-feeding. Acta Obstet Gynecol Scand. 1984;126 (Suppl.):11.

139 **Wilson JT.** Production and characteristics of breast milk. In: Wilson JT. Drugs in Breast Milk. Sydney: ADIS Press; 1981:4.

140 **Wilson JT.** Pharmacokinetics of drug excretion. In: Wilson JT, ed. Drugs in Breast Milk. Sydney: ADIS Press; 1981:15,31.

141 **Dailey JW.** Anticoagulant and cardiovascular drugs. In: Wilson JT, ed. Drugs in Breast Milk. Sydney: ADIS Press; 1981:61.

142 **Lawrence RA.** Breast-Feeding. A Guide For the Medical Profession. St Louis: The C.V. Mosby Company; 1980.

143 **FDA.** Federal Register. 1980;44:37434.

144 **Wilson JT.** Pharmacokinetics of drug excretion. In: Wilson JT, ed. Drugs in Breast Milk. Sydney: ADIS Press; 1981:16.

145 **Committee on Drugs.** American Academy of Pediatrics. The transfer of drugs and other chemicals into human milk. Pediatrics. 1994;93:137.

146 **Boutroy MJ et al.** To nurse when receiving acebutolol: is it dangerous for the neonate? Eur J Clin Pharmacol. 1986;30:737.

147 **Schmimmel MS et al.** Toxic effects of atenolol consumed during breast feeding. J Pediatr. 1989;114:476.

148 **Matheson I et al.** Infant rash caused by paracetamol in breast milk? Pediatrics. 1985;76:651.

149 **Soderman P et al.** Acetazolamide excretion into human breast milk. Br J Clin Pharmacol. 1984;17:599.

150 **Lau RJ et al.** Unexpected accumulation of acyclovir in breast milk with estimation of infant exposure. Obstet Gynecol. 1987;69:468.

151 **Meyer LJ et al.** Acyclovir in human breast milk. Am J Obstet Gynecol. 1988;158:586.

152 **Yurchak AM, Jusko WJ.** Theophylline secretion into breast milk. Pediatrics. 1976;57:518.

153 **McKenna WJ et al.** Amiodarone therapy during pregnancy. Am J Cardiol. 1983;51:1231.

154 **Pitcher D et al.** Amiodarone in pregnancy. Lancet. 1983;1:597.

155 **Steiner E et al.** Amphetamine secretion in breast milk. Eur J Clin Pharmacol. 1984;27:123.

156 **Clark JH, Wilson WG.** A 16-day-old breast-fed infant with metabolic acidosis caused by salicylate. Clin Pediatr (Phila). 1981;20:53.

157 **Anderson PO.** Drug use during breast-feeding. Clin Pharm. 1991;10:594.

158 **Mortimer EA Jr.** Drug toxicity from breast milk? Pediatrics. 1977;60:780.

159 **Briggs GG et al.** Excretion of bupropion in breast milk. Ann Pharmacother. 1993;27:431.

160 **Devlin RG, Fleiss PM.** Selective resistance to the passage of captopril into human milk. Clin Pharmacol Ther. 1980;27:250.

161 **Devlin RG, Fleiss PM.** Captopril in human blood and breast milk. J Clin Pharmacol. 1981;21:110.

162 **Akintonwa A et al.** Placental and milk transfer of chloroquine in humans. Ther Drug Monit. 1988;10:147.

163 **Edstein MD et al.** Excretion of chloroquine, dapsone and pyrimethamine in human milk. Br J Clin Pharmacol. 1986;22:733.

164 **Wiles DH et al.** Chlorpromazine levels in plasma and milk of nursing mothers. Br J Clin Pharmacol. 1978;5:272.

165 **Matheson I et al.** Presence of chlorprothixene and its metabolites in breast milk. Eur J Clin Pharmacol. 1984;27:611.

166 **Somogyi A, Gugler R.** Cimetidine excretion into breast milk. Br J Clin Pharmacol. 1979;7:627.

167 **Giamarellou H et al.** Pharmacokinetics of three newer quinolones in pregnant and lactating women. Am J Med. 1989;87(Suppl. 5A):49S.

168 **Cover DL, Mueller BA.** Ciprofloxacin penetration into human breast milk: a case report. Ann Pharmacother. 1990; 24:703.

169 **Gardner DK et al.** Simultaneous concentrations of ciprofloxacin in breast milk and in serum in mother and breast-fed infant. Clin Pharm. 1992;11:352.

170 **De Vries EGE et al.** Excretion of platinum into breast milk. Lancet. 1989;1:497.

171 **Kok THHG et al.** Drowsiness due to clemastine transmitted in breast milk. Lancet. 1982;1:914.

172 **Browne SG, Hogerzeil LM.** "B663" in the treatment of leprosy. Preliminary report of a pilot trial. Lepr Rev. 1962;33:6.

173 **Schimmell MS et al.** Toxic neonatal effects following maternal clomipramine therapy. J Toxicol Clin Toxicol. 1991;29:479.

174 **Hartikainen-Sorri A-L et al.** Pharmacokinetics of clonidine during pregnancy and nursing. Obstet Gynecol. 1987;69:598.

175 **Shannon M et al.** Cocaine exposure among children seen at a pediatric hospital. Pediatrics. 1989;83:337.

176 **Chasnoff IJ et al.** Cocaine intoxication in a breast-fed infant. Pediatrics. 1987; 80:836.

177 **Milunsky JM, Milunsky A.** Breast-feeding during colchicine therapy for familial Mediterranean fever. J Pediatr. 1991;119:164.

178 **Lewis GJ et al.** Successful pregnancy in a renal transplant recipient taking cyclosporin A. Br Med J (Clin Res). 1983;286:603.

179 **Flechner SM et al.** The presence of cyclosporine in body tissues and fluids during pregnancy. Am J Kidney Dis. 1985;5:60.

180 **Lowenstein BR et al.** Successful pregnancy and vaginal delivery after heart transplantation. Am J Obstet Gynecol. 1988;158:589.

181 **Ziegenhagen DJ et al.** Pregnancy under cyclosporine administration after renal transplantation. Dtsch Med Wochenschr. 1988;113:260.

182 **Ellsworth AJ et al.** Disopyramide and N-monodesalkyldisopyramide in serum and breast milk. Drug Intell Clin Pharm. 1989;23:56.

183 **MacKintosh D, Buchanan N.** Excretion of disopyramide in human breast milk. Br J Clin Pharmacol. 1985;19:856.

184 **Barnett DB et al.** Disopyramide and its N-monodesalkyl metabolite in breast milk. Br J Clin Pharmacol. 1982; 14:310.

185 **Hoppu K et al.** Disopyramide and breast feeding. Br J Clin Pharmacol. 1986;21:553.

186 **Matheson I et al.** Respiratory depression caused by N-desmethyldoxepin in breast milk. Lancet. 1985;2:1124.

187 **Kemp J et al.** Excretion of doxepin and N-desmethyldoxepin in human milk. Br J Clin Pharmacol. 1985;20:497.

188 **Snider DE Jr, Powell KE.** Should women taking antituberculosis drugs breast-feed? Arch Intern Med. 1984; 144:589.

189 **Little RE et al.** Maternal alcohol use during breast-feeding and infant mental and motor development at one year. N Engl J Med. 1989;321:425.

190 **Courtney TP et al.** Excretion of famotidine in breast milk. Br J Clin Pharmacol. 1988;26:639P.

191 **Kanto JH et al.** Placental transfer and breast milk levels of flunitrazepam. Curr Ther Res. 1979;26:539.

192 **Kanto JH.** Use of benzodiazepines during pregnancy, labour and lactation, with special reference to pharmacokinetic considerations. Drugs. 1982;23:354.

193 **Isenberg KE.** Excretion of fluoxetine in human breast milk. J Clin Psychiatry. 1990;51:169.

194 **Kirk L, Jorgensen A.** Concentration of cis(z)-flupenthixol in maternal serum, amniotic fluid, umbilical cord serum, and milk. Psychopharmacology (Berlin). 1980;72:107.

195 **Matheson I, Skjaeraasen J.** Milk concentrations of flupentixol, nortriptyline and zuclopenthixol and between-breast differences in two patients. Eur J Clin Pharmacol. 1988;35:217.

196 **Ostensen M et al.** Excretion of gold into human breast milk. Eur J Clin Pharmacol. 1986;31:251.

197 **Stewart RB et al.** Haloperidol excretion in human milk. Am J Psychiatry. 1980;137:849.

198 **Whalley LJ et al.** Haloperidol secreted in breast milk. Br Med J (Clin Res). 1981;282:1746.

199 **Sylvester RK et al.** Excretion of hydroxyurea into milk. Cancer. 1987;60:2177.

200 **Townsend RJ et al.** A study to evaluate the passage of ibuprofen into breast milk. Drug Intell Clin Pharm. 1982;16:482. Abstract.

201 **Weibert RT et al.** Lack of ibuprofen secretion into human milk. Clin Pharm. 1982;1:457.

202 **Townsend RJ et al.** Excretion of ibuprofen into breast milk. Am J Obstet Gynecol. 1984;149:184.

203 **Mehta PS et al.** Congenital iodide goiter and hypothyroidism: a review. Obstet Gynecol Surv. 1983;38:237.

204 **Postellon DC, Aronow R.** Iodine in mother's milk. JAMA. 1982;247:463.

205 **Harclerode J.** The effect of marijuana on reproduction and development. Natl Inst Drug Abuse Res Monogr Ser. 1980;31:137.

206 **Arena JM.** Drugs and chemicals excreted in breast milk. Pediatr Ann. 1980;9:452.

207 **Perez-Reyes M, Wall ME.** Presence of delta-9-tetrahydrocannabinol in human milk. N Engl J Med. 1982;307:819.

208 **Tennes K et al.** Marijuana: prenatal and postnatal exposure in the human. Natl Inst Drug Abuse Res Monogr Ser. 1985;59:48.

209 **Rao TS.** Does mebendazole inhibit lactation? N Z Med J. 1983;96:589.

210 **Edstein MD et al.** Excretion of mefloquine in human breast milk. Chemotherapy (Basel). 1988;34:165.

211 **Centers for Disease Control.** Recommendations for the prevention of malaria among travelers. MMWR. 1990;39:1.

212 **Nelis GF.** Diarrhea due to 5-aminosalicylic acid in breast milk. Lancet. 1989;1:383.

213 **Lewis PJ et al.** Controlled trial of metoclopramide in the initiation of breast feeding. Br J Clin Pharmacol. 1980;9:217.

214 **Pelkonen O et al.** Metoclopramide in breast milk and newborn. Acta Physiol Scand. 1982;(Suppl. 502):62. Abstract.

215 **Kauppila A et al.** Metoclopramide and breast feeding: transfer into milk and the newborn. Eur J Clin Pharmacol. 1983;25:819.

216 **Ilett KF et al.** Excretion of metrizamide in milk. Br J Radiol. 1981;54:537.

217 **Erickson SH et al.** Metronidazole in breast milk. Obstet Gynecol. 1981;57:48.

218 **Clements CJ.** Metronidazole and breast feeding. N Z Med J. 1980;92:329.

219 **Jamali F et al.** Naproxen excretion in breast milk and its uptake by suckling infant. Drug Intell Clin Pharm. 1982;16:475. Abstract.

220 **Jamali F, Stevens DRS.** Naproxen excretion in milk and its uptake by the infant. Drug Intell Clin Pharm. 1983;17:910.

221 **Ehrenkranz RA et al.** Nifedipine transfer into human milk. J Pediatr. 1989;114:478.

222 **Obermeyer BD et al.** Secretion of nizatidine into human breast milk after single and multiple doses. Clin Pharmacol Ther. 1990;47:724.

223 **Witter FR, Smith RV.** The excretion of pentoxifylline and its metabolites into human breast milk. Am J Obstet Gynecol. 1985;151:1094.

224 **Kaufman KR et al.** PCP in amniotic fluid and breast milk: case report. J Clin Psychiatry. 1983;44:269.

225 **Katz FH, Duncan BR.** Entry of prednisone into human milk. N Engl J Med. 1975;293:1154.

226 **McKenzie SA et al.** Secretion of prednisone into breast milk. Arch Dis Child. 1975;50:894.

227 **Ost L et al.** Prednisolone excretion in human milk. J Pediatr. 1985;106:1008.

228 **Pittard WB III, Glazier H.** Procainamide excretion in human milk. J Pediatr. 1983;102:631.

229 **Dailland P et al.** Intravenous propofol during cesarean section: placental transfer, concentrations in breast milk, and neonatal effects. A preliminary study. Anesthesiology. 1989;71:827.

230 **Low LCK et al.** Excretion of carbimazole and propylthiouracil in breast milk. Lancet. 1979;2:1011.

231 **Kampmann JP et al.** Propylthiouracil in human milk. Lancet. 1980;1:736.

232 **Findlay JWA et al.** Pseudoephedrine and triprolidine in plasma and breast milk of nursing mothers. Br J Clin Pharmacol. 1984;18:901.

233 **Holdiness MR.** Antituberculosis drugs and breast-feeding. Arch Intern Med. 1984;144:1888.

234 **Hardell LI et al.** Pyridostigmine in human breast milk. Br J Clin Pharmacol. 1982;14:565.

235 **Clyde DF et al.** Transfer of pyrimethamine in human milk. J Trop Med Hyg. 1956;59:277.

236 **Hill LM, Malkasian GD Jr.** The use of quinidine sulfate throughout pregnancy. Obstet Gynecol. 1979;54:366.

237 **Riley AJ et al.** Transfer of ranitidine to biological fluids: milk and semen. In: Misiewicz JJ, Wormsley KG, eds. Proceedings of the 2nd International Symposium on Ranitidine. London, Oxford: Medicine Publishing Foundation; 1981:78.

238 **O'Hare MF et al.** Sotalol as a hypotensive agent in pregnancy. Br J Obstet Gynaecol. 1980;87:814.

239 **Wagner X et al.** Coadministration of flecainide acetate and sotalol during pregnancy: lack of teratogenic effects, passage across the placenta, and excretion in human breast milk. Am Heart J. 1990;119:700.

240 **Hackett LP et al.** Excretion of sotalol in breast milk. Br J Clin Pharmacol. 1990;29:277.

241 **Lonnerholm G, Lindstrom B.** Terbutaline excretion into breast milk. Br J Clin Pharmacol. 1982;13:729.

242 **Boreus LO et al.** Terbutaline in breast milk. Br J Clin Pharmacol. 1982;13:731.

243 **Stec GP et al.** Kinetics of theophylline transfer to breast milk. Clin Pharmacol Ther. 1980;28:404.

244 **Berlin CM.** Excretion of methylxanthines in human milk. Semin Perinatol. 1981;5:389.

245 **Sagraves R et al.** Tolmetin in breast milk. Drug Intell Clin Pharm. 1985;19:55.

246 **Verbeeck RK et al.** Excretion of trazodone in breast milk. Br J Clin Pharmacol. 1986;22:367.

247 **Reyes MP et al.** Vancomycin during pregnancy: does it cause hearing loss or nephrotoxicity in the infant? Am J Obstet Gynecol. 1989;161:977.

248 **Anersen HJ.** Excretion of verapamil in human milk. Eur J Clin Pharmacol. 1983;25:279.

249 **Anderson P et al.** Verapamil and norverapamil in plasma and breast milk during breast feeding. Eur J Clin Pharmacol. 1987;31:625.

250 **Aaes-Jorgensen T et al.** Zuclopenthixol levels in serum and breast milk. Psychopharmacology. 1986;90:417.

251 **Hall JG et al.** Maternal and fetal sequelae of anticoagulation during pregnancy. Am J Med. 1980;68:122–20.

252 **Nageotte MP et al.** Anticoagulation in pregnancy. Am J Obstet Gynecol. 1981;141:472.

253 **Hahn CLA.** Pulsatile heparin administration in pregnancy: a new approach. Am J Obstet Gynecol. 1986;155:283.

254 **Hanson JW, Buehler BA.** Fetal hydantoin syndrome: current status. J Pediatr. 1982;101:816.

255 **Buehler BA et al.** Prenatal prediction of risk of the fetal hydantoin syndrome. N Engl J Med. 1990;322:1567.

256 **Janz D.** Antiepileptic drugs and pregnancy: altered utilization patterns and teratogenesis. Epilepsia. 1982;23 (Suppl. 1):S53.

257 **Biale Y, Lewenthal H.** Effect of folic acid supplementation on congenital malformations due to anticonvulsive drugs. Eur J Obstet Gynecol Reprod Biol. 1984;18:211.

258 **Hiilesmaa VK et al.** Serum folate concentrations during pregnancy in women with epilepsy: relation to antiepileptic drug concentrations, number of seizures, and fetal outcome. Br Med J (Clin Res). 1983;287:577.

259 **Nakane Y et al.** Multi-institutional study on the teratogenicity and fetal toxicity to antiepileptic drugs: a report of a collaborative study group in Japan. Epilepsia. 1980;21:633.

260 **Paulson GW, Paulson RB.** Teratogenic effects of anticonvulsants. Arch Neurol. 1981;38:140.

261 **Guignard J-P, Gouyon J-B.** Adverse effects of drugs on the immature kidney. Biol Neonate. 1988;53:243.

262 **Norton ME et al.** Neonatal complications after the administration of indomethacin for preterm labor. N Engl J Med. 1993;329:1602.

263 **Schoenfeld A et al.** Antagonism of antihypertensive drug therapy in pregnancy by indomethacin? Am J Obstet Gynecol. 1989;161:1204.

264 **Hansten PD, Horn JR.** Drug Interactions and Updates Quarterly. Vancouver, WA: Applied Therapeutics Inc; 1995:452.

265 **Troche BI.** The methylene-blue baby. N Engl J Med. 1989;320:1756.

266 **Nicolini U, Monni G.** Intestinal obstruction in babies exposed in utero to methylene blue. Lancet. 1990;336:1258.

267 **Van Der Pol JG et al.** Jejunal atresia related to the use of methylene blue in genetic amniocentesis in twins. Br J Obstet Gynaecol. 1992;99:141.

268 **McFadyen I.** The dangers of intra-amniotic methylene blue. Br J Obstet Gynaecol. 1992;99:89.

Gynecological Disorders

Rosalie Sagraves
Nancy A Letassy

Vaginitis 46-2
Assessing Self-Dosed Vulvovaginal Candidiasis
(See Table 46.1) 46-2
Signs and Symptoms of Vulvovaginal Candidiasis 46-2
Diagnosis (See Table 46.2) 46-3
Vulvovaginal candidiasis 46-3
Bacterial vaginosis (BV) (See Table 46.3) 46-3
Trichomonas vaginitis (See Chapter 64) 46-4
Physiologic Vaginal Discharge (See Table 46.2) 46-4
Susceptibility to Vulvovaginal Candidiasis 46-4
Treatment 46-4
Vulvovaginal candidiasis (See Table 46.4) 46-4
Vaginally administered imidazoles and triazoles ... 46-4
Nystatin 46-6
Oral imidazoles 46-6
Adverse effects of imidazoles and triazoles 46-6
Patient counseling 46-6
Recurrent vulvovaginal candidiasis 46-6
Vulvovaginal candidiasis during pregnancy 46-7
Bacterial vaginosis 46-7
Toxic Shock Syndrome (TSS) 46-7
Menstrual TSS (See Figure 46.1 and Table 46.5) 46-7
Nonmenstrual TSS 46-8
Signs and Symptoms (See Table 46.5) 46-8
Laboratory Tests 46-9
Treatment 46-9
Risk Factors and Prevention 46-10
Tampon use 46-10
Contraceptive sponge 46-10
Dysmenorrhea 46-10
Signs and Symptoms 46-11
Pathogenesis 46-11
Treatment 46-11
General management 46-11
Combination oral contraceptives (COC) 46-12
Nonsteroidal anti-inflammatory drugs (NSAID)
(See Table 46.6) 46-12
Mechanism of action (See Figure 46.2) 46-12
Choice of agent (See Table 46.6) 46-13
Ibuprofen 46-13
Other NSAIDs 46-13
Adverse effects 46-14
Contraindications 46-14
Duration of therapy 46-14
Other Agents 46-14
Premenstrual Syndrome (PMS) 46-14
Signs and Symptoms (See Table 46.7) 46-14
Diagnosis (See Tables 46.8 and 46.9) 46-15
Treatment 46-16
Fluoxetine 46-16
Alprazolam 46-16
Progestins 46-16
Combination oral contraceptives 46-16
Pyridoxine 46-17
Mefenamic acid 46-17
Spironolactone and metolazone 46-17

Gonadotropin-releasing hormone (GnRH)
agonists 46-18
Bromocriptine and danazol 46-18
Other agents 46-18
Endometriosis 46-18
Pathogenesis 46-18
Signs and Symptoms (See Table 46.10) 46-19
Treatment 46-20
Definitive surgery 46-20
Conservative surgery 46-20
Danazol 46-20
Gonadotropin-releasing hormone agonists
(See Table 46.11) 46-21
Estrogen-progestin combination 46-21
Progestin therapy 46-21
Expectant management 46-21
Clinical Application 46-21
Danazol 46-22
Dosing 46-22
Duration of therapy 46-22
Adverse effects (See Table 46.12) 46-22
GnRH agonists 46-23
Dosing (See Table 46.11) 46-23
Adverse effects 46-23
Hypoestrogenic effects 46-23
Bone demineralization 46-23
The Climacteric and Postmenopause 46-23
Pathophysiology 46-24
Target Tissues Affected by Decreased Estrogen 46-24
Hot Flushes 46-24
Signs and symptoms 46-24
Treatment 46-25
Oral estrogens (See Table 46.13
and Figure 46.3) 46-25
Transdermal estradiol 46-26
Clonidine 46-26
Megestrol acetate 46-26
Transdermal estradiol versus oral estrogens 46-26
Genitourinary Atrophy 46-26
Signs and symptoms 46-26
Treatment 46-27
Vaginally administered estrogens 46-27
Oral and transdermal estrogens 46-27
Primary Osteoporosis 46-27
Incidence and Fracture Sites 46-27
Pathophysiology 46-27
Changes in bone mass 46-27
Classification (See Table 46.14 and Figure 46.4) 46-28
Risk Factors (See Table 46.14) 46-28
Gender, race, heredity, and body build 46-28
Mobility 46-28
Calcium 46-28
Cigarette smoking and alcohol ingestion 46-29
Potential risks (e.g., excessive caffeine
ingestion) 46-29

(Continued)

Drugs 46-29
Disease 46-29
Prevention 46-29
  Premenopausal women 46-29
    Vitamin D 46-29
    Exercise 46-29
    Calcium (See Tables 46.15 and 46.16) 46-29
  Postmenopausal women 46-30
    Vitamin D 46-30
    Exercise 46-30
    Calcium 46-30
  Estrogen replacement 46-31
    Effect on bone mass 46-31
    Duration of therapy 46-31
    Dosing (See Table 46.13) 46-31
    Contraindications 46-31
    Risks 46-32
      Breast cancer 46-32
      Endometrial adenocarcinoma 46-32

      Thromboembolic disease 46-32
      Cholelithiasis 46-32
      Hypertension 46-32
  Benefits 46-32
    Cardiovascular disease 46-32
  Adverse effects 46-32
    Use with progestin 46-32
Treatment 46-33
  Calcium 46-33
  Estrogens 46-33
  Vitamin D 46-33
  Exercise and prevention of falls 46-33
  Thiazides 46-33
  Sodium fluoride 46-34
  Calcitonin 46-34
  Anabolic steroids 46-34
  Etidronate 46-34

There are many medical problems unique to women. Gynecologic infections may occur in women of all ages; however, they occur primarily in young women during their reproductive years. The most common infections encountered are vaginitis, toxic shock, and pelvic inflammatory disease (PID). Several gynecologic problems that occur in menstruating women are dysmenorrhea, premenstrual syndrome, and endometriosis. During the climacteric, the transition between reproductive and nonreproductive years, women begin to experience several problems related to declining estrogen concentrations, including hot flushes and genitourinary atrophy. The most significant postmenopausal condition is osteoporosis, although women are at higher risk postmenopausally for cardiac disease and breast cancer.

Vaginitis

A vaginal infection is one of the most common reasons that women seek gynecological care. Of these, the three most commonly occurring infections are bacterial vaginosis (40%–50% of cases); *Candida* vulvovaginitis (20%–25% of cases); and *Trichomonas* vaginitis (15%–20% of cases).[1] Bacterial vaginosis (BV) is a polymicrobial infection that is characterized microbiologically by the presence of increased numbers of *Gardnerella vaginalis* in association with organisms such as *Mycoplasma hominis*, *Mobiluncus* species, and various *Bacteroides* species, and a decrease in lactobacilli. Of women diagnosed as having *Candida* vulvovaginitis, the causative organism is *C. albicans* in 85% to 90% of cases with *Torulopsis glabrata* and *C. tropicalis* accounting for most of the remaining cases.[1] Information on trichomonas vaginitis may be found in Chapter 64: Sexually Transmitted Diseases.

Assessing Self-Dosed Vulvovaginal Candidiasis

1. L.L., a 23-year-old female, comes to your pharmacy to purchase an over-the-counter (OTC) antifungal agent to relieve vaginal symptoms that she believes are caused by a vaginal yeast infection. Before purchasing an antifungal agent, L.L. asks you which product she should purchase. You want to be assured that she probably has a vaginal yeast infection. What questions would you ask to obtain helpful information?

Some of the questions that you might ask L.L. to gain needed information are listed in Table 46.1. It is important to ask questions of a woman who believes she has a yeast infection to determine if it is appropriate to treat herself with an antifungal agent (e.g., clotrimazole or miconazole) or if she should be referred to a physician.

L.L. should be reminded that OTC antifungal agents are to be used by women who previously were diagnosed by their physicians as having vulvovaginal candidiasis and who have vaginal symptoms previously experienced. (Also see Questions 13 and 14 of Chapter 1: Assessment of Therapy and Pharmaceutical Care.)

Signs and Symptoms of Vulvovaginal Candidiasis

2. L.L. tells you that she has had 2 episodes of vaginal yeast infections; the most recent one was approximately 1 year ago. She was seen by her gynecologist on both occasions and was diagnosed as having a vulvovaginal candidiasis that subsequently responded to antifungal therapy. When questioned further, L.L. tells you that she currently is experiencing vaginal and vulvar itching, vaginal soreness, and vulvar burning ac-

Table 46.1	Questions to Gain Information About Possible Vulvovaginal Candidiasis[a]

What symptoms are you experiencing currently? (See Question 1)

Have you previously been diagnosed by a physician as having a vaginal yeast infection? (See Question 1)

What symptoms did you experience with that previous yeast infection? Are the symptoms you are experiencing now the same or similar to those you had with that previous infection? (See Questions 1–4)

If you were treated previously for a vaginal infection, what antifungal agent did you use? For how long was it used? Was it effective?

Did you experience any adverse effects associated with the use of the antifungal agent? (See Question 8)

Are you pregnant? (See Question 5)

Do you have any medical problems? (See Question 5)

Are you taking any medications? (See Question 5)

Do you have allergies?

Do you use any vaginal preparations (e.g., feminine hygiene sprays or douches)? (See Questions 4 and 5)

If you have sexual intercourse, what contraceptive method do you use? Does your sexual partner use a condom? (See Question 4)

Are you a "candy binger"? (See Question 9)

You also might ask questions about tight-fitting clothes, nylon undergarments, swimming, etc., especially in warm weather. (See Questions 5 and 9)

[a] A questionnaire also might be helpful in collecting information from the patient.

companied by a thick, white vaginal discharge that has the consistency of cottage cheese. She has been unable to have intercourse because of pain. These all are symptoms that she experienced with her previous vaginal yeast infections. L.L. has no underlying major health problems. Her current medications include oral tetracycline for acne and Ortho-Novum 1/35 for birth control. She has regular menstrual cycles and her last menstrual period was 4 days ago. What clinical manifestations does L.L. exhibit that are consistent with the presence of vulvovaginal candidiasis? What are other common manifestations?

L.L. exhibits signs and symptoms associated with vulvovaginal candidiasis which include vulvar and vaginal pruritus, vaginal soreness, vulvar burning, and dyspareunia (painful coitus or intercourse). She also has a thick, white vaginal discharge that may be attributed to a candidal infection. Vulvar pruritus occurs in most symptomatic patients, but many women do not have a vaginal discharge or, if present, it is minimal.[2] Typically, the vaginal discharge is a nonodorous, highly viscous, white discharge that may vary in consistency from cottage cheese-like in character to a watery discharge.[2] Symptoms may be worse before menses and may decline with the onset of menses.[2]

If L.L. had been examined by her gynecologist, she might have been noted to have vulvar edema and erythema. A speculum examination could have revealed the presence of a bright red vagina with patches of white, curd-like plaques. In addition, patients with vulvovaginal candidiasis may have geographic erythema or small fissures on the vulva and external dysuria caused by urine irritating the infected vulva.[2]

Diagnosis

3. How can candidal vulvovaginitis be differentiated from other vaginal infections?

It is especially important to help a woman determine if she has vulvovaginal candidiasis because the inappropriate use of an OTC antifungal agent could delay the treatment of another vaginal infection such as bacterial vaginosis. Therefore, clinicians in all areas of practice should be knowledgeable about the signs and symptoms of vulvovaginal candidiasis and other common vaginal infections.

Vulvovaginal Candidiasis

Clinical symptoms alone may be a poor predictor of a candidal infection, but the physical appearance of the vaginal discharge may be helpful if it is a highly viscous, white, curd-like or cottage cheese-appearing discharge that is nonodorous and has a normal pH (pH ≤4.5).[2] The quantity of the discharge may be scanty to profuse. Some women with candidiasis exhibit only vaginal erythema with minimal discharge or an increased amount of normal-appearing secretion. (Table 46.2 lists characteristics of discharges associated with vulvovaginal candidiasis, vaginal trichomoniasis, and bacterial vaginosis.)

The vaginal discharge can be examined for the presence of *C. albicans* microscopically as a wet mount or saline preparation, but examination using 10% potassium hydroxide (KOH) is more reliable in diagnosing the presence of germinated yeast.[2] The presence of hyphae or budding spores that are indicative of a candidal

infection may be identified in approximately 75% of women diagnosed as having this fungal infection. Additionally, the discharge usually will contain numerous large gram-positive rods, lactobacilli. Vaginal cultures are not used routinely for diagnosis but may be useful in diagnosing women with atypical symptoms and negative microscopy.[1]

The mere presence of *C. albicans* in the vagina is not necessarily consistent with an infection because this organism can be isolated from the genital tracts of 10% to 55% of asymptomatic, healthy women of child-bearing age.[2] Of these asymptomatic women with positive cultures, approximately 25% to 40% are colonized with *C. albicans*.[2] It is the proliferation of this organism that causes vulvovaginitis and the symptoms that are observed.

Bacterial Vaginosis (BV)

Women diagnosed as having bacterial vaginosis usually have increased numbers of organisms in their vaginal secretions with *G. vaginalis* (noted in the vaginal secretions of up to 99% of women with BV) being most common.[3] This organism may play a role in the development of BV or it may be a precipitating factor. Other organisms observed include *Mycoplasma hominis* (reported in 58%–76% of women with BV), *Mobiluncus* species (reported in up to 96% of women with BV), and various *Bacteroides* species.[3,4] In addition, various species of *Prevotella* as well as Porphyromonas and *U. urealyticum* may be present. Women with BV have decreased numbers of facultative (hydrogen peroxide-producing) lactobacilli that help maintain vaginal acidity which is important in preventing vaginal infections.

Many women diagnosed as having BV are asymptomatic or have mild symptoms that include vaginal pruritus and burning. They may have a vaginal discharge described as a thin, foul-smelling (fishy odor), homogenous, white to gray discharge with an increased pH (see Table 46.2). The infection is classified as a vaginosis rather than a vaginitis because there is little vaginal inflammation and symptoms usually are mild. Diagnosis usually is based upon Amsel's criteria (see Table 46.3).[5] Of the included criteria, the presence of clue cells (vaginal epithelial cells whose borders are obscured by adhering bacteria) and an amine odor appear to be the best indicators of BV.[4]

Vaginal cultures for *G. vaginalis* may not always be helpful because greater than 55% of asymptomatic women are colonized with *G. vaginalis*.[4] The presence of clue cells on Papanicolaou smear (Pap smear) has a sensitivity of 90% and a specificity of 97% for the presence of BV in women who have clinical symptoms associated with this infection.[4] On Gram's stain, the appearance of gram-positive *G. vaginalis*, gram-negative coccobacilli, curved rods (*Mobiluncus sp.*), clue cells, and the absence of lactobacilli is indicative of BV.[4] A scoring system using a scale from 0 to 10 (score ≥7 being indicative of BV) that is based upon the presence of previously mentioned organisms and the lack of lactobacilli has been used successfully for diagnosing BV.[4] A Gram's stain is less subjective than most criteria for BV and is a good adjunct to the clinical diagnosis. Other diagnostic measures include a rapid di-

Table 46.2		Characteristics of Vaginal Discharge[1,2,6]		
Characteristics	**Normal**	**Candidiasis**	**Trichomoniasis**	**Bacterial Vaginosis**
Color	White	White	Yellow-green	White to gray
Odor	Nonodorous	Nonodorous	Fishy smell	Fishy smell
Consistency	Floccular	Floccular	Homogeneous	Homogeneous
Viscosity	High	High	Low	Low
pH	≤4.5	≤4.5	≥4.5	>4.5
Other characteristics	—	Curdlike	Frothy	Thin

Table 46.3	Modified Amsel's Criteria for the Diagnosis of Bacterial Vaginosis[5]

At least 3 of the following signs must be present for diagnosis:
Homogeneous discharge
Fishy amine odor when 10% KOH[a] is added (sniff test)
Clue cells (i.e., >20% on wet mount)
Vaginal pH >4.5
Absence of lactobacilli on wet mount

[a] KOH = Potassium hydroxide.

agnostic test that uses the presence of proline aminopeptidase activity for BV diagnosis and gas-liquid chromatography to detect organic acids produced as metabolic by-products of organisms that are found in the vaginal secretions of women with BV.

Bacterial vaginosis primarily occurs in women during child-bearing years and is detected equally in pregnant and nonpregnant women. A history of multiple sexual partners, concurrent or prior trichomoniasis infection, and the use of an intrauterine device (IUD) for birth control have been associated with BV. Higher occurrence rates have been noted in women diagnosed in sexually transmitted disease clinics, but there is controversy regarding the linkage of BV to sexual activity.[4]

Trichomonas Vaginitis

Information on trichomonas vaginitis may be found in Chapter 64: Sexually Transmitted Diseases.

Physiologic Vaginal Discharge

4. Do women, such as L.L., who have an increased vaginal discharge always have a vaginal infection?

Although the possibility of vaginal infection must be addressed when a woman presents with an increased vaginal discharge, there are other conditions which are associated with an increased discharge. First, a physiologic discharge must be distinguished from a pathologic discharge. Physiologic discharges characteristically are nonodorous, white, highly viscous or floccular, and acidic (pH ≤4.5). (See Table 46.2.) Physiologic discharges may become more profuse at midcycle secondary to cervical mucus or increased vaginal epithelial cells. Other conditions resulting in excessive vaginal discharges include retention of foreign bodies (e.g., tampons); allergic reactions to vaginal spermicidal agents, products used for douching, and condoms; or the presence of cervicitis.

Susceptibility to Vulvovaginal Candidiasis

5. What groups of women are most susceptible to candidiasis? Would L.L. fit into a high-risk group for vulvovaginal candidiasis?

Women are most susceptible to vulvovaginal candidiasis during child-bearing years, and 75% of all women experience at least one episode with 40% to 50% of these women having a second recurrence.[6] Approximately 5% of women who have vulvovaginal candidiasis will have repeated, recurrent candidal episodes.[6] Predisposing host factors for increased C. albicans vaginal colonization include pregnancy; uncontrolled diabetes mellitus; use of high-estrogen-containing oral contraceptives, broad spectrum antibiotics, cytotoxic agents, or corticosteroids; or being immunocompromised. Vulvovaginal candidiasis usually is not acquired from sexual intercourse.[6]

Candida albicans colonization occurs in approximately 10% to 50% of pregnant women, but only 15% to 43% of these women will be symptomatic.[7] Etiologies for increased colonization and symptomatic vulvovaginal candidiasis during pregnancy, espe-

cially the third trimester, include high vaginal glycogen concentrations (an excellent carbohydrate source for C. albicans), increased germination of vaginal yeast, and an increased binding affinity of vaginal epithelial cells for C. albicans.[1,2] All of these possible etiologies are associated with increased estrogen concentrations during pregnancy. An increased incidence of vaginal colonization and symptomatic vulvovaginitis in women with uncontrolled or poorly controlled diabetes mellitus may be related to elevated urine glucose concentrations.[1] Women with depressed cell-mediated immunity because of disease [e.g., cancer, human immunodeficiency virus (HIV) infection, acquired immunodeficiency syndrome] or secondary to the use of immunosuppressive drugs (e.g., cytotoxic agents, corticosteroids) may have increased susceptibility to candidal vulvovaginitis.[1]

L.L. was taking tetracycline, a broad spectrum antibiotic, which may have increased her risk for developing vulvovaginal candidiasis. Women taking broad spectrum antibiotics (e.g., tetracycline, ampicillin, cephalosporins) are at increased risk for C. albicans overgrowth because of the suppression of the normal vaginal flora, including lactobacillus, which are protective against C. albicans. L.L. was using a low estrogen-containing oral contraceptive, but symptomatic candidiasis usually occurs at the same rate in oral contraceptive users as nonusers, especially when users take low-dose oral contraceptives.[1,8]

Factors that may predispose a woman to candidal vulvovaginitis include swimming in chlorinated pools and the use of perfumed toilet paper, feminine hygiene sprays, or commercially available douches.[1,2] Wearing nylon undergarments or other tight-fitting, poorly ventilated clothing has been shown to increase a woman's risk for symptomatic vulvovaginitis. The use of various types of contraceptives (e.g., IUD, sponge, diaphragm, spermicidal agents) and a high frequency of sexual intercourse may be risk factors.[1,2] High carbohydrate diets or "candy binges" may influence the incidence of candidiasis.[1,2]

Treatment

Vulvovaginal Candidiasis

6. What vaginally administered therapy might be effective for L.L.'s vulvovaginal candidiasis?

L.L. is an appropriate candidate for OTC clotrimazole or miconazole antifungal therapy (see Table 46.4) because she has had a previous vaginal yeast infection with symptoms similar to those she currently is experiencing. In addition, L.L. is not pregnant nor does she have any underlying medical conditions such as diabetes mellitus: conditions for which she would need medical referral for a possible yeast infection. L.L. should check with her physician about whether she should continue oral tetracycline or switch to another oral antimicrobial or a topical product.

Vaginally Administered Imidazoles and Triazoles. If L.L. were examined by her gynecologist, the physician's choices would be for L.L. to purchase an OTC product to be used for seven days or to have a prescription filled for an imidazole or triazole product available for single-dose or three-day vaginal candidiasis therapy (see Question 7 for information about oral prescription therapy for vulvovaginal candidiasis). L.L.'s infection should respond to any of these regimens. In women with extensive vulvar involvement, the vaginal cream is preferred over the vaginal suppositories or tablets.[9] OTC antifungal products for vaginal use include clotrimazole (FemCare, Gyne-Lotrimin, Mycelex G, generics) available as vaginal tablets or creams and miconazole (Monistat 7, generics) which is available as a vaginal suppository or cream. Some products include an antifungal cream for external use. All OTC regimens are to be used for seven days. Final product selection for

Table 46.4		Products Available for the Treatment of Vulvovaginal Candidiasis[a]	
Drug	Availability	Trade Names	Dosing Regimens
OTC Products[b]			
Clotrimazole	1% vaginal cream	Gyne-Lotrimin; Mycelex-7; FemCare; various generics	Administer 1 applicatorful intravaginally Q HS for 7 consecutive days
	100 mg vaginal tabs	Gyne-Lotrimin; Mycelex-7; FemCare; various generics	Insert 1 tab intravaginally Q HS for 7 consecutive days
Miconazole	2% cream[c]	Monistat 7; various generics	Administer 1 applicatorful intravaginally Q HS for 7 consecutive days
	100 mg vaginal suppositories[c]	Monistat 7	Insert 1 suppository intravaginally Q HS for 7 consecutive days
	100 mg vaginal suppositories[c] (with 2% topical cream)	Monistat 7 Combination Pack	Insert 1 suppository intravaginally Q HS for 7 consecutive days; apply topical cream to affected areas BID (morning and night) for 7 consecutive days
Prescription Products			
Butoconazole	2% vaginal cream[c]	Femstat	*Nonpregnant women:* Administer 1 applicatorful intravaginally Q HS for 3 consecutive days; may extend to 6 days of therapy if necessary *Pregnant women during 2nd and 3rd trimesters:* Administer 1 applicatorful intravaginally Q HS for 6 consecutive days
Clotrimazole	500 mg vaginal tab	Mycelex-G	Insert 1 tab intravaginally, preferably at HS for 1 dose only
	500 mg vaginal tab (with 1% topical cream)	Gyne-Lotrimin Combination Pack; Mycelex Twin Pack	Insert 1 tab intravaginally, preferably at HS, for 1 dose and apply topical cream to affected areas BID (morning and night) for 7 consecutive days
Fluconazole	150 mg oral	Diflucan tab	Take 1 tab PO for 1 dose only
Miconazole	200 mg vaginal suppositories[c]	Monistat 3	Insert 1 suppository intravaginally Q HS for 3 consecutive days
	200 mg vaginal suppositories[c] (with 2% topical cream)	Monistat Dual-Pak	Insert 1 suppository intravaginally Q HS for 3 consecutive days; apply topical cream to affected areas BID (morning and night) for 7 consecutive days
Nystatin	100,000 U vaginal tab	Mycostatin; various generics	Insert 1 tab intravaginally Q HS for 14 consecutive days
Terconazole	0.4% vaginal cream	Terazol 7	Administer 1 applicatorful intravaginally Q HS for 7 consecutive days
	0.8% vaginal cream	Terazol 3	Administer 1 applicatorful intravaginally Q HS for 3 consecutive days
	80 mg vaginal suppositories[c]	Terazol 3	Insert 1 suppository intravaginally Q HS for 3 consecutive days
Tioconazole	6.5% vaginal cream[c]	Vagistat-1	Administer 1 applicatorful intravaginally at HS for 1 dose only

[a] The Centers for Disease Control (CDC) recommends 3- and 7-day courses of an imidazole or triazole; single-dose therapy should be used in mild cases where compliance may not be good.
[b] OTC = Over the counter.
[c] The CDC states that the use of vaginally administered oil-based preparations may weaken latex products such as condoms and diaphragms.

L.L. should be based upon efficacy, cost, response or failure to previous therapy, and L.L.'s preference for dosage form. She also may prefer a nonoil-based product if condoms or a diaphragm are used for contraception (see Table 46.4).

Vaginally administered imidazoles and triazoles are effective in the treatment of vulvovaginal candidiasis because microbiological cure rates exceed 85% of women who complete a full course of therapy.[1,2,9] Cure rates for the various clotrimazole and miconazole products used over the counter are comparable. For example, in a study comparing clotrimazole and miconazole, cure rates one and four weeks after therapy completion were 84.4% and 75% for clotrimazole 1% vaginal cream and 85.4% and 74.5% for miconazole 2% vaginal cream.[10]

In addition to OTC clotrimazole products, it is available on a prescription basis as a 500 mg vaginal tablet for single-dose therapy, especially for women with mild vaginal candidiasis symptoms and for those in whom compliance may be a problem. Several studies have shown that its efficacy is similar to three- or six-day courses of one or two 100 mg clotrimazole vaginal tablets.[11–13] An open multicenter trial found no difference in treatment outcome one week (response rate: 88%) and four weeks (90%) after treat-

ment in women diagnosed as having mild or severe vulvovaginal candidiasis who were treated with one 500 mg clotrimazole vaginal tablet.[14] The Centers for Disease Control (CDC) recommend that single-dose therapy "should probably be reserved for cases of uncomplicated mild-to-moderate vulvovaginal candidiasis."[6]

A miconazole vaginal tampon (Monistat 5) available on a prescription basis was being test-marketed in California at the time this chapter was written. The effectiveness of the tampon appears unaffected by menstruation, but this medicated tampon should not be used primarily to absorb menstrual flow.[15] In addition, the miconazole vaginal tampon is not recommended for use during pregnancy. (See Table 46.4 for additional information.)

Butoconazole (Femstat) is an imidazole antifungal agent available on a prescription basis as a 2% vaginal cream. When administered intravaginally for three nights, it is as effective as miconazole 2% vaginal cream, clotrimazole 1% cream, or clotrimazole 200 mg (administered as two 100 mg vaginal tablets).[16–19] Although the length of therapy for miconazole or clotrimazole, the specific products studied, type of cure rates addressed (i.e., clinical, microbiological, or a combination of both), length of follow-up (usually 1–4 weeks), and the type of study varied, all investigators reported no significant differences in cure rates or adverse effects among the agents tested.[16–19]

Terconazole (Terazol) is an imidazole derivative classified as a triazole, which is structurally similar to ketoconazole. The efficacy of clotrimazole 200 mg ovula (available in Sweden) administered intravaginally daily for three days was compared to terconazole 80 mg suppositories also administered for three days and to terconazole 240 mg suppositories administered as a single dose for vulvovaginal candidiasis.[20] The investigators noted cure rates of 84%, 84%, and 92% based upon symptoms and 80%, 79%, and 80% based upon cultures, respectively. At four weeks, 5% of the patients in the clotrimazole group and 5% in the 80 mg terconazole group had relapsed; 16% in the 240 mg terconazole group relapsed in this same time period. Other investigators[21] compared terconazole 160 mg depot vaginal suppositories (available in Finland) and clotrimazole 500 mg vaginal tablets administered as single-dose therapy for vulvovaginal candidiasis. Cure rates based upon cultures one week posttherapy were 86% and 68%, respectively; at four weeks, rates were 88% and 100%, respectively. Based upon available studies, terconazole appears effective for vaginal candidiasis.

Tioconazole (Vagistat) 6.5% ointment administered as a single vaginal dose appears as effective as clotrimazole 100 mg vaginal tablets administered for three days.[22] Symptom relief for a four week follow-up period was 84% and 85%, respectively; cure rates based upon culture results were 59% and 62%, respectively. Patients in the tioconazole group experienced significantly more local irritation or itching when compared to those in the clotrimazole group.

Nystatin. Cure rates for imidazoles and triazoles are higher than those for nystatin (Mycostatin, Nilstat, various generics), a polyene antifungal agent. It is available as 100,000 unit vaginal tablets and should be administered intravaginally for 10 to 14 days. Because of lower cure rates (75% versus 80%),[1] nystatin is not considered a drug of choice by the CDC.[6]

7. Oral Imidazoles. Can orally administered imidazoles be used to treat an acute vulvovaginal candidiasis infection such as the one L.L. is experiencing? If so, how effective are they?

Fluconazole (Diflucan) administered as a single 150 mg oral dose is the only oral antifungal agent currently approved by the Food and Drug Administration (FDA) for the treatment of acute vulvovaginal candidiasis.[23] In two studies, median time for the relief of symptoms was one day and two days after beginning therapy;[24,25] if symptoms do not decrease within three to five days, the patient should be re-evaluated. In an open multicenter clinical trial, 88% (591 of 669 women) preferred oral antifungal therapy; this may increase patient compliance because of the need for only a single dose of an oral medication.[26] Itraconazole (200 mg/day for 3 days or 400 mg administered as a single dose) and ketoconazole (400 mg/day for 5 days) also have been studied for the treatment of vulvovaginal candidiasis.[27–29] All have been shown to be effective in achieving a clinical and microbiological cure.[1,27–29]

8. Adverse Effects of Imidazoles and Triazoles. What adverse effects might L.L. experience from the administration of an imidazole or triazole antifungal agent?

When used vaginally, imidazoles and triazoles are associated with minimal adverse reactions. Many of the adverse effects associated with vaginal administration are similar to the symptoms women report that are associated with the candidiasis infection. Thus, it may be hard to differentiate the symptoms of the disease from adverse drug effects. If the symptoms seem to worsen after therapy is started, the woman should contact her physician or other health care provider. In addition, if the patient's symptoms have not improved within three days of beginning therapy, the patient should contact her physician to rule out more severe disease, the treatment of the wrong disease, or drug-related adverse effects. Adverse effects commonly associated with vaginally administered miconazole therapy include vulvovaginal irritation, itching, and burning (2%–6.6%).[30] Other less common complaints include headaches, pelvic cramps, vaginal burning, and skin rashes. Possible adverse effects associated with clotrimazole vaginal administration include vulvovaginal irritation, burning, erythema, and pruritus. Mild abdominal complaints including cramps and bloating have been reported.[31,32] Irritation or burning in sexual partners also has been reported. Vulvovaginal pruritus, burning, soreness, and swelling are the adverse effects most commonly associated with butoconazole administration.[33] Adverse reactions most commonly reported for terconazole include headaches, genital pain, burning, and pruritus.[34] Fever and chills also have been reported. Burning (6%) and itching (5%) were the most common adverse effects associated with tioconazole therapy. Vaginal pain, discharge, and dryness; vulvar edema and swelling; dysuria, dyspareunia, and nocturia also have been observed (all <1%).[35]

Disadvantages of fluconazole 150 mg oral administration include headache (13%), nausea (7%), and abdominal pain (6%).[23] Common adverse effects associated with ketoconazole therapy include nausea and vomiting, diarrhea, abdominal pain, and pruritus; headache, somnolence, dizziness, photophobia, and other neuropsychiatric effects also have been reported. Anaphylaxis rarely occurs and hepatotoxicity has been reported to occur in 1 in 10,000 ketoconazole users.[1] Adverse effects reported for itraconazole are similar to those noted for ketoconazole including abnormalities in liver function tests (LFTs).

9. Patient Counseling. If L.L. elects to use an OTC vaginal antifungal product, what information should you supply when counseling her about product use?

Counsel L.L. to read the patient information supplied with the antifungal agent. The importance of completing a full course of therapy even if her symptoms subside before seven days should be emphasized; she should continue the medication even if she has or begins menstruation.[9] Counsel L.L. to see her physician in the following circumstances: symptoms persist beyond three days or if symptoms are not relieved completely after seven days of therapy; she develops symptoms that signal a more severe problem such as abdominal pain, fever, a foul-smelling or bloody vaginal discharge; or another yeast infection recurs within two months.

Review the details of product administration and instruct her to disassemble the applicator (if one is used for drug administration) and rinse it after each use. A sanitary napkin can be used to prevent staining of her underwear due to the leakage of the antifungal product. Also, remind L.L. that certain vaginal preparations are oil-based and may weaken condoms or diaphragms (see Table 46.4).

It is common to advise women like L.L. to avoid wearing tight-fitting, unventilated underwear (e.g., nylon panties or panty hose) and tight-fitting jeans since a warm, moist environment may favor fungal growth.[1,2,9] However, a study addressing risk factors for vulvovaginal candidiasis found no relationship between the type of underwear worn and the incidence of vulvovaginal candidiasis.[36] L.L. also could be alerted to the possible relationship between candidiasis and swimming in a chlorinated pool and candy binging.[1,2,9]

Recurrent Vulvovaginal Candidiasis

10. L.L. develops another case of vaginal candidiasis 1 month later. How should she be treated?

Most women have only occasional episodes of vulvovaginal candidiasis, but approximately 5% have recurrent candidiasis. First, confirm the diagnosis of recurrent vulvovaginal candidiasis and treat the underlying risk factor such as uncontrolled diabetes mellitus. Keep in mind that recurrent vulvovaginal candidiasis can be an early warning of HIV infection. Therapy may be aimed at "control rather than cure" with many women requiring long-term prophylaxis.[1]

Currently, there is no one treatment of choice for recurrent vulvovaginal candidiasis. The following information is provided about therapeutic regimens, vaginal and oral, that have been used for recurrence. Nystatin or clotrimazole have been administered vaginally in combination with oral nystatin, but intestinal recolonization recurred when oral therapy was stopped.[37] Intermittent clotrimazole (500 mg vaginal suppositories) has been administered on a monthly basis to prevent recurrence.[38] This regimen was effective for three months, but thereafter was only modestly effective. The investigators stated that more frequent clotrimazole administration on an intermittent basis might be more effective. Oral ketoconazole has been recommended for its efficacy and convenience, but relapse rates increase with time after ketoconazole therapy is stopped.[39,40] This was noted in a prospective, placebo-controlled study where women with recurrent candidiasis were enrolled in a low-dose oral ketoconazole (100 mg/day), placebo, or intermittent oral ketoconazole (400 mg/day) group for five days each month, beginning with menses (all regimens were administered for 6 months after the patients had received an initial course of ketoconazole 400 mg/day for 2 weeks). After six months, 28.6% of the placebo group (n = 21), 71.4% of the intermittent ketoconazole group (n = 21), and 95.2% of the low-dose ketoconazole group (n = 21) remained asymptomatic. Six months later, only 23.8% of the placebo group, 42.9% of the intermittent group, and 52.4% of the low-dose group were asymptomatic. Thus, ketoconazole appeared useful for the prevention of recurrent candidiasis, but relapse rates increased with time after drug withdrawal. Although there were few adverse effects reported during the study, ketoconazole has more adverse effects associated with its use than do vaginally administered antifungal agents.[40]

Oral lactobacillus and lactobacillus-containing yogurt have been used with some success, but only small numbers of women have been enrolled in studies, and none of the studies were randomized, double-blinded, placebo-controlled trials.[41] Boric acid capsules (600 mg) inserted high in the vagina have been used with some success but they are messy to use.[9] No adverse effects were reported, but boric acid toxicity has been reported to occur with topical administration and from use of irrigation solutions. Gentian violet preparations have limited use in treating candidiasis.[9] They are messy to use and may leave stains on clothing and bed linens and they can cause local irritation and edema.

Vulvovaginal Candidiasis During Pregnancy

11. Pregnant women are at increased risk for vulvovaginal candidiasis. Are there teratogenic risks associated with the use of imidazole or triazole preparations?

When miconazole is used for vulvovaginal candidiasis, small amounts of the drug may be absorbed vaginally.[31] Therefore, the manufacturer recommends that the drug not be used during the first trimester of pregnancy unless the risks and benefits for mother and fetus have been considered. No known congenital malformations associated with the vaginal use of the drug during pregnancy have been reported.[42] Miconazole is classified as a category B drug for fetal risk.[42] This classification, based upon a definition set forth by the FDA, means that no teratogenic effects have been observed in animal studies, but no controlled studies have been undertaken in pregnant women in the first trimester of pregnancy.[42]

Although clotrimazole appears poorly absorbed vaginally, manufacturers recommend that the drug not be used during the first trimester of pregnancy unless the risks and benefits for mother and fetus have been considered.[31,32] No congenital malformations have been reported to be associated with vaginally administered clotrimazole,[42] and it also is classified as a category B drug.[42] Butoconazole, fluconazole, terconazole, and tioconazole all are designated as category C drugs by their respective manufacturers.[23,33-35] Category C classification means animal studies have revealed adverse effects in the fetus, but no controlled studies have been conducted in pregnant women.[42]

Bacterial Vaginosis

12. If L.L. had explained that she had a thin, yellow-colored vaginal discharge that had a fishy smell with no other symptoms, what most likely would be L.L.'s problem? What would you tell L.L. to do? What would be the treatment of choice for L.L.'s problem?

Based upon the symptoms that L.L. is describing, it does not appear that she has vulvovaginal candidiasis but rather bacterial vaginosis (see Table 46.2). Because bacterial vaginosis can be treated with medications available only by prescription, L.L. cannot be treated with OTC medications and should be referred to her physician. Diagnosis is made based upon criteria listed in Table 46.3. Nonpregnant women diagnosed as having BV who are symptomatic and pregnant, with or without symptoms, should be treated although treatment in asymptomatic pregnant women has been debated. Because BV has been associated with premature rupture of the membranes, preterm labor, and preterm delivery, asymptomatic as well as symptomatic pregnant women may require treatment.[6] Randomized controlled trials have not determined if therapy would decrease BV-associated problems that can occur during pregnancy.[6]

The CDC recommends metronidazole (Flagyl) 500 mg orally twice daily for seven days for the treatment of BV in nonpregnant women.[6] As alternatives, the CDC recommends metronidazole 2 gm as a single dose; clindamycin (Cleocin) cream 2%, one applicatorful (5 gm) intravaginally at bedtime for seven days; metronidazole (MetroGel) gel 0.75%, one applicatorful (5 gm) intravaginally, two times daily for five days; or clindamycin 300 mg orally twice daily for seven days.[6] Vaginal administration may be preferred for patients with mild to moderate disease because systemic absorption is relatively minimal.[6] Because metronidazole is contraindicated during the first trimester of pregnancy, clindamycin vaginal cream is the preferred treatment and is recommended even over oral clindamycin because it offers decreased fetal drug exposure.[6] The CDC does not recommend the routine treatment of asymptomatic sex partners.

Toxic Shock Syndrome (TSS)

Toxic shock syndrome is an acute, life-threatening multisystem illness, associated with *Staphylococcus aureus*, which was first described in seven children in 1978.[43] The patients presented with acute fever, headache, vomiting, diarrhea, sore throat, conjunctival hyperemia, and rash which progressed to shock and multiple organ dysfunction.

Menstrual TSS

In 1980 toxic shock syndrome received worldwide media attention after 55 cases of menstrually related TSS were reported to the CDC.[44] More than 2500 cases which met the CDC's definition for TSS (see Table 46.5) were reported by April 1984.[45,46] Of those cases, approximately 95% were females, and 84% were associated with menstruation when the menstrual status was known. In those women with menstrual TSS where the catamenial product (i.e., tampons, sanitary napkins) used was known, 99% were tampon

Table 46.5	CDC Case Definition for TSS[a,47]

Fever (>38.9 °C)

Rash (diffuse macular erythroderma)

Desquamation of rash (1–2 weeks after onset of illness; particularly palms and soles)

Hypotension (systolic BP <90 mm Hg for adults; <5th percentile by age for children; orthostatic syncope)

Plus involvement of at least 3 of the following organ systems:
Mucous membranes (oropharyngeal, conjunctival, or vaginal)
Muscular (severe myalgia or creatine phosphokinase level >2 times UNL[a])
GI (vomiting or diarrhea)
Renal (BUN or SrCr >2 times UNL or >5 WBC/hpf without UTI)
Hepatic (total bilirubin, AST, or ALT >2 times UNL)
Hematologic (platelets <100,000/mm[3])
CNS (disorientation, altered mental status when temperature and BP are normal)

Negative blood, throat, and cerebrospinal fluid

Negative serology for Rocky Mountain spotted fever, measles and leptospirosis

[a] ALT = Alanine aminotransferase; AST = Aspartate aminotransferase; BP = Blood pressure; BUN = Blood urea nitrogen; CDC = Centers for Disease Control; CNS = Central nervous system; GI = Gastrointestinal; hpf = High-power field; SrCr = Serum creatinine; TSS = Toxic shock syndrome; UNL = Upper normal levels; UTI = Urinary tract infection; WBC = White blood cell.

users.[45,46] Cases reported to the CDC peaked at 130 to 140 monthly in 1980 and gradually declined thereafter.[45,47] (See Figure 46.1.) Eighty-five percent of the menstrual TSS patients were between 15 and 34 years of age; 60% were between 15 and 24 years of age.[46] Incidence rates of 6.2 to 16 per 100,000 women for menstrual TSS were reported during the early 1980s.[48] The variation in rates may reflect geographic differences. Additionally, a majority of menstrual TSS cases (81%–98%) have occurred in white women.[48] The current incidence of menstrual TSS in the U.S. is 1 to 3 per 100,000 women.[49]

Menstrual TSS has been associated with tampon use during menstruation in the presence of vaginal colonization or infection with a specific strain of S. aureus that elaborates an exoprotein toxin designated as toxic shock syndrome toxin-1 (TSST-1).[49] The toxin gains systemic access through the vagina or wounds. Many women with menstrual TSS do not have antibodies, or have low antibody titers to TSST-1, and may not develop titers until they have had two or more episodes of TSS.[49] Usually, antibodies to TSST-1 increase with age, and they have been found to be present in 90% of the population by age 25 years.[49] The formation of antibodies following TSS varies, and persons who do not attain adequate antibody concentrations are prone to relapse.

A study by the CDC in 1980 revealed an increased risk of menstrual TSS when a superabsorbent type of tampon (Rely) was used.[47] (The product contained polyester foam in small cubes along with carboxymethylcellulose.) Rely was removed from the market in 1980 and other tampons were modified to eliminate carboxymethylcellulose. In 1985 products containing polyacrylate were removed because of a possible association with TSS. This risk may be associated with the tampon's chemical composition and high absorbency for fluid and various ions, including magnesium.[49] (Also see Question 16.)

Nonmenstrual TSS

Nonmenstrual toxic shock syndrome occurs in both men and women primarily between the ages of 15 and 44 years, but case-fatality ratios for this type of TSS are higher for both sexes after age 45.[48] The incidence of nonmenstrual TSS has remained rather constant since 1980.[49] Nonmenstrual TSS appears to be associated with S. aureus, but ≥70% of the isolates from patients with nonmenstrual TSS produce TSST-1.[49] It has been suggested that other S. aureus isolates associated with this type of TSS may produce enterotoxins which may account for their toxicity.[49]

Signs and Symptoms

13. R.R., a previously well 22-year-old female, is admitted to the hospital delirious and febrile. Two days before admission she developed diarrhea, malaise, muscle pain, and weakness. One day before admission she complained of a severe headache, developed chills, and became increasingly disoriented as the day progressed. She had started her menstrual period 3 days before her hospital admission.

Physical examination reveals a 50 kg female with blood pressure (BP) 90/50 mm Hg, pulse 110 beats/min, respirations 30/min, and temperature 40 °C. Ophthalmologic examination reveals bilateral conjunctivitis, and otolaryngologic examination reveals a red, inflamed pharynx with a red, strawberry-appearing tongue. There is upper abdominal tenderness on abdominal examination and an inflamed vaginal mucosa with a purulent discharge on pelvic examination; a putrid-smelling tampon was removed. A diffuse, macular erythroderma was observed on her trunk, hands, and feet.

Admitting laboratory values include the following: serum electrolytes are sodium (Na) 139 mEq/L (Normal: 135–145); potassium (K) 3.5 mEq/L (Normal: 3.5–5.0); chloride (Cl) 101 mEq/L (Normal: 100–106); bicarbonate (HCO$_3^-$) 12 mEq/L (Normal: 24–28); pH 7.25 (7.35–7.45); pCO$_2$ 28 mm Hg (Normal: 34–45); blood urea nitrogen (BUN) 45 mg/dL (Normal: 8–25); serum creatinine (SrCr) 2 mg/dL (Normal: 0.6–1.5); glucose 90 mg/dL (Normal: 70–110); aspartate aminotransferase (AST) 90 U/mL (Normal: 10–40); serum alanine aminotransferase (ALT) 85 U/mL (Normal: 10–40); total bilirubin 2.2 mg/dL (Normal: 0.2–1.0); hematocrit (Hct) 35% (Normal: 37%–48%); hemoglobin (Hgb) 10.5 gm/dL (Normal: 12–16); white blood cell (WBC) count 14,000/mm^3 (Normal: 4300–10,800) with 85% polymorphonuclear neutrophils (PMNs), 5% bands, and 10% lymphocytes (Normal: 40%–60%, 0%, 20%–40%); platelets 80,000/mm^3 (Normal: 200,000–400,000). Urinalysis (UA) reveals 6 WBC/high-power field (hpf) (Normal: up to 1–2 WBC/hpf), +2 protein (Normal: 0), and pH 5.0 (Normal: 4.6–8.0). Blood, urine, vaginal, nares, and stool specimens were sent for Gram's stain and culture. Blood also was sent to confirm the presence of TSST-1. What clinical manifestations in R.R. are consistent with TSS? What are other common manifestations? [SI units: Na 139 mmol/L (Normal: 135–145); K 3.5 mmol/L (Normal: 3.5–5.0); Cl 101 mmol/L (Normal: 100–106); bicarbonate 12 mmol/L (Normal: 24–28); pCO$_2$ 3.7 kPa (Normal: 4.5–6.0); BUN 16.1

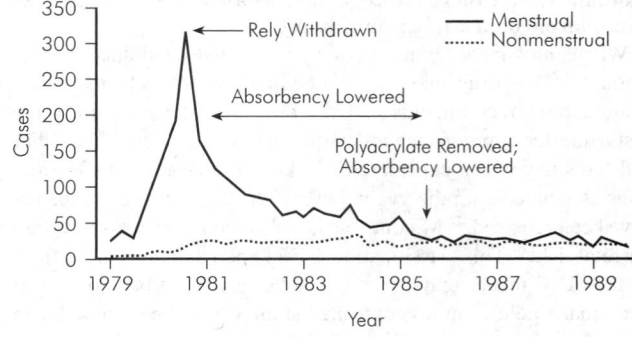

Fig 46.1 Reported Cases of Toxic Shock Syndrome by Quarter
Includes only cases meeting the case definition from the Centers for Disease Control. U.S., January 1, 1979 to March 31, 1990. Reprinted with permission from reference 312.

mmol/L (Normal: 2.8–8.9); SrCr 176.8 µmol/L (Normal: 50–132.6); glucose 5.0 mmol/L (Normal: 3.9–6.1); total bilirubin 37.6 µmol/L (Normal: 3.4–18); WBC 14,000 × 10^6 cells/L (Normal: 4300–10,800 × 10^6); platelets 80 × 10^9/L (Normal: 200–400 × 10^9)]

The CDC established a TSS case definition (see Table 46.5) which has been used since 1980 for reporting cases. Other definitions also have been proposed that are less restrictive and facilitate the inclusion of patients with less severe presentations of TSS.

R.R. is a young female with a multisystem illness which meets the CDC clinical criteria for TSS. She was a previously healthy young woman who developed fever, myalgia, and vomiting before admission. R.R. recently started her menstrual period and had a foul-smelling tampon in place during vaginal examination. She also had a purulent-smelling vaginal discharge which was sent for a Gram's stain. Vaginal discharges and cervical exudates similar to those noted for R.R. have been reported for patients with menstrual TSS.[50]

R.R. presented with a temperature greater than 38.9 °C, a systolic blood pressure of 90 mm Hg, and a diffuse macular erythroderma. She had not experienced desquamation of her rash but this usually does not begin until one week after onset of the illness (range: 1–3 weeks).[50] When peeling occurs, it may involve the fingers, toes, palms, and soles or it may be generalized. Desquamation is followed by rapid re-epithelization without scarring. Hypotension associated with TSS, which may have a rapid onset, appears to be related to decreased vascular tone and the leakage of fluid from the intravascular into the interstitial space. The fluid has a high protein content, which may account for the hypoproteinemia and hypoalbuminemia observed in patients with TSS. These changes may be due directly to *S. aureus* toxins such as TSST-1 or the presence of interleukin-1 (IL-1) and tumor necrosis factor (TNF).[49,51] The cause of the erythroderma currently is unclear. It may be caused directly by a toxin or result from the "opening of the microcirculation."[51]

R.R. also had more than three organ systems involved. Such involvement may be a direct result of TSST-1 or secondary to her hypotension. Her mucous membrane involvement included an inflamed pharynx (reported incidence: 73%), a strawberry-appearing tongue (50%), conjunctivitis (60%), and an inflamed vaginal mucosa (40%).[52] R.R.'s musculoskeletal involvement consisted of diffuse myalgia, muscle weakness, and pain, which commonly are associated with TSS.[50,52] Muscle symptoms such as myalgias may be caused by toxins or the release of IL-1 and TNF.[50] Gastrointestinal (GI) complaints included diarrhea, which occurred two days before admission, and upper abdominal tenderness noted on physical examination. Vomiting and diarrhea, which usually occur early in the illness, have been reported in approximately 90% of cases.[52] Diarrhea may be due to the direct effect of the exotoxin on the gut wall.[50] Patients may have abdominal tenderness with or without guarding, abdominal distention, hypoactive bowel sounds, and signs of ileus. Hepatomegaly, pancreatitis, and fecal incontinence also have been reported.[52] Liver involvement is common in patients with TSS with approximately 50% having some increase in their liver function tests. The most likely causes for increased LFTs are decreased organ perfusion, increased injury due to toxin, or secondary to TNF of IL-1.[50]

Neurological involvement noted in R.R. includes headache and disorientation. Other neurological problems associated with TSS include encephalopathy, confusion, agitation, somnolence, photophobia, psychomotor retardation, and seizures.[50] Lumbar puncture examination, if performed, generally reveals spinal fluid with normal glucose and protein concentrations and low WBC counts.[50] Computed tomography (CT) scans usually are normal even when the patient has edema or encephalopathy.[50]

Although R.R. did not have clinical manifestations of renal or hepatic involvement, she did have abnormalities in associated laboratory values (see Question 14). Additionally, patients such as R.R. who may need large quantities of intravenous (IV) fluids for the treatment of their TSS can develop capillary leak syndrome, adult respiratory distress syndrome, and pleural effusions.[50]

Patients with TSS may experience a decompensation in their cardiac function, and hemodynamic changes have been observed. Additionally, patients may experience changes in their electrocardiograms, such as flattened T waves, diffuse nonspecific ST-T wave changes, and a diffuse loss of voltage.[51] Cardiac dysfunction most likely is a result of "capillary leak, tissue vascular congestion, interstitial edema, and minimal perivascular mononuclear cell inflammation seen in other tissues" that may be mediated by a toxin or TNF.[51]

Laboratory Tests

14. What laboratory data obtained from R.R. are consistent with TSS?

R.R. has a metabolic acidosis (pH 7.25; bicarbonate 12 mEq/L; pCO_2 28 mm Hg) with an anion gap [139 − (101 + 12) = 26 mEq/L] which is seen in greater than 75% of TSS patients.[51,52] R.R. also has an increased BUN, serum creatinine (reported incidence: 65% in patients with TSS), AST (77%), ALT (48%), and total bilirubin (58%) which are consistent with TSS.[52] She may be anemic with a hematocrit of 35% and hemoglobin of 10.5 gm/L. Anemia has been reported in approximately 60% of patients with TSS.[52] R.R. also has leukocytosis with a left shift and thrombocytopenia which have been observed in TSS patients.[50] Her urinalysis reveals a pyuria (6 WBC/hpf) and proteinuria which have been reported in approximately 75% of TSS patients.[50] Other common abnormalities reported in TSS patients include hypokalemia, hypocalcemia, hypophosphatemia, hypoproteinemia, hypoalbuminemia, elevated lactic dehydrogenase, elevated creatine phosphokinase, prolonged prothrombin time, prolonged partial thromboplastin time, and microhematuria.[50]

Blood, cerebrospinal fluid, and throat cultures are negative for *S. aureus* in the majority of TSS patients, but the organism may be found in vaginal or wound cultures. TSST-1 or one of several enterotoxins may be found in blood if specimens are evaluated for toxins. An increase in serum antibody to TSST-1 in a patient such as R.R. who has demonstrative clinical signs and symptoms of TSS would help support the diagnosis of TSS. There are no rapid methods to determine if a strain of *S. aureus* can produce TSST-1, and only research laboratories presently are able to provide such information or determine serum antibody titers to TSST-1.[50] Negative serological tests for Rocky Mountain spotted fever, measles, and leptospirosis will eliminate these illnesses as possible causes for R.R.'s illness. Kawasaki's Disease, staphylococcal scarlet fever, and streptococcal scarlet fever must be eliminated as possible causes for the illness. Additionally, a toxic-like syndrome due to Group A streptococcus also must be ruled out.[50,53]

Treatment

15. What treatment modalities must be considered for R.R.?

There is no standard therapy for toxic shock syndrome, and treatment must be individualized. Initial physical and laboratory examination with aggressive therapy to maintain blood pressure and organ perfusion are necessary for the survival of patients like R.R. who have severe TSS. Additionally, the removal of a vaginal tampon or other foreign body may decrease the production and spread of staphylococcal toxin.

A patient may require 5 to 10 L of IV colloid and/or crystalloid during the first day.[54] Fluid therapy should be monitored through a central venous pressure line or a Swan-Ganz catheter in critically ill patients.[54] If an infection focus is identified, it should be drained.[54] Parenteral administration of a β-lactamase-resistant antibiotic such as oxacillin, nafcillin, vancomycin, or a cephalosporin is recommended as soon as the diagnosis is made. R.R. should receive intravenous antibiotic therapy until she can take an oral antibiotic. Therapy should be continued for seven to ten days.[52,54] β-lactamase-resistant antibiotics do not shorten the course of the acute illness, but they may lower the risk of bacteremia and decrease the rate of TSS recurrence.[51,52] The risk of recurrence has been reported to be as high as 29% to 34%, but as low as 2% when a β-lactamase-resistant antibiotic was administered during the acute episode and tampon use was discontinued.[55]

Corticosteroids (e.g., methylprednisolone 10–30 mg/kg Q 8–12 hours),[54] vasopressor agents, and various types of blood products also may be needed for individual patients.

Mechanical ventilation and renal dialysis may be necessary for selected patients. The use of intravenous immune globulin (IVIG) may be used in severely ill patients or those who do not appear to be responding to therapy.[54]

Risk Factors and Prevention

16. How does tampon use during menses increase the risk of TSS? How can menstrual TSS be prevented?

Tampon Use

Although many questions are unresolved concerning the association between tampon use and the development of menstrual TSS, several theories have been proposed. A tampon may trap menstrual fluid in the vagina, creating a culture media for staphylococcal growth. The amount of trapping may be associated with the type of fiber used and/or the absorbency of the tampon. Another theory associates staphylococci toxin production with increased oxygen supplied to the anaerobic vagina by tampons.[56] Kass[57] theorizes that fibers used in some tampons linked to TSS may have absorbed magnesium as well as fluid, thus increasing toxin production by specific strains of staphylococci. Early in the menses, when the menstrual flow is significant, sufficient magnesium is present in vaginal fluid to minimize toxin production, but as the menstrual flow declines, fibers in tampons may remove magnesium so that a low magnesium environment results, which is ideal for toxin production. This hypothesis is consistent with the following observation: "maximal attack rate of TSS is on the fourth menstrual day; presumably when menstrual flow is relatively low."[57] Additionally, women who are sexually active are less prone to develop TSS. The reason for sex-linked protection may be the high magnesium concentrations found in human semen which may protect the female sex partner.[57] Kass has recommended that magnesium be added to tampons, even those made from highly absorbent polyacrylate, to decrease toxin production without decreasing absorbency.[57]

Although the risk of developing menstrual TSS is low, the relative risk for tampon users is 32.8 times greater than for nonusers with a range of 18.7 to 57.8, depending upon the product.[58] A woman can decrease her risk of developing TSS by using other catamenial products such as sanitary napkins (pads) rather than tampons during menses. If tampons are used, a woman should select the lowest absorbency product that provides adequate protection. She also should alternate the use of tampons with pads. Manufacturers' guidelines for tampon absorbency and product labeling has been mandated by the FDA.[59] The FDA regulations standardize descriptive terms used by manufacturers so that terms for tampon absorbency such as "junior" absorbency tampon are the same from brand to brand. Junior tampons have been designated as tampons that absorb ≤6 gm of menstrual fluid, regular absorbency refers to products that absorb 6 to 9 gm of menstrual fluid; super absorbency, 9 to 12 gm; and super plus absorbency, 12 to 15 gm.[59]

Patient education is extremely important in the prevention of TSS. A woman who uses tampons should be counseled by her physician and pharmacist about symptoms associated with TSS, such as fever, rash, dizziness, and fainting. If symptoms occur, she should remove her tampon and seek medical attention.

A woman who has experienced an acute TSS episode should refrain from future tampon use since recurrence rates have been reported to be as high as 29% to 34%.[55] If a woman does not develop antibodies to TSST-1 after the initial bout, she is at significant risk for recurrence. Some women have experienced as many as 6 to 12 episodes of TSS.[51] The risk for recurrence also may be reduced by administering oral β-lactamase–resistant antibiotics during menses. The use of rifampin or intravenous immune globulin also has been suggested to decrease recurrence rates in women unresponsive to the previously mentioned antibiotic therapy. IVIG would be recommended primarily for women who did not mount an antibody response to TSST-1 after bouts of TSS.[51]

Contraceptive Sponge

The use of vaginal contraceptive sponges has been associated with the development of TSS. The relative risk rate may be similar to that for tampon use, but the case-fatality rate is low (0.1–1 per 100,000 woman-years) when compared to birth-related deaths (7 per 100,000 woman-years) for 15- to 19-year-olds who used no method of birth control.[60] To decrease the risk of TSS associated with the use of contraceptive sponges, women who have had menstrual TSS or who are postpartum should avoid their use. Also, contraceptive sponges should not be used during menses or left in place longer than 30 hours.[60] If symptoms associated with TSS occur, the patient should remove the sponge and seek medical advice. The use of diaphragms also has been associated with TSS; conversely, the use of oral contraceptives has been associated with a decreased incidence of TSS.[52]

A study by Schwartz et al. demonstrated an increased risk of nonmenstrual TSS when barrier contraceptive methods are employed.[61] The risk of developing TSS associated with sponge use had an odds ratio of 10.5 compared to matched controls; for diaphragm use, the odds ratio was 11.7; for cervical cap use, the odds ratio was 8. Even with increased risk rates associated with barrier contraceptive methods, incidences for developing TSS are low.

Dysmenorrhea

Primary dysmenorrhea is painful menstruation that occurs during ovulatory cycles and is due to factors intrinsic to the uterus rather than underlying pelvic pathology. Primary dysmenorrhea must be differentiated from secondary dysmenorrhea caused by pelvic inflammatory disease; endometriosis; pelvic congestion syndrome; adenomyosis; complications associated with IUD use; ovarian cysts; uterine polyps, adhesions, and fibroids; cervical strictures or stenosis.

The prevalence of primary dysmenorrhea ranges from 6% to 80%[62,63] (average: 50%),[64] with most women having symptoms for up to three days (usually 1–2 days).[64] It is the most frequent cause of time lost from school or work among young women, with approximately 600 million work hours lost annually in the U.S.[65] Primary dysmenorrhea is most prevalent in women 20 to 24 years of age. Its prevalence decreases with age, although it appears to decrease more rapidly in married than unmarried women.[65] Dysmenorrhea-related symptoms also are observed more frequently among working women, but it does not appear to be occupation-related.

Signs and Symptoms

17. J.J., a 15-year-old female, complains of severe cramping pain that is associated with her menstrual cycles. The pain begins with the onset of her menstrual flow and has occurred monthly for the past 10 months. J.J. states that her first menstrual period was at age 14. The pain usually is cramp-like starting in the pelvic area with radiation to her back and legs. Additionally, she may experience a headache and feel extremely tired. J.J. denies nausea, vomiting, or diarrhea. She also states that her symptoms last for 1–2 days but are most severe during the first 12–24 hours; they subside somewhat with the use of aspirin. She usually takes two 325 mg tablets when her pain begins and then 2 tablets Q 4–6 hr PRN. She has taken no other medications for her symptoms and has no known allergies to medications. She has no other medical problems. Her physical examination was within normal limits. What clinical manifestations in J.J. are consistent with primary dysmenorrhea? What are other common manifestations associated with this menstrually related problem?

The diagnosis of primary dysmenorrhea is based primarily upon a patient's symptoms and her response to therapy rather than a negative physical examination for pelvic diseases which could result in secondary dysmenorrhea.[65] J.J.'s symptoms which are typical of primary dysmenorrhea include cramping pain in the suprapubic area which may radiate into the back and/or thighs, headache, and fatigue. Other symptoms include nausea, vomiting, diarrhea, nervousness, dizziness, or syncope.[65,66] Nausea and vomiting may occur in 89% of women with primary dysmenorrhea; fatigue in 85%; diarrhea in 60%; backache in 60%; and headache in 45%.[66]

J.J. first experienced the pain one year after menarche. This is consistent with primary dysmenorrhea which usually commences within 6 to 12 months after menarche when ovulation becomes regular; it occurs only with ovulatory cycles.[65,67,68] The time sequence of J.J.'s pain also fits the pattern of dysmenorrhea with pain typically beginning within 12 hours before menstrual flow, becoming most severe for 2 to 24 hours, and continuing for 24 to 72 hours.[62,66,68] The pain, which often is characterized as "crampy," typically decreases with age, after becoming sexually active (sexual intercourse), and childbirth (although childbirth does not necessarily end dysmenorrhea).[65,67] J.J. had a normal gynecological examination which also is consistent with primary dysmenorrhea. The diagnosis of primary dysmenorrhea in J.J. most likely will be confirmed by her response to appropriate drug therapy such as a prostaglandin synthetase inhibitor or a combination oral contraceptive (COC).

Pathogenesis

18. What is the etiology of the symptoms of primary dysmenorrhea that J.J. is experiencing?

Intrauterine pressure monitoring techniques indicate that uterine activity is cyclical in response to variations in ovarian hormonal production and endometrial prostaglandin concentrations that occur during various phases of the normal menstrual cycle. During the menstrual phase (menses) in women with normal menstrual cycles, basal uterine tone (resting tone) is at its lowest (less than 10 mm Hg), active pressure is highest ($\approx$120 mm Hg), and uterine contraction rate is at its lowest (3–4 contractions per 10-minute interval).[66] Women with primary dysmenorrhea consistently do not show a single abnormality in uterine activity but may have one or more of the following problems: increased resting pressure, in-

creased active pressure, increased rate of uterine contraction, or dysrhythmic uterine activity.[66] Decreased uterine blood flow resulting in hypoxia and ischemia appears to be a consequence of increased abnormal uterine activity.[65] The production and release of endometrial prostaglandins during menstruation are increased in women with primary dysmenorrhea, and they may stimulate uterine contractility resulting in hypoxia, ischemia, and pain.[65,66]

Evidence for prostaglandin involvement in the pathogenesis of primary dysmenorrhea was established when the exogenous administration of either prostaglandin F$_2$-α (PGF$_2\alpha$) or prostaglandin E$_2$ (PGE$_2$) produced pain and uterine contractions similar to those observed in patients with primary dysmenorrhea.[64,65] Either prostaglandin will induce nausea, vomiting, and diarrhea, which are common clinical findings in women with primary dysmenorrhea. Increased concentrations of PGF$_2\alpha$, PGE$_2$ and the ratio of PGF$_2\alpha$ to PGE$_2$ occur in the endometrial and menstrual fluids of women with primary dysmenorrhea.[62–65,68] PGF$_2\alpha$ concentrations are highest in the endometrium at the end of an ovulatory cycle. This supports the observation that primary dysmenorrhea occurs with ovulatory cycles and explains the effectiveness of oral contraceptives in decreasing associated symptoms.[65] PGF$_2\alpha$ is a vasodilator and a potent stimulator of smooth muscle contraction which has been shown to stimulate uterine contractions resulting in ischemia and pain. PGE$_2$ is a vasodilator and a potent platelet disaggregator. Additionally, nonsteroidal anti-inflammatory drugs (NSAIDs) which inhibit prostaglandin synthesis have been shown to be effective in the treatment of primary dysmenorrhea.

Cold exposure also may be a cause of primary dysmenorrhea. This may occur because cold temperatures cause vasoconstriction and increase prostaglandin production.[69] Women with intrauterine devices often suffer from dysmenorrhea-like symptoms which may result from the increased production of prostaglandins by leukocyte infiltration near the IUD. These women may respond to NSAIDs, but one also must remember that a patient with an IUD in place is at risk for pelvic inflammatory disease, IUD perforation, or an unplanned pregnancy, which might result in similar symptoms.

Because only 80% to 85% of patients believed to have primary dysmenorrhea respond to therapy, the remaining patients may be diagnosed incorrectly or they may have other factors contributing to their symptoms.[65] For example, some women with primary dysmenorrhea symptoms have normal concentrations of PGF$_2\alpha$ but increased leukotriene concentrations which are known to stimulate uterine contractions and symptoms of dysmenorrhea. These patients probably will not respond to NSAIDs because these drugs do not inhibit the excessive production of leukotrienes.[65]

Treatment

General Management

19. Since the manifestations of primary dysmenorrhea appear to be associated with elevated concentrations of prostaglandins, are prostaglandin synthetase inhibitors the only treatment modality needed for J.J.'s problem?

J.J.'s therapy should be based upon her specific symptoms, response to previous therapy, and any adverse effects associated with that therapy. J.J.'s previous therapy consisted only of aspirin, which was somewhat effective. A therapy plan should include education about primary dysmenorrhea, its proposed etiology, and various treatment modalities currently employed. Exercise has reduced dysmenorrhea-related symptoms. Possible reasons for this include the suppression of prostaglandin release, an increased release of endorphins, or the shunting of blood away from the uterus.[69] Exercise also may decrease stress which may exacerbate dysmenorrhea.[70] Because dysmenorrhea has been linked to diet, lowering dietary fat also may decrease symptoms.[69] For most women with primary dysmenorrhea, including J.J., nonpharmaceutical measures including exercise programs, relaxation techniques, and dietary modifications usually are adjunctive; patients usually require drug therapy as well. Transcutaneous electrical nerve stimulation (TENS) may be helpful. It appears that TENS provides analgesia for dysmenorrhea by decreasing the individual's ability to perceive pain.[71] The use of TENS in association with ibuprofen may give better results than placebo or TENS alone.[72] Psychotherapy may be necessary in some cases when pain becomes so overwhelming that a woman cannot cope with her normal daily routine.

Combination Oral Contraceptives (COC)

20. Would the use of a COC be an appropriate therapeutic choice for J.J.?

If J.J. desires a birth control method, she may benefit from the use of combination oral contraceptives which are effective in controlling dysmenorrhea symptoms in greater than 90% of women.[66] Relief of symptoms usually occurs within three to six months after beginning hormonal therapy.[65] If symptoms do not abate, a prostaglandin synthetase inhibitor alone or in combination with an oral contraceptive may be effective. If pain does not respond to either course of therapy, laparoscopy may be necessary to determine the cause. If J.J. has no need for contraception, she may not wish to take a pill for three weeks each month for a problem that occurs only two to three days monthly. Also, adverse effects associated with oral contraceptive use must be considered. One study addressing this issue reported a 33% incidence of adverse effects, including nausea, acne, breakthrough bleeding, breast soreness, and depression, in women using oral contraceptives for primary dysmenorrhea.[73] However, this study did not address the use of low-dose estrogen combination oral contraceptives in dysmenorrheic patients. (See Chapter 43: Contraception.)

Combination oral contraceptives reduce prostaglandin concentrations in menstrual fluid below normal by either decreasing the volume of menstrual fluid or suppressing ovulation.[74,75] During an anovulatory cycle, progesterone concentrations needed for the biosynthesis of prostaglandins are diminished. This further helps decrease prostaglandin concentrations in menstrual fluid.

Nonsteroidal Anti-Inflammatory Drugs (NSAID)

21. Mechanism of Action. J.J.'s gynecologist decides to start her on ibuprofen 200 mg PO at the beginning of menses, followed by 200 mg Q 4–6 hr thereafter for the 2–3 days she experiences dysmenorrhea. J.J. also is told that the dose may be adjusted later if she does not receive adequate relief from her symptoms. By what mechanism do the NSAIDs act to decrease prostaglandin concentrations in a primary dysmenorrhea patient like J.J.?

To understand the mechanisms by which ibuprofen and other NSAIDs act to decrease prostaglandin concentrations in women with primary dysmenorrhea, it is important to have a basic knowledge of prostaglandin biosynthesis. Prostaglandins, leukotrienes, thromboxanes, and prostacyclin are synthesized via the arachidonic acid pathway (see Figure 46.2). Free, unesterified fatty acids such as arachidonic acid (derived from phospholipids, cholesterol, and triglycerides) are precursors for prostaglandin synthesis. Arachidonic acid may be synthesized from phospholipids found in cell membranes of the menstruating uterus through the conversion of phospholipids by phospholipase A_2. It may be metabolized by lipoxygenase to 5-hydroperoxyeicosatetranoic acid, which is converted to leukotrienes, or by cyclooxygenase to unstable cyclic endoperoxides (PGG_2 and PGH_2). Cyclic endoperoxides are converted to prostacyclin (PGI_2), thromboxane A_2, and the prostaglandins $PGF_2\alpha$ and PGE_2 by the action of prostacyclin synthetase, thromboxane synthetase, or isomerase reductase, respectively.[66,76]

Currently there are two major categories of NSAIDs, the carboxylates and the enolic acids. The carboxylates [subgrouped into salicylic acids, indole acetic acids, propionic acids, and fenamates (see Table 46.6)] inhibit cyclooxygenase and are denoted Type I prostaglandin synthetase inhibitors (Type I PG inhibitors). Enolic acids (pyrazolones and oxicams) are Type II prostaglandin inhibitors (Type II PG inhibitors) which work on the arachidonic acid cascade beyond cyclic endoperoxide formation at the level of the isomerase reductase step in PGE_2 and $PGF_2\alpha$ formation.[66,76] The enolic acids are less effective for primary dysmenorrhea because they do not suppress the production of cyclic endoperoxides which are uterotoxic substances.[66] Therefore, Type I PG inhibitors are the agents of choice because they relieve dysmenorrhea-related symptoms by decreasing endometrial and menstrual fluid prostaglandin concentrations.[65,74,75] Additionally, they may relieve pain through their analgesic effects.

Fig 46.2   Biosynthesis of Prostaglandins

Table 46.6		NSAIDs and Dosing Regimens for Primary Dysmenorrhea[a,66,67]		
Carboxylates	Drugs	Dosages	Dosing Regimen	Approved for Primary Dysmenorrhea
Salicylic acids	Aspirin Various[b]	325, 500, 650, 975 mg	500–600 mg PO Q 4–6 hr	No
Indole acetic acids	Diclofenac Cataflam[c]	50 mg (as potassium)	50 mg PO TID; some patients may need a 1st dose of 100 mg followed by 50 mg TID; generally should not exceed 150 mg/day	Yes
Propionic acids	Ibuprofen Advil[b] Motrin IB[b] Nuprin[b] Motrin[c] Rufen[c] and other Rx and OTC products	200 mg 200 mg 200 mg 300, 400, 600, 800 mg 400, 600, 800 mg	400 mg PO Q 4–6 hr[d]	Yes
	Ketoprofen Orudis[c] and other Rx products	25, 50, 75 mg	25–50 mg Q 6–8hr	Yes
	Naproxen Naprosyn[c] and other Rx products	250, 375, 500 mg	500 mg PO 1st dose; 250 mg PO Q 6–8 hr (max: 1250 mg/day)	Yes
	Naproxen sodium Aleve[b] Anaprox[c] and other Rx products	200 mg (220 mg naproxen sodium) 250 mg (275 mg naproxen sodium), 500 mg (550 mg naproxen sodium)	550 mg (naproxen sodium) PO 1st dose; 275 mg (naproxen sodium) PO Q 6–8 hr; max: 1375 mg/day (naproxen sodium)[e]	Yes
Fenamates	Flufenamic acid	Only available in Europe	100–200 mg PO Q 8 hr	No
	Meclofenamate sodium Meclomen[c]	50, 100 mg	100 mg TID for up to 6 days	Yes
	Mefenamic acid Ponstel[c]	250 mg	500 mg PO 1st dose; 250 mg PO Q 6 hr for 2–3 days	Yes

[a] NSAID = Nonsteroidal anti-inflammatory drug; OTC = Over the counter.
[b] OTC product.
[c] Rx product available by prescription.
[d] Dosing recommended for dysmenorrhea when using the prescription product is higher than the OTC dosing of 200 mg Q 4–6 hr; may wish to start with the OTC dosing when an OTC product is used.
[e] Dosing recommended for dysmenorrhea when using the prescription product is higher than the OTC dosing of 220 mg Q 8–12 hr; may wish to start with the OTC dosing when an OTC product is used.

In addition to the effects that all Type I PG inhibitors share, individual NSAIDs may have other effects. Mefenamic acid (Ponstel) is a fenamate NSAID approved for use in women with primary dysmenorrhea. It is a potent Type I PG inhibitor which also appears to antagonize the action of formed prostaglandins at receptor sites.[68,77,78] This dual effect of mefenamic acid may increase its efficacy substantially in the treatment of primary dysmenorrhea. Other Type I PG inhibitors also are used to control primary dysmenorrhea-related symptoms (see Table 46.6). In addition to its prostaglandin synthetase inhibition, indomethacin may antagonize the action of prostaglandin at receptor sites but to a lesser degree than mefenamic acid.[68,78] Naproxen sodium appears to stabilize lysosomal membranes, decreasing the initiation of the arachidonic synthesis cascade and prostaglandin formation.[79] Other NSAIDs also may have additional mechanisms of action but further studies are needed to elucidate them.

22. Was the selection of ibuprofen appropriate for J.J.? What criteria should be used to select an NSAID for primary dysmenorrhea? What adverse effects can be expected?

Choice of Agent

Ibuprofen. The selection of ibuprofen to relieve J.J.'s primary dysmenorrhea symptoms is a good one. The choice usually is based upon effectiveness, incidence of adverse effects, and FDA approval for this specific indication. Using these criteria, either a fenamate or a propionic acid derivative should be instituted ini-

tially. However, ibuprofen (e.g., Advil, Motrin IB, Nuprin) frequently is used initially because of its OTC status.

Other NSAIDs. Aspirin in doses of 500 to 650 mg four times a day appears no better than placebo in that moderate or complete pain relief is achieved in only 21% to 30% of women with primary dysmenorrhea.[66,67,80] In contrast, excellent, marked, or complete pain relief was reported for 42% to 87% of women using ibuprofen in seven clinical trials, with 13% to 39% having only slight to no pain relief;[81] others have reported relief rates of 66% to 100%[66] and 61% to 84%.[67] Sixteen studies evaluated the efficacy of naproxen (Naprosyn) or naproxen sodium (Anaprox) for dysmenorrhea. Excellent, marked, or complete pain relief was experienced by 13% to 92% of women while 7% to 38% had only slight to no pain relief.[81] Dawood[66] reported pain relief in 78% to 90% of patients treated with naproxen sodium.

Excellent, significant, or complete pain relief was achieved in 86% to 94% of patients with primary dysmenorrhea receiving mefenamic acid in three studies.[81] Between 4% and 14% of the patients in two of these three studies reported only slight or no pain relief.[81] In other studies, moderate or complete relief was achieved in 93%[66] and 43% to 100%[67] of subjects receiving mefenamic acid. A range of 58% to 80% of patients included in ten clinical trials reported from good to excellent or complete dysmenorrhea pain relief when receiving indomethacin (Indocin).[81] Others have reported moderate to complete relief in 73% to 90%[74] and 73% to

75%[67] of subjects taking indomethacin. Thus, all of the NSAIDs discussed (except for aspirin) appear to decrease dysmenorrhea pain. Ketoprofen (Orudis) has been shown to be more effective than placebo and as effective as naproxen.[82] Additionally, initial ketoprofen doses of 50 mg were more effective than 25 mg doses.[82]

Adverse Effects

Similar types of adverse effects have been reported for all NSAIDs and are primarily gastrointestinal, central nervous system (CNS), or allergic in nature. GI-related adverse effects include nausea, vomiting, indigestion, anorexia, diarrhea, constipation, abdominal pain, melena, and bloating. Central nervous system adverse effects include headache, vertigo, dizziness, visual disturbances, depression, drowsiness, irritability, excitation, insomnia, fatigue, tremors, and confusion. Patients also can experience hypersensitivity reactions, including bronchospasm, asthma, anaphylaxis, and acute respiratory distress. Patients who have experienced any of these reactions with salicylate use are not candidates for NSAID therapy. Rashes also have been reported with NSAID use. Additionally, adverse effects also may involve cardiovascular, hepatic, renal, or hematologic systems.[66] (See Chapter 41: Rheumatic Disorders.)

The prevalence of adverse effects associated with NSAIDs is similar for all NSAIDs used for dysmenorrhea, except for indomethacin which has a higher rate. In a review of NSAIDs used for primary dysmenorrhea, the incidence of adverse effects associated with various agents was as follows: ibuprofen, 0% to 12%; naproxen, 0% to 21%; naproxen sodium, 6% to 15%; mefenamic acid, 6% to 10%; and indomethacin, 0% to 56%.[67]

The greatest incidence of adverse effects was reported in Owen's review.[81] One hundred thirty-four adverse effects per 33 cycles of use occurred in 12 clinical trials evaluating indomethacin in 350 women with primary dysmenorrhea. The adverse effects most frequently noted with ibuprofen and fenamate use were GI-related, while CNS-related adverse effects predominantly were associated with naproxen and indomethacin.[81]

Effectiveness, incidence of adverse effects, FDA approval for primary dysmenorrhea and over-the-counter availability should be considered when selecting an initial NSAID for dysmenorrhea.

Contraindications

23. Are there any contraindications that should be considered before J.J.'s NSAID therapy is initiated?

The primary contraindications to the use of NSAIDs include a history of hypersensitivity to salicylates or previously used NSAIDs or active or chronic ulcer disease. Additionally, NSAIDs should be avoided by patients with underlying renal disease. J.J. did not have any problems with aspirin nor did she have any medical problems that would preclude her from using an NSAID.

Duration of Therapy

24. When should J.J. begin taking ibuprofen and for what length of time?

Since the absorption and onset of action of NSAIDs are relatively rapid, it usually is unnecessary to start treatment before the onset of the monthly menses.[75] This practice decreases the likelihood that a sexually active woman will take the drug when she is pregnant. The NSAID should be initiated at the beginning of menses and continued for up to three days because prostaglandin release is highest for the first 48 hours after the menstrual flow starts.[66,75] Women who do not get adequate symptom relief using this method may begin therapy when their basal body temperature declines before menses.[83] Loading doses are not always suggested because there are little data available supporting such use. A course of therapy should be tried for at least three months. If symptoms

are not relieved or if they become worse even when NSAID doses are adjusted upward or other NSAIDs (or an oral contraceptive agent) are tried, then a laparoscopic examination may become necessary.[65]

Other Agents

25. Are there any other drugs that are recommended for primary dysmenorrhea?

Currently, only NSAIDs and COCs are recommended for treating women with primary dysmenorrhea. Calcium channel blockers have been used when other agents have failed, but they should be used only in selected patients because there are so little data supporting such use.[64] These drugs appear to decrease dysmenorrhea by reducing uterine hyperactivity.[64]

Premenstrual Syndrome (PMS)

Signs and Symptoms

26. J.K., a 22-year-old female, visits her family physician complaining of significant mood changes that occur the week before her menstrual cycle. She experiences increased irritability, sadness, and sensitivity to rejection; crying episodes for no apparent reason; an intense desire to be alone and avoid contact with friends, family, and coworkers; and increased fatigue and appetite for sweets. Sometimes these feelings lead to verbal outbursts of extreme anger that have caused problems at home and at work. During this time, her breasts swell, she feels bloated, and gains 2–3 pounds. These symptoms usually subside the 1st day or 2 after her menses begins. For 2–3 weeks after her menstrual period, she is her "normal, usual self." Her menstrual cycles are regular, occurring every 28–30 days with a light flow lasting 3–4 days.

Pelvic, cardiovascular, and neurological examinations are normal. The following laboratory results are within normal limits: complete blood count (CBC) with differential, serum electrolytes, thyroid function tests, serum glucose, liver function tests, and urinalysis. She has a class I (normal) Pap smear and a serum pregnancy test is negative. She has no history of an affective disorder. Her physician makes a preliminary diagnosis of PMS. What is PMS and what symptoms does J.K. have that are consistent with the diagnosis of this syndrome?

Premenstrual syndrome is an ill-defined problem with no standard definition. The term is applied broadly to a number of behavioral and somatic symptoms that occur cyclically during the late luteal phase of the menstrual cycle and disappear shortly after the onset of menses. Most menstruating women report minor changes

Table 46.7	Common PMS Symptoms[a,98]
Physical Complaints	**Behavioral and Psychological Complaints**
Abdominal bloating	Anger
Acne	Anxiety
Ankle edema	Crying
Backache	↓ efficiency or work performance
Breast swelling and/or tenderness	↓ judgment
Constipation	↓ feeling of well-being
Diarrhea	Depression, sadness, or hopelessness
Fatigue, hypersomnia, insomnia	
Headache	Difficulty concentrating
Joint and muscle pain	Irritability
↑ cravings for sweet or salty food	Loneliness, social withdrawal
Nausea and vomiting	Restlessness, agitation
Weight gain	Tension

a PMS = Premenstrual syndrome.

in mood and some physical changes during the premenstruum but are not disabled by these symptoms. This phenomenon termed by some as the "premenstrual molimina" is considered a normal physiological occurrence.[84] However, women with PMS report symptoms severe enough to interfere with their work responsibilities and/or social relationships, create legal difficulties, entertain suicidal ideations, or seek medical help for physical complaints.[85] An estimated 3% to 5% of women report PMS symptoms that are temporarily disabling.[86,87]

The etiology of PMS is unknown. No significant differences in serum concentrations of estradiol, progesterone, follicle-stimulating hormone (FSH), or luteinizing hormone (LH) have been found in women with PMS compared to controls.[88] Changes in prolactin concentrations, once thought to be a potential cause of PMS, have not been found to be significantly different in women with or without PMS.[89,90] Nor have any significant differences been found in thyroid-stimulating hormone response to thyrotropin-releasing hormone[89] or dexamethasone suppression tests (disorders which are associated with depression).[91] Women with PMS have decreased concentrations of β-endorphins[92,93] and decreased platelet serotonin uptake,[94] although these findings are not always consistent[95] nor are these alterations associated only with the luteal phase. There is much interest in the influence of neurotransmitters on the symptomatology of PMS, but much of the work is preliminary; therefore, more information is necessary to ascertain their role in the etiology of PMS.

The question has been raised whether or not the luteal phase is necessary for PMS to occur, a long-held criteria for the diagnosis of this condition. Schmidt et al. administered mifepristone (a progesterone antagonist) or placebo to 18 women with PMS to induce menses.[96] The women also received human chorionic gonadotropin (HCG) (to maintain the corpus luteum, progesterone production and thus, a luteal phase) or placebo. Women receiving mifepristone and placebo entered a follicular phase of the menstrual cycle. There was a significant increase in the severity of PMS symptoms recorded by all groups whether or not they received HCG during the seven days following mifepristone. Two possible explanations for these findings have been proposed: 1) PMS is a separate cyclical disorder that is synchronized to the menstrual cycle but can be dissociated from it; and 2) biological triggers that lead to PMS symptoms occur earlier than the luteal phase.

While much work has been done to rule out excess or deficient hormonal concentrations as the cause of PMS, the pathophysiologic abnormality of PMS has yet to be defined. Current research focuses on the influence of gonadal steroids on neurotransmitters, identification of biological triggers, and behavior regulation.[97]

Over 150 nonspecific symptoms have been reported during the premenstrual phase. (See Table 46.7.) J.K.'s symptoms are consistent with PMS.

Diagnosis

27. How is the diagnosis of PMS determined in patients like J.K.?

Since PMS is a diagnosis of exclusion, a thorough physical examination should be performed to rule out dysmenorrhea, ovarian cysts, uterine fibroids, galactorrhea, thyroid dysfunction, and endometriosis, conditions which may produce symptoms similar to those observed in PMS. A medical, gynecological, obstetrical, menstrual, and psychiatric history should be taken. There is a high association of a lifetime history of affective disorders and PMS; therefore, the possibility that the woman has an underlying affective disorder that is exacerbated during the premenstruum should be ruled out.[99–101]

One of the difficulties in diagnosing PMS in the past was the lack of standard diagnostic criteria. This leads to a great degree of variance among patient groups, difficulty assessing the results of drug therapy trials, and establishing the biologic basis of this condition. In an effort to standardize the diagnosis of PMS for research and clinical purposes, the American Psychiatric Association developed criteria for a subset of women with PMS who experience primarily mood changes. They use the term late luteal phase dysphoric disorder (LLPDD) or premenstrual dysphoric disorder.[102] (See Table 46.8.) Based upon these criteria, a diagnosis of PMS requires a one-year history of symptoms associated with the majority of the menstrual cycles and prospective documentation of symptoms during the luteal phase for at least two cycles. At least five of the listed symptoms must be sufficiently severe to interfere seriously with the patient's work or personal relationships. Women with affective disorders that are exacerbated during the luteal phase and those who experience physical symptoms predominantly are excluded by these criteria. These criteria have been difficult to apply for many reasons. There is no standard, valid self-assessment tool to confirm impairment; the degree of change in symptoms between the follicular and luteal phases has not been defined; and it is not understood how the process of reporting symptoms itself affects the outcome of the study.[103–105] The National Institute of Mental Health set the degree of symptom change between the lu-

Table 46.8	Diagnostic Criteria for Premenstrual Dysphoric Disorder[a]

A. In most menstrual cycles during the past year, symptoms listed in B occurred during the last week of the luteal phase and remitted within a few days after onset of the follicular phase. In menstruating females, these phases correspond to the week before and a few days after the onset of menses. (In nonmenstruating females who have had a hysterectomy, the timing of the luteal and follicular phases may require measurement of circulating reproductive hormones)

B. At least 5 of the following symptoms have been present for most of the time during each symptomatic late luteal phase, with at least 1 of the symptoms being either number 1, 2, 3, or 4:

  1) Marked affective lability (e.g., feeling suddenly sad, tearful, irritable, or angry)

  2) Persistent and marked anger or irritability

  3) Marked anxiety, tension, feelings of being "keyed up" or "on edge"

  4) Markedly depressed mood, feelings of hopelessness, or self-deprecating thoughts

  5) ↓ interest in usual activities (e.g., work, friends, hobbies)

  6) Easily fatigued or marked lack of energy

  7) Subjective sense of difficulty in concentration

  8) Marked change in appetite, overeating, or specific food cravings

  9) Hypersomnia or insomnia

  10) Other physical symptoms (e.g., breast tenderness or swelling, headaches, joint or muscle pain, a sensation of "bloating," weight gain)

C. The disturbance seriously interferes with work or with usual social activities or relationships with others

D. The disturbance is not merely an exacerbation of the symptoms of another disorder, such as major depression, panic disorder, dysthymia, or a personality disorder (although it may be superimposed on any of these disorders)

E. Criteria A, B, C, and D are confirmed by prospective daily self-ratings during at least 2 symptomatic cycles (the diagnosis may be made provisionally before this confirmation)

[a] Adapted from reference 102.

teal and follicular phases at 30% in an effort to standardize this measure.[106] However, this guideline is not used in all studies evaluating premenstrual dysphoric disorder. In the Diagnostic and Statistical Manual of Mental Disorders, Fourth Edition, the criteria for diagnosis essentially are unchanged.[102]

Thus, to confirm a diagnosis of premenstrual dysphoric disorder, J.K. should keep a daily diary for two consecutive menstrual cycles to demonstrate a temporal relationship between her symptoms and the luteal phase and to document the severity of these symptoms (see Table 46.9). Additionally, she should indicate the presence of menstrual flow, weight, and daily basal body temperature readings to help determine when ovulation occurs. The diary establishes a baseline for each patient and documents the most troublesome symptoms. Once therapy is selected for these symptoms, the diary aids in assessing patient response.[107]

Treatment

28. Using J.K.'s diary (see Table 46.9) and the criteria for LLPDD, assess her symptoms and recommend treatment.

A review of J.K.'s diary reveals that her symptoms are related to the luteal phase because they begin after ovulation and end with menses. She has at least five symptoms required for the diagnosis of LLPDD or premenstrual dysphoric disorder: fatigue, irritability, inability to concentrate, breast tenderness, and bloating. These symptoms are graded severe and show at least a 30% change in severity.

Selecting therapy to treat PMS is difficult because the etiology is unknown. Most clinicians select drug therapy to relieve or diminish the most severe or troublesome symptoms. Since the major symptoms experienced by J.K. are related to changes in mood and behavior, then a psychotropic is the most reasonable category of medication to initiate. Several psychotropic agents have been evaluated in the treatment of affective symptoms of PMS including alprazolam, fluoxetine, clomipramine, buspirone, nortriptyline, and fenfluramine. Clonidine and verapamil, while not classified as psychotropics, also have been used to decrease the behavioral symptoms related to PMS.

Fluoxetine, a serotonin uptake inhibitor, has been evaluated in randomized, double-blind, placebo-controlled trials for the treatment of severe PMS. Wood et al. administered fluoxetine 20 mg/day or placebo for three months each in a crossover design to eight women who met the criteria for severe PMS.[108] Fluoxetine was significantly better than placebo in relieving symptoms of tension, depression, anger, fatigue, and confusion in seven of eight women. Side effects commonly associated with fluoxetine (headache, insomnia, anxiety, nausea, and dizziness) were similar in the placebo and active drug phase of the study. Stone et al. evaluated fluoxetine 20 mg/day versus placebo for three months in 20 women who met the criteria for LLPDD.[109] Symptoms of labile affect, irritability, anxiety, depression, anhedonia, fatigue, and difficulty concentrating were reduced significantly in the treatment group as compared to the placebo group. Physical symptoms were not relieved significantly by fluoxetine. Side effects associated with fluoxetine included fatigue, decreased appetite, insomnia, and difficulty achieving orgasm, all of which disappeared in nine out of ten subjects after two to three months of use. While the fluoxetine trials have involved small numbers of women, these results are very promising for the mood and behavioral changes associated with PMS.

Alprazolam. The efficacy of alprazolam in significantly relieving anxiety and depression relative to placebo in patients with PMS has been demonstrated in two double-blind, placebo-controlled, crossover trials. Harrison et al. gave titrated doses of alprazolam (0.25–5 mg/day; average daily dose: 2.25 mg) to 52 women with

moderate to severe PMS symptoms during the luteal phase.[110] There was a high attrition rate secondary to daytime sedation or poor response. Thus, only 30 women completed at least two months out of three of each treatment phase of the crossover design. Eighteen of these women were judged to be alprazolam responders according to the Clinical Global Impressions Scale. Smith et al. gave alprazolam 0.25 mg three times daily to 22 women with moderate to severe PMS during the luteal phase and compared this to placebo.[111] Of the 14 women who finished the study, alprazolam was more effective than placebo in alleviating anxiety and depression-related symptoms. In both studies, the dose of alprazolam was tapered to avoid withdrawal side effects and daytime sedation was the dose-limiting side effect.

In contrast to the findings above, Schmidt et al. found no significant difference between alprazolam and placebo in relieving anxiety or depression in 22 women with LLPDD.[112] Alprazolam was titrated from 0.75 to 2.25 mg/day during the luteal phase and tapered over three days after menses started. Ten out of 22 women could not tolerate doses greater than 0.75 mg/day due to sedation. Differences between the trials include dose and a higher percentage of women with affective disorders in Harrison's trials who may have been more alprazolam-responsive. Thus, while there is some evidence that alprazolam is effective in the treatment of anxiety and depression, there is substantial dose-limiting sedation and a need to taper the dose to avoid withdrawal symptoms.

Other psychotropic medications reported to be beneficial in the treatment of PMS have not been evaluated extensively. Trials investigating the use of buspirone,[113] nortriptyline,[114] clomipramine,[115] and fenfluramine[116] have demonstrated significant reduction of affective symptoms related to PMS as compared to placebo. Successful use of clonidine in the treatment of PMS has been noted in case reports and in one small crossover study which demonstrated a significant decrease in mood-related symptoms such as irritability and aggression.[117–119] Verapamil also has been reported to relieve symptoms of irritability, agitation, and hostility in two women with severe, disabling PMS.[120,121] Further investigations using larger study populations diagnosed according to established criteria are needed to establish the efficacy and safety of these medications in the general population of women with severe PMS.

29. What other therapeutic modalities are available to treat symptoms of PMS and what evidence exists to support their use?

Progestins. Progesterone suppositories (100–400 mg twice daily) have been advocated for use in PMS by many clinicians based upon the favorable results in open clinical trials; however, double-blind, placebo-controlled studies show no significant difference between placebo and progesterone.[122–125] Despite these findings, progesterone therapy still is prescribed widely as a first-line agent for women with PMS.[126] The extemporaneously prepared suppositories are administered vaginally or rectally. The most common side effects are vaginal spotting or bleeding, weight change, loss of libido, monilial infections, anal tenderness, flatulence, and diarrhea. Synthetic progestins, such as norethisterone and medroxyprogesterone acetate given orally, also have been evaluated for the treatment of PMS without significant results.[127] Cyclical progestin administration has resulted in the development of symptoms very similar to those of PMS.[128] Currently, there are no well-designed studies supporting the use of progestins for PMS symptoms.

Combination Oral Contraceptives (COC). Contradictory results have been reported by investigators evaluating the use of combination oral contraceptives in the treatment of PMS symptoms. Morris and Udry found no significant difference between the effects of placebo or oral contraceptives on women's sense of well-

Table 46.9	Menstrual Cycle Daily Diary Chart

Month 1

Grading Severity of Symptoms:
1 = Mild; general awareness of discomfort but does not interfere with daily activities
2 = Moderate symptoms present; interferes with activities but not disabling
3 = Severe; symptoms disabling, unable to meet daily social, family, or work obligations

Each Day:
1) List the major symptoms (mood, physical, emotional, behavioral) that you experience during your menstrual cycle
2) Grade the severity of the symptom
3) Record daily weight
4) Record basal body temperature
5) Check the days of the cycle when menstrual flow occurs

Day of Month	1	2	3	4	5	6	7	8	9	10	11	12	13	14	15	16	17	18	19	20	21	22	23	24	25	26	27	28	29	30	31
Day of Cycle	18	19	20	21	22	23	24	25	26	27	28	1	2	3	4	5	6	7	8	9	10	11	12	13	14	15	16	17	18	19	20
Menses												•	•	•	•	•															
Breast Tenderness and Pain				1	1	1	1	1	1	1	1																				
Sadness/Depression				1	2	3	3	3	3	3	3	2	1																		
Fatigue				3	3	3	3	3	3	3	3	2	1																		
Irritability					2	2	3	3	3	3	3																				
Inability to Concentrate							2	2	3	3	3																				
Daily Weight	130	130	130	130	130	130	130	130	130	130	130	131	131	131	130	130	130	130	130	130	129	129	129	128	128	129	128	128	128	128	128
Basal Body Temperature	98.0	98.2	98.0	98.2	98.0	98.0	98.2	97.8	98.0	97.8	97.6					97.8	97.8	97.6	97.8	97.6	97.8	97.8	97.6	97.4	98.4	98.0	98.4	98.6	98.0	98.2	98.0

Month 2

Day of Month	1	2	3	4	5	6	7	8	9	10	11	12	13	14	15	16	17	18	19	20	21	22	23	24	25	26	27	28	29	30
Day of Cycle	21	22	23	24	25	26	27	28	1	2	3	4	5	6	7	8	9	10	11	12	13	14	15	16	17	18	19	20	21	22
Menses									•	•	•	•																		
Breast Tenderness and Pain				1	1	1	1	1	1																					
Sadness/Depression		1	2	3	3	3	3	3	2	1																				
Fatigue		2	3	3	3	3	3	2	1																					
Irritability	1	2	2	2	3	3	3	3	2	2	1																			
Inability to Concentrate			1	1	2	2	3	3																						
Daily Weight	128	128	128	128	128	128	128	129	129	129	128	128	128	128	128	128	128	128	128	128	128	128	128	129	128	128	128	128		
Basal Body Temperature	98.0	98.2	98.4	98.0	98.2	97.8	98.0	97.4				97.6	97.6	97.8	97.8	97.6	97.8	97.6	97.6	97.6	97.2	97.2	97.0	98.4	98.6	98.0	98.2	98.2	98.0	

being over the three treatment cycles.[129] Two studies evaluating the effects of oral contraceptives on mood changes found a tendency toward greater symptom relief in those using progestin-dominant pills compared to women using estrogen-dominant pills.[130,131] Graham and Sherwin conducted a three-month prospective, placebo-controlled, randomized trial evaluating a triphasic oral contraceptive with a fixed estrogen dose and variable progestin dose in 82 women.[132] Of the 59 women who completed the trial, the COC significantly decreased breast pain and edema. Women in the active treatment group who had prospectively confirmed premenstrual depression reported greater improvement in energy levels, less work impairment, and decreased hypersomnia. However, there was no significant difference between placebo and COC in the relief of mood symptoms.

Pyridoxine. Five double-blind, placebo-controlled studies (2 of which also were crossover in design) have evaluated the use of pyridoxine in women with PMS.[133–137] None of these controlled trials found pyridoxine to be more effective than placebo for the treatment of PMS symptoms. The daily dose of pyridoxine used ranged from 50 to 500 mg, exceeding the recommended daily adult requirement of 2 to 4 mg. Sensory neuropathies (ataxia, perioral numbness and paresthesia of the extremities) secondary to pyridoxine use have been reported in patients consuming daily doses as low as 100 mg.[138–140] Because of the lack of efficacy and the potential for toxicity, pyridoxine cannot be recommended for the treatment of PMS.

Mefenamic acid 250 to 500 mg every eight hours administered during the luteal phase for up to six months has been reported to significantly improve a wide variety of PMS symptoms when compared to placebo.[141–143] However, mood symptoms were not improved consistently. Symptoms responsive and unresponsive to mefenamic acid are inconsistent among the studies. All studies exceeded the manufacturer's recommendation that the drug be used for no more than seven consecutive days due to reports of hematologic and renal toxicity associated with chronic, continuous use. There is no evidence to support the use of mefenamic acid in women with LLPDD, but it may have a place for women who experience physical symptoms related to PMS.

Spironolactone and metolazone both have been evaluated in double-blind, placebo-controlled, crossover trials for the treatment of PMS symptoms. O'Brien et al. found that spironolactone 100 mg/day administered on days 18 to 26 of the menstrual cycle significantly decreased mood symptoms and abdominal bloating compared to placebo.[144] Vellacott et al. also reported a decrease in complaints of bloating but no change in other symptoms.[145] Burnet et al. found no significant difference between placebo and 100 mg/day of spironolactone taken on days 5 to 25 of each cycle.[146] How these investigators diagnosed PMS was not addressed; therefore, patient selection was difficult to evaluate and compare to the first two studies. Werch and Kane administered metolazone 1 to 5 mg/day to 33 women beginning seven days before menses and continuing until menstrual flow ceased.[147] Weight gain was decreased significantly in patients receiving metolazone compared to patients receiving placebo. The majority of women receiving metolazone 5 mg/day experienced excessive diuresis with resulting weakness and electrolyte disturbances. Short-course, low-dose diuretic therapy may be appropriate for women who experience a documented, significant weight gain during the luteal phase.

Gonadotropin-Releasing Hormone (GnRH) Agonists have been found to effectively eliminate many of the physical symptoms of PMS. Most of the studies are open-labeled due to the difficulty of blinding the subjects and investigators to the administration and side effects of the GnRH agonists. Freeman et al. administered leuprolide 3.75 mg intramuscularly (IM) every month for three months in seven women with PMS.[148] There was a significant decrease in swelling, depression, nervous tension, breast tenderness, anxiety, and loss of control when the third treatment month was compared to the pretreatment phase. Irritability, crying, food cravings, and fatigue were not relieved by leuprolide. Reduction in physical and mood-related symptoms also have been reported with buserelin[149] and goserelin.[150] Some women report a worsening of PMS symptoms during the first month which may be related to declining estradiol concentrations.

Adverse effects related to the GnRH agonists are related to their hypoestrogenic action. (See Question 36.) Increased rate of bone loss is the duration-limiting factor. (See Question 38.) In an effort to decrease the hypoestrogenic side effects and decrease or prevent bone loss, some clinicians have combined GnRH agonist therapy with a combination of estrogen and progestin (see Question 38). Mortola et al. combined subcutaneous histrelin 100 µg/day with estrogen (days 1–25) or medroxyprogesterone (days 16–25) or a combination of estrogen and medroxyprogesterone versus placebo in eight women with PMS.[151] Histrelin alone resulted in a 75% improvement in symptom scores and histrelin with combination hormonal steroids resulted in a 60% improvement in symptom scores. In contrast, GnRH agonist with either estrogen or medroxyprogesterone alone did not improve symptoms compared to placebo. While the addition of hormonal steroids did not worsen PMS symptoms, there was no report of amelioration of adverse effects and no evaluation of this therapy on bone demineralization. The use of GnRH agonists in PMS cannot be recommended for the general population of women with PMS given the limited experience with its use and the potential for osteoporosis and cardiovascular disease associated with the hypoestrogenic state.

Bromocriptine and Danazol. Bromocriptine mesylate has been shown to relieve cyclical mastodynia in several double-blind trials.[152–155] Pain relief occurs with doses of 5 to 7.5 mg/day which usually are initiated at midcycle and continued until the onset of menses. The most common side effects are nausea, vomiting, dizziness, and headaches. Danazol 200 to 400 mg/day also has improved cyclical breast pain significantly in women with PMS in two double-blind, placebo-controlled trials.[156,157] The occurrence and severity of danazol side effects (see Question 35) resulted in high withdrawal rates in these studies.

Other Agents. Numerous other agents have been used to relieve PMS-related symptoms but there is little or no support for their use. These include tamoxifen, lithium, atenolol, evening primrose oil, magnesium, and calcium.[158]

Endometriosis

Endometriosis is the presence of functioning, proliferating endometrial tissue outside the uterine cavity. It may occur anywhere in the body, but it most commonly is limited to the pelvic structures. It is difficult to estimate the true incidence of endometriosis because the disease can exist without significant symptoms and current diagnosis requires visual affirmation of lesions during surgery. The best estimate of the incidence of endometriosis in women 15 to 44 years of age in the general population is 1% to 5%;[159] however, until a reliable noninvasive marker is developed for the diagnosis of endometriosis, the true incidence remains unknown.

Endometriosis occurs almost exclusively in menstruating women; it rarely is observed before puberty, after menopause, or in women with amenorrhea.

Pathogenesis

The etiology of endometriosis is uncertain. Several theories have been proposed to explain the histological changes associated with this disease. The transport theory suggests that viable endometrial tissue is delivered and implanted in the abdomen and other areas of the body by retrograde menstruation through the fallopian tubes or by hematogenous or lymphatic spread.[160] This theory accounts for the presence of endometrial plaques on the organs located in the pelvic and abdominal cavities (the most common sites for endometriosis) and at distant sites such as the lungs and the extremities. It does not explain why only a few women develop endometriosis when retrograde menstruation is an almost universal phenomenon nor does it explain the more rare occurrences of endometriosis in men or nonmenstruating women. The coelomic metaplasia theory proposes that stimulation (by an as-yet-unidentified substance) of the ovarian epithelium and the mesothelium of the pelvic peritoneum can result in their transformation into Müllerian elements which then give rise to endometrial tissue.[161] This theory has been criticized for its failure to explain the predominance of the disease in women, the primary occurrence of the disease in the pelvis, and the age distribution of the disease.[162] Both of these theories account for some aspects of endometriosis but fail to explain all of its features.

A growing body of literature documents the role of the immune system in the pathogenesis of endometriosis. Women with this disease have altered cell-mediated and humoral immune function that can be found locally in the peritoneal fluid and in the systemic circulation. Documented changes in the immune system of women with endometriosis include autoantibodies to the endometrium,[163] abnormal polyclonal B cell activation,[164] increased complement concentrations,[165] activated macrophages,[166] and decreased natural killer cell activity.[167] Characteristics of endometriosis are similar to other autoimmune diseases which include changes in the immune system, a disproportionate occurrence in females, multiorgan involvement, a genetic linkage, and a predisposition to concomitant autoimmune diseases.[168] The alterations in the immune system may be responsible for the increased infertility and miscarriage rates associated with endometriosis. Consequently, there is interest in the use of immune modulators to improve pregnancy rates in these women.[169,170]

Once endometrial implants are established, hormones are necessary for their continued growth. Endometrial implants appear to respond to ovarian hormones in a manner similar to normal endometrium because both possess estrogen, progesterone, and androgen receptors. (See Chapter 43: Contraception for the effects of estrogens and progestin on the endometrium.) A study of the effects of estrogen and progesterone replacement therapy on endometrial implants in the peritoneum of castrated female monkeys found that the growth of the endometrial implants was supported by estrogen alone, progesterone alone, and the combination of estrogen and progesterone, but endometrial growth atrophied when hormonal replacement was withheld.[171] Pharmacologic treatment of endometriosis is based upon this hormonal response: danazol, GnRH agonist progestins, and estrogen-progestin combination all cause endometrial tissue to atrophy.

The responsiveness of endometrial implants to ovarian hormones plays a role in the pathology of endometriosis. Withdrawal of estrogen and progesterones causes the endometrial implants to bleed, leading to an inflammatory response in the adjacent tissues.

Repetitive cycles of bleeding and inflammation lead to the development of scar tissue and adhesions between adjacent peritoneal tissues. On laparoscopy, these areas of involvement appear as multiple hemorrhagic foci composed of endometrial epithelium, stroma, and glands. Ovarian endometriosis usually involves the formation of endometriomas, blood-filled cysts (''chocolate cysts'') ranging in size from microscopic to 10 cm. Nodules may form on uterosacral ligaments. Fibrosis usually is present with the endometrial implants, and extensive adhesions may form between pelvic structures.[172]

Signs and Symptoms

30. J.B., a 27-year-old female, has been married for 3 years; she has not attempted to become pregnant. Her chief complaints are severe pelvic pain associated with menstruation and mild to moderate pelvic pain associated with some nonmenstrual days. Her menstrual history reveals menarche at age 10 with regular cycles of 26–27 days' duration and heavy menses for 6–7 days. She experiences lower abdominal cramping and a dull backache with her menstrual periods. The occurrence of this pain has been increasing in severity and frequency over the past several months. Recently, she has begun to experience some pain during sexual intercourse.

A physical examination of J.B. is normal except that on pelvic examination, there is diffuse uterine and adnexal tenderness and multiple, tender nodes palpated along the uterosacral ligament. J.B. is scheduled for a laparoscopy the following week. Laparoscopic examination of the pelvis and lower abdomen reveals endometriotic lesions. The involvement of the endometriosis is staged as moderate according to the Revised American Fertility Society Classification of Endometriosis. What subjective and objective evidence in J.B. is compatible with endometriosis?

J.B.'s age and her nulliparity are consistent with the characteristics of women with endometriosis. Although endometriosis has been diagnosed in women of all ages, it most commonly occurs in women in their late 20s and early 30s who have delayed pregnancy or who have infrequent pregnancies. The majority of women diagnosed with endometriosis are nulliparous; however, approximately 30% to 40% are multiparous.[173,174]

J.B.'s chief complaints are progressive dysmenorrhea and dyspareunia. These symptoms, though not specific for this disease, are the most common presenting complaints associated with endometriosis. Dysmenorrhea, usually described as acquired, begins when the woman is in her 20s or 30s and progresses in severity. This pain may be an aching, cramping, or a pressure sensation located in the pelvic area or low back. The pain may occur premenstrually, menstrually, or throughout the menstrual cycle. Less commonly, women may report pain during sexual intercourse (dyspareunia). These women usually have a fixed, retroverted uterus or endometriosis located in the posterior fornix of the vagina or along the uterosacral ligaments.[172]

Although infertility is not an apparent problem in J.B., it is a common problem associated with endometriosis and may be the problem that brings the woman to the physician. The etiology of endometriosis-associated infertility is unknown. Proposed mechanisms that have yet to be elucidated include physical distortion of the pelvic architecture, chronic inflammation secondary to immunological changes, ovulatory dysfunction, and postconception events.[175] Distortion of the internal genitalia is thought to be a primary contributor to infertility in women with moderate to severe endometriosis. The etiology of infertility in women with minimal to mild disease and no anatomical alterations has not been determined. Attention is focusing on the role of the immune response, but the cause and effect have not been established.

J.B.'s menstrual pattern is characteristic of women with endometriosis. Cramer et al. compared the menstrual characteristics of white women with endometriosis to controls. Women with endometriosis were more likely to have shorter cycle lengths (≤ 27 days), longer duration of menses (≥ 7 days), heavier menstrual flow, and greater frequency of dysmenorrhea as compared to controls.[176] Other symptoms associated with endometriosis depend upon the organs affected. If the intestines are involved, painful defecation or rectal bleeding may be present. Hematuria, dysuria, and cyclic flank pain may occur with bladder or ureter involvement. On rare occasions, hemoptysis that occurs during menstruation may be present if endometrial lesions are located in the pleura.[177] (See Table 46.10.)

J.B.'s physical findings of uterine and adnexal tenderness and multiple tender nodes in the area of the uterosacral ligament are common clinical findings in women with endometriosis. Other physical findings that may be present in women with endometriosis are a fixed, retroverted uterus; adnexal enlargement; fixed ovarian masses; nodules in the area of the posterior fornix of the vagina; and pelvic tenderness. Physical findings may be absent if the lesions are small and few in number.[172]

Because some of these symptoms and physical findings of endometriosis can be associated with other gynecologic conditions or diseases, a definitive diagnosis of endometriosis can be made only by laparoscopy or laparotomy, which allows direct visualization of the pelvic and abdominal structures and the opportunity to biopsy the lesions.[172] Laparoscopy allows staging of the disease, which aids in selecting the appropriate method of treatment. Staging endometriosis currently is done at the time of surgery according to the Revised American Fertility Society Classification of Endometriosis. The stages are minimal (Stage I), mild (Stage II), moderate (Stage III), and severe (Stage IV). Staging is determined by an accumulated point total. Points are assigned based upon the

Table 46.10	Location of Endometriosis and Associated Symptoms[178,179]
Sites	**Symptoms**
Most Common	
Pelvic	
Cervix	Abnormal uterine bleeding
Ovaries	Dysmenorrhea
Peritoneum	Dyspareunia
Rectovaginal septum	Infertility
Uterosacral ligaments	Pelvic pain
Intestinal	
Abdominal scars	Intestinal obstruction
Sigmoid colon	Midabdominal pain
Small intestines	Nausea
	Painful defecation
	Rectal bleeding
Urinary Tract	
Bladder	Cyclic flank pain
Ureter	Hematuria
	Hydronephrosis
	Hydroureter
Least Common	
Miscellaneous	
Breasts	Hemoptysis
Diaphragm	Sciatica
Extremities	Subarachnoid bleeding
Gall bladder	
Pleura	
Sciatic notch	
Spleen	
Stomach	
Subarachnoid space	

location of the endometrial lesions, the size of the lesions, the presence of adhesions, the extent of the adhesions, and the degree of obliteration of the posterior cul-de-sac.[180] This classification system has been criticized because it does not include the presence of microscopic disease, the biochemical changes in the peritoneal fluid, the metabolic activity of the lesions, nor distant extrapelvic sites.[181,182] The classification system does not predict infertility or pelvic pain, aid in treatment selection or outcomes, or predict recurrence of disease. Inconsistencies in staging the disease between observers and an inability to reproduce staging by the same observers using this classification system are other drawbacks.[183] The need for a noninvasive procedure for diagnosing endometriosis has been mentioned already. Two such tests currently are being investigated: an immunoradiometric assay to detect CA-125 and an immunofluorescence technique to identify endometrial autoantibodies.[184,185] CA-125 is an antigen that has been detected in ovarian epithelial cancers and endometrial tissues, but it has a low sensitivity for endometriosis, making it impractical as a screening tool; however, the detection of antiendometrial antibodies in women with endometriosis has been shown to be highly sensitive and specific for endometriosis.

Treatment

31. What therapeutic approaches are available for the management of J.B.'s endometriosis?

Therapy for endometriosis should be individualized for each patient after carefully considering the following factors: the patient's age, extent of the disease, severity of symptoms, duration of infertility, and the patient's desire for fertility. The goals of treatment are to relieve symptoms and, if desired, to preserve the woman's childbearing potential. The modalities currently available to treat endometriosis include definitive and conservative surgery; hormonal therapy with estrogen-progestin combinations or progestins alone to induce pseudopregnancy; danazol, gestrinone, or the gonadotropin releasing hormone agonists to induce pseudomenopause; and expectant management. With the exception of surgical removal of the uterus and ovaries, all modes of treatment should be considered temporizing methods only because the disease and symptoms will recur with time after surgery or once pharmacologic therapy is discontinued.

Infertility attributed to endometriosis is a diagnosis that is made after other causes of infertility such as female genital tract defects, ovarian defects, and male factors have been ruled out. It is known that pharmacologic therapy and surgery will relieve most of the symptoms of endometriosis, and it once was believed that these interventions also would improve a woman's chances of conceiving.[186–188] However, most studies reporting improved pregnancy rates with pharmacologic treatment have been criticized for failure to include placebo treatment groups.[189,190] Several prospective, randomized, placebo-controlled clinical studies of women with minimal to mild endometriosis have reported no significant differences in pregnancy rates between the treatment and placebo groups.[191–193] Hughes et al. performed a meta-analysis on controlled trials assessing the effect of pharmacologic therapy and laparoscopic ablation on pregnancy outcome.[194] In controlled trials evaluating the effect of ovulation suppression therapy (danazol, gestrinone, or medroxyprogesterone) on endometriosis-associated infertility, no significant difference in outcome was found when compared to placebo or no treatment. Results of studies comparing combination oral contraceptives, GnRH agonists or gestrinone with danazol also failed to show any beneficial effect on pregnancy outcome. Analysis of laparoscopy versus danazol or no treatment did show treatment benefit in favor of surgery but the heterogeneity

of the studies casts some doubt on their combination. Larger randomized controlled trials are needed to demonstrate the benefits of this treatment. Pooled data from trials assessing the combination of laparoscopy and danazol did not show any benefit to improving pregnancy rates by the addition of danazol.

Definitive Surgery. In definitive surgery, the patient undergoes a total abdominal hysterectomy and bilateral salpingo-oophorectomy, which eliminates the risk of recurrence of the disease. This radical surgery is reserved for women who have no desire for future conception or who have intractable pain unresponsive to hormonal therapy or conservative surgery.[172] Since the majority of women with endometriosis are premenopausal, hormone replacement therapy (HRT) has been recommended after surgery to relieve symptoms secondary to the hypoestrogenic state and to delay the development of osteoporosis. Short-term therapy with 0.625 mg/day of conjugated estrogens usually is effective and does not appear to stimulate any residual endometriosis remaining after surgery.[195] It should be kept in mind when considering HRT that the follow-up time to evaluate HRT in women after definitive surgery for endometriosis has been relatively short. There are no studies to evaluate the recurrence of endometriosis in women on HRT after several years.

Conservative Surgery. Surgery via laparoscopy or laparotomy is necessary to establish the diagnosis of endometriosis. At the time of diagnosis, endometriotic lesions can be ablated and adhesions or endometriomas can be removed to relieve symptoms, restore normal pelvic architecture, and preserve child-bearing potential.[196,197]

Danazol (Danocrine), a synthetic derivative of 17-α-ethinyl testosterone, is used to induce a psuedomenopausal state by suppressing the release of luteinizing hormone and follicle-stimulating hormone from the anterior pituitary. It inhibits the enzymes involved in ovarian steroidogenesis and increases the metabolic clearance of estradiol; in addition, danazol has immunosuppressive activity that decreases autoantibody titers directed at endometrial antigens.[198] The net effect of danazol therapy is the creation of a hypoestrogenic, hypoprogestogenic environment resulting in anovulation, amenorrhea, and atrophy of the endometrium and endometrial implants.

The goal of danazol therapy is to provide symptomatic relief. Using endoscopy, Dmowski and Cohen documented that danazol causes regression of endometriosis with a concurrent decrease in symptoms.[186] Up to 95% of women using danazol for moderate to severe endometriosis may have significant improvement in dysmenorrhea, pelvic pain, dyspareunia, and menorrhagia.[199] Danazol usually is administered in doses of 400 to 800 mg/day for six to nine months depending upon the severity of the disease. There are problems associated with danazol therapy, however, including a high incidence of side effects, a high rate of disease recurrence once therapy is discontinued, and the high cost of therapy. Most women placed on danazol therapy experience some side effects (see Question 35); however, most adverse reactions are well tolerated with few women having to discontinue therapy. In 12% to 18% of women with mild to moderate disease, endometriotic lesions were present when another laparoscopy was performed six months after therapy was stopped.[188] Recurrent pain occurred in 38% of women six to nine months following discontinuation of therapy.[187]

Danazol has immunosuppressive activity in women with endometriosis, decreasing autoantibody titers and inhibiting lymphocyte proliferation.[200,201] These findings are consistent with changes in the immune response observed when danazol is used to treat systemic lupus erythematosus,[202] idiopathic thrombocytopenia purpura,[203] adenomyosis,[204] and hereditary angioneurotic edema.[205] The importance of this effect will be determined as the role of the immune system in the pathogenesis of endometriosis is delineated. Neither hormonal therapy nor the GnRH agonists alter the immune response.

Another testosterone derivative, gestrinone, not approved for use in the U.S., is available in other countries for the treatment of endometriosis. Its long duration of action allows for twice-weekly dosing. Side effects are very similar to danazol and are related to the androgenic effects of the drug.[206]

Gonadotropin-Releasing Hormone Agonists (nafarelin, leuprolide, goserelin, buserelin, and histrelin) are being investigated for the treatment of endometriosis.[207] Nafarelin and leuprolide are the only GnRH agonists with approved FDA labeling for pelvic pain and implant shrinkage in endometriosis. Dosing regimens for these drugs are listed in Table 46.11. GnRH agonists prevent the pulsed release of endogenous GnRH from the hypothalamus which in turn stimulates the release of FSH and LH. Continuous use of these agents results in a decline in serum estradiol concentrations to the range found in menopausal women (<30–45 pg/mL). Adverse effects of the GnRH agonists are secondary to the hypoestrogenic state and include hot flushes, vaginal dryness, decreased libido, and significant loss of trabecular bone mass during therapy (see Question 36). Recurrence of disease and symptoms occurs after treatment is completed. Five years after treatment, Waller and Shaw found a cumulative recurrence rate of 53.4% for all patients treated with buserelin, nafarelin, or goserelin.[208] Women with greater disease severity experienced the higher recurrence rates. In studies comparing nafarelin,[209,210] buserelin,[211] goserelin,[212] and leuprolide[213] with danazol, the GnRH agonists were as effective as danazol in reducing endometriotic growth and relieving symptoms.

Estrogen-Progestin Combination. In the past, high doses of combination oral contraceptives for six to nine months were used to induce a pseudopregnant state.[214] Because of the adverse effects associated with high doses of estrogens, this therapeutic intervention was replaced with danazol. Treatment of endometriosis with low-dose combination oral contraceptives (<35 μg of ethinyl estradiol) has been suggested,[215] but studies documenting its effectiveness compared to other treatment modalities are limited. Vercellini et al. compared 3.6 mg of goserelin depot administered every 28 days to the cyclic use of a monophasic oral contraceptive containing ethinyl estradiol 20 to 30 μg and desogestrel 150 μg/tablet for six months in women with all stages of endometriosis.[216] The majority of women in this study had mild endometriosis. Both groups experienced significant reductions in dyspareunia, dysmenorrhea, and nonmenstrual pain. The only statistical difference between groups was greater relief of dyspareunia with goserelin. The effect of either regimen on endometriotic lesions was not established with a second laparoscopy. The use of combination oral contraceptives is considered second-line therapy but may be useful in young women who have mild symptoms and do not desire immediate conception.[217]

Progestin Therapy. Medroxyprogesterone has been used both orally and intramuscularly to decrease pelvic pain in women with all stages of endometriosis. In oral doses of 30 to 50 mg/day for three to four months, diminution or disappearance of pelvic pain and tenderness occurs within a few days of initiation.[218,219] Intramuscular administration of medroxyprogesterone acetate 100 mg every two weeks for eight weeks followed by 200 mg monthly for four months also provides pain relief.[215] The suppression of the hypothalamic-pituitary-gonadal axis persists for six to twelve months following discontinuation of IM medroxyprogesterone acetate; therefore, women who wish to conceive soon after therapy should be treated with the oral form. Adverse effects include breakthrough or cyclic bleeding (30%), average weight gain of 1.5 kg (60%), edema or bloating (60%), and anxiety and irritability (20%).[219] A 58% decrease in high-density lipoprotein (HDL) was found in women receiving IM medroxyprogesterone 150 mg every two weeks for six months.[220] No change in low-density lipoprotein (LDL) was reported. There are no data available on the lipid effects of oral medroxyprogesterone or lower doses of parenteral medroxyprogesterone. Today, it is used primarily as a second-line agent for women in the U.S. who cannot tolerate danazol or GnRH agonist therapy. However, in other countries, such as the Netherlands, it is the first pharmacologic treatment of choice because it is considered to be the most cost effective.[178]

Expectant Management. It has not been established that danazol, GnRH agonists, oral contraceptives, or the progestins increase the conception rate in women with minimal to mild disease.[194] Current recommendations for management of women who fall into this category include reassurance, emotional support, antiprostaglandins for pelvic pain, and a "wait-and-see" approach for six to twelve months depending upon the woman's age and duration of fertility. If the woman does not conceive within this time period, then the next step is assisted conception with ovarian stimulation.[221]

Clinical Application

32. J.B. wants relief from pelvic pain and wishes to delay conception at this time. What is the treatment of choice?

Based upon current knowledge, the treatment of choice for J.B. is unclear. Surgical ablation of visible endometriotic lesions, removal of endometriomas, and adhesions can be done at the time of diagnosis; however, the relationship between these lesions and the etiology of endometriosis-related pelvic pain is not established. Short-term follow-up showed pain relief in 82% of women one year after surgery;[222] however, that number decreased to 66% at five years.[223] Surgery, like medical management of endometriosis, is palliative and not curative.[217]

There is no clear consensus on the choice of pharmacologic therapy, criteria for use, or patient selection. Pharmacologic therapy with danazol, GnRH agonists, oral contraceptives, and pro-

Table 46.11		GnRH Agonists[a]	
GnRH Agonist (Brand Name)	Strength	Dosage Form	Dosage Regimen
Nafarelin (Synarel)	2 mg/mL delivers 200 μg/spray	Intranasal	200–400 μg BID
Leuprolide (Lupron)	3.75, 7.5 mg	IM depot	3.75 mg/month
Goserelin (Zoladex)	3.6 mg	SQ implant	3.5–7.5 mg/month
Buserelin[b] (Suprefact)	1 mg/mL delivers 200 μg/spray	Intranasal	400 μg TID
	1 mg/mL	SQ inj	500 μg Q 8 hr for 7 days followed by a maintenance dose of 200 μg/day
Histrelin (Supprelin)	120 μg/0.6 mL 300 μg/0.6 mL 600 μg/0.6 mL	SQ inj	100 μg/day

[a] GnRH = Gonadotropin-releasing hormone; SQ = Subcutaneous.
[b] Not available in the U.S.

gestins relieves endometriosis-related pain and appears to be equally efficacious but differs in their side effect profiles. However, the studies evaluating these agents were open-label, nonrandomized trials without placebo control groups. Treatment usually is continued for six months but this is an arbitrary duration; shorter and longer periods have not been evaluated. Other treatment issues that need to be addressed include the efficacy and safety of retreatment of women whose symptoms return, the pre- and postoperative roles of pharmacologic agents, and therapeutic direction in women who fail to respond to a particular agent. As the pathogenesis of endometriosis is better understood, well-constructed studies will be needed to evaluate the efficacy of current and future treatment options.

Given that there is no clear-cut treatment of choice for J.B., the advantages and disadvantages of the different pharmacologic agents should be discussed with her so that she can make a decision regarding treatment of her endometriosis.

33. J.B. is 5′2″ and weighs 100 pounds. She does not smoke and only drinks alcohol occasionally. She does not have a regular exercise program and her calcium intake is inadequate based upon dietary recall. She has no risk factors for the development of cardiovascular disease. How does this information assist in the selection of therapy?

J.B. has several risk factors that increase the likelihood that she will develop osteoporosis. (See Question 45.) Given the increased bone loss associated with the GnRH agonists and the fact that she has no risk factors for the development of heart disease, danazol, or medroxyprogesterone is a reasonable choice for J.B.

Danazol

34. Because J.B. wants relief from pelvic pain but wishes to delay conception at this time, her physician recommends she try danazol therapy. How should danazol therapy be managed in J.B.?

Dosing. The initial dosage recommendation for danazol therapy was 400 mg twice a day, but later studies found that doses of 400 and 600 mg/day relieved symptoms and produced amenorrhea.[224,225] Unfortunately, the lower doses did not decrease the incidence of adverse reactions. Women taking doses less than 400 mg/day took longer to achieve amenorrhea or gain symptomatic relief compared to women taking ≥400 mg/day.[225]

Duration of Therapy. The optimal duration of danazol therapy has not been determined, but most investigators evaluate six months of therapy. Clinicians usually treat patients for six to nine months depending upon the severity of the disease and patient response. Women with severe disease may require longer treatment periods.

J.B. can be started on 200 mg twice a day; this dose should be increased by 200 mg monthly until amenorrhea is achieved or a total daily dose of 800 mg is attained. Doses greater than 800 mg/day should not be prescribed because insufficient data exist to support the use of these doses. Danazol should be initiated on the first day of the menstrual cycle (day 1 is the first day of menstrual flow). J.B. should be advised to use a nonhormonal contraceptive while on danazol therapy because ovulation may occur in women taking lower doses, and virilization of female fetuses occurred in women who became pregnant while taking this drug. J.B. should experience relief of symptoms within one to two months. Dysmenorrhea usually is the first symptom to disappear, followed by dyspareunia and pelvic pain. Analgesics and antiprostaglandin agents may be used to relieve dysmenorrhea in the interim if needed (see Questions 21–25). While J.B. is on danazol, she should be monitored for relief of symptoms and amenorrhea as evidence of response to therapy and for the appearance of adverse effects.

35. Adverse Effects. J.B. returns to the clinic 6 weeks after beginning danazol therapy. She has experienced a significant decrease in pelvic pain and dysmenorrhea; however, she complains of a 10-pound weight gain, muscle soreness, facial acne flares, oily skin, hot flushes, and mild fatigue. A lipid profile shows a significant increase in LDL and a decrease in HDL from baseline values. What subjective and objective evidence in J.B. is compatible with the adverse effects of danazol therapy?

The majority of women (85%–94%) experience some adverse reactions to danazol therapy.[199,225,226] (See Table 46.12.) These side effects, which do not appear to be dose-related, usually are mild, transient, and well tolerated by the majority of women; however, they have been severe enough to cause 3% to 7% of women to discontinue the drug.[188,191,224,225]

The common side effects of danazol therapy are related to its androgenic and antiestrogenic activity. Weight gain, an androgenic effect, is the most common complaint of patients receiving danazol. Weight gains greater than ten pounds are reported commonly, and gains of up to 20 to 30 pounds or more are not infrequent.[224,225] Weight gain usually is most rapid in the first two months of therapy and generally plateaus by the fourth month.[225] Other androgenic side effects include acne, oily skin and hair, hirsutism, and deepening voice.

The hot flushes J.B. has reported are secondary to the antiestrogenic effects of danazol. Other side effects related to this hypoestrogenic state are similar to those reported by postmenopausal women and include irregular vaginal bleeding, decreased breast size, and vaginal dryness. Other common side effects are muscle cramps and a generalized maculopapular skin rash which may require discontinuation of the drug.

Danazol decreases high-density lipoprotein cholesterol by 48% and increases low-density lipoprotein by 19% to 41% during treatment; values return to pretreatment levels within one month after therapy is withdrawn. This effect on plasma lipids is undesirable, but probably is clinically insignificant considering the short-term use of this drug. J.B.'s lipid profile should be re-evaluated after danazol is discontinued to ensure that these concentrations return to baseline values.[227]

Table 46.12	Incidence of Adverse Effects with Danazol[187,188,224,225,227]
Androgenic Effects	
Weight gain	12%–84%
Oily skin/hair	11%–45%
Acne	15%–39%
Hirsutism	8%–26%
Voice deepening	3%–12%
Antiestrogenic Effects	
↓ breast size	34%–54%
Hot flushes	5%–50%
Vaginal dryness	9%
Abnormal vaginal bleeding	9%
Irritability	3%
Miscellaneous Effects	
Muscle cramps	6%–57%
Edema	5%–55%
Depression	2%–51%
↓ libido	16%
Nausea	13%
Skin rash	2%–9%
Headache	3%–6%
Diarrhea	3%
Hair loss	3%

The severity of the side effects J.B. is experiencing and her willingness to continue therapy should be assessed. The side effects that occur in women taking danazol must be weighed against the relief of endometriosis symptoms. If J.B. is willing to tolerate these side effects, she should be encouraged to continue therapy.

GnRH Agonists

36. C.B., a 30-year-old female, with significant pelvic pain secondary to moderate endometriosis, had good pain relief secondary to surgical ablation of endometriotic lesions 3 years ago but her symptoms have returned. She has no cardiovascular risk factors and no risk factors for the development of osteoporosis. She wishes to try a trial of GnRH agonists. How should GnRH agonist therapy be managed in C.B.?

Dosing. All of the GnRH agonists on the market have been evaluated in clinical trials for efficacy in the treatment of endometriosis; however, only leuprolide and nafarelin have FDA-approved labeling. Contraindications to use are hypersensitivity to the drug, pregnancy, breast-feeding, and undiagnosed vaginal bleeding. Leuprolide is available as an IM depot monthly injection while nafarelin is available in an intranasal dosage form administered daily (see Table 46.11). These products have not been compared to each other in clinical trials but have proven to be as effective in treatment of endometriosis related pelvic pain as danazol.[209,210,213] Patient preference can guide product selection. Leuprolide requires an every-28-day IM injection while nafarelin is initiated at a dose of 200 μg twice daily with one spray in one nostril in the morning and one spray in the other nostril in the evening. If menses does not stop after two months, then the dose of nafarelin can be increased to 800 μg/day. Strict compliance with daily inhalations is critical to the effectiveness of this product. Missed doses can result in breakthrough bleeding or ovulation and pregnancy. For sexually active women, a nonhormonal contraceptive should be used during GnRH agonist therapy.[228] Duration of therapy is six months without interruption. Menses usually returns within one to two months after a GnRH agonist has been discontinued. C.B., as all women, should be monitored for resolution of dysmenorrhea, dyspareunia, and pelvic pain.

Adverse effects. C.B. should be informed of the adverse effects she may experience with GnRH agonist therapy. Adverse effects of the GnRH agonists are related to the hypoestrogenic state they induce. (See Question 37.) The incidence of side effects reported with these products are hot flushes, 90%; sleep disturbances secondary to hot flushes, 72%; headache, 19%; vaginal dryness, 18%; emotional lability, 15%; and decreased libido, 14%.[209,210] Adverse effects reported in less than 10% of women include myalgias, reduced breast size, edema, seborrhea, weight gain, and hirsutism.[228] No significant changes in LDL or HDL cholesterol were observed in nafarelin clinical trials.[209,229] No changes in hepatic function have been reported with GnRH agonist therapy.[209,210] Significant decreases in polymorphonuclear leukocytes (lowest nadir reported: 2500/mL) have been reported in women using nafarelin.[230] Neutrophils decreased from an average of 4000/mL to 2900/mL after six months of nafarelin 1000 μg/day; no increased susceptibility to infections was noted after discontinuation of nafarelin, and neutrophil counts returned to normal. Women with rhinitis who require a topical decongestant should be advised to administer it at least 30 minutes after the nafarelin dose to decrease the potential for reducing drug absorption.[228] Significant bone loss has been associated with the use of GnRH agonists. (See Question 38.)

37. Hypoestrogenic Effects. Can anything be done for C.B. to ameliorate the hypoestrogenic effects of the GnRH agonists?

The addition of a progestin to GnRH agonist therapy to decrease the hypoestrogenic effects has been evaluated in several small trials. Medroxyprogesterone 20 to 30 mg/day did not reduce the subjective reports of hot flushes;[231] however, the addition of norethindrone to histrelin did result in a significant decrease in the number of women complaining of hot flushes.[232] A second study evaluating the combination of norethindrone and leuprolide found a significant decrease in vasomotor symptoms and vaginal dryness in women taking both medications as opposed to those taking the GnRH agonist only.[233] While the information regarding the combination of a progestin and a GnRH agonist is promising, larger well-designed trials are needed.

38. Bone Demineralization. Is the bone loss associated with GnRH agonists significant?

Several studies have demonstrated a significant bone loss associated with GnRH agonist therapy that is evident within three months of administration.[234–238] In contrast, other investigations have demonstrated no significant bone loss associated with these agents.[239–241] This discrepancy is attributed to the techniques used to determine bone mass and the bone sites measured. Quantitated computerized tomography is preferred over dual photon absorptiometry because it is not affected by calcified soft tissue and provides a volumetric calculation of bone density.[242] Results between studies also can vary depending upon the bone site measured since the proportion of cortical and trabecular bone differ among sites.

Studies using quantitated computerized tomography found bone loss to be significant with a continuing decline for the duration of treatment.[234–236] There was a 5.9% to 12.8% decrease in vertebral bodies; the bone loss was dose-related and there was a good correlation with the average estradiol concentrations attained. Whether bone loss is reversible is unclear. In some studies, bone loss completely reversed six months after treatment.[236,237] Another trial reported a partial reversal with a remaining deficit at six months[235] and two other studies showed no reversal at the six-month follow-up.[234,238]

The evidence for bone loss with variable reversibility currently limits the duration of GnRH agonist therapy and retreatment for recurring symptoms. The addition of a progestin to GnRH agonist therapy to prevent bone loss has been evaluated.[233] Twenty women with endometriosis were placed on IM depot leuprolide 3.75 mg every 28 days for six months. The women were assigned randomly to receive 5 to 10 mg/day of norethindrone or placebo. A decrease in bone density was found in both groups; however, women assigned to the norethindrone group had a significantly lower bone loss. At the six-month follow-up, a reversal of bone loss back to baseline occurred only in the women who received norethindrone. Eldred et al. failed to demonstrate any protective effect on bone loss when up to 2.45 mg of norethisterone was added to nafarelin therapy.[243] Although the preliminary results are ambiguous, further investigation of combination therapy to prevent bone loss is warranted.

The Climacteric and Postmenopause

The climacteric is the phase in the feminine aging process between the reproductive and nonreproductive years, usually occurring between the fifth and sixth decade. It is characterized by waning ovarian function and decreasing estrogen concentrations. Menopause is the last spontaneous episode of physiological uterine bleeding and may occur several years after the beginning of the climacteric.

Although age at puberty has declined steadily and longevity has increased, the average age of women at menopause has remained approximately 50.4 years for centuries.[244] Thus, women today may spend one-third of their lives with reduced ovarian hormonal concentrations; 75% to 85% may develop symptoms secondary to this hormonal decline. Age at menopause does not appear to be influenced by race, physical characteristics, age at menarche, age at last pregnancy, socioeconomic status, or alcohol consumption. Cigarette smoking may decrease age at menopause. This may be related to a direct effect of nicotine on the central nervous system or ovaries or an increase in hormonal metabolism.[245]

Pathophysiology

The climacteric occurs in response to declining estrogen secretion from ovarian follicles with age. Throughout life, the number and function of the ovarian follicles decrease secondary to ovulation and follicular atresia so that ovarian weight decreases from 14 gm during the fourth decade to approximately 5 gm postmenopausally.[245] The remaining follicles require higher concentrations of follicle-stimulating hormone for follicular maturation; without maturation, estradiol-17β (E_2) production, ovulation, and progesterone secretion do not occur. Estradiol serum concentrations fall from a mean of 120 to 18 ng/L after menopause,[245] which leads to lengthening menstrual intervals, anovulation, oligomenorrhea, and dysfunctional uterine bleeding (all clinical manifestations of the approaching menopause).[244]

The earliest pituitary-ovarian axis change during the climacteric is an elevated serum FSH concentration which continues to increase after menopause, eventually exceeding serum luteinizing hormone concentrations which also are elevated. Both gonadotropins reach their maximum concentrations two to three years after menopause. Although gonadotropin concentrations may be many times those observed during the reproductive years, residual ovarian follicles become refractory to gonadotropin stimulation. A declining ovarian production of estradiol-17β leads to lower circulating estradiol concentrations, an alteration in the cyclic estrogen pattern, and a decreased negative feedback to the hypothalamic-pituitary axis.[244,245]

After menopause, the primary estrogen no longer is estradiol but a less potent estrogen, estrone, which is derived primarily from the peripheral conversion of the androgen, androstenedione. As ovarian secretion declines at menopause, increased aromatization of adrenally derived androstenedione to estrone occurs. The aromatase enzyme may be found in fat, liver, and hypothalamic nuclei[246] with a conversion rate that is proportional to body weight.

Postmenopausally, approximately 40 μg of estrone and 6 μg of estradiol are produced daily while, premenopausally, daily estrone production ranges from 80 to 300 μg and estradiol production rates range from 80 to 500 μg.[245] Estradiol concentrations in the postmenopausal woman are due primarily to the conversion of estrone to estradiol. It is of interest that estrogen concentrations do not vary in a cyclical fashion as they do in women who are in their reproductive years.

Ovarian progesterone production also is diminished during the climacteric so that progesterone concentrations after menopause are equivalent to concentrations seen in the follicular phase of the ovarian cycle during the reproductive years.[244] Since these low progesterone plasma concentrations may be insufficient to oppose even low estrogen concentrations, estrogenic effects may be unopposed after menopause. Androgen production remains high during the climacteric, but the overall concentration is decreased from 1500 pg/mL (observed during the reproductive years) to approximately 800 pg/mL.[245] Testosterone is produced by the ovary and adrenal glands and by the extraglandular conversion of androstenedione in premenopausal women. After menopause, ovarian production accounts for at least 50% of circulating testosterone.[245]

Target Tissues Affected by Decreased Estrogen

Clinical symptoms in the climacteric period primarily are associated with an estrogen deficiency which directly affects target tissues, including the hypothalamic-pituitary axis, the ovary, endometrial lining of the uterus, vaginal epithelium, skin, and bone.[244,245,247] Symptom complexes which have been shown to improve with estrogen therapy are vasomotor symptoms (including hot flushes), genitourinary atrophy, and osteoporosis. Estrogen therapy also is protective against coronary heart disease.[248] Studies suggest that the risk for coronary heart disease may be decreased approximately 50%.[248]

Hot Flushes

Signs and Symptoms

39. D.R., a 50-year-old female, has been having sudden feelings of warmth over her chest accompanied by a patchy flushing of her skin for the past month. She now visits her physician because she has been waking up shivering from a perspiration-drenched gown nightly for the past week. D.R. also has noticed a warm sensation after drinking coffee or wine. She denies any current medication use. She has not had a menstrual period for at least 6 months. Her physical examination was normal for a 50-year-old female. What is the assessment based upon the data provided for D.R.?

It appears that D.R. is experiencing hot flushes (hot flashes), a vasomotor symptom associated with the climacteric. Approximately 75% to 85% of all women in the climacteric years will suffer from hot flushes.[244,245] At least 75% initially will suffer from hot flushes in the first menopausal year, with symptoms lasting for one year in 80% but for longer than five years in 25% of women.[245] Of women who have had a bilateral oophorectomy before menopause, 37% to 50% also will experience hot flushes.[245]

Symptoms include a feeling of warmth in the chest, neck, and facial areas which may be accompanied by visible red flushing. The term "flash" may be used to explain a patient's feeling at the beginning of the vasomotor episode while the "flush" is the true physical vasomotor episode that can be recorded using skin conductance studies.[249] The flushes characteristically are episodic rather than continuous. Women also may experience other vasomotor symptoms including headaches, dizziness, palpitations, nausea, vomiting, diaphoresis, and night sweats.[245,250] Insomnia and sleep deprivation associated with hot flushes may result in fatigue, nervousness, irritability, forgetfulness, inability to concentrate, and depression. An increased environmental temperature, the ingestion of hot liquids or alcohol, and mental stress also may provoke hot flushes.

Associated with the hot flushes is a rapid skin temperature elevation which may last from 10 to 15 minutes, longer than the 2.4 to 4.7 minute range for the duration of hot flushes.[250,251] Additionally, changes in basal metabolic rate, heart rate, and blood pressure as well as increased blood velocity in peripheral blood vessels (such as those in the fingers) have been observed during hot flushes.[249,250]

40. What are the underlying causes of the hot flushes associated with the climacteric?

The hot flush may result from changes that occur in the hypothalamic thermoregulatory center. Estrogen deficiency may cause a downward resetting of the central hypothalamic thermostat which leads to heat dissipation through vasodilation and perspiration at relatively low body temperature. Hot flushes occur and the core body temperature declines.[249,252]

The exact trigger for hot flushes is unknown, but there clearly is an association between the development of hot flushes and declining estrogen concentrations that occur during the climacteric. Conjugated estrogens are more effective than placebo in reducing hot flushes, but when exogenous estrogen is withdrawn, hot flushes promptly resume.[249] Investigators have shown objectively that eth-

Table 46.13	Hormone Replacement Therapy[273]
Drug (Brand Name)	Minimum Daily Dosage to Prevent Bone Loss
Estrogens	
Conjugated estrogens[a] (Premarin)	0.625 mg
Estropipate[a] (piperazine estrone sulfate) (Ogen)	0.625 mg
Ethinyl estradiol[b] (Estinyl)	0.02 mg
Micronized estradiol[a] (Estrace)	0.5 mg
Estradiol transdermal system[a] (Estraderm)	0.05 mg/24-hr patch applied twice weekly
Progestins	
Medroxyprogesterone acetate[b] (various generic and brand name products)	2.5 mg for continuous regimens or 5 or 10 mg for sequential regimens
Norethindrone/norethindrone acetate[b] (various brand name products)	2.5 mg for continuous and sequential regimens

[a] Approved by the FDA for prevention and treatment of osteoporosis.
[b] Not approved by the FDA for prevention and treatment of osteoporosis.

inyl estradiol reduces hot flushes by measuring changes in finger temperature; subjectively, symptoms are eliminated.[252] Nevertheless, it appears that low estrogen concentrations do not cause hot flushes independently. London and Hammond[245] believe there are no differences in total estrogen or luteinizing hormone concentrations between women who experience hot flushes and those who do not. Instead, they postulate that there are differences in concentrations of biologically active estrogen (i.e., estrogen not bound to sex hormone-binding globulin) that crosses into the central nervous system. Estrogen deficiency in the CNS may then affect the neurons in the hypothalamus that produce hot flushes.[245]

Hot flushes occur with pulsatile increases in LH serum concentrations, but these luteinizing pulsations do not appear responsible for the flushes. Instead, it is likely that factors triggering LH release also initiate the flushes. For example, gonadal failure may increase hypothalamic norepinephrine which increases GnRH and subsequently, LH. Norepinephrine has been shown to play roles in central thermoregulatory function and the release of GnRH from the hypothalamus. Since both GnRH neurons and the thermoregulatory centers are in close proximity in the hypothalamus, catecholamine may be the link between pulsatile LH release and the occurrence of hot flushes.[245,249]

Declining estrogen concentrations in the CNS also may be associated with decreased opioid concentrations in the CNS.[245] A lowering of opioid concentrations or an alteration in the ratio of norepinephrine to opioid may result in the lability of the thermoregulatory center. Symptoms of opiate withdrawal are similar to those noted by women who experience hormonal decline during menopause. This similarity adds additional support to the notion that declining gonadal estrogen concentrations are associated with falling endogenous opioid activity.[245,249] Decreased concentrations of serotonin in the CNS or a change in the ratio of norepinephrine to serotonin may be responsible for symptoms such as insomnia, fatigue, and depression noted by postmenopausal women.[245]

Treatment

41. What therapeutic modalities might benefit D.R.?

Oral Estrogens. Menopausal hot flushes are responsive to estrogen therapy. The most effective estrogen dose for the relief of vasomotor instability-related symptoms varies with a woman's level of estrogen deprivation. Treatment for a patient such as D.R. could begin with a low dose of oral estrogen such as 0.3 or 0.625

mg of conjugated estrogens (Premarin)[253] or an equivalent dose of another oral estrogen. (See Table 46.13 for estrogen products used for hormone replacement.) The dose should be adjusted until the lowest dose that will control symptoms is achieved. Estrogen may be administered on a continuous or a cyclical basis (e.g., 25 days a month). Although continuously administered estrogen and progestin may result in variable patterns of breakthrough bleeding for the first four to six months of therapy, amenorrhea should occur in 60% to 65% of women thereafter. Continuous administration may be preferred because it should increase patient compliance in women who prefer to have as little estrogen-associated bleeding as possible, and it may result in less menopausal-associated symptoms.[254] For these and other possible methods for estrogen and progestin administration, see Figure 46.3.

Women such as D.R. with an intact uterus should receive a progestin for at least 12 days a month along with estrogen replacement therapy (ERT). This is to decrease the risk for endometrial hyperplasia and a possible fourfold to eightfold increase in endometrial cancer associated with unopposed estrogen use.[254,255] The incidence of endometrial hyperplasia is approximately 4% when progestins are administered seven days monthly, 2% when used for ten days a month, and 0% when used 12 days monthly.[256] Oral progestins commonly used to antagonize the endometrial effects of estrogen replacement are divided into two classes, the C-19-nortestosterone derivatives and C-21 derivatives. Medroxyprogesterone acetate (Provera) which is the progestin most commonly used in the U.S. in hormone replacement therapy regimens is a C-21 derivative. Data suggest that 5 to 10 mg of oral medroxyprogesterone acetate is needed daily for at least 12 days monthly to prevent endometrial hyperplasia when used in cyclical regimens while 2.5 to 5 mg/day are recommended when used in continuous regimens.[257,258] Although not as effective for the relief of hot flushes as estrogen, a progestin alone may be used if a patient is unable to tolerate estrogens. (See Figure 46.3 for various estrogen-progestin regimens.)

Since hot flushes are self-limiting, estrogen therapy should be discontinued as soon as possible, usually within 6 to 12 months, unless the woman needs to continue estrogen for other postmenopausal problems. Estrogen therapy should be tapered gradually because abrupt withdrawal may result in recurrence of vasomotor

Fig 46.3 Treatment Regimens for Estrogen-Progestogen Therapy X = Normal flow; S = Spotting or light flow. Reprinted with permission from reference 273.

symptoms. Before estrogen therapy is started, a baseline histologic evaluation of the endometrium may be performed to rule out the presence of endometrial hyperplasia or adenocarcinoma. If either is revealed, estrogen therapy should not be instituted. Obtaining a baseline histologic evaluation may not always be possible, especially in women who are extremely estrogen deficient and have little, if any, endometrial lining. While on estrogen therapy, abnormal vaginal bleeding would be reason for a biopsy.

Transdermal Estradiol. As an alternative to oral ERT, D.R. might use an estradiol transdermal system available as Estraderm 0.05 (each 10 cm^2 system contains 4 mg of estradiol and delivers 0.05 mg/day) or Estraderm 0.1 (each 20 cm^2 system contains 8 mg of estradiol and delivers 0.1 mg/day). If D.R. wants to use a transdermal system, she should be started on the lower dose, and only if her symptoms do not abate should she be switched to the other system. D.R. needs to be informed that the transdermal system (patch) should be applied twice weekly for at least three weeks each month for the relief of vasomotor symptoms. The patch should be applied to a clean, dry area on the trunk such as the abdomen rather than the breasts or to skin that is oily, abraded, or irritated. In addition, the old patch should be removed before applying the new one.

The effects of 0.05 mg and 0.1 mg of transdermal estradiol are similar to those produced by 0.625 mg and 1.25 mg of conjugated estrogens, respectively;[259,260] however, three to four weeks of therapy are necessary for women to receive a full therapeutic effect from transdermal estradiol delivery.[261] (See Question 42.)

Clonidine appears more effective in reducing menopausal flushes than placebo, but it is less effective than hormone replacement therapy.[249] Hot flushes may be reduced by clonidine's ability to selectively stimulate postsynaptic α_2-receptors found in both the vasomotor center of the medulla oblongata and in the hypothalamus; this ultimately may decrease norepinephrine release.[250] Doses of 0.1 to 0.2 mg orally twice a day of clonidine have been used, but side effects are common.[245] Other medications including beta blockers, androgens, and verapamil have been used with some success.

Megestrol Acetate. Doses of megestrol acetate 20 mg orally twice daily resulted in an 85% reduction of hot flushes compared to a 21% reduction when placebo was used.[200] This was noted in a group of 97 women and 66 men who experienced hot flushes secondary to breast cancer or prostate cancer treatment, respectively. Thus, for women who are experiencing hot flushes secondary to cancer chemotherapy, or the results thereof, megestrol acetate appears to be an alternative to the use of estrogen which is relatively contraindicated in this patient group because of a possibility to increase tumor growth.[200] Thus, the short-term use of progestins such as megestrol acetate (Megace) in doses of 20 to 40 mg/day, depot medroxyprogesterone acetate (Depo-Provera) in doses of 50 to 150 mg every one to three months, and medroxyprogesterone (various manufacturers) in doses of 10 mg/day have been effective in decreasing hot flushes in women unable take estrogen.[262]

42. Transdermal Estradiol Versus Oral Estrogens. Are there any advantages or potential advantages associated with the use of transdermal estradiol over the use of oral estrogens for vasomotor symptoms?

Estrogens administered orally are metabolized primarily to estrone because of a significant hepatic first-pass effect which does not occur when estrogens are administered transdermally, vaginally, or parenterally. This first-pass effect produces elevations of hepatic factors such as renin substrate, sex hormone-binding globulin, cortisol-binding globulin activity, and thyroxine-binding globulin that are not elevated significantly in women using trans-

dermal estrogen.[260] The significance of these elevations is poorly understood, but increased renin substrate and an alteration in clotting factors did not appear to increase the risk of hypertension or coagulation problems in women using oral agents. Estrogens given orally or transdermally generally do not change plasma lipid concentrations significantly. However, conjugated estrogen 1.25 mg significantly decreased total cholesterol and low-density lipoprotein and increased high-density lipoprotein and the HDL:LDL ratio.[260] These latter effects are known to be protective against coronary heart disease.[248,260] Additionally, FSH and LH serum concentrations were reduced significantly in postmenopausal women who used transdermal estradiol (0.05, 0.1, or 0.2 mg/day) or oral conjugated estrogens (0.625 or 1.25 mg/day), but the highest dosage of each hormonal agent did not reduce serum concentrations to levels seen in premenopausal women.[260]

Genitourinary Atrophy

Signs and Symptoms

43. R.J., a 60-year-old female who has remarried recently, complains of debilitating pain associated with intercourse. She also complains of vaginal dryness during intercourse, pain and urgency on urination, and occasional nocturia. Upon physical examination, she is noted to have sparse, gray pubic hair. Her labia minora has a pale, dry appearance while the labia majora appears flattened. Her vagina is small with a pale, dry epithelium. Vaginal and urine specimens were obtained for cultures. Direct endometrial sampling also was performed for cytologic and histologic studies. How would you assess R.J.'s problem?

R.J. appears to be experiencing symptoms associated with genitourinary atrophy, a problem that begins as estrogen levels decline. The vulva, vagina, uterus, urethra, and trigone of the bladder all are sensitive to changes in circulating estrogens and are prone to atrophic changes as estrogen stimulation diminishes with age. The vagina decreases in size and loses its rugal pattern; its mucosa becomes pale, thin, and dry. The labia minora shrinks in size while the labia majora is flattened because of decreased subcutaneous fat and tissue elasticity.[245] Thus, the postmenopausal vagina is traumatized more easily with intercourse. Postmenopausal women who engage in regular coital activity have less atrophic vaginal changes compared to women of similar age and estrogen levels who do not have intercourse regularly.[263] Also, postmenopausal women who have breaks in their sexual intercourse patterns, such as that experienced by R.J. between the death of her first husband and remarriage, tend to have dyspareunia (painful coitus) with the resumption of intercourse. A Swedish survey of 902 postmenopausal women (average age: 61 years) reported that 38% experienced vaginal dryness and/or dyspareunia; 15% had vaginal pruritus, pain, or discharge; 29% experienced urinary incontinence; and 13% had chronic urinary tract infections.[264]

Changes in vaginal pH from 4.5 to 5 (observed during the reproductive years) to 6 to 8 after menopause may predispose women such as R.J. to increased bacterial colonization and possible infectious vaginitis. Therefore, a vaginal culture for possible bacterial related vaginitis may be needed, although R.J.'s problem probably is atrophic vaginitis.

Secondary to declining estrogen concentrations, atrophic changes also occur in the urethra and bladder trigone, which predispose postmenopausal women to the urethral syndrome, a recurrent nonbacterial urethritis. Symptoms associated with the syndrome include increased dysuria (painful urination), frequency and urgency of urination, postvoid dribbling, and nocturia.[244,245] R.J. is experiencing many of these symptoms. It also is important to obtain a urine culture because the urinary symptoms R.J. is exhibiting may not be attributed entirely to the urethral syndrome. The incidence of bacteriuria which may cause these symptoms also is increased in postmenopausal women (7%–10% versus 4% in pre-menopausal women).[245]

Stress incontinence is another common problem in older women that can cause significant discomfort and embarrassment. Incontinence may be acute or chronic, and some patients experience both forms. Chronic urinary incontinence can be divided into overflow incontinence, urge incontinence, and stress incontinence with the latter type being the one for which estrogen administration may be helpful. In addition to estrogen administration, other therapeutic modalities for women with stress incontinence include pelvic floor exercises, biofeedback, α-adrenergic agonists such as pseudo-ephedrine or phenylpropanolamine which increase smooth muscle tone and surgery.[265]

Several mechanisms have been postulated for the effects of estrogen on the urethra. Estrogen may increase the numbers of estrogen and α-adrenoreceptors in the urethra; cellular proliferation, and thus, the thickness of the urethral mucosa; the strength of the musculature involved in urethral closure pressure; and abdominal pressure transmission to the urethra.[265] The optimal estrogen dose, route of administration, or length of therapy is unknown, but conjugated estrogens given at doses of 0.3 to 1.25 mg/day have improved this condition.[265]

Treatment

44. What therapeutic approach might be used to decrease the vaginal and urinary symptoms R.J. is experiencing?

Vaginally Administered Estrogens. Symptoms associated with genitourinary atrophy respond to either local or systemic estrogen therapy.[245] Estrogens reverse vaginal epithelial thinning and decrease the vaginal pH. Various estrogen creams have been compared. The vaginal use of estrone, estradiol, and conjugated estrogens all abated symptoms associated with atrophic vaginitis. Although 0.625 or 1.25 mg/day of vaginally administered conjugated estrogens decreases symptoms associated with atrophic vaginitis, 0.3 mg administered vaginally also results in symptomatic relief and a 70% increase in the superficial vaginal epithelial cell count.[266] Since hormonal therapy should begin with the lowest dose that will relieve symptoms, 0.3 to 0.625 mg of conjugated estrogen cream (or an equivalent dose of another vaginally administered estrogen cream) should be prescribed initially. The cream should be applied daily for one to three months, then intermittently for the relief of symptoms.[245] Therapy should be discontinued as soon as possible unless it is needed for other menopausal problems.

Before estrogen therapy is started, histologic evaluation of the endometrium may be performed to rule out the presence of endometrial hyperplasia or adenocarcinoma. If either is observed, estrogen therapy should not be started. (Also see Questions 51–53 for discussions of risks, benefits, contraindications, and adverse effects associated with estrogen replacement therapy.)

Oral and Transdermal Estrogens. Oral or transdermal estrogen administration is an alternative to vaginal administration if the patient does not wish to use a vaginal cream or if she needs ERT for other postmenopausal problems such as the prevention or treatment of osteoporosis. The urinary symptoms which R.J. has been experiencing also may respond to ERT if they are caused by the urethral syndrome.

Primary Osteoporosis

Osteoporosis is a decrease in bone density without a change in the chemical composition or a reduction of expected bone mass. As a result of this decreased bone mass, minor traumatic events, such as a fall from a standing position or rolling over in bed, can produce fractures.

Incidence and Fracture Sites

Osteoporosis is a major health problem which affects approximately 25 million Americans, the majority of whom are women.[247] Annually, 1.5 million osteoporosis-related fractures occur in elderly Americans.[247] Fracture sites predominantly include the vertebrae, distal radius (Colles' fracture), and hips. Statistically, 32% of women and 17% of men living to age 90 will suffer at least one osteoporosis-related fracture.[267] The risk of a hip fracture occurring during the lifetime of an average adult white female (estimated life expectancy: 80 years) is approximately 15%; for an average white male (estimated life expectancy: 75 years) the estimated risk is 5%.[268] Patients who suffer hip fractures have a 12% to 20% higher mortality rate when compared with normal individuals of the same sex and similar age.[268] Additionally, hip fractures result in a multitude of complications for the elderly including prolonged hospitalization, decreased independent living, depression, and fears concerning future falls and lifelong disability. Vertebral fractures may be painless or result in pain that usually lasts less than three months. The initiating injury may be as minor as a cough or turning over in bed. Vertebral collapse or deformity may result in loss of height, kyphosis (dowager's hump), abdominal protuberance, decreased pulmonary function, and chronic back pain.

The annual cost for treating osteoporosis and osteoporosis-related fractures in the U.S. currently exceeds $10 billion and is projected to double in the next 30 years if prevention and early intervention measures do not reduce the incidence.[269] Thus, it is staggering to consider the potential impact osteoporosis may have on the health care system in the twenty-first century.

Pathophysiology

Structurally, bone may be either cortical or trabecular, with the adult skeleton containing 80% cortical and 20% trabecular (cancellous) bone.[268] Dense cortical bone forms the outer shell of the skeleton while porous trabecular bone forms the interior structures in a honeycombed fashion. The proportions of cortical and trabecular bone vary at different sites in the skeleton, with cortical bone predominating in long bones (≈90%) except at their ends which predominantly are trabecular. Trabecular bone is predominant in the vertebrae (greater than 66%) and distal forearms (50%–70%).[268,270] A balance between osteoblast and osteoclast activity results in a continuous remodeling process with osteoclasts resorbing bone while osteoblasts help reform bony surfaces and fill bony cavities.

Changes in Bone Mass

Bone mass peaks during the third decade.[267] After 35 to 40 years of age, cortical bone gradually decreases 0.3% to 0.5% yearly in both women and men.[271] Following menopause, cortical bone loss increases to 2% to 3% yearly and is superimposed on age-related bone loss; this loss then gradually decreases over eight to ten years until annual bone loss is similar to premenopausal rates.[271] This accelerated bone loss occurs after natural menopause and surgical oophorectomy. Trabecular bone loss begins between the ages of 30 and 35 with yearly decreases in women of 0.6% to 0.8% (linear decrease) or 2.4% (curvilinear decrease).[271,272] It appears that age-related trabecular losses in women begin earlier, even a decade earlier, than cortical bone loss. Thus, early trabecular bone loss in conjunction with postmenopausal decreases in cortical bone may lead to increased vertebral and distal forearm fractures which predominate early after menopause.[271] Additionally, women may be at increased risk for osteoporosis because throughout life they have 30% less bone mass than men of similar age.[267]

Classification

Osteoporosis may be classified as Type I, II, or III. Type I or "Postmenopausal Osteoporosis" is associated with increased trabecular bone loss. It occurs primarily in women during the first three to six years after menopause but may continue for up to 20 years following menopause and is manifested by vertebral fractures, distal radius fractures, and increased tooth loss (secondary to osteoporosis of the mandible). It has a female:male ratio of 6:1[272] and may occur earlier in women who have had an oophorectomy.

Type II or "Senile Osteoporosis" occurs in both women and men older than age 70 with a female:male ratio of 2:1.[272] Cortical and trabecular bone loss are proportional. Elderly patients are at greatest risk for hip, pelvic, and vertebral fractures. Thus, women ages 50 to 75 are at increased risk for Type I osteoporosis, while older women (>70) are more prone to Type II-associated fractures.

Type III or "Secondary Osteoporosis" occurs secondarily to the use of various medications or the presence of particular disease states (see Table 46.14 and Question 45). This type of osteoporosis can occur at any age and is equally common in men and women.

Bone remodeling is a continuous process that occurs in discrete skeletal foci called "bone-remodeling units."[247] This process begins with bone resorption that is initiated by osteoclasts excavating the lacuna that are found on the surface of trabecular bone or it occurs when cavities are formed in cortical bone. (See Figure 46.4.) Thereafter, bone formation occurs as osteoblasts gradually refill the spaces that were created during the resorption process.[247] A decline in serum estrogen concentrations that occurs after menopause initiates bone loss at an accelerated rate ("high turnover bone loss") in patients with Type I osteoporosis. In these patients, the osteoclasts create a deeper than normal resorption cavity that is not refilled completely by the osteoblasts. In elderly patients with Type II osteoporosis, the osteoblasts are unable to refill normal bone cavities created by the osteoclasts. This type of abnormal bone remodeling is termed "low turnover bone loss." High turnover bone loss that most often is seen in postmenopausal women usually is more damaging than bone loss that occurs in the elderly (i.e., low turnover bone loss). The former also results in a significant loss of trabecular bone.[247]

Risk Factors

45. T.J., a 28-year-old thin, white, single woman, is worried about developing osteoporosis. Her 75-year-old maternal

Fig 46.4 The Bone Remodeling Cycle at the Cellular Level In normal young adults (top panels), the bone removed by the osteoclasts (left) is replaced completely by the osteoblasts (right). In high turnover bone loss (middle panels), such as that which occurs in women soon after menopause, the osteoclasts create a deeper resorption cavity that is not refilled completely. In low turnover bone loss (bottom panels), such as that which occurs with aging, the osteoclasts create a resorption cavity of normal or decreased depth, but the osteoblasts fail to refill it. Reprinted by permission of The New England Journal of Medicine (372;621, 1992).

grandmother has osteoporosis and recently, her postmenopausal mother (age 53) was told that she was at increased risk for osteoporosis. T.J. is 5′ 2″ tall, weighs 108 pounds, and is in good health. She jogs and occasionally does aerobic exercise. Her diet typically consists of cereal for breakfast, a sandwich for lunch, and meat with vegetables for dinner. Her only milk consumption consists of ½ cup of skim milk used for her cereal. She occasionally has a dairy product for lunch or dinner. T.J. takes no medications except a daily multiple vitamin which contains 400 IU of vitamin D; she does not use a calcium supplement. She denies cigarette smoking and occasionally drinks alcohol at social functions. Is T.J. at increased risk for developing osteoporosis?

Table 46.14 lists endogenous and exogenous risk factors that are associated with the development of osteoporosis. T.J. has several risk factors which could increase her risk for osteoporosis. She is a white female of small stature and low weight, has a positive family history, and has a low calcium intake.

Gender, Race, Heredity, and Body Build. White and Asian women in the U.S. are at greater risk for osteoporosis because of their lower bone mass than are men or blacks of either gender.[269,273] Women small in stature, such as T.J., and those proportionally underweight for height are at increased risk for osteoporosis.[269,273] The significance of heredity as a risk factor for osteoporosis is being studied. It has been proposed that approximately 75% of the genetic effect on an individual's chance to develop osteoporosis is due to a particular allelic variant in the gene that is responsible for encoding the 1,25-dihydroxyvitamin D receptor.[274] This initial study suggests that heredity is very important in the development of osteoporosis, but other studies are needed to confirm these results and to separate genetic from environmental influences.

Mobility. Immobility resulting from prolonged bedrest (especially in the elderly) has been associated with decreased bone mass. Conversely, weight-bearing exercise prevents further reduction and helps restore both cortical and trabecular bone loss.[267,268,273] Exercise throughout life helps maintain skeletal mass and may help reduce bone loss even in postmenopausal women.[273]

Calcium. The amount of calcium needed by women to achieve and help maintain optimal bone mass has been debated for many years. The current recommended dietary allowance (RDA) for elemental calcium for nonpregnant, nonlactating women is 800 mg/day, but others, such as those in attendance at the National

Table 46.14	Risk Factors Associated with the Development of Osteoporosis
Endogenous	**Exogenous**
↑ age	Sedentary lifestyle
Female gender	↓ mobility
Caucasian or Asian	Low calcium intake
Heredity	Excessive alcohol problems
Small stature	Cigarette smoking
Low weight	Predisposing medical problems (e.g., chronic liver disease, chronic renal failure, hyperthyroidism, primary hyperparathyroidism, Cushing's syndrome, GI[a] resection, or malabsorption)
Early menopause or oophorectomy	
	Drugs (e.g., corticosteroids, long-term anticonvulsant therapy, excessive use of aluminum-containing antacids, long-term high-dose heparin, furosemide, excessive levothyroxine therapy)

a GI = Gastrointestinal.

Institutes of Health (NIH) Consensus Panel on Osteoporosis, recommended 1000 mg/day of elemental calcium for premenopausal women and postmenopausal women receiving estrogen and 1500 mg for postmenopausal women not receiving estrogen replacement.[267] To address the issue of what is an adequate amount of calcium for women of various ages, the NIH convened The Consensus Development Conference on the Optimal Calcium Intake.[275] The recommendations from this conference included the need for adolescents and young adults to age 24 to ingest 1200 to 1500 mg of elemental calcium to meet their calcium needs. Women between the ages of 25 and 50 need a daily calcium intake of 1000 mg/day while postmenopausal women or those over age 50 should ingest 1500 mg/day of calcium.

Cigarette Smoking and Alcohol Ingestion. Although T.J. does not smoke and only occasionally ingests alcohol, it is important to include questions concerning cigarette and alcohol use when obtaining a medication history from an individual at risk for osteoporosis. Women who smoke, especially those who are thin, are at increased risk for fractures compared to nonsmokers.[268,276,277] Additionally, premenopausal smokers have lower estrogen serum concentrations and undergo menopause earlier than nonsmokers while postmenopausal smokers using exogenous estrogen have lower serum concentrations than expected.[277] In addition, smoking may negate some of the benefits from estrogen replacement therapy on bone. Excessive alcohol use by both women and men may predispose them to osteoporosis, but it is unclear whether moderate alcohol consumption has an effect on bone mass. The mechanism appears to be a direct effect of alcohol on osteoblasts, resulting in decreased bone formation.[278]

Potential Risks. It is postulated that *excessive caffeine ingestion* may increase the risk of osteoporosis. A lifetime ingestion of caffeine has been shown to decrease bone mineral density (BMD) in postmenopausal women. In a study in which 980 postmenopausal women were enrolled, BMD was decreased in the hip and lumbar spine as demonstrated by dual energy x-ray absorptiometry.[279] Those women who have ingested the equivalent of two cups of coffee daily throughout their adult lives were at an increased risk for decreased BMD, but the deleterious effect of caffeine on bones could be offset by the daily drinking of one or more glasses of milk. *High-protein diets* may increase urinary calcium excretion by reducing tubular reabsorption but this effect appears to be a minor effect.[268,272]

Drugs. Corticosteroids, phenytoin, aluminum-containing antacids, and long-term high-dose heparin therapy have been associated with the development of Type III osteoporosis (see Table 46.14 for other medications that may predispose a patient to osteoporosis). Long-term corticosteroid use predisposes patients to fractures primarily by decreasing trabecular bone mass.[268] The mechanism by which this occurs is complex. It may be due to "a direct inhibition of osteoblasts, a decrease in intestinal absorption and renal tubular reabsorption of calcium, and an inhibition of bone collagen synthesis."[273] Phenytoin (Dilantin), when used long-term, may increase the catabolism of vitamin D and its active metabolites to inactive forms: this then may decrease calcium absorption from the gastrointestinal tract.[273] Aluminum-containing antacids may affect calcium balance.[268] Heparin, when administered at high doses (15,000 units/day) for long time periods, may inhibit the conversion of vitamin D renally.[280]

Disease. Patients with a variety of different diseases may be at higher risk than the population as a whole for Type III osteoporosis (see Table 46.14 for specific diseases). In addition, women who have undergone oophorectomy before menopause are at high risk for developing osteoporosis at a younger age.

Prevention

Premenopausal Women

46. Although T.J. is premenopausal, what recommendations could be made to decrease her future risk of developing osteoporosis?

Since T.J. is premenopausal, she should take steps to prevent future osteoporosis. Thus, her course of action should be to maximize her peak bone mass and prevent or decrease bone loss. This may be accomplished by maintaining adequate calcium and vitamin D intakes, and developing a lifelong exercise program.

Vitamin D requirements for adults range from 200 to 400 IU/day (current RDA: 200 IU/day for nonpregnant women over age 24) which T.J. should obtain from her diet and exposure to sunlight. T.J. could increase her dietary vitamin D intake by adding more milk to her diet (1 quart contains 400 IU of vitamin D and 1200 mg of elemental calcium).[273] Additionally, she has been taking a multiple vitamin which contains 400 IU of vitamin D. Current studies do not show that increased vitamin D helps to prevent osteoporosis; however, higher than recommended doses may lead to toxicity.

Exercise. T.J. should be encouraged to participate regularly in weight-bearing exercises such as jogging, walking, running, biking, tennis, or weight lifting and to continue exercise appropriate for her age throughout life, because weight-bearing exercise is important for the maximization and maintenance of bone mass even in postmenopausal women.[281] Aerobic training also is important in controlling weight, increasing cardiorespiratory endurance, and decreasing the risk for cardiovascular disease.[281]

Young women such as T.J. should be informed that excessive exercise may cause amenorrhea. Women with exercise-induced amenorrhea have been reported to have decreased lower lumbar mineralization and a high propensity for running-related fractures; they also may be at increased risk for developing early osteoporosis.[282,283]

Calcium. T.J.'s diet should be calcium-enriched to ensure that she receives at least 800 mg/day of elemental calcium to meet the current RDA, but she should be encouraged to ingest 1000 mg/day as recommended during the recent NIH Consensus Development Conference on Optimal Calcium Intake.[275] Optimally, calcium should be from dietary sources.[275] Because dairy products are the major source of dietary calcium in the U.S., T.J. should select low-fat dairy products to decrease her caloric intake and minimize her fat intake when possible. If T.J. were lactose intolerant, she could select dairy products containing lactase. Although nondairy sources may contain lower amounts of calcium, they may be included in a diet plan to increase calcium content, especially when a woman cannot or will not use dairy products. Salmon, sardines, and dark green leafy vegetables are good sources of calcium.[284,285] (See Table 46.15 for the calcium content of some selected foods.)

If T.J. is unable to meet her daily calcium requirement from dietary sources, she can use a calcium supplement. Table 46.16 lists the percentage of elemental calcium available from selected calcium salts.

47. Which calcium salt should be recommended for T.J.?

Currently, not enough data are available to make a definitive decision as to which calcium salt is the best (see Table 46.16 for information about various calcium salts). Sheikh et al. demonstrated no significant difference in the absorption of calcium (range: 27%–39%) from various salts (acetate, carbonate, citrate, gluconate, and lactate) or milk in eight healthy, fasting male subjects who ingested 500 mg of elemental calcium from each of the previously mentioned sources.[286] Recker[287] reported that calcium ranged from 21% to 26% for ten healthy, postmenopausal females

Table 46.15	Calcium Content of Selected Foods[284,285]	
Food	Serving Size	Calcium (mg)
Dairy Products		
Milk, dry nonfat	1 cup	350–450
Yogurt, low fat	1 cup	345
Milk, skim	1 cup	303
Milk, whole	1 cup	250–350
Cheese, cheddar	1 oz	211
Cheese, cottage	1 cup	211
Cheese, American	1 oz	195
Ice cream or ice milk	½ cup	50–150
Fish		
Sardines, in oil	8 med	354
Salmon, canned (pink)	3 oz	167
Vegetables		
Spinach, fresh cooked	½ cup	245
Broccoli, cooked	1 med spear	205
Collards, turnip greens	½ cup	175
Kale	½ cup	50–150

who each ingested 250 mg of ^{45}Ca-labeled elemental calcium from whole milk, chocolate milk, yogurt, imitation milk, cheese, and calcium carbonate. Individuals with achlorhydria have decreased calcium absorption from insoluble calcium carbonate, but calcium absorption was normalized when subjects ingested calcium carbonate with a meal rather than during a fasting state.[288] Elderly individuals, especially those with osteoporosis, also may experience poor calcium absorption because of decreased gastric acid secretion which occurs with aging. Additionally, older individuals, especially those over age 70, have impaired calcium absorption associated with decreased 1,25-dihydroxyvitamin D$_3$ serum concentrations[289] and decreased estrogen concentrations. Thus, older individuals may require increased calcium intakes to prevent a negative calcium balance. This increased need also may be met by the use of a soluble calcium supplement such as calcium citrate because it is absorbed better than calcium carbonate at higher gastric pHs. If calcium carbonate is the selected supplement, it should be taken in divided doses with meals to increase absorption.[288,290]

Young adults, such as T.J., normally can increase calcium absorption when calcium intake is low. Therefore, T.J. should not have a problem with calcium absorption. A calcium carbonate-containing product should be suggested because it currently is the most frequently used calcium supplement, has a high elemental calcium content, and is inexpensive. If T.J. needs a supplement, she should be advised to take it in divided doses with meals to increase absorption.[288,290] She also should be told to avoid taking her calcium concomitantly with fiber or drugs such as tetracycline. She should be informed that the most common adverse effects associated with calcium use are constipation, GI irritation, and flatulence. Additionally, doses exceeding current recommendations could result in hypercalcemia, hypercalciuria, and possibly, urinary stones. If T.J. or any family member has a history of urinary stones, she should be under close medical supervision while taking calcium.

Postmenopausal Women

48. T.J.'s mother, M.J., also is a woman of small stature and low weight. She occasionally walks in the evenings but otherwise exercises little. She currently is taking a calcium supplement to maintain a total calcium intake of about 1 gm/day. She takes no medications except an occasional aspirin for headaches. M.J. was a smoker but stopped in her late twenties; she rarely drinks alcohol. She is in good health and has had no gynecological surgery or major diseases. Her last menstrual period was approximately 6 months ago. Her menstrual periods were regular until 2 years ago when she began experiencing irregularity. The results of a recent quantitative CT scan showed decreased vertebral bone mass. She recently discussed the possibility of starting ERT with her gynecologist. What recommendations for therapy should be made to a postmenopausal woman such as M.J. for the prevention of osteoporosis?

M.J. shares similar risk factors with her daughter, but additionally, she is early in the postmenopausal phase and was a previous smoker.

Vitamin D. Like T.J., it is important for M.J. to have an adequate vitamin D intake from her diet and exposure to sunlight. Although the RDA for vitamin D is 200 IU for women over age 24, it has been recommended that postmenopausal women such as M.J. should ingest 400 to 800 IU/day of vitamin D.[290] This may be achieved from a diet that contains appropriate amounts of vitamin D or from the ingestion of a daily multiple vitamin containing vitamin D.

Exercise. M.J. should begin an exercise program appropriate for her age and physical condition because exercise (and in particular weight-bearing exercise) in conjunction with an appropriate vitamin D and calcium intake is important for maintaining healthy bones. However, the impact of weight-bearing exercise on bone mass and fracture rates in postmenopausal women is debated.[269,273,291] In addition, exercise improves muscular function and agility. Exercise that is both aerobic and weight-bearing has a positive effect on bones and cardiovascular health.[269]

Calcium. Because of her postmenopausal status and the presence of other risk factors, M.J. should increase her current intake of calcium to 1500 mg/day as recommended by the NIH Consensus Development Conference on Optimal Calcium Intake to prevent future bone loss.[275]

Although calcium has antiresorptive activity, its role in the prevention and treatment of osteoporosis is currently unclear. In 16 of 19 studies performed before 1993 where calcium intake in postmenopausal women was known, bone mineral density decline was slowed or stopped.[292] Calcium significantly reduced loss of BMD in women who were five or more years postmenopausal. It appears that in the first five years after menopause, the sharp estrogen decline is responsible for BMD loss and not calcium insufficiency.[292] BMD can be slowed or stopped with a total daily calcium intake of at least 900 mg.[293,294] Reid et al. compared the use of supplemental calcium (1000 mg daily) and dietary calcium intake (mean: 1750 mg/day) versus a daily dietary intake of 750 mg and placebo. The calcium supplements significantly slowed loss of total body BMD as well as loss from particular sites such as the legs, trunk, and lumbar spine.[294] Thus, in the initial period after menopause, calcium alone is not an alternative to estrogen in the prevention of osteoporosis. However, calcium supplementation is important in

Table 46.16	Percentage of Calcium in Various Salts
Salt	% Calcium
Calcium carbonate	40
Tricalcium phosphate (calcium phosphate, tribasic)	39
Calcium chloride	27
Dibasic calcium phosphate dihydrate	23
Calcium citrate	21
Calcium lactate	13
Calcium gluconate	9

delaying BMD loss in women, especially those who are at least five years postmenopausal. (See Questions 45–47 for a further discussion of calcium requirements, supplementation, and product selection.)

Estrogen Replacement

Estrogen prophylaxis should be considered for M.J. because she is at risk for osteoporosis. Standard roentgenograms (x-rays) are not useful for the early detection of osteoporosis because bone density must be decreased by 20% to 30% before it can be detected. Therefore, it has been suggested that postmenopausal women at increased risk for osteoporosis be screened for decreased bone density at potential fracture sites (especially vertebrae in early menopause) using quantitative computed tomography, dual-photon absorptiometry (DPA), single-photon absorptiometry (SPA), or another similar radiographic technique.[226] The precision of these methods has improved considerably, but screening remains rather expensive. Women found to have low bone density then could be started on estrogen prophylaxis. If screening techniques are unavailable or a physician elects not to use them, the postmenopausal woman who is at high risk for osteoporosis should be given estrogen prophylaxis with close follow-up. Thus, because M.J. is postmenopausal, has low vertebral density, and has multiple risk factors for osteoporosis, she is to be started on estrogen prophylactically.

49. Effect on Bone Mass. What effect does estrogen have on the bone mass in a postmenopausal woman such as M.J.?

Estrogen replacement therapy is the most effective modality that can be used to prevent osteoporosis in postmenopausal women.[267] Vertebral bone mass has been shown to increase in women with known osteoporosis who receive ERT; this leads to decreased fracture rates.[295] The effect of estrogen on bone is related primarily to its antiresorptive activity; nevertheless, during initial phases of ERT, bone mass may be increased. As bone resorption is decreased, bone formation declines to equal resorption, which results in bone mass stabilization.[272] The interplay between estrogens and receptors located on osteoblasts results in the secretion of a "chemical mediator that inhibits osteoclasts."[273]

50. When should M.J. begin ERT? For what length of time should she continue therapy? What dosage should be used?

Duration of Therapy. The greatest benefits on bone density from ERT in women between menopause and age 75 occur when therapy is begun as soon after menopause as possible and is continued throughout a woman's life. New information from the Framingham Study indicates that the effect of estrogen on bone density wanes in women who have used estrogen for a mean of 11 years after menopause.[296] It has been estimated that 10% to 15% of a woman's bone mass is estrogen-dependent.[297] For women who do not begin estrogen use postmenopausally, their bone density initially will decline 30% between the ages of 50 and 80.[297] This decline postmenopausally occurs at a rate of 2% per year for approximately five years and about 1% per year thereafter. If a woman begins ERT, but stops thereafter, she will have the same rapid bone density loss (i.e., 2% per year) following the discontinuation of ERT that would mirror the rate of loss she would have had after menopause if she had not started ERT. Thereafter, bone loss would proceed at approximately 1% annually.[297]

Because estrogen effects on bone loss decrease after hormonal therapy is discontinued, lifelong use of ERT is advocated for high-risk patients under close medical supervision.[297] For individuals who do not wish to take estrogen throughout their lives, another approach would be to use ERT early on for menopausal symptoms and then reinstitute it later in life to slow bone loss and prevent fractures, for example hip fractures, that occur more frequently in those over 75 years of age.[297] Additionally, long-term estrogen use

in postmenopausal women is advocated for its beneficial effects in the prevention of cardiovascular disease, especially coronary heart disease. (See Question 52.)

Dosing. Conjugated estrogens (Premarin) is the estrogenic preparation most frequently used in the U.S. for the prevention of osteoporosis. Doses of 0.625 or 1.25 mg doses of conjugated estrogens, or the equivalent doses of another estrogen supplement, are effective for the prevention of osteoporosis;[273] however, since the daily dose of estrogen should be as low as possible to minimize risks but high enough to permit a maximum benefit, 0.625 mg orally is the preferred dose. (See Table 46.13 for estrogen preparations and doses.) The NIH Consensus Panel recommended initiating conjugated estrogens at a dose of 0.625 mg/day orally on a cyclical basis.[267] The dose then could be modified if needed. Such a course of therapy (0.625 mg/day of conjugated estrogens) could be recommended for M.J. Estrogen would be given cyclically for 25 days each month, and a progestin would be taken for the last 12 days of each estrogen cycle.[273] Alternatively, the progestin could be given at the beginning of the cycle for the first 12 days. Estrogen and progestin therapy may be combined and given continuously rather than cyclically because it induces amenorrhea in 60% to 65% of women after six months of hormone replacement therapy.[273] Other methods for HRT include "continuous sequential" and "cyclic combined" (see Figure 46.3). The continuous sequential regimen typically is used as an alternative to the cyclic sequential regimen when a woman experiences adverse effects from a lack of estrogen on the days when no estrogen is taken.[273] The cyclic combined regimen may be recommended for the early control of breakthrough bleeding. In some cases, breakthrough bleeding diminishes even after one month of HRT.[254,273]

The administration of conjugated estrogens in a dose of 0.3 mg currently is not recommended for the prevention of osteoporosis. Nevertheless, bone loss was prevented in postmenopausal women when only 0.3 mg of conjugated estrogens was administered with 1500 mg of calcium.[298] Other studies are needed to confirm these findings.

Transdermal estradiol and various oral estrogens are approved for osteoporosis (see Table 46.13) and represent alternative treatment modalities. Women treated with transdermal estradiol had a positive gain in bone density, decreased bone turnover, and maintained serum estradiol concentrations at levels usually noted during the follicular phase of the menstrual cycle.[299] Studies of larger groups of women are needed to confirm these results. (See Questions 41 and 42 for information concerning transdermal estradiol.) Histologic evaluation of the endometrium should be performed if possible before initiating estrogen therapy and annually thereafter or as needed for abnormal bleeding or spotting.

51. Contraindications. What contraindications are there to the use of ERT in a postmenopausal woman such as M.J.? Would any of these prohibit the use of ERT in M.J.?

Contraindications to ERT include current pregnancy; a history of or existing thrombophlebitis or thromboembolic disease; known or suspected breast or endometrial cancer; undiagnosed abnormal genital bleeding; or acute, active hepatic disease.[273] Some data suggest that ERT may not increase a woman's risk for venous thrombosis[273,300] and the use of ERT in women with a history of breast or other hormone-dependent cancers currently is under debate. Therefore, alternative therapies are recommended for those with a history of these types of cancers until more definitive data enable practitioners to appropriately weigh the risks and benefits of ERT in these individuals.[301]

Relative contraindications to postmenopausal HRT use include hypertension, diabetes mellitus, severe varicose veins, depression, or hepatic or renal disease.[302,303]

M.J. is in good health and does not appear to have any contra-indications to estrogen replacement therapy. She should have a physical examination (including endometrial sampling) before estrogen replacement therapy is started and undergo periodic endometrial evaluation while receiving estrogen therapy.

52. Risks. **M.J. asks if she will be at increased risk for cancer or heart disease if she receives ERT for the next 10–15 years. What are the risks associated with ERT in a postmenopausal woman such as M.J.? Are there any benefits from ERT besides osteoporosis prevention?**

Although there is concern that ERT may increase the risk of *breast cancer*, it appears that the greatest risk in a postmenopausal woman with an intact uterus, such as M.J., is *endometrial adenocarcinoma*. Additionally, an increased prevalence of *thromboembolic disorders*, *cholelithiasis*, and *abnormal glucose tolerance* have been reported in postmenopausal women receiving ERT. Estrogen use in postmenopausal women does not appear to increase hypertension and is protective against cardiovascular disease such as myocardial infarction. Some risks associated with estrogens used for oral contraception do not apply to the use of estrogens as part of HRT in older women. Perhaps differences in the types of estrogens used for these two purposes may be responsible for the differing risk rates.

Breast Cancer. Because many studies have reported increases, decreases, or no change in the incidence of breast cancer in postmenopausal women who were "ever-users" of estrogens versus those who were "never-users," Grady et al. reviewed studies and meta-analyses to explore this issue.[304] They calculated a relative risk for breast cancer in the "ever-user" category as 1.01 compared to "never-users." Available data do not indicate that the risk is influenced by differences in estrogen doses or treatment regimens.[304] A relative risk of 1.3 was calculated for women who used ERT for at least 15 years compared to "nonusers." Current data suggest that estrogen use postmenopausally probably does not increase the risk of breast cancer. Nevertheless, a woman using estrogen replacement therapy should examine her breasts regularly and be followed by her physician. The effect of using an estrogen and progestin on the risk of breast cancer currently is unknown because adequate data are unavailable to calculate a relative risk among "ever-users" to "never-users."[304]

Endometrial Adenocarcinoma. Estrogenic receptors in the endometrium respond to exogenous estrogen stimulation by proliferation and hyperplasia of the endometrium. Approximately 12% of women with an intact uterus who use ERT without concomitant progestin will experience endometrial hyperplasia. Additionally, 1.6% to 25% of women with endometrial hyperplasia will develop endometrial adenocarcinoma.[244]

The relative risk of endometrial adenocarcinoma in women receiving estrogen replacement therapy is estimated to be between 4 and 8 and appears to be dose- and duration-related.[255,273] The use of a progestin for the last 10 to 12 days of the estrogen replacement cycle decreases the risk of endometrial cancer.[273,305] This benefit results from the ability of progestins to antagonize the estrogenic proliferative effects on the endometrium and to reverse endometrial hyperplasia.[244]

Thromboembolic Disease. A review of clinical studies has shown both increased and no effects on coagulation factors when various estrogens were used in postmenopausal women.[244] Large, well-designed, controlled studies are needed to determine the thromboembolic potential associated with estrogen replacement therapy. Women with an increased risk for thromboembolic disease should refrain from estrogen use or use estrogen with caution.

Cholelithiasis. A relative risk of 2.5 for cholelithiasis has been reported for postmenopausal women receiving estrogens.[244] *Ab-*

normal glucose tolerance associated with the use of conjugated estrogens, mestranol, quinestrol, and ethinyl estradiol for replacement therapy has resulted in elevated glucose serum concentrations, but these abnormalities rarely progressed to diabetes mellitus. Nevertheless, a diabetic woman using estrogens should be monitored closely.

The use of transdermal estrogen may be of benefit for women who are at risk for thrombophlebitis, pulmonary embolism, intravascular clotting, or cholelithiasis. This potential benefit would be related to avoidance of the hepatic first-pass effect. However, the patient may not benefit from the positive effects on the lipid profile associated with oral estrogens.[294]

Hypertension. A review of epidemiologic studies and clinical trials failed to show a significant association between estrogen use and hypertension.[304] In fact, blood pressure does not appear to increase among women receiving ERT although a small number of women may experience increases in blood pressure when ERT is initiated.[304]

Benefits. Cardiovascular Disease. There appears to be no increased risk for coronary heart disease in women using estrogen replacement therapy. In fact, case-control studies and large cohort studies have shown estrogen use to be protective with relative risk rates of 0.5 to 0.65 which equates with a decrease in coronary heart disease of 35% to 50%.[273,304] Thus, a protective effect may be associated with the favorable effects of oral estrogens on the lipid profile (see Question 42). After menopause, women have increased concentrations of low-density lipoprotein which may increase their risk for cardiovascular disease. The use of estrogen replacement therapy has resulted in decreased concentrations of LDL with increased concentrations of HDL.[273] Other actions of estrogen on the cardiovascular system that may be beneficial include a decrease in platelet adhesiveness and a direct effect on coronary artery receptors that may result in vasodilation.[255]

53. Adverse Effects. **What potential adverse effects of estrogen replacement therapy should be discussed with M.J.?**

M.J. should be aware of estrogen-related adverse effects including nausea, vomiting, dizziness, weight gain, breast tenderness, and breast enlargement. The prevalence of nausea and vomiting secondary to ethinyl estradiol has been reported to be 6% to 10%, but these adverse effects occur less frequently in women using nonsynthetic estrogens.[244]

A woman with an intact uterus, such as M.J., who may receive estrogen replacement therapy alone or in combination with a progestin must be educated about the possible return of uterine bleeding because this is the main reason that women stop taking HRT. Estrogens used alone result in dose-dependent uterine bleeding. Women who received 1.25 mg/day of conjugated estrogens were reported to have a 2% to 12% incidence of bleeding while those receiving 0.625 mg/day had a 1% to 4% incidence.[244] The addition of a progestin cyclically may increase the incidence of uterine bleeding but may normalize the bleeding pattern and reduce breakthrough bleeding. The continuous administration of both hormones at low doses may decrease the incidence of bleeding, but breakthrough bleeding may continue for approximately six months until the endometrium becomes atrophic.[244,273]

54. Use with Progestin. **If M.J. is to be started on progestin therapy, as well as ERT, what progestin should be used?**

The dose and specific progestin to use currently are under debate. Medroxyprogesterone acetate, the most commonly used progestin in the U.S. for hormone replacement therapy, is effective and does not appear to decrease the positive effects of estrogens on serum lipid concentrations. Studies have shown that 2.5 mg of medroxyprogesterone acetate administered continuously or 2.5, 5, or 10 mg administered cyclically with conjugated estrogens decreased total cholesterol and LDL with modest rises in HDL.[257,258] At least 12 days of progestin use each month is needed to reduce the incidence of endometrial hyperplasia (see Question 41).[306]

Treatment

55. T.J.'s 75-year-old grandmother, M.B., was diagnosed as having osteoporosis 5 years ago when she broke her distal forearm. Additionally, she has lost 2″ in height (current height 5′ and weight 100 pounds) and has mild kyphosis. M.B. denies severe back pain but occasionally uses aspirin for mild back pain. The results of a recent quantitative CT scan revealed significantly decreased vertebral and forearm bone mass. M.B. had her last menstrual period before her hysterectomy approximately 25 years ago. Her only major medical problem is mild congestive heart failure (CHF) for which she receives hydrochlorothiazide 25 mg/day PO and digoxin 0.125 mg/day PO. Additionally, M.B. takes conjugated estrogens 0.625 mg PO days 1–25 each month and calcium carbonate 1500 mg/day in divided doses with meals. What changes, if any, should be made in her treatment plan? What other medications might be considered for the treatment of osteoporosis?

It appears that M.B. has Type I osteoporosis but currently is in the age range for developing Type II osteoporosis. Since she already has lost trabecular bone from the forearm and spine, her treatment plan should be aimed at preventing further bone loss.

Calcium and estrogens both are classified as antiresorptive agents and work to decrease bone mass demineralization. Calcium supplementation can slow or prevent further bone loss, especially cortical bone loss that occurs with Type II osteoporosis. M.B.'s calcium intake should be at least 1500 mg/day. Studies by Dawson-Hughes[293] and Reid et al.[294] have demonstrated that bone mass demineralization can be slowed or stopped if adequate calcium is ingested in older postmenopausal women. (See Question 48.) As noted previously, older individuals with osteoporosis may have decreased calcium absorption because of lower gastric acid secretion, decreased 1,25-dihydroxyvitamin D_3 serum concentrations, and decreased endogenous estrogen serum concentrations.[268,288,289] To overcome this problem, M.B. should continue taking her calcium in divided doses with meals or use a more soluble calcium product such as calcium citrate.[275,288,289]

Estrogens. Long-term estrogen use is advocated more frequently, not only for the prevention but also for the treatment of osteoporosis. Riggs and Melton[272] advocate estrogen replacement therapy for women with Type I osteoporosis even if they are 10 to 15 years postmenopausal. They state that estrogen replacement may not decrease bone loss in women who already have Type II osteoporosis because those individuals already have lost significant amounts of bone and no longer lose bone (primarily cortical) at an accelerated rate. Today many gynecologists are recommending long-term estrogen use because the beneficial effects on bone decrease rapidly after estrogen therapy is stopped.[297] Additionally, estrogen replacement is beneficial in reducing cardiovascular disease in postmenopausal women.

Thus, it appears that estrogen replacement therapy should be continued because M.B. currently has only significant Type I osteoporosis. She also may benefit from the cardiovascular protective effects of estrogen and will not be at risk for endometrial adenocarcinoma since she has had a hysterectomy. She is on an appropriate dose of conjugated estrogens and does not need concomitant progestin because she no longer has an intact uterus.

Vitamin D. Although there is no current recommended dietary allowance for vitamin D specified for elderly women, M.B. should maintain a vitamin D intake of at least 200 to 400 IU/day from her diet or a multivitamin containing 400 IU of vitamin D. Hearney has recommended 400 to 800 IU/day for postmenopausal wom-

en.[292] Patients receiving vitamin D require calcium supplementation to ensure calcium availability for absorption. Additionally, because patients receiving high doses of vitamin D can develop vitamin D toxicity, the NIH Consensus Panel recommended that patients not consume more than 600 to 800 IU/day of vitamin D without close medical supervision.[267]

The vitamin D metabolite, 1,25-dihydroxyvitamin D_3 (Rocaltrol), can normalize calcium absorption and reduce the incidence of vertebral fractures; it also is associated with hypercalcemia and hypercalciuria. Additionally, 1,25-dihydroxyvitamin D_3 can stimulate, rather than decrease, the rate of bone turnover.[306] Doses range from 0.25 to 1 μg/day. A patient receiving 1,25-dihydroxyvitamin D_3 should have serum and urinary calcium concentrations routinely monitored. Because 1,25-dihydroxyvitamin D_3 is not used routinely for osteoporosis and M.B.'s osteoporosis appears stable, she currently is not a candidate for such therapy.

Exercise and Prevention of Falls. M.B. should continue exercise appropriate for her age to help maintain bone mass. Additionally, the prevention of falls also should be considered as part of M.B.'s therapy plan because falls often result in fractures. (See Questions 45 and 46.) Other therapeutic modalities that may be used in the treatment of osteoporosis include inhibitors of bone resorption and agents that stimulate bone formation (see Tables 46.17 and 46.18). Many of these agents currently are not FDA-approved for any indication or not specifically for the treatment of osteoporosis.

Thiazides. M.B. currently is receiving hydrochlorothiazide for mild CHF, but thiazides have been shown to increase calcium retention. Whether this effect has long-term benefit on calcium balance is debated. Transbol et al.[307] reported no bone loss for six months in postmenopausal women receiving bendroflumethiazide,

Table 46.17	Inhibitors of Bone Resorption[a,b]	
Drug (Brand Name)	Dosing Regimens	Adverse Effects
Biphosphonates		
Alendronate sodium[c] (Fosamax)	Various doses are being used in studies; no dosage has been established yet to prevent fractures	GI intolerance at doses >10 mg/day
Etidronate disodium[d] (Didronel)	Various doses have been used in studies (e.g., 400 mg/day PO on intermittent schedule of 2 weeks on, 13 weeks off)	—
Pamidronate (Aredia)	Available in the U.S. as an IV form for hypercalcemia;[d] PO form available in Europe, has been used for treating osteoporosis at doses of 150 mg/day PO for 1 year[c]	Nausea associated with PO administration
Calcitonin salmon (Calcimar, Miacalcin)	100 IU/day IM, SQ (100 IU BID intranasal)[c]	Flushing, nausea, vomiting, rash, local irritation with IM or SQ administration
Calcitrol[d] (Rocaltrol)	0.25 μg PO BID; need to adjust using serum calcium concentrations	Hypercalcemia, hypercalciuria, and renal stones

a Adapted with permission from reference 273.
b FDA = Food and Drug Administration; GI = Gastrointestinal.
c Investigational drug and currently not FDA-approved for any indication.
d Not currently approved by the FDA for the prevention or treatment of osteoporosis.

Table 46.18	Stimulators of Bone Formation[a,b]	
Drug	Dosing Regimens	Adverse Effects
Anabolic steroids[c]	Various doses (e.g., nandrolone decanoate 50 mg IM Q 2–3 weeks)	Androgenic effects in women (e.g., hirsutism); ↑ LDL:HDL cholesterol ratio; may aggravate sleep-related breathing disorders
Synthetic human parathyroid hormone[d]	400–750 U/day SQ for 1 week (study data)	Transient redness and itching at injection site
Recombinant human IGF-1[d]	160 μg/day SQ for 1 week (study data)	No adverse effects observed to date
Sodium fluoride[c]	Various doses reportedly have been used in studies (e.g., 75 mg/day PO with calcium 1500 mg/day; 25 mg PO BID of slow-release sodium fluoride given in cycles of 12 months on and 2 months off with sodium fluoride being administered with calcium 400 mg/day [309]	Nausea, lower extremity pain, ↓ cortical bone density, ↑ skeletal fragility and incidence of nonvertebral fractures

[a] Adapted with permission from reference 273 with the addition of reference 309.
[b] HDL = High-density lipoprotein; IGF-1 = Insulin-like growth factor-1; IM = Intramuscular; LDL = Low-density lipoprotein; SQ = Subcutaneous.
[c] Not currently approved by the FDA for the prevention or treatment of osteoporosis.
[d] Investigational drug not currently FDA-approved for any indication.

but bone mineral content was not significantly different in women receiving the drug compared to control subjects after two years. Controlled prospective studies are needed to determine whether thiazides have long-term effects on bone mineral content and, if so, whether these effects are dose-, duration-, or sex-dependent. Thus, M.B.'s thiazide therapy may have a positive effect on her bone mineral content.

Since M.B. has a history of fractures, she should continue calcium supplementation, estrogen replacement, and adequate vitamin D intake. Other medications such as fluoride, calcitonin, diphosphonates, and anabolic steroids may be considered for osteoporotic patients with complications who may not be optimally managed on an antiresorptive regimen similar to M.B.'s.

Sodium fluoride, 40 to 80 mg/day, has been shown to increase trabecular bone mass by directly affecting osteoblasts, but the newly formed bone has less strength than normal bone.[272] Calcium supplementation in conjunction with fluoride administration may help to prevent mineralization abnormalities which can occur when fluoride is used without an adequate calcium intake.[272] Riggs et al.[308] demonstrated that fluoride (75 mg/day) in conjunction with a calcium supplement (1500 mg/day) increased trabecular (cancellous) bone but not cortical bone. Additionally, the number of new fractures experienced by women receiving fluoride was similar to the number experienced by women in a matched placebo group; the number of nonvertebral fractures was higher in the former group. Gastrointestinal irritation and pain in the lower extrem-

ities were the most frequently reported adverse effects. Some of the adverse effects associated with fluoride therapy may be decreased if fluoride is used in lower doses. Pak et al.[309] demonstrated the positive effects of slow-release sodium fluoride (25 mg twice a day, orally) given for two 14 month cycles with a washout period (2 months) between cycles when compared to women receiving placebo. Both groups also received calcium citrate 400 mg twice daily. Those in the fluoride group had increased femoral neck density (4.1% and 2.1% during the 2 study periods) while fracture rates were decreased.

Calcitonin acts directly on osteoclasts to decrease bone resorption primarily in vertebral and femoral sites and appears to be most effective on trabecular bone.[269,272] In addition, calcitonin may have an analgesic effect in patients with acute fractures. It is effective in reducing corticosteroid-induced osteoporosis.[269] Currently, it is available for injection as calcitonin-salmon (Calcimar and Miacalcin) and calcitonin-human (Cibacalcin) in the U.S., but it is available as a nasal spray in some countries. Calcitonin-salmon is approved for postmenopausal osteoporosis and may become available in the U.S. Adverse effects associated with calcitonin therapy are uncommon, but flushing, nausea, and vomiting as well as local irritation at the injection site have been reported.[273] The drug is inconvenient to administer because it is available only for parenteral use and is relatively expensive.

Anabolic steroids are not used commonly in women for the treatment of osteoporosis because of their adverse effects even though they have been shown to increase total body calcium; however, the incidence of vertebral fractures in postmenopausal women receiving concomitant calcium supplementation was not decreased.[310] Adverse effects include increased facial hair, acne, hoarseness, and increased LDL to HDL.[273]

Etidronate (Didronel) is a biphosphonate available in the U.S. that inhibits bone resorption mediated by osteoclasts. Watts et al.[311] published a prospective randomized, double-blind, placebo-controlled study that evaluated the effectiveness of etidronate given cyclically over a two-year time span. The investigators enrolled 429 women with postmenopausal osteoporosis to participate in the study. The women were assigned randomly to one of four groups: in group 1, women received placebo and placebo; group 2, phosphate and placebo; group 3, placebo and etidronate; group 4, phosphate and etidronate. Therapy cycles were repeated eight times. Bone density of the vertebral column was followed by sequential dual-photon absorptiometry. After two years, women in groups 3 and 4 had significant increases in spinal bone density, but phosphate administration did not seem to increase the effectiveness of the etidronate.

When 66 women with postmenopausal osteoporosis were placed into either an etidronate group (n = 33) or a placebo group (n = 33) in a double-blind study, the etidronate group (400 mg/day for 2 weeks followed by a 13-week drug-free period which was repeated for a total of 150 weeks) was more effective than placebo. Women who received etidronate had a decreased rate of vertebral bone loss after three years of therapy.

Future treatment for osteoporosis may include transdermal estrogen, nasal synthetic calcitonin administration, additional biphosphonates, and recombinant human insulin-like growth factor produced by recombinant-DNA technology.

References

1   **Sobel JD.** Vulvovaginitis. Dermatol Clin. 1992;10:339.

2   **Sobel JD.** Candidal vulvovaginitis. Clin Obstet Gynecol. 1993;36:153.

3   **Hill GB.** The microbiology of bacterial vaginosis. Am J Obstet Gynecol. 1993; 169:450.

4   **Biswas MK.** Bacterial vaginosis. Clin Obstet Gynecol. 1993;36:166.

5   **Amsel R et al.** Non-specific vaginitis: diagnostic criteria and microbial and epidemiologic associations. Am J Med. 1983;74:14.

6   **Centers for Disease Control and Prevention.** 1993 Sexually Transmitted Diseases Treatment Guidelines. MMWR. 1993;42(RR-14).

7   **Rubin A.** Vaginitis. In: Rivlin ME et al., eds. Manual of Clinical Problems in Obstetrics and Gynecology. Boston: Little, Brown and Co; 1990:284.

8   **Davidson F, Oates JK.** The pill does not cause ''thrush.'' Br J Obstet Gynaecol. 1985;92:1265.

9   **Reed BD, Eyler A.** Vaginal infections: diagnosis and management. Am Fam Physician. 1993;47:1805.

10 **Lebherz TB et al.** A comparison of the efficacy of two vaginal creams for vulvovaginal candidiasis, and correlations with the presence of *Candida* species in the perianal area and oral contraceptive use. Clin Ther. 1983;5:409.

11 **Lebherz T et al.** Efficacy of single-versus multiple-dose clotrimazole therapy in the management of vulvovaginal candidiasis. Am J Obstet Gynecol. 1985;152:965.

12 **Fleury F et al.** Therapeutic results obtained in vaginal mycoses after single-dose treatment with 500 mg clotrimazole vaginal tablets. Am J Obstet Gynecol. 1985;152:968.

13 **Floyd R, Hodgson C.** One-day treatment of vulvovaginal candidiasis with a 500-mg clotrimazole vaginal tablet compared with a three-day regimen of two 100-mg vaginal tablets daily. Clin Ther. 1986;8:181.

14 **Goormans E et al.** One-dose therapy of Candida vaginitis. Chemotherapy. 1982;28(Suppl. 1):106.

15 **Olin EW, ed.** Monistat 5 (Miconazole) Tampon—released in California. Drug Newsletter. 1994;13:56.

16 **Bradbeer CS et al.** Butoconazole and miconazole in treating vaginal candidiasis. Genitourin Med. 1985;61:270.

17 **Brown D Jr et al.** Butoconazole vaginal cream in the treatment of vulvovaginal candidiasis. Comparison with miconazole nitrate and placebo. J Reprod Med. 1986;31:1045.

18 **Kaufman RH et al.** Comparison of three-day butoconazole treatment with seven-day miconazole treatment for vulvovaginal candidiasis. J Reprod Med. 1989;34:479.

19 **Hajman AJ.** Vulvovaginal candidiasis: comparison of 3-day treatment with 2% butoconazole nitrate cream and 6-day treatment with 1% clotrimazole cream. J Int Med Res. 1988;16:367.

20 **Kjaeldgaard A, Larsson B.** Single-blind comparative clinical trial of short-term therapy with terconazole versus clotrimazole vaginal tablets in vulvovaginal candidiasis. Curr Ther Res. 1985;38:939.

21 **Vartiainen E, Widholm O.** Single-dose therapy of vulvovaginal candidiasis: comparison of terconazole and clotrimazole. Curr Ther Res. 1988;44:185.

22 **Stien GE et al.** Single-dose tioconazole compared with 3-day clotrimazole treatment in vulvovaginal candidiasis. Antimicrob Agents Chemother. 1986;29:969.

23 **Pfizer Roerig.** Diflucan package insert. New York, NY: July 1994.

24 **A comparison of single-dose oral fluconazole with 3-day intravaginal clotrimazole in the treatment of vaginal candidiasis: report of an international multicentre trial.** Br J Obstet Gynaecol. 1989;96:226.

25 **Brammer KW.** Treatment of vaginal candidiasis with single oral dose of fluconazole. Eur J Clin Microbiol Infect Dis. 1988;7:364.

26 **Phillips RJM et al.** An open multicentre study of the efficacy and safety of fluconazole 150 mg in the treatment of vaginal candidiasis in general practice. Br J Clin Pract. 1990;44:219.

27 **Bloch B, Smythe E.** Ketoconazole in the treatment of vaginal candidiasis. S Afr Med J. 1985;67:178.

28 **Bingham JS.** Single blind comparison of ketoconazole 200 mg oral tablets and clotrimazole 100 mg vaginal tablets and 1% cream in treating acute candidosis. Br J Vener Dis. 1984;60:175.

29 **Cauwenbergh G.** Itraconazole: the first orally active antifungal for single-day treatment of vaginal candidosis. Cur Therapeutic Research. 1987;41:210.

30 **Ortho Pharmaceutical Corp.** Monistat 3 package insert. Raritan, NJ: 1989.

31 **Schering Corp.** Gyne-Lotrimin package insert. Kenilworth, NJ: 1986.

32 **Miles Pharmaceuticals.** Mycelex-G package insert. West Haven, CT: 1988.

33 **Syntex Laboratories Inc.** Femstat package insert. Palo Alto, CA: 1988.

34 **Ortho Pharmaceutical Corp.** Terazol 7 package insert. Raritan, NJ: 1992.

35 **Fujisawa Corp.** Vagistat package insert. Philadelphia, PA: 1989.

36 **Foxman B.** The epidemiology of vulvovaginal candidiasis: risk factors. Am J Public Health. 1990;80:329.

37 **Milsom I, Forssman L.** Repeated candidiasis: reinfection or recrudescence? A review. Am J Obstet Gynecol. 1985;152:956.

38 **Sobel JD et al.** Clotrimazole treatment of recurrent and chronic *Candida* vulvovaginitis. Obstet Gynecol. 1989;73:330.

39 **Sobel JD.** Recurrent vulvovaginal candidiasis: a prospective study of the efficacy of maintenance ketoconazole therapy. N Engl J Med. 1986;315:1455.

40 **Fong IW et al.** Lack of in vitro resistance of Candida albicans to ketoconazole, itraconazole and clotrimazole in women treated for recurrent vaginal candidiasis. Genitourin Med. 1993;69:44.

41 **McGroarty JA.** Probiotic use of lactobacilli in the human female urogenital tract. FEMS Immunol Med Microbiol. 1993;6:251.

42 **Briggs GG et al.** Drugs in Pregnancy and Lactation. Baltimore, MD: Williams & Wilkins; 1994.

43 **Todd J et al.** Toxic-shock syndrome associated with phage-group-1 *staphylococci*. Lancet. 1978;2:1116.

44 **Centers for Disease Control.** Toxic-shock syndrome—United States. MMWR. 1980;29:229.

45 **Reingold AL.** Epidemiology of toxic-shock syndrome—United States, 1960–1984. MMWR. 1984;33(Suppl. 3SS):19SS.

46 **Reingold AL.** Toxic shock in the United States of America: epidemiology. Postgrad Med J. 1985;61(Suppl. 1):23.

47 **Centers for Disease Control.** Follow-up on toxic-shock syndrome. MMWR. 1980;29:441.

48 **Broome CV.** Epidemiology of toxic shock syndrome in the United States: overview. Rev Infect Dis. 1989; 11(Suppl. 1):S14.

49 **Reingold AL.** Toxic shock syndrome: an update. Am J Obstet Gynecol. 1991; 165:1236.

50 **Freedman JD, Beer DJ.** Expanding perspectives on the toxic shock syndrome. Adv Intern Med. 1991;36:363.

51 **Chesney PJ.** Clinical aspects and spectrum of illness of toxic shock syndrome: overview. Rev Infect Dis. 1980;11(Suppl. 1):S1.

52 **Wagner GP.** Toxic shock syndrome: a review. Am J Obstet Gynecol. 1983; 146:93.

53 **Erstad B et al.** Toxic shock-like syndrome. Pharmacotherapy. 1992;12:23.

54 **Todd JK.** Therapy of toxic shock syndrome. Drugs. 1990;39:856.

55 **Helgerson SE et al.** Toxic shock syndrome in Oregon: risk of recurrence. JAMA. 1984;252:3402.

56 **Wagner G et al.** Tampon-induced changes in vaginal oxygen and carbon dioxide tensions. Am J Obstet Gynecol. 1984;148:147.

57 **Kass EH.** Magnesium and the pathogenesis of toxic shock syndrome. Rev Infect Dis. 1989;11(Suppl. 1):S167.

58 **Berkley SF et al.** The relationship of tampon characteristics to menstrual toxic shock syndrome. JAMA. 1987; 258:917.

59 **Food and Drug Administration.** Medical devices; labeling for menstrual tampons; ranges of absorbency. Fed Regist. 1989;54:43766.

60 **Reingold AL.** Toxic shock syndrome and the contraceptive sponge. JAMA. 1986;255:242.

61 **Schwartz B et al.** Nonmenstrual toxic shock syndrome associated with barrier contraceptives: report of a case-control study. Rev Infect Dis. 1989;11(Suppl. 1):S43.

62 **Primary dysmenorrhoea.** Lancet. 1980;1:800. Editorial.

63 **Dingfelder JR.** Primary dysmenorrhea treatment with prostaglandin inhibitors: a review. Am J Obstet Gynecol. 1981;140:874.

64 **Akerlund M.** Modern treatment of dysmenorrhea. Acta Obstet Gynecol Scand. 1990;69:563.

65 **Dawood Y.** Nonsteroidal anti-inflammatory drugs and changing attitudes toward dysmenorrhea. Am J Med. 1988;84(Suppl. 5A):23.

66 **Dawood MY.** Dysmenorrhea. J Reprod Med. 1985;30:154.

67 **Wenzloff NJ, Shimp L.** Therapeutic management of primary dysmenorrhea. Drug Intell Clin Pharm. 1984;18:22.

68 **Mackinnon GL, Parker WA.** Current concepts in the management of primary dysmenorrhea. Can Pharm J. 1982; 115:3.

69 **Avant RF.** Dysmenorrhea. Prim Care. 1988;15:549.

70 **Metheny WP, Smith RP.** The relationship among exercise, stress, and primary dysmenorrhea. J Behav Med. 1989;12:569.

71 **Smith RP, Heltzel JA.** Interrelation of analgesia and uterine activity in women with primary dysmenorrhea; a preliminary report. J Reprod Med. 1991;36:260.

72 **Dawood MY, Ramos J.** Transcutaneous electrical nerve stimulation (TENS) for the treatment of primary dysmenorrhea: a randomized crossover comparison with placebo TENS and ibuprofen. Obstet Gynecol. 1990;75:656.

73 **Kremser E, Mitchell GM.** Treatment of primary dysmenorrhea with a combined type of oral contraceptive—a double-blind study. J Am Coll Health. 1971;19:195.

74 **Chan WY, Dawood MY.** Prostaglandin levels in menstrual fluid of non-dysmenorrheic and of dysmenorrheic subjects with and without oral contraceptive or ibuprofen therapy. Adv Prostaglandin Thromboxane Res. 1980;8:1443.

75 **Chan WY et al.** Prostaglandin in primary dysmenorrhea: comparison of prophylactic and non-prophylactic treatment with ibuprofen and use of oral contraceptive. Am J Med. 1981;70:535.

76 **Smith RP.** Non-steroidal anti-inflammatory drugs: drugs for dysmenorrhea. IMJ. 1986;169:22.

77 **Budoff PW.** Mefenamic acid therapy in dysmenorrhea. Adv Prostaglandin Thromboxane Res. 1980;8:1449.

78 **Budoff PW.** Use of mefenamic acid in the treatment of primary dysmenorrhea. JAMA. 1979;241:2713.

79 **Segre EJ.** Naproxen sodium (Anaprox). Pharmacology, pharmacokinetics and drug interactions. J Reprod Med. 1980;25:222.

80 **Rosenwaks Z, Seegar-Jones G.** Menstrual pain: its origin and pathogenesis. J Reprod Med. 1980;25:207.

81 **Owen PR.** Prostaglandin synthetase inhibitors in the treatment of primary dysmenorrhea. Am J Obstet Gynecol. 1984;148:96.

82 **Mehlisch DR.** Double-blind crossover comparison of ketoprofen, naproxen, and placebo in patients with primary dysmenorrhea. Clin Ther. 1990;12:398.

83 **Benassi L et al.** An attempt at real prophylaxis of primary dysmenorrhea:

comparison between meclofenamate sodium and naproxen sodium. Clin Exp Obstet Gynecol. 1993;10:102.

84 **Reid RL.** Premenstrual syndrome. N Engl J Med. 1991;324:1208. Editorial.

85 **Mortola JF.** Issues in the diagnosis and research of premenstrual syndrome. Clin Obstet Gynecol. 1992;35: 587.

86 **Woods NF et al.** Prevalence of perimenstrual symptoms. Am J Public Health. 1982;72:1257.

87 **Rivera-Tovar AD, Frank E.** Late luteal phase dysphoric disorder in young women. Am J Psychiatry. 1990;147: 1634.

88 **Rubinow DR et al.** Changes in plasma hormones across the menstrual cycle in patients with menstrually related mood disorder and in control subjects. Am J Obstet Gynecol. 1988;158:5.

89 **Casper RF et al.** Thyrotropin and prolactin responses to thyrotropin-releasing hormone in premenstrual syndrome. J Clin Endocrinol Metab. 1989; 68:1.

90 **Steiner M et al.** Plasma prolactin and severe PMS. Psychoneuroendocrinology. 1984;9:29.

91 **Roy-Byrne PP et al.** Cortisol response to dexamethasone in women with premenstrual syndrome. Neuropsychobiology. 1986;16:61.

92 **Chuong C et al.** Neuropeptide levels in premenstrual syndrome. Fertil Steril. 1985;44:760.

93 **Hamilton JA, Gallant S.** Premenstrual symptom changes and plasma β-endorphin/β-lipotropin throughout the menstrual cycle. Psychoneuroendocrinology. 1988;13:505.

94 **Ashby CR et al.** Alteration of platelet serotonergic mechanisms and monoamine oxidase activity in premenstrual syndrome. Biol Psychiatry. 1988;24: 225.

95 **Malmgren R et al.** Platelet serotonin uptake and effects of vitamin B₆— treatment in premenstrual tension. Neuropsychobiology. 1987;18:83.

96 **Schmidt PJ et al.** Lack of effect of induced menses on symptoms in women with premenstrual syndrome. N Engl J Med. 1991;324:1174.

97 **Rubinow DR.** The Premenstrual Syndrome. New Views. JAMA. 1992;268: 1908.

98 **Reid RL.** Premenstrual syndrome. Curr Probl Obstet Gynecol Fertil. 1985;8:1.

99 **Halbreich U, Endicott J.** Relationship of dysphoric premenstrual changes to depressive disorders. Acta Psychiatr Scand. 1985;71:331.

100 **MacKenzie TB et al.** Lifetime prevalence of psychiatric disorders in women with perimenstrual difficulties. J Affect Disord. 1986;10:15.

101 **Pearlstein TB et al.** Prevalence of axis I and axis II disorders in women with late luteal phase dysphoric disorder. J Affect Disord. 1990;20:129.

102 **American Psychiatric Association.** Diagnostic and Statistical Manual of Mental Disorders 4th ed. Washington, DC: American Psychiatric Association; 1994.

103 **Hurt SW et al.** Late luteal phase dysphoric disorder in 670 women evaluated for premenstrual complaints. Am J Psychiatry. 1992;149:525.

104 **Gallant SJ et al.** Using daily ratings to confirm premenstrual syndrome/late luteal phase dysphoric disorder. Part I. Effects of demand characteristics and expectations. Psychosom Med. 1992; 54:149.

105 **Gallant SJ et al.** Using daily ratings to confirm premenstrual syndrome/late luteal phase dysphoric disorder. Part II. What makes a "real" difference? Psychosom Med. 1992;54:167.

106 **National Institute of Mental Health.** NIMH Premenstrual Syndrome Workshop Guidelines, April 14–15, 1983. Rockville, MD: National Institute of Mental Health; 1983.

107 **Gath D, Iles S.** Treating the premenstrual syndrome. Ask the woman to keep a diary. Br Med J. 1988;297:237.

108 **Wood SH et al.** Treatment of premenstrual syndrome with fluoxetine: a double-blind, placebo-controlled, crossover study. Obstet Gynecol. 1992;80: 339.

109 **Stone AB et al.** Fluoxetine in the treatment of late luteal phase dysphoric disorder. J Clin Psychiatry. 1991;52:290.

110 **Harrison WM et al.** Treatment of premenstrual dysphoria with alprazolam and placebo. Psychopharmacol Bull. 1987;23:150.

111 **Smith S et al.** Treatment of premenstrual syndrome with alprazolam: results of a double-blind, placebo-controlled, randomized crossover clinical trial. Obstet Gynecol. 1987;70:37.

112 **Schmidt PJ et al.** Alprazolam in the treatment of premenstrual syndrome. A double-blind, placebo-controlled trial. Arch Gen Psychiatry. 1993;50:467.

113 **Rickels K et al.** Buspirone in treatment of premenstrual syndrome. Lancet. 1989;1:777. Letter.

114 **Harrison WM et al.** Treatment of premenstrual depression with nortriptyline: a pilot study. J Clin Psychiatry. 1989;50:136.

115 **Sundblad C et al.** Clomipramine effectively reduces premenstrual irritability and dysphoria: a placebo-controlled trial. Acta Psychiatr Scand. 1992;85:39.

116 **Brzezinski AA et al.** d-Fenfluramine suppresses the increased calorie and carbohydrate intakes and improves the mood of women with premenstrual depression. Obstet Gynecol. 1990;76: 296.

117 **Price WA, Giannini AJ.** The use of clonidine in the premenstrual tension syndrome. J Clin Pharmacol. 1984;24: 463.

118 **Nilsson LC et al.** Clonidine for relief of premenstrual syndrome. Lancet. 1985;2:549.

119 **Giannini AJ et al.** Clonidine in the treatment of premenstrual syndrome: a subgroup study. J Clin Psychiatry. 1988;49:62.

120 **Price WA, Giannini AJ.** Verapamil in the treatment of premenstrual syndrome: case report. J Clin Psychiatry. 1986;47:213.

121 **Deicken RF.** Verapamil treatment of premenstrual syndrome. Biol Psychiatry. 1988;24:689.

122 **Andersch B, Hahn L.** Progesterone treatment of premenstrual tension—a double-blind study. J Psychosom Res. 1985;2:489.

123 **Maddocks S et al.** A double-blind placebo-controlled trial of progesterone vaginal suppositories in the treatment of premenstrual syndrome. Am J Obstet Gynecol. 1986;154:573.

124 **Freeman E et al.** Ineffectiveness of progesterone suppository treatment for premenstrual syndrome. JAMA. 1990; 264:349.

125 **Corney RH et al.** Comparison of progesterone, placebo and behavioral psychotherapy in the treatment of premenstrual syndrome. J Psychosom Obstet Gynaecol. 1990;11:211.

126 **Rossignol AM, Phillips MJ.** Obstetricians' and gynecologists' beliefs and preferred modes of treatment for women diagnosed with premenstrual symptoms. Womens Health Issues. 1992;2:26.

127 **West CP.** Inhibition of ovulation with oral progestins—effectiveness in premenstrual syndrome. Eur J Obstet Gynecol Reprod Biol. 1990;34:110.

128 **Norris RV.** Progesterone for premenstrual tension. J Reprod Med. 1983;28: 509.

129 **Morris NM, Udry JR.** Contraceptive pills and day-by-day feelings of well-being. Am J Obstet Gynecol. 1972; 113:763.

130 **Kutner SJ, Brown WL.** Types of oral contraceptives, depression and premenstrual symptoms. J Nerv Ment Dis. 1972;155:153.

131 **Cullberg J.** Mood changes and menstrual symptoms with different gestagen/oestrogen combinations. Acta Psychiatr Scand. 1972;236(Suppl.):1.

132 **Graham CA, Sherwin BB.** A prospective treatment study of premenstrual symptoms using a triphasic oral contraceptive. J Psychosom Res. 1992; 36:257.

133 **Abraham GE, Hargrove JT.** Effect of vitamin B₆ on premenstrual symptomatology in women with premenstrual tension syndrome: a double-blind crossover study. Infertility. 1980;3:155.

134 **Stokes J, Mendels J.** Pyridoxine and premenstrual tension. Lancet. 1972;1: 1177.

135 **Williams MJ et al.** Controlled trials of pyridoxine in the premenstrual syndrome. J Int Med Res. 1985;13:174.

136 **Hagen I et al.** No effect of vitamin B₆ against premenstrual tension: a controlled clinical study. Acta Obstet Gynecol Scand. 1985;64:667.

137 **Kendall KE, Schnurr PP.** The effects of vitamin B₆ supplementation on premenstrual syndrome. Obstet Gynecol. 1987;70:145.

138 **Schaumburg H et al.** Sensory neuropathy from pyridoxine abuse. A new megavitamin syndrome. N Engl J Med. 1983;309:445.

139 **Parry GJ, Bredesen DE.** Sensory neuropathy with low-dose pyridoxine. Neurology. 1985;35:1466.

140 **Dalton K, Dalton MJ.** Characteristics of pyridoxine overdose neuropathy syndrome. Acta Neurol Scand. 1987; 76:8.

141 **Wood C, Jakubowicz D.** The treatment of premenstrual symptoms with mefenamic acid. Br J Obstet Gynaecol. 1980;87:627.

142 **Mira M et al.** Mefenamic acid in the treatment of premenstrual syndrome. Obstet Gynecol. 1986;68:395.

143 **Gunston KD.** Premenstrual syndrome in Cape Town. Part II. A double-blind placebo-controlled study of the efficacy of mefenamic acid. S Afr Med J. 1986;70:159.

144 **O'Brien PMS et al.** Treatment of premenstrual syndrome by spironolactone. Br J Obstet Gynaecol. 1979;86:142.

145 **Vellacott ID et al.** A double blind placebo controlled evaluation of spironolactone in premenstrual syndrome. Curr Med Res Opin. 1987;10:450.

146 **Burnet RB et al.** Premenstrual syndrome and spironolactone. Aust N Z J Obstet Gynaecol. 1991;31:366.

147 **Werch A, Kane RE.** Treatment of premenstrual tension with metolazone: a double-blind evaluation of a new diuretic. Curr Ther Res. 1976;19:565.

148 **Freeman EW et al.** Gonadotropin-releasing hormone agonist in treatment of premenstrual symptoms with and without comorbidity of depression: a pilot study. J Clin Psychiatry. 1993;54:192.

149 **Muse KN.** Clinical experience with the use of GnRH agonists in the treatment of premenstrual syndrome. Obstet Gynecol Suvr. 1989;44:317.

150 **West CP et al.** Modification of symptoms of the premenstrual syndrome during ovarian suppression with goserelin (Zoladex) depot—potential for research and clinical investigation. J Psychosom Obstet Gynaecol. 1989;10: 79.

151 **Mortola JF et al.** Successful treatment of severe premenstrual syndrome by combined use of gonadotropin-releasing hormone agonist and estrogen/progestin. J Clin Endocrinol Metab. 1991; 72:252A.

152 **Mansel RE.** A double-blind trial of the prolactin-inhibitor bromocriptine in painful benign breast disease. Br J Surg. 1978;65:724.

153 **Anderson AN et al.** Effect of bromocriptine on the premenstrual syndrome: a double-blind clinical trial. Br J Obstet Gynaecol. 1977;84:370.

154 **Andersch B.** Bromocriptine and premenstrual symptoms: a survey of double-blind trials. Obstet Gynecol Scand. 1983;38:643.

155 **Kullander S, Svanberg L.** Bromocriptine treatment of the premenstrual syndrome. Acta Obstet Gynecol Scand. 1979;58:373.

156 **Watts JF et al.** A clinical trial using danazol for the treatment of premenstrual tension. Br J Obstet Gynecol. 1987;94:30.

157 **Gilmore DH et al.** Danol for premenstrual syndrome: a preliminary report of a placebo-controlled double-blind study. J Int Med Res. 1985;123:129.

158 **Moline ML.** Pharmacologic strategies for managing premenstrual syndrome. Clin Pharm. 1993;12:181.

159 **Barbieri RL.** Etiology and epidemiology of endometriosis. Am J Obstet Gynecol. 1990;162:565.

160 **Ridley JH.** The validity of Sampson's theory of endometriosis. Am J Obstet Gynecol. 1962;62:777.

161 **Suginami H.** A reappraisal of the coelomic metaphasia theory by reviewing endometriosis occurring in unusual sites and instances. Am J Obstet Gynecol. 1991;165:214.

162 **Olive DL, Schwartz LB.** Endometriosis. N Engl J Med. 1993;328:1759.

163 **Badawy SZA et al.** Autoimmune phenomena in infertile patients with endometriosis. Obstet Gynecol. 1984;63:271.

164 **Gleicher N et al.** Is endometriosis an autoimmune disease? Obstet Gynecol. 1987;70:115.

165 **Meek SC et al.** Autoimmunity in infertile patients with endometriosis. Am J Obstet Gynecol. 1988;158:1365.

166 **Halme J et al.** Altered maturation and function of peritoneal macrophages: possible role in pathogenesis of endometriosis. Am J Obstet Gynecol. 1987;156:783.

167 **Oosterlynck DJ et al.** The natural killer activity of peritoneal fluid lymphocytes is decreased in women with endometriosis. Fertil Steril. 1992;58:292.

168 **Gleicher N, Pratt D.** Abnormal (auto)immunity and endometriosis. Int J Gynecol Obstet. 1993;40(Suppl.):S21.

169 **Gleicher N.** Endometriosis: a new approach is needed. Hum Reprod. 1992;7:821.

170 **Simon C et al.** Glucocorticoid treatment decreases sera embryotoxicity in endometriosis patients. Fertil Steril. 1992;58:284.

171 **DiZerega GS et al.** Endometriosis: role of ovarian steroids in initiation, maintenance and suppression. Fertil Steril. 1980;33:649.

172 **Talbert LM, Kauma SM.** Endometriosis. In: Scott JR et al., eds. Danforth's Obstetrics and Gynecology. Philadelphia: JB Lippincott Co.; 1990:845.

173 **Williams TJ, Pratt JH.** Endometriosis in 1000 consecutive celiotomies: incidence and management. Am J Obstet Gynecol. 1977;129:245.

174 **Chatman DL.** Endometriosis in the black woman. Am J Obstet Gynecol. 1976;125:987.

175 **Surrey ES, Halme J.** Endometriosis as a cause of infertility. Obstet Gynecol Clin North Am. 1989;16:79.

176 **Cramer DW et al.** The relation of endometriosis to menstrual characteristics, smoking, and exercise. JAMA. 1986;255:1904.

177 **Merrill JA.** Endometriosis. In: Scott JR et al., eds. Danforth's Obstetrics and Gynecology. Philadelphia: JB Lippincott Co.; 1990:995.

178 **Luciano AA, Metzger DA.** Endometriosis—what can medical therapy offer? Br J Clin Prac. 1991;72(Autumn Suppl.):14.

179 **Luciano AA, Pitkin RM.** Endometriosis: approaches to diagnosis and treatment. Surg Annu. 1984;16:297.

180 **Buttram VC.** Evolution of the revised American Fertility Society classification of endometriosis. Fertil Steril. 1985;43:347.

181 **Damario MA, Rock JA.** New considerations for the classification of endometriosis. Int J Gynecol Obstet. 1993;40(Suppl.):S9.

182 **Candiani GB et al.** Mild endometriosis and infertility: a critical review of epidemiologic data, diagnostic pitfalls, and classification limits. Obstet Gynecol Surv. 1991;46:374.

183 **Hornstein MD et al.** The reproducibility of the revised American Fertility Society classification of endometriosis. Fertil Steril. 1993;59:1015.

184 **Barbieri RL et al.** Elevated serum concentrations of CA-125 in patients with advanced endometriosis. Fertil Steril. 1986;45:630.

185 **Wild RA et al.** Antiendometrial antibodies versus CA-125 for the detection of endometriosis. Fertil Steril. 1989;52:59.

186 **Dmowski WP, Cohen MR.** Antigonadotropin (danazol) in the treatment of endometriosis. Evaluation of post treatment fertility and three-year follow-up data. Am J Obstet Gynecol. 1978;130:41.

187 **Puleo JB, Hammond CB.** Conservative therapy of endometriosis externa: the effects of danazol therapy. Fertil Steril. 1983;40:164.

188 **Daniell JF, Christianson C.** Combined laparoscopic surgery and danazol therapy for pelvic endometriosis. Fertil Steril. 1981;35:521.

189 **Olive DL, Haney AF.** Endometriosis-associated infertility: a critical review of therapeutic approaches. Obstet Gynecol Surv. 1986;41:538.

190 **Evers JLH.** The pregnancy rate of the no-treatment group in randomized clinical trials of endometriosis therapy. Fertil Steril. 1989;52:906. Editorial.

191 **Seibel MM et al.** The effectiveness of danazol on subsequent fertility in minimal endometriosis. Fertil Steril. 1982;38:534.

192 **Bayer SF et al.** Efficacy of danazol therapy for minimal endometriosis in infertile women, a prospective randomized study. J Reprod Med. 1988;33:179.

193 **Butler L et al.** Collaborative study of pregnancy rates following danazol therapy of stage I endometriosis. Fertil Steril. 1984;41:373.

194 **Hughes et al.** A quantitative overview of controlled trials in endometriosis-associated infertility. Fertil Steril. 1993;59:963.

195 **Hammond BC, Maxson SW.** Current status of estrogen therapy for the menopause. Fertil Steril. 1982;37:5.

196 **Younger JB.** Endometriosis. Curr Opin Obstet Gynecol. 1993;5:333.

197 **Nezhat C et al.** Surgery for endometriosis. Curr Opin Obstet Gynecol. 1991;3:385.

198 **el-Roeiy A et al.** Danazol but not gonadotropin-releasing hormone agonists suppresses autoantibodies in endometriosis. Fertil Steril. 1988;50:864.

199 **Mandanes AE, Farber M.** Danazol. Ann Intern Med. 1982;96:625.

200 **Loprinzi CL et al.** Megestrol acetate for the prevention of hot flashes. N Engl J Med. 1994;331:347.

201 **Hill JA et al.** Immunosuppressive effects of danazol in vitro. Fertil Steril. 1987;48:414.

202 **Agnello V et al.** Preliminary observations on danazol therapy of systemic lupus erythematosus: effects on DNA antibodies, thrombocytopenia and complement. J Rheumatol. 1983;10:682.

203 **Ahn YS et al.** Danazol for the treatment of idiopathic thrombocytopenic purpura. N Engl J Med. 1983;308:1396.

204 **Ota H et al.** Effects of danazol at the immunologic level in patients with adenomyosis, with special reference to autoantibodies: a multi-center cooperative study. Am J Obstet Gynecol. 1992;167:481.

205 **Gelfand JA et al.** Treatment of hereditary angioedema with danazol: reversal of clinical and biochemical abnormalities. N Engl J Med. 1976;295:1444.

206 **Coutinho EM.** Therapeutic experience with gestrinone. Prog Clin Biol Res. 1990;323:233.

207 **Shaw RW.** The role of GnRH analogues in the treatment of endometriosis. Br J Obstet Gynecol. 1992;99 (Suppl. 7):9.

208 **Waller KG, Shaw RW.** Gonadotropin-releasing hormone analogues for the treatment of endometriosis: long-term follow-up. Fertil Steril. 1993;59:511.

209 **The Nafarelin European Endometriosis Trial Group.** Nafarelin for endometriosis: a large-scale, danazol-controlled trial of efficacy and safety, with 1-year follow-up. Fertil Steril. 1992;57:514.

210 **Henzl MR et al.** Administration of nasal nafarelin as compared with oral danazol for endometriosis. A multicenter double-blind comparative clinical trial. N Engl J Med. 1988;318:485.

211 **Jelley RY.** Multicentre open comparative study of buserelin and danazol in the treatment of endometriosis. Br J Clin Pract. 1987;41(Suppl. 48):64.

212 **Shaw RW.** An open randomized comparative study of the effect of goserelin depot and danazol in the treatment of endometriosis. Fertil Steril. 1992;58:265.

213 **Wheeler JM et al.** Depot leuprolide versus danazol in treatment of women with symptomatic endometriosis. Am J Obstet Gynecol. 1992;167:1367.

214 **Metzger DA, Luciano AA.** Hormonal Therapy of Endometriosis. Obstet Gynecol Clin North Am. 1989;16:105.

215 **Moghissi KS.** Pseudopregnancy induced by estrogen-progestogen or progestogens alone in the treatment of endometriosis. Prog Clin Biol Res. 1990;323:221.

216 **Vercellini P et al.** A gonadotropin-releasing hormone agonist versus a low-dose oral contraceptive for pelvic pain associated with endometriosis. Fertil Steril. 1993;60:75.

217 **Rock JA, Moutos DM.** Endometriosis: the present and future—an overview of treatment options. Br J Obstet Gynecol. 1992;99(Suppl. 7):1.

218 **Moghissi KS, Boyce CR.** Management of endometriosis with oral medroxyprogesterone acetate. Obstet Gynecol. 1976;47:265.

219 **Luciano AA et al.** Evaluation of oral medroxyprogesterone acetate in the treatment of endometriosis. Obstet Gynecol. 1988;72:323.

220 **Fahraeus L et al.** Lipoprotein changes during treatment of pelvic endometriosis with medroxyprogesterone acetate. Fertil Steril. 1986;45:503.

221 **Taylor PJ, Kredentser JV.** Nonsurgical management of minimal and moderate endometriosis to enhance fertility. Int J Fertil. 1992;37:138.

222 **Nezhat C et al.** Videolaseroscopy and laser laparoscopy in gynaecology. Br J Hosp Med. 1987;38:219.

223 **Redwine DB.** Treatment of endometriosis-associated pain. Infertil Reprod Med Clin North Am. 1993;3:697.

224 **Buttram VC et al.** Treatment of endometriosis with danazol: report of a 6-year prospective study. Fertil Steril. 1985;43:353.

225 **Biberoglu KO, Behrman SJ.** Dosage aspects of danazol therapy in endometriosis: short-term and long-term effectiveness. Am J Obstet Gynecol. 1981;139:645.

226 **Barbierio RL et al.** Danazol in the treatment of endometriosis: analysis of 100 cases with a 4-year follow-up. Fertil Steril. 1982;37:737.

227 **Burry KA et al.** Metabolic changes during medical treatment of endometriosis: nafarelin acetate versus danazol. Am J Obstet Gynecol. 1989;160:1454.

228 **Syntex Laboratories, Inc.** Synarel product information. Palo Alto, CA: 1990 Feb.

229 **Burry KA et al.** Metabolic changes during medical treatment of endometriosis: nafarelin acetate versus danazol. Am J Obstet Gynecol. 1989;160:1454.

230 **Monroe SE et al.** Dose-dependent inhibition of pituitary-ovarian function during administration of a gonadotropin-releasing hormone agonistic analog (nafarelin). J Clin Endocrinol Metab. 1986;63:1334.

231 **Cedar MI et al.** Treatment of endometriosis with a long-acting gonadotropin-releasing hormone agonist plus medroxyprogesterone acetate. Obstet Gynecol. 1990;75:641.

232 **Steingold KA et al.** Treatment of endometriosis with a long-acting gonadotropin-releasing hormone agonist. Obstet Gynecol. 1987;69:403.

233 **Surrey ES, Judd HL.** Reduction of vasomotor symptoms and bone mineral density loss with combined norethindrone and long-acting gonadotropin-releasing hormone agonist therapy of symptomatic endometriosis: a prospective randomized trial. J Clin Endocrinol Metab. 1992;75:558.

234 **Dawood MY et al.** Cortical and trabecular bone mineral content in women with endometriosis: effect of gonadotropin-releasing hormone agonist and danazol. Fertil Steril. 1989;52:21.

235 **Whitehouse RW et al.** The effects of nafarelin and danazol on vertebral trabecular bone mass in patients with endometriosis. Clin Endocrinol (Oxf). 1990;33:365.

236 **Matta WH et al.** Reversible trabecular bone density loss following induced hypo-estrogenism with GnRH analogue buserelin in premenopausal women. Clin Endocrinol (Oxf). 1988;29:45.

237 **Johansen JS et al.** The effect of a gonadotropin-releasing hormone agonist analog (nafarelin) on bone metabolism. J Clin Endocrinol Metab. 1988;67:701.

238 **Nencioni P et al.** Gonadotropin releasing hormone agonist therapy and its effect on bone mass. Gynecol Endocrinol. 1991;5:49.

239 **Comite F et al.** Reduced bone mass in reproductive-aged women with endometriosis. J Clin Endocrinol Metab. 1989;69:837.

240 **Matta WH et al.** Hypogonadism induced by luteinizing hormone-releasing agonist analogues: effects on bone density of premenopausal women. Br Med J. 1987;294:1523.

241 **Damewood MD et al.** Interval bone mineral density with long-term gonadotropin-releasing hormone agonist suppression. Fertil Steril. 1989;52:596.

242 **Dawood MY.** Impact of medical treatment of endometriosis on bone mass. Am J Obstet Gynecol. 1993;168:674.

243 **Eldred JM et al.** A randomized double blind placebo controlled trial of the effects on bone metabolism of the combination of nafarelin acetate and norethisterone. Clin Endocrinol (Oxf). 1992;37:354.

244 **Hammond CB, Maxson WS.** Estrogen replacement therapy. Clin Obstet Gynecol. 1986;29:407.

245 **London SN, Hammond CB.** The climacteric. In: Scott JR et al., eds. Danforth's Obstetrics and Gynecology. Philadelphia: JB Lippincott; 1990:853.

246 **Mishell DR Jr.** Is routine use of estrogen indicated in postmenopausal women? An affirmative view. J Fam Pract. 1989;29:406.

247 **Riggs BL, Melton LJ III.** The prevention and treatment of osteoporosis. N Engl J Med. 1992;327:620.

248 **Wenger NK et al.** Cardiovascular health and diseases in women. N Engl J Med. 1993;329:247.

249 **Rebar R, Spitzer IB.** The physiology and measurement of hot flushes. Am J Obstet Gynecol. 1987;156:1284.

250 **Abdalla HI.** Pathophysiology of hot flushes. Obstet Gynecol Surv. 1985;40:338.

251 **Molnar GW.** Body temperature during menopausal hot flashes. J Appl Physiol. 1975;38:499.

252 **Tataryn IV et al.** Objective techniques for the assessment of postmenopausal hot flushes. Obstet Gynecol. 1981;57:340.

253 **Ryan KJ.** Postmenopausal estrogen use. Annu Rev Med. 1982;33:171.

254 **Gambrell RD Jr.** Update on hormone replacement therapy. Am Fam Physician. 1992;46(Suppl. 5):87S.

255 **Dumesic DA.** Current perspective in the management of menopausal and post-menopausal women (clinical conference). J Clin Pharmacol. 1992;32:774.

256 **Whitehead MI et al.** The role and use of progestogens. Obstet Gynecol. 1990;75:59S.

257 **Clisham PR et al.** Comparison of continuous versus sequential estrogen and progestin therapy in postmenopausal women. Obstet Gynecol. 1991;77:241.

258 **Weinstein L et al.** Evaluation of a continuous combined low-dose regimen of estrogen-progestin for treatment of the menopausal patient. Am J Obstet Gynecol. 1990;162:1534.

259 **Powers MS et al.** Pharmacokinetics and pharmacodynamics of transdermal dosage forms of 17 β-estradiol; comparison with conventional oral estrogens used for hormone replacement. Am J Obstet Gynecol. 1985;152:1099.

260 **Chetkowski RJ et al.** Biologic effects of transdermal estradiol. N Engl J Med. 1986;314:1615.

261 **Haas S et al.** The effect of transdermal estradiol on hormone and metabolic dynamics over a six-week period. Obstet Gynecol. 1988;71:671.

262 **McGuffey EC.** Treating hot flashes. Am Pharm. 1994;NS35:14.

263 **Leiblum S et al.** Vaginal atrophy in the postmenopausal woman: the importance of sexual activity and hormones. JAMA. 1983;249:2195.

264 **Iosif CS, Bekassy Z.** Prevalence of genitourinary symptoms in the late menopause. Acta Obstet Gynecol Scand. 1984;63:257.

265 **Erush SC.** Estrogens in the treatment of stress incontinence. Pharmacol Ther. 1993 (July):709.

266 **Cutler WB, Garcia C-R.** The Medical Management of Menopause and Premenopause. Philadelphia, PA: JB Lippincott; 1984.

267 **Peck WA et al.** Consensus conference. Osteoporosis. JAMA. 1984;252:799.

268 **Cummings SR et al.** Epidemiology of osteoporosis and osteoporotic fractures. Epidemiol Rev. 1985;7:178.

269 **Consensus development conference: prophylaxis and treatment of osteoporosis.** Am J Med. 1991;90:107.

270 **Riggs BL et al.** Changes in bone mineral density of the proximal femur and spine with aging: differences between the postmenopausal and senile osteoporosis syndromes. J Clin Invest. 1982;70:716.

271 **Mazess RB.** On aging bone loss. Clin Orthop. 1982;165:239.

272 **Riggs BL, Melton LJ III.** Involutional osteoporosis. N Engl J Med. 1986;314:1676.

273 **Sagraves R et al.** Therapeutic options for osteoporosis. APhA Special Report. Washington, DC: American Pharmaceutical Association; 1993.

274 **Morrison NA et al.** Prediction of bone density from vitamin D receptor alleles. Nature. 1994;367:284.

275 **National Institutes of Health.** Consensus Development Conference statement: optimal calcium intake. Bethesda, MD: National Institutes of Health, June 6–8, 1994.

276 **Kiel DP et al.** Smoking eliminates the protective effect of oral estrogens on the risk for hip fracture among women. Ann Intern Med. 1992;116:716.

277 **Morley JE et al.** UCLA geriatric grand round: osteoporosis. J Am Geriatr Soc. 1988;36:845.

278 **Farley JR et al.** Direct effects of ethanol on bone resorption and formation in vitro. Arch Biochem Biophys. 1985;238:305.

279 **Barrett-Connor E et al.** Coffee-associated osteoporosis offset by daily milk consumption. JAMA. 1994;271:280.

280 **Aarskog D et al.** Heparin-induced inhibition of 1,25-dihydroxyvitamin D formation. Am J Obstet Gynecol. 1984;148:1141.

281 **Shangold MM.** Exercise in the menopausal woman. Obstet Gynecol. 1990;75:53S.

282 **Heath H.** Athletic women, amenorrhea and skeletal integrity. Ann Intern Med. 1985;102:258.

283 **Drinkwater BL et al.** Bone mineral content of amenorrheic and eumenorrheic athletes. N Engl J Med. 1984;311:277.

284 **Calcium supplements.** Med Lett Drugs Ther. 1989;31:101.

285 **Willis J.** Please pass that woman some more calcium and iron. FDA Consum. 1984;18:6.

286 **Sheikh MS et al.** Gastrointestinal absorption of calcium from milk and calcium salts. N Engl J Med. 1987;317:532.

287 **Recker RR.** Calcium absorbability from milk products, and imitation milk, and calcium carbonate. Am J Clin Nutr. 1988;47:93.

288 **Recker RR.** Calcium absorption and achlorhydria. N Engl J Med. 1985;313:70.

289 **Gallagher JC et al.** Intestinal absorption and serum vitamin D metabolites in normal subjects and osteoporotic patients: effects of age and dietary calcium. J Clin Invest. 1979;64:729.

290 **Heaney RP.** Calcium in the prevention and treatment of osteoporosis. J Intern Med. 1992;231:169.

291 **Prince RL et al.** Prevention of postmenopausal osteoporosis: a comparative study of exercise, calcium supplementation, and hormone-replacement therapy. N Engl J Med. 1991;325:1189.

292 **Heaney RP.** Thinking straight about calcium. N Engl J Med. 1993;328:503.

293 **Dawson-Hughes B et al.** A controlled trial of the effect of calcium supplementation on bone density in postmenopausal women. N Engl J Med. 1990;323:878.

294 **Reid IR et al.** Effect of calcium supplementation on bone loss in postmenopausal women. N Engl J Med. 1993;328:460.

295 **Lufkin EG et al.** Treatment of postmenopausal osteoporosis with transdermal estrogen. Ann Intern Med. 1992;117:1.

296 **Felson DT et al.** The effect of postmenopausal estrogen therapy on bone density in elderly women. N Engl J Med. 1993;329:1141.

297 **Ettinger B et al.** The waning effect of postmenopausal estrogen therapy on osteoporosis. N Engl J Med. 1993;329:1192.

298 **Ettinger B et al.** Menopausal bone loss can be prevented by low-dose estrogen combined with calcium supplements. In: Update on Postmenopausal Osteoporosis. New York: Biomedical Information; 1984:63.

299 **Ribot C et al.** Preventive effects of transdermal administration of 17 beta-estradiol on postmenopausal bone loss: a 2-year prospective study. Obstet Gynecol. 1990;75(Suppl.):42S.

300 **Devor M et al.** Estrogen replacement therapy and the risk of venous thrombosis. Am J Med. 1992;92:275.

301 **Hutchison-Williams, Gutmann JN.** Estrogen replacement therapy (ERT) in high-risk cancer patients. Yale J Biol Med. 1991;64:607.

302 **Wyeth-Ayerst Laboratories.** Premarin package insert. Philadelphia: 1990 Mar.

303 **Ciba Pharmaceutical CO.** Estraderm package insert. Summitt, NJ: 1991 Sept.

304 **Grady D et al.** Hormone therapy to prevent disease and prolong life in postmenopausal women. Ann Intern Med. 1992;117:1016.

305 **MacDonald PC.** Estrogen plus progestin in postmenopausal women—Act II. N Engl J Med. 1986;315:959.

306 **Gallagher JC et al.** 1,25-dihydroxyvitamin D₃: short- and long-term effects on bone and calcium metabolism in patients with postmenopausal osteoporosis. Proc Natl Acad Sci USA. 1982;79:3325.

307 **Transbol I et al.** Thiazide for the postponement of postmenopausal bone loss. Metabolism. 1982;31:383.

308 **Riggs BL et al.** Effect of fluoride treatment on the fracture rate in postmenopausal women with osteoporosis. N Engl J Med. 1990;322:802.

309 **Pak CYC et al.** Slow-release sodium fluoride in the management of postmenopausal osteoporosis. A randomized controlled trial. Ann Intern Med. 1994;120:625.

310 **Need AG et al.** Effects of nandrolone decanoate and antiresorptive therapy on vertebral density in osteoporotic postmenopausal women. Arch Intern Med. 1989;149:57.

311 **Watts NB et al.** Intermittent cyclical etidronate treatment of postmenopausal osteoporosis. N Engl J Med. 1990;323:73.

312 **Centers for Disease Control.** Reduced incidence of menstrual toxic shock syndrome—United States, 1980–1990. MMWR. 1990;39:421–23.

Thyroid Disorders

Betty J Dong

Overview 47-1
Thyroid Function Tests (See Table 47.1) 47-3
  Overview 47-3
  Measurements of Free and Total Serum
    Hormone Levels 47-3
    Free thyroxine (FT$_4$), free thyroxine index (FT$_4$I),
      free triiodothyronine index (FT$_3$I) 47-3
    Total thyroxine (TT$_4$), total
      triiodothyronine (TT$_3$) 47-5
  Tests of the Hypothalamic-Pituitary-Thyroid Axis 47-5
    Sensitive thyroid-stimulating hormone (TSH) 47-5
    Thyrotropin-releasing hormone (TRH) 47-5
  Tests of Gland Function 47-5
    Radioactive iodine uptake (RAIU) 47-5
    Scan 47-5
  Tests of Autoimmunity 47-5
    Antithyroglobulin (ATgA) and antimicrosomal
      (AMA) antibodies 47-5
    Thyroid-receptor antibodies (TRab) 47-6
  Miscellaneous Tests 47-6
    Thyroglobulin 47-6
    Cholesterol 47-6
    Exophthalmometer 47-6
  Clinical Application and Interpretation 47-7
    Euthyroidism 47-7
    Amiodarone 47-8
Hypothyroidism (See Table 47.4) 47-8
  Clinical Presentation (See Table 47.3): Anemia 47-8
  Treatment with Thyroid Hormones 47-8
    Thyroid hormone products (See Table 47.5) 47-8
    Desiccated thyroid 47-9
    Levothyroxine or L-thyroxine 47-9
    Triiodothyronine 47-10
    Liotrix 47-10
    Thyroxine 47-10
    Dosage 47-10
    Monitoring therapy 47-10
    Triiodothyronine 47-11
    Parenteral dosing 47-11
    In pregnancy 47-11
    Congenital hypothyroidism (See Table 47.6) 47-11
    Unresponsiveness to thyroid therapy 47-12
  Myxedema Coma 47-13
    Clinical presentation 47-13
    Treatment 47-13
  With Congestive Heart Failure (CHF) 47-14
    Clinical presentation 47-14
    Treatment 47-14
  In the elderly 47-15
Hyperthyroidism 47-15
  Clinical Presentation (See Table 47.7 and 47.8) 47-15

Hypoprothrombinemia 47-15
  Warfarin metabolism 47-15
  Thioamide effects 47-16
Response to Digoxin 47-16
Cardioversion 47-16
Thyrotoxicosis: Clinical presentation 47-17
Iodides 47-17
Treatment Modalities (See Table 47.9) 47-18
  Thioamides 47-18
  Surgery 47-18
  Radioactive iodine (RAI) 47-18
  Ipodate 47-18
Treatment with Thioamides 47-18
  Propylthiouracil (PTU) 47-18
    Versus methimazole 47-18
    Dosing and administration 47-20
    Monitoring therapy 47-20
    Duration of therapy 47-20
  Precautions 47-20
  Adjunctive therapy 47-21
  Adverse effects 47-21
    Thioamide rash 47-21
    Hepatitis 47-21
    Agranulocytosis 47-22
  Preoperative preparation 47-22
  Single daily dosing 47-22
  Remission 47-23
  In pregnancy 47-24
Treatment with RAI 47-24
  Pretreatment 47-24
  Onset of effects 47-24
  Iatrogenic hypothyroidism 47-25
Ophthalmopathy 47-25
  Clinical presentation 47-26
  Management 47-26
Thyroid Storm 47-26
  Clinical presentation 47-26
  Treatment 47-26
    Decrease in synthesis and release of hormones 47-26
    Reversal of the peripheral effects of hormones
      and catecholamines 47-26
    Supportive treatment of vital functions 47-26
    Elimination of precipitating causes of storm 47-26
Drug-Induced Thyroid Disease 47-26
  Lithium and antidepressants 47-26
  Iodides and amiodarone 47-27
Nodules 47-28
  "Hot" Nodule 47-28
  "Cold" Nodule 47-28
  Nontoxic Multinodular Goiter 47-28

Thyroid disease is common, affecting approximately 5% to 15% of the general population. Females are three to four times more likely than males to develop any type of thyroid disease. The typical thyroid disorders emphasized in this chapter include hypothyroidism, hyperthyroidism, and nodular disease. Thyroid cancer is discussed briefly. The reader is referred to standard medical textbooks for more detailed medical and diagnostic information.

Triiodothyronine (T$_3$) and thyroxine (T$_4$) are the two biologically active thyroid hormones produced by the thyroid gland in response to hormones released by the pituitary and hypothalamus.

The hypothalamic thyrotropin-releasing hormone (TRH) stimulates release of thyrotropin [i.e., thyroid-stimulating hormone (TSH)] from the pituitary in response to low circulating levels of thyroid hormone. TSH in turn promotes hormone synthesis and release by increasing thyroid activity. When sufficient synthesis has occurred, high circulating thyroid hormone levels block further production by inhibiting TSH release. The intrapituitary deiodination of T_4 to T_3 also plays a critical role in the inhibition of TSH secretion.[1] As the serum concentrations of thyroid hormone decrease, the hypothalamic-pituitary centers again become responsive by releasing TRH and TSH.

T_3 is four times more potent than T_4, but its serum concentration is lower. T_4 is the major circulating hormone secreted by the thyroid. In contrast, about 80% of the total daily T_3 production results from the peripheral conversion of T_4 to T_3 through deiodination of T_4. T_4 has intrinsic biological activity and does not function solely as a prohormone. Approximately 35% to 40% of secreted T_4 is converted peripherally to T_3; another 45% of secreted T_4 undergoes peripheral conversion to inactive reverse T_3 (rT_3). Certain drugs and diseases can modify the conversion rate of T_4 to T_3 and decrease the serum T_3 levels (see Table 47.2 and Question 2).

T_3 and T_4 exist in the circulation in the free (active) and protein-bound (inactive) forms. About 99.97% of circulating T_4 is bound: 70% to thyroxine-binding globulin (TBG), 15% to thyroxine-binding prealbumin (TBPA), and the rest to albumin. Only 0.03% exist as the free form. This affinity for plasma proteins accounts for T_4's slow metabolic degradation and long half-life ($t\frac{1}{2}$) of seven days. In contrast, T_3 is considerably less strongly bound to plasma proteins (99.7%); about 0.3% exists as free hormone. The lower protein-binding affinity of T_3 accounts for its threefold greater metabolic potency and its shorter half-life of one and one-half days.

Hypothyroidism is a clinical syndrome that results from a deficiency of thyroid hormone. The prevalence of hypothyroidism in females is 1.4% to 2% and 0.1% to 0.2% in males. The incidence increases in the elderly (age >60 years) to 6% of women and 2.5% of men. Hypothyroidism can be caused by either primary (thyroid gland) or secondary (hypothalamic-pituitary) malfunction. Primary hypothyroidism is more common than secondary causes.

Hashimoto's thyroiditis, an autoimmune disorder, is the most frequent cause of primary hypothyroidism and appears to have a strong genetic predisposition. The pathogenesis of Hashimoto's thyroiditis results from an impaired immune surveillance causing dysfunction of normal ''suppressor'' T lymphocytes and excessive production of thyroid antibodies by ''helper'' T lymphocytes. The destruction of thyroid cells by circulating thyroid antibodies produces an underlying defect or block in the intrathyroidal, organobinding of iodide. As a result, inactive hormones or insufficient amounts of active hormones are synthesized and this eventually produces hypothyroidism. However, the clinical presentation of Hashimoto's thyroiditis can be quite variable, depending upon the time of patient diagnosis. Although the typical presentation is hypothyroidism and goiter (thyroid gland enlargement), patients can present with hypothyroidism and no goiter, with euthyroidism and a goiter, or rarely (<5%), hyperthyroidism (Hashi-toxicosis). Hashimoto's thyroiditis might be related to Graves' disease, a frequent cause of hyperthyroidism. Both diseases share similar clinical features: positive antibody titers, a goiter with lymphocytic infiltration of the gland, a familial tendency, and a predilection for women; both diseases can co-exist in the same gland, thyrotoxicosis can precede the onset of Hashimoto's hypothyroidism, and the end result of Graves' hyperthyroidism often is hypothyroidism. These common clinical features suggest that Graves' disease and Hashimoto's thyroiditis might be the same disease manifesting in different ways.

Other frequent causes of hypothyroidism are presented in Table 47.4 and include iatrogenic destruction of the gland after radioiodine therapy or surgery and hypothyroidism secondary to nontoxic multinodular goiter. Drug-induced hypothyroidism from iodides, amiodarone, and lithium occurs in susceptible individuals (i.e., Hashimoto's thyroiditis) with a pre-existing thyroid abnormality.

The typical symptoms of *hypothyroidism* include weight gain, fatigue, sluggishness, cold intolerance, constipation, heavy menstrual periods, and muscle aches. A goiter might or might not be present. Patients with end-stage hypothyroidism, or myxedema coma, also can present with hypothermia, confusion, stupor or coma, carbon dioxide retention, hypoglycemia, hyponatremia, and ileus. Symptoms of ''slowing down'' would be expected because thyroid hormone is essential for the function and maintenance of all body systems and metabolic processes. In general, the more severe the degree of hypothyroidism is, the greater the number of clinical findings. The exception is the elderly patient with hypothyroidism who often presents with minimal or atypical symptoms (e.g., weight loss, deafness, tinnitus, carpal tunnel syndrome). Patients with mild and subclinical hypothyroidism also might have few or no symptoms. Laboratory findings diagnostic for overt hypothyroidism include an elevated TSH and low free thyroxine levels; for subclinical or early hypothyroidism, an elevated TSH and normal free thyroxine level. The common clinical symptoms, physical findings, and laboratory abnormalities of overt hypothyroidism are summarized in Table 47.3.

Levothyroxine is the preferred thyroid replacement preparation of choice. Several brand and generic preparations are available and interchangeable in the majority of patients. The signs and symptoms of hypothyroidism can be reversed easily in most patients by the administration of levothyroxine at average oral replacement doses of 1.6 to 1.7 µg/kg/day. Exceptions include the elderly, patients with severe and long-standing hypothyroidism, and patients with cardiac disease in whom administration of full replacement doses might cause cardiac toxicity. In such patients, minute thyroxine doses should be started initially and the dosage titrated upward as tolerated; complete reversal of hypothyroidism might not be indicated or possible. In myxedema coma, intravenous (IV) therapy with large initial doses of levothyroxine (e.g., 400 µg) is necessary to increase the active free hormone level by saturating the empty thyroid binding sites, and to prevent the 60% to 70% mortality rate. The goal of therapy is to reverse the signs and symptoms of hypothyroidism and normalize the TSH and free thyroxine levels. Overreplacement of levothyroxine (manifested by low serum concentrations of TSH) is associated with osteoporosis and cardiac changes. The optimal thyroxine replacement dosage must be administered for a minimum of six to eight weeks before steady-state levels are reached. Evaluation of thyroid function tests before this time are misleading and should be interpreted correctly. Once euthyroid, laboratory tests can be monitored every three to six months for the first year, and then yearly thereafter. Medications that interfere with thyroxine absorption (e.g., iron, aluminum hydroxide) should be avoided.

Hyperthyroidism or thyrotoxicosis is the hypermetabolic syndrome that occurs from an excessive quantity of thyroid hormone. Hyperthyroidism is common, affecting about 2% of females and about 0.1% of males. The prevalence of hyperthyroidism in the elderly varies between 0.5% to 2.3%, but accounts for 10% to 15% of all thyrotoxic patients, depending upon the population studied.

Graves' disease is the most frequent cause of hyperthyroidism. Toxic autonomous nodular goiters, both multi- and uninodular, account for a large proportion of the remaining causes. Other causes of hyperthyroidism are outlined in Table 47.8. Graves' disease is an autoimmune disorder characterized by one or more of the following features: hyperthyroidism, diffuse goiter, ophthalmopathy (exophthalmos), dermopathy (pretibial myxedema), and acropachy (thickening of fingers or toes). The production of excessive quantities of thyroid hormone is attributed to a circulating IgG immunoglobulin or thyroid-receptor antibody (TRab) which has TSH-like ability to stimulate hormone synthesis. The abnormal production of TRab by helper T-lymphocytes results from a deficiency of normal suppressor T-cell lymphocytes. The peak incidence of Graves' disease occurs in the third or fourth decade of life, the duration of the disease is unknown, and its clinical course is characterized by remission and relapse.

The classic symptoms of hyperthyroidism, summarized in Table 47.7, mimic a hypermetabolic state and include nervousness, heat intolerance, palpitations, weight loss despite increased appetite, insomnia, proximal muscle weakness, frequent bowel movements, amenorrhea, and emotional lability. Often, these symptoms are present for 3 to 12 months before the diagnosis is made. The typical symptoms often are absent in the elderly patient, producing a masked or "apathetic" picture. Because the clinical presentation of hyperthyroidism in the elderly is atypical, occult hyperthyroidism always must be considered, especially in patients with new or worsening cardiac findings (e.g., atrial fibrillation). Untreated hyperthyroidism can progress to thyroid storm, a life-threatening form of hyperthyroidism characterized by "exaggerated" symptoms of thyrotoxicosis and the acute onset of high fever (*sine qua non*). The diagnosis of hyperthyroidism is confirmed by a high serum concentration of free thyroxine and/or an undetectable TSH level. The presence of positive thyroid antibodies confirms an autoimmune etiology for the hyperthyroidism (e.g., Graves').

The three major options for the treatment of hyperthyroidism include antithyroid drugs (thioamides), radioiodine, and surgery. All three treatments are effective and the treatment of choice is influenced by the etiology of the hyperthyroidism, the size of the goiter, presence of ophthalmopathy, presence of concomitant disorders (e.g., cardiac), likelihood of pregnancy, patient age, patient preference, and physician bias. Elderly patients, and those with cardiac disease, ophthalmopathy, and hyperthyroidism secondary to a toxic multinodular goiter are treated best with radioactive iodine. Surgery is preferable if there are obstructive symptoms or suspicion of concomitant malignancy. Pregnant patients can be managed by thioamides or surgery in the second trimester; radioactive iodine is absolutely contraindicated.

The thioamides are used as primary therapy for hyperthyroidism and as adjunctive short-term therapy to produce euthyroidism before surgery or radioactive iodine. The thioamides [e.g., methimazole and propylthiouracil (PTU)] act primarily to prevent further hormone synthesis but do not affect existing stores of thyroid hormone. Therefore, hyperthyroid symptoms will continue for four to six weeks after beginning thioamide therapy, and initial treatment with beta blockers or iodides often is required for symptomatic relief. The onset of action of PTU is more rapid than methimazole because propylthiouracil has an additional mechanism of action to inhibit the peripheral conversion of T_4 to T_3. Therefore, PTU is the thioamide of choice in thyroid storm. Propylthiouracil also is the drug of choice in pregnancy and during breast-feeding because it crosses the placenta less than methimazole, is not teratogenic, and is not secreted in breast milk. Otherwise, methimazole is preferred over PTU to enhance compliance because it can be dosed once daily whereas PTU must be given two to three times daily. The duration of treatment is empiric and thioamides generally are prescribed for 12 to 18 months in hopes of long-term spontaneous remission once the drug is discontinued. Although thioamides maintain euthyroidism, thioamides do not change the natural

course of the disease; and spontaneous remission, once treatment is discontinued, is poor. The combination of thioamide and thyroxine therapy might increase the likelihood of remission once treatment is discontinued. The major adverse effects from thioamides include skin rash, gastrointestinal (GI) complaints, agranulocytosis, and hepatitis. Cross-sensitivity between the thioamides is not complete and the alternative drug can be used if rash or gastrointestinal complaints do not resolve.

Nodular goiters, both multinodular and uninodular, are very common thyroid problems. The estimated prevalence is 4% to 5% of the adult population. The etiology of thyroid nodules is unknown although TSH stimulation, iodine deficiency, goitrogens (e.g., iodides, lithium, amiodarone), and radiation exposure are contributory. The nodular goiter usually is found upon routine physical examination in asymptomatic and euthyroid individuals. However, patients can present with hyperthyroidism due to autonomous functioning "hot" nodules, overt hypothyroidism, or obstructive symptoms of dysphagia and respiratory difficulty. Malignancy must be considered if there is recent growth in a single or dominant nodule, if there is a history of thyroid irradiation, or if there is a strong family history of medullary thyroid carcinoma. Thyroid function tests, including a TSH, free thyroxine level, and antibodies should be obtained. A fine needle aspiration (FNA) of the thyroid nodule helps to determine the possibility of malignancy: the character of the nodular goiter can be evaluated by a radioactive iodine uptake, ultrasound, or magnetic resonance imaging. Treatment options include surgery, radioactive iodine, thyroid replacement therapy if necessary to correct hypothyroidism, and TSH suppression therapy using levothyroxine dosages of 2.2 µg/kg/day. All goitrogens should be removed if possible. Thyroid suppression therapy is used to prevent further growth of a benign nodular goiter but it is not very effective in reducing or normalizing the goiter. The goal of thyroxine suppression therapy is a suppressed but detectable TSH to prevent further gland stimulation. However, thyroid suppression therapy might not be indicated if the dangers from supraphysiologic dosages of thyroxine (e.g., osteoporosis and the potential for cardiac arrhythmias) exceed the benefits of nodular suppression. Toxic multinodular goiters have a small risk of malignancy and rarely undergo spontaneous remission so that definitive treatment with radioactive iodine is required. Surgery is indicated for any goiters with a high risk of malignancy and any obstructive or respiratory symptoms.

Thyroid Function Tests

The principal laboratory tests recommended in the initial evaluation of thyroid disorders include the sensitive TSH and the free thyroxine level (FT_4).[2,3] If a direct measure of the free thyroxine level is not available, the estimated free thyroxine index (FT_4I) can provide comparable information. Measurement of only the total T_4 (TT_4) should not be used because it is not as reliable as the FT_4 or FT_4I when alterations in thyroid-binding globulin or nonthyroidal illnesses exist. Positive thyroid antibodies identify the presence of an autoimmune thyroid disorder. Adjuncts to the above tests include the total T_3(TT_3), radioactive iodine uptake (RAIU) and Scan, thyroid-receptor antibody, and miscellaneous tests such as the exophthalmometer, cholesterol, fine needle aspiration biopsy, and thyroglobulin (see Table 47.1).

Measurements of Free and Total Serum Hormone Levels

Free Thyroxine (FT_4), Free Thyroxine
Index (FT_4I), Free Triiodothyronine Index (FT_3I)
The FT_4 by equilibrium dialysis is the most accurate method available for direct measurement of the free T_4. A number of two-step labeled hormone analog methods for determining the FT_4 exist

Table 47.1		Common Thyroid Function Tests[a]		
Tests	Measures	Normals[b]	Assay Interference	Comments
Measurement of Circulating Hormone Levels				
FT$_4$	Direct measurement of free thyroxine	*Dialysis method:* 9–24 pmol/L *Analog method:* 0.6–2.1 ng/dL	No interference by alterations in TBG	Most accurate determination of FT$_4$ levels; might be higher than normal in patients on thyroxine replacement
FT$_4$I	Calculated free thyroxine index	*T$_4$ uptake method:* 6.5–12.5 *TT$_4$ x RT$_3$U method:* 1.3–3.9	Euthyroid sick syndrome (See Question 2)	Estimates direct FT$_4$ measurement; compensates for alterations in TBG
TT$_4$	Total free and bound T$_4$	5.0–11.0 µg/dL	Alterations in TBG (See Table 47.2)	Specific and sensitive test if no alterations in TBG
TT$_3$	Total free and bound T$_3$	88–160 ng/dL	Alterations in TBG levels; T$_4$ to T$_3$ (See Table 47.2). Euthyroid sick syndrome (See Question 2)	Useful in detecting early, relapsing, and T$_3$ toxicosis. Not useful in evaluation of hypothyroidism
RT$_3$U	Indirect measure of saturation of TBG binding sites; does not measure either T$_3$ or T$_4$ levels directly	26%–35%	Alterations in TBG levels (See Table 47.2)	Can be used to calculate FT$_3$I and FT$_4$I
Tests of Thyroid Gland Function				
RAIU	Iodine utilization by the gland after trace dose of either I^{123} or I^{131}	5 hr = 5%–15% 24 hr = 15%–35%	False decrease with excess iodide intake; false elevation with iodide deficiency	Useful in hyperthyroidism to determine RAI dose in Graves'. Does not provide information regarding hormone synthesis
Scan	Gland size, shape, and tissue activity after I^{123} or Tc^{99}m	—	I^{123} scan blocked by antithyroid/thyroid medications	Useful in nodular disease to detect "cold" or "hot" areas
Tests of Hypothalamic-Pituitary-Thyroid Axis				
TSH	Pituitary TSH level	0.5–5.5 µU/mL	Dopamine, glucocorticoids, metoclopramide, thyroid hormone, amiodarone (See Table 47.2)	Most sensitive index for hyperthyroidism, hypothyroidism, and replacement therapy
TRH	Pituitary TSH responsiveness	5–25 µU/mL rise from baseline TSH 30 min after 400 mg IV TRH (protirelin)	Thyroid hormone, depression. See TSH interferences	Only useful in the diagnosis of secondary hypothyroidism
Tests of Autoimmunity				
ATgA	Antibodies to thyroglobulin	<10%	Nonthyroidal autoimmune disorders	Present in autoimmune thyroid disease; undetectable during remission
AMA	Antibodies to microsomal antigen by TRC agglutination	Titers <1:100	Nonthyroidal autoimmune disorders	More sensitive of the two antibodies. Titers detectable even after remission
TRab	Thyroid receptor IgG antibody	Titers negative	—	Confirms Graves' disease; detects risk of neonatal Graves'
Miscellaneous				
Thyroglobulin	Colloid protein of normal thyroid gland	5–25 ng/dL	Goiters; inflammatory thyroid disease	Marker for recurrent thyroid cancer or metastases in thyroidectomized patients

[a] AMA = Antimicrosomal; ATgA = Antithyroglobulin; FT$_4$ = Free thyroxine; FT$_4$I = Free thyroxine index; IV = Intravenous; RAIU = Radioactive iodine uptake; RT$_3$U = Resin triiodothyronine uptake; T$_3$ = Triiodothyronine; T$_4$ = Thyroxine; TBG = Thyroxine-binding globulin; TRab = Thyroid-receptor antibodies; TRC = Tanned red cell; TRH = Thyrotropin-releasing hormone; TSH = Thyroid-stimulating hormone; TT$_4$ = Total thyroxine; TT$_3$ = Total triiodothyronine.
[b] At University of California labs.

but can be of variable accuracy in different clinical settings. In contrast, direct measurement of the free T$_3$ level is expensive and unnecessary because the calculated index correlates well with the actual T$_3$ level. The free thyroxine index and the free triiodothyronine index are indirect estimations of the free levels of T$_4$ and T$_3$. Calculation of the free T$_4$ or free T$_3$ index is most helpful when TBG levels are abnormal. These indirect calculated values correct for the latter clinical situations and correlate favorably with the true thyroid status as derived from direct measurement of actual free hormone levels. Unfortunately, these indices do not correct for changes ob-

served in patients with "euthyroid sick" nonthyroidal illnesses whose binding affinity for the TBG is altered. In these circumstances, the FT$_4$ by dialysis or by analog method is preferable.

The results of the FT$_4$I often are reported so that calculations by the clinician are not required. In contrast, calculations are required to determine the FT$_3$I. The traditional method of estimating the T$_4$ index is to multiply the Resin T$_3$ Uptake (RT$_3$U) by the TT$_4$. A newer and more accurate method to calculate the FT$_4$I is to divide the TT$_4$ by the T$_4$ "uptake." The free T$_3$ index can be calculated similarly using either method. It is important to identify which method (RT₃U or T₄ "uptake") is used to determine the free T_4 or T_3 index, since the normal values will be significantly different.

Total Thyroxine (TT₄), Total Triiodothyronine (TT₃)

The total serum T_4 and total serum T_3 are fairly sensitive and specific measures of both free and bound (total) serum T_4 and T_3. They also are free from iodine interferences. Since the bound fraction is the major fraction measured, situations which change the hormone's affinity for TBG or the TBG level will influence the results. For example, falsely elevated levels of TT_4 and TT_3 are common in the euthyroid pregnant female (see Question 4). Additionally, the TT_3 often is low in the elderly and in many acute and chronic nonthyroidal illnesses because the peripheral conversion of T_4 to T_3 is decreased (see Questions 2 and 3). Therefore, careful interpretation of these tests is necessary in situations which alter thyroid hormone binding or TBG levels. (See Table 47.2.) The TT_4 is most useful when used to evaluate thyroid disorders in patients without existing alterations in thyroid protein binding. The TT_3 is subject to the same interferences as the TT_4. The TT_3 is particularly helpful in detecting early relapse of Graves' disease and in confirming the diagnosis of hyperthyroidism despite normal TT_4 levels. TT_3 is not a good indicator in hypothyroidism.

Tests of the Hypothalamic-Pituitary-Thyroid Axis.

Sensitive Thyroid-Stimulating Hormone (TSH)

The serum thyroid-stimulating hormone or thyrotropin by immunometric assay is the most sensitive test used to evaluate thyroid function.[2,3] TSH secreted by the pituitary is elevated in early or subclinical hypothyroidism (when thyroid hormone levels apparently are normal) and when thyroid hormone replacement therapy is inadequate. This is because low free hormone levels stimulate the pituitary to synthesize increased amounts of TSH. Unfortunately, the test does not distinguish primary hypothyroidism (thyroid failure), which is characterized by elevated TSH levels, from secondary (pituitary or hypothalamus failure) hypothyroidism. In the latter instance, the sensitive assay may show low normal TSH levels. The sensitive TSH assay, unlike the older insensitive assay, also is capable of quantitating both the upper and lower limits of normal so that a suppressed TSH level is highly suggestive of hyperthyroidism or exogenous thyroid overreplacement. Therefore, the TSH level eliminates the need for further TRH testing in patients with suspected hyperthyroidism.

However, the TSH is not entirely specific for thyroid disease and can be abnormal in euthyroid individuals with nonthyroidal illnesses and in individuals receiving drugs that can interfere with TSH secretion. TSH secretion is suppressed physiologically by dopamine which antagonizes the stimulatory effects of TRH. Therefore, dopaminergic agonists and antagonists can alter TSH secretion. Dopamine (Intropin),[2,45] levodopa (Sinemet),[6,7] bromocriptine (Parlodel),[8] and glucocorticoids[2,9] inhibit TSH secretion; while metoclopramide (Reglan)[10,11] and domperidone (Motilium)[12] increase TSH secretions in euthyroid and hypothyroid individuals (see Question 5).

Thyrotropin-Releasing Hormone (TRH)

Thyrotropin-releasing hormone, administered as synthetic protirelin, measures pituitary TSH responsiveness because TRH released from the hypothalamus normally stimulates TSH production.[13] A test dose of 400 μg TRH is given as an intravenous bolus and serum TSH levels are determined just before and 30 minutes after the injection. Normally, a prompt rise of 5 to 25 mIU/mL in TSH levels from baseline is expected by 30 minutes; in men over the age of 40, a smaller rise of 3 mIU/mL is expected. In patients with hypothalamic hypothyroidism, the pituitary responds sluggishly to exogenous TRH and produces a slow but continuous rise

in TSH. In hypopituitary hypothyroidism, no TSH response to TRH would be expected. Thus, the TRH test can help differentiate hypopituitary from hypothalamic hypothyroidism. The TRH offers no additional information from the TSH in the evaluation of hyperthyroidism (see Table 47.1).

Tests of Gland Function

Radioactive Iodine Uptake (RAIU)

The radioactive iodine uptake is a measure of iodine utilization by the gland. A tracer dose of I^{123} or I^{131} is administered, and the radioactivity of the gland is measured at 5 and 24 hours after ingestion. The normal values of this test depend upon the sufficiency of dietary iodine in various geographical areas. In some hyperthyroid patients, uptake values will peak within the first few hours after the tracer dose is administered and the uptake then will fall progressively to lower, even subnormal levels. Therefore, the uptake of the RAIU should be measured at 5 and 24 hours so that those patients with rapid turnover of iodine will not be missed.

The RAIU indirectly reflects the need for iodine and thyroid function. As a measurement of thyroid activity, the test has a clinical accuracy of 70% to 90% and is more accurate in the hyperthyroid than in the hypothyroid ranges.

Any condition which affects the thyroid requirement for iodine will alter the RAIU. Therefore, iodine deficiency resulting from rigorous diuretic therapy or from iodine-deficient diets will reflect a falsely increased uptake due to replenishment of depleted total iodide pools. Conversely, dilution of total body iodide pools with exogenous iodide sources (e.g., contrast dyes) will result in a falsely low RAIU.

The RAIU is elevated in hyperthyroid states and early hypothyroidism when the failing hypothyroid gland is trying to compensate through increased hormone synthesis. A low RAIU is seen in hypothyroidism and thyrotoxicosis factitia. An RAIU usually is obtained when radioactive iodine therapy for Graves' disease is considered.

Scan

A scan of the gland is performed simultaneously with the RAIU or after ingestion of technetium Tc 99ᵐ pertechnetate. The scan provides information concerning gland size and shape and identifies hypermetabolic (hot) and hypometabolic (cold) areas. The possibility of carcinoma must be considered if cold areas are present. A scan should be considered in the patient with nodular thyroid disease.

Tests of Autoimmunity

Antithyroglobulin (ATgA) and
Antimicrosomal (AMA) Antibodies

Antithyroglobulin and antimicrosomal antibodies to the thyroid gland are detected by radioimmunoassay and by the tanned red cell (TRC) agglutination method, respectively. The presence of these antibodies indicates the existence of an autoimmune process, although the nature of the problem is undetermined. About 60% to 70% of patients with Graves' disease and 95% of patients with Hashimoto's thyroiditis will have positive antibodies to both thyroid antigens. The presence of positive antibodies alone does not indicate thyroid disease, since 5% to 10% of asymptomatic individuals, as well as individuals with other nonthyroidal autoimmune disorders, will have positive antibodies.

Clinically, the AMA seems to be more specific than ATgA in assessing disease activity. Although both antibodies are elevated during acute flares of the disease, lower titers of AMA remain positive during quiescent periods of the disease while antithyroglobulin levels revert to negative.

Table 47.2	Factors Which Can Significantly Alter Thyroid Function Tests in Euthyroid Patients[a,c,2,3,17]
↑ TBG Binding Capacity	**Drugs/Situations[b]**
↑ TT_4	Estrogens,[2,17] tamoxifen[28]
↑ TT_3	Oral contraceptives[2,17]
↓ RT_3U	Heroin[29]
Normal TSH	Methadone maintenance[29]
Normal FT_4I, FT_4	Genetic ↑ in TBG
Normal FT_3I, FT_3	Clofibrate
	Active hepatitis[17]
↓ TBG Binding Capacity/Displacement T_4 from Binding Sites	
↓ TT_4	Androgens
↓ TT_3	Salicylates,[17,22,23] disalcid,[22] salsalate[23]
↑ RT_3U	High-dose furosemide[17]
Normal TSH	↓ TBG synthesis-cirrhosis/hepatic failure[17]
Normal FT_4I, FT_4	Nephrotic syndrome[17]
Normal FT_3I, FT_3	Danazol[24]
	Glucocorticoids[17]
↓ Peripheral $T_4 \rightarrow T_3$ conversion	
↓ TT_3	PTU
Normal TT_4	Propranolol[158]
Normal FT_4I, FT_4	Glucocorticoids[17]
Normal TSH	
↓ Pituitary and Peripheral $T_4 \rightarrow T_3$	
↓ TT_3	Ipodate, iopanoic acid[136–138]
↑ TT_4	Amiodarone[30–32]
↑ TSH (transient)	Euthyroid sick syndrome[16–20]
↑ FT_4I	
↑ T_4 Clearance by Enzyme Induction/↑ Fecal Loss	
↓ TT_4	Phenytoin[25–27]
↓ FT_4I	Phenobarbital[25]
Normal FT_4	Carbamazepine[25]
Normal or ↑ TT_3	Cholestyramine, colestipol[78,79]
Normal or ↑ TSH	Rifampin[25]
↓ TSH Secretion	Dopamine[3,4,6]
	Levodopa[3–7]
	Glucocorticoids[3,9,17]
	Bromocriptine[8]
	Octreotide[17]
↑ TSH	Metoclopramide[10,17]
	Domperidone[12]

[a] FT_3 = Free triiodothyronine; FT_4 = Free thyroxine; FT_3I = Free triiodothyronine index; FT_4I = Free thyroxine index; PTU = Propylthiouracil; RT_3U = Resin triiodothyronine uptake; TBG = Thyroxine-binding globulin; T_3 = Triiodothyronine; T_4 = Thyroxine; TSH = Thyroid-stimulating hormone; TT_3 = Total triiodothyronine; TT_4 = Total thyroxine.

[b] See references for more complete information.

[c] See Question 14 for further explanation.

Thyroid-Receptor Antibodies (TRab)

Thyroid receptor antibodies are IgG immunoglobulins which are present in Graves' disease. Like TSH, these immunoglobulins can stimulate the thyroid gland to produce thyroid hormones; they are present in virtually all patients with Graves' disease. Very high titers of TRab are useful in the diagnosis of otherwise asymptomatic Graves' disease (i.e., exophthalmos), in predicting the risk of relapse of Graves' disease upon medication discontinuation, and in predicting the risk of congenital hyperthyroidism in infants through transplacental passage of TRab from the pregnant Graves' mother.[14,15] Otherwise, the TRab is expensive and offers no additional information in the patient with typical Graves' disease presentation.

Miscellaneous Tests

Thyroglobulin

Thyroglobulin is the colloid protein secreted by the thyroid gland and normally is measured in the serum by radioimmunoassay. Thyroglobulin is nonspecific and is elevated whenever the thyroid is inflamed or enlarged (goiter). Therefore, thyroglobulin levels are nondiagnostic except in patients who have undergone a thyroidectomy for malignancy. Since the thyroglobulin level usually is undetectable in these patients, an elevated thyroglobulin indicates recurrent cancer and/or metastases.[2]

Cholesterol

In hypothyroid individuals, the serum concentration of cholesterol is high because its rate of degradation is decreased in relation to its synthesis. Conversely, the serum concentration of cholesterol is low in hyperthyroid patients. However, since many extrathyroidal factors influence the serum concentration of cholesterol, this test is an imprecise reflection of thyroid status.

Exophthalmometer

The exophthalmometer is an instrument used to measure the extent of protrusion of the ophthalmic globe beyond the orbital notch. This is a fairly precise and reproducible measurement that is used to monitor the progression or regression of Graves' ophthalmopathy. Normal readings are less than 20 mm but the normal range varies among different ethnic groups.

Clinical Application and Interpretation

Euthyroidism

1. R.K., a 42-year-old obese female, is admitted to the hospital because of increasing fatigue, sluggishness, shortness of breath (SOB), and pitting edema of the legs over the past 3 weeks. Bilateral pleural effusions found on chest x-ray indicate a worsening of her congestive heart failure (CHF). Her other medical problems include cirrhosis of the liver, diabetes, and chronic bronchitis for which she takes tolbutamide (Orinase) and Lugol's solution TID.

Pertinent physical findings include a palpable but normal size thyroid, bibasilar rales, cardiomegaly, hepatomegaly, 4+ pitting edema, and normal deep tendon reflexes (DTRs). A diagnosis of increasing CHF secondary to hypothyroidism is suspected based upon the following laboratory findings: cholesterol 385 mg/dL; RAIU at 24 hr = 13% (Normal: 15%–35%); Scan: normal-sized gland with homogenous uptake; TT_4 1.4 μg/dL (Normal: 5–11); RT_3U 35% (Normal: 26%–35%); TT_3 22 ng/dL (Normal: 88–160); TSH 4 mIU/mL (Normal: 0.5–5.5); FT_4I 0.5 (Normal: 6.5–12.5); AMA = negative; ATgA 3% (Normal: <3%). Evaluate and explain R.K.'s thyroid status based upon her clinical and laboratory findings. [SI units: cholesterol 9.96 mmol/L; TT_4 18 nmol/L; TT_3 0.3 nmol/L; TSH 4 mU/L]

Although low output failure can be a presenting sign of hypothyroidism, the normal TSH definitely indicates that R.K. is euthyroid despite the confusing results of her other thyroid function tests. The depressed RAIU is consistent with her history of iodide ingestion and dilution of total iodide pools. The low TT_4, TT_3, and FT_4I may be explained by her cirrhosis and "euthyroid sick syndrome." (See Question 2.) The absence of thyroid antibodies, the normal scan, and the presence of normal deep tendon reflexes further substantiate the diagnosis of euthyroidism. In this case, the elevated cholesterol level is not secondary to hypothyroidism.

2. Assess the results and explain the significance of the TT_4, FT_4I, RT_3U, and TT_3 values seen in R.K.

R.K.'s thyroid function test results are consistent with the "euthyroid sick syndrome." Abnormal thyroid function tests frequently are found in euthyroid patients with a wide variety of systemic diseases, including acute and chronic starvation, acute infections, acute psychiatric disorders, asymptomatic and symptomatic human immunodeficiency virus (HIV) disease, and chronic cardiac, pulmonary, renal, hepatic, and neoplastic diseases.[16–21] This "euthyroid sick syndrome" occurs in 37% to 70% of chronically ill or hospitalized patients and must be recognized to prevent unnecessary and dangerous hormone replacement.[21] In general, the more ill the patient, the greater is the degree of abnormal thyroid function findings, even though the patient has no thyroid abnormality.

Typical changes include a normal or low TT_4, a normal or low calculated FT_4I despite normal free thyroxine levels when determined by equilibrium dialysis, an RT_3U that is not markedly increased; a normal or borderline-high compensatory TSH as patients recover from illness, a low total TT_3 ($\approx$15 to 20 ng/dL), and a high reverse T_3 (rT_3). These changes are explained by alterations in the peripheral conversion of T_4 to T_3 and by complex abnormalities in the hypothalmic-pituitary-thyroid relationships. The low serum T_3 levels and high inactive, reverse T_3 are due to decreased activity of 5-deiodinase, an enzyme which is necessary for the peripheral conversion of T_4 to T_3. Impaired protein synthesis of thyroid-binding prealbumin and an increase in the proportion of a lower-binding-capacity form of TBG can account for the low serum hormone levels, but the concomitant increase in the free hormone concentrations maintains a euthyroid state. Furthermore, circulating substances that inhibit the binding of T_4 and T_3 to the serum-binding proteins might be present.

However, less often, a modestly elevated TT_4 and calculated FT_4I are found in patients with acute viral hepatitis, psychiatric disorders, renal failure, and progression of HIV disease.[16,17] The T_3 usually is normal but can be low in critically ill patients. Modest elevations in hormonal binding affinity and increased synthesis of thyroxine-binding globulins explain these changes.

Interestingly, several studies have shown a strong inverse correlation between mortality and total serum T_4 and T_3 levels.[19,20] Of 86 hospitalized intensive care patients, 84% of those with a serum T_4 of less than 3 μg/dL died, while only 15% of those with a serum T_4 value greater than 5 μg/dL died. Decreases in serum T_3 values developed only in critically ill patients with HIV and *Pneumocystis carinii* infections.[18] During recovery, TSH levels increase and serum hormone levels start to normalize. Therefore, reversal of the hormone indices is associated with a favorable outcome.

In summary, T_4 and T_3 measurements are of limited value in the diagnosis of thyroid dysfunction in patients with significant nonthyroidal illness. A normal or near normal TSH is paramount in establishing the existence of euthyroidism in sick patients with nonthyroidal illness. No thyroid hormone treatment is indicated in patients like R.K. Thyroxine therapy is not beneficial, and by inhibiting TSH, is detrimental to normal thyroid recovery.[21] The abnormal laboratory findings should reverse when R.K.'s nonthyroidal illness is corrected. The slightly elevated TSH should be repeated to confirm euthyroidism once R.K. has recovered.

3. J.R., a 45-year-old male, complains of fatigue, dry skin, and constipation. His other medical problems include alcoholism for 10 years; cirrhosis; grand mal seizures treated with phenytoin (Dilantin) 300 mg/day and phenobarbital 90 mg at night; and rheumatoid arthritis for which he takes aspirin 325 mg, 20 tablets/day.

The results of his thyroid function tests are as follows: TT_4 4.2 μg/dL, RT_3U 40%, and TSH 2.5 mIU/mL. How should these laboratory findings be interpreted? What factors are responsible for the observed changes? [SI units: TT_4 54 nmol/L; TSH 2.5 mU/L]

Despite the presence of hypothyroid symptoms (e.g., fatigue, dry skin, constipation) and the low serum hormone values, J.R. is euthyroid as evidenced by the normal TSH level. If secondary hypothyroidism is suspected, a TRH test should be performed.

A number of factors could account for J.R.'s decreased TT_4 and increased resin uptake.[17] Anti-inflammatory doses of salicylates and salicylate derivatives (i.e., disalcid, salsalate) can displace thyroxine from both TBG and TBPA, causing decreased values for TT_4. RT_3U values are increased. Salsalate can produce significant falls of TT_4 and TT_3 values into the hypothyroid ranges. Free T_4 estimates and TSH values also are altered transiently. Cirrhosis, stress, severe infections, and hereditary factors can decrease TBG and TBPA synthesis to produce the above laboratory findings. A medication history for other drugs such as androgens[24] or glucocorticoids[17] which also could produce this picture should be obtained (see Table 47.2).

The anticonvulsants [phenytoin, phenobarbital, valproic acid (Depakene), carbamazepine (Tegretol)] and rifampin can affect serum thyroid hormone levels.[25–27] Patients on long-term phenytoin therapy have a 30% to 40% decrease in both total and free T_4 serum concentrations. This is due to a reduction in intestinal thyroxine absorption and an increase in the metabolism (nondeiodination) of thyroxine. Although phenytoin displaces thyroxine from its binding sites *in vitro*, this is not responsible for the changes in thyroxine levels seen *in vivo*. The reduced serum thyroxine levels do not seem to be accompanied by increased TSH levels in euthyroid patients, although elevated TSH levels and hypothyroidism have been reported during phenytoin therapy in patients requiring levothyroxine replacement.[26,27] Serum T_3 levels are normal or slightly decreased. Carbamazepine and valproic acid are reported to have similar but less potent effects on thyroid function.[25] Rifampin also results in subnormal concentrations of free T_4. Phenobarbital can increase T_4 uptake by the liver and increase the fecal excretion of thyroxine. Serum binding of thyroid hormones is unaffected by phenobarbital.

In summary, J.R. is taking several drugs which can further compromise the already low serum thyroxine levels resulting from his liver disease. The free thyroxine index, as previously described, should be calculated to correct for alterations in protein binding. Both the normal TSH and FT_4I confirm euthyroidism.

4. S.T., a 23-year-old, sexually active female who is taking only birth control pills, comes to clinic complaining of extreme nervousness, diaphoresis, and scanty menstrual periods. Although she appears healthy, the possibility of hyperthyroidism is entertained on the basis of a TT_4 of 16 µg/dL, an RT_3U of 23%, an FT_4 of 16 pmol/L, and a TSH of 1.2 mIU/mL. Based upon this information, what would be a reasonable assessment of S.T.'s thyroid status? [SI units: TT_4 206 mmol/L; TSH 1.2 mU/L]

The normal free thyroxine by equilibrium dialysis (FT_4), the normal TSH level, and a calculated normal free thyroxine index confirm that S.T. is not hyperthyroid. The elevated TT_4 and the depressed resin uptake are consistent with increased TBG levels observed in individuals with acute hepatitis, pregnant women, or in persons taking estrogen, oral contraceptives or tamoxifen,[2,3,17,28] heroin, or methadone.[29] Since TBG and, therefore, bound T_4 levels are increased by estrogens in S.T., total serum T_4 measurements will be elevated falsely. Conversely, since there is an absolute increase in the amount of thyroxine binding sites available, the RT_3U will be decreased. However, thyroid function tests should return to normal two to four weeks after discontinuation of oral contraceptives, although two to four months might be required. Progesterone-only oral contraceptives do not appear to affect protein binding; consequently, they do not alter thyroid function tests.

Amiodarone

5. J.P., a 55-year-old female, has a 3-month history of progressive tremors, dizziness, and ataxia. Two months ago she had a silent myocardial infarction (MI) complicated by malignant ventricular ectopy which was responsive only to amiodarone (Cordarone) therapy. Her other medical problems include parkinsonism, insulin-dependent diabetes, and diabetic gastroparesis. Her current medications include amiodarone, insulin, metoclopramide (Reglan), bromocriptine (Parlodel), and levodopa/carbidopa (Sinemet). Physical examination of the thyroid was unremarkable. Thyroid function tests show a TT_4 of 14.5 µg/dL, an FT_4I of 5.2, a TSH of 4.8 mIU/mL, a TT_3 of 100 ng/dL, and negative thyroid antibodies. How should J.P.'s laboratory values be interpreted? [SI units: TT_4 187 nmol/L; TSH 4.8 mU/L; TT_3 1.5 mmol/L]

Although the symptoms of tremors, dizziness, and weight loss are suggestive of hyperthyroidism, the normal TT_3, negative antibodies, normal TSH, and normal physical examination make this diagnosis unlikely. A toxic reaction to amiodarone is a likely etiology of J.P.'s symptoms. Her drug therapy also is responsible for some of the laboratory findings.

Amiodarone produces complex changes in thyroid function tests which can cause diagnostic confusion if not interpreted properly.[30-32] Since it can block both the peripheral and pituitary conversion of T_4 to T_3, the resultant increased TSH secretion increases both the TT_4 and FT_4I. There is a less dramatic decrease in the TT_3 in euthyroid patients on amiodarone. The TSH is transiently elevated above baseline values during the first few weeks of therapy due to the pituitary T_4 to T_3 block; these levels should return to normal in ≤ 3 months. If thyroid function tests do not return

to normal, then amiodarone-induced thyroid disease should be considered. (See Question 53.)

The other drugs J.P. is taking, bromocriptine, levodopa, and metoclopramide, also add to the diagnostic confusion. Although these drugs do not affect the actual circulating hormone levels, they affect the dopaminergic system which controls both TSH and TRH secretion.[4,17] Infusions of dopamine can decrease both TSH secretion and the TSH response to TRH in euthyroid and hypothyroid individuals. Therefore, dopamine agonists such as bromocriptine and levodopa can decrease the TSH response in hypothyroidism.[6,8,17] Conversely, dopamine antagonists such as metoclopramide or domperidone can elevate TSH levels even in hypothyroid patients.[10,12,17] Fortunately, the alterations in TSH and in the TRH stimulation test caused by these agents usually are not substantial enough to obscure the true thyroid abnormality completely.

Hypothyroidism

Clinical Presentation: Anemia

6. M.W., a 70 kg, 23-year-old voice student, thinks that her neck has become "fatter" over the past 3 to 4 months. She has gained 20 pounds, feels mentally sluggish, tires easily, and finds that she is unable to hit the high notes as she has before. Upon physical examination, a puffy facies, yellowish skin, delayed DTRs, and a firm, enlarged thyroid are noted. Laboratory data include: TT_4 4 µg/dL, RT_3U 25%, TSH 20 mIU/mL, ATgA 55%, antimicrosomal by TRC 1:2500, Hematocrit (Hct) 33%, Hemoglobin (Hgb) 12 gm/dL, RBC 3500/mm³, mean corpuscular volume (MCV) 104 µm³. An RAIU at 24 hours was 7%. Assess M.W.'s thyroid status based upon her clinical and laboratory findings. [SI units: TT_4 52 nmol/L; TSH 20 mU/L; Hct 0.33; Hgb 120 mg/L; RBC 3.5×10^{12}/L; MCV 104 fL]

M.W. presents with many of the clinical features of hypothyroidism as presented in Table 47.3.[33] These include weight gain, mental sluggishness, easy fatigability, lowering of the voice pitch, a puffy facies, a yellowish tint of the skin, delayed deep tendon reflexes, and an enlarged thyroid. The diagnosis of hypothyroidism is substantiated by her laboratory findings of a borderline low TT_4 and RT_3U, a low FT_4I, an elevated TSH value, positive antibodies, and a low radioactive iodine uptake.

The presence of a firm goiter and thyroid antibodies, as well as clinical symptoms of hypothyroidism, strongly suggest Hashimoto's thyroiditis. She has no history of prior antithyroid drug use, surgery, or radioactive iodine treatment, which are the most common causes of iatrogenic hypothyroidism. She also is not taking any known goitrogens or drugs known to cause hypothyroidism. (See Table 47.4.)

M.W. also appears to have a macrocytic anemia. Anemia can be expected in hypothyroidism because thyroid hormones stimulate erythropoiesis. Three major types of anemia[34] have been observed in hypothyroidism: 1) A mild normochromic, normocytic anemia is found in 25% of hypothyroid patients. It is unresponsive to iron therapy but is reversed easily by thyroid administration. 2) A hypochromic, microcytic anemia appears in 4% to 15% of hypothyroid patients. Contributing factors may include achlorhydria and menorrhagia. This anemia will respond to iron therapy without correction of the hypothyroidism. 3) A macrocytic anemia, as observed in M.W., also may appear in hypothyroidism. Folate deficiency and pernicious anemia have been implicated; treatment with folate and B_{12}, respectively, corrects the anemia.

Treatment with Thyroid Hormones

Thyroid Hormone Products

7. What thyroid preparation should be used to treat M.W.'s hypothyroidism? Are there significant differences, advantages,

Table 47.3	Clinical and Laboratory Findings of Primary Hypothyroidism[a]	
Symptoms	Physical Findings	Laboratory
General: weakness, tiredness, lethargy, fatigue	Thin brittle nails	↓ TT₄
	Thinning of skin	↓ FT₄I
	Pallor	↓ FT₄
Cold intolerance	Puffiness of face, eyelids	↓ TT₃
Headache		↓ FT₃I
Loss of taste/smell	Yellowing of skin	↑ TSH
Deafness	Thinning of outer eyebrows	Positive antibodies (in Hashimoto's)
Hoarseness		
Absence of sweating	Thickening of tongue	RAIU <10%
Modest weight gain	Peripheral edema	↑ cholesterol
Muscle cramps, aches, pains	Pleural/peritoneal/pericardial effusions	↑ CPK
		↓ Na
Dyspnea	↓ DTRs	↑ LDH
Slow speech	"Myxedema heart"	↑ AST
Constipation	Bradycardia (↓ HR)	↓ Hct/Hgb
Menorrhagia	Hypertension	
Galactorrhea	Goiter (primary hypothyroidism)	

a AST = Aspartate aminotransferase; CPK = Creatinine phosphokinase; DTRs = Deep tendon reflexes; FT₃I = Free triiodothyronine index; FT₄I = Free thyroxine index; Hct = Hematocrit; Hgb = Hemoglobin; HR = Heart rate; LDH = Lactate dehydrogenase; Na = Sodium; RAIU = Radioactive iodine uptake; TT₃ = Total triiodothyronine; TT₄ = Total thyroxine.

or disadvantages among the various generic and brand formulations of thyroid hormones?

The principal goals of thyroid hormone therapy are to attain and maintain a euthyroid state. Thyroid preparations (see Table 47.5) are synthetic (levothyroxine, L-triiodothyronine, liotrix) or natural (desiccated thyroid). The latter come from animal tissues.

Desiccated thyroid (USP) is derived from pork thyroid glands, although beef and sheep also are used. There is no justification for starting patients today on desiccated thyroid.[35] The United States Pharmacopoeia (USP) requires only that desiccated thyroid contain between 0.17% and 0.23% organic iodine by weight. These requirements do not seem stringent enough because potency may vary with changes in the proportion of the two active hormones (T₃ and T₄) or with changes in the amount of organic iodine present.[36,37] This variable potency seems to be particularly true of generic formulations as compared to the biologically standardized Armour brand of desiccated thyroid.[36,37] Inactive desiccated thyroid preparations which contain negligible amounts of T₃ and T₄ or even iodinated casein instead of active hormone have been identified in various brands sold in retail pharmacies and in over-the-counter products found in health food stores.[37-39] Likewise, preparations with greater-than-expected activity resulting from an abnormally high T₃ content have resulted in thyrotoxicosis. Allergic reactions to the animal protein also might occur. Additionally, desiccated thyroid suffers from two problems inherent to all T₃-containing preparations. Since T₃ is absorbed more rapidly than T₄, supraphysiologic elevations in plasma T₃ levels occur after oral ingestion which can produce mild thyrotoxic symptoms in some patients. TT₄ levels are low during T₃ administration and, if misinterpreted, can result in the erroneous administration of more hormone. These problems with T₃ are missed easily unless T₃ levels are monitored routinely. Since significant amounts of T₄ are converted to T₃ peripherally, there is no advantage or need to administer T₃ orally.

Prolonged storage of desiccated thyroid preparations may result in loss of potency but this instability probably is not as important as once thought.[37] Since the only apparent advantage of desiccated thyroid is its low cost, it should not be considered the drug of

choice for replacement therapy.[35] Patients already maintained on desiccated thyroid should be encouraged to change to L-thyroxine (T₄). Although 60 mg (1 gr) of desiccated thyroid theoretically is equal in potency to 75 to 100 µg of T₄,[36,40] this equivalency may not hold true if the desiccated thyroid preparation is less active than its labeled content. The patient's weight also should be considered when switching therapy (see Question 8).

The synthetic thyroid preparations differ from one another in their relative potencies, onsets of action, and biological half-lives.

Levothyroxine or L-thyroxine (Synthroid, Levothroid, Levoxine, Various) is the thyroid replacement of choice.[41] Its advantages include stability, uniform potency, relatively low cost, and lack of an allergenic foreign protein content. The long half-life of seven days permits once-a-day dosing and allows for the creation of special convenience schedules, such as omission of medication on weekends. The mean absorption of a commonly used branded preparation is 81%.[42] Spuriously low absorption values noted in earlier studies resulted from an overestimation of levothyroxine tablet content.

Several proprietary and generic levothyroxine preparations are available. The two brand name levothyroxine products (i.e., Synthroid, Levothroid) are similar in hormone content, consistency, and stability, and are interchangeable in most patients.[43,44] However, no data are available about the bioavailability and equivalency of less costly generic preparations. Generic preparations generally were considered not bioequivalent to brand name preparations based upon previous reports of subpotent (i.e., contained less than their labeled levothyroxine content) tablets.[45-47] However, subpotent preparations no longer are a problem since the USP required all manufacturers to monitor their levothyroxine tablet content and tablet-to-tablet consistency by high performance liquid chromatography.[42,48] Before the adoption of these 1984 USP guidelines, levothyroxine preparations, including Synthroid, contained 20% more or less than their stated content.[45-47] Because levothyroxine products are more uniform, generic substitution of brand name products can be considered if routine monitoring by the FT₄ or FT₄I and TSH tests are available.

Table 47.4	Causes of Hypothyroidism

Nongoitrous[a,b]
Primary hypothyroidism[c]
  Idiopathic atrophy
  Iatrogenic destruction of the thyroid
    Surgery
    RAI therapy
    X-ray therapy
  Postinflammatory thyroiditis
  Cretinism
Secondary hypothyroidism
  Deficiency of TSH due to pituitary dysfunction
  Deficiency of TSH due to hypothalamic dysfunction

Goitrous Hypothyroidism[d]
  Dyshormonogenesis: defect in hormone synthesis, transport, or action
  Hashimoto's thyroiditis
  Drug-induced: iodides, lithium, thiocyanates, phenylbutazone, sulfonylureas, amiodarone
  Congenital cretinism: maternally-induced
  Iodide deficiency
  Natural goitrogens: rutabagas, turnips, cabbage

a No gland enlargement.
b RAI = Radioactive iodine; TSH = Thyroid-stimulating hormone.
c Dysfunction of the gland.
d Enlargement of the thyroid gland.

Table 47.5 — Thyroid Preparations[a]

Drug/Dosage Forms	Composition	Dosage Equivalent	Comments
Thyroid USP (Armour) Tab: 0.25, 0.5, 1, 1.5, 2, 3, 4, and 5 gr	Desiccated hog, beef, or sheep thyroid gland. Standardized iodine content	1 gr[b]	Unpredictable T_4:T_3 ratio; supraphysiologic elevations in T_3 levels might produce toxic symptoms. Armour brand preferred
L-thyroxine (Levoxine, Synthroid, Levothroid, Various) Tab: 0.025, 0.050, 0.075, 0.088, 0.112, 0.125, 0.137, 0.15, 0.175, 0.2, and 0.3 mg Inj: 200 and 500 µg	Synthetic T_4	60 µg[b]	Stable, predictable potency; well absorbed. More potent than desiccated thyroid. When changing from >2 gr desiccated thyroid to L-T_4 a lower dosage of L-T_4 might be needed to avoid toxicity. Weight should be considered in dosing (1.6–1.7 µg/kg/day)
L-triiodothyronine (Cytomel) Tab: 5, 25, and 50 µg Inj: 10 µg/mL (Triostat)	Synthetic T_3	25–37.5 µg	Complete absorption. Requires multiple daily dosing. Toxicity similar to all T_3-containing products. See Desiccated thyroid comments
Liotrix (Thyrolar) Tab: 0.25, 0.5, 1, 2, and 3 gr	60 µg T_4:15 µg T_3 50 µg T_4:12.5 µg T_3	Thyrolar-1	No need for liotrix since T_4 is converted to T_3 peripherally. Expensive, stable, and predictable content

[a] gr = Grain; Inj = Injection; T_3 = Triiodothyronine; T_4 = Thyroxine; Tab = Tablet.
[b] 60 mg (1 gr) of desiccated thyroid = 60 µg of T_4.[40]

Triiodothyronine (Cytomel) is not recommended for routine thyroid hormone replacement because of the problems identified earlier with T_3 administration (see Desiccated Thyroid). Although T_3 is well absorbed, it has a relatively short half-life (1.5 days) necessitating multiple daily dosing to insure a uniform response. Other disadvantages include higher expense and a greater potential for cardiotoxicity. Its primary use is in patients who require short-term hormone replacement therapy and as a diagnostic agent in the T_3 suppression test. If used, therapy should be monitored by use of TSH and TT_3 levels.

Liotrix (Thyrolar) is a combination of synthetic T_4 and T_3 in a physiologic ratio of 4:1. This preparation is subject to the same disadvantages common to all T_3-containing preparations. It also is stable and potent, but it is more expensive than other thyroid preparations. Because there is no need to administer T_3 orally, this is an obsolete and expensive preparation and should not be recommended. Patients should be changed to an equivalent dosage of levothyroxine.

Thyroxine

8. Dosage. What would you recommend as appropriate starting and maintenance doses of thyroxine for M.W.?

The maintenance dosage for M.W. can be estimated from her weight. With the reformulation[42] of Synthroid in 1982 and with the availability of more consistent and more potent levothyroxine products, a downward trend from earlier dosage recommendations is necessary to avoid subtle toxicities such as osteoporosis and the consequences of subclinical hyperthyroidism.[41,49–53] Average replacement doses of 1.6 to 1.7 µg/kg/day (e.g., 100 to 125 µg) are sufficient to normalize the TSH.[41,54] In one study, 80% of patients receiving more than 125 µg/day of L-thyroxine were not clinically hyperthyroid, but their dose was too high as indicated by a blunted TSH response to the TRH stimulation test.[54] These current guidelines are especially important in elderly patients who might require less thyroxine than their younger counterparts and who are particularly sensitive to minute changes in thyroxine doses (see Question 10). Additionally, patients who were started on replacement doses of L-thyroxine before 1983 should have their dose re-evaluated and adjusted downward if necessary to normalize the TSH and avoid subclinical toxicity.[93–97]

How fast thyroxine replacement can proceed will depend upon the likelihood of producing cardiac toxicity in susceptible individuals. Minute doses of T_4 can increase heart rate, stroke volume, oxygen consumption, and cardiac workload before euthyroidism occurs. Since M.W. has no risk factors (see Question 20) which increase the potential for cardiotoxicity and which require small dosage increments (e.g., old age, cardiac disease, long duration of hypothyroidism), she can be started on an estimated full replacement dose of 0.125 mg/day of L-thyroxine (70 kg × 1.7 µg/kg/day = 0.12 mg). An alternate, more conservative approach would be to start with a lower dose of 0.1 mg/day for six to eight weeks, check the FT_4I and TSH tests, and, in the absence of toxicity, increase the dose to 0.125 mg/day. The appropriate replacement dose should normalize the TSH and FT_4 or FT_4I and reverse clinical symptoms of hypothyroidism. Small changes in dosage can be achieved if needed by monthly titration. Generally, dosing changes should not exceed monthly increments of 12.5 to 25 µg/day.

9. Monitoring Therapy. Two weeks after starting levothyroxine therapy, M.W. continues to complain of tiredness, fatigue, and difficulty singing. Thyroid function tests show a TT_4 of 14 µg/dL and an FT_4 of 20 pmol/L. What therapeutic options are available? How should M.W.'s thyroid function tests be interpreted? [SI unit: TT_4 180 nmol/L]

Clinical improvement in the signs and symptoms of hypothyroidism as well as normalization of laboratory parameters are appropriate therapeutic endpoints. If the replacement dose is sufficient, some reversal of signs and symptoms should occur after two to three weeks; maximal effects should occur after four to six weeks. However, symptoms such as anemia and hair and skin changes may not reverse for several months.[33]

An FT_4 and TSH should be checked about six weeks after the initiation of therapy because T_4 has a half-life of seven days, and three to four half-lives are needed to reach steady-state levels. Levels obtained before this time (as in M.W.) may be misleading and should be interpreted cautiously.

Patients with hypothyroidism of greater than one year's duration might not achieve steady-state levels for six or more months after initiation of T_4 therapy. In severely myxedematous patients, a transiently elevated T_4 level might occur at six weeks because thyroxine's metabolic clearance is decreased by the hypometabolic state of hypothyroidism.[55]

About 20% of levothyroxine-treated patients may develop an elevated TT_4 concentration and FT_4 without overt clinical signs of hyperthyroidism.[41,42,46,56] Despite these elevated levels, the patients usually are euthyroid as evidenced by a normal TT_3 level, a decreased T_3:T_4 ratio, and a normal TSH. Since the ratio of T_3:T_4 released from a functioning thyroid gland is higher than the ratio of T_3:T_4 obtained from peripheral conversion, an elevated T_3:T_4 ratio should be observed in hyperthyroidism. Rendell and Salmon noted the T_3:T_4 ratio in levothyroxine-treated patients was 15:18, greater than 22 in hyperthyroid patients and about 20 in euthyroid patients (not on thyroxine).[56] As expected, levothyroxine-treated patients with both an elevated TT_4 and an elevated TT_3 also had symptoms of hyperthyroidism. Thus, the serum T_3 and TSH appear to be the best indicators of euthyroidism in levothyroxine-treated patients.

In conclusion, if an elevated TT_4 and FT_4 are noted without any symptoms of thyrotoxicosis (as in M.W.), the dosage should not be adjusted downward; rather, a TT_3 and TSH should be obtained to evaluate excessive dosing. Both should be in the normal range with the correct dosing.[57] An excessively suppressed TSH confirms a dosage that is too high. In M.W., a repeat FT_4 and TSH should be checked after six weeks of replacement before any therapeutic changes are made.

Triiodothyronine

10. C.B., a 65-year-old female, complains of fatigue and vague muscular aches and pains which she attributes to insufficient thyroid medication. Upon physical examination, the thyroid gland is palpable but not enlarged, and DTRs were 2+ and brisk. Her dose of triiodothyronine (Cytomel) was increased from 25 μg TID to 50 μg TID about 2 weeks ago based upon the results of a recent TT_4 of 1.4 μ/dL. She denies taking any other medications. Is C.B.'s hormone replacement appropriate? [SI unit: TT_4 18 nmol/L]

As noted earlier, Cytomel is not the drug of choice for thyroid replacement. The use of levothyroxine would simplify her dosing regimen and facilitate monitoring.

The low TT_4 did not justify increasing C.B.'s dose of Cytomel. Since she is receiving T_3, the TT_4 which is a measure of bound T_4, always will be low and will never reach normal levels. In fact, her vague complaints may be related to hyperthyroidism since she is receiving the equivalent of 0.2 to 0.3 mg of levothyroxine daily. TSH and TT_3 are most useful in monitoring patients receiving T_3 therapy. A suppressed TSH and an elevated TT_3 would indicate hyperthyroidism. It is important to remember that in the elderly, hyperthyroidism might not always produce symptoms due to an "apathetic" sympathetic system.

Levothyroxine should be initiated cautiously in elderly patients since underlying asymptomatic arteriosclerotic heart disease might be present and aggravated (see Questions 19 and 20). In general, elderly patients require smaller replacement dosages (approximately ≤1.6 μg/kg/day of thyroxine) than their younger counterparts.[41,58-60] Doses of ≤50 μg/day of T_4 were common in patients over age 60. However, this lower T_4 dose is not universal for all elderly subjects.[61] It is unclear why older patients need lower doses, but it has been suggested that the lower requirements are due to an age-related decrease in thyroxine degradation rates.[62] Because dosage requirements change with age, patients should be reassessed every year to determine if the original dosage prescribed still is appropriate.

In C.B., who had been on T_3 without any evidence of cardiac toxicity, a less cautious approach in switching to thyroxine can be used. A conservative, empirical levothyroxine dosage of 68 μg/day (40 kg × 1.6 μg/kg/day) is an appropriate dosing endpoint for C.B. The Cytomel should be discontinued and T_4 initiated in a dose of 50 μg/day; this dose can be adjusted as needed based upon C.B.'s symptoms and thyroid function tests. After T_3 therapy is discontinued, its effects will disappear over three to five days. In

contrast, T_4 levels rise slowly over four to five days, so that no overlap in T_3 administration is necessary to prevent hypothyroidism.

11. Parenteral Dosing. G.F., a 70-year-old male with long-standing hypothyroidism, has been receiving L-thyroxine 0.2 mg/day. He currently is in the hospital with a stroke and paralysis has left him unable to swallow oral medications. What is a reasonable method of administering thyroid hormone to G.F.?

Since L-thyroxine has a half-life of seven days, administration can be delayed for up to one week, assuming G.F. is able to resume oral intake at that time.[63,64] However, if parenteral administration is required, L-thyroxine is available as an intramuscular (IM) or IV injection. The IV route is preferred because IM absorption may be slow and unpredictable, particularly if the circulation is compromised. Since the oral absorption of T_4 is approximately 80%,[42] parenteral doses should be adjusted downward.

12. In Pregnancy. P.K., a 35-year-old female, takes L-thyroxine 0.1 mg/day for Hashimoto's thyroiditis. Laboratory tests show a TT_4 of 5 μg/dL and a RT_3U of 25%. She is 6 weeks pregnant. What dosing adjustments will be required because of P.K.'s pregnancy? [SI unit: TT_4 64 nmol/L]

Women with primary hypothyroidism on thyroxine therapy will need a larger dosage of thyroxine when they are pregnant.[65,66] Often there are no clinical symptoms of hypothyroidism and the free thyroxine index will be in the normal range. Evidence of subclinical hypothyroidism and increased thyroxine requirements will be detected only by an elevated TSH level. Previously, it was thought that few women required an upward dosage adjustment to maintain euthyroidism and that no adjustment in dosage was required.

Patients should be followed closely during pregnancy and the TSH should be evaluated monthly during the first trimester. Most patients will require a 45% increase in their baseline thyroxine requirements to maintain adequate replacement.[65,66] The goal should be a normal TSH and maintenance of the FT_4 or FT_4I in the upper limits of normal. Because TBG is elevated, the TT_4 should be kept above the normal range and is not the best indicator of replacement therapy.

It is unclear if inadequately treated maternal hypothyroidism poses any risk to the developing fetus because normal children have been born to myxedematous mothers.[67] On the other hand, abnormal fetal development secondary to poor placental maturation, spontaneous abortions, congenital defects, mental retardation, and an increased rate of still births have been associated with maternal hypothyroidism. Since thyroid hormone does not cross the placenta in significant amounts, the effect of maternal hypothyroidism on the fetus (if it occurs) must be indirect. There is a small risk of congenital hypothyroidism if maternal antibodies from Hashimoto's thyroiditis cross the fetal circulation. The infant's cord blood should be assayed at birth to assure that TSH is normal and that the child is euthyroid.

P.K.'s low TT_4 and RT_3U are of concern. The TT_4 should be much higher and the RT_3U lower due to pregnancy-associated increases in TBG. The calculated FT_4I of 1.25 also is somewhat low. The TSH level should be obtained and the dosage of T_4 should be increased to 0.125 mg after ruling out the possibility of patient noncompliance. The TSH should be repeated in six weeks, and the dosage should be adjusted as needed to keep the TSH in the normal range. After delivery, the dosage should be reduced to prepregnancy levels and the FT_4 and TSH rechecked to ensure euthyroidism.

Congenital Hypothyroidism

13. P.K. delivered a healthy baby, T.K., at term without difficulty. T.K.'s postpartum serum T_4 level was 5 μg/dL and TSH

was 15 mIU/mL. At home T.K. became lethargic, had a weak cry, sucked poorly, and failed to thrive. Assess the situation (include a treatment plan and prognosis). How is mental development affected? [SI units: T$_4$ 64 nmol/L; TSH 15 mU/L]

T.K.'s symptoms are suggestive of congenital hypothyroidism; although in the majority of infants, the clinical signs and symptoms are so subtle and nonspecific that they are missed easily until the child is several months old. The early clinical findings include prolonged jaundice, skin mottling (cutis marmorata), lethargy, poor feeding, constipation, hypothermia, hoarse cry, large fontanels, distended abdomen, hypotonia, slow reflexes, and pig-like facies. Respiratory difficulties, delayed skeletal maturation, and choking (but not palpable goiter) may be present. These infants also are at risk for additional congenital defects or complications.[68-70] Mass neonatal screening programs have been successful in detecting congenital hypothyroidism within the first month of life before clinical manifestations are apparent and before irreversible changes occur.[71]

The postpartum low serum T$_4$ concentration and elevated TSH level in T.K. should be verified. An elevated TSH greater than 20 mIU/mL normally can occur shortly after birth and no treatment is necessary. Transient hypothyroidism also can result from intrauterine exposure to thioamides or excess iodides. Thyroid function tests normalize after one to three weeks without treatment.[71] The diagnosis should be confirmed by a low serum T$_4$, a low free T$_4$, and an elevated TSH concentration during the next few days. In hypothyroid patients, serum T$_3$ concentrations often are in the normal range and are not helpful. It is important to note that normal serum T$_4$ concentrations are higher in the first few weeks of life and gradually return to normal by two to four months of life. The FT$_4$I may also be elevated until 12 months of age. Because of these confusing changes, thyroid serum levels should be compared to the normal range for the approximate postnatal age.

Thyroid hormones play a critical role in normal growth and development, particularly of the central nervous system (CNS) during the first three years of life. If untreated, dwarfism and irreversible mental retardation occur. T.K.'s normal mental and physical development will be determined by the age at which treatment is started, the adequacy with which treatment is maintained, and the etiology of the initial athyreosis.[69-72]

Sodium levothyroxine is the preparation of choice for replacement. T$_4$ tablets can be crushed and mixed with either breast milk or formula; suspensions are not stable and should not be used. T$_3$ also can be used, but this form is less desirable because its short half-life causes a greater fluctuation in plasma levels (see Table 47.5).

The replacement dose of T$_4$ varies according to the age of the infant and presence of risk factors.[68-72] Infants can be started safely on full replacement doses unless the infant has underlying heart disease or is extremely sensitive to the effects of thyroid hormones. In these infants, small reduced doses of T$_4$ ($\approx$25% to 33% of the recommended dose) can be started and increased gradually by similar increments until the therapeutic dose is achieved.

The average replacement dose of T$_4$ during the first three months of life is approximately 10 to 15 µg/kg/day; this drops to about 6 to 8 µg/kg/day at three to six months of age.[68,71,72] A larger initial dosage of T$_4$ (10 to 15 µg/kg/day) might be necessary in neonates with more severe congenital disease to normalize T$_4$ concentrations earlier in an effort to improve IQ values.[72] In the full-term healthy infant, an average initial T$_4$ dose of 37.5 to 50 µg/day is appropriate. The recommended replacement dose decreases with age and is shown in Table 47.6.

Mental development and attainment of normal adult height do not seem to be affected if adequate thyroxine treatment to achieve a serum thyroxine level greater than 10 µg/dL is initiated before three months of age.[69-72] Newborns detected by screening programs who start therapy within the first four to six weeks of life have IQs (mean: 100 to 109) that are similar to the control populations.[68-70,72] The mean intelligence quotient drops if treatment is started between six weeks and three months (mean: 95); and between three and six months (mean: 75). When treatment is delayed until six months to one year of age, normal mental development is impaired despite subsequent treatment (mean IQ: 55). Higher IQs also were found in children who had a mean serum T$_4$ level greater than 14 µg/dL in the first year of therapy.[69] Neurologic deficits also are more likely to occur in infants whose thyroid replacement is delayed or inadequate [as evidenced by a serum T$_4$ <8 µg/dL within 30 days of therapy and delayed suppression (18 to 24 months) of the TSH into the normal range]. Additional risk factors for a low IQ and poor motor and speech skills despite adequate therapy include clinical signs of hypothyroidism during fetal life, more marked chemical hypothyroidism at birth (T$_4$: <2 µg/dL), thyroid aplasia, and retarded bone age.[68,70,72]

The adequacy of thyroid replacement is monitored best by maintenance of serum T$_4$ concentrations in the 10 to 14 µg/dL range and suppression of the TSH toward the normal range (i.e., 20 µU/mL). Although TSH suppression is the most reliable index of adequate replacement in older children, normalization of the TSH should not be used as the sole monitoring parameter in infants because the TSH may remain elevated for months, even with proper or excessive thyroid hormone replacement.[71-73] Adequate treatment should suppress serum TSH to normal after three to four months of therapy. Earlier normalization of the TSH level often produces symptoms of hypermetabolism (hyperactivity and irritability) and should be watched for carefully. Overtreatment should be avoided to prevent brain dysfunction, acceleration of bone age, and premature craniosynostosis. Normal growth and development also should be a treatment goal. Other clinical endpoints include an improvement in activity level, skin color, temperature, facial appearance, and reversal of other symptoms and signs of hypothyroidism.

Unresponsiveness to Thyroid Hormone

14. R.T., a 45-year-old female, complains of weight gain, heavy menses, sluggishness, and cold intolerance. Her present medical problems include Hashimoto's thyroiditis treated with desiccated thyroid 4 gr QD; hypercholesterolemia treated with cholestyramine (Questran) 4 gm QID; anemia treated with FeSO$_4$ 325 mg BID; and a history of peptic ulcer disease treated with antacids and sucralfate 1 gm BID. Her laboratory data include a cholesterol serum concentration of 280 mg/dL, a TSH of 21 µU/mL, an FT$_4$ of 8 pmol/L, and positive ATgA and AMA antibodies. R.T. admits that she has increased her dosage of thyroid because she feels better on the higher dose. Why is R.T. apparently unresponsive to thyroid therapy? [SI units: cholesterol 7.2 nmol/L; TSH 21 mU/L]

Table 47.6	T$_4$ Recommended Replacement Dose^a
Age	Daily µg/kg T$_4$
3–6 months	10–15
6–12 months	5–7
1–10 years	3–6
>10 years	2–4

^{a} T$_4$ = Thyroxine.

R.T.'s complaints and laboratory values confirm hypothyroidism which has been treated inadequately despite thyroid therapy. Possible causes of therapeutic failure include noncompliance, error in diagnosis, poor absorption, inactive medication, rapid metabolism, and tissue resistance.[37–39,74,75] The last two factors are extremely rare, and noncompliance and error in diagnosis do not appear to be reasonable explanations in R.T. The most likely explanations are poor bioavailability and an inactive preparation. There is no history of surgical bowel resection or GI disorders (e.g., steatorrhea, malabsorption) that can interfere with the enterohepatic circulation of orally administered thyroid and lead to excessive fecal loss.[76,77] Evidence for incomplete absorption of the hormone can be obtained by comparing R.T.'s response to oral and parenteral thyroxine. Inactive desiccated thyroid preparations which contain small amounts of T_4 and T_3, or even iodinated casein instead of active hormone, have been identified.[37–39] R.T. also is taking numerous medications (i.e., cholestyramine, iron sulfate, antacids, sucralfate) that can interfere with thyroid absorption if these medications are administered at the same time.[78–83] Since cholesterol resin binders (e.g., cholestyramine, colestipol) and iron can bind thyroid and delay its absorption, R.T. should be questioned about the time of administration of her thyroid and then instructed to take her thyroid at least six hours apart from these two other medications.[78–80] Other cholesterol-lowering agents (e.g., lovastatin) also might interfere with thyroid absorption.[81] Aluminum-containing products (i.e., antacids, sucralfate) should be discontinued because separating the concurrent administration of thyroid and the aluminum-containing preparations does not correct this interaction.[82,83] R.T. should be changed to an aluminum-free antacid (e.g., Riopan) and, if necessary, a H_2-receptor antagonist. After R.T. has been instructed on the proper times of administration for her thyroid medication and cholestyramine, her thyroid replacement should be changed to an appropriate dose of L-thyroxine. R.T.'s therapeutic response and thyroid function tests should be re-evaluated in six to eight weeks.

15. Could R.T.'s hypothyroidism be responsible for her hypercholesterolemia?

Type IIa hypercholesterolemia is the most common lipid abnormality in patients with primary hypothyroidism.[84] Although the rate of cholesterol synthesis is normal in hypothyroid individuals, the rate of cholesterol clearance is decreased. Similarly, slow removal of triglycerides may result in hyperlipidemia. Hypercholesterolemia frequently is observed before the appearance of clinical hypothyroidism. Treatment with thyroxine alone should lower the cholesterol levels if there are no other contributing etiologies.[84]

Myxedema Coma

Clinical Presentation

16. R.B., a 65-year-old, agitated female alcoholic, arrived at the emergency room complaining of chest pain unrelieved by nitroglycerin (NTG). Her medical problems include alcoholic cardiomyopathy, angina, and hypothyroidism. Although she has been advised repeatedly to take her thyroxine regularly, R.B. continues to take it sporadically. An FT_4I drawn 4 months ago was 1.0. Chlorpromazine (Thorazine) 25 mg IM and morphine sulfate 10 mg IM were given for the agitation. After the injection, the nurse noticed increased mental depression, lethargy, and shallow breathing. R.B.'s oral temperature was 34.5 °C, and she exhibited chills and shakes. What is your assessment of R.B.'s subjective and objective data?

R.B. has several symptoms consistent with myxedema coma. Myxedema coma is the end stage of long-standing, uncorrected hypothyroidism.[85,86] The classic features are hypothermia, delayed DTRs, and an altered sensorium which ranges from stupor to coma.

Other predominant features include hypoxia, carbon dioxide retention, severe hypoglycemia, hyponatremia, and paranoid psychosis.[85,86] Typical physical findings (see Table 47.3) include a puffy face and eyelids, a yellowish discoloration of the skin, and loss of the lateral eyebrows. Pleural and pericardial effusions and cardiomegaly can be present. Since myxedema coma frequently occurs in the elderly female, it often is difficult to distinguish the signs and symptoms from senility or other disease states, as illustrated by R.B.

Precipitating factors include cold weather or hypothermia; stress (e.g., surgery, infection, trauma); coexisting disease states such as myocardial infarction, diabetes, hypoglycemia, or fluid and electrolyte abnormalities (especially hyponatremia); and medications such as respiratory depressants and diuretics.

Chlorpromazine and morphine might be responsible for what appears to be impending myxedema coma in R.B. In severely myxedematous patients, respiratory depressants (anesthetics, narcotic analgesics, phenothiazines, sedative-hypnotics) alone or in combination with the hypothermic effects of the phenothiazines can aggravate the pre-existing hypothermia and carbon dioxide retention to precipitate myxedema coma.[85,86] Tranquilizers such as chlorpromazine should not be given; small doses of less depressive sedative-hypnotics such as the benzodiazepines should be used only when absolutely necessary. Myxedematous patients also are inherently sensitive to the respiratory depressant effects of narcotic analgesics, especially morphine. A dose as small as 10 mg may induce coma in a hypothyroid patient or cause death in a patient who already is comatose. If morphine is required, the dose should be decreased to one-third to one-half the usual analgesic dose and the respiratory rate should be monitored closely.

Treatment

17. What would be a reasonable therapeutic plan for the management of R.B.'s myxedema coma?

Emergency treatment of myxedema coma is directed toward thyroid replacement, maintenance of vital function, and elimination of precipitating factors. Despite immediate and aggressive therapy with large replacement doses of thyroid, mortality rates of 60% to 70% are common.[85,86]

It is controversial which hormone preparation, T_4 or T_3, is the drug of choice in myxedema coma because there are no comparative trials. T_3, although potentially more cardiotoxic, has been recommended because its more rapid onset might reverse coma faster, and the peripheral conversion from T_4 to the biologically active T_3 might be inhibited in severe systemic disease.[87–89] T_4 alone, T_3 alone, or a combination of the two all have been successful in the treatment of myxedema coma. However, levothyroxine generally is regarded as the hormone of choice because there is greater clinical experience with T_4 than with T_3. Also, mortality has occurred despite the higher T_3 levels achieved after T_3 administration.[90] T_3 might be considered after failure to T_4 or if there is concomitant systemic illness (e.g., heart failure) in which failure of conversion from T_4 to T_3 is likely. Supraphysiologic elevations in T_3 levels occur only after oral administration but are not seen after IV T_3 infusion.

L-thyroxine 400 to 500 μg IV should be given initially to saturate the TBG and raise the serum T_4 level to 6 to 7 μg/dL.[85,86,90–92] This initial dose can be adjusted depending upon the patient's size and other restrictive factors. The initial dosage for R.B. might be decreased to 300 μg because of her cardiac disease. If the proper dosage is given, consciousness, restoration of vital signs, and decreased TSH levels should occur within 24 hours.

Maintenance doses should be titrated to the patient's clinical response. Because myxedema can impair oral absorption, the IV route is preferred to assure adequate drug concentrations. Oral administration is permitted once gastrointestinal function returns to normal. The smallest dosage (in the absence of untoward effects) administered should be 50 to 100 µg/day of T_4 or 10 to 15 µg of T_3 every 12 hours.[85,86,89,90,92]

Supportive measures include assisted ventilation, glucose for hypoglycemia, restriction of fluids for hyponatremia, and the use of blood or plasma expanders to prevent circulatory collapse and to maintain blood pressure. The use of blankets to treat R.B.'s hypothermia is not advised since vasodilation will occur and further compromise the cardiovascular components of shock. Although steroids have not been shown to be clearly beneficial in primary myxedema, they may be life-saving in patients with hypopituitarism presenting as myxedema coma. Since it is difficult to distinguish between primary and secondary myxedema, hydrocortisone 50 to 100 mg every six hours should be given empirically.[85,86]

Appropriate measures should be taken to relieve R.B.'s chest pain while ruling out the possibility of a myocardial infarction. The use of a narcotic antagonist such as naloxone also may be beneficial in this particular instance because it can reverse the effects of the morphine. Naloxone also can arouse comatose patients intoxicated with alcohol.[93]

Hypothyroidism with Congestive Heart Failure (CHF)

Clinical Presentation

18. E.B., a 45-year-old female, is admitted with complaints of substernal pressure and chest pain, SOB, dyspnea on exertion, and orthopnea. Other subjective and objective data suggest CHF complicated by MI. Significant past medical history reveals exertional angina and Graves' disease, which was treated with RAI ablation 3 years ago. There has been no recurrence of symptoms.

Upon physical examination, cardiomegaly, diastolic hypertension, obesity, facial edema and puffiness, delayed DTRs, and pretibial edema are noted. Pertinent laboratory findings include a TT_4 (RIA) of 1.8 µg/dL; RT_3U of 15%; TSH of 50 mIU/mL; creatinine kinase of 150 IU/L; aspartate aminotransferase (AST) of 80 U/L; and a lactate dehydrogenase (LDH) of 250 IU/L. A chest x-ray reveals cardiomegaly and pericardial effusions, and an electrocardiogram (ECG) shows bradycardia and flattened T-waves with ST depression. Diuretics, nitrates, and digitalis are instituted. E.B. improves symptomatically but her cardiac abnormalities are not reversed. Why do these clinical findings suggest hypothyroidism?
[SI units: TT_4 23 nmol/L; TSH 50 mU/L; creatinine kinase 2.5 µkat/L; AST 1.33 µkat/L; LDH 4.16 mkat/L]

E.B.'s abnormal thyroid function tests, symptoms, physical findings, and history of RAI therapy confirm the presence of severe hypothyroidism. "Myxedema heart" can be confused with low-output CHF since the symptoms are similar: cardiomegaly, dyspnea, edema, pericardial effusions, and an abnormal cardiogram.[33,94] Therefore, hypothyroidism should be excluded in all patients with new or worsening symptoms of cardiovascular disease. Although hypothyroidism alone rarely causes congestive heart failure, it is likely to worsen an underlying cardiac condition. The cardiac damage from hypothyroidism results from deposition of mucopolysaccharides in the myocardium.

Although E.B.'s enzyme elevations (i.e., AST, CK, LDH) are suggestive of an MI, they all may be moderately or significantly increased from chronic skeletal or cardiac muscle damage or from decreased enzyme clearance from hypothyroidism. The enzymes can be fractionated to determine their origin.

Treatment

19. What might be the effect of hypothyroidism on the cardiac treatment and status of E.B.?

If E.B.'s cardiac abnormalities are caused by hypothyroidism rather than organic disease, adequate doses of thyroxine will restore the heart size, normalize the diastolic blood pressure, reverse the ECG findings, and normalize the serum enzyme elevations within two to four weeks. However, improvement in myocardial function occurs only at doses of 50 to 75 µg/day of thyroxine which may be tolerated poorly by cardiac patients.[94]

The relationship between the altered lipid metabolism of hypothyroidism and increased risk of atherosclerosis is controversial and poorly documented.[95] Interestingly, angina pectoris and myocardial infarction are rather uncommon among hypothyroid patients.[94,96] Theoretically, the hypometabolic state associated with hypothyroidism may protect the ischemic myocardium by reducing metabolic demands. However, hypothyroidism actually aggravates subendocardial ischemia during an acute MI by decreasing erythrocyte production of 2,3 diphosphoglycerate which shifts the oxyhemoglobin dissociation curve to the left. This effect further diminishes oxygen delivery to already ischemic tissues.

Angina might develop or worsen with the institution of thyroxine therapy,[96-98] so doses should be titrated carefully (see Question 20). In the absence of organic disease, digitalis is ineffective and even may be harmful. Hypothyroid patients show an increased sensitivity to digitalis, and digitalis toxicity is possible unless the maintenance dose is decreased.[99] (See Question 25.) Nitrates may precipitate hypotension and/or syncope in hypothyroid patients because these patients have a low circulating blood volume and their response to vasodilation can be exaggerated. Furthermore, if beta blockers are required, the cardioselective beta blockers are preferred. The noncardioselective beta blockers have produced coronary spasm by exacerbating the increased norepinephrine levels and alpha-adrenergic tone found in hypothyroidism.

20. How aggressively should thyroid hormone therapy be initiated in a patient like E.B. who has angina? What is the hormone replacement of choice in patients with cardiac disease?

Patients with long-standing hypothyroidism, arteriosclerotic cardiac disease, or advanced age tend to be extremely sensitive to the cardiac effects of thyroid hormone. Initiation of normal or even subtherapeutic doses in these individuals might result in severe angina, myocardial infarction, cardiac failure, or sudden death. These effects underscore the need to replace thyroid cautiously, and sometimes suboptimally, to avoid cardiac toxicity.[96-98]

The angina and cardiac status should be controlled as well as possible before initiating thyroxine therapy. Cardiac catheterization is warranted in the poorly controlled angina patient to assess the coronary artery status accurately before starting hormone therapy. Coronary bypass to control the angina has been performed safely in the hypothyroid patient with minimal complications. This procedure may allow institution of full replacement doses without cardiotoxicity.[98,100,101]

For E.B., thyroxine should be initiated cautiously with minute amounts (12.5 to 25 µg) of T_4 and increased by similar increments of T_4 every two to six weeks as tolerated. The rapidity with which the increments can proceed is determined by how well each increased dose is tolerated. If cardiac toxicity occurs, therapy should be stopped immediately. Once symptoms resolve, therapy can be restarted using smaller dosage increments, and longer intervals between dosage adjustments. If cardiac symptoms recur, further thyroxine therapy should be stopped pending further cardiac evaluation. In some patients with severe cardiac sensitivity, complete euthyroidism might never be achieved. In these patients, the correct replacement dosage is a compromise between prevention of myxedema and avoidance of cardiac toxicity.[96]

E.B.'s clinical status and electrocardiogram should be monitored closely during the titration period and thyroxine should be discontinued or decreased at the first sign of cardiac deterioration. It is not useful to routinely monitor thyroid function tests (e.g., TSH or FT_4) during the titration period because the tests will remain low until adequate replacement is achieved. Thyroid function tests should be obtained once maximally tolerated or estimated euthyroid dosages are achieved.

Triiodothyronine (Cytomel) has been suggested by some to be the agent of choice in patients with cardiac abnormalities. The onset of action of T_3 is one to three days as compared to three to five days for T_4. After therapy is withdrawn, the effects of T_3 dissipate in three to five days, while seven to ten days are needed for T_4. Thus, if toxicity occurs, the effects of T_3 will disappear rapidly upon cessation of therapy, a theoretical advantage in the cardiac patient. Nevertheless, T_3 is not recommended because its greater potency requires finer and more difficult dosage titration to insure smooth and uniform blood levels. Furthermore, the high serum T_3 levels which occur after oral administration might cause more cardiac toxicity, especially angina.

Hypothyroidism In the Elderly

21. M.P., a 93-year-old healthy female, comes in for her regular checkup. Her only complaints include very dry skin and some constipation which she treats with prune juice. She has no other medical problems, takes no other medications, and has no known allergies. Routine screening laboratory tests are within normal limits except for a TT_4 of 6.5 μg/dL, an FT_4 of 16 pmol/L, and a TSH of 15 mIU/mL. Discuss whether M.P. requires thyroid treatment based upon her clinical presentation and laboratory findings. [SI units: TT_4 84 nmol/L; TSH 15 mU/L]

M.P.'s thyroid function tests are within the lower limits of normal except for an elevated TSH level. Thyroid disease, especially hypothyroidism or subclinical hypothyroidism, is common among the elderly, especially females.[102-108] In the elderly, hypothyroidism often presents atypically with signs and symptoms reflecting dysfunction of any part of the body.[103,104,108] Subclinical hypothyroidism (normal thyroxine and free thyroxine levels but an elevated TSH) probably represents the early stages of thyroid failure. In one study, 20% of healthy asymptomatic people greater than 60 years of age had elevated TSH levels.[103]

Patients with subclinical hypothyroidism often are considered to be asymptomatic, but subtle hypothyroid symptoms can be elicited by intensive questioning.[105] Although E.B. has the typical hypothyroid symptoms of dry skin and constipation, the presentation often is atypical and missed easily because the symptoms are attributed to normal aging. Hypothyroid elderly patients tend to present with a limited number of nonspecific symptoms: failure to thrive, mental confusion, weight loss with poor appetite, incontinence, depression, inability to walk, carpal tunnel syndrome, deafness, ileus, anemia, and hyponatremia. Therefore, routine TSH screening is advisable.[102-108]

Treatment of elderly patients with subclinical hypothyroidism requires an assessment of the risks versus benefits of therapy. Thyroid therapy carries the risk of unmasking cardiac disease in elderly patients who may have underlying coronary artery disease. Nevertheless, thyroid replacement is indicated in patients with symptoms of mild hypothyroidism or symptoms suggestive of abnormal myocardial contractility.[105-107] It is unclear whether patients with asymptomatic subclinical hypothyroidism and normal cardiac function warrant therapy.

Since M.P. has dry skin and is constipated, therapy is indicated if tolerated.

Hyperthyroidism

Clinical Presentation

22. S.K., a 38-year-old female, is admitted for a possible MI. Her complaints include chest pain which is unrelieved by NTG, nervousness, palpitations, muscle weakness, weight loss despite an increased appetite, and epistaxis; she also bruises easily. Her other medical problems include: deep venous thrombosis treated with warfarin (Coumadin) 5 mg/day, last prothrombin time (PT) was 18 seconds and an INR of 1.8; angina treated with NTG 0.4 mg; and CHF treated with digoxin (Lanoxin) 0.25 mg/day.

Physical examination reveals a thin, flushed, hyperkinetic, nervous female. Blood pressure (BP) is 180/90 mm Hg; pulse is 130 beats/min, irregularly irregular; respiratory rate is 30 breaths/min; temperature is 37.5 °C. Other pertinent findings include a lid lag with stare, minimal proptosis with tearing, decreased visual acuity, a diffusely enlarged thyroid gland without nodules, a bruit in the left lobe of the thyroid, positive jugular venous distension (JVD), bibasilar rales, warm moist skin with multiple bruises, new onset atrial fibrillation, slight diarrhea, hepatomegaly, acropachy, 2+ pitting edema, a fine tremor, proximal muscle weakness, and irregular scant menses.

Laboratory data include TT_4 30 μg/dL; RT_3U 45%; RAIU at 24 hr 80%; PT 40 sec; an INR of 4.8; AMA 1:6400; ATgA 65%; alkaline phosphatase 200 U/L; total bilirubin 1.1 mg/dL; AST 60 U/L; alanine aminotransferase (ALT) 55 U/L; Scan: diffusely enlarged gland, 3 to 4 times normal size. What subjective and objective data are suggestive of hyperthyroidism in S.K.? [SI units: TT_4 386 nmol/L; alkaline phosphatase 3.3 μkat/L; total bilirubin 19 μmol/L; AST 1 mkat/L; ALT 0.92 μkat/L]

S.K. presents with many of the clinical and laboratory features[109] associated with an increased metabolic state resulting from excessive thyroxine (see Table 47.7). Her ophthalmic symptoms are consistent with Graves' disease and include lid lag (lid falls behind the movement of the eye and a narrow white rim of sclera becomes visible between the upper lid and cornea producing a ''staring'' appearance); proptosis (protrusion of the eyeball); and decreased visual acuity. The bruit, palpitations, atrial fibrillation, CHF (JVD, bibasilar rales, edema, hepatomegaly), diarrhea, irregular scant menses, nervousness, tremor, muscle weakness, weight loss despite increased appetite, increased perspiration, and flushing of the skin are consistent with a hypermetabolic state. Together with S.K.'s symptoms, a diagnosis of Graves' disease is confirmed by an elevated TT_4, RT_3U, FT_4I, and RAIU; positive antibodies; and a goiter on scan. This probably is aggravating her cardiac status and other medical problems. See Table 47.8 for a list of the causes of hyperthyroidism.

Hypoprothrombinemia

23. What factors contribute to S.K.'s hypoprothrombinemia? What effect could this have on her subsequent drug treatment?

The hypoprothrombinemia and bleeding observed in S.K. most likely are related to an exaggerated response to warfarin. This may be related to a decrease in the hepatic metabolism of warfarin (secondary to hepatic congestion), but it is more likely that S.K.'s findings are due to the combined effects of hyperthyroidism and warfarin on vitamin K-dependent clotting factors.

Warfarin Metabolism

Warfarin metabolism and the metabolism of vitamin K-dependent clotting factors can be altered by thyroid status. Net circulating levels of vitamin K-dependent clotting factors generally are not altered in hyperthyroid patients because both the synthesis and catabolism of these clotting factors are increased. However,

Table 47.7	Clinical and Laboratory Findings of Hyperthyroidism[a]

Symptoms
Heat tolerance
Weight loss common; or weight gain due to ↑ appetite
Palpitations
Pedal edema
Diarrhea/frequent bowel movements
Amenorrhea/light menses
Tremor
Weakness, fatigue
Nervousness, irritability, insomnia

Physical Findings
Thinning of hair (fine)
Proptosis, lid lag, lid retraction, stare, chemosis, conjunctivitis, periorbital edema, loss of extraocular movements
Diffusely enlarged goiter, bruits, thrills
Wide pulse pressure
Pretibial myxedema
Plummer's nails[b]
Flushed, moist skin
Palmar erythema
Brisk DTRs

Laboratory Findings
↑ TT_4
↑ TT_3
↑ FT_4I/FT_4
↑ FT_3I
Suppressed TSH
⊕ TRab
⊕ ATgA
⊕ AMA
RAIU >50%
↓ cholesterol
↑ alkaline phosphatase
↑ calcium
↑ AST

[a] AMA = Antimicrosomal; AST = Aspartate aminotransferase; ATgA = Antithyroglobulin; DTRs= Deep tendon reflexes; FT_4 = Free thyroxine; FT_3I = Free triiodothyronine index; FT_4I = Free thyroxine index; TRab = Thyroid-receptor antibodies; TSH = Thyroid-stimulating hormone; TT_3 = Total triiodothyronine; TT_4 = Total thyroxine; RAIU = Radioactive iodine uptake.
[b] The fingernail separates from its matrix, but only 1 or 2 nails generally are affected.

an enhanced anticoagulant response occurs when the warfarin-induced decrease in clotting factor synthesis is combined with the hyperthyroidism-induced increase in clotting factor catabolism.[110,111] This may explain S.K.'s elevated prothrombin time, bruising, and history of epistaxis.

The opposite is true in hypothyroidism where there is a decrease in both metabolism and synthesis of clotting factors. In hypothyroid patients, the response to oral anticoagulants is delayed because the clotting factors are catabolized more slowly.[110,111] Therefore, thyrotoxic patients will need less warfarin, while myxedematous patients will require more warfarin to achieve the same hypoprothrombinemic response. The anticoagulant response to warfarin should be monitored carefully in patients with thyroid abnormalities and the dose adjusted as the thyroid status changes with therapy.

Thioamide Effects

Since S.K.'s hyperthyroidism most likely will be treated with a thioamide, caution must be exercised. Treatment of hyperthyroid patients with thioamides, especially propylthiouracil, has been associated with hypoprothrombinemia, thrombocytopenia, and bleeding, albeit rarely.[112] These drugs can depress the bone marrow as well as the synthesis of clotting factors II, VII, III, IX, X, and XIII; vitamin K and prothrombin times may remain depressed for up to two months after discontinuation of therapy. The effects of thioamides on the clotting factors and vitamin K may be due to a subclinical hepatic alteration in synthesis or to hepatotoxicity (see Question 37).[113–117] Symptoms occur two weeks to 18 months after starting therapy. The bleeding is responsive to vitamin K or blood transfusions. (Also see Question 30 for further discussion of treatment with thioamides.)

Response to Digoxin

24. After treatment with RAI, S.K.'s daily dose of digoxin was increased to 0.5 mg because of persistent atrial fibrillation. After 6 weeks she returns with complaints of nausea and vomiting. The gland remains palpable but is decreased considerably in size. The ECG shows ST depression, atrioventricular (AV) block, and occasional bigeminy. Assess these subjective and objective data.

S.K.'s symptoms of nausea and vomiting, together with the ECG changes of AV block and bigeminy, strongly suggest digitalis toxicity. Although a high dose of digoxin is appropriate while a patient is thyrotoxic, continuation of this same dose as the hyperthyroidism resolves increases the likelihood of digitalis toxicity.

25. Why was such a large dose of digoxin required initially? What other options can be used to control the ventricular rate?

The atrial fibrillation of hyperthyroidism often is resistant to digitalis. When euthyroid patients with atrial fibrillation were given digitalis before and after exogenous T_3 administration, the daily dose of digoxin required to maintain a ventricular rate of 70 was increased from 0.2 to 0.8 mg after T_3 administration.[118] Higher dosages of digoxin without side effects might be tolerated better by the hyperthyroid individual.[118,119] Nevertheless, the goal of digoxin therapy should be a higher target heart rate (i.e., 110 to 120 beats/min) than that achieved with digoxin in the euthyroid individual with atrial fibrillation to minimize cardiac toxicity. If additional rate control is required, beta blockers or calcium channel blockers can be added. Unless contraindicated by myocardial dysfunction or bronchospasm, beta blockers rather than calcium channel blockers are preferred because they are more effective in controlling the ventricular rate and are less likely to cause hypotension.[120]

This apparent resistance to digitalis is attributed to intrinsic changes in myocardial function, to an increased volume of distribution (V_d) for digoxin, and to an increased glomerular filtration of the glycoside.[99,119] Conversely, hypothyroid patients are inordinately sensitive to the effects of digitalis and require smaller doses to achieve a therapeutic response. Regardless of the mechanism, one should be aware that higher-than-normal doses might be required in patients with thyrotoxicosis, and that the initial dosage should be reduced as the hyperthyroid state resolves.

Cardioversion

26. If the atrial fibrillation persists, when should cardioversion be attempted in S.K.? Is other treatment indicated?

Table 47.8	Causes of Hyperthyroidism

Graves' disease (toxic diffuse goiter)

Toxic uninodular goiter (Plummer's disease)

Toxic multinodular goiter

Nodular goiter with hyperthyroidism due to exogenous iodine (Jod-Basedow)

Exogenous thyroid excess through self-administration (factitious hyperthyroidism)

Tumors (thyroid adenoma, follicular carcinoma, thyrotropin-secreting tumor of the pituitary, and hydatidiform mole with secretion of a thyroid-stimulating substance)

Since S.K. received radioactive iodine six weeks ago, her thyroid function tests should be rechecked to determine her present thyroid status. Cardioversion, either medical or electrical, should not be attempted if she is still toxic because the success rate is low. Atrial fibrillation spontaneously reverts to normal sinus rhythm (NSR) in about three-fourths of patients within three weeks of control of the hyperthyroidism.[121]

Spontaneous conversion is highly unlikely if the duration of the hyperthyroidism-induced atrial fibrillation exceeds 13 months or if the atrial fibrillation persists after four months of euthyroidism.[121] Patients with underlying heart disorders (except CHF) also are less likely to spontaneously convert to NSR. Patients who meet these criteria are candidates for cardioversion at about the sixteenth week after achieving euthyroidism. Age and the duration of thyrotoxicosis are important determinants of successful cardioversion. NSR is maintained in about 50% of patients after cardioversion.[121]

S.K. should be maintained on warfarin because there is a high prevalence of systemic embolization in thyrotoxic patients with atrial fibrillation.[94,121] Anticoagulation should be started when the atrial fibrillation is first diagnosed and continued until S.K. is euthyroid and in NSR. This is especially true for the younger patients at low risk of bleeding with Coumadin. The risks versus benefits of anticoagulation should be weighed before therapy (see Chapter 12: Thrombosis). Since an increased sensitivity to warfarin is observed, close monitoring is warranted.[111]

Thyrotoxicosis: Clinical Presentation

27. C.R., a 27-year-old female, has a 3-month history of intermittent heat intolerance, sweats, tremor, and severe muscle weakness which has limited her ability to climb stairs. Her weight has increased due to increased appetite. She also is bothered by the pounding of her heart and some minor difficulty in swallowing. There is a positive family history of thyroid disease, but she denies taking any thyroid medications or having had any radiation to her neck. C.R. previously received iodide drops with improvement in her symptoms, but her disease recurred despite continued administration. Her other medical problems include diabetes, which is controlled with diet; and arthritis, which is treated with aspirin 5.4 gm/day. She has a history of noncompliance with her clinic visits.

Pertinent physical findings include a BP of 180/90 mm Hg, a pulse of 110 beats/min, hyperreflexia, lid lag, and a diffusely enlarged thyroid gland which is about 4 times normal (about 100 gm). Available laboratory data include the following: TT_4 15 µg/dL, TSH <0.01 mIU/mL, AMA 1:3200, ATgA = 25%, and blood glucose 350 mg/dL. Assess these subjective and objective data. [SI units: TT_4 193 nmol/L; TSH <0.01 mU/L; blood glucose 19.4 mmol/L.]

C.R.'s clinical findings verify the presence of an autoimmune hyperthyroid state. However, the serum TT_4, and FT_4I are elevated only slightly and are disproportionately low relative to the severity of her symptoms, the undetectable TSH level, and her other laboratory findings. The possibility of a variant type of hyperthyroidism known as T_3-toxicosis should be considered. The clinical features include signs and symptoms of thyrotoxicosis, normal or borderline levels of TT_4 and FT_4I, an undetectable TSH level, and elevated T_3 levels. The latter occurs through preferential secretion and peripheral conversion of T_4 to T_3. A T_3 level should be obtained to establish the diagnosis.

Asymptomatic elevations of T_3 levels often precede elevation of T_4 levels and the development of overt hyperthyroidism. T_3-toxicosis probably represents an early stage of classical T_4-toxicosis and is useful for early diagnosis or as an early indicator of

relapse following discontinuation of thioamide therapy. The decreased TT_4 also could be explained by displacement of T_4 from TBG by aspirin (see Question 3).

Iodides

28. Why were the iodide drops initially effective in improving C.R.'s symptomatology but later ineffective? When are iodides indicated? What is their mechanism of action?

Iodides have several effects: they inhibit thyroid hormone release; they block iodotyrosine and iodothyronine synthesis by blocking organification; and they decrease the vascularity of the thyroid gland.[122] However, large doses may accentuate hyperthyroidism because they provide a marked increase in available substrate for hormone synthesis (see Question 55).[122–125]

The inhibitory effect of exogenous iodides on the intrathyroidal organification of iodides is known as the Wolff-Chaikoff effect. This represents an inherent autoregulatory function of the normal gland to prevent excessive hormone synthesis in the event of a large iodide load. The Wolff-Chaikoff effect occurs when intrathyroidal concentrations of iodides reach a critical level and this is not overcome by TSH stimulation. However, as illustrated by C.R., the gland can "escape" from this block even with continued iodide use. The gland "escapes" by decreasing iodide transport or by "leaking" iodide. Both of these mechanisms decrease the critical intrathyroidal iodide level, thereby decreasing the block to organification. This effect is illustrated by C.R. Therefore, iodides should not be used as primary therapy for Graves' disease.

Conversely, some patients are very responsive to iodide therapy. These include: a) patients who already have high intrathyroidal iodine stores (i.e., "hot nodules," Graves' disease); b) patients with underlying defects in organic binding mechanisms (i.e., Hashimoto's); c) patients on lithium; d) patients with Graves' disease made euthyroid with RAI or surgery.

These patients are so sensitive that small doses of iodide can elicit the Wolff-Chaikoff effect resulting in either amelioration of hyperthyroid symptoms or precipitation of hypothyroidism.[122–126] For this reason, patients with recurrent hyperthyroidism following surgery or RAI often can be managed with iodides alone.[126]

The most important pharmacological effect of iodides is their ability to promptly inhibit thyroid hormone release when doses of ≥6 mg/day are given.[122,124] The mechanism is unknown, but it is not related to the Wolff-Chaikoff effect which may take several weeks to manifest. Unlike the Wolff-Chaikoff effect, this effect can be overcome partially by an increase in TSH secretion. Thus, the normal gland can escape in 7 to 14 days because inhibition of thyroid hormone release stimulates a reflex increase in TSH secretion. Since patients with hyperthyroidism experience an improvement in symptoms within two to seven days of initiation of therapy, inhibition of hormone release must be the predominant mechanism of action for the iodides. This rapid onset is the reason why iodides are used in the treatment of thyroid storm and as an ameliorative measure while awaiting the onset of the therapeutic effects of thioamides or RAI.

Large doses of iodides also are used two weeks before thyroid surgery to increase the firmness of the thyroid gland by decreasing its size, vascularity, and friability. Iodides facilitate a smoother, less complicated surgery and decrease postoperative complications by inducing a euthyroid state.[122,124]

Stable iodine can be administered orally either as an unpleasant tasting Lugol's solution (5% iodine and 10% potassium iodide), containing 8 mg/drop of iodide, or as the more palatable saturated solution of potassium iodide (SSKI), containing 50 mg/drop of iodide. The minimum effective daily dose is 6 mg,[127] although larger doses (e.g., 5 to 10 drops QID of SSKI) are administered frequently.

The advantages of iodide therapy are that it is simple, inexpensive, relatively nontoxic, and there is no glandular destruction. Disadvantages include "escape," accentuation of thyrotoxicosis, allergic reactions, relapse after discontinuation of treatment, and subsequent interference with RAI if used before therapy.

Treatment Modalities

29. What are the advantages and disadvantages of the different treatment modalities available for C.R.?

The three major treatment modalities for Graves' related hyperthyroidism are the thioamides, RAI, and surgery (see Table 47.9).[128-132] In most cases, any of these three modalities can be used, and it is controversial which is the most effective therapy. A survey among experts treating uncomplicated hyperthyroidism shows considerable variation in choice of therapy selected.[130] Often, the final decision is empiric, depending upon the physician's available resources and the patient's desires. Elderly patients, and those with cardiac disease, concomitant ophthalmopathy, and hyperthyroidism due to a toxic multinodular goiter are treated best with radioactive iodine. Surgery is the preferred therapy when obstructive symptoms are present or malignancy is suspected.

Thioamides

The thioamides are the preferred treatment for children, pregnant women, and young adults with uncomplicated Graves' disease.[128-130,133] This is the only treatment that leaves the thyroid gland intact and does not carry the added risk of hypothyroidism often associated with RAI or surgery.

Since the thyrotoxicosis of Graves' disease might be self-limiting, thioamides are used to control the symptoms until spontaneous remission hopefully occurs. Thioamides also should be given before treatment with RAI or surgery to deplete the gland of stored thyroid hormone and prevent subsequent thyroid storm. Although hyperthyroidism from toxic nodules also will respond to thioamides, more definitive therapy (surgery or RAI) is needed since these other conditions do not undergo spontaneous remission.

Disadvantages of thioamide therapy include the large number of tablets required, patient compliance, possible drug toxicity, the long duration of treatment, and the low incidence of remission after discontinuation of therapy (see Questions 43 and 44).

There are several potential drawbacks to the use of thioamides in C.R. Her relatively large gland and severe disease make the prognosis for spontaneous remission somewhat less favorable. A delay in the onset of thioamide's effect may be expected if intraglandular stores of thyroid have been increased by her prior iodide therapy. Furthermore, her noncompliance and difficulty swallowing may necessitate another means of treatment.

Surgery

Surgery is considered the treatment of choice when:[128,130,132,134] 1) malignancy is suspected; 2) esophageal obstruction, evidenced by difficulty swallowing, is present; 3) respiratory difficulties are present; 4) contraindications to the use of thioamides (e.g., allergy) or radioactive iodine (e.g., pregnancy) exist; or 5) a large goiter is present which regresses poorly on RAI or thioamide therapy.

If C.R.'s minor difficulty in swallowing persists due to poor regression of goiter size with drug therapy, then surgery is a reasonable alternative. If surgery is contemplated, it is imperative that C.R. be brought to surgery in a euthyroid state to prevent rapid postoperative rises in T$_4$ levels and subsequent thyroid storm (see Question 39).[128,132,134]

Subtotal thyroidectomy is effective and successful in over 90% of patients with Graves' disease. Subtotal thyroidectomy poten-

tially avoids the predictable risk of hypothyroidism associated with total thyroidectomy; however, the risk of recurrent hyperthyroidism increases in proportion to the amount of residual thyroid tissue remaining.[132,134] Recurrent thyrotoxicosis following subtotal thyroidectomy should be treated with RAI because the incidence of surgical complications increases with a second surgery.

Surgical treatment of hyperthyroidism is safe and effective in the hands of an experienced and competent surgeon, when the patient is adequately prepared for surgery. The disadvantages to the surgical approach are expense, hospitalization, hypothyroidism, the small risk of postoperative complications, and the patient's fear of surgery (see Question 39).

Radioactive Iodine (RAI)

Radioactive iodine is the preferred treatment for: 1) debilitated, cardiac, or elderly patients who are poor surgical candidates; 2) patients who fail to respond to drug therapy or who experience adverse drug reactions; and 3) patients who develop recurrent hyperthyroidism after surgery.[128,130,131]

Pregnancy is an absolute contraindication to RAI therapy. The use of RAI also has been restricted to adults over an arbitrary age of 20 to 35 years because it was feared that RAI could result in genetic damage or neoplasia. However, after more than 25 years of clinical experience with RAI, it generally is accepted as a safe and effective treatment.[128,131] There is no reported evidence of genetic damage after I[131] ingestion and the dose of radiation to the gonads is less than three rads, which is comparable to other radiographic diagnostic tests (e.g., barium enemas).[135] The incidence of leukemia or malignancy is no higher in recipients of I[131] when compared to thyrotoxic patients treated with drugs or surgery.[131]

Radioactive iodine is painless, effective, economical, and quick, but fear of radiation and the high incidence of hypothyroidism may deter its use. RAI could be used safely in this nonpregnant young patient. However, C.R.'s prior use of iodides has diluted her total iodide pools. Thus, it will be impossible to achieve therapeutic thyroid concentrations of RAI for as long as three to six months.

Ipodate

The radiographic iodinated contrast agents, iopanoic acid (Telepaque) and sodium ipodate (Oragrafin), are effective short-term antithyroid agents.[136-139] These iodinated agents inhibit the peripheral T$_4$ to T$_3$ conversion and release iodide to inhibit thyroid hormone secretion. The onset of therapeutic effect is more rapid than that with the thioamides.[137] After administration of 0.5 to 1 gm/day orally, a rapid decline in T$_3$ concentrations and significant clinical improvement occurs within three to seven days. Within 24 hours, ipodate decreases serum T$_3$ levels by 58% and T$_4$ levels by 20% and is more effective than 600 mg of PTU which decreases T$_3$ levels by only 23% within 24 hours.[137] Ipodate appears to be a useful adjunct to thioamides in the early treatment of severe hyperthyroidism. However, relapse of the hyperthyroidism occurs after one month despite continued administration; subsequent response to thioamides also might be impaired.[138] Thus, it would be reasonable to consider these agents in severely thyrotoxic or storm patients who are allergic to thioamides. They also may be effective as preoperative agents. Preliminary evidence also indicates that ipodate may not prevent the retention of I[131] to the same extent as iodides.[137]

Treatment with Thioamides

Propylthiouracil (PTU)

30. Versus Methimazole. C.R. is started on PTU 200 Q 8 hr after a baseline FT$_4$I and TSH level have been obtained. Three

Table 47.9		Treatment for Hyperthyroidism[a]		
Modality	Drug/Dose	Mechanism of Action	Toxicity	Indication
Primary Treatment				
Thioamides				
PTU 50 mg tab; rectal formulation can be made[209]	100–200 mg PO Q 6–8 hr (*max:* 1200 mg/day) for 6–8 weeks or until euthyroid; then maintenance of 50–150 mg QD PO	Blocks organification of hormone synthesis, blocks peripheral conversion of T_4 to T_3 (PTU only)	Skin rashes, GI symptoms, arthralgias, ↑ transaminases, hepatitis, agranulocytosis	DOC in pregnancy, thyroid storm, breast-feeding. Combination with thyroxine might ↑ efficacy
Methimazole (Tapazole) 5, 10 mg tab; rectal suppositories can be made[208]	Methimazole 30–40 mg PO QD or in 2 divided doses (*max:* 60 mg/day) for 6–8 weeks or until euthyroid, then maintenance of 5–10 mg/day PO	Similar to PTU except does not block conversion of T_4 to T_3	Similar to PTU; cholestatic jaundice	Thioamide DOC because QD dosing and better compliance. Alternative to PTU in pregnancy. Not DOC in breast-feeding or thyroid storm. Combination with thyroxine might ↑ efficiency
Surgery	Preoperative preparation with iodides, thioamides, ipodate, or propranolol before surgery. See specific operative agent	Subtotal or total thyroidectomy	Hypothyroidism, cosmetic scarring, hypoparathyroidism, risks of surgery, and anesthesia, vocal cord damage	Obstruction, choking, malignancy, pregnancy in 2nd trimester, contraindication to RAI or thioamides
RAI	I^{131} radioactive isotope; 80–100 µCi/gm thyroid tissue. Average dose = ≈10 mCi. Pretreatment with corticosteroids indicated in patients with ophthalmopathy	Destruction of the gland	Hypothyroidism; worsening of ophthalmopathy; fear of radiation-induced leukemia; genetic damage; malignancy; rarely, radiation sickness	Adults, elderly patients who are poor surgical risks or have cardiac disease; patients with a history of prior thyroid surgery; contra-indications to thioamide usage
Adjuncts to Primary Usage				
Iodinated contrast dye Ipodate (Oragrafin) Iopanoic acid (Telepaque)	0.5–1 gm QD–QOD PO	Blocks T_4 to T_3 conversion. Release of iodides to block hormone secretion from thyroid gland	Same as iodides	Alternative to thioamide for rapid control of hyperthyroidism, symptomatic relief of symptoms, adjuncts to surgery, thioamides, and possibly RAI. Escape occurs with chronic usage
Iodides Lugol's Solution 8 mg/drop (5% iodine, 10% potassium iodide); Saturated (SSKI) 50 mg/drop)	5–10 drops TID PO for 10–14 days before surgery. Minimum effective dose 6 mg/day	↓ vascularity of gland and ↑ firmness; blocks release of thyroid hormone	Hypersensitivity reactions, skin rashes, mucous membrane ulcers, anaphylaxis, metallic taste, rhinorrhea, parotid and submaxillary swelling; fetal goiters and death	Preoperative preparation before surgery; thyroid storm, provides symptomatic relief of symptoms. *Do not use before RAI or chronically during pregnancy*
Beta blockers Propranolol or equivalent beta blocker. *Avoid those with ISA*	Propranolol 10–40 mg PO Q 6 hr or PRN to control HR <100 beats/min. IV 0.5–1 mg slowly	Blocks effects of thyroid hormone peripherally, no effect on underlying disease. blocks T_4 to T_3 conversion	Related to beta blockade; bradycardia, CHF, blocks hyperglycemic response to hypoglycemia, bronchospasm, CNS symptoms at high doses; fetal bradycardia	Symptomatic relief while awaiting onset of thioamides, RAI; preop-erative preparation for surgery; thyroid storm
Calcium channel blockers	Diltiazem 120 mg TID–QID PO or verapamil 80–120 mg TID–QID PO PRN to control HR <100 beats/min	Blocks effects of thyroid hormone peripherally, no effect on underlying disease	Bradycardia, peripheral edema, CHF, headache, flushing, hypotension, dizziness	Alternative for symptomatic relief of hyperthyroid symptoms in patients unable to tolerate beta blockers
Corticosteroids	Prednisone or equivalent corticosteroid 50–140 mg/day PO in divided doses. IV hydro-cortisone 50–100 mg Q 6 hr or equivalent for thyroid storm	↓ TRab, suppression of inflammatory process; blocks T_4 to T_3 conversion	Complications of steroid therapy	Ophthalmopathy, thyroid storm (use IV steroid), pretibial myxedema, pretreatment before RAI therapy in patients with ophthalmopathy

[a] CHF = Congestive heart failure; CNS = Central nervous system; DOC = Drug of choice; GI = Gastrointestinal; HR = Heart rate; ISA = Intrinsic sympathomimetic activity; IV = Intravenous; PTU = Propylthiouracil; RAI = Radioactive iodine; Tab = Tablet.

weeks later, she angrily complains that her symptoms are worse and that the medication is not working. She reluctantly admits missing doses because of difficulty swallowing, nausea, vomiting, diarrhea, fatigue, a cough, and a sore throat. What are the advantages of using either PTU or methimazole in the treatment of hyperthyroidism?

Both thioamides are effective in treating hyperthyroidism. The antithyroid effectiveness of the thioamides primarily depends upon their ability to block the organification of iodines, thereby inhib-iting thyroid hormone synthesis.[128,129] Thyroid autoantibody syn-thesis also may be suppressed.[140,141] In most hyperthyroid situa-tions, methimazole should be considered the drug of choice over PTU because methimazole may improve patient compliance and ease of administration.[142,143]

Methimazole is more likely to be effective when administered initially as a single dose compared to the multiple-dose regimen required with PTU to achieve a euthyroid state.[144-146] Although a single-dose regimen of PTU has been used acutely,[146] it is most effective when given in divided doses (see Question 40). Compared to PTU, methimazole also is less expensive, requires daily ingestion of fewer numbers of tablets, and is not associated with a bitter tablet taste. However, PTU is preferred over methimazole in thyroid storm because it also blocks the peripheral conversion of T_4 to T_3; this effect is not shared by methimazole. Within 24 to 48 hours after PTU administration, a 25% to 40% reduction in peripheral T_3 production is seen which contributes to PTU's therapeutic effectiveness. A significantly greater fall in the T_3 concentration and the T_3:T_4 ratio can be demonstrated in hyperthyroid patients treated acutely with PTU and iodine than with methimazole and iodides. Lastly, PTU also is preferred over methimazole in pregnant or breast-feeding patients (see Question 43).

31. Why was the thioamide therapy ineffective in C.R.? Was the dose of PTU appropriate?

The inadequate response in C.R. suggests noncompliance with the thioamides or a delayed response due to prior iodide loading of the gland.

The onset of action of the thioamides is slow because they block the synthesis rather than the release of thyroid hormone.[129] Therefore, hormone secretion will continue until the glandular stores of hormone are depleted. If adequate doses were given, some improvement of clinical symptoms should be noted after two or three weeks.

Dosing and Administration. The dose of PTU is appropriate. Initially, high blocking doses of PTU (300 to 800 mg/day, depending upon the severity of the toxicosis) should be given in three to four divided doses, as in C.R.[128,129] Rarely, doses of 1200 mg/day of PTU or its equivalent may be required in patients with severe disease or storm. Equipotent doses of methimazole (which is 10 times more potent than PTU on a mg per mg basis) also can be used. However, it usually is unnecessary to use more than 40 mg/day of methimazole to restore a euthyroid state.[142,144,145] Toxicity also is less common (see Question 38). True resistance to thioamides is rare; thus, most cases of unresponsiveness are due to poor patient compliance as illustrated by C.R.[143]

C.R.'s compliance also is hindered by the frequency of PTU administration. The serum half-life of PTU is short ($\approx$1.5 hours) but it is the intrathyroidal drug concentrations that should determine the dosing intervals because they are most clearly related to the drug's antithyroid effects[129] (see Question 40). PTU must be dosed every six to eight hours initially, or as frequently as every four hours in cases of severe hyperthyroidism and thyroid storm. In contrast, methimazole has a serum half-life of six to eight hours, remains in the thyroid for 20 hours, and has a duration of activity of up to 40 hours.[147,148]

If C.R. is taking her PTU as directed, then an increase in the PTU dosage to 200 mg every six hours is reasonable. However, noncompliance often is difficult to ascertain and is more likely when multiple daily doses are required.[143] The best option for C.R. is to change to 30 to 40 mg of methimazole, given once daily to improve compliance, or divided into two doses to decrease GI distress. After methimazole is given for four to six weeks or until euthyroidism is achieved, the daily dosage can be reduced gradually by 25% to 30% monthly to a dosage that maintains euthyroidism, usually 5 to 10 mg/day of methimazole or 50 to 150 mg/day of PTU. If C.R. remains hyperthyroid despite adequate doses of thioamides, then the most likely reason is noncompliance.

32. Monitoring Therapy. What additional objective baseline data should be obtained to monitor both the efficacy and toxicity of PTU?

Before thioamides are administered, a baseline FT_4 and TSH should be obtained. A baseline white blood cell count (WBC) with differential also can help differentiate the leukopenia associated with hyperthyroidism from drug-induced leukopenia and/or agranulocytosis (see Question 38). A repeat FT_4 and TSH should be obtained after four to six weeks on therapy and four to six weeks after any change in the dosing regimen. Once euthyroid on maintenance dosages, thyroid function tests can be obtained every three to six months.

33. Duration of Therapy. How long should C.R. be continued on thioamide treatment?

Traditionally, thioamide therapy is continued for one to two years despite the lack of data regarding the optimal treatment period. The goal of treatment is to control the symptoms of Graves' disease until spontaneous remission occurs. Graves' disease will remit spontaneously in about 25% to 30%. Since it is unknown when or if remission will occur, it is understandable why the optimal duration of therapy is unclear. Short-term therapy has produced remission rates of about 39% which is comparable to that observed in some studies using conventional long-term treatment.[149-151] Therefore, short-term therapy (i.e., <6 months, given until the patient is euthyroid) has been advocated to save time, money, and improve compliance without sacrificing the therapeutic outcome. However, longer follow-ups of patients receiving short-term therapy note disappointing remission rates of 23%, similar to that obtained with spontaneous remission.[150,151]

The majority of data support a longer course of treatment. Although rates of remission might be low, higher remission rates of 60% to 85% often are reported after treatment durations of 18 months or longer.[149-151] These conflicting results underscore the fact that the optimal treatment period is subject to large patient variability and is dependent upon the likelihood of spontaneous remission rather than on the actual duration of drug therapy alone. It is on this basis that many caution against overenthusiastic adoption of short-term treatment with thioamides. Thus, longer treatment periods of one to two years are justifiable in compliant patients. Therapy can be reinstituted if hyperthyroidism reappears shortly after therapy is discontinued. Thioamides also can be continued indefinitely if there are no side effects and treatment with either radioactive iodine or surgery is not desired. In C.R., this goal might not be achievable, given her history of noncompliance.

Precautions

34. Can thioamide therapy affect any of C.R.'s pre-existing medical conditions?

Thyrotoxicosis can activate or intensify diabetes, primarily by increasing the basal hepatic glucose production and the metabolism of insulin.[152,153] Therefore, effective therapy with thioamides may restore control of C.R.'s diabetes.

C.R.'s arthritis should not be affected by the PTU, although both PTU and methimazole are associated with the development of lupus, lupus-like syndromes, and vasculitis.[129,154-157] These adverse drug reactions are rare; the incidence is less than 0.1%. Lupus-like syndromes include skin ulcers, splenomegaly, migratory polyarthritis, pleuritis and pericarditis, periarteritis, and renal abnormalities. Serological abnormalities also may occur with these connective tissue disorders and include hyperglobulinemia, positive LE preparations, and positive antinuclear antibodies. Recovery occurs with adequate steroid therapy and withdrawal of the thioamides. Since cross-reaction between methimazole and PTU is likely to occur, patients exhibiting these reactions should be treated with surgery or RAI. C.R.'s treatment should be monitored with this lupus-like adverse effect in mind, but the occurrence of this syndrome is so infrequent that a trouble-free course of therapy can be anticipated.

Adjunctive Therapy

35. What adjunctive therapy might help to alleviate some of C.R.'s symptoms while awaiting the onset of thioamide effects?

Iodides (see Question 28), β-adrenergic blocking agents, or calcium channel blockers can be used acutely to ameliorate some of C.R.'s symptoms. Ipodate also can be used (see Question 29). Since iodides previously were ineffective in C.R., a beta blocker should be tried.

β-adrenergic blocking agents rapidly decrease the nervousness, palpitations, fatigue, weight loss, diaphoresis, heat intolerance, and tremor associated with thyrotoxicosis, probably because many of the signs and symptoms mimic sympathetic overactivity.[158,159] An increase in the number of β-adrenergic receptors rather than an elevation in catecholamine levels probably is responsible for this overactivity.[158,159] Since the underlying disease process and thyroid hormone levels are not affected significantly by beta blockers, patients generally remain mildly symptomatic and fail to gain weight. For this reason, they should not be used as the sole treatment for thyrotoxicosis.

All beta blockers are effective in alleviating the hyperthyroid symptoms, but propranolol (Inderal) is the only beta blocker that inhibits peripheral conversion of T_4 to T_3.[158] Thyroid function tests generally are not affected except for a mild decrease in T_3 level.

In summary, beta blockers are: 1) effective adjuncts in the management of thyroid storm; 2) useful preoperatively to prepare patients for surgery; and 3) useful in the management of thyrotoxicosis during pregnancy.[158,160,161] Surprisingly, propranolol also improves many of the neuromuscular manifestations of hyperthyroidism, including thyrotoxic periodic paralysis.[162]

Diltiazem or verapamil appears to be an effective alternative to beta blockers, especially when they are contraindicated.[120,163,164] Doses of diltiazem 120 mg three to four times a day can be tried. Other calcium channel blockers (i.e., dihydropyridine derivatives) might not be effective.

Since C.R. is a diabetic by history, the effects of β-adrenergic blocking drugs in patients with diabetes must be considered. (Also see Chapter 48: Diabetes Mellitus.) If beta blockers are instituted, a cardioselective beta blocker would be a better choice. Otherwise, ipodate, diltiazem, or a retrial of iodides is warranted.

36. Propranolol 40 mg BID is prescribed for C.R. Why might this dose be inappropriate for her?

The effects of thyrotoxicosis on propranolol pharmacokinetics and plasma levels are complex.[158,165] The elimination half-life and volume of distribution of propranolol did not change when hyperthyroid patients became euthyroid. However, the systemic clearance of total and free propranolol was significantly greater when patients were hyperthyroid than when they had become euthyroid. Plasma protein binding of propranolol was reduced when patients were thyrotoxic. In another study, the metabolic clearance rates and volume of distribution of propranolol were higher in 15 thyrotoxic patients than in matched euthyroid controls. Furthermore, plasma propranolol levels were lower in thyrotoxic patients and these levels increased once euthyroidism was achieved. Others have noted no significant differences in propranolol levels between thyrotoxic and euthyroid patients. Large variations in propranolol levels exist between individuals who receive identical doses of propranolol and these large intraindividual variations probably account for some of the discrepancies in these studies. The pharmacokinetics of atenolol and metoprolol also are changed in hyperthyroidism.[158,165]

Because the data are so conflicting, the appropriate dose should be based upon objective signs of improvement such as a reduction in heart rate. A dosage of 40 mg twice a day should be started initially and the dose increased as needed to maintain the heart rate less than 100 beats/minute.

Adverse Effects

37. Thioamide Rash. A pruritic area over the pretibial aspects of both legs as well as several maculopapular erythematous patches and abdominal tenderness were noticed during C.R.'s physical examination. Do these reactions require the discontinuation of her PTU?

Although C.R. may be experiencing a drug rash from PTU, pretibial myxedema or the dermopathy of Graves' disease also may be a possibility due to the location of the pruritic area. About 4% of patients with Graves' disease who exhibit infiltrative exophthalmos also have dermatological changes. The skin is thickened, erythematous, and nonpitting due to mucopolysaccharide infiltration and accentuation of hair follicles. Pruritus or pain may be present. Treatment includes topical corticosteroids, control of the Graves' disease, and reassurance.

Both PTU and methimazole can produce a maculopapular pruritic rash in 5% to 6% of treated patients.[129,166] The rash can occur at any time but is more common early in therapy. If the rash is mild, drug therapy can be continued while the patient is treated symptomatically with an antihistamine and a topical steroid; such rashes generally subside spontaneously. Alternatively, another thioamide can be substituted because cross-sensitivity to this side effect is uncommon. If the rash is urticarial or is associated with other systemic manifestations of a drug reaction (e.g., fever, arthralgias), thioamides should be stopped and nondrug treatment considered.

Hepatitis. C.R.'s symptoms of nausea, vomiting, diarrhea, fatigue, and abdominal tenderness require further evaluation. Her symptoms could be consistent with mild gastrointestinal side effects from her PTU therapy or with impending thyroid storm from noncompliance. (See Question 49.) Taking the PTU after meals or changing to methimazole could improve medication intolerance and improve compliance.[117,166] However, the possibility of drug-induced hepatitis should be considered. PTU-induced hepatotoxicity typically is hepatocellular in nature but cholestasis, hepatic necrosis, and fulminant hepatic failures have been reported.[113,115,116] Transient elevations in transaminases occur in approximately 30% of asymptomatic patients within the first two months of PTU therapy and do not require drug discontinuation.[113] Dosage reduction of the PTU to maintenance levels normalizes the liver enzymes in three months despite drug continuation. However, PTU should be stopped immediately in patients with clinical symptoms of hepatitis to ensure complete recovery. The mechanism of PTU-induced hepatotoxicity appears to be autoimmune because circulating autoantibodies and *in vitro* peripheral lymphocyte sensitization to PTU have been found.[115] Overt hepatitis typically occurs during the first two months of PTU therapy and is not dose related. In contrast, methimazole typically produces a cholestatic jaundice picture and might be more common in patients receiving higher dosages (i.e., >40 mg/day).[114,116,166] In patients with thioamide-induced hepatitis, changing to the alternative thioamide is not recommended because fatalities have been reported upon rechallenge. In such patients, either radioactive or surgery should be used.

The thyroid function tests, transaminases, and bilirubin should be checked in C.R. and the PTU stopped until these results are available. Routine monitoring of liver function tests is not recommended because patients can be asymptomatic. However, routine monitoring might be indicated in patients with a history of liver disease and risk factors for hepatitis (e.g., alcohol usage). All patients receiving thioamides should be questioned closely during the first two months of therapy for symptoms of hepatitis and hepatic function tests obtained if appropriate.

38. Agranulocytosis. **Assess C.R.'s complaints of sore throat and cough.**

C.R.'s complaints should not be dismissed casually because they might be indicative of PTU-induced agranulocytosis. Agranulocytosis (defined as <500/mm³ of neutrophils) is the most severe adverse hematological reaction associated with the thioamides and should be considered strongly in C.R.[129,166–169] In contrast, drug-induced leukopenia usually is transient, is not associated with impending agranulocytosis, and is not an indication to discontinue thioamide therapy. An accurate history should be obtained from C.R. The clinician should be alert particularly for a temperature of ≥101 °F for two or more days, malaise, or other flu-like findings that appeared temporally with her sore throat. If subjective or objective data are consistent with agranulocytosis, the PTU should be discontinued immediately until the results of a repeat WBC with a differential are reported. Traditionally, routine serial determinations of WBC counts are not recommended for monitoring the development of agranulocytosis because the onset is so abrupt. Instead, patients should be instructed to immediately report rash, fever, sore throat, or any flu-like symptoms. However, one study suggests that weekly monitoring of the WBC with a differential during the first three months of antithyroid therapy might identify asymptomatic patients with agranulocytosis before infection occurs.[167]

The prevalence of agranulocytosis is about 0.5% but ranges from 0.5% to 6%.[129,166–169] The risk factors for agranulocytosis are unknown. There is no predilection for either gender and the reaction may be idiosyncratic or dose related. Some reports suggest that patients over the age of 40 years or those on high-dose methimazole (>40 mg/day) might be more susceptible than those on any dosage of PTU. Although controversial, patients receiving low-dose methimazole (<40 mg/day) might be at less risk than those receiving high or conventional doses of PTU.[129,166–169]

Agranulocytosis typically develops within the first three months of treatment, although it can occur at any time and as late as 12 months after starting thioamide therapy.[129,166–169] A delayed reaction is more common with methimazole therapy than with PTU. In 55 patients who developed agranulocytosis on thioamides, the duration of PTU therapy (17.7 ± 9.7 days) was significantly shorter than that of methimazole therapy (36.9 ± 14.5 days).[167] The mechanism of thioamide-induced agranulocytosis is unknown. Both an allergic (idiosyncratic) and toxic type (dose related) reaction have been suggested. An autoimmune reaction with circulating antineutrophil antibodies and lymphocyte sensitization to antithyroid drugs has been demonstrated.[170] Death usually results from overwhelming infection.

If agranulocytosis is diagnosed, the drug should be discontinued, the patient monitored for signs of infection, and antibiotics instituted if necessary. Data suggest that glucocorticoids and granulocyte colony-stimulating factor might help shorten the recovery period.[171–173] If the patient recovers, granulocytes begin to reappear in the periphery within a few days to three weeks; a normal granulocyte count occurs shortly thereafter.[167,171–173]

Although some cases of granulocytopenia have resolved with substitution or continuation of thioamides, the risks of drug rechallenge clearly outweigh the benefits and other treatments should be instituted. Switching to an alternate thioamide also should be avoided since little is known regarding the cross-sensitivity between these agents.[167]

In summary, all patients receiving thioamide therapy should be well educated regarding the signs and symptoms of agranulocytosis. If these symptoms develop, they should be advised to contact their physician. If they are unable to reach their own physician, patients should inform the emergency physician that they are taking thioamides and a WBC with differential should be obtained. Routine monitoring of a WBC and differential is not recommended until further studies justify that it is indicated and cost effective.

Preoperative Preparation

39. C.R.'s PTU is discontinued because she developed agranulocytosis and hepatitis, and surgery is scheduled when her granulocytes return to normal. What preoperative thyroid preparation is needed for C.R. before thyroidectomy? What postoperative complications are associated with thyroidectomy?

C.R. should be in a euthyroid state at the time of surgery to avoid precipitation of thyroid storm and enhanced morbidity. Generally, iodides (see Question 28), thioamides, or propranolol can be used.[132,134,158] The combination of iodides and propranolol may be more effective than either used alone.[160] Propranolol used alone has been associated with thyroid crises postoperatively[158] and may be less effective than iodides in decreasing gland friability and vascularity.

Ipodate can be used instead of iodides since iodides are released with ipodate administration. In a comparison of ipodate and Lugol's in 46 preoperative patients, those on ipodate required less preparation time and bled less during surgery (see Question 28).[139]

Since C.R. received only one week of thioamide therapy, it is likely that her gland still contains large stores of hormone; therefore, pretreatment is necessary.

In addition to the risks of anesthesia and surgery, postoperative complications include hypoparathyroidism, adhesions, laryngeal nerve damage, infection, and poor wound healing.[132] The risks of hypothyroidism are higher during the first year after surgery, although there is an insidious rise in incidence over the following ten years. The incidence of hypothyroidism ranges from 6% to 75%[132,134] and is related inversely to the amount of remnant tissue left behind. Transient hypothyroidism one to six months postoperatively is common; thereafter, permanent hypothyroidism is likely.[134]

Single Daily Dosing

40. J.R., a 23-year-old male with newly diagnosed Graves' disease, remains hyperthyroid after 6 weeks of PTU 200 mg TID. He admits he has trouble remembering to take it 3 times a day and desires a more simplified regimen. Could J.R. be placed on a single daily dose of PTU?

Although a single daily dose of PTU can be used as initial therapy, multiple daily doses of PTU are recommended because they are more effective in controlling the hyperthyroidism.[146,174] The success rate of this approach depends upon the size of the gland and the severity of the disease. According to various studies, euthyroid states are achieved in 39% to 68% of hyperthyroid patients treated with single-dose PTU.[146,174,175] However, single daily doses of PTU are effective once the patient is made chemically euthyroid through multiple dosing. In contrast, several clinical studies have documented that a single daily dose of methimazole is as effective as multiple daily doses in over 90% of treated patients.[144,145,148,176]

The usual single daily doses prescribed are ≥300 mg of PTU,[175] 30 to 60 mg of methimazole,[117,144,145] or 30 to 60 mg of carbimazole. Although low-dose methimazole (10 to 15 mg QD) is effective in producing euthyroidism and produces fewer side effects than higher dosages, 30 to 40 mg/day of methimazole is recommended as the initial dosage because more patients will achieve euthyroidism in six weeks than on the low dose regimen.[145,176]

Methimazole is the preferred agent for once-a-day dosing because of its longer intrathyroidal duration of action (20 hours).[148] However, PTU is preferable in very toxic patients (i.e., thyroid storm) because it acts more rapidly due to its ability to block the extrathyroidal conversion of T_4 to T_3. In spite of its short plasma half-life of four to six hours, a single 30 mg dose of methimazole has a duration of action of 40 hours.[147] The duration of action of PTU is unknown but it is shorter than methimazole. Apparently, the duration of action of the antithyroid agents correlates best with the size of the dose and the intrathyroidal concentration of the drug.[147,148]

J.R. should be changed to 30 to 40 mg of methimazole given once daily. Thyroid function tests should be obtained after four to six weeks and the dosage reduced as necessary to maintain euthyroidism. An effective single daily dose regimen of methimazole should increase patient acceptance and compliance.

Remission

41. B.D., a 30-year-old female, has been maintained on PTU 100 mg BID for over 2 years. Her PTU has been discontinued twice in the past, and each time her hyperthyroidism recurred. She refuses either surgery or RAI therapy. Although she is clinically euthyroid on the PTU, her gland is larger than normal size and never decreased in size on therapy. Recent laboratory tests showed an FT_4 of 14 pmol/L and a TSH level of 4.5 mIU/mL. Levothyroxine 0.1 mg/day was initiated. Why was thyroxine added to B.D.'s PTU therapy? [SI unit: TSH 4.5 mU/L]

There are several reasons why addition of thyroxine might be helpful in B.D. Thyroid supplements are used with high-dose blocking regimens of thioamides to prevent hypothyroidism.[117] In this case, thyroxine might have been added to help decrease the size of the goiter which is stimulated by TSH production. TSH secretion is stimulated by PTU suppression of hormone synthesis. The reported FT_4 is normal and thus of no value in supporting this assumption. However, the high normal TSH level suggests that TSH stimulation is contributing to the size of her goiter. The easiest solution to this problem is to decrease the high maintenance dose of PTU; in cases where titration of the proper dose of PTU is difficult, the combination of T_4 and PTU is reasonable.

A major reason for the addition of thyroxine to her PTU therapy is to increase her chance of remission once thioamides are discontinued. Purportedly, TSH suppression with thyroxine decreases antigen release from the gland and, thereby, decreases TSH receptor antibody titers. Low or absent TSH receptor antibody titers are correlated with a higher likelihood of remission (see Question 42). In one study, the combination of levothyroxine and maintenance doses of thioamides given for one year, followed by an additional year of levothyroxine alone significantly decreased the risk of relapse once thioamides were discontinued.[177] After patients were made euthyroid on 30 mg of methimazole for six months, the daily addition of 100 µg of thyroxine to 10 mg of methimazole caused a significant and further reduction in TSH receptor antibody titers than in patients who were maintained on methimazole alone. The thyroxine-treated patients also had a lower TSH level and a lower rate of recurrence (1.7%) within three years after all therapy was discontinued than those on methimazole therapy alone (recurrence rate: 34.7%).

If combination therapy is used, patients should be euthyroid on 30 to 40 mg/day of methimazole, or equivalent dosages of PTU, before levothyroxine is added. High-dose methimazole or PTU can be continued for six months with the addition of levothyroxine; thereafter, dosages of thioamides should be reduced to maintenance levels. Levothyroxine should be added in a dosage (i.e., 75 to 100 µg) that maintains euthyroidism and normalizes the TSH level. The combination should be given together for a minimum of one year before the thioamide is discontinued. Levothyroxine then should be given alone for one year thereafter. Patients should be monitored closely for hyperthyroidism from the addition of exogenous levothyroxine therapy.

Although combined therapy might be justifiable in B.D. since she already has had two relapses off therapy, combined treatment carries the risk of added toxicity, greater expense, and closer laboratory monitoring. Further studies are needed to confirm the possible protective effects of levothyroxine supplementation before it can be recommended as routine therapy.

42. What subjective or objective data in B.D. would influence her remission rate and justify a longer course of thioamide therapy?

Long-term remission rates achieved with the thioamides are quite disappointing. Remission rates after discontinuing therapy range from 14% to 75%,[117,141,149-151,176,177] although relapse rates as high as 80% occur. Permanent remission usually is rare if the follow-up period is long enough.[178,179] Why some patients remain in remission while others relapse upon discontinuation of the thioamides is unclear, although patients who remain euthyroid for more than 10 to 15 years after discontinuing therapy probably have concomitant autoimmune thyroiditis (i.e., Hashimoto's).[180] In other words, the natural course of Graves' hyperthyroidism might be eventual hypothyroidism regardless of the treatment modality used. Studies on thioamides have shown divergent results on the value of predictive factors for relapse and remission.

The duration of treatment (see Question 33), the dosage of thioamides, and the addition of thyroxine might influence the remission rate by changing the basic underlying abnormality of Graves' disease.[117,149-151,176-178] Numerous studies show that titers of thyroid receptor antibody or thyroid-stimulating immunoglobulins (TSI) fall during therapy with the thioamides but are unchanged during therapy with placebo or beta blockers.[141] Patients with detectable titers at the end of thioamide therapy are at a higher risk of relapse within one to two years. Combination therapy with thyroxine also results in lower TRab titers and better remission rates (see Question 41).[177] In one study, high-dose therapy with either PTU (mean: 693 mg/day) or methimazole (mean: 60 mg/day), given for 10 to 20 months, resulted in lower TSI titers and a higher remission rate than conventional therapy (75.4% versus 41.6%).[117] Unfortunately, a higher incidence of side effects, including arthralgias, dermatitis, gastritis, and hepatotoxicity, but not hematological toxicity, occurred with the high-dose regimen.

A number of clinical features might be predictive of a higher rate of remission and identify patients who deserve a longer trial of drug treatment before changing to RAI or surgery. These clinical features include: 1) smaller goiter; 2) mild symptoms of short duration; 3) a reduction in goiter size during treatment; 4) return of thyroid suppressibility; and 5) a normal TRH test.[179,181-183]

It has been suggested that genetic factors also might be important in determining relapse and the duration of therapy because a high prevalence of HLA antigens, B8, DR3, and possibly DR5 occurs in Graves' disease.[183,184] Although the absence of HLA antigens might indicate that drug treatment ultimately will be successful, detection of these antigens have not been reliably predictive of the clinical outcome.

Increased dietary intake of iodide might decrease the effectiveness of thioamides and increase the likelihood of relapse. A retrospective review correlated better remission rates with the decline in dietary iodide intake but further confirmation is needed.[181]

B.D.'s large goiter reduces her chance of remission with longer therapy. Thyroxine should be added (see Question 41). Although thioamide therapy can be continued indefinitely to control the thyrotoxicosis if there is no evidence of drug toxicity, surgery or radioactive iodine therapy should be considered seriously for B.D. who already has received PTU for over two years. Alternative therapy is especially crucial if she plans to be pregnant within the next few years (see Question 43).

In Pregnancy

43. N.N., a 32-year-old female who is 3 months pregnant, is referred for management of her Graves' disease. What are the therapeutic ramifications of managing thyrotoxicosis during pregnancy?

Hyperthyroidism develops in 0.02% to 1.4% of the pregnant population and often precedes conception.[67,185] Symptoms of thyrotoxicosis typically are ameliorated during the second and third trimesters and exacerbated early in the postpartum period.[67,185,186] Treatment is crucial to prevent damage to the fetus and to maintain pregnancy. Radioactive iodine, chronic iodide therapy, and iodine-containing compounds are contraindicated during pregnancy since these will cross the placenta to produce fetal goiter and athyreosis.[67,122] As little as 12 mg/day of iodide has produced neonatal goiter and death. The long-term use of propranolol also should be avoided because it is associated with fetal respiratory depression, a small placenta, intrauterine growth retardation, impaired response to anoxia, and postnatal bradycardia and hypoglycemia.[187] However, if rapid control of hyperthyroidism is required, short-term use (<1 week) of propranolol or the iodides is safe.[67,187]

Either surgery or the thioamides are the treatments of choice for hyperthyroidism in the pregnant patient. Surgery is safe during the second trimester with adequate preoperative preparation. During the last trimester, thioamides are preferred since surgery can precipitate spontaneous abortion. PTU generally is considered the thioamide of choice based upon anecdotal reports of methimazole causing reversible congenital scalp defects (aplasia cutis).[185,188] However, in patients allergic to PTU, methimazole is a viable alternative because no excess occurrence of this defect is noted in larger studies.[189,190] (Also see Chapter 45: Teratogenicity and Drugs in Breast Milk.)

The thioamides cross the placenta and are active against the fetal thyroid. PTU crosses the least because it is highly protein bound.[185] However, serum PTU concentrations are higher in the cord than in the mother's serum suggesting that PTU is cleared more slowly by the fetus.[191] Therefore, fetal hypothyroidism and goiter can develop when large doses are administered to the mother, even if the mother is hyperthyroid.[67,188,192,193]

To avoid goiter and suppression of the fetal thyroid gland, which begins to function at about 12 to 14 weeks of gestation, PTU usually is prescribed in minimally effective doses. The patient is initiated on maximum doses of 150 to 300 mg/day or as necessary to achieve euthyroidism and then tapered to 50 to 100 mg/day for the remainder of the pregnancy. Some patients can discontinue thioamides in the second half of pregnancy.[185] Such modest doses of PTU provide satisfactory control of maternal hyperthyroidism and should not cause clinically evident thyroid dysfunction in the neonate.

Nevertheless, a small but significant reduction in neonatal serum thyroxine occurs even when small (100 to 200 mg) doses of PTU are administered during pregnancy to mothers with Graves' disease.[192–194] It is unclear whether this mild, transient reduction in serum thyroxine causes long-term impairment of mental development or is otherwise detrimental to the newborn. To date, no significant differences in intellectual development have been noted between children exposed to PTU or methimazole *in utero* and their unexposed siblings. However, children exposed *in utero* to more than 300 mg/day of PTU had a lower IQ.[195,196]

Although transient fetal or neonatal hypothyroidism does not appear to be a major threat to the baby, it is advisable to maintain the mother in a mildly hyperthyroid state.[192] Mild maternal hyperthyroidism seems to be well tolerated, but maternal hypothyroidism is poorly tolerated by both the mother and fetus (also see Question 12). Laboratory indices should be maintained in the upper ranges of normal since normal thyroid function tests are suggestive of hypothyroidism during pregnancy (high TBG and TBPA levels).

It is not rational to add thyroid hormone to the mother's regimen to prevent fetal goiter or hypothyroidism because thyroid hormones do not reach the fetal circulation. Thyroid supplementation only complicates treatment of maternal hyperthyroidism by increasing PTU requirements which can further compromise fetal thyroid hormone production.[193,197] If the mother has not been thyrotoxic throughout pregnancy, a normal infant can be expected. All pregnant patients with a history of, or active, autoimmune thyroid disease (i.e., Graves', Hashimoto's) should be screened during pregnancy for thyroid-receptor antibodies to evaluate the risk of neonatal hyperthyroidism.[67] Lastly, PTU also is the drug of choice in the lactating mother.[198] Methimazole, propranolol, and iodides are secreted in breast milk and should be avoided.[67,147] (Also see Chapter 45: Teratogenicity and Drugs in Breast Milk.)

Treatment with RAI

Pretreatment

44. B.J., a 35-year-old female, has newly diagnosed Graves' disease complicated by CHF and angina. PTU was discontinued after 1 week because of severe granulocytopenia. After a few days treatment with Lugol's solution, 5 drops/day, B.J. received RAI therapy. Six months later, she still is symptomatic. Evaluate B.J.'s therapy before RAI therapy.

Severely hyperthyroid patients, hyperthyroid patients with cardiac disease, and those who are debilitated or elderly should receive antithyroid treatment before RAI therapy. The goal of pretreatment is to deplete stored thyroid hormone. This minimizes postRAI hyperthyroidism (which occurs the first 10 days after I[131] administration) and thyroid storm which is caused by leakage of hormones from the damaged thyroid gland.[86,128,131,199] Other hyperthyroid patients can be treated safely with RAI without pretherapy.

Lugol's solution should not have been given before RAI because iodides decrease the effectiveness of this therapy by decreasing the gland's uptake of RAI. This effect of iodides persists for several weeks. Iodides can be used for one to seven days after RAI treatment if they are needed to rapidly control symptoms of hyperthyroidism.[126]

The thioamides can be used before RAI therapy to achieve a euthyroid state, but they should be discontinued three days before and for one to seven days after treatment to facilitate optimum uptake and retention of I[131] by the gland. Pretreatment with thioamides can lower the cure rate and increase the need for subsequent doses of RAI.[200] β-adrenergic blocking agents can be used before, during, and after RAI therapy without interfering with its uptake.

B.J. remains symptomatic because pretreatment with the iodides decreased the effectiveness of RAI therapy. Propranolol should be given to B.J. before RAI therapy to ameliorate symptoms of hyperthyroidism since she has received only a short course of thioamide. Iodides might be preferable to propranolol following RAI therapy if B.J.'s congestive heart failure worsens.

Onset of Effects

45. B.J. still is symptomatic 2 weeks after a second dose of RAI. When can she expect to experience the therapeutic effects of RAI therapy?

Although some benefits from RAI therapy are evident within one month, three to six months generally are required for maximal effects.[128,131] Euthyroidism occurs in approximately 60% of patients treated with a single nonablative dose of RAI; the remaining 40% become euthyroid after two or more doses. This slow onset is a disadvantage, but symptomatic control can be obtained quickly by administration of a β-adrenergic blocking agent, ipodate, or iodide starting 1 to 14 days after the I^{131} dose.[126,128,158] Iodides are less preferable if a second dose of RAI is necessary. Thioamides also can be given, although their therapeutic effects are delayed for three to four weeks.

At least three months should elapse before a second radioactive dose of iodide is administered, and most recommend six months to a year's wait before repeating I^{131} administration unless the patient remains severely thyrotoxic. It is inadvisable to give a second dose before the major effects of the first dose have become apparent. Although the use of iodides before RAI in B.J. may have decreased the amount of I^{131} retained by her thyroid, it still is advisable to wait at least three months before a second dose is given.

Iatrogenic Hypothyroidism

46. S.D., a 54-year-old female, returns to thyroid clinic after being lost to follow-up for 6 months. She initially received RAI 3 years ago but required a repeat dose of RAI 1 year ago for recurrence of hyperthyroidism. She currently has no other medical problems and is on no medications. She is a mildly obese, puffy-faced female wrapped in several layers of clothing. She complains of fatigue and lack of energy. Her reflexes are delayed and her skin is cool and dry. What is a likely explanation for her symptoms?

S.D.'s clinical presentation and history are compatible with hypothyroidism secondary to RAI therapy. An FT_4 and a TSH level would confirm this diagnosis. Iatrogenic hypothyroidism is the major complication of I^{131} therapy, although transient hypothyroidism may be seen in the first three to six weeks after RAI therapy.[201] The incidence of iatrogenic myxedema often is reported as 7% to 8% but it increases at a constant rate of 2.5% per year.[131] The reported prevalence of this complication ranges from 26% to 70% after 1 to 14 years.[126,131,201]

The best predictor of eventual hypothyroidism is the dose of I^{131} administered. Prevention of iatrogenic hypothyroidism is directed toward calculation of a dose that will produce neither recurrent hyperthyroidism nor hypothyroidism. Unfortunately, when lower doses of I^{131} were used to avoid hypothyroidism, the cure rate was reduced but the incidence of hypothyroidism was unaffected. Thus, the appearance of iatrogenic hypothyroidism may be inevitable with time. However, hypothyroidism is managed easily and is an acceptable therapeutic endpoint. Since hypothyroidism after RAI therapy is latent and often insidious, patients should be made aware of this and monitored closely at monthly intervals for subsequent hypothyroidism. Awareness of a transient hypothyroidism soon after RAI therapy should minimize the institution of unnecessary hormone replacement.

Ophthalmopathy

Clinical Presentation

47. H.R., a 50-year-old female, first developed "large eyes with stare," weakness, diaphoresis, and thyroid enlargement in 1970. She was diagnosed as having Graves' disease and treated with RAI with some regression of eye symptoms. Although she is clinically euthyroid, physical examination revealed severe bilateral conjunctival edema and injection, proptosis of the right eye, incomplete lid closure, and decreased visual acuity. She complains of photophobia, tearing, and extreme irritation which is worse after smoking cigarettes. What is the association of H.R.'s ocular changes with Graves' disease?

H.R. presents with symptoms consistent with the infiltrative ophthalmopathy of Graves' disease.[14,202] The eye signs of Graves' disease are the most striking abnormality of this disorder. Rarely, euthyroid ophthalmopathy can occur without any evidence of hyperthyroidism. Fortunately, severe ophthalmopathy only occurs in 3% to 5% of patients, while 25% to 50% have some eye findings. Smokers often have higher levels of thyroid-receptor antibodies and more severe ophthalmopathy.[203] The eye involvement can occur at any time and usually is bilateral. The ocular symptoms usually subside or remain stable once the patient is euthyroid; however, some cases will progress during the euthyroid period or following treatment of the hyperthyroidism (see Question 48).[204]

It is unknown why the eye and its muscles are attacked in Graves' disease. Histologic examination reveals lymphocytic infiltration, increased mucopolysaccharide content, fat, and water in all retrobulbar tissue. Ocular symptoms include edema, chemosis, excessive lacrimation, photophobia, corneal protrusion (proptosis), scarring, ulceration, extraocular muscle paralysis with loss of eye movements, and blindness from retinal and optic nerve damage.

Management

48. Was previous treatment of H.R.'s hyperthyroidism appropriate? How should her current ocular symptoms be managed?

The optimal treatment of the hyperthyroidism and its effect on the course of ophthalmopathy is controversial and conflicting. Mild and minimal eye symptoms have worsened after RAI and thyroidectomy. Therefore, the concomitant use of corticosteroids is indicated before RAI therapy in those with any degree of ocular involvement to prevent further deterioration of their eye symptoms.[204,205] On the other hand, some clinicians suggest that gland ablation or surgical removal is preferable because it removes the antigen source and prevents progression of the ophthalmopathy. Thioamides might improve eye symptoms through an immunosuppressive mechanism of action and control of the hyperthyroidism. No differences in eye symptoms were noted in patients receiving either the combination of thioamides and thyroxine or thioamides alone.[206] Regardless of the treatment used, control of the hyperthyroidism often will improve most eye findings except for proptosis.

In H.R. prednisone should have been started before her RAI treatment and continued for 10 to 14 days or until the eye symptoms improve.

Since the pathophysiology of the ophthalmopathy is unclear, treatment is limited to symptomatic and empiric measures once the patient is euthyroid. H.R. also should be encouraged to stop smoking to prevent progression of her ophthalmopathy.[203]

Periorbital edema and chemosis are worse in the morning after being in the horizontal position; elevation of the head of the bed and treatment with diuretics and salt restriction may be helpful. Protective glasses can relieve photophobia and external irritation. Topical corticosteroid drops are effective in decreasing local irritation, but they should be used cautiously since they increase the risk of infection. Ocular irritants such as smoke and dust should be avoided. Bothersome symptoms (e.g., dry eye, redness, tearing) due to eyelid retraction can be managed temporally by the use of 2% guanethidine eye drops until the hyperthyroidism resolves.[202] Incomplete lid closure predisposes the patient to corneal scarring and ulceration, so lubricant eyedrops should be applied several times daily and at night to keep the bulbs moist. Taping the eyelids shut at night helps prevent drying and scarring. Lateral surgical closure of the lids (tarsorrhaphy) may be required to improve lid closure.

When the ophthalmopathy is severe and progressive, an aggressive approach is necessary. Systemic corticosteroids can produce dramatic or marginal results in the emergency treatment of progressive exophthalmos associated with decreasing visual acuity. Prednisone in doses of 35 to 80 mg/day often is effective, although doses as large as 100 to 140 mg/day may be necessary.[14,202] Pain, irritation, tearing, and other subjective complaints often respond within 24 hours of administration. Therapy for days to weeks is necessary for improvement of eye muscle and optic nerve function disturbances. Initial large doses should be tapered rapidly once the desired response is obtained to minimize adverse effects. Subconjunctival and retrobulbar injections of steroids are not as effective.

X-ray therapy to the orbit also relieves congestive and inflammatory symptoms.[14,202] The combination of orbital irradiation and systemic steroids may be required to achieve maximal benefits. Plasmapheresis and immunosuppressive agents, such as cyclophosphamide, azathioprine, cyclosporine, and methotrexate, also have been used with success.[14,202]

When the above measures and thyroid ablation fail to arrest the progression of visual loss and exophthalmos, then surgical decompression should be considered.

Thyroid Storm

Clinical Presentation

49. H.L., a 48-year-old female, is admitted to the hospital with a 3-week history of fatigue, weakness, dyspnea on exertion, SOB, palpitations, and inability to keep food and liquids down. One year before admission she began noticing a preference for cold weather and an increase in nervousness and emotional lability. After her husband died a few days ago, she experienced increased nausea and vomiting, irritability, insomnia, tremor, and a 104 °F fever which she attributed to an upper respiratory tract infection. She denies any current medication. Her laboratory data obtained on admission included a FT$_4$ of 60 pmol/L and an undetectable TSH level. Assess H.L.'s subjective and objective data.

The presentation is consistent with thyroid storm, a life-threatening medical emergency which might have been precipitated by the death of her husband. The clinical manifestations of thyroid storm[86,207] include the acute onset of high fever (*sine qua non*), tachycardia, tachypnea, and involvement of the following organ systems: cardiovascular (tachycardia, pulmonary edema, hypertension, and shock); CNS (tremor, emotional lability, confusion, psychosis, apathy, stupor, and coma); GI (diarrhea, abdominal pain, nausea and vomiting, liver enlargement, jaundice, and nonspecific elevations of bilirubin and PT). Hyperglycemia was a clinical finding in 12 out of 18 episodes.

Thyroid storm develops in about 2% to 8% of hyperthyroid patients. The pathogenesis of thyroid storm is not well understood, but the condition can be described as an "exaggerated" or decompensated form of thyrotoxicosis. The term "decompensated" implies failure of body systems to adequately resist the effects of thyrotoxicosis. It is not attributed solely to the release of massive quantities of hormones which can occur after surgery or following RAI therapy. Catecholamines also play an important role; the increased quantities of thyroid hormone in conjunction with increased sympathetic and adrenal output contribute to many of the manifestations of thyroid storm. Although thyroid hormones exert an independent effect, many of the symptoms of hyperthyroidism are ameliorated by catecholamine-blocking agents such as propranolol, reserpine, and guanethidine. Calcium channel blockers also are effective.[120,163,164]

Treatment

50. What treatment plan (including route of administration) should be initiated promptly in H.L.?

Accurate, continuous, and immediate treatment can decrease the mortality of thyroid storm significantly. Mortality rates as low as 7% and survival rates as high as 50% are reported. Treatment of thyroid storm should be directed against four major areas.[86,207]

Decrease in Synthesis and Release of Hormones. Large doses of thioamides, preferably PTU 600 to 1200 mg/day or methimazole 60 to 120 mg/day, should be given orally in divided doses. If H.L. is unable to take oral doses, then a rectal formulation of PTU or methimazole, which is as effective as the oral route, can be administered.[208,209] There is no commercial parenteral preparation available for either drug, limiting their use by the IV route. Unfortunately, extemporaneous preparation of an IV formulation using water soluble methimazole is not possible because sterile methimazole no longer is available from the manufacturer. Theoretically, PTU is the thioamide of choice since it acts more rapidly than methimazole by blocking the peripheral conversion of T$_4$ to T$_3$, a dominant source of the hormone.

Iodides, which rapidly block further release of intraglandular stores of thyroxine, should be given at least one hour after thioamide administration. Given in this way, the substrate for hormone synthesis is not increased and one avoids blocking thioamide's therapeutic effect. Iodides can be administered orally as Lugol's solution 30 drops/day. Such a combination often ameliorates symptoms within one day.

Reversal of the Peripheral Effects of Hormones and Catecholamines. β-adrenergic blocking drugs are the preferred agents to decrease the tachycardia, agitation, tremulousness, and other symptoms of excessive adrenergic stimulation seen in thyroid storm. Propranolol is the beta blocker of choice because its clinical efficacy in storm is well documented and because it inhibits the peripheral conversion of T$_4$ to T$_3$.[158,207] Furthermore, propranolol is effective in patients refractory to reserpine and guanethidine. If rapid effects are necessary, propranolol 1 mg by slow IV push can be given every five minutes to lower the heart rate to between 90 to 110 beats/minute. A 5 to 10 mg/hour IV infusion can be given to maintain the desired heart rate. Otherwise, oral propranolol 40 mg every six hours can be given instead. The dose can be doubled every 12 hours until a therapeutic response is obtained.

Catecholamine depleting agents, such as reserpine and guanethidine, have been used successfully in storm, but their use has been replaced by beta blockers. Reserpine in doses of 1 to 3 mg IM/IV every eight hours or guanethidine 20 to 50 mg orally every eight hours can be tried. Intravenous reserpine is preferred over the IM injection since absorption from intramuscular sites is poor, particularly if circulatory collapse is present.

Supportive Treatment of Vital Functions. This may include sedation, oxygen, intravenous glucose, vitamins, treatment of infections with antibiotics, digitalization to maintain the cardiac status, rehydration, and treatment of hyperpyrexia with cooling blankets, sponge baths, and the judicious use of antipyretics. Since hypoadrenalism often is suspected, hydrocortisone 100 to 200 mg IV every six hours should be given. Since pharmacologic doses of steroids acutely depress serum T$_3$ levels, a beneficial effect in storm, their routine use is recommended.[86,207]

Elimination of Precipitating Causes of Storm. Factors associated with the induction of thyroid storm include infection (most common), trauma, inadequate preparation before thyroidectomies, surgical operations, stress, diabetic acidosis, pregnancy, emboli, abrupt discontinuation of antithyroid medications, drug therapy, and RAI therapy.[134,135,199,207]

Drug-Induced Thyroid Disease

Lithium and Antidepressants

51. D.A., a 56-year-old male, complains of sluggishness, cold intolerance, fatigue, and a "rundown" feeling which doctors attribute to the depressive phase of his bipolar affective illness. He previously had been well controlled on imipramine (Tofranil) 300 mg/day, but lithium carbonate (Eskalith) 900 mg/day was added 4 months ago because of unreasonable mirthfulness and uncontrollable gift-buying tendencies. Upon physical ex-

amination, a puffy face and a large goiter are prominent findings. What is a reasonable assessment of these subjective and objective data?

Thyroid function tests (i.e., TSH, FT$_4$) should be obtained to evaluate the possibility of lithium and possibly imipramine-induced hypothyroidism and goiter. If appropriate, thyroxine should be initiated. Although the incidence of goiter and hypothyroidism in the manic depressive population is unknown, the incidence of baseline elevated TSH might be higher than in the general population; one study reported an incidence of 15%.[210]

The antithyroid effects of lithium were noted first in manic depressive patients. The exact mechanism of lithium's effect on the gland is unclear, although it is highly concentrated by the gland. Similar to the iodides, chronic lithium therapy inhibits the release of thyroid hormone from the gland. The fall in serum T$_4$ and T$_3$ hormone levels leads to a compensatory and transient increase in serum TSH levels until a new steady state is achieved.[210-212]

The incidence of subclinical hypothyroidism (i.e., increased TSH level) occurs in approximately 19% of patients on chronic lithium therapy.[210-212] Typically, the serum thyroid hormone levels decrease and the TSH levels increase during the first few months of treatment, with return to pretreatment levels after one year. In one study, TSH levels increased within ten days after starting therapy.[212] Normalization of the TSH level is less likely to occur in individuals with positive thyroid antibodies before lithium therapy. Induction of thyroid antibody positivity and increases in baseline antibody titers also occur after chronic lithium therapy. Because abnormal thyroid function tests can be transient, a longer period of observation is justified before starting thyroid hormone therapy in patients with subclinical hypothyroidism.

Lithium-induced goiter, with or without hypothyroidism, appears in a small percentage of the population after five months to two years of therapy.[210,213,214] Overt hypothyroidism develops most often during the first two years of treatment in women with a history of positive antibodies before lithium therapy. A direct goitrogenic effect of lithium might explain the occurrence of euthyroid goiter. The goiters respond to discontinuation of lithium or to suppression with thyroid hormone despite continuation of lithium therapy. Surgical removal of the goiter is required if there are local obstructive symptoms. In D.A.'s case, imipramine could be exerting an additive or synergistic antithyroid effect with lithium since antithyroid effects also have been associated with this drug.

Most patients with lithium-induced thyroid abnormalities have a prior history of compromised thyroid function (e.g., Hashimoto's thyroiditis), positive thyroid antibodies before lithium therapy, or a strong family history of thyroid disease.[210-214] Therefore, baseline thyroid function tests (i.e., FT$_4$, TSH) and antibodies should be obtained before the initiation of lithium therapy and rechecked every six months thereafter or more frequently if clinically indicated. Patients also should be questioned about a positive history or family history for thyroid disease and the concurrent use of other, potentially goitrogenic medications (e.g., tricyclic antidepressants, iodides, iodinated expectorants).

52. A.B., a 66-year-old, otherwise healthy male, is admitted for evaluation of new onset atrial fibrillation. His only other medical problem is a history of bipolar manic depression treated with lithium for 1 year. However, A.B. discontinued the lithium 1 month before hospitalization without the knowledge of his physician. His laboratory studies are within normal limits except for a TT$_3$ of 380 ng/dL. What is the potential cause of A.B.'s atrial fibrillation?

Atrial fibrillation may be the only manifestation of thyrotoxicosis in elderly patients.[94,104,159] Thyrotoxicosis is reported following lithium withdrawal and A.B.'s atrial fibrillation most likely

is the result of excessive thyroid hormone activity. Lithium's antithyroid action is substantial and is comparable to that of the thioamides; T$_4$ levels decline by 20% to 35%. Therefore, A.B.'s underlying hyperthyroidism probably has been unmasked by his discontinuation of the lithium.

Although lithium is not considered the standard of care for hyperthyroidism, it is recommended as an adjunct to RAI therapy in patients allergic to conventional treatment modalities because it does not interfere with I^{131} uptake. Furthermore, lithium can increase I^{131} retention by decreasing its rate of elimination from the gland.[210,212,215] The increased thyroidal half-life of I^{131} by lithium is beneficial in localizing the dose of radiation to the gland.[215]

Because clinical experience with lithium in the treatment of thyrotoxicosis is limited and because it has such a narrow therapeutic index, its use should be restricted to situations where rapid suppression of thyroid hormone secretion is needed and thioamides, iodides, and ipodate are contraindicated. It should not be considered an alternative to thioamides, only an adjunct.

Iodides and Amiodarone

53. C.Y., a 54-year-old male with chronic obstructive airways disease (COAD), presents with a 6-month history of weakness, fatigue, tremor, heat intolerance, palpitations, and cardiac tachyarrhythmias, previously controlled for the last 2 years on amiodarone 400 mg/day. Upon physical examination a 50 gm multinodular gland is present which C.Y. says has "been there forever." He denies any family history of thyroid disease or ingestion of any thyroid medication. An iodinated expectorant recently was started for his COAD. His current complaints began after an intravenous pyelogram (IVP). What might be responsible for C.Y.'s hyperthyroid symptoms?

The iodine load from the IVP, the iodinated expectorant, or from the amiodarone could be responsible for C.Y.'s hyperthyroid symptoms.[30-32,122-125] Iodide-induced hyperthyroidism, known as the Jod-Basedow phenomenon, was described first in the 1800s when patients residing in iodide-deficient areas became toxic when given adequate iodide supplementation. Other reports have appeared since. Both T$_3$ toxicosis and classical T$_4$ toxicosis have occurred following iodide ingestion or injection of roentgenographic contrast media.

Although it is presumed that both iodide deficiency and a multinodular goiter, as in C.Y., are essential for the production of the Jod-Basedow phenomenon, patients residing in iodide-sufficient areas and euthyroid patients with supposedly normal glands and no history or family history of thyroid disease also might be at risk following administration of iodides.[122-125]

Amiodarone can cause hypo- or hyperthyroidism in susceptible individuals due to its high iodine content.[30-32,216] There are 12 mg (37%) of free iodine released per 400 mg dose of amiodarone. Patients with multinodular goiters who lose the ability to turn off organification of iodide with increasing iodide loads (Wolff-Chaikoff effect) are most likely to develop iodide-induced thyrotoxicosis. Conversely, patients with positive antibodies or with underlying Hashimoto's thyroiditis who are unable to escape from the Wolff-Chaikoff block are most likely to develop hypothyroidism.

Amiodarone-induced hypothyroidism may occur at any time during the course of therapy and does not appear to be related to the cumulative dose. A normal FT$_4$ along with a persistently elevated TSH are consistent with amiodarone-induced hypothyroidism which occurs in 6% to 10% of long-term users. The hypothyroidism responds readily to thyroxine therapy and the amiodarone often can be continued.[30-32,216]

In contrast, the development of amiodarone-induced thyrotoxicosis is unpredictable, and occurs early and suddenly during the course of therapy so that routine monitoring of TFTs often is not useful. It often is difficult to treat due to the long half-life of the drug (22 to 55 days) and to the large amounts of preformed hormone within the thyroid induced by the massive iodine load.[30-32,216] A destructive type of thyroiditis with excess release of thyroid hormone also may contribute to amiodarone-induced hyperthyroidism.[217] An elevated TT_3 level, an undetectable TSH level, and the presence of clinical symptoms consistent with hyperthyroidism are the best indicators of amiodarone-induced thyrotoxicosis which occurs in 1% to 5% of long-term users. Worsening of tachyarrhythmias may be the first clinical clue to amiodarone-induced thyrotoxicosis.

Radioactive iodine ablation is not a viable option in patients with amiodarone-induced thyrotoxicosis because the high plasma iodine levels will suppress therapeutic uptake of the I^{131}. Although the combined use of methimazole and potassium perchlorate as well as steroids may be useful, resistance also has been reported.[216-219] The best option appears to be surgery which rapidly controls the thyrotoxicosis and allows continued therapy with amiodarone. Even though most of these patients have underlying cardiac disorders, surgery generally is uneventful and complications minimal.[220]

Large doses of iodides should be avoided in patients with nontoxic multinodular goiters who are predisposed to thyrotoxicosis. (See Questions 5 and 28.)

Nodules

"Hot" Nodule

54. N.S., a 20-year-old female, noted a "lump" in the right side of her neck. There is no history of irradiation, no family history of thyroid disease, no local symptoms, and no symptoms suggestive of hypo- or hyperthyroidism. The right lobe of the thyroid is occupied by a 3 × 3 cm firm, immovable nodule, while the left lobe is barely palpable. All thyroid function tests are within normal limits although the gland is not suppressible. A scan shows a large "hot" nodule occupying the right lobe and a nonexistent left lobe. How should N.S.'s single "hot nodule," or Plummer's disease be managed?

"Hot" nodule is a term used to describe a "hyperfunctioning" or iodine-concentrating area of the thyroid as shown on scan; it appears as an area of greater density than the rest of the gland. The hyperfunctioning autonomous nodule typically suppresses activity in the remainder of the gland, but it need not produce clinical or chemical evidence of hyperthyroidism and may remain unchanged for years. Some nodules may develop into toxic goiters, causing overt symptoms of toxicosis. Most "hot" nodules are benign; malignancies rarely are reported.[221]

Treatment of the "hot" nodule depends upon the existing clinical situation. If the "hot" nodule is suppressing the other lobe of the thyroid, is not causing toxic symptoms, and is the only source of thyroid production, the patient should be left alone and monitored closely for signs of toxicity. If the gland is not suppressed by the functioning "hot" nodule, then thyroid suppression therapy is indicated to avoid further nodule growth and stimulation by TSH.[221,223] A toxic "hot" nodule is best treated surgically or with RAI ablation. Because they do not spontaneously resolve, antithyroid drugs are not the treatment of choice. Since the normal thyroid tissue is suppressed, RAI is concentrated only by the "hot" nod-

ule, sparing the suppressed tissue. After treatment, the suppressed tissue should begin functioning again.

"Cold" Nodule

55. P.L., a 29-year-old female, is found to have a left thyroid nodule upon routine physical examination. She has no history of neck irradiation, no family history of thyroid disease, and no symptoms suggestive of hypo- or hyperthyroidism. A firm, nontender 1.0 cm nodule occupies the left lobe of the gland. Thyroid function tests are within normal limits. The scan shows a "cold" nodule and the echogram reveals a solid mass ruling out the possibility of a cyst. An FNA shows a benign colloid nodule. Antibodies are negative. What is the significance of a "cold nodule"?

A "cold" nodule is a "hypofunctioning" area of the thyroid which fails to collect radioiodine. It is depicted on the scan as a lighter or less dense area. The differential diagnosis includes Hashimoto's thyroiditis, benign adenomas, cysts, and malignant tumors. The absence of antibodies and solidarity of the mass by echo rules out the possibility of cyst or Hashimoto's thyroiditis. Most "cold" nodules turn out to be benign adenomas rather than cancers. The results of the fine needle aspiration also suggest a benign lesion. However a benign biopsy in a suspicious nodule or in a patient with risk factors for malignancy does not absolutely eliminate the possibility of malignancy. In these patients, surgery is recommended. The incidence of malignancy in a "cold" nodule varies between 10% and 20%.[221] A history of irradiation increases the likelihood of cancer in a nodule and surgery is recommended in these instances.[222] The nature of the nodule is important. Fixation of the nodule to the strap muscles or trachea, a hard bulging mass, any pain or tenderness, or voice hoarseness can indicate malignancy.

Nontoxic Multinodular Goiter

56. G.D., a 35-year-old female, is referred for a "goiter" discovered on routine physical examination. She denies any symptoms of hyper- or hypothyroidism or any history of irradiation. Her grandmother had hypothyroidism and a goiter. A large "lumpy bumpy" gland is present but she has no problem with breathing or swallowing. The assessment is a nontoxic multinodular goiter. How should this be managed?

Nontoxic multinodular goiter is a common finding in about 5% of the population.[221] In low-risk patients, long-standing asymptomatic nodules which have not exhibited recent growth are likely to be benign and can be followed or excised surgically for cosmetic reasons. If the patient develops symptoms (swallowing or respiratory difficulty), surgery is the treatment of choice. Thyroxine suppression therapy to decrease TSH stimulation should be considered to prevent further growth if the patient has no cardiac contraindications. Thyroxine does not return the gland to normal size but prevents further goiter enlargement.[221,223] Some gland shrinkage should be noted three to six months following the initiation of thyroxine 0.1 to 0.2 mg/day to suppress the TSH to undetectable levels. If so, maintenance therapy should be continued. If the nodules grow on thyroxine therapy, surgery should be considered. The dangers of long-term suppressive therapy include osteoporosis and cardiac changes.[49-53] *Note:* Nodular responsiveness to thyroxine does *not* rule out malignancy.

References

1 Larsen PR. Thyroid-pituitary interaction feedback regulation of thyrotropin secretion by thyroid hormones. N Engl J Med. 1982;306:23.

2 Bayer MF. Effective laboratory evaluation of thyroid status. Med Clin North Am. 1991;75:1.

3 Surks MI et al. ATA guidelines for use of laboratory tests in thyroid disorders. JAMA. 1990;263:1529.

4   **Kaptein EM et al.** Prolonged dopamine administration and thyroid hormone economy in normal and critically ill subjects. J Clin Endocrinol Metab. 1980;51:387.

5   **Feek CM et al.** Influence of thyroid status on dopaminergic inhibition of thyrotropin and prolactin secretion: evidence for an additional feedback mechanism in the control of thyroid hormone secretion. J Clin Endocrinol Metab. 1980;51:585.

6   **Minozzi M et al.** Effect of L-dopa on plasma TSH levels in primary hypothyroidism. Neuroendocrinology. 1975;17:147.

7   **Verges B et al.** Ultrasensitive TSH assay and antiparkinsonian treatment with levodopa. J Neurol Neurosurg Psychiatry. 1992;55:1210. Letter.

8   **Miyai K et al.** Inhibition of thyrotropin and prolactin secretion in primary hypothyroidism by 2-Br-;oba;cb-ergocryptine. J Clin Endocrinol Metab. 1974;39:391.

9   **Brabant A et al.** The role of glucocorticoids in the regulation of thyrotropin. Acta Endocrinol (Copenh). 1989;121:95.

10 **Healy DL, Burger HG.** Increased prolactin and thyrotropin secretion following oral metoclopramide: dose-response relationships. Clin Endocrinol (Oxf). 1977;7:195.

11 **Scanlon MF et al.** Catecholaminergic interactions in the regulation of thyrotropin (TSH) secretions in man. J Endocrinol Invest. 1980;3:125.

12 **Delitala G et al.** Domperidone, an extracerebral inhibitor of dopamine receptors, stimulates thyrotropin and prolactin release in man. J Clin Endocrinol Metab. 1980;50:1127.

13 **Jackson IMD.** Thyrotropin-releasing hormone. N Engl J Med. 1982;306:145.

14 **Burch HB, Wartofsky LW.** Graves' ophthalmopathy. Current concepts regarding pathogenesis and management. Endocr Rev. 1993;14:747.

15 **Zakarija M et al.** Clinical significance of assay of thyroid-stimulating antibody in Graves' disease. Ann Intern Med. 1980;93:28.

16 **Wartofsky L, Burman KD.** Alterations in thyroid function in patients with systemic illness: the "euthyroid sick syndrome." Endocr Rev. 1982;3:164.

17 **Cavalieri RR.** The effects of nonthyroid disease and drugs on thyroid function tests. Med Clin North Am. 1991;75:27.

18 **LoPresti JS.** Unique alterations of thyroid hormone indices in the acquired immunodeficiency syndrome (AIDS). Ann Intern Med. 1989;110:970.

19 **Slag MF et al.** Hypothyroxinemia in critically ill patients as a predictor of high mortality. JAMA. 1981;245:43.

20 **Kaptein EM et al.** Relationships of altered thyroid hormone indices to survival in nonthyroidal illnesses. Clin Endocrinol (Oxf). 1982;16:565.

21 **Brent GA, Hershman JM.** Thyroxine therapy in patients with severe nonthyroidal illnesses and low serum thyroxine concentrations. J Clin Endocrinol Metab. 1986;63:1.

22 **Kabadi UM, Danielson S.** Misleading thyroid function tests and several homeostatic abnormalities induced by "disalcid" therapy. J Am Geriatr Soc. 1987;35:255.

23 **McDonnell RJ.** Abnormal thyroid function test results in patients taking salsalate. JAMA. 1992;267:1242.

24 **Graham RL, Gambrell RD.** Changes in thyroid function tests during danazol therapy. Obstet Gynecol. 1980;55:395.

25 **Curran PG, Degroot LJ.** The effect of hepatic enzyme-inducing drugs on thyroid hormones and the thyroid gland. Endocr Rev. 1991;12:135.

26 **Blackshear JL et al.** Thyroxine replacement requirements in hypothyroid patients receiving phenytoin. Ann Intern Med. 1983;99:341.

27 **Kushnir M et al.** Hypothyroidism and phenytoin intoxication. Ann Intern Med. 1985;102:341.

28 **Gordon D et al.** The effect of tamoxifen therapy on thyroid function tests. Cancer. 1986;58:1422.

29 **English TN et al.** Abnormalities in thyroid function associated with chronic therapy with methadone. Clin Chem. 1988;34:2202.

30 **Figge HL, Figge J.** The effects of amiodarone on hormone function: a review of the physiology and clinical manifestations. J Clin Pharmacol. 1990;30:588.

31 **Singh BN.** Amiodarone and thyroid function: clinical implications during antiarrhythmic therapy. Am Heart J. 1983;106:857.

32 **Nademanee K et al.** Amiodarone and thyroid function. Prog Cardiovasc Dis. 1989;31:427.

33 **Sawin CT.** Hypothyroidism. Med Clin North Am. 1985;69:989.

34 **Fein HG et al.** Anemia in thyroid disease. Med Clin North Am. 1975;59:1133.

35 **Cooper DS.** Thyroid hormone treatment: new insights into an old therapy. JAMA. 1989;261:2694. Editorial.

36 **Rees-Jones RW, Larsen PR.** Triiodothyronine and thyroxine content of desiccated thyroid tablets. Metabolism. 1977;26:1213.

37 **Rees-Jones RW et al.** Hormonal content of thyroid replacement preparations. JAMA. 1980;243:549.

38 **Csako GA et al.** Therapeutic potential of two over-the-counter thyroid hormone preparations. Drug Intell Clin Pharm. 1990;24:26.

39 **Sawin CT, London MH.** "Natural desiccated thyroid, a health food" thyroid preparation. Arch Intern Med. 1989;149:2117.

40 **Sawin CT et al.** A comparison of thyroxine and desiccated thyroid in patients with primary hypothyroidism. Metabolism. 1978;27:1518.

41 **Mandel SJ et al.** Levothyroxine therapy in patients with thyroid disease. Ann Intern Med. 1993;119:492.

42 **Fish LH et al.** Replacement dose, metabolism, and bioavailability of levothyroxine in the treatment of hypothyroidism. N Engl J Med. 1987;316:764.

43 **Hennessey JV et al.** The equivalency of two L-thyroxine preparations. Ann Intern Med. 1985;102:770.

44 **Blouin RA et al.** Biopharmaceutical comparison of two levothyroxine sodium preparations. Clin Pharm. 1989;8:588.

45 **Dong BJ et al.** The nonequivalence of levothyroxine products. Drug Intell Clin Pharm. 1986;20:77. Letter.

46 **Sawin CT et al.** Oral thyroxine: variation in biologic action and tablet content. Ann Intern Med. 1984;100:641.

47 **Stoffer SS, Szpunar WE.** Potency of current levothyroxine preparations evaluated by high-performance liquid chromatography. Henry Ford Hosp Med J. 1988;36:64.

48 **Carmeyer NR, Wolfson BB.** Possible leaching of diethylphthalate into levothyroxine sodium tablets. Am J Hosp Pharm. 1991;48:735.

49 **Paul TL et al.** Long-term L-thyroxine therapy is associated with decreased hip bone density in premenopausal women. JAMA. 1988;259:3137.

50 **Ross DS et al.** Subclinical hyperthyroidism and reduced bone density as a possible result of prolonged suppression of the pituitary-thyroid axis with L-thyroxine. Am J Med. 1987;82:1167.

51 **Bell GM et al.** The effect of minor increments in plasma thyroxine on heart rate and urinary sodium excretion. Clin Endocrinol (Oxf). 1983;18:511.

52 **Stall GM et al.** Accelerated bone loss in hypothyroid patients overtreated with L-thyroxine. Ann Intern Med. 1990;113:265.

53 **Ross DS.** Subclinical hyperthyroidism: possible dangers of overzealous thyroxine replacement therapy. Mayo Clin Proc. 1988;63:1223.

54 **Hennessey JV et al.** L-thyroxine dosage: a reevaluation of therapy with contemporary preparations. Ann Intern Med. 1986;105:11.

55 **Brown ME, Refetoff S.** Transient elevation of serum thyroid hormone concentration after initiation of replacement therapy in myxedema. Ann Intern Med. 1980;92:491.

56 **Rendell M, Salmon D.** "Chemical hyperthyroidism": the significance of elevated serum thyroxine levels in L-thyroxine treated individuals. Clin Endocrinol (Oxf). 1985;22:693.

57 **Grund FM, Niewoehner CB.** Hyperthyroxinemia in patients receiving thyroid replacement therapy. Arch Intern Med. 1989;149:921.

58 **Rosenbaum RL, Barzel US.** Levothyroxine replacement dose for primary hypothyroidism decreases with age. Ann Intern Med. 1982;96:53.

59 **Sawin CT et al.** Aging and the thyroid. Decreased requirements for thyroid hormone in older hypothyroid patients. Am J Med. 1983;75:206.

60 **Davis FB et al.** Estimation of a physiologic replacement dose of levothyroxine in elderly patients with hypothyroidism. Arch Intern Med. 1984;144:1752.

61 **Kabadi UM.** Variability of L-thyroxine replacement dose in elderly patients with primary hypothyroidism. J Fam Pract. 1987;24:473.

62 **Miralles-Garcia JM et al.** Thyroxine and triiodothyronine kinetics and extra thyroidal peripheral conversion rate of thyroxine to triiodothyronine in healthy elderly humans. Horm Metab Res. 1981;13:626.

63 **Bernstein RS et al.** Intermittent therapy with L-thyroxine. N Engl J Med. 1969;281:1444.

64 **Sekadde CR et al.** Administration of thyroxin once a week. J Clin Endocrinol Metab. 1974;39:759.

65 **Mandel SJ et al.** Increased need for thyroxine during pregnancy in women with primary hypothyroidism. N Engl J Med. 1990;323:91.

66 **Kaplan MN.** Monitoring thyroxine treatment during pregnancy. Thyroid. 1992;2:147.

67 **Burrow GN.** Thyroid function and hyperfunction during gestation. Endocr Rev. 1993;14:194.

68 **LaFranchi S.** Diagnosis and treatment of hypothyroidism in children. Compr Ther. 1987;13(10):20.

69 **Heyerdahl S et al.** Intellectual development in children with congenital hypothyroidism in relation to recommended thyroxine treatment. J Pediatr. 1991;118:850.

70 **Rovet J et al.** Intellectual outcome in children with fetal hypothyroidism. J Pediatr. 1987;110:700.

71 **American Academy of Pediatrics, American Thyroid Association.** Newborn screening for congenital hypothyroidism: recommended guidelines. Pediatrics. 1987;80:745.

72 **Fisher DA, Foley BL.** Early treatment of congenital hypothyroidism. Pediatrics. 1989;83:785.

73 **Abusrewil SSA et al.** Serum thyroxine and thyroid stimulating hormone concentrations after treatment of congenital hypothyroidism. Arch Dis Child. 1988;63:1368.

74 **Kaplan MM et al.** Partial peripheral resistance to thyroid hormone. Am J Med. 1981;70:1115.

75 **Ain KB et al.** Pseudomalabsorption of levothyroxine. JAMA. 1991;266:2118.

76 **Hays MT.** Thyroid hormone and the gut. Endocr Res. 1988;14:203.

77 **Stone E et al.** L-thyroxine absorption in patients with short bowel. J Clin Endocrinol Metab. 1984;59:134.

78 **Northcutt RC et al.** The influence of cholestyramine on thyroxine absorption. JAMA. 1969;208:1857.

79 **Harmon SM, Seifert CF.** Levothyroxine-cholestyramine interaction reemphasized. Ann Intern Med. 1991;115:658. Letter.

80 **Campbell NRC et al.** Ferrous sulfate reduces thyroxine efficacy in patients with hypothyroidism. Ann Intern Med. 1992;117:1010.

81 **Demke DM.** Drug interaction between thyroxine and lovastatin. N Engl J Med. 1991;321:1341. Letter.

82 **Sperber AD, Liel Y.** Evidence for interference with the intestinal absorption of levothyroxine sodium by aluminum hydroxide. Arch Intern Med. 1992;152:183.

83 **Havrankova J, Lahaie R.** Levothyroxine binding by sucralfate. Ann Intern Med. 1992;117:445. Letter.

84 **O'Brien T et al.** Hyperlipidemia in patients with primary and secondary hypothyroidism. Mayo Clin Proc. 1993;68:860.

85 **Nicoloff JT, LoPresti JS.** Myxedema coma. A form of decompensated hypothyroidism. Endocrinol Metab Clin North Am. 1993;22:279.

86 **Gavin LA.** Thyroid crises. Med Clin North Am. 1991;75:179.

87 **MacKerrow SD et al.** Myxedema-associated cardiogenic shock treated with intravenous triiodothyronine. Ann Intern Med. 1992;117:1014.

88 **Pereira VG et al.** Management of

myxedema coma: report on three successfully treated cases with nasogastric or intravenous administration of triiodothyronine. J Endocrinol Invest. 1982;5:331.

89 Ladenson PW et al. Rapid pituitary and peripheral tissue responses to intravenous L-triiodothyronine in hypothyroidism. J Clin Endocrinol Metab. 1983;56:1252.

90 Hylander B, Rosenqvist U. Treatment of myxedema coma. Factors associated with fatal outcome. Acta Endocrinol (Copenh). 1985;108:65.

91 Kaptein EM et al. Acute hemodynamic effect of levothyroxine loading in critically ill hypothyroid patients. Arch Intern Med. 1986;146:662.

92 Ariot S et al. Myxoedema coma: response of thyroid hormones with oral and intravenous high-dose L-thyroxine treatment. Intensive Care Med. 1991; 17:16.

93 Lyon LJ et al. Reversal of alcoholic coma by naloxone. Ann Intern Med. 1982;96:464.

94 Ladenson PW. Recognition and management of cardiovascular disease related to thyroid dysfunction. Am J Med. 1990;88:638.

95 Becker C. Hypothyroidism and atherosclerotic heart disease: pathogenesis, medical management and the role of coronary artery bypass surgery. Endocr Rev. 1985;6:432.

96 Levine D. Compromise therapy in the patient with angina pectoris and hypothyroidism. Am J Med. 1980;69:411.

97 Myerowitz PD. Diagnosis and management of the hypothyroid patient with chest pain. J Thorac Cardiovasc Surg. 1983;86:57.

98 Hay ID. Thyroxine therapy in hypothyroid patients undergoing coronary revascularization: a retrospective analysis. Ann Intern Med. 1981;95:456.

99 Doherty JE et al. Digoxin metabolism in hypo- and hyperthyroidism. Ann Intern Med. 1966;64:489.

100 Ladenson PW. Complications of surgery in hypothyroid patients. Am J Med. 1984;77:261.

101 Weinberg AD et al. Outcome of anesthesia and surgery in hypothyroid patients. Arch Intern Med. 1983;143:893.

102 Sawin CT et al. The aging thyroid: the use of thyroid hormone in older persons. JAMA. 1989;261:2653.

103 Robuschi G et al. Hypothyroidism in the elderly. Endocr Rev. 1987;8:142.

104 Isley WL. Thyroid dysfunction in the severely ill and the elderly. Forget the classic signs and symptoms. Postgrad Med. 1993;94:111,127.

105 Cooper DS et al. L-thyroxine therapy in subclinical hypothyroidism. Ann Intern Med. 1984;101:18.

106 Drinka PJ, Nolten WE. Subclinical hypothyroidism in the elderly: to treat or not to treat. Am J Med Sci. 1988; 295:125.

107 Nystrom E. A double-blind cross-over 12 month study of L-thyroxine treatment of women with "sub-clinical" hypothyroidism. Clin Endocrinol. 1988; 29:63.

108 Tachman ML, Guthrie GP Jr. Hypothyroidism: diversity of presentation. Endocr Rev. 1984;5:456.

109 Spaulding SW, Lippes H. Hyperthyroidism. Causes, clinical features, and

diagnosis. Med Clin North Am. 1985; 69:937.

110 Loeliger EA et al. The biological disappearance rate of prothrombin factors VII IX X from plasma in hypo- hyperand during fever. Thromb Diath Haemorrh. 1964;10:267.

111 Hansten PD. Oral anticoagulants and drugs which alter thyroid function. Drug Intell Clin Pharm. 1980;14:331.

112 Lipsky JJ, Gallego MO. Mechanism of thioamide antithyroid drug associated hypoprothrombinemia. Drug Metabol Drug Interact. 1988;6:317.

113 Liaw Y et al. Propylthiouracil induced hepatic injury. Ann Intern Med. 1993; 118:424.

114 Ozenne G et al. Carbimazole-induced acute cholestatic hepatitis. J Clin Gastroenterol. 1989;11:95.

115 Fong PC et al. Propylthiouracil hypersensitivity with circumstantial evidence for drug-induced reversible sensorineural deafness. A case report. Horm Res. 1991;35:132.

116 Vitug AC, Goldman JM. Hepatotoxicity from antithyroid drugs. Horm Res. 1985;21:229.

117 Romaldini JH et al. Comparison of effects of high and low dosage regimens of antithyroid drugs in the management of Graves' hyperthyroidism. J Clin Endocrinol Metab. 1983;57:563.

118 Frye RL, Braunwald E. Studies on digitalis III: the influence of triiodothyronine on digitalis requirement. Circulation. 1961;23:376.

119 Morrow DH et al. Studies on digitalis—influence of hyper- and hypothyroidism on the myocardial response to ouabain. J Pharmacol Exp Ther. 1963;140:324.

120 Clozel JP et al. Effects of propranolol and of verapamil on heart rate and blood pressure in hyperthyroidism. Clin Pharmacol Ther. 1984;36:64.

121 Nakazawa HK et al. Management of atrial fibrillation in the post-thyrotoxic state. Am J Med. 1982;72:903.

122 Woeber KA. Iodine and thyroid disease. Med Clin North Am. 1991;75: 169.

123 Becker CB, Gordon JM. Iodinated glycerol and thyroid dysfunction. Four cases and review of the literature. Chest. 1993;103:188.

124 Silva JE. Effects of iodine and iodine-containing compounds on thyroid function. Med Clin North Am. 1985;69: 881.

125 Fradkin JE, Wolff J. Iodide-induced thyrotoxicosis. Medicine (Baltimore). 1983;62:1.

126 Ross DS et al. Use of adjunctive potassium iodide after radioactive iodine (^{131}I) treatment of Graves' hyperthyroidism. J Clin Endocrinol Metab. 1983;57:250.

127 Friend DG. Iodide therapy and the importance of quantitating the dose. N Engl J Med. 1960;263:1358.

128 McDougall IR. Graves' disease. Current concepts. Med Clin North Am. 1991;75:79.

129 Cooper DS. Medical progress. Antithyroid drugs. N Engl J Med. 1984; 311:1353.

130 Wartofsky LW et al. Differences and similarities in the diagnosis and treatment of Graves' disease in Europe, Ja-

pan, and the United States. Thyroid. 1991;1:129.

131 Graham GD, Burman KD. Radioiodine treatment of Graves' disease. An assessment of its potential risks. Ann Intern Med. 1986;105:900.

132 Weber CA, Clark OH. Surgery for thyroid disease. Med Clin North Am. 1985;69:1097.

133 Hamburger J. Management of hyperthyroidism in children and adolescents. J Clin Endocrinol Metab. 1985;60: 1019.

134 Mansberger AR Jr. One hundred years of surgical management of hyperthyroidism. Ann Surg. 1988;207: 724.

135 Robertson J, Gorman CA. Gonadal radiation dose and its genetic significance in radioiodine therapy of hyperthyroidism. J Nucl Med. 1976;17:826.

136 Der-Chung S et al. Long-term treatment of Graves' hyperthyroidism with sodium ipodate. J Clin Endocrinol Metab. 1985;61:723.

137 Wu SY et al. Comparison of sodium ipodate (Oragrafin) and propylthiouracil in early treatment of hyperthyroidism. J Clin Endocrinol Metab. 1982;54: 630.

138 Martino E et al. Therapy of Graves' disease with sodium ipodate is associated with a high recurrence rate of hyperthyroidism. J Endocrinol Invest. 1991;14:847.

139 Berghout A et al. Sodium ipodate in the preparation of Graves' hyperthyroid patients for thyroidectomy. Horm Res. 1989;31:256.

140 Murakami M et al. Improvement of immunologic abnormalities associated with hyperthyroidism of Graves' disease during methimazole treatment. Horm Metab Res. 1988;20:235.

141 Teng CS, Yeung RTT. Changes in thyroid-stimulating antibody activity in Graves' disease treated with antithyroid drugs and its relationship to relapse: a prospective study. J Clin Endocrinol Metab. 1980;50:144.

142 Cooper DS. Which antithyroidal drug? Am J Med. 1986;80:1165.

143 Cooper DS. Propylthiouracil levels in patients unresponsive to large doses. Evidence of poor patient compliance. Ann Intern Med. 1985;102:328.

144 Roti E et al. Methimazole and serum thyroid hormone concentrations in hyperthyroid patients: effects of single and multiple daily doses. Ann Intern Med. 1989;111:181.

145 Shiroozu A et al. Treatment of hyperthyroidism with a small single daily dose of methimazole. J Clin Endocrinol Metab. 1986;63:125.

146 Greer MA et al. Treatment of hyperthyroidism with a single daily dose of propylthiouracil. N Engl J Med. 1965; 272:888.

147 Cooper DS et al. Methimazole pharmacology in man: studies using a newly developed radioimmunoassay for methimazole. J Clin Endocrinol Metab. 1984;58:473.

148 Jansson R et al. Intrathyroid concentrations of methimazole in patients with Graves' disease. J Clin Endocrinol Metab. 1983;57:129.

149 Allannic H et al. Antithyroid drugs and Graves' disease: a prospective randomized evaluation of the efficacy of

treatment duration. J Clin Endocrinol Metab. 1990;70:675.

150 Tamai H et al. Thioamide therapy in Graves' disease: relation of relapse rate to duration of therapy. Ann Intern Med. 1980;92:488.

151 Bouma DJ et al. Follow-up comparison of short term versus one year antithyroid drug therapy for the toxicosis of Graves' disease. J Clin Endocrinol Metab. 1982;64:1138.

152 Nijs HG et al. Increased insulin action and clearance in hyperthyroid newly diagnosed IDDM patient. Restoration to normal with antithyroid treatment. Diabetes Care. 1989;12:319.

153 Jap TS et al. Insulin secretion and sensitivity in hyperthyroidism. Horm Metab Res. 1989;21:261.

154 Carrasco MD et al. Cutaneous vasculitis associated with propylthiouracil therapy. Arch Intern Med. 1987;147: 1677.

155 Dolman KM et al. Vasculitis and antineutrophil cytoplasmic autoantibodies associated with propylthiouracil therapy. Lancet. 1993;342:651.

156 Snergy WJ, Caldwell DS. Polymyositis after propylthiouracil treatment for hyperthyroidism. Ann Rheum Dis. 1988;47:340.

157 Vasily DB, Tyler WB. Propylthiouracil-induced cutaneous vasculitis: case presentation and review of the literature. JAMA. 1980;23:458.

158 Geffner DL, Hershman JM. Beta-adrenergic blockade for the treatment of hyperthyroidism. Am J Med. 1992;93: 61.

159 Polikar R et al. The thyroid and the heart. Circulation. 1993;87:1435.

160 Feek CM et al. Combination of potassium iodide and propranolol in preparation of patients with Graves' disease for thyroid surgery. N Engl J Med. 1980;302:883.

161 Rubin PC. Beta blockers in pregnancy. N Engl J Med. 1981;305:1323.

162 Olson BR et al. Hyperthyroid myopathy and the response to treatment. Thyroid. 1991;1:137.

163 Milner MR et al. Double-blind crossover trial of diltiazem versus propranolol in the management of thyrotoxic symptoms. Pharmacotherapy. 1990;10: 100.

164 Roti E et al. The effect of diltiazem, a calcium channel-blocking drug, on cardiac rate and rhythm in hyperthyroid patients. Arch Intern Med. 1988;148: 1919.

165 Feely J. Clinical pharmacokinetics of beta-adrenoreceptor blocking drugs in thyroid disease. Clin Pharmacokinet. 1983;8:1.

166 Werner MC et al. Adverse effects related to thioamide drugs and their dose regimen. Am J Med Sci. 1989;297:216.

167 Tajiri J et al. Antithyroid drug-induced agranulocytosis. The usefulness of routine white blood cell count monitoring. Arch Intern Med. 1990;150: 621.

168 Cooper DS et al. Agranulocytosis associated with antithyroid drugs. Effects of patient age and drug dose. Ann Intern Med. 1983;98:26.

169 Tamai H et al. Methimazole-induced agranulocytosis in Japanese patients with Graves' disease. Clin Endocrinol. 1989;30:525.

170 **Wall JR et al.** In vitro immunosensitivity to propylthiouracil, methimazole, and carbimazole in patients with Graves' disease: a possible cause of antithyroid drug-induced agranulocytosis. J Clin Endocrinol Metab. 1984; 58:868.

171 **Tajiri J et al.** Granulocyte colony-stimulating factor treatment of antithyroid drug-induced granulocytopenia. Arch Intern Med. 1993;153:509.

172 **Heinrich B et al.** Methimazole-induced agranulocytosis and granulocyte-colony stimulating factor. Ann Intern Med. 1989;111:621.

173 **Hamada N et al.** Effect of corticosteroids in 10 cases of methimazole-induced agranulocytosis. Endocrinol Jpn. 1981;28:823.

174 **Gwinup G.** Prospective randomized comparison of propylthiouracil. JAMA. 1978;239:2457.

175 **Kammer H, Srinivasan K.** Use of antithyroid drugs in a single daily dose: treatment of diffuse toxic goiter. JAMA. 1969;209:1325.

176 **Reinwein D et al.** A prospective randomized trial of antithyroid drug dose in Graves' disease therapy. J Clin Endocrinol Metab. 1993;76:1516.

177 **Hashizume K et al.** Administration of thyroxine in treated Graves disease. Effects on the level of antibodies to thyroid-stimulating hormone receptors and on the risk of recurrence of hyperthyroidism. N Engl J Med. 1991;324: 947.

178 **Hedley AJ et al.** Antithyroid drugs in the treatment of hyperthyroidism of Graves' disease: long-term follow-up of 434 patients. Clin Endocrinol (Oxf). 1989;31:209.

179 **Lippe BM et al.** Hyperthyroidism in children treated with long-term medical therapy: twenty-five percent remission every two years. J Clin Endocrinol Metab. 1987;64:1241.

180 **Tamai H et al.** The mechanism of spontaneous hypothyroidism in patients with Graves' disease after antithyroidism drug treatment. J Clin Endocrinol Metab. 1987;64:718.

181 **Solomon BL et al.** Remission rates with antithyroid drug therapy: continuing influence of iodine intake? Ann Intern Med. 1987;107:510.

182 **Laurberg P et al.** Goiter size and outcome of medical treatment of Graves' disease. Acta Endocrinol (Copenh). 1986;111:39.

183 **Schleusener H et al.** Prospective multicentre study on the prediction of relapse after antithyroid drug treatment in patients with Graves' disease. Acta Endocrinol (Copenh). 1989;120:689.

184 **Allannic H et al.** A prospective study of the relationship between relapse of hyperthyroid Graves' disease after antithyroid drugs and HLA haplotype. J Clin Endocrinol Metab. 1983;57:719.

185 **Hamburger JI.** Diagnosis and management of Graves' disease in pregnancy. Thyroid. 1992;2:219.

186 **Amino N et al.** Aggravation of thyrotoxicosis in early pregnancy and after delivery in Graves' disease. J Clin Endocrinol Metab. 1982;55:108.

187 **Momotani N et al.** Effects of iodine on thyroid status of fetus versus mother in treatment of Graves' disease complicated by pregnancy. J Clin Endocrinol Metab. 1992;75:738.

188 **Mujtaba Q, Burrow GN.** Treatment of hyperthyroidism in pregnancy with propylthiouracil and methimazole. Obstet Gynecol. 1975;46:282.

189 **Momotani N et al.** Maternal hyperthyroidism and congenital malformation in the offspring. Clin Endocrinol (Oxf). 1984;20:695.

190 **Van Dijke CP et al.** Methimazole, carbimazole, and congenital skin defects. Ann Intern Med. 1987;106:60. Letter.

191 **Gardner DF et al.** Pharmacology of propylthiouracil (PTU) in pregnant hyperthyroid women: correlation of maternal PTU concentrations with cord serum thyroid function tests. J Clin Endocrinol Metab. 1986;62:217.

192 **Momotani N et al.** Antithyroid drug therapy for Graves' disease during pregnancy. Optimal regimen for fetal thyroid status. N Engl J Med. 1986; 315:24.

193 **Cheron RG et al.** Neonatal thyroid function after propylthiouracil therapy for maternal Graves' disease. N Engl J Med. 1981;304:525.

194 **Lamberg BA et al.** Treatment of maternal hyperthyroidism with antithyroid agents and changes in thyrotropin and thyroxine in the newborn. Acta Endocrinol (Copenh). 1981;97:186.

195 **Eisenstein A et al.** Intellectual capacity of subjects exposed to methimazole or propylthiouracil in utero. Euro J Pediatr. 1992;151:558.

196 **Burrow GN et al.** Intellectual development in children whose mothers received propylthiouracil during pregnancy. Yale J Biol Med. 1978;51:151.

197 **Ramsay I et al.** Thyrotoxicosis in pregnancy: results of treatment by antithyroid drugs combined with T4. Clin Endocrinol (Oxf). 1983;18:73.

198 **Momotani N et al.** Recovery from foetal hypothyroidism: evidence for the safety of breast feeding while taking propylthiouracil. Clin Endocrinol. 1989;31:591.

199 **McDermott MT et al.** Radioiodine-induced thyroid storm: case report and literature review. Am J Med. 1983;75: 353.

200 **Marcocci C et al.** A reappraisal of the role of methimazole and other factors on the efficacy and outcome of radioactive therapy of Graves' hyperthyroidism. J Endocrinol Invest. 1990;13: 513.

201 **Sawers JSA et al.** Transient hypothyroidism after iodine-131 treatment of thyrotoxicosis. J Clin Endocrinol Metab. 1980;50:226.

202 **Char DH.** The ophthalmopathy of Graves' disease. Med Clin North Am. 1991;75:97.

203 **Prummel MF, Wiersinga WM.** Smoking and the risk of Graves' disease. JAMA. 1993;269:479.

204 **Bartalena L et al.** Use of corticosteroids to prevent the progression of Graves' ophthalmopathy following radioactive iodine treatment for hyperthyroidism. N Engl J Med. 1989;321: 1349.

205 **Marcocci C et al.** Relationship between Graves' ophthalmopathy and type of treatment of Graves' hyperthyroidism. Thyroid. 1992;2:171.

206 **Bromberg N et al.** The evolution of Graves' ophthalmopathy during treatment with antithyroid drug alone and combined with triiodothyronine. J Endocrinol Invest. 1992;15:191.

207 **Raber JH.** The pharmacotherapy of thyroid storm. Drug Intell Clin Pharm. 1980;14:344.

208 **Nabil N et al.** Methimazole: an alternative route of administration. J Clin Endocrinol Metab. 1982;54:180.

209 **Walter RM Jr, Bartle WR.** Rectal administration of propylthiouracil in the treatment of Graves' disease. Am J Med. 1990;88:69.

210 **Salata R, Klein I.** Effects of lithium on the endocrine system. A review. J Lab Clin Med. 1987;110:130.

211 **Bocchetta A et al.** The course of thyroid abnormalities during lithium treatment: a two-year follow-up study. Acta Psychiatr Scand. 1992;86:38.

212 **Lombardi G et al.** Effects of lithium treatment on hypothalamic-pituitary-thyroid axis: a longitudinal study. J Endocrinol Invest. 1993;16:259.

213 **Vincent A et al.** Early onset of lithium-associated hypothyroidism. J Psychiatr Neurosci. 1993;18:74.

214 **Perrild H et al.** Thyroid function and ultrasonically determined thyroid size in patients receiving long-term lithium treatment. Am J Psychiatry. 1990;147: 1518.

215 **Pons F et al.** Lithium as an adjunct of I^{131} uptake when treating patients with well-differentiated thyroid carcinoma. Clin Nucl Med. 1987;12:644.

216 **Trip MD et al.** Incidence, predictability, and pathogenesis of amiodarone-induced thyrotoxicosis and hypothyroidism. Am J Med. 1991;91:507.

217 **Roti E et al.** Thyrotoxicosis followed by hypothyroidism in patients treated with amiodarone. A possible consequence of a destructive process in the thyroid. Arch Intern Med. 1993;153: 886.

218 **Martino E et al.** Treatment of amiodarone associated thyrotoxicosis by simultaneous administration of potassium perchlorate and methimazole. J Endocrinol Invest. 1986;9:201.

219 **Reichert JN, deRooy HAM.** Treatment of amiodarone-induced hyperthyroidism with potassium perchlorate and methimazole during amiodarone treatment. Br Med J (Clin Res). 1989;298: 1547.

220 **Brenan MD et al.** Amiodarone-associated thyrotoxicosis: experience with surgical management. Surgery. 1987; 102:1062.

221 **Greenspan FS.** The problem of the nodular goiter. Med Clin North Am. 1991;75:195.

222 **Maxon HR.** Radiation-induced thyroid disease. Med Clin North Am. 1985;69: 1049.

223 **Gharib HG et al.** Suppressive therapy with levothyroxine for solitary thyroid nodules. N Engl J Med. 1987;317:70.

Diabetes Mellitus

Mary Anne Koda-Kimble
Betsy A Carlisle

Definition and Classification (See Table 48.1) 48-2
    Type I diabetes (IDDM) 48-3
    Type II diabetes (NIDDM) 48-3
        Syndrome X (insulin resistance syndrome)
        (See Figure 48.1) 48-3
        Nonobese NIDDM 48-4
        Obese NIDDM 48-4
            Impaired insulin secretion 48-4
            Tissue resistance 48-4
            Hepatic glucose production 48-4
Carbohydrate Metabolism 48-4
    Postprandial glucose metabolism in the
        nondiabetic individual 48-4
    Fasting glucose metabolism in the
        nondiabetic individual 48-4
Signs and Symptoms 48-5
Diagnosis (See Table 48.2) 48-5
    Urine glucose 48-5
Long-Term Complications and their Relationship
    to Glucose Control 48-6
    Macrovascular disease 48-6
        Coronary heart disease 48-6
        Peripheral vascular disease (PVD) 48-6
    Ocular complications 48-6
    Nephropathy 48-6
    Neuropathy 48-7
        Autonomic neuropathy 48-7
Prevention 48-7
    Cyclosporine 48-7
    Nicotinamide 48-7
    Insulin prophylaxis 48-7
Treatment 48-7
    Diet 48-7
        Artificial sweeteners 48-8
        Alcohol 48-8
    Exercise 48-8
    Drugs 48-8
    Overall goals of therapy 48-8
Methods of Monitoring Glycemic Control 48-8
    Urine glucose tests 48-8
    Fasting plasma glucose (FPG) 48-8
    Home blood glucose monitoring (HBGM) 48-9
    Glycosylated hemoglobin (HbA$_{1c}$)
    (See Table 48.5) 48-9
        Clinical use 48-10
    Fructosamine 48-10
Insulin 48-10
    Types of Insulin (See Table 48.6) 48-10
    Absorption, Distribution, and Elimination 48-10
    Time Course of Activity
    (See Tables 48.7 to 48.9) 48-11
        Short-acting insulins 48-11
        Intermediate-acting insulins 48-12
        Long-acting insulins 48-12
    Insulin Immunogenicity 48-12
        Purity 48-12
        Species source: beef, pork, and human 48-12

Human Insulin 48-12
    Technology 48-12
    Pharmacokinetics 48-12
Insulin Concentration 48-12
Treatment of Type I Diabetes:
Clinical Use of Insulin 48-13
    Treatment Goals (See Table 48.10) 48-13
    Intensive Insulin Therapy
    (See Tables 48.11 and 48.12) 48-14
        Insulin pumps 48-14
            Continuous subcutaneous insulin infusion 48-15
        Multiple daily injections
        (See Tables 48.13 to 48.15) 48-15
    Clinical Use of Insulin 48-16
        Agitation 48-17
        Measurement 48-17
        Injection 48-18
        Rotation of injection sites 48-18
        Home blood glucose testing
        (See Tables 48.16 to 48.21) 48-18
        Stability of mixed insulins 48-21
            NPH-regular 48-21
            Lente-regular 48-21
            Phosphate-buffered regular-lente 48-22
        Evaluating fasting hyperglycemia 48-22
            Somogyi effect 48-23
        Midmorning hyperglycemia 48-23
        Supplementary insulin doses 48-23
            Compensatory insulin doses 48-24
            Anticipatory insulin supplements 48-24
        Sick day management (See Table 48.22) 48-24
        Dawn phenomenon 48-24
    Adverse Effects of Insulin 48-25
        Hyperinsulinemia 48-25
        Insulin reactions: defective counterregulation 48-25
        Signs and symptoms/treatment of hypoglycemia .. 48-26
            Simple sugars (See Table 48.23) 48-26
            Glucagon 48-27
        Dermatologic complications of insulin 48-27
            Lipoatrophy 48-27
            Lipohypertrophy 48-27
            Local skin reactions (See Table 48.24) 48-27
            Dose change with switch to a human insulin 48-28
    Insulin Stability 48-28
            Flocculation 48-28
            Temperature 48-28
Factors Altering Response to Insulin 48-29
Exercise and Insulin Requirements
    (See Table 48.25) 48-29
Insulin Requirements in Renal Failure 48-29
Sliding Scale Method of Insulin Dosing 48-30
    Perioperative management 48-30
    Bedside glucose measurement 48-31
Honeymoon Period 48-31
Alternate Routes of Administration 48-32

(Continued)

Injection aids 48-32
Jet injectors 48-32
Automatic injection aids 48-32
Pen injectors 48-32
External insulin infusion pumps
(See Question 3) 48-32
Implantable insulin infusion pumps 48-32
Intranasal insulin 48-32

Immunotherapy and Pancreatic Transplants 48-32
Pancreatic transplants 48-32
Islet cell transplantation 48-33
Immunosuppressive therapy 48-33

Diabetic Ketoacidosis (DKA) 48-33
Treatment 48-34
Fluids 48-34
Sodium 48-34
Potassium 48-34
Phosphate therapy 48-34
Insulin 48-34
Insulin adsorption 48-35
Sodium bicarbonate 48-35

Oral Hypoglycemic Agents 48-36
Biguanides 48-36
Sulfonylureas 48-36
Mechanism of action 48-36
Pancreatic effects 48-36
Extrapancreatic effects 48-36
First- and second-generation sulfonylureas
(See Table 48.26) 48-36
Pharmacokinetics of sulfonylureas 48-37
Tolbutamide 48-38
Chlorpropamide 48-38
Acetohexamide 48-38
Tolazamide 48-38
Glipizide 48-38
Glyburide 48-38
Pharmacokinetic drug interactions
(See Table 48.27) 48-38

Treatment of Patients with NIDDM 48-39
Clinical Presentation 48-39
Urine Glucose Tests 48-40
Clinical Use of Sulfonylureas 48-40
Contraindications 48-41
Secondary failure 48-41
Insulin in Patients with NIDDM 48-41
Combined use of oral sulfonylureas and insulin ...48-42
Premixed regular and NPH insulin 48-42
Cost-saving measures 48-43
Reuse of insulin syringes 48-43
Strip splitting 48-43

Adverse Effects of the Sulfonylureas 48-43
Gastrointestinal Effects 48-43
Hematologic Effects 48-43
Miscellaneous Adverse Effects 48-43

Dermatologic Reactions 48-43
Syndrome of Inappropriate ADH (SIADH) 48-44
Hepatotoxicity 48-44
Cardiovascular Effects 48-44
Hypoglycemia 48-44
Sulfonylurea Use in Special Situations 48-45
Renal Dysfunction 48-45
Hepatic Dysfunction 48-45
Diabetes in the Elderly (See Table 48.28) 48-45
Treatment of Diabetic Complications 48-46
Painful Diabetic Peripheral Neuropathy (DPN)
(See Table 48.29) 48-46
Tight glycemic control 48-47
Aldose reductase inhibitors (ARIs) 48-47
Simple analgesics 48-47
Psychotropic drugs 48-47
Carbamazepine 48-48
Other agents 48-48
Capsaicin treatment 48-48
Diabetic Gastroparesis 48-48
Metoclopramide 48-49
Cisapride 48-49
Erythromycin 48-49
Metoclopramide side effects 48-50
Hypertension (See Table 48.30) 48-50
Diuretics 48-50
Beta-adrenergic blockers 48-51
Central and peripheral sympatholytic agents 48-51
Vasodilators 48-52
ACE inhibitors 48-52
Calcium channel antagonists 48-52
Alpha-adrenergic antagonists 48-52
Diabetic Nephropathy 48-52
Coronary Heart Disease (See Table 48.31) 48-53
Bile acid sequestrants 48-54
Fibric acid derivatives 48-54
HMG-CoA reductase inhibitors 48-54
Niacin 48-54
Drug-Induced Hyperglycemia (See Table 48.32) ..48-54
Sympathomimetics 48-54
Corticosteroids 48-54
Drug-Induced Hypoglycemia (See Table 48.33) 48-55
Decreased Carbohydrate Intake 48-55
Age 48-56
Renal Failure 48-56
Hepatic Dysfunction 48-56
Ethanol 48-56
Salicylates 48-56
Hypoglycemic effects 48-56
Antiplatelet effects 48-57
Pentamidine 48-57
Quinine 48-57
Ritodrine and Other Betamimetic Agents 48-58
Nonspecific Beta Blocking Agents 48-58

Definition and Classification

Diabetes is a syndrome that is caused by a relative or an absolute lack of insulin. Clinically, it is characterized by symptomatic glucose intolerance as well as alterations in lipid and protein metabolism. Over the long term, these metabolic abnormalities—particularly hyperglycemia—contribute to the development of complications such as retinopathy, nephropathy, and neuropathy. There is considerable evidence that, clinically and genetically, diabetes is a heterogeneous group of disorders.

Diabetes mellitus is a major public health problem in the U.S.; there are approximately 13 million patients with diabetes, of whom one-half are diagnosed. This represents about 5.2% of the population. The prevalence of Type I diabetes (insulin-dependent diabetes mellitus or IDDM) is 160 per 100,000 population; the prevalence of Type II diabetes (noninsulin-dependent diabetes mellitus or NIDDM) is approximately 6670 per 100,000 population. The prevalence of Type II diabetes is higher in blacks, Hispanics, Native Americans, and women.

Compared to the general population, the mortality rate for persons who develop diabetes before age 15 is 11 times greater; it is two to three times greater for individuals whose diabetes is diagnosed after age 40. Both the incidence and prevalence of diabetes increase dramatically with age. For example, the prevalence of "self-reported diabetes" is 1.6% among persons 18 to 34 years of age and 12.5% among persons 65 and 74 years of age.[2] In the U.S., diabetes is present in almost 17% of the white population 65 to 74 years of age. Gestational diabetes occurs in approximately 2% to 4% of pregnant women in the U.S.

Approximately $90 billion are spent each year for both direct and indirect costs of diabetes. In 1992, the direct costs for medical care were about $45 billion, $37 billion of which represented inpatient care and $1.2 billion of which represented outpatient prescription drugs. Thus, considerable effort has been directed toward early diagnosis and metabolic control of patients with diabetes in an effort to prevent or minimize the complications of this condition.[1-3]

The National Diabetes Data Group classifies diabetes on the basis of its clinical presentation (see Table 48.1).[4] However, because the precise pathophysiology of this condition is poorly understood, patients may present with characteristics which typify both Type I and Type II disease.

Type I Diabetes (IDDM)

Approximately 5% to 10% of the diabetic population has Type I diabetes [insulin-dependent diabetes mellitus (IDDM)]. At clinical presentation, these patients have little or no pancreatic reserve, have a tendency to develop ketoacidosis, and require exogenous insulin to sustain life. Symptoms generally develop over one to two months or over a few days. Although the onset appears to be abrupt, evidence now exists for a several-year-long preclinical period during which immune markers in Type I diabetes can be detected. Children 10 to 14 years of age have the highest incidence of Type I diabetes, although the age at onset can occur between 9

months and 28 years of age. In adults, the incidence of Type I diabetes peaks in the fifth decade. This form of diabetes is associated closely with certain histocompatibility antigens (HLA-DR3 or HLA-DR4) and the presence of circulating islet cell antibodies.[5,6]

Within days or weeks following the initial diagnosis, many Type I diabetic patients experience an apparent remission which is reflected by decreased blood glucose concentrations and markedly decreased insulin requirements. This is called the "honeymoon period" because it only lasts for a few months. During this time, patients should be maintained on insulin even if the dose is very low, since interrupted treatment is associated with a greater incidence of resistance and allergy to insulin. (See Question 23.)

Type II Diabetes (NIDDM)

Individuals with Type II diabetes [noninsulin-dependent diabetes mellitus (NIDDM)] comprise approximately 90% of the diabetic population. Unlike persons with Type I diabetes, these patients retain some pancreatic reserve and generally can be treated with diet, exercise, and oral agents. Nevertheless, a considerable number of these individuals eventually may require insulin for control of their symptoms.

Syndrome X (Insulin Resistance Syndrome). Patients with Type II diabetes are characterized predominantly by resistance to the action of insulin rather than an absolute insulin deficiency. A strong association has been observed between Type II diabetes and a variety of disorders including obesity, atherosclerosis, hyperlipidemia, and hypertension (see Figure 48.1).[7] This relationship was investigated by Dr. Gerald Reaven who refers to this association as Syndrome X or *insulin resistance syndrome*.[8] In the presence of insulin resistance, glucose utilization by tissues is impaired and excess glucose accumulates in the circulation. This hyperglycemia stimulates the pancreas to produce more insulin in an effort to overcome the insulin resistance. The simultaneous elevation of both glucose and insulin is strongly suggestive of the presence of insulin resistance.

Either the insulin resistance itself or the compensatory hyperinsulinemia that results from insulin resistance may be the fundamental underlying pathophysiologic process responsible for the

Table 48.1		Type I and Type II Diabetes
Characteristics	Type I	Type II
Other Names	Insulin-dependent diabetes mellitus (IDDM); previously, juvenile-onset diabetes mellitus	Noninsulin-dependent diabetes mellitus (NIDDM); previously, adult onset diabetes mellitus
Percent of Diabetic Population	5%–10%	90%
Age at Onset	Usually <30 yr; peaks at 12–14 yr; rare before 6 mon; some adults develop Type I during the 5th decade	Usually >40 yr
Pancreatic Function	Usually none, although some residual C-peptide can sometimes be detected at diagnosis, especially in adults	Insulin present in low, "normal," or high amounts
Pathogenesis	Associated with certain HLA types; presence of islet cell antibodies suggests autoimmune process	Defect in insulin secretion; tissue resistance to insulin; ↑ hepatic glucose output
Family History	Generally not strong	Strong
Obesity	Uncommon unless "overinsulinized"	Common (60%–90%)
History of Ketoacidosis	Often present	Rare, except in circumstances of unusual stress
Clinical Presentation	Moderate to severe symptoms which generally progress relatively rapidly (days–weeks): polyuria, polydipsia, fatigue, weight loss, ketoacidosis	Mild polyuria, fatigue; often diagnosed on routine physical or dental examination
Treatment	Insulin Diet Exercise	Diet Exercise Sulfonylureas Biguanides (metformin is the only agent available in the US) Insulin

Fig 48.1 Syndrome of insulin resistance depicting the metabolic cascade beginning with acquired (obesity) or inherited [non-insulin-dependent diabetes mellitus (NIDDM)] insulin resistance leading to hyperinsulinemia and eventual hypertension, dyslipidemia, and atherosclerosis. Reprinted with permission from reference 7.

frequent occurrence of these diseases in the same patient.[9] The concept of a single defect explaining this cluster of disorders is the subject of considerable discussion and research activity.

The onset of Type II diabetes is gradual, and symptoms generally are mild. Because these patients have sufficient insulin concentrations to prevent lipolysis, there is usually no history of ketosis except in situations of unusual stress (e.g., infections or trauma). There is a stronger family history of diabetes in this group than in individuals with Type I diabetes. Circulating islet cell antibodies are absent, and there is no association with certain human lymphocyte antigen (HLA) types.[10]

Patients with NIDDM exhibit varying degrees of tissue resistance to insulin, impaired insulin secretion, and increased basal hepatic glucose production. Subclassifications of these patients have been suggested based upon weight, age of onset, and insulin levels. The most commonly used division of this class of diabetic patients is based upon weight.[4,11]

Nonobese NIDDM. This group comprises approximately 10% of the Type II diabetic population. Typically, they develop a mild form of diabetes during childhood, adolescence, or as young adults (usually <25 years of age) and their insulin levels are low in response to a glucose challenge. Included in this group are patients with *maturity onset diabetes of the young (MODY)*. This form of diabetes is associated with a strong family history which suggests an autosomal dominant transmission. At presentation, symptoms may be moderate to severe with or without ketosis. However, unlike Type I diabetes, the disease generally is mild and controlled easily with low doses of insulin (<40 U), diet, or oral agents. This form of diabetes can be associated with a low prevalence of diabetic complications. Many individuals with this form of diabetes may be classified erroneously as having Type I diabetes based upon age at onset. A mild form of diabetes which is controlled easily in a young adult who has a strong family history of diabetes is strongly suggestive of MODY. The pathogenesis and heterogeneous nature of MODY have been reviewed extensively.[12]

Obese NIDDM. Obese individuals with noninsulin-dependent diabetes constitute the majority of the diabetic population and 60% to 90% of the Type II diabetic population. Although this is the most common form of diabetes, its pathogenesis is the least understood. As noted above, patients with NIDDM have defects in insulin secretion, tissue responsiveness to insulin, and hepatic glucose production.[10]

Impaired Insulin Secretion. Although basal levels of insulin may be normal or high in this population, pulsatile insulin delivery is absent, the beta cell loses its ability to respond to elevated glucose concentrations, and first- or early-phase insulin release in response to glucose often is reduced. Furthermore, in patients with severe hyperglycemia, the amount of insulin secreted in response to glucose is diminished.[156]

Tissue Resistance. Most patients also exhibit decreased tissue responsiveness to insulin. Increasing evidence suggests that decreased peripheral glucose uptake and utilization in muscle is the primary site of insulin resistance. This resistance may be secondary to decreased numbers of insulin receptors on the cell surface or defects in insulin action which follows receptor binding. The latter have been termed ''postreceptor'' or ''postbinding'' defects. The causes of these defects are unknown, but they must be related to the degree of metabolic abnormality, since they may be reversed with improved glycemic control.

Hepatic Glucose Production. In many patients with NIDDM, hepatic glucose production also is increased; this defect correlates with the level of fasting hyperglycemia. Theoretically, overeating stimulates secretion of large amounts of insulin which, in turn, ''down-regulates'' or decreases the number of insulin receptors on the surface of the target organ. This leads to insulin resistance and, when the pancreas is unable to secrete sufficient insulin to overcome tissue resistance, hyperglycemia. Since high insulin levels cause hunger and promote lipogenesis, the obese patient with diabetes often finds himself in a vicious cycle which can be broken only through decreased caloric intake and weight loss.

Carbohydrate Metabolism

An understanding of the signs and symptoms associated with diabetes is based upon a knowledge of glucose metabolism and the metabolic effects of insulin in diabetic and nondiabetic subjects during the fed (postprandial) and fasting (postabsorptive) states.

Homeostatic mechanisms maintain blood glucose concentrations between 60 and 160 mg/dL. A minimum concentration of 40 to 60 mg/dL is required to provide adequate fuel for the central nervous system (CNS), which uses glucose as its primary energy source and is independent of insulin for glucose utilization. When blood glucose concentrations exceed the reabsorptive capacity of the kidneys ($\approx$180 mg/dL), glucose spills into the urine resulting in a loss of calories and water. Muscle and fat also use glucose as a major source of energy, but these tissues require insulin. If glucose is unavailable, these tissues are able to use other substrates such as amino acids and fatty acids for fuel.

Postprandial Glucose Metabolism in the Nondiabetic Individual

After food is ingested, blood glucose concentrations rise and stimulate insulin release. Insulin is the key to efficient glucose utilization. It promotes the uptake of glucose, fatty acids, and amino acids and their conversion to storage forms in most tissues. In muscle, insulin promotes the uptake of glucose and its storage as glycogen. It also stimulates the uptake of amino acids and their conversion to protein. In adipose tissue, glucose is converted to free fatty acids and stored as triglycerides. Insulin also prevents a breakdown of these triglycerides to free fatty acids, a form which may be transported to other tissues for utilization. The liver does not require insulin for glucose transport, but insulin facilitates the conversion of glucose to glycogen.

Fasting Glucose Metabolism in the Nondiabetic Individual

As blood glucose concentrations drop toward normal during the fasting state, insulin release is inhibited. Simultaneously, a number of counterregulatory hormones which oppose the effect of insulin and promote an increase in blood sugar are released (glucagon, epinephrine, growth hormone, and glucocorticoids). As a result, several processes maintain a minimum blood glucose concentration for the CNS. Glycogen in the liver is broken down into glucose (glycogenolysis); amino acids are transported from muscle to liver where they are converted to glucose through gluconeogenesis; there is a diminished uptake of glucose by insulin-dependent tissues to conserve glucose for the brain; and finally, triglycerides are broken down into free fatty acids which are used as alternative fuel sources.

Signs and Symptoms

In a patient with diabetes, blood glucose concentrations remain high after a meal because the uptake, utilization, and storage of glucose by adipose tissue and muscle are diminished secondary to an absolute or relative lack of insulin. Because glucose is inaccessible to cells (even though blood glucose concentrates are high), fasting metabolism is triggered. This further increases blood glucose concentrations through glycogenolysis and gluconeogenesis. If glucose concentrations exceed the renal threshold, glucose spills into the urine, taking water with it by the process of osmosis. As a result of the loss of calories and water, patients experience symptoms of polyuria, polydipsia, fatigue, and profound weight loss despite normal or excessive food intake (polyphagia). Since glucose provides an excellent medium for microorganisms, patients with diabetes also may present with recurrent respiratory, vaginal, and other infections. Muscle begins to metabolize glycogen for fuel, and the liver begins to metabolize free fatty acids which are released in response to epinephrine and low insulin concentrations. An absolute lack of insulin may cause excessive mobilization of free fatty acids to the liver, where they are metabolized to ketones. This can result in ketonemia, ketonuria, and ultimately, ketoacidosis. Patients with high blood glucose concentrations also may experience blurred vision secondary to osmotically induced changes in the lens of the eye.

It should be emphasized that weight loss and ketoacidosis primarily occur in poorly controlled Type I (IDDM) diabetic individuals. Persons with NIDDM frequently have mild symptoms related to elevated blood glucose concentrations (fatigue, polyuria, vaginal infections) but rarely develop ketoacidosis because insulin is present in sufficient amounts to suppress lipolysis. Furthermore, weight loss is uncommon in these individuals because relatively high endogenous insulin levels promote lipogenesis.

Diagnosis

It is relatively simple to diagnose diabetes in individuals who present with the classic signs and symptoms and have a plasma glucose concentration of 200 mg/dL or higher. The diagnosis is more confusing in those patients who are asymptomatic but have glucosuria or hyperglycemia on routine examination. In these individuals, the diagnosis is based upon the efficiency with which they utilize glucose following the ingestion of a standard glucose load [Oral Glucose Tolerance Test (OGTT)]. Various groups, including the World Health Organization and National Diabetes Data Group, have established criteria for the diagnosis of diabetes based upon the OGTT. The criteria developed by the National Diabetes Data Group[4] have been adopted by the American Diabetes Association (ADA) (see Table 48.2). For nonpregnant individuals of any age, a diagnosis of diabetes can be made if at least one of the following is present:

- The patient presents with classical signs and symptoms of diabetes (polyuria, polydipsia, ketonuria, rapid weight loss)

Table 48.2	Normal and Diabetic Plasma[a] Glucose Levels in mg/dL (mmol/L) for the Oral Glucose Tolerance Test		
	Fasting	½, 1, 1½ hr	2 hr
Normal	<115 (6.4)	<200 (11)	<140 (7.8)
Impaired Glucose Tolerance (IGT)	<140 (7.8)	≥200 (11)	140–200 (7.8–11)
Diabetes (Non-pregnant adult)	≥140 (7.8)	≥200 (11)	≥200 (11)

[a] Equivalent *venous whole blood* glucose concentrations are ≈12%–15% lower. *Arterial* samples are higher than venous samples postprandially because glucose has not yet been removed from peripheral tissues. *Capillary whole blood* samples contain a mixture of arterial and venous blood. Fasting levels will be equivalent to whole blood venous samples. One hour following a 100 gm glucose load, capillary samples may be 30–40 mg/dL higher than venous samples.

and has an unequivocally high fasting (≥140 mg/dL) or random (≥200 mg/dL) venous plasma glucose concentration.

- A fasting plasma glucose concentration is greater than or equal to 140 mg/dL on two or more occasions.

- Following a standard oral glucose challenge (75 gm glucose for an adult or 1.75 gm/kg for a child), the venous plasma glucose concentration is greater than or equal to 200 mg/dL at two hours and greater than 200 mg/dL at least one other time in between (0.5, 1, 1.5 hr).

Individuals with fasting plasma glucose values or OGTT values that are intermediate between normal and those considered diagnostic of diabetes are considered to have ''*impaired glucose tolerance*.'' (see Table 48.2). These individuals are not given the diagnosis of diabetes since this can have broad social, psychological, and economic implications.

Many factors can impair glucose tolerance or increase plasma glucose, and these must be eliminated as a source of abnormal results before a firm diagnosis of diabetes is made. For example, an individual who has not fasted for a minimum of ten hours may have an elevated fasting plasma glucose; one who has fasted too long (>16 hr) or has ingested insufficient carbohydrates before testing may have an impaired glucose tolerance. Patients who are tested for glucose tolerance during or soon after an acute illness (e.g., a myocardial infarction) may be diagnosed improperly because of the presence of high concentrations of counterregulatory hormones which increase glucose concentrations; glucose tolerance often returns to normal in these individuals. Pregnancy, other forms of stress, and lack of physical activity can affect the glucose tolerance similarly. Many drugs may alter glucose tolerance due to their effects upon insulin release and tissue response to insulin and through direct cytotoxic effects upon the pancreas. These are discussed in more detail in Questions 67, 73, and 75 and listed in Table 48.32. Drugs and other chemicals also may falsely elevate the plasma glucose concentrations through interference with specific analytical methods. A detailed list of factors which may alter oral glucose test results can be found in reference 4.

Urine Glucose

The measurement of glucose in the urine may be used to screen individuals for diabetes, but its presence is not diagnostic because glucosuria may occur when the renal threshold for glucose is decreased (as in pregnancy) or when there are other sugars and interfering substances in the urine.[4] Conversely, the absence of glucose in the urine does not rule out diabetes in individuals with elevated renal thresholds (e.g., the elderly). The use of urine glucose as a monitoring tool is discussed later in this introduction and in Question 42.

Long-Term Complications and their Relationship to Glucose Control

The longer-term sequelae of diabetes account for the majority of the morbidity and mortality in the diabetic population. The relationship between hyperglycemia and the development of chronic microvascular diabetes complications such as retinopathy, nephropathy, and neuropathy has been debated for years. Theoretically, tight blood glucose control should reduce complications in Type I diabetes if the underlying cause is hyperglycemia; however, results from individual studies have been inconsistent. A meta-analysis of 16 short-term, randomized trials revealed intensive blood glucose control significantly reduced the risk of diabetic retinopathy and nephropathy progression.[13]

Results of the Diabetes Complications and Control Trial (DCCT) definitively established that intensive treatment of IDDM can prevent or slow the onset of long-term diabetes complications including retinopathy, nephropathy, and neuropathy.[14] The DCCT, a multicenter, randomized study involving 1441 Type I diabetic patients aged 13 to 39 years was designed to determine whether the complications of diabetes could be reduced or prevented with intensive insulin therapy aimed at achieving euglycemia. Patients were randomized to receive conventional therapy versus intensive insulin therapy and followed for a mean of 6.5 years. Patients in the conventional treatment group received one to two insulin injections per day, performed daily blood glucose monitoring, and returned to clinic every three months. Patients in the intensive treatment group were initiated on insulin in the hospital. They were given three or more insulin injections per day or used an insulin pump, performed blood glucose tests four or more times per day, and had weekly to monthly clinic visits.

Intensive treatment reduced the risk of clinically meaningful retinopathy by 34% to 76% and neuropathy by 60%. The development of microalbuminuria decreased by 39% and clinical grade albuminuria by 54%. Thus, patients treated with intensive therapy experienced a significant decrease in the incidence of long-term microvascular complications.

Patients with NIDDM were not studied; however, the American Diabetes Association believes analogous results can be achieved in this group by striving for goals similar to intensive treatment while considering age, capabilities, and concurrent disease states.[15]

Macrovascular Disease

Compared to the general population, macrovascular disease (coronary heart disease, stroke, and peripheral vascular disease) occurs at an earlier age and with greater frequency in patients with diabetes. However, approximately 20% to 25% of all patients with diabetes never develop severe macrovascular complications. On this basis, some believe that the propensity for developing these complications is to some extent genetically determined.

Coronary heart disease is the leading cause of premature death in the Type II population. Among males and females who were 40 to 45 years of age at the time of diagnosis, 42% of males and 39% of females died from coronary heart disease by age 70. Comparable figures for those without diabetes were 23% for males and 10% for females. Thus, the lower prevalence for heart disease normally observed in women is eliminated by diabetes.[16,17] These sobering figures point to the importance of minimizing or eliminating all other preventable risk factors for cardiovascular disease in patients

with diabetes (i.e., smoking, hypertension, hypercholesterolemia, obesity) through the prescription of exercise, diet, and appropriate medications.[18]

Peripheral vascular disease (PVD) can cause intermittent claudication, skin ulcers, and gangrene. One-half of all nontraumatic amputations are performed in patients with diabetes. PVD occurs in 16% to 58% of the diabetic population, approximately four times that of the nondiabetic population. The prevalence of this condition increases with age, duration of diabetes, and the presence of risk factors such as hypertension or smoking.[16,19,20]

Signs and symptoms of peripheral vascular disease include leg pain, which is relieved by rest; cold feet; nocturnal leg pain, which is relieved by dangling the feet over the bed or walking; absent pulses; loss of hair on the foot and toes; and gangrene. Treatment of this condition includes elimination and treatment of risk factors such as smoking, hypertension, and hyperglycemia; exercise, the mainstay of therapy; and surgery.[18] Vasodilator drugs and antiplatelet agents[21] have not been effective, but pentoxifylline (Trental), a hemorheological agent, may improve walking distance and rest pain.[22] Patients should be thoroughly educated regarding proper foot care.

Ocular Complications

Ocular disorders related to diabetes are the leading cause of new cases of legal blindness in Americans, 5800 of whom become blind each year from the disease.[16] Patients with diabetes may experience blurred vision associated with poor diabetic control. They also may develop senile-type cataracts at an early age and a type of glaucoma which is relatively resistant to treatment. The most common ocular complication, however, is diabetic retinopathy, which usually appears after 15 to 20 years and may occur in up to 80% of diabetic individuals. Current theories addressing the possible causes of this complication have been thoroughly reviewed.[23] Microvascular disease characterized by thickening of the capillary membrane may be the underlying lesion for two forms of retinopathy. The first and most common presentation is a *nonproliferative retinopathy* characterized by microaneurysms which may progress to hard yellow exudates, signifying chronic leakage; retinal edema; and punctate hemorrhage. This form of retinopathy may be associated with loss of central vision, but generally is associated with an excellent visual prognosis. Focal laser photocoagulation of the retina in patients with nonproliferative diabetic retinopathy and macular edema decreases the likelihood of visual loss by 50%.[24]

A second, less common presentation is *proliferative retinopathy*. This form is characterized by neovascularization (presumably due to retinal hypoxia) and occurs in approximately 45% of people with Type I diabetes and in 15% of people with Type II diabetes who have had the disease for 15 years. Neovascularization ultimately leads to fibrosis, vitreous hemorrhage, and retinal detachment. Photocoagulation therapy may arrest progression and decrease loss of vision associated with neovascularization.[24,25] Since hypertension, smoking, uremia, and perhaps, hyperglycemia may lead to more rapid progression of the retinopathy, every effort should be made to eliminate these risk factors.

Nephropathy

Diabetic nephropathy, characterized by nephrotic syndrome and azotemia, accounts for 30% of all patients with end-stage renal disease and is a major cause of death in patients with Type I diabetes.[26] Treatment consists of early detection through screening for microalbuminuria and correction of existing hypertension which can accelerate deterioration of renal function. The management of diabetes in a patient with microalbuminuria is considered in Question 69. The management of end-stage renal disease is discussed in Chapter 29: Acute Renal Failure and Chapter 30: Chronic Renal Failure.

Neuropathy

Diabetic neuropathy may be a consequence of metabolic disturbances in the neurons or secondary to microangiopathy affecting the capillary supply to neurons. Clinically, the neuropathy presents as a peripheral neuritis or autonomic insufficiency. Symptomatic *peripheral neuropathy* may occur in 25% of patients with diabetes. It is characterized by paresthesia and pain in the lower extremities which may be mild or severe and unrelenting; decreased vibration sense; decreased ankle and knee jerks; and decreased nerve conduction velocity. The decreased sensation associated with peripheral neuropathy contributes to the progression of foot injuries and infections which may go unnoticed by the patient until they are severe.[27] The treatment of painful peripheral neuropathy is considered in Questions 61 through 63.

Autonomic neuropathy may present as gastroparesis with the feeling of fullness and nausea (see Question 64); urinary retention; impotence in males (manifested as retrograde ejaculation or an inability to attain an erection); postural hypotension; and diarrhea with incontinence of stool.[27] The presence of autonomic insufficiency may have profound effects on the patient's response to vasodilating drugs and ability to counteract hypoglycemia.

Prevention

Because the clinical symptoms of Type I diabetes mellitus are the overt expression of an insidious pathogenic process that begins years earlier, investigators are focusing attention on strategies that alter the natural history of the disease. First-degree relatives of individuals with Type I diabetes mellitus are at an increased risk of developing the disease and can be identified by the appearance of immune markers which may herald the disease by many years.[6] This has led to attempts at immune intervention at the prediabetes stage.

Cyclosporine

Studies using cyclosporine in patients with new-onset diabetes have demonstrated its effect on the preservation of beta-cell function; however, responses have been transient (see Question 33). Cyclosporine has been used in two subjects before the clinical onset of diabetes and both subjects demonstrated improvement in beta cell function.[28,29] However, potential nephrotoxicity is a major concern with cyclosporine usage.

Nicotinamide

Nicotinamide is thought to serve as a free radical scavenger, thereby limiting DNA and beta-cell damage. Oral nicotinamide (150 to 300 mg/yr of age/day) was administered to 14 children with prediabetes.[30] The evolution of diabetes was compared to eight untreated historical controls. After 30 months of follow-up, 5 of the 14 patients in the nicotinamide group had developed diabetes versus all of the eight untreated subjects.

Insulin Prophylaxis

Insulin prophylaxis may provide beta-cell rest, making beta cells less susceptible to immune attack. In one study,[31] insulin therapy was given to five first-degree relatives with prediabetes consisting of a five-day course of intravenous (IV) insulin every nine months combined with daily, low-dose subcutaneous insulin. Seven patients with prediabetes who were offered treatment but declined therapy served as a control group. Diabetes developed in six of the seven untreated comparison subjects versus only one of the five treated patients.

In 1994, the National Institutes of Health (NIH) announced it would undertake a large-scale clinical trial examining the effectiveness of insulin prophylaxis in individuals identified as being predisposed to develop Type I diabetes within five years. Ten diabetes centers nationwide are currently recruiting 830 relatives of patients with Type I diabetes to be screened for the presence of two specific antibodies associated with eventual development of IDDM. The study will be conducted over five to seven years.

The ultimate goal of these efforts is to prevent the development of overt Type I diabetes mellitus in those individuals identified as being at risk for developing the disease while utilizing strategies that are both safe and specific. Studies to date have failed to demonstrate a clear clinical benefit of such intervention since what has been achieved thus far, regardless of the immunotherapeutic agent used, is a prolongation of the "honeymoon period" (see Question 31). It also must be kept in mind that prediction for the development of clinical diabetes must be accurate to avoid the possibility of exposing an individual to risks inherent in any preventative intervention. An extensive review of strategies to prevent Type I diabetes is provided in reference 6.

Treatment

There are three major components to the treatment of diabetes: diet, drugs (insulin and oral hypoglycemic agents), and exercise. Each of these components interacts with the others to the extent that no assessment and modification of one can be made without a knowledge of the other two.

Diet

Diet plays a crucial role in the therapy of all individuals with diabetes. The American Diabetes Association's recommendations for a diabetic diet reflect new information regarding the differential glycemic effects of carbohydrates, the effect of fibers on carbohydrate absorption, and the effect of diet on cardiovascular disease.[32] The goals of a diabetic diet are:

- To provide adequate calories to maintain normal growth and development of a young diabetic and ideal body weight (IBW) in other patients with diabetes. For obese Type II diabetes, this means a calorie-restricted diet (500 to 1000 kilocalories below the daily requirement).

- To provide adequate calories at times which match the peak action of exogenously administered insulin. This means *regularly scheduled* meals and snacks to prevent hypoglycemic reactions in individuals taking insulin.

- To normalize glucose concentration and lipid levels. This is in an effort to delay or prevent long-term complications of diabetes and to contribute to a normal pregnancy and delivery for women with diabetes.

- To minimize acute excursions in blood glucose concentrations. The amount of carbohydrates in the diet has been liberalized to 55% to 60% of the total calories. Previously, use of *complex carbohydrates* was emphasized and most recommended against the use of simple sugars. However, studies now indicate that some complex carbohydrates can produce plasma glucose responses comparable to equivalent amounts of sucrose. The glycemic response induced by complex carbohydrates varies widely and can be influenced by the type of carbohydrate ingested (e.g., rice versus potato), the preparation (e.g., wheat in bread versus wheat in pasta), or the concurrent ingestion of other foods.[33] In view of these findings, the ADA has liberalized its recommendations regarding *simple sugars*. Now, a "modest amount of sucrose and other refined sugars may be acceptable, contingent upon metabolic control and body weight." Since *soluble fibers* may slow the absorption of carbohydrates and ameliorate their glycemic effect, unrefined carbohydrates with fiber are recommended.

- To prevent cardiovascular disease (a major cause of morbidity and mortality in patients with diabetes) the fat content has been restricted to less than 30% of the total calories, and *cholesterol* intake has been restricted to less than 300 mg/day for patients with normal plasma cholesterol concentrations. More severe restrictions may be indicated for individuals with hypercholesterolemia. *Sodium* intake is restricted to 3000 mg/day except in individuals with hypertension in whom restriction may be more severe.
- To assure adequate growth and nutrition, protein intake is 0.8 gm/kg. This amount may be liberalized in pregnant and lactating women or elderly subjects and restricted in patients with diabetic nephropathy or individuals with hepatic encephalopathy.

Other dietary recommendations relate to the use of artificial sweeteners and alcohol.

Artificial Sweeteners. The use of both noncaloric sweeteners (saccharin and aspartame) and caloric sweeteners (sorbitol and fructose) is acceptable in the dietary management of patients with diabetes. A patient whose diet is calorically restricted should be warned that the sweeteners used in many foods labeled "dietetic" provide substantial calories. Furthermore, excessive intake of sorbitol-sweetened foods (e.g., 30 to 50 gm/day) may produce an osmotically induced diarrhea.

Alcohol. The ADA does not prohibit the use of small amounts of alcohol in the diabetic diet, although its caloric contribution and hypoglycemic effect must be considered. (See Question 77.)

Some clinicians have questioned the clinical value of a complex dietary prescription.[33] All agree that patients on insulin should take food regularly and that obese individuals with Type II diabetes are likely to benefit from caloric restriction and moderate weight loss. However, the use of diets highly restricted in cholesterol content and high in fiber have been questioned as has the use of complex food exchanges. Instead, individualized prescriptions which take into account the patient's ethnic preferences, socioeconomic status, and lifestyle have been recommended.

Exercise

Exercise generally increases the utilization of glucose, which is provided initially from the breakdown of muscle glycogen and, subsequently, from hepatic glycogenolysis and gluconeogenesis. These effects are mediated through norepinephrine, epinephrine, growth hormone, cortisol, and glucagon along with the suppression of insulin secretion. In insulin-dependent patients, hyperglycemia, normoglycemia, or hypoglycemia can occur secondary to exercise depending upon the degree of control, recent administration of insulin, and food intake. (See Question 26.)

In the noninsulin-dependent diabetic population, there is generally a decrease in the plasma glucose concentration, although symptomatic hypoglycemia is uncommon. Since diabetic individuals are predisposed to cardiovascular disease, more attention has been paid to the metabolic response of the diabetic patient to exercise. In general, moderate, regular exercise is highly recommended for individuals with Type II diabetes treated with diet and/or oral agents and encouraged in individuals taking insulin if special precautions are taken. (See Question 26.) Exercise in patients taking insulin must be tempered by increased food intake,

delayed administration of insulin, decreased doses of insulin, or a combination of these maneuvers.

Drugs

Insulin, along with diet, is crucial to the survival of individuals with Type I diabetes and plays a major role in the therapy of individuals with Type II diabetes when their symptoms cannot be controlled with diet alone or together with oral antidiabetic agents. Insulin also is used in patients with Type II diabetes during periods of intercurrent illness or stress (e.g., surgery, pregnancy). The use of oral sulfonylureas is reserved for the treatment of patients with Type II diabetes whose symptoms cannot be controlled with diet and exercise alone. The clinical use of these agents and the complications associated with their use are discussed later in this chapter.

Overall Goals of Therapy

Specific therapeutic endpoints vary with different viewpoints on diabetic control and the methods used to monitor diabetic therapy (i.e., urine glucose, blood glucose, HbA$_{1c}$). These are discussed in appropriate sections of this chapter. However, there are some overall goals of therapy agreed to by most diabetologists. Since there is presently no cure for diabetes, the overall goals are as follows:

- Try to keep patients free of symptoms associated with hyperglycemia (polyuria, polydipsia, weight loss, fatigue, recurrent infection, ketoacidosis) or hypoglycemia.
- Try to maintain patients as close to euglycemia as possible without exposing them to an undue risk of hypoglycemia. This effort is aimed at preventing or slowing progression of the chronic complications associated with diabetes. It assumes that these complications are, to some extent, related to glucose toxicity.
- In children, normal growth and development should be maintained.
- Eliminate or minimize all other cardiovascular risk factors.
- Try to integrate patients into the health care team through intensive education. Many studies have demonstrated that the diabetic patient's knowledge and understanding of this disease can have a tremendous influence on overall diabetic control. (See Table 48.3.)

Methods of Monitoring Glycemic Control

In addition to monitoring signs and symptoms associated with hyperglycemia, hypoglycemia, and the long-term complications of diabetes, several chemical measurements may be used by the patient and clinician to directly or indirectly assess glycemic control. The advantages and limitations of various measurements of glucose control have been reviewed extensively.[34]

Urine Glucose Tests

Urine glucose concentrations correlate so poorly with blood glucose concentrations that urine glucose tests are now used only for patients who cannot or will not test blood glucose concentrations. Advantages and disadvantages of urine glucose tests as well as their clinical use are discussed in Question 42.

Fasting Plasma Glucose (FPG)

Fasting plasma glucose concentrations (normal FPG = 3.9 to 6.4 mmol/dL or 70 to 115 mg/dL) commonly are used to assess diabetic control because this is when glucose concentrations are most reproducible. Before the advent of home blood glucose monitoring, clinicians commonly extrapolated the serial results of these concentrations to overall diabetic control. Two-hour postprandial

Table 48.3	Areas of Patient Education

Diabetes: Describe the pathogenesis and the complications associated with this condition

Hyperglycemia: Signs and symptoms

Ketoacidosis: Signs and symptoms. What do ketones in the urine mean?

Hypoglycemia: Signs, symptoms, treatment (See Table 48.23)

Exercise: Effect on blood glucose concentrations and insulin dose (See Table 48.25)

Diet: See text

Insulins:
Injection technique
Types of insulin (animal source, NPH, Reg)
Onset and peak actions
Storage
Stability (look for crystallization and precipitation)

Home blood glucose testing: (See Table 48.17)

Interpretation of home blood glucose testing results

Foot care: Inspect feet daily; wear well-fitted shoes; avoid self-care of ingrown toenails, corns, or athlete's foot; see a podiatrist

Sick-day management: (See Table 48.22)

Cardiovascular risk factors: Smoking, high blood pressure, obesity, elevated cholesterol

Importance of annual ophthalmologic examinations

(2 HPP) glucose concentrations also are used to assess diabetic control when fasting glucose concentrations are within normal limits. In nondiabetic individuals, glucose concentrations generally return to normal by this time. Fasting plasma glucose concentrations generally reflect glucose derived from hepatic glucose production since this is the primary source of glucose in the postabsorptive state. Two-hour postprandial concentrations primarily reflect the efficiency of insulin-mediated glucose uptake by peripheral tissue. Since any glucose concentration is subject to alteration by factors such as diet, drugs, and stress, measurement at a single point in time should not be used to assess a patient's overall control.

Most laboratories measure glucose concentrations in the *plasma* rather than whole blood because these values are not subject to changes in the hematocrit. Whole blood glucose concentrations are approximately 15% *lower* than plasma glucose concentrations because glucose is not distributed into hemoglobin. (See Table 48.4).

Home Blood Glucose Monitoring (HBGM)

The advent of blood glucose monitoring has made euglycemia both pre- and postprandially an achievable goal (70 to 140 mg/dL). For the first time, patients and their physicians are able to assess directly the effects of drug doses, dietary patterns, exercise, and illness on blood glucose concentrations. In the ideal world, home blood glucose monitoring would replace urine glucose tests as the day-to-day monitoring test of choice for all patients with diabetes. Practically, however, HBGM is expensive, invasive, and technique-dependent. Further, to achieve maximum benefit with HGBM, both the clinician and the patient must be motivated and willing to spend the time required to understand its use in achieving glycemic control. Selection and use of home blood glucose testing materials are discussed in Questions 10 and 11. Patients in whom home blood glucose monitoring is particularly valuable include:[35]

- **Unstable Type I Diabetic Patients.** HBGM provides the unstable insulin-dependent patient with several benefits. Instant feedback provides an increased sense of control and motivation, and frequent blood glucose measurements

help the patient correlate diet, exercise, and insulin dose with blood glucose concentrations. Most importantly, HBGM can improve control in unstable patients.

- **Pregnant Patients and Determining the Need for Insulin Initiation in Gestation Diabetes Mellitus (GDM).** Infant morbidity and mortality may be associated with the mother's overall glucose control. Utilizing HBGM, the diabetic mother who achieves normoglycemia before conception and throughout pregnancy improves her chances of delivering a live, healthy infant. Evolving evidence suggests HBGM may aid in the identification of a subset of women with GMD, thus impacting on fetal outcome by earlier initiation of insulin therapy.

- **Patients Having Difficulty Recognizing Hypoglycemia.** Acute anxiety attacks or signs and symptoms associated with a rapidly falling blood glucose concentration may mimic a true hypoglycemic reaction. This can be evaluated easily by measuring a blood glucose concentration. Over time, many patients with diabetes may have a sluggish counterregulatory response to hypoglycemia. These individuals may be unable to recognize a hypoglycemic reaction because they are asymptomatic. Routine HBGM is essential in these individuals. (See Question 21.)

- **Patients with an Abnormal or Unstable Renal Threshold.** Although the average renal threshold for glucose is approximately 180 mg/dL, the thresholds vary greatly among individuals (see Question 42). HBGM should be used in patients with high renal thresholds or in those with urinary retention.

- **Patients Who Are on Intensive Insulin Therapy.** Individuals who are on multiple daily doses of insulin or those using an insulin pump should use HBGM to evaluate the adequacy of their insulin regimen and to check for hypoglycemic or hyperglycemic reactions. (See Question 11.) Knowledge of preprandial, bedtime, and nocturnal blood glucose concentrations is essential in determining basal and preprandial insulin requirements. A decrease in the frequency of HBGM to less than four times daily has been associated with a worsening of glycemic control.

- **Patients with Impaired Color Vision.** Many color blind patients who are unable to visually read urine or blood glucose strips are able to read the digital read-out provided on reflectance colorimeters.

Glycosylated Hemoglobin HbA$_{1c}$

Before the measurement of glycosylated hemoglobin (GH) was available, clinicians only could infer overall blood glucose control by extrapolating information from fasting or random blood glucose measurements. The introduction of GH made possible an accurate assessment of glucose control over a definite time period. Hemo-

Table 48.4	Conversion of Plasma Glucose Concentrations (mg/dL) to Whole Blood Glucose Values or to mmol/L

Conversion to Equivalent Whole Blood Glucose Concentrations (mg/dL)

$$\text{Whole Blood Glucose (mg/dL)} = \text{Plasma Glucose (mg/dL)} \times 0.85$$

Conversion to mmol/L

$$\text{Plasma Glucose (mmol/L)} = \frac{\text{Plasma Glucose (mg/dL)}}{18}$$

globin A_{1c} (HbA_{1c}) is measured most widely because it comprises the majority of glycosylated hemoglobin and is the least affected by recent fluctuations in blood glucose.[2] HbA_{1c} measures the percentage of hemoglobin that has been irreversibly glycosylated at the N terminal amino group of the beta chain; its value is determined by the plasma glucose level and the life span of a red blood cell ($\approx$120 days). Thus, HbA_{1c} is an indicator of glycemic control over the preceding two to three months.[36,37] In patients without diabetes, HbA_{1c} comprises approximately 4% to 6% of the total hemoglobin. Values may be three times this level in patients with diabetes.

"Normal values" for HbA_{1c} are established by each laboratory. This relates to the different methodologies used, the different components of hemoglobin A that are measured, and the lack of a reference value. Since a 1% change in the glycosylated hemoglobin can represent a 25 to 35 mg/dL change in the mean blood glucose concentration,[37] it is important to follow relative changes in HbA_{1c} values measured by a single laboratory. (Note: The terms glycosylation and glucosylation are used interchangeably in the literature.)

Alterations in red blood cell (RBC) survival such as hemoglobinopathies, anemias, acute or chronic blood loss, and uremia may affect HbA_{1c} values, resulting in inaccurate indications of glycemic control. Antioxidants such as vitamins C and E also may interfere with the glycosylation process (See Table 48.5).[38,39] In the unstable, uncontrolled diabetic patient, measurements of glycosylated hemoglobin may be altered by an intermediate, labile form of glycosylated hemoglobin (Pre A_{1c}) unless samples are treated to remove this fraction;[37] all assays used should include this step. Affinity chromotography appears to be unaffected.[40]

The advantages of the glycosylated hemoglobin are that it can be measured without any special patient preparation (e.g., fasting) and its levels generally are not subject to acute changes in insulin dosing, exercise, or diet. Normalization of the glycosylated hemoglobin may be the simplest way for the clinician to evaluate whether euglycemia has been achieved. However, HbA_{1c} does *not* replace the day-to-day monitoring of blood glucose concentrations for the purpose of evaluating acute changes in blood glucose concentrations and altering insulin doses.[35]

Table 48.5	Factors Affecting HbA$_{1c}$[a]
Cause	**Effect on HbA$_{1c}$**
Alterations in RBC Survival	
Hemoglobinopathies	Decreased
Anemias	
Hemolytic	Decreased
Iron deficiency	Decreased[b]
Blood loss	Decreased
Assay Interference[a]	
Uremia	Increased or no change[c,d]
Hemodialysis	No change[c]
Antioxidants	Decreased[e]

[a] HbA$_{1c}$ = Glycosylated hemoglobin; RBC = Red blood cell.
[b] For patients receiving iron replacement therapy. Normal levels would be expected in untreated patients.
[c] Interference seen in assays utilizing HPLC (high pressure liquid chromatography) and electroendosmosis. Affinity chromatography appears unaffected.
[d] Carbamylated hemoglobin = 0.063% of total hemoglobin is formed for every 1 mmol/L of serum urea.
[e] Reported with vitamins C (1 gm/day) and E (1200 mg/day). Possible mechanism is competitive inhibition of hemoglobin glycosylation.

Clinical Use. Currently, the glycosylated hemoglobin value is used as an adjunct in assessing glycemic control in patients with diabetes. Often, it is used to verify clinical impressions related to glucose control and patient compliance. (See Question 20.) Some also have suggested the use of glycosylated hemoglobin values for diabetes screening and diagnosis; however, until the test is standardized and more studies are completed, it cannot be recommended for these purposes. Glycosylated hemoglobin should be measured at least semiannually in patients with diabetes and preferably quarterly in insulin-treated diabetic patients with poor metabolic control.[41]

Fructosamine

Fructosamine (FA) measures the glycosylation of a variety of serum proteins, including serum albumin, which accounts for more than half of the total glycated plasma proteins.[42] The half-life of albumin is approximately 14 to 20 days; therefore, FA provides an indication of glycemic control over a shorter time frame (1 to 3 weeks) than does the HbA_{1c}.[43] The normal range for FA is 2 to 2.8 mmol/L. Fructosamine levels may be useful as an adjunct to HbA_{1c} in determining whether a patient is improving or worsening in the short term.[44] Fructosamine has been proposed as a screening test for gestational diabetes, but increased protein turnover rates during pregnancy may limit this use.[45]

The exact role of fructosamine in monitoring diabetes control requires further study. Currently its use should be reserved for those cases in which HbA_{1c} concentrations are unreliable (see Table 48.5) or when short-term changes in blood glucose control (over 1 to 2 weeks) must be assessed. In most cases, HbA_{1c} remains the preferred marker of glycemic control.

Insulin

Types of Insulin

There are three basic types of insulin, each with different physical and chemical properties: regular, the lentes, and the protamine insulins. *Regular insulin*, an unmodified soluble insulin solution, is absorbed quickly from a subcutaneous site and is the fastest acting insulin available. Because it is the only insulin that is a solution, it is the only one that can be administered intravenously. All of the other insulins are suspensions.

Regular insulin has been modified to produce other insulin types that are absorbed more slowly from the subcutaneous site, thus increasing the time-course of activity. An excess of protamine in this product significantly delays the absorption and biologic activity of this insulin. *Neutral protamine hagedorn* (NPH, also called isophane) insulin is a mixture of regular and protamine zinc insulin with an intermediate-acting activity.

The lente insulins are zinc-insulin mixtures. *Semilente*, a short-acting insulin, is an amorphous precipitate of insulin with zinc ions. *Ultralente*, a long-acting insulin, is composed of insoluble zinc-insulin crystals. *Lente* insulin, a 30:70 mixture of semilente and ultralente insulins, is intermediate in activity. (See Table 48.6.)

Absorption, Distribution, and Elimination

After subcutaneous injection, insulin is absorbed directly into the bloodstream, bypassing the lymphatics. The rate-limiting step of insulin activity after subcutaneous administration is absorption from the subcutaneous site, which depends upon the type of insulin administered as well as a multitude of other factors. While subcutaneous absorption generally follows a simple exponential course, absorption is highly irregular. Coefficients of variation for the time until 50% of the insulin dose is absorbed are approximately 25%

Table 48.6		Insulins Available in the U.S.	
Type/Duration of Action	Animal Source/ Manufacturing Process	Brand Name	Manufacturer
Short-Acting			
Regular			
Standard	Beef/Pork	Regular Iletin I	Lilly
Purified	Pork	Regular Iletin II	Lilly
	Pork	Regular Purified Pork Insulin	Novo Nordisk
Human	Recombinant DNA	Humulin R	Lilly
		Novolin R[b,c]	Novo Nordisk
	Semisynthetic	Velosulin BR[a]	Novo Nordisk
Intermediate-Acting			
NPH (Isophane Insulin Suspension)			
Standard	Beef/Pork	NPH Iletin I	Lilly
Purified	Pork	Pork NPH Iletin II	Lilly
	Pork	NPH Purified (N)	Novo Nordisk
Human	Recombinant DNA	Humulin N	Lilly
		Novolin N[b]	Novo Nordisk
Lente (Insulin Zn Suspension)			
Standard	Beef/Pork	Lente Iletin I	Lilly
Purified	Pork	Lente Iletin II (Pork)	Lilly
	Pork	Lente (L) Purifed Pork Insulin	Novo Nordisk
Human	Recombinant DNA	Humulin L	Lilly
		Novolin L[b]	Novo Nordisk
NPH/Regular Mixture (70%/30%)			
Human	Recombinant DNA	Humulin 70/30	Lilly
		Novolin 70/30[b,c]	Novo Nordisk
NPH/Regular Mixture (50%/50%)			
Human	Recombinant DNA	Humulin 50/50	Lilly
Long-Acting[d]			
Ultralente (Insulin Zn Suspension, Extended)			
Human	Recombinant DNA	Humulin U Ultralente	Lilly

a Phosphate buffered product. Preferred for use in insulin pumps.
b FDA approval of a recombinant DNA product using yeast occurred in July 1991. The semisynthetic product has been phased out of the market.
c These products also available in 1.5 cc cartridges for use in "pen" delivery devices: Novolin Pen and as prefilled syringes.
d Eli Lilly and Company discontinued its Iletin II beef products in September 1993.

within and up to 50% between patients for all insulins studied.[46] A primary cause of this variation is changes in blood flow.

In the bloodstream, insulin exists in free form and, in patients who have developed circulating IgG insulin-binding antibodies, in equilibrium with these insulin-antibody complexes. Antibodies may prolong or blunt the onset of activity and prolong the biologic half-life of insulin.[46,47]

Insulin is degraded at both renal and extra-renal (liver and muscle) sites. Degradation also takes place at the receptor cell level after internalization of the insulin receptor complex. The kidney clears 30% to 80% of insulin (greater in diabetic than nondiabetic patients) from the systemic circulation.[45] After insulin is filtered by the glomerular capillaries, more than 99% is reabsorbed by the proximal tubules and then is degraded in glomerular capillary cells and postglomerular peritubular cells. (Also see Question 27.) For additional information about insulin pharmacokinetics, the reader is referred to several thorough reviews.[46–49]

Time Course of Activity

Insulin products can be categorized by their durations of activity into short-acting, intermediate-acting, and long-acting insulins. The onset of action, peak effect, and duration of action of each of these insulins are displayed in Table 48.7. However, in applying these data the clinician must realize that most were obtained through the measurement of insulin levels and glycemic responses of normal, healthy volunteers to pharmacologic doses of insulin in the fasting state or in well-controlled diabetics stabilized in a met-

abolic ward. In actuality, there is tremendous inter- and intrasubject variation in response to insulin.[46] This is because there are numerous factors that may alter an individual patient's time pattern of insulin response including the formation of insulin antibodies, dose, exercise, site of injection, massage of the injection site, ambient temperature, and interactions between insulins that have been mixed together. (See Table 48.8 and Question 14.) A knowledge of when one might expect the various insulins to exert their effects, however, is absolutely essential to the rational manipulation of insulin doses. Insulin pharmacokinetics are summarized in Table 48.9.

Short-Acting Insulins

Regular and Semilente insulins are the rapid-onset, short-acting insulins. Most standard textbooks indicate that regular insulin has an onset of action of 30 to 60 minutes, a peak effect at two to four hours, and a duration of action of five to seven hours (see Table 48.7). However, in Type I diabetic persons who have used regular insulin for several months or years, the effects of short-acting insulin may be delayed significantly.[47] Semilente insulin has a somewhat delayed onset and peak action relative to regular insulin and a considerably longer duration of activity.[53] For this reason, it fell into disuse and was removed from product lines. The 30 to 60 minute onset of action requires proper timing of premeal regular insulin. So that patients can have greater flexibility in their lifestyle, insulin analogues which are more rapidly absorbed and with peak actions that more closely simulate physiologic insulin relative to

Table 48.7	Comparison of Insulin Preparations[a]			
Insulin	Onset (hr)	Peak (hr)	Duration (hr)	Appearance
Regular	½–1	2–4	5–7	Clear
NPH	1–2	6–14	24+	Cloudy
Lente	1–3	6–14	24+	Cloudy
Ultralente[b]	6	18–24	36+	Cloudy

a The onset, peak, and duration of insulin activity may vary considerably from times listed in this table. See text and Table 48.8.

b Human ultralente may have a shorter duration of action. Some patients require BID dosing.

meals are under study.[319] For example, Lilly soon will seek approval of Lys-Pro Human insulin in Europe.

Intermediate-Acting Insulins

NPH (isophane) and Lente insulins are the intermediate-acting insulins. Both have an onset of action of approximately two hours, a peak effect of approximately 6 to 14 hours, and a duration of approximately 24 hours. Again, it must be emphasized that this pattern of response is at best a generalization. Patients may have a variable pattern of response to both NPH and lente insulins over time. Up to 80% of these day-to-day fluctuations in blood glucose responses can be accounted for by variation in the absorption of the intermediate-acting insulins.[46]

Long-Acting Insulins

Ultralente insulin is a long-acting insulin preparation. This insulin has a long onset of activity (6 hr), a delayed peak action (18 to 24 hr), and a prolonged duration of activity (36 hr). This time course of activity is not very useful in suppressing acute glucose challenges related to meals. However, with the interest in mimicking the physiologic release of insulin, long-acting insulin has been used (in combination regimens with frequent, short-acting insulin injections) to supply low, "basal" levels of insulin between meals. (See Question 4 and Table 48.13.) Unfortunately, human ultralente's "peak" action often requires twice daily administration of lower doses to achieve a smoother effect. Insulin analogues which have a more prolonged effect without "peaks" are under investigation.[319]

Insulin Immunogenicity

Before 1982, various insulin products available on the market differed significantly with respect to their ability to stimulate IgG insulin antibody formation. Because contaminants virtually have been eliminated from current products, there is much less antibody formation. Consequently, immunologically-mediated sequelae, such as lipodystrophy, hypersensitivity, and immunologic insulin resistance, now occur less frequently.[47] (See Questions 23 and 24.)

Insulin antibodies also can alter insulin pharmacokinetics. Usually, insulin antibodies delay insulin activity, but high levels also may produce extreme swings of hyperglycemia and hypoglycemia in some patients.[47] The latter may be due to the erratic release of free insulin from antibodies. Although it also has been hypothesized that antibodies or immune complexes may contribute to certain late complications of diabetes such as nephropathy, there is little evidence to substantiate these claims.

Purity

Most of the impurities found in older insulins (proinsulin, glucagon, somatostatin, pancreatic polypeptide, and other noninsulin material) have been eliminated from current insulin products. Although IgG antibodies are stimulated by the insulin molecule itself (even highly purified animal and human insulins are immunogenic), the increased antigenic response to these older insulins was due mainly to impurities. Technological advances such as gel filtration and ion-exchange chromatography virtually have eliminated proinsulin and other noninsulin contaminants from insulin products. In the early 1980s, the Food and Drug Administration (FDA) required that "purified" insulins contain no more than 10 ppm proinsulin. At that time, there was a wide variation of proinsulin contamination between different products. Currently, however, all insulin products contain far less than 10 ppm proinsulin and therefore can be considered purified; minor differences in purity between different products are now unlikely to be clinically significant.

Species Source: Beef, Pork, and Human

Because proinsulin contamination virtually has been eliminated from insulin products, species source is now the primary immunogenic determinant. Beef (or mixed beef-pork) products are more immunogenic than pork insulin; beef insulin differs from human insulin by three amino acids, while pork insulin differs by only one amino acid. Pure beef products are no longer manufactured in the U.S.

Purified pork insulin is slightly more immunogenic than commercially available human insulin; however, the difference between these insulins is subtle. In most new diabetic patients, human insulin consistently produces less antibody response than purified pork insulin, albeit the difference often is slight and probably clinically unimportant.[47]

Human Insulin

Technology

Human insulins currently are produced by two different technologies: biosynthesis and semisynthesis. Biosynthetic insulin is of recombinant DNA origin. The genetic code for human proinsulin is inserted into the plasmid (genetic material) of *E.coli* bacteria (Lilly) or yeast (Novo Nordisk) which then produce human proinsulin. The connecting peptide (C-peptide) is then enzymatically cleaved from proinsulin. After purification, the end product is identical to human insulin.

Semisynthetic insulin (Novo-Nordisk) is manufactured through enzymatic conversion of pork insulin. Alanine is substituted for threonine at the terminal end of the pork insulin molecule. This product will be replaced by the more recently approved recombinant DNA product.

Pharmacokinetics

The pharmacokinetic, blood glucose-lowering, and metabolic effects of human insulin are identical to those of pork insulin after *intravenous* administration. However, human insulin may be absorbed slightly more quickly or have a shorter duration of activity than pork insulin after *subcutaneous* injection. Although this difference appears to be slight, transfer studies have demonstrated higher morning fasting blood glucose concentrations or other signs of deteriorating control in patients transferred from an animal-source insulin to a human insulin.[53] Human insulin is more soluble than pork insulin, and this increased solubility is thought to shorten its duration of activity. Adjustments in the ratio, amounts, or timing of insulin administration may be necessary in some patients who are transferred from an animal-source insulin to a human insulin.

Insulin Concentration

Most patients taking insulin are now using U-100 insulin (100 U/cc). Patients requiring very low doses should be advised to use "low dose" syringes for accurate measurement. (See Question 8.)

Table 48.8	Factors Altering Onset and Duration of Insulin Action[a]
Factor	**Comments**
Route of Administration	Onset of action more rapid and duration of action shorter for IV>IM>SQ[50,51,59]
	Intranasal insulin has more rapid onset and shorter duration than SQ insulin, resembling IV pharmacokinetics[116,117]
Factors Altering Clearance	
Renal Function	Renal failure ↓ insulin clearance. May prolong and intensify action of exogenous and endogenous insulin[49,50]
Insulin Antibodies	IgG antibodies bind insulin as it is absorbed and release it slowly, thereby delaying and/or prolonging its effect[47,56]
Subcutaneous Enzyme	Rare. Patients with SQ insulin-degrading enzymes are resistant to SQ administration, but are responsive to IV and other routes of administration. Variable, physiologic SQ degradation also occurs[50,53]
Thyroid Function	Hyperthyroidism ↑ clearance, but also ↑ insulin action, making control difficult. Patients stabilize as they become euthyroid[52]
Factors Altering SQ Absorption	Factors that ↑ SQ blood flow ↑ absorption rates of regular insulin. Effect on intermediate and long-acting insulins minimal
Site of Injection	Rate of absorption fastest from the abdomen, intermediate from the arm, and slowest from the thigh:[46,48,54]

Site	$t\frac{1}{2}$ Absorption (min)
Abdomen	87 ± 12
Arm	141 ± 23
Hip	153 ± 28
Thigh	164 ± 15

Exercise of Injected Area	Strenuous exercise of an injected area within 1 hr of injection can ↑ absorption rate. Rate of absorption of regular insulin ↑, but little effect on intermediate-acting insulin[46,55,60]
Ambient Temperature	Heat (e.g., hot weather, hot bath, sauna) ↑ absorption rate. Cold has opposite effect[46,53,60]
Local Massage	Massaging injected area for 30 min substantially ↑ absorption rate of regular insulin as well as longer-acting insulins[60]
Smoking	Controversial. Vasoconstriction may ↓ absorption rate[60]
Jet Injectors	Insulin absorption more rapid, probably secondary to ↑ surface area for absorption[114,115]
Lipohypertrophy	Insulin absorption is delayed from lipohypertrophic sites[58]
Insulin Preparation	More soluble forms of insulin are absorbed more rapidly and have shorter durations of action. (See Table 48.7 and text.) Human insulin may have shorter action than animal species (See text)[53]
Insulin Mixtures	The short-acting properties of regular insulin may be lost if mixed with PZI or lente insulins. (See Table 48.21 and Question 13)[47,73]
Insulin Concentration	More dilute solutions (e.g., U-40, U-10) are absorbed more rapidly than more concentrated forms (U-100, U-500)[53,57]
Insulin Dose	Lower doses are absorbed more rapidly and have a shorter duration of action than larger doses

[a] IV = Intravenous; IM = Intramuscular; SQ = Subcutaneous; IgG = Immunoglobulin G.

For special cases, patients can dilute U-100 insulin with Insulin Diluting Solution which is available on special request from Eli Lilly and Co. Patients requiring exceptionally high doses may require the use of a more concentrated insulin (U-500), also available from Lilly.

Treatment of Type I Diabetes: Clinical Use of Insulin

1. A.H., a slender, 18-year-old female, is referred to the Diabetic Clinic by the University Student Health Service because a routine physical examination revealed glucosuria; a random plasma glucose ordered subsequently was 250 mg/dL. About 4 weeks before this visit, A.H. moved across the country to attend college, her first time away from home. In retrospect, she has noted polydipsia, nocturia (3 times/night), fatigue, and a 12-lb weight loss over this period, which she has attributed to the anxiety associated with her move away from home and adjustment to her new environment. Her past medical history is remarkable for recurrent upper respiratory infections and 3 cases of vaginal monilia over the past 6 months. Her family history is negative for diabetes, and she takes no medications.

Physical examination is within normal limits. Her weight is 50 kg and her height is 5′4″. Laboratory results are as follows: FPG 280 mg/dL (Normal: <115 mg/dL); HbA₁c 14% (Normal:
4%–6%); urine glucose and ketones as measured by Keto-Diastix 2% and trace, respectively. On the basis of the above history and laboratory findings, a presumptive diagnosis of Type I diabetes is made.

Which findings are consistent with this diagnosis in A.H.?
[SI units: random plasma glucose 13.9 mmol/L; FPG 15.5 mmol/L (Normal: <6.4 mmol/L); HbA₁c 0.14 (Normal: 0.04–0.06)]

A.H. meets several of the diagnostic criteria for diabetes. She has classic symptoms of the disease (polyuria, polydipsia, weight loss, glucosuria, fatigue, recurrent infections) and a random plasma glucose greater than 200 mg/dL as well as a fasting plasma glucose which exceeds 140 mg/dL. (See Table 48.2.) The elevated glycosylated hemoglobin also is consistent with diabetes mellitus. Features of A.H.'s history that are consistent with Type I diabetes in particular include the relatively acute onset of symptoms in association with a major life event (moving away from home); ketones in the urine; negative family history; and a relatively young age at onset.

Treatment Goals

2. A.H. will be started on insulin therapy on this visit. What are the goals of therapy? Will normoglycemia prevent the development or progression of long-term complications?

In the early 1990s, most diabetologists were leaning toward normoglycemia as an ideal goal of insulin therapy, although there was

Table 48.9	Insulin Pharmacokinetics[a,35,46]
Clearance	
Total clearance	700–800 mL/min
Hepatic clearance	300–400 mL/min
Renal clearance	190–270 mL/min
IV Infusion	
Elimination follows multicompartment model	
$t\frac{1}{2}$ for 3 compartments are as follows: 2.3–2.4 min; 14 min; 133 min	
Insulin action most closely corresponds to last compartment. Therefore, it is unnecessary to adjust the dose more often than Q 2 hr	
SQ Administration of Regular Insulin[b]	
Intermittent Boluses	
$t\frac{1}{2}$ (absorption: 70–120 min)	
$t\frac{1}{2}$ (elimination: 53 min)	
SQ: approximately 4 × the hourly dose	
SQ Infusion	
Steady state achieved in 6–8 hr[46]	
If infusion is discontinued, check for rise in glucose ketones after 2 or 3 hr. Since there is no SQ pool, effects dissipate quickly	
SQ Administration of Intermediate-Acting Insulins[b]	
NPH $t\frac{1}{2}$ (absorption) 12–19 hr	

[a] IV = Intravenous; SQ = Subcutaneous; $t\frac{1}{2}$ = Half-life; NPH = Isophane insulin suspension.

[b] Insulin absorption varies by 25% within the same individual and 50% among individuals. See Table 48.8 for factors which influence absorption.

still some debate about the relationship between hyperglycemia and the progression and development of long-term complications. As discussed earlier in the introduction to this chapter, the results of the Diabetes Control and Complications trial (DCCT) convincingly demonstrated that lowering blood glucose concentrations through intensive insulin therapy (IIT) in persons with Type I diabetes slows or prevents the development of microvascular complications.[14] Thus, the American Diabetes Association now advocates "tight control" which it defines as "blood glucose levels equal to or better than those achieved in the intensively treated group in the DCCT trial."[15]

The original goal of intensive insulin therapy in the DCCT was to achieve glucose levels as close to the nondiabetic range as possible. (See Table 48.10.) However, the investigators were unable to achieve these ideal targets in the intensive insulin therapy group: mean HbA_{1c} levels were 7.2% (normal: 6%) and mean fasting glucose concentrations were 155 mg/dL (normal: <140 mg/dL). Thus, intensive insulin therapy does not necessarily lead to the attainment of euglycemia and most patients will require individualized glycemic goals.[14,63]

It is important to understand that intensive insulin therapy involves a *complete* program of diabetes management[64] which includes a balanced food intake, exercise, daily home blood glucose monitoring, and insulin adjustments based upon these factors. (See Table 48.11.) Since the patient is the key member of the team, A.H. must be highly motivated and able to learn about the complex metabolic interplay between insulin and lifestyle.

Higher target glucose concentrations are advisable for patients with a history of recurrent, severe hypoglycemia or hypoglycemic unawareness. Also, patients with established renal insufficiency, proliferative retinopathy, severe neuropathy, and other advanced complications are not likely to be improved significantly by tight control. (See Questions 20 and 21 and Table 48.15.)

In summary, A.H. is a newly diagnosed Type I diabetic patient who has not yet developed any signs or symptoms of long-term

complications. If she is a willing and motivated patient, normoglycemia is a reasonable long-term goal. This goal should be achieved gradually over several months with intensive insulin therapy, diet, education, and strong clinical support. If A.H. is unwilling to pursue such a rigorous approach at this time or is unwilling to test her blood glucose concentrations, a more conservative approach will have to be used. One may have to resort to occasional blood glucose concentrations, random blood glucose concentrations and glycosylated hemoglobin determinations every three to six months. A desirable goal is a HbA_{1c} 1% to 2% above the normal range with rare hypoglycemic reactions.

Intensive Insulin Therapy

Insulin Pumps

3. What methods of insulin administration currently are available to implement intensive insulin therapy?

Most methods of insulin delivery used in intensive insulin therapy are predicated upon mimicking normal insulin secretion as closely as possible.[65] However, since so many factors affect the subcutaneous absorption of insulin and diabetic control, none of the current regimens is ideal. (See Tables 48.8 and 48.12 and Questions 3 through 5.) Furthermore, none of the insulins have pharmacodynamic profiles that allow one to simulate the "basal-bolus" model described below. Some argue that euglycemia will not be achievable until insulin is administered directly into the portal vein or in a way that bypasses the peripheral circulation initially, thereby mimicking its physiologic release into the portal circulation. Administering insulin subcutaneously or intravenously produces peripheral hyperinsulinemia and relatively low levels of insulin in the hepatic vein.

Nevertheless, clinicians have had to work with the tools available to mimic pancreatic release of the hormone.[65] In the nondiabetic individual, the pancreas secretes boluses of insulin in response to snacks and meals. Between meals and throughout the night, the pancreas secretes small amounts of insulin which are sufficient to suppress lipolysis and hepatic glucose output (basal insulin). Two methods have been used to achieve a similar pattern of insulin release: 1) continuous subcutaneous infusion of insulin

Table 48.10	Goals of Intensive Insulin Therapy[a]		
Target Blood Glucose Values	Ideal[b] (mg/dL)	Acceptable[c] (mg/dL)	Pregnancy (mg/dL)
Fasting	70–120	70–140	60–90
Preprandial	70–105	70–130	60–105
1 hr postprandial	100–160	100–180	70–140
2 hr postprandial	80–120	80–150	60–120
2–4 a.m.	70–100	70–120	>60
HbA_{1c}[d]	<6%	≤7–8%	<6%
Urine ketones[e]	Absent	Rare	Rare

[a] Modified and extrapolated from references 14 and 63. Intensive insulin therapy is a complete therapeutic program of diabetes management and requires a team approach. (See Table 91.10.)

[b] Ideal values approximate those seen in nondiabetic individuals and are included for illustrative purposes only.

[c] Acceptable values should be individualized and are attainable in appropriate patients without creating an undue risk of hypoglycemia. These results are similar to the results achieved in the DCCT trial. These values may be inappropriate for patients with hypoglycemic unawareness, counterregulatory insufficiency, angina pectoris, or other complicating features.

[d] HbA_{1c} = Glycosylated hemoglobin. Normal values vary; normalize to laboratory.

[e] Does not apply to Type II patients.

Table 48.11	Components of Intensive Insulin Therapy[a,b]

Multicomponent insulin regimen

Balance of food intake, exercise, and insulin dosage

Daily, multiple self-monitoring of blood glucose levels

Patient self-adjustment of food intake and insulin dosage with use of supplemental regular insulin according to a predetermined plan

Individualized target blood glucose and HbA_{1c} levels

Frequent contact between patient and diabetes team

Intensive patient education

Psychologic support

Regular objective assessment (as measured by HbA_{1c})

[a] Modified from reference 64.
[b] HbA_{1c} = Glycosylated hemoglobin.

(CSII) through insulin infusion pumps and 2) multiple daily doses of insulin (MDI). (See Question 4.)

Continuous Subcutaneous Insulin Infusion. Insulin pumps are available in open loop and closed loop (artificial pancreas) systems.[66] The *closed loop system* (e.g., Biostater, Ames) consists of three components: a battery-operated pump, a computer that controls the rate of insulin delivery, and a glucose sensor which feeds back into the computer. Thus, like that released by the pancreas, the amount of insulin released by the pump is determined by the blood glucose concentration. The system delivers glucose as well as insulin. Because the system is not portable, it is used in patients who are ketoacidotic, undergoing surgery, or are acutely ill. It also is used in diabetic individuals with complicated pregnancies during the last trimester and during labor and delivery. In all of these situations, insulin requirements may fluctuate drastically. Insulin usually is delivered intravenously, but it also may be delivered subcutaneously or intraperitoneally.[114]

The *open loop system* (Insulin Pump) is composed of a battery-operated pump and a computer that can program the pump to deliver predetermined amounts of insulin from a reservoir to a subcutaneously inserted catheter or needle. These systems are portable and designed to deliver basal amounts of insulin throughout the day (≈ 1 U/hr) as well as meal-related boluses that can be initiated by the patient 30 minutes before food ingestion. The basal insulin infusion rate may be varied, depending upon the situation. Many patients find it advantageous to decrease the basal rate during the middle of the night when nocturnal hypoglycemia is most likely to occur. The basal rate also may be increased before awakening to avoid hyperglycemia due to the ''dawn phenomena.'' These adjustments are not possible with conventional insulin regimens. Remote-controlled implantable pumps that deliver insulin intravenously or intraperitoneally are under study.[67]

Multiple Daily Injections

4. Describe how insulin injections can be administered to A.H. in a way which mimics the physiologic release of insulin from the pancreas.

Diabetologists have been experimenting with various split-dose regimens (see Table 48.13) which are intended to mimic the release of insulin from the pancreas.[68] A total daily dose of insulin is estimated empirically or according to guidelines similar to those listed in Table 48.14.[61] The total daily dose of insulin then is split into several doses.[68]

Method 1 A regimen commonly used involves injecting a mixture of intermediate-acting and regular insulin twice daily before breakfast and before dinner. Ideally, the morning dose of regular insulin takes care of the breakfast meal; the morning dose of NPH takes care of the noon meal; the evening dose of regular insulin takes care of the evening meal; and the evening dose of NPH provides basal insulin levels during the night and takes care of any evening snack which is ingested. Because patients in the DCCT used three to four injections per day to achieve tight control, this method no longer can be considered ''intensive insulin therapy.''

Method 2 is a variation of the above method. It is the same except that the evening dose of intermediate-acting insulin is given as a third injection at bedtime. This delays the peak effect so that it occurs at approximately 7:00 a.m. By administering the intermediate-acting insulin at bedtime, nocturnal hypoglycemia is minimized and peak insulin activity is shifted to a time when the patient will be ingesting food. This method may be useful in patients in whom nocturnal hypoglycemia and fasting hyperglycemia are particularly troublesome.

Method 3 consists of three equal doses of regular insulin before meals and a dose of intermediate-acting insulin at bedtime to provide basal insulin levels during the night. This regimen gives the patient more flexibility with regard to the timing and size of his meals.

Method 4 is an alternative to Method 3 and uses long-acting insulin (ultralente) in the morning or twice daily to provide basal insulin levels throughout the day along with three doses of regular

Table 48.12	Factors Which Can Alter Blood Glucose Control

Diet

Insufficient calories (e.g., alcoholism, eating disorders, anorexia, nausea, and vomiting)

Overeating (e.g., during the holidays)

Irregularly-spaced or delayed meals

Dietary content (e.g., fiber, carbohydrate content)

Physical Activity

See Table 48.23 and Question 26

Stress

Infection

Surgery/trauma

Psychological

Drugs

See Tables 48.27 and 48.28

Hormonal Changes

Menstruation: glucose concentrations may $\uparrow$ premenstrually and return to normal postmenses

Pregnancy

Puberty: hyperglycemia probably related to high growth hormone levels

Gastroparesis

Delays gastric emptying time. Peak insulin action and meal-related glucose excursions may become mismatched

Altered Insulin Pharmacokinetics

See Table 91.7

Insulin Injection Technique

Measuring

Timing

Technique

Inactive Insulin

Outdated insulin

Improperly stored insulin (heat or cold)

Crystallized insulin

Table 48.13				Multiple Daily Dosing Regimens[a]	
Time of Insulin Administration[b]	7 a.m. Before Breakfast	11 a.m. Before Lunch	6 p.m. Before Dinner	11 p.m. Bedtime	Comments
Method 1	NPH:Reg (2/3)	—	NPH:Reg (1/3)	—	Lente can be substituted for NPH. A 2:1 ratio of NPH:Reg is commonly recommended but clinically, a ratio approaching 1:1 may be needed to control midmorning hyperglycemia
Method 2	NPH:Reg (2/3)	—	Reg (1/6)	NPH (1/6)	When NPH administration is delayed until bedtime, the peak effect occurs around breakfast time rather than 2–3 a.m. when hypoglycemia is unlikely to be noticed. Further, some residual action remains which can minimize the midmorning hyperglycemia associated with breakfast
Method 3	Reg (1/4)	Reg (1/4)	Reg (1/4)	NPH (1/4)	This method provides premeal boluses of insulin. The evening dose of NPH is used to suppress glycogenolysis and lipolysis which occur during the fasting state
Method 4	Reg (1/5) Ultralente (1/5)	Reg (1/5)	Reg (1/5) Ultralente (1/5)	—	Long-acting insulins should be given as separate injections, since excess zinc contained in this product binds regular insulin

[a] Fractions in parentheses represent fraction of total daily dose (see Table 48.14) administered at that time of day.
[b] The division of doses listed in this table should be used as a guide to the initation of intensive split-dose insulin therapy. Each patient must closely monitor blood glucose concentrations, and doses of the appropriate insulin must be adjusted accordingly. (See Questions 15–18.)

insulin before meals. This method theoretically provides insulin in exactly the same way as the insulin pump (basal levels + 3 meal boluses). In doing so, it offers some of the same advantages of the pump in that it permits some degree of flexibility in the patient's lifestyle. For example, if a diabetic patient chooses to skip a meal, he omits a premeal bolus; if he chooses to eat a larger meal than usual, he increases his premeal bolus. Similar dose adjustments can be made to accommodate exercise patterns and acute illnesses. The excess zinc in ultralente binds regular insulin; therefore, they should be administered in separate syringes. Furthermore, to minimize the "peak" effects of ultralente and to assure 24-hour basal insulin levels, twice-daily administration may be needed. This is particularly true for human ultralente which has a shorter duration of action than beef ultralente, a product that was discontinued in the U.S. in 1994.

5. Is A.H. a candidate for intensive insulin therapy? Should she use the pump or multiple insulin injections?

Indications for intensive insulin therapy are listed in Table 48.15. If A.H. is motivated to control her blood glucose concentrations, she would be an ideal candidate for intensive insulin therapy. She is a newly diagnosed diabetic who has not yet developed the long-term complications of diabetes and would be in the best position to derive the potential benefits of normoglycemia. Assuming A.H. will be able to comply with intensive insulin therapy, individualized target blood glucose levels that strive for the best level of glucose control possible without placing her at an undue

risk for hypoglycemia should be prescribed. She must be willing to test her blood glucose concentrations four or more times daily and inject herself three to four times daily or learn about the use and care of an insulin pump. She also must be willing to keep meticulous records and participate in an extensive education program which should enable her to adjust her insulin doses based upon blood glucose concentrations, physical activity, and diet.

The American Diabetes Association currently recommends that the use of insulin pumps be limited to highly motivated, compliant individuals under the guidance of a health care team trained and knowledgeable in their use.[69] This is underscored by reports of ketoacidosis, hypoglycemia, dermatologic complications, and mechanical complications associated with insulin pump use.[68,70,71] Although pumps offer the patient flexibility with regard to meal schedules and travel, there is no evidence that they achieve better glucose control than intensive split-dose insulin regimens.[68]

In summary, the cost ($3500 for the pump alone),[72] complications associated with their use; lack of evidence that these devices achieve superior control to multiple insulin injections; and the technical complexity of their operation limit the use of insulin pumps to a small fraction of insulin-requiring patients at this time. The methods by which insulin doses are established and altered in patients using the insulin pump have been described by others.[68] A.H. should be initiated on multiple daily doses of insulin at this time. The overall goals of intensive insulin therapy are listed in Table 48.10.

Clinical Use of Insulin

6. How should multiple dose insulin therapy be initiated in A.H.?

There is no generally accepted approach to the initiation of multiple-dose insulin therapy in newly diagnosed patients. A conservative total daily dose of insulin is estimated empirically or according to guidelines similar to those listed in Table 48.14. This total daily dose generally is split initially into two doses: two-thirds in the morning and one-third before dinner. Some diabetologists prefer to begin with NPH, optimize the NPH doses, and then add short-acting insulin if needed later. Others initiate the patient on mixed doses of NPH and regular insulin twice daily. On an out-

Table 48.14	Usual Total Daily Dose of Insulin[a,61,68]	
		Dose (U/kg)
Type I:	Initial dose	0.5–0.8
Type I:	Honeymoon phase	0.2–0.5
Type I:	With ketosis: during illness; adolescents in growth phase	1–1.5
Type II:	With insulin resistance	0.7–2.5

[a] This is an initial dose. Many patients on split dose therapy often require up to 1.2 U/kg. Insulin doses may change over time. The weight used is actual body weight, not ideal body weight.

Table 48.15	Intensive Insulin Therapy: Indications and Precautions

Patient selection criteria

Type I, otherwise healthy patients (>13 yr of age) who are highly motivated and compliant individuals. Must be willing to test blood glucose concentrations 4 times daily and inject 2–4 doses of insulin daily

Diabetic women who plan to conceive

Pregnant diabetic patients

Patients poorly-controlled on conventional therapy

Technical ability to test blood glucose concentrations

Intellectual ability to interpret blood glucose concentrations and adjust insulin doses appropriately

Access to trained and skilled medical staff to direct treatment program and provide close supervision

Avoid or use cautiously in patients who are predisposed to severe hypoglycemic reactions or in whom such reactions could be fatal

Patients with counterregulatory insuffiency

Type I diabetes for ≥15 years (not all patients)

β-adrenergic blocker therapy

Autonomic insufficiency

Adrenal or pituitary insufficiency

Patients with coronary or cerebral vascular disease (Note: Counterregulatory hormones may have adverse effects in these individuals)

Unreliable, noncompliant individuals including those who abuse alcohol or drugs and those with psychiatric disorders

patient basis, this latter approach may be somewhat impractical in that the patient will have to learn how to mix insulins in addition to several other skills on the first visit. One also should be aware that administration of two-thirds of the dose in the morning assumes consumption of two-thirds of the total daily calories at breakfast and lunch. This may not hold true for many patients.

During the initial visit, A.H. will need to learn how to inject her insulin (see Question 9); how to test her blood glucose (see Table 48.17); how and when to test her urine for ketones; and how to recognize and treat hypoglycemia (see Table 48.23). She also will need to understand the importance of eating regularly and avoiding simple sugars. One must be extremely cautious not to overload A.H. with information on the first visit. It is important to be sensitive to the psychological impact of this diagnosis, address her major concerns, and provide only that information which is absolutely essential before the next visit. (Also see Table 48.3.)

A reasonable first approach in A.H. is to provide a total daily dose of 24 U of NPH (≈0.5 U/kg) divided into two doses: 16 U one-half hour before breakfast and 8 U one-half hour before dinner.

7. Should NPH or lente insulin be prescribed? Should A.H. be initiated on human insulin?

Most clinicians use NPH and lente insulins interchangeably. The onset of action, maximum effect, and duration of these two insulins are basically the same, although lente may be slightly slower in onset and have a slightly longer effect than NPH. Some have supported the use of lente insulin because it does not contain protamine, a protein which is rarely antigenic. However, rare allergic reactions to both protamine and zinc (contained in lente insulins) have been reported.[73]

There is evidence that the rapid onset of regular insulin is more likely to be retained when mixed with NPH as opposed to lente insulin (see Question 14). Since it is likely that A.H. eventually will be administering a mixture of regular insulin and intermediate-acting insulin, these authors favor the initial use of NPH insulin.

A.H. should be initiated on human insulin, the least antigenic form of insulin. The objective is to minimize insulin antibody formation, since antibodies mediate immunologic complications of insulin (see Questions 23 and 24) and alter the onset and duration of action of insulins.[47]

Biosynthetic and semisynthetic human insulins may be used interchangeably. The biosynthetic form of human insulin may have a slightly more rapid onset of action and a slightly shorter duration of action. However, since there are so many variables that can alter the onset, duration, and action of insulin, this difference is unlikely to be clinically important. (Also see the introductory section on insulin and Table 48.8.)

Although purified pork insulin has low antigenicity, it is slightly more antigenic than human insulin. Since it also is more expensive than human insulin, there rarely is any indication for its use.

8. What kind of insulin syringe should be prescribed for A.H.?

Virtually all patients with diabetes now use plastic disposable insulin syringes because they do not require repeated sterilization before use.

Tremendous improvements have been made in needles and syringes so that insulin injections are relatively painless if proper technique is used. The needles are finer (27-, 28-, and 29-gauge), sharper, and lubricated for ease of insertion. Less pain is associated with the smaller, 28- or 29-gauge needles. The ''dead space'' (measurable space at the hub of the needle) has been virtually eliminated so that mixing and measuring problems previously associated with its presence are no longer a concern. The length of needles is ½″ or ⅝″; the longer needle is used when back leakage of insulin occurs and in obese diabetic patients.

Manufacturers produce 1 cc, ½ cc, ¼ cc, and ³⁄₁₀ cc syringes for U-100 insulin. For patients such as A.H. using less than 40 U of insulin per injection, the ½ cc (low-dose) syringe is preferred. These syringes have a smaller caliber barrel so that the highly concentrated U-100 insulin can be measured more accurately. They also provide scales which allow the patient to measure insulin in one-unit increments. Syringes with ¼ cc and ³⁄₁₀ cc capacities are recommended for pediatric and insulin-sensitive patients using small amounts of insulin (<25 U) before meals and snacks.

A ½ cc U-100 insulin syringe with a ½″, 28- or 29-gauge needle should be prescribed for A.H. Cost and patient preference will govern the brand selected. Subjectively, patients can ''feel'' the difference between different brands, or they may prefer the ''ease of bubble removal,'' physical characteristics, or packaging of one syringe over another.[72]

9. How should A.H. be instructed to measure and inject her NPH insulin?

Agitation. All insulins, with the exception of regular insulin, are suspensions and must be agitated before they are withdrawn from the vial. A new, unused vial of NPH or lente insulin may require vigorous agitation to loosen the sediment which may have become packed with storage. Otherwise, the vial should be rolled between the palms of the hand to minimize foaming.

Measurement. A.H. first should withdraw the plunger to the level of insulin she intends to inject (16 U); then she should insert the needle into the vial and inject 16 U of air to prevent creation of a vacuum within the vial. The vial then should be inverted with the syringe inserted, and 16 U of NPH should be withdrawn. The bevel of the needle should be well below the surface of the insulin to avoid withdrawing air or bubbles into the syringe.

The barrel of the syringe should be held at eye level to check for the presence of air bubbles and to allow for accurate placement of the plunger tip at the 16-unit mark. If bubbles are present, they should be removed by tapping the syringe gently to coax the bubbles to the top of the barrel where they can be injected back into the insulin vial.

Injection. The patient now should prepare an area for injection. Alcohol swabs may be used to clean the rubber stopper of the insulin vial and the area of injection. To inject the insulin subcutaneously, A.H. should be instructed to firmly pinch up the area to be injected (this creates a firm surface for the injection) and to quickly insert the needle perpendicularly into the center of this area. The syringe should be held toward the middle or back of the barrel like a pencil with the bevel pointed upward. Anxious patients have a tendency to "choke" the hub of the syringe, and this prevents proper needle insertion. A 45° angle of injection may be used for infants and thin or emaciated individuals who have little subcutaneous fat.

Before injecting the insulin, the plunger can be pulled back to determine whether the needle has been inserted inadvertently into a vein or artery. (Patients report that this occurs rarely and thus frequently skip this step.) If no blood appears in the barrel, the insulin may be injected. The skin should be released before the insulin syringe is withdrawn, and pressure should be applied at the site of injection with an alcohol swab, cotton, or finger to prevent back leakage of the insulin as the needle is removed. The site should not be massaged, as this may accelerate the absorption and onset of action of insulin. (See Table 48.8.)

Various maneuvers have been used to assist patients who are anxious about self-injection. These include application of ice cubes to the site and the use of spring-loaded devices which automatically insert the needle with light pressure (e.g., Inject-Ease, Palco; Auto-jector, Ulster Scientific Inc.). (See Question 32.) However, these approaches generally are unnecessary once the patient realizes that injections are relatively pain-free with proper technique.

Rotation of Injection Sites. Previously, patients were advised to rotate injection sites between the arms, thighs, abdomen, and buttocks. However, this practice was questioned by Koivisto and Felig[54] who noted that differences in the rate of insulin absorption from these sites resulted in altered glucose control. Now the ADA recommends that insulin injections be rotated within the same anatomical region to avoid this effect.[74] These authors prefer the abdominal area since absorption from this site is least affected by exercise. Alternatively, A.H. can be instructed to rotate her morning injection within one region (e.g., the thigh) and her evening injection in another anatomical region. This will minimize the variables which can alter her response to insulin.

Rotating injection sites originally was recommended to avoid the lipodystrophic effect of insulin; however, since insulin has been purified, these complications are less frequent and the importance of rotation is less critical. Repetitive use of the same site of injection, however, may result in lipohypertrophy (see Question 23), and it does toughen the skin, making needle penetration more difficult. Furthermore, insulin absorption from lipohypertrophic sites can be delayed.[58]

Home Blood Glucose Testing

10. Should A.H. perform home blood glucose testing? What types of home blood glucose monitoring tests are available, and what are the major differences between them? How accurate are results obtained from home blood glucose testing?

The advent of home glucose monitoring revolutionized the management of diabetes mellitus by providing a simple and portable method for periodic and repeated measurement of blood glucose in the ambulatory care setting. The ADA recommends self-monitoring of blood glucose (SMBG) for insulin-treated patients.[35] It is felt to be especially important in 1) pregnancy complicated by diabetes; 2) patients with unstable diabetes; 3) patients with a propensity to severe ketosis or hypoglycemia; 4) patients prone to hypoglycemia who may not experience the usual warning symptoms; 5) patients on intensive insulin regimens; and 6) patients with abnormal renal glucose thresholds. Since A.H. is being initiated on insulin therapy with the goal of normoglycemia, she should perform SMBG.

Home blood glucose testing has been widely accepted by both patients and clinicians. Since home blood glucose testing materials constitute a multimillion dollar business, the market has been flooded with a multitude of reflectance meters and chemically impregnated strips which measure blood glucose concentrations based upon the glucose oxidase reaction. The technology in this area is changing rapidly, and it is likely that several new devices will be introduced each year.

Currently, all devices use strips and can be categorized into those which require the patient to wipe off the blood after a specified time period and those which are self-timing and require no patient action after the blood is placed on the strip. The latter methods are much less technique-dependent and thus remove this variable as a source of error.

Several factors should be taken into account when evaluating a new device. The primary considerations are ease of use, accuracy relative to a reference standard, reliability, and cost.[75] Convenience factors include meter size, volume of blood required for testing, capacity of the meter to store blood glucose values (memory), testing time, size of readout, general availability of strips, ability to read strips visually to verify meter results, ability to turn off audible signals, and availability of technical support. Some devices are less reliable for use in anemic patients (e.g., renal transplant patients) and all function most reliably within certain temperature ranges (usually 60 to 95 °F) and humidity (generally <90%) conditions. Strips are sensitive to light, moisture, and temperature extremes and must be stored and handled with care. Table 48.16 compares and contrasts selected glucose meters.

Several generic strips have become available (First Choice, Quick Check One) offering patients an inexpensive solution to the cost of frequent monitoring. These generic strips supposedly are compatible with several meters; however, these authors are unaware of any studies confirming their accuracy and question the validity of these strips since brand name strips are calibrated by the manufacturer. If a patient wishes to try a generic brand of strips, the authors suggest the patient perform blood glucose determination at the same time as a laboratory determination to ensure the strips are providing accurate results.

Patient education regarding testing procedures, the importance of recording results, and test times are critical. Ultimately, A.H. should be taught how to use blood glucose values to adjust her insulin dose, dietary intake, and exercise pattern. (See Table 48.17.)

According to the ADA Consensus Statement, currently available meters are precise enough to allow the patient to utilize results for diabetes management.[106] However, several factors can affect the accuracy of meter results (most commonly, equipment malfunction and human error). Problems with a meter can be detected by performing a quality-control test once weekly and with each vial of strips. Human error includes problems such as: difficulty obtaining a sufficient drop of blood or incorrect timing and removal of blood from the strip. Table 48.18 lists other factors which may affect results obtained. Clinicians using blood glucose reagent strips in the hospital or clinic should keep in mind that blood glucose concentrations determined by these methods are approximately 10% to 15% less (depending upon the patient's hematocrit) than con-

Table 48.16 Features of Selected Blood Glucose Meters

Meter (Manufacturer)	Strip	BG Range (mg/dL)	Test Time (sec)	Memory Capacity (#)	Ease of Calibration	Comments
Meters That Use Strips: Timing and Wiping or Blotting Required						
Accu-Chek III (Boehringer Mannheim)	Chemstrips BG	20–500	120	20	Bar-encoded strip	Strip can be read visually as a back up; quantitative
Glucometer 3 (Ames)	Glucofilm	20–500	60	1 (Most recent test)	Single button	Strip can be read visually as a back up; qualitative; inexpensive; disposable after 15,000 tests; strip must be wiped, not blotted
Glucometer M+ (Ames)	Glucofilm	20–500	60	338 tests	Single button	Allows patient input of insulin, diet, and exercise. Optional Glucofacts modem available to generate reports for MD and chart
Meters That Use Strips: No Wiping/Timing Required						
Accu-Chek Easy (Boehringer Mannheim)	Easy Test Strip	20–500	15–60	30	Insert Easy Key Code Chip	Strip can be read visually as a back up; qualitative
One Touch II (Lifescan)	One Touch Strips	0–600	45	250	Single button	Very simple to calibrate and use. Patients with poor vision have difficulty finding target area for blood sample. Strip cannot be read visually as a back up if the meter fails. Voice package available for the blind. Requires frequent cleaning with multiple uses
Pen 2 [Companion 2 (formerly Exactech)] Pen 2/Companion 2 Sensor Electrodes	Medisense	20–600	20	10	Bar-encoded strip	Smallest meters on the market (size ≈ pen and credit card). Measures current generated from glucose oxidase reaction. Difficult to read result if vision impaired. Strip cannot be read visually
Glucometer Elite (Ames)	Glucometer Elite Strips	40–500	60	1 (Most recent test)	Bar-encoded strip	Electrochemical method. Electrodes protected by hard plastic coating. Strip cannot be read visually
CheckMate (Cascade Medical)	CheckMate BG Strip	40–400	60–90	40	Bar-encoded strip	Electrochemical method. Pen-size. Built-in lancet. Auto-start. Strip cannot be read visually
One Touch Basic (Lifescan)	One Touch Strip	0–600	45	1 (Most recent test)	Single button	Electrochemical method. Strip cannot be read visually
Accu-Chek Advantage (Boehringer Mannheim)	Advantage Strip	20–600	40	100	Insert Key Code Chip	Electrochemical method. Large, easy-to-read display. Stores time and date of test. Strip cannot be read visually
Glucometer Encore (Ames)	Glucometer Encore Strips	10–600	15–60	10	Single button	Requires occasional cleaning. Glucose oxidase method

Table 48.17	Home Blood Glucose Testing: Areas of Patient Education

When and how often to test

Technique

How and when to calibrate the machine

Review all "buttons" and their purposes. Identify battery case. Review cleaning procedures

Preparation

1) Calibrate machine

2) Turn machine on

3) Prepare all materials: tissue, strip, lancet

4) Remember to close the lid of the strip container immediately. Strips exposed to air and moisture deteriorate rapidly

5) Wash hands with warm water. *Dry thoroughly.* A wet finger causes blood to spread rather than form a drop. Milk the finger from the base to insure an adequate flow of blood. Some patients use a rubber band as a tourniquet

6) Lance the tip of the finger. Avoid the balls of the finger where nerves are concentrated

7) Hold the finger *below* the heart with the lanced area pointing toward the floor

8) Once a sufficient amount of blood is available *quickly* cover the *entire* pad or designated area with blood. Do not touch the pad with your fingers

9) For strips requiring removal of blood, begin timing immediately, and at the appropriate time, quickly wipe *all* the blood from the strip with cotton or tissue. This may take 2–3 blots. Newer devices allow the patient to use smaller amounts of blood and eliminate the wiping procedure, thereby eliminating the need for accurate timing

10) Place the developed strip into the machine *or* visually read the strip at the appropriate time. *Note:* Strips are inserted into the One Touch and Pen 2 machines *before* blood is applied

Importance of recording results in a log book to bring to all physician visits. Patient also should include information regarding alterations in diet or exercise

Interpreting results to achieve normoglycemia

current plasma glucose concentrations reported by the laboratory. Nevertheless, if home blood glucose testing values are inconsistent with the patient's symptoms, other sources of error should be suspected. (See Tables 48.4 and 48.18 and Question 30.) Periodically, A.H.'s technique should be reviewed since clinical decisions are based upon the patient's blood glucose testing record.

11. How often should A.H. be instructed to test her blood glucose concentrations?

The objective of frequent blood glucose testing is to determine whether normoglycemia has been achieved and to assess the action of specific insulin doses. Ideally, patients should test their blood glucose concentration before meals, 90 to 120 minutes after meals, at bedtime, and, occasionally, at 3:00 a.m. (i.e., 8 times daily). Practically, however, most patients are unable to comply with such a rigorous regimen. At the minimum, A.H. should test her blood glucose concentrations four to five times daily: before each meal and at bedtime. She also should set her alarm for 3:00 a.m. two or three times per week and test her blood glucose at that time. Blood glucose concentrations measured at these times more or less correspond to the peak action of short- and intermediate-acting insulins administered at various times of the day, enabling the clinician to evaluate the effect of various insulin components on meals and to identify nocturnal hypoglycemia. (See Table 48.19.) For ex-

ample, the blood glucose measured before dinner will reflect the action of A.H.'s morning dose of NPH on food she has eaten for breakfast and lunch, as well as hepatic glucose production between meals.

The importance of frequent blood glucose testing cannot be overemphasized. When the frequency of blood glucose testing falls below four times daily, glucose control deteriorates to baseline levels. This is because complete profiles are no longer available and it is impossible to adjust insulin doses based upon random blood glucose concentrations.[68] If patients refuse to test four times daily, they should be encouraged to test four times daily on representative days of the week or to test at different times of the day each day so that a weekly profile can be developed. A.H. also should be encouraged to test her blood glucose concentration any time she is feeling unusual or to evaluate the effect of unusual circumstances on her blood glucose concentration (e.g., physical exercise, a large holiday meal, examinations, a family crisis).

12. A.H. was instructed to inject herself BID with NPH insulin: 16 U before breakfast and 8 U before dinner. She was asked to test her blood glucose QID (before meals and at bedtime), to record her results and other unusual events or symptoms during the day, and to bring her records to the clinic. One week later, trends in her blood glucose concentrations were as follows:

Time	Glucose Concentration (mg/dL)
7 a.m.	180
12 p.m.	240
5 p.m.	150
11 p.m.	160

Occasional 3 a.m. tests averaged 160 mg/dL. A.H.'s urine sugar and acetone are 1% and negative, respectively. Subjectively, A.H. feels a bit better, but she still urinates 2–3 times nightly. Her weight has remained stable for the past week. How should these results be interpreted, and how should A.H.'s in-

Table 48.18	Factors That Can Alter Home Blood Glucose Test Results: Troubleshooting

- Machine is improperly calibrated[a]
- Strips are out-of-date or have been stored improperly[b]
- An inadequate amount of blood was applied or smeared onto the strip[b]
- For strips which require blotting or wiping
  The strip was improperly blotted[a]
  Too much force applied to strip[b]
  Blood removed too early or contact time with reagent otherwise shortened[b]
  Blood removed beyond the specified time[c]
- Meter is dirty[a]
- Battery is low[a]
- Test is performed outside of temperature and humidity operating conditions[a]
- Hct[d] is low[c] or high[b]
- Dehydration[b]
- Hyperosmolar, nonketotic state[b]
- Lipemia[a]
- High levels of ascorbic acid or salicylates (rare)[b]

[a] Effect unpredictable.
[b] Values tend to be lower.
[c] Values tend to be higher.
[d] Hct = Hematocrit.

Table 48.19	Interpreting Home Blood Glucose Concentrations[a]	
Test Time	Target Insulin Dose	Target Meal/Snack
Prebreakfast (Fasting)	Predinner/bedtime intermediate or long-acting insulin	Bedtime snack
Prelunch	Prebreakfast regular insulin	Breakfast/midmorning snack
Predinner	Prebreakfast intermediate-acting insulin and/or prelunch regular insulin	Lunch/midafternoon snack
Bedtime	Predinner regular insulin	Dinner
3 a.m. or later	Predinner intermediate-acting insulin	Dinner/bedtime snack

[a] Considerations: 1) Assumes a normal meal pattern. For patients who travel, have odd working or sleeping hours, or irregular meal patterns, these rules may not apply. 2) Assumes administration 30–60 min before meals and a normal pattern of insulin response. See Table 48.8 for factors which can alter insulin absorption and response. 3) If prebreakfast concentrations are high, rule out reactive hyperglycemia (Somogyi reaction or posthypoglycemic hyperglycemia). Consider contribution of "dawn" phenomenon as well. Whenever blood glucose concentrations are high, consider reactive hyperglycemia (excessive insulin doses). 4) Consider accuracy of reported test results: a) Do they correlate with HbA$_{1c}$ and patient's signs and symptoms? b) What is the patient's compliance? Could results be fabricated? c) Is patient's technique appropriate? Check timing, adequate blood sample, machine, strips, calibration, removal of blood. (See Table 48.18.) d) Are insulin kinetics altered? (See Table 48.8.) e) Meals: consider content, quality, and regularity.

sulin dose be altered? **The initial goal of therapy is to achieve preprandial blood glucose concentrations of <180 mg/dL and to eliminate symptoms of hyperglycemia.** [SI units: blood glucose 7 a.m. 9.9 mmol/L, 12 p.m. 13.3 mmol/L, 5 p.m. 8.3 mmol/L, 11 p.m. and 3 a.m. 8.9 mmol/L]

Health care providers should use the data obtained from self-monitoring to 1) set glycemic goals, 2) develop recommendations for pharmacological therapy, 3) evaluate the effectiveness of pharmacological therapy, 4) instruct patients to interpret and respond to blood glucose patterns, 5) evaluate the impact of dietary factors on glycemic control, 6) modify therapy during acute/intercurrent illness or whenever patients receive medications known to affect glycemic control, 7) modify the management plan in response to change in activity levels, and 8) identify hypoglycemic unawareness.[35]

Before using A.H.'s blood glucose results to adjust her insulin dose, it is important to observe and reassess her testing technique. One also should determine if there were any unusual circumstances in her life, diet, or exercise patterns over the past week which might have affected her response to insulin. Once these have been ruled out as confounding factors, one can begin making gross adjustments in A.H.'s insulin dose, realizing that fine tuning will be impossible until a consistent diet and exercise pattern have been instituted.

Several principles must be kept in mind whenever blood glucose tests are used to adjust a patient's basic insulin dose. (See Table 48.20.) Since many factors may alter a patient's response to insulin, it is important to base insulin doses upon blood glucose concentration *trends* measured over a minimum of three days. The only exception to this rule would be the use of supplemental insulin doses during periods of illness or stress. (See Questions 17 and 18.) Results of home blood glucose testing should be evaluated in conjunction with other parameters such as glycosylated hemoglobin and periodic laboratory blood glucose measurements.

The split dose of NPH is inadequately controlling A.H.'s symptoms and blood glucose concentrations. She is achieving some response in the late afternoon, but the delayed onset of NPH action and inadequate total daily dose have resulted in poor control of her blood glucose concentrations overall. The blood glucose concentration of 160 mg/dL at 3:00 a.m. indicates that rebound hyperglycemia is an unlikely cause of her high fasting levels. (See Questions 15 and 19.) As an initial step toward control, A.H.'s evening dose of NPH could be increased in an attempt to control her fasting hyperglycemia.

If A.H. is capable and ready to learn how to mix short-acting and intermediate-acting insulins, another approach may be used:

- Increase the total daily dose of insulin slightly since her overall control is poor (e.g., 0.6 U/kg × 50 kg = 30 U).

- Split the dose of insulin so that approximately two-thirds (21 U) is administered in the morning and one-third (9 U) is administered in the evening.

- Provide a 2:1 ratio of NPH:regular insulin in the morning (14 U/7 U) and evening (6 U/3 U).

If this approach is used, it is essential that A.H. incorporate a bedtime snack into her diet and test her blood glucose concentrations periodically at 3:00 a.m. in the morning to assure that she does not suffer from nocturnal hypoglycemia.

13. A.H. is quite anxious to get her diabetes under control and agrees to mix her insulins. How should she be instructed to measure and withdraw this insulin mixture?

The procedure used to mix and withdraw NPH and regular insulin is basically the same as that described in Question 9. The major difference is that an adequate volume of air must be injected into the NPH vial *before* the regular insulin is measured and withdrawn. Also, regular insulin is measured and withdrawn into the insulin syringe *first* to avoid contamination of the vial of regular insulin with NPH. Contamination with NPH ultimately will alter the NPH:Reg ratio which is administered. When patients withdraw NPH or lente insulin first, the vial of regular insulin eventually becomes cloudy. In contrast, contamination of the NPH insulin with regular insulin probably is insignificant because the protamine contained in NPH can bind the regular insulin. (See Question 14.) The procedure which A.H. should use to mix her insulins is described below, using her morning dose as an example.

- After dispersing the NPH insulin suspension, inject 14 U of air into the NPH vial and withdraw the needle.

- Inject 7 U of air into the regular insulin vial, and withdraw the 7 U of insulin as described in Question 9.

- Insert the needle into the NPH vial, and pull the plunger down to the 21 unit mark (14 U of NPH + 7 U of regular).

Stability of Mixed Insulins

14. Will mixing NPH with regular insulin blunt the rapid action of regular insulin? How stable are other insulin mixtures?

NPH-Regular. The onset and duration of action of regular and NPH insulin administered as a mixture are similar to those which are observed when the two insulins are administered by separate injection. The pharmacodynamic profiles of these insulins are retained in premixed preparations stored in vials or syringes for three months.[77,78] This is so even though protamine in NPH binds regular insulin *in vitro*.

Lente-Regular. In contrast to the NPH-regular mixtures, the rapid action of regular insulin is blunted significantly when premixed with lente insulin. The excess zinc in lente preparations binds the regular insulin, converting it to an intermediate-acting form. This effect is observed even when the two insulins are mixed just before injection; however, the clinical importance of this effect seems to be minimal.[48,77,79] Similar changes occur when regular insulin is mixed with *ultralente* insulin.[53]

Phosphate-Buffered Regular-Lente. When phosphate-buffered regular insulin (Velosulin BR-Novo Nordisk) is mixed with lente insulin, the phosphate binds with zinc and converts lente insulin to rapid-acting regular insulin.[68,80]

Evaluating Fasting Hyperglycemia

15. A.H. is instructed to inject 14 U NPH/7 U Reg before breakfast and 6 U NPH/3 U Reg before dinner. Two weeks later, A.H. returns to the clinic with the following blood glucose trends:

Time	Glucose Concentration (mg/dL)
7 a.m.	160
12 p.m.	130
5 p.m.	110
11 p.m.	90–120
3 a.m.	60–70

Subjectively, A.H. feels substantially better. Her energy level is beginning to return to normal, and her nocturia actually has diminished. She occasionally gets up 1 or 2 times nightly to urinate. Her weight remains the same, and she has begun to develop some consistency in her dietary patterns with the help of a dietitian. The glycosylated hemoglobin from her last visit is 12%. The new goal is to achieve blood glucose concentrations <150 mg/dL preprandially. Evaluate A.H.'s blood glucose values. What are possible causes of A.H.'s fasting hyperglycemia?

[SI units: blood glucose 7 a.m. 8.9 mmol/L, 12 p.m. 7.2 mmol/L, 5 p.m. 6.1 mmol/L, 11 p.m. 5.0–6.7 mmol/L, 3 a.m. 3.3–3.9 mmol/L]

Table 48.21	Compatibility of Insulin Mixtures	
Mixture	Proportion	Comments
Regular + NPH	Any proportion	See Questions 14 and 25. The excess protamine in NPH and excess zinc in lente insulins combine with regular insulin and may potentially reduce or delay the activity of regular insulin. The interaction is concentration- and time-dependent. It does not appear to be clinically significant for NPH:regular mixtures, but may be important for lente:regular insulin mixtures. Phosphates in phosphate-buffered regular insulins bind zinc in lente insulins to form short-acting insulin
Regular + Lente	<1:1	
Regular + Normal Saline	Any proportion	Use within 2–3 hr of preparation
Regular + Insulin diluting solution	Any proportion	Stable indefinitely

A.H.'s prelunch, predinner, and bedtime blood glucose concentrations have improved considerably, indicating that her morning dose of regular insulin, morning dose of NPH, and evening dose of regular insulin are adequate. (See Table 48.19.) Her fasting plasma glucose concentration remains elevated, and her prelunch concentration could be improved. When evaluating morning hyperglycemia, several causes must be considered:[83]

- An insufficient dose of evening NPH. If the evening dose of NPH is insufficient, hepatic glucose output during the fasting state will be excessive, thereby producing hyperglycemia.

Table 48.20	Guidelines for Dosing Insulin

Basic Insulin Dose

First adjust the basic insulin dose (i.e., the dose that the patient will be instructed to take daily). This assumes that diet and physical activity are stable. Set a reasonable goal initially. This may mean the upper limits of the acceptable concentrations may be high initially (e.g., <200 mg/dL). Move towards a more ideal goal slowly.

Only adjust insulin doses if a *pattern* of response is observed under stable diet and exercise circumstances. That is, the same response to insulin is observed for ≥3 days. It is important to verify the stability of diet and exercise. Consider adjusting these variables as well.

Unless all levels are >200 mg/dL, try to adjust one component of insulin therapy at a time.

Start with the insulin component affecting the fasting blood glucose concentration. This glucose level often is the most difficult to control and frequently affects all other glucose concentrations measured throughout the day.

Adjust the basic insulin dose by 1–2 U at a time. The amount prescribed is based upon the individual patient's response to insulin. This can be determined by looking at the patient's total daily dose on a U/kg basis. (See below and Table 48.14.)

Supplementary Insulin Doses

Once the basic dose of insulin has been established, supplemental doses of *regular* insulin can be prescribed to correct excessive *preprandial* glucose concentrations. For example if the goal is 140 mg/dL, and the glucose value is 190 mg/dL, administer an additional unit of regular insulin. Supplemental doses also can be used when the patient is ill (See Table 48.22)

Algorithms for supplemental doses are based upon the patient's sensitivity to insulin. Generally, they are in the range of 1–2 U for every 50 mg/dL *above* the goal. If values exceed 200 mg/dL, consider delaying the meal by another 20–30 min (i.e., 60 min after injection)

If premeal glucose concentrations are <60–70 mg/dL, the dose of regular insulin administered before the meal is ↓ 1–2 U; insulin administration is delayed until just before the meal; the meal includes 10 gm of glucose if the value is <50 mg/dL

If supplemental doses before a given meal are required for ≥3 days, the basic insulin dose should be adjusted appropriately. For example, if a patient requires 2 U before lunch for ≥3 days, 2 U should be added to the prebreakfast dose of regular insulin

Anticipatory Insulin Doses

The basic insulin dose is increased or decreased based upon the anticipated effects of diet or physical activity

Increase regular insulin by 1.5–2 U for each additional 20 gm of carbohydrate ingested (e.g., holiday meal) or decrease the usual dose by 1–2 U if the meal is smaller than usual

See Table 48.25 for recommended insulin adjustments for exercise

- An insufficient duration of action of the evening dose of NPH. (See below.)
- Reactive hyperglycemia in response to a nocturnal hypoglycemic episode (Somogyi effect).
- An excessive bedtime snack.
- The dawn phenomenon (see Question 19).

Somogyi Effect. The presence of normoglycemia at bedtime and a low blood glucose concentration at 3:00 a.m. are consistent with a possible rebound hyperglycemia reaction in the morning (posthypoglycemic hyperglycemia; Somogyi effect). Theoretically, this effect is secondary to an excessive increase in glucose production by the liver which is activated by insulin-counterregulatory hormones such as cortisol, glucagon, epinephrine, and growth hormone.[65] The waning effects of the evening dose of NPH insulin also may contribute since insulin is needed to suppress hepatic glucose output during the fasting state.[81] The existence of rebound hyperglycemia has been questioned.[65,82–84] However, as Gerich[83] points out, the studies' findings can be explained by the absence of counterregulatory responses in some patients or hyperinsulinemia, which counteracts the effects of glucagon, epinephrine, and cortisol. Asymptomatic nocturnal hypoglycemia can occur in 33% of patients taking evening doses of insulin and may account for morning hyperglycemia in more than 10% of patients. Another potential consequence of nocturnal hypoglycemia is prolonged insulin resistance as signified by high postbreakfast glucose concentrations. In correcting the nocturnal hypoglycemia, normalization of A.H.'s fasting hyperglycemia also may be achieved. The following are therapeutic options:

- Decrease the evening dose of NPH by 2 to 3 U and have A.H. continue to monitor blood glucose concentrations at 3:00 a.m. in the morning.
- If A.H. is willing to give herself three injections of insulin, shift the evening injection of NPH (6 U) from predinner to bedtime. This effectively shifts the peak action of NPH to the early morning when she will be awake.[70,81] This peak action also corresponds to the dawn phenomenon (see Question 19) and the breakfast meal.

Midmorning Hyperglycemia

16. Evaluate A.H.'s 12 p.m. blood glucose concentration.

Midmorning hyperglycemia frequently represents the maximum glucose excursion in patients with diabetes and often is the most difficult to manage. The following are possible explanations for midmorning hyperglycemia:

- An insufficient dose of regular insulin before breakfast.
- Poor synchrony between meal intake and insulin action. This could be caused by administration of insulin just before or after meals or a delayed onset of action of regular insulin due to binding with intermediate-acting insulin or insulin-blocking antibodies.[47] The latter two explanations are unlikely in A.H. As discussed in Question 14, lente insulin, but not NPH insulin, is more likely to delay the pharmacologic response to regular insulin. Since A.H. is a newly diagnosed patient with diabetes, it is unlikely that she has yet developed significant concentrations of insulin blocking antibody.
- An insufficient dose of evening NPH insulin to suppress hepatic glucose production (glycogenolysis and gluconeogenesis) during the fasting state or the dawn phenomenon. (See Question 19.)
- Excessive carbohydrate ingestion at breakfast.

When evaluating midmorning hyperglycemia, it is important to remember that the fasting plasma glucose concentration can contribute up to 50% of this plasma glucose excursion. Therefore, the primary approach to the control of hyperglycemia may be to normalize the fasting glucose concentration.

This should be the approach in A.H. If control of fasting hyperglycemia does not correct midmorning hyperglycemia, the following interventions may be considered:

- Increase the dose of regular insulin before breakfast.
- Inject the morning dose of insulin 45 to 60 minutes before breakfast in an attempt to match peak insulin concentrations with postmeal glucose excursions. If this maneuver is used, the patient should be warned of possible hypoglycemia before breakfast.
- If lente insulin is being used as the intermediate-acting insulin, consider switching the patient to NPH insulin.
- Alter the carbohydrate content of the diet. This may include decreasing the amount of carbohydrate in the breakfast meal, changing the type of carbohydrate ingested, or adding fiber to that meal to minimize glucose excursions.

Supplementary Insulin Doses

17. A.H. agrees to give herself 3 injections of insulin as follows: 14 U NPH/7 U Reg before breakfast; 3 U Reg before dinner; and 6 U NPH at bedtime. Two weeks later she brings in her blood glucose concentration records which read as follows:

Time	Glucose Concentration (mg/dL)
7 a.m.	110–120
12 p.m.	80–110
5 p.m.	90–110
11 p.m.	90–110
3 a.m.	80–110

A.H. feels that she is now "back to normal." She has no signs or symptoms of hyperglycemia, and her weight has remained stable. Occasionally, her preprandial blood glucose concentrations inexplicably exceed the new goal of 120 mg/dL. Evaluate A.H.'s blood glucose trends. How should occasional preprandial glucose concentrations which exceed the desired goal of 120 mg/dL be managed? [SI units: blood glucose 7 a.m. 6.1–6.7 mmol/L, 12 p.m. 4.4–6.1 mmol/L, 5 p.m. 5.0–6.1 mmol/L, 11 p.m. 5.0–6.1 mmol/L, 3 a.m. 4.4–6.1 mmol/L]

A.H.'s blood glucose concentrations indicate that her basic insulin regimen is adequate to achieve the overall goal of preprandial blood glucose concentrations of less than 120 mg/dL. Note that correction of A.H.'s fasting plasma glucose concentration ultimately corrected her midmorning hyperglycemia. In fact, if one were to evaluate A.H.'s blood glucose concentrations from the previous visit, it is evident that the prebreakfast dose of regular insulin was working. (See Question 15.) That is, even though the absolute blood glucose concentration at midmorning was high, it was 30 mg/dL less than the fasting glucose concentration of 160 mg/dL. This domino effect on blood glucose concentrations emphasizes the importance of correcting one blood glucose concentration at a time.

Once the basic dose of insulin has been established, one can begin to teach A.H. how to adjust her dose of insulin when preprandial blood glucose concentrations fall above or below the range of blood glucose concentrations which have been established as her goal of therapy (70 to 120 mg/dL). There are two types of supplementary doses that are used in this situation: compensatory insulin doses and anticipatory insulin doses.[68]

Compensatory insulin doses are used to compensate for unusually high or low preprandial blood glucose concentrations. To re-emphasize, this assumes there are no unusual changes in the patient's diet or exercise patterns. Generally, the patient is instructed to give herself an additional one or two units of *regular* insulin for every 30 to 50 mg/dL increment above the desired blood glucose concentration. Conversely, if the preprandial blood glucose concentration falls below 60 to 70 mg/dL, the patient is instructed to decrease her dose of regular insulin by one to two units.

Supplemental doses must be individualized for each patient. The patient's sensitivity to insulin, as reflected by her total daily dose on a unit/kg basis is a major determinant of any algorithm developed. A.H. is relatively sensitive to insulin. Thus, a conservative algorithm of one unit of insulin for every 50 mg/dL excursion above her goal of 120 mg/dL is a reasonable place to begin. If this dose of insulin is insufficient, one can increase the dose of insulin or decrease the blood glucose excursion required per unit of insulin dose. Supplementary insulin doses also are used for sick day management. (See Question 18.) The following is an example of an algorithm for A.H.:

Glucose Concentrations (mg/dL)	Regular Insulin
<70	1 U less
70–120	Usual dose
120–170	1 U extra
170–220	2 U extra
220–270	3 U extra
270–320*	4 U extra

*(Check urine ketones. If urine ketones are positive and blood glucose concentrations remain above 240 mg/dL for ≥12 hours, call the physician for directions.)

Anticipatory insulin supplements are prescribed in anticipation of an immediate event which is likely to alter a patient's response to insulin. This includes an unusually large or small meal or exercise. (See Table 48.12 and Question 26.)

Sick Day Management

18. A.H.'s diabetes has been well controlled on 3 daily doses of insulin. However, 2 days ago, she began to develop signs and symptoms consistent with the flu. She has been anorexic and nauseated and now has begun to vomit; consequently, her food intake has been minimal. Should A.H. discontinue her insulin in view of the fact that she cannot eat at this time?

Insulin requirements always increase in the presence of an infection or acute illness, even if the food intake is diminished. Insulin-dependent diabetic patients such as A.H. commonly decrease or eliminate insulin doses under these circumstances, and it is just in this setting that ketoacidosis occurs.

Therefore, A.H. should be instructed to maintain her usual dose of insulin and test her blood glucose concentration every three to four hours; the latter is particularly important if she has become less compliant. If blood glucose concentrations are above the usual range, supplemental doses of regular insulin should be administered according to a prescribed algorithm. Usually, 1 to 2 units of regular insulin for each 30 to 40 mg/dL increment above the target goal is administered every three to four hours. A.H. also should be instructed to test her urine for ketones if the blood glucose concentration exceeds 240 mg/dL. She should call her physician if her blood glucose concentration remains above 240 mg/dL after three supplementary insulin doses or if she begins to develop signs and

symptoms related to ketoacidosis (polyuria, polydipsia, dehydration, ketonuria, and a fruity breath). (Also see Question 34.) A.H. also should attempt to maintain her fluid, mineral, and carbohydrate intake with easily digested food and fluids. (See Table 48.22.)[61]

Dawn Phenomenon

19. R.D., a 37-year-old male, has had diabetes since age 14. Over the past 2 years he has been reasonably well controlled on the following insulin regimen: 20 U NPH/10 U Reg before breakfast; 10 U Reg before dinner; and 10 U NPH at bedtime.

On this regimen, his blood glucose concentrations for the past 2 weeks have been as follows:

Time	Glucose Concentration (mg/dL)
7 a.m.	150
12 p.m.	110
5 p.m.	110–120
11 p.m.	130
3 a.m.	110

What are the likely causes of R.D.'s fasting hyperglycemia?
[SI units: blood glucose 7 a.m. 8.3 mmol/L, 12 p.m. 6.1 mmol/L, 5 p.m. 6.1–6.7 mmol/L, 11 p.m. 7.2 mmol/L, 3 a.m. 6.1 mmol/L]

As discussed in Question 15, fasting hyperglycemia may be the result of insufficient doses of insulin in the evening, a decline in the effect of insulin over time, and possibly, reactive hyperglycemia. In R.D.'s case, the dawn phenomenon also must be considered.[87] The dawn phenomenon is a rise in the blood glucose concentration which occurs between 4:00 and 8:00 a.m. following a physiologic nadir in the blood glucose concentration that occurs between 12:00 and 3:00 a.m. This 30 to 40 mg/dL increase in the morning blood glucose concentration cannot be attributed to increases in counterregulatory hormones secondary to an antecedent hypoglycemic event, but it may be secondary to rising growth hormone levels. This phenomenon is inconsistently observed in individuals with Type I and Type II diabetes as well as nondiabetic individuals; furthermore, it is inconsistently present from one day to the next.[83-86]

R.D.'s 3:00 a.m. blood glucose concentration indicates that post hypoglycemic hyperglycemia is an unlikely etiology of his fasting hyperglycemia. Thus, the modest increase in his blood glucose concentration between 3:00 a.m. and 8:00 a.m. may be attributed to the waning effects of insulin or the dawn phenomenon. In both cases, an *increase* in R.D.'s evening NPH dose would be indicated. In patients treated with constant subcutaneous infusions of insulin, the pump may be programmed to increase the basal infusion rate

Table 48.22	Sick Day Management[61]

1) Continue taking your basic dose of insulin *even* if you are not eating well or have nausea or vomiting

2) Test your blood glucose more frequently: every 3–4 hr

3) If indicated, give yourself *supplemental* doses of regular insulin: for example 1–2 U for every 30–50 mg/dL over an agreed-upon target glucose concentration (e.g., 150 mg/dL). Supplemental doses must be individualized based upon the patient's sensitivity to insulin

4) Begin testing your urine for ketones

5) Try to drink plenty of fluid (½ cup/hr for adults) and maintain your caloric intake (50 gm carbohydrate every 4 hr). Foods such as jello, uncarbonated soft drinks, crackers, soup, and soda may be used

6) Call a physician if your blood glucose concentration remains above 240 mg/dL or your urine ketones remain high after 2–3 supplemental doses of insulin

at approximately 12:00 midnight. Because it takes three to four hours to observe a biological response following a change in the infusion rate, the response would occur at approximately 3:00 a.m. to 4:00 a.m. when the dawn phenomenon begins.[68]

Since the dawn phenomenon varies from day to day, increasing R.D.'s NPH dose may increase his risk of nocturnal hypoglycemia. Thus, it is important that he continue to monitor occasional blood glucose concentrations at 3:00 a.m.

Adverse Effects of Insulin

Hyperinsulinemia

20. G.O., a 42-year-old, slightly overweight (5'11", 180 lb) male, has had a history of IDDM for 19 years. G.O.'s medical care was sporadic until 1 year ago when he referred himself to a diabetes clinic because he was beginning to develop pain and numbness in his feet. At that time, he was poorly controlled on a single daily dose of 45 U of NPH insulin. He had not been testing his urine or blood glucose concentrations, and his HbA$_{1c}$ was 13%.

On physical examination, G.O. was found to have an elevated blood pressure [(BP) 160/94 mm Hg], background retinopathy, and decreased pedal pulses. There was decreased sensation to vibration and pin prick in both feet. G.O. complained of impotence and "shooting pains" in both legs. A 24-hour collection of urine protein contained 1.5 gm of albumin.

G.O. was treated with multiple daily doses of insulin. Over the last several months, he has been treated with the following regimen: 12 U Lente/10–12 U Reg before breakfast; 10–12 U Reg before lunch; and 24 U Lente at bedtime. Blood glucose concentrations have been as follows:

Time	Glucose Concentration (mg/dL)
7 a.m.	100–150
12 p.m.	280
5 p.m.	40–280

Over the past year, G.O.'s HbA$_{1c}$ has decreased to 7.2%. Currently, he has approximately 5 hypoglycemic reactions per week, primarily in the late afternoon and evenings. He has found that he can avoid nocturnal hypoglycemia by eating a large bedtime snack. Over the past 3 months, he has gained 15 lb. Evaluate G.O.'s overall control. What interventions are indicated at this time? [SI units: blood glucose 7 a.m. 5.5–8.3 mmol/L, 12 p.m. 15.5 mmol/L/L, 5 p.m. 2.2–15.5 mmol/L; HbA$_{1c}$ = 0.72]

G.O. illustrates one of the major hazards of intensive insulin therapy: hypoglycemia and hyperinsulinemia.[48,68] The signs and symptoms of overinsulinization in G.O. include:

- A total daily insulin dose of almost 0.9 U/kg. This dose is unusual in a patient with Type I diabetes.

- A weight gain over the past several months. This is secondary to the anabolic effects of insulin as well as G.O.'s increased carbohydrate intake to match his high insulin doses.

- Frequent hypoglycemic reactions.

- An apparently "brittle" situation (i.e., blood glucose concentrations which fluctuate wildly between hypoglycemia and hyperglycemia). In G.O.'s case, high blood glucose concentrations may represent reactive hyperglycemia or overtreatment of hypoglycemic episodes.

- Normal glycosylated hemoglobin levels indicate mean blood glucose concentrations which must be within the normal range even though the patient has recorded numerous high blood glucose concentrations. DCCT patients treated with intensive insulin therapy experienced hypo-

glycemic episodes three times more often than patients treated with standard insulin therapy.[14] This is particularly ominous in patients with defects in glucose counterregulation. (See Question 21.)

G.O. should be managed by gradually decreasing his insulin doses. Since most of his reactions are occurring in the late afternoon and evening, the morning dose of intermediate-acting insulin should be adjusted first. Changing his intermediate-acting insulin from lente to NPH insulin also should be considered, since the excess zinc in the lente insulin may be converting some of the short-acting insulin to an intermediate-acting form. (See Question 14.) The bedtime dose of intermediate-acting insulin also should be reduced since the patient has reported episodes of nocturnal hypoglycemia. Conservative reduction in the insulin dose (10%) should minimize hyperglycemia and ketonemia. Thus, a total reduction to 6 to 7 U (e.g., a reduction in the morning dose of intermediate-acting insulin to 10 U and a reduction in the bedtime intermediate-acting insulin to 20 U) could be recommended.

G.O. also should begin testing his glucose concentrations at 3:00 a.m., and he should be taught to treat his hypoglycemic episodes appropriately. (See Question 22.) If he is capable, an algorithm for adjusting his preprandial regular insulin doses should be provided to minimize hypoglycemic and hyperglycemic reactions. An example of an algorithm which may be appropriate for G.O. follows:

Glucose Concentrations (mg/dL)	Change Dose of Regular Insulin by:
<50	−2 U
<80	−1 U
80–140	no change
140–170	+1 U
170–200	+2 U
200–230	+3 U
>230	+4 U

G.O. should be instructed to take regular insulin before each meal and adjust his dose according to the above algorithm. It will be important that he record the actual dose he administers before each meal and bring the record to clinic so that his basic dose of insulin can be more finely tuned.

Insulin Reactions: Defective Counterregulation

21. M.M., a 35-year-old, unemployed male, has had IDDM since the age of 3. As a consequence of the diabetes, he has developed proliferative retinopathy and progressive diabetic nephropathy [current serum creatinine (SrCr) = 3.0 mg/dL]. M.M. has an erratic lifestyle. Because he does not work, he often stays out late at night and sleeps late into the morning. His insulin is injected whenever he awakens, and his meals are irregularly spaced. Each time he comes to clinic, he brings with him a complete log of glucose concentrations which range from 80–140 mg/dL. He has 2–3 severe hypoglycemic reactions a month which require emergency treatment with IV glucose. On several occasions, his blood glucose concentration has been 20 mg/dL. M.M.'s last HbA$_{1c}$ was 12%. M.M. says he adheres to the following insulin regimen: 18 U NPH/11 U Reg before breakfast; 10 U Reg before lunch; and 14 U NPH at bedtime.

On this visit, M.M. comes with his girlfriend. He has a large gash on his nose which occurred when he lost consciousness while pushing his stalled car 3 days ago. This occurred around 1:30 p.m. He was unable to eat lunch at the usual hour because he had problems with his car. Assess M.M.'s blood glucose control. How should he be managed? [SI units: SrCr 265 μmol/L; blood glucose 4.4–7.8 mmol/L; HbA$_{1c}$ 0.12]

M.M. illustrates a patient with Type I diabetes who has defective glucose counterregulation and, as a result, is unable to counteract a hypoglycemic reaction effectively. He also is an example of a patient who should *not* be treated with intensive insulin therapy. (See Table 48.15.)[68]

- M.M. clearly is noncompliant. His lifestyle is erratic, he eats irregularly, and his reported blood glucose concentrations (80 to 140 mg/dL) do not correspond with his high glycosylated hemoglobin value. This may indicate that M.M.'s technique is incorrect or that he simply fills in the log with fictitious numbers before he comes to the clinic. Irregular entries in different colored inks usually indicate authentic records.

- M.M. has developed advanced, long-term complications which are unlikely to be reversed by intensive insulin therapy. In fact, proliferative retinopathy may actually worsen with intensive insulin therapy initially.[68]

- In the DCCT study, severe hypoglycemic reactions were three times more common in patients treated with intensive insulin therapy and nocturnal hypoglycemia accounted for 41% of the total hypoglycemic episodes.[14] In patients with defective counterregulation, the risk of severe hypoglycemia may be 25 times higher than in patients with adequate counterregulatory mechanisms treated with intensive insulin therapy.[65] M.M. is at great risk for death secondary to hypoglycemia which accounts for approximately 4% of deaths in patients with IDDM.

The primary hormones which are secreted in response to a low blood glucose concentration are glucagon and epinephrine. In patients who have had IDDM for more than two to five years, a deficiency in glucagon secretion is a relatively consistent finding. These patients must rely upon epinephrine to reverse low blood glucose concentrations. Unfortunately, approximately 40% of patients with long-standing IDDM (8 to 15 years) have defective epinephrine secretion as well and this may be related to the development of autonomic neuropathy. Patients whose diabetes is controlled closely with intensive insulin therapy also have reduced counterregulatory hormone responses to hypoglycemia. As illustrated by M.M., patients with defective epinephrine secretory responses also lose the warning signs and symptoms of hypoglycemia.[65] Consequently, their hypoglycemic reactions may go unnoticed and untreated until they lose consciousness. M.M. should be managed as follows:

- Since his waking, sleeping, and eating patterns are highly irregular, he should be treated with an insulin regimen which addresses his lifestyle. For example, he could be instructed to give himself regular insulin one-half hour before he actually intends to eat. A dose of NPH could be given before his first meal to supply basal levels of insulin between meals. Evening doses of NPH should be eliminated because of the danger of severe hypoglycemic reactions.

- Since M.M. has no warning symptoms for hypoglycemia, the importance of regular blood glucose testing should be emphasized. When blood glucose testing was reviewed with M.M., it was discovered that his eyesight was so poor that he was unable to distinguish between the right and wrong side of the strip. Furthermore, because he had lost his depth of field, he was unable to place a drop of blood onto the center of the pad. To address this situation, M.M.'s girlfriend was taught how to perform blood glucose testing.

- M.M.'s girlfriend also was taught how to inject glucagon in the event that she found him unconscious.

All of these maneuvers diminished the frequency of M.M.'s severe hypoglycemic reactions. On the whole, his blood glucose concentrations were maintained below 180 mg/dL and he remained relatively free of hyperglycemic symptoms. M.M.'s glycosylated hemoglobin using this insulin regimen was 10.5%.

Signs and Symptoms/Treatment of Hypoglycemia

22. How should M.M. be taught to assess and manage any hypoglycemic reactions which may occur? Could his use of human insulin be blunting his symptoms of hypoglycemia?

Hypoglycemia is defined as a blood glucose concentration of less than 50 mg/dL and its occurrence is potentially fatal if it is not recognized and promptly treated. Approximately 10% of patients treated with insulin develop at least one severe, disabling episode of hypoglycemia per year. Virtually all patients treated with insulin experience a hypoglycemic reaction at one time or another.[65]

The signs and symptoms associated with hypoglycemia include blurred vision, generalized sweating, tremor, intense hunger, sweaty palms, a cold feeling, headache, palpitation, and piloerection. Diminished cerebral function is indicated by lethargy, confusion, agitation, and nervousness. Ultimately, convulsions, with stupor, and coma can occur. Tingling of the lips and tongue are common complaints of patients who develop insulin reactions at night. These patients also may complain of headache and difficulty arising in the morning.[65] It is important to note that early warning symptoms of hypoglycemia vary from patient to patient. Thus, it is important that M.M. studies and learns to recognize his earliest warning symptoms. Patients generally can recall prodromal symptoms following recovery from a severe hypoglycemic reaction.

Unfortunately, many patients (M.M. may be one of them) have no warning symptoms of hypoglycemia. These patients are said to have "hypoglycemia unawareness" because they have no awareness of blood glucose concentrations below 50 mg/dL. In these individuals, loss of consciousness, seizures, or irrational behavior may be the first objective signs of exceedingly low blood glucose concentrations. This situation occurs in patients with long-standing diabetes who have defects in the counterregulatory secretion of both glucagon and epinephrine.[65] The glycemic threshold for symptoms also is lowered in patients on intensive insulin therapy whose glucose concentrations have been lowered to normal or near-normal levels.[65] Some isolated European reports have suggested that patients switched from animal source to human insulin developed asymptomatic and fatal hypoglycemia. However, current evidence does not support the hypothesis that the asymptomatic nature of these episodes was related to the insulin source.[88,89]

These authors occasionally have seen patients who "feel" hypoglycemic after their blood glucose concentrations have been normalized with intensive insulin therapy. We encourage patients to test their blood glucose concentrations any time they "feel unusual" to verify a low blood glucose concentration. M.M. should treat the symptoms only if he is truly hypoglycemic.

Simple Sugars. Most hypoglycemic reactions are managed readily with the equivalent of 10 to 20 gm of glucose. (See Table 48.23 for examples of carbohydrate sources containing 10 gm of glucose.) If the blood concentration remains low after 15 minutes, the patient should ingest another 10 to 20 gm of carbohydrate. This "quick" source of sugar should be followed by a small complex carbohydrate/protein snack to provide a continual source of glucose if a meal is not scheduled within the next one to two hours. Most patients with diabetes have a tendency to overtreat hypogly-

Table 48.23	Hypoglycemia[a]

Definition

Blood glucose concentration <50 mg/dL; patient may or may not be symptomatic. Blood glucose <40 mg/dL; patient generally symptomatic. Blood glucose <20 mg/dL can be associated with seizures and coma

Signs and Symptoms

Blurred vision, sweaty palms, generalized sweating, tremulousness, hunger, confusion, anxiety, circumoral tingling and numbness. Patients vary with regard to their symptoms. Behavior can be confused with inebriation. Patients become combative and use poor judgment

Nocturnal hypoglycemia: nightmares, restless sleep, profuse sweating, morning headache, morning "hangover." In one study, 80% of patients with nocturnal hypoglycemia had no symptoms

Clinical Considerations

Irregular eating patterns

↑ physical exercise

Gastroparesis: (delayed gastric emptying time)

Defective counterregulatory responses

Excessive oral sulfonylureas

Drugs (See Table 48.28)

Treatment

10–20 gm rapidly-absorbed carbohydrate. Repeat in 15–20 min if glucose concentration remains <60 mg/dL or patient is symptomatic. Follow with complex carbohydrate/protein snack if meal time is not imminent

Examples of food sources which provide 10 gm of carbohydrate:

Orange juice; regular, nondiet soda	½ cup
Apple juice	⅓ cup
Grape juice	¼ cup
Sugar	2 tsp or 2 cubes
Lifesavers	5–6 pieces
B/D glucose tablets	2 tablets

If unconscious:
Glucagon 1 mg, SQ, IM, or IV (Mean response time: 6.5 min)
Glucose 25 gm IV (Dextrose 50%–50 cc)
(Mean response time: 4 min)

[a] SQ = Subcutaneous; IM = Intramuscular; IV = Intravenous.

cemic reactions with, for example, large quantities of juice or several candy bars. This should be discouraged since overcorrection ultimately will result in hyperglycemia.[65]

M.M.'s friends also should be taught how to recognize symptoms of hypoglycemia. Often, patients with diabetes ignore early warning symptoms of hypoglycemia and progress to a point where they lose the judgment needed to treat the condition. If the patient has not yet become combative, friends may encourage the ingestion of a "quick" carbohydrate source.

Glucagon. A 1 mg dose of glucagon should be kept on hand for management of M.M.'s hypoglycemia if he becomes unconscious. Glucagon can be injected by the subcutaneous, intramuscular, or intravenous route. The subcutaneous and intramuscular route are equally effective, but in the emergency room (ER) situation, intravenous administration can produce significantly higher blood glucose concentrations within the first five to ten minutes.[65] Patients who are given glucagon should be positioned so that their face is turned toward the floor to prevent aspiration in the event of vomiting. As soon as the patient awakens (10 to 25 minutes), he should be fed.

If glucagon is unavailable, M.M. should be taken to the emergency room where he can be treated with intravenous glucose (≈25 gm) or glucagon.

Each time M.M. has a hypoglycemic reaction, he must determine its cause and take preventive or corrective action. This entails assessment of his diet (did he skip or delay a meal or change its content?), exercise pattern, and time of insulin administration and dose. If hypoglycemic reactions consistently occur at a certain time of the day, he should determine whether this corresponds to the maximum effect of one of his insulin doses and reduce that insulin dose by 1 to 2 U. Alternatively, he can add a supplemental snack to that part of the day.

Dermatologic Complications of Insulin

23. R.C. is a 27-year-old female whose Type I diabetes was diagnosed 8 years ago. Currently, she is well controlled on split doses of standard insulins. Her primary concerns on this visit are the unsightly indentations present on the anterior aspects of her thighs where she injects her insulin. On physical examination, extensive areas of lipoatrophy as well as mild lipohypertrophy are noted on the anterior, lateral, and posterior aspects of her thighs. On history, R.C. recalls that when she first began using insulin she developed "red, itchy" spots at the sites of insulin injection which have since disappeared. What are the causes of R.C.'s dermatologic history and findings? How can they be managed?

Lipodystrophy secondary to the use of insulin may present in two ways, both of which are evident in R.C.: as atrophy (subcutaneous concavities caused by wasting of fat tissue) and as hypertrophy (tumorous-like fat pads at the sites of injection).

Lipoatrophy occurs most commonly in young women (as illustrated by R.C.) and children and is believed to have an immune pathogenesis. The reported prevalence of lipoatrophy has fallen as insulin products have become more pure. While approximately 15% of patients using conventional, unpurified insulins developed this problem, it is now a rare phenomenon.[47] R.C. has been using a standard insulin product that contains beef insulin, the most antigenic product.

Lipoatrophy can be treated by injecting human or purified pork insulin directly into the margins of the lipoatrophic site. Improvement begins in four weeks and complete recovery should be attained in three to six months. This form of therapy has been found to be 90% to 100% successful, but atrophy may recur unless insulin is reinjected into the same site every three to four weeks.[53]

Lipohypertrophy. R.C. also exhibits mild areas of lipohypertrophy that probably are caused by the lipogenic effects of insulin. Most cases occur after many months or years of repeated injections into the same site and may be self-perpetuating because the site of injection becomes anesthetized. Proper rotation of the injection sites may result in spontaneous regression of these lipomas but surgical resection may be needed in extreme cases. As expected, the injection of "purified" insulins into the affected site does not appear to improve this form of lipodystrophy and, in fact, cases of lipohypertrophy have been associated with their use.[53]

Local Skin Reactions. R.C. also has a history of local skin reactions to insulin. Before insulin was purified, local erythema, pain, swelling, and itching were much more common. Although the prevalence has decreased considerably, even pork and human insulin can cause occasional local and systemic allergic reactions.[90,91] Insulin dimers, zinc, and protamine may be the source of "insulin" allergies.[53] The reactions occur in one of four forms: 1) an immediate wheal/flare reaction; 2) an immediate reaction followed in four to eight hours by erythema and induration (most common); 3) a delayed reaction which occurs 12 to 24 hours following injection; and 4) Arthus reactions.[53] Frequently, as illustrated by R.C., spontaneous desensitization to insulin occurs by the time the first vial of insulin is completed (3 weeks to 3 months)

Table 48.24	Indications for Human or Purified Pork Insulin
Indications for Patients Who Have	**Comments**
Local or systemic insulin allergies	Some cases of systemic allergy resolve when patients are switched to human or purified pork insulin. There is a decreased prevalence of local allergic reactions to these insulins. However, occasional systemic allergic reactions to purified insulins may occur, indicating that they also have some inherent antigenicity
Immunologically-based insulin resistance	When insulin resistance is due to the presence of excessive circulating insulin antibodies, the use of human or purified pork insulin may be beneficial
Lipodystrophies	Lipoatrophy often responds to more purified insulins and, in fact, has been reported to develop during their use
Temporary requirements for insulin	Because interrupted insulin therapy is associated more frequently with the development of local or systemic allergy and immunologic resistance, many diabetologists recommend the use of human or purified pork insulins for patients who require insulin only temporarily. These situations include gestational diabetes, insulin requirements during hyperalimentation, and in Type II diabetics requiring insulin during surgery or major stress

and the local reaction subsides. If the reaction persists or is particularly bothersome, the patient should be switched to human insulin. (See Table 48.24.)

For resistant cases, oral antihistamines or small doses of a glucocorticoid mixed in the same syringe with insulin (dexamethasone, 1 mg/U insulin) can be tried.

Fortunately, *systemic allergic reactions* to insulin are exceedingly rare. When they do occur, desensitization is the primary form of treatment. Similarly, *insulin resistance* (insulin dose requirements >200 U/day) caused by high titers of IgG blocking antibodies also is rare and has been reported only in patients using animal-source insulins. Patients generally respond when they are switched to human insulin. Both of these conditions most commonly occur in patients who have had a history of interrupted insulin therapy.[53,93]

24. Dose Change with Switch to a Human Insulin. R.C. agrees to use a human insulin in an attempt to resolve the disfiguring lipoatrophy of both legs. Will a change of insulin dose be necessary?

As previously discussed, human insulin may be absorbed more quickly and may have a slightly shorter duration of action than insulin from animal sources. However, there are so many variables that affect insulin response that the slight difference in pharmacokinetics between human and animal insulins is not enough to alter the dose prophylactically.

In the late 1970s and early 1980s, reduced insulin requirements were reported in Europe when patients were changed from a conventional beef or beef/pork insulin to a "purified" pure pork insulin. Presumably this was due to decreased levels of insulin-binding antibodies produced by the less antigenic insulin product. The reduced requirements prompted the European manufacturers to warn clinicians to reduce initial doses by 20%, especially when patients used doses exceeding 40 U. However, in the U.S., where the change in insulin purity was less pronounced, dramatic changes in dose requirements were not observed.[92] The differences in purity between the many insulins currently available are now insignifi-

cant; therefore, except in rare instances where patients have high titers of animal-source insulin, dosage adjustments should not be necessary when switching among insulins.

A specific dose change should not be made initially in R.C.'s regimen. However, she should be instructed to monitor her diabetic control closely for the first few weeks after changing to a human insulin because a modification in her insulin regimen may become apparent.

Insulin Stability: Factors Altering Control

25. T.M., a 31-year-old farmer, has had IDDM for 20 years. He has been relatively well controlled on split-mixed doses of regular and NPH human insulin over the past years. During the winter and spring seasons, his blood glucose concentrations have ranged from 90–140 mg/dL, and the HbA$_{1c}$ measured at his last clinic visit 3 months ago was 8.5%. It is now August. For the past 2 months, T.M. has noticed that his diabetes is not under good control. His blood glucose concentrations vary widely from concentrations as low as 60 mg/dL to as high as 240 mg/dL. He has no explanation for this. On inspection, his vial of regular insulin is cloudy and there is a white precipitate clinging to the NPH vial, giving it a frosted appearance. Both vials are ≈one-third full. What factors may be contributing to T.M.'s poor glycemic control? [SI units: blood glucose concentrations 5.0–7.8 mmol/L; HbA$_{1c}$ 0.085]

Many factors may be contributing to T.M.'s poor control. These are discussed below.

Insulin Stability. Both of T.M.'s insulin vials have changed in appearance. T.M. should be instructed not to use his regular insulin if it becomes cloudy, thickened, or if it contains small, thread-like or other solid particles. As discussed in Question 13, the cloudiness may be caused by contamination of regular insulin with NPH. If T.M. reuses his syringes, this also may be caused by the silicone oil that is used to coat needles of disposable syringes.[94] The latter may denature the insulin, reducing its pharmacologic effect.

Flocculation. Occasionally, purified pork or human NPH flocculates or crystallizes onto the insulin bottle.[95] This results in a significant loss of potency with insulin concentrations in the remaining suspensions varying from 6 to 64 U/mL (labeled 100 U/mL). This phenomenon can occur "overnight," generally after three to six weeks of use. Incorporation of additional zinc into these preparations during the manufacturing process has minimized this problem. Nevertheless, all patients should be warned to inspect their vials carefully before each injection and to avoid the use of any insulin which has changed in appearance. Unused insulin in these vials may be exchanged for a new vial at most pharmacies.

Temperature. All commercially available insulins are stable for several months at room temperature (68 to 75 °F) for 18 to 24 months. Nevertheless, refrigeration is recommended by the manufacturers. In practice, most patients store vials currently in use at room temperature because injection of cold insulin is uncomfortable. The United States Pharmacopeia (USP) recommends that patients discard vials which have not been completely used in one month if they are kept at room temperature.

The stability of insulin at temperatures of 75 to 100 °F is unknown, but all insulins lose significant potency within one to two months at 100 °F. Patient T.M. lives in an area where temperatures frequently exceed 100 °F during the summer months. Therefore, it is important that he not store his insulin in an automobile or in the sun where it may be subject to deterioration. It also is of interest that many wholesale drug distributors do not take special precautions when delivering insulins to pharmacies during the summer months. Thus, exposure to high temperatures during these months may alter the potency and actions of insulins. Freezing apparently does not affect the potency of insulin, but may cause aggregation of the precipitate. This could alter the absorption kinetics of the preparation.[53,96]

Factors Altering Response to Insulin. Many other factors may be altering T.M.'s response to insulin. The heat in the summer months may increase circulation to the injected site, thus increasing the onset and shortening the duration of action of his insulin. Exercise of the injected limb may affect insulin action similarly. During the summer months, farmers typically are more physically active and as a consequence, require less insulin than usual. Other factors which may alter insulin action are listed in Tables 48.8 and 48.12.

Exercise and Insulin Requirements

26. J.S., a 17-year-old, nonobese, Type I diabetic, was diagnosed at age 12. He currently is moderately well controlled on 2 daily doses of insulin (7 U Reg/14 U NPH in the morning and 7 U Reg/7 U NPH in the evening). His HbA$_{1c}$ is 10%, and his blood glucose levels before meals range from 150–190 mg/dL. Fasting blood glucose concentrations in the clinic range from 130–170 mg/dL. He has rare hypoglycemic reactions which are associated with skipped meals, and he generally is compliant with his prescribed diet. What effect is jogging likely to have on his diabetic control? What precaution, if any, should he take? [SI units: HbA$_{1c}$ 0.10; blood glucose before meals 5.0–10.5 mmol/L; FPG 7.2–9.4 mmol/L]

Exercise has varying effects on plasma glucose levels in patients such as J.S. taking insulin. In the resting state, muscle derives approximately 10% of its metabolic requirement from glucose. In contrast, almost all of the muscle's metabolic requirements are derived from glucose during moderate to heavy exercise. Muscle glycogen stores are depleted quite rapidly after which glucose is derived from the peripheral circulation. To meet the increased glucose demands, hepatic glycogenolysis and gluconeogenesis increase. This is mediated primarily through suppression of insulin secretion and increased secretion of counterregulatory hormones such as glucagon. Low, permissive levels of insulin are required for glucose utilization by the muscle. In nondiabetic individuals, hepatic glucose output and peripheral utilization are balanced such that euglycemia is maintained during exercise.[97]

In a patient like J.S., exercise may cause hyperglycemia or hypoglycemia if he does not take proper precautions. If J.S. is insulin-deficient when he commences exercise, hepatic glucose output will be increased, but peripheral utilization will be decreased and hyperglycemia will ensue. Thus, patients like J.S. with insulin-dependent diabetes mellitus should not exercise if their blood glucose concentrations equal or exceed 250 to 300 mg/dL, since these levels usually indicate insulin deficiency.[25,96,184]

Conversely, excess insulin will enhance peripheral utilization of glucose by muscle and suppress hepatic glucose output. Both can contribute to hypoglycemia. Hypoglycemia is more likely to occur in patients whose blood glucose concentrations are normal or low just before exercise. Thus, if J.S.'s blood glucose concentration is normal or low before he begins exercise, he should take a carbohydrate snack (10 to 20 gm) and/or decrease his dose of regular insulin.[61]

It is less well appreciated that peripheral glucose utilization remains high after exercise has been discontinued. This is thought to be related to the replenishment of glycogen stores in the liver and muscle. Thus, if appropriate adjustments are not made in diet and insulin dose following exercise, hypoglycemia can occur 10 to 12 hours thereafter.[98]

If J.S. injects insulin into his thigh, jogging may enhance insulin absorption. The absorption of regular insulin is increased when it is administered just before exercise (within 5 minutes) but it does not appear to be affected if injected 30 to 40 minutes before exercise. Absorption of the intermediate-acting insulins is less likely to be augmented by exercise.[46,55,60] Some have suggested that insulin be injected at a site that is not exercised, for example the abdomen, to minimize this effect.

In summary, J.S. should be encouraged to exercise at least 30 to 40 minutes after insulin injection. He should test his blood glucose concentrations before, during, and after exercise and adjust his insulin doses and food intake accordingly. (See Table 48.25.) Regular exercise may increase tissue sensitivity to insulin and eventually lower J.S.'s insulin requirements. Vigorous exercise is contraindicated in patients with retinal or vitreous hemorrhages since retinal detachment may occur.

In obese individuals with noninsulin-dependent diabetes mellitus who are treated with diet, exercise is unlikely to cause hypoglycemia. An extremely low calorie diet (<800 calories) which also is low in carbohydrates may decrease an individual's exercise endurance because muscle glycogen stores are not maintained.[97] Patients with NIDDM who are treated with sulfonylureas or insulin may become hypoglycemic if insulin levels are high enough to increase peripheral utilization of glucose and suppress hepatic glucose output. Thus, individuals who are normoglycemic before exercise should consider increasing their carbohydrate intake.[99] Since patients with NIDDM do not have an absolute lack of insulin, they are less likely to become hyperglycemic in response to exercise.

Insulin Requirements in Renal Failure

27. M.B., a 32-year-old female, has had IDDM for 15 years. Over the past 2 years, a gradual deterioration of her renal function, as reflected by increased urinary protein, SrCr, and blood urea nitrogen (BUN) values, has been observed. What are the anticipated effects of decreased renal function on M.B.'s insulin requirements?

The effects of renal failure on insulin requirements are complex and, under various circumstances, insulin requirements may increase or decrease. The kidney is the most important site of extrahepatic insulin metabolism and excretion. Renal clearance of in-

Table 48.25	Exercise in Patients with Diabetes

1) Test blood glucose concentrations before, during, and after exercise

2) For moderate exercise (e.g., bicycling or jogging for 30–45 min), ↓ the preceding dose of regular insulin by 30%–50%. If glucose concentration is normal or low before exercise, supplement the diet with a snack containing 10–15 gm of carbohydrate

3) To avoid ↑ absorption of regular insulin by exercise, inject into the abdomen or exercise 30 min–1 hr following injection

4) Individuals with low glycogen stores may be predisposed to the hypoglycemic effects of exercise. Examples include alcoholics, fasted individuals, or patients on extremely hypocaloric (<800 cal), low carbohydrate (<10 gm/day) diets

5) Patients taking insulin are more susceptible to hypoglycemia than those taking sulfonylureas. Patients with NIDDM treated with diet are unlikely to develop hypoglycemia

6) Watch for postexercise hypoglycemia. Individuals who have been exercising during the day (e.g., skiing) should ↑ their carbohydrate intake and test their blood glucose concentration during the night to detect nocturnal hypoglycemia. Hypoglycemia can occur 8–15 hr following exercise

7) If the glucose concentration >240–300 mg/dL, the patient should not exercise. This indicates severe insulin deficiency. These patients are predisposed to hyperglycemia secondary to exercise

8) Patients with severe proliferative retinopathy or retinal hemorrhage should avoid jarring exercise or exercise which involves moving the head below the waist

sulin is 190 to 270 mL/minute, approximately two-thirds of hepatic clearance (320 to 400 mL/min). In nondiabetic individuals, approximately 40% to 50% of insulin secreted endogenously is extracted by the liver before it reaches the peripheral circulation.[50] Since exogenous insulin is delivered directly to the periphery, the kidney plays a more important role in its elimination. Insulin is filtered by the glomerulus and reabsorbed in the proximal tubules where it is destroyed enzymatically. The kidney also clears insulin from the peritubular circulation.[49,100] At that site, insulin can enhance the reabsorption of sodium which may account for the edema occasionally observed following the initiation of insulin therapy in some individuals.

Diminished renal function can be accompanied by decreased clearance of endogenous and exogenous insulin, resulting in increased plasma concentrations of insulin. Therefore, one might expect that M.B.'s insulin requirements may diminish as her renal disease progresses. Rabkin et al.[101] showed that patients with moderate degrees of renal failure [glomerular filtration rate (GFR) over 22.5 mL/min] remove 39% of insulin from arterial plasma, similar to normal subjects. In contrast, patients with severe renal insufficiency (GFR <6 mL/min) have a marked reduction in insulin removal from arterial plasma (9%). Decreased insulin clearance in conjunction with the anorexia, nausea, and decreased food intake associated with uremia can lead to hypoglycemia in such individuals. In some diabetic patients, particularly those with residual endogenous insulin secretion (Type II), glucose tolerance may normalize as renal function diminishes, eliminating the need for insulin.

In contrast, severe uremia is associated with glucose intolerance. This appears to be related to tissue resistance to insulin secondary to an unknown factor which can be removed by dialysis. Other factors which may alter blood glucose control in patients with renal failure include dialysis against glucose-containing dialysates and high-dose glucocorticoids in patients who have undergone renal transplantation.[113]

As M.B.'s renal failure progresses through various stages of severity, many alterations in her insulin dose should be anticipated. During this time, M.B. should monitor her blood glucose concentrations closely and adjust her insulin according to an algorithm. (See Table 48.20 and Question 28.)

Sliding Scale Method of Insulin Dosing

28. A.G., a 27-year-old, 60 kg female with a 15-year history of IDDM, was admitted for an abdominal hysterectomy. She has been moderately well controlled on a split-mixed dose of NPH and Regular insulin: 18 U NPH/8 U Reg before breakfast and 12 U NPH/6 U Reg before dinner. Her surgery is scheduled in ≈24 hours. Orders are written to give A.G. nothing by mouth (NPO) and to begin maintenance fluids (5% dextrose/0.45% saline with 20 mEq KCl) at a rate of 125 mL/hr. She is to receive her usual dose of insulin, and supplemental doses of insulin are to be given according to a "rainbow schedule." What is meant by the "rainbow" or "sliding-scale" method of insulin dosing?

These terms refer to a method of adjusting doses of subcutaneous *regular* insulin according to blood glucose test results. "Rainbow" schedules or sliding scales typically are used for hospitalized diabetic patients whose insulin requirements may vary drastically because of stress (e.g., infections, surgery, any acute illness), inactivity, or variable caloric intake. However, as previously noted, sliding scales also are used routinely by Type I patients on intensive insulin therapy.

Previously, insulin doses were based upon urine test results measured by the copper reduction method (Clinitest). Since various glucose concentrations in the urine produced different colors, this

dosing method was referred to as the "rainbow" schedule, a term which is still in occasional use. Today, blood glucose concentrations can be measured easily at the bedside and serve as a more precise guide to the determination of insulin doses. Typically, blood glucose concentrations are measured every four hours, and insulin is administered as prescribed. Sliding scales should be individualized to the patient's known sensitivity to insulin and adjusted according to her response. Generally, for patients like A.G. on usual total daily doses, 1 to 2 U of regular insulin are administered for every 30 to 50 mg/dL above a predetermined target glucose concentration (e.g., 180 mg/dL). (See Tables 48.20 and 48.22 and Question 18.)

29. Perioperative Management. How should A.G.'s diabetes be managed perioperatively?

Perioperative management of a patient with diabetes is complex because so many variables can influence the patient's insulin requirements. Many approaches to the management of such patients have been suggested in the literature and include:[103–105]

● The administration of one-third to one-half the total daily dose as intermediate-acting insulin before surgery and postoperatively along with a 5% dextrose solution at a rate of 100 to 200 mL/hour. This is accompanied by supplemental regular insulin dosed subcutaneously according to blood glucose concentrations.

● Administration of a combined insulin and glucose infusion at a fixed rate. A popular solution is 20 U of regular insulin and 20 mEq KCl in each liter of 10% dextrose in water administered at a rate of 100 mL/hour.

● Administration of a separate continuous insulin infusion (IV) and glucose (usually dextrose 5% in water at 100 to 125 mL/hour) delivered by dedicated pumps to allow for independent adjustments of each.

The last of these options seems most reasonable. It eliminates the uncertain pharmacokinetics of subcutaneously administered intermediate-acting insulin and, unlike option two, acknowledges that glucose utilization and insulin response may be altered in such patients. Insulin infusion must be started at least two to three hours before the surgery to titrate to the desired level of glucose control. To successfully monitor and regulate the insulin infusion regimen, an accurate bedside measurement of blood glucose levels is mandatory. Watts et al.[103] recommend a solution of D₅W/0.45% NaCl with KCl 20 mEq/L at 100 mL/hour. An insulin solution is prepared separately and piggybacked into the same infusion line. Other fluid and electrolyte requirements are administered through a separate line. Patients are initiated at an arbitrary infusion rate of 1.5 U/hour. Blood glucose concentrations are measured at the bedside using blood glucose reagent strips and reflectometers, and the infusion is adjusted according to the following algorithm:

Blood Glucose (mg/dL)	Insulin Infusion Adjustment (U/hr)	Other
<80	−0.5	+12.5 gm glucose IV
80–119	−0.5	—
120–180	no change	—
180–240	+0.5	—
>240	+0.5	+8 U IV

This method was used postoperatively in 24 diabetic patients who had been treated with various insulin regimens preoperatively.[90] Within eight hours, the mean glucose concentration was within the target range of 120 to 180 mg/dL; 93% of all blood glucose concentrations were between 80 and 240 mg/dL, and 57% were between 120 and 180 mg/dL. These results are superior to those obtained by other methods described above. The mean insulin infusion rate was 2 U/hour and ranged from 0.5 to 5.0 U/hour. The insulin infusion is continued until the patient's oral intake is stabilized. When switching a patient over to subcutaneous insulin, regular insulin is administered one-half hour before meals. The principles of perioperative care of diabetes have been reviewed nicely, and these authors suggest institution of similar therapy preoperatively.[104,105]

Thus, A.G.'s usual dose of insulin should be discontinued, and she should be initiated on an insulin infusion that is adjusted according to an algorithm similar to the one suggested above. Throughout the perioperative period, she should receive a minimum of 100 gm glucose daily to prevent starvation ketosis. If bedside measurements of glucose are impossible, any of the options suggested may be used.

30. Bedside Glucose Measurement. The use of algorithms to adjust the dose of IV infusions of insulins requires frequent bedside measurement of capillary glucose concentration by nurses. What are the potential problems with this procedure? How can these be minimized?

The ADA advocates the use of bedside blood glucose monitoring in hospitals to adjust the insulin doses.[106] This procedure eliminates repeated venipuncture if personnel are trained properly and appropriate quality control procedures are put into place. It is well documented that specially trained health professionals as well as patients can obtain capillary glucose concentrations which correlate well with concurrently measured laboratory values.[107]

A study by the FDA, however, suggests user-procedural errors may cause inaccurate results in capillary blood glucose monitoring (CBGM) and, if used as the basis for regimen adjustment, may endanger health.[108] These authors know of instances in which blood glucose concentrations were overestimated resulting in excessive insulin doses and hypoglycemia. Inaccurate capillary glucose measurements may have several causes:

- Improper technique. Many methods used to test blood glucose at the bedside are extremely technique-dependent. (See Question 10.) Even if nursing personnel are properly trained, skills can deteriorate if they are practiced infrequently.
- Improper maintenance and calibration of the machine. Unless the meters are properly cleaned and calibrated, their accuracy can deteriorate. Some meters may also be sensitive to environmental conditions such as temperature and light.
- Deteriorated strips. All the strips used to test capillary blood glucose concentrations are extremely sensitive to moisture. If containers are not tightly sealed, strips can deteriorate quite rapidly.
- If a visual method is used, it is important not to interpolate blood glucose concentrations which exceed 240 mg/dL, since beyond this concentration, the glucose concentration differences between each color block are quite large. For example, when a nurse incorrectly interpolated between the 400 mg/dL and 800 mg/dL color blocks on a Chemstrips bG vial, an overdose of insulin was administered to a patient in error. Even when meters are used, levels higher than 400 mg/dL should be verified by the laboratory.
- Swabbing the finger with iodine can falsely elevate the blood glucose tests[111] and intravenous dopamine can inhibit the reaction resulting in false low glucose concentrations.[112]

A national steering committee for quality assurance in capillary blood glucose monitoring (NSCQA) was formed to develop consensus guidelines for training users of CBGM and to increase user access to training and education.[109] A summary of suggested guidelines for training health care professionals are as follows:

- Healthcare professionals should be trained by a qualified trainer, such as a representative of the manufacturer.
- Training should include explanations of all aspects of monitor use and maintenance and should be accompanied by written and visual reference material.
- Under supervision of the instructor, trainees should perform the test (with control solutions) until they get three consecutive results that are within control range and do not differ more than 10% from one another. In addition, trainees should perform the procedure with their own blood until two consecutive values within 10% of one another at glucose levels ≥80 mg/dL are obtained.
- Instruction should be reassessed 30 days after training and annually thereafter. Instructors should be requalified annually or whenever new technology is introduced. Reassessment may be accomplished by a peer review or participation in a proficiency program.

To avoid other potential pitfalls, these authors also suggest the following:

- Use the simplest, most convenient method available that offers pre-established hospital quality assurance programs and eliminates the possibility of cross-contamination of blood among patients.
- There should be written policies and procedures for test performance, quality control, standardization, and calibration of the meters.
- Develop a regular schedule for cleaning and calibrating machines. Date the bottles of strips when they are opened and discard them after 10 to 15 days of use. Alternatively, use individually packaged strips.
- For each patient on bedside glucose monitoring, obtain a laboratory sample once daily in an unstable patient and two to three times weekly in moderately well-controlled patients to verify capillary glucose readings. Cohen et al.[110] suggest that one rely strictly on clinical laboratory measurements when a patient's glucose concentrations are less than 75 mg/dL or greater than 325 mg/dL. Caution also should be used in interpreting results in patients with severe anemia or polycythemia.
- Records should be kept to include the patient's name, date, and test result to correlate with documented quality control results.

Honeymoon Period

31. S.C. is a 33-year-old, slightly overweight male (5'11", 198 lb) who, 6 weeks before this clinic visit, presented to the ER with a 20-lb weight loss, a blood glucose concentration of 380 mg/dL, and "large" amounts of ketones in his urine. His HbA$_{1c}$ measured at that time was 15.7%. According to S.C., he was given IV fluids and insulin and sent home with instructions to inject himself with 30 U of Novolin 70/30 (70% NPH/30% Reg) BID.

Since his older brother has had diabetes for several years, he is somewhat familiar with the condition. He read books about diabetes and began treating himself with a 2000 calorie diet. Within 1 week, he began experiencing hypoglycemic reactions and decreased the Novolin 70/30 on his own to 20 U BID. One week later, he again reduced his Novolin 70/30 to 10

U BID because of recurrent hypoglycemic reactions. Within 1 month, he had weaned himself off insulin entirely. He now presents to clinic with a fasting blood glucose of 90 mg/dL. He has been off insulin for 2 weeks, and blood glucose concentrations measured at home range between 80–130 mg/dL. Does S.C. have diabetes mellitus? [SI units: initial blood glucose 21.0 mmol/L; FPG 5.0 mmol/L; home blood glucose 4.4–7.2 mmol/L; HbA$_{1c}$ 0.157]

Yes. It is quite likely that S.C. has Type I diabetes even though his age at onset is somewhat older than the typical case. This is indicated by the relatively rapid onset of symptoms, ketonuria, and a 20 pound weight loss. The elevated glycosylated hemoglobin and random blood glucose also are consistent with the diagnosis of diabetes.

S.C. was sent home on a reasonable dose of insulin (0.66 U/kg); however, his institution of a low calorie diet, increased activity after discharge, and the honeymoon period no doubt contributed to his decreased requirement for insulin.

Approximately 20% to 30% of individuals with Type I diabetes go into a remission phase (honeymoon period) within days to weeks of their diagnosis.[113] During this time, which can last for weeks to months, C-peptide can be measured, indicating a return of pancreatic function; insulin requirements may diminish partially or completely. Although it is tempting to discontinue insulin, diabetes invariably recurs. To minimize the possibility of inducing insulin allergy secondary to intermittent insulin exposure and to avoid engendering a sense of false hope in S.C. that his disease has been cured, many clinicians would continue insulin even if the doses were minuscule. S.C. should be followed closely for rising blood glucose concentrations.

Alternate Routes of Administration

32. Injection Aids. **Since S.C. already has discontinued his insulin, a decision is made to follow him for recurrent signs and symptoms of diabetes. S.C. understands that his symptoms are likely to return; however, he fears needles and would like to avoid injections if at all possible. Are there other modes of insulin administration which are available for S.C.?**

Several alternative devices and routes of administration of insulin have been explored. These include jet injectors, intranasal insulin, spring-loaded injectors, and pen injectors.[72]

Jet Injectors. These devices shoot a stream of insulin into the subcutaneous tissue under high pressure. Probably because the insulin is exposed to a larger subcutaneous surface area, it is absorbed more rapidly and has a shorter duration of action.[114] This pharmacokinetic profile is considered to be more physiologic. However, administration may be associated with stinging, bruising, and ''deep pain'' following administration, and the devices are bulky, expensive ($500 to $925),[72] and technically difficult for many to manipulate. For these reasons, they are not used widely. Examples of these devices include Medi-Jector II (Derata), Preci-Jet 50 (Ulster Scientific), and Vita-Jet (British American Medical).

Automatic Injection Aids. Several spring-loaded devices have been developed which automatically insert the needle of a loaded syringe by simple depression of a button or pressure of the device against the skin. The insulin then is administered manually by pressing the plunger. These devices can facilitate insulin injection in hard-to-reach areas such as the back of the arm or the buttocks. They also are convenient for arthritic patients and can minimize injection anxiety by camouflaging the needle. These devices are relatively inexpensive ($20 to $50) and may be useful for S.C. Examples include the injectomatic (Kendall-Futuro), Autojector (Ulster-Scientific), the Busher Automatic Injection (B-D), and Inject-Ease (Palco).[72]

Pen Injectors are convenience items which eliminate the need to carry syringes and insulin vials separately. Examples of these devices include the Novolin Pen, manufactured by Novo Nordisk and Accupen (Ulster). Many of these devices are available in Europe, and it is likely that more will become available in the U.S. soon. Both pens hold prefilled, disposable insulin cartridges which resemble fountain pen refills; regular, NPH, and 70/30 insulins are available for use in these devices. The pens come with disposable needles and deliver insulin in two-unit (Novolin Pen) increments.

The NovoPen which has been discontinued was suited particularly for use in Type I patients taking small doses of regular insulin before meals and snacks together with NPH or Ultralente insulin separately to provide their basal insulin levels. It was not useful for patients who are taking individualized mixtures of intermediate and short-acting insulins. It was imperative that all patients who used the NovoPen prime the device before each use to assure that insulin is injected. The Novolin Pen is useful for Type II patients who have been prescribed relatively simple, uncomplicated insulin regimens such as single or twice daily doses of NPH or 70/30 insulin. Some patients who find manipulating syringes and vials difficult can easily be taught to use the Novolin Pen. This device provides auditory and sensory cues and thus can be used by the visually impaired as well.

External Insulin Infusion Pumps. These devices were discussed in Question 3 and have been reviewed extensively.[114]

Implantable Insulin Infusion Pumps. These devices deliver insulin intravenously or intraperitoneally at variable rates established by a remote-controlled device.[67,114] A difficulty with all implantable insulin infusion devices is that commercially available insulins are unstable at body temperature for prolonged periods. Insulins which are stable under such conditions are currently under study.

Intranasal Insulin. The intranasal administration of insulin by aerosol has been studied experimentally. Insulin administered by this route has a pharmacokinetic profile which more closely resembles the intravenous administration of regular insulin than the subcutaneous administration. That is, the onset of action is more rapid (within 15 minutes), and the duration of action is shorter. Thus, intranasal insulin may potentially be used in place of subcutaneous regular insulin before meals, but a subcutaneous injection of intermediate or long-acting insulin still will be needed to supply basal needs.

There are still some problems associated with intranasal insulin administration. First, high concentrations of surfactants must be used to assure bioavailability of the insulin. These surfactants can be irritating to the nasal mucosa, and no one knows what their long-term effects will be. Secondly, since bioavailability is so poor ($\approx$10% SC insulin), insulin administration by this route is still prohibitively expensive. Finally, the bioavailability of these insulin preparations in patients using other intranasal medications and whose nasal passages are clogged or inflamed is unknown.[48,116,117]

In summary, with the exception of the injection aids, none of the above is a viable alternative for S.C. He should be reassured and instructed how to inject his insulin when it is reinstituted.

Immunotherapy and Pancreatic Transplants

33. S.C. read a newspaper article which suggested his diabetes could be cured with immunotherapy or a pancreatic transplant. Are either of these methods viable alternatives for S.C.?

Pancreatic Transplants

More than 3100 pancreas transplants had been performed worldwide by the end of 1990; of these, 550 were done in the U.S. The graft functional survival rate for those performed between 1987 and 1990 was 54% (i.e., the patients were normoglycemic and required no insulin). This rate now approaches 60% in pancreas-only cases and 77% in patients with combined kidney-pancreas transplants.[121] One-year survival of such patients is about 90%.[118]

Successful pancreas transplantation is currently the only treatment of Type I diabetes that establishes an insulin-independent state with HbA$_{1c}$ levels in the normal range for as long as the graft functions. The largest experience with pancreatic transplantation to date has been in patients with advanced nephropathy receiving a simultaneous kidney transplantation. Pancreas transplantation prevents the appearance and progression of diabetic glomerular lesions in the transplanted kidney which can occur in diabetic patients receiving kidney transplants alone.[119] The addition of a pancreas transplantation to a kidney transplantation also has been shown to halt the progression of diabetic polyneuropathy.[120] Advanced retinopathy, however, has not been altered in recipients of simultaneous pancreas/kidney transplants, although retinopathy tends to stabilize in patients with long-term functioning grafts versus continued deterioration of retinopathy in those patients with failed grafts.[121] Pancreas transplantation following kidney transplantation constitutes the second largest experience to date. Kidney transplantation may be performed before a pancreatic transplantation in a patient eligible to receive a kidney from an HLA-identical sibling because of the long-term success rate of such a procedure from an immunologic standpoint. Pancreatic transplantation alone in a patient with diabetes mellitus without evidence of secondary complications remains controversial since the disadvantage of exogenous insulin therapy is replaced with risks of the transplantation procedure itself and the complications of immunosuppression.

Islet cell transplantation

Islet cell transplantation, currently an investigational procedure, has been performed in only a small number of patients to date.[118,122,123,320] A few patients have achieved transitory insulin independence and one patient has demonstrated insulin independence for more than one year.[124] Five patients who received autologous transplants remained insulin-independent for 1 to 7.5 years.[32] Islet cell transplantation, if proven successful, offers potential advantages over pancreas transplantation because it requires a minor surgical procedure; islet cells potentially can be altered *in vitro* to obviate the need for posttransplant immunosuppression; and the supply of animal islet cells for transplantation would be much greater than that of whole human glands. Many questions regarding islet cell transplantation, however, remain to be answered. These relate to isolation, separation, culture, and preparation of islet cells; sites and methods of transplantation; and protection from immune rejection.

Once strategies that have fewer adverse consequences than existing regimens are developed, islet cell transplants may become a more viable alternative to exogenous insulin as a treatment for diabetes mellitus before secondary complications develop. Since S.C. has been diagnosed with diabetes only recently and has not yet developed complications, a pancreatic transplant cannot be recommended at this time.

Immunosuppressive Therapy

Since there is strong evidence that an autoimmune process underlies the pathogenesis of IDDM,[5] several groups have investigated the potential beneficial effects that immunosuppressive therapy may have on the course of IDDM. Many immunosuppressive drugs have been used,[125,126] but cyclosporine has been used most frequently and is the most promising of all agents studied. Several open-labeled, uncontrolled studies[127] and two randomized, placebo-controlled trials[128,129] have looked at the effect of cyclosporine in patients with recently-diagnosed, insulin-dependent diabetes mellitus. These studies used doses of 7.5 to 10 mg/kg/day, adjusting doses on the basis of side effects and cyclosporine blood concentrations. The controlled studies suggest that the remission rate in the cyclosporine-treated groups is greater than that of the placebo group: approximately 25% after one year versus 2% to 10% for the placebo group. Others have reported remissions in up to 40%, but these do not last for more than one year in 50% to 60% of treated patients.[127] Remissions are more likely to occur in patients with mild symptoms who are treated early (within 2 to 6 weeks of diagnosis).[125,127] Diabetes recurs if cyclosporine is discontinued; thus, at this point, it would seem that long-term immunosuppressive therapy is required to maintain remission. However, early follow-up of patients who experienced remission, albeit for less than a year, suggests they are controlled more easily on lower insulin doses and have higher residual C-peptide levels (an indication of endogenous insulin secretion) than those patients who failed to respond to cyclosporine. Since cyclosporine therapy is associated with potential irreversible nephropathy, the risks versus the benefits of long-term therapy remain in question. If the risks of immunosuppressive therapy can be minimized in the future, this may be a viable therapeutic alternative for newly diagnosed patients with IDDM such as S.C. Other approaches to modulating the immune system are discussed in the Introduction: Prevention.

Diabetic Ketoacidosis (DKA)

34. J.L., a 25-year-old, 60 kg female with an 8-year history of IDDM, is moderately well controlled on 24 U NPH plus 10 U Reg Q AM. She is brought by her family to the ER where she complains of abdominal tenderness, nausea, and vomiting. According to her family, J.L. was well until 1.5 days ago when she awoke with nausea, vomiting, diarrhea, and chills. Since she was unable to eat, she omitted her usual morning dose of insulin. Her gastrointestinal (GI) symptoms progressed, and she was brought to the ER when she became lethargic.

Physical examination reveals an ill-appearing female who is lethargic but responsive. Her temperature is 37 °C. Skin turgor is poor, mucous membranes are dry, and her eyeballs are shrunken and soft. J.L.'s lungs are clear, but respirations are deep and her breath has a fruity odor. Cardiac examination is within normal limits.

In the supine position, J.L.'s pulse rate is 115 beats/min and her BP is 105/60 mm Hg. In the upright position, her pulse increased to 140 beats/min and her BP dropped to 85/40 mm Hg. There is mild, diffuse tenderness over her abdomen.

Laboratory results on admission disclosed the following: blood glucose 750 mg/dL; Na 148 mEq/L; potassium (K) 5.4 mEq/L; Cl 106 mEq/L; HCO$_3$ 6 mEq/L; creatinine 2.0 mg/dL; Hgb 14.7 gm/dL; Hct 49%; white blood cell (WBC) count 15,000/mm^3 with 3% bands, 70% polymorphonuclear neutrophils, and 27% lymphocytes; serum ketones were moderate at 1:10 dilution. The urinalysis showed 2% glucose, moderate ketones, pH 5.5, and a specific gravity of 1.029. There were no WBCs, RBCs, bacteria, or casts. Arterial blood gas (ABG) results were as follows: pH 7.05, pCO$_2$ 20 mm Hg, pO$_2$ 120 mm Hg. What supports the diagnosis of DKA in J.L.? [SI units: blood glucose 41.6 mmol/L; Na 148 mmol/L; K 5.4 mmol/L; Cl 106 mmol/L; HCO$_3$ 6 mmol/L; creatinine 176.8 μmol/L; Hgb 147 gm/L; Hct 0.49; WBC count 15 × 10^9/L with 0.03 bands; polymorphonuclear neutrophils 0.70; lymphocytes 0.27; pCO$_2$ 2.6 kPa; pO$_2$ 16.0 kPa]

The fact that J.L. has insulin-dependent diabetes puts her at risk for developing ketoacidosis. An absolute or relative insulin deficiency promotes lipolysis and metabolism of free fatty acids to beta-hydroxybutyrate, acetoacetic acid, and acetone in the liver. Excess glucagon enhances gluconeogenesis and impairs peripheral ketone utilization. Stress can contribute to the development of DKA by stimulating release of insulin-counterregulatory hormones such as glucagon, catecholamines, glucocorticoids, and growth hormone. Common stress factors include infection, pregnancy, pancreatitis, trauma, hyperthyroidism, and an acute myocardial infarction.

J.L. presented with symptoms of nausea, vomiting, diarrhea, and chills and these are suggestive of an acute viral gastroenteritis. Patients such as J.L. commonly discontinue their insulin in this setting which further predisposes them to the development of diabetic ketoacidosis. (See Question 18.)

As illustrated by J.L., patients with DKA present with moderate to high serum glucose concentrations secondary to decreased peripheral utilization and increased hepatic production. This increases serum osmolality which initially shifts fluid from the intracellular to the intravascular compartment. When glucose concentrations exceed the renal threshold, osmotic diuresis ensues and water, sodium, potassium, and other electrolytes are depleted. J.L. also has lost fluid and electrolytes from vomiting and diarrhea. Eventually, as losses exceed input, the patient becomes dehydrated (dry mucous membranes, dry skin, soft shrunken eyeballs, increased hematocrit) and intravascular volume becomes depleted (orthostatic blood pressure and pulse changes).

Evidence of excessive ketone production in J.L. includes ketonuria, ketonemia, and the characteristic fruity odor of acetone on the breath. Elevated levels of these organic acids increase the anion gap and decrease the pH and carbonate levels. The respiratory rate is increased to compensate for the metabolic acidosis leading to hypercapnia.[130-132]

Treatment

35. How should J.L. be treated?

Treatment of patients with DKA is aimed at correction of intravascular volume, dehydration, fluid and electrolyte losses, and hyperosmolarity (hyperglycemia).

Fluids

Rapid correction of fluid loss is most crucial. The usual fluid deficit approximates 6 to 10 L or 10% of body weight in most patients with DKA. Whether normal saline or half-normal saline should be used is controversial. Some authors recommend hypotonic saline on the basis that water loss is relatively greater than that of salt in this situation. Others favor isotonic saline to protect intravascular volume and prevent shock. Generally, normal saline is used unless the patient is hypernatremic or has significant renal dysfunction.[131,132]

J.L. has evidence of significant dehydration and intravascular volume depletion. A rough calculation indicates that approximately 6 to 7 L will be needed (10% of body weight). Typically, fluids are replaced at the rate of 1 L/hour for the first three to four hours; during the first hour, 2 L may be infused. When the blood pressure and serum sodium are normal, fluids can be switched to half-normal saline at a rate of 250 to 500 mL/hour. When serum glucose concentrations approach 250 to 300 mg/dL, solutions should be changed to 5% glucose in half-normal saline. Glucose is added to prevent hypoglycemia and cerebral edema which can occur if the osmolality is reduced too rapidly. The use of dextrose also allows for continued insulin administration which is required to resolve the ketoacidosis.[131,132] (See Question 38.) These recommendations for fluid replacement must be adjusted in the elderly or those with compromised renal or myocardial function. In these patients, fluid administration must be titrated against central venous pressure. (See Chapter 18: Intensive Care Therapeutics.)

Sodium

Total body sodium usually is depleted by 7 to 10 mEq/kg of body weight in patients with DKA. In assessing serum sodium in these patients, it is important to remember that false low values may be reported as a result of hyperglycemia and hypertriglyceridemia. A corrected sodium value may be obtained by adding 1.6 to 2 mEq/L to the observed value for every 100 mg/dL glucose above 200 mg/dL. Sodium is replaced adequately with normal saline.[131]

Potassium

Potassium balance is altered markedly in patients with DKA because of combined urinary and GI losses. Invariably, total potassium is depleted; however, the serum potassium concentration may be high, normal, or low depending upon the degree of acidosis and volume contraction. Usual potassium deficits in this situation average 3 to 5 mEq/kg of body weight, although they may be as high as 10 mEq/kg.[131,132] Thus, J.L. will need approximately 200 to 350 mEq of potassium to replenish her body stores, assuming her normal weight is 70 kg. In patients whose initial serum potassium concentrations are elevated, supplementation is withheld for the first hour or until serum levels begin to drop. An adequate urine output also should be established before potassium supplements are initiated; however, a low serum potassium in the face of pronounced acidosis suggests severe potassium depletion requiring early, aggressive therapy to prevent life-threatening hypokalemia during treatment. The latter can occur from dilution, continued urinary losses, correction of acidosis, and insulin-mediated cellular uptake. In these cases, initial intravenous solutions should contain KCl 20 to 60 mEq/L.

J.L.'s admission laboratory data reveal a slightly elevated serum creatinine (most likely prerenal azotemia). This, in conjunction with a high-normal serum potassium concentration, weighs in favor of withholding potassium until serum levels begin to decline and urine output increases. Potassium levels generally begin to decrease in one to two hours, but if the patient is given bicarbonate a decline may occur more rapidly. Once potassium levels begin to fall, 20 to 40 mEq should be added to each liter of fluid.

Phosphate Therapy

The need for phosphate in the treatment of DKA is controversial. Phosphate is lost as the result of increased tissue catabolism, impaired cellular uptake, and enhanced renal excretion. Like other electrolytes, serum levels initially may appear normal even though body stores are depleted. Profound hypophosphatemia can decrease cardiac output, alter mental status, and produce tissue hypoxia and hemolysis. Prospective, randomized studies have shown no particular advantage of phosphate therapy in the treatment of DKA.[132] In fact, overzealous replacement can result in hypomagnesemia or hypocalcemia. Nevertheless, if phosphate concentrations drop to 1 mg/dL or less, 40 to 60 mEq of phosphate can be replaced as potassium phosphate. The available preparation contains 60 mEq of potassium and phosphorous per 15 cc vial. Subsequent phosphate rarely is required but may be administered based upon serum phosphate determinations.

Insulin

36. What is an appropriate insulin dose and route of administration for J.L.?

The appropriate dose of insulin needed to manage patients with DKA has been debated. Before the late 1970s, this disorder was traditionally treated with large, intermittent doses of insulin administered by the intravenous, intramuscular, or subcutaneous route (50 to 200 U Q 2 to 4 hr). In the late 1970s, several investigators demonstrated that low doses of insulin administered by the intramuscular or intravenous route could be used successfully to treat DKA (2 to 10 U/hr).[132]

Despite differences in study design, similar observations were noted by all investigators studying the low-dose insulin regimens: 1) serum glucose declines at a fairly constant rate of approximately 75 to 100 mg/dL/hour, and large insulin doses do not cause a more rapid decline; 2) correction of ketosis and ketoacidosis lags behind that of serum glucose, usually by several hours; 3) low-dose intravenous and intramuscular regimens appear to be equally effective in resolving hyperglycemia and acidosis; and 4) low-dose regimens are associated with considerably less hypoglycemia and hypokalemia than regimens using large doses of insulin.

The objective of low-dose insulin is to achieve insulin concentrations in the high physiologic range (100 to 200 µU/mL). This can be achieved with IV insulin infusion rates of 0.1 U/kg/hour or 5 to 10 U/hour of regular insulin intramuscularly. Physiologic concentrations can be achieved in 20 to 30 minutes following intravenous infusion and after 2.5 hours following intramuscular administration. Typically, loading doses of 0.1 U/kg intravenously or 20 U intramuscularly have been administered. Since the initial half-life of IV insulin is four to five minutes, an intravenous loading dose is optional; however, since the absorption half-life of intramuscular insulin is two hours, a loading dose is advisable if this route is used.[130-132]

These authors recommend insulin administration by continuous intravenous infusion because effective blood levels can be established rapidly and altered almost instantaneously. This route also avoids the potential for erratic absorption from the intramuscular site which may occur in patients who are severely volume depleted. Thus, for J.L., an intravenous bolus dose of 6 U (optional) followed by an infusion of 6 U/hour would be appropriate. The insulin should be infused separately from the fluids being used to replace volume so that its rate can be adjusted independently. A solution with an insulin concentration of 0.1 U/mL can be obtained by adding 50 U of regular insulin to 500 mL of normal saline. If a dose of 0.1 U/kg is used, the infusion rate is equivalent to the patient's weight in kg (in J.L., 60 mL/hr). If J.L.'s plasma glucose concentration remains unchanged after two hours, the infusion rate should be doubled. As noted earlier, as the glucose concentration falls to 250 to 300 mg/dL, the insulin infusion rate should be decreased and a 5% dextrose solution should be instituted.

37. Insulin Adsorption. Is the adsorption of insulin onto IV bottles and infusion sets clinically significant?

The magnitude of insulin adsorption onto intravenous bags or bottles and infusion sets varies with the concentration of insulin and the duration of the infusion. The degree of adsorption ranges from 20% to 70%.[133-135] Although the addition of human serum albumin in a concentration of 1.25 to 3.5 mg/dL to the insulin infusion mixture decreases insulin adsorption to 5% or less, the high price of human serum albumin makes this approach unrealistic.[134] Furthermore, insulin infusions without the addition of protein have produced significant plasma insulin serum concentrations; thus, the clinical significance of insulin adsorption is questionable. This problem can be minimized without the addition of protein by running 50 to 100 mL of the solution containing more than 5 U/100 mL of insulin through the tubing before it is administered to the patient.[134] Clinicians should be aware of the potential decrease in bioavailability and monitor the patient for an appropriate response.

Sodium Bicarbonate

38. J.L. was treated with fluids, electrolytes, and insulin as discussed in previous questions. Laboratory and clinical data 4 hours after therapy are as follows: pH 7.1, blood glucose 400 mg/dL, K 3.8 mEq/L, creatinine 3.1 mg/dL, and serum ketones strongly positive at a 1:40 dilution. Her BP was 120/70 mm Hg with no orthostatic changes. Urine output over the last 3 hours has been 500 mL. Since serum ketones have increased, should J.L. receive more insulin? Should she receive bicarbonate therapy? [SI units: blood glucose 22 mmol/L; K 3.8 mmol/L; creatinine 274 µmol/L]

The assumption that ketosis is worse in J.L. is incorrect. In DKA, low levels of insulin and elevated glucagon levels promote the metabolism of free fatty acids in the liver to acetoacetate and beta-hydroxybutyrate. The standard nitroprusside reaction test for ketones measures only acetoacetate, even though beta-hydroxybutyrate is the more important ketone. The conversion of acetoacetic acid to beta-hydroxybutyrate is coupled closely with the NADH:NAD ratio. If this ratio is high (as in the presence of alcohol) so much beta-hydroxybutyrate may be formed that acetoacetate is virtually undetectable; thus, the absence of ketones in the serum does not rule out ketoacidosis.

Conversely, treatment with insulin begins to suppress lipolysis and fatty acid oxidation; NAD is regenerated shifting the reaction back in favor of acetoacetate.[131] Thus, even though there appears to be higher concentrations of ketones in the serum, J.L.'s declining blood glucose concentration, improved bicarbonate concentrations, and improved acid-base and cardiovascular responses indicate that she is responding appropriately. Therefore, no change in the insulin dose is indicated. It is important to emphasize that the glucose concentrations will normalize before ketones (4 to 6 hours versus 6 to 12 hours) because the latter metabolize more slowly. For this reason, it is important to continue insulin to maintain suppression of lipolysis until plasma and urine ketones have cleared.

The use of sodium bicarbonate in patients with DKA has been controversial.[131,132] Most investigators discourage its routine use, reserving it for patients with severe acidemia (pH <7.0) or those in clinical shock. It has been shown that coma is correlated most closely to blood glucose concentrations (>700 mg/dL) and hyperosmolality (calculated osmolality >340 mOsm/kg).[131] Furthermore, a randomized, prospective study showed that bicarbonate did not affect recovery in patients with severe diabetic ketoacidosis (arterial pH 6.9 to 7.14).[136] Thus, even though J.L.'s acidosis seemed severe on admission (pH 7.05, bicarbonate 6 mEq/L, Kussmaul respirations), bicarbonate was not administered. It is apparent that with fluid and insulin therapy alone, her acidosis is beginning to improve.

39. What is the expected course of diabetic ketoacidosis in J.L.?

After 3 L of fluid and a constant insulin infusion of 6 U/hour for three hours, J.L.'s glucose concentration had dropped to 500 mg/dL and she had no orthostatic blood pressure changes. Potassium (40 mEq/L) was added to her fluids which were administered at a reduced rate of 300 mL/hour.

Three hours later, the glucose concentration had dropped to 350 mg/dL and her pH had increased to 7.21. The serum potassium remained low-normal at 3.4 mEq/L, and serum sodium increased to 151 mEq/L. In view of these changes, the IV infusion fluid was changed to half-normal saline with 5% dextrose to which 40 mEq/L of potassium were added. The rate was slowed to 250 mL/hour, and the insulin infusion was decreased to 4 U/hour.

Four hours later (10 hours following admission), the blood glucose was 235 mg/dL and the serum potassium was 3.5 mEq/dL. The intravenous fluids were changed to 5% dextrose with 40 mEq/L of KCl, administered at a rate of 250 mL/hour, and the regular insulin infusion was decreased to 2 U/hour. J.L. continued to improve over the next 12 hours, and she began taking full oral liquids by the second hospital day. At that time, her IV infusion rate was decreased to 200 mL/hour but her insulin infusion was continued.

Approximately 24 hours after admission, J.L.'s blood glucose concentration was 175 mg/dL; potassium was 4.6 mEq/L; and sodium was 144 mEq/L. There were no ketones in the plasma. The urine contained 1% glucose and moderate amounts of ketones. Intravenous fluids were discontinued and regular insulin was administered subcutaneously one hour before the insulin infusion was discontinued. J.L. continued to receive regular insulin subcutaneously every four hours according to a sliding scale (see Question 28). Thirty-six hours after admission, J.L. was given her usual dose of NPH and regular insulin and was sent home for follow-up in the clinic.

Oral Hypoglycemic Agents

Individuals with Type II diabetes are treated with diet, exercise, oral hypoglycemic agents, and insulin. Before addressing the clinical use of oral agents, an overview of their mechanisms of action and pharmacokinetics will be presented.

Biguanides

Two drugs belong to the biguanide class of oral hypoglycemic agents: phenformin and metformin. Phenformin was available in the U.S. until 1977, when it was withdrawn by the FDA because of its association with fatal lactic acidosis. Today, metformin (Glucophage) is accepted as the biguanide of choice in Europe and Canada and was released for use in the U.S. in 1995.

The biguanides are described more accurately as antihyperglycemic agents. Although they lower blood glucose concentrations in diabetics, they do not cause hypoglycemia in nondiabetic individuals. Their mechanism of action remains undetermined. Unlike the oral sulfonylureas, they do not stimulate the release of insulin from the pancreas. They may decrease or slow the GI absorption of carbohydrates; increase the peripheral utilization of glucose; enhance insulin binding to its receptors; or decrease hepatic glucose output. All of these actions have been proposed and disputed. Other beneficial effects of metformin include an improved lipid profile [increased high density lipoprotein (HDL), decreased low density lipoprotein (LDL), decreased triglycerides (TG)], and modest weight loss, or at least, no weight gain. In contrast to phenformin, metformin rarely has been associated with lactic acidosis. The few patients in which this event has been reported had renal, liver, or cardio-respiratory contraindications to the use of biguanides.[137,138] Nevertheless, patients should be warned to bring symptoms of lactic acidosis to the attention of their physician: weakness, malaise, and heavy and labored breathing. (See Update on page 48-58.)

The actions of metformin offer potential advantages as monotherapy in the obese Type II diabetes mellitus patient who has failed diet therapy. In addition to countering hyperglycemia without the development of weight gain, metformin does not exacerbate hyperinsulinemia. Because its mechanism of action appears to be clearly different from that of the sulfonylureas, metformin also is used in combination with the sulfonylureas when primary or secondary failure occurs. Combined metformin-sulfonylurea therapy has been reported to lower basal glucose concentrations approximately 20% more than with sulfonylureas alone.[139]

Metformin is administered with meals (0.5 to 0.850 gm TID). It has a half-life of two to four hours and is eliminated entirely by the kidney unmetabolized. Transient side effects include diarrhea and other GI disturbances such as abdominal discomfort, metallic taste, nausea, and anorexia. These disturbances can be minimized by taking the drug with meals and slowly increasing the dose (e.g., 0.5 BID initially). Patients with renal impairment, hepatic disease, or a history of lactic acidosis should be excluded from therapy.[137]

Sulfonylureas

Sulfonylureas are used in patients with NIDDM who have failed diet and exercise therapy. (See Questions 43 through 45.)

Mechanism of Action

Pancreatic Effects. Sulfonylureas stimulate the release of insulin from pancreatic beta cells and enhance beta cell sensitivity to glucose. A specific sulfonylurea receptor which is linked closely to the ATP-sensitive potassium ion channel has been identified on the beta cell. It has been proposed that sulfonylureas inhibit this channel, blocking the efflux of potassium. This lowers the membrane potential causing depolarization. As a consequence, the voltage-dependent calcium channels open, increasing intracellular calcium concentrations. Calcium ultimately stimulates insulin secretion.[142] With the possible exception of glipizide, insulin levels tend to return to baseline values after a few months of continued use, although chronic administration of sulfonylureas increased glucose-induced insulin secretion for decades in one small study.[144] Nevertheless, sulfonylureas continue to exert beneficial effects on glucose tolerance and this has stimulated investigators to look for "extrapancreatic" mechanisms of action.

Extrapancreatic Effects. Sulfonylureas can normalize the increased hepatic glucose production which is primarily responsible for fasting hyperglycemia in patients with NIDDM. They also may partially reverse insulin resistance in the peripheral tissues that is caused by receptor and postreceptor defects. The receptor defect is due to decreased numbers of insulin receptors on insulin target tissues, while the postreceptor defect renders tissues insensitive to the insulin-receptor complex. Whether these "extrapancreatic" effects of the sulfonylureas are direct effects of these agents or are secondary to improved insulin release and lower glucose concentrations remains to be established.[140] Failure of Type I patients to respond to sulfonylureas and the failure to locate (to date) a specific sulfonylurea receptor on target tissues favors the view that these are indirect effects of these agents. In any case, it is clear that in patients treated with sulfonylureas, tissues become more responsive to lower concentrations of endogenous insulin.

As noted above, sulfonylureas have no beneficial effects on the glucose tolerance of pancreatectomized or Type I diabetic individuals who have no pancreative reserve. Their use, therefore, should be reserved for symptomatic, Type II diabetic patients who are unable to achieve control on diet alone.

First- and Second-Generation Sulfonylureas

The four first-generation sulfonylureas are acetohexamide (Dymelor), chlorpropamide (Diabinese), tolazamide (Tolinase), and tolbutamide (Orinase). Although these drugs are considered equally effective, each differs with respect to its pharmacokinetic properties and, to a lesser extent, its adverse effect profile. (See the following discussion and Table 48.26.)

Second-generation sulfonylureas were first introduced into the U.S. in May, 1984. These include glipizide (Glucotrol) and glyburide (DiaBeta, Micronase). These agents are approximately 100 times more potent than the first-generation drugs on a mg for mg basis; however, there is no evidence that they are more effective clinically. Like tolazamide, these agents have a relatively favorable side effect profile and have a duration of activity that requires no more than one or two daily doses. The basis upon which specific agents are selected for patients is discussed in Questions 44 and 53 through 55. For extensive references regarding glipizide and glyburide, the reader is referred to several key reviews.[140,141,144,145]

Table 48.26 Oral Antidiabetic Pharmacokinetic Data

Drug (Brand Names) Available Tablet Strengths	Approximate Equivalent Therapeutic Dose	Usual Minimum and Maximum Daily Dose/ How Divided	Mean t½ (hr)	Approximate Duration of Activity (hr)	Metabolism and Excretion	Comments
First-Generation Sulfonylureas						
Acetohexamide (Dymelor) 250, 500	500	0.25–1.5 gm QD or BID	6	12–18	Activity of metabolite >parent drug. Metabolite excreted, in part, by kidney	Caution in elderly and patients with renal disease. Significant uricosuric effects
Chlorpropamide (Diabinese) 100, 250	250	0.1–0.5 gm QD	35+	24–72	Inactive and weakly active metabolites; 20% excreted unchanged; varies widely	Caution in elderly and patients with renal impairment. Highest frequency of side effects relative to other sulfonylureas
Tolazamide (Tolinase) 100, 250, 500	250	0.2–1 gm QD or BID	7	12–24	Some metabolites with moderate activity excreted via kidney	Active metabolites may accumulate in renal failure
Tolbutamide (Orinase) 250, 500	1000	0.5–3 gm BID or TID	7	6–12	Metabolized to compounds with negligible activity	No special precautions. Shortest acting sulfonylurea
Second-Generation Sulfonylureas						
Glipizide (Glucotrol) 5, 10	5–10	2.5–40 mg QD or BID[a]	3	12–24	Metabolized to inactive compounds	No special precautions. Daily dose >15 mg should be divided. Dose 30 min before meals
Glipizide extended-release (Glucotrol XL) 5	5	5–20 mg QD	4–13	24	Same as glipizide	Use with caution in patients with pre-existing gastro-intestinal narrowing due to possible obstruction
Glyburide (Diabeta, Micronase) 1.25, 2.5, 5	5	1.25–20 mg QD or BID[a]	4–13	12–24 (See Question 48)	Metabolized to inactive/weakly inactive compounds; ½ excreted in urine and ½ in feces	Caution in elderly patients with renal failure, and others predisposed to hypoglycemia. Daily doses >10 mg should be divided
Micronized Glyburide (Glynase PresTab) 1.5, 3	3	1.0–12 mg QD	4	24	Metabolized to inactive/weakly inactive compounds; ½ excreted in urine and ½ in feces	Daily doses >6 mg should be divided. ↑ bioavailability relative to original formulation, resulted in reduced dose
Biguanides						
Metformin (Glucophage) 500, 850	N/A	0.5–2.5 gm BID or TID	Unknown. t½ ≈3 hr. Multiple daily doses required	6–12	Excreted unchanged in urine	Avoid in patients with renal failure or those who could be pre-disposed to lactic acidosis (e.g., alcoholics; cardio-respiratory disorders)

[a] These are maximum doses indicated by the manufacturers. Studies indicate that maximum insulin responses and glucose lowering effects occur at doses of 10 mg/day.[147,148]

Pharmacokinetics of Sulfonylureas

The biopharmaceutic and pharmacokinetic parameters of the individual agents have been reviewed extensively and are summarized in the following text and in Table 48.26.[140,141,144,145]

It should be emphasized that the duration of hypoglycemic activity is related to the half-life of these compounds only in very general terms and may correlate poorly in some cases. All sulfonylureas are highly protein bound (90% to 100%) mainly to albumin, although various binding characteristics have been demonstrated. Food does not impair the extent of drug absorption but may delay the peak effect of some agents.

Little information exists regarding the dose-response relationship between sulfonylureas and their blood glucose-lowering effect. A long-term comparison study of glyburide and glipizide showed little or no improvement in glucose control at dosages of >10 mg/day of either agent.[146] Single-dose and short-term studies with glipizide have demonstrated an increased blood glucose-lowering effect up to 10 mg daily.[147,148] A placebo-controlled, double-blind study examining the effect of glipizide 10, 20, or 40 mg/day in patients with Type II diabetes revealed the maximal insulin response and blood glucose-lowering effect was achieved with a dose of 10 mg/day.[148] These data suggest that sulfonylureas operate within a narrow range of plasma concentrations that may be achieved with low dosages of the drug; therefore, a need to re-evaluate recommended maximum doses of sulfonylureas exists. A patient no longer responding to increased doses of a sulfonylurea may need to be switched to insulin before reaching the maximum dose recommended by the manufacturers (20 mg for glyburide, 40 mg for glipizide).

Tolbutamide is the sulfonylurea with the shortest duration of action (6 to 12 hours). It is metabolized rapidly and totally in the liver to very weakly active or inactive compounds (carboxytolbutamide and hydroxytolbutamide) which are excreted in the urine. The average half-life of tolbutamide is about seven hours but varies considerably among individuals (range: 4 to 25 hours), suggesting genetic variability in the way this drug is metabolized.[140,141] Multiple daily dosing (BID to TID) is usually necessary so that tolbutamide is less desirable for noncompliant individuals. Tolbutamide more effectively normalizes postprandial hyperglycemia when it is given at least 30 minutes before, rather than with, a meal.[149]

Chlorpropamide is the longest acting sulfonylurea (24 to 72 hours) and is approximately 80% metabolized in the liver to inactive and weakly active compounds. The average amount of drug that is excreted unchanged (20%) varies considerably (range: 10% to 60%). This variance, at least in part, is due to changes in urine pH. Chlorpropamide is a weak acid (pKa 4.8) and its ionization is pH dependent. In one study, alkalinization of the urine increased the urinary excretion of chlorpropamide fourfold, and its mean serum half-life decreased to one-fourth the initial value (from 49.7 to 12.8 hours). Conversely, urine acidification reduced renal excretion of the drug and prolonged the mean serum half-life to 68.5 hours.[150] The average half-life of chlorpropamide is approximately 36 hours, though values vary widely from subject to subject. The mean ($\pm$ SD) chlorpropamide half-life in one study was 38 ± 10 hours in young, nondiabetic subjects and 99 ± 50 hours in older diabetic patients. This variation was attributed to differences in nonrenal clearance and volume of distribution.[151]

Because of its variable renal excretion, long serum half-life, and long duration of hypoglycemic activity, use of chlorpropamide has fallen and should be avoided in the elderly or in patients with renal impairment. (See Question 53.)

Acetohexamide is an intermediate-acting (12 to 18 hours) sulfonylurea which principally is metabolized and eliminated as L-hydroxyhexamide, a compound with greater activity than the parent drug. About 50% of L-hydroxyhexamide is excreted in the urine; the rest is metabolized further to an inactive compound. While the mean half-life of the parent drug is 1.3 hours, the mean half-life of L-hydroxyhexamide is about five hours. Thus, the hypoglycemic activity of acetohexamide is due mainly to its active metabolite. Like chlorpropamide, it is a poor choice for the elderly or patients with renal impairment and is no longer widely used.

Tolazamide is the newest of the first-generation sulfonylureas and has an intermediate duration of activity (12 to 24 hours). It is metabolized to several compounds, at least one of which retains partial activity; all are excreted in the urine. The half-life of the active drug is about seven hours.

Glipizide is an intermediate-acting second-generation agent with a half-life of two to four hours, but a duration of action of 12 to 24 hours. Many patients, especially those receiving small to inter-mediate daily doses of this drug (<20 mg), require only one dose per day. Glipizide is extensively metabolized by the liver to inactive products that are eliminated primarily by the kidney.[140,141,143] Food delays the rate of absorption of glipizide but not its bioavailability.[152] Administration 30 minutes before meals has been suggested, but this has been disputed by a group who noted no acute effects of this drug in patients who had been taking it chronically.[153]

Glyburide (or glybenclamide) is an intermediate-acting second-generation agent similar to glipizide. The half-life is approximately 1.5 to 4 hours following single dose studies and up to 13.7 hours following chronic administration for six weeks.[318] Nevertheless, as with glipizide, the duration of action lasts for up to 24 hours in many patients, allowing single-daily dosing with small to intermediate doses (<15 mg). Glyburide is metabolized completely by the liver to several inactive or weakly active metabolites (now studied in humans), half of which are excreted in the urine and the remainder eliminated via the biliary tract.[140,141,145] Unlike glipizide, food does not delay the rate or extent of absorption of glyburide. The time of ingestion relative to meals appears to be unimportant in patients on chronic therapy.[153]

Pharmacokinetic Drug Interactions

Drug interactions with oral sulfonylureas have a pharmacodynamic or pharmacokinetic basis. Pharmacodynamic interactions occur with drugs that alter glucose tolerance intrinsically through their effects on insulin secretion, glucose production, and peripheral glucose utilization. These are discussed in the sections on drug-induced hypoglycemia and hyperglycemia. Pharmacokinetic interactions occur when drugs alter the absorption, metabolism, elimination, or protein binding of the sulfonylureas.

Most of the reported pharmacokinetic drug interactions with the sulfonylureas involve chlorpropamide and tolbutamide because these are the oldest agents and were once the most commonly prescribed and studied. However, since most of the clinically significant interactions occur with drugs that alter liver metabolism or urinary excretion, possible interactions with all of the sulfonylureas must be anticipated even though the outcomes may be quite different. For example, a drug that inhibits the hepatic metabolism of tolbutamide can increase its hypoglycemic activity; conversely, the same drug actually may diminish the hypoglycemic activity of acetohexamide by inhibiting formation of its active metabolite. This hypothesis has not been tested.

The second-generation sulfonylureas, glipizide and glyburide, are dosed in mg rather than gm quantities, and thus may be less likely to interact with other drugs on a pharmacokinetic basis; this has yet to be established. Glipizide and glyburide also differ from the first-generation agents in that they are highly bound to albumin at non-ionic rather than ionic sites.[140,141] On this basis, it has been suggested that these agents are unlikely to interact with other highly protein-bound drugs such as phenylbutazone, salicylates, or certain sulfonamide antibiotics, which have been reported to enhance the effects of the first-generation sulfonylureas. However, these highly protein-bound drugs appear to interact with the sulfonylureas by altering their hepatic metabolism as well. (See Table 48.27.) Therefore, glipizide and glyburide should be used cautiously with drugs reported to interact with the first-generation sulfonylureas.

The many potential pharmacokinetic interactions reported with the sulfonylureas have been reviewed extensively, and only the more important or clinically significant interactions are included in Table 48.27. Additional discussions and primary references for these interactions can be found in several sources.[154]

Table 48.27	Pharmacokinetic Drug Interactions With Sulfonylureas[a,b]
Drugs	**Comments**
Drugs Increasing Sulfonylurea Effect	
Chloramphenicol	↓ tolbutamide hepatic metabolism and ↑ t½ 2–3-fold. Possible prolongation of chlorpropamide t½
Clofibrate	May displace sulfonylureas from proteins, ↓ insulin resistance, ↓ renal tubular secretion of chlorpropamide
Heparin	Heparin may have significantly prolonged glipizide hypoglycemia in 1 unconvincing case report. Needs confirmation
Methyldopa	↑ mean tolbutamide t½ by 24% in 1 study
Cimetidime	↓ tolbutamide hepatic metabolism by 17% in 1 study. Ranitidine had no effect
Nonsteroidal Anti-Inflammatory Drugs	Sulfinpyrazone and phenylbutazone ↓ tolbutamide hepatic metabolism and ↑ t½ 2–3-fold. Enhanced hypoglycemia secondary to acetohexamide (↓ renal excretion of active metabolite) and chlorpropamide also reported. Severe, fatal hypoglycemia can occur. Ibuprofen, naproxen, sulindac, and tolmetin do not affect sulfonylurea disposition
Salicylates	Limited and indirect documentation (primarily *in vitro*) that salicylates may ↑ sulfonylurea activity through protein-binding displacement or inhibition of active renal tubular secretion (Also see Question 78 for discussion of intrinsic hypoglycemic effects)
Sulfonamide Antimicrobials	Co-trimoxazole ↓ tolbutamide metabolism and ↑ t½ by 30% in 1 study. Severe hypoglycemia with glyburide and chloropropamide reported rarely. Sulfisoxazole also rarely associated with tolbutamide- and chlorpropamide-induced severe hypoglycemia
Warfarin	No evidence that warfarin affects sulfonylurea disposition; however, dicumarol ↑ tolbutamide (and possibly chlorpropamide) t½ 3–4 fold, probably by ↓ hepatic metabolism. Sulfonylureas do not appear to alter patient response to the anticoagulants
Drugs Decreasing Sulfonylurea Effect	
Alcohol	Chronic ethanol use ↑ tolbutamide hepatic metabolism 2-fold. Conversely, short-term ethanol infusions ↓ tolbutamide clearance by 50%. (Also see Question 77)
Rifampin	↑ tolbutamide and glyburide metabolism, thereby ↓ t½ and plasma drug concentrations
Other Drugs	
Phenytoin	Unknown effects on sulfonylureas; however, tolbutamide transiently ↑ free phenytoin concentrations through protein-binding displacement by approximately 45% in 1 study
Cyclosporine	May compete with glipizide for cytochrome P450 hydroxylation. Necessitated a 20%–30% dosage reduction of cyclosporine in 2 case reports. (See reference 155)

[a] For additional references and more detailed discussion, see reference 154.

[b] t½ = Half-life.

Treatment of Patients with NIDDM

Clinical Presentation

40. L.H., a 65-year-old, moderately obese female (5′5″ and 160 lb), was referred to the diabetes clinic when her gynecologist, who had been treating her for recurrent monilial infections, noted the presence of glucose on routine urinalysis. Subsequently she was found to have an FPG of 150 mg/dL and 167 mg/dL on 2 separate occasions. L.H. denies any symptoms of polyphagia or polyuria, although she has been more thirsty than usual. She does complain of lethargy and often takes afternoon naps. Over the past year, she has gained 10 lb.

L.H.'s other medical problems include rheumatoid arthritis, which is well controlled on 3.6 gm/day of aspirin, and recurrent urinary tract infections which are treated with ampicillin. L.H. smokes 1 pack of cigarettes per day and her family history is significant for a sister (also overweight), aunt, and grandmother with diabetes.

Laboratory assessment reveals an FPG of 147 mg/dL; aglycosuria (Diastix); plasma triglycerides of 600 mg/dL; and an HbA₁c of 11% (Normal: 4%–7%). All other values are within normal limits. L.H. is given the diagnosis of NIDDM. What features in L.H.'s history and physical examination are consistent with this diagnosis? How should she be managed at this time? [SI units: plasma glucose 8.1 mmol/L; plasma triglycerides 6.77 mmol/L; HbA₁c 0.11 (Normal: 0.04–0.07)]

The features of L.H.'s history that are consistent with NIDDM include a fasting plasma glucose concentration of 140 mg/dL or higher on more than one occasion, obesity, age over 40, family history of diabetes, and elevated HbA₁c. Diagnosis on routine examination and mild signs and symptoms of hyperglycemia, in-

cluding increased thirst, lethargy, recurrent monilial infections and hypertriglyceridemia, also are typical in patients with NIDDM. (See Tables 48.1 and 48.2.)

L.H.'s symptoms are mild and her fasting plasma glucose concentrations are moderately high. Therefore, she should be treated initially with diet and exercise. Since obesity is associated with increased tissue resistance to endogenous insulin, L.H. should be strongly encouraged to decrease her caloric intake and lose weight. When signs and symptoms are mild, diet alone can correct glucose intolerance. L.H. also should space her meals by four to five hours. In patients with mild and moderate forms of the condition, insulin release is delayed, but the amount of insulin released may be sufficient to reduce postprandial blood glucose concentrations to normal; however, in contrast to nondiabetic individuals, this may take four to five hours rather than one to two hours.

41. What are the goals of therapy for L.H. and other patients with NIDDM?

The ADA recommends that otherwise healthy patients with NIDDM strive to achieve tight control based upon the results of the DCCT.[15] Advanced age or significant cerebrovascular or coronary artery disease should be considered a relative contraindication to tight control in NIDDM due to the serious consequences of hypoglycemia (see Table 48.10). The goal of tight control is to prevent long-term vascular complications, the major cause of morbidity and mortality in this group.

Several diabetologists have thoughtfully questioned the wisdom of extrapolating results of the DCCT to NIDDM patients because the study population included only young, nonobese, normotensive, Type I individuals who were predominantly white. This stands in stark contrast to the typical NIDDM population. Furthermore, the study set out to determine the effects of normoglycemia on the prevention and progression of microvascular disease. Type II patients also develop microvascular complications which ought to respond favorably to glycemic control. Nevertheless, macrovascular disease is the primary cause of death in this population and its underlying pathogenesis may or may not be related to hyperglycemia per se. Although lower low density lipoprotein (LDL) cholesterol levels were noted in the intensively treated group, these findings could not be extrapolated to a decrease in the number of macrovascular events in future years. Some have worried that hyperinsulinemia associated with intensive insulin therapy actually could accelerate atherosclerosis (see discussion of Syndrome X in the Introduction of this chapter) or increase the risk of cardiovascular events and that accompanying hypoglycemia endangers those with existing cardiovascular disease. These views are summarized and analyzed by Colwell[322] who suggests a more aggressive stance toward glycemic control than that which has been previously practiced and attention to reduction of risk factors for cardiovascular disease (e.g., the daily intake of aspirin). However, in patients who have failed diet and oral agents, he questions whether the benefits of normoglycemia achieved through intensive insulin therapy override the potential risks of therapy. Other studies in progress are likely to provide data which will more clearly guide treatment in the future.

Biochemical indices used to evaluate metabolic control in Type II patients are similar to those used for Type I patients and include fasting and postprandial blood glucose concentrations, fasting cholesterol and triglyceride levels, and the glycosylated hemoglobin. If L.H. is capable and motivated, she should be encouraged to use home blood glucose testing. (See Tables 48.10 and 48.31.)

L.H.'s acute symptoms should improve as her glucose intolerance normalizes. Normalization of all metabolic abnormalities also should minimize L.H.'s risk for vascular complications. However, weight loss and elimination of other cardiovascular risk factors such as smoking and hypertriglyceridemia also is essential.

Urine Glucose Tests

42. L.H. is reluctant to test her blood glucose concentrations. What are the advantages and disadvantages of urine glucose tests relative to home blood glucose monitoring (HBGM)?

Urine glucose tests were once the primary tools used to monitor diabetic control. However, urine testing quickly is becoming outmoded with the advent of easy-to-use HBGM methods. Urine glucose testing is inexpensive, painless, and noninvasive; nevertheless, because there are so many disadvantages to its use, urine testing now is recommended only for diabetic patients who cannot or will not use HBGM (still a large fraction of patients).[62] Disadvantages of urine glucose testing include poor correlation between urine glucose and blood glucose concentrations, inconvenience, and the inability to verify hypoglycemia.

Urine glucose tests are positive only when blood glucose concentrations exceed the renal threshold (180 mg/dL). Therefore, a negative test may reflect a blood glucose concentration which ranges from 0 to 180 mg/dL. In view of this, some clinicians recommend that insulin-treated patients "aim" for trace amounts of glucose in their urine to avoid hypoglycemia. This virtually assures consistent hyperglycemia. Patients like L.H. with NIDDM who are treated with oral agents are at such low risk for hypoglycemia that they should "aim" for negative urine glucose concentrations at all times.

The most serious disadvantage of urine glucose tests is that they correlate poorly with concurrent blood glucose concentrations.[157]

This is because urine glucose concentrations are influenced by a patient's renal threshold for glucose, urinary retention, urine dilution or concentration, drug interference, and accurate testing. Furthermore, changes in urine glucose concentrations often lag behind changes in blood glucose concentrations.

Renal thresholds vary greatly from patient to patient which makes interpretation of urine tests even more difficult. In one study of 65 insulin-dependent diabetic patients, the renal threshold ranged from 54 to 180 mg/dL (mean: 130 mg/dL). Renal thresholds tend to rise with age and with decreasing renal function and may increase to greater than 300 to 400 mg/dL.[158] Ideally, when a patient is started on urine glucose testing, simultaneous blood glucose concentrations and second-voided urine glucose concentrations should be measured to determine the patient's renal threshold for glucose. Considering the disadvantages associated with urine glucose testing, every effort should be made to encourage L.H. to perform blood glucose monitoring.

Clinical Use of Sulfonylureas

43. Despite several attempts at diet management, L.H. only lost 2–3 lb and FPG concentrations began to rise over 3 months to 180–220 mg/dL. Urine glucose records reveal glucosuria in 75% of the urines tested and a repeat HbA$_{1c}$ is 12.5%. L.H. now complains of nocturia (2 to 3 times nightly) and a definite increase in fluid intake. She feels extremely fatigued and "doesn't have the energy to do anything." Are sulfonylureas or insulin indicated at this time? Is L.H. likely to respond to the sulfonylureas? [SI units: plasma glucose 10.0–12.2 mmol/L; HbA$_{1c}$ 0.125]

Patients like L.H. with moderate to severe NIDDM have varying degrees of beta cell dysfunction and tissue resistance to insulin. In these individuals, pulsatile insulin secretion and first-phase insulin release are absent, and the pancreas is "blind" or unresponsive to high glucose concentrations. Because target tissues are less responsive to insulin, hepatic glucose output typically is increased and patients may require higher concentrations of insulin to achieve the same degree of peripheral glucose utilization. At this stage, oral sulfonylureas, metformin and insulin work equally well. Which mode of therapy is selected depends upon patient and physician preference.[62,159,160]

As NIDDM progresses to its most severe form (fasting plasma glucose >250 to 300 mg/dL; preprandial glucose concentrations ≥200 mg/dL), the pancreas secretes low levels of insulin and postreceptor (postbinding) defects in insulin activity become more important. Postreceptor defects are characterized by a decrease in maximum responsiveness of tissues to any level of insulin. At this point, intensive insulin therapy is indicated. If glucose concentrations can be normalized, postreceptor defects and pancreatic responsiveness to glucose can be improved. Occasionally, patients who are brought into control with intensive insulin therapy can be switched back to oral agents.[140] This may be related to the hypothesis that high glucose concentrations in and of themselves may be toxic to the beta cells and peripheral tissues (glucotoxicity).[156]

Given the choice between oral and parenteral therapy, most patients select oral agents. L.H. was no exception. Patients who are most likely to respond favorably to oral sulfonylureas are recently diagnosed, within 110% to 160% of ideal body weight, and have a fasting plasma glucose of less than 180 mg/dL. If patients have been treated with insulin, those whose requirements are less than 40 U/day (indicating endogenous pancreatic reserve) are most likely to respond.[140] L.H. fulfills many of these criteria, but she is overweight and has a fasting plasma glucose concentration that is greater than 180 mg/dL. Thus, her initial response to oral agents cannot be predicted. Approximately two-thirds to three-fourths of those patients who meet all the criteria specified above will achieve satisfactory control initially. The remainder (16% to 36%) fail to respond to a one-month trial of maximum therapeutic doses and are considered primary failures.[140]

Contraindications

L.H. has no contraindications to the use of sulfonylureas which include:

- IDDM,
- pregnant or lactating women (see Chapter 45: Teratogenicity and Drugs in Breast Milk),
- patients with documented hypersensitivity to sulfonylureas,
- patients with severe hepatic or renal dysfunction, and
- patients with severe, acute intercurrent illness (infection, MI), surgery, or other stress during which control fluctuates.

A viable option to sulfonylureas is metformin which is now available in the U.S. (See discussion of Biguanides and Update.)

44. Which oral sulfonylurea should be used in L.H.? How should she be dosed?

There is little evidence that any particular oral sulfonylurea is more effective than another in properly selected patients with NIDDM. However, there are differences in duration of action and side effects which should be considered in the selection of these agents. The highest incidence of adverse effects is associated with chlorpropamide which causes intolerance to alcohol ("Antabuse reactions"), water retention, and prolonged hypoglycemia. Acetohexamide is metabolized to active products which can accumulate in patients with decreased renal function.[140] For these reasons, we recommend against the routine use of these two agents. Tolbutamide is the shortest-acting of the sulfonylureas and generally is dosed two to three times daily. For patients in whom compliance is a problem, this agent is not recommended.

Of the first-generation agents, tolazamide has several advantages. It has an intermediate activity so that control usually can be achieved with one dose and in some cases two doses per day. However, its duration of action is not so prolonged that accumulation is likely to result in severe hypoglycemic episodes. One should be cautious of its use, however, in patients with creatinine clearances of less than 30 mL/minute since its metabolites are mildly active.[161]

Glipizide and glyburide are second-generation agents. Although they are approximately 100 times more potent on a mg for mg basis, there is no evidence that they are more effective than first-generation agents.[140,167] Glipizide is metabolized to inactive products and has an intermediate duration of action. Like tolazamide, many patients can be controlled on single daily doses, but twice daily doses are recommended for patients who require more than 15 mg.

Clinically, glyburide has a longer duration of action than glipizide. Unlike other sulfonylureas, glyburide may accumulate inside beta cells, which could account for its long duration of action despite its short half-life.[161] This is consistent with the observation that fasting plasma insulin concentrations are higher in patients treated with glyburide than those treated with glipizide.[162] In contrast, postprandial insulin concentrations are higher in patients treated with glipizide than those treated with glyburide. It is on this basis that some clinicians believe that glyburide may be more effective in patients with fasting hyperglycemia, whereas glipizide may be more effective in patients with postprandial hyperglycemia. Because glyburide has a long duration of action, it is associated more frequently with severe, prolonged hypoglycemia than is glipizide. For this reason, it should be used cautiously in frail, elderly

individuals or those, who for any reason, are predisposed to hypoglycemia. (See Questions 53 and 58.)

For L.H., tolazamide, glipizide, or glyburide would be the agents of choice. She should be initiated on low doses (e.g., 100 to 250 gm tolazamide; 5 mg glipizide; or 1.25 to 2.5 mg glyburide) once daily. Every one to two weeks the dose can be increased until the therapeutic goals are achieved or maximum doses of these agents have been reached. (See Table 48.26.) Increasing the dose of sulfonylureas beyond the maximum dose does not increase the therapeutic effect, but places the patient at higher risk for adverse effects. The manufacturers recommend twice daily dosing of these agents once a specified dose has been exceeded; whether this actually is necessary has not been documented. Many clinicians recommend taking these agents 30 minutes before meals so that the onset of action more closely matches food absorption;[140] this may be less important in patients taking these agents chronically, particularly for the intermediate and longer acting agents.[153] If GI intolerance occurs, these agents should be taken with food.

Secondary Failure

45. L.H. was encouraged to maintain her diet and was placed on tolazamide 250 mg/day. She did well for ≈2 years (FPGs 130–150 mg/dL; consistently negative urine tests; HbA$_{1c}$ 8%–9%; asymptomatic) until 2 months ago when she was hospitalized for pneumonia. During her hospitalization, fasting and random plasma glucose concentrations ranged from 370–450 mg/dL and she was managed with insulin.

L.H. was discharged on tolazamide 500 mg/day and, for the past 4 weeks, she has been taking 500 mg BID. Since she has been discharged from the hospital, L.H. has begun to spill glucose in her urine, and her FPG concentrations have been rising gradually (200–250 mg/dL) despite increasing doses of tolazamide. On this clinic visit, her FPG is 320 mg/dL and she again complains of extreme fatigue, polyuria, polydipsia, and recurrent vaginal infections. Assess L.H.'s recent and past diabetic history and therapy. [SI units: plasma glucose concentrations 7.2–8.3, 20.5–25.0, 11.1–13.9, and 17.8 mmol/L; HbA$_{1c}$ 0.08–0.09]

L.H.'s history is consistent with secondary failure to treatment with the sulfonylureas which is characterized by progressively poor diabetic control that occurs following a one-month to several-year period of good response. This phenomenon is fairly common and occurs at a rate of about 5% to 10% per year in patients who initially are well controlled on these agents.[62,140]

The etiology of secondary failure is unknown, but it may be related to progression of the disease with pancreatic failure; poor dietary compliance; exogenous diabetogenic factors such as obesity, illness, or drugs;[303] or tachyphylaxis to the oral sulfonylurea (see Tables 48.12 and 48.32).[163] Treatment includes identifying and correcting any diabetogenic factor; switching the patient to another oral sulfonylurea (although this is not effective in the majority of cases);[165] adding metformin;[139] adding an evening dose of intermediate or long-acting insulin (see Question 47); or switching the patient to insulin.[62,165]

Insulin in Patients with NIDDM

46. Metformin was added to maximum doses of glipizide and this improved L.H.'s FPG and HbA$_{1c}$ modestly for about 6 months. She remained symptomatic, however, and it was decided then to consider insulin. How should L.H. be switched from oral agents to insulin? Is it reasonable to use insulin in combination with oral sulfonylurea therapy?

Some have suggested that the addition of basal insulin may bring patients who are poorly controlled on oral agents under control.[140,166,168] They recommend daytime dosing of the oral sulfonylureas in conjunction with ultralente insulin in the evening or

NPH at bedtime to suppress hepatic glucose output during the post-absorptive state [Bedtime Insulin Daytime Sulfonylureas (BIDS)].

However, it is common clinical practice to treat patients who have responded poorly to the oral agents with insulin alone.[62,140,167] The switch to insulin may be made abruptly, but one should be aware of the prolonged action of chlorpropamide and glyburide in patients taking these agents and use more conservative doses initially.

Since glipizide has an intermediate duration of action and metformin a short duration of action, it is unlikely that any residual effects will remain beyond one day. Even if they do, L.H. is in such poor control that any effect is unlikely to be clinically important. Therefore, L.H. can be instructed to discontinue her glipizide and metformin immediately and begin insulin therapy. Insulin dosing procedures are the same as those described for patients with IDDM in Questions 5 and 15 through 18, except that L.H.'s total daily dose of insulin may be higher on a U/kg basis due to insulin tissue resistance. (See Table 48.14.)

Typically, Type II patients are initiated on single or twice daily doses of intermediate-acting insulin. Although a single dose usually is administered before breakfast, bedtime doses have been advocated by others[166–168] on the grounds that this method is more likely to lower the fasting plasma glucose. If the fasting glucose level is lower, they reason, postprandial excursions also will be lower, leading to an overall decrease in mean plasma glucose concentrations. Like Type I patients, patients with severe Type II disease may require regular insulin before meals to minimize postprandial excursions. One should be aware that when high doses of insulin are used, patients have difficulty losing weight. This is secondary to the anabolic effects of insulin and hunger that can occur in association with low glucose concentrations. There also is concern about the potential atherogenic consequences of chronically elevated insulin levels.[167,168]

Combined Use of Oral Sulfonylureas and Insulin

47. Over a period of 6 weeks, L.H. is moderately well controlled on BID doses of NPH and regular insulin; 45 U NPH/15 U regular in the a.m. and 20 U NPH/10 U Reg in the p.m. She now uses HBGM; fasting blood glucose concentrations range from 140–160 mg/dL, and preprandial blood glucose concentrations range from 120–200 mg/dL. Despite what she considers earnest attempts to comply with her diabetic diet, she has gained 5 lb since her last visit 4 weeks ago. Is it rational to add oral sulfonylureas to L.H.'s therapy?

Several investigators have explored the beneficial effects of sulfonylureas used in combination with insulin and the results of their work have been thoughtfully and critically reviewed.[140,167,168] Originally, combined therapy was based upon the hypothesis that the extrapancreatic effects of the sulfonylureas might enhance the action of exogenously administered insulin. It has since been demonstrated that the primary beneficial effect of the sulfonylureas when used in combination with insulin can be attributed to the enhanced secretion of endogenous insulin, resulting in more effective suppression of hepatic glucose production and lower fasting plasma glucose.[167,169] This is corroborated by the observation that the addition of sulfonylureas to insulin therapy in patients with true IDDM (i.e., no C-peptide) generally has no effect on glucose control.[170,171]

Placebo-controlled and uncontrolled studies indicate that in some patients with NIDDM who have failed treatment with sulfonylurea and insulin therapy alone, the addition of sulfonylureas to insulin may improve fasting plasma glucose concentrations and glycosylated hemoglobin values modestly (40 to 50 mg/dL and 1% to 2%, respectively). This may or may not be accompanied by a modest decrease in insulin requirement (≈25%). Since many pa-

tients treated in these studies were not optimally controlled on insulin before combination therapy was instituted, it is impossible to tell whether combination therapy was more effective than intensive insulin regimens. Furthermore, most studies assessed the effectiveness of combined therapy for four or fewer months. In those few studies that have been carried out for a longer period, beneficial effects diminish or are lost at six months.[172] Other potential drawbacks of combination therapy include increased costs, complex therapeutic regimens, and a higher incidence of hypoglycemic reactions. Few studies have addressed the comparative efficacy of adding insulin to maximal doses of sulfonylurea versus insulin alone. Such studies could help clarify the clinical approach to the management of secondary failure to the sulfonylureas. Question 59 addresses the use of combination therapy in the elderly population.

The patient most likely to benefit from combination therapy is slightly obese, has a relatively short duration of NIDDM, and has preserved beta cell function. Genuth recommends that combination therapy be considered in Type II patients taking over 100 units or greater than 1 U/kg of insulin daily whether or not they are well controlled. Addition of sulfonylureas in the well-controlled patient may allow one to decrease the total daily dose, thereby minimizing the potential risks of hyperinsulinemia (weight gain and atherogenesis). The addition of sulfonylureas in patients who are poorly-controlled on high insulin doses may improve their symptoms and biochemical indices.[167]

In both these instances, sulfonylureas should be discontinued after 8 to 12 weeks if there is no improvement in glucose control in the first instance or decreased insulin requirements in the second instance. L.H. is poorly-controlled on insulin doses of 1.3 U/kg/day and she clearly is having difficulty maintaining her weight on such high doses. In her case, it may be worthwhile to add a sulfonylurea in an attempt to improve her glucose control and, perhaps, decrease her insulin requirements. She can be started on 5 mg/day glipizide or glyburide, and this dose should be adjusted upward at one- to two-week intervals to a maximum of 10 mg/day. L.H. should be warned to watch for symptoms of hypoglycemia. The combined use of metformin and insulin has not been studied extensively, but is rational on the basis of mechanism of action.

Premixed Regular and NPH Insulin

48. L.H. has difficulty mixing her NPH and regular insulin. Even with repeated education, she continues to make dosing errors and her vial of regular insulin is consistently clouded. What are options for L.H.?

There are several options for individuals who have difficulty mixing NPH and regular insulin. The first is to prescribe a fixed, mixed dose of NPH and regular insulin. In the U.S., fixed mixtures of NPH and regular insulin in a 70:30 ratio and a 50:50 ratio are available. (See Table 48.6.) In Europe, many other fixed ratios are available. The biggest advantage of premixed insulins is convenience, especially for patients who administer their injections away from home. Another important advantage is accuracy. As L.H. illustrates, a large percentage of patients make errors in drawing up insulin, especially the elderly. Ideally, the ratio of NPH and regular insulin should be individualized for each patient. Practically, however, there are occasional patients in whom the fixed mixed products must be used to provide both the rapid-acting action of regular insulin and the more prolonged action of NPH. It has been established that the onset and duration of action of these fixed mixtures is identical to that achieved when regular insulin and NPH in the same doses are administered by separate injection. Additionally, it is now possible to purchase prefilled syringes containing a fixed mixture of NPH and regular insulin in a 70:30 ratio. (See Table 48.6.)

If L.H. is eligible for visiting nursing services or if she lives with someone who can be taught how to mix insulins, several syringes can be predrawn for her and placed in the refrigerator. Insulin stored in this way is stable for up to three months.[78]

Cost-Saving Measures

49. A.M., a 45-year-old NIDDM patient, has been using insulin for the past 5 years. She injects herself twice daily and tests her blood glucose by the visual method with Chemstrips bG. In the course of her visit, she discloses that she reuses her disposable insulin syringes 3–4 times before discarding them and cuts her Chemstrips in half with cuticle scissors so that she can get twice as many tests from a single bottle. Should these practices be discouraged?

Reuse of Insulin Syringes. Those who work with patients with diabetes know that they are extremely resourceful in cutting their health care costs. Two frequently encountered practices are the reuse of disposable syringes and strip splitting. In a survey of 254 adult insulin users, 45% reused their syringes for an average of four days, 16% refrigerated their syringes between uses, and 35% wiped their needles with alcohol. Dullness was the major reason for changing to a new syringe.[173] Borders et al. examined approximately 2800 injection sites, and no infection was noted.

The ADA does not discourage syringe reuse and recommends that patients discard syringes into puncture-resistant, disposable containers if they are dull, bent, or have come in contact with surfaces other than the skin. They do not recommend refrigeration or wiping the needle with alcohol between uses, only recapping. Patients who reuse their syringes should inspect their skin for signs of infection.[174]

Strip Splitting. Another common practice among patients is to cut strips in half lengthwise to double the number of glucose tests per bottle. This has been such a common practice that a commercial strip-splitter is now available. Spraul et al.[175] demonstrated that visual reading of split test strips was as reliable as reading uncut test strips. Strips halved by a commercial strip splitter or scissors were equally reliable. Therefore, we do not discourage this practice among our patients. However, split strips cannot be used in reflectance colorimeters. A commercial device which theoretically adapts a machine for reading split strips is available; however, there are no studies verifying the reliability of readings using this device. Until such studies are available, we strongly recommend against this practice.

Adverse Effects of the Sulfonylureas

Adverse effects attributed to the sulfonylureas generally are infrequent and mild, and less than 2% of patients discontinue these agents because of side effects. In general, the type, incidence, and severity of reported side effects are similar for all the sulfonylureas. An important exception is chlorpropamide, which has several unique adverse effects. (See Questions 53 and 54.) The most frequently reported adverse reactions to the sulfonylureas include:

- GI symptoms (see below),
- blood dyscrasias (see below),
- dermatologic reactions (see Question 50),
- alcohol intolerance (see below),
- hyponatremia or syndrome of inappropriate antidiuretic hormone secretion (SIADH) (see below),
- hepatotoxicity (see Question 51),
- hypothyroidism (Also see Chapter 47: Thyroid Disorders),
- cardiovascular effects (UGDP Study) (see Question 52), and
- hypoglycemia (see Question 53).

Gastrointestinal Effects

The GI effects usually are manifested as nausea, fullness, or heartburn and appear to be dose-related. In the majority of cases, they can be relieved by reducing the dose or instructing the patient to take the drug with meals. In many cases, these complaints resolve over time with continued use of the same dose.

Hematologic Effects

The sulfonylureas rarely have been ($<0.1\%$) associated with a variety of hematologic disorders, including: leukopenia, neutropenia, thrombocytopenia, pancytopenia, agranulocytosis, aplastic anemia, pure red-cell aplasia, and hemolytic anemia. Almost all of the reported cases have been due to chlorpropamide or tolbutamide.

Sulfonylurea-induced agranulocytosis and pancytopenia can be fatal. Other hematologic effects generally are reversible after the drug is withdrawn. Sulfonylurea-induced immune hemolysis can be caused by the "innocent bystander" mechanism, which is abrupt in onset and causes severe hemolysis, or the hapten mechanism, which generally is subacute in onset (may take months or years to develop) and moderate in severity. All of these serious hematologic reactions are very rare, with the possible exception of hapten-mediated hemolytic anemia. Patients can develop only a mild anemia, and the diagnosis of drug-induced hemolysis can then be missed.[176]

Miscellaneous Adverse Effects

An Antabuse-like reaction is known to occur in patients taking oral sulfonylurea drugs, but is most frequently associated with chlorpropamide, occurring in approximately one-third of all patients receiving it.

The flushing reaction seen so often with chlorpropamide is rare with other sulfonylureas. Less than 5% of diabetic patients treated with tolbutamide report a flushing reaction with alcohol; the prevalence for other sulfonylureas is even less. The second-generation sulfonylureas, glipizide and glyburide, have been associated with a flushing reaction only in a few rare reports.[178]

Rare reports in the literature of serious idiosyncratic reactions include: pulmonary infiltration, eosinophilia or eosinophilic pneumonia, nephrotic syndrome, pseudomembranous colitis, and optic neuropathy. Rare cases of Wernicke's encephalopathy induced by hypoglycemic agents also have been reported.[159] Correction of hyperglycemia increases the short-term use of glucose in the tissues. In an alcoholic or malnourished patient with borderline thiamine reserves, this can cause acute thiamine depletion and induce Wernicke's encephalopathy. This effect is similar to administering an exogenous glucose load to a patient with thiamine deficiency, which is well-known to cause this encephalopathy.

Dermatologic Reactions

50. F.M., a 68-year-old female, was found to have NIDDM on routine examination 8 months ago. She was treated with chlorpropamide despite a history of an allergic reaction to sulfisoxazole and began to develop a mild, pruritic maculopapular rash 3 weeks later. She eventually was treated with glyburide for 6 months. The rash progressed to severe erythroderma with exfoliation and hypopigmentation. Eventually, F.M. was hospitalized for her progressive dermatitis. At that time, glyburide was discontinued, high-dose prednisone was initiated to treat the dermatitis, and insulin treatment was begun. What kinds of skin reactions have been attributed to the sulfonylureas? Is the use of sulfonylureas contraindicated in F.M.? Was it appropriate to treat F.M. with another sulfonylurea?

Pruritus and/or rash are among the most commonly reported side effects attributed to the sulfonylureas. The majority are minor and reversible within 2 to 14 days if the offending drug is discontinued. There have been occasional reports of spontaneous clearing despite continuation of therapy, and rashes also have been noted to increase in severity following discontinuation of therapy.

The rash, which usually is maculopapular, erythematous, and discrete in nature, generally involves the face, neck, upper trunk, and proximal portion of the arms. It may or may not be preceded or accompanied by pruritus. Infrequently, patients may develop erythema multiforme, exfoliative dermatitis, Stevens-Johnson syndrome, photosensitivity reactions, and lichenoid eruptions.

Because sulfonylureas have a sulfa-like structure, many authors have suggested that their use be avoided in those patients allergic to sulfonamides. Unless a severe reaction is documented, however, there is probably not a contraindication to the use of sulfonylureas in this situation, since the prevalence of cross-sensitivity among various sulfonamides is about 17% and the structure of sulfonylureas differs from sulfonamides. Some patients who have developed rash to one sulfonylurea have been managed successfully with another sulfonylurea. However, cross-sensitivity among the sulfonylureas also has been documented and is said to be common.

Because F.M.'s initial reaction was mild, a trial with another sulfonylurea was appropriate; however, glyburide should have been discontinued as soon as it was evident that F.M.'s rash was not regressing.

Syndrome of Inappropriate ADH (SIADH)

Chlorpropamide, and to a much lesser extent, tolbutamide, may enhance the release of antidiuretic hormone (ADH) centrally, enhance the effect of ADH on the kidney, and override the inhibitory effects of waterloading on ADH release resulting in SIADH. This antidiuretic effect has been used clinically to treat diabetes insipidus.[179]

Symptoms of SIADH are secondary to hyponatremia and include weakness, headaches, nausea, vomiting, disorientation, confusion, stupor, and, in extreme cases, coma. The diagnostic criteria include hyponatremia, a normal state of hydration, and urine osmolality exceeding serum osmolality.[140]

Chlorpropamide-induced SIADH is rare in patients without other risk factors which include: old age, congestive heart failure, and concurrent diuretic use. Symptoms usually occur several days to weeks after an increase in dose, usually to greater than 500 mg/day. Therapeutic waterloads for urinary tract infections and cancer chemotherapy also should be used cautiously in patients taking chlorpropamide.[140,180]

In contrast to chlorpropamide and tolbutamide, glipizide, glyburide, tolazamide, and acetohexamide have a mild diuretic effect.

Hepatotoxicity

51. Four weeks following the initiation of chlorpropamide therapy (500 mg/day), E.T., a 61-year-old woman with NIDDM, develops a fever and complains of nausea, vomiting, and a pruritic rash. Her urine has turned dark, and her stools are clay-colored. She seeks medical advice at the urging of friends who have noted her yellow complexion. Initial laboratory tests indicate that she has an elevated serum bilirubin, alkaline phosphatase, and eosinophil count. Could E.T.'s signs and symptoms be related to her chlorpropamide therapy? If so, could they be alleviated by changing to another sulfonylurea?

Mildly elevated liver function tests that are completely reversible have been associated with all of the sulfonylureas; hepatotoxicity with clinical jaundice also has been well documented. Of the commercially available preparations, chlorpropamide has been implicated most frequently (estimated incidence of 0.5% to 1.5%),[181]

although hepatotoxicity also has been associated with tolbutamide, acetohexamide, tolazamide, and glyburide.

As illustrated by E.T., hepatotoxic reactions to sulfonylureas are characterized primarily by intrahepatic cholestasis with infrequent cellular damage. Since many are hypersensitivity reactions, fever, rash, and eosinophilia are common.[181-183]

In most cases, mild hepatic biochemical changes are seen within one to two weeks after the drug is initiated, with symptoms developing within two to five weeks. Most reactions are reversible within one to two months after the drug is discontinued. Occasionally, a more severe chronic liver disease may persist.[182] Although there have been reports of patients who respond favorably when rechallenged at a lower dose or switched to a different sulfonylurea, others have experienced recurrence of hepatotoxicity.

Therefore, E.T. should be treated with diet and insulin, and chlorpropamide should be discontinued immediately. If oral therapy is absolutely necessary once the patient is asymptomatic, a sulfonylurea other than chlorpropamide can be tried, but the patient must be monitored closely.

Cardiovascular Effects

52. The package insert for all sulfonylureas includes a special warning on increased risk of cardiovascular mortality. What is the basis of this warning? Are sulfonylureas contraindicated in patients with cardiovascular disease?

The FDA required that all manufacturers of sulfonylureas include the above warning on the basis of an unexpected finding of the University Group Diabetes Program (UGDP) study in 1970. This was a cooperative, prospective study to evaluate the effectiveness of antidiabetic therapy in preventing vascular and other late complications of diabetes in mild Type II patients. Unexpectedly, twice as many cardiovascular deaths occurred in the tolbutamide-treated group as in the placebo- and insulin-treated groups.[184]

Following publication of the UGDP results, a great controversy regarding the study's validity and clinical implications appeared in both the professional and lay press; these are summarized elsewhere.[167] A major impact of the study was to cause the medical community to reappraise a therapeutic tool which it previously had taken for granted and to place greater emphasis on diet and exercise. Growing evidence that normalization of glucose concentrations may, in fact, delay long-term complications and the failure of others to find higher cardiovascular mortality[167] have caused a resurgence in the use of these agents. Current evidence indicates that the benefits of sulfonylureas far outweigh their risks in Type II patients with cardiovascular disease. On this basis, their use is not contraindicated in this group of patients.

Hypoglycemia

53. C.A., a 68-year-old female who has had a 20-year history of NIDDM and a 5-year history of mild renal failure (creatinine 1.5 mg/dL; BUN 30 mg/dL) is admitted to the hospital in a coma. According to her daughter, C.A.'s diabetes has been well controlled over the past several months with chlorpropamide 750 mg/day (she took her last dose ≈9 hours before admission). Three days before admission she developed anorexia, nausea, and vomiting in association with the flu and became progressively lethargic. Laboratory results on admission are as follows: plasma glucose 20 mg/dL; SrCr 3.0 mg/dL; BUN 80 mg/dL. What is C.A.'s diagnosis? Were there any predisposing factors? [SI units: creatinine 132.6 and 265.2 µmol/L; BUN 10.7 and 28.6 mmol/L; plasma glucose 1.1 mmol/L]

C.A. has developed a case of severe hypoglycemia secondary to chlorpropamide. Hypoglycemia is the most common (incidence 2.4/100 patients/year) and potentially severe (4% to 7% mortality) adverse effect of the sulfonylureas. The incidence and severity of this effect increase with the duration of action and potency of the agents. Thus, the incidence of severe, prolonged hypoglycemia secondary to chlorpropamide and glyburide is about twice as high as that for glipizide and about five times as high for tolbutamide.[83,140,185] As discussed in the section on drug-induced hypoglycemia later in this chapter, sulfonylureas account for almost all cases of drug-induced hypoglycemia in individuals over age 60.

Most cases of sulfonylurea-induced hypoglycemia occur in patients who are predisposed to hypoglycemia in some way, and C.A. is no exception. She is an elderly woman with renal impairment who was on relatively high doses of an agent, a portion of which is excreted unchanged in the urine. Even in the face of decreased carbohydrate intake (anorexia and vomiting), she continued to take her usual dose of chlorpropamide. The decreased intake and vomiting probably led to dehydration and further compromised renal function.

Since chlorpropamide and glyburide have a long duration of action, hypoglycemia induced by these agents may last for several hours or days. Therefore, patients such as C.A. must be hospitalized and treated with continuous glucose infusions until oral intake resumes. Otherwise, severe hypoglycemia may recur.

Sulfonylurea Use in Special Situations
Renal Dysfunction

54. Chlorpropamide has been withheld and C.A.'s kidney function is stabilized [creatinine clearance (Cl$_{Cr}$) = 35 mL/min]. Because she lives alone and has impaired eyesight secondary to cataracts and a severe case of arthritis, insulin treatment is impractical. Oral hypoglycemics are to be continued. What is the agent of choice? [SI unit: Cl$_{Cr}$ 5.83 mL/s]

Once C.A.'s plasma glucose concentrations and renal function have been stabilized, reinstitution of antidiabetic therapy must be considered. Sulfonylurea compounds that are eliminated unchanged or are metabolized to active products that depend upon the kidney for elimination (acetohexamide, chlorpropamide glyburide, tolazamide) should be avoided in the elderly and patients with decreased renal function. Sulfonylureas that are completely metabolized to inactive or weakly active products may be used (i.e., glipizide or tolbutamide). Although glyburide is unlikely to accumulate in patients with a Cl$_{Cr}$ greater than 30 mL/minute, it should be used cautiously in C.A. because of its association with severe hypoglycemic reactions. Furthermore, even patients who are not taking sulfonylureas are more likely to experience hypoglycemic reactions if they have renal insufficiency; therefore, any oral hypoglycemic agent should be initiated at a low dose and titrated slowly. C.A. should be instructed to eat regularly, since skipped meals may result in recurrent hypoglycemia.[161,186]

Hepatic Dysfunction

55. B.R., a 60-year-old male with cirrhosis of the liver, is found to have diabetes mellitus. Glipizide 10 mg QD is initiated. How will B.R.'s liver function affect the disposition of glipizide and his response to this agent?

Because hepatic metabolism is the primary route of elimination for most sulfonylureas, including glipizide, patients with hepatic disease should be expected to have an exaggerated response to those drugs metabolized to less active products (acetohexamide is the exception).

Tolbutamide is the sulfonylurea that has been studied most extensively with respect to liver disease. In a double-blind, placebo-controlled trial of 50 cirrhotic patients, hypoglycemia was a complication in 20% of the tolbutamide-treated group.[187] Tolbutamide elimination half-life in subjects with cirrhosis has been reported to be increased or unaltered in different studies.[188] A complicating

factor is that alcohol can induce hepatic enzymes, markedly increasing tolbutamide metabolism in alcoholic cirrhotic patients.

Liver disease can be a separate predisposing factor for severe, prolonged hypoglycemia because glycogenolysis and gluconeogenesis are impaired; thus, sulfonylureas are relatively contraindicated for cirrhotic patients. If they are used, shorter-acting agents are preferred and small initial doses should be used. For B.R., glipizide should be initiated at a dose no greater than 2.5 mg/day and increased if needed by 2.5 mg increments at no less than weekly intervals.

Diabetes in the Elderly

56. J.M. is a frail, 82-year-old, unresponsive male who is brought to the ER. According to J.M.'s family, he has become increasingly confused, dizzy, and lethargic with a recent weight loss of 10 lb. Fasting serum chemistry reveals the following: Na 128 mEq/L (Normal: 135–145 mEq/L), glucose 798 mg/dL (Normal: 70–110 mg/dL), and serum osmolality 374 mOsm/L (Normal: 280–295 mOsm/kg H$_2$O). His serum is negative for ketones. Upon physical examination, J.M. has poor skin turgor, dry mucous membranes, and is responsive only to deep pain. His BP is 90/60 mm Hg with a pulse of 96 beats/min. He is noted to have rales at the left lower base of his lung and a chest x-ray confirms pneumonia. Despite aggressive fluid replacement, J.M.'s blood glucose remains consistently >250 mg/dL and his HbA$_{1c}$ is 11% (Normal: ≤6%). What special factors contribute to the atypical presentation of an elderly diabetic as seen in J.M.? What is the incidence of Type II diabetes mellitus in the elderly? [SI units: Na 128 mmol/L (Normal: 135–145 mmol/L); glucose 44.3 and >13.9 mmol/L (Normal: 3.9–6.1 mmol/L); serum osmolality 374 mmol/kg; HbA$_{1c}$ 0.11]

Diabetes in the elderly often has an atypical presentation and for this reason, it frequently is underdiagnosed and undertreated.[189] (See Table 48.28 for a comparison of presenting symptoms for diabetes mellitus in the elderly compared to younger patients.) Approximately one-half of patients who initially present in hyperosmolar coma have not been diagnosed previously with diabetes, as demonstrated by J.M.

Several factors predispose the elderly to hyperosmolar, nonketotic coma. Failure of the mu-opioid drinking system that occurs with aging results in an inability to recognize thirst.[191] This hypodipsia may interact with the hyperosmolar diuresis from an elevated blood glucose to produce dehydration as evidenced in J.M. Demented individuals who are unable to ask for fluid are particularly prone to this. Early on, high renal thresholds also may prevent or minimize polyuria secondary to hyperglycemia. Other precipitating factors for the development of hyperosmolar, nonketotic coma include: infection, drugs (hydrochlorothiazide, propranolol or glucocorticoids) and other acute illnesses (e.g., myocardial infarction, GI bleeding, pancreatitis).

Because patients with Type II diabetes have some residual insulin production, they are protected against ketone production. Measurements of serum ketones and blood pH differentiate this

Table 48.28	Presentation of Diabetes Mellitus in the Elderly Compared to Younger Patients	
Metabolic Abnormality	Symptoms in Young Patients	Symptoms in Elderly Patients
↑ serum osmolality	Polydipsia	Dehydration, confusion, delirium
Glycosuria	Polyuria	Incontinence
Catabolic state due to insulin deficiency	Polyphagia	Weight loss, anorexia

condition from diabetic ketoacidosis (see Question 34). J.M. presents with several symptoms of hyperosmolar nonketotic dehydration including: osmolality >330 mOsm, plasma glucose >600 mg/dL, decreased skin turgor, hypotension, and the absence of serum ketones. His pneumonia was probably the precipitating factor. While the mortality rate for this disorder is 3% in patients under 50 years of age, it increases to 30% for those over 50.[192] Treatment involves rapid intravenous hydration, replacing one half of the water deficit in the first five hours using 1 L/hr of normal saline. The administration rate is then reduced to 250 to 500 mL/hr until adequate hydration has been established.[190] Insulin may be given simultaneously, if indicated, to correct the hyperglycemia more rapidly. Rehydration has been sufficient to correct J.M.'s metabolic imbalance, allowing his diabetes control to be addressed now.

Diabetes mellitus currently represents one of the major chronic disorders affecting the elderly population, occurring in 18% of persons between the ages of 65 and 70 years of age and in 40% of patients 80 years of age or greater. The elderly comprise 48% of the population with ''noninsulin dependent'' or Type II diabetes and account for approximately 63% of the total spent on health care for patients with Type II diabetes. Currently, 14.5% of nursing home patients have diabetes.[193]

57. What are the goals of therapy for J.M.?

The basic principles of management are to maintain J.M.'s blood glucose between 100 and 140 mg/dL and avoid hypoglycemia. Since the majority of elderly patients have Type II diabetes, dietary and exercise programs are the initial steps in therapy. While weight loss is essential in the management of Type II diabetes, the elderly usually are not excessively overweight upon presentation. Use of an ADA diet currently is being questioned because it can be expensive and may result in malnutrition. Therefore, exclusion of free sugars from the diet appears to be sufficient in this patient population. Weight reduction is recommended only if the patient is 20% or more overweight. Exercise has been shown to increase wellbeing[194] and glucose stability in the elderly while decreasing their propensity to fall. Exercise also improves blood pressure, the lipid profile, hypercoagulability, and bone density. Twenty minutes of brisk walking three times weekly to raise the heart rate to 100 to 120 beats per minute is recommended. For patients with arthritis, aquatic exercise may be substituted. Before such an exercise program is initiated, careful cardiovascular evaluation via stress testing is mandatory to avoid myocardial ischemia or the acceleration of retinopathy.[195]

58. What considerations should be made in selecting an oral hypoglycemic agent for J.M.? Are the elderly at greater risk for developing hypoglycemia?

There are several age-associated problems with the use of oral hypoglycemic agents. Hepatic blood flow and oxidative metabolism are decreased with aging, resulting in prolonged half-lives of hepatically metabolized drugs. Serum albumin is reduced in the elderly and this affects the highly-protein-bound first generation sulfonylureas, resulting in increased serum levels of free drug.[195] Response to hypoglycemic counterregulatory hormones is diminished in the elderly, resulting in prolonged hypoglycemia.[196] Decreased renal function and mass that occurs with aging decreases the clearance and increases the half-lives of oral agents excreted renally, specifically acetohexamide, chlorpropamide, glyburide, and metformin. Chlorpropamide (Diabinese) should be avoided in the elderly population due to its long half-life (≥35 hours) and high incidence of hyponatremia.[197] Glyburide (Micronase, Dia-Beta) and glipizide (Glucotrol), the second generation oral hypoglycemics, may be preferred for use in the elderly because they are nonionically bound to serum albumin, reducing the potential for drug interactions in an elderly patient taking several medica-

tions. Unlike glyburide, glipizide has no pharmacologically active metabolites and this may lessen the risk of hypoglycemia in this patient population. (See Table 48.26 for specific prescribing information for these agents.)

Others factors also predispose the elderly to hypoglycemia. Anorexia is very common in the elderly and can result in malnutrition. This can lead to irregular or inadequate food intake and hypoglycemia in patients taking sulfonylureas or insulin. Other factors include ill-fitting dentures, difficulty in chewing and swallowing, decreased ability or interest in cooking, impaired taste, and lack of companionship during meals.

59. If J.M. does not respond to an oral hypoglycemic, should insulin therapy be considered? What about combination therapy?

Use of insulin is reserved for those patients with Type II diabetes in whom dietary modification and oral hypoglycemic agents fail to control glucose levels or in those whose initial fasting blood glucose exceeds 300 mg/dL. The approach is similar to younger patients and should not be viewed as an undue hardship for the elderly. With proper training, elderly patients are able to self-administer their insulin. Split-dose insulin therapy has been shown to be more efficacious in achieving euglycemia and also avoids complications arising from single daily doses. The elderly have been shown to make a 10% to 20% error rate when drawing up their insulin doses.[198] Aids which can help ensure the correct dosage administration include: a syringe magnifier, insulin dosage gauge, premixed insulin, or predrawn syringes. The patient's ability to draw up the correct dosage should be assessed at each clinic visit.

Studies of combination therapy with insulin and sulfonylureas have been performed in middle-aged diabetic patients only. Combination therapy in the elderly would increase the number of medications and increase the risk of hypoglycemia. Therefore, combination therapy currently is not recommended in the elderly population.

60. Should J.M. be instructed to perform home blood glucose monitoring?

Since the signs and symptoms of hypoglycemia in the elderly often are very subtle, an accurate assessment of glycemic control is necessary. Urine glucose testing often is prescribed for the elderly because of the perceived hardship of blood testing. However, elevations of the renal threshold for glucose and altered bladder function that occur with aging result in a poor correlation between urine and blood glucose concentrations. Elderly patients who test their blood glucose have demonstrated improvements in wellbeing, knowledge regarding diabetes, and glycemic control.[199] Clinicians should review the various blood glucose meters available, keeping in mind that elderly patients have decreased agility and reduced vision. The patient's ability to perform home glucose monitoring and visual acuity must be evaluated since retinopathy produces a blue-green color vision disturbance which can result in misinterpretation of test results that rely upon color changes in the test pad.[193]

In conclusion, the diagnosis and management of diabetes in the elderly remains a challenge. Careful surveillance for its unique presentation in the elderly will confirm the diagnosis. Diet and exercise remain the cornerstones of management; however, persistently elevated blood glucose levels may require the addition of a sulfonylurea agent or insulin with careful monitoring.[200]

Treatment of Diabetic Complications
Painful Diabetic Peripheral Neuropathy (DPN)

61. A.D., a 58-year-old man with diabetes of 6 years duration, has been reasonably well controlled with diet and tola-

zamide as evidenced by a recent HbA$_{1c}$ of 8% (Normal: 4%–6%). However, over the past 6 months, A.D. has complained of increasing bilateral foot and leg pain, described as a burning or aching sensation. What role does glycemic control play in the development and progression of diabetic neuropathy? Is there any benefit from the use of aldose reductase inhibitors? What initial steps can be taken to alleviate A.D.'s neuropathy?

Painful diabetic peripheral neuropathy is a common complication of diabetes that usually involves the lower extremities. It ranges from mild paresthesias to severe pain that can become incapacitating and refractory to analgesic therapy. Although a multitude of drugs have been recommended for the treatment of DPN, few have been proven to be clinically effective.

Tight Glycemic Control

The relationship between glycemic control and nerve function has been debated for years. Intensive glycemic control may have beneficial effects on nerve function in diabetic patients.[201] Similar results were seen in small studies conducted over short time periods. Evidence from the DCCT confirms previous data indicating that near-normal control of blood glucose helps delay the development and progression of diabetic neuropathy.[14] Only 3% of patients without evidence of neuropathy at baseline developed DPN at five years versus 10% of patients in the conventional treatment group. Intensive therapy led to reversal of diabetic peripheral neuropathy in the secondary intervention cohort by 57%. Therefore, A.D.'s glycemic patterns should be reviewed to evaluate whether his current glucose control can be improved.

Aldose Reductase Inhibitors (ARIs)

Theories regarding the pathogenesis of diabetic neuropathies include: 1) nerve ischemia leading to hypoxia; 2) nonenzymatic glycosylation of proteins; 3) abnormalities of sorbitol and myo-inositol metabolism and 4) increased platelet aggregability. The most popular theory proposed thus far is an accumulation of sorbitol and fructose in peripheral nerve cells with a corresponding reduction in nerve myo-inositol concentrations.

Aldose reductase is an enzyme that enhances the conversion of glucose to sorbitol via the sorbitol (or polyol) pathway; sorbitol then is converted to fructose. Although glucose is metabolized preferentially to glucose-6-phosphate via the hexokinase pathway, elevated glucose concentrations saturate hexokinase in some tissues and activate aldose reductase. Theoretically, this may lead to tissue accumulation of sorbitol, other sugar alcohols, and fructose. Aldose reductase is found in many tissues including the retina, cornea, lens, kidney, placenta, erythrocytes, brain, muscle, liver, and peripheral nerves. Its most profound effects appear to be in the Schwann cell which is responsible for the formation of myelin, the fatty substance forming the sheath surrounding many nerve fibers.[202] When glucose concentrations are high, sorbitol and fructose accumulate within the Schwann cell, producing an osmotic gradient that in turn causes cellular edema, necrosis, and degeneration of the myelin sheath. Myo-inositol is a six carbon alcohol found in nerve cells that serves as a substrate for the synthesis of inositol phospholipids which are responsible for maintaining the integrity and ion channels of neuronal membranes.[202] Increased concentrations of glucose and sorbitol prevent uptake of myo-inositol, thus decreasing the synthesis of inositol phospholipids. In addition, increased sorbitol and decreased myo-inositol concentrations alter the metabolism of myo-inositol which affects the structure of the sodium-potassium ATPase complex, decreasing nerve conduction velocity with eventual axonal injury.[203]

Aldose reductase inhibitors are the only agents currently being developed that block the progression of peripheral neuropathies. Early clinical trials with aldose reductase inhibitors demonstrated very modest increases in conduction velocity with possible subjective benefits. However, more recent investigations have taken different approaches and there is a clear sign of efficacy for aldose reductase inhibitors with improvements that are structural and functional in nature. This was first demonstrated with *sorbinil*. Sima et al.[204] demonstrated diminished ultrastructural signs of degeneration and increased numbers of regenerating profiles in sural nerves of treated patients versus the placebo group. The authors suggested sorbinil may improve the neuropathologic lesions of diabetic peripheral neuropathy. However, sorbinil has been associated with a high incidence of hepatotoxicity and further studies involving this aldose reductase inhibitor have been suspended.

The largest trials to date have been performed with *tolrestat*. The most convincing evidence of efficacy with tolrestat has resulted from a follow-up to a large double-blind trial which demonstrated modest efficacy from the use of tolrestat over four to five years against deficient parameters of nerve conduction.[205] Patients who had received the drug were allowed to continue for 12 months on tolrestat (200 to 400 mg/day) or switch to placebo. Patients given placebo showed a clear worsening of pain and a relatively brisk deterioration of conduction velocities in four nerves. The tolrestat group showed stability of these variables. A structural examination of efficacy for tolrestat also was performed with results similar to the previous sorbinil trial.[204] Tolrestat treatment was associated with an increase in the ultrastructural regeneration of sural nerve biopsies.[206] Unlike sorbinil, tolrestat appears to be relatively free of side effects with only 2% of patients developing reversible liver abnormalities and occasional dizziness.[207] Other aldose reductase inhibitors under study include ponalrestat and epalrestat. Aldose reductase inhibitors may be most beneficial if given prophylactically or before the development of advanced neuropathic complications; however, additional study is required to further delineate their role in therapy. Some investigations provide hope for the efficacy of aldose reductase inhibitors in the treatment and prevention of diabetic neuropathy in the future.

Simple Analgesics

A.D.'s neuropathy may respond to simple analgesics or nonsteroidal anti-inflammatory agents (NSAIDs). Aspirin, sulindac, and indomethacin have chemical characteristics similar to aldose reductase inhibitors and high doses of these agents inhibit aldose reductase.[208,209] The analgesic selected for A.D. should be based upon a history of responsiveness to these agents as well as their duration of action and side effect profiles. Common side effects include GI upset and bleeding, renal and hepatic toxicity, and CNS effects such as dizziness and confusion. Therefore, these agents should be used cautiously in patients with a history of ulcer disease or renal dysfunction.

62. Despite successful attempts to improve A.D.'s glucose control, he continues to complain of increasing pain which has become so severe that he is unable to work. The pain is more intense at night and he has become so sensitive to touch that he can barely tolerate bedcovers on his feet or legs. His pain has not responded to trials of aspirin or sulindac. Within the past 2 months, A.D. has become severely depressed about his pain and diabetes, with somatic complaints of early morning awakening, weight loss, constipation, and generalized fatigue. What further steps can be taken to manage A.D.'s neuropathy?

Psychotropic Drugs

Because A.D.'s neuropathy has become incapacitating and is not relieved by analgesics, serious consideration should be given to the use of an antidepressant drug, with or without the addition of a phenothiazine. Tricyclic antidepressants (TCAs) have been shown to be effective in the treatment of painful diabetic neuropathy in patients with both normal and depressed moods. Possible mechanisms for pain relief include: 1) inhibition of reuptake of serotonin and noradrenaline, and 2) a "quinidine-like" local analgesic effect.[210]

Amitriptyline and imipramine are the most commonly used TCAs and have demonstrated the most favorable results for DPN.[211–213] Daily doses used in studies have been low to moderate (25 to 150 mg) and the onset of analgesia occurs in one to four weeks. Some studies have used a combination of tricyclic agents and a phenothiazine to achieve greater pain efficacy; however, results have been conflicting.[213,214] To minimize side effects, attempts should be made to use antidepressants alone.

A typical regimen of amitriptyline (Elavil) 75 mg at bedtime and fluphenazine (Prolixin) 1 mg three times a day was begun in A.D. with moderate relief of pain within one week. Both psychologic and somatic complaints of depression lessened dramatically. Over the next few weeks, amitriptyline was tapered to 25 mg at bedtime and fluphenazine to 1 mg twice a day, but further attempts to reduce the dose resulted in a flareup of his leg pain. Most of the adverse effects of psychotropic drug therapy (sedation, anticholinergic effects, extrapyramidal reactions, cardiovascular effects) are dose-related except for tardive dyskinesia. Patients with autonomic neuropathy are at increased risk for complications. Elderly patients are more sensitive to the adverse effects of TCAs and should be initiated on lower doses with close supervision. A.D. should continue treatment for as long as necessary to control pain, but periodic attempts should be made to reduce the dose and discontinue drug therapy. Trazodone also has been reported to be effective and is a reasonable option for patients who require an antidepressant with less anticholinergic or cardiac side effects.[210]

In conclusion, psychotropic drugs are not always effective for the treatment of painful DPN and have many chronic adverse effects. Nevertheless, in a patient such as A.D. with severe painful DPN refractory to analgesics who also is severely depressed, these drugs probably represent the treatment of choice. Drugs and doses should be tailored individually to the patient.

63. If A.D. had been unresponsive to psychotropic drug therapy, what other drugs are available to treat painful diabetic neuropathy? How effective are they?

Carbamazepine

Carbamazepine is effective in relieving the paresthesias, and particularly the pain, of some patients with severe DPN.[215,216] Doses have varied from 100 mg three times daily to 200 mg four times daily. Dizziness and drowsiness are common but often transient, and GI disturbances or dermatologic reactions are observed in 5% to 10% of patients. However, many diabetic patients do not respond to therapy and, like the psychotropic drugs, carbamazepine should be reserved for cases of painful DPN resistant to other measures. An appropriate initial trial would be 100 mg three times daily for several weeks. If needed, the dose may be increased slowly as tolerated.

Phenytoin (Dilantin) generally is not considered to be of value in the treatment of diabetic neuropathy.[217,218] One problem is that toxicity (such as macrocytic anemia, gingival hyperplasia, and ataxia) often develops before a therapeutic effect is seen. Furthermore, phenytoin potentially decreases insulin secretion in Type II patients.

Other Agents

Mexiletine and lidocaine are two antiarrhythmic drugs that are beneficial in the treatment of resistant neuropathy.[219,220] However, because of inconsistent therapeutic benefits and an increased risk of side effects, these agents are reserved for cases which cannot be treated successfully with other, less toxic agents.

Pentoxifylline is a rheological agent that decreases blood viscosity by increasing erythrocyte flexibility, which in turn enhances tissue oxygenation. Subjective improvement has been reported[221] and a six-center clinical investigation currently is ongoing to determine the safety and efficacy of pentoxifylline in the treatment of diabetic peripheral neuropathy.

Clonidine (Catapres) has been examined because it causes peripheral vasodilation and peripheral vasodilation may decrease neuronal ischemia. Early reports of efficacy have been disappointing; however, the authors concluded that a responsive subgroup may have been missed and suggested a larger study.[221]

Capsaicin Treatment

Topical application of 0.075% capsaicin (Axsain), the active ingredient in hot peppers, is used to treat postherpetic neuralgia and has been recommended for diabetic neuropathy. This nonprescription preparation enhances the release and prevents the reaccumulation of substance P in nerve terminals of type C nociceptive fibers. In this way, it impedes the conduction and transmission of peripheral pain impulses. A multicenter, double-blind, vehicle-controlled study evaluated the effect of treatment with capsaicin versus placebo on the quality of life of 277 diabetic patients with painful diabetic neuropathy.[223] Patients randomly were assigned to receive either 0.075% capsaicin cream or vehicle cream which they applied four times daily to the painful area associated with neuropathy. The effects of pain on the quality of life were evaluated by functional capacity scales, which rated the interference of pain with working, sleeping, walking, participating in recreational activities, and other activities. Patients in the capsaicin group showed significantly greater improvements in pain status versus placebo (69.5% versus 53.4%, p = 0.012). Improvement in walking, working, sleeping, and participating in recreational activities also reached statistical significance. The response of patients treated with vehicle cream was attributed to massaging the painful area during cream application. Burning was the most frequently described side effect in both groups (63% of capsaicin-treated patients versus 17% of patients in the vehicle group). Note: a very high placebo effect is typical of all pain studies. Because capsaicin acts to deplete substance P from nerve fiber terminals, initial high levels are released from the fibers, resulting in a burning and stinging sensation. Capsaicin may be useful in diabetic patients intolerant of oral medications. Patients should be advised that benefit from capsaicin may not occur for several weeks. Patients should use gloves or an applicator to apply capsaicin and avoid contact with the eyes or mucous membranes.

In conclusion, the treatment of DPN continues to center around providing symptomatic relief. The use of TCAs or carbamazepine continues to provide the best analgesic effect. A variety of other medications may provide relief in refractory patients (See Table 48.29 for a suggested sequence of drug selection in the treatment of DPN.)

Diabetic Gastroparesis

64. H.D. is a 36-year-old man with a 20-year history of insulin-dependent diabetes. He is in poor control (HbA$_{1c}$ 12%) and complains of frequent, severe hypoglycemic reactions which "don't make sense. I have insulin reactions right after I eat, but later on, my glucose concentrations are sky high." H.D. presents to the diabetes clinic with a 2-month history of nausea, postprandial fullness, and occasional vomiting, all of which are unrelieved by antacids. H.D. also has peripheral neuropathy involving both his hands and feet and manifestations of autonomic neuropathy (impotence and orthostatic hypotension). An upper GI series was ordered to rule out peptic ulcer disease and reflux esophagitis, but a preliminary diagnosis of

Table 48.29	Suggested Sequence for the Treatment of Painful Diabetic Neuropathy[a]

Preventative Measures

1) Tight glycemic control

2) Aldose reductase inhibitors[b]

Treatment Measures

1) First line

   a) Physical measures (body stockings, TENS)

   b) Simple analgesics (aspirin, acetaminophen, NSAIDs)

   c) Psychotropic agents (amitriptyline, imipramine)

2) Refractory cases

   a) Anticonvulsants (carbamazepine, phenytoin)

   b) Antiarrhythmics[b] (mexiletine, lidocaine)

[a] NSAIDs = Nonsteroidal anti-inflammatory drugs; TENS = Transcutaneous nerve stimulation.
[b] Currently investigational only.

diabetic gastroparesis was made. What is diabetic gastroparesis and how should H.D. be treated?

Diabetic gastroparesis, or gastroparesis diabeticorum, is one of the most common GI complications of diabetes mellitus (along with constipation, diarrhea, and fecal incontinence). Caused by delayed gastric emptying, the symptoms range from early satiety, bloating, or prolonged postprandial fullness to severe gastric retention with nausea, vomiting, abdominal pain, or bezoar formation. Impaired gastric emptying is caused by abnormal motility of the stomach or a reduction of cyclic motor complex activity in the intestine. Impaired diabetic control with "unexplained" hypoglycemia may result from the disrupted delivery of food to the intestine; that is, glucose delivery does not correspond with insulin action. Many patients with diabetic gastroparesis, like H.D., have been insulin-dependent for many years and also have evidence of peripheral and autonomic neuropathies, although cause and effect relationships have not been clearly demonstrated.

Metoclopramide

If therapy is indicated, H.D. should receive a trial of metoclopramide (Reglan), 10 mg orally four times daily, 30 minutes before meals and at bedtime. Although treatment may not eliminate all symptoms, it should minimize most of his complaints.[224–227] Metoclopramide is the first satisfactory treatment available for diabetic gastroparesis. In fact, metoclopramide seems to be effective in relieving symptoms of gastroparesis irrespective of the cause (diabetes, vagotomy, gastric surgery, idiopathic).[228] If oral therapy is ineffective, metoclopramide may be effective in suppository form (not commercially available).[228]

Metoclopramide affects gut motility through indirect cholinergic stimulation of the gut muscle.[225] However, symptomatic improvement does not always correlate with improved gastric emptying, which implies that the effectiveness of metoclopramide also is due to its centrally-mediated antiemetic activity.[224,225,227]

Cisapride

Cisapride (Propulsid) stimulates GI motility by enhancing the physiologic release of acetylcholine from postganglionic nerve endings of the myenteric plexus in GI smooth muscle. Cisapride currently is approved for the treatment of gastroesophageal reflux symptoms but has been examined for use in the treatment of diabetic gastroparesis. Oral cisapride (20 mg) increases both solid and liquid emptying in patients with diabetic gastroparesis.[229] However, results of long-term clinical trials using cisapride in the treatment of diabetic gastroparesis have produced equivocal results.

Interpretation of these results is hampered by flaws in the studies which include a lack of a controlled design and the inclusion of patients with gastroparesis of various etiologies. Long-term administration of cisapride, 20 mg three times daily for 3 to 13 months, enhanced solid emptying and reduced the frequency and severity of symptoms in six gastroparetic patients (1 diabetic origin).[230] Twenty-one patients with gastroparesis (9 diabetic and 12 idiopathic origin) received cisapride 10 mg three times daily in an open trial.[231] After 12 months of therapy, gastric emptying of both solids and liquids was enhanced; however, improved symptoms were demonstrated only in those patients with diabetes. These results were confirmed by a case study where correction of both gastric emptying and symptoms were attained for more than one year.[232] Currently, only four placebo-controlled, double-blind trials have been conducted exclusively in patients with diabetic gastroparesis. Cisapride, 10 mg three times daily, was significantly more effective than placebo in shortening gastric emptying time of a radiolabelled solid meal in 18 insulin-dependent patients.[233] Cisapride 40 mg daily versus placebo significantly increased the rate of gastric emptying of solid and liquid meals in insulin-dependent diabetics with gastroparesis.[229] Another long-term study, however, failed to demonstrate a statistically significant difference in relief of symptoms between cisapride and placebo.[234]

A study comparing cisapride and metoclopramide versus placebo demonstrated no significant effect of any treatment on gastric emptying or whole-gut transit over six months, although a trend towards reduced nausea and vomiting was noted with metoclopramide and reduced epigastric fullness with cisapride.[235] This supports previous suggestions that symptomatic benefits of metoclopramide may be due to its central effect. Concern has been expressed that metoclopramide may become less effective with time[236,237] while objective improvement may persist for at least one year on chronic treatment with cisapride.[231]

Prolonged placebo-controlled, crossover trials are warranted to confirm the long-term efficacy of cisapride in the treatment of diabetic gastroparesis. Cisapride may, however, provide an alternative when limited efficacy or side effects preclude the use of metoclopramide.

Erythromycin

Intravenous erythromycin normalized and oral erythromycin improved gastric emptying times in ten diabetic subjects with gastroparesis. A single dose of erythromycin lactobionate 200 mg was infused immediately following a standard meal, and erythromycin ethylsuccinate 250 mg was given three times daily 30 minutes before meals for four weeks. None of the patients experienced side effects, but symptomatic relief was noted by many. Three experienced fewer hypoglycemic attacks that had been caused by the mismatch between insulin action and food absorption, and two who had been restricted to tube feedings were able to resume oral intake. Erythromycin's gastrokinetic action probably is related to its ability to mimic the effects of motilin on gastric motility. It binds to motilin receptors on GI smooth muscle membranes and acts as an agonist.[238] The effects of erythromycin (250 mg TID) and metoclopramide (10 mg TID) were compared on gastric emptying and symptoms of gastroparesis in a single-blind, crossover study of 13 diabetic patients with delayed gastric emptying.[239] While both agents significantly improved gastric emptying half-life and meal retention percentages at 60 to 90 minutes following treatments, no significant differences were found between the effects of erythromycin and metoclopramide. However, the symptom score following three weeks of erythromycin therapy was significantly less than the postmetoclopramide therapy score (p <0.05). The authors concluded erythromycin appears to be an alternative to metoclopramide in the treatment of diabetic gastroparesis and may provide greater symptomatic relief. If longer-term, placebo-controlled studies show equally promising results, erythromycin and related macrolides may offer a therapeutic option for patients with this condition.

65. Metoclopramide Side Effects. H.D.'s symptoms of gastroparesis were reduced by metoclopramide. However, 3 weeks later he complains of involuntary spasms of his neck and facial muscles. Could this be due to metoclopramide? What are the side effects and precautions for use of this drug?

H.D. is complaining of a dystonic reaction secondary to metoclopramide. Like the antipsychotic drugs, metoclopramide inhibits dopamine activity in the central nervous system. Reversible extrapyramidal side effects such as akinesias, akathisias, and dystonic reactions occur in at least 1% of patients.[225–227] Potentially irreversible tardive dyskinesia may occur rarely after chronic metoclopramide therapy.[240] If long-term therapy is considered, the potential for tardive dyskinesia warrants drug-free periods to determine if therapy is still necessary. H.D.'s dystonic reaction can be controlled with an injectable or oral anticholinergic drug such as diphenhydramine or benztropine.

Other side effects of metoclopramide usually are mild and reversible.[225] Drowsiness and lassitude are not uncommon, and GI disturbances may occur due to the drug's effect on gut motility. The latter usually are not reported as an adverse effect in patients with gastroparesis, however. Galactorrhea and menstrual disorders are caused by prolactin release, which is a result of dopamine receptor blockade in the CNS.[225] Metoclopramide should be used cautiously in patients with Parkinson's disease or patients taking psychotropic agents or other drugs with dopamine antagonist activity.

Hypertension

66. L.S. is a 46-year-old, obese male with an 8-year history of NIDDM. His current problems include a BP of 155/103 mm Hg (documented on 3 occasions), mild background retinopathy, and sexual impotence, which he now admits has troubled him for the last few years. Physical examination reveals decreased pedal pulses bilaterally and an amputated toe on the right foot. The fasting blood glucose is 120 mg/dL, and fasting cholesterol and triglyceride levels are 240 mg/dL and 160 mg/dL, respectively. L.S. has normal electrolyte values and proteinuria (50 mg/dL urine albumin by Micral). His only medication is glipizide 10 mg/day. Describe the pathogenesis of hypertension in patients like L.S. Why is it important to treat L.S.'s hypertension? What must be considered in selecting an antihypertensive agent for L.S.? [SI units: FPG 6.7 mmol/L; fasting cholesterol 6.21 mmol/L; triglyceride 1.81 mmol/L]

Hypertension is the main determinant of life expectancy and complications in diabetic patients[241] and determines the evolution of diabetic nephropathy and retinopathy, in particular.[242] It occurs twice as frequently in patients with diabetes mellitus versus the nondiabetic population and approximately 50% of those with diabetes ultimately become hypertensive. Patients with Type I diabetes usually are normotensive in the absence of nephropathy, but blood pressures rise one to two years following the onset of incipient nephropathy as indicated by microalbuminuria (see discussion of nephropathy: Question 71). Thus, hypertension in the Type I diabetic patient usually is of renal parenchymal origin.

The relationship between hypertension and Type II diabetes is more complex and is not as closely correlated to the presence of nephropathy. Hypertension may be present for years or decades in these patients before overt diabetes mellitus is demonstrable.

Hyperinsulinemia may contribute to the pathogenesis of hypertension by decreasing renal excretion of sodium, stimulating activity

of and tissue response to the sympathetic nervous system, and increasing peripheral vascular resistance through vascular hypertrophy.[3] The latter effect is thought to be related to insulin's growth-promoting action. As noted previously, hyperinsulinemia may be associated with atherogenesis and abnormal lipid profiles which include hypertriglyceridemia, increased very low density lipoprotein (VLDL) cholesterol, and decreased HDL cholesterol.[243–245]

Aggressive therapy of hypertension is essential in patients like L.S. because: 1) cardiovascular events are the major cause of death in these individuals and hypertension constitutes a separate risk factor for these events and 2) hypertension increases the risk of development and rate of progression of long-term diabetic complications including nephropathy and retinopathy, both of which are evident in L.S.

The new information linking insulin resistance and hyperinsulinemia to hypertension has implications for the nonpharmacologic therapy of patients like L.S. Weight reduction and exercise decrease insulin resistance (and therefore hyperinsulinemia) and will be effective in lowering the blood pressure. Dietary sodium restriction addresses the increased total body sodium found in these patients secondary to increased sodium retention.

If more conservative measures are unsuccessful and drugs must be instituted, one must keep in mind that many of the drugs traditionally used as first-line antihypertensive therapy actually can worsen the underlying metabolic abnormalities present in patients like L.S.: insulin resistance, hyperinsulinemia, abnormal lipid profiles, and hyperglycemia. Furthermore, diabetic patients will be particularly sensitive to some of the common side effects of these agents which can mimic or exaggerate symptoms of many diabetic complications. These include, for example, compromised peripheral or renal blood flow, orthostatic hypotension, and impotence. Finally, patients who have lost their glucagon response to hypoglycemia rely upon the sympathetic system for recovery. Drugs which block this system mask the symptoms of and prolong recovery from hypoglycemic attacks. Thus, one should select an agent for L.S. which will have minimal adverse effects on his metabolic profile and existing diabetic complications.

67. Which antihypertensive agents are likely to adversely affect L.S.'s metabolic profile or his diabetic complications?

Adverse effects of antihypertensive agents which are of particular importance to patients with diabetes are summarized in Table 48.30. (Also see Chapter 10: Essential Hypertension and the index for more extensive discussions of these agents throughout this text.) This section addresses those drugs for which adverse consequences in patients with diabetes are well documented.

Diuretics

Thiazides and other diuretics which cause hypokalemia can worsen hyperglycemia and increase the risk of hyperosmolar, nonketotic coma, although the magnitude of diuretic-induced hyperglycemia generally is small and does not present an apparent therapeutic problem in most patients. Nevertheless, the underlying mechanism of this effect, peripheral insulin resistance, is of concern in light of the new-found association between this defect and hypertension. This, together with the atherogenic lipid profiles associated with diuretics, has caused clinicians to call the use of these agents into question in that their net effect may be to increase the risk of cardiovascular morbidity and mortality.[243,247,248] (Also see Chapter 10: Essential Hypertension and Chapter 9: Dyslipidemias.) Therefore, unless the patient has edema or other specific indications for diuretics, their use is not recommended. A suitable alternative would be the diuretic, indapamide which, in a usual antihypertensive dose of 2.5 mg daily, has neutral effects on glucose tolerance and lipoprotein metabolism. Low doses (≤25 mg of hydro-

Table 48.30			Antihypertensive Agents: Important Adverse Effects in Patients with Diabetes[a]			
Drug	Blood Glucose	Lipid Profile	Impotence	Insulin Sensitivity	Proteinuria	Comments
Preferred Antihypertensive Agents[b]						
ACE inhibitors	↑	Neutral	Rare	↑	↓	May cause hyperkalemia in patients with impaired renal function
Calcium Channel Blockers	None	Neutral	Rare	No effect	Variable	Nifedipine potentially may worsen proteinuria
α-Adrenergic Blockers	None or ↑	↓ LDL-Chol ↑ HDL-Chol ↓ TG	Rare	↑	Unknown	First-dose hypotension
Second-Line Antihypertensive Agents[c]						
Thiazide Diuretics	↑	↑ Chol ↑ TG	+	↓	↓	Hypokalemia can ↓ insulin secretion, cause tissue resistance, and promote arrhythmias. Diabetogenic effects most prevalent in NIDDM. To minimize metabolic effects, do not exceed 25 mg/day HCTZ or use indapamide 2.5 mg/dL
β-Adrenergic Blockers	↓↑	↑ TG ↓ HDL	+	↓	↓	Can prolong and mask hypoglycemic symptoms (most important in patients on insulin and with long-term IDDM). Response to counterregulatory hormones may be exaggerated due to unopposed α effects (e.g., arrhythmias, hypertension). Cardioselective agents may be preferable. Hyperosmolar nonketotic coma may occur in patients with endogenous insulin. Unopposed α effects may ↓ peripheral circulation
Central Adrenergic Inhibitors	None	None	+ +	No effect	No effect	Sedation, depression, dry mouth, sodium retention, orthostasis
Peripheral Adrenergic Inhibitors	None	None	+ + +	No effect	No effect	Orthostasis; sodium retention usually requires addition of thiazides
Vasodilators	None	None	Rare	No effect	No effect	Tachycardia and sodium retention require addition of thiazide and beta blocker

[a] ACE inhibitors = Angiotensin-converting enzyme inhibitors; Chol = Cholesterol; HDL-Chol = High density lipoprotein cholesterol; HCTZ = Hydrochlorothiazide; IDDM = Insulin-dependent diabetes mellitus; LDL-Chol = Low density lipoprotein cholesterol; NIDDM = Noninsulin-dependent diabetes mellitus; TG = Triglycerides.

[b] These agents are preferred because they have minimal adverse metabolite effects. Agents are listed in general order of use; individualize selection to patient needs.

[c] These agents are not contraindicated, but are not preferred because of adverse effects on glucose and lipid metabolism or sexual function.

chlorothiazide equivalent), when indicated, are recommended, since higher doses are most likely to cause metabolic disturbances without enhancing the antihypertensive efficacy of these agents.[243–248]

Beta-Adrenergic Blockers

There are several reasons to avoid beta-adrenergic blockers in patients like L.S. with diabetes. First, all of these agents can *impair glucose tolerance, worsening diabetic control.* This includes cardioselective agents and those with intrinsic sympathomimetic activity, although they appear to have the least pronounced effects. Beta blockers decrease insulin secretion and increase insulin resistance, and these effects are additive with those of thiazides.[247,249] Beta blockers without intrinsic sympathomimetic activity (ISA) lower serum HDL cholesterol by about 7%.[249]

Beta-adrenergic blockers may alter the severity, rate of recovery, and warning signs of hypoglycemic episodes by opposing the hyperglycemic effect of epinephrine, which can be the most important counterregulatory hormone in Type I patients who have lost their glucagon response. Many warning symptoms of hypoglycemia are caused by epinephrine. Thus, hypoglycemic tachycardia or palpitations are suppressed in a significant proportion of patients. Hunger, irritability, confusion, and tremor are variably affected; however, sweating is increased and may remain as the only warning signal.

Again, cardioselective agents may not mask symptoms to the same degree. Nevertheless, any diabetic patients for whom these agents are prescribed should be warned that they may experience a change in their hypoglycemic symptoms.

Beta-adrenergic blockers may alter the hemodynamic response to hypoglycemia, resulting in exaggerated hypertension. Epinephrine released in response to hypoglycemia normally raises the systolic blood pressure. Beta blockade by both nonselective and cardio-selective agents can result in unopposed alpha-mediated vasoconstriction and serious hypertensive episodes.[251]

Beta-adrenergic blockers may impair peripheral circulation. Several cases of gangrene in the extremities of patients receiving propranolol have been reported and those, like patient L.S., with impaired peripheral circulation are predisposed. The effect is related to blockade of beta receptor-mediated vasodilation and unopposed alpha vasoconstrictor effects in situations where circulation of sympathomimetic amines is high.

Central and Peripheral Sympatholytic Agents

Although there have been rare reports of hyperglycemia associated with these agents (particularly clonidine which may inhibit insulin secretion by stimulating α₂-adrenergic receptors in the pancreas), sympatholytic drugs have little adverse effect on the metabolic profile of patients with diabetes.[252–254] However, their use is not favored because the orthostatic hypotension and impotence they cause can be particularly onerous in patients with existing neuropathies. This is certainly true in L.S.'s case. These agents also cause sodium retention, often requiring the addition of diuretics for continued effectiveness.

Vasodilators

These agents generally are not used because tachycardia and sodium retention require combined use with thiazides and beta-adrenergic blockers.

68. Which antihypertensive agents can be recommended to treat L.S.'s hypertension if more conservative measures fail?

The three groups of antihypertensive agents which are favored currently by many clinicians for use in patients with diabetes include the angiotensin-converting enzyme (ACE) inhibitors, the calcium channel antagonists, and the alpha-adrenergic antagonists.

ACE Inhibitors

Captopril and enalapril have no adverse effects on glucose tolerance or lipid profiles, and captopril actually may enhance insulin-mediated glucose utilization.[248] These agents also have no effect on sexual function and may paradoxically improve proteinuria associated with diabetic nephropathy.[253,255] (See Nephropathy: Question 69.) Both of these latter effects are of particular importance in L.S. who already complains of impotence and has protein in his urine. (See Chapter 10: Essential Hypertension for discussion of therapeutic use of these agents.)

Calcium Channel Antagonists

While certain calcium antagonists may elicit subtle effects on glucose control, fasting and postprandial blood glucose values have mostly been stable. Nifedipine was reported to exert a mild hyperglycemic effect in hypertensive diabetics.[256] Thus, verapamil or diltiazem may be preferable agents. Nifedipine also may have disadvantages with regard to proteinuria due to conflicting reports regarding a possible increase in proteinuria.[257] This may be explained in part by the lack of dihydropyridine calcium channels in the efferent arterioles.[258] Like the ACE inhibitors, these agents have no adverse effect on serum lipids and cause no impotence. This, together with their relatively mild adverse effect profiles, makes them suitable for use in patients with diabetes.[246]

Alpha-Adrenergic Antagonists

Prazosin, like the ACE inhibitors, has no adverse effects on the glucose profiles of patients with diabetes and actually may enhance the effect of insulin on peripheral tissues.[246,250] The alpha-adrenergic antagonists have demonstrated a modest lipid-lowering effect, reducing LDL-cholesterol concentrations by approximately 8%. Adverse effects associated with these agents also are relatively mild, with the exception of first-dose orthostasis which can be minimized by instructing the patient to take the first dose at bedtime.

Lisinopril 10 mg daily, was chosen for initial treatment of L.S. because of its relative lack of adverse effects and potential beneficial effects on proteinuria. If this drug is ineffective or cannot be tolerated at maximum doses, these authors would consider switching to doxazosin or a calcium channel blocker.

Diabetic Nephropathy

Diabetic nephropathy is the most common cause of newly diagnosed end-stage renal disease (ESRD) in the U.S. today.[259] It is second only to hypertensive nephropathy as the primary diagnosis for patients receiving renal replacement therapy under Medicare funding at an estimated cost of three billion dollars annually.[259] Approximately 80% of patients with Type I diabetes mellitus develop nephropathy 10 to 15 years following diagnosis[260] and nephropathy in Type II diabetes is associated with an increase in cardiovascular mortality.[261] Our understanding and management of diabetic nephropathy have changed, and new information indicates that diabetic nephropathy may be prevented or delayed.

Thickening of the glomerular capillary basement membranes is the hallmark of diabetic nephropathy. Diffuse deposition of basement membrane-like material expands the mesangium. This process narrows the capillary lumina, impedes blood flow, and reduces the filtering surface in the glomerulus. Poor glucose control increases intraglomerular pressure which results in glomerular hyperfiltration. Hyperfiltration then is followed by microalbuminuria with minimal glomerulosclerosis, which still is potentially reversible. If appropriate therapy is not initiated, overt proteinuria occurs and the patient usually progresses to nephrotic syndrome.

Factors that correlate with progression of diabetic renal disease include the presence of hypertension and microalbuminuria. Lipid abnormalities also have been identified as a possible mediator in the progression of initial glomerular injury to glomerulosclerosis.[275] Currently, it is recommended that diabetic patients be screened for microalbuminuria annually after five years of diabetes or onset of puberty.[262]

69. A.C., a 28-year-old female with a 13-year history of IDDM, has been reasonably well controlled with 2 insulin injections per day. A random urine sample performed at this clinic visit is positive for microalbuminuria using Micral (Boehringer Mannheim) and her BP is elevated to 142/95 mm Hg. How is microalbuminuria detected? How should A.C.'s results be interpreted?

Microalbuminuria is present when urinary albumin excretion (UAE) exceeds 20 to 200 μg/min or 30 to 300 mg/24 hours.[263] Albumin excretion levels above 30 mg/day or 0.2 mg albumin/1.0 mg creatinine are considered abnormal. A patient is considered at risk for the development of nephropathy when microalbuminuria is found in two of three urine samples collected consecutively within six months. A.C. should be re-evaluated for microalbuminuria. An assessment of albumin excretion with a timed urine collection or a collection that is related to creatinine excretion should be performed in A.C.

70. How do the current tests available for the detection of microalbuminuria compare? How are the tests performed?

Traditional urine dipsticks generally register "positive" for albumin once the UAE is ten times the normal rate. Newly developed immunochemical methods such as Micral allow the detection of much lower concentrations of urinary albumin.[262] Albumin binds to antibody contained in a color-substrate pad, and the intensity of the color produced is proportional to the albumin concentration in the urine. The color formed after five minutes is compared to a reference chart on the vial, reflecting albumin concentrations ranging from 20 to 100 mg/dL. Micral has been shown to be a sensitive and specific screening tool but is semi-quantitative and critically time-dependent.[264] Contact with the urine for less than the recommended five seconds or reading the result before five minutes results in an underestimation of the albumin concentration. Only fresh urine samples should be assayed, since falsely low results occur when samples that have been frozen and thawed are tested. Microbumintest (Ames) is equally sensitive but less specific because other urine proteins contribute to the colorimetric reaction.[265] Albusure (Cambridge Life Sciences) is a latex bead agglutination test which also compares favorably with Micral;[264] however, both of these latter tests require drop-wise addition of urine and reagents and thus, are not as simple to perform as Micral.

71. How should A.C.'s elevated blood pressure and microalbuminuria be managed?

Hypertension accelerates the decline in renal function which can progress to end-stage renal failure. Thiazides and beta blockers have been used for blood pressure control and thus, have significantly attenuated the progression of diabetic renal disease; however, these agents adversely affect blood glucose and lipid values. Studies suggest that angiotensin-converting enzyme (ACE) inhibitors and certain calcium antagonists may provide beneficial effects on nephropathy beyond conventional blood pressure control.[266]

ACE inhibitors block the formation of angiotensin II, resulting in dilation of both afferent and efferent arterioles in the glomerulus. In addition, ACE inhibitors increase levels of vasodilatory prostaglandins PGI2 and PGE2, which reduces glomerular permeability. This reduction in permeability correlates with a reduction in urinary albumin excretion. Use of captopril in insulin-dependent patients with a mean albumin excretion rate of 90 μg/minute decreased albuminuria significantly while lowering blood pressure slightly.[267]

ACE inhibitors also exert this beneficial effect on urine albumin in normotensive diabetics. Treatment with enalapril prevented the development of overt nephropathy in normotensive diabetic patients with microalbuminuria in a placebo-controlled trial.[268] The efficacy of captopril in postponing nephropathy was reported in a four-year trial of 44 normotensive Type I diabetic patients with persistent microalbuminuria. Approximately 33% of the untreated group developed diabetic nephropathy while none of the patients in the treatment group developed nephropathy. Systemic blood pressure, glomerular filtration rate and HbA$_{1c}$ remained virtually unchanged in both groups.[268] Fifty-two NIDDM patients with persistent microalbuminuria randomized to receive enalapril 5 mg daily versus placebo for four years were evaluated. Twenty-six of the patients had hypertension well controlled on nifedipine (30 mg/day) and also were randomized to enalapril or placebo therapy. A significant reduction in urinary albumin excretion (UAE) was observed in all patients who received enalapril, whereas no significant change occurred in either placebo group.[269] A prospective, double-blind, randomized, multicenter clinical trial was performed to determine whether captopril was effective in slowing the progression of diabetic nephropathy independent of its effect on blood pressure.[270] Patients aged 18 to 49 years with Type I diabetes were eligible for inclusion in the study if they had a urinary protein excretion of 500 mg/24 hours or more and a serum creatinine of 2.5 mg/dL or less. A total of 409 patients were randomized to receive captopril 25 mg three times daily or placebo. Hypertension was treated in both groups with various agents, including thiazides and beta blockers. Patients treated with captopril had a 50% reduction in the risk of death and kidney failure and a 48% reduction in the risk of doubling serum creatinine. Patients with advanced kidney disease appeared to benefit the most from treatment with captopril. Those with an initial serum creatinine of 2.0 and 1.5 mg/dL had a 78% and 55% reduced risk of doubling serum creatinine, respectively, compared to those patients with a serum creatinine level of 1.0 mg/dL who had a 17% risk. The magnitude of blood pressure reduction in the two treatment groups was comparable; therefore, the beneficial effect of captopril was not explained by the small differences in the level of blood pressure control between the two groups. A meta-regression analysis of the literature also supports the conclusion that ACE inhibitors reduce proteinuria and preserve GFR independently of changes in systemic blood pressure in the patient with diabetes.[272]

Based upon evidence to date, the FDA granted approval for captopril to be used in the treatment of nephropathy (as evidenced by microalbuminuria) in patients with Type I diabetes.

Some controversy exists with regard to the intrarenal effects of the various calcium antagonists. These agents induce substantial afferent arteriolar vasodilation; however, their effects on efferent arteriolar resistance remains controversial. Verapamil and diltiazem exert hemodynamic and antiproteinuric effects comparable to the ACE inhibitors.[266] The dihydropyridine class of calcium antagonists, of which nifedipine has been the most widely studied, has not been associated with a consistent decrease in urinary albumin excretion.[266] This may be explained in part by the lack of dihydropyridine calcium channels in the efferent arterioles.[270]

In summary, A.C. should be counseled regarding nonpharmacologic measures for blood pressure control and an ACE inhibitor should be considered if her blood pressure and microalbuminuria do not return to normal.

72. What further steps can be taken to delay or possibly prevent the development of diabetic nephropathy in A.C.?

Detection of microalbuminuria should prompt re-evaluation of M.B.'s glycemic control. HbA$_{1c}$ values above 9.5% correlate with glomerular hyperfiltration and subsequent nephropathy. Stricter glycemic control using more intensified treatment with twice-daily insulin or insulin pumps ameliorates early renal hyperfiltration[271] and should be considered in A.C. Dietary protein restriction (0.4 to 0.7 gm/kg/day) slowed renal function decline in one human study. The exact role of protein restriction in the prevention of diabetic nephropathy, however, remains to be determined.

Coronary Heart Disease

Cardiovascular disease is three times more common in the diabetic population versus the nondiabetic population and is the main cause of death in patients with Type II diabetes mellitus.[273] In 1988, more than half of all diabetes-related deaths were caused by cardiovascular disease. Of those deaths, 61% were attributable to ischemic heart disease (IHD) and 14% to stroke.[274]

Tissue resistance to insulin-mediated glucose homeostasis may be an important factor in predisposing susceptible persons to atherosclerosis and its clinical manifestations, including diabetes.[277] Theoretically, the resulting hyperglycemia (even if transient) leads to glycosylation of lipoproteins, hemoglobin, and proteins of the arterial wall. These advanced glycosylated end products (AGEs) may damage endothelial or smooth muscle cells of the arterial wall, initiating the atherosclerotic process.[276]

The most common lipid abnormality in Type II diabetes is hypertriglyceridemia with low levels of HDL cholesterol.[278] Poor control of Type I diabetes also is associated with elevated LDL cholesterol levels as well as hypertriglyceridemia.[279] All these lipid abnormalities contribute to the risk for cardiovascular disease.

Adults with diabetes should be screened annually for serum lipoprotein levels, including triglycerides, total cholesterol, LDL and HDL.[280] A total cholesterol level of less than 200 mg/dL is acceptable in patients with diabetes who have no evidence of macrovascular disease or other cardiovascular risk factors. Triglyceride levels of less than 200 mg/dL and LDL cholesterol levels of less than 130 mg/dL are desirable. Patients who already have evidence of macrovascular disease are at greatest risk for developing heart disease. In these individuals, triglyceride levels should be reduced to 150 mg/dL and LDL cholesterol levels maintained at 100 mg/dL or less (see Table 48.31).

73. A.L., a 58-year-old, mildly obese female recently was diagnosed with Type II diabetes. She was treated initially with diet and eventually controlled with glyburide. Recent laboratory values include an FPG of 130 mg/dL, HbA$_{1c}$ of 7.0% (Normal: 4%–6%), a triglyceride level of 650 mg/dL with a total cholesterol of 160 mg/dL, and HDL of 20 mg/dL (Normal: 27–67 mg/dL). How should A.L. be treated? [SI units: FPG 7.2 mmol/L; HbA$_{1c}$ 0.07; triglycerides 7.34 mmol/L; total cholesterol 4.14 mmol/L; HDL 0.52 mmol/L (Normal: 0.7–1.7)]

Diet and exercise are cornerstones in the management of dyslipidemia in patients with diabetes. Weight loss is associated with improvements in insulin sensitivity and glucose control, as well as a reduction in triglycerides, total cholesterol and LDL cholesterol. Physical activity enhances weight loss and increases HDL cholesterol levels. Thus, A.L.'s diet and exercise habits should be reassessed and instruction in both reinforced as appropriate. Blood glucose control should be optimized with diet, exercise, and oral agents or insulin when indicated. But as illustrated by A.L., the attainment of diabetes control in patients with Type II diabetes does not necessarily correct lipid abnormalities. Insulin resistance may be the underlying cause of elevated lipids in these patients and efforts should be devoted to reversing insulin resistance as well. Since A.L.'s FPG and HbA$_{1c}$ values indicate that she has achieved diabetes control, a lipid-lowering agent is warranted if she does not respond to nonpharmacologic treatment.

Bile Acid Sequestrants

Bile acid sequestrants primarily lower total and LDL cholesterol levels with little effect on HDL cholesterol. These agents can elevate triglyceride levels and may be problematic as monotherapy for patients like A.L. with mild to moderate hypertriglyceridemia. Low doses of bile acid sequestrants may be useful as adjunctive therapy when combined with a fibric acid derivative.

Fibric Acid Derivatives

Gemfibrozil and clofibrate currently are the only fibric acid derivatives available in the U.S. These drugs activate lipoprotein lipase causing a reduction in triglycerides and increased HDL cholesterol. They exert a variable but generally modest LDL cholesterol-lowering effect. Clofibrate is used infrequently due to an increased incidence of gall bladder disease associated with its use, but gemfibrozil may be useful in patients like A.L. with predominant hypertriglyceridemia..

HMG-CoA Reductase Inhibitors

Simvastatin, pravastatin, lovastatin, and fluvastatin inhibit HMG-CoA reductase, a key regulatory enzyme for cholesterol biosynthesis. As a result, hepatic cholesterol synthesis declines and a twofold increase in surface LDL particle receptors is seen; this increases LDL cholesterol clearance. However, these agents have only marginal effects on triglycerides and HDL cholesterol levels, a drawback in A.L.'s case.

Niacin

Niacin effectively lowers LDL cholesterol. However, it increases both fasting and postprandial hyperglycemia. Garg et al. observed a 21% increase in HbA$_{1c}$ concentrations, a 16% increase in mean plasma glucose concentrations, and marked glycosuria during niacin therapy in 13 patients with Type II diabetes treated with niacin de-

Table 48.31	Suggested Lipid Levels for Adult Diabetics[a,b]			
	Chol (mg/dL)	HDL-Chol (mg/dL)	LDL-Chol (mg/dL)	TG (mg/dL)
Acceptable	<200	—	<130	<200
Borderline	200–239	—	130–159	200–399
High-Risk for CHD	≥240	≤35	≥160	≥400

[a] CHD = Coronary heart disease; Chol = Cholesterol; HDL-Chol = High density lipoprotein cholesterol; LDL-Chol = Low density lipoprotein cholesterol; TG = Triglycerides.

[b] Modified from reference 280. Patients with diabetes should be screened annually for lipoprotein levels. Patients with evidence of macrovascular disease are at greatest risk for developing heart disease. LDL cholesterols of 100 mg/dL and triglyceride levels of 150 mg/dL should be attained in these patients.

spite improvement in lipoprotein concentrations.[281] In another study, 6% of patients without diabetes developed clinical diabetes requiring treatment while receiving niacin during a 2.5 year period.[282] Although precise mechanisms by which this occurs are unknown, it may be due to accentuation of insulin resistance.[283,284] Therefore, its use as first-line therapy for dyslipidemia in diabetics is not recommended.

Since hypertriglyceridemia is the main abnormality in A.L.'s lipid profile, gemfibrozil should be given in a dose of 600 mg twice daily to attain a triglyceride level of less than 200 mg/dL. (See Chapter 9: Dyslipidemias for a more detailed discussion of these agents.)

Drug-Induced Hyperglycemia

Important diabetogenic drugs are discussed in Questions 74 and 75 and tabulated in Table 48.32. Other drugs that have been reported to produce hyperglycemia but are clinically less significant are discussed briefly in Question 76.

Sympathomimetics

74. R.C., a 41-year-old, insulin-dependent diabetic, is well controlled on split doses of regular and NPH insulin and has been taking pseudoephedrine 30 mg QID for 7 days and Robitussin DM 10 mL QID (which contains 2.8 gm/mL sugar and 1.4% alcohol) for a cold. Recently, glucose concentrations have been higher than usual. Can pseudoephedrine or the cough preparation be the cause of his poor control? Discuss the use of adrenergic agents, sympathomimetics, and cough preparations in diabetic patients.

Over-the-counter (OTC) drug products such as decongestants and diet aids which contain sympathomimetics carry warning labels that caution against their use in diabetic patients. Standard sugar- and ethanol-containing cough preparations also carry such warning labels. However, clinically significant glucose intolerance probably is very infrequent. It is well established that parenterally administered epinephrine increases blood glucose concentrations secondary to increased glycogenolysis and gluconeogenesis. Other sympathomimetics generally do not have as potent an effect on blood glucose as epinephrine and their use usually does not pose a practical problem in diabetic patients. Nevertheless, therapeutic to high oral doses of phenylephrine caused hyperglycemia and acetonuria in three nondiabetic children.[285-587] Furthermore, the effects of sympathomimetics on blood pressure must be considered in many patients with diabetes.

High doses of beta-adrenergic agonists, such as terbutaline (Brethine, Bricanyl) and ritodrine (Yutopar), which are used to inhibit preterm labor, can cause maternal hyperglycemia and even ketoacidosis in pregnant patients.[288] Intravenous infusions of salbutamol (albuterol) also have caused hyperglycemia and ketoacidosis in diabetic and nondiabetic patients.[289,290] The effects of two cough syrup formulations (1 with sugar and alcohol and 1 without) were examined on the metabolic control of 20 NIDDM patients and found no difference in pretherapy and posttherapy glucose values with either formula.[291]

Pseudoephedrine or the cough preparation may be aggravating R.C.'s diabetic control, although at these low to normal therapeutic doses it is quite unlikely. The stress related to R.C.'s underlying cold is more likely to be impairing his glucose tolerance than these low doses of sympathomimetic agents or the sugar contained in the cough syrup.

Corticosteroids

75. A.L., a 37-year-old, obese female with systemic lupus erythematosus (SLE), has been taking 60 mg/day of prednisone

Table 48.32		Important Diabetogenic Drugs[a,b]	
Drug	Significance	Significance	See Question
Beta-Adrenergic Blockers	++	↓ insulin secretion, ↓ tissue sensitivity to insulin	67
Calcium Antagonists	+	↓ insulin secretion	68
Diazoxide	+++	↓ insulin secretion, ↓ glucose utilization	68
Diuretics	+++	↓ tissue sensitivity to insulin	67
Glucocorticoids	+++	↑ gluconeogenesis, ↓ tissue sensitivity to insulin	75
L-Asparaginase	++	↓ insulin synthesis	
Nicotinic Acid (Niacin)	++	↓ tissue sensitivity to insulin	
Oral Contraceptives	++	↓ tissue sensitivity to insulin	
Pentamidine	+++	Toxic to pancreatic beta-cells. Hypoglycemia occurs initially	80
Phenytoin	++	↓ insulin secretion	
Rifampin	+	↓ tissue sensitivity to insulin	
Sympathomimetics	++	↑ glycogenolysis, ↑ gluconeogenesis	74

[a] See Question 76 for other drugs reported to cause drug-induced hyperglycemia.

[b] + Possibly important; limited or conflicting reports or studies. ++ Clinically significant. +++ Clinically significant effect of substantial prevalence and/or magnitude.

for 6 months. During this period her weight has increased by 30 lb and she has developed glycosuria. She was referred to the diabetes clinic where her FPG was found to be 190 mg/dL. There was 1% glucose in her urine and no ketones. Physical examination shows a 5'2", 150 lb, depressed female with truncal obesity and an acneiform rash. Her mother and one sister have diabetes mellitus. How do corticosteroids contribute to diabetes mellitus? How should A.L. be treated?

The term ''steroid diabetes'' was first used to describe the hyperglycemia and glycosuria seen in patients with Cushing's syndrome. Now it is associated more commonly with exogenously administered glucocorticoids and has been a side effect of parenteral, oral, and even topical therapy.[292] Corticosteroids are one of the most common drug groups that unmask latent diabetes or aggravate pre-existing disease, and they may produce hyperglycemia and overt diabetes in individuals who are not otherwise predisposed.

Corticosteroids increase hepatic gluconeogenesis and decrease tissue responsiveness to insulin. Although steroid-induced diabetes generally is mild and rarely associated with ketonemia, a wide spectrum of severity may be encountered from asymptomatic, abnormal glucose tolerance tests to difficult-to-control, insulin-dependent disease. The onset of glucose tolerance can occur within hours to days, or after months to years of chronic therapy. The effect generally is considered to be dose-dependent and usually is reversible upon discontinuation of the drug; reversal may take several months.[293,294]

Patients such as A.L. on chronic corticosteroid therapy require frequent blood glucose monitoring. Mild diabetes in obese individuals, as in A.L.'s case, sometimes can be controlled by diet, but may require exogenous insulin supplementation or sulfonylurea therapy. A known diabetic whose condition is aggravated by glucocorticoids should modify treatment appropriately to restore control. It is important to anticipate the need to modify insulin or sulfonylurea therapy as corticosteroid doses are increased or decreased.

76. What other drugs have been reported to cause hyperglycemia?

There are a number of other drugs that cause hyperglycemia or glucose intolerance in normal or diabetic patients. These drugs include: oral contraceptives,[295,296] phenytoin,[297] L-asparaginase,[298] amiodarone,[299,300] synthetic salmon calcitonin,[300,301] cimetidine,[302]

lithium,[303] morphine,[303] neuroleptics,[304] nicotinic acid,[281] and rifampin,[307] among others. The evidence for these drugs is limited to small studies and case reports. The effects of pentamidine are discussed in Questions 79 and 80, and those of beta blockers are addressed in Question 67.

Drug-Induced Hypoglycemia

The clinical presentation and treatment of hypoglycemia occurring in patients taking insulin has been discussed. (See Question 21.) This section addresses the circumstances and mechanisms by which other drugs can induce hypoglycemia. The symptoms of hypoglycemia are the same, but the condition may be underdiagnosed if it occurs in the context of other clinical situations which also may cause coma (e.g., acute alcohol or salicylate intoxication; head injury). Patients should be treated with IV glucose followed by glucose infusions for as long as three to five days. Since the effect of many of these drugs is long-acting, severe episodes may recur unless the patient is treated over a prolonged period.

Seltzer comprehensively reviewed all reported cases of drug-induced hypoglycemia from 1940 to late 1988.[185] Sulfonylureas accounted for over 70% of cases, particularly in the adult population. Most all cases of hypoglycemia reported in newborns occurred in those whose mothers had been treated with ritodrine or other betamimetics, propranolol, or sulfonylureas. In children up to two years of age, salicylates were the primary cause, and alcohol accounted for most cases in children through age eight. Insulin or sulfonylureas were identified as the primary cause of hypoglycemia in patients age 11 through 30, but interestingly, about one-half of these were suicide attempts in nondiabetic individuals. Alcohol again becomes an important cause of drug-induced hypoglycemia between the ages of 30 and 50. As expected, sulfonylureas and insulin alone or in combination with other hypoglycemic agents become more frequent causes of hypoglycemia after age 40. Several factors predispose individuals to drug-induced hypoglycemia, and it is the unusual case that is not associated with one of these.

Decreased Carbohydrate Intake

Decreased carbohydrate intake is the most frequently reported predisposing factor in cases of drug-induced hypoglycemic coma. Decreased carbohydrate intake ultimately results in depletion of liver glycogen. Because hepatic glycogenolysis is essential to the maintenance of plasma glucose concentrations in the fasting state, its depletion can cause excessive hypoglycemia in a patient taking a hypoglycemic agent. Acute decreases in carbohydrate intake, secondary to nausea and vomiting for example, are most important in individuals who have marginal glycogen stores due to irregular eating habits (e.g., alcoholics, elderly individuals).

Age

The number of cases of drug-induced hypoglycemia per decade appears to be approximately the same between the ages of 11 and 50 and increases markedly thereafter. The elderly most likely are predisposed because their renal function is physiologically diminished (see below) and they have a greater tendency toward irregular eating patterns.

Renal Failure

Renal impairment may predispose individuals to drug-induced hypoglycemia by several mechanisms. First, endogenous and exogenous insulin clearance is impaired because the kidney is responsible for metabolic degradation of approximately 30% to 80% of insulin.[306] Second, many of the drugs that cause hypoglycemia rely upon the kidney for elimination of unchanged drug or active metabolites. Therefore, patients with renal failure may accumulate these active substances. Third, patients who are uremic often become nauseated and anoretic and may voluntarily decrease their carbohydrate intake. The effects of different degrees of renal failure on carbohydrate metabolism are complex and are discussed in Question 27.

Hepatic Dysfunction

The liver is the primary source of plasma glucose during the fasting state: first, through glycogenolysis and second, through gluconeogenesis. Impairment of liver function therefore may alter these counterregulatory effects. The liver also is responsible for the metabolism, and, in some cases, the inactivation of drugs that induce hypoglycemia. If this function is impaired, active drug or metabolite may accumulate, thereby exaggerating the drug's effect on plasma glucose. Drugs that have been well-described to cause hypoglycemia are discussed in Questions 77 through 80 and tabulated in Table 48.33. Other drugs that are poorly documented and are less likely to cause clinical hypoglycemia are discussed briefly in Question 81.

Ethanol

77. C.F., a 22-year-old female newly diagnosed with IDDM, enjoys a glass or 2 of wine with her evening meal. What effect does alcohol have on a diabetic patient, particularly one using insulin? Is alcohol contraindicated in C.F. or any person with diabetes?

Clinicians often are reluctant to permit the use of alcoholic beverages in patients with diabetes. However, barring contraindications that are similar in the nondiabetic and diabetic alike (e.g., alcoholism, hypertriglyceridemia, gastritis, pancreatitis, pregnancy), a diabetic can safely enjoy a moderate alcohol intake as long as certain precautions are taken. For an in-depth discussion, the reader is referred to two comprehensive reviews of alcohol and diabetes, parts of which are summarized below.[309,310]

As noted above, alcohol is one of the most common causes of profound and lethal hypoglycemic coma in children and adults. This is caused primarily by decreased gluconeogenesis, an important source of glucose in the fasting state and in individuals with depleted liver glycogen stores. Hypoglycemia most often occurs in individuals drinking large amounts of ethanol chronically. However, it can follow binge drinking and even moderate alcohol intake in subjects who are fasting or who otherwise have depleted glycogen stores.[185]

The concomitant use of insulin or a sulfonylurea with alcohol can increase the risk of hypoglycemic coma in diabetic patients. Furthermore, there is a danger that hypoglycemia can be mistaken for intoxication in a patient who has been drinking alcohol. The failure to recognize and treat hypoglycemia in this setting has led to death and irreparable brain damage.[185] Separately, alcohol intoxication may impair judgment, a skill critical to the maintenance of glycemic control, particularly in patients taking insulin.

Alcohol has other effects in people with diabetes which may be important to consider. Excessive and chronic alcohol ingestion can impair glucose tolerance and produce hyperglycemia, but this is of limited clinical significance outside the alcoholic population. This level of alcohol intake also can induce pancreatitis which may secondarily cause diabetes mellitus. Chronic alcohol ingestion decreases the half-life of tolbutamide, probably through enzyme induction, and patients taking chlorpropamide may experience a flush reaction. (See Table 48.27.)

With the above in mind, alcohol can be included in C.F.'s diet with the following caveats:

- Never drink on an empty stomach and do not substitute alcohol for food. Drink just before, with, or directly after a meal. Sip slowly and make a drink last a long time. This decreases the risk for hypoglycemia.

- Drink in moderation: no more than 2 oz of ethanol equivalents per day once or twice weekly: 8 oz wine, 24 oz beer, 3 oz distilled liquor. Be aware of your own sensitivity to the intoxicating effects of ethanol and adjust consumption downward, if needed. This is particularly important for insulin-dependent patients.

- Avoid drinks that contain large amounts of sugar, such as liqueurs, sweet wines, and sugar-containing mixes. Instead, consider dry wines, light beers, and distilled spirits. Not only does the simple sugar content add an additional source of glucose and calories to the diet, but ethanol ingested with simple sugar-containing mixers enhances reactive hyperglycemia.

- Remember to count the calories in alcohol [cal = (0.8)(proof)(ounces)]; substitute 1 oz of alcohol for two fat exchanges.

- Be aware that the symptoms of alcohol intoxication and hypoglycemia are similar. If hypoglycemia is mistaken for intoxication by others, treatment can be delayed.

- Be aware of alcohol-sulfonylurea drug interactions, specifically, the alcohol-induced enzyme induction of tolbutamide metabolism and the chlorpropamide-alcohol flush reaction.

Salicylates

78. M.C. is a 52-year-old woman with NIDDM controlled on diet and chlorpropamide 250 mg/day. She has evidence of diabetic nephropathy with a creatinine of 2.2 mg/dL. Her complaints of joint pain, early morning fatigue, and joint stiffness of both hands are diagnosed as rheumatoid arthritis, and she is to start on aspirin 3.9 gm/day. Will aspirin therapy affect M.C.'s diabetic control? Is there an interaction between aspirin and oral sulfonylureas? Discuss the implications of salicylate use in persons with diabetes. [SI unit: creatinine 194.48 μmol/L]

Hypoglycemic Effects

Although hypoglycemia secondary to salicylate intoxication in children generally is well recognized, it is less well appreciated that salicylates can predictably decrease blood glucose concentrations at anti-inflammatory concentrations (25 to 35 mg/dL) and

Table 48.33		Important Drugs That Can Cause Hypoglycemia[a,b]	
Drug	Significance	Mechanism/Comments	See Question
Anabolic Steroids	+	Complex metabolic effects. Only certain steroids studied	
Beta-Adrenergic Blockers	++	↓ glycogenolysis, ↓ warning signs	
Disopyramide	++	Unknown	
Ethanol	+++	↓ gluconeogenesis	77
Insulin	+++	↑ glucose utilization	21,22
Pentamidine	+++	↑ insulin release	79
Quinine	++	Possible ↑ insulin release. High doses needed	
Salicylates	++	↑ insulin secretion among others. High doses needed	78
Sulfonamide Antibiotics	+	Rare reaction with renal failure and/or high doses	
Sulfonylureas	+++	Stimulate insulin release; extrapancreatic effects	53, Table 48.27

[a] See Question 81 for other drugs reported to induce hypoglycemia.
[b] + Possibly important; rare, limited, or conflicting studies. + + Clinically significant. + + + Clinically significant effect of substantial prevalence and/or magnitude.

doses (4 to 6 gm/day in adults).[185] This effect may be due to an increased insulin response to glucose and an increased peripheral utilization of glucose.[310] In six diabetic subjects, 6 gm of aspirin daily decreased the mean fasting plasma glucose concentration from 371 to 128 mg/dL after ten days of therapy.[312] Thus, high doses of salicylates may add to the blood glucose-lowering effects of sulfonylureas intrinsically or, in some cases, enhance the effects of some sulfonylureas through protein displacement. (See Table 48.27.)

Antiplatelet Effects

Some evidence suggests that the progression of diabetic vascular complications, and retinopathy in particular, may be related to the increased platelet aggregation observed in diabetics. On this basis, it has been postulated that aspirin or other prostaglandin inhibitors that inhibit platelet aggregation may halt or slow the progression of vascular complications. However, the only large randomized, double-blind, placebo-controlled trial to date that has studied the effects of antiplatelet agents on vascular endpoints (vascular mortality and amputations) failed to demonstrate a beneficial effect in the drug-treated group.[21] Nevertheless, daily intake of low doses of aspirin for its prophylactic effects on stroke and cardiovascular events is safe and unlikely to have a hypoglycemic effect.

Because M.C. is predisposed to the hypoglycemic effects of salicylates by several mechanisms, she should be initiated on a lower dose. Alternatively, another anti-rheumatic agent could be used, or her sulfonylurea dose could be adjusted downward. Furthermore, in view of her decreased renal function, discontinuing chlorpropamide in favor of a safer sulfonylurea or insulin should be strongly considered (see Question 53).

Pentamidine

79. M.H., a 29-year-old bisexual male with acquired immunodeficiency syndrome (AIDS), was admitted with progressive dyspnea, fevers, and diffuse pulmonary infiltrates. A diagnosis of *Pneumocystis carinii* pneumonia (PCP) was made, and therapy was started with IV trimethoprim-sulfamethoxazole (TMP-SMX). This drug was discontinued after 2 days of therapy due to a severe allergic reaction, and IV pentamidine isethionate was begun at a dose of 4 mg/kg/day. After 9 days of pentamidine therapy, M.H. was found unconscious, flaccid, and unresponsive to deep pain. His blood glucose was 17 mg/dL. Can pentamidine cause severe hypoglycemia? [SI unit: blood glucose 0.9 mmol/L]

It is well recognized that pentamidine, a biguanide derivative, can cause hypoglycemia, and this usually occurs several days to two weeks following initiation of pentamidine treatment.[185,313] It can be sudden, recurrent, and life-threatening.

In one series of 37 patients with AIDS who received pentamidine isethionate for the treatment of PCP, approximately 25% of patients developed symptomatic hypoglycemia; the mean nadir was 38 mg/dL (range: 20 to 55 mg/dL).[312] The onset of hypoglycemia averaged 11 days after initiation of therapy, and in some patients hypoglycemia persisted for several days after pentamidine was discontinued. Most patients respond adequately to hypertonic glucose infusions, although oral diazoxide also has been used successfully.[185]

80. Three weeks after M.H. was discharged, he returned to the hospital with a 7-day history of progressive polyuria, polydipsia, weight loss, and severe fatigue. His FPG concentration was 440 mg/dL. M.H. has no history of diabetes mellitus. What could be the cause of his hyperglycemia? [SI unit: FPG 24.4 mmol/L]

Pentamidine is a selective beta-cell toxin which produces an early cytolytic release of insulin resulting in initial hypoglycemia. This is followed by beta-cell destruction and insulin deficiency which results in drug-induced diabetes mellitus. Diabetes mellitus can follow the hypoglycemic episode within a few days, but its appearance more often is delayed by several weeks or even months. Many patients become insulin-dependent, and the effect probably is irreversible.[185,312] [Also see Chapter 68: Human Immunodeficiency Virus (HIV) Infection.]

Blood glucose concentrations were screened in 128 immunocompromised patients who received pentamidine to treat *Pneumocystis carinii* pneumonia. Of these, 48 or 38.9% developed glucose abnormalities: hypoglycemia (7), hypoglycemia followed by diabetes (18); and diabetes only (23). Relative to their counterparts who did not develop these reactions, these patients received higher doses of pentamidine, had higher creatinine levels, and were more severely anoxic.[323]

81. What other drugs have been reported to cause hypoglycemia?

Quinine/Quinidine

Quinine administered orally or parenterally (≈600 mg Q 8 hr) stimulates insulin secretion and causes symptomatic hypoglycemia in about 10% of patients treated for falciparum malaria,[185,314] although the importance of the effect has been questioned.[314,315] Interestingly, large single doses of quinine (500 mg and 1000 mg of the base) also have stimulated hyperinsulinemia and hypoglycemia in healthy patients and patients with malaria.[316] These investigators theorize that many of the signs and symptoms of classical cinchonism, common to both quinine and quinidine, may be due to hypoglycemia. More studies are needed to substantiate this theory. Hypoglycemia also has been reported infrequently in patients using quinine for muscle cramps at a conventional dose of 300 mg at bedtime;[317] however, a well documented case of quinine-mediated hypoglycemia occurred in a patient who had repeated episodes of symptomatic hypoglycemia while taking quinine 325 mg given four times daily for leg cramps.[317]

Ritodrine and Other Betamimetic Agents

Ritodrine and other betamimetic agents which have been used for tocolysis (fenoterol, terbutaline, isoxsuprine) can induce hypoglycemia in the infants of mothers who have received these agents. This effect is secondary to augmented insulin secretion in the newborn which has been stimulated by the maternal hyperglycemia induced by these agents. (See Question 74.) This can last for several days following delivery. Infants born to mothers who have received these agents within 36 hours of delivery should be monitored carefully for hypoglycemia. Hypoglycemia should be considered in the differential diagnosis whenever CNS symptoms are present or when there are other signs of persistent betamimetic activity such as hypotension and tachycardia.[185] (Also see Chapter 44: Obstetrics.)

Nonspecific Beta Blocking Agents

Nonspecific beta blocking agents such as propranolol have been implicated in cases of prolonged hypoglycemia, usually in patients taking insulin. (See Question 67.) In the nondiabetic population, drug-induced hypoglycemia has been reported in patients on dialysis and in neonates born to mothers taking these agents before delivery.

Many other drugs (e.g., antipsychotics, disopyramide, lidocaine, lithium, sulfonamides, penicillamine, tricyclic antidepressants) occasionally have been associated with hypoglycemia. These are included in Seltzer's review of the subject[185] and in Hansten and Horn's discussion of drugs which interact with antidiabetic agents.[154] In different studies, anabolic steroids have been reported to impair glucose tolerance or induce hyperglycemia or, conversely, to reduce fasting plasma glucose concentrations.

Update

The Role of Metformin in the Treatment of NIDDM

As this publication went to press, metformin was approved to treat Type II diabetes by the FDA. The authors expect that metformin will be most commonly added to sulfonylurea therapy in patients no longer responsive to the latter, as illustrated below. However, it is rational to consider metformin as a first-line agent in the treatment of Type II diabetes because it may reverse or ameliorate the underlying pathogenesis of the disease: insulin resistance. The reader also is referred to the discussion of biguanides on page 48-36.

U1. N.H., a 46-year-old, mildly obese male with NIDDM, has been treated with diet, exercise, and glyburide 20 mg/day. His medical history is significant for recurrent deep venous thromboses and hyperlipidemia. He currently smokes 2 packs of cigarettes per day. His laboratory values on this routine clinic visit are as follows: Fasting plasma glucose 185 mg/dL; HbA$_{1c}$ 9.3%; and 4+ glucose in the urine. These results are consistent with his last visit 2 months ago when he refused initiation of insulin. Now that metformin is available, could it be used instead of insulin? How should N.H. be managed?

Diet and exercise should be reinforced and continued and every effort should be made to eliminate or minimize all cardiovascular risk factors since macrovascular disease is the primary cause of mortality in patients like N.H. with NIDDM. These include tobacco use, hyperlipidemia, and obesity. As discussed on page 48-3 and in Question 41, insulin resistance in NIDDM can lead to hyperinsulinemia and a necessity for high doses of exogenous insulin, which may have detrimental cardiovascular effects. In contrast, metformin seems to decrease insulin resistance thereby decreasing hepatic glucose output and increasing glucose utilization in the periphery. For these reasons, metformin is preferred over insulin in N.H. and should be *added* to his current glyburide regimen. Furthermore, N.H. has no risk factors for lactic acidosis (e.g., renal, liver, or cardiorespiratory disease) which would contraindicate the use of metformin.

N.H. should be initiated on metformin, 500 mg twice daily with meals, and monitored for gastrointestinal side effects such as bloating, anorexia, abdominal discomfort, nausea, and metallic taste. These symptoms often dissipate with time and can be minimized if the dose is titrated up to the maximum dose (850 mg TID) slowly as tolerated. One can expect to see an additional lowering of the blood glucose by 20% or more and the HbA$_{1c}$ by 1.4% to 3.3%.[139] Other benefits may include an improved lipid profile and some weight loss. Although it is unlikely that lactic acidosis will develop, N.H. should be warned to bring to the attention of his physician any symptoms of this condition which include shortness of breath, weakness, or malaise. In patients who have failed to respond to maximum doses of sulfonylureas, one cannot expect a good response to metformin alone and a response cannot be expected in patients whose glycemic control has deteriorated severely (e.g., FPG >240 mg/dL). These patients are likely to have a high level of insulin resistance and may have lost pancreatic reserve. If N.H. fails to respond adequately to the combination therapy, both oral agents should be discontinued and insulin initiated.

References

1 **CDC.** Surveillance for diabetes mellitus—United States, 1980–1989. MMWR. 1993;42:1.

2 **CDC.** Regional variation in diabetes mellitus prevalence—United States, 1988 and 1989. MMWR. 1990;39:806.

3 **American Diabetes Association.** Diabetes 1993 Vital Statistics. Alexandria, VA: ADA; 1993.

4 **National Diabetes Data Group.** Classification and diagnosis of diabetes mellitus and other categories of glucose metabolism. Diabetes. 1979;28:1039.

5 **Rossini AA et al.** Immunopathogenesis of diabetes mellitus. Diabetes Review. 1993;1:43.

6 **Skyler JS, Marks JB.** Immune intervention in type I diabetes mellitus. Diabetes Review. 1993;1:15.

7 **DeFronzo RA.** Insulin resistance, hyperinsulinemia, and coronary artery disease: a complex metabolic web. J Cardiovasc Pharmacol. 1992;20(Suppl. 11):S1–S16.

8 **Reaven GM.** Resistance to insulin-stimulated glucose uptake and hyperinsulinemia: Role in non-insulin-dependent diabetes, high blood pressure, dyslipidemia and coronary heart disease. Diabetes Metab. 1991;17:78.

9 **Haffner SM et al.** Prospective analysis of the insulin-resistance syndrome (syndrome X). Diabetes. 1992;41:715.

10 **DeFronzo RA.** The triumvirate: beta-cell, muscle, liver: a collusion responsible for NIDDM. Diabetes. 1988;37:667.

11 **Karam JH.** Diabetes mellitus, hypoglycemia, and lipoprotein disorders. In: Krupp MA et al., eds. Current Diagnosis and Treatment. Los Altos: Lange Medical Publications; 1985:761.

12 **Fajans SS.** Scope and heterogeneous nature of MODY. Diabetes Care. 1990; 13:49–64.

13 **Wang PH et al.** Meta-analysis of effects of intensive blood-glucose control on late complications of type I diabetes. Lancet. 1993;341:1306.

14 **The Diabetes Control and Complications Trial Research Group.** The effect of intensive treatment of diabetes

on the development and progression of long-term complications in insulin-dependent diabetes mellitus. N Engl J Med. 1993;329:977–86.

15 **ADA Position Statement.** Implications of the diabetes control and complications trial. Diabetes Care. 1993; 16:1517.

16 **Carter Center of Emory University.** Closing the gap. The problem of diabetes mellitus in the United States. Diabetes Care. 1985;8:391.

17 **Krolewski AS et al.** Onset, course, complications, and prognosis of diabetes mellitus. In: Marble A et al., eds. Joslin's Diabetes Mellitus. Philadelphia: Lea and Febiger; 1985:251.

18 **ADA Consensus Statement: Role of cardiovascular risk factors in prevention and treatment of macrovascular disease in diabetes.** Diabetes Care. 1993;16:72.

19 **Bild DE et al.** Lower extremity amputation in people with diabetes: epidemiology and prevention. Diabetes Care. 1989;12:24–31.

20 **Levin ME, Sicard GA.** Peripheral vascular disease in the person with diabetes. In: Rifkin H, Porte D Jr, eds. Diabetes Mellitus: Theory and Practice. 4th ed. New York: Elsevier; 1990: 768–91.

21 **Colwell JA et al.** Veterans administration cooperative study on antiplatelet agents in diabetic patients after amputation for gangrene: II. effects of aspirin and dipyridamole on atherosclerotic vascular disease rates. Diabetes Care. 1986;9:140.

22 **Ward A, Clissold SP.** Pentoxifylline, a review of its pharmacodynamic and pharmacokinetic properties and therapeutic efficacy. Drugs. 1987;34:50.

23 **Merimee TJ.** Diabetic retinopathy: a synthesis of perspectives. N Engl J Med. 1990;322:978–83.

24 **Singerman LJ.** Early-treatment diabetic retinopathy report: good news for diabetic patients and health care professionals. Diabetes Care. 1986;9: 426. Editorial.

25 **Klein R et al.** New management concepts for timely diagnosis of diabetic retinopathy treatable by photocoagulation. Diabetes Care. 1987;10:633.

26 **Drury P, Watkins P.** Diabetic renal disease and its prevention. Clin Endocrinol. 1993;38:445.

27 **Greene DA et al.** Diabetic neuropathy. In: Rifkin H, Porte D Jr, eds. Diabetes Mellitus: Theory and Practice. 4th ed. New York: Elsevier; 1990:710.

28 **Levy-Marchal C et al.** Cyclosporin administration reverses abnormalities in a prediabetic child. Diabetes. 1984; 33:183A. Abstract.

29 **Assan R et al.** Treatment of a glucose intolerant pre-type I diabetic twin with cyclosporin. Diabetes Res Clin Pract. 1991;14(Suppl. 1):S51. Abstract.

30 **Elliott RB, Chase HP.** Prevention or delay of type I (insulin-dependent) diabetes mellitus in children using nicotinamide. Diabetologia. 1991;34:362.

31 **Keller RJ et al.** Insulin prophylaxis in individuals at high risk of type I diabetes. Lancet. 1993;341:927.

32 **ADA Position Statement.** Nutritional recommendations and principles for individuals with diabetes mellitus. Diabetes Care. 1995;18(Suppl. 1):16.

33 **Wood FC Jr.** Is diet the cornerstone in management of diabetes? N Engl J Med. 1986;315:1224.

34 **Service JF et al.** Measurements of glucose control. Diabetes Care. 1987;10: 225.

35 **ADA Consensus Statement.** Self-monitoring of blood glucose. Diabetes Care. 1994;17:81.

36 **Bunn HF.** Nonenzymatic glycosylation of protein: relevance to diabetes. Am J Med. 1981;70:325–30.

37 **National Diabetes Data Group.** Report of the expert committee on glycosylated hemoglobin. Diabetes Care. 1984;7:602.

38 **Ceriello A et al.** Vitamin E reduction of protein glycosylation in diabetes: new prospect for prevention of diabetic complications? Diabetes Care. 1991; 14:68.

39 **Davie SJ et al.** Effect of vitamin C on glycosylation of proteins. Diabetes. 1992;41:167–73.

40 **Weykamp CW et al.** Interference of carbamylated and acetylated hemoglobins in assays of glycohemoglobin by HPLC, electrophoresis, affinity chromatography and enzyme immunoassay. Clin Chem. 1993;39:138.

41 **ADA Position Statement.** Standards of medical care for patients with diabetes mellitus. Diabetes Care. 1995; 18(Suppl. 1):8–15.

42 **Schleicher ED et al.** Specific glycation of albumin depends on its half life. Clin Chem. 1993;39:625–28.

43 **Armbruster DA.** Fructosamine: structure, analysis and clinical usefulness. Clin Chem. 1987;33:2153–163.

44 **Winocur P et al.** Relative clinical usefulness of glycosylated serum albumin and fructosamine during short term changes in glycemic control in IDDM. Diabetes Care. 1989;12:665–772.

45 **Suhonen L et al.** Correlation of HbAlc, glycated serum proteins and albumin and fructosamine with the 24-h glucose profile of insulin-dependent pregnant diabetics. Clin Chem. 1989; 35:922.

46 **Binder C et al.** Insulin pharmacokinetics. Diabetes Care. 1984;7:188.

47 **Van Haeften TW.** Clinical significance of insulin antibodies in insulin-treated diabetic patients. Diabetes Care. 1989;12:641–48.

48 **Zinman B.** The physiologic replacement of insulin. An elusive goal. N Engl J Med. 1989;321:363–70.

49 **Rabkin R et al.** The renal metabolism of insulin. Diabetologia. 1984;27:351.

50 **Turnheim K.** Basic aspects of insulin pharmacokinetics. In: Brunetti P, Waldhausl WK, eds. Advanced Models for the Therapy of Insulin-Dependent Diabetes. New York: Raven Press; 1987:91.

51 **Vaag A et al.** Variation in absorption of NPH insulin due to intramuscular injection. Diabetes Care. 1990;13:74–6.

52 **Nijs HGT et al.** Increased insulin action and clearance in hyperthyroid newly diagnosed IDDM patient. Restoration to normal with antithyroid treatment. Diabetes Care. 1989;12:319.

53 **Nolte MS.** Insulin therapy in insulin-dependent (type I) diabetes mellitus. Endocrinol Metab Clin North Amer. 1992;21:281.

54 **Koivisto VA, Felig P.** Alterations in insulin absorption and in blood glucose control associated with varying insulin injection sites in diabetic patients. Ann Intern Med. 1980;92:59.

55 **Koivisto VA et al.** Effect of leg exercise on insulin absorption in diabetic patients. N Engl J Med. 1978;1:479.

56 **Paulsen EP et al.** Insulin resistance caused by massive degradation of subcutaneous insulin. Diabetes. 1979;28: 640.

57 **Chantelau E et al.** Absorption of subcutaneously administered regular human and porcine insulin in different concentrations. Diabetes Metab. 1985; 11:106.

58 **Young RJ.** Diabetic lipohypertrophy delays insulin absorption. Diabetes Care. 1984;7:479.

59 **Thow JC et al.** Effect of raising injection-site skin temperature on isophane (NPH) insulin crystal dissociation. Diabetes Care. 1989;12:432–34.

60 **Koivisto VA.** Various influences on insulin absorption. Neth J Med. 1985; 28(Suppl. 1):25.

61 **Sperling MA, ed.** Physician's Guide to Insulin-Dependent (Type I) Diabetes: Diagnosis and Treatment. Alexandria, VA: American Diabetes Association; 1988.

62 **Lebovitz H, ed.** Physician's Guide to Non-Insulin-Dependent (Type II) Diabetes: Diagnosis and Treatment. 2nd ed. Alexandria, VA: American Diabetes Association; 1988.

63 **Hirsch IB, Herter CD.** Intensive insulin therapy: part II. Multicomponent insulin regimens. Am Fam Physician. 1992;45:2643.

64 **Hirsch IB, Herter CD.** Intensive insulin therapy: part I. Basic principles. Am Fam Physician. 1992;45:2141.

65 **Cryer PE, Gerich JE.** Hypoglycemia in insulin-dependent diabetes mellitus: insulin excess and defective glucose counterregulation. In: Rifkin H, Porte D Jr, eds. Diabetes Mellitus: Theory and Practice. 4th ed. New York: Elsevier; 1990:526–46.

66 **Rizza RA.** Treatment options for insulin-dependent diabetes mellitus: a comparison of artificial pancreas, continuous subcutaneous insulin, and multiple daily injections. Mayo Clin Proc. 1986; 61:796.

67 **Duckworth WC et al.** Why intraperitoneal delivery of insulin with implantable pumps in NIDDM? Diabetes. 1992;41:657.

68 **Hirsch IB et al.** Intensive insulin therapy for treatment of type I diabetes mellitus. Diabetes Care. 1990;13:1265–283.

69 **ADA Position Statement.** Continuous subcutaneous insulin infusion. Diabetes Care. 1995;18(Suppl. 1):33.

70 **Mecklenberg RS, Guinn RN.** Complications of insulin pump therapy. The effect of insulin preparation. Diabetes Care. 1985;8:367.

71 **Mecklenberg RS et al.** Acute complications associated with insulin infusion pump therapy. JAMA. 1984;252:3255.

72 **1993 Consumer Issue.** Diabetes Forecast. 1993;Oct:48.

73 **Gin H, Aubertin J.** Generalized allergy due to zinc and protamine in insulin preparation treated with insulin pump. Diabetes Care. 1987;10:789.

74 **ADA Position Statement.** Insulin administration. Diabetes Care. 1995;18 (Suppl. 1):29.

75 **Updike SJ et al.** Laboratory evaluation of new reusable blood glucose sensor. Diabetes Care. 1988;11:801.

76 **ECRI Scientific Staff.** Blood glucose monitors. Health Devices. 1988;17: 253.

77 **Jawadi MH, Ho LS.** Stability and reproducibility of the biologic activity of premixed short-acting and intermediate-acting insulin. Am J Med. 1986;81: 467.

78 **Peters AL, Davidson MB.** Effect of storage on action of NPH and regular insulin mixtures. Diabetes Care. 1987; 10:799.

79 **Turnbridge FKE et al.** Double-blind crossover trial of isophane (NPH)— and lente-based insulin regimens. Diabetes Care. 1989;12:115.

80 **Personal communication.** Nordisk USA. Rockville, MD: 1986.

81 **Sherwin RS et al.** Lessons from glucose monitoring at night. Diabetes Care. 1987;10:249.

82 **Tordjman KM et al.** Failure of nocturnal hypoglycemia to cause fasting hyperglycemia in patients with insulin-dependent diabetes mellitus. N Engl J Med. 1987;317:1552.

83 **Gerich JE.** Glucose counterregulation and its impact on diabetes mellitus. Diabetes. 1988;37:1608.

84 **Bolli GB et al.** Nocturnal blood glucose control in type I diabetes. Diabetes Care. 1993;16(Suppl. 3):71.

85 **Bolli GB, Gerich JE.** The "dawn phenomenon"—a common occurrence in both non-insulin-dependent and insulin-dependent diabetes mellitus. N Engl J Med. 1984;310:746.

86 **Campbell PJ et al.** Pathogenesis of the dawn phenomenon in patients with insulin-dependent diabetes mellitus. N Engl J Med. 1985;312:1473.

87 **Bolli GB et al.** Physiology of overnight glucose homeostasis and pathophysiology of the dawn phenomenon in type I diabetes. In: Brunetti P, Waldhausl WK, eds. Advanced Models for the Therapy of Insulin-Dependent Diabetes Mellitus. New York: Raven Press; 1987:23.

88 **Cryer PE.** Human insulin and hypoglycemia unawareness. Diabetes Care. 1990;13:536.

89 **Gorden P.** Human insulin and hypoglycemia. N Engl J Med. 1990;322: 1007. Letter.

90 **Patrick AW, Williams G.** Adverse effects of exogenous insulin. Drug Saf. 1993;8:427.

91 **Janachek DA.** Allergic reactions to purified pork insulin. Drug Intell Clin Pharm. 1983;17:818.

92 **Galloway JA.** Insulin treatment for the early 80's. Facts and questions about old and new insulins and their usage. Diabetes Care. 1980;3:615.

93 **Galloway JA, deShazo RD.** Insulin chemistry and pharmacology: insulin allergy, resistance and lipodystrophy. In: Rifkin H, Porte D Jr, eds. Diabetes Mellitus: Theory and Practice. 4th ed. New York: Elsevier; 1990:497.

94 **Bernstein R.** Clouding and deactivation of clear (regular) human insulin: association with silicone oil from disposable syringes. Diabetes Care. 1987; 10:786.

95 **Benson EA et al.** Flocculated humulin N insulin. N Engl J Med. 1987;316:1026.

96 **Storvick W et al.** Effect of storage temperature on stability of commercial insulin preparations. Diabetes. 1968; 17:499.

97 **Vranic M et al.** Metabolic implications of exercise and physical fitness in physiology and diabetes. In: Rifkin H, Porte D Jr, eds. Diabetes Mellitus: Theory and Practice. 4th ed. New York: Elsevier; 1990:198.

98 **McDonald MJ.** Postexercise late-onset hypoglycemia in insulin-dependent diabetic patients. Diabetes Care. 1987; 10:584.

99 **Kemmer FW et al.** Mechanism of exercise-induced hypoglycemia during sulfonylurea treatment. Diabetes. 1987; 36:1178.

100 **Rubenstein AH et al.** Role of the kidney in insulin metabolism and excretion. Diabetes. 1968;17:161.

101 **Rabkin R et al.** Effect of renal disease on renal uptake and excretion of insulin. N Engl J Med. 1970;282:182.

102 **Rabkin R et al.** The renal metabolism of insulin. Diabetologia. 1984;27:351.

103 **Watts NB et al.** Postoperative management of diabetes mellitus: steady-state glucose control with bedside algorithm for insulin adjustment. Diabetes Care. 1987;10:722.

104 **Hirsch IB, McGill JB.** Role of insulin in management of surgical patients with diabetes mellitus. Diabetes Care. 1990;13:980.

105 **Gavin LA.** Perioperative management of the diabetic patient. Endocrinol Metab Clin North Am. 1992;21:457.

106 **ADA Position Statement.** Bedside blood glucose monitoring in hospitals. Diabetes Care. 1993;16(Suppl. 2):38.

107 **Godine JE et al.** Bedside capillary glucose measurement by staff nurses in a general hospital. Am J Med. 1986;80: 803.

108 **Kelly RI et al.** Human factors in self-monitoring of blood glucose. In: Food and Drug Administration Contractors Report. Washington, DC: U.S. Govt. Printing Office; April 1990.

109 **The National Steering Committee for Quality Assurance in Capillary Blood Glucose Monitoring.** Proposed strategies for reducing user error in capillary blood glucose monitoring. Diabetes Care. 1993;16:493.

110 **Cohen FE et al.** Potential danger of extending SMBG techniques to hospital wards. Diabetes Care. 1986;9:320.

111 **Feingold K et al.** Iodine-induced artifacts in home blood glucose measurements. Diabetes Care. 1983;6:317.

112 **Keeling AB, Schmidt P.** Dopamine influence on whole-blood glucose reagent strips. Diabetes Care. 1987;10: 532.

113 **Agner T et al.** Remission in IDDM: prospective study of basal C-peptide and insulin dose in 268 consecutive patients. Diabetes Care. 1987;10:164.

114 **Selam JL, Charles MA.** Devices of insulin administration. Diabetes Care. 1990;13:955.

115 **Koda-Kimble MA, Rotblatt MD.** Diabetes mellitus. In: Young LY, Koda-Kimble MA, eds. Applied Therapeutics. The Clinical Use of Drugs. 4th ed. Vancouver: Applied Therapeutics; 1988:1663. (More extensive references available in this edition.)

116 **Salzman R et al.** Intranasal aerosolized insulin. N Engl J Med. 1985;312: 1078.

117 **Frauman AG et al.** Long-term use of intranasal insulin in insulin-dependent diabetic patients. Diabetes Care. 1987; 10:573.

118 **American Diabetes Association.** Pancreas transplantation for patients with diabetes mellitus. Diabetes Care. 1993; 16(Suppl. 2):49.

119 **Bilous RW et al.** The effects of pancreas transplantation on the glomerular structure of renal allografts in patients with insulin-dependent diabetes. N Engl J Med. 1989;321:80–5.

120 **Kennedy WR et al.** Effects of pancreatic transplantation on diabetic neuropathy. N Engl J Med. 1990;322:1031–037.

121 **Kendall DM, Robertson RP.** Pancreas transplantation in diabetes mellitus: consequences for glucose homeostasis and secondary complications. Practical Diabetology. 1993;March:14.

122 **Scharp DW et al.** Results of our first nine intraportal islet allografts in type I, insulin-dependent diabetic patients. Transplantation. 1991;51:76–85.

123 **Lacy PE.** Status of islet cell transplantation. Diabetes Rev. 1993;1:76.

124 **Warnock GL et al.** Long-term follow-up after transplantation of insulin-producing pancreatic islets into patients with type I (insulin-dependent) diabetes mellitus. Diabetologia. 1992;35: 89–95.

125 **Herold KC, Rubenstein AH.** Immunosuppression for insulin-dependent diabetes mellitus. N Engl J Med. 1988; 318:701.

126 **Silverstein J et al.** Immunosuppression with azathioprine and prednisone in recent-onset insulin-dependent diabetes mellitus. N Engl J Med. 1988; 319:599.

127 **Bougneres PF et al.** Limited duration of remission of insulin dependency in children with recent overt type I diabetes treated with low-dose cyclosporine. Diabetes. 1990;39:1264.

128 **Feutren G et al.** Cyclosporin increases the rate and length of remissions in insulin-dependent diabetes of recent onset: results of a multicentre double-blind trial. Lancet. 1986;2:119.

129 **The Canadian-European Randomized Control Trial Group.** Cyclosporin-induced remission of IDDM after early intervention. Diabetes. 1988; 37:1574.

130 **Luzi L et al.** Metabolic effects of low-dose insulin therapy on glucose metabolism in diabetic ketoacidosis. Diabetes. 1988;37:1470.

131 **Siperstein M.** Hyperosmolar coma and ketoacidosis. In: New Concepts of Diabetes Management. No. 8. New York: HP Publishing; 1987.

132 **Kreisburg RA.** Diabetic ketoacidosis. In: Rifkin H, Porte D Jr, eds. Diabetes Mellitus: Theory and Practice. 4th ed. New York: Elsevier; 1990:591.

133 **Hirsch JL et al.** Clinical significance of insulin adsorption by polyvinylchloride infusions systems. Am J Hosp Pharm. 1977;34:583.

134 **Peterson L et al.** Insulin adsorbance to polyvinylchloride surfaces with implications for constant infusion therapy. Diabetes. 1976;25:72.

135 **Petty G et al.** Insulin adsorption by glass infusion bottles, polyvinylchloride infusion containers and intravenous tubing. Anesthesiology. 1974;40:400.

136 **Morris LR et al.** Bicarbonate therapy in severe diabetic ketoacidosis. Ann Intern Med. 1986;105:836.

137 **Bailey CJ.** Biguanides and NIDDM. Diabetes Care. 1992;15:755.

138 **Wu MS et al.** Effect of metformin on carbohydrate and lipoprotein metabolism in NIDDM patients. Diabetes Care. 1990;13:1.

139 **Hermann LS et al.** Therapeutic comparison of metformin and sulfonylurea alone and in various combinations: a double-blind controlled study. Diabetes Care. 1994;17:1100.

140 **Groop LC.** Sulfonylureas in NIDDM. Diabetes Care. 1992;15:737.

141 **Marchetti P, Navalesi R.** Pharmacokinetic-pharmacodynamic relationships of oral hypoglycemic agents: an update. Clin Pharmacokinet. 1989;16: 100.

142 **Malaisse WF, Lebrun P.** Mechanisms of sulfonylurea-induced insulin release. Diabetes Care. 1990;113(Suppl. 3):9.

143 **Fajans S, Brown M.** Administration of sulfonylureas can increase glucose-induced insulin secretion for decades in patients with maturity-onset diabetes of the young. Diabetes Care. 1992;16: 1254–261.

144 **Lebovitz HE.** Glipizide: a second-generation sulfonylurea hypoglycemic agent. Pharmacotherapy. 1985;5:63.

145 **Feldman JM.** Glyburide: a second-generation sulfonylurea hypoglycemic agent. Pharmacotherapy. 1985;5:43.

146 **Groop LC et al.** Effect of sulfonylurea on glucose-stimulated insulin secretion in healthy and non-insulin dependent diabetic subjects: a dose-response study. Acta Diabetol. 1991;28:162.

147 **Wahlin-Boll E et al.** Impaired effect of sulfonylurea following increased dosage. Eur J Clin Pharmacol. 1982; 22:21.

148 **Stenman S et al.** What is the benefit of increasing the sulfonylurea dose? Ann Intern Med. 1993;118:169.

149 **Samanta A et al.** Improved effect of tolbutamide when given before food in patients on long-term therapy. Br J Clin Pharmacol. 1984;18:647.

150 **Karkkainen S et al.** Urine pH is important for chlorpropamide elimination. Diabetes Care. 1983;6:313.

151 **Arrigoni L et al.** Chlorpropamide pharmacokinetics in young healthy adults and older diabetic patients. Clin Pharm. 1987;6:162.

152 **Wahlin-Boll E et al.** Bioavailability, pharmacokinetics and effects of glipizide in type 2 diabetes. Clin Pharmacokinet. 1982;7:363.

153 **Faber OK et al.** Acute actions of sulfonylurea drugs during long-term treatment of NIDDM. Diabetes Care. 1990;13(Suppl. 3):26.

154 **Hansten PD, Horn JR.** Drug Interactions & Updates Quarterly. Vancouver, WA: Applied Therapeutics; 1993.

155 **Chidester PD, Connito DJ.** Interaction between glipizide and cyclosporine: report of two cases. Transplant Proc. 1993;25:2136.

156 **Leahy JL.** Natural history of beta-cell dysfunction in NIDDM. Diabetes Care. 1990;13:992.

157 **Ohlsen P et al.** Discrepancies between glucosuria and home estimate of blood glucose in insulin-treated diabetes mellitus. Diabetes Care. 1980;3:178.

158 **Walford S et al.** The influence of renal threshold on the interpretation of urine tests for glucose in diabetic patients. Diabetes Care. 1980;3:672.

159 **Martin DB.** Type II diabetes. Insulin versus oral agents. N Engl J Med. 1986;20:1314.

160 **UK Prospective Diabetes Study II.** Reduction of HbA$_{1c}$ with basal insulin supplement, sulfonylurea, or biguanide therapy in maturity-onset diabetes. Diabetes. 1985;34:793.

161 **Melander A et al.** Sulfonylureas: why, which, and how? Diabetes Care. 1990; 13(Suppl. 3):18.

162 **Groop L et al.** Comparison of pharmacokinetics metabolic effects and mechanisms of action of glyburide and glipizide during long-term treatment. Diabetes Care. 1987;10:671.

163 **Karam JH et al.** Selective unresponsiveness of pancreatic beta-cells to acute sulfonylurea stimulation during sulfonylurea therapy in NIDDM. Diabetes. 1986;35:1314.

164 **Lev JD et al.** Glyburide and glipizide treatment of diabetic patients with secondary failures to tolazamide and chlorpropamide. Diabetes Care. 1987; 10:679.

165 **Genuth S.** Management of the adult onset diabetic with sulfonylurea drug failure. Endocrinol Metab Clin North Am. 1992;21:351.

166 **Riddle MC, Hart JS.** Which patients might benefit from combining a sulfonylurea with insulin? Diabetes Care. 1985;8:204.

167 **Genuth S.** Insulin use in NIDDM. Diabetes Care. 1990;13:1240.

168 **Turner RC, Homan RR.** Insulin use in NIDDM: rationale based on pathophysiology of disease. Diabetes Care. 1990;13:1011.

169 **Simonson DC et al.** Effect of glyburide on glycemic control, insulin requirement, and glucose metabolism in insulin-treated diabetic patients. Diabetes. 1987;36:136.

170 **RAR.** Combined sulfonylurea and insulin therapy in insulin-dependent diabetes: research or clinical practice. Diabetes Care. 1985;8:511. Editorial.

171 **Gurenberger G et al.** Sulfonylureas do not affect insulin binding or glycemic control in insulin-dependent diabetics. Diabetes. 1982;31:890.

172 **Casner PR.** Insulin-glyburide combination therapy for non-insulin dependent diabetes mellitus: a long-term double-blind, placebo-controlled trial. Clin Pharmacol Ther. 1988;44:594.

173 **Borders LM et al.** Traditional insulin-use practices and the incidence of bacterial contamination and infection. Diabetes Care. 1984;7:121.

174 **ADA Position Statement.** Insulin administration. Diabetes Care. 1995;18 (Suppl. 1):29.

175 **Spraul M et al.** Less expensive, reliable blood glucose self-monitoring. Diabetes Care. 1987;10:357.

176 **Kopicky JA, Packman CH.** The mechanisms of sulfonylurea-induced immune hemolysis: case report and review of the literature. Am J Hematol. 1986;23:283.

177 **Kwee IL, Nakada T.** Wernicke's encephalopathy induced by tolazamide. N Engl J Med. 1983;309:599.

178 **Wolfsthal SD, Wiser TH.** Chlorpropamide and an antabuse-like reaction. Ann Intern Med. 1985;103:158.

179 **Early LE.** Chlorpropamide antidiuresis. N Engl J Med. 1971;284:103.

180 **Kadowski T et al.** Chlorpropamide-induced hyponatremia: incidence and risk factors. Diabetes Care. 1983;6:468.

181 **Schneider HL et al.** Chlorpropamide hepatotoxicity: report of a case and review of the literature. Am J Gastroenterol. 1984;79:721.

182 **Nakao NL et al.** A case of chronic liver disease to tolazamide. Gastroenterology. 1985;89:192.

183 **Goodman RC et al.** Glyburide-induced hepatitis. Ann Intern Med. 1987; 106:837.

184 **University Group Diabetes Program: a study of the effects of hypoglycemic agents on vascular complications in patients with adult-onset diabetes I.** Design, methods, and baseline results. II. Mortality results. Diabetes. 1970;19:747.

185 **Seltzer H.** Drug-induced hypoglycemia. A review of 1418 cases. Endocrinol Metab Clin North Am. 1989;18: 163.

186 **Pearson JG et al.** Pharmacokinetic disposition of 14 C-glyburide in patients with varying renal function. Clin Pharmacol Ther. 1986;39:318.

187 **Gulati PD et al.** A double-blind trial of tolbutamide in cirrhosis of the liver. Am J Dig Dis. 1967;12:42.

188 **Ueda H et al.** Disappearance rate of tolbutamide in normal subjects and in diabetes mellitus. Liver cirrhosis, and renal disease. Diabetes. 1963;12:414.

189 **Gambert SR.** Atypical presentation of diabetes mellitus in the elderly. Clin Geriatr Med. 1990;6:721.

190 **Wachtel TJ.** The diabetic hyperosmolar state. Clin Geriatr Med. 1990;6: 797.

191 **Silver AJ, Morley JE.** The role of the opioid system in hypodipsia of aging. Clin Res. 1989;37:90A.

192 **Morley JE et al.** Diabetes mellitus in elderly patients: is it different? Am J Med. 1987;83:533–44.

193 **Morley JE, Perry HM.** The management of diabetes mellitus in older individuals. Drugs. 1991;41:548–65.

194 **Rosenthal MJ et al.** UCLA geriatric grand rounds: diabetes in the elderly. J Am Geriatr Soc. 1987;35:435–47.

195 **Greenblatt DJ.** Reduced serum albumin concentrations in the elderly: a report from the Boston Collaborative Drug Surveillance Program. J Am Geriatr Soc. 1979;27:20.

196 **Bresnick GH et al.** Urinary glucose testing inaccuracies among diabetic patients. Arch Ophthalmol. 1984;102: 1489–496.

197 **Melander A et al.** Sulphonylurea antidiabetic drugs an update of their clinical pharmacology and rational therapeutic use. Drugs. 1989;37:58–72.

198 **Kerson CM, Baile GR.** Do diabetic patients inject accurate doses of insulin? Diabetes Care. 1981;4:333–37.

199 **Gilden JL.** Benefits from self-monitoring of blood glucose. Consultant. 1988; 28:29.

200 **Carlisle B.** Diabetes in the elderly: factors to consider. Pharm Times. 1992; 11:130.

201 **American Neurological Association.** Does improved control of glycemia prevent an ameliorate diabetic polyneuropathy? Ann Neurol. 1986;19:288.

202 **Tomlinson DR.** Aldose reductase inhibitors and the complications of diabetes mellitus. Diabetes Med. 1993;10: 214.

203 **Greene DA et al.** Sorbitol, phosphoinositides, and sodium-potassium-ATPase in the pathogenesis of diabetic complications. N Engl J Med. 1987; 316:599.

204 **Sima AAF et al.** Regeneration and repair of myelinated fibers in sural-nerve biopsy specimens from patients with diabetic neuropathy treated with sorbinil. N Engl J Med. 1988;319:548.

205 **Gonen B et al.** The effect of withdrawal of tolrestat, aldose reductase inhibitor, on signs, symptoms and nerve function in diabetic neuropathy. Diabetologia. 1991;34(Suppl. 2):A153. Abstract.

206 **Greene DA et al.** Biochemical and morphometric response to tolrestat in human diabetic nerve. Diabetologia. 1990;33(Suppl):A92. Abstract.

207 **Ryder S et al.** Human safety profile of tolrestat: an aldose reductase inhibitor. Drug Development Research. 1987;11: 131.

208 **Kirchain WR, Rendell MS.** Aldose reductase inhibitors. Pharmacotherapy. 1990;10:326.

209 **Miller LG, Prichard JG.** Current issues in NSAID therapy. Prim Care. 1990;17:589.

210 **Sindrup SH et al.** The mechanism of action of antidepressants in pain treatment: controlled crossover studies in diabetic neuropathy. Clin Neuropharmacol. 1992;15(Suppl. 1):380A.

211 **Kvinesdal B et al.** Imipramine treatment of painful diabetic neuropathy. JAMA. 1984;251:1727.

212 **Gomez-Perez FJ et al.** Nortriptyline and fluphenazine in the symptomatic treatment of diabetic neuropathy. A double-blind cross-over study. Pain. 1985;23:395.

213 **Mendel CM et al.** A trial amitriptyline and fluphenazine in the treatment of painful diabetic neuropathy. JAMA. 1986;255:637.

214 **Egbunike IG, Chaffee BJ.** Antidepressants in the management of chronic pain syndromes. Pharmacotherapy. 1990;10:262.

215 **Charkrabarti AK et al.** Diabetic peripheral neuropathy. Nerve conduction studies before, during, and after carbamazepine therapy. Aust N Z J Med. 1976;6:565.

216 **Rull HA et al.** Symptomatic treatment of peripheral diabetic neuropathy with carbamazepine (Tegretol). Double-blind crossover trial. Diabetologia. 1969;5:215.

217 **Ellenberg M.** Treatment of diabetic neuropathy with diphenylhydantoin. N Y State J Med. 1968;68:2653.

218 **Saudek CD et al.** Phenytoin in the treatment of diabetic symmetrical polyneuropathy. Clin Pharmacol Ther. 1977;22:196.

219 **Dejgard A et al.** Mexiletine for treatment of chronic painful diabetic neuropathy. Lancet. 1988;2:9.

220 **Bach FW et al.** The effect of intravenous lidocaine on nociceptive processing in diabetic neuropathy. Pain. 1990; 40:29.

221 **Cohen KL et al.** Lack of effect of clonidine and pentoxifylline in short-term therapy of diabetic peripheral neuropathy. Diabetes Care. 1990;13:1074.

222 **Cohen KL, Harris S.** Pentoxifylline and diabetic neuropathy. Ann Intern Med. 1987;107:600.

223 **Capsaicin Study Group.** Effect of treatment with capsaicin on daily activities of patients with painful diabetic neuropathy. Diabetes Care. 1992;15:159.

224 **Schade RR et al.** Effect of metoclopramide on gastric liquid emptying in patients with diabetic gastroparesis. Dig Dis Sci. 1985;30:10.

225 **Brown CK, Khanderia U.** Use of metoclopramide, domperidone and cisapride in the management of diabetic gastroparesis. Clin Pharm. 1990;9:357.

226 **McCallum RW et al.** A multicenter placebo-controlled clinical trial of oral metoclopramide in diabetic gastroparesis. 1983;6:463.

227 **Ricci DA et al.** Effect of metoclopramide in diabetic gastroparesis. J Clin Gastroenterol. 1985;7:25.

228 **Trapnell BC et al.** Metoclopramide suppositories in the treatment of diabetic gastroparesis. Arch Intern Med. 1986;146:2278.

229 **Horowitz M et al.** Effect of cisapride on gastric and esophageal emptying in insulin-dependent diabetes mellitus. Gastroenterology. 1987;92:1899.

230 **McCallum et al.** Chronic oral cisapride therapy increases solid meal gastric emptying and improves symptoms in patients with gastroparesis. Gastroenterology. 1987;92:1525.

231 **Abell TL et al.** Long-term efficacy of oral cisapride in symptomatic upper gut dysmotility. Dig Dis Sci. 1991;36:616.

232 **Horowitz M, Roberts AP.** Long-term efficacy of cisapride in diabetic gastroparesis. Am J Med. 1990;88:195.

233 **Champion MC et al.** Cisapride improves symptoms and solid phase gastric emptying in diabetic gastroparesis. Diabetes. 1988;37(Suppl. 1):84A.

234 **Havelund T et al.** Effect of cisapride on gastroparesis in patients with insulin-dependent diabetes mellitus: a double-blind controlled trial. Acta Med Scand. 1987;222:339.

235 **DeCaestecker JS et al.** Evaluation of oral cisapride and metoclopramide in diabetic autonomic neuropathy; an eight-week, double-blind crossover study. Aliment Pharmacol Ther. 1989;3:69.

236 **Loo FD et al.** Gastric emptying in patients with diabetes mellitus. Gastroenterology. 1984;86:485.

237 **Schade R et al.** Effect of metoclopramide on gastric liquid emptying in patients with diabetic gastroparesis. Dig Dis Sci. 1985;30:10.

238 **Janssens J et al.** Improvement of gastric emptying in diabetic gastroparesis by erythromycin. Preliminary studies. N Engl J Med. 1990;322:1028.

239 **Erbas T et al.** Comparison of metoclopramide and erythromycin in the treatment of diabetic gastroparesis. Diabetes Care. 1993;26:1511.

240 **Breibart W.** Tardive dyskinesia associated with high-dose intravenous metoclopramide. N Engl J Med. 1986; 315:518.

241 **Ritz E.** Hypertension in diabetic nephropathy: prevention and treatment. Am Heart J. 1993;125:1514–519.

242 **Borch-Johnsen K et al.** The effect of proteinuria on relative mortality in type I (insulin-dependent) diabetes mellitus. Diabetologia. 1985;28:590–96.

243 **DeFronzo RA.** Diabetes and hypertension: from research to practice. Conclusions. Diabetes Spectrum. 1990;3:325.

244 **Pollare T et al.** Insulin resistance is a characteristic feature of primary hypertension independent of obesity. Metabolism. 1990;39:167.

245 **Kaplan NM.** Hyperinsulinemia in diabetes and hypertension. Clinical Diabetes. 1991;9:1.

246 **The Working Group on Hypertension in Diabetes.** Statement on hypertension in diabetes mellitus. Arch Intern Med. 1987;147:83.

247 **Swislocki ALM et al.** Insulin resistance, glucose intolerance and hyperinsulinemia in patients with hypertension. Am J Hypertens. 1989;2:419.

248 **Pollare T et al.** A comparison of the effects of hydrochlorothiazide and captopril on glucose and lipid metabolism in patients with hypertension. N Engl J Med. 1989;321:868.

249 **Pollare T et al.** Sensitivity to insulin during treatment with atenolol and metoprolol: a randomized double-blind study of the effects on carbohydrate and lipoprotein metabolism in hypertensive patients. Br Med J (Clin Res). 1989;298:1152.

250 **Pollare T et al.** Application of prazosin is associated with an increase of insulin sensitivity in obese patients with hypertension. Diabetologia. 1988;31: 415.

251 **Shepherd AMM et al.** Hypoglycemia-induced hypertension in a diabetic patient on metoprolol. Ann Intern Med. 1981;94:357.

252 **Josselson J, Sadler JH.** Nephrotic-range proteinuria and hyperglycemia associated with clonidine therapy. Am J Med. 1986;80:545.

253 **Parving H-H et al.** Protection of kidney function and decrease in albuminuria by captopril in insulin-dependent diabetics with nephropathy. Br Med J (Clin Res). 1988;297:1086.

254 **Marre M et al.** Prevention of diabetic nephropathy with enalapril in normotensive diabetics with microalbuminuria. Br Med J (Clin Res). 1988;297:1092.

255 **Keane WF et al.** Angiotensin-converting enzyme inhibitors and progressive renal insufficiency: current experience and future directions. Ann Intern Med. 1989;111:503.

256 **Chellingsworth MC et al.** The effects of verapamil, diltiazem, nifedipine and propranolol on metabolic control in hypertensives with non-insulin dependent diabetics mellitus. J Hum Hypertens. 1989;3:35.

257 **Demarie BK, Bakris GL.** Effects of different calcium antagonists on proteinuria associated with diabetes mellitus. Ann Intern Med. 1990;113:987.

258 **Carmines PK et al.** Direct evidence for voltage gated calcium channels in afferent but not efferent arterioles from rabbit kidney. Am J Hypertens. 1992; 5:13A. Abstract.

259 **U.S. Renal Data System.** USRDS 1989 annual data report. Bethesda, MD: The National Institutes of Health, National Institute of Diabetes and Digestive Diseases, 1989 Aug.

260 **Mogensen CE, Christensen CK.** Predicting diabetic nephropathy in insulin-dependent patients. N Engl J Med. 1984;311:89.

261 **Mogensen CE.** Microalbuminuria predicts clinical proteinuria and early mortality in maturity-onset diabetes. N Engl J Med. 1984;310:356.

262 **ADA Position Statement.** Standard of medical care. Diabetes Care. 1995; 18(Suppl. 1):8.

263 **Mogensen CE et al.** Microalbuminuria: an early marker of renal involvement in diabetes. Uremia Invest. 1985; 9:85.

264 **Marshall SM et al.** Micral-Test strips evaluated for screening for albuminuria. Clin Chem. 1992; 38:588.

265 **Tai J, Tze WJ.** Evaluation of microbumintest reagent tablets for screening of microalbuminuria. Diabetes Res Clin Pract. 1990;9:137.

266 **Demarie BK, Bakris GL.** Different effects of calcium antagonists on proteinuria in diabetic man. Ann Intern Med. 1990;113:987.

267 **Marre M et al.** Prevention of diabetic nephropathy with enalapril in normotensive diabetics with microalbuminuria. Br Med J. 1988;297:1092.

268 **Mathiesen ER et al.** Efficacy of captopril in postponing nephropathy in normotensive insulin dependent diabetic patients with microalbuminuria. Br Med J. 1991;303:81.

269 **Sano T et al.** Effects of long-term enalapril treatment of persistent microalbuminuria in well-controlled hypertensive and normotensive NIDDM patients. Diabetes Care. 1994;17:420.

270 **Carmines PK et al.** Direct evidence for voltage gated calcium channels in afferent but not efferent arterioles from rabbit kidney. Am J Hypertens. 1992; 5:13A. Abstract.

271 **Reichard P, Rosenqvist U.** Nephropathy is delayed by intensified insulin treatment in patients with insulin-dependent diabetes mellitus and retinopathy. J Intern Med. 1989;226:81.

272 **Kasiske BL et al.** Effect of antihypertensive therapy on the kidney in patients with diabetes: a meta-regression analysis. Ann Intern Med. 1993;118: 129.

273 **Barrett-Connor E, Orchard T.** Diabetes and heart disease. In: Harris MI, Hammon RF, eds. National Diabetes Data Group. Diabetes in America. Bethesda: US Department of Health and Human Services, 1984:1–41.

274 **CDC.** Surveillance for diabetes mellitus—United States, 1980–1989. MMWR. 1993;42:1.

275 **Moored JF et al.** Lipid nephrotoxicity in chronic progressive glomerular and tubulointerstitial disease. Lancet. 1982; 1:1309.

276 **Kohn RA et al.** Collagen aging in vitro by non-enzymatic glycosylation and browning. Diabetes. 1984;33:57–9.

277 **Donahue RP, Orchard TJ.** Diabetes mellitus and macrovascular complications. Diabetes Care. 1993;15:1141.

278 **Stern MP, Hafner SM.** Dyslipidemia in type II diabetes. Diabetes Care. 1991;14:1144.

279 **Ginsberg HN.** Lipoprotein physiology in nondiabetic and diabetic states. Diabetes Care. 1991;14:839.

280 **ADA Consensus Statement.** Detection and management of lipid disorders in diabetes. Diabetes Care. 1995;18 (Suppl. 1):86.

281 **Garg A, Grundy SM.** Management of dyslipidemia in NIDDM. Diabetes Care. 1990;13:153.

282 **Brown G et al.** Regressing coronary artery disease as a result of intensive lipid-lowering therapy in men with high levels of apolypoprotein B. N Engl J Med. 1990;323:1289–298.

283 **Miettinen TA et al.** Glucose tolerance and plasma insulin in man during acute and chronic administration of nicotinic acid. Acta Med Scand. 1969;186:247–53.

284 **Kahn SE et al.** Increased beta-cell secretory capacity as mechanism for islet adaptation to nicotinic acid-induced insulin resistance. Diabetes. 1989;38: 562–68.

285 **Baker L et al.** Hyperglycemia and acetonuria simulating diabetes. Am J Dis Child. 1966;3:59.

286 **Inoue S.** Effects of epinephrine on asthmatic children. J Alter. 1967;40: 337.

287 **Porte D Jr.** Sympathomimetic regulation of insulin secretion. Its relation to diabetes mellitus. Arch Intern Med. 1969;123:253.

288 **Souney PF et al.** Pharmacotherapy of preterm labor. Clin Pharm. 1983;2:29.

289 **Gundogdu AS et al.** Comparison of hormonal and metabolic effects of salbutamol infusion in normal subjects and insulin-requiring diabetics. Lancet. 1979;2:1317.

290 **Leslie D et al.** Salbutamol-induced diabetic ketoacidosis. Br Med J. 1977;2: 768. Letter.

291 **LeMar H, Georgitis W.** Effect of cold remedies on metabolic control of NIDDM. Diabetes Care. 1993;16:426.

292 **Gomez EC et al.** Induction of glycosuria and hyperglycemia by topic corticosteroid therapy. Arch Dermatol. 1976;112:1559.

293 **Davies DM, ed.** Textbook of Adverse Drug Reactions. 3rd ed. Oxford: Oxford University Press; 1985:354.

294 **McMahon M et al.** Effects of glucocorticoids on carbohydrate metabolism. Diabetes Metab Rev. 1988;4:17.

295 **Perlman JA et al.** Oral glucose tolerance and the potency of contraceptive progestins. J Chronic Dis. 1985;38: 857.

296 **Spellacy WN.** Carbohydrate metabolism prospectively studied in women using a low-estrogen oral contraceptive for six months. Contraception. 1979; 20:137.

297 **Carter BL et al.** Phenytoin-induced hyperglycemia. Am J Hosp Pharm. 1981;38:1508.

298 **Rao SP, Castells S.** Hyperglucagonemia in L-asparaginase-induced diabetes mellitus. Am J Pediatr Hematol Oncol. 1986;8:83.

299 **Politi A et al.** Can amiodarone induce hyperglycemia and hypertriglyceridaemia? Br Med J (Clin Res). 1984;285: 288.

300 **Pollak PT, Sam M.** Acute necrotizing pneumonitis and hyperglycemia after amiodarone therapy. Am J Med. 1984; 76:935.

301 **Evans IMA et al.** Hyperglycaemic effect of synthetic salmon calcitonin. Lancet. 1978;1:280.

302 **Lahtela JT et al.** The effect of liver microsomal enzyme-inducing and inhibiting drugs on insulin-mediated glucose metabolism in man. Br J Clin Pharmacol. 1986;21:19.

303 **Kondzieilla JR et al.** Diabetic ketoacidosis associated with lithium: case report. J Clin Psychiatry. 1985;46:492.

305 **Gulgliano D.** Increased glycosylated haemoglobin A1 in opiate addicts: evidence for hyperglycaemic effect of morphine. Diabetologia. 1982;22:379.

306 **Tollefson G, Lesar T.** Nonketotic hyperglycemia associated with loxapine and amoxapine; case report. J Clin Psychiatry. 1983;44:347.

307 **Atkin SL et al.** Increased insulin requirement in a patient with type I diabetes on rifampin. Diabetic Med. 1993; 10:392. Letter.

308 **Rabkin R et al.** The renal metabolism of insulin. Diabetologia. 1984;27:351.

309 **McDonald J.** Alcohol and diabetes. Diabetes Care. 1980;5:629.

310 **Franz MJ.** Diabetes mellitus; considerations in the development of guidelines for the occasional use of alcohol. J Am Diet Assoc. 1983;83:147.

311 **Baron SH.** Salicylates as hypoglycemic agents. Diabetes Care. 1982;5:64.

312 **Gilgore SG.** The influence of salicylates on hyperglycemia. Diabetes. 1960;9:392.

313 **Stahl-Bayliss CM et al.** Pentamidine-induced hypoglycemia in patients with the acquired immune deficiency syndrome. Clin Pharmacol Ther. 1986;39: 271.

314 **White NJ et al.** Severe hypoglycemia and hyperinsulinemia in falciparum malaria. N Engl J Med. 1988;309:61.

315 **Taylor TE et al.** Blood glucose levels in Malawian children before and during administration of intravenous quinine for severe falciparum malaria. N Engl J Med. 1988;319:1040.

316 **Phillips RE et al.** Hypoglycemia and antimalarial drugs: quinidine and release of insulin. Br Med J (Clin Res). 1986;292:1319.

317 **Limburg PJ et al.** Quinine-induced hypoglycemia. Ann Intern Med. 1993; 119:218.

318 **Jaber LA et al.** Comparison of pharmacokinetics and pharmacodynamics of short-term and long-term glyburide therapy in NIDDM. Diabetes Care. 1994;17:1300.

319 **Galloway JP.** New directions in drug development: mixtures, analogues, and modeling. Diabetes Care. 1993;16 (Suppl. 3):17.

320 **Pyzdrowski KL et al.** Preserved insulin secretion and independence in recipients of islet autografts. N Engl J Med. 1992;327:220.

321 **Schreiber M et al.** Ketoacidosis: emphasis on acid-base aspects. Diab Rev. 1994;2:98.

322 **Colwell JA.** DCCT findings. Applicability and implications for NIDDM. Diab Res. 1994;2:277.

323 **Assan R et al.** Pentamidine-induced derangements of glucose homeostasis: determinants of renal failure and drug accumulation. Diabetes Care. 1995;18:47.

Eye Disorders

Steven R Abel

Ocular Anatomy and Physiology (See Figure 49.1) 49-1
Glaucoma 49-2
  Intraocular Pressure (IOP) 49-2
  Ocular Hypertension 49-3
  Open-Angle Glaucoma 49-3
  Angle-Closure Glaucoma 49-3
Primary Open-Angle Glaucoma (POAG) 49-3
  Predisposing Factors 49-3
    Anticholinergic drugs 49-3
    Adrenergic drugs 49-3
    Corticosteroids (See Question 25) 49-17
    Other drugs 49-3
  Treatment 49-4
    Initial therapy (See Table 49.1 and Figure 49.2) 49-4
      Pilocarpine 49-4
      Epinephrine 49-4
      Timolol 49-4
      Levobunolol 49-4
      Betaxolol 49-7
      Metipranolol 49-7
      Carteolol 49-7
      Timoptic XE 49-7
    Patient education 49-7
    Nasolacrimal occlusion 49-8
    Alternative therapy 49-8
      Pilocarpine Ocusert 49-8
      Pilocarpine 4% gel 49-8
      Carbachol 49-8
      Anticholinesterase agents 49-8
        Echothiophate iodide 49-8
        Adverse effects 49-9
    Surgery 49-9
    Timolol and epinephrine 49-9
      Combined therapy 49-9
      Comparison with betaxolol and epinephrine 49-9
      Drug interactions 49-9
      Adverse effects 49-10
  Postoperative therapy 49-10
  Epinephrine products 49-10
  Dipivefrin 49-10
  Carbonic anhydrase inhibitors (See Table 49.2) ...49-10
    Adverse effects 49-10
    Topical carbonic anhydrase inhibitors 49-11
  Other drugs 49-11
Angle-Closure Glaucoma (See Table 49.3) 49-11
  Treatment 49-11
    Hyperosmotic Agents 49-11
Ocular Side Effects of Drugs (See Table 49.4) 49-12
Ocular Emergencies 49-12
  Chemical Burns 49-12
  Other Ocular Emergencies 49-12
Common Ocular Disorders 49-16
  Stye (Hordeolum) 49-16
  Conjunctivitis 49-16
    Acute bacterial conjunctivitis (pink-eye) 49-16
    Allergic conjunctivitis 49-16
  Corneal Ulcers 49-17
Ophthalmic Corticosteroids 49-17
  Comparison of Preparations (See Table 49.5) 49-17
  Adverse Effects 49-17
    Increased intraocular pressure (See Table 49.6) 49-17
    Cataracts 49-18
Systemic Side Effects from Ophthalmic Medication 49-18
Ocular Nonsteroidal Anti-Inflammatory Drugs (NSAIDs) (See Table 49.7) 49-18
Ocular Herpes Simplex Virus (HSV) Infections ...49-18
  Treatment 49-18
    Idoxuridine (IDU) 49-19
    Vidarabine (Vira-A) 49-19
    Trifluridine (Viroptic) 49-19
    Acyclovir 49-20

An understanding of primary ocular disorders requires some knowledge of ocular anatomy and physiology. Vaughn provides a comprehensive discussion in his text.[1] The following review will assist the practitioner in understanding conditions covered in this chapter.

Ocular Anatomy and Physiology

The eyeball is approximately one inch in diameter and is highly complex. It is housed in the orbital cavity formed by two bony orbits that serve as sockets which are lined with fat to protect the eyeball. Six ocular muscles allow for movement of the eyeball. (See Figure 49.1.)

The outer coat of the eye is comprised of the sclera, conjunctiva, and cornea. The sclera is the white, dense, fibrous protective coating. It is covered by a thin layer of loose connective tissue, the episclera, which contains blood vessels to nourish the sclera. The conjunctiva is a mucous membrane that covers the anterior portion of the eye and lines the eyelids. The cornea is the transparent, avascular tissue which functions as a refractive and protective window membrane through which light rays pass en route to the retina. The corneal epithelium and endothelium are lipophilic and the centrally located stroma is hydrophilic. These three corneal layers are particularly important because they affect drug penetration through the cornea. The best penetration through the intact cornea is accomplished with biphasic preparations, or those that are both fat and water soluble.

The choroid, ciliary body, and iris are known collectively as the uveal tract. The iris is a colored, circular membrane suspended between the cornea and the crystalline lens. It functions to control the amount of light that enters the eye. The choroid lies between the sclera and retina. It is comprised largely of blood vessels which nourish the retina. The ciliary body is adherent to the sclera and contains the ciliary muscle and ciliary processes. The ciliary muscle contracts and relaxes the zonular fibers which hold the crystalline lens in place. The ciliary processes are responsible for the

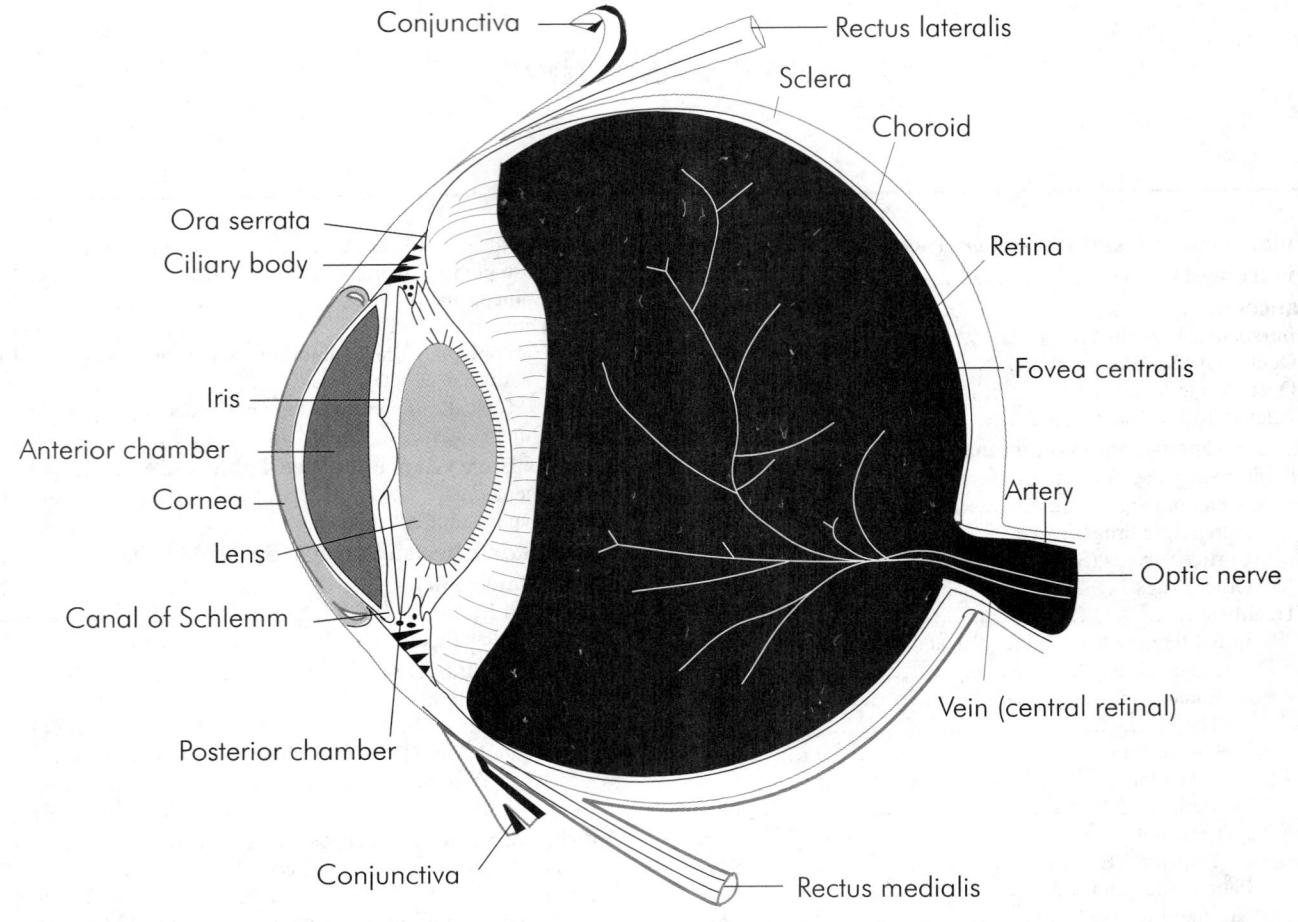

Fig 49.1 Anatomy of the Human Eye Adapted from artwork courtesy of Burroughs Wellcome.

secretion of aqueous humor, a clear liquid which occupies the anterior chamber. The anterior chamber is bounded anteriorly by the cornea and posteriorly by the iris; the posterior chamber lies between the posterior iris and the crystalline lens.

The inner segment of the eye contains the retina with the optic nerve. The retina contains all sensory receptors for light transmission. The optic nerve transmits visual impulses from the retina to the brain.

The crystalline lens, aqueous humor, and vitreous assist the cornea with the process of refraction. The lens has an inner nucleus which is surrounded by the cortex; this, in turn, is enveloped by an outer capsule. The only lens-related disorder discussed in this review is drug-induced opacification (cataract formation). Disorders involving the aqueous humor will be discussed in the section on glaucoma. The primary function of the vitreous is to maintain the shape of the eye.

The eyelids and eyelashes are the outermost means of protection for the eye. The eyelids contain various sebaceous and sweat glands which may become infected or inflamed, contributing to a variety of ocular disorders.

The eye is innervated by both the sympathetic and parasympathetic nervous systems. Parasympathetic fibers originating from the oculomotor nerve in the brain innervate the ciliary muscle and sphincter pupillae muscle which constricts the pupil. Therefore, parasympathomimetic (cholinergic) agents cause miosis (pupillary contraction) and parasympatholytic (anticholinergic) agents cause mydriasis (pupillary dilation) and cycloplegia. Cycloplegia is pa-

ralysis of the ciliary muscle and zonules that results in decreased accommodation (adjustment of the lens curvature for various distances) and blurred vision. Tear secretion by the lacrimal glands also is a parasympathetic function.

Sympathetic fibers from the superior cervical ganglion in the spinal cord innervate the dilator pupillae muscle, the blood vessels of the ciliary body, the episclera, and the extraocular muscles. Sympathomimetics cause mydriasis without affecting accommodation. The exact role of the sympathetic nervous system in glaucoma and its treatment is not understood fully. Postulated adrenergic innervation is discussed in Question 8.

Glaucoma
Intraocular Pressure (IOP)

Glaucoma, a condition characterized by an increase in intraocular pressure, is a disease primarily of middle age; an estimated 2% of all individuals over the age of 40 have glaucoma. However, it may occur in other age groups, including children. IOP is influenced by the production of aqueous humor by the ciliary processes and the outflow of aqueous humor through the trabecular meshwork. Applanation tonometry is used to measure the IOP; it is based upon the pressure required to flatten a small area of the central cornea. Generally, an IOP of 10 to 20 mm Hg is considered normal. An IOP of 22 mm Hg or more should arouse suspicion of glaucoma, although a more rare form of glaucoma is associated with a low IOP.

Ocular Hypertension

Ocular hypertension has been defined as an IOP greater than 21 mm Hg, normal visual fields, normal optic discs, open angles, and the absence of any ocular disease contributing to the elevation of IOP. Only a small percentage of patients with ocular hypertension develop open-angle glaucoma. A pathologic cupping of the optic nerve occurs with glaucoma so that diagnosis often can be made by inspection of the optic disc with an ophthalmoscope. Other provocative and confirmatory tests for open-angle glaucoma include tonography and a water-drinking test, but these are used rarely.

Open-Angle Glaucoma

Open-angle glaucoma accounts for approximately 90% of all primary glaucoma. In primary open-angle glaucoma (POAG), aqueous humor outflow from the anterior chamber constantly is subnormal, while the IOP may vary in the course of a day from normal to significantly elevated pressures.[2] The decreased outflow appears to be due to degenerative changes in outflow channels such as the trabecular meshwork and Schlemm's canal and tends to worsen with the passage of time.[1,2] In rare cases, the outflow is normal even during a phase of elevated IOP, and the elevation appears to be due to hypersecretion of aqueous humor.[2]

The onset of POAG usually is gradual and asymptomatic. A defect in the visual field examination may be present in early glaucoma, but loss of peripheral vision usually is not seen until late in the course of the disease. Visual field defects correlate well with changes in the optic disc and help in differentiating glaucoma from ocular hypertension in patients with increased IOP. Studies indicate that patients with normal visual fields and an IOP between 22 and 30 mm Hg have no greater than a 5% likelihood of developing visual field loss over periods of up to ten years.[3]

Angle-Closure Glaucoma

Examination of the anterior chamber angle by gonioscopy, utilizing a corneal contact lens, magnifying device (such as a slit lamp microscope), and light source, assists in differentiating between open-angle and angle-closure glaucoma. Angle-closure glaucoma comprises approximately 5% of all primary glaucoma. In angle-closure glaucoma, there is no abnormal resistance to aqueous humor outflow. The sole cause of the elevated IOP is closure of the anterior chamber angle.[2]

Angle-closure glaucoma, a medical emergency, usually presents as an acute attack with a rapid increase in IOP, blurring or sudden loss of vision, appearance of haloes around lights, and pain which often is severe. Patients predisposed to angle-closure glaucoma should not have their pupils dilated during an ophthalmic examination and should be educated regarding the signs and symptoms of angle closure. Acute attacks may terminate without treatment, but if the IOP remains high, irreparable damage to the optic nerve may occur.[1] In chronic angle closure, the closure is gradual and the patient may be asymptomatic until the glaucoma is in an advanced state.[2] Permanent medical management of acute or chronic angle-closure is difficult, and surgical procedures (such as peripheral iridectomies) often are required to improve the prognosis.

Primary Open-Angle Glaucoma (POAG)
Predisposing Factors

1. M.H., a 52-year-old female, presented for routine ophthalmic examination. Visual acuity without correction was 20/40 OD (right eye) and 20/80 OS (left eye). Tonometry measured an IOP of 36 mm Hg OU (both eyes). Ophthalmoscopy revealed physiologic cupping of the optic discs OU, and visual field examination revealed a nerve fiber bundle defect consistent with glaucoma. Pupils were normal OU, and gonioscopy indicated that anterior chamber angles were open OU; there were no signs of cataract formation. M.H. related a positive family history for glaucoma and presently is being treated for hypertension, congestive heart failure (CHF), and asthma. Her medications include:

Amitriptyline	75 mg HS
Chlorpheniramine	4 mg Q 6 hr PRN
Digoxin	0.25 mg QD
Furosemide	40 mg BID
Nitroglycerin (NTG)	1/150 gm SL PRN
Theophylline SR	300 mg Q 12 hr

Findings upon examination indicate that M.H. has POAG. What other factors may predispose M.H. to an increased IOP?

Primary open-angle glaucoma is thought to be determined genetically, and M.H. has a positive family history.[1,2] In addition, she is taking several medications which have been associated with increases in IOP.

Anticholinergic Drugs

The majority of reports dealing with drug-induced increases in IOP center around precipitation of angle-closure glaucoma by topical mydriatic/cycloplegic agents (anticholinergics). In eyes with open-angle glaucoma, topical anticholinergics can significantly increase resistance to aqueous humor outflow and elevate IOP while the anterior chamber remains grossly open.[4] As part of any routine ophthalmic examination, the pupils are dilated with a mydriatic/cycloplegic (unless otherwise contraindicated). The IOP always is measured before this procedure, so the use of these agents would not have influenced the IOP readings in M.H.

If systemic anticholinergic agents are administered in doses sufficient to cause pupillary dilatation, the risk of precipitating angle closure increases. However, it is unlikely that these agents will aggravate open-angle glaucoma unless the amount reaching the eye is sufficient to cause cycloplegia.[4] Consideration must be given to medications with anticholinergic side effects (antihistamines, benzodiazepines, diopyramide, phenothiazines, tricyclic antidepressants), although literature documentation of glaucoma potentiation is scarce. M.H. is receiving chlorpheniramine as needed (PRN) and amitriptyline at bedtime (HS), but her pupil examination is normal with no evidence of mydriasis or cycloplegia. Therefore, it is highly unlikely that these medications contributed to her increased IOP.

Adrenergic Drugs

Adrenergic agents such as central nervous system (CNS) stimulants, vasoconstrictors, appetite suppressants, and bronchodilators may produce minimal pupillary dilatation. These have no proven adverse influence on IOP in either normal eyes or eyes with open-angle glaucoma. Consequently, the use of theophylline in M.H. also is an unlikely source of the increased IOP.[5]

Other Drugs

No conclusive evidence for the production of angle-closure glaucoma by vasodilators has ever been published, although slight increases in IOP have been reported.[6] Use of NTG as needed in M.H. is not a cause for concern. There have been isolated reports of other medications causing mydriasis in glaucoma patients. These include muscle relaxants (carisoprodol), monoamine oxidase inhibitors, fenfluramine, ganglionic blocking agents, salicylates, oral contraceptives, and chlorpropamide (Diabinese).[7] Succinylcholine, ketamine, and caffeine have been associated with increases in IOP.[6,8] Alpha-chymotrypsin has been reported to increase IOP in patients who have received the medication during operative procedures; these patients' outflow channels probably were obstructed by debris generated from use of the enzyme.[9] Corticosteroid-induced IOP elevation is discussed in Question 25. Should M.H. require administration of any other medications associated with increases in IOP, potential adverse effects may be avoided by routine follow-up.

Treatment

Initial Therapy

2. How should therapy for POAG be initiated in M.H.? How effective are the different classes of agents and what are their major side effects?

Table 49.1 outlines topical agents commonly used in the treatment of glaucoma. The practitioner has three options available as initial therapy of POAG: pilocarpine, epinephrine, or a topical beta blocker. Figure 49.2 provides an algorithm of the medical management of glaucoma.

Pilocarpine historically has been an initial treatment of choice. Therapy usually is begun using lower concentrations (0.5% to 1%), one drop administered four times a day. Pilocarpine is a direct-acting cholinergic (parasympathomimetic) that causes contraction of ciliary muscle fibers attached to the trabecular meshwork and scleral spur. This opens the trabecular meshwork to enhance aqueous humor outflow. There also may be a direct effect upon the trabecular meshwork. Pilocarpine causes miosis by contraction of the iris sphincter muscle, but the miosis is not related to the decrease in IOP. The onset of miosis is rapid, occurring in 10 to 15 minutes, while IOP decreases within one hour; the duration of action is four to eight hours. Melanin in the iris is a binding site for pilocarpine; therefore, its effects upon IOP may be decreased in heavily pigmented eyes.[3]

Epinephrine is a sympathomimetic agent that stimulates both alpha and beta receptors. In the past, it was thought that stimulation of alpha receptors caused an increase in aqueous humor outflow, while stimulation of beta-receptors caused a decrease in the production of aqueous humor. However, studies have concluded that the opposite is true. It is the beta-adrenergic activity which is responsible for increasing aqueous humor outflow. This is the probable basis of epinephrine's ability to lower IOP.[204,205] The alpha-adrenergic effect predominantly decreases the inflow of aqueous humor which is not as significant as the increase in aqueous humor outflow.[204,205] The exact mechanism of action is discussed further in Question 9. When used alone, epinephrine produces a 30% to 35% decrease in the rate of aqueous humor production, while use in conjunction with carbonic anhydrase inhibitors may produce a 65% to 70% decrease.[3] Epinephrine often is used in younger patients or patients with cataracts where miosis and the resultant decreased vision from cholinergic agents are a problem. Epinephrine is a first-line drug in the therapy of POAG, but is used most often as a second agent in combination rather than as the initial single agent for therapy.

Systemic effects, including tachycardia, hypertension, and faintness, occur rarely with epinephrine.[10] As with timolol, patients in whom systemic effects could potentiate pre-existing problems should be monitored closely.

Timolol accounts for approximately 70% of all glaucoma medications used.[11] Timolol (Timoptic) and other beta-adrenergic blockers appear to lower IOP by decreasing aqueous humor production. Some studies have demonstrated a slight effect upon the facility of outflow, but this does not seem to be significant.[12,13] Concentrations or dosages exceeding one drop of 0.5% timolol administered twice a day do not produce further significant decreases in IOP.[14] Therapy usually is initiated with a 0.25% solution administered as one drop twice a day. Monocular administration of timolol has resulted in equal bilateral IOP reduction and may reduce the cost of therapy and side effects in some patients.[15] An escape phenomenon, or tachyphylaxis, has been seen with timolol. If a patient has a large initial decrease in IOP, the IOP often will stabilize at a lesser reduction in approximately four to six weeks.[16,17] The long-term safety and efficacy of timolol has been described in adult and pediatric patients.[18,19] Timolol has been shown to be at least as effective as pilocarpine and epinephrine and may be more efficacious in diurnal IOP control.[20,21]

Because M.H. has a history of CHF and asthma, she should not be initiated on timolol. Timolol has been associated with a reduction of resting pulse rate and worsening of CHF,[22,23] although the change in pulse rate generally is slight (5 to 8 beats/minute). Pulmonary effects such as dyspnea, airway obstruction, and pulmonary failure also have occurred.[24–26] Timolol has been reported to produce corneal anesthesia after chronic administration in susceptible individuals.[206,211] Uveitis is another side effect which has been reported rarely in patients receiving ophthalmic timolol.[212,213] However, a cause-and-effect relationship has not been implied or demonstrated for this reported reaction.[212,213]

Systemic absorption of timolol has been studied in rabbits and humans following topical administration.[27,28] Affrime et al. found that plasma levels of timolol were not detected in most human subjects following topical administration; however, a level of 9.6 ng/mL was detected in one subject.[28] In ten patients over age 60 receiving chronic topical timolol therapy, the baseline mean plasma timolol level was 0.34 ng/mL, increasing to 1.34 ng/mL one hour after administration of one drop of 0.5% timolol.[29] When punctal occlusion was practiced, the mean one-hour plasma timolol level diminished to 0.9 ng/mL.

The beta-blocking plasma concentration of timolol has been estimated to be about 5 to 10 ng/mL.[17] Although systemic absorption following topical administration does not appear to be significant in most cases, care should be taken when timolol is used in patients with sinus bradycardia, CHF, and pulmonary disease. Systemic side effects may be exaggerated in the elderly secondary to inadvertent overdosing associated with poor administration technique (see Question 4).

A milk sample from a nursing mother was obtained one and one-half hours after administration of one drop of 0.5% topical timolol.[31] The drug level in milk was 5.6 ng/mL versus a concomitant plasma concentration of 0.93 ng/mL. Therefore, timolol should be used cautiously in nursing mothers.

Based upon M.H.'s past medical history which includes asthma and congestive heart failure, pilocarpine 1%, administered four times a day is the recommended initial therapy.

3. Betaxolol, levobunolol, metipranolol, carteolol, and Timoptic XE are all topical beta blockers which also are indicated for treatment of open-angle glaucoma and ocular hypertension. Do these agents offer advantages over timolol in the treatment of M.H.'s glaucoma?

All of the ocular beta blockers have the same basic mechanism of action. Ophthalmic beta blockers reduce the IOP by blocking the beta adrenoreceptors in the ciliary epithelium of the eye causing a fall in aqueous humor production. Timolol was the first ocular beta blocker marketed and has been used most widely; therefore, all of the newer agents are compared to timolol for safety and effectiveness.

Levobunolol is a β_1- and β_2-adrenergic antagonist. The ocular hypotensive effect of levobunolol has been demonstrated in single- and multiple-dose studies, the latter a three-month study utilizing every 12-hour administration.[32,33] Average IOP reduction was approximately 9 mm Hg with 0.5% or 1% solutions in the multiple dose study.[33]

Table 49.1		Common Topical Agents Used in the Treatment of Open-Angle Glaucoma		
Generic	Mechanism	Strength	Usual Dose	Comments
Miotics				
Pilocarpine (Isopto-Carpine)	Parasympathomimetic	0.25%–10% 4% (ointment) 20–40 µg/hr (ocusert)	1–2 drops TID–QID ¼ inch in cul-de-sac QD Weekly	Long-term proven effectiveness. Little rationale for use of concentrations >4% or administration more frequently than Q 4 hr. Side effects of miosis with decreased vision and brow ache are frequent sources of patient complaints. Once daily administration of ointment may ↑ compliance. Effectiveness over 24 hr should be assessed in patients receiving the ointment. Ointment may cause a visual haze and blurred vision
Carbachol (Isopto-Carbachol)	Parasympathomimetic	0.75%–3%	1–2 drops TID–QID	Used in patients allergic to or intolerant of other miotics. May be used as frequently as Q 4 hr. Corneal penetration is enhanced by benzalkonium chloride in commercial preparations. Side effects are similar to pilocarpine
Echothiophate Iodide (Phospholine Iodide)	Anticholinesterase	0.03%–0.25%	1 drop BID	Most used anticholinesterase agent. Long duration, although usually dosed BID which enhances compliance. Solutions are relatively unstable. Side effects similar to pilocarpine, especially in concentrations >0.06%. ↑ cataract formation has been associated with its use
Mydriatics				
Epinephrine (Glaucon, Eppy/N, Epitrate)	Sympathomimetic	0.25%–2%	1 drop BID	Good response often seen with use of lower concentrations (0.5%–1%). Bitartrate salt contains ½ labeled strength in epinephrine free base equivalent. BID dosage enhances compliance. Cosmetic complaints associated with use include hyperemia and pigment deposits on the cornea and conjunctiva. Not recommended for use in aphakic patients due to 20%–30% incidence of cystoid macular edema
Dipivefrin (Propine)	Sympathomimetic	0.1%	1 drop BID	Prodrug of epinephrine associated with ↓ in systemic side effects if absorbed. BID dosage enhances compliance
Beta Blockers				
Betaxolol [Betoptic (solution), Betoptic S (suspension)]	Sympatholytic	0.25% (suspension) 0.5% (solution)	1 drop BID	Effective with few associated ocular side effects. BID dosage enhances compliance. May be the ocular beta blocker of choice in patients with pre-existing CHF or pulmonary disease, due to β_1 specificity. Patient response may be less than that seen with timolol
Carteolol (Ocupress)	Sympatholytic	1%	1 drop BID	Effective with few associated side effects. BID dosage enhances compliance. Use with caution in patients with pre-existing CHF or pulmonary disease
Levobunolol (Betagan)	Sympatholytic	0.25%–0.5%	1 drop QD–BID	Effective with few associated ocular side effects. QD–BID dosage enhances compliance. Use with caution in patients with pre-existing CHF or pulmonary disease
Metipranolol (OptiPranolol)	Sympatholytic	0.3%	1 drop BID	Effective with few associated side effects. BID dosage enhances compliance. Use with caution in patients with pre-existing CHF or pulmonary disease
Timolol (Timoptic)	Sympatholytic	0.25%–0.5%	1 drop BID	Effective with few associated ocular side effects. BID dosage enhances compliance. Use with caution in patients with pre-existing CHF or pulmonary disease. Proven long-term effectiveness, with well-defined side effect profile
Timoptic XE	Sympatholytic	0.25%–0.5%	1 drop QD	New once-daily timolol formulation. The ophthalmic vehicle, gellan gum (Gelrite)

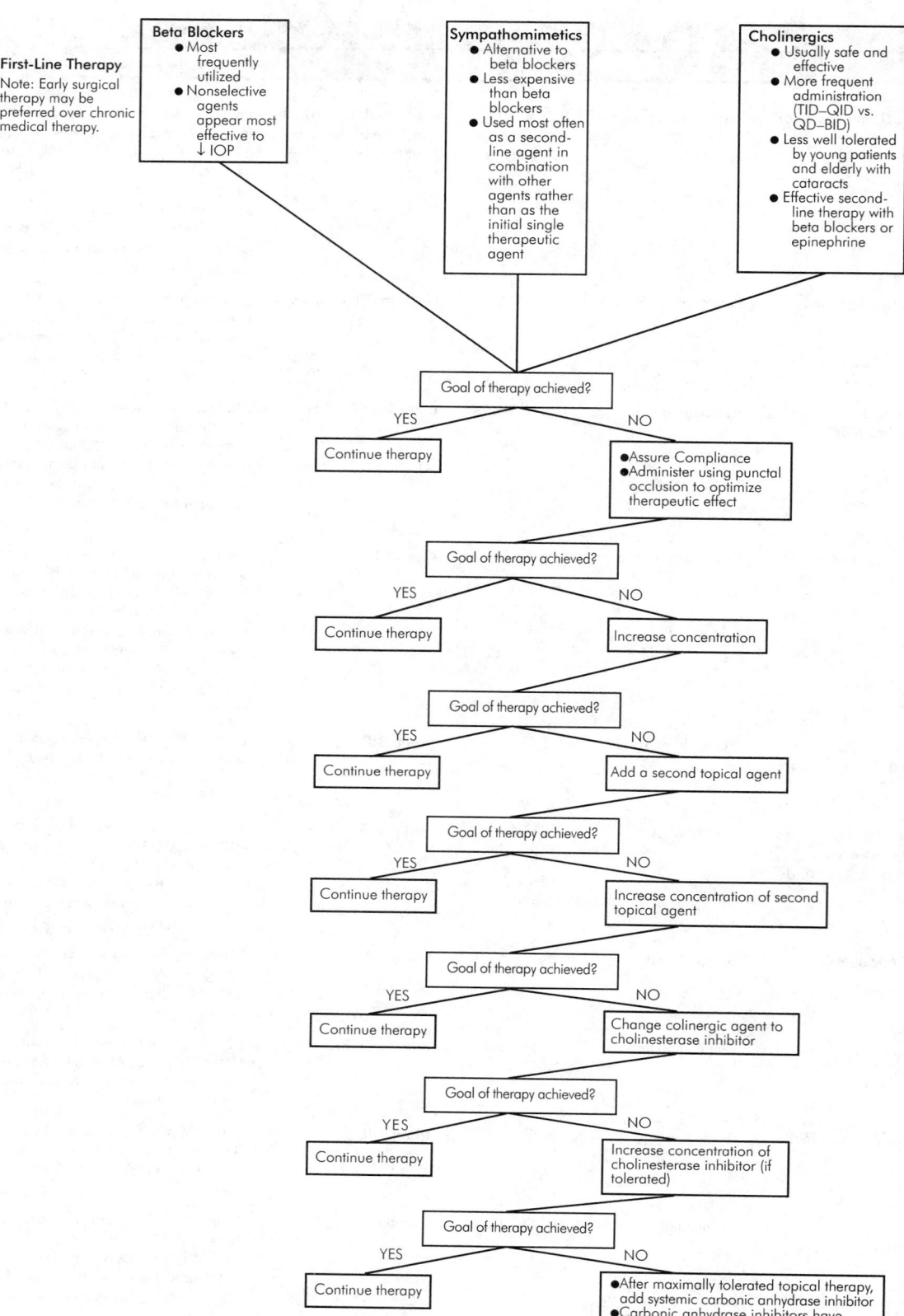

Fig 49.2   Medical Management of Glaucoma

Levobunolol, in concentrations of 0.5% and 1%, was compared to timolol 0.5% in four studies ranging from one month to two years duration.[34,35] Both medications were administered twice daily. Ocular hypotensive effects and the incidence of adverse reactions were similar for both agents in each study. Slight to significant decreases in heart rate were noted for both agents.

Levobunolol is marketed as a once- or twice-daily treatment regimen. A three-month study comparing levobunolol 0.5% once daily with twice daily administration demonstrated that the regimens provided similar reductions in IOP.[217] Wandel et al. compared once-daily levobunolol and timolol at various concentrations; levobunolol demonstrated greater effectiveness over the three-month study period.[218] However, Silverstone conducted a study comparing timolol and levobunolol 0.25% administered once daily and both agents were shown to be equally effective.[219] Levobunolol has been reported to be more expensive than timolol whether it is administered once or twice daily.[220]

Betaxolol is a selective β_1-adrenergic blocker. In concentrations of 0.125% to 0.5%, betaxolol has been shown to effectively reduce IOP up to 35% from baseline for treatment periods of up to two and one-half years.[36–38]

In comparative studies, betaxolol 0.5% and timolol 0.5% administered twice daily were effective in decreasing IOP with similar side effect profiles including slight but insignificant decreases in systolic and diastolic blood pressure (BP).[38–40] In these studies, timolol was slightly but not significantly more effective in decreasing IOP, with fewer patients requiring adjunctive therapy for adequate IOP control. In a six-month trial, betaxolol was compared with timolol in concentrations of 0.25% and 0.5%.[41] The median IOP was consistently and significantly lower in the timolol group than in the betaxolol group, and more betaxolol patients required adjunctive therapy. Thus, while these studies confirm the efficacy of betaxolol in decreasing IOP, the magnitude of decrease may not be as great as with timolol.

Betaxolol 1% has been shown to exhibit fewer cardiovascular side effects than timolol 0.5% in healthy volunteers.[42] It also is better tolerated than timolol in patients with reactive airway disease and asthma and should be considered for use when topical beta blocker therapy is indicated in patients such as M.H.[43,44] However, betaxolol has been associated with adverse pulmonary and cardiac side effects; therefore, it must be used with caution in patients with pulmonary or cardiac disease.[221,222] Additionally, ocular burning and stinging has been associated more frequently with betaxolol and metipranolol than with the other topical beta blockers.[223]

Metipranolol is a nonselective beta-blocking agent which effectively lowers IOP in patients with open-angle glaucoma and ocular hypertension. Metipranolol, in concentrations ranging from 0.1% to 0.6%, has been comparable to timolol 0.25% to 0.5% in reducing IOP in patients with open-angle glaucoma.[207,208] Single-dose metipranolol 0.1% and 0.3% and timolol 0.25% did not change significantly resting heart rate or the resting or exercise mean blood pressure.[209] Timolol significantly reduced exercise tachycardia. Metipranolol 0.6% and levobunolol 0.5% administered twice daily caused mean IOP reductions of about 7 mm Hg (29%).[210] Insignificant reductions in heart rate and blood pressure were observed in each group. Metipranolol was associated with a greater incidence of stinging or burning upon administration than other beta blockers. Topical metipranolol appears to offer no advantage over timolol or levobunolol in the treatment of glaucoma. Like timolol, metipranolol reportedly produces corneal anesthesia which occurs within one minute of instillation and returns to baseline after ten minutes.[211] Metipranolol has been withdrawn from clinical use in the United Kingdom because it has been associated with granu-

lomatous anterior uveitis. This adverse effect was thought to be related to the introduction of irradiated plastic containers.[224] However, a rechallenge study supports metipranolol as the responsible agent for these inflammatory reactions.[225] The seven patients who participated in the metipranolol rechallenge study were included in a study that evaluated the pattern of IOP in glaucomatous eyes with and without metipranolol-induced adverse reactions.[226] There was a significant secondary elevation (57.6%) in IOP in patients with metipranolol-associated adverse reactions.[226] Metipranolol has been cited as the most cost-effective agent in treating POAG; however, the increased frequency of ocular burning and stinging and granulomatous anterior uveitis may limit its use.

Carteolol, the most recently marketed ocular beta blocker, is a nonselective beta-blocking agent which has partial beta-agonist activity. Partial beta-agonist activity or intrinsic sympathomimetic activity (ISA) theoretically should minimize the bronchospastic, bradycardic, and hypotensive effects associated with other ocular beta blockers.[227] Several studies comparing carteolol and timolol have failed to demonstrate a clinical difference in the effects of these two agents on cardiovascular or pulmonary function.[111,228,229] More studies are needed to determine the clinical significance of partial beta-agonist activity.

In comparative studies, carteolol 1% and timolol 0.25% administered twice daily for one month were equally effective in reducing IOP.[111] There were significantly fewer patients reporting adverse effects, specifically ocular irritation, in the carteolol treatment group.[111] Other studies also have reported comparable effectiveness with carteolol and timolol.[228,229]

Timoptic XE is a timolol ophthalmic gel-forming solution which is administered once daily. The ophthalmic vehicle, gellan gum (Gelrite), is a solution which forms a clear gel in the presence of mono or divalent cations.[230] This ion activated gelation prolongs precorneal residence time and increases ocular bioavailability, allowing timolol to be administered once daily.[230] A preliminary 24-week study compared Timoptic XE 0.5% once daily and Timoptic solution 0.5% twice daily and found both formulations to be equally effective in lowering IOP.[231]

Patient Education

4. Based upon her past medical history, pilocarpine 1%, 1 drop OU QID, is ordered for M.H. How should M.H. be instructed regarding proper use of her pilocarpine and expected therapeutic side effects?

Merck, Sharp, and Dohme suggests a method of administration of Timoptic that is effective for administering eye drops from all types and sizes of plastic ophthalmic dropper bottles. M.H. should be instructed to hold the inverted pilocarpine bottle between her thumb and middle finger. The index finger is left free to depress the bottom of the container, releasing one drop for the dose. With a little practice, this technique is easy to master. The lower eyelid should be drawn downward with the index finger of the opposite hand or pinched between the thumb and index finger to form a pouch. The patient should look up and administer the drug into the pouch.

Patients must be encouraged to continue regular use of their medications for effective treatment of glaucoma. Since chronic glaucoma is a silent disease, like hypertension, there is little positive reinforcement to continue therapy; the only noticeable effects are drug side effects. It is best to administer pilocarpine every six hours, a schedule consistent with its duration of action (see Table 49.1).

M.H. should be warned that pilocarpine (and other miotics) may cause ciliary spasm that may result in brow ache and myopia which presents as blurred vision. Since miosis also decreases vision in poor light, night driving may be hazardous for patients. Miotics also have been associated with retinal detachments, especially in aphakic eyes (eyes from which the crystalline lens has been removed).[45]

Systemic, cholinergic effects such as nausea, vomiting, sweating, salivation, and diarrhea have been associated with the use of all miotics, although most reports have been associated with use of the anticholinesterase agents.[46,47] M.H. should report any of these side effects to her physician. As discussed in Question 5, occlusion of the puncta (through the application of slight pressure to the inner core of the eye with the finger during administration) may decrease systemic absorption of ophthalmic drugs and decrease the incidence of side effects.

Nasolacrimal Occlusion

5. Does nasolacrimal occlusion (punctal occlusion) significantly influence systemic absorption or alter the therapeutic effects of antiglaucoma medications?

Systemic side effects may be minimized by decreasing drug loss through the nasolacrimal system into the posterior nasopharynx. Nasolacrimal occlusion is a technique that markedly decreases the amount of drug absorbed systemically.[214] The influence of nasolacrimal occlusion on levels of topically applied antiglaucoma medications has been studied in the human eye.[214–216] Ellis et al. studied the influence of nasolacrimal occlusion on aqueous humor concentrations of timolol in eyes of patients undergoing cataract surgery.[215] A single drop of ophthalmic timolol 0.5% was instilled at various times before surgery. Nasolacrimal occlusion was applied for five minutes and aqueous humor was collected at the beginning of cataract surgery. Drug levels were significantly greater in samples obtained 15, 90, and 180 minutes after timolol administration in patients receiving nasolacrimal occlusion. The average measured maximum aqueous humor timolol concentration of 1.66 µg/mL in the occlusion group was significantly greater than 0.85 µg/mL in the nonocclusion group. The area under the curve was 1.7 times greater in patients receiving nasolacrimal occlusion. This indicates that nasolacrimal occlusion will increase timolol aqueous humor concentrations for hours following instillation.[215]

Nasolacrimal occlusion is effective and may provide maximum drug effect utilizing lower drug concentrations and less frequent administrations. Zimmerman et al. determined that 1% and 2% pilocarpine significantly decreased intraocular pressure at 6, 8, and 12 hours after instillation when nasolacrimal occlusion was performed.[214] Similarly, carbachol 1.5%, 3%, and the combination of timolol 0.25% and carbachol 1.5% every 12 hours also were maximally effective at 12 hours utilizing nasolacrimal occlusion.[214] Timolol reduced IOP by 15% and maintained this reduction at 24 hours in 92% of patients in whom nasolacrimal occlusion was performed, compared to 55% in whom nasolacrimal occlusion was not performed.[214] When utilizing nasolacrimal occlusion, Zimmerman suggests starting pilocarpine and carbachol treatment with 2% every 12 hours and 1.5% every 12 hours, respectively.[214] The treatment then can be adjusted according to the patient's response. Timolol can be administered every 24 hours if nasolacrimal occlusion is performed.[214] If nasolacrimal occlusion is used consistently and properly, maximal drug effect can be achieved with reduced frequency and with half of the concentrations typically used. Nasolacrimal occlusion should be incorporated into patient counseling for instillation of all eye drops.[214] Nasolacrimal occlusion is accomplished by placing a finger over the inner canthus (''corner'' of the eye closest to the nose). This also has been referred to as occlusion of the puncta. (See Question 6.)

Alternative Therapy

6. Two weeks after initiation of therapy, M.H. returns for follow-up. Her IOP measures 32 mm Hg OD and 30 mm Hg OS. She denies noncompliance (confirmed by miotic pupils) and has no complaints of intolerable side effects. How should therapy be altered? Are there alternative dosage forms or drugs that can be used?

The concentration of pilocarpine may be increased and the dosage schedule made more frequent to achieve continuous pressure-lowering effects. Concentrations that exceed 4% and administration more frequently than every four hours offer little increased advantage in controlling IOP.[3]

Based upon recently published data, nasolacrimal occlusion should be recommended before increasing the dose of pilocarpine. Nasolacrimal or punctal occlusion consists of application of finger pressure over the inner canthus of the eye. Pressure is applied for three to five minutes during and after drug instillation.

Initial follow-up usually occurs within four weeks. If the patient has been compliant and the pressure response is not optimal, the concentration likely will be increased at this time. Patients who are unstable will be followed at one- to three-month intervals. Stable patients usually are evaluated every six months.

Pilocarpine Ocusert. The pilocarpine Ocusert, an elliptically shaped unit designed to fit in the conjunctival cul-de-sac, is available in two strengths which release 20 or 40 µg/hour for one week. This dosage form increases compliance in some patients and better controls the IOP. However, the Ocusert system may cause discomfort and retention in the eye may be difficult in some patients.

Pilocarpine 4% gel effectively reduces IOP for 18 to 24 hours following a single administration.[48,49] Average IOP control with the once-daily gel formulation has been equal to or slightly less than that achieved with pilocarpine drops administered four times a day.[49,50] Johnson et al. observed development of a superficial haze with gel treatment exceeding eight weeks.[49] Although the haze produced no symptoms, its long-term consequences are unknown. The convenience of a once-daily dosage form was noted in patients receiving the gel.

Carbachol is used most frequently when intolerance to pilocarpine develops. In addition to having direct cholinergic effects, carbachol is more resistant to cholinesterase than pilocarpine. Added benefits include increased release of acetylcholine from parasympathetic nerve terminals and a weak anticholinesterase effect. Carbachol preparations contain banzalkonium chloride as a preservative, which also enhances the otherwise very poor corneal penetration of the drug. Carbachol should be administered three times a day.

Anticholinesterase Agents. If control of IOP is not achieved with optimal use of pilocarpine, anticholinesterase agents usually are prescribed as second-line therapy. Anticholinesterase agents inhibit the enzyme cholinesterase, thereby increasing the amount of acetylcholine and its naturally occurring cholinergic effects. Physostigmine (Eserine) is a reversible cholinesterase inhibitor and was the first medication used in the treatment of glaucoma. It is prescribed rarely because chronic use has been associated with allergic irritation and follicular hypertrophy of the palpebral conjunctiva.[3] Physostigmine is sensitive to both heat and light and oxidizes to a pink or rusty color, indicating that it should be discarded. Other reversible cholinesterase inhibitors include neostigmine (3% to 5%, administered every four to six hours) and demecarium (Humorsol), which has a much longer duration of action than physostigmine.

Echothiophate iodide (Phospholine Iodide) is an irreversible cholinesterase inhibitor which primarily inactivates pseudocholinesterase and secondarily inhibits true cholinesterase. Echothiophate iodide is the most widely used cholinesterase inhibitor for open-angle glaucoma and would be the best alternative for M.H. if maximal doses of pilocarpine are ineffective. It is marketed as a powder plus diluent because of product instability. Following reconstitution, the product is stable for 30 days at room temperature or six months under refrigeration. Echothiophate iodide has a long duration of action which affords better control of IOP; however, the side effects of miosis and myopia are more constant. Concentrations higher than 0.06% are associated with a significant increase in subjective complaints such as the previously mentioned brow ache.[51] (See Question 4.)

Another irreversible cholinesterase inhibitor, isoflurophate [diisopropyl fluorophosphate (DFP)] is used occasionally in open-angle glaucoma associated with aphakia. In general, anticholinesterase agents that are used in open-angle glaucoma have a long duration of action (see Table 49.1) but are dosed on a twice a day, every 12 hours schedule.

7. Adverse Effects. Several weeks later, M.H. is switched to echothiophate iodide, 1 drop BID. Are there any adverse effects associated with the use of this agent?

Miotics, primarily cholinesterase inhibitors, have been associated with the formation of iris cysts. These may be prevented by the use of phenylephrine in combination with the cholinesterase inhibitor.[52] Also, there is considerable clinical evidence that cataracts occur more frequently and progress more rapidly in patients over 50 years of age treated with echothiophate iodide. The initial changes consist of clusters of small vacuoles located in the anterior subcapsular region, giving a characteristic mossy appearance.[3] Similar changes have been noted in patients treated with demecarium or isofluorphate. Such changes may occur in 8% to 10% of nonglaucomatous eyes and in a similar percentage of eyes treated with pilocarpine or carbachol, but they are seen in up to 60% of eyes treated with echothiophate iodide for more than six months.[53–55] Following continuous therapy for three years, about 50% of treated eyes demonstrate a loss of visual acuity due to lens changes. Initially, visual acuity may not be affected, and most cases do not progress when therapy is stopped at the early stage.[3] Because of these effects, anticholinesterases often are reserved for aphakic glaucomatous patients; exceptions include patients such as M.H. in whom beta blockers must be used cautiously. If M.H.'s response to echothiophate iodide is unsatisfactory or if visual changes and intolerance occur, a trial of pilocarpine plus a beta blocker or epinephrine (along with careful monitoring in view of her underlying disease states) is warranted.

Surgery

8. J.W. has been treated for POAG with echothiophate iodide in 0.06% and timolol 0.5%, 1 drop OU BID. He is to be admitted to the hospital in the near future for an exploratory laparotomy under general anesthesia. Should the glaucoma therapy be continued up to the time of surgery?

Cholinesterase inhibitors decrease levels of pseudocholinesterase, the enzyme responsible for the hydrolysis and metabolism of succinylcholine and procaine.[56,57] Reports have appeared in the literature substantiating potentiation of these agents by concomitant use of cholinesterase inhibitors.[58,59] Therefore, J.W.'s echothiophate therapy should be changed to pilocarpine two to four weeks before the surgical procedure. Patients receiving cholinesterase inhibitors who exhibit signs of cholinergic overdose should be managed with pralidoxime and atropine.

Timolol and Epinephrine

9. Combined Therapy. S.H. has been treated with timolol 0.5%, 1 drop OU BID for approximately 8 weeks. IOP control has proven inadequate, and epinephrine hydrochloride 1%, 1 drop OU BID, has been added to his regimen. Are these two agents synergistic in the treatment of glaucoma?

Pharmacologically, timolol and epinephrine should be antagonistic. The additive effect of concurrent administration of timolol

and epinephrine is controversial. However, several reports have reached the general consensus that there is a small additive effect when timolol and epinephrine are coadministered.[204,232] Goldberg et al. conducted a short-term study in 1980 which found timolol to cause a greater reduction in IOP when added to epinephrine therapy than when epinephrine is added to timolol therapy.[60] An initial timolol dose often produces a large reduction in IOP, only to diminish in a few days.[60] It also is known that patients can develop tolerance to a beta blocker over time.

Korey et al. have expanded on Goldberg's short-term study conducted in 1980.[60,232] Korey et al. conducted a 90-day clinical trial of the concurrent administration of topical 0.5% timolol maleate and topical 2% epinephrine hydrochloride in ocular hypertensive subjects.[232] This study demonstrated that the ocular hypotensive effects of timolol and epinephrine are partially additive on a long-term (90-day) basis. Epinephrine became more effective and timolol less effective during the three months of therapy.[232] Epinephrine causes an initial increase in aqueous formation and improvements in outflow facility develop slowly over a period of time.[232] This may explain the results of the short-term study by Goldberg in 1980.

Other authors have suggested that the major therapeutic action of adrenergic agonists on outflow facility is fully blocked by timolol when epinephrine and timolol are used in combination.[204] The small additive effect probably is a result of the secondary alpha effect of epinephrine on inflow after the beta receptors in the ciliary processes have been blocked by the antagonist.[204] Nevertheless, the partial additive effects of epinephrine and timolol may be considered worthwhile for some patients.[204]

10. Comparison with Betaxolol and Epinephrine. Is the synergistic activity of epinephrine and betaxolol comparable to epinephrine and timolol?

In contrast to timolol, an outflow facility effect of adrenergic agents appears to be preserved in combination treatment regimens using betaxolol.[204] Allen and Epstein conducted a four-week study of epinephrine on IOP and facility of outflow when administered concurrently with timolol or betaxolol. Aqueous humor outflow did not improve when epinephrine was added to timolol therapy and there was not a significant additional reduction in IOP.[205] In contrast, the administration of epinephrine with betaxolol therapy provided a statistically significant additional decrease in IOP and outflow facility improved significantly. This study suggests that the lack of significant beta$_2$-blockade may be a prerequisite for an effective and therapeutic increase in outflow facility following treatment with epinephrine. Further studies are needed to confirm this hypothesis.

11. Drug Interactions. Are there other potentially significant interactions among drugs used to treat glaucoma and other agents?

In general, drugs with different pharmacologic actions appear to be at least partially additive in treating glaucoma. There is no rationale for combining agents with similar pharmacological action e.g., two parasympathomimetics, sympathomimetics). It is thought that such combinations are likely to increase adverse reactions.

In addition to epinephrine, timolol has additive effects with dipivefrin,[64,65] miotics, and carbonic anhydrase inhibitors.[66,67] Concomitant use of timolol and pilocarpine may achieve adequate control of IOP with twice a day administration of each drug.[58,69] Dipivefrin and echothiophate also are additive.[70]

Topical timolol has been shown to complicate digoxin toxicity in a 91-year-old woman.[71] Bradycardia has been observed secondary to an interaction between quinidine and ophthalmic timolol.[72] In addition, bradycardia with asystole has been observed in a patient receiving topical timolol plus oral verapamil.[73]

12. Adverse Effects. **Following 2 weeks of therapy with timolol and epinephrine, S.H. complains of "red eyes." Could this be due to the medications? Have additional adverse effects been reported with these preparations? How can these be avoided?**

Conjunctival hyperemia has been seen with timolol, although allergic conjunctivitis and conjunctival vessel vasoconstriction with rebound hyperemia have been associated more frequently with epinephrine therapy.

Other adverse effects associated with epinephrine include permanent corneal and conjunctival pigmentation which may occur in patients using epinephrine for longer than one year.[74,75] Hypersensitivity and supersensitivity with long-term use also have been reported with epinephrine.[76,77] A burning sensation upon administration of epinephrine preparations can be minimized by use of the borate salt which has a pH more compatible with the eye.[78] Discolored solutions of epinephrine should be discarded.

Ocular side effects associated with timolol include superficial punctate keratitis, corneal anesthesia, allergic blepharoconjunctivitis, and dry-eye syndrome.[79] Additional systemic side effects include palpitations, hypotension, and syncope, as well as CNS effects such as lightheadedness, mental depression, and disorientation.[24] Dermatologic reactions (rash, alopecia) and gastrointestinal upset have been reported.[80] There have been reports of hypoglycemia, worsening of myasthenia gravis in two patients, transient amaurosis fugax, sexual dysfunction, and respiratory distress and postoperative apnea in children.[81-87] The puncta may be occluded with the finger following administration to decrease the possibility of systemic absorption. Although timolol has been used effectively in many patients without significant side effects, the clinician should realize that topical timolol is not free of adverse local and systemic effects.

Postoperative Therapy

13. C.W., a 66 year-old female with a 10-year history of POAG, recently had cataract surgery. Before surgery, she was treated with pilocarpine 4%, 1 drop OU QID, and epinephrine hydrochloride 1%, 1 drop OU BID. Should this therapy be continued postoperatively?

Epinephrine should not be reinstituted, since macular edema will develop in 20% to 30% of aphakic patients treated with this agent.[3] Initial symptoms include blurring and distortion of vision which may occur within a few weeks to months. The maculopathy is reversible if therapy is stopped, and improvement usually is seen within one month, although it may take six or more weeks to recover maximum vision. C.W. should be treated with miotics and/or beta blockers.

Epinephrine Products

14. K.V., a 58-year-old woman, presents with a prescription for Glaucon 2%. The pharmacist informs her that he only stocks Epitrate 2% and he would like to substitute that product. Are these two preparations therapeutically equivalent?

The two are not equivalent. Glaucon is the hydrochloride salt of epinephrine, and Epitrate is the bitartrate salt. Eppy/N, epinephryl borate also is available. The 2% bitartrate salt contains 1.1% epinephrine free base equivalent, while the 1% concentration of the borate or hydrochloride salt is equivalent to 1% epinephrine free base. The bitartrate salt of epinephrine is used in the various pilocarpine-epinephrine combination products. There have been no significant therapeutic or toxic differences between the salts when used in equivalent concentrations.

Dipivefrin

15. What is dipivefrin (Propine)?

Dipivefrin, a prodrug, is hydrolyzed rapidly to epinephrine following its administration. It is more lipophilic than epineph-

rine, and this enhances its corneal penetration. Theoretically, use of the prodrug will produce the desired therapeutic effect with fewer side effects. Dipivefrin, available as a 0.1% solution which is administered twice a day, produces reductions in IOP that are comparable to 1% to 2% epinephrine.[88] Studies have shown the dipivefrin is better tolerated than epinephrine. However, reports of side effects similar to those occurring with epinephrine have been serious enough to require discontinuation of dipivefrin in certain cases.[89,90]

Liesegang reported the development of bulbar conjunctival follicles in 12 patients who received prolonged dipivefrin therapy for POAG;[91] these disappeared within one month after dipivefrin was discontinued. Five patients subsequently were treated successfully with epinephryl borate while others received no dipivefrin replacement or different therapy. The author suggests that this is an irritant reaction unique to dipivefrin, not a reaction to the preservatives or an allergic reaction.

Carbonic Anhydrase Inhibitors

16. B.A. is a 59-year-old male with a 6-year history of POAG which remained uncontrolled despite treatment with pilocarpine 4%, 1 drop OU Q 4 hr; epinephrine hydrochloride 2%, 1 drop OU BID; and timolol 0.5%, 1 drop OU BID. One month ago, echothiophate iodide 0.25% was prescribed in place of the pilocarpine. The IOP remains 36 mm Hg OU. How should B.A. be managed?

Maximal medical therapy for POAG utilizes topical agents plus carbonic anhydrase inhibitors. Table 49.2 lists available carbonic anhydrase inhibitors, their onset, duration of action, and usual doses. Acetazolamide (Diamox) is the carbonic anhydrase inhibitor most frequently used to treat POAG; it also is used in acute angle-closure glaucoma (see Question 19). Carbonic anhydrase occurs in high concentrations in the ciliary processes and retina of the eye. The exact mechanism by which carbonic anhydrase inhibitors lower IOP is not understood, but it is felt that these agents act to buffer an acid residue which may be present in secretory cells as a result of production of an alkaline aqueous humor. The net effect may be a 40% to 60% decrease in aqueous humor secretion, although it may be balanced by up to a 40% decrease in aqueous humor outflow.[1,92]

17. Adverse Effects. **If a carbonic anhydrase inhibitor is added to B.A.'s therapy, what side effects can be anticipated?**

Side effects commonly associated with carbonic anhydrase inhibitors are a frequent source of patient intolerance. Such effects include paresthesias (often transient) and gastrointestinal intolerance (anorexia, weight loss). Drowsiness, malaise, and depression may be overlooked and attributed to causes other than carbonic anhydrase inhibitor therapy. Administration of supplemental sodium acetate may reduce these symptoms in about 50% of patients treated with carbonic anhydrase inhibitors.[94] A metallic taste has been associated with carbonic anhydrase inhibitors, as have ureteral colic, hypokalemia, renal calculi formation, loss of libido, and systemic acidosis.[95-97] Metabolic acidosis has been seen less frequently with dichlorphenamide (Daranide), and formation of renal calculi is thought to be less with methazolamide (Neptazane) because there is no interference with urinary citrate excretion.[3]

Rarely, patients may develop dermatitis, myopia, agranulocytosis, and aplastic anemia. These side effects may be related to the fact that carbonic anhydrase inhibitors are sulfonamides.[98] Carbonic anhydrase inhibitors may cause alkalinization of the urine and complicate therapy with agents dependent upon urine pH for excretion or reabsorption. In patients treated with carbonic anhydrase inhibitors, the results of gonioscopy may be invalid, as these agents cause some widening of the anterior chamber angle.[2]

Table 49.2	Carbonic Anhydrase Inhibitors Used in Treatment of Glaucoma				
Agent	Strength	Onset (min)	Peak (hr)	Duration (hr)	Usual Dose
Acetazolamide injection	500 mg	5–10	—	2	500 mg
Acetazolamide tablets	125 mg 250 mg	120	4	6–8	250 mg QID
Acetazolamide sequels	500 mg	120	8–18	22–30	500 mg BID
Dichlorphenamide	50 mg	30	2–4	6–12	50 mg TID
Ethoxyzolamide	125 mg	90	3–4	7	125 mg QID
Methazolamide	50 mg	120	4–8	10–12	50 mg TID

Topical Carbonic Anhydrase Inhibitors. It is estimated that only about half of all patients with glaucoma can tolerate long-term systemic treatment with the carbonic anhydrase inhibitors in full dose.[233] The high incidence of drug-induced side effects probably contributes substantially to poor medication compliance.[233] To avoid the systemic side effects, investigators have researched the topical application of these drugs. Topical carbonic anhydrase inhibitors studied in the 1950s failed to reduce IOP; thus, research was abandoned for more than 20 years.[233] The topical route was ineffective in the earlier studies because the drug is not lipid soluble and has poor penetration through the lipophilic corneal epithelium.[234] Recently, there has been renewed interest in the development of an active topical carbonic anhydrase inhibitor.

A topical aminozolamide gel lowers IOP but causes a high incidence of bulbar infection and follicular conjunctivitis.[234,235] Other more promising topical carbonic anhydrase inhibitors that have been developed include MK 927, MK 417 (Sezolamide), and MK 507 (Dorzolamide). MK 417 is the more potent S-enantiomer of the racemic compound MK 927. In initial human studies, sezolamide produced a slightly greater decrease in IOP than MK 927.[234,236] Dorzolamide is the most potent topical carbonic anhydrase inhibitor that has been developed thus far. It is specific for carbonic anhydrase isoenzyme II, the isoenzyme present in ciliary processes. It appears to be more active in lowering IOP in primary open-angle glaucoma and ocular hypertension and may be somewhat better tolerated than sezolamide. Lippa et al. compared the efficacy of dorzolamide and sezolamide in a double-masked, randomized, placebo-controlled study in 82 patients with POAG or ocular hypertension.[237] Dorzolamide was somewhat more active than sezolamide, with a peak mean IOP reduction of 26.2% for dorzolamide and 22.5% for sezolamide. The difference between the treatments was not statistically significant. Effective topical carbonic anhydrase inhibitors are likely to be available in the near future. These agents have the potential to eliminate many of the intolerable side effects of systemic carbonic anhydrase inhibitors and offer an additional treatment option in patients with POAG or ocular hypertension.

Other Drugs

18. What other agents have been investigated for the management of open-angle glaucoma?

Ross demonstrated that topical isoproterenol caused a decrease in IOP that most likely was related to a decreased production of aqueous humor.[99] Krupin has shown that topical prazosin lowers IOP in rabbit eyes, and this effect appears to be due to a decreased production of aqueous humor.[100] Oral propranolol (Inderal), in doses of 20 to 40 mg administered three to four times a day, has been used in the long-term management of glaucoma.[101] In doses of 40 to 60 mg twice a day, oral propranolol plus pilocarpine 2% three times a day had ocular hypotensive effects comparable to

topical timolol 0.5% twice a day plus pilocarpine.[102] When both beta blockers were combined, a further additive effect was seen in more than half of the treated patients. Oral nadolol (Corgard) 20 to 40 mg every day was equivalent to timolol 0.25% to 0.5% twice a day in lowering IOP.[103]

Topical guanethidine has been shown to decrease IOP by decreasing aqueous humor production and has been used alone and in combination in the treatment of open-angle glaucoma.[104–107] Apraclonidine, an alpha agonist used to control or prevent post-surgical elevations in IOP which occur following argon laser trabeculoplasty or iridotomy, decreases IOP in patients with ocular hypertension or mild POAG.[108] Topical clonidine has been shown to decrease IOP while 1% delta-9-tetrahydrocannabinol was no different than placebo in its effect on IOP in 23 human volunteers.[109,110] Topical prostaglandin F-2 alpha-1-isopropylester has been shown to reduce IOP in normal volunteers.[112] Topical angiotensin-converting enzyme (ACE) inhibitors and verapamil 1.25 mg/mL have reduced IOP in patients with ocular hypertension and POAG.[113,114]

Angle-Closure Glaucoma
Treatment

19. D.H., a 72-year-old male, presents to the emergency room (ER) with an intensely red right eye, a "steamy" appearing cornea, complaints of haloes around lights, and extreme pain. A diagnosis of acute angle-closure glaucoma is made. How should D.H. be managed?

D.H. should be seen by an ophthalmologist since acute angle-closure glaucoma is a medical emergency. Medical treatment usually consists of pilocarpine 2% to 4%, one drop every five minutes for four to six administrations. It is recommended that the puncta be covered during administration to decrease the possibility of systemic absorption. Stronger miotics are contraindicated as they may potentiate angle-closure.[3] Topical timolol also has been used in acute angle-closure glaucoma, frequently in combination with pilocarpine.

Hyperosmotic Agents

Hyperosmotic agents act by creating an osmotic gradient between the plasma and ocular fluids.[120] Those agents which are confined to the extracellular fluid space (e.g., mannitol) provide greater effect on blood osmolality at the same dosage than do agents distributed in total body water.[120] Intravenously administered drugs provide a faster, somewhat greater effect than oral agents. Palatability may be a problem with oral agents and can be improved by serving these agents over crushed ice or with lemon juice or cola flavoring.

Orally, 50% glycerin is the usual drug of choice, and is administered in dosages of 1 to 1.5 gm/kg.[115] Isosorbide is an alternative, especially in diabetics because it is not metabolized to provide calories.[116] Ethyl alcohol (2 to 3 mL/kg) has been proven effective and may be helpful in emergency situations when other agents are unavailable.[117] Parenterally, mannitol is the drug of choice. It is administered in doses of 1 to 2 gm/kg, is not metabolized to provide calories, and may be used in patients with renal failure.[118,119]

Primary side effects of hyperosmotic agents include headache, nausea, vomiting, diuresis, and dehydration. It is important that the patient not be allowed to drink because this will counteract the osmotic effects of these agents. Precipitation of pulmonary edema and CHF have been reported with hyperosmotic agents, and an allergic reaction has been reported with mannitol.[121,122]

Acetazolamide (Diamox) 500 mg IV frequently is administered in addition to hyperosmotic agents (see Table 49.3).

Ocular Side Effects of Drugs

20. B.C., a 58-year-old male, has a history of hypertension managed with hydrochlorothiazide 50 mg/day. He takes amiodarone 800 mg/day for a cardiac arrhythmia and chlorpheniramine 12 mg BID PRN for allergies. One week ago, chlorpromazine 25 mg TID was added to his medication regimen. He complains of occasional blurred vision. Could these symptoms be related to his medications?

All of the drugs B.C. is taking have been associated with ocular side effects. Thiazide diuretics have been associated with acute myopia that may last from 24 to 48 hours.[123,124] However, hydrochlorothiazide is an unlikely cause of B.C.'s blurred vision considering its recent onset.

Amiodarone can cause keratopathy, but it is asymptomatic.[125,126] A high percentage of patients who receive this drug develop microdeposits within the corneal epithelium which resemble the verticillate keratopathy induced by chloroquine.[125] These corneal deposits are bilateral, dose and duration related, reversible, and unassociated with visual symptoms.

The primary ocular side effect associated with chlorpromazine is lens deposits. These deposits are rare when the total dose of chlorpromazine ingested is less than 500 gm.[123,124] During the past week B.C. could have received a maximum of 525 mg, assuming the medication was taken as prescribed. When lens deposits occur, they often do not affect vision appreciably.[123,124] This, along with the short duration of therapy, suggests that chlorpromazine lens deposits are not a cause of B.C.'s visual complaints. However, phenothiazines have anticholinergic side effects, and the blurred vision may be associated with mydriasis produced by chlorpromazine.

B.C. may be one of the approximately 1% of the population that experiences blurred vision with chlorpheniramine. This effect has been seen in patients receiving 12 to 14 mg/day.[123,124]

Table 49.4 outlines some of the more common ocular side effects associated with systemic medications. Each case should be evaluated individually and alternative therapy considered in intolerant patients.

Ocular Emergencies
Chemical Burns

21. S.J., a 24-year-old construction worker, has splashed an unidentified chemical in his eyes and enters a nearby pharmacy complaining of burning in both eyes. Should the pharmacist attempt to treat S.J. or refer him to the ER?

Chemical burns require immediate attention. The immediate treatment is copious irrigation using the most accessible source of water (e.g., shower, faucet, drinking fountain, hose, bathtub). After at least five minutes of initial irrigation, S.J. should be taken immediately to the ER. A water-soaked towel or cloth should be kept on his eyes during transport.

Other Ocular Emergencies

Health care professionals often are approached by patients with acute ocular problems. Before briefly reviewing these conditions, it is necessary to stress that patients should be referred to an ophthalmologist if the practitioner has even the slightest doubt regarding proper therapy. It generally is difficult to effectively evaluate the severity of ocular disorders without the benefit of training or a thorough ophthalmologic work-up.

In addition to chemical burns, there are other cases which can be considered ocular emergencies requiring immediate treatment.[1] Included in this listing is corneal trauma from abrasion or foreign bodies. Often the patient will complain of a gritty, scratchy feeling and will be aware of a foreign body's presence. Patients with corneal ulcers also should see an ophthalmologist immediately. The corneal tissue is an excellent culture medium for bacteria such as *Pseudomonas aeruginosa*, and therapy should be initiated as soon as possible to avoid corneal perforation and possible loss of the eye.[1]

Generally, cases of conjunctivitis are not emergency situations with the exception of gonococcal conjunctivitis. In suspected cases, the patient should see an ophthalmologist to avoid potential corneal perforation.[1] Patients with symptoms of red, tender, swollen eyelids with exophthalmos and mild pain may be suffering from orbital cellulitis or endophthalmitis which require immediate treatment with systemic antibiotics.

Signs and symptoms of acute angle-closure glaucoma, an ocular emergency, are reviewed in Question 19. Severe iritis causes extreme pain and photophobia and requires prompt treatment. Visual

(*Text continues on page 49-16*)

Table 49.3				Hyperosmotic Agents				
Generic	Mode of Admin.	Strength	Onset	Peak	Duration	Dose	Ocular Penetration	Distribution[a]
Urea	IV	30%	30–45 min (at 90–120 drops/min)	1 hr	5–6 hr	1–1.5 gm/kg	Good	TBW
Mannitol	IV	5%, 10%, 15%, 20%	30–60 min	1 hr	6–8 hr	1–2 gm/kg	Very poor	E
Glycerin	PO	50%	10–30 min	30 min	4–5 hr	1–1.5 gm/kg	Poor	E
Isosorbide	PO	45%	10–30 min	1 hr	5 hr	1.5–2 gm/kg	Good	TBW
Sodium ascorbate	IV	20%	70 min	1–2 hr	12 hr	2–5 mL/kg	Good	TBW
Ethyl Alcohol	PO	50%	—	—	—	2–3 mL/kg	Good	TBW

[a] TBW = Total body water; E = Extracellular water.

Table 49.4	Ocular Side Effects of Systemic Medications	
Drug Class	**Effect(s)**	**Clinical Remarks**
Analgesics		
Ibuprofen	Reduced vision	Rare; blurred vision has been reported in patients taking from four 200 mg tablets/week to 6 tablets/day. Changes in color vision rarely have been reported
Narcotics, including pentazocine	Miosis	Miosis often with morphine in normal doses: slight with other agents. The effect is secondary to CNS action on the pupilloconstrictor center[123,124]
	Tearing Irregular pupils Paresis of accommodation Diplopia	These effects are associated with narcotic withdrawal[123,124]
Antiarrhythmics		
Amiodarone	Keratopathy	Dose- and duration-related; resembles chloroquine keratopathy. Corneal deposits are bilateral, reversible, and unassociated with visual symptoms. Patients taking 100–200 mg/day have only minimal deposits. Deposits will occur in almost 100% of patients receiving 400 mg/day[123–126]
	Cataracts	Previously reported as insignificant, anterior subcapsular lens opacities have been associated with amiodarone therapy. Rarely, such opacities may progress, increasing in density and in the diffuse distribution of the deposits, ultimately covering an area somewhat larger than the undilated pupil's aperture. The mechanism for this effect is unclear, but like chlorpromazine, amiodarone is a photosensitizing agent. Given that the lens changes are limited largely to the pupillary aperture, light exposure may result in the lens changes
Anticholinergics		
Atropine Idicyclomine Glycopyrrolate Propantheline Scopolamine Trihexyphenidyl	Mydriasis Cycloplegia ↓ accommodation Photophobia	Systemic and transdermal anticholinergic agents may cause mydriasis and, less frequently, cycloplegia. Mydriasis may precipitate angle-closure glaucoma. Photophobia is related to the mydriasis. Accommodation ↓ for near objects[123,124,127]
Anticonvulsants		
Carbamazepine	Diplopia Blurred vision	Ocular adverse reactions when dosage >1–2 gm/day; disappear when dosage↓[123]
Phenytoin	Nystagmus Cataracts	Nystagmus in patients with high blood levels (>20 μg/mL); rarely occurs with other hydantoins. Cataracts may occur rarely with prolonged therapy[123, 124]
Trimethadione	Visual glare	A prolonged glare or dazzle occurs when eyes are exposed to light. The glare is reversible, occurs at the retinal level, and is more common in adolescents and adults; rarely in young children[123,124]
Anesthetics		
Propofol	Inability to open eyes	6 of 50 patients undergoing ENT procedures using standardized anesthesia with propofol were unable to open their eyes either spontaneously or in response to verbal commands. This effect lasted between 3–20 min after the end of anesthetic administration. 2 patients showed complete loss of ocular motility. This was a transient, myasthenic-like weakness
Antidepressants		
Tricyclic antidepressants (TCAs)	Mydriasis Cycloplegia	Mydriasis is most common ocular side effect of TCAs. Cycloplegia is rare. Reports of precipitation of angle-closure glaucoma[123,124]
Fluoxetine	Eye tics	Administration of fluoxetine 20–40 mg/day has been associated with paroxysmal contractions of the muscles around the lateral aspect of the eye. This effect occurred 3–4 weeks after initiation of fluoxetine therapy and resolved within 2 weeks of discontinuation
Antihistamines		
Chlorpheniramine	Blurred vision	Blurred vision occurs rarely (≈1% of patients taking 12–14 mg/day)[123,124]
	Mydriasis ↓ lacrimal secretions	Rare[123,124]
Antihypertensives		
Clonidine	Miosis	Miosis is seen in overdose[124]
	Dry itchy eyes	Rare[124]
Diazoxide	Lacrimation	About 20% experience lacrimation that may continue after drug is discontinued[123]
Guanethidine	Miosis Ptosis Conjunctivitis Blurred vision	Sporadically documented. 1 study reported a 17% incidence of blurred vision in patients taking guanethidine 70 mg/day[123,124]

Continued

Table 49.4	Ocular Side Effects of Systemic Medications (Continued)	
Drug Class	Effect(s)	Clinical Remarks
Reserpine	Miosis	Miosis is slight, but can last up to 1 week after a single dose[123,124]
	Conjunctivitis	Common, secondary to dilation of conjunctival blood vessels[123,124]
Anti-Infectives		
Amantadine	Corneal lesions	Diffuse, white punctate subepithelial corneal opacities have been reported, occasionally associated with superficial punctate keratitis. Onset has been 1–2 weeks after initiation of therapy with doses of 200–400 mg/day. Resolves with drug discontinuation
Chloramphenicol	Optic neuritis	Rare unless a total dose of 100 gm and duration >6 weeks are exceeded. Vision usually improves after the drug is discontinued[123,124]
Chloroquine	Corneal deposits	Some patients using ordinary doses may develop corneal deposits in a few months. The deposits are visible with use of a biomicroscope, appear as white-yellow in color, but are of no consequence[123,124]
	Retinopathy (macular degeneration)	Serious retinopathy when total dose >100 gm. Usually develops after 1–3 years; can occur in 6 months. Visual loss may be peripheral, with progression to central vision loss and disturbance of color vision. Rarely, effects such as blurred vision are seen earlier when larger doses (500–700 mg/day) are used. Macular changes may progress after drug is discontinued. These agents concentrate in pigmented tissue[123,124]
Ethambutol	Retrobulbar neuritis	At doses of 15 mg/kg/day, virtually void of ocular side effects. Such effects are rare at doses of 25 mg/kg/day for a duration of a few months. Patients treated for prolonged periods should have routine visual examinations including visual fields. Most effects are reversible after the drug is discontinued[123,124]
Gentamicin	Pseudotumor cerebri	Rare, but has been well documented with secondary papilledema and visual loss[123,124]
Isoniazid	Optic neuritis	Prevalence not well defined, but appears to be significantly less than peripheral neuritis. Evaluation difficult since most patients malnourished, chronic alcoholics, or receiving multiple medications. Pre-existing eye disease does not appear to be a predisposing factor[123,124]
Nalidixic acid	Visual sensations	Most common ocular side effect. Main feature a brightly-colored appearance of objects; occurs soon after the drug is taken. Although quinolone antibiotics are nalidixic acid derivatives, they have rarely been associated with these ocular side effects[123,124]
	Visual loss	Temporary effect (30 min–3 days)
	Papilledema	Primarily in infants and young children and secondary to ↑ intracranial pressure; reversible upon withdrawal of the drug
Sulfonamides	Myopia	Acute and reversible; most common ocular side effect[123,124]
	Conjunctivitis	Primarily with topical sulfathiazole, 4% incidence between the 5th and 9th day of therapy[123,124]
	Optic neuritis	Even in low dosages. Usually reversible with complete recovery of vision[123,124]
	Photosensitivity	Associated with use of sulfisoxazole lid margin therapy[133,134]
Tetracyclines	Myopia	Appears to be acute, transient, and rare[123,124]
	Papilledema	More frequently in children and infants than adults; rare[123,124]
Anti-Inflammatory Agents (Also see Analgesics; Corticosteroids)		
Gold	Corneal Conjunctival deposits	Deposition in the conjunctiva and superficial cornea more common than in the lens or deep cornea. Incidence in cornea of 40%–80% in total doses of 1.5 gm; visual acuity is unaffected. One reported case following oral therapy[123]
Indomethacin	↓ vision	Rare; also changes in color vision have been rarely reported[123,124]
Phenylbutazone	↓ vision	Most common ocular side effect with this drug may be due to ↑ lens hydration[123,124]
	Conjunctivitis Retinal hemorrhage	Occurs less frequently than ↓ vision. The conjunctivitis may be associated with development of Stevens-Johnson syndrome or an allergic reaction[123,124]
Antilipemic Agents		
Lovastatin	Cataracts	The crystalline lenses of hypercholesteremic patients were assessed before and after 48 weeks of treatment with lovastatin, 20–80 mg/day. Statistical analyses of the distribution of cortical, nuclear, and subcapsular opacities at 48 weeks showed no significant differences between placebo and lovastatin-treated groups. Visual acuity assessments also were not significantly different among the groups
Antineoplastic Agents		
Busulfan	Cataracts	Reported with high doses[123,124]

Continued

Table 49.4	Ocular Side Effects of Systemic Medications (Continued)	
Drug Class	**Effect(s)**	**Clinical Remarks**
Carmustine	Arterial narrowing Nerve fiber-layer infarcts Intraretinal hemorrhages	These ocular side effects are not well established. Evidence of delayed bilateral ocular toxicity developed in 2 of 50 patients treated with high-dose IV carmustine (800 mg/m^2). Symptoms of ocular toxicity became evident 4 weeks after IV treatment. Evidence of delayed ocular toxicity (mean onset 6 weeks) ipsilateral to the site of infusion developed in 7 of 10 patients treated with intra-arterial carotid doses of carmustine to a cumulative minimum of 450 mg/m^2 in 2 treatments[136]
Cytarabine	Keratoconjunctivitis Ocular burning Photophobia Blurred vision	Corneal toxicity and conjunctivitis have been reported with high-dose (3 gm/m^2) therapy[137,138]
Doxorubicin	Conjunctivitis Excessive tearing	May last for several days following treatment[123,124]
Fluorouracil	Ocular irritation Lacrimation	Reversible and seldom interfere with continued therapy[123,124]
Tamoxifen	Corneal opacities ↓ vision Retinopathy	Generally occur in patients taking higher than normal doses for 12–18 months[123,135]
Vinca alkaloids (especially vincristine)	Extraocular muscle paresis (EMP) Ptosis	The onset of EMP or paralysis may be seen as early as 2 weeks. Dose-related. Most recover fully when drug is discontinued[123,124]
Barbiturates	Miosis Mydriasis Disturbances in ocular movement Ptosis	Most significant ocular side effects occur in chronic users or in toxic states. Pupillary responses are variable; miosis seen most frequently except in toxicity when mydriasis predominates. Nystagmus and weakness in extraocular muscles may be seen. Chronic abusers have a characteristic ptosis[123,124]
Calcium Channel Blockers	Blurred vision Transient blindness	Primarily blurred vision; transient blindness at peak concentrations has been observed in several patients[123]
Corticosteroids	Cataracts	Posterior subcapsular cataracts have been associated with systemic corticosteroids. ↑ in patients who have received >15 mg/day of prednisone or its equivalent daily for periods >1 year.[123,124] Rare reports of bilateral posterior subcapsular cataracts associated with nasal aerosol or inhalation of beclomethasone dipropionate have been received. Most patients had received therapy for >5 years, often in higher than the recommended dosage. About 40% of patients also were receiving systemic corticosteroids. (Also see Question 26)
	↑ intraocular pressure	More common with topical corticosteroids than with systemic therapy. Of little consequence in patients without pre-existing glaucoma. Glaucoma patients should be monitored routinely if receiving systemic corticosteroids.[123,124] (See Question 25)
	Papilledema	Intracranial hypertension or pseudotumor cerebri from systemic corticosteroids has been well documented. The incidence appears to be greater in children than in adults; primarily associated with chronic therapy
Digitalis	Altered color vision, visual acuity	Changes in color vision. A glare phenomenon, and a snowy appearance in objects have been associated primarily with digitalis intoxication. In a small number of cases, reversible reduction in visual acuity has been noted. Also associated with changes in the visual fields[123,124]
	↓ intraocular pressure	Digitalis derivatives can ↓ intraocular pressure, but clinical use for glaucoma is not practical as the therapeutic systemic dose for this effect is very near the toxic dose[123,124]
Diuretics Carbonic anhydrase inhibitors Thiazides	Myopia	Acute myopia that may last from 24–48 hr. Probably caused by an ↑ in the anteroposterior diameter of the lens which may be reversible even if drug use continued[123,124]
Estrogens Clomiphene	Blurred vision Mydriasis Visual field changes Visual sensations	5% to 10% experience ocular side effects. Blurred vision is the most common effect, although visual sensations such as flashing lights, distortion of images, and various colored lights (primarily silver) may occur[123,124]
Oral contraceptives	Optic neuritis Pseudotumor cerebri Retrobulbar neuritis	Quite rare. In patients with retinal vascular abnormalities, use of OCs is questionable. There are numerous other possible ocular side effects associated with these agents, and further documentation is required[123,124]

Continued

Table 49.4		Ocular Side Effects of Systemic Medications (Continued)
Drug Class	Effect(s)	Clinical Remarks
Hypouricemics Allopurinol	Cataracts	Conflicting reports have suggested allopurinol may be associated with anterior and posterior lens capsule changes and with anterior subcapsular vacuoles. 42 cases of cataracts have been reported; these have been observed primarily in age groups in whom normal lens aging changes would not be expected. No cause and effect relationship has been proven[123,129–132]
Immune Modulators Interleukin 2	Visual deficits	Interleukin 2 visual complications have occurred during the 1st or 2nd treatment cycle, usually within 5–6 days of initiation of therapy. Ocular symptoms included diplopia, binocular negative scotomata (isolated areas of varying size and shape in which vision is absent or depressed. These are not perceived ordinarily but would be apparent upon completion of a visual field examination), and palinopsia (abnormal recurring visual imagery). In most cases, treatment was continued for the entire planned duration of therapy. Symptoms resolved after discontinuation
Phenothiazines Chlorpromazine	Deposits on the lens	Rare when total dose <0.5 kg. Visible after a total dose of 1 kg in most cases; incidence may ↑ to 90% after 2.5 kg or more. Usually, deposits do not affect vision appreciably. The cornea and conjunctiva may be affected after the lens shows pigment changes[123,124]
	Retinal pigment deposits	The number of reported cases is small; further documentation is necessary[123,124]
Thioridazine	Pigmentary retinopathy	Primarily associated with maximal daily dosages or average doses >1000 mg. Daily dosages up to 600 mg are relatively safe; 600–800 mg is uncertain, but rarely suspect. If >800 mg/day is used, periodic ophthalmoscopic examinations may uncover problems before visual acuity is compromised[123,124]

a CNS = Central nervous system; ENT = Ear, nose, and throat; OCs = Oral contraceptives.

loss, whether sudden, complete, or transient, or flashes of light may signify various potentially damaging ocular disorders including retinal artery occlusion, optic neuritis, amaurosis fugax, or retinal detachment. The patient should be evaluated by an ophthalmologist as soon as possible. Referral also is recommended for patients with pupil disorders, diplopia, nystagmus, or ocular hemorrhage.

Common Ocular Disorders

Stye (Hordeolum)

Sties are infections of the hair follicles or sebaceous glands of the eyelids. The most common infecting organism is *Staphylococcus aureus*. Treatment consists of hot, moist compresses and topical antibiotics (e.g., sulfacetamide). Over-the-counter products should not be recommended. Sties that do not respond to warm compresses within a few days should be evaluated by an ophthalmologist.

Conjunctivitis

Conjunctivitis is a common external eye problem which involves inflammation of the conjunctiva. The symptoms are a diffusely reddened eye with purulent or serous discharge accompanied by itching, smarting, stinging, or a scratching, "foreign body" sensation. Patients with pain, decreased vision, unequal distribution of redness, irregular pupils, or opacity should be referred immediately to an ophthalmologist, as these are signs of more serious eye disease.

Conjunctivitis can be bacterial, fungal, parasitic, viral, or allergic in origin. Most cases of bacterial conjunctivitis are caused by *S. aureas*, pneumococcus (in temperate climates), or *Haemophilus aegypticus* (in warm climates), although a number of other organisms may be responsible. The infection usually starts in one eye and is spread to the other by the hands. It also may be spread to other persons. Unlike bacterial conjunctivitis, corneal infections can obliterate vision rapidly; therefore, accurate diagnosis is important.

Acute Bacterial Conjunctivitis (Pink-Eye)

22. L.T. is a 6-year-old male with diffuse bilateral conjunctival redness that has been present for 2 days. A crusting discharge is deposited on his lashes and the corners of his eyes. His vision is normal and his pupils are round and equal. The diagnosis of acute bacterial conjunctivitis is made, and sodium sulfacetamide 10% ophthalmic drops, 2 drops OU Q 2 hr while awake, are prescribed. What other measures should be employed? What instructions should his parents receive?

Although treatment of typical bacterial conjunctivitis such as this is empirical, a culture should be obtained. Other ophthalmic antibiotic drops or ointments such as neomycin-polymyxin-B-gramicidin combination (Neosporin) also are used in these situations. Proper management of this infection also includes mechanical cleaning of the eyelids and hygienic measures which avoid spreading the infection to other children. The deposits should be removed as often as possible with moist cotton swabs or cotton-tipped applicators. A mild baby shampoo can be used to moisten the applicator. Firm adherent crusts may be softened with warm, moist compresses. Because this material is infectious, it should be disposed of in a sanitary fashion. The common use of washcloths by several individuals will spread bacterial conjunctivitis.

Allergic Conjunctivitis

23. N.V., a 10-year-old female, has had redness OU accompanied by "hay fever" for the past 2 months (June and July). There is no crusting on her eyelids, and her vision is normal; she rubs her eyes frequently because they itch. What treatments are available for N.V.'s allergic conjunctivitis?

Topical vasoconstrictors may be used to treat hyperemia, but they should not be used excessively since rebound congestion may occur. Antihistamine tablets or syrup will give considerable but temporary relief. The ideal treatment would be removal of the allergen, but this usually is impossible when the conjunctivitis is secondary to seasonal allergies. Topical corticosteroids provide dramatic relief, but their use must be limited because of potential adverse effects (see Ophthalmic Corticosteroids).

Sodium cromoglycate, a drug which inhibits the release of histamine in response to antigen, may be effective as an alternative for those who fail to respond to more conservative measures. However, commercially available sodium cromoglycate has been in short supply and solutions must be compounded for ophthalmic use. Lodoxamide tromethamine is a mast cell stabilizer with a mechanism of action similar to sodium cromoglycate. Comparative studies have documented that lodoxamide tromethamine 0.1% is at least as effective as sodium cromoglycate 2% to 4% in treating allergic ocular disorders including vernal keratoconjunctivitis.[230,231] Patients in these studies demonstrated more rapid and greater response when treated with lodoxamide, one drop four times a day.

Corneal Ulcers

24. T.S. presents with a diagnosis of bacterial corneal ulcer OD and prescriptions for "fortified gentamicin" and cefazolin eye drops which are not commercially available. What is the rationale for this therapy?

The initial choice of therapy for bacterial corneal ulcers frequently is based upon gram stain and clinical impression of the severity of the ulcer. Single or combination antimicrobial therapy may be prescribed. While there are many commercially available antimicrobial products, some clinicians feel that these products contain antimicrobial concentrations that are too low to effectively treat bacterial corneal ulcers.[185,186]

Topical antimicrobials for the treatment of bacterial corneal ulcers may be prepared from parenteral antimicrobials or by the addition of parenteral antimicrobials to "fortify" commercially available products. Commonly prescribed products include bacitracin 5000 to 10,000 U/mL, cefazolin 33 to 100 mg/mL, gentamicin or tobramycin 9.1 to 13.6 mg/mL, and vancomycin 25 to 50 mg/mL. "Fortified gentamicin" usually is prepared by adding 80 mg of parenteral gentamicin to the commercially available gentamicin ophthalmic solution. The final concentration of this solution is 13.6 mg/mL. Cefazolin ophthalmic solution is prepared by reconstituting 500 mg parenteral cefazolin with 2 mL sterile normal saline. Two milliliters of artificial tear solution are removed from a commercially available 15 mL bottle and replaced with the 2 mL reconstituted cefazolin solution. This results in a final cefazolin concentration of 33 mg/mL. Comprehensive guidelines for preparation of such products are included in *Extemporaneous Ophthalmic Preparations*.[203] Therapy initially may be administered as frequently as every 15 to 30 minutes with extension of intervals as the ulcer resolves.[185,186]

Ophthalmic Corticosteroids
Comparison of Preparations

The various topical ophthalmic corticosteroid preparations are described in Table 49.5. The salt form affects the ability of the preparation to penetrate the cornea; biphasic salts penetrate the intact cornea better than water-soluble salts. However, ability to penetrate the cornea does not indicate increased therapeutic effectiveness. Prednisolone acetate 1% and fluorometholone acetate 0.1% have the best anti-inflammatory effects.[139–141,187]

Adverse Effects
Increased Intraocular Pressure

25. L.P. has been treated with topical prednisolone acetate 1%, 1 drop OU QID for 8 weeks. Before therapy, IOP measured 16 mm Hg OU, but on the last follow-up visit, readings were 26 mm Hg OD and 22 mm Hg OS. Assess these observations.

It is likely that L.P.'s elevated intraocular pressure is related to topical steroid therapy. Armalay and Becker et al. have shown that three genetically distinct subgroups of random populations respond with various increases in IOP associated with the administration of topical corticosteroid preparations (see Table 49.6).[142,143] One retrospective follow-up assessment indicated that 13% of high corticosteroid responders developed POAG and 63.8% developed ocular hypertension. No low responders developed POAG, and only 2.4% developed ocular hypertension.[144] Although corticosteroid-induced increases in IOP are associated most frequently with topical preparations, systemic corticosteroids may cause a similar response, although the magnitude is somewhat less.[145]

Table 49.5		Corticosteroids for Ophthalmic Use		
Agent	Salt Form	Strength	Dosage Form	% Decrease in Corneal Inflammation
Clobetasone	Butyrate	0.1%	—a	26%
	Butyrate	0.5%	—	44%
Dexamethasone	Alcohol (Maxidex, Decadron)	0.1%	Suspension	40%
	Na phosphate (Decadron)	0.1%	Solution	19%
	Na phosphate	0.05%	Ointment	12%
Fluorometholone	—	0.1%	Suspension	31%
	—	0.25%	Suspension	35%
	Acetate (Flarex)	0.1%	Suspension	48%
Prednisolone	Acetate (Econopred, Pred Mild)	0.12%	Suspension	34%
	Acetate (Econopred Plus, Pred Forte)	1.0%	Suspension	52%
	Na phosphate (Inflamase Mild)	0.12%	Solution	23%
	Na phosphate (Inflamase Forte)	1.0%	Solution	28%

a There is no dosage form commercially available yet in the United States.

Table 49.6				IOP Response to Topical Steroids in Random Populations			
Author	Parameter of Response	No. of Subjects	Low	Medium	High	Mean
Armalay[142]	↑ of pressure in eye medicated with 0.1% dexamethasone	80	≤5 mm Hg 66%	6–15 mm Hg 29%	≥16 mm Hg 5%	5.5 mm Hg
Becker[143]	Final pressure in eye medicated for 6 weeks with 0.1% betamethasone	50	≤19 mm Hg 70%	20–30 mm Hg 26%	≥32 mm Hg 4%	17.0 mm Hg
	Time to maximum response	—	2 weeks	4 weeks	4 weeks	—

Topical corticosteroids exert their effects by decreasing aqueous humor outflow, while systemic corticosteroids may increase aqueous humor production.[145] The effects on IOP apparently are unrelated to the corticosteroid's ability to penetrate the cornea. Dexamethasone has been associated with the greatest IOP increase.[146] Fluorometholone and less potent medrysone have been associated with small, although sometimes significant, increases in IOP.[147,188] The pressure response often, but not always, is reversible upon discontinuation of the offending agent. In those subjects with prolonged IOP elevation, glaucomatous field defects are more likely to develop in corticosteroid-responsive patients.[148]

Cataracts

26. G.A., who had asthma, has been taking prednisone 10 mg/day for 1 year. A routine ophthalmic examination revealed early cataract formation. Could this be related to the prednisone?

Yes. Both oral and topical corticosteroids may cause cataracts. Available data show an approximate 23% incidence of posterior subcapsular cataract (PSC) formation in patients treated with 10 to 16 mg/day of prednisone orally or its equivalent for one year or more.[149,150] There is an estimated 70% or greater occurrence of PSC in patients treated with dosages in excess of 16 mg/day over the same time period. Patients receiving less than 10 mg/day prednisone or its equivalent are unlikely to develop PSC, although some contend that the concept of a "safe" dose should be abandoned because of variable patient sensitivity to this side effect.[151] As illustrated by G.A., the cataracts cause few subjective complaints and little measurable decrease in visual acuity. Although systemic corticosteroids primarily are implicated, use of topical corticosteroids also has been associated with PSC formation.[152] Patients treated with every-other-day corticosteroids may be at lower risk for PSC formation.[153] Any patient receiving long-term corticosteroids should receive routine ophthalmic follow-up.

Systemic Side Effects from Ophthalmic Medication

27. J.F., a 62-year-old female, received 1 drop of phenylephrine 10% in each eye to dilate the pupils. Shortly after administration, her BP increased to 210/130 mm Hg for 5 minutes, and she became confused. Are reactions of this type common in patients receiving topical phenylephrine? Have other topical ophthalmic medications been associated with systemic effects?

One group of investigators reported 33 cases of possible adverse effects associated with topical phenylephrine 10%.[154] However, when phenylephrine 10% or tropicamide (Mydriacyl) 1% was administered to 150 patients in a double-blind study, no statistically significant differences between experimental and control groups with respect to blood pressure or pulse rate were observed.[155] Care should be taken when phenylephrine 10% is administered in patients with hypertension or cardiac abnormalities in whom systemic absorption could be hazardous. No similar reports have been associated with topical use of phenylephrine 2.5%.

In addition to the previously mentioned systemic effects of cholinergic agents (Question 4), epinephrine (Question 2), and timolol (Question 2) side effects such as psychosis have been associated with topical atropine, cyclopentolate (Cyclogyl), and scopolamine.[156–158] There also have been reports of death associated with topical atropine.[179] Ataxia has been seen with use of homatropine, while only a single report of unconsciousness has been associated with the use of tropicamide.[159,160]

Topical chloramphenicol-polymyxin-B sulfate ophthalmic ointment has been associated with bone marrow aplasia following intermittent use for four months.[161] A cushingoid reaction has been reported in a 30-month-old female treated with dexamethasone alcohol (Maxidex) four times a day in both eyes for 14 months.[162]

Ocular Nonsteroidal Anti-Inflammatory Drugs (NSAIDs)

28. W.A. is scheduled to undergo cataract extraction with implantation of an intraocular lens. Preoperative orders include administration of flurbiprofen 0.03% to inhibit intraoperative miosis. The formulary only includes diclofenac 0.1%. Is this a suitable alternative to flurbiprofen?

Within the eye, prostaglandins produce various effects including miosis, increased vascular permeability of the blood-ocular barrier, conjunctival hyperemia, and changes in IOP.[189] Ocular instillation of NSAIDs provides ocular tissue levels adequate to inhibit prostaglandin synthesis and reduce these prostaglandin-mediated ocular effects.[189] Commercially available ocular NSAIDs include the phenylacetic acid derivative, diclofenac, and the phenylalkanoic acids flurbiprofen, ketorolac, and suprofen. (See Table 49.7.) These agents are well tolerated, but there is transient burning and stinging upon installation. While the ocular NSAIDs share a similar mechanism of action, there is considerable variability in their studied and approved indications. Published data suggest there are minor clinical differences among these agents which probably are insignificant. In this case, diclofenac is likely to be an acceptable alternative to flurbiprofen, despite the lack of an approved indication for inhibition of intraoperative miosis. Table 49.7 provides an overview of ocular NSAIDs.

Ocular Herpes Simplex Virus (HSV) Infections

Treatment

29. P.B., a 34-year-old male, presents with a 2-week history of a red, irritated left eye with watery discharge. Recently, vision in his left eye became blurred, and he complained of light

sensitivity. **A slit lamp examination with rose bengal stain revealed a multibranched corneal epithelial defect. This dendritic ulcer is the hallmark of ocular *Herpes simplex* (Type I) infection. What is the therapy of choice?**

There are approximately 300,000 to 500,000 cases of corneal herpes each year.[163] Before 1962, the standard form of therapy for epithelial herpetic keratitis was debridement, in which the margins of the corneal ulcers are scraped to remove the virus-laden cells.

Idoxuridine (IDU)

In 1962, the antimetabolite idoxuridine (Stoxil) was marketed. IDU is structurally similar to thymidine and alters DNA synthesis of the herpes simplex virus. IDU is applied topically to the eye in the form of a 0.1% solution or 0.5% ointment.

Since continued presence of the antimetabolite IDU is necessary to inhibit multiplication of HSV, the recommended dose is one drop of solution in each infected eye every hour during the day and every two hours throughout the night until improvement is confirmed by ophthalmic examination. The dose then may be reduced to one drop every two hours during the day and every four hours throughout the night. IDU therapy should be continued for three to five days after healing is complete to prevent recurrence of the infection. Alternatively, IDU ointment may be applied four to five times daily as single-agent therapy or as a nighttime medication when the solution is used during the day.

Idoxuridine therapy is efficacious: approximately 80% to 85% of initial dendritic ulcers resolve within two weeks.[164] Since IDU does not penetrate well into and through the cornea, it has no proven effectiveness in the treatment of herpetic iritis or stromal keratitis.

Patients occasionally experience ocular irritation, pain, inflammation, and photophobia following topical administration of IDU. A temporary visual haze may occur in patients using the ointment form as would be expected from the use of any ocular ointment. IDU therapy also may cause contact dermatitis, punctate epithelial keratopathy, follicular conjunctivitis, and thickening of the lid margins associated with stenosis of the lacrimal canaliculi. IDU's major disadvantage may be that it also is incorporated into host DNA, thus inhibiting the replication of normal, noninfected cells. This nonselectivity actually could delay healing of the dendritic lesions as normal cells may regenerate at a slower rate. The emergence of IDU-resistant strains, the potential for toxicity, and the inability of IDU to prevent recurrence of latent infection led to the search for more effective and less toxic antiherpetic agents.

Vidarabine (Vira-A)

Vidarabine was the second clinically useful drug to be developed for use against ocular HSV infections. Its exact mechanism of antiviral activity has not been determined, although the primary effect, like that of IDU, appears to be inhibition of DNA synthesis.[165] Vidarabine is similar to IDU with respect to its effect on epithelial herpes keratitis.

Vidarabine is available as a 3% ophthalmic ointment for administration into the conjunctival sac. Approximately one-half inch of ointment should be applied five times daily (at three-hour intervals) until re-epithelialization has occurred. An additional seven days of treatment at reduced dosages (e.g., twice daily) is advised to prevent recurrence of the infection.

Adverse reactions associated with topical vidarabine are similar to those described for IDU, including increased lacrimation, foreign body sensation, burning, and ocular irritation. Vidarabine appears to interfere less with the growth of normal cells as the corneal epithelium heals. Vidarabine has been proven especially beneficial in patients who are hypersensitive to IDU or who are infected with IDU-resistant viral strains.

Trifluridine (Viroptic)

At the present time, trifluridine is the drug of choice for the treatment of ocular herpes.[166] *In vitro*, trifluridine's mechanism of action is similar to IDU. Trifluridine also inhibits thymidylate synthase, an enzyme required for DNA synthesis. The actual *in vivo* antiviral effects of trifluridine have not been determined.

Trifluridine is available as a 1% ophthalmic solution. One drop should be instilled into the affected eye every two hours while awake with a maximum daily dose of nine drops. Following re-epithelialization, application of trifluridine should be continued for

Table 49.7	Ocular Non-Steroidal Anti-Inflammatory Drugs	
Indication	**Drug**	**Dose(s)**
Inhibition of intraoperative miosis	Flurbiprofen 0.03%[a,190]	1 drop Q 30 min beginning 2 hr before surgery
	Suprofen 1%[a,191]	2 drops 3, 2, and 1 hr before surgery
	Diclofenac 0.1%[192]	3 reported regimens: 1 drop Q 15–30 min for 4 doses; 1 drop TID for 2 days preoperatively; or 1 drop at 2 hr, 1 hr, and 15 min before surgery
Anti-inflammatory postcataract surgery	Diclofenac 0.1%[a,193]	1 drop BID–QID including 24-hr preoperative administration
	Ketorolac 0.5%[194]	1 drop TID beginning 1 day before surgery
Prevention/treatment of cystoid macular edema	Diclofenac 0.1%[192]	2 drops 5 times preoperatively followed by 1 drop 3–5 times daily
	Ketorolac 0.5%[195–197]	1 drop TID–QID including 24-hour preoperative administration
	Suprofen 1%[198]	2 drops every hour for 3 hr before surgery and Q 4 hr while awake thereafter
Ocular inflammatory conditions (iritis, iridocyclitis, episcleritis)	Diclofenac 0.1%[192]	1 drop QID
Seasonal allergic conjunctivitis	Ketorolac 0.5%[a,199]	1 drop QID
Contact-lens associated giant papillary conjunctivitis	Suprofen 1%[200,201]	2 drops QID
Vernal conjunctivitis	Suprofen 1%[202]	2 drops QID

[a] Approved indication.

an additional seven days at a reduced dosage of one drop every four hours while awake with a minimum of five drops daily. Continuous administration for periods exceeding 21 days is not recommended because of potential ocular toxicity.

Clinical trials have proven trifluridine to be more effective than IDU and vidarabine. Approximately 96% of treated herpetic corneal ulcers are healed within two weeks.[167] Therapeutic levels of trifluridine can be found in the aqueous humor after topical administration of a 1% solution enhancing its possible effectiveness in the treatment of stromal keratitis and uveitis.[163] Other advantages of trifluridine include its effectiveness in treating HSV infections resistant to IDU and/or vidarabine and its lack of cross-toxicity or allergenicity with these agents.[167]

Despite the apparent superiority of trifluridine over its antiviral predecessors, it is not without disadvantages. Trifluridine is activated by noninfected corneal cells and is incorporated into cellular as well as viral DNA. Punctate lesions in the corneal epithelium are clinical manifestations of trifluridine cytotoxicity.[168] Yet these effects seem to occur less frequently than with IDU and vidarabine.

Acyclovir

In vitro studies (plaque inhibition assays) have found acyclovir to have five to ten times the activity of IDU and trifluridine and more than 100 times the activity of vidarabine against several strains of Type I and Type II Herpes simplex virus.[169] In experimental (rabbit) Herpes simplex keratitis, 3% acyclovir ointment was significantly more effective than 0.5% IDU and 3% vidarabine ointments in healing established herpes epithelial ulcerations at a faster rate and in eliminating the virus.[170] Rabbit ocular models were used because of their similarity to human eyes. Other rabbit studies have shown similarities in the activities of acyclovir, IDU, vidarabine, and trifluridine in therapy of superficial dendritic ulcers.[163,171,172] As with rabbit models, ulcerative corneal epithelial lesions in humans appear to respond similarly to acyclovir, IDU, and trifluridine, with no statistically significant differences evident in most studies.[173] Acyclovir's apparent superiority lies in its lack of toxicity to normal host cells. Administered systemically, acyclovir shows promise in the management of latent herpes viral infections.[164] Based upon its high degree of viral specificity and apparent lack of toxicity, acyclovir presents a potentially important addition to currently available ocular antiviral arsenal. However, since no ophthalmic preparation currently is available, trifluridine is the drug of choice. (For more information on acyclovir and acyclovir resistance see Chapters 68: Human Immunodeficiency Virus (HIV) Infection and 70: Viral Infections.)

Acknowledgment

We gratefully acknowledge Suellyn Jacko-Sorenson's contributions to this chapter.

References

1   **Vaughan D et al.** General Ophthalmology. 13th ed. Norwalk, CT: Appleton and Lange; 1992.

2   **Chandler PA et al.** Glaucoma. 3rd ed. Philadelphia: Lea and Febiger; 1986.

3   **Kolker AE et al.** Becker-Shaffer's Diagnosis and Therapy of the Glaucomas. 6th ed. St. Louis: CV Mosby; 1989.

4   **Grant WM.** Action of drugs on movement of ocular fluids. In: Annual Reviews of Pharmacology. 9th vol. Palo Alto: Annual Reviews Inc.; 1969:85.

5   **Grant WM.** Ocular complications of drugs. JAMA. 1969;207:2089.

6   **Grant WM.** Systemic drugs and adverse influence on ocular pressure. In: Symposium on Ocular Therapy. 3rd vol. St. Louis: CV Mosby; 1968:57.

7   **Davies DM.** Textbook of Adverse Drug Reactions. New York: Oxford University Press; 1977.

8   **Dukes M.** Meyler's Side Effects of Drugs, annual 1. Amsterdam: Excerpta Medica; 1977.

9   **Kirsch R.** Glaucoma following cataract extraction associated with use of alpha-chymotrypsin. Arch Ophthalmol. 1964;72:612.

10   **Ballin N et al.** Systemic effects of epinephrine applied topically to the eye. Invest Ophthalmol. 1966;5:125.

11   **Novack GD.** Ophthalmic beta-blockers since timolol. Surv Ophthalmol. 1987;31:307.

12   **Zimmerman T et al.** Timolol and facility of outflow. Invest Ophthalmol Vis Sci. 1977;16:623.

13   **Sonntag JR et al.** Effect of timolol therapy on outflow facility. Invest Ophthalmol Vis Sci. 1978;17:293.

14   **Zimmerman TJ et al.** Timolol: dose response and duration of action. Arch Ophthalmol. 1977;95:605.

15   **Kwitko GM et al.** Bilateral effects of long-term monocular timolol therapy. Am J Ophthalmol. 1987;104:591.

16   **Boger WP et al.** Long-term experience with timolol ophthalmic solution in patients with open-angle glaucoma. Ophthalmology. 1978;85:259.

17   **Heel RC et al.** Timolol: a review of its therapeutic efficacy in the topical treatment of glaucoma. Drugs. 1979;17:38.

18   **Goethals M.** Ten-year follow-up of timolol-treated open-angle glaucoma (summary). Surv Ophthalmol. 1989; 33:S463.

19   **Zimmerman TJ et al.** Safety and efficacy of timolol in pediatric glaucoma. Surv Ophthalmol. 1983;28:262.

20   **Boger WP et al.** Clinical trials comparing timolol ophthalmic solution to pilocarpine in open-angle glaucoma. Am J Ophthalmol. 1978;86:8.

21   **Moss AP et al.** A comparison of the effects of timolol and epinephrine on intraocular pressure. Am J Ophthalmol. 1978;86:489.

22   **Britman NA.** Cardiac effects of topical timolol. N Engl J Med. 1979;300:566.

23   **Kim JW et al.** Timolol-induced bradycardia. Anesth Analg. 1980;59:301.

24   **McMahon CD et al.** Adverse effects experienced by patients taking timolol. Am J Ophthalmol. 1979;88:736.

25   **Guzman CA.** Exacerbation of bronchorrhea induced by topical timolol. Am Rev Respir Dis. 1980;121:899.

26   **Jones FC et al.** Exacerbation of asthma by timolol. N Engl J Med. 1979;301:270.

27   **Schmitt CJ et al.** Penetration of timolol into the rabbit eye. Arch Ophthalmol. 1980;98:547.

28   **Affrime MD et al.** Dynamics and kinetics of ophthalmic timolol. Clin Pharmacol Ther. 1980;27:471.

29   **Passo MS et al.** Plasma timolol in glaucoma patients. Ophthalmology. 1984; 91:1361.

30   **Hayes LP et al.** Timolol side effects and inadvertent overdosing. J Am Geriatr Soc. 1989;37:261.

31   **Lustgarten JS, Podos SM.** Topical timolol and the nursing mother. Arch Ophthalmol. 1983;101:1381.

32   **Partamian LG et al.** A dose-response study of the effect of levobunolol on ocular hypertension. Am J Ophthalmol. 1983;95:229.

33   **Bensinger RE et al.** Levobunolol: a three-month efficacy study in the treatment of glaucoma and ocular hypertension. Arch Ophthalmol. 1985;103:375.

34   **Berson FG.** Levobunolol compared with timolol for the long-term control of elevated intraocular pressure. Arch Ophthalmol. 1985;103:379.

35   **Berson FG et al.** Levobunolol: a beta-adrenoreceptor antagonist effective in the long-term treatment of glaucoma. Ophthalmology. 1985;92:1271.

36   **Radius RL.** Use of betaxolol in the reduction of elevated intraocular pressure. Arch Ophthalmol. 1983;101:898.

37   **Caldwell DR et al.** Effects of topical betaxolol in ocular hypertensive patients. Arch Ophthalmol. 1984;102: 539.

38   **Levy NS et al.** A controlled comparison of betaxolol and timolol with long-term evaluation of safety and efficacy. Glaucoma. 1985;7:54.

39   **Berry DP et al.** Betaxolol and timolol: a comparison of efficacy and side effects. Arch Ophthalmol. 1984;102:42.

40   **Stewart RH et al.** Betaxolol vs. timolol: a six-month double-blind compar-ison. Arch Ophthalmol. 1986;104:46.

41   **Allen RC et al.** A double-masked comparison of betaxolol vs. timolol in the treatment of open-angle glaucoma. Am J Ophthalmol. 1986;101:535.

42   **Atkins JM et al.** Cardiovascular effects of topical beta-blockers during exercise. Am J Ophthalmol. 1985;99: 173.

43   **Weinreb RN et al.** Long-term betaxolol therapy in glaucoma patients with pulmonary disease. Am J Ophthalmol. 1988;106:162.

44   **VanBuskirk EM et al.** Betaxolol in patients with glaucoma and asthma. Am J Ophthalmol. 1986;101:531.

45   **Alpar JJ.** Miotics and retinal detachment. Ann Ophthalmol. 1979;11:395.

46   **Ellis PP.** Systemic effects of locally applied anticholinesterase agents. Invest Ophthalmol Vis Sci. 1966;5:146.

47   **Hiscox PEA et al.** Cardiac arrest occurring in a patient on echothiophate iodide therapy. Am J Ophthalmol. 1965;60:425.

48   **Stewart RH et al.** Long acting pilocarpine gel: a dose response in ocular hypertensive subjects. Glaucoma. 1984; 6:182.

49   **Johnson DH et al.** One-year multicenter clinical trial of pilocarpine gel. Am J Ophthalmol. 1984;97:723.

50   **Goldberg I et al.** Efficacy and patient acceptance of pilocarpine gel. Am J Ophthalmol. 1979;88:843.

51   **Harris LS.** Dose response analysis of echothiophate iodide. Arch Ophthalmol. 1971;86:502.

52   **Chin NB et al.** Iris cysts and miotics. Arch Ophthalmol. 1964;71:611.

53   **Shaffer R et al.** Anticholinesterase drugs and cataracts. Am J Ophthalmol. 1966;62:613.

54 deRoetth A. Lens opacities in glaucoma patients on phospholine iodide therapy. Am J Ophthalmol. 1966;62: 619.

55 Axelsson U et al. The frequency of cataract after miotic therapy. Acta Ophthalmol (Copenh) 1966;44:421.

56 Wahl JW et al. Echothiophate iodide. Am J Ophthalmol. 1965;60:419.

57 deRoetth A et al. Blood cholinesterase activity of glaucoma patients treated with phospholine iodide. Am J Ophthalmol. 1966;62:834.

58 Pantuck EF. Echothiophate iodide eye drops and prolonged response to suxamethonium. Br J Anaesth. 1966;38: 406.

59 Gesztes T. Prolonged apnea after suxamethonium injection associated with eye drops containing an anticholinesterase agent. Br J Anaesth. 1966;38: 408.

60 Goldberg I et al. Timolol and epinephrine. A clinical study of ocular interactions. Arch Ophthalmol. 1980;98: 484.

61 Thomas JV. Ocular adrenergic receptor sites pertinent to aqueous humor dynamics. Ann Ophthalmol. 1980;12:96.

62 Cyrlin MN et al. Additive effect of epinephrine to timolol therapy in primary open angle glaucoma. Arch Ophthalmol. 1982;100:414.

63 Knupp JA et al. Combined timolol and epinephrine therapy for open angle glaucoma. Surv Ophthalmol. 1983;28: 280.

64 Keates EU, Stone RA. Safety and effectiveness of concomitant administration of dipivefrin and timolol. Am J Ophthalmol. 1981;91:243.

65 Cebon L et al. Experience with dipivalyl epinephrine: its effectiveness alone or in combination and its side effects. Aust J Ophthalmol. 1983;11:159.

66 Kass MA. Efficacy of combining timolol with other antiglaucoma medications. Surv Ophthalmol. 1983;28:274.

67 Berson FG, Epstein DL. Separate and combined effects of timolol maleate and acetazolamide in open-angle glaucoma. Am J Ophthalmol. 1981;92:788.

68 Airaksinen PJ et al. A double-masked study of timolol and pilocarpine combined. Am J Ophthalmol. 1988;104:587.

69 Soderstrom MB et al. Timolol-pilocarpine combined vs. timolol and pilocarpine given separately. Am J Ophthalmol. 1989;107:465.

70 Mindel JS et al. Dipivefrin and echothiophate: efficacy of combined use in human beings. Arch Ophthalmol. 1981; 99:1583.

71 Rynne MV. Timolol toxicity: ophthalmic medication complicating systemic disease. J Maine Med Assoc. 1980;71: 82.

72 Dinai Y et al. Bradycardia induced by interaction between quinidine and ophthalmic timolol. Ann Intern Med. 1985; 103:890.

73 Sinclair NI, Benzie JL. Timolol eye drops and verapamil—a dangerous combination. Med J Aust. 1983;1:548.

74 Corwin ME et al. Conjunctival melanin depositions. Arch Ophthalmol. 1963;69:317.

75 Cleasby G et al. Epinephrine pigmentation of the cornea. Arch Ophthalmol. 1967;78:74.

76 Aronson SB et al. Ocular hypersensi-

tivity to epinephrine. Invest Ophthalmol Vis Sci. 1966;5:75.

77 Flach A et al. Supersensitivity to topical epinephrine after long-term epinephrine therapy. Arch Ophthalmol. 1980;98:482.

78 Vaughan D et al. A new stabilized form of epinephrine for the treatment of open-angle glaucoma. Arch Ophthalmol. 1961;66:232.

79 VanBuskirk EM. Corneal anesthesia after timolol maleate therapy. Am J Ophthalmol. 1979;88:739.

80 Munroe EP et al. Systemic side effects associated with the ophthalmic administration of timolol. Drug Intell Clin Pharm. 1985;19:85.

81 Angelo-Nielsen K. Timolol topically and diabetes mellitus. JAMA. 1980; 244:2263.

82 Shavitz S. Timolol and myasthenia gravis. Am J Ophthalmol. 1979;242: 1611.

83 Coppeto JR. Timolol-associated myasthenia gravis. Am J Ophthalmol. 1984;98:244.

84 Coppeto JR. Transient ischemic attacks and amaurosis fugax from timolol. Ann Ophthalmol. 1985;17:64.

85 Fraunfelder FT, Meyer SM. Sexual dysfunction secondary to topical ophthalmic timolol. JAMA. 1985;253: 3092.

86 Williams T, Ginther WH. Hazard of ophthalmic timolol. N Engl J Med. 1982;306:1485.

87 Bailey PL. Timolol and postoperative apnea in neonates and young infants. Anesthesiology. 1984;61:622.

88 Theodore J et al. External ocular toxicity of dipivalyl epinephrine. Am J Ophthalmol. 1979;88:1013.

89 Kohn AN et al. Clinical comparison of dipivalyl epinephrine and epinephrine in the treatment of glaucoma. Am J Ophthalmol. 1979;87:196.

90 Yablonski ME et al. Dipivefrin use in patients with intolerance to topically applied epinephrine. Arch Ophthalmol. 1977;95:2157.

91 Liesegang TJ. Bulbar conjunctival follicles associated with dipivefrin therapy. Ophthalmology. 1985;92:228.

92 Galin MA et al. Acetazolamide and outflow facility. Arch Ophthalmol. 1966;76:493.

93 Thomas RP et al. Acetazolamide and ocular tension. Am J Ophthalmol. 1965;60:241.

94 Arrigg CA et al. The influence of supplemental sodium acetate on carbonic anhydrase inhibitor-induced side effects. Arch Ophthalmol. 1981;99:1969.

95 Pepys MB. Acetazolamide and renal stone formation. Lancet. 1970;1:837.

96 Parfitt AM. Acetazolamide and sodium bicarbonate-induced nephrocalcinosis and nephrolithiasis. Arch Intern Med. 1969;124:736.

97 Wallace TR et al. Decreased libido—a side effect of carbonic anhydrase inhibitors. Ann Ophthalmol. 1979;11: 1563.

98 Werblin TP et al. Aplastic anemia and agranulocytosis in patients using methazolamide for glaucoma. JAMA. 1979; 241:2817.

99 Ross RA et al. Effects of topically applied isoproterenol on aqueous dynamics in man. Arch Ophthalmol. 1979;83: 39.

100 Krupin T et al. Effect of prazosin on aqueous humor dynamics in rabbits. Arch Ophthalmol. 1980;98:1639.

101 Ohrstrom A et al. Long-term treatment of glaucoma with systemic propranolol. Am J Ophthalmol. 1978;86: 340.

102 Ohrstrom A et al. Oral and topical adrenergic beta-receptor blockers in glaucoma treatment. Acta Ophthalmol. 1984;62:681.

103 Williamson J et al. Comparative efficacy of orally and topically administered beta blockers for chronic simple glaucoma. Br J Ophthalmol. 1985;69: 41.

104 Bonomi L et al. Outflow facility after guanethidine sulfate administration. Arch Ophthalmol. 1967;78:337.

105 Romano J et al. Evaluation of a 5% guanethidine and 0.5% adrenaline mixture (Ganda 5/05) and of a 3% guanethidine and 0.5% adrenaline mixture (Ganda 3/05) in the treatment of open-angle glaucoma. Br J Ophthalmol. 1979;63:52.

106 O'Connor MA, Mooney DJ. The additional pressure-lowering effect in patients with glaucoma of pilocarpine 2%, adrenaline 1%, or guanethidine 3% with adrenaline 0.5% and timolol 0.25%: a double-blind crossover study. Trans Ophthalmol Soc U K. 1983;103:588.

107 Hoyng PF, Verbey NLJ. Timolol vs. guanethidine-epinephrine formulations in the treatment of glaucoma. Arch Ophthalmol. 1984;102:1788.

108 Abrams DA et al. A limited comparison of apraclonidine's dose response in subjects with normal or increased intraocular pressure. Am J Ophthalmol. 1989;108:230.

109 Hodapp E et al. The effect of topical clonidine on intraocular pressure. Arch Ophthalmol. 1981;99:1208.

110 Jay WM, Green K. Multiple-drop study of topically applied 1% delta-9-tetrahydrocannabinol in human eyes. Arch Ophthalmol. 1983;101:591.

111 Scoville B et al. A double-masked comparison of carteolol and timolol in ocular hypertension. Am J Ophthalmol. 1988;105:150.

112 Kerstetter JR et al. Prostaglandin F2 alpha-1-isopropylester lowers intraocular pressure without decreasing aqueous humor flow. Am J Ophthalmol. 1988;105:30.

113 Constad WH et al. Use of an angiotensin converting enzyme inhibitor in ocular hypertension and primary open-angle glaucoma. Am J Ophthalmol. 1988;105:674.

114 Abelson M et al. Sustained reduction of intraocular pressure in humans with the calcium channel blocker verapamil. Am J Ophthalmol. 1988;105:155.

115 Drance SM. Effect of oral glycerol on intraocular pressure in normal and glaucomatous eyes. Arch Ophthalmol. 1964;72:491.

116 Becker B et al. Isosorbide: an oral hyperosmotic agent. Arch Ophthalmol. 1967;78:147.

117 Obstbaum SA et al. Low-dose oral alcohol and intraocular pressure. Am J Ophthalmol. 1973;76:926.

118 Adams RE et al. Ocular hypotensive effect of intravenously administered mannitol. Arch Ophthalmol. 1963;69: 55.

119 Smith EW et al. Reduction of human intraocular pressure with intravenous mannitol. Arch Ophthalmol. 1962;68: 734.

120 Galin MA et al. Ophthalmological use of osmotic therapy. Am J Ophthalmol. 1966;62:629.

121 D'Alena P et al. Adverse effects after glycerol orally and mannitol parenterally. Arch Ophthalmol. 1966;75:201.

122 Spaeth GL et al. Anaphylactic reaction to mannitol. Arch Ophthalmol. 1967;78:583.

123 Fraunfelder FT. Drug-Induced Ocular Side Effects and Drug Interactions. Philadelphia: Lea and Febiger; 1976.

124 Grant WM. Toxicology of the Eye. 2nd ed. Springfield: Charles C. Thomas; 1974.

125 D'Amico DJ et al. Amiodarone keratopathy: drug-induced lipid storage disease. Arch Ophthalmol. 1981;99:257.

126 Kaplan LJ, Cappaert WE. Amiodarone keratopathy: correlation to dosage and duration. Arch Ophthalmol. 1982; 100:601.

127 Hamill MB et al. Transdermal scopolamine delivery system and acute angle-closure glaucoma. Ann Ophthalmol. 1983;1:1011.

128 Bar S et al. Presenile cataracts in phenytoin-treated epileptic patients. Arch Ophthalmol. 1983;101:422.

129 Fraunfelder FT et al. Cataracts associated with allopurinol therapy. Am J Ophthalmol. 1982;94:137.

130 Lerman S et al. Allopurinol therapy and cataractogenesis in humans. Am J Ophthalmol. 1982;94:141.

131 Jick H, Brandt DE. Allopurinol and cataracts. Am J Ophthalmol. 1984;98: 355.

132 Rudy MA et al. Lack of photosensitization of ocular tissues by allopurinol. Arch Ophthalmol. 1981;99:2030.

133 Flach A. Photosensitivity to sulfisoxazole ointment. Arch Ophthalmol. 1981; 99:609.

134 Flach AJ et al. Photosensitivity to topically applied sulfisoxazole ointment. Arch Ophthalmol. 1982;100:1286.

135 Gerner EW. Ocular toxicity of tamoxifen. Ann Ophthalmol. 1989;21:420.

136 Shingleton BJ et al. Ocular toxicity associated with high-dose carmustine. Arch Ophthalmol. 1981;100:1766.

137 Hopen G et al. Corneal toxicity with systemic cytarabine. Am J Ophthalmol. 1981;91:500.

138 Smollen KW et al. Non-hematologic toxicities from high-dose cytarabine: analysis of seven patients and development of a monitoring guide. PharmFax. 1984;13:4.

139 Leibowitz H et al. Bioavailability and effectiveness of topically administered corticosteroids. Trans Am Acad Ophthalmol Otolaryngol. 1975;79:78.

140 Leibowitz H et al. Anti-inflammatory effectiveness in the cornea of topically administered prednisolone. Invest Ophthalmol Vis Sci. 1974;13:757.

141 Kupferman A et al. Therapeutic effectiveness of fluorometholone in inflammatory keratitis. Arch Ophthalmol. 1975;93:1011.

142 Armalay MF. Statistical attributes of the steroid hypertensive response in the clinically normal eye. Invest Ophthalmol. 1965;4:187.

143 Becker B et al. Glaucoma and corti-

costeroid provocative testing. Arch Ophthalmol. 1965;74:621.

144 **Lewis JM et al.** Intraocular pressure response to topical dexamethasone as a predictor for the development of primary open-angle glaucoma. Am J Ophthalmol. 1988;106:607.

145 **Godel V et al.** Systemic steroids and ocular fluid dynamics II: systemic versus topical steroids. Acta Ophthalmol (Copenh). 1972;50:664.

146 **Cantrill HL et al.** Comparison of in vitro potency of corticosteroids with ability to raise intraocular pressure. Am J Ophthalmol. 1975;79:1012.

147 **Stewart RH et al.** Intraocular pressure response to topically administered fluorometholone. Arch Ophthalmol. 1979;97:2139.

148 **Kitazawa Y, Horie T.** The prognosis of corticosteroid-responsive individuals. Arch Ophthalmol. 1981;99:819.

149 **Oglesby RB et al.** Cataracts in rheumatoid arthritis patients treated with corticosteroids: description and differential diagnosis. Arch Ophthalmol. 1961;66:519.

150 **Oglesby RB et al.** Cataracts in patients with rheumatic diseases treated with corticosteroids: further observations. Arch Ophthalmol. 1961;66:625.

151 **Skalka HW, Prchal JT.** Effect of corticosteroids on cataract formation. Arch Ophthalmol. 1980;98:1773.

152 **Yablonski MF et al.** Cataracts induced by topical dexamethasone in diabetics. Arch Ophthalmol. 1975;94:474.

153 **Sevel D et al.** Lenticular complications of long-term steroid therapy in children with asthma and eczema. J Allergy Clin Immunol. 1977;60:215.

154 **Fraunfelder FT et al.** Possible adverse effects from topical ocular 10% phenylephrine. Am J Ophthalmol. 1978;85:447.

155 **Brown MN et al.** Lack of side effects from topically administered 10% phenylephrine eye drops: a controlled study. Arch Ophthalmol. 1980;98:487.

156 **Morton HG.** Atropine intoxication: its manifestations in infants and children. J Pediatr. 1939;14:755.

157 **Marks HH.** Psychotogenic properties of cyclopentolate. JAMA. 1963;186:430.

158 **Freund M et al.** Toxic effects of scopolamine eye drops. Am J Ophthalmol. 1970;70:637.

159 **Hoefnagel D.** Toxic effects of atropine and homatropine eye drops in children. N Engl J Med. 1961;264:168.

160 **Wahl JW.** Systemic reaction to tropicamide. Arch Ophthalmol. 1969;82:320.

161 **Abrams SM et al.** Marrow aplasia following topical application of chloramphenicol eye ointment. Arch Intern Med. 1980;140:576.

162 **Musson K.** Cushingoid status: induced by topical steroid medication. J Pediatr Ophthalmol Strabismus. 1968;5:33.

163 **Kaufman HE.** Herpetic keratitis. Invest Ophthalmol Vis Sci. 1978;17:941.

164 **Kaufman HE.** Antimetabolite drug therapy in herpes simplex. Ophthalmology. 1980;87:135.

165 **Bauer DJ et al.** Treatment of experimental herpes simplex keratitis with acycloguanosine. Br J Ophthalmol. 1979;63:429.

166 **Kaufman HE.** Antiviral update. Ophth AAO. 1979;86:131.

167 **Pavan-Langston DR, Foster CS.** Trifluorothymidine and idoxuridine therapy of ocular herpes. Am J Ophthalmol. 1977;84:818.

168 **McGill J et al.** Some aspects of the clinical use of trifluorothymidine in the treatment of herpetic ulceration of the cornea. Trans Ophthalmol Soc U K. 1974;94:342.

169 **Collins P, Bauer DJ.** The activity in vitro against herpes virus of 9-(2-hydroxyethoxymethyl) guanine (acycloguanosine), a new antiviral agent. J Antimicrob Chemother. 1979;5:431.

170 **Pavan-Langston DR et al.** Acyclic antimetabolite therapy of experimental herpes simplex keratitis. Am J Ophthalmol. 1978;86:618.

171 **Falcon MG, Jones BR.** Acycloguanosine: antiviral activity in the rabbit cornea. Br J Ophthalmol. 1979;63:422.

172 **Shiota J et al.** Efficacy of acycloguanosine against herpetic ulcers in rabbit cornea. Br J Ophthalmol. 1979;63:425.

173 **Coster DJ et al.** A comparison of acyclovir and idoxuridine as treatment for ulcerative herpetic keratitis. Br J Ophthalmol. 1980;64:763.

174 **Moore CD et al.** Evaluation of corneal contact lenses. In: Girard LJ, ed. Corneal Contact Lenses. 2nd ed. St. Louis: CV Mosby; 1978:12.

175 **Fraunfelder FT, Meyer SM.** Amantadine and corneal deposits. Am J Ophthalmol. 1990;110:96.

176 **Flach AJ, Dolan BJ.** Amiodarone-induced lens opacities: an 8-year follow-up study. Arch Ophthalmol. 1990;108:1668.

177 **Fraunfelder FT, Meyer SM.** Posterior subcapsular cataracts associated with nasal or inhalation corticosteroids. Am J Ophthalmol. 1990;109:489.

178 **Cunningham M et al.** Eye tics and subjective hearing impairment during fluoxetine therapy. Am J Psychiatry. 1990;147:947.

179 **Nicastro NJ.** Visual disturbances associated with over-the-counter ibuprofen in three patients. Ann Ophthalmol. 1989;29:447.

180 **Friedman DI et al.** Neuro-ophthalmic complications of interleukin 2 therapy. Arch Ophthalmol. 1991;109:1679.

181 **Laties AM et al.** Expanded clinical evaluation of lovastatin (EXCEL) study results II. Assessment of the human lens after 48 weeks of treatment with lovastatin. Am J Cardiol. 1991;67:447.

182 **Marsch SCU, Schaefer HG.** Problems with eye opening after propofol anesthesia. Anesth Analg. 1990;70:115.

183 **Caldwell DR et al.** Efficacy and safety of lodoxamide 0.1% vs cromolyn sodium 4% in patients with vernal keratoconjunctivitis. Am J Ophthalmol. 1992;113:632.

184 **Fahy GT et al.** Randomized double-masked trial of lodoxamide and sodium cromoglycate in allergic eye disease. A multicentre study. Eur J Ophthalmol. 1992;2:144.

185 **Baum JL.** Initial therapy of suspected microbial corneal ulcers: antibiotic therapy based on prevalence of organisms. Surv Ophthalmol. 1979;24:97.

186 **Jones DB.** Initial therapy of suspected microbial corneal ulcers: specific antibiotic therapy based on corneal smears. Surv Ophthalmol. 1979;24:97.

187 **Leibowitz HM et al.** Comparative anti-inflammatory efficacy of topical corticosteroids with low glaucoma-inducing potential. Arch Ophthalmol. 1992;110:118.

188 **Stewart RH et al.** Ocular pressure response to fluorometholone acetate and dexamethasone sodium phosphate. Cur Eye Res. 1984;3:835.

189 **Flach AJ.** Cyclo-oxygenase inhibitors in ophthalmology. Surv Ophthalmol. 1992;36:259.

190 **Allergan America.** Ocufen package insert. Hormigueros, PR: 1992.

191 **Alcon Laboratories, Inc.** Profenal package insert. Fort Worth, TX: 1989 March.

192 **Goa KL, Chrisp P.** Ocular diclofenac: a review of its pharmacology and clinical use in cataract surgery, and potential in other inflammatory ocular conditions. Drugs Aging. 1992;2:473.

193 **CIBA Vision Ophthalmics.** Voltaren Ophthalmic package insert. Atlanta, GA: 1991 August.

194 **Flach AJ et al.** The effect of ketorolac tromethamine solution in reducing postoperative inflammation after cataract extraction and intraocular lens implantation. Ophthalmology. 1988;95:1279.

195 **Flach AJ et al.** Effectiveness of ketorolac tromethamine 0.5% ophthalmic solution for chronic aphakic and pseudophakic cystoid macular edema. Am J Ophthalmol. 1987;103:479.

196 **Flach AJ et al.** Prophylaxis of aphakic cystoid macular edema without corticosteroids. Ophthalmology. 1990;97:1253.

197 **Flach AJ et al.** Improvement in visual acuity in chronic aphakic and pseudophakic cystoid macular edema after treatment with topical 0.5% ketorolac tromethamine. Am J Ophthalmol. 1991;112:514.

198 **Rosenthal AL et al.** Clinical evaluation of suprofen in cataract surgery. Paper presented to 25th International Congress of Ophthalmology. Rome, Italy: 1986 May 4.

199 **Tinkelman DG et al.** Double-masked, paired-comparison clinical study of ketorolac tromethamine 0.5% ophthalmic solution compared with placebo eyedrops in the treatment of seasonal allergic conjunctivitis. Surv Ophthalmol. 1993;38(Suppl.):133.

200 **Ballas Z et al.** Clinical evaluation of ketorolac tromethamine 0.5% ophthalmic solution for the treatment of seasonal allergic conjunctivitis. Surv Ophthalmol. 1993;38(Suppl.):141.

201 **Wood TS et al.** Suprofen treatment of contact lens-associated giant papillary conjunctivitis. Ophthalmology. 1988;95:822.

202 **Buckley DC et al.** Treatment of vernal conjunctivitis with suprofen, a topical non-steroidal anti-inflammatory agent. Invest Ophthalmol Vis Sci. 1986;27:29.

203 **Reynolds LA, Closson RG, eds.** Extemporaneous Ophthalmic Preparations. Applied Therapeutics, Vancouver, WA: 1993.

204 **Polansky JR.** Beta-adrenergic therapy for glaucoma. Int Ophthalmol Clin. 1990;20:219–26.

205 **Allen RC, Epstein DL.** Additive effect of betaxolol and epinephrine in primary open angle glaucoma. Arch Ophthalmol. 1986;104:1178–184.

206 **Van Buskirk EM.** Corneal anesthesia after timolol maleate therapy. Am J Ophthalmol. 1979;88:739–43.

207 **Battershill PE, Sorkin EM.** Ocular metipranolol: a preliminary review of its pharmacodynamic and pharmacokinetic properties, and therapeutic efficacy in glaucoma and ocular hypertension. Drugs. 1988;36:601.

208 **Mills KB, Wright G.** A blind randomized cross-over trial comparing metipranolol 0.3% with timolol 0.25% in open-angle glaucoma: a pilot study. Br J Ophthalmol. 1986;70:39.

209 **Bacon PJ et al.** Cardiovascular responses to metipranolol and timolol eyedrops in healthy volunteers. Br J Clin Pharmacol. 1989;27:1.

210 **Krieglstein GK et al.** Levobunolol and metipranolol: comparative ocular hypotensive efficacy, safety, and comfort. Br J Ophthalmol. 1987;71:250.

211 **Draeger J, Winter R.** The local anaesthetic action of metipranolol versus timolol in patients with healthy eyes. In: Merte, ed. Metipranolol. New York: Springer-Verlag Wien; 1983:76–84.

212 **Akingbehin T, Villada JR.** Metipranolol-associated granulomatous anterior uveitis. Br J Ophthalmol. 1991;75:519–23.

213 **Zimmerman TJ et al.** Side effects of timolol. Surv Ophthalmol. 1983;28(Suppl.):243–49.

214 **Zimmerman TJ et al.** Therapeutic index of pilocarpine, carbachol, and timolol with nasolacrimal occlusion. Am J Ophthalmol. 1992;114:1–7.

215 **Ellis PP et al.** Effect of nasolacrimal occlusion on timolol concentrations in the aqueous humor of the human eye. J Pharm Sci. 1992;81:219–20.

216 **Urtti A, Salminen L.** Minimizing systemic absorption of topically administered ophthalmic drugs. Surv Ophthalmol. 1993;37:435–56.

217 **Rakofsky SI et al.** A comparison of the ocular hypotensive efficacy of once-daily and twice-daily levobunolol treatment. Ophthalmology. 1989;96:8–11.

218 **Wandel T et al.** Glaucoma treatment with once-daily levobunolol. Am J Ophthalmol. 1986;101:298–304.

219 **Silverstone D et al.** Evaluation of once-daily levobunolol 0.25% and timolol 0.25% therapy for increased pressure. Am J Ophthalmol. 1991;112:56–60.

220 **Ball SF, Scheider E.** Cost of β-adrenergic receptor blocking agents for ocular hypertension. Arch Ophthalmol. 1992;110:654–57.

221 **Harris LS et al.** Respiratory difficulties with betaxolol. Am J Ophthalmol. 1986;102:274. Letter.

222 **Ball S.** Congestive heart failure from betaxolol. Arch Ophthalmol. 1987;105:320. Editorial.

223 **Brooks AMV, Gillies WE.** Ocular β-blockers in glaucoma management. Drugs Aging. 1992;2:208–21.

224 **Anon.** Dr. Mann on metipranolol difference. Scrip. 1991;1601:26.

225 **Akingbehin T et al.** Metipranolol-induced adverse reactions: I. The rechallenge study. Eye. 1992;6:277–79.

226 **Akingbehin T, Villada JR.** Metipranolol-induced adverse reactions: II. Loss

of intraocular pressure control. Eye. 1992;6:280–83.

227 **James IM.** Pharmacologic effects of beta-blocking agents used in the management of glaucoma. Surv Ophthalmol. 1989;33(Suppl.):453–54.

228 **Stewart WC et al.** A 3-month comparison of 1% and 2% carteolol and 0.5% timolol in open-angle glaucoma. Graefes Arch Clin Exp Ophthalmol. 1991;229:258–61.

229 **Brazier DJ, Smith SE.** Ocular and cardiovascular response to topical carteolol 2% and timolol 0.5% in healthy volunteers. Br J Ophthalmol. 1988;72:101–03.

230 **Rozier A et al.** Gelrite: a novel, ion-activated, in situ gelling polymer for ophthalmic vehicles. Effect on bioavailability of timolol. Int J Pharm. 1989;57:163–68.

231 **Shedden AH et al.** Multiclinic, double-masked study of 0.5% Timoptic-XE once daily versus 0.5% Timoptic twice daily. Ophthalmology. 1993;100:111.

232 **Korey MS et al.** Timolol and epinephrine: long-term evaluation of concurrent administration. Arch Ophthalmol. 1982;100:742–45.

233 **Kass MA.** Topical carbonic anhydrase inhibitors. Am J Ophthalmol. 1989;107:280–82.

234 **Hurvitz LM et al.** New developments in the drug treatment of glaucoma. Drugs. 1991;41:514–32.

235 **Kalina PH et al.** 6-amino-2-benzothiazole-sulfonamide: the effect of topical carbonic anhydrase inhibitor on aqueous humor formation in the normal eye. Ophthalmology. 1988;95:772–77.

236 **Bron A et al.** Multiple-dose efficacy comparison of the two topical carbonic anhydrase inhibitors sezolamide and MK-927. Arch Ophthalmol. 1991;109:50–3.

237 **Lippa EA et al.** MK-507 versus sezolamide. Comparative efficacy of two topically active carbonic anhydrase inhibitors. Ophthalmology. 1991;98:308–12.

Headache

Brian K Alldredge

Prevalence 50-1
Classification (See Table 50.1) 50-1
  Migraine headaches 50-2
  Cluster headaches 50-2
  Tension-type headaches 50-2
  Other headache types 50-2
  Acute headaches 50-2
  Subacute headaches 50-2
Pathophysiology 50-3
Drug Therapy 50-3
Migraine Headache 50-3
Pathophysiology 50-3
Signs and Symptoms 50-4
  Migraine with and without aura 50-4
Diagnostic Tests 50-5
Therapeutic Considerations 50-5
  Abortive therapy 50-5
  Aggravating factors (See Table 50.3) 50-5
    Oral contraceptives 50-5
Abortive Therapy 50-6
  Ergotamine tartrate 50-6
    Caffeine 50-6
    Route of administration 50-6
    Contraindications 50-6
    Adverse effects 50-6
      Antiemetics 50-6
    Treatment failure 50-7
  Ergonovine maleate and isometheptene 50-7
  Nonsteroidal anti-inflammatory drugs (NSAIDs) ... 50-7
  Sumatriptan (See Figure 50.1) 50-7
Intractable Migraine (See Table 50.4) 50-8
  Dihydroergotamine (DHE) 50-8
  Sumatriptan 50-8
  Chlorpromazine 50-8

Narcotic analgesics 50-9
Prednisone 50-9
Prophylactic Therapy (See Tables 50.5 and 50.6) 50-9
  Criteria for use 50-9
  Propranolol 50-10
    Dosing 50-10
  Methysergide 50-11
    Contraindications 50-11
    Adverse effects 50-11
  Amitriptyline 50-11
    Dosing 50-12
  Valproate 50-12
  Calcium channel blockers 50-12
    Verapamil 50-12
    Nifedipine and diltiazem 50-12
    Nimodipine 50-13
Cluster Headache 50-13
Pathophysiology 50-13
Signs and Symptoms 50-13
Abortive Therapy 50-14
  Ergotamine tartrate 50-14
  Oxygen 50-14
  Sumatriptan 50-14
  Other therapeutic interventions 50-14
Prophylactic Therapy (See Table 50.7) 50-15
  Prednisone 50-15
  Ergotamine 50-15
  Methysergide 50-15
  Lithium carbonate 50-15
Tension-Type Headache 50-15
Pathophysiology 50-16
General Management and Abortive Therapy 50-16
  Analgesics 50-16
  Nondrug techniques 50-16
Prophylactic Therapy 50-16

Clinical features and drug therapy of the common headache syndromes are presented in this chapter. Proposed pathophysiological features of the major headache types also are presented to provide the reader an understanding of the rationale for current and future therapies.

Prevalence

Migraine headache affects nearly ten million persons in the United States[1] and is the fourth most common symptom reported at outpatient medical visits.[2] Overall, the prevalence of headache is highest in adolescence and early adulthood and declines with age through the elderly years.[3,4] Despite numerous potential causes of headaches, over 90% of patients with a chief complaint of continuous or sporadically recurring headaches are eventually diagnosed as having either tension-type or migraine headache.[5]

Classification

Headache is a symptom that can be caused by many disorders. For example, head pain can result from traction, displacement, or inflammation of pain-sensitive structures within the head or can be due to disorders of extracranial structures such as the eyes, ears, or sinuses. Such headaches may be referred to as having an "organic" etiology. Conversely, many patients experience recurring headache without any recognizable cause.

Depending upon the cause, headache may be manifested in a variety of ways or may be accompanied by other associated signs or symptoms. A comprehensive classification scheme of the different types of headaches, modified from the International Headache Society (IHS) is shown in Table 50.1.[6] Readers are referred to the IHS classification report for the comprehensive headache classification scheme and a detailed description of the specific diagnostic features of each headache type. This classification scheme is useful for grouping headaches with similar clinical features or etiologies. Headache must be accurately evaluated and classified because this symptom may reflect an ominous problem such as the presence of a brain tumor or a much more benign process such as muscle tension. Moreover, effective intervention depends upon a correct diagnosis.

Migraine Headaches

Migraine headaches usually develop over a period of minutes to hours progressing from a dull ache to a more intense pulsating pain that worsens with each pulse. The headache usually begins in the frontotemporal region and may radiate to the occiput and neck; it may occur unilaterally or bilaterally. Migraine headaches often are accompanied by nausea and vomiting and may last for up to 72 hours. These headaches usually are alleviated by relaxation in a dark room and sleep. Migraine is more common in females than males. Migraine headaches are divided into those with and without an aura. The term, *aura*, refers to the complex of focal neurologic symptoms (e.g., alterations in vision or sensation) that initiate or accompany a migraine attack. Migraine may be precipitated by a variety of dietary, pharmacological, hormonal, or environmental factors.

Cluster Headaches

Cluster headaches derive their name from a characteristic pattern of recurrent headaches that are separated by periods of remission which last from months to even years. During those periods when clusters of headaches are experienced, the headaches usually occur at least once daily. The headache generally is unilateral, occurs behind the eye, reaches maximal intensity over several minutes, and lasts for less than three hours. Unilateral lacrimation, rhinorrhea, and facial flushing may accompany the cluster headache. During cluster periods, headache is commonly precipitated by alcohol, naps, and vasodilating drugs. In contrast to migraine headaches, cluster headaches are more common in males than females.

Tension-Type Headaches

A dull, persistent headache, occurring bilaterally in a hatband distribution around the head is characteristic of tension-type headaches. The headache is usually not debilitating and may fluctuate in intensity throughout the day. Tension-type headaches often occur during or after stress; however, chronic tension-type headaches may persist for months even in the absence of recognizable stress. Skeletal muscle overcontraction, depression, and occasionally nausea may accompany the headache. Prodrome neurologic symptoms do not occur in association with tension-type headache. More detailed descriptions of migraine, cluster, and tension-type headaches appear in following sections of this chapter.

Other Headache Types

In addition to migraine, cluster, and tension-type headaches, patients may also experience headache associated with head trauma, vascular disorders, central nervous system infection [including human immunodeficiency virus (HIV)], or metabolic disorders. Examples of these and other headache types are given in Table 50.1.

The length of time that a patient has experienced headaches provides highly useful information for assessing the nature and etiology of the headaches. A new severe headache in a patient without a previous history is the most useful single piece of information for identifying potentially destructive intracranial or extracranial causes of headache. Such headaches may develop suddenly, over a period of hours to days (acute headache), or more gradually over days to months (subacute headache).

Acute Headaches

Acute headaches can be symptomatic of subarachnoid hemorrhage, stroke, meningitis, or intracranial mass lesion (e.g., brain tumor, hematoma, abscess). The headache that accompanies subarachnoid hemorrhage is typically severe (often described by the patient as the "worst headache of my life"), and may occur in conjunction with alteration of mental status and focal neurologic signs. The headache of meningitis is usually bilateral and develops

Table 50.1	Classification of Headache[6]

Migraine
Migraine without aura
Migraine with aura
Complicated migraine

Tension-Type Headache
Episodic tension-type headache
Chronic tension-type headache

Cluster Headache
Episodic cluster headache
Chronic cluster headache

Miscellaneous Headaches Unassociated with Structural Lesion (e.g., cold stimulus headache, benign exertional headache)

Headache Associated with Head Trauma
Acute post-traumatic headache
Chronic post-traumatic headache

Headache Associated with Vascular Disorders
Acute ischemic cerebrovascular disease (TIA or stroke)
Intracranial hematoma
Subarachnoid hemorrhage
Unruptured vascular malformation
Arteritis
Carotid or vertebral artery pain
Venous thrombosis
Arterial hypertension

Headache Associated with Nonvascular Intracranial Disorder (e.g., high or low cerebrospinal fluid pressure, intracranial infection, or neoplasm)

Headache Associated with Substances or Their Withdrawal (e.g., withdrawal from alcohol, caffeine, ergotamine, narcotics; also see Table 77.3)

Headache Associated with Noncephalic Infection (e.g., viral or bacterial infection)

Headache Associated with Metabolic Disorder (e.g., hypoxia, hypercapnia, hypoglycemia, dialysis)

Headache or Facial Pain Associated with Disorder of Cranium, Neck, Eyes, Ears, Nose, Sinuses, Teeth, Mouth, or Other Facial or Cranial Structures (e.g., cervical spine, acute glaucoma, refractive errors, acute sinus headache)

Cranial Neuralgias, Nerve Trunk Pain and Deafferentation Pain (e.g., compression, demyelination, infarction, or inflammation of cranial nerves)

Headache Not Classifiable

gradually over hours to days; symptoms such as fever, photophobia, and positive meningeal (Kernig's and Brudzinski's) signs often accompany the meningeal headache. Although the acute onset of headache associated with coughing, sneezing, straining, or change in head position is commonly thought to indicate a cranial mass lesion with cerebrospinal fluid pathway obstruction, several varieties of exertional headache are benign.[7,8]

Subacute Headaches

Subacute headaches may be a sign of increased intracranial pressure, intracranial mass lesion, temporal arteritis, sinusitis, or trigeminal neuralgia (i.e., tic douloureux). Trigeminal neuralgia usually occurs after the age of 40 and is more common in women than men. The pain usually occurs along the second or third divisions of the trigeminal (facial) nerve and lasts only moments. Trigeminal neuralgia is characterized by sudden, intense pain which recurs paroxysmally, often in response to triggers such as talking, chewing, or shaving.

The clinical manifestations of headache, as described above, focus on the onset, frequency, duration, site, sex of the patient, distribution, and other unique characteristics of the head pain. A comprehensive medical history and physical examination of the patient often provide sufficient information to make an adequate assessment of a patient's headache complaint, and may enable the practitioner to rule out headache as a manifestation of more serious illness. Physical examination of the patient suffering from the common, benign forms of headache (e.g., migraine, cluster, and tension-type headaches) is usually normal. When the medical history of the patient is suggestive of an organic cause of headache, a more extensive evaluation, with referral or consultation by a neurologist, is necessary.

Pathophysiology

Intracranially, only a limited number of structures are sensitive to pain. The most important pain-sensitive structures within the cranium are the proximal portions of the cerebral arteries, large veins, and the venous sinuses.[9] Headache may result from either dilation, distention, or traction of the large intracranial vessels. The brain itself is pain-insensitive. Referred pain from inflammation of frontal or maxillary sinuses, or refractive errors of the eye are potential, though over-diagnosed, causes of headache.[10] Scalp arteries and muscles are also capable of registering pain and have been implicated in the pathophysiology of migraine and tension-type headache. Extracranially, most of the structures outside the skull (e.g., periosteum, eye, ear, teeth, skin, deeper tissues) have pain afferents. In general, pain can be produced by activation of peripheral pain receptors (nociceptors); injury to central or peripheral nervous systems; or displacement of the pain-sensitive structures mentioned above.

The "gate-control" theory of pain has been used as a biochemical model to explain the pathophysiology of headache.[10] Alterations in serotonin (5-hydroxytryptamine) balance have been demonstrated and used in support of this theory. When serotonin is released from descending projections of brain stem nuclei, it activates interneurons that inhibit the transmission of pain impulses. The inhibitory action of these interneurons is mediated by enkephalin activation of presynaptic opiate receptors. Serotonin thus acts as an inhibitory neurotransmitter for neurons that receive and propagate pain impulses. The peripheral alterations of serotonin activity and the effect of serotonin on the caliber of cerebral blood vessels may also be important to the pathogenesis of vascular headache.

Drug Therapy

Drug therapy for headache is divided into two major categories: 1) abortive therapy to provide relief during an acute headache attack and 2) prophylactic therapy to prevent or reduce the severity of recurrent headaches. The majority of people with infrequent tension-type headaches self-medicate with over-the-counter (OTC) analgesics to abort the acute event and do not require prophylactic therapy. By contrast, migraine and cluster headache sufferers who experience frequent headaches and who respond poorly to abortive measures are good candidates for preventative therapy.

Although analgesics are often useful for the treatment of episodic tension-type headaches, most patients with migraine and all patients with cluster headaches require other abortive measures. Ergot alkaloids (e.g., ergotamine and dihydroergotamine) are the most frequently prescribed agents for relief of migraine and cluster headaches; they are available in oral, sublingual, rectal, and parenteral dosage forms.

Antidepressant agents (e.g., amitriptyline) are useful for the prophylactic treatment of migraine and tension-type headaches. Since many patients suffer from mixed headache types, these agents can be useful for patients who might otherwise require preventative polytherapy. Other agents useful for migraine headache prophylaxis include beta blocking agents (e.g., propranolol), calcium channel blocking agents (particularly verapamil), and valproate. Although calcium channel blocking drugs and valproate are also effective for prophylaxis against episodic cluster headaches, corticosteroids (e.g., prednisone) and methysergide often are preferred for their greater efficacy.

Migraine Headache

The word migraine comes from the Greek "hemicrania" and historically was used to describe unilateral headaches with associated symptoms. More recently, the International Headache Society described migraine as follows. Migraine is an "idiopathic, recurring headache disorder manifesting in attacks lasting 4 to 72 hours. Typical characteristics of [migraine] headache are unilateral location, pulsating quality, moderate or severe intensity, aggravation by routine physical activity, and association with nausea, photo- and phonophobia."[6] Migraine headaches are subclassified according to the presence or absence of aura symptoms. Most persons who suffer from migraine do not experience aura symptoms. In those patients with aura, visual symptoms are most common. Complicated migraine is a less common type of migraine in which the neurologic symptoms are more pronounced or disabling; in some cases the aura symptoms may outlast the headache itself. Table 50.2 outlines the predominant types of complicated migraine. While patients with persistent symptoms should be thoroughly evaluated by a neurologist, permanent neurologic sequelae after migraine are rare even for patients with complicated migraine.

Pathophysiology

Past theories of pathogenesis have focused on alterations in cranial vessel diameter and blood flow as the primary cause of migraine. In this "vascular hypothesis," focal neurologic symptoms preceding or accompanying the headache were proposed to be caused by vasoconstriction and reduction in cerebral blood flow. The headache was proposed to have been caused by a compensatory vasodilation with displacement of pain-sensitive intracranial

Table 50.2	Types of Complicated Migraine[6]

Migraine with Prolonged Aura
Aura symptoms lasting >60 min but <1 wk

Familial Hemiplegic Migraine
Aura with hemiparesis; identical attacks in a first-degree relative

Basilar Migraine
Aura symptoms arising from brain stem or occipital lobes (e.g., dysarthria, vertigo, ataxia, decreased level of consciousness)

Ophthalmoplegic Migraine
Paresis of one or more ocular cranial nerves

Retinal Migraine
Aura symptoms with monocular scotoma or blindness lasting <1 hr

Status Migrainosus
Migraine headache lasting >72 hr despite treatment

Migrainous Infarction
Aura symptoms lasting longer than 7 days

structures. Although blood flow is decreased during the aura of migraine,[11] other observations do not support the vascular hypothesis. The headache phase of migraine with aura has been shown to begin while blood flow is reduced[11] and migraine without aura is not associated with alterations in regional cerebral blood flow.[12] Furthermore, some drugs that are effective for migraine treatment have no discernible effect on blood vessels.

More recent evidence suggests that the pain of migraine is generated centrally and involves serotonergic and adrenergic pain-modulating systems.[13] This theory is supported by evidence which demonstrates neural control of the cranial circulation. The noradrenergic locus ceruleus, trigeminal nerve, and nucleus raphe dorsalis have all been shown to modulate cerebral blood flow in experimental models[14] and the alterations simulate those found in migraineurs.[15]

Biochemical and hormonal changes may also play a role in migraine pathogenesis. Although alterations in free fatty acids,[16] prostaglandins,[17] histamine,[18] catecholamines,[19] substance P,[20] neuroexcitatory amino acids,[21] and serotonin (5-HT) have been demonstrated, 5-HT is most frequently implicated in the pathophysiology of migraine.[13,15] Plasma 5-HT levels decrease by nearly one-half during a migraine attack[22] with a corresponding rise in the urinary excretion of 5-hydroxyindoleacetic acid,[23] the primary metabolite of 5-HT. Also, reserpine, a drug which depletes 5-HT from body stores, has been found to induce a stereotypical headache in migraineurs and a dull discomfort in patients not prone to migraine.[22,24] An intravenous (IV) injection of 5-HT was effective for relieving both reserpine-induced and spontaneous migraine headache.[22,24] The therapeutic effects of drugs that stimulate 5-HT$_1$ receptors (e.g., dihydroergotamine and sumatriptan), antagonize 5-HT$_2$ receptors (e.g., methysergide, cyproheptadine), prevent 5-HT reuptake (e.g., amitriptyline), or release (e.g., calcium channel blockers) or inhibit brain stem serotonergic raphe neurons (e.g., valproate) all lend support to the hypothesis that 5-HT is an important mediator of migraine.

In summary, the pathophysiology of migraine probably involves cerebrovascular changes as well as alterations in peripheral or central 5-HT activity. These effects may be mediated by a central mechanism involving brain stem noradrenergic and serotonergic neurotransmission.

Signs and Symptoms

Migraine With and Without Aura

1. J.Y., a 29-year-old female, presents to the clinic with a five-month history of left-sided pulsatile head pain recurring on a weekly basis. Her headaches are usually preceded by unformed flashes of light bilaterally and a sensation of lightheadedness. The ensuing pain is always unilateral and is commonly associated with nausea, vomiting, and photophobia. The headache is not relieved by two tablets of either aspirin 325 mg or ibuprofen 200 mg and will usually last all day unless she is able to lie in a dark room and sleep. The headaches usually interfere with her ability to continue work. J.Y. is unable to identify any external factors which precipitate a migraine attack. Both J.Y.'s mother and grandmother also were affected by migraine headaches. Past medical history is unremarkable and J.Y. denies any other medical problems. Current medications include only the OTC analgesics for headache and the contraceptive Ortho-Novum 1/35. General physical and neurologic examinations are within normal limits.

What subjective and objective data from the above description are consistent with a diagnosis of migraine with aura?

Given J.Y.'s headache description, normal physical examination, and age of onset, she is most likely suffering from migraine with aura; a benign, though quite uncomfortable disorder.

Approximately 18% of females and 6% of males in the United States suffer from migraine headaches.[25] The usual age of onset of migraine headaches is 15 to 35 years; after the age of 50, the onset of new migraine headaches is less common and would be suggestive of organic pathology. Although influenced by physiological and environmental factors, migraine headaches occur more frequently among first-degree relatives suggesting a hereditary basis for this disorder.[26] J.Y.'s gender (female), age (29 years), and positive family history are compatible with these aspects of migraine.

In the assessment of headache, the site or location of the pain, the quality of the pain, duration and time course of the pain, and the conditions that provoke or palliate the pain should be considered.

The site or location of head pain can provide the clinician with clues as to potential for an organic cause (e.g., lesions in the frontal sinuses, eyes, ears, teeth, or cerebral arteries). Pain, however, often is referred from other regions and the location of pain can provide misleading information. Thus, the site of head pain need not be related to the apparent site of the focal neurological symptoms that accompany migraine with aura. Head pain may be either unilateral or bilateral, and the pain need not recur on the same side if unilateral. In fact, 50% of patients with unilateral headache report that either side of the head may be affected during any individual migraine attack.[27]

The quality of migraine head pain usually begins as a dull ache that intensifies over a period of minutes or hours to a throbbing headache which worsens with each arterial pulse. The headache, if untreated, lasts from several hours to as long as three days, or until the patient sleeps. The pain usually is of sufficient intensity to interfere with daily activities. Although migraine headaches seldom occur more often than once every few weeks, there is great interpatient variability in the frequency of occurrence. A patient may experience only several migraines in a lifetime, while others may suffer several headaches weekly on a chronic basis. J.Y., like half of all patients with migraine, describes headaches which recur between one to four times monthly.[27] In this patient, the quality of the pain (i.e., interferes with J.Y.'s ability to continue work); the duration and the time course of the pain (i.e., usually lasts all day); and the conditions that palliate the pain (i.e., lie in a dark room and sleep) are all compatible with the description of migraine headaches.

Aura symptoms are focal neurologic features that precede or accompany the headache in about 10% of migraine sufferers. When they precede the headache, aura symptoms usually begin ten minutes to one hour before the onset of head pain. Lightheadedness and photopsia (unformed flashes of light) are frequently reported, and were described by J.Y. before the onset of her head pain. Visual disturbances, such as scotoma (an isolated area within the visual field where vision is absent), occur in 30% of migraine patients. At times, the scotoma are preceded only by a sensation that something is wrong with vision which cannot be more specifically characterized. At other times, the scotoma may be preceded by other visual distortions (e.g., the "halves of peoples' faces were vertically displaced in such a way that one eye appeared to be a centimeter or two lower than the other").[28] When scotoma are surrounded by a shiny pattern they are termed "scintillating scotoma." These scintillating scotoma can have "the visual quality of images in the kaleidoscopes we looked into as children, with the difference that the scotoma are silvery instead of multicolored as in the toy."[28] "Fortification spectrum" is the term used to describe slowly enlarging scotoma surrounded by bright zigzagging patterns which are said to resemble the pattern seen at the top of a fort. The presence of these visual disturbances suggests that the visual cortex in the occipital lobe of the brain might serve as the sight of origin for some migraine attacks.[29] Other neurological symptoms of cortical origin (e.g., paresthesias, temporal lobe symptoms) occur less commonly in patients who suffer from migraine with aura. J.Y.'s physical and neurological examinations were within normal limits. The nausea and vomiting that were experienced by J.Y. accompany migraine headaches (with or without aura) in 90% of patients. The vomiting is occasionally followed by a gradual resolution of migraine symptoms. Diarrhea may also occur.

In summary, J.Y.'s history and relative lack of important physical findings are compatible with a diagnosis of migraine with aura.

Diagnostic Tests

2. What further laboratory or diagnostic tests should be ordered for J.Y.?

Headaches are common medical complaints and evaluation of these headaches with sophisticated diagnostic procedures [e.g., computed tomography (CT), magnetic resonance imaging (MRI) scans] are generally unnecessary in the uncomplicated migraine patient. Since J.Y.'s headaches are not of recent origin, not progressive, and unassociated with traumatic injury or persistent neurological deficits, CT or MRI scanning procedures should be unnecessary. Her headaches are unaccompanied by fever or nuchal rigidity, and she does not present with headache described as being "the worst headache of my life"; therefore, a lumbar puncture would not likely be of diagnostic value since meningitis or subarachnoid hemorrhage is unlikely. The signs and symptoms experienced by J.Y., as described in the answer to Question 1, are typical of migraine with aura. The most important diagnostic evaluations of patients presenting with headache should be based upon a thorough medical history and physical examination. The role of costly or invasive diagnostic procedures is limited to their usefulness in detecting other, more serious disorders which may manifest as migrainous headache.

Therapeutic Considerations

3. What should be the general approach to the treatment of J.Y.'s headache attacks?

In recent years, the concept that headaches can be classified into distinct types with unrelated pathophysiologic features has been challenged. Patients will frequently complain of more than one type of headache or will report symptoms or recurrence patterns which are inconsistent with a single diagnosis. Since the selection of therapy is based primarily upon the characteristics of headache gathered from the history, the practitioner needs to be flexible in his choice of treatments when the features do not fit within classical definitions. Even for patients with well-defined headache types, specific therapies may alleviate pain in only 50% to 80% of patients. Still, with careful monitoring of therapeutic response and optimization of effective treatments, patients with a wide variety of headache complaints can be successfully managed with relatively few drugs.

Abortive Therapy

The general approach to treatment of acute migraine headache attacks is one of pharmacotherapy aimed at relief of migraine headache pain and associated symptoms. Such a treatment plan may include: 1) 5-HT receptor agonists (e.g., ergot derivatives or sumatriptan), 2) analgesics, 3) sedatives, and 4) antiemetic drug therapy, depending upon the exact nature of the patient's complaint. A combination treatment program utilizing all of the above forms

of treatment in a quiet, comfortable atmosphere is successful in as many as 90% of migraine patients.[30]

Aggravating Factors

Clinicians should always search for factors that might precipitate migraine attacks in their patients before initiating drug therapy. Although J.Y. could not associate her migraine attacks with any external events, the factors listed in Table 50.3 should be discussed with J.Y. in hopes that their elimination or avoidance may improve her headaches; however, complete relief, even in patients who can clearly identify such precipitants, is unlikely.

4. J.Y. recalls being told by her gynecologist that headaches are a possible side effect of oral contraceptive use. She initially started oral contraceptives two years ago and did not associate the medication with the recent onset of migraine attacks. Why should the use of Ortho-Novum 1/35 be discontinued in J.Y.?

Oral contraceptives may either worsen or precipitate migraine attacks in women without a previous history of this problem.[31] Although headaches usually arise within the first few months of oral contraceptive use, headaches developing after several years have been described.[32] It is, possible, therefore, that J.Y.'s headaches are worsened or even caused by Ortho-Novum 1/35 and a change in contraceptive method would be indicated.

The frequency of headaches that are induced by oral contraceptives may correlate with the estrogen content.[33] The use of a lower potency estrogen product may decrease the frequency of migraine attacks. Women with migraine symptoms while on birth control pills, however, may be at increased risk for stroke[34,35] and their continued use is best avoided in these patients. When oral contraceptives are discontinued, 30% to 40% of women[36] notice an improvement in their headaches, although several months may elapse before a benefit is realized.[33] An alternate form of birth control should be recommended for J.Y. and the frequency of her headaches should be monitored for detection of an improvement in this problem.

Table 50.3	Factors Which May Precipitate Migraine Headache
Stress	
Emotion	
Glare	
Hypoglycemia	
Altered sleep pattern	
Menses	
Exercise	
Alcohol	
Carbon monoxide	
Excess caffeine use or withdrawal	
Foods containing:	
MSG[a] [e.g., Chinese food, canned soups, seasonings (e.g., Johnny's Seasoning Salt)]	
Tyramine (e.g., red wine, ripened cheeses)	
Nitrites (e.g., cured meat products)	
Phenylethylamine (e.g., chocolate, cheese)	
Aspartame (e.g., artificial sweeteners, diet sodas)	
Drugs[215]	
Excess analgesic use or withdrawal	
Estrogens (e.g., oral contraceptives)	
Cocaine	
Nitroglycerin	

[a] MSG = Monosodium glutamate.

Abortive Therapy

Ergotamine Tartrate

5. What would be an appropriate drug of first choice for the treatment of J.Y.'s acute headaches?

Ergotamine tartrate (Bellergal-S, Cafergot) is the drug of choice for treatment of acute migraine headaches unresponsive to non-narcotic analgesics. About 50% to 70% of migraine sufferers will benefit from ergotamine given during an acute attack.[37] Ergotamine is highly specific for migraine and cluster headaches; only occasionally are other types of headaches affected by this drug.

The pharmacologic actions of ergotamine and other ergot derivatives are complex and, in some cases, mutually antagonistic. Ergotamine has both vasoconstrictive and vasodilatory effects although vasodilatation occurs with high doses in animals and is unlikely to occur in man with therapeutic use.[38] Ergotamine also interacts with 5-HT, dopamine, and noradrenaline receptors. The serotonergic and vasoconstrictive properties likely mediate ergotamine's beneficial effects in the acute management of migraine headache.

Ergotamine should be given at the first sign of a migraine attack in a dosage which is effective and acceptable to the patient. If administration is delayed until the headache is firmly established, ergotamine is rarely effective and other therapies (e.g., dihydroergotamine, chlorpromazine, or narcotic analgesics) are usually required.

6. Why is caffeine added to some ergotamine products (e.g., Cafergot)?

Caffeine is combined with ergotamine in several preparations and was originally added to potentiate the vasoconstrictive properties of ergotamine.[39] Subsequent studies have shown that caffeine improves intestinal ergotamine absorption[40] and potentiates the pain relief properties of analgesics.[41] However, it should be kept in mind that caffeine's stimulant effect may prevent the sleep which is beneficial to many migraine sufferers.

7. What ergotamine dosage form should be prescribed for an acute migraine attack in J.Y.?

Route of Administration. Ergotamine tartrate is available for oral, sublingual, rectal, or parenteral use. The rectal and sublingual routes of administration bypass the portal circulation, avoid first-pass metabolism, and are more bioavailable than the oral route of administration; however, documentation of improved efficacy is lacking.[42,43] A metered-dose inhaler containing ergotamine tartrate was previously marketed in the United States, but this product has been withdrawn.

J.Y.'s next acute migraine attack should be treated with a sublingual ergotamine preparation because it is convenient to use and has a faster onset of action than oral ergotamine.[44] Acute migraine attacks also are associated with decreased gastric motility.[45] This phenomenon is presumably responsible for the impaired oral absorption of aspirin and ergotamine when given during an acute migraine attack.[46,47] Delayed drug absorption during a migraine attack occurs independent of associated nausea or vomiting and is primarily related to headache severity.[48] The usual ergotamine dosage (when given by either oral, sublingual, or rectal routes) is 1 to 4 mg given immediately and followed by 1 to 2 mg at half-hour intervals to a maximum of 6 mg/attack or 10 mg/week.

8. What are the contraindications to the use of an ergotamine-containing product in J.Y.?

Contraindications to the use of ergot alkaloids include cardiovascular disease, sepsis, liver and kidney disease, pregnancy, breast-feeding, and concomitant use of triacetyloleandomycin or erythromycin.[37] The latter drugs can inhibit the metabolism of ergotamine and may potentiate the toxicity of this agent.[49] The vasoconstrictive effects of ergotamine can be particularly harmful to the patient with these pre-existing conditions. Although hypertension is occasionally listed as a contraindication to ergotamine use, usual therapeutic doses of ergotamine used for migraine therapy have minimal effects on blood pressure, and hypertension need not be a contraindication to its occasional use.[50]

Concerns about using vasoconstrictors such as ergotamine during the aura of migraine when focal neurologic deficits may be due to cerebral ischemia have not been validated. Human studies have found no alteration in regional cerebral blood flow after parenteral administration of either ergotamine or dihydroergotamine and their use during the prodrome is not contraindicated.[51–54] In summary, there are no contraindications to the use of ergotamine in J.Y.

9. Adverse Effects. What can be done to minimize ergotamine-induced gastric disturbances in J.Y. who already experiences nausea and vomiting associated with migraine attacks?

Gastrointestinal (GI) disturbances can be a limiting factor to the use of ergotamine for headache therapy. Nausea, vomiting, and anorexia are common, dose-dependent ergotamine adverse effects which may worsen the GI symptoms that frequently accompany acute migraine headaches. These gastrointestinal symptoms after ergotamine usage are likely due to central dopamine receptor agonism at the chemoreceptor trigger zone.[55] Since these effects are centrally mediated, they can occur after administration of ergotamine by any bioavailable route. Patients are reluctant to continue therapy if their initial experience with the medication has been unpleasant; therefore, patients should be educated as to the potential for this adverse effect. Clinicians can also take measures to minimize migraine-associated and ergotamine-induced gastrointestinal upset.

One technique useful for minimizing ergotamine-induced GI upset is to determine the smallest dose of ergotamine that will elicit gastrointestinal distress in a patient during a headache-free interval. For example, if the suppository form of ergotamine is being used, the patient can be instructed to insert one-fourth of a suppository at hourly intervals until nausea develops. The total dosage is then reduced by one-fourth of a suppository and used as the initial dose for subsequent migraine attacks.[50] The same technique can be utilized for patients using oral or sublingual ergotamine by splitting the tablets in half.

Antiemetics. Adjunctive antiemetic therapy can effectively reduce the GI upset that is associated with migraine headaches. Although phenothiazine antiemetics can provide symptomatic relief from nausea, they also can reduce GI motility and further impair absorption of medication taken orally.[56] Metoclopramide (Reglan) is the antiemetic of choice in migraine.[57] The recommended dose is 10 mg orally taken as soon as possible. While the drug has no direct antimigraine effect,[58] it does provide symptomatic relief from nausea and vomiting while enhancing the oral absorption of medications taken during the migraine attack.[56] Unfortunately, metoclopramide is not available in a suppository dosage form.

Given J.Y.'s complaint of nausea and vomiting during migraine attacks, adjunctive antiemetic therapy with metoclopramide should be initiated. If the oral absorption of metoclopramide is likely to be impaired because of vomiting, prochlorperazine (Compazine) 25 mg suppositories should be used. J.Y. should be instructed on how to predetermine her maximal tolerated dose of sublingual ergotamine such that this drug does not provoke nausea or vomiting.

10. Ortho-Novum 1/35 was discontinued, and J.Y. was given a diaphragm with instructions on its proper use. She was also given a prescription for ergotamine tartrate (Ergostat) 2 mg SL and metoclopramide 10 mg. At her follow-up clinic visit one month later, J.Y. reported only moderate relief from migraine headache with Ergostat. She also reported a transient

tingling sensation in her legs which she associated with Ergostat use. Do these symptoms of peripheral vasoconstriction warrant the discontinuation of ergotamine therapy in J.Y.?

The peripheral vasoconstrictive effects of ergotamine most commonly involve the lower extremities and are often characterized by coldness, decreased distal pulses, and a tingling sensation. Continuous paresthesias, limb pain, venous thrombosis, or gangrene necessitating amputation are more severe consequences of ergotamine therapy.[59] Although some of these symptoms may occur with therapeutic doses in hypersensitive individuals,[55] they are most commonly associated with overdose or excessive therapeutic use of ergotamine.

Beta-adrenergic receptor blocking agents, commonly used in migraine prophylaxis, occasionally can potentiate the vasoconstrictive effects of ergotamine.[60,61] Their concomitant use is not contraindicated; however, patients should be closely monitored for the signs and symptoms of peripheral vasoconstriction.

Symptoms of acute arterial insufficiency should be managed by discontinuation of ergotamine. If this intervention is ineffective, aggressive vasodilator therapy with sodium nicotine,[62] tolazoline,[63] nitroprusside,[64] or nitroglycerin[65] may be warranted.

J.Y. should be questioned regarding the exact use of Ergostat during her migraine headaches. If maximum daily or weekly dosing restrictions have not been followed, J.Y. should be educated as to their importance. It is probably unnecessary to discontinue ergotamine therapy in J.Y. based upon her report of transient tingling of lower extremities. Acute vascular insufficiency is the most worrisome consequence of ergotamine's peripheral vasoconstrictive effects; however, most episodes are preceded by persistent paresthesias or claudication pain. J.Y. should be told to limit Ergostat usage to 6 mg/attack and 10 mg/week, and to report persistent tingling or leg pain immediately to her physician.

11. J.Y. was asked to record the number, frequency, severity, and duration of her migraine headaches so that an accurate assessment of her abortive migraine therapy could be made at her next clinic visit. She has done so and her diary suggests that Ergostat has not improved her headaches with respect to any of the parameters noted. Should the diagnosis of migraine headache be reconsidered? What alternative therapies are available for aborting these migraine attacks?

Treatment Failure. Given the variable response rate of acute migraine headache to ergotamine, it is not reasonable to exclude the diagnosis of migraine based on a negative outcome. It must also be determined that J.Y. is using her medication appropriately before alternative therapies are considered.

Possible reasons for failure of sublingual ergotamine to relieve migraine headaches may include: using the medication too late in the headache attack; swallowing the sublingual tablet; vomiting before the drug is absorbed; or rebound headaches caused by overuse of ergotamine. Rebound headache after discontinuation of long-term, daily ergotamine usage is a common phenomenon. These rebound headaches respond to larger ergotamine doses, but ultimately, the headaches become more frequent and other symptoms of ergotamine overuse become apparent. This cycle of overmedication and resultant headache can render patients refractory to other useful forms of headache treatment.[66]

If the patient does not respond to an oral or sublingual dosage form of ergotamine, a trial with ergotamine rectal suppositories may be successful.[48] The rectal administration of ergotamine is associated with a higher rate of success (i.e., about 70%) than the oral or sublingual routes of administration (about 50% to 60% effective).[67] This difference may be due to improved bioavailability of ergotamine when administered rectally.[68] Substituting ergotamine suppositories for Ergostat would be a reasonable alternative for J.Y. since her response to Ergostat has been poor.

Ergonovine Maleate and Isometheptene

Other drugs which have been used to abort migraine headaches, and may be considered as alternatives for J.Y., include ergonovine maleate, isometheptene-containing products, nonsteroidal anti-inflammatory drugs, and sumatriptan. Ergonovine maleate (Ergotrate) is an ergot alkaloid which is sometimes preferred to ergotamine tartrate because of its relative lack of gastrointestinal and peripheral vasoconstrictive effects. Ergonovine, however, is also less effective than ergotamine and would be an inappropriate alternative for J.Y. Isometheptene, a sympathomimetic amine, is combined with acetaminophen and a sedative (dichloralphenazone) in the product of Midrin. This combination is as effective as oral ergotamine in the treatment of acute migraine headaches[69,70] and, in many patients, better tolerated. Although the contraindications to Midrin are similar to those of ergotamine, severe adverse effects are less common.[71] Patients unresponsive to ergotamine products occasionally will respond to Midrin; therefore, this product could be a reasonable alternative for aborting J.Y.'s acute headaches. The usual dosage of Midrin is two capsules taken immediately followed by one additional capsule every hour until the headache is relieved. Subsequent migraine attacks can be managed by administering the same total dose of Midrin that was effective in treating the previous headache; however, no more than five Midrin capsules should be taken within a 12-hour period.[69]

Nonsteroidal Anti-Inflammatory Drugs (NSAIDs)

NSAIDs may also provide symptomatic relief of migraine headaches for some patients unresponsive to ergotamine. Naproxen,[72] tolfenamic acid,[73] ketoprofen,[74] and diclofenac[75] have all been used successfully despite the lack of formal approval for the treatment of migraine by the Food and Drug Administration (FDA). If NSAIDs are to be used in the abortive treatment of migraine, the concomitant administration of metoclopramide can enhance the absorption of the NSAIDs and provide more effective and rapid pain relief.[46,76]

The prescription of NSAIDs to patients with frequent migraine headaches should be undertaken with caution. Analgesic overuse is common in these patients and may be responsible for perpetuating chronic head pain. Additionally, analgesic abuse is a common cause of failure of the usual abortive treatment measures (e.g., ergotamine).[71] Successful abortive and prophylactic treatment of migraine headache in patients with a history of analgesic overuse necessitates detoxification from the abused agents.[77]

Sumatriptan

Sumatriptan (Imitrex) is a structural analogue of 5-HT that was approved by the FDA for the abortive treatment of migraine headache (See Figure 50.1). Unlike the ergot alkaloids (e.g., dihydroergotamine) which stimulate serotonergic, dopaminergic, and noradrenergic receptors, sumatriptan has selective agonist activity at $5\text{-}HT_{1D}$ subtype receptors; this is the most common 5-HT receptor in the human brain and is thought to predominate in the carotid circulation.[78]

Sumatriptan has been found to be effective in the acute treatment of migraine after oral,[79] intravenous,[80] subcutaneous,[81] and intranasal[82] administration when compared to placebo or other antimigraine drugs. At this time, only the subcutaneous dosage form has received FDA approval. After a 6 mg subcutaneous dose of sumatriptan, 70% to 79% of patients had their migraine headaches abolished or significantly reduced at one hour.[82,83] At two hours the response rate increased to approximately 90%.[83] Sumatriptan 6 mg subcutaneously can be readministered within one hour if the first injection is ineffective,[84] although some studies have failed to show a benefit from the second injection.[82,83] Unlike ergotamine,

Fig 50.1   Structures of 5-HT (Serotonin) and Sumatriptan.

which needs to be given at the earliest sign of a migraine attack for maximal benefit, sumatriptan is effective when given four hours or longer after the onset of headache.[83] No studies have yet been published which compare subcutaneous sumatriptan to ergotamine or dihydroergotamine, the agents currently preferred for abortive treatment of migraine attacks. Oral sumatriptan is the next dosage form likely to receive approval in the United States. In placebo-controlled trials, 100 mg oral sumatriptan relieved migraine headache in 51% to 67% of patients.[85,86] In other trials, oral sumatriptan was found to be more effective than a single dose of 2 mg ergotamine with caffeine (Cafergot)[87] and the combination of metoclopramide 10 mg plus aspirin 900 mg.[88] In addition to relieving the pain of migraine headache, sumatriptan is also effective for ameliorating the associated symptoms of migraine such as nausea, vomiting, and photophobia in 80% to 90% of patients.[83]

Overall, sumatriptan has been very well tolerated in premarketing studies and this feature may offer a significant advantage over ergot alkaloids in selected patients. Most adverse effects with sumatriptan are dose related and transient. After subcutaneous administration of sumatriptan the most common adverse events are mild pain or redness at the site of injection.[89] These injection site reactions occur in 40% of patients and usually resolve within 60 minutes.[89] Other adverse effects associated with sumatriptan include mild sensations of heaviness (8%) or pressure in the head (6%), tingling (9%), and bodily warmth (9%).[89] Another complication of sumatriptan use is recurrent migraine headache. In about 40% of patients, migraine headache recurs within 24 hours after initial successful treatment with sumatriptan.[90] This phenomenon may be related to the short half-life of the drug (2 hr), and the recurrent headache may respond to repeat doses of sumatriptan.[90]

In early studies with an oral dispersible tablet formulation of sumatriptan, patients commonly reported an unpleasant taste. A new film-coated tablet has been developed and should avoid this problem. Although sumatriptan's receptor specificity suggests it may be less likely to cause significant cardiovascular effects, it has been associated with possible myocardial ischemia in one patient[89] and transient chest pain with ST segment alterations on electrocardiogram (ECG) in two patients with prior histories of cardiac ischemia.[91,92] In the majority of patients who report a transient sensation of chest tightness or pressure after subcutaneous sumatriptan, no accompanying ECG abnormalities are seen.[90] Nonetheless, sumatriptan should be avoided in patients with a history of cardiac ischemia.

Sumatriptan is a valuable addition to the agents currently available for the abortive treatment of migraine headache. However, given the high cost of subcutaneous sumatriptan ($\approx$\$28 per injec-

tion, wholesale cost), it seems reasonable to reserve this drug for patients who fail to respond to, or are intolerant of, other abortive agents including ergotamine, dihydroergotamine, and isomethepene-containing products. Direct comparative trials with these agents are necessary to further clarify the optimal use of sumatriptan.

J.Y.'s headaches have failed to respond to sublingual ergotamine and moderate doses of aspirin and ibuprofen. A trial with an alternate NSAID may be considered (e.g., naproxen 750 mg followed by 250 mg as needed to a maximum dose of 1250 mg/24 hour period). Likewise, sumatriptan may be considered, but it is a less optimal choice because of its high cost. An isomethepene-containing product, such as Midrin, is a good choice in J.Y. It may be effective when ergotamine has failed, is less expensive than sumatriptan, and may be more likely to provide relief than another NSAID.

Intractable Migraine

12. J.Y. used Midrin as directed, for her next migraine headache attack; however, the headache continued to worsen throughout the day until she could no longer work. After vomiting twice, J.Y. was taken to the emergency room (ER) by a friend. The diagnosis of intractable migraine was made. How should J.Y. be treated?

Dihydroergotamine (DHE)

Intractable migraine usually requires parenteral therapy with ergot derivatives, sumatriptan, or potent narcotic analgesics. Dihydroergotamine (DHE 45) 1 mg subcutaneously[93] or intramuscularly,[94] or 0.75 mg intravenously,[95] is particularly effective in the treatment of acute and intractable migraine headaches and thereby reduces the necessity for narcotic analgesics. If ineffective, a second dose of DHE should be administered 30 to 45 minutes later. An intravenous antiemetic (prochlorperazine 5 to 10 mg or metoclopramide 10 mg) should be administered 15 to 30 minutes before DHE to minimize the GI side effects of this agent. Experimental use of dihydroergotamine nasal spray suggests promise for this dosage form once it is available.[96] Intramuscular administration of ergotamine tartrate 0.5 mg is also effective; however, ergot-related side effects are more severe with ergotamine tartrate than with dihydroergotamine. Ergotamine tartrate administered by the oral, sublingual, or rectal routes is unlikely to be effective in this setting.

Sumatriptan

Sumatriptan 6 mg subcutaneously is also effective for the treatment of established migraine.[83] If the first injection does not provide relief at one hour, a second injection may be administered; however, the daily dosage should not exceed 12 mg.[84] An auto-injector device is available and may be preloaded to simplify subcutaneous self-administration of sumatriptan during an acute attack. The manufacturer warns that sumatriptan should not be administered within 24 hours of ergot alkaloids due to the potential for prolonged vasospastic reactions.[84]

Chlorpromazine

Chlorpromazine (Thorazine) given parenterally is also an effective abortive agent for acute migraine headache that is unresponsive to ergotamine or oral analgesics.[97] This agent has both antiemetic and pain-relieving properties and has gained increased acceptance in emergency rooms as a pharmacologic alternative to potent narcotic analgesics such as meperidine. In a double-blind, controlled trial, intravenous chlorpromazine (0.1 mg/kg) provided more effective pain relief from intractable migraine than meperidine (0.4 mg/kg) plus dimenhydrinate.[98] Chlorpromazine 1 mg/kg intramuscularly has also been shown to relieve migraine headache more effectively than placebo.[99] Intravenous prochlorperazine edisylate (Compazine) (10 mg) was also found to be effective in one controlled trial and may have a lower risk of orthostatic hypotension than chlorpromazine; however, this treatment requires further study.[100]

Narcotic Analgesics

Parenteral narcotic analgesics also effectively relieve intractable migraine headache pain; however, they should generally be reserved for second- or third-line therapy after patients have failed to respond to parenteral dihydroergotamine, sumatriptan, or chlorpromazine. Emergency room treatment of headache with narcotics is a common antecedent to iatrogenic drug addiction.[101] In some emergency rooms that deal with a large number of drug-seeking patients, the use of synthetic narcotic agonist/antagonists (e.g., butorphanol, nalbuphine) has been advocated for treatment of intractable migraine.[102,103] In a comparison with intramuscular butorphanol and intramuscular meperidine plus hydroxyzine, the superiority of intravenous DHE plus metoclopramide was clearly demonstrated.[102]

Prednisone

Prednisone 40 to 60 mg orally for three to five days, or dexamethasone 4 to 16 mg intramuscularly, may be used as alternate treatments for intractable migraine and presumably work by suppressing the sterile perivascular inflammation of resistant headache.[71,104] Table 50.4 summarizes the agents commonly used for the treatment of acute migraine headaches.

J.Y. should be treated with intramuscular or intravenous prochlorperazine (5 mg) or metoclopramide (10 mg) followed by dihydroergotamine 1 mg subcutaneously or intramuscularly, or 0.75 mg intravenously. If the headache persists after 30 to 45 minutes, the dihydroergotamine dose may be readministered. If this regimen is ineffective, parenteral meperidine 75 to 100 mg, sumatriptan 6 mg subcutaneously, or chlorpromazine 1 mg/kg intramuscularly would be reasonable alternatives.

Prophylactic Therapy

13. J.Y. returns to the clinic six weeks later for follow-up. Her current medications include: Midrin, metoclopramide, and acetaminophen with codeine. Acetaminophen with codeine 30 mg (#20) was prescribed by the emergency room physician who treated her single episode of intractable migraine. Since that episode, about half of her headaches have promptly responded to Midrin. The remainder of her attacks have been aborted with two acetaminophen with codeine tablets and rest. Her only concern is that these resistant headaches occur about twice monthly and necessitate her taking the rest of the day off from work. J.Y. reports no adverse effects to Midrin or metoclopramide.

What further treatment should be recommended to reduce the frequency and severity of J.Y.'s migraine attacks?

Criteria for Use

J.Y.'s present drug regimen is effectively aborting about half of her migraine attacks. The frequency of her disabling, drug-resistant headaches, however, is sufficient to warrant additional therapy that is directed toward preventing migraine attacks. Prophylactic migraine treatment not only reduces the frequency of migraine attacks, but also may reduce the severity of ensuing headaches or render them more responsive to abortive measures. The usual cri-

Table 50.4			Drug Treatment of Acute Migraine Headache[a]		
Drug	Route[c]	Dose	Contraindications[b]	Adverse Effects[b]	Comments[b]
Ibuprofen (Motrin) or other NSAIDs	PO	400–800 mg	Aspirin or NSAID-related bronchospasm	N, V, bleeding, renal dysfunction	First-line therapy. Acetaminophen may also be effective
Ergotamine tartrate (Cafergot, Ergostat)	PO, SL, PR	1–4 mg stat, then 1–2 Q 30 min to max of 6 mg/attack or 10 mg/wk	CV disease, sepsis, liver or kidney disease, arterial insufficiency, pregnancy, breast feeding, concomitant macrolide use	N, V, anorexia, limb paresthesias or pain	Use at HA onset for max effect. ↓ N and V by using smallest effective dose
Isometheptene/ dichloralphenazone/ acetaminophen (Midrin)	PO	2 cap stat, then 1 cap Q hr to max 5 cap/12 hr	See Ergotamine tartrate. Avoid in patients taking MAOIs	N, V, dizziness, drowsiness	As effective as ergotamine tartrate
Sumatriptan (Imitrex)	SQ	6 mg stat; may repeat in 1 hr	Ischemic heart disease, within 24 hr of ergot alkaloids	Heavy sensation in head or chest, tingling, pain at injection site	Effective and well tolerated. Cost limits widespread use. Reserve for intractable migraine or patients intolerant of other abortive agents
Chlorpromazine (Thorazine)	IM	1 mg/kg	CV disease, history of seizures	Extrapyramidal reactions, sedation, hypotension	For intractable migraine. Also has antiemetic properties
Morphine (or meperidine)	IM	5–10 mg	↑ ICP or head trauma with funduscopic changes	Sedation, hypoventilation	For intractable migraine
Metoclopramide (Reglan)	PO, IM	10 mg stat	GI hemorrhage or obstruction; pheochromocytoma	Extrapyramidal reactions, sedation, restlessness	For adjunctive antiemetic therapy. Prochlorperazine also effective

[a] See text for references and additional details.
[b] CV = Cardiovascular; GI = Gastrointestinal; HA = Headache; ICP = Intracranial pressure; MAOIs = Monoamine oxidase inhibitors; N = Nausea; NSAID = Nonsteroidal anti-inflammatory drug; V = Vomiting.
[c] IM = Intramuscular; PO = Oral; PR = Rectal; SL = Sublingual; SQ = Subcutaneous.

teria for migraine prophylaxis are: 1) headaches that occur twice monthly or more; 2) disabling headaches that occur less frequently but are unresponsive to usual abortive measures; 3) patients in whom abortive agents are contraindicated; and 4) headaches that occur in predictable patterns.[10,50] Given the frequency with which J.Y. continues to experience migraine headaches and the detrimental effect they have on her job performance, prophylactic migraine therapy is warranted.

Various prophylactic agents have been advocated for reducing the frequency and/or severity of migraine headaches. For many of these drugs, it is impossible to make an adequate assessment of efficacy based upon the available literature. Therapeutic trials often are not optimally designed to establish the relative usefulness of a given drug to others within the current armamentarium of prophylactic agents. For example, the efficacy of newer therapies may be continually compared with placebo rather than to other agents whose effectiveness is well documented; dosages are often suboptimal; or the duration of therapy may be insufficient to document maximal efficacy. Ideally, the evaluation of migraine drug therapy should be based upon double-blind, controlled, crossover trials with optimal dosage titration (to effect, toxicity, or established maximum dosing recommendations) and with sufficient wash-out periods to minimize ambiguous results. Many prophylactic therapy recommendations are not so well grounded. Table 50.5 contains a list of the more well-established drugs used for migraine headache prophylaxis.

Propranolol

Propranolol (Inderal) is the drug of first choice for migraine prophylaxis because of its safety, efficacy, favorable adverse effect profile, and the large number of studies which support its effectiveness.[105] Although the effectiveness of propranolol in the prophylaxis of migraine is well established, not all individuals respond to this treatment.[105–111] When propranolol is used appropriately, 50% to 80% of patients obtain complete or partial relief from migraine attacks;[105,111,112] most patients who initially respond to pro-

pranolol continue to benefit without any evidence of drug tolerance.[111] The effectiveness of propranolol is comparable to that of methysergide,[113] the agent previously considered the drug of choice for migraine prophylaxis and the standard by which other therapies are often judged.

The mechanism by which propranolol exerts its antimigraine effects is unknown. It was generally assumed, without evidence to support the hypothesis, that β-receptor blockade prevented the vasodilatory phase of migraine; however, propranolol has no significant effect upon cerebral blood flow.[114] The mechanism of action may be related to the drug's effects on the serotonergic system.[115,116] Propranolol has a high affinity for serotonin receptors[116] and has been shown to inhibit platelet uptake of serotonin in vivo and in vitro.[117]

Despite the lack of FDA approval for migraine prophylaxis, other β-adrenergic blocking drugs such as timolol[118] and the cardioselective agents, metoprolol[119] and atenolol,[120,121] have been found to be equally as efficacious as propranolol in double-blind, crossover trials. In parallel treatment trials, nadolol (Corgard)[122] has also been effective. Nadolol and atenolol are appropriate therapeutic alternatives for patients intolerant of propranolol's central nervous system adverse effects. The lack of efficacy demonstrated for pindolol[123] and acebutolol[124] may be related to their intrinsic sympathomimetic activity; these agents should not be used.

14. Dosing. What dose of propranolol should be prescribed for J.Y.?

Propranolol 40 to 320 mg/day in two to four divided doses is effective in the prophylaxis of migraine headaches.[50,105] Since the dosage range is wide, propranolol therapy should be initiated with 20 mg two to three times a day; this dose can be increased gradually at weekly intervals to a maximum of 320 mg/day.[10] Once the daily dosage of propranolol required to control headaches is established, patient compliance may be improved by changing to a long-acting oral dosage form (e.g., Inderal LA). Although the usual dosage for migraine prophylaxis is 80 to 240 mg/day, up to 30%

Table 50.5		Drugs Commonly Used for Migraine Headache Prophylaxis[a]		
Drug	Dose	Dosage Forms/Strengths[b]	Effectiveness	Comments
Propranolol (Inderal)	20 mg BID–TID. Gradually ↑ dose at weekly intervals to effect or max of 320 mg/day	Tab: 10, 20, 40, 60, 80, 90 mg ER Cap: 60, 80, 120, 160 mg	50%–80% obtain complete or partial relief. Comparable to methysergide	Drug of first choice for prophylaxis because of safety, efficacy, and tolerability. Atenolol, metoprolol, nadolol, and timolol also effective
Amitriptyline (Elavil)	25 mg HS. ↑ by 25 mg/day at weekly intervals to max 150 mg/day. Most should benefit from 50–75 mg/day	Tab: 10, 25, 50, 75, 100, 150 mg	Effectiveness comparable to propranolol and methysergide	Effective for prophylaxis of migraine and tension-type headache. Fluoxetine and nortriptyline also effective
Verapamil (Isoptin, Calan)	80 mg TID. If needed, ↑ dose gradually to max of 480 mg/day	Tabs: 40, 80, 120 mg ER Cap: 120, 240 mg ER Tab: 180, 240 mg	50% obtain complete or partial relief	Delay of 1–2 months for maximal effect. Efficacy of nifedipine and diltiazem questionable
Valproate (Depakote)	250 mg BID. ↑ by 250 mg/day at weekly intervals to effect or adverse effects. Most should benefit from 1000–2000 mg/day	Cap:[c] 250 mg DR Tab:[d] 125, 250, 500 mg SCaps: 125 mg	50% obtain complete or partial relief	Well tolerated. Additional studies needed to confirm effectiveness
Methysergide (Sansert)	2–8 mg/day in 3–4 divided daily doses to be taken with food	Tab: 2 mg	60%–70% obtain complete or partial relief	Use limited by propensity for frequent and sometimes severe adverse effects. Drug holidays should be planned every 6 months

[a] See text for references and additional details.
[b] Tab = Tablets; ER = Extended release; Cap = Capsules; DR = Delayed release; SCap = Sprinkle capsules containing coated particles.
[c] Valproic acid capsules.
[d] Divalproex sodium delayed release tablets.

of patients prophylactically treated with propranolol would not have benefited in one clinical study of 865 patients if the propranolol dosage had not been titrated to a maximum of 320 mg/day.[112] Although most propranolol responders will experience relief within four to six weeks of beginning therapy,[50] in some cases, three to six months may be required before maximal benefit is realized.[112] Tolerance to the antimigraine effects of propranolol was not detected in one 12-month study.[111]

Since propranolol is the prophylactic agent of choice in migraine and J.Y. has no pre-existing disease states that would prohibit its use, she should be started at a low dosage with gradual titration to either therapeutic response, side effects, or a maximum dose of 320 mg/day. Several months may be required before optimal results are achieved.

Methysergide

15. G.W., a 46-year-old male with an 11-year history of migraine without aura, comes to clinic with a complaint of epigastric distress for the past two days. Current medications include: Fiorinal (aspirin 325 mg, butalbital 50 mg, caffeine 40 mg) two capsules PO at headache onset; methysergide (Sansert) 2 mg PO TID; and Theo-Dur 300 mg PO BID. G.W.'s headaches are notable for bilateral, throbbing, temporal head pain and the absence of associated GI or focal neurologic symptoms. Migraine prophylaxis with methysergide has resulted in a reduction of headache frequency from three headaches monthly to about one headache every two to three months. A review of G.W.'s medical record reveals that methysergide therapy was initiated two years ago and that a drug holiday was not taken. Past medical history includes asthma since adolescence, with frequent emergency room visits for exacerbation of symptoms and a three-year history of painful lower extremity peripheral vascular disease (PVD).

Why is methysergide an appropriate (or inappropriate) alternative to propranolol prophylaxis of migraine in this asthmatic patient with PVD?

Methysergide, a semisynthetic ergot alkaloid with peripheral serotonin antagonist properties, is one of the most effective agents for migraine prophylaxis;[125,126] previously it was the standard by which newer therapies were often judged. Its use is limited, however, by a propensity for frequent, and sometimes severe, side effects.

Within the usual dosage range of 2 to 8 mg in three to four daily divided doses, as many as 40% of patients treated with methysergide will experience side effects. Adverse effects are severe enough to require discontinuation in 10% of patients.

Contraindications. Like other ergot alkaloids, methysergide has peripheral vasoconstrictive properties that may preclude its use in some patients. Contraindications to methysergide use include PVD, coronary artery disease, thrombophlebitis, and pregnancy. Even when such precautions are kept in mind, some patients will experience side effects attributable to the drug's vasoconstrictive properties (e.g., coldness, numbness, or tingling of the extremities or even anginal pain).

Given G.W.'s history of peripheral vascular disease, methysergide is not an appropriate agent for migraine prophylaxis. Although G.W. had a history of PVD before methysergide was initiated, the continued use of this drug may have aggravated his condition. G.W.'s methysergide should be tapered immediately and an alternative treatment regimen initiated.

16. Adverse Effects. **In addition to G.W.'s history of PVD, what is another reason for discontinuing his methysergide therapy and how should it be tapered?**

Retroperitoneal, endocardial, and pleuropulmonary fibrosis are severe complications of methysergide. Fibrosis has developed after 7 to 79 months of methysergide therapy and has been associated with doses in excess of 8 mg/day.[50] Since most fibrotic complications have been reported following long-term, uninterrupted use of methysergide,[127,128] drug-free holidays of three to four weeks are recommended after each six-month treatment period to minimize this risk. The discontinuation of methysergide, however, should be gradual to avoid the rebound vascular headache that can occur after abrupt discontinuation. Patients on long-term therapy should be counseled to report any flank pain, dysuria, or chest pain to their physician. During each patient visit, cardiac auscultation should be performed. An intravenous pyelogram and chest x-ray also should be obtained after six months of therapy to monitor for the development of fibrosis. When the therapeutic benefits of methysergide become evident (approximately three to four weeks after initiation of therapy) the dose of this drug should be reduced to the minimum effective amount.[50]

Since G.W. has received methysergide continuously for two years without a drug holiday, he is at risk for developing methysergide fibrosis. The methysergide should be discontinued in G.W. because of the risk of drug-induced fibrosis and because of his history of peripheral vascular disease. His methysergide therapy should be gradually tapered to discontinuation over a three-week period to avoid migraine headache rebound. Subsequently, another form of prophylactic therapy should be initiated for G.W.

17. G.W. has been experiencing nausea for the past two days. What is one approach to resolving these GI complaints?

Gastrointestinal distress is the most common side effect to methysergide therapy; however, the discomfort is usually mild and disappears within the first several days to weeks of therapy. GI distress can be minimized by administering methysergide doses with food and by avoiding rapid increases in dose. Since G.W. has received methysergide therapy for two years and his gastrointestinal complaints appear to be of recent origin, other potential causes for GI distress should be investigated. Methysergide can also activate latent peptic ulcer disease,[126] presumably by increasing gastric acid secretion.[129] However, G.W. has no known history of ulcer disease and his gastrointestinal complaint does not specifically suggest this complication.

G.W.'s GI distress may be the result of gastritis or peptic ulcer disease caused by the aspirin component in Fiorinal (G.W. receives 650 mg aspirin with each two capsule Fiorinal dose). The nausea also could be due to theophylline toxicity. These potential causes of G.W.'s nausea should be evaluated. A laboratory determination of G.W.'s hemoglobin (Hgb) concentration and evaluation of his stools for occult blood would be helpful in assessing aspirin-induced gastritis with blood loss. A serum theophylline concentration also should be obtained. A more detailed history that focuses on the relationship of nausea to medication use or other concurrent illness may also provide useful information for assessing G.W.'s gastrointestinal distress.

18. What drug should be prescribed in place of methysergide for prevention of G.W.'s migraine attacks?

Amitriptyline

Amitriptyline (Elavil) is effective for prevention of both migraine and tension-type headaches. It may be the drug of choice for patients whose symptoms suggest features of both headache types (i.e., mixed tension-type/migraine headaches).[128] Since G.W. has pre-existing medical problems that prohibit the use of both propranolol and methysergide, amitriptyline would be a reasonable alternative for migraine prophylaxis.

In a double-blind, placebo-controlled cross-over study, amitriptyline was as effective as propranolol.[130] Amitriptyline also was as effective as methysergide based upon comparative results from previous studies.[131] The mechanism of amitriptyline's antimigraine effect is independent of its antidepressant activity[130,132] and has been proposed to be related to its ability to block the reuptake of serotonin at central sites.[50] However, other antidepressant agents which block 5-HT reuptake (e.g., clomipramine) have been ineffective for migraine prophylaxis.[133] Amitriptyline and other antidepressants have been reported to down-regulate 5-HT receptors, although this effect has been inconsistent in published reports.[134]

Dosing. G.W. should be treated with 25 mg amitriptyline at bedtime. This nightly dose can be increased at weekly intervals by 25 mg until the maximum dose of 150 mg/day is reached. The majority of patients achieve optimal benefit from 50 to 75 mg/day of amitriptyline; doses greater than 150 mg/day are unlikely to produce better results.[50] Two-thirds of patients note a decrease in the number of headaches within seven days of starting amitriptyline therapy, but a six-week trial is warranted before the drug should be considered ineffective.[131,132]

Fluoxetine (Prozac)[135] and nortriptyline (Aventyl)[50] are also effective for prevention of migraine; however, their effectiveness in preventing migraine headaches is not as well established as that for amitriptyline. Preliminary observations suggest that imipramine and trazodone are ineffective.[50]

Valproate

Valproate (Depakote), an antiepileptic drug shown to effectively prevent migraine headaches,[142] is gaining popularity as a prophylactic agent in some centers. In a randomized, double-blind, parallel treatment comparison of valproate (titrated to trough serum concentrations of 70 to 120 µg/mL) or placebo, 48% of valproate-treated patients had a 50% or greater reduction in the frequency of migraine.[143] Further studies are needed to establish the role of valproate in prophylactic migraine therapy. Amitriptyline would be the preferred agent for treating G.W.'s migraine headaches.

19. S.A. is a 41-year old female with a two-year history of disabling migraine headaches (with aura) occurring two to three times weekly. She is currently using Ergostat (sublingual ergotamine) for abortive therapy but she usually requires 4 mg ergotamine to abort each attack and the clinic physician is concerned about cumulative ergotamine toxicity if she overuses this drug. Past medical history includes depression with three suicide attempts and a history of polydrug abuse. She has failed prophylactic therapy with propranolol and valproate. Her physician wishes to avoid antidepressants because of her psychiatric history and methysergide due to its side effect profile. What other prophylactic therapies are available?

Some of the less established therapies occasionally recommended for migraine prophylaxis are listed in Table 50.6. Evaluative reports for some of these agents do not meet the criteria for establishing a clear benefit in migraine. In general, a significant reduction of headache frequency in 50% of patients should be demonstrated before a drug can be said to be more effective than placebo. Placebo response rates for migraine and other painful conditions range from 30% to 50%[10,136,137] and may be maintained over several months.[137] This significant effect should also be considered when evaluating studies of migraine therapy.

Calcium Channel Blockers

20. A trial with a calcium channel blocker is suggested by S.A.'s physician to reduce the frequency and severity of migraine attacks. Which of the currently available calcium channel blockers should be chosen for prophylaxis of S.A.'s migraine headaches?

Calcium channel blockers influence the final common pathway of vascular reactivity by altering calcium flux across smooth muscle. Hormone and neurotransmitter secretion are also calcium-dependent processes that can be altered by calcium channel blockers.[138] Whether the efficacy of calcium antagonists in migraine

Table 50.6	Other Drugs for Migraine Headache Prophylaxis	
Drug	Dose/Day (Oral)	Comments
Aspirin[154]	325 mg QOD	Additional studies needed to document effectiveness
Clonidine[155–157]	0.1–0.2 mg BID–TID	No benefit found in some studies
Cyproheptadine[71]	4–8 mg TID–QID (adults)	Particularly useful for migraine in children
Ergonovine maleate[50,158]	0.2 mg TID–QID during menses or continuously	Effective for menstrual migraine and when other prophylactic agents contraindicated. Recommended by some authors as a first-line prophylactic agent
Naproxen sodium[71]	275–550 BID	Effective for menstrual migraine. Effective as an abortive agent
Phenelzine[71,159]	15 mg TID–QID	Caution when used simultaneously with antidepressants and beta blockers
Phenytoin[50]	200–400 mg QD	Benefits in children and adults established by uncontrolled studies

therapy is due to their vasoactive properties or modulation of neurotransmitter release or action is unknown.

Verapamil (Isoptin, Calan) is the calcium channel blocker of choice for S.A.'s treatment since its effectiveness has been most extensively demonstrated by blinded, cross-over, placebo-controlled studies. Most patients respond to verapamil at doses of 240 to 320 mg/day; therefore, treatment can be initiated with an 80 mg dose three times a day and increased to 80 mg four times a day after one week. Observable benefits from this treatment may not be apparent for three to eight weeks; as a result, verapamil should be continued for at least two months to properly evaluate response to therapy. This is one of the limiting properties of calcium channel antagonists and a major reason why verapamil is not considered a drug of first choice for migraine prophylaxis.[50] If an adequate response is not achieved in this interval, the verapamil dose can be increased weekly by increments of 80 mg to a maximum of 480 mg/day. Sustained-release (SR) formulations of verapamil (Calan SR, Isoptin SR) are available and often useful for improving patient compliance with long-term therapy. Headache frequency, intensity, and duration are reduced in 50% of patients treated with verapamil.[139–141] Patients who suffer from migraine with or without aura respond equally well.[139,140] Although tolerance to the antimigraine effects of calcium antagonists has occurred within the first several months of therapy, an increase in dosage may restore headache control.[189,217] Verapamil should be used as a second- or third-line prophylactic agent when β-adrenergic receptor blockers and antidepressants are ineffective or contraindicated.

Nifedipine and Diltiazem. Nifedipine (Procardia) and diltiazem (Cardizem) are other calcium antagonists that have been used for the treatment of migraine.[189,144,145] Although preliminary experience suggested that nifedipine was effective, a double-blind, cross-over study found nifedipine to be no more effective than placebo for preventing migraine headaches with aura. This study was designed to detect a 50% reduction in migraine frequency during treatment.[146] The effectiveness of diltiazem is based upon two open-label studies with no control treatment.[144,147] As yet, no placebo-controlled, crossover studies have been reported. On the basis of current evidence, neither nifedipine nor diltiazem can be recommended for prophylaxis of migraine headache until other, better-established therapies (see Table 50.5) have been adequately tried and yielded unsatisfactory results.

Nimodipine (Nimotop) is a newer calcium antagonist with marked selectivity for the cerebral vasculature.[148] The drug is approved only for improvement of neurologic deficits following aneurysmal subarachnoid hemorrhage. Results from double-blind, placebo-controlled trials have been inconsistent in showing a benefit of nimodipine for preventing migraine headaches.[149-152] In most studies, the dose of oral nimodipine was 40 mg given three times daily.[150-152] Unfortunately, no studies are available which compare nimodipine to β-adrenergic receptor blocking agents, methysergide, or antidepressant drugs; therefore, the appropriate place of nimodipine in migraine prophylaxis is yet to be determined. In light of the modest benefit in most trials and the high cost of this drug, nimodipine should be reserved for patients who are candidates for calcium antagonist therapy but have not responded adequately to verapamil. The manufacturer of nimodipine has abandoned efforts to obtain FDA approval for this agent in the treatment of migraine due to the modest benefit suggested by clinical trials.[153]

S.A. should be started on verapamil 80 mg three times a day with gradual dosage titration to side effects, cessation of migraine attacks, or a maximum dose of 480 mg/day. A two-month trial may be necessary to demonstrate optimal therapeutic effect. Prophylactic therapy for migraine should be continued for three to six months. If a satisfactory response is achieved, the prophylactic agent should be gradually discontinued over several weeks to assess the continued need for this mode of therapy.[71]

Cluster Headache

Cluster headache is a relatively infrequent headache disorder which derives its name from the characteristic pattern of headache recurrence; headaches tend to occur nightly over a relatively short period of time (i.e., several weeks or months), followed by a long period of complete remission. Cluster headaches occur more commonly in males than females. There may be a seasonal predilection to cluster attacks with the spring and fall being common times for headache recurrence. Headaches are usually of short duration and present as severe, unrelenting, unilateral pain occurring behind the eye with radiation to the territory of the ipsilateral trigeminal nerve (temple, cheek, or gum). Associated aura symptoms are uncommon.

The different clinical characteristics between cluster and migraine headaches (e.g., sex ratio, periodicity of attacks, duration of headaches, aura symptoms) suggest that these two types of vascular headaches are different clinical entities.[160]

Pathophysiology

The pathophysiology of cluster headache is undetermined. As in migraine, vascular, neurogenic, metabolic, and humoral factors have been proposed to play a role in cluster headache pathogenesis. Precipitation of headaches during a cluster period by vasodilators and response to vasoconstrictors suggests an underlying vascular component. During a cluster headache, thermography shows increased periorbital heat emission ipsilateral to the head pain.[161] Also, patients commonly report flushing in the same area and these observations suggest that extracranial vasodilation occurs in cluster headache. However, intracranial blood flow studies fail to show

consistent changes during a cluster attack[162-164] and the alterations in extracranial blood flow follow the onset of head pain[165] suggesting that vasodilation occurs in response to some other initiating stimulus.

Observations which suggest a neural component to cluster headache include the occurrence of headache in the distribution of the trigeminal nerve, accompanying autonomic symptoms and the fact that headache precedes extracranial vasodilation. Stimulation of the trigeminal nerve results in the release of substance P and vasoactive polypeptides, vasodilation, and pain.[166] These features implicate the trigeminovascular system in cluster headache pathogenesis; however, a coherent theory to explain the symptoms, periodicity, and circadian regularity of cluster headaches remains elusive.

Signs and Symptoms

21. R.H. is a 31-year-old male with a three-year history of episodic cluster headache. He has been headache-free for the past year but today states that the headaches are returning in their characteristic fashion. He reports abrupt onset of right-sided retro-orbital pain with occasional superimposed knife-like "jabs" which increase in intensity over several minutes to a severe, unrelenting pain which lasts about 90 minutes. The headache then gradually subsides. Associated symptoms include right-sided lacrimation, conjunctival injection, and rhinorrhea. He denies any premonition of ensuing headache or GI upset during the attacks. Physical examination during a cluster headache shows right eyelid droop and pupillary miosis. R.H.'s cluster periods characteristically last about two months and usually recur once or twice yearly. The first headache of the current bout awoke R.H. from a short nap. R.H. expects to suffer one or two such headaches daily as this has been the usual pattern during each cluster period. Previous cluster headaches have been symptomatically treated with aspirin and codeine 30 mg; however, R.H. reports only modest relief with this treatment approach. R.H.'s past medical history is unremarkable. He does not use tobacco but admits to occasional social drinking.

What subjective and objective evidence in this case are consistent with a diagnosis of cluster headaches?

R.H.'s sex, age of onset, quality and intensity of headache pain, periodicity of headache attacks, and associated symptoms all support the diagnosis of cluster headaches.

Cluster headaches affect males more commonly than females by a ratio of 5:1,[161,167] and have their usual onset between the second and fourth decades of life.[167] R.H.'s sex (male) and age of onset (28 years) are compatible with these aspects of cluster headaches.

Recurrent cluster headaches are usually severe, throbbing, and affect the same side of the head. Occasionally, cluster headaches may involve the entire hemicranium. The pain starts abruptly, often waking the patient from sleep, reaches maximum intensity over 5 to 15 minutes, and usually lasts 45 to 60 minutes.[161] Cluster periods often last from two to three months and recur once or twice yearly.[161] Patients suffering from chronic cluster headaches have bouts that last 12 months or longer. R.H.'s headache quality (severe, unrelenting pain), site (unilateral), evolution and resolution pattern (worsens over several minutes and resolves within 90 minutes), and periodicity of attacks (one or two headaches occurring daily for about two months followed by a period of remission that lasts about one year) are all compatible with the usual character of cluster headaches.

Associated features may include ipsilateral lacrimation, injected conjunctiva, and rhinorrhea or blocked nasal passage. A partial Horner's syndrome (ptosis with miosis) occurs in one-third of patients and is often the only abnormal physical finding during a cluster headache. Nausea, vomiting, and focal neurological symptoms are often absent. Associated symptoms reported by R.H. during headache attacks (e.g., lacrimation, rhinorrhea, conjunctival injection) and the absence of gastrointestinal or neurologic disturbances are also compatible with the diagnosis of cluster headaches.

During a cluster period, headaches may be precipitated by alcohol (even in small amounts), vasodilators, stress, warm weather, missed meals, and excessive sleep. Therefore, during the current cluster period, R.H. should be counseled to avoid all alcohol and daytime naps.

Abortive Therapy

22. What abortive measures are available for symptomatic treatment of individual headaches during R.H.'s current cluster period?

The treatments of choice for abortive treatment of cluster headaches are oxygen inhalation and ergotamine tartrate.[161,168] The expense and inconvenience of having oxygen inhalation apparatus close at hand make ergotamine a more acceptable treatment modality for some patients.

Ergotamine Tartrate

Inhalational, sublingual, and parenteral routes of ergotamine administration are preferred for aborting an attack because of their rapid onset of action.[169] Ergotamine by inhalation or sublingual administration is effective in 70% to 80% of patients[170,171] and traditionally these routes of administration have been preferred. Unfortunately, no inhaled ergotamine product is currently being marketed in the United States, and the product is likely to remain unavailable. Thus, sublingual ergotamine would be preferred for initial therapy in R.H. if oxygen inhalation is impractical. Sublingual ergotamine 1 mg taken every five minutes, up to 3 mg over a 15-minute period, was effective in 70% of patients studied in one report,[172] and would be an appropriate regimen to use in R.H. Ergotamine tartrate 2 mg given rectally also can be effective if given early in the attack.[170] Since few patients are willing to inject themselves, parenteral administration of ergotamine is usually reserved for inpatient treatment of cluster headache. Ergotamine tartrate 0.5 mg and dihydroergotamine (DHE) 1 mg given intramuscularly are equally effective; DHE is better tolerated.[170]

Oxygen

Oxygen inhalation is preferred not only for in-hospital treatment of cluster headache but also for use by some patients at home or at work. Oxygen is also useful for patients with frequent cluster headaches who would otherwise exceed maximum dosing restrictions of ergotamine.[173] The benefits of oxygen inhalation at 7 L/min for 15 minutes, are superior to placebo[174] and equal to those of ergotamine[172] in relieving cluster headaches. Additionally, oxygen is very fast-acting with the majority of patients experiencing headache relief within seven minutes of beginning inhalation.[172] The mechanism of oxygen's effect is unknown but has been proposed to be related to a direct vasoconstrictive action.[168]

Sumatriptan

Sumatriptan 6 mg subcutaneously has also been shown to effectively relieve cluster headache in one double-blind, placebo-controlled trial. Seventy-four percent of attacks responded to sumatriptan compared to 26% of placebo-treated attacks.[175] An additional injection of 6 mg does not appear to give better headache relief.[168] Until sumatriptan is compared to ergot alkaloids or oxygen inhalation, its use should be reserved for selected cluster headache patients who do not obtain relief from these therapies.

Other Therapeutic Interventions

Cluster headaches also can be relieved by less commonly utilized therapeutic interventions such as dexamethasone 8 mg orally,[161] methoxyflurane inhalation (10 to 15 drops applied to a handkerchief and inhaled for several seconds),[50] somatostatin intravenous infusion (25 μg/min for 20 minutes),[176] and local anesthesia with either topical application of 1 mL of 4% lidocaine hydrochloride[177] or 0.3 mL of a 5% to 10% solution of cocaine hydrochloride[178] to the ipsilateral sphenopalatine fossa. Preliminary results with intranasal DHE for the treatment of cluster headaches suggest that the intensity of headaches is reduced;[179] trials with larger intranasal doses are needed to establish the optimal use of DHE.

Orally administered narcotic analgesics are usually ineffective in cluster headache[161] and R.H. has suffered several cluster periods with inadequate therapy. Improved response can be expected with the use of a more effective agent with a faster onset of action. Either sublingual ergotamine or oxygen can be recommended depending upon availability and patient preference.

Table 50.7		Drugs Commonly Used for Acute Treatment of Cluster Headache[a]				
Drug	Route[c]	Dose[b]	Contraindications	Adverse Effects[b]	Comments
Ergotamine tartrate (Ergostat, Cafergot)	SL, PR	1–2 mg at HA onset. May repeat in 5 min (SL only). Do not exceed 6 mg/attack or 10 mg/wk	CV disease, sepsis, liver or kidney disease, arterial insufficiency, pregnancy, breast feeding, concomitant macrolide use	N, V, anorexia, limb paresthesias or pain	SL ergotamine may have faster onset of effect. ↓ N and V by using smallest effective dose
Oxygen	Inhalation	7 L/min for 15 min	—	—	Fast onset of effect. Equally effective as ergotamine tartrate
Dihydroergotamine (DHE-45)	SQ, IM, IV	1 mg (SQ, IM) or 0.75 mg (IV) stat; may repeat in 45 min	CV disease, sepsis, liver or kidney disease, arterial insufficiency, pregnancy, breast feeding	N, V, limb paresthesias or pain	More effective and faster onset than SL or PR ergotamine. Premedicate with antiemetic (e.g., metoclopramide or prochlorperazine)
Sumatriptan (Imitrex)	SQ	6 mg at HA onset	Ischemic heart disease, within 24 hr of ergot alkaloids	Heavy sensation in head or chest, tingling, pain at injection site	Not an FDA-approved indication. Costly but well tolerated

[a] See text for references and additional details.
[b] HA= Headache; N = Nausea; V = Vomiting.
[c] IM= Imtramuscular; IV = Intravenous; PR = Rectal; SL = Sublingual; SQ = Subcutaneous.

Table 50.8	Drugs for Prophylaxis of Cluster Headache[a]		
Drug	Dose/Day[b]	Route[c]	Comments[b]
Ergotamine tartrate (Cafergot, Ergostat)[50]	0.25–0.5 mg BID–TID 5 days/wk	SQ	Effective when given 30 min before anticipated cluster HA
	1–2 mg BID or HS for nocturnal HA. Max 12 mg/wk	PO, SL, PR	
Indomethacin (Indocin)[50,207]	50 mg TID	PO	Effective for chronic cluster HA
Lithium carbonate[183,184,208]	600–1500 mg	PO	Drug of choice for chronic cluster HA. Effective in 80% of patients
Methysergide (Sansert)[170,181]	2 mg TID–QID	PO	Effective in 65%–70% of patients with episodic cluster HA. Less effective for chronic cluster HA
Prednisone[50,170,180,181]	40 mg QID × 2 days, then taper by 5 mg/day to maintenance dose of 15–30 mg QID	PO	A first-line agent for episodic cluster HA. More effective and faster-acting than methysergide. Benefits usually within 48 hr. Best for short bouts of cluster HA because of long-term adverse effects
Triamcinolone (Aristocort)[50]	4–8 mg QID	PO	May be useful in patients unresponsive to prednisone
Valproate (Depakote)[142]	600–2000 mg/day divided TID–QID	PO	Effective in 73% of patients in 1 open trial
Verapamil (Isoptin, Calan)[145,208]	240–480 mg/day divided TID–QID	PO	Nifedipine and nimodipine also effective. Further study needed to confirm efficacy

[a] See text for references and additional details.
[b] HA= headache.
[c] PO = Oral; PR = Rectal; SL = Sublingual; SQ = Subcutaneous.

Prophylactic Therapy

23. What therapeutic agents are available for prophylaxis of headache for R.H. during an active cluster period?

Pharmacotherapy aimed at prevention of cluster headaches during an active period should be considered if symptomatic therapy is ineffective, intolerable, or if headaches occur more frequently than twice daily. Table 50.7 contains a list of available drugs for cluster headache prophylaxis.

Prednisone

Prednisone provides relief from episodic cluster headache in 50% to 75% of patients[180,181] and is superior to methysergide in both episodic and chronic cluster types.[181] Prednisone also has a faster onset of action than many other agents used for cluster headache prophylaxis.[71] The beneficial effect is usually evident within 48 hours of initiating treatment.[50] Corticosteroids are best used for short bouts of cluster headaches because of the side effects associated with prolonged use.

Ergotamine

Ergotamine's use as a prophylactic agent is particularly attractive when headache recurrence follows a predictable pattern (e.g., nocturnal attacks). Prophylactic administration at bedtime or at least 30 minutes before the anticipated headache often will prevent the attack.[161]

Methysergide

Methysergide is effective in 65% to 70% of patients with episodic cluster headache and can be used for cluster periods of less than three months' duration without the same degree of concern for fibrotic complications because of the anticipated shorter period of drug exposure.[170,181] A limitation to the use of methysergide as the sole prophylactic agent for cluster headache is the delay in symptomatic response which may be up to two weeks in some patients. Chronic cluster headache responds less dramatically to methysergide and other agents are preferred.[170] Calcium channel blockers may be effective,[145,182,217] and some authors recommend their use as first-line prophylactic therapy.[161] Beta blockers, anti-

depressants, and carbamazepine have no proven usefulness in the treatment of cluster headaches.[50]

Lithium Carbonate

Lithium carbonate is effective in preventing episodic cluster headache in 80% of patients and is the drug of choice for prevention of chronic cluster headaches.[170,183,184] Benefits from lithium prophylaxis are observable one to two weeks after initiation of therapy,[50,183,184] and these benefits are maintained with long-term use.[185] Lithium serum levels associated with efficacy in cluster headache prophylaxis are usually between 0.6 and 1.2 mEq/L;[161] however, lower levels (0.3 to 0.8 mEq/L) may also be effective.[186] Adverse effects from long-term lithium use (e.g., renal toxicity) are discussed in Chapter 77: Mood Disorders II: Bipolar Affective Disorders.

R.H. should be evaluated at his next clinic visit for response to abortive ergotamine therapy. Prompt consideration should be given to the above additional treatments if suppression of the cluster period is warranted. In general, once response to a suppressive agent has been established and maintained for at least two weeks, attempts can be made to discontinue the drug. Treatment should be reinstituted if headaches recur.

Tension-Type Headache

Tension-type headache is the most common headache type with a lifetime prevalence of 88% in women and 69% in men.[187] Tension-type headaches (previously known as tension or muscle contraction headaches) are usually characterized by a dull aching sensation bilaterally which occurs in a hatband distribution around the head. The pain is usually mild to moderate in severity and has a nonpulsating quality.[188] Tension-type headaches are not associated with aura symptoms, nor are they accompanied by nausea, vomiting, or photophobia.[6] The headache is usually not of sufficient intensity to interfere with daily activities but may be a nuisance by virtue of its persistent nature. Headache frequency varies widely between patients. Chronic tension-type headache sufferers may have headache continuously for months or even years.

Pathophysiology

The throbbing pain associated with migraine headaches is not characteristic of tension-type headaches,[6] although it may occur in one-fourth of tension-type headache sufferers when the pain becomes severe.[50] Such patients may be diagnosed more appropriately as having a mixed tension-type/migraine headache disorder.[192] Indeed, in recent years the traditional boundaries distinguishing migraine from tension-type headaches have become less clear. Headache features such as neck muscle contraction and precipitation by stress were previously thought to be specific for tension-type headaches but are now recognized to occur in migraine as well.[189]

For many years, excessive muscle contraction with constriction of pain-sensitive extracranial structures was thought to be the cause of tension-type headache.[190] More recent evidence shows no correlation between muscle contraction and the presence of tension-type headache.[191] Abnormal vascular reactivity was also thought to play a role in tension-type headache but temporal muscle blood flow is unaltered compared to controls.[191] Platelet 5-HT content is lower in patients with chronic tension-type headache suggesting that migraine and tension-type headaches share some pathophysiologic features.[188]

Tension-type headaches also may be associated with depression,[192] repressed hostility, or resentment.[193] These psychological associations, however, may be the result of the chronic pain syndrome rather than a cause or feature of the headache disorder. Patients with recurrent tension-type headaches probably do not experience more frequent stressful events, but may employ less effective coping strategies in stressful situations.[194]

General Management and Abortive Therapy

24. K.B., a 27-year-old female financial analyst, presents to her general practitioner with a complaint of recurring headaches that worsened when she started her current job. Before this time she had experienced infrequent headaches which she associated with periods of stress. The headaches would occur three to four times yearly, were of a constant, dull, or ''pressing'' character, and were present around the entire head. Recently, headaches of similar character have been occurring about one to two times weekly, usually toward the end of her work day. The pain usually lasts the rest of the day but varies in intensity. Occasionally, a headache will be present upon awakening in the morning as well. K.B. denies GI and aura symptoms associated with her headaches. She has noticed that relaxation and alcohol ingestion seem to relieve these headaches; however, aspirin and acetaminophen have been ineffective. Her blood pressure is 120/74 mm Hg; her physical and neurological examinations are completely normal.

What measures should be taken to relieve K.B.'s headaches? What is an appropriate goal for treatment?

As in the treatment of other chronic headache disorders, a cure for recurrent tension-type headache is unlikely. K.B. should clearly understand that the goal of treatment is a reduction in the frequency and severity of headache. Drug therapy and relaxation techniques are the primary means by which tension-type headaches are treated.

Analgesics

Analgesics are the drugs of choice for treatment of acute tension headache attacks.[188] The initial choice of an analgesic should be based upon the severity of the pain. Acetaminophen, aspirin, and NSAIDs are often effective, although their benefits may be short-lived. Acetaminophen 1000 mg provides equal relief from moderately severe tension-type headache when compared to 650 mg aspirin; both are superior to placebo.[195] Ibuprofen is as effective

as aspirin for relief from tension headache discomfort, and side effects with both 400 and 800 mg ibuprofen are less common than with aspirin.[196] Naproxen sodium (Anaprox) 550 mg is more effective than placebo and acetaminophen 650 mg for relieving the pain of tension-type headache.[188] The potency of some analgesics may be enhanced by combination with an antihistamine (e.g., doxylamine).[197] Since the relative potencies of non-narcotic analgesics are equivalent, the choice between agents should be guided by cost and patient preference.

Sedatives (e.g., butalbital),[50] anxiolytics (e.g., meprobamate,[198] diazepam),[199] and skeletal muscle relaxants (e.g., orphenadrine) have also been used to treat tension-type headache and occasionally, patients respond to their concomitant use when an analgesic alone affords insufficient relief.

Nondrug Techniques

Nondrug techniques such as massage, hot baths, acupuncture, and various relaxation methods can provide relief from tension headache and are often effective adjuncts to drug therapy.[200] The literature both supports and refutes the effectiveness of acupuncture,[10,201] EMG biofeedback,[202–204] and other relaxation techniques in the therapy of tension-type headache. The utility of biofeedback and other relaxation techniques is based upon the premise that voluntary control of muscle contraction could benefit the headache sufferer. These techniques are most successful in young, episodic headache sufferers who are motivated to apply the techniques as instructed.[205]

A nonsteroidal anti-inflammatory agent (e.g., ibuprofen) would be an appropriate recommendation for therapy of K.B.'s tension-type headaches because of her previous inadequate responses to aspirin and acetaminophen. Drug use should be carefully monitored because analgesic abuse in patients with frequently recurring tension headache is a primary factor in the perpetuation of chronic pain syndromes.[206]

Prophylactic Therapy

25. Ibuprofen 400 mg Q 4–6 hr PRN headache was prescribed for acute relief of K.B.'s recurrent tension-type headaches. At her next scheduled follow-up visit, K.B. reported moderate relief with ibuprofen but complained of GI upset with each dose, even when taken with food. Since headaches have been occurring more frequently, her use of ibuprofen has also increased. What prophylactic agents are available for continuous suppression of K.B.'s tension-type headaches?

Antidepressants are the most useful group of agents in the prophylaxis of tension-type and mixed-type headaches. Amitriptyline (Elavil) is considered the drug of choice because it is most effective,[209] 65% of patients improved by more than 50% and 25% became headache-free in an early report.[192] The effective daily dose of amitriptyline for most patients is 50 to 100 mg, though up to 300 mg/day may be required.[50] Response to amitriptyline does not require a history of depressive symptoms, and benefit to the tension-type headache sufferer is usually evident within two to ten days.[50] Amitriptyline should be initiated at a dose of 25 mg/day at bedtime and increased gradually as needed to allow for the development of tolerance to the sedative and anticholinergic side effects of this drug. About 7% of patients discontinue amitriptyline because of side effects.[10] Although there is less experience with their use, doxepin (Sinequan),[210] imipramine (Tofranil),[5,211] maprotiline (Ludiomil),[212] and protriptyline (Vivactil)[213] are also effective in tension-type headache prophylaxis. Like amitriptyline, these agents have significant anticholinergic activity. If an agent with less anticholinergic activity is desired, fluoxetine (Prozac) or desipramine (Norpramin) may be used.[214,215]

Given K.B.'s increasing frequency of tension-type headache and her intolerance to moderate doses of ibuprofen, prophylactic treatment with amitriptyline would be appropriate. A starting dose of 25 mg nightly, increasing by 25 mg at one-week intervals to a maintenance dose of 75 mg/day should be prescribed, at which time headache response can be assessed and the dose increased as necessary. If effective, amitriptyline should be continued for three to four months before gradually decreasing the dose until the drug is completely discontinued. Therapy should be reinstituted if headaches return.

Since the dividing line between migraine and tension-type headache is often vague, the entire range of migraine drugs may be tried in refractory cases of tension-type headache or when symptoms suggest a mixed tension-type/migraine headache disorder.

References

1 **Stang PE, Osterhaus JT.** Impact of migraine in the United States: data from the national health interview survey. Headache. 1993;33:29.

2 **Kroenke K, Mangelsdorf D.** Common symptoms in ambulatory care: incidence, evaluation, therapy and outcome. Am J Med. 1989;86:262.

3 **Cook NR et al.** Correlates of headache in a population-based cohort of elderly. Arch Neurol. 1989;46:1338.

4 **Linet MS et al.** An epidemiologic study of headache among adolescents and young adults. JAMA. 1989;26:2211.

5 **Lance JW et al.** Investigations into the mechanism and treatment of chronic headache. Med J Aust. 1965;2:909.

6 **Headache Classification Committee of the International Headache Society.** Classification and diagnostic criteria for headache disorders, cranial neuralgias and facial pain. Cephalalgia. 1988;8(Suppl. 7):1–96.

7 **Symonds CP.** Cough headache. Brain. 1956;79:557.

8 **Rooke ED.** Benign exertional headache. Med Clin North Am. 1968;52:801.

9 **Ray BS, Wolff HG.** Experimental studies on headache. Pain sensitive structures of the head and their significance in headache. Arch Surg. 1940;41:813.

10 **Lance JW.** Mechanism and Management of Headache. 4th ed. London: Butterworths Scientific; 1982.

11 **Olesen J et al.** Timing and topography of cerebral flow, aura and headache during migraine attacks. Ann Neurol. 1990;28:791.

12 **Olesen J et al.** The common migraine attack may not be initiated by cerebral ischemia. Lancet. 1981;2:438.

13 **Silberstein SD.** Advances in understanding the pathophysiology of headache. Neurology. 1992;42(Suppl. 2):6.

14 **Lance JW et al.** Contribution of experimental studies to understanding the pathophysiology of migraine. In: Sandler M, Collins G, eds. Migraine: a spectrum of ideas. Oxford: Oxford University Press, 1990:21.

15 **Lance JW.** Current concepts of migraine pathogenesis. Neurology. 1993; 43(Suppl. 3):S11.

16 **Anthony M.** Plasma-free fatty acids and prostaglandin E1 in migraine and stress. Headache. 1976;16:58.

17 **Carlson LA et al.** Clinical and metabolic effects of different doses of prostaglandin in E1 in man. Acta Med Scand. 1968;183:423.

18 **Anthony M, Lance JW.** Histamine and serotonin in cluster headache. Arch Neurol. 1971;25:225.

19 **Hsu LKG et al.** Early morning migraine. Nocturnal plasma levels of catecholamines, tryptophan, glucose, and free fatty acids and sleep encephalographs. Lancet. 1977;2:447.

20 **Moskowitz MA.** The neurobiology of vascular head pain. Ann Neurol. 1984; 16:157.

21 **Ferrari MD et al.** Neuroexcitatory plasma amino acids are elevated in migraine. Neurology. 1990;40:1582.

22 **Anthony M et al.** Plasma serotonin in migraine and stress. Arch Neurol. 1967; 16:544.

23 **Curran DA et al.** Total plasma serotonin, 5-hydroxyindoleacetic acid and p-hydroxy-m-methoxymandelic acid excretion in normal and migrainous subjects. Brain. 1965;88:997.

24 **Kimball RW et al.** Effect of serotonin in migraine patients. Neurology. 1960; 10:107.

25 **Stewart WF et al.** Prevalence of migraine headache in the United States: relation to age, income, race, and other sociodemographic factors. JAMA. 1992; 267:64.

26 **Russell MB et al.** Familial occurrence of migraine without aura and migraine with aura. Neurology. 1993;43:1369.

27 **Selby G, Lance JW.** Observations on 500 cases of migraine and allied vascular headache. J Neurol Neurosurg Psychiatry. 1960;23:23.

28 **Creditor MC.** Me and migraine. N Engl J Med. 1982;307:1029.

29 **Olesen J et al.** Focal hyperemia followed by spreading oligemia and impaired activation of rCBF in classical migraine. Ann Neurol. 1981;9:344.

30 **Wilkinson M.** Treatment of the acute migraine attack—current status. Cephalalgia. 1983;3:61.

31 **Stang PE et al.** Incidence of migraine headache: a population-based study in Olmstead County, Minnesota. Neurology. 1992;42:1657.

32 **Ryan RE.** A controlled study of the effect of oral contraceptives on migraine. Headache. 1978;17:250.

33 **Bousser MG, Massiou H.** Migraine in the reproductive cycle. In: Olesen J et al., eds. The headaches. New York: Raven Press, 1993:413.

34 **Benson MD, Rebar RW.** Relationship of migraine headache and stroke to oral contraceptive use. J Reprod Med. 1986; 31:1082.

35 **Collaborative Group for the Study of Stroke in Young Women.** Oral contraceptives and stroke in young women; associated risk factors. JAMA. 1975; 231:718.

36 **Dennerstein L et al.** Headache and sex hormone therapy. Headache. 1978;18:146.

37 **Tfelt-Hansen P, Johnson ES.** Ergotamine. In: Olesen J et al, eds. The headaches. New York: Raven Press, 1993:313.

38 **Fozard JR.** The animal pharmacology of drugs used in the treatment of migraine. J Pharm Pharmacol. 1975;27:297.

39 **Moyer JH et al.** The effect of theophylline and ethylene diamine (aminophylline) and caffeine on cerebral hemodynamics and cerebrospinal fluid pressure in patients with hypertension headaches. Am J Med Sci. 1952;224:377.

40 **Schmidt R, Franchamps A.** Effect of caffeine on intestinal absorption of ergotamine in man. Eur J Clin Pharmacol. 1974;7:213.

41 **Laska EM et al.** Caffeine as an analgesic adjuvant. JAMA. 1984;251:1711.

42 **Sutherland JM et al.** Buccal absorption of ergotamine. J Neurol Neurosurg Psychiatry. 1974;37:1116.

43 **Tfelt-Hansen P et al.** Clinical pharmacology of ergotamine studied with a high performance liquid chromatographic method. In: Rose FC, ed. Advances in Migraine Research and Therapy. New York: Raven Press; 1982: 173.

44 **Crooks J et al.** Clinical trial of inhaled ergotamine tartrate in migraine. Br Med J. 1964;1:221.

45 **Carstairs LS.** Headache and gastric emptying time. Proc R Soc Med. 1958; 51:790.

46 **Volans GN.** Absorption of effervescent aspirin during migraine. Br Med J (Clin Res). 1974;2:265.

47 **Orton D.** Ergotamine tartrate levels in migraine, ergotamine tartrate overdose, and normal subjects using a radioimmunoassay. Proceedings of the Migraine Trust International Symposium. London: 1976 Sept 16–17.

48 **Raskin NH.** Acute and prophylactic treatment of migraine: practical approaches and pharmacologic rationale. Neurology. 1993;43(Suppl. 3):S39.

49 **Krupp P, Haas G.** Effects indesirables et interactions medicamenteuse des alcaloides de L'ergot de seigle. J Pharmacol. 1979;10:401.

50 **Raskin NH.** Headache. 2nd ed. New York, NY: Churchill-Livingstone; 1988.

51 **Hachinski V et al.** Ergotamine and cerebral blood flow. Stroke. 1978;9:594.

52 **Andersen AR et al.** The effect of ergotamine and dihydroergotamine on cerebral blood flow in man. Stroke. 1987;18:120.

53 **Edmeads J.** Ergotamine and the cerebral circulation. Hemicrania. 1976;7:6.

54 **Simar D, Paulson OB.** Cerebral vasomotor paralysis during migraine attack. Arch Neurol. 1973;29:207.

55 **Rall TW.** Drugs affecting uterine motility. In: Gilman AG et al, eds. Goodman and Gilman's the pharmacological basis of therapeutics, 8th ed. New York: Pergamon Press, 1990:933.

56 **Tokola RA.** The effect of metoclopramide and prochlorperazine on the absorption of effervescent paracetamol in migraine. Cephalalgia. 1988;8:139.

57 **Tfelt-Hansen P, Johnson ES.** Antiemetic and prokinetic drugs. In: Olesen J et al, eds. The headaches. New York: Raven Press, 1993:343.

58 **Tfelt-Hansen P et al.** A double-blind study of metoclopramide in the treatment of migraine attacks. J Neurol Neurosurg Psychiatry. 1980;43:369.

59 **Blau JN et al.** Ergotamine tartrate overdosage. Br Med J (Clin Res). 1979;1:265.

60 **Baumrucker JF.** Drug interaction—propranolol and cafergot. N Engl J Med. 1973;288:916.

61 **Venter CP et al.** Severe peripheral ischaemia during concomitant use of beta blockers and ergot alkaloids. Br Med J (Clin Res). 1984;289:288.

62 **Young JR, Humphries AW.** Severe arteriospasm after use of ergotamine tartrate suppositories. JAMA. 1961; 175:1141.

63 **Greenberg DJ, Hallert JW.** Lower extremity ischemia due to combined drug therapy for migraine. Postgrad Med. 1982;72:103.

64 **Dierckx RA et al.** Intraarterial sodium nitroprusside infusion in the treatment of severe ergotism. Clin Neuropharmacol. 1986;9:542.

65 **Tfelt-Hansen P et al.** Treatment of ergotism with nitroglycerin infusion. In: Rose FC, ed. Advances in Migraine Research and Therapy. New York: Raven Press; 1982;199.

66 **Saper JR, Jones M.** Ergotamine tartrate dependency: features and possible mechanism. Clin Neuropharmacol. 1986;9:244.

67 **Saper J.** Headache Disorders: Current Concepts and Treatment Strategies. Littleton, MA: Wright-PSG Publishers; 1983.

68 **Ala-Hurula V et al.** Systemic availablity of ergotamine tartrate after oral, rectal and intramuscular administration. Eur J Clin Pharmacol. 1979;15:51.

69 **Diamond S.** Treatment of migraine with isometheptene, acetaminophen, and dichloralphenazone combination: a double-blind, crossover trial. Headache. 1976;15:282.

70 **Yuill GM et al.** A double-blind crossover trial of isometheptene mucate compound and ergotamine in migraine. Br J Clin Pract. 1972;26:76.

71 **Saper JR.** Chronic headache syndromes. Neurol Clinics. 1989;7:387.

72 **Sargent JD et al.** Aborting a migraine attack: naproxen sodium v ergotamine plus caffeine. Headache. 1988;28:263.

73 **Larsen BH et al.** Randomized double-blind comparison of tolfenamic acid and paracetamol in migraine. Acta Neurol Scand. 1990;81:464.

74 **Kangasneimi P, Kaaja R.** Ketoprofen and ergotamine in acute migraine. J Intern Med. 1992;231:551.

75 **Karachalios GN et al.** Treatment of acute migraine attack with diclofenac sodium: a double-blind study. Headache. 1992;32:98.

76 **Volans GN.** Migraine and drug absorption. Clin Pharmacokinet. 1978;3:313.

77 **Hering R, Steiner TJ.** Abrupt outpatient withdrawal of medication in analgesic-abusing migraineurs. Lancet. 1991;337:1442.

78 **Petrouka SJ.** Sumatriptan in acute migraine: pharmacology and review of world experience. Headache. 1990 (Suppl. 2):554.

79 **Multinational Oral Sumatriptan and Cafergot Comparative Study Group.** A randomized, double-blind comparison of sumatriptan in the acute treatment of migraine. Eur Neurol. 1991;31:314.

80 **Perrin VL et al.** Overview of initial clinical studies with intravenous and oral GR43175 in acute migraine. Cephalalgia. 1991;9(Suppl. 9):63.

81 **Cady RK et al.** Treatment of acute migraine with subcutaneous sumatriptan. JAMA. 1991;265:2831.

82 **Finnish Sumatriptan Group and the Cardiovascular Clinical Research Group.** A placebo-controlled study of intranasal sumatriptan for the acute treatment of migraine. Eur Neurol. 1991;31:332.

83 **The Subcutaneous Sumatriptan International Study Group.** Treatment of migraine attacks with sumatriptan. N Engl J Med. 1991;325:316.

84 **Glaxo, Inc.** Imitrex package insert. Research Triangle Park, NC:1993, January.

85 **Oral Sumatriptan Dose-Defining Study Group.** Sumatriptan; an oral dose-defining study. Eur Neurol. 1991;31:300.

86 **Goadsby PJ et al.** Oral sumatriptan in acute migraine. Lancet. 1991;338:782.

87 **Multinational Oral Sumatriptan and Cafergot Comparative Study Group.** A randomized, double-blind comparison of sumatriptan in the acute treatment of migraine. Eur Neurol. 1991;31:314.

88 **Oral Sumatriptan and Aspirin Plus Metoclopramide Comparative Study Group.** A study to compare oral sumatriptan with oral aspirin plus oral metoclopramide in the acute treatment of migraine. Eur Neurol. 1992;32:177.

89 **Brown EG et al.** The safety and tolerability of sumatriptan: an overview. Eur Neurol. 1991;31:339.

90 **Saxena PR, Tfelt-Hansen P.** Sumatriptan. In: Olesen J et al, eds. The headaches. New York: Raven Press, 1993;329.

91 **Abrahamsen B, Christiansen BD.** Angina pectoris after administration of sumatriptan. Ugeskr Læger. 1992;154:3602.

92 **Willett F et al.** Coronary vasospasm induced by subcutaneous sumatriptan. Br Med J. 1992;304:1415.

93 **Klapper JA, Stanton J.** Clinical experience with patient administered subcutaneous dihydroergotamine mesylate in refractory headaches. Headache. 1992;32:21.

94 **Saadah HA.** Abortive headache therapy with intramuscular dihydroergotamine. Headache. 1992;32:18.

95 **Callaham M, Raskin N.** A controlled study of dihydroergotamine in the treatment of acute migraine headache. Headache. 1986;26:168.

96 **Mondell B et al.** Dihydroergotamine nasal spray in the acute treatment of migraine headache. Clin Pharmacol Ther. 1989;45:161. Abstract.

97 **McEwen JI et al.** Treatment of migraine with intramuscular chlorpromazine. Ann Emerg Med. 1987;16:758.

98 **Lane PL et al.** Comparative efficacy of chlorpromazine and meperidine with dimenhydrinate in migraine headache. Ann Emerg Med. 1989;18:360.

99 **McEwen J et al.** Treatment of migraine with intramuscular chlorpromazine. Ann Emerg Med. 1987;16:758.

100 **Jones J et al.** Randomized double-blind trial of intravenous prochlorperazine for the treatment of acute headache. JAMA. 1989;261:1174.

101 **Lane PL, Ross R.** Intravenous chlorpromazine-preliminary results in acute migraine. Headache. 1985;25:302.

102 **Belgrade MJ et al.** Comparison of single-dose meperidine, butorphanol, and dihydroergotamine in the treatment of vascular headache. Neurology. 1989;39:590.

103 **Tek D.** The effectiveness of nalbuphine and hydroxyzine for the emergency treatment of severe headache. Ann Emerg Med. 1987;16:308.

104 **Rapoport AM, Silberstein SD.** Emergency treatment of headache. Neurology. 1992;42(Suppl. 2):43.

105 **Holroyd KA et al.** Propranolol in the management of recurrent migraine: a meta-analytic review. Headache. 1991;31:333.

106 **Weber RB, Reinmuth OM.** The treatment of migraine with propranolol. Neurology. 1972;22:366.

107 **Wideroe TE, Vigander T.** Propranolol in the treatment of migraine. Br Med J (Clin Res). 1974;1:699.

108 **Diamond S, Medina JL.** Double-blind study of propranolol for migraine prophylaxis. Headache. 1976;16:24.

109 **Forssman B et al.** Propranolol for migraine prophylaxis. Headache. 1976;16:238.

110 **Stensrud P, Sjaastad O.** Short-term clinical trial of propranolol in racemic form (Inderal), d-propranolol and placebo in migraine. Acta Neurol Scand. 1976;53:229.

111 **Diamond S et al.** Long-term study of propranolol in the treatment of migraine. Headache. 1982;22:268.

112 **Rosen JA.** Observations on the efficacy of propranolol for the prophylaxis of migraine. Ann Neurol. 1983;13:92.

113 **Behan PO, Reid M.** Propranolol in the treatment of migraine. Practitioner. 1980;224:201.

114 **Olesen J et al.** Isoproterenol and propranolol: ability to cross the blood-brain barrier and effects on cerebral circulation in man. Stroke. 1978;9:344.

115 **Middlemiss DN et al.** Direct evidence for an interaction of beta-adrenergic blockers with the 5-HT receptor. Nature. 1977;267:289.

116 **Hiner BC et al.** Antimigraine drug interactions with 5-hydroxytryptamine 1A receptors. Ann Neurol. 1986;19:511.

117 **Lingjaerde O.** Platelet uptake and storage of serotonin. In: Essman WD, ed. Serotonin in Health and Disease. Vol. 4. New York: Spectrum; 1977;139.

118 **Tfelt-Hensen P et al.** Timolol vs. propranolol vs. placebo in common migraine prophylaxis: a double-blind multicenter trial. Acta Neurol Scand. 1984;69:1.

119 **Olsson JE et al.** Metoprolol and propranolol in migraine prophylaxis: a double-blind multicenter study. Acta Neurol Scand. 1984;70:160.

120 **Stensrud P, Sjaastad O.** Comparative trial of Tenormin (atenolol) and Inderal (propranolol) in migraine. Headache. 1980;20:204.

121 **Forssman B et al.** Atenolol for migraine prophylaxis. Headache. 1983;23:188.

122 **Ryan SE et al.** Nadolol: its use in the prophylactic treatment of migraine. Headache. 1983;23:26.

123 **Sjaastad O, Stensrud P.** Clinical trial of β-receptor blocking agent LB-46 in migraine prophylaxis. Acta Neurol Scand. 1972;48:124.

124 **Nanda RN et al.** A double-blind trial of acebutolol for migraine prophylaxis. Headache. 1978;18:20.

125 **Curran DA, Lance JW.** Clinical trial of methysergide and other preparations in the management of migraine. J Neurol Neurosurg Psychiatry. 1964;27:463.

126 **Curran DA et al.** Methysergide. Res Clin Stud Headache. 1967;1:74.

127 **Graham JR et al.** Inflammatory fibrosis associated with methysergide therapy. Res Clin Stud Headache. 1967;1:123.

128 **Gommersall JD, Stuart A.** Amitriptyline in migraine prophylaxis. Changes in pattern of attacks during a controlled clinical trial. J Neurol Neurosurg Psychiatry. 1973;36:684.

129 **Caldara R et al.** Effect of two antiserotominergic drugs, methysergide and metergoline, on gastric acid secretion and gastrin release in healthy man. Eur J Clin Pharmacol. 1980;17:13.

130 **Ziegler DK et al.** Migraine prophylaxis: a comparison of propranolol and amitriptyline. Arch Neurol. 1987;44:486.

131 **Couch JR, Hassanein RS.** Amitriptyline in migraine prophylaxis. Arch Neurol. 1979;36:695.

132 **Couch JR et al.** Amitriptyline in the prophylaxis of migraine. Effectiveness and relationship of antimigraine and antidepressant drugs. Neurology. 1976;26:121.

133 **Langohr HD et al.** Clomipramine and metoprolol in migraine prophylaxis—a double-blind crossover study. Headache. 1985;25:107.

134 **Heninger GR, Charney DS.** Mechanism of action of antidepressant treatments: implications for the etiology and treatment of depressive disorders. In: Meltzer HY, ed. Psychopharmacology: the third generation of progress. New York: Raven Press, 1987;535.

135 **Adly C et al.** Fluoxetine prophylaxis of migraine. Headache. 1992;32:101.

136 **Beecher HK.** The powerful placebo. JAMA. 1955;159:1602.

137 **Couch JR et al.** The long-term effect of placebo on migraine. Neurology. 1987;27(Suppl. 1):238. Abstract.

138 **Reuter M.** Calcium channel modulation by neurotransmitters, enzymes and drugs. Nature. 1983;301:569.

139 **Markely HG et al.** Verapamil in prophylactic therapy of migraine. Neurology. 1984;34:973.

140 **Solomon GD et al.** Verapamil prophylaxis of migraine. JAMA. 1983;250:2500.

141 **Solomon GD.** Comparative efficacy of calcium antagonist drugs in the prophylaxis of migraine. Headache. 1985;25:368.

142 **Hering R, Kuritzky A.** Sodium valproate in the prophylactic treatment of migraine: a double-blind study versus placebo. Cephalalgia. 1992;12:81.

143 **Saper J et al.** Safety and efficacy of divalproex sodium in the prophylaxis of migraine headache: a multicenter, double-blind, placebo-controlled trial. Neurology. 1993;43(Suppl. 2):A401.

144 **Smith R, Schwartz A.** Dilitazem prophylaxis in refractory migraine. N Engl J Med. 1984;310:1327.

145 **Meyer JS, Hardenberg J.** Clinical effectiveness of calcium entry blockers in prophylactic treatment of migraine and cluster headaches. Headache. 1983;23:266.

146 **McArthur JC et al.** Nifedipine in the prophylaxis of classic migraine: a cross-over, double-masked, placebo-controlled study of headache frequency and side effects. Neurology. 1989;39:284.

147 **Riopelle RJ, McCans JL.** A pilot study of the calcium antagonist diltiazem in migraine syndrome prophylaxis. J Can Sci Neurol. 1982;9:269.

148 **Flaim SF.** Comparative pharmacology of calcium blockers based on studies of vascular smooth muscle. In: Flaim SF, Zelig R, eds. Calcium Blockers: Mechanism of Action and Clinical Applications. Baltimore: Urban & Schwarzenberg;1982:155.

149 **Havanka-Kannianinen H et al.** Efficacy of nimodipine in the prophylaxis of migraine. Cephalalgia. 1984;5:39.

150 **Gelmer HJ.** Nimodipine, a new calcium antagonist, in the prophylactic treatment of migraine. Headache. 1983;23:106.

151 **Stewart DJ et al.** Effect of prophylactic administration of nimodipine in patients with migraine. Headache. 1988;28:260.

152 **Ansell E et al.** Nimodipine in migraine prophylaxis. Cephalalgia. 1988;8:269.

153 **Personal communication, RJ Taylor, Ph. D.;** Professional Services Department, Miles Inc.

154 **Buring JE et al.** Low-dose aspirin for migraine prophylaxis. JAMA. 1990;264:1711.

155 **Stensrud P, Sjaastad O.** Clonidine (Catapres)—a double-blind study after long-term treatment with the drug in migraine. Acta Neurol Scand. 1976;53:233.

156 **Mondrup K, Moller CE.** Prophylactic treatment of migraine with clonidine. Acta Neurol Scand. 1977;56:405.

157 **Boisen E et al.** Clonidine in the prophylaxis of migraine. Acta Neurol Scand. 1978;58:288.

158 **Gallagher RM.** Menstrual migraine and intermittent ergonovine therapy. Headache. 1989;29:366.

159 **Anthony M, Lance JW.** Monoamine oxidase inhibition in the treatment of migraine. Arch Neurol. 1969;21:263.

160 **Ekborn K.** A clinical comparison of cluster headache and migraine. Acta Neurol Scand. 1970;41(Suppl.):7.

161 **Mathew NT.** Cluster headache. Neurology. 1992;42(Suppl. 2):22.

162 **Sakai F, Meyer JS.** Regional cerebral haemodynamics during migraine and cluster headaches measured by the 133 Xe inhalation method. Headache. 1978; 18:122.

163 **Sakai F, Meyer JS.** Abnormal cerebrovascular reactivity in patients with migraine and cluster headache. Headache. 1979;19:257.

164 **Krabbe AA et al.** Tomographic determination of cerebral blood flow during attacks of cluster headache. Cephalalgia. 1984;4:17.

165 **Drummond PD, Lance JW.** Thermographic changes in cluster headache. Neurology. 1984;34:1292.

166 **Buzzi MG et al.** Morphological effects of electrical trigeminal ganglion stimulation on intra and extracranial vessels. Soc Neurosci. 1990;16:160. Abstract.

167 **Manzoni GC et al.** Cluster headache—clinical findings in 180 patients. Cephalalgia. 1983;3:21.

168 **Ekbom K, Sakai F.** Tension-type headache, cluster headache and miscellaneous headaches; management. In: Olesen J et al, eds. The headaches. New York: Raven Press, 1993:591.

169 **Ekbom K et al.** Optimal routes of administration of ergotamine tartrate in cluster headache patients. A pharmacokinetic study. Cephalalgia. 1983;3:15.

170 **Kudrow L.** Cluster headache: mechanisms and management. Oxford: Oxford University Press; 1980.

171 **Graham JR et al.** Aerosol ergotamine tartrate for migraine and Horton's syndrome. N Engl J Med. 1960;263:802.

172 **Kudrow L.** Response of cluster headache attacks to oxygen inhalation. Headache. 1981;21:1.

173 **Janks JF.** Oxygen for cluster headaches. JAMA. 1978;239:191.

174 **Fogan L.** Treatment of cluster headache. A double-blind comparison of oxygen vs. air inhalation. Arch Neurol. 1985;42:362.

175 **The sumatriptan cluster headache study group.** Treatment of acute cluster headache with sumatriptan. N Engl J Med. 1991;325:322.

176 **Sicuteri F et al.** Pain relief by somatostatin in attacks of cluster headache. Pain. 1984;18:359.

177 **Kittrelle JP et al.** Cluster headache. Local anesthetic abortive agents. Arch Neurol. 1985;42:496.

178 **Barre F.** Cocaine as an abortive agent in cluster headache. Headache. 1982; 22:69.

179 **Andersson PG, Jespersen LT.** Dihydroergotamine nasal spray in the treatment of attacks of cluster headache. A double-blind trial versus placebo. Cephalalgia. 1986;6:51.

180 **Couch JR, Ziegler DK.** Prednisone therapy for cluster headache. Headache. 1978;18:219.

181 **Kudrow L.** Comparative results of prednisone, methysergide, and lithium therapy in cluster headache. In: Greene R, ed. Current Concepts in Migraine Research. New York: Raven Press; 1978:159.

182 **DeCarolis P et al.** Nimodipine in episodic cluster headache: results and methodological considerations. Headache. 1987;27:397.

183 **Damasio H, Lyon L.** Lithium carbonate in the treatment of cluster headaches. J Neurol. 1980;224:1.

184 **Ekbom K.** Lithium for cluster headache: review of the literature and preliminary results of long-term treatment. Headache. 1981;21:132.

185 **Savoldi F et al.** Lithium salts in cluster headache treatment. Cephalalgia. 1983;(Suppl. 1):79.

186 **Manzoni GC et al.** Lithium carbonate in cluster headache: assessment of its short- and long-term therapeutic efficacy. Cephalalgia. 1983;3:109.

187 **Rassmussen BK et al.** Epidemiology of headache in a general population—a prevalence study. J Clin Epidemiol. 1991;44:1147.

188 **Silberstein SD.** Tension-type and chronic daily headache. Neurology. 1993;43:1644.

189 **Meyer JS et al.** Migraine and cluster headache treatment with calcium antagonists supports a vascular pathogenesis. Headache. 1985;25:358.190. Tunis MM, Wolff HG. Studies on headache. Cranial artery vasoconstriction and muscle-contraction headache. Arch Neurol Psychiatry. 1954;71:425.

191 **Langemark M et al.** Temporal muscle blood flow in chronic tension-type headache. Arch Neurol. 1990;47:654.

192 **Lance JW, Curran DA.** Treatment of chronic tension headache. Lancet. 1964;1:1236.

193 **Kolb LC.** Psychiatric aspects of the treatment of headache. Neurology. 1963;13:34.

194 **Holm JE et al.** The role of stress in recurrent tension headache. Headache. 1986;26:160.

195 **Peters BH et al.** Comparison of 650 mg aspirin and 1,000 mg acetaminophen with each other, and with placebo in moderately severe headache. Am J Med. 1983;74(6A):36.

196 **Diamond S.** Ibuprofen versus aspirin and placebo in the treatment of muscle contraction headache. Headache. 1983; 23:206.

197 **Gawel MJ et al.** Evaluation of analgesic agents in recurring headache compared with other clinical pain models. Clin Pharmacol Ther. 1990;47:504.

198 **Friedman AP.** The treatment of chronic headache with meprobamate. Ann N Y Acad Sci. 1957;67:882.

199 **Weber MB.** The treatment of muscle contraction headaches with diazepam. Curr Ther Res. 1973;15:210.

200 **Jay GW et al.** The effectiveness of physical therapy in the treatment of chronic daily headaches. Headache. 1989;29:156.

201 **Hansen PE, Hansen JH.** Acupuncture treatment of chronic tension headache—a controlled cross-over trial. Cephalalgia. 1985;5:137.

202 **Nuchterlein K, Holroyd J.** Biofeedback in the treatment of tension headache: current status. Arch Gen Psychiatry. 1980;37:866.

203 **Bakal D, Kaganov J.** Muscle contraction and migraine headache: psychophysiologic comparison. Headache. 1977;17:208.

204 **Andrasik F, Holroyd KA.** Specific and nonspecific effects in the biofeedback treatment of tension headache: 3-year follow-up. J Consult Clin Psychol. 1983;51:634.

205 **Solbach P, Sargent J.** An analysis of home practice patterns for non-drug headache treatments. Headache. 1989; 29:528.

206 **Black RG.** The chronic pain syndrome. Surg Clin North Am. 1975;55: 999.

207 **Watson CPN, Evans RJ.** Chronic cluster headache: a review of 60 patients. Headache. 1987;27:158.

208 **Bussone gm et al.** Double blind comparison of lithium and verapamil in cluster headache prophylaxis. Headache. 1990;30:411.

209 **Diamond S, Baltes BJ.** Chronic tension headache treated with amitriptyline: a double-blind study. Headache. 1971;11:110.

210 **Morland TJ et al.** Doxepin in the prophylactic treatment of mixed ''vascular'' and tension headache. Headache. 1979;19:382.

211 **Lance JW, Curran DA.** Treatment of chronic tension headache. Lancet. 1964;1:1236.

212 **Fogelholm R, Murros K.** Maprotiline in chronic tension headache: a double-blind cross-over study. Headache. 1985;25:273.

213 **Diamond S.** Management of headaches: focus on new strategies. Postgrad Med. 1990;87:189.

214 **Bussone GM et al.** Effectiveness of fluoxetine on pain and depression in chronic headache disorders. In: Nappi GM et al, eds. Headache and depression: serotonin pathways as a common clue. New York: Raven Press; 1991: 265.

215 **Diamond S, Freitag FG.** The use of fluoxetine in the treatment of headache. Clin J Pain. 1989;5:200.

216 **Pereira Monteiro JM.** Headache associated wtih single use substances. In: Olesen J, Tfelt-Hansen P, Welch KMA, eds. The Headaches. New York: Raven Press, 1993:343.

217 **Meyer JS et al.** Clinical and hemodynamic effects during treatment of vascular headaches with verapamil. Headache. 1984;24:313.

218 **Gilman AG et al, eds.** Goodman and Gilman's The Pharmacological Basis of Therapeutics, 8th ed. New York: Pergamon Press, 1990:933

Parkinson's Disease

John F Flaherty
Barry E Gidal

Clinical Features 51-1
Etiology 51-1
Pathophysiology 51-2
Clinical Presentation 51-2
Staging of Parkinson's (See Table 51.1) 51-2
Treatment (See Table 51.2) 51-3
Anticholinergics 51-3
Initial therapy 51-3
Comparison of commonly used agents
(See Table 51.3) 51-3
Adverse effects 51-3
Amantadine 51-4
Mechanism of action 51-4
Efficacy 51-4
Initiation of therapy 51-4
Adverse effects 51-4
Monitoring therapy 51-5
Livedo reticularis 51-5
Levodopa (See Figure 51.1) 51-5
Efficacy 51-5
Sinemet: advantages and disadvantages
(See Figure 51.1) 51-5
Initiation of therapy 51-5
Carbidopa/levodopa (Sinemet) dosing 51-7

Levodopa response fluctuations 51-7
Controlled-release Sinemet 51-7
Adverse effects: mental changes 51-8
Drug holiday 51-8
Interference with laboratory tests 51-9
Dopamine Agonists (See Figure 51.2) 51-10
Bromocriptine 51-10
Efficacy 51-10
Dosing 51-10
Adverse effects 51-11
Pergolide 51-11
Adverse effects 51-11
Lisuride 51-12
Monoamine Oxidase-B (MAO-B) Inhibitors 51-12
Selegiline 51-12
Mechanism of action 51-12
Efficacy 51-12
Use to slow disease progression 51-12
Antioxidant Therapy 51-13
Adjunctive Treatment of Parkinsonian Tremor 51-13
β-adrenergic blockers 51-13
Surgery 51-13
Levodopa Treatment Failure 51-13
Misdiagnosis 51-13
Drug interactions 51-14

Clinical Features

Parkinson's disease, like epilepsy and migraine headaches, is a neurological disorder in which drug therapy plays a role of central importance. Parkinson's disease is a chronic, progressive disorder of motor function primarily of middle to late life. Although first described as the "shaking palsy" by James Parkinson in 1817, it was not until recently that major breakthroughs in understanding the neurochemistry and pathophysiology of this disorder have led to more effective drug therapies.[1] Most cases of Parkinson's disease are of unknown etiology, referred to as idiopathic parkinsonism; however, a parkinsonian syndrome has been associated with viral encephalitis, neurotoxins, and neuroleptic drugs.[1] Additionally, other neurologic disorders such as benign essential tremor and progressive supranuclear palsy share symptoms similar to Parkinson's disease as part of their clinical presentation. Unless otherwise stated, all references to Parkinson's disease in this chapter refer to the idiopathic type.

The age at onset of Parkinson's disease is variable, usually between 50 to 80 years.[2,3] In a retrospective study of 802 patients, a mean age at onset of 55 years was noted; in two-thirds of patients the disease began between the ages of 50 to 69 years. Men and women are affected equally.[2,3] The prevalence of Parkinson's disease is about 100 cases per 100,000 population and the incidence is estimated at 20 cases per 100,000 people annually.[3] An estimated one million Americans, or 1% of the population over the age of 65, presently suffer from Parkinson's disease.[3,4] Parkinsonian symptoms are insidious in onset. These symptoms progress over time such that within 10 to 20 years total immobility can result despite drug treatment.[4] Since the introduction of levodopa, currently the most effective treatment available, mortality rates for patients with Parkinson's disease have decreased, approaching those of the general population.[3,5] Death usually is not due to the disease itself, but rather to complications related to immobility (e.g., aspiration pneumonia, cardiovascular and cerebrovascular disease).[2]

Etiology

Many theories have been advanced regarding the etiology of Parkinson's disease. Environmental and genetic factors have been discussed most frequently. Hereditary factors do not appear to play a major role as evidenced by studies carried out in twins.[9] Environmental factors have been implicated since it was discovered that many patients developed a parkinsonian syndrome following the epidemic of encephalitis lethargica in the U.S. between 1919 and the early 1930s.[1] Attempts to isolate a virus as a causative agent of the disease have been unsuccessful. Renewed interest in environmental factors has resurfaced with the discovery that ingestion of a meperidine analog, 1-methyl-4-phenyl-1,2,3,6-tetrahydropyridine (MPTP), causes irreversible parkinsonism.[10] It also is now recognized that the byproducts of dopamine metabolism (e.g., hydrogen peroxide) can lead to the production of free radicals which cause peroxidation of cell membranes and ultimately cell death. Thus, the most attractive hypothesis at present is that exposure to an environmental contaminant resembling MPTP (or possible MPTP itself) superimposed upon the normal loss of nigrostriatal dopamine, which occurs with the aging process, may result in the clinical manifestations of Parkinson's disease.[11,12]

Pathophysiology

Parkinson's disease is a disorder of the extrapyramidal system of the brain involving, in particular, the basal ganglia. The extrapyramidal system is involved with maintaining posture and muscle tone as well as with regulating voluntary smooth motor activity. In Parkinson's disease, for reasons not clearly understood, there is a loss of melanin containing cells within the substantia nigra.[6] The pigmented neurons within the substantia nigra have dopaminergic fibers which project into the neostriatum and globus pallidus. Together, the substantia nigra, neostriatum, and globus pallidus comprise the basal ganglia. In Parkinson's disease there is a progressive loss of the inhibitory neurotransmitter, dopamine, in the nigrostriatal tracts and a relative increase in the excitatory neurotransmitter acetylcholine.[6-8]

The pathologic hallmark of Parkinson's disease is the presence of Lewy bodies, or intraneuronal inclusion bodies within the dopaminergic cells of the substantia nigra.[4,6] It is generally felt that an 80% loss of dopaminergic neurons must occur before Parkinson's disease becomes clinically recognizable.[4,6]

The imbalance between dopamine and acetylcholine is primarily responsible for the manifestations of the disease and drug therapy is directed toward correcting this imbalance. To attribute the disease solely to an imbalance between these two neurotransmitters is an oversimplification, since decreases in other neurotransmitters such as norepinephrine and serotonin also are present in the parkinsonian brain. These deficiencies also play an important role in the pathophysiology of this disorder.[7,8]

There are two major families of dopamine receptors in the central nervous system, D1 and D2 receptors. D2 receptors (specifically D2A) are involved with mediating the therapeutic effect of levodopa and the dopamine agonists (Dopamine Agonists). The precise role of D1 receptors is less well understood, and it is unclear whether stimulation of D1 receptors results in beneficial or detrimental (e.g., dyskinesias) effects.[4,7]

Clinical Presentation

1. L.M., a 65-year-old, right-handed male artist, presents to the neurology clinic complaining of difficulty painting because of unsteadiness in his right hand. He also complains of increasing difficulty getting out of chairs and tightness in his arms and legs. His wife claims that he has become more "forgetful" lately and L.M. admits that his memory does not seem to be as sharp. His past medical history is significant for depression for the past year, gout (currently requiring no treatment), constipation, and benign prostatic hypertrophy. On physical examination, L.M. was noted to be a well-developed, well-nourished male who displayed a notable lack of normal changes in facial expression and spoke in a soft, monotone voice. A strong body odor was noted. Examination of his extremities revealed a slight "ratchet-like" rigidity in both arms, and a mild tremor was present in his hands. His gait was slow, but otherwise normal, with a slightly bent posture. His balance was determined to be normal. His genitourinary examination was remarkable only for prostatic enlargement. The remainder of L.M.'s physical examination and laboratory studies were within normal limits. What signs and symptoms suggestive of Parkinson's disease are present in L.M.?

Establishment of the diagnosis of Parkinson's disease is based entirely upon clinical symptoms.[4,7] The four classical features of Parkinson's disease are easily recognized and consist of *tremor*, *rigidity*, *bradykinesia*, and *postural disturbances*. Tremor, which is most often the first symptom observed, is nearly always initially unilateral. Frequently, the tremor is of a "pill-rolling" type involving the thumb and index finger; is present at rest; worsens under fatigue or stress; and is absent with purposeful movement

or when asleep.[2,4,8] Muscular rigidity resulting from increased muscle tone often manifests as a "cogwheel" or "ratchet" (catch-release) type of motion when an extremity is moved passively. It is due to the action of opposing muscle groups.[2,4,8] Bradykinesia, or a poverty of spontaneous movements, often is evidenced by a "masked facies," or blank stare and is associated with reduced eye blinking.[2,4,8] As the disease progresses, difficulty initiating and terminating steps results in a hurried or festinating gait; the posture becomes stooped (simian posture) and postural reflexes are impaired.[2,4,8] Symptoms which were unilateral upon initial presentation, often become bilateral and more severe as the disease progresses.[4]

L.M. presents with many of the classic symptoms of Parkinson's disease. A noticeable tremor is present, along with decreased manual dexterity as evidenced by his difficulty handling a paintbrush. Rigidity ("ratcheting" of the arms), bradykinesia (slowness of movement), and a mask-like facial expression also are present. Although he has a partially stooped posture, it is difficult to attribute this entirely to the disease, since postural changes commonly occur with advancing age.[4]

There are numerous associated features of parkinsonism. Handwriting abnormalities occur frequently, particularly micrographia.[2,4,8] This abnormality would be particularly troublesome to L.M. who is an artist. Signs of autonomic nervous system dysfunction, such as drooling (sialorrhea) and seborrhea may occur which can be particularly embarrassing to the patient.[4,8] The foul body odor exhibited by L.M. could be ascribed to excess sebum production. Speech disturbances, often manifesting as a soft, monotone voice may, on occasion, be one of the first symptoms noted.[2,4,13] Dysphagia and constipation are the most common gastrointestinal complaints encountered.[1] While it is possible to attribute L.M.'s constipation to Parkinson's disease, other causes must first be ruled out. Sensory complaints such as numbness and paresthesia can occur and may be misdiagnosed if other classical features of the disease are absent.[4] In a few patients, psychiatric disturbances, such as nervousness, anxiety, and depression occur.[2,4] L.M. has a history of depression which could possibly be due to Parkinson's disease. Finally, the prevalence of dementia among parkinsonian patients ranges from 10% to 30%, and many neurologists consider dementia part of the clinical syndrome of Parkinson's disease in a small subgroup of patients.[14] The "forgetfulness" and decrease in memory described by L.M. could be early signs of dementia and warrant close observation.

Staging of Parkinson's

2. What are the stages of Parkinson's disease? At what stage of disease is L.M.?

There is tremendous variability in the symptomatology and progression of symptoms among parkinsonian patients. In order to assess the degree of disability and determine the disease's rate of progression relative to treatment, various scales have been developed. The most common of these is the Hoehn and Yahr scale (see Table 51.1).[2] In general, patients in stages I and II of Parkinson's disease have mild disease that does not interfere with activities of daily living or work and usually requires no treatment. In stage III disease, daily activities are restricted somewhat and employment may be significantly affected unless effective treatment is initiated. These patients usually can be managed with anticholinergics or amantadine (see Table 51.2).[4,7] Care must be exercised not to broadly generalize, but rather to approach each patient individually. For example, a neurosurgeon's practice may be severely impaired by even a mild tremor and he may require treatment earlier than stage III. Judging by the symptoms L.M. is displaying, he

Table 51.1	Staging of Disability in Parkinson's Disease[2]
Stage I	Unilateral involvement only; minimal or no functional impairment
Stage II	Bilateral involvement, without impairment of balance
Stage III	Evidence of postural imbalance; some restriction in activities; capable of leading independent life; mild to moderate disability
Stage IV	Severely disabled, unable to walk and stand unassisted; markedly incapacitated
Stage V	Restricted to bed or wheelchair unless aided

would probably be placed in stage II or III. His symptoms are bilateral in nature and are interfering with his ability to paint, thus affecting his livelihood. He is otherwise able to live independently and would benefit from treatment. Many patients in stage III, and most patients in stage IV, require levodopa therapy [with a peripheral decarboxylase inhibitor (Sinemet)] and often in combination with a dopamine agonist such as bromocriptine (Parlodel) or, in some cases, selegiline (Deprenyl). Patients with end-stage disease (stage V) are severely incapacitated and because of extended disease progression, often do not respond well to treatment.

Treatment

An overview of the management of patients with Parkinson's disease is presented in Table 51.2. There is no known cure for parkinsonism; therefore, treatment is only symptomatic.

Although no cure presently exists, there is exciting new evidence that treatment of early states (stages I to II) with the monoamine oxidase-B (MAO-B) inhibitor, selegiline, may slow progression of the disease. (See Question 24.) The development and implementation of a long-term individualized treatment plan usually is characterized by frequent dosage adjustments over time because of the chronicity and progressive nature of this disease. Although the majority of this chapter is devoted to the drug therapy of Parkinson's disease, the importance of supportive care cannot be overemphasized. Exercise and physiotherapy can be beneficial at the earlier stages to improve mobility, increase strength, and enhance well-being. Speech therapy may be helpful and psychological support often is necessary in dealing with depression and other related problems. Newly diagnosed patients need to be educated about what to expect from the disease and the various forms of treatment available. Additionally, enlisting the support of family members is vitally important in establishing an overall effective therapeutic plan.

Anticholinergics

3. Initial Therapy. The decision is made to initiate therapy for L.M. Should he be given an anticholinergic or amantadine?

The choice of whether to begin therapy with anticholinergic drugs or amantadine (Symmetrel) is controversial. Anticholinergic drugs have been used to treat Parkinson's disease since 1867, when it was discovered that symptoms were improved by the belladonna derivative, hyoscyamine (scopolamine).[15] These drugs remained the mainstay of treatment until the late 1960s when amantadine and levodopa were introduced.

The anticholinergics work by blocking the excitatory neurotransmitter, acetylcholine, in the substantia nigra. Early in the course of the disease when dopamine depletion is not substantial, this form of therapy can be beneficial.[15,16] Anticholinergics improve tremor and rigidity more than bradykinesia, postural imbalance, or gait disturbances which appear later in the course of the

disease and are the most disabling symptoms.[8,16] Overall, only about a 25% improvement in symptoms can be expected with anticholinergic therapy.[8,17] Many patients gain additional benefits from combining anticholinergics with amantadine or levodopa in the later stages of the disease. Although L.M. could be treated with either an anticholinergic or amantadine as initial therapy for his Parkinson's disease, amantadine would be preferable for the reasons presented in the answer to Question 5.

4. Comparison of Commonly Used Agents. What are the most commonly used anticholinergic agents in Parkinson's disease? How are they administered?

The anticholinergic drugs of most value in Parkinson's disease are the synthetic agents which are more centrally selective than atropine and scopolamine (see Table 51.3).[8] The most commonly used anticholinergics are trihexyphenidyl and benztropine. The antihistamines, diphenhydramine and orphenadrine, and the phenothiazine, ethopropazine, have significant anticholinergic properties and are useful in parkinsonism.

While no single agent has been proven superior to another in well designed clinical trials, patients who do not respond to one anticholinergic may respond to another. Many neurologists may prefer one agent over another simply on the basis of having more experience with a particular drug. Benztropine, biperiden, and diphenhydramine are available in an injectable form, but the oral route is preferred unless for some reason the patient cannot take anything by mouth.

The dosage ranges of the anticholinergics are listed in Table 51.3. Therapy should be initiated with small doses that can be increased slowly as tolerated.[8,17] A response should be evident within days after starting therapy. Anticholinergics are often useful as adjunctive therapy with amantadine or levodopa; however, to ensure better tolerance, the dosage should be reduced when therapy with these agents is begun. Anticholinergics should never be abruptly discontinued because this has led to "withdrawal" reactions, characterized by an immediate worsening of parkinsonian symptoms in a number of patients.[18]

5. Adverse Effects. What are the side effects of anticholinergics? How might these impact the choice of therapy in L.M.?

Table 51.2	Overview of the Management of Parkinson's Disease

Drug Therapy
Mild to Moderate Symptoms
    Anticholinergics
    Amantadine (Symmetrel)
    Monoamine oxidase B inhibitors
        Selegiline (Deprenyl)

Moderate to Severe Symptoms
    Levodopa with carbidopa (Sinemet)
    Dopamine agonists
        Bromocriptine (Parlodel)
        Pergolide (Permax)
        Lisuride (investigational)
    Monoamine oxidase B inhibitors
        Selegiline (Deprenyl)

Supportive Care
    Exercise
    Physical therapy
    Psychological support
    Speech therapy
    Antiemetics [domperidone (investigational)]
    Beta-blockers (for tremor)

Surgery
    Stereotaxic thalamotomy (for tremor)
    Fetal substantia nigra implants

Table 51.3   Anticholinergic Drugs in Parkinson's Disease

Drug (Brand Name)	Dosage Forms[a]	Daily Dosage Range
Benztropine (Cogentin)	Tab: 0.5, 1, and 2 mg Inj: 2 mg/2 mL	1–3 mg QD–BID
Biperiden (Akineton)	Tab: 2 mg Inj: 5 mg/mL	2 mg TID–QID
Cycrimine (Pagitane)	Tab: 1.25 and 2.5 mg	1.25–5 mg TID
Ethopropazine (Parsidol)	Tab: 10 and 50 mg	10–150 mg QID
Procyclidine (Kemadrin)	Tab: 5 mg	2.5–5 mg TID–QID
Trihexyphenidyl (Artane)	Tab: 2 and 5 mg Liq: 2 mg/5 mL	1–5 mg TID
Antihistamines Diphenhydramine (Benadryl)	Cap: 25 and 50 mg Liq: 12.5 mg/5 mL Inj: 50 mg/mL	25–50 mg TID–QID
Orphenadrine (Disipal)	Tab: 50 mg	50 mg TID–QID

[a] Inj = Injection; Liq = Liquid; Tab = Tablet.

Anticholinergics produce both peripherally and centrally mediated side effects. Peripheral side effects such as dry mouth, blurred vision, constipation, and urinary retention are frequent and bothersome.[8,15,17] Anticholinergics can increase intraocular pressure and should be avoided in patients with angle closure glaucoma. The central nervous system (CNS) side effects of confusion, impairment of recent memory, hallucinations, and delusions, are usually the most disturbing.[8,15,17,18] Parkinsonian patients are more prone to anticholinergic side effects due to increased age, intercurrent illness, and the impaired cognition experienced by some individuals.[8,17,18] If a patient experiences significant CNS side effects, doses of the anticholinergic drug should be reduced or possibly, discontinued. The antihistamines, diphenhydramine and orphenadrine, may be better tolerated in these individuals.

Given his history and clinical presentation, L.M. probably should not be given an anticholinergic for initial therapy. He presented with signs of intellectual impairment which may worsen on anticholinergic therapy. L.M. also has prostatic hyperplasia that could result in urinary retention if exacerbated by anticholinergic drugs. The mydriasis and cycloplegia associated with these drugs could interfere with his ability to paint unless corrected with pilocarpine eye drops. Finally, his constipation also could be aggravated by anticholinergic drugs. He could be started on diphenhydramine 25 mg three times a day and should be monitored for therapeutic and adverse responses to this medication. For the reasons above and those discussed below, amantadine would be a better choice of therapy.

Amantadine

6. How does amantadine work in Parkinson's disease?

Amantadine, an antiviral agent, was discovered by accident to have antiparkinson activity when a patient given the drug for influenza experienced a remission in her tremor, rigidity, and bradykinesia.[19] Shortly thereafter, clinical trials documented its effectiveness when used alone and in combination with levodopa to treat mild forms of Parkinson's disease.[20–22]

Mechanism of Action. The precise mechanism of action of amantadine for the treatment of parkinsonism is not entirely understood, but it probably augments dopamine release from presynaptic nerve terminals and possibly inhibits dopamine reuptake into storage granules.[23] Others have suggested an anticholinergic mechanism of action since certain anticholinergic-type side effects are exhibited by the drug.[18]

Efficacy. When 351 parkinsonian patients at various stages of the disease were treated with amantadine 200 mg/day for $\geq$60 days an overall positive response was noted in 64% of patients studied.[20] Response was greater (79%) in patients also receiving levodopa and less (48%) in those on amantadine alone. About half of the patients experienced a loss of efficacy 30 to 60 days after initiation of therapy.[20] Similar results were reported in subsequent long-term, double-blind, placebo-controlled trials involving smaller numbers of patients.[21,22] Amantadine is effective in improving all of the symptoms of parkinsonian disability in about 50% of patients, usually within days after starting therapy; however, a substantial number of patients develop tachyphylaxis within one to three months. Temporary withdrawal, discontinuation, and subsequent reinstitution of amantadine at a later date can result in improved benefit in some individuals.[22]

7. Initiation of Therapy. The decision is made to begin L.M. on amantadine. How should therapy be initiated?

Amantadine is noted for its simplicity in dosing. For L.M., therapy should be started with one 100 mg capsule taken with breakfast; an additional 100 mg capsule can be taken with lunch five to seven days after the initiation of the drug.[20] The dosage can be increased to a maximum of 300 mg/day; however, doses greater than 200 mg/day are rarely necessary and pose a greater risk of adverse effects. The second dose is best taken in the early afternoon to minimize the likelihood of insomnia. Amantadine also is available in a liquid preparation which is advantageous for individuals with dysphagia. The liquid formulation allows for more subtle dosage adjustments, but such adjustments are rarely necessary.

Amantadine is renally excreted and doses need to be reduced in patients with renal impairment[24] (see Table 51.4.). Because the elimination half-life is about seven days in patients with end-stage renal disease, a loading dose of 200 mg on the first day of therapy is recommended for patients with significant renal impairment.[24] Insignificant amounts of amantadine are removed by hemodialysis.[24] While L.M. does not relate any history of renal dysfunction, baseline blood urea nitrogen (BUN) and serum creatinine concentrations should be evaluated before therapy is initiated.

8. How should therapy with amantadine be monitored?

Adverse Effects. Side effects of amantadine are relatively infrequent and mainly involve the gastrointestinal, cardiovascular, and central nervous systems. In one large scale study, at least one side effect was experienced by 15% of patients, while 9% had two or

Table 51.4   Amantadine Dosing Guidelines in Renal Impairment[24]

Cl_{Cr} (mL/min/1.73 m^2)	Suggested Maintenance Regimen
>80	100 mg BID
60	200 mg/100 mg alternate days
50	100 mg/day
40	100 mg/day
30	200 mg twice weekly[a]
20	100 mg thrice weekly
≤10	200 mg/100 mg alternating Q 7 days[b]

[a] Loading dose of 200 mg recommended on the first day for Cl_{Cr} <30 mL/min.
[b] Includes patients maintained on thrice-weekly hemodialysis.

more adverse effects.[20] Amantadine was discontinued due to side effects in only 5% of patients.[20] Central nervous system (CNS) complaints are seen most frequently and include dizziness, confusion, disorientation, depression, nervousness, irritability, insomnia, and hallucinations.[17,20,21,25] Convulsions have been observed on rare occasions with very high doses ($\approx$800 mg/day), particularly in patients with renal impairment.[17,25] Amantadine does have some anticholinergic-like properties, and patients concomitantly receiving anticholinergics appear to experience a greater degree of CNS side effects.[18,20,25] Dry mouth, nausea, vomiting, cramps, diarrhea, and constipation are less frequently encountered.[17,20,21,25] Amantadine can cause mild elevations in BUN and alkaline phosphatase which are not believed to be of clinical importance.[21,25]

Monitoring Therapy. Thus, L.M. should be watched carefully for gastrointestinal and CNS complaints. The gastrointestinal side effects can be managed by taking the drug with food. Signs of central nervous system stimulation, such as insomnia can be minimized by taking the second dose at noon, rather than in the evening. Because of his advancing age, BUN and serum creatinine concentrations should be evaluated periodically (e.g., every 3 months).

9. Livedo Reticularis. **After 2 months of amantadine 200 mg/day, L.M. has experienced good relief of symptoms, but now presents to the clinic complaining of a purplish-red mottling of the skin which began on the thighs and quickly spread to involve his lower legs. He denies itching or pain associated with these lesions, but is clearly quite disturbed by them. Also of note on physical examination is slight pitting edema of the lower extremities. What is the likelihood that this reaction is the result of L.M.'s amantadine?**

Livedo reticularis, a rose colored mottling of the skin usually involving the lower extremities (but can involve the upper extremities as well), can occur in up to 80% of patients receiving amantadine.[20–22,25] Livedo reticularis can be observed as early as two weeks after initiating amantadine therapy. This adverse effect persists until therapy is discontinued, often intensifying to a blackish-purple color.[21] It is more commonly observed in women, when higher doses (>200 mg/day) are prescribed, and is worse upon standing and in colder climates.[21,25] Livedo reticularis is believed to be due to local release of catecholamines which cause vasoconstriction and alter the permeability of cutaneous blood vessels.[18] The consequences of livedo reticularis are entirely cosmetic. Since this adverse effect is benign, discontinuation of therapy is unnecessary. Livedo reticularis eventually will subside after amantadine therapy is stopped.

Ankle edema occurs in up to 10% of patients, usually in association with livedo reticularis; it may contribute to congestive heart failure and related problems.[17,25] Elevation of the legs, diuretic therapy, and possibly a dose reduction of amantadine should alleviate the edema. Since L.M. is only experiencing mild ankle edema and does not have a significant cardiac history, elevation of his legs is probably all that is necessary. He should be continued on amantadine 200 mg/day because this is currently providing beneficial relief of symptoms.

Levodopa

10. **L.M. has responded very well to amantadine for the past 4 months with an increased ability to paint and carry on the activities of daily life. However, over the past few weeks he has noticed a gradual worsening in his symptoms and once again is having difficulty holding a paint brush. He currently complains of feeling more "tied up," has more difficulty getting out of a chair, and his posture is slightly more stooped. Otherwise, he is able to carry out most of his daily activities without a lot of difficulty. Why should levodopa, be considered for the treatment of L.M.'s Parkinson's disease at this time?**

Levodopa (Larodopa, Dopar), without question, has revolutionized the treatment of Parkinson's disease. Although the most rational approach to treating parkinsonism is to replenish depleted dopamine in the brain, dopamine itself does not cross the blood-brain barrier. In high doses, levodopa, an inert neutral amino acid with no known pharmacologic action of its own, penetrates into the brain where it is converted to dopamine.[26] Early trials by Cotzias[27,28] and Barbeau[29] demonstrating significant (often dramatic) improvement in all the cardinal features of the disease, soon led to further studies which clearly established levodopa as the drug of choice for long-term treatment of Parkinson's disease.[30,31]

Efficacy. In an early open trial involving 86 patients, 79% experienced $\geq$50% improvement in all their symptoms when given an average levodopa dose of 4.8 gm/day.[29] Only 8 of the 79 patients (10%) failed therapy, two of these due to side effects.[29] Similar findings were reported in another study of 100 patients.[30] A dramatic improvement (>75%) in bradykinesia, rigidity, and tremor was observed in 33 patients.[30] Most patients show an initial response to levodopa by five weeks; however, an average of four months is required before maximum benefits are seen. The prolonged period of titration to maximum response is necessary because most patients have difficulty tolerating the large doses required.[29,30]

11. Sinemet: Advantages and Disadvantages. **What are the advantages/disadvantages of Sinemet over levodopa alone?**

Although levodopa is highly effective, its use is not without problems. High doses are required because significant amounts are peripherally (extracerebrally) metabolized by the enzyme, aromatic L-amino acid (dopa) decarboxylase, to dopamine. These high doses result in many undesirable side effects such as nausea, vomiting, and anorexia (50% of patients); postural hypotension (30% of patients); and cardiac arrhythmias (10% of patients).[17,25,26,29,30] Additionally, mental disturbances (see Question 16) are encountered in 15% of patients and abnormal involuntary movements (dyskinesias) can be seen in up to 55% of patients during the first six months of levodopa treatment.[17,26,29,30]

By combining levodopa with a dopa decarboxylase inhibitor which does not penetrate the blood-brain barrier, a decrease in the peripheral conversion of levodopa to dopamine can be achieved, while the desired conversion within the basal ganglia remains unaffected (see Figure 51.1).[32–34] The two peripheral decarboxylase inhibitors in clinical use are benserazide (unavailable in the U.S.) and carbidopa.[33] Sinemet is the fixed combination of carbidopa and levodopa and is available in ratios of 1:4 (Sinemet 25/100) and 1:10 (Sinemet 10/100 and 25/250).[33] A controlled release product (Sinemet-CR) is available in a ratio of 25/100 and 50/200.

Combining levodopa with carbidopa enhances the amount of dopamine available to the brain and, thereby, allows the dose of levodopa to be decreased by 80%. This combination also shortens the time needed for the process of gradually increasing the levodopa dose to achieve maximal effects by several weeks because carbidopa substantially decreases levodopa-induced nausea and vomiting.[33,34] Cardiac arrhythmias are lessened and postural hypotension may be slightly improved.[33,34] Disadvantages of the combination include earlier and more frequent occurrences of dyskinesias and no change in the incidence of mental side effects.[17,32–34] Additionally, Sinemet is more expensive than levodopa by itself. Overall, the advantages of Sinemet far outweigh the disadvantages such that nearly all patients are given this form of treatment rather than levodopa alone.

12. Initiation of Therapy. **L.M. does not have severe disability at this time. Should he be started on levodopa therapy now or should it be reserved for a later date when symptoms are more severe?**

Fig 51.1 Schematic Representation of the Peripheral Decarboxylation of Levodopa When Given Alone (a) and With a Peripheral Decarboxylase Inhibitor (b) When combined with a decarboxylase inhibitor, less drug is required and more levodopa reaches the brain. Reproduced with permission from reference 34.

The question of when to begin levodopa remains somewhat of a controversial issue in the treatment of Parkinson's disease.[35-37] Despite initial hopes to the contrary, levodopa therapy does not alter the progression of the disease. Studies have proven that with long-term use, the efficacy of levodopa decreases.[30,31] Because Parkinson's disease is a progressive disorder, it is unclear whether the decrease in levodopa effectiveness is due to progression of the disease (i.e., neuronal destruction is so extensive that levodopa is no longer adequately converted to dopamine) or due to a finite period of usefulness of the drug itself, regardless of the extent of disease.

The most convincing argument for early levodopa therapy comes from studies carried out by Markham and Diamond.[38,39] When different groups of patients were compared for duration of levodopa treatment (irrespective of length of symptoms before initiation of levodopa), significant differences were observed between the groups in terms of disability scores (i.e., subjects with the shortest symptom duration were the least disabled). Conversely, when the subjects were matched for duration of symptoms (irrespective of treatment duration), similar disability scores were found for the groups. These results strongly implicate duration of the disease, rather than duration of therapy as the reason for loss of levodopa efficacy.

There is, however, evidence that long-term levodopa therapy itself often leads to altered therapeutic response. The explanation for the loss of efficacy with long-term therapy may be related in part to alterations in dopamine receptor activity or interference by dopamine metabolites.[36,37,40] This concept is supported by the fact that temporary levodopa withdrawal (drug holiday) can lead to

improvement in levodopa response.[41] After two years or more of levodopa, a substantial number of patients develop response fluctuations (''on-off'' and ''wearing off'' effects).[26,31,33,34] These response fluctuations are only associated with long-term levodopa use; therefore, delaying the initiation of therapy will delay the onset of these problems.

It also has been suggested that chronic levodopa therapy actually may accelerate the neuro-degenerative process through formation of free radicals via dopamine metabolism.[40] Free radicals can cause oxidative damage to lipid cell membranes. Thus, metabolism of either endogenous dopamine, or dopamine derived from levodopa, may induce an ''oxidative stress'' and, thereby, contribute to neuronal damage.[4,40] Although intriguing, evidence to support this hypothesis is limited and the ''oxidative stress'' issue remains controversial.

Given the above considerations, the optimal time to initiate levodopa therapy must be individualized. Most neurologists agree that there is little reason to start levodopa until the patient is clearly bothered (socially, vocationally, or otherwise) by the disease. Before levodopa is started, patients must fully understand the nature of the disease and what to expect with long-term therapy. L.M. should be seriously considered for levodopa therapy because his disease has progressed enough to threaten job performance. L.M. has developed tachyphylaxis to amantadine; however, if amantadine is withdrawn for a month or so and reinstituted along with levodopa, further benefit may be derived.[20] Response fluctuations may be encountered sooner, but these can be managed by various means (see Question 14).

13. *Carbidopa/Levodopa (Sinemet) Dosing.* **The decision is made to begin L.M. on carbidopa/levodopa (Sinemet). How is Sinemet dosed?**

About 75 to 100 mg/day of carbidopa is necessary to saturate peripheral dopa decarboxylase.[33,34] Giving higher amounts of carbidopa than this is usually unnecessary and more costly. Therapy should be initiated with Sinemet 25/100 at a dose of one tablet three times a day. The dosage may then be increased by 100 mg levodopa every day or every other day as tolerated. The best approach to dosing carbidopa/levodopa is to titrate up to a maximum response while attempting to avoid dyskinesias. If dyskinesias occur at doses needed for maximum response (as is frequently the case), the dose can be decreased slightly to alleviate dyskinetic activity while minimizing a recrudescence of the disease. The goal of optimizing therapy lies in balancing the most therapeutic dose with that which does not produce an unacceptable degree of side effects. Therefore, for best results, long-term follow up with frequent subtle dosage adjustments is the preferred approach. Most patients respond to levodopa doses of 750 to 1000 mg/day when given with carbidopa. When levodopa doses are more than 750 mg/day, patients such as L.M. can be switched from the 1:4 ratio of carbidopa/levodopa to the 1:10 ratio to prevent providing excessive amounts of decarboxylase inhibitor. For example, if L.M. needed 800 mg of levodopa per day, two Sinemet 10/100 tablets four times daily could be given. Some clinicians would consider the addition of bromocriptine (see Question 19) after the daily levodopa dose has been increased to more than 600 mg because bromocriptine can provide comparable benefits to that achieved by higher levodopa doses and is associated with fewer side effects.[7,99,100]

14. *Levodopa Response Fluctuations.* **L.M. had a dramatic improvement in all of his parkinsonian symptoms with the initiation of levodopa therapy. After 2 months of treatment he began to experience dyskinesias. These usually occurred 1 to 2 hours after a dose and were manifested by facial grimacing, lip smacking, tongue protrusion, and rocking of the trunk. These dyskinetic effects have been lessened by gradually decreasing his dosage of Sinemet, but have not totally cleared.**

After 3 years of levodopa therapy, more serious problems began to emerge. In the mornings, L.M. often experiences immobility. Nearly every day, he has periods (lasting for a few minutes) in which he is unable to move, followed by a sudden "switch" to a fluid-like state often associated with dyskinetic activity. He continues to take Sinemet QID (Sinemet 25/250), but only gains symptomatic relief for about 3–4 hours following a dose. Also, the response to a given dose varies and is often less in the afternoon. At times, he becomes "frozen" particularly when he needs to board an elevator or is required to move quickly. What are possible explanations for these alterations in clinical response?

For most patients, the initial response to levodopa is quite favorable. This early phase of therapy is termed the "honeymoon period." Although variable, the "honeymoon period" may last for up to three to five years.[139] However, after the initial period of stability, many patients experience fluctuations in motor response with long-term levodopa use. Response fluctuations are seen in 50% of parkinsonian patients after two or more years of therapy.[42,43,139] Often categorized as the "on-off" effect, this designation does not accurately describe the different varieties of altered responses observed. In attempting to describe response fluctuations, it is important to separate those effects due to the disease and those due to the drug. Because levodopa is a short-acting agent with an elimination half-life of about 1.5 hours, much of the effect from the evening dose is absent upon awaking in the morning.[34] For this reason, it is not surprising that L.M. is experiencing a period of immobility upon arising. This is alleviated in most patients shortly after taking the morning dose. The degree of response may vary over the course of a day, with good periods of relief often seen in the morning and early evening and poor periods in the late afternoon and late evening.[33]

Two of the more common response fluctuations are the true "on-off" effect and the "wearing off" or "end-of-dose deterioration" effect. The true "on-off" effect is described as random fluctuations from mobility to the parkinsonian state appearing suddenly as if a switch has been turned. These fluctuations can last from minutes to hours and increase in frequency and intensity with time. Eventually, many end-stage patients experience either mobility with severe dyskinesias or complete immobility.[33,42] In most patients this effect bears no clear-cut relation to the timing of the dose or levodopa serum levels.[44] The "wearing off" or "end-of-dose" effect is a more predictable effect which occurs at the latter part of the dosing interval following a period of relief; it can be improved by various means such as shortening the dosing interval or by adjunctive dopamine agonist therapy.

The explanations for these motor responses are not entirely clear. Incomplete delivery of dopamine to central receptors is at least partially responsible: variations in the rate and extent of levodopa absorption; dietary substrates (e.g., large neutral amino acids) which compete with cerebral transport mechanisms; and competition for receptor binding by levodopa metabolites can explain these variable responses to levodopa.[45–47] Furthermore, early in the course of the disease sufficient dopaminergic neurons remain which can store dopamine derived from levodopa administration. These neurons act as a "buffer" against fluctuating levodopa concentrations. With disease progression, the buffering capacity of these neurons is diminished and motor response becomes more dependent upon fluctuations in synaptic dopamine concentrations.[48,49]

15. *Controlled-Release Sinemet.* **L.M. is to be converted from immediate-release Sinemet to Sinemet CR because of his continuing motor fluctuations. How useful is controlled-release Sinemet in improving levodopa response fluctuations? How should L.M.'s immediate-release Sinemet be converted to Sinemet CR?**

The ability to partially alleviate response fluctuations by using continuous infusions of levodopa has prompted the development of slow-release carbidopa/levodopa formulations in attempts to assure a smoother, more sustained delivery of drug.[47,50,51] Sinemet CR contains 25 mg carbidopa and 100 mg levodopa or 50 mg carbidopa and 200 mg levodopa in an erodible polymer matrix which retards dissolution in gastric fluids. By gradually dissolving, Sinemet CR permits a more gradual absorption of levodopa and more sustained plasma concentrations of levodopa in comparison to standard Sinemet. Because of the sustained-release properties of Sinemet CR, the dosing interval can be extended and the number of doses per day can be decreased.[50,51] The end-of-dose deterioration ("wearing off") effect is improved in many patients by virtue of the slower rate of plasma levodopa decline. Peak dose dyskinesias may improve in some patients because Sinemet CR administration lowers peak plasma concentrations. Furthermore, the bioavailability of controlled-release Sinemet is about 30% less than immediate-release Sinemet. Accordingly, L.M.'s dosage of Sinemet CR will most likely need to be increased. His late afternoon or early evening dose of Sinemet CR, however, could be reduced moderately to minimize the risk of evening dyskinesias. Treatment with Sinemet CR also might improve sleeping patterns by virtue of decreasing the frequency of nocturnal awakenings. Sinemet CR doses for L.M. should not be adjusted more frequently than three to five day intervals because the slow-release characteristics of this formulation provide a more prolonged effect.

There are a few disadvantages of controlled-release Sinemet. The delay in reaching maximum effect, which is particularly a problem in the morning, is unacceptable to some patients. To manage this problem, patients can either take their morning dose of Sinemet CR one hour before arising, or can supplement their regimen with a dose of conventional-release product in the morning. With repeated dosing of Sinemet CR, levodopa can accumulate over the course of the day resulting in severe dyskinesias later in the day in some cases. Furthermore, controlled-release Sinemet is more expensive than standard Sinemet.

The clinical response to levodopa therapy may be improved by modification of dietary protein ingestion. Levodopa is actively transported across the blood brain barrier by the large neutral amino-acid transport system. This transport system also facilitates the blood-to-brain transport of amino acids such as L-leucine, L-isoleucine, L-valine, and L-phenylalanine. Levodopa and these neutral amino acids compete for transport mechanisms, and high plasma concentrations of these amino acids can decrease brain concentrations of levodopa.[132] Overall reduction, or redistribution of the total daily dietary protein intake (i.e., having L.M. consume most of his dietary protein at the evening meal) may improve levodopa response fluctuations.[133] Patients generally are instructed to take immediate-release Sinemet 30 minutes before or 60 minutes after meals for maximal effect. This relationship of dosing around a meal probably is less important with the controlled-release formulation. Nevertheless, it would be prudent to take Sinemet CR at about the same time each day to facilitate compliance.

Other means for improving levodopa response fluctuations include the use of adjunctive agents such as the dopamine agonists and selegiline. In severe cases, continuous duodenal infusion of levodopa[52] and continuous subcutaneous infusion of the dopamine agonist, lisuride,[53] have shown potential usefulness.

If L.M. prefers not to convert to Sinemet CR, his condition may be improved by taking his daily doses of immediate-release Sinemet in shorter dosing intervals while avoiding substantial increases in the daily dosage which could worsen his dyskinesias. Taking his morning dose before arising from bed or adding a long-acting dopamine agonist like bromocriptine or pergolide may help with early morning problems and smooth out other response fluctuations.

16. Adverse Effects: Mental Changes. L.M. has become notably more depressed often feeling helpless and hopeless. At times he does not even feel like getting out of bed in the morning and he does not have much of an appetite. He feels increasingly confused at times and has trouble remembering things that recently happened. In addition to these complaints, L.M. reports that he often has vivid dreams and on occasion experiences visual hallucinations. To what extent is levodopa contributing to these mental problems? How should they be managed?

A number of psychiatric side effects have been associated with levodopa therapy. These include confusion, depression, restlessness and overactivity, psychosis, hypomania, and vivid dreams.[54] Mental side effects occur in approximately 20% of patients receiving levodopa, but incidences vary. In one early study, confusion, hallucinations, or vivid dreams occurred in 16% and depression in 11% of 80 patients treated with levodopa.[29] Another group encountered mental changes in 51% of patients given levodopa for five years.[31] The combination of levodopa with a decarboxylase inhibitor has little effect on the incidence of mental disturbances.[34] Patients predisposed to levodopa-induced mental disturbances include those with underlying or pre-existing psychiatric disorders and those receiving high doses for prolonged periods.[54]

An organic confusional state with disorientation, which may progress to toxic delirium, is the most commonly observed mental side effect.[54] This side effect can be exacerbated by concurrent anticholinergic or amantadine therapy. Because of its ability to improve disease symptoms and profoundly impact neurologic function, levodopa often produces an elevation in mood, but this is not always the case. Depression, often out of proportion to the degree of neurologic impairment, is another commonly observed finding and may in some instances precede motor dysfunction.[14,54] This disorder may be linked to a decrease in serotonin metabolism as evidenced by decreased 5-hydroxyindoleacetic acid (5-HIAA) concentrations in the cerebrospinal fluid of depressed parkinsonian patients.[55] While a few individuals like L.M. may experience depression, a number of patients receiving levodopa experience psychomotor excitation.[54] Symptoms associated with psychomotor activation include overactivity, restlessness, and agitation.[54] Similarly, hypomania has been reported in up to 8% of patients, and is characterized by grandiose thinking, flight of ideas, tangential thinking, and poor social judgment.[54] Normal sexual activity often is restored with improved motor function; however, hypersexuality and libido are increased in about 1% of levodopa treated patients.[29,54] The hypersexuality is most likely an associated feature of levodopa-induced hypomania.[54] Psychotic behavior, often in the form of paranoid delusions and visual or olfactory hallucinations, is seen less frequently.[29,54]

From the symptoms described by L.M., a number of levodopa-associated mental disturbances are likely present. He has a predisposition for these particular side effects because he presented with underlying depression, confusion, and disturbances of cognition. In general, most of the mental disturbances are dose related and can be lessened by a reduction in dosage. This may be impractical for L.M. because a return of parkinsonian symptoms can be anticipated.

In some cases, depression in parkinsonian patients can be treated successfully with antidepressant drugs.[18,56-58] Care must be exercised, however, because a number of drugs (see Question 27), including the tricyclic antidepressants, may adversely interact with levodopa (see Table 51.5).[58-64,68,69] Hypertensive crisis has been reported with levodopa and imipramine, particularly when an insufficient amount of carbidopa is administered (see Table 51.5).[58] The tricyclic antidepressants also possess significant anticholinergic properties which may delay gastric emptying and increase levodopa degradation in the gut.[60,64] In addition, these properties may result in additive toxicity in patients concomitantly receiving anticholinergics or in patients like L.M. who have conditions that can be exacerbated by anticholinergic therapy. Nonselective monoamine oxidase inhibitors (MAOIs), such as phenelzine (Nardil) and tranylcypromine (Parnate), are used to treat certain types of depressive disorders; however, these should be avoided in patients on levodopa because of the significant risk of hypertensive crisis (see Table 51.5).[68,69] Selegiline selectively binds to type-B MAO receptors in the CNS and does not cause a hypertensive reaction.[70] Depression is related to serotonin metabolism; therefore, other classes of antidepressants which act specifically on serotonergic mechanisms such as fluoxetine (Prozac) or trazodone (Desyrel), could be employed to treat depression in parkinsonian patients.[18,55,56] Thus, L.M. may be treated with fluoxetine 20 mg at bedtime, increased to 80 mg/day as necessary. He should be observed carefully for adverse effects or changes in parkinsonian symptoms.

17. Drug Holiday. What is the current status of "drug holidays" in the management of Parkinson's disease?

Table 51.5		Levodopa Drug Interactions[a,b]	
Drug	Interaction	Mechanism	Comments
Anticholinergics[60]	↓ levodopa effect	↓ gastric emptying, thus ↑ degradation of levodopa in gut, and ↓ amount absorbed	Watch for ↓ levodopa effect when anticholinergics used in doses sufficient to ↓ GI motility. When anticholinergic therapy discontinued in a levodopa patient, watch for signs of levodopa toxicity. Anticholinergics can relieve symptoms of parkinsonism and might offset the reduction of levodopa bioavailability. Overall, interaction of minor significance
Benzodiazepines[71]	↓ levodopa effect	Mechanism unknown	Use together with caution; discontinue if interaction observed
Ferrous sulfate[72]	↓ levodopa oral absorption by 50%	Formation of chelation complex	Avoid concomitant administration
Food	↓ levodopa effect	Large, neutral amino acids compete with levodopa for intestinal absorption	Although levodopa usually taken with meals to slow absorption and ↓ central emetic effect, high protein diets should be avoided (see Question 15)
MAOIs[68–70] (e.g., phenelzine, tranylcypromine)	Hypertensive crisis	↑ peripheral dopamine and norepinephrine	Avoid using together; selegiline and levodopa used successfully together. Carbidopa might minimize hypertensive reaction to levodopa in patients receiving an MAOI
Methyldopa[61,62]	↑ or ↓ levodopa effect	Acts as central and peripheral decarboxylase inhibitor	Observe for response, may need to switch to another antihypertensive
Metoclopramide[65,66]	↓ levodopa effect	Central dopamine blockade	Avoid using together; domperidone, a peripheral dopamine blocking antiemetic preferred[c]
Moclobemide	↑ adverse effects (e.g., nausea, headache)	Not established	Although MAO-B is more important than MAO-A in the metabolism of dopamine, an MAO-A inhibitor such as moclobemide may have some effect on dopamine response
Neuroleptics[63] (e.g., butyrophenones, phenothiazines)	↓ levodopa effect	Central blockade of dopamine neurotransmission	Important interaction, avoid using these drugs together
Papaverine	↓ levodopa effect	Unknown; might block dopamine receptors	Should be avoided. Therapeutic response to levodopa returns 5–10 days after papaverine discontinued
Phenytoin[67]	↓ levodopa effect	Mechanism unknown	Avoid using together if possible
Pyridoxine[59]	↓ levodopa effect	↑ peripheral decarboxylation of levodopa	Not observed when levodopa given with carbidopa
Reserpine[61]	↓ levodopa effect	Central dopamine depletion	Clinical evidence lacking, best to avoid if possible
Tacrine	↓ levodopa effect	↑ central cholinergic activity	Try to avoid combination. Doses of tacrine and/or antiparkinson drugs may need to be adjusted if used concomitantly
TCAs[b,58,64]	↓ levodopa effect	↑ levodopa degradation in gut due to delayed emptying	TCAs and levodopa have been used successfully together, use with caution

[a] For more information regarding these and other levodopa drug interactions, see Hansten PD, Horn JR. Drug Interactions & Updates Quarterly. Applied Therapeutics, Inc. Vancouver: 1995.
[b] MAOI = Monoamine oxidase inhibitor; MAO-A = Monoamine oxidase A; MAO-B = Monoamine oxidase B; TCAs = Tricyclic antidepressants.
[c] Not available in the U.S.

The concept of a drug holiday in Parkinson's disease was first prompted by observations of improved response in patients whose levodopa therapy was temporarily discontinued while undergoing surgical procedures or for other reasons.[41] Defined as a brief period of drug withdrawal, the drug holiday has been attempted in the past as a means of improving response and minimizing side effects in patients on long-term levodopa therapy.[41,73,74] It is theorized that long-term levodopa use results in "down regulation" of dopamine receptors.[36,41] The drug holiday is believed to exert a beneficial effect by allowing striatal dopamine receptors to be "resensitized."[41]

While some studies have demonstrated a temporary benefit, other studies show no improvement in motor performance or side effect profile at six months and one year following a ten-day period of levodopa withdrawal.[73–75]

Drug holidays can pose substantial risks. The immobility experienced by patients during the withdrawal period can have devastating psychological and physiological consequences. Drug holidays require hospitalization and careful observation for complications of immobility such as deep venous thrombosis, aspiration pneumonia, and decubitus ulcer formation.[41,74] Also, potentially fatal hyperpyrexic reactions have been reported.[76]

Because of the serious complications and the lack of sustained improvement, a drug holiday should not be considered for L.M.

18. Interference with Laboratory Tests. L.M. returned to the neurology clinic for his routine follow-up visit and had a panel of laboratory tests performed. Laboratory results are as follows: electrolytes (sodium, potassium, chloride, CO_2) were within normal limits, BUN 22 mg/dL, creatinine 0.9 mg/dL, complete blood count (hemoglobin, hematocrit, white blood cell count) were within normal limits, uric acid 8.0 mg/dL, aspartate aminotransferase (AST) 45 IU, alanine aminotransferase (ALT) 55 IU, alkaline phosphatase 190 mg/dL, fasting glucose 190 mg/dL, with "trace" glucose and 1+ ketones on urinalysis. Which of these laboratory results may be affected by levodopa therapy? [SI units: uric acid 475.84 μmol/L; AST 45 U/L; ALT 55 U/L; glucose 10.55 mmol/L]

A number of the laboratory abnormalities displayed by L.M. may be related to levodopa therapy. Levodopa has been associated with asymptomatic elevations in serum uric acid levels.[29,77,78] Levodopa-induced elevations in uric acid levels are believed to be due to interfering substances produced by levodopa metabolism (DOPAC) creating "false elevations" when determined by the colorimetric method.[77] These do not occur when the uricase method is used.[77] Gout has occurred in two patients receiving levodopa who had no apparent history of the disease. The relationship between levodopa and gout is unclear; however, given his history of gout, L.M. should be watched for signs and symptoms of an acute gouty attack (see Chapter 40: Gout and Hyperuricemia).

Mild elevations in BUN have been observed that may improve with hydration.[29] Elevations in AST, ALT, lactate dehydrogenase, bilirubin, and alkaline phosphatase all have been reported.[29,34] Levodopa can increase fasting blood sugar and may decrease glucose tolerance, but a direct correlation between levodopa and diabetes has not been established.[34,79] False positive "trace" readings have been seen in the absence of glucosuria when urine is tested by the copper reductase method (Clinitest), and false negative readings in the presence of glucosuria can occur with the glucose oxidase method (Clinistix, Tes-Tape).[80,81] False negative readings with Tes-Tape can be averted by holding the tape vertically and reading the uppermost region of the strip.[80,81] Finally, false positive readings for urine ketones may result with the Ketostix and Labstix testing methods.[82]

Dopamine Agonists

The need for alternative drug therapies in Parkinson's disease became evident once declining efficacy and response fluctuations were encountered with long-term levodopa therapy. Because of the indirect means by which levodopa exerts its dopaminergic activity, investigators searched for agents which could directly stimulate dopamine receptors, thus bypassing degenerated neurons. This led to the discovery of the dopamine agonists (see Figure 51.2).[83,84] The dopamine agonists work by directly stimulating postsynaptic dopamine receptors within the corpus striatum. There are two types of postsynaptic receptors, D1 and D2 receptors. Stimulation of D2 receptors is largely responsible for antiparkinson activity, while the precise role of the D1 receptors remains uncertain.[7,83] In addition to D1 and D2 receptors, presynaptic dopaminergic receptors also are involved with regulating the synthesis and release of dopamine through feedback inhibition. Although the dopamine agonists differ slightly from each other in terms of their affinities for dopamine receptors, these agents produce essentially the same clinical effects when used to treat Parkinson's disease.[7]

As a class, the dopamine agonists represent the most effective therapy currently available for patients experiencing long-term problems with levodopa.[85] They are also effective alone in earlier forms of the disease.[4,7,84,85] The dopamine agonists in present use are derived from the ergoline class of ergot alkaloids and include bromocriptine,[85-100] pergolide,[102-109] and lisuride[110-114] (see Table 51.2 and Figure 51.2).

Bromocriptine

19. L.M. continues to have a gradual worsening in symptoms. Bromocriptine therapy is to be started. How effective is bromocriptine in the treatment of Parkinson's disease?

Bromocriptine (Parlodel) is a semisynthetic ergot alkaloid which was initially approved for use as a prolactin inhibitor for conditions such as amenorrhea, galactorrhea, and infertility.[86,87] It has been used to treat parkinsonism since the early 1970s. The dopamine agonist properties of bromocriptine are primarily due to its ability to stimulate postsynaptic D2 receptors.[83]

Efficacy. Bromocriptine has been studied in Parkinson's disease by numerous investigators.[88-100] These investigations can be divided into two major areas. The first area, encompassing many of the earlier studies, involves the administration of bromocriptine to patients with moderate to severe parkinsonism maintained on levodopa.[84-86,88-91] These studies clearly demonstrate improvement in clinical response in up to 75% of patients treated with bromocriptine.[85,88,89] Improvement in response fluctuations (primarily end-of-dose deterioration) also occurs in approximately 60% of cases.[85,88,89] Rigidity, tremor, and bradykinesia seem to respond equally well.

The second area of bromocriptine use is as "de novo," or sole therapy (without levodopa), usually in the earlier stages of the disease.[84,85,92-96] The majority of these investigations have utilized lower doses of bromocriptine and demonstrate improvement in disability in approximately 60% of patients.[85,94-97] Substantial improvement in patients with response oscillations was noted.[85,94,96] Declining efficacy is seen with early "de novo" bromocriptine therapy, such that by two years many patients will require the addition of levodopa for optimal results.[92,95,96] The Parkinson's Disease Research Group in the United Kingdom is conducting a prospective, randomized trial comparing levodopa (with benserazide, a decarboxylase inhibitor), levodopa with selegiline, and bromocriptine in patients with early, mild Parkinson's disease. Results from an interim analysis revealed similar efficacy in reducing parkinsonian disability; however, significantly more patients receiving bromocriptine experienced adverse reactions (primarily gastrointestinal and psychiatric) resulting in a higher withdrawal rate from the study.[98] Another approach for treating early Parkinson's disease is to combine low-dose bromocriptine with low-dose levodopa (500 to 600 mg/day) in the early stages of the disease in an attempt to prolong the usefulness of both agents and minimize side effects associated with long-term, high-dose levodopa.[7,99,100]

20. Dosing. What is the most effective way to dose bromocriptine?

Determination of optimal dosing strategies for bromocriptine has evolved gradually as clinicians have gained more experience with the drug. A compilation of results from 27 papers encom-

Fig 51.2 Chemical Structures of the Dopamine Agonists Bromocriptine, Pergolide, and Lisuride. Reproduced with permission from reference 102.

passing 790 patients treated with bromocriptine has allowed the question of dose to be more closely addressed.[85] Results from studies using low doses (<30 mg/day) of bromocriptine alone versus those using high doses (usually between 30 to 80 mg/day) alone show improvement in 58% versus 62% of cases, respectively.[85] Side effects leading to discontinuation of therapy were encountered in 9% and 27% of patients in the low- and high-dose groups, respectively. Similarly, 71% of patients given low-dose bromocriptine with levodopa improved, compared to 58% given high-dose therapy together with levodopa.[85] Adverse effects causing discontinuation of therapy were observed in 26% of low-dose and 32% of high-dose patients when combined with levodopa. While these results seem to favor the use of lower doses, patients receiving higher doses often had the disease for a longer duration and tended to have more advanced symptoms.[85] Thus, the dose required for optimal therapeutic response is most likely a function of the severity of illness.[97] Therefore, the goal of bromocriptine therapy is to keep the dose as low as possible recognizing that as the disease progresses, higher doses may be required. An important consideration in keeping the dose of bromocriptine as low as possible concerns the high cost of therapy, especially for doses above 50 mg/day.

The best approach to dosing bromocriptine is to start low and slowly titrate upward. For L.M., therapy should be initiated at 1.25 mg/day at bedtime and increased by 2.5 mg every two to four weeks. It may take months to achieve optimum results.[93,95]

21. Adverse Effects. What are the side effects of bromocriptine? How can these be managed?

Bromocriptine therapy is associated with a number of potentially serious side effects. *Mental changes* are most commonly experienced, occurring in up to 40% of patients.[85,86] Most notable of these mental effects are visual hallucinations which may be related to the lysergic acid moiety in the chemical structure of the drug (see Figure 51.2).[86] Confusion, paranoid delusions, and mania are all associated with bromocriptine use and may persist for weeks after the drug is discontinued.[86] As with levodopa, mental effects are more pronounced in patients with underlying psychiatric disturbances.[85,86]

Orthostatic hypotension with dizziness is the next most frequently observed side effect.[85-87] *Nausea*, with or without vomiting, can be a significant problem, particularly with higher doses. While the nausea with bromocriptine is less severe than that associated with levodopa given alone, it is more severe than levodopa combined with carbidopa.[86,87] Administering bromocriptine with food may partially alleviate this problem. With continued use, many patients develop tolerance to the hypotensive and gastrointestinal side effects of bromocriptine.

Peripheral vascular effects are uncommonly associated with bromocriptine (<5% of patients) and are probably due to the mild alpha-blocking properties of the drug. These vascular adverse effects include digital vasospasm, Raynaud's phenomenon, and angina; all are usually reversible with discontinuation of therapy.[85,86] Erythromelalgia, an unusual vascular complaint characterized by redness, warmth, tenderness, and edema of the legs, occurs uncommonly in patients on bromocriptine. This side effect may improve with a decrease in dose and reverses when the drug is stopped.[86]

Dyskinesias occur in up to 80% of patients receiving bromocriptine for the treatment of parkinsonism; this adverse effect is not as common in patients receiving this drug for the treatment of other disorders.[86,87] These abnormal involuntary movements are similar to those seen with levodopa, and include orofacial dyskinesias, facial grimacing, and choreic movements of the trunk and limbs.[85,86] Bromocriptine-induced dyskinesias are improved by decreasing the dose; however, this may worsen control of the disease.

Finally, bromocriptine has been associated in rare instances with *pleuropulmonary fibrosis*, similar to that seen with methysergide, another ergot alkaloid.[102] Chest x-rays should be checked on all bromocriptine treated patients with abnormalities on pulmonary examination.[86,102] Hypertension, seizures, fatal cerebrovascular accident (stroke), and acute myocardial infarction have occurred rarely in women receiving bromocriptine for postpartum lactation.

22. How do pergolide and lisuride compare to bromocriptine?

Pergolide

Pergolide is a synthetic ergoline derivative with pharmacologic properties differing from bromocriptine. (See Table 51.2 and Figure 51.2.) Pergolide exerts an antiparkinson effect through direct stimulation of both D1 and D2 postsynaptic receptors.[17,84,103] Pergolide also differs from bromocriptine in that it is more potent and longer acting.[84,102,103]

In open trials, the addition of pergolide improves parkinsonian disability in up to 75% of patients with advanced Parkinson's disease who no longer respond satisfactorily to levodopa.[84,103,107] In double-blind, placebo-controlled trials, a significant placebo effect has been observed, but improvements greater than could be attributed to placebo alone, are elicited.[103,104] Pergolide has been compared to bromocriptine in patients with advanced parkinsonism in a randomized, double-blind trial with similar results.[102] These studies indicate that like bromocriptine, pergolide is an effective adjunctive agent in patients on long-term levodopa. Improvements induced by pergolide are greatest at one month, but begin to decline after six months of therapy. By the second year of therapy, most patients on pergolide fail to show improvement over pretreatment values.[84,103,104,107] Early responders to pergolide tend to experience more prolonged benefit with the drug.[104] Small numbers of patients given pergolide alone, showed some minor improvements; however, these were inferior to those obtained with levodopa.[104,105]

A major advantage of pergolide is its ability to improve response fluctuations in levodopa treated patients. This benefit of pergolide directly relates to its potency and prolonged duration of action.[104-107] Improvements in "end-of-dose" deterioration respond more favorably than the "on-off" phenomenon.[104,105] A mean improvement of 120% in the number of hours the patients were "on" has been observed from various trials performed to date.[84,105] Pergolide also can improve disability during "off" periods.[104-107] As a result, its long duration of action may make it especially advantageous for managing cases of early morning akinesia if the dose is taken at bedtime. This property could be of benefit to L.M. who suffers from this effect. Finally, a few studies suggest that pergolide can be efficacious in up to 50% of patients showing unresponsiveness, decreased responsiveness over time, or intolerance to bromocriptine.[103,108]

Adverse effects of pergolide are similar to those of bromocriptine.[17,102,103] Although in some studies up to 40% of patients had to discontinue pergolide therapy because of unacceptable side effects, this estimate is probably high and only about 25% of patients will have trouble with this drug.[84,103] As with bromocriptine, the higher incidence of side effects may be the result of escalating the dose too rapidly. The incidence of mental changes with pergolide appears to be similar to other dopamine agonists.[102,103,108]

Nausea and vomiting occur, particularly upon initiation of therapy, and may lessen with time.[103] Orthostasis and other cardiovascular effects may be more frequent with pergolide than with other dopamine agonists.[84,105] Cardiac arrhythmias were a concern in the early period of clinical trials; however, well designed studies using careful cardiac monitoring techniques have demonstrated that although pergolide causes a mild bradycardia, no significant arrhythmogenic properties are seen in patients without underlying cardiac problems.[109] Angina has been seen in 2% to 13% of patients in some trials.[103] Pergolide should be administered cautiously in patients with cardiac arrhythmias or angina. Dyskinesias may worsen when pergolide is added to levodopa, but can be managed by decreasing the levodopa dose if tolerated.[103–105] Peripheral vascular side effects also occur with pergolide,[103] and erythromelalgia has been reported.[103] Pergolide shares similarities in chemical structure with lergotrile, a hepatotoxic agent, and mild elevations in hepatic enzymes have been observed.[102,104] To date, serious hepatotoxicity has not been encountered with pergolide.

Therapy with pergolide should be started with 0.05 to 0.1 mg/day given at bedtime and slowly increased by 0.05 to 0.15 mg increments every third day to a maximum of 6 mg/day. Most patients respond to doses between 2 to 4 mg/day, with a few requiring doses as high as 10 mg/day. A daily dose ratio for bromocriptine to pergolide of 13:1 has been suggested from comparative studies.[102]

Lisuride

Lisuride (see Table 51.2 and Figure 51.2) is a water soluble, semisynthetic ergoline derivative that directly stimulates postsynaptic D2 receptors as well as serotonergic receptors in the brain stem.[17,83] Lisuride is superior to placebo and is effective in up to 70% of patients when combined with levodopa.[84,110–113] Lisuride also improves response fluctuations and decreases the frequency and severity of "off" periods.[83,84,111,113] Similar improvements in tremor, rigidity, and gait and postural disturbances for lisuride, bromocriptine, and pergolide suggest that these drugs probably are equivalent.[102,112] As with other dopamine agonists, decreased efficacy is seen with time.[84] The high water solubility of lisuride permits continuous subcutaneous administration which may be beneficial for patients with severe response fluctuations.[53,114] Presently lisuride is not commercially available in the U.S., but can be obtained through participation in National Institute of Health-sponsored clinical trials.

The adverse effects of lisuride are essentially the same as those associated with bromocriptine and pergolide.[17,84,124] In clinical studies, therapy had to be stopped because of side effects in an average of 27% of patients.[84]

Lisuride is dosed in an identical manner to pergolide. Therapy should be started with 0.05 mg/day and increased slowly to a maximum daily dose of between 5 to 10 mg/day.[110–113] Most patients require doses of 2 to 5 mg/day.[84]

Monoamine Oxidase-B (MAO-B) Inhibitors

Selegiline

23. What type of antiparkinson drug is selegiline and what place does it have in the treatment of Parkinson's disease?

Mechanism of Action. Selegiline (also referred to as deprenyl) is a monoamine oxidase inhibitor (MAOI) which irreversibly inhibits MAO type B (see Table 51.2).[18,70] Two different types of MAOs are present: type A which oxidatively deaminates catecholamines such as serotonin, norepinephrine, and tyramine and MAO type B which, among other things, is responsible for the metabolism of dopamine.[18,70,115] Within the brain, approximately 80% of MAO activity is due to MAO type B.[70] The antiparkinson activity of selegiline lies in its ability to act centrally to prevent the destruction of endogenous and exogenously administered dopamine.[70] Because selegiline selectively binds to MAO type B, it does not, in usual doses, produce a hypertensive reaction ("cheese effect") in the presence of dietary tyramine or other catecholamines.[4,7,18,70]

Efficacy. Selegiline has been studied in Parkinson's disease since 1975. Although results have been variable, selegiline can improve the "wearing off" effect of levodopa in 50% to 70% of patients

and may allow as much as a 30% reduction in the total daily dose of levodopa.[116,117] The "on-off" effect is less responsive to the addition of selegiline.[116,117] Minimal improvement is seen when selegiline is used alone in early forms of the disease, and the drug is also of little benefit in patients with severe disease.[116,117] Overall, the benefits of selegiline are only modest and tolerance to the beneficial effects is seen with long-term use.[116]

Selegiline is well tolerated by most patients, provided it is not given late in the evening when excess stimulation from metabolites (L-methamphetamine and L-amphetamine) can cause insomnia and other psychiatric side effects.[70,115] Importantly, the potency of the L-amphetamine metabolites of selegiline is only one-tenth that of the d-isomeric form found in commercial amphetamine products (e.g., dextroamphetamine). The administered form of selegiline is the L-isomer. The usual dose of selegiline is 10 mg/day given in 5 mg doses in the morning and early afternoon.[115]

24. Use to Slow Disease Progression. Can selegiline actually slow the progression of L.M.'s Parkinson's disease?

Attention has been focused on selegiline as an agent which could conceivably slow the progression of Parkinson's disease.[11,12,115,118–122] Birkmayer[118] was the first to suggest that the addition of selegiline to levodopa therapy leads to increased life expectancy; however, the data supporting this assertion were uncontrolled and retrospective in nature.

With the discovery of parkinsonism developing in addicts who ingested 1-methyl-4-phenyl-1,2,3,6-tetrahydropyridine (MPTP), a synthetic meperidine analog, exciting new information regarding the pathophysiology and potential for new forms of treatment began to emerge.[11,119] With the isolation and identification of this compound came the development of superior animal models in which it was found that the neurotoxicity associated with MPTP is not due to MPTP itself, but rather the oxidized product, 1-methyl-4-phenylpyridinium ion (MPP$^+$), a compound which can persist for long periods in the brain.[119] The conversion of MPTP to its neurotoxic metabolite MPP$^+$ is a two-step process mediated in part by MAO-B.[119,120] In animals, pretreatment with selegiline protects against neuronal damage following the administration of MPTP.[121]

If Parkinson's disease is caused by an environmental toxin similar to MPTP (or perhaps MPTP itself) then it is conceivable that treatment with MAO-B inhibitors, such as selegiline, might retard neuronal degeneration. Furthermore, as the brain dopamine content declines in parkinsonian patients, a compensatory increase in dopamine generation and metabolism by remaining neurons generates free radicals which also are capable of causing neuronal damage.[12,122] Anti-oxidative therapy aimed at decreasing the activity of these free radicals also may prove to be beneficial. At present, the only well-documented data regarding the value of antioxidants are from the DATATOP studies described below.

Several studies have now been published that demonstrate beneficial effects of selegiline in early Parkinson's disease.[115,122,123] The Deprenyl And Tocopherol Antioxidative Therapy Of Parkinsonism (DATATOP) Study was initiated by the Parkinson Study Group to test the hypothesis that the combined use of both an MAO-B inhibitor (selegiline) and an antioxidant (alpha-tocopherol) early in the course of the disease may slow disease progression.[122,123] The principal outcome measure was the length of time that patients could go before requiring levodopa therapy (an indication of disease progression). Results of this study demonstrated that early treatment with selegiline 10 mg/day delayed the need to start levodopa therapy by approximately nine months as compared to patients given placebo.[123] The controversy now exists as to whether selegiline possesses neuroprotective properties which may slow disease progression, or whether the DATATOP study results merely reflect mild symptomatic benefit from the drug. Patients given selegiline also had a significantly lower risk of having to give up full-time employment.[123]

Regardless of the exact mechanism, results from the DATATOP study suggest that the early use of selegiline can delay the need for levodopa therapy in patients with untreated disease, perhaps by retarding disease progression. It is unclear whether the drug can slow disease progression in patients like L.M. who have more advanced disease. Until more information becomes available, selegiline should only be considered for supportive therapy in L.M. Its efficacy in reducing the ''wearing off'' effect is modest at best and selegiline is not very effective in controlling the ''on-off'' effect which L.M. has been experiencing. Thus, for L.M., selegiline does not appear to offer any advantages over bromocriptine or other dopamine agonists, except perhaps a lower incidence of CNS side effects.

Antioxidant Therapy

25. What is the role of antioxidants (e.g., vitamin E) in the treatment of Parkinson's disease?

If free radical generation is important in the pathophysiology of Parkinson's disease, then adjunctive therapy with antioxidant drugs early in the course of disease may offer some benefit. The most comprehensive evaluation of antioxidant therapy for Parkinson's disease has come from the DATATOP Study.[122,123,140] In this study, patients were assigned to one of four treatment regimens: alpha-tocopherol (2000 IU/day) and selegiline placebo, selegiline 10 mg/day and alpha-tocopherol placebo, selegiline and alpha-tocopherol active treatments, or placebos. After approximately 14 months of follow-up, the results indicated that while selegiline had a beneficial effect (described above), there was no significant additional benefit derived from tocopherol therapy.[140] Thus, despite promising preliminary observations, data are lacking to currently support their routine use.

Adjunctive Treatment of Parkinsonian Tremor

26. L.M. has gained additional improvement in rigidity, bradykinesia, and posture as well as improvement in the ''on-off'' and ''wearing off'' effects, with the combination of Sinemet (carbidopa/levodopa) and bromocriptine. He has experienced little if any improvement in tremor, which at present is one of the most debilitating symptoms of his disease. What are other therapies for severe parkinsonian tremor?

Parkinsonian tremor is often less responsive to dopaminergic therapy than other symptoms. There also can be a great deal of interpatient variability in the frequency and amplitude of parkinsonian tremor. Tremor can be worsened by peripheral factors, such as catecholamine release, often in association with stress or anxiety, as well as central factors inherent to the disease.[124]

β-Adrenergic Blockers. Adjunctive therapy with β-adrenergic blockers (see Table 51.2) in double-blind, placebo-controlled trials improves parkinsonian tremor in approximately 50% of individuals.[124,125] An early study of propranolol (Inderal) showed subjective and objective improvement of 54% in resting tremor, 32% in postural tremor, and 54% in intention tremor at a maximum dose of 240 mg/day.[124] Nadolol (Corgard) treatment did not affect the frequency, but significantly reduced the amplitude of tremor in the patients studied.[125] These results suggest that beta blocker therapy can be safe and effective in selected individuals with debilitating tremor.

L.M. may benefit from a trial of beta blocker for his tremor. Nadolol would be the preferred choice for a number of reasons. Because nadolol is less lipophilic than propranolol, it does not penetrate across the blood-brain barrier as well, and thus is less

likely to cause CNS side effects, such as depression which has been a problem for L.M.[125] Also, nadolol can be dosed once daily because it has a longer half-life than propranolol. L.M. is already taking a number of medications at frequent intervals over the course of a day; therefore, the simplicity of giving the drug once daily has appeal. Therapy can be initiated with 40 to 60 mg/day and increased weekly to a maximum of 320 mg/day. The dosage should be reduced if bradycardia or hypotension are encountered.

Surgery has played a role in the management of Parkinson's disease, particularly in the treatment of parkinsonian tremor (see Table 51.2). Before the introduction of levodopa, Parkinson's disease was primarily viewed as a surgically treated condition. With the current availability of effective drug therapies, the importance of surgical intervention has lessened. In patients with mild forms of parkinsonism where bradykinesia and gait disturbances are absent, many patients with debilitating tremor and rigidity can benefit from stereotaxic thalamotomy.[126] In one study, patients experienced decreased ''off time'' and decreased levodopa-dyskinesias for at least one year after ventral pallidotomy.[141] In another study, stereotaxic surgery had abolished tremor in 90% of parkinsonian patients (n = 60) two years after the procedure and the tremors were still absent ten years following the procedure.[126] When using standard measurements of Parkinson's disease disability, there was a 9% to 68% improvement following posteroventral pallidotomy and ratings of activities of daily living improved by an average of more than 70%.[142] Stereotaxic pallidotomy, therefore, can be a viable option for patients with medically intractable Parkinson's disease. The disadvantages of these procedures are the significant risks associated with major neurosurgical procedures.

Attention has been directed toward surgical treatment of Parkinson's disease by transplanting fetal dopaminergic neurons directly into dopamine depleted regions of the basal ganglia in the hopes of providing a localized infusion of dopamine from these cells (Table 51.2).[127] While some patients may derive a significant, albeit modest, clinical response sufficient to allow a reduction in levodopa dosage, this procedure must still be considered experimental.[134,135]

Finally, several reports suggest a beneficial effect of the neuroleptic clozapine (Clozaril) on parkinsonian symptoms.[143] Although the precise mechanisms are not well understood, low doses of clozapine can reduce severity of levodopa dyskinesias,[136] improve resting tremor,[137] and modulate the severity of levodopa-induced motor fluctuations (i.e., ''on-off'').[138] Given the potential for serious toxicity (agranulocytosis) to clozapine, and the preliminary nature of these findings, indiscriminate use of adjunctive clozapine should be discouraged until more data are available.

Levodopa Treatment Failure

27. J.B., an 80-year-old retired pharmacist, presents to his local doctor complaining of a tremor in both hands. He was begun on Sinemet 25/100 TID and this dose was gradually increased to 100 mg carbidopa/1000 mg levodopa per day with little if any improvement in symptoms. J.B. has a long history of adult onset diabetes controlled by diet and diabetic gastroparesis managed with metoclopramide 10 mg PO TID. He has been feeling ''run down'' lately and started taking ferrous sulfate to increase his energy. J.B. also is anxious at times and takes diazepam 5 mg PO Q 6 hr PRN. Otherwise, J.B. is healthy except that he occasionally forgets things. His family history is significant for diabetes and his father also suffered from ''tremors.'' What is the explanation for J.B.'s lack of response to levodopa therapy?

Misdiagnosis. As previously mentioned, the vast majority of parkinsonian patients show at least a partial response to levodopa when given in therapeutic doses. In fact, the response to levodopa is so predictable that many neurologists consider a lack of response strong evidence that the patient may be suffering from a neurologic disorder other than Parkinson's disease.[4,128,129] Since the diagnosis of Parkinson's disease usually is made entirely on clinical grounds, it is possible that J.B. does not actually have the disease. He may be suffering from another disorder with similar clinical features such as benign essential tremor.[4,128,129] While a further diagnostic work-up is warranted, this diagnosis is supported by the bilateral nature of his tremors along with a significant family history of tremor.[4]

Another important reason for levodopa failure is inadequate dosage.[129] Most patients respond to levodopa doses of ≤1000 mg/day when given as Sinemet; however, the response to levodopa in parkinsonian patients is highly variable with some patients requiring much higher doses.[129] Many elderly patients take numerous medications and some individuals, like J.B., have difficulty with memory; thus compliance may be a significant problem.

Drug Interactions. There are many drugs which can interact with levodopa to decrease it effectiveness (see Table 51.5).[58-72,129] A number of drugs possess central dopamine blocking properties which can interfere with the dopaminergic effects of levodopa. Most notable of these are the neuroleptic drugs such as the phenothiazines (e.g., chlorpromazine, fluphenazine, and the antiemetic, prochlorperazine), the butyrophenones (e.g., haloperidol), and the thioxanthenes (e.g., thiothixene).[63] Antihypertensive medications, such as reserpine[61] and methyldopa,[61,62] are known to decrease levodopa response. Metoclopramide, an agent used to treat diabetic gastroparesis and nausea can, on occasion, produce central dopamine blockade leading to decreased levodopa effect.[65,66] J.B. is receiving metoclopramide and if possible it should be discontinued. Domperidone, an antiemetic similar to metoclopramide, (not yet available in the U.S.) does not cross the blood-brain barrier, and thus does not adversely interact with levodopa.[101] Before the combination of levodopa with carbidopa was available, a significant interaction existed between pyridoxine (vitamin B6) and levodopa.[59] Pyridoxine, as a precursor for the enzyme, dopa decarboxylase, can increase the peripheral metabolism of levodopa leaving less drug available for penetration into the brain.[59] This interaction is of little significance when levodopa is combined with a peripheral decarboxylase inhibitor.[33,34,59] A study

in healthy volunteers has shown that ferrous sulfate 325 mg can decrease levodopa absorption by a factor of 50% through chelation of iron by levodopa.[72] Thus, unless absolutely necessary, iron therapy should be discontinued in J.B. Other agents which can decrease levodopa effect include phenytoin[67] and the benzodiazepines.[71] J.B. currently is taking diazepam for anxiety. A careful drug history should be taken to assess how often he is taking this drug. If he requires regular intake to relieve anxiety, an alternative agent should be substituted.

Finally, many patients show a response to levodopa, but are unable to take the drug chronically because of intolerable side effects.[129,130] Every effort should be made to minimize the levodopa dose, while maximizing clinical response. Adjunctive agents should be considered as discussed above. These often allow a substantial reduction in levodopa dose and subsequently improve tolerance.

Patients taking selegiline should avoid, or use cautiously the selective serotonergic reuptake inhibitors, such as fluoxetine. The potential for inducing hypomania can occur with concomitant fluoxetine and selegiline.[131]

The key to successful management of the patient with Parkinson's disease requires a thorough knowledge of the various treatment modalities available coupled with an individualized approach which takes into account the needs and concerns of the patient.[129,130]

Note To The Reader

The Parkinson's Educational Program (PEP USA), a nonprofit national association was founded in 1982 to provide services for individuals with Parkinson's disease and their family members. PEP USA believes that by providing information about Parkinson's disease they can heighten public awareness and motivate people to take action to improve the methods of treatment for this devastating disease. Books, newsletters, and video and audio tapes as well as aids for easier living can be ordered through PEP USA for a reasonable charge. PEP Support Groups have been established throughout the U.S. For a listing of the support groups in your area and a complete publications/products catalog contact PEP USA; 3900 Birch Street #105; Newport Beach, California 92660. (Toll free telephone number: 1-800-344-7872.)

References

1 Duvoisin R. History of parkinsonism. Pharmacol Ther. 1987;32:1.
2 Hoehn MM, Yahr MD. Parkinsonism: onset, progression, and mortality. Neurology. 1967;17:427.
3 Rajput AH et al. Epidemiology of parkinsonism: incidence, classification, and mortality. Ann Neurol. 1984;16:278.
4 Standaert DG, Stern MB. Update on the management of Parkinson's disease. Med Clin North Am. 1993;77:169.
5 Joseph C et al. Levodopa in Parkinson disease: a long-term appraisal of mortality. Ann Neurol. 1978;3:116.
6 Mann DMA, Yates PO. Pathogenesis of Parkinson's disease. Arch Neurol. 1982;39:545.
7 Calne DB. Treatment of Parkinson's disease. N Engl J Med. 1993;329:1021.
8 Ervin WG, Turco TF. Current concepts in clinical therapeutics: Parkinson's disease. Clin Pharm. 1986;5:742.

9 Ward CD et al. Parkinson's disease in 65 pairs of twins and in a set of quadruplets. Neurology. 1983;33:815.
10 Ballard PA et al. Permanent human parkinsonism due to 1-methyl-4-phenyl-1,2,3,6-tetrahydropyridine (MPTP): seven cases. Neurology. 1985;35:949.
11 Langston JW. MPTP: insights into the etiology of Parkinson's disease. Eur Neurol. 1987;26(Suppl. 1):2.
12 Tanner CM. The role of environmental toxins in the etiology of Parkinson's disease. Trends Neurosci. 1989;12:49.
13 Critchley EMR. Speech disorders in parkinsonism: a review. J Neurol Neurosurg Psychiatry. 1981;44:751.
14 Agid Y et al. Parkinson's disease and dementia. Clin Neuropharmacol. 1986;9(Suppl. 2):S22.
15 Calne DB. The role of various forms of treatment in the management of Parkinson's disease. Clin Neuropharmacol. 1982;5(Suppl. 1):S38.
16 Lieberman AN. Parkinson's disease.

Compr Ther. 1986;12:25.
17 Quinn NP. Anti-parkinsonian drugs today. Drugs. 1984;28:236.
18 Lang AE. Treatment of Parkinson's disease with agents other than levodopa and dopamine agonists: controversies and new approaches. Can J Neurol Sci. 1984;11(Suppl.):210.
19 Schwab RS et al. Amantadine in the treatment of Parkinson's disease. JAMA. 1969;208:1168.
20 Schwab RS et al. Amantadine in Parkinson's disease. JAMA. 1972;222:792.
21 Timberlake WH, Vance MA. Four-year treatment of patients with parkinsonism using amantadine alone or with levodopa. Ann Neurol. 1978;3:119.
22 Fahn S, Isgreen WP. Long-term evaluation of amantadine and levodopa combination in parkinsonism by double-blind crossover analyses. Neurology. 1975;25:695.
23 Stromberg U et al. On the mode of

action of amantadine. J Pharm Pharmacol. 1970;22:959.
24 Aoki FY, Sitar DS. Clinical pharmacokinetics of amantadine hydrochloride. Clin Pharmacokinetic. 1988;14:35.
25 Parkes JD. Adverse effects of antiparkinsonian drugs. Drugs. 1981;21:341.
26 Yahr MD. Levodopa. Ann Intern Med. 1975;83:677.
27 Cotzias GC et al. Aromatic amino acids and modification of parkinsonism. N Engl J Med. 1967;267:374.
28 Cotzias GC et al. Modification of parkinsonism—chronic treatment with L-dopa. N Engl J Med. 1969;280:337.
29 Barbeau A. L-dopa therapy in Parkinson's disease. Can Med Assoc J. 1969;101:791.
30 McDowell F et al. Treatment of Parkinson's syndrome with L-dihydroxyphenyl-alanine (levodopa). Ann Intern Med. 1970;72:29.
31 Sweet RD, McDowell FH. Five years'

treatment of Parkinson's disease with levodopa. Ann Intern Med. 1975;83:456.

32 **Papavasiliou PS et al.** Levodopa in parkinsonism: potentiation of central effects with a peripheral inhibitor. N Engl J Med. 1972;285:8.

33 **Boshes B.** Sinemet and the treatment of parkinsonism. Ann Intern Med. 1981;94:364.

34 **Pinder RM et al.** Levodopa and decarboxylase inhibitors: a review of their clinical pharmacology and use in the treatment of parkinsonism. Drugs. 1976;11:329.

35 **Markham CH, Diamond SG.** Modification of Parkinson's disease by long-term levodopa treatment. Arch Neurol. 1986;43:405.

36 **Fahn S, Bressman SB.** Should levodopa therapy for parkinsonism be started early or late? Evidence against early treatment. Can J Neurol Sci. 1984;11(Suppl.):200.

37 **Melamed E.** Initiation of levodopa therapy in parkinsonian patients should be delayed until advanced stages of the disease. Arch Neurol. 1986;43:402.

38 **Markham CH, Diamond SG.** Evidence to support early levodopa therapy in Parkinson's disease. Neurology. 1981;31:125.

39 **Markham CH, Diamond SG.** Long-term follow-up of early dopa treatment in Parkinson's disease. Ann Neurol. 1986;19:365.

40 **Olanow CW.** An introduction to the free radical hypothesis in Parkinson's disease. Ann Neurol. 1992;32:S2.

41 **Kofman OS.** Are levodopa "drug holidays" justified? Can J Neurol Sci. 1984;11(Suppl.):206.

42 **Sweet RD, McDowell FH.** Plasma dopa concentrations and the "on-off" effect after chronic treatment of Parkinson's disease. Neurology. 1974;24:953.

43 **Melamed E.** Early-morning dystonia. A late side effect of long-term levodopa therapy in Parkinson's disease. Arch Neurol. 1979;36:308.

44 **Tolosa ES et al.** Patterns of clinical response and plasma dopa levels in Parkinson's disease. Neurology. 1975;25:177.

45 **Nutt JG et al.** The "on-off" phenomenon in Parkinson's disease. Relation to levodopa absorption and transport. N Engl J Med. 1984;310:483.

46 **Quinn N et al.** Complicated response fluctuations in Parkinson's disease: response to intravenous infusion of levodopa. Lancet. 1982;2:412.

47 **Hardie RJ et al.** On-off fluctuations in Parkinson's disease. Brain. 1984;107:487.

48 **Fabbrini G et al.** Motor fluctuations in Parkinson's disease: central pathophysiologic mechanisms. Ann Neurol. 1988;24:366.

49 **Fabbrini G et al.** Levodopa pharmacokinetic mechanisms and motor fluctuations in Parkinson's disease. Ann Neurol. 1987;21:370.

50 **Friedman JH et al.** An open trial of controlled release carbidopa/L-dopa (Sinemet CR) for the treatment of mild to moderate Parkinson's disease. Clin Neuropharmacol. 1989;12:220.

51 **Hutton JT et al.** Multicenter controlled study of Sinemet CR vs Sinemet

(25/100) in advanced Parkinson's disease. Neurol. 1989;39(Suppl. 2):67.

52 **Kurth MC et al.** Double-blind, placebo-controlled, crossover study of duodenal infusion of levodopa/carbidopa in Parkinson's disease patients with 'on-off' fluctuations. Neurol. 1993;43:1698.

53 **Obeso JA et al.** Lisuride infusion pump: a device for the treatment of motor fluctuations in Parkinson's disease. Lancet. 1986;1:467.

54 **Goodwin FK.** Psychiatric side effects of levodopa in man. JAMA. 1971;218:1915.

55 **Mayeux R et al.** Altered serotonin metabolism in depressed patients with Parkinson's disease. Neurology. 1984;34:642.

56 **Nausieda PA et al.** Serotonergically active agents in levodopa-induced psychiatric toxicity reactions. Adv Neurol. 1983;37:23.

57 **Pelton EW, Chase TN.** L-dopa and the treatment of extrapyramidal disease. Adv Pharmacol Chemother. 1975;13:253.

58 **Edwards M.** Adverse interaction of levodopa with tricyclic antidepressants. Practitioner. 1982;226:1447.

59 **Leon AS et al.** Pyridoxine antagonism of levodopa in parkinsonism. JAMA. 1971;218:1924.

60 **Algeri S et al.** Effect of anticholinergic drugs on gastrointestinal absorption of L-dopa in rats and man. Eur J Pharmacol. 1976;35:293.

61 **Cotzias GC et al.** L-dopa in Parkinson's syndrome. N Engl J Med. 1969;281:272.

62 **Strang RR.** Parkinsonism occurring during methyldopa therapy. Can Med Assoc J. 1966;95:928.

63 **Tarsy D.** Neuroleptic-induced extrapyramidal reactions: classification, description, and diagnosis. Clin Neuropharmacol. 1983;6(Suppl. 1):S9.

64 **Morgan JP et al.** Imipramine-mediated interference with levodopa absorption from the gastrointestinal tract in man. Neurology. 1975;25:1029.

65 **Yamamoto M et al.** Metoclopramide-induced parkinsonism. Clin Neuropharmacol. 1987;10:287.

66 **Buchholz D, Kariya S.** Metoclopramide-induced parkinsonism. Arch Neurol. 1983;40:528.

67 **Mendez JS et al.** Diphenylhydantoin blocking of levodopa effects. Arch Neurol. 1975;32:44.

68 **Friend DG et al.** The action of L-dihydroxyphenylalanine in patients receiving nialamide. Clin Pharmacol Ther. 1965;6:362.

69 **Hunter KR et al.** Monoamine oxidase inhibitors and L-dopa. Br Med J. 1970;3:388.

70 **Youdim MBH.** Pharmacology of MAO-B inhibitors: mode of action of (-) deprenyl in Parkinson's disease. J Neural Transm. 1986;22(Suppl.):91.

71 **Yosselson-Superstine S, Lipman AG.** Chlordiazepoxide interaction with levodopa. Ann Intern Med. 1982;96:259.

72 **Campbell NRC, Hasinoff B.** Ferrous sulfate reduces levodopa bioavailability: chelation as a possible mechanism. Clin Pharmacol Ther. 1989;45:220.

73 **Weiner WJ et al.** Drug holiday and management of Parkinson disease. Neurology. 1980;30:1257.

74 **Goetz CG et al.** Drug holiday in the management of Parkinson disease. Clin Neuropharmacol. 1982;5:351.

75 **Mayeux R et al.** Reappraisal of temporary levodopa withdrawal ("drug holiday") in Parkinson's disease. N Engl J Med. 1985;313:724.

76 **Maesner JE.** Transient levodopa withdrawal in Parkinson's disease. Clin Pharm. 1987;6:22.

77 **Cawein MJ.** False rise in serum uric acid after L-dopa. N Engl J Med. 1969;281:1489.

78 **Honda H, Gindin A.** Gout while receiving levodopa for parkinsonism. JAMA. 1972;219:55.

79 **Sirtori CR et al.** Metabolic responses to acute and chronic L-dopa administration in patients with parkinsonism. N Engl J Med. 1972;287:729.

80 **Rotblatt MD, Koda-Kimble MA.** Review of drug interference with urine glucose tests. Diabetes Care. 1987;10:103.

81 **Feldman JM, Lebovitz HE.** Levodopa and tests for urinary glucose. N Engl J Med. 1970;283:1053.

82 **Cawein MJ et al.** Levodopa and tests for ketonuria. N Engl J Med. 1970;283:659.

83 **Lieberman AN et al.** D-1 and D-2 agonists in Parkinson's disease. Can J Neurol Sci. 1987;14(Suppl.):466.

84 **Lieberman AN et al.** Management of levodopa failures: the use of dopamine agonists. Clin Neuropharmacol. 1986;9(Suppl. 2):S9.

85 **Lieberman AN, Goldstein M.** Bromocriptine in Parkinson disease. Pharmacol Rev. 1985;37:217.

86 **Parkes JD.** Bromocriptine in the treatment of parkinsonism. Drugs. 1979;17:365.

87 **Vance ML et al.** Drugs five years later—bromocriptine. Ann Intern Med. 1984;100:78.

88 **Calne DB et al.** Long-term treatment of parkinsonism with bromocriptine. Lancet. 1978;1:735.

89 **Lieberman AN et al.** Bromocriptine in Parkinson disease: further studies. Neurology. 1979;29:363.

90 **Kartzinel R, Calne DB.** Studies with bromocriptine Part 1. "On-off" phenomena. Neurology. 1976;26:508.

91 **Kartzinel R et al.** Studies with bromocriptine Part 2. Double-blind comparison with levodopa in idiopathic parkinsonism. Neurology. 1976;26:511.

92 **Lees AJ, Stern GM.** Sustained bromocriptine therapy in previously untreated patients with Parkinson's disease. J Neurol Neurosurg Psychiatry. 1981;44:1020.

93 **Tolosa E et al.** Low-dose bromocriptine in the early phases of Parkinson's disease. Clin Neuropharmacol. 1987;10:169.

94 **Teychenne PF et al.** Bromocriptine: low-dose therapy in Parkinson disease. Neurology. 1982;32:577.

95 **Staal-Schreinemachers AL et al.** Low-dose bromocriptine therapy in Parkinson's disease: double-blind, placebo-controlled study. Neurology. 1986;36:291.

96 **Grimes JD, Delgado MR.** Bromocriptine: problems with low-dose de novo therapy in Parkinson's disease. Clin Neuropharmacol. 1985;8:73.

97 **Larsen TA et al.** Severity of Parkin-

son's disease and the dosage of bromocriptine. Neurology. 1984;34:795.

98 **Parkinson's Disease Research Group in the United Kingdom.** Comparisons of therapeutic effects of levodopa, levodopa and selegiline, and bromocriptine in patients with early, mild Parkinson's disease: three year interim report. Br Med J. 1993;307:469.

99 **Rinne UK.** Early combination of bromocriptine and levodopa in the treatment of Parkinson's disease: a 5 year follow-up. Neurology. 1987;37:826.

100 **Rinne UK.** Combined bromocriptine-levodopa therapy early in Parkinson's disease. Neurology. 1985;35:1196.

101 **Parkes JD.** Domperidone and Parkinson's disease. Clin Neuropharmacol. 1986;9:517.

102 **LeWitt PA et al.** Comparison of pergolide and bromocriptine therapy in parkinsonism. Neurology. 1983;33:1009.

103 **Langtry HD, Clissold SP.** Pergolide. A review of its pharmacological properties and therapeutic potential in Parkinson's disease. Drugs. 1990;39:491.

104 **Ahlskog JE, Muenter MD.** Treatment of Parkinson's disease with pergolide: a double-blind study. Mayo Clin Proc. 1988;63:969.

105 **Lieberman AN et al.** Further studies with pergolide in Parkinson disease. Neurology. 1982;32:1181.

106 **Ahlskog JE, Muenter MD.** Pergolide: long-term use in Parkinson's disease. Mayo Clin Proc. 1988;63:979.

107 **Goetz CG et al.** Chronic agonist therapy for Parkinson's disease: a 5-year study of bromocriptine and pergolide. Neurology. 1985;35:749.

108 **Factor SA et al.** Parkinson's disease: an open label trial of pergolide in patients failing bromocriptine therapy. J Neurol Neurosurg Psychiatry. 1988;51:529.

109 **Kurlan R et al.** Double-blind assessment of potential pergolide-induced cardiotoxicity. Neurology. 1986;36:993.

110 **Rinne UK.** Lisuride, a dopamine agonist in the treatment of early Parkinson's disease. Neurology. 1989;39:336.

111 **Lieberman AN et al.** Lisuride combined with levodopa in advanced Parkinson disease. Neurology. 1981;31:1466.

112 **LeWitt PA et al.** Lisuride vs bromocriptine treatment in Parkinson disease: a double-blind study. Neurology. 1982;32:69.

113 **Giovannini P et al.** Lisuride in Parkinson's disease. Four-year follow-up. Clin Neuropharmacol. 1988;11:201.

114 **Obeso JA et al.** Subcutaneous administration of lisuride in the treatment of complex motor fluctuations in Parkinson's disease. J Neural Transm. 1988;27(Suppl.):17.

115 **Tetrud JW, Langston JW.** The effect of deprenyl (Selegiline) on the natural history of Parkinson's disease. Science. 1989;245:519.

116 **Golbe LI.** Deprenyl as symptomatic therapy in Parkinson's disease. Clin Neuropharmacol. 1988;11:387.

117 **Elizam TS et al.** Selegiline as an adjunct to conventional levodopa therapy in Parkinson's disease. Arch Neurol. 1989;46:1280.

118 **Birkmayer W et al.** Increased life expectancy resulting from addition of L-deprenyl to Madopar treatment in Parkinson's disease: a long-term study. J Neural Transm. 1985;64:113.

119 **Snyder SH, D'Amato RJ.** MPTP: a neurotoxin relevant to the pathophysiology of Parkinson's disease. Neurology. 1986;36:250.

120 **Markey SP et al.** Intraneuronal generation of a pyridinium metabolite may cause drug-induced parkinsonism. Nature. 1984;311:464.

121 **Heikkila TE et al.** Protection against the dopaminergic neurotoxicity of 1-methyl-4-phenyl-1,2,5,6-tetrahydropyridine by monoamine oxidase inhibitors. Nature. 1984;311:467.

122 **Parkinson Study Group.** DATATOP: a multicenter controlled clinical trial in early Parkinson's disease. Arch Neurol. 1989;46:1052.

123 **Parkinson Study Group.** Effect of deprenyl on the progression of disability in early Parkinson's disease. N Engl J Med. 1989;321:1364.

124 **Owen DAL, Marsden CD.** Effect of adrenergic beta-blockade on parkinsonian tremor. Lancet. 1965;2:1259.

125 **Foster NL et al.** Peripheral beta-adrenergic blockade treatment of parkinsonian tremor. Ann Neurol. 1984;16:505.

126 **Kelly PJ, Gillingham FJ.** The long-term results of stereotaxic surgery and L-dopa therapy in patients with Parkinson's disease. J Neurosurg. 1980;53:332.

127 **Ahlskog JE.** Cerebral transplantation for Parkinson's disease: current progress and future prospects. Mayo Clin Proc. 1993;68:578.

128 **Calne DB, Stoessl AJ.** Early parkinsonism. Clin Neuropharmacol. 1986;9(Suppl. 2):S3.

129 **Duvoisin RC.** Management of patients who fail to respond to levodopa therapy. Clin Neuropharmacol. 1982;5(Suppl. 1):S13.

130 **Klawans HL.** What to do when Sinemet fails: part 1. Clin Neuropharmacol. 1984;7:121.

131 **Hansten PD, Horn JR.** Drug Interactions & Updates Quarterly. Vancouver, WA: Applied Therapeutics, Inc.; 1995.

132 **Alexander GM et al.** Effect of plasma levels of larger neutral amino acids and degree of parkinsonism on the blood-to-brain transport of levodopa in naive and MPTP parkinsonian monkeys. Neurology. 1994;44:1491.

133 **Braco F et al.** Protein redistribution diet and antiparkinsonian response to levodopa. Eur Neurol. 1991;31:68.

134 **Freed CR et al.** Survival of implanted fetal dopamine cells and neurological improvement 12 to 46 months after transplantation for Parkinson's disease. N Engl J Med. 1992;327:1549.

135 **Spencer DD et al.** Unilateral transplantation of human mesencephalic tissue into the caudate nucleus of patients with Parkinson's disease. N Engl J Med. 1992;327:1541.

136 **Bennet JP et al.** Suppression of dyskinesias in advanced Parkinson's disease: part II. Increasing clozapine doses suppress dyskinesias and improve Parkinson's symptoms. Neurology. 1993;43:1551.

137 **Friedman JH et al.** Clozapine responsive tremor in Parkinson's disease. Mov Disord. 1990;5:225.

138 **Arevalo GJ, Gershank OS.** Modulatory effect of clozapine on levodopa response in Parkinson's disease: a preliminary study. Mov Disord. 1993;8:349.

139 **Wooten GF.** Progress in understanding the pathophysiology of treatment-related fluctuations in Parkinson's disease. Ann Neurol. 1988;24:363.

140 **Parkinson Study Group.** Effects of tocopherol and deprenyl on the progression of disability in early Parkinson's disease. N Engl J Med. 1993;328:176.

141 **Fazzini E et al.** Unilateral ventral pallidotomy in patients with Parkinson's disease: one year follow-up. Neurology. 1994;44:A323.

142 **Laitinen LV et al.** Leskels posteroventral pallidotomy in the treatment of Parkinson's disease. J Neurosurg. 1992;76:53–61.

143 **Pfeiffer C, Wagner ML.** Clozapine therapy for Parkinson's disease and other movement disorders. Am J Hosp Pharm. 1994;51:3047.

Seizure Disorders

Rex S Lott

Incidence, Prevalence, and Epidemiology 52-1
Terminology, Classification, and Diagnosis
  of Epilepsies 52-2
  Classification of seizures and epilepsies
    (See Table 52.1) 52-2
  Epileptic syndromes (See Table 52.2) 52-2
Diagnosis 52-3
Treatment 52-3
  Nonpharmacologic treatment of epilepsy 52-3
  Avoidance of potential seizure precipitants 52-4
  Antiepileptic drug (AED) therapy 52-4
    Choice of AED (See Table 52.3) 52-4
    Therapeutic endpoints 52-4
    Serum drug concentrations 52-4
      Relation to dosage 52-4
      Relation to clinical response 52-5
      Indications for use 52-5
      Interpretation of serum concentrations 52-5
    Monotherapy versus polytherapy 52-6
    Duration of therapy and discontinuation of AEDs
      (See Table 52.5) 52-6

**Clinical Assessment and Treatment of
Seizure Disorders** 52-7
  Complex Partial Seizures with Secondary
  Generalization 52-7
    Diagnosis 52-7
    Decision to use AED therapy 52-7
    Choice of AED 52-8
    Carbamazepine therapy 52-8
      Initiation and dosage 52-8
      Hematologic toxicity 52-8
        Routine hematologic testing 52-8
      Hepatotoxicity 52-9
      Pharmacokinetics and autoinduction
        of metabolism 52-9
      Bioequivalence of generic dosage forms and
        effects of storage on bioequivalence 52-9
      Carbamazepine intoxication and carbamazepine-
        induced hyponatremia 52-10
      Treatment failure and alternate AEDs 52-11
    Antiepileptic drugs in development
      (See Table 52.7) 52-13
    Lamotrigine therapy (Also see Question 9) 52-13
      Initiation and dosage titration 52-13
      Side effects and possible interaction with
        carbamazepine 52-14
    Gabapentin therapy (Also see Question 9) 52-14
      Initiation and dosage titration 52-14
      Patient instructions 52-14
    Phenytoin therapy 52-14
      Initiation and dosage 52-14
      Patient information (Also see Question 18) 52-15
      Accumulation pharmacokinetics 52-15

Oral loading doses 52-15
Phenytoin intoxication 52-15
Bioequivalence of dosage forms 52-16
Extended-release dosage forms 52-16
Intramuscular (IM) phenytoin and phenytoin
  prodrug (Fosphenytoin) 52-16
Adverse effects 52-17
  Gingival hyperplasia 52-17
  Encephalopathy 52-17
  Choreiform movement disorders 52-18
  Neurotoxicity 52-18
Interaction with valproate 52-18
Absence Seizures 52-19
  Choice of medication and initiation of
  ethosuximide therapy (See Table 52.8) 52-19
    Patient/caregiver education 52-19
    Therapeutic monitoring 52-19
    Precipitation of generalized tonic-clonic
      seizures (See Question 28) 52-19
Generalized Tonic-Clonic Seizures
  Accompanying Absence Seizures 52-19
    Assessment regarding need for alteration in AED
      therapy and choice of alternative AED 52-20
    Valproate Therapy 52-20
      Initiation and dosage 52-20
      Dosage forms 52-21
      Pharmacokinetics and serum concentration
        monitoring 52-21
      Hepatotoxicity 52-22
        Routine liver function tests (LFTs) 52-22
  Febrile Seizures 52-22
    Incidence and classification 52-22
    Treatment of acute seizure 52-23
    Prophylaxis and choice of AED 52-23
AED Drug Interactions and Adverse Effects 52-24
  Carbamazepine-Erythromycin Interaction 52-24
  Valproate-Carbamazepine Interaction
    (Also see Question 41) 52-24
  Valproate-Related Thrombocytopenia 52-24
  Skin Rash: Hypersensitivity Reactions to AEDs ... 52-25
  AED-Oral Contraceptive Interaction 52-26
  Teratogenicity 52-26
Status Epilepticus (SE) 52-27
  Characteristics and Pathophysiology 52-27
  General Treatment Measures and AED Therapy ... 52-27
    Parenteral phenytoin 52-28
      Loading dose 52-28
      Intravenous administration 52-28
  Maintenance Therapy 52-29
  Alternative Therapies for Refractory Status
    Epilepticus 52-29

Incidence, Prevalence, and Epidemiology

Approximately 10% of the population will experience a seizure at some time. Up to 30% of all seizures are caused by central nervous system (CNS) disorders or insults (e.g., meningitis, trauma, tumors, and exposure to toxins); these seizures may become recurrent and require chronic treatment with antiepileptic drugs (AEDs). Reversible conditions such as alcohol withdrawal, fever, and metabolic disturbances may cause isolated seizures that usually do not require long-term AED therapy. Between 0.5% and 1% of the U.S. population have recurrent epileptic seizures.[1]

Terminology, Classification, and Diagnosis of Epilepsies

Classification of Seizures and Epilepsies

An *epileptic seizure* is the "clinical manifestation presumed to result from an abnormal and excessive discharge of a set of neurons in the brain. The clinical manifestation consists of sudden and transitory abnormal phenomena that may include alterations of consciousness, motor, sensory, autonomic, or psychic events perceived by the patient or observer." *Epilepsy* is a "condition characterized by recurrent (≥ 2) epileptic seizures, unprovoked by any immediate identified cause."[2] Nomenclature associated with epilepsy and epileptic seizures has undergone revision.[1,3,4] The current International Classification of Epileptic Seizures is shown in Table 52.1. Older terms such as "grand mal" and "petit mal" are still commonly used, and this may sometimes create confusion in the clinical setting.

Generalized tonic-clonic (grand mal) seizures are a common seizure type. The patient loses consciousness and falls at the onset. Simultaneously, tonic muscle spasms begin and may be accompanied by a cry that results from air being forced through the larynx. There is then a period of bilateral, repetitive clonic movements. Following the clonic phase, patients return to consciousness but remain lethargic and may be confused for varying periods of time (postictal state). Urinary incontinence occurs commonly. *Primary generalized tonic-clonic seizures* affect both cerebral hemispheres from the outset. *Secondarily generalized tonic-clonic seizures* begin as either simple or complex partial seizures. The aura described by some patients before a generalized tonic-clonic seizure actually represents an initial partial seizure that may spread to become a secondarily generalized seizure. Identification of secondarily generalized tonic-clonic seizures is important; some AEDs more effectively control primary generalized seizures than secondarily generalized seizures, and partial seizures are often more difficult to control with currently available AEDs.[5,6]

Absence (petit mal) seizures occur primarily in children and often disappear at puberty; affected patients may develop a second type of seizure. Absence seizures consist of episodes of brief loss of consciousness. *Simple (typical) absence seizures* are not accompanied by motor symptoms; *atypical (complex) absence seizures* may be accompanied by automatisms, muscle twitching, myoclonic jerking, or autonomic manifestations. Although consciousness is lost, patients do not fall during absence seizures. Patients are unaware of their surroundings and will have no recall of events during the seizure. Consciousness returns immediately when the seizure ends, and there is no postictal confusion. Differentiation of atypical absence seizures from complex partial seizures may be difficult if only observation of episodes is available; identification of a focal abnormality by electroencephalogram (EEG) often is necessary to identify complex partial seizures. This distinction is important to proper selection of AEDs.

Simple partial (focal motor or sensory) seizures are localized in a single cerebral hemisphere or portion of a hemisphere. There is no loss of consciousness. A variety of motor, sensory, or psychic manifestations may occur. A single part of the body may twitch or the patient may experience only an unusual sensory experience.

Complex partial (psychomotor or temporal lobe) seizures result from spread of focal discharges to partially involve the other cerebral hemisphere. Consciousness is impaired and patients may exhibit complex, but inappropriate behavior (automatisms) such as lip smacking, picking at clothing, or aimless wandering. There is often a period of brief postictal lethargy or confusion.

Epileptic Syndromes

Seizures can be classified based upon seizure type as shown in Table 52.1 or can be described as epileptic syndromes that may include etiology (if known), precipitating factors, age of onset, characteristic EEG patterns, severity, chronicity, family history, and prognosis. Accurate diagnosis of an epileptic syndrome often will guide the clinician regarding the need for drug therapy, the choice of appropriate medication and the likelihood of successful treatment.[1,4,7,8] Many epileptic syndromes have been defined, and a complete listing is beyond the scope of this chapter. Several of these syndromes are, however, of interest with respect to application of pharmacotherapy (see Table 52.2).[8] *Juvenile myoclonic epilepsy* is an hereditary disorder characterized by generalized tonic-clonic seizures (frequently occurring upon awakening or precipitated by sleep deprivation or alcohol intake), mild myoclonic seizures which are most prominent in the morning, and, occasionally absence seizures. The EEG pattern is characteristic and is distinct from patterns typically seen in absence epilepsy. Juvenile myoclonic epilepsy responds extremely well to several antiepileptic drugs; valproate is usually the preferred medication. Despite the excellent response to medication, discontinuation of AED treatment usually is unsuccessful.[11,14] *Lennox-Gastaut syndrome* involves mixed seizures (tonic, generalized tonic-clonic, partial seizures, atypical absence, and frequent atonic seizures) which begin early in life; the syndrome almost always is associated with brain damage, mental retardation, and other developmental disabilities. There is a characteristic EEG pattern that is distinct

Table 52.1	International Classification of Epileptic Seizures[1,3,4]

Partial Seizure (Local or Focal)
  Simple Partial Seizures (Without Impairment of Consciousness)
    Motor symptoms
    Special sensory or somatosensory symptoms
    Autonomic symptoms
    Psychic symptoms

  Complex[a] Partial Seizures (With Impairment of Consciousness)
    Progressing to impairment of consciousness
      With no other features
      With features as in simple partial seizures
      With automatisms
    With impaired consciousness at onset
      With no other features
      With features as in simple partial seizures
      With automatisms

  Partial Seizures Which Evolve to Generalized Seizures
    Simple partial seizures evolving to generalized seizures
    Complex partial seizures evolving to generalized seizures
    Simple partial seizures evolving to complex partial seizures to generalized seizures

Generalized Seizures (Convulsive or Nonconvulsive)
  Absence Seizures
    Typical seizures (Impaired consciousness only)
    Atypical absence seizures
  Myoclonic Seizures
  Clonic Seizures
  Tonic Seizures
  Tonic-Clonic Seizures
  Atonic (Astatic or Akinetic) Seizures

Unclassified Epileptic Seizures
  All seizures that cannot be classified because of inadequate or incomplete data and some which cannot be classified in previously described categories

[a] Complex implies organized, high-level activity.

Table 52.2		Selected Epileptic Syndromes[a,8–13]	
Syndrome	Seizure Patterns and Characteristics	Preferred AED Therapy	Comments
Juvenile Myoclonic Epilepsy	Myoclonic seizures often precede generalized tonic-clonic seizures. Myoclonic and generalized tonic-clonic episodes upon awakening. Absence seizures also common. ↓ sleep, fatigue, and alcohol commonly precipitate seizures	Valproic acid. Phenytoin or carbamazepine as adjuncts to valproate in resistant cases. Carbamazepine reported to exacerbate seizures in some patients	5%–10% of all epilepsies. 85%–90% response to valproate. Lifelong therapy usually needed. High relapse rate with attempts to discontinue AED therapy
Lennox-Gastaut Syndrome	Generalized seizures: atypical absence, atonic/akinetic, myoclonic and tonic most common. Abnormal interictal EEG with slow spike-wave pattern. Cognitive dysfunction and mental retardation. Status epilepticus common	Valproic acid, benzodiazepines. Felbamate may be effective; potential hematologic toxicity limits use. Poorly responsive to AEDs	Oversedation with aggressive AED trials may increase ↑ seizure frequency. Tolerance to benzodiazepines limits their usefulness
Childhood Absence Epilepsy (True Petit Mal)	Typical absences often in clusters of multiple seizures (pyknolepsy). Tonic-clonic seizures in ≈ 40%. Onset usually between ages 4–8. Significant genetic component. EEG shows classic 3 Hz spike-wave pattern	Ethosuximide or valproic acid	80%–90% response rate to AED therapy. Good prognosis for remission. Tonic-clonic seizures may persist
Reflex Epilepsy	Tonic-clonic seizures most common. Induced by flicker or patterns (photosensitivity) most commonly. Reading also may precipitate partial seizures affecting the jaw which may generalize. Some cases involve precipitation of underlying seizures; some seem primary	AED specific to underlying seizures. Avoidance of precipitating stimuli when possible. Valproic acid usually effective for cases of spontaneous seizures precipitated by photosensitivity	Relatively rare. Seizures may be precipitated by television or video games
Temporal Lobe Epilepsy	Complex partial seizures with automatisms. Simple partial seizures (auras) very common; secondary generalized seizures occur in 50%	Carbamazepine, phenytoin, valproic acid. Gabapentin, lamotrigine	Often incompletely controlled with current AEDs. Emotional stress may precipitate seizures; psychiatric disorders seen with temporal lobe epilepsy

[a] AED = Antiepileptic drug; EEG = Electroencephalogram.

from patterns seen with other seizure disorders. Seizures associated with Lennox Gastaut syndrome often are refractory to AED therapy, and affected children often must wear helmets to minimize injuries associated with almost daily falls with seizures. Affected patients suffer frequent episodes of status epilepticus and often are stuporous because of recurrent seizure activity. In addition, there is risk of chronic intoxication with AEDs resulting from attempts to control refractory seizures with multiple medications.[12] Characteristics of other selected epilepsy syndromes are described in Table 52.2.

Diagnosis

Optimum treatment of seizure disorders requires accurate classification (diagnosis) of seizure type and appropriate choice and use of medications. Seizure classification may be straightforward if an adequate history and description of the clinical seizure are available. Physicians often are not available for observation of patients' seizures; thus family, teachers, nurses, and others who have frequent direct contact with patients should learn to accurately observe and objectively describe and record these events. The onset, duration, and characteristics of a seizure should be described as completely as possible. Several aspects of the events surrounding a seizure may be especially significant: the patient's behavior before the seizure (e.g., did the patient complain of feeling ill or describe an unusual sensation); deviation of the eyes or head to one side or localization of convulsive activity to one portion of the body; presence of impaired consciousness; loss of continence; and the patient's behavior following the seizure (e.g., was there any postictal confusion). Those who observe a seizure should be strongly discouraged from labeling the seizure and should be encouraged to describe the event fully and objectively.

Accurate seizure diagnosis and identification of the type of epilepsy or epileptic syndrome also depend upon neurological examination, medical history, and techniques such as electroencephalography, computerized tomography (CT), and magnetic resonance imaging (MRI). The EEG often is critical for identifying specific seizure types. CT scans are routinely used to assess newly diagnosed patients, especially when partial seizures may be due to smaller focal lesions. Magnetic resonance imaging may locate brain lesions or anatomical defects that are missed by conventional x-rays or CT scans.[15]

Treatment

Early control of epileptic seizures is important, as it allows normalization of patients' lives and prevents acute physical harm and long-term morbidity associated with recurrent seizures.[16] In addition, early control of tonic-clonic seizures is associated with a reduced likelihood of seizure recurrence.[17] Early control of epileptic seizures also correlates with successful discontinuation of AED treatment after long-term seizure control.[18–24]

Nonpharmacologic Treatment of Epilepsy

Alternatives or adjuncts to pharmacotherapy may be important in some patients. Surgery has become recognized as an extremely useful form of treatment in selected patients. Depending upon the epileptic syndrome and procedure performed, up to 90% of patients treated surgically may improve or become seizure free. Surgery is being advocated as early therapy for some patients with specific epileptic syndromes such as Lennox-Gastaut Syndrome or Mesial Temporal Lobe Epilepsy. Early surgical intervention may prevent or lessen neurologic deterioration and developmental delay that often are associated with these forms of epilepsy.[25] Dietary modification occasionally is used to treat seizures that are not completely responsive to AEDs. In most circumstances, dietary modification consists of use of a ketogenic diet: this low-carbohydrate, high-fat diet results in persistent ketosis which is believed to play a major role in the therapeutic effect. Ketogenic diets, while potentially beneficial, are not commonly utilized; however, occasionally they are used as adjuncts to ongoing AED treatment.[26,27]

Avoidance of Potential Seizure Precipitants

It is not possible to generalize regarding environmental and lifestyle precipitants of seizure activity in persons with epilepsy. Individual patients or caregivers may identify specific circumstances such as stress, sleep deprivation, or ingestion of excessive amounts of caffeine or alcohol which increase the likelihood of seizure occurrence. Patients with seizure disorders should be advised to avoid any activities which seem to precipitate seizures; as always, the goal is adequate seizure control with as little alteration in quality of life as possible.

Antiepileptic Drug (AED) Therapy

Seizure disorders most often are treated with pharmacotherapy. Therefore, patient education regarding medications and consultation among health professionals regarding techniques for optimal use of AEDs are essential to quality patient care. Optimal AED therapy may completely control seizures in 60% to 95% of patients.[7,28–30] Optimization of drug therapy is dependent upon several factors. Choice of appropriate AED, individualization of dosing, and limitation of polydrug therapy are perhaps the most important.

Choice of AED. Most antiepileptic drugs have a narrow spectrum of efficacy, therefore, choice of appropriate drug therapy for a specific patient is dependent upon accurate classification of seizures and, if possible, diagnosis of epileptic syndrome. Additionally, the risks of common side effects and potential toxicity must be considered when an AED is selected. Preferred drugs for specific types of seizures and common epileptic syndromes are listed in Tables 52.2 and 52.3. While certain drugs are preferred choices, the identification of the most effective drug for a particular patient may be

a process of trial and error; trials of several medications may be necessary before therapeutic success is achieved.

Therapeutic Endpoints. The individual patient's response to AED treatment (i.e., seizure frequency and severity, presence and severity of symptoms of dose-related toxicity) must be the major focus for assessment of therapy. In general, the goal of AED treatment is administration of sufficient medication to completely control seizure recurrence without producing significant dose-related side effects. Careful titration of doses to achieve the desired level of seizure control is the mainstay of optimization of therapy. Realistically, this goal may be compromised for a large number of patients; it may not be possible to completely prevent recurrence of seizure activity without producing intolerable adverse effects. Thus, the therapeutic endpoints actually achieved will vary among patients; optimization of AED therapy for a specific person is highly dependent upon individualization of the drug therapy regimen to the needs and lifestyle of that individual. It is rarely optimum to administer "standard" or "usual" doses of an AED to a patient or to adjust doses to achieve a "therapeutic blood level" without paying due consideration to the effect of the dose or serum concentration on the patient's condition and quality of life. As with many chronic conditions requiring maintenance drug therapy, participation of the patient in development and evaluation of a therapeutic plan is extremely important. Patients should be educated regarding the expected positive and negative effects of their AED therapy, and they must be encouraged to communicate with their health care provider regarding their responses to prescribed antiepileptic drugs.

Serum Drug Concentrations: Relation to Dosage. Wide availability of AED serum concentration determinations has had a significant impact on the treatment of seizure disorders. There is a poor correlation between the administered maintenance dose of an AED and the resulting steady-state serum concentration. Administration of "usual therapeutic doses," even when calculated on the basis of body weight, is equally likely to produce subtherapeutic, appropriately therapeutic, or potentially intoxicating serum

Table 52.3	Antiepileptic Drugs Useful for Various Seizure Types[a,30–33]			
Primary Generalized Tonic-Clonic	**Secondarily Generalized Tonic-Clonic**	**Simple or Complex Partial**	**Absence**	**Myoclonic, Atonic/Akinetic**
Most Effective With Least Toxicity				
Valproate	Carbamazepine	Carbamazepine	Ethosuximide	Valproate
Phenytoin	Phenytoin	Phenytoin	Valproate	Clonazepam
Carbamazepine	Valproate	Valproate		(Lamotrigine)[b]
	(Gabapentin)[b]	(Gabapentin)[b]		
	(Lamotrigine)[b]	(Lamotrigine)[b]		
Effective, But Often Cause Unacceptable Toxicity				
Phenobarbital	Phenobarbital	Clorazepate	Clonazepam	(Felbamate)[c]
Primidone	Primidone	Phenobarbital	Trimethadione	
(Felbamate)[c]	(Felbamate)[c]	Primidone		
		(Felbamate)[c]		
Of Little Value				
Ethosuximide	Ethosuximide	Ethosuximide	Phenytoin	
Trimethadione	Trimethadione	Trimethadione	Carbamazepine	
			Phenobarbital	
			Primidone	

[a] Drugs are listed in general order of preference within each category. Recommendations by various authorities may differ, especially regarding the relative place of valproate and the role of phenytoin as a first-line AED. Many authorities now discourage the use of phenobarbital and primidone.

[b] The place of gabapentin and lamotrigine is yet to be determined. They are placed on this table only to indicate the types of seizures for which they appear to be effective. Much more clinical experience is needed before their roles as possible primary AEDs are clarified.

[c] The place of felbamate is yet to be determined. It is placed on this table only to indicate the types of seizures for which it appears to be effective. Much more clinical experience is needed before felbamate's role as a possible primary AED is clarified. Felbamate has been associated with aplastic anemia and hepatic failure; until a possible causative role is clarified, felbamate cannot be recommended for treatment of epilepsy unless all other, potentially less toxic treatment options have been exhausted.

concentrations. Interindividual variation in hepatic metabolic capacity probably accounts for most of this variability. There is a much better correlation between serum concentrations and both therapeutic response and toxic symptoms.

Relation to Clinical Response. Proper use and interpretation of AED serum concentrations is important for optimizing treatment regimens in epilepsy.[34,35] An individual patient's clinical response to AED treatment (i.e., seizure frequency and severity, presence of symptoms of dose-related toxicity) must be the major focus for assessment of therapy. Neither therapeutic effects nor toxic symptoms are "all or none"; in most situations, there are gradations of efficacy and toxicity. Upward dose adjustments and titration to AED serum concentrations within and occasionally above the "therapeutic range" may markedly improve therapeutic responses without producing significant toxicity.[35,36] Individual patients often differ dramatically in their response to a particular serum drug concentration; therefore, "therapeutic" serum concentrations should only be considered as guidelines for treatment. Seizure type and other clinical variables such as the number of seizures occurring before control is achieved may significantly influence the serum drug concentrations required for seizure control. For example, complete control of simple or complex partial seizures requires serum concentrations of carbamazepine (Tegretol) 27% higher than those needed for complete control of generalized tonic-clonic seizures; similar figures for phenytoin (Dilantin) and phenobarbital were 64% and 11%, respectively.[5,6] Likewise, many patients may be controlled with serum drug concentrations below the usual "therapeutic" range.[37]

Indications for Use. Measurement of serum drug concentrations often provides clinically useful information in the following situations:

- *Uncontrolled seizures* despite administration of greater than average doses. Serum concentrations of AEDs may help distinguish drug resistance from subtherapeutic drug concentrations due to malabsorption, noncompliance, or rapid metabolism.

- *Seizure recurrence* in a previously controlled patient. This often is due to noncompliance with the prescribed medication regimen.

- *Documentation of intoxication.* In patients who develop signs or symptoms of dose-related AED toxicity, documentation of the dose and serum concentration of the responsible drug is helpful.

- *Assessment of patient compliance.* Although monitoring AED serum concentrations often is recommended to assess patient compliance with therapy, conclusions must be based upon comparisons with previous steady-state serum concentrations that reflected reliable intake of a given dose of AED.

- *Documentation of desired results* from a dose change or other therapeutic maneuver (e.g., administration of a loading dose). When patients are receiving multiple AEDs, serum concentrations of all drugs should be measured following a change in the dose of one drug because changes in the serum concentration of one drug frequently change the pharmacokinetic disposition of other drugs.

- *Assessment of therapy in patients with infrequent seizures.* Serum AED concentrations usually are much less important than seizure frequency as a monitoring parameter; however, in patients with infrequent seizures, it may be desirable to initiate maintenance doses of medication that are sufficient to produce steady-state serum concentrations

well within the drug's usual therapeutic range. This approach enhances the likelihood of successful drug therapy although the initial dosage and resultant serum concentration may be higher than actually necessary.

- *When precise dosage changes are required.* On occasion, very small changes in the dose of a drug (e.g., phenytoin) may result in large changes in both the serum concentration and clinical response. Additionally, cautious titration of dosage and serum concentration may be necessary to avoid intoxication. Knowledge of the serum drug concentration before the dosage change may allow the clinician to select a more appropriate new maintenance dose.

Frequent, "routine" determinations of serum antiepileptic drug concentrations are costly and generally not warranted for patients whose clinical status is stable. There may be a tendency for clinicians to focus attention on normal variability in serum concentrations rather than on the patient's clinical status; as a result, unnecessary dosage adjustments may be made to make serum concentrations "fit" the "normal range." Therefore, the results of individual serum concentration determinations must be evaluated carefully to decide whether a significant, clinically meaningful change has occurred.[38]

Interpretation of Serum Concentrations. Several factors may alter the relationship between AED serum concentration and the patient's response to the drug. Any time there is an apparent change in serum concentration, pharmacokinetic factors (see Table 52.4) should be considered (along with the patient's clinical status) before a decision is made to adjust AED dosage based upon a new serum concentration. *Laboratory variability* may cause minor fluctuations in reported AED serum concentrations. Under the best conditions, reported values for serum concentrations may be within ± 10% of "true" values.[39,40] Therefore, the magnitude of any apparent change must be considered. *Therapeutic ranges are not well established for some drugs* (e.g., valproate and carbamazepine). Published "therapeutic ranges" may have been determined in small numbers of patients or may more accurately represent "average serum concentrations" at "usual doses." As an example, many clinicians now agree that "pushing" valproate serum concentrations up to 150 to 200 µg/mL may be beneficial for some patients; these higher concentrations are not consistently associated with specific toxicity symptoms.[41-44] Nevertheless, most laboratories report 50 to 100 µg/mL as a "therapeutic range" for valproate. *Inappropriate sample timing* may result in inconsistent and clinically meaningless changes in AED serum concentrations. Generally, serum concentrations of AEDs should not be measured until a minimum of four to five half-lives have elapsed since initiation of therapy or a dosage change. Blood samples should be obtained in the morning before any doses of AED have been taken; this practice will provide reproducible, postabsorptive (i.e., "trough") serum concentrations. On occasion, especially for rapidly-absorbed drugs with short half-lives (e.g., valproate), determination of peak serum concentrations may help assess possible toxic symptoms. *Interindividual variability* in response to a given serum concentration of medication is seen frequently. Excellent therapeutic response or even symptoms of intoxication may be associated with AED serum concentrations that are classified as "subtherapeutic."[45] *Active metabolites* of AEDs usually are not measured when serum concentrations are determined.[40,46] Alterations in the relative proportion of parent drug and active metabolite may result in an apparent alteration in the relationship between serum concentration of the parent drug and the patient's response. *Binding to serum proteins* is significant for some antiepileptic drugs (e.g., phenytoin, valproate). Changes in protein binding to

Table 52.4					Pharmacokinetic Properties of Antiepileptic Drugs		
Drug	Oral Absorption	Half-Life (hr)	Time to Steady State[a]	Dosage Schedule	Usual Therapeutic Serum Concentration	Plasma Protein Binding	Volume of Distribution
Carbamazepine	90%–100%	*Chronic*: 5–25	2–4 days	BID–TID	5–12+ µg/mL	75% (50–90)	0.8–1.6 L/kg
Ethosuximide	90%–100%	*Pediatric*: 30 *Adult*: 60	5–10 days	QD (BID)	40–100 µg/mL	0%	0.7 L/kg
Felbamate	>90%	12–20	3–4 days	BID–TID	Not determined	24%	0.7–0.8 L/kg
Gabapentin	40%–60%; ↓ with ↑ dose size	*Normal renal function*: 5–9; ↑ with ↓ renal function	*Normal renal function*: 1–1.5 days	TID–QID (Q 6–8 hr)	>2 µg/mL (proposed)	0%	≈0.8 L/kg
Lamotrigine	90%–100%	*Monotherapy*: 24–29 *Enzyme inducers*: 15 *VPA[b] enzyme inhibition*: 59	4–9 days	QD	≤5 µg/mL (proposed)	55%	0.9–1.2 L/kg
Phenobarbital	90%–100%	2–4 days	8–16 days	QD	15–40 µg/mL	50%	0.5–0.6 L/kg
Phenytoin	90%–100%	Varies with dose	5–30+ days	QD (BID)	10–20 µg/mL	95%	0.5–0.7 L/kg
Primidone	90%–100%	3–12	12–48 hr	BID–TID	5–15 µg/mL (15–40 µg/mL for derived phenobarbital)	<50%	0.4–1.1 L/kg
Valproate	100%	10–16	2–3 days	BID–QID	50–150+ µg/mL (?)	90+%	0.09–0.17 L/kg

[a] Based upon 4 half-lives. This lag time should allow determination of steady-state serum concentrations within limits of most assay sensitivities.
[b] VPA = Valproic acid.

albumin may result from drug interaction, renal failure, or changes in nutritional status. These changes may alter the usual relationship between the measured total drug concentration (bound and unbound to plasma proteins) and the unbound (pharmacologically active) drug concentration. This change may not be apparent when total serum concentrations are measured. Determination of serum concentrations of free (i.e., unbound) AEDs is available from many commercial laboratories; these determinations are expensive and results may not be available for several days. In situations where significant changes in protein binding may occur, determination of free concentrations of AEDs may provide additional useful information for adjustment of doses or interpretation of symptom changes in patients.[39,40]

Monotherapy Versus Polytherapy. Historically, seizure disorders have been treated with multiple AEDs (polytherapy). A second, third, or even fourth drug was added when seizures were incompletely controlled with a single AED. Occasionally, therapy was initiated with two AEDs for a single seizure type (e.g., phenytoin and phenobarbital for generalized tonic-clonic seizures). Evaluation of the effectiveness of multiple drug therapy in recent years has shown little advantage of this practice for most patients. Use of a single drug at optimum tolerated serum concentrations produces excellent therapeutic results and minimal side effects in up to 80% of patients. Addition of a second AED significantly improves seizure control in only 10% to 20% of patients.[47,48] Reduction or elimination of existing polytherapy in patients with long-standing seizure disorders often lessens or eliminates cognitive impairment and other side effects: seizure control actually may improve.[47,49–52]

Most experts advocate the use of monotherapy (i.e., use of a single AED) whenever possible. Successful monotherapy may require higher than usual antiepileptic drug doses that may produce serum concentrations above the upper limit of the "usual therapeutic range."[30,53] Addition of a second drug may be necessary in some patients; however, polytherapy usually should be reserved for patients with multiple seizure types or for patients in whom

first-line AEDs have produced significant partial improvement when "pushed" to maximum tolerated doses.[30,50]

Use of multiple AEDs creates several disadvantages that must be weighed against possible benefits. Seizure control may not significantly improve; in fact, this author's experience and information from studies in which patients were converted from polytherapy to monotherapy indicate that, even with use of an optimum AED, seizure control may be worsened by polytherapy regimens.[52,53] Patient expenses for medications and for increased laboratory monitoring may increase significantly with polytherapy: drug interactions among AEDs may complicate assessment of serum concentrations and patient response. Patient compliance often is worsened when multiple medications are prescribed. Adverse effects often increase with the use of multiple AEDs because the side effects of many of these drugs are additive.

Duration of Therapy and Discontinuation of AEDs. A diagnosis of epilepsy no longer necessitates a commitment to lifelong drug therapy. Several long-term studies have examined the prognosis of epilepsy following drug discontinuation; AED therapy may be successfully withdrawn from some patients after a seizure-free period of two to five years.[18–24] Seizures recurred in only 12% to 36% of patients who were followed for up to 23 years after AED withdrawal. Therefore, many patients whose epilepsy is completely controlled with medication can successfully stop therapy after a seizure-free period of at least two years.

Discontinuation of medications is advantageous for economic, medical, and psychosocial reasons. Costs associated with physician visits, serum concentration determinations, and the medications themselves are eliminated. The risk of adverse effects from long-term medication use is eliminated, and patients can expect fewer lifestyle restrictions. There are also risks associated with attempts to withdraw AED therapy; reappearance of seizure activity may result in status epilepticus, loss of driving privileges, employment difficulties, or physical injury.

Risk factors for seizure recurrence following discontinuation of AEDs also have been identified in observational studies; unfortunately, there is not complete agreement between studies as to the nature and importance of specific risk factors. Opinions and data also differ regarding the optimal duration of the seizure-free period before discontinuation of AEDs is attempted. Nevertheless, there is at least some consensus regarding certain factors that may predict a higher risk of seizure recurrence. (See Table 52.5 for a summary of these risk factors.)[18-24,54,55]

In nonemergency situations, AEDs should be withdrawn slowly; if a patient receives multiple drugs, each drug should be withdrawn separately. Too rapid withdrawal may result in status epilepticus. Clinical studies of AED discontinuation usually used a two- to three-month withdrawal schedule for each drug. There is no specific information which identifies an optimum safe rate of withdrawal of AEDs. One study[56] compared withdrawal of individual drugs over a six-week period and a nine-month period and found no difference in seizure recurrence between the groups. Another study compared seizure frequencies in patients withdrawn from carbamazepine rapidly (over 4 days) and in patients withdrawn more slowly (over 10 days).[57] Significantly more generalized tonic-clonic seizures occurred when carbamazepine was withdrawn rapidly; complex partial seizures, however, did not occur at a higher rate with rapid withdrawal. Therefore, withdrawal of each AED over at least six weeks would seem to be a safe approach to discontinuation of medication. Gradual withdrawal is recommended even for medications such as phenobarbital that have long half-lives and should theoretically be "self-tapering." In the author's experience, gradual reduction of medications such as phenobarbital is associated with a significantly higher success rate. Appearance of seizures during medication withdrawal is not necessarily an indication for reinstitution of maintenance therapy; many patients who experience seizures during drug withdrawal will remain seizure free after complete withdrawal.[22] At least some seizures that occur during withdrawal may result from the withdrawal process itself or from other causes such as infection and are not related to reappearance of the underlying seizure disorder.[52]

Clinical Assessment and Treatment of Seizure Disorders
Complex Partial Seizures with Secondary Generalization
Diagnosis
1. A.R. is a 14-year-old, 40 kg, female high school student. Her 8-year-old brother has a seizure disorder and experiences

Table 52.5	Risk Factors Possibly Predicting Seizure Recurrence Following AED Withdrawal[a,18–24,54,55]

- <2 yr seizure-free before withdrawal
- Onset of seizures after age 12
- History of atypical febrile seizures
- Family history of seizures
- >2–6 yr before seizures controlled
- Large number of seizures (>30) before control or total of >100 seizures
- Partial seizures (simple or complex)
- History of absence seizures
- Abnormal EEG persisting throughout treatment
- Slowing on EEG before medication withdrawal
- Presence of organic neurologic disorder
- Moderate to severe mental retardation
- Withdrawal of valproate or phenytoin (higher rate of recurrence than withdrawal of other AEDs)

a AED = Antiepileptic drug; EEG = Electroencephalogram.

absence spells and generalized tonic-clonic seizures. A.R. had 3 febrile seizures when she was 3 years old. She received phenobarbital prophylaxis, "off and on" according to her parents, for about 6 months following her 2nd febrile seizure. Since then, she had no reported seizures until 24 hours before admission. At that time she had a "convulsion" at school shortly after arriving for her first class of the morning. A teacher who witnessed the episode describes her as behaving "oddly" before the seizure. She abruptly got up from her classroom desk and began to walk clumsily toward the door; she bumped into several desks and did not respond to the teacher's attempts to redirect her back to her seat. After approximately 1 minute of this behavior, she fell to the floor and experienced an apparent generalized tonic-clonic seizure that lasted for approximately 90 seconds. During the episode, she was incontinent of urine and was described as "turning kind of blue." Following this episode, A.R. was transported to the hospital.

On arrival at the hospital, A.R. appeared drowsy and confused. Laboratory studies including complete blood count (CBC), serum glucose, electrolytes, drug/alcohol screen, and a lumbar puncture were normal. Physical examination and complete neurological evaluation were normal. An EEG showed diffuse slowing with focal epileptiform discharges in the left temporal area; it was interpreted as abnormal. There was no history of recent illness or injury, although A.R. had stayed up late several nights recently studying for an examination.

A second seizure occurred in the hospital approximately 18 hours following the episode at school. The nursing staff's description of the episode was similar to that provided by the observers at school. After recovery from each episode, A.R. had no memory of events during the seizures; she only remembered a "funny feeling" in her stomach and a "buzzing" in her head before she lost consciousness. She describes having these feelings "a couple of times" in the past; she attributed them to "just getting dizzy" and had not reported them to her parents. After these previous episodes, A.R. described feeling "mixed up" and groggy for a few minutes. What subjective and objective features of A.R.'s seizures are consistent with a diagnosis of complex partial seizures with secondary generalization?

A.R.'s clinical pattern of observed seizure activity (an apparent aura preceding her generalized tonic-clonic seizures), her history of apparent complex partial seizures that were not accompanied by generalized seizures, and the findings of focal abnormal activity on EEG are all typical of this diagnosis. The occurrence of postictal confusion and grogginess is also common after both generalized tonic-clonic and complex partial seizures. In the past, A.R.'s description of "a funny feeling" or a "buzzing" in her head would have been attributed to an aura; it is now recognized that, these feelings and her unusual or inappropriate behavior, represent a complex partial seizure that subsequently generalized. The clinical features accompanied by her EEG findings also help rule out possible atypical absence seizures; atypical absence may be confused with complex partial epileptic syndromes based upon only clinical presentation. In both syndromes, patients may briefly appear to lose contact with their surroundings and display automatisms and mild clonic movements during seizure activity. In A.R.'s case, the EEG and the occurrence of generalized tonic-clonic seizures during her episodes would rule out atypical absence as a likely possibility.

Decision to Use AED Therapy
2. What factors should be considered in a decision to treat A.R.'s seizures with antiepileptic medication?

Once a diagnosis of epileptic seizures is established, the decision to treat with medication is based upon the likelihood of recurrence. The need for AED therapy after a single seizure is controversial, however, recurrence of generalized tonic-clonic seizures is less likely if antiepileptic drug therapy is initiated following the first generalized tonic-clonic seizure.[17] Therefore, at least for this one specific seizure type, there is support for early use of AEDs. It is not known whether this information applies to other types of seizures. Clinical wisdom, however, holds that "seizures beget seizures," and most experts advocate early treatment of epileptic seizures (i.e., after a first or second unprovoked seizure).

In A.R.'s case, the potential benefits of immediate introduction of AED therapy appear to outweigh potential risks. She experienced complex partial seizures followed by secondarily generalized tonic-clonic seizures. Recurrences of seizure activity are likely to result in social embarrassment and interference with her participation in activities typical of a person her age. If her seizures are not controlled, she faces future limitation of her driving privileges and may face barriers to employment. While AED therapy is associated with risks, these risks probably are outweighed by the potential benefits.

Choice of AED

3. Discuss the AEDs commonly used for A.R.'s seizure type. Based upon the subjective and objective data available, recommend a first choice antiepileptic medication for A.R. and a plan for initial dosing of this medication.

Phenytoin and carbamazepine are currently considered first choice AEDs for complex partial seizures with secondarily generalized tonic-clonic seizures (see Table 52.2).[31,32,48] Valproate (Depakene/Depakote), in some studies, is effective for both generalized and complex partial seizures.[58–60] While valproate presently is used as a second-line agent for treatment of partial seizures by many clinicians, its usefulness is becoming more widely recognized. Clorazepate (Tranxene) is useful primarily in situations where an adjunctive medication is required because of incomplete response to primary drugs; its usefulness is limited by the common development of tolerance and by its prominent sedative effects.[61] Phenobarbital and primidone (Mysoline) are less commonly used than in the past. While both drugs are effective, the rate of side effects is high and, as a result, long term adherence to therapy by patients is difficult.[31] Felbamate (Felbatol), gabapentin (Neurontin), and lamotrigine (Lamictal) are effective for control of partial seizures (with or without secondary generalization); however, most experience with these drugs has been obtained when they are used as second-line agents that are added to existing drugs when initial therapy is unsuccessful. Gabapentin and lamotrigine appear to be safe and usually well tolerated; the usefulness of felbamate is, however, limited owing to its potential for serious hematologic and hepatic toxicity (see below).

Carbamazepine has several advantages over phenytoin which make it a preferred agent in the opinion of many clinicians. Carbamazepine is less sedating than phenytoin for many patients; it is not associated with dysmorphic effects such as hirsutism, acne, gingival hyperplasia, and coarsening of facial features. Carbamazepine's pharmacokinetic profile also makes dosage regimen adjustment easier. In A.R.'s case, several of these advantages for carbamazepine may be significant. The lack of cosmetic side effects may be especially significant to this young patient as she will potentially be taking medication for many years. Reduced sedation may be important with respect to her school performance. In recent years there has been a great deal of focus on the relative cognitive effects of AEDs.[62] Initial studies comparing cognitive effects of phenytoin and carbamazepine found a significantly higher rate of cognitive impairment with phenytoin therapy as measured by neuropsychological tests of motor performance, learning, attention, and memory.[63] Based upon these studies and clinical observation, phenytoin has gained a reputation for causing significant impairment of function. More recent studies and re-analysis of data from

the initial studies have revealed that much of the cognitive impairment attributed to phenytoin could be explained by elevations in phenytoin serum concentrations and overemphasis of neuropsychological tests involving motor function.[64–66] Actual differences between these two drugs usually are subtle and difficult to detect; nevertheless, many clinicians and patients prefer carbamazepine to phenytoin because of its presumed lesser effects on cognition and motor function.

Carbamazepine Therapy

Initiation and Dosage. Acutely, administration of full therapeutic maintenance doses of carbamazepine often causes excessive side effects such as nausea, vomiting, diplopia, and significant sedation. Therefore, carbamazepine therapy should be initiated gradually and patients should be allowed time to acclimate to the effects of the drug. Final dosing requirements are difficult to anticipate in individual patients. A reasonable starting dose of carbamazepine for A.R. would be 100 mg twice a day; her dose could be increased by 100 to 200 mg/day every 7 to 14 days. The rapidity of upward dose adjustments will depend upon A.R.'s tolerance for the drug and the frequency of seizure recurrence. Serum concentrations of carbamazepine may be helpful in assessing adequacy of dosage after A.R. is receiving usual therapeutic doses of the drug. Reasonable target serum concentrations of carbamazepine would be approximately 6 to 8 µg/mL.[6,35,40]

4. Carbamazepine has been associated with hematologic and hepatic toxicities. What is the incidence and significance of these potential toxicities? How should A.R. be monitored for their occurrence?

Hematologic Toxicity. Aplastic anemia and agranulocytosis have occurred in association with carbamazepine therapy.[67,68] Several cases have been fatal; however, most cases occurred in older patients treated for trigeminal neuralgia. Many patients were receiving other medications, and occasionally, the reports were incomplete; thus, assessment of a causal role for carbamazepine is difficult.[69,70] Severe blood dyscrasias from carbamazepine seem quite rare (estimated prevalence of <1/50,000) and have predominantly occurred in nonepileptic patients. There has been a notable lack of severe hematological toxicity in various published series and clinical trials in patients with epilepsy.

Leukopenia is relatively common in patients taking carbamazepine. It is usually mild, and often reverses despite continued administration of the drug.[71,72] Total leukocyte counts may fall below 4,000 cells/mm^3 in some patients, but differentials and platelet and erythrocyte counts remain normal. Symptoms (e.g., fever, sore throat) which might suggest early stages of agranulocytosis do not occur. This author has worked with several patients who developed persistent leukopenia while receiving carbamazepine; total WBC counts occasionally fell below 3,000 cells/mm^3, but differentials remained normal. No other hematological parameters were affected, and patients were asymptomatic. There is no information to support a dosage relationship for carbamazepine-associated hematological disorders, and this reaction is believed to be idiosyncratic.

Routine Hematologic Testing. Laboratory monitoring of A.R.'s hematological status is recommended during carbamazepine therapy. The likelihood of early detection of cases of aplastic anemia or agranulocytosis through frequent blood counts is very low, however, and such monitoring is costly.[71,73] Since hematologic toxicity from carbamazepine primarily occurs early in therapy, complete blood counts should be obtained before therapy and at monthly intervals during the first two months of therapy; thereafter, a yearly or every other year CBC, WBC differential, and platelet count should be sufficient.

Hepatotoxicity. Carbamazepine-related liver damage appears to be extremely rare despite frequent mention as a potential problem and strong warnings in the package insert.[74,75] Hepatic adverse reactions are believed to be idiosyncratic or immunologically based. Aggressive laboratory monitoring of liver function tests (LFTs) probably is unnecessary.[73] Alkaline phosphatase concentrations often are elevated in patients taking carbamazepine (and other AEDs). This is believed to result from hepatic enzyme induction and is not necessarily evidence for hepatic disease.[76]

In summary, the hepatic and hematologic toxicities of carbamazepine are quite rare. While they are potentially serious, they are best monitored on clinical grounds rather than by ongoing, intensive laboratory testing. Patients and their families or significant caregivers should be aware that the appearance of unusual symptoms (e.g., jaundice, abdominal pain, excessive bruising/bleeding, or sudden onset of severe sore throat with fever) should be reported to a health professional. Baseline (pretherapy) determination of A.R.'s hepatic and hematologic status possibly followed by monthly follow-up testing for two to three months probably will be sufficient.[71,73] Thereafter, a CBC and a liver function battery should probably be evaluated only every one to two years unless signs or symptoms of hepatic or hematologic disorders are observed.

5. Pharmacokinetics and Autoinduction of Metabolism. Over the following 6 weeks, A.R.'s carbamazepine dose was gradually increased to 400 mg BID (20 mg/kg/day). Until the last dose increase, she had been experiencing 1 or 2 complex partial seizures weekly; she had had only 1 generalized tonic-clonic seizure since her hospitalization. One week following initiation of this dose, her serum carbamazepine concentration was 9 µg/mL just before her first dose of the day. No seizures occurred for 4 weeks and she tolerated the medication well. Subsequently, she again began experiencing 1 seizure weekly. A repeated measurement of her serum carbamazepine concentration was 6 µg/mL. How might this change in serum concentration and recurrence of seizure activity be explained?

Several factors may account for this change. One should always consider the possibility of poor compliance with the medication regimen when serum concentrations and/or clinical response change unexpectedly. This should be investigated and A.R. and her family should be educated regarding the importance of regular medication intake if necessary.

The observed changes in A.R.'s carbamazepine serum concentrations also are characteristic of this drug's pharmacokinetic behavior. Carbamazepine is a potent inducer of hepatic enzymes and accelerates its own metabolism and the metabolism of many other drugs. Carbamazepine's half-life following single acute doses is approximately 35 hours; with chronic dosing, its half-life decreases to 15 to 25 hours. This induction of metabolism may be further enhanced by combined administration of carbamazepine and other enzyme inducing AEDs: with polytherapy, carbamazepine's half-life may be as short as six to ten hours.[40] This increase in clearance necessitates increased doses of carbamazepine to maintain target serum concentrations. Autoinduction of carbamazepine metabolism appears to be dose or serum concentration related. Approximately one month may be required for the autoinduction process to reach completion after an increase in carbamazepine dose.[77]

Assuming that compliance was not the main problem, A.R.'s carbamazepine dose should be increased. The drug's pharmacokinetics tend to generally be linear with respect to acute dosage changes.[78] A 50% increase in dose to 1200 mg/day should re-establish seizure control with a serum concentration of approximately 9 µg/mL. Some decrease in this concentration should be anticipated after autoinduction has reached completion; depending upon A.R.'s clinical status, further upward dosage adjustment may be necessary.

6. Bioequivalence of Generic Dosage Forms and Effects of Storage on Bioequivalence. A.R.'s dose was increased to 600 mg BID. Four weeks later, she was still experiencing approximately 1 complex partial seizure weekly. A repeat serum carbamazepine concentration was reported as 6.5 µg/mL. Upon questioning, A.R. denied missing doses of medication and a tablet count confirmed apparent accurate drug intake. A.R. relates that she experiences some mild nausea following her doses, but she has not vomited. It is noted that her pharmacist has begun substituting generic carbamazepine tablets for the Tegretol that was previously dispensed. What role, if any, might this change in carbamazepine tablet brand have played in the failure of A.R.'s serum concentrations to increase as expected? What other factors might be considered in explaining this situation?

Several manufacturers have marketed generic carbamazepine tablets. Bioavailability data supplied by the manufacturers are based upon single dose or very short multiple-dose studies. Therefore, it is impossible to completely predict the results of a change from Tegretol to generic carbamazepine for maintenance therapy in an individual patient.[79] Available bioavailability data and the author's experience with institutionalized patients with severe seizure disorders suggest that generic carbamazepine preparations currently on the market may be substituted for Tegretol with little need for dosage adjustment. Nevertheless, significant differences in dissolution rates and absorption characteristics between generic carbamazepine and brand-name Tegretol have been reported.[46,80] In A.R.'s case, substitution of generic carbamazepine may be a possible cause for the lower-than-expected serum concentrations. Re-adjustment of her dose and avoidance of changing between manufacturers of carbamazepine might alleviate this problem.

A.R. or her parents also should be questioned regarding the quantities of carbamazepine tablets on hand and the storage conditions for the medication. Storage of 200 mg carbamazepine tablets under conditions of high humidity may result in hardening of these tablets, poor dissolution properties, and decreased absorption of drug. Up to one-third of the efficacy of carbamazepine may be lost with continuous exposure to 97% humidity at room temperature for 14 days. This loss of efficacy may be even more pronounced with generic carbamazepine.[46] Chewable 100 mg tablets do not appear to be affected by humidity in the same way. Many patients purchase large quantities of medication and store their prescriptions in the bathroom or kitchen where conditions of high humidity often exist. If A.R. is taking carbamazepine that has been affected by humidity, this would account for the failure of her serum concentrations to increase. To avoid this problem, the Food and Drug Administration (FDA) has recommended that carbamazepine be dispensed only in tightly closed containers. Physicians are urged to prescribe carbamazepine in small quantities, and manufacturers and pharmacists are urged to market or dispense this medication in containers of ≤100 tablets. Unit dose packaging also may help avoid this problem.[81]

Another factor may be partly responsible for the failure of A.R.'s serum concentrations to increase. Carbamazepine absorption appears somewhat capacity-limited; as larger single doses are administered, smaller fractions of the administered dose may be absorbed.[82] Twice-daily administration of carbamazepine, when relatively large doses must be used, may be reducing A.R.'s capacity to absorb the drug. Changing to a three times daily or even four times daily dosing schedule may result in improved absorption, increased serum concentrations, and improved clinical response. Additionally, A.R.'s transient nausea also may improve;

this side effect may be caused by direct irritation from the large quantities of carbamazepine ingested or by elevated peak serum concentrations of the drug.

In conclusion, it is impossible to identify a single cause for the unexpected serum concentration results in A.R. Use of a generic substitute for Tegretol and capacity-limited absorption may be playing a role. Poor compliance cannot be completely ruled out despite accurate tablet counts, especially when the medication causes the patient physical discomfort. Patients may go to elaborate lengths to conceal inaccurate drug intake. While multiple daily dosing regimens may make patient compliance more difficult, changing A.R.'s regimen to a three or even four times daily schedule may reduce nausea and improve absorption.

7. Carbamazepine Intoxication and Carbamazepine-Induced Hyponatremia. A.R.'s regimen was changed to 400 mg TID and her seizure frequency decreased to approximately 1 every 2–3 months. She continued to receive generic carbamazepine. Steady-state trough serum concentrations were consistently reported as 10–11 μg/mL. She was not experiencing any significant side effects other than occasional mild nausea following doses; this was prevented if she took her medication with food. Following a generalized tonic-clonic seizure, her physician decided to increase her carbamazepine to 1600 mg/day (400 mg a.m., 400 mg noon, 400 mg late afternoon, and 400 mg HS) in an attempt to further control her seizures. Ten days after the dose increase, A.R. began complaining of nausea, double vision, dizziness, a mildly unsteady gait, and an inability to concentrate. Discuss the possible explanations for A.R.'s new symptoms. What further information should be obtained to assess this situation?

The carbamazepine intoxication syndrome is not as well defined nor as closely correlated with serum concentrations as intoxication with other AEDs such as phenytoin. Therefore, carbamazepine intoxication is defined primarily by symptoms: serum concentrations may not help in its confirmation.[35,83,84] A.R.'s current complaints are similar to those commonly associated with elevated serum carbamazepine concentrations; the same symptoms may, however, occur at much lower concentrations. Gastrointestinal intolerance (e.g., A.R.'s nausea) may occur at low doses and limit therapy despite "subtherapeutic" serum concentrations. Determination of a carbamazepine serum concentration would be helpful at this time to document concentrations which produce symptoms of intoxication in A.R.

Carbamazepine also may cause "paradoxical intoxication" at serum concentrations of ≥ 20 μg/mL. This condition is characterized by increased seizure frequency, and is similar to paradoxical intoxication occasionally seen with markedly elevated serum concentrations of phenytoin.[83] Accumulation of carbamazepine's active metabolite, carbamazepine-10,11-epoxide (CBZ-E), also may result in increased seizure activity without other symptoms of intoxication in some patients despite usual serum concentrations of the parent compound.[85] This is most likely to occur in patients receiving other drugs (usually AEDs such as valproate and felbamate) which inhibit the metabolism of CBZ-E. Mental retardation also may be a predisposing factor for this form of intoxication. While A.R. does not seem especially predisposed to this adverse reaction to carbamazepine and CBZ-E, her recent dose increase may have resulted in a significant elevation in CBZ-E serum concentrations; measurement of CBZ-E concentrations is indicated as part of the laboratory assessment of her present condition.

Hyponatremia associated with syndrome of inappropriate antidiuretic hormone (SIADH) also should be evaluated as a possible cause of A.R.'s symptoms. SIADH is a well documented adverse reaction to carbamazepine.[86] This condition is less likely to occur in children.[87] Symptoms associated with water intoxication can resemble those exhibited by A.R. Affected patients usually will complain of headache, nausea, vomiting, and dizziness; in more severe cases, confusion and increased seizure activity may occur. This symptom pattern may be mistakenly attributed to carbamazepine intoxication. The mechanism by which carbamazepine produces hyponatremia is unclear. It was believed that the drug stimulates release of antidiuretic hormone (ADH) from the pituitary, but this mechanism has been questioned. Carbamazepine may act directly on the kidney to increase sodium loss, or it may cause resetting of osmoreceptors.[88,89] While this effect is predictable enough for carbamazepine to be used in the treatment of some forms of diabetes insipidus, clinically significant water intoxication in patients treated with carbamazepine is uncommon. Nevertheless, laboratory monitoring often reveals depression of serum sodium concentrations in many patients receiving this drug. The effect of carbamazepine on ADH probably is dependent upon serum concentration.[90] SIADH may be less common in patients who receive both phenytoin and carbamazepine; phenytoin appears to counteract the antidiuretic effect of carbamazepine in some, but not all, affected patients.[90-92] This may result from either inhibition of ADH release or stimulation of carbamazepine metabolism by phenytoin; the relative contribution of each effect has not been determined. A.R.'s serum electrolytes should be measured to evaluate the possible role of hyponatremia in causing her current symptoms.

When significant SIADH related to carbamazepine therapy is identified, the condition usually can be treated successfully by dosage reduction and mild fluid restriction. Discontinuation of carbamazepine and substitution of an alternate AED may be necessary in some patients. Demeclocycline (Declomycin) has been used successfully to manage some cases of carbamazepine-induced SIADH.[88] Demeclocycline inhibits activation of ADH-sensitive adenyl cyclase in the distal renal tubules and collecting ducts. Some patients may respond positively to increased sodium intake.[89]

8. A.R.'s serum concentrations of carbamazepine and CBZ-E were 14 μg/mL and 3.1 μg/mL (usual range: 0.4–4.0 μg/mL), respectively. At the same time, a serum sodium (Na) concentration was 130 mEq/L, chloride (Cl) was 94 mEq/L, potassium (K) was 3.8 mEq/L, BUN was 9 mg/dL, and albumin was 3.2 gm/dL. A CBC and a 12-panel chemistry screen were otherwise normal. On the basis of the subjective and objective information available, recommend a plan for management of A.R.'s condition. [SI units: Na 130 mmol/L; Cl 94 mmol/L; K 3.8 mmol/L; 3.21 mmol/L of urea; albumin 32 gm/L]

While A.R.'s serum sodium concentration is somewhat low, it is not sufficiently reduced to account for her symptoms. Significant symptoms usually are not seen until serum sodium concentrations are below 120 to 125 mEq/L. The temporal relationship between A.R.'s symptom onset and dosage increase and the elevated carbamazepine serum concentration suggest CNS intoxication from carbamazepine as the cause of her symptoms. Neither the serum concentration of CBZ-E nor the ratio of CBZ-E to carbamazepine serum concentrations are unusually elevated; however, CBZ-E may be contributing to A.R.'s apparent intoxication syndrome by exerting effects which are additive with those of carbamazepine. A.R.'s carbamazepine dosage regimen should be adjusted. The pattern of her symptoms, however, also should be evaluated before a decision is made to reduce the total daily dose. If the symptoms occur two to four hours following dosage administration, it may be possible to alleviate them by further dividing her daily dosage or altering the pattern of dosage administration.[84,93] Transient intoxication associated with peak serum concentrations is relatively common with carbamazepine. It is possible that a sustained-release dosage form of this AED will be available in the future and that this preparation will help alleviate toxic symptoms associated with peak serum concentrations while allowing less frequent administration of medication. Should further division of A.R.'s doses prove unsuccessful or impractical, then reduction in her total daily dose to an intermediate level of 1400 mg/day may relieve her intoxication while still producing improved seizure control. No additional alteration in A.R.'s regimen is necessary to control her reduced serum sodium concentration. Should her daily dose of carbamazepine be reduced, this change will minimize the effect of the drug on her water excretion.

9. Treatment Failure and Alternate AEDs. **R.H., a 17-year-old, 53 kg, female, has experienced simple partial seizures, complex partial seizures, and secondarily generalized tonic-clonic seizures for the past 2 years. She was unable to tolerate treatment with phenytoin (severe gingival hyperplasia, hypertrichosis, and mental "dullness") or valproate (persistent GI distress, tremor, and a weight gain of 8 kg). In addition, neither phenytoin nor valproate was dramatically effective for reduction of her seizures at tolerable serum concentrations. She currently receives carbamazepine 600 mg TID. Over the past 3 months, while being treated with carbamazepine, she has had approximately 5 simple partial seizures, 3 complex partial seizures, and 1 generalized tonic-clonic seizure following a complex partial seizure episode. This represents an approximately 30% reduction in her frequency of seizures. She tolerates her present dose of carbamazepine, but she has experienced significant drowsiness, GI upset, and mental confusion at higher doses. Her most recent serum concentration of carbamazepine was 14 μg/mL. What are possible therapeutic options for R.H.? Evaluate the newer AEDs and their possible usefulness for R.H.**

R.H. is exhibiting a partial response to maximally tolerated doses of carbamazepine. An alteration in her current antiepileptic drug regimen appears to be indicated. She has been unable to tolerate other preferred medications due to side effects. Valproate often is effective for control of partial seizures and now is considered a useful alternative to medications such as carbamazepine and phenytoin.[60] R.H.'s prominent CNS side effects (e.g., persistent drowsiness) with other AEDs would make many clinicians reluctant to consider medications such as phenobarbital, primidone, clorazepate, or clonazepam as either alternatives or adjunctive agents to her current carbamazepine regimen. Use of one of the newer AEDs as adjunctive medication may be of value for R.H.

Three AEDs recently have been marketed in the U.S. Felbamate (Felbatol), gabapentin (Neurontin), and lamotrigine (Lamictal) (see Table 52.6) are each indicated for treatment of partial seizures with or without secondary generalization. All three of these newer agents have been effective as "add-on" or adjunctive medications in patients who do not respond to other AEDs.[94-102] Felbamate has been evaluated intensively in controlled trials for treatment of seizures associated with Lennox-Gastaut syndrome and shown to be effective;[103] limited experience with lamotrigine suggests that this drug also may be effective in this syndrome.[104,105] Gabapentin has not yet been formally evaluated for treatment of seizures in Lennox-Gastaut syndrome. Felbamate also has been effective when used as monotherapy;[96] results of monotherapy trials with gabapentin and lamotrigine are not yet available. Animal screening tests and limited clinical reports have suggested a broad spectrum of efficacy for lamotrigine and felbamate;[94,104,105] both drugs may prove useful in other seizure types such as absence. None of these newer AEDs are as sedating for patients as the older medications such as phenobarbital or phenytoin. Felbamate, in fact, has been associated with insomnia and irritability in a significant proportion of treated patients.

Common side effects for the newer medications are described in Table 52.6. Gabapentin, to date, has not been associated with serious side effects.[255] The most serious side effect associated with lamotrigine has been skin rash which occurs in approximately 10% of treated patients. Widespread, maculopapular rashes appear during the first few days of lamotrigine therapy and may progress to erythema multiforme. These rashes resolve rapidly when lamotrigine is discontinued. Coadministration of valproate with lamotrigine may increase the likelihood of dermatologic reactions.[104,106,107] Side effects have been prominent during felbamate therapy; patients may experience headaches, insomnia, and gastrointestinal effects such as nausea, vomiting, anorexia, and weight loss. Interactions between felbamate and other AEDs may make therapeutic monitoring of patients difficult. Felbamate reduces the clearance of phenytoin, valproate, and probably phenobarbital; it also reduces the clearance of carbamazepine-10,11-epoxide while, apparently, increasing conversion of carbamazepine to the epoxide metabolite.[108-110] Clinically, this latter effect may create a somewhat paradoxical situation: patients may experience symptoms of carbamazepine intoxication (including increased seizure activity)[85] with carbamazepine serum concentrations lower than those found before addition of felbamate: CBZ-E serum concentrations usually will be elevated in these situations. Felbamate's usefulness has been seriously limited by its association with several cases of aplastic anemia and hepatic failure. Some cases of felbamate-associated aplastic anemia and hepatotoxicity were fatal. Preliminary information indicates that aplastic anemia may appear at any time during therapy. A conservative, preliminary estimate of the occurrence rate is 1 case per 2000 to 5000 patients treated.[111] Too few cases of hepatic failure associated with felbamate therapy have been reported to allow conclusions regarding characteristics of this potential adverse effect and risk factors for its development. Frequent monitoring of liver function tests is recommended in conjunction with observation of treated patients for clinical signs and symptoms suggesting liver damage.[112] Until the relationship between felbamate therapy and aplastic anemia and hepatic failure is clarified and guidelines for safe use of this drug are identified, the place of felbamate in the treatment of epilepsy is uncertain.

The newer AEDs have somewhat different pharmacokinetic profiles from those seen with older agents. Gabapentin is excreted entirely by the kidneys as unchanged drug and it is not significantly bound to serum albumin. Gabapentin has a relatively short half-life and should be dosed three times daily.[113,114] Felbamate undergoes both hepatic metabolism and renal excretion as unchanged drug. Phenytoin and carbamazepine induce the hepatic metabolism of felbamate and lower steady-state felbamate concentrations.[94] Lamotrigine is primarily eliminated by hepatic glucuronidation and excretion of metabolites in the urine. Lamotrigine's hepatic metabolism may be induced by other AEDs such as carbamazepine and phenytoin. When lamotrigine is coadministered with enzyme-inducing drugs its half-life decreases from approximately 24 hours to 15 hours. Valproate inhibits lamotrigine metabolism causing increases in half-life and serum concentrations.[115] Patients treated with both lamotrigine and carbamazepine may experience more nausea, drowsiness, and ataxia; this, in part, may result from an increase in serum concentrations of carbamazepine-10,11-epoxide.[116]

On the basis of efficacy and side effect characteristics, either gabapentin or lamotrigine could be considered for use as adjunctive therapy for R.H. In young, active individuals such as R.H. initial sedation might prove to be problematic; however, it is not clear that either gabapentin or lamotrigine predictably causes more initial sedation. Gabapentin's short half-life and the associated need

Table 52.6		Drugs Used for the Treatment of Partial and Generalized Tonic-Clonic Seizures[a]	
AED	**Regimen**	**Adverse Effects**	**Comments**
Carbamazepine (Tegretol)	Initial 200 mg BID (adults) or 100 mg BID (children) and ↑ weekly until therapeutic response or target serum concentrations. Usual maintenance doses 7–15 mg/kg/day in adults; 10–40 mg/kg/day in children	GI upset, sedation, visual disturbance may limit dosage. Severe blood dyscrasias extremely rare (<1/50,000). Mild leukopenia more common. Laboratory monitoring of little value. Hepatotoxicity rare. May cause SIADH	Usually little sedation and minimal interference with cognitive function or behavior. Preferred by most for partial or secondarily generalized seizures
Phenytoin (Dilantin)	Initiate at maintenance dose of 4–5 mg/kg/day (300–400 mg/day). Titrate on basis of clinical response and target serum concentration. 3–4 weeks between dose ↑ recommended because of potentially slow accumulation	Nystagmus, ataxia, sedation, mental changes usually predictable from serum concentrations. Gum hyperplasia, hirsutism common. Osteomalacia uncommon. Seizure frequency may ↑ with markedly ↑ serum concentrations. Peripheral neuropathy, pseudolymphoma, hypersensitivity with liver damage rare	Clearance and t½ change with dose. Small ↑ in dose (30 mg capsule dosage form) recommended as therapeutic range approached. Suspension and chewable tablets contain free acid form of phenytoin; capsules contain sodium phenytoin (converts to 92% of free acid form). Cautious use of suspension; dose measurement and potential mixing difficulties. IM administration not recommended. Potential precipitation in IV solutions. Dilute in small volume of normal saline and administer IV using 0.45–0.22 micron filter. Administer IV at <50 mg/min
Valproate (Depakene, Depakote)	See Table 52.8		
Phenobarbital	Initial 1 mg/kg/day; titrate to therapeutic response or target serum concentration. 2–3 weeks between dose ↑	Sedation (chronic), behavior disturbances common, especially in children. Possibly impairs learning and intellectual performance. Osteomalacia uncommon	Considered outmoded for antiepileptic therapy in most patients. Questionable benefit for prophylaxis of febrile seizures; adverse effects outweigh benefits. IV use for refractory status epilepticus. 10–20 mg/kg IV at <100 mg/min; caution when used with diazepam for status epilepticus because of additive cardiovascular and respiratory depression
Primidone (Mysoline)	Initial 5–15 mg/kg/day; then titrate to therapeutic response or target serum concentration. 2–3 weeks between dose ↑	Sedation, ataxia, GI toxicity common with initial therapy. Essentially similar profile to phenobarbital	Considered outmoded for antiepileptic therapy in most patients. Majority of antiepileptic effect from phenobarbital as metabolite. Expensive with less favorable side effect profile
Felbamate (Felbatol)	Initial 1200 mg/day (15 mg/kg). ↑ Q 7 days by 1200 mg/day (15 mg/kg/day). Current maximum recommended dose of 3600 mg/day. Therapeutic serum concentrations not yet defined	Nausea, anorexia, and headache common with initial add-on therapy; much less frequent with monotherapy. Insomnia may occur. Associated with cases of aplastic anemia and hepatotoxicity. Fatalities reported. Careful monitoring of patients necessary	Significant inhibition of metabolism of other AEDs; doses of existing drugs should be ↓ 20%–30% with addition of felbamate. May have positive effect on mental status and functioning
Gabapentin (Neurontin)	Initial 300 mg/day with titration to 900–1800 mg/day over 1–2 weeks. Up to 2400 mg/day or higher may be needed for some patients. Owing to short t½, TID or QID dosing recommended	Sedation, dizziness, and ataxia relatively common with initiation of therapy. Gabapentin therapy usually not associated with prominent side effects	Primarily excreted unchanged by kidneys. No significant interactions with other AEDs or other drugs identified to date. Absorption dose dependent; fraction absorbed ↓ as size of individual dose ↑
Lamotrigine (Lamictal)	*When added to enzyme inducers alone:* Initiate at 50 mg QD HS. May start at 50 mg BID. Daily dose can be ↑ by 50–100 mg Q 7–14 days. Usual maintenance doses of 400–500 mg/day. Doses up to 700 mg/day have been used. BID dosing may be necessary with enzyme inducer cotherapy. *When added to valproate alone:* Initiate at 25 mg QOD HS. Daily dose can be ↑ by 25 mg Q 14 days. Usual maintenance doses of 100–200 mg/day. *When added to valproate and enzyme inducers:* Initiate at 25 mg QOD HS. Daily dose can be ↑ by 25 mg Q 14 days. Usual daily doses of 100–200 mg/day	Dizziness, diplopia, sedation, ataxia, and blurred vision. Common with initiation of therapy; limit speed of titration. Rash in ≈10% of treated patients; may be more common with coadministration with valproate	Significant ↑ in clearance of lamotrigine when coadministered with enzyme inducers such as carbamazepine. Significant ↓ in clearance when coadministered with valproate; valproate appears to inhibit metabolism of lamotrigine. Lamotrigine may ↑ concentrations of carbamazepine 10,11-epoxide; may be responsible for ↑ CNS side effects when lamotrigine is used with carbamazepine. Slow, gradual titration of dose may reduce risk of skin rash

[a] AEDs = Antiepileptic drugs; CNS = Central nervous system; GI = Gastrointestinal; SIADH = Syndrome of inappropriate antidiuretic hormone secretion; t½ = Half-life.

for R.H. to take several doses during the day might decrease her compliance with a prescribed treatment regimen. Other AEDs in development may become available in the near future (see Table 52.7). Several of these drugs (e.g., vigabatrin, tiagabine, and topiramate) may become additional alternatives or adjuncts to established medications for treatment of partial seizures.

Lamotrigine Therapy

10. Initiation and Dosage Titration. R.H. is to be started on lamotrigine as adjunctive therapy to her carbamazepine. Outline a treatment plan for initiation and monitoring of therapy for R.H. What should R.H. and her family be told about this medication and how to use it properly?

Lamotrigine therapy should be initiated with slow upward dosage titration to minimize early sedative effects and reduce the likelihood of skin rash. Initial doses of 50 mg/day given at bedtime are recommended; the daily dose can be increased by 50 mg every 7 to 14 days. Usual doses of lamotrigine are approximately 400 mg/day, although there is some experience with doses of up to 700 mg/day. A patient's ability to tolerate this medication ultimately

will determine dosage limitations. Onset of side effects such as nausea, diplopia, ataxia, and dizziness may prevent further dose increases. Lower initial doses (25 mg/every other day) with more conservative increases (i.e., by 25 mg/day every 2 weeks) have been recommended for patients who are receiving valproate when lamotrigine is added. Valproate's inhibition of lamotrigine metabolism results in significantly lower lamotrigine dosage requirements; side effects appear to be much more common with lamotrigine doses above 200 mg when it is administered with valproate monotherapy.

As R.H. is currently receiving carbamazepine, induction of liver enzymes is likely to increase her dosage requirements for lamotrigine and allow a less conservative dosage titration. An initial dose of 50 mg/day with increases of 50 mg/day every one to two weeks should be recommended. R.H. should be instructed to take the medication daily at bedtime. She also should be told that she may feel drowsy and possibly experience headache and upset stomach, but that these side effects usually disappear with ongoing therapy. R.H. should contact her physician or other health professional if

Table 52.7	Antiepileptic Drugs in Development[a],[107],[117–123],[256]			
Drug	**Efficacy/Seizure Types**	**Pharmacokinetics**	**Dosage**	**Adverse Effects and Drug Interactions**
Vigabatrin (Sabril)	Partial and secondarily generalized	F >60%; Vd = 0.6–0.8 L/kg; no protein binding; 60%–70% renal excretion; t½ = 5–7 hr. Serum concentrations probably not helpful; irreversible inhibitor of GABA-transaminase	2000–4000 mg/day; QD dosing sufficient	Sedation, dizziness, fatigue common with add-on therapy. Psychosis uncommon but may be severe. May precipitate absence seizures. No drug interactions reported
Tiagabine (TGB)	Partial and secondarily generalized; other types undetermined	F ≈ 100%; t½ = 4.5–13.5 hr (monotherapy); t½ ↓ by enzyme-inducing AEDs. 96% protein bound	Up to 80 mg/day. TID or QID dosing probably required	Drowsiness, dizziness, headache, tremor common. No metabolic or hematologic adverse effects noted. Hepatic clearance ↑ by enzyme-inducing drugs (e.g., phenobarbital, phenytoin, carbamazepine). Potential for protein-binding displacement interactions with other highly-bound drugs
Topiramate (TPM)	Partial; possible efficacy in secondarily generalized	Well-absorbed orally; F ≥80%; t½ = 20–24 hr; ≈ 50% renal elimination. 9%–17% protein bound	Slow dosage titration to minimize dose-related side effects. Usual doses of 300–900 mg/day. TID dosing	Sedation, confusion, paresthesias, and cognitive dysfunction. No drug interactions reported
Oxcarbazepine (OCBZ) (Trileptal)	Partial and secondarily generalized	Pro-Drug. Converted to active monohydroxy derivative (MHD) of carbamazepine. F ≈100%; t½ (MHD) = 8–13 hr; low protein binding; not metabolized via epoxide pathway	≈50% higher than carbamazepine doses when converting from carbamazepine to oxcarbazepine. 600–1200 mg/day; BID–TID	Fatigue, headache, ataxia, and dizziness. May cause hyponatremia. Rash less common than with carbamazepine. Does not appear to induce hepatic enzymes. Few drug interactions noted. May reduce plasma levels of estrogens
Fosphenytoin (Cerebyx)	Convulsive status epilepticus; partial and secondarily generalized; parenteral replacement for oral phenytoin	Rapidly and completely absorbed after IM administration. IV/IM administration well-tolerated with ↓ venous/tissue irritation. Rapid conversion to phenytoin. Disposition pharmacokinetics same as phenytoin	Fosphenytoin 75 mg = 50 mg sodium phenytoin. Doses calculated in terms of phenytoin equivalents	Same as phenytoin. Less tissue/venous irritation when given parenterally. Same as phenytoin

[a] AED = Antiepileptic drug; F = Bioavailability; GABA = Gamma-aminobutyric acid; IM = Intramuscular; IV = Intravenous; MHD = Monohydroxy derivative; t½ = Half-life; Vd = Volume of distribution.

severe side effects occur which make it difficult to take the medication; this is especially important if she should develop a skin rash.

11. Side Effects and Possible Interaction with Carbamazepine. Two days after her dose of lamotrigine was increased to 300 mg/day (12 weeks after beginning therapy), R.H. noticed that her vision was blurring; she also complained of feeling dizzy and having difficulty maintaining her balance. Previously she had experienced only mild, occasional nausea. She had continued to experience seizures at approximately the same frequency she had before initiation of Lamotrigine. Her physician had encouraged her to continue taking the medication and explained that it would take time to increase the dose to possibly effective levels. Serum concentrations of carbamazepine and CBZ-E were 13.5 µg/mL and 3.1 µg/mL, respectively. Do these new side effects represent treatment failure with lamotrigine? If not, how might these new side effects be managed?

It is possible that R.H.'s seizure disorder is unresponsive to lamotrigine therapy and that her side effects may limit further dose increases. Her present side effects, on clinical grounds, might represent either carbamazepine intoxication or lamotrigine side effects. Since R.H. tolerated the same carbamazepine serum concentration previously, her symptoms may represent lamotrigine "intoxication." Nevertheless, it may be of some value to determine a lamotrigine serum concentration to aid in further assessing her situation. While a usual "therapeutic range" for lamotrigine serum concentrations has not been established, evidence from clinical trials indicates that serum lamotrigine concentrations up to 5 µg/mL have been free of toxicity.[107] If R.H.'s serum lamotrigine concentration is below 5 µg/mL, her symptoms may be related to the apparent interaction between lamotrigine and carbamazepine reported by some authors.[106] Side effects experienced by some patients taking both drugs seem to be related to carbamazepine rather than lamotrigine and can be relieved by carbamazepine dose reduction. Subsequently, it may be possible to further increase lamotrigine doses. As determination of serum lamotrigine concentrations is not yet widely available and reporting of results may be delayed for several days, this situation also could be assessed and possibly managed by empirically decreasing R.H.'s carbamazepine dose by 200 to 400 mg/day and observing the effect on her side effects.

Gabapentin Therapy

12. Initiation and Dosage Titration. R.H.'s carbamazepine dose was reduced to 1400 mg/day and a serum lamotrigine concentration was determined. After 5 days her symptoms persisted, and she continued to have seizures. The serum lamotrigine concentration was 4.1 µg/mL. A decision was made to abandon lamotrigine therapy and institute treatment with gabapentin. Recommend a plan for initiation of gabapentin treatment of R.H.

R.H.'s apparent lamotrigine-related side effects continued and did not respond to a reduction in her carbamazepine dose. Since a higher carbamazepine dose was used previously and produced a partial response for R.H., the dose of carbamazepine should be returned to 1800 mg/day. Her lamotrigine dose should be reduced in an effort to alleviate her side effects. There is little specific information available to allow one to determine how safely lamotrigine can be discontinued. As a general rule, rapid discontinuation of AEDs is not recommended in other than emergency situations. Therefore, immediate reduction of R.H.'s lamotrigine dose to 200 mg/day would seem reasonable. This dose could then be reduced in decrements of 50 to 100 mg every week until lamotrigine was discontinued.

Gabapentin treatment can be instituted immediately for R.H. There is no evidence that gabapentin interacts with other AEDs,

and R.H. is continuing to have seizures. Therefore, discontinuation of lamotrigine during initiation of gabapentin should not create difficulties in the assessment of R.H.'s response. Gabapentin should be initiated at a dose of 100 mg three times daily, and R.H. should be instructed to space the three daily doses as evenly as possible. Gabapentin has a relatively short half-life and even spacing of doses may improve the antiepileptic response by reducing fluctuations in serum and brain concentrations. The manufacturer of gabapentin recommends that no more than 12 hours elapse between doses. R.H.'s daily gabapentin dose can be increased by 300 mg every one or two days, according to her tolerance of side effects, until her daily dose reaches at least 900 mg. While there may be a significant response to a dose of 900 mg/day, many patients require doses of 1800 to 2400 mg/day of gabapentin.[123,124] As the drug reaches steady-state quickly, upward dosage changes frequently can be made based upon the R.H.'s tolerance of side effects and her seizure frequency. At present, there is no well defined relationship between serum concentrations of gabapentin and therapeutic response or symptoms of intoxication. Preliminary information indicates that serum concentrations above 2 µg/mL may be associated with an improved therapeutic response.[124] Therefore, R.H.'s dose should be titrated to maximum tolerated levels which are required to control her seizure activity. There is limited published experience with gabapentin doses as high as 3600 mg/day.[125]

Patient Instructions. R.H. should be informed that, while she is being started on gabapentin, she may experience side effects similar to those she had with lamotrigine, but that they should be temporary. A great deal of reassurance and encouragement may need to be given along with this information to help ensure that R.H. adheres to her treatment regimen. Many patients become discouraged when multiple trials of medication are necessary and side effects are prominent. This may result in their expressing feelings of being "guinea pigs" and becoming uncooperative with therapeutic plans.

Phenytoin Therapy

13. J.N., an 18-year-old, 88 kg male college student, was diagnosed as having epilepsy. He experiences generalized tonic-clonic seizures which last approximately 2 minutes approximately 3 times monthly. Before his seizures, J.N. describes a "churning" feeling in his abdomen; this is followed by involuntary right-sided jerking of his upper extremities during which J.N. is awake and aware of his surroundings. His seizures have been observed and described well both by his family and by nursing staff who cared for him during a brief hospitalization following his first seizure. An EEG showed diffuse slowing with focal epileptiform discharges in the left temporal area; it was interpreted as abnormal. No correctable cause for his seizure disorder was identified despite a thorough workup. He has no other medical conditions and takes no routine medications. He was treated initially with carbamazepine up to 600 mg/day. He was unable to tolerate the medication because of nausea and diplopia despite serum concentrations of only 5 µg/mL. His physician has elected to implement a therapeutic trial of phenytoin for J.N. Recommend an initial dose and describe the information which should be provided to J.N. regarding his new medication.

Initiation and Dosage. Selection of a nontoxic, therapeutic dose of any drug is difficult in the absence of information regarding the drug's disposition in the individual patient (i.e., prior doses and resulting steady-state serum concentrations and clinical response). Although average doses and resulting serum concentrations often are quoted, there is significant interpatient variability. Phenytoin serum concentrations of ≥10 µg/mL will be achieved in many adults receiving 4 to 5 mg/kg/day of phenytoin; however, either subtherapeutic or potentially toxic concentrations also may occur in significant numbers.[39] Therefore, careful monitoring of patient response is necessary to help ensure effective, nontoxic therapy. An initial dose of 400 mg/day would be appropriate for J.N. This represents a dose of approximately 4.5 mg/kg/day.

Patient Information. In addition to the name and strength of the medication and instructions for when and how it should be taken, J.N. should be informed that he initially may experience some initial mild sedation from phenytoin. He should be cautioned that symptoms such as blurred or double vision, dysarthria ("thick" tongue), dizziness, or staggering may indicate that his dose is too high; he should be instructed to notify his physician, pharmacist, or other health professional of these symptoms. It is also a good idea to inform patients, at the beginning of therapy, that adjustments of medication dosage and possibly medication changes may be necessary before medication is stabilized. This may help patients avoid the feeling that they are a "guinea pig" upon whom the doctor is continually experimenting.

14. Accumulation Pharmacokinetics. What are the characteristics of phenytoin accumulation pharmacokinetics? When should phenytoin serum concentrations be determined in J.N.?

Phenytoin exhibits dose-dependent (Michaelis-Menten or capacity-limited) pharmacokinetics; therefore, the usual pharmacokinetic concepts of "clearance" and "half-life" are meaningless. The apparent half-life of phenytoin changes with dose and serum concentration. Thus, the time required to reach a new steady state after alteration in dosage is difficult to predict as it depends upon the dose itself and the patient's pharmacokinetic parameters, Vmax and Km.[39] Vmax is a kinetic constant representing the maximum rate of phenytoin elimination from the body. Km is the Michaelis Constant; it is the serum concentration at which the rate of elimination is one-half of Vmax. Values for these parameters vary widely among patients; as a result, patterns of phenytoin accumulation and the time required to achieve steady state also are variable. Many clinicians assume that phenytoin's apparent half-life is approximately 24 hours, and wait five to seven days before assessing the patient's clinical response and measuring serum phenytoin concentrations. Both clinical studies[126] and model simulations[127] using observed values for Km and Vmax indicated that up to 30 days may be required for serum concentrations to reach 90% of the steady state resulting from a dose of 4 mg/kg/day. Occasionally such a dose may exceed a patient's Vmax; the result is accumulation of extremely high serum phenytoin concentrations with probable intoxication. If doses sufficient to produce steady-state serum concentrations of 10 to 15 µg/mL are given, 5 to 30 days may be required to achieve 90% of these concentrations.[39,127] One should not assume that steady state has been reached unless widely-spaced, serial serum concentrations indicate that accumulation has ceased. Alterations in phenytoin dosage before steady state has been reached may result in marked fluctuations in serum concentrations and the patient's clinical status. In this author's experience, such situations occur frequently in practice and result in unnecessary confusion and expense.

Given the variability in phenytoin's accumulation pharmacokinetics, a reasonable approach to timing of serum concentration measurements would involve weekly serum concentration determinations during the first month of treatment to detect either excessive accumulation or subtherapeutic dosing. Even though serum concentrations appear stable and are in the usual therapeutic range after one month, continued slow accumulation may occur. Close monitoring of phenytoin serum concentrations is still advisable after this period. As always, serum concentrations in J.N. must be interpreted in the context of his clinical response.

15. Oral Loading Doses. Would a loading dose be of value for J.N. to reduce the potential delay in achieving a "therapeutic" serum concentration of phenytoin? How large a loading dose should be used and how should it be administered?

Administration of a loading dose would allow therapeutic serum concentrations of phenytoin to be achieved more rapidly. More rapid control of J.N.'s seizure activity also would result. As he is active and pursuing an education, more rapid seizure control may be a significant therapeutic goal. Available studies of oral phenytoin loading indicate that doses of approximately 18 mg/kg will achieve serum concentrations approaching the usual therapeutic range after approximately eight hours in most patients.[128,129] Loading doses appear to be better tolerated when administered in divided doses over four or more hours. GI upset appears to the most common side effect related to this procedure. Cardiac side effects (e.g., sinus bradycardia, shortened PR intervals) have been observed rarely; they were not related to serum phenytoin concentrations and their significance is uncertain.[130]

Oral phenytoin absorption after large doses is unpredictably slow and it may be less complete than after smaller doses.[131] While potentially therapeutic serum concentrations usually are seen after approximately eight hours, peak concentrations may not occur for up to 60 hours following administration of large single doses.[39,130,131] Record et al. estimated that 18 mg/kg given in three doses over six hours would produce serum concentrations of 13 to 20 µg/mL 12 hours after completion of loading.[132] No rigorous clinical evaluations of this recommendation are available, although these suggested doses compare well with intravenous loading regimens. Intravenous loading doses of 18 mg/kg will maintain phenytoin serum concentrations above 10 µg/mL for 24 hours.[133]

While administration of an oral loading dose to J.N. is pharmacokinetically sound and has certain therapeutic advantages, practical difficulties in monitoring an ambulatory patient for potential complications may indicate caution in recommending such a procedure. Additionally, as J.N. had difficulty tolerating carbamazepine, it may be difficult to justify exposing him to the potential neurologic side effects of a phenytoin loading dose. A more practical approach with a lower risk of complications involves administration of 1.5 to 2 times the prescribed maintenance dose for the first two or three days of treatment. Serum phenytoin concentrations should be checked on the day following completion of such a "miniloading" and weekly thereafter.

16. Phenytoin Intoxication. J.N. was given phenytoin 200 mg a.m. and 400 mg p.m. for 3 days. A phenytoin serum concentration drawn the morning of the 4th day was reported as 12 µg/mL. No seizures had occurred, and there were no side effects other than mild morning sedation. He was then instructed to take only 400 mg at bedtime. One week later, his phenytoin concentration was reported as 18 µg/mL. Mild nystagmus on far lateral gaze was noted, but J.N. had no subjective complaints and remained seizure-free. After 3 weeks, J.N. complained of double vision and feeling "drunk" and "unsteady." Significant nystagmus was present. His phenytoin concentration was 24 µg/mL. How should J.N.'s phenytoin dosage be altered?

J.N.'s signs and symptoms in conjunction with the phenytoin serum concentration indicate mild phenytoin intoxication. Dosage reduction is indicated. As there is no indication that steady state has been achieved, techniques for estimating J.N.'s Vmax and Km cannot be readily employed; the size of any dose reduction must be determined empirically.

Reduction of J.N.'s dose to 360 or 330 mg/day would be reasonable. This dosage reduction can be accomplished using 30 mg phenytoin capsules along with the usual 100 mg capsules. A larger reduction may result in a dramatic fall in serum concentrations with some risk of loss of seizure control. Many clinicians also would have J.N. omit one day's dose of phenytoin before beginning the new maintenance dose. This would accelerate the decline in phenytoin serum levels. Following this dosage change, clinical response and serum concentrations should be monitored closely. It is possible that the new maintenance dose may still be excessive; if J.N.'s Vmax for phenytoin is low, continued accumulation of drug may occur and serum concentrations may continue to increase despite the dose reduction.[39]

17. Bioequivalence of Dosage Forms. S.D. is a 24-year-old male state hospital patient with a history of complex partial and secondarily generalized tonic-clonic seizures. On his present phenytoin dose of 300 mg/day, his serum phenytoin concentrations have ranged from 3.2–13.5 µg/mL. Control of his seizures also fluctuates widely correlating well with plasma concentrations of phenytoin. Nurses suspect S.D. of "cheeking" his phenytoin capsules, and his phenytoin has been changed to suspension form to reduce opportunities for this behavior. Discuss differences in bioavailability and biopharmaceutic among phenytoin dosage forms. Based upon these differences, what would be an appropriate dose of phenytoin suspension for S.D.?

Surreptitious refusal to take medications is a frequent problem in psychiatric patients. In addition, elderly, physically handicapped, or pediatric patients may have difficulty swallowing capsules. In these situations, phenytoin suspension is potentially useful.

There are no reported significant differences in bioavailability between phenytoin (i.e., Dilantin, Parke-Davis) suspension and capsules; in addition, chewable phenytoin tablets (i.e., Dilantin Infatabs) are equally well absorbed.[39] The suspension and chewable tablets, however, contain phenytoin free acid; capsules contain sodium phenytoin. Unlike many drugs, phenytoin products are labeled with their contents listed as either phenytoin acid or sodium phenytoin rather than in terms of active drug. Therefore, phenytoin capsule products contain only 92% of the labeled content as phenytoin acid (i.e., a 100 mg sodium phenytoin capsule contains only 92 mg of phenytoin acid). Because small changes in dose may result in dramatic changes in phenytoin serum concentrations and clinical response, this difference in phenytoin content should be considered when dosage forms are changed.[134] This difference in phenytoin content also accounts for apparent differences in bioavailability perceived by some clinicians when patients are changed from phenytoin capsules to either tablets or suspension.

If it is assumed that 300 mg of phenytoin capsules is a therapeutic daily dose for S.D., an appropriate dose of phenytoin suspension would be approximately 92% of 300 mg or 275 mg. This would be 11 mL of the adult phenytoin suspension containing 125 mg/5 mL. It is important to ensure that the proper form of phenytoin suspension is prescribed and dispensed. Two strengths of phenytoin suspension are available; the "pediatric" suspension contains 30 mg/5 mL, while the "adult" suspension contains 125 mg/5 mL.

18. Patient Information. What special instructions should be provided to S.D. or the nursing staff to ensure proper, efficacious administration of this medication?

In the author's experience, use of phenytoin suspension often results in unstable phenytoin serum concentrations and seizure control. This instability has been attributed to rapid settling of suspension between doses; however, significant between-dose or long-term settling does not appear to explain the clinical instability in patients receiving this dosage form. More likely, observed fluctuations in patients' status result from inconsistent or improper dose measurement.[135,136] An accurate dosage measuring device such as an oral syringe should be provided with phenytoin suspension. Patients or caregivers should be informed of the importance of accurate dose measurement and discouraged from using household measures such as "teaspoons." The person measuring the dose should be instructed to thoroughly shake the container before measuring each dose. Crushed chewable phenytoin tablets may provide better clinical stability and acceptable ease of administration in situations where use of phenytoin suspension is considered.

19. Extended-Release Dosage Forms. Is there any need to alter the frequency of phenytoin administration when phenytoin suspension is used for S.D.?

The FDA requires phenytoin capsule preparations to be labeled as either "prompt" or "extended" on the basis of their rates of dissolution and absorption. Only extended phenytoin products are recommended for once daily dosing. Presumably, use of rapidly absorbed preparations as single daily doses will result in wide fluctuation of phenytoin serum concentrations between doses and cause either loss of seizure control or toxicity.

Published documentation of significant differences in phenytoin serum concentrations and clinical response resulting from the use of rapidly- versus slowly-absorbed preparations during maintenance therapy is lacking.[137] A single dose study in normal volunteers compared the absorption characteristics and bioavailability of phenytoin extended-release capsules and phenytoin suspension.[138] There were no significant differences in bioavailability or pharmacokinetics between the two dosage forms, and once-daily administration of properly measured phenytoin suspension is feasible on the basis of pharmacokinetic characteristics. Most studies of the feasibility of single daily phenytoin doses have used Parke-Davis' Kapseals.[139,140] The likely effects of absorption rate and dosing interval on steady-state phenytoin serum concentration have been examined using a Michaelis-Menten pharmacokinetic model.[141] Predicted fluctuations resulting from use of rapidly-absorbed products administered once daily are not likely to be clinically significant unless the patient requires a very high daily dose or has a low therapeutic index. Although the rate of phenytoin absorption does not appear to be of major clinical significance to therapy, extent of absorption (relative bioavailability) may dramatically affect steady-state serum concentrations and clinical response. Dose-dependent pharmacokinetics magnify the effects of even minor changes in bioavailability or variations in drug content between dosage forms.[142] Therefore, the clinical significance of differences in absorption rates for oral phenytoin preparations is yet to be determined, but, at present, it appears to be minor.[137,141,143] In situations where there is concern regarding possible fluctuations in serum concentrations, use of a twice daily dosing schedule should alleviate any potential problems.

S.D. can probably be adequately managed with administration of his phenytoin suspension as a single daily dose. His clinical response and serum concentrations should be monitored to detect significant effects of the suspension or dosage schedule on seizure control.

20. Intramuscular (IM) Phenytoin and Phenytoin Prodrug (Fosphenytoin). S.D. has been stabilized while receiving 275 mg/day of phenytoin as suspension. Serum drug concentrations are stable at 10–12 µg/mL, and he has had no seizures for 2 months. S.D. has been transferred to the acute medical unit following a 2-day history of anorexia, nausea, occasional vomiting, and abdominal pain accompanied by diarrhea. He is now nothing per os (NPO). IM phenytoin has been ordered. Discuss the biopharmaceutical differences between PO and IM phenytoin and devise a dosage regimen and plan for use of IM phenytoin in S.D.

Intramuscular administration of phenytoin generally is not recommended, especially in situations requiring either rapid onset of effect or long-term therapy. Injectable phenytoin is highly alkaline (pH 12) and potentially very irritating to tissue. Following IM injection, the drug may precipitate at the injection site because of the change in pH. As a result, phenytoin crystals form a repository or depot from which the drug is slowly absorbed.[144-146] There may be injection site discomfort, although severe muscle damage does not seem to occur.[146] As parenteral phenytoin products contain only 50 mg/mL of sodium phenytoin, multiple injections of a maximum of 2 to 3 mL each will be necessary in most patients. Absorption is approximately 93% complete from IM sites, but it is prolonged for three to five days.[144]

Conversion to intramuscular phenytoin requires careful dosage adjustment based upon cumbersome calculations. It is unpleasant for patients and carries risks of either over- or underdosage. This drug should be administered intravenously if possible whenever oral administration is not feasible. (See Questions 48 and 49 for discussion of IV phenytoin administration.)

In the near future, an alternative to IM administration of phenytoin probably will become available. Fosphenytoin (phenytoin prodrug) is currently undergoing phase III clinical trials and appears to be a safe and effective preparation. Fosphenytoin is a phosphate ester of phenytoin which is water soluble. Its solubility allows this preparation to be administered parenterally without the need for solubilization using propylene glycol or the adjustment of pH. Therefore, fosphenytoin may be administered either IM or IV with less risk of tissue damage, venous irritation, or cardiovascular and respiratory adverse effects associated with parenteral administration of phenytoin.[147] After administration, the prodrug is rapidly absorbed and converted to phenytoin by phosphatase enzymes. When this preparation becomes available, it may allow a practical method for IM administration of phenytoin.[148]

21. Adverse Effects: Gingival Hyperplasia. **M.N., a 10-year-old boy receiving 150 mg/day of phenytoin as chewable tablets, is to be fitted with braces for his teeth. He currently exhibits moderate gingival hyperplasia resulting in difficulty maintaining oral hygiene and associated with halitosis. Discuss phenytoin-related gingival hyperplasia and possible management techniques which may be helpful for M.N.**

Gum hyperplasia related to phenytoin is common and troublesome. Prevalence is estimated at up to 90%,[149] depending upon the rating system used and the degree of gum change rated as hyperplastic. A realistic prevalence estimate is probably 40% to 50% of treated patients.[150] Prevalence and incidence rates, however, are misleading because the occurrence and severity of hyperplasia are related to the dose and serum concentration of phenytoin.[150,151] Gingival hyperplasia is of obvious cosmetic importance. Also, as in M.N. formation of pockets of tissue leads to difficulties with oral hygiene; severe halitosis may result.

The mechanism of phenytoin-induced gingival hyperplasia is not well understood. The drug is excreted in saliva, and there is a correlation between saliva phenytoin concentrations and hyperplasia; however, this correlation may simply reflect higher serum concentrations producing greater pharmacologic effect. Phenytoin may stimulate gingival mast cells to release heparin and other mediators. These mediators may encourage synthesis of excessive amounts of new connective tissue by fibroblasts. Local irritation due to dental plaque and food particles may further stimulate this process. Some patients may be especially predisposed to gum hyperplasia because they accumulate higher concentrations of phenytoin in gum tissue.[150,151]

There are three approaches to treatment of existing hyperplasia:[151] 1) dosage reduction or discontinuation of phenytoin (and replacement with an alternate AED), if possible, will permit partial or complete reversal of hyperplasia. 2) surgical gingivectomy will correct the problem temporarily, but hyperplasia eventually recurs. 3) oral physiotherapy (periodontal treatment) eliminates local irritants and maintains oral hygiene. As M.N. is to be fitted with braces which will further complicate oral hygiene, institution of some form of treatment for existing hyperplasia and prevention of further tissue enlargement are important. Assuming phenytoin is producing adequate seizure control, a combination of gingivectomy and follow-up periodontal treatment may be the best approach.

Theoretically, use of chewable phenytoin tablets in M.N. may aggravate hyperplasia. Exposure of gingiva to high localized concentrations of phenytoin may result from braces holding tablet fragments in close physical contact with gum tissue. The significance of this relationship, however, is questionable. If M.N. is able to swallow capsules, a change to this dosage form may be beneficial and usually will be less expensive. The most appropriate dose of phenytoin sodium capsules for M.N. would be 160 mg/day. If chewable tablets are used, having M.N. rinse and swallow after each dose may eliminate potential problems. Use of phenytoin suspension also may be a theoretically useful option. Drug particles, however, may still be retained by the braces, and maintenance of uniform dosage may be more difficult.

Oral hygiene programs appear to effectively reduce the degree and severity of gingival hyperplasia when they are initiated before phenytoin therapy.[151] Patients who are beginning phenytoin therapy should be educated as to the role of oral hygiene in diminishing this side effect. The use of dental floss, gum stimulators, and Water Pik-type appliances may be beneficial adjuncts to other oral hygiene techniques.

22. Encephalopathy. **G.R. is a 53-year-old male with primary generalized epilepsy characterized by occasional tonic-clonic seizures. His phenytoin dose was recently increased from 300 mg/day to 400 mg/day in response to an increase in seizure frequency. At 300 mg/day, his serum phenytoin concentration was 11 lg/mL. After 3 weeks at the new dose, G.R. is brought to the physician by his sister who reports that he has become confused, staggers, and has developed "funny" movements of his face and arms. In addition, he has experienced several unusual seizures over the past few days which consist of arching his neck and back for 10–20 seconds with mild clonic movements of both arms. Abnormal facial and arm movements are noted to consist of rapid, jerky random movements of the arms and repetitive rolling tongue movements accompanied by facial grimacing. G.R. is oriented to time and place. No nystagmus is seen. What is the relationship of G.R.'s symptoms to his phenytoin therapy?**

G.R. is probably experiencing phenytoin encephalopathy, an acute change in mental status and seizure frequency which may accompany elevated phenytoin serum concentrations. His choreiform movements also may be a result of phenytoin intoxication.[152] Based upon his previous serum concentration and the magnitude of the recent dose increase, intoxication with phenytoin is likely and should be confirmed by a serum phenytoin concentration determination. In addition, a complete neurologic examination should be performed to rule out other potential causes for G.R.'s sudden change in neurologic status.

Increased seizure frequency and a change in seizure pattern to include manifestations of opisthotonos may accompany phenytoin encephalopathy. The actual frequency with which seizures occur during phenytoin intoxication is controversial.[153-155] Changes in mental status (e.g., confusion and delirium) frequently accompany the increase in seizure activity. While this syndrome is probably much less common than classical phenytoin intoxication (i.e., nystagmus, ataxia, CNS depression), clinicians should be alert for its possible occurrence. On clinical grounds, one may be tempted to further increase the phenytoin dosage in an effort to control the increased seizures, while dose reduction is actually the appropriate method of correcting the situation. The absence of nystagmus in some cases further complicates assessment. Nystagmus may not appear until phenytoin concentrations fall.[152]

Choreiform movement disorders are an uncommon complication of phenytoin therapy. Affected patients are often mentally retarded or have functional or structural CNS impairment. Patients also may exhibit dystonia and asterixis.[152,156] The movement disorders usually are reversible after discontinuation of phenytoin. Other AEDs also may cause dyskinesias as a part of an intoxication syndrome.[157]

23. *Neurotoxicity.* **G.R.'s serum phenytoin concentration was reported as 32 μg/mL. The neurological evaluation was otherwise negative. After the daily dose of phenytoin was reduced to 360 mg, his mental symptoms cleared and the choreiform movements disappeared. No seizures occurred during the following 8 weeks. He continued to complain of being mildly "unsteady" on his feet. Nystagmus on far lateral gaze appeared. Serum phenytoin was decreased to 24 μg/mL. As G.R.'s seizures are apparently under complete control, is there any problem maintaining him on mildly intoxicating doses of phenytoin? Does prolonged intoxication with phenytoin increase the likelihood of permanent neurologic impairment?**

Patients chronically maintained on intoxicating doses of phenytoin appear to be at some risk for developing irreversible cerebellar damage or peripheral neuropathy. Cerebellar degeneration resulting in symptoms such as dysarthria, ataxic gait, intention tremor, and muscular hypotonia is of particular concern.[152,158] Generalized seizures also may cause cerebellar degeneration secondary to hypoxia. For this reason, there is controversy concerning the relative importance of phenytoin in the development of this condition. Nevertheless, a number of cases involved patients without hypoxic seizures.[158,159]

Symptomatic phenytoin-related peripheral neuropathy is rare, although electrophysiologic evidence of impaired neuronal conduction may be found in a large number of patients.[152,160] Symptomatic patients may complain of paresthesias, muscle weakness, and occasional muscle wasting. Knee and ankle tendon reflexes are absent in 18% of patients on long-term phenytoin therapy; the upper limbs are affected rarely. Although areflexia may be irreversible,[161] electrophysiologic abnormalities may be closely related to excessive serum phenytoin concentrations and are reversible following dose reduction or discontinuation.[159]

In G.R., the general discomfort of mild phenytoin intoxication and the potential for producing cerebellar degeneration would appear to dictate an alteration in therapy. The phenytoin dose should be reduced to 330 mg/day, because this dose may produce adequate seizure control without toxic symptoms. Should seizures recur at this lower dose, it may be advisable to attempt to treat G.R. with an alternate AED.

24. Interaction with Valproate. **G.R.'s phenytoin dose was reduced to 330 mg/day. Over the following 6 weeks, serum phenytoin concentrations decreased to 18 μg/mL and there was complete reversal of neurotoxic symptoms. G.R. has once again begun to experience generalized tonic-clonic seizures twice monthly. His seizures appear to be primary; there is no aura, and there are no focal changes on EEG. His physician decided to initiate treatment with divalproex (Depakote). The therapeutic goal is to titrate divalproex to achieve seizure control and subsequently discontinue phenytoin. Divalproex was started at 250 mg TID and, over 3 weeks, increased to 1000 mg BID. At the next office visit, G.R. complained of again feeling "unsteady" on his feet. Nystagmus on far lateral gaze was again noted. Serum concentrations of valproic acid and phenytoin were 62 μg/mL and 15 μg/mL, respectively. A complete laboratory screening battery showed no abnormalities other than a serum albumin concentration of 3.0 gm/dL. How might**

the interaction between valproate (divalproex) and phenytoin have caused these symptoms? How should this interaction be managed? [SI unit: 30 gm/L]

The interaction between valproate and phenytoin is often troublesome because clinical manifestations of the interaction may not correlate with serum drug concentrations. Valproate potentially has two effects on phenytoin's pharmacokinetic disposition; the clinical results of this interaction will vary among individuals depending upon the magnitude of each effect and the patient's ability to metabolize phenytoin. Valproate displaces phenytoin from binding sites on serum albumin causing an increase in the free fraction of phenytoin. For some patients, there is no net clinical effect of this displacement because metabolism of phenytoin increases and free serum concentrations of phenytoin return to their predisplacement levels. Under these circumstances, total serum phenytoin concentration would be reduced while the free fraction would remain elevated. If a patient's serum concentration of phenytoin is high enough to approach saturation of metabolic enzymes, the increase in metabolism of unbound phenytoin may not occur. As a result, unbound concentrations of phenytoin may remain elevated, and total serum phenytoin concentrations may change only slightly or even increase. Valproate also is capable of inhibiting the metabolism of several drugs, including phenytoin. This effect may cause an increase in both unbound and total serum phenytoin concentrations.[162–164] Owing to the complexity of mechanisms involved in this interaction, prediction of the clinical or pharmacokinetic effect of addition of valproate to phenytoin therapy is extremely difficult. Clinicians should be aware that there is a possibility of a significant, persistent increase in the serum concentration of unbound, pharmacologically active phenytoin. The clinical status of the patient must be monitored carefully; determination of free (unbound) serum phenytoin concentrations may provide information helpful in assessing reasons for any changes observed in clinical status. Most clinical laboratories can provide analysis of free serum phenytoin concentrations, although samples may need to be sent to an outside reference laboratory resulting in a delay of several days before results are available.

In G.R.'s case, it appears likely that the addition of valproate has caused unbound phenytoin serum concentrations to increase significantly. This interaction usually is not observed unless serum valproate concentrations approach 100 μg/mL. G.R.'s slightly reduced serum albumin level may account for this interaction's occurrence. In the presence of a reduced serum albumin concentration, binding sites for phenytoin and valproate are already limited; therefore, displacement interactions such as this are more likely to occur. G.R.'s symptoms are identical to those he exhibited previously while intoxicated on phenytoin; they are not characteristic of symptoms associated with initiation of valproate therapy. The elevation in unbound serum phenytoin concentration has the same effect as an increase in his phenytoin dose. G.R.'s total phenytoin serum concentration of 15 μg/mL is misleading because it does not reflect the increased free fraction and free concentration of phenytoin. A free phenytoin serum concentration should be determined to help in assessing this situation. As there may be a delay in receiving the results of this laboratory test, G.R.'s phenytoin dose should be reduced empirically to alleviate his toxicity. A reduction of at least 30 mg/day in G.R.'s dose would be appropriate.

25. G.R.'s phenytoin dose was held for 1 day and then reduced to 300 mg/day. Within 3 days his symptoms had improved significantly. The serum concentration of free phenytoin was reported as 2.4 μg/mL (usual therapeutic range: 1.0–2.0 μg/mL). As G.R. remained seizure-free, his phenytoin dose was tapered by 30 mg/day to 40 mg/day every week in an effort to eliminate phenytoin and employ divalproex monother-

apy. What effect is discontinuation of phenytoin likely to have on G.R.'s valproate serum concentrations and his clinical response? How should G.R. be monitored during this reduction?

The interaction between phenytoin and valproate also involves stimulation of valproate metabolism. Induction of hepatic metabolic enzymes by phenytoin may significantly increase the clearance of valproate.[165] During concomitant therapy, larger doses of valproate will be required to achieve effective serum concentrations. Upon discontinuation of an enzyme inducer such as phenytoin, valproate serum concentrations may increase significantly as clearance decreases. In this author's experience, discontinuation of phenytoin (and other enzyme inducing drugs such as carbamazepine) is not always associated with a gradual stepwise increase in valproate serum concentrations. Instead, valproate concentrations may increase only slightly until phenytoin is discontinued completely. Subsequently, there may be striking increase in valproate concentrations as hepatic metabolism returns to normal levels. G.R. should be monitored for clinical signs and symptoms which may indicate excessive serum valproate concentrations (see below). In addition, measurement of serum concentrations of valproate will allow detection of excessive elevations. While elevated valproate serum concentrations do not always indicate intoxication, they may be useful as guidelines for reduction in the dose of divalproex which G.R. receives. If his seizures remain well controlled, the dose of divalproex can be reduced to the lowest level necessary to produce serum concentrations which are therapeutic for G.R. During phenytoin reduction, valproate serum concentrations should be monitored every one to two weeks. Following complete discontinuation of phenytoin, this pattern of monitoring should be continued for at least an additional four to eight weeks. G.R. also should be instructed to report any signs or symptoms which may be due to excessive valproate serum concentrations (e.g., GI symptoms such as nausea, tremor, or drowsiness).[166]

Absence Seizures

Choice of Medication and Initiation of Ethosuximide Therapy

26. T.D., a 7-year-old, 25 kg girl, is reported by her teacher to have 3–4 episodes of "staring" daily. Each spell lasts 5–10 seconds. There are no convulsive movements although her eyelids appear to flutter during the episodes. She is fully alert afterward. T.D.'s school performance is somewhat below average, despite an IQ of 125. An EEG shows 3/second spike-wave activity. Typical absence epilepsy is diagnosed. A physical examination and laboratory evaluation are normal, and there are no other positive findings on neurologic examination. What drug should be prescribed for T.D., and how should therapy with this drug be initiated?

Only a small number of drugs are routinely used for treatment of absence epilepsy (see Tables 52.2 and 52.8). At present, ethosuximide (Zarontin) and valproate are the primary drugs available in the U.S., and both drugs are equally effective against absence seizures. Trimethadione (Tridione) was formerly used, but it is less effective and is associated with a high rate of neurologic side effects and risk of hematologic toxicity.[167] Ethosuximide is presently considered the drug of first choice for treatment of absence seizures by most authorities. Controlled trials have demonstrated its efficacy, and it is potentially less toxic than valproate. In comparison to ethosuximide, valproate is more likely to cause significant nausea and initial drowsiness; it is more expensive than ethosuximide; and it is more likely to interact with other AEDs. Valproate usually is reserved for patients with absence seizures who do not respond to ethosuximide.[168] Clonazepam (Klonopin), a benzodiazepine, often is effective for control of absence seizures. Therapy with this

drug is limited by prominent CNS side effects (sedation, ataxia, and mood changes) and development of tolerance to its antiepileptic effect after long-term use.[169] Clonazepam is considered a third-choice drug for treatment of absence by most authorities.

Ethosuximide therapy should be initiated for T.D. at a dose of 15 to 20 mg/kg/day or 250 mg twice daily. The daily dose can be increased by 250 mg every 10 to 14 days as necessary to control seizures. Since the average half-life of ethosuximide in children is ≥30 hours, a delay of 10 to 14 days between dosage increments allows approximately seven days for achievement of steady state and seven days for assessment of response.[40]

Patient/Caregiver Education. Educating T.D. and her parents regarding the importance of regular administration of the drug is extremely helpful in assuring successful therapy. Noncompliance is common in patients taking AEDs, and rapid discontinuation of these drugs (often secondary to noncompliance) may precipitate status epilepticus. The concept that medication controls rather than cures the seizure disorder should be strongly reinforced. It is also critical to inform both the parents and T.D. that a therapeutic response may not occur immediately and that dosage adjustments may be necessary to establish an effective dose with minimal side effects.

27. Therapeutic Monitoring. What subjective or objective clinical data should be monitored in T.D. for evidence of ethosuximide's therapeutic and adverse effects?

Serum concentrations of 40 to 100 µg/mL of ethosuximide are considered necessary for therapeutic benefits, however, a clearly-defined toxicity syndrome does not seem to develop when ethosuximide serum concentrations are greater than 100 µg/mL. Thus, a gradual and cautious increase in the dose of ethosuximide when serum concentrations are already beyond the upper limits of the usual therapeutic range may allow further response in resistant patients. Although ethosuximide traditionally is administered in divided doses, its long half-life allows successful use of single daily doses for many patients. Clinicians should be alert to acute side effects of nausea and vomiting that are associated with large single doses of ethosuximide; should these occur, divided daily doses may be necessary.[40]

Laboratory monitoring for idiosyncratic hematologic toxicity from ethosuximide often is recommended. Ethosuximide may cause neutropenia in approximately 7% of patients. Although this reaction often is transient even if the drug is continued, rare patients may develop fatal pancytopenia. Presumably, early detection of neutropenia through periodic determination of a complete blood count will allow discontinuation of the drug and potential reversal of this adverse effect.[170] These hematologic reactions, however, can occur unpredictably at any time during therapy and often will be missed by routine laboratory monitoring. Patient/caregiver education regarding signs and symptoms associated with leukopenia and pancytopenia (e.g., sudden onset of severe sore throat with oral lesions, easy bruisability, increased bleeding tendency) and instructions to consult with the physician if these symptoms occur may be more important than laboratory monitoring.[73]

T.D.'s parents should be informed that nausea or sedation may occur with initiation of ethosuximide. Tolerance to these effects usually develops, although temporary dose reductions may be necessary. Subtle degrees of sedation may persist throughout therapy and may not be recognized until the drug has been discontinued and alertness improves.

Generalized Tonic-Clonic Seizures
Accompanying Absence Seizures

28. Three months later, T.D.'s absence spells have been reduced to a frequency of 1 every 2 weeks with an ethosuximide

Table 52.8	Common Drugs for the Treatment of Absence Seizures[a]		
AED	Regimen	Adverse Effects	Comments
Valproate (Depakene, Depakote)	Initial 5–10 mg/kg/day (sprinkle caps or syrup); then ↑ by 5–10 mg/kg/day weekly to therapeutic effect or target serum concentration. Manufacturer's recommended usual maximum dose of 60 mg/kg/day often must be exceeded clinically (especially for patients receiving enzyme-inducing AEDs) to achieve optimum clinical results	GI upset, appetite stimulation, and weight gain common. Serious hepatotoxicity extremely rare with monotherapy and in patients >2 yr	Enteric-coated tablets or capsules preferred oral dosage forms because of ↓ GI toxicity. Time to peak serum concentrations delayed for 3–8 hr with enteric coating; longer delay if given with food; serum concentrations must be interpreted carefully. Also effective against primarily generalized tonic-clonic seizures
Ethosuximide (Zarontin)	Initial 20 mg/kg/day or 250 mg QD or BID; then ↑ by 250 mg/day Q 2 weeks to therapeutic effect or target serum concentration	GI upset and sedation common with large single dose, especially on initiation of therapy. Daily divided doses may be necessary despite long t½. Leukopenia (mild, transient) in up to 7%; serious hematologic toxicity extremely rare	Parents/patient should be informed GI effects and sedation may occur but tolerance usually develops. No good evidence that ethosuximide precipitates tonic-clonic seizures. Up to 50% of patients with absence may develop tonic-clonic seizures independent of ethosuximide

[a] AED = Antiepileptic drug; GI = Gastrointestinal.

dose of 750 mg/day and a serum concentration of 85 µg/mL. Initial drowsiness has almost disappeared, and nausea was alleviated by administering doses with food. She has, however, experienced 2 tonic-clonic convulsions in the past month. Both seizures were witnessed by her parents and well described: there were no apparent auras or signs of focal seizure activity; each episode lasted from 3–4 minutes and apparently consisted of typical tonic-clonic activity. T.D. was incontinent of urine on both occasions, and there was marked postictal confusion and drowsiness. Physical examination and laboratory testing showed no abnormalities. A repeat EEG continued to show infrequent 3/second spikes and waves; no abnormal focal discharges were noted. What is the relationship between T.D.'s tonic-clonic seizures and ethosuximide therapy?

It is commonly believed and often stated in the literature that ethosuximide may precipitate or worsen tonic-clonic seizures; however, this effect has not been clearly demonstrated. As many as 50% of patients who initially present with absence seizures also develop tonic-clonic seizures.[171] In the past, it was common practice to add phenobarbital or phenytoin to ethosuximide therapy to prevent this occurrence. Livingston et al.[172] found that 80.5% of their patients treated with a drug specific for absence spells developed "grand mal" seizures, while only 36% did so while receiving combined therapy. On the other hand, Browne and Mirsky[171] point out that a child with absence seizures who has not yet had a tonic-clonic seizure has only a 25% chance of doing so in the future. In addition, routine use of drugs for prophylaxis of tonic-clonic seizures may increase the risk of toxicity and potentially reduce patients' compliance with medication regimens. Sedative drugs, especially phenobarbital, actually may aggravate absence seizures in some patients.[173]

In summary, the subsequent occurrence of generalized tonic-clonic seizures is common in patients who initially develop absence spells. It is not possible to assess the causative role of ethosuximide for this development in T.D.

Assessment Regarding Need for Alteration in AED Therapy and Choice of Alternative AED

29. What alterations are indicated in T.D.'s drug therapy because of the appearance of generalized tonic-clonic seizures?

Drug therapy for prevention of further tonic-clonic seizures would seem indicated at this time. Phenobarbital, phenytoin, carbamazepine, or valproate might be considered for use in T.D.'s case. Owing to her age and sex, many clinicians would avoid using phenytoin because of its dysmorphic and cosmetic side effects. Phenobarbital may cause sedation and behavioral disturbances (see

below) and may aggravate coexisting absence seizures. Carbamazepine is now considered by many experts to be the drug of first choice for secondarily generalized tonic-clonic seizures and some cases of primary tonic-clonic seizures in children. It lacks many of the troublesome, common side effects associated with phenobarbital and phenytoin; in young children with primary generalized tonic-clonic seizures, carbamazepine may be preferred over valproate because it is less likely to induce serious hepatotoxicity.[1] Carbamazepine, however, is not effective for control of absence seizures. Therefore, it is likely that both valproate and carbamazepine would be needed by T.D. Carbamazepine also has been occasionally associated with exacerbation of seizures (including atonic, myoclonic, and absence seizures) in children with mixed seizure disorders who exhibit bilaterally synchronous 2.5 to 3 cycle per second discharges on EEG.[174,175] The need for polytherapy and the possible risk of seizure exacerbation might make carbamazepine less attractive as a treatment option for T.D.

Valproate is an effective agent for control of both absence and primarily generalized tonic-clonic seizures.[30,176] In T.D., the difference in potential efficacy for tonic-clonic seizures between carbamazepine and valproate may be significant. She appears to have primary generalized tonic-clonic convulsions; focal signs (e.g., unilateral or single limb involvement) were not observed by the parents and focal discharges (e.g., isolated abnormal electrical activity localized to one portion of the brain) were not found on the EEG. While neither observation completely rules out secondarily generalized tonic-clonic seizures, this likelihood seems low. Therefore, valproate may offer some advantages over carbamazepine in terms of efficacy. In addition, both of T.D.'s seizure types potentially could be controlled with a single medication.

Valproate Therapy

30. Initiation and Dosage. T.D.'s physician elects to use valproate. The therapeutic goal is control of her seizures with valproate alone. What procedure should be followed regarding discontinuation of ethosuximide and initiation of valproate?

Techniques used by clinicians to substitute one AED for another depend largely upon experience and judgment. Generally, it is best to attain potentially therapeutic doses/serum concentrations of a new medication before attempting to discontinue the previous drug. Ethosuximide has a relatively long half-life, while valproate's half-life is quite short. Therefore, potentially steady-state serum concentrations can be established and evaluated rapidly; evaluations of the effects of decreases in ethosuximide dosage must await the prolonged elimination of this drug. Once desired serum concentrations of valproate are achieved, the ethosuximide dosage can be reduced gradually by 250 mg/day every two to four weeks. This prolonged process of gradually decreasing the dose of ethosuximide should allow sufficient time for attainment of a new steady state with each dosage decrease of ethosuximide and appropriate evaluation of T.D.'s response at each new steady-state plateau.

Valproate should be initiated at 125 mg twice daily. Valproic acid syrup or divalproex sodium (Depakote tablets or Depakote Sprinkle capsules) can be used. Divalproex usually is preferred because it is enteric coated and causes significantly fewer gastrointestinal side effects than plain valproic acid. T.D.'s starting dose of approximately 8 mg/kg/day is more conservative than that recommended by the manufacturer; lower initial doses are less likely to cause acute side effects (e.g., drowsiness and GI upset). Weekly dose increases of 5 to 10 mg/kg/day of valproate usually are well tolerated and would be appropriate for T.D. More rapid upward titration may be desirable if tonic-clonic seizures are recurring frequently. The maximum currently recommended dose of valproate is 60 mg/kg/day. Many patients, especially those receiving enzyme-inducing drugs (e.g., carbamazepine or phenytoin), will require higher-than-recommended doses to achieve adequate serum concentrations and clinical effect; other patients may respond at much lower doses. Valproate should be titrated in T.D. to produce a "target" serum concentration of approximately 75 µg/mL. As ethosuximide is withdrawn, the valproate dose can be further adjusted on the basis of seizure frequency and side effects.

31. Dosage Forms. Three months later, T.D. has been taking sodium valproate syrup, 250 mg TID for 3 weeks. Ethosuximide was discontinued 2 weeks ago; at that time, a valproate serum level just before her morning dose was 68 µg/mL. She has not experienced generalized tonic-clonic seizures for 6 weeks but continues to have an absence spell every 2–3 weeks. T.D. complains of nausea, epigastric burning pain, and occasional vomiting lasting for approximately 1 hour following her doses of valproate. All recent laboratory tests were within normal limits. Administration of the drug with meals is only partially helpful. What alterations can be made in T.D.'s dosing regimen to relieve these symptoms and possibly improve seizure control?

T.D. appears to be an excellent candidate for the use of divalproex (Depakote). This enteric-coated tablet preparation of a complex salt of valproic acid has almost entirely replaced other solid dosage forms of valproate owing to the much lower occurrence of gastrointestinal side effects. Capsules containing enteric-coated beads of divalproex (Depakote Sprinkles 125 mg) also are available; the capsule contents can be dispersed in food for administration to children or others who have difficulty swallowing tablets or capsules. Additionally, doses of 62.5 mg can be approximated by using the "cap" end of the capsule to measure one-half of the contents. Syrup forms of valproate should be avoided unless extremely small doses are required (e.g., infants) or patients are unable to swallow. Valproate syrup has an unpleasant taste, and its rapid absorption increases the likelihood of acute, dose-related side effects such as nausea. Patients with feeding tubes in place may be given opened Depakote Sprinkles through their feeding tubes; however, patients with certain types of feeding gastrostomies should be assessed frequently for possible leakage at the insertion point. This complication may occur because of adherence of undissolved medication beads to the exterior of the feeding tube. This complication seems more likely when the sprinkle formulation is administered through "button"-type gastrostomy feeding tubes; use of divalproex sprinkles should be avoided in such patients.[177]

Administration of divalproex tablets results in delayed rather than prolonged absorption of valproate; therefore, these tablets are not a sustained-release product formulation. When patients are switched from nonenteric-coated formulations to divalproex tablets, the frequency of administration should not be decreased. The sprinkle formulation, apparently owing to the presence of large numbers of enteric-coated beads, effectively acts as a sustained-release dosage form, and may be administered less frequently without producing unacceptable fluctuations in serum concentrations.

Bioavailability data and widespread clinical experience indicate that all dosage forms of valproate are completely absorbed; therefore, dosage forms can be interconverted at the same total daily dosage of medication.[178,179] Therefore, T.D.'s valproate syrup should be replaced with an equal daily dose of divalproex tablets. Divalproex should be administered on a three times daily dosing schedule. The results of this change should be apparent within approximately one week. By that time, significant relief from GI side effects should have occurred. It may then be possible to increase the dose of divalproex to approximately 1000 mg/day in an effort to improve control of both absence and generalized tonic-clonic seizures.

32. Pharmacokinetics and Serum Concentration Monitoring. Two weeks later, T.D. returns for follow-up. Her GI symptoms have almost completely disappeared. She has been taking divalproex 250 mg with breakfast and lunch and 375 mg with a bedtime snack for the past week. She has had no seizures in the past 2 weeks and complains of no side effects. A valproate serum level before her morning dose today was reported as 117 µg/mL (considerably higher than her previous valproate level of 68 µg/mL). The laboratory reports that duplicate determinations of this level agreed within 5 µg/mL. T.D. denies taking her medication incorrectly; her parents support this, and the tablet count in her prescription bottle is correct. She has taken no other drugs except a multivitamin. How can this disproportionate increase in her valproate serum concentration be explained and what is its clinical significance? Does valproate exhibit dose-dependent pharmacokinetics?

Changes in valproate serum concentrations of this nature are, in this author's experience, relatively common when divalproex is used. They are probably not the result of saturable, dose-dependent metabolism as is seen with phenytoin; instead, these changes are more readily explained by the absorption characteristics of divalproex tablets. Peak serum concentrations of valproate after administration of divalproex may be delayed for three to eight hours, and administration of food may further delay absorption.[180] Additionally, there appears to be significant diurnal fluctuation in both the rate and extent of absorption of divalproex. Absorption may be reduced by approximately one-third and peak plasma concentrations may be delayed for up to 12 hours for divalproex doses administered in the evening.[46] Twelve to fifteen hours probably elapsed between the administration of T.D.'s last dose and blood sampling; therefore, the currently-reported blood level may more closely approximate a peak concentration. Previous blood levels, determined while she was receiving rapidly-absorbed valproate syrup, are more likely to have been "trough" concentrations. T.D.'s compliance with her prescribed dosage regimen also may have increased because of the change in dosage form and reduced side effects; her previous serum concentrations may not have reflected administration of the prescribed dose.

Other pharmacokinetic factors may have moderated this unusual increase in valproate concentrations. There is inherent fluctuation in these concentrations throughout the day in a pattern which does not reflect the timing of doses.[181] This fluctuation may be partially related to changes in serum concentrations of endogenous fatty acids. Fatty acids displace valproate from protein binding sites.[41]

Valproate's hepatic clearance is restrictive (i.e., valproate has a low extraction ratio and its clearance is limited by the free fraction of drug in blood); therefore, protein binding displacement increases plasma concentration of free drug and clearance. As a result, total serum concentrations decrease. Valproate also exhibits dose-dependency in its binding to serum proteins. As concentrations approach 70 to 80 µg/mL, binding sites on albumin molecules become saturated, and the free fraction of drug in plasma increases.[40,178] This effect also increases valproate clearance and reduces total serum concentrations. Both of these effects may actually "dampen" the apparent increase in plasma concentrations seen in T.D. When one also considers the poorly established "therapeutic range" for this drug, it becomes apparent that monitoring serum concentrations is a less useful tool in valproate therapy than in treatment with other AEDs.[41,178]

The clinical significance of T.D.'s elevated valproate serum concentrations is minimal. She is not experiencing any symptoms suggestive of valproate toxicity, and it is too soon following the dose increase to assess the effect of this change on her seizure frequency. Therefore, alteration in her drug therapy is presently unnecessary and might only confuse evaluation of her response to this drug. She should be observed for an additional four to six weeks to evaluate seizure frequency before further alterations in her dosing regimen are considered. The presence of these apparently elevated valproate levels should not discourage further increases in her dose as long as she is tolerating the medication and such increases are justified on the basis of seizure frequency.

33. Hepatotoxicity. Two months later, T.D. is taking 500 mg of divalproex BID with meals. She has had no absence spells for 5 weeks and no generalized tonic-clonic seizures for 10 weeks. Yesterday her valproate plasma concentration was 132 µg/mL. In addition, her alanine aminotransferase (ALT) was 32 IU/mL (Normal: 6–14) and her aspartate aminotransferase (AST) was 41 IU/mL (Normal: 7–17). All other laboratory tests [bilirubin, alkaline phosphatase, lactate dehydrogenase (LD), prothrombin time, and serum albumin] were normal. T.D.'s LFTs have been monitored monthly since she began taking valproate, and they were previously normal. Physical examination was negative for scleral icterus, abdominal pain, or other signs of liver disease. Discuss these laboratory abnormalities and physical findings in relation to possible valproate-induced hepatotoxicity in T.D. [SI units: ALT 32 U/L (Normal: 6–14); AST 41 U/L (Normal: 7–17)]

Liver damage related to valproate therapy appears to be caused by accumulation of directly hepatotoxic metabolites of valproate (probably 4-en-valproate) in certain individuals.[182,183] These metabolites may be formed in larger quantities in patients who also receive enzyme-inducing drugs such as phenobarbital. The majority of cases of fatal hepatotoxicity have occurred in very young (<2 years) patients with neurologic and metabolic abnormalities who also suffered from severe, difficult-to-control seizures and who were taking multiple AEDs.[182–187] Liver damage occurs early in therapy and symptomatically resembles fulminant hepatitis with hepatic failure. Patients may experience vomiting, drowsiness, lethargy, anorexia, edema, and jaundice; these symptoms often precede laboratory evidence of hepatic damage. Liver biopsies in affected individuals show evidence of hepatic necrosis and steatosis. Laboratory findings consist of dramatic elevations of AST, total bilirubin, and serum ammonia; coagulation disturbances accompanied by prolonged prothrombin times; low fibrinogen concentrations; and thrombocytopenia also may be observed. Death results from hepatic failure or a Reye's-like syndrome.[183,185,188]

Asymptomatic elevations in liver enzymes (such as those found in T.D.) occur commonly during the first six months of treatment

with valproate and usually are not associated with severe and potentially fatal valproate-induced hepatotoxicity. These changes in aminotransferase usually disappear without alteration in therapy; in some cases, temporary dosage reduction is followed by normalization of laboratory tests within four to six weeks.[183,185] In the absence of systemic symptoms or other signs of significant liver damage, it is unlikely that the laboratory abnormalities observed in T.D. represent severe liver toxicity from valproate. As T.D. is responding well to valproate therapy, the only change in therapy warranted at this time would be a small (e.g., 125 mg/day) reduction in divalproex dose. Laboratory testing probably should be repeated in four to six weeks to assess the effect of this dose change. T.D. and her family should be educated regarding the possible signs and symptoms of valproate-induced liver damage and instructed to consult with their physician if these symptoms are noted.

34. *Routine Liver Function Tests (LFTs).* What is the usefulness of routinely monitoring LFTs in patients receiving valproate?

Serious hepatotoxicity related to valproate therapy is extremely rare. Dreifuss et al.[185,186] estimate that less than 0.002% of valproate-treated patients developed fatal hepatotoxicity between 1985 and 1986. This compares with an incidence of 0.01% between 1978 and 1984.[184] The lower recent incidence (despite much wider use of valproate) is attributed to increased valproate monotherapy and reduced use of this drug in high-risk patients such as the very young (see Table 52.8). The majority of cases of fatal hepatotoxicity occur in children less than ten years of age. In children less than two years old who receive AED polytherapy, the incidence of this complication is 1/500 to 1/800. Because asymptomatic, apparently benign elevations in liver enzymes are common early in therapy with valproate and symptoms of liver damage often precede laboratory changes, frequent liver function tests during early valproate therapy are unlikely to allow detection of serious hepatotoxicity.[73,183–185,189] Additionally, this type of laboratory monitoring adds significantly to the cost of therapy while providing little benefit for patients. Education of caregivers and/or patients regarding potential symptoms of hepatotoxicity with careful observation and follow-up by health professionals is recommended as the most effective method for monitoring for this drug-induced illness. Especially careful monitoring should be provided for predisposed individuals (i.e., very young children with associated neurologic abnormalities and/or those receiving polytherapy). In predisposed patients, marked increases in hepatic function tests that are noted early in therapy may be clinically significant. At the onset of symptoms suggesting this condition, laboratory testing may help confirm its presence. Practitioners who feel compelled to perform frequent laboratory testing for liver dysfunction on the basis of manufacturer's package insert recommendations should be cautious not to overinterpret common, transient, and apparently benign elevations in aminotransferases or ammonia levels.

Febrile Seizures

Incidence and Classification

35. J.J., a 14-month-old female, is brought to the ER after having a generalized tonic-clonic convulsion lasting approximately 10 minutes. The episode occurred in association with an upper respiratory infection. Upon arrival in the ER, her temperature was 39.5 °C rectally. She was alert at that time; all laboratory and neurologic findings, including lumbar puncture, were normal. J.J. has no history of neurologic abnormality. Her 7-year-old brother suffers from both absence and generalized tonic-clonic seizures. What is the relationship between febrile seizures and epilepsy? How may J.J.'s convulsion be classified on the basis of the data available?

Up to 5% of children have a febrile seizure between six months and six years of age.[190] *Simple febrile seizures* occur with a fever of ≥38 °C in previously normal children less than five years of age. They last less than 15 minutes and have no focal features. The associated seizure does not arise from CNS pathology. *Complex febrile seizures* show focal characteristics or are prolonged. The child may or may not have previous neurologic abnormalities, but the fever itself is not secondary to central nervous system pathology. *Febrile status epilepticus* consists of continuous or serial tonic-clonic seizures lasting more than 30 minutes without return of consciousness. The fever does not originate in the central nervous system. *Seizures with fever* occur in association with febrile illnesses and may be of any type or duration. The previous neurologic status of the patient may or may not have been normal. This category is most commonly used to classify symptomatic seizures associated with neurologic conditions such as meningitis. The risk of occurrence of afebrile seizures following one or more febrile seizures is two to three times greater than in the general population. A family history of afebrile seizures, a complicated initial seizure, and pre-existing neurologic abnormality are risk factors associated with the later development of chronic epilepsy.[191]

J.J.'s seizure appears to be a typical simple febrile seizure that developed in association with her upper respiratory tract infection. The lack of previous neurologic abnormality and normal findings on lumbar puncture and laboratory evaluation help to affirm this assessment.

Treatment of Acute Seizure

36. How should J.J.'s febrile seizures be treated?

Since J.J.'s seizure activity is stable at present, immediate antiepileptic therapy is not required. Nevertheless, measures to reduce her elevated temperature should be initiated immediately to reduce the risk of further seizures. Acetaminophen and tepid sponge baths usually are helpful.

If patients experience prolonged or repeated febrile seizures, either phenobarbital (15 mg/kg loading dose by slow IV) or diazepam (Valium 0.3 mg/kg IV at 1 mg/minute) may be administered.[191] If long-term prophylactic treatment for febrile seizures is anticipated, phenobarbital may be preferred for acute treatment.

Prophylaxis and Choice of AED

37. On the basis of the subjective and objective data available for J.J., is AED therapy indicated on a long-term basis? What are the benefits and risks of AED prophylaxis for febrile seizures?

Long-term treatment of simple febrile seizures remains controversial. Up to 54% of affected patients will have recurrent febrile seizures. Risk of recurrence is even higher when the first episode occurs before 13 months of age. While it has been believed that recurrent, multiple, or severe febrile seizures can cause temporal lobe lesions that result in complex partial (temporal lobe) epilepsy, data available from epidemiologic studies do not support this belief.[190] The efficacy of prophylactic AEDs for prevention of chronic epilepsy following febrile seizures has not been evaluated.[192] Thus, the primary potential benefit of long-term AED therapy would be prevention of recurrence of febrile seizures.

A National Institute of Health (NIH) Consensus Development Conference in 1980 recommended that prophylactic medication after a first febrile seizure be considered when one of the following risk factors were present: 1) focal or prolonged seizures; 2) neurological abnormalities; 3) afebrile seizures in a first-degree relative; 4) age less than one year; and 5) multiple febrile seizures occurring within 24 hours.[193] A reanalysis of published studies has,

however, questioned these recommendations, because the NIH Consensus Statement risk factors were not strong predictors of febrile seizure recurrence.[192] Only early age (<1 year) at first febrile seizure and a family history of febrile seizures reliably predicted a significant increase in the risk of repeat febrile seizures. AED prophylaxis should be considered only when multiple risk factors or other medical conditions which place the patient at special risk are present. Complex febrile seizures or febrile status epilepticus should be treated with chronic AED therapy, as these episodes represent significant neurologic dysfunction even though they do not necessarily increase the risk of febrile seizure recurrence.[191,192]

The efficacy and risk-benefit profile of AED prophylaxis for febrile seizures also have been questioned.[194] A reanalysis of published British trials of both valproate and phenobarbital for febrile seizure prophylaxis found that neither drug was reliably effective.[195] Although phenobarbital has been considered to be at least partially effective, the high rate of side effects (40%) preclude recommending its use. When the effects on intelligence of phenobarbital versus placebo prophylaxis for febrile seizures in young children were compared against NIH Consensus Statement risk factors for recurrence, IQ scores were significantly lower in children treated with phenobarbital.[196] This effect persisted for at least six months following discontinuation of drug therapy. In addition, there was no statistically significant reduction in the recurrence rate of febrile seizures in children treated with phenobarbital. However, approximately one-third of those patients who experienced recurrent febrile seizures were noncompliant with phenobarbital therapy. This study's design and findings have been criticized on the basis of patient selection and "crossing over" of patients from the control group to the study group.[197] Further confirmation of these findings may be needed to more fully establish the role of phenobarbital.

AED prophylaxis for febrile seizures is probably not warranted for J.J., even though she is at risk for both development of epilepsy and recurrence of febrile seizures. There is no evidence that medication will significantly affect the first of these conditions. Phenobarbital and valproate are the only AEDs that have been considered useful for febrile seizure prophylaxis and even their efficacy is being seriously questioned. Phenobarbital's use for this purpose is difficult to justify when one considers the risk of potential learning impairment. In addition, phenobarbital therapy is associated with hyperactivity and behavioral disturbance in up to 75% of children receiving the drug.[62,198,199]

J.J.'s age places her at higher risk of valproate-related hepatotoxicity, and this risk probably outweighs any potential benefit from treatment with this drug. Close medical follow-up of J.J. is warranted. In addition, her parents should be instructed to institute antipyretic measures (i.e., acetaminophen and tepid sponge baths) at the onset of any febrile illness. Many febrile seizures occur early in the course of an illness before fever is detected,[191] nevertheless, early vigilance by her parents and early antipyretic therapy may help prevent further febrile seizures. An additional measure which may be employed is the intermittent administration of oral diazepam (Valium) at the onset of a febrile illness. Doses of 0.33 mg/kg orally every eight hours appear to be effective in reducing the recurrence rate of febrile seizures.[200] Diazepam should be initiated as soon as a febrile illness appears and continued until J.J. has been afebrile for 24 hours. Side effects are common when DZP is used in this manner; approximately one-third of patients will experience ataxia, lethargy, or irritability. These and other common CNS side effects such as dysarthria and insomnia may confuse assessment of the condition of children with febrile illnesses.

AED Drug Interactions and Adverse Effects
Carbamazepine-Erythromycin Interaction

38. J.N., a 17-year-old male, is treated with carbamazepine 600 mg/day for complex partial seizures. He is presently well controlled with serum carbamazepine concentrations of 8 µg/mL. He developed an upper respiratory infection assessed as probable streptococcal pharyngitis. Because J.N. is allergic to penicillin, erythromycin 333 mg TID with meals for 10 days was prescribed. Four days after beginning erythromycin therapy, J.N. complains that, although his upper respiratory symptoms are improving, he is constantly drowsy and is experiencing dizziness and double vision. He also complains of nausea and has vomited once this morning. He receives no other routine medication, although he did take approximately 5 doses of 2 tablets of Extra Strength Tylenol (acetaminophen 500 mg/tablet) during the initial stage of his current illness for fever and general discomfort. What is the relationship between J.N.'s symptoms and the potential interaction between carbamazepine and erythromycin? How might this interaction be further assessed and managed at this point?

Inhibition of hepatic metabolism of carbamazepine by erythromycin may result in dramatic elevations in carbamazepine serum concentrations and precipitation of intoxication.[201,202] J.N.'s symptoms are consistent with carbamazepine toxicity, although erythromycin therapy may be contributing to his gastrointestinal symptoms. While dramatic elevation of carbamazepine serum concentrations is not consistently seen, susceptible patients may exhibit a twofold increase in serum levels. Determination of a carbamazepine serum concentration is indicated to help confirm probable toxicity and assess the magnitude of the interaction. Erythromycin is believed to inhibit metabolic conversion of carbamazepine to its epoxide metabolite with a resulting decrease in carbamazepine clearance. This potential interaction is commonly encountered in practice and represents a significant risk factor for precipitation of carbamazepine intoxication.

Management of this interaction at this point is somewhat difficult; prevention of the interaction by avoiding the use of erythromycin whenever possible is usually the best clinical strategy. As J.N. is allergic to penicillin, alternatives to erythromycin for treatment of his presumed streptococcal infection are limited. Replacement of erythromycin with clindamycin should provide adequate antibiotic therapy with no risk of further interaction with carbamazepine. One or two doses of carbamazepine could be held to allow carbamazepine serum concentrations to decrease to pre-erythromycin levels and correct J.N.'s present intoxication. An alternative approach would be to reduce J.N.'s carbamazepine dose, based upon his present serum level, for the duration of erythromycin therapy. This approach may be more difficult to manage; the time required for erythromycin-induced metabolic inhibition to subside when the antibiotic is stopped is unpredictable. With either approach to management of this interaction, J.N.'s clinical status will need to be monitored carefully. Further adjustment of carbamazepine dosage may be required and repeat serum level determinations may be helpful.

Valproate-Carbamazepine Interaction

39. D.H., a 21-year-old, 84 kg male, was taking carbamazepine 1400 mg/day (600 mg Q AM and 800 mg HS) for treatment of generalized tonic-clonic seizures. Despite carbamazepine serum concentrations of 14 µg/mL, he continued to have 1 seizure every 6–8 weeks. Higher serum levels have produced toxicity symptoms. Valproate (divalproex) was recently added and gradually increased to a dose of 1000 mg TID; the therapeutic goal was replacement of carbamazepine with valproate. At this dose, D.H. again experienced symptoms of carbama-

zepine intoxication (double vision, unsteady gait, and drowsiness) although his carbamazepine serum concentration was reported as 12 µg/mL. Valproate serum levels were 40 µg/mL and 43 µg/mL on 2 occasions. D.H. has continued to experience seizures at his previous rate. He appears to be compliant with his prescribed medication regimen. How can D.H.'s symptoms and failure to achieve therapeutic valproate levels be explained on the basis of an interaction between his two AEDs?

Difficulty in achieving serum valproate concentrations adequate for improvement in seizure control frequently is encountered in patients who receive concomitant therapy with potent enzyme inducers such as carbamazepine. Clinicians frequently note that it is difficult to administer doses of valproate large enough to achieve desired serum levels under these circumstances.[164,40] Serum concentrations of valproate in patients receiving carbamazepine may be only approximately 50% of those expected on the basis of single dose pharmacokinetic studies.

D.H.'s symptoms of carbamazepine intoxication at plasma levels which were previously tolerated suggest possible accumulation of carbamazepine-10,11-epoxide. Valproate may inhibit epoxide hydrolase and cause accumulation of serum concentrations of CBZ-E sufficient to exert significant pharmacologic effects, including intoxication. This author has personally observed a patient receiving both valproate and carbamazepine who developed serum concentrations of CBZ-E which were equal to the concentration of carbamazepine itself (both compounds were measured at ≈12 µg/mL) and experienced significant intoxication. Determination of the serum concentration of carbamazepine and its epoxide should help confirm the clinical impression. Unfortunately, the assay for CBZ-E is not readily available in many clinical laboratories. Significant delay in receiving results is common owing to the need for most laboratories to refer samples to outside reference laboratories.

40. What recommendations can be made for alteration in D.H.'s drug therapy regimen to alleviate the effects of this drug interaction and enhance his therapeutic response to his medication?

On clinical/empirical grounds, D.H.'s dose of carbamazepine should be reduced; this would seem especially appropriate since the therapeutic goal was replacement of carbamazepine with valproate. Dose reduction will result in a decrease in serum concentrations of both carbamazepine and CBZ-E and improvement in symptoms of intoxication. An initial decrease of 10% to 20% (200 mg) of D.H.'s daily carbamazepine dose would be reasonable. Subsequently, his carbamazepine dose can be tapered using reductions of 200 mg every one to two weeks. During tapering of carbamazepine, D.H. should be monitored carefully for increased seizure activity. Upward adjustment of his divalproex dose and/or slowing of the reduction of the carbamazepine dose may be necessary to maintain adequate seizure control.

Valproate-Related Thrombocytopenia

41. D.H.'s symptoms improved significantly within 3 days of reduction of his carbamazepine dose to 1200 mg/day. A CBZ-E serum concentration was not determined. His carbamazepine dose was reduced by 200 mg/day in weekly steps; there was no increase in seizure activity. A serum valproate concentration after his carbamazepine dose reached 600 mg/day was reported as 53 µg/mL. At that time he had not had a seizure in approximately 6 weeks. A serum valproate concentration was repeated when his carbamazepine dose reached 200 mg/day and was 58 µg/mL. Three weeks following discontinuation of carbamazepine, D.H. noted the onset of tremor affecting his hands and a "fuzzy sensation in his head" accompanied by difficulty in concentrating on tasks. His serum

valproate concentration was reported as 126 µg/mL. In addition, a CBC showed a platelet count of 60,000/mm³ cells; no other abnormalities were seen. No bleeding tendencies were noted and D.H. denied symptoms or signs of easy bruisability or unusual bleeding. Previous CBCs had been normal. Is this pattern of increase in valproate serum concentrations consistent with the loss of carbamazepine-related enzyme induction? What is the relationship between D.H.'s new symptoms, his reduced platelet count and the elevation in his valproate serum concentration? [SI unit: 60 × 10⁹/L]

D.H.'s valproate serum concentrations were expected to increase with "de-induction" of hepatic microsomal enzymes while carbamazepine was being discontinued. The pattern and timing of "de-induction" are not consistently predictable. While one might anticipate a somewhat linear increase in valproate concentrations as enzyme inducers such as carbamazepine are gradually reduced, it is not unusual for valproate levels to remain relatively constant until one to two weeks after discontinuation of enzyme inducers.[164] Therefore, patients should be monitored for signs or symptoms of possible valproate intoxication during and for several weeks after such a discontinuation process; clinicians and patients should be aware that dosage adjustment may not be required until the enzyme inducing drug has been completely discontinued. The magnitude of the increase observed in D.H. is somewhat unusual, although this author has observed similar patterns in patients.

D.H.'s new symptoms appear to be consistent with mild to moderate intoxication by valproate. Tremor is a relatively common side effect of valproate which is likely to appear as serum concentrations exceed approximately 80 µg/mL.[40] This side effect may be troublesome for some patients as the tremor is usually an intention tremor which worsens with physical activity. In most patients, dose reduction will improve or eliminate tremor. Some workers have successfully counteracted this side effect with propranolol therapy in doses similar to those used to treat essential tremor.[166] The neurologic symptoms exhibited by D.H. also are typically seen with valproate intoxication. All of these symptoms are reversible with dosage reduction.

Reductions in platelet counts are not rare in valproate-treated patients. Significant thrombocytopenia with bleeding manifestations is extremely uncommon.[203,204] The mechanism underlying thrombocytopenia is not known; there is evidence for both a dose- or serum concentration-related effect[204] and an immunologic mechanism.[205] Affected patients usually can be continued on valproate therapy at reduced doses without adverse effects. The author has observed two patients who developed marked valproate-related thrombocytopenia without bleeding complications; both cases were associated with dramatic increases in valproate serum concentrations following discontinuation of enzyme-inducing drugs. In one of these patients there appeared to be a significant relationship between valproate serum concentrations and platelet counts.

Both the neurologic symptoms and thrombocytopenia exhibited by D.H. probably can be successfully corrected by reducing his dose of divalproex. The magnitude of dose reduction will need to be determined by titration using remission of symptoms and normalization of his platelet count as endpoints. Periodically rechecking valproate serum concentrations will help to establish a safe upper limit dose and serum levels for D.H. Ongoing monitoring also will be important for several weeks as the process of "de-induction" of hepatic enzymes may not yet be complete. Further dose reductions may be necessary as this process reaches completion and D.H.'s valproate clearance gradually decreases. Reduction of D.H.'s dose to 2000 mg/day should approximate serum concentrations between those which were previously subtherapeutic and those which are causing his current adverse effects.

Skin Rash: Hypersensitivity Reactions to AEDs

42. R. S., a 34-year-old black male, has been taking phenytoin, 200 mg BID, for the past 7 weeks to control complex partial and secondarily-generalized tonic-clonic seizures. Seizures began approximately 4 months ago following surgical evacuation of a subdural hematoma. Today he appeared at the walk-in clinic and complained of an "itchy rash" which had begun 2 days ago. He described "feeling lousy" for the past week. On examination he is febrile (38.5 °C orally). There was a maculopapular, scaly, erythematous rash over his upper extremities and torso and the mucous membranes of his mouth appeared to be mildly inflamed. Cervical lymphadenopathy was noted and the liver was found to be enlarged and tender. R.S. also related that his urine had become very dark in the last 2 days and that his stools were light colored. What is the significance of R.S.'s skin rash and other signs and symptoms? Are these likely to be related to his phenytoin therapy?

Skin rash is a relatively common (2% to 3% of patients) side effect related to AED therapy. It is most commonly associated with phenytoin, lamotrigine, carbamazepine, and phenobarbital. The majority of cases are relatively mild, but severely affected patients may develop Stevens-Johnson Syndrome and/or a full-blown hypersensitivity syndrome accompanied by severe hepatic damage. In R.S.'s case, the skin rash is accompanied by signs and symptoms suggesting hepatic involvement. Fever, lymphadenopathy, and apparent inflammation of mucous membranes also suggest a possible hypersensitivity reaction to phenytoin with multisystem involvement and the potential for progression to Stevens-Johnson Syndrome. Viral infection (e.g., hepatitis, influenza, infectious mononucleosis) should be considered and ruled out as a possible cause of R.S.'s symptoms before they are attributed to phenytoin therapy.[149,206–209]

Phenytoin hypersensitivity syndrome is most commonly seen in adults and is more likely to affect blacks.[207] Typically, patients with this syndrome present with complaints of fever, skin rash, and lymphadenopathy during the first two months of phenytoin therapy. Hepatomegaly, splenomegaly, jaundice, and bleeding manifestations such as petechial hemorrhage also are relatively common. Laboratory manifestations usually include leukocytosis with eosinophilia, elevated serum bilirubin, and elevated AST and ALT. When a phenytoin hypersensitivity reaction includes significant hepatotoxicity, fatality may occur in as many as 38% of affected patients.[206]

There appears to be a high likelihood that R.S. has developed a severe reaction to phenytoin; the clinical manifestations and the timing of their appearance along with his race and age are typical of this reaction. Phenytoin should be discontinued immediately pending diagnostic clarification (i.e., evaluation for other possible causes of his symptoms such as viral illness). R.S. should be hospitalized for further diagnostic evaluation and treatment. Treatment of phenytoin-related hypersensitivity and hepatotoxicity is symptomatic and supportive. Intensive therapy with corticosteroids has commonly been used, although there is little objective evidence for beneficial effects of this treatment. Potential complications of this reaction include sepsis and hepatic failure; these conditions should be treated specifically.

43. R.S. was hospitalized and treated with oral prednisone and topical corticosteroids. Other potential causes for his condition were ruled out and his signs and symptoms were attributed to phenytoin hypersensitivity. His fever resolved within 5 days; the skin rash became exfoliative but resolved without infectious complications. Laboratory parameters began to normalize after 10 days. While he was hospitalized, R.S. experienced 3 episodes of generalized seizure activity which were treated with acute administration of IV lorazepam. R.S. was

afebrile at the time these episodes occurred. What information regarding the pathogenesis of phenytoin hypersensitivity and hepatotoxicity can be used to guide selection of an alternate AED for R.S.?

Further administration of phenytoin to R.S. is contraindicated on the basis of his history of a severe hypersensitivity reaction to this drug. Re-administration of phenytoin to similar patients has resulted in rapid recurrence of severe symptoms of this syndrome. While the mechanism of this reaction is not fully understood, research implicates reactive epoxide metabolites (arene oxides) of phenytoin (and other chemically similar AEDs) as possible causative agents for hypersensitivity reactions. Affected patients purportedly are predisposed genetically to the development of hypersensitivity possibly because a relative deficiency of epoxide hydrolase enzymes allows the accumulation of toxic concentrations of reactive epoxide metabolites. These reactive metabolites are believed to exert a direct cytotoxic effect and/or to interact with cellular macromolecules, thereby functioning as haptenes which stimulate an immunologic reaction.[210-213] Carbamazepine, phenytoin, and phenobarbital all are metabolized by similar pathways and converted to reactive arene oxides. It is hypothesized that carbamazepine-induced liver damage also may result from the effects of accumulation of reactive epoxide metabolites; these reactive metabolites are different from the 10,11-epoxide metabolite which accumulates during carbamazepine therapy. For this reason, these drugs potentially cross-react in susceptible patients. Cases of apparent cross-reactivity between phenytoin and phenobarbital or carbamazepine have been documented.[214-216] Additionally, both carbamazepine and phenobarbital may produce hypersensitivity reactions similar to those seen with phenytoin. This potential for cross-reactivity should be considered when an alternative AED is selected for R.S. Valproate has been suggested as the preferred alternative AED for patients who have developed hypersensitivity reactions to phenytoin.[215] Valproate is not metabolized to epoxides and also is chemically dissimilar to all other AEDs. Since valproate often shows good efficacy for complex partial seizures with secondary generalization, it would seem to be a safe and potentially effective alternate AED for R.S. Ethotoin (Peganone) is a hydantoin derivative with an antiepileptic spectrum similar to that for phenytoin. While it is infrequently used by most clinicians, published case reports indicate that it might be safely used as an alternative to phenytoin for patients who develop hypersensitivity reactions.[214]

AED-Oral Contraceptive Interaction

44. P.Z., a 26-year-old female, experiences complex partial and secondarily generalized tonic-clonic seizures. She is taking phenytoin 400 mg/day (serum level: 11 μg/mL), carbamazepine 800 mg/day (serum level: 5.3 μg/mL), and divalproex 2000 mg/day (serum level: 48 μg/mL). She currently reports having 2 or 3 partial seizures and 1 generalized seizure every 3–4 months. Despite treatment with Lo/Ovral (norgestrel 0.3 mg with ethinyl estradiol 30 μg), she has just learned she is pregnant. Her last menstrual period was 6 weeks ago. What is the relationship between P.Z.'s apparent contraceptive failure and her anticonvulsant therapy?

There have been several reports of reduced efficacy of oral contraceptives in patients receiving various AEDs.[89,218] These reports describe both breakthrough bleeding and pregnancy. In a small retrospective study, the relative risk of "pill" failure (i.e., pregnancy) was up to 25 times greater in women taking AEDs.[218] Enzyme induction by AEDs such as phenobarbital, phenytoin, and carbamazepine is believed to accelerate metabolism of steroid hormones and reduce their effect. This effect is not associated with valproate, lamotrigine, or gabapentin therapy.[89,116,117] Some AEDs

also stimulate synthesis of sex hormone binding globulin (SHBG). Increased binding of steroid contraceptive hormones to SHBG would result in lower concentrations of unbound, biologically active hormones and reduced contraceptive efficacy.[89,219] The effects of newer AEDs (lamotrigine, felbamate, and gabapentin) on concentrations of SHBG have not been determined as yet. The use of higher estrogen dose oral contraceptives has been recommended to help overcome this interaction,[217] but there is insufficient information to permit evaluation of this practice.[220] In addition, estrogens may exacerbate seizures in some women, and higher estrogen doses may increase the risk of serious side effects related to oral contraceptives.[221]

Assuming P.Z. was taking her contraceptive on a regular basis, it is possible that her AEDs are responsible for "the pill's" failure. Patients receiving AEDs should be informed that this interaction may occur and advised concerning the use of alternative contraceptives. The use of oral contraceptives containing higher doses of estrogen may offset this interaction, but there is little information available to guide clinicians in assessing adequacy of oral contraceptive dosage; it is not clear whether breakthrough bleeding is correlated with reduced contraceptive efficacy.[217] (Also see Chapter 43: Contraception.)

Teratogenicity

45. What are the risks of teratogenic effects from P.Z.'s medications? What steps might be taken to minimize these risks?

P.Z.'s child is at a relatively high risk of congenital malformations. There has been exposure to two potentially teratogenic drugs: estrogen/progestin combination oral contraceptives and antiepileptics (also see Chapter 45: Teratogenicity and Drugs in Breast Milk). Exposure to oral contraceptives is associated with limb reduction defects, cardiovascular abnormalities, skeletal malformations, and a variety of other abnormalities.[222]

All major AEDs are now believed to have teratogenic effects.[223] While animal data regarding the teratogenic potential of lamotrigine, felbamate, and gabapentin are encouraging, the teratogenic potential of these drugs in humans is not known at this time. Carbamazepine was previously felt to offer a lower risk of teratogenicity than other AEDs; however, both the pattern and risk of malformations secondary to carbamazepine are comparable to those associated with phenytoin.[224] Some controversy persists regarding the relative contributions of parental epilepsy itself, genetic influences, and drug therapy.[225,226] The risk of major congenital malformations (e.g., facial clefts, cardiac septal defects) in children exposed to AEDs *in utero* may be as high as two to three times the baseline risk in the general population.[223,227,228] However, syndromes consisting of multiple, often minor abnormalities associated with prenatal exposure to AEDs appear to exist, and these syndromes may be more common than one would expect on the basis of relative risk figures developed for isolated major malformations. Additionally, maternal epilepsy increases the risk of complications of pregnancy, pre- or postnatal infant mortality, premature birth, low infant birth weight, and symptoms of withdrawal from antiepileptic medication.[227]

Most AEDs, with the exception of valproate are now believed to exert their teratogenic effects (and possibly other adverse effects such as hepatotoxicity) partly via reactive epoxide metabolites.[229,230] Enhancement of the formation of these metabolites via hepatic enzyme induction (e.g., by carbamazepine or phenobarbital) or inhibition of their breakdown (e.g., through inhibition of epoxide hydrolase by valproate) increases the risk of teratogenicity. Combined administration of enzyme inducers and valproate (specifically the combination of carbamazepine, phenobarbital, and valproate with or without phenytoin) is associated with an especially high risk of teratogenicity.[231] Additionally, each of the present major AEDs has been associated with production of congenital malformations when administered alone. Valproate and phenytoin (and possibly other AEDs) also appear to interfere with folic acid metabolism; this effect may be responsible for a portion of the congenital malformations observed with these drugs.[223,232,233]

Minimization of drug-related risks in the pregnant epileptic patient and fetus may be possible.[223,234] Extensive guidelines have been formulated by an international panel of experts. If feasible, before conception, seizure control should be optimized using the AED of first choice for the prospective mother's seizure type/epilepsy syndrome. Monotherapy at the lowest effective dose is the goal of optimization. Maintenance of adequate folic acid stores before conception and during fetal organogenesis is also important. Folic acid supplementation can reduce the risk of congenital neural tube malformations in infants at risk who are born to women without epilepsy; however, folate supplementation does not reliably reduce the teratogenic effects of AEDs. Nevertheless supplementation of folic acid and ensuring adequate folate levels is recommended. During pregnancy, serum levels of AEDs (including free serum levels for highly protein bound drugs) should be monitored closely; alterations in protein binding, volumes of distribution, and drug clearance occur during pregnancy. Necessary dose adjustments may aid in preventing the increased seizure frequency seen in approximately 25% of pregnant epileptics.[235] Falls and anoxia associated with uncontrolled seizure activity may increase the risk of congenital malformations.

In P.Z., one can presume that significant exposure of the fetus to any teratogenic influence of AEDs has already occurred. The primary concern at this point would be optimization of seizure control. Any major alterations in P.Z.'s antiepileptic regimen should be made cautiously to avoid precipitation of seizures. An attempt to convert P.Z. to monotherapy may be beneficial; phenytoin and carbamazepine exert both therapeutic antiepileptic effects and teratogenic effects via the same mechanisms.[224,236] Based upon P.Z.'s seizure type and current AED serum concentrations, elimination of valproate (divalproex) with an attempt to optimize carbamazepine or possibly phenytoin may improve therapy and produce better seizure control.

Status Epilepticus (SE)
Characteristics and Pathophysiology

46. V.S., a 22-year-old, 85 kg male, was recently diagnosed as having idiopathic epilepsy. For the past 3 months, he has been treated with 600 mg/day of carbamazepine which completely eliminated his generalized tonic-clonic seizures. His steady-state carbamazepine serum concentration was 10 µg/mL. While at his parents' home, he had 2 tonic-clonic seizures, each lasting 3–4 minutes. On arrival at the hospital (approximately 30 min after the first seizure began), he was noted to be only semiconscious. His BP was 197/104 mm Hg, his pulse was 124 beats/min, respirations were 23/min, and his body temperature was 37.5 °C rectally. Shortly after his arrival, another generalized tonic-clonic seizure began. How does V.S.'s current condition meet accepted diagnostic criteria for status epilepticus? What are the risks to V.S. associated with status epilepticus?

Status epilepticus exists if there is "more than 30 minutes of (1) continuous seizure activity or (2) two or more sequential seizures without full recovery of consciousness between seizures."[237] As V.S. has had three seizures within slightly more than 30 minutes and remains unconscious, his present condition meets this definition. V.S. is experiencing generalized convulsive SE; this is the

most common type and is associated with the greatest risk of physical and neurologic damage. SE also may be characterized by nonconvulsive seizures that produce a persistent state of impaired consciousness or by partial seizures (motor or sensory) which may not interfere with consciousness.

Uncontrolled convulsive SE may cause severe metabolic and hemodynamic alterations. V.S.'s vital signs (tachycardia, elevated BP, increased respiratory rate, and elevated body temperature) are typical of those seen in patients with SE. Prolonged, severe muscle contractions and CNS dysfunction from uncontrolled seizure discharges result in hyperthermia, cardiorespiratory collapse, myoglobinuria, renal failure, and neurologic damage. Neurologic damage also may occur with nonconvulsive SE; neurologic sequelae of status epilepticus are related to the excessive electrical activity and resulting alterations in brain tissue metabolism. When seizure activity persists longer than approximately 30 minutes, there is a higher likelihood of failure of mechanisms which regulate cerebral blood flow; this failure accompanies dramatic increases in brain metabolism and demand for glucose and oxygen. Failure to meet metabolic demands of brain tissue results in accumulation of lactate and necrosis. Peripherally, there also is accumulation of lactate and alterations in serum glucose and electrolytes. After 30 minutes of seizure activity, the body often fails to compensate for increased metabolic demands, and cardiovascular collapse may occur.[238,239] For these reasons, SE is considered a medical emergency which requires immediate treatment to prevent or lessen both physical and neurologic damage. Mortality in adults with SE may be as high as 30%;[237] fatal outcome is often the result of the injury or condition which precipitated status epilepticus (e.g., CNS tumor, CNS infection, trauma). Long-term neurologic consequences of severe SE are thought to include cognitive impairment, memory loss, and worsening of seizure disorders. However, the effect of SE on cognitive function is not clearly established; cognitive impairment may result from the neurologic disorder underlying SE rather than from status epilepticus itself.[240]

General Treatment Measures and AED Therapy

47. How should V.S.'s status epilepticus be treated?

The immediate therapeutic concern in V.S. is to ensure ventilation and terminate current seizure activity. If possible, an airway should be placed; however, this may not be possible while the patient is convulsing. Objects (e.g., spoons, tongue blades) should never be forced into the mouth of a seizing patient. If airway placement is impossible, V.S. should be positioned on his side to allow drainage of saliva and mucus from the mouth and prevent aspiration. An intravenous line should be established using normal saline, and blood for serum chemistry (especially glucose and electrolytes) determinations, AED serum concentrations, and toxicology screens should be obtained. Thiamine 100 mg or vitamin B complex should be given intravenously. This should be followed by 25 gm of glucose (50 mL of 50% dextrose solution) by IV push; these maneuvers will correct any hypoglycemia which may be responsible for SE. Glucose administration should be preceded by IV thiamine 100 mg or vitamin B complex to prevent possible development of Wernicke's encephalopathy.[237]

Intravenous administration of either diazepam (Valium) or lorazepam (Ativan) is effective for rapid termination of seizure activity in status epilepticus.[241,242] Owing to diazepam's higher lipid solubility, it redistributes from the CNS to peripheral tissues rapidly after administration; this results in a short duration of action (<60 minutes). Lorazepam's lower lipid solubility prevents rapid redistribution and accounts for its longer effective duration of action. Lorazepam is effective for up to 72 hours.[243,244] Owing to this longer duration, lorazepam is now the preferred benzodiazepine for immediate treatment of SE in many centers. Repeated doses of lorazepam have been associated with development of tachyphylaxis; and lorazepam may be less effective in patients who have received chronic maintenance doses of benzodiazepines.[245,246] At adequate doses, the onset of antiepileptic activity and efficacy of lorazepam and diazepam are equal.[241]

Diazepam usually is administered as an initial dose of 10 mg IV; the usual initial dose of lorazepam is 4 mg IV. Lorazepam may cause significant venous irritation and the manufacturer recommends dilution with an equal volume of normal saline solution or water for injection before IV administration. Doses of either lorazepam or diazepam should be repeated after five to ten minutes if seizure activity has not stopped. Efficacy of either drug depends upon rapid achievement of high serum/CNS concentrations. Lorazepam can be administered IV push over two minutes; the rate of diazepam injection should be limited to approximately 2 mg/minute to minimize the risk of cardiorespiratory toxicity related partly to the propylene glycol solvent used in parenteral solutions of diazepam.[247] Diazepam has been administered as rapidly as 5 mg/minute without excessive toxicity. While both diazepam and lorazepam may be administered intramuscularly, this route should not be used for treatment of SE.[237] It is unlikely that either drug would achieve serum concentrations necessary for termination of seizure activity when administered IM; this is especially true for diazepam which is absorbed very slowly and erratically from intramuscular gluteal sites.[248] Both lorazepam and diazepam are relatively safe drugs. Their primary adverse effects are sedation, hypotension, and respiratory arrest.[242] These side effects are usually short-lived and, when adequate facilities are available for assisted ventilation and administration of fluids, they usually can be managed without major risk to the patient. Respiratory depression occurs most commonly in patients who receive multiple IV medications for control of status epilepticus.

Parenteral Phenytoin

48. V.S. was given lorazepam 4 mg IV. Seizure activity ceased 5 minutes after the injection was completed. What drug should be administered to V.S. for prolonged control of seizures? What is an appropriate dose, route, and method of administration?

Continued effective seizure control is important for patients who experience SE. In the past, when diazepam was the benzodiazepine predominantly used for immediate control of SE, a long-acting primary AED such as phenytoin was routinely administered at the same time to ensure continued suppression of seizure activity. Routine use of phenytoin has been somewhat de-emphasized with increased use of lorazepam;[237] lorazepam's apparent longer duration of effect may make routine use of intravenous phenytoin less necessary. Nevertheless, phenytoin is still used in conjunction with both lorazepam and diazepam by many centers.

Phenytoin is considered the long-acting anticonvulsant of choice for most patients with generalized convulsive status epilepticus.[242] Extensive clinical experience with the use of intravenous loading doses of phenytoin has established its efficacy and safety. Phenytoin causes much less sedation and respiratory depression than drugs such as phenobarbital when it is used in conjunction with intravenous diazepam.[237,247] V.S.'s maintenance carbamazepine therapy produced moderate serum concentrations and was previously effective. In the absence of obvious precipitating factors such as head trauma, CNS infection, or drug/alcohol abuse, SE, in a patient with a history of epilepsy, most commonly results from poor compliance with maintenance medication. Therefore, intravenous use of phenytoin to produce therapeutic serum concentra-

tions is a good choice for re-establishment of effective AED therapy for V.S. Status epilepticus is uncommonly the first presentation of idiopathic epilepsy.

Loading Dose. Although V.S. presumably has existing serum concentrations of carbamazepine, he should be given a full intravenous therapeutic loading dose of phenytoin 18 mg/kg (1500 mg). This should establish a serum phenytoin concentration of approximately 23 µg/mL.[133] Serum concentrations should remain above 10 µg/mL for approximately 24 hours; this will allow time for determination of the patient's serum carbamazepine concentration and estimation of an appropriate maintenance dose of oral carbamazepine. In this setting, the use of intravenous phenytoin is a temporary measure. V.S.'s previous positive response to carbamazepine indicates that he should continue to receive this drug as oral maintenance medication.

Intravenous phenytoin can be administered by direct injection into a running intravenous line. The rate of administration should be no faster than 50 mg/minute to minimize the risk of hypotension and acute cardiac arrhythmias. Cardiovascular status [BP, electrocardiogram (ECG)] should be monitored closely during administration. Hypotension or ECG abnormalities usually reverse if administration of phenytoin is slowed or stopped temporarily.[133]

49. Intravenous Administration. V.S.'s physician is reluctant to administer this dose of phenytoin by direct IV injection. What are the guidelines for phenytoin administration by intravenous infusion?

Practical difficulties associated with administration of phenytoin by direct IV push undoubtedly have contributed to its low usage rate. In many hospitals or other facilities, direct intravenous injections must be administered by a physician, and many physicians would be unwilling to commit the 30 to 45 minutes necessary to administer V.S.'s loading dose at a safe rate. In addition, the rate of direct intravenous administration is very difficult to control, and there is potential risk of too rapid administration resulting in cardiac toxicity.

There has been a great deal of controversy concerning the compatibility of phenytoin injection with IV solutions. Phenytoin's chemical properties (weakly acidic with a pKa of 8 and low water solubility) require that the commercial injectable dosage form of sodium phenytoin be dissolved in a mixture of 40% propylene glycol and 10% alcohol; the pH of the final product is adjusted to approximately 12 with sodium hydroxide. Addition of the preparation to intravenous fluids dilutes the drug's solvent system and reduces pH. A possible result would be precipitation of free phenytoin. However, a number of studies indicate that phenytoin may be diluted, preferably in small total volumes, with saline solution.[249,250] Despite formation of crystals in many solutions, measured phenytoin concentrations are essentially identical to those predicted. Thus, dilution of the required volume of phenytoin injection in approximately 100 to 500 mL of 0.45% or 0.9% saline should provide an appropriate solution for intravenous administration. An in-line filter of 0.45 to 0.22 micron pore size may be used to prevent the infusion of crystals.[249] The administration rate should be limited to ≤50 mg/minute. This method of administration is both safe and effective when the infusion rate is monitored carefully. Burning pain at the IV infusion site, hypotension, and cardiac arrhythmias may occur during infusion and appear to be related to the infusion rate. These side effects may be relieved by either slowing or temporarily stopping the IV infusion.[251,252] Availability of fosphenytoin in the future may simplify the administration of phenytoin to patients with SE by reducing the risk of side effects associated with administration of the currently available preparation of parenteral phenytoin.

Maintenance Therapy

50. Following administration of IV phenytoin, no further seizures occurred. The laboratory reported that serum chemistries were all normal. Carbamazepine serum concentration was 5 µg/mL on admission. A serum phenytoin concentration determined 1 hour after administration of the IV loading dose was 24 µg/mL. How should V.S.'s maintenance therapy with anticonvulsants be altered?

The reduced serum concentration of carbamazepine appears to confirm the role of noncompliance in this episode of status epilepticus. As V.S. was previously well controlled on 600 mg/day, this also would be a reasonable maintenance dose at this time. Administration of maintenance doses should be resumed as soon as V.S. is able to take oral medication. This will allow re-establishment of therapeutic carbamazepine serum concentrations before phenytoin serum concentrations become subtherapeutic. Repeat determination of serum carbamazepine concentration should be performed after two to three days of monitored intake or sooner if seizure activity should recur. V.S. should be counseled regarding the importance of taking his medication according to directions.

Alternative Therapies for Refractory Status Epilepticus

51. What other medications are useful for treatment of status epilepticus which does not respond to benzodiazepines and/or phenytoin?

Phenobarbital may be useful for treatment of SE in patients who cannot tolerate phenytoin or in whom phenytoin has proven ineffective. It also is recommended for patients who continue to seize following administration of appropriate loading doses of phenytoin. Patients who receive phenobarbital after being treated with intravenous benzodiazepines should be monitored closely for respiratory depression, as this effect of these drugs may be additive. Equipment and personnel to provide ventilatory assistance should be available.[237] Administration of intravenous phenobarbital may cause hypotension which may necessitate discontinuation of administration of the drug or the use of pressor agents. Intramuscular administration of phenobarbital results in slow absorption, and this route of administration is not recommended for treatment of SE. An initial dose of 20 mg/kg given intravenously at a rate no faster than 100 mg/minute is recommended.[237]

Pentobarbital or other anesthetic barbiturates are administered for treatment of refractory SE which has not responded to more conservative measures including phenobarbital. Marked respiratory depression is expected with this therapy; patients will require intubation and mechanical ventilation. In addition, vasopressors such as dopamine or dobutamine may be required to control hypotension. Constant EEG monitoring also is required to assess the effect of the drug. Pentobarbital is given as a loading dose (10 to 25 mg/kg IV over 1 hour) and is followed by an intravenous infusion of approximately 1.5 mg/kg/hour or greater. The dose and infusion rate are adjusted to produce either a flat or a burst-suppression EEG pattern.[242,253] Most protocols for pentobarbital coma recommend attempts at gradually reducing the dose of medication after 12 to 24 hours of treatment. If clinical or EEG seizure activity recurs, the dose is increased again to produce continued EEG suppression. Pentobarbital coma may be continued for several days in some patients.

Several other drugs have been used for treatment of refractory SE. Experience with these agents is somewhat limited. *Midazolam* (Versed), a short-acting anesthetic benzodiazepine has been used by intravenous infusion (0.1 to 0.4 mg/kg/hour based upon EEG response) after a loading dose of 0.2 mg/kg.[254] *Valproate* has been used for treatment of refractory SE. As there has not been a parenteral form of this drug available, the syrup form has been administered either rectally or via nasogastric tube. At present, information available regarding this use of valproate is largely anecdotal. An intravenous formulation of valproate currently is undergoing clinical trials, and may be evaluated for the treatment of SE.[242] *Lidocaine* (Xylocaine) by intravenous infusion at a rate of 1.5 to 3.5 mg/kg/hour following a bolus dose of 100 mg (1 to 2 mg/kg) also has been employed as an alternative agent for patients refractory to standard drugs for SE.[242] *General anesthesia* with agents such as halothane or isoflurane also is used occasionally for refractory cases.

References

1 **Scheuer ML, Pedley TA.** The evaluation and treatment of seizures. N Engl J Med. 1990;323:1468.

2 **Commission on Epidemiology and Prognosis, International League Against Epilepsy.** Guidelines for epidemiologic studies on epilepsy. Epilepsia. 1993;34:592.

3 **Commission on Classification and Terminology of the International League Against Epilepsy.** Proposal for revised clinical and electroencephalographic classification of epileptic seizures. Epilepsia. 1981;22:489.

4 **Penry JK, ed.** Epilepsy: Diagnosis Management Quality of Life. New York: Raven Press; 1986:4.

5 **Schmidt D, Haenel F.** Therapeutic plasma levels of phenytoin, phenobarbital, and carbamazepine: individual variation in relation to seizure frequency and type. Neurology. 1984;34:1252.

6 **Schmidt D et al.** The influence of seizure type on the efficacy of plasma concentrations of phenytoin, phenobarbital, and carbamazepine. Arch Neurol. 1986;43:263.

7 **Dreifuss FE.** Classification of epileptic seizures and the epilepsies. Pediatr Clin North Am. 1989;36:265.

8 **Dreifuss FE.** The epilepsies: clinical implications of the international classification. Epilepsia. 1990;31(Suppl. 3):S3.

9 **Mikati MA, Holmes GL.** Temporal lobe epilepsy. In: Wyllie E, ed. The Treatment of Epilepsy: Principles and Practice. Philadelphia: Lea & Febiger; 1993:513.

10 **Berkovic SF.** Childhood absence epilepsy and juvenile absence epilepsy. In: Wyllie E, ed. The Treatment of Epilepsy: Principles and Practice. Philadelphia: Lea & Febiger; 1993:547.

11 **Serratosa JM, Delgado-Escueta AV.** Juvenile myoclonic epilepsy. In: Wyllie E, ed. The Treatment of Epilepsy: Principles and Practice. Philadelphia: Lea & Febiger; 1993:552.

12 **Farrell K.** Secondary generalized epilepsy and Lennox-Gastaut syndrome. In: Wyllie E, ed. The Treatment of Epilepsy: Principles and Practice. Philadelphia: Lea & Febiger; 1993:604.

13 **Zifkin BG, Andermann F.** Epilepsy with reflex seizures. In: Wyllie E, ed. The Treatment of Epilepsy: Principles and Practice. Philadelphia: Lea & Febiger; 1993:614.

14 **Asconape J, Penry JK.** Some clinical and EEG aspects of benign juvenile myoclonic epilepsy. Epilepsia. 1984; 25:108.

15 **Holmes GL.** Electroencephalographic and neuroradiologic evaluation of children with epilepsy. Pediatr Clin North Am. 1989;36:395.

16 **Browne TR, Feldman RG.** Epilepsy: an overview. In: Browne TR, Feldman RG, eds. Epilepsy: Diagnosis and Management. Boston: Little Brown; 1983:1.

17 **First Seizure Trial Group.** Randomized clinical trial on the efficacy of antiepileptic drugs in reducing the risk of relapse after a first unprovoked tonic-clonic seizure. Neurology. 1993;43:478.

18 **Dean JC, Penry JK.** General principles: discontinuation of antiepileptic drugs. In Levy R et al., eds. Antiepileptic Drugs. New York: Raven Press; 1989:133.

19 **Holowach J et al.** Prognosis in childhood epilepsy: follow-up study of 148 cases in which therapy had been suspended after prolonged anticonvulsant

20 **Thurston JH et al.** Prognosis in childhood epilepsy: additional follow-up of 148 children 15 to 23 years after withdrawal of anticonvulsant therapy. N Engl J Med. 1982;306:831.

21 **Emerson R et al.** Stopping medication in children with epilepsy: predictors of outcome. N Engl J Med. 1981;304:1125.

22 **Todt H.** The late prognosis of epilepsy in childhood: results of a prospective follow-up study. Epilepsia. 1984;25:137.

23 **Callaghan N et al.** Withdrawal of anticonvulsant drugs in patients free of seizures for two years: a prospective study. N Engl J Med. 1988;318:942.

24 **Matricardi M et al.** Outcome after discontinuation of antiepileptic drug therapy in children with epilepsy. Epilepsia. 1989;30:582.

25 **Engel J Jr.** Update on surgical treatment of the epilepsies: summary of the second international palm desert conference on the surgical treatment of the epilepsies (1992). Neurology. 1993;43:1612.

26 **Dodson WE et al.** Management of sei-

control. N Engl J Med. 1972;286:169.

zure disorders: selected aspects. J Pediatr. 1976;89(Part II):695.

27 **Kinsman SL et al.** Efficacy of the ketogenic diet for intractable seizure disorders: a review of 58 cases. Epilepsia. 1992;33:1132.

28 **Delgado-Escueta AV et al.** The treatable epilepsies. N Engl J Med. 1983; 308(Pt. 1):1508.

29 **Reynolds EH.** Early treatment and prognosis of epilepsy. Epilepsia. 1987; 28:97.

30 **Pellock JM.** Efficacy and adverse effects of antiepileptic drugs. Pediatr Clin North Am. 1989;36:435.

31 **Mattson RH et al.** Comparison of carbamazepine, phenobarbital, phenytoin, and primidone in partial and secondarily generalized tonic-clonic seizures. N Engl J Med. 1985;313:145.

32 **Mattson RH et al.** A comparison of valproate with carbamazepine for the treatment of complex partial seizures and secondarily generalized tonic-clonic seizures in adults. N Engl J Med. 1992;327:765.

33 **Troupin AS.** Epilepsy with generalized tonic-clonic seizures. In: Wyllie E, ed. The Treatment of Epilepsy: Principles and Practice. Philadelphia: Lea and Febiger; 1993:584.

34 **Beardsley RS et al.** Anticonvulsant serum levels are useful only if the physician appropriately uses them: an assessment of the impact of providing serum level data to physicians. Epilepsia. 1983;24:330.

35 **Choonara IA, Rane A.** Therapeutic drug monitoring of anticonvulsants: state of the art. Clin Pharmacokinet. 1990;18:318.

36 **Dodson WE.** Level off. Neurology. 1989;39:1009. Editorial.

37 **Hayes G, Kootsikas ME.** Reassessing the lower end of the phenytoin therapeutic range: a review of the literature. Ann Pharmacother. 1993;27:1389.

38 **Commission on Antiepileptic Drugs, International League Against Epilepsy.** Guidelines for therapeutic monitoring on antiepileptic drugs. Epilepsia. 1993;34:585.

39 **Tozer TN, Winter ME.** Phenytoin. In: Evans WE et al., eds. Applied Pharmacokinetics: Principles of Therapeutic Drug Monitoring. 3rd ed. Vancouver: Applied Therapeutics, Inc.; 1989: 25-1.

40 **Levy RH, et al.** Carbamazepine, valproic acid, phenobarbital, and ethosuximide. In: Evans WE et al., eds. Applied Pharmacokinetics: Principles of Therapeutic Drug Monitoring. 3rd ed. Vancouver: Applied Therapeutics, Inc.; 1989:26-1.

41 **Chadwick DW.** Concentration-effect relationships of valproic acid. Clin Pharmacokinet. 1985;10:155.

42 **Bourgeois BFD.** Valproate: clinical use. In: Levy RH et al., eds. Antiepileptic Drugs. New York: Raven Press; 1989:633.

43 **Ohtsuka Y et al.** Treatment of intractable childhood epilepsy with high-dose valproate. Epilepsia. 1992;33:158.

44 **Hurst DL.** Expanded therapeutic range of valproate. Pediatr Neurol. 1987;3: 342.

45 **Woo E et al.** If a well-stabilized epileptic patient has a subtherapeutic antiepileptic drug level, should the dose be increased? A randomized prospective study. Epilepsia. 1988;29:129.

46 **Cloyd JC.** Pharmacokinetic pitfalls of present antiepileptic medications. Epilepsia. 1991;32(Suppl. 5):S53.

47 **Schmidt D.** Reduction of two-drug therapy in intractable epilepsy. Epilepsia. 1983;24:368.

48 **Smith DB et al.** Results of a nationwide veterans administration cooperative study comparing the efficacy and toxicity of carbamazepine, phenobarbital, phenytoin, and primidone. Epilepsia. 1987;28(Suppl. 3):S50.

49 **Thompson PJ, Trimble MR.** Anticonvulsant drugs and cognitive functions. Epilepsia. 1982;23:531.

50 **Albright P, Bruni J.** Reduction of polypharmacy in epileptic patients. Arch Neurol. 1985;42:797.

51 **Prevey ML et al.** Improvement in cognitive functioning and mood state after conversion to valproate monotherapy. Neurology. 1989;39:1640.

52 **Mirza WU et al.** Results of antiepileptic drug reduction in patients with multiple handicaps and epilepsy. Drug Invest. 1993;5:320.

53 **Reynolds EH, Shorvon SD.** Monotherapy or polytherapy for epilepsy? Epilepsia. 1981;22:1

54 **Shinnar S et al.** Discontinuing antiepileptic drugs in children with epilepsy: a prospective study. Ann Neurol. 1994;35:534.

55 **Berg AT, Shinnar S.** Relapse following discontinuation of antiepileptic drugs: a meta-analysis. Neurology. 1994;44:601.

56 **Tennison M et al.** Discontinuing antiepileptic drugs in children: a comparison of a six-week and a nine-month taper period. N Engl J Med. 1994;330: 1407.

57 **Malow BA et al.** Carbamazepine withdrawal: effects of taper rate on seizure frequency. Neurology. 1993;43:2280.

58 **Reynolds EH et al.** Valproate versus carbamazepine for seizures. N Engl J Med. 1993;328:207.

59 **Penry JK, Dean JC.** Valproate monotherapy in partial seizures. Am J Med. 1988;84(Suppl. 1A):14.

60 **Chadwick D.** Valproate in the treatment of partial epilepsies. Epilepsia. 1994;35(Suppl. 5):S96.

61 **Wilensky AJ, Friel PN.** Benzodiazepines: clorazepate. In: Levy RH et al., eds. Antiepileptic Drugs. New York: Raven Press; 1989:805.

62 **Vining EPG.** Cognitive dysfunction associated with antiepileptic drugs. Epilepsia. 1987;28(Suppl. 2):S18.

63 **Dodrill CB, Troupin AS.** Psychotropic effects of carbamazepine in epilepsy: a double-blind comparison with phenytoin. Neurology. 1977;27:1023.

64 **Dodrill CB, Troupin AS.** Neuropsychological effects of carbamazepine and phenytoin: a reanalysis. Neurology. 1991;41:141.

65 **Meador KJ et al.** Comparative cognitive effects of carbamazepine and phenytoin in healthy adults. Neurology. 1991;41:1537.

66 **Aldenkamp AP et al.** Withdrawal of antiepileptic medication in children—effects on cognitive function: the multicenter Holmfrid study. Neurology. 1993;43:41.

67 **Franceschi M et al.** Fatal aplastic anemia in a patient treated with carbamazepine. Epilepsia. 1988;29:582.

68 **Hawson GAT et al.** Agranulocytosis after administration of carbamazepine. Med J Aust. 1980;1:82. Letter.

69 **Pisciotta AV.** Hematologic toxicity of carbamazepine. Adv Neurol. 1975;11: 355.

70 **Pisciotta AV.** Carbamazepine: hematological toxicity. In: Woodbury DM et al., eds. Antiepileptic Drugs. New York: Raven Press; 1982;533.

71 **Hart RG, Easton JD.** Carbamazepine and hematologic monitoring. Ann Neurol. 1982;11:309.

72 **Graves NM, Bodor MC.** Carbamazepine-induced leukopenia. Drug Therapy. 1989;August:56.

73 **Camfield C et al.** Asymptomatic children with epilepsy: little benefit from screening for anticonvulsant-induced liver, blood, or renal damage. Neurology. 1986;36:838.

74 **Horowitz S et al.** Hepatotoxic reactions associated with carbamazepine therapy. Epilepsia. 1988;29:149.

75 **Hadzic N et al.** Acute liver failure induced by carbamazepine. Arch Dis Child. 1990;65:315.

76 **Livingston S et al.** Carbamazepine (Tegretol) in epilepsy: nine-year follow-up study with special emphasis on untoward reactions. Dis Nerv System. 1974;35:103.

77 **Tomson T et al.** Relationship of intraindividual dose to plasma concentration of carbamazepine: indication of dose-dependent induction of metabolism. Ther Drug Monit. 1989;11:533.

78 **Sanchez A et al.** Steady-state carbamazepine concentration-dose ratio in epileptic patients. Clin Pharmacokinet. 1986;11:41.

79 **Oles KS, Gal P.** Bioequivalency revisited: Epitol versus Tegretol. Neurology. 1993;43:2435.

80 **Gilman JT et al.** Carbamazepine toxicity resulting from generic substitution. Neurology. 1993;43:2696.

81 **Anon.** Carbamazepine deterioration. FDA Drug Bull. 1990;20(Apr):2.

82 **Troupin AS.** Carbamazepine re-examined. In: Pedley TA, Meldrum BS, eds. Recent Advances in Epilepsy: I. New York: Churchill Livingstone; 1983:47.

83 **Masland RL.** Carbamazepine: neurotoxicity. In: Woodbury DM et al., eds. Antiepileptic Drugs. New York: Raven Press; 1982:521.

84 **Gram L, Jensen PK.** Carbamazepine: toxicity. In: Levy RH et al., eds. Antiepileptic Drugs. New York: Raven Press; 1989:555.

85 **So EL et al.** Seizure exacerbation and status epilepticus related to carbamazepine-10,11-epoxide. Ann Neurol. 1994;35:743.

86 **Nanji AA.** Drug-induced electrolyte disorders. Drug Intell Clin Pharm. 1983;17:175.

87 **Helin I et al.** Serum sodium and osmolality during carbamazepine treatment in children. Br Med J. 1977;2: 558.

88 **Ringel RA, Brick JF.** Perspective on carbamazepine-induced water intoxication: reversal by demeclocycline. Neurology. 1986;36:1506.

89 **Ramsay RE, Slater JD.** Effects of antiepileptic drugs on hormones. Epilepsia. 1991;32(Suppl. 5):S60.

90 **Lahr MB.** Hyponatremia during carbamazepine therapy. Clin Pharmacol Ther. 1985;37:693.

91 **Perucca E, Richens A.** Water intoxication produced by carbamazepine and its reversal by phenytoin. Br J Clin Pharmacol. 1980;9:302P.

92 **Sordillo P et al.** Carbamazepine-induced syndrome of inappropriate antidiuretic hormone secretion: reversal by concomitant phenytoin therapy. Arch Intern Med. 1978;138:299.

93 **Hoppener RJ et al.** Correlation between daily fluctuations of carbamazepine serum levels and intermittent side effects. Epilepsia. 1980;21:341.

94 **Graves NM.** Felbamate. Ann Pharmacother. 1993;27:1073.

95 **Leppik IE et al.** Felbamate for partial seizures: results of a controlled clinical trial. Neurology. 1991;41:1785.

96 **Sachdeo R et al.** Felbamate monotherapy: controlled trial in patients with partial onset seizures. Ann Neurol. 1992;32:386.

97 **Bourgeois B et al.** Felbamate: a double-blind controlled trial in patients undergoing presurgical evaluation of partial seizures. Neurology. 1993;43:693.

98 **US Gabapentin Study Group No. 5.** Gabapentin as add-on therapy in refractory partial epilepsy: a double-blind, placebo-controlled, parallel-group study. Neurology. 1993;43: 2292.

99 **US Gabapentin Study Group.** The long-term safety and efficacy of gabapentin (Neurontin) as add-on therapy in drug-resistant partial epilepsy. Epilepsy Res. 1994;18:67.

100 **UK Gabapentin Study Group.** Gabapentin in partial epilepsy. Lancet. 1990;335:1114.

101 **Matsuo F et al.** Placebo-controlled study of the efficacy and safety of lamotrigine in patients with partial seizures. Neurology. 1993;43:2284.

102 **Messenheimer J et al.** Lamotrigine therapy for partial seizures: a multicenter, placebo-controlled, double-blind, cross-over trial. Epilepsia. 1994;35: 113.

103 **The Felbamate Study Group in Lennox-Gastaut Syndrome.** Efficacy of felbamate in childhood epileptic encephalopathy (Lennox-Gastaut syndrome). N Engl J Med. 1993;328:29.

104 **Schlumberger E et al.** Lamotrigine in treatment of 120 children with epilepsy. Epilepsia. 1994;35:359.

105 **Yuen AWC.** Lamotrigine: a review of antiepileptic efficacy. Epilepsia. 1994; 35(Suppl. 5):S33.

106 **Betts T.** Clinical use of lamotrigine. Seizure. 1992;1:3.

107 **Leppik IE.** Antiepileptic drugs in development: prospects for the near future. Epilepsia. 1994;35(Suppl. 4):S29.

108 **Graves NM et al.** Effect of felbamate on phenytoin and carbamazepine serum concentrations. Epilepsia. 1989; 30:225.

109 **Wagner ML et al.** The effect of felbamate on valproate disposition. Epilepsia. 1991;32(Suppl. 3):15.

110 **Albani F et al.** Effect of felbamate on plasma levels of carbamazepine and its metabolites. Epilepsia. 1991;32:130.

111 **Costin JC.** Important drug warning.

Dear Doctor Letter. Wallace Laboratories. August 26, 1994.

112 **Costin JC.** Important drug warning. Dear Doctor Letter. Wallace Laboratories. September 21, 1994.

113 **McLean MJ.** Clinical pharmacokinetics of gabapentin. Neurology. 1994; 44(Suppl. 5):S17.

114 **Goa KL, Sorkin EM.** Gabapentin: a review of its pharmacological properties and clinical potential in epilepsy. Drugs. 1993;46:409.

115 **Yuen AWC et al.** Sodium valproate acutely inhibits lamotrigine metabolism. Br J Clin Pharmacol. 1992;33:511.

116 **Richens A.** Safety of lamotrigine. Epilepsia. 1994;35(Suppl. 5):S37.

117 **Harden CL.** New antiepileptic drugs. Neurology. 1994;44:787.

118 **Kalviainen R et al.** Place of the newer antiepileptic drugs in the treatment of epilepsy. Drugs. 1993;46:1009.

119 **Grant SM, Faulds D.** Oxcarbazepine: a review of its pharmacology and therapeutic potential in epilepsy, trigeminal neuralgia and affective disorders. Drugs. 1992;43:873.

120 **Bialer M.** Comparative pharmacokinetics of the newer antiepileptic drugs. Clin Pharmacokinet. 1993;24:441.

121 **Ramsay RE, Slater JD.** Antiepileptic drugs in clinical development. Epilepsy Res. 1993;(Suppl. 10):45.

122 **Bebin M, Bleck TP.** New anticonvulsant drugs: focus on flunarizine, fosphenytoin, midazolam and stiripentol. Drugs. 1994;48:153.

123 **Ramsay RE.** Clinical safety and efficacy of gabapentin. Neurology. 1994; 44(Suppl. 5):S23.

124 **Sivenius J et al.** Double-blind study of gabapentin in the treatment of partial seizures. Epilepsia. 1991;32:539.

125 **Parke-Davis.** Neurontin package insert. Morris Plains, NJ: 1994 January.

126 **Allen JP et al.** Phenytoin cumulation kinetics. Clin Pharmacol Ther. 1979; 26:445.

127 **Ludden TM et al.** Rate of phenytoin accumulation in man: a simulation study. J Pharmacokinetics Biopharm. 1978;6:399.

128 **Osborn HH et al.** Single-dose oral phenytoin loading. Ann Emerg Med. 1987;16:407.

129 **Goff DA et al.** Absorption characteristics of three phenytoin sodium products after administration of oral loading doses. Clin Pharm. 1984;3:634.

130 **Evans RP et al.** Phenytoin toxicity and blood levels after a large oral dose. Am J Hosp Pharm. 1980;37:232.

131 **Jung D et al.** Effect of dose on phenytoin absorption. Clin Pharmacol Ther. 1980;28:479.

132 **Record KE et al.** Oral phenytoin loading in adults: rapid achievement of therapeutic plasma levels. Ann Neurol. 1979;5:268.

133 **Cranford RE et al.** Intravenous phenytoin: clinical and pharmacokinetic aspects. Neurology. 1978;28:874.

134 **Ludden TM et al.** Sensitivity analysis of the effect of bioavailability or dosage form content on mean steady state phenytoin concentration. Ther Drug Monitoring. 1991;13:120.

135 **Sarkar MA et al.** The effects of storage and shaking on the settling properties of phenytoin suspension. Neurology. 1989;39:207.

136 **Rankine DA, Sadler RM.** Phenytoin suspension. Neurology. 1989;39:1644. Letter.

137 **Sawchuk RJ et al.** Rapid and slow release phenytoin in epileptic patients at steady state: comparative plasma levels and toxicity. J Pharmacokinet Biopharm. 1982;10:365.

138 **Fitzsimmons WE et al.** Single dose comparison of the relative bioavailability of phenytoin suspension and extended capsules. Epilepsia. 1986;27: 464.

139 **Haerer AF, Buchanan RA.** Effectiveness of single daily doses of diphenylhydantoin. Neurology. 1972;22:1021

140 **Cooks DA et al.** Control of epilepsy with a single daily dose of phenytoin sodium. Br J Clin Pharmacol. 1975;2: 449.

141 **Sawchuk RJ et al.** Steady-state plasma concentrations as a function of the absorption rate and dosing interval for drugs exhibiting concentration-dependent clearance: consequences for phenytoin therapy. J Pharmacokinet Biopharm. 1979;7:543.

142 **Mikati M et al.** Double-blind randomized study comparing brand-name and generic phenytoin monotherapy. Epilepsia. 1992;33:359.

143 **Tindula RJ et al.** Generic phenytoin versus Dilantin for once-a-day dosing. Am J Hosp Pharm. 1981;38:1114.

144 **Kostenbauder HB et al.** Bioavailability and single-dose pharmacokinetics of intramuscular phenytoin. Clin Pharmacol Ther. 1975;18:449.

145 **Serrano EE et al.** Plasma diphenylhydantoin values after oral and intramuscular administration of diphenylhydantoin. Neurology. 1973;23:311.

146 **Serrano EE et al.** Intramuscular administration of diphenylhydantoin: histologic follow-up studies. Arch Neurol. 1974;31:276.

147 **Jamerson BD et al.** Venous irritation related to intravenous administration of phenytoin versus fosphenytoin. Pharmacotherapy. 1994;14:47.

148 **Leppik IE et al.** Phenytoin prodrug: preclinical and clinical studies. Epilepsia. 1989;30(Suppl 2):S22.

149 **Silverman AK et al.** Cutaneous and immunologic reactions to phenytoin. J Am Acad Dermatol. 1988;18:721.

150 **Butler RT et al.** Drug-induced gingival hyperplasia: phenytoin, cyclosporine, and nifedipine. J Am Dent Assoc. 1987;114:56.

151 **Stinnett E et al.** New developments in understanding phenytoin-induced gingival hyperplasia. J Am Dent Assoc. 1987;114:814.

152 **Reynolds EH.** Phenytoin: Toxicity. In: Levy RH et al., eds. Antiepileptic Drugs. New York: Raven Press; 1989: 241.

153 **Stilman N, Masdeu JC.** Incidence of seizures with phenytoin toxicity. Neurology. 1985;35:1769.

154 **Dashieff RM et al.** Seizures and phenytoin toxicity. Neurology. 1986; 36:1411.

155 **Osorio I et al.** Phenytoin-induced seizures: a paradoxical effect at toxic concentrations in epileptic patients. Epilepsia. 1989;30:230.

156 **Choonara IA, Rosenbloom L.** Focal dystonic reactions to phenytoin. Dev Med Child Neurol. 1984;26:667.

157 **Chadwick D et al.** Anticonvulsant-induced dyskinesias: a comparison with dyskinesias induced by neuroleptics. J Neurol Neurosurg Psychiatry. 1976;39: 1210.

158 **McLain LW Jr et al.** Cerebellar degeneration due to chronic phenytoin therapy. Ann Neurol. 1980;7:18.

159 **Rapport RL et al.** Phenytoin-related cerebellar degeneration without seizures. Ann Neurol. 1977;2:437.

160 **So EL, Penry JK.** Adverse effects of phenytoin on peripheral nerves and neuromuscular junction: a review. Epilepsia. 1981;22:467.

161 **Lovelace RE, Horwitz SJ.** Peripheral neuropathy in long-term diphenylhydantoin therapy. Arch Neurol. 1968;18: 69.

162 **Kutt H.** Phenytoin: interactions with other drugs. In: Levy RH et al., eds. Antiepileptic Drugs. New York: Raven Press; 1989:215.

163 **May T, Rambeck B.** Fluctuations of unbound and total phenytoin concentrations during the day in epileptic patients on valproic acid comedication. Ther Drug Monitoring. 1990;12:124.

164 **Mattson RH, Cramer JA.** Valproate: interactions with other drugs. In: Levy RH et al., eds. Antiepileptic Drugs. New York: Raven Press; 1989:621.

165 **Levy RH, Koch KM.** Drug interactions with valproic acid. Drugs. 1982; 24:543.

166 **Dreifuss FE.** Valproate: toxicity. In: Levy RH et al., eds. Antiepileptic Drugs. New York: Raven Press; 1989: 643.

167 **Booker HE.** Trimethadione. In: Levy RH et al., eds. Antiepileptic Drugs. New York: Raven Press; 1989:715.

168 **Mattson RH.** General principles: selection of therapy. In: Levy RH et al., eds. Antiepileptic Drugs. New York: Raven Press; 1989:103.

169 **Sato S.** Benzodiazepines: clonazepam. In: Levy RH et al., eds. Antiepileptic Drugs. New York: Raven Press; 1989: 765.

170 **Browne TR.** Ethosuximide (Zarontin) and other succinimides. In: Browne TR, Feldman RG, eds. Epilepsy: Diagnosis and Management. Boston: Little Brown; 1983:215.

171 **Browne TR, Mirsky AF.** Absence (petit mal) seizures. In: Browne TR, Feldman RG, eds. Epilepsy: Diagnosis and Management. Boston: Little Brown; 1983:61.

172 **Livingston S et al.** Petit mal epilepsy: results of a prolonged follow-up study of 117 patients. JAMA. 1965;194:227.

173 **Penry JK et al.** Refractiveness of absence seizures and phenobarbital. Neurology. 1971;31:158.

174 **Snead OC, Hosey LC.** Exacerbation of seizures in children by carbamazepine. N Engl J Med. 1985;313:916.

175 **Shields WD, Saslow E.** Myoclonic, atonic and absence seizures following institution of carbamazepine therapy in children. Neurology. 1983;33:1487.

176 **Wilder BJ, Rangel RJ.** Review of valproate monotherapy in the treatment of generalized tonic-clonic seizures. Am J Med. 1988;84(Suppl. 1A):7.

177 **Jones-Saete C et al.** External leakage from feeding gastrostomies in patients receiving valproate sprinkle. Epilepsia. 1992;33:692.

178 **Zaccara G et al.** Clinical pharmacokinetics of valproic acid—1988. Clin Pharmacokinet. 1988;15:367.

179 **Cloyd JC et al.** Comparison of sprinkle versus syrup formulations of valproate for bioavailability, tolerance, and preference. J Pediatr. 1992;120: 634.

180 **Fischer JH et al.** Effect of food on the serum concentration profile of enteric-coated valproic acid. Neurology. 1988; 38:1319.

181 **Bauer LA et al.** Valproic acid clearance: unbound fraction and diurnal variation in young and elderly adults. Clin Pharmacol Ther. 1985;37:697.

182 **Tennison MB et al.** Valproate metabolites and hepatotoxicity in an epileptic population. Epilepsia. 1988;29:543.

183 **Eadie MJ et al.** Valproate-associated hepatotoxicity and its biochemical mechanisms. Med Toxicol. 1988;3:85.

184 **Dreifuss FE et al.** Valproic acid hepatic fatalities: a retrospective review. Neurology. 1987;37:379.

185 **Dreifuss FE et al.** Valproic acid hepatic fatalities. II. US experience since 1984. Neurology. 1989;39:201.

186 **Dreifuss FE.** Valproic acid hepatic fatalities: revised table. Neurology. 1989;39:1558. Letter.

187 **Scheffner E et al.** Fatal liver failure in 16 children with valproate therapy. Epilepsia. 1988;29:530.

188 **Willmore LJ.** Clinical manifestations of valproate hepatotoxicity. In: Levy RH, Penry JK, eds. Idiosyncratic Reactions to Valproate: Clinical Risk Patterns and Mechanisms of Toxicity. New York: Raven Press; 1991;3.

189 **Willmore LJ et al.** Valproate toxicity: risk-screening strategies. J Child Neurol. 1991;6:3.

190 **Sofijanov N et al.** Febrile convulsions and later development of epilepsy. Am J Dis Child. 1983;137:123.

191 **Oullette EM.** Febrile Seizures. In: Browne TR, Feldman RG, eds. Epilepsy: Diagnosis and Management. Boston: Little Brown; 1983:315.

192 **Berg AT et al.** Predictors of recurrent febrile seizures: a metaanalytic review. J Pediatr. 1990;116:329.

193 **Freeman JM.** Febrile seizures: a consensus of their significance, evaluation, and treatment. Pediatrics. 1980;66: 1009.

194 **Fischbein CA et al.** Diazepam to prevent febrile seizures. N Engl J Med. 1993;329:2033. Letter.

195 **Newton RW.** Randomized controlled trials of phenobarbitone and valproate in febrile convulsions. Arch Dis Child. 1988;63:1189.

196 **Farwell JB et al.** Phenobarbital for febrile seizures—effects on intelligence and on seizure recurrence. N Engl J Med. 1990;322:364.

197 **Holmes GL et al.** Panel discussion. Epilepsia. 1991;32(Suppl. 5):S80.

198 **Committee on Drugs.** Behavioral and cognitive effects of anticonvulsant therapy. Pediatrics. 1985;76:644.

199 **Hanzel TE et al.** A case of phenobarbital exacerbation of a preexisting maladaptive behavior partially suppressed by chlorpromazine and misinterpreted as chlorpromazine efficacy. Res Dev Disabil. 1992;13:381.

200 **Rosman NP et al.** A controlled trial of diazepam administered during febrile

illnesses to prevent recurrence of febrile seizures. N Engl J Med. 1993;329: 79.

201 **Wroblewski BA et al.** Carbamazepine-erythromycin interaction: case studies and clinical significance. JAMA. 1986;255:1165.

202 **Miles MV, Tennison MB.** Erythromycin effects on multiple-dose carbamazepine pharmacokinetics. Ther Drug Monit. 1989;11:47.

203 **Loiseau P.** Sodium valproate, platelet dysfunction, and bleeding. Epilepsia. 1981;22:141.

204 **Neophytides AN et al.** Thrombocytopenia associated with sodium valproate treatment. Ann Neurol. 1979;5:389.

205 **Barr RD et al.** Valproic acid and immune thrombocytopenia. Arch Dis Childhood. 1982;57:681.

206 **Dreifuss FE, Langer DH.** Hepatic considerations in the use of antiepileptic drugs. Epilepsia. 1987;28(Suppl. 2): S23.

207 **Smythe MA, Umstead GS.** Phenytoin hepatotoxicity: a review of the literature. DICP. 1989;23:13.

208 **Howard PA et al.** Phenytoin hypersensitivity syndrome: a case report. DICP Ann Pharmacother. 1991;25: 929.

209 **Pelekanos J et al.** Allergic rash due to antiepileptic drugs: clinical features and management. Epilepsia. 1991;32: 554.

210 **Spielberg SP et al.** Predisposition to phenytoin hepatotoxicity assessed in vitro. N Engl J Med. 1981;305:722.

211 **Gerson WT et al.** Anticonvulsant-induced aplastic anemia: increased susceptibility to toxic drug metabolites in vitro. Blood. 1983;61:889.

212 **Shear NH, Spielberg SP.** Anticonvulsant hypersensitivity syndrome: in vitro assessment of risk. J Clin Invest. 1988;82:1826.

213 **Pirmohamed M et al.** Detection of an autoantibody directed against human liver microsomal protein in a patient with carbamazepine hypersensitivity. Br J Clin Pharmacol. 1992;33:183.

214 **Engel JN et al.** Phenytoin hypersensitivity: a case of severe acute rhabdomyolysis. Am J Med. 1986;81:928.

215 **Reents SB et al.** Phenytoin-carbamazepine cross-sensitivity. DICP. 1989; 23:235.

216 **Ettinger AB et al.** Use of ethotoin in phenytoin-related hypersensitivity reactions. J Epilepsy. 1993;6:29.

217 **Mattson RH et al.** Use of oral contraceptives by women with epilepsy. JAMA. 1986;256:238.

218 **Coulam CB, Annegers JF.** Do anticonvulsants reduce the efficacy of oral contraceptives? Epilepsia. 1979;20: 519.

219 **Barragry JM et al.** Effect of anticonvulsants on plasma testosterone and sex hormone binding globulin levels. J Neurol Neurosurg Psychiatry. 1978;41: 913.

220 **Elkington KW et al.** Use of oral contraceptives by women with epilepsy. JAMA. 1986;256:2961.

221 **Mattson RH, Cramer JA.** Epilepsy, sex hormones, and antiepileptic drugs. Epilepsia. 1985;26(Suppl. 1):S40.

222 **Nora JJ et al.** Exogenous progestogen and estrogen implicated in birth defects. JAMA. 1978;240:837.

223 **Delgado-Escueta AV, Janz D.** Consensus guidelines: preconception counseling, management, and care of the pregnant woman with epilepsy. Neurology. 1992;42(Suppl. 5):149.

224 **Jones KL et al.** Pattern of malformations in the children of women treated with carbamazepine during pregnancy. N Engl J Med. 1989;320:1661.

225 **Friis ML et al.** Facial clefts among epileptic patients. Arch Neurol. 1981;38: 227.

226 **VanDyke DC et al.** Family studies in fetal phenytoin exposure. J Pediatr. 1988;113:301.

227 **Yerby MS.** Problems and management of the pregnant woman with epilepsy. Epilepsia. 1987;28(Suppl. 3):S29.

228 **Janz D.** Antiepileptic drugs and pregnancy: altered utilization patterns and teratogenesis. Epilepsia. 1982;23 (Suppl. 1):S53.

229 **Lindhout D.** Pharmacogenetics and drug interactions: role in antiepileptic-drug-induced teratogenesis. Neurology. 1992;42(Suppl. 5):43.

230 **Finnell RH et al.** Clinical and experimental studies linking oxidative metabolism to phenytoin-induced teratogenesis. Neurology. 1992;42(Suppl 5): 25.

231 **Kaneko S et al.** Teratogenicity of antiepileptic drugs: analysis of possible risk factors. Epilepsia. 1988;29:459.

232 **Dansky LV et al.** Mechanisms of teratogenesis: folic acid and antiepileptic therapy. Neurology. 1992;42(Suppl. 5):32.

233 **Wegner C, Nau H.** Alteration of embryonic folate metabolism by valproic acid during organogenesis: implications for mechanism of teratogenesis. Neurology. 1992;42(Suppl. 5):17.

234 **Commission on Genetics, Pregnancy, and the Child, International League Against Epilepsy.** Guidelines for the care of epileptic women of childbearing age. Epilepsia. 1989;30:409.

235 **Schmidt D et al.** Change of seizure frequency in pregnant epileptic women. J Neurol Neurosurg Psychiatry. 1983;46: 751.

236 **Buehler BA et al.** Prenatal prediction of risk of the fetal hydantoin syndrome. N Engl J Med. 1990;322:567.

237 **Dodson WE et al.** Treatment of convulsive status epilepticus: recommendations of the Epilepsy Foundation of America's Working Group on Status Epilepticus. JAMA. 1993;270:854.

238 **Wasterlain CG et al.** Pathophysiologic mechanisms of brain damage from status epilepticus. Epilepsia. 1993;34(Suppl. 1).S37.

239 **Lothman E.** The biochemical basis and pathophysiology of status epilepticus. Neurology. 1990;40(Suppl. 2): 13.

240 **Dodrill CB, Wilensky AJ.** Intellectual impairment as an outcome of status epilepticus. Neurology. 1990;40.

241 **Leppik IE et al.** Double-blind study of lorazepam and diazepam for status epilepticus. JAMA. 1983;249:1452.

242 **Ramsay RE.** Treatment of status epilepticus. Epilepsia. 1993;34(Suppl. 1): S71.

243 **Levy RJ, Krall RL.** Treatment of status epilepticus with lorazepam. Arch Neurol. 1984;41:605.

244 **Lacey DJ et al.** Lorazepam therapy of status epilepticus in children and adolescents. J Pediatr. 1986;108:771.

245 **Treiman DM.** The role of benzodiazepines in the management of status epilepticus. Neurology. 1990;40(Suppl. 2):32.

246 **Crawford TO et al.** Lorazepam in childhood status epilepticus and serial seizures: effectiveness and tachyphylaxis. Neurology. 1987;37:190.

247 **Browne TR.** Status epilepticus. In: Browne TR, Feldman RG, eds. Epilepsy: diagnosis and management. Boston: Little Brown; 1983:341.

248 **Hillestad L et al.** Diazepam metabolism in normal man. I. Serum concentration and clinical effects after intravenous, intramuscular and oral administration. Clin Pharmacol Ther. 1974;16:479.

249 **Cloyd JC et al.** Concentration-time profile of phenytoin after admixture with small volumes of intravenous fluids. Am J Hosp Pharm. 1978;35:45.

250 **Salem RB et al.** Investigation of the crystallization of phenytoin in normal saline. Am J Hosp Pharm. 1980;14: 605.

251 **DelaCruz FG et al.** Efficacy of individualized phenytoin sodium loading doses administered by intravenous infusion. Clin Pharm. 1988;7:219.

252 **Vozeh S et al.** Intravenous phenytoin loading in patients after neurosurgery and in status epilepticus: a population pharmacokinetic study. Clin Pharmacokinet. 1988;14:122.

253 **Yaffe K, Lowenstein DH.** Prognostic factors of pentobarbital therapy for refractory generalized status epilepticus. Neurology. 1993;43:895.

254 **Kumar A, Bleck TP.** Intravenous midazolam for the treatment of refractory status epilepticus. Crit Care Med. 1992; 20:483.

255 **Browne TR.** Efficacy and safety of gabapentin. In: Chadwick D, ed. New Trends in Epilepsy Management: The Role of Gabapentin. New York: Royal Society of Medicine Services Limited; 1993:47.

256 **Connelly JF.** Vigabatrin. Ann Pharmacother. 1993;27:197.

Cerebrovascular Disorders

Timothy E Welty

Definitions 53-1
    Cerebrovascular disease 53-1
    Transient ischemic attack (TIA) 53-1
    Reversible ischemic neurological deficit (RIND) ... 53-1
    Cerebral infarction 53-1
    Cerebral hemorrhage 53-1
Epidemiology 53-2
Pathophysiology 53-2
    Thrombotic events (See Figures 53.1 and 53.2) 53-2
    Intracerebral hemorrhage 53-3
General Treatment Principles 53-3
Transient Ischemic Attacks (TIAs) 53-3
Clinical Presentation (See Table 53.2) 53-3
Risk Factors 53-4
Treatment 53-4
    Goals of therapy 53-4
    Surgical interventions 53-4
        Carotid endarterectomy (CEA) 53-4
    Drug therapy (See Table 53.3) 53-6
        Aspirin 53-6
            Patient education (See Question 10) 53-8
        Dipyridamole 53-7
        Sulfinpyrazone 53-7
        Ticlopidine 53-8
        Warfarin/anticoagulants 53-8
Cerebral Infarction and Ischemic Stroke 53-9
Clinical Presentation and Diagnostic Tests 53-9

Treatment 53-9
    Heparin 53-10
    Heparinoids 53-10
    Ancrod 53-11
    Thrombolytics 53-11
Preservation of Central Nervous System Function 53-12
    Hemodilution 53-12
    Corticosteroids 53-12
    21-aminosteroids 53-12
    Calcium channel blockers 53-12
        Nimodipine 53-13
        Nicardipine and PY108-068 53-13
    Ganglioside GM-1 53-13
Complications 53-13
Prognosis 53-13
Rehabilitation 53-13
Subarachnoid Hemorrhage 53-14
Clinical Presentation and Classification
    (See Table 53.4) 53-14
Complications (Also see Table 53.5) 53-14
    Rebleeding 53-14
    Hydrocephalus 53-14
    Delayed cerebral ischemia (vasospasm) 53-14
        Calcium channel blockers 53-15
        Nimodipine 53-15
        Nicardipine 53-15
    Seizures 53-15
        Phenytoin 53-15

Definitions

Cerebrovascular disease is a broad term encompassing a variety of disorders affecting the blood vessels of the central nervous system (CNS). These disorders result from either inadequate blood flow to the brain (i.e., cerebral ischemia) with subsequent infarction of the involved portion of the CNS or from hemorrhages into the parenchyma or subarachnoid space of the CNS and subsequent neurological dysfunction. A variety of terms have been used to describe cerebrovascular events, but the four most commonly used terms are defined below. It should be noted that this chapter does not include discussions on traumatic head injuries or increased intracranial pressure.

Transient Ischemic Attack (TIA). A transient ischemic attack describes the clinical condition in which a patient experiences a temporary focal neurological deficit such as slurred speech, aphasia, weakness or paralysis of a limb, or blindness. These symptoms are rapid in onset and temporary in nature, lasting less than 24 hours (usually only 2 to 15 minutes). The exact clinical presentation depends upon the portion of the cerebrovascular tree (e.g., carotid artery, vertebrobasilar artery, or both) affected by diminished or absent blood flow. Transient ischemic attacks frequently result from emboli which break away from distant blood clots. These emboli are then dissolved by the fibrinolytic system, allowing re-establishment of blood flow and return of neurologic function.

Reversible Ischemic Neurological Deficit (RIND). A RIND is similar to a TIA, since the neurological deficits associated with the ischemic event are temporary. However, when a patient experiences a RIND the deficit improves over no more than 72 hours and may not completely resolve. This is in contrast to a TIA where the patient regains normal neurological function within 24 hours. During a RIND the patient experiences a loss of blood flow to a portion of the brain, usually due to an embolic or thrombotic clot. Neurological function is regained as the clot is slowly lysed or collateral blood flow to the affected area of the brain replaces the lost flow.

Cerebral Infarction. A cerebral infarction is described as a permanent form of neurological disorder with symptoms similar to a TIA or a RIND. The patient with a cerebral infarction presents with fixed neurological deficits caused by the death of neurons in a focal area of the brain. The two primary causes of infarction and persistent ischemia are atherosclerosis or an embolus to cerebral arteries. Cerebral infarctions can present in three forms: stable, improving, or progressing. A *stable infarction* describes the condition when the neurological deficit is permanent, will not improve and will not deteriorate. An *improving infarction* is marked by return of previously lost neurological function over several days or weeks. Finally, a *progressing infarction* is one in which the patient's neurological status continues to deteriorate following the initial onset of focal deficits.

Cerebral Hemorrhage. This cerebrovascular disorder involves escape of blood from the vasculature into the brain and its surrounding structures. The leakage of blood causes clinical symptoms similar to those associated with a TIA or infarction. The neurological damage that is associated with TIAs or cerebral infarction results from the lack of blood flow to a given portion of the brain.

In a cerebral hemorrhage, the initial neurological deficits are due to the direct irritant effects of blood that is in direct contact with brain tissue. Primary causes of a cerebral hemorrhage include subarachnoid hemorrhage, arteriovenous malformation (AVM), hypertensive hemorrhage, and trauma.

The term "stroke" or "paralytic stroke" is commonly used by lay people to describe a sudden neurological affliction that usually is related to the cerebral blood supply. A "stroke," therefore, can be due to cerebral ischemia, infarction, or hemorrhage, and usually implies permanent neurological deficits.

Epidemiology

Annually, about 500,000 individuals in the U.S. experience a cerebral infarction and about 150,000 will die due to the neurological destruction. Cerebrovascular disease is the third most common cause of death and is one of the more commonly encountered causes of neurological dysfunction.[1] This nevertheless represents a dramatic decrease in the mortality rate of ischemic stroke from 88.8 per 100,000 population in 1950 to 30.1 per 100,000 in 1988 (the last available data). There is an important difference in mortality rates for ischemic stroke between blacks and whites. The mortality rate for black men is 57.9 per 100,000 and 46.6 per 100,000 for black women, while the mortality rate for white men is 30 per 100,000 and 25.6 per 100,000 for white women. The precise reasons for these differences are unclear, but geographic, economic, and social factors have been speculated.[2] In addition the incidence of other risk factors like hypertension, diabetes, and hypercholesterolemia is higher in blacks.

Atherosclerotic disease of large arteries (e.g., carotid arteries, vertebrobasilar arteries) is responsible for about 60% of cerebral ischemia and infarctions. Disease of penetrating arteries that are responsible for oxygenation and nutrition of the CNS account for another 20%; cardiogenic causes (e.g., atrial fibrillation) account for 15%; and the remaining 5% are due to unusual causes such as infection or inflammation of arteries.[3]

There is a strong relationship between TIA and cerebral infarction; however, the precise incidence of a TIA progressing to infarction is unclear. Studies of transient ischemic attacks associated with carotid artery stenosis have shown that 2% to 50% will progress to subsequent cerebral infarction.[4] Differing classifications of patients, poor documentation of atheromatous lesions, and varying periods of follow-up account for the rather wide range of study results. Overall, about 4% to 8% of patients experiencing a TIA will have an ischemic stroke in each year following the initial TIA.[5,6]

Definite risk factors for cerebral infarction are listed in Table 53.1. Less certain risk factors include oral contraceptive use, diet, abnormal blood lipids, personality, pregnancy, and geographical location.[7] A key element in the management of stroke is the elimination or control of risk factors. The first step in managing a patient with a TIA, RIND, or cerebral infarction is control of risk factors. All other therapies for stroke prophylaxis or treatment are secondary to control or elimination of risk factors.

Hemorrhage into the brain accounts for 10% of all strokes.[6] Hypertensive hemorrhage is the most frequent cause of intracerebral hemorrhages (ICHs) with 46% of ICHs being due to hypertension.[8] Subarachnoid hemorrhage occurs in about 26,000 individuals annually and carries a mortality rate of approximately 50%. Victims of this disorder are usually 20 to 70 years old and 20% to 50% of the survivors will suffer permanent neurological deficits.[9,10] The majority of neurological deficits will be due not to the original hemorrhage, but to complications of rebleeding or hydrocephalus or problems from delayed cerebral ischemia. A less

Table 53.1	Definite Risk Factors for Ischemic Stroke
Lifestyle Risk Factors	Pathophysiologic Risk Factors
Age (older)	Blood pressure differences between arms[a]
Alcohol abuse	Cardiac disease[b]
Cigarette smoking	Carotid bruit[c]
Drug abuse	Diabetes mellitus
Genetic factors	Hypertension
Males	↑ fibrinogen
	↑ hematocrit
	Migraine headaches[d]
	Sickle cell disease[e]
	Retinal emboli[f]
	Transient ischemic attacks (past history)

[a] This may indicate an aortic obstruction involving or prior to carotid artery.

[b] Atrial fibrillation especially is associated with stroke due to the potential for embolism. However, the presence of cardiovascular disease is associated with peripheral and cerebrovascular disease.

[c] A carotid bruit indicates a blood flow defect in the carotid artery and usually is associated with a carotid artery thrombus. This increases the risk for small emboli to go to the brain.

[d] Migraine headaches are caused by strong vasoconstriction. In especially severe cases, the constriction of the cerebral arteries results in cerebral ischemia and stroke.

[e] Ischemic events are common in sickle cell disease due to clumping of red blood cells in arterioles and capillaries, restricting blood flow.

[f] Since the retinal artery is supplied from the carotid artery, an embolus to the retina usually is indicative of a carotid artery thrombus.

common cause of ICH is an arteriovenous malformation, usually resulting from a congenital defect or trauma.

Pathophysiology

Thrombotic Events

Usually, the neurological sequelae of cerebral ischemia or infarction directly result from an embolic or thrombotic source. A clot may form in the heart, along the wall of a major cerebral vessel (e.g., carotid or basilar artery), or in arteries penetrating deep into the central nervous system. If the clot is located in the vicinity of the infarction, it is considered to be a thrombus; however, when the clot has migrated to the CNS from a distant source, it is considered to be an embolus. Either can diminish or block blood flow to the affected area of the CNS.

The majority of clots, embolic and thrombotic, that affect the cerebral vasculature are arterial in origin. These are fibrin clots, also known as *white thrombi*, evolving from a complex series of events (see Figure 53.1). Tissue injury or turbulent blood flow cause the release of adenosine diphosphate (ADP), thrombin, epinephrine, and a variety of other substances to stimulate platelet migration. Exposure of collagen and other subendothelial surfaces of the blood vessel wall results in adhesion of platelets to the damaged vessel wall. Additional granular release of ADP causes increased adhesion of platelets and the formation of platelet aggregates.[11]

As platelets adhere and aggregate, phospholipase is activated leading to the splitting of arachidonic acid from platelet membrane phospholipid. This begins a cascade of events ultimately ending in the formation of thromboxane A_2 (TXA_2) and prostacyclin. Prostacyclin inhibits platelet aggregation and is a powerful vasodilator, while TXA_2 is a potent inducer of platelet release and aggregation. Prostacyclin is formed in and released from arterial and venous walls. TXA_2 is formed in and released from the platelet. A delicate balance between these two compounds controls thrombogenesis. When a clot is formed it can either embolize to the cerebral vasculature or occlude a cerebral artery.

When neurons become ischemic, excitatory neurotransmitters such as N-methyl-D-aspartate (NMDA) and glutamate are released. An excess of these neurotransmitters causes neurons to rapidly and repeatedly discharge, compromising the survival of damaged neurons around the area of infarction. This increased neuronal activity results in extreme metabolic demands, disrupts neuronal homeostasis, and synergistically increases the effects of hypoxia. Especially vulnerable to ischemic effects are neurons in the middle layers of the cerebral cortex, portions of the hippocampus (CA-1 and subiculum regions), a structure running parallel to the parahippocampal gyrus, and Purkinje cells in the cerebellum (see Figure 53.2).[12]

In addition, ischemia results in rapid intracellular influx of calcium that also is destructive to the neurons. Both voltage-dependent and chemical-dependent calcium channels are unable to act as a gate to prevent calcium influx. Intracellular stores of calcium ions also are disrupted causing release of calcium into the cytoplasm. Increased concentration of calcium ions causes destruction of the cellular lipoprotein portion of the cell membrane. This results in an inability of the cell to maintain intracellular homeostasis and eventually causes neuronal death.[13,14]

These events, the release of excitatory neurotransmitters and increased intracellular calcium concentrations, occur rapidly following ischemia. Unless the neurons are quickly supplied with oxygen, glucose, and other metabolic substrates they will die, resulting in permanent neurological damage.

Intracerebral Hemorrhage

Cerebral aneurysms, arteriovenous malformations (AVM), hypertension, and adverse drug reactions are the four major causes of intracerebral hemorrhage. Intracerebral hemorrhage into the subarachnoid space can result from weakened blood vessel walls (i.e., aneurysms) caused by congenital defects, trauma, infection, and hypertension. Blood can leak slowly from the involved vessel or the aneurysm may rupture suddenly. The direct contact of blood with brain tissue irritates and damages brain cells. Rebleeding, hydrocephalus, and delayed cerebral ischemia frequently will occur after the aneurysm first ruptures, further worsening the patient's neurological function.

Arteriovenous malformations, due to congenital causes or traumatic injury, and uncontrolled hypertension also can cause devastating intracerebral bleeding. Occasionally, intracerebral hemorrhages are the result of adverse reactions to drugs, such as anticoagulants, thrombolytics, and sympathomimetics.[4]

General Treatment Principles

Rapid recognition of stroke symptoms and the immediate initiation of treatment is essential to the management of ischemic or hemorrhagic stroke. The pharmacological management of cerebrovascular disease requires a precise diagnosis. It is vital to differentiate between an ischemic stroke and a hemorrhagic stroke, since an inaccurate diagnosis can lead to the use of drugs that may cause severe morbidity or mortality. Anticoagulation may be beneficial in certain types of ischemic stroke, but would be disastrous in a hemorrhagic stroke. Interventions to prevent and treat ischemic strokes are directed at reducing risk factors, eliminating or modifying the underlying pathological process, reducing secondary brain damage, and rehabilitation.

Transient Ischemic Attacks (TIAs)

Clinical Presentation

1. J.S., a 55-year-old 5'6" tall male weighing 85 kg, experienced a rapidly progressive paralysis of his right arm and slurred speech yesterday. These symptoms lasted for 15–20 minutes and resolved rapidly. His neurological examination is entirely normal and he denies any feeling of weakness. He smokes 2 packs of cigarettes a day and drinks 3–6 cans of beer each evening. His physical examination is entirely normal except for a left carotid bruit which was first noted 2 years ago. His blood pressure (BP) is 165/100 mm Hg and he has a long history of hypertension. His hemoglobin (Hgb) is 16.5 gm/dL (Normal: 12–16), hematocrit (Hct) is 51% (Normal: 42–52), and a total serum cholesterol concentration is 275 mg/dL. A Doppler examination of his carotid arteries shows a 90% stenosis on the left and a 40% stenosis on the right. What subjective and objective data in J.S.'s history are consistent with a TIA? [SI units: Hgb 165 gm/L (Normal: 120–160; Hct 0.51 (Normal: 0.42–0.52); cholesterol 7.11 mmol/L]

A transient ischemic attack can present with any type of neurological deficit. The presentation is determined entirely by the location of the involved arteries and the portion of the brain they supply (see Figure 53.3). For example, if the affected artery provides circulation to the motor strip in the left hemisphere of the brain, the expected result would be impairment of the right side of the body. Symptoms of TIA may include paresis or paralysis of one or more limbs, slurred speech, blurred vision, blindness (amaurosis fugax), facial droop, or difficulty in swallowing (see Table 53.2). The patient will rarely lose consciousness. Symptoms always resolve within 24 hours and there is no residual focal neurological deficit. Most often the neurological deficits last for only 2 to 15 minutes and neurological function rapidly returns to normal.

J.S.'s rapid onset of right arm paralysis and slurred speech is suggestive of a left carotid lesion. The 15 to 20 minute duration of these symptoms and the entirely normal neurological exami-

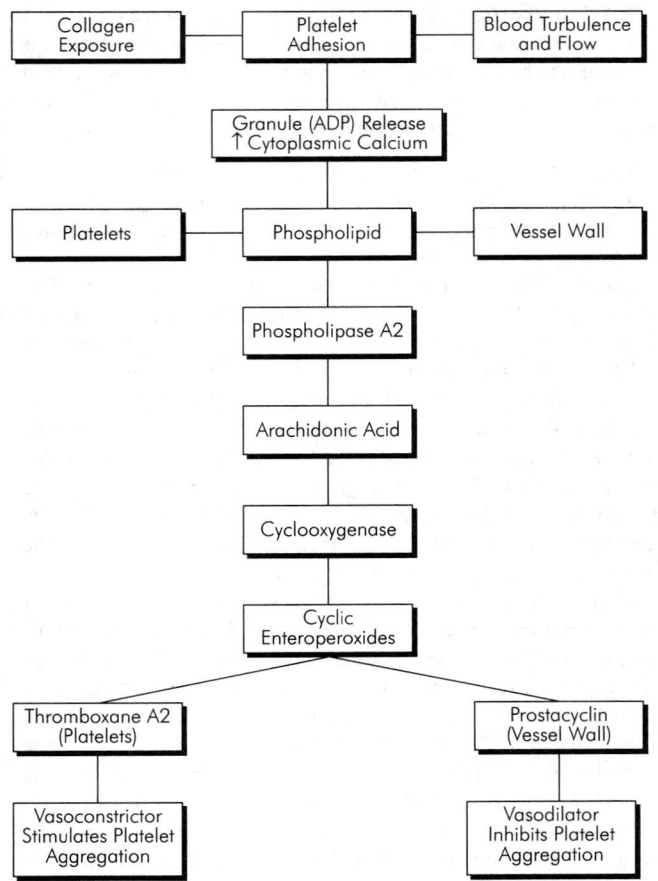

Fig 53.1 Arachidonic acid cascade and platelet plug formation

Fig 53.2 A Sagittal Section of the Cerebral Hemisphere Showing the Major Anatomical Landmarks

nation on the day subsequent to these symptoms also are compatible with a TIA. The left carotid bruit heard on physical examination is consistent with a left-sided process. The high serum cholesterol concentration suggests an atherosclerotic lesion as a possible cause of his TIA.

Right-sided neurological deficits generally suggest a left-sided cerebral lesion because motor and sensory neuronal tracts cross over in the midbrain. Thus, the left hemisphere of the cerebral cortex controls the right or contralateral side of the body. CNS lesions occurring below the midbrain will cause ipsilateral neurological deficits. J.S.'s right arm paralysis, therefore, suggests a left-sided cerebral lesion above the midbrain.

Risk Factors

2. How can risk factors for J.S. be limited to prevent another TIA?

J.S. has several major risk factors for TIA and ischemic stroke (see Table 53.1): a smoking history, alcohol consumption, obesity, older age, male gender, hypercholesterolemia, and hypertension. He should be instructed and counseled to change his lifestyle by discontinuing his smoking, limiting his alcohol consumption, reducing his weight, and increasing his physical exercise. Hypoxia and hypercarbia induced by cigarette smoking may have caused his increased hematocrit, and his high serum cholesterol and obesity suggest the need for dietary changes. Aggressive reduction of risk factors should limit the recurrence of a TIA.

Since approximately 90% of strokes are due to uncontrolled hypertension, blood pressure control is vital for stroke prevention; an increased risk for stroke is associated with both systolic and diastolic hypertension.[15] The goals of antihypertensive therapy should be a systolic blood pressure less than 140 mm Hg and a diastolic pressure less than 90 mm Hg.[16] Since the 1960s, the control of hypertension has been shown repeatedly to decrease the risk of stroke and has proved to be of significant pharmacoeconomic benefit.[17-20]

Thus, continued management of J.S.'s hypertension is imperative; however, his blood pressure should be reduced gradually. A sudden or dramatic decrease in blood pressure could compromise cerebral perfusion and result in a decreased level of consciousness

or infarction. The degree of his carotid artery stenosis will contribute to the problem of decreased perfusion if the blood pressure is decreased rapidly. A mild degree of hypertension may be temporarily acceptable because of the extent of carotid stenosis.

Treatment

Goals of Therapy

3. What are the initial and long term goals in treating J.S.?

The immediate goal is to re-establish adequate blood flow in his diseased cerebral vessels. Longer range objectives are to prevent re-occlusion, decrease the risk of future symptomatic TIAs, and ultimately to prevent a cerebral infarction.[21]

Surgical Interventions

4. What nonpharmacological interventions might be available to prevent another TIA? What would be the best choice for J.S.?

A variety of surgical interventions are available to prevent TIA or infarction. These are designed to either remove the source for an embolism or improve circulation to ischemic areas of the brain.

Carotid endarterectomy (CEA) is a common surgical procedure for correcting atheromatous lesions that are responsible for causing a TIA. In this procedure the carotid artery is surgically exposed and the atheromatous plaque is excised. Balloon angioplasty also can improve blood flow through a stenosed artery. During this procedure a catheter with a small deflated balloon is placed in the stenosed artery and the atherosclerotic lesion is pressed into the arterial wall when the balloon is inflated.

CEA should be reserved for patients with an ulcerated lesion or stenotic clot that occludes ≥70% of blood flow in the carotid artery. Use of CEA in these patients may result in a 60% reduction in stroke risk over the subsequent two years.[22-24] In addition CEA has been associated with reducing the risk of functional impairment of patients with TIA or partial strokes with ipsilateral high-grade carotid stenosis.[25] The use of CEA in individuals with 30% to 69% stenosis has not been thoroughly studied. Generally, carotid endarterectomy is not indicated in patients who have permanent neurological deficits or total occlusion of the carotid artery.[26,27] Vertebral-to-carotid artery transposition for vertebral stenosis and

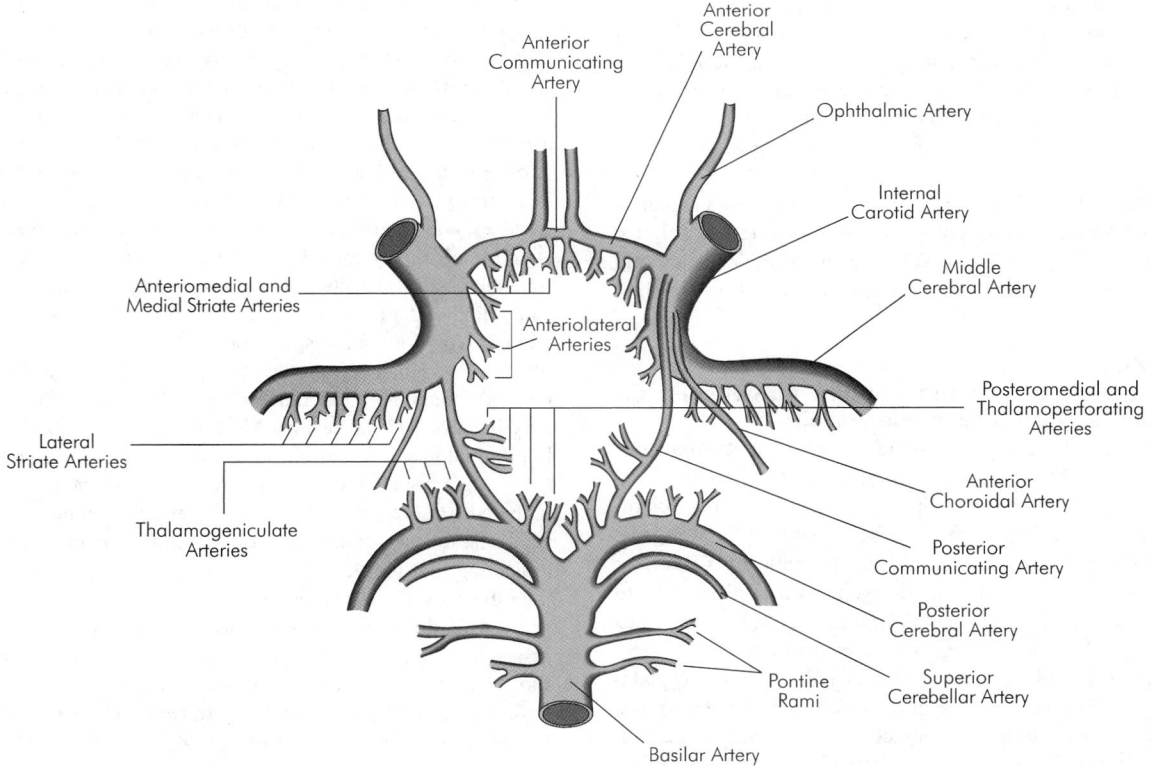

Fig 53.3   A View of the Major Cerebral Arteries Seen From the Base of the Brain and in Relation to the Circle of Willis   The middle artery primarily supplies the motor and sensory strips of the parietal lobe; the posterior cerebral artery primarily supplies the occipital lobe; and the anterior artery primarily supplies the frontal lobe.

Table 53.2	Symptoms Associated with Transient Ischemic Attacks		
Symptom	Right Carotid	Left Carotid	Vertebrobasilar
Aphasia	Possible	Yes	No
Ataxia	No	No	Yes
Blindness	Right	Left	Right or left
Clumsiness	Yes	Yes	Yes
Diplopia	No	No	Yes
Dysarthria	Yes	Yes	No
Paralysis	Left side	Right side	Any limb
Paresthesia	Left side	Right side	Any limb
Vertigo	No	No	Yes

vertebral endarterectomy for vertebral artery stenosis are surgical interventions that generally have been abandoned because of questionable benefits and high morbidity.[28,29]

A major concern following CEA is the problem of re-stenosis. Over the first year after CEA, 25% of patients will redevelop a stenotic lesion, with more than half of these causing a greater than 50% reduction in carotid blood flow.[30] Initial studies indicated that combination therapy with aspirin 325 mg/day and dipyridamole 75 mg three times a day would decrease the rate of re-stenosis.[31,32] However, a subsequent randomized, placebo-controlled study using this regimen in post-CEA patients did not substantiate the earlier findings. Harker and colleagues showed that a greater than 50% stenotic lesion developed in 26% of treated patients and in 12% of placebo patients.[33] There were similar findings for stenotic lesions of 20% to 50%. Since dipyridamole has been shown repeatedly to be ineffective in preventing thrombus formation, it is presumed that aspirin also is ineffective in preventing re-stenosis following CEA.

J.S. should undergo CEA for his left carotid lesion as soon as possible. The lesion on the right should be monitored closely for continued progression. If further TIAs occur or the right carotid stenosis is ≥70% he should have a CEA performed on the right carotid artery.

Drug Therapy

5. Aspirin. What role does aspirin have in preventing the progression of a TIA to an ischemic stroke?

Since platelets play a key role in the formation of atheromatous clots (see Figure 53.1), various antiplatelet drugs, such as aspirin,[34–44] sulfinpyrazone,[31,45] dipyridamole,[32,46,47] and ticlopidine,[48,49] have been tried to prevent ischemic strokes. These agents generally work by either preventing the formation of TXA_2 or increasing the concentration of prostacyclin. This action seeks to re-establish the proper balance between these two substances, thus preventing the adhesion and aggregation of platelets.

Due to its wide availability and well understood actions on platelet function, aspirin has been the most widely tested agent for use in preventing transient ischemic attack and ischemic stroke. Aspirin primarily acts by irreversibly inactivating platelet cyclooxygenase.[50] Inactivation of cyclooxygenase decreases platelet aggregation, prevents release of vasoactive substances, and prolongs the bleeding time. These changes are due to suppression of TXA_2 synthesis by cyclooxygenase. Since binding of cyclooxygenase by the acetyl component of acetylsalicylic acid [(ASA) aspirin] is irreversible and the platelet cannot synthesize new protein, platelet function is altered for the duration of the platelet's life, usually five to seven days. Aspirin's ability to prevent clot formation and sub-

sequent embolic or thrombotic events also can be attributed to an inhibition of TXA_2 vasoconstriction, activation of fibrinolysis, inhibition of synthesis of vitamin K-dependent clotting factors, and inhibition of lipooxygenase pathways.

In addition to its action on platelet cyclooxygenase, high concentrations of aspirin also inhibit prostacyclin synthesis in the walls of blood vessels. Since prostacyclin inhibits platelet aggregation, depletion of prostacyclin could result in an undesirable increase in aggregation of platelets. However, depletion of prostacyclin is not prolonged because the vascular endothelium is able to synthesize new enzymes. Higher doses of aspirin (1.3 gm/day) also may decrease vascular plasminogen activator thereby enhancing thrombus formation.[51–53] For this reason, aspirin should be dosed carefully.

At least 15 randomized trials have studied aspirin alone or in combination with other antiplatelet drugs in the prevention of cerebrovascular events. Over 13,000 patients were included in these studies and seven of these trials compared aspirin with placebo.[36] Patients were enrolled in these studies for as long as five years after experiencing a vascular event (i.e., TIA, stroke, unstable angina, or myocardial infarction). Follow-up periods lasted from one to six years. The incidence of cerebrovascular accidents (CVAs) ranged from 7% to 23%: the aspirin-treated patients experienced an average 22% decrease in risk of a stroke compared to those receiving placebo. Of these 15 trials, only four reported no statistically significant benefit with aspirin, and these four studies involved small numbers of patients. These data clearly show that aspirin is effective for preventing stroke in patients who have a history of cerebrovascular events.

In ten trials which considered only TIA or stroke patients, there was a 24% reduction in the incidence of nonfatal stroke associated with the use of antiplatelet agents. A statistically significant benefit from aspirin was demonstrated in all but two of these studies. When considered in total, it is overwhelmingly conclusive that aspirin reduces the risk of stroke and death in patients who have experienced a previous TIA or stroke. Even though this fact has been firmly established, questions about the ideal dose, gender differences, and its efficacy relative to ticlopidine have been debated.

In initial studies considering the use of aspirin in stroke prevention, the positive effects were seen primarily in men. The Canadian study did not demonstrate any benefit of aspirin in women, and the United Kingdom TIA study only showed minimal benefit in women.[31,40] However, the incidence of stroke is lower in women; thus, a greater preponderance of men in both study populations may have biased the results. More recent studies have attempted to eliminate gender bias and have produced differing results. The European Stroke Prevention Study and the French AICLA study included a more equal balance of men and women.[32,39] In both studies, the risk reduction rate was equal for men and women, indicating that the benefit of aspirin in stroke prevention extends to both sexes. Caution must be exercised when interpreting stroke study data since women have lower stroke rates, making it necessary to include larger numbers and longer follow-up periods to show the benefit of aspirin or other antiplatelet drugs.

6. If J.S. had been taking aspirin regularly before this event, would he have been at a lower risk for developing a TIA or stroke?

The data for primary prevention (i.e., prophylactic treatment in previously asymptomatic individuals) is controversial. In a study of 22,071 male physicians who took 325 mg of aspirin or placebo every other day for five years, there was not a reduced incidence of stroke.[54,55] This group of individuals who had no previous history of cerebrovascular disease experienced 217 strokes, 119 in the aspirin group and 98 in the placebo group. In addition, there was an increased risk of cerebrovascular events due to hemorrhage in

Table 53.3 — Drugs for Transient Ischemic Attacks and Ischemic Stroke[a]

Drug	Indication	Action	Dose	Adverse Reaction
Aspirin	Prophylaxis	Antiplatelet	325–900 mg/day	Diarrhea, gastric ulcer, GI upset
Dexamethasone	Not indicated	Glucocorticoid	NA	—
Dextran	Not indicated	Hemodilution; antiplatelet	NA	—
Dipyridamole	Not indicated	Antiplatelet	NA	—
Heparin	Stroke in progression	Anticoagulant	Titrate to PTT 1.5–2 × baseline	Bleeding, thrombocytopenia, petechiae
Nimodipine	Subarachnoid hemorrhage	Calcium channel blocker	60 mg PO Q 6 hr	Hypotension
Sulfinpyrazone	Not indicated	Antiplatelet	NA	—
Ticlopidine	Prophylaxis	Antiplatelet	500 mg/day	Diarrhea; neutropenia; rash
Warfarin	Cardiogenic emboli	Anticoagulant	Titrate to INR 2–3	Bleeding, bruising, petechiae

[a] GI = Gastrointestinal; NA = Not available; PT = Prothrombin time; PTT = Partial thromboplastin time; INR = International normalized ratio.

the aspirin group. The results of this study indicate that aspirin should be withheld until after an individual experiences a TIA or stroke.

Additional studies supporting the use of aspirin in previously asymptomatic patients are lacking.[187] Two long-term, longitudinal studies are currently underway, but results from these trials have not been published.[188]

7. What dose of aspirin should be used for J.S.?

Doses of aspirin used in clinical trials have ranged from 50 to 1500 mg/day. In a meta-analysis of placebo-controlled studies using 900 to 1500 mg/day of aspirin compared to similar studies using 300 to 325 mg/day, there was a 23% reduction in the risk of cerebrovascular events in patients receiving 900 to 1500 mg/day and a 24% reduction in risk in patients receiving 300 to 325 mg/day.[36] More direct studies of aspirin dosing have been attempted and have produced conflicting results. A Dutch trial in 3131 patients showed a 14.7% frequency of nonfatal stroke or nonfatal myocardial infarction in patients receiving 30 mg of aspirin a day and a 15.2% frequency in patients receiving 283 mg of aspirin a day, a nonsignificant difference between these two doses.[56] The Swedish Aspirin Low-Dose Trial (SALT) showed an 18% reduction in stroke in patients taking 75 mg of aspirin daily compared to placebo.[57] Two other studies have shown that increasing doses of aspirin have increased effects on platelet aggregation. Helgason and colleagues compared the effects of 325, 650, 975, and 1300 mg of aspirin a day in stroke patients.[58] Platelet aggregation studies were performed to determine the effects of aspirin. Eighty-five of 107 patients achieved complete suppression of aggregation at a daily dose of 325 mg. An additional five patients responded at 650 mg/day, and only one more responded at 975 mg/day. There was no further response at 1300 mg. Similar findings were reported by Tohgi and colleagues.[59]

In a large retrospective cohort study, Bornstein and colleagues found no benefit with aspirin doses less than 500 mg/day.[60] A total of 2231 patients admitted to the hospital with a diagnosis of stroke were enrolled in the study. For one cohort aspirin dose and date of first stroke were matched, another cohort matched age, sex, and date of first stroke, and the third cohort matched age, sex, dates of first stroke, and aspirin dose. When cohorts were compared, age and sex did not influence the effectiveness of aspirin in preventing stroke. However, there was a clear association between decreased risk of stroke and aspirin doses greater than 500 mg/day. The retrospective nature of this trial limits the usefulness of these findings, but they do tend to support the need to use higher doses of aspirin for stroke prevention.

A more recent meta-analysis of all published trials of antiplatelet agents did show that aspirin doses of 75 to 325 mg/day were effective in preventing stroke.[61] The advantage of this study is that 145 trials representing 100,000 patients were evaluated. However, all patients in these trials had survived a stroke, TIA, or myocardial infarction before being started on an antiplatelet agent. It did not address the use of antiplatelet agents before a cerebrovascular event.

Until more conclusive evidence for lower doses of aspirin is available, the recommended dose is 325 to 975 mg/day. The goal is to use the lowest effective aspirin dose to prevent recurrent transient ischemic attacks or stroke and to limit the gastrointestinal side effects of aspirin.[62] Thus, J.S. should be started on an aspirin dose of 325 mg/day and the dose should be increased only if he experiences repeated symptoms of a TIA.

8. Dipyridamole. Should dipyridamole be used alone or in combination with aspirin for J.S.? Would sulfinpyrazone offer any advantages over dipyridamole?

Two pharmacologic actions of dipyridamole prompted investigations into its use in preventing TIAs and ischemic stroke. *In vitro* data suggest that dipyridamole weakly inhibits platelet aggregation and platelet phosphodiesterase.[63] In addition, increased platelet survival has been noted subsequent to administration of dipyridamole in patients and animals suffering from platelet consumptive disorders.[64,65] Dipyridamole also has potential vasodilating properties through its inhibition of adenosine uptake in vascular smooth muscle.

These pharmacodynamic actions of dipyridamole, however, have not been substantiated in clinical trials that used dipyridamole for the management of stroke.[36] At least five clinical studies have used dipyridamole in combination with aspirin and one trial compared dipyridamole alone to placebo. These trials consistently showed that the combination of dipyridamole and aspirin did not further decrease the risk of a cerebrovascular event when compared to aspirin alone. When dipyridamole was compared to placebo, the incidences of TIA and stroke were similar in both treatment groups. Since there is no apparent benefit of dipyridamole in preventing TIA or stroke, it is not recommended for J.S.

Sulfinpyrazone (Anturane) inhibits platelet function by reversibly binding to cyclooxygenase. Studies that used sulfinpyrazone either as a single agent or in combination with aspirin have not shown it to be of benefit in reducing TIA.[36] For this reason, sulfinpyrazone is no longer recommended for use in the management of transient ischemic attack.

9. Ticlopidine. What are the risks and benefits of using ticlopidine instead of aspirin in J.S.?

Ticlopidine (Ticlid) is an antiplatelet agent approved only for the prevention of TIA and stroke in patients with a prior cerebral thrombotic event. By inhibiting ADP-induced platelet aggregation, its activity differs from aspirin.[66,67]

A randomized, double-blind, placebo-controlled, multicenter trial, the Canadian American Ticlopidine Study (CATS), provides evidence that ticlopidine significantly reduces the risk of stroke.[45] One thousand seventy-two patients were enrolled to receive either 500 mg of ticlopidine a day (in 2 divided doses) or an identical placebo. Patients were enrolled between one week and four months after a thromboembolic stroke and were followed at four-month intervals for a maximum of three years. In the ticlopidine group, 53 patients experienced another stroke, while 88 patients experienced a stroke in the placebo group. This represents a risk reduction of 30.2% for all vascular events and 33.5% reduction for stroke. Stratification by gender did not demonstrate a difference between males and females. At all evaluation points, the number of vascular events was significantly less in the ticlopidine group.

The Ticlopidine Aspirin Stroke Study Group (TASS), a triple-blind (the patient, physician, and drug company were unaware of the randomization) multicenter study evaluated 3069 patients who received either 500 mg/day of ticlopidine or 1300 mg/day of ASA.[46] Individuals greater than 40 years of age who had suffered a TIA or minor stroke within the past three months were eligible for enrollment into this study. Follow-up was at four-month intervals and lasted for as long as five years. The ticlopidine-treated group experienced an early and sustained reduction in stroke incidence. Death from any cause, including stroke, occurred in 306 patients receiving ticlopidine and 349 patients receiving ASA. Stroke occurred in 172 patients on ticlopidine and 212 patients on ASA. Thus, risk was reduced by 12% for all events when ticlopidine was compared to ASA and by 21% for stroke. Again, the risk was reduced for both sexes.

One subgroup analysis from the TASS study yielded interesting findings in regards to the efficacy of ticlopidine in nonwhite patients.[68] Over one year, 5.5% of 312 nonwhite patients who received ticlopidine suffered a nonfatal stroke or death from any cause, compared to 10.6% of 291 nonwhite aspirin-treated patients. This represents a 48.1% risk reduction associated with ticlopidine relative to aspirin in nonwhite patients. Note the 21% risk reduction in the total study population described above. Another important finding in this subgroup analysis is that none of the neutropenia cases occurred in nonwhite patients. Although these findings give strong evidence for an improved response with ticlopidine in nonwhite patients, direct comparative studies are needed.

There was a significantly higher occurrence of peptic ulcer for patients receiving ASA in the TASS. Diarrhea occurred in 20% to 22% of patients on ticlopidine and resulted in discontinuation of the drug in 1% to 6% of patients. Although there were no life-threatening dermatological complications, 12% to 15% of patients experienced a rash and approximately 5% discontinued ticlopidine. The total serum cholesterol increased by 9% in patients on ticlopidine; but the ratio of high-density lipoprotein to total cholesterol ratio was unchanged.

A more disturbing reaction, neutropenia, developed in about 1% to 2% of patients on ticlopidine in both the CATS and TASS studies. Severe neutropenia [absolute neutrophil count (ANC) <450/mm^3] usually appears in the first three months of therapy and is reversible when the drug is discontinued. One episode of neutropenia-associated infection was reported in the CATS study. In the TASS group, mild-to-moderate neutropenia (ANC 450 to 1200/mm^3) was reported, but ticlopidine was not discontinued in

these patients. As a result of the rather high potential for this adverse reaction, a complete blood count should be performed every two weeks for the first three months of therapy.

Both the CATS and TASS studies indicate that ticlopidine is effective in reducing the risk for TIA and stroke in patients who have previously experienced a cerebrovascular event. It is more effective than ASA, and the reduced risk of gastrointestinal bleeding is to its advantage. Neutropenia and the marked increased cost associated with ticlopidine (both for the drug itself and for laboratory monitoring) limit its use. Ticlopidine should be reserved for individuals who have failed aspirin therapy or who are intolerant of aspirin due to allergy or gastrointestinal bleeding. At this time, its use also should be limited to patients who have experienced a TIA or stroke.

J.S. is clearly at risk for additional TIAs or an ischemic stroke. The most important element in reducing this risk is to change his lifestyle. However, since J.S. has experienced a TIA, he should be placed on an antiplatelet agent. He does not have any definite contraindications to aspirin, so it should be initiated at a dose of 325 mg/day as previously described. This dose should minimize the potential for gastrointestinal problems and provide adequate prophylaxis for TIA or stroke. Ticlopidine should be considered only if J.S. is unable to tolerate aspirin.

10. *Aspirin: Patient Education.* **The physician decides to begin J.S. on aspirin 325 mg/day. How should he be counseled on the use of aspirin? Should J.S. be advised to discontinue ASA before surgical and dental procedures?**

Even low doses of aspirin may cause gastric erosions and gastric ulcers. J.S. should be instructed to take aspirin with the largest meal of the day, inform his physician of any epigastric pain and seek medical attention at the first sign of any gastric bleeding (e.g., dark stools). Enteric-coated aspirin may cause less gastric upset than uncoated aspirin formulations.

J.S. should inform all of his physicians and dentist that he is taking aspirin on a daily basis. The decision to discontinue aspirin is at the discretion of his physician or dentist. This decision is based upon the possibility of bleeding complications from the procedure and the risk of J.S. having a TIA while off aspirin. If the aspirin is to be discontinued it should be stopped for at least five to seven days before the procedure and at least a week after the procedure. Platelet function can be evaluated by a bleeding time, which would demonstrate when the antiplatelet activity of aspirin had abated.

11. Warfarin/Anticoagulants. When would an anticoagulant such as warfarin be considered instead of aspirin for a patient such as J.S.? What situations make anticoagulants more desirable?

Original studies using warfarin for stroke prophylaxis were performed before the development of modern study methodologies and did not show a significant benefit.[69–72] The results of these studies are confounded by the high levels of anticoagulation, poor management of hypertension, and the lack of computerized tomography (CT) imaging to distinguish hemorrhagic from ischemic strokes. Such inadequacies make these trials useless in evaluating the role of warfarin in stroke prophylaxis.

There are no recent studies that prove the superiority of anticoagulants to antiplatelet agents in preventing TIA or stroke. Three small Swedish studies were reported in the 1980s.[73–75] In these studies, the combined incidence of stroke for antiplatelet agents was 13% compared to 10% for anticoagulants.[76] None of the studies individually showed a statistically significant difference. However, these studies were too small to avoid a Type II error (i.e., missing a significant difference when one truly exists).

Long-term anticoagulation appears to reduce the risk of stroke in patients who have previously suffered myocardial infarction. A study performed by the Anticoagulants in the Secondary Prevention of Events in Coronary Thrombosis (ASPECT) Research Group randomized 3404 patients to receive oral anticoagulants (nicoumalone or phenprocoumon) or placebo within six weeks of discharge from the hospital for myocardial infarction.[77] Prothrombin times were maintained in the range of 2.8 to 4.8 international normalized ratio (INR) for patients treated with anticoagulants. Cerebrovascular events (stroke, intracranial bleeding) occurred in 62 of 1704 patients receiving placebo compared to 37 of 1700 patients receiving an anticoagulant. This difference was significant. However, 73 patients on anticoagulants had a major bleeding complication compared to 19 patients on placebo.

Anticoagulants may have a role in patients who continue to have TIAs or minor strokes despite adequate antiplatelet therapy.[78] In addition, anticoagulants may be preferred when the affected region of the brain is the pons or medulla (since the consequences of further events in this region would be devastating for the individual) and in patients who have previously had a myocardial infarction. Thus, J.S. should not be anticoagulated unless he has recurrent TIAs while taking aspirin or ticlopidine as prescribed.

A clear exception to the avoidance of anticoagulants is the case of TIA or stroke from an embolic event arising from a clot of cardiac origin in patients with atrial fibrillation. Numerous studies have clearly shown that warfarin prevents embolic cerebrovascular events in patients with nonvalvular atrial fibrillation.[79-85] In these studies, the warfarin dose was adjusted to maintain a prothrombin time (PT) INR of 1.5 to 4.5. The Stroke Prevention in Atrial Fibrillation (SPAF) trial included aspirin combined with warfarin in one study arm and indicated that some benefit may be derived by combining antiplatelet agents with anticoagulants.[86] Since this study was not designed to answer this question, a follow-up study was performed and showed no difference between warfarin and aspirin in preventing stroke in atrial fibrillation.[87] A meta-analysis of the studies using warfarin or aspirin in atrial fibrillation failed to demonstrate any benefit from aspirin.[88] Further work needs to be done comparing warfarin and aspirin for prevention of stroke in atrial fibrillation.

Cerebral Infarction and Ischemic Stroke
Clinical Presentation and Diagnostic Tests

12. P.C., a 65-year-old male, is admitted through the emergency room (ER) after suddenly collapsing to the ground and experiencing a brief loss of consciousness. He regained consciousness by the time he arrived in the ER 1 hour after the initial event. Both right extremities are flaccid. He is unable to speak, but is capable of understanding instructions (i.e., expressive aphasia). Gross ophthalmologic examination indicates right-sided neglect (inability of his eyes to track to the right or acknowledge the right side of his body). His BP is 175/105 mm Hg; other vital signs are normal. Laboratory studies are all within normal limits. By the next day his neurological status is unchanged and he is diagnosed as having an ischemic stroke. What diagnostic tests and evaluations will be helpful in guiding P.C.'s therapy?

A careful diagnosis of ischemic stroke is key to guiding further therapy. Since hemorrhagic or ischemic cerebrovascular events cause similar symptoms, the etiology of the altered neurological status must be determined. Therapy should not be initiated until an accurate diagnosis is made.

Basic laboratory and diagnostic tests should be performed to exclude such noncerebrovascular causes, as metabolic or toxicologic derangements, or infections, for the neurological compromise that P.C. has experienced. These tests include a routine serum chemistry profile (electrolytes, BUN, SrCr, hepatic enzymes, cal-

cium, phosphorus, magnesium, albumin), complete blood count, and toxicology screen. Coagulation studies, including a prothrombin time and partial thromboplastin time (PTT), should be done to provide baseline values for potential anticoagulation or thrombolytic therapy. Additionally, a thorough physical, neurological, and mental status examination should be performed. The neurological examination in particular usually will allow a localization of the lesion in the CNS. Besides providing important information for diagnosis of the neurological compromise, these tests will provide baseline data for ongoing assessment of P.C.'s progress and recovery.

However, the etiology of a stroke is difficult to discern based solely upon a physical and neurological examination. As a result, computer-assisted tomography or magnetic resonance imaging commonly are used to assist in the evaluation of these patients. An MRI is preferred to a CT due to its superior tissue contrast, ability to obtain images in multiple planes, absence of artifacts caused by bone, vascular imaging capabilities, absence of ionizing radiation, and safer contrast medium.[89] Another advantage of the MRI is that it facilitates performance of a magnetic resonance angiogram allowing visualization of the cerebrovasculature and possible identification of the precise location of the thrombus or embolus. Within the first 24 hours of an ischemic stroke, an MRI is clearly more sensitive than a CT. An MRI will identify 82% of ischemic lesions in the 24 hours following the initial event compared to 58% for a CT. However, an MRI is not reliable within the first eight hours. After 48 hours the MRI and CT are equally effective in detecting ischemic infarcts. The primary disadvantage of the MRI is that it is more sensitive to artifacts and less practical in unstable patients. Also, a CT is often the only imaging test available and is acceptable in emergency situations.

P.C. should have either a CT or MRI before initiation of anticoagulation, thrombolytic agents, or other therapies that may increase his risk of bleeding. A follow-up CT or MRI in five to seven days is useful to determine the extent of neurological damage resulting from the ischemic stroke.

Positron emission tomography (PET) scanning of the CNS can be utilized to demonstrate the ischemic changes associated with a stroke. A PET image displays areas of cerebral hypometabolism following administration of a specially labeled metabolic substrate like glucose. A PET image of the CNS has the capability of picturing the primary region of the stroke, the marginally ischemic region (penumbra) surrounding the infarction, and secondary metabolic changes in areas of the CNS that are distant from the primary infarction, but connected through neuronal pathways.

Angiographic, Doppler, or sonographic examination of the cerebral vasculature may be helpful in identifying the location of the vascular lesion. These tests usually are performed after the patient has been stabilized. A lumbar puncture (LP) with collection of cerebrospinal fluid (CSF) for evaluation may be helpful in identifying the presence of blood in the CNS. In the presence of suspected increased intracranial pressure, a lumbar puncture should be avoided because of the potential for tentorial herniation (i.e., passage of the cerebral peduncles, the ventral half of the midbrain, through the tentorial notch, the portion of the dura mater that supports the occipital lobes and covers the cerebellum, resulting in blockage of blood flow to the cerebral cortex).

Treatment

13. What general treatment interventions should be made for P.C.?

In addition to the general supportive therapy needed for a hospitalized patient, several issues are important to the proper management of a stroke patient. Careful attention should be given to fluid and electrolyte control. Excessive hydration or inadequate sodium supplementation may result in hyponatremia, thereby forcing fluid into neurons to further increase the damage from ischemia. Also, hyponatremia can produce seizures which increases the metabolic demand on compromised neurons. Thus, it is advisable to initiate fluid therapy with a solution containing at least 0.45% saline.

Another metabolic parameter that must be followed carefully is the serum glucose concentration, since hyperglycemia may adversely affect ischemic infarction outcomes. In a study of 39 ischemic stroke patients, Kushner and colleagues showed that those subjects who had a serum glucose level ≥155 mg/dL had significantly worse clinical outcomes.[90] PET scanning in these patients confirmed increased metabolic compromise associated with hyperglycemia. If hyperglycemia is detected, appropriate insulin therapy should be initiated to keep the serum glucose concentration less than 155 mg/dL as much as possible.

Caution should be exercised in acutely controlling P.C.'s blood pressure, since decreasing the blood pressure too rapidly will compromise cerebral blood flow and expand the region of ischemia and infarction. Thus, mild hypertension should be maintained for one to two days after the stroke onset. The blood pressure can then be brought under control with an antihypertensive agent such as a calcium channel antagonist or angiotensin-converting enzyme inhibitor.

The general daily needs of the patient should be assessed and provided on an as-needed basis. These include nutrition, urination, defecation, and prevention of decubitus ulcers. Neurological deficits will compromise the ability of many patients to adequately meet these needs, increasing the need for medical assistance.

Heparin

14. Should anticoagulation with heparin be initiated in P.C.?

Patients must be selected carefully for anticoagulant therapy based upon the rate of stroke progression, degree of stroke progression, and etiology of the ischemia (i.e., embolic versus thrombotic). In patients with an ischemic stroke that is progressing, as evidenced by worsening neurological deficits, anticoagulation may be indicated. Once an intracerebral hemorrhage has been ruled out as a cause for P.C.'s neurological changes, either heparin or warfarin therapy may be indicated.

As reported in early studies, anticoagulation with heparin in patients with progressive ischemic stroke can reduce the stroke progression by 25% to 50% when compared to patients not receiving heparin.[91-96] Heparin therapy, however, had no significant influence on mortality rates in these original studies. More recent studies have failed to substantiate the positive benefits of heparin on stroke progression.[97-99] Due to major differences in methodology, populations, and outcome measures in these studies, the value of anticoagulation in progressing stroke is still open to question and decisions to treat are at the discretion of the individual practitioner. In summary, stroke in progression is an acceptable, although not absolute, indication for the use of heparin.

If heparin therapy is to be used for stroke in progression, guidelines for dosing are similar to those for other indications. A 50 to 70 units/kg loading dose should be given as a bolus dose, followed by a maintenance infusion of 10 to 25 units/kg/hour. The heparin maintenance infusion is then titrated to maintain the patient's PTT at 1.5 to 2 times the baseline PTT. Occasionally, warfarin will be initiated as a follow-up to heparin therapy. Warfarin should be started as soon as possible after beginning heparin. The heparin infusion should continue until the patient's INR is elevated to 2 to 3 times the patient's baseline value. When warfarin is started for

this indication it usually is continued for one to six months. (See Chapter 12: Thrombosis for a more detailed discussion of heparin.)

Some practitioners advocate the use of heparin in stable embolic stroke based upon the theory that it could prevent further embolic events. In ischemic strokes due to embolic etiologies there is approximately a 10% risk of further embolic events in the first two weeks.[100] However, there is a 20% risk of embolic brain infarctions converting spontaneously to hemorrhagic lesions, and heparin alone can cause hemorrhagic conversion in 1.4% to 24% of treated patients.[70] Because of these complications, heparin use is not advised in ischemic stroke due to embolism. Similarly, anticoagulation is probably of no benefit in patients who have a completed ischemic stroke. In fact, full dose heparin actually may put these patients at an increased risk of bleeding.[86]

As noted above, the major complication of anticoagulation is bleeding. This is of particular concern because heparin may cause an ischemic stroke to evolve into a hemorrhagic stroke.[101,102] If an intracerebral hemorrhage does develop, it usually will occur within the first 24 hours after the initiation of heparin therapy or when the PTT is greater than two times the baseline value. Therefore, patients must be selected carefully and heparin dosing must be monitored closely.

If heparin had been initiated immediately, it may have benefited P.C. since it is possible his stroke was progressing as evidenced by his continued neurological deterioration in the emergency room. However, since P.C.'s neurological examination has been stable for 24 hours, heparin should be discontinued (if it was started) because it can induce cerebral bleeding.

Heparinoids

15. Would low-molecular-weight heparin (LMWH) or heparinoids have a role in P.C.'s ischemic stroke management?

Low-molecular-weight heparin is approved for deep venous thrombosis (DVT) prevention in patients undergoing hip surgery and may be a potential alternative to be used in stroke management.[103] (See Chapter 12: Thrombosis for a more complete discussion of LMWH.) The lower risk of hemorrhage, lower risk of thrombocytopenia, and prolonged half-life of LMWH compared to conventional heparin makes it an attractive alternative.[104] Low-molecular-weight heparin does have an improved safety profile, but the incidence of hemorrhages is dose dependent.[105]

Independent of its effect on stroke progression, LMWH may prevent further embolic events in high-risk patients following ischemic stroke by reducing the incidence of deep venous thrombosis.[106,107] Prins and associates studied a LMWH, "Kabi-2165," as prophylaxis for DVT in stroke patients.[106] A total of 60 patients were studied in this double-blind, placebo-controlled randomized trial with 30 patients in each group. There were six cases of deep venous thrombosis in the LMWH group and 15 cases in the placebo group, a significant difference. There were no differences in the number of deaths or hemorrhagic events between groups. A similar study was done in seven Canadian university-affiliated hospitals.[107] Patients received either 750 units of anti-factor Xa twice daily or a different LMWH ("Org-10172") or 5000 units of unfractionated heparin subcutaneously twice daily. Deep venous thrombosis occurred in 9% of LMWH patients and in 31% of unfractionated heparin patients. This represented a 71% risk reduction associated with LMWH use. There was no difference in the number of hemorrhagic events. Based upon these studies, P.C. should receive DVT prophylaxis with a low-molecular-weight heparin.

A second potential use for LMWH is in the management of the stroke. A preliminary two-phase study investigated the use of a LMWH, "Org-10172," for acute ischemic stroke. In phase I, five different dosages were considered in a dose-ranging study.[108] All patients completed the study with only minor bleeding events, epistaxis, or heme-positive stools reported as adverse reactions. None of the patients had died at three months and 50% of the patients had a complete recovery. Phase II of this study evaluated the LMWH in 57 stroke patients.[109] Each patient received the low-molecular-weight heparin in a loading dose of 2500 units followed by a three-staged infusion: 600 units/hour for four hours, 400 units/hour for 12 hours, and then 300 units/hour for the remainder of the seven day course. Only two patients had died at the seven day point and six patients had expired at three months. At the three month evaluation, 40% were significantly improved compared to their admission examination. Three patients had major hemorrhagic events: one experienced severe gastrointestinal bleeding and two died after hemorrhagic conversion of large cardioembolic ischemic strokes. At this time, LMWH should not be used to treat acute ischemic stroke until the results of an ongoing multicenter trial have been reported.

Ancrod

16. What is ancrod? Can it be used to treat an acute stroke?

Derived from the venom of the Malayan pit viper snake, ancrod cleaves fibrinogen in a way similar to thrombin.[110] This produces a circulating soluble ancrod-fibrin complex that is not cross-linked and may stimulate tissue plasminogen activator (tPA) activation from vascular endothelium. Ancrod leads to fibrinolysis soon after its administration and is rarely associated with significant bleeding complications. This low risk of hemorrhagic complications makes ancrod especially attractive for use in ischemic stroke.

In a study which compared low-molecular-weight dextran and mannitol alone or in combination with ancrod, Hossman and colleagues observed ancrod induced hypofibrinogenemia for two weeks.[111] An equal number of patients (15) were in each group and there was a more rapid neurological improvement in patients receiving ancrod, based upon an arbitrary rating scale. There were only two deaths in the ancrod group compared to five in the control group.

Pollack and colleagues conducted a pilot study of ancrod in acute, developing ischemic stroke.[112] Twenty patients were randomized to receive either normal saline or ancrod, 0.5 units/kg in normal saline over six hours. There was a rapid onset of ancrod action, as shown by decreases in functional plasminogen activator inhibitor within one hour and significant elevations in fibrin degradation products within three to four hours. Both the placebo and ancrod were administered for seven days. Patients were followed for three months and there were no bleeding or rethrombosis complications noted with ancrod. Ancrod-treated patients showed a greater improvement in their stroke scores. Even though ancrod shows some promise for the treatment of ischemic stroke, additional studies are needed to determine its role in the treatment of ischemic stroke.

Thrombolytics

17. Would thrombolytic agents be useful to treat P.C.'s acute ischemic stroke?

The critical primary event in a thromboembolic stroke is the development of an acute thrombus. Prospective cerebral angiography has demonstrated an arterial occlusion corresponding to the area of acute deficit in more than 90% of cases.[113] Occlusion of cerebral arteries does not cause complete ischemia since collateral circulation from other arterial sources provides unstable and incomplete circulation to the ischemic region of the brain.[114] To maintain normal neuronal electrical activity, a blood flow of at least 15 to 18 mL/100 gm of brain tissue/minute is needed.[115] Neuronal

membrane function is maintained even when blood flow falls below 10 mL/100 gm/minute. When blood flow falls below this threshold, membrane failure and neuronal death occur. However, when blood flow is sustained in the range of 10 to 18 mL/100 gm/minute, irreversible cellular damage may occur. The judicious use of thrombolytic agents allows blood flow to be restored to rates necessary for maintenance of neuronal homeostasis and electrical function.

Blood flow must be restored quickly after the event. Experimental studies in dogs and cats have shown that when blood flow is restored within two to three hours there are no neurological deficits.[116] Occlusions lasting three to seven hours produce permanent neurological damage, but are far less severe than those associated with a sustained occlusion. Based upon these studies, it appears that rapid administration of a thrombolytic agent to a patient experiencing an acute ischemic stroke is required to minimize the neurological damage.

A number of early studies using various thrombolytic agents were performed before CT scanning was available. Because ischemic and hemorrhagic stroke were difficult to differentiate, the findings of these studies are confusing. In 1958, Sussman and Fitch first attempted to use plasmin in stroke.[117] Of the three patients treated with plasmin, only one showed neurological improvement and the other two did not improve. Following this initial report, a number of short reports and small studies used plasmin, streptokinase, or urokinase in an attempt to achieve recanalization of occluded cerebral arteries.[118–124] From 15% to 52% of patients treated in these studies experienced significant improvements with these thrombolytic agents. However, 33% to 52% of patients expired despite treatment. Due to the uncertain results and high mortality rates, additional studies evaluating thrombolytic agents were not pursued.

Since CT scans have become widely available, there has been a renewed interest in the use of thrombolytic agents, particularly in tissue plasminogen activator. Animal studies have substantiated that tPA effectively restores cerebral blood flow and limits neurological damage.[125–128] In addition to these studies, an animal trial of tPA and streptokinase in simulated middle cerebral artery stroke showed that microscopic hemorrhage was present in the brains of all animals regardless of the therapy they received.[129] Gross cerebral hemorrhages were not found in animals who received early thrombolytic therapy (within 1 hour of the initial event) but were a complication of both tPA and streptokinase when treatment was delayed for 24 hours. These data suggest that delaying delivery of the thrombolytic drug increases the risk of life-threatening hemorrhage.

There have been a few reports of tPA use in humans for the treatment of acute stroke. A pilot study of tPA administered within 90 minutes of the initial stroke event was performed by Brott and colleagues.[130] In this study, 74 patients were randomized to seven different tPA doses ranging from 0.35 mg/kg to 1.08 mg/kg. In 30% of patients, major neurological improvement was observed two hours after initiation of the tPA therapy; 46% had improved at 24 hours. Improvement in neurological function was not dose related, but a total of three patients receiving higher tPA doses had intracranial hemorrhages that led to neurological deterioration. No hemorrhagic events occurred in patients receiving less than 0.85 mg/kg. Part II of this pilot study evaluated tPA use in acute stroke 91 to 180 minutes after the event.[131] In this group of 20 patients, only 15% experienced a significant improvement in neurological function at 24 hours. This study also showed there is a 17% risk of intracerebral hemorrhage in patients receiving ≥0.85 mg/kg of tPA. Two additional pilot studies using either 100 mg or 0.85

mg/kg of tPA administered over 60 minutes demonstrated similar findings.[132,133] In the Danish study, arterial patency was evaluated and 10 of 12 patients showed reperfusion.

Since 0.18% to 0.78% of patients receiving tPA for acute myocardial infarction have an intracerebral hemorrhage, this is a major concern when using tPA for stroke.[134] Hemorrhagic conversion of ischemic stroke compounds this concern. One study has directly evaluated this potential for tPA in stroke.[135] In this study, of 32 patients who received 100 mg of tPA over 90 minutes within an average of 226 minutes after the onset of symptoms, three (9%) of the patients had hemorrhagic conversion of the ischemic stroke; all three patients died. Another 6% of patients had major non-intracranial hemorrhagic events. At 24 hours, 53% of the patients had complete or partial reperfusion of the occluded artery. In another study, del Zoppo and colleagues carefully evaluated the hemorrhagic conversion of ischemic stroke in an efficacy study of tPA for stroke. They found the primary factor associated with hemorrhagic conversion was treatment started later than 3.5 hours after the onset of symptoms.[136]

Only pilot studies on the use of tPA have been published at this time. Although the data from these studies are incomplete, they have elucidated several important concepts with regard to the use of tPA for ischemic stroke.

- Treatment with tPA should be initiated as soon as possible after the onset of stroke symptoms, preferably within 90 minutes.
- Rapid diagnosis and immediate administration of tPA increases its efficacy and may limit the potential for hemorrhagic conversion of ischemic stroke.
- The dose of tPA should not exceed 0.85 mg/kg administered over 60 minutes, since higher doses increase the risk of intracranial hemorrhage.

Even though tPA is not approved for this indication and more studies are needed, P.C. might benefit from the administration of tPA. He has received medical attention within the first two hours after his onset of symptoms and has no other risks for major hemorrhagic events. If the CT scan is negative for an intracerebral hemorrhage and his physician is familiar with the use of tPA for this indication, P.C. is a candidate for receiving this drug.

Preservation of Central Nervous System Function

Preservation of marginally ischemic regions of the brain is an active area of investigation. Hemodilution, corticosteroids, calcium channel blockers, 21-aminosteroids, and ganglioside GM1 are therapeutic interventions that have been studied to retain CNS function in the ischemic penumbra. None of these interventions are approved for this indication, but some may hold promise for future interventions.

Hemodilution

18. What is the rationale for hemodilution therapy in ischemic stroke? Should this therapeutic approach be recommended for P.C.?

Based upon a direct relationship between a lowered hematocrit and decreased blood viscosity, various colloid and crystalloid solutions have been administered to ischemic stroke patients.[137] Initial studies indicated that volume expansion might be useful, but larger, more recent trials have not supported the original findings.[138,139] These conflicting results can be attributed to late initiation of therapy, varying protocols for hemodilution and hypervolemia, different goals for reduction of the hematocrit, and the possibility that only specific subgroups of patients might benefit. One trial has indicated that only patients who present with overt signs of dehydration respond favorably to hemodilution therapy.[140] Hemodilution remains a questionable practice in ischemic stroke and would not be recommended in P.C.'s management.

A typical hemodilution regimen would utilize albumin or plasma-protein fraction to decrease the hematocrit to 30% to 35% or to maintain a pulmonary capillary wedge pressure of 14 to 18 mm Hg. Hetastarch is relatively contraindicated due to the possibility of hemorrhage associated with its use.

19. How might corticosteroids and 21-aminosteroids (lazeroids) help to preserve cerebral function? Is there any evidence that they actually are effective?

Corticosteroids

Corticosteroids have been used to treat stroke on the theory that decreasing edema and swelling of the brain will increase cerebral blood flow to ischemic regions. Dexamethasone (4 to 20 mg Q 6 hr) was commonly used because it has substantial anti-inflammatory effects without mineralocorticoid activity; however, multiple studies have shown that corticosteroids are ineffective in treating of cerebral infarction or hemorrhagic stroke.[141–146] The lack of efficacy of steroids might be explained by inflammation of dead neurons rather than in marginally ischemic neurons. The use of corticosteroids is relatively contraindicated in these patients because of possible increases in morbidity and mortality.[106] Although corticosteroids are ineffective in the treatment of cerebral infarction or hemorrhagic stroke, they clearly are effective in acute cases of spinal cord injuries and some space occupying tumors of the brain.

21-Aminosteroids

During ischemia a variety of processes generate oxygen-free radicals which in turn initiate lipid peroxidation.[147–149] The availability of an unpaired electron in the outer atomic orbit of these radicals make them highly reactive with other substances. The allylic hydrogen between adjacent double-bonds in the unsaturated fatty acid that form phospholipid membranes of the neuron are especially vulnerable to oxidation by free oxygen radicals. Oxidation of phospholipid membranes contribute significantly to neuronal destruction. Iron facilitates the initiation of this reaction and actually may catalyze its ongoing process.

The 21-aminosteroids (lazeroids), derivatives of methylprednisolone, are potent inhibitors of lipid peroxidation.[150] Studies of 21-aminosteroids in gerbil stroke models have shown these agents to be extremely effective for focal and global ischemia.[151] Similar findings have been observed in subarachnoid hemorrhage models.[152,153] Initial pharmacokinetic studies with tirilazad mesylate, a 21-aminosteroid, have shown that doses of up to 6.0 mg/kg/day in four divided doses for up to five days are well tolerated.[154] Clinical studies of efficacy in ischemic stroke and subarachnoid hemorrhage have been undertaken with tirilazad mesylate, but definitive results in humans are unavailable.

Calcium Channel Blockers

20. What is the rationale for using calcium channel blockers in ischemic stroke? Are they indicated for use in P.C.?

Studies of the pathophysiologic responses of the CNS to ischemia have demonstrated that calcium influx into neurons is responsible for much of the cellular destruction associated with ischemia. Since calcium influx into the neuron is modulated both by voltage-dependent channels and neurotransmitter-dependent channels, calcium channel blockers that penetrate the CNS could be useful for limiting the neurologic damage associated with an ischemic stroke. In addition, the calcium channel blockers have been shown to increase blood flow into ischemic regions of the brain.

Nimodipine. The calcium channel antagonist, nimodipine, can significantly improve neurological outcomes and mortality rates when administered within 24 hours of an ischemic stroke.[155] In one study of 186 patients, there was an 8.6% mortality rate in the nimodipine-treated group compared to a 20.4% mortality rate in the placebo group. Stratification according to gender indicated a significant difference in males, but not in females. Using a standardized evaluation scale, neurological outcomes were assessed by the investigators; significant improvements occurred in the nimodipine group. Nimodipine doses of 30 mg orally every six hours for 28 days were used in this trial.

Four other studies failed to substantiate this first study. The TRUST study group evaluated nimodipine 120 mg/day in 1215 patients in a double-blind, randomized trial.[156] Based upon two stroke rating scales and mortality rates there was no difference between nimodipine and placebo. The other two studies concluded that orally administered nimodipine was not effective for the treatment of acute ischemic stroke.[157,158] Finally a randomized, double-blind, placebo-controlled study of nimodipine (120 mg/day for 21 days) in 350 patients showed no improvement with nimodipine.[189]

Nicardipine PY108-068. Two other calcium channel antagonists, nicardipine and PY108-068, have been studied in the acute management of stroke.[190–192] These trials indicate that these calcium channel antagonists may be of some benefit, but their small size makes them inconclusive.

The precise place of calcium channel blockers in the management of acute ischemic stroke has not been fully elucidated. An important key to their use seems to be early initiation of therapy (i.e., within 6 to 8 hours following the stroke). Newer agents more selective for the cerebrovasculature may have value in treating ischemic stroke. In conclusion, calcium channel blockers are probably not indicated in P.C. Their use in subarachnoid hemorrhage is discussed in Question 26.

Ganglioside GM-1

21. Are gangliosides useful in ischemic stroke? Would P.C. be a candidate for gangliosides?

Monosialotetrahexosyl ganglioside GM-1 is a constituent of mammalian neuronal cell membranes that is important for axonal growth, differentiation, and repair.[193,194] As such, it accelerates regeneration of neuronal tissue in cooperation with nerve growth factor. It is thought to facilitate the short-term recovery and reduce the mortality associated with cerebrovascular injury. One clinical study with monosialoganglioside (ganglioside GM-1) in ischemic stroke is ongoing.[159] A second study has been completed.[160] In this study, 792 patients received one of two placebo-controlled regimens; 200 mg of GM-1 or a placebo IV within five hours of the onset of stroke symptoms, or 100 mg of GM-1 IV 12 hours later and 100 mg of GM-1 IM daily for days two through ten. Overall survival was the same among all groups, but neurological improvement was more rapid in the patients treated with GM-1. This difference existed only for the patients who received GM-1 within four hours of the onset of stroke symptoms. Three patients receiving GM-1 had to discontinue the medication due to fever or increased liver function tests. Although these findings are encouraging the efficacy of GM-1 in treating stroke is yet to be determined.

Complications

22. What complications associated with stroke might P.C. experience?

Agitation, delirium, stupor, coma, cerebral edema, or increased intracranial pressure are other symptoms that can be associated with ischemic stroke. These symptoms correlate with the specific blood vessels that are affected, and the development of these complications in P.C. would depend upon the progression of his stroke.

Seizures may occur in up to 20% of stroke patients. Pneumonia, pulmonary edema, cardiac arrest, deep vein thrombosis, and arrhythmias frequently are associated with ischemic stroke and should be managed as they occur. In P.C., these may occur soon after his stroke or be related to a rapidly developing neurological event such as further infarction, hemorrhage, or severe cerebral edema. Pneumonia or DVT are related primarily to inactivity, and the risk of these events will increase the longer P.C. remains immobile.

Stroke patients frequently experience psychological reactions. The most common psychiatric complication is depression, occurring in 40% to 50% of patients.[161] The severity of depression varies from mild to major depressive episodes. If the depression interferes with recovery and the rehabilitative process, it should be managed with the use of a selective serotonin reuptake inhibitor or nortriptyline. When combined with severe psychomotor depression or agitation, methylphenidate may be helpful in treating the psychiatric accompaniments of stroke.[162] Due to P.C.'s hypertension, methylphenidate should be used with careful blood pressure monitoring.

Prognosis

23. After 7 days in the hospital, P.C.'s neurological status is stabilized. Will further neurological improvements be realized?

Neurological deficits in stroke patients are not considered to be stable or fixed until at least 8 to 12 months have elapsed. During this time, neurological function may return, but rarely to normal.[163] The prognosis following ischemic stroke depends upon a variety of factors including age, hypertension, coma, cardiopulmonary complications, hypoxia, and neurogenic hyperventilation. Infarction of the middle cerebral artery, however, is associated with a poor chance for recovery. Therefore, it is possible that P.C. might experience further neurological improvement.

Rehabilitation

24. As P.C. enters rehabilitation, what interventions will aid his recovery?

Rehabilitation efforts for P.C. are directed at managing daily functions and enhancing existing neurological function. Considerations for daily functions include activities of daily living and bowel and bladder management through balanced pharmacologic interventions. Efforts should be made to allow P.C. to function independently with activities of daily living. Enhancement of existing neurological function includes elimination of drugs that may compromise P.C.'s memory and mental function. These include benzodiazepines, major tranquilizers, and sedating antiepileptic drugs. Studies indicate that judicious use of amphetamines or methylphenidate may help in the rehabilitation process.[164] In P.C., stimulants should be used cautiously due to his hypertension.

Spasticity of the affected limb may present a problem for P.C. Since spasticity often is localized to a single limb after ischemic stroke, it frequently responds to regional motor nerve blocks with lidocaine or phenol. Aggressive physical therapy is also essential to the management of spasticity. Systemic antispasticity agents like baclofen, dantrium, or diazepam are not used routinely because of the risk for toxicity. They generally are used only when spasticity is bilateral or unresponsive to other therapies.

Other less common impediments to P.C.'s recovery include decubitus ulcers, hypercalcemia, and heterotopic ossification (e.g., the laying down and calcification of a bone matrix in muscle surrounding major joints). Prevention through meticulous skin care is the key to the management of pressure ulcers. Hypercalcemia and heterotopic ossification can be prevented by mobilizing P.C. as soon as possible after the stroke, or they may be treated with etidronate (Didronel).

Subarachnoid Hemorrhage
Clinical Presentation and Classification

25. R.A., a 65-year-old female, suddenly collapsed in the bathroom of her home. An ambulance was immediately called and upon arrival at the ER she had regained consciousness. She complained of a severe headache and kept dropping off to sleep during the examination. Nuchal rigidity (i.e., a stiff and painful neck when flexed) and mild mental confusion with regard to place also were observed. A CT scan demonstrated blood in the subarachnoid space and in her ventricles. A cerebral angiogram demonstrated a posterior communicating artery aneurysm. Electrolytes, coagulation studies, and blood counts were within normal limits. What classification scales are used to evaluate the severity of the hemorrhage and how are they related to therapy?

Various rating scales have been utilized in the clinical setting to evaluate and categorize patients with a subarachnoid hemorrhage. The Hunt and Hess scale (see Table 53.4) and the Subarachnoid Hemorrhage Grading Scale of the World Federation of Neurological Surgeons are used most commonly.[165,166] Patients who fall into the higher grades (indicating a more severe hemorrhage) have a poorer prognosis and are generally less responsive to pharmacologic interventions. R.A. would most likely be classified as having a Hunt and Hess grade II or III subarachnoid hemorrhage.

Complications

26. R.A.'s neurological status deteriorated about 3 days after admission. What complications may be responsible for these changes?

Following the initial hemorrhagic event, there are three major complications that usually are responsible for neurological changes. *Rebleeding* from an aneurysm occurs in 20% of patients, usually within the first 48 hours after the initial event. In some cases, rebleeding can happen as long as 14 days later. From 24 hours to weeks after the hemorrhage, *hydrocephalus* (i.e., accumulation of CSF within the ventricular system of the brain) may be caused by blood interrupting CSF flow through the ventricles and reabsorption of cerebrospinal fluid through the arachnoid villa. Another 20% to 40% of patients will develop *delayed cerebral ischemia*, usually within 5 to 12 days following the initial hemorrhage. Delayed ischemia caused by vasospasm of the cerebral vessels is evidenced by development of new neurological deficits and confirmed by a cerebral angiogram. At least one-half of these individuals will die or experience permanent neurological damage. About 5% to 15% of patients have seizures.

Table 53.4	Hunt and Hess Scale for Rating Severity of Subarachnoid Hemorrhage
Grade	Description
I	Minor headache, minor neck stiffness
II	Severe headache, severe neck stiffness, cranial nerve signs, photophobia
III	Drowsiness, confusion, mild paresis, mild dysphasia
IV	Stupor or sopor, moderate to severe hemiparesis, dysphasia
V	Coma, decerebrate rigidity, symptoms of acute midbrain syndrome

Table 53.5	Therapy for Subarachnoid Hemorrhage Complications		
Rebleeding	Hydrocephalus	Delayed Ischemia[a]
Surgical clip	Ventricular drain	Nimodipine 60 mg Q 4 hr × 21 days
Aminocaproic acid 5 gm loading dose 2–4 mg/hr	Ventricular-peritoneal shunt	Hypervolemia PCWP[a] 12–15 mm Hg
		Hypertension Systolic BP 170–220 mm Hg

[a] BP = Blood pressure; PCWP = Pulmonary capillary wedge pressure.

27. How should each of these complications (rebleeding, hydrocephalus, vasospasm, and seizures) be managed in R.A.? Are calcium channel blockers more effective in treating subarachnoid hemorrhage than ischemic stroke?

Rebleeding

Surgical clipping of the aneurysm is the best method to prevent rebleeding. If early surgery is contraindicated or unavailable, antifibrinolytic therapy with epsilon aminocaproic acid (EACA) may be instituted. EACA blocks the activation of plasminogen and inhibits the action of plasmin on the fibrin clot. EACA enhances hemostasis when fibrinolysis contributes to bleeding and stabilizes the clot that has formed around the ruptured aneurysm. The incidence of rebleeding is decreased from 20% to 30% to 10% to 15% by EACA.[160,167,168] However, delayed cerebral ischemia occurs more frequently in patients receiving EACA.[162] It is unclear whether this is a direct effect of EACA or whether more individuals survive to experience delayed cerebral ischemia. EACA usually is given as a 5 gm intravenous bolus followed by a continuous infusion of 1 to 2 gm/hour. Doses can be adjusted to maintain serum concentrations of 200 to 400 µg/mL. R.A. may benefit from receiving EACA as soon as a subarachnoid hemorrhage is diagnosed, and it should be continued until surgical clipping can be performed or for at least two weeks after the initial hemorrhage. It is preferable to surgically repair the aneurysm as soon as possible after R.A. is admitted to the hospital.

Hydrocephalus

The only effective treatment for hydrocephalus is surgical intervention. If a CT scan demonstrates hydrocephalus, a ventricular drain should be surgically placed after the aneurysm has been clipped. When hydrocephalus becomes a chronic problem, the drain can be replaced with a permanent ventriculoperitoneal shunt.

Ventriculitis is a common complication of a ventricular drain and it is most likely caused by staphylococci or gram-negative bacteria. Antibiotic therapy for this complication should consist of an intravenous agent (e.g., chloramphenicol, ceftriaxone, ampicillin, penicillin, vancomycin, ceftazidime, cefuroxime, nafcillin, rifampin) that readily crosses the blood-brain barrier with inflamed meninges.[169] Alternatively, gentamicin and vancomycin can be instilled through the ventricular drains directly to the site of infection.[163,170] The antibiotic solution is prepared using a sterile powder for injection that is free of preservatives. Gentamicin 4 to 8 mg or vancomycin 5 to 20 mg is instilled once a day. Systemic and intraventricular antibiotics should be continued until three consecutive CSF cultures are free of bacterial growth.

Delayed Cerebral Ischemia (Vasospasm)

The occurrence of delayed cerebral ischemia probably is due to vasospasm of the cerebral blood vessels. Current therapy for delayed ischemia is not optimal and rather confusing. Volume expansion with normal saline or plasma protein fraction usually is initiated when focal neurological changes develop, with the goal of maintaining a pulmonary capillary wedge pressure of 15 to 20 mm Hg.[171–174] Some clinicians may institute hypervolemia therapy in anticipation of delayed cerebral ischemia. If the neurological deficits are not reversed with hypervolemia, systolic blood pressure can be increased to as high as 200 to 220 mm Hg using dopamine or norepinephrine. A high systolic pressure allows the brain to redirect flow to ischemic areas, and such therapy is often continued for 7 to 14 days.

Calcium Channel Blockers: Nimodipine. Nimodipine also is indicated for the prevention of delayed cerebral ischemia in patients with a subarachnoid hemorrhage. Its mechanisms of action may include preventing cerebral vasospasm that is responsible for delayed ischemia, inhibiting calcium influx into ischemic neurons, or re-establishing cerebrovascular autoregulation (i.e., the ability of the brain to control blood flow in accordance with metabolic needs).

Nimodipine has been administered in clinical studies intravenously, orally, or topically (i.e., direct application to the brain's surface and the cerebral vasculature during surgery). Currently, only the oral form is available for use in the U.S. Of six initial studies that included a total of 468 patients who received nimodipine parenterally,[175–180] only one reported a reduced incidence of vasospasm.[175] However, in three these neurological outcomes were improved relative to the investigators' previous experience.[173,177,178] Only one study found no improvement in outcome.[174] All of these studies were open-labeled and without placebo control.

The more recent studies of nimodipine in subarachnoid hemorrhage have used oral formulations. In these studies, a total of 1038 patients were given nimodipine prophylactically according to double-blind, placebo-controlled, randomized protocols.[181–184] Each study utilized the Hunt and Hess grading scale and CT scans that were independently graded according to severity of the hemorrhage and the amount of subarachnoid blood present. Several different scales were used to assess neurological outcome. Angiographic improvement was not significantly different in patients treated with nimodipine or placebo, but neurological outcomes improved significantly in nimodipine-treated patients who presented with a Hunt and Hess grade I to III subarachnoid hemorrhage. In another study, nimodipine significantly benefited patients with poor-grade aneurysm (grades III to V). Nimodipine 60 to 90 mg every four hours for 21 days was initiated within the first 96 hours after the original subarachnoid hemorrhage in these patients. No trial has compared the efficacy of nimodipine to hypervolemia therapy and interventions to increase systolic blood pressure. Nimodipine's approved dose is 60 mg orally every six hours.

Nicardipine. Another calcium channel antagonist, nicardipine, has the advantage of being available in a parenteral form. The results of a double-blind, placebo-controlled trial with nicardipine were reported by Haley and colleagues.[185] A total of 906 patients in 41 centers received either nicardipine 0.15 mg/kg/hour or placebo as a continuos intravenous infusion for 14 days after presenting with a subarachnoid hemorrhage. Patients in both groups had comparable symptoms and severity at onset, but more patients in the placebo group received hypervolemia therapy or treatment to induce hypertension. Forty-six percent of patients receiving placebo had demonstrated vasospasm and 32% of nicardipine patients had vasospasm. There were no differences in the mortality rates or neurological outcomes between the two groups. Results from this study are difficult to interpret because more placebo patients received hypervolemia and hypertensive therapy. Further work with nicardipine is needed.

R.A. should receive nimodipine 60 mg orally every four hours for 21 days, since she was diagnosed within several hours of her subarachnoid hemorrhage.

Seizures

Phenytoin. Seizures occur in approximately 9% of patients experiencing a subarachnoid hemorrhage. Only two factors associated with subarachnoid hemorrhage have been identified as predictive of seizures: rebleeding or large amounts of cisternal blood on CT scan.[186]

Phenytoin often is used for seizure prophylaxis. However, there are no trials that have investigated the efficacy of phenytoin in preventing seizure in patients with subarachnoid hemorrhage. The usual dose of phenytoin is 15 to 20 mg/kg administered as an intravenous bolus at a rate no greater than 50 mg/minute. A maintenance dose of 5 to 7 mg/kg/day either orally or intravenously is titrated to maintain steady-state serum concentrations of 10 to 20 µg/mL. Phenytoin usually is continued for one to two years unless the patient experiences seizures. Since there is a 5% to 20% risk of seizures for R.A., she should receive phenytoin prophylactically. Carbamazepine is an acceptable alternative, but a parenteral form of the drug is unavailable.

References

1 **Gunby P.** Cardiovascular diseases remain nation's leading cause of death. JAMA. 1992;267(3):335.

2 **Caplan LR.** Strokes in African-Americans. Circulation. 1991;83:558.

3 **Barnett HJM.** Stroke prevention and treatment. Milestones, perspectives and challenges. In: Plum F, Pulsinelli W, eds. New York: Raven Press; 1985: 27–41.

4 **Brust JCM.** Transient ischemic attacks: natural history and anticoagulation. Neurology. 1977;27:701.

5 **Whisnant JP et al.** Transient ischemic attacks in a community: Rochester, MN, 1955 through 1969. Mayo Clin Proc. 1973;48:194.

6 **Goldner JC et al.** Long-term prognosis of transient ischemic attacks. Stroke. 1971;2:160.

7 **Whisnant JP et al.** Classification of cerebrovascular disease III. Stroke. 1990;21(4):637.

8 **Furlan AJ et al.** The decreasing incidence of primary intracerebral hemorrhage: a population study. Ann Neurol. 1979;5:367.

9 **Pakarinen S.** Incidence, etiology, and prognosis of primary subarachnoid hemorrhage: a study based on 589 cases diagnosed in a defined urban population during a defined period. Acta Neurol Scand. 1967;43(Suppl. 29):1.

10 **Weir B.** Aneurysms affecting the nervous system. Baltimore: Williams & Wilkins; 1987:19–53.

11 **Didisheim P et al.** Actions and clinical status of platelet-suppressive agents. Semin Hematol. 1978;15:55.

12 **Collins RC et al.** Selective vulnerability of the brain: new insights into the pathophysiology of stroke. Ann Intern Med. 1989;110:992.

13 **Uematsu D et al.** *In vivo* measurement of cytosolic-free calcium during cerebral ischemia and reperfusion. Ann Neurol. 1988;24:420.

14 **Siesjo BK.** Cellular calcium metabolism, seizures and ischemia. Mayo Clin Proc. 1986;61:299.

15 **Kannel AB et al.** Epidemiological assessment of the role of blood pressure in stroke. The Framingham study. JAMA. 1978;214:301.

16 **Havas S et al.** Report of the New England task force on reducing heart disease and stroke risk. Public Health Rep. 1989;104:134.

17 **Veterans Administration Cooperative Study Group.** Effects of treatment on morbidity in hypertension. JAMA. 1967;202:102834.

18 **Veterans Administration Cooperative Study Group.** Effects of treatment on morbidity in hypertension II. JAMA. 1970; 213:114352.

19 **Smith GT.** The economics of hypertension and stroke. Am Heart J. 1990; 119:725.

20 **Nissinen A et al.** Cost effectiveness of the Noteth Karelia hypertension programme 1972–1977. Med Care. 1986; 24:767–80.

21 **Feinberg WM et al.** Guidelines for the management of transient ischemic attacks from the Ad Hoc Committee on Guidelines for the Management of Transient Ischemic Attacks of the Stroke Council of the American Heart Association. Circulation. 1994; 89:2950.

22 **North American Symptomatic Carotid Endarterectomy Trial Collab-**

orators. Beneficial effect of carotid endarterectomy in symptomatic patients with high-grade carotid stenosis. N Engl J Med. 1991;325:445.

23 **European Carotid Surgery Trialists' Collaborative Group.** MRC European Carotid Surgery Trial: interim results for symptomatic patients with severe (70%–90%) or mild (0%–29%) carotid stenosis. Lancet. 1991;337:1235.

24 **Veterans Affairs Cooperative Studies Program 309 Trialist Group.** Carotid endarterectomy and prevention of cerebral ischemia in symptomatic carotid stenosis. JAMA. 1991;26:3289.

25 **Haynes RB et al.** Prevention of functional impairment by endarterectomy for symptomatic high-grade carotid stenosis. JAMA. 1994;271:1256.

26 **Easton JD et al.** Diagnosis and management of ischemic stroke. Part 1. Threatened stroke and its management. Curr Probl Cardiol. 1983;8:1.

27 **Chambers BR et al.** Outcome in patients with asymptomatic bruits. N Engl J Med. 1986;315:860.

28 **Chater N et al.** Microsurgical vascular bypass for occlusive cerebrovascular disease: current status. Adv Neurol. 1977;16:121.

29 **The EC/IC Bypass Study Group.** Failure of extracranial-intracranial arterial bypass to reduce the risk of ischemic stroke: results of an international randomized trial. N Engl J Med. 1985; 313:1191.

30 **Bernstein EF et al.** Life expectancy and late stroke following carotid endarterectomy. Ann Surg. 1983;198:80.

31 **Hess et al.** Drug-induced inhibition of platelet function delays progression of peripheral occlusive arterial disease. Lancet. 1985;200:74.

32 **Chesebro JH et al.** Antiplatelet therapy in coronary disease progression: reduced infarction and new lesion formation. Circulation. 1989;80(Suppl.II): II-266.

33 **Harker LA et al.** Failure of aspirin plus dipyridamole to prevent restenosis after carotid endarterectomy. Ann Intern Med. 1992;116:731.

34 **Barnett HJM et al.** The Canadian Cooperative Study Group: a randomized trial of aspirin and sulfinpyrazone in treated stroke. N Engl J Med. 1978; 299:53.

35 **Boussere MG et al.** "AICLA" controlled trial of aspirin and dipyridamole in the secondary prevention of atherothrombotic cerebral ischemia. Stroke. 1983;14:15.

36 **Sorenson PS et al.** Acetylsalicylic acid in the prevention of stroke in patients with reversible cerebral ischemic attacks. A Danish Cooperative Study. Stroke. 1983;14:15.

37 **Fields WS et al.** Controlled trial of aspirin in cerebral ischemia: Part II: surgical group. Stroke. 1978;9:309.

38 **Fields WS et al.** Controlled trial of aspirin in cerebral ischemia. Stroke. 1977;8:301.

39 **Antiplatelet Trialists' Collaboration.** Secondary prevention of vascular disease by prolonged antiplatelet treatment. Br. Med J (Clin Res Ed). 1988; 290:320.

40 **Ruenther R, Dorndorf W.** Aspirin in patients with cerebral ischemia and normal angiograms or nonsurgical lesions: the results of a double-blind trial. In: Breddin K et al., eds. Acetylsalicylic acid in cerebral ischemia and coronary heart disease. Stuttgart: Schattauer; 1978;97.

41 **Swedish Cooperative Study.** High-dose acetylsalicylic acid after cerebral infarction. Stroke. 1987;18:325.

42 **European Stroke Prevention Study Group.** ESPS: principal end points. Lancet. 1987;2:1351.

43 **UK-TIA Study Group.** United Kingdom transient ischaemic attack (UK-TIA) aspirin trial: interim results. Br Med J. 1988;296:315.

44 **UK-TIA Study Group.** The United Kingdom transient ischemic attack (UK-TIA) aspirin trial: final results. J Neurol Neurosurg Psychiatry. 1991;54: 1044.

45 **Roden S et al.** Transient cerebral ischemic attacks—management and prognoses. Postgrad Med J. 1981;57: 237.

46 **Acheson J et al.** Controlled trial of dipyridamole in cerebral vascular disease. Br Med J. 1969;1:614.

47 **The American-Canadian Cooperative Study Group.** Persantine-aspirin trial in cerebral ischemia. Part II. Endpoint results. Stroke. 1985;16:406.

48 **Gent M et al.** The Canadian-American ticlopidine (CATS) in thromboembolic stroke. Lancet. 1989;2:1215.

49 **Hass WK et al.** A randomized trial comparing ticlopidine hydrochloride with aspirin for the prevention of stroke in high risk patients. N Engl J Med. 1989;321:501.

50 **Roth GJ et al.** Acetylation of prostaglandin synthetase by aspirin. Proc Natl Acad Sci USA. 1975;73:3073.

51 **Levin RI et al.** Aspirin inhibits vascular plasminogen activity in vivo. J Clin Invest. 1984;74:571.

52 **Kelton JG et al.** Thrombogenic effect of high dose aspirin in rabbits: relationship to inhibition of vessel wall synthesis. J Clin Invest. 1978;62:892.

53 **Zimmerman R et al.** The paradoxical thrombogenic effect of aspirin in experimental thrombosis. Thromb Res. 1979;16:843.

54 **Steering Committee of the Physicians' Health Study Research Group.** Preliminary report: findings from the aspirin component of the ongoing Physicians' Health Study. N Engl J Med. 1988;318:262.

55 **Steering Committee of the Physicians' Health Study Research Group.** Final report on the aspirin component of the ongoing physicians' health study. N Engl J Med. 1989;321: 129.

56 **The Dutch TIA Trial Study Group.** A comparison of two doses of aspirin (30 mg versus 283 mg a day) in patients after a transient ischemic attack or minor ischemic stroke. N Engl J Med. 1991;325:1261.

57 **The SALT Collaborative.** Swedish aspirin low-dose trial (SALT) of 75 mg aspirin as secondary prophylaxis after cerebrovascular ischemic events. Lancet. 1991;338:1345.

58 **Helgason CM et al.** Aspirin response and failure in cerebral infarction. Stroke. 1993;24:345.

59 **Tohgi H et al.** Effects of low-to-high doses of aspirin on platelet aggregability and metabolites of thromboxane A_2 and prostacyclin. Stroke. 1992;23: 1400.

60 **Bornstein NM et al.** Failure of aspirin treatment after stroke. Stroke. 1994;25: 275.

61 **Antiplatelet Trialists' Collaboration.** Collaborative overview of randomized trials of antiplatelet therapy-I: prevention of death, myocardial infarction, and stroke by prolonged antiplatelet therapy in various categories of patients. Brit Med J. 1994;308:83–108.

62 **Matachar DB et al.** Medical treatment for stroke prevention. Stroke. 1994; 121:41.

63 **Pedersen AK et al.** The human pharmacology of platelet inhibition. Pharmacokinetics relevant to drug action. Circulation. 1985;72:1164.

64 **Harker LA et al.** Platelet and fibrinogen consumption in man. N Engl J Med. 1972;287:999.

65 **Harker LA et al.** Experimental arterial thromboembolism in baboons. Mechanism, quantitation and pharmacological prevention. J Clin Invest. 1979;64: 559.

66 **Lecrubier C et al.** Study of platelet aggregation induced by platelet activating factor (PAF) after administration of ticlopidine or aspirin. Agents Actions. 1983;13:77.

67 **Vargrafting BB et al.** Present concepts on the mechanisms of platelet aggregation. Biochem Pharmacol. 1981; 30:263.

68 **Weisberg LA et al.** The efficacy and safety of ticlopidine and aspirin in non-whites: analysis of a patient subgroup from the ticlopidine aspirin stroke study. Neurology. 1993;43:27.

69 **Pearce JMS et al.** Long-term anticoagulant therapy in transient ischemic attacks. Lancet. 1965;1:6.

70 **Baker RN et al.** Anticoagulation therapy in cerebral infarction. Neurology. 1962;12:823.

71 **Baker RN.** An evaluation of anticoagulant therapy in the treatment of cerebrovascular disease. Report of the Veterans Administration Cooperative Study of Atherosclerosis. Neurology. 1961;11:132.

72 **Baker RN et al.** Transient ischemic attacks—a report of anticoagulant treatment. Neurology. 1966;16:841.

73 **Olsson JE et al.** Anticoagulant vs. antiplatelet therapy as a prophylactic against cerebral infarction in transient ischemic attacks. Stroke. 1980;11:4.

74 **Buren A, Ygge J.** Treatment program and comparison between anticoagulants and platelet aggregation inhibitors after transient ischemic attack. Stroke. 1981;12:578.

75 **Garde A et al.** Treatment after transient ischemic attacks. A comparison between anticoagulant drug and inhibition of platelet aggregation. Stroke. 1983;14:677.

76 **Sherman DG et al.** Antithrombotic therapy for cerebrovascular disorders. Chest. 1992;102(Suppl.):529S.

77 **Anticoagulants in the Secondary Prevention of Events in Coronary Thrombosis (ASPECT) Research Group.** Effect of long-term oral anticoagulant treatment on mortality and cardiovascular morbidity after myocardial infarction. Lancet. 1994;343:499.

78 **Rothrock JF, Hart RG.** Antithrombotic therapy in cerebrovascular disease. Ann Intern Med. 1991;115:885.

79 **Stroke Prevention in Atrial Fibrillation Study Group Investigators.** The Stroke Prevention in Atrial Fibrillation Study: patient characteristics and final results. Circulation. 1991;84:527.

80 **Stroke Prevention in Atrial Fibrillation Study Group Investigators.** Predictors of Thromboembolism: I. Clinical features of patients at risk. Ann Intern Med. 1992;116:1.

81 **Stroke Prevention in Atrial Fibrillation Study Group Investigators.** Predictors of thromboembolism: II. Echocardiographic features of patients risk. Ann Intern Med. 1992;116:6.

82 **Peterson P et al.** Placebo-controlled, randomized trial of warfarin and aspirin for prevention of thromboembolic complications in chronic atrial fibrillation: the Copenhagen AFASAK Study. Lancet. 1989;1:175.

83 **The Boston Area Anticoagulation Trial for Atrial Fibrillation Investigators.** The effect of low-dose warfarin on the risk of stroke in patients with nonrheumatic atrial fibrillation. N Engl J Med. 1990;323:1505.

84 **Connolly SJ et al.** Canadian Atrial Fibrillation Anticoagulation (CAFA) Study. J Am Coll Cardiol. 1991;18: 349.

85 **Ezekowitz MD, SPINAF Investigators.** Interim analysis of the VA Cooperative Study: stroke prevention in nonrheumatic atrial fibrillation. Circulation. 1991;84 (Suppl. II):450. Abstract.

86 **Miller VT et al.** Ischemic stroke in patients with atrial fibrillation: effects of aspirin according to stroke mechanism. Neurology. 1993;43:32.

87 **Stroke Prevention in Atrial Fibrillation Investigators.** Warfarin versus aspirin for prevention of thromboembolism in atrial fibrillation: Stroke Prevention in Atrial Fibrillation II Study. Lancet. 1994;343:687–91.

88 **Atrial Fibrillation Investigators.** Risk factors for stroke and efficacy of antithrombotic therapy in atrial fibrillation. Arch Intern Med. 1994;154:1449–57.

89 **Edelman RR, Warach S.** Magnetic resonance imaging (first of two parts). N Engl J Med. 1993;328:708.

90 **Kushner M et al.** Relation of hyperglycemia early in ischemic brain infarction to cerebral anatomy, metabolism, and clinical outcome. Ann Neurol. 1990;28:129.

91 **Fisher CM.** Use of anticoagulants in cerebral thrombosis. Neurology. 1958; 8:311.

92 **Carter AB.** Anticoagulant treatment in progressing stroke. Br Med J. 1961;2: 70.

93 **Fisher CM.** Anticoagulant therapy in cerebral thrombosis and cerebral embolism. A national cooperative study, interim report. Neurology. 1961;11: 119.

94 **Duke RJ et al.** Intravenous heparin for the prevention of stroke progression in acute stable stroke: a randomized controlled trial. Ann Intern Med. 1986; 105:825.

95 **Weksler BB et al.** Anticoagulation in cerebral ischemia. Stroke. 1983;14: 658.

96 **Genton E et al.** Cerebral ischemia: the role of thrombosis and of antithrombotic therapy: Study Group on Antithrombotic Therapy. Stroke. 1977;8:150.

97 **Slivka A, Levy D.** Natural history of progressive ischemic stroke in a population treated with heparin. Stroke. 1990;21:1657.

98 **Duke RJ et al.** Clinical trial of low-dose subcutaneous heparin for the prevention of stroke progression. In: Reivich M, Hurting HI, eds. Cerebrovascular Diseases. New York: Raven Press; 1983:399.

99 **Haley EC Jr et al.** Failure of heparin to prevent progression in progressing ischemic infarction. Stroke. 1988;19:10.

100 **Cerebral Embolism Task Force.** Cardiogenic brain embolism. Arch Neurol. 1986;43:71.

101 **Babikian VL et al.** Intracerebral hemorrhage in stroke patients anticoagulated with heparin. Stroke. 1989;20:1500.

102 **Hornig CR et al.** Hemorrhagic cerebral infarction—a prospective study. Stroke. 1986;17:179.

103 **Gordon DL et al.** Low-molecular-weight heparins and heparinoids and their use in acute or progressing ischemic stroke. Clin Neuropharmacol. 1990;13:522.

104 **Hirsh J.** Rationale for development of low-molecular-weight heparins and their clinical potential in the prevention of post-operative venous thrombosis. Am J Surg. 1991;161:512.

105 **ten Cate H et al.** Randomized double-blind placebo controlled safety study of a low molecular weight heparinoid in patients undergoing transurethral resection of the prostate. Thromb Haemost. 1987;57:92.

106 **Prins MH et al.** Prophylaxis of deep venous thrombosis with a low-molecular-weight heparin (Kabi 2165/Fragmin) in stroke patients. Haemostasis. 1989;19:245.

107 **Turpie AGG et al.** A low-molecular-weight heparinoid compared with unfractionated heparin in the prevention of deep vein thrombosis in patients with acute ischemic stroke. Ann Intern Med. 1992;117:353.

108 **Biller J et al.** A dose escalation study of ORG 10172 (low molecular weight heparinoid) in the treatment of acute cerebral infarction. Neurology. 1989; 39:262.

109 **Massey EW et al.** Heparinoid ORG 10172 in stroke. Ann Neurol. 1988;24: 130.

110 **Levine SR, Brott TG.** Thrombolytic therapy in cerebrovascular disorders. Prog Cerebrovasc Dis. 1992;34:235.

111 **Hossman V et al.** Controlled trial of Ancrod in ischemic stroke. Arch Neurol. 1983;40:803.

112 **Pollak VE et al.** Ancrod causes rapid thrombolysis in patients with acute strokes. Am J Med Sci. 1990;299:319.

113 **Solis OJ et al.** Cerebral angiography in acute cerebral infarction. Rev Interam Radiol. 1977;2:19.

114 **Symon L et al.** The concept of thresholds of ischaemia in relation to brain structure and function. J Clin Pathol Suppl (R Coll Pathol.). 1977;30(Suppl. II):149.

115 **Sharbrough FW et al.** Correlation of continuous electroencephalograms with cerebral blood flow measurements during carotid endarterectomy. Stroke. 1973;4:674.

116 **Sundt TM Jr et al.** Restoration of middle cerebral artery flow in experimental infarction. J Neurosurg. 1969;31:311.

117 **Sussman BJ, Fitch TS.** Thrombolysis with fibrinolysin in cerebral arterial occlusion. JAMA. 1958;167:1705.

118 **Herndon RM et al.** Thrombolytic treatment in cerebrovascular thrombosis. In: MacMillan RL, Mustard JF, eds. Anticoagulants and Fibrinolysis. Philadelphia: Lea & Febiger; 1961:154.

119 **Meyer JS et al.** Anticoagulants plus streptokinase therapy in progressive stroke. JAMA. 1963;189:373.

120 **Clarke RL, Clifton EE.** The treatment of cerebrovascular thrombosis and embolism with fibrinolytic agents. Am J Cardiol. 1960;30:546.

121 **Fletcher A et al.** A pilot study of urokinase therapy in cerebral infarction. Stroke. 1976;7:135.

122 **Meyer JS et al.** Therapeutic thrombolysis in cerebral thromboembolism. Double-blind evaluation of intravenous plasmins therapy in carotid and middle cerebral arterial occlusion. Neurology. 1963;13:927.

123 **Herndon RM et al.** Fibrinolysin therapy in thrombotic diseases of the nervous system. J Mich St Med Soc. 1960; 59:1684.

124 **Larcan A et al.** Indications des thrombolytiques au cours des accidents vasculaires cerebraux thrombosants traites par ailleurs par O.H.B. (2ATA). Therapie. 1977;32:259.

125 **Zivin JA et al.** Tissue plasminogen activator reduces neurological damage after cerebral embolism. Science. 1985;230:1289.

126 **Del Zoppo GJ et al.** Intracerebral hemorrhage following r-tPA infusion in a primate stroke model. Stroke. 1988;19:134. Abstract.

127 **Perar PL, Greer CA.** The effect of intravenous tissue-type plasminogen activator in a rat model of embolic cerebral ischemia. Yale J Biol Med. 1987; 60:233.

128 **Kissel P et al.** Digital angiographic quantification of blood flow dynamics in embolic stroke treated with tissue-type plasminogen activator. J Neurosurg. 1987;67:399.

129 **Slivka A, Pulsinelli W.** Hemorrhagic complications of thrombolytic therapy in experimental stroke. Stroke. 1987; 18:1148.

130 **Brott TG et al.** Urgent therapy for stroke Part I. Pilot study of tissue plasminogen activator administered within 90 minutes. Stroke. 1992;23:632.

131 **Haley EC Jr et al.** Urgent therapy for stroke Part II. Pilot study of tissue plasminogen activator administered 91–180 minutes from onset. Stroke. 1992; 23:641.

132 **Overgaard K et al.** Thrombolytic therapy in acute ischemic stroke: a Danish pilot study. Stroke. 1993;24:1439.

133 **Haley EC et al.** Pilot randomized trial of tissue plasminogen activator in acute ischemic stroke. Stroke. 1993;24:1000.

134 **Sloan MA, Gore JM.** Ischemic stroke and intracranial hemorrhage following thrombolytic therapy for acute myocardial infarction: a risk-benefit analysis. Am J Cardiol. 1992;69:21A.

135 **von Kummer R, Hacke W.** Safety and efficacy of intravenous tissue plasminogen activator and heparin in acute middle cerebral artery stroke. Stroke. 1992;23:646.

136 **del Zoppo GJ et al.** Hemorrhagic transformation following tissue plasminogen activator in experimental cerebral infarction. Stroke. 1990;21:596.

137 **Thomas DJ.** Hemodilution in acute stroke. Stroke. 1985;16:763.

138 **Scandinavian Stroke Study Group.** Multicenter trial of hemodilution in acute ischemic stroke I. Results in the total patient population. Stroke. 1987; 18:691.

139 **Strand T et al.** A randomized controlled trial of hemodilution therapy in acute ischemic stroke. Stroke. 1984;15: 980.

140 **Goslinga MD et al.** Custom-tailored hemodilution with albumin and crystalloids in acute ischemic stroke. Stroke. 1992;23:181.

141 **Bauer RB et al.** Dexamethasone as treatment in cerebrovascular disease. A controlled study in acute cerebral infarction. Stroke. 1973;4:547.

142 **Norris JW.** Steroid therapy in acute cerebral infarction. Arch Neurol. 1976; 33:69.

143 **Dyken M et al.** Evaluation of cortisone in the treatment of cerebral infarction. JAMA. 1956;162:1531.

144 **Mulley et al.** Dexamethasone in acute stroke. Br Med J. 1978;2:994.

145 **Norris JW et al.** High-dose steroid treatment in cerebral infarction. Br Med J (Clin Res). 1986;292:21.

146 **Poungvarin N et al.** Effects of dexamethasone in primary supratentorial intracerebral hemorrhage. N Engl J Med. 1987;315:1229.

147 **Halliwel B.** Oxidants and human disease: some new concepts. FASEB J. 1987;1:358.

148 **Southern PA, Powis G.** Free radicals in medicine II. Involvement in human disease. Mayo Clin Proc. 1988;63:390.

149 **Braughler JM, Hall ED.** Central nervous system trauma and stroke: I. Biochemical considerations for oxygen radical formation and lipid peroxidation. Free Radic Biol Med. 1989;6.

150 **Braughler JM et al.** Novel 21-aminosteroids as potent inhibitors of iron dependent lipid peroxidation. J Biol Chem. 1987;262:10438.

151 **Hall ED et al.** The 21-aminosteroid lipid peroxidation inhibitor U74006F protects against cerebral ischemia in gerbils. Stroke. 1988;19:997.

152 **Asano T et al.** Possible participation of free radical reactions initiated by clot lysis in the pathogenesis of vasospasm after subarachnoid hemorrhage. In: Wilkins RH, ed. Cerebral Arterial Spasm. Baltimore: Williams & Wilkins; 1980:190.

153 **Hall ED, Travis MA.** Effects of the non-glucocorticoid 21-aminosteroid U7006F on progressive brain hypoperfusion following experimental subarachnoid hemorrhage. Exp Neurol. 1988;1102:244.

154 **Fleishaker JC et al.** Evaluation of the pharmacokinetics and tolerability of tirilazad mesylate, a 21-aminosteroid free radical scavenger: II. Multiple-dose administration. J Clin Pharmacol. 1993;33:182.

155 **Gelmers HJ et al.** A controlled trial of nimodipine in acute ischemic stroke. N Engl J Med. 1988;318:203.

156 **Trust Study Group.** Randomized, double-blind, placebo-controlled trial of nimodipine in acute stroke. Lancet. 1990;336:1205.

157 **Bogousslavsky J et al.** Double-blind study of nimodipine in non-severe stroke. Eur Neurol. 1990;30:23.

158 **Kramer G et al.** Nimodipine German Austrian Stroke Trial. Neurology. 1990;40(Suppl. 1):415.

159 **Rocca WA et al.** Design and baseline results of the monosialoganglioside early stroke trial. Stroke. 1992;23:519.

160 **Lenzi GL et al.** Early treatment of stroke with monosialoganglioside GM-1: efficacy and safety results of an early stroke trial. Stroke. 1994;25: 1552–558.

161 **Catapano F, Galderisi S.** Depression and cerebral stroke. J Clin Pyschiatry. 1990;5 (Suppl. 9):9.

162 **Mooney GF, Haas LJ.** Effect of methylphenidate on brain injury-related anger. Arch Phys Med Rehabil. 1993;74: 153.

163 **Dombovy ML.** Stroke: clinical course and neurophysiologic mechanisms of recovery. Crit Rev Phys Rehab Med. 1991;2:171.

164 **Crisostomo EA et al.** Evidence that amphetamine with physical therapy promotes recovery of motor function in stroke patients. Ann Neurol. 1988;23: 94.

165 **Biller J et al.** Management of aneurysmal subarachnoid hemorrhage. Curr Concept Cerebrovasc Dis Stroke. 1988;23:13.

166 **Adams HP et al.** Antifibrinolytic therapy in patients with aneurysmal subarachnoid hemorrhage: a report of the cooperative aneurysmal study. Arch Neurol. 1981;38:25.

167 **Vermeulen M et al.** Antifibrinolytic treatment in subarachnoid hemorrhage. N Engl J Med. 1984;311:432.

168 **Hijdra A et al.** Prediction of delayed cerebral ischemia, rebleeding, and outcome after aneurysmal subarachnoid hemorrhage. Stroke. 1988;19:1250.

169 **Fan-Harvard P et al.** Treatment and prevention of infections of cerebrospinal shunts. Clin Pharm. 1987;6:866.

170 **Bayston R et al.** Intraventricular vancomycin in the treatment of ventriculitis associated with cerebrospinal fluid shunting and drainage. J Neurol Neurosurg Pyschiatry. 1987;50:1419.

171 **Kassell NJ et al.** Treatment of ischemic deficits from vasospasm with intravascular volume expansion and induced arterial hypertension. Neurosurgery. 1982;11:337.

172 **Kosnik EJ et al.** Postoperative hypertension in the management of patients with intracranial arterial hypertension. J Neurosurg. 1976;45:148.

173 **Awad IA et al.** Clinical vasospasm after subarachnoid hemorrhage: response to hypervolemic hemodilution and arterial hypertension. Stroke. 1987;18: 365.

174 **Otsubo H et al.** Normovolaemic induced hypertension therapy for cerebral vasospasm after subarachnoid heamorrhage. Acta Neurochir (Wien). 1990;103:18.

175 **Ljunggren B et al.** Outcome in 60

consecutive patients treated with early aneurysm operation and intravenous nimodipine. J Neurosurg. 1984;61:861.

176 **Grotenhuis JA et al.** Intracarotid slow bolus injection of nimodipine during angiography for treatment of cerebral vasospasm after SAH. J Neurosurg. 1984;61:231.

177 **Auer LM.** Acute operation and preventative nimodipine improves outcome in patients with ruptured cerebral aneurysms. Neurosurgery. 1984;15:57.

178 **Auer LM et al.** Nimodipine and early aneurysm operation in good-condition SAH patients. Acta Neurochir (Wien). 1986;82:7.

179 **Boker et al.** Clinical experiences in the prevention of ischaemic neurological deficits after subarachnoid hemorrhage with nimodipine. In: Auer LM, ed. Timing of Aneurysm Surgery. Berlin: Walter de Gruyter; 1985:535.

180 **Baumann H et al.** Experiences with nimodipine in combination with postoperative hypertensive, hypervolemic treatment in the management of ruptured intracranial aneurysms. In: Auer LM, ed. Timing of Aneurysm Surgery. Berlin: Walter de Gruyter; 1985:561.

181 **Allen GS et al.** Cerebral arterial spasm—a controlled trial of nimodipine in patients with subarachnoid hemorrhage. N Engl J Med. 1983;308:619.

182 **Petruk KC et al.** Nimodipine treatment in poor-grade aneurysm patients—results of a multicenter double-blind placebo-controlled trial. J Neurosurg. 1988;68:505.

183 **Phillippon J et al.** Prevention of vasospasm in subarachnoid hemorrhage: a controlled study with nimodipine. Acta Neurochir (Wien). 1986;82:110.

184 **Pickard JD et al.** Effect of oral nimodipine on cerebral infarction and outcome after subarachnoid hemorrhage: British aneurysm nimodipine trial. Br Med J (Clin Res Ed). 1989;289:636.

185 **Haley EC et al.** A randomized controlled trial of high dose intravenous nicardipine in aneurysmal SAH—a report of the cooperative aneurysmal study. J Neurosurg. 1993;78:537.

186 **Hasan D et al.** Epileptic seizures after subarachnoid hemorrhage. Ann Neurol. 1993;33:286.

187 **Matchar DB et al.** Medical treatment for stroke prevention. Ann Intern Med. 1994;121:41–53.

188 **Sila CA.** Prophylaxis and treatment of stroke: the state of the art in 1993. Drugs. 1993;45:329–37.

189 **Kaste M et al.** A randomized, double-blind, placebo-controlled trial of nimodipine in acute ischemic stroke. Stroke. 1994;25:1348–353.

190 **Rosenbaum D et al.** Early treatment of ischemic stroke with a calcium antagonist. Stroke. 1991;22:437.

191 **Rosenbaum DM et al.** Pilot study of nicardipine for acute ischemic stroke. Angiology. 1990:1017.

192 **Oczkowski WJ et al.** A double-blind, randomized trial of PY108-068 in acute ischemic cerebral infarction. Stroke. 1989;20:604.

193 **Wiegandt H.** The gangliosides. In: Agranoff BW, Aprison MH, eds. Advances in Neurochemistry. New York: Plenium Press. 1982;4:149.

194 **Schengrund CL.** The roles of gangliosides in neural differentiation and repair. A perspective. Brain Res Bull. 1990;24:131.

Principles of Infectious Diseases

B Joseph Guglielmo

Approaching the Problem 54-1
Establishing the Presence of an Infection 54-1
  Fever.. 54-2
  Leukocytosis 54-2
Establishing the Severity of an Infection 54-2
  Pathogenesis of Sepsis (See Figure 54.1) 54-3
  Hemodynamic Changes 54-2
  Cellular Changes 54-3
  Respiratory Changes 54-3
  Hematological Changes 54-3
  Neurological Changes 54-3
Problems in the Diagnosis of an Infection 54-4
  Confabulating Variables 54-4
  Drug Effects 54-4
  Fever.. 54-4
    Disease-induced 54-4
    Drug-induced 54-4
Establishing the Site of the Infection 54-5
Determining Likely Pathogens 54-5
  Classification of Organisms (See Table 54.1) 54-4
  Likely Organisms at Sites of Infections
  (See Table 54.2) 54-5
Microbiological Tests and Susceptibility
  of Organisms 54-6
  Gram's Stain (Also see Table 54.1) 54-6
  Potassium Hydroxide (KOH) Stain 54-6
  Acid-Fast Bacilli (AFB) Stain 54-6
  Classification of Antibacterials (See Table 54.3) 54-7
  Susceptibilities of Aerobic Gram-Positives
  (See Table 54.4) 54-8
  Susceptibilities of Aerobic Gram-Negatives
  (See Table 54.5) 54-8
  Susceptibilities of Anaerobic Organisms
  (See Table 54.6) 54-9
  Antimicrobial Drugs of Choice (See Table 54.7) 54-10
  Culture and Susceptibility Testing 54-6
    Disk diffusion 54-6
    Broth dilution 54-6

Minimum Inhibitory Concentration (MIC) 54-7
Minimum Bactericidal Concentration (MBC) 54-7
Serum Bactericidal Test (SBT) 54-7
Determination of Isolate Pathogenicity 54-7
Antimicrobial Toxicities 54-9
  Adverse Effects and Toxicities (See Table 54.8) 54-9
  Concomitant Disease States 54-9
Antimicrobial Costs of Therapy 54-9
Route of Administration 54-12
Antimicrobial Dosing 54-12
  Dosing Guidelines (See Table 54.9) 54-15
  Site of Infection 54-12
  Anatomical and Physiological Barriers 54-12
  Route of Elimination 54-12
    Dosing of aminoglycosides (See Figure 54.2) 54-18
    Dosing of vancomycin (See Figure 54.3) 54-19
  Patient Age 54-12
  Fever and Inoculum Effect 54-12
Postantibiotic Effect (PAE) 54-14
  Once-Daily Dosing of Aminoglycosides 54-17
Antimicrobial Protein Binding 54-18
Antimicrobial Failure 54-18
  Antibiotic Specific Factors 54-18
    Drug resistance 54-18
    Superinfection 54-18
  Concurrent Therapy 54-18
    Indifference 54-19
    Synergism 54-19
    Antagonism 54-19
  Pharmacological Factors 54-19
    Subtherapeutic dosing 54-19
    Reduced oral absorption 54-19
    Site of infection 54-19
    Inadequate duration of therapy 54-19
  Host Factors 54-19
    Prosthetic material 54-19
    Diabetes 54-19
    Immune status 54-19

Approaching the Problem

The proper selection of antimicrobial therapy is based upon a number of factors. Disease states (malignancy, autoimmune disease) and drugs can mimic infection, it is, therefore, important to first clearly establish the presence of an infectious process before initiating therapy. Once infection has been documented, the most likely site of infection must be identified. Signs and symptoms (e.g., erythema associated with cellulitis) direct the clinician to the likely source. Since certain pathogens are known to be associated with a specific site of infection, therapy often can be directed against these organisms. Additional laboratory tests, including the Gram's stain, serology, and antimicrobial susceptibility testing generally identify the primary pathogen. While a number of antimicrobials potentially can be considered, clinical efficacy, adverse effect profile, pharmacokinetic disposition, and cost considerations ultimately guide the choice of therapy. Once an agent has been selected, the dosage must be based upon the size of the patient, site of infection, route of elimination, and other factors.

Establishing the Presence of an Infection

1. R.G., a 63-year-old male in the intensive care unit, underwent emergent resection of his large bowel. He has been intubated throughout his postoperative course. On the 20th day of hospitalization, R.G. suddenly became confused, his blood pressure (BP) dropped to 70/30 mm Hg with a heart rate of 130 beats/min. His extremities were cold upon touch and he presented with circumoral pallor. His temperature increased to 40 °C (axillary) and his respiratory rate was noted to be 24 breaths/min. Copious amounts of yellow-green secretions were suctioned from his endotracheal tube.

Physical examination revealed sinus tachycardia with no rubs or murmurs. Rhonchi with decreased breath sounds were observed on auscultation. The abdomen was distended and

R.G. complains of new abdominal pain. No bowel sounds can be heard and the stool is guaiac positive. Urine output from the Foley catheter has been 10 mL/hr for the last 2 hours. Erythema is noted around the central venous catheter.

Chest x-ray reveals bilateral lower lobe infiltrates, and urinalysis reveals >50 white blood cells/high power field (WBCs/HPF), few casts, and a specific gravity of 1.015. Blood, tracheal aspirate, and urine cultures are pending. Other laboratory values include: sodium (Na) 131 mEq/L, phosphate (K) 4.1 mEq/L, chloride (Cl) 110 mEq/L, CO_2 16 mEq/L, blood urea nitrogen (BUN) 58 mg/dL, creatinine 3.8 mg/dL (increased from 0.9 mg/dL at admission), and glucose 320 mg/dL. The serum albumin is 2.1 gm/dL, hemoglobin (Hgb) 10.3 gm/dL, hematocrit (Hct) 33%, and the WBC is 15,600/mm^3 with bands present. Platelets are 40,000/mm^3 with a prothrombin time (PT) of 18 seconds. His erythrocyte sedimentation rate (ESR) is 65 mm/hr. What signs and symptoms exhibited by R.G. are consistent with infection? [SI units: Na 131 mmol/L; K 4.1 mmol/L; Cl 110 mmol/L; CO_2 16 mmol/L; BUN 20.71 mmol/L of urea; creatinine 335.92 and 7.56 μmol/L, respectively; glucose 17.76 μmol/L; albumin 235.62 μmol/L; Hgb 103 gm/L; Hct 0.33; WBC 15.6 × 10^9; platelets 40 × 10^9; ESR 65 mm/hr]

R.G. is demonstrating numerous signs and symptoms which are consistent with an infectious process. R.G. has both an increased white blood cell count (15,600/mm^3), as well as a ''shift to the left'' (bands are present on the differential). An increased white blood cell count commonly is observed with infection, particularly with bacterial pathogens. The white blood cell differential in patients with a bacterial infection often demonstrates a ''shift to the left'' (i.e., presence of immature neutrophils) suggesting that the bone marrow is responding to an infectious insult. However, it is important to note that infection is not always associated with leukocytosis. Overwhelming sepsis can cause a decreased white blood cell count: some patients may become neutropenic secondary to infection. In less acute infection (e.g., subacute bacterial endocarditis, abscesses), the white blood cell count may remain within the normal range. Since the abscess is a localized lesion, less bone marrow response would be anticipated; thus, the white blood cell count may not increase in these patients.

R.G.'s fever is 40 °C by axillary measurement. Fever is a common manifestation of infection, with oral temperatures generally greater than 38 °C. Oral and axillary temperatures tend to be approximately 0.4 °C lower compared to rectal measurement.[1] As a result, R.G.'s temperature would be expected to be 40.4 °C if his temperature had been taken rectally. In general, rectal measurement of temperature is a more reliable determination of fever. Some patients with overwhelming infection, however, may present with hypothermia and temperatures less than 36 °C. Furthermore, patients with localized infections (e.g., uncomplicated urinary tract infection, chronic abscesses) may be afebrile.

The bilateral lower lobe infiltrates on R.G.'s chest x-ray, the presence of copious amounts of yellow-green secretions from his endotracheal tube, and the erythema surrounding his central venous catheter also are compatible with an infectious process. Furthermore, R.G. has the additional signs and symptoms described below that also are consistent with sepsis.

Establishing the Severity of an Infection

2. What signs and symptoms manifested by R.G. are consistent with a serious systemic infection?

The term ''sepsis'' has been a poorly described syndrome; however, sepsis generally suggests more systemic infection associated with the presence of pathogenic micro-organisms or their toxins in the blood. A uniform system for defining the spectrum of disorders associated with sepsis is needed.[2]

The pathogenesis of sepsis is complex (see Figure 54.1) and only partially understood.[2-4] Gram-negative aerobes produce endotoxin which results in a cascade of endogenous mediator release, including tumor necrosis factor (TNF), interleukins-1 and 6, platelet activating factor (PAF), and various other substances from mononuclear phagocytes and other cells. While this initial stimulus commonly is associated with gram-negative endotoxin, other substances, including gram-positive exotoxin and fungal cell wall constituents also may be associated with cytokine release. After release of TNF, interleukin-1 and PAF, arachidonic acid is metabolized to form leukotrienes, thromboxane A_2, and prostaglandins, particularly prostaglandin E_2 and prostaglandin I_2. Interleukin-1 and interleukin-6 activate the T cells to produce interferon, interleukin-2, interleukin-4, and granulocyte-macrophage colony stimulating factor. Increased endothelial permeability ensues. Subsequently, the endothelium releases two hemodynamically active substances: endothelium-derived relaxing factor (EDRF) and endothelin-l. Activation of the complement cascade (fragments C3a and C5a) follows with additional vascular abnormalities and neutrophil activation. Other potentially important agents in this cascade include adhesion molecules, kinins, thrombin, myocardial depressant substance, beta-endorphin and heat shock protein. The net result of the above cascade is a number of hemodynamic, renal, acid-base, and other disorders.

Hemodynamic Changes. Critically ill patients often have central intravenous lines in place for measuring cardiac output and systemic vascular resistance (SVR). A normal systemic vascular resistance of 800 to 1200 dyne·sec·cm^{-5} may fall to 500 to 600 dyne·sec·cm^{-5} or less with septic shock because of intense vasodilation. In response to this vasodilation, the heart reflexly increases cardiac output from its normal 4 to 6 L/minute to as much as 11 to 12 L/minute in septic patients. This increase in cardiac output primarily is due to an increased heart rate: stroke volume is unchanged or decreased due to the hypovolemic state. Although the heart rate is increased on the basis of reflex tachycardia, a chronotropic response also takes place due to stress-induced catecholamine release (norepinephrine, epinephrine). Thus, the cardiac output will increase in response to arterial vasodilation, however, this increase generally is insufficient to overcome the vasodilatory state and hypotension ensues. In overwhelming septic shock, myocardial depression results in a decreased cardiac output. The combination of decreased cardiac output and decreased systemic vascular resistance can make hypotension unresponsive to pressors and intravenous fluids. R.G. does have hemodynamic evidence of being in septic shock. He is hypotensive (BP 70/30 mm Hg), and he is experiencing tachycardia (rate 130 beats/minute), presumably in response to significant vasodilation and catecholamine release.

While vasodilation commonly occurs in sepsis, hemodynamic changes are not equal throughout the vasculature. Some vascular beds constrict, resulting in maldistribution of blood flow. Significant amount of blood is shunted away from the kidneys, mesentery, and extremities.

Normal urine output of approximately 0.5 to 1.0 mL/kg/hour (30 to 70 mL/hour for a 70 kg patient) can decrease to less than 20 mL/hour in sepsis. The urine output for R.G. has decreased to 10 mL/hour, consistent with sepsis-induced perfusion abnormalities. Decreased blood flow to the kidney, as well as mediator-induced microvascular failure can cause acute tubular necrosis (ATN). R.G.'s uremia (BUN 58 mg/dL) and his increased serum creatinine concentration (3.8 mg/dL) are consistent with decreased renal perfusion secondary to sepsis. When sepsis has progressed to septic shock, blood flow to most major organs is decreased. De-

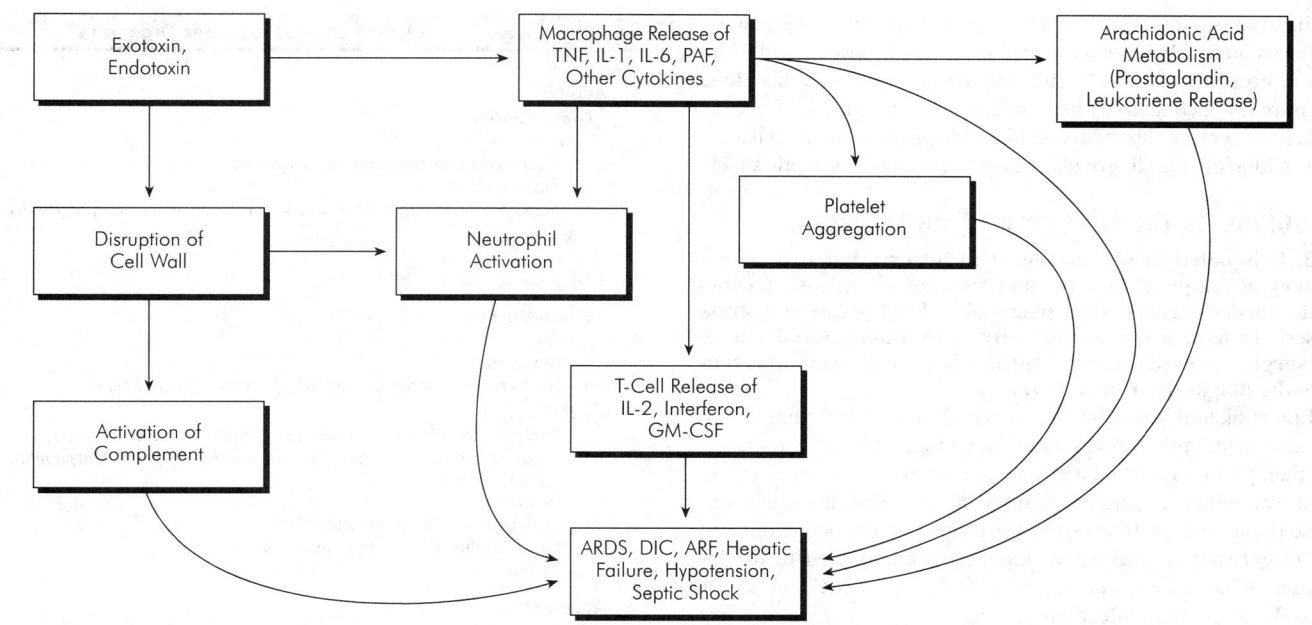

Fig 54.1 The Sepsis Cascade TNF = Tumor necrosis factor; IL-1 = Interleukin-1; IL-6 = Interleukin-6; GM-CSF = Granulocyte macrophage colony stimulating factor; ARDS = Acute respiratory distress syndrome; DIC = Disseminated intravascular coagulopathy; PAF = Platelet activating factor; ARF = Acute renal failure.

creased blood flow to the liver may result in ''shock liver,'' during which time liver function tests, including the alanine aminotransferase (ALT), aspartate aminotransferase (AST), and alkaline phosphatase, become elevated. The liver function tests for R.G. are not available, however, his serum albumin concentration is low (2.1 gm/dL) and his prothrombin time of 18 seconds is prolonged. Decreased blood flow to the musculature classically is characterized by cool extremities, and decreased blood flow to the brain can result in decreased mentation. Note R.G. is confused, his extremities are cold, and the area around his mouth appears pale. All these signs and symptoms provide strong evidence that he is in septic shock.

Cellular Changes. The sepsis syndrome is associated with significant abnormalities in cellular metabolism. Glucose intolerance commonly is observed in sepsis, and patients with previously normal blood glucose levels may experience sudden increases in blood sugar. In some cases, an increase in glucose may be one of the first signs of an infectious process. R.G.'s increased blood glucose concentration (320 mg/dL) is, therefore, consistent with sepsis. Another sensitive indicator of sepsis-associated inflammation is the erythrocyte sedimentation rate. The ESR is a nonspecific test which commonly is elevated in a variety of inflammatory states, including infection. The ESR can be used to determine the progression of infection; currently R.G.'s ESR is elevated at 65 mm/hour. With appropriate management of infection, the ESR would be expected to decrease; inadequate treatment would be associated with persistent elevation of the erythrocyte sedimentation rate.

Respiratory Changes. Production of organic acids, such as lactate, increased glycolysis, decreased fractional extraction of oxygen, and abnormal delivery-dependent oxygen consumption are observed.[4] This increase in lactic acid results in metabolic acidosis with accompanying decreased serum bicarbonate levels. The lungs normally respond in a compensatory manner with an increased respiratory rate (tachypnea), resulting in an increased elimination of arterial carbon dioxide. R.G.'s acid-base status is consistent with sepsis-associated metabolic acidosis (CO_2 16 mEq/L) and compensatory respiratory alkalosis (respiratory rate 24/minute).

While not currently present in R.G., a late complication of the above mentioned sepsis cascade is acute respiratory distress syndrome (ARDS). ARDS initially was described as noncardiogenic pulmonary edema with severe hypoxemia caused by right to left intrapulmonary shunting due to atelectasis and edema-filled alveoli. While the exact cause of ARDS has not been determined, the primary pathophysiology is a breakdown in the natural integrity of the alveolar-capillary network in the lung.[6] In the early phase of ARDS, patients have severe alveolar edema with large numbers of inflammatory cells, primarily neutrophils. The chronic phase of ARDS (10 to 14 days after development of the syndrome) is associated with significant lung destruction. Emphysema, pulmonary vascular obliteration, and fibrosis commonly are observed. Severe ARDS is associated with arterial oxygen level/fraction of inspired oxygen (PaO_2/FiO_2) ratios of less than 100, low lung compliance, and need for high positive end expiratory pressure (PEEP) and other respiratory maneuvers. At the present time the treatment for this syndrome primarily is supportive, including mechanical ventilation, high inspired oxygen, and PEEP. The mortality associated with ARDS is high, approximating 50%.[7] While R.G. currently does not have acute respiratory distress syndrome, the severity of his septic episode strongly suggests he may develop this complication in the next few days.

Hematological Changes. Disseminated intravascular coagulation (DIC) is a well-recognized sequelae of sepsis. Huge quantities of clotting factors and platelets are consumed in DIC as widespread clotting takes place throughout the circulatory system. As a result, the prothrombin time and the activated partial thromboplastin time (aPTT) are prolonged and the platelet count commonly is decreased in sepsis. Decreased fibrinogen levels and increased fibrin split products generally are diagnostic for DIC. The prothrombin time of 18 seconds and the decreased platelet count of 40,000/mm[3] in R.G. are consistent with sepsis-induced disseminated intravascular coagulation.

Neurological Changes. Central nervous system (CNS) changes, including lethargy, disorientation, confusion, and psychosis, predominate in sepsis. Altered mental status is well-recognized with infections of the central nervous system, such as meningitis and brain abscess. However, it is important to note that these changes are also commonly observed with other sites of sepsis. On the 20th day of hospitalization, R.G. suddenly became confused, his blood pressure dropped, and his heart rate increased. Thus, R.G.'s CNS effects as well as his hematological, respiratory, hemodynamic, and cellular effects all provide substantial evidence of septic shock.

Problems in the Diagnosis of an Infection

3. It is noted in his past medical history that R.G. has a history of temporal arteritis and seizures chronically treated with corticosteroids and phenytoin. Perioperative "stress doses" of hydrocortisone recently were administered due to his surgical procedure. What medications or disease states confuse the diagnosis of infection?

Confabulating Variables. A variety of factors, including major surgery, acute myocardial infarction, and initiation of corticosteroid therapy are associated with an increased white blood cell count. However, unlike infection, a "shift to the left" does not occur with these disease states. In R.G. the stress dose of hydrocortisone and his recent surgical procedure might have contributed to the increased WBC count. The presence of bands in R.G., however, strongly suggests an infectious process.

Drug Effects. The ability of *corticosteroids* to mimic or mask infection is noteworthy. Corticosteroids are associated with an increased white blood cell count as well as glucose intolerance when therapy is initiated or when doses are increased. Furthermore, some patients experience corticosteroid-induced mental status changes which may complicate the diagnosis of a septic infection, which can be accompanied by decreased mentation. While corticosteroids mimic infection, they also have the ability to mask infection. Bowel perforation in a patient with ulcerative colitis would result in significant peritoneal contamination. However, concomitant corticosteroids, due to their potent anti-inflammatory effects, may reduce the classic findings of peritonitis. Furthermore, corticosteroids can reduce and sometimes ablate the febrile response. Thus, these corticosteroid-treated patients may be asymptomatic, but at great risk for gram-negative septic shock.

Another example of the influence of corticosteroids on the diagnosis of infection relates to neurosurgical procedures. Dexamethasone is a corticosteroid commonly used to reduce the inflammation and swelling associated with neurosurgical procedures. Certain neurosurgical procedures are associated with significant trauma to the meninges, however, the patient often is asymptomatic while receiving high-dose dexamethasone. When the dexamethasone dose is decreased, the patient subsequently may experience classic meningismus, including stiff neck, photophobia, and headache. The lumbar puncture may demonstrate cloudy cerebrospinal fluid (CSF), an elevated WBC, high CSF protein, and low CSF glucose. While the signs and symptoms are consistent with infectious meningitis, this disease state is considered aseptic meningitis (i.e., inflammation of the meninges without an infectious etiology).[11] Certain drugs may cause aseptic meningitis, including OKT3,[12] nonsteroidal anti-inflammatory agents, and sulfonamides.

Fever also is consistent with autoimmune diseases, such as lupus erythematosus and temporal arteritis.[8,9] Neoplasms, such as leukemia and lymphoma, also may present with low-grade fevers, similar to that observed in an infectious process. One evaluation of fever of unknown origin (FUO) in community hospitals demonstrated a 25% incidence of FUO due to cancer.[9] Other diseases associated with fever include sarcoidosis, chronic liver disease, and familial Mediterranean fever. Acute myocardial infarction, pulmonary embolism, and postoperative pulmonary atelectasis are commonly associated with an elevated temperature. Factitious fever or self-induced disease must be considered in certain patients.

Table 54.1	Classification of Infectious Organisms[a]

Bacteria
  Aerobic
    Gram-Positive
      Cocci
        Streptococci: pneumococcus, *Streptococcus viridans*
        Enterococcus
        Staphylococci: *Staphylococcus aureus, Staphylococcus epidermidis*
      Rods (bacilli)
        Corynebacterium
        Listeria
    Gram-Negative
      Cocci
        Moraxella
        Neisseria (*Neisseria meningitidis, Neisseria gonorrhoeae*)
      Rods (bacilli)
        Enterobacteriaceae (*Escherichia coli, Klebsiella, Enterobacter, Citrobacter, Proteus, Serratia, Salmonella, Shigella, Morganella, Providencia*)
        Pseudomonas
        Helicobacter (Campylobacter)
        Haemophilus (Coccobacilli morphology)
        Legionella
  Anaerobic
    Gram-Positive
      Cocci
        Peptococcus
        Peptostreptococcus
      Rods (bacilli)
        Clostridia (*Clostridium perfringens, Clostridium tetani*)
        Proprionibacterium acnes
    Gram-Negative
      Cocci
        None
      Rods (bacilli)
        Bacteroides (*Bacteroides fragilis, Bacteroides melaninogenicus*)
        Fusobacterium

Fungi
  Aspergillus, candida, coccidioides, cryptococcus, histoplasma, Mucor, tinea, trichophyton, torulopsis

Viruses
  Influenza, hepatitis A, B, C, D human immunodeficiency virus, rubella, herpes, cytomegalovirus, respiratory syncytial virus, Epstein-Barr virus

Chlamydiae
  Chlamydia trachomatis
  Chlamydia psittaci
  Chlamydia pneumoniae (TWAR)
  LGV [(lymphogranuloma venereum) disease caused by *Chlamydia trachomatis* of immunotype L1-L3)]

Rickettsiae
  Rocky Mountain Spotted Fever, Q fever

Ureaplasma

Mycoplasmas
  Mycoplasma pneumoniae, Mycoplasma hominis

Spirochetes
  Treponema pallidum, Borrelia burgdorferi (Lyme disease)

Mycobacteria
  Mycobacterium tuberculosis
  Mycobacterium avium intracellulare

[a] Adapted from Handbook of Applied Therapeutics.

After infection, autoimmune disease, and malignancy have been ruled out, drug fever should be considered. Drugs, including certain antimicrobials (e.g., amphotericin B) and phenytoin have been associated with drug fever. Drug fever generally occurs after seven to ten days of therapy and resolves within 48 hours of the drug's discontinuation.[10] Some clinicians claim that patients with drug fever generally feel "well" and are unaware of their fever. Re-challenge with the offending agent usually results in recurrence of fever within hours of administration. However, it is important to reinforce that drug fever should be considered a diagnosis of exclusion. Drug fever should be considered only after eliminating the presence of other disease states. (Also see Chapter 6: Anaphylaxis and Drug Allergy.)

Neoplasms may be radiographically indistinguishable from an abscess. An example of this dilemma is the differential diagnosis of toxoplasmosis versus lymphoma in acquired immunodeficiency syndrome (AIDS) patients with CAT scan-documented brain lesions. One method for diagnosis is the use of empiric therapy versus *Toxoplasmosis gondii*. If the lesions appear to be unresponsive to therapy, the presumptive diagnosis of malignancy can be made.

In summary, R.G. has an autoimmune disease, temporal arteritis, which has been reported to be associated with fever. Similarly, his corticosteroid administration and phenytoin use may confuse the diagnosis of infection. His other signs and symptoms, however, strongly suggest that R.G.'s problems are of an infectious etiology.

Establishing the Site of the Infection

4. What are the most likely sources of R.G.'s infection?

Independent of the presumed site of infection, a blood culture should be drawn to demonstrate the presence of bacteremia. After blood cultures are sampled, a thorough physical examination generally documents the source of infection. Urosepsis, the most common cause of nosocomial infection, may be associated with dysuria, flank pain, and abnormal urinalysis.[13] Tachypnea, increased sputum production, altered chest x-ray, and hypoxemia may direct the clinician toward a pulmonary source. Evidence for an infected intravenous (IV) line would include pain, erythema, and purulent discharge around the IV catheter. Other potential sites of infection include the peritoneum, pelvis, bone, and central nervous system. R.G. is demonstrating a number of possible sites of infection. The copious production of yellow-green sputum, tachypnea, and the altered chest x-ray suggest the presence of pneumonia. The abdominal pain, absent bowel sounds, and recent surgical procedure, however, require ruling out an intra-abdominal source.[14] Lastly, the abnormal urinalysis (>50 WBC/HPF) and the redness around the central venous catheter suggest other sites of infection.

Determining Likely Pathogens

5. What are the most likely pathogens associated with R.G.'s infection(s)?

As described above, R.G. has a number of possible sources of infection. The suspected pathogens are dependent upon the presumed site of infection. Table 54.1 provides a classification of infectious organisms (e.g., gram-positive, gram-negative, aerobic, anaerobic) and Table 54.2 lists the most likely organisms associated with sites of infection. Determination of the most likely infectious agent is not only associated with the site of infection, but also upon certain host factors. As an example, bacterial pneumonia may be caused by a variety of pathogens, including *Streptococcus pneumoniae*, *Enterobacteriaceae*, and atypical pathogens (e.g., *Legionella pneumophila*).[15] Empiric antimicrobial therapy directed against all the above organisms, however, is unnecessary. A number of host factors must be evaluated in order to streamline therapy against the most likely pathogens. If the pneumonia is community-acquired, *Streptococcus pneumoniae*, *Haemophilus influenzae*, and *Moraxella catarrhalis* may predominate.[16] However, in nosocomial (hospital, nursing home) pneumonia, gram-negative enterics (e.g., *Escherichia coli*, *Klebsiella* species, *Enterobacter* species, and *Pseudomonas aeruginosa*) become more significant patho-

Table 54.2	Site of Infection: Suspected Organisms[b]
Site/Type of Infection[a]	Suspected Organisms
Respiratory	
Pharyngitis	Group A streptococci
Bronchitis, otitis	Haemophilus influenzae, Streptococcus pneumoniae, Moraxella catarrhalis
Acute sinusitis	Streptococcus pneumoniae, Haemophilus influenzae, Moraxella catarrhalis
Chronic sinusitis	Anaerobes, Staphylococcus aureus
Epiglottitis	Haemophilus influenzae
Pneumonia	
Community-acquired	
Normal host	*Streptococcus pneumoniae*, viral, mycoplasma
Aspiration	Normal aerobic and anaerobic mouth flora
Pediatrics	*Streptococcus pneumoniae, Haemophilus influenzae*
COAD	*Streptococcus pneumoniae, Haemophilus influenzae*
Alcoholic	*Streptococcus pneumoniae, Klebsiella*
Hospital-acquired	
Aspiration	Mouth anaerobes, gram-negative aerobic rods, *Staphylococcus aureus*
Neutropenic	Fungi, gram-negative aerobic rods, *Staphylococcus aureus*
AIDS	Fungi, pneumocystis, *Legionella, Nocardia, Streptococcus pneumoniae*
Urinary Tract	
Community-Acquired	*Escherichia coli*, other gram-negative rods, *Staphylococcus aureus, Staphylococcus epidermidis*, enterococci
Hospital-Acquired	Resistant gram-negative rods, enterococci
Skin/Soft Tissue	
Cellulitis	Group A streptococci, *Staphylococcus aureus*
IV catheter site	*Staphylococcus aureus, Staphylococcus epidermidis*
Surgical wound	*Staphylococcus aureus*, gram-negative rods
Diabetic ulcer	*Staphylococcus aureus*, gram-negative aerobic rods, anaerobes
Furuncle	*Staphylococcus aureus*
Intra-Abdominal	*Bacteroides fragilis, Escherichia coli*, enterococci
Gastroenteritis	*Salmonella, Shigella, Helicobacter, Clostridium difficile*, amoeba, Giardia, viral, enterotoxigenic-hemorrhagic *Escherichia coli*
Endocarditis	
Subacute	*Streptococcus viridans*
Acute	
IV drug abuser	*Staphylococcus aureus*, gram-negative aerobic rods, enterococci, fungi
Prosthetic valve	*Staphylococcus epidermidis* (prosthetic valve)
Osteomyelitis/Septic Arthritis	*Staphylococcus aureus*, gram-negative aerobic rods
Meningitis	
<2 months	*Escherichia coli*, group B streptococci, *Listeria*
2 months–12 years	*Haemophilus influenzae, Streptococcus pneumoniae, Neisseria meningitidis*

Continued

Table 54.2	Site of Infection: Suspected Organisms[b] (Continued)
Site/Type of Infection[a]	**Suspected Organisms**
Adults	*Streptococcus pneumoniae, Neisseria meningitidis*, gram-negative aerobic rods
Hospital-acquired	*Streptococcus pneumoniae, Neisseria meningitidis*, gram-negative aerobic rods
Post-neurosurgery	*Staphylococcus aureus*, gram-negative rods

[a] AIDS = Acquired immunodeficiency syndrome; COAD = Chronic obstructive airways disease; IV = Intravenous.
[b] Adapted from Handbook of Applied Therapeutics.

gens. If the pneumonia is considered to be a result of a gastric aspiration, mouth anaerobes empirically must be covered. In nosocomial pneumonia, knowledge of the hospital-specific flora is important. If *Escherichia coli* is the most commonly isolated pathogen at a given institution, antimicrobials, such as first- or second-generation cephalosporins, can be used. If *Pseudomonas aeruginosa* or *Enterobacter cloacae* predominate, then alternative therapy is necessary. A thorough evaluation of antimicrobial exposure also is necessary. Recent use of antimicrobials is more likely to result in infection due to resistant gram-negative organisms (e.g., AIDS patients or transplant recipients receiving suppressive trimethoprim-sulfamethoxazole therapy). Age of the patient is also an important determinant in the epidemiology of infection. Meningitis in a neonate is commonly caused by Group B streptococci, *Escherichia coli*, and *Listeria monocytogenes*, whereas, these bacteria are uncommon pathogens in normal adults. Concomitant diseases, such as chronic obstructive airways disease (COAD) or alcohol and intravenous drug abuse, also can influence the selection of certain pathogens. As an example, patients with COAD-associated bronchitis or pneumonia are more likely to be infected by *Streptococcus pneumoniae, Haemophilus influenzae*, and *Moraxella catarrhalis*. Chronic alcoholics are more likely to have infection caused by enteric gram-negative pathogens, such as *Klebsiella* species when compared with normal patients.

Immune status is an important predictor of likely pathogens. Human immunodeficiency virus (HIV)-positive individuals or those patients receiving cyclosporine and corticosteroids have lymphocyte deficiency-associated infections, including those due to cytomegalovirus, *Pneumocystis carinii*, atypical mycobacteria, and *Cryptococcus neoformans*. Leukemics and neutropenic patients are at risk for infection due to aerobic gram-negative bacilli, including *Pseudomonas aeruginosa* and fungi.

In the case of R.G., the abdomen, respiratory tract, urinary tract, and intravenous catheter are all potential sites of infection. Intra-abdominal infection is likely caused by gram-negative enterics and *Bacteroides fragilis*: nosocomial urinary tract infection is usually secondary to aerobic gram-negative rods. R.G.'s pneumonia possibly is due to gram-negative bacilli, staphylococci, and a variety of other organisms. Furthermore, his use of corticosteroids may predispose him to infection due to more opportunistic organisms, including Legionella, *Pneumocystis carinii*, and fungi. Lastly, his intravenous catheter infection suggests infection due to staphylococci, including *Staphylococcus epidermidis* and *Staphylococcus aureus*.

Microbiological Tests and Susceptibility of Organisms

6. A Gram's stain of R.G.'s tracheal aspirate demonstrates gram-negative bacilli. What tests may assist with the identification of the pathogen(s)?

Once the site of infection has been determined and host defense and other epidemiologic factors have been evaluated, additional tests can be performed to identify the pathogen. Some tests can be performed which provide immediate information to guide selection of the initial antimicrobial regimen. The **Gram's stain** involves the use of crystal violet solution and iodine which results in bacteria staining gram-positive or gram-negative; some organisms are gram-variable. In addition, the shape of the organism (cocci, bacilli) is readily apparent with the use of the Gram's stain. Streptococci and staphylococci are gram-positive cocci, whereas, *Escherichia coli, Enterobacter cloacae*, and *Pseudomonas aeruginosa* appear as gram-negative bacilli (Table 54.1).[17]

If the Gram's stain of the tracheal aspirate demonstrates gram-positive cocci in clusters, empiric antistaphylococcal therapy is indicated. In contrast, if the Gram's stain shows gram-negative rods, antimicrobials with activity versus these pathogens are indicated. Similar to the Gram's stain in bacterial infection, the India ink and **potassium hydroxide (KOH) stains** are helpful in the identification of certain fungi. The **acid-fast bacilli (AFB) stain** is critical in the diagnosis of infection due to *Mycobacterium tuberculosis* or atypical mycobacteria. In R.G. the Gram's stain suggests that antimicrobials active against gram-negative bacilli should be utilized. Table 54.3 provides a classification of antibacterials (e.g., different generations of cephalosporins). Tables 54.4, 54.5, and 54.6 list *in vitro* susceptibilities of aerobic gram-positive organisms, gram-negative aerobes, and anaerobic organisms, respectively.

Culture and susceptibility testing provides for final identification of the pathogen, as well as information regarding the possible effectiveness of various antimicrobials. While these tests provide more information than the Gram's stain, they generally require 18 to 24 hours to complete. After the pathogen has been identified, Table 54.7 can be used in conjunction with an institution's specific susceptibility studies to select the most appropriate antimicrobial. (Repeated use of this table would help the reader to recall the drugs of choice for specific microorganisms.)

Disk Diffusion. The most widely utilized tests for bacterial susceptibility are the disk diffusion and the broth dilution methods. The disk diffusion (Kirby-Bauer) technique utilizes an agar plate on which an inoculum of the organism is placed. After inoculation, several antimicrobial laden disks are placed upon the plate and evidence for bacterial growth is observed after 18 to 24 hours. If the antimicrobial is active versus the pathogen, a zone of inhibition of growth is observed around the disk. As per guidelines provided by the National Committee for Clinical Laboratory Standards (NCCLS), the diameter of inhibition is reported as susceptible, intermediate, or resistant.

Broth Dilution. The broth dilution method involves placement of a bacterial inoculum into several tubes or wells filled with broth. Serial dilutions of antimicrobials (e.g., nafcillin 0.5, 1.0, and 2.0 μg/mL) are placed in the respective wells. Bacteria are allowed to incubate for 18 to 24 hours, after which the wells are examined for bacterial growth. If the well is cloudy, bacterial growth has taken place, suggesting resistance to the antimicrobial at that concentration. As an example, if bacterial growth is observed with *Staphylococcus aureus* at 0.5 μg/mL of nafcillin, but not at 1.0 μg/mL, then 1.0 μg/mL would be considered the minimum inhibitory concentration (MIC) for nafcillin versus *Staphylococcus aureus*. Similar to the disk diffusion method, the NCCLS provides guidelines,[18] which account for the pharmacokinetic characteristics of an antimicrobial to determine whether the MIC should be reported as susceptible, moderately susceptible, or resistant. It is important to note that MIC interpretations are both organism- and antimicrobial-specific. As an example, ciprofloxacin achieves serum concentrations of 1 to 4 µg/mL and ceftriaxone achieves peak serum concentrations of 100 to 150 µg/mL: an MIC of 4 µg/mL for *Escherichia coli* would be interpreted as resistant to ciprofloxacin and susceptible to ceftriaxone. Although these tests provide an accurate assessment of *in vitro* susceptibility, the time delay (18 to 24 hours) can hinder streamlining of therapy. Some rapid diagnosis culture and susceptibility tests may provide similar information within hours, however, these are somewhat less accurate than standard susceptibility testing. While susceptibility testing is relatively well standardized for aerobic gram-negative and gram-positive organisms, its utility is debated for anaerobes[19] and fungi.[20] In general, most institutions do not perform susceptibility testing for anaerobes.

The consensus of the NCCLS and other experts is that anaerobic isolates from blood, bone, and joint sources, brain abscesses, empyemic fluid, and other body fluids that are normally sterile should be considered for susceptibility testing. Isolates from other sources should be considered for testing only if the physician feels the results are clearly indicated in the given patient.[19] While progress has been made in developing a standardized test for determination of fungal susceptibility, the primary emphasis has been with *Candida* species and other yeasts. Little data exist regarding standardized susceptibility testing for molds.[20]

The **minimum inhibitory concentration (MIC)** is the minimum concentration at which an antimicrobial inhibits the growth of the organism: the test does not provide information whether the organism is actually killed. In some disease states (e.g., endocarditis, meningitis), bactericidal therapy may be necessary. The **minimum bactericidal concentration (MBC)** is the test which can be utilized to determine the killing activity associated with an antimicrobial. The MBC is determined by taking an aliquot from each clear MIC tube and subsequently subcultured onto agar plates. The concentration at which no significant bacterial growth is observed on these plates is considered to be the MBC.

The **serum bactericidal test (SBT)** occasionally is utilized as an *in vivo* test of antimicrobial activity.[21] The test may have utility in assessing the treatment of more severe infections, such as endocarditis (see Chapter 57: Endocarditis) and osteomyelitis. A blood sample is taken from a patient receiving an antibiotic and this blood sample is serially diluted, utilizing Mueller-Hinton broth (e.g., 1:2, 1:4, 1:8, 1:16) and subsequently inoculated with the infecting organism. After 18 to 24 hours the samples are visually inspected for evidence of bacterial growth. If no growth is observed at dilutions of 1:8 and 1:16, but growth is seen at 1:32 and above, the serum is considered to be ''inhibitory'' at 1:16. Similar to the MIC methodology, the clear tubes define the inhibitory titers, however, it is unknown whether bactericidal concentrations have been achieved. As a result, aliquots of each of the clear tubes are subplated onto agar. If significant bacterial growth is observed at 1:16, but not at 1:8 or less, then the serum is considered to be bactericidal at 1:8. The NCCLS considers as appropriate, ''peak'' SBTs of 1:8 to 1:16 and ''trough'' SBTs of 1:4 to 1:8. While the SBT provides an *in vivo* test of antibacterial activity, the practical utility of the test is debated at the present time.

Determination of Isolate Pathogenicity

7. *Serratia marcescens* grows from a culture of R.G.'s tracheal aspirate and the decision to treat this organism is based upon whether the isolate is a true pathogen. How does one determine the difference between true bacterial infection versus colonization or contamination?

A positive culture may represent colonization, contamination, or infection. Colonization indicates that bacteria are present at the

Table 54.3	Classification of Antibacterials[a]
Beta-Lactam Antibiotics	**Beta-Lactam Antibiotics**
Cephalosporins	**Penicillins** *(continued)*
1st-Generation	*Carboxypenicillins*
cefadroxil (Duricef)	carbenicillin (Geocillin)
cefazolin (Ancef)	ticarcillin (Ticar)
cephalexin (Keflex)	
cephalothin (Keflin)	*Ureidopenicillins*
cephapirin (Cefadyl)	mezlocillin (Mezlin)
cephradine (Anspor)	piperacillin (Pipracil)
2nd-Generation	*Combination with Beta-*
cefaclor (Ceclor)	*Lactamase Inhibitors*
cefamandole (Mandol)	Augmentin (amoxicillin
cefmetazole (Zefazone)	plus clavulanic acid)
cefonicid (Monocid)	Timentin (ticarcillin plus
ceforanide (Precef)	clavulanic acid)
cefotetan (Cefotan)	Unasyn (ampicillin plus
cefoxitin (Mefoxin)	sulbactam)
cefprozil (Cefzil)	Zosyn (piperacillin plus
cefuroxime (Zinacef)	tazobactam)
cefuroxime axetil (Ceftin)	**Aminoglycosides**
loracarbef (Lorabid)	amikacin (Amikin)
3rd-Generation	gentamicin (Garamycin)
cefixime (Suprax)	neomycin (Mycifradin)
cefoperazone (Cefobid)	netilmicin (Netromycin)
cefotaxime (Claforan)	streptomycin
cefpodoxime proxetil (Vantin)	tobramycin (Nebcin)
ceftizoxime (Cefizox)	**Protein Synthesis Inhibitors**
ceftriaxone (Rocephin)	azithromycin (Zithromax)
ceftazidime (Fortaz)	clarithromycin (Biaxin)
4th-Generation	clindamycin (Cleocin)
cefepime (Maxipime)	chloramphenicol
Carbacephems	(Chloromycetin)
loracarbef (Lorabid)	erythromycin (Erythrocin)
	tetracyclines (doxycycline,
Monobactams	minocycline, tetracycline)
aztreonam (Azactam)	**Folate Inhibitors**
Penems	sulfamethoxazole (Gantanol)
carbapenems	sulfonamides [sulfisoxazole
Primaxin (imipenem plus	(Gantrisin)]
cilastatin)	trimethoprim (Trimpex)
meropenem	trimethoprim-
Penicillins	sulfamethoxazole (Bactrim,
Natural Penicillins	Septra)
penicillin G	**Quinolones**
penicillin V	ciprofloxacin (Cipro)
Aminopenicillins	difloxacin
ampicillin (Omnipen)	enoxacin (Penetrex)
amoxicillin (Amoxil)	lomefloxacin (Maxaquin)
bacampicillin (Spectrobid)	norfloxacin (Noroxin)
hetacillin (Verspen)	ofloxacin (Floxin)
Penicillinase-Resistant	pefloxacin
Penicillins	sparfloxacin
isoxazolyl penicillins	tosufloxacin
(dicloxacillin, oxacillin,	**Vancomycin (Vancocin)**
cloxacillin)	**Teicoplanin**
nafcillin (Unipen)	**Dalfopristin/Quinupristin**
	(Synercid)
	Metronidazole (Flagyl)

[a] Adapted from *Handbook of Applied Therapeutics.*

site, but are not actively causing infection. Poor sampling techniques or inappropriate handling of specimens can result in contamination. Infection, colonization, and contamination might all be applicable to R.G. If a suction catheter was used for a sample of R.G.'s tracheal aspirate, the infecting organism likely would be cultured; however, other flora in the oropharynx (but not associated with infection) would also appear in the culture medium (colonization). Furthermore, if the sample is not handled aseptically by the clinician or the microbiology laboratory, bacterial contamination is likely. In summary, culture results do not necessarily identify only the actual pathogens. In R.G., the *Serratia* may be a path-

Table 54.4	In Vitro Antimicrobial Susceptibility: Aerobic Gram-Positive Cocci[f]					
Drugs	Staphylococcus aureus	Staphylococcus aureus (MR)[a]	Staphylococcus epidermidis	Staphylococcus epidermidis (MR)[a]	Streptococci[b]	Enterococci[c]
Ampicillin	+	—	+	—	++++	++++
Augmentin	++++	+	++++	—	++++	++++
Aztreonam	—	—	—	—	—	—
Cefazolin	++++	—	++++	—	++++	—
Cefoxitin/cefotetan	++	—	++	—	++++	—
Cefuroxime	++++	—	++++	—	++++	—
Ciprofloxacin (ofloxacin)[d]	+++	++	+++	++	+	++
Clindamycin	++++	+	++++	+	+++	—
Cotrimoxazole	++++	+++	++++	+	++++	+
Erythromycin (azithromycin/clarithromycin)	++	—	+	—	++++	
Imipenem	++++	+	++++		++++	++
Mezlocillin	+	—	+	—	++++	++++
Nafcillin	++++	—	++++	—	++++	—
Penicillin	+	—	+	—	++++	++++
Teicoplanin	++++	++++	++++	++++	++++	++++
TGC[e]	+++	—	++	—	++++	—
Ticarcillin	+	—	+	—	++++	+
Timentin	++++	—	++++	—	++++	+
Unasyn	++++	—	++++	—	++++	++++
Vancomycin	++++	++++	++++	++++	++++	++++
Zosyn	++++	—	++++	—	++++	++++

[a] MR = Methicillin resistant.
[b] Nonenterococcal streptococci.
[c] In vitro susceptibility may not provide adequate information and serious infections. Usually requires combination therapy (e.g., ampicillin and an aminoglycoside) for serious infection.
[d] Ofloxacin generally is more active than ciprofloxacin versus staphylococci and streptococci.
[e] TGC = Cefotaxime, ceftizoxime, ceftriaxone, cefoperazone. Ceftazidime has comparatively inferior antistaphylococcal activity. Ceftizoxime may be less active versus pneumococci.
[f] Adapted from Handbook of Applied Therapeutics.

Table 54.5	In Vitro Antimicrobial Susceptibility: Gram-Negative Aerobes[a]							
Drugs	Escherichia coli	Klebsiella pneumoniae	Enterobacter cloacae	Proteus mirabilis	Serratia marcescens	Pseudomonas aeruginosa	Haemophilus influenzae	Haemophilus influenzae[b]
Ampicillin	++	—	—	+++	—	—	++++	—
Augmentin	+++	++	—	++++	—	—	++++	++++
Aztreonam	++++	++++	+	++++	++++	+++	++++	++++
Cefazolin	+++	+++	—	++++	—	—	+	—
Cefepime	++++	++++	+++	++++	++++	++++	++++	++++
Cefoperazone	+++	+++	+	++++	++++	++	++++	++++
Ceftazidime	++++	++++	+	++++	++++	++++	++++	++++
Cefuroxime	+++	+++	+	++++	+	—	++++	++++
Ciprofloxacin	++++	++++	++++	++++	++++	++++	++++	++++
Cotrimoxazole	+++	+++	++++	++++	+++	—	++++	++++
Gentamicin	++++	++++	++++	++++	++++	+++	++	++
Imipenem	++++	++++	++++	+++	++++	++++	++++	++++
Mezlocillin	++	+++	++	+++	+++	++	+++	—
Piperacillin	++	+++	++	+++	+++	+++	+++	—
TGC[c]	++++	++++	+	++++	++++	+	++++	++++
Ticarcillin	++	+	++	+++	+++	++	+++	—
Timentin	+++	++	++	++++	+++	++	++++	++++
Tobramycin	++++	++++	++++	++++	+++	++++	++	++
Unasyn	+++	+++	—	++++	++	—	++++	++++
Zosyn	++++	++++	++	++++	++++	+++	++++	++++

[a] Adapted from Handbook of Applied Therapeutics.
[b] Beta-lactamase producing strains.
[c] TGC = Cefotaxime, ceftizoxime, ceftriaxone.

| Table 54.6 | | Antimicrobial Susceptibility: Anaerobes[a] | | |
Drugs	*Bacteroides fragilis*	Peptococcus	Peptostreptococcus	Clostridia
Ampicillin	+	++++	++++	+++
Aztreonam	—	—	—	—
Cefazolin	—	++++	++++	—
Cefepime	+	++	++	+
Cefotaxime	++	+++	+++	+
Cefoxitin	+++	+++	+++	+
Ceftazidime	—	+	+	+
Ceftizoxime	+++	+++	+++	+
Ciprofloxacin	+	+	+	+
Clindamycin	+++	++++	++++	++
Imipenem	++++	++++	++++	++
Metronidazole	++++	++++	++	+++
Penicillin	+	++++	++++	+++
Timentin	++++	+++	+++	+++
Unasyn	++++	++++	++++	+++
Vancomycin	—	+++	+++	+++
Zosyn	++++	++++	+++	+++

[a] Adapted from Handbook of Applied Therapeutics.

ogen, contaminant, or colonizer. Nevertheless, considering the severity of R.G.'s illness, treatment directed against this pathogen would be necessary.

Antimicrobial Toxicities

8. In light of the positive culture for *Serratia*, his increased respiratory secretions, and a worsening chest x-ray, T.G.'s lungs are considered the primary source of infection. In this particular case, the *Serratia marcescens* is susceptible to ciprofloxacin; therefore, ciprofloxacin 400 mg IV Q 12 hr is prescribed. Erythromycin 1.0 gm IV Q 6 hr is added to provide empiric coverage versus atypical pathogens such as *Legionella*. Reviewing R.G.'s medical record, gastric intolerance to both ciprofloxacin and erythromycin is noted. What steps should be taken to facilitate the safe use of these agents?

Adverse Effects and Toxicities. Before the initiation of therapy, it is important to elicit an accurate *drug and allergy history*. When "allergy" has been reported by the patient, it is necessary to determine whether the reaction was intolerance, toxicity, or true allergy (see Chapter 6: Anaphylaxis and Drug Allergy). Table 54.8 lists the most common adverse effects and toxicities associated with antimicrobial therapy. As an example, gastric intolerance due to oral erythromycin is common, however, this adverse effect does not represent an allergic manifestation or toxicity due to the drug. As a result, if intravenous erythromycin was necessary for the treatment of presumed Legionella pneumonitis, the drug could be used. True toxicity (e.g., hearing loss) has been associated with erythromycin with doses greater than 2 gm/day especially in the presence of concomitant renal or hepatic failure.[22] Since R.G. has an increased serum creatinine concentration and is receiving 4 gm/day, he is at higher risk for erythromycin toxicity. Erythromycin-induced ototoxicity differs from the gastrointestinal side effects in that the effects on the ear are dose related. Thus, lower doses of erythromycin could be utilized in a patient at high risk for ototoxicity or with a past history of auditory problems. On the other hand, if the patient had experienced a true severe allergic reaction, (e.g., bronchospasm or anaphylaxis), then the drug would be contraindicated.

Concomitant Disease States. Knowledge of concomitant disease states also should be considered in the selection of therapy. Elderly patients with hearing deficits are poor candidates for potentially ototoxic aminoglycoside therapy. Diabetics or patients with kidney transplants may be better treated with intravenous fluconazole than nephrotoxic amphotericin B in candidemia. Patients with a pre-existing seizure history should not receive imipenem, if less toxic therapy can be utilized. In summary, the toxicological profile must be taken into account in the selection of antimicrobial therapy. If properly dosed, erythromycin and ciprofloxacin can be safely prescribed in R.G.

Antimicrobial Costs of Therapy

9. What factors should be included in calculating the cost of R.G.'s ciprofloxacin therapy?

The true cost of antimicrobial therapy is difficult to quantitate.[23] Although acquisition cost traditionally has been the primary factor in the overall cost of therapy, drug administration labor costs (i.e., nursing and pharmacy), and the use of intravenous sets, piggyback bags, and infusion control devices must be included in the analysis. As a result, a drug which must be administered several times daily, such as penicillin, will incur increased administration costs compared to one which only requires once-a-day dosing.

Some drugs, such as aminoglycosides, are associated with increased laboratory costs (e.g., aminoglycoside serum concentrations, serum creatinine, audiometry), that are not anticipated with other agents,[24] such as the third-generation cephalosporins and quinolones. Similarly, drugs with high potential for misuse or toxicity may be associated with increased costs due to monitoring (e.g., drug utilization evaluation, pharmacokinetic monitoring). Although ciprofloxacin would be expected to be associated with relatively few laboratory costs, its broad spectrum of activity[25] and potential for misuse might result in increased monitoring costs.

Costs which are difficult to quantitate include the cost of failure of therapy and the cost of antimicrobial toxicity. Ineffective or toxic therapy can result in prolongation of hospitalization, and interventions, such as hemodialysis,[24] mechanical ventilation, and intensive care unit admission. The net effect of these latter costs can be significantly greater than the acquisition and administration costs of antimicrobial therapy.

In summary, determination of the true cost of antimicrobial therapy, including ciprofloxacin, is complex. Acquisition cost, IV bags, infusion controllers, and labor must be incorporated into the anal-

Table 54.7	Antimicrobials of Choice in the Treatment of Bacterial Infection		
Organism	**Drug of Choice**	**Alternatives**	**Comments**
Aerobes			
Gram-Positive Cocci			
Streptococcus pyogenes (Group A *streptococci*)	Penicillin	Erythromycin, cephalosporin	
Streptococcus pneumoniae	Penicillin	Erythromycin, cephalosporin, trimethoprim-sulfamethoxazole, doxycycline	The pneumococcus usually is susceptible to penicillin. The incidence of penicillin-resistant pneumococci is ≈5%. Penicillin-resistant pneumococci also may demonstrate resistance to other agents, including erythromycin, tetracyclines, and cephalosporins
Enterococcus faecalis	Ampicillin ± gentamicin	Vancomycin ± gentamicin; teicoplanin ± gentamicin	Most commonly isolated enterococcus (80%–85%). Most reliable antienterococcal agents are ampicillin (penicillin, mezlocillin, piperacillin), vancomycin, and teicoplanin. Monotherapy generally inhibits but does not kill the enterococcus. Aminoglycosides must be added to ampicillin or vancomycin to provide bactericidal activity. Ampicillin resistance and, less frequently, vancomycin resistance is increasing. High-level aminoglycoside resistance takes place
Enterococcus faecium	Vancomycin ± gentamicin	Teicoplanin ± gentamicin	Second most common enterococcal organism (10%–20%) and is more likely than *E. faecalis* to be resistant to multiple antimicrobials. Most reliable agents are vancomycin and teicoplanin. Monotherapy generally inhibits but does not kill the enterococcus. Aminoglycosides must be added to provide bactericidal activity. Ampicillin and vancomycin resistance is common. High-level aminoglycoside is common
Staphylococcus aureus	Nafcillin	Cefazolin, vancomycin, clindamycin, trimethoprim-sulfamethoxazole	≈10%–15% of isolates inhibited by penicillin. Most isolates susceptible to nafcillin, cephalosporins, trimethoprim-sulfamethoxazole and clindamycin. 1st-generation cephalosporins are equal to nafcillin. Most 2nd- and 3rd-generation cephalosporins adequate in the treatment of infection (exceptions include ceftazidime and cefonicid). Methicillin-resistant *S. aureus* must be treated with vancomycin or teicoplanin; however, trimethoprim-sulfamethoxazole or minocycline can be used
(Nafcillin-resistant)	Vancomycin	Teicoplanin, trimethoprim-sulfamethoxazole, minocycline	
Staphylococcus epidermidis	Nafcillin	Cefazolin, vancomycin, clindamycin	Large percentage of isolates are beta-lactam-, clindamycin-, and trimethoprim-sulfamethoxazole-resistant. Most reliable agents are vancomycin and teicoplanin. Rifampin active and can be used in conjunction with other agents; however, monotherapy with rifampin is associated with development of resistance
(Nafcillin-resistant)	Vancomycin	Teicoplanin, quinolone	
Gram-Positive Bacilli			
Diphtheroids	Penicillin	Cephalosporin	
Corynebacterium jeikeium	Vancomycin	Erythromycin, quinolone	
Listeria monocytogenes	Ampicillin (± gentamicin)	Trimethoprim-sulfamethoxazole	
Gram-Negative Cocci			
Moraxella catarrhalis	Trimethoprim-sulfamethoxazole	Amoxicillin-clavulanic acid, erythromycin, doxycycline, 2nd-/3rd-generation cephalosporin	
Neisseria gonorrhoeae	Quinolone, cefixime	Ceftriaxone	2nd-generation cephalosporins active
Neisseria meningitidis	Penicillin	3rd-generation cephalosporin	
Gram-Negative Bacilli			
Campylobacter fetus	Imipenem	Gentamicin	
Campylobacter jejuni	Quinolone, erythromycin	Tetracycline	
Enterobacter	Trimethoprim-sulfamethoxazole	Quinolone, imipenem, gentamicin	Not predictably inhibited by cephalosporins; imipenem, quinolones, trimethoprim-sulfamethoxazole, and aminoglycosides most active agents

Continued

Table 54.7	Antimicrobials of Choice in the Treatment of Bacterial Infection (Continued)		
Organism	**Drug of Choice**	**Alternatives**	**Comments**
Escherichia coli	3rd-generation cephalosporin	1st- or 2nd-generation cephalosporin, gentamicin	1st- and 2nd-generation cephalosporins active
Haemophilus influenzae	3rd-generation cephalosporin	2nd-generation cephalosporin, trimethoprim-sulfamethoxazole, beta-lactamase inhibitor combinations	2nd-generation cephalosporins active
Helicobacter pylori	Tetracycline + metronidazole + bismuth subsalicylate	Amoxicillin + metronidazole + bismuth subsalicylate	
Klebsiella pneumoniae	3rd-generation cephalosporin	1st- or 2nd-generation cephalosporin, gentamicin, trimethoprim-sulfamethoxazole	1st- and 2nd-generation cephalosporins active
Legionella	Erythromycin ± rifampin	Doxycycline, ciprofloxacin	
Proteus mirabilis	Ampicillin	1st-generation cephalosporin, trimethoprim-sulfamethoxazole	1st- and 2nd-generation cephalosporins active
Other *Proteus*	3rd-generation cephalosporin	β-lactamase inhibitor combination, aminoglycoside, trimethoprim-sulfamethoxazole	2nd-generation cephalosporins active
Pseudomonas aeruginosa	Antipseudomonal penicillin (or ceftazidime) ± aminoglycoside	Quinolone, imipenem ± aminoglycoside	Most active agents include aminoglycosides, imipenem, ceftazidime, cefepime, aztreonam, quinolones, and the extended-spectrum penicillins
Salmonella typhi	Quinolone	Ceftriaxone, trimethoprim-sulfamethoxazole	
Serratia marcescens	3rd-generation cephalosporin	Trimethoprim-sulfamethoxazole, aminoglycoside	3rd-generation cephalosporins active
Shigella	Quinolone	Trimethoprim-sulfamethoxazole, ampicillin	
(Xanthomonas) maltophilia *Stenotrophomonas*	Trimethoprim-sulfamethoxazole	Ceftazidime, minocycline, quinolone, beta-lactamase inhibitor combination	
Anaerobes			
Bacteroides fragilis	Metronidazole	Clindamycin, beta-lactamase inhibitor combinations, imipenem	Most active agents (95%–100%) include metronidazole, the beta-lactamase inhibitor combinations (ampicillin-sulbactam, piperacillin-tazobactam, ticarcillin-clavulanic acid), and imipenem. Clindamycin, cefotoxitin, cefotetan, cefmetazole, ceftizoxime, and the antipseudomonal penicillins (piperacillin, mezlocillin) have good activity, but not to the degree of metronidazole. Aminoglycosides and aztreonam inactive
Clostridia difficile	Metronidazole	Vancomycin	
Fusobacterium	Penicillin	Metronidazole, clindamycin	
Other oropharyngeal *Bacteroides*	Penicillin	Metronidazole, clindamycin	Most beta-lactams active (exceptions include aztreonam, nafcillin, ceftazidime). If beta-lactamase producing, clindamycin should be added
Peptostreptococcus	Penicillin	Clindamycin, cephalosporin	Most beta-lactams active (exceptions include aztreonam, nafcillin, ceftazidime)
Other			
Actinomycetes			
Actinomyces israelii	Penicillin	Tetracycline	
Nocardia	Trimethoprim-sulfamethoxazole	Amikacin, minocycline, imipenem	
Chlamydiae			
Chlamydia trachomatis	Doxycycline	Erythromycin, azithromycin	
Chlamydia pneumoniae (TWAR strain)	Doxycycline	Erythromycin	
Mycoplasma			
Mycoplasma pneumoniae	Erythromycin, doxycycline	Azithromycin, clarithromycin	

Continued

Table 54.7	Antimicrobials of Choice in the Treatment of Bacterial Infection (Continued)		
Organism	Drug of Choice	Alternatives	Comments
Spirochetes			
Borrelia burgdorferi	Doxycycline	Ampicillin, 2nd- or 3rd-generation cephalosporin	
Treponema pallidum	Penicillin	Doxycycline	

ysis. While difficult to estimate, other costs, including antibiotic toxicity and failure of therapy also should be included.

Route of Administration

10. Oral ciprofloxacin was considered for the treatment of R.G.'s presumed *Serratia* pneumonia, however, the IV route was prescribed. Why is the oral administration of ciprofloxacin reasonable (or unreasonable) in R.G.?

The selection of the proper route of antibiotic administration is dependent upon many factors, including severity of infection, bioavailability, and other patient factors. In those patients who appear "septic," blood flow often is shunted away from the mesentery and extremities, resulting in unreliable bioavailability from the gastrointestinal tract or muscles. As a result, hemodynamically unstable patients should receive antimicrobials intravenously to ensure therapeutic antimicrobial levels. Furthermore, some drug interactions can result in subtherapeutic serum concentrations (e.g., reduced bioavailability associated with concomitant quinolone and antacid administration and the decreased absorption of ketoconazole or itraconazole with concurrent H_2-blocker therapy).

R.G. is clinically septic with a possible *Serratia* pneumonia. Considering his unstable state, the bioavailability of oral ciprofloxacin cannot be guaranteed; thus, he should be treated with intravenous antimicrobials.

Antimicrobial Dosing

11. What dose of IV ciprofloxacin should be given to R.G.? What factors must be taken into account in the selection of a proper antimicrobial dose?

The choice of dosing regimen should be based upon many factors. Table 54.9 provides a guide for the dosing of more commonly administered antimicrobials. Selection of the appropriate dose should be based upon information which documents the efficacy of the dose in the treatment of infection. Patient-specific factors, including weight, site of infection, and route of elimination also must be considered in the selection of dose. The weight of the patient is important, particularly for those agents with a low therapeutic index (e.g., aminoglycosides, vancomycin, flucytosine): these drugs should be dosed on a mg/kg/day basis (see Figure 54.2). Other agents with a more favorable adverse effect profile, such as cephalosporins, are less likely to require weight-specific dosing.

Site of Infection. The site of infection also results in differing dosage requirements. An uncomplicated urinary tract infection requires low antimicrobial doses due to the high urinary drug concentrations that are achieved. In contrast, a more serious systemic infection, such as pyelonephritis, requires increased antimicrobial doses to achieve therapeutic drug levels in tissue and in serum.

Anatomical and physiological barriers also must be considered in the evaluation of a dosing regimen. For example, penetration into the central nervous system necessitates high doses to ensure adequate antimicrobial concentrations at the site of infection.[26]

Vitreous humor[27] and the prostate gland[28] are additional sites in which therapeutic antimicrobial concentrations are more difficult to achieve.

Route of elimination must also be considered in the dosage calculation. In general, antimicrobials are either eliminated via the kidney or nonrenally (metabolic/biliary). Renal function can be estimated via 24-hour urine collection or with equations, such as that of Cockcroft and Gault:[29]

$$Cl_{Cr} = \frac{(140 - Age)(Weight\ in\ kg)}{72 \times SrCr}$$

A number of anti-infectives are eliminated renally (see Table 54.10). Most beta-lactams are eliminated by the kidney with certain exceptions. Ceftriaxone, cefoperazone, most antistaphylococcal penicillins (e.g., nafcillin, oxacillin, dicloxacillin), and most extended spectrum penicillins (e.g., piperacillin, mezlocillin) are eliminated both renally and nonrenally. Aminoglycosides, vancomycin, acyclovir, and ganciclovir are extensively cleared by the kidney. Thus, dosage adjustment is recommended for these drugs in patients with renal failure (see Table 54.9 and Figures 54.2 and 54.3). Azithromycin, clindamycin, and metronidazole are metabolized primarily by the liver and, as a result, do not accumulate appreciably in end-stage renal disease. While renal function can be approximated with the use of the Cockcroft-Gault equation (or similar equation), hepatic function is more difficult to evaluate. No standard liver function test (AST, ALT, alkaline phosphatase) has been demonstrated to correlate well with hepatic drug clearance. Some tests, such as prothrombin time and albumin, are markers of hepatic function; however, even these tests do not clearly predict drug clearance.

Patient Age. Most dosing information has been derived from a younger, relatively healthy patient population; however, total drug clearance for a number of antimicrobials may be decreased in neonatal and geriatric patients. As a result, the age of the patient may be an important factor in the selection of a proper dose.

Fever and Inoculum Effect. The impact of other factors on the selection of an antimicrobial dose is less clear. Fever increases and decreases blood flow to mesenteric, hepatic, and renal organ systems[30] and can either increase or decrease drug clearance. Inoculum effect also may be a factor in the selection of a dosing regimen because it is associated with an increase in the MIC of the organism in response to increasing bacterial concentrations.[31] As an example, piperacillin may demonstrate an MIC of 8.0 µg/mL versus *Pseudomonas aeruginosa* at a concentration of 10^5 colony forming units/mL (CFU/mL); however, at 10^9 CFU/mL, the minimum inhibitory concentration may increase to 32 to 64 µg/mL. This phenomenon is well recognized, particularly with beta-lactamase producing bacteria treated with beta-lactam antimicrobials. The more beta-lactamase stable the antimicrobial, the less the influence of inoculum effect. Aminoglycosides, quinolones, and imipenem appear to be less affected by the inoculum effect than beta-lactams. The inoculum effect probably is most relevant in the treatment of

Table 54.8		Antibiotic Adverse Effects and Toxicities[a,b]
Antibiotic	**Adverse Effects**	**Comments**
Beta-lactams, (penicillin, cephalosporins, monobactams, penems)	*Allergic*: anaphylaxis, urticaria, serum sickness, rash, fever	Many patients will have "ampicillin rash" with no cross-reactivity with any other penicillins. Most common in patients with mononucleosis or those receiving allopurinol. Likelihood of IgE-mediated cross-reactivity between penicillins and cephalosporins ≈3%–7%. Extensive cross-reactivity between penicillins and imipenem. No cross-reactivity between aztreonam and penicillins
	Diarrhea	Particularly common with ampicillin, Augmentin, ceftriaxone, and cefoperazone. Pseudomembranous colitis can occur with most antimicrobials
	Hematologic: anemia, thrombocytopenia, antiplatelet activity, hypothrombinemia	Hemolytic anemia more common with higher doses. Antiplatelet activity most common with the antipseudomonal penicillins and high serum levels of other beta-lactams
		Hypothrombinemia more often associated with those cephalosporins with the methyltetrazolethiol side chain (cefamandole, cefotetan, cefoperazone, cefmetazole, moxalactam). Reaction preventable and reversible with vitamin K
	Hepatitis	Most common with oxacillin. Biliary sludging and stones reported with ceftriaxone
	Phlebitis	
	Seizure activity	Associated with high levels of beta-lactams, particularly penicillins and imipenem
	Potassium load	Penicillin G (K+)
	Sodium load	Ticarcillin, ticarcillin-clavulanic acid
	Nephritis	Most common with methicillin; however, reported for most other beta-lactams
	Neutropenia	Nafcillin
	Disulfiram reaction	Associated with cephalosporins with methyltetrazolethiol side chain (cefamandole, cefotetan, cefoperazone, cefmetazole, moxalactam)
	Hypotension, nausea	Associated with fast infusion of imipenem
Aminoglycosides (gentamicin, tobramycin, amikacin, netilmicin)	Nephrotoxicity	Averages 10%–15% incidence. Generally reversible, usually occurs after 5–7 days of therapy. *Risk factors*: dehydration, age, dose, duration, concurrent nephrotoxins, liver disease
	Ototoxicity	1%–5% incidence, often irreversible. Both cochlear and/or vestibular toxicity occur. Netilmicin may be less ototoxic than other aminoglycosides
	Neuromuscular paralysis	Rare, most common with large doses administered via intraperitoneal instillation or in patients with myasthenia gravis
Macrolides (erythromycin, azithromycin, clarithromycin)	Nausea, vomiting, "burning" stomach	Oral administration. Azithromycin and clarithromycin associated with less nausea than erythromycin
	Cholestatic jaundice	Reported for all erythromycin salts, most common with estolate
	Ototoxicity	Most common with high doses in patients with renal and/or hepatic failure
Clindamycin	Diarrhea	Most common adverse effect. High association with pseudomembranous colitis
Tetracyclines	Allergic	Rash, anaphylaxis, urticaria, fever
	Photosensitivity	
	Teeth/bone deposition and discoloration	Avoid in pediatrics
	Gastrointestinal	Nausea, diarrhea
	Hepatitis	Primarily with high IV doses of tetracycline in pregnancy or the elderly
	Renal (azotemia)	Tetracyclines have antianabolic effect and should be avoided in patients with ↓ renal function. Less with doxycycline
	Vestibular	Associated with minocycline
Vancomycin	Ototoxicity	Primarily with high serum levels (>50 µg/mL)
	Nephrotoxicity	Little to no nephrotoxicity observed with current preparations of vancomycin. May ↑ nephrotoxicity of aminoglycosides
	Hypotension, flushing	Associated with rapid infusion of vancomycin. Appears dose related (more common with 1 gm dose compared to 500 mg)
	Phlebitis	Needs large volume dilution
Sulfonamides	Gastrointestinal	Nausea, diarrhea
	Hepatic	Cholestatic hepatitis, ↑ incidence in AIDS
	Rash	Exfoliative dermatitis, Stevens-Johnson syndrome. More common in AIDS
	Bone marrow	Neutropenia, thrombocytopenia. More common in AIDS
	Kernicterus	Due to ↑ unbound drug in the neonate. Premature liver unable to conjugate bilirubin. Sulfonamide displace bilirubin from protein, resulting in excessive free sulfonamide and kernicterus
Chloramphenicol	Anemia	Idiosyncratic irreversible aplastic anemia (rare). Reversible dose-related anemia
	Gray syndrome	Due to inability of neonates to conjugate chloramphenicol

Continued

Table 54.8	Antibiotic Adverse Effects and Toxicities[a,b] (Continued)	
Antibiotic	**Adverse Effects**	**Comments**
Quinolones (ciprofloxacin, enoxacin, norfloxacin, ofloxacin)	GI	Nausea, vomiting, diarrhea
	Drug interactions	↓ oral bioavailability with multivalent cations
	CNS	Altered mental status, confusion, seizures
	Cartilage toxicity	Teratogenic in animal model. Avoid in children, however, may be safe in cystic fibrosis
Antifungals		
Amphotericin B	Nephrotoxicity	Common. May be dependent upon patient Na load. ↓ dose or QOD dosing may result in improvement of renal function. Caution with concomitant nephrotoxins (e.g., aminoglycosides, cyclosporine)
	Hypokalemia	Predictable. Probably due to renal tubular excretion of potassium. More common in patients receiving concomitant ticarcillin, mezlocillin, piperacillin
	Hypomagnesemia	Less commonly observed than hypokalemia
	Anemia	Long-term adverse effect. Similar to anemia of chronic disease. Treatable with transfusion
Flucytosine	Neutropenia, thrombocytopenia	Secondary to metabolism of flucytosine to fluorouracil. More commonly observed with flucytosine levels >100 µg/mL. More common in AIDS patients
	Hepatitis	Usually moderate ↑ in LFTs. Rarely clinical hepatitis
Ketoconazole (fluconazole, itraconazole)	Drug interactions	↓ oral bioavailability of ketoconazole and itraconazole with ↑ gastric pH
	Hepatitis	Ranges from mild ↑ in LFTs to occasional fatal hepatitis. May be less common with newer imidazoles/triazoles (e.g., fluconazole, itraconazole)
	Gynecomastia	More common with high dose (>400 mg/day). Less common with fluconazole and itraconazole. ↓ libido, azoospermia
Antivirals		
Acyclovir	Phlebitis	Due to poor solubility of IV preparation. Reported in 1%–20% of cases
	Renal failure	Low solubility acyclovir associated with renal. Dehydrated patients as well as rapid infusions predispose to toxicity
	CNS	1% incidence in AIDS. ↑ incidence with dose in >10 mg/kg/day
Didanosine (ddI)	Pancreatitis	Fatalities reported
	Peripheral neuropathy	Dose related
	↑ uric acid	
Zalcitabine (ddC)	Peripheral neuropathy	Dose related, delayed, often severe
	Mucocutaneous	Early in the course of therapy
Foscarnet	Nephrotoxicity	Occurs in up to 60% of patients. May be prevented with normal saline bolus before dose. Frequent monitoring of renal function imperative
	Mineral and electrolyte abnormalities	↑ and ↓ calcium/phosphate may be observed. Hypocalcemia, hypo- and hyperphosphatemia, hypomagnesemia, hypokalemia. ↑ risk of cardiomyopathy and seizures
	Anemia	Anemia in 33%; usually manageable with transfusions and discontinuation of foscarnet
	Nausea, vomiting	
Ganciclovir	Neutropenia, thrombocytopenia	↑ incidence in AIDS. ↑ incidence with doses in excess of 10 mg/kg/day
	Hepatitis	Usually mild to moderate ↑ in LFTs
Stavudine (D4T)	Peripheral nephrotoxicity	
Zidovudine (AZT)	Anemia, neutropenia	Anemia at 2–4 weeks occasionally with ↑ MCV. Neutropenia appears later (6–8 weeks)
	General	Severe headache, nausea, insomnia, myalgia, lethargy

[a] AIDS = Acquired immunodeficiency syndrome; CNS = Central nervous system; GI = Gastrointestinal; IV = Intravenous; LFTs = Liver function tests; MCV = Mean corpuscular volume; Na = Sodium.
[b] Adapted from Handbook of Applied Therapeutics.

a bacterial abscess, where extremely high concentrations of bacteria would be expected. As a result, those antimicrobials that are more susceptible to the inoculum effect may require increased drug doses for optimal outcome in the treatment of abscesses.

In summary, R.G. normally would be given an intravenous dose of ciprofloxacin at 400 mg every 12 hours. However, his reduced renal function suggests that his dose should be decreased to 200 to 300 mg every 12 hours.

Postantibiotic Effect (PAE)

12. R.G.'s respiratory status remains unchanged, thus, the ciprofloxacin and erythromycin are discontinued and cefotax-

Table 54.9		University of California San Francisco Adult Antimicrobial Dosing Guidelines[f]					
Drug	Max Daily IV Dose[a]	Cl$_{Cr}$	Dialysis[b]	t½ (hr) Normal	t½ (hr) ESRD	Hepatic Failure Dosage
Acyclovir	30 mg/kg	*>50 mL/min:*[c] *Herpes simplex infections*: 5 mg/kg/dose Q 8 hr. *HSV encephalitis/Herpes zoster*: 10 mg/kg/dose Q 8 hr *10–50 mL/min: Herpes simplex infections*: 5 mg/kg/dose Q 12–14 hr. *HSV encephalitis/ Herpes zoster:* 10 mg/kg/dose Q 12–24 hr *<10 mL/min:*[d] *Herpes simplex infections*: 2.5 mg/kg Q 24 hr. *HSV encephalitis/Herpes zoster*: 5 mg/kg Q 24 hr	D[e]	2.3–3.2	20	No change
Amikacin	See Fig. 54.2		D[e]	2–3	36–82	No change
Amphotericin B	1.5 mg/kg	*>50 mL/min:*[c] 0.3–1.0 mg/kg *10–50 mL/min*: No change *<10 mL/min:*[d] No change	ND	15 days	Unchanged	No change
Ampicillin	12 gm	*>50 mL/min:*[c] 1–2 gm Q 6–8 hr *10–50 mL/min*: 1–1.5 gm Q 6 hr *<10 mL/min:*[d] 1 gm Q 8–12 hr	MD[e]	1–1.3	20	No change
Aztreonam	8 gm	*>50 mL/min:*[c] 1–2 gm Q 6–8 hr *10–50 mL/min*: 1–2 gm Q 8–12 hr *<10 mL/min:*[d] 1 gm Q 12–24 hr	MD[e]	1.3–2.2	6–9	No change
Cefazolin	8 gm	*>50 mL/min:*[c] 1–2 gm Q 8 hr *10–50 mL/min*: 0.5–1.5 gm Q 12 hr *<10 mL/min:*[d] 0.5–1.0 gm Q 24 hr	MD[e]	1.8–2.6	12–40	No change
Cefotaxime	12 gm	*>50 mL/min:*[c] 1–2 gm Q 6–12 hr *10–50 mL/min*: 1–2 gm Q 8–12 hr *<10 mL/min:*[d] 0.5–1 gm Q 12 hr	MD[e]	0.9–1.1	2.3–3.5	Limited data
Cefotetan	6 gm	*>50 mL/min:*[c] 1–2 gm Q 12 hr *10–50 mL/min*: 1–2 gm Q 24 hr *<10 mL/min:*[d] 0.5–1 gm Q 24 hr	MD[e]	3–4.2	13	No change
Cefoxitin	12 gm	*>50 mL/min:*[c] 1–2 gm Q 6–8 hr *10–50 mL/min*: 1–2 gm Q 12–24 hr *<10 mL/min:*[d] 0.5–1 gm Q 24 hr	MD[e]	0.7–0.8	12–24	No change
Ceftazidime	6 gm	*>50 mL/min:*[c] 1–2 gm Q 8 hr *10–50 mL/min*: 1–2 gm Q 12–24 hr *<10 mL/min:*[d] 0.5 gm Q 24 hr	D[e]	1.6–2.0	13–25	No change
Ceftizoxime	12 gm	*>50 mL/min:*[c] 1–2 gm Q 8–12 hr *10–50 mL/min*: 1–2 gm Q 12–24 hr *<10 mL/min:*[d] 0.5 gm Q 24 hr	MD[e]	1.4–1.7	19–35	No change
Ceftriaxone	4 gm	*>50 mL/min:*[c] 1–2 gm Q 12–24 hr *10–50 mL/min*: 1–2 gm Q 24 hr *<10 mL/min:*[d] 1–2 gm Q 24 hr	ND	5–8	12–17[g]	Limited data
Cefuroxime	9 gm	*>50 mL/min:*[c] 0.75–1.5 gm Q 8 hr *10–50 mL/min*: 0.75–1.5 gm Q 12–24 hr *<10 mL/min:*[d] 0.75–1.5 gm Q 24 hr	MD[e]	1.1–1.7	15–17	No change
Ciprofloxacin	800 mg	*>50 mL/min:*[c] 200–400 mg Q 12 hr *10–50 mL/min: 30–50 mL/min:* No change. *10–30 mL/min:* 100–300 mg Q 12 hr *<10 mL/min:*[d] 100–200 mg Q 12 hr	SD	4	8.5	No change
Clindamycin	4.8 gm	*>50 mL/min:*[c] 600–900 mg Q 6–8 hr *10–50 mL/min*: No change *<10 mL/min:*[d] No change	ND	2–4	1.6–3.4	600–900 mg Q 8–12 hr
Erythromycin	4 gm	*>50 mL/min:*[c] 500–1000 mg Q 6 hr *10–50 mL/min*: No change *<10 mL/min:*[d] No change	SD	1.4–2.0	4	500–1000 mg Q 8 hr
Ethambutol	25 mg/kg (PO)	*>50 mL/min:*[c] 15 mg/kg QD *10–50 mL/min*: 7.5–10 mg/kg QD *<10 mL/min:*[d] 5 mg/kg QD	SD	3.1	98	No change
Fluconazole	400 mg	*>50 mL/min:*[c] 100–400 mg Q 24 hr *10–50 mL/min*: 50–200 mg Q 24 hr *<10 mL/min:*[d] 50–100 mg Q 24 hr	MD[e]	30	98	No change

Continued

Table 54.9		University of California San Francisco Adult Antimicrobial Dosing Guidelines[f] (Continued)				
Drug	Max Daily IV Dose[a]	Cl_{Cr}	Dialysis[b]	t½ (hr) Normal	t½ (hr) ESRD	Hepatic Failure Dosage
Flucytosine	150 mg/kg (PO)	*>50 mL/min:*[c] 12.5–37.5 mg/kg/dose Q 6 hr *10–50 mL/min: 25–50 mL/min:* 12.5–37.5 mg/kg Q 12 hr. *10–25 mL/min:* 12.5–37.5 mg/kg Q 24 hr *<10 mL/min:*[d] 12.5–25 mg/kg Q 24 hr	D[e]	4–6	30–70	No change
Ganciclovir	10 mg/kg	*>50 mL/min:*[c] *>80 mL/min:* 5 mg/kg/dose Q 12 hr. *50–79 mL/min:* 2.5 mg/kg/dose Q 12 hr *10–50 mL/min:* 1.25–2.5 mg/kg/dose Q 12–24 hr *<10 mL/min:*[d] 1.25 mg/kg Q 24 hr	D[e]	2.5–3.6	11.5–28	No change
Gentamicin	See Fig. 54.2		D[e]	1.5–3.0	20–24	No change
Imipenem	(4 gm) 50 mg/kg	*>50 mL/min:*[c] 5–10 mg/kg Q 6–8 hr *10–50 mL/min:* 5–10 mg/kg Q 8–12 hr *<10 mL/min:*[d] 5–10 mg/kg Q 12 hr	MD[e]	0.8–1.3	2.9–3.7	No change
Isoniazid	300 mg	*>50 mL/min:*[c] 300 mg *10–50 mL/min:* No change *<10 mL/min:*[d] No change	D[e]	0.5–4	8	200 mg QD
Ketoconazole	800 mg (PO)	*>50 mL/min:*[c] 200–400 mg QD *10–50 mL/min:* No change *<10 mL/min:*[d] No change	ND	3.8	Unchanged	Limited data
Metronidazole	4 gm	*>50 mL/min:*[c] 500 mg Q 8 hr *10–50 mL/min:* 500 mg Q 8 hr *<10 mL/min:*[d] 500 mg Q 12 hr	D[e]	6–14	8–15	500 mg Q 12 hr
Nafcillin	12 gm	*>50 mL/min:*[c] 1–2 gm Q 4–6 hr *10–50 mL/min:* No change *<10 mL/min:*[d] No change	ND	1–1.5	1.9	1–1.5 gm Q 4–6 hr
Nitrofurantoin	400 mg (PO)	*>50 mL/min:*[c] 50–100 mg Q 6 hr *10–50 mL/min:* Avoid *<10 mL/min:*[d] Avoid	N/A	N/A	N/A	N/A
Penicillin G	30 MU	*>50 mL/min:*[c] 2–3 MU Q 4 hr *10–50 mL/min:* 1–2 MU 4–6 hr *<10 mL/min:*[d] 1 MU Q 6 hr	MD[e]	0.4–0.9	4–10	No change
Pentamidine	4 mg/kg	*>50 mL/min:*[c] 3–4 mg/kg Q 24 hr *10–50 mL/min:* No change *<10 mL/min:*[d] No change	ND	5–9 days	No data	No change
Piperacillin	24 gm	*>50 mL/min:*[c] 3–4 gm Q 4–6 hr *10–50 mL/min:* 3–4 gm Q 6 hr *<10 mL/min:*[d] 2–3 gm Q 8 hr	MD[e]	0.8–1.4	3–6	Limited data
Pyrazinamide	35 mg/kg (PO)	*>50 mL/min:*[c] 20–25 mg/kg/day *10–50 mL/min:* No change *<10 mL/min:*[d] No change	No data	9–10	Unchanged	ND
Rifampin	600 mg	*>50 mL/min:*[c] 600 mg QD *10–50 mL/min:* No change *<10 mL/min:*[d] No change	ND	2.5–5	2–5	450 mg QD[h]
Tobramycin	See Fig. 54.2		D[e]	1.3–2.2	33–70	No change
Trimethoprim-sulfamethoxazole	20 mg/kg TMP	*>50 mL/min:*[c] *Systemic GNR infection:* 10 mg TMP/kg/day divided Q 6–12 hr. *Pneumocystis carinii pneumonia:* 12–20 mg TMP/kg/day divided Q 6–12 hr *10–50 mL/min: Systemic GNR infection:* 5–7.5 mg TMP/kg/day divided Q 12–24 hr. *Pneumocystis carinii pneumonia:* 10–15 mg TMP/kg/day divided Q 12–24 hr *<10 mL/min:*[d] *Systemic GNR infection:* 2.5–5.0 mg TMP/kg/day Q 24 hr. *Pneumocystis carinii pneumonia:* 5–10 mg TMP/kg/day divided Q 24 hr	SD/MD	*TMP:* 8–12 *SMX:* 9–11	*TMP:* 24–62 *SMX:* 9–15 *SMX-metabolite:* 22–50	No change

Continued

Table 54.9		University of California San Francisco Adult Antimicrobial Dosing Guidelines[f] (Continued)					
Drug	Max Daily IV Dose[a]	Cl_{Cr}	Dialysis[b]	t½ (hr) Normal	t½ (hr) ESRD	Hepatic Failure Dosage
Vancomycin	See Fig. 54.1		ND: conventional HD; MD: high flux[e]	9–11	129–190	No change

ime and gentamicin are started empirically. The use of a constant IV infusion of cefotaxime is being considered in R.G. In addition the use of single daily dosing of gentamicin is being discussed. What is the rationale for these approaches and would either be advantageous for R.G.?

The *in vivo* bactericidal activities of beta-lactams, such as cefotaxime, show minimal enhancement with increasing drug concentrations. Activity appears to correlate better with duration of exposure to beta-lactam levels above the MIC than on the magnitude of drug concentration.[32] The animal model suggests that beta-lactam antimicrobials should be dosed such that their serum levels always exceed the MIC of the pathogen.[33,34] This observation appears to be most critical in the neutropenic model, in which the use of a constant infusion more reliably inhibits bacterial growth when compared with traditional intermittent dosing. An additional benefit of the use of constant infusions of beta-lactams is that smaller daily doses appear to be as effective as higher doses administered intermittently. However, other than this latter outcome, it is unclear whether constant infusions have any distinct advantages or disadvantages when compared to usual dosing of beta-lactams.

Aminoglycosides traditionally have been administered every 8 to 12 hours to achieve peak serum gentamicin levels of 5 to 8 µg/mL to ensure efficacy in the treatment of serious gram-negative infection.[35,36] Gentamicin troughs of greater than 2 µg/mL have been associated with an increased risk for nephrotoxicity.[36,37] These studies attempting to correlate efficacy and toxicity with serum levels and the association of peaks or troughs with clinical outcomes have been questioned.[38] Vancomycin peaks generally have been recommended to be less than 50 µg/mL and troughs 5 to 10 µg/mL;[39–41] however, the validity of these recommendations also is debated.

A number of antimicrobials (e.g., aminoglycosides) have been associated with a pharmacodynamic phenomenon known as a post-antibiotic effect. PAE can be defined as delayed regrowth of bacteria following exposure to an antibiotic[42,43] (i.e., continued suppression of normal growth in the absence of antibiotic levels above the MIC of the organism). As an example, if *Pseudomonas aeruginosa* is cultured in broth, it will multiply to a concentration of ≥10^9 CFU/mL. If piperacillin is added in a concentration above the minimum inhibitory concentration of the organism, a reduction in the bacterial concentration is observed. When piperacillin is re-

moved from the broth, immediate bacterial growth takes place. Some clinicians suggest that beta-lactam antibiotics always must be present in concentrations above the MIC due to this growth pattern. If the above experiment is repeated with gentamicin, a reduction in bacterial CFUs is observed. In contrast with beta-lactam antibiotics, if the gentamicin is removed from the system, a lag period of two to six hours takes place before characteristic bacterial growth occurs. This lag period is defined as the PAE. A postantibiotic effect also has been observed with quinolones and imipenem versus gram-negative organisms. While most beta-lactam antibiotics, such as antipseudomonal penicillins or cephalosporins, do not exhibit PAE with gram-negative organisms, PAE has been demonstrated with gram-positive pathogens, such as *Staphylococcus aureus.*

Once-Daily Dosing of Aminoglycosides. As a result of PAE and other pharmacodynamic factors, certain antimicrobials may be dosed less frequently in the treatment of infection. The greatest clinical experience has been with the aminoglycosides in the treatment of gram-negative infection.[44–46] Earlier data suggest that the maximal aminoglycoside peak level/MIC ratio correlates well with clinical response. Thus, the higher the achievable peak, the more likely a favorable outcome. As a result of PAE, it is possible that aminoglycosides may be dosed less frequently than previously thought. In several studies once-daily dosing of aminoglycosides in the treatment of gram-negative infection is equally efficacious to traditional dosing. As an example, netilmicin administered either as a single dose given every 24 hours was compared to the same daily dose divided every eight hours in the treatment of severe bacterial infection.[44] Concomitant ceftriaxone was given to all patients. Clinical efficacy was identical with both dosing regimens. The overall incidence of nephrotoxicity was 16% in each group; however, nephrotoxicity was observed earlier in therapy with the divided dose regimen when compared to the single daily dose. Auditory toxicity was documented in one patient treated with conventional dosing and in two patients treated with once-daily doses.

It is important to note that single daily dosing of aminoglycosides has been investigated only in those patients with normal renal function. In addition, few critically ill patients have been treated with this nontraditional regimen. Thus, those patients in septic shock as well as severely immune compromised patients are not candidates for once-daily dosing. Lastly, considering that peak

Aminoglycoside Dosing Chart

1. Select loading dose in mg/kg (using IBW) to provide peak plasma levels in range listed below for desired aminoglycoside.

Aminoglycoside	Usual Loading Doses	Expected Peak Plasma Levels
Tobramycin Gentamicin	1.5–2.0 mg/kg	4–10 µg/mL
Amikacin Kanamycin	5.0–7.5 mg/kg	15–30 µg/mL

2. Select maintenance dose (as percentage of chosen loading dose) to continue peak plasma levels indicated above according to desired dosing interval and the patient's corrected creatinine clearance.[a]

Percentage of Loading Dose Required For Dosage Interval Selected

Cl_{Cr} (mL/min)	$t\frac{1}{2}$[c] (hr)	8 hr (%)	12 hr (%)	24 hr (%)
90	3.1	84	—	—
80	3.4	80	91	—
70	3.9	76	88	—
60	4.5	71	84	—
50	5.3	65	79	—
40	6.5	57	72	92
30	8.4	48	63	86
25	9.9	43	57	81
20	11.9	37	50	75
17	13.6	33	46	70
15	15.1	31	42	67
12	17.9	27	37	61
10[b]	20.4	24	34	56
7	25.9	19	28	47
5	31.5	16	23	41
2	46.8	11	16	30
0	69.3	8	11	21

[a] Calculate corrected creatinine clearance (Cl_{Cr}) as:

$$Cl_{Cr} \text{ male} = \frac{(140 - age)(wt \text{ in kg})}{(72)(SrCr)}$$

$$Cl_{Cr} \text{ female} = 0.85 \times Cl_{Cr} \text{ male}$$

[b] Dosing for patients with changing renal function, obesity, or volume overload, should be guided by measured serum levels.

[c] Alternatively, one-half of the chosen loading dose may be given at an interval approximately equal to the estimated $t\frac{1}{2}$.

Fig 54.2 Dosing Chart for Amikacin, Kanamycin, Gentamicin, and Tobramycin Reprinted with permission from Ann Intern Med.

gentamicin/tobramycin levels associated with a 6 mg/kg dose of gentamicin are high (20 to 25 µg/mL) and troughs low (<1.0 µg/mL), the monitoring of serum aminoglycoside concentrations is not recommended with this regimen.

In summary, the use of a constant intravenous infusion of cefotaxime is possible in R.G., however, the benefit of this mode of administration is not clear. Considering the severity of R.G.'s infection and his elevated creatinine, he is not a candidate for single daily dosing of aminoglycosides (i.e., 5 to 6 mg/kg Q 24 hr). Independent of aminoglycoside-associated postantibiotic effect, his current renal function will result in a reduced gentamicin dose in the treatment of his infection.

Antimicrobial Protein-Binding

13. Ceftriaxone (Rocephin), rather than cefotaxime (Claforan), is being considered for the treatment of R.G.'s infection. It is noted that ceftriaxone is more highly protein bound than cefotaxime. Why is protein binding important in the selection of therapy?

Free (i.e., unbound), rather than total drug levels are best correlated with antimicrobial activity.[47] The degree of protein binding may have important clinical consequences in some patients. Cham-

bers et al.[48] reported treatment failures with the highly protein-bound cefonicid (98% protein bound) in patients with endocarditis caused by *Staphylococcus aureus*. Despite achievable serum drug concentrations well above the MIC of the organism, breakthrough bacteremia occurred in three of four patients. However, while total drug concentrations greatly exceeded the minimum inhibitory concentration of the pathogen, free concentrations were consistently below the level necessary to inhibit bacterial growth. Similar experiences have been reported with teicoplanin (98% protein bound).[49] Thus, clinical cure appears to be more likely if unbound antibiotic concentrations exceed the MIC of the infecting organism. Although ceftriaxone is 85% to 90% protein-bound, the free concentrations probably remain far above the MIC of the *Serratia*. Therefore, protein binding considerations are unlikely to be important in the treatment of R.G.'s infection.

Antimicrobial Failure

14. Antibiotic Specific Factors. Despite "appropriate" treatment, R.G. is unresponsive to antimicrobial therapy. What antibiotic-specific factors may contribute to "antimicrobial failure"?

Antimicrobials may "fail" for a variety of reasons, including patient-specific host factors, drug/dosage selection, and concomitant disease states. One of the most common reasons for antimicrobial failure is **drug resistance**.[50-52] A number of clinically important pathogens have been associated with emergence of resistance over the past decade, including *Mycobacterium tuberculosis*,[53] Enterococci,[54] gram-negative rods,[55] *Staphylococcus aureus*,[56] *Streptococcus pneumoniae*,[57] and others.

Development of resistance, while less common than initial resistance, may also account for failure to respond to therapy. Cephalosporin-susceptible *Enterobacter cloacae* may appear to be susceptible to a cephalosporin, however, beta-lactamase production can result in development of resistance to the agent.[58] **Superinfection** also may play a role in the unsuccessful treatment of infection. Superinfection is isolation of a new pathogen resistant to the previous antimicrobial regimen. If R.G.'s ceftriaxone-treated *Serratia* pneumonia subsequently worsens and a tracheal aspirate is positive for *Pseudomonas aeruginosa*, then superinfection has occurred.

Concurrent Therapy. Most infections can be treated with monotherapy (e.g., an *Escherichia coli* wound infection is treatable with a cephalosporin). However, some infections require two-drug therapy for successful outcome, including enterococcal endocarditis and certain *Pseudomonas aeruginosa* infections. Hilf and colleagues[59] studied 200 consecutive patients with *Pseudomonas*

Table 54.10	Influence of Renal Disease on Antimicrobial Accumulation

None to Mild

Azithromycin, cefoperazone, ceftriaxone, chloramphenicol, clarithromycin, clindamycin, cloxacillin, dicloxacillin, didanosine, doxycycline, erythromycin, ketoconazole, metronidazole, nafcillin, oxacillin, pentamidine, sulfamethoxazole, zalcitabine, zidovudine

Mild to Moderate

Cefotaxime, ciprofloxacin, clavulanic acid, imipenem, mezlocillin, norfloxacin, piperacillin, Zosyn

Significant

Acyclovir, amikacin, amoxicillin, ampicillin, aztreonam, cefadroxil, cefamandole, cefazolin, cefepime, cefixime, cefonicid, ceforanide, cefotetan, cefoxitin, ceftazidime, ceftizoxime, cefuroxime, cephalexin, cephalothin, flucytosine, foscarnet, ganciclovir, gentamicin, methicillin, netilmicin, ofloxacin, penicillin G, teicoplanin, tetracycline, ticarcillin, tobramycin, trimethoprim, Unasyn, vancomycin

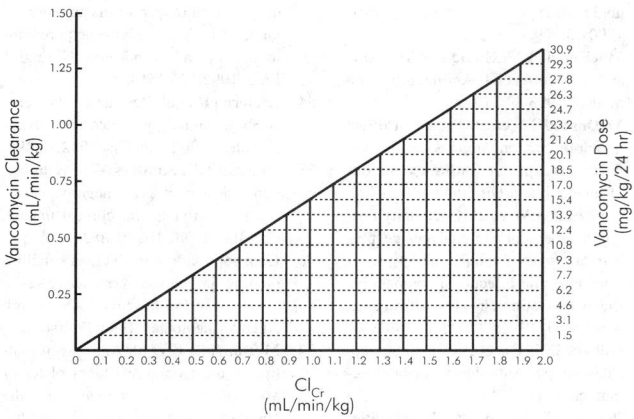

Fig 54.3 Reduced Dosage Nomogram for Vancomycin in Patients with Impaired Renal Failure as derived by Moellering et al. Reprinted with permission from Ann Intern Med. 1981;94:343.

aeruginosa bacteremia and demonstrated a 47% mortality in those patients receiving monotherapy (antipseudomonal beta-lactam or aminoglycoside) versus 27% if two-drug therapy was utilized. Thus, use of monotherapy can contribute to antimicrobial failure in certain infections.

If two antimicrobials are utilized in the treatment of infection, one of three sequelae will result: indifference, synergism, or antagonism.[60] **Indifference** occurs when the antimicrobial effect of Drug A plus that of Drug B equals the anticipated sum activity of Drug A + Drug B. **Synergism** occurs when the addition of Drug A to Drug B results in a total antibiotic activity greater than the expected sum of the two agents. **Antagonism** has occurred if the addition of Drug A to Drug B results in a combined activity less than the sum of Drug A + Drug B. An example of antagonism is the combination of imipenem with a less beta-lactamase stable beta-lactam, such as piperacillin.[61] Certain organisms, including *Pseudomonas aeruginosa* or *Enterobacter cloacae* can be induced to produce beta-lactamases.[55] If *Pseudomonas aeruginosa* is exposed to imipenem and piperacillin, the large amounts of generated beta-lactamase degrades and inactivates: antagonism has resulted. Antagonism is not unique to antibacterials: ketoconazole may antagonize amphotericin B in the treatment of *Aspergillus* infection.[62]

15. Pharmacologic Factors. What pharmacologic or pharmaceutic factors may be implicated in failure of therapy?

Subtherapeutic dosing regimens are commonplace especially for those agents with a low therapeutic index, such as the aminoglycosides. For example, a serious gram-negative pneumonitis may not respond to therapy if the achievable peak gentamicin serum levels are only 3 to 4 μg/mL.[35] Considering that only 20% to 30% of the aminoglycoside penetrates into bronchial secretions, only 0.5 to 1.0 μg/mL may exist at the site of infection,[63] a level that may be inadequate in the treatment of pneumonia. As another example, the use of an aminoglycoside "loading dose" is particularly critical in those patients with renal failure because it may be several days before a therapeutic level is achieved (see Chapter 2: Clinical Pharmacokinetics). Yet another reason for subtherapeutic levels could be attributable to **reduced oral absorption** secondary to drug interactions (e.g., ciprofloxacin with antacids or sucralfate).

Site of infection also contributes to antimicrobial failure. Most antimicrobials concentrate in the urine resulting in therapeutic levels, even with low doses. However, in some cases, antimicrobial penetration to the site of infection may be inadequate. Examples of these infections include meningitis, prostatitis, and endophthalmitis. Agents which have been proven to penetrate into the site of infection are required for a favorable outcome.

Another potential reason for antimicrobial failure may be **inadequate duration of therapy**. A woman with a first-time uncomplicated cystitis may respond adequately to a single dose of an antibiotic. However, a patient with recurrent urinary tract infection is not a candidate for this therapy. Failure would be expected with the use of a single dose in these patients.

16. Host Factors. What host factors potentially contribute to the failure of antimicrobial therapy?

A number of host factors may limit the ability of an antibiotic to cure infection. Infection of **prosthetic material** (e.g., IV catheters, prosthetic hip replacement, mechanical cardiac valves, and vascular grafts) is difficult to eradicate without removal of hardware. In most cases, surgical intervention is necessary. In order to adequately treat R.G.'s intravenous catheter infection, removal of his central line probably would be required. Similar to removal of prostheses, large undrained abscesses are difficult, if not impossible, to treat with antimicrobial therapy. These infections generally require surgical drainage for successful outcome.

Diabetic foot ulcer cellulitis may not respond adequately to antimicrobial therapy. Reasons for antimicrobial failure in patients with diabetes include poor wound healing as well as significant peripheral vascular disease that reduces the delivery of antibiotics to the site of infection.

Immune status, particularly neutropenia or lymphocytopenia, contributes to outcome in the treatment of infection. Profoundly neutropenic patients with disseminated *Aspergillus* infections are unlikely to respond to amphotericin B therapy. Similarly, AIDS patients with low CD4 lymphocyte counts are unable to eradicate a variety of infections, including cytomegalovirus, atypical mycobacteria, and cryptococcus.

Once the above factors have been eliminated as causes for antimicrobial failure, noninfectious etiologies must be ruled out. As discussed previously, malignancy, autoimmune disease, drug fever, and other diseases must be evaluated.

References

1 **Cranston WI et al.** Oral, rectal and esophageal temperatures and some factors affecting them in man. J Physiol. 1954;126:347.

2 **Parrillo JE, moderator.** Septic shock in humans. Advances in the understanding of pathogenesis, cardiovascular dysfunction, and therapy. Ann Intern Med. 1990;113:227.

3 **Bone RC.** The pathogenesis of sepsis. Ann Intern Med. 1991;115:457.

4 **Parrillo JE.** Pathogenic mechanisms

of septic shock. N Engl J Med. 1993; 328:1471.

5 **Ashbaugh DG et al.** Acute respiratory distress in adults. Lancet. 1967;2:319.

6 **Wiener-Kronish JP et al.** The adult respiratory distress syndrome: definition and prognosis, pathogenesis and treatment. Br J Anaesth. 1990;65:107.

7 **Murray JF et al.** Mechanisms of acute respiratory failure. Am Rev Respir Dis. 1977;115:1071.

8 **Arbo MJ et al.** Fever of nosocomial

origin: etiology, risk factors, and outcomes. Am J Med. 1993;95:505.

9 **Kazanjian PH.** Fever of unknown origin: review of 86 patients treated in community hospitals. Clin Infect Dis. 1992;15:968.

10 **Lipsky BA, Hirschmann JV.** Drug fever. JAMA. 1981;245:851.

11 **Ross D et al.** Differentiation of aseptic and bacterial meningitis in postoperative neurosurgery patients. J Neurosurg. 1988;69:669.

12 **Martin MA et al.** Nosocomial aseptic meningitis associated with administration of OKT3. JAMA. 1988;259:2002.

13 **Brumfitt W.** Progress in understanding urinary tract infections. J Antimicrob Chemother. 1991;27:9.

14 **Gorbach SL.** Intraabdominal infections. Clin Infect Dis. 1993;17:961.

15 **Edelstein PH.** Legionnaires' disease. Clin Infect Dis. 1993;16:741.

16 **Carbon C, Leophonte P.** Management of community-acquired pneumonia. J Antimicrob Chemother. 1993;32:1.

17 Mandell GL et al., eds. Principles and Practice of Infectious Diseases. 3rd ed. Churchill Livingstone, Inc.; 1990.

18 National Committee for Clinical Laboratory Standards. Performance standards for antimicrobial susceptibility testing. National Committee for Clinical Laboratory Standards. Villanova, PA: 1994.

19 Rosenblatt JE, Brook I. Clinical relevance of susceptibility testing of anaerobic bacteria. Clin Infect Dis. 1993; 16(Suppl. 4):S446.

20 Galgiani JH. Susceptibility testing of fungi: current status of the standardization process. Antimicrob Agents Chemother. 1993;37:2517.

21 Wolfson JS, Swartz MN. Serum bactericidal activity as a monitor of antibiotic therapy. N Engl J Med. 1985; 312:968.

22 Haydon RC et al. Erythromycin ototoxicity: analysis and conclusions based on 22 case reports. Otolaryngol Head Neck Surg. 1984;92:678.

23 Guglielmo BJ, Brooks GF. Antimicrobial therapy. Cost-benefit considerations. Drugs. 1989;38:473.

24 Eisenberg JM et al. What is the cost of nephrotoxicity associated with aminoglycosides? Ann Intern Med. 1987;107:900.

25 Campoli-Richards DM et al. Ciprofloxacin. A review of its antibacterial activity, pharmacokinetic properties and therapeutic use. Drugs. 1988;35: 373.

26 Thea D et al. Use of antibacterial agents in infections of the central nervous system. Infect Dis Clin North Am. 1989;3:553.

27 Barza M. Antibacterial agents in the treatment of ocular infection. Infect Dis Clin North Am. 1989;3:533.

28 Drach GW. Prostatitis. Man's hidden infection. Urol Clin North Am. 1975; 2:499.

29 Cockcroft DW, Gault MH. Prediction of creatinine clearance from serum creatinine. Nephron. 1976;16:31.

30 Mackowiak PA. Influence of fever on pharmacokinetics. Rev Infect Dis. 1989;11:804.

31 Brook I. Inoculum effect. Rev Infect Dis. 1989;11:361.

32 Craig WA, Ebert SC. Continuous infusion of beta-lactam antibiotics. Antimicrob Agents Chemother. 1992;36: 2577.

33 Roosendaal R et al. Continuous infusion versus intermittent administration of ceftazidime in experimental Klebsiella pneumoniae pneumonia in normal and leukopenic rats. Antimicrob Agents Chemother. 1986;30:403.

34 Baaker-Woudenberg IAJM, Roosendaal R. Impact of dosage regimens on the efficacy of antibiotics in the immunocompromised patient. J Antimicrob Chemother. 1988;21:145.

35 Moore RD et al. Association of aminoglycoside levels with therapeutic outcome in gram-negative pneumonia. Am J Med. 1984;77:657.

36 Mattie H. Determinants of efficacy and toxicity of aminoglycosides. J Antimicrob Chemother. 1989;24:281.

37 Matske GR et al. Controlled comparison of gentamicin and tobramycin nephrotoxicity. Am J Nephrol. 1983;3: 11.

38 McCormack JP, Jewesson PJ. A critical reevaluation of the "therapeutic range" of aminoglycosides. Clin Infect Dis. 1992;14:320.

39 Cheung RP, Dipiro JT. Vancomycin: an update. Pharmacotherapy. 1986;6: 153.

40 Cimino MA et al. Relationship of serum antibiotic concentrations to nephrotoxicity in cancer patients receiving concurrent aminoglycoside and vancomycin therapy. Am J Med. 1987;83: 1091.

41 Rybak MJ et al. Nephrotoxicity of vancomycin, alone and with an aminoglycoside. J Antimicrob Chemother. 1990;25:679.

42 MacKenzie FM, Gould IM. The postantibiotic effect. J Antimicrob Chemother. 1993;32:519.

43 McDonald PJ et al. Persistent effect of antibiotics on Staphylococcus aureus after exposure for limited periods of time. J Infect Dis. 1977;135:217.

44 ter Braak EW et al. Once-daily dosing regimen for aminoglycoside plus beta-lactam combination therapy of serious bacterial infections: comparative trial with netilmicin plus ceftriaxone. Am J Med. 1990;89:58.

45 Gilbert DN. Once-daily aminoglycoside therapy. Antimicrob Agents Chemother. 1991;35:399.

46 Parker SE, Davey PG. Practicalities of once-daily aminoglycoside dosing. J Antimicrob Chemother. 1993;31:4.

47 Lam YWF et al. Effect of protein binding on serum bactericidal activities of ceftazidime and cefoperazone in healthy volunteers. Antimicrob Agents Chemother. 1988;32:298.

48 Chambers HF et al. Failure of a once-daily regimen of cefonicid for treatment of endocarditis due to Staphylococcus aureus. Rev Infect Dis. 1984; 6(Suppl. 4):S870.

49 Greenberg RN. Treatment of bone, joint, and vascular-access-associated gram-positive bacterial infections with teicoplanin. Antimicrob Agents Chemother. 1990;34:2392.

50 Cohen ML. Epidemiology of drug resistance: implications for a post-antimicrobial era. Science. 1992;257:1050.

51 Murray BE. Problems and dilemmas of antimicrobial resistance. Pharmacotherapy. 1992;12(Suppl.):86S.

52 Jacoby GA, Archer G. New mechanisms of bacterial resistance to antimicrobial agents. N Engl J Med. 1991; 324:601.

53 Edlin BR et al. An outbreak of multidrug-resistant tuberculosis among hospitalized patients with the acquired immunodeficiency syndrome. N Engl J Med. 1992;326:1514.

54 Leclercq R et al. Resistance of enterococci to aminoglycosides and glycopeptides. Clin Infect Dis. 1992;15:495.

55 Sanders CC, Sanders WE. Beta-lactam resistance in gram-negative bacteria: global trends and clinical impact. Clin Infect Dis. 1992;15:824.

56 Georgopapadakou NH. Penicillin-binding proteins and bacterial resistance to beta-lactams. Antimicrob Agents Chemother. 1993;37:2045.

57 McDougal LK et al. Analysis of multiple antimicrobial-resistant isolates of Streptococcus pneumoniae from the United States. Antimicrob Agents Chemother. 1992;36:2176.

58 Chow JW et al. Enterobacter bacteremia: clinical features and emergence of antibiotic resistance during therapy. Ann Intern Med. 1991;115:585.

59 Hilf M et al. Antibiotic therapy for Pseudomonas aeruginosa bacteremia: outcome correlations in a prospective study of 200 patients. Am J Med. 1989; 87:540.

60 Fantin B, Carbon C. In vivo antibiotic synergism: contribution of animal models. Antimicrob Agents Chemother. 1992;36:907.

61 Bertram MA, Young LS. Imipenem antagonism of the in vitro activity of piperacillin against Pseudomonas aeruginosa. Antimicrob Agents Chemother. 1984;26:272.

62 Schaffner A, Frick PG. The effect of ketoconazole on amphotericin B in a model of disseminated aspergillosis. J Infect Dis. 1985;151:902.

63 Smith BR, LeFrock JC. Bronchial tree penetration of antibiotic. Chest. 1983;904.

64 Ann Intern Med. 1978;89(Part I): 612–618.

Antimicrobial Prophylaxis for Surgical Procedures

Laurie L Briceland

B Joseph Guglielmo

Risk Factors for Infection 55-1
Classification of Surgical Wounds
(See Table 55.1) 55-1
Principles of Surgical Antimicrobial
Prophylaxis 55-1
    Decision to Use Antimicrobial Prophylaxis 55-1
    Timing of Antimicrobial Administration 55-2
    Route of Administration 55-2

Duration of Administration 55-4
Signs of Wound Infection 55-4
Selection of an Antimicrobial Agent
    (Also see Questions 1 and 5 for Colorectal Surgery, 8 for
    Cardiac, 9 for Cesarean Section, 13 for Orthopedic,
    and 14 for Appendectomy) 55-4
Risks of Indiscriminate Antimicrobial Use 55-5
Optimizing Surgical Antimicrobial Prophylaxis 55-5

Prophylactic antibiotics are used widely in surgical procedures and account for up to 50% of total antibiotic usage in many hospitals.[1,2] The purpose of surgical antibiotic prophylaxis is to reduce the prevalence of postoperative wound infection (about 5% of surgical cases overall) at or around the surgical site.[3] Such surgical wound infections reportedly extend the duration of hospitalization by at least one week at an annual cost of more than 1.5 billion dollars nationwide.[4,5] By preventing surgical wound infections, prophylactic antimicrobial agents have the potential to decrease patient morbidity and hospitalization costs for many surgical processes that pose significant risk of infection (e.g., appendectomy); however, the benefits of prophylaxis are controversial and not justified for some surgical procedures (e.g., urological operations in patients with sterile urine).[6] Consequently, the inappropriate or indiscriminate use of prophylactic antibiotics can increase the risk of drug toxicity, selection of resistant organisms, and costs.

Risk Factors for Infection

The development of postoperative wound infection is related to the degree of bacterial contamination during surgery, the virulence of the infecting organism, and host defenses. Operative and environmental factors also may increase the risk of postoperative wound infection.

Bacterial contamination may occur from *exogenous* sources (e.g., the operative team, instruments, airborne organisms) or from *endogenous* sources [e.g., the patient's microflora of the skin, respiratory, genitourinary, gastrointestinal (GI) tract].[7,8] Infection control procedures to minimize all sources of bacterial contamination, including patient and surgical team preparation, operative technique, and wound care are compiled in Centers for Disease Control-directed guidelines for surgical wound infection.[8]

The risk of postoperative wound infection also is affected by host factors such as extremes of age, obesity, malnutrition, and comorbid states, including diabetes mellitus, remote infection, and immunosuppressive therapy.[7,9] Additionally, the longer the preoperative hospital stay and the surgical procedure are, the greater is the likelihood of developing a postoperative wound infection, presumably as a result of nosocomial bacterial acquisition in the former and the greater amount of bacterial contamination occurring over time in the latter instance.[7]

Another major risk factor for infection is the skill of the surgeon(s). Farber et al.[10] reported that postoperative wound infection rates were related inversely to the frequency of performing a surgical procedure; thus, hospitals with the highest frequency of surgical procedures have the lowest incidence of postoperative infection.

Based upon the aforementioned risk factors for infection, the decision of whether or not a given patient should receive antimicrobial prophylaxis is multifactorial. Many experts recommend that antimicrobial prophylaxis should be given for surgical procedures with increased frequency of infection or in which an infection would result in catastrophic consequences, or in patients with impaired host resistance to infection.[11] A widely used surgical wound classification system to assist in this decision-making process follows.

Classification of Surgical Wounds

From 1960 to 1964, the National Academy of Sciences National Research Council conducted a landmark study of surgical wound infections and formulated a widely used standard classification of surgical wounds based upon the risk of intraoperative bacterial contamination (see Table 55.1).[7] Current recommendations for surgical prophylaxis pertain to clean surgeries involving implantation of prosthetic material, clean-contaminated surgeries, and select contaminated wounds. Antimicrobial therapy for most contaminated and all dirty surgeries where infection already is established is considered ''treatment'' instead of prophylaxis, and will not be presented further in this chapter. Table 55.2 lists suspected pathogens and recommendations for site-specific prophylactic antimicrobial regimens; a detailed examination of clinical trials supporting these recommendations is presented elsewhere.[6]

Principles of Surgical Antimicrobial Prophylaxis

Decision to Use Antimicrobial Prophylaxis

1. M.R., a 72-year-old female, is admitted to hospital with severe abdominal pain, nausea and vomiting, and temperature of 102.8 °F. A diagnosis of acute cholecystitis is made, and M.R. is scheduled for biliary tract surgery (cholecystectomy). Why is antimicrobial prophylaxis warranted for M.R.?

Biliary tract surgery is considered a clean-contaminated procedure and, therefore, carries a risk of surgical wound infection approaching 10% (see Tables 55.1 and 55.2). Prophylaxis for biliary tract surgery is limited to ''high-risk'' procedures, which include age greater than 70 years, acute cholecystitis, obstructive jaundice, or common duct stones.[13] Thus, prophylaxis is warranted in M.R., who falls into at least two high risk categories (i.e., age > 70 years and acute cholecystitis).

Table 55.1	National Research Council Wound Classification[3,7]	
Classification	Criteria[a]	Infection Rate (%)
Clean	No acute inflammation or entry into GI, respiratory, GU, or biliary tracts; no break in aseptic technique occurs; wounds primarily closed	<5
Clean-contaminated	Elective, controlled opening of GI, respiratory, biliary, or GU tracts without significant spillage; clean wounds with major break in sterile technique	<10
Contaminated	Penetrating trauma (<4 hr old); major technique break or major spillage from GI tract; acute, nonpurulent inflammation	15–20
Dirty	Penetrating trauma (>4 hr old); purulence or abscess (active infectious process); preoperative perforation of viscera	30–40

[a] GI = Gastrointestinal; GU = Genitourinary.

2. An order for "cefazolin 1 gm IV on call to operating room (OR)" is written for M.R. Why is this an appropriate (or inappropriate) antibiotic selection?

The selected prophylactic agent should be directed against likely infecting organisms (see Table 55.2) but need not eradicate every potential pathogen. Cefazolin has been proven effective for most surgical procedures, including biliary tract surgery, keeping in mind that the goal of prophylaxis is to decrease bacterial counts below critical levels necessary to cause infection. Broad-spectrum agents such as third-generation cephalosporins should be avoided for prophylaxis because such drastic alterations of microbial flora would promote the emergence of microbial resistance to these otherwise valuable agents.

Timing of Antimicrobial Administration

3. Why is the administration time for this antimicrobial appropriate (or inappropriate) for M.R.?

Classic animal studies of Burke and colleagues[14,15] clearly demonstrated the need for therapeutic antibiotic concentrations in the bloodstream and vulnerable tissue at the time of wound contamination. Bacteria were most likely to enter the tissue beginning with the initial surgical incision and continuing until the wound was closed; and antibiotics administered more than three hours after bacterial contamination were ineffective in minimizing the development of wound infection.[14,15] This two- to three-hour period after the surgical incision was deemed the "effective" or "decisive" period for prophylaxis when the animal wound was most susceptible to the beneficial effects of the antibiotic. This decisive period for administration of prophylactic antibiotics subsequently has been confirmed in humans.[16,17] For maximal efficacy, an antibiotic should be present in therapeutic concentrations at the incision site as early as possible during the decisive period continuing until the wound is closed. Since an antibiotic administered postoperatively cannot achieve therapeutic concentrations during the decisive period, such timing of surgical "prophylaxis" is of no benefit in preventing postoperative wound infections and infection

rates will be similar to those of patients who receive no antibiotics.[17] An exception in which postincision administration sometimes is justified is in cesarean incisions because the incidence of postcesarean section endometritis is decreased significantly by postoperative administration of antibiotics.[13]

Based upon these study results, prophylactic antibiotics should be administered *before* the surgical procedure. It currently is recommended that prophylactic antibiotics be administered preoperatively in the operating room before the induction of anesthesia.[12,13] Prophylactic antibiotics are most effective when given during the two-hour period before the surgical incision, and rates of infection increase significantly if antibiotics are administered more than two hours preoperatively or any time postoperatively.[18]

The "on call" prescribing practice for surgical prophylaxis, as in M.R., has fallen into disfavor because the time between antibiotic administration and the actual incision may exceed two hours and, therefore, may result in subtherapeutic antibiotic concentrations during the decisive period.[19,20] M.R.'s cefazolin should be ordered preoperatively, and should be administered in the operating room no earlier than two hours before the operative procedure.

4. Will M.R. require the administration of a second dose of cefazolin during the scheduled surgical procedure?

The duration of the surgical procedure and the half-life of the administered antibiotic should be considered when determining whether or not an additional postoperative dose is necessary to maintain adequate antibiotic concentrations at the operative site. Studies have indicated an inverse relationship between the efficacy of short-acting antibiotics and the duration of the surgical procedure; as operative time increases, so does the incidence of postoperative infection.[21,22] Cefazolin, with a half-life of approximately 1.8 hours, is effective in a single preoperative dose for most surgical procedures. For prolonged procedures lasting more than four hours, additional intraoperative doses should be administered every four to eight hours for the duration of the procedure,[13] especially if an antibiotic with a short half-life, such as cefoxitin, has been administered.

M.R. should only require an additional intraoperative cefazolin dose in the event of a prolonged (>4 hour) surgical procedure.

Route of Administration

5. G.B., a 55-year-old female recently diagnosed with carcinoma of the large bowel, is admitted to hospital for an elective colorectal surgical resection; the surgery is expected to last at least 5 hours. Physical examination reveals a cachectic female with a 9 kg weight loss over the previous 3 months (current weight: 60 kg). Increased frequency of bowel movements and chronic fatigue were noted; all other systems were normal. Laboratory data included: hemoglobin (Hgb) 10.4 gm/dL, hematocrit (Hct) 29.7%, prothrombin time (PT) 15 sec (Normal: 11–13). Stool guaiac was positive. Vital signs were within normal limits. G.B. was taking no medications and had no history of drug allergies. The following orders were written to begin at home on the day before surgery:

1. **Clear liquid diet**
2. **Mechanical bowel cleansing with polyethylene glycol-electrolyte lavage solution (CoLyte, GoLytely)**
3. **Neomycin sulfate 1 gm and erythromycin 1 gm PO at 1:00 p.m., 2:00 p.m., and 11:00 p.m.**

Comment on the appropriateness of the oral route of administration of antibiotic prophylaxis for G.B. [SI units: Hgb 104 gm/L; Hct 0.297]

Table 55.2	Suggested Prophylactic Antimicrobial Regimens for Surgical Procedures[a]		
Procedure	Predominant Organism(s)	Antibiotic Regimen (Alternative)	Adult Preoperative IV Dose
Clean			
Cardiac (all with sternotomy, cardiopulmonary bypass)	S. aureus, S. epidermidis	Cefazolin (Vancomycin)	1 gm (1 gm)
Vascular (aortic resection, groin incision, prosthesis)	S. aureus, S. epidermidis, gram-negative enterics	Cefazolin (Vancomycin)	1 gm (1 gm)
Orthopedic (total joint replacement, internal fixation of fractures)	S. aureus, S. epidermidis	Cefazolin (Vancomycin)	1 gm (1 gm)
Neurosurgery	S. aureus, S. epidermidis	Cefazolin (Vancomycin)	1 gm (1 gm)
Clean-Contaminated			
Head and neck	S. aureus, oral anaerobes, streptococci	Cefazolin (Clindamycin)	1 gm (600 mg)
Gastroduodenal (only for procedures entering stomach)	Gram-negative enterics, S. aureus, mouth flora	Cefazolin	1 gm
Colorectal	Gram-negative enterics, anaerobes (B. fragilis)	Oral neomycin/erythromycin base (IV Cefoxitin or Cefotetan)	1 gm each at 1, 2, and 11 p.m. day before surgery (1 gm of either)
Appendectomy (uncomplicated)	Gram-negative enterics, anaerobes (B. fragilis)	Cefoxitin (Cefotetan)	1 gm (1 gm)
Biliary tract (only for "high-risk" procedures)	Gram-negative enterics, Enterococcus faecalis, clostridia	Cefazolin	1 gm
Cesarean section	Group B streptococci, enterococci, anaerobes, gram-negative enterics	Cefazolin	1 gm after umbilical cord clamped
Hysterectomy	Group B streptococci, enterococci, anaerobes, gram-negative enterics	Cefazolin	1 gm

[a] Adapted with permission from references 6, 12, and 13.

In general, oral administration of surgical antimicrobial prophylaxis is not recommended because of unreliable or poor absorption of oral agents in the anesthetized bowel. Oral agents, however, function very effectively as gastrointestinal decontaminants because high intraluminal drug concentrations are sufficient to decrease bacterial counts.[23] The concentration of bacteria in the colon may approach 10^{13} bacteria/mm^3 and colorectal procedures, such as the one G.B. will undergo, carry a relatively high risk of postoperative infection. Antimicrobial regimens with activity against the mixture of aerobic and anaerobic bacteria which comprise the fecal flora (*Esherichia coli* and other *Enterobacteriaceae, Bacteroides fragilis*) are effective in preventing postoperative wound infections.[24,25]

The most widely used oral antimicrobial regimen directed against the fecal flora is 1 gm each of the nonabsorbable antibiotics, neomycin sulfate (for gram-negative aerobes) and erythromycin base (for anaerobes), given one day before surgery at the times indicated for G.B.[17,26] Mechanical bowel cleansing, such as with polyethylene glycol-electrolyte lavage solution, must precede this regimen; the purpose of such bowel purging is to evacuate the colonic contents as completely as possible to decrease colonic bacterial counts. Effective oral alternatives to neomycin plus erythromycin include metronidazole with or without neomycin or with kanamycin, or kanamycin plus erythromycin;[24,25] however, clinical situations which would warrant the use of such alternatives over the well-established neomycin-erythromycin regimen are practically nonexistent. Thus, the regimen selected for G.B. is highly appropriate.

6. The surgical resident has canceled the oral neomycin-erythromycin bowel regimen for G.B. Instead, he orders cefoxitin (Mefoxin) 1 gm IV preoperatively. Why is (or is not) this change in therapy an effective and rational choice for G.B.?

Numerous parenteral regimens, specifically with agents that possess both aerobic and anaerobic activity, are effective as surgical prophylaxis in colorectal procedures.[25] The second-generation cephalosporins with significant anaerobic activity (e.g., cefoxitin, cefotetan) are superior to first-generation cephalosporins which lack sufficient anaerobic activity.[27,28] However, experts who have evaluated many studies of oral or parenteral colorectal regimens have concluded that oral regimens are superior to parenteral based upon the finding that the infection rate was reduced to less than 5% in 48% of oral regimens versus 26% of parenteral regimens evaluated.[6]

Thus, while both intravenous and oral regimens are effective in colorectal surgical prophylaxis, the parenteral route of administration, selected based upon physician preference, may be less effective. Furthermore, the cefoxitin order for G.B. would be unacceptable if the surgery takes longer than 3.5 hours (the relatively short half-life of cefoxitin could render G.B. antibiotic-free and would predispose her to infection).[29] For prolonged procedures (greater than ≈3 hours) such as anticipated for G.B., an alternative agent with a longer half-life (e.g., cefotetan) or a second dose of cefoxitin should be administered. However, cefotetan may be a poor choice for G.B. because of cefotetan's propensity to cause hypoprothrombinemia with or without associated bleeding episodes: this effect is attributed in part to the N-methylthiotetrazole side chain in the chemical structure of cefotetan. G.B. currently has an increased prothrombin time, so it would be prudent to avoid cefotetan. Thus, for G.B., the importance and efficacy of established oral prophylactic regimens (plus bowel cleansing) should be stressed to the resident.

7. The surgical resident has reconsidered the cefoxitin order and decided to prescribe both the oral and parenteral prophylactic regimens for G.B. Will the combination significantly reduce the rate of postoperative wound infection as compared to either regimen administered singly?

While the coadministration of both oral and parenteral prophylactic regimens occurs commonly in practice (88% of one survey's respondents),[30] data in support of this practice are inadequate, presumably because a study of large numbers of patients would be required to document a further decrease in already low infection rates ($\approx$5% to 10%).[31] Rectal surgical procedures, however, are associated with a higher infection rate (than colonic procedures) and an oral plus parenteral antimicrobial prophylaxis combination is superior to orally administered regimens alone in reducing infection rates;[29] therefore, some experts recommend a combination of oral and parenteral antimicrobial prophylaxis for rectal surgery.[6]

Thus, there is no supporting evidence for combination oral plus parenteral therapy for colon surgery prophylaxis in G.B., although the standard of practice often dictates its use.[30]

Duration of Administration

8. L.G., a 28-year-old male with a history of rheumatic heart disease, has a 12-year history of a heart murmur consistent with mild mitral stenosis and mitral regurgitation. Over the last 4 months his murmur has become much more prominent. Additionally, he has developed severe dyspnea with light physical activity and 3+ pitting edema over both lower legs. Physical examination is notable for coarse rales and an S₃ gallop. For the past 6 weeks he has been maintained on digoxin and diuretics without significant relief of his shortness of breath (SOB). The cardiothoracic surgeon recommends mitral valve replacement and orders the following surgical antibiotic prophylaxis regimen: cefazolin 1 gm IV preoperatively, then Q 8 hr × 48 hours. Why is cefazolin the most appropriate antimicrobial for L.G.? Why was prophylaxis only ordered for 48 hours?

While the incidence of postoperative wound infection for cardiothoracic procedures is low (<5%), the devastating consequences of a postoperative endocarditis (following valve replacement) and mediastinitis or sternal osteomyelitis (following sternotomy) warrant careful antimicrobial prophylaxis.[32] Organisms of concern for cardiothoracic surgery include *Staphylococcus aureus* and *Staphylococcus epidermidis* (see Table 55.2); based upon these potential pathogens, successful prophylactic regimens include cefazolin (Ancef), cefamandole (Mandol), and cefuroxime (Zinacef).[33] When cefazolin has been compared to cefuroxime or cefamandole, a statistical trend in favor of the second-generation cephalosporins has been noted and collective wound infection rates were slightly higher in the cefazolin group.[34-36] In contrast, a comparison of prophylactic cefazolin and cefuroxime in patients undergoing open heart surgery noted a significantly greater incidence of sternal wound infection and mediastinitis in the cefuroxime group.[37] Furthermore, equal efficacy between the two agents was noted in yet another study.[38] In conclusion, cefazolin probably is at least as effective as second-generation cephalosporins; therefore, the choice of agent should be based upon an institution's antimicrobial susceptibility and cost data. Hospital-specific antimicrobial resistance patterns are especially important in determining the incidence of *methicillin-resistant S. aureus* (MRSA) or *methicillin-resistant S. epidermidis* (MRSE); vancomycin is the drug of choice for prophylaxis of such organisms.[39]

In three surveys of antimicrobial prophylaxis in cardiothoracic surgery, second-generation cephalosporins were used in approximately 30% of cases in each survey; however, cefazolin remained the widely used, time-honored mainstay of prophylaxis, having been used in approximately 50% of cases in each survey.[13,33,40,41] Thus, the cefazolin prophylaxis selected for L.G. is acceptable, provided MRSA and MRSE are not of concern in his institution.

With regard to duration, the shortest effective prophylactic course of antibiotics should be used (i.e., single-dose preopera-

tively or no >24 hours postoperatively for most procedures). Single-dose prophylaxis, a viable option for many surgical procedures (see Question 9), is controversial for cardiac procedures.[32] In practice, cardiothoracic antimicrobial prophylaxis often is continued 48 hours after surgery,[12] as in L.G., or until all chest tubes and/or IV lines are removed.[33] There is no benefit to prolonging prophylaxis to greater than 48 hours, and such use should be discouraged.[42] The duration of antimicrobial prophylaxis ordered for L.G. is appropriate.

9. G.J., a 27-year-old female, is admitted to the obstetrics unit at term with her first pregnancy. She is scheduled for a cesarean section because the baby is breeched. Cefazolin 1 gm IV to be administered postcord-clamp and Q 8 hr for 24 hours is ordered. Why was this surgical prophylaxis inappropriate?

As noted previously, the shortest effective duration of prophylaxis is desired. In the past, five- or six-day antimicrobial regimens were used, but 24-hour regimens have since been proven as effective as these longer regimens.[43,44] Actually, a single cefazolin dose administered after the umbilical cord is clamped seems to be sufficient in preventing postoperative wound infections in cesarean section.[45,46] Single-dose prophylaxis is less costly[47] and minimizes the development of bacterial resistance.[48] Thus, G.J. should receive the single dose of cefazolin after the cord has been clamped without the three additional doses.

Single-dose prophylaxis also is effective in a variety of GI tract, orthopedic, and gynecologic procedures.[22] A single dose of an antibiotic with a short half-life, however, may provide insufficient antimicrobial coverage during a prolonged surgical procedure and repeated intraoperative dosing or selection of agent with longer half-life is recommended when the duration of surgery is long.

Signs of Wound Infection

10. G.J. is discharged on the fifth hospital day and instructed to carefully observe her cesarean-section incision site for signs of infection. What are the typical signs of wound infection? What is the typical time course for signs of wound infection to become manifest?

The majority of surgical wound infections involve the incision site. Typically, an infected incision site wound will be red, inflamed, and purulent. The purulent drainage should be cultured to identify the causative pathogen and to direct antimicrobial therapy. Empiric therapy directed against the most likely pathogens (see Table 55.2) should be instituted while awaiting culture and sensitivity test results. While most incision site infections will be clinically apparent shortly after surgery, some deep-seated infections present indolently over weeks to months by which time an abscess may have developed.[7]

Selection of an Antimicrobial Agent

11. L.T., a 46-year-old female, has a recent history of abnormal uterine bleeding and vaginal discharge. Endometrial biopsy is positive for squamous cell carcinoma. There is no evidence of invasive disease. The diagnosis is carcinoma *in situ*, and a vaginal hysterectomy is scheduled. What would be a good surgical prophylaxis antimicrobial regimen for L.T.?

The selection of a prophylactic regimen should incorporate such factors as the agent's microbiological activity against the most likely potential pathogens encountered during the surgical procedure (see Table 55.2), pharmacokinetic characteristics (e.g., half-life), inherent toxicity, potential to promote the emergence of resistant strains of bacteria, and cost.

The usefulness of antimicrobial prophylaxis in vaginal hysterectomies is well established and is directed against vaginal microflora, including gram-positive and gram-negative aerobes and anaerobes (see Table 55.2). The narrowest spectrum efficacious agent is desired, keeping in mind that the goal of prophylaxis is not to eradicate every potential pathogen, but to reduce bacterial counts below a critical level necessary to cause infection. Cefazolin has been proven to be an effective prophylactic agent for vaginal hysterectomies when compared against broad-spectrum agents such as moxalactam and ceftriaxone (Rocephin).[49,50] This indicates that a broader spectrum agent with anaerobic activity (which cefazolin lacks) is unwarranted.[51] Furthermore, cefazolin exhibits a favorable toxicity profile and possesses a relatively long half-life ($\approx$1.8 hours) such that a single dose has proved prophylactic efficacy.[52] Cefazolin also is considerably less expensive compared to broader spectrum agents. Thus, L.T. should receive cefazolin 1 gm IV preoperatively.

12. Because cefoxitin has an increased spectrum of activity against the anaerobe *B. fragilis*, it is being considered as an alternative to cefazolin prophylaxis for L.T. Comment on the appropriateness of this proposed change in prophylaxis.

The second- and third-generation cephalosporins are not more effective than the first-generation cephalosporins for surgical prophylaxis in vaginal hysterectomy or gastroduodenal, biliary, and colorectal surgery.[53] Cefoxitin is more costly and no more efficacious than cefazolin and should not be used for surgical prophylaxis for L.T.

13. S.N., a 57-year-old female with rheumatoid arthritis and degenerative joint disease, has been admitted for insertion of a prosthesis in her left hip (total hip arthroplasty). She has an allergy to penicillin (hives, SOB). What should be prescribed for S.N. for surgical prophylaxis during her total hip arthroplasty?

Cefazolin is the preferred prophylactic agent for orthopedic procedures (see Table 55.2). Although the risk of cefazolin cross-allergenicity to penicillin is minimal, S.N. experienced a significant penicillin allergy (hives, shortness of breath); therefore, an alternative prophylactic agent definitely is appropriate. The organisms most likely to cause postoperative infection after total hip replacement are *S. aureus* and *S. epidermidis* (see Table 55.2). Nafcillin, cefazolin, and vancomycin possess excellent activity against these potential pathogens; however, nafcillin clearly must be avoided because of the penicillin allergy. Thus, the preferred agent for S.N. is vancomycin.

Preoperative IV vancomycin 1 gm should be administered slowly, over at least 60 minutes. This slow rate of infusion is necessary to reduce the risk of infusion-related hypotension, which poses particular danger during anesthesia induction and has been reported to cause cardiac arrest.[54] The vancomycin should be continued postoperatively every 12 hours for two additional doses.[6]

14. B.K., an 18-year-old female, complains of severe acute belly pain and nausea; the pain is localized to the periumbilical region. B.K. has a temperature of 39.5 °C. After initial examination by her pediatrician, she is admitted to hospital with presumed appendicitis and an exploratory laparotomy is scheduled. What surgical antimicrobial prophylaxis should be ordered for B.K.?

As with colorectal surgery, the most likely infecting organisms in appendectomy are *Bacteroides* species and gram-negative enterics (see Table 55.2). Upon surgical inspection, if the appendix appears normal (uninflamed, without perforation), then antimicrobial prophylaxis is unnecessary. If the appendix is inflamed without perforation, a single preoperative antibiotic dose is necessary; however, if the appendix is perforated or gangrenous (complicated), infection is already established and postoperative treatment is warranted. Unfortunately, the status of the appendix cannot be determined before surgery; therefore, all patients should receive at least one dose of an appropriate antibiotic preoperatively. After surgical inspection of the appendix,[6] the decision can be made as to the necessity of postoperative antibiotic therapy.

Based upon the pathogens likely to be encountered, an antimicrobial agent with both aerobic and anaerobic activity is desired for surgical prophylaxis in this situation. Cefoxitin (Mefoxin) is the most extensively studied and recommended cephalosporin for surgical prophylaxis during an appendectomy; however, cefotetan (Cefotan), ceftizoxime (Cefizox), cefmetazole (Zefazone), or cefotaxime (Claforan) are acceptable alternatives.[6] B.K. could receive cefoxitin 1 gm IV preoperatively, with a second dose administered if the procedure exceeds three hours.

Risks of Indiscriminate Antimicrobial Use

15. Upon surgical exploration, B.K. was found to have uncomplicated (nonperforated, nongangrenous) appendicitis; however, cefoxitin therapy was continued for 3 days for unclear reasons. What are the risks of indiscriminate use of antimicrobials for surgical prophylaxis?

The risks to a given patient include the potential for adverse effects and superinfection. The administration of any beta-lactam agent poses the risk of a hypersensitivity reaction, and many antibiotics, including cefoxitin such as in B.K., are known to predispose patients to *Clostridium difficile*-associated disease.[55,56] Additionally, widespread or prolonged use of antimicrobial agents increases the potential for the development or selection of resistant organisms in a given patient or other patients who may acquire a pathogen nosocomially.[57]

Optimizing Surgical Antimicrobial Prophylaxis

Antibiotic control strategies have improved the appropriate use of antimicrobial agents for surgical prophylaxis. The implementation of an automatic stop-order policy for surgical prophylaxis has reduced the duration of antimicrobial prophylaxis dramatically. These stop-order policies can be printed directly onto an antibiotic order form.[58,59] Surveys indicate that 37% to 71% of institutions use an antibiotic automatic stop order, with the most common surgical prophylaxis duration being 24 hours.[41,60] In one early study, the creation of an antibiotic order form with an automatic stop order after two days of surgical prophylaxis reduced the mean duration of surgical prophylaxis from 4.9 to 2.9 days.[58] One experience noted that the duration of surgical prophylaxis exceeded the recommended 24 hours in only 4% to 18% of cases.[59] Both of these examples demonstrate significant improvement in the use of antimicrobial prophylaxis. At one time, about 80% of prophylactic antibiotic usage for surgical procedures occurred either too soon (>2 hours before surgery) or for too long (>24 hours postoperatively).[1]

The pharmacy department of health organizations has the responsibility to optimize the timing, choice, and duration of antimicrobial surgical prophylaxis.[61–64] In one program, computer-assisted monitoring of the duration of surgical prophylaxis helped to identify and automatically discontinue inappropriately long courses of surgical antimicrobial prophylaxis, significantly reduced the average number of antibiotic doses administered, and generated reduced costs without jeopardizing clinical outcomes.[63] Similar cost savings can be achieved by orchestrating changes within an institution aimed at reducing the duration and frequency of prophylactic surgical antibiotic administration.[62] Staff in a surgical satellite pharmacy corrected a problem of too early preoperative antibiotic administration (88% of cases exceeded recommended guidelines) and demonstrated the value of proactive interventions achievable by pharmaceutical care.[61]

References

1 Shapiro M et al. Use of antimicrobial drugs in general hospitals: patterns of prophylaxis. N Engl J Med. 1979;301:351.

2 Gilbert DN. Current status of antibiotic prophylaxis in surgical patients. Bull NY Acad Med. 1984;60:340.

3 Cruse PJE et al. The epidemiology of wound infection: a 10-year prospective study of 62,939 wounds. Surg Clin North Am. 1980;60:27.

4 Haley RW et al. Extra charges and prolongation of stay attributable to nosocomial infections: a prospective interhospital comparison. Am J Med. 1981;70:51.

5 Wenzel RP. Preoperative antibiotic prophylaxis. N Engl J Med. 1992;326:337.

6 ASHP Commission on Therapeutics. ASHP therapeutic guidelines on antimicrobial prophylaxis in surgery. Clin Pharm. 1992;11:483.

7 Ad Hoc Committee of the Committee on Trauma, Division of Medical Sciences. National Academy of Sciences-National Research Council. Postoperative wound infections: the influence of ultraviolet irradiation of the operating room and various other factors. Ann Surg. 1964;160(Suppl. 2):1.

8 Polk HC et al. Guidelines for prevention of surgical wound infection. Arch Surg. 1983;118:1213.

9 DiPiro JT et al. The prophylactic use of antimicrobials in surgery. Curr Probl Surg. 1983;20:69.

10 Farber BF et al. Relation between surgical volume and incidence of postoperative wound infection. N Engl J Med. 1981;305:200.

11 Lewis RT. Antibiotic prophylaxis in surgery. Can J Surg. 1981;24:561.

12 Page CP et al. Antimicrobial prophylaxis for surgical wounds: guidelines for clinical care. Arch Surg. 1993;128:79.

13 Anon. Antimicrobial prophylaxis in surgery. The Medical Letter. 1993;35:91.

14 Miles AA et al. The value and duration of defence reactions of the skin to the primary lodgement of bacteria. Br J Exp Pathol. 1957;38:79.

15 Burke JF. Effective period of preventive antibiotic action in experimental incisions and dermal lesions. Surgery. 1961;50:161.

16 Polk HC et al. Postoperative wound infection: a prospective study of determinant factors and prevention. Surgery. 1969;66:97.

17 Stone HH et al. Antibiotic prophylaxis in gastric, biliary and colonic surgery. Ann Surg. 1976;184:443.

18 Classen DC et al. The timing of prophylactic administration of antibiotics and the risk of surgical-wound infection. N Engl J Med. 1992;326:281.

19 Nix DE et al. Cephalosporins for surgical prophylaxis: computer projections of intraoperative availability. South Med J. 1985;78:962.

20 Galanduik S et al. Re-emphasis of priorities in surgical antibiotic prophylaxis. Surg Gynecol Obstet. 1989;169:219.

21 Shapiro M et al. Risk factors for infection at the operative site after abdominal or vaginal hysterectomy. N Engl J Med. 1982;307:1661.

22 DiPiro JT et al. Single dose systemic antibiotic prophylaxis of surgical wound infections. Am J Surg. 1986;152:552.

23 Bartlett JG et al. Veterans administration cooperative study on bowel preparation for elective colorectal operations. Ann Surg. 1978;188:249.

24 DiPiro JT et al. Antimicrobial prophylaxis in surgery: part 1. Am J Hosp Pharm. 1981;38:320.

25 Guglielmo BJ et al. Antibiotic prophylaxis in surgical procedures: a critical analysis of the literature. Arch Surg. 1983;118:943.

26 Nichols RL et al. Effect of preoperative neomycin-erythromycin intestinal preparation on the incidence of infectious complications following colon surgery. Ann Surg. 1973;178:453.

27 Hoffman CEJ et al. Use of perioperative cefoxitin to prevent infection after colonic and rectal surgery. Ann Surg. 1981;193:353.

28 Lewis RT. Are first generation cephalosporins effective for antibiotic prophylaxis in elective surgery of the colon? Can J Surg. 1983;26:504.

29 Coppa G et al. Factors involved in antibiotic selection in elective colon and rectal surgery. Surgery. 1988;104:853.

30 Solla J et al. Preoperative bowel preparation: a survey of colon and rectal surgeons. Dis Colon Rectum. 1990;33:154–59.

31 Condon RE et al. Efficacy of oral and systemic antibiotic prophylaxis in colorectal operations. Arch Surg. 1983;118:496.

32 Ariano RE et al. Antimicrobial prophylaxis in coronary bypass surgery: a critical appraisal. DICP. 1991;25:478.

33 Woods M et al. Antibiotic prophylaxis in cardiothoracic surgery: results of a second survey. Hosp Pharm. 1990;25:643.

34 Slama T et al. Randomized comparison of cefamandole, cefazolin and cefuroxime prophylaxis in open-heart surgery. Antimicrob Agents Chemother. 1986;29:744.

35 Kaiser A et al. Efficacy of cefazolin, cefamandole, and gentamicin as prophylactic agents in cardiac surgery. Ann Surg. 1987;206:791.

36 Geroulanos S et al. Antimicrobial prophylaxis in cardiovascular surgery. Thorac Cardiovasc Surg. 1987;35:199.

37 Doebbeling B et al. Cardiovascular surgery prophylaxis: a randomized, controlled comparison of cefazolin and cefuroxime. J Thorac Cardiovasc Surg. 1990;99:981–89.

38 Conklin C et al. Determinants of wound infection incidence after isolated coronary artery bypass surgery in patients randomized to receive prophylactic cefuroxime or cefazolin. Ann Thorac Surg. 1988;46:172.

39 Gelfand MS et al. Cefamandole versus cefonicid prophylaxis in cardiovascular surgery: a prospective study. Ann Thorac Surg. 1990;49:435.

40 Woods M et al. Survey of antimicrobial prophylaxis in cardiovascular surgery. Poster presented at 43rd ASHP Annual Meeting. Denver, CO: 1986 June.

41 Woods M et al. Antibiotic prophylaxis in cardiothoracic surgery 1990: results of a third survey. Hosp Pharm. 1992;27:404.

42 Goldmann DA et al. Cephalothin prophylaxis in cardiac valve surgery. A prospective, double-blind comparison of two-day and six-day regimens. J Thorac Cardiovasc Surg. 1977;73:470.

43 D'Angelo LJ et al. Short-versus long course prophylactic antibiotic treatment in cesarean section patients. Obstet Gynecol. 1980;55:583.

44 Scarpignato C et al. Short term vs long term cefuroxime prophylaxis in patients undergoing emergency cesarean section. Clin Ther. 1982;5:186.

45 Jacobi P et al. Single-dose cefazolin prophylaxis for cesarean section. Am J Obstet Gynecol. 1988;158:1049.

46 Crombleholme WR. Use of prophylactic antibiotics in obstetrics and gynecology. Clin Obstet Gynecol. 1988;31:466.

47 Smith KS et al. Multidisciplinary program for promoting single prophylactic doses of cefazolin in obstetrical and gynecological surgical procedures. Am J Hosp Pharm. 1988;45:1338.

48 Kaiser AB. Antimicrobial prophylaxis in surgery. N Engl J Med. 1986;315:1129.

49 Hemsell D et al. Moxalactam versus cefazolin prophylaxis for vaginal hysterectomy. Am J Obstet Gynecol. 1983;147:379.

50 Hemsell D et al. Ceftriaxone or cefazolin prophylaxis for the prevention of infection after vaginal hysterectomy. Am J Surg. 1984;148(4A):22.

51 Houang ET. Antibiotic prophylaxis in hysterectomy and induced abortion: a review of the evidence. Drugs. 1991;41:19.

52 Hemsell DL et al. Single dose prophylaxis for vaginal and abdominal hysterectomy. Am J Obstet Gynecol. 1987;157:498.

53 DiPiro JT et al. Prophylactic parenteral cephalosporins in surgery. Are the newer agents better? JAMA. 1984;252:3277.

54 Dajee H et al. Profound hypotension from rapid vancomycin administration during cardiac operation. J Thorac Cardiovasc Surg. 1984;87:145.

55 Block BS et al. Clostridium difficile-associated diarrhea follows perioperative prophylaxis with cefoxitin. Am J Obstet Gynecol. 1985;87:145.

56 Cannon SR et al. Pseudomembranous colitis associated with antibiotic prophylaxis in orthopaedic surgery. J Bone Joint Surg. 1988;70B:600.

57 Moellering RC. Interaction between antimicrobial consumption and selection of resistant bacterial strains. Scand J Infect Dis. 1990;(Suppl. 70):18.

58 Durbin WA et al. Improved antibiotic usage following introduction of a novel prescription system. JAMA. 1981;246:1796.

59 Lipsy RJ et al. Design, implementation, and use of a new antimicrobial order form: a descriptive report. Ann Pharmacother. 1993;27:856.

60 Lesar TS et al. Survey of antibiotic control policies in University Hospital Consortium members. Poster presented at 28th Annual ASHP Midyear Clinical Meeting. Orlando, FL: 1993 Dec 9.

61 Peterson CD et al. Pharmacist monitoring of the timing of preoperative antibiotic administration. Am J Hosp Pharm. 1990;47:384.

62 Peterson CD et al. Reducing prophylactic antibiotic costs in cardiovascular surgery: the role of the clinical pharmacist. DICP. 1985;19:134.

63 Evans RS et al. Reducing the duration of prophylactic antibiotic use through computer monitoring of surgical patients. DICP Ann Pharmacother. 1990;24:351.

64 Michael KA et al. Impact of a pharmacist/physician cooperative target drug monitoring program on prophylactic antibiotic prescribing in obstetrics and gynecology. Hosp Pharm. 1992;27:213.

Central Nervous System Infections

John F Flaherty

Review of Central Nervous System (CNS)
Anatomy and Physiology 56-1
  Meninges 56-1
  Cerebrospinal Fluid (CSF) 56-2
  Blood-Brain Barrier (See Figure 56.1) 56-2
Meningitis 56-2
  Microbiology (See Table 56.1) 56-3
  Pathogenesis and Pathophysiology (See Figure 56.2) 56-3
  Diagnosis and Clinical Features 56-4
    Clinical and laboratory features of bacterial
      meningitis (See Table 56.2) 56-4
    Cerebrospinal fluid examination
      (See Table 56.3) 56-5
    Microbiologic evaluation 56-6
  Treatment Principles 56-6
    Antimicrobial penetration into the cerebrospinal
      fluid (See Table 56.4 and Figure 56.3) 56-6
    Empiric therapy for childhood meningitis
      (See Table 56.5) 56-7
    Dosing considerations (See Table 56.6) 56-7
    Adjunctive corticosteroid therapy 56-8
  Haemophilus influenzae Meningitis 56-10
    Definitive therapy (See Table 56.7) 56-10
    Monitoring therapy 56-10
    Ceftriaxone-induced biliary pseudolithiasis 56-11
    Duration of therapy (See Table 56.8) 56-12
    Prevention of *H. influenzae* type b (Hib)
      meningitis 56-12
      Chemoprophylaxis of household contacts 56-12
      Hib vaccination recommendations
        (See Table 56.9) 56-12
  Streptococcus pneumoniae Meningitis 56-12
    Clinical features, predisposing factors,
      and diagnosis 56-12
  Empiric therapy in adults 56-13
  Corticosteroid therapy for adult meningitis 56-14
  Treatment of penicillin-resistant
    pneumococcal meningitis 56-14
  Prevention of meningitis 56-14
Gram-Negative Bacillary Meningitis 56-15
  Epidemiology 56-15
  Predisposing factors 56-15
  Microbiology 56-15
  Clinical features 56-15
  Treatment of gram-negative bacillary meningitis ..56-15
  Treatment of *Enterobacter* meningitis 56-16
    Duration of therapy 56-17
Staphylococcus epidermidis Meningitis/Ventriculitis ...56-17
  Clinical presentation of CSF shunt infections 56-17
  Treatment of CSF shunt infections 56-17
    Glycocalyx 56-17
    Vancomycin therapy 56-18
    Intraventricular and intravenous dosing
      of vancomycin 56-18
Brain Abscess 56-18
  Epidemiology 56-18
  Predisposing Factors (See Table 56.10) 56-19
  Staging 56-19
  Microbiology (See Table 56.10) 56-19
  Clinical and Radiologic Features 56-19
  Treatment 56-20
    Surgical techniques 56-20
    Antimicrobial penetration into brain abscess 56-20
    Antibiotic therapy (See Table 56.10) 56-21
    Adjunctive corticosteroid therapy 56-21
    Adjunctive anticonvulsant therapy 56-21
    Monitoring therapy 56-21

The pharmacotherapy of central nervous system (CNS) infections presents a tremendous challenge to the clinician. CNS infections often are caused by virulent pathogens. These infections occur in an area of the body in which antibiotic penetration often is limited and where host defenses are absent or inadequate. Thus, morbidity and mortality from infections of the CNS remain high despite the availability of highly potent, bactericidal antibiotics. In a review of 445 adult patients treated for bacterial meningitis at the Massachusetts General Hospital between 1962 to 1988, the mortality rates were 25% and 35% for community-acquired and hospital-acquired cases, respectively.[1] The overall case fatality rate of 25% did not change significantly over the 27-year period of the study. Although eradication of bacteria is essential, it is only one of the variables that affect mortality from CNS infections. In an attempt to improve morbidity and mortality statistics, the pathophysiologic mechanisms of CNS infections are being further scrutinized.[2-4] For example, the beneficial effects of corticosteroids in bacterial meningitis continue to be evaluated.[5]

A number of infectious processes can occur within the CNS (e.g., meningitis, encephalitis, meningoencephalitis, brain abscess, subdural empyema, and epidural abscess).[6,7] In addition, placement of prosthetic devices into the CNS [e.g., cerebrospinal fluid

(CSF) shunts for management of hydrocephalus] frequently are complicated by infection.[8] Many etiologic agents are capable of inducing CNS infections including bacteria, viruses, fungi, and certain parasites. This chapter will focus primarily on bacterial infections of the CNS with an emphasis on the pharmacotherapy of bacterial meningitis and brain abscess. [Also see Chapters 67: Infections in Immunocompromised Hosts and 68: Human Immunodeficiency Virus (HIV) Infection for presentations pertaining to CNS infections in these unique populations.]

Review of Central Nervous System (CNS) Anatomy and Physiology
Meninges

Proper therapy of central nervous system infections first requires an understanding of the anatomic and physiologic characteristics of this region. The brain and spinal cord are ensheathed by a protective covering known as the meninges, and suspended in cerebrospinal fluid which acts as a ''shock absorber'' to outside trauma.[9,12] The meninges consist of three layers of fibrous tissue: the *pia mater*, *arachnoid*, and *dura mater*. The pia mater is the innermost thin, delicate membrane layer of the meninges that closely adheres to the contours of the brain. Separating the pia mater from the more loosely enclosed arachnoid membrane is the subarachnoid space where the CSF resides. The pia mater and arachnoid, known collectively as the leptomeninges, lie interior to the dura mater, a tough outer membrane which adheres to the periosteum and vertebral column.[9,10] Meningitis is a term describing inflammation (often due to infection) of the subarachnoid space, while subdural empyema refers to a collection of purulent material (pus) in the region separating the dura and arachnoid.[7,9] Abscesses also can form outside the dural space (epidural abscess), often with devastating consequences.[7]

Cerebrospinal Fluid (CSF)

Cerebrospinal fluid is produced and secreted by the choroid plexus in the lateral ventricles, and to a lesser extent by choroid plexuses located within the third and fourth ventricles.[11,12] The choroid plexus is histologically similar to renal tubules and removes organic acids (including penicillins) from the CSF via active transport mechanisms. These transport processes can be inhibited by probenecid (Benemid) administration.[10] Cerebrospinal fluid flows unidirectionally from the lateral ventricles through the foramina of the third and fourth ventricles into the subarachnoid space then over the cerebral hemispheres, and downward into the spinal canal. CSF is absorbed through villous projections (arachnoid villi) into veins, primarily the cerebral venous sinuses.[11,12] About 550 mL/day of cerebrospinal fluid is produced, with complete exchange occurring every three to four hours.[11,12] The flow of CSF is unidirectional from the ventricles to the intralumbar space; therefore, intrathecal injection of antibiotics results in little, if any, antibiotic that reaches the cerebral ventricles.[13,14] This unidirectional flow of cerebrospinal fluid presents a problem because ventriculitis commonly occurs in conjunction with bacterial meningitis. Direct intraventricular instillation of antibiotics, usually by means of a reservoir, is preferable in the setting of ventriculitis (also see Question 21).[13,14]

In adults, infants, and children, the volume of CSF is approximately 150 mL, 40 to 60 mL, and 60 to 100 mL, respectively.[11,12] Knowledge of approximate CSF volume facilitates estimation of the cerebrospinal fluid concentration of a drug subsequent to intrathecal administration. For example, administration of gentamicin 5 mg (5000 µg) intrathecally should result in a CSF concentration of roughly 33 µg/mL in an adult shortly after administration.

The composition of CSF differs from other physiological fluids. The pH of CSF is slightly acidic (normal pH: 7.3), and, with the exception of chloride ion, electrolyte concentrations are slightly less than those in serum.[11,12] Under normal conditions the protein concentration in CSF is less than 50 mg/dL, CSF glucose values are approximately 60% those of plasma, and few if any white blood cells (WBCs) are present (<5 cells/mm^3).[11,12] When the meninges become inflamed (i.e., in meningitis), the composition of the CSF is altered. In particular, the protein concentration in the CSF increases, and the glucose concentration in the CSF usually declines with meningitis. Therefore, careful evaluation of CSF chemistries is useful when establishing a diagnosis of meningitis.

Blood-Brain Barrier

The blood-brain barrier plays a crucial role in protecting the brain and maintaining homeostasis within the CNS.[11,15,16] There actually are two distinct barriers that exist within the brain: the blood-CSF barrier and the blood-brain barrier.[15,16] The *blood-CSF barrier* is located in the choroid plexus and circumventricular organs (e.g., area postrema) and is characterized morphologically by fenestrated (porous) capillaries (see Figure 56.1).[15] This arrangement allows proteins and other molecules (including antibiotics) to pass freely into the immediate interstitial space. Diffusion of substances into the cerebrospinal fluid is restricted by tightly fused ependymal cells lining the ventricular side of the choroid plexus (see Figure 56.1).[15] Cerebral capillary endothelial cells comprise the blood-brain barrier which separates blood from the interstitial fluid of the brain. Unlike capillaries in other areas of the body, the capillary endothelia of the brain are packed closely together, forming "tight junctions" which in effect produces a barrier physiologically similar to a continuous lipid bilayer.[15] The surface area of the blood-brain barrier is over 5000 times greater than that of the blood-CSF barrier; thus, the blood-brain barrier plays a more essential role in protecting the brain and regulating its chemical composition.[11,15] Many antimicrobials traverse the blood-brain barrier with difficulty, particularly agents having low lipid solubility (see below).[16]

Meningitis

Meningitis is the most common type of CNS infection. The signs and symptoms associated with bacterial meningitis usually are acute in onset, evolving over a few hours.[6] Prompt recognition and early institution of therapy are essential to ensuring beneficial outcomes. In contrast, a diverse group of infectious (e.g., viruses, fungi, and mycobacteria) and noninfectious (e.g., chemical irritants) agents produce a meningitic picture often of a less acute or

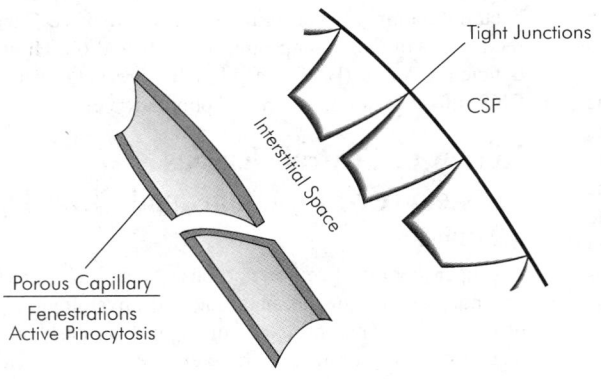

A. Capillary Surface Area = 1

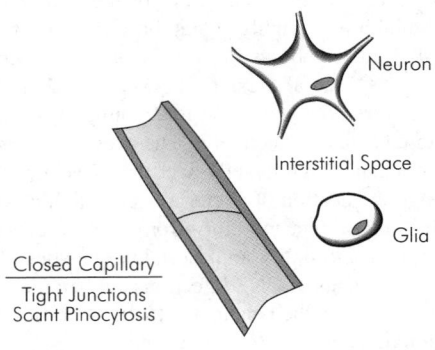

B. Capillary Surface Area = 5000

Fig 56.1   The Two Membrane Barrier Systems in the CNS: The Blood-CSF Barrier (A) and the Blood-Brain Barrier (B)   See text for a description of each barrier. Reproduced with permission from reference 15.

chronic nature.[17] On occasion, such "aseptic" causes can produce signs and symptoms nearly indistinguishable from acute bacterial meningitis.[6,17] Drugs that can induce aseptic meningitis include trimethoprim-sulfamethoxazole (TMP-SMX), antirejection monoclonal antibody muromonab (OKT3), azathioprine, and nonsteroidal anti-inflammatory drugs (NSAIDs) such as ibuprofen, naproxen, and sulindac.[17]

Microbiology

The bacterial etiologies of meningitis correlate very well with age and underlying conditions such as head trauma or recent neurosurgery (see Table 56.1).[18-20] Generally, meningitis is a disease of the very young and very old: the majority of cases occur in children under two years of age and in elderly adults.[18,19] Neonates (infants <2 months) especially are at a high risk of developing meningitis. Meningitis in neonates most often is caused by group B streptococci (*Streptococcus agalactiae*), or coliform organisms such as *Escherichia coli*.[18,19,21] These highly virulent pathogens usually are acquired during passage through the birth canal, or from the hospital environment, and are associated with significant morbidity and mortality, particularly in premature infants.[18,19,21] Case fatality rates of over 20% and 30% have been reported for meningitis due to group B streptococci and gram-negative bacilli, respectively.[18] *Listeria monocytogenes* is another important and frequently overlooked pathogen in neonates.[18,19,22] Because *L. monocytogenes* is resistant to many antimicrobial agents, including third-generation cephalosporins, selection of initial (empiric) therapy in neonates must be approached with this pathogen in mind.[22]

Infants more than one month of age and children less than four years of age are at the highest risk for meningitis. In this age group, the disease is caused predominantly by three pathogens: *Haemophilus influenzae*, *Streptococcus pneumoniae*, and *Neisseria meningitidis*.[18,19] Up to 45% of all cases of meningitis in the U.S. before 1985 were due to *H. influenzae* type b (Hib);[19] however, from 1987 through 1993, Hib meningitis cases in children less than five years of age decreased by 95%.[23,24] This reduction in *H. influenzae*-induced meningitis roughly correlates with the widespread vaccination of children against invasive *H. influenzae* disease with the Hib polysaccharide-protein conjugate vaccines. Invasive *H. influenzae* infection now is considered a vaccine-preventable disease in the U.S. and is targeted for elimination by 1996.[24]

In adults and children given the conjugated Hib vaccine, community-acquired meningitis most often is caused by *S. pneumoniae* (the pneumococcus), and *Neisseria meningitidis* (the meningococcus).[4,18,19] Meningococci more commonly are implicated in individuals between 5 to 30 years of age, whereas the pneumococcus is the predominant pathogen in adults more than 30 years of age.[18] Traditionally, both of these organisms have been highly susceptible to penicillin G [minimum inhibitory concentration (MIC) <0.1 µg/mL]. Pneumococcal strains showing relative penicillin resistance (MIC >0.1 ≤1.0 µg/mL) and high level resistance (MIC ≥2.0 µg/mL), however, are becoming a problem in many areas of the world, including the U.S.[2,25] Optimum therapy for resistant pneumococci is controversial and is discussed in greater detail in Question 14.

The elderly also are prone to developing meningitis, and infection-related mortality in this population often is higher than in other age groups.[18,19,26] For example, the case-fatality rate for pneumococcal meningitis in children less than five years of age is 5%; whereas, the case-fatality rate in the elderly is 31%.[19] Patients with advanced age are most susceptible to meningitis from pneumococci and meningococci; however, enteric gram-negative bacilli

Table 56.1	Microbiology of Bacterial Meningitis
Age Group or Predisposing Condition	Most Likely Organisms[a]
Neonates (<2 months)	Group B Streptococcus (*S. agalactiae*), *E. coli* and other gram-negative bacilli (*Klebsiella, Serratia* species), *L. monocytogenes*
Infants and children (2 months–10 yr)	*H. influenzae, S. pneumoniae, N. meningitidis*
Children and adults (>10–30 yr)	*N. meningitidis, S. pneumoniae*
Adults (30–60 yr)	*S. pneumoniae, N. meningitidis*
Elderly (>60 yr)	*S. pneumoniae, N. meningitidis, E. coli, Klebsiella* species, and other gram-negative bacilli, *L. monocytogenes*
Postneurosurgical	*S. aureus*, gram-negative bacilli (e.g., *E. coli, Klebsiella* species), *S. epidermidis*[b]
Closed head trauma	*S. pneumoniae, H. influenzae*
Open head trauma	*S. aureus*, gram-negative bacilli (e.g., *E. coli, Klebsiella* species)

[a] Organisms listed in descending order of frequency.
[b] Most commonly seen in association with prosthetic devices (e.g., cerebrospinal fluid shunts).

(e.g., *E. coli, Klebsiella pneumoniae*) also are isolated occasionally.[18,19,26] Furthermore, *L. monocytogenes* also is a problem pathogen in the elderly, especially in immunocompromised patients.[18,19,22,26,27]

Meningitis following neurosurgical procedures or open trauma to the head most often is caused by enteric gram-negative bacilli (predominantly *E. coli*, and *K. pneumoniae*), and to a lesser extent staphylococci, particularly *Staphylococcus aureus*.[1,20,27] Postneurosurgical meningitis occasionally may be caused by resistant pathogens such as *Enterobacter* species and *Pseudomonas aeruginosa*, often with devastating consequences.[20,28-30] In addition, patients requiring ventriculostomy or placement of CSF shunts can develop infections of these prosthetic devices by coagulase-negative staphylococci (e.g., *S. epidermidis*) or diphtheroids.[8,20] Closed-head trauma, particularly when associated with CSF rhinorrhea or otorrhea, can lead to pneumococcal meningitis or to a lesser extent *Haemophilus influenzae* meningitis.[20]

Pathogenesis and Pathophysiology

While many issues remain under investigation, the steps leading up to the development of meningitis and the underlying pathophysiologic processes involved have become more clearly understood.[2,4] In general, meningitis can develop from *hematogenous* spread of organisms (the most common mechanism), by *contiguous* spread from a parameningeal focus (e.g., sinusitis or otitis media), or by direct bacterial *inoculation* as occurs with head trauma or neurosurgery.

The list of pathogens causing bacterial meningitis is relatively short because only bacteria possessing certain virulence factors are capable of invading the meninges. Specifically, the presence of a polysaccharide capsule and other cell surface structures (e.g., pili) are necessary for bacteria to evade host defenses and gain entry into the subarachnoid space.[2-4] Once in CSF, virulence factors contained within the cell wall (e.g., lipopolysaccharide or endotoxin in the case of *H. influenzae*) initiate a complex cascade of events culminating in neurological damage.[2,3] These cell wall substances trigger release of various cytokines which act as mediators of the inflammatory response.[2–4]

Colonization of mucosal surfaces is a necessary first step in the pathogenesis of meningitis (see Figure 56.2).[3,4] The polysaccharide capsule and pili or fimbriae on the bacterial cell surface allow attachment to oro- or nasopharyngeal mucosa.[2–4] Secretion of protease enzymes that neutralize the protective activity of mucosal IgA, and intrinsic resistance to ciliary clearance mechanisms allow meningeal pathogens to adhere to, and penetrate through the epithelial surface and enter the intravascular space.[3] Presence of a capsule prevents binding by the alternative complement pathway and prolongs survival within the bloodstream.[3,4] Eventually, organisms achieve sufficient numbers such that invasion of the blood-brain barrier becomes possible. The exact mechanism of bacterial invasion of the blood-brain barrier is not well understood; however, bacteria probably adhere to cerebral capillary endothelia or perhaps the epithelium of the choroid plexus.[3,4]

Once bacteria gain entry into the CSF, host defenses are inadequate to contain the infection and bacteria replicate rapidly. Humoral immunity (both complement and immunoglobulin) essentially is absent within the CSF.[2–4] In addition, opsonic activity in CSF is negligible, and although leukocytosis ensues shortly after bacterial invasion, phagocytosis also is inefficient.[3,4] This relative immunodeficiency state, therefore, necessitates initiation of bactericidal therapy.[2]

Inflammation of the meninges is initiated by contents within the bacterial cell wall.[2–4] Specifically, gram-negative bacteria possess lipopolysaccharide, or endotoxin, and gram-positive bacteria contain teichoic acid in their cell walls. Release of lipopolysaccharide (or teichoic acid) induces production and secretion of inflammatory cytokines such as interleukin-1 (IL-1), interleukin-6 (IL-6), prostaglandin E_2, and tumor necrosis factor (TNF) from astrocytes, endothelial cells, and circulating monocytes.[3,4] These cytokines play an essential role in promoting the adherence of leukocytes to cerebral capillary endothelial cells and also facilitate the migration of leukocytes into the CSF.[2,3] Upon attachment to brain endothelium, leukocytes release toxic oxygen products which damage en-

dothelial cells causing increased pinocytotic activity, widening of tight junctions, and eventually increased blood-brain barrier permeability (see Figure 56.2).[2–4]

Inflammation of the blood-brain barrier allows the influx of albumin and consequently, vasogenic cerebral edema.[2,3] The brain edema combined with obstruction of CSF outflow increases intracranial pressure and alters cerebral blood flow.[3] Altered cerebral blood flow is a problem in that it often is coupled with a loss of cerebrovascular autoregulation. Hyper- or hypoperfusion of the brain secondary to increases or decreases in systemic blood pressure, respectively, ultimately may result in neuronal injury, cerebral ischemia, and irreversible brain damage.[3] Adjunctive corticosteroids can substantially reduce inflammation and subsequent neurological sequelae of meningitis.[2,5]

The inflammatory response in meningitis also can be aggravated by some antibiotics, notably penicillins and cephalosporins.[2,31] When the beta-lactam antibiotics lyse bacterial cell walls, large amounts of cell wall products are liberated early in the course of disease and these contents of bacterial cell walls amplify the inflammatory response.[31] The long-term benefits of beta-lactam therapy far outweigh such transient detrimental effects; however, use of less rapidly bacteriolytic agents may be of theoretical advantage.[2] The proinflammatory effect of beta-lactam antibiotics is attenuated by concomitant corticosteroid therapy.[2,5]

Neurologic sequelae develop in one-third to one-half of patients with bacterial meningitis.[32–34] The type and severity of neurologic complications vary with the specific infecting organism, the severity of the infection, and the susceptibility of the host. In children, pneumococcal meningitis carries the highest risk of permanent neurological sequelae, particularly sensorineural hearing loss.[6,34] In a long-term prospective study of 185 children with acute bacterial meningitis, permanent hearing loss occurred in 6%, 10.5%, and 31% of children with meningitis due to H. influenzae, N. meningitidis, and S. pneumoniae, respectively.[34] Although seizures are fairly common upon initial presentation, long-term epilepsy occurs in approximately 7% of patients.[32] Other important long-term complications include spastic paraparesis, behavioral disorders, and learning deficits.[32]

Diagnosis and Clinical Features

Clinical and Laboratory
Features of Bacterial Meningitis

1. S.C., an 11-month-old male, is brought to the emergency room (ER) by his mother with complaints of a fever of 102 °F, irritability, lethargy, and new onset of seizures. S.C. was in his usual state of good health until last night when he awoke crying. When S.C.'s mother went in to investigate, she noticed her son begin to stiffen up and rock back and forth in his bed. Being unable to arouse her son at that time, S.C.'s mother rushed him to the hospital. S.C.'s past medical history is noncontributory except for an episode of otitis media diagnosed 2 weeks ago and treated with oral amoxicillin suspension. His mother discontinued the amoxicillin after 5 days of treatment when she noticed S.C. developing diarrhea and what was described as a faint skin rash. S.C., his mother and father, and his 3-year-old brother recently moved to the U.S. S.C.'s vaccination history currently is unknown.

Upon physical examination S.C. was in marked distress having a temperature of 40 °C, a blood pressure (BP) of 90/60 mm Hg, and respiratory rate of 32 breaths/min. His weight upon admission was 10 kg. Upon neurologic examination, there was evidence of nuchal rigidity, and he was lethargic and difficult to arouse. Brudzinski's and Kernig's signs were positive. Upon head, eyes, ears, nose, and throat (HEENT) examination, S.C. was photophobic (he squinted severely when a light was shone

Fig 56.2 Schematic Summary of the Pathogenesis and Pathophysiology of Bacterial Meningitis Adapted from references 2 and 4.

in his eyes), but had no evidence of papilledema. There was slight erythema surrounding his right ear, with no purpuric lesions visible on the skin and no evidence of a rash. The remainder of S.C.'s examination was essentially normal.

Blood drawn for laboratory tests revealed the following: sodium (Na) 128 mEq/L, potassium (K) 3.2 mEq/L, chloride (Cl) 100 mEq/L, bicarbonate (HCO_3^-) 25 mEq/L, blood urea nitrogen (BUN) 16 mg/dL, serum creatinine (SrCr) 0.6 mg/dL, and serum glucose 80 mg/dL. A WBC count of 18,000 cells/mm³ with 95% polymorphonuclear cells (PMN) and 5% lymphocytes was present, while the hemoglobin (Hgb), hematocrit (Hct), and platelet count all were within normal limits. What clinical and laboratory features does S.C. display that are suggestive of meningitis? [SI units: Na 128 mmol/L; K 3.2 mmol/L; Cl 100 mmol/L; HCO_3^- 25 mmol/L; BUN 5.7 mmol/L; SrCr 53.04 μmol/L; serum glucose 4.44 mmol/L; WBC count 18 × 10⁹/L]

S.C.'s presentation contains many features typical of acute bacterial meningitis. For example, S.C. was in good health until he awoke at night and was confused and disoriented. When symptoms present abruptly and evolve quickly over a period of several hours, an acute bacterial process is a strong possibility.[35,36] S.C. has several predisposing factors for the development of meningitis (e.g., young age, a questionable vaccination history, a recent episode of inadequately treated otitis media).[1,33]

The clinical features of bacterial meningitis are summarized in Table 56.2.[1,6,20,35,36] The most common symptoms include the triad of fever, stiff neck (nuchal rigidity), and altered mental status.[1,6,35] When all three of these features are present, as is the case with S.C., meningitis should be strongly suspected. Other less commonly seen signs and symptoms include headache, photophobia (unusual intolerance to light), and focal neurologic deficits including cranial nerve palsies.[1,6,35,36] A positive Brudzinski's sign (reflex flexion of the hips and knees produced upon flexion of the neck when lying in the recumbent position), and Kernig's sign (pain upon extension of the hamstrings when lying supine with the thighs perpendicular to the trunk) provide physical evidence of meningeal irritation.[37] Brudzinski's and Kernig's signs both were positive in S.C. Seizures occur upon initial presentation in 15% to 30% of patients and may be either focal or generalized in nature.[1,6,32] S.C.'s rocking back and forth motion while being unarousable is consistent with a seizure. The presence of seizures or severely depressed mental status (i.e., obtundation or coma) generally are associated with a poorer prognosis.[1,6,32] Headache, nausea, vomiting, photophobia, and papilledema upon eye examination all suggest increased intracranial pressure.[6,35,36] When these symptoms or focal neurologic deficits are present, a computerized tomographic (CT) scan is recommended before lumbar puncture in order to rule out an intracranial mass.[6,35,36] Although controversial, brain herniation may occur when lumbar puncture is performed in such patients because of the pressure changes induced within the cranial vault.[38] As is clearly evident, S.C. has many of the clinical features associated with acute bacterial meningitis.

Table 56.2	Signs and Symptoms of Acute Bacterial Meningitis
Fever	Anorexiaᵇ
Nuchal rigidity (stiff neck)	Headache
Altered mental status	Photophobia
Seizures	Nausea and vomiting
Brudzinski's signᵃ	Focal neurologic deficits
Kernig's signᵃ	Septic shock
Irritabilityᵇ	

ᵃ See text for description of sign.
ᵇ Symptoms seen in infants with meningitis.

High fever, stiff neck, altered mentation, photophobia, positive Kernig's and Brudzinski's signs, and new onset of seizures all are consistent with bacterial meningitis. Furthermore, the low blood pressure (hypotension) and increased respiratory rate are characteristic findings in severe, life-threatening types of bacterial infection (e.g., septic shock, meningitis) and are likely the result of endotoxin release.

The signs and symptoms of meningitis differ in the very young and very old in comparison to older children and adults.[6,21,26,33] In neonates, signs of meningeal irritation may be absent and often fever, irritability, and poor feeding are the only symptoms manifested.[6,21] Fullness of the fontanelle in infants also may reflect raised intracranial pressure which occurs with meningitis.[6,34] S.C. is only 11 months old which makes accurate assessment of his mental status difficult. Irritability (crying), as was manifested by S.C., is an important finding which suggests an altered mental status.

In elderly patients, many of the classic signs of meningeal irritation are absent, and the disease presentation can be more subtle.[6,26,35] Therefore, given the grave consequences of a misdiagnosis, clinicians caring for infants and elderly patients must have a particularly high index of suspicion for meningitis.

Laboratory evaluation of meningitis should include serum chemistries and hemogram as well as a detailed examination of the cerebrospinal fluid.[6,12,35] The peripheral WBC count often is markedly elevated in acute bacterial meningitis, usually with a left shift evident on differential analysis; however, this finding is nonspecific and occurs in many acute inflammatory and infectious diseases. S.C. has a marked leukocytosis with a predominance of polymorphonuclear cells on differential examination. A low serum sodium value, which is present in S.C., is reflective of the syndrome of inappropriate antidiuretic hormone (SIADH), a frequent complication of acute bacterial meningitis.[4,6] SIADH is an important finding in meningitis in that, if present, SIADH contributes to a worsening of cerebral edema.[4,6]

The abrupt onset of S.C.'s clinical symptoms is consistent with an acute bacterial process. Fungal and viral etiologies for his meningitis seem less likely. Given his age (11 months) and the community-acquired nature of the infection, the most likely pathogens for meningitis are *H. influenzae*, *N. meningitidis*, and *S. pneumoniae*. The absence of petechiae or purpuric lesions argues against *N. meningitis* as the causative pathogen as this finding frequently is present with meningococcemia or meningococcal meningitis. S.C.'s recent history of inadequately treated otitis media makes infection with either *H. influenzae* or *S. pneumoniae* a more likely possibility. To make an accurate clinical and microbiologic diagnosis in S.C., it is necessary to obtain cerebrospinal fluid for analysis. Thus, a lumbar puncture is required as soon as possible.

Cerebrospinal Fluid Examination

2. The resident in the ER performs a lumbar puncture which yielded the following: opening pressure 300 mm CSF, CSF glucose 20 mg/dL, protein 250 mg/dL, WBC count 1200 cells/mm³ with 90% PMNs, 4% monohistiocytes, and 6% lymphocytes. The CSF red blood cell (RBC) count was 50/mm³. A stat Gram's stain of CSF revealed numerous WBCs, but no organisms. CSF, blood, and urine cultures are pending. What CSF findings in S.C. are consistent with a diagnosis of bacterial meningitis? [SI units: CSF glucose 1.1 mmol/L; protein 2.5 gm/L; WBC 1200 × 10⁶ cells/L; RBC 5 × 10⁶/L]

Careful examination of the cerebrospinal fluid is essential to confirm the diagnosis of meningitis.[12] Table 56.3 compares the typical findings in CSF obtained from patients with acute bacterial meningitis with those seen with fungal or viral etiologies.[6,17,35] In acute bacterial meningitis, the CSF is purulent, containing numer-

Table 56.3		CSF Findings in Various Types of Meningitis[a]		
Microbial Etiology	WBC Count (cells/mm^3)	Predominant Cell Type	Protein	Glucose
Bacterial	>500	PMN	Elevated	↓
Fungal	10–500	MN	Elevated	Variable
Viral	10–200	PMN or MN	Variable	Normal

[a] CSF = Cerebrospinal fluid; MN = Mononuclear cells; PMN = Polymorphonuclear neutrophils; WBC = White blood cell.

ous white blood cells (usually >500 cells/mm^3) with a predominance of PMNs, and often is turbid in appearance.[12,35] CSF protein nearly always is elevated, usually greater than 100 mg/dL, and the CSF glucose concentration is low, either less than 50 mg/dL, or less than 50% of a simultaneously obtained serum glucose value.[12,13] In contrast, CSF obtained in viral and fungal cases of meningitis usually is clear in appearance and characterized by a much lower WBC (<100 cells/mm^3) with a mononuclear or lymphocyte predominance.[17,35] While the CSF protein concentration often is elevated, it also may be normal, on occasion.[17] A variable effect is observed with CSF glucose.[17]

Although considered experimental at the present time, tumor necrosis factor concentrations in CSF are much higher in patients with bacterial meningitis compared to normal controls or patients with nonbacterial causes of meningitis.[3,39] TNF was elevated in 42 of 51 (82%) mostly adult patients with bacterial meningitis, and only was elevated in 5 of 78 (6%) of patients with nonbacterial meningitis.[39] The ability to detect elevated TNF in CSF is greatest early in the course of disease because TNF levels quickly revert to normal within a period of hours to a few days after the onset of infection. Given the good predictive value of this test (sensitivity 82%; specificity 96%), measurement of TNF eventually may become an important parameter for diagnosing and monitoring meningitis.[39]

Microbiologic Evaluation

Microbiologic evaluation should include examination of CSF by Gram's stain and culture as well as cultures obtained from other potential sites of infection (e.g., blood, sputum, urine).[6,35] The Gram's stain of the CSF is positive in over 50% of cases of acute bacterial meningitis and is an extremely useful test to help direct initial (empiric) antimicrobial therapy.[6,12,35] The presence of organisms on smear is indicative of a high bacterial inoculum (i.e., inoculum >10^5 colony forming units/mL) and is associated with more fulminant disease.[2] The absence of organisms on Gram's stain by no means rules out infection but does make selection of empiric therapy more difficult. S.C. has a negative Gram's stain which may be the result of previous antibiotic therapy or the early detection of disease. Given the negative CSF Gram's stain result, S.C. must receive antibacterial therapy broad enough to cover all pathogens associated with meningitis in his age group until results from his CSF culture are available (usually within 24 to 48 hours). CSF culture nearly always is positive in purulent meningitis and the presence of any organism in this normally sterile fluid must always be taken seriously.[6,35,40] In a few instances, particularly when prior antibiotic therapy has been given, CSF cultures are negative in a patient who clearly appears to have meningitis.[12,33,40] In this setting, newer diagnostic tests such as latex particle agglutination are available which reliably detect antigens of H. influenzae, S. pneumoniae, N. meningitidis, E. coli (K-1 capsular antigen), and group b streptococci in CSF.[39] Latex particle agglutination should be considered for S.C., especially if his cultures

fail to yield any growth. Finally, results from cultures of other sites such as the blood, urine, and sputum (when appropriate) can yield very useful microbiological information.[35,40]

Cerebrospinal fluid findings in S.C. also strongly support the diagnosis of bacterial meningitis. He has a markedly elevated opening CSF pressure, CSF leukocytosis (with a predominance of PMNs), an elevated cerebrospinal fluid protein concentration, and a depressed CSF glucose value. A small amount of red blood cells is present in cerebrospinal fluid which suggests contamination with peripheral blood caused by the traumatic nature of the lumbar puncture. Precise identification of the offending organism is not possible until CSF culture results are available.

Treatment Principles

Prompt institution of appropriate antimicrobial therapy is essential when treating meningitis.[35] When choosing antimicrobial therapy, a number of factors must be considered. First, antibiotics selected must penetrate adequately into CSF.[13,16,41] In addition, the regimen chosen must have potent activity against known or suspected pathogens and exert a bactericidal effect.[16,41,42]

Antimicrobial Penetration into the Cerebrospinal Fluid

Another important factor is that during purulent meningitis the number of bacteria in the CSF often is much higher than the standard inoculum of approximately 10^5 colony forming units/mL used in routine antimicrobial susceptibility testing.[16,42] As a result, extrapolation of in vitro sensitivity results to clinical efficacy is difficult, particularly for antimicrobials susceptible to an inoculum effect (i.e., an increase in MIC with an increase in inoculum size). Cefuroxime (Zinacef) for example, is affected by an inoculum effect against H. influenzae, and extended-spectrum penicillins (e.g., piperacillin and mezlocillin) are affected similarly by enteric gram-negative bacilli.[16,43] In addition, some antimicrobials (e.g., aminoglycosides, fluoroquinolones) have reduced bactericidal activity in the acidic milieu of purulent CSF.[16,42,44,45] For example, gentamicin has an MBC of 1 µg/mL against E. coli at a pH of 7.35, and a decrease in the pH to 7.0 results in an eightfold increase in MBC.[45] This may partially explain why aminoglycoside therapy of gram-negative bacillary meningitis is suboptimal, even when direct intrathecal therapy is given.[27,30]

The ability of antimicrobials to penetrate into CSF is affected by lipid solubility, degree of ionization, molecular weight, protein binding, and susceptibility to active transport systems operative within the choroid plexus.[13,16,44,46] In general, penetration of most antibiotics into CSF is increased when the meninges are inflamed. Although the optimum degree of CSF penetration has not been worked out entirely, experiments in the rabbit meningitis model indicate that bactericidal effects are maximal when CSF antibiotic concentrations exceed the MBC of the infecting pathogen by 10- to 30-fold.[16,42]

Table 56.4 summarizes the CSF penetration characteristics of various antimicrobials during acute bacterial meningitis.[13,14,41,44,47,48] Chloramphenicol, metronidazole, and trimethoprim are highly lipophilic compounds and penetrate into CSF extremely well, achieving high concentrations even when meningeal inflammation is absent.[13,41,48] Rifampin also has good CSF penetration and, because of this, often is combined with vancomycin for treatment of coagulase-negative staphylococcal infections in the CNS.[8,41,48] Because beta-lactams and aminoglycosides usually are ionized at physiologic pH, they are more polar and do not penetrate into CSF as well. Beta-lactams penetrate poorly when the meninges are intact; however, when the meninges are inflamed, most penicillins and the third-generation cephalosporins achieve

Table 56.4	CSF Penetration Characteristics of Various Antimicrobials[a]

Very Good[b]
Chloramphenicol, metronidazole, rifampin, TMP-SMX

Good[c]
Penicillins: Penicillin G, ampicillin, mezlocillin, nafcillin, piperacillin,
 ticarcillin
Other Beta-lactams: Aztreonam, clavulanic acid, imipenem, sulbactam
Cephalosporins: Cefepime, cefotaxime, ceftazidime, ceftizoxime,
 ceftriaxone, cefuroxime
Fluoroquinolones: Ciprofloxacin, ofloxacin

Fair to Poor[d]
Aminoglycosides: Amikacin, gentamicin, tobramycin
Other agents: Azithromycin, clarithromycin, clindamycin, erythromycin,
 vancomycin

> [a] CSF = Cerebrospinal fluid; TMP-SMX = Trimethoprim-sulfamethoxazole.
> [b] Penetrate CSF well regardless of meningeal inflammation.
> [c] Adequate CSF penetration achieved when the meninges are inflamed.
> [d] Penetration often inadequate even when the meninges are inflamed.

CSF concentrations sufficient to treat meningitis (≈10% to 30% of simultaneously obtained serum concentrations).[13,41,46-48] An additional factor working against maintenance of therapeutic CSF concentrations of beta-lactams is the active transport system of the choroid plexus which pumps these organic acids out of the CSF.[16]

The aminoglycosides have a low therapeutic index and adequate CSF concentrations are difficult to achieve with intravenous (IV) dosing alone without risking significant toxicity.[14,41] Furthermore, the acidic nature of purulent CSF reduces antimicrobial activity of the aminoglycosides.[45] Thus, when aminoglycoside therapy is initiated for adults with CNS infections, concomitant intrathecal therapy is required.[14,49] Direct instillation of aminoglycosides into the ventricles is preferred; however, this approach requires the surgical insertion of a reservoir (e.g., Ommaya reservoir) which often is not possible, particularly in the early stages of bacterial meningitis.[16,41] Thus, at the very least, patients requiring aminoglycosides for meningitis should receive daily intralumbar injections until clinical improvement is seen and CSF cultures are sterilized.[14,16]

The degree of serum protein binding correlates well with the extent of CSF penetration,[16,46] and this relationship for selected cephalosporin antibiotics is depicted in Figure 56.3.[46] Cefoperazone and ceftriaxone are highly bound to serum proteins and, as a consequence, are more confined to the intravascular space and not as readily available for CSF penetration as cefotaxime and ceftazidime which are protein bound to a lesser extent. Although cefoperazone penetrates the CSF inconsistently and is best avoided for meningitis,[47] ceftriaxone achieves sustained, reliable bactericidal activity within the CSF despite its high protein binding.[41,47] Ceftriaxone has been successful in the treatment of meningitis in both pediatrics and adults for many years.[5,47,50]

Vancomycin and polymyxin B do not diffuse well across the blood-CSF barrier primarily because of their large molecular size.[13,16,41,48] Therapeutic concentrations in CSF are attained with systemic vancomycin therapy when the meninges are inflamed; however, in selected circumstances, concomitant intralumbar or intraventricular therapy also may be necessary.[8,41] The commonly prescribed antimicrobials, clindamycin and erythromycin penetrate the CSF poorly,[13,41,48] and they have limited usefulness due to their bacteriostatic mode of action.

Finally, fluoroquinolones, such as ciprofloxacin and ofloxacin, penetrate reasonably well into CSF on a percentage basis (≈20% to 30%); however, the concentrations attained are fairly low

(≤1 µg/mL) when standard doses are administered.[41,44] Given the potential neurotoxicity of the quinolones and their reduced potency against gram-positive bacteria, these agents have limited usefulness in treating meningitis.

Empiric Therapy for Childhood Meningitis

3. What constitutes appropriate initial empiric therapy for childhood meningitis? What would be appropriate for S.C.?

Results from culture and sensitivity testing of cerebrospinal fluid take ≥24 hours to become available; therefore, empiric therapy must be instituted promptly to provide coverage of potential pathogens. The initial antimicrobial regimen should take into consideration the age of the patient, any predisposing conditions that might make the patient vulnerable to increased morbidity and mortality, results from CSF Gram's stain, history of allergy, and the presence of organ dysfunction. Table 56.5 gives recommendations for empiric antimicrobial therapy for acute bacterial meningitis.[4,6,19,35,36,49-51]

S.C. is 11 months old and has a negative CSF Gram's stain; therefore, therapy with a third-generation cephalosporin such as ceftriaxone (Rocephin) or cefotaxime (Claforan) is preferred. Either of these two agents will provide excellent coverage of the most likely pathogens in this age group (*H. influenzae, S. pneumoniae,* and *N. meningitidis*).[18,19,51] Of these three pathogens, *H. influenzae* is most likely given the uncertainty of S.C.'s vaccination status against *H. influenzae* type b. The recent episode of otitis media also implicates *H. influenzae* as well as *S. pneumoniae. N. meningitidis*, although possible, is less likely in the absence of common clinical features such as a petechial rash.[6,35] Thus, initiation of antibiotic therapy with ceftriaxone would be appropriate for S.C. at this time.

Use of a cephalosporin in this case is appropriate even though S.C. is questionably allergic (skin rash) to amoxicillin. Patients with penicillin allergy carry a 5% to 12% risk of cross-reactivity when cephalosporins are prescribed.[52] In this setting, the type of reaction to penicillin is important to consider.[52] Patients with a history of accelerated hypersensitivity reactions [e.g., hives, shortness of breath (SOB), or anaphylaxis] to penicillins should not be prescribed cephalosporins because the risk of cross-reactivity is too high. Conversely, a benign skin rash would not contraindicate use of a cephalosporin. If S.C. had experienced an accelerated reaction to penicillin, chloramphenicol would be the best alternative choice (see Table 56.5).[4,6,51]

Dosing Considerations

In general, therapy of meningitis requires the use of high doses of antimicrobials administered by the intravenous route. Table 56.6

Fig 56.3 Relationship Between Serum Protein Binding and CSF Penetration for Selected Cephalosporin Antibiotics Reproduced with permission from reference 46.

Table 56.5	Empiric Therapy for Bacterial Meningitis	
Age Group or Predisposing Condition	Recommended Therapy	Alternative Therapy
Neonates (<2 months)	Ampicillin and cefotaxime	Ampicillin and gentamicin
Infants and children (2 months–10 yr)	Cefotaxime[a] + vancomycin	Cefotaxime[a] + rifampin
Older children and adults (10–60 yr)	Cefotaxime[a] + vancomycin	Cefotaxime + rifampin
Elderly (>60 yr)	Ampicillin, cefotaxime,[a] and vancomycin	Ampicillin, cefotaxime, and rifampin
Postneurosurgical	Nafcillin and cefotaxime[a] ± gentamicin	Vancomycin and cefotaxime[a] ± gentamicin
Open head trauma	Nafcillin and cefotaxime[a]	Vancomycin and cefotaxime[a]

[a] Ceftriaxone is an acceptable alternative.

lists the recommended dosing regimens for treatment of CNS infections.[4,6,8,14,49,51,53] S.C. should receive ceftriaxone in a dose of 100 mg/kg/day given in one or two doses.[6,50,51] A ceftriaxone regimen of 500 mg intravenously every 12 hours is reasonable for S.C. The elimination half-life of ceftriaxone is long (usually between 6 to 8 hours) and once-daily dosing is feasible. Many clinicians, however, prefer to administer ceftriaxone on a twice-daily schedule[4,51] because the majority of published trials used the twice daily regimen, and such a schedule reduces the potential for prolonged periods of subtherapeutic CSF concentrations if a dose is delayed or inadvertently missed.[4] Nevertheless, the Food and Drug Administration (FDA) has approved use of the once-daily dosing regimen of ceftriaxone for treatment of pediatric meningitis.[54]

Adjunctive Corticosteroid Therapy

4. What is the rationale for adjunctive corticosteroid therapy in acute bacterial meningitis and why would it be appropriate for S.C.? How should dexamethasone be dosed and monitored for S.C.?

Corticosteroids are used for a wide variety of inflammatory conditions with varying results. Corticosteroids, particularly dexamethasone, can reduce cerebral edema and lower intracranial pressure;[55] however, early studies evaluating the efficacy of corticosteroids in bacterial meningitis failed to demonstrate any beneficial effects.[56,57] These studies were not designed very well, and importantly, hearing loss was not a routinely monitored complication. Given the recent elucidation of the pathophysiologic mechanisms of meningeal inflammation and the important role of cytokine mediators in this process, attention has been refocused on adjunctive corticosteroid therapy for meningitis.

The rationale for steroid therapy in meningitis stems from the fact that steroids reduce the synthesis and release of the proinflammatory cytokines TNF-α and IL-1β from monocytes and astrocytes.[3-5] These two cytokines play a central role in initiating the cascade of events leading to neuronal tissue damage and the development of neurological sequelae. Early use of steroids now has been shown in several studies to reduce neurologic complications, particularly sensorineural hearing loss.[5,58-61]

The efficacy and safety of adjunctive dexamethasone therapy were evaluated in two separate prospective, double-blind, placebo-controlled trials involving 200 infants and children with meningitis due primarily to *H. influenzae* type b.[5] Antibiotic therapy differed in the two studies and consisted of cefuroxime (100 patients; Study 1) and ceftriaxone (100 patients; Study 2). Dexamethasone (0.15 mg/kg IV Q 6 hr for 4 days) or matching saline placebo were administered 30 minutes to several hours following institution of antibiotics. After 24 hours of therapy, patients receiving dexamethasone showed a significant elevation in CSF glucose and reductions in CSF protein and lactate values compared to the placebo

recipients.[5] In addition, the number of days patients remained febrile was two times longer for placebo-treated versus dexamethasone-treated patients. There was no difference noted in the rate of CSF sterilization between the placebo and dexamethasone groups, indicating that steroid therapy did not adversely impair antibacterial activity.[5]

Moderate to severe hearing impairment occurred significantly less often in the dexamethasone-treated patients compared to saline controls (3% versus 15%, respectively; p <0.01).[5] Furthermore, hearing aids were required in a substantially higher percentage of patients randomized to the placebo group (14% versus 1%, respectively; p <0.001). The dexamethasone regimen was well tolerated: however, two patients developed gastrointestinal (GI) bleeding severe enough to require blood transfusion.[5]

A limitation of the above study design was that corticosteroid therapy was not begun until after antibiotic therapy was initiated. Experimental studies suggest that for optimum results, steroids should be started either just before, or coincident with, antimicrobial therapy.[3] To address the benefits of early dexamethasone therapy, another randomized, double-blind, placebo-controlled trial involving 101 infants and children with bacterial meningitis was undertaken.[59] All patients were treated with cefotaxime and the dexamethasone regimen employed was identical to the previous study. In this trial, the first dose of dexamethasone was given 15 to 20 minutes before starting cefotaxime. Compared to placebo treatment, patients receiving dexamethasone had lower opening cerebrospinal fluid pressures when measured at 12 hours, fewer days of fever, and significantly better Glasgow coma scores at 24 hours.[59] Furthermore, with dexamethasone treatment, CSF glucose, protein, and lactate values were much closer to being normal by 24 hours. Significantly higher numbers of placebo-treated patients developed neurologic sequelae such as ataxia, hearing loss, and seizures.[59] As in the previous study, moderate or severe hearing loss and requirement of a hearing aid occurred significantly more often in patients given placebo.

These studies taken together provide convincing evidence for the beneficial effects of adjunctive dexamethasone therapy. The risks associated with short-term (4 day) steroid therapy are low and are far outweighed by the benefit of a reduction in neurological complications. All children with bacterial meningitis, therefore, should receive concomitant dexamethasone therapy.[2,4,58] Thus, S.C. should receive dexamethasone therapy at a dose of 0.15 mg/kg given intravenously every six hours. For S.C., this would be 1.5 mg every six hours with the first dexamethasone dose given 15 minutes before initiating ceftriaxone therapy.

Although the vast majority of patients studied had disease due to *H. influenzae*, it is reasonable to assume that disease caused by other meningeal pathogens (e.g., pneumococci or meningococci) would respond similarly.[2,58,61] The benefit of corticosteroid therapy in adults has not been systematically studied, but an uncontrolled study suggests benefits similar to those observed in children.[61] Until more data are available, the utility of dexamethasone in adults with meningitis currently is unknown. In instances of overwhelming infection (as manifested by profoundly altered mental status), or when high bacterial inocula are present (as reflected by a positive CSF Gram's stain), dexamethasone therapy should be seriously considered.[2] For such patients, the risk of neurologic complications is much greater than the potential for adverse drug effects.

The efficacy of lower dexamethasone doses or a shorter treatment duration has not been well studied.[2,58,60] A placebo-controlled multicenter European study resulted in excellent drug tolerance with dexamethasone 0.15 mg/kg IV every 12 hours for just two days.[60] Similarly, a randomized trial involving 118 children with bacterial meningitis (primarily caused by N. meningitidis and H. influenzae) compared two days versus four days of therapy with dexamethasone (using a daily dose of 0.15 mg/kg IV Q 6 hr) and failed to detect any differences in clinical response, neurologic sequelae, or audiologic abnormalities between the two groups.[58] Although not statistically significant, there was a trend toward less GI bleeding in patients who were treated for only two days.[58] Because very few patients with pneumococcal meningitis were enrolled in the latter study, it is unclear whether a shorter course of dexamethasone is appropriate in such patients. Given the findings of these two well-designed trials,[58,60] it appears reasonable to treat S.C. with dexamethasone for a duration of two days.

Potential adverse effects associated with dexamethasone include GI bleeding, mental status changes (e.g., euphoria or encephalopathy), increases in blood glucose, and possibly elevations in blood pressure.[5,55-60] For S.C., the complete blood count (CBC), serum chemistries, and stool guaiac test should be monitored daily while he is receiving dexamethasone. He also should be questioned about possible gastrointestinal upset and assessed for changes in mental status (e.g., confusion, combativeness). Given the short duration of therapy (2 days) that S.C. is receiving, abrupt discontinuation of dexamethasone without tapering is appropriate when steroid therapy is completed.

Another issue to consider is whether dexamethasone, a potent anti-inflammatory agent, reduces the ability of some antimicrobials (e.g., the beta-lactams) to penetrate across the blood-brain barrier into cerebrospinal fluid. Since CSF penetration of the penicillins, cephalosporins, and other beta-lactams is greatest when the meninges are inflamed, there is a hypothetical concern that concomitant dexamethasone may reduce CSF concentrations of these agents resulting in reduced efficacy. Data to support or refute this hypothesis are limited. While LeBel et al. did not directly measure antibiotic concentrations in cerebrospinal fluid, the authors did not observe any significant differences in CSF bactericidal activity (a test in which CSF is serially diluted and tested for activity against the infecting pathogen) in steroid-treated versus placebo-treated children.[5] Furthermore, children given dexamethasone had similar, if not better, clinical responses (e.g., shorter duration of fever) than placebo controls,[5] and the rate of CSF sterilization was no different.[5,58,60]

Other adjunctive therapies aimed at reducing neurologic complications of meningitis currently under active investigation include NSAIDs, pentoxyfylline, and intrathecal monoclonal antibodies targeted at the lipopolysaccharide (i.e., Lipid A) region of

Table 56.6	Suggested Antibiotic Dosing Regimens for Treatment of Central Nervous System Infections[a]				
	Daily Dose[b]			Dosing Interval (hr)	
Antibiotic	Neonates[c]	Children	Adults	Neonates	Children/Adults
Penicillins					
Ampicillin	100–200 mg/kg	200–300 mg/kg	12 gm	8–12	4–6
Nafcillin	100–150 mg/kg	150–200 mg/kg	12 gm	8–12	4–6
Penicillin G	0.1–0.2 million units/kg	0.15–0.2 million units/kg	20–24 million units	8–12	4–6
Piperacillin	150-300 mg/kg	250–300 mg/kg	16–20 gm	8–12	4–6
Cephalosporins					
Cefotaxime	100–150 mg/kg	200 mg/kg	12 gm	8–12	4–6
Ceftizoxime	100–150 mg/kg	200 mg/kg	12 gm	8–12	6–8
Ceftriaxone	NR	100 mg/kg	4 gm	—	12–24
Ceftazidime	100–150 mg/kg	150–200 mg/kg	8–12 gm	8–12	6–8
Aminoglycosides[f]					
Gentamicin	5–7.5 mg/kg[d,e]	—	5–6 mg/kg[d,e]	12	8–12
Tobramycin	5–7.5 mg/kg[d,e]	—	5–6 mg/kg[d,e]	12	8–12
Amikacin	15–30 mg/kg[d,e]	—	15–25 mg/kg[d,e]	12	8–12
Chloramphenicol	NR	75–100 mg/kg	4–6 gm	—	6
Metronidazole	—	30 mg/kg	1.5–2 gm	—	6–8
TMP-SMX	—	12–15 mg/kg[g]	12–15 mg/kg[g]	—	8
Vancomycin	20–30 mg/kg	40–60 mg/kg[h]	2–3 gm[h] or 20–30 mg/kg[h]	12	8–12

[a] CNS = Central nervous system; NR = Not recommended for therapy; TMP-SMX = Trimethoprim-sulfamethoxazole.
[b] Recommended daily dose when renal and hepatic function are normal.
[c] Infants <1 month old; lower end of dosage range applies to neonates ≤7 days old.
[d] Dose should be individualized based upon serum level monitoring.
[e] Concurrent intrathecal therapy not recommended for neonatal meningitis.
[f] Concurrent intrathecal doses of 5–10 mg (gentamicin, tobramycin), or 20 mg (amikacin) often required when treating gram-negative bacillary meningitis.
[g] Dose is based upon the trimethoprim component.
[h] Concurrent intrathecal doses of 5–20 mg recommended if response to intravenous therapy is inadequate.

the gram-negative cell wall.[2,62,63] If results from clinical trials prove favorable, viable alternatives to corticosteroids eventually may exist. Until such a time, steroids remain the most useful means for reducing neurologic complications of meningitis and represent the only viable option for use in S.C.

Haemophilus influenzae Meningitis

Definitive Therapy

5. Twenty-four hours after admission, S.C.'s culture results from his blood and CSF samples are available. The CSF culture is growing *H. influenzae*, negative for beta-lactamase. *H. influenzae* (beta-lactamase-negative) also is present in both of 2 collected blood cultures. What modification in S.C.'s antimicrobial therapy is necessary at this time?

Once culture and sensitivity results become available, definitive therapy can be instituted, oftentimes with a single agent (see Table 56.7).[4,6,28–30,51] As suspected, S.C.'s CSF culture is positive for *H. influenzae*. An important concern when treating meningitis caused by this organism is whether the isolate produces beta-lactamase. Ampicillin is the drug of choice for beta-lactamase-negative strains. In contrast, beta-lactamase-producing strains are always resistant to ampicillin.[6,19] Approximately 30% of *H. influenzae* type b isolates causing meningitis in the U.S. produce beta-lactamase, although there is substantial geographic variability.[19] Either ceftriaxone or cefotaxime are recommended for beta-lactamase positive isolates because *H. influenzae* resistance to these agents is rare.[4,6,51]

Cefuroxime, a second-generation cephalosporin, also has activity against beta-lactamase-positive Hib; however, cefuroxime is less effective against this organism than third-generation cephalosporins.[43,64,65] In a prospective, randomized trial involving 106 children with acute bacterial meningitis, 12% of patients receiving cefuroxime had positive CSF cultures after 18 to 24 hours versus 2% of those who received ceftriaxone (p = 0.11), and 17% of cefuroxime-treated patients developed moderate to severe hearing loss compared to only 4% of those receiving ceftriaxone (p = 0.05).[64] Nearly identical findings to these also were noted in a retrospective analysis of four comparative trials of children treated with cefuroxime (159 patients) and ceftriaxone (174 patients) for bacterial meningitis.[65] The reason for the inferiority of cefuroxime relative to ceftriaxone most likely is related to reduced potency, and the presence of an inoculum effect (described above).[43]

Although the isolate causing meningitis in S.C. is negative for beta-lactamase, his questionable history of amoxicillin rash makes the use of ampicillin worrisome. Therefore, therapy previously begun with ceftriaxone should be continued.

Monitoring Therapy

6. What subjective and objective data should be monitored to evaluate efficacy and toxicity of treatment of patients with meningitis and what specifically should be monitored for S.C.?

The monitoring of patients with meningitis is similar in many respects to other infectious diseases. Clinical signs and symptoms attributable to the disease, such as fever, altered mental status, and stiff neck need to be checked periodically throughout the day and monitored for resolution. S.C. should have his temperature checked and his mental status assessed at least four times a day. Accurate assessment of S.C.'s mental status can be difficult because of his young age. His baseline level of mentation should be evaluated (e.g., whether he is awake and alert, or lethargic and difficult to arouse). If awake and alert, S.C. should be observed for irritability as this often is the only sign of altered mentation. S.C. should be questioned for orientation (i.e., asked if he knows where he is, what his name is, and whether he is able to recognize his mother or other

Table 56.7	Definitive Therapy for Bacterial Meningitis[a]	
Pathogen	**Recommended Treatment**	**Alternative Agents**
H. influenzae		
Beta-lactamase-negative	Ampicillin	Cefotaxime[b]
Beta-lactamase-positive	Cefotaxime[b]	Chloramphenicol
N. meningitidis	Penicillin G or ampicillin	Cefotaxime[b] or chloramphenicol
S. pneumoniae	*Penicillin-sensitive:*[c] Penicillin G or ampicillin	Cefotaxime[b] or chloramphenicol
	Intermediately penicillin-resistant:[c] Vancomycin + cefotaxime[b]	Cefotaxime[b] and rifampin
	Highly penicillin-resistant:[c] Vancomycin + cefotaxime ± rifampin	
S. agalactiae	Penicillin G or ampicillin + gentamicin	Cefotaxime[b] or chloramphenicol
L. monocytogenes	Ampicillin ± gentamicin	TMP-SMX
Enterobacteriaceae		
E. coli, Klebsiella species	Cefotaxime[b]	Piperacillin + gentamicin[d]
Enterobacter, Serratia species	TMP-SMX	Piperacillin + gentamicin,[d] or ciprofloxacin,[e] or imipenem[e]
P. aeruginosa	Ceftazidime + tobramycin[d]	Piperacillin + tobramycin, or ciprofloxacin,[e] or imipenem[e]
S. aureus		
Penicillinase-producing	Nafcillin or oxacillin	Vancomycin[d]
Methicillin-resistant (MRSA)	Vancomycin[d] ± rifampin	TMP-SMX[e] ± rifampin
S. epidermidis	Vancomycin[d] ± rifampin	TMP-SMX[e] ± rifampin

[a] TMP-SMX = Trimethoprim-sulfamethoxazole; MIC = Minimum inhibitory concentration.
[b] Ceftriaxone also may be used.
[c] Penicillin-sensitive strains defined as having MIC ≤0.1 µg/mL; intermediately resistant strains MIC >0.1–1.0 µg/mL; highly resistant strains MIC ≥2.0 µg/mL.
[d] Concomitant intrathecal therapy often required for optimal response.
[e] Limited experience or efficacy data for the agent against with this pathogen.

family members). In general, signs of clinical improvement should be evident within 24 to 48 hours for most uncomplicated cases of acute bacterial meningitis;[5,6,35,64] and the corticosteroid therapy that S.C. is receiving may accelerate the clinical response even further.[5,59]

S.C. also should undergo laboratory monitoring for his meningitis. A complete blood count with a differential examination, serum electrolytes (e.g., Na, K, Cl, bicarbonate), blood glucose, and renal function tests (e.g., BUN, SrCr) should be performed daily.

Abnormal electrolyte results may require monitoring more frequently than once a day. Laboratory abnormalities such as leukocytosis and hyponatremia, may take longer to normalize than clinical symptoms. If S.C. develops severe SIADH, as manifested by serum sodium values ≤120 mEq/L with altered mental status or seizures, fluid restriction and short-term (i.e., 6 to 12 hours) intravenous administration of 3% sodium chloride may be necessary.

CSF chemistries usually normalize after several days, although CSF protein may remain elevated for a week or more.[6,35] With effective therapy, the CSF culture usually is sterile after about 18 to 24 hours of therapy.[5,59,64] Delays in CSF sterilization are associated with a higher propensity for neurologic complications.[4,30] If S.C. responds to therapy in a straightforward manner, there is no need for him to undergo a repeat lumbar puncture. However, if the response is inadequate as evidenced by persistent fever, and/or deteriorating mental status, S.C. will require a repeat lumbar puncture to re-examine CSF parameters.[6,35]

In addition to monitoring therapeutic response, side effects of the antimicrobial regimen also need to be assessed frequently. Meningitis therapy requires high doses, making the likelihood of encountering adverse effects much greater. Currently, S.C. is being treated with ceftriaxone, a cephalosporin antibiotic. Beta-lactam antibiotics such as ceftriaxone frequently are used in meningitis therapy because of their high efficacy and excellent tolerance. Adverse effects most frequently associated with ceftriaxone include hypersensitivity reactions, mild pain and phlebitis at the injection site, and gastrointestinal complaints.[66] S.C. should be observed daily for the presence of a skin rash or evidence of an accelerated allergic reaction (e.g., hives, wheezing). The intravenous catheter site should be observed daily for any evidence of redness, tenderness, or pain upon palpation of the vein. S.C. should be watched closely for loose stools or diarrhea. While diarrhea is a common side effect of most antimicrobials, this adverse effect is more likely to occur with ceftriaxone given that approximately 40% to 50% of a dose is excreted unchanged into the bile. Mild diarrhea usually not requiring discontinuation of therapy occurs in 23% to 41% of children receiving ceftriaxone for meningitis therapy.[50,64] Less common, but of concern is the potential for antibiotic-associated colitis.[66,67] If S.C. experiences diarrhea which is persistent, particularly if accompanied by fever and abdominal cramping, he should have a stool sample tested for toxin to *Clostridium difficile*. If positive, oral therapy, preferably metronidazole, should correct the problem (see Chapter 60: Gastrointestinal Infections).

Ceftriaxone-Induced Biliary Pseudolithiasis

7. After 5 days of treatment, the nurse caring for S.C. notes that his appetite is markedly diminished and he complains of an upset stomach. Upon physical examination, S.C. was afebrile and alert and oriented. Examination of S.C.'s abdomen revealed "guarding," with pain localized in the right upper-quadrant area. Laboratory data at this time are: WBC count 6000 cells/mm³, Hgb 12.5 gm/dL, Hct 34%, platelets 120,000/mm³, Na 135 mEq/L, K 3.6 mEq/L, Cl 98 mEq/L, aspartate aminotransferase (AST) 35 U/L, alanine aminotransferase (ALT) 33 U/L, alkaline phosphatase 110 MU/dL, total bilirubin 1.2 mg/dL, and amylase 70 U/L. A stool guaiac is negative. What could be possible causes of S.C.'s abdominal discomfort? [SI units: WBC 6 × 10⁹ cells/L; Hgb 125 gm/L; Hct 0.34; platelets 120 × 10⁹/L; Na 135 mmol/L; K 3.6 mmol/L; Cl 98 mmol/L; AST 33 U/L; ALT 33 U/L; alkaline phosphatase 110 U/L; total bilirubin 20.5 μmol/L; amylase 70 U/L]

There are a number of possible etiologies for the abdominal discomfort that S.C. is experiencing. His corticosteroid therapy may have caused an acute GI bleed. This is unlikely given that the dexamethasone was discontinued three days ago and S.C.'s hemo-

globin and hematocrit values are in the low-normal range. If an acute GI bleed had occurred recently, these parameters would be expected to be much lower. The negative stool guaiac result also argues strongly against a GI bleed. Acute pancreatitis is unlikely given the normal amylase result. Viral or drug-induced hepatitis is another possibility, but is unlikely to be the cause of the pain given that the AST, ALT, and bilirubin results are within normal limits. An intra-abdominal process (e.g., bowel obstruction, infection) also is a possibility. Given that S.C. currently is afebrile and has a normal WBC count, a new infectious process seems improbable. Other causes such as acute cholecystitis or appendicitis require further diagnostic evaluation.

8. An abdominal ultrasound is performed on S.C. which reveals the presence of sludge in the gallbladder. What is the significance of this finding in S.C. and how should this abnormality be managed?

The abnormality on S.C.'s abdominal ultrasound provides an explanation for the right upper quadrant pain he is experiencing. S.C. has what appears to be a condition known as biliary pseudolithiasis (i.e., biliary "sludging"). Biliary sludging can occur in conditions of gallbladder hypomotility (e.g., recent surgery, burns, total parenteral nutrition), and in some instances can be drug-induced. S.C. has been receiving ceftriaxone for treatment of his meningitis, a drug which can cause biliary pseudolithiasis.[68-71]

Antibiotic-associated biliary pseudolithiasis is a unique adverse effect seen almost exclusively with ceftriaxone.[66] The predominance of biliary excretion which occurs with ceftriaxone results in very high concentrations of the drug in gallbladder bile.[68] In selected circumstances, the biliary concentration of ceftriaxone may exceed solubility limits resulting in formation a fine, granular precipitate (i.e., sludge).[68] The formation of sludge in gall bladder bile following ceftriaxone therapy differs in composition and ultrasonic features from true gallstones.[64,69] Studies performed *in vitro* reveal the precipitate to be composed of a ceftriaxone:calcium complex, the formation of which is dose dependent.[68,70] Given the high doses required for meningitis therapy, it is not surprising that this adverse effect has occurred in S.C.[64,69] In the comparative randomized trial between ceftriaxone and cefuroxime cited above, evidence of biliary pseudolithiasis on abdominal ultrasonography was observed in 16 of 35 (46%) patients who received ceftriaxone, and in none of 35 patients receiving cefuroxime.[64] Pseudolithiasis usually appears three to ten days following the start of therapy, and in the majority of instances is clinically asymptomatic. Symptoms similar to acute cholecystitis are evident in some individuals and include nausea with or without vomiting and abdominal right upper-quadrant pain. Although he has not vomited yet, S.C.'s symptoms fit this description. Approximately 10% to 20% of patients with evidence of biliary sludging on ultrasound display symptoms in association with this abnormality.[69,71]

Prompt recognition and discontinuation of ceftriaxone therapy is required to effectively manage biliary pseudolithiasis. Before this complication of ceftriaxone therapy was recognized, a few individuals underwent cholecystectomies. Such an intervention rarely, if ever, is necessary as the condition nearly always is reversible. Once S.C.'s ceftriaxone is discontinued, the condition should resolve gradually over a period of weeks to months. The clinical symptoms S.C. is experiencing should disappear within a few days.[69,71] Cefotaxime can be substituted for ceftriaxone given the lack of association of this agent with biliary complications and the equivalent efficacy of these two agents.[59,66] For S.C., the cefotaxime dose would be 500 mg IV every six hours (see Table 56.6). Chloramphenicol also could be considered. Although only bacteriostatic against most bacteria, chloramphenicol has bactericidal activity against the three common meningeal pathogens, *H. influenzae*, *S. pneumoniae*, and *N. meningitidis*.[6,16,30,72] Chloramphenicol has excellent CSF penetration and frequently was used before the commercial availability of third-generation cephalosporins.[6,35,72] Aplastic anemia, an extremely rare but potentially fatal complication of therapy, has served to drastically limit the use of chloramphenicol.[72] More commonly, dose-related bone marrow suppression occurs which can be minimized by maintaining peak serum concentrations of chloramphenicol below 25 µg/mL.[72] The recommended dose of chloramphenicol is 75 to 100 mg/kg/day given intravenously in four divided doses.[51]

Duration of Therapy

9. What is the recommended duration of antimicrobial therapy for *H. influenzae* meningitis and for how long should S.C. be treated?

The optimum duration of therapy for meningitis is difficult to ascertain because few trials have been designed to address this issue.[73] While general guidelines exist, the decision to discontinue therapy should be individualized based upon the response to therapy, presence of complicating factors (e.g., immunosuppression), and the specific causative pathogen. Table 56.8 lists the recommended treatment durations for uncomplicated cases of bacterial meningitis according to the specific pathogen.[6,51,53,73] Patients like S.C. with meningitis due to *H. influenzae* should be treated for seven to ten days.[51,73] Complicated cases such as those with delayed CSF sterilization require therapy for longer periods (up to 2 or more weeks).

S.C. had been responding well to the ceftriaxone therapy and if S.C. continues to respond well to the cefotaxime regimen outlined above, there is no need for additional oral antibiotics upon discharge from the hospital. It is doubtful that an oral second- or third-generation cephalosporin would achieve sufficient concentrations within the CSF to offer any benefit and such an approach might increase the risk of antibiotic-related side effects. S.C. should be watched carefully for a possible relapse (e.g., the reappearance of signs and symptoms of meningitis), which would require readmission to the hospital for further evaluation and intravenous antibiotic therapy.

Prevention of H. influenzae Type b (Hib) Meningitis

10. S.C. is ready to be discharged home. How can the potential spread of Hib disease be prevented in persons with whom S.C. has contact?

Chemoprophylaxis of Household Contacts. Despite an excellent response to therapy, S.C. still may harbor *H. influenzae* type b in his nasopharynx and could transmit this organism to individuals with whom he has close contact.[74] Chemoprophylaxis to reduce nasopharyngeal carriage of Hib, therefore, is indicated for S.C. and for contacts within his household.[74,75] In this context, a household contact is defined as someone who resides with or has spent ≥4 hours for at least five of the past seven days with S.C. preceding

the development of disease.[74] In households where contacts less than four years of age reside, chemoprophylaxis should be undertaken for all individuals who fit this definition regardless of age or immune status.[74,75] Children in this high-risk group (<4 years) are 100 to 600 times more likely to become infected with Hib than members of the general population.[75] Older persons with adequate immunity are at low risk of disease, but can become colonized with Hib and transmit the organism to other more susceptible individuals. S.C. has a three-year-old brother who is at risk for invasive Hib disease and should receive chemoprophylaxis. Also, the children of nurses or nursing students at the hospital who have been caring for S.C. also are at risk for acquiring the organism and may benefit from chemoprophylaxis. Because the risk of secondary disease is greatest in the period surrounding exposure, chemoprophylaxis should be instituted as soon as possible. Reduction of nasopharyngeal carriage of Hib is accomplished with rifampin given once daily in a dosage of 20 mg/kg/day (up to a maximum of 600 mg) for four days.[74,75] S.C. should be given rifampin 200 mg orally once daily for four days. A suspension containing 10 mg/mL of rifampin (which requires extemporaneous compounding) is required to deliver a 200 mg (20 mL) dose to S.C.

Hib Vaccination Recommendations. As stated previously, the vaccination status of S.C. is unknown and must be ascertained. If vaccination against Hib has not yet occurred, S.C. should receive one of the Hib protein conjugate vaccines promptly, despite his having an episode of invasive disease.[76] Despite an episode of meningitis, many children fail to develop an adequate antibody response to Hib.[74,76] Given the tremendous success that conjugated Hib vaccines have had on reducing the incidence of Hib meningitis in the U.S., all children more than two months of age should receive the vaccination series with one of the three commercially available products.[76] HbOC (HibTITER) is a product which links polyribosylribitol phosphate (PRP), the antigen derived from Hib purified capsular polysaccharide, with a carrier protein (CRM$_{197}$) derived from a mutated variant of the diphtheria toxin protein, while PRP-OMP (PedvaxHIB), links PRP with the outer membrane complex protein of *N. meningitidis*.[74,76] The third product, PRP-T (ActHIB), is a PRP-tetanus toxoid conjugate. The linkage of PRP with a carrier protein is necessary in order to elicit an adequate immune response in children less than 15 months of age.[74,77] HbOC and PRP-OMP have been licensed since 1988 and 1989, respectively. In 1990, both products received FDA approval for use in infants ≥2 months of age. PRP-T was approved for use in infants ≥2 months of age by the FDA in early 1993. All three of these conjugate vaccines are regarded as equally effective.[23,24,76,77] Table 56.9 outlines the vaccination schedule for HbOC, PRP-OMP, and PRP-T as recommended by the Centers for Disease Control Advisory Committee on Immunization Practices.[76] Because S.C. now is 11 months of age, he needs to be placed on a modified schedule consisting of two doses of vaccine at least two months apart, followed by a booster dose at 15 months of age. In general, the vaccines are well tolerated with fever, redness, and swelling at the injection site being the most frequent adverse effects (seen in <4% of patients).[24,74,77]

Streptococcus pneumoniae Meningitis

Clinical Features, Predisposing Factors, and Diagnosis

11. A.L., a 56-year-old male with a long history of alcohol abuse, is admitted to the ER febrile and unresponsive. Over the past several days, A.L. has experienced intermittent episodes of fever, chills, with SOB and a worsening productive cough. A friend came to visit A.L. today and, upon finding him unarousable, called 911. After reviewing his old medical records, it is noted that A.L. suffers from hypertension, adult-

Table 56.8	Duration of Therapy for Bacterial Meningitis[4,35,49,73]	
Etiology		**Duration of Therapy (days)**
H. influenzae		7–10
N. meningitidis		7
S. pneumoniae		10–14
Group B streptococci (*S. agalactiae*)		14–21
L. monocytogenes		14–21
Gram-negative bacilli		14–21

Table 56.9	Recommended Vaccination Schedule for *Haemophilus influenzae* Protein Conjugated Vaccines				
	Schedule				
Vaccine (Trade Name)	2 Months	4 Months	6 Months	12 Months	15 Months
HbOC (HibTITER)	Dose 1	Dose 2	Dose 3	—	Booster
PRP-T (ActHIB)	Dose 1	Dose 2	Dose 3	—	Booster
PRP-OMP (PedvaxHIB)	Dose 1	Dose 2	—	Booster	—

onset diabetes mellitus, peptic ulcer disease (PUD), and chronic obstructive airways disease (COAD). A splenectomy was performed 10 years ago following trauma to the abdomen. A.L. is divorced and lives alone in a low-income apartment. He has no known drug allergies. His records show him to be a smoker for over 30 years. Current medications include hydrochlorothiazide 50 mg PO QD, sustained-release theophylline (Theodur) 300 mg PO TID, glipizide 5 mg PO BID, famotidine 20 mg PO HS, and ciprofloxacin 250 mg PO BID PRN cough and increased sputum production.

Upon admission to the ER, A.L. had a temperature of 40 °C, BP of 90/50 mm Hg, and pulse and respiratory rates of 115 beats/min and 25 breaths/min, respectively. His weight is 59 kg. A.L. was unresponsive but withdrew all extremities to painful stimuli. His pupils were equal and sluggishly reactive to light; papilledema and evidence of meningismus were present. Wheezes and crackles were heard throughout both lung fields with dense consolidation noted in the left lower lobe. The remainder of his physical examination was noncontributory.

Stat laboratory tests revealed a WBC count of 18,000 cells/mm^3 (with 80% PMNs, 15% bands, 3% lymphocytes, and 2% basophils), Hgb and Hct of 10.5 gm/dL and 33 gm/dL, respectively, and a platelet count of 250,000/mm^3. Serum chemistries were significant for a K of 3.0 mEq/L; glucose of 250 mg/dL; AST and ALT of 190 mg/dL and 140 mg/dL, respectively; BUN of 35 mg/dL; and SrCr of 2.4 mg/dL. The prothrombin time was high normal and an albumin was 3.1 mg/dL. A stat blood alcohol level of 100 mg/dL was reported, and a urine toxicology screen was negative. A.M.'s serum theophylline concentration was 18 mg/dL. Also of note, a stool guaiac test was positive.

A CT scan showed no evidence of mass lesions or cerebral hematoma. Lumbar puncture yielded the following: CSF opening pressure 200 mm Hg, protein 120 mg/dL, glucose 100 mg/dL, WBC count 8500 cells/mm^3 (92% PMNs, 4% mono-histiocytes, and 4% lymphocytes), and RBC count 400/mm^3. Gram-positive, lancet-shaped diplococci were visible on CSF Gram's stain. In addition, a sputum Gram's stain revealed numerous WBCs, few epithelial cells, and numerous gram-positive cocci in pairs, and short chains. Blood, CSF, urine, and sputum cultures are pending. What are the clinical and laboratory features of pneumococcal meningitis? What features of pneumococcal meningitis are present in A.L.? [SI units: WBC 18 × 10^9 cells/L with 0.8 PMNs, 0.15 bands, 0.03 lymphocytes, and 0.02 basophils; Hgb 105 gm/L; platelets 250 × 10^9/L; K 3.0 mmol/L; glucose 13.9 mmol/L; BUN 12.5 mmol/L urea;SrCr 212 μmol/L; glucose 5.5 mmol/L; WBC 8500 × 10^6 cells/L; RBC 400 × 10^6/L]

A.L. presents to the emergency room with many signs and symptoms suggestive of pneumococcal meningitis. A.L. is 56 years old and *S. pneumoniae* is the most common bacterial etiology for meningitis in adults over 30 years of age (see Table 56.1).[18,19] As is evidenced by A.L.'s presentation, invasive pneumococcal disease frequently is associated with significant morbidity, and mortality rates remain high.[19] Over the past several years, the incidence of *S. pneumoniae* meningitis in the U.S. has ranged consistently from 1.2 to 2.8 cases per 100,000 population per year.[18,19,23] Predisposing factors to invasive pneumococcal disease include ad-

vanced age, alcoholism, chronic pulmonary disease, and sickle cell disease.[6,35,74] In addition, individuals infected with the human immunodeficiency virus (HIV), those with Hodgkin's disease, and patients who have undergone kidney, liver, or bone marrow transplantation also appear to be at higher risk.[6,74,78,79] Patients with CSF otorrhea or rhinorrhea induced by closed head trauma or neurosurgical procedures are more prone to develop pneumococcal meningitis as well.[20,74,79]

A.L. has many predisposing factors of pneumococcal meningitis. He is of low socioeconomic status, has a long history of alcohol abuse, has had a splenectomy, and suffers from diabetes and COAD. Underlying COAD is an important predisposing factor in that chronic colonization with pneumococci occurs in such patients. Intermittent use of ciprofloxacin by A.L. for acute exacerbations of COAD is unjustified. The poor activity of this antibiotic against *S. pneumoniae* is likely to select out for infection due to this organism. Furthermore, ciprofloxacin can increase serum theophylline concentrations via inhibition of metabolism: another important reason why this agent is not a good choice.[80]

A diagnosis of pneumococcal meningitis in A.L. is supported by the high fever, stiff neck (meningismus), and altered mental status. He is unresponsive which is a definite negative prognostic factor.[1,6] Results from CSF chemistries and microbiologic analysis are highly suggestive of pneumococcal meningitis. A.L. has an elevated opening CSF pressure with a markedly elevated CSF protein and WBC count (and notably a predominance of neutrophils on differential examination). The seemingly normal CSF glucose (100 gm/dL) is misleading because A.L. is a diabetic. The calculated ratio of CSF to serum glucose for A.L. is less than 50% which is consistent with acute bacterial meningitis (see Table 56.3). The presence of gram-positive, ''lancet shaped'' diplococci in pairs on the cerebrospinal fluid Gram's stain strongly supports the diagnosis of pneumococcal disease. The signs and symptoms of pneumococcal pneumonia (cough, SOB, increased sputum production, and pulmonary consolidation), as well as the sputum Gram's stain result also lend support for a diagnosis of invasive pneumococcal infection.

Empiric Therapy in Adults

12. What empiric therapy is appropriate for A.L. at this time?

Until culture results are available, the recommended antibiotic in this situation is penicillin G (see Table 56.5).[4,6,35] The dose usually is 20 to 24 million units/day in adults with normal renal function (see Table 56.6). However, A.L. has renal impairment which requires that he receive a reduction in penicillin dosage. One of the most useful methods for dosing penicillin G in renal compromise is by use of the following equation:[81]

$$\frac{\text{Dose}}{\text{(in million units/day)}} = \left(\frac{\text{Calculated Creatinine Clearance}}{7} \right) + 3.2$$

This equation should be used only when the calculated creatinine clearance is less than 40 mL/minute.[81] For A.L., who has a calculated creatinine clearance of 30 mL/minute (according to the method of Cockcroft and Gault), the daily dose would be approximately 8 million units/day, or 2 million units given every six hours. This revised regimen should provide penicillin serum concentrations similar to those achieved with high-dose therapy when kidney function is normal. Failure to appropriately adjust the dosage is equivalent to providing "massive" doses of penicillin which may result in hyperkalemia (if the potassium-containing preparation is used), and possibly seizures or encephalopathy.[81]

In patients unable to tolerate penicillin G, the best alternatives are ceftriaxone or cefotaxime (see Table 56.5).[4,6] First-generation cephalosporins (e.g., cefazolin) have good activity against pneumococci, but limited CSF penetration makes these agents poor choices for therapy.[41,47] Conversely, the third-generation agent, ceftazidime, penetrates well into CSF, but its usefulness is limited by reduced activity against pneumococci in comparison to other third-generation agents.[46,47] Cefuroxime also has good pneumococcal activity, but as previously mentioned, is inferior to ceftriaxone and cefotaxime.[64] Vancomycin has more limited and variable CSF penetration as well as the possibility of ototoxicity or nephrotoxicity.[41,82] Therefore, vancomycin should be reserved for situations of resistance or penicillin intolerance. Trimethoprim-sulfamethoxazole has excellent CSF penetration characteristics and is active against many (but not all) strains of S. pneumoniae; however, limited experience exists with this product for treatment of pneumococcal meningitis.[41,83]

Corticosteroid Therapy for Adult Meningitis

13. Why should A.L. receive corticosteroid therapy in addition to his antibiotic therapy?

The issue of adjunctive corticosteroid therapy for A.L. needs to be addressed. As previously stated, the efficacy of dexamethasone in adults with meningitis has not been studied adequately.[2] With this in mind, clinicians must weigh the potential benefits of steroids against the risk associated with this form of therapy. Clearly, A.L. presents with profoundly altered mental status, and signs and symptoms consistent with a fulminant course of disease. Given that he is unarousable, hypotensive, and tachycardic, A.L. likely will be admitted to the intensive care unit. Thus, his age, underlying medical problems, and deteriorating clinical status all point to a poor prognosis and argue for the use of adjunctive dexamethasone. Conversely, A.L. is diabetic and has an elevated glucose concentration. He also suffers from peptic ulcer disease, which may be active given that he is anemic and has a positive stool guaiac result. High-dose dexamethasone therapy may cloud A.M.'s sensorium making mental status assessment more difficult. Although each of these latter issues are a concern, none appear to be so critical as to preclude the use of corticosteroids.[2] Therefore, dexamethasone given in a dose of 8 mg (≈0.15 mg/kg) intravenously every six hours should be instituted before starting penicillin G therapy and continued for up to four days, provided that the diagnosis of bacterial meningitis is confirmed. To control blood glucose, a sliding scale dosing schedule of regular insulin is recommended. A.L.'s peptic ulcer disease should be properly worked up and treated if necessary.

Treatment of Penicillin-Resistant Pneumococcal Meningitis

14. Results from A.L.'s CSF, blood, and sputum cultures now are available and are positive for S. pneumoniae at each site. Sensitivity testing in CSF revealed an MIC of 1.0 μg/mL to penicillin, 0.5 μg/mL to cefotaxime and ceftriaxone, 0.25 μg/mL to vancomycin, and 8 μg/mL to chloramphenicol. How is penicillin-resistant pneumococcal meningitis treated and what therapy is indicated for A.L.?

Unfortunately, A.L. has become infected with a strain of S. pneumoniae that is resistant to penicillin. Resistance among pneumococci to penicillin G has become an important concern worldwide and in the U.S.[2,25,84] For this reason, susceptibility testing is now recommended to be performed on all pneumococcal isolates obtained from sterile sites (e.g., blood, CSF).[2,84] For treatment of meningitis caused by strains relatively resistant to penicillin (defined as an MIC between 0.1 and 1.0 μg/mL), either ceftriaxone or cefotaxime are the most useful agents because many of these isolates retain cephalosporin sensitivity.[2,8,85] Management of invasive pneumococcal infections in sites other than CSF (e.g., lungs, bloodstream) usually can be accomplished by increasing the dose of penicillin G to 20 to 24 million units/day. This approach is not possible with meningitis caused by relatively resistant strains, because further increases in the penicillin dose are likely to produce unacceptable neurotoxicity. Vancomycin and chloramphenicol are potential options; however, relapses and clinical failures have been reported with both of these agents when given alone.[84,86,87] As can be seen in A.L., many penicillin-resistant pneumococcal isolates also are resistant to chloramphenicol (defined as an MIC >4 μg/mL) and even against susceptible isolates, chloramphenicol may fail to elicit a bactericidal effect.[2,84,86,87] Third-generation cephalosporins cannot be relied upon for treatment of meningitis caused by strains fully resistant to penicillin (MIC ≥2.0 μg/mL), because reduced cephalosporin sensitivity frequently occurs (MICs range from 2 to 8 μg/mL to both cefotaxime and ceftriaxone). As a result, breakpoints for cephalosporin susceptibility to S. pneumoniae in cerebrospinal fluid have been revised. By the new criteria, strains with MICs ≤1 μg/mL to cefotaxime or ceftriaxone are considered sensitive, and MICs ≥2 μg/mL are defined as resistant.[88] Reduced activity of ceftriaxone and cefotaxime against penicillin-resistant pneumococci affects the therapeutic ratio achieved in CSF and is the likely explanation for reports of clinical failures.[84,85] Optimum therapy for fully penicillin-resistant pneumococcal meningitis presently is unclear. Vancomycin alone in high dosage (3 to 4 gm/day in adults) has been suggested.[2,84,86] The combination of vancomycin and ceftriaxone is superior to either agent given alone in a rabbit model of penicillin-resistant pneumococcal meningitis.[89] Ceftriaxone or vancomycin combined with rifampin also may be superior to either drug given alone.[84,86] Thus, until more information is available, the combination of ceftriaxone or cefotaxime with vancomycin represents the most reasonable approach to therapy for penicillin-resistant pneumococcal meningitis.

A.L. has pneumococcal meningitis due to a strain that is relatively resistant to penicillin G. Thus, penicillin G must be discontinued, and given the sensitivity results described above, cefotaxime or ceftriaxone should be started immediately. Ceftriaxone 2 gm given intravenously every 12 hours is a reasonable choice for A.L. It is not necessary to combine rifampin or vancomycin with ceftriaxone because the isolate is very sensitive to ceftriaxone. However, if he fails to respond to this regimen within 24 to 48 hours, combination therapy should be reconsidered.

Prevention of Meningitis

15. Should A.L. receive pneumococcal vaccine? How effective is vaccination in preventing invasive pneumococcal disease?

The pneumococcal vaccine (Pneumovax 23, Pnu-Immune 23) provides protection against invasive pneumococcal disease.[74,75,79] The vaccine is composed of purified capsular polysaccharide antigens of 23 serotypes of S. pneumoniae which are responsible for causing approximately 88% of the bacteremic pneumococcal disease in the U.S.[74,79] Individuals like A.L. who are at high risk for pneumococcal infection should be given the vaccine. Persons with chronic cardiopulmonary diseases, diabetes, alcoholism, cirrhosis, CSF leaks, asplenia, and those over 65 years of age should be vaccinated with the pneumococcal vaccine.[79] Immunocompromised patients such as those with Hodgkin's disease, lymphoma, multiple myeloma, chronic renal failure, patients who have undergone organ transplantation, and HIV-infected individuals also are at high risk for pneumococcal disease and should receive the vaccine.[79] Unfortunately, immunocompromised patients often fail to mount an immune response sufficient to fully protect against infection.[74,79,90] Patients with asymptomatic HIV disease respond more favorably to the vaccine than those with advanced acquired immunodeficiency syndrome (AIDS).[90] The antibody response in children less than two years of age also is poor or absent and the vaccine is not recommended for these young children.[74] Thus, given his underlying medical condition (splenectomy) and history of alcoholism, A.L. should receive the pneumococcal vaccine. A single dose is all that is required; subsequent doses may be necessary in five or more years.

Gram-Negative Bacillary Meningitis

16. R.R., a 40-year-old, 80 kg male, is admitted to the hospital for a cervical laminectomy with vertebral fusion. His surgical procedure was complicated by a dural tear. On the 3rd postoperative day, drainage at his surgical excision site was noted and R.R. was febrile to 38.2 °C. A Gram's stain of the drainage revealed few gram-positive cocci and moderate gram-negative bacilli. Therapy with IV cefazolin 1 gm Q 8 hr was begun. The following morning, R.R. was oriented to person, place, and time, but was slightly obtunded and had a temperature of 40 °C. Neck stiffness could not be assessed because of his recent surgery. A magnetic resonance imaging (MRI) scan of the head and neck was negative, and lumbar puncture yielded a CSF WBC count of 3000 cells/mm³ (95% PMNs), glucose 20 mg/dL, and protein 280 mg/dL. CSF Gram's stain showed numerous large gram-negative rods. What important clinical and laboratory features of gram-negative bacillary meningitis are manifested by R.R.? [SI units: WBC 3 × 10⁹ cells/L; glucose 1.11 mmol/L; protein 2.8 gm/L]

Epidemiology

R.R. has developed gram-negative meningitis as a complication of his recent neurosurgical procedure. Although gram-negative bacilli do not cause meningitis nearly as often as *H. influenzae*, *S. pneumoniae*, and *N. meningitidis*, they remain important pathogens both in the community and hospital setting.[1,18,19,27,30,53] During an eight-year period covering 1972 to 1979, 158 cases of gram-negative bacillary meningitis were reported to the New York City Health Department, or approximately 20 cases per year for the population of eight million.[27] Of 493 episodes of meningitis occurring over a 27-year period (1962 to 1988), at the Massachusetts General Hospital, enteric gram-negative bacilli accounted for 33% of all nosocomial episodes, and 3% of community-acquired cases.[1] Historically, mortality rates from gram-negative bacillary meningitis have been extremely high, ranging from 40% to 70%; however, with the availability of newer antimicrobials such as third-generation cephalosporins, fatalities have declined to less than 40%.[18,27,30,53] Increasing resistance among certain gram-negative bacilli, such as *Enterobacter* species and *Pseudomonas aeruginosa*, present a therapeutic dilemma in that mortality associated with these pathogens is high and therapeutic options are fewer.[28,29]

Predisposing Factors

Individuals at greatest risk for gram-negative bacillary meningitis include neonates, the elderly, and debilitated individuals, patients with open trauma to the head, and individuals like R.R. undergoing neurosurgical procedures.[18–20,27,53] Although meningitis is a rare complication of clean neurosurgical procedures (e.g., craniotomy, laminectomy), the consequences can be devastating when it does happen.[1,20,91]

Microbiology

E. coli and *K. pneumoniae* are the most common gram-negative bacteria causing meningitis and comprise about two-thirds of all cases.[30,53,91] *E. coli* is the most common gram-negative etiology of neonatal meningitis, while *K. pneumoniae* is isolated more often in the adult population.[21,30,53,91] The remaining one-third of cases are divided evenly among *Proteus*, *Serratia*, *Enterobacter*, and *Salmonella* species, *P. aeruginosa*, and other less commonly encountered bacilli.[30,53,91]

Clinical Features

In general, clinical laboratory features of gram-negative bacillary meningitis are similar to other types of bacterial meningitis.[21,35,53,91] Because of high virulence, gram-negative bacillary meningitis often is a fulminant, rapidly progressive disease. An exception to this rule is meningitis following neurosurgery.[20] As is evidenced by R.R.'s clinical presentation, postneurosurgical gram-negative bacillary meningitis can present in a more subtle fashion. In such patients, many of the symptoms of meningitis (e.g., altered mental status, stiff neck) are masked by underlying neurological disease. Thus, a high index of suspicion is warranted in the postsurgical setting. In addition to gram-negative bacilli, staphylococci also are associated with postneurosurgical meningitis.[20] The presence of what looks like staphylococci on R.R.'s wound drainage fluid is of concern; however, the abundance of gram-negative rods on his CSF Gram's stain supports the latter as being the most likely causative pathogen.

Treatment of Gram-Negative Bacillary Meningitis

17. What would be appropriate therapy for gram-negative bacillary meningitis in R.R.?

Fewer choices are available for treatment of gram-negative bacillary meningitis than for other meningitides. Ampicillin is active only against *E. coli*, *P. mirabilis*, and *Salmonella* species, but low potency and a high likelihood of resistance severely limit its use.[30,53,91] Chloramphenicol has broad gram-negative activity (except against *P. aeruginosa*) but is only bacteriostatic in activity against enteric bacilli.[30] Chloramphenicol treatment of gram-negative bacillary meningitis historically has been associated with excessively high mortality.[27,30,53,91] Aminoglycosides are limited by the inability to achieve therapeutic CSF concentrations, as well as reduced activity in the acidic milieu of purulent CSF.[14,16,30,49] Intrathecal administration allows therapeutic CSF concentrations to be achieved; however, repeated administration often is complicated by painful arachnoiditis, and even with this approach, mortality rates are high (>40%).[14,53] Extended-spectrum penicillins (e.g., piperacillin) are active against most gram-negative rods but require combination therapy with aminoglycosides for optimum results.[53] By far, the third-generation cephalosporins represent the most useful group of agents for treating gram-negative bacillary meningitis given their high potency against many enteric gram-negative bacilli and good CSF penetration. Experience with these agents spanning over a decade has a resulted in the third-generation cephalosporins becoming the drugs of choice for gram-negative bacillary meningitis.[4,30,92]

Empiric therapy for R.R. should include a third-generation cephalosporin such as cefotaxime, ceftriaxone, or ceftazidime (see Table 56.5).[4,20,51] These three have excellent activity against *E. coli* and *K. pneumoniae* and are active against other enteric gram-negative bacilli as well.[30,92] Ceftazidime is the only agent active against *P. aeruginosa* and is the drug of choice in this setting (see Table 56.7).[4,29,46] Resistance to third-generation cephalosporins among species of *Enterobacter, Citrobacter,* and *Serratia* is problematic such that these drugs cannot be relied upon for the treatment of meningitis caused by these pathogens.[28–30,92] With this in mind, empiric therapy of gram-negative meningitis in situations where resistance is more likely to be encountered (e.g., nosocomial or postneurosurgical meningitis) also should consist of an aminoglycoside [both IV and intrathecal (IT)], at least until susceptibility results become available. Of the third-generation cephalosporins currently available, the most experience has been accumulated with cefotaxime.[30,92,93] Success rates of over 80% have been documented with cefotaxime, primarily for gram-negative bacillary meningitis due to *E. coli* or *K. pneumoniae.*[30,92,93] Ceftriaxone has comparable efficacy to cefotaxime and is considered a good alternative.[30] Ceftizoxime penetrates CSF to about the same extent as cefotaxime and has virtually the same spectrum of activity, but published experience with this agent is limited.[30,94] Nonetheless, there is no compelling evidence to suggest that ceftizoxime is inferior to cefotaxime or ceftriaxone, and, therefore, it represents another therapeutic option. Cefoperazone should not be considered for gram-negative bacillary meningitis because of erratic CSF penetration, and inferior potency in comparison to the other third-generation cephalosporins.[30,47]

For R.R., cefazolin should be discontinued, and treatment with cefotaxime (3 gm IV Q 6 hr) should be instituted. The choice of cefotaxime for empiric therapy is appropriate while waiting for results from culture and sensitivity testing. Until these results are available, combination therapy with cefotaxime and an aminoglycoside (gentamicin) is warranted. The dose of intravenous gentamicin should be designed to achieve high peak serum concentrations (i.e., >6 µg/mL) while maintaining trough concentrations below 2 µg/mL (see Table 56.6). To assure optimum concentrations of gentamicin in CSF, a 5 to 10 mg intrathecal dose of gentamicin also must be administered daily until clinical improvement is noted.[13,14,53] Gentamicin is commercially available in a 2 mg/mL, preservative-free solution for intrathecal use. Thus, R.R. should receive a 5 mg intrathecal dose administered in a total volume of 2.5 mL. The most practical way to provide intrathecal gentamicin to R.R. is by performing a lumbar puncture each day and administering the drug by intralumbar injection. This also will allow daily sampling of CSF for monitoring purposes and repeat culturing. While intraventricular administration of gentamicin ideally would be the most effective approach, insertion of a ventricular reservoir (e.g., Ommaya reservoir) is not appropriate at this time given that R.R. just recently has undergone major spinal surgery, and it is not clear yet whether prolonged therapy is required.

It is important to make the distinction between aminoglycoside therapy for gram-negative bacillary meningitis in neonates versus adults. In adults, results from clinical trials support the use of combined intravenous and intrathecal therapy for reasons described above.[30,53] In neonates, however, combined intraventricular and intravenous gentamicin produces higher mortality rates than intravenous gentamicin alone.[95] The reason for the poor clinical outcomes associated with direct instillation of gentamicin into ventricular fluid is unclear. Initially, the increased mortality was attributed to increased trauma related to repeated insertion of the intrathecal needle into the infant's fontanelle. More recent evidence suggests that the direct intraventricular injection of aminoglycoside can cause an abrupt release of inflammatory cytokines (TNF and IL-1) from mononuclear cells that could have led to enhanced neurological sequelae.[96] Whatever the reason, intraventricular and intrathecal therapy should not be given to neonates

with gram-negative bacillary meningitis (see Tables 56.5 and 56.6)[51] without due consideration of this increased risk.

Treatment of Enterobacter Meningitis

18. Culture results from R.R.'s wound drainage and CSF both are positive for *E. cloacae*. Sensitivity data reveal resistance to ceftriaxone, cefotaxime, ceftazidime, piperacillin, aztreonam, and chloramphenicol. Drugs to which the isolate is sensitive include imipenem, TMP-SMX, gentamicin, tobramycin, and ciprofloxacin. What alteration in antimicrobial therapy is most appropriate for R.R. at this time?

Treatment of meningitis caused by *Enterobacter* and related species (e.g., *Serratia, Citrobacter* species) presents a challenge in that resistance is encountered more commonly.[28,30,92] Furthermore, some isolates which are sensitive to third-generation cephalosporins can become resistant during therapy by virtue of possessing inducible, type I beta-lactamases.[28] Thus, in contrast to gram-negative bacillary meningitis due to *E. coli* and *Klebsiella* species, alternative therapies are needed when treating meningitis due to *Enterobacter, Serratia, Citrobacter,* and *Pseudomonas* species. Based upon the sensitivity profile of R.R.'s infecting strain, it is apparent that an extended-spectrum penicillin (e.g., piperacillin) would not be appropriate. Aztreonam, a monobactam antibiotic with good CSF penetration and gram-negative activity comparable to ceftazidime, also unfortunately is inactive against R.R.'s infecting strain.[97] The isolate is sensitive to imipenem; however, the higher propensity for seizures compared to other beta-lactams (including penicillin G) argues against the use of imipenem for R.R.[98–100] Ciprofloxacin, a fluoroquinolone antibiotic, offers the attractive features of excellent *in vitro* potency against gram-negative bacilli (including *Enterobacter* and *Pseudomonas* species) and reasonable CSF penetration;[44,101] however, experience with ciprofloxacin in meningitis is limited.[44] Furthermore, fluoroquinolones also are associated with adverse CNS effects, including the potential to cause seizures.[102] TMP-SMX has excellent activity against most gram-negative bacteria with the exception of *P. aeruginosa* and penetrates into CSF especially well.[41,48,83] Thus, after consideration of the above options, TMP-SMX appears to be the best choice of therapy for R.R. Cefotaxime should be discontinued and therapy started with TMP-SMX 15 mg/kg/day (based upon the trimethoprim component) given intravenously in three divided doses.[4,53,83] For R.R., this would be a dose of 400 mg (trimethoprim component) given every eight hours. Because of poor aqueous solubility, intravenous TMP-SMX must be prepared such that each 80 mg (5 mL) of TMP-SMX injectable solution is diluted with 75 to 125 mL of 5% dextrose in water. For R.R., 400 mg of TMP-SMX would be administered in approximately 500 mL of D₅W and each dose infused over one hour. Whether or not to discontinue gentamicin in R.R. at this time is less clear. While there are no data demonstrating superiority of TMP-SMX combined with aminoglycosides over TMP-SMX alone, there is *in vitro* evidence of synergy which may be of theoretical advantage.[103]

A review of antibiotic therapy for *Enterobacter* meningitis supports the contention that TMP-SMX is the most useful therapy currently available.[28] Although uncontrolled and retrospective in design, infection was cured in seven of seven patients receiving TMP-SMX, compared to 21 of 32 (65%) patients treated solely with third-generation cephalosporins. In all 11 instances of clinical failure, development of resistance during therapy was encountered.[28] In an earlier report describing TMP-SMX treatment of bacterial meningitis, including eight cases of gram-negative bacillary meningitis due to organisms known to be moderately susceptible to third-generation cephalosporins (2 cases each of *E. cloacae, S. marcescens,* and *C. diversus;* 1 case each of *Proteus vulgaris* and

Morganella morganii), clinical and bacteriological cures were observed in all instances.[83] In contrast, TMP-SMX therapy failed to produce a cure in six cases of gram-negative bacillary meningitis due to *E. coli* (4 cases), and *K. pneumoniae* (2 cases) despite documented sensitivity to the drug combination. Thus, TMP-SMX appears to be most useful for treatment of gram-negative bacillary meningitis caused by organisms only moderately susceptible to third-generation agents, while cefotaxime or ceftriaxone remain the drugs of choice for meningitis caused by *E. coli* and *K. pneumoniae* (see Table 56.7).

Duration of Therapy. The optimum duration of therapy for gram-negative bacillary meningitis has not been clearly established. Because of high mortality and morbidity associated with these pathogens and the reduced susceptibility of enteric pathogens to antimicrobial agents, a longer duration of therapy of 14 to 21 days has been suggested (see Table 56.8).[51,53,91] Given that R.R. does not appear to have a fulminant case of gram-negative bacillary meningitis, a 14-day course of therapy would be acceptable provided he responds adequately to TMP-SMX therapy.

Staphylococcus Epidermidis Meningitis/Ventriculitis

Clinical Presentation of CSF Shunt Infections

19. T.A., a 21-year-old female with a history of congenital hydrocephalus, is admitted to the neurosurgery unit for worsening mental status and fever. T.A. has a prior history of multiple revisions and placements of intraventricular shunts for control of hydrocephalus. Currently she has a ventriculo-peritoneal (VP) shunt which was placed 1 month ago and previously had been functioning normally. Over the past few days, T.A. has developed worsening obtundation, stiff neck, and a fever of 39.5 °C. A CT scan performed today reveals enlarged ventricles consistent with acute hydrocephalus.

T.A.'s past medical history is noncontributory except for a seizure disorder for which she takes phenytoin 400 mg PO HS. She also takes Lo-Ovral for birth control. T.A. is allergic to sulfa drugs (severe skin rash). Her weight upon admission is 132 pounds.

Laboratory analysis was significant for a WBC count of 14,000 cells/mm³, with a differential of 85% PMNs, and 10% lymphocytes; and BUN and SrCr values of 19 mg/dL and 0.9 mg/dL, respectively.

A tap of T.A.'s shunt was performed and ventricular fluid obtained which was notable for a total protein of 100 mg/dL, glucose of 40 mg/dL, and a WBC count of 200 cells/mm³ (85% PMNs, 10% lymphocytes). Gram's stain of the ventricular fluid showed numerous gram-positive cocci in clusters. What are the subjective and objective findings of CSF shunt infections and what manifestations of this type of infection are present in T.A.? [SI units: WBC 14 × 10⁹ cells/L with 0.85 PMNs and 0.1 lymphocytes; BUN 6.8 mmol/L urea; SrCr 80 μmol/L; total protein 1.0 gm/L; glucose 2.2 mmol/L; WBC 200 × 10⁶ cells/L with 0.85 PMNs and 0.1 lymphocytes]

T.A. appears to have meningitis with ventriculitis secondary to infection of her ventriculo-peritoneal shunt. The most important means for managing hydrocephalus involves the use of devices which divert (shunt) CSF from the cerebral ventricles to other areas of the body such as the peritoneum (VP shunts), or atrium (VA shunts).[8,104,105] This approach alleviates increased CSF pressure and substantially reduces morbidity and mortality.[104,105] Unfortunately, infection of these devices is a frequent cause of shunt malfunction, as seen in T.A. The reported incidence of CSF shunt infections varies from 2% to 39% (usually between 10% to 11%), and depends upon patient factors, surgical technique, and the type and duration of the procedure performed (i.e., shunt revision versus placement of a new device).[104–106] T.A., who has been hydrocephalic since birth, and has a prior history of multiple shunt procedures, is at high risk for such an infection to occur.

Clinical symptoms associated with infected CSF shunts vary widely from asymptomatic colonization to fulminant ventriculitis with meningitis.[104–106] Fever is common, and in many instances, may be the only presenting symptom.[104] CSF findings also are slightly different in shunt infection compared to acute meningitis. Specifically, the WBC count usually is not as substantially elevated, the decrease in CSF glucose is less pronounced, and the protein value may be normal or slightly elevated.[104,105] CSF culture is positive in most patients not receiving concurrent antibiotics.[104,105] T.A.'s clinical presentation, CSF findings, and radiographic evidence of hydrocephalus are highly suggestive of the presence of a VP shunt infection. She is febrile and has altered mental status. The presence of a stiff neck strongly suggests meningeal involvement. Evaluation of T.A.'s ventricular fluid reveals a slightly elevated WBC count with a predominance of polymorphonuclear neutrophils, an elevated protein concentration, and a slightly lower than normal glucose concentration.

Organisms which comprise the skin microflora are the most common etiologies for CSF shunt infections.[104–107] Staphylococci account for 75% of all cases, with two-thirds of these caused by coagulase-negative staphylococci (usually *S. epidermidis*), and one-third due to *S. aureus*.[106,107] Other less commonly encountered pathogens include diphtheroids, enterococci, and *Propionibacterium acnes* (an anaerobic diphtheroid). Enteric gram-negative bacilli are responsible for a small percentage of cases, usually developing when the distal end of the shunt is inserted improperly into the peritoneal cavity.[106,107] The identification of gram-positive cocci in clusters on CSF Gram's stain strongly suggests that T.A. has a staphylococcal shunt infection. Determination of the coagulase status of the isolate will allow differentiation between *S. aureus* and *S. epidermidis*.

Treatment of CSF Shunt Infections

20. Results from culture and sensitivity testing of T.A.'s ventricular fluid are positive for *S. epidermidis*. The isolate is resistant to nafcillin, but sensitive to cefazolin, vancomycin, rifampin, and TMP-SMX. How should T.A.'s CSF shunt infection be managed?

In order for T.A.'s CSF shunt infection to be optimally managed, a combined medical-surgical approach is required.[104,107,108] Antibiotic therapy directed against the causative organism, while essential, often is inadequate by itself. On average, cure rates of less than 40% are found with antibiotic therapy alone.[107] In contrast, antibiotic therapy with surgical removal of the infected device is associated with clinical cures in excess of 80%.[107] Since many patients cannot tolerate the complete removal of their shunt for very long, externalization of the distal end of the shunt, or shunt removal and placement of an external drainage device often are necessary while systemic antibiotics are being administered. The presence of an externalized device permits sequential sampling of ventricular fluid and also provides a convenient means for daily intraventricular administration of antibiotics (see below).

Glycocalyx. Although *S. epidermidis* is not as virulent a pathogen as *S. aureus*, it is extremely difficult to eradicate this organism from prosthetic devices (e.g., CSF shunts). Many strains of *S. epidermidis* produce a mucous film or "slime-layer" known as glycocalyx.[109] The presence of glycocalyx allows the staphylococcus to tightly adhere to the silastic shunt material and protects against phagocytosis.[109,110] As would be expected, antibiotic failures are much more likely to occur with slime-producing strains of *S. epidermidis*.

Vancomycin is the drug of choice for treatment of shunt infections due to *S. epidermidis* and should be instituted immediately in T.A.[8,104,110] This is because a high percentage (>60%) of coagulase-negative staphylococci are resistant to methicillin (e.g., MRSE). Furthermore, methicillin-resistant staphylococci (both MRSA and MRSE) also are resistant to cephalosporins, despite the appearance of sensitivity to these agents with *in vitro* testing (as is evident with T.A.). Cephalosporin treatment of infection due to such strains is associated with failures and cannot be recommended. T.A.'s isolate also is sensitive to TMP-SMX, as is the case with many strains of MRSE (and also MRSA);[8] however, TMP-SMX must be avoided because T.A. is allergic to this drug combination. While many staphylococcal isolates (both *S. epidermidis* and *S. aureus*) are susceptible to rifampin, monotherapy with this drug is not recommended due to rapid emergence of resistance. Combination therapy with vancomycin and rifampin may be synergistic and sometimes is employed.

21. Vancomycin Therapy. What would be an appropriate dose of vancomycin therapy in T.A.? What subjective or objective data should be monitored to evaluate the efficacy and toxicity of the treatment?

Vancomycin therapy for T.A.'s CSF shunt infection requires the use of higher than usual doses.[8,51,111] The same is true for treatment of other types of staphylococcal CNS infections. For adults like T.A., vancomycin doses of 20 to 30 mg/kg/day up to a maximum of 2 gm/day have been suggested; however, higher doses may be required in patients with fulminant disease (see Table 56.6).[8,51,86,111] For children with meningitis or infected shunts, the recommended dose for vancomycin is 40 to 60 mg/kg/day, given intravenously in two to four divided doses (see Table 56.6).[8,51] Although specific recommendations are lacking, it is reasonable to target serum trough concentrations of vancomycin toward the higher end of the target range (i.e., $\approx$15 μg/mL). With an every 12 hour dosing schedule, peak serum concentrations (obtained at least 1 hour following a 1-hour infusion) will approach or possibly exceed 40 μg/mL. It is unlikely, however, that peak serum concentrations of more than 60 μg/mL will be observed. Although the potential for toxicity may be greater, higher than usual vancomycin serum concentrations are warranted to better insure adequate penetration into CSF.[86,111]

T.A. weighs 132 pounds and, therefore, should be started on a vancomycin regimen of 1 gm IV every 12 hours ($\approx$30 mg/kg/day), given that her renal function is normal. Alternatively, the dose could be calculated using population estimates of vancomycin pharmacokinetic parameters to achieve a trough serum concentration of 15 μg/mL. In either case, trough (and possibly peak) serum concentrations should be obtained at steady-state to assess whether the initial dosing regimen is adequate.

Anecdotal evidence suggests that very high doses of vancomycin ($\geq$3 gm/day in adults with normal renal function) are associated with an increased risk of ototoxicity.[86,112] Given that hearing loss also is a potential sequela of meningitis, this observation is difficult to verify. Another potential complication of high dose vancomycin therapy is the greater likelihood of inducing the "Red Man Syndrome."[113,114] This adverse effect manifested by flushing, and pruritus with or without hypotension is related directly to the amount of drug infused over a given period of time.[113] The Red Man Syndrome usually can be avoided or minimized by administering vancomycin doses of $\geq$1000 mg in 250 mL of solution (either D$_5$W or normal saline), and infusing over at least one hour. If Red Man Syndrome is observed, slowing of the infusion rate often results in amelioration of symptoms.[113] Pretreatment with antihistamines (diphenhydramine or hydroxyzine) also can be of benefit in that the proposed mechanism of Red Man Syndrome at least partially involves histamine release.[114]

Another consideration for T.A. is the addition of rifampin to her vancomycin regimen. This is based upon the excellent staphylococ-

cal activity of rifampin, its good CSF penetration, and the potential for synergy between these two agents.[8,104] Whether or not rifampin plus vancomycin is superior to vancomycin alone has not been determined. For T.A., it is best to avoid rifampin because evidence supporting its efficacy is weak, and she currently is taking phenytoin and birth control pills. Rifampin is a potent inducer of hepatic microsomal enzymes which can lower serum phenytoin concentrations (possibly resulting in seizure activity), and increase the possibility of an unplanned pregnancy (from reduced birth control pill effectiveness).

22. Intraventricular and Intravenous Dosing of Vancomycin. Should T.A. receive intraventricular vancomycin therapy? If so, what would be an appropriate dose?

T.A. has a long history of hydrocephalus and will require placement of an external drainage device following removal of her VP shunt. This makes intraventricular administration of vancomycin possible and such treatment should be instituted promptly. The range of doses used in the literature varies from 5 to 20 mg/day. There is no evidence to suggest that doses higher than 10 mg/day provide more effective therapy and the toxicity associated with this intrashunt therapy is unknown. Given this, an intraventricular vancomycin dose of 10 mg/day is recommended for T.A. to start with, and serial (daily) cultures of CSF are recommended to monitor her response to therapy. Some authors suggest that intraventricular vancomycin doses should be adjusted to achieve trough CSF vancomycin concentrations of at least 5 μg/mL, or CSF bactericidal activity of at least 1:8 against the infecting strain.[8,104] Until more information is available, measurement of vancomycin trough concentrations in CSF appears to be more appropriate to perform than CSF bactericidal titers, and serial trough levels should be obtained in T.A. Thus, T.A. should receive combined intravenous and intraventricular vancomycin therapy as described above. Therapy should be continued for at least ten days following documented sterilization of her ventricular fluid, at which time a new VP shunt can be placed.[104,107]

In contrast to T.A.'s situation, vancomycin therapy for patients with staphylococcal meningitis not associated with a CSF shunt or indwelling ventricular catheter is more problematic. Intrathecal vancomycin, while preferable, requires either daily lumbar puncture (for intralumbar therapy) or surgical placement of an intraventricular reservoir. Because of this, therapy frequently is instituted with intravenous vancomycin alone.[86,111] If the response to therapy within the first 24 to 48 hours is inadequate, intrathecal vancomycin therapy in doses ranging from 5 to 20 mg/day is recommended.[86,111] In fulminant cases of staphylococcal meningitis, however, intrathecal vancomycin should be instituted as quickly as possible (i.e., with the first lumbar puncture) to optimize the response to therapy.

Brain Abscess
Epidemiology

Although not nearly as common as meningitis, abscesses of the brain parenchyma (brain abscess) remain an important type of CNS infection. The incidence of brain abscess has not varied since the preantibiotic era and is estimated to account for 1 in 10,000 hospital admissions.[115] On a busy neurosurgical service, between four to ten cases a year typically are seen.[115,116] For reasons which are not entirely clear, men appear to be more likely to develop abscesses within the brain than women.[115,117] Brain abscess can occur at any age, but the median age ranges from 30 to 40 years, with approximately 25% of cases occurring in children.[115,118,119]

Despite advances in antimicrobial therapy over the past several decades, mortality rates from brain abscess remained over 40%

until just recently. Developments in imaging techniques such as CT and MRI scanning, which allow early recognition of abscesses and the ability to serially monitor the radiographic response to antimicrobial therapy, have had the most profound impact on reducing morbidity and mortality from brain abscess.[115,116,120] In a review of 102 cases of bacterial abscesses occurring over a 17-year period, mortality was 41% in the period before 1975 (preCT scan era), compared to 6% during 1975 to 1986 when CT scanning became routinely available.[116] With the combined medical-surgical approach currently recommended for management of bacterial brain abscess, mortality rates continue to average less than 10%.[115,116,120]

Predisposing Factors

Brain abscesses most commonly arise from a contiguous suppurative source of infection (e.g., sinusitis, otitis, mastoiditis, or dental infections).[115,117,121] Abscesses occurring as a complication of sinusitis are more common in the U.S. than abscesses arising from otitic or dental sources.[115] The formation of a single abscess cavity usually is found when infection develops from a contiguous source. In addition, the abscess nearly always is formed in close proximity to the primary focus of infection (see Table 56.10).[115,121] For example, abscesses of sinusitic origin more commonly involve the frontal lobe, while otitic infections frequently lead to temporal lobe abscess formation.[121] Brain abscess also occurs as a consequence of metastatic spread of organisms from a primary site of infection (e.g., lung abscess, endocarditis, osteomyelitis, pelvic, and intra-abdominal infections).[115,117] In children, cyanotic congenital heart disease is a common predisposing factor for brain abscess.[118,119] Multiple abscesses suggest a metastatic source of infection.[115] As with meningitis, brain abscess occurs as an infrequent complication of head trauma or neurosurgery.[10,115,121] No identifiable source (cryptogenic abscess) is detected in as many as 25% of cases.[115,121]

Staging

Once an intracranial focus of infection is established, the evolution of brain abscess involves two distinct stages: the cerebritis stage and that of capsule formation.[117,120] The cerebritis stage evolves gradually over first nine to ten days of infection and is characterized by an area of marked inflammatory infiltrate containing a necrotic center, surrounded by an area of cerebral edema.[117,120] Capsule formation occurs about 10 to 14 days after initiation of infection, and once formed, the capsule continues to thicken over a period of weeks.[117,120] Estimation of the stage of abscess development has important implications for therapy. While it is best to wait until the capsule is fully formed before attempting

any type of surgical intervention, antimicrobial therapy alone may resolve the infection if discovered in the early cerebritis stage.[120]

Microbiology

The microbiology of brain abscess is distinctly different from that of meningitis. Streptococci are implicated in 60% to 70% of cases and include anaerobic as well as microaerophilic streptococci of the *S. milleri* group.[115,121,122] Other anaerobes, particularly *Bacteroides* species (including *B. fragilis*) are found in up to 40% of cases, usually in mixed culture.[115,121] In recent years, staphylococci appear to be decreasing and enteric gram-negative bacteria are increasing as etiologic agents of bacterial brain abscess.[115] Although somewhat imprecise, there is a reasonable correlation between the various predisposing conditions and the microbiologic etiology of brain abscess (see Table 56.10).[115,116,119,121]

In the immunocompromised patient, a diverse group of microorganisms are capable of inducing abscesses within the brain. In patients with AIDS, *Toxoplasma gondii* is by far the most common infectious etiology of focal brain lesions.[123] Transplant patients and those receiving immunosuppressive therapy are susceptible to infection from *Nocardia* species.[124] In Mexico and other Central American countries, cysticercosis remains a frequent cause of intracerebral infection.[125]

Clinical and Radiologic Features

23. L.Y., a 40-year-old male, is brought to the ER by a friend with complaints of severe headache, fever, weakness in his left arm and leg, and increasing drowsiness.

Over the past week, L.Y. has suffered from headaches which have gradually worsened in intensity and from intermittent episodes of fever. Despite getting plenty of sleep, L.Y. states that he has been feeling increasingly drowsy over the past several days. When he noticed weakness in his left arm and difficulty concentrating this morning, he called a friend and asked to be taken in for evaluation.

Medical history reveals L.Y. to have chronic sinusitis treated with a variety of oral antibiotics. His last episode of sinusitis was about 1 month ago and was treated with a 10-day course of cephalexin. He denies any nausea or vomiting and has not experienced any seizures in the recent past. L.Y. was tested for HIV 6 months ago and the result of his antibody test was negative. He takes no current medications, denies smoking and use of recreational drugs, and drinks alcohol only on social occasions a few times a month. L.Y. states that he has no known drug allergies.

Physical examination reveals L.Y. to be in mild distress, with a temperature of 38.2 °C. He was slightly lethargic and oriented to person and place, but not time (0 × 2). The strength in L.Y.'s left arm and left leg are 3/5 and 4/5, respectively. The

Table 56.10	Predisposing Conditions, Microbiology, and Recommended Therapy for Bacterial Brain Abscess		
Predisposing Condition	**Usual Location of Abscess**	**Most Likely Organisms**	**Recommended Therapy**
Contiguous Site			
Otitic infection	Temporal lobe or cerebellum	Streptococci (anaerobic and aerobic), *B. fragilis*, gram-negative bacilli	Penicillin G + metronidazole + cefotaxime
Sinusitis	Frontal lobe	Streptococci (predominantly), *Bacteroides* species, gram-negative bacilli, *S. aureus*, *Haemophilus* species	Penicillin G + metronidazole + cefotaxime
Dental infection	Frontal lobe	*Fusobacteria* species, *Bacteroides* species, and streptococci	Penicillin G + metronidazole
Primary Infection			
Head trauma or neurosurgery	Related to site of wound	Gram-negative bacilli, staphylococci, streptococci, diphtheroids	Nafcillin + cefotaxime

remainder of his neurologic examination is grossly normal. L.Y. described moderate pain upon palpation of his frontal sinuses, and a purulent discharge is noted.

Laboratory evaluation shows a WBC count of 8000 cells/mm³ (70% PMNs, 25% lymphocytes, 5% monocytes), Hgb and Hct values of 14.5 gm/dL and 47%, respectively, and a platelet count of 120,000/mm³. Serum chemistries are within normal limits, and his BUN and SrCr are 16 mg/dL and 1.2 mg/dL, respectively. L.Y.'s erythrocyte sedimentation rate (ESR) is 40 mm/hr.

A CT scan with contrast dye reveals a right frontal ring-enhancing lesion with a small amount of surrounding cerebral edema. L.Y. now is admitted to the neurosurgery unit for further evaluation and treatment. What clinical signs and symptoms does L.Y. display which are suggestive of bacterial brain abscess? How can brain abscess be diagnosed in L.Y.? [SI units: WBC 8 × 10⁹ cells/L with 0.7 PMNs, 0.25 lymphocytes, and 0.05 monocytes; Hgb 145 gm/L; Hct 0.4; platelets 120 × 10⁹/L; BUN 5.7 mmol/L urea; SrCr 106.1 μmol/L; ESR 40 mm/hr]

L.Y. has presented to the emergency room with many signs and symptoms suggestive of bacterial brain abscess. He is 40 years old and a male, both of which place him in a group with the highest likelihood to have a brain abscess. In contrast to the diffuse nature of meningitis, brain abscess presents as a focal neurologic process.[115,116] Notable in L.Y.'s presentation is left-sided (arm and leg) weakness. Symptoms of brain abscess range in severity from indolent to fulminant, and in the majority of patients, the duration of symptoms at the time of presentation is ≤2 weeks.[115,116,118] Headache is the most common symptom of brain abscess occurring in approximately 70% of cases. L.Y.'s clinical manifestations gradually have become worse over the past week, and his worsening headaches, increasing drowsiness, and difficulty in concentrating all are consistent with bacterial brain abscess. L.Y. presents with the classic triad of fever, headache, and focal neurologic deficits. While this triad should always be looked for, less than one-half of patients with confirmed bacterial brain abscess present in this manner.[115,116,119] The absence of fever does not rule out infection; fever is found in ≤50% of patients.[115,116] Focal neurologic deficits are present in approximately 50% of patients, and vary in nature and severity in relation to the location and size of the abscess and surrounding cerebral edema.[115,116,119] While L.Y. does not elicit a history of seizure activity, approximately one-third of patients experience seizures, which usually are partial in nature frequently with secondary generalization.[115,119] Papilledema and nuchal rigidity occur in less than 25% of cases and often are not useful in confirming the diagnosis. Symptoms associated with a contiguous focus of infection should always be looked for, and in some situations, may predominate the clinical picture.[115,116] L.Y. has a history of sinus infection, and the pain on palpation of his sinuses coupled with the purulent sinus drainage suggest active infection at this site.

As can be seen from L.Y.'s test results, laboratory evaluation usually is not very helpful when diagnosing brain abscess. L.Y. does not have a peripheral leukocytosis, but he does have elevated erythrocyte sedimentation rate. Lack of an elevation in peripheral WBC count does not rule out brain abscess as this parameter frequently is normal in patients with intracranial suppuration. The ESR often is elevated in brain abscess; however, this test is nonspecific and, therefore, only indirectly supports the diagnosis.

L.Y. did not undergo a lumbar puncture and for good reason. Lumbar puncture is contraindicated for diagnosing brain abscess.[38,115,116] The diagnostic yield from cerebrospinal fluid is low because chemistries (e.g., protein, glucose, WBC) usually are normal and culture of the cerebrospinal fluid in patients with brain abscess is unlikely to yield the causative pathogen. More impor-

tantly, performing a lumbar puncture in patients with space-occupying lesions of the brain may produce cerebral herniation as a consequence of the shifting pressure gradient induced within the cranial vault following insertion of the lumbar puncture needle.[38]

Of paramount importance is the abnormality detected on the computed tomography scan of L.Y.'s brain. When dye is injected before the CT scan, brain abscesses will appear to "ring enhance." Furthermore, cerebral edema can be identified as a variable hypodense region immediately surrounding the abscess cavity. As stated earlier, CT and MRI scanning techniques have revolutionized the diagnosis and treatment of brain abscess.[115,116,120] The superiority of CT versus MRI is unclear; however, MRI is more sensitive in detecting cerebritis than CT, and MRI can be helpful in ruling out (or ruling in) an abscess when the CT scan is negative.[115,120] Assessment of the size and location of the lesion is possible with both techniques, which is invaluable in deciding which surgical intervention is indicated. Additionally, serial radiographic studies enable the evaluation of response to antimicrobial therapy over time.[116,120] In general, a good correlation exists between the clinical and radiologic response to therapy of bacterial brain abscess.

Treatment

24. How should L.Y.'s brain abscess be managed?

Surgical Techniques

A combined medical-surgical approach is the best form of therapy for L.Y.'s brain abscess.[115,120] Response rates to antimicrobial therapy alone have been disappointing, and with a few exceptions, surgical intervention is necessary to ensure optimum results. Medical therapy is indicated when multiple abscesses are present; when the abscess cavity is not accessible surgically; for patients who are poor surgical candidates; and as an option when the size of the abscess is small (<4 cm).[115,120,126] There are two types of surgical approaches for brain abscess: stereotaxic needle aspiration and craniotomy for abscess excision.[120] Stereotaxic aspiration of abscess contents can be performed under local anesthetic and produces lower morbidity and mortality than craniotomy.[120] Such an approach is highly effective, except possibly when multiloculated abscesses are present.[120] Craniotomy enables complete excision of the abscess cavity which often allows a shorter duration of antimicrobial therapy. However, craniotomy carries a much higher risk of complications than stereotaxic aspiration.[120] Both techniques are effective, and the decision regarding which procedure is most appropriate must be individualized.

Antimicrobial Penetration into Brain Abscess

Antimicrobial therapy is an essential component of brain abscess therapy.[121] Penetration of antibiotics into brain abscess fluid has not been studied as carefully as penetration into CSF, and as discussed above, the barrier involved is different (see Figure 56.1).[15] Penicillins and cephalosporins penetrate adequately into abscess fluid, but certain agents, like penicillin G, may be susceptible to degradation by enzymes present within the abscess milieu.[115,121,127–129] Third-generation cephalosporins are believed to sufficiently penetrate into the abscess based largely upon CSF data, and are good choices when gram-negative bacteria are present.[115,129] Chloramphenicol penetrates very well into brain abscesses and has been used extensively in the past.[115,121,127] Chloramphenicol has excellent anaerobic activity, but also can be degraded (deacetylated) in purulent abscess fluid.[115] Metronidazole achieves abscess fluid concentrations equal to, or in excess of, serum levels and is bactericidal against strict anaerobes. The unique mechanism of action of metronidazole makes it particularly useful in the necrotic core of the cavity where the oxidation-reduction potential is low and bacteria replicate slowly or are dormant. For these reasons, metronidazole now has supplanted chloramphenicol for treatment of bacterial brain abscess.[115] Although data are limited, vancomycin and imipenem appear to penetrate sufficiently into brain abscess fluid.[115,131] While specific abscess penetration data are unavailable, successful treatment of cerebral nocardiosis with TMP-SMX and CNS toxoplasmosis with clindamycin suggests that these compounds also achieve adequate penetration into cerebral abscess cavities.[123,124]

Antibiotic Therapy

The decision regarding when to institute antibiotic therapy depends upon the status of the patient and the stage of abscess development. For patients diagnosed during the cerebritis stage where a well-circumscribed capsule has not formed yet, surgery should be delayed, and antimicrobial therapy begun for patients with significant symptoms.[115,120] If capsule formation already has taken place, it is better to delay initiation of antibiotics until after surgery in order to increase the microbiologic yield from tissue and fluid obtained. In situations when the disease is fulminant, antibiotics must be instituted promptly and surgical intervention performed as quickly as possible.[115,120]

L.Y.'s clinical presentation is suggestive of an advanced brain abscess. The presence of "ring enhancement" on CT and the onset of symptoms for two weeks are evidence in support of this. Because he is not critically ill, antibiotic therapy should be delayed until surgery is performed. Specimens obtained from the surgical procedure should be sent for aerobic and anaerobic culture and stat Gram's stain.

Initial antibiotic therapy for brain abscess needs to be sufficiently broad to cover the most likely pathogens (see Table 56.10).[115,117,119,121] In most cases, a combination of high dose penicillin G and metronidazole is indicated. Penicillin will cover aerobic, anaerobic, and microaerophilic streptococci, while metronidazole will provide coverage for strict anaerobes, including *Bacteroides* species. In situations where gram-negative bacilli are suspected or documented, such as abscesses related to otitis, head trauma, or neurosurgery, a third-generation cephalosporin is indicated.[115] Staphylococcal abscesses should be treated with nafcillin or vancomycin.[115,117,131]

For L.Y., therapy with penicillin G 4 million units IV every four hours and metronidazole 500 mg IV every eight hours should be started postoperatively (see Table 56.6). Because his abscess appears to be of sinusitic origin, the likelihood of gram-negatives being present is reduced. If there is evidence of gram-negative bacteria on Gram's stain of abscess fluid, therapy with cefotaxime 3 gm IV every six hours also should be included. Trimethoprim-sulfamethoxazole is an alternative if the organism is resistant to cefotaxime; however, the large fluid volume required (particularly when 5% dextrose in water is used) for intravenous TMP-SMX administration may contribute to a worsening of cerebral edema.[115] Antimicrobial therapy for L.Y. should be revised once results from culture and sensitivity testing are available.

Adjunctive Corticosteroid Therapy

Adjunctive corticosteroid therapy for bacterial brain abscess is controversial.[115,120] Steroids may interfere with antibiotic penetration into abscesses and obscure interpretation of serial CT scans when assessing response to therapy.[115,120] Therefore, steroids are indicated only where significant cerebral edema is present, particularly when accompanied by rapid neurological deterioration.[115,120] L.Y. should not be begun on dexamethasone given that his mental status is only mildly depressed and the cerebral edema seen on CT scan is not massive.

Adjunctive Anticonvulsant Therapy

L.Y. has shown no signs of seizure activity thus far and, therefore, does not require anticonvulsant therapy. Anticonvulsants, however, should be used in the acute setting when seizures are present.[115,120] Agents with activity against partial and complex partial seizures are preferred (e.g., phenytoin, carbamazepine). The long-term use of anticonvulsants depends upon whether or not seizure activity persists. There is insufficient information regarding how long to continue anticonvulsants in such cases; therefore, discontinuation of these agents must be individualized.

No formal guidelines are available regarding the optimum duration of therapy for bacterial brain abscess. Given the serious nature of the infection and the difficulty associated with antibiotic penetration, therapy with high-dose intravenous therapy should continue for at least four to six weeks.[115,120] In an attempt to ensure complete eradication of infection, some experts recommend following this with a prolonged period (2 to 6 months) of oral antibiotic therapy provided agents are available with good oral absorption and activity against the offending pathogens.[115]

Monitoring Therapy

25. How should the therapy L.Y. is receiving be monitored for response and toxicity?

L.Y. should continue on antibiotic therapy for at least four weeks and serial (i.e., weekly or biweekly) CT scans should be obtained to evaluate abscess resolution. His clinical response to therapy also should be assessed daily. If therapy is effective, L.Y. should experience a gradual improvement in his mental status (e.g., he will become more alert and oriented) over a period of several days. L.Y.'s headaches and hemiparesis (weakness in his arm and leg) also should resolve eventually; however, it may take a week or longer to see a complete resolution of symptoms.[115,117] In general, radiologic improvement (i.e., reduction in abscess size) correlates reasonably well with clinical response, but not always.[115,117,120] Persistent symptoms or a failure to detect a reduction in abscess size on CT scan (or the appearance of new abscesses) may indicate improper antimicrobial therapy or warrant the need for additional surgery.[115,120] Repeated surgical intervention with appropriate reculturing may be required in some instances to optimize therapy.

Adverse effects associated with the penicillin G therapy that L.Y. is receiving are similar to other beta-lactam antibiotics. Seizures are a potential complication when high doses of penicillin are employed in the presence of a mass lesion in the brain.[6,81,100,132] L.Y. should be observed closely by those providing care and questioned regularly for any evidence of seizure activity. Metronidazole usually is well tolerated, but also has the potential to cause neurotoxicity.[115,130,132,133] The most common neurotoxic reaction seen with metronidazole is peripheral neuropathy.[132] L.Y. should be assessed for the presence of numbness or tingling in his hands or feet. Seizures, although uncommon, occasionally can occur with metronidazole.[132] If L.Y. experiences peripheral neuropathy or seizures, a switch to chloramphenicol would be most appropriate. Other adverse effects associated with metronidazole include mild nausea, brownish discoloration of the urine, and the potential for disulfiram-like reaction with concomitant ethanol ingestion.[133] L.Y. should be counseled regarding the possibility of gastric upset, discoloration of the urine, and he should be strongly cautioned to avoid alcoholic beverages while receiving metronidazole. Given his young age, the absence of significant underlying diseases, and the relative early detection of L.Y.'s brain abscess, there is every reason to expect a good response to his treatment, and eventually, a complete resolution of his abscess.

56–22

Infectious Disorders

References

1 **Durand ML et al.** Acute bacterial meningitis in adults. N Engl J Med. 1993;328:21.

2 **Quagliarello VJ, Scheld WM.** New perspectives on bacterial meningitis. Clin Infect Dis. 1993;17:603.

3 **Quagliarello VJ, Scheld WM.** Bacterial meningitis: pathogenesis, pathophysiology, and progress. N Engl J Med. 1992;327:864.

4 **Tunkel AR et al.** Bacterial meningitis: recent advances in pathophysiology and treatment. Ann Intern Med. 1990; 112:610.

5 **Lebel MH et al.** Dexamethasone therapy for bacterial meningitis. N Engl J Med. 1988;319:964.

6 **Overturf GD.** Pyogenic bacterial infections of the CNS. Neurol Clin. 1986; 4:69.

7 **Silverberg AL, DiNubile MJ.** Subdural empyema and cranial epidural abscess. Med Clin North Am. 1985;69: 361.

8 **McLauren RL, Frame PT.** Treatment of cerebrospinal fluid shunts. Rev Infect Dis. 1987;9:595.

9 **Romanes GJ.** Cunningham's Textbook of Anatomy. 12th ed. New York: Oxford University Press; 1981:28.

10 **Greenlee JE.** Anatomic considerations in central nervous system infections. In: Mandell GL et al., eds. Principles and Practice of Infectious Diseases. 3rd ed. NY: Churchill Livingstone; 1990: 732.

11 **Gagnong WF.** Review of Medical Physiology. 16th ed. Norwalk, CT: Appleton and Lange; 1993:551.

12 **Bonadio WA.** The cerebrospinal fluid: physiologic aspects and alterations associated with bacterial meningitis. Pediatr Infect Dis J. 1992;11:423.

13 **Allinson RR, Stach PE.** Intrathecal drug therapy. Drug Intell Clin Pharm. 1978;12:347.

14 **Kaiser AB, McGee ZA.** Aminoglycoside therapy of gram-negative bacillary meningitis. N Engl J Med. 1975; 293:1215.

15 **Pardridge WM et al.** Blood-brain barrier: interface between internal medicine and the brain. Ann Intern Med. 1986;105:82.

16 **Scheld WM.** Drug delivery to the central nervous system: general principles and relevance to therapy for infections of the central nervous system. Rev Infect Dis. 1989;11 (Suppl. 7):S1669.

17 **Katzman M, Ellner JJ.** Chronic meningitis. In: Mandell GL et al., eds. Principles and Practice of Infectious Diseases. 3rd ed. NY: Churchill Livingstone; 1990:755.

18 **Schlech WF III et al.** Bacterial meningitis in the United States, 1978 through 1981. JAMA. 1985;253:1749.

19 **Wenger JD et al.** Bacterial meningitis in the United States, 1986: report of a multistate surveillance study. JAMA. 1990;162:1316.

20 **Tenney JH.** Bacterial infections of the central nervous system in neurosurgery. Neurol Clin. 1986;4:91.

21 **Unhanand M et al.** Gram-negative enteric bacillary meningitis: a twenty-one-year experience. J Pediatr. 1993; 122:15.

22 **Gellin BG, Broome CV.** Listeriosis. JAMA. 1989;261:1313.

23 **Adams WG et al.** Decline of childhood *Haemophilus influenzae* type b (Hib) disease in the Hib vaccine era. JAMA. 1993;269:221.

24 **Anon.** Progress toward elimination of *Haemophilus influenzae* type b disease among infants and children—United States 1987–1993. MMWR. 1994;43: 144.

25 **McDougal LK et al.** Analysis of multiple antimicrobial-resistant isolates of *Streptococcus pneumoniae* from the United States. Antimicrob Agents Chemother. 1992;36:2176.

26 **Choi C.** Bacterial meningitis. Clin Geriatr Med. 1992;8:889.

27 **Cherubin CE et al.** Listeria and gram-negative bacillary meningitis in New York City, 1972–1979. Am J Med. 1981;71:199.

28 **Wolff MA et al.** Antibiotic therapy for enterobacter meningitis: a retrospective review of 13 episodes and review of the literature. Clin Infect Dis. 1993;16:772.

29 **Fong IW, Tomkins KB.** Review of *Pseudomonas aeruginosa* meningitis with special emphasis on treatment with ceftazidime. Rev Infect Dis. 1985; 7:604.

30 **Cherubin CE et al.** Treatment of gram-negative bacillary meningitis: role of the new cephalosporin antibiotics. Rev Infect Dis. 1982;4(Suppl.): S453.

31 **Tauber MG et al.** Antibiotic therapy, endotoxin concentrations in cerebrospinal fluid, and brain edema in experimental *Escherichia coli* meningitis in rabbits. J Infect Dis. 1987;156:456.

32 **Pomeroy SL et al.** Seizures and other neurologic sequelae of bacterial meningitis in children. N Engl J Med. 1990; 323:1651.

33 **Taylor HG et al.** The sequelae of *Haemophilus influenzae* meningitis in school-age children. N Engl J Med. 1990;323:1657.

34 **Dodge PR et al.** Prospective evaluation of hearing impairment as a sequelae of acute bacterial meningitis. N Engl J Med. 1984;311:869.

35 **Perfect JR.** Meningitis: pitfalls in diagnosis and treatment. Hosp Med. 1987;(June):110.

36 **Keroack MA.** The patient with suspected meningitis. Emerg Med Clin North Am. 1987;5:807.

37 **Verghese A, Gallemore G.** Kerning's and Brudzinski's signs revisited. Rev Infect Dis. 1987;9:1187.

38 **Addy DP.** When not to do a lumbar puncture. Arch Dis Child. 1987;62: 873.

39 **Glimaker M et al.** Tumor necrosis factor-alpha (TNF-alpha) in cerebrospinal fluid from patients with meningitis of different etiologies: high levels of TNF-alpha indicate bacterial meningitis. J Infect Dis. 1993;167:882.

40 **Edberg SC.** Conventional and molecular techniques for the laboratory diagnosis of infections of the central nervous system. Neurol Clin. 1986;4:13.

41 **Thea D, Barza M.** Use of antibacterial agents in infections of the central nervous system. Infect Dis Clin North Am. 1989;3:553.

42 **Tauber MG, Sande MA.** Principles in the treatment of bacterial meningitis. Am J Med. 1984(Suppl. May 15):224.

43 **Arditi M et al.** Cefuroxime treatment failure and *Haemophilus influenzae* meningitis: case report and review of the literature. Pediatrics. 1989;84:132.

44 **Scheld WM.** Quinolone therapy for infections of the central nervous system. Rev Infect Dis. 1989;11(Suppl. 5): S1194.

45 **Scheld WM et al.** Comparison of netilmicin with gentamicin in the therapy of experimental Escherichia coli meningitis. Antimicrob Agents Chemother. 1978;13:899.

46 **Norrby SR.** Role of cephalosporins in the treatment of bacterial meningitis. Am J Med. 1985;79(Suppl. 2A):56.

47 **Cherubin CE et al.** Penetration of newer cephalosporins into cerebrospinal fluid. Rev Infect Dis. 1989;11:526.

48 **Norrby SR.** A review of the penetration of antibiotics into CSF and its clinical significance. Scand J Infect Dis Suppl. 1978;14:296.

49 **Bolan G, Barza M.** Acute bacterial meningitis in children and adults. Med Clin North Am. 1985;69:231.

50 **Del Rio M et al.** Ceftriaxone versus ampicillin and chloramphenicol for treatment of bacterial meningitis in children. Lancet. 1983;1:1241.

51 **Plotkin SA et al.** Treatment of bacterial meningitis. Pediatrics. 1988;81: 904.

52 **Saxon A et al.** Immediate hypersensitivity reactions to beta-lactam antibiotics. Ann Intern Med. 1987;107:204.

53 **Rahal JJ, Simberkoff MS.** Host defense and antimicrobial therapy in adult gram-negative bacillary meningitis. Ann Intern Med. 1982;96:468.

54 **Roche Laboratories.** Rocephin Package insert. Nutley, NJ: 1994 Jan.

55 **Fishman R.** Steroids in the treatment of brain edema. N Engl J Med. 1982; 306:359.

56 **deLemos RA, Haggerty RJ.** Corticosteroids as an adjunct to treatment in bacterial meningitis. Pediatrics. 1969; 44:30.

57 **Belsey MA et al.** Dexamethasone in the treatment of acute bacterial meningitis: the effect of study design on the interpretation of results. Pediatrics. 1969;44:503.

58 **Syrogiannopoulos GA et al.** Dexamethasone therapy for bacterial meningitis in children: 2- versus 4-day regimen. J Infect Dis. 1994;169:853.

59 **Odio CM et al.** The beneficial effects of early dexamethasone administration in infants and children with bacterial meningitis. N Engl J Med. 1991;324: 1525.

60 **Schaad UB et al.** Dexamethasone therapy for bacterial meningitis in children. Lancet. 1993;342:457.

61 **Girgis NI et al.** Dexamethasone treatment for bacterial meningitis in children and adults. Pediatr Infect Dis J. 1989;8:848.

62 **Saez-Llorens X, McCracken GH.** Mediators of meningitis: therapeutic implications. Hosp Pract. 1991;(Jan. 15):68.

63 **Tuomanen E et al.** Nonsteroidal anti-inflammatory agents in the therapy for experimental pneumococcal meningitis. J Infect Dis. 1987;155:985.

64 **Schaab UB et al.** A comparison of ceftriaxone and cefuroxime for the treatment of bacterial meningitis in children. N Engl J Med. 1990;322:141.

65 **Lebel MH et al.** Comparative efficacy of ceftriaxone and cefuroxime for treatment of bacterial meningitis. J Pediatr. 1989;114:1049.

66 **Neu HC.** Third-generation cephalosporins: safety profiles after 10 years of clinical use. J Clin Pharmacol. 1990; 30:396.

67 **Kelly CP et al.** *Clostridium difficile colitis.* N Engl J Med. 1994;330:257.

68 **Shiffman ML et al.** Pathogenesis of ceftriaxone-associated biliary sludge. Gastroenterology. 1990;99:1772.

69 **Schaad UB et al.** Reversible ceftriaxone-associated biliary pseudolithiasis in children. Lancet. 1988;2:1411.

70 **Park HZ et al.** Ceftriaxone-associated gallbladder sludge. Gastroenterology. 1991;100:1665.

71 **Heim-Duthoy KL et al.** Apparent biliary pseudolithiasis during ceftriaxone therapy. Antimicrob Agents Chemother. 1990;34:1146.

72 **Feder HM et al.** Chloramphenicol: a review of its use in clinical practice. Rev Infect Dis. 1981;3:479.

73 **Radetsky M.** Duration of treatment in bacterial meningitis: a historical inquiry. Pediatr Infect Dis J. 1990;9:2.

74 **Lieberman JM et al.** Prevention of bacterial meningitis. Infect Dis Clin North Am. 1990;4:703.

75 **Ebert SC et al.** ASHP therapeutic guidelines on nonsurgical antimicrobial prophylaxis. Clin Pharm. 1990;9: 423.

76 **Immunization Practices Advisory Committee.** *Haemophilus* b conjugate vaccines for prevention of *Hemophilus influenzae* type b disease among infants and children two months of age and older. MMWR. 1991;40:1.

77 **Ward JI et al.** *Haemophilus influenzae* type b vaccines: lessons for the future. Pediatr. 1988;81:886.

78 **Redd SC et al.** The role of human immunodeficiency virus infection in pneumococcal bacteremia in San Francisco residents. J Infect Dis. 1990;162: 1012.

79 **Immunization Practices Advisory Committee.** Pneumococcal polysaccharide vaccine. MMWR. 1989;38:64.

80 **Polk RE.** Drug-drug interactions with ciprofloxacin and other fluoroquinolones. Am J Med. 1989;87(Suppl. 5A): 76S.

81 **Bryan SC, Stone WJ.** "Comparably massive" penicillin G therapy in renal failure. Ann Intern Med. 1975;82:189.

82 **Farber BF, Moellering RC.** Retrospective study of the toxicity of preparations of vancomycin from 1974 to 1981. Antimicrob Agents Chemother. 1983;23:138.

83 **Levitz RE, Quintiliani R.** Trimetho-prim-sulfamethoxazole for bacterial meningitis. Ann Intern Med. 1984;100: 881.

84 **Friedland IR, McCracken GH.** Management of infections caused by antibiotic-resistant *Streptococcus pneumoniae*. N Engl J Med. 1994;331:377.

85 **John CC.** Treatment failure with use of a third-generation cephalosporin for penicillin-resistant pneumococcal meningitis: case report and review. Clin Infect Dis. 1994;18:188.

86 **Viladrich PF et al.** Evaluation of vancomycin therapy for therapy of adult pneumococcal meningitis. Antimicrob Agents Chemother. 1991;35:2467.

87 **Friedland IR, Klugman KP.** Failure of chloramphenicol therapy in penicillin-resistant pneumococcal meningitis. Lancet. 1992;339:405.

88 **NCCLS.** Performance standards for antimicrobial susceptibility testing. Document M100-S5. 1994;14:16. NCCLS, Vilanova, Pennsylvania.

89 **Friedland IR et al.** Evaluation of antimicrobial regimens for treatment of experimental penicillin- and cephalosporin-resistant pneumococcal meningitis. Antimicrob Agents Chemother. 1993;37:1630.

90 **Rodriguez-Barradas MC et al.** Antibody to capsular polysaccharides of *Streptococcus pneumoniae* after vaccination of human immunodeficiency virus-infected subjects with 23-valent pneumococcal vaccine. J Infect Dis. 1992;165:553.

91 **Berk SL, McCabe WR.** Meningitis caused by gram-negative bacilli. Ann Intern Med. 1980;93:253.

92 **Corrado ML et al.** Designing appropriate therapy in the treatment of gram-negative bacillary meningitis. JAMA. 1982;248:71.

93 **Cherubin CE, Eng RHK.** Experience with the use of cefotaxime in the treatment of bacterial meningitis. Am J Med. 1986;80:398.

94 **Overturf GD et al.** Treatment of bacterial meningitis with ceftizoxime. Antimicrob Agents Chemother. 1984;25: 258.

95 **McCracken GH et al.** Intraventricular gentamicin therapy in gram-negative bacillary meningitis in infancy. Lancet. 1980;1:787.

96 **Swartz MN.** Intraventricular use of aminoglycosides in the treatment of gram-negative bacillary meningitis: conflicting views. J Infect Dis. 1981; 143:293.

97 **Lentnek AL, Williams RR.** Aztreonam in the treatment of gram-negative bacterial meningitis. Rev Infect Dis. 1991;13(Suppl. 7):S586.

98 **Wong VK et al.** Imipenem/cilastatin treatment of bacterial meningitis in children. Pediatr Infect Dis J. 1991;10: 122.

99 **Calandra G et al.** Factors predisposing to seizures in seriously ill infected patients receiving antibiotics: experience with imipenem/cilastatin. Am J Med. 1988;84:911.

100 **Eng RHK et al.** Seizure propensity with imipenem. Arch Intern Med. 1989;149:1881.

101 **Wolff M et al.** Penetration of ciprofloxacin into cerebrospinal fluid of patients with bacterial meningitis. Antimicrob Agents Chemother. 1987;31:899.

102 **Hooper DC, Wolfson JS.** Fluoroquinolone antimicrobial agents. N Engl J Med. 1991;324:384.

103 **Parsley TL et al.** Synergistic activity of trimethoprim and amikacin against gram-negative bacilli. Antimicrob Agents Chemother. 1977;12:349.

104 **Gardner P et al.** Infections of central nervous system shunts. Med Clin North Am. 1985;69:297.

105 **Yogev R Davis AT.** Neurosurgical shunt infections. A review. Childs Brain. 1980;6:74.

106 **Schoenbaum SC et al.** Infections of cerebrospinal fluid shunts: epidemiology, clinical manifestations, and therapy. J Infect Dis. 1975;131:543.

107 **Yogev R.** Cerebrospinal fluid shunt infections: a personal view. Pediatr Infect Dis J. 1985;4:113.

108 **Walters BC et al.** Cerebrospinal fluid shunt infection. J Neurosurg. 1984;60: 1014.

109 **Younger JJ et al.** Coagulase-negative staphylococci isolated from cerebrospinal fluid shunts: importance of slime production, species identification, and shunt removal to clinical outcome. J Infect Dis. 1987;156:548.

110 **Shapiro S et al.** Origin of organisms infecting ventricular shunts. Neurosurgery. 1988;22:868.

111 **Gump DW.** Vancomycin for treatment of bacterial meningitis. Rev Infect Dis. 1981;3(Suppl.):S289.

112 **Brummett RE, Fox KE.** Vancomycin- and erythromycin-induced hearing loss in humans. Antimicrob Agents Chemother. 1989;33:791.

113 **Polk RE et al.** Vancomycin and the red-man syndrome: pharmacodynamics of histamine release. J Infect Dis. 1988;157:502.

114 **Sahai J et al.** Influence of antihistamine pretreatment on vancomycin-induced red-man syndrome. J Infect Dis. 1989;160:876.

115 **Wispelwey B, Scheld WM.** Brain abscess. Clin Neuropharmacol. 1987;10: 483.

116 **Mampalam TJ, Rosenblum ML.** Trends in the management of bacterial brain abscesses: a review of 102 cases over 17 years. Neurosurgery. 1988;23: 451.

117 **Yoshikawa TT, Quinn W.** The aching head. Intracranial suppuration due to head and neck infections. Infect Dis Clin North Am. 1988;2:265.

118 **Patrick, Kaplan SL.** Current concepts in the pathogenesis and management of brain abscesses in children. Pediatr Clin North Am. 1988;35:625.

119 **Saez-Llorens X et al.** Brain abscess in infants and children. Pediatr Infect Dis J. 1989;8:449.

120 **Rosenblum ML et al.** Controversies in the management of brain abscesses. Clin Neurosurg. 1986;33:603.

121 **de Louvois J.** The bacteriology and chemotherapy of brain abscess. J Antimicrob Chemother. 1978;4:395.

122 **Gossling J.** Occurrence and pathogenicity of the *Streptococcus milleri* group. Rev Infect Dis. 1988;10:257.

123 **Luft BJ, Remington JS.** Toxoplasmic encephalitis in AIDS. Clin Infect Dis. 1992;15:211.

124 **Simpson GL et al.** Nocardial infections in the immunocompromised host: a detailed study in a defined population. Rev Infect Dis. 1981;3:492.

125 **Del Brutto OH et al.** Therapy for neurocysticercosis: a reappraisal. Clin Infect Dis. 1993;17:730.

126 **Rosenblum ML et al.** Nonoperative treatment of brain abscesses in selected high-risk patients. J Neurosurg. 1980; 52:217.

127 **Black P et al.** Penetration of brain abscess by systemically administered antibiotics. J Neurosurg. 1973;38:705.

128 **de Louvois J, Hurley R.** Inactivation of penicillin by purulent exudates. Br Med J. 1977;1:998.

129 **Yamamoto M et al.** Penetration of intravenous antibiotics into brain abscesses. Neurosurgery. 1993;33:44.

130 **Warner JF et al.** Metronidazole therapy of anaerobic bacteremia, meningitis, and brain abscess. Arch Intern Med. 1979;139:167.

131 **Levy RM et al.** Vancomycin penetration of a brain abscess: case report and review of the literature. Neurosurgery. 1986;18:632.

132 **Snavely SR, Hodges GR.** The neurotoxicity of antibacterial agents. Ann Intern Med. 1984;101:92.

133 **Smilack JD et al.** Tetracyclines, chloramphenicol, erythromycin, clindamycin, and metronidazole. Mayo Clin Proc. 1991:66:1270.

Endocarditis

Daniel P Healy

Annie Wong-Beringer

Pathogenesis 57-1
Epidemiology 57-2
Predisposing Factors 57-2
Bacteriology 57-2
Site of Involvement 57-2
Classification 57-2
Streptococcus viridans **Endocarditis** 57-3
Clinical Presentation 57-3
Diagnosis (See Tables 57.2 and 57.3) 57-4
Blood cultures 57-4
Adjunctive imaging studies 57-4
Antimicrobial Therapy (See Table 57.4) 57-4
General principles 57-4
High-dose penicillin for four weeks 57-6
High-dose penicillin for four weeks plus
an aminoglycoside for two weeks 57-6
High-dose penicillin plus an aminoglycoside
for two weeks 57-6
Regimen selection 57-6
Staphylococcus epidermidis **Prosthetic Valve**
Endocarditis (PVE) 57-7
Etiology 57-7
Prophylaxis 57-8
Cephalosporins 57-8
Vancomycin 57-8
Adverse effects 57-8
Administration 57-9
Antimicrobial Therapy (See Table 57.5) 57-9
Staphylococcus aureus **Endocarditis** 57-9
Intravenous Drug Abuser versus Nonabuser 57-9
Antimicrobial Therapy 57-9
Methicillin-sensitive *S. aureus* (MSSA) 57-9
Penicillin allergic patients 57-11
Combination therapy 57-11

Methicillin resistant *S. aureus*
(MRSA): vancomycin 57-11
Dosing 57-11
Enterococcal Endocarditis 57-11
Antimicrobial Therapy (See Table 57.6) 57-11
Antibiotic synergy 57-11
Streptomycin resistant 57-12
Gentamicin resistant 57-12
Gentamicin 57-12
Dosing 57-12
In combination with vancomycin 57-12
Duration of therapy 57-13
Increased nephrotoxicity with vancomycin
combination therapy 57-13
Glycopeptide resistance 57-14
Ramoplanin 57-15
Streptogramin 57-15
Fungal Endocarditis Due to *Candida albicans* 57-15
Prognosis and Treatment 57-15
Combination therapy 5-FC and amphotericin B 57-16
Alternative antifungals 57-16
Gram-Negative Bacillary Endocarditis due
to *Pseudomonas aeruginosa* 57-16
Prevalence 57-16
Antimicrobial Therapy 57-17
Culture-Negative Endocarditis 57-17
Empiric Therapy 57-17
Prophylactic Therapy 57-18
Rationale and Recommendations
(See Tables 57.4 and 57.5) 57-18
Dental and upper respiratory tract procedures 57-18
Gastrointestinal and genitourinary
tract procedures 57-18
Indications and Choice of Agent 57-18
Home Intravenous (IV) Antibiotic Therapy 57-19

Pathogenesis[1,2]

Infective endocarditis is a microbial infection of the heart valves or other endocardial tissue and usually is associated with an underlying cardiac defect. The pathogenesis of endocarditis involves a complex series of events which ultimately result in the formation of an infected platelet-fibrin thrombus on the valve surface. This thrombus is called a vegetation.

The first step in the formation of the vegetation involves modification of the endocardial surface which is normally nonthrombogenic. In patients with rheumatic heart disease, endocardial injury occurs as a result of immune complex deposition or hemodynamic disturbances. Valvular insufficiency caused by aortic stenosis or ventricular septal defects can produce regurgitant blood flow, high pressure gradients, or narrow orifices, resulting in turbulence and endocardial damage.

Once the endocardial surface of the valve is traumatized, small sterile thrombi consisting of platelets and fibrin are deposited,

forming the lesion called nonbacterial thrombotic endocarditis (NBTE). NBTE occurs most commonly on the atrial surfaces of the mitral and tricuspid valves and on the ventricular surface of the aortic valve.

Nonbacterial thrombotic endocarditis serves as a nidus for microbial colonization during periods of bacteremia (see Table 57.1 for a list of procedures that cause bacteremia). Organisms such as *Streptococcus viridans, Enterococci* species, *Staphylococcus aureus, Staphylococcus epidermidis, Pseudomonas aeruginosa*, and *Candida albicans* possess adherence factors that facilitate their colonization. Once the nonbacterial thrombotic endocarditis lesion becomes colonized by micro-organisms, the surface is rapidly covered with a sheath of fibrin and platelets. This avascular encasement provides an environment protected from host defenses and is conducive to further bacterial replication and vegetation growth. Progression of the infection can be interrupted at any time by various host defense mechanisms which include: blocking antibodies that interfere with bacterial adherence, serum bactericidal complement activity, hemodynamic forces that dislodge poorly ad-herent bacteria, and circulating prophylactic antibiotics.

The vegetation is thought to propagate by continuous reseeding of the thrombus by circulating organisms. As the vegetation en-larges, it takes on a laminar appearance due to the alternating layers of bacteria and platelet-fibrin deposits. The bacterial colony count can be as high as 10^9 to 10^{10} bacteria/gm of valvular vegetation.

Endocarditis can result in life-threatening hemodynamic distur-bances and embolic episodes. Without antimicrobial therapy and surgical intervention, infective endocarditis is virtually 100% fatal.

Epidemiology[1,3,4,151]

Infective endocarditis is a relatively uncommon disease that ac-counts for approximately 10,000 to 15,000 new cases per year in the U.S.[151] While the overall incidence has remained relatively unchanged over the past 30 years, the frequency of cases in intra-venous (IV) drug abusers and those with prosthetic heart valves appears to be increasing. The mean patient age reportedly has in-creased from less than 30 years in the 1920s to about 55 years today. This upward shift in age is thought to be largely related to advances in the field of cardiothoracic surgery. Men are affected more often than women (roughly 2:1), and the disease remains uncommon in children.

Predisposing Factors[1,3,4,151]

Rheumatic heart disease was at one time the most frequent un-derlying cardiac defect associated with endocarditis; however, the predominant defect in documented cases of endocarditis currently is mitral valve prolapse and infection of prosthetic valves.[151] In addition, a growing population of IV drug abusers and a larger number of compromised hospitalized patients who are subjected to intravenous access procedures (e.g., IV catheterization, central venous catheterization for hyperalimentation, dialysis, and other shunt procedures) have resulted in a proportionate increase in the number of cases seen in these groups. Congenital heart defects such as patent ductus arteriosus, ventricular septal defect, coarctation of the aorta, and tetralogy of Fallot are underlying causes in about 10% of the cases. Degenerative cardiac lesions and idiopathic sub-aortic stenosis also have been associated with the development of endocarditis. The actual contribution of these lesions is unknown. In addition, as many as one-third of all patients have no recogniz-able underlying cardiac disease.

Bacteriology[1,3–5,151]

Streptococci are infecting organisms in about 60% of all cases of infective endocarditis: *Streptococcus viridans* (50% to 60%) and *Streptococcus bovis* (10%). Staphylococci cause an estimated 20% to 35% of the cases, and 80% to 90% of these are due to *S. aureus*. *Enterococcus faecalis* accounts for about 10% to 20% of the cases. Endocarditis in narcotic addicts often is due to *S. aureus*, whereas prosthetic valve endocarditis is more commonly caused by coag-ulase-negative staphylococci such as *Staphylococcus epidermidis*. Gram-negative bacilli and fungi together account for less than 10% of all endocarditis cases and usually are associated with IV drug abuse, valvular prostheses, and hospital-acquired intravenous ac-cess procedures. Endocarditis caused by anaerobes and other or-ganisms is rare. Polymicrobial infective endocarditis (caused by ≥2 organisms), while uncommon in the typical patient, is being recognized more frequently in IV drug abusers and postoperative patients. *Candida* species, *S. aureus*, *Pseudomonas aeruginosa*, *Serratia marcescens*, and nongroup D streptococci are the organ-isms involved most frequently.

Site of Involvement[1,2,6]

The site of heart valve involvement is determined by the un-derlying cardiac defect and the infecting organism. The mitral valve is affected in more than 85% of cases caused by *S. viridans* when rheumatic heart disease is the underlying abnormality. The tricuspid valve is the common site of involvement in staphylococ-cal endocarditis associated with IV drug abuse. In addition, more than one heart valve may be affected simultaneously. Overall the mitral valve is affected in about 86% of the cases, followed by the aortic (55%), tricuspid (20%), and pulmonic (1%) valves.

Classification[1]

In the past, infective endocarditis commonly was classified as either "acute bacterial endocarditis" (ABE) or "subacute bacterial endocarditis" (SBE), based upon the presentation and course of the untreated disease. The acute form, caused by relatively path-ogenic organisms such as *Staphylococcus aureus*, *Streptococcus pyogenes*, *Streptococcus pneumoniae* (pneumococcus), and *Neis-seria gonorrhoeae*, is characterized by high fevers, a "septic" ap-

Table 57.1	Conditions and Procedures for Antibiotic Prophylaxis[a,b]

Cardiac Conditions

Prophylaxis Recommended
- Prosthetic cardiac valves, including bioprosthetic and homograft valves
- Previous bacterial endocarditis, even in the absence of heart disease
- Most congenital cardiac malformations
- Rheumatic and other acquired valvular dysfunction, even after valvular surgery
- Hypertrophic cardiomyopathy
- Mitral valve prolapse with valvular regurgitation

Prophylaxis Not Recommended
- Isolated secundum atrial septal defect
- Surgical repair without residua beyond 6 months of secundum atrial septal defect, ventricular septal defect, or patent ductus arteriosus
- Previous coronary artery bypass graft surgery
- Mitral valve prolapse without valvular regurgitation[c]
- Physiologic, functional, or innocent heart rumors
- Previous Kawasaki disease without valvular dysfunction
- Previous rheumatic fever without valvular dysfunction
- Cardiac pacemakers and implanted defibrillators

Dental or Surgical Procedures

Prophylaxis Recommended
- Dental procedures known to induce gingival or mucosal bleeding, including professional cleaning
- Tonsillectomy and/or adenoidectomy
- Surgical operations that involve intestinal or respiratory mucosa
- Bronchoscopy with a rigid bronchoscope
- Sclerotherapy for esophageal varices
- Esophageal dilatation
- Gallbladder surgery
- Cystoscopy
- Urethral dilatation
- Urethral catheterization if urinary tract infection is present[d]
- Urinary tract surgery if urinary tract infection is present[d]
- Prostatic surgery
- Incision and drainage of infected tissue[d]
- Vaginal hysterectomy
- Vaginal delivery in the presence of infection[d]

Continued

Table 57.1	Conditions and Procedures for Antibiotic Prophylaxis^a,b (Continued)

Prophylaxis Not Recommended

- Dental procedures not likely to induce gingival bleeding, such as simple adjustment of orthodontic appliances or fillings above the gum line
- Injection of local intraoral anesthetic (except intraligamentary injections)
- Shedding of primary teeth
- Tympanostomy tube insertion
- Endotracheal intubation
- Bronchoscopy with a flexible bronchoscope, with or without biopsy
- Cardiac catheterization
- Endoscopy with or without gastrointestinal biopsy
- Cesarean section
- In the absence of infection for urethral catheterization, dilatation and curettage, uncomplicated vaginal delivery, therapeutic abortion, sterilization procedures, or insertion or removal of intrauterine devices

a This table lists selected procedures and conditions but is not meant to be all-inclusive.
b Adapted with permission from reference 119.
c Individuals who have a mitral valve prolapse associated with thickening and/or redundancy of the valve leaflets may be at increased risk for bacterial endocarditis, particularly men ≥45 years of age.
d In addition to prophylactic regimen for genitourinary procedures, antibiotic therapy should be directed against the most likely bacterial pathogen.
e In patients who have prosthetic heart valves, a previous history of endocarditis, or surgically constructed systemic-pulmonary shunts or conduits, physicians may choose to administer prophylactic antibiotics even for low-risk procedures that involve the lower respiratory, genitourinary, or gastrointestinal tracts.

pearance, systemic toxicity, and leukocytosis. The progression of the untreated disease is fulminant, resulting in death within several days to less than six weeks. Subacute bacterial endocarditis tends to develop in persons with pre-existing valvular disease and classically is caused by *S. viridans*, and more recently, *S. epidermidis*. Unlike the acute form, symptoms of subacute bacterial endocarditis begin insidiously and include weakness, fatigue, low grade fever, night sweats, anorexia, and weight loss, as well as other nonspecific complaints. Untreated SBE generally results in death within six weeks to three months.

There are two major problems associated with this classification. First, there is considerable overlap between acute and subacute bacterial endocarditis with respect to the clinical presentation and the course of disease. Second, this classification ignores many non-bacterial causes of endocarditis such as chlamydiae, rickettsiae, and fungi. Consequently, this classification system has been abandoned, although the terminology often is still used. The current system is based upon the causative organism and is preferable since it provides information regarding the probable course of the disease, the likelihood for underlying heart disease, and the appropriate antimicrobial regimens to employ.

Streptococcus Viridans Endocarditis
Clinical Presentation

1. A.G., a 57-year-old 60 kg male with chief complaints of fatigue, a persistent low grade fever, night sweats, arthralgias, and a 7 kg unintentional weight loss, was admitted to University Hospital for evaluation. Visual inspection revealed a cachectic, ill-appearing male in no acute distress. Physical examination on admission was significant for a grade III/VI diastolic murmur with mitral regurgitation (insufficiency), a temperature of 100.2 °F, conjunctival petechiae, subungual splinter hemorrhages, and Janeway lesions on the soles of both feet. There was no evidence of Roth spots, Osler's nodes, or nail clubbing. The remainder of his physical examination was unremarkable. A.G.'s past medical history is significant for rheumatic fever at age 8 and more recently, a dental procedure involving the extraction of 4 wisdom teeth. The history of his present illness is noteworthy for the development of the above-mentioned symptoms about 2 weeks after the dental procedure ($\approx$2 months before admission). His only current medication is ibuprofen 600 mg QID.

Relevant laboratory results include the following: hemoglobin (Hgb) 11.4 gm/dL; hematocrit (Hct) 34%; reticulocyte count 0.5%; white blood cell (WBC) count 85,000/mm^3 with 65% polys and 1% bands; blood urea nitrogen (BUN) 21 mg/dL; and serum creatinine (SrCr) 1.8 mg/dL. A urinalysis (UA) revealed 2+ proteinuria and 10–20 red blood cells (RBCs) per high power field (HPF). The erythrocyte sedimentation rate (ESR) on admission was elevated at 66 mm/hr and the rheumatoid factor (RF) was positive. The results of a 2-dimensional echocardiogram were unrevealing.

To establish the diagnosis of infective endocarditis, 5 blood cultures were obtained over 48 hours. The first 3 cultures obtained on day 1 are all reported to be growing alpha-hemolytic streptococci. While definitive confirmation and speciation of the organism is being performed, A.G. is started on penicillin G, 2 million units IV Q 4 hr (12 million units/day) and gentamicin, 120 mg (loading dose) followed by 60 mg Q 12 hr. Antimicrobial susceptibility results are pending. What clinical manifestations and laboratory abnormalities in A. G. are consistent with infective endocarditis? [SI units: Hgb 114 gm/L; Hct 0.34; reticulocyte count 0.005; WBC count 85 × 10^9/L with 0.65 polys and 0.01 bands; BUN 7.5 mmol/L of urea; and SrCr 159 μmol/L]

The clinical presentation of infective endocarditis is highly variable and can involve almost any organ system.[7] A.G. appears pale and chronically ill and represents the typical patient with subacute disease (e.g., that due to *S. viridans*). Nonspecific complaints consistent with endocarditis in A.G. include fatigue, weight loss, fever, night sweats, and arthralgias.[6] Only fever is present in the majority (90%) of patients with endocarditis. The fever is characteristically low grade and remittent, with peaks in the afternoon and evening. The temperature rarely exceeds 103 °F in subacute disease.[7] Musculoskeletal complaints such as arthralgias, myalgias, and back pain are common and may mimic rheumatic disease. Other symptoms can include lethargy, anorexia, malaise, nausea, and vomiting.[1] Because signs and symptoms are nonspecific and subtle, diagnosis often is difficult. In addition, the time from bacteremia to diagnosis often is prolonged as a result of the insidious progression of symptoms.[1,7]

The temporal relationship between A.G.'s dental procedure and the onset of symptoms make it the most obvious cause of bacteremia and subsequent endocarditis. Although it is assumed that prophylactic antibiotics were administered before the procedure, endocarditis can develop despite apparently adequate chemoprophylaxis.[8]

A.G. is noted to have a diastolic murmur with mitral insufficiency, a finding consistent with endocarditis caused by *S. viridans*. **Cardiac murmurs** are present in more than 85% of patients with endocarditis. However, murmurs frequently are absent in patients with acute disease (e.g., staphylococcal endocarditis), right-sided disease (e.g., endocarditis in IV drug abusers), or mural infection.[1]

A.G. exhibits several peripheral manifestations of infective endocarditis including conjunctival petechiae, Janeway lesions, and splinter hemorrhages. Overall, peripheral manifestations are found in 10% to 50% of cases, but none are pathognomonic for infective endocarditis. **Mucocutaneous petechial lesions** of the conjunctiva, mouth, or pharynx are present in 20% to 40% of patients, especially in those with long-standing disease. These lesions generally are small, nontender, and hemorrhagic in appearance and occur as a result of vasculitis or peripheral embolization. **Janeway lesions** are painless, hemorrhagic, macular plaques most commonly found on the palms and soles. **Splinter hemorrhages** are nonspecific findings that appear as red to brown linear streaks in the proximal portion of the fingers or toe nails. Other findings can include **Roth spots** (small, flame-shaped retinal hemorrhages with pale white centers found near the optic nerve) and **Osler's nodes** (purplish, nonhemorrhagic, painful nodules that develop on the subcutaneous pads of the fingers and toes or on palms and soles). **Clubbing** (broadening and thickening) of the nails also may be observed in patients with prolonged disease.[1,7,9]

Several laboratory findings are consistent with infective endocarditis in A.G. A low hemoglobin and hematocrit with normal red cell indices suggest anemia of chronic disease. Of patients with subacute disease, 70% to 90% will have a normochromic, normocytic **anemia** as part of their initial presentation. **Leukocytosis** with a left shift, while not evident in A.G., commonly is seen in those with acute, fulminant disease such as staphylococcal endocarditis. The erythrocyte sedimentation rate nearly always is elevated in infective endocarditis, but is nonspecific and may be associated with a number of other disease entities. Rheumatoid factor (an IgM antiglobulin) and circulating immune complexes can be detected in the majority of patients with long-standing disease, but both are nonspecific findings.[1]

Major embolic episodes and infarction involving the kidney, spleen, lung, and carotid artery may develop as **secondary complications** in up to one-third of cases.[1] A.G. presently exhibits some degree of renal damage as evidenced by moderate hematuria and proteinuria. Erythrocyte and leukocyte cast formation also may be present. Alteration in A.G.'s renal function (increased BUN and creatinine) probably is a result of immune complex deposition (diffuse glomerulonephritis) or secondary to renal embolization (focal glomerulonephritis). Fortunately, renal impairment usually is reversible with the institution of effective antimicrobial therapy.[10]

Splenomegaly, while not part of A.G.'s findings, occurs in 20% to 60% of all cases and is seen more commonly in patients with a prolonged subacute presentation. Neurological manifestations such as headache, mental change, aphasia, ataxia, hemiplegia, or seizures can occur in 20% to 40% of the cases and may be the only major presenting symptoms. Neurological signs make the diagnosis of bacterial endocarditis difficult to establish and are associated with a much higher mortality rate.[1,7]

More than 90% of the patients who exhibit a new regurgitant murmur will develop some degree of congestive heart failure (CHF), a major complication and the primary cause of death in patients with endocarditis.[10,11] Mitral valve injury caused by *S. viridans* generally is better tolerated hemodynamically than aortic valve injury due to staphylococci.[10] Although A.G. has no apparent signs of overt heart failure, he should be monitored closely for the development of hemodynamic instability.

Diagnosis

2. How was the diagnosis of infective endocarditis established in A.G.?

Blood Cultures

Although A.G.'s past medical history (rheumatic fever, recent dental procedure) and clinical presentation are highly suggestive of infective endocarditis, the definitive diagnosis can be made only with microbiological identification of the causative organism.[1]

Bacteremia secondary to endocarditis is continuous and low grade; more than 50% of the cultures have only 1 to 30 bacteria/mL. Despite the low concentration of organisms, bacteremia (when present) results in at least one of the first two blood cultures being positive in 95% of cases.[1,12] Administration of antibiotics within the previous two weeks may significantly decrease this yield.[13]

To minimize the risk of blood culture contamination, proper collection is extremely important. Each sample of blood (minimum of 10 mL from adults and 5 mL from children) should be obtained by separate venipuncture following a thorough cleansing of the skin. Multiple bottles filled with blood from a single venipuncture should be regarded as a single blood culture. Blood for culture should never be drawn through an indwelling catheter.[14]

Three to five blood cultures should be obtained over the first 24 to 48 hours.[1] In a "stable" patient such as A.G. who has had the disease for several weeks or months, it is important it establish the exact microbiological etiology before initiating antimicrobial therapy. Patients who are acutely ill should have empiric therapy started as soon as the appropriate cultures are obtained to avoid further valvular damage or other complications.[1,14] Three separate samples for blood culture (by separate venipuncture) obtained over 15 to 20 minutes will result in the isolation of the causative organism in virtually all cases.[12]

Adjunctive Imaging Studies

Echocardiography has become widely accepted as a noninvasive adjunct for diagnosing infective endocarditis, especially in culture-negative and fungal endocarditis. It is an extremely valuable test in identifying valvular vegetations, perivalvular abscesses, and valve destruction. Vegetations can be visualized with conventional transthoracic echocardiography in about 30% to 80% of patients with endocarditis,[129-131] and echocardiography using transesophageal imaging has increased the diagnostic accuracy significantly. When properly utilized, the latter can detect valvular vegetations with a sensitivity better than 95%[129,132] and it is up to eight times more sensitive than transthoracic imaging for detection of intracardiac abscesses.[129,132] However, because of the variable sensitivity associated with echocardiography, there is a high rate of false negative results, particularly in the setting of mechanical prosthetic valve endocarditis.[15,133]

In summary, infective endocarditis should be suspected in any patient who has a documented fever and heart murmur. Prior cardiac disease, the presence of peripheral manifestations, splenomegaly, various laboratory abnormalities, and a positive echocardiography further strengthen the diagnosis, but microbiological documentation is clearly the most important factor in confirming the presence of infective endocarditis. Disease entities with overlapping clinical presentation and laboratory abnormalities should be excluded using the appropriate tests.[1]

New criteria have been proposed for the diagnosis of endocarditis.[179] They are listed in Tables 57.2 and 57.3. A.G. possesses two major criteria (positive blood cultures and evidence of new valvular regurgitation) and several minor criteria (fever, predisposing heart condition, vascular and immunologic phenomena), therefore, he meets the diagnostic criteria for "definite" infective endocarditis.[179]

Antimicrobial Therapy

General Principles

3. What would be a reasonable duration of antibiotic therapy for A.G.? When are serum bactericidal titers (SBTs) useful in the management of bacterial endocarditis?

The avascular nature of the vegetation results in an environment that is devoid of normal host defenses (e.g., phagocytic cells and

Table 57.2	Proposed New Criteria for Diagnosis of Infective Endocarditis[a]

Definite Infective Endocarditis
Pathologic Criteria

- Micro-organisms: Demonstrated by culture or histology in a vegetation, *or* in a vegetation that has embolized, *or* in an intracardiac abscess, *or*
- Pathologic lesions: Vegetation or intracardiac abscess present, confirmed by histology showing active endocarditis

Clinical criteria, using specific definitions listed in Table 57.3

- 2 major criteria, *or*
- 1 major criteria and 3 minor criteria, *or*
- 5 minor criteria

Possible Infective Endocarditis

- Findings consistent with infective endocarditis that fall short of "definite," but not "rejected"

Rejected

- Firm alternate diagnosis for manifestations of endocarditis, *or*
- Resolution of manifestations of endocarditis, with antibiotic therapy for ≤4 days, *or*
- No pathologic evidence of infective endocarditis at surgery *or* autopsy, after antibiotic therapy for ≤4 days

[a] Adapted with permission from Durack et al. Diagnosis of infective endocarditis. Am J Med. 1994;46:203.

complement): this permits uninhibited growth of bacteria.[2] Therefore, to successfully eradicate the causative organism, high-doses of a parenterally administered, bactericidal antibiotic generally are administered for four to six weeks.[19] For some infections, it may be necessary to use two antibiotics to achieve synergistic activity against the organism.[20] For example, the addition of an aminoglycoside to penicillin results in a more rapid and complete bactericidal effect against the enterococcus.[21] (See Question 16 for a more detailed discussion of synergy.)

Once an organism has been identified, its *in vitro* susceptibility pattern is determined by the minimum inhibitory concentration (MIC) for various antibiotics. The minimum bactericidal concentration (MBC) also should be determined since truly tolerant organisms may not respond as well to therapy (see Question 15).[19,22] Treatment of endocarditis requires bactericidal activity; therefore, the serum concentration of the antibiotic must greatly exceed the MBC for the particular organism. For endocarditis caused by *S. viridans*, this usually is achieved without much problem since most isolates (90%) are sensitive to penicillin at an MIC of less than 0.2 μg/mL; corresponding MBCs are, at most, one or two tube dilutions higher.[19,23,24]

The serum bactericidal titer, commonly called a "Schlicter" test, is an *in vitro* modification of the minimum bactericidal concentration test. It measures the killing activity of the patient's serum (containing antibiotic) against the isolated organism.[25] To perform the test, a known inoculum of the patient's organism is added to serial dilutions of the patient's serum. The SBT is the highest dilution that kills 99% to 100% of the inoculum. The combination of a very sensitive, nontolerant organism (low MIC and low MBC) and a high concentration of a bactericidal antibiotic will produce a high SBT.[25,26] Not surprisingly, positive response rates correlate well with the attainment of high serum bactericidal titers.

There is a great deal of controversy surrounding the appropriate SBT required for successful treatment of bacterial endocarditis.[20] This is due, in part, to the lack of standardization of the serum bactericidal titer test.[27] In one large multicenter study using a standardized method, peak titers (dilutions) of ≥1:64 and trough titers

of ≥1:32 were needed to satisfactorily predict bacteriologic cure in all patients.[28] The serum bactericidal titer was a poor predictor of failure, since many patients who were cured had much lower serum bactericidal titers (e.g., <1:8). Until an accepted, standardized method is established, the SBT value for a given patient should be interpreted with caution. In spite of the inconclusive results, the antibiotic dosage (or selection) should be adjusted to achieve a peak (and if possible trough) level of antibiotic which is bactericidal at a serum dilution ≥1:8.[19,20,29–31]

The serum bactericidal titer test appears to be most useful in the following situations: 1) when endocarditis is due to relatively resistant organisms (e.g., relatively penicillin resistant *S. viridans* MIC >0.1 and <0.5 μg/mL) where a synergistic combination of antibiotics might be beneficial; 2) when response to therapy has been suboptimal; and 3) when less well-established regimens are used for treatment.[25,31] The SBT also may be useful to assess the effect on therapy of a change from parenteral to oral dosing, a change in dose or dosing interval, or the addition of other drugs.

Blood samples for determining the peak SBT are drawn about 30 minutes following completion of a 30 to 60 minute intravenous infusion or 60 to 90 minutes after intramuscular (IM) or oral ad-

Table 57.3	Definitions of Terminology Used in the Proposed New Criteria

Major Criteria
Positive blood culture for infective endocarditis

- Typical micro-organisms for infective endocarditis from 2 separate blood cultures
  - Viridans streptococci,[a] *Streptococcus bovis*, HACEK group,[b] *or*
  - Community-acquired *Staphylococcus aureus* or enterococci, in the absence of a primary focus, *or*
- Persistently positive blood culture, defined as recovery of a micro-organism consistent with infective endocarditis from:
  1) Blood cultures drawn more than 12 hr apart, *or*
  2) All of 3 or a majority of ≥4 separate blood cultures, with 1st and last drawn at least 1 hr apart

Evidence of endocarditis involvement

- Positive echocardiogram for infective endocarditis
  1) Oscillating intracardiac mass, on valve or supporting structures, *or* in the path of regurgitant jets, *or* on implanted material, in the absence of an alternative anatomic explanation, *or*
  2) Abscess, *or*
  3) New partial dehiscence of prosthetic valve, *or*
- New valvular regurgitation (increase or change in pre-existing murmur not sufficient)

Minor Criteria

- *Predisposition*: Predisposing heart condition or intravenous drug use
- Fever ≥38 °C (100.4 °F)
- *Vascular Phenomena*: Major arterial emboli, septic pulmonary infarcts, mycotic aneurysm, intracranial hemorrhage, conjunctival hemorrhages, Janeway lesions
- *Immunologic Phenomena*: Glomerulonephritis, Osler's nodes, Roth spots, rheumatoid factor
- *Microbiologic Evidence*: Positive blood culture but not meeting major criterion as noted previously,[c] or serologic evidence of active infection with organism consistent with infective endocarditis
- *Echocardiogram*: Consistent with infective endocarditis but not meeting major criterion as note previously

[a] Including nutritional variants.
[b] HACEK = *Hemophilus* sp., *Actinobacillus actinomycetemcomitans, Cardiobacterium hominis, Eikenella* sp., and *Kingella kingae.*
[c] Excluding single positive cultures for coagulase-negative staphylococci and organisms that do not cause endocarditis.

ministration of the antibiotic. Samples for trough SBT should be obtained just before the administration of the next antibiotic dose.[25] If more than one antibiotic is used (e.g., penicillin and an aminoglycoside), the peak SBT should be determined one hour after a time when the time for administration of both antibiotics coincides; and the trough SBT should be determined just before the less frequently administered antibiotic is given.[25] In addition, antibiotic drug concentrations should be at steady state before samples are collected for SBT determinations.[25]

4. What antibiotic regimens are most useful for the treatment of S. viridans endocarditis?

Patients with endocarditis caused by penicillin-sensitive strains of *S. viridans* and nonenterococcal Group D streptococci (e.g., *S. bovis*; MIC <0.1 µg/mL) can be treated with any one of three possible regimens.[31,32] The suggested regimens (see Table 57.4) are associated with cure rates of 95% to 99% and include: 1) high-dose parenteral penicillin for four weeks; 2) high-dose parenteral penicillin for four weeks combined with an aminoglycoside (usually gentamicin or streptomycin) for the first two weeks; and 3) two weeks of combined therapy with high-dose parenteral penicillin and an aminoglycoside.[33–36]

High-Dose Penicillin for Four Weeks

The intravenous administration of 10 to 20 million units/day of penicillin G for four weeks resulted in a cure rate of 100% for 66 patients with nonenterococcal streptococcal endocarditis.[33] Another study using penicillin alone reported relapse in only 2 of 49 patients; however, both patients who relapsed received less than four weeks of therapy.[37] The large range of 10 to 20 million units/day of penicillin is recommended to allow for flexibility in dosing based upon the patient's level of renal function and disease severity.

High-Dose Penicillin for Four Weeks
Plus an Aminoglycoside for Two Weeks

The combination of two weeks of streptomycin (or gentamicin) with four weeks of penicillin is synergistically bactericidal for most streptococci, including enterococci (see Question 16).[20,34] This *in vitro* synergy also has been correlated with a more rapid rate of eradication of *S. viridans* from cardiac vegetations in the rabbit model of endocarditis.[38] Whether an aminoglycoside in combination with penicillin is needed in humans is controversial since both regimens result in high cure rates and prospective comparative trials have not been performed.[31] In other words, for most patients with endocarditis due to penicillin-sensitive streptococci, it is unknown whether the increased risk of ototoxicity and nephrotoxicity secondary to an aminoglycoside is offset by any clinically significant advantage of the synergistic combination.

High-Dose Penicillin Plus an
Aminoglycoside for Two Weeks

A shortened combination regimen consisting of procaine penicillin G (1.2 million units IM Q 6 hr) and streptomycin (500 mg IM Q 6 hr) for two weeks is an effective alternative to the previously described regimens. The reported cure rate in 104 patients treated at the Mayo Clinics with this regimen was 99%.[34,35] Based upon available data, the two-week regimen appears to be efficacious for uncomplicated cases of *S. viridans* endocarditis. It is not currently recommended for patients with long-standing disease (>3 months), prosthetic valve infections, or those infected with nutritionally-deficient strains of *S. viridans* or penicillin resistant strains (MIC >0.2 µg/mL).[31,32]

Patients allergic to penicillin should be treated with vancomycin (500 mg IV Q 6 hr or 1000 mg IV Q 12 hr) for four weeks. In patients who have experienced minor reactions to penicillins (e.g.,

a delayed rash), a first-generation cephalosporin such as cefazolin (1 to 2 gm Q 6 to 8 hr) may be cautiously substituted. Although the addition of an aminoglycoside to a cephalosporin or vancomycin enhances bactericidal activity *in vitro*, it is unknown whether the addition of an aminoglycoside confers any additional clinical benefit.[31]

The risk of relapse may be higher in patients who have had symptoms for longer than three months before the initiation of treatment.[37,39] As a result, these patients should be treated with four weeks of penicillin combined with an aminoglycoside for the first two weeks.[31,32]

Nutritionally-deficient *S. viridans* are slow growing, fastidious organisms that have *in vitro* susceptibility patterns similar to other strains of *S. viridans*, but infections with these organisms are associated with a higher rate of relapse.[32,40] These slow growing bacteria are responsible for approximately 10% of the cases of *S. viridans* endocarditis. Because many of these organisms require the addition of vitamin B_6 (pyridoxal HCl) to the culture media for laboratory growth, an initial diagnosis of culture-negative endocarditis may be reported.[40] The animal model of endocarditis indicates that a penicillin-aminoglycoside (streptomycin or gentamicin) combination is significantly better than penicillin alone in reducing the bacterial counts of these organisms.[40] All patients infected with a nutritionally-deficient strain should receive two weeks of gentamicin or streptomycin with four weeks of penicillin. Patients with prosthetic valve endocarditis caused by *S. viridans* should be treated with penicillin for four weeks combined with an aminoglycoside for the first two weeks.[31,32]

Regimen Selection

5. What factors must be considered in selecting the regimen of choice for A. G.? Which regimen should be used for A.G.?

For the majority of cases of endocarditis due to penicillin-sensitive *S. viridans* (in patients not allergic to penicillin), all three of the above regimens are equally acceptable; therefore, the choice should be based upon their relative advantages and disadvantages. The two-week regimen is the most cost effective since it reduces the length of hospitalization by two weeks. Both the two-week regimen and four-week combined regimen have the disadvantage of possible ototoxicity and nephrotoxicity secondary to aminoglycoside administration. Therefore, it may be prudent to use four weeks of penicillin (alone) in elderly individuals (over 65 years) and those with impaired renal or vestibular function. The combined regimen consisting of penicillin for four weeks supplemented with an aminoglycoside for the first two weeks is preferred for patients infected with nutritionally-deficient variants of streptococci, relatively penicillin resistant strains, those with prosthetic valve infections, and individuals with long-standing disease.[31,32]

Assuming the *S. viridans* isolated from A.G. is not resistant to penicillin and he has no other complicating factors, any one of the suggested regimens would be appropriate. Since there is no compelling reason to use the four-week regimens, the two-week penicillin/aminoglycoside regimen is the most economical choice. Although A.G. has mild renal impairment, this is most likely secondary to the endocarditis and should improve once adequate antimicrobial therapy has been instituted. A.G. was begun on 12 million units/day of penicillin G which would be reasonable for his age and mild renal impairment. If nephrotoxicity is a major concern in A.G., switching from gentamicin to streptomycin or using penicillin alone for four weeks would be reasonable. If gentamicin is used, A.G.'s dose should be adjusted appropriately and he should be evaluated frequently for signs of toxicity. Periodic peak and trough aminoglycoside concentrations should be monitored.

Table 57.4	Suggested Regimens for Therapy for Endocarditis Due to *Streptococci viridans* and *Streptococci bovis*ᵃ	
Antibiotic	Dose and Routeᵇ	Duration

Penicillin-Susceptible (Minimum Inhibitory Concentration ≤0.1 μg/mL)

Nonpenicillin Allergic Patients

1) Aqueous crystalline penicillin Gᶜ	*Adult*: 10–20 million units/24 hr IV either continuously or in 6 equally divided doses *Pediatric*: 150,000–200,000 units/kg/24 hr IV (*max*: 20 million units/24 hr) either continuously or in 6 equally divided doses	4 weeks
2) Aqueous crystalline penicillin Gᵈ	*Adult*: 10–20 million units/24 hr IV either continuously or in 6 equally divided doses *Pediatric*: 150,000–200,000 units/kg/24 hr IV (*max*: 20 million units/24 hr) either continuously or in 6 equally divided doses	2–4 weeks
With streptomycinᵉ	*Adult*: 7.5 mg/kg IM (*max*: 500 mg) Q 12 hr *Pediatric*: 15 mg/kg IM (*max*: 500 mg) Q 12 hr	2 weeks
or		
With gentamicinᵉ	*Adult*: 1 mg/kg IM or IV (*max*: 80 mg) Q 8 hr *Pediatric*: 2–2.5 mg/kg IV (*max*: 80 mg) Q 8 hr	2 weeks

Penicillin Allergic Patients

1) Cefazolinᶠ,�g	*Adult*: 1 gm IM or IV Q 8 hr *Pediatric*: 80–100 mg/kg/24 hr IM or IV (*max*: 3 gm/24 hr) in equally divided doses Q 8 hr	4 weeks
2) Vancomycinʰ	*Adult*: 30 mg/kg/24 hr IV in 2 or 4 equally divided doses (*max*: 2 gm/24 hr unless serum levels monitored) *Pediatric*: 40 mg/kg/24 hr IV in 2 or 4 equally divided doses (*max*: 2 gm/24 hr unless serum levels monitored)	4 weeks

Relatively Penicillin G Resistant (Minimum Inhibitory Concentration >0.1 μg/mL and <0.5 μg/mL)ⁱ

Aqueous crystalline penicillin G	*Adult*: 20 million units/24 hr IV either continuously or in 6 equally divided doses *Pediatric*: 200,000–300,000 units/kg/24 hr IV (*max*: 20 million units/24 hr) either continuously or in 6 equally divided doses	4 weeks
With Streptomycinʲ	*Adult*: 7.5 mg/kg IM (*max*: 500 mg) Q 12 hr *Pediatric*: 15 mg/kg IM Q 12 hr	2 weeks
or		
With Gentamicinʲ	*Adult*: 1 mg/kg IM or IV (*max*: 80 mg/kg) Q 8 hr *Pediatric*: 2–2.5 mg/kg IM or IV (*max*: 80 mg) Q 8 hr	2 weeks

ᵃ Adapted with permission from reference 31.

ᵇ Antibiotic doses for patients with impaired renal function should be modified appropriately. Vancomycin dose should be reduced in patients with renal dysfunction; cephalosporin dose may need to be reduced in patients with moderate to severe renal dysfunction.

ᶜ Preferred in most patients over 65 years of age and in those with impairment of the 8th nerve or of renal function.

ᵈ Or procaine penicillin G, 1.2 million units IM Q 6 hr. Procaine penicillin G is not recommended for treatment of endocarditis due to *streptococci viridans* in children.

ᵉ Should be given in addition to penicillin. If regimen 3 is selected, streptomycin or gentamicin should be given for the first 2 weeks. Peak streptomycin levels of ≈20 μg/mL and peak gentamicin levels of ≈3 μg/mL are desirable. Dosing of aminoglycosides on a mg/kg basis will produce higher serum concentrations in obese than in lean patients. Relative contraindications to use of aminoglycosides are age >65 years and renal or 8th nerve impairment.

ᶠ Streptomycin or gentamicin may be added to cephalothin or cefazolin for first 2 weeks in doses recommended for nonpenicillin allergic patients.

�g There is potential cross-allergenicity between penicillins and cephalosporins. Cephalosporins should be avoided in patients with immediate-type hypersensitivity to penicillin.

ʰ Peak serum concentrations of vancomycin should be obtained 1 hour after infusion and should be in the range of 30–45 μg/mL for BID dosing and 20–30 μg/mL for QID dosing. Trough serum concentrations should be obtained within half an hour of the next dose and be in the range of 5–15 μg/mL. Vancomycin or aminoglycosides given on a mg/kg basis will produce higher serum concentrations in obese than in lean patients.

ⁱ Cefazolin (with an aminoglycoside for the first 2 weeks) or vancomycin alone can be used in patients whose penicillin hypersensitivity is not of the immediate type. Vancomycin also can be used in patients with immediate penicillin allergy. Antibiotic doses should be modified appropriately for patients with impaired renal function.

ʲ Streptomycin or gentamicin should be given in addition to penicillin for the first 2 weeks. Peak streptomycin levels of 20 μg/mL and peak gentamicin levels of about 3 μg/mL are desirable. For the rare *Streptococcus viridans* with an MIC ≥0.5 μg/mL of penicillin G, aminoglycoside therapy should be continued for 4 weeks with appropriate monitoring of serum levels of streptomycin or gentamicin. Aminoglycosides given on a mg/kg basis will produce higher serum concentrations in obese than in lean patients.

Staphylococcus Epidermidis: Prosthetic Valve Endocarditis (PVE)

Etiology

6. F.T., a 65-year-old male, presents with chief complaints of anorexia, fever, chills, and weight loss. His past medical history is significant for replacement of his mitral and aortic heart valves (both porcine) 1 year ago for aortic stenosis, mitral regurgitation, and mitral stenosis secondary to rheumatic heart disease. One month later he was readmitted with fever, a right pleural effusion, a pericardial friction rub, and pericarditis. The impression at that time was either post-pericardotomy syndrome or Dressler's syndrome. F.T. was sent home on anti-inflammatory agents, but failed to improve. After continued complaints of anorexia, nausea, chills, and fever to 101 °F, he returned to the hospital. On readmission his physical examination was noteworthy for a systolic ejection murmur at the left sternal border and 3+ pedal edema. Blood cultures were obtained and routine laboratory studies were performed. His history and clinical presentation were strongly suggestive of prosthetic valve endocarditis. What are the most likely etiologic agents responsible for prosthetic valve endocarditis in F.T.?

Prosthetic valve endocarditis is a life-threatening infectious complication of artificial heart valve insertion.[41] While the frequency of this infection is low (see Question 7), it is associated with significant morbidity and mortality.[42] The prevalence of complications resulting in death has been as high as 20% to 40%.[41] Prosthetic valve endocarditis is categorized as early or late depending upon the onset of clinical manifestations following cardiac surgery.[43] Early prosthetic valve endocarditis occurs up to one year following surgery and is thought to represent infection acquired during placement of the valve. It usually is caused by skin organisms which were implanted into the valve annulus (suture site where the valve is attached to cardiac muscle) at the time of surgery.[43] The most common organisms cultured from patients like F.T. with early prosthetic valve endocarditis are coagulase-negative staphylococci [primarily *S. epidermidis* (30%) of which most are resistant to methicillin], *S. aureus* (10% to 20%), and gram-negative bacilli (10% to 20%). Miscellaneous organisms such as diphtheroids and fungi account for the remainder.[42] In contrast, late prosthetic valve endocarditis, representing infection of the valve leaflet, is caused by the same organisms that are responsible for native valve endocarditis.[41]

Prophylaxis

7. What measures can be taken to prevent early prosthetic valve endocarditis?

The overall frequency of early prosthetic valve endocarditis, despite antibiotic prophylaxis, is 1% to 4%.[41] Complications are severe and include valve dehiscence, acute heart failure, dysrhythmias, and outflow obstruction. Although antibiotic prophylaxis before valve surgery (a "clean" procedure) has not been proven to reduce the frequency of early prosthetic valve endocarditis, it is indicated nevertheless, since the complications of infection are catastrophic. Animal data indicate that antibiotic prophylaxis reduces the infection rate.[44]

Cephalosporins

The antimicrobial regimen which has been used most commonly for prophylaxis consists of a first-generation cephalosporin, such as cefazolin, given in the operating room at the time of anesthesia, or at the time the patient is called to the operating room ("on call"). Administration in the operating room is preferable, since higher concentrations are achieved. Cephalosporins are frequently selected since they are active against most strains of *S. aureus*. Historically, they also were active against coagulase-negative staphylococci; however, the current incidence of methicillin (and cephalosporin) resistance among coagulase-negative staphylococci is as high as 80% for nosocomial isolates.[42,43] Resistance is thought to be due to an altered penicillin binding protein (PBP 2a); thus, cross resistance to all other beta-lactams is expected.[45] This latter point is an area of active research, since it has implications for prophylaxis and treatment.

The prophylactic administration of second-generation cephalosporins, cefuroxime (Zinacef) and cefamandole (Mandol), resulted in a lower incidence of postoperative wound infections (not prosthetic valve endocarditis) due to *S. aureus* when compared to cefazolin;[46,47] however, the results were not sufficiently impressive to displace the more common practice of using cefazolin.[30,41] Since *S. aureus* usually is considered equally sensitive to the above three drugs, the explanation for these disparate findings is unclear. Improved stability to some staphylococcal beta-lactamases for the second-generation cephalosporins has been proposed as a possible explanation.[48,49]

When a first-generation cephalosporin cannot be used, vancomycin is the alternative prophylactic agent of choice. It is the only currently available agent which is reliably active against *S. aureus* (including methicillin resistant isolates) and coagulase-negative staphylococci.

When vancomycin (Vancocin), cefazolin (Ancef), and cefamandole (Mandol) were administered for surgical prophylaxis in 321 patients undergoing cardiac or major vascular operations,[174] the overall surgical wound infection rates were 3.6%, 12.3%, and 11.5% (p = 0.05), respectively. Furthermore, there were no thoracic wound infections in the vancomycin group versus 7% (p = 0.04) in the cefazolin group and 4% in those receiving cefamandole. Due to vancomycin's superiority over the two cephalosporins it could be considered as the prophylactic agent for the following situations: 1) prosthetic valve replacement[151] and implantation of prosthetic grafts; 2) any cardiovascular procedure in which the patient recently has received broad-spectrum antimicrobial therapy and is likely to be colonized with cephalosporin resistant staphylococci or enterococci; and 3) cardiovascular procedures in centers experiencing outbreaks or a high endemic rate of surgical infection with methicillin resistant staphylococci. While the effectiveness of vancomycin prophylaxis appeared better than that afforded by cefazolin, hypotension developed in eight patients treated with vancomycin, two patients treated with cefazolin (p = 0.06), and in none treated with cefamandole. Five of the eight patients, however, were able to continue on vancomycin after slowing the rate of infusion to greater than one hour or pretreating with diphenhydramine (Benadryl).

Investigational agents with good activity against methicillin resistant staphylococci include teicoplanin, daptomycin, and the fluoroquinolones; however, efficacy of these drugs in this setting remains unproven.[134]

Vancomycin

8. What are the disadvantages for the routine use of vancomycin as a prophylactic agent?

Since the frequency of prosthetic valve endocarditis is low, it would be nearly impossible to demonstrate a statistically significant decrease in its incidence following the use of vancomycin as compared to conventional agents. Thus, the decision to use vancomycin rests upon its superior *in vitro* activity for *methicillin resistant staphylococci*. However, there are compelling arguments against the use of vancomycin in this specific setting.[41] First, the cost of vancomycin and the monitoring of serum concentrations is significantly more than the cost of first-generation cephalosporins. Second, although resistance to vancomycin has been reported only rarely,[51] increasing usage likely will increase resistance and limit its future utility. Finally, the potential for toxicity of vancomycin, especially hypotension, is a major concern.[50]

In summary, the most appropriate prophylactic antibiotic for valve-replacement surgery is controversial. The decision should be based upon conditions at each institution such as the infection rate, the types of organisms recovered, the number of procedures performed, and the feasibility of implementing effective infection control measures.

9. Adverse Effects. What is the most common infusion-related adverse effect associated with vancomycin, and how can it be minimized?

The most common adverse effect associated with vancomycin administration is the so-called "red man" or "red neck" syndrome.[52] This syndrome most commonly causes erythema of the head and upper torso, pruritus, urticaria, and in some cases, hypotension.[53] It is mediated, in part, by histamine release and the severity of the reaction is proportional to the quantity released (see Chapter 6: Anaphylaxis and Drug Allergy). The total dose of vancomycin administered and the rate of infusion are major determinants of the reaction frequency and its severity. This reaction can be minimized when vancomycin is administered over at least one hour. Nevertheless, cutaneous manifestations of the vancomycin-induced ''red man syndrome'' still can occur with a one-hour infusion; however, hypotension is uncommon.[50,52,53]

Several drugs used perioperatively and in anesthesia also cause histamine release; therefore, the possibility of additive toxicity with vancomycin cannot be dismissed. Most of the serious reactions caused by vancomycin have occurred in patients scheduled for surgery. Vancomycin-induced hypotension occurred in 7% of patients scheduled for cardiothoracic surgery despite the one-hour infusion time.[50]

10. Administration. **If vancomycin is used prophylactically to prevent prosthetic valve endocarditis, when should it be administered relative to the time of surgery?**

Vancomycin cannot practically be given in the operating room because it must be administered by infusion over one hour; and ''on-call'' administration may not provide sufficient time for the vancomycin infusion to achieve adequate serum and tissue levels. Vancomycin therapeutic serum concentrations during surgery can be reliably maintained if the 15 mg/kg dose is infused over one hour just before initiation of anesthesia.[50]

Antimicrobial Therapy

11. What are the treatment options for F.T.?

As noted earlier, F.T. most likely is infected with coagulase-negative staphylococci. For those rare coagulase-negative staphylococci which remain sensitive to beta-lactams (<20%), a penicillinase resistant penicillin (nafcillin or oxacillin) is the drug of choice (see Table 57.5).[54] For the treatment of prosthetic valve endocarditis caused by methicillin resistant, coagulase-negative staphylococci, vancomycin remains the cornerstone of therapy.[43] Virtually all staphylococci remain sensitive to vancomycin at concentrations of less than 5 μg/mL, and the reported resistant isolates are noteworthy for their infrequency.[51]

The major unresolved question concerning the treatment of prosthetic valve endocarditis caused by methicillin resistant, coagulase-negative staphylococci is whether more than one antibiotic should be used. In a retrospective review of 75 episodes of prosthetic valve endocarditis caused by *methicillin resistant Staphylococcus epidermidis (MRSE)*,[54] 21 of 26 patients treated with vancomycin were cured compared to 10 of 20 patients who were treated with a beta-lactam antibiotic (p = 0.05); however, the addition of either rifampin or an aminoglycoside to vancomycin appeared to produce superior results (18 of 20 cured) compared to vancomycin alone (3 of 6 cured, p = 0.06). A subsequent prospective multicenter study compared the efficacy of six weeks of vancomycin plus rifampin with and without gentamicin for the first two weeks for the treatment of prosthetic valve endocarditis caused by *methicillin resistant S. epidermidis*.[55] The emergence of rifampin resistant strains during therapy was reduced by the addition of gentamicin (6 of 15 versus 0 of 8, p = 0.04). Based upon current data, a three-drug regimen (vancomycin, gentamicin, and rifampin) appears to be optimal for the medical treatment of prosthetic valve endocarditis caused by *methicillin resistant S. epidermidis*, although toxicity would be expected to be greater. When isolates of *methicillin resistant S. epidermidis* are gentamicin resistant, this three-drug regimen would not be reasonable. In addition, most patients who responded to medical treatment also required valve replacement surgery.[43,56]

Staphylococcus Aureus Endocarditis
Intravenous Drug Abuser versus Nonabuser

12. T.J., a 36-year-old male with a long history of IV drug abuse, was admitted to the hospital 4 months after being re- leased from the state prison. His chief complaints on admission were fever, night sweats, pleuritic chest pain, shortness of breath (SOB), dyspnea on exertion (DOE), and fatigue. Physical examination was remarkable for a temperature of 101.2 °F, splenomegaly, and a pansystolic ejection murmur at the left sternal border, best heard during inspiration. Chest x-ray revealed diffuse nodular infiltrates. Significant laboratory results included: WBC count 14,000/mm³ with 65% polys and 5% bands; Hgb 13.1 gm/dL; Hct 39%; and an ESR of 55 mm/hr (Westergren). Infective endocarditis was suspected. Blood cultures were obtained and 6 out of 6 samples were positive for coagulase-positive cocci, later identified as methicillin-sensitive *S. aureus*. How does the clinical presentation and prognosis of endocarditis in the intravenous drug abuser differ from that of the nonabuser? [SI units: WBC 14 × 10⁹/L with 0.65 polys and 0.05 bands; Hgb 131 gm/L; Hct 0.39]

The presentation, pathophysiology, and prognosis of endocarditis in those who acquire the disease secondary to IV drug abuse differ from that in nonabusers.[57] Although *S. aureus* is the pathogen in approximately 30% of all cases of native valve endocarditis, this organism is the most common cause of endocarditis (60% to 90%) in the drug abuser.[58] *S. aureus* is part of the normal skin flora and is introduced when the illicit drug is injected. It is hypothesized that insoluble agents used to ''cut'' the drug damage the normal heart valve, preparing the surface for bacterial adherence and growth.

The following are differences between addicts and nonaddicts with *S. aureus* endocarditis: the addict group 1) was significantly younger; 2) had fewer underlying diseases; 3) had more right-sided (tricuspid) involvement in contrast to the predominance of left-sided disease in the nonaddict; 4) was less likely to suffer from heart failure or central nervous system (CNS) complications; 5) exhibited fewer signs of peripheral involvement; and 6) had a lower incidence of death.[57]

Antimicrobial Therapy

13. What are the therapeutic options for treating *S. aureus* endocarditis in T.J.?

Methicillin-Sensitive S. aureus (MSSA)

Whether the *S. aureus* is methicillin-sensitive or methicillin resistant is the major determinant of the antibiotic selected to treat T.J.'s endocarditis. T.J. is infected with MSSA. The therapy of choice for methicillin-sensitive strains is a penicillinase resistant penicillin, such as nafcillin or oxacillin[56] (see Table 57.5). Penicillin G rarely is appropriate since nearly all isolates of *S. aureus* produce penicillinase. Methicillin itself rarely is used because it is associated with a high incidence of interstitial nephritis.

Prospective, randomized, clinical trials have established that four to six weeks of therapy with high-dose (12 gm/day) nafcillin is effective in the majority of patients.[56,59,60] Intravenous drug addicts, for the reasons previously identified, have a higher response rate to appropriate therapy compared to nonaddicts, and four weeks of therapy is probably adequate. In one study, 31 addicts were successfully treated with 16 days of parenteral therapy followed by 26 days of oral dicloxacillin.[61]

Addicts with uncomplicated right-sided endocarditis caused by methicillin-sensitive *S. aureus* can be treated successfully with an abbreviated course of therapy.[62] In one study, 47 of 50 patients (94%) were cured after treatment with the combination of IV nafcillin (1.5 gm Q 4 hr) and tobramycin (1 mg/kg Q 8 hr) for a total of two weeks. Surprisingly, two of three patients in this study who were treated with vancomycin relapsed, resulting in early termination of this arm of study.

Table 57.5	Treatment of Staphylococcal Endocarditis[a]	
Antibiotic	Dose and Route[b]	Duration
In the Absence of Prosthetic Material[b]		
Methicillin-Susceptible Staphylococci		
Nonpenicillin Allergic Patients		
Nafcillin	*Adult:* 2 gm IV Q 4 hr	4–6 weeks
or	*Pediatric:* 150–200 mg/kg/24 hr IV (*max:* 12 gm/24 hr) in 4–6 equally divided doses	
Oxacillin	*Adult:* 2 gm IV Q 4 hr	4–6 weeks
	Pediatric: 150–200 mg/kg/24 hr IV (*max:* 12 gm/24 hr) in 4–6 equally divided doses	
With optional addition of gentamicin[c,d]	*Adult:* 1 mg/kg IM or IV (*max:* 80 mg) Q 8 hr *Pediatric:* 2–2.5 mg/kg IV (*max:* 80 mg) Q 8 hr	3–5 days
Penicillin Allergic Patients		
1) Cefazolin[e]	*Adult:* 2 gm IV Q 8 hr	4–6 weeks
	Pediatric: 80–100 mg/kg/24 hr IV (max: 6 gm/24 hr) in equally divided doses Q 8 hr	
With optional addition of gentamicin[c]	*Adult:* See Nonpenicillin allergic patient *Pediatric:* See Nonpenicillin allergic patient	4–6 weeks
2) Vancomycin[c,f,h]	*Adult:* 30 mg/kg/24 hr IV in 2 or 4 equally divided doses (*max:* 2 gm/24 hr unless serum levels monitored) *Pediatric:* 40 mg/kg/24 hr IV in 2 or 4 equally divided doses (*max:* 2 gm/24 hr unless serum levels monitored)	4–6 weeks
Methicillin-Resistant Staphylococci		
Vancomycin[c,f,h]	*Adult:* 30 mg/kg/24 hr IV in 2 or 4 equally divided doses (*max:* 2 gm/24 hr unless serum levels monitored) *Pediatric:* 40 mg/kg/24 hr IV in 2 or 4 equally divided doses (*max:* 2 gm/24 hr unless serum levels monitored)	4–6 weeks
In the Presence of Prosthetic Valve or Other Prosthetic Material[g]		
Methicillin-Resistant Staphylococci		
Vancomycin[c,f]	*Adult:* 30 mg/kg/24 hr IV in 2 or 4 equally divided doses (max: 2 gm/24 hr unless serum levels monitored) *Pediatric:* 40 mg/kg/24 hr IV in 2 or 4 equally divided doses (*max:* 2 gm/24 hr unless serum levels monitored)	≥6 weeks
With rifampin[i]	*Adult:* 300 mg PO Q 8 hr	≥6 weeks
and	*Pediatric:* 20 mg/kg/24 hr PO (*max:* 900 mg/24 hr) in 2 equally divided doses	
With gentamicin[c,j,k]	*Adult:* 1 mg/kg IM or IV (*max:* 80 mg) Q 8 hr *Pediatric:* 2–2.5 mg/kg/24 hr IV (*max:* 80 mg) Q 8 hr	2 weeks
Methicillin-Susceptible Staphylococci		
Nafcillin or oxacillin[l]	*Adult:* 2 gm IV Q 4 hr *Pediatric:* 150–200 mg/kg/24 hr (*max:* 12 gm/24 hr) in 4–6 equally divided doses	≥6 weeks
With rifampin[i]	*Adult:* 300 mg PO Q 8 hr	≥6 weeks
and	*Pediatric:* 20 mg/kg/24 hr PO (*max:* 900 mg/24 hr) in 2 equally divided doses	
With gentamicin[c,j,k]	*Adult:* 1 mg/kg IM or IV (*max:* 80 mg) Q 8 hr *Pediatric:* 2–2.5 mg/kg IV (*max:* 80 mg) Q 8 hr	2 weeks

[a] Adapted with permission from reference 31.

[b] Antibiotic doses should be modified appropriately for patients with impaired renal function. For treatment of endocarditis due to penicillin-susceptible staphylococci (MIC ≤0.1 µg/mL), aqueous crystalline penicillin G (Table 57.4, first regimen) should be used for 4–6 weeks instead of nafcillin or oxacillin. Shorter antibiotic courses have been effective in some drug addicts with right-sided endocarditis due to *S. aureus.* See text for comments on use of rifampin.

[c] Dosing of aminoglycosides and vancomycin on a mg/kg basis will give higher serum concentrations in obese than in lean patients.

[d] Benefit of additional aminoglycoside has not been established. Risk of toxic reactions due to these agents is increased in patients >65 years of age or those with renal or 8th nerve impairment.

[e] There is potential cross-allergenicity between penicillins and cephalosporins. Cephalosporins should be avoided in patients with immediate-type hypersensitivity to penicillin. (See Chapter 6: Anaphylaxis and Drug Allergy.)

[f] Peak serum concentrations of vancomycin should be obtained 1 hour after infusion and be in the range of 30–45 µg/mL for BID dosing and 20–30 µg/mL for QID dosing. Trough serum concentrations should be obtained within half an hour of the next dose and be in the range of 5–15 µg/mL. Each vancomycin dose should be infused over 1 hour.

[g] Vancomycin and gentamicin doses must be modified appropriately in patients with renal failure.

[h] See text for consideration of optional addition of gentamicin.

[i] Rifampin is recommended for therapy of infections due to coagulase-negative staphylococci. Its use in coagulase-positive staphylococcal infections is controversial. Rifampin increases the amount of warfarin sodium required for antithrombotic therapy.

[j] Serum concentration of gentamicin should be monitored and dose should be adjusted to obtain a peak level of ≈3 µg/mL.

[k] Use during initial 2 weeks. See text on alternative aminoglycoside therapy for organisms resistant to gentamicin.

[l] First-generation cephalosporins or vancomycin should be used in penicillin-allergic patients. Cephalosporins should be avoided in patients with immediate-type hypersensitivity to penicillin and those infected with methicillin-resistant staphylococci.

Ten addicts with uncomplicated right-sided endocarditis caused by methicillin-sensitive *S. aureus*[63] were treated successfully with oral rifampin (300 mg Q 12 hr) for the first seven days followed by 21 days of oral ciprofloxacin (750 mg Q 12 hr). These findings require confirmation in randomized trials before such an abbreviated oral regimen can be recommended.

Penicillin-Allergic Patients. Treatment of the penicillin-allergic patient with *S. aureus* endocarditis is somewhat controversial. First-generation cephalosporins have been used with some success for the treatment of patients with mild penicillin allergy; however, treatment failures with cefazolin are difficult to explain satisfactorily.[64] The stability of cefazolin when exposed to staphylococcal beta-lactamase has been proposed as a mechanism for these failures.[48,49] Until further data are available, vancomycin should be used to treat the penicillin-allergic patient with endocarditis caused by *S. aureus*.

14. Combination Therapy. Will the addition of another antibiotic enhance T.J.'s response to nafcillin?

An enhanced response to combination therapy in the experimental animal model of methicillin-sensitive *S. aureus* endocarditis has prompted clinical trials to evaluate whether the addition of gentamicin to nafcillin confers any additional benefit. The combination of nafcillin and gentamicin resulted in a more rapid clearing of organisms from the blood; however, the response rates were similar to patients treated with nafcillin alone.[59,60] As expected, the group receiving gentamicin had a higher incidence of nephrotoxicity. Thus, for the routine management of endocarditis due to methicillin-sensitive *S. aureus*, the addition of a second drug does not appear to offer additional benefit. The addition of rifampin may be indicated in the patient who remains bacteremic or in the patient who fails to improve clinically (usually the nonaddict).[56]

Methicillin Resistant S. aureus (MRSA): Vancomycin

15. How would T.J.'s therapy differ if he were infected with a methicillin resistant strain of *S. aureus*?

Although endocarditis due to *methicillin resistant S. aureus* is relatively uncommon, it occurs in some communities of IV drug abusers with a much higher frequency. As a nosocomial pathogen, *methicillin resistant S. aureus* also can cause endocarditis in the hospitalized patient.

Failure to correctly identify the organism's susceptibility may result in disastrous consequences. *Methicillin resistant Staphylococcus aureus* may be mistaken for sensitive strains when routine susceptibility testing methods are used. Therefore, detailed procedures for identifying these organisms have been published.[65] Methicillin resistance is heterotypic; in other words, only one in every 10^6 organisms will be resistant. The resistance mechanism is similar to that already discussed for *S. epidermidis* (see Question 7). As a result, *methicillin resistant S. aureus* should be considered resistant to all beta-lactam antibiotics.[43]

Dosing. The treatment of choice for *methicillin resistant S. aureus* endocarditis is vancomycin, for which no resistant strains of *S. aureus* have been identified. Vancomycin 2 gm/day in divided doses for a total of four to six weeks is recommended for adults with normal renal function. Peak serum vancomycin concentrations of 25 to 40 μg/mL one hour after a one-hour infusion of 1 gm should provide maximal benefit at a low frequency of toxicity.[66] Subjects with body weights markedly different from 70 kg are likely to have concentrations above or below the recommended guidelines, so that administration of 30 mg/kg/day (in divided doses) may be appropriate for these individuals.

The addition of a second drug, such as an aminoglycoside or rifampin, for the routine management of endocarditis caused by methicillin resistant *S. aureus* is unnecessary,[56] and the coadmin-

istration of vancomycin with an aminoglycoside increases the potential for additive or synergistic nephrotoxicity (see Question 21).[67,135] Trimethoprim-sulfamethoxazole has been used successfully in a limited number of patients with right-sided native valve endocarditis due to susceptible strains of *S. aureus* and may be an alternative to vancomycin.[56,68] However, a recent study of experimental staphylococcal endocarditis found trimethoprim-sulfamethoxazole to be inferior to cloxacillin, vancomycin, and teicoplanin.[180]

Penicillins, cephalosporins, and vancomycin are bactericidal for *S. aureus*. However, some *S. aureus* demonstrate marked resistance, called "tolerance," to this killing effect. Tolerance is manifested by a high MBC to MIC ratio (MBC usually >8 times the MIC) or a decreased rate of kill.[69]

At one time, there was a great deal of concern regarding these tolerant organisms, since optimal treatment of endocarditis requires bactericidal antibiotics; however, clinical studies evaluating the response of tolerant versus nontolerant strains to beta-lactam therapy were equivocal.[69] In retrospect, inconsistency in the laboratory identification of tolerant strains and a general lack of agreement on the definition of tolerance may have contributed to confusion. It is possible, for example, that tolerance may be a laboratory phenomenon of little clinical relevance.

Since the majority of *S. aureus* strains do not demonstrate tolerance when careful studies are performed, it is unnecessary to routinely screen for tolerant strains. If the facilities are available, it may be appropriate to study clinical isolates which are associated with unexplained treatment failures. If truly tolerant strains are identified, a second drug such as rifampin should be added.

Although vancomycin is the drug of choice for methicillin resistant *S. aureus* endocarditis, patients with methicillin-sensitive *S. aureus* endocarditis seem to respond less rapidly to vancomycin than to semisynthetic penicillins (e.g., nafcillin).[176] The mean duration of bacteremia in patients with methicillin-sensitive *S. aureus* endocarditis has been reported to be 3.4 days for nafcillin alone and 2.9 days for the combination of nafcillin and gentamicin.[57,59] The median duration of bacteremia for methicillin resistant *S. aureus* endocarditis was seven days for vancomycin alone and nine days for vancomycin with rifampin.[176] While the bacteremia with methicillin resistant *S. aureus* isolates responds slower than methicillin-sensitive *S. aureus* isolates to the antibiotics of choice, most patients respond to therapy without complications.

Enterococcal Endocarditis

Antimicrobial Therapy

Antibiotic Synergy

16. G.S., a 35-year-old female, has complained of anorexia, weight loss, and fever for the past 2 months. Her past medical history is significant for an aortic aneurysm with insufficiency that resulted in an aortic valve replacement (porcine) 3 years before admission. Approximately 2 months before admission, G.S. had a cesarean section followed by a tubal ligation. She did not receive antibiotic prophylaxis for either procedure.

Physical examination revealed a thin female (5′0″, 48 kg) in no acute distress with evidence of a systolic heart murmur, splinter hemorrhages, and petechiae on her soft palate. Her temperature at that time was 100.2 °F.

Her WBC was 14,000/mm³ with a slight left shift; all other laboratory results were within normal limits. She was not on any medications and she has a documented allergy to penicillin (rash, urticaria, and wheezing). The impression at that time was probable bacterial endocarditis. Four sets of blood cultures were obtained that later grew streptococci. Biochemical testing subsequently identified the organism as an enterococcus

(*Enterococcus faecalis*) highly resistant to streptomycin (MIC >2000 µg/mL). Antibiotic therapy with gentamicin (50 mg IV Q 8 hr) and vancomycin (1000 mg IV Q 12 hr) was begun. Why are two antibiotics prescribed for the treatment of enterococcal endocarditis in G.S.? [SI unit: WBC 14 × 10⁹/L]

Enterococci, unlike streptococci, are inhibited, but not killed by penicillin or vancomycin alone.[21,70,71] The synergistic combination of penicillin (or ampicillin, piperacillin, or vancomycin) and an aminoglycoside is required to produce the desired bactericidal effect.[20,72] An antibiotic regimen is synergistic when a combination of antibiotics lowers the MIC to at least one-fourth the minimum inhibitory concentration of either drug alone.[73] The mechanism of synergy against enterococci is due to an increased cellular uptake of the aminoglycoside in the presence of agents that inhibit cell wall synthesis[74] (e.g., beta-lactams and vancomycin). Since G.S. is allergic to penicillin, vancomycin was prescribed with an aminoglycoside. Relapse rates are unacceptably high if penicillin is used alone for the treatment of enterococcal endocarditis.[21,75–78] The addition of an aminoglycoside to penicillin therapy markedly increases the sterilization rate of vegetations in animal studies.[76,77] Several clinical studies have since demonstrated the efficacy of penicillin plus streptomycin therapy for enterococcal endocarditis.[78–80]

Unlike penicillin G and ampicillin, cephalosporins and the penicillinase resistant penicillins are *not* synergistic with aminoglycosides; consequently, they should not be used to treat enterococcal endocarditis.[20,76,81]

17. G.S. has enterococcal endocarditis caused by strains exhibiting high-level resistance to streptomycin. Why would (or would not) treatment with gentamicin achieve the desired synergy with vancomycin in G.S. with enterococcus highly-resistant to streptomycin?

Streptomycin Resistant. The combination of streptomycin and penicillin is synergistic for most enterococci that are sensitive to streptomycin (MIC <2000 µg/mL).[19,20] However, as many as 40% of all enterococci are highly resistant to streptomycin (MIC >2000 µg/mL) and the combination is not synergistic for isolates demonstrating this high-level resistance to streptomycin.[82] In contrast, gentamicin in combination with penicillin, ampicillin, or vancomycin is synergistic for most blood isolates of enterococci, regardless of their susceptibility to streptomycin.[1,20,72] For this reason, gentamicin in combination with penicillin (or ampicillin) commonly is prescribed for all cases of enterococcal endocarditis as it was for G.S. Nevertheless, the number of actual clinical failures to the combination of penicillin and streptomycin for enterococcal endocarditis due to streptomycin resistant isolates is very small.[75] Despite the high prevalence of these strains (40%), only three failures to penicillin and streptomycin therapy were found in the literature.[84]

In summary, the significance of high-level streptomycin resistance in human endocarditis is unknown. Several authorities recommend the use of gentamicin with penicillin only for those strains which are highly resistant to streptomycin or when relapse occurs following streptomycin-penicillin therapy for streptomycin-sensitive strains.[20,31,32,83,85,86] Table 57.6 lists the suggested regimens for the treatment of enterococcal endocarditis.

Gentamicin Resistant. Until fairly recently, enterococci exhibiting high-level resistance to gentamicin were uncommon. However, about 15% of the clinical isolates of *E. faecalis* and up to 50% of *E. faecium* are resistant to gentamicin.[87,88,171] It is anticipated that the prevalence of these isolates will continue to increase. In one medical center, high-level resistance to gentamicin was observed in 55% of enterococci found in its patients.[87] In those cases, all available aminoglycosides should be tested with penicillin (or am-

picillin) for synergistic bactericidal activity. Because enterococcal endocarditis caused by isolates resistant to all aminoglycosides has been rare thus far, firm recommendations for these infrequent cases are not available.[31,38,89] However, in the absence of conclusive data, some groups favor long-term (8 to 12 weeks) therapy with high-dose penicillin (20 to 40 million units/day IV in divided doses) or ampicillin (2 to 3 gm IV Q 4 hr) for treatment of these multiply resistant enterococci. Ampicillin plus the beta-lactamase inhibitor sulbactam (Unasyn) would be substituted for beta-lactamase-producing, high-level gentamicin resistant enterococci.

Gentamicin

18. Dosing. What is the optimal dosage of gentamicin for G.S.?

Since patients with enterococcal endocarditis require prolonged therapy with aminoglycosides, the optimum serum concentration should minimize toxicity without jeopardizing clinical cure. Early *in vitro* data indicated that there was no significant difference between 5 µg/mL and 3 µg/mL of gentamicin in enterococcicidal activity; however, there were significant differences between 3 µg/mL and 1 µg/mL.[90] In the rat model of endocarditis, the bacterial counts in vegetations at five and ten days were compared between those treated with low-dose (1 mg/kg IM BID) and those treated with high-dose (5 mg/kg IM BID) gentamicin with penicillin.[91] There was no difference in the bacterial counts at five days; however, bacterial counts at ten days were significantly lower in the rats receiving the high-dose regimen. In contrast, results in the rabbit model showed no difference in the amount of bacteria per gram of vegetation between high- and low-dose gentamicin treatment groups.[92]

The only study comparing high-dose (>3 mg/kg/day) and low-dose (<3 mg/kg/day) gentamicin with penicillin in humans with enterococcal endocarditis evaluated 56 patients with enterococcal endocarditis seen over a 12-year period (36 with streptomycin-susceptible and 20 with streptomycin resistant infections).[86] The relapse rate of patients infected with streptomycin resistant organisms (n = 20) was not significantly different between the high- and low-dose treatment groups (n = 10 each). Furthermore, patients who received the higher doses of gentamicin experienced a greater prevalence of nephrotoxicity (10/10 versus 2/10, p <0.001). Mean peak and trough concentrations of gentamicin in the patients who received the high doses were 5 µg/mL and 2.1 µg/mL, respectively. Corresponding levels for patients receiving the low-dose regimen were 3.1 µg/mL and 1 µg/mL.

These data suggest that a gentamicin dosage of 3 mg/kg/day is adequate for the majority of patients with uncomplicated enterococcal endocarditis. However, because of conflicting animal data and the lack of sufficient human data, dosing guidelines for treatment of streptomycin resistant strains have not been established. Until more definitive data are available, the dosing of aminoglycosides should be individualized on a case-by-case basis.[83,86]

Based upon available data, it would be reasonable to start G.S. on a gentamicin dosage of 1 mg/kg every eight hours (assuming his renal function is normal) and maintain peak concentrations of 3 to 5 µg/mL and trough concentrations less than 1 µg/mL.

19. In Combination with Vancomycin. Why was vancomycin used in combination with gentamicin in G.S.? Is this combination effective against enterococci?

G.S. has a history of penicillin allergy. Most clinicians favor a combination of vancomycin and gentamicin for the penicillin-allergic patient with enterococcal endocarditis, although vancomycin plus streptomycin is a suitable alternative as well.[19,20,31,32,86] The combination of vancomycin and gentamicin demonstrates bactericidal synergy for about 95% of enterococci strains. In contrast,

Table 57.6	Therapy for Endocarditis Due to Enterococci (or to *Streptococci viridans* with an MIC ≥0.5 µg/mL)[a,b]	
Antibiotic	Dose and Route	Duration
Nonpenicillin-Allergic Patient		
1) Aqueous crystalline penicillin G	*Adult*: 20–30 million units/24 hr IV given continuously or in 6 equally divided doses *Pediatric*: 200,000–300,000 units/kg/24 hr IV (*max*: 30 million units/24 hr) given continuously or in 6 equally divided doses	4–6 weeks
With gentamicin[c,d,e] *or*	*Adult*: 1 mg/kg IM or IV (*max*: 80 mg) Q 8 hr *Pediatric*: 2–2.5 mg/kg IM or IV (*max*: 80 mg) Q 8 hr	4–6 weeks
With streptomycin[c,e,f]	*Adult*: 7.5 mg/kg IM (*max*: 500 mg) Q 12 hr *Pediatric*: 15 mg/kg IM (*max*: 500 mg) Q 12 hr	4–6 weeks
2) Ampicillin	*Adult*: 12 gm/24 hr IV given continuously or in 6 equally divided doses *Pediatric*: 300 mg/kg/24 hr IV (*max*: 12 gm/24 hr) in 4–6 equally divided doses	4–6 weeks
With gentamicin[c,d,e] *or*	*Adult*: 1 mg/kg IM or IV (*max*: 80 mg) Q 8 hr *Pediatric*: 2–2.5 mg/kg IM or IV (*max*: 80 mg) Q 8 hr	4–6 weeks
With streptomycin[c,e,f]	*Adult*: 7.5 mg/kg IM (*max*: 500 mg) Q 12 hr *Pediatric*: 15 mg/kg IM (*max*: 500 mg) Q 12 hr	4–6 weeks
Penicillin-Allergic Patients[g] Vancomycin[h]	*Adult*: 30 mg/kg/24 hr IV in 2 or 4 equally doses (*max*: 2 gm/24 hr unless serum levels monitored) *Pediatric*: 40 mg/kg/24 hr IV in 2 or 4 equally divided doses (*max*: 2 gm/24 hr unless serum levels monitored)	4–6 weeks
With gentamicin[c,d,e] *or*	*Adult*: 1 mg/kg IM or IV (*max*: 80 mg) Q 8 hr *Pediatric*: 2–2.5 mg/kg IM or IV (*max*: 80 mg) Q 8 hr	4–6 weeks
With streptomycin[c,e,f]	*Adult*: 7.5 mg/kg IM or IV (*max*: 500 mg) Q 12 hr *Pediatric*: 15 mg/kg IM (*max*: 500 mg) Q 12 hr	4–6 weeks

[a] Adapted with permission from reference 31.

[b] Antibiotic doses should be modified appropriately in patients with impaired renal function.

[c] Choice of aminoglycoside depends upon resistance level of infecting strain. Enterococci should be tested for high-level resistance (Streptomycin: MIC ≥2000 µg/mL, Gentamicin: MIC ≥500 µg/mL).

[d] Serum concentration of gentamicin should be monitored and dose adjusted to obtain a peak level of ≈3 µg/mL.

[e] Dosing of aminoglycosides and vancomycin on a mg/kg basis will give higher serum concentrations in obese than in lean patients.

[f] Serum concentrations of streptomycin should be monitored if possible and dose adjusted to obtain a peak level of ≈20 µg/mL.

[g] Desensitization should be considered; cephalosporins are not satisfactory alternatives.

[h] Peak serum concentrations of vancomycin should be obtained 1 hour after infusion and be in the range of 30–45 µg/mL for BID dosing and 20–30 µg/mL for QID dosing. Trough serum concentrations should be obtained within half an hour of the next dose and be in the range of 5–15 µg/mL. Each dose should be infused over 1 hour.

the vancomycin-streptomycin combination demonstrates bactericidal synergy for about 65% of enterococci.[93] Since G.S. has prosthetic valve endocarditis, she should receive approximately 30 mg/kg/day or roughly 1.5 gm/day (750 mg Q 12 hr) of vancomycin in combination with gentamicin (3 mg/kg/day). Serum levels of vancomycin and gentamicin should be monitored as previously discussed. (See Question 3.)

Duration Therapy

20. How long should G.S. be treated?

Historically, enterococcal endocarditis has been treated with penicillin plus an aminoglycoside for six weeks; the overall cure rate with this regimen is about 85%.[20,81] Data indicate that four weeks of therapy is probably adequate for most patients with enterococcal endocarditis.[31,32,84,86] Nine of nine patients with uncomplicated enterococcal endocarditis treated for four weeks were cured and none relapsed.[84] Other studies have reported similar results.[86]

However, patients with complicated courses should receive six weeks of therapy. These include patients infected with streptomycin resistant organisms (such as G.S.); those who have had symptoms for longer than three months before the initiation of antibiotics; and patients with prosthetic value endocarditis (such as G.S.).[31,81,83,86,88] Some clinicians recommend six weeks of therapy

for all patients in whom the duration of illness cannot be firmly established; this accounts for many patients who present with subacute disease.[94]

Increased Nephrotoxicity with Vancomycin Combination Therapy

21. Is the combination of vancomycin and an aminoglycoside more nephrotoxic than either drug alone?

The incidence of nephrotoxicity associated with vancomycin administration (alone) in humans is thought to be minimal or nonexistent.[95,96] However, in the rat model, the combination of vancomycin and tobramycin produced more severe renal injury than that observed with either agent alone (p <0.005).[97]

A retrospective study evaluated 100 patient courses of vancomycin between 1974 and 1981.[67] Nephrotoxicity was evident in 5% of patients treated with vancomycin alone and in 35% of patients treated with the combination of vancomycin and an aminoglycoside. Clinical significance of this study is difficult to interpret because the study was retrospective and did not include an aminoglycoside control group.

Subsequent prospective investigations have reported conflicting results regarding the increased incidence of nephrotoxicity when vancomycin and an aminoglycoside are used concomitantly. However, those later studies either did not include an aminoglycoside control group or the numbers of patients in the comparative groups were too small to provide statistically significant results.[98,99,136] In a more recent three-arm study involving over 200 patients,[135] nephrotoxicity was found in 5% of patients who received vancomycin alone, 22% of those receiving vancomycin with an aminoglycoside, and 11% of those receiving an aminoglycoside alone. The study was well-designed in that unlike previous studies, an aminoglycoside control group was included for comparison on the incidence of nephrotoxicity. Patients in whom increases in the serum creatinine concentration may have been a result of clinical conditions and patients who received drugs known to alter renal function were excluded in the analysis of this study. Serial serum vancomycin and aminoglycoside concentrations as well as duration of therapy were reported and analyzed. The authors concluded that vancomycin trough concentrations greater than 10 µg/mL and vancomycin concurrent therapy with an aminoglycoside were risk factors associated with increased incidence of nephrotoxicity. Based upon the study data it is difficult to ascertain the precise risk of nephrotoxicity relative to specific vancomycin trough concentrations greater than 10 µg/mL. This issue needs to be studied further because a trough concentration in the range of 10 to 15 mg/L is advocated for the treatment of prosthetic valve staphylococcal endocarditis.[56]

Thus, based upon the above studies, it appears that an increased incidence of nephrotoxicity is likely when vancomycin and an aminoglycoside are given concomitantly. However, the issue of trough serum vancomycin concentration as it relates to the risk of developing nephrotoxicity in combined therapy remains uncertain.

Glycopeptide Resistance
22. How do enterococci develop vancomycin resistance and what are the therapeutic implications when managing a patient with glycopeptide resistant enterococcal endocarditis?
The therapeutic challenges faced as a result of endocarditis caused by enterococci exhibiting high-level resistance to aminoglycosides are further compounded by the newly acquired resistance of enterococci to glycopeptide antibiotics such as vancomycin. Since 1988, a number of reports have documented vancomycin resistance among enterococci, particularly *E. faecium*.[152,153] The percentage of nosocomial enterococci reported as resistant to vancomycin in the U.S. subsequently has increased from 0.3% in 1989 to 7.9% in 1993.[154] Enterococcal isolates from intensive care units increased even more dramatically, from 0.4% to 13.6%, over the same time period. More importantly, epidemiologic studies conducted by the Centers for Disease Control's (CDC) National Nosocomial Infections Surveillance system have indicated that the mortality is significantly higher in patients with bloodstream infections due to vancomycin resistant isolates as compared to vancomycin-susceptible enterococci (36% versus 16% mortality).[154]

Of the various species of enterococci, *E. faecium* is more likely to exhibit resistance to glycopeptides as compared to *E. faecalis*. Glycopeptide resistant enterococci synthesize abnormal precursors of peptidoglycan that lower the binding affinity of glycopeptides to peptidoglycans.[155] The vancomycin resistant enterococci can be broadly classified into three separate phenotypes: A, B, and C, based upon three structurally different genes and gene products (e.g., altered ligases).[156] The majority (≈70%) of resistant enterococci are of the VanA phenotype which are resistant to high levels of both vancomycin (MIC >256 µg/mL) and teicoplanin (MIC >16 µg/mL).[157,158] Expression of resistance is inducible, usually plasmid-mediated, and transferable to other organisms via conjugation. The VanB strains exhibit moderate vancomycin resistance (MIC 16 to 64 µg/mL), but remain susceptible to teicoplanin (MIC ≤2 µg/mL). Overall, the VanC isolates are the least resistant (van-

comycin MIC 8 to 16 µg/mL; teicoplanin MIC ≤2 µg/mL) due to chromosomal-mediated constitutive expression (i.e., not inducible like VanA and VanB); however, VanC isolates usually are associated with the much less common *E. gallinarum* and *E. casseliflavus* infections.[155-158]

Several studies have suggested that prior vancomycin use is a risk factor for the development of resistant enterococci.[159,160] At least one outbreak of resistant enterococci occurred after restoration of vancomycin to the empiric regimen in febrile hemodialysis patients.[152] Since the use of prophylactic vancomycin has been increasing steadily since the mid 1980s, perhaps it should not be surprising to see increased resistance to this class of compounds.

The emergence of vancomycin resistant *E. faecium* causing serious infections is indeed worrisome since few therapeutic alternatives exist for an organism for which synergistic combinations are required for bactericidal activity and a clinical cure. As might be anticipated with an organism that is still a relatively uncommon cause of serious infection, well-established guidelines for antimicrobial therapy are not available. To date, there are no published articles in which investigators report on their experience in a large series of patients infected with glycopeptide resistant enterococci. As a result, practitioners must make patient-care decisions using the available data from *in vitro* synergy studies, experimental models of endocarditis, and scattered case reports. In addition, glycopeptide resistant isolates often exhibit concomitant high-level resistance to aminoglycosides and/or high level resistance to beta-lactams (e.g., ampicillin, penicillin) secondary to either beta-lactamase production or alteration in the target penicillin binding proteins.

The MICs of other cell wall inhibitors (e.g., beta-lactams, daptomycin, ramoplanin) generally are not significantly modified as a result of enterococcal resistance to glycopeptides.[157] In fact, combinations of vancomycin or teicoplanin with beta-lactam antibiotics often exhibit synergy against VanB and, to a lesser extent, VanA isolates.[157] A triple combination regimen consisting of high-dose penicillin (40 µg/mL), vancomycin (10 µg/mL), and gentamicin (4 µg/mL) is relatively effective against a VanA strain of *E. faecium* in a rabbit model of endocarditis.[161] The infecting isolate did not produce lactamase, but was highly resistant (MIC/MBC in µg/mL) to both penicillin (128/256) and vancomycin (1024/>1024), with low-level (normal) resistance to gentamicin (32/64). *In vitro* studies indicated that strain-to-strain differences in the susceptibility of VanA isolates to the synergistic effects of penicillin-vancomycin combinations was dependent upon the level of beta-lactam resistance of each strain.[161,162] In other words, there was more of a synergistic effect (i.e., lowering of MIC) in isolates exhibiting a low level of resistance to penicillin as compared to those displaying high level resistance. A systematic evaluation of this triple drug regimen in patients has not yet been evaluated. However, this regimen would seem a rational option in the patient infected with a VanA or VanB isolate that is also highly resistant to beta-lactams provided that the isolate does not display high-level resistance to gentamicin and that a synergistic effect between penicillin (or ampicillin) and vancomycin can be demonstrated *in vitro*.[161] Based upon their *in vitro* and animal data, Caron et al. also cautioned practitioners that the triple therapy approach might lead to the emergence of subpopulations inherently resistant to the synergistic effect of the penicillin-vancomycin combination.[161] Clinically, this phenomenon might be more likely to result in therapeutic failure for infections, such as endocarditis, in which a high bacterial burden is present in the vegetation.

In patients infected with a VanB isolate, one could utilize teicoplanin in combination with gentamicin (or other active aminoglycoside), however such strains have a known propensity to develop constitutive resistance to teicoplanin during therapy, making the strains resistant to all glycopeptides.[163] In addition, the free levels of teicoplanin (and daptomycin) that are required for synergy with an aminoglycoside sufficient to cure experimental endocarditis caused by a VanA or VanB strain of *E. faecium,* may not be readily achievable in humans.[164]

In one epidemic of vancomycin resistant (MIC 500 µg/mL), gentamicin-susceptible (MIC 12.5 µg/mL) *E. faecium,* the combination of ciprofloxacin (MIC 3.13 µg/mL) plus gentamicin and rifampin (MIC 0.098 µg/mL) was found to be bactericidal *in vitro*.[159] Although both patients who received this combination died of their underlying diseases, blood cultures were found to be sterile several days after completing a 14-day course of therapy. The same team of investigators later studied the above isolates in a rat model of endocarditis and found the ciprofloxacin-gentamicin-rifampin regimen to be effective at reducing the bacterial burden in the vegetation.[165] However, a small residual population of enterococci remained following the standard five days of therapy which subsequently resulted in relapse. It was concluded that a longer course of therapy might further improve the efficacy of this regimen.

Ramoplanin, a lipoglycodepsipeptide antibiotic, has *E. faecium* isolates. It exhibited concentration-dependent bactericidal activity against multiple *E. faecium* isolates that were highly resistant to vancomycin or penicillin alone or to combinations of these antibiotics with gentamicin.[166] Unfortunately, due to poor parenteral tolerance, ramoplanin may be developed only for nonsystemic administration to eradicate colonization. Efforts to develop other related compounds with better systemic tolerance are likely. Novobiocin in combination with a fluoroquinolone (ciprofloxacin or ofloxacin) has been successful in animal studies and *in vitro* against these glycopeptide resistant enterococci.[167,168] Like ramoplanin, novobiocin has toxicity limitations as well as problems with resistance. In addition, like teicoplanin and daptomycin, novobiocin is highly protein bound and may not achieve adequate free plasma levels with nontoxic doses. Currently, novobiocin is only available as an oral formulation. Recent *in vitro* data suggest that clinofloxacin, an investigational fluoroquinolone, in combination with ampicillin is bactericidal against many multidrug resistant *E. faecium* isolates.[175] While several antibiotic combinations look promising *in vitro* and in preliminary animal models of endocarditis, few data are currently available in humans.

Streptogramin. Perhaps the most promising investigational agent for treating glycopeptide resistant enterococci is a parenteral streptogramin (Synercid, RP 59500, Rhone-Poulenc Rorer) that belongs to the antibiotic family of macrolides-lincosamides-streptogramins. It exists as a fixed combination of quinupristin (RP 57669, 30%) and dalfopristin (RP 54476, 70%). The combination is synergistic for glycopeptide resistant enterococci with an MIC_{90} of 2 µg/mL. The fixed product generally is bactericidal for enterococci with minimum inhibitory concentrationss about two to three tube dilutions higher than the MICs.[171] Recommended dosing of 7.5 mg/kg every 8 to 12 hours (depending upon severity of infection) produces peak serum concentrations of about 5 µg/mL.[178] Currently, the predominant adverse events that can be anticipated include liver function test abnormalities and peripheral vein irritation. As a result, liver function tests are recommended to be obtained once a week during therapy. In addition, the dose should be diluted up to 500 to 750 mL, as long as the entire infusion can be given in one hour.[178] Anectdotally, we have successfully used Synercid at the University of Cincinnati in three patients over a two-month period who were either infected with a VanA or VanB isolate as well as in one patient who exhibited a true allergy to both vancomycin and teicoplanin (nonglycopeptide resistant strain).

While the search continues for an optimal antimicrobial regimen to treat glycopeptide resistant enterococci, considerable efforts also should be directed toward the rapid identification of these isolates and limiting their nosocomial transmission. Therefore, in addition to consulting infectious diseases specialists for input on these cases, the infection control team also should be informed immediately so that efforts can be made to prevent an epidemic outbreak. Several outbreaks of resistant enterococci have implicated patient-to-patient and staff-to-patient dissemination.[159,160] Surveillance cultures indicated that about 22% of patients and 7% of staff members who were tested were colonized with resistant strains. Infection control interventions including strict hand washing, bathing with chlorhexidine, cohorting infected and colonized patients, and employee education controlled the outbreak after several weeks.[160]

Due to the increasing frequency of multidrug resistant enterococci and their endemic nature in many institutions, enterococci cultured from the blood of patients (especially in intensive care units) probably should be routinely evaluated for high-level resistance to penicillins, aminoglycosides, and vancomycin.[154] The National Committee for Clinical Laboratory Standards (NCCLS) has recommended changes in the disk diffusion testing methodology to increase the accuracy of detecting VanA and VanB strains.[154] Susceptible strains are those with inhibition zone diameters of ≥ 15 mm, as tested with vancomycin or teicoplanin 30 µg disks.[155] Zone diameters less than 15 mm should prompt the determination of exact MICs. The NCCLS also is assessing a vancomycin resistance screen test using 6 µg/mL of vancomycin in brain-heart infusion agar. Resistant blood isolates should subsequently be evaluated for drug susceptibility by setting up synergy panels of various antibiotics in an effort to find a therapeutic combination that might be bactericidal *in vivo*. Serum bactericidal titers may be particularly helpful in assessing the *in vivo* performance of various clinically untested combination regimens against resistant enterococci. The duration of therapy for most causes of endocarditis is largely empiric. Therefore, an argument could be made for a longer treatment course (>6 weeks) since the risk of treatment failure is higher with these resistant isolates. Patients receiving antimicrobial therapy for these highly resistant enterococci should be aggressively evaluated in a clinic after completing therapy to assess outcome and identify early relapse. A strong argument also could be made for early valve replacement in cases where a multidrug resistant enterococci are isolated and the patient's initial clinical response is poor.[169]

The lack of optimal regimens to treat this increasingly prevalent multidrug resistant organism is indeed alarming, but perhaps the biggest fear is that these enterococci may serve as a reservoir of resistance genes for other organisms, in particular staphylococci. Although clinical strains of vancomycin resistant *S. aureus* (VRSA) have not been reported, laboratory evidence suggests that transfer of the VanA gene from enterococci to *S. aureus* can occur to produce a vancomycin resistant *S. aureus*.[154] The selective pressure provided by increasing vancomycin use, both for prophylaxis and treatment, is certainly present. Since there has already been at least one reported case of a VanB enterococcal bacteremia developing while on vancomycin prophylaxis,[170] it is probably just a matter of time before such antibiotic pressure also results in widespread infections caused by vancomycin resistant staphylococci.

Fungal Endocarditis Due to *Candida Albicans*
Prognosis and Treatment

23. B.G., a 35-year-old male heroin addict, was admitted to University Hospital with chief complaints of pleuritic chest pain and DOE. Physical examination revealed a cachectic male with the following positive findings: temperature of 104 °F, a

diastolic regurgitant heart murmur heard loudest during inspiration, splenomegaly, and pharyngeal petechiae. Funduscopic examination was noncontributory. On chest x-ray, there were several pulmonary infiltrates with cavitation. UA was significant for microscopic hematuria and RBC casts. An echocardiogram demonstrated vegetations on both the tricuspid and aortic heart valves. B.G. had evidence of moderate heart failure, although his hemodynamic status at that time was "stable." Six sets of blood cultures were drawn over 2 days and broad-spectrum empiric coverage consisting of vancomycin, gentamicin, and ceftazidime was initiated. Two days later, 2 of the cultures grew *C. albicans* and a diagnosis of fungal endocarditis was established. What is B.G.'s prognosis and how should his fungal endocarditis be managed?

Fungal endocarditis is a life-threatening infection with a grave prognosis that is generally very difficult to diagnose and even more difficult to treat.[100] The majority of cases are caused by *Candida* and *Aspergillus* species. Fungal endocarditis occurs primarily in IV drug abusers, patients with prosthetic heart valves, immunocompromised patients, those with intravenous catheters, or individuals receiving broad-spectrum antibiotics.[101]

Management of fungal endocarditis generally requires early valve replacement and aggressive fungicidal therapy with a combination of high-dose amphotericin B (usually 0.5 to 1 mg/kg/day IV) and 5-flucytosine (Ancobon) 150 mg/kg/day orally.[100,101] These antifungal agents should be prescribed for B.G. and his broad-spectrum antibiotic coverage with vancomycin, gentamicin, and ceftazidime discontinued.

B.G.'s clinical presentation and chest x-ray indicate that fragments of vegetation have already embolized to his lungs and possibly to other vital organs (e.g., spleen, kidneys). Because of the morbidity and mortality associated with major emboli and valvular insufficiency, B.G.'s aortic valve should be replaced and his tricuspid valve should be excised (valvulectomy without replacement) within 48 to 72 hours after antifungal therapy has been initiated. Delaying surgery beyond this timeframe can increase B.G.'s risk of mortality.[10,100]

The prognosis for B.G. is dismal even with proper medical and surgical treatment. The rate of relapse is high and may occur as long as 20 months after completion of antifungal therapy.[100–102] Mortality is also unacceptably high. In one series, only 6 of 11 patients with fungal endocarditis survived ≥2 years and only one of the six survived ≥5 years.[100] The majority of deaths in drug abusers with endocarditis are secondary to heart failure, a finding already evident in B.G.[1,11] In addition, replacement of a heart valve for fungal endocarditis in a heroin addict carries a significant risk of late morbidity and mortality.[100] It is unlikely that B.G. will stop abusing IV drugs; therefore, he will be at increased risk for the subsequent development of prosthetic valve endocarditis and its associated complications.

Combination Therapy 5-FC and Amphotericin B

24. Why is it important to treat B.G.'s fungal endocarditis with the combination of 5-FC with amphotericin B? What is the optimal duration of therapy?

The importance of adding 5-FC (Ancobon) to amphotericin B (Fungizone) therapy has not been adequately studied, however, the poor prognosis associated with fungal endocarditis warrants the administration of 5-FC, despite its potential for causing bone morrow suppression and hepatotoxicity[100] (see Chapter 67: Infections in Immunocompromised Hosts for a discussion of amphotericin B and 5-FC). The vegetations from his tricuspid or aortic heart valves already have broken off and caused pulmonary cavitation and possibly splenomegaly. His clinical presentation is consistent with a potentially fatal outcome; therefore, his blood isolates should be tested for *in vitro* susceptibility to amphotericin, 5-FC, and to both of these drugs in combination. Fungi resistant to 5-FC alone may still be susceptible to the synergistic effect of the 5-FC-amphotericin B combination.[103] If the organism is resistant to 5-FC and *in vitro* synergy between these two antifungals is lacking, continued treatment with 5-FC is not indicated.[1,100]

The optimal dose and duration of antifungal therapy of fungal endocarditis have not been determined by clinical studies; however, postoperative treatment with amphotericin B and 5-flucytosine (if it has *in vitro* activity) for a minimum of six weeks (total dose: 1.5 to 3 gm of amphotericin B) is the current standard.[1,100,101] Poor penetration of amphotericin B into heart valve tissue necessitates prolonged fungicidal therapy for B.G.[102]

Nephrotoxicity due to amphotericin is often a serious dose-limiting factor to completion of therapy, particularly in patients who require a prolonged treatment course (see Chapter 67: Infections in Immunocompromised Hosts). Alternative antifungal agents may need to be considered in patients who experience significant renal toxicities.

Alternative Antifungals

25. If B.G. experiences significant toxicities due to prolonged combination treatment with amphotericin and 5-FC, what alternative antifungal agent(s) can be used in the treatment of his fungal endocarditis?

Fluconazole (Diflucan) is a relatively new triazole compound active against *Candida* species, particularly *C. albicans* and *C. parapsilosis*. It also has a favorable toxicity profile compared to amphotericin and 5-FC.[137] Prolonged combination treatment with amphotericin and 5-FC often is limited by nephrotoxicity, bone marrow suppression, and/or hepatic damage. Thus, limited experimental and clinical experience using fluconazole in the treatment of candidal endocarditis has been accumulating.

Fluconazole is effective in eradicating cardiac fungal vegetations due to *C. albicans* and *C. parapsilosis* in a rabbit model.[138] Successful experience with fluconazole treatment of fungal endocarditis in humans has been described in only a few case reports.[139–143] Fluconazole-treated endocarditis patients were either intolerant of amphotericin or poor surgical candidates who required suppressive antifungal therapy after completion of a course of amphotericin therapy. Various *Candida* species (i.e., *C. albicans*, *C. parapsilosis*, and *C. tropicalis*) were treated with 200 to 600 mg of fluconazole daily over a period of 45 days to six months or until death. Fluconazole therapy reduced or completely removed all cardiac vegetations and resolved clinical symptoms. However, due to the lack of adequate clinical experience, the use of fluconazole in treating fungal endocarditis cannot be advocated except in situations where significant toxicities from amphotericin preclude continued therapy or lifelong suppressive antifungal therapy is needed in patients who are poor surgical candidates.

Gram-Negative Bacillary Endocarditis due to *Pseudomonas aeruginosa*

Prevalence

26. Fourteen months after completing his course of antifungal therapy, B.G. was readmitted to the hospital with a 48-hour history of fever, shaking chills, rigors, and night sweats. His vital signs at that time were blood pressure 100/60 mm Hg, pulse 120 beats/min, respirations 24/min, and temperature 103.7 °F. A new-onset systolic murmur was noted on auscultation. Two-dimensional echocardiography revealed 2 small vegetations located on the prosthetic valve. Empiric therapy consisting of amphotericin B, 5-FC, vancomycin, and gentamicin was initiated. Three blood cultures drawn on the day

of admission were positive for *Pseudomonas aeruginosa* with the following antibiotic susceptibilities (MIC): gentamicin (8 µg/mL), tobramycin (2 µg/mL), piperacillin (64 µg/mL), and ceftazidime (8 µg/mL).

The presumptive diagnosis of prosthetic valve endocarditis due to *P. aeruginosa* was made. Why was the finding of pseudomonas not unexpected in B.G.?

The prevalence of endocarditis caused by gram-negative organisms has increased significantly in recent years, especially in IV drug abusers (e.g., B.G.) and patients with prosthetic heart valves. Gram-negative organisms are responsible for about 15% to 20% of endocarditis cases in these populations.[104] The majority of gram-negative endocarditis cases are caused by *Pseudomonas* species, *Serratia marcescens*, and *Enterobacter* species, although a wide variety of other gram-negative organisms have been known to cause endocarditis.[104,105,144-147] In addition, there appears to be a geographical clustering of certain organisms causing endocarditis in narcotic addicts.[106] For example, most cases reported in the Detroit area are due to *P. aeruginosa* while cases in San Francisco addicts are caused by *S. marcescens*.[107,108,148] In the narcotic addict with gram-negative endocarditis, the tricuspid, aortic, and mitral valves are involved in 50%, 45%, and 40% of cases, respectively.[104]

Antimicrobial Therapy

27. How should B.G.'s gram-negative endocarditis be treated and monitored?

The amphotericin B, 5-flucytosine, vancomycin, and gentamicin that were initiated empirically for B.G. pending the outcome of culture and sensitivity results should now be discontinued because *P. aeruginosa* has been cultured from B.G.'s blood. Proper antibiotic selection for the treatment of gram-negative endocarditis should depend upon the results of antimicrobial susceptibility and synergy testing. A bactericidal combination of antibiotics usually is required to provide *in vivo* synergy and to prevent resistant subpopulations from emerging during therapy.[1,20] B.G., therefore, should be treated with ceftazidime (2 gm IV Q 8 hr) with concurrent high-dose tobramycin (3 mg/kg IV Q 8 hr). The duration of therapy is not well defined, but most authorities recommend four to six weeks.[1,105,107] Despite the problems associated with interpretation of the serum bactericidal test as a monitoring tool (see Question 3), therapy should be tailored to achieve a trough titer of at least 1:8.[20] Since B.G. should be receiving both ceftazidime and tobramycin on the same schedule (every 8 hours), the trough titer should be drawn just before dose administration. Finally, the infected valve should be surgically excised for the reasons previously discussed.

Endocarditis caused by *P. aeruginosa* (as in B.G.) should be treated for at least six weeks with a combination of an aminoglycoside and an antipseudomonal penicillin (ticarcillin or piperacillin) or cephalosporin (ceftazidime).[107] The combination of an antipseudomonal penicillin and an aminoglycoside is synergistic in the rabbit model of *P. aeruginosa* endocarditis,[109] and clinical experience has confirmed this finding in the addict population. Combination therapy with high doses of tobramycin or gentamicin (8 mg/kg/day) has been associated with a significantly higher cure rate and lower mortality rate compared to an older, ''low-dose'' regimen (2.5 to 5 mg/kg/day).[107,110] Aminoglycoside doses which produce peak serum concentrations of tobramycin (and gentamicin) in excess of 12 µg/mL should be prescribed to ensure maximum efficacy; therefore, high-dose tobramycin should be selected for B.G. For obvious reasons, peak and trough aminoglycoside concentrations should be routinely monitored in all patients receiving high-dose therapy for gram-negative bacillary endocardi-

tis. The choice of aminoglycoside is somewhat arbitrary, but the decision should be based upon its *in vitro* activity of the organism, relative toxicity potential, and cost.[20] In B.G.'s case, tobramycin should be selected over gentamicin because the isolated organism exhibited greater susceptibility to this aminoglycoside. Generally *P. aeruginosa* is more susceptible to tobramycin than to gentamicin. Thus, it is not at all surprising that the *P. aeruginosa* in B.G.'s blood cultures had a 2 µg/mL MIC for tobramycin compared to the 8 µg/mL MIC for gentamicin.

Data on the use of ceftazidime for the treatment of *P. aeruginosa* endocarditis is limited; however, it should be preferred over piperacillin in B.G. on the basis of its greater *in vitro* activity and good penetration into cardiac valvular tissue.[111]

A number of compounds such as imipenem (Primaxin), aztreonam (Azactam), and ciprofloxacin (Cipro) have demonstrated excellent *in vitro* activity against many of the gram-negative organisms causing endocarditis; however, data evaluating their clinical efficacy in the treatment of endocarditis currently are lacking.[112-114]

Culture-Negative Endocarditis

28. B.G.'s history, clinical presentation, and imaging studies are strongly suggestive of infective endocarditis. If his blood cultures had been negative after 48 hours of incubation, the working diagnosis would have been culture-negative endocarditis. What are the possible reasons for culture-negative endocarditis and what measures should be taken to establish a microbiological etiology?

The proportion of patients with culture-negative endocarditis has diminished considerably, presumably as a result of improved microbiological culture techniques. However, there are still patients who have negative cultures in the face of clinically-apparent endocarditis.[115]

The prior administration of antimicrobials is thought to account for the majority of cases of culture-negative endocarditis.[115,116] B.G.'s blood cultures may remain negative for several days to weeks if he has taken antibiotics recently.[116] The use of antibiotic absorbance resins or the addition of beta-lactamases to the blood sample may remove or inactivate some antibiotics.[117,118]

The presence of slow-growing and fastidious organisms such as gram-negative bacilli in the Hemophilus-Actinobacillus-Cardiobacterium-Eikenella-Kingella group (HACEK), pyridoxal-dependent streptococci, Brucella, Coxiella, Chlamydiae, strict anaerobes, and fungi should be pursued in culture-negative patients. This usually is accomplished by the use of special culture media or by obtaining appropriate serologic acute and convalescent titers. Blood cultures should be saved for at least three weeks to detect the presence of slow-growing organisms.[115]

Empiric Therapy

29. Assume that the causative organism remains unidentified. Recommend an antimicrobial regimen for the empiric treatment of B.G.'s presumed culture-negative endocarditis.

In the hemodynamically stable patient, antibiotic therapy should be withheld until positive blood cultures are obtained.[29] Based upon B.G.'s clinical presentation and echocardiographic findings, empiric antibiotics should be initiated as soon as necessary cultures have been collected. Since staphylococci and gram-negative bacilli account for the majority of organisms responsible for endocarditis in the narcotic addict with a prosthetic heart valve, B.G. should be started on a regimen consisting of an antistaphylococcal penicillin such as nafcillin, an aminoglycoside, and a third agent with gram-negative coverage such as piperacillin (or other ureidopenicillin). Since B.G. may be experiencing a relapse due to *C. albicans*, the addition of amphotericin B and flucytosine would be appropriate. If B.G. is from an area where methicillin resistant staphylococci are prevalent, vancomycin should be substituted for nafcillin. A third-generation cephalosporin such as ceftriaxone or ceftazidime could be substituted for piperacillin depending upon the gram-negative pathogens common to the region and their anticipated susceptibilities. The regimen, which contains an aminoglycoside and piperacillin, also will provide coverage for enterococci.

The clinical status of B.G. and positive echocardiogram indicate that early surgical valve excision and replacement are necessary.[16] Cultures obtained from excised valve may result in identification of the causative organism. His antimicrobial regimen may need to be altered if and when subsequent culture information becomes available. Other noninfective conditions, such as atrial myxoma, marasmic endocarditis, and rheumatic fever, may mimic culture-negative endocarditis and should be excluded from the differential diagnosis with the appropriate tests.[1]

Prophylactic Therapy

Rationale and Recommendations

30. B.B., a 74-year-old male with poor dentition, is scheduled to have all of his remaining teeth extracted for subsequent fitting of dentures. His past medical history is significant for numerous infections of the oral cavity with abscess formation and mitral stenosis with mild insufficiency. His only current medications are digoxin (Lanoxin) 0.125 mg/day and furosemide (Lasix) 40 mg Q AM. What is the rationale for antibiotic prophylaxis?

Since infective endocarditis is associated with significant mortality and long-term morbidity, prevention in susceptible individuals is of paramount importance.[1] Unfortunately, it is estimated that less than 10% of all cases are, theoretically, preventable.[44]

The incidence of endocarditis in patients undergoing procedures known to cause significant bacteremia, even in the absence of antibiotic prophylaxis, is low. In addition, endocarditis may develop following the administration of seemingly appropriate chemoprophylaxis. Therefore, it is not surprising that the efficacy of prophylaxis has never been established through placebo-controlled clinical trials. Approximately 6,000 patients would be necessary to demonstrate a statistical difference (if one exists) between untreated controls and a group receiving prophylaxis.[44]

In the absence of conclusive clinical data from prospective trials, recommendations for antibiotic prophylaxis have been based largely on *in vitro* susceptibility data, evaluation of antibiotic regimens using animal models of endocarditis, and anecdotal experiences.[8,41,44,119–122]

Most authorities recommend antibiotic prophylaxis for patients at risk who are undergoing procedures associated with significant bacteremia. Table 57.1 lists the more common conditions and procedures for which antibiotic prophylaxis is currently recommended.

Prophylactic antibiotics are thought to provide protection by decreasing the number of organisms reaching the damaged heart valve from a primary source. Thus, antibiotics theoretically prevent bacterial multiplication on the valve and interfere with bacterial adherence to the cardiac lesion.[2,8]

The 1990 American Heart Association (AHA) recommendations for antibiotic prophylaxis before common medical procedures are outlined in Table 57.7.[119] Compared to previous (1984) guidelines,[120] the current recommendations place less emphasis on parenteral administration and are considerably less complicated.

Dental and Upper Respiratory Tract Procedures[119]

Antibiotic prophylaxis is recommended in susceptible individuals (see Table 57.1) undergoing any dental procedure that is likely to result in gingival bleeding, including routine professional cleaning. Simple adjustment of orthodontic appliances and spontaneous shedding of deciduous teeth do not require the administration of chemoprophylaxis. Endotracheal intubation also does not require prophylactic therapy.

Antimicrobial prophylaxis should be directed against the viridans group of streptococci because these organisms are the most common cause of endocarditis following dental procedures. Surgical procedures involving the upper respiratory tract (e.g., tonsillectomy/adenoidectomy, biopsy of respiratory mucosa, rigid bronchoscopy) may cause transient bacteremia with organisms that have similar antibiotic susceptibilities to those which occur after dental procedures; therefore, the same regimens are suggested. Amoxicillin is currently recommended for oral prophylaxis in susceptible individuals undergoing dental or upper respiratory tract surgery. Oral erythromycin or clindamycin is recommended for penicillin (amoxicillin)-allergic patients. High-risk patients, such as those with prosthetic heart valves, should receive parenteral antibiotics to provide the widest margin of safety possible. However, unlike past recommendations of the AHA, the current guidelines allow for use of an oral regimen in high-risk patients because of the logistical and financial barriers that have historically resulted in poor compliance with parenteral regimens.[121] In addition, other countries have accumulated considerable experience using oral regimens in patients with prosthetic heart valves without apparent failure. Patients who already are receiving continuous low-dose penicillin therapy for the secondary prevention of rheumatic fever should receive oral erythromycin, clindamycin, or a parenteral regimen to adequately protect them against strains of *S. viridans* that have become relatively-resistant to penicillin and amoxicillin.

Gastrointestinal and Genitourinary Tract Procedures[119]

The most common organisms responsible for bacteremia following gastrointestinal or genitourinary procedures are gram-negative aerobes, *E. faecalis* (enterococcus), and anaerobes. Gram-negative organisms and anaerobes only rarely cause endocarditis; therefore, in the majority of cases requiring prophylaxis, therapy should be directed against enterococci. Although the use of ampicillin and an aminoglycoside (gentamicin) is still suggested to achieve synergy and bactericidal activity against enterococci in high-risk patients (e.g., those with a prosthetic heart valve, those who have had endocarditis previously, and those taking oral penicillin for rheumatic fever prophylaxis), "low-risk" patients may receive an oral 3 gm dose of amoxicillin one hour before the procedure and 1.5 gm six hours later. The allowance of an oral prophylactic regimen without an aminoglycoside for these procedures is different from past AHA and Medical Letter recommendations, presumably in an attempt to increase compliance and safety. Patients allergic to penicillin should receive a combination of vancomycin and gentamicin.

Indications and Choice of Agent

31. Is prophylactic antibiotic therapy indicated for B.B.? If so, which antibiotic(s) should be used?

Based upon the current recommendations, B.B. is a candidate for antibiotic prophylaxis. The mitral valve stenosis and insufficiency place him in a higher risk category (as compared to other populations) for developing endocarditis. He also is scheduled to have all of his remaining teeth extracted, a procedure likely to result in bacteremia. According to Table 57.7, B.B. should receive a single 3 gm oral dose of amoxicillin one hour before the procedure and an additional dose of 1.5 gm six hours later. Since some degree of gastrointestinal upset would be expected following such

Table 57.7	Endocarditis Prophylaxis Regimen for Patients Who Are at Risk[a]
Drug	**Dose**
Dental, Oral, or Upper Respiratory Tract Procedures[b]	
Standard Regimen[c,d]	
Amoxicillin	3 gm PO 1 hr before procedure; then 1.5 gm 6 hr after initial dose
Amoxicillin/Penicillin-Allergic Patients[c]	
Erythromycin[g]	Erythromycin ethylsuccinate 800 mg, or erythromycin stearate 1 gm, PO 2 hr before procedure; then half dose 6 hr after initial dose
Or Clindamycin	300 mg PO 1 hr before procedure; then 150 mg 6 hr after initial dose
Alternative Regimens[e]	
Patients Unable to Take Oral Medications	
Nonpenicillin Allergic	
Ampicillin	IV or IM ampicillin 2 gm 30 min before procedure; then IV or IM or ampicillin, 1 gm, or PO amoxicillin 1.5 gm, 6 hr after initial dose
Ampicillin/Amoxicillin/Penicillin Allergic	
Clindamycin	300 mg IV 30 min before procedure; then IV or PO 150 mg 6 hr after initial dose
High-Risk Patients	
Not Candidates for Standard Regimen	
Ampicillin, gentamicin, and amoxicillin	IV or IM ampicillin 2 gm, plus gentamicin 1.5 mg/kg (max: 80 mg), 30 min before procedure followed by amoxicillin 1.5 gm PO 6 hr after initial dose; alternatively, the parenteral regimen may be repeated 8 hr after initial dose
Ampicillin/Amoxicillin/Penicillin-Allergic Patients	
Vancomycin	1 gm IV over 1 hr, starting 1 hr before procedure; no repeat dose necessary
Genitourinary/Gastrointestinal Procedures[f]	
Standard Regimen	
Ampicillin, gentamicin, and amoxicillin	IV or IM ampicillin 2 gm, plus gentamicin 1.5 mg/kg (max: 80 mg), 30 min before procedure; followed by amoxicillin 1.5 gm PO 6 hr after initial dose, alternatively, the parenteral regimen may be repeated once 8 hr after initial dose
Ampicillin/Amoxicillin/Penicillin-Allergic Patients	
Vancomycin and gentamicin	Vancomycin, 1 gm IV over 1 hr, plus gentamicin 1.5 mg/kg (max: 80 mg) IV or IM, 1 hr before procedure; may be repeated once 8 hr after initial dose
Alternative Low-Risk Patient Regimen	
Amoxicillin	3 gm PO 1 hr before procedure; then 1.5 gm 6 hr after initial dose

[a] Adapted with permission from reference 119.
[b] Includes those with prosthetic heart valves and other high-risk patients.
[c] Initial pediatric doses are as follows: amoxicillin 50 mg/kg; erythromycin ethylsuccinate or erythromycin stearate 20 mg/kg; and clindamycin 10 mg/kg. Follow-up doses should be ½ the initial dose. **Total pediatric dose should not exceed total adult dose.** The following weight ranges also may be used for the initial pediatric dosing of amoxicillin: <15 kg, 750 mg; 15–30 kg, 1500 mg; and >30 kg, 3000 mg (full adult dose).
[d] A 2 gm amoxicillin dose will provide adequate amoxicillin serum concentrations for endocarditis prophylaxis with fewer gastrointestinal complaints than the 3 gm dose.[173]
[e] Initial pediatric doses are as follows: ampicillin 50 mg/kg; clindamycin 10 mg/kg; gentamicin 2 mg/kg; and vancomycin 20 mg/kg. Follow-up doses should be ½ the initial dose. **Total pediatric dose should not exceed total adult dose.** No initial dose is recommended in this table for amoxicillin (25 mg/kg is the follow-up dose).
[f] Initial pediatric doses are as follows: ampicillin 50 mg/kg; amoxicillin 50 mg/kg; gentamicin 2 mg/kg; and vancomycin 20 mg/kg. Follow-up doses should be ½ the initial dose. **Total pediatric dose should not exceed total adult dose.**
[g] Although the dose of erythromycin ethylsuccinate recommended by the AHA is probably adequate for prophylaxis, the dose equivalent to 1 gm of the stearate would be 1.6 gm before procedure and 800 mg after 6 hr. Pediatric dose = 30 mg/kg initially, followed by 15 mg/kg 6 hr later.[128] **Total pediatric dose should not exceed total adult dose.**

a 3 gm oral dose, the dentist should make sure B.B. does not experience vomiting. In such a case, in-office administration of parenteral ampicillin (with or without gentamicin) would be advisable to ensure adequate prophylaxis before his oral extraction procedure. When the blood levels and tolerability of 2 and 3 gm oral amoxicillin doses were compared in a crossover study involving 30 adult volunteers,[173] the 2 gm doses resulted in adequate serum levels; concentrations six hours after dosing were well above the MICs for most oral streptococci. Furthermore, no adverse effects were noted with the 2 gm dose versus a 10% incidence of GI complaints with the 3 gm dose. Since a 2 gm dose of amoxicillin will provide adequate endocarditis prophylaxis for dental, oral, or upper respiratory tract procedures with minimal gastrointestinal upset, the current 3 gm recommendation may change upon further analyses or other confirming studies.

Home Intravenous (IV) Antibiotic Therapy

32. T.M., a 48-year-old female, developed *S. viridans* endocarditis following a dental procedure. Her past medical history is significant for rheumatic heart disease and chronic renal insufficiency (measured Cl_{Cr} = 50 mL/min). She is hemodynamically stable and has no evidence of vegetation by echocardiography. She is currently on day 7 of therapy with penicillin G, 2 MU IV Q 4 hr. The plan is to continue penicillin therapy for a total of 4 weeks. What are the considerations for using home IV therapy for the treatment of infective endocarditis? Is T.M. a candidate for home antibiotic therapy?

The successful use of home intravenous antibiotic therapy for the patient with endocarditis has been described, although the number of patients treated is relatively small compared to those treated for osteomyelitis.[126] The advantages of home therapy include economic benefits to the hospital for early discharge [the diagnosis-related-group (DRG) allocation for endocarditis is 18.4 days, which is shorter than the usual recommended duration of therapy] and the potential for greater acceptance by the patient.[3]

However, home treatment of endocarditis is not without risk. Patients must be hemodynamically stable before discharge and free from the risk of sudden valve rupture. The drug abuser is obviously not a candidate for home treatment, nor is the patient receiving frequent doses of medication. Some patients with streptococcal or staphylococcal endocarditis may be successfully switched from a penicillin to vancomycin while in the hospital to allow for a more feasible twice daily outpatient administration. The successful management of any infection amenable to home treatment requires careful patient evaluation for suitability and coordination of the health care provided by key personnel.

T.M. represents the typical patient with uncomplicated streptococcal endocarditis. If the sole reason for continued hospitalization is to receive intravenous antibiotics, she is a potential candidate for home therapy. This assumes that she can be successfully switched to twice daily (or probably once daily) vancomycin administration.

Vancomycin is traditionally recommended as an alternative agent for penicillin-allergic patients. In the case of T.M., the ease of administration due to less frequent dosing (once or twice daily) makes vancomycin an attractive option for home intravenous antibiotic therapy. However, adequate venous access, infusion-related side-effects, and serum drug level monitoring are potential problems with using vancomycin in the home care setting. Ceftriaxone has been considered as a possible option for outpatient therapy of uncomplicated endocarditis caused by penicillin-susceptible streptococci. The excellent in vitro activity, of ceftriaxone and its long half-life of six to nine hours allow once a day administration. The feasibility of IM administration of ceftriaxone also obviates the need for an IV access; thus, avoiding any potential line-related complications when administered in the outpatient setting.

Clinical experience with the use of ceftriaxone in the treatment of patients with penicillin-susceptible streptococcal endocarditis was described in two open-labelled studies.[149–150] All infecting strains of streptococci in the studies were inhibited by ceftriaxone at an MIC of ≥ 0.25 µg/mL. Ceftriaxone was given at a dose of 2 gm once daily for a period of four weeks to most patients, with 15 receiving ceftriaxone for two weeks followed by amoxicillin 1 gm four times daily for two weeks. A majority of the patients received therapy predominantly as outpatients. All patients (n = 30) reported in this study responded favorably to treatment with ceftriaxone or ceftriaxone followed by amoxicillin.[149] Patients with cardiovascular risk factors such as heart failure, severe aortic insufficiency, or evidence of recurrent thromboembolic events were excluded from the study. Only one probable relapse was noted at three months after therapy with presentation of febrile syndrome, elevated sedimentation rate, and negative bacterial blood culture. A more recent uncontrolled study extended the favorable results of the above study.[150] Treatment was completed in 55 of 59 patients. Patients were followed for four months up to five years after the end of treatment with no clinical signs or laboratory evidence of relapse. Seventy-one percent of patients completed therapy without complications; however, ten required valve replacement secondary to hemodynamic deterioration or recurrent emboli while four required a change in therapy due to drug allergy. Adverse effects were minor; however, neutropenia was noted in three patients which resolved after cessation of therapy.

Due to the lack of controlled trials comparing the efficacy of ceftriaxone against penicillin with or without an aminoglycoside in the treatment of penicillin-susceptible streptococcal endocarditis, ceftriaxone cannot be routinely recommended as treatment of choice. Until more data are available, particularly in patients with hemodynamic or embolic complications, ceftriaxone should only be considered in patients such as T.M. where home antibiotic therapy is a treatment option and who are hemodynamically stable with no evidence of vegetation.

The feasibility of home therapy would depend upon consideration of the following additional factors: 1) patient willingness; 2) adequate venous access; 3) psychosocial stability; 4) accessibility to medical care if an emergency occurs; 5) ability to train T.M. (proper aseptic technique, catheter site care, antibiotic preparation, recognition of untoward effects of the antibiotic, and recognition of symptoms associated with worsening infection); and 6) whether her insurance carrier will cover home intravenous therapy. The above can only be accomplished with the multidisciplinary involvement of the infectious disease physician, a social worker, a pharmacist, specialty nurse, and the patient.[127] Home care, outpatient care, and other options will be used increasingly because health care reform mandates the decreased utilization of tertiary care facilities when possible.

References

1 **Scheld WM, Sande MA.** Endocarditis and intravascular infections. In: Mandell GL et al., eds. Principles and Practice of Infectious Diseases. 4th ed. New York: John Wiley and Sons; 1995:740.

2 **Sullman PM et al.** Pathogenesis of endocarditis. Am J Med. 1985;78(6B):110.

3 **Kaye D.** Changing pattern of infective endocarditis. Am J Med. 1985;78(6B):157.

4 **Kaye D.** Definitions and demographic characteristics. In: Kaye D, ed. Infective Endocarditis. Baltimore: University Park Press; 1976:1.

5 **Saravolatz LD et al.** Polymicrobial endocarditis: an increasing clinical entity. Am Heart J. 1978;95:163.

6 **Pelletier LL, Petersdorf RG.** Infective endocarditis: a review of 125 cases from the University of Washington Hospitals, 1963–72. Medicine (Baltimore). 1977;56:287.

7 **Hermans PE.** The clinical manifestations of infective endocarditis. Mayo Clin Proc. 1982;57:15.

8 **Durack DT.** Current issues in prevention of infective endocarditis. Am J Med. 1985;78(6B):149.

9 **Lerner PI, Weinstein L.** Infective endocarditis in the antibiotic era. N Engl J Med. 1966;274:199.

10 **Snow RM, Cobbs CG.** Treatment of complications of infective endocarditis. In: Kaye D, ed. Infective Endocarditis. Baltimore: University Park Press; 1976:213.

11 **Weinstein L.** Life-threatening complications of endocarditis and their management. Arch Intern Med. 1986;146:953.

12 **Belli J, Waisbren BA.** The number of blood cultures necessary to diagnose most cases of bacterial endocarditis. Am J Med Sci. 1956;50:91.

13 **Prazin GL et al.** Blood culture positivity: suppression by outpatient antibiotic therapy in patients with bacterial endocarditis. Arch Intern Med. 1982;142:263.

14 **Mandell GL.** The laboratory in diagnosis and management. In: Kaye D, ed. Infective Endocarditis. Baltimore: University Park Press; 1976:155.

15 **Mintz GS, Kotler MN.** Clinical value and limitations of echocardiography: its use in the study of patients with infective endocarditis. Arch Intern Med. 1980;140:1022.

16 **Alsip SG.** Indications for cardiac surgery in patients with acute infective endocarditis. Am J Med. 1985;78(6B):138.

17 **Wiseman J et al.** Gallium-67 myocardial imaging for the detection of bacterial endocarditis. Radiology. 1976;120:135.

18 **Welton DE et al.** Value and safety of

cardiac catheterization during active infective endocarditis. Am J Cardiol. 1979;44:1306.

19 **Wilson WR, Geraci JE.** Antibiotic treatment of infective endocarditis. Ann Rev Med. 1983;34:413.

20 **Sande MA, Scheld WM.** Combination antibiotic therapy of bacterial endocarditis. Ann Intern Med. 1980;92:390.

21 **Watanakunakorn C.** Penicillin combined with gentamicin or streptomycin: synergism against enterococci. J Infect Dis. 1971;124:581.

22 **Pulliam L et al.** Penicillin tolerance in experimental streptococcal endocarditis. Lancet. 1979;2:957.

23 **Bourgault AM et al.** Antimicrobial susceptibilities of species of viridans streptococci. J Infect Dis. 1979;140:316.

24 **Gallis HA.** Viridans and beta-hemolytic (nongroup A, B, and D) strepto-

cocci. In: Mandell GL et al., eds. Principles and Practice of Infectious Diseases. 3rd ed. New York: John Wiley and Sons; 1990:1563.

25 Wolfson JS, Swartz MN. Serum bactericidal activity as a monitor of antibiotic therapy. N Engl J Med. 1985; 312:968.

26 Marcon MJ, Bartlett RC. Laboratory evaluation of the serum dilution test in serious staphylococcal infection. Am J Clin Pathol. 1983;80:176.

27 Reller LB, Stratton CW. Serum dilution test for bactericidal activity. IL Standardization and correlation with antimicrobial assays. J Infect Dis. 1977; 136:196.

28 Weinstein MP et al. Multicenter collaborative evaluation of a standardized serum bactericidal test as a prognostic indicator in infective endocarditis. Am J Med. 1985;78:262.

29 Wilson WR et al. General considerations in the diagnosis and treatment of infective endocarditis. Mayo Clin Proc. 1982;57:31.

30 Carrizosa J, Kaye D. Antibiotic concentrations in serum, serum bactericidal activity, and results of therapy of streptococcal endocarditis in rabbits. Antimicrob Agents Chemother. 1977; 12:479.

31 Bisno AL et al. Antimicrobial treatment of infective endocarditis due to viridans streptococci, enterococci and staphylococci. JAMA. 1989;261:1471.

32 Wilson WR, Geraci JE. Treatment of streptococcal infective endocarditis. Am J Med. 1985;78(6B):128.

33 Karchmer AW et al. Single-antibiotic therapy for streptococcal endocarditis. JAMA. 1979;241:1801.

34 Wilson WR et al. Short-term intramuscular therapy with procaine penicillin plus streptomycin for infective endocarditis due to viridans streptococci. Circulation. 1978;57:1158.

35 Wilson WR et al. Short-term therapy for streptococcal infective endocarditis: combined intramuscular administration of penicillin and streptomycin. JAMA. 1981;245:360.

36 Wolfe JC, Johnson WD Jr. Penicillin-sensitive streptococcal endocarditis: in vitro and clinical observations on penicillin-streptomycin therapy. Ann Intern Med. 1974;81:178.

37 Malacoff RF et al. Streptococcal endocarditis (nonenterococcal, nongroup A): single vs combination therapy. JAMA. 1979;241:1807

38 Sande MA, Irvin RG. Penicillin-aminoglycoside synergy in experimental streptococcus viridans endocarditis. J Infect Dis. 1974;129:572.

39 Phair JP, Tan JS. Therapy of streptococcus viridans endocarditis. In: Kaplan EL, Taranta AV, eds. Infective endocarditis—an American Heart Association Symposium. Dallas: American Heart Association; 1977:55.

40 Henry NK et al. Antimicrobial therapy of experimental endocarditis caused by nutritionally variant viridans group streptococci. Antimicrob Agents Chemother. 1986;30:465.

41 Bayer AS et al. Current concepts in prevention of prosthetic valve endocarditis. Chest. 1990;97:1203–207.

42 Threlkeld M, Cobbs GG. Infectious complications of prosthetic valves and intravascular devices. In: Mandell GL et al., eds. Principles and Practice of Infectious Diseases. 3rd ed. New York: John Wiley and Sons; 1990:706–15.

43 Archer GL. Staphylococcus epidermidis and other coagulase-negative staphylococci. In: Mandell GL et al., eds. Principles and Practice of Infectious Diseases. 3rd ed. New York: John Wiley and Sons. 1990:1511.

44 Durack DT. Prophylaxis of infective endocarditis. In: Mandell GL et al., eds. Principles and Practice of Infectious Diseases. 3rd ed. New York: John Wiley and Sons; 1990:716–21.

45 Hartman B, Tomasz A. Altered penicillin-binding proteins in methicillin-resistant strains of Staphylococcus aureus. Antimicrob Agents Chemother. 1981;19:726.

46 Slama T et al. Randomized comparison of cefamandole, cefazolin, and cefuroxime prophylaxis in open heart surgery. Antimicrob Agents Chemother. 1986;29:744.

47 Kaiser AB et al. Efficacy of cefazolin, cefamandole, and gentamicin as prophylactic agents in cardiac surgery. Ann Surg. 1987;206:791.

48 Sabath LD. Reappraisal of the antistaphylococcal activities of first-generation (narrow-spectrum) and second-generation (expanded-spectrum) cephalosporins. Antimicrob Agent Chemother. 1989;33:407–11.

49 Kernodle DS et al. Failure of cephalosporins to prevent Staphylococcus aureus surgical wound infections. JAMA. 1990;263:961–11.

50 Maki DG et al. Comparative study of cefazolin, cefamandole and vancomycin for surgical prophylaxis in cardiac and vascular surgery. In press.

51 Schwalbe RS et al. Emergence of vancomycin resistance in coagulase-negative staphylococci. N Engl J Med. 1987;316:927.

52 Polk RE et al. Vancomycin and the red man syndrome: pharmacodynamics of histamine release. J Infect Dis. 1988; 157:520–27.

53 Southorn PA et al. Adverse effects of vancomycin administered in the perioperative period. Mayo Clin Proc. 1986;61:721.

54 Karchmer AW et al. Staphylococcus epidermidis causing prosthetic valve endocarditis: microbiological and clinical observations as guides to therapy. Ann Intern Med. 1983;98:447.

55 Karchmer AW, Archer GL. The endocarditis study group. Methicillin-resistant Staphylococcus epidermidis prosthetic valve endocarditis. 24th Interscience Conference on Antimicrobial Agents and Chemotherapy. Washington, DC: 1984 October. Abstract 476.

56 Karchmer AW. Staphylococcal endocarditis: laboratory and clinical basis for antibiotic therapy. Am J Med. 1985; 78(6B):116.

57 Chambers HF et al. The National Collaborative Endocarditis Study Group. Staphylococcus aureus endocarditis: clinical manifestations in addicts and nonaddicts. Medicine (Baltimore). 1983;62:170.

58 Thompson RL. Staphylococcal infective endocarditis. Mayo Clin Proc. 1982;57:106.

59 Korzeniowski O, Sande MA. The National Collaborative Endocarditis Study Group: combination antimicrobial therapy for Staphylococcus aureus endocarditis in patients addicted to parenteral drugs and nonaddicts. Ann Intern Med. 1982;97:496.

60 Abrams G et al. Single or combination therapy of staphylococcal endocarditis in intravenous drug abusers. Ann Intern Med. 1979;90:789.

61 Parker RH. Fossieck BE. Intravenous followed by oral antimicrobial therapy for staphylococcal endocarditis. Ann Intern Med. 1980;93:832.

62 Chambers HF et al. Right-sided endocarditis in intravenous drug abusers two-week combination therapy. Ann Intern Med. 1988;104:619–24.

63 Drown RJR et al. Treatment of right-sided Staphylococcus aureus endocarditis in intravenous drug abusers with ciprofloxacin and rifampin. Lancet. 1989:1071–073.

64 Bryant RE, Alford RH. Unsuccessful treatment of staphylococcal endocarditis with cefazolin. JAMA. 1978;239: 1130.

65 McDougal LK, Thornsberry CE. New recommendations for disc diffusion antimicrobial susceptibility tests for methicillin-resistant hetero-resistant staphylococci. J Clin Microbiol. 1984;19:482.

66 Healy DP et al. Comparison of steady-state pharmacokinetics of two-dosage regimens of vancomycin in normal volunteers. Antimicrob Agents Chemother. 1987;31:393.

67 Faber BF, Moellering RC Jr. Retrospective study of the toxicity of preparations of vancomycin from 1974 to 1981. Antimicrob Agents Chemother. 1983;23:138.

68 Markowitz N et al. Comparative efficacy and toxicity of trimethoprim-sulfamethoxazole versus vancomycin in the therapy of serious S. aureus infections. 23rd Interscience Conference on Antimicrobial Agents and Chemotherapy. Las Vegas, NV: 1983 October. Abstract 638.

69 Sherris JC. Problems in in vitro determination of antibiotic tolerance in clinical isolates. Antimicrob Agents Chemother. 1986;30:633.

70 Wilkowske CJ. Enterococcal endocarditis. Mayo Clin Proc. 1982;57:101.

71 Wilkowske CJ et al. Antibiotic synergism: enhanced susceptibility of group D streptococci to certain antibiotic combinations. Antimicrob Agents Chemother. 1970;10:195.

72 Drake TA, Sande MA. Studies of the chemotherapy of endocarditis: correlation of in vitro, animal model, and clinical studies. Rev Infect Dis. 1983; 5(Suppl. 2):S345.

73 Krogstad DJ, Moellering RC Jr. Antimicrobial combinations. In: Lorian V, ed. Antibiotics in Laboratory Medicine. Baltimore: Williams and Wilkins; 1986:537.

74 Moellering RC Jr, Weinberg AN. Studies on antibiotic synergisms against enterococci II: effect of various antibiotics on the uptake of C14-labeled streptomycin by enterococci. J Clin Invest. 1971;50:2580.

75 Hook EW et al. Antimicrobial therapy of experimental enterococcal endocarditis. Antimicrob Agents Chemother. 1975;8:564.

76 Abrutyn E et al. Cephalothin-gentamicin synergism in experimental enterococcal endocarditis. J Antimicrob Chemother. 1987;4:153.

77 Carrizosa J, Kaye D. Antibiotic synergism in enterococcal endocarditis. J Lab Clin Med. 1976;88:132.

78 Mandell GL et al. An analysis of 38 patients observed at New York Hospital—Cornell Medical Center. Arch Intern Med. 1970;125:258.

79 Serra P et al. Synergistic treatment of enterococcal endocarditis. Arch Intern Med. 1975;137:1562.

80 Koenig GM, Kaye D. Enterococcal endocarditis. Report of nineteen cases with long-term follow-up data. N Engl J Med. 1961;264:257.

81 Kaye D. Treatment of enterococcal endocarditis in experimental animals and in man. In: Bisno AL, ed. Treatment of Infective Endocarditis. New York: Grune and Stratton; 1981:97.

82 Moellering RC Jr et al. Prevalence of high-level resistance to aminoglycosides in clinical isolates of enterococci. Antimicrob Agents Chemother. 1970; 10:335.

83 Kaye D. Antibiotic treatment of streptococcal endocarditis. Am J Med. 1980;69:650.

84 Tompsett R, Berman W. Enterococcal endocarditis: duration and mode of treatment. Trans Am Clin Assoc. 1977; 89:49.

85 Scheld WM, Mandell GL. Enigmatic enterococcal endocarditis. Ann Intern Med. 1984;100:904

86 Wilson WR et al. Treatment of streptomycin-susceptible and streptomycin-resistant enterococcal endocarditis. Ann Intern Med. 1984;100:816.

87 Zervos MJ et al. Nosocomial infection by gentamicin-resistant Streptococcus faecalis: an epidemiological study. Ann Intern Med. 1987;106:687.

88 Murray BE. The life and times of the enterococcus. Clin Microbiol Rev. 1990;3:46.

89 Hoffman SA, Moellering RC Jr. The enterococcus: ''Putting the bug in our ears.'' Ann Intern Med. 1987;106:757.

90 Matsumoto JY et al. Synergy of penicillin and decreasing concentrations of aminoglycosides against enterococci from patients with infective endocarditis. Antimicrob Agents Chemother. 1980;18:944.

91 Carrizosa J, Levison ME. Minimal concentrations of aminoglycosides that can synergize with penicillin in enterococcal endocarditis. Antimicrob Agents Chemother. 1981;20:405.

92 Wright AJ et al. Influence of gentamicin dose size on the efficacies of combinations of gentamicin and penicillin in experimental streptomycin-resistant enterococcal endocarditis. Antimicrob Agents Chemother. 1982;22: 972.

93 Watanakunakorn C, Bakie C. Synergism of vancomycin-gentamicin and vancomycin-streptomycin against enterococci. Antimicrob Agents Chemother. 1973;4:120.

94 Hook EW, Guerrant RL. Therapy of infective endocarditis. In: Kaye D, ed. Infective Endocarditis. Baltimore: University Park Press; 1976:167.

95 Fekety R. Vancomycin. Med Clin North Am. 1982;66:175.

96 Wilhelm MP. Vancomycin. Mayo Clin Proc. 1991;66:1165–170.

97 Wood CA et al. Vancomycin enhancement of experimental tobramycin nephrotoxicity. Antimicrob Agents Chemother. 1986;30:20.

98 Mellor JA et al. Vancomycin toxicity: a prospective study. J Antimicrob Chemother. 1985;15:253.

99 Sorrell TC, Collignon PJ. A prospective study of adverse reactions associated with vancomycin therapy. J Antimicrob Chemother. 1985;16:235.

100 Rahal JJ Jr, Simberkoff MS. Treatment of fungal endocarditis. In: Bisno AL, ed. Treatment of Infective Endocarditis. New York: Grune and Stratton; 1981:135.

101 Rubinstein E et al. Fungal endocarditis: analysis of 24 cases and review of the literature. Medicine. 1975;54: 331.

102 Rubinstein E et al. Tissue penetration of amphotericin B in Candida endocarditis. Chest. 1974;66:376.

103 Shadomy S et al. In vitro studies with combinations of 5-fluorocytosine and amphotericin B. Antimicrob Agents Chemother. 1975;8:117.

104 Cannon HJ, Cobbs CG. Infective endocarditis drug addicts. In: Kaye D, ed. Infective Endocarditis. Baltimore: University Park Press; 1976:111.

105 Watanakunakorn C. Antimicrobial therapy of endocarditis due to less common bacteria. In: Bisno AL, ed. Treatment of Infective Endocarditis. New York: Grune and Stratton; 1981: 123.

106 Reiner NE. Regional pathogens in endocarditis. Ann Intern Med. 1976;84: 613.

107 Reyes MP, Lerner AM. Current problems in the treatment of infective endocarditis due to Pseudomonas aeruginosa. Rev Infect Dis. 1983;5:314.

108 Mills J, Crew D. Serratia marcescens endocarditis: a regional illness associated with intravenous drug abuse. Ann Intern Med. 1976;84:29.

109 Archer G, Fekety FR. Experimental endocarditis due to pseudomonas aeruginosa. II. Therapy with carbenicillin and gentamicin. J Infect Dis. 1977;136: 327.

110 Reyes MP et al. Treatment of patients with pseudomonas endocarditis with high-dose aminoglycoside and carbenicillin therapy. Medicine (Baltimore). 1978;57:57.

111 Frank U. Penetration of ceftazidime into heart valves and subcutaneous and muscle tissue of patients undergoing open-heart surgery. Antimicrob Agents Chemother. 1987;31:813.

112 Dickinson G et al. Efficacy of imipenem/cilastatin in endocarditis. Am J Med. 1985;78(6A):117.

113 Scully BE, Neu HC. Use of aztreonam in the treatment of serious infection due to multiresistant gram-negative organisms, including Pseudomonas aeruginosa. Am J Med. 1985;78:251.

114 Strunk RW et al. Comparison of ciprofloxacin with azlocillin plus tobramycin in the therapy of experimental Pseudomonas aeruginosa endocarditis. Antimicrob Agents Chemother. 1985; 28:428.

115 Van Scoy RE. Culture negative endocarditis. Mayo Clin Proc. 1982;57:149.

116 Pesanti EL, Smith IM. Infective endocarditis with negative blood cultures; an analysis of 52 cases. Am J Med. 1979;66:43.

117 Washington JA II. The role of the microbiology laboratory in the diagnosis and antimicrobial treatment of infective endocarditis. Mayo Clin Proc. 1982;57: 22.

118 Munro R et al. Is the antimicrobial removal device a cost-effective addition to conventional blood cultures? J Clin Pathol. 1984;37:348.

119 Dajani AS et al. Prevention of bacterial endocarditis. Recommendations by American Heart Association (AHA). JAMA. 1990;264:2919.

120 Shulman ST et al. Prevention of bacterial endocarditis: a statement for health professionals by the Committee on Rheumatic Fever and Infective Endocarditis of the Council on Cardiovascular Disease in the Young. Circulation. 1984;70:1123A.

121 Anon. Prevention of bacterial endocarditis. Med Lett Drugs Ther. 1986;28: 22.

122 Antibiotic prophylaxis of infective endocarditis recommendations from the endocarditis working party of the British Society for Antimicrobial Chemotherapy. Lancet. 1990;335:88.

123 Oakley CM. Single-dose oral amoxicillin for prophylaxis of bacteraemia, associated with dental surgery. Br Heart J. 1981;45:343.

124 Kaye D. Prophylaxis for infective endocarditis. Ann Intern Med. 1986;104: 419.

125 Brooks RG et al. Hospital survey of antimicrobial prophylaxis to prevent endocarditis in patients with prosthetic heart valves. Am J Med. 1988;84(Part 2):617–21.

126 Poretz DM. Home management of antibiotic therapy. Curr Clin Top Infect Dis. 1989;10:27.

127 Rehm SJ, Weinstein AJ. Home intravenous antibiotic therapy: a team approach. Ann Intern Med. 1983;99:388.

128 McMorrow J, Nahata MC. Prevention of bacterial endocarditis. JAMA. 1991;265:687–88. Letter.

129 Lukes AS et al. Diagnosis of infective endocarditis. Infect Dis Clin N Amer. 1993;7:1.

130 Drexler M et al. Diagnostic value of two-dimensional transoesophageal versus transthoracic echocardiography in patients with infective endocarditis. Eur Heart J. 1987;8(Suppl. J):303.

131 Daniel WG et al. Conventional and transoesophageal echocardiography in the diagnosis of infective endocarditis. Eur Heart J. 1987;8(Suppl. J):287.

132 Daniel WG et al. Improvement in the diagnosis of abscesses associated with endocarditis by transesophageal echocardiography. N Engl J Med. 1991; 324:795.

133 Murphy JG, Foster-Smith K. Management of complications of infective endocarditis with emphasis on echocardiographic findings. Infect Dis Clin N Amer. 1993;7:153.

134 Megran DW. Enterococcal endocarditis. Clin Infect Dis. 1992;15:63–71.

135 Rybak MJ et al. Nephrotoxicity of vancomycin, alone and with an aminoglycoside. J Antimicrob Chemother. 1990;25:679–87.

136 Downs NJ. Mild nephrotoxicity associated with vancomycin use. Arch Intern Med. 1989;149:1777–781.

137 Terrell CL, Hughes CE. Antifungal agents used for deep-seated mycotic infections. Mayo Clin Proc. 1992;67:69.

138 Longman LP et al. Efficacy of fluconazole in prophylaxis and treatment of experimental candida endocarditis. Rev Infect Dis. 1990;12(Suppl. 3):S294.

139 Isalska BJ, Stanbridge TN. Fluconazole in the treatment of candidal prosthetic valve endocarditis. Br Med J. 1988;297:178.

140 Martino P, Cassone A. Candidal endocarditis and treatment with fluconazole and granulocyte-macrophage colony-stimulating factor. Ann Intern Med. 1990;112:966. Letter.

141 Roupie E et al. Fluconazole therapy of candidal native valve endocarditis. Eur J Clin Microbiol Infect Dis. 1991;10: 458. Letter.

142 Venditti M et al. Fluconazole treatment of catheter-related right-sided endocarditis caused by Candida albicans and associated with endophthalmitis and folliculitis. Clin Infect Dis. 1992; 14:422.

143 Hernandez JA et al. Candidal mitral endocarditis and long-term treatment with fluconazole in a patient with human immunodeficiency virus infection. Clin Infect Dis. 1992;15:1062. Letter.

144 Ellner JJ et al. Infective endocarditis caused by slow-growing, fastidious, gram-negative bacteria. Medicine. 1979;58:145.

145 Cohen PS et al. Infective endocarditis caused by gram-negative bacteria: a review of the literature, 1945–1977. Prog Cardiovasc Dis. 1980;22:205.

146 von Graevenitz A. Endocarditis due to nonfermentative gram-negative rods. An updated review. Eur Heart J. 1987; 8(Suppl. J):331.

147 Tunkel AR et al. Enterobacter endocarditis. Scand J Infect Dis. 1992;24: 233.

148 Cooper R, Mills J. Serratia endocarditis. A follow-up report. Arch Intern Med. 1980;140:199.

149 Stamboulian D et al. Antibiotic management of outpatients with endocarditis due to penicillin-susceptible streptococci. Rev Infect Dis. 1991;13 (Suppl. 2):S160.

150 Francioli P et al. Treatment of streptococcal endocarditis with a single daily dose of ceftriaxone sodium for 4 weeks. JAMA. 1992;267:264.

151 Bayer AS. Infective endocarditis. Clin Infect Dis. 1993;17:313–22.

152 Uttley AHC et al. Vancomycin-resistant enterococci. Lancet. 1988;319: 157.

153 LeClercq RE et al. Plasmid-mediated resistance to vancomycin and teicoplanin in Enterococcus faecium. N Engl J Med. 1988;1:157.

154 Anon. Nosocomial enterococci resistant to vancomycin—United States, 1989–1993. Morbid Mortal Weekly Report. 1993;42:597.

155 Courvalin P. Resistance of enterococci to glycopeptides. Antimicrob Agents Chemother. 1990;34:2291.

156 Arthur M, Courvalin P. Genetics and mechanisms of glycopeptide resistance in enterococci. Antimicrob Agents Chemother. 1993; 37:1563.

157 LeClercq R et al. Resistance of enterococci to aminoglycosides and glycopeptides. Clin Infect Dis. 1992;15:495.

158 Shales DM et al. Emerging antimicrobial resistance and the immunocompromised host. Clin Infect Dis. 1993; 17(Suppl. 2):S527.

159 Livornese LL et al. Hospital-acquired infection with vancomycin-resistant Enterococcus faecium transmitted by electronic thermometers. Ann Intern Med. 1992;117:112.

160 Handwerger S et al. Nosocomial outbreak due to Enterococcus faecium resistant to vancomycin, penicillin, and gentamicin. Clin Infect Dis. 1993;16: 750.

161 Caron F et al. Triple combination penicillin-vancomycin-gentamicin for experimental endocarditis caused by a highly penicillin- and glycopeptide-resistant isolate of Enterococcus faecium. J Infect Dis. 1993;168:681.

162 Caron F et al. Triple combination penicillin-vancomycin-gentamicin for experimental endocarditis caused by a moderately penicillin- and highly glycopeptide-resistant isolate of Enterococcus faecium. J Infect Dis. 1991;164: 888.

163 Hayden MK et al. In vivo development of teicoplanin resistance in a VanB Enterococcus faecium isolate. J Infect Dis. 1993;167:1224.

164 Caron F et al. Daptomycin or teicoplanin in combination with gentamicin for treatment of experimental endocarditis due to a highly glycopeptide-resistant isolate of Enterococcus faecium. Antimicrob Agents Chemother. 1992; 36:2611.

165 Whitman MS et al. Antibiotic treatment of experimental endocarditis due to vancomycin- and ampicillin-resistant Enterococcus faecium. Antimicrob Agents Chemother. 1993;37:2069.

166 Johnson CC et al. Bactericidal activity of ramoplanin against antibiotic-resistant enterococci. Antimicrob Agents Chemother. 1992;36:2342.

167 French P et al. In vitro activity of novobiocin against multiresistant strains of Enterococcus faecium. Antimicrob Agents Chemother. 1993;37:2736.

168 Landman D et al. Novel antibiotic regimens against Enterococcus faecium resistant to ampicillin, vancomycin, and gentamicin. Antimicrob Agents Chemother. 1993;37:1904.

169 Herman DJ, Gerding DN. Screening and treatment of infections caused by resistant enterococci. Antimicrob Agents Chemother. 1991;35:215.

170 Poüdras P et al. Bacteremia due to vancomycin-resistant Enterococcus faecium of VanB phenotype during prophylaxis with vancomycin. Clin Infect Dis. 1992;15:752.

171 Ruoff KL et al. Species identities of enterococci isolated from clinical specimens. J Clin Microbiol. 1990;28:435.

172 Wells VD et al. Infections due to beta-lactamase-producing, high-level gentamicin-resistant Enterococcus faecalis. Ann Intern Med. 192;116:285.

173 Dajani AS et al. Oral amoxicillin as prophylaxis for endocarditis: what is the optimal dose? Clin Infect Dis. 1994;18:157.

174 **Maki DG et al.** Comparative study of cefazolin, cefamandole, and vancomycin for surgical prophylaxis in cardiac and vascular operations. J Thorac Cardiovasc Surg. 1992;104:1423.

175 **Burney S et al.** Activity of clinafloxacin against multi-drug resistant Enterococcus faecium. Antimicrob Agents Chemother. 1994;38:1668.

176 **Levine DP et al.** Slow response to vancomycin or vancomycin plus rifampin in methicillin-resistant *Staphylococcus aureus* endocarditis. Ann Intern Med. 1991;115:674.

177 **Fass RJ.** In vitro activity of RP 59500, a semisynthetic injectable pristinamycin, against staphylococci, streptococci, and enterococci. Antimicrob Agents Chemother. 1991;35:553–59.

178 **Investigator's brochure, Synercid; Rhone-Poulenc Rorer, revised October 27, 1993.**

179 **Durack DT et al.** New criteria for diagnosis of infective endocarditis: utilization of specific echocardiographic findings. Am J Med. 1994;96:200.

180 **DeGórgolas M et al.** Treatment of experimental endocarditis due to methicillin-susceptible or methicillin-resistant Staphylococcus aureus with trimethoprim-sulfamethoxazole and antibiotics that inhibit cell wall synthesis. Antimicrob Agents Chemother. 1995;39:953.

181 **Voorn GP et al.** Role of tolerance in cloxacillin treatment of experimental *Staphylococcus aureus* endocarditis. J Infect Dis. 1991;163:640.

Respiratory Tract Infections

George S Jaresko
Donald P Alexander

Upper Respiratory Tract Infections 58-1
  Otitis Media 58-1
  Bronchial Infections 58-2
    Acute bronchitis 58-2
    Chronic bronchitis 58-2
      Clinical presentation 58-2
      Microbiology 58-2
      Antibiotic therapy 58-3
      Antibiotic prophylaxis 58-3
      Immunoprophylaxis 58-3
Pneumonia 58-4
  Normal Respiratory Tract Defenses 58-4
  Risk Factors 58-4
  Clinical Presentation 58-5
  Determination of Etiologic Agent (See Table 58.2) 58-5
  Treatment 58-5
  Complications of Infection 58-6
  Community-Acquired Pneumonia 58-6
    Clinical presentation 58-6
    Treatment (See Table 58.4) 58-7
    Penicillin 58-7
    Alternative antimicrobial therapy 58-7
    Drugs of choice 58-7
  Aspiration Pneumonia 58-8

Predisposing factors 58-8
Clinical course 58-8
Treatment 58-8
  Antimicrobial therapy (See Question 36
    and Table 56.8) 58-9
Clinical presentation (See Table 56.5) 58-9
Microbiology (See Tables 56.6 and 56.7) 58-9
Hospital-Acquired Pneumonia 58-11
  Risk factors 58-11
  Treatment 58-11
    Empiric antibiotic therapy 58-11
    Broad-spectrum beta-lactams 58-12
    Aminoglycosides 58-12
    Bronchial penetration of antibiotics 58-12
    Locally administered antibiotics: prophylaxis 58-13
    Aerosolized antibiotics 58-13
      Administration 58-13
      Bronchial and serum concentrations 58-13
      Adverse effects 58-13
Pneumonia in Cystic Fibrosis (CF) 58-14
  Special treatment considerations 58-14
    Microbiology 58-14
    Dosing considerations 58-14
    Local antibiotic administration 58-14

Infection of the respiratory tract continues to be the most frequent and important cause of short-term illness in the U.S. It is typically the first infection to occur after birth, with pneumonia being the sixth leading cause of death and the number one infectious disease cause of death in the U.S.[1,2] Respiratory tract infections occur more frequently than they are reported and are often thought of as inconveniences of life; however, they are responsible for more days of bed disability, restricted activity, and lost time from work and school than any other category of reported acute illness in America. Respiratory infections account for more than 40% of the disability days secondary to acute illness,[2] and pneumonia and influenza are among the ten leading causes of death in the population overall with 80% to 90% of deaths occurring in the elderly (≥65 years).[3,4] An estimated 2.2 million people, worldwide, die yearly because of acute respiratory infections.[5] Eighty thousand people died in the U.S. in 1990 directly due to pneumonia or influenza. The actual number is much larger since this figure does not include individuals that died from pneumonia that had other diseases [e.g., human immunodeficiency virus (HIV), tobacco, alcohol].[3]

The financial impact associated with respiratory infections is in excess of 15 billion dollars yearly in direct treatment costs.[1] The indirect costs of respiratory infections (e.g., losses in personal income and productivity) would add substantially to this figure, but are difficult to quantitate. The treatment of respiratory infections in the ambulatory setting is estimated to be ten billion dollars a year, two-thirds of the total estimated cost in this area. These figures largely underestimate the financial impact of treating ambulatory respiratory infections. Statistics reported by the National Health Interview Survey estimate that 182 million episodes of respiratory infection occur for which no medical attention is sought.[2] Often, individuals with respiratory infections try home remedies or over-the-counter (OTC) medications for relief of their symptoms and only seek medical advice or treatment when these efforts fail. The estimated cost associated with the use of OTC medications in this population will contribute an additional $456 million annually to the treatment of respiratory infections.[1]

This chapter addresses the concepts relevant to the treatment of upper and lower respiratory tract bacterial infections. In addition, several important therapeutic issues regarding the use of drugs in the treatment of respiratory tract infections will be discussed. Respiratory tract infections caused by viruses (see Chapter 70: Viral Infections) and fungi (see Chapter 69: Fungal Infections) are presented elsewhere in this book, as are the unique features of respiratory tract infections in immunocompromised hosts (see Chapter 67: Infections in Immunocompromised Hosts) and *Pneumocystis carinii* [see Chapter 68: Human Immunodeficiency Virus (HIV) Infection].

Upper Respiratory Infections
Otitis Media

Acute otitis media is defined as the presence of fluid in the middle ear caused by infection, allergy, or anatomic or functional alterations of the middle ear or eustachian tube. Second to hypertension as the most frequently mentioned principal diagnosis, acute otitis media accounts for 3.5% of all office visits (≈24.5 million visits) and is the most common primary diagnosis for children under 15 years of age.[6] It occurs most commonly in infancy and early childhood. Approximately one-half of infants will have at least one episode of acute otitis media in the first year of life; by three years of age, 71% of children will have at least one episode of acute otitis media and one-third will have three or more episodes.[7] Acute episodes often follow viral respiratory infections during the winter season; infections with respiratory syncytial virus, influenza virus (type A or B), and adenovirus are associated with a greater risk of otitis media.[8,9] Although otitis occurs in adults and children, it more commonly affects children and the presentation of this topic is found in Chapter 97: Pediatric Infectious Diseases. Similarly, epiglottitis and croup are presented in Chapter 97: Pediatric Infectious Diseases.

Bronchial Infections

Acute Bronchitis

1. F.A., a 35-year-old female, presents with a persistent cough following an acute respiratory viral infection which began 7 days ago. Although the nasal stuffiness and sore throat resolved 3 or 4 days ago, the cough has persisted and her sputum has become thick and mucoid in appearance; a burning, substernal pain is associated with each coughing episode. F.A. is presently afebrile. Coarse rales and rhonchi are heard on physical examination of her chest and a tentative diagnosis of acute bronchitis is made. How should F.A. be managed?

Uncomplicated (acute) bronchitis is an inflammatory condition of the tracheobronchial tree that most often is associated with a generalized respiratory infection during the winter months. Viruses associated with acute bronchitis include rhinovirus, coronavirus, influenza, and adenovirus. Lower respiratory tract infection with *Mycoplasma pneumoniae* also is associated with episodes of bronchitis. As in F.A., cough, with or without sputum production, is the most prominent clinical feature of this disease. It usually begins early in the course of the respiratory infection and may persist after the acute viral infection is resolved. The initial dry, unproductive cough eventually may progress to one with a productive mucoid sputum.

The treatment of acute bronchitis is directed at symptomatic control of cough, maintenance of adequate hydration, and the intermittent administration of antipyretics for fever and aches accompanying influenza syndrome. Antibiotics are not indicated for the treatment of viral bronchitis. Bronchitis due to *M. pneumoniae* or secondary bacterial pathogens such as *Streptococcus pneumoniae* may require the use of antimicrobial therapy (i.e., erythromycin or penicillin, respectively). Patients with underlying pulmonary disease [i.e., asthma, chronic obstructive airways disease (COAD)] are especially at risk for a secondary bacterial infection.

Chronic Bronchitis

2. Clinical Presentation. M.J., a 54-year-old male with a 40 year, 1 pack/day smoking history, has a 7-year history of emphysema. He reports 2 cupfuls of whitish-clear, occasionally mucoid sputum per day; the largest amount is coughed up in the morning upon arising. He has a raspy voice and a crackling cough which frequently interrupts his talking. Two days ago, M.J. noticed that his sputum had increased in volume and had changed in appearance. A sputum sample which was yellowish-green, tenacious, and obviously purulent was sent for culture; the Gram's stain showed few epithelial cells, moderate white cells, few gram-positive cocci and gram-negative rods with no predominant organisms. M.J. denies fever or chills and had no signs of bronchopneumonia; the chest x-ray is negative for pneumonia. M.J. has experienced similar episodes 3 or 4 times per year. What signs and symptoms in M.J.'s history are consistent with chronic bronchitis?

Chronic bronchitis is an inflammatory condition of the tracheobronchial tree in which chronic cough and excessive production

of sputum are the prominent features. By definition, patients who cough up sputum daily or on most days over three or more consecutive months for more than two successive years have chronic bronchitis. M.J. meets these criteria. This definition of chronic bronchitis usually does not include those patients with reversible airway disease caused by chronic or recurrent asthma. Chronic obstructive airway disease with emphysema may be present in many of these patients and often complicates the clinical presentation of bronchitis. Bronchitis is more common in men than women and more common after the age of 40 than earlier recognized.[15]

Three important factors are associated with the pathophysiology of chronic bronchitis: cigarette smoking, infection, and environmental exposure to dust and fumes. In M.J., cigarette smoking is an important factor associated with his disease. However, not all patients with chronic bronchitis have a history of smoking and 6% to 10% of nonsmoking men will have persistent cough and sputum production.[15] Smoking is an irritant to the respiratory airways and may stimulate the mucus-secreting goblet cells found in major and smaller bronchi. The increased amount of mucus is not readily cleared from smaller peripheral airways creating airflow resistance; this also accounts for the large volume of sputum cleared from larger airways.

3. Has M.J.'s bronchitis worsened? Is he likely to have an infection?

There are few objective signs of worsening of bronchitis when temporally-related infections are not documented. The most reliable sign of worsening bronchitis is the patient's observation that his or her sputum has changed in amount, color, or consistency as in M.J. These changes in sputum have been used as presumptive evidence of infection, but similar changes in sputum have been reported without documented infection. As illustrated by M.J., most patients have neither systemic symptoms of chills and fever, nor leukocytosis. Some patients report shortness of breath, fatigue, chest tightness, or an increasing cough with dyspnea as their only complaints.

Microbiology. It is difficult to determine the role of bacteria recovered in cultures of sputum and bronchial fluid from patients with chronic bronchitis. It is believed that bronchial fluid from individuals without bronchitis and other lung diseases is sterile, but the methods of fluid collection cannot eliminate contamination with oral flora.[16] *S. pneumoniae* and nontypable *Haemophilus influenzae* are commonly recovered from routine sputum cultures of patients with chronic bronchitis. Since one or both of these organisms are found in 30% to 50% of sputum specimens, they can be considered baseline microbial flora in most patients. The isolation of these organisms is common during quiescent periods and usually does not markedly increase during an exacerbation. However, a quantitative increase in *S. pneumoniae* during an acute exacerbation is correlated with sputum purulence.[17] This association has not been shown for nontypable *H. influenzae*. Other bacteria cultured from sputum samples of patients with chronic bronchitis include *M. pneumoniae* (1% to 10%) and *Moraxella catarrhalis* (5% to 25%).[18]

The correct interpretation of a Gram's stain of a sputum sample is dependent upon whether the sample to be examined is a sample of sputum rather than saliva. Sputum, by definition, represents matter ejected from the lungs or bronchi and should contain at most a few white blood cells upon microscopic examination. A good sputum sample also should not have large numbers of epithelial cells when examined microscopically. In contrast, saliva often contains large numbers of epithelial cells. The consideration of the numbers of epithelial cells or of white blood cells (WBCs) is important because debilitated patients with a pulmonary infection often have difficulty in performing the physical maneuvers necessary to eject sputum from the lungs or bronchi. Treatment of a bronchial infection must be directed at organisms found in the pulmonary tree rather than at organisms commonly found in the oral cavity. In the case of M.J., the Gram's stain would be interpreted as a good specimen (because of the low number of epithelial cells). The fact that there are moderate amounts of WBCs is consistent with infection, especially with a change in the volume and appearance of his sputum. The finding of few gram-positive and gram-negative organisms with no predominant organism suggests some oral flora contamination but also is consistent with pneumonia caused by an atypical pathogen.

The relationship between viral and/or bacterial infection and acute exacerbations of bronchitis in patients with obstructive lung disease is unclear. Although respiratory infections disturb the function of the smaller airways in normal patients, there is no evidence that lung function declines more rapidly in patients with chronic disease with frequent acute exacerbations.[17] Documented infection contributes to the acute decompensation of chronically ill patients and is an important cause of morbidity and mortality.

4. Antibiotic Therapy. Should M.J. be given antibiotic therapy to treat his acute episode?

Controversy exists regarding the use of antibiotics for acute exacerbations of chronic bronchitis. Moderately ill patients without pneumonia, such as M.J., usually do not require antibiotics to treat exacerbations of chronic bronchitis.[19]

Instead, M.J. should be well hydrated and treated with scheduled postural drainage exercises to help mobilize the excessive mucus and improve his pulmonary function. If he does not improve within three or four days, an antibiotic effective against *S. pneumoniae* and *H. influenzae* should be prescribed. Treatment of choice is amoxicillin 250 or 500 mg orally three times daily. Although susceptibility of type B *H. influenzae* varies geographically (10% to 40% resistance reported), most *H. influenzae* causing pulmonary infections in adults are nontypable (i.e., encapsulated) and sensitive to amoxicillin or ampicillin. Because the endpoint for the treatment of chronic bronchitis is unclear, a seven to ten day course of antibiotics usually is prescribed. The choice and use of alternative antibiotics should be guided by an appropriate interpretation of the sputum culture, the patient's clinical condition, and cost of the antibiotic therapy. The indiscriminate use of antibiotics is discouraged.

One alternative therapy would be a macrolide [i.e., erythromycin 250 or 500 mg PO TID or QID, clarithromycin (Biaxin) 250 mg (500 mg for *H. influenzae*) PO BID, azithromycin (Zithromax) 500 mg on day 1 followed by 250 mg PO QD]. Advantages of a macrolide include improved activity against ampicillin-resistant *H. influenzae* (especially with clarithromycin) and improved spectrum of activity against the often coexisting pathogen *M. catarrhalis*. Both newer macrolides (i.e., azithromycin and clarithromycin) have less nausea and vomiting associated with them and can be given less frequently (once or twice daily, respectively) than erythromycin. These newer macrolides, however, are much more expensive and should be reserved for patients known to be noncompliant or in patients that cannot tolerate the gastrointestinal effects of erythromycin. The major advantage and role for azithromycin is as a single dose treatment regimen for *Chlamydia trachomatis* (see Chapter 64: Sexually Transmitted Diseases).

5. M.J.'s sputum culture results are positive for *M. catarrhalis*; should the recovery of *M. catarrhalis* in the sputum culture alter the choice of antibiotic therapy?

The recovery of *M. catarrhalis* in sputum cultures from patients with acute exacerbations of chronic bronchitis has increased in the last few years and follows a seasonal distribution, primarily during the late fall and winter months.[18] A large proportion of these isolates (40% to 75%) produce beta-lactamase and are resistant to many oral penicillins and cephalosporins.[10–13] Therapy with erythromycin, doxycycline, amoxicillin with clavulanic acid (Augmentin), cefuroxime axetil (Ceftin), cefixime (Suprax), ciprofloxacin (Cipro), or trimethoprim-sulfamethoxazole (TMP-SMX) would be effective (preference is determined by susceptibility results, cost, and convenience). While this organism is likely to be sensitive to ciprofloxacin and other fluoroquinolones, the quinolones should be considered third-line agents and should not be used as empiric therapy in the treatment of community-acquired respiratory tract infections. This rationale is due to the disproportionate number of clinical failures when respiratory tract infections, especially with *S. pneumonia*, have been treated with a quinolone.

M.J.'s *M. catarrhalis* is susceptible to all of the therapies listed. He should be treated (author's preference) with TMP-SMX DS (double strength tablet containing TMP 160 mg and SMX 800 mg) one tablet orally twice daily because TMP-SMX is effective, is convenient with a twice daily dosing regimen, is inexpensive, and has a favorable side effect profile.

6. Antibiotic Prophylaxis. What strategies should be considered in the use of antibiotic prophylaxis if M.J. develops frequent exacerbations?

Prophylactic antibiotic therapy decreases the number of acute exacerbations of bronchitis in patients with frequent episodes, but has not been helpful in those patients such as M.J. who have infrequent exacerbations.[15] Antibiotic therapy does not alter the rate of decline in pulmonary function.[20]

Patients in whom prophylactic antibiotics are used should receive them during critical periods when they are most susceptible to acute exacerbations of bronchitis. For example, daily doses of antibiotics four days a week during the winter months may be helpful,[21] or, a seven-day course of antibiotics at the first sign of a "chest cold."

7. Immunoprophylaxis. Should M.J. receive immunoprophylaxis against infection?

Patients such as M.J. with chronic bronchitis should be strongly encouraged to receive a yearly influenza immunization. Because the influenza strain(s) causing infection differs each year, the patient should be immunized with the current vaccine. Other groups that should be immunized annually include the elderly and individuals that are at high risk for exposure (i.e., teachers, day care and health care personnel). Since patients with chronic bronchitis are susceptible to all of the respiratory viruses, only limited protection can be provided by administering the currently available vaccine.

The value of the pneumococcal vaccine is less clear and should be individualized in each patient with chronic pulmonary disease. It has been suggested that persons with chronic pulmonary disease may benefit from the administration of the pneumococcal vaccine, although a critical analysis of the literature has not clearly demonstrated benefit of its use in this population.[21,22] It remains unclear whether the number of acute exacerbations of chronic bronchitis is altered with the use of the vaccine. However, since the incidence of side effects associated with pneumococcal vaccine is usually mild and uncommon, M.J. should receive it. Unlike the influenza vaccine, the 23 subtype-pneumococcal vaccine should be given only once in a lifetime.

The use of vaccines would not be expected to provide any protection against *H. influenzae* colonization in patients with chronic bronchitis because the strains recovered from these individuals are nontypable strains of *H. influenzae*, not type B. Therefore, M.J. should not be given this vaccine.

Pneumonia

Pneumonia is an inflammation of the lung parenchyma which is caused by infection. Since pneumonia is not a reportable disease and since most community-acquired infections are treated as outpatients, it is difficult to determine the true incidence of this infection and its related morbidity. Of those patients hospitalized for pneumonia, patient mortality varies with the type and number of underlying diseases, age of the patient, complications that occur during the hospitalization, and type of bacteria causing pneumonia. Table 58.1 summarizes the mortality associated various bacterial pneumonias.

Normal Respiratory Tract Defenses

8. A.T., an 85-year-old male, is admitted to the hospital from a local nursing home with fever, increased sputum production, tachypnea, and complaints of a knife-like chest pain which is made worse by coughing and breathing. Pertinent past medical history includes a right-sided stroke with partial paralysis and a 12-year history of chronic bronchitis. A.T. regularly produces 2 cups of sputum a day and continues to smoke 2.5 packs/day of cigarettes. He has been taking tetracycline 250 mg BID prophylactically for the past 14 months.

Physical examination reveals an elderly man lying restlessly in bed. Vital signs are as follows: blood pressure (BP) 145/88 mm Hg, heart rate (HR) 105 beats/min, and temperature 38.5 °C. Chest examination revealed slight splinting on the right side with inspiration and fine crackling rales in the lower base of the right lung. Examination of the left lung was normal.

Significant laboratory results include: WBC count 16,200 cells/mm^3 (Normal: 5000–10,000); differential polymorphonuclear neutrophils (PMNs) 82% (Normal: 45–79), bands 9% (Normal: 0–5), lymphocytes 8% (Normal: 16–47); Hct 45% (Normal: 37–47); arterial blood gases (ABGs) pH 7.46 (Normal: 7.38–7.45), pO$_2$ 68 mm Hg (Normal: 80–100), pCO$_2$ 36 mm Hg (Normal: 38–45), HCO$_3$ 24 mEq/L (Normal: 22–26). Gram's stain: <10 epithelial cells, 20–25 PMNs, predominance of pleomorphic gram-negative rods. What are the normal respiratory defenses against infection? [SI units: WBC count 16.2 × 10^9/L (Normal: 5–10); differential PMNs 0.82 (Normal: 0.45–0.79), bands 0.09 (Normal: 0–0.05), lymphocytes 0.08 (Normal: 0.16–0.47); Hct 0.45 (Normal: 0.37); pO$_2$ 9.06 kPa (Normal: 10.66–13.33); pCO$_2$ 4.8 kPa (Normal: 5.07–6)]

Preservation of normal respiratory tract function involves a complex system of local pulmonary lung defenses. Anatomical, functional, and mechanical barriers protect the tracheobronchial tree from inert particle and microbial invasion. In addition, an intricate system of cellular and humoral immune host defenses contribute to maintain the respiratory tract free of infection. Intrinsic defects in these normal defenses predispose the patient to respiratory infections.[23,24]

The hairs lining the nasal passages, ciliated epithelial cells on mucosal surfaces, production of mucus, salivary enzymes, and the mechanical process of swallowing help decrease and prevent the passage of foreign material into the lower respiratory tract. Disease states, environmental factors, and age may alter the integrity and influence the function of these barriers.

Alterations in normal oropharyngeal flora by disease or antibiotics permit colonization of the oropharynx with more pathogenic bacteria. Colonization of the oropharynx in itself is not predictive of infection but predisposes the patient who may aspirate oropharyngeal secretions to infection.

Neurological diseases and altered states of consciousness which result in the loss of control of epiglottal and laryngeal function predispose the patient to recurrent episodes of aspiration of upper respiratory tract secretions. Without an intact cough or gag reflex, the volume of upper respiratory secretions reaching the lower airways may exceed the local lung defenses, resulting in an unfavorable environment, and increase the risk for infection. Patients at risk include any patient with altered consciousness secondary to disease or drugs (e.g., alcoholics, stroke victims, substance abusers, epileptics, surgical patients receiving general anesthesia, head injury patients, patients with any illness associated with obtundation).

A functioning mucociliary transport system, which traps and removes foreign material from the lower respiratory tract, is critical to the protection of the lungs. Diseases that alter mucus production and ciliary function severely compromise the body's ability to defend against infection.

Finally, defects in the cellular and humoral immune response will severely compromise the host to invading pathogens. These defenses include the pulmonary macrophages residing within the alveoli, polymorphonuclear leukocytes, immunoglobulin and complement present in lung tissue. Deficiency of the latter substances is associated with an increase in the prevalence of infection with encapsulated organisms (i.e., *S. pneumoniae*, *H. influenzae*). These substances enhance the body's defense against bacterial invaders by functioning as opsonins to improve the efficiency of phagocytosis.

In the normal state, the lungs are repeatedly inoculated with micro-organisms from the upper airway and inhaled aerosols, but pneumonia rarely occurs.[25] It is through defects in one or more of the above mechanisms that the lung is exposed to an increased inoculum of micro-organisms for a sufficient period of time to cause marked inflammatory changes resulting in pneumonia.

Risk Factors

9. What factors present in A.T.'s case make him susceptible to pulmonary infection?

Stroke, with neurologic loss of epiglottal function and cough reflex, predisposes A.T. to recurrent aspiration of upper airway secretions. Upon aspiration, secretions enter the lower airway where altered ciliary function caused by chronic bronchitis, age, and smoking, do not permit effective removal of these secretions. Pooling of these secretions results in the accumulation of a sufficient inoculum of bacteria to overcome the ability of the alveolar macrophage to eliminate the bacteria and prevent the establishment of infection. Ultimately, inflammatory changes with local edema and cellular destruction occur in the lung tissue. The inflammatory process and mediators released from macrophages recruit polymorphonuclear leukocytes from the blood stream. These cells contribute to additional tissue damage in the normal course of containing the infective process.

Table 58.1	Incidence of Mortality Due to Pneumonia Relating to Bacterial Source	
Bacterial Source	**Mortality^a**
Gram-Positive	
Streptococcus sp.	10%–40%
Staphylococcus sp.	30%–50%
Gram-Negative	
All sources	30%–100%
Including *Pseudomonas aeruginosa*	50%–100%
Other	
Legionella pneumophila	15%–25%
Mycoplasma pneumoniae	Uncommon

^{a} Higher in patients with severe underlying disease and advanced age.

Most bacterial pneumonias probably result from the entry of pathogenic bacteria present in the upper respiratory tract into the lung. In the healthy state, the bacterial flora of the oropharynx are the organisms normally present in the mouth and upper respiratory tract. This flora consists of a mixture of aerobic bacteria including *streptococci* species, *S. pneumoniae*, *Klebsiella pneumoniae*, and anaerobic bacteria including *Peptococcus* species, *Peptostreptococcus* species, *Fusobacterium* species, and various *Bacteroides* species including *Bacteroides melaninogenicus* and *Bacteroides fragilis*.[26]

The suppression of normal flora with the administration of broad-spectrum antibiotics (such as tetracycline in A.T.) and the physiological state of the host are the major factors which can alter oropharyngeal flora.[27,28] These factors facilitate the colonization of the oropharynx with significant numbers of pathogenic gram-negative aerobic bacteria and *staphylococci*. Gram-negative rods are cultured from the sputum in 2% to 18% of healthy individuals, but the numbers of recovered organisms are usually small.[29,30]

Gram-negative bacilli are also common in the oropharyngeal secretions of patients with moderate to severe acute and chronic illnesses who have had no exposure to broad-spectrum antibiotics.[31,37] Patients admitted to the hospital with acute illnesses are rapidly colonized with gram-negative organisms. Approximately 20% are colonized on the first hospital day, and the number of patients colonized increases with the duration of hospitalization and severity of illness.[28] Approximately 35% to 45% of hospitalized patients[28] and up to 100% of critically ill patients[30] will be colonized within three to five days of admission.

The elderly, such as A.T., also have a higher prevalence of oropharyngeal colonization. Colonization increases with the level of dependence: gram-negative bacteria are recovered from the oropharyngeal cultures of 9% of the elderly living in apartments and 60% of elderly in acute hospital wards.[32] Altered pulmonary clearance resulting from a decrease in mucociliary transport also has been found in the elderly. Other features contributing to the increase in colonization and pneumonia in the elderly include a decrease in cell-mediated immunity, altered immunoglobulin production and antibody response, and an increase in the severity of underlying diseases.[33] Evidence suggests that colonization of the upper respiratory tract with gram-negative bacteria correlates with the development of infection.[28,30,31]

Colonization of the lower respiratory tract is well established in patients, such as A.T., with chronic bronchitis.[16] These patients are susceptible to recurrent episodes of bronchitis which are believed to be related to or associated with an infectious etiology. Whether a positive sputum culture represents a true pulmonary infection or simple colonization of the respiratory tract is difficult to determine. Additional data from the patient's history, physical examination, and laboratory tests are needed to interpret the positive sputum culture.

Clinical Presentation

10. What clinical signs, symptoms, and laboratory tests are consistent with pneumonia in A.T.?

A.T. has many signs and symptoms of pneumonia. Fever, tachypnea, tachycardia, a productive cough, and a change in the amount or character of the sputum are common in patients with pneumonia. A.T. gives a history of pleuritic (knife-like) chest pain and examination of the chest shows splinting and an inspiratory lag on the right side during inspiration. All these signs are suggestive of a pneumonic process and usually are present on the affected side. Decreased breath sounds, dullness on chest percussion, and vowel tone changes (E to A) found during auscultation

of the chest also are highly suggestive of a consolidation process. The chest x-ray is important in identifying and/or confirming a pulmonary infiltrate in patients with respiratory infections. A.T.'s white blood cell count is elevated with a left shift in the cell differential (predominance of PMNs and bands); this is consistent with bacterial infection. Patients also may be mildly hypoxemic as illustrated by A.T.

Determination of Etiologic Agent

11. How can the etiologic organism be determined?

Gram's stain and sputum culture of appropriately collected sputum are the mainstays in identifying the etiologic organisms of acute pneumonias. The sputum should be examined and the color, consistency, amount, and odor should be recorded. Empiric antibiotic therapy is based upon bacterial morphology or Gram's stain before the culture results become available 24 to 48 hours later.

Most often, sputum is collected by having the patient cough and expectorate lower respiratory tract secretions into a collection container; however, because the secretions must pass through the mouth, they may become contaminated with mouth flora. Specimens containing greater than 10 epithelial cells/low power field (LPF) usually are not considered acceptable for analysis.[34] If there is a predominant organism on Gram's stain, empiric therapy can be directed toward the most probable organism (see Table 58.2). Patients with risk factors for pneumonia (e.g., elderly, hospitalized, chronically ill), frequently are colonized by multiple pathogens and a sputum culture is seldom helpful in identifying the specific causative organism.[106] In these cases, physical examination, chest x-ray, and changes in sputum production and quality continue to be the cornerstone for the diagnosis of pneumonia.

If a patient is unable to give an acceptable sputum specimen after three to four attempts, transtracheal aspiration, bronchoscopy, or open lung biopsy can be used to obtain sputum or tissue samples for laboratory analysis. However, these procedures are not without risk and should be used only when the etiology is crucial for diagnosis.

Treatment

12. How should A.T. be treated?

A.T. should be started empirically on antibiotics pending identification of the bacteria causing the pneumonia. The choice of

Table 58.2	Most Likely Pathogens to Consider When Evaluating a Sputum Gram's Stain with a Predominant Organism and PMNs[a]	
	Community-Acquired	Hospital-Acquired
Gram-Positive Cocci		
Pairs, small chains	*S. pneumoniae*	
Clusters		*S. aureus*
Gram-Negative rods		*P. aeruginosa* *Enterobacter cloacae*
Pleomorphic, hearty	*H. influenzae*	
Pleomorphic, thin		*Fusobacterium sp.*
Short, plump	*K. pneumoniae*	
Gram-Positive and Gram-Negative with PMNs	Aspiration	Aspiration
No Organism Seen	*Mycoplasma* *Legionella* Tuberculosis	*Legionella*

[a] PMNs = Polymorphonuclear neutrophils.

antibiotic should be guided by the results of the sputum Gram's stain, patient age, prior medical history, concomitant diseases, prior place of residence, and clinical signs and symptoms. If no sputum is available for Gram's stain, antibiotics active against possible or probable bacterial pathogens are selected. Since A.T. has a diagnostic Gram's stain, empiric therapy should be directed at *H. influenzae* pneumonia. Since A.T. was treated with tetracycline before admission, one can assume this pathogen is resistant to all tetracyclines. The tetracyclines should not be used for the treatment of *H. influenzae* because large numbers of *H. influenzae* are resistant.[107] Tetracycline, therefore, should not be continued in A.H.

With A.T.'s age and paralysis history, aspiration pneumonia (see Question 21) is possible and may require expansion of empiric therapy to include anaerobes. Of some concern is the possibility of nosocomial flora predominating at the nursing home, but, in this case, the Gram's stain still has the greatest influence on selecting initial antimicrobial therapy. Ampicillin 1 gm intravenously (IV) every six hours; gentamicin 100 mg IV now, followed by 70 mg IV every eight hours; and clindamycin 900 mg IV every eight hours could be initiated empirically.

In contrast to respiratory tract infections in children, the prevalence of ampicillin-resistant *H. influenzae* in adults is <5%.[14,107,108] Nevertheless, the selection of an antibiotic regimen that would be effective even against ampicillin-resistant *H. influenzae* would be reasonable in this case because of the need to also treat A.T. for possible aspiration pneumonia. Given these considerations, monotherapy (versus the above mentioned three drug therapy) with ampicillin/sulbactam (Unasyn), ticarcillin/clavulanate (Timentin), or piperacillin/tazobactam (Zosyn) would be effective against most anaerobes and beta-lactamase producing *H. influenzae*, would be cost-effective, and less labor intensive in administering to A.T.

Although practitioners frequently are reluctant to modify therapy, especially if a patient is improving, a change in therapy may be justified if the clinician believes in the reliability of the culture and sensitivity results and if the redirected therapy will be better for the patient (i.e., disrupt normal flora less, lower cost, less side effects) or for society (influence on institutional resistance patterns). Antibiotics usually are administered for 10 to 14 days or for at least five days after the patient becomes afebrile.

Ancillary therapy of pneumonia includes supplemental oxygen if needed for hypoxia and mechanical ventilation if acute respiratory failure occurs. Treatment of A.T.'s pleuritic chest pain may require the use of analgesics such as morphine or nonsteroidal anti-inflammatory drugs; however, if narcotics are used, their effects on respiration should be followed closely. A.T.'s fluid status should be evaluated and managed appropriately.

Complications of Infection

13. What complications of pneumonia should be anticipated in A.T.?

Pneumonia may result in the development of anatomically local or distant complications. In the lung, atelectasis may occur during the acute phase of infection or during the resolution phase. The affected areas usually clear with coughing and deep breathing but they may become fibrotic if atelectasis persists for prolonged periods. Lung abscess is an infrequent complication of pneumonia and is found most often in patients with aspiration pneumonia or in situations where the patient has delayed seeking medical attention for pneumonia. Lung abscess in a patient with these risk factors most commonly is caused by anaerobic gram-negative bacteria (e.g., beta-lactamase producing *Bacteroides* species, *Fusobacterium* species) or anaerobic gram-positive bacteria (e.g., *Peptostrep-*

tococcus species, microaerophilic *streptococci*). Treatment with metronidazole or clindamycin *plus* high dose penicillin G (10 to 20 million units/day IV) has been effective. Although not examined in rigorous clinical trials, imipenem (Primaxin) or a beta-lactamase inhibitor combination (i.e., ampicillin/sulbactam, ticarcillin/clavulanate, piperacillin/tazobactam) also should be highly effective and would be excellent treatment alternatives. If a lung abscess is due to hematogenous spread, *staphylococci*, gram-negative bacilli or gram-negative anaerobes often are implicated and the treatment regimen needs to be directed towards these probable pathogens. Duration of treatment for lung abscess is longer than for pneumonia and usually requires two to four months of therapy.

Parapneumonic effusions may occur as a result of lower respiratory tract infections. Infection within the lung causes an altered permeability of the visceral pleura resulting in the accumulation of sterile fluid in the pleural space. Bacterial infiltration into this fluid makes the effusion difficult to treat with antibiotics alone and may require needle aspiration for resolution. Only complicated pleural effusions require drainage. If the effusion does not resolve, polymorphonuclear leukocytes infiltrate the fluid; this is followed by fibrin deposition which results in fluid loculation and empyema formation. Surgical placement of a chest tube for drainage, in addition to antibiotic therapy, often is required for successful treatment of empyemas.

In addition to local complications of pneumonia, metastatic infections may occur secondary to bacteremia. Bacteremia, which reflects the body's inability to contain the infection, is a poor prognostic sign. The true incidence of bacteremia resulting from bacterial pneumonias is unknown but it is estimated to occur in approximately 20% to 30% of cases. The finding of a positive blood culture in a patient with pneumonia usually is associated with an increased incidence of morbidity and a worse overall prognosis.

Community-Acquired Pneumonia

Clinical Presentation

14. D.A., a 55-year-old male, is seen in the emergency room (ER) with the chief complaint of severe right-sided chest pain. Two hours earlier, he felt feverish and experienced a "teeth-chattering" chill. Shortly after this episode, his chest began hurting; the pain has increased in intensity over the last 30 minutes to the point where it is now quite difficult for him to breathe. He has a productive cough and his sputum is pinkish or "rusty" in appearance. His respirations are shallow and rapid. Significant past medical history only includes a flu-like syndrome which began 7 days ago.

Table 58.3	Etiologies and Relative Incidence of Community-Acquired Bacterial Pneumonia[1–4]
Pathogen	Relative Incidence (%)
Streptococcus pneumoniae	25–60
Legionella sp.	1–16[a,b]
Hemophilus influenzae	4–15
Moraxella catarrhalis	NA[c]
Staphylococcus aureus	2–10[d]
Gram-negative bacilli	7–18[d]
Mycoplasma pneumoniae	NA[e]

[a] True incidence unknown; incidence is influenced by geographic location.
[b] ↑ in middle-aged patients with chronic diseases.
[c] True incidence unknown; ↑ incidence of bronchopulmonary infections in patients with chronic lung disease.
[d] ↑ incidences in patients with alcoholism and in nursing homes.
[e] True incidence unknown; most treated as outpatients.

On physical examination, D.A.'s BP is 140/82 mm Hg, HR 106 beats/min, respirations 32/min, and temperature 38.2 °C. Chest examination reveals that D.A. is tachypneic and favors his right side with inspiration. He has light crackling rales over his right lung base on auscultation and complains of tenderness and dullness to percussion in the same area. There is no nuchal rigidity, joint pain or swelling, or abdominal complaints.

Laboratory results are as follows: WBC count 18,600 cells/mm^3 (Normal: 5000–10,000) with a cell differential as follows: PMNs 88%, bands 10%, lymphocytes 2%. Hct is 42.5%. The chest x-ray shows a patchy infiltrate in the right lung accompanied by a mild pleural effusion. Gram's stain of the sputum reveals multiple gram-positive cocci in pairs (diplococci). D.A. is admitted to the hospital with the diagnosis of pneumococcal pneumonia. What features in D.A.'s case are consistent with pneumococcal pneumonia? [SI units: WBC count 18.6×10^9/L with PMNs 0.88, bands 0.10, lymphocytes 0.02; Hct 0.425]

D.A. presents with many of the classical signs of *S. pneumoniae* pneumonia. Pneumococcal pneumonia is a disease of the middle-aged and elderly but it is also an important cause of pneumonia in infants, children, and young adults. The sudden rapid onset of dramatic rigor, pleuritic chest pain, a rust-colored sputum with gram-positive diplococci, and leukocytosis is consistent with pneumococcal pneumonia. Pneumococcus is the pathogen for 25% to 60% of all community-acquired bacterial pneumonias and frequently follows a viral illness. Tachypnea, fever, tachycardia, the chest examination, and chest x-ray findings represent an acute pulmonary process.

Table 58.3 lists the etiologies and prevalence of the community-acquired bacterial pneumonias.

Treatment

15. Penicillin. How should D.A. be treated? (See Table 58.4.)

Penicillin susceptibility should be tested on all pneumococcal isolates. Highly sensitive *S. pneumoniae* isolates will have penicillin minimum inhibitory concentrations (MICs) less than 0.12 μg/mL. If an isolate is resistant (i.e., MIC is ≥2 μg/mL) the patient needs to be treated with parenteral vancomycin. Most hospitalized pneumonia patients should be treated with intravenous antimicrobials. In a randomized trial, penicillin G 20 million units/day given as a continuous infusion was no more effective than 600,000 units of procaine penicillin given intramuscularly (IM) twice a day.[35] Although not frequently used, intramuscular procaine penicillin is a proven cost-effective alternative to intravenous penicillin for the patient with uncomplicated, highly susceptible *S. pneumoniae* pneumonia. Therapy usually is continued for 7 to 14 days. Oral antibiotics may be substituted after the patient has been afebrile for at least two days.

Patients with evidence of metastatic infection (e.g., meningitis, empyema, shock, arthritis, and endocarditis), or complicated infection (e.g., multilobar, elderly, underlying chronic disease) should receive intravenous penicillin 20 million units/day. Young reliable adults with relatively mild symptoms can be treated with oral penicillin (e.g., Pen VK 500 mg QID) as outpatients. The duration of therapy depends upon how rapidly the patient responds but is at least one week. An outpatient's progress should be followed frequently by telephone.

Alternative Antimicrobial Therapy. In those patients allergic to penicillin, alternative antibiotics should be prescribed. If the patient's allergic reaction to penicillin was mild (i.e., a maculopapular rash without difficult breathing), the chance for cross-reactivity to a cephalosporin is low. A first-generation cephalosporin such as cefazolin is administered every eight hours. In patients with mild disease, 1 gm of cefazolin administered IV could be followed with oral cephalexin or cephradine, 500 mg four times a day. Erythromycin, 500 mg orally four times a day, is also an acceptable al-

Table 58.4	Antimicrobial Therapy for Community-Acquired Pneumonia	
Bacterial Source	Antibiotic of Choice	Alternatives
Streptococcus pneumonia	Aqueous penicillin G or procaine penicillin	Cefazolin, erythromycin, penicillin V (PO), ampicillin, amoxicillin (PO)
Mycoplasma pneumoniae	Erythromycin (IV, PO)	Doxycycline (IV, PO)
Haemophilus influenzae		
Beta-lactamase negative	Ampicillin *or* Amoxicillin	2nd- or 3rd-generation cephalosporins *or* TMP-SMX
Beta-lactamase positive	Nonantipseudomonal 3rd-generation cephalosporins	TMP-SMX, amoxicillin/clavulanic acid
Moraxella catarrhalis	Erythromycin	Beta-lactamase inhibitor combination, clarithromycin (Claritin) or azithromycin (Zithromax), quinolones, TMP-SMX, amoxicillin/clavulanic acid, nonantipseudomonal 3rd-generation cephalosporins
Legionella pneumophila	Erythromycin	Doxycycline, ciprofloxacin (Cipro), ofloxacin (Floxin)
Klebsiella sp.	1st-generation cephalosporin	Aminoglycosides, TMP-SMX
Escherichia coli	1st-generation cephalosporin	Aminoglycosides, TMP-SMX

^{a} TMP-SMX = Trimethoprim-sulfamethoxazole.

ternative to penicillin. Although erythromycin is available in several different forms and salts, the most cost-effective regimen should be used.

16. Drugs of Choice. What are the drugs of choice for the treatment of other community-acquired pneumonias?

H. influenzae has long been recognized as a significant pulmonary pathogen in infants and children. In recent years, *H. influenzae* also has been recognized as a significant pulmonary pathogen in adults. This trend may be related to the fact that the population is growing older and the number of patients with chronic lung diseases is increasing. Most of the isolates of *H. influenzae* are nontypable strains and demonstrate a low incidence of beta-lactamase production (12.5%).[36]

Legionella pneumophila contributes significantly to the incidence of community-acquired pneumonia. Patients with altered immunological function (e.g., elderly) and chronic diseases (e.g., COAD) are most susceptible to infection with this organism.

M. catarrhalis now is recognized to be a significant pulmonary pathogen in patients with chronic pulmonary diseases. The recovery of this organism shows a seasonal distribution, encountered largely during the late fall and winter months. (See Question 4 for further discussion of this topic.)

Gram-negative pneumonia in the community setting is increasing in incidence. Most cases of pneumonia occur in patients who reside in nursing homes and long-term care facilities. In addition, the frequency of gram-negative pneumonia, often with *K. pneumoniae*, in the alcoholic patient is well recognized.

Aspiration Pneumonia

Predisposing Factors

17. R.G., a 38-year-old male, was brought to the ER after he was found unconscious, lying on his right side near a pool of vomitus, in a local municipal park. R.G. has a long history of binge drinking and has been admitted to the ER frequently for problems related to his alcoholism. Upon admission R.G.'s vital signs were: BP 100/60 mm Hg, pulse 110 beats/min, respirations 32 breaths/min, and temperature 38.0 °C. There is a strong odor of alcohol and vomitus on his breath. R.G.'s overall mental status is depressed; he has intermittent periods of disoriented talking and uncoordinated motor movements.

On examination of his chest, crackling rales were heard in the middle and lower right lung fields; the left fields were clear. An ABG was drawn on room air: pH 7.46, pO_2 52 mm Hg, pCO_2 35 mm Hg, and HCO_3 24 mEq/L. Laboratory data include: WBC count 12,000 cells/mm³; differential PMNs 68%, bands 8%, and lymphocytes 24%. During a period of consciousness, the physician obtained a sputum specimen from R.G. for Gram's stain and culture. A chest x-ray revealed density changes consistent with interstitial infiltrates in the dependent segments of the middle and lower right lung. A tentative diagnosis of aspiration pneumonitis is made. What factors predispose R.G. to aspiration pneumonitis? How can the aspirated material cause pneumonitis? [SI units: pO_2 6.93 kPa; pCO_2 4.67 kPa; WBC count 12×10^9/L with PMNs 0.68, bands 0.08, and lymphocytes 0.24]

Several factors in R.G.'s history make him susceptible to aspiration. Alcohol intoxication has depressed his mental status and cough and gag reflex which may have led to his aspiration of his vomitus. Table 58.5 lists many conditions which commonly predispose individuals to aspiration. Leading this list are those conditions which cause or contribute to an altered state of consciousness. The specific effect of the aspirated material on the lungs depends upon the quantity and quality of the material aspirated. The latter can be categorized into three types: direct pulmonary toxin, particulate matter, and infected inoculum.[37,38]

There are several toxic materials that cause pneumonitis, the most common of which is gastric acid. When gastric acid enters the lungs, the sequence of events has been likened to a chemical burn. The aspirated secretions are neutralized rapidly over the first few minutes and this is accompanied by a shift of fluid into the involved area of the lung. An estimated 96% of patients will demonstrate signs of respiratory compromise within one hour of aspiration, and 100% within two hours. The two immediate consequences of aspiration of gastric acid are rapid, profound hypoxia and shock secondary to massive fluid shifts into lung tissue. In addition, atelectasis, hemorrhage, and pulmonary edema may occur.[37] Approximately 45% of normal adults aspirate oropharyngeal secretions during deep sleep and 70% of patients with depressed consciousness aspirate pharyngeal secretions.[39] Other toxic materials causing aspiration pneumonitis include hydrocarbons, mineral oil, bile, alcohol, and animal fats.[38]

Gastric juice has a pH of 2.5 or below and contains few to no bacteria.[40,41] However, after the initial insult the patient will frequently develop a secondary bacterial pneumonia following a several day period of improvement.[42] The infection is due primarily to aspiration of oropharyngeal contents in a setting of diminished host defenses caused by the chemical pneumonitis.

A second category of aspirated material is fluid containing various amounts of bacteria. Oropharyngeal secretions are the most frequent source of this material. Bacterial pneumonia results when the normal host lung defenses have been damaged or altered and when the inoculum of the bacteria exceeds the body's ability to contain and eliminate the bacterial inoculum. Infection due to aspirated bacteria may result in a pneumonia ranging from little or no tissue destruction, necrotizing pneumonia, lung abscess, or empyema.

A third category of aspirated material consists of particulate matter. When relatively large particles are aspirated, sudden aphonia, cyanosis, and respiratory distress occur; the patient can progress rapidly toward death. Smaller particles may reach the lower airways causing local irritation with bronchospasm. If these particles are not removed, bacterial infection may occur. Many of these cases occur in young children following the ingestion of coins, peanuts, teeth, vegetables, or other small particles. Rapid removal of these particles usually results in the rapid reversal of symptoms without significant sequelae.

Clinical Course

18. What is the expected clinical course of aspiration pneumonia in R.G.?

The clinical course of a patient like R.G. who has aspirated gastric contents and/or oropharyngeal secretions is variable; three courses have been identified. Shock will occur in 20% to 30% of patients with documented aspiration;[40,43] respiratory function continues to deteriorate in many of these patients and approximately 25% die. Mortality rates may be higher in severely ill patients.[44] Early clinical signs and symptoms of gastric aspiration include fever, tachypnea, rales, cough, cyanosis, wheezing, apnea, and shock. A second group of patients will resolve the pneumonitis completely over a few days to weeks without complication. A third group will develop bacterial pneumonia following an initial period of improvement.

Treatment

19. How should R.G. be treated?

R.G.'s initial treatment should primarily consist of supportive measures. Attention should be directed toward respiratory support and correction of his fluid and electrolyte status. In addition, any particulate matter present in the airways should be removed.

Pulmonary edema secondary to massive fluid shifts into the lung can contribute to a decrease in the intravascular volume. If this occurs, aggressive supportive therapy with ventilation, oxygen supplementation, and fluid replacement is indicated.

Table 58.5	Predisposing Conditions in Aspiration Pneumonia[a]

Alterations of Consciousness
  Alcoholism
  Seizure disorders
  General anesthesia
  Cerebrovascular accident
  Drug intoxication
  Head injury
  Severe illness with obtundation

Impaired Swallowing Mechanism
  Neurological disorders
  Esophageal dysfunction

Nasogastric Feeding

Tracheotomy

Endotracheal Tube

Periodontal Disease

[a] Reprinted with permission from Klein RS, Steinbiegl NH. Seminars in Infectious Disease, Vol. 5, Thieme Medical Publishers, New York: 1983.

The use of corticosteroids to reduce inflammation in the setting of aspiration pneumonia is not warranted. There are no well designed studies and much of the data supporting their use is anecdotal. Animal studies also have not conclusively shown benefit from the administration of steroids. In one published report, the use of steroids in treatment of aspiration in humans, actually may have been harmful.[45] No difference was found in the mortality rate between the two groups but the incidence of gram-negative pneumonia was more frequent in those patients receiving steroids. Therefore, if steroids are used in patients with aspiration pneumonia, their potential risks must be weighed against their unproven benefit. Since bacteria play little or no role in the initial events following aspiration, antibiotic therapy should be withheld until bacterial involvement is established.

Prophylactic antibiotics are not beneficial in this setting and may contribute to a change in the oropharyngeal flora which may, in turn, predispose the patient to pneumonia secondary to resistant bacterial organisms. On the other hand, if the patient has been hospitalized for more than three days and then aspirates, empiric antimicrobial therapy often is justified especially if the patient is elderly, debilitated, or is felt to be deteriorating clinically.

Clinical Presentation

20. R.G.'s pulmonary symptoms improved during the next 3 days, but now he has a temperature of 38.5 °C with an increase in sputum production. How should he be assessed?

Patients like R.G. with mild aspiration pneumonia usually resolve their respiratory difficulties within a few days following the insult. If an infection occurs, there is occasionally a short period of clinical improvement before signs and symptoms present. Criteria used to identify bacterial pneumonia following aspiration include: 1) a new fever or a significant temperature rise from the patient's baseline, 2) a new or extending pulmonary infiltrate on x-ray after the initial 36 to 48 hour period, 3) an increase in WBCs or a change in the differential WBC count, 4) a change in sputum characteristics with purulence, and 5) the presence of pathogenic bacteria in a transtracheal aspirate.

Microbiology

21. What bacterial organisms are likely to be responsible for R.G.'s infectious pneumonia?

In the setting of aspiration pneumonitis, the bacterial pathogen is difficult to predict because large numbers of potential bacterial pathogens are present in sputum.

Most cases of aspiration pneumonia are caused by a wide spectrum of gram-positive and gram-negative anaerobic and aerobic bacteria representing the complex microbial flora of the oropharynx and upper gastrointestinal tract. In approximately one-half of cases, aerobic bacteria have been recovered and in 60% to 90% of

Table 58.7		Etiology of Aspiration-Associated Lung Infections[33,59]		
	No. of Patients	Anaerobes Only	Aerobes Only	Mixed
Community-acquired	54	32 (59%)	5 (10%)	17 (31%)
Hospital-acquired	47	8 (18%)	17 (36%)	22 (47%)

cases, anaerobes have been recovered.[28,46] Tables 58.6 and 58.7 list the most common bacteria recovered from patients with aspiration pneumonia. One can see that a large percentage of community-acquired aspiration pneumonias are caused by anaerobes alone, followed by mixed or polymicrobial etiologies. In contrast, a larger percentage of hospital-acquired aspiration pneumonias are caused by aerobic bacteria; they also are usually polymicrobial in nature. The aerobic bacteria recovered from patients with hospital-acquired aspiration pneumonia include *S. aureus*, various *Enterobacteriaceae*, and *P. aeruginosa*. The difference in the aerobic bacteria found in these two settings is not surprising since hospitalized patients readily colonize their oropharynx within days following admission. Understanding the differences in the bacterial etiology in these two settings facilitates the selection of antimicrobial therapy. The bacterial etiology of aspiration pneumonia in children is similar to that of adults.[47,48]

When a patient develops aspiration pneumonia in the community setting, mouth anaerobes and gram-positive aerobic bacteria such as Group A *Streptococcus*, *S. pneumoniae*, and *S. aureus* are the most common pathogens. However, some patients with community-acquired aspiration pneumonia are more susceptible to gram-negative pathogens because of oropharyngeal colonization. These individuals include alcoholics (as in the case of R.G.), elderly patients housed in long-term care nursing facilities,[33] patients receiving enteral feedings,[49] and patients treated chronically with antacids and/or H_2-receptor antagonists, such as cimetidine or ranitidine. In the latter individuals, gram-negative flora are recovered from the stomach because they are better able to survive in a more alkaline pH.[40,50,51] In addition, the oropharynx of these individuals frequently is colonized with the same bacteria found in the gastric flora.[52] In those patients in which this occurred, 60% developed gram-negative pneumonia. Limited information suggests that the use of sucralfate reduces bacterial colonization of the stomach of critically ill patients while maintaining adequate stress ulcer prophylaxis.[53,54] Although sucralfate might lower the incidence and mortality of nosocomial pneumonia in patients requiring mechanical ventilation, more study is needed.

Treatment

22. Antimicrobial Therapy. How should antibiotics be used in aspiration pneumonia? How should R.G. be treated?

Antibiotic therapy should be selected on the basis of several criteria: the clinical setting in which the aspiration occurred, knowledge of the patient's past medical history, the Gram's stain of a reliably obtained sputum, and aerobic and anaerobic culture results of lower respiratory tract secretions. Table 58.8 lists common antibiotics and dosages used to treat aspiration pneumonia.

As noted above, anaerobes are often the sole or dominant bacteria involved in patients with community-acquired aspiration pneumonia. Most of these cases of pneumonia respond well to high dose intravenous penicillin G.[55] Other penicillins that may be used intravenously in high doses are ampicillin, ticarcillin, mezlocillin,

Table 58.6	Bacteriology of Aspiration Pneumonia

Community-Acquired Pneumonia

Streptococcus pneumoniae	*Fusobacterium sp.*
Peptococcus sp.	*Bacteroides melaninogenicus*
Peptostreptococcus sp.	*Bacteroides sp.*
Microaerophilic streptococci	*Streptococcus sp.*

Special Patients [Alcoholics, Diabetics (± Nursing Home Residents)]

Staphylococcus aureus	*Escherichia coli*
Klebsiella pneumoniae	Anaerobes included above

Hospital-Acquired Pneumonia

Pseudomonas aeruginosa	*Escherichia coli*
Staphylococcus aureus	*Enterobacter cloacae*
Streptococcus pneumoniae	*Serratia marcescens*
Anaerobes included above	Other gram-negative bacilli

Table 58.8	Suggested Antimicrobial Dosages for Treatment of Aspiration Pneumonia[a]			
	Adult		Pediatric[b]	
Drug	Dose	Interval (hr)	Total Daily Dose (mg/kg/24 hr)	Interval (hr)
Penicillins				
Ampicillin	1–2 gm	Q 4–6	100–200	Q 4–6
Mezlocillin	2–3 gm	Q 4–6	200–300	Q 4–6
Nafcillin	1–2 gm	Q 4–6	100–200	Q 4–6
Penicillin (procaine) (IM)	0.6–1.2 million units	Q 12	50,000 units	Q 12
Penicillin G (for anaerobic infection)	1–2 million units	Q 4–6	50,000–100,000 units	Q 4–6
Piperacillin	2–5 gm	Q 4–8	200–300	Q 4–6
Ticarcillin	2–3 gm	Q 4–6	200–300	Q 4–6
Other Antibacterials				
Aztreonam	1–2 gm	Q 8–12	50–100	Q 6–8
Chloramphenicol	250–500 mg	Q 6–8	50–100	Q 6–8
Ciprofloxacin	400 gm	Q 12	—	—
Clindamycin	600–900 mg	Q 6–8	25–40	Q 6–8
Doxycycline	100 mg	Q 12	—	—
Erythromycin	250–500 mg	Q 6	40	Q 6
Imipenem	0.25–1 gm	Q 6–8	60	Q 6
Metronidazole	500 mg	Q 8	25–60	Q 8–12
TMP-SMX[c]	10 mg/kg	Q 12	10 mg	Q 12
Vancomycin	500–1000 mg	Q 6–12	40	Q 6–12
Cephalosporins				
Cefamandole	1–2 gm	Q 4–6	—	—
Cefazolin	1–2 gm	Q 8	50–100	Q 8
Cefoperazone	1–2 gm	Q 8–12	50–100	Q 8–12
Cefotaxime	1–2 gm	Q 6–8	50–100	Q 6–8
Cefotetan	1–2 gm	Q 8–12	—	—
Cefoxitin	1–2 gm	Q 4–6	50–100	Q 4–6
Ceftazidime	1–2 gm	Q 8–12	50–100	Q 8–12
Ceftizoxime	1–2 gm	Q 8–12	50–100	Q 8–12
Ceftriaxone	1–2 gm	Q 12–24	50–75	Q 12–24
Cefuroxime	0.75–1.5 gm	Q 6–8	50–100	Q 6–8
Aminoglycosides				
Amikacin	5–7.5 mg/kg	Q 8–12	15–30	Q 8–12
Gentamicin	1.7 mg/kg	Q 8	6–7.5	Q 8
Tobramycin	1.7 mg/kg	Q 8	6–7.5	Q 8

[a] Intravenous doses administered over 30–60 min; in patients with normal clearance.
[b] Infants and children >1 month.
[c] TMP-SMX = Trimethoprim-sulfamethoxazole. TMP-SMX dosed at 10 mg/kg of TMP.

piperacillin, and beta-lactamase inhibitor combinations. These agents have been used with reasonable success in community-acquired aspiration but are usually more expensive than penicillin G and have a higher incidence of side effects associated with their use. Treatment of aspiration pneumonia in the elderly, patients from extended care facilities, patients with extensive past medical histories, and alcoholics (as in the case of R.G.) should include an aminoglycoside since gram-negative bacterial colonization may be present. If the infection possibly involves S. aureus, a penicillinase-resistant penicillin should be added to the regimen, or an alternative therapy with a beta-lactamase inhibitor combination should be used.

Aspiration pneumonia in the hospital setting, where colonization of the oropharynx is more prevalent, should be treated with a regimen that treats both gram-negative pathogens and anaerobes. P. aeruginosa should be considered when selecting a regimen only if the unit (e.g., intensive care unit) has a recognized problem with cross-contamination of the pathogen or if the patient is at high risk (i.e., neutropenic patients or moderate-to-severe thermal injury pa-

tients). This combination of antibiotics should be started initially and modified when the results of the sputum culture are known. Penicillinase-resistant penicillins, such as nafcillin, do not consistently inhibit anaerobes well enough to be used alone in the setting of aspiration pneumonia.[56] Therefore, these agents should be used to provide antibacterial coverage for aerobic gram-positive pathogens only.

In patients with community-acquired pneumonia the selection of a cephalosporin should be based upon its ability to effectively inhibit anaerobes inhabiting the oropharynx (e.g., Peptostreptococcus, Peptococcus). Clindamycin is an effective alternative in the treatment of aspiration pneumoniae. Metronidazole also has been used to treat anaerobic pleuropulmonary infections,[57,58] but the results have been mixed due in part to the severity of infections treated (e.g., lung abscess). Metronidazole effectively inhibits gram-negative obligate anaerobic bacteria, such as B. fragilis and other Bacteroides species, but fails to effectively inhibit facultative anaerobic bacteria, such as Peptococcus species and Peptostreptococcus species.[59]

Parenteral antibiotics should be continued until the patient has clinically responded to the therapy as evidenced by defervescence, decrease in sputum production, decreasing total WBC count, and resolution of the left shift in the cell differential. Oral antibiotics may then be instituted and continued for two to four weeks. In patients with lung abscesses, six weeks of antibiotic therapy may be needed. Although several oral antibiotics have been used in this setting: (e.g., penicillin V, ampicillin, amoxicillin, cephradine, cephalexin, and clindamycin), only metronidazole or Augmentin are likely to be appropriate oral agents for anaerobic lung infections.

Hospital-Acquired Pneumonia

Risk Factors

23. A.A., a 68-year-old male, is admitted to the hospital from an extended care nursing facility because of an acute change in mental status, fever, dyspnea with respiratory difficulty, cough, and sputum production.

His past medical history is notable for a right-sided cerebrovascular accident which left him with residual weakness, insulin dependent diabetes mellitus since the age of 10, and a recent *Escherichia coli* urinary tract infection which was treated with oral TMP-SMX DS for ten days. Because of poor nutrition, A.A. has been receiving nutritional supplements through a flexible nasogastric feeding tube for the past 2 months.

Physical examination reveals a restless, elderly man with the following vital signs: BP 147/87 mm Hg, pulse 110 beats/min, respirations 28 breaths/min, temperature 39 °C. His head is without obvious trauma and his neck is supple. Examination of the chest demonstrated crackling rales with diminished breath sounds in the middle and upper right lung fields. The chest x-ray shows pulmonary infiltrate involving the right middle and upper lobes of the right lung with lobar consolidation. Because A.A. is relatively uncooperative and cannot give a good sputum specimen, a specimen of lower respiratory tract secretions was collected by transtracheal aspiration. This specimen was sent to the laboratory for Gram's stain and culture.

The Gram's stain showed 3+ gram-negative rods with 4+ neutrophils. ABGs showed that A.A. had a PaO₂ of 34 mm Hg on room air; his current PaO₂ is 52 mm Hg 80–100 with 4 L/min of supplemental oxygen. Other laboratory values include: an Hct 39%; WBC count 16,000 cells/mm³; PMNs 88%, bands 10%, lymphocytes 2%; blood urea nitrogen (BUN) 12 mg/dL (Normal: 7–20); and creatinine 1.0 mg/dL (Normal: 0.8–1.2).

Medications upon admission include oral cimetidine (Tagamet) 300 mg QID. A tentative diagnosis of a hospital-acquired gram-negative pneumonia is made. A.A. is intubated and placed on a ventilator to provide respiratory assistance and improve oxygen delivery. In addition, IV fluids were started to maintain a urine output of 50 mL/hr. What are the risk factors for pneumonia in A.A.? [SI units: PaO₂ 4.53 and 6.93 kPa, respectively; Hct 0.39; WBC count 16 × 10⁹/L, PMNs 0.88, bands 0.1, lymphocytes 0.02; BUN 4.28 mmol/L of urea (Normal: 2.5–7.14); creatinine 88.4 μmol/L (Normal: 70.72–106.08)]

Although A.A. is just now being admitted to the hospital, he is given a diagnosis of hospital-acquired pneumonia because he lives in a large nursing home which generally will have flora similar to a hospital and he has a Gram's stain that is consistent with a gram-negative pneumonia. Other factors associated with the risk of developing hospital-acquired pneumonia include: prior or present administration of antibiotics, chronic cardiopulmonary diseases, intubation, immunosuppression, and age (neonates and the elderly). In addition to the above, an important contributing factor in the cause of a pneumonia is colonization of the oropharynx.

Several factors may contribute to the colonization of A.A.'s oropharynx with gram-negative bacteria. A.A. is disabled because of a cerebrovascular accident which has left him with right-sided weakness; this chronic condition also may predispose him to changes in oropharyngeal flora. A.A. is prone to aspiration of these secretions because the residual effects of the stroke and nasogastric tube used for nutritional support have decreased his airway protection. Finally, an altered immune response in diabetics and elderly can further contribute to the establishment of a respiratory infection in A.A.[60-62]

The use of drugs that inhibit the production of gastric acid, such as cimetidine, increases the possibility of oropharyngeal colonization.[51,52] Finally, the use of broad-spectrum antibiotics may inhibit many of the normal bacteria which resided in the oropharynx and reduce bacterial interference which keeps other pathogenic bacteria at a low level.[63] When these normal flora bacteria are inhibited, gram-negative bacteria and other multiply-resistant bacteria are permitted to colonize the oropharynx.

Patients residing in nursing homes have an increased incidence of nosocomial pneumonias. These patients have higher incidences of oropharyngeal colonization with gram-negative bacteria. In addition, poor infection control practices contribute to the cross contamination of patients with pathogenic bacteria.[64]

Treatment

24. Empiric Antibiotic Therapy. How should antibiotic therapy be started in A.A.?

After a specimen of the lower respiratory tract secretions has been collected for Gram's stain and other potential sites of infection have been cultured, empiric therapy should be started with a combination of antibiotics whose spectrum of activity covers all of the potential bacterial pathogens. Table 58.9 lists the bacteriology of hospital-acquired pneumonia. As can be seen, gram-negative bacteria are important pathogens in hospital-acquired pneumonia, either alone or in combination with other bacteria. In a study of the bacteriology of hospital-acquired pneumonias nearly one-half of the specimens collected yielded more than one potential pathogen.[65] Other significant pathogens of hospital-acquired pneumonia are *P. aeruginosa*, *S. aureus*, and *S. pneumoniae*.

Because of the high mortality associated with hospital-acquired pneumonia, aggressive broad-spectrum empiric antibiotic therapy should be started and then modified when the results of sputum culture are known. The choice of empiric antibiotic therapy should be guided by the results of the Gram's stain and an analysis of the patient's risk factors for oropharyngeal colonization or altered pulmonary host factors. When these are present, as in the case of A.A., infection due to gram-negative bacteria should be considered.

If culture results are negative or inconclusive (because of known specimen contamination with mouth flora) the patient's response to the initial antibiotic therapy should be considered in determining

Table 58.9	Common Bacterial Pathogens Causing Hospital-Acquired Pneumoniaᵃ
Staphylococcus aureus	10%–20%
Enterobacteriaceae	50%
Escherichia coli	
Klebsiella pneumoniae	
Enterobacter sp.	
Acinetobacter sp.	
Pseudomonas sp.	20%
Legionella sp.	50%ᵇ

ᵃ Reprinted with permission from Ravel Press, New York. Bergogne-Berezine E. Pharmacokinetics antibiotics in respiratory infections. In: Respiratory Infections: Diagnosis and Management; 1983.
ᵇ Estimate: sporadic outbreaks and cluster.

whether or not to modify the antibiotic regimen. If the patient responds to the initial therapy, those antibiotics should be continued. If the patient is not responding to the initial antibiotic therapy, one should consider whether: 1) the pneumonia may be caused by pathogenic bacteria not covered in the initial choice of antibiotic therapy; 2) the dose of antibiotic is sufficient to reach the infected site and control the infection; and 3) any other factors are responsible for the failure of the patient to respond to their therapy. Such factors include poor pulmonary clearance of necrotic tissue and cellular debris, lung abscesses, and severely altered host defenses with a rapidly fatal underlying disease.

Knowledge of the potential pathogens and the local institution's bacteria antibiotic sensitivities permits the rational selection of initial empiric therapy which should include a combination of antibiotics with broad spectrum antibacterial coverage, including antipseudomonal activity. This regimen usually includes one to two agents active against enteric gram-negative bacilli. Many successful combinations are available and the choice depends upon individual hospital sensitivities and total cost of the antibiotic regimen. Therapy is continued until the patient has been afebrile for two to three days, the white blood cell count has decreased and the left shift has resolved, and the chest x-ray findings have stabilized or resolved.

It is unknown if all patients with hospital-acquired gram-negative pneumonia require continued combination antibiotic therapy. Patients with neutropenia associated with severe underlying diseases, rapidly fatal diseases, and infections caused by *P. aeruginosa* respond better to combination antibiotic therapy than to a single antibiotic. This is especially true if the antibiotics are synergistic. The potential advantages of combination antibiotic therapy include a broad antibacterial coverage, improved bactericidal activity because of synergy between the agents and suppression of resistance that may develop to one of the antibiotics.

In summary, A.A. could be empirically started on gentamicin 2 mg/kg IV now, then 1.7 mg/kg every 12 hours. The dosing interval, τ, should be determined based upon estimates of creatinine clearance and *a priori* pharmacokinetic estimates targeting peaks of 8 to 10 µg/mL and troughs of 1 to 1.5 µg/mL. Serum concentrations should be monitored and the dose adjusted to achieve target concentrations. In addition, piperacillin 3 gm IV every four hours or ceftizoxime 2 gm every 12 hours should be started. When culture results are known, the antibiotic regimen can be modified and individualized for the patient. A.A.'s clinical response should be monitored to determine whether the selected antibiotics are effective in treating this infection. These would include a decrease in temperature and heart rate, resolution of left shift, and decreases in the WBC count. Mental status and sensorium are good monitoring parameters in older individuals. Other signs and symptoms of pneumonia also should begin to resolve as well.

25. Broad-Spectrum Beta-Lactams. Can the broad spectrum beta-lactam antibiotics such as ceftizoxime (Cefizox) be used alone in lieu of the combination antibiotic regimen to treat A.A.'s pneumonia?

In the past, the aminoglycosides have been considered the antibiotics of choice in the treatment of nosocomial gram-negative infections. However, the availability of a large number of antibiotics with broad spectrum antibacterial coverage has challenged the role of aminoglycosides as the agents of choice for these infections. Many of the newer antibiotics have been studied in the treatment of hospital-acquired pneumonias and are effective. Monotherapy with newer beta-lactam antibiotics is a useful alternative choice to the aminoglycosides in the treatment of patients with gram-negative pneumonia which does not involve *P. aeruginosa*. However, when choosing empiric therapy for a suspected pneu-

monia that may include *Pseudomonas* and/or for a documented pneumonia involving *Pseudomonas*, combination therapy remains the treatment of choice.

26. Aminoglycosides. What pharmacokinetic and pharmacodynamic characteristics must be considered in the dosing of aminoglycosides in patients with hospital-acquired pneumonia?

Individualization of aminoglycoside dosing is required in patients receiving these drugs.[66-68] The efficacy and toxicity of aminoglycosides correlates with aminoglycoside plasma concentrations and therapeutic outcome in patients with gram-negative pneumonia.[69] Patients in whom one hour postinfusion peak plasma concentrations exceeded 7 µg/mL had successful outcomes more often than those with lower plasma concentration. These results suggest that all patients with should be dosed individually and monitored using aminoglycoside plasma concentrations.

Despite the use of individualized aminoglycoside dosing, morbidity and mortality due to gram-negative pneumonia remains high. This is because the success of antibiotic therapy depends upon the ability of the antibiotic to reach the site of infection and remain biologically active. Concentrations of the aminoglycosides in bronchial secretions range from 1 to 5 µg/mL ($\approx$30% to 40% of serum concentrations) two to four hours after parenteral administration.[70] These concentrations may be insufficient to inhibit most gram-negative bacteria in this setting, especially *Pseudomonas*.

In addition, the bioactivity of the aminoglycosides is influenced by the local tissue pH. A 2- to 16-fold increase in the minimal inhibitory concentration of most gram-negative bacteria occurs when the pH is decreased from 7.4 to 6.8.[71] Therefore, more antibiotic would have to be present in an acidic environment to inhibit the bacteria. The bacterial sensitivity patterns of penicillins and cephalosporins are influenced little by pH over a range of 6 to 8. The pH of endobronchial fluid in patients with normal lung physiology and pneumonia show that the pH of the endobronchial fluids averages 6.6 in these patients with and without infection. Therefore, to achieve the aminoglycoside concentrations needed to exceed the MICs of most gram-negative bacteria in bronchial secretions, much larger doses of parenteral antibiotics will be required.

Inactivation of the aminoglycosides at the site of infection also has been demonstrated. The aminoglycosides bind to purulent exudates and cellular debris and this inactivates their antimicrobial effects.[72-74] In summary, the aminoglycosides penetrate poorly into bronchial secretions and are less active at the site of infection because of local pH effects and binding to cellular debris. Thus, higher doses must be used which may, in turn, place patients at higher risk for ototoxicity and nephrotoxicity.

27. Bronchial Penetration of Antibiotics. What factors govern the penetration of antibiotics into bronchial secretions? Is penetration into bronchial secretions critical to the effectiveness of an antibiotic used in the treatment of pneumonia?

An important factor to consider in the selection of an antibiotic to be used in the treatment of pneumonia is its ability to reach the site of infection, whether this is lung tissue or the bronchopulmonary secretions. Antibiotic concentrations in bronchial secretions do not necessarily reflect the lung tissue concentrations, but do represent the ability of the antibiotic to cross the bronchoalveolar barrier.[70]

Many factors govern the transfer of antibiotics in respiratory tissue and secretions. These involve anatomical, physicochemical, and host factors that influence drug penetration.[70] Active transport mechanisms for drugs have not been identified in respiratory tissues; therefore, passive diffusion is responsible for the transfer of antibiotics into respiratory tissue. The latter is determined by the ability of the antibiotic to reach high free concentrations in the serum. Because the transfer of an antibiotic into tissue may be slower than its elimination from the serum, and because elimination of the antibiotic from the tissue site occurs more slowly than from the serum, serum concentrations do not necessarily reflect antimicrobial concentrations in lung tissue. These two factors also significantly influence the interpretation of antibiotic concentrations in respiratory secretions.

The results of many studies investigating the penetration of antibiotics into bronchial secretions should be interpreted cautiously. These studies have analyzed the amount of antibiotic present in samples of expectorated sputum or saliva and may significantly underestimate the amount of antibiotic present in respiratory secretions. The use of fiberoptic bronchoscopy with a protected sampling device has been helpful in the study of antibiotic penetration into respiratory secretions, but this procedure is impractical in the routine management of patients with pneumonia.

28. Locally Administered Antibiotics: Prophylaxis. Can locally administered antibiotics be used to prevent gram-negative pneumonias?

The morbidity and mortality from hospital-acquired gram-negative pneumonia has not been reduced despite aggressive treatment with high dose parenteral antibiotics. This may be the result of poor antibiotic penetration into the bronchial secretins and the local conditions at the site of infection that reduce the activity of the antibiotic. For this reason, several investigators have studied the efficacy of endotracheally instilled or aerosolized antibiotics in preventing gram-negative pneumonias in patients at risk for oropharyngeal colonization.[75-79] Most of the patients treated were seriously ill individuals who were admitted to the intensive care unit; many of the patients were unconscious and had a tracheotomy to provide long-term ventilatory support. In these studies, endotracheally instilled and aerosolized antibiotics significantly reduced oropharyngeal colonization with gram-negative pathogens and the incidence of pneumonia. However, several studies have shown that these prophylactic regimens also can result in the emergence of antibiotic resistant gram-negative organisms in respiratory secretions.[77-79] Pneumonias which occurred in patients receiving the prophylactic regimens often were caused by pathogens resistant to the prophylactic antibiotic. In summary, endotracheally instilled and aerosolized antibiotics can be used to prevent or reduce oropharyngeal colonization in high risk patients when used for short periods of time with close microbiologic monitoring. Routine and long-term use should be avoided since resistant pathogens can emerge.

29. Aerosolized Antibiotics. Can aerosolized antibiotics be used to treat patients with gram-negative pneumonias?

The efficacy of locally administered antibiotics in the treatment of bronchopneumonia has been studied to a limited extent.[80] Klastersky et al. compared the effects of endotracheally instilled gentamicin alone versus intramuscular gentamicin alone in patients with pneumonia. A favorable outcome occurred in all seven patients receiving endotracheally instilled gentamicin versus only two of eight patients receiving intramuscular gentamicin.

In a second study, these investigators compared the effects of endotracheally instilled sisomicin (an aminoglycoside) versus placebo in a similar patient population.[81] All patients received systemic antibiotics consisting of parenteral sisomicin and carbenicillin. A more favorable outcome occurred in those patients receiving endotracheally instilled sisomicin versus placebo: 78% and 45%, respectively. In those patients in whom the infecting organism was sensitive to both carbenicillin and sisomicin, a more favorable response occurred than in those patients receiving endotracheal sisomicin versus placebo: 79% to 54%, respectively. When the infecting organism was sensitive to sisomicin only, a favorable

outcome occurred in 79% versus 28%, respectively. The development of resistant organisms was not a problem in either case.

In a third study, these same investigators compared the effects of parenteral mezlocillin and endotracheally administered sisomicin with and without parenteral sisomicin to determine whether concomitant parenteral aminoglycoside was needed.[82] The clinical outcome of both groups was similar; however, resistant bacteria were isolated from the sputum of the groups administered endotracheal sisomicin without parenteral administration. This finding strongly supports the recommendation that this form of therapy be reserved for those patients who are unresponsive to maximal doses of parenteral therapy. Local antibiotic administration also could be used in conjunction with parenteral antibiotics when further increases in the dose of parenteral antibiotics could place the patient at risk for significant systemic toxicities.

30. Administration. How is the local antibiotic therapy administered?

Local antibiotic therapy may be administered by direct endotracheal instillation or aerosolization. The antibiotic usually is diluted with normal saline before administration. In the case of direct instillation, gentamicin/tobramycin 40 to 80 mg or amikacin (Amikin) 500 mg is diluted in 5 to 10 mL of normal saline and instilled directly into the trachea through a catheter which has been inserted for its administration or through an endotracheal tube used for mechanical ventilation. The patient is then rotated from side to side to promote distribution. Delivery of the antibiotic into the oropharynx by aerosolization is accomplished by use of an atomizer or nebulizers to deliver the antibiotic to the lungs. The dosage of antibiotic used for aerosolization is the same as for endotracheal instillation except that the drug is diluted in a smaller volume (1 to 3 mL).

31. Bronchial and Serum Concentrations. What concentration of aminoglycoside can be achieved in bronchial secretions by this route of administration and is any of the antibiotic absorbed?

The concentration of the aminoglycoside in bronchial secretions after parenteral administration (IV or IM) is low and usually ≤ 2 µg/mL.[70] When the aminoglycosides are delivered by either endotracheal instillation or aerosolization, bronchial fluid antibiotic concentrations are substantially higher.[83-86] Bronchial fluid concentrations are significantly higher when the aminoglycosides are given by endotracheal instillation than by aerosol. These values usually exceed 200 µg/mL and remain elevated for the dosing interval;[85] when aerosolization is used, bronchial fluid concentrations usually exceed 20 µg/mL.[84,85]

Absorption of the aminoglycosides from the lung differs with the method of local administration employed. Various doses of aminoglycosides have been administered which makes quantification of the amount of the drug absorbed difficult. When 80 mg of gentamicin is administered by endotracheal instillation, serum concentrations above 2.5 µg/mL are achieved, suggesting that a substantial amount of the administered drug is absorbed.[77,83,84] Approximately 10% to 15% of the dose administered by endotracheal instillation is excreted into the urine.[87] When similar doses of antibiotic are administered by aerosolization, serum concentrations are low or undetectable; approximately 2% to 5% of the dose is excreted into the urine. The amount of drug absorbed from local administration to the lungs has significance in that it will influence how serum antibiotic concentrations are monitored and interpreted. In addition, patients with renal dysfunction will accumulate the drug which may contribute to systemic toxicities.

32. Adverse Effects. What adverse effects are associated with local antibiotic administration?

As noted earlier, the emergence of antibiotic resistant bacteria is of major concern since these may be responsible for subsequent bacterial infections. This phenomenon is more frequently associated with aerosol antibiotic administration for prophylaxis.

Endotracheal instillation or aerosolization of antibiotics may cause cough, bronchial irritation, and, in some individuals, bronchospasm. These effects most often have been associated with polymyxin-B and have resulted in episodes of acute respiratory failure.[88,89] Polymyxin can stimulate the release of histamine which is believed to be responsible for these adverse effects; it also can decrease ventilatory function.[88] The aminoglycosides have been relatively well tolerated, although minor alterations in ventilatory function have been reported.[90]

Although studies evaluating the incidence of aminoglycoside nephrotoxicity and ototoxicity associated with local antibiotic administration are unavailable, the incidence should be low. Patients with renal dysfunction may accumulate this drug and serum concentrations of the aminoglycoside should be monitored.

Pneumonia in Cystic Fibrosis (CF)

Special Treatment Considerations

33. K.P., an 18-year-old male with CF, has been well until 3 days ago when he noticed "chest tightness" and a progressive deterioration of pulmonary function requiring supplemental oxygen. Other symptoms include an increased cough with sputum production, a decreased appetite, and weight loss.

On physical examination K.P. is a cachectic young male in moderate respiratory distress. Vital signs include: BP 110/60 mm Hg, pulse 120 beats/min, respirations 35 breaths/min, and temperature 38.5 °C. Examination of the chest reveals an increased chest diameter with diffuse bilateral rales; there are no wheezes. Height 64″, weight 42 kg, and serum creatinine (SrCr) 1.0 mg/dL. Are there special considerations in the treatment of pneumonia in patients with cystic fibrosis? [SI unit: 88.4 μmol/L]

Cystic fibrosis is a genetically linked disease affecting exocrine gland secretions throughout the body.[91] (Also see Chapters 98: Bronchopulmonary Dysplasia and 100: Cystic Fibrosis.) Progressive pulmonary disease is the major determinant of the morbidity and mortality of patients with this illness. The presence of airway mucus plugging is likely to contribute to the development of significant respiratory dysfunction and the establishment of infection; recurrent respiratory infections play a major role in the pathogenesis of the chronic pulmonary disease seen in these patients.

Microbiology. Early in the disease, S. aureus is an important pathogen but later, colonization and infection with P. aeruginosa frequently develops. Multiple bacterial isolates with differing antimicrobial sensitivity patterns often are found.[92] Additionally, infection with Pseudomonas cepacia is emerging as a significant problem in patients with CF.[93,94] Whether P. cepacia is a pathogen in these patients is difficult to determine since many patients recover from acute infections despite the fact that this organism is inadequately covered by the antibiotic regimen prescribed. Most strains demonstrate variable sensitivity patterns to many of the presently used antibiotics. Therefore, antibiotic therapy should be based upon known in vitro sensitivity testing.

Vigorous chest percussion with postural drainage and systemic antibiotics have been the mainstay of therapy in the treatment of pulmonary infections in patients with CF. It is unclear whether combination antibiotic therapy is required to treat these patients, but it frequently is used to treat gram negative pulmonary infections in CF patients. Combination therapy usually consists of an aminoglycoside and an extended-spectrum penicillin (e.g., ticarcillin), ureidopenicillin (e.g., mezlocillin, piperacillin), or third-

generation cephalosporin (e.g., ceftazidime, cefoperazone). The effectiveness of antibiotics with in vitro activity against P. aeruginosa (e.g., aztreonam, ciprofloxacin, imipenem) alone or in combination with other antibiotics appears to be similar to other antibiotics.

Dosing Considerations. Altered drug elimination in CF patients has been reported for several different types of drugs.[95-98] Jusko et al. studied the pharmacokinetics of dicloxacillin in patients with CF and reported that the total body clearance and renal clearance of this drug were increased. In another study, when specific techniques to assess the glomerular infiltration rate were used, tobramycin renal clearance was not increased out of proportion to the glomerular filtration rate. These results suggest that alterations in the nonrenal clearance are responsible for the aminoglycosides.[95] In summary, it is likely that patients with CF will require higher doses to achieve therapeutic plasma concentrations of some antibiotics. Therefore, doses must be carefully individualized.

34. Local Antibiotic Administration. Since such high doses or parenteral aminoglycosides are required in CF patients, can aerosolized aminoglycosides be used instead?

Aerosolized antibiotics have been advocated for cystic fibrosis patients with acute pulmonary infections.[99-102] Intravenous administration has several limiting factors in patients with CF. Because most antibiotics penetrate variably into lung tissue, they usually are administered in maximal doses to facilitate passive diffusion. The use of these high doses of antibiotics also increases the risk of systemic toxicity. Inhaled antibiotics have the potential advantage of delivering large concentrations of antibiotics to the site of infection. In addition, the administration of aerosolized antibiotics produces negligible serum concentrations in CF patients which should reduce the risk of systemic toxicity.

However, aerosolized antibiotics have several potential problems associated with their use. The prolonged administration of inhaled antibiotics selects out resistant organisms in the bronchial airways. This may have deleterious consequences because of the recurrent nature of their pulmonary infections. To be effective, the antibiotic must be delivered to the site of infection and to reach the alveoli, particles should be less than two micrometers in diameter. Most commercially available nebulizers generate particles between 2.5 and 4.5 micrometers in diameter,[103] and these are deposited primarily in the oropharynx and smaller airways. Also, studies using radioisotope labeled aerosolized particles have shown that there is a heterogeneous pattern of deposition in CF patients,[104] which may limit the therapeutic effectiveness of this delivery route. Bronchospasm has been reported to occur in patients given aerosolized gentamicin and this may limit the delivery of antibiotic to the site of infection. Although nephrotoxicity and ototoxicity have not been associated, or are expected, with the administration of aerosolized aminoglycosides, the data are limited. Long-term administration studies have not been performed.

To date, there are no well controlled studies evaluating the effectiveness of aerosolized antibiotics in CF patients. Stephens et al. administered aerosolized tobramycin along with parenteral antibiotics and reported that the clinical outcomes of those receiving the combination of parenteral and aerosolized antibiotics did not differ from those receiving parenteral antibiotics alone.[100] Steinkamp et al. evaluated the clinical effectiveness of long-term tobramycin aerosol therapy in 14 cystic fibrosis patients.[102] The best clinical outcomes as a result of this prophylactic intervention were found in individuals defined as moderately ill and having milder lung disease. Drug toxicity and the incidence of selecting resistant organisms were minimal in the study population. Although aerosolized antibiotics have reportedly resulted in a slower rate of pulmonary function decline in uncontrolled trials,[105] these positive results are difficult to separate from the natural course of CF which is characterized by marked variability in the rate of lung function deterioration.

In summary, aerosolized antibiotics should not be used in the routine management of patients with CF. However, this route can be used as an adjunct to parenteral therapy in patients with severe, acute exacerbations of pulmonary infections which are unresponsive to maximal parenteral doses.

The optimal dose of aerosolized antibiotics is unknown. The most frequently used dose in CF patients is 2.5 mg/kg of gentamicin or tobramycin and 12 mg/kg of amikacin two to three times daily.

References

1 **Dixon RE.** Economic costs of respiratory tract infections in the United States. Am J Med. 1985;78(Suppl. 6B): 45.

2 **U.S. Department of Commerce, Bureau of the Census:** Statistical Abstract of the United States. 113th ed. Washington, D.C.: U.S. Government Printing Office; 1993.

3 **McGinnis JM, Foege WH.** Actual causes of death in the United States. JAMA. 1993;270:2207.

4 **Lui KJ, Kendal AP.** Impact of influenza epidemics on mortality in the United States from October 1972 to May 1985. Am J Public Health. 1987; 77:712.

5 **Chretien J et al.** Acute respiratory infections in children: burden during the first five years of life. N Engl J Med. 1984;310:982.

6 **Center for Disease Control.** Office visits for otitis media: United States, 1975–1990. Advance Data. 1992;214: 1–9.

7 **Teele DW et al.** Epidemiology of otitis media in children. Ann Otol Rhinol Laryngol. 1980;89(Suppl. 68):5.

8 **Henderson FW et al.** A longitudinal study of respiratory viruses and bacteria in the etiology of acute otitis media with effusion. N Engl J Med. 1982; 306:1377.

9 **Klein BS et al.** The role of respiratory syncytial virus and other viral pathogens in acute otitis media. J Pediatr. 1982;101:16.

10 **Berman SA et al.** Otitis media in infants less than 12 weeks of age: differing bacteriology among in-patients and out-patients. J Pediatr. 1978;93:453.

11 **Thomsen J et al.** Penicillin and acute otitis: short- and long-term results. Ann Otol Rhinol Laryngol. 1980;89(Suppl. 68):271.

12 **Bluestone CD.** Chronic otitis media with effusion. Pediatr Infect Dis. 1982; 1:180.

13 **Bennett FC et al.** Middle ear function in learning-disabled children. Pediatrics. 1980;66:254.

14 **Saginur R, Bartlett JG.** Antimicrobial drug susceptibility of respiratory isolates of Haemophilus influenzae from adults. Am Rev Respir Dis. 1980;122: 61.

15 **Reynolds HY.** Chronic bronchitis and acute infectious exacerbations. In: Mandell GL et al., eds. Principles and Practice of Infectious Diseases. 3rd ed. New York: John Wiley and Sons; 1990:531.

16 **Haas H et al.** Bacterial flora of the respiratory tract in chronic bronchitis: comparison of transtracheal, fiberbronchoscopic, and oropharyngeal sampling methods. Am Rev Respir Dis. 1977;116:41.

17 **Gump DW et al.** Role of infection in chronic bronchitis. Am Rev Respir Dis. 1976;113:465.

18 **Pollard JA et al.** Incidence of *Moraxella catarrhalis* in the sputa of patients with chronic lung disease. Drugs. 1986:31(Suppl. 3):103.

19 **Nicotra MB et al.** Antibiotic therapy of acute exacerbations of chronic bronchitis. A controlled study using tetracycline. Ann Intern Med. 1982;97:18.

20 **Fletcher CM et al.** Value of chemoprophylaxis and chemotherapy in early chronic bronchitis. A report to the medical research council by their working party on trials of chemotherapy in early chronic bronchitis. Br Med J. 1966;1: 1317.

21 **Recommendations of the Immunization Practices Advisory Committee (ACIP).** Pneumococcal polysaccharide vaccine. MMWR. 1989;38:64.

22 **Williams JH, Moser KM.** Pneumococcal vaccine and patients with chronic lung disease. Ann Intern Med. 1986;104:106.

23 **Pennington JE.** Respiratory tract infections: intrinsic risk factors. Am J Med. 1984;76(Suppl. 5A):34.

24 **Skerett SJ.** Host defenses against respiratory infections. Med Clin North Am. 1994;78:941.

25 **Toews GB.** Pulmonary clearance of infectious agents. In: Pennington JE, ed. Respiratory Infections: Diagnosis and Management. New York: Raven Press; 1983:31.

26 **Lorber B, Swenson R.** Bacteriology of aspiration pneumonia. A prospective study of community- and hospital-acquired cases. Ann Intern Med. 1974; 81:329.

27 **Petersdorf RG et al.** A study of antibiotic prophylaxis in unconscious patients. N Engl J Med. 1957;257:1001.

28 **Tillotson JR, Finland M.** Bacterial colonization and clinical super-infection of the respiratory tract complicating antibiotic treatment of pneumonia. J Infect Dis. 1969;119:597.

29 **Rosenthal S, Tager IB.** Prevalence of gram-negative rods in the normal pharyngeal flora. Ann Intern Med. 1975; 83:355.

30 **Johanson WG et al.** Changing pharyngeal bacterial flora of hospitalized patients. N Engl J Med. 1969;28:1137.

31 **Johanson WG et al.** Nosocomial respiratory infections with gram-negative bacilli. The significance of colonization of the respiratory tract. Ann Intern Med. 1972;77:701.

32 **Valenti WM et al.** Factors predisposing to oropharyngeal colonization with gram-negative bacilli in the aged. N Engl J Med. 1978;298:1108.

33 **Verghese A, Berk SL.** Bacterial pneumonia in the elderly. Medicine (Baltimore). 1983;62:271.

34 **Murray PR, Washington JA.** Microscopic and bacteriologic analysis of expectorated sputum. Mayo Clin Proc. 1975;50:339.

35 **Brewin A et al.** High-dose penicillin therapy and pneumococcal pneumonia. JAMA. 1974;230:409.

36 **Wallace RJ et al.** Ampicillin, tetracycline, and chloramphenicol resistant *Haemophilus influenzae* in adults with chronic lung disease: relationship of resistance to prior antimicrobial therapy. Am Rev Respir Dis. 1988;137:695.

37 **Klein RS, Steigbigel NH.** Aspiration pneumonia. Semin Infect Dis. 1983;5: 274.

38 **Bartlett JG, Gorbach SL.** The triple threat of aspiration pneumonia. Chest. 1975;68:560.

39 **Huxley EJ et al.** Pharyngeal aspiration in normal adults and patients with depressed consciousness. Am J Med. 1978;64:564.

40 **Gianella RA et al.** Gastric acid barrier to ingested microorganisms in man: studies *in vivo* and *in vitro*. Gut. 1972; 13:251.

41 **Drasar BS et al.** Studies on the intestinal flora. I. The bacterial flora of the gastrointestinal tract in health and achlorhydric persons. Gastroenterology. 1969;56:71.

42 **Bynum LJ, Pierce AK.** Pulmonary aspiration of gastric contents. Am Rev Respir Dis. 1976;114:1129.

43 **LeFrock JL et al.** Aspiration pneumonia: a ten-year review. Am Surg. 1979;45:305.

44 **Landay MJ et al.** Pulmonary manifestations of acute aspiration of gastric contents. Am J Roentgenol. 1978;131: 587.

45 **Wolfe JE et al.** Effects of corticosteroids in the treatment of patients with gastric aspiration. Am J Med. 1977;63: 719.

46 **Bartlett JG et al.** The bacteriology of aspiration pneumonia. Am J Med. 1974;56:202.

47 **Brook I.** Percutaneous transtracheal aspiration in the diagnosis and treatment of aspiration pneumonia in children. J Pediatr. 1980;96:1000.

48 **Brook I, Finegold SM.** Bacteriology of aspiration pneumonia in children. Pediatrics. 1980;65:1115.

49 **Pingleton SD et al.** Enteral nutrition in patients receiving mechanical ventilation: multiple sources of tracheal colonization include the stomach. Am J Med. 1986;80:827.

50 **Drasar BS et al.** Studies of the intestinal flora. Gastroenterology. 1969;56: 71.

51 **Muscroft TJ et al.** The microflora of the postoperative stomach. Br J Surg. 1981;68:560.

52 **DuMoulin GC et al.** Aspiration of gastric bacteria in antacid-treated patients: a frequent cause of postoperative colonization of the airway. Lancet. 1982; 1:242.

53 **Tryba M.** Risk of acute stress bleeding and nosocomial pneumonia in ventilated intensive care unit patients: sucralfate versus antacids. Am J Med. 1987;83(Suppl. 3B):117.

54 **Driks MR et al.** Nosocomial pneumonia in intubated patients given sucralfate as compared with antacids of histamine type 2 blockers. N Engl J Med. 1987;317:1376.

55 **Bartlett JG, Gorbach SL.** Treatment of aspiration pneumonia and primary lung abscess. Penicillin G vs clindamycin. JAMA. 1975;234:935.

56 **Busch DF et al.** Susceptibility of respiratory tract anaerobes to orally administered penicillins and cephalosporins. Antimicrob Agents Chemother. 1976;10:713.

57 **Sanders CV et al.** Metronidazole in the treatment of anaerobic infections. Am Rev Respir Dis. 1979;120:337.

58 **Perlino CA.** Metronidazole vs clindamycin treatment of anaerobic pulmonary infection. Arch Intern Med. 1981; 141:1424.

59 **Ingham HR et al.** The activity of metronidazole against facultatively anaerobic bacteria. J Antimicrob Chemother. 1980;6:343.

60 **Mackowiak PA et al.** Pharyngeal colonization by gram-negative bacilli in aspiration-prone persons. Arch Intern Med. 1978;138:1224.

61 **Johanson WG et al.** Association of respiratory tract colonization with adherence of gram-negative bacilli to epithelial cells. J Infect Dis. 1979;139: 667.

62 **Johanson WG et al.** Bacterial adherence to epithelial cells in bacillary colonization of the respiratory tract. Am Rev Respir Dis. 1980;121:55.

63 **Sprunt K, Redman W.** Evidence suggesting importance of role of interbacterial inhibition in maintaining balance of normal flora. Ann Intern Med. 1968; 68:579.

64 **Garibaldi RA et al.** Infections among patients in nursing homes. Policies, prevalence, and problems. N Engl J Med. 1981;305:731.

65 **Bartlett JG et al.** Bacteriology of hospital-acquired pneumonia. Arch Intern Med. 1986;146:868.

66 **Barza M et al.** Predictability of blood levels of gentamicin in man. J Infect Dis. 1975;132:165.

67 **Zaske DE et al.** Wide interpatient variations in gentamicin dose require-

ments for geriatric patients. JAMA. 1982;248:3122.

68 **Flint LM et al.** Serum level monitoring of aminoglycoside antibiotics. Arch Surg. 1985;120:99.

69 **Moore RD et al.** Association of aminoglycoside plasma levels with therapeutic outcome in gram-negative pneumonia. Am J Med. 1984;77:657.

70 **Bergogne-Berezin E.** Pharmacokinetics of antibiotics in respiratory secretion. In: Pennington JE, ed. Respiratory Infections: Diagnosis and Management. New York: Ravel Press; 1983:461.

71 **Bodem CR et al.** Endobronchial pH. Relevance of aminoglycoside activity in gram-negative bacillary pneumonia. Am Rev Respir Dis. 1983;127:39.

72 **Vaudaux P.** Peripheral inactivation of gentamicin. J Antimicrob Chemother. 1981;8(Suppl. A):17.

73 **Levy J et al.** Bioactivity of gentamicin in purulent sputum from patients with cystic fibrosis or bronchiectasis: comparison with activity in serum. J Infect Dis. 1983;148:1069.

74 **Mendelman PM et al.** Aminoglycoside penetration, inactivation, and efficacy in cystic fibrosis sputum. Am Rev Respir Dis. 1985;132:761.

75 **Greenfield S et al.** Prevention of gram-negative bacillary pneumonia using aerosol polymyxin as prophylaxis. I. Effect on the colonization pattern of the upper respiratory tract of seriously ill patients. J Clin Invest. 1973;52:2935.

76 **Klick JM et al.** Prevention of gram-negative bacillary pneumonia using polymyxin aerosol as prophylaxis. II. Effect on the incidence of pneumonia in seriously ill patients. J Clin Invest. 1975;55:514.

77 **Klastersky J et al.** Endotracheally-administered gentamicin for the prevention of infections of the respiratory tract in patients with tracheostomy: a double-blind study. Chest. 1974;65:650.

78 **Feeley TW et al.** Aerosol polymyxin and pneumonia in seriously ill patients. N Engl J Med. 1975;293:471.

79 **Klastersky J et al.** Endotracheal antibiotics for the prevention of tracheobronchial infections in tracheotomized unconscious patients. Chest. 1975;68:302.

80 **Klastersky J et al.** Endotracheal gentamicin in bronchial infections in patients with tracheostomy. Chest. 1972;61:117.

81 **Klastersky J et al.** Endotracheally-administered antibiotics for gram-negative bronchopneumonia. Chest. 1979;75:586.

82 **Sculier JP et al.** Effectiveness of mezlocillin and endotracheally-administered sisomicin with or without parenteral sisomicin in the treatment of gram-negative bronchopneumonia. J Antimicrob Chemother. 1982;9:63.

83 **Lake KB et al.** Combined topical pulmonary and systemic gentamicin: the question of safety. Chest. 1975;68:62.

84 **Baran D et al.** Concentration of gentamicin in bronchial secretions of children with cystic fibrosis or tracheostomy. Int J Clin Pharmacol. 1975;12:336.

85 **Odio W et al.** Concentrations of gentamicin in bronchial secretions after intramuscular and endotracheal administration. J Clin Pharmacol. 175;15:518.

86 **Stillwell PC et al.** Endotracheal tobramycin in gram-negative pneumonitis.

Drug Intell Clin Pharm. 1988;22:577.

87 **Klastersky J, Thys JP.** Local antibiotic therapy for bronchopneumonia. In: Pennington JE, ed. Respiratory Infections: Diagnosis and Management. New York: Raven Press; 1983:481.

88 **Dickie KJ, de Groot WJ.** Ventilatory effects of aerosolized kanamycin and polymyxin. Chest. 1974;63:694.

89 **Wilson FE.** Acute respiratory failure secondary to polymyxin-B inhalation. Chest. 1981;79:237.

90 **Dally MB et al.** Cystic fibrosis. Ventilatory effects of aerosol gentamicin. Thorax. 1978;33:54.

91 **Wood RE et al.** Cystic fibrosis. Am Rev Respir Dis. 1976;113:833.

92 **Thomassen MJ et al.** Multiple isolates of *Pseudomonas aeruginosa* with differing antimicrobial susceptibility patterns from patients with cystic fibrosis. J Infect Dis. 1979;140:873.

93 **Isles A et al.** *Pseudomonas cepacia* infection in cystic fibrosis: an emerging problem. J Pediatr. 1984;104:206.

94 **Tablan OC et al.** *Pseudomonas cepacia* colonization in patients with cystic fibrosis: risk factors and clinical outcome. J Pediatr. 1985;107:382.

95 **Jusko WJ et al.** Enhanced renal excretion of dicloxacillin in patients with cystic fibrosis. Pediatrics. 1975;56:1038.

96 **Ziemniak JA et al.** The bioavailability of pharmacokinetics of cimetidine and its metabolites in juvenile cystic fibrosis patient: age-related differences as compared to adults. Eur J Clin Pharmacol. 1984;26:183.

97 **Isles A et al.** Theophylline disposition in cystic fibrosis. Am Rev Respir Dis. 1983;127:417.

98 **Levy J et al.** Disposition of tobramycin

in patients with cystic fibrosis: a prospective controlled study. J Pediatr. 1984;105:117.

99 **Hodson ME et al.** Aerosol carbenicillin and gentamicin treatment of *Pseudomonas aeruginosa* infection in patients with cystic fibrosis. Lancet. 1981;2:1137.

100 **Stephens D et al.** Efficacy of inhaled tobramycin in the treatment of pulmonary exacerbations in children with cystic fibrosis. Pediatr Infect Dis. 1983;2:209.

101 **Cooper DM et al.** Comparison of intravenous and inhalation antibiotic therapy in acute pulmonary deterioration in cystic fibrosis. Am Rev Respir Dis. 1985;131:A242.

102 **Steinkamp G et al.** Long-term tobramycin aerosol therapy in cystic fibrosis. Pediatr Pulmonol. 1989;6:91.

103 **Swift DL.** Aerosols and humidity therapy. Generation and respiratory deposition of therapeutic aerosols. Am Rev Respir Dis. 1980;122:71.

104 **Alderson PO et al.** Pulmonary disposition of aerosols in children with cystic fibrosis. J Pediatr. 1974;84:479.

105 **MacLusky I et al.** Inhaled antibiotics in cystic fibrosis: is there a therapeutic effect? J Pediatr. 1986;108:861.

106 **Dal Nogare AR.** Nosocomial pneumonia in the medical and surgical patient. Med Clin North Am. 1994;78:1081.

107 **Kauffman CA et al.** Antimicrobial resistance of Haemophilus species in patients with chronic bronchitis. Am Rev Respir Dis. 1979;120:1382.

108 **Wallace RJ et al.** Haemophilus influenzae infections in adults: characterization of strains by serotypes, biotypes, and beta-lactamase production. J Infect Dis. 1981;144:101.

Tuberculosis

Earl S Ward, Jr

Etiology 59-1	Thrombocytopenia 59-8
Transmission 59-1	Miscellaneous reactions 59-8
Pathogenesis 59-1	Acute renal failure 59-8
Infection 59-2	Drug interactions 59-8
Clinical disease 59-2	INH-Rifampin 59-8
Clinical Risk Factors 59-2	Hepatotoxicity 59-8
Incidence 59-2	Hepatitis 59-9
Diagnosis 59-2	Ethambutol 59-9
Signs and Symptoms 59-2	Optic neuritis 59-9
Subjective findings 59-2	**Special Treatment Considerations** 59-9
Objective findings 59-2	The Elderly 59-9
Misdiagnosis 59-2	Incidence 59-9
PPD Skin Test 59-2	Diagnosis 59-9
Treatment of Active Disease 59-3	Treatment 59-10
Initial Therapy 59-3	Adverse drug effects 59-10
Multiple Drug Therapy 59-3	Multidrug-Resistant Organisms 59-10
Continuation 59-4	Acquired Immunodeficiency Syndrome (AIDS) 59-11
Monitoring Drug Therapy 59-5	PPD and treatment 59-11
Subjective symptoms 59-5	Preventive therapy 59-11
Objective signs 59-5	Pregnancy 59-11
Preventive Treatment 59-7	Teratogenicity 59-12
Adverse Drug Effects 59-7	Therapeutic abortion 59-12
Isoniazid (INH) 59-7	Pediatrics 59-12
Hepatitis 59-7	Extrapulmonary Tuberculosis and Tuberculous
Peripheral neuropathy 59-8	Meningitis 59-12
Allergic reactions 59-8	Treatment 59-13
Other reactions 59-8	Corticosteroids 59-13
Drug interactions 59-8	**Booster Phenomenon (PDD Skin Test)** 59-13
Rifampin 59-8	**Bacillus of Calmette and Guerin (BCG) Vaccine** ...59-13
Flu-like syndrome 59-8	

Etiology

Tuberculosis (TB) is a bacterial infection caused by the organism, *Mycobacterium tuberculosis*. In humans, the lung is the most common site of infection, although numerous other sites (meninges, bones, joints, peritoneum, genitourinary tract, skin) can become infected. If unrecognized or left untreated, infection may progress to clinical disease (tuberculosis) which can lead to lung necrosis and cavitation. Furthermore, a person with untreated pulmonary tuberculosis is infectious and can transmit the organism to those with whom he is in close contact.[1]

M. tuberculosis is an aerobic bacillus that resists decolorization by acid alcohol after staining with basic fuchsin. For this reason, the organism often is referred to as an ''acid-fast'' bacillus (AFB). The bacillus thrives in environments where the oxygen tension is relatively high such as the apices of the lung, the renal parenchyma, and the growing ends of bones.[1]

Transmission

Tubercle bacilli are transmitted by aerosolized droplets expectorated from a person with pulmonary tuberculosis. These droplets are small enough (<10 microns) to remain airborne for a considerable period of time. Transmission of these particles can be prevented by adequate room ventilation, ultraviolet light, and proper chemotherapy of the infected individual.[1-3] Tubercle bacilli are not transmitted on objects such as dishes, clothing, or bedding.

Family household contacts, especially children, and individuals working or living in an enclosed environment (e.g., hospitals, nursing homes, prisons) with an infected person are at major risk for becoming infected.

Pathogenesis

Infected aerosol droplets are inhaled into the lungs; their small size allows them to reach the respiratory bronchioles and alveoli where infection may establish. The initial infection usually occurs in the lower segment(s) of the lung. In the nonimmune (susceptible) host, the bacilli initially multiply unopposed by normal host defense mechanisms. Tubercle bacilli that are taken into the macrophage during phagocytosis may remain viable for extended periods of time. These organisms then enter the lymphatic system and may disseminate to other organs of the body. Two to eight weeks after infection, a specific T lymphocyte-mediated immune response should develop and prevent further multiplication of these bacilli. The T lymphocytes release lymphokines which stimulate the release of lysosomal enzymes from macrophages. These enzymes destroy some bacilli, but also damage host tissues in the process. The outcome of this immune response is usually tissue healing with granuloma formation. The bacilli and macrophages contained in the granuloma may survive and remain dormant for many years (dormant infection). These granulomas may break down in later years and produce pulmonary or extrapulmonary clinical disease.[4–7] Persons previously infected with tubercle bacilli usually are protected from reinfection by immunity mediated by the sensitized T lymphocytes. This protection may decrease significantly with advancing age.

Infection. A clear distinction should be made between infection and clinical disease (tuberculosis). Infection occurs when the bacilli are harbored in the body. There are no x-ray changes or symptoms, and bacteriologic studies are negative. Infection is suspected when the tuberculin skin test (PPD-Mantoux) is reactive.

Clinical disease (tuberculosis) occurs when deficient host defense mechanisms allow the infection to progress to one or more organs until clinical symptoms, x-ray changes, or positive bacteriologic studies are produced. The absolute diagnosis of tuberculosis is made by the isolation of *M. tuberculosis* from sputum, spinal fluid, urine, or tissue biopsy.[5,6] Because the organism grows so slowly, it takes six to eight weeks for this culture to become positive. The risk of developing clinical disease following infection is about 10%.[3,8] About 5% of infected persons will develop active disease within one year. In another 5% the progression from infection to active disease will occur later. Approximately 30% of human immunodeficiency virus (HIV) infected patients will develop clinical disease immediately following infection.

Clinical Risk Factors

Certain risk factors such as crowded living conditions, diabetes mellitus, silicosis, gastrectomy, intestinal bypass surgery, alcohol abuse, chronic renal failure, hematologic disease, reticuloendothelial disease, corticosteroid use, intravenous (IV) drug abuse, and infection with HIV increase a person's chances of developing clinical disease.[1,4,9,10]

Incidence

There has been a dramatic decline in the incidence of tuberculosis since 1900 which is largely due to effective chemotherapy and early recognition of source cases. The number of cases in the U.S. continually declined until 1985. Since 1985 the number of tuberculosis cases has continued to increase.[11] In 1992, a total of 26,673 cases of tuberculosis were reported to the Centers for Disease Control (CDC). This represents a 1.5% increase in the number of cases reported in 1991. This is due in part to the increased number of cases reported in association with HIV infected persons. The largest increase in TB cases occurred in the 25 to 44 year age group. This increase primarily is due to persons who have HIV infection. Increases in TB occurred in every racial/ethnic group except nonHispanic whites and American Indians/Alaskan Natives. The case rate in persons ≥65 years of age is 18.7 cases per 100,000 compared to approximately 10.5 cases per 100,000 average. The incidence rate in nursing homes is even higher and is estimated to be 234 cases per 100,000.[12] The number of cases in children less than five years has increased by 36% since 1985. The number of homeless people with latent tuberculosis infection is estimated to be between 18% to 51%.[13,14]

In 1987, an advisory committee was established by the Department of Health and Human Services to provide recommendations for the elimination of tuberculosis in the U.S. This plan urges establishment of a national goal of TB elimination (<1 case per million of population) by the year 2010. This plan incorporates identification of populations more susceptible to TB infection, the use of biotechnology in diagnosis and treatment, and computer telecommunication to track cases.[15]

Since tuberculosis can be effectively treated on an outpatient basis, the responsibility for treatment has shifted to health departments, community hospitals, private physicians, and community pharmacies. The need for early recognition and treatment necessitates that all practitioners become familiar with the tuberculosis disease process and principles of treatment. Proper monitoring of the patient for clinical improvement, adverse drug reactions, and medication compliance is critical to a successful treatment outcome.

Diagnosis

Signs and Symptoms

1. **M.W., a 36-year-old female, is admitted to the hospital with a 2-month history of cough which has recently become productive. She also is experiencing fatigue, night sweats, and has lost 10 pounds. Other medical problems include diabetes mellitus, which is controlled with 10 units of NPH insulin daily, and poor nutritional status secondary to frequent dieting. M.W. works as a volunteer in a nursing home several days a week. Recently it was discovered that 2 patients that she had been caring for had undiagnosed tuberculosis.**

Physical examination was normal but M.W.'s chest x-ray revealed bibasilar infiltrates. A PPD skin test and sputum collections for cultures and sensitivity and a smear for AFB were ordered as part of M.W.'s diagnostic work-up. Initial laboratory tests were within normal limits.

The result of her PPD skin test, read at 48 hours, was a palpable induration of 14 mm. Her sputum smear was positive for AFB, and additional sputum cultures for *M. tuberculosis* were ordered to confirm a diagnosis of active disease. What subjective and objective findings does M.W. have that are consistent with tuberculosis?

Subjective Findings. M.W.'s history of cough (which gradually became productive), bibasilar infiltrates, fatigue, and night sweats is consistent with the classic symptoms of tuberculosis.[1,5] The cough is usually nonproductive in the early stages but may later become productive. The sputum may contain blood (hemoptysis) in patients with advanced cavitary disease. Anorexia, along with frequent dieting, has resulted in a weight loss. Other symptoms may include fever, pleuritic pain, and general malaise. Many patients with pulmonary tuberculosis (active disease) have no acute symptoms, and cases often are found following routine chest x-rays for another illness. Since many of these symptoms often occur in persons with pre-existing pulmonary disease or pneumonia, they often are overlooked and not attributed to tuberculosis.

Objective Findings. M.W. has a chest x-ray consistent with a lower respiratory tract infection, a positive sputum smear for AFB, and a positive PPD skin test (14 mm).

Misdiagnosis. A report from a private urban hospital showed that over a one-year span almost 50% of the cases of active tuberculosis were misdiagnosed because classic symptoms were absent.[16] More than one-third of the patients with active tuberculosis had no sweats, chills, or malaise, and fewer than 50% had fever. Cough was evident in 80% of these patients, but only 25% had hemoptysis. Although dullness over the apices of the lungs and post-tussive rales are expected in tuberculosis, fewer than one-third of the above patients had any abnormal pulmonary signs upon physical examination. Similarly, tuberculosis was not suspected in 42% of patients with active disease in a community hospital.[17] The lack of specific clinical symptoms underscores the importance of skin testing, sputum smears for AFB, and chest x-rays as diagnostic tools in those suspected to have tuberculosis.

PPD Skin Test

2. **What is the PPD skin test? How should the results be interpreted in M.W.?**

The PPD skin test (Mantoux method) is a diagnostic tool used for the detection of infection with *M. tuberculosis*. The abbreviation PPD refers to the purified protein derivative of *M. tuberculosis* which is prepared from a culture of tubercle bacilli. The solutions are available as 1, 5, or 250 tuberculin units (TU)/0.1 mL. The skin test (formerly referred to as intermediate-strength PPD) is performed by injecting 0.1 mL of solution containing 5 TU intradermally into the flexor surface of the upper forearm.[18] The solution should be administered immediately after its withdrawal from the vial.

When a mycobacterial infection occurs, a delayed hypersensitivity reaction to the tubercle bacillus or to its components develops in the host. This reaction usually develops within two to eight weeks after initial infection.[19] Upon re-exposure to the tuberculin antigen (PPD skin test), the host's immune system responds with a characteristic inflammatory reaction at the site of exposure. The skin test will remain positive throughout M.W.'s life. She should not be retested.

M.W.'s reaction is positive (14 mm). She has no history of a previously positive PPD skin test. A palpable induration of greater than 5 mm diameter, 48 to 72 hours after administration is considered to be a positive reaction in a person with a history of exposure to a person with active TB, chest x-ray changes, or suspected HIV infection.[10,20,21] Use Figure 59.1 to estimate the likelihood of new infection with *M. tuberculosis*.[10]

A reaction size of 10 mm may be used in persons with increased risk for TB but no history of exposure. It is important to emphasize that it is the induration, not the erythematous zone which is measured. The induration represents a localized thickening of the skin which is caused by edema and accumulation of sensitized lymphocytes.[1] Indurations less than 10 mm in size may be due to infections secondary to other mycobacteria which crossreact with the *M. tuberculosis* antigen. These crossreacting mycobacteria are common in many areas of the U.S., especially the Southeast area of the country.[18]

M.W.'s positive reaction to 5 TU-PPD alone does not imply clinical disease. It merely signifies that she has been infected previously with *M. tuberculosis*. However, since she also has symptoms which are consistent with tuberculosis and a positive sputum smear for AFB, a preliminary diagnosis of active disease can be made. To confirm this diagnosis, *M. tuberculosis* must be isolated from the sputum.

3. Should M.W. be tested for HIV infection?

Yes. Tuberculosis may be the first manifestation of HIV infection.[22] Approximately 37% of HIV-infected patients develop tuberculosis within five months compared to 5% of exposed persons with an intact immune defense.[3,23,24] A complete discussion of tuberculosis and HIV infection can be found in Question 21. [Also see Chapter 68: Human Immunodeficiency Virus (HIV) Infection.]

4. Would a negative tuberculin skin test have eliminated the possibility of infection with *M. tuberculosis* in M.W.? Should patients suspected of having tuberculosis and exhibiting a negative skin test with 5 TU-PPD be tested with 250 TU-PPD (formerly referred to as second-strength)?

A negative skin test may be the result of a testing error. However, it most frequently occurs in individuals who 1) have had no prior infection with *M. tuberculosis*; 2) have only recently been infected; or 3) are anergic.

Testing error may be due to variability in performance and interpretation of the Mantoux test. In a study of 1036 persons who received two injections of 5 TU-PPD from the same vial (one in each arm), 14.5% had a greater than 10 mm reaction in one arm but less than a 10 mm reaction in the other arm.[25]

Anergy or decreased ability to respond to antigens may be due to severe debility, old age, high fever, sarcoidosis, corticosteroids, immunosuppressive drugs, hematological disease, HIV infections, overwhelming disseminated (miliary) tuberculosis, recent viral in-

fection, or vaccination. The nutritional status of the patient is also of concern, since the number of positive skin tests in patients with tuberculosis infection increases with the correction of malnutrition.[26] If anergy is suspected, control skin tests (*Candida*, mumps) also should be performed. If the control tests are positive and the PPD test is negative, infection with *M. tuberculosis* is not likely.

A "false-negative" reaction may occur in 15% to 20% of persons infected with *M. tuberculosis*.[1] In a study by Nash et al., 25% of acutely ill patients with active pulmonary tuberculosis failed to respond to 5 TU-PPD. The majority of these patients responded to the 250 TU test.[26] Therefore, a negative response to 5 TU in M.W. would not have excluded infection with *M. tuberculosis*.

The use of the 250 TU/0.1 mL PPD for persons who have not responded to 5 TU is not recommended by the CDC because these results cannot be interpreted using the American Thoracic Society Guidelines and may be misleading.[5,27] This position has been challenged by practitioners who believe that the 250 TU test is an important diagnostic tool in acutely ill patients suspected of having tuberculosis.[28] This test may be of diagnostic value in patients with large pleural effusions secondary to infection with *M. tuberculosis*. The 5 TU skin test is often negative in these individuals, but the 250 TU skin test is nearly always positive.[1] The 250 TU skin test also may be useful in patients with clinical findings consistent with tuberculosis who have responded negatively to 5 TU-PPD.

Treatment of Active Disease
Initial Therapy

5. How should treatment be initiated in M.W. pending the results of the sputum culture and sensitivity? Will she be able to transmit infection during treatment? Her HIV test was negative.

Effective treatment of tuberculosis requires a period of intensive drug therapy with at least two bactericidal drugs that are active against the organism. There are three options available for treatment of M.W. (see Table 59.1).[29] M.W., with uncomplicated pulmonary tuberculosis, should be started on isoniazid (INH) 300 mg, rifampin 600 mg, and pyrazinamide 15 to 30 mg/kg in a single daily dose. Doses of rifampin less than 600 mg a day in combination with the INH may be less effective in treating pulmonary tuberculosis. Ethambutol 15 to 25 mg/kg/day also may be used empirically until organism sensitivities are known.[29,30] The initial phase of treatment should last eight weeks until the sputum culture is negative for AFB.

The addition of pyrazinamide (to the INH and rifampin regimen) 15 to 30 mg/kg/day for the first two months will allow a decrease in treatment duration to six months with very successful results.[31] The INH and rifampin must be continued for an additional four months.

M.W., who is a diabetic and has a poor nutritional status, also should be placed on pyridoxine 10 to 50 mg/day because she may be at greater risk for the development of isoniazid-induced peripheral neuritis (see Question 11).[1,32]

Symptoms should improve within four weeks. She should cease to be infectious about two to four weeks after chemotherapy has been initiated, at which time the number of organisms in her sputum should be significantly reduced. If there are no complications from her drug therapy or disease, M.W. may be released from the hospital as soon as her symptoms resolve.

Multiple Drug Therapy

6. Why is multiple drug therapy indicated for the treatment of active disease? What is the role of each drug in the treatment of tuberculosis?

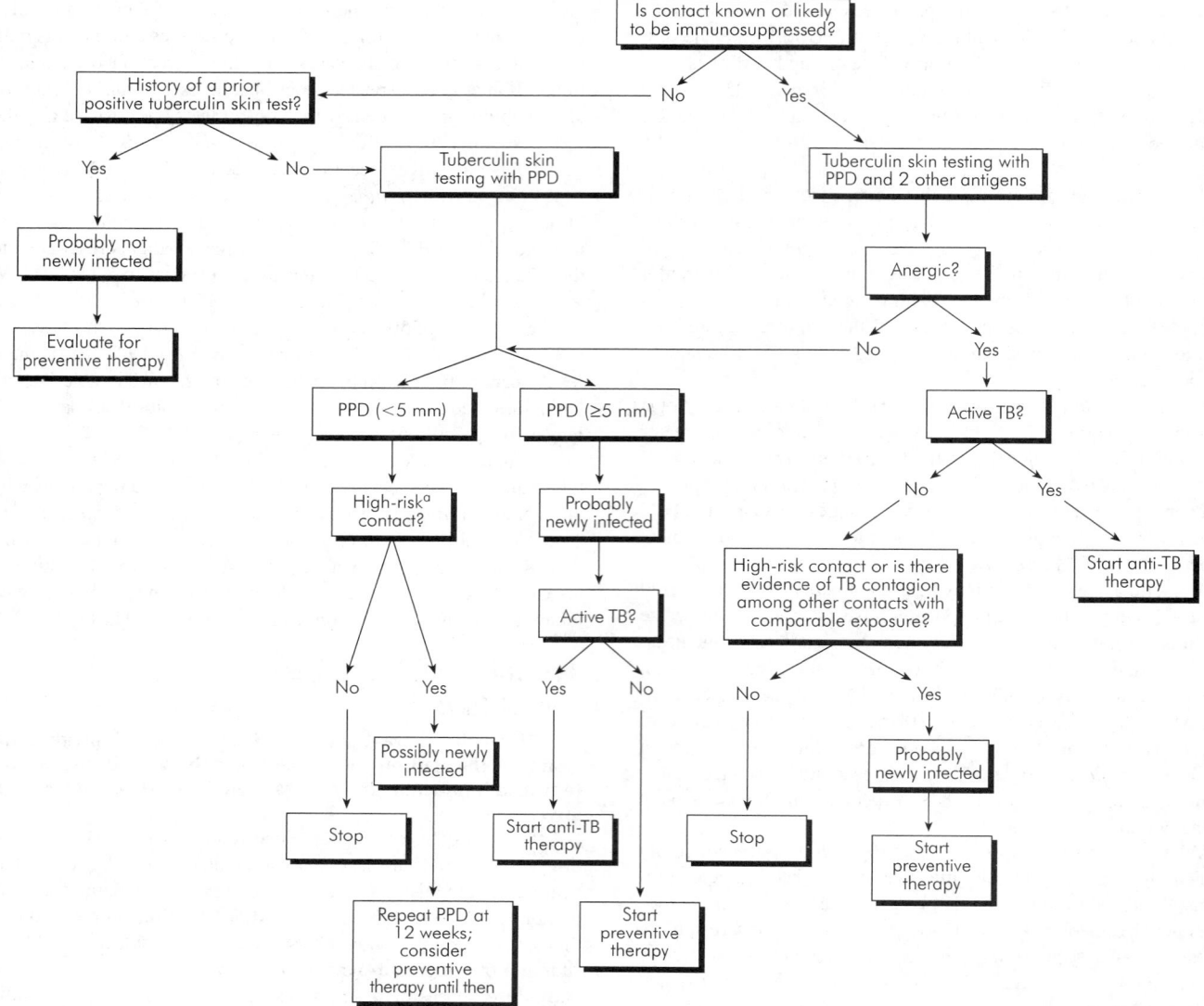

Fig 59.1   Estimating the Likelihood of New Infection with *Mycobacterium tuberculosis* and Preventive Therapy Decision-Making for Contacts of Infectious Tuberculosis Cases   PPD = Purified Protein Derivative. ° Members of the immediate family, close social contacts, or others who shared the same indoor environment with an infectious TB patient for substantial periods. Reprinted from reference 10.

Multiple drug therapy is needed to prevent the development of resistant strains of tubercle bacilli and to sterilize the sputum and lesions as quickly as possible. The drugs available for the treatment of tuberculosis vary in their ability to accomplish these tasks.[33]

Drugs that are effective against tubercle bacilli can be divided into two groups: primary and secondary (see Table 59.2). The foundation of treatment should be with primary drugs such as isoniazid, rifampin, pyrazinamide, and ethambutol. Both INH and rifampin are bactericidal against the fast growing extracellular bacilli in the lung cavity. Rifampin also has activity against intracellular organisms which usually are dormant but undergo periods of active growth (slow multipliers).[33] This ability to penetrate and destroy the slow-growing, persistent intracellular organisms makes rifampin extremely valuable in short-course chemotherapy regimens.[34]

Pyrazinamide is effective against intracellular bacilli, the growth of which is partially inhibited by the acidic environment within the macrophage. It is very effective in sterilizing lesions when used in the first two months of treatment.[35,36] Pyrazinamide must be prescribed if the duration of treatment is to be less than nine months.

Ethambutol is bacteriostatic at low doses and bactericidal at higher doses. It is moderately effective against the fast growing

bacilli. It has very little sterilizing activity and is primarily used to prevent the emergence of drug-resistant organisms.[31,33]

Streptomycin is active against the fast-multiplying extracellular organisms and is very effective when given daily for two months followed by two to three times weekly thereafter.[37] Intramuscular (IM) injections of streptomycin are painful and may decrease patient compliance. Also, like all aminoglycosides, streptomycin can cause ototoxicity and renal toxicity.

The other drugs used in the treatment of tuberculosis (capreomycin, kanamycin, cycloserine, ethionamide, aminosalicylic acid) usually are reserved for cases involving drug-resistant organisms, treatment failures, extrapulmonary tuberculosis, drug toxicity, or patient intolerance to the other agents.

Continuation

7. Six weeks later M.W.'s sputum cultures were found to be positive for *M. tuberculosis*. Sensitivity tests showed that the organism was sensitive to the current drug regimen, INH and rifampin. What drug regimen should be used for continued therapy of M.W.? How long should treatment be maintained?

For years, isoniazid 300 mg/day combined with ethambutol 15 to 25 mg/kg/day for 18 to 24 months was the recommended treatment for tuberculosis. Streptomycin 1 gm/day IM was used for the first two months to prevent the development of INH-resistant organisms.[1] Successful treatment of uncomplicated tuberculosis can now be completed in six months if INH, rifampin, and pyrazinamide are used for the first two months. If drugs other than INH and rifampin are used in the initial phase, treatment must be continued for 18 to 24 months.[31,38–41] If pyrazinamide is not used for the first two months along with INH and rifampin, therapy must be continued for nine months. Most uncomplicated tuberculosis can be treated in six months if pyrazinamide is added to the INH and rifampin regimen in the first two months and drug compliance and organism susceptibility can be assured.

Drugs used in the continuation phase of treatment can be administered daily, or two or three times weekly[42] (see Table 59.1). One study demonstrated the effectiveness of a regimen consisting of INH 300 mg and rifampin 600 mg daily for one month followed by INH 900 mg and rifampin 600 mg twice weekly for eight additional months.[42] Three months after beginning therapy, 95% of all patients studied had negative sputum cultures. In a more recent study of 1028 patients with positive cultures for tuberculosis, the same investigators found that 95% of those individuals completing the above drug regimen were cured.[42] There was a 2.1% relapse rate and only 2.8% of patients failed to convert their sputum to negative cultures for *M. tuberculosis*.

Twice-weekly administration of INH (900 mg) and rifampin (600 mg) is recommended for M.W. because this approach requires fewer doses of rifampin and should result in substantial cost savings.[42] Treatment should be continued for a total of six months or until the sputum cultures have been negative for three months. Pyridoxine 10 to 50 mg/day should be continued throughout the treatment period.

Monitoring Drug Therapy

8. What subjective and objective findings should be followed to ensure therapeutic efficacy and minimize drug toxicity? Should M.W. be followed closely after completion of her treatment regimen?

Subjective Symptoms. M.W. should be questioned about the occurrence of adverse reactions secondary to the isoniazid and rifampin (see Table 59.2). Specifically, she should be asked about gastrointestinal complaints of anorexia, nausea, or vomiting which may be an indication of possible hepatitis. Since she has diabetes and is at greater risk for the development of peripheral neuritis, she should be questioned about numbness and tingling in her extremities. Isoniazid-induced peripheral neuritis, however, should not be a problem in M.W. because she is being maintained on pyridoxine. M.W. also should be examined for and questioned about petechiae, bruises, or hematuria, since thrombocytopenia may be more commonly associated with twice-weekly rifampin therapy.[42]

In a study of twice-weekly INH-rifampin therapy, the incidence of side effects was 10.3%.[42] Major side effects such as hepatitis and hematologic disturbances accounted for 3.2% of the adverse effects, while minor effects such as gastrointestinal problems, rash, and fever accounted for 7.1% of reactions.

Objective Signs. A pretreatment complete blood count, platelet count, blood urea nitrogen (BUN), hepatic enzymes (serum aminotransferase), and bilirubin should be determined. These should be repeated if the patient experiences any evidence of drug toxicity or is at greater risk of developing toxicity.

M.W. is over 35 years of age and is at increased risk for the development of INH- and/or rifampin-induced hepatotoxicity. Therefore, serum aminotransferase levels should be monitored monthly at least initially. This recommendation is controversial in that many practitioners prefer to monitor serum aminotransferase levels only when the patient experiences symptoms consistent with hepatitis.[31,42]

Sputum cultures and smears for acid-fast bacilli should be ordered every two to four weeks initially and then monthly after the sputum cultures become negative. With appropriate therapy, sputum cultures should become negative in about two to three months.[43] In a CDC surveillance report involving 11,410 tuberculosis patients, 75% had converted to a negative sputum cultures within six months. Within this group of patients, however, were many individuals treated with clinical regimens other than INH and rifampin, individuals infected with drug-resistant organisms,

Table 59.1	Regimen Options for the Initial Treatment of TB Among Children and Adults[a,b]			
	TB Without HIV Infection			
	Option 1	Option 2	Option 3	TB With HIV Infection
	Administer daily INH, RIF, and PZA for 8 weeks followed by 16 weeks of INH and RIF daily or 2–3 times/week[c] in areas where the INH resistance rate is not documented to be <4%. EMB or SM should be added to the initial regimen until susceptibility to INH and RIF is demonstrated. Continue treatment for at least 6 months and 3 months beyond culture conversion. Consult a TB medical expert if the patient is symptomatic or smear or culture positive after 3 months	Administer daily INH, RIF, PZA, and SM or EMB for 2 weeks followed by 2 times/week[c] administration of the same drugs for 6 weeks (by DOT), and subsequently, with 2 times/week administration of INH and RIF for 16 weeks (by DOT). Consult a TB medical expert if patient is symptomatic or smear or culture positive after 3 months	Treat by DOT, 3 times/week[c] with INH, RIF, PZA, and EMB or SM for 6 months.[d] Consult a TB medical expert if patient is symptomatic or smear or culture positive after 3 months	Options 1, 2, or 3 can be used, but treatment regimens should continue for a total of 9 months and at least 6 months beyond culture conversion

[a] Reprinted with permission from MMRW. 1993;42 (no. RR-7):1.

[b] DOT = Directly observed therapy; EMB = Ethambutol; HIV = Human immunodeficiency virus; INH = Isoniazid; PZA = Pyrazinamide; RIF = Rifampin; SM = Streptomycin.

[c] All regimens administered 2 or 3 times/week should be monitored by directly observed therapy for the duration of therapy.

[d] The strongest evidence from clinical trials is the effectiveness of all 4 drugs administered for the full 6 months. There is weaker evidence that SM can be discontinued after 4 months if the isolate is susceptible to all drugs. The evidence for stopping PZA before the end of 6 months is equivocal for the 3 times/week regimen and there is no evidence on the effectiveness of this regimen with EMB for less than the full 6 months.

Table 59.2 Drugs Used in the Treatment of Tuberculosis[b]

Drug/Daily Dose	Twice Weekly Dose	Peak Serum Concentrations[103] (µg/mL)	Primary Adverse Effects	Dosage Adjustment in Renal Impairment	Comments
Primary Drugs					
Isoniazid *Adult:* 5 mg/kg (*max:* 300 mg) *Child:* 10–20 mg/kg (*max:* 300 mg)	*Adult:* 15 mg/kg (*max:* 900 mg) *Child:* 20–40 mg/kg (*max:* 900 kg)	3–5	Peripheral neuropathy, hepatitis, skin rashes, fever arthralgia, hypersensitivity reactions	No	Peripheral neuropathy preventable by pyridoxine 10–15 mg. ↑ serum levels of phenytoin. Hepatitis more common in older patients and alcoholics
Rifampin *Adult:* 600 mg *Child:* 10–20 mg/kg (*max:* 600 mg)	*Adult:* 600 mg *Child:* 10–20 mg/kg (*max:* 600 mg)	8–20	Hepatitis, thrombocytopenia, renal failure, "flu-like" syndrome, cutaneous reactions	No	Red discoloration of body secretions (perspiration, saliva, urine). Induces hepatic metabolism of warfarin, corticosteroids, diazepam, quinidine, oral contraceptives, methadone, ketoconazole, propranolol, sulfonylureas
Pyrazinamide *Adult:* 15–30 mg/kg (*max:* 2 gm) *Child:* 15–30 mg/kg (*max:* 2 gm)	50–70 mg/kg (*max:* 4 gm)	20–60	Hepatitis, fever, skin rashes, arthralgia, GI disturbance, fever, hyperuricemia	Yes	AST monthly
Ethambutol *Adult:* 15–25 mg/kg (*max:* 2.5 gm)	50 mg/kg (*max:* 2.5 gm)	3–5	Optic neuritis, skin rashes, drug fever, hyperuricemia	Yes	Routine vision tests of questionable value. 50% excreted unchanged in urine
Secondary Drugs					
Streptomycin *Adult:* 15 mg/kg IM (max: 1 gm) ≥60 years: 0.5 gm IM	25–30 mg/kg IM (*max:* 1.5 gm)	35–45	Vestibular and/or auditory dysfunction or 8th nerve, renal dysfunction, skin rashes, neuromuscular blockade	Yes	Audiometric and neurological examinations recommended. 60%–80% excreted unchanged in urine. Monitor renal function
Capreomycin *Adult:* 15–30 mg/kg IM (*max:* 1 gm IM)		35–45	See Streptomycin	Yes	See Streptomycin
Kanamycin *Adult:* 15–30 mg/kg IM (*max:* 1 gm)		35–45	Auditory dysfunction (see streptomycin)	Yes	See Streptomycin
Cycloserine *Adult:* 15–20 mg/kg (*max:* 1 gm)		20–35	CNS toxicity (psychosis and seizures), headache, tremor, fever, skin rashes	Yes	Contraindicated in epileptic patients. Some toxicity preventable by pyridoxine. 65% excreted unchanged in urine
Ethionamide *Adult:* 15–20 mg/kg (*max:* 1 gm)		1–5	GI irritation (50%), hepatitis (especially diabetics), gynecomastia, impotence, postural hypotension, difficulty in diabetic management	No	Must be given with meals and antacids. AST monthly
Para-aminosalicylic acid[a] *Adult:* 4–6 gm BID *Child:* 75 mg/kg BID		40–70	GI upset (10%), anemia in G6PD deficient patients, skin rashes, fever, hepatitis, hypothyroidism	Yes	Must be taken with meals, or antacids. 80% excreted into urine
Ciprofloxacin *Adult:* 750 mg BID		3–5	Nausea		
Ofloxacin *Adult:* 400 mg BID		8–10	Nausea		

[a] Available from the Centers for Disease Control.
[b] AST = Aspartate aminotransferase; CNS = Central nervous system; G6PD = Glucose-6 phosphate dehydrogenase; GI = Gastrointestinal; IM = Intramuscular.

and immunocompromised patients. The patients receiving INH-rifampin regimens were 100% sputum negative within six months of initiation of treatment.

Follow-up usually is not required after the successful completion of chemotherapy with INH and rifampin.[45] However, since most relapses occur during the first six months after treatment is completed, the patient should be re-examined at six months or at the first sign of any symptoms suggestive of tuberculosis. Chest x-rays are indicated only if there are signs and symptoms consistent with recurrence of active disease.[45]

Preventive Treatment

9. M.W.'s 38-year-old husband, S.W., is skin tested with 5 TU strength PPD to determine if he is infected with *M. tuberculosis*. He has a 10 mm reaction to the skin test which is classified as "positive." He does not have any clinical symptoms or x-ray findings suggestive of tuberculosis at this time. Is he at risk of developing active disease? What are the current recommendations for using INH as preventive therapy? Should S.W. be treated?

S.W. is at great risk of becoming infected, because he is a household contact of a patient with active disease and has a positive skin test. (See Table 59.3.) During the first year after infection of the source case, a household contact's risk of developing active disease is 5% if upon initial evaluation, the household contact has a positive tuberculin skin test.

Preventive therapy of tuberculosis with isoniazid decreases the bacterial population in those taking the drug. Therefore, INH "preventive therapy" actually is used to treat an infection and is not simply considered prophylactic therapy. Such therapy reduces future morbidity from tuberculosis in the groups at high risk for the development of active disease. High-risk persons treated with INH had a 60% reduction in bacteriologically proven disease over a seven-year period when compared to persons receiving a placebo.[46] In one trial, INH preventive therapy reduced the incidence of clinical disease by 70% to 80% during the year of treatment.[47] There was an overall reduction of 50% lasting at least 20 years. The benefits of preventive therapy usually outweigh the risks of iatrogenic drug reactions because every person with a positive PPD skin test reaction is at risk for developing clinical disease throughout his lifetime.[48]

S.W. is infected, but does not have tuberculosis at present. He should be placed on isoniazid 300 mg/day, given as a single daily dose, for six months.[20,51] Even though he has a higher chance of developing liver damage (2.3%) because of his age, he also has a high risk for developing tuberculosis. In this case, the benefits of preventive treatment outweigh the possible risks of hepatitis. S.W. should be educated and questioned frequently about the clinical symptoms of hepatitis which often are associated with gastrointestinal complaints. Pretreatment serum aminotransferase and bilirubin levels should be assessed to rule out pre-existing liver disease. The need for monthly or routine monitoring of these values is controversial.

Adverse Drug Effects

Isoniazid (INH)

10. Hepatitis. After 2 months of INH therapy, S.W. was found to have an aspartate aminotransferase (AST) level of 130 U/L (Normal: 7–40). Discuss the presentation, prognosis, and mechanism of INH hepatitis. What are the risks factors for developing hepatitis? Should INH be discontinued to prevent further liver damage? [SI unit: 130 U/L]

Approximately 10% to 20% of isoniazid recipients develop elevated liver enzymes.[52] However, most patients with mild, sub-

Table 59.3	High Priority Candidates for Tuberculosis Preventive Therapy[a,c]

Preventive therapy should be recommended for the following persons with a positive tuberculin test, regardless of age:

1) Persons with known or suspected HIV infection[b]
2) Close contacts of persons with infectious TB[b]
3) Recent tuberculin skin test converters (≥10 mm increase within a 2-yr period for those <35 yr of age; ≥15 mm increase for those ≥35 yr of age)
4) Persons with past TB, as demonstrated by abnormal chest radiographs that show fibrotic lesions likely to represent old, healed TB
5) Persons with medical conditions that have been reported to increase the risk of TB (e.g., diabetes, prolonged corticosteroid therapy, immunosuppressive therapy, some IV hematologic and reticuloendothelial disease, IV drug use, end-stage renal disease, and clinical situations associated with rapid weight loss)

Preventive therapy should be recommended for the following persons in high-incidence groups with a positive tuberculin test who are <35 yr of age and do not have additional risk factors:

1) Foreign-born persons from high-prevalence countries (e.g., Latin America, Asia, and Africa)
2) Medically underserved low-income populations, including high-risk racial or ethnic minority populations, especially blacks, Hispanics, and American Indians/Alaska natives
3) Residents of facilities for long-term care (e.g., correctional institutions, nursing homes, and mental institutions)

Infected persons <35 yr of age with no additional risk factors for TB should be given a lower priority for prevention efforts than persons in the groups listed above

---

a Reprinted with permission from reference 136.
b Persons in these categories may be given preventive therapy in the absence of a positive tuberculin test in some circumstances.
c HIV = Human immunodeficiency virus; IV = Intravenous; TB = Tuberculosis.

clinical hepatic damage do not progress to overt hepatitis and recover completely even while continuing INH therapy. In contrast, continuation of INH in patients with clinical symptoms may result in severe hepatocellular toxicity which is associated with a higher fatality rate than that of patients whose INH was discontinued immediately.[52,53] The risk of death from TB is estimated to be 11 times higher than the risk of death from INH hepatitis.[54]

Isoniazid-induced hepatitis is clinically, biochemically, and histologically indistinguishable from viral hepatitis.[52] Viral hepatitis, however, primarily affects young adults, while INH hepatitis occurs most frequently in older patients.[55] The development of INH hepatitis has been linked to several factors including acetylator phenotype, age, daily alcohol consumption, and concurrent rifampin use. Additionally women may be at higher risk of death especially during the postpartum period.[56]

The mechanisms responsible for INH hepatotoxicity remain unclear. Previously, it was thought that rapid acetylators had a greater risk for INH hepatitis than slow acetylators. Rapid acetylators of INH form monoacetylhydrazine, a compound which can cause liver damage, more rapidly than slow acetylators.[57,58] However, rapid acetylators also would eliminate this compound at a faster rate, and this should equalize the risk of toxicity between slow and fast acetylators.[59] One study demonstrated a different incidence of hepatitis between Asian males and females. Since both groups were fast acetylators, this study suggests that hepatitis is probably due to factors other than acetylator phenotype.[60] Thus, it appears that acetylator status alone does not explain the development of INH hepatitis.

Age and concurrent daily alcohol ingestion are probably more significant factors to consider in the development of INH hepatitis.[60] Progressive liver damage is rare in individuals less than 20 years of age. It occurs in approximately 0.3% of individuals between the ages of 20 to 34 years; 1.2% of those between the ages of 35 to 49 years; and 2.3% of persons ≥50 years of age.

There is some doubt as to whether biochemical monitoring of liver function is of value in the detection of liver toxicity secondary to INH. The American Thoracic Society and the CDC do not recommend routine liver function tests unless there are symptoms suggestive of hepatitis. However, of 1000 patients receiving isoniazid, 47 out of 64 patients with extremely high AST levels were asymptomatic. Subclinical hepatic injury occurs early in treatment and is reversible during the first three months if detected early with routine liver function tests.[61] High-risk individuals (e.g., daily alcohol consumers, persons over age 35, women, those taking other hepatotoxic drugs, those with liver disease) should be followed with routine liver function tests.[50] INH should be temporarily discontinued if the AST level exceeds three to five times the normal value.

Since S.W.'s AST is three times the upper range of the normal value and he is over 35 years old, INH should be discontinued temporarily until the levels return to normal.[62] At that time, INH should be resumed and the laboratory tests rechecked. If the AST increases again, the drug should be discontinued and S.W. should be followed frequently for development of tuberculosis. In addition to laboratory monitoring, S.W. should be reminded of the importance of reporting any gastrointestinal symptoms which might suggest hepatitis. Of all patients with INH hepatitis, 55% experience gastrointestinal symptoms such as nausea, anorexia, vomiting, and abdominal discomfort. Some patients (35%) complain of a viral-like illness, and others are asymptomatic until the onset of jaundice (10%). Other patients have had hepatomegaly (33%), hyperbilirubinemia (25%), and prolonged prothrombin times (35%).[52]

11. C.M., a 50 kg, 35-year-old female, is being treated for active disease with INH 1200 mg and rifampin 900 mg twice weekly. Is 1200 mg of INH twice-weekly an appropriate dose for a 50 kg patient? What INH side effects, other than hepatotoxicity, should be anticipated?

C.M. should be receiving 900 mg rather than 1200 mg of INH. High doses usually result in more INH side effects and should be reduced whenever possible. The incidence of adverse reactions to INH is estimated to be 5.4%.[38,63,64]

Peripheral Neuropathy. Rarely, isoniazid may cause a direct, dose-dependent peripheral neuropathy. As many as 20% of patients may experience this problem when the dose exceeds 6 mg/kg/day.[32] The peripheral neuropathy results from the competitive inhibition of pyridoxine by INH. Clinically, the patient usually experiences numbness or tingling in the feet or hands. Since this side effect is most common in alcoholic, diabetic, and malnourished patients, these patients should always receive pyridoxine 10 to 50 mg/day. Other patients probably do not need pyridoxine unless they receive more than 6 mg/kg/day of INH.

Allergic reactions consisting of arthralgia, skin rash, swelling of the tongue, and fever also can occur.[30,65] Isoniazid also has been associated with arthritic symptoms[66] and lupus erythematosus; in as many as 50% of patients, positive tests for antinuclear antibodies have been noted.[67]

Other reactions that may occur with INH are dry mouth, epigastric distress, CNS stimulation and depression, psychoses, hemolytic anemia, pyridoxine-responsive anemia, and agranulocytosis.[32,68]

Drug Interactions. In addition to the previously mentioned adverse reactions, INH inhibits the hepatic metabolism of phenytoin resulting in increased plasma phenytoin levels. Patients receiving these two drugs should be observed for signs of phenytoin toxicity such as nystagmus, ataxia, or drowsiness. Plasma phenytoin levels

should be followed periodically so that the dose can be adjusted if necessary.[62] INH also inhibits the metabolism of diazepam, but rifampin has the opposite effect: INH-rifampin combination therapy stimulates the metabolism of diazepam.[64,70]

Rifampin

12. One month after beginning her twice-weekly, directly observed therapy (DOT), C.M. developed symptoms of myalgias, malaise, and anorexia. Laboratory data were normal except for a slightly decreased platelet count. Could C.M.'s symptoms be related to her drug therapy? What adverse reactions other than hepatotoxicity should be anticipated in a patient receiving rifampin?

Flu-Like Syndrome. A flu-like syndrome has been reported in about 1% of patients receiving intermittent rifampin administration. This syndrome is rarely seen with usual doses of 600 mg twice-weekly, but the incidence increases with doses greater than 900 mg. The incidence also increases if the dosage interval is increased to one week or longer.[71–73] Unless the symptoms are severe, discontinuation of the drug is unnecessary. Since C.M. is receiving rifampin 900 mg twice-weekly, it would be advisable to decrease the dose to 600 mg and administer rifampin daily until the symptoms subside. Twice-weekly therapy may then be resumed as long as the dose of rifampin does not exceed 600 mg.

Thrombocytopenia. The platelet count should be monitored closely, since thrombocytopenia is also more frequently associated with intermittent rifampin administration.[72,74,75] A reduction in the rifampin dose and a change to daily therapy should prevent any further decrease in C.M.'s platelet count. However, if her platelets continue to decrease, rifampin should be discontinued immediately.

Miscellaneous Reactions. In addition to the side effects associated with high-dose, intermittent therapy, 3% to 4% of patients taking normal doses may experience adverse reactions.[74] The most common of these are nausea, vomiting, fever, and rash. Other reactions to rifampin include the hepatorenal syndrome, hemolysis, leukopenia, and anemia.[32] The development of these reactions would require discontinuation of the drug.

Acute renal failure also has occurred rarely with rifampin.[76–78] This hypersensitivity reaction may occur with both intermittent and daily administration and may last as long as 12 months.[72] Rifampin should be discontinued and other drugs such as pyrazinamide and ethambutol should be given in reduced doses. However, both rifampin and isoniazid may be given in normal dosages to patients with pre-existing renal failure.[79,80]

Another problem associated with rifampin is due to its chemical makeup. It is an orange-red crystalline powder which is distributed widely in body fluids. As a result it may discolor saliva, tears, urine, and sweat. Patients using rifampin should be cautioned not to use soft contact lenses because of possible discoloration.

Drug Interactions. Rifampin is also a potent enzyme inducer; it increases the metabolism of corticosteroids, oral contraceptives, quinidine, diazepam, ketoconazole, propranolol, metoprolol, sulfonylureas, and warfarin.[32,62,81–84] It may be necessary to increase the doses of these drugs while the patient is receiving rifampin. Women who are taking rifampin and oral contraceptives should use an alternative birth control method.

INH-Rifampin

13. Does the combination of INH and rifampin cause hepatotoxicity more frequently than either drug alone? Is this combination contraindicated in alcoholic patients?

Hepatotoxicity. Some evidence suggests that the combination of INH and rifampin may lead to a greater incidence of hepatotoxicity in some patients.[75] Rifampin, like INH, may cause elevated liver enzymes and possibly, hepatotoxicity. It is most likely to produce cholestasis during the first month of treatment. An increase in alkaline phosphatase and bilirubin may indicate rifampin-induced toxicity.[75] In short-course regimens with isoniazid and rifampin, the incidence of hepatotoxicity appears to be higher in patients who are slow acetylators. One possible explanation is that the threshold for hydrazine elimination (a major metabolite of INH and a known hepatotoxin) is exceeded when increased amounts of this metabolite are formed as a result of rifampin enzyme induction.

Older patients, alcoholics, and those with pre-existing liver disease also may be more susceptible to the development of hepatotoxicity.[85] However, the use of rifampin and isoniazid is not contraindicated in alcoholic patients.[86]

Hepatitis. Development of active hepatitis is the primary contraindication to INH-rifampin combination therapy.[39] If the AST increases three to five times above normal, both INH and rifampin should be discontinued temporarily until laboratory values return to normal. Isoniazid should then be resumed at a lower dosage and gradually increased to 300 mg a day. Rifampin also may be restarted at a lower dosage and gradually increased to 600 mg. Alternatively, ethambutol 15 to 25 mg/kg/day may be substituted for rifampin, but if rifampin is discontinued from the regimen, therapy must be extended to at least 18 to 24 months. Serum aminotransferase levels should probably be determined weekly during the first month after therapy is resumed. Thereafter, monthly determinations should be adequate. Another approach would be to use the combination of rifampin, ethambutol, and streptomycin.

Ethambutol

14. Optic Neuritis. S.E., a 65-year-old female, was placed on INH 300 mg/day, rifampin 600 mg/day, pyrazinamide 900 mg/day, and ethambutol 1200 mg/day for initial treatment of tuberculosis. Two months after the initiation of therapy, she began to complain of blurred vision. A routine eye examination and visual field tests resulted in a diagnosis of optic neuritis. There was no evidence of glaucoma, cataract, or retinal damage. Laboratory tests were within normal limits except for an elevated serum uric acid (9.7 mg/dL) and an elevated serum creatinine [(SrCr) 1.4 mg/dL]. There were no symptoms of joint pain associated with the elevated serum uric acid and no past history of gout. Her calculated creatinine clearance (Cl$_{Cr}$) based upon her weight of 60 kg was 50 mL/min. Could the visual problem and increased uric acid levels be related to her medications? [SI units: uric acid 576.96 μmol/L; SrCr 123.76 μmol/L; Cl$_{Cr}$ 0.83 mL/s]

S.E.'s decrease in visual acuity is compatible with ethambutol-induced optic neuritis. This condition is characterized by central scotomas, loss of green color vision, or less commonly, a peripheral vision defect. The intensity of these ocular effects is related to the duration of continued therapy after decreased visual acuity is first noted.[32,62] The optic neuritis is dose and duration related. The optic neuritis is rare at doses of 15 mg/kg but has occurred.[87–89] The incidence is estimated to be 6% for doses of 25 mg/kg and increases to 15% for doses greater than 35 mg/kg. Recovery is usually complete when the drug is discontinued.

The optic neuritis manifested in S.E. is probably due to the use of a higher dose (20 mg/kg) in the presence of mildly-impaired renal function (estimated Cl$_{Cr}$ 50 mL/minute). Since ethambutol adds no additional benefit to the INH-rifampin regimen after the first two months unless resistant organisms are suspected, it should be discontinued. Because ethambutol is partially excreted by the kidney (50%), her dosage interval for ethambutol should have been increased based upon the decline in creatinine clearance. If the Cl$_{Cr}$

is 10 to 50 mL/minute the interval should be increased to 24 to 36 hours; if it is less than 10 mL/minute it should be increased to 48 hours.[79] Her visual acuity should be monitored closely through periodic eye examinations and she should be instructed to contact her physician immediately if she experiences any further visual changes.

S.E.'s elevated serum uric acid also may be attributed to her ethambutol as well as a decline in her renal function. Approximately 50% of the patients receiving ethambutol experience an increase in serum uric acid due to decreased renal excretion.[90] The hyperuricemia also may be due to pyrazinamide. Pyrazinamide decreases the tubular secretion of urate. Asymptomatic hyperuricemia secondary to drugs usually does not require treatment. (See Chapter 40: Gout and Hyperuricemia.)

Special Treatment Considerations
The Elderly

15. G.H., a 75-year-old male recently confined to a nursing home, becomes disoriented, refuses to eat, and has a productive cough. Physical examination reveals a thin man who is having slight difficulty breathing. Laboratory findings are essentially normal with the exception of a slightly elevated BUN 25 mg/dL (Normal: 10–20) and SrCr 1.3 mg/dL (Normal: 0.6–1.0). A chest x-ray reveals infiltrates in the right lower lobe; he has a history of congestive heart failure which is well controlled. Blood, urine, and sputum samples are sent for culture and sensitivity; the initial Gram's stain is negative. Since the nursing home has recently had 2 cases of tuberculosis (active disease), a PPD test and sputum smear for AFB are ordered as well. The PPD skin test is 11 mm and the sputum is positive for AFB. G.H.'s admission skin test was negative. Discuss the presentation of tuberculosis in the elderly and the appropriate treatment of active disease in G.H. Is the incidence of drug side effects greater in the elderly? Should other patients in close contact with G.H. receive INH preventive therapy? [SI units: BUN 8.93 mmol/L of urea (Normal: 3.57–7.14); SrCr 114.92 μmol/L (Normal: 53.04–88.4)]

Incidence. The incidence of new tuberculosis infections has increased in the geriatric population living in nursing homes. The case rate of 39.2 per 100,000 is greater than that of elderly patients living at home (18.7 per 100,000).[11,91] Although active disease in this population has been attributed to a decrease in the immune system followed by reactivation of an earlier infection, active disease is a common, endemic infection in nursing homes in patients with no previous immunity (negative skin test) to *M. tuberculosis*.[92,93]

The incidence of positive skin tests increases after patients have been in the nursing home over one month. Therefore, all patients entering a home should be tested with 5 TU-PPD. If the initial test is negative and a source case is present in the home (as illustrated by this case) this test should be repeated in one month. The rate of tuberculin skin test conversion (from negative to positive tests) in this population is approximately 5%. If these recent converters are not treated with INH, approximately 5.9% will progress from infection to active disease.

Diagnosis. The diagnosis of tuberculosis in elderly patients may be extremely difficult since specific symptoms are often absent and elderly patients may describe their symptoms poorly. The chest x-ray and PPD test may be the only clues indicating the presence of a tuberculosis infection.[94,95] Frequently, the chest x-ray is atypical, resembling pneumonia or worsening heart failure. If the patient's clinical disease is caused by granuloma breakdown (reactivation), the chest x-ray often shows apical infiltrates or nodules. However, if the disease is progressing from an initial infection, as in the case of G.H., lower lobe infiltrates may be present.

Treatment. Since G.H. has clinical symptoms of a respiratory infection, positive sputum smears for AFB, and a positive skin test, he should be treated with a multiple drug regimen for active disease. His initial drug regimen should include isoniazid 300 mg, rifampin 600 mg, and pyrazinamide 15 to 30 mg/kg/day daily for eight weeks. The continuation treatment program should consist of INH 900 mg and rifampin 600 mg twice weekly for a total of six months. He also should receive pyridoxine 10 to 50 mg/day.

Adverse Drug Effects. The incidence of side effects, especially hepatic toxicity, is higher for elderly patients; approximately 10% of elderly patients receiving isoniazid for preventive therapy may need to discontinue the drug.[12] Therefore, serum aminotransferase levels should be monitored monthly and G.H. should be observed clinically for signs of hepatitis.

Isoniazid also may cause hyperexcitability in elderly patients. This usually can be prevented by dividing the dose (100 mg TID).[94] Rifampin given twice weekly may cause a higher incidence of "flu-like" symptoms in elderly patients. Since potential drug interactions with INH and rifampin are possible, any medication added to the patient's regimen should be carefully evaluated. Ethambutol may cause optic neuritis even at the lower doses in the presence of an age-related decline in renal function. G.H. has an increased serum creatinine and should be watched carefully.

Preventive therapy of patients with positive skin tests (no clinical disease) with INH 300 mg daily for six months is essential if a source case is present in the nursing home.[92] Stead et al. reported only one case of active disease in patients receiving preventive therapy compared to 69 cases in untreated patients. In patients with recently-converted skin tests, one patient in the group receiving preventive INH developed active disease compared to 45 who received no treatment.[12]

Multidrug-Resistant Organisms

16. M.S., a 22-year-old Asian male, is admitted to the hospital very ill with signs and symptoms of pneumonia. He is coughing and his x-ray indicates bilateral infiltrates. He is placed in respiratory isolation pending the results of sputum testing for _M. tuberculosis_. He states that he was diagnosed with tuberculosis 3 months ago and begun on a regimen of INH, rifampin, and pyrazinamide. He stopped taking his medication after 1 month. He is HIV negative. What is the likelihood of drug resistance?

Drug-resistant organisms have become increasingly prevalent over the past several years.[10,20,96] There is approximately a 9% incidence of resistant organisms in the U.S. The highest reason for resistance is noncompliance. Patients that sporadically take their medications can lead to susceptible _M. tuberculosis_ becoming resistant to multiple drugs within a few months. Other factors that contribute to this increased development of drug-resistance are inappropriate treatment regimens, inadequate dosages, and poor absorption of drugs.[97,98] These resistant organisms can be transmitted to persons who have never received treatment.

Multiple drug resistance (resistant to both INH and rifampin) has been reported with increasing frequency in hospitalized patients and prisons which underscores the potential for nosocomial transmission of multidrug-resistant organisms.[100] The majority of these cases (96%) occurred in HIV-infected patients. Health care workers caring for these patients also have been infected.[101]

M.S. is a typical example of the problem of treatment failure due to noncompliance and the development of resistant organisms. He also may have acquired resistant organisms from the person who infected him with tuberculosis.

17. How should M.S. be treated?

His current regimen should be evaluated and drug susceptibility determined. Current drug susceptibility testing in most institutions

is slow (6 to 8 weeks). This can decrease to three weeks with the use of the BACTEC system. A new regimen should contain at least four drugs and possibly more depending upon the severity of the disease.

If resistance to INH and rifampin is suspected, M.S. should be started on a regimen of pyrazinamide, ethambutol, ofloxacin (400 mg BID) or ciprofloxacin (750 mg BID), and amikacin (15 mg/kg/day) pending the results of susceptibility testing (see Table 59.4).[102] Treatment would need to be continued for 18 to 24 months. In one study, the average hospital stay was seven months and the patients received an average of 5.7 drugs.[97] Surgical resection of the lung may be indicated for some cases.[104]

Ciprofloxacin and ofloxacin have been used in treatment of resistant organisms for as long as eight years with little toxicity.[103] Resistance has developed if used in inappropriate regimens.

18. L.W., the 26-year-old roommate of M.S., is recently found to be HIV positive. Currently he does not have symptoms of tuberculosis. His PPD skin test is 6 mm. What is the possibility that M.S. has infected L.W. with drug-resistant _M. tuberculosis_? How should he be managed?

There is a high risk that L.W. is infected with drug-resistant _M. tuberculosis_. HIV-infected persons are much more likely to be-

Table 59.4	Potential Regimens for Patients with Tuberculosis with Various Patterns of Drug Resistance[a]		
Resistance	Suggested Regimen	Duration of Therapy	Comments
Isoniazid, streptomycin, and pyrazinamide	Rifampin; pyrazinamide; ethambutol; amikacin[b]	6–9 months	Anticipate 100% response and <5% relapse rate[36]
Isoniazid and ethambutol (± streptomycin)	Rifampin; pyrazinamide; ofloxacin or ciprofloxacin; amikacin[b]	6–12 months	Efficacy should be comparable to above regimen
Isoniazid and rifampin (± streptomycin)	Pyrazinamide; ethambutol; ofloxacin or ciprofloxacin; amikacin[b]	18–24 months	Consider surgery
Isoniazid, rifampin, and ethambutol (± streptomycin)	Pyrazinamide; ofloxacin or ciprofloxacin; amikacin;[b] Plus 2[c]	20 months after conversion	Consider surgery
Isoniazid, rifampin, and pyrazinamide (± streptomycin)	Ethambutol; ofloxacin or ciprofloxacin; amikacin;[b] Plus 2[c]	24 months after conversion	Consider surgery
Isoniazid, rifampin, pyrazinamide, and ethambutol (± streptomycin)	Ofloxacin or ciprofloxacin; amikacin[b]; plus 2[c]	24 months after conversion	Surgery, if possible

[a] Reprinted with permission from reference 137.
[b] If there is resistance to amikacin, kanamycin, and streptomycin, capreomycin is a good alternative. Injectable agents usually are continued for 4–6 months if toxicity does not intervene. All the injectable drugs are given daily (or twice or thrice weekly) and may be administered intravenously or intramuscularly.
[c] Potential agents from which to choose: ethionamide, cycloserine, or aminosalicylic acid. Others that are potentially useful but of unproved utility include clofazimine and amoxicillin-clavulanate. Clarithromycin, azithromycin, and rifabutin are unlikely to be active.

come infected than persons who are immunocompetent. His risk is estimated to be 113 times that of a person with no known risk factors.[10]

Since L.W. is at high risk of infection with multidrug-resistant organisms, he should be started on two drugs for preventive therapy.[10] He could be started on ethambutol 15 to 25 mg/kg/day and pyrazinamide 25 to 30 mg/kg/day for 12 months. Another possible regimen would be pyrazinamide and either ciprofloxacin 750 mg twice daily or ofloxacin 400 mg twice daily. The specific regimen for L.W. also takes into consideration the drug susceptibility results of his roommate, M.S.

19. If L.W. had acquired immunodeficiency syndrome (AIDS), would his prognosis be worse?

If L.W. developed multidrug-resistant tuberculosis and had AIDS, his risk of death would increase to 72% to 89% even with aggressive multidrug treatment.[105] Most patients progressed to tuberculosis immediately after infection and died within 4 to 19 weeks. In one study, the median survival time for AIDS patients with multidrug-resistant tuberculosis was 1.5 months compared to 14.8 months for HIV-infected patients without AIDS.

20. T.G., a 25-year-old Hispanic female who just arrived in the U.S. from Mexico, is admitted to the hospital with cough, hemoptysis, and fever. She has a positive PPD skin test and her sputum smear is positive for AFB. She is HIV negative. She has taken prednisone 20 mg/day for 1 month following an acute exacerbation of asthma. She also is receiving a sustained-release theophylline preparation, 200 mg Q 12 hr. Her serum theophylline level is 12 µg/mL. What effects do steroids have on the development of tuberculosis? How should T.G. be treated? [SI unit: 6.66 µmol/L]

Steroids interfere with the ability of monocytes to kill organisms which may increase the patient's susceptibility to tuberculosis. Their effects on the immune response also may depress tuberculin reactivity, resulting in a false-negative PPD skin test.[106] Persons infected with tuberculosis who are receiving steroids are at greater risk for developing clinical tuberculosis. Even though steroids may depress skin reactivity to tuberculin, thereby masking TB, it is possible to have a positive reaction to PPD.[107]

T.G. has a greater chance for infection with drug-resistant organisms since she is from an area with a higher incidence of drug-resistant tuberculosis. She should be started on INH, rifampin, pyrazinamide, and ethambutol until the susceptibility tests are available. If the organisms are susceptible, she can be treated with a standard six-month regimen (Option 1, 2, or 3 in Table 59.1) until the sputum is negative for *M. tuberculosis* for three months. If she has resistant organisms, her drug regimen should be changed according to the guidelines in Table 59.4.

T.G. also may require an adjustment of her prednisone and theophylline dosages, because rifampin may decrease their effectiveness by increasing their metabolism.[82]

Acquired Immunodeficiency Syndrome (AIDS)

21. F.R., a 32-year-old male with recently diagnosed AIDS, is experiencing mild pleuritic chest pain with a productive cough. He also has experienced weight loss, fatigue, and night sweats over the past week. A chest x-ray reveals bilateral infiltrates. Sputum samples are ordered for a smear (AFB × 3) and culture. The AFB smear is positive. A PPD skin test is ordered and the result is 6 mm and his CD4 is 150. He is currently receiving ciprofloxacin 500 mg Q 12 hr for his productive cough and zidovudine for his HIV. What is the frequency of tuberculosis in a patient with AIDS? How effective is skin testing in the diagnosis of tuberculosis infection? How should F.R. be treated?

HIV infects helper-T-cells leading to a decrease in cell-mediated immunity. This absence of immunity allows for the development of tuberculosis in a person previously infected with *M. tuberculosis*.[22,23,29,108–110,136]

The lungs are most frequently affected (74% to 79% of cases); however, extrapulmonary disease also occurs much more frequently than in patients without HIV infection (45% to 72% versus 17.5%).[110,111] Patients with AIDS have a much greater chance of extrapulmonary disease when compared to an asymptomatic HIV-infected person.

Infection with *M. tuberculosis* may be difficult to distinguish from other HIV-related pulmonary opportunistic infections (*Pneumocystis carinii*, *M. avium-intracellulare*). Tuberculosis often precedes other opportunistic pulmonary infections and should be ruled out in any patient with HIV infection.[108]

PPD and Treatment. A PPD-skin test should be applied to HIV-infected patients. Nevertheless, only about 30% to 50% of patients with AIDS and tuberculosis will respond to a PPD skin test with an induration of greater than 10 mm. Therefore, some clinicians consider an induration of greater than 5 mm as being a positive reaction to the skin test in this population.[10] F.R.'s reaction to PPD (6 mm) should be considered positive. Based upon his symptoms and positive AFB smear, he should be placed on multiple drug therapy. F.R. should receive INH, rifampin, pyrazinamide, and ethambutol initially. Drug resistance should be expected until susceptibilities are determined. After two months, if there is no drug resistance, he can be treated with isoniazid and rifampin daily or two to three times a week for a total of nine months. He should be treated until the sputum is negative for at least six months. If resistant organisms are isolated, he should be managed according to the guidelines in Table 59.4.

Zidovudine may be used safely in combination with his medications for tuberculosis.[114] A further exacerbation of anemia by zidovudine is very common in patients with low baseline hemoglobin values. A temporary discontinuation or dosage reduction of zidovudine may be required.

The quinolone antibiotics, ciprofloxacin and ofloxacin, are active against mycobacteria including *M. tuberculosis*[103,135] and penetrate rapidly into mammalian cells. These two features are critical in treating intracellular pathogens such as *M. tuberculosis*. *In vitro* studies do not show any cross resistance with other antimycobacterial drugs.

There is a possibility of anaphylactoid drug reaction to rifampin and ciprofloxacin in HIV-infected patients.[112] In the absence of other respiratory pathogens, ciprofloxacin should be discontinued in F.R.

22. Preventive Therapy. Why should N.M., an HIV-infected person with a positive PPD skin test and no clinical symptoms, receive preventive treatment?

The risk of developing clinical disease is substantial in N.M. INH 300 mg/day for 12 months is recommended for N.M.[10] A few clinicians suggest that these patients receive INH for life because eventual failure of the immune system will allow infection to progress to active disease.[108] The reliability and safety of INH preventive therapy in this group of patients will need to be assessed.

Pregnancy

23. E.F., a 25-year-old female who is being treated with INH 15 mg/kg and rifampin 600 mg twice a week for uncomplicated pulmonary tuberculosis, thinks she might be pregnant. Her obstetrician is concerned about the possible teratogenic effects of INH and rifampin and urges her to have a therapeutic abortion. Are these drugs teratogenic? Should a therapeutic abortion be recommended?

Teratogenicity. Isoniazid, rifampin, ethambutol, and streptomycin have all been reported to be teratogenic in animals, but no direct correlation with human malformation has been reported. Animal data may suggest a teratogenic potential, but because of genetic and environmental differences, these data cannot always be extrapolated to humans.[115] Ideally, all drugs should be discontinued during pregnancy. However, offspring of women with untreated pulmonary tuberculosis reportedly have a higher incidence of congenital defects than offspring of women receiving treatment.[116] Furthermore, the untreated patient is a community health hazard and has a greater chance of dying from tuberculosis herself.

A comprehensive review of the literature by Snider et al. reveals that INH, rifampin, and ethambutol are all relatively safe to use during pregnancy in normal dosages.[117] Treatment can be started with all three drugs and should be continued for nine months.[1] Pyrazinamide should be reserved for cases of suspected drug-resistance since the risk of teratogenicity has not been evaluated. All pregnant women receiving INH also should receive pyridoxine 50 to 100 mg/day because of the possibility of CNS toxicity. Rifampin has only been used in a small number of pregnant patients. The incidence of limb malformations was slightly increased but was not statistically different from the control population; several infants also were reported to have hypoprothrombinemia or an increased tendency to hemorrhage.

Streptomycin should not be used during pregnancy except as a last alternative because it has been associated with mild to severe ototoxicity in the infant. This ototoxicity can occur throughout the gestational period and is not confined to the first trimester. With the exception of streptomycin ototoxicity, the occurrence of birth defects in women being treated for TB with the above agents is no greater than that of healthy pregnant women. (See Table 59.5.)

Therapeutic abortion is not necessary in a patient with tuberculosis who becomes pregnant. The benefits versus the risks should be discussed with E.F., and she should decide whether to continue the pregnancy or to have a therapeutic abortion. When the baby is born, E.F. may breast-feed while continuing her medication. Drug concentrations are small and cause neither toxicity, nor provide sufficient concentration for the treatment or prevention of tuberculosis.[117]

Pediatrics

24. A.M., a 3-year-old black male, is suspected of having tuberculosis. His father has been receiving treatment for tuberculosis for the last 2 months. A.M. has a productive cough, fever, and general malaise. His sputum is positive for AFB and his PPD skin test is positive (10 mm). What is the incidence of tuberculosis in children? How should A.M. be treated?

Tuberculosis is increasing in children less than 15 years of age.[11] There was a 36.1% increase in the number of cases (5.5 cases per 100,000) from 1985 to 1992 in the 0- to 4-year-old group.

A.M. should be started on INH 10 to 20 mg/kg/day, rifampin 10 to 20 mg/kg/day, and pyrazinamide 15 to 30 mg/kg/day.[29] Ethambutol should be avoided in A.M. since it would be difficult to assess his visual acuity. If resistance is suspected, ethambutol 15 to 25 mg/kg/day or streptomycin 20 to 30 mg/kg/day should be added to the regimen until susceptibility of the organism to INH, rifampin, and pyrazinamide is known.

If resistance is not suspected in A.M. and is confirmed by susceptibility testing, he should receive the INH, rifampin, and pyrazinamide daily for eight weeks. He can then continue to take the INH and rifampin daily or two to three times a week (directly observed) for an additional four months. The dosage for isoniazid and rifampin in a two to three times a week regimen would be 20 to 40 mg/kg/dose and 10 to 20 mg/kg/dose, respectively.

A.M. should be examined carefully for signs and symptoms of hepatitis. The incidence of hepatitis from INH and rifampin in children may occur six times more frequently than in children receiving other medications with INH.[119] Most of the hepatitis occurred within the first three months of therapy and generally was associated with higher than recommended doses of INH or rifampin.

Extrapulmonary Tuberculosis and Tuberculous Meningitis

25. R.U., a 64-year-old male, is brought to the emergency room following a 4-day period during which he became progressively disoriented, febrile to 105 °F, and obtunded. He also had severe headaches during this time. Physical examination revealed some nuchal rigidity and a positive Brudzinski sign (neck resistant to flexion). An initial diagnosis of possible meningitis was made and a lumbar puncture ordered. The cerebrospinal fluid (CSF) appeared turbid, and laboratory analysis revealed an elevated protein concentration of 200 mg/dL, a decreased glucose concentration of 30 mg/dL, and a white blood cell (WBC) count of 500/mm³ (85% lymphocytes). A Gram's stain of the spinal fluid and a sputum smear for AFB were negative; other laboratory tests were within normal limits. A diagnosis of tuberculous meningitis was made. Discuss the presentation and prognosis of tuberculous meningitis. How should R.U. be treated? [SI units: WBC count 500 × 10⁹/L (0.85 lymphocytes)]

Tuberculous meningitis is only one of the extrapulmonary complications of infection with *M. tuberculosis*. One of the most frequent forms of extrapulmonary tuberculosis involves the lymph nodes (other sites of infection were mentioned in the introduction). Successful treatment of extrapulmonary tuberculosis may be accomplished in nine months with an acceptable relapse rate.[111,120] It also may be possible to treat many of these extrapulmonary infections in six months except in cases of lymphadenitis and bone infections. Since specimens for culture and sensitivity may be difficult or impossible to obtain from a site, response to treatment must be based upon clinical and radiographic improvement.

Tuberculous meningitis in older persons usually is caused by hematogenous dissemination of the tubercle bacilli from a primary site, usually the lungs. In its early stages, tuberculous meningitis often is confused with aseptic meningitis, since the Gram's stain is negative.[111]

The most common symptoms of tuberculous meningitis are headache, fever, restlessness, irritability, nausea, and vomiting. A positive Brudzinski sign and neck stiffness may be present. As

Table 59.5	Pregnancy Outcomes Among Women Receiving Antituberculosis Therapy and in a Normal Population[a,f]			
Drug	Spontaneous Abortion (%)	Still-birth	Premature Birth	Malformed Infant (%)
Isoniazid	0.34	0.61	1.88	1.09
Ethambutol	0.16	0.78	4.08	2.19
Rifampin	1.67	2.15	0.48	3.35
Streptomycin	0.97	0.0	0.0	16.91
Normal populations	6.8[b]	2.2[c]	7.1[c]	1.4–6.0[d] 2.3–13.8[e]

[a] Rates expressed as percentages of all conceptions that were not electively aborted.
[b] Based upon fetal deaths at 12–20 weeks gestation.[138]
[c] Based upon Collaborative Perinatal Study data for whites.[139]
[d] Based upon reports in 16 series of malformations noted at birth.[140]
[e] Cumulative rates of malformations detected by 5 years of age.[140]
[f] Reprinted with permission. Snider DE et al. Treatment of tuberculosis during pregnancy. Am Rev Respir Dis. 1980;122;65.

illustrated by R.U., the CSF is usually turbid with increased protein and decreased glucose concentrations. There is an increase in the CSF white blood cell count with a predominance of lymphocytes. Acid-fast bacilli are cultured from the CSF in only about 20% to 37% of cases.[111,121]

Early recognition and treatment is essential to a favorable outcome. In a study by Kennedy et al., four of five patients whose treatment was delayed for seven or more days died.[121] Treatment usually must be based upon a suspected diagnosis of tuberculous meningitis and must be started before culture and sensitivity reports are received. At least three drugs should be used, since irreversible brain damage or death may occur as soon as two weeks after the onset of infection (not clinical symptoms).[122]

Treatment should be initiated in R.U. with INH 300 mg/day, rifampin 600 mg/day, and pyrazinamide 15 to 30 mg/kg/day for the first two months.[29,120] If drug resistance is suspected, treatment should be initiated with a four-drug regimen of INH, rifampin, ethambutol, and pyrazinamide for two months. Both isoniazid and rifampin penetrate into the cerebrospinal fluid and reduce the morbidity and mortality associated with tuberculous meningitis. Ethambutol should be used in the highest dosage to achieve bactericidal concentrations in the CSF. Streptomycin penetrates into the cerebrospinal fluid poorly even with inflamed meninges.[123,124] (See Table 59.6 for a list of the most commonly-used drugs and their CSF concentrations.)

Extensive experience with short-course chemotherapy of extrapulmonary disease indicates that successful treatment can be accomplished within nine months (relapse rate: 0.7%; treatment failure: 1.5%). After the initial phase of treatment (8 weeks), R.U. should receive either daily INH and rifampin or two to three times a week (directly observed) treatment for a total of six months.[120] Some experts extend the duration of treatment to nine months. In addition, pyridoxine 50 mg/day should be given to R.U. to prevent the occurrence of peripheral neuritis secondary to INH. It also should be remembered that rifampin may impart a red to orange color to the spinal fluid.

Corticosteroids. The use of corticosteroids in the initial treatment of tuberculous meningitis to reduce the intracranial pressure associated with cerebral edema is questionable. Prednisone 60 to 80 mg/day is recommended in patients who are in a coma or in those who have subarachnoid block or spinal fluid pressures greater than 300 mm Hg.[1] The dose of prednisone can be tapered slowly after symptoms subside. Corticosteroids may reduce the mortality and frequency of neurologic sequelae in patients with a positive CSF culture for *M. tuberculosis.*[125] Corticosteroids are not indicated for R.U. at this time.

Booster Phenomenon (PPD Skin Test)

26. S.N., a 50-year-old male hospital employee receiving his initial tuberculin skin test (PPD-Mantoux), had a 7 mm reaction. Because of his age and previous hospital employment, it was decided to retest him in 1 week to rule out any "booster" effect. The result of the repeated skin test was 12 mm. He denied exposure to persons with clinical tuberculosis. What is the significance of this reaction? Should S.N. be placed on INH preventive therapy?

Some persons experience a marked increase in size of a tuberculin skin test reaction which may not be due to *M. tuberculosis* infection.[126] This reaction, or "booster" phenomenon, is not fully understood but may be due to a remote tuberculosis mycobacteria, infection with other mycobacteria, or prior Bacillus of Calmette and Guerin (BCG) vaccination. The tuberculin skin test itself can stimulate an increase in reaction size when tests are performed every one to two years. The incidence of this reaction appears to increase with age and can occur as soon as one week after a previous test.[127,128] Therefore, S.N.'s reaction may not represent infection with *M. tuberculosis.*

Since serial tuberculin testing is recommended for hospital employees, it becomes important to distinguish a possible booster reaction from a recent infection with *M. tuberculosis.* Some hospitals advocate the use of two-step skin testing in *new* employees.[129,130] Persons who exhibit an increase from less than 10 mm to greater than 10 mm, as in the case of S.N., may be mistaken for a recent converter and given INH preventive therapy unnecessarily. To determine if a reaction is due to "boosting" rather than an infection, a second identical skin test should be administered 7 to 21 days after the first. The results of this test should be read in 48 to 72 hours. If the repeat test is positive (>10 mm), the reaction should be classified as a booster reaction and the subject should not be treated with INH. If the repeat test is less than 10 mm but changes to positive (with a 6 mm increase) after one year, the person should be classified as a recent converter and managed according to the recommendations in Table 59.4. One report suggested using a 15 mm induration as the appropriate baseline in hospital employees tested annually.[131]

The increase in reaction size in S.N. is probably due to the booster effect. Since he is over 35 years old, he would not be a candidate for INH preventive therapy. S.N. should be given a repeat skin test next year and evaluated as described above. He should not receive a two-step test in the future since this is only done on initial evaluation of an employee.

Bacillus of Calmette and Guerin (BCG) Vaccine

27. C.T., a 25-year-old female refugee from Cambodia, was given a routine physical examination upon entering this country. As part of this examination, she received a tuberculin skin test with 5 TU strength PPD. The result of this test was positive with an induration of 12 mm. She denied previous treatment for tuberculosis, but remembered receiving a tuberculosis vaccine (BCG) several years ago. What is BCG vaccine? Does this positive skin test indicate infection with *M. tuberculosis*?

Table 59.6		Tuberculosis Meningitis Cerebrospinal Fluid Concentrations[a,b]			
Drug	Dose	C$_{max}$ (mg/dL)	MIC (mg/dL)	T$_{max}$ (hr)	% Serum Concentration
Isoniazid	1.8–3.1 mg/kg	1.77–4.10	0.05–0.20	3.25–4.25	100
Rifampin	600 mg	0.24–2.40	0.5	3–6	6–30
Ethambutol	15–35 mg/kg	0.30–4.21	1–2	—	10–54
Pyrazinamide	3 gm	50	20	5	100

a Adapted with permission from reference 141.
b C$_{max}$ = Maximum CSF concentration with inflamed meninges; MIC = Minimum inhibitory concentration; T$_{max}$ = Time to achieve maximum CSF concentration.

BCG is a vaccine derived from a strain of bovine mycobacterium. It is used in many foreign countries with a high incidence of tuberculosis to prevent the disease in persons who are tuberculin negative (no immunity to tuberculosis infection). There are many different BCG vaccines available worldwide, and all of them differ with respect to immunogenicity, efficacy, and reactogenicity.[18] These factors may account for the varied degrees of protection afforded by the vaccine. In trials conducted in the U.S., the protective effect derived from BCG vaccine ranged from 0% to 80%.[132]

Prior vaccination with BCG usually results in a positive tuberculin skin test. It is impossible to differentiate between a positive skin test due to BCG and that due to infection with *M. tuberculosis*.[132] Therefore, C.T. should be treated as though she has a positive tuberculin skin test according to the guidelines outlined in Table 59.4. Since she is from an area of the world with a high drug-resistance rate, the possibility of infection with organisms that are resistant to INH also should be considered. (See Question 16.)

Adverse reactions to the BCG vaccine vary according to the type, dose, and age of the vaccine. Osteomyelitis, prolonged ulceration at the vaccination site, lupoid reactions, lymphadenitis, disseminated BCG infection, and death have all been reported.[133,134]

BCG vaccine is not recommended for use in the routine prophylaxis of tuberculosis in the U.S. The risk of exposure to tuberculosis in this country is relatively low, and other methods of control (e.g., treatment of high risk groups) usually are adequate. BCG vaccine should only be used in persons who are tuberculin negative and are repeatedly exposed to highly infectious, untreated patients with active tuberculosis.[132]

References

1 **Daniel TM et al.** Tuberculosis. In: Wilson JD et al., eds. Harrison's Principles of Internal Medicine. 12th ed. New York: McGraw-Hill; 1991:637.

2 **Iseman MD.** A leap of faith: what can we do to curtail institutional transmission of tuberculosis? Ann Intern Med. 1992;117:251.

3 **Murray JF.** The white plague. Down and out or up and coming? Am Rev Respir Dis. 1989;140:1788.

4 **Farer LS.** The public health aspects of tuberculosis. Semin Respir Med. 1981; 2:175.

5 **American Thoracic Society/Centers for Disease Control.** Diagnostic standards and classification of tuberculosis. Am Rev Respir Dis. 1990;142:725.

6 **Glassroth J et al.** Tuberculosis in the 1980's. N Engl J Med. 1980;302:1441.

7 **Sbarbaro JA.** Tuberculosis. Med Clin North Am. 1980;64:417.

8 **Barnes PF et al.** Tuberculosis in patients with human immunodeficiency virus infection. N Engl J Med. 1991; 324:1644.

9 **Centers for Disease Control.** Tuberculosis—United States—1985 and the possible impact of human T-lymphotropic virus type III/Lymphadenopathy-associated virus infection. MMWR. 1986;35:74.

10 **Centers for Disease Control.** Management of persons exposed to multidrug-resistant tuberculosis. MMWR. 1992;41(RR-11):61.

11 **Centers for Disease Control.** Tuberculosis morbidity—United States, 1992. MMWR. 1993;42:696.

12 **Stead WW et al.** Tuberculosis as an endemic and nosocomial infection among elderly in nursing homes. N Engl J Med. 1985;312:1483.

13 **Schieffelbein CW et al.** Tuberculosis control among homeless population. Arch Intern Med. 1988;148:1843.

14 **Centers for Disease Control.** Prevention and control of tuberculosis among homeless persons. Recommendations of the Advisory Council on the elimination of tuberculosis. MMWR. 1992; 41(No. RR-5):13.

15 **Centers for Disease Control.** A strategic plan for the elimination of tuberculosis in the United States. MMWR. 1989;38(Suppl. S-3).

16 **MacGregor RR.** A year's experience with tuberculosis in a private urban teaching hospital in the post sanatorium era. Am J Med. 1975;58:221.

17 **Counsel SR et al.** Unsuspected pulmonary tuberculosis in a community teaching hospital. Arch Intern Med. 1989;149:1274.

18 **Reichman LB.** Tuberculin skin testing: the state of the art. Chest. 1979; 76(Suppl.):764.

19 **Daniel T et al.** Improving methods for detecting infected persons at risk of developing disease. Am Rev Respir Dis. 1986;134:409.

20 **Snider DE.** Recognition and elimination of tuberculosis. Adv Intern Med. 1993;38:169.

21 **Centers for Disease Control.** Screening for tuberculosis and tuberculosis infection in high risk populations and the use of preventive therapy for tuberculosis in the United States. Recommendations of the Advisory Council for the elimination of tuberculosis. MMWR. 1990;39(No. RR-8):1.

22 **Centers for Disease Control.** Tuberculosis and human immunodeficiency virus infections: Recommendations of the Advisory Committee for the elimination of tuberculosis. MMWR. 1989; 38:236.

23 **Daley CL et al.** An outbreak of tuberculosis with accelerated progression among persons infected with the human immunodeficiency virus. An analysis using restriction-fragment-length-polymorphisms. N Engl J Med. 1992; 326:231.

24 **Dooley SW et al.** Nosocomial transmission of tuberculosis in a hospital unit for HIV-infected patients. JAMA. 1991;267:2632.

25 **Chaparas SD.** Tuberculin test: variability with the Mantoux procedure. Am Rev Respir Dis. 1985;132:175.

26 **Nash DR et al.** Anergy in pulmonary tuberculosis. Chest. 1980;77:32.

27 **Snider DE.** The tuberculin skin test. Am Rev Respir Dis. 1982;125:108.

28 **Riebel W.** The 250-TU PPD and second-strength skin tests. N Engl J Med. 1983;309:246.

29 **Centers for Disease Control.** Initial therapy for tuberculosis in the era of multidrug-resistance: Recommendations of the Advisory Counsel for the

elimination of tuberculosis. MMWR. 1993;42(No. RR-7):1.

30 **Stead WW et al.** Contribution of a third drug to various two drug regimens in the treatment of tuberculosis. Am Rev Respir Dis. 1980;121:463. Abstract.

31 **Snider DE et al.** Standard therapy for tuberculosis. Chest. 1985;87(Suppl.): 117S.

32 **Mandell GL et al.** Antimicrobial agents: drugs used in the chemotherapy of tuberculosis and leprosy. In: Gilman AG et al., eds. The Pharmacological Basis of Therapeutics. 8th ed. New York: McMillan; 1990:1146.

33 **Mitchison DA.** Basic mechanisms of chemotherapy. Chest. 1969;76 (Suppl.): 771.

34 **Dickinson JM et al.** Experimental models to explain the high sterilizing activity of rifampin in the chemotherapy of tuberculosis. Am Rev Respir Dis. 1981;123:376.

35 **Jindani A et al.** The bactericidal activity of drugs in patients with pulmonary tuberculosis. Am Rev Respir Dis. 1980;121:939.

36 **Fox W.** Wither short-course chemotherapy? Br J Dis Chest. 1981;75:331.

37 **Stradling P et al.** Twice-weekly streptomycin plus isoniazid for tuberculosis. Am Rev Respir Dis. 1981;123:367.

38 **Moulding TS et al.** The treatment of tuberculosis. Semin Respir Med. 1981; 2:215.

39 **Dutt AK et al.** Short-course treatment regimens for patients with tuberculosis. Arch Intern Med. 1980;140:827.

40 **Dutt AK et al.** Present chemotherapy for tuberculosis. J Infect Dis. 1982; 146:698.

41 **American Thoracic Society and the Centers for Disease Control.** Guidelines for short-course tuberculosis chemotherapy. Am Rev Respir Dis. 1980; 121:611.

42 **Dutt AK et al.** Short-course chemotherapy for tuberculosis with mainly twice-weekly isoniazid and rifampin. Am J Med. 1984;77:233.

43 **American Thoracic Society.** Treatment of tuberculosis and tuberculosis infection in adults and children. Am Rev Respir Dis. 1986;134:355.

44 **Centers for Disease Control.** Bacteriologic conversion of sputum among

tuberculosis patients—United States. MMWR. 1985;34:747.

45 **Centers for Disease Control.** Follow-up on guidelines for short-course tuberculosis chemotherapy. MMWR. 1980; 29:183.

46 **Falk A et al.** Prophylaxis with isoniazid in inactive tuberculosis. Chest. 1978; 77:44.

47 **Ferebee SH.** Controlled chemoprophylaxis trials in tuberculosis: a general review. Adv Tuberc Res. 1970;17:28.

48 **Taylor WC et al.** Should young adults with a positive tuberculin test take isoniazid? Ann Intern Med. 1981;94:808.

49 **Comstock GW.** Evaluating isoniazid preventive therapy: the need for more data. Ann Intern Med. 1981;94:817. Editorial.

50 **Bailey WC et al.** Preventive treatment of tuberculosis. Chest. 1985;87 (Suppl.): 1285.

51 **Centers for Disease Control.** The use of preventive therapy in the United States. MMWR. 1990;39(RR-8):9.

52 **Mitchell JR et al.** Isoniazid liver injury—clinical spectrum, pathology, and probable pathogenesis. Ann Intern Med. 1976;84:181.

53 **Maddrey WC et al.** Isoniazid hepatitis. Ann Intern Med. 1973;79:1.

54 **Snider DE.** Isoniazid-associated hepatitis deaths: a review of available information. Am Rev Respir Dis. 1992; 146:1643. Letter.

55 **Comstock GW et al.** The competing risks of tuberculosis and hepatitis for adult tuberculin reactors. Am Rev Respir Dis. 1975;11:573.

56 **Snider DE, Caras GJ.** Isoniazid-associated hepatitis deaths: a review of available information. Am Rev Respir Dis. 1992;145:494.

57 **Ellard GA.** Variations between individuals and populations in the acetylation of isoniazid and its significance for the treatment of pulmonary tuberculosis. Clin Pharmacol Ther. 1976;19: 610.

58 **Dickenson DS et al.** The effect of acetylation status on isoniazid hepatitis. Am Rev Respir Dis. 1977;115(Suppl.): 395.

59 **Ellard GA et al.** The hepatic toxicity of isoniazid among rapid and slow acetylators of the drug. Am Rev Respir Dis. 1978;118:628.

60 **Kopanoff DE et al.** Isoniazid-related hepatitis. Am Rev Respir Dis. 1976; 117:991.

61 **Black M.** Isoniazid and the liver. Am Rev Respir Dis. 1974;110:1.

62 **Van Scoy RE, Wilkowske CJ.** Antituberculous agents. Mayo Clin Proc. 1992;67:179.

63 **Van Scoy RE et al.** Antituberculous agents. Mayo Clin Proc. 1983;58:233.

64 **Coleman LT et al.** Pharmacist as a primary care provider in a tuberculosis clinic. Am J Hosp Pharm. 1983;40:278.

65 **Jacobs NF et al.** Spiking fever from isoniazid simulating a septic process. JAMA. 1977;238:1759.

66 **Good AE et al.** Rheumatic symptoms during tuberculosis therapy, a manifestation of isoniazid toxicity. Ann Intern Med. 1965;63:800.

67 **Alarcon-Segovia D.** Drug-induced lupus syndromes. Mayo Clin Proc. 1969; 44:664.

68 **Girling DJ.** Adverse effects of antituberculosis drugs. Drugs. 1982;23:56.

69 **Ochs HR et al.** Diazepam interactions with antituberculosis drugs. Clin Pharmacol Ther. 1981;29:671.

70 **Hauser MJ et al.** Interactions of isoniazid with foods. Drug Intell Clin Pharm. 1982;16:617.

71 **Dutt AK et al.** Treatment of pulmonary tuberculosis with short-course, intermittent chemotherapy using rifampin-isoniazid. Am Rev Respir Dis. 1977;115(Suppl.):296.

72 **Sanders WE.** Rifampin. Ann Intern Med. 1976;85:82.

73 **Zierski M et al.** Side-effects of drug regimens used in short-course chemotherapy for pulmonary tuberculosis: a controlled clinical study. Tubercle. 1980;61:41.

74 **Girling DJ.** Adverse reactions to rifampicin in antituberculosis regimens. J Antimicrob Chemother. 1977;3:115.

75 **Aquinas SM et al.** Adverse reactions to daily and intermittent rifampicin regimens for pulmonary tuberculosis in Hong Kong. Br Med J (Clin Res). 1972;1:765.

76 **Nessi R et al.** Acute renal failure after rifampin: a case report and survey of the literature. Nephron. 1976;16:148.

77 **Warrington RJ et al.** Insidious rifampin-associated renal failure with light-chain proteinuria. Arch Intern Med. 1977;137:924.

78 **Ransal VK et al.** Prolonged renal failure after rifampin. Am Rev Respir Dis. 1977;116:137.

79 **Bennett WM et al.** Drug therapy in renal failure: dosing guidelines for adults. Ann Intern Med. 1980;93(Pt. 1): 62.

80 **Andrew OT et al.** Tuberculosis in patients with end-stage renal disease. Am J Med. 1980;68:59.

81 **Skilnick JL et al.** Rifampicin, oral contraceptives, and pregnancy. JAMA. 1976;236:1382.

82 **Zilly W et al.** Pharmacokinetic interactions with rifampin. Clin Pharmacokinet. 1977;2:61.

83 **Twum-Barima Y et al.** Quinidine rifampin interaction. N Engl J Med. 1981; 304:1466.

84 **Englehard D et al.** Interaction of ketoconazole with rifampin and isoniazid. N Engl J Med. 1984;311:1681.

85 **Gronhagen-Riska C et al.** Predisposing factors in hepatitis induced by isoniazid-rifampin treatment of tuberculosis. Am Rev Respir Dis. 1978;118: 461.

86 **Cross FS et al.** Rifampin-isoniazid therapy of alcoholic and nonalcoholic tuberculosis patients in a U.S. Public Health Service cooperative therapy trial. Am Rev Respir Dis. 1980;122: 349.

87 **Citron KM.** Ocular toxicity from ethambutol. Thorax. 1986;41:737.

88 **Schlid HS, Fox BC.** Rapid-onset reversible ocular toxicity from ethambutol therapy. Am J Med. 1991;90:404.

89 **Alvarez KL, Krop LC.** Ethambutol-induced ocular toxicity revisited. Ann Pharmacother. 1993;27:102. Letter.

90 **Postlethwaite AE et al.** Hyperuricemia due to ethambutol. N Engl J Med. 1972;286:761.

91 **Centers for Disease Control.** Prevention and control of tuberculosis in facilities providing long-term care to the elderly. Recommendation of the Advisory Committee for elimination of tuberculosis. MMWR. 1990;39(No. RR-10):7.

92 **Marain JP et al.** Epidemic tuberculosis in a nursing home: a retrospective cohort study. J Am Geriatr Soc. 1985; 33:258.

93 **Dutt AK, Stead WW.** Tuberculosis. Clin Geriatr Med. 1992;8:761.

94 **Nagami P et al.** Management of tuberculosis in elderly person. Compr Ther. 1984;10:57.

95 **Rudd AJ.** Tuberculosis and the aged. J Am Geriatr Soc. 1985;33:566.

96 **Snider DE et al.** Drug-resistant tuberculosis. Am Rev Respir Dis. 1991;144: 732.

97 **Goble M et al.** Treatment of 171 patients with pulmonary tuberculosis resistant to INH and rifampin. N Engl J Med. 1993;328:527.

98 **Berning SE et al.** Malabsorption of antituberculosis medications by a patient with AIDS. N Engl J Med. 1992; 327:1817.

99 **Centers for Disease Control.** Follow-up on drug-resistant tuberculosis—Mississippi. MMWR. 1980;29:602.

100 **Edlin BR et al.** An outbreak of multidrug-resistant tuberculosis among hospitalized patients with the acquired immunodeficiency syndrome. N Engl J Med. 1992;326:1514.

101 **Centers for Disease Control.** Nosocomial transmission of multidrug-resistant tuberculosis to health care workers and HIV infected patients in an urban hospital—Florida. MMWR. 1990;39: 718.

102 **Iseman MD.** Treatment of multidrug-resistant tuberculosis. N Engl J Med. 1993;329:784.

103 **Heifets LB, Lindholm-Levy PJ.** Bacteriostatic and bactericidal activity of ciprofloxacin and ofloxacin against Mycobacterium tuberculosis and Mycobacterium avium complex. Tubercle. 1987;68:267.

104 **Iseman MD et al.** Surgical intervention in the treatment of pulmonary disease caused by drug-resistant mycobacterium tuberculosis. Am Rev Respir Dis. 1990;141:623.

105 **Fischl MA et al.** Clinical presentation and outcome of patients with HIV infection and tuberculosis caused by multiple drug resistant bacilli. Ann Intern Med. 1992;117:184.

106 **Fauci AS et al.** Glucocorticosteroid therapy: mechanisms of action and clinical considerations. Ann Intern Med. 1976;84:304.

107 **Centers for Disease Control.** Tuberculosis in a school teacher—Pennsylvania. MMWR. 1980;29:589.

108 **Chaisson RE et al.** Tuberculosis and human immunodeficiency virus infection. J Infect Dis. 1989;159:96.

109 **Mehta JB, Morris F.** Impact of HIV infection on mycobacterial disease. Am Fam Physician. 1992;45:2203.

110 **Theuer CP.** Tuberculosis in patients with human immunodeficiency virus infection. West J Med. 1989;150:700.

111 **Girling DJ et al.** Extrapulmonary tuberculosis. Br Med Bull. 1988;44:738.

112 **Wurtz RM et al.** Anaphylactoid drug reaction to ciprofloxacin and rifampin in HIV-infected patients. Lancet. 1989; (April 29):955.

113 **Mitchison DA et al.** Influence of initial drug resistance on the response to short-course chemotherapy of pulmonary tuberculosis. Am Rev Respir Dis. 1986;133:423.

114 **Antoniskis D et al.** Combined toxicity of zidovudine and antituberculosis chemotherapy. Am Rev Respir Dis. 1992; 145:430.

115 **Jacobs RF et al.** Management of tuberculosis in pregnancy and the newborn. Clin Perinatol. 1988;15:305.

116 **Warkany J.** Antituberculosis drugs: teratogen update. Teratology. 1969;20: 133.

117 **Snider DE et al.** Treatment of tuberculosis during pregnancy. Am Rev Respir Dis. 1980;122:76.

118 **Vallejo J, Starke J.** Tuberculosis and pregnancy. Clin Chest Med. 1992;13: 693.

119 **Centers for Disease Control.** Adverse drug reactions among children treated for tuberculosis. MMWR. 1980;29:589.

120 **Dutt AK.** Treatment of extrapulmonary tuberculosis. Sem Respir Infect. 1989;4:225.

121 **Kennedy DH et al.** Tuberculous meningitis. JAMA. 1979;241:264.

122 **Oill PA et al.** Infectious disease emergencies. Part 1. Patients presenting with an altered state of consciousness. West J Med. 1976;125:36.

123 **Davidson PT, Le HQ.** Drug treatment of tuberculosis— 1992. Drugs. 1992; 43–651.

124 **Holdness MR.** Cerebrospinal fluid pharmacokinetics of the antituberculosis drugs. Clin Pharmacokinet. 1985; 10:532.

125 **Girgis NI et al.** Dexamethasone adjunctive treatment for tuberculosis meningitis. Pediatr Infect Dis J. 1991; 10–179.

126 **Comstock GW et al.** Tuberculin conversions: true or false. Am Rev Respir Dis. 1978;118:215.

127 **Thompson JN et al.** The booster phenomenon in serial tuberculin testing. Am Rev Respir Dis. 1979;119:587.

128 **Richards NM et al.** Tuberculin test conversions during repeated skin testing associated with sensitivity to nontuberculosis mycobacteria. Am Rev Respir Dis. 1979;120:59.

129 **Snider DE et al.** Tuberculin skin testing of hospital employees: infection, "boosting," and two-step testing. Am J Infect Control. 1984;12:305.

130 **Ktsanes UK et al.** The cumulative risk of tuberculin skin test conversion for five years of hospital employment. Am J Public Health. 1986;76:65.

131 **Bass JB et al.** Choosing an appropriate cutting point for conversion in annual tuberculin skin testing. Am Rev Respir Dis. 1985;132:379.

132 **Centers for Disease Control.** Recommendations of the Public Health Service Advisory Committee on Immunization Practices: BCG vaccine. MMWR. 1979;28:241.

133 **MacKay A et al.** Fatal disseminated BCG infection in an 18-year-old boy. Lancet. 1980;2:1332.

134 **Centers for Disease Control.** Disseminated mycobacterium bovis infection from BCG vaccination of a patient with acquired immunodeficiency syndrome. MMWR. 1985;34:227.

135 **Leysen DC et al.** Mycobacterial and the new quinolones. Antimicrob Agents Chemother. 1989;33:1.

136 **Snider DE.** Adv Intern Med. 1993;38: 169.

137 **Iseman MD.** N Engl J Med. 1993;239: 784.

138 **Werner EE et al.** The childern of Kauai. Honolulu: University of Hawaii Press. 1971.

139 **Niswander KR, Gordon M.** The women and their pregnancies. Washington, DC: USGPO; 1972:40.

140 **Hakasalo JK.** Cumulative detection rates of congenital malformation in a 10-year study. Acta Pathol Microbiol Scand (A). 1973;242 (Suppl):12.

141 **Holdness MR.** Cerebrospinal fluid pharmacokinetics of the antituberculosis drugs. Clin Pharmacokinet. 1985; 10:532.

Gastrointestinal Infections

Larry H Danziger
Gail S Itokazu

Pathophysiology 60-1
Treatment 60-1
  Rehydration therapy 60-1
  Antimicrobial (see Table 60.1) 60-2
  Opiate and atropine derivatives 60-2
  Kaolin-pectin/aluminum hydroxide 60-2
Predisposing Factors (See Table 60.2) 60-2
Travelers' Diarrhea 60-2
  Treatment (See Table 60.3) 60-3
    Nonantibiotics 60-3
    Antimicrobials 60-4
      Trimethoprim-sulfamethoxazole (TMP-SMX) 60-4
      Fluoroquinolones 60-4
      Aztreonam 60-4
  Combination therapy 60-4
  Prophylaxis 60-4
    Bismuth subsalicylate 60-4
    Trimethoprim or TMP-SMX 60-5
    Doxycycline 60-5
    Fluoroquinolones 60-5
    Microbiologic consequences of prophylaxis 60-5
  Recommendations For Treatment and Prophylaxis
  (see Table 60.3) 60-5
  Clinical Assessment 60-6
    Treatment 60-6
      General management 60-6
    Prophylaxis 60-6
Cryptosporidiosis 60-7
Pathophysiology 60-7
Diagnosis 60-7
Clinical Presentation 60-7
Treatment 60-7
  Spiramycin 60-7
  Paromomycin 60-7

Food Poisoning 60-8
Enterohemorrhagic *Escherichia* coli
(*E. coli* 0157:H7) 60-8
  Clinical Presentation 60-8
  Transmission 60-9
  Diagnosis 60-9
  Treatment 60-9
    Antibiotics 60-9
    Antimotility and antidiarrheal agents 60-10
  Prevention 60-10
Antibiotic-Associated Pseudomembranous
Colitis (AAPMC) 60-10
  Pathophysiology (See Table 60.5) 60-10
  Clinical Presentation and Diagnosis 60-10
  Treatment 60-11
    Vancomycin 60-11
    Metronidazole 60-11
    Bacitracin 60-11
    Exchange resins 60-11
    Antidiarrheal agents 60-11
    Teicoplanin 60-11
    Parenteral drugs (See Question 21) 60-12
  Recurrence 60-11
    Treatment (see Table 60.5) 60-11
***Campylobacter* Infections** 60-12
Viral Gastroenteritis 60-12
Helicobacter Infections 60-13
Salmonella Gastroenteritis 60-13
  Gastroenteritis, Enteric Fever, and Chronic Carrier 60-13
  Prevention 60-14
Shigella Gastroenteritis 60-14
  Treatment 60-14

Pathophysiology

Infections of the gastrointestinal tract (GI) are among the most common of infectious diseases. These infections are a major source of morbidity and mortality throughout the world. Acute infectious gastroenteritis associated with diarrhea is the leading cause of death in children less than four years of age.

These illnesses may be caused by bacterial, viral, or protozoal pathogens (see Table 60.1). Although many pathogens cause gastrointestinal disease, most produce a similar syndrome of diarrhea, fever, nausea, and vomiting. The most severe gastrointestinal infections are caused by bacterial pathogens. Unlike other infections, these diseases are caused by alterations in the intestinal microflora rather than introduction of a pathogen into a normally sterile site. Endogenous microflora consisting of anaerobes such as bacteroides, anaerobic streptococci, and clostridia normally inhabit the large intestine at a concentration of 10^{11} organisms per gram.[1] Bacterial gastrointestinal infections often are associated with a relative predominance of aerobic organisms in the large intestine.[1]

Bacterial diarrheas may be characterized as either being invasive or toxigenic (noninvasive). Infections caused by invasive pathogens generally are associated with abdominal pain, fever, head-ache, myalgias, and other systemic symptoms. Noninvasive illnesses generally are characterized by few symptoms and the lack of fever. Noninvasive organisms, such as *Escherichia coli* release substances into the lumen of the intestine which lead to irritation, inflammation, and net fluid loss. These pathogens colonize the small bowel epithelium without invading the mucosa. Two types of enterotoxins produced by *E. coli* are heat-labile (LT) and heat-stable (ST) toxins, which activate intestinal adenylate cyclase or guanylate cyclase, respectively.[1] Invasive organisms such as *Salmonella* and *Shigella* penetrate the intestinal mucosa, causing inflammation, necrosis, diarrhea, and depending upon the pathogen, systemic complications such as fever, bacteremia, and lymphatic invasion.

Treatment

Rehydration Therapy. The most disastrous consequences of gastrointestinal infections are related to fluid losses. Regardless of etiology, the primary goal of drug therapy is prevention or reversal of fluid and electrolyte losses and metabolic complications of the gastroenteritis. Rehydration therapy should accompany or precede antibiotic therapy in patients with moderate to severe fluid losses. Significant dehydration and uncontrolled diarrhea are indications

Table 60.1		Predisposing Factors, Symptoms, and Therapy of Gastrointestinal Infections		
Pathogen	Predisposing Factors	Symptoms	Diagnostic Evaluations	Therapy[a,b]
Salmonella (nontyphoid)	Ingestion of contaminated poultry, raw milk, custards and cream fillings; foreign travel	Nausea, vomiting, diarrhea, cramps, fever, tenesmus *Incubation*: 12–36 hr	Fecal leukocytes, stool culture	Ampicillin, TMP-SMX, chloramphenicol, ciprofloxacin
Shigella	Ingestion of contaminated food, foreign travel Minimum infective dose: 10–100 organisms	Fever, dysentery, cramps, tenesmus *Incubation*: 12–24 hr	Fecal leukocytes	TMP-SMX, ciprofloxacin, tetracycline, chloramphenicol,[c] norfloxacin, ciprofloxacin
Campylobacter	Daycare centers, contaminated eggs, raw milk, foreign travel	Mild to severe diarrhea; fever, systemic malaise *Incubation*: 72 hr	Fecal leukocytes, stool culture	Erythromycin, tetracycline, ciprofloxacin, chloramphenicol[c]
Clostridium difficile	Antibiotics, antineoplastics	Mild to severe diarrhea, cramps	*C. difficile* toxin, *C. difficile*, culture, colonoscopy	Metronidazole, vancomycin, bacitracin, binding resins
Staphylococcal food poisoning	Contaminated meat, milk, exposed foods	Nausea, diarrhea; onset <4 hr, resolves in 24–48 hr *Incubation*: 2–4 hr	Stool cultures	Supportive only
Travelers' diarrhea (*E. coli*)	Contaminated food (vegetables and cheese), water, foreign travel	Nausea, vomiting, mild to severe diarrhea, cramps *Incubation*: 16–48 hr	Stool culture	TMP-SMX, bismuth subsalicylate, doxycycline (prophylaxis), ciprofloxacin, norfloxacin, ofloxacin
Escherichia coli enterohemorrhagic (*E. coli* 0157:H7)	Beef, raw milk, water	Diarrhea, headache, bloody stools *Incubation*: 48–96 hr	Stool cultures on MacConkey's sorbitol	Ciprofloxacin, doxycycline, TMP-SMX
Cryptosporidiosis	Immunosuppression, daycare centers, contaminated water, animal handlers	Mild to severe diarrhea (chronic or self-limited); large fluid	Small bowel biopsy, special stool cultures[d]	Paromomycin, spiramycin
Viral gastroenteritis	Community-wide outbreaks, contaminated food	Nausea, diarrhea (self-limited), cramps *Incubation*: 16–48 hr	Special viral studies	Supportive only

[a] See text for doses and duration of therapy.
[b] TMP-SMX = Trimethoprim-sulfamethoxazole.
[c] Not all cases require antibiotic therapy.
[d] Sheathers' flotation method.

for hospitalization.[2] In the U.S., most severe dehydration is managed in the hospital with intravenous fluids and electrolytes. Commercial preparations such as Lytren, Pedialyte, and Infalyte for oral rehydration therapy may be appropriate for mild to moderate diarrhea but they do not contain enough glucose or electrolytes to adequately treat severe dehydration. For severe dehydration in the absence of parenteral therapy, a formula has been developed by the World Health Organization.[2] It supplies water, glucose, and electrolytes and is effective because sodium absorption is accelerated in the presence of glucose.[3–5] Once dehydration is corrected, high-sodium formulas should be diluted to prevent hypernatremia or edema.[6]

Antimicrobial use depends upon the type and severity of gastrointestinal infection. Diarrhea alone is often an effective physiologic response to pathogenic organisms and toxins. Antibiosis is necessary if the host is immunocompromised or if normal enteric defenses are absent (see Table 60.1). The selection of a specific antimicrobial will be influenced by the differing and changing patterns of bacterial resistance in various areas of the world.[7]

Opiate and Atropine Derivatives. Historically, opiate and atropine derivatives have been promoted for relief of diarrhea. These agents decrease jejunal motor activity and increase rectal sphincter tone. Despite symptomatic relief with these agents, inhibition of peristalsis prevents the removal of the pathogen; may lead to toxic megacolon; and can exacerbate *Salmonella* and *Shigella* gastroenteritis.[8] Such agents do not eliminate the need for fluids and electrolytes and should be avoided in patients with high fever, dysentery, and antibiotic-associated pseudomembranous colitis. They

may be used sparingly in mild cases of diarrhea with painful cramps and no fever, but they should not be used for more than three days under any circumstances.[9,10]

Kaolin-pectin/aluminum hydroxide preparations may solidify stool but do not affect the frequency of infectious diarrhea[11] or reduce intestinal fluid losses. Bismuth subsalicylate (Pepto Bismol) is effective in travelers' diarrhea and under certain circumstances may be considered an alternative to antibiotic agents. However, large doses of bismuth subsalicylate may lead to salicylate toxicity and its complications.

Predisposing Factors

A number of systemic pharmacologic agents may predispose patients to or exacerbate infectious diarrhea. These include H_2 blockers, suspension-type antacids, antibiotics, and immunosuppressive agents (see Table 60.2). When evaluating any patient with gastroenteritis, the clinician should first assess the relevance of other drugs and systemic diseases on the GI tract. Most drug-induced disease results from an imbalance of benign and pathogenic flora. Agents that alter gastric acidity compromise gut defenses by allowing viable pathogens to pass into the small intestine. Others, such as corticosteroids, have a direct effect on the immunologic defenses of the small and large intestine.

Travelers' Diarrhea

Travelers' diarrhea is a syndrome familiar to persons from industrialized countries who are exposed to the endogenous enteric flora of developing countries in Latin America, Asia, and Africa.

Travelers' diarrhea also encompasses diarrhea occurring within seven to ten days after returning from a developing area: this time frame reflects the incubation period of most enteropathogens.[12] The definition of travelers' diarrhea has not been entirely consistent between studies; however, most would agree with the definition of three or more loose unformed stools per day plus at least one symptom of enteric infection (i.e., abdominal pain or cramps, nausea, vomiting, fever, dysentery, fecal urgency, and tenesmus of ≤72 hours duration).[12] Except for the requirement of a symptom of enteric infection, the same criteria for travelers' diarrhea applies to infants.[177]

The syndrome spreads by fecally-contaminated sources that contain enterotoxins which are not inactivated by cooking or processing.[13] The microbiologic etiology of travelers' diarrhea is dependent upon the area of interest, as well as the season of the year. For example, while enterotoxigenic *Escherichia coli* is common in Latin America and Africa, *Campylobacter* is an important cause of infectious diarrhea in Mexico and southeast Asia during the winter or dry seasons.[12] Less frequently, other pathogens such as *Shigella* (5% to 15%), *Salmonella*, *Aeromonas* species (especially in Thailand), *Plesiomonas* species, *Vibrio parahaemolyticus* (from raw fish), rotavirus, and Norwalk virus also are cultured from stool specimens.[13] As many as 20% to 50%[27,28] of cases of diarrhea lack a specific pathogen while others may be caused by multiple strains.[13,204] Immunity to native pathogenic strains may be acquired if the traveler remains in the affected area for at least one year.[14,15]

Treatment

The ideal therapy for travelers' diarrhea should have a rapid effect, minimal adverse reactions, no effect on normal colonic flora, and should not promote the development of resistant organisms. Several nonantibiotic and antibiotic options are available for the treatment of travelers' diarrhea (see Table 60.3). Selection of the most appropriate regimen should take several factors into consideration including the: severity of illness; suspected pathogen and its susceptibility to antimicrobials; age and past medical history of the patient; and whether or not the patient is pregnant. Of the various therapies, loperamide (Imodium) has the fastest onset of action. Treatment with antibiotics alone or antibiotics plus antimotility agents results in improvement or cure within 24 hours in many patients,[16,21] and at 48 hours as many as 90% are improved or fully recovered.[16]

Nonantibiotics

Bismuth subsalicylate (Pepto Bismol) and loperamide are effective, nonantibiotic approaches to the management of travelers' diarrhea.[22] Of the two agents, loperamide has a faster onset of action, as the efficacy of bismuth subsalicylate may be delayed for as long as four hours.[22] Experimentally, bismuth subsalicylate may be beneficial for the treatment (and prevention) of travelers' diarrhea because of its antisecretory effect on the GI tract and its antimicrobial activity against enteropathogens.[23] The antisecretory effect may be

Table 60.2	Pharmacologic Agents Which May Promote Gastrointestinal Infection
Drug	Mechanism
Antacids, H₂ blockers	↑ gastric pH; viable pathogens passed to lower gut
Antibiotics	Eradication of normal (anaerobic) flora
Antidiarrheals	↓ gut motility; bacterial growth
Immunosuppressives	Inhibition of gut immune defenses

Table 60.3	Prophylaxis and Therapy of Travelers' Diarrhea in Adults[a]	
Drug	Prophylaxis[b]	Treatment
Bismuth subsalicylate	2 tab chewed with meals and HS (8 tab/day)	1 oz Q 30 min for a total dose of 8 oz/day
Loperamide	—	4 mg load, followed by 2 mg after each loose stool (*max:* 16 mg/day)
TMP-SMX[c]	160–800 mg/day	320–1600 mg once, or 160–800 mg BID for 3 days
Doxycycline	100 mg/day	—
Trimethoprim	200 mg/day	—
Norfloxacin	400 mg/day	400 mg BID for 3 days
Ciprofloxacin	500 mg/day	500 mg BID for 3 days
Ofloxacin	300 mg/day	300 mg BID for 3 days

[a] Adapted from reference 40. Many cases of travelers' diarrhea require neither prophylaxis nor therapy.
[b] While in endemic area, and continuing for 1–2 days after returning home, but not to exceed >3 weeks.
[c] Trimethoprim-sulfamethoxazole.

due to the binding of bismuth subsalicylate to enterotoxins such as those elaborated by enterotoxigenic *E. coli* (ETEC) or *Cholera vibrios*, thus preventing the binding of these toxins to their receptor sites in the gastrointestinal tract. In addition, the salicylate component of bismuth subsalicylate may exhibit an antisecretory effect by inhibition of prostaglandin synthesis; or by stimulation of sodium and chloride reabsorption, thereby reducing intestinal secretions. Antimicrobial activity of bismuth subsalicylate has been demonstrated against enteropathogens such as enterotoxigenic *E. coli*, *Salmonella* species, *Campylobacter jejuni*, and *Clostridium difficile*.[24]

Loperamide decreases gastrointestinal motility by altering the intestinal musculature, resulting in an increased gut capacity and prolonged transit time of intestinal contents.[25] Animal studies also suggest an antisecretory effect.[25] A major concern with the use of antimotility agents in infectious diarrhea is that they may aggravate disease caused by invasive enteropathogens such as *Shigella* and *Campylobacter*. In experimentally induced *Shigella* infection, diphenoxylate-atropine (Lomotil) significantly prolonged the illness compared to the placebo.[8] Furthermore, shock and enterocolitis occurred in children with watery diarrhea who were given loperamide. Thus, as a precaution, most trials evaluating loperamide exclude patients with symptoms suggestive of invasive diarrhea, (i.e., frankly bloody stools or temperatures above 39 °C).[21,25,26] Despite these exclusion criteria, patients with nondysenteric *Shigella* eventually do receive loperamide. Fortunately, in these patients, loperamide has not been found to cause significant prolongation of illness, although there was a tendency for these patients to electively take trimethoprim sulfamethoxazole (TMP-SMX) if they felt worsening of their illness at 12 hours.[22] Other investigators also document a worsening of gastroenteritis due to *Shigella* when patients were treated with TMP-SMX and loperamide.[16,21] Given the controversy surrounding the use of antimotility drugs in travelers' diarrhea, antimotility agents are not recommended in patients with high fever or blood in the stool, and they should be discontinued if symptoms persist for more than 48 hours.[27]

Bismuth subsalicylate[22,28,29] and loperamide[22,25] are effective in the treatment of travelers' diarrhea. Compared to placebo, bismuth subsalicylate 30 to 60 mL (4.2 to 8.2 gm bismuth subsalicylate) every half-hour for eight doses beginning at the onset of symptoms significantly decreased the number of unformed stools between 4 and 48 hours after initiation of treatment.[28] When separated out by probable pathogen, only study participants with diarrhea due to enterotoxigenic E. coli benefited by a reduction in the number of unformed stools. Symptoms of enteric infection (nausea, abdominal pain, or cramps) also were significantly decreased within 24 hours.[28] The higher dose of bismuth subsalicylate was used in participants with more severe illness (≥5 unformed stools in the preceding 24 hours) while the lower dose was used in patients with less severe gastroenteritis (≤3 unformed stools in the preceding 24 hours).

Compared to placebo, patients given a two day regimen of liquid bismuth subsalicylate (525 mg Q 30 minutes, maximum of 8 doses/day) had a moderate but significantly decreased duration of diarrhea.[29] A one to two day regimen of Pepto-Bismol (30 mL every half-hour for 8 doses) was compared to loperamide (4 mg load, followed by a 2 mg capsule after an unformed stool, maximum of 8 capsules/day) in over 200 travelers acquiring diarrhea in Latin America.[22] Patients treated with loperamide had fewer unformed stools 4 to 48 hours after treatment was initiated. Loperamide is a safe and effective alternative to bismuth subsalicylate for nondysenteric travelers' diarrhea.

Zaldaride maleate, an intestinal calmodulin inhibitor with antisecretory activity that decreases the severity and duration of travelers' diarrhea,[30] is in clinical study.

Antimicrobials

Compared to placebo, antibiotics decrease the duration of travelers' diarrhea from 59 to 93 hours to 16 to 30 hours.[12]

Trimethoprim/Sulfamethoxazole (TMP-SMX). About 70% to 95% of moderate to severe cases of travelers' diarrhea will respond to broad-spectrum antimicrobial agents which are active against E. coli, Salmonella species, or Shigella species.[31] Trimethoprim/sulfamethoxazole has been used extensively because of its broad-spectrum activity, ease of administration, and relatively safe profile. A five-day course of trimethoprim 200 mg orally four times a day, TMP-SMX 160/800 mg orally twice a day, or placebo was given to American students visiting Mexico who developed diarrhea (≥4 unformed stools/day or ≥3 stools in 8 hours).[32] Students who received either trimethoprim or TMP-SMX benefited considerably.[32] TMP-SMX, however, is not active against Campylobacter and should not be used in areas where this organism is an important cause of gastroenteritis.

Fluoroquinolones. Norfloxacin,[33] ciprofloxacin,[34] ofloxacin (300 mg BID for 3 to 5 days),[35] and fleroxacin (400 mg/day for 1 to 2 days),[36] also are effective treatments for travelers' diarrhea. Review of these studies revealed that the conventional definition of diarrhea[12] was not always used,[23,36] and that the longer duration of therapy did not seem to influence the efficacy of therapy.[35,36]

Specifically, compared to placebo, norfloxacin (Noroxin) 400 mg twice daily for three days significantly decreased the frequency of diarrhea in travelers to Africa, Asia, or Latin America: 73.9% (n = 46) versus 37.5% (n = 48).[33] A significant increase in resistance of E. coli to doxycycline after treatment with norfloxacin was noted. Ciprofloxacin (Cipro) 500 mg orally twice a day and TMP-SMX (160/800 mg PO BID) were equally effective therapies in 191 adults with travelers' diarrhea acquired in Mexico.[34]

Aztreonam. In contrast to placebo, oral aztreonam 100 mg three times a day for five days significantly decreased the duration of travelers' diarrhea from 84 hours to 44 hours (p = 0.0001).[37] Since less than 1% of aztreonam is absorbed after oral administration, it may be useful in circumstances in which systemic bioavailability may be undesirable (e.g., pregnancy, children who should not re-

ceive fluoroquinolones, individuals with significant hepatic or renal dysfunction). An oral formulation of aztreonam is not commercially available in the U.S.

Combination Therapy

Two[21,26] of four studies which evaluated the efficacy of loperamide plus an antibiotic demonstrated a significant advantage of the combination over therapy with either agent alone. The other two studies[16,38] demonstrated only marginal to no benefit of combination therapy. The dose of loperamide in all four studies was 4 mg load, followed by 2 mg after each unformed bowel movement, to a maximum of 16 mg/day.

Specifically, loperamide plus TMP-SMX (320/1600 mg load, followed by 160/800 mg BID for 5 doses)[26] or TMP-SMX (160 mg/800 mg BID for 3 days)[21] was significantly better than single or multiple doses of antibiotic, loperamide alone, or placebo in achieving the desired therapeutic endpoints. In the first study,[26] 75% of patients recovered from diarrhea within 12 hours of initiating therapy versus about 33 hours for the other treatment regimens (p <0.01). In the second study, compared to placebo, TMP-SMX plus loperamide decreased the duration of diarrhea within one hour of initiating treatment, versus 59 hours for placebo-treated patients.[21] The large difference in time to achieve clinical endpoints within each of these studies is likely due to the fact that ETEC was the predominant pathogen in one study,[21] while Shigella species (a more invasive pathogen) was more common in the other trial.[26]

Overall, data with ciprofloxacin plus loperamide were less impressive than with TMP-SMX. In one study, loperamide had a negligible effect on duration of illness when Campylobacter and Shigella were the most common enteropathogens.[38] In another study, a single 500 mg dose of ciprofloxacin plus loperamide was not more advantageous over ciprofloxacin 500 mg twice a day for three days.[16] In both of these ciprofloxacin studies, an enteric symptom of infection was not required of patients and the recommended definition of traveler's diarrhea[12] was not met.

Prophylaxis

A consensus conference on travelers' diarrhea did not recommend the prophylactic use of antibiotics because of the potential for: 1) side effects from antimicrobials; 2) development of other infections (e.g., antibiotic-associated colitis and Candida vaginitis); and 3) development of antimicrobial resistance; although this would be less likely to be a concern in developing countries with widespread, over-the-counter availability of antibiotics. In addition, no underlying disease is significantly worsened by a bout of travelers' diarrhea to warrant the aforementioned risks; and the treatment of travelers' diarrhea with antibiotics should it occur, is very successful. Nevertheless, prophylaxis could be considered in travelers' with repeated episodes of diarrhea, decreased gastric acidity, or with underlying diseases that would result in poor toleration of diarrhea [e.g., inflammatory bowel disease, acquired immunodeficiency syndrome (AIDS), diabetes, and chronic renal failure].[27]

If initiated, antimicrobial prophylaxis should be started on the first day in the country being visited; continued for two days after exposure but not for more than three weeks (see Table 60.3).[40,41]

Bismuth Subsalicylate

Both a liquid and tablet formulation of bismuth subsalicylate effectively prevent travelers' diarrhea. The tablet form is convenient and is more effective when the same total daily dose (2.1 gm/day) is administered in four divided doses versus two divided doses, 65%[42] and 32%,[43] respectively.

Bismuth subsalicylate 60 mL orally four times a day will prevent diarrhea if it is begun when the traveler arrives in the foreign area and is continued for several weeks or until the traveler leaves.[44] American students traveling to Mexico and treated prophylactically with two tablets of bismuth subsalicylate (262 mg/tablet) four times a day for three weeks experienced significantly less diarrhea than students given placebo [7/51 (14%) versus 23/58 (40%), respectively].[42] In contrast, bismuth subsalicylate twice a day for a mean of 16.1 days, was only half as effective as the four times a day regimen.[43]

Trimethoprim or TMP-SMX

TMP-SMX (Bactrim, Septra) is an effective prophylactic agent against travelers' diarrhea. American students given TMP-SMX 160/800 mg/day orally or TMP 200 mg/day orally for two weeks developed diarrheal illness significantly less frequently than those given placebo.[45] TMP-SMX also was superior to trimethoprim alone. Skin rash was the most common adverse effect, occurring in 2% of patients. An earlier study using twice the dose of TMP-SMX resulted in a 14% incidence of drug-related skin rash and no increase in benefits.[46] Resistant gram-negative bacterial strains were noted in the stools of some subjects who took trimethoprim or TMP-SMX.[46]

Doxycycline

Doxycycline is another broad-spectrum antibiotic used for prophylaxis of travelers' diarrhea because of its long half-life and excretion into the gut.[205] As with TMP-SMX, doxycycline in doses of 100 mg/day is superior to placebo for prevention of travelers' diarrhea.[47] However, increasing resistance of enteropathogens to doxycycline limits the usefulness of this drug in many parts of the world. Because photosensitivity is an adverse reaction of doxycycline, the drug probably should be avoided by patients traveling to sunny areas. Doxycycline also should not be given to pregnant women or children less than eight years of age.

Fluoroquinolones

The fluoroquinolones (ciprofloxacin, norfloxacin, ofloxacin, enoxacin) are orally-active against many enteropathogens. Two controlled trials which administered either placebo or norfloxacin 400 mg once a day to military personnel[48] or students[49] for 7 to 14 days documented significantly fewer cases of diarrhea with antimicrobial therapy, 2% to 7% versus 26% to 61%. Similarly, compared to placebo, norfloxacin 200 mg twice daily for 15 days also significantly decreased the incidence of diarrhea in travelers to "high risk" (Africa, Asia, Latin America) areas, but not to "low risk" (Mediterranean Europe and the Canary Islands) areas of the world. In this latter study, norfloxacin afforded a 70% protection rate from the development of gastrointestinal illness.[50]

Consistent with the data for norfloxacin, ciprofloxacin 500 mg once a day for seven days was significantly more effective than placebo in preventing travelers' diarrhea in volunteers visiting Tunisia for eight days.[51] Diarrhea occurred in 4% (n = 25) versus 64% (n = 28) of the subjects treated with ciprofloxacin and placebo, respectively; the first dose of medication was administered on the day before departure.

Few side effects have been associated with fluoroquinolones. Cutaneous reactions and photosensitivity have been reported.

Microbiologic Consequences of Prophylaxis

Several studies suggest widespread antimicrobial prophylaxis promotes the development of antibiotic-resistant bacterial strains. Such strains were first noted in patients using trimethoprim or TMP-SMX prophylactically for chronic urinary tract infections.[52-55] Resistant enteric flora also can develop rapidly after exposure to TMP-SMX in the gut. Students who received a two-week course of TMP or TMP-SMX showed resistant Enterobacteriaceae in their stool samples, a significant change when compared to stool samples taken before the onset of therapy and placebo controls.[56] These strains also were resistant to numerous other antibiotics including ampicillin, tetracycline, and streptomycin. Despite the development of resistance, TMP and TMP-SMX were still effective prophylactic agents; demonstrating that the spread of resistance does not always imply the spread of pathogenicity. This is corroborated by Sack et al. who found that doxycycline could prevent travelers' diarrhea in areas with endemic doxycycline-resistant *E. coli*.[57] In another survey, 71% of diarrheal stool samples from civilian and military personnel in the Far East contained enteric flora resistant to one or more broad-spectrum antibiotics.[58] These isolates also could transfer antibiotic resistance and pathogenicity to recipient *E. coli*.

Campylobacter species resistance to fluoroquinolones also has been reported. In 1989, quinolone resistance to *Campylobacter* species was 6% in Sweden and 11% in the Netherlands.[59] During treatment protocols of infectious diarrhea, development of resistance to norfloxacin was noted in six of nine patients with persisting *Campylobacter* species,[60] and two cases of relapse of travelers' diarrhea were associated with the development of *Campylobacter* resistance following a single dose of ciprofloxacin.[32] Fluoroquinolone resistance should be monitored carefully, as widespread resistance would limit the future utility of this class of antimicrobials.

Antibiotic prophylaxis also may increase the risk of severe, unrelated enteric infections. The removal of normal enteric flora from the gut eliminates an important defense against infection. Some authors have speculated that serious *Shigella* or *Salmonella* gastroenteritis may be more likely to occur following antimicrobial prophylaxis of travelers' diarrhea.[61]

Recommendations for Treatment and Prophylaxis

Travelers' diarrhea is generally a relatively mild (although inconvenient) and self-limiting disease that requires only symptomatic treatment and careful hygiene. Patients should be treated symptomatically with uncontaminated fruit juices, caffeine-free carbonated beverages, and salted crackers. If the patient desires rapid relief of mild symptoms, an antimotility agent may be used. Such agents may work faster than bismuth subsalicylate preparations.[22] Loperamide 4 mg may be given after the first unformed stool followed by one capsule (2 mg) after each unformed stool up to a maximum of 16 mg/day.[20] The most common adverse effect of bismuth subsalicylate is constipation, occurring in one-third of patients.[44] Black tongue and stools, encephalopathy,[62] and tinnitus also may occur with bismuth subsalicylate. Salicylate absorption may be a significant problem for elderly patients; those with renal dysfunction; those already taking aspirin products; or patients with bleeding disorders. Otherwise normal individuals may benefit from the convenience of a solid dosage form while avoiding adverse reactions and potential induction of resistance with antibiotics.

Antibacterials are appropriate only if diarrhea is moderate to severe (see Table 60.3). High-risk patients (e.g., those with immune dysfunction, achlorhydria, gastric resection, or those taking antacids) may benefit from prophylactic antibiotics. The most commonly used antibiotics, TMP-SMX or doxycycline may become ineffective as resistant strains evolve. Fluoroquinolones are effective for both the prophylaxis and treatment of travelers' diarrhea; however, they are currently not recommended for use in children. Drug-related complications such as rash (TMP-SMX) and photosensitivity (doxycycline) are infrequent but may be potentially serious, especially in a foreign environment.

The few travelers who fail to respond to these measures and whose symptoms include persistent malaise, fever, or bloody diarrhea may have systemic involvement requiring medical attention and antibiotic therapy.

Clinical Assessment

Treatment

1. E.J. and B.R., two healthy male pharmacy students, are spending their summer vacation traveling through the interior areas of Mexico. Except for a daily iron supplement which B.R. takes to "keep his strength up," neither traveler takes any medications. On the morning of the third day of their trip, B.R. complains of malaise and abdominal cramps. This soon progresses to frequent diarrheal stools (6–8 a day) with fever and chills. The next day he notes some improvement and blames the illness on jet lag. Afraid of dehydration, he continues to drink lots of tap water and iced tea. Why is B.R.'s illness consistent with traveler's diarrhea?

The incidence of infection is highest during the first week of arrival to the area,[16] with symptoms typically occurring within 24 to 48 hours following exposure to contaminated sources. Symptoms include cramps (60%), fever and/or vomiting (10%), bloody stools (15%), nausea, chills, and myalgias.[12,17,18] B.R. had been traveling for three days and his symptoms are consistent with traveler's diarrhea.

Diarrhea can range from one or two loose stools per day or may be severe enough to mimic a case of cholera with voluminous rice-water stools.[19] Left untreated, travelers' diarrhea is a self-limiting illness, with most travelers experiencing four to five loose or watery stools per day for three to five days.[12] As many as 60% of travelers with mild disease are well by the second day; about 20% will be confined to bed for one to two days; and 8% to 15% may be ill for longer than one week.[177] Rarely is travelers' diarrhea a life-threatening infection.

2. General Management. How should B.R. approach treating his diarrhea?

Although B.R.'s concern about dehydration is appropriate, his plan to increase his intake of contaminated tap water and iced tea is likely to prolong his symptoms. The first step is to avoid continued contamination. Common fecally-contaminated sources include tap water, ice cubes, raw milk, unpeeled fruits and vegetables, uncooked foods, raw seafood, and unreliable restaurants and street vendors. The two travelers should immediately change their eating habits to avoid these infectious sources. They should eat well-cooked foods and drink boiled or commercially-bottled beverages.

3. Forty-eight hours after the onset of diarrhea, B.R.'s symptoms have not improved. Afraid that he will not be able to sightsee or visit the beach, he considers trying the TMP-SMX tablets that his companion has brought along. He would like to take 1 double strength tablet BID for at least 3 days. His companion, however, disagrees with B.R.'s decision, suggesting he wait an additional 48–72 hours for the diarrhea to subside. What would be your approach to the therapy for B.R.'s attack of travelers' diarrhea?

Before using any agent for travelers' diarrhea, the severity of the attack must be assessed.[20] Although B.R. does not feel well enough to enjoy his vacation, he shows no signs of severe systemic complications or dehydration. Such symptoms would include highly concentrated, low volume urine; orthostatic hypotension; tachycardia; altered mental status; poor skin turgor; dry mucus membranes; persistent fever; malaise, and myalgias. Although B.R's moderate case of diarrhea has only slightly improved, it

should resolve within 24 to 72 hours if he avoids contaminated food or drink. B.R. should, therefore, avoid antibiotics and continue an uncontaminated diet as tolerated. Therapy should be instituted if symptoms persist; if he shows signs of dehydration and other systemic complications; or if there are any underlying disorders compromising normal gut defenses.

4. Listening to his companion, B.R. decided not to take the TMP-SMX and has diligently avoided ingesting contaminated foods and beverages. However, 72 hours later his diarrhea has increased to 10–12 watery stools per day and he is still having fevers and chills. Because he has not gotten better, and feels somewhat weaker, B.R. decides that antibiotics are indicated. He proposes to take ciprofloxacin which he has brought along. How should B.R. assess his treatment plan?

Both TMP-SMX and ciprofloxacin are effective therapies for travelers' diarrhea acquired in Mexico. Both are active against enterotoxigenic *E. coli* which is an important cause of travelers' diarrhea in Mexico.[40] However, *Campylobacter* which is also an important pathogen (particularly during the winter months and in the coastal areas of Mexico) is usually susceptible to ciprofloxacin, but not to TMP-SMX.[40] However, since B.R. and his companion are traveling during the summer months and in the noncoastal areas of Mexico, *Campylobacter* would be less likely. In addition, B.R. would have to be very conscientious to avoid taking ciprofloxacin at the same time as his iron supplement because of a significant reduction in the bioavailability of the antibiotic when taken concurrently with cations such as iron, aluminum, magnesium, and calcium.[208] Thus, in this setting TMP-SMX would be a good choice for B.R.

Prophylaxis

5. Upon hearing of the travel adventures of B.R. and E.J., 2 other classmates, J.G. and T.M., begin to make plans to vacation through the interior areas of Mexico where they would like to spend lots of time in the sun. However, they would like to avoid any bouts of travelers' diarrhea and wish to use something to prevent diarrhea (e.g., 1 double-strength TMP-SMX tablet/day) while in Mexico. Except for migraines for which T.M. will take 1–2 gm/day of aspirin, both travelers have no significant past medical history. What would be your recommendation regarding the need for antibiotic prophylaxis?

J.G.'s and T.M.'s concern about acquiring diarrhea is justified and nondrug prophylactic measures to avoid pathogens by carefully selecting food and drink should be undertaken. Even if prophylactic agents are used, the rate of recurrence of diarrhea will depend upon their dietary habits. For example, eating food purchased from street vendors or restaurants was associated with significantly more diarrhea than self-cooked meals even in patients using prophylactic bismuth subsalicylate.[39] Although antibiotics prevent 80% to 90% of travelers' diarrhea that would occur without prophylaxis,[40] they should be reserved for special situations where the risk of travelers' diarrhea outweighs the risk of adverse drug reactions, increased bacterial resistance, and excess expense.

6. Despite your recommendation not to use medications for the prevention of travelers' diarrhea, J.G. and T.M. insist on some drug regimen. What options exist for them?

For the reasons cited in Question 4, TMP-SMX would be a reasonable agent for the prophylaxis of travelers' diarrhea for J.G. and T.M. This antimicrobial agent would be preferable to agents such as doxycycline or fluoroquinolones which will predispose them to phototoxicity, particularly since they plan to spend lots of time in the sun. Phototoxicity has been reported in 2.4% to 10% of patients taking lomefloxacin, and reports of phototoxicity with ciprofloxacin also are available.[209]

While bismuth subsalicylate is also effective prophylaxis against travelers' diarrhea, it would not be the best agent for T.M. because concurrent administration with aspirin would increase her risk for salicylate toxicity.

Cryptosporidiosis

Pathophysiology

Cryptosporidiosis, a diarrheal disease occurring in both normal and immunocompromised patients, is caused by *Cryptosporidium parvum*, a coccidian, protozoan parasite, similar to toxoplasma. This organism was previously thought to infect animals only;[63] however, in the 1980s it was recognized as a significant pathogen in humans. The most severe form of this disease occurs in the immunocompromised patient. A less severe form occurs in the immunocompetent host (most often after traveling to the Caribbean or Africa) or in animal handlers. Cryptosporidiosis is the cause of severe gastroenteritis in about 15%[64] of human immunodeficiency virus (HIV) patients in the U.S. and up to 30% to 50% of Haitians and Africans with HIV.[65]

Infection usually is confined to the epithelial surfaces of the GI tract. Immunocompetent patients experience acute diarrhea, painful abdominal cramps, and nausea that usually resolve within ten days. However, patients with immune disorders may have a cholera-like syndrome with profuse watery diarrhea resulting in fluid losses of up to 10 L/day, malabsorption, and weight loss.[66–68] Although the disease requires only symptomatic intervention in normal hosts, cryptosporidiosis should be considered in any patient presenting with a several day history of watery diarrhea.[69]

Cryptosporidiosis is transmitted via the fecal-oral route. In addition to animal contact, spread may occur through patient contact, contaminated water supplies, contaminated milk, or day-care centers.[70,71]

Diagnosis

Diarrhea is a common manifestation in HIV patients; and *Cryptosporidium* is one of the most easily identified causes of diarrhea in these patients. Identification of the *Cryptosporidium* oocyte in a stool specimen is the "gold standard" of the differential diagnosis. The most specific and sensitive method for the diagnosis uses a commercially available fluorescein-labeled IgG monoclonal antibody (Meridan Diagnostics, Cincinnati, Ohio).

Clinical Presentation

7. L.S., a 30-year-old male, was admitted with complaints of abdominal cramps, diarrhea, and anorexia. This was only slightly responsive to diphenoxylate/atropine (Lomotil) and stool output exceeded 5 L/day for 2 weeks. A 15 kg weight loss also was noted. Six months earlier L.S. had been diagnosed as having HIV syndrome. On admission he was cachectic and severely dehydrated. Stool specimens were negative for blood, mucus leukocytes, bacteria, ova, and parasites but a small bowel biopsy later showed cryptosporidium. Cryptosporidial oocysts were later found in the stool. What patient characteristics suggest cryptosporidial infection in L.S.?

L.S. is an immunocompromised host at risk for numerous GI infections. Other possible etiologies include parasitic diarrhea (e.g., *Giardia lamblia*, *Isospora belli*), fungal overgrowth, or viruses. Human cryptosporidiosis is characterized by profuse watery diarrhea, cramping abdominal pain, and weight loss. Nausea, vomiting, and myalgias also are often present, but fever is relatively uncommon. Although the large fluid and weight losses reported are characteristic of cryptosporidiosis, dysentery and cholera also may cause similar outputs. Cryptosporidiosis also is typically un-

responsive to normal doses of antidiarrheals. However, this organism could have been easily isolated from the stool and a small bowel biopsy would have been unnecessary for diagnosis.

Physical examination usually will reveal signs of dehydration as seen in L.S. Fecal examination often discloses mucus, usually without blood or leukocytes. The cachexia seen in these patients is due to the malabsorption of B_{12}, fats, and carbohydrates.

Treatment

8. What antibiotic and supportive therapy should be prescribed for L.S.?

At present cryptosporidiosis is the only opportunistic infection in HIV patients for which there is no specific therapy.[72] Many different agents have been tried without any effect. However, some antimicrobial agents (spiramycin, clarithromycin, azithromycin, and paromomycin) may be of limited value. Eradication of this disease in HIV patients has proven difficult at best. Therefore, the goal of therapy is to suppress the cryptosporidiosis or treat the relapses and avoid dehydration, malnutrition, and electrolyte imbalances.

L.S. requires fluids, electrolytes, nutrition, and antibiotics. Although weight gain may occur with an enteral regimen, a cryptosporidiosis-related malabsorption syndrome has been noted and some patients may require total parenteral nutrition until diarrhea is controlled.[73]

Spiramycin

Cryptosporidiosis does not respond to the usual antiprotozoal agents such as metronidazole (Flagyl), thiabendazole (Mintezol), pyrimethamine-sulfadiazine, TMP-SMX, or pentamidine.[74] However, spiramycin, a macrolide antibiotic similar to erythromycin, has been used in Europe and Canada.[75] After receiving spiramycin, 1 gm orally three times a day, five HIV patients in this study had complete resolution of diarrhea and four had symptomatic improvement. Durations of therapy ranged from 1 to 16 weeks, depending upon the persistence of cryptosporidial oocysts in the stool. Unfortunately, treatment failures are common. Spontaneous remissions do occur even in HIV patients, making evaluation of therapy difficult in small patient populations.[76] In one study,[77] 28 of 37 immunocompromised patients (almost all having HIV) responded favorably to spiramycin 1 gm three times a day. Favorable response was defined as a reduction in the daily number of bowel movements to less than 50% of baseline and less than five. However, even if no cure is achieved, spiramycin may still control symptoms even if the pathogen persists.[78] Spiramycin is not commercially available in the U.S., but is obtainable as an orphan drug through the National Information Center for Orphan Drugs and Rare Diseases. Adverse effects, which include nausea, vomiting, diarrhea, epigastric pain, paresthesias, and acute colitis, are rare.[78,79]

Paromomycin

Paromomycin is readily available and is effective in the treatment of cryptosporidiosis in patients with AIDS.[80–82] Paromomycin is a broad spectrum, nonabsorbable aminoglycoside, similar to neomycin and kanamycin. More than 99% of the drug remains within the gastrointestinal tract after an oral dose. Paromomycin is commercially available from Parke Davis (Humatin) and is approved for the treatment of *Entameba histolytica*.

When paromomycin 1500 to 2000 mg/day was given for a median of 14 days to 12 HIV patients, 23 episodes of cryptosporidial diarrhea were successfully treated in these 12 patients.[81] Gastrointestinal disease was confirmed by stool examination or biopsy. All patients except one had over five stools daily. Complete response was defined as improvement in symptoms, elimination of diarrhea and weight gain. In a randomized, blinded-controlled trial in 11 AIDS patients with confirmed cryptosporidial diarrhea, patients received either placebo or paromomycin 500 mg every six hours for 14 days.[82] Efficacy was assessed by microbiological and clinical response. None of the patients randomized to placebo responded to therapy. In the paromomycin-treated patients there was one complete response and four partial responders. The mean time to response was 4.5 days. No adverse reactions were noted and excellent patient acceptance of therapy was noted.

Antidiarrheal agents such as kaolin plus pectin (Kaopectate), bismuth subsalicylate (Pepto Bismol), diphenoxylate (Lomotil), opiates, and loperamide (Imodium) are worth a trial. Moderate to high doses of loperamide (8 to 16 mg/day) sometimes can reduce diarrheal output and provide symptomatic relief until eradication or remission. Octreotide (Sandostatin), a long-acting parenteral analogue of somatostatin, has resulted in an adequate response to therapy in 76% of 21 patients with cryptosporidiosis when patients received 100 to 250 µg every eight hours subcutaneously.[83]

L.S. should receive a course of paromomycin 500 mg every six hours for 14 days as initial therapy. Serial stool samples should be checked for the presence of oocytes every two weeks during paromomycin therapy. If the diarrhea resolves and oocytes are not being shed, therapy can be discontinued and L.S. monitored closely. If he is still shedding oocytes or the diarrhea has not completely resolved, paromomycin 500 mg every six hours should be continued for another 14 days. Subsequently, paromomycin can be increased to 750 mg every six hours if still needed. For those patients who relapse after successfully completing a course of therapy, retreatment with paromomycin as described above is recommended. Unfortunately, many patients will maintain a biliary or other reservoir of *Cryptosporidium* and will relapse overtime. If L.S. continues to shed the *Cryptosporidium* oocyst and has multiple relapses, he may have to be maintained on paromomycin indefinitely.

Food Poisoning

Food poisoning is caused by the ingestion of food contaminated with bacteria or their toxins, parasites, viruses, or chemicals. Of the food-borne disease outbreaks reported to the Centers for Disease Control between 1972 and 1976, *Salmonella* species, *Staphylococcus aureus*, *Clostridium botulinum*, and *Clostridium perfringens* represented the four most common known causes of food poisoning.[138] Nonmicrobial food poisoning may be caused by mushrooms (Amanita, Psilocybe species), fish (ciguatera, scombroid, shellfish contaminants), and heavy metals (copper, tin, zinc, cadmium).[139-141] The syndromes of food-poisoning are characterized by acute onset (within 72 hours), abdominal cramps, vomiting, diarrhea, or neurologic complications.

Clues to the etiology of food poisoning include the details of the clinical syndrome which evolves, type of food ingested, season, and geographical location. For example, nausea and vomiting within one to six hours of consuming contaminated foods high in protein (ham, poultry, potato and egg salads, and cream-filled pastries) should lead to a strong suspicion of food poisoning due to *S. aureus* or *Bacillus cereus* (short incubation). These bacteria cause disease by preformed enterotoxins in food, thus accounting for the rapid onset of symptoms.

In contrast, *C. perfringens* should be suspected in a patient presenting with abdominal cramps and diarrhea occurring within 8 to 16 hours after consumption of contaminated meat (particularly beef and poultry) and gravies.[142]

9. E.P., a 55-year-old male, attended his company's annual picnic on a warm summer day in July. He was otherwise healthy except for mild hypertension. The evening following this picnic, he became nauseated and had several bouts of vomiting and watery stools which continued throughout the night. The next morning the symptoms had improved although he felt quite weak and light-headed. What may have caused this problem? How should it be treated?

The timing and severity of E.P.'s ailment are characteristic of an acute, self-limited problem. E.P.'s complaints are characteristic of food poisoning associated with improperly prepared or stored food. Staphylococcal contamination often occurs in the spring or summer and may contaminate ham, poultry, eggs, salads, or pastries that are stored where bacteria can proliferate.[142,143]

Since the majority of these outbreaks are self-limited in otherwise healthy patients, therapy is largely supportive. Antiperistaltic drugs should not be used because these would inhibit elimination of the toxin. Since E.P.'s symptoms have already subsided, most of the toxin has been eliminated.

Botulism, ciguatera (especially in tropical and subtropical areas), scombroid, or mushroom poisonings often produce life-threatening neurological manifestations such as paralysis, paresthesias, or hallucinations. Antibiotics are ineffective because the disease is caused by toxins. Acute or intensive care with an available antitoxin often is necessary.

E.P. should be reassured that he probably has a self-limiting case of food poisoning, and he should be warned not to eat improperly-stored or contaminated foods, including perishable foods exposed to warm temperatures for extended periods of time.

Enterohemorrhagic
Escherichia coli (E. coli 0157:H7)

Enterohemorrhagic *Escherichia coli* (also referred to as EHEC or Verotoxin-producing *E. coli*) is a broad term for strains of *E. coli* that produce Shiga-like toxins. These toxins are thought to be responsible for the hemolytic uremic syndrome (HUS) and thrombotic thrombocytopenic purpura (TTP) that accompany the gastroenteritis. This organism can cause clinical illness ranging from asymptomatic infection, mild and nonbloody diarrhea, hemorrhagic colitis, or hemolytic uremic syndrome and thrombotic thrombocytopenia purpura.[212] In the U.S., *E. coli* 0157:H7 is the most common serotype identified as causing this infection.[211] Acquisition of *E. coli* 0157:H7 is more common during the summer months and in specific geographical locations such as Washington, Minnesota, Canada, and Argentina.[211]

Enterohemorrhagic *E. coli* is spread primarily by contaminated beef products and milk and occasionally by fresh-pressed apple cider[213] and water.[214] The risk for *E. coli* 0157:H7 gastroenteritis is greater in children between the ages of two to ten years,[211] the elderly,[215] patients with a previous gastrectomy,[215] and females.[216] Person-to-person-transmission of the organism is responsible for secondary spread of enterohemorrhagic *E. coli*.

The incubation period for *E. coli* 0157:H7 infection ranges from five to eight days.[215] Watery diarrhea and abdominal cramping is later followed by streaks of blood or grossly bloody diarrhea; fever usually is absent.[211] The diarrhea usually lasts 9.1 ± 2 days in children and is longer than the 6.6 ± 1.1 days in adults.[217]

Therapy for enterohemorrhagic *E. coli* infection is primarily supportive. Antimotility agents should be avoided because of their potential to worsen the progression of the disease and the role of antibiotic therapy is controversial.

Clinical Presentation

10. P.J., a 3-year-old female, celebrated the fourth of July holiday with her family at a new fast-food restaurant in Seattle,

Washington. All the children ordered hamburgers and chocolate shakes, while the adults ordered fish and soft drinks. Four days later, P.J. was noted to have some watery diarrhea and complained of "stomach pains." The next day, the diarrhea was noted to contain some blood. Since this illness seems to be similar to an episode of diarrhea P.J. experienced about a year ago from which she recovered without incident, her parents decided it was not sufficiently severe to take her to her pediatrician. However, 5 days later P.J. has not improved and now has a temperature of 39 °C, dark urine, and decreased urine output. P.J. is taken to her pediatrician who noted P.J. was lethargic, pale, and had several bruises on her extremities. Blood tests reveal the following: blood urea nitrogen (BUN) 150 mg/dL (Normal: 5–25), serum creatinine (SrCr) 6 mg/dL (Normal: 0.3–0.7), serum potassium (K) 6.8 mEq/L (Normal: 3.5–5.5), white blood cell (WBC) count 20,000 × 10^9L (Normal: 5000–15,000), hemoglobin (Hgb) 5 gm/dL (Normal: 11–13), platelets 50,000 cells/mm³ (Normal: 150,000–350,000), and urinalysis shows hematuria and proteinuria. A stool specimen is negative for fecal leukocytes and a culture for GI pathogens is pending. The presumptive diagnosis for P.J. is enterohemorrhagic gastroenteritis complicated by the onset of HUS. What features of P.J.'s case are suggestive of enterohemorrhagic gastroenteritis that progressed to HUS? [SI units: BUN 53.55 mmol/L urea (Normal: 1.79–8.93); SrCr 530.4 μmol/L (Normal: 26.52–62.88); K 6.8 mmol/L (Normal: 3.5–5.5); WBC count 20 × 10^9/L (Normal: 5–15); Hgb 50 gm/L (Normal: 110–130); platelets 50 × 10^9/L (Normal: 150–350)]

Enterohemorrhagic gastroenteritis, particularly that caused by serotype *E. coli* 0157:H7 generally involves ingestion of undercooked ground beef or contaminated milk. A major outbreak of enterohemorrhagic gastroenteritis occurred in Washington state during the summer of 1993. The majority of these cases involved a fast-food restaurant chain that presumedly failed to heat the internal temperature of the hamburger patty sufficient to kill the pathogenic *E. coli* 0157:H7 strain. Several hundred people were affected by the gastroenteritis, many developed hemolytic uremic syndrome, several required dialysis, and a few died. Since hemolytic-uremic syndrome commonly appears during the winter months, Seattle pediatricians quickly suspected that the summer appearance of multiple cases of hemolytic uremic syndrome was unusual and justified an intensive search for the etiology of these cases. Due to their diligence, several tons of contaminated beef were seized and the state health department was able to limit the potential for significantly more numbers of people who might have become infected.

The typical clinical presentation of EHEC involves a four-day incubation period (range: 5 to 8 days), abdominal cramps, and watery nonbloody diarrhea that progresses to bloody diarrhea. It is, therefore, noteworthy that P.J. ate a hamburger at a fast-food restaurant in the summer, four days before the onset of her "stomach pains" and did not have blood in her diarrhea until the day after the onset of her diarrhea. Fever also is usually absent and P.J. did not develop a temperature of 39 °C until about five days after her onset of diarrhea. The progression of enterohemorrhagic *E. coli* gastroenteritis to hemolytic uremic syndrome typically becomes apparent about one week after the onset of diarrhea[215,218] and occurs in the summer months.[220]

The *E. coli* 1057:H7 gastroenteritis progresses to hemolytic uremic syndrome in about 10% of children[219] and in as many as 22% of adults.[215] Hemolytic uremic syndrome is characterized by the triad of microangiopathic hemolytic anemia, thrombocytopenia, and renal failure. On physical examination, P.J.'s pale appearance and the bruises on her extremities are consistent with anemia and thrombocytopenia, respectively. The P.J.'s dark urine perhaps results from the color imparted from bilirubin because of red cell lysis. P.J.'s decreased urine output and increased serum creatinine and BUN concentrations are suggestive of renal failure; and the absence of fecal leukocytes is consistent with infection caused by *E. coli* 0157:H7.[211]

Transmission

11. Why is it important to determine whether other family members also are having GI symptoms?

Since outbreaks of *E. coli* 0157:H7 gastroenteritis are linked to a common contaminated source(s), the source(s) must be identified to prevent further spread of infection and to identify other likely infected individuals. The Washington state outbreak in 1993 involved several cases of presumedly person to person transmission, therefore, the siblings and daycare playmates of P.J. also need to be evaluated. The potential for the progression of gastroenteritis to hemolytic uremic syndrome and thrombotic thrombocytopenia purpura is especially ominous because about 3% to 5% of children[219] and as many as 88% of elderly nursing home patients die from hemolytic uremic syndrome.[215] P.J.'s siblings especially need to be evaluated because they too ate similar food at the same fast-food restaurant. Their hamburgers perhaps were cooked at a sufficient temperature to kill the organism or perhaps their ground beef was from a different batch of prepared hamburger patties. Whether P.J.'s siblings and friends indeed ate the same food or whether P.J. was more susceptible to infection by the enterohemorrhagic *E. coli* is unknown without additional interviews and more patient-specific data.

Diagnosis

12. The results from the culture of P.J.'s stool specimen indicate that it is negative for *E. coli* 0157:H7. Does this mean she is not infected with this organism?

Although it is possible that P.J. does not have infection with *E. coli* 0157:H7, her history of present illness and clinical and laboratory manifestations are consistent with gastroenteritis due to EHEC that is now complicated by the onset of hemolytic uremic syndrome. Stool cultures may be negative because they were obtained more than six days after the onset of illness. Isolation of *E. coli* 0157:H7 has been found to be much more likely when stool cultures are obtained within six days of the onset of illness.[222] Sorbitol-MacConkey agar can be used as a screening test for *E. coli* 0157:H7, since unlike most *E. coli* found in stool, *E. coli* 0157:H7 does not ferment sorbitol.

Treatment

Antibiotics

13. Would antibiotics be a useful adjunct in the management of *E. coli* 0157:H7 infection?

The effect of antibiotics on the clinical course of *E. coli* 0157:H7 enteritis is controversial. Much interest has focused on the effect of antibiotics on the progression of gastroenteritis to hemolytic uremic syndrome. In one retrospective assessment[223] and one prospective[224] study, antibiotics did not increase the risk of hemolytic uremic syndrome. In another retrospective analysis, the administration of antibiotics, recognized to be effective for *Shigella* diarrhea, for more than 24 hours decreased the progression of enterohemorrhagic *E. coli* gastroenteritis to hemolytic uremic syndrome;[220] however, TMP-SMX increased the risk of progression to HUS[218] or increased the mortality.[215] Analysis of reports on the adverse influence of antibiotics on the course of *E. coli* 0157:H7 gastroenteritis must include an assessment of whether the population who received the antibiotics were more severely ill.[215,218] In light of these inconclusive studies, prospective, dou-

Table 60.4	Treatment of Shigella Infections[a,b]	
Drug	**Adults**	**Children[b]**
Ampicillin	500 mg QID	100 mg/kg/day (4 divided doses)
TMP-SMX[c]	160–800 mg BID	10 mg/kg/day TMP (2 divided doses)
Nalidixic acid	1 gm QID	55 mg/kg/day (4 divided doses)
Ciprofloxacin	500 mg BID	Not recommended
Norfloxacin	400 mg BID	Not recommended
Enoxacin	200 mg BID	Not recommended

a Adapted from reference 183. Duration of therapy for all agents listed is 5 days. Single dose therapies have been effective; see question 8.
b Fluoroquinolones are not approved for use in children.
c TMP-SMX = Trimethoprim-sulfamethoxazole.

ble-blind trials are needed to resolve the issue of whether antibiotic treatment for this infection is warranted.

Antimotility and Antidiarrheal Agents

14. Would antimotility or antidiarrheal agents be of benefit for *E. coli* 0157:H7 gastroenteritis?

The use of antidiarrheal agents for more than 24 hours can increase the risk of progression of *E. coli* 0157:H7 gastroenteritis to hemolytic uremic syndrome.[220] By reducing bowel motility, antimotility agents presumably decrease the clearance of organisms and increase the absorption of toxins;[220] however, the precise explanation for the increased risk is unknown.

Prevention

15. P. J. is discharged from the hospital without sequelae from this ordeal. What precautions can be taken to prevent infection with *E. coli* 0157:H7?

Since thorough cooking will kill this organism, meat should be well cooked (i.e., juices from meat should not be pink but should be clear) and unpasteurized milk products should not be ingested. Although thorough cooking of meats should be adequate, one outbreak of *E. coli* 0157:H7 gastroenteritis from precooked meat patties has been reported.[225] If infection occurs, person to person transmission may be prevented by good hygiene. Finally, passive or active immunoprophylaxis may be possible in the future.[226]

Antibiotic-Associated Pseudomembranous Colitis (AAPMC)

Pathophysiology

Antibiotic-associated pseudomembranous colitis is an uncommon, but potentially serious adverse reaction to almost any oral or parenteral antibiotic that alters colonic flora (see Table 60.5).[69] AAPMC is a specific form of *Clostridium difficile* pseudomembranous colitis. *C. difficile* pseudomembranous colitis may be caused by almost any antimicrobial agent and even some antineoplastic agents (see Table 60.5). Although many antibiotic agents cause gastrointestinal distress and diarrhea, AAPMC is a specific syndrome caused by an overgrowth of toxigenic strains of *C. difficile*. *C. difficile* is a toxin producing, spore forming anaerobe. Approximately 5% of normal adults carry this organism in their feces, but in small numbers.[145]

Clindamycin often is cited as a common predisposing antibiotic; however, it does not cause antibiotic-associated pseudomembranous colitis more frequently than ampicillin or cephalosporins (see Table 60.5).[146,147] AAPMC may occur less frequently after exposure to erythromycin, penicillins, tetracycline, or TMP-SMX.[147,148]

Although anaerobic bacteria are normal colonic inhabitants, this disease is directly related to the presence of *C. difficile* and its cytotoxins which disrupt mucosal integrity.[75] Spread occurs when contaminated hospital personnel or equipment expose susceptible patients.[150–153] Therefore, enteric isolation precautions are recommended to avoid further nosocomial infection.[154,155]

Clinical Presentation and Diagnosis

16. B.W., a 35-year-old female, is admitted to County Hospital with a diagnosis of bacterial meningitis. Upon arrival, she began a 2-week course of cefotaxime (Claforan) 1 gm IV Q 4 hr. On the day 12 of therapy, she noted abdominal cramping and pain, fever of 38.5 °C, and frequent loose stools. The diarrhea continued and blood appeared in the stools. The physician, suspecting pseudomembranous colitis, ordered stool cultures and began vancomycin 500 mg PO Q 6 hr. How would you differentiate antibiotic-associated pseudomembranous colitis from antibiotic-induced diarrhea in B.W.?

All of B.W.'s gastrointestinal symptoms are typical of antibiotic-associated pseudomembranous colitis.[155] The most common symptom is diarrhea, and in 10% blood can be found in the diarrheal stool.[155] Other common features include crampy abdominal pain, a leukocytosis, and an average temperature of 100 to 101 °F but fevers occasionally may reach as high as 105 °F. In approximately 50% of cases fecal leukocytes may be seen. Hypovolemia, dehydration, and hypoalbuminemia also may occur as a consequence of antibiotic-associated pseudomembranous colitis. Symptoms may appear from a few days after the start of therapy to ten weeks after discontinuation of the offending agent.[155,156]

Antibiotic-associated pseudomembranous colitis is a subset within the broader category of *C. difficile* colitis which includes colonization of newborns and patients who are being treated with antineoplastics, immunosuppressives, or antibiotics. *C. difficile* produces at least two antigenically distinct toxins. Toxin A is a lethal enterotoxin and toxin B is described as a cytotoxin. Positive diagnosis is confirmed by the isolation of *C. difficile* or its toxins from symptomatic patients. A positive *C. difficile* toxin assay is found in almost 100% of patients with AAPMC.[148] Culture of *C. difficile* also may be performed but identification takes several days, making the *C. difficile* toxin assay the preferred laboratory test.[157] ELISAs (rapid enzyme-linked immunosorbent assays) which rapidly detect both *C. difficile* toxins A and B are commonly used.[145] The diagnosis of AAPMC is most accurately made via endoscopy. Colonoscopy often is performed, but it is not manda-

Table 60.5	Antibiotics and Antineoplastic Agents Associated with Pseudomembranous Colitis[229]	
Antibiotics		
Amoxicillin		Methicillin
Amphotericin B		Metronidazole
Ampicillin[a]		Nafcillin
Carbenicillin		Neomycin
Cephalosporins[a,b]		Penicillin G
Chloramphenicol		Penicillin V
Clindamycin[a]		Rifampin
Cloxacillin		Trimethoprim-sulfamethoxazole
Erythromycin		Tetracycline
Gentamicin		Ticarcillin
Lincomycin		Tobramycin
Antineoplastic Agents		
Cyclophosphamide		Fluorouracil
Doxorubicin		Methotrexate

a Most frequently associated with pseudomembranous colitis.
b Includes cefazolin, cefotaxime, cefuroxime, cefoxitin, cefamandole, cephalexin, cephalothin, cephaloridine, cephradine, and moxalactam.

tory because characteristic pseudomembranes may be scattered throughout the colon and can be missed on examination.

Treatment

17. Why was vancomycin selected for therapy of B.W.'s antibiotic-associated pseudomembranous colitis and is it the best choice in this situation?

The first step in the management of most drug-related adverse reactions is to remove the offending drug. Discontinuation of B.W.'s antimeningitis therapy would, however, constitute incomplete therapy of this life-threatening disease. Therefore, drug therapy for her meningitis must continue while she receives therapy directed against *C. difficile*. Discontinuation or alteration of antibiotics is warranted for less severe infections. Antibiotic-associated pseudomembranous colitis resolves in approximately 25% of patients with fluid and electrolyte replacement and discontinuation of the offending agent.

Vancomycin. Severe cases of AAPMC must be treated with an anti-clostridial antibiotic. Vancomycin, metronidazole, and bacitracin have all been used with varying success (see Table 60.6). Some clinicians consider a seven to ten day course of vancomycin (125 to 500 mg PO QID) first-line therapy; however, many now prefer metronidazole because of lower cost.[147,155,158,160] This vancomycin regimen produces fecal concentrations that are several hundred times the concentration needed to inhibit toxin-producing strains of *C. difficile*.[158,161] Diarrhea or cramping usually subside within two to four days after onset of therapy and stool toxin titers become negative within one week. Although oral vancomycin is considered nonsystemic, measurable serum concentrations have been found in patients with both normal and compromised renal function.[162,163]

Metronidazole is equally as effective as vancomycin in the treatment of antibiotic-associated pseudomembranous colitis. In one study, no significant differences in relapse rates or treatment failures were noted among 94 patients receiving ten days of vancomycin or metronidazole.[164] Many clinicians prefer metronidazole (250 mg PO QID or 500 mg PO TID) as the drug of choice because of its significantly lower cost of therapy, unless the patient is critically ill. The use of vancomycin as drug of first choice in the critically ill patient has not been substantiated by any clinical trials and the definition of "critically ill" needs clarification. Metronidazole also has been successful in AAPMC patients who fail repeated courses of vancomycin.[165] Unlike vancomycin, metronidazole is absorbed systemically and must be excreted through the biliary tract before it reaches the site of infection, thus exposing the patient to the possibility of some systemic side effects. The most common adverse reactions include GI upset, metallic taste, dizziness, and irritability.[166] Rarely, disulfiram-like reactions will occur when alcohol is ingested concurrently with metronidazole. Reversible and rare peripheral neuropathies and seizures may occur when high doses are given for long periods.

Metronidazole probably would be preferable to vancomycin for treatment of B.W.'s AAPMC because of its considerably lower cost (see Table 60.6) and comparable effectiveness. Despite considerable clinical experience, vancomycin is no longer the agent of choice because of its high cost, bitter taste, and reports of relapse in up to 39% of its patients. Therefore, a ten-day course of metronidazole 500 mg three times daily should be initiated for B.W.

18. What other therapies are useful in the treatment of patients with AAPMC?

Bacitracin 25,000 units (about 500 mg) four times daily also has been used successfully but the published experience is lim-

Table 60.6	Costs of Drug Therapy for Antibiotic-Associated Pseudomembranous Colitis	
Drug	Regimen	Cost[a]
Bacitracin	25,000 units QID × 10 days	$85.75/10 days
Metronidazole (generic)	500 mg TID × 10 days	$2.34/10 days
Vancomycin (generic)	500 mg TID × 10 days	$173/10 days

[a] AWP Red Book 1995.

ited.[167,168] Bacitracin often is not readily available, the taste is unpleasant, and some strains of *C. difficile* are resistant to bacitracin.[169] When oral bacitracin 25,000 units four times a day was compared to vancomycin 500 mg four times a day in 30 patients who had *C. difficile* toxin isolated from the stool, bacitracin was significantly less effective than vancomycin in the eradication of *C. difficile* and its toxin from the stool.

Exchange resins such as cholestyramine presumably bind clostridial toxins.[171] Tedesco[172] successfully treated 11 patients with recurrent AAPMC (1 to 3 relapses) utilizing a tapering course of oral vancomycin with colestipol. Six weeks after therapy all of the patients were asymptomatic. A favorable response also was observed in a 4- and a 19-month-old treated with a prolonged course of cholestyramine with or without oral vancomycin.[173] Despite encouraging results in a few studies, these agents do not eradicate the pathogenic organisms and should be considered only for minor cases.[174]

Antidiarrheal Agents. Opiates and other antiperistaltic agents should be avoided in patients with AAPMC. Although these types of drugs may promote relief from the diarrheal symptoms, the GI tract may be damaged because of delayed toxin removal. Some cases of antibiotic-associated pseudomembranous colitis have deteriorated during therapy with antimotility medications.[175]

Teicoplanin is an investigational glycopeptide with good *in vitro* activity against *C. difficile*-associated disease.[176]

Recurrence

19. B.W. was discharged after successfully completing both her cefotaxime and metronidazole regimens. One week later she noted the return of abdominal pain and diarrhea. Her clinic physician assumed that this could not be related to AAPMC because she had responded to metronidazole. What is the likelihood that AAPMC has recurred? What would be appropriate therapy?

Relapse of antibiotic-associated pseudomembranous colitis is frequent despite the extreme sensitivity of *C. difficile* to antibiotics, the absence of metronidazole or vancomycin-resistant strains, and easily achievable bactericidal concentrations. Relapses occur in 10% to 20% of patients regardless of which antimicrobial has been selected for therapy.[167,177] Relapses generally occur one to four weeks after treatment has been discontinued and result either from the germination of dormant spores or reinfection with *C. difficile* from some external source.

Treatment

20. How should patients, such as B.W., who relapse after therapy for AAPMC be treated?

Relapses respond well to retreatment with either vancomycin or metronidazole if treatment is begun early enough. Patients whose symptoms do not improve after vancomycin can be treated successfully with metronidazole.[165] Similarly, those who fail metronidazole therapy may respond to vancomycin.[178,179] However, retreatment of relapses with the same drug also has been effective. Despite the number of documented successes, both vancomycin[180] and metronidazole under certain circumstances, actually may cause AAPMC.[181-183]

Some patients suffer from multiple relapses. No ideal treatment has yet been identified for these patients. Different approaches have been tried including a four to six week course with vancomycin after which the dose is tapered over a one to two month period[184] or the use of cholestyramine or other resins to bind the toxins after antimicrobial therapy has been finished. A combination of vancomycin and rifampin (600 mg PO BID) also has been used successfully for recurring AAPMC.[185]

An appropriate approach to B.W.'s relapse would be another seven to ten day course of metronidazole. Vancomycin can be a viable alternative despite its higher cost, bitter taste, and higher relapse rate.

21. Parenteral Drugs. If B.W. were unable to take oral antibiotics, what parenteral agents are available to treat her antibiotic-associated pseudomembranous colitis?

Adequate colonic antibiotic levels are necessary for treatment of AAPMC. If the oral route is inappropriate, the clinician must choose an agent that is either secreted or excreted into the gastrointestinal tract in its active form. Intravenous vancomycin would not be suitable in this situation because it is not secreted into the GI tract. Metronidazole is eliminated by both renal and hepatic routes and bactericidal concentrations equal to serum have been found in bile.[166] Although bacitracin also is eliminated throughout the biliary tract, the parenteral form is significantly more toxic than metronidazole.

Clinically, there are a few cases in which intravenous metronidazole (500 mg Q 6 to 8 hr)[186-188] or intravenous vancomycin (1 to 2 gm/day)[158,189] have been used to treat AAPMC. Bolton et al.[186] demonstrated that bactericidal concentrations of metronidazole were achievable in stool samples from patients with acute disease. Three patients with diarrhea who had a positive C. difficile culture and toxin assay were successfully treated. Kleinbeld et al.[187] described one C. difficile toxin-positive patient who became negative within a few days of IV metronidazole therapy. The patient subsequently completed therapy with oral metronidazole. In contrast, Guzman et al.[188] reported an unsuccessful attempt to treat AAPMC with IV metronidazole in a patient with an adynamic ileus. Vancomycin 500 mg IV every six hours cleared the toxin from the stool and improved AAPMC in one patient.[189] On the other hand, after IV vancomycin 1 gm/day, Tedesco et al.[158] were not able to detect vancomycin in a stool sample obtained from a colostomy, and eradication of C. difficile toxin was not achieved. In summary, the efficacy of IV metronidazole or vancomycin in the treatment of AAPMC is based upon limited anecdotal reports. Fekety[190] has recommended that if oral therapy is not possible, both IV metronidazole (500 mg IV Q 6 to 8 hr) and vancomycin be instituted. In adults, vancomycin 500 mg four times daily or metronidazole 500 mg every eight hours can be given through a nasogastric tube, via ileostomy or colostomy (if present), or by rectal enema. However, the efficacy of vancomycin (or metronidazole) enemas in patients with antibiotic-associated pseudomembranous colitis has not been established.

Campylobacter Infections

Campylobacter organisms are highly motile, comma shaped gram-negative bacilli. *Campylobacter pylori* and *Campylobacter fetus* now are recognized as the major causes of *Campylobacter* enteritis. Gastrointestinal disorders associated with *Campylobacter jejuni* are now recognized as the most common cause of bacterial diarrhea. *Campylobacter* enteritis occurs more frequently than either *Salmonella* and *Shigella* gastroenteritis.[191] Although newly recognized, the pathogen frequently is found in domestic animals and human infection may occur following consumption of improperly cooked or unpasteurized foods.[191]

22. M.U., a 25-year-old female college student, noted the onset of abdominal discomfort and headache late one evening. She reported eating fried chicken at a fast-food restaurant the evening of the initial episode. Early the next morning, she became febrile to 39 °C and then developed, chills, severe cramps, and numerous watery bowel movements that progressed to bloody stools. These symptoms continued for about 1 day and finally diminished 72 hours after the onset of the illness. C. jejuni was recovered from a stool sample taken by M.U.'s physician. About 1 week later, M.U. had another 3-day bout of the same illness, but she recovered uneventfully without drug therapy. What are the risk factors and symptoms of Campylobacter enteritis? Is antimicrobial therapy necessary?

Campylobacter enteritis may affect any age group but infection seems to be most common in children less than five years of age. Infection has been linked to ingestion of contaminated foods (usually poultry), unpasteurized milk, and contaminated water. Symptoms of *Campylobacter* enteritis are first noticed 24 to 72 hours following exposure. Several distinct features may suggest *Campylobacter*, including fever, malaise, waxing and waning of GI symptoms with recurrences of increasing severity, and bloody stools.[1]

Campylobacter enteritis usually is self-limited in normal adults and does not require antibiotics. The ideal treatment regimen for *Campylobacter* enteritis has not yet been delineated. When 15 adults and children with *Campylobacter* enteritis received 250 mg erythromycin four times a day for five days, the course of the disease and time to recovery was unaffected despite the rapid eradication of *Campylobacter* from the stool. Since it remains unclear whether erythromycin is significantly better than placebo, otherwise healthy patients should not receive erythromycin for an initial, uncomplicated episode. *In vitro* data have shown ciprofloxacin to be the most potent agent against *Campylobacter* when compared to erythromycin, TMP-SMX, nalidixic acid, doxycycline, and others.[193] Other anecdotal data suggest that chloramphenicol, aminoglycosides, and tetracycline may be effective in the treatment of this infection. Typically most strains of *Campylobacter* are resistant to penicillin, cephalosporins, and vancomycin.

Viral Gastroenteritis

Gastrointestinal illness that remains undiagnosed by usual means may be due to viral pathogens. Viral gastrointestinal infections afflict both adults and children and are the second leading cause of illness in this country, second only to viral respiratory illness.[198,199,207]

Clinical manifestations of acute viral gastroenteritis may range from mild illness of short duration to severe dehydration, especially in infants and young children. The two most important viral pathogens are Norwalk virus and rotavirus. Rotavirus may cause as many as 50% of all cases of infantile enteritis requiring hospitalization, and the Norwalk virus causes approximately one-third of all episodes of viral gastroenteritis in the U.S., occurring primarily among older children, adolescents, and adults.[199,200]

As with most viral illnesses, therapy is largely supportive until immune defenses remove the viral load. Since the morbidity and mortality associated with the viral gastroenteritides is primarily due to electrolyte imbalance and dehydration, supportive therapy is aimed at correcting these deficits.[228] The pathogen often affects whole communities, often in fall or winter.[201] Shellfish may be reservoirs for Norwalk virus especially if they are eaten raw or if they are improperly cooked.[201]

23. M.T., a 14-year-old female, has just begun babysitting for the neighborhood children. Before the Thanksgiving holiday, she had the opportunity to babysit M.K. and L.T., 1-year-olds from different families. While one of the children, M.K. was well, the other child, L.T. began having some watery diarrhea, fever, and vomiting. Despite having one ill child, the evening was uneventful, which M.T. attributed in part to her efficient system of changing diapers (i.e., changing both diapers at the same time). Two days later, M.K. (who was initially well) also began to have the same GI symptoms as L.T. Could M.K.'s illness have been acquired while at the babysitter's? What features of this case are characteristic of viral gastroenteritis caused by rotavirus?

It is very likely that M.K. acquired her gastrointestinal illness while at the babysitter's. The child with the watery diarrhea, fever, and vomiting was probably infected with the rotavirus. Since this virus is spread by the fecal-oral route, M.T.'s efficient system of changing diapers also played a role in transmitting the virus to M.K.

Features of this case which are characteristic of rotavirus gastroenteritis include the incubation period of 48 hours, occurrence during the cooler months of the year, and age of the children.[227] In the U.S., gastrointestinal illness caused by rotavirus is greatest in children six months to two years of age and is more common in the cooler months (October to April).[227] The GI symptoms also are characteristic of rotavirus infection.[228]

24. After hearing about the viral GI illness of the second child, M.T. wanted to know what she could do to prevent this from happening again. What would be your recommendation?

Since rotavirus is spread by the fecal-oral route, preventing the spread of this virus to others is directed at hygienic measures such as proper handwashing and disposal of contaminated items.[228] M.T. should be instructed to change the diaper of each child separately and to rigorously wash her hands each time. She should also use a washable surface as a changing table and clean it with disinfectant between uses. Some investigators have attempted to synthesize rotavirus vaccines.[202] Presently, their results are encouraging but it is too premature to determine their usefulness.[202,203]

Helicobacter Infections

Helicobacter pylori (previously *Campylobacter pylori*) is a small spiral shaped gram-negative rod. This pathogen is uniquely adapted for survival in the acidic environment of the stomach and is now known to be a cause of infection of the GI tract. *H. pylori* infection has now been firmly linked with antral gastritis, peptic ulcer disease, and possibly some gastric cancers.[194–196] About 95% to 100% of patients with peptic ulcer disease are infected with *H. pylori* (see Chapter 23: Upper Gastrointestinal Disorders).

Salmonella Gastroenteritis

Most cases of Salmonella infection in humans are acquired by the ingestion of contaminated food or water. Sources for Salmonella include poultry (chickens, turkeys, ducks), poultry products (eggs), meats (especially beef and pork), and dairy products (raw milk, powdered milk). Of the many Salmonella serotypes that have been identified, the most common are *S. typhimurium*, *S. enteritidis*, and *S. heidelberg*.[84] Salmonella infections frequently are divided into four major syndromes [i.e., bacteremia, localized infection, enterocolitis (gastroenteritis), enteric fever (classically caused by *S. typhi*), and the chronic carrier state].[84] This section will focus upon the latter three syndromes.

Enterocolitis is the most common form of Salmonella infection. Illness usually begins 6 to 48 hours after ingestion of contaminated food or water, with clinical manifestations that include diarrhea, nausea, vomiting, headache, fever, chills, and myalgias. Although loose stools (without blood) of moderate volume are a common finding, fulminant, bloody diarrhea also has been reported. Diarrhea generally persists for less than seven days.

Enteric fever is a clinical syndrome which classically is caused by *S. typhi*, although other Salmonella such as *S. paratyphi A* may cause this infection. When caused by *S. typhi*, enteric fever is referred to as typhoid fever. Manifestations of enteric fever include fever, headache, prostration, cough, splenomegaly, rash, and leukopenia.

Chronic carriage of Salmonellae is defined as the excretion of a Salmonella species for ≥1 year after an infection with this organism, or after initial isolation of Salmonellae from stool.[84] Eradication of Salmonella from chronic carriers is an important public health concern, as these individuals are the major reservoir for subsequent transmission of infection.

Gastroenteritis, Enteric Fever, and Chronic Carrier

24. R.G., a 3-year-old male, was taken to the ER by his mother because his fever and diarrhea of several days duration did not improve with fluids and Kaopectate. There, she was told that Salmonella had been found in R.G.'s stools. R.G. was hospitalized and hydrated with IV solutions but was not given any medications. Was R.G. properly treated?

Since Salmonella gastroenteritis is generally a self-limiting illness, supportive therapies (i.e., fluids and electrolytes) are the mainstay of treatment.[85] Antimicrobials usually are not indicated unless there is evidence of dissemination of infection beyond the GI tract. Besides being a self-limiting illness, additional reasons not to use antimicrobials as part of the management of uncomplicated Salmonella gastroenteritis are that: 1) antibiotics generally have not been proven to decrease the duration of illness; 2) antibiotics may actually prolong fecal excretion of pathogens; 3) they may increase the rate of relapse; 4) they may exacerbate asymptomatic infections by eradicating competitive natural flora; 5) they may promote widespread resistance to antibacterials; and 6) antibiotics will place patients at risk for side effects associated with drug therapy.[86–92]

Despite the aforementioned arguments against the use of antibiotics in Salmonella gastroenteritis, there is some information which suggests that antibiotics may be beneficial; however, a closer look at the data reveals suboptimal study designs or additional, undesirable effects of antimicrobial therapy.[93–97] For example, although TMP-SMX produced symptomatic relief in patients with Salmonella gastroenteritis, there was no placebo group for comparison.[95] Ciprofloxacin 500 mg or norfloxacin 400 mg both administered twice daily for the treatment of bacterial diarrhea of various etiologies (including Salmonella) either shortened the duration of diarrhea (1.9 versus 3.4 days)[98] or demonstrated bacterial eradication in more than 98% of patients.[97] Unfortunately, 4/16 (25%) patients with Salmonella gastroenteritis had bacteriologic relapses within three weeks after treatment,[98] and stool cultures may have been obtained too early after the completion of treatment (12 hours to 5 days) for accurate determination of bacterial eradication.[97] Finally, compared to placebo, norfloxacin (400 mg PO BID for 5 days) was clinically more effective than placebo in patients with acute diarrhea; however, there was a delay in the elimination of Salmonella in the norfloxacin treated patients.[60] More disturbing in this study was the isolation of norfloxacin-resistant Salmonella species in six of nine patients treated with this antibiotic.[60]

Treatment of convalescent carriers of Salmonella with antibiotics also has been tried in order to eliminate potential sources for future outbreaks of infection, however, the validity of this hypothesis is not well documented.[98] The efficacy of ciprofloxacin 500 to 750 mg orally twice daily for 7 to 14 days in this setting is controversial. For example, although ciprofloxacin was an effective adjunctive measure in the control of an outbreak of Salmonella gastroenteritis,[99] another study documented bacteriologic relapse in 7/11 (64%) subjects within three weeks of therapy, some of whom experienced a longer duration of excretion of Salmonella species.[100] Furthermore, norfloxacin (400 mg BID) was not effective in shortening the carrier stage during an outbreak of *S. typhimurium* gastroenteritis.[101]

Patients such as R.G. with mild to moderate episodes of Salmonella gastroenteritis require only symptomatic treatment. High-risk patients (failure to thrive infants, immunocompromised hosts) may benefit from antibiotics even if disease is mild because antimicrobial therapy may prevent systemic spread.[102] When antibiotics are indicated for gastroenteritis, ampicillin, TMP-SMX, third-generation cephalosporins, and the fluoroquinolones are effective therapies.[83,103,104]

In contrast to the management of uncomplicated enterocolitis, antimicrobial treatment of enteric fever will shorten the duration of illness.[84] At least two weeks of antimicrobial therapy are recommended. Depending upon susceptibility patterns in specific areas of the world, chloramphenicol, ampicillin, amoxicillin, TMP-SMX, and third-generation cephalosporins are effective therapies. Open studies also have demonstrated the efficacy of ciprofloxacin and ofloxacin in the management of enteric fever,[105,106] and a small sample of patients also were effectively treated with a short course (3 days) of parenteral ceftriaxone; further confirmation of this data is necessary.[107]

Although most patients excrete viable organisms for only three to four weeks following recovery, 1% to 3% will become chronic carriers of *S. typhi*, harboring organisms in the biliary tract.[84] Abnormal biliary tracts or cholelithiasis often are associated with the chronic carrier state. If the diseased gallbladder is surgically removed, high dose ampicillin (6 to 8 gm/day) is recommended immediately before and two weeks following surgery.[84] Treatment is unnecessary in asymptomatic patients. If surgery is contraindicated, and if the patient remains symptomatic or is a public health problem, sterilization of the gall bladder may be achieved by using antibiotics that concentrate in the biliary tract and that are active against Salmonella. Cure of the chronic carrier state has been achieved in 50% to 90% of patients treated with various antimicrobials.[96,108–110] Various oral therapies for chronic carriers which have been recommended include ampicillin 1.5 gm four times a day plus probenecid for six weeks,[111] ampicillin 2 gm four times a day, amoxicillin 2 gm three times a day, or TMP-SMX 160/800 mg twice a day for at least four weeks in patients with normal gallbladder function.[112] A limited number of chronic carriers treated with ciprofloxacin (500 to 750 mg BID for 3 to 4 weeks)[113–115] or norfloxacin (400 mg BID for 4 weeks)[116] were cured at follow-up 10 to 12 months later.

Prevention

Recently, an oral vaccine for the prevention of typhoid fever has been licensed for use in the U.S.[117] However, since the vaccine is not fully protective, good hygiene still is necessary for the prevention of Salmonella infections.

Shigella Gastroenteritis

Shigella are gram-negative bacilli which cause intestinal disease primarily by penetration of the colonic mucosa; which is followed by multiplication within the mucosa and subsequent destruction of the superficial tissue.[118] In addition, the production of toxins probably plays a role in the tissue destruction associated with this infection, as well as the watery diarrhea seen during the early stages of the illness.[118] Gastroenteritis due to Shigella is a leading cause of pediatric diarrhea in both industrialized and under-developed areas of the world.[119] Spread of Shigella is via direct patient contact, contaminated food and water, or houseflies.[119] Most outbreaks occur in institutional settings such as day care centers or long-term care facilities, which in part is explained by the fact that only a small inoculum of organisms (as few as 200 viable cells) can cause disease in healthy adults.[118] Left untreated, gastroenteritis due to Shigella is usually self-limiting, with clinical illness lasting approximately seven days.[118] Early on in this infection patients present with fever, abdominal cramping, and voluminous watery diarrhea; symptoms suggestive of infection involving the small bowel. These symptoms are then followed by a decrease in fever, decrease in the volume of stool (which also becomes bloody and mucoid), fecal urgency, and tenesmus.

Treatment

Antimicrobial therapy decreases the duration and severity of illness associated with Shigella gastroenteritis.[120,124] Since infection is usually self-limiting, one approach to therapy is to treat only moderate or severe cases with antibiotics.[121,122] In contrast, other experts feel that shigellosis should be treated in order to prevent person-to-person transmission and subsequent morbidity in other individuals.[118]

Most studies which evaluated the efficacy of antimicrobials for the treatment of gastroenteritis due to Shigella utilized a five-day course of therapy; although single dose regimens also have been effective. Selection of a specific antimicrobial agent for shigellosis in part is based upon the safety of the antibiotic, changing susceptibility patterns of these organisms to antibiotics, and cost of therapy. Agents which have been found to be efficacious for the treatment of gastroenteritis due to Shigella include trimethoprim (200 mg BID for 5 days),[123] chloramphenicol,[118] tetracycline,[124] ampicillin,[121,125] TMP-SMX,[127,200] nalidixic acid,[118–126] and more recently, the fluoroquinolones[24] (see Table 60.4). Chloramphenicol should be used as a last alternative because of potentially severe side effects which include dose-related and nondose-related blood dyscrasia.

The increasing frequency of strains of Shigella which are resistant to conventional antimicrobials[7,127] is a worldwide problem which is not only limited to developing countries. A recent study demonstrated that 20% of TMP-SMX-resistant Shigella in the U.S. were associated with foreign travel.[128] Although the fluoroquinolones maintain antibacterial activity against strains of Shigella which are resistant to conventional antimicrobials; unfortunately, the current cost of these agents will limit their routine availability in developing countries.[24] Nevertheless, several studies demonstrate the efficacy of the fluoroquinolones in adults with gastroenteritis due to various species of Shigella. A five-day course of ciprofloxacin 500 mg twice a day[120] or norfloxacin 400 mg twice daily[129] were found to be clinically as effective as the comparative regimens of ampicillin 500 mg four times daily and nalidixic acid 1 gm three times daily, respectively, in patients with shigellosis. The only significant difference between these therapies was that bacterial eradication from stool was significantly better with norfloxacin on day three of the study.[129]

In an effort to shorten the duration of therapy for shigellosis, a strategy which would improve compliance and decrease the cost of therapy, several investigators have evaluated the efficacy of a single dose of antibiotic in the management of this infection. Single doses of tetracycline (2.5 gm)[124] or trimethoprim (600 mg)[123] have been found effective. More recently, a single 800 mg dose of norfloxacin (n = 29) was as effective as a standard five-day regimen of TMP-SMX (160/800 mg) twice a day (n = 26) in adult outpatients infected primarily with *S. flexneri*; however, both agents appeared to be less effective in subjects with more severe illness.[130] A single 1 gm dose of oral ciprofloxacin was found to be as effective as a conventional five-day regimen of ciprofloxacin 500 mg twice daily in adults with gastroenteritis due to Shigella species, however, the efficacy did not extend to *S. dysenteriae* type 1.[131] The authors postulated that the reduced clinical efficacy of a single dose of ciprofloxacin (as compared to a 5-day course of ciprofloxacin) against *S. dysenteriae* type 1 may be related to the reduced antimicrobial activity against this particular species of Shigella (in comparison to other species of Shigella).

Although the use of antimotility agents in shigellosis is not recommended in the treatment of dysentery,[8] a recent study demonstrated the efficacy and lack of adverse clinical consequences of ciprofloxacin (500 mg BID for 3 days) with loperamide (4 mg load, followed by 2 mg after each loose stool for a maximum of 16 mg/day) in adults with bacillary dysentery.[132] In this study, compared to a regimen consisting of placebo plus ciprofloxacin, the addition of loperamide to ciprofloxacin significantly decreased the median duration of diarrhea and number of stools in patients with dysentery due to Shigella, an effect which was not observed in patients with dysentery due to other enteric pathogens.

Currently, the fluoroquinolones are not recommended in children because lesions on cartilage tissue have been reported in animals.[104] However, a Scientific Working Group of the World Health Organization[133] concluded that further clinical studies with quinolones in children would be appropriate for two reasons. First, since very high concentrations of these agents are achieved in the feces, it is possible that one or two doses, a dosage which is much smaller than that used in animal trials, may constitute effective therapy. Second, nalidixic acid currently is approved for use in children and in some areas is considered the drug of choice for shigellosis; no reports of major adverse effects have been associated with this drug. Furthermore, nalidixic acid has been found to be effective for the treatment of shigellosis in children.[126]

Finally, beta-lactam compounds which have been found to be effective treatment for shigellosis include a five-day course of intramuscular ceftriaxone (50 mg/kg/day) in children[153] and amdinocillin pivoxil.[24] Amoxicillin may be ineffective despite serum concentrations that exceed those of ampicillin.[135] Other lesser-known agents that have been used successfully but are not widely recognized include furazolidone (unavailable in the U.S.) and bicozamycin.[135,136]

References

1 **Gorbach SL.** Infectious diarrhea. In: Sleisenger MH, Fortran JS, eds. Gastrointestinal Diseases. 3rd ed. Philadelphia: WB Saunders; 1983:925.

2 **Greenough WB, Maung-U K.** Oral rehydration therapy. In: Michael Field, ed. Diarrheal Diseases. New York: Elsevier Science Publishing; 1991.

3 **Esposito G et al.** Influence of the transport of amino acids on glucose and sodium transport across the small intestine of the rat. Experientia. 1964;20: 122.

4 **Schults SG, Zausky R.** Interactions between active sodium transport and active amino acid transport in isolated rabbit ileum. Nature. 1965;205:292.

5 **Pierce NF et al.** Replacement of water and electrolyte losses in cholera by an oral-electrolyte solution. Ann Intern Med. 1969;70:1173.

6 **Anonymous.** Oral fluids for rehydration. Med Lett Drugs Ther. 1987;29:63.

7 **Murray BE.** Resistance of Shigella, Salmonella and other selected enteric pathogens to antimicrobial agents. Rev Inf Dis. 1986;8(Suppl. 2):172.

8 **DuPont HL, Hormick RB.** Adverse effects of Lomotil therapy in Shigellosis. JAMA. 1973;226:1525.

9 **Satterwhite TK, DuPont HL.** Infectious diarrhea in office practice. Med Clin North Am. 1983;67:203.

10 **Hart LL.** Constipation and diarrhea. In: Katcher BSet al., eds. Applied Therapeutics: The Clinical Use of Drugs. 3rd ed. Vancouver: Applied Therapeutics, Inc.; 1983:101.

11 **Portnoy BL et al.** Antidiarrheal agents in the treatment of acute diarrhea in children. JAMA. 1976;236:844.

12 **Ericsson CD et al.** Travelers' diarrhea: approaches to prevention and treatment. Clin Infect Dis. 1993;16:616.

13 **Gorbach SL et al.** Travelers' diarrhea. Consensus development statement. National Institutes of Health. 1985;5:1.

14 **MacDonald KL, Cohen M.** Epidemiology of travelers' diarrhea. Rev Inf Dis. 1986;8(Suppl. 2):S117.

15 **DuPont HL et al.** Diarrhea of travelers to Mexico. Am J Epidemiol. 1977;105: 37.

16 **Taylor DN et al.** Treatment of travelers' diarrhea: ciprofloxacin plus loperamide compared with ciprofloxacin alone. Ann Intern Med. 1991;114:731.

17 **Lifshitz F et al.** Carbohydrate intolerance in infants with diarrhea. J Pediatr. 1971;79–760.

18 **Borgstrom B et al.** Studies of intestinal digestion and absorption in the human. J Clin Invest. 1957;36:1521.

19 **Merson MH et al.** Disease due to enterotoxigenic *Escherichia coli* in Bangladesh adults: clinical aspects and a controlled trial of tetracycline. J Infect Dis. 1980;141:702.

20 **DuPont HL et al.** Chemotherapy and chemoprophylaxis of travelers' diarrhea. Ann Intern Med. 1985;102:260.

21 **Ericsson CD et al.** Treatment of travelers' diarrhea with sulfamethoxazole and trimethoprim and loperamide. JAMA. 1990;263:257.

22 **Johnson PC et al.** Comparison of loperamide with bismuth subsalicylate for the treatment of acute travelers' diarrhea. JAMA. 1986;255:757.

23 **Gorbach SL.** Bismuth therapy in gastrointestinal diseases. Gastroenterology. 1990;99:863.

24 **Salam MA et al.** Antimicrobial therapy for shigellosis. Clin Infect Dis. 1991;13(Suppl. 4):S332.

25 **Van Loon FPL et al.** Double-blind trial of loperamide for treating acute watery diarrhea in expatriates in Bangladesh. Gut. 1989;30:492.

26 **Ericsson CD et al.** Optimal dosing of trimethoprim-sulfamethoxazole when used with loperamide to treat travelers' diarrhea. Antimicrob Agents Chemother. 1992;36:2821.

27 **Travelers' diarrhea.** JAMA. 1985; 253:2700. Consensus Conference.

28 **DuPont HL et al.** Symptomatic treatment of diarrhea with bismuth subsalicylate among students attending a Mexican university. Gastroenterology. 1977;73:715.

29 **Steffen R et al.** Travelers' diarrhea in West Africa and Mexico: fecal transport systems and liquid bismuth subsalicylate for self-therapy. J Infect Dis. 1988;157:1008.

30 **DuPont HL et al.** Zaldaride maleate, an intestinal calmodulin inhibitor, in the therapy of travelers' diarrhea. Gastroenterology. 1993;104:709.

31 **Sack RB.** Antimicrobial prophylaxis of travelers' diarrhea: a summary of studies using doxycycline or trimethoprim and sulfamethoxazole. Scand J Gastroenterol. 1983;84(Suppl.):111.

32 **DuPont HL et al.** Treatment of travelers' diarrhea with trimethoprim/sulfamethoxazole and with trimethoprim alone. N Engl J Med. 1982;307:841.

33 **Wistrom J et al.** Short-term self-treatment of travelers' diarrhea with norfloxacin: a placebo-controlled study. J Antimicrob Chemother. 1989;23:905.

34 **Ericsson CD et al.** Ciprofloxacin or trimethoprim/sulfamethoxazole as initial therapy for travelers' diarrhea. Ann Intern Med. 1987;106:216.

35 **DuPont HL et al.** Five versus three days of ofloxacin therapy for travelers' diarrhea: a placebo controlled study. Antimicrob Agents Chemother. 1992; 36:87.

36 **Steffen R et al.** Efficacy and toxicity of fleroxacin in the treatment of travelers' diarrhea. Am J Med. 1993;94 (Suppl. 3A):182.

37 **DuPont HL et al.** Oral aztreonam for bacterial diarrhea in travelers to Mexico. JAMA. 1992;267:1932.

38 **Petruccelli BP et al.** Treatment of travelers' diarrhea with ciprofloxacin and loperamide. J Infect Dis. 1992;165: 557.

39 **Ericsson CD et al.** The role of location of food consumption in the prevention of travelers' diarrhea in Mexico. Gastroenterology. 1980;79:812.

40 **DuPont HL et al.** Prevention and treatment of travelers' diarrhea. N Engl J Med. 1993;328:1821.

41 **Advice for travelers.** Med Lett Drugs Ther. 1992;34:41.

42 **DuPont HL et al.** Prevention of travelers' diarrhea by the tablet formulation of bismuth subsalicylate. JAMA. 1987; 257:1347.

43 **Steffen R et al.** Prevention of travelers' diarrhea by the tablet form of bismuth subsalicylate. Antimicrob Agents Chemother. 1986;29:625.

44 **DuPont HL, Sullivan P.** Prevention of travelers' diarrhea (emporiatric enteritis): prophylactic administration of subsalicylate bismuth. JAMA. 1980; 243:237.

45 **DuPont HL et al.** Prevention of travelers' diarrhea with trimethoprim/sulfamethoxazole and trimethoprim alone. Gastroenterology. 1983;84:75.

46 **DuPont HL et al.** Prevention of travelers' diarrhea with trimethoprim/sulfamethoxazole. Rev Inf Dis. 1982;4: 533.

47 **Sack DA et al.** Prophylactic doxycycline for travelers' diarrhea. N Engl J Med. 1978;298:758.

48 **Scott DA et al.** Norfloxacin for the prophylaxis of travelers' diarrhea in U.S. military personnel. Am J Trop Med Hyg. 1990;42:160.

49 **Johnson PC et al.** Lack of emergence

of resistant fecal flora during successful prophylaxis of travelers' diarrhea with norfloxacin. Antimicrob Agents Chemother. 1986;30:671.

50 **Wistrom J et al.** Norfloxacin versus placebo for prophylaxis against travelers' diarrhea. J Antimicrob Chemother. 1987;20:563.

51 **Rademaker CMA et al.** Results of a double-blind placebo-controlled study using ciprofloxacin for prevention of travelers' diarrhea. Eur J Clin Microbiol Infect Dis. 1989;8:690.

52 **Person NJ et al.** Emergence of trimethoprim resistant enterobacteria in patients receiving long-term cotrimoxazole for the control of intractable urinary tract infection. Lancet. 1979;2:1205.

53 **Towner KJ et al.** Increasing importance of plasmid-mediated trimethoprim resistance in enterobacteria: two six-month clinical surveys. Br Med J (Clin Res). 1980;280:517.

54 **Houvinen P, Toivanen P.** Trimethoprim resistance in Finland after three years' use of plain trimethoprim. Br Med J (Clin Res). 1980;280:72.

55 **Dornbusch K, Toivanen P.** Effect of trimethoprim or trimethoprim/sulfamethoxazole usage on the emergence of trimethoprim resistance in urinary tract pathogens. Scand J Infect Dis. 1981;13:203.

56 **Murray BE et al.** Emergence of high-level trimethoprim resistance in fecal *Escherichia coli* during administration of trimethoprim or trimethoprim/sulfamethoxazole. N Engl J Med. 1982;306:130.

57 **Sack RB et al.** Doxycycline prophylaxis of travelers' diarrhea in Honduras, an area where resistance to doxycycline is common among enterotoxigenic *Escherichia coli*. Am J Trop Med Hyg. 1984;33:460.

58 **Echeverria P et al.** Antimicrobial resistance and enterotoxin production among isolates of *Escherichia coli* in the far east. Lancet. 1978;2:589.

59 **Endtz HP et al.** Quinolone resistance in campylobacter isolated from man and poultry following the introduction of fluoroquinolones in veterinary medicine. J Antimicrob Chemother. 1991;27:199.

60 **Wistrom J et al.** Empiric treatment of acute diarrheal disease with norfloxacin. A randomized, placebo-controlled study. Ann Intern Med. 1992;117:202.

61 **Guerant RL et al.** Doxycycline for travelers' diarrhea: risks and benefits. N Engl J Med. 1978;299–683.

62 **Mendelowitz PC et al.** Bismuth absorption and myoclonic encephalopathy during bismuth subsalicylate therapy. Ann Intern Med. 1990;112:140.

63 **Navin TR, Juraneck DD.** Cryptosporidiosis: clinical, epidemiological, and parasitological review. Rev Inf Dis. 1984;6:313.

64 **Laughon BE et al.** Prevalence of enteric pathogens in homosexual men with and without acquired immunodeficiency syndrome. Gastroenterology. 1988;94:984–91.

65 **Soave R.** Cryptosporidiosis and isosporiasis in patients with AIDS. Infect Dis Clin North Am. 1988;2:485–93.

66 **Case records of Massachusetts General Hospital.** Case 39-1985. N Engl J Med. 1985;313:805.

67 **D'antonio RG et al.** A waterbourne outbreak of cryptosporidiosis in normal hosts. Ann Intern Med. 1985;103:886.

68 **Wolfson JS, Richter JM.** Cryptosporidiosis in immunocompetent patients. N Engl J Med. 1985;312:1278.

69 **DuPont HL.** Cryptosporidiosis and the healthy host. N Engl J Med. 1985;312:1319.

70 **Borman S.** Accidental infection of a researcher with human cryptosporidium. J Infect Dis. 1983;148:772.

71 **Centers for Disease Control.** Cryptosporidiosis among children attending day care centers: Georgia, Pennsylvania, Michigan, California, New Mexico. MMWR. 1984;33:599.

72 **Gellin BG, Save R.** Coccidian infections in AIDS: Toxoplasmosis, cryptosporidiosis and Isosporiasis. Med Clin North Am. 1992;76:205–34.

73 **Mata L et al.** Cryptosporidiosis in children from highland Costa Rica rural and urban areas. Am J Trop Med Hyg. 1984;33:24.

74 **Soave R et al.** Cryptosporidiosis in homosexual men. Ann Intern Med. 1984;100:504.

75 **Portnoy D et al.** Treatment of intestinal cryptosporidiosis with spiramycin. Ann Intern Med. 1984;101:202.

76 **Armstrong DA et al.** Treatment of infections in patients with the acquired immunodeficiency syndrome. Ann Intern Med. 1985;103:738.

77 **Moskovitz BL et al.** Spiramycin therapy for cryptosporidial diarrhea in immunocompromised patients. J Antimicrob Therapy. 1988;22(Suppl. B):189.

78 **Center for Disease Control update: treatment of cryptosporidiosis in patients with acquired immunodeficiency syndrome (AIDS).** MMWR. 1984;33:117.

79 **Decaux GM, Devroede C.** Acute colitis related to spiramycin. Lancet. 1978;2:993.

80 **Clezy K et al.** Paromomycin for the treatment of cryptosporidial diarrhea in AIDS patients. AIDS. 1991;5:1146.

81 **Gathe J et al.** Treatment of gastrointestinal cryptosporidiosis with paromomycin. In: Program and abstracts: VI International conference on AIDS (San Francisco). San Francisco: University of California; 1990:2121.

82 **Kanyok T et al.** Preliminary results of a randomized, blinded, control study of paromomycin versus placebo for the treatment of cryptosporidial diarrhea in AIDS patients. IX Intl Conf AIDS IVth STD World Congress. Berlin, Germany: 7–11 June 1993. Abstract 5969.

83 **Romeu J et al.** Efficacy of octreotide in the management of chronic diarrhea in AIDS. AIDS. 1991;5:1495–499.

84 **Hook EW.** Salmonella species (including typhoid fever). In: Mandell et al., eds. Principles and Practice of Infectious Diseases. 3rd ed. New York: Churchill Livingstone; 1990:1700.

85 **Gianella RA, Formal SB.** Pathogenesis of salmonellosis. J Clin Invest. 1973;52:441.

86 **Asenkoff B, Benett JV.** Effect of antibiotic therapy in acute salmonellosis on the fecal excretion of salmonella. N Engl J Med. 1969;281:636.

87 **Rosenthal SJ.** Exacerbation of salmonella gastroenteritis due to ampicillin. N Engl J Med. 1969;280:147.

88 **Clementi KJ.** Treatment of salmonella carriers with trimethoprim/sulfamethoxazole. Can Med Assoc J. 1975;28:1343.

89 **Dixon JMS.** Effect of antibiotic treatment on duration and excretion of *Salmonella typhimurium* by children. Br Med J (Clin Res). 1965;2:1343.

90 **Rosenstein BJ.** Salmonellosis in children: epidemiologic and therapeutic considerations. J Pediatr. 1967;70:1.

91 **Nelson JD et al.** Treatment of salmonella gastroenteritis with ampicillin, amoxicillin, or placebo. Pediatrics. 1980;65:1125.

92 **Wilcox MH et al.** Quinolones and salmonella gastroenteritis. J Antimicrob Chemother. 1989;23:789.

93 **Abrams IF et al.** A salmonella Newport outbreak in a premature nursery with a one-year follow-up: effect of ampicillin following bacteriologic failure of response to kanamycin. Pediatrics. 1966;37:616.

94 **Enat R et al.** Treatment of *Salmonella typhimurium* salmonellosis. Lancet. 1978;2:638.

95 **Geddes AM et al.** Evaluation of trimethoprim/sulfamethoxazole in the treatment of salmonella infections. Br Med J. 1971;3:451.

96 **Kaye D et al.** Treatment of chronic enteric carriers of *Salmonella typhosa* with ampicillin. Ann NY Acad Sci. 1967;145:429.

97 **Asperilla MO et al.** Quinolone antibiotics in the treatment of salmonella infections. Rev Inf Dis. 1990;12:873.

98 **Jewes LA.** Antimicrobial therapy of non-typhi salmonella and shigella infection. J Antimicrob Chemother. 1987;19:557.

99 **Ahmad F et al.** Use of ciprofloxacin to control a salmonella outbreak in a long-stay psychiatric hospital. J Hosp Infect. 1991;17:171.

100 **Neill MA et al.** Failure of ciprofloxacin to eradicate convalescent fecal excretion after acute salmonellosis: experience during an outbreak in health care workers. Ann Intern Med. 1991;114:195.

101 **Carlstedt G et al.** Norfloxacin treatment of salmonellosis does not shorten the carrier stage. Scand J Infect Dis. 1990;22:553.

102 **Sanders DY et al.** Chronic salmonellosis in infancy. Clin Pediatr (Phila). 1974;8:640.

103 **Kazemi M et al.** A controlled trial comparing sulfamethoxazole, trimethoprim, ampicillin and no therapy in the treatment of salmonella gastroenteritis in children. J Pediatr. 1973;83:646.

104 **The choice of antimicrobial drugs.** Med Lett Drugs Ther. 1992;34:49.

105 **Ramirez CA et al.** Open, prospective study of the clinical efficacy of ciprofloxacin. Antimicrob Agents Chemother. 1985;28:128.

106 **Wang F et al.** Treatment of typhoid fever with ofloxacin. J Antimicrob Agents Chemother. 1989;23:785.

107 **Lasserre R et al.** Three-day treatment of typhoid fever with two different doses of ceftriaxone, compared to 14-day therapy with chloramphenicol: a randomized trial. J Antimicrob Chemother. 1991;28:765.

108 **Phillips WE.** Treatment of chronic typhoid carriers with ampicillin. JAMA. 1971;217:913.

109 **Nolan CM et al.** Treatment of typhoid carriers with amoxicillin. JAMA. 1978;239:2352.

110 **Pichler H et al.** Treatment of chronic carriers of *Salmonella typhi* and *Salmonella paratyphi* b with trimethoprim-sulfamethoxazole. J Infect Dis. 1973;128(Suppl.):S743.

111 **Guerrant RL.** Salmonella infections. In: Braunwald E et al., eds. Harrison's Principles of Internal Medicine. 11th ed. New York: McGraw-Hill; 1987:592.

112 **Dunagan WC et al.** Antimicrobials and infectious diseases. In: Dunagan WC et al., eds. Manual of Medical Therapeutics. 26th ed. Boston: Little, Brown; 1989:237.

113 **Diridl G et al.** Treatment of chronic salmonella carriers with ciprofloxacin. Eur J Clin Microbiol. 1986;5:260. Letter.

114 **Sammalkorpi K et al.** Treatment of chronic salmonella carriers with ciprofloxacin. Lancet. 1987;2:164. Letter.

115 **Ferreccio C et al.** Efficacy of ciprofloxacin in the treatment of chronic typhoid carriers. J Infect Dis. 1988;157:1235.

116 **Gotuzzo E et al.** Use of norfloxacin to treat chronic typhoid carriers. J Infect Dis. 1988;157:1221.

117 **Woodruff BA et al.** A new look at typhoid vaccination: information for the practicing physician. JAMA. 1991;265:756.

118 **DuPont HL.** Shigella species (bacillary dysentery). In: Mandell GL et al., eds. Principles and Practice of Infectious Diseases. 3rd ed. New York: Churchill Livingstone; 1990:1716.

119 **Rennels MB et al.** Classical bacterial diarrhea: perspectives and update: Salmonella, Shigella, *Escherichia coli*, Aeromonas, and Plesiomonas. Pediatr Infect Dis. 1985;5:S91.

120 **Bennish ML et al.** Therapy for shigellosis. ii. Randomized, double-blind comparison of ciprofloxacin and ampicillin. Infect Dis. 1990;162:711.

121 **Gilman RH et al.** Randomized trial of high and low dose ampicillin therapy for treatment of severe dysentery due to *Shigella dysenteriae* type I. Antimicrob Agents Chemother. 1980;17:402.

122 **Weissman JB et al.** Changing needs in the antimicrobial therapy of shigellosis. J Infect Dis. 1973;127:611.

123 **Oldfield EC et al.** Empirical treatment of *shigella* dysentery with trimethoprim: five-day course versus single dose. Am J Trop Med Hyg. 1987;37:616.

124 **Pickering LK et al.** Single-dose tetracycline therapy for shigellosis in adults. JAMA. 1978;239:853.

125 **Haltalin KS et al.** Comparison of orally absorbable and nonabsorbable antibiotics in shigellosis: a double-blind study with ampicillin and neomycin. J Pediatr. 1968;72:708.

126 **Salam MA et al.** Therapy for shigellosis. I. Randomized, double-blind trial of nalidixic acid in childhood shigellosis. J Pediatr. 1988;113:901.

127 **Bennish ML et al.** Antimicrobial resistance of shigella isolates in Bangladesh, 1983–1990: increasing frequency of strains multiply resistant to ampicillin, trimethoprim-sulfamethox-

azole, and nalidixic acid. Clin Infect Dis. 1992;14:1055.

128 **Tauxe RV et al.** Antimicrobial resistance of shigella isolates in the USA: the importance of international travelers. J Infect Dis. 1990;162:1107.

129 **Rogerie F et al.** Comparison of norfloxacin and nalidixic acid for treatment of dysentery caused by *Shigella dysenteriae* type 1 in adults. Antimicrob Agents Chemother. 1986;29:883.

130 **Gotuzzo E et al.** Comparison of single-dose treatment with norfloxacin and standard 5-day treatment with trimethoprim-sulfamethoxazole for acute shigellosis in adults. Antimicrob Agents Chemother. 1989;33:1101.

131 **Bennish ML et al.** Treatment of shigellosis: iii. Comparison of one- or two-dose ciprofloxacin with standard 5-day therapy. Ann Intern Med. 1992; 117:727.

132 **Murphy GS et al.** Ciprofloxacin and loperamide in the treatment of bacillary dysentery. Ann Intern Med. 1993;118: 582.

133 **Fontaine O.** Antibiotics in the management of shigellosis in children: what role for the quinolones? Rev Inf Dis. 1989;11(Suppl. 5):S1145.

134 **Varsano I et al.** Comparative efficacy of ceftriaxone and ampicillin for treatment of severe shigellosis in children. J Pediatr. 1991;118:627.

135 **Nelson JD, Haltalin KS.** Amoxicillin less effective than ampicillin against shigella *in vitro* and *in vivo*: relationship of efficacy to activity in serum. J Infect Dis. 1974;129(Suppl.):S222.

136 **DuPont HL et al.** Furazolidone versus ampicillin in the treatment of travelers' diarrhea. Antimicrob Agents Chemother. 1984;26:160.

137 **Ericsson CD et al.** Bicozamycin, a poorly absorbable antibiotic, effectively treats travelers' diarrhea. Ann Intern Med. 1983;98:20.

138 **Hughes JM et al.** Food-borne disease. In: Mandell GL et al., eds. Principles and Practice of Infectious Diseases. 3rd ed. New York: Churchill Livingstone; 1990:893.

139 **Centers for Disease Control.** Illness associated with elevated levels of zinc in fruit punch: New Mexico. MMWR. 1983;32:257.

140 **Barker WH, Runte V.** Tomato juice-associated gastroenteritis, Washington and Oregon, 1969. Am J Epidemiol. 1972;76:219.

141 **Hughes JM, Merson MH.** Fish and shellfish poisoning. N Engl J Med. 1976;295:1117.

142 **Hall HE, Angelotti R.** *Clostridium perfringens* in meat and meat products. Appl Microbiol. 1965;13:352.

143 **Sheagen JN.** Staphylococcus aureus: the persistent pathogen. N Engl J Med. 1984;310:1437.

144 **Chang TW, Gorbach SL.** Rapid identification of *Clostridium difficile* by toxin detection. J Clin Microbiol. 1982; 15:465.

145 **Fekety R, Shah A.** Diagnosis and treatment of *Clostridium difficile* colitis. JAMA. 1993;269:71–5.

146 **Tedesco FJ et al.** Clindamycin-associated colitis: a prospective study. Ann Intern Med. 1974;81:429.

147 **Silva J et al.** Inciting and etiologic agents of colitis. Rev Inf Dis. 1984; 6(Suppl.):S214.

148 **Chang TW.** Antibiotic-associated injury to the gut. In: Berk JE et al., eds. Bockus' Gastroenterology. 4th ed. Philadelphia: WB Saunders; 1985: 2583.

149 **Taylor NS et al.** Comparison of two toxins produced by *Clostridium difficile*. Infect Immun. 1981;3:1036.

150 **Mulligan ME et al.** Contamination of a hospital environment by *Clostridium difficile*. Curr Microbiol. 1979;3:173.

151 **Pierce PF Jr et al.** Antimicrobial-associated pseudomembranous colitis: an epidemic investigation of a cluster of cases. J Infect Dis. 1982;145:269.

152 **Fekety R et al.** Epidemiology of antibiotic-associated colitis: isolation of *Clostridium difficile* from the hospital environment. Am J Med. 1981;70:906.

153 **Kim K et al.** Isolation of *Clostridium difficile* for the environment and contacts of patients with antimicrobial-associated colitis. J Infect Dis. 1981;143: 42.

154 **Burdon DW.** *Clostridium difficile*: the epidemiology and prevention of hospital-acquired infections. Infection. 1982;10:203.

155 **Tedesco FJ.** Pseudomembranous colitis: pathogenesis and therapy. Med Clin North Am. 1982;66:655.

156 **Silva J, Fekety R.** Clostridial and antimicrobial enterocolitis. Ann Rev Med. 1981;32:327.

157 **George WL et al.** Selective and differential media for isolation of *Clostridium difficile*. J Clin Microbiol. 1979;9:214.

158 **Tedesco F et al.** Oral vancomycin for antibiotic-associated pseudomembranous colitis. Lancet. 1978;2:226.

159 **Lettau LA.** Oral fluoroquinolone therapy in *clostridium difficile* enterocolitis. JAMA. 1988;260:2216. Letter.

160 **Fekety R et al.** Treatment of antibiotic-associated *clostridium difficile* colitis with oral vancomycin: comparison of two-dosage regimens. Am J Med. 1989;86:15.

161 **Keighley MRD et al.** Randomized controlled trial of vancomycin for pseudomembranous colitis and postoperative diarrhea. Br Med J. 1978;2: 1667.

162 **Dudley NM et al.** Absorption of vancomycin. Ann Intern Med. 1984;101: 144.

163 **Spizter PG, Eliopoulous GM.** Systemic absorption of vancomycin in a patient with pseudomembranous colitis. Ann Intern Med. 1984;100:523.

164 **Teasly DG et al.** Prospective randomized study of metronidazole versus vancomycin for clostridium-associated diarrhea and colitis. Lancet. 1983;2: 1043.

165 **Eglinton GS et al.** Pseudomembranous colitis unresponsive to oral vancomycin therapy. South Med J. 1982;75: 1279.

166 **Goldman P.** Metronidazole. N Engl J Med. 1980;303:1212.

167 **Chang TW et al.** Bacitracin treatment of antibiotic-associated pseudomembranous colitis and diarrhea caused by *Clostridium difficile* toxin. Gastroenterology. 1980;78:1584.

168 **Tedesco FJ.** Bacitracin therapy in antibiotic-associated pseudomembranous colitis. Dig Dis Sci. 1980;25:783.

169 **Fekety R et al.** Antibiotic associate colitis: effects of antibiotics on the disease in hamsters. Rev Inf Dis. 1979;1: 386–96.

170 **Dudley MN et al.** Oral bacitracin versus vancomycin therapy for *Clostridium difficile*-induced diarrhea. Arch Intern Med. 1986;146:1101.

171 **Keigley MRB.** Antibiotic-associated pseudomembranous colitis: pathogenesis and management. Drugs. 1980;20: 49.

172 **Tedesco FJ.** Treatment of recurrent antibiotic-associated pseudomembranous colitis. Am J Gastroenterology. 1982; 77:220.

173 **Pruksananonda P et al.** Multiple relapses of *clostridium difficile*-associated diarrhea responding to an extended course of cholestyramine. Pediatr Infect Dis J. 1989;8:175.

174 **Tedesco FJ et al.** Therapy of antibiotic-associated pseudomembranous colitis. J Clin Gastroenterol. 1979;1:51.

175 **Novak E et al.** Unfavorable effect of atropine-diphenoxylate therapy in the therapy of lincomycin diarrhea. JAMA. 1976;235:1451–455.

176 **DeLalla F et al.** Treatment of *clostridium difficile*-associated disease with teicoplanin. Antimicrob Agents Chemother. 1989;33:1125.

177 **Bartlett JG et al.** Symptomatic relapse after oral vancomycin therapy of antibiotic-associated pseudomembranous colitis. Gastroenterology. 1980;78:431.

178 **Cherry RD et al.** Metronidazole, and alternate therapy for antibiotic-associated colitis. Gastroenterology. 1982; 82:849.

179 **Portnoy D et al.** Pseudomembranous colitis; multiple relapses after treatment with metronidazole. Can Med Assoc J. 1981;124:1603.

180 **Hecht J, Olinger E.** *Clostridium difficile* colitis secondary to intravenous vancomycin. Dig Dis Sci. 1989;34: 148–49.

181 **Saginur R et al.** Colitis associated with metronidazole therapy. J Infect Dis. 1980;141:772.

182 **Kappas HA et al.** Diagnosis of pseudomembranous colitis. Br Med J (Clin Res). 1978;1:675.

183 **Daly J, Chowdory KVJ.** Pseudomembranous colitis secondary to metronidazole. Dig Dis Sci. 1983;28:573.

184 **Tedesco F et al.** Approach to patients with multiple relapses of antibiotic associated pseudomembranous colitis. Am J Gastroenterol. 1985;80:867–68.

185 **Buggy BP et al.** Therapy of relapsing *Clostridium difficile*-associated diarrhea and colitis with the combination of vancomycin and rifampin. Clin Gastroenterol. 1987;9:155.

186 **Bolton RP et al.** Faecal metronidazole concentrations during oral and intravenous therapy for antibiotic-associated colitis due to *clostridium difficile*. Gut. 1986;27:1169.

187 **Kleinfeld DI et al.** Parenteral therapy for antibiotic-associated pseudomembranous colitis. J Infect Dis. 1988;157: 389. Letter.

188 **Guzman R et al.** Failure of parenteral metronidazole in the treatment of pseudomembranous colitis. J Infect Dis. 1988;158:1146. Letter.

189 **Donta ST et al.** Cephalosporin-associated colitis and *Clostridium difficile*. Arch Intern Med. 1980;140:574.

190 **Fekety R.** Antibiotic-associated colitis. In: Mandell GL et al., eds. Principles and Practice of Infectious Diseases. 3rd ed. New York: Churchill Livingstone; 1990:863.

191 **Blaser MJ, Berkowitz ID.** *Campylobacter enteritis*: clinical and epidemiological features. Ann Intern Med. 1979;91:179.

192 **Anders BJ et al.** Double-blind placebo-controlled study of erythromycin for treatment of *Campylobacter enteritis*. Lancet. 1982;1:131.

193 **Fliegelman RM et al.** Comparative *in vitro* activities of twelve antimicrobial agents *Campylobacter* species. Antimicrob Agents Chemother. 1985;27:429.

194 **Hornick RB.** Peptic ulcer disease: a bacterial infection? N Engl J Med. 1987;316:1598–599.

195 **Blase MJ.** *Helicobacter pylori* and the pathogenesis of gastroduodenal inflammation. J Infect Dis. 1990;161:626–31.

196 **Moss S, Calam J.** *Helicobacter pylori* and peptic ulcers: the present position. Gut. 1992;33:289–92.

197 **Tytgat GN et al.** *Helicobacter pylori* infection and duodenal ulcer disease. Gastroenterol Clin North Am. 1993;22: 127–39.

198 **Lerner AM.** Enteric viruses. In: Petersdorf RG et al., eds. Harrison's Principles of Internal Medicine. 10th ed. New York: McGraw Hill; 1983:1125.

199 **Christensen H.** Human viral gastroenteritis. Clin Micro Rev. 1989;2:51.

200 **Davidson GP.** Viral diarrhea. Clin Gastroenterol. 1986;15:39.

201 **Blacklow NR, Cuckor G.** Viral gastroenteritis. N Engl J Med. 1981;304: 397.

202 **Edelman R.** Prevention and treatment of infectious diarrhea: speculation on the next ten years. Am J Med. 1985; 78(Suppl. 6B):99.

203 **Vesikari T et al.** Protection of infants against rotavirus diarrhea by RIT 4237, attenuated bovine rotavirus strain vaccine. Lancet. 1983;2:977.

204 **Gorbach SL.** Travelers' diarrhea. N Engl J Med. 1976;236:844.

205 **Barza M, Schiefe RT.** Antimicrobial spectrum, pharmacology, and therapeutic use of antibiotics. Part 1: tetracyclines. Am J Hosp Pharm. 1977;34: 49.

206 **DuPont HL.** Nonfluid therapy and selected chemoprophylaxis of acute diarrhea. Am J Med. 1985;78(Suppl. 6B):81.

207 **Hedberg CW.** Outbreaks of foodborne and waterborne viral gastroenteritis. Clin Microbiol Rev. 1993;6: 199.

208 **Radandt JM et al.** Interactions of fluoroquinolones with other drugs: mechanisms, variability, clinical significance, and management. Clin Infect Dis. 1992;14:272.

209 **Allen JE.** Drug-induced photosensitivity. Clin Pharm. 1993;12:580.

210 **Sperber SJ et al.** Salmonellosis during infection with human immunodeficiency virus. Rev Infect Dis. 1987;9: 925.

211 **Braden C et al.** Diarrhea-and dysentery-causing *Escherichia coli*. In: Feigin RD et al., eds. Pediatric Infectious Diseases. 3rd ed. Philadelphia: WB Saunders; 1992:607.

212 **Griffin PM et al.** Illnesses associated with *escherichia coli* 0157:H7 infections. Ann Intern Med. 1988;109:705.

213 **Besser RE et al.** An outbreak of diarrhea and hemolytic uremic syndrome from *escherichia coli* 0157:H7 in fresh-pressed apple cider. JAMA. 1993;269:2217.

214 **Swerdlow DL et al.** A waterborne outbreak in Missouri of *escherichia coli* 0157:H7 associated with bloody diarrhea and death. Ann Intern Med. 1992;117:812.

215 **Carter AO et al.** A severe outbreak of *escherichia coli* 0157:H7-associated hemorrhagic colitis in a nursing home. N Engl J Med. 1987;317:1496.

216 **Cimolai N et al.** Gender and the progression of *escherichia coli* 0157:H7 enteritis to haemolytic uraemic syndrome. Arch Dis Child. 1991;66:171.

217 **Pai CH et al.** Sporadic cases of hemorrhagic colitis associated with *escherichia coli* 0157:H7: clinical, epidemiologic and bacteriologic features. Ann Intern Med. 1984;101:738.

218 **Pavia AT et al.** Hemolytic-uremic syndrome during an outbreak of *escherichia coli* 0157:H7 infections in institutions from mentally retarded persons: clinical and epidemiologic observations. J Pediatr. 1990;116:544.

219 **Center for Disease Control.** *Escherichia coli* 0157:H7 outbreak-California, July 1993. MMWR. 1994;43:213.

220 **Cimolai N et al.** Risk factors for the progression of *Escherichia coli* 0157:H7 enteritis to hemolytic-uremic syndrome. J Pediatr. 1990;116:589.

221 **Martin DL et al.** The epidemiology clinical aspects of the hemolytic uremic syndrome in Minnesota. N Engl J Med. 1990;323:1161.

222 **Tarr PI et al.** *Escherichia coli* 0157:H7 and the hemolytic uremic syndrome: importance of early cultures in establishing the etiology. J Infect Dis. 1990;162:553.

223 **Cimolai N et al.** Antibiotics for *Escherichia coli* 0157:H7 enteritis? (correspondence). J Antimicrob Chemother. 1989;23:807.

224 **Proulx F et al.** Randomized, controlled trial of antibiotic therapy for *Escherichia coli* 0157:H7 enteritis. J Pediatr. 1992;121:299.

225 **Belongia EA et al.** An outbreak of *Escherichia coli* 0157:H7 colitis associated with consumption of precooked meat patties. J Infect Dis. 1991;164:338.

226 **Cleary TG.** *Escherichia coli* that cause hemolytic uremic syndrome. Infect Dis North Am. 1992;6:163.

227 **Center for Disease Control.** Viral agents of gastroenteritis. MMWR. 1990;39:1.

228 **Kapikian AZ et al.** Viral gastrointestinal infections. In: Feigin RD et al., eds. Pediatric Infectious Diseases. 3rd ed. Philadelphia: WB Saunders; 1992:655.

229 **Gross MH.** Management of antibiotic-associated pseudomembranous colitis. Clin Pharm. 1985;4:304.

Intra-Abdominal Infections

Peggy L Carver

Karen A Kostiuk

Infections of the Biliary Tract 61-1
  Cholangitis and Cholecystitis 61-1
    Clinical presentation and diagnosis 61-2
    Bacteriology 61-2
    Antimicrobial therapy 61-2
      Biliary concentrations 61-3
Primary Peritonitis 61-3
  Spontaneous Bacterial Peritonitis (SBP) 61-4
    Signs and symptoms 61-4
  Primary Peritonitis in Cirrhotics 61-4
    Pathogenesis 61-4
    Antimicrobial therapy 61-4
      Empiric 61-4
      Therapeutic endpoints 61-5
    Risk factors 61-5
  Continuous Ambulatory Peritoneal Dialysis
  (CAPD)-Associated Peritonitis 61-5
    Pathogenesis 61-5
    Antimicrobial therapy 61-5
Secondary Peritonitis 61-7
  Pathogenesis and Epidemiology 61-7
  Normal Gastrointestinal Flora (See Figure 61.1) 61-7

Diagnosis 61-7
  Signs and symptoms of infection 61-7
  Infecting pathogens (See Table 61.3) 61-8
Antimicrobial Therapy 61-9
  Empiric therapy (See Tables 61.4 and 61.5) 61-9
  Beta-lactam antibiotics 61-10
  Single agent therapy 61-11
  Enterococcal infection 61-13
  Anaerobic bacteria 61-13
    Resistance to antianaerobic antimicrobial agents .. 61-14
    Susceptibility testing 61-14
  Antimicrobial irrigations 61-15
  Duration of therapy 61-15
Intra-Abdominal Abscess 61-15
  Microbiology 61-15
  Penetration of antimicrobial agents into
    the peritoneum 61-16
Antifungal Therapy: Treatment of *Candida*
  (See Question 14) 61-14
Infections Following Abdominal Trauma 61-16
  Antimicrobial Therapy 61-16
    Penetrating trauma (See Table 61.6) 61-16
    Appendectomy 61-16

Despite the introduction of newer, more potent antimicrobial agents and improvements in diagnostic and surgical techniques, the treatment of intra-abdominal infections remains a therapeutic challenge. Improvements in radiographic techniques which allow better localization of abscesses and early drainage, improved nutritional management, and the selection of appropriate antimicrobial agents all contribute to a decrease in mortality from intra-abdominal infection. Mortality ranges from an average of 3.5% in patients with early infection following penetrating abdominal trauma to more than 60% in patients with well established intra-abdominal infections that result in multiple organ failure.[1,2]

Intra-abdominal infections are those contained within the peritoneal cavity which extends from the undersurface of the diaphragm to the floor of the pelvis or the retroperitoneal space. Intra-abdominal infections may present as localized infections, a diffuse inflammation throughout the peritoneum, or infections in visceral organs such as the liver, biliary tract, spleen, pancreas, or female pelvic organs. Abscesses may form in any of the potential spaces within the abdomen, between bowel loops, or in the solid organs. If localization of the infection site is delayed, multiple organ failure, which is associated with a high mortality, is likely to occur.[3]

Antimicrobial therapy should be selected on the basis of the microbiology of the infecting pathogens, *in vitro* susceptibility data, an understanding of the pharmacokinetic and pharmacodynamic properties of the antimicrobial agents, and the results of well-designed clinical trials.[2,3] Although the efficacy of many antimicrobial agents has been evaluated, poor study design, differences in patient populations, and the severity of disease make comparisons between clinical trials difficult.

Infections of the Biliary Tract
Cholangitis and Cholecystitis

Cholangitis is defined as inflammation of the biliary ductal system. When acute cholangitis was first described by Charcot[198] in 1877 it was considered a life-threatening disease associated with a 100% mortality rate if not treated surgically. Since then, considerable progress has been made in early diagnosis and management with a subsequent reduction in the mortality rate. Several prognostic factors have been identified which predict mortality. Those at risk for developing cholangitis include patients with acute renal failure, hepatic abscesses, cirrhosis, post-percutaneous transhepatic cholangiography (PTC), females, and patients over the age of 50.[198–200] Acute cholangitis can develop from an infectious, chemical, ischemic, or idiopathic process. Historically, the most common cause of biliary obstruction resulting in cholangitis has been cholelithiasis obstructing the common bile duct.[201] Other principal etiologies of obstruction include biliary tract surgery complicated by stricture, parasitic infections, and neoplasm of either the biliary system (cholangiocarcinoma) or head of the pancreas (adenocarcinoma).

Under normal conditions, bile is a sterile fluid; however, bacterial colonization of the biliary tract by enteric bacteria can occur in patients with biliary pathology, especially those patients with gallstone disease.[198] Colonization of the biliary tree, or bactibilia, is associated with the obstruction to the outflow of bile.[201] In acute infectious cholangitis, the progression of obstruction leads to biliary stasis and proliferation of bacteria within the biliary tree. Once infection occurs, increased pressure and edema results in increased permeability of the surrounding tissues and promotes systemic spread of bacteria resulting in sepsis.[199]

Cholecystitis is an inflammation of the gallbladder and is associated with obstruction of the cystic duct, which normally drains the contents of the gall bladder into the common bile duct. The pathogenesis of infection is similar in both cholangitis and cholecystitis, as biliary stasis results in bacterial proliferation and subsequent infection.

Clinical Presentation and Diagnosis

1. L.K., a 59-year-old female, presents to the hospital with a 2-day history of abdominal pain and tenderness, localized to the right upper quadrant, fever to 102 °F, and rigors. She complains of nausea with 3 episodes of emesis occurring in the last 24 hours. L.K. appears jaundiced and reports dark colored urine. Her laboratory values are as follows: white blood cell (WBC) count 15 × 10³/mm³, with a shift to the left; serum creatinine (SrCr) 1.9 mg/dL; total bilirubin 4 mg/dL; and alkaline phosphatase 220 U/L. What evidence of cholangitis exists in L.K.? How does cholecystitis differ from cholangitis? [SI units: WBC count 15 × 10⁹/L; SrCr 167.96 µmol/L; total bilirubin 119.7 mmol/L]

Acute cholangitis presents with varying degrees of severity. The clinical presentation ranges from mild discomfort, resolving with conservative management to overwhelming sepsis. Charcot's triad is the classical description of cholangitis and is characterized by three signs: fever, jaundice, and abdominal pain.[198] The clinical signs and symptoms of cholangitis, as exemplified by L.K., include high fevers (exceeding 38.5 °C), chills, jaundice, and abdominal pain. Abdominal pain localized to the right upper quadrant is often the presenting symptom and is accompanied by nausea and vomiting. In severe cases of cholangitis, bacteremia may occur leading to septic shock.

Laboratory evidence of cholangitis reveals leukocytosis, an elevated white blood cell (WBC) count, with a left shift of neutrophils or predominance of immature forms. L.K. is demonstrating a WBC count of 15 × 10³/mm³, with a shift to the left, consistent with cholangitis. Abnormal laboratory values may include an elevated bilirubin level (usually in the range of 2 to 4 mg/dL) and elevated alkaline phosphatase, liver transferases, and amylase levels. L.K. has a total bilirubin of 4 mg/dL and alkaline phosphatase of 220 U/L.

Clinical and laboratory findings of acute cholecystitis are similar to those of acute cholangitis. Both diseases are associated with leukocytosis, fever, acute right upper quadrant pain and tenderness, nausea and vomiting, and elevations in liver transferases, total bilirubin, alkaline phosphatase, and amylase levels. The differences between the diseases are subtle but patients with cholecystitis generally present with milder fevers, with temperatures of 38 to 38.5 °C; prominent rebound tenderness and guarding during physical examination; minimal elevations in bilirubin, alkaline phosphatase, and amylase; and less frequent development of jaundice (10% of patients). Radiologic diagnosis includes ultrasonography which reveals distention of the gall bladder often with stones. Conversely, patients with cholangitis generally have an increase in the diameter of the common bile duct, however, no increase in gall bladder size.

Bacteriology

2. Which organisms are likely to be associated with infection in L.K.? Are blood cultures helpful in identifying the pathogen(s)?

The most prevalent biliary tract pathogens include *Escherichia coli*, *Klebsiella sp.*, *Enterococcus*, *Proteus sp.*, *Enterobacter cloacae*, and anaerobes, including *Bacteroides fragilis*.[199,201] Improved culture methods have documented that anaerobes are common pathogens in acute cholangitis[201] and frequently are involved in polymicrobic infections.[198] Other possible pathogens include

Pseudomonas aeruginosa, *Streptococcus viridans*, and *Staphylococcus aureus*. Bacteriologic findings are similar in infectious cholecystitis,[201] however, anaerobes are infrequent pathogens.

Obstruction of the common bile duct results in increased ductal pressure, forcing proliferating bacteria through the hepatic sinusoids into the systemic circulation.[199] As a result, blood cultures obtained from a patient with signs of systemic infection, such as rigors and hypotension, are often positive.

A three step approach is suggested in the treatment of acute biliary tract infections: 1) drainage of the biliary tree by either surgery or interventional radiology; 2) appropriate antibacterial therapy; and 3) supportive measures.[198,201] Treatment of both cholecystitis and cholangitis requires drainage of obstructed biliary fluid.[199] In patients with cholangitis, endoscopic retrograde cholangiopancreatography (ERCP) is used to relieve biliary ductal system blockage by removing the obstructive stone or stricture in the common bile duct. Cholecystitis requires removal of the gall bladder (cholecystectomy), or drainage (cholecystostomy) in older, more debilitated patients.[199] Endoscopic or surgical treatment of the obstruction often is necessary to avoid recurrences.[198] The timing of surgery in patients with uncomplicated cholecystitis remains controversial.[201] Many support delaying surgery until after the acute attack subsides with conservative management. Others support early surgery claiming that a relatively benign presentation may mask complications. No difference in morbidity has been observed between early and delayed surgical intervention.[202]

Antimicrobial Therapy

3. Based upon the expected pathogens, what empiric antimicrobial therapy should be suggested for L.K.?

Treatment of cholangitis must be started empirically and should be directed at the most likely pathogens: enteric gram-negative bacilli, enterococci, and anaerobes. Combination therapy with an aminoglycoside or second- or third-generation cephalosporin, plus metronidazole or clindamycin, and possibly ampicillin (for enterococcal coverage) has been used empirically in the treatment of cholangitis. A more specific antibiotic regimen should be substituted when culture and sensitivity results are available.

The most widely studied regimen for the empiric treatment of cholangitis has been the combination of a penicillin with an aminoglycoside. Although several authors support this regimen, aminoglycosides have been associated with renal and cochlear toxicity and require close monitoring of drug levels and parameters of renal function. Furthermore, the risk of renal toxicity has been suggested to be greater in the elderly, the jaundiced, and the septic patient.[203] As a result, less toxic antibacterials have been studied in the treatment of biliary tract infections. Muller and associates[204] conducted a prospective, randomized trial comparing the efficacy and toxicity of three treatment groups: 1) ampicillin and tobramycin, 2) cefoperazone, and 3) piperacillin. One hundred and six patients with cholecystitis, cholangitis, or both were enrolled. The clinical cure rates with ampicillin plus tobramycin, cefoperazone, and piperacillin were 85%, 95%, and 95% respectively, in patients with acute cholecystitis. Interestingly, the clinical cure rates for cholangitis differed between regimens. The combination of ampicillin plus tobramycin was significantly better than cefoperazone, but not significantly different than piperacillin. Nephrotoxicity developed in 10% of patients with cholangitis treated with an aminoglycoside, compared to only 3% in patients who received cefoperazone or piperacillin. The authors concluded that patients with acute cholangitis should be treated with piperacillin to avoid the nephrotoxicity of conventional aminoglycoside therapy.

In vitro data suggest that aminoglycosides and third-generation cephalosporins demonstrate the most reliable *in vitro* activity versus biliary tract pathogens.[205] Cefoperazone, a third-generation cephalosporin, was compared with ampicillin plus tobramycin for severe biliary tract infections.[206] Sixty-four patients were treated with either cefoperazone 2 gm every 12 hours, or ampicillin 1 gm every four hours plus tobramycin 1.5 mg/kg every eight hours after a 2 mg/kg loading dose. Cefoperazone and the combination therapy were equally effective in the cure of infection. However, microbiologic cure was achieved in a significantly greater number of patients receiving cefoperazone (94%) compared with the combination (62%). Limited eradication of micro-organisms with ampicillin plus tobramycin was considered to be due to the fact that 51% of isolates were resistant to ampicillin, compared to only 1% of isolates to cefoperazone. Three patients had an increase in serum creatinine in the ampicillin plus tobramycin group, which returned to normal when therapy was discontinued. The overall clinical and bacteriological cure rates observed with cefoperazone support its use as an alternative to standard therapy.

Successful monotherapy also has been reported with mezlocillin, piperacillin, and imipenem.[81,207,208] Gerecht and associates evaluated mezlocillin, a broad-spectrum ureidopenicillin, compared to ampicillin plus gentamicin for cholangitis. Twenty-four patients received mezlocillin, 4 gm every six hours, while 22 patients were treated with ampicillin 1 gm every four hours and gentamicin 1.5 mg/kg every eight hours. Eighty-three percent of patients in the mezlocillin group were cured compared to 41% of patients in the ampicillin plus gentamicin group and there were fewer toxic and adverse effects noted in the mezlocillin group. The authors concluded that the difference in cure rates between the two groups was due to high serum and bile concentrations of mezlocillin compared to ampicillin and gentamicin. The authors support the use of mezlocillin alone for cholangitis claiming it was more effective, less toxic, and less expensive than ampicillin plus gentamicin. Another way to explain the difference in efficacy may be that only 45% of the aerobic gram-negative bacilli recovered from patients were susceptible to ampicillin whereas all isolates were susceptible to mezlocillin.[207]

Recently, cefepime, a new parenteral broad-spectrum cephalosporin, was prospectively compared to gentamicin plus mezlocillin for the treatment of biliary tract infections.[209] Cefepime was administered parenterally at 2 gm every 12 hours versus gentamicin at 1.5 mg/kg every eight hours plus mezlocillin at 3 gm every four hours. All patients treated with gentamicin plus mezlocillin and 97.5% of patients treated with cefepime were cured. Cefepime provides yet another alternative for the treatment of biliary tract infections.

Aminoglycoside therapy should be avoided in L.K. for several reasons: her age, elevated serum creatinine, and hyperbilirubinemia place her at higher risk for the development of aminoglycoside-induced nephrotoxicity.[203] Alternatively, a less toxic, broad-spectrum agent which has adequate coverage for common biliary tract pathogens should be considered. The benefits of combination therapy are not clearly understood, therefore, L.K. should be treated with monotherapy. Possible choices include a ureidopenicillin, third-generation cephalosporin, or beta-lactamase inhibitor combination.

4. Biliary Concentrations. **The medical resident on the primary service caring for L.K. would prefer to use an antibiotic which concentrates in the bile. What is the benefit of using an antibiotic that is excreted into bile?**

Common bile duct obstruction is a factor that affects and may prevent the entry of antibiotics into the bile.[210,211] The need for high biliary concentrations of antibiotics in the treatment of cholangitis is unclear.[207,210,211] Several authors have investigated the excretion of antibiotics into bile. Table 61.1 summarizes the con-

Table 61.1	Concentration in Bile Relative to Serum[a]	
Bile Less Than Serum	Bile Equal To Serum	Bile Greater Than Serum
Penicillin G	Ampicillin	Nafcillin
Phenoxypenicillins	Mezlocillin	Cefamandole
Amoxicillin	Cefazolin	Cefoxitin
Cefuroxime	Cefotaxime	Cephradine
Ceftazidime	Gentamicin	Cefoperazone
Ceftizoxime	Amikacin	Cefotetan
Vancomycin	Sulfamethoxazole	Erythromycin
		Clindamycin
		Doxycycline
		Metronidazole
		Rifampin

[a] Adapted with permission from references 198 and 210.

centrations of several antibiotics in bile relative to serum.[198,210] Nagar et al. reviewed the biliary excretion of several antibiotics and concluded that a number of antibiotics with excellent *in vitro* susceptibility are poorly excreted into bile yet are clinically effective. They question the benefit of high biliary concentrations of antibiotics.[210]

Prospective studies which compare highly excreted versus moderately excreted antibiotics have been conducted. Keighley and colleagues[211] conducted a randomized controlled trial in 150 patients undergoing biliary operations. They compared the prophylactic administration of gentamicin, which achieves adequate concentrations in the serum only, with rifamide, an antibiotic almost entirely excreted in the bile, versus a control. Rifamide reached extremely high levels in bile but low serum levels in the absence of obstruction. On the other hand, rifamide levels were subtherapeutic in both bile and serum in patients with obstruction. Rifamide-treated patients had a comparable rate of postoperative infection compared to controls. In the gentamicin group, bile levels were extremely low but therapeutic serum levels were achieved with an associated significant reduction in wound infections, 22% to 6%, and septicemia, 14% to 2%, when compared to controls. They concluded that serum levels are of more value than biliary levels to reduce the septic complications of biliary tract surgery. Furthermore, these authors[211] and others[201] conclude that biliary excretion of any antibiotic is minimal in the presence of obstruction.

Primary Peritonitis

Peritonitis is an inflammation of the peritoneal lining which occurs in response to chemical irritation or bacterial invasion; this chapter addresses infectious peritonitis only. The etiology of peritonitis is important because it can determine the treatment approach. Most often, peritonitis is secondary to contamination of the peritoneum by gastrointestinal (GI) bacteria that have been released by inflammation, perforation, or trauma; this is termed ''secondary peritonitis.'' Some clinicians use the term ''tertiary'' or ''persistent'' peritonitis to describe a subgroup of patients with intra-abdominal infection with a higher morbidity and mortality.[1] Less frequently, patients develop primary or ''spontaneous'' bacterial peritonitis that has no apparent connection with an intra-abdominal event (e.g., appendicitis). In this form of peritonitis, there is no obvious intra-abdominal source of bacterial contamination.

Primary peritonitis often is associated with alcoholic cirrhosis, occurring in up to 12% of patients with chronic liver disease and ascites; however, it also is associated with other postnecrotic liver diseases (including hepatitis, cryptogenic cirrhosis, cardiac cirrhosis, and biliary cirrhosis), nephrosis, and peritoneal dialysis. In adults, the presence of peritoneal fluid appears to be an essential factor for the development of spontaneous bacterial peritonitis (SBP); end-stage liver disease need not be present.[4,5] Thus, spontaneous bacterial peritonitis also has been reported in patients with nephrotic syndrome, malignancies, congestive heart failure, and severe viral hepatitis.

Spontaneous Bacterial Peritonitis (SBP)

Signs and Symptoms

Spontaneous bacterial peritonitis generally is characterized by fever, chills, vomiting, abdominal pain, signs of peritoneal irritation, and impending shock and hepatic coma. In contrast to secondary peritonitis which is generally an acute event, this process can develop over a period of days to weeks. Bowel sounds become hypoactive, and rebound tenderness appears as the abdominal pain becomes progressively more severe.[5] However, these signs are not invariably present, and asymptomatic bacterial ascites sometimes occurs.[4,5] Although some authors have suggested that a cloudy ascitic fluid with an elevated leukocyte count is indicative of peritoneal infection, others consider this indicator unreliable and rely on a positive peritoneal fluid culture for diagnosis.[1]

Primary Peritonitis In Cirrhotics

Pathogenesis

5. R.S., a 47-year-old male with Laennec's (alcohol-related) cirrhosis and massive abdominal ascites, presents with a 4-day history of fever, decreasing mental status, decreased urine output, and abdominal pain. Ascitic fluid obtained by paracentesis was cloudy. What organisms are likely to be cultured from R.S.'s ascitic fluid?

Enteric bacteria, most commonly *Escherichia coli*, are recovered in approximately two-thirds of patients with spontaneous bacterial peritonitis; and nonenteric organisms, usually *S. pneumoniae* or other streptococci, are recovered in the other one-third of patients. Staphylococci, anaerobes, and microaerophilic organisms are reported infrequently. Anaerobes, when present, are almost invariably seen in the setting of a polymicrobial infection. Bacteremia occurs in 30% to 40% of patients.[5,6]

Although the pathogenesis of spontaneous bacterial peritonitis is unclear, several mechanisms have been suggested. In cirrhotics such as R.S., hematogenous spread is the most likely route of infection. In advanced cirrhosis, more than 80% of portal blood flow may bypass the liver, permitting circulating bacteria to bypass the hepatic reticuloendothelial filtering system, a major site for their removal from the blood.[5]

Breaks in the intestinal mucosa also may serve as a source of bacteremia. Congestion of the splanchnic veins and lymphatics due to portal hypertension may result in inflammation and edema of the bowel wall and a decreased local resistance to bacterial invasion. Alternatively, irritation or inflammation of the bowel wall may occur secondary to the diarrhea frequently present in cirrhotics. Finally, there are qualitative and quantitative abnormalities in the distribution of intestinal bacteria in cirrhotic patients.[5] Gastrointestinal procedures such as endoscopy or paracentesis also may predispose patients to the development of spontaneous bacterial peritonitis. Under certain circumstances, bacteria are known to cross the intact intestinal wall. As early as 1950, Schweinburg et al.[7] demonstrated that ^{14}C-labeled *E. coli* passed from the bowel into the peritoneal cavity of dogs after the introduction of hypertonic solutions into the peritoneum. More recently, bacterial translocation from the GI tract to mesenteric lymph nodes following the administration of broad-spectrum antimicrobials has been demonstrated in a rat model. Translocation of *E. coli* is most frequently

demonstrated, although *Enterococcus faecalis* also can be cultured. Bacteria are transported from the mesenteric lymph nodes to the peritoneal cavity or visceral organs via the bloodstream.[7,9]

The lymphatic system also may play an important role in the pathogenesis of spontaneous peritonitis. When a pure suspension of *E. coli* is injected into the peritoneal cavity of an animal, these bacteria appear within the diaphragmatic lymphatics within six minutes, suggesting that absorption of bacteria via the regional lymphatic system is a primary local defense mechanism of the peritoneum. Therefore, any disruption in the ability of the lymphatic system to remove bacteria may contribute to the development of peritonitis. Bacteria also can flow out of the lymphatic system. For example, bacteria removed from the blood by the liver may contaminate hepatic lymph and pass through the permeable lymphatic walls into the ascitic fluid.[8,9]

A second local defense mechanism of the peritoneum is its capacity to exude opsonins, polymorphonuclear cells (PMNs) and macrophages into the peritoneal cavity, where phagocytosis and destruction of bacteria can take place. In cirrhotics, this host defense mechanism is compromised because macrophages phagocytize bacteria poorly and the large fluid volume present in ascites may prevent phagocytosis of bacteria.[9]

In children, spontaneous bacterial peritonitis occurs primarily in females and almost exclusively in children less than ten years of age. Although pre-existing cirrhosis may be present, peritonitis generally occurs following necrotic liver disease, nephrotic syndrome, or urinary tract infections, and the infecting organisms are almost invariably *S. pneumoniae* or beta-hemolytic streptococci. In the preantibiotic era, primary peritonitis accounted for about 10% of all pediatric abdominal emergencies. It now accounts for less than 1% to 2% of cases, perhaps because of the widespread use of antimicrobials for minor upper respiratory tract illness. Many investigators believe that in pediatric cases, bacteria are spread hematogenously to the peritoneal cavity from a remote focus of infection, such as the respiratory tract. The spread of *S. pneumoniae* from the vagina may explain the higher frequency of spontaneous bacterial peritonitis in the female pediatric population. The possibility of transfallopian spread also is suggested by the development of primary peritonitis in women with intrauterine devices (IUDs) and gonococcal or chlamydial perihepatitis (Fitz-Hugh-Curtis syndrome).[5,9]

Antimicrobial Therapy

6. What antimicrobial therapy should be considered for R.S. pending ascitic fluid culture results? How long should therapy be continued and how should the response to therapy be monitored?

Empiric. There are no prospective studies that have established the optimal antimicrobial therapy, the appropriate duration of therapy, or criteria for termination of antimicrobial therapy for spontaneous bacterial peritonitis.[8] A Gram's stain of spun ascitic fluid may be helpful in selecting empiric antimicrobial therapy. If unspun fluid is examined, the Gram's stain will be negative unless greater than 10^5 bacteria/mL are present.[8] Empiric therapy generally is aimed at likely pathogens, primarily *E. coli* and other gram-negative enteric bacteria. Ampicillin or a first-generation cephalosporin plus an aminoglycoside can be used until culture and sensitivity data are available.[10-19] Single-agent therapy with cefotaxime is also efficacious and avoids the risk of nephrotoxicity associated with aminoglycoside use.[16,20] The use of prophylactic antimicrobial therapy with broad-spectrum agents such as norfloxacin has been advocated by some investigators.[21] However, the risk and benefits of such therapy must be evaluated carefully in this patient population.[18,21]

In a prospective, randomized study, 32 cirrhotic patients with ascites received prophylactic norfloxacin, 400 mg/day orally, throughout their hospitalization while 31 patients in the control group were not given prophylaxis.[21] The treated group experienced a significantly lower incidence of spontaneous bacterial peritonitis (0%) compared to the untreated group (22.5%). In a double-blind study in 80 cirrhotic patients,[15] norfloxacin prophylaxis was compared to placebo in the prevention of recurrence of spontaneous bacterial peritonitis. Prophylactic administration of norfloxacin resulted in selective intestinal decontamination by eliminating aerobic gram-negative bacilli. The incidence of recurrent spontaneous bacterial peritonitis was significantly lower in the treatment group (12%) compared to the control (35%). Long-term selective decontamination, therefore, is effective and safe in preventing recurrent spontaneous bacterial peritonitis in cirrhotic patients.

Concerns have been raised regarding the rapid emergence of resistance with norfloxacin prophylaxis in cirrhotic patients. Thirty-one hospitalized patients with alcoholic cirrhosis and ascites were studied to determine the influence of prophylactic norfloxacin on fecal flora and the development of resistant bacteria. Norfloxacin was given at 400 mg/day to all patients. Quantitative stool cultures were carried out before treatment, weekly initially, and then every two weeks. The number of Enterobacteriaceae was reduced to undetectable levels during treatment. There was no effect on anaerobes or enterococci. Sixteen patients (51.6%) developed fluoroquinolone-resistant isolates during treatment, occurring at 14 and 43 days of treatment. Prophylactic antibiotics for selective decontamination, therefore, should not be routinely used because of the risk of resistance.[194]

Therapeutic Endpoints. In a prospective study of the decline in ascitic fluid PMN count during therapy for spontaneous bacterial peritonitis, a PMN count of 250 cells/mm^3 was determined to be a suitable endpoint for termination of antibiotic therapy.[13] Patients treated on the basis of polymorphonuclear cell counts were treated for a significantly shorter period of time than patients who received "conventional" therapy in which the therapeutic endpoint was determined on an empirical basis. Mortality correlated with the severity of underlying liver disease rather than the duration of antibiotic therapy.

Risk Factors

The short-term outcome of spontaneous bacterial peritonitis is associated with increasing hepatic encephalopathy, the absence of gastrointestinal pain at admission, the presence of greater than 85% granulocytes in peripheral blood or ascitic fluid, a total bilirubin greater than 8 mg/dL, and a serum albumin less than 2.5 gm/dL. A temperature greater than 38 °C which is indicative of relatively intact host defense mechanisms, and is associated with increased survival. Although they occur less frequently, enteric bacteremias are associated with a significantly higher mortality than infections caused by nonenteric pathogens. Rapid death (≤7 days from onset of SBP) correlates with the acute onset of liver disease, hepatomegaly, increased serum bilirubin concentrations, increased serum creatinine concentrations, and increased peripheral white blood cell counts.[20]

R.S. should receive empiric therapy with antimicrobial agents that are effective against *E. coli, S. pneumoniae,* and other common gram-negative enteric pathogens such as *Klebsiella sp.* Antimicrobial therapy should be tailored to the specific bacteria when culture and sensitivity results are available.

Continuous Ambulatory Peritoneal Dialysis (CAPD)-Associated Peritonitis

7. S.K., a 23-year-old female with diabetes mellitus and end-stage renal disease, has undergone CAPD daily for the past year. She presents with abdominal pain and a cloudy dialysate fluid. Against which bacteria should empiric antimicrobial therapy be directed? How should antimicrobial agents be administered?

Pathogenesis

Approximately 80% of patients undergoing CAPD develop peritonitis during the first year of dialysis, and recurrent infection occurs in 20% to 30% of patients. Infections are caused primarily by gram-positive bacteria, with coagulase-negative staphylococci responsible for approximately 40% of all infections. Gram-negative bacteria are isolated in approximately 25% of cases, while anaerobes, fungi, and mycobacteria constitute the remainder of the commonly observed pathogens. The source of most gram-positive infections is generally the patients' own skin flora.[22,23] The source and portal of entry of other bacteria are unclear, although transmural migration of bacteria has been suggested, and continuous spread from the skin along the peritoneal dialysis cuff to the peritoneum has been demonstrated.[5,25] Patients may present with abdominal pain and tenderness, but fever is not a consistent finding. Often, the only clue to the presence of infection is a cloudy dialysate although bacteria may be seen on examination of a centrifuged specimen of dialysate.[24] Fortunately, the majority of patients do not become bacteremic.[24]

Antimicrobial Therapy

The optimal antimicrobial regimen and appropriate dose, route, and duration of therapy for the treatment of CAPD-associated peritonitis are unclear due to a paucity of randomized, controlled trials. In general, empiric antibiotic therapy should be directed against both gram-positive and facultative gram-negative enteric bacteria until cultures of peritoneal fluid are available. After IV administration, most antimicrobial agents reach therapeutic concentrations within the peritoneal cavity. Intraperitoneal administration of antibiotics also can be employed, since this produces high concentrations of antibiotics at the site of infection. Most agents readily cross the peritoneal membrane, with 50% to 80% of the intraperitoneal dose reaching the systemic circulation. Approximately 70% to 80% of patients can be treated on an outpatient basis with intravenous and/or intraperitoneal instillation of antimicrobials.

Revised treatment recommendations for continuous ambulatory peritoneal dialysis-associated peritonitis provide a systematic approach for antimicrobial management, antibiotic selection, dosing guidelines, duration of therapy, and prophylaxis.[195] Empiric coverage of gram-positive and gram-negative organisms with vancomycin plus an aminoglycoside or third-generation cephalosporin is recommended. If gram-positive organisms are isolated (e.g., *S. aureus, S. epidermidis,* or streptococci) vancomycin alone is recommended. If *Enterococcus* is identified, an intraperitoneal dose of an aminoglycoside should be added to the vancomycin. In 10% to 15% of cases, cultures may be negative. If there is no evidence of a gram-negative infection and the patient is improving after five days of empiric coverage, vancomycin alone should be continued. If a single gram-negative organism is cultured, the recommended therapy is an aminoglycoside or third-generation cephalosporin. Alternatively, if susceptible, an extended-spectrum penicillin (e.g., piperacillin) can be used in place of the aminoglycoside to minimize the risk of toxicity. If an anaerobic gram-negative organism is cultured, anaerobic coverage with metronidazole should be added. For infections due to *P. aeruginosa,* double coverage is recommended, such as piperacillin plus an aminoglycoside. Table 61.2 lists antimicrobial dosing guidelines for the treatment of peritonitis associated with CAPD.[195]

Table 61.2	Pharmacokinetics of Antibiotics in CAPD Patients and Proposed Regimens for the Treatment of CAPD Peritonitis[a,b]					
	Half-life (hr)				Maintenance Dose[c]	
	Normal	ESRD	CAPD	Initial Dose (mg/2 L bag)	Intermittent (mg/2 L bag/dosing interval)	Continuous (mg/2 L bag)
Aminoglycosides						
Amikacin	1.6	39	40	500	120/day	12–24
Gentamicin	2.2	53	32	70–140	40/day	8–16
Netilmicin	2.1	42	18	70–140	40/day	8–16
Tobramycin	2.5	58	36	70–140	40/day	8–16
Cephalosporins						
First generation						
Cefazolin	2.2	28	30	500–1000	1000/day	250–500
Cefonicid	4.0	68	50	250	ND	50
Cephradine	0.9	12	ND	500	ND	250
Cephalexin	0.8	19	9	1000 PO	500 QID PO	NA
Second generation						
Cefamandole	1.0	10	8.0	1000	1000/day	500
Cefmenoxime	1.3	11.3	6.0	2000	1000/day	100
Cefoxitin	0.8	20	15	1000	ND	200
Cefuroxime	1.3	18	15	1000	400/day IV/PO	150–400
Third generation						
Cefixime	3.2	11.5	15	400 PO	400/day PO	NA
Cefoperazone	1.8	2.3	2.2	2000	ND	400–1000
Cefotaxime	0.9	2.5	2.4	2000	2000/day	500
Ceftazidime	1.8	26	13	1000	1000/day	250
Ceftizoxime	1.6	28	11	1000	1000/day	250
Ceftriaxone	8.0	15	12	1000	1000/day	250–500
Penicillins						
Azlocillin	0.9	5.1	ND	500	ND	500
Mezlocillin	1.0	4.3	ND	3000 IV	3000 BID IV	500
Piperacillin	1.2	3.9	2.4	4000 IV	4000 BID IV	500
Ticarcillin	1.2	15	ND	1000–2000	2000 BID	250
Quinolones						
Ciprofloxacin	4.0	8.0	11	500 PO	500 TID PO	50
Fleroxacin	13	27	27	800 PO	400/day PO	NA
Ofloxacin	7.0	30	25	400 PO	200/day PO	NA
Vancomycin and Others						
Vancomycin	6.9	161	92	1000–2000	1000–2000/7 days	30–50
Teicoplanin	50	260	260	400	400 BID	40[d]
Aztreonam	2.0	7.0	9.3	1000	1000/day	500
Clindamycin	2.8	2.8	ND	300	ND	300
Erythromycin	2.1	4.0	ND	ND	500 QID PO	150
Metronidazole	7.9	7.7	11	500 PO/IV	500 TID PO/IV	ND
Minocycline	15.5	20	ND	NA	100 BID PO	NA
Rifampin	4.0	8.0	ND	600 PO	600/day PO	NA
Antifungal Agents						
Amphotericin B	360	360	ND	NA	20–30 QD IV	2–8
Flucytosine	4.2	115	ND	2000–3000 PO	1000 QD PO	NA
Fluconazole	22	125	72	NA	150 mg Q 2 day	ND
Ketoconazole	2.0	1.8	2.4	400 PO	200–800/day PO	NA
Miconazole	24	25	ND	200	ND	100–200
Combinations						
Ampicillin-Sulbactam	Amp: 1.3 Sul: 1.0	Amp: 15 Sul: 19	Amp: 9.5 Sul: 9.7	Amp: 1000–2000 Sul: 1000–2000	Amp: 1000 BID Sul: 1000 BID	Amp: 100 Sul: 100
Imipenem-Cilastatin	Imi: 0.9 Cil: 0.8	Imi: 3.0 Cil: 15	Imi: 6.4 Cil: 19	Imi: 1000 Cil: 500–1000	Imi: 500 BID Cil: 500 BID	Imi: 200 Cil: 100–200
TMP-SMX	TMP: 14 SMX: 10	TMP: 33 SMX: 13	TMP: 34 SMX: 14	TMP: 320 PO SMX: 1600 PO	TMP: 320/1–2 days PO SMX: 1600/1–2 days PO	TMP: 80 SMX: 400

[a] Reprinted with permission from reference 195.

[b] BID = Twice a day; CAPD = Continuous ambulatory peritoneal dialysis; ESRD = creatinine clearance <10 mL/min, patient not on dialysis; IV = Intravenous; NA = Not applicable; ND = No data; PO = oral; QID = Four times a day; TID = Three times a day; TMP-SMX = Trimethoprim-sulfamethoxazole.

[c] Dose per 70 kg adult. The route of administration is intraperitoneal unless otherwise specified. The pharmacokinetic data and proposed dosage regimens presented here are based upon published literature reviewed through April 1992. There is no evidence that mixing different antibiotics in dialysis fluid (except for aminoglycosides and penicillins) is deleterious for the drugs or patients. Do not use the same syringe to mix antibiotics.

[d] This is in each bag × 7 days, then in 2 bags/day × 7 days, and then in 1 bag/day × 7 days.

Secondary Peritonitis

Pathogenesis and Epidemiology

Secondary peritonitis usually occurs following contamination of the peritoneal cavity or its surrounding structures by intestinal contents.[3] In this setting, factors that interfere with the normal clearance of bacteria from the peritoneal cavity[18,26,27] or potentiate their virulence can enhance the development of secondary peritonitis. Intra-abdominal infections most often occur following perforation of the gastrointestinal tract (e.g., appendicitis, diverticulitis, perforated ulcer, colonic carcinoma). However, inflammatory bowel disease, pancreatitis, cholangitis, intestinal infarction, and hepatobiliary tract infection also can result in contamination of the peritoneal cavity and peritonitis.[3,28,29] Intra-abdominal infection following elective surgery occurs most often following colon resection, and less commonly after elective gynecologic or upper GI tract surgery.[28,29]

Dissemination of infection within the peritoneal cavity depends upon five major factors: 1) the location and size of the primary leak; 2) nature of the underlying disease or injury; 3) presence of adhesions from previous operations; 4) duration of the current disease; and 5) efficiency of the host's immune system.[28,29] The most frequently reported type of intra-abdominal infection is generalized peritonitis following penetrating or blunt abdominal trauma.

Localization of intra-abdominal infections without eradication of bacteria results in intraperitoneal, retroperitoneal, or visceral abscesses.[28,29] Intraperitoneal abscesses occur most often in the right lower quadrant in association with appendicitis or a perforated duodenal ulcer, while retroperitoneal abscesses usually are associated with diseases or trauma of the kidney, pancreas, or spine. Visceral abscesses generally are found in the liver, but may occasionally occur in the pancreas, spleen, or kidney. More than 50% of liver abscesses are associated with either cholangitis or appendicitis.[28,29]

Normal Gastrointestinal Flora

Since intra-abdominal infections result from perforation of the intestinal tract, the normal flora of the perforated segment of the intestinal tract determine the initial bacterial inoculum. (See Figure 61.1.) In patients with normal GI tract function, the stomach is sparsely populated by bacteria, mainly facultative gram-positive organisms derived from the oropharynx.[3,19] The stomach of fasting individuals contains very few bacteria (i.e., less than 100 colony-forming units (CFU)/mL) due to the combined effects of gastric motility and the bactericidal activity of normal gastric fluid which has a pH of 1 to 2.[2] The bacterial population of the stomach can be altered by drugs or diseases that increase gastric pH or decrease gastric motility. Thus, patients with bleeding or obstructing duodenal ulcers, gastric ulcers, or gastric carcinomas have an increased number of oral anaerobes and facultative gram-negative bacteria colonizing the stomach. In addition, infections following upper GI tract surgery tend to be more common among patients in whom acidity and motility of the GI tract are compromised.[28,29]

The upper small intestine (duodenum and jejunum) usually contains $<10^3$ CFU/mL of lactobacilli, streptococci, and oral anaerobes such as *Fusobacterium* and *Bacteroides* species (not including *B. fragilis*). The lower small intestine serves as a transitional zone between the sparsely populated stomach and the abundant microbial flora of the colon. The biliary tree is generally sterile, although colonization with aerobic gram-negative bacilli (particularly *E. coli* and *Klebsiella*) and enterococci is more likely in patients with acute cholecystitis, jaundice, or biliary tract stones and in patients over 70 years of age.[24] In the proximal small bowel,

10^3 to 10^4 CFU/mL of facultative gram-negative and gram-positive species are encountered. As the distal ileum is approached, the quantity and species of bacteria increase due to the effects of increasing alkalinity, the presence of bile, and decreased oxygen tension.[2,28] In the distal ileum, bacterial counts average 10^3 to 10^7 CFU/mL, and gram-negative bacteria begin to outnumber gram-positive organisms. Substantial numbers of anaerobic bacteria are present, including *Bacteroides sp.*, streptococci, lactobacilli, and gram-positive nonspore-forming anaerobes.[30,31]

The large bowel harbors more than 400 bacterial species and 10^{10} to 10^{12} CFU/gm of colonic contents, of which anaerobic bacteria (particularly *Bacteroides sp.*) predominate.[30,31] In the distal colon, bacterial counts average 10^{12} CFU/gm of feces, with anaerobes outnumbering other organisms by a ratio of 1000:1. Although large numbers of *Clostridia*, anaerobic cocci, and nonspore-forming anaerobic rods are present, the most prevalent anaerobes are *Bacteroides sp.*, particularly *B. thetaiotaomicron*.[32,33] Among the facultative anaerobes, *E. coli* and various streptococci (especially enterococci) predominate. Nearly one-third of the fecal dry weight consists of viable bacteria.[31]

Given these differences in regional microflora populations, it is not surprising that trauma to the colon (which contains large numbers of bacteria) carries a much higher risk of intra-abdominal infection than trauma to the stomach or jejunum.[3] Solid organs, such as the liver and spleen, rarely harbor any significant endogenous microflora, a factor which likely accounts for the low rate of infection ($<5\%$) following injury to these organs.[31]

Diagnosis

8. T.R. is a 63-year-old male with colonic carcinoma. One day after undergoing surgical resection of the colon, he develops a fever to 102 °F, shaking chills, and abdominal pain. Does he have an intra-abdominal infection? What bacteria should be considered as potential pathogens if T.R. has an intra-abdominal infection?

Signs and Symptoms of Infection

The diagnosis of localized intra-abdominal infection may be difficult, despite the presence of signs and symptoms typical of severe infection. The patient may experience pain and voluntary guarding of the abdomen, with shallow, rapid respirations. Generalized abdominal pain usually is followed by a rigid, "board-like" tensing of the abdominal muscles.[24,34] Inflammation around the intestines and peritoneal cavity results in local paralysis and reflex rigidity of the abdominal wall muscles and the diaphragm, inhibiting respiration and the absorption of potentially toxic bacteria.[2] Bowel sounds may be faint or absent with concomitant abdominal distention, nausea, and vomiting. Fever of 100 to 103 °F usually is present with tachycardia and decreased urine output secondary to fluid loss into the peritoneum. These signs usually are accompanied by an elevated WBC count of 15,000 to 20,000/mm³ with a predominance of neutrophils ("left shift"). The hematocrit (Hct) and blood urea nitrogen (BUN) may be elevated due to dehydration. Initially, patients are usually alkalotic due to vomiting and hyperventilation, but in the later stages of peritonitis acidosis usually occurs. Untreated peritonitis will result in generalized sepsis and hypovolemic shock. Dehydration with hypovolemic shock is the major cause of mortality in the early stage of peritonitis.[24]

The infected material should be Gram's-stained immediately to identify potential pathogens. The presence of pleomorphic gram-negative bacilli, a strong odor, or tissue gas are strongly suggestive of infection with anaerobes, particularly *B. fragilis*.[29,32–35] Cultures utilizing appropriate media for the isolation of both facultative and anaerobic bacteria should be performed before antimicro-

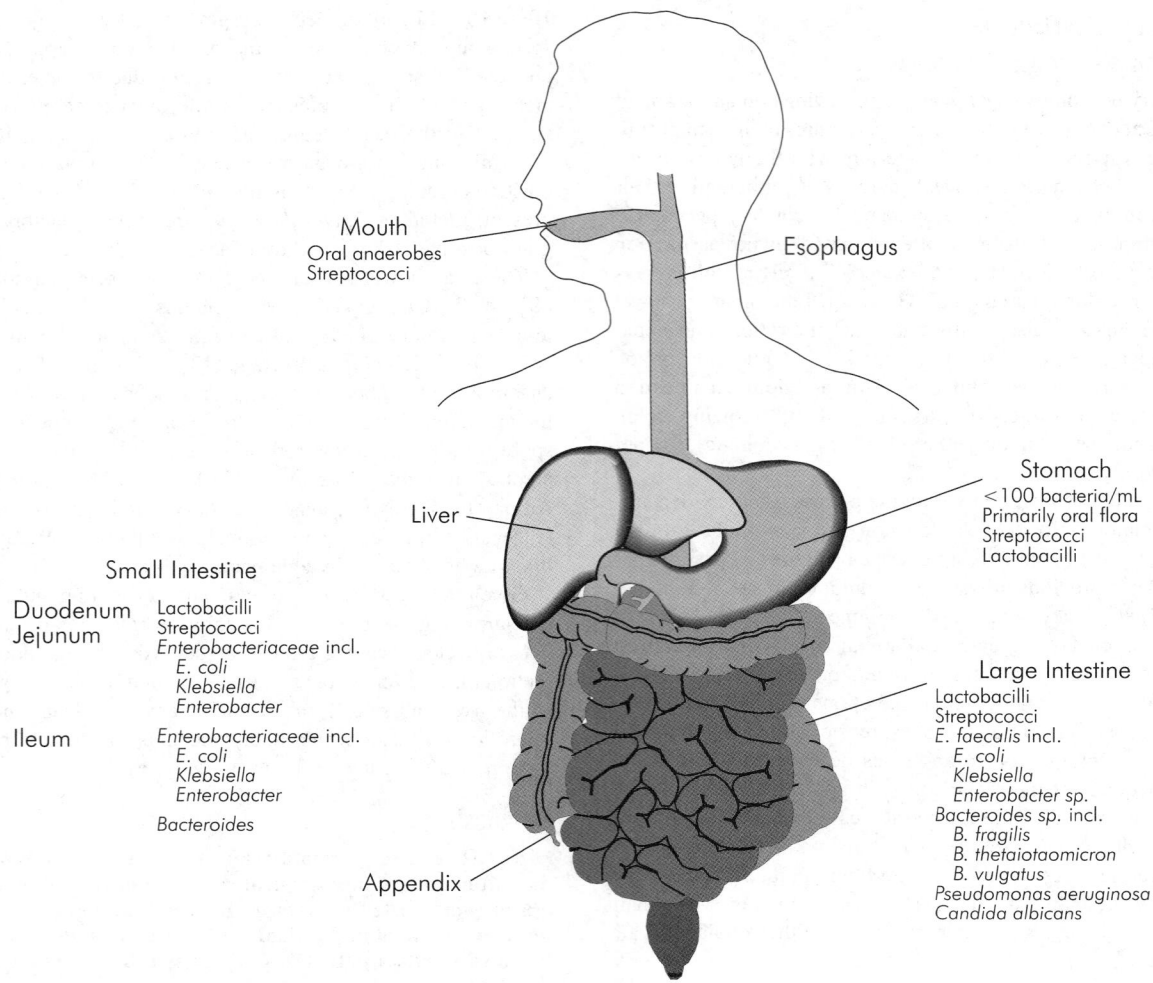

Fig 61.1   Microflora of the Gastrointestinal Tract

bial therapy is initiated. Plain abdominal radiograms or sonography may help to localize sites of intra-abdominal abscesses.

Infecting Pathogens

The microbiology of intra-abdominal infection was first documented more than 40 years ago[36] when anaerobic and facultative gram-negative bacteria were identified in patients with appendicitis. The availability of more advanced techniques for the collection and processing of anaerobic specimens has increased our awareness and understanding of the role of obligate anaerobes in the pathogenesis of intra-abdominal infections.[28,29] Studies consistently document a mixed culture of aerobes and anaerobes. The polymicrobic nature of intra-abdominal infections is illustrated by the observation that an average of five different species (two facultative and three obligate anaerobic bacteria) can be cultured from infected sites; in some patients, as many as 15 different species can be cultured.[3,28,29,37,38]

The most commonly isolated facultative bacterium is *E. coli*, which is found in approximately 60% of cultures. A variety of other gram-negative bacteria also are isolated, including *Klebsiella sp.*, *Proteus sp.*, *Enterobacter sp.*, and *P. aeruginosa* (see Table 61.3). Highly antibiotic-resistant strains of *P. aeruginosa*, *Serratia marcescens,* and *Acinetobacter sp.* often are isolated from patients who develop intra-abdominal infections while hospitalized.[28,29,37] *B. fragilis* is the most important anaerobe recovered from intra-abdominal sites, accounting for 40% to 56% of *Bacteroides* iso-

lates recovered. *B. thetaiotaomicron*, which generally exhibits much greater *in vitro* resistance to second- and third-generation cephalosporins than *B. fragilis*, accounts for 13% to 23% of isolates.[28] The *B. thetaiotaomicron*, however, are much less virulent than *B. fragilis* despite their greater numbers. Anaerobic cocci (peptococci and peptostreptococci) and facultative gram-positive cocci such as enterococci frequently are isolated.[37,38] Although it rarely is isolated in pure culture from intra-abdominal infections, *B. fragilis* is the most commonly isolated anaerobe found in blood culture samples following bacteremia from intra-abdominal infection.[3,29]

Animal models of intra-abdominal infection have been used to clarify the roles of various bacteria on mortality and abscess formation. When a standardized inoculum of rat colonic contents was placed into the peritoneal cavity of Wistar rats, untreated rats developed a biphasic condition that was initially characterized by an acute peritonitis that was associated with a 37% mortality rate: all surviving rats developed intra-abdominal abscesses. *E. coli* was the numerically dominant organism obtained from peritoneal exudate in early peritonitis, whereas *B. fragilis* was dominant in the abscesses found later in the course of infection. Blood cultures taken during the peritonitis stage were positive for *E. coli* in the majority of animals, while *B. fragilis* and *Fusobacterium* were routinely isolated from peritoneal abscesses; *E. coli* and enterococci were present in lower concentrations. Rats treated with gentamicin, a drug active against aerobic gram-negative bacteria but not anaerobes, survived the initial peritonitis and septicemia, but continued to develop abscesses. Animals treated with clindamycin, which has activity against gram-positive and gram-negative anaerobic bacteria but not against gram-negative aerobic bacteria, developed peritonitis and septicemia with a mortality rate similar to that of untreated controls, but survivors did not develop abscesses.

Later studies[37,40] further clarified the roles of coliforms and anaerobes. E. coli, enterococci, B. fragilis, and Fusobacterium varium alone and in all possible combinations were inoculated in an experimental intra-abdominal abscess model in Wistar rats. After gelatin capsules containing the test organisms were implanted in the peritoneum of rats, mortality rates and the frequency of intraabdominal abscess formation were measured. Mortality was restricted to the animals receiving E. coli as one of the implanted species and correlated linearly with the size of the bacterial inoculum. Thus, coliforms were implicated as the cause of the acute lethality associated with intra-abdominal infections. No abscesses were detected in any of the animals challenged with a single microbial species. Abscess formation correlated with the inoculation of one facultative strain and one anaerobic strain; inoculation of anaerobes alone or E. coli in combination with Enterococcus failed to produce abscesses. These results suggest that synergy between anaerobic and facultative bacteria is important in abscess formation, and that coliform bacteria are responsible for early mortality in intra-abdominal infections, while anaerobic bacteria are primarily responsible for the late complication of intra-abdominal abscess formation.

Several possible mechanisms have been proposed to explain the increased virulence of the combination of facultative and anaerobic bacteria: 1) Production of enzymes by one bacteria may permit tissue invasion by the other bacteria. A similar mechanism has been demonstrated in staphylococcal infections, where production of hyaluronidase by staphylococci permits the invasion of tissue by microaerophilic streptococci.[37] 2) Critical growth factors or nutrients produced by one organism may permit survival of another pathogen at the site of infection. 3) Aerobic bacteria may lower local oxygen concentrations and the oxidation-reduction potential producing the appropriate environment for the replication of anaerobic species. This mechanism is supported by in vitro studies demonstrating that the infective dose of anaerobic streptococci is significantly reduced when the inoculum is supplemented with chemical reducing agents. 4) One organism may protect another

from natural host defenses. For example, B. fragilis reduces opsonization of E. coli by leukocytes.[37,41]

B. fragilis possesses a unique capsular polysaccharide external to the outer membrane.[42,43] Although many Bacteroides species possess capsules or capsule-like material located on the surface, only the capsular polysaccharide of B. fragilis appears capable of potentiating abscesses.[44,45] Implantation of encapsulated B. fragilis or heat-killed, encapsulated B. fragilis in rats resulted in abscess formation in most recipients, whereas unencapsulated B. fragilis strains seldom produced this effect unless they were combined with another organism.[46] Implantation of purified capsular material alone or in conjunction with unencapsulated strains also resulted in abscess formation. Similar experiments employing capsular material from E. coli or S. pneumoniae did not produce abscesses. Immunization of rats with B. fragilis capsular polysaccharide protected them against abscess formation following challenge with B. fragilis, but failed to provide protection when pooled cecal contents were used as inoculae.[47-53] Thus, the virulence of B. fragilis appears to be related to the capsular polysaccharide and may explain the preponderance of B. fragilis isolated from abscesses, in contrast to other Bacteroides species such as B. vulgatus and B. thetaiotaomicron, which outnumber B. fragilis in normal colonic flora by two logs.[31,54,55] Although the precise portion of the capsule responsible for virulence is unknown, studies indicate that immunization with capsular polysaccharide provides a T cell-dependent immunity to abscess development when animals are challenged with B. fragilis.[44-46]

In summary, T.R. is likely to have an intra-abdominal infection caused by mixed flora, containing both aerobic and anaerobic bacteria. His current clinical status, highlighted by an elevated temperature and shaking chills, is probably secondary to the presence of facultative gram-negative bacteria such as E. coli, Proteus, Klebsiella, or Enterobacter. P. aeruginosa, Candida sp., or other resistant bacteria are less likely to be present unless T.R. has recently undergone prolonged hospitalization or received broadspectrum antimicrobial agents.

Antimicrobial Therapy

Empiric Therapy

9. Based upon clinical studies, what empiric antimicrobial therapy is appropriate for T.R. at this time? What are the limitations of existing studies?

Therapy for intra-abdominal infection should include surgical intervention and drainage, antimicrobial therapy directed at facultative gram-negative bacteria and obligate anaerobes, fluid therapy, and support of vital functions. Although surgical debridement and drainage are crucial to the success of therapy, appropriate antimicrobial therapy clearly decreases the morbidity and mortality associated with this disease.[2,24,56,57]

In general, antimicrobial agents should be started before any surgical procedures in the presence of an intra-abdominal infection. The parenteral route is recommended to ensure adequate systemic and tissue concentrations, especially in patients in whom shock or poor perfusion of the muscles or GI tract precludes the use of oral or intramuscular routes of administration. Doses that ensure adequate tissue concentrations of drug at the site of infection should be used.[58,59] Antimicrobial therapy should be started immediately after appropriate specimens (e.g., blood, peritoneal fluid, abscess drainage) are obtained for culture and sensitivity. Therefore, antimicrobial therapy is generally empiric, based upon the expected pathogens at the site of infection.[60]

Table 61.3	Bacteriology of Peritonitis and Intra-Abdominal Abscess[2,26,29,34]
Bacteria	**% of Patients**
Facultative and Aerobic	
Escherichia coli	56–66
Proteus sp.	11–26
Klebsiella or Enterobacter sp.	8–29
Pseudomonas aeruginosa	3–15
Streptococci (including enterococci)	12–47
Staphylococci	7
Anaerobes	
Bacteroides fragilis	40–93
Other Bacteroides sp.	25–59
Peptococci	13–28
Peptostreptococci	14–31
Clostridium sp.	9–58
Fusobacterium sp.	11–32

Studies conducted in animal models of intra-abdominal infection have clearly demonstrated that optimal decreases in mortality and residual abscess formation are obtained by the use of antimicrobial regimens directed against both facultative and anaerobic components of the infection. Antimicrobial agents effective against the facultative component prevent early mortality, but do not alter abscess formation. Conversely, antimicrobial agents directed against anaerobes do not prevent early mortality, but survivors do not develop abscesses.

Optimal antimicrobial therapy has not been established by well-designed clinical trials. Despite marked differences in the antimicrobial spectrum of newer agents, no significant differences in clinical efficacy have been demonstrated. Nevertheless, several groups have published guidelines for the appropriate use of antibiotics for the treatment of intra-abdominal infection.[58,59] These recommendations are based upon in vitro activity, experience in animal models, and the results of clinical trials.

The guidelines identify the most common isolates that cause intra-abdominal infections and antibiotic selection.[21] For mild to moderate community-acquired intra-abdominal infections, monotherapy (e.g., cefoxitin[196]) is recommended. For infections of increased severity, imipenem/cilastatin alone[81] or metronidazole in combination with a cephalosporin (cefotaxime or cefoxitin), or aztreonam, or an aminoglycoside, is recommended.[196,197] The antimicrobial regimen should provide coverage against facultative and anaerobic gram-negative bacilli such as E. coli and B. fragilis, respectively, since they are the most common intra-abdominal pathogens.[58,59]

Solomkin et al.[63] identified a number of deficiencies in antibiotic study design common to most published antimicrobial trials, including: 1) failure to enroll ''high-risk'' or critically ill patients in whom high failure rates might be anticipated; 2) enrollment based solely upon bacterial contamination of the peritoneum rather than patients with established infection; 3) nonuniform criteria and reporting of infectious diagnosis, premorbid health status, severity of infection, outcome of therapy, or reasons for treatment failure; and 4) failure to enroll sufficient numbers of patients to detect true differences between regimens (i.e., a large beta error). Many of the studies are not prospective, randomized, double-blind, or (for ethical reasons) placebo-controlled trials (see Table 61.4).[63]

Antimicrobial regimens should evaluate patients with a single disease entity who experience a substantial failure rate following standard therapy. Clinical trials should enroll sufficient numbers of patients to detect true differences in outcome. Investigators must utilize appropriate randomization techniques to avoid bias in patient assignment and employ a standardized method of stratifying patient factors known to affect the outcome of therapy, including premorbid health status, severity of illness, and type of infection.[63] Several surgical infection stratification systems, such as the Acute Physiologic Assessment and Chronic Health Evaluation (APACHE) score, have been proposed and evaluated in an effort to standardize the stratification of patient factors and severity of illness: the use of patient-standardized scoring systems would allow clinical trials at one institution to be compared with those at other centers[60,64–66] and allow more accurate correlation of the risk of mortality to severity of illness.

Clindamycin combined with gentamicin is generally the ''standard'' antimicrobial therapy to which other treatment regimens for intra-abdominal infections should be compared.[64,67–71] Although this regimen is clearly efficacious, the potential for nephrotoxicity secondary to aminoglycosides and clindamycin-associated enterocolitis have led investigators to search for alternative therapies.[72] Table 61.5 lists the antimicrobial regimens found to be efficacious

for the treatment of intra-abdominal infections in randomized, controlled clinical trials.[73–83] Imipenem/cilastatin (Primaxin), a carbapenem combined with an inhibitor of imipenem metabolism, has a broad spectrum of activity versus gram-positive, facultative gram-negative, and obligate anaerobes. In a randomized controlled trial imipenem/cilastatin was significantly more effective than tobramycin plus clindamycin ($p = 0.043$) for the treatment of intra-abdominal infection.[81] The failure rate for patients treated with tobramycin plus clindamycin was significantly higher ($p = 0.018$) than the imipenem/cilastatin treated group and was associated with a persistence of facultative gram-negative organisms. The investigators attribute the significantly high failure rate to the four day delay in achieving maximum peak aminoglycoside levels and recommend imipenem/cilastatin for treatment of intra-abdominal infections. In another randomized trial, piperacillin/tazobactam (Zosyn) was superior to imipenem/cilastatin in patients with intra-abdominal infections ($p = 0.005$). There were four failures in the piperacillin/tazobactam group while 18 failures were noted in the imipenem/cilastatin group. A possible explanation for the difference in clinical cure and failure rate can be attributed to the lower dose of imipenem (500 mg Q 8 hr) used in this trial.[82] A variety of other regimens, tested in nonrandomized or unblinded comparative trials, were found to be as efficacious as the combination of clindamycin and gentamicin (see Table 61.4).[84–89]

Therapy with an agent with activity against P. aeruginosa is desirable if the infectious process develops while the patient is hospitalized or has received broad-spectrum antimicrobials.

Beta-Lactam Antibiotics

10. Can a beta-lactam antibiotic be used to treat T.R.'s infection?

The use of beta-lactam antimicrobials in mixed-flora infections is associated with a higher failure rate than aminoglycoside-based combinations. However, the primary reason for these failures is a lack of activity against anaerobic flora rather than a lack of activity against facultative gram-negative bacteria.[2,59] In studies employing a beta-lactam in combination with clindamycin, metronidazole, or a beta-lactam with activity against B. fragilis (e.g., cefoxitin or imipenem-cilastatin), equivalent cure rates have been demonstrated.[90–103]

Advantages of aminoglycosides include their ability to kill stationary-phase (nondividing) bacteria as long as protein synthesis is occurring. Bacterial killing is rapid and persists even in the presence of sublethal concentrations of drug and immediate regrowth of the bacteria is prevented by this ''postantibiotic effect.'' A similar effect is not observed against gram-negative bacteria when beta-lactams are utilized, although a postantibiotic effect has been observed with imipenem-cilastatin against P. aeruginosa and with penicillin against gram-positive bacteria.[59]

Bartlett and colleagues[45,54,56] compared a variety of beta-lactams in two different animal models of intra-abdominal infection. In a model employing intraperitoneal inoculation of pooled rat cecal contents, all antimicrobial agents tested reduced the lethality associated with the acute peritonitis stage. However, there was a significant difference in the incidence of intra-abdominal abscesses between antimicrobial agents, which correlated well with their in vitro activity against B. fragilis.[54] Optimal results, obtained with cefotaxime, cefoxitin, moxalactam, and carbenicillin, were not statistically different from results obtained with clindamycin therapy alone. Results with cephalothin, cefazolin, and cefamandole were statistically superior to untreated controls, but less efficacious than the above agents. In this model, all animals received a similar inoculum of pooled rat cecal contents. Therefore, variations in results

Table 61.4	Comparative Trials for the Treatment of Intra-Abdominal Infections[a]	
Investigator	Antimicrobial Regimen	Comments
Combination Therapy Trials		
Stone[84]	Metronidazole + gentamicin Cefamandole + erythromycin	Not blinded or placebo-controlled. Similar efficacy for all 3 regimens (95%) but recurrence of sepsis less with metronidazole + gentamicin
Lennard[87]	Chloramphenicol + gentamicin	No significant difference in efficacy
Harding[124]	Chloramphenicol + ticarcillin Metronidazole + gentamicin Cefoxitin + tobramycin Ceftizoxime	All regimens equally efficacious but not all studies conducted simultaneously. Small number of patients
Luke[11]	Ceftriaxone + metronidazole Ampicillin + netilmicin + metronidazole	Ceftriaxone regimen more effective. Not blinded or placebo-controlled
Single-Agent Therapy		
Gonzenbach[90]	Imipenem/cilastatin	Not blinded or placebo-controlled
Schentag[94]	Moxalactam	Clindamycin + tobramycin combination more nephrotoxic. Clinical response equivalent. Moxalactam associated with hypoprothrombinemia. Not blinded (after patients enrolled in study)
Henry[85]	Aztreonam + clindamycin	Favorable clinical response in 90% of patients. Not blinded, randomized, or placebo-controlled
Solomkin[91]	Imipenem/cilastatin	Not blinded or placebo-controlled. No difference in mortality
Scandinavian Study Group[92]	Imipenem/cilastatin	Imipenem superior to clindamycin + gentamicin. Not blinded, randomized, or placebo-controlled. Failures: 9/86 (gentamicin/clindamycin), 2/77 (imipenem)
Drusano[97]	Cefoxitin	36/46 patients cured with cefoxitin. 33/44 patients cured with clindamycin/aminoglycoside
Busuttil[96]	Cefamandole	Failures more common in cefamandole group
Stone[98]	Moxalactam Cefotaxime Cefoperazone	Trials not run concurrently. Not blinded or placebo-controlled. 83% cure for cephalosporin regimens, 73% for clindamycin/gentamicin
Harding[99]	Chloramphenicol + ticarcillin	

[a] All studies were prospective, comparative trials.

that might be observed with inoculae composed of bacteria with different susceptibilities may not be detected.[52]

Further work was performed by these investigators in a subcutaneous abscess model utilizing 15 different strains of *B. fragilis* in an effort to define the comparative efficacy of a variety of antimicrobial agents against *B. fragilis*. Quantitative cultures of bacteria from abscess sites were utilized to compare the efficacy of each agent. Clindamycin, moxalactam, and cefoxitin were significantly more effective than carbenicillin, thienamycin, cefotaxime, or ceftizoxime in reducing mean colony forming units of *B. fragilis* cultured from abscess sites. Results with ceforanide, cephalothin, ampicillin, and cefoperazone were not significantly different from untreated controls, although the activity of cefoperazone was significantly improved by the addition of a beta-lactamase inhibitor. The investigators reported a reasonably good correlation between *in vitro* and *in vivo* activity of the agents, stability to *B. fragilis* beta-lactamase, and penetration of the agent into abscess sites.[54]

These animal models employed a standard inoculum in order to produce a uniform mortality rate of 35% to 45% in untreated controls. However, other investigators have utilized animal models employing larger inoculums (e.g., human feces) which resulted in much higher mortality rates.[61,62] Extrapolation of these methods to the clinical setting may not produce the same results.[52,56]

The use of beta-lactams is not entirely problem-free. *B. fragilis* produces chromosomal beta-lactamases which inactivate most beta-lactams. Notably, cefoxitin and imipenem-cilastatin are resistant to this beta-lactamase. Although currently available beta-lactams can be combined with beta-lactamase inhibitors such as clavulanic acid, sulbactam, and tazobactam, they have little activity against the chromosomal type I beta-lactamases seen in some *Enterobacteriaceae*.[59] Fortunately, these bacteria are uncommon in community-acquired infections.

Risk factors that predispose patients to the acquisition of multiresistant bacteria include: 1) the presence of bacteria such as *P. aeruginosa*, *Enterobacter cloacae*, *Providencia*, and indole-positive *Proteus* species; 2) a large inoculum; and 3) poor blood flow at the site of infection. The net result of these risk factors is exposure of the bacteria to low concentrations of antibiotic for a prolonged period of time. Since most beta-lactams do not possess a postantibiotic effect against gram-negative bacteria, lack of efficacy and the development of resistance are more likely. In any inoculum of bacteria, a small percentage of bacteria are likely to be resistant; a large inoculum enhances the possibility that these resistant bacteria are able to survive.[59]

T.R. should receive antimicrobial therapy with activity against facultative gram-negative bacteria and anaerobes, including *B. fragilis*. The use of an aminoglycoside in combination with clindamycin, metronidazole, or cefoxitin provides effective and appropriate antimicrobial therapy.

Single Agent Therapy

11. The surgery team is concerned about the potential for nephrotoxicity associated with regimens that include an aminoglycoside. Is single-agent therapy appropriate to treat T.R.'s infection?

Table 61.5			Randomized, Controlled Trials for the Treatment of Intra-Abdominal Infections[a]				
				Outcome of Therapy			
Investigator	# of Patients	Antimicrobial Regimen[b]		Improvement (%)	Cure (%)	Failure (%)	Comments

Comparative Trials

Investigator	# of Patients	Antimicrobial Regimen[b]	Improvement (%)	Cure (%)	Failure (%)	Comments
Smith[73,74] (1980, 1983)	23	CM 600 mg IV Q 8 hr + Tob 1.5 mg/kg IV Q 8 hr[c]	3/23 (13%)	17/23 (73.9%)	3/23 (13%)	CM dose lower than most other studies
	35[d]	Metro 500 mg IV Q 8 hr + Tob 1.5 mg/kg IV Q 8 hr[c]	0/35 (0%)	29/35 (82.9%)	6/35 (17.1%)	
Tally[75] (1981)	37	CFX 1.5–3 gm IV Q 6 hr[c] ± Amik 5 mg/kg IV Q 8 hr[c]	10/37 (27%)	24/37 (64.9%)	3/37 (8.1%)	
	37	CM 600–900 mg IV Q 6 hr + Amik 5 mg/kg IV Q 8 hr[c]	9/37 (24.3%)	20/37 (54.1%)	8/37 (21.6%)	
Kirkpatrick[76] (1983)	25[e]	Metro 500 mg IV Q 8 hr + Tob 1– 1.5 mg/kg IV Q 8 hr	2/25 (8%)	20/25 (80%)	3/25 (12%)	No adjustment of aminoglycoside concentrations
	28	CM 800 mg IV Q hr + Tob 1–1.5 mg/kg IV Q 8 hr	1/28 (3.6%)	24/28 (85.7%)	3/25 (12%)	Very small number of patients enrolled
Canadian Metronidazole-Clindamycin Study Group[78] (1983)	72	Metro 500 mg IV Q 8 hr + Gent 1.5 mg/kg IV Q 8 hr[c]	8/72 (11.1%)	60/72 (83.3%)	4/72 (5.5%)	Equivalent efficacy for both regimens
	69	CM 600–800 mg IV Q 8 hr; Gent 1.5 mg/kg IV Q 8 hr[c]	8/69 (11.6%)	58/69 (84.1%)	3/69 (4.3%)	Gent adjusted to produce peak serum concentration of 5 mg/L, trough <2 mg/L
Malangoni[77] (1985)	59	CFX 3 gm IV Q 6 hr	Not stated	49/59 (83.1%)	10/59 (16.9%)	Clinical failure more common in "high-risk" patients (19/21 failures) with colonic, gastroduodenal, postoperative, appendiceal sources. Number of improved patients not reported. Single blind study
	53	CM 600 mg IV Q 6 hr + Tob 1.5 mg/kg IV Q 8 hr[c]	Not stated	42/53 (79.2%)	11/53 (20.8%)	
Study Group of Intra-Abdominal Infections[79] (1986)	46	Amp/S	4/46 (8.7%)	36/46 (78.3%)	6/46 (13%)	Not placebo-controlled but double-blinded
	37	CM 600 mg IV Q 6 hr + Gent 1.5 mg/kg IV Q 8 hr[c]	3/37 (8.1%)	33/37 (89.2%)	1/37 (2.7%)	
Walker[83] (1993)	96	Amp/S 2 gm/1 gm IV Q 6 hr	—	84/96 (88%)	12/96 (13%)	
	101	CFX 2 gm IV Q 6 hr	—	80/101 (79%)	21/101 (21%)	
Solomkin[81] (1990)	81	Imi 500 mg IV Q 8 hr	—	67/81 (83%)	14/81 (17%)	Multicenter trial; Imi significantly more effective than CM/tob
	81	Tob 1.5 mg/kg IV Q 8 hr; CM 600 mg IV Q 6 hr	—	57/81 (70%)	24/81 (30%)	
Brismar[82] (1992)	55	Pip/T 4 gm/500 mg IV Q 8 hr	1/55 (2%)	50/55 (91%)	2/55 (4%)	Pip/T significantly more effective than Imi
	58	Imi 500 mg IV Q 8 hr	0/58 (0%)	40/58 (69%)	2/58 (3%)	

Noncomparative Trials

Investigator	# of Patients	Antimicrobial Regimen[b]	Improvement (%)	Cure (%)	Failure (%)	Comments
LeFrock[80] (1983)	15	CFX 2 gm IV Q 6 hr	2/15 (13.6%)	10/15 (66.6%)	3/15 (20%)	
	17	Mezlo 5 gm IV Q 6 hr	2/17 (11.8%)	12/17 (76.4%)	2/17 (11.8%)	

[a] All studies were prospective, randomized, and blinded with specific outcome criteria and appropriate statistical analysis.
[b] Antibiotics were as follows: CFX = Cefoxitin; CM = Clindamycin; Gent = Gentamicin; Tob = Tobramycin; Amp/S = Ampicillin/Sulbactam; Metro = Metronidazole; Amik = Amikacin; Mezlo = Mezlocillin; Imi = Imipenem + cilastatin; Pip/T = Piperacillin + tazobactam.
[c] Dosage adjusted for body weight, renal function, and/or aminoglycoside serum concentrations (when applicable).
[d] 34 patients received 35 courses of therapy.
[e] One patient could not be evaluated.

A number of potent, broad-spectrum antimicrobials have been evaluated as single agents for the treatment of intra-abdominal infections (see Table 61.5).[90–103] Second- and third-generation cephalosporins, imipenem-cilastatin, ampicillin/sulbactam, and aztreo-nam have all been compared with combination drug regimens containing aminoglycosides. In general, these single drug regimens appear to be as efficacious as combination therapy; however, many of the patients enrolled in these studies were neither critically ill nor at high risk for peritonitis. In addition, insufficient numbers of patients were studied to reliably detect any differences between these regimens.[59]

When selecting a single agent for therapy, its activity against common gram-negative bacteria and anaerobes, including *B. fragilis*, as well as its stability to beta-lactamase should be considered. T.R. is a "high-risk" patient because he has been exposed to a heavy bacterial inoculum resulting from colonic perforation. Therefore, he should be continued on combination therapy until the results of blood and peritoneal fluid cultures are available.

Enterococcal Infection

12. T.R.'s peritoneal fluid cultures reveal a mixed infection with *E. coli*, *B. fragilis*, *Candida albicans*, and *Enterococcus*. Should he receive additional antimicrobial therapy active against enterococcus?

While *Enterococcus* is frequently cultured in patients with secondary peritonitis, its pathogenicity has been questioned, and there is ambivalence regarding the necessity for antimicrobial coverage for this organism.[104,105] *Enterococcus* can potentially cause serious disease infections (e.g., endocarditis, urinary tract infections), although it often has been considered relatively nonvirulent in the setting of polymicrobial infections such as intra-abdominal abscess.[104]

An important issue is whether empiric treatment should have included antibiotics directed specifically against *Enterococcus*, particularly when it would have required the addition of a third or fourth drug to the patient's antimicrobial regimen. Some investigators believe that *E. faecalis* (previously known as *Streptococcus faecalis*) is a commensal organism that need not be treated in most clinical settings. They point to clinical studies in which the use of antibiotic regimens lacking *in vitro* activity against *E. faecalis* have been successful.[24,106] Other investigators feel that the pathogenicity of *E. faecalis* lies in its ability to synergize with anaerobes to form abscesses[106,107] and believe that it should be treated.

One reason *E. faecalis* is not regarded as a pathogen in mixed infections is that enterococcal bacteremia following therapy with agents with no activity against this organism is presumably rare. However, several investigators have noted that "breakthrough bacteremia" during therapy is not as uncommon as it was once presumed, and although enterococcemia from an abdominal source is relatively unusual, it carries a very high mortality.[104,106–108] Enterococcal bacteremia has been observed, albeit infrequently, following therapy with some antibiotics ineffective against *E. faecalis*, such as cephalosporins or an aminoglycoside plus clindamycin.[24,104,106,107] However, it is possible that the increased use of indwelling urinary catheters and intravascular devices may have contributed to the bacteremia. Furthermore, these studies still fail to establish the pathogenicity of the organism because the patients usually are severely debilitated. Thus, enterococcal bacteremia may be a symptom of a compromised host status rather than a cause.[104]

E. faecalis does not produce acute mortality, bacteremia, or abscesses in animal models for intra-abdominal infections when inoculated in pure culture.[37,38,55] However, when a facultative organism is inoculated in combination with an anaerobic species, abscesses develop. Synergy between enterococci and *B. fragilis* also has been noted by Hite et al.[109] and Brook.[110] *Enterococcus* may enhance the virulence of anaerobes by altering the oxidation-reduction potential of the local environment.[37,38,104] Matlow et al.[111] injected *E. coli*, *B. fragilis*, and *Clostridium perfringens* with or without *E. faecalis* into the peritoneum of rats. The presence of *E. faecalis* in the original inoculum was associated with death or the development of large abscesses when these two endpoints were

examined together, although there was no statistically significant difference in mortality alone. They concluded that *E. faecalis* may synergize with other bacterial pathogens in intra-abdominal sepsis to augment morbidity and possibly mortality.

In contrast to the above, Bartlett et al.[54] concluded that *E. faecalis* did not play an important role in their rat model despite its frequent presence in mixed flora at infected sites. Combination therapy directed at *E. faecalis* (e.g., penicillin plus an aminoglycoside) did not produce significantly different mortality rates compared to treatment with either penicillin or an aminoglycoside alone. Weinstein[38] found that polymicrobial peritonitis in the rat could be successfully treated with a combination of gentamicin and clindamycin despite the presence of *E. faecalis*.

Approximately 90% of strains of *E. faecalis* are inhibited by penicillin G, ampicillin, or vancomycin.[111,112] Unlike most other streptococci, these organisms are resistant to most antimicrobial agents, including the majority of beta-lactams. The relatively high minimum inhibitory concentrations (MICs) required for most beta-lactams have been related to a decreased affinity of certain enterococcal penicillin-binding proteins for these agents. Although aminoglycosides are inactive against enterococci *in vitro*, the addition of an aminoglycoside to cell wall-active agents such as penicillin, ampicillin, vancomycin, or extended-spectrum penicillins results in synergistic activity against the *Enterococcus*, with rapid, complete, bactericidal activity. The mechanism of this synergy appears to be facilitation of aminoglycoside entry into the bacterial cell by the disruptive effect of cell wall-active antimicrobial agents. Notably, however, cephalosporins lack activity against enterococci, even when used in combination with aminoglycosides.[104,112]

The question of whether to provide antimicrobial activity against *E. faecalis* is complicated by reports of an increased incidence of high-level gentamicin resistance in enterococci. High-level resistance to gentamicin is now endemic in many regions of the U.S.[104,113] Organisms possessing this resistance possess aminoglycoside-modifying enzymes and generally are resistant to all other aminoglycosides. Since the resistance is plasmid mediated, it usually is transferable and invariably entails the loss of bactericidal synergy between the aminoglycosides and penicillins or vancomycin.[104,112] In a 1986 study,[113] 33% of newly-hospitalized patients were colonized with gentamicin-resistant enterococci at initial culture (all had been hospitalized before entry into the study) and an additional 10% acquired resistant isolates during the study. Gentamicin-resistant enterococci were believed to have contributed to one-third of all deaths, and the acquisition of the resistant strains by patients appeared to be related to previous antibiotic exposure.[104,112,113] Factors that seemed to be related to infection with a gentamicin-resistant strain included treatment with cephalosporins or aminoglycosides within the preceding three months, perioperative antibiotic prophylaxis, prior surgical procedures, and longer hospitalizations.[113]

Beta-lactamase producing strains of enterococci resistant to gentamicin which are not inhibited by usual concentrations of ampicillin or penicillin are increasingly isolated, particularly at tertiary care institutions. Addition of a beta-lactamase inhibitor such as clavulanic acid or sulbactam is required in order to achieve inhibitory activity.[104,112]

Anaerobic Bacteria

13. The surgical resident selects cefoxitin plus gentamicin for the treatment of T.R.'s intra-abdominal infection. Is the anaerobic activity of this regimen required?

The need for antimicrobial therapy active against anaerobic bacteria in the treatment of intra-abdominal infections is well accepted. Early studies demonstrated decreased mortality rates in regimens employing an antimicrobial agent with activity against *B. fragilis* as compared with regimens that did not possess activity against this pathogen.[58,59]

With the introduction of broad-spectrum antimicrobial agents with *in vitro* activity against *B. fragilis*, the choice of a specific antianaerobic agent has become more complex. It is important to evaluate the results of well designed clinical trials in addition to *in vitro* susceptibility data. Chloramphenicol, clindamycin, cefoxitin, cefotetan, moxalactam, ceftizoxime, metronidazole, ampicillin plus sulbactam, ticarcillin, mezlocillin, piperacillin, doxycycline, and imipenem all possess good activity against *B. fragilis*. A number of clinical studies have demonstrated that the majority of these agents are as efficacious as the "gold standard" therapy with clindamycin plus an aminoglycoside.

The presence or absence of *in vitro* activity against anaerobic bacteria does not always correlate with *in vitro* results. For example, despite its lack of activity against *E. coli*, Bartlett[55] demonstrated that the mortality rate of rats treated with metronidazole alone was only 10%, as compared with a mortality rate of 42% in rats treated with clindamycin alone. Clinical trials also have shown that treatment with metronidazole resulted in eradication of resistant coliforms as well as susceptible anaerobes from infected sites.[54,114] More extensive studies with the rat model demonstrated a reduction in the incidence of *E. coli* bacteremia during treatment with metronidazole, but only when susceptible anaerobic bacteria were included in the inoculum. Similar results were noted with mixed cultures *in vitro*; the rate of killing of *B. fragilis* can be enhanced by the presence of *E. coli*, and under anaerobic conditions, metronidazole can suppress the growth of *E. coli*.[114–125] It is theorized that anaerobic bacteria may convert metronidazole to metabolites with activity against *E. coli*, since the concentration of parent drug decreases during incubation with *E. coli*.[55,114] A similar effect on *E. coli* is not seen when clindamycin is tested. As animal studies and clinical trials have not consistently demonstrated a difference in the efficacy of clindamycin versus metronidazole combination therapy in the treatment of intra-abdominal infections, the clinical implications of these *in vitro* findings are unclear.[126–129]

Similarly, a discrepancy between *in vitro* activity and *in vivo* efficacy of chloramphenicol against *B. fragilis* is theorized to be due to inactivation of chloramphenicol by enzymatic reduction of the nitro group by anaerobic bacteria. Because this inactivation is slow, the organisms appear susceptible by usual laboratory susceptibility testing methods.[55,56]

Resistance to Antianaerobic Antimicrobial Agents. Unfortunately, there is a significant problem of increasing resistance to antimicrobial agents among anaerobic bacteria. The susceptibility of *B. fragilis* to a variety of antimicrobial agents has been studied by a number of investigators. Multiple mechanisms of resistance are encountered, and resistance rates differ among various geographic areas of the U.S.[32,117] Furthermore, there is some disagreement as to the correlation between *in vitro* and *in vivo* activity and the clinical effectiveness of some antimicrobials, particularly with regard to newer cephalosporins.[32] In most cases, inadequate numbers of patients have been studied with each drug to correlate clinical outcome with *in vitro* susceptibility, although numerous studies have demonstrated that agents with good *in vitro* activity against a broad range of anaerobic pathogens are more likely to produce favorable results than less active agents. The role of surgical drainage, debridement, underlying disease states, and antimicrobial pharmacokinetics and pharmacodynamics cannot always be assessed. Therefore, given the multitude of other factors that influence therapeutic success or failure, it may be difficult to correlate specific susceptibility data with clinical outcome in individual cases.[32]

Susceptibility Testing. Despite a number of existent methods for susceptibility testing, there are problems with reproducibility and a lack of comparability between methods and/or inability to grow all significant anaerobes with each method.[117–120] For a number of drugs, there may be clustering of a significant percentage of susceptibility test endpoints at or near the proposed breakpoints. Since the variability in most dilution tests is one, twofold dilution, this could result in large differences in the reporting of the numbers of susceptible versus resistant isolates.[32]

The Working Group on Anaerobic Susceptibility Testing of the National Committee for Clinical Laboratory Standards (NCCLS) has suggested that susceptibility testing should be performed in four settings: 1) to determine patterns of susceptibility of anaerobes to new antimicrobial agents; 2) to periodically monitor susceptibility patterns on a geographic basis; 3) to periodically monitor susceptibility patterns in local institutions; and 4) to assist occasionally in the management of individual patients.[32,118,119] Strains which are felt to merit testing include the *Bacteroides* group and *C. perfringens*. Antimicrobials such as metronidazole, chloramphenicol, imipenem, and beta-lactam/beta-lactamase inhibitor combinations, to which anaerobes are essentially universally susceptible, should not be tested. Sensitivity testing is recommended for penicillin G, certain wide-spectrum penicillins, cefoxitin, cefotetan, and clindamycin.[118,120]

As most anaerobes are cultured in the setting of mixed flora, isolation of individual components of a complex mixture can be time consuming. In addition, most anaerobes are very slow growing, and it may take days to weeks for a definitive culture and sensitivity report. If specimens are not collected and transported in optimal media or in a timely fashion, inaccurate or misleading results may be reported. The methods for susceptibility testing of anaerobic bacteria are not well standardized, and many hospital laboratories do not have the necessary funds or expertise to perform extensive culture and sensitivity testing.[116] Therefore, empiric therapy often must be aimed at the most likely pathogens and the clinician must be aware of their usual sensitivity patterns at the institution.[32]

Antifungal Therapy: Treatment of *Candida*

14. Should T.R.'s antimicrobial therapy include an agent with antifungal activity?

The need to treat *Candida sp.* as a solitary isolate or as part of a polymicrobial infection is controversial. Certainly, *Candida* has the potential to cause peritonitis, intraperitoneal abscesses, and subsequent candidemia. Many investigators favor early, aggressive therapy with parenteral administration of 500 to 1000 mg amphotericin B over 10 to 14 days.[130–132] However, concern over the toxicity of amphotericin is warranted, and the risk/benefit ratio must be assessed carefully for each patient. The use of newer antifungal agents such as fluconazole may offer decreased toxicity in these patients. However, the potential risk of the development of resistance must be addressed in clinical trials.

In patients undergoing continuous ambulatory peritoneal dialysis, *Candida* can attach to the peritoneal catheter; thus, even prolonged antimicrobial therapy with amphotericin B (parenteral and locally instilled) may not eradicate the infection. There are other problems. Penetration of amphotericin B into the peritoneal fluid is minimal because it is extensively bound to serum protein, and intraperitoneal instillation of amphotericin B often is irritating to the mucosa. Antifungal therapy appears to merely suppress the infection, and removal of the catheter may be required to eradicate the infection.[25] Peritoneal dialysate concentrations of fluconazole following daily oral administration of 100 mg results in peritoneal fluid concentrations that approximate 60% of simultaneous serum concentrations. However, the results of clinical trials are not yet available.[133]

T.R. should be treated with an antimicrobial regimen that has activity against gram-negative coliforms and anaerobes. If the clinician desires additional activity against *E. faecalis*, this can be accomplished by the use of a penicillin plus an aminoglycoside (e.g., ampicillin/sulbactam and an aminoglycoside). Therapy with an intravenous antifungal agent is not warranted at this time, unless positive blood cultures for *Candida* are isolated or T.R. fails to respond to appropriate antimicrobial therapy.

Antimicrobial Irrigations

15. T.R.'s physicians wish to irrigate the peritoneum with aminoglycosides to achieve high local concentrations. Is irrigation with antimicrobial agents rational or effective in the treatment of intra-abdominal infections?

Some clinicians are reluctant to irrigate the peritoneal cavity for fear of spreading local infection, further damaging the mesothelium, diluting opsonins, or suspending bacteria in a fluid medium where they are less amenable to phagocytosis. However, most animal studies demonstrate that gravity and the movement of the diaphragm during respiration spread bacteria throughout the peritoneal cavity even in the absence of irrigation. In addition, free circulation of fluids within the peritoneal cavity facilitates lymphatic clearance of micro-organisms and toxins.[67,115]

Most clinicians agree that the peritoneum should be cleared of gastric mucin, bile, blood, necrotic tissue, and other substances that could promote the development of intra-abdominal abscesses.[67,134] In the preantibiotic era, local irrigation with saline decreased the mortality associated with intra-abdominal calamities dramatically. These promising results encouraged surgeons to add antibiotics directly to the irrigating solutions, on the theory that direct application would provide the highest possible concentration of antibiotic at the site of infection.[135-142]

Although data are limited, systemic antibiotic therapy and antibiotic irrigations appear to be equally efficacious for both the prevention and treatment of postoperative infections.[67,139-142] Hunt[136] randomized patients to one of three perioperative regimens. All patients received potassium penicillin G 2 million units IV every six hours and gentamicin 5 mg/kg every 24 hours, perioperatively and for a minimum of seven days postoperatively. Group 1 patients received no peritoneal irrigation, group 2 patients received intraoperative irrigation with 2 to 10 L of lactated Ringer's injection, and group 3 patients received both intraoperative and postoperative irrigation. There were no significant differences in mortality among the three groups. Noon and associates[142] were unable to demonstrate any difference in the incidence of mortality or intraperitoneal abscess formation between patients receiving normal saline irrigation and IP kanamycin plus bacitracin.

The potential for systemic toxicity resulting from systemic absorption of antimicrobial agents from the peritoneal cavity often is ignored or unrecognized by clinicians. Most antimicrobials are readily absorbed from mucosal surfaces, especially when they are inflamed. When large volumes of irrigating solution containing antibiotics are used (especially in combination with IV doses) systemic drug concentrations can markedly exceed the therapeutic range. Neuromuscular blockade, renal failure, and ototoxicity have been reported following absorption of aminoglycosides from mucosal surfaces. Although a greater margin of safety exists for the newer penicillins and cephalosporins, the potential for toxicity is still of concern.[135]

At this time, there are few data to support the superiority of antibiotic-containing irrigating solutions over systemic therapy.[135]

Given the potential for systemic toxicity secondary to absorption of antimicrobial agents from the peritoneum, the paucity of controlled trials documenting the efficacy of this method of administration, and the proven efficacy of systemic therapy, it seems prudent to use systemic therapy alone for the treatment of intra-abdominal infections. If irrigation of contaminated tissue is desired, antibiotic-free dialysate should be utilized.[135,141]

Duration of Antimicrobial Therapy

16. How long should T.R. receive antimicrobial therapy?

Recommendations for the duration of therapy for intra-abdominal infection vary from five to seven days, and depend primarily upon the patient's clinical response to therapy.[1,58,59] In general, antimicrobial therapy should be continued until the patient's temperature, WBC count, and differential are within normal limits.[1,2]

A longer duration of therapy may be required to prevent relapse because host defenses may be inadequate to eradicate bacteria from sequestered sites or areas of tissue necrosis. Antimicrobial penetration of abscesses or necrotic tissue may be inadequate and not all areas are accessible to surgical drainage. Longer therapy may be justified if the patient remains febrile, resistant bacteria are isolated, or a focus of infection persists.[24]

Intra-Abdominal Abscess

17. Two weeks postoperatively, T.R. develops abdominal pain and begins to drain purulent material from his abdominal wound. An intra-abdominal abscess is visualized by plain films. How did this abscess develop? What are your considerations in the selection of appropriate antimicrobial agents?

Abscesses are collections of necrotic tissue, bacteria, and white blood cells, that form over a period of days to years. They generally result from chronic inflammation and the body's attempt to localize organisms and toxic substances by formation of an avascular fibrous wall. This isolates bacteria and the liquid core from opsonins and antimicrobial agents.

Microbiology

Abscesses pose a therapeutic challenge because they typically contain large bacterial inoculums (10^7 to 10^9 CFU/mL) that are likely to include small subpopulations of resistant bacteria.[58] Furthermore, the rate of penetration of antibiotics into abscesses is hindered by the low surface-to-volume ratio and the presence of a fibrous capsule. Once antimicrobials penetrate the abscess, several factors can decrease their effectiveness. Dead bacteria and other debris present in an abscess can bind to antimicrobial agents, reducing effective drug concentrations, and the low redox potential decreases the oxygen-dependent transport of aminoglycosides into bacteria. In addition, release of lysosomal enzymes decreases the pH to as low as 5.7 which, in turn, decreases the intrinsic activity of aminoglycosides and erythromycin.[3,143,144]

Many anaerobic bacteria produce beta-lactamase which inactivates most penicillins and cephalosporins, with the exception of cefoxitin and imipenem. The effectiveness of newer agents that are administered in combination with a beta-lactamase inhibitor, such as clavulanic acid or sulbactam, needs to be studied further. Inactivation of clindamycin was demonstrated in an animal model utilizing intraperitoneal capsules inoculated with *B. fragilis*. The mechanism for this inactivation is unclear.[145]

Although surgical debridement and drainage of T.R.'s abscess is crucial, adjunctive therapy with antimicrobial agents is warranted. The optimal antimicrobial agent must rapidly penetrate the abscess in adequate concentrations; resist inactivation by low pH, enzymes, or cellular debris; and possess the appropriate antimicrobial spectrum in order to provide optimal activity in the treatment of intra-abdominal abscesses.[3]

Penetration of Antimicrobial Agents into the Peritoneum

Burke[146] demonstrated that adequate antibiotic concentrations need to be present at the site of infection at the time of bacterial contamination, because the effective period of antibiotic action is restricted to the initial few hours after the arrival of bacteria in tissue.[146–148]

The penetration of antimicrobial agents into tissues or abscess cavities depends upon 1) the serum to tissue fluid concentration gradient, 2) binding of the antimicrobial to serum and tissue proteins, 3) diffusibility of the drug, based upon its molecular size and pKa, and 4) lipid solubility.[149] In general, the beta-lactam antimicrobials have been shown to achieve peritoneal tissue fluid concentrations that exceed typical MICs for most commonly-encountered facultative gram-negative and anaerobic bacteria.[148–153]

Despite inactivation of 57% of the drug, clindamycin concentrations in peritoneal fluid are 31.8% of simultaneous serum concentrations.[145] Although aminoglycosides penetrate the peritoneal fluid in low but adequate concentrations, they function poorly in acidic or hypoxic environments. Nevertheless, clinical trials have failed to disclose evidence of a difference in efficacy between combination antibiotic regimens which do and do not contain an aminoglycoside, even in studies in seriously ill patients and in patients whose initial cultures harbor beta-lactam resistant bacteria.[72]

Infections Following Abdominal Trauma

Risk factors for infection following penetrating abdominal trauma include the number, type, and location of injuries; the presence of hypotension; large transfusion requirements; prolonged operation; advanced age; and the mechanism of injury.[28,29,33,154,155]

Most investigators stress the importance of instituting antimicrobial therapy as close to the time of trauma as possible. Fullen et al.[156] demonstrated a significant reduction in the incidence of postoperative infections when antibiotics were administered before laparotomy, compared with those patients whose antibiotics were initiated during or after surgery.

Antimicrobial Therapy

Penetrating Trauma

18. J.K., a 23-year-old male, is admitted to the emergency room following a gunshot wound to the stomach, colon, and right thigh. He is to undergo emergency laparotomy. What antimicrobial therapy is appropriate at this time?

As with other types of intra-abdominal infections, the use of antibiotics active against both aerobic and anaerobic pathogens has become the cornerstone of therapy for peritoneal contamination following penetrating abdominal trauma.[28]

Thadepalli et al.[154] compared the efficacy of clindamycin plus gentamicin (an antimicrobial combination with activity against most enteric aerobes, facultative anaerobes, and strict anaerobes) to cephalothin plus kanamycin (a regimen lacking anaerobic coverage) and found that significantly more patients developed infections in the cephalothin/kanamycin group. In addition, these patients had anaerobic bacteria recovered from infectious sites.

Comparative trials of antimicrobial agents in patients who have sustained penetrating trauma to the abdomen (usually from knife or gunshot wounds) generally have compared newer therapies to a "standard" regimen of clindamycin in combination with an aminoglycoside. Many of the newer second- and third-generation cephalosporins have been studied, as they offer the potential for decreased toxicity and lower cost. In several comparative trials, single drug therapy with cefoxitin or moxalactam was as effective

as the combination of clindamycin or metronidazole plus an aminoglycoside.[94,157] However, in evaluating these studies, it is important to note that the majority of patients did not sustain injuries to the colon, where the risk of infection is highest. Several studies included patients with perforations of the colon and rectum or colonic perforation alone; cephalothin or clindamycin in combination with an aminoglycoside were equally efficacious. These trials suffer from many of the same common design flaws outlined by Solomkin et al.[63] regarding antimicrobial therapy for intra-abdominal infections. At this time, the results of only four prospective, randomized, double-blind, comparative studies are available (see Table 61.6).[33,158–160] The remaining studies are retrospective,[156,161,162] or are not placebo-controlled,[161–169] randomized,[156,163,170] or blinded.[156,162,163,165,167,170,171] They also may lack appropriate statistical analysis or sufficient numbers of subjects to enable detection of significant differences between treatment regimens.[144,154,156,165]

The appropriate duration of antimicrobial therapy after penetrating gastrointestinal trauma probably is dependent upon the time elapsed since injury. In trauma cases, injury and contamination occur before antibiotics can be administered; therefore, adequate antimicrobial tissue concentrations are not present at the time of contamination. For this reason, some authorities have suggested that antimicrobial therapy constitutes treatment rather than prevention of infection and that it should be continued for a longer period of time.[154] Some investigators believe that if antimicrobial therapy is initiated within three to four hours of the initial trauma, prolonged antimicrobial therapy is unnecessary because the bacterial infection is not well established and most infectious complications can be avoided.

The shortest duration of therapy that has been shown to be effective has been 12 hours. Several investigators have demonstrated in a prospective, randomized fashion that short-course (≥ 48 hours) antimicrobial therapy is as efficacious as five- to seven-day courses of therapy if antimicrobial therapy is promptly instituted.[159,162,163,171] Several other trials (noncomparative) have had low infection rates using a 48-hour regimen.[164] If the initial dose of antibiotic is administered more than three to four hours after injury, therapy should be continued for three to seven days, because the incidence of infection in this circumstance is high.

Since antimicrobial therapy carries a risk of adverse reactions and the development of resistance and is costly, short-term therapy seems warranted if it can be instituted soon after the injurious event.[173]

Appendectomy

19. K.S. is a 13-year-old female with a 2-day history of periumbilical pain migrating to the right lower quadrant, abdominal distension, fever to 102 °F, diarrhea, and decreased bowel sounds. The WBC count is $16.1 \times 10^3/mm^3$. A presumptive diagnosis of acute appendicitis is made. What antimicrobial therapy is indicated and how long should it be continued?

Although appendicitis was responsible for 58% of intra-abdominal infections and 35% of the mortality from 1896 to 1925, it currently accounts for only about 15% of infections and 0% to 8% of mortality.[134,172]

A variety of antimicrobial agents are effective in the treatment of peritoneal contamination associated with acute appendicitis.[34,173–193] Unfortunately, the majority of studies employed patients without gangrenous or perforated appendices, which are associated with the highest risk of infection. In several well designed randomized, placebo-controlled trials the combination of clindamycin plus an aminoglycoside has been compared to imipenem, cefamandole, cefotaxime, moxalactam, cefoperazone, cef-

Table 61.6			Randomized, Controlled Trials for the Treatment of Penetrating Intra-Abdominal Trauma[a]					
	# of Patients[b]						Intra-Abdominal	
Investigator	NC	C	Antimicrobial Regimen[c]	Duration of Therapy	Wound Infections (%)	Intra-Abdominal Infection (%)	Other Infectious Complications[d]	Comments
Comparative Studies								
O'Donnell[159] (1978)	45	15 (I)	Carb 6 gm IV Q 6 hr	>6 days	5/60 (8.3%)	0/60 (0%)	6/60 (10%)	
	51	15 (II)	CM 600 mg IV Q 6 hr + Gent 80 mg IV Q 8 hr	>6 days	3/66 (4.5%)	0/66 (0%)	5/66 (7.7%)	
Martinez[158] (1979)	0	29 (I)	CM 600 mg IV Q 6 hr + K 1 gm then 0.5 gm IM Q 12 hr	72 hr	2/29 (6.9%)	1/29 (3.4%)	Not stated	Aminoglycoside concentrations not adjusted during therapy
	0	18 (II)	Ceph 3 gm then 2 gm IV Q 6 hr + K 1 gm then 0.5 gm IM Q 12 hr	72 hr	1/18 (5.5%)	1/18 (5.5%)	Not stated	Irrigation with polymyxin B/bacitracin
	0	13 (III)	CM 600 mg IV Q 6 hr + Gent 80 mg IV Q 8 hr	72 hr	1/13 (7.7%)	1/13 (7.7%)	Not stated	Unclear if blinded study
Nichols[33] (1984)	30	40 (I)	CFX 2 gm IV Q 6 hr + P	5 days	8/70 (11.4%)	3/70 (4.3%)	3/70 (4.3%)	Antibiotic irrigation in ≈3% of patients
	40	35 (II)	CM 600 mg IV Q 6 hr + Gent 1.7 mg/kg IV Q 8 hr	5 days	10/75 (13.3%)	5/75 (6.7%)	2/75 (2.7%)	
Noncomparative Studies								
Crenshaw[160] (1978)	32	17 (I)	CFM 2 gm IV Q 6 hr	≥72 hr	3/49 (6.1%)	Not stated	Not stated	Single-blind study
	29	16 (II)	Ceph 2 gm IV Q 6 hr + Tob 1 mg/kg IV Q 8 hr	≥72 hr	4/45 (8.9%)	Not stated	Not stated	Average duration of treatment 5.5 days

[a] All studies were prospective, randomized, and blinded with specific outcome criteria and appropriate statistical analysis.

[b] NC = Patients with noncolonic gastrointestinal tract injuries; C = Patients with colonic injury.

[c] Antibiotics were as follows: Carb = Carbenicillin; CFM = Cefamandole; CFX = Cefoxitin; Ceph = Cephalothin; CM = Clindamycin; Gent = Gentamicin; K = Kanamycin; P = Placebo; Tob = Tobramycin.

[d] Included patients with septicemia, peritonitis, or other infection judged to be related to trauma.

oxitin, aztreonam plus clindamycin, or cefepime, ticarcillin-clavulanate, ampicillin plus sulbactam or metronidazole. These agents were found to be as efficacious as the "gold standard."[173,174,176–179,182,183] These studies enrolled patients with gangrenous or perforated appendices who were afebrile for 48 hours and involved treatments ranging in duration from single dose therapy[177] to ≥3 days.[173,174] A number of other less well controlled trials have examined the efficacy of a variety of agents, including cefoxitin, cefazolin, penicillin G, ampicillin, moxalactam, cefamandole, cefoperazone, or cefotaxime alone or in combination with metronidazole and generally found them to be efficacious. However, many of these trials were not randomized, comparative, or placebo-controlled and many specifically excluded high-risk patients.[175,180,181,184–193]

Overall, the studies justify the use of single-agent therapy with any of the above beta-lactams that possess antimicrobial activity directed at both gram-negative aerobes and anaerobes.[1] The appropriate duration of therapy is not as clear. In patients with uncomplicated appendicitis, single-dose therapy is probably sufficient. Further studies are needed to support the use of single-dose therapy in patients with gangrenous or perforated appendicitis.

K.S. should receive a preoperative dose of any of the above beta-lactam antimicrobials with activity against facultative gram-negative and anaerobic bacteria. Cost, availability, potential side effects, and ease of administration can be used to guide selection of a specific agent. If a gangrenous or perforated appendix is found during surgery, antimicrobial therapy should be continued for a minimum of three days and until K.S. is afebrile for 48 hours.

References

1 **Sawyer MD, Dunn DL.** Antimicrobial therapy of intra-abdominal sepsis. Infect Dis North Am. 1992;6:545.

2 **Sirinek KR.** Management of intra-abdominal infections. Pharmacotherapy. 1991;11(2 Pt. 2):99S.

3 **Tally FP, Gorbach SL.** Therapy of mixed anaerobic-aerobic infections.

Lessons from studies of intra-abdominal sepsis. Am J Med. 1985;78(Suppl. 6A):145.

4 **Rimland D, Hand WL.** Spontaneous peritonitis: a reappraisal. Am J Med Sci. 1987;293:285.

5 **Conn HO, Fessel JM.** Spontaneous bacterial peritonitis in cirrhosis: varia-

tions on a theme. Medicine. 1971;50: 161.

6 **Targan SR et al.** Role of anaerobic bacteria in spontaneous peritonitis of cirrhosis. Am J Med. 1977;62:397.

7 **Schweinburg FB et al.** Transmural migration of intestinal bacteria. N Engl J Med. 1950;242:747.

8 **Fong TL et al.** Polymorphonuclear cell count response and duration of antibiotic therapy in spontaneous bacterial peritonitis. Hepatology. 1989;9:423.

9 **Edmiston CE Jr, Condon RE.** Bacterial translocation. Surg Gynecol Obstet. 1991;173(1):73.

10 **Gomez-Jimenez J et al.** Randomized

trial comparing ceftriaxone with cefonicid for treatment of spontaneous bacterial peritonitis in cirrhotic patients. Antimicrob Agents Chemother. 1993; 37(8):1587.

11 Runyon BA et al. Short-course versus long-course antibiotic treatment of spontaneous bacterial peritonitis. A randomized controlled study of 100 patients. Gastroenterology. 1991;100(6): 1737.

12 Mihas AA et al. Spontaneous bacterial peritonitis in cirrhosis: clinical and laboratory features, survival and prognostic indicators. Hepatogastroenterology. 1992;39(6):520.

13 Llovet JM et al. Short-term prognosis of cirrhotics with spontaneous bacterial peritonitis: multivariate study. Am J Gastroenterol. 1993;88(3):388.

14 Andreu M et al. Risk factors for spontaneous bacterial peritonitis in cirrhotic patients with ascites. Gastroenterology. 1993;104(4):1133.

15 Gines P et al. Norfloxacin prevents spontaneous bacterial peritonitis recurrence in cirrhosis: results of a double-blind, placebo-controlled trial. Hepatology. 1990;12(4 Pt. 1):716.

16 Toledo C et al. Spontaneous bacterial peritonitis in cirrhosis: predictive factors of infection resolution and survival in patients treated with cefotaxime. Hepatology. 1993;17(2):251.

17 Grange JD et al. Amoxicillin-clavulanic acid therapy of spontaneous bacterial peritonitis: a prospective study of twenty-seven cases in cirrhotic patients. Hepatology. 1990;11(3):360.

18 Holland DJ, Sorrell TC. Antimicrobial therapy and prevention of spontaneous bacterial peritonitis. J Gastroenterol Hepatol. 1993;8(4):370.

19 Felisart J et al. Cefotaxime is more effective than is ampicillin-tobramycin in cirrhotics with severe infections. Hepatology. 1985;5:457.

20 Hoers JC et al. Spontaneous bacterial peritonitis. Hepatology. 1982;2:399.

21 Soriano G et al. Selective intestinal decontamination prevents spontaneous bacterial peritonitis. Gastroenterology. 1991;100(2):477.

22 Peterson PK et al. Current concepts in the management of peritonitis in patients undergoing continuous ambulatory peritoneal dialysis. Rev Infect Dis. 1987;9:604.

23 Rubin J et al. Peritonitis during continuous ambulatory peritoneal dialysis. Ann Intern Med. 1980;92:7.

24 DePiro JT et al. Current concepts in clinical therapeutics: intra-abdominal infections. Clin Pharm. 1986;5:34.

25 Horton MW et al. Treatment of peritonitis in patients undergoing continuous ambulatory peritoneal dialysis. Clin Pharm. 1990;9:102.

26 Lorber B, Swenson RM. The bacteriology of intra-abdominal infections. Surg Clin North Am. 1975;55:1349.

27 Danziger L, Hassan E. Antimicrobial prophylaxis of gastrointestinal surgical procedures and treatment of intra-abdominal infections. Drug Intell Clin Pharm. 1987;21:406.

28 Nichols RL. The treatment of intra-abdominal infections in surgery. Diagn Microbiol Infect Dis. 1989;12(Suppl. 4):S195.

29 Nichols RL. Infections following gastrointestinal surgery: intra-abdominal abscess. Surg Clin North Am. 1980;60: 197.

30 Drasar BS et al. Studies on the intestinal flora. I. The bacterial flora of the gastrointestinal tract in healthy and achlorhydric persons. Gastroenterology. 1969;56:71.

31 Simon GL, Gorbach SL. Intestinal flora in health and disease. Gastroenterology. 1984;86:174.

32 Finegold SM. Anaerobes: problems and controversies in bacteriology, infections, and susceptibility testing. Rev Infect Dis. 1990;12(Suppl. 2):S223.

33 Nichols RL et al. Risk of infection after penetrating abdominal trauma. N Engl J Med. 1984;311:1065.

34 Gorbach SL. Treatment of intra-abdominal infection. Am J Med. 1984: 107.

35 Liavag I. Intra-abdominal infections: etiology, clinical manifestations, diagnosis, and treatment. Scand J Gastroenterol. 1983;85:26.

36 Altemeier WA. The bacterial flora of acute perforated appendicitis with peritonitis. Ann Surg. 1938;107:517.

37 Onderdonk AB et al. Microbial synergy in experimental intra-abdominal abscess. Infect Immun. 1976;13:22.

38 Weinstein WM et al. Antimicrobial therapy of experimental intra-abdominal sepsis. J Infect Dis. 1975;132:282.

39 Weinstein WM et al. Experimental intra-abdominal abscesses in rats: development of an experimental model. Infect Immun. 1974;10:1250.

40 Onderdonk AB et al. Experimental intra-abdominal abscesses in rats: quantitative bacteriology of infected animals. Infect Immun. 1974;10:1256.

41 Onderdonk AB et al. Use of a model of intra-abdominal sepsis for studies of the pathogenicity of Bacteroides fragilis. Rev Infect Dis. 1984;6(Suppl. 1): S91.

42 Joiner KA et al. Host factors in the formation of abscesses. J Infect Dis. 1980;142:40.

43 Lindner JG et al. Intracellular polysaccharide of Bacteroides fragilis. J Gen Microbiol. 1979;111:93.

44 Onderdonk AB et al. Animal model system for studying virulence of and host response to Bacteroides fragilis. Rev Infect Dis. 1990;12(Suppl. 2): S169.

45 Louie TJ et al. Therapy for experimental intra-abdominal sepsis: comparison of four cephalosporins with clindamycin plus gentamicin. J Infect Dis. 1977;135(Suppl.):518.

46 Onderdonk AB et al. The capsular polysaccharide of Bacteroides fragilis as a virulence factor: comparison of the pathogenic potential of encapsulated and unencapsulated strains. J Infect Dis. 1977;136:82.

47 Kasper DL et al. Protective efficacy of immunization with capsular antigen against experimental infection with Bacteroides fragilis. J Infect Dis. 1979; 140:724.

48 Shapiro ME et al. Cellular immunity to Bacteroides fragilis capsular polysaccharide. J Exp Med. 1982;154: 1188.

49 Connolly JC et al. The effect of capsular polysaccharide and lipopolysaccharide of Bacteroides fragilis on poly-

morph function and serum killing. J Med Microbiol. 1984;17:259.

50 Brook I. Encapsulated anaerobic bacteria in synergistic infections. Microbiol Rev. 1986;50:452.

51 Kasper DL, Onderdonk AB. Infection with Bacteroides fragilis: pathogenesis and immunoprophylaxis in an animal model. Scand J Infect Dis. 1982;31(Suppl.):28.

52 Kasper DL. Bacterial capsule— old dogmas and new tricks. J Infect Dis. 1986;153:407.

53 Kasper DL et al. Protective efficacy of immunization with capsular antigen against experimental infection with Bacteroides fragilis. J Infect Dis. 1979; 140:724.

54 Bartlett JG et al. Relative efficacy of B-lactam antimicrobial agents in two animal models of infections involving Bacteroides fragilis. Rev Infect Dis. 1983;5(Suppl. 2):S338.

55 Bartlett JG et al. Therapeutic efficacy of 29 antimicrobial regimens in experimental intra-abdominal sepsis. Rev Infect Dis. 1981;3:535.

56 Brook I. Inoculum effect. Rev Infect Dis. 1989;11:361.

57 Pollock AV. Nonoperative antiinfective treatment of intra-abdominal infections. World J Surg. 1990;14:227.

58 Bohnen JMA et al. Guidelines for clinical care: anti-infective agents for intra-abdominal infection. A Surgical Infection Society Policy Statement. Arch Surg. 1992;127:83.

59 Solomkin JS et al. Evaluation of new anti-infective drugs for the treatment of intra-abdominal infections. Infectious Diseases Society of America and the Food and Drug Administration. Clin Infect Dis. 1992;15(Suppl. 1):S33.

60 Holzheimer RG et al. Intra-abdominal infections: classification, mortality, scoring and pathophysiology. Infection. 1991;19(6):447.

61 Lahnborg G et al. Efficacy of different antibiotics in the treatment of experimentally induced intra-abdominal sepsis. J Antimicrob Chemother. 1982; 10:497.

62 Nichols RL et al. Efficacy of parenteral antibiotics in the treatment of experimentally induced intra-abdominal sepsis. Rev Infect Dis. 1979;1:302.

63 Solomkin JS et al. Antibiotic trials in intra-abdominal infections. A critical evaluation of study design and outcome reporting. Ann Surg. 1984;200: 29.

64 Meakins JL et al. A proposed classification of intra-abdominal infections. Arch Surg. 1984;119:1372.

65 Dellinger EP et al. Surgical infection stratification system for intra-abdominal infection. Arch Surg. 1985;120:21.

66 Nystrom P et al. Proposed definitions for diagnosis, severity scoring, stratification, and outcome for trials on intra-abdominal infection. World J Surg. 1990;14:148.

67 Hau T et al. Irrigation of the peritoneal cavity and local antibiotics in the treatment of peritonitis. Surg Gynecol Obstet. 1983;156:25.

68 Drusano GL. Role of pharmacokinetics in the outcome of infections. Antimicrob Agents Chemother. 1988;32: 289.

69 Collier J et al. A multicentre compar-

ison of clindamycin and metronidazole in the treatment of anaerobic infections. Scand J Infect Dis Suppl. 1981; 26:96.

70 Stone HH et al. Incidence and significance of intraperitoneal anaerobic bacteria. Ann Surg. 1975;181:705.

71 Bartlett JG et al. Empiric treatment with clindamycin and gentamicin of suspected sepsis due to anaerobic and aerobic bacteria. J Infect Dis. 1977; 135(Suppl.):S80.

72 Ho JL, Barza M. Role of aminoglycoside antibiotics in the treatment of intra-abdominal infection. Antimicrob Agents Chemother. 1987;31:485.

73 Smith JA et al. Prospective, randomized, double-blind comparison of metronidazole and tobramycin with clindamycin and tobramycin in the treatment of intra-abdominal sepsis. Ann Surg. 1980;192:213.

74 Smith JA et al. Metronidazole in the treatment of intra-abdominal sepsis. Surgery. 1983;93(Part 2):217.

75 Tally FP et al. A randomized comparison of cefoxitin with or without amikacin and clindamycin plus amikacin in surgical sepsis. Ann Surg. 1981;193: 318.

76 Kirkpatrick JR et al. Double-blind comparison of metronidazole plus gentamicin and clindamycin plus gentamicin in intra-abdominal infection. Surgery. 1983;93:215.

77 Malangoni MA et al. Treatment of intra-abdominal infections is appropriate with single-agent or combination therapy. Surgery. 1985;98:648.

78 Canadian Metronidazole-Clindamycin Study Group. Prospective, randomized comparison of metronidazole and clindamycin, each with gentamicin, for the treatment of serious intra-abdominal infection. Surgery. 1983;93: 221.

79 Study Group of Intra-abdominal Infections. A randomized controlled trial of ampicillin plus sulbactam vs. gentamicin plus clindamycin in the treatment of intra-abdominal infections: a preliminary report. Rev Infect Dis. 1986;8(Suppl. 5):S583.

80 LeFrock JL et al. In vitro and in vivo comparison of mezlocillin and cefoxitin. J Antimicrob Chemother. 1983;11 (Suppl. C):83.

81 Solomkin JS et al. Results of a multicenter trial comparing imipenem/cilastatin to tobramycin/clindamycin for intra-abdominal infections. Ann Surg. 1990;212:581.

82 Brismar B et al. Piperacillin-tazobactam versus imipenem-cilastatin for treatment of intra-abdominal infections. Antimicrob Agents Chemother. 1992;36(12):2766.

83 Walker AP et al. Efficacy of a beta-lactamase inhibitor combination for serious intra-abdominal infections. Ann Surg. 1993;217(2):115.

84 Stone HH, Fabian TC. Clinical comparison of antibiotic combinations in the treatment of peritonitis and related mixed aerobic-anaerobic surgical sepsis. World J Surg. 1980;4:415.

85 Henry SA. Overall clinical experience with aztreonam in the treatment of intra-abdominal infections. Rev Infect Dis. 1985;7(Suppl. 4):S729.

86 Mehtar S et al. A non-comparative

study of parenteral ampicillin and sulbactam in intra-thoracic and intra-abdominal infections. J Antimicrob Chemother. 1986;17:389.

87 Lennard ES et al. Stratified outcome comparison of clindamycin-gentamicin vs chloramphenicol-gentamicin for treatment of intra-abdominal sepsis. Arch Surg. 1985;120:889.

88 Luke M et al. Ceftriaxone/metronidazole is more effective than ampicillin/netilmicin/metronidazole in the treatment of bacterial peritonitis. Eur J Surg. 1991;157(6-7):397.

89 Hackford AW et al. Prospective study comparing imipenem-cilastatin with clindamycin and gentamicin for the treatment of serious surgical infections. Arch Surg. 1988;123:322.

90 Gonzenbach HR et al. Imipenem (N-F thienamycin) versus netilmicin plus clindamycin. A controlled and randomized comparison in intra-abdominal infections. Ann Surg. 1987;205:271.

91 Solomkin JS et al. Randomized trial of imipenem/cilastatin versus gentamicin and clindamycin in mixed flora infections. Am J Med. 1985;78(Suppl. 6A):85.

92 Imipenem/cilastatin versus gentamicin/clindamycin for treatment of serious bacterial infections. Report from a Scandinavian Study Group. Lancet. 1984;1:868.

93 Stone HH et al. Clinical comparison of cefotaxime versus the combination of gentamicin plus clindamycin in the treatment of peritonitis and similar polymicrobial soft-tissue surgical sepsis. Clin Ther. 1981;4(Suppl. A):67.

94 Schentag JJ et al. A randomized clinical trial of moxalactam alone versus tobramycin plus clindamycin in abdominal sepsis. Ann Surg. 1983;198:35.

95 Leaper DJ et al. Treatment of acute bacterial peritonitis: a trial of imipenem/cilastatin against ampicillin-metronidazole-gentamicin. Scand J Infect Dis. 1987;52(Suppl.):7.

96 Busuttil RW et al. A comparative study of cefamandole versus gentamicin plus clindamycin in the treatment of documented or suspected bacterial peritonitis. Surg Gynecol Obstet. 1984;158:1.

97 Drusano GL et al. A prospective randomized controlled trial of cefoxitin versus clindamycin-aminoglycoside in mixed anaerobic-aerobic infections. Surg Gynecol Obstet. 1982;154:715.

98 Stone HH et al. Third-generation cephalosporins for polymicrobial surgical sepsis. Arch Surg. 1983;118:193.

99 Harding GKM et al. Prospective, randomized comparative study of clindamycin, chloramphenicol, and ticarcillin, each in combination with gentamicin, in therapy for intra-abdominal and female genital tract sepsis. J Infect Dis. 1980;142:384.

100 Busuttil RW et al. A comparative study of cefamandole versus gentamicin plus clindamycin in the treatment of documented or suspected bacterial peritonitis. Surg Gynecol Obstet. 1984;158:1.

101 Birolini D et al. Aztreonam plus clindamycin vs. tobramycin plus clindamycin for the treatment of intra-abdominal infections. Rev Infect Dis. 1985;7(Suppl. 4):S724.

102 Tornqvist A. Antibiotic treatment during surgery for diffuse peritonitis: a prospective randomized study comparing the effects of cefuroxime and of a cefuroxime and metronidazole combination. Br J Surg. 1985;72:261.

103 DiPiro JT, Bowden TA. A comparison of monobactam antibiotics in surgical infections. Am J Surg. 1989;157:607.

104 Murray BE. B-lactamase-producing enterococci. Antimicrob Agents Chemother. 1992;36(11):2355.

105 Ruoff KL. Recent taxonomic changes in the genus Enterococcus. Eur J Clin Microbiol Infect Dis. 1990;9:75.

106 Dougherty SH. Role of enterococcus in intra-abdominal sepsis. Am J Surg. 1984;148:308.

107 Dougherty SH et al. 'Breakthrough' enterococcal septicemia in surgical patients. Arch Surg. 1983;118:232.

108 Maki DG, Agger WA. Enterococcal bacteremia: clinical features, the risk of endocarditis, and management. Medicine (Baltimore). 1988;67:248.

109 Hite KE et al. Synergism in experimental infections with nonsporulating anaerobic bacteria. J Infect Dis. 1949;84:1.

110 Brook I. Effect of Streptococcus faecalis on the growth of Bacteroides species and anaerobic cocci in mixed infection. Surgery. 1988;103:107.

111 Matlow AG et al. Pathogenicity of enterococci in a rat model of fecal peritonitis. J Infect Dis. 1989;160:142.

112 Courvalin P. Resistance of enterococci to glycopeptides. Antimicrob Agents Chemother. 1990;34(12):2291.

113 Zervos MJ et al. High-level resistance to gentamicin in Streptococcus faecalis: risk factors and evidence for exogenous acquisition of infection. J Infect Dis. 1986;153:1075.

114 Onderdonk AB et al. Activity of metronidazole against Escherichia coli in experimental intra-abdominal sepsis. J Antimicrob Chemother. 1979;5:201.

115 Dunn DL, Simmons RL. The role of anaerobic bacteria in intra-abdominal infections. Rev Infect Dis. 1984;6(Suppl. 1):S139.

116 Tally FP et al. Mechanisms of resistance and resistance transfer in anaerobic bacteria: factors influencing antimicrobial therapy. Rev Infect Dis. 1984;6(Suppl. 1):S260.

117 Cuchural GJ et al. Susceptibility of the Bacteroides fragilis group in the United States: analysis by site of isolation. Antimicrob Agents Chemother. 1988;32:717.

118 Thornsberry C. Antimicrobial susceptibility testing of anaerobic bacteria: review and update on the role of the National Committee for Clinical Laboratory Standards. Rev Infect Dis. 1990;12(Suppl. 2):S218.

119 Brown WJ. National committee for clinical laboratory standards agar dilution susceptibility testing of anaerobic gram-negative bacteria. Antimicrob Agents Chemother. 1988;32:385.

120 Ohm-Smith MJ et al. Occurrence of clindamycin-resistant anaerobic bacteria isolated from cultures taken following clindamycin therapy. Antimicrob Agents Chemother. 1986;30:11.

121 Eykyn SJ, Phillips I. Metronidazole in surgical infections. J Antimicrob

Chemother. 1978;4(Suppl. C):75.

122 Ingham HR et al. Interactions between micro-organisms and metronidazole. J Antimicrob Chemother. 1982;10:84.

123 Ingham HR et al. Enhancement of activity of metronidazole by Escherichia coli under sub-optimal anaerobic conditions. J Antimicrob Chemother. 1981;8:475.

124 Soriano F et al. Reciprocal antimicrobial synergism between Escherichia coli and Bacteroides fragilis in the presence of metronidazole. J Clin Pathol. 1982;35:1150.

125 Ingham HR et al. The activity of metronidazole against facultatively anaerobic bacteria. J Antimicrob Chemother. 1980;6:343.

126 Brook I. In vitro susceptibility and in vivo efficacy of antimicrobials in the treatment of Bacteroides fragilis-Escherichia coli infection in mice. J Infect Dis. 1989;160:651.

127 Bartlett JG et al. Relative efficacy and critical interval of antimicrobial agents in experimental infections involving Bacteroides fragilis. Arch Surg. 1983;118:181.

128 Wexler HM et al. In vitro efficacy of sulbactam combined with ampicillin against anaerobic bacteria. Antimicrob Agents Chemother. 1985;27:876.

129 Gisby J, Beale AS. Comparative efficacies of amoxicillin-clavulanic acid and ampicillin-sulbactam against experimental Bacteroides fragilis-Escherichia coli mixed infections. Antimicrob Agents Chemother. 1988;32:1830.

130 Bayer AS et al. Candida peritonitis: report of 22 cases and review of the English literature. Am J Med. 1976;61:832.

131 Marsh PK et al. Candida infections in surgical patients. Ann Surg. 1983;198:42.

132 Sobel JD. Candida infections in the intensive care unit. Crit Care Clin. 1988;4:325.

133 Levine J et al. Fungal peritonitis complicating continuous ambulatory peritoneal dialysis: successful treatment with fluconazole, a new orally active antifungal agent. Am J Med. 1989;86:825.

134 Farthmann EH, Schoffel U. Principles and limitations of operative management of intra-abdominal infections. World J Surg. 1990;14:210.

135 Carver P. Postoperative use of antibiotic irrigations. Clin Pharm. 1987;6:352.

136 Hunt JL. Generalized peritonitis. To irrigate or not to irrigate the abdominal cavity. Arch Surg. 1982;117:209.

137 Lally KP, Nichols RL. Various intraperitoneal irrigation solutions in treating experimental fecal peritonitis. South Med J. 1981;74:789.

138 Rambo WM. Irrigation of the peritoneal cavity with cephalothin. Am J Surg. 1972;123:192.

139 Benjamin JB, Volz RG. Efficacy of a topical antibiotic irrigant in decreasing or eliminating bacterial contamination in surgical wounds. Clin Orthop. 1984;184:114.

140 Burnett WE et al. The treatment of peritonitis using peritoneal lavage. Ann Surg. 1957;145:675.

141 Roth RM et al. Antibiotic irrigations.

A plea for controlled clinical trials. Pharmacotherapy. 1985;5:222.

142 Noon GP et al. Clinical evaluation of peritoneal irrigation with antibiotic solution. Surgery. 1967;62:73.

143 Bryan LE et al. Mechanism of aminoglycoside antibiotic resistance in anaerobic bacteria: Clostridium perfringens and Bacteroides fragilis. Antimicrob Agents Chemother. 1979;15:7.

144 Rowlands BJ et al. Penetrating abdominal trauma: the use of operative findings to determine length of antibiotic therapy. J Trauma. 1987;27:250.

145 Simon GL et al. Penetration of clindamycin into experimental infections with Bacteroides fragilis. J Antimicrob Chemother. 1981;8:59.

146 Burke JF. The effective period of preventive antibiotic action in experimental incisions and dermal lesions. Surgery. 1961;50:161.

147 Bergamini TM, Polk CH Jr. The importance of tissue antibiotic activity in the prevention of operative wound infection. J Antimicrob Chemother. 1989;23:301.

148 Kaplan O et al. Penetration of prophylactic antibiotics into peritoneal fluid. Am J Surg. 1989;157:585.

149 Gerding DN, Hall WH. The penetration of antibiotics into peritoneal fluid. Bull NY Acad Med. 1975;51:1016.

150 Wittman DH, Schassan HH. Penetration of eight B-Lactam antibiotics into the peritoneal fluid. Arch Surg. 1983;118:205.

151 Gerding DN et al. Antibiotic concentrations in ascitic fluid of patients with ascites and bacterial peritonitis. Ann Intern Med. 1977;86:708.

152 Van Etta LL et al. Effect of the ratio of surface area to volume on the penetration of antibiotics into extravascular spaces in an in vitro model. J Infect Dis. 1982;146:423.

153 Joiner KA et al. Antibiotic levels in infected and sterile subcutaneous abscess in mice. J Infect Dis. 1981;143:487.

154 Thadepalli H et al. Abdominal trauma, anaerobes, and antibiotics. Surg Gynecol Obstet. 1973;137:270.

155 Wilson RF et al. Predicting and preventing infection after abdominal vascular injuries. J Trauma. 1989;29:1371.

156 Fullen WD et al. Prophylactic antibiotics in penetrating wounds of the abdomen. J Trauma. 1972;12:282.

157 Tally FP et al. A randomized prospective study comparing moxalactam and cefoxitin with or without tobramycin for the treatment of serious surgical infections. J Antimicrob Chemother. 1986;29:244.

158 Martinez OV et al. Antibiotic prophylaxis in penetrating colorectal injuries: the comparative effectiveness of clindamycin and cephalothin in combination with an aminoglycoside. Am Surg. 1979;45:378.

159 O'Donnell V et al. Evaluation of carbenicillin and a comparison of clindamycin and gentamicin combined therapy in penetrating abdominal trauma. Surg Gynecol Obstet. 1978;147:525.

160 Crenshaw C et al. A prospective random study of a single agent versus combination antibiotics as therapy in

penetrating injuries of the abdomen. Surg Gynecol Obstet. 1983;156:289.

161 **Nailathambi MN et al.** Aggressive definitive management of penetrating colon injuries: 136 cases with 3.7 percent mortality. J Trauma. 1984;24:500.

162 **Oreskovich MR et al.** Duration of preventive antibiotic administration for penetrating abdominal trauma. Arch Surg. 1982;117:200.

163 **Gentry LO et al.** Perioperative antibiotic therapy for penetrating injuries of the abdomen. Ann Surg. 1984;200:561.

164 **Jones RC et al.** Evaluation of antibiotic therapy following penetrating abdominal trauma. Ann Surg. 1985;201:576.

165 **Moore FA et al.** Preoperative antibiotics for abdominal gunshot wounds. A prospective, randomized study. Am J Surg. 1983;146:762.

166 **Rowlands BJ, Ericsson CD.** Comparative studies of antibiotic therapy after penetrating abdominal trauma. Am J Surg. 1984;148:791.

167 **Nelson RM et al.** Single-antibiotic use for penetrating abdominal trauma. Arch Surg. 1986;121:153.

168 **Bivins BA et al.** Antibiotics for penetrating abdominal trauma: a prospective comparative trial of single agent cephalosporin therapy versus combination therapy. Diagn Microbiol Infect Dis. 1989;12:113.

169 **Ericsson CD et al.** Prophylactic antibiotics in trauma: the hazards of underdosing. J Trauma. 1989;29:1356.

170 **Hofstetter SR et al.** A prospective comparison of two regimens of prophylactic antibiotics in abdominal trauma: cefoxitin versus triple drug. J Trauma. 1984;24:307.

171 **Stone HH et al.** Prophylactic and preventive antibiotic therapy: timing, duration, and economics. Ann Surg. 1979;189:691.

172 **Berne TV et al.** A clinical comparison of cefepime and metronidazole versus gentamicin and clindamycin in the antibiotic management of surgically treated advanced appendicitis. Surg Gyn Obstet. 1993;177:S18.

173 **Heseltine PNR et al.** Imipenem therapy for perforated and gangrenous appendicitis. Surg Gynecol Obstet. 1986;162:43.

174 **Heseltine PN et al.** Perforated and gangrenous appendicitis: an analysis of antibiotic failure. J Infect Dis. 1983;148:322.

175 **Berne TV et al.** Surgically-treated gangrenous or perforated appendicitis. A comparison of aztreonam and clindamycin versus gentamicin and clindamycin. Ann Surg. 1987;205:133.

176 **The Danish multicenter study group.** A Danish multicenter study: cefoxitin versus ampicillin—metronidazole in perforated appendicitis. Br J Surg. 1984;71:144.

177 **Foster MC et al.** A randomized comparative study of sulbactam plus ampicillin vs. metronidazole plus cefotaxime in the management of acute appendicitis in children. Rev Infect Dis. 1986;8(Suppl. 5):S634.

178 **Lau WY et al.** Randomized, prospective, and double-blind trial of new beta-lactams in the treatment of appendicitis. Antimicrob Agents Chemother. 1985;28:639.

179 **Lau WY et al.** Cefoxitin versus gentamicin and metronidazole in prevention of post-appendectomy sepsis: a randomized, prospective trial. J Antimicrob Chemother. 1986;18:613.

180 **Miholic HJ et al.** Metronidazole plus cefazolin versus cefazolin in gangrenous and perforated appendicitis in childhood—a prospective randomized trial. Z Kinderchir. 1983;38:159.

181 **Saario TL et al.** Comparison of cefuroxime and gentamicin in combination with metronidazole in the treatment of peritonitis due to perforation of the appendix. Acta Chir Scand. 1983;149:423.

182 **Winslow RE et al.** Acute nonperforating appendicitis. Arch Surg. 1983;118:651.

183 **Busuttil RW et al.** Effect of prophylactic antibiotics in acute nonperforated appendicitis: a prospective, randomized, double-blind clinical study. Ann Surg. 1981;194:502.

184 **Lou MA et al.** Comparison of cefamandole and carbenicillin in preventing sepsis following penetrating abdominal trauma. Am Surg. 1985;51:580.

185 **Bates T et al.** Timing of prophylactic antibiotics in abdominal surgery: trial of a pre-operative versus an intra-operative first dose. Br J Surg. 1989;76:52.

186 **Bivins BA et al.** Preventative antibiotics for penetrating abdominal trauma—single agent or combination therapy? Drugs. 1988;35(Suppl. 2):100.

187 **Gutierrez C et al.** Study of appendicitis in children treated with four different antibiotic regimens. J Pediatr Surg. 1987;22:865.

188 **Yellin AE et al.** The role of *Pseudomonas* species in patients treated with ampicillin and sulbactam for gangrenous and perforated appendicitis. Surg Gynecol Obstet. 1985;161:303.

189 **Foster MC et al.** Perioperative prophylaxis with sulbactam and ampicillin compared with metronidazole and cefotaxime in the prevention of wound infection in children undergoing appendectomy. J Pediatr Surg. 1987;22:869.

190 **Altemeir WA.** The pathogenicity of the bacteria of appendicitis peritonitis. Surgery. 1942;11:374.

191 **Fan ST et al.** Once daily administration of netilmicin compared with thrice daily, both in combination with metronidazole, in gangrenous and perforated appendicitis. J Antimicrob Chemother. 1988;22:69.

192 **Elmore JR et al.** The treatment of complicated appendicitis in children. What is the gold standard? Arch Surg. 1987;122:424.

193 **Berne TV et al.** Antibiotic management of surgically treated gangrenous or perforated appendicitis. Comparison of gentamicin and clindamycin versus cefamandole versus cefoperazone. Am J Surg. 1982;144:8.

194 **Dupeyron C et al.** Rapid emergence of quinolone resistance in cirrhotic patients treated with norfloxacin to prevent spontaneous bacterial peritonitis. Antimicrob Agents Chemother. 1994;38(2):340.

195 **Keane WF et al.** Peritoneal dialysis-related peritonitis treatment recommendations 1993 update. Perit Dial Int. 1993;13:14–28

196 **Malangoni MA et al.** Treatment of intra-abdominal infections is appropriate with single-agent or combination antibiotic therapy. Surgery 1985;98(4):648.

197 **Lau WY et al.** Prophylaxis of postappendicectomy sepsis by metronidazole and cefotaxime; a randomized, prospective and double blind trial. Br J Surg. 1983;70:670.

198 **Sinanan MN.** Acute cholangitis. Infect Dis Clin North Am. 1992;6(3):571.

199 **Keighley MRB et al.** Antibiotic treatment of biliary sepsis. Surg Clin North Am. 1975;55(6):1379.

200 **Gigot JF et al.** Acute cholangitis: multivariate analysis of risk factors. Ann Surg. 1989;209:435.

201 **Munro R, Sorrell TC.** Biliary sepsis reviewing treatment options. Drugs. 1986;31:449.

202 **Jarvinen HJ, Hastbacka J.** Early cholecystectomy for acute cholecystitis. Ann Surg. 1980;191(4):501.

203 **Pitt HA et al.** Consequences of preoperative cholangitis and its treatment on the outcome of operation for choledocholithiasis. Surgery. 1983;94(3):447.

204 **Muller EL et al.** Antibiotics in infections of the biliary tract. Surg Gynecol Obstet. 1987;165(4):285.

205 **Maluenda et al.** Bacteriological study of choledochal bile in patients with common bile duct stones, with or without acute suppurative cholangitis. Hepatogastroenterology. 1989;36:132.

206 **Bergeron MG et al.** Cefoperazone compared with ampicillin plus tobramycin for severe biliary tract infections. Antimicrob Agents Chemother. 1988;32(8):1231.

207 **Gerecht WB et al.** Prospective randomized comparison of mezlocillin therapy alone with combined ampicillin and gentamicin therapy for patients with cholangitis. Arch Intern Med. 1989;149:1279.

208 **Thompson JE et al.** Broad spectrum penicillin as an adequate therapy for acute cholangitis. Surg Gynecol Obstet. 1990;171(4):275.

209 **Thompson JE et al.** Cefepime for infections of the biliary tract. Surg Gynecol Obstet. 1993;177:30.

210 **Nagar H, Berger SA.** The excretion of antibiotics by the biliary tract. Surg Gynecol Obstet. 1984;158:601.

211 **Keighley MRB et al.** Antibiotics in biliary disease: the relative importance of antibiotic concentrations in the bile and serum. Gut. 1976;17:495.

Acute and Chronic Hepatitis

Robin L Corelli

Acute Viral Hepatitis 62-1
    Causative Agents and Characteristics
    (See Tables 62.1 and 62.2) 62-1
        Hepatitis A 62-2
            Modes of transmission 62-2
            Serologic events 62-2
            Diagnosis 62-2
        Hepatitis B 62-2
            Modes of transmission 62-2
            Serologic events 62-2
            Diagnosis (See Table 62.3) 62-3
        Hepatitis C 62-3
            Modes of transmission 62-3
            Serologic events 62-3
            Diagnosis 62-3
        Hepatitis D 62-3
            Modes of transmission 62-3
            Serologic events 62-3
            Diagnosis 62-3
        Hepatitis E 62-3
    Clinical Features and Serologic Markers 62-3
    Treatment 62-4
        Bed rest and diet 62-5
        Drug Therapy 62-5
    Adjustments of Medication Doses (See Table 62.4) 62-5
    Guidelines to Prevent Hepatitis B Transmission 62-5
    Immunoprophylaxis 62-6
        Pre-exposure prophylaxis 62-6
            Hepatitis A 62-6
                Immune globulin 62-6
                Vaccine 62-6
            Hepatitis B vaccine 62-6
                Dosing regimen (See Table 62.5) 62-6
                Efficacy 62-7

                Non-responders 62-7
                Interchangeability of HBV vaccines 62-7
                Duration of response 62-8
                Indications 62-8
            Universal hepatitis B vaccination
            (See Table 62.6) 62-8
                Adverse effects 62-8
        Postexposure prophylaxis 62-8
            Hepatitis B (See Table 62.7) 62-8
                Percutaneous exposure (See Table 62.8) 62-8
                Sexual exposure 62-9
                Perinatal exposure 62-9
            Hepatitis A 62-9
            Hepatitis C, D, and E 62-10
Chronic Hepatitis 62-10
    Overview (See Table 62.9) 62-10
        Definitions 62-10
        Clinical features 62-10
        Diagnosis 62-10
    Clinical Presentation and Diagnosis 62-11
    Treatment of Chronic Hepatitis B 62-11
        Goals of therapy 62-11
        Drug therapy 62-12
            Interferons 62-12
                Efficacy 62-12
                Predictors of response 62-12
                Adverse effects 62-12
                Dosing 62-12
            Corticosteroids 62-12
            Other agents 62-13
    Treatment of Chronic Hepatitis C 62-13
    Treatment of Chronic Hepatitis D 62-13
    Treatment of Autoimmune Chronic Hepatitis 62-14

Acute Viral Hepatitis

Acute viral hepatitis probably is the most common cause of liver disease and jaundice in the world. It is the third most frequently reported category of infectious diseases in the U.S., exceeded only by gonorrhea and chicken pox. The case definition for acute viral hepatitis used by the Viral Hepatitis Surveillance Program operated by the Centers for Disease Control (CDC) includes: 1) an illness with a discrete date of onset and 2) jaundice or increased serum aminotransferase concentrations greater than two and one-half times the upper limit of normal. Specific serologic tests can differentiate each type of hepatitis.[1]

Causative Agents and Characteristics

At least five distinct agents are responsible for viral hepatitis. These viruses are identified by the letters A through E as follows: *type A hepatitis* caused by hepatitis A virus (HAV), *type B hepatitis* caused by hepatitis B virus (HBV), *type C hepatitis* caused by hepatitis C virus (HCV), delta *hepatitis* caused by the HBV-associated hepatitis D virus (HDV), and *type E hepatitis* caused by hepatitis E virus (HEV). (See Table 62.1.) All of these agents pri-

marily affect the liver and have the potential to cause inflammation and necrosis of hepatocytes. The viruses differ in their immunologic characteristics and epidemiological patterns. (See Table 62.2.) Fecal-oral transmission is the primary mode of infection for hepatitis A and E. In contrast, this route of transmission is not observed with hepatitis B, C, and D. Percutaneous transmission is characteristic of hepatitis B, C, and D, but is observed rarely with hepatitis A or E.

Another important difference concerns the existence of a long-term carrier state resulting in chronic infection and an increased risk of cirrhosis and primary hepatocellular carcinoma. Data suggest that neither hepatitis A nor hepatitis E infections result in the development of chronic hepatitis. However, patients with hepatitis B, C, or D are at risk for chronic infection and the development of chronic liver disease.

Several other viruses primarily affect nonhepatic organ systems and may secondarily induce a hepatitis-like syndrome. These include the Epstein-Barr virus (infectious mononucleosis), cytomegalovirus, herpes simplex viruses, varicella-zoster virus, and rubella, rubeola, and mumps viruses.

Table 62.1	Hepatitis Nomenclature		
Hepatitis Type	Antigen	Corresponding Antibody	Comments[a]
A	Hepatitis A virus (HAV)	Hepatitis A antibody (antiHAV)	RNA virus; present in stool and serum early in course of hepatitis A
B	Hepatitis B surface antigen (HBsAg)	Hepatitis B surface antibody (antiHBs)	DNA virus; found in serum in >90% of patients with acute hepatitis B. AntiHBs appears following infection and confers immunity
	Hepatitis B core antigen (HBcAg)	Hepatitis B core antibody (antiHBc)	AntiHBc detected in serum during and after acute infection
	Hepatitis Be antigen (HBeAg)	Hepatitis Be antibody (antiHBe)	HBeAg correlates with infectivity; suggestive of active viral replication
C	Hepatitis C antigen (HCAg)	Hepatitis C antibody (antiHCV)	RNA virus; cause of post-transfusion NANB hepatitis
D	Hepatitis delta antigen (HDAg)	Hepatitis delta antibody (antiHDV)	Defective RNA virus; requires presence of HBsAg
E	Hepatitis E antigen (HEAg)	Hepatitis E antibody (antiHEV)	RNA virus present in stool; cause of enteric NANB hepatitis

[a] NANB = NonA, nonB.

Hepatitis A

Hepatitis A virus is a single-stranded RNA virus with a capsid structure consisting of four virion proteins. The antibody response to HAV (antiHAV) is directed against the antigenic determinants of these proteins.

Modes of Transmission. Hepatitis A virus infection is transmitted by the fecal-oral route when a susceptible person ingests food, water, milk, or shellfish contaminated by feces containing the virus. Spread of the virus is facilitated by poor hygiene, substandard sanitation, and crowding. Hepatitis A occurs readily within families, among institutionalized persons, and in the military. HAV also is spread more readily among promiscuous homosexual males and in young children within day care centers.[2,3] Due to the lack of an asymptomatic carrier state for hepatitis A and a brief incubation period, percutaneous transmission is rare.[4]

Serologic Events. Antibodies to HAV can be detected by radioimmunoassay and enzyme immunoassay during acute illness when serum concentrations of hepatic aminotransferases are increased and when fecal shedding of HAV is occurring. The presence of antiHAV indicates previous or ongoing infection with HAV. The initial antibody response consists of antiHAV of the IgM class which usually persist for three to six months. IgG antiHAV serum concentrations become detectable during the recovery phase of the illness and confer lifelong immunity to hepatitis A.[5]

Diagnosis. There are two types of commercially available antiHAV tests. One is nonspecific and detects all classes of antiHAV (IgM and IgG); the other is specific for IgM antiHAV. Testing for IgM antiHAV is the method of choice to establish the diagnosis of acute HAV infection because this test will be positive at the time the patient presents with clinical illness. A negative IgM antibody test effectively rules out acute HAV infection in an individual with normal immune function. The nonspecific test for all classes of antiHAV should be used only to determine the HAV exposure status of a patient because a positive test result represents either acute infection (in which case the specific IgM antiHAV test also will be positive) or immune antibodies persisting from a previous HAV infection.

Hepatitis B

Unlike HAV, which has only one serotype and causes a self-limited infection, HBV is antigenically complex and results in an acute illness with or without a chronic disease state. HBV is a double-stranded DNA virus originally known as the Dane particle. There are three antigenic determinants associated with HBV. On the surface of HBV is an antigen called the hepatitis B surface antigen (HBsAg). Inside the surface coat of the intact hepatitis B virion is an internal nucleocapsid core which expresses hepatitis B core antigen (HBcAg). The hepatitis Be antigen (HBeAg) is a secreted product of the nucleocapsid core of HBV.

Modes of Transmission. Percutaneous inoculation is the primary route of HBV transmission. The virus can be transmitted in contaminated blood or blood products, by IV drug abuse, tattooing, ear-piercing, acupuncture, hemodialysis, and accidental needle sticks. Sporadic cases also have been attributed to nonpercutaneous transmission via small breaks in the skin or mucous membranes. Although HBsAg is found in saliva, tears, sweat, semen, vaginal secretions, breast milk, cerebrospinal fluid, ascites, pleural fluid, synovial fluid, gastric juice, urine, and rarely, feces of HBsAg-positive persons, only semen, saliva, and serum actually have been shown to contain infectious HBV in experimental transmission studies.[6]

The three modes of HBV transmission that have the greatest impact are: 1) percutaneous transmission via contaminated blood, blood products, or instruments; 2) sexual contact; and 3) perinatal (vertical) transmission from a HBsAg-positive mother to her infant.

Serologic Events. Within the first several weeks following exposure, HBsAg appears in the blood and is present for several weeks before serum concentrations of aminotransferases increase and symptoms become apparent. Clinical illness usually follows HBV exposure by one to three months. HBsAg can be detected in serum until the clinical illness resolves. The antibody to HBsAg (antiHBs) often appears after a short ''window'' period during which neither HBsAg nor antiHBs are detectable. AntiHBs persist for years after HBV infection, conferring immunity to reinfection.

HBeAg is detectable early during the acute phase of the disease and persists in chronic hepatitis B infection. HBeAg is a marker of active HBV replication and its presence correlates with circulating HBV particles. The presence of both HBeAg and HBsAg indicates a high level of viral replication and infectivity. AntiHBe becomes detectable as HBeAg levels decline in acute or chronic hepatitis B. The appearance of antiHBe suggests resolution of HBV infection.

The most reliable marker of active HBV replication is the presence of HBV DNA in serum which is detectable early during the course of acute HBV infection. Persisting levels of HBV DNA indicate ongoing infection and a high degree of active viral replication and infectivity.

Hepatitis B core antigen does not circulate freely in the bloodstream and is not measured. AntiHBc, the antibody directed against

HBcAg, usually is detected one to two weeks after the appearance of HBsAg and just before the onset of clinical symptoms and persists for life. The detection of IgM antiHBc is the most sensitive diagnostic test for acute HBV infection. During the recovery phase of infection, the predominant form of antiHBc is in the IgG class. The presence of this antibody suggests prior or ongoing infection with HBV. Patients immunized against HBV do not develop antiHBc; therefore, the presence of this antibody differentiates successful vaccination from actual HBV infection.

Up to 10% of patients acutely infected with HBV remain chronically infected. In these patients, HBsAg remains detectable indefinitely and antiHBs fails to appear.

Diagnosis. The presence of HBsAg in serum is diagnostic for HBV infection. In 5% to 10% of acute cases in which the HBsAg levels fall below sensitivity thresholds of current assays, the presence of IgM antiHBc in serum confirms a recent acute hepatitis B infection.[7] Common serologic patterns of HBV infection are depicted in Table 62.3.

Hepatitis C

Before the development of methods to identify HCV, the majority of post-transfusion hepatitis cases were designated as nonA, nonB (NANB) hepatitis. HCV is recognized now as the most common cause of chronic NANB transfusion-associated hepatitis.[8,9] HCV is an RNA virus related to the flaviviruses, a family that includes the yellow fever virus.

Modes of Transmission. HCV appears to be readily transmitted parenterally;[9] other modes of transmission (e.g., sexual[10] and perinatal[11]) have been reported but occur to a lesser extent than with HBV. Before the use of routine blood screening, the incidence of acute HCV infection among transfusion recipients in the 1970s was approximately 5% to 10%.[12] Current blood screening techniques which include surrogate tests [measurement of alanine aminotransferase (ALT) and antiHBc in donor blood] to exclude high-risk donations have reduced the risk to less than 1%.[13] More sensitive second-generation antiHCV assays are under development that will decrease the risk even further.

Serologic Events. AntiHCV antibodies usually are detected in serum late during the course of acute hepatitis C. However, in many cases, seroconversion may take up to a year or longer following exposure to HCV. AntiHCV is detectable in serum for a variable length of time after acute infection. AntiHCV is not protective and its presence does not differentiate between acute, chronic, or resolved infection.

Diagnosis. A diagnosis of acute hepatitis C can be made in a patient with symptoms of acute hepatitis and a positive antiHCV

titer. A history of parenteral blood exposure (drug abuse, blood transfusions, needle stick) also would substantiate the diagnosis of HCV.

Hepatitis D

The delta virus is a defective RNA virus that can replicate only in the presence of HBsAg. Delta infection may be acquired simultaneously in a patient with acute hepatitis B infection (coinfection) or it may occur in a patient with chronic hepatitis B who is a carrier of HBsAg (superinfection). Infection with HDV can lead to both acute and chronic forms of hepatitis.[14]

Modes of Transmission. Hepatitis D virus is transmitted by the same routes as HBV and represents a potential infectious hazard to patients susceptible to hepatitis B and chronic hepatitis B carriers.[14] Since infection by the HDV requires the presence of active hepatitis B virus, prevention of hepatitis B infection will prevent HDV infection in a susceptible patient.

Serologic Events. Hepatitis D antigen (HDV-Ag) is found primarily in hepatocytes and is detected only rarely in serum, thus routine testing for HDV-Ag is not done. AntiHDV antibodies appear late during acute delta hepatitis and usually are not detectable while the patient is symptomatic. The current assay for antiHDV antibody is nonspecific and detects both IgM and IgG antibodies. AntiHDV antibody is not protective and is present in high titers in patients with chronic delta hepatitis.

Diagnosis. The diagnosis of acute delta hepatitis can be established in a patient with symptoms of hepatitis and positive HBsAg and antiHDV titers. Coinfection can be differentiated from superinfection by the presence of IgM antiHBc suggesting simultaneous acute HBV infection.

Hepatitis E

Hepatitis E virus has been recognized as the etiologic agent of epidemic or enterically transmitted NANB hepatitis. The disease has been associated with acute epidemic hepatitis in Third World countries, particularly in India, Africa, and Asia.[15] Infection with HEV does not lead to chronic hepatitis or a carrier state. HEV is transmitted by the fecal-oral route and is associated with contaminated food and water sources. Currently, serologic tests for HEV are not commercially available. The diagnosis of HEV is reserved for those patients with symptoms of acute hepatitis who have traveled recently to an endemic area and have negative serologic markers for acute hepatitis A, B, and C.

Clinical Features and Serologic Markers

The symptoms of acute viral hepatitis caused by HAV, HBV, HCV, HDV, and HEV are similar. The onset of symptoms in HBV

Table 62.2		Comparison of the Etiologic Forms of Viral Hepatitis			
	Hepatitis A	Hepatitis B	Hepatitis C	Hepatitis D	Hepatitis E
Causative agent	HAV	HBV	HCV	HDV	HEV
Mode of transmission	Fecal-oral; contaminated food, water	Parenteral; sexual; maternal-neonatal	Parenteral	Parenteral	Fecal-oral
Incubation period (mean)	15–45 days (30)	28–180 days (80)	15–160 days (50)	21–140 days (35)	15–65 days (42)
Onset	Sudden	Insidious	Insidious	Insidious	Sudden
Complete recovery	95%–99%	85%–95%	50%	90%	99%
Chronic hepatitis	0%	1%–10%	50%	1%–5%	0%
Carrier state	No	Yes	Yes	Yes	No
Cirrhosis	0%	<4%	10%–20%	1%–5%	0%

HBsAg	HBeAg	AntiHBs	AntiHBe	AntiHBc[a]	Interpretation
+	+	–	–	±	Incubation period
+	+	–	–	+ (IgM)	Acute HBV infection (typical case); chronic HBV carrier with high infectivity
–	–	+	±	+ (IgG)	Recovery from HBV infection
+	±	–	±	+ (IgG)	Chronic HBV carrier; chronic hepatitis B
–	–	+	–	–	Successful immunization with HBV vaccine

Table 62.3 — Common Serologic Patterns of Hepatitis B Virus Infection

[a] IgG = Immunoglobulin G; IgM = Immunoglobulin M.

and HCV usually is more insidious than that seen with HAV infection. Generally, symptoms are present several days to a week or more before the onset of jaundice. These consist of nonspecific influenza-like symptoms including malaise, fatigue, arthralgias, fever, headache, anorexia, nausea, and vomiting. Abdominal pain is common and is associated with hepatomegaly. Transient rashes also are observed in some patients. After this prodromal phase, patients may enter an icteric phase with symptoms including clay-colored stools, darkened urine, scleral icterus, and frank jaundice. Mild pruritus is common in jaundiced patients. Abnormalities in laboratory tests consist of rising levels of serum aminotransferases [usually ALT >aspartate aminotransferase (AST)], elevated bilirubin (usually <10 mg/dL) and mild elevations in alkaline phosphatase and prothrombin time (PT). The white blood cell (WBC) count, hematocrit (Hct), and hemoglobin (Hgb) usually are within normal limits. The icteric phase can persist from days to weeks. Complete normalization of laboratory tests following recovery from infection may take up to four months.

1. H.L., a 24-year-old female dental student, presents to the student health center with acute onset of jaundice. She was in good health until 1 week ago, when she noted a headache, loss of appetite, persistent nausea, fatigue, and low-grade fevers ranging between 99° to 101°F. She attributed these symptoms to the flu and took acetaminophen with plenty of fluids. Her symptoms persisted and later included generalized arthralgias and myalgias. Yesterday her urine appeared to be "cola-colored," and she experienced mild epigastric pain. This morning she noted jaundice of her eyes and skin and sought medical attention.

H.L.'s past medical and family histories are unremarkable. Her social history includes occasional alcoholic beverages on weekends. She denies travel outside of the U.S. There is no history of needle use or transfusions, and no known exposure to hepatitis. Her current medications include Ortho-Novum 1/35 (1 mg norethindrone/35 μg ethinyl estradiol) daily and diazepam 5 mg PO HS PRN temporal mandibular joint (TMJ) pain. She has been taking her oral contraceptive for years without problems and has not taken diazepam for "several months."

Physical examination was significant for a well-developed, well-nourished female in no acute distress. She was alert and oriented. Her temperature was 99 °F. Her sclerae and skin were icteric and her abdomen was positive for a tender, enlarged liver with a palpable spleen tip.

Laboratory tests revealed: Hgb 13 gm/dL; Hct 40%; WBC 6000 cells/mm³; AST 320 U/L (Normal: 5–40); ALT 360 U/L (Normal: 5–40); alkaline phosphatase 86 U/mL (Normal: 21–91); total bilirubin 3.2 mg/dL (Normal: 0.2–1.0); direct bilirubin 1.5 mg/dL (Normal: 0–0.2). The albumin, PT, blood glucose, and electrolytes all were within normal limits. H.L. had a negative test for IgM antiHAV, antiHCV, and HBsAg but was notably positive for IgM antiHBc. What clinical features and serological markers of viral hepatitis are evident in H.L.?

[SI units: Hgb 130 gm/L; Hct 0.40; WBC 6000 × 10⁹ cells/L; AST 320 U/L (Normal: 5–40); ALT 360 U/L (Normal: 5–40); alkaline phosphatase 86 U/L (Normal: 21–91); total bilirubin 54.72 μmol/L (Normal: 3.42–17.1); direct bilirubin 25.65 μmol/L (Normal: 0–4)]

H.L. presents with classic signs and symptoms of acute viral hepatitis. Her early influenza-like symptoms including fever, headache, nausea, anorexia, arthralgias, and myalgias are observed commonly in patients with acute viral hepatitis. The darkening in the color of her urine yesterday can be attributed to the presence of bilirubin; and this generally occurs shortly before the onset of jaundice. H.L. should be questioned about the presence of pale stools (light, gray, or yellow-colored) as this usually is observed during the icteric phase. Her physical examination findings of hepatosplenomegaly and scleral icterus are strongly suggestive of viral hepatitis. The results of H.L.'s liver function tests [LFTs (i.e., marked elevations in AST, ALT, and bilirubin)] are consistent with viral hepatitis.

Serologic testing is commonly used to establish the diagnosis of viral hepatitis. For patients presenting with signs and symptoms of acute viral hepatitis, an initial serologic work-up should include: IgM antiHAV, IgM antiHBc, HBsAg, and antiHCV. H.L. has a negative IgM antiHAV which rules out a current or recent HAV infection. Similarly, a negative antiHCV test makes acute HCV infection unlikely although these antibodies often are detectable only late in the disease process. A positive HBsAg in an acutely symptomatic patient with elevated liver enzymes is diagnostic of acute HBV infection. Failure to demonstrate HBsAg in H.L. with the clinical and laboratory findings of viral hepatitis does not exclude the diagnosis since the elevated titers may have disappeared by the time she became symptomatic.

The diagnostic test to confirm HBV infection in a patient with negative HBsAg is the detection of IgM antiHBc. H.L. has a positive IgM antiHBc test, indicating a diagnosis of acute HBV infection.

Treatment

2. Outline a rational treatment plan for H.L.'s acute viral hepatitis.

Acute viral hepatitis usually is a self-limited disease that does not require specific therapy. Many treatments have been recommended for acute viral hepatitis, but it is unlikely that any of them alter the course of the disease. Since evidence that the different types of hepatitis respond differently to various treatment regimens is sparse, recommendations regarding management apply equally to all acute viral hepatitis infections.

The patient with viral hepatitis may be treated at home if symptoms are mild to moderate and regular medical evaluation is possible. Hospitalization is required for patients with complications of hepatic insufficiency including encephalopathy or hemorrhage secondary to hypoprothrombinemia. H.L. has no signs of fulminant hepatic failure. She is alert and oriented, has no signs of bleeding and a normal PT. Her current clinical condition suggests she may be managed safely at home. During the illness, the serum concentration of aminotransferase and bilirubin, along with a prothrombin time, should be tested periodically until the liver enzyme concentrations return to normal.

In H.L., repeat testing of HBsAg and antiHBs will aid in documenting recovery from acute HBV infection. Seroconversion from HBeAg to antiHBeAg indicates that the infection is resolving and infectivity has fallen to a low level. A percutaneous liver biopsy is not necessary in the diagnosis of a typical case of acute viral hepatitis. Liver biopsy would be considered if disease persisted beyond three months or if ascites, edema, or hepatic encephalopathy developed. H.L. is acutely ill but in stable condition and, thus, a liver biopsy is not indicated at this time.

Bed Rest and Diet

Strict bed rest has not been shown to improve the rate of recovery from acute viral hepatitis. Controlled trials conducted among young servicemen have shown that even heavy physical exercise in the recovery period does not result in more frequent relapse or progression to chronic disease.[16,17] H.L. should continue her normal activities as much as possible while avoiding physical exhaustion. Since she is a dental student, she should not participate in direct patient care-related activities during the acute phase of her illness.

No evidence is available that a particular dietary regimen will shorten or ameliorate the course of acute viral hepatitis. H.L. should be encouraged to eat a generally well-balanced, nutritious diet. Severe nausea and vomiting may necessitate intravenous (IV) fluid and electrolyte replacement in some patients. H.L. should be advised to abstain from alcohol during the acute phase of the disease. Following resolution of symptoms and serum biochemical abnormalities, moderate alcohol intake no longer is contraindicated.

Drug Therapy

3. What drug therapy can be used to treat acute viral hepatitis B in H.L.?

Pharmacologic interventions in the management of acute hepatitis B have been disappointing. Early studies demonstrated a transient decrease in serum aminotransferase activity and bilirubin concentration in patients treated with corticosteroids. However, a higher incidence of relapse[18,19] and mortality[20–22] was observed in later studies in patients receiving corticosteroids in comparison to untreated patients. Other therapies including hepatitis B immune globulin (HBIG)[23] and α-interferon[24] have been ineffective in the management of acute viral hepatitis secondary to HBV. No data substantiate that vitamin therapy alters the course of viral hepatitis, although vitamin K administration should be considered in patients with an elevated prothrombin time. Vitamin K is not indicated for H.L. at the present time because her PT is within normal limits.

Adjustment of Medication Doses

4. Should H.L.'s medications be adjusted during the acute phase of hepatitis B infection?

Dosage adjustments for hepatically eliminated drugs in the setting of liver disease are difficult to predict. This is due to the complexity of hepatic metabolism that involves numerous oxidative and conjugative pathways which are variably affected in hepatic disease. In renal disease, creatinine serves as an endogenous marker to predict the clearance of renally eliminated drugs. Unfortunately, in hepatic disease, there are no reliable endogenous markers to accurately predict drug hepatic clearance. Laboratory

Table 62.4	Half-Life Data for Various Agents in Acute Viral Hepatitis Compared to Normal Controls[a]	
	$t\frac{1}{2}$ (hr)	
Drug	Normal Controls	Acute Viral Hepatitis
Acetaminophen[26]	2.1	3.2
Aspirin[26]	0.4	No change
Chlordiazepoxide[27]	11.1	91
Chloramphenicol[28]	4.6	11.6
Clofibrate[29]	17.5	No change
Diazepam[30]	37.2	74.5
Lidocaine[31]	3.7	6.4
Lorazepam[32]	21.7	No change
Meperidine[33]	3.4	7
Nitrendipine[34]	2.2	No change
Norfloxacin[35]	4.3	No change
Oxazepam[36]	5.1	No change
Phenobarbital[37]	86	No change
Phenytoin[38]	13.2	No change
Quinine[39]	10	17
Rifampin[40]	2.5	6.5
Theophylline[41]	7.7	19.2
Tolbutamide[42]	5.9	4.0
Warfarin[43]	25	No change

[a] No change = No statistically significant difference between patients with acute viral hepatitis and normal controls; $t\frac{1}{2}$ = Half-life.

tests that approximate the synthesis functions of the liver (albumin, PT) and biliary clearance (bilirubin) commonly are used to estimate the degree of hepatic impairment, but these tests are not dependable in predicting alterations in pharmacokinetic parameters for hepatically metabolized drugs.

Due to the difficulty in predicting hepatic drug clearance, unnecessary and potentially hepatotoxic medications are best avoided during the acute phase of the illness. When drug therapy is indicated with agents that undergo hepatic elimination, it is prudent to use the lowest doses possible to achieve the desired therapeutic effect.

There are limited data regarding the use of medications in the setting of acute viral hepatitis. An early study showed there were no increases in morbidity or mortality in women who continued to take oral contraceptives during acute hepatitis[25] and, thus, H.L. may continue her oral contraceptives. Data from small pharmacokinetic studies in patients with acute viral hepatitis[26–43] are shown in Table 62.4. H.L. should be advised to discontinue diazepam (Valium) as this medication undergoes extensive hepatic biotransformation and limited data suggest this agent accumulates in the setting of acute viral hepatitis.[30] If H.L. should require drug therapy for an attack of temporal mandibular joint pain, she should either decrease the diazepam dose or consider using an alternative agent (e.g., lorazepam) that does not accumulate in acute viral hepatitis.[32]

Guidelines to Prevent Hepatitis B Transmission

5. What precautions should be taken by H.L. to prevent the transmission of HBV to her patients?

The risk of a health care worker transmitting HBV to a patient is extremely low; however, there are case reports of such transmission. These cases usually involved laceration of a nongloved health care worker during an invasive procedure allowing percutaneous transfer of blood to the patient.[44,45] The CDC published guidelines for the prevention of HBV transmission to patients during exposure-prone invasive procedures in 1991. The guidelines recommend that all health care workers adhere to universal precautions including the appropriate use of hand washing, protective barriers, and care in the use and disposal of needles and other sharp instruments. Also included is the recommendation that health care workers who are infected with HBV (and are HBeAg-positive) not perform exposure-prone invasive procedures until they have sought counsel from an expert panel and been advised under what circumstances, if any, they may continue these procedures. This would include informing prospective patients of the health care worker's serological status before they undergo exposure-prone invasive procedures.[46] H.L., as a dental student, would be expected to perform exposure-prone procedures in her practice (e.g., root canals, tooth extractions), thus posing a slight but possible risk to her patients. She should refrain from direct patient care activity while she is acutely ill. Following resolution of the acute HBV infection, she may participate in patient care with meticulous adherence to universal precautions in her practice.

Immunoprophylaxis

Immunoprophylaxis may be passive, active, or a combination of both. In passive immunization, temporary protective antibody in the form of immune globulin (IG) is administered. In active immunization, a vaccine is administered to induce the formation of protective antibody. Prophylaxis can be administered before exposure (pre-exposure prophylaxis) or after exposure has occurred (postexposure prophylaxis).

Pre-exposure Prophylaxis

6. Hepatitis A. M.D., a 30-year-old, 60 kg surgical resident, is preparing for a 2-week vacation to Thailand. What pre-exposure prophylactic regimen should M.D. receive for HAV?

Immune globulin is an injectable solution containing a full complement of antibodies normally present in human serum. Immune globulin is manufactured by cold ethanol fractionation of pooled plasma collected from at least 1000 human donors and provides adequate levels of antiHAV. Passive immunity afforded by the immune globulin is effective in both pre-exposure and postexposure prophylaxis of HAV.

Pre-exposure prophylaxis is recommended for international travelers visiting undeveloped countries where the risk of contracting hepatitis A is high. In general, the risk of infection increases with the duration of travel and is highest for those who visit rural areas or frequently eat or drink in settings of poor sanitation. M.D. should be advised to avoid potentially contaminated water or food (i.e., uncooked shellfish or uncooked fruits and vegetables that have been peeled), or beverages with ice.[47]

For travelers visiting high-risk areas, a single dose of immune globulin 0.02 mL/kg body weight is recommended if travel is for less than three months. M.D. is traveling to a high-risk area for a short period of time and should receive 0.02 mL/kg (1.2 mL) of immune globulin as an intramuscular (IM) injection preferably in the gluteal region before his trip if primary immunization with hepatitis A vaccine cannot be completed at least two weeks before expected exposure to HAV.

Vaccine. A vaccine for hepatitis A (Havrix) is now available for IM injection into the deltoid region. HAV vaccine should not be given gluteally because of possible suboptimal response. This for-

malin-inactivated vaccine is well tolerated and highly effective when given to adults as a single IM dose of 1440 EL units [referenced to a standard using an enzyme-linked immunosorbent assay (ELISA) expressed as EL units]. While data suggest a single dose is effective, a three-dose schedule may confer optimal protection.[49] Primary immunization for children 2 to 18 years of age consists of two doses each containing 360 EL units given one month apart. A booster dose is recommended between 6 to 12 months after initiation of the primary course to ensure the highest antibody titers. Hepatitis A vaccine is effective for pre-exposure prophylaxis of hepatitis A in high-risk groups (e.g., frequent travelers, military personnel, international workers). Since this hepatitis A vaccine is available, M.D. should receive the vaccine if time allows.

7. Hepatitis B Vaccine. P.G., a 55-year-old female nursing student, is going to start her clinical rotations. She has no history of hepatitis and has not yet been immunized. She is 5'2" and weighs 80 kg. What prophylactic regimen should P.G. receive to prevent hepatitis secondary to HBV?

The first available HBV vaccine was manufactured from the pooled plasma of asymptomatic HBsAg carriers. This plasma-derived vaccine (Heptavax-B) has not been available since 1991. The currently available vaccines are manufactured using recombinant DNA technology. Both Recombivax HB (10 mg HBsAg/mL) and Engerix-B (20 mg HBsAg/mL) are yeast-derived HBV vaccines that induce an immunologic response similar to the plasma-derived vaccine. Since P.G. will come in contact with potentially infectious bodily secretions during her rotations, she should be immunized against hepatitis B with either Recombivax HB or Engerix-B.

Dosing Regimen. The recommended doses of the currently available hepatitis B vaccines are shown in Table 62.5. The usual vaccination schedule uses a three-dose regimen. The first dose is followed one month later by a second dose, and the third dose is administered six months after the initial dose. The first two doses function as priming doses and induce antiHBs in greater than 85% of normal individuals. The third dose serves as a booster dose and markedly increases the antiHBs titer, thus conferring optimal protection. The third dose can be administered up to 12 months after the initial dose with comparable efficacy. A four-dose series has been approved for high-risk patients in whom rapid protection is desired. If this schedule is followed, the last dose at 12 months is necessary to ensure protective antibody titers.

The recommended doses for the yeast-derived recombinant hepatitis B vaccines were based upon dose-response studies that determined the optimal dose necessary to achieve protective antibody titers. Dose response studies with Recombivax HB in healthy adults using 1.25, 2.5, 5, 10, and 20 µg of HBsAg all elicited an immune response. Those patients receiving the 10 or 20 µg dose developed substantially higher antibody titers than those receiving lower doses. No significant difference was observed between the 10 µg or 20 µg dose; thus, the 10 µg dose was selected as the standard adult dose of Recombivax HB. Similar analyses were performed to determine the 5 µg adolescent and 2.5 µg pediatric dosages.[51] Dose response trials with Engerix-B demonstrated an optimal immune response at higher dosages. The reason for the differing doses necessary to elicit an adequate immune response is unknown. Some have speculated that differences in the manufacturing process (yeast culture, purification methods) may influence the immunogenicity of the final product. For this reason, hepatitis B vaccines produced by different manufacturers may not be equally immunogenic on a microgram for microgram basis.[52] Relative potency comparisons are not clinically important because comparative trials using Recombivax HB and Engerix-B in the recommended dosages have demonstrated equivalent immunoge-

Table 62.5	Recommended Doses of Currently Licensed Hepatitis B Vaccines[75]	
Group[b]	Recombivax HB[a] Dose (µg)(mL)	Engerix-B[b] Dose (µg)(mL)
Infants of HBsAg-negative mothers and children <11 yr	2.5 (0.25)	10 (0.5)
Infants of HBsAg-positive mothers; prevention of perinatal infections	5 (0.5)	10 (0.5)
Children and adolescents 11–19 yr	5 (0.5)	20 (1.0)
Adults ≥20 yr	10 (1.0)	20 (1.0)
Dialysis patients and other immuno-compromised hosts	40 (1.0)[c]	40 (2.0)[d]

[a] Both vaccines are administered routinely in a 3 dose series at 0,1, and 6 months. Engerix-B also has been licensed for a dose series administered at 0, 1, 2, and 12 months.
[b] HBsAg = Hepatitis B surface antigen.
[c] Special formulation.
[d] Two 1.0 mL doses administered at 1 site, in a 4-dose schedule at 0, 1, 2, and 6 months.

nicity and tolerability. P.G. can be immunized with either product provided she receives the manufacturer's recommended dosage with each injection.

Hepatitis B vaccine should be administered as an IM injection in the deltoid muscle of adults and children or in the anterolateral thigh muscle of neonates and infants. The immunogenicity of hepatitis B vaccine is significantly lower when injections are given in the buttocks probably because the greater amount of fat tissue in the buttocks inhibits interfacing of vaccine and antigen-recognition leukocytes. The results of a small vaccination series suggest that healthy adults who do not respond to HBV injection to the buttocks have a significantly higher response when vaccinated in the arm.[54] P.G. should be immunized with either Recombivax HB (10 µg) or Engerix-B (20 µg) administered as a 1 mL IM injection in the deltoid muscle.

Efficacy. The plasma-derived HBV vaccine (e.g., Heptavax-B) provides a detectable immune response in greater than 90% of individuals receiving the three-dose vaccination series.[55–63] Recombinant yeast-derived vaccines (e.g., Recombivax HB and Engerix-B) produce similar results.[64] While a measurable immune response is readily achieved with the current HBV vaccine, a quantitative titer of circulating antiHBs necessary to prevent infection has not been substantiated clearly. A protective antibody response has been defined as antiHBs levels ≥10 milliinternational units/mL.[47] This threshold was derived from early HBV vaccine trials in homosexual men where it was observed that vaccine recipients with serum antibody levels ≥10 sample ratio units (SRU) were protected from HBV infection.[58,59,61,65] A serum antibody level of 10 SRU is roughly equivalent to 10 milliinternational units/mL when the international standard is used.[66] For this reason, an antiHBs level of ≥10 milliinternational units/mL is considered to be a protective antibody titer. Although HBV infections have occurred in vaccine recipients with a detectable immune response, almost all infections have been subclinical and identified only through the presence of antiHBc. These infections have been limited largely to patients with no response or a poor response to vaccination.[60,61]

8. *Nonresponders.* **P.G. has completed her 3-dose vaccination series with Engerix-B. During routine hepatitis serology testing performed before volunteering for a drug study, it was found that P.G. is antiHBs negative. Why did P.G. not respond to the hepatitis B vaccine and how should she be managed?**

Two important determinants of vaccine efficacy appear to be the age at vaccination and underlying immune function. In healthy recipients, the immune response to vaccination decreases with advancing age. In one study, 99% of patients age 0 to 19 years, 93% of those age 20 to 49 years, and 73% of those more than 50 years of age achieved protective antiHBs levels (≥10 SRU) after three doses of the hepatitis B vaccine.[63] Immunocompromised patients including those receiving hemodialysis[67] or infected with human immunodeficiency virus (HIV)[68] tend to respond poorly to the HBV vaccine. Patients who smoke or are obese also may have a reduced response to HBV vaccine.[69,70] P.G. has two risk factors for a poor response to the hepatitis B vaccine: she is more than 50 years of age and she is moderately obese (her ideal body weight for her height is ≈50 kg).

Vaccine recipients who respond poorly to hepatitis B vaccine have been classified either as *relative nonresponders* (hyporesponders) who probably can be protected by additional doses of vaccine, or as *true nonresponders*. True nonresponders are rare. Patients with an inadequate initial response to the HBV vaccine series should be revaccinated. Eighty percent of hyporesponders (antiHBs levels <10 milliinternational units/mL) develop a protective level following a single booster injection[71] or after repeating the entire three-dose series.[65] Revaccination of nonresponders (no detectable antiHBs) is less successful and protective levels, if achieved, are not sustained.[72] P.G. should be revaccinated with a booster dose of hepatitis B vaccine. Her antiHBs levels can be rechecked one month after the injection. If she still has not responded, it is reasonable to administer an additional two injections to complete a second vaccination series.

9. *Interchangeability of HBV Vaccines.* **T.M., a 32-year-old male hospital laboratory technician, received the first 2 doses of hepatitis B vaccine with Recombivax HB. He has relocated recently and is due for the 3rd injection. The employee health service at his new job uses only Engerix-B for hepatitis B vaccination. Can hepatitis B vaccines produced by different manufacturers be used interchangeably?**

While it is recommended that patients receive the complete vaccination series with the same product, data suggest this is not absolutely necessary to induce a protective antibody titer. In a study to determine if a hepatitis B vaccination series initiated with Recombivax HB could be completed with Engerix-B, healthy adults received 10 µg of Recombivax HB at baseline and one month. At six months, the subjects were randomized to receive either Engerix-B 20 µg or Recombivax HB 10 µg. One month after the third dose, 100% of those who had received Engerix-B and 92% of those who had received Recombivax HB had protective antiHBs levels.[73]

Chan et al. studied the booster response to either recombinant hepatitis B vaccine or plasma-derived vaccine in children who had been vaccinated originally with the plasma-derived product (Heptavax-B). Children were randomized to either 5 µg of the plasma-derived vaccine or 20 µg of Engerix-B. One month after the booster injection, all vaccine recipients had marked elevations in their antiHBs titers suggesting recombinant hepatitis B vaccines elicit an adequate booster response in individuals who originally received the plasma-derived vaccine.[74] According to the Immunization Practice Advisory Committee (ACIP) in the U.S., the immune response from one or two doses of a vaccine produced by one manufacturer, when followed by subsequent doses from a different manufacturer, is comparable with that resulting from a full course of vaccination with a single vaccine.[75]

T.M. may complete the hepatitis B vaccine series with Engerix-B provided he receives the recommended dosage of 20 µg administered as a 1 mL IM injection to the deltoid region. This dose will markedly increase his circulating antiHBs titer, thus conferring optimal protection from HBV infection.

10. *Duration of Response.* **Does T.M. require a booster injection for sustained protection from HBV infection?**

The duration of vaccine-induced immunity has been evaluated in several long-term studies.[63,65,76,77] The duration of detectable antiHBs appears to be proportional to the peak antibody response achieved after vaccination. Protective serum concentrations of hepatitis B antibodies were observed in 58% to 83% of patients successfully vaccinated after five years. In a nine-year follow-up study, 73% of patients receiving two or three doses of plasma-derived HBV vaccine had protective antiHBs levels ≥10 milli-international units/mL.[76] The ACIP does not recommend booster doses of vaccine except for patients receiving chronic hemodialysis. For these patients, the ACIP recommends annual testing of antiHBs levels and booster doses when levels are less than 10 milliinternational units/mL.[75] Based upon available evidence, T.M. does not require a scheduled booster dose of hepatitis B vaccine.

11. Why is it appropriate for T.M. to be vaccinated with hepatitis B vaccine and who should be vaccinated with this vaccine?

Indications. The ACIP has recommended pre-exposure hepatitis B vaccination for the following high-risk groups: health care workers with exposure to blood, staff of institutions for the developmentally disabled, hemodialysis patients, recipients of blood products, household and sexual contacts of HBV-carriers, international travelers to HBV endemic areas, injecting drug users, sexually active homosexual men, and inmates of long-term correctional facilities.[75] Since T.M. is a hospital laboratory technician, he is at high risk for exposure to hepatitis B and should be vaccinated.

Universal Hepatitis B Vaccination. In addition to the above listed high-risk groups, all infants should receive hepatitis B vaccination. This recommendation is based upon data that suggest the current strategy of vaccinating only high-risk persons has had little impact in decreasing the incidence of HBV disease. High-risk individuals (injecting drug users, persons with multiple sexual partners) generally are not vaccinated before they begin engaging in high-risk behaviors. Additionally, many individuals who become infected have no identifiable risk factors for infection and thus would not be recognized as candidates for vaccination. A program designed to immunize children before they initiate high-risk behaviors is likely to have a greater impact in reducing future HBV infections. As a means to achieve this goal, the hepatitis B vaccine now is incorporated into the existing pediatric vaccination schedule. The first dose is administered during the newborn period (preferably before the infant is discharged from the hospital) but no later than two months of age.[75] The recommended vaccination schedule is shown in Table 62.6. It is anticipated that this universal vaccination program will reduce the incidence of acute hepatitis B and hepatitis B-associated chronic liver disease in the future.

Adverse Effects. HBV vaccination generally has been well tolerated. The most common side effect is pain at the injection site, observed in 10% to 20% of patients. Transient febrile reactions occur in less than 5% of recipients, and other reactions including nausea, rash, headache, myalgias, and arthralgias are observed in less than 1% of recipients.

12. Is universal vaccination with hepatitis B vaccine cost effective?

Table 62.6	Recommended Schedules of Hepatitis B Vaccination for Infants Born to HBsAg-Negative Mothers[75]
Hepatitis B Vaccine	**Age of Infant**
Option 1	
Dose 1	Birth (before hospital discharge)
Dose 2	1–2 months[a]
Dose 3	6–18 months[a]
Option 2	
Dose 1	1–2 months[a]
Dose 2	4 months[a]
Dose 3	6–18 months[a]

[a] Hepatitis B vaccine can be administered simultaneously with diphtheria-tetanus-pertussis, *Haemophilus influenza* type b conjugate, measles-mumps-rubella, and oral polio vaccines.

Universal hepatitis B vaccination, although expensive to initiate, is expected to be a cost-effective public health measure over time by decreasing morbidity and mortality associated with HBV disease. A cost-effective analysis compared universal vaccination to maternal screening and selective vaccination of high-risk newborns. In this analysis, the incremental cost per year of life saved was reduced substantially with implementation of a universal vaccination program.[78] Another analysis determined that the most cost-effective hepatitis B vaccination strategy involves a combination of immunizing high-risk newborns and all adolescent children. This model includes screening of all pregnant women before delivery with vaccination of neonates born to HBsAg-positive mothers. Additionally, all adolescents would be vaccinated at age ten before entering middle school or junior high school. Implementation of this hepatitis B vaccine program predicted a cost of $375 per year of life saved. This compares favorably with current medical interventions including renal transplantation at $7500 per year of life saved or cholestyramine therapy for hyperlipidemia at $65,250 per year of life saved.[79]

Preliminary evaluations suggest a more widespread hepatitis B vaccination program is comparable to many existing health care interventions from a cost-effective standpoint. Universal hepatitis B vaccination appears to be a reasonable addition to the existing pediatric immunization schedule.

Postexposure Prophylaxis for Viral Hepatitis

13. Hepatitis B: *Percutaneous Exposure.* **K.N., a 26-year-old female medical student, presents to the emergency room (ER) after accidentally sticking herself with a contaminated needle while drawing blood from an HBsAg-positive patient. K.N. had not been vaccinated previously and had no known prior episodes of hepatitis or liver disease. Her tetanus status is current. She weighs 56 kg. How should K.N. be managed for percutaneous exposure to hepatitis B?**

The wound should be examined, cleansed, and dressed. Additionally, following exposure to HBV, prophylactic treatment with hepatitis B vaccination and possibly passive immunization with hepatitis B immune globulin should be considered. The ACIP recommendations for postexposure immunoprophylaxis following hepatitis B exposure are shown in Table 62.7.

K.N.'s percutaneous exposure warrants active immunization with HBV and passive immunization with hepatitis B immune globulin. The source of K.N.'s exposure is HBsAg-positive and K.N. had not been vaccinated previously with the hepatitis B vaccine. She should receive a single dose of hepatitis B immune globulin 0.06 mL/kg (3.4 mL) as an IM injection in either the gluteal or deltoid region as soon as possible after exposure and preferably within 24 hours. Hepatitis B immune globulin is prepared from plasma of individuals preselected for high titer antiHBs. The antiHBs of hepatitis B immune globulin in the U.S. is 1:100,000 as determined by radioimmunoassay. Hepatitis B immune globulin is superior to immune globulin in the prevention of hepatitis B infection following percutaneous exposure.[80] K.N. also should receive active immunization with intramuscular hepatitis B vaccine (at a separate site) simultaneously with hepatitis B immune globulin. The second and third doses are given one month and six months later. Passively acquired antibodies against hepatitis B virus from hepatitis B immune globulin or immune globulin will not interfere with active immunization via hepatitis B vaccine.[81]

If the HBsAg status of the donor source of K.N.'s accidental needle stick was unknown, recommendations for prophylaxis of HBV infection are dependent upon whether the donor source is at high risk or at low risk for being HBsAg-positive. Donor sources considered high risk for being HBsAg-positive include male homosexuals, IV drug abusers, patients undergoing hemodialysis, residents of mental institutions, immigrants from areas where HBV is endemic, household contacts of HBV carriers, and patients with acute, unconfirmed hepatitis. Additional ACIP recommendations for hepatitis B prophylaxis following percutaneous exposure are shown in Table 62.8.

14. *Sexual Exposure.* **What are the current recommendations for an individual who has had sexual contact with an HBsAg-positive person?**

Sexual transmission of hepatitis B is an important cause of HBV infections, accounting for up to 66% of all new cases annually. Passive immunization with a single 5 mL dose of hepatitis B immune globulin was found to be highly effective in preventing hepatitis B infection following sexual exposure when compared to a control globulin (with no antiHBs activity).[82] The CDC recommends that susceptible persons exposed to HBV through sexual contact with a person who has acute or chronic HBV infection should receive postexposure prophylaxis with 0.06 mL/kg of hepatitis B immune globulin as a single intramuscular dose within 14 days of the last exposure. Patients also should receive the standard three-dose immunization series with hepatitis B vaccine beginning at the time of hepatitis B immune globulin administration.[83]

15. *Perinatal Exposure.* **S.L., a 3.2 kg male, was just born to an HBsAg-positive mother. Is S.L. at risk for acquiring HBV infection and how should he be managed?**

In many Asian and developing countries, perinatal (vertical) transmission accounts for the majority of hepatitis B infections. Infants born to HBV-infected mothers have a greater than 85% risk of acquiring HBV during the perinatal period.[84] Of those who become infected, 80% to 90% become chronic HBsAg carriers.[85–87] While fulminant cases have been reported, most hepatitis infections in neonates are asymptomatic. In contrast, the long-term consequences of chronic HBsAg carriage in neonates are profound. Chronic hepatitis B infection is associated with chronic liver disease and has been clearly implicated as a major risk factor in the development of primary hepatocellular carcinoma.[88,89]

Mothers who are chronic carriers of hepatitis B, although not acutely infected, pose the risk of transmitting the hepatitis B virus to their infants. The risk is related to the presence of HBsAg and HBeAg (suggesting a high degree of viral replication and infectivity). The likelihood that S.L. will develop HBV infection is very high. S.L. requires immediate therapy with hepatitis B immune globulin (to provide immediate high titers of circulating antiHBs) and simultaneous vaccination with hepatitis B vaccine (to induce long-lasting protective immunity). Screening pregnant women for the presence of HBeAg and administration of hepatitis B immune globulin and hepatitis B vaccine is 85% to 98% effective in preventing HBV infection and the chronic carrier state.[84,85,87,90,91] This compares with a 71% efficacy rate for administration of hepatitis B immune globulin alone.[86] Simultaneous administration of hepatitis B immune globulin and hepatitis B vaccine does not adversely affect the production of antiHBs in neonates.[85,87]

Infants born to mothers who are HBsAg-positive should receive simultaneous IM injections of the appropriate doses of hepatitis B vaccine (see Table 62.5) and hepatitis B immune globulin (0.5 mL) within 12 hours of birth. The injections should be administered at separate sites. S.L. should receive hepatitis B immune globulin (0.5 mL) as soon as possible after birth administered as an IM injection. He also should receive 0.5 mL of either Recombivax HB (5 μg) or Engerix-B (10 μg) as an IM injection at a separate site.

16. What if the HBsAg status of S.L.'s mother was unknown?

The ACIP has developed recommendations for the prevention of perinatal HBV infection. This includes the routine testing of all pregnant women for HBsAg during an early prenatal visit. HBsAg testing should be repeated late in the pregnancy for women who are HBsAg-negative but who are at high risk of HBV infection or who have had clinically apparent hepatitis. Women admitted for delivery who have not had prenatal HBsAg testing should have blood drawn for testing. While test results are pending, the infant should receive hepatitis B vaccine within 12 hours of birth, in a dose appropriate for infants born to HBsAg-positive mothers (see Table 62.5). If the mother is found later to be HBsAg-positive, her infant should receive hepatitis B immune globulin as soon as possible and within seven days of birth. The second and third doses should be administered at one and six months, respectively. If the mother is found to be HBsAg-negative, her infant should continue to receive hepatitis B vaccine as part of the routine vaccination series in the dose appropriate for hepatitis HBsAg-negative mothers[75] (see Table 62.5).

17. *Hepatitis A.* **L.W., a 26-year-old male, recently was diagnosed with HAV infection. He currently attends college and works part-time as a shop assistant. He is married with an infant son. Which contacts of L.W. require postexposure prophylaxis for HAV?**

A serologic test for the detection of antiHAV is available but not routinely performed because screening is more costly than a dose of immune globulin and would delay its administration. The ACIP recommends a single intramuscular dose of immune globulin, 0.02 mL/kg as soon as possible, for postexposure prophylaxis of hepatitis A. Administration of immune globulin within two weeks of exposure to HAV is 80% to 90% effective in preventing acute HAV infection.[92,93]

Table 62.7	Guide to Postexposure Immunoprophylaxis for Exposure to Hepatitis B Virus[75,83]
Type of Exposure	**Immunoprophylaxis[a]**
Perinatal	Vaccination + HBIG
Sexual	Vaccination + HBIG
Household contact	
Chronic carrier	Vaccination
Acute case	None unless known exposure
Acute case, known exposure	HBIG ± vaccination
Infant (<12 months) acute case in primary caregiver	HBIG + vaccination
Inadvertent (percutaneous/permucosal)	Vaccination ± HBIG

[a] HBIG = Hepatitis B immunoglobulin.

Table 62.8	Recommendations for Hepatitis B Prophylaxis Following Percutaneous Exposure[75]		
	Treatment When Source Is Found to Be		
Exposed Person	HBsAg-Positive	HBsAg-Negative	Unknown or Not Tested
Unvaccinated	Administer HBIG x 1[a] and initiate hepatitis B vaccine	Initiate hepatitis B vaccine[b]	Initiate hepatitis B vaccine[b]
Previously vaccinated Known responder	Test exposed person for antiHBs[c] 1) If inadequate, hepatitis B vaccine booster dose 2) If adequate, no treatment	No treatment	No treatment
Known nonresponder	HBIG x 1[a] as soon as possible, repeat in 1 month *OR* HBIG x 1,[a] plus 1 dose of hepatitis B vaccine	No treatment	If known high-risk-source, may treat as if source were HBsAg positive
Response unknown	Test exposed person for antiHBs[c] 1) If inadequate, HBIG x 1[a] plus hepatitis B vaccine booster dose 2) If adequate, no treatment	No treatment	Test exposed person for antiHBs[c] 1) If inadequate, hepatitis B vaccine booster dose 2) If adequate, no treatment

[a] HBIG dose 0.06 mL/kg IM.
[b] For dosing information, see Table 62.5.
[c] Adequate antiHBs is ≥10 milliinternational units.

In most cases, when given early, immune globulin prevents both clinical and subclinical HAV illness.[94] Protection following immune globulin administration is immediate and complete. The natural infection with HAV is prevented but long-lasting immunity to HAV does not develop.

Immune globulin is recommended for close personal contacts (i.e., family and household contacts) and institutional contacts (i.e., prisons and institutions for the developmentally disabled) of patients with acute HAV. L.W.'s wife and infant son should receive prophylactic administration of IG. Prophylaxis is not recommended for casual contacts at work or school. In outbreaks of acute HAV in day care centers, postexposure prophylaxis of children, staff, and family members of infected children has been shown to minimize the spread of HAV. Unless exposed persons can be identified and treated within two weeks of exposure in food-borne outbreaks of hepatitis A, widespread prophylaxis with immune globulin is not recommended.[47]

18. Hepatitis C, D, and E. **Guidelines for postexposure prophylaxis for hepatitis A and hepatitis B have been presented in Questions 13 to 17, but what guidelines are available for patients exposed to hepatitis C, D, and E?**

Although the benefit of immune globulin for postexposure prophylaxis of HCV has not been established, 0.06 mL/kg of immune globulin may be administered as soon as possible to individuals following percutaneous exposure to HCV-infected blood.[47] No specific recommendations for other types of HCV exposure are available at the present time. Currently, no postexposure prophylaxis is available for hepatitis D and E.

Chronic Hepatitis

Definition. Chronic hepatitis is an inflammatory condition of the liver that involves ongoing hepatocellular necrosis for at least six months. The etiologies of chronic hepatitis are shown in Table 62.9. The most common cause of chronic hepatitis is chronic viral hepatitis caused by HBV or HCV. Drug-induced and autoimmune chronic hepatitis occur less frequently, while metabolic disorders and HDV chronic hepatitis are relatively rare.

Chronic hepatitis has been categorized into two distinct forms, including chronic persistent hepatitis (CPH) and chronic active hepatitis (CAH). A liver biopsy is necessary to differentiate these types of chronic hepatitis. CPH is the most common form of chronic hepatitis and usually is an asymptomatic condition with minimal risk of progression to cirrhosis or hepatic failure. Conversely, CAH is characterized by the presence of symptoms, marked alterations in liver function tests, and derangement in liver histology. The risk of progression to cirrhosis, frank hepatic failure, primary hepatocellular carcinoma, and death is much greater with CAH.

Clinical Features. Patients with CPH generally present with modest increases in the serum concentrations of aminotransferase and bilirubin. Patients with CAH may present with a variety of clinical features ranging from asymptomatic illness with minor liver function abnormalities to fulminant hepatic failure. Clinical manifestations include fatigue, jaundice, malaise, anorexia, and low-grade fever. Extrahepatic manifestations may be observed and include arthralgias, arthritis, neuropathy, thyroiditis, glomerulonephritis, vasculitis, skin rash, thrombocytopenia, amenorrhea, acne, hirsutism, and gynecomastia. Extrahepatic features are particularly common in the autoimmune form of chronic hepatitis.

Diagnosis. A liver biopsy is necessary to establish the diagnosis of chronic active hepatitis or chronic persistent hepatitis. Histologic examination of liver tissue in CPH generally reveals chronic inflammatory infiltration of the portal areas with little or no fibrosis. CAH is characterized by inflammation extending beyond the portal areas into surrounding hepatic structures with extensive necrosis and fibrosis.

The diagnostic evaluation of a patient with the presumptive diagnosis of chronic hepatitis also should include hepatitis serologies. The appropriate tests include HBsAg and antiHCV. If HBsAg is present, further testing for HBeAg and HBV DNA are indicated to document the presence of active viral replication and assess the viral load. Testing for antiHDV also should be performed in patients with hepatitis B to evaluate the possibility of coexisting delta hepatitis. If the hepatitis serology is negative, rare but treatable causes of chronic active hepatitis should be excluded. These include alcoholic liver disease, Wilson's disease, α-antitrypsin deficiency, and drug-induced chronic active hepatitis. Drugs associated with reversible chronic active hepatitis syndrome include methyldopa,[95] nitrofurantoin,[96] isoniazid,[97] and rarely, sulfonamides[98] and propylthiouracil.[99]

Following exclusion of the above conditions, the patient should be evaluated for the presence of circulating immunologic markers associated with the autoimmune (idiopathic) form of chronic hepatitis. These tests include antismooth-muscle antibody, antimitochondrial antibody, antinuclear antibody titers, and increased serum immunoglobulins.

Clinical Presentation and Diagnosis

19. C.R., a 28-year-old male, presents to the ER with jaundice and complaints of incapacitating fatigue and vague intermittent abdominal pain for the past month. C.R. has a history of hepatitis B diagnosed 2 years before admission. He also has a seizure disorder sustained after a motorcycle accident 10 years before admission, for which he takes phenytoin 400 mg PO HS.

C.R.'s social history is significant for a history of IV drug abuse (none for 5 years) and alcohol abuse (none for 2 years). Several weeks ago C.R. noted darkening of his urine and yellowing of his eyes.

Physical examination revealed a thin man in no apparent distress. He was afebrile, and blood pressure, heart rate, and respiratory rate were within normal limits. Moderate scleral icterus was noted. The abdomen was soft and nondistended. The liver was enlarged, nontender, and smooth with an edge palpable 5 cm below the costal margin and a span of 15 cm. The spleen was palpable. The cardiac, pulmonary, neurologic, and extremity exams all were within normal limits.

The laboratory evaluation was significant for the following: Hct 44%, Hgb 15 gm/dL, WBC count 8.8 cells/mm^3, platelets 225,000/mm^3 (Normal: 150,000–300,000); PT 15.4 sec (Control: 12 sec), international normalized ratio 1.8; AST 326 U/L (Normal: 5–40); ALT 382 U/L (Normal: 5–40), alkaline phosphatase 142 U/mL (Normal: 21–91); total bilirubin 4.2 mg/dL (Normal: 0.1–1.2); albumin 2.8 gm/dL (Normal: 3.5–4.5); phenytoin 11 mg/L (Normal: 10–20). Hepatitis serologic tests were positive for HBsAg, HBeAg, and antiHBc and negative for IgM antiHBc, IgM antiHAV, and antiHCV. A liver biopsy revealed periportal inflammation, piecemeal and bridging necrosis consistent with CAH. What clinical findings does C.R. have that support the diagnosis of chronic active hepatitis?

[SI units: Hct 0.44; Hgb 150 gm/L; WBC count 8.8 × 10^9 cells/L; AST 326 U/L (Normal: 5–40); ALT 382 U/L (Normal: 5–40); alkaline phosphatase 142 U/L (Normal: 21–91); total bilirubin 71.8 μmol/L (Normal: 1.7–20.5); albumin 28 gm/L (Normal: 35–45); phenytoin 43.6 μmol/L (Normal: 40–80)]

Table 62.9	Etiologies of Chronic Hepatitis

Viral Infections
Hepatitis viruses (B, C, D)
CMV[a]
Epstein-Barr virus
Rubella virus

Drug-Induced
Methyldopa
Nitrofurantoin
Isoniazid
Sulfonamides
Propylthiouracil

Metabolic Disorders
Wilson's disease
α$_1$-antitrypsin deficiency

Autoimmune Hepatitis

[a] CMV = Cytomegalovirus.

The chronic occurrence of jaundice and hepatosplenomegaly with markedly elevated AST and ALT in a young patient such as C.R. is suggestive of chronic hepatitis. Although alcoholic hepatitis secondary to long-term alcohol abuse and phenytoin-induced hepatotoxicity also would be consistent with these clinical features, he has been treated with phenytoin for about ten years and his serologic tests are positive for HBV.

The serum concentrations of aminotransferase and bilirubin in C.R. are increased and his hepatitis serologies are suggestive of chronic hepatitis B. Serum concentrations of aminotransferase can range from slightly abnormal to markedly elevated, with ALT concentrations generally greater than AST concentrations. Hepatitis serology with positive HBsAg and HBeAg suggest on-going viral replication and a high degree of infectivity. Serum bilirubin concentrations greater than 3.0 mg/dL are common, serum concentrations of alkaline phosphatase usually are increased, and the prothrombin time may be prolonged. Patients such as C.R. with a prolonged PT and low serum albumin concentration generally have a more severe form of chronic hepatitis.

The liver biopsy is important for the diagnosis, treatment, and prognosis of patients with chronic hepatitis. C.R.'s liver biopsy revealed the classic triad of periportal inflammation, piecemeal and bridging necrosis. The liver biopsy and hepatitis serologic test results are consistent with a diagnosis of chronic active hepatitis B.

Treatment of Chronic Hepatitis B

20. Does C.R. require treatment for CAH secondary to hepatitis B?

The decision to treat C.R. is dependent upon the severity of symptoms, the serum biochemistries, and the liver biopsy results. Symptom-free patients with moderate elevations in aminotransferases and liver biopsies demonstrating mild CAH probably should not be treated. These patients should be monitored every three to six months with routine serum biochemistries and by liver biopsy at yearly intervals.

C.R. has evidence of severe CAH. He is symptomatic with jaundice, severe fatigue, and abdominal pain. The results of his liver function tests suggest his disease is advanced (decreased albumin, elevated PT). He should be treated to reduce the replication of HBV, resolve the hepatocellular damage, and prevent long-term adverse hepatic sequelae.

Goals of Therapy

21. What are the goals of therapy for CAH secondary to HBV?

Progression of chronic active hepatitis to cirrhosis is thought to be related to continued replication of the hepatitis B virus. Loss of active viral replication usually is associated with a decrease in infectivity, a reduction in inflammatory cells within the liver, and a fall of serum aminotransferase activities into the normal range. The disappearance of detectable HBeAg and HBV DNA is considered an indicator of loss of active viral replication.

The goal of therapy in chronic HBV infection is eradication of viral carriage. Successful viral eradication will resolve on-going hepatocellular damage and the development of cirrhosis and hepatocellular carcinoma. Clinical trials for chronic HBV infection have used the following markers as endpoints for successful therapy: seroconversion from HBeAg positive to HBeAg negative (with appearance of antiHBe), reductions in serum aminotransferase activity, elimination of circulating HBV DNA, and improvement in liver histology. The elimination of HBsAg (termination of HBV carrier state) has been difficult to achieve in clinical trials.

Drug Therapy

22. Interferons. **What drug therapy should C.R. receive for the treatment of HBV-associated CAH?**

The most effective agents in the treatment of chronic hepatitis B have been the interferons. The interferons are a family of proteins that possess complex antiviral, antineoplastic, and immunomodulating activities. There are three classes of interferons (α, β, γ) that are secreted endogenously by different cells in response to foreign stimuli. *alpha-interferon* is produced by peripheral monocytes, macrophages, and B-lymphocytes in response to viral infection. *beta-interferon* is produced by fibroblasts and epithelial cells in response to viral infection. *gamma-interferon* is produced by T-lymphocytes and differs from both α- and β-interferons in that it possesses more immunoregulatory effects than antiviral effects. To date, α-interferon is the most widely studied agent in the treatment of chronic hepatitis B infection.

There are two formulations of α-interferon produced by recombinant DNA technology. Interferon α-2a (Roferon-A) and interferon α-2b (Intron-A) differ by a single amino acid substitution. The clinical significance of this difference is unknown. While both agents have been used in the treatment of chronic hepatitis B infection, most of clinical data is with interferon α-2b.

Efficacy. Alpha-interferon is effective in the treatment of chronic hepatitis B.[100–104] Approximately 45% of patients receiving α-interferon experience a virologic response (clearance of HBeAg and HBV DNA) compared to 9% of untreated controls. Normalization of ALT values is observed in 47% of α-interferon-treated patients versus 13% in untreated controls. Clearance of HBsAg occurs in only 10% to 15% of patients after completion of therapy.[100–104] However, in a long-term follow-up study of patients responding to α-interferon, delayed clearance of HBsAg was observed in 65% of patients three years after completion of therapy.[105] Relapse after successful therapy is rare. No long-term follow up data are available to demonstrate reductions in cirrhosis or hepatocellular cancer in patients receiving α-interferon therapy. For these reasons, a trial with interferon is reasonable for C.R.

23. *Predictors of Response.* **Why is C.R. likely to respond to α-interferon therapy?**

Certain patient variables can predict the response to therapy with α-interferon. The most reliable predictor of a positive response to α-interferon appears to be the pretreatment level of HBV DNA. Patients with HBV DNA levels less than 200 pg/mL are more likely to respond to therapy than those with higher levels.[103] Other predictors of a positive response include a short duration of disease, negative HIV status, high pretreatment aminotransferase levels, and active liver disease demonstrated by liver biopsy.[106]

C.R. is a reasonable candidate for α-interferon therapy. His liver biopsy is consistent with active disease, he has high pretreatment aminotransferase levels, and his duration of chronic hepatitis is short. Before initiating α-interferon, a serum HBV DNA level and serologic testing for HIV should be performed to assist in the evaluation of C.R.'s response to therapy.

24. *Adverse Effects.* **What adverse effects to α-interferon should be monitored in C.R.?**

Adverse effects associated with α-interferon therapy are common. These have been categorized as early side effects which rarely limit the use of interferon and late side effects which may necessitate dose reduction or discontinuation of therapy altogether.[107] The early side effects of α-interferon therapy generally appear hours after administration and resemble an influenza-like syndrome with fever, chills, anorexia, nausea, myalgias, fatigue, and headache. Virtually all patients receiving α-interferon experience these toxicities and they tend to resolve after repeated exposure to the drug. Administration of α-interferon at bedtime may decrease the severity of early side effects. Acetaminophen can be used to treat early side effects of α-interferon therapy but should be limited to ≤2 gm/day to minimize the risk of hepatotoxicity. The late side effects usually are observed after two weeks of therapy and are more serious. These toxicities limit the use of α-interferon and include worsening of the influenza-like syndrome, alopecia, bone marrow suppression, bacterial infections, thyroid dysfunction (both hypo- and hyperthyroidism), and psychiatric disturbances (depression, anxiety, delirium). C.R. should be questioned at each clinic visit about new or worsening symptoms as well as any changes in mood or the ability to perform daily tasks of living. Additional monitoring parameters include a complete blood count with differential and platelet count after weeks one and two of therapy and monthly thereafter during treatment.

25. *Dosing.* **What dose of α-interferon should C.R. receive?**

Interferon doses of 2.5 to 10 million units can be administered subcutaneously (SQ) daily or three times weekly for 1 to 12 months. The manufacturer of interferon α-2b recommends 30 to 35 million units per week, administered subcutaneously or intramuscularly as 5 million units/day or 10 million units three times weekly for 16 weeks. Some authorities believe that thrice weekly administration of α-interferon is associated with more severe flu-like symptoms and headache when compared to daily administration. In contrast, severe bone marrow suppression tends to occur less often with thrice weekly administration.[108] C.R. has normal WBC and platelet counts and initially should receive interferon α-2b as a 5 million units SQ injection daily for 16 weeks. The SQ route of administration is preferred in C.R. to decrease the possibility of hematoma formation because his prothrombin time is prolonged.

The dose should be decreased by 50% if granulocyte or platelet counts decline to less than 750/mm^3 and 50,000/mm^3, respectively.[109] Profound thrombocytopenia (<30,000/mm^3) or neutropenia (<500/mm^3); serious changes in mood or behavior; and intractable nausea, vomiting, or fatigue warrant the immediate discontinuation of α-interferon.

26. Corticosteroids. **C.R.'s hepatologist is considering a course of prednisone before initiating α-interferon therapy. What is the therapeutic rationale for this therapy?**

Long-term treatment of chronic hepatitis B with corticosteroids no longer is used because randomized, controlled trials consistently have demonstrated corticosteroid-treated patients experience a worsening of serologic, biochemical, and histological parameters and a higher incidence of complications and death when compared to untreated controls.[110–112] Despite these data, corticosteroids have been administered short term as priming agents for antiviral therapy with interferons. It is known that corticosteroids augment HBV replication[113] and induce immunosuppression by decreasing the activity of cytotoxic T-cells. It has been proposed that high-dose corticosteroid administration with abrupt discontinuation induces a "rebound" immune state with enhanced T-cell function. Theoretically, this should improve the antiviral activity of α-interferon leading to enhanced clearance of HBV.

A large multicenter trial examined the dose-dependent effects of interferon α-2b and the role of prednisone pretreatment in the management of chronic hepatitis B.[103] Patients were randomized to one of the four following regimens: interferon 5 million units/day for 16 weeks; interferon 1 million units/day for 16 weeks; prednisone 60 mg/day tapered to 20 mg/day over six weeks followed by interferon 5 million units/day for 16 weeks or placebo. Of the 41 patients treated with 5 million units of interferon, 15 (37%) cleared HBeAg and HBV DNA from serum. This was significantly better than that observed in the 1 million units interferon (17%) and placebo (7%) groups. Patients treated with a short course of prednisone before interferon therapy had a response rate of 36% which was similar to 5 million units interferon alone, suggesting that pretreatment with prednisone is not beneficial. A subgroup of patients was identified (with baseline ALT <100 U/L) who had a higher (but not statistically significant) response rate with combination therapy than with interferon alone. Other trials have failed to demonstrate a significant effect of steroid pretreatment on the response rate to interferon.[104,114]

Available data do not support the routine use of prednisone priming therapy with interferon in the treatment of chronic hepatitis B. Limited evidence suggests patients with serum ALT values less than 100 U/L may respond to combination therapy but this requires further study. C.R. has a serum ALT value of 382 U/L and is not likely to benefit from adjunctive priming corticosteroid therapy.

27. Other Agents. If C.R. does not respond to α-interferon, what alternative therapies are available?

A variety of agents have been studied in the treatment of chronic hepatitis B. Early trials with adenine arabinoside (vidarabine, ARA-A) and the aqueous-soluble monophosphate derivative (vidarabine phosphate, ARA-AMP) showed early promise.[115,116] These agents no longer are used as they are only marginally effective and have an unacceptably high incidence of neurotoxicity.[117,118]

The inability of interferon therapy alone to affect a cure of chronic hepatitis B has led to numerous combinations of interferon with other agents. Adenine arabinoside,[119] zidovudine,[120] interleukin-2,[121] levamisole,[122] and acyclovir[123] in combination with α-interferon are no better than interferon alone and may be more toxic. Other agents being considered in the therapy of chronic hepatitis B include thymosin[124] and sargramostim.[125] Some suggest treating nonresponders with a second course of α-interferon at higher doses.[108]

Treatment of Chronic Hepatitis C

28. What treatments are effective in the management of CAH in patients with chronic hepatitis C?

Chronic hepatitis develops in approximately half of patients with acute hepatitis C infection. Of those patients chronically infected with HCV, approximately 10% to 20% develop cirrhosis. The lack of specific immunoprophylaxis and significant morbidity and mortality associated with chronic HCV infection highlight the need for effective antiviral therapy. Early treatment of chronic hepatitis C with prednisone[126] and acyclovir[127] proved to be ineffective. Currently, symptomatic patients with active chronic hepatitis C infection are managed with α-interferon based upon controlled studies that document clinical effectiveness in the majority of treated patients.[128-131]

In the largest trial published to date, patients with chronic hepatitis C were randomly assigned to 3 million units or 1 million units of interferon α-2b three times weekly for 24 weeks or placebo.[128] Response to therapy was assessed by serial measurements of ALT values and liver biopsy results before and after treatment. Of 58 patients treated with 3 million units of α-interferon, 22 (38%) had a complete response (normalization of ALT values) compared to 9 of 57 (16%) patients treated with 1 million units α-interferon and 2 of 51 (4%) untreated controls. Improvement in liver histology was noted in 52% and 29% of patients treated with 3 million units and 1 million units of α-interferon, respectively. The responses to α-interferon were rapid (generally within 12 weeks). Therapy was well tolerated with flu-like symptoms observed in

30% to 50% of treated patients. Unfortunately, relapse was common and was observed in 50% of patients six months after discontinuation of α-interferon.

Overall, 40% to 50% of patients receiving 3 million units of α-interferon for 24 weeks experience complete normalization of ALT values.[128,130,131] Histologic improvement has been observed in several studies comparing interferon treated patients to untreated controls; however, a sustained response is observed only in 10% to 25% of treated patients.[128-131] The current recommendation is to treat patients with chronic hepatitis C (with elevated aminotransferases and evidence of CAH on liver biopsy) with interferon α-2b 3 million units three times a week SQ for six months. If reductions in ALT values have not been observed after three months of therapy, α-interferon can be discontinued.

Higher doses of α-interferon may result in a more sustained response. Patients receiving 10 million units of interferon α-2b six times weekly for two weeks followed by 10 million units three times weekly for 12 weeks experienced a sustained biochemical response, with 55% of patients achieving normalized ALT values six months after discontinuation of therapy.[132] Maintenance therapy with low doses of interferon (1 million units three times weekly for 24 weeks) is ineffective in preventing relapse in patients who have responded to an initial treatment course of α-interferon.[133] Pretreatment with prednisolone before α-interferon therapy does not improve the initial response to therapy but may increase the duration of response.[134]

Ribavirin has been studied as an alternative to interferon in the management of chronic hepatitis C. Small controlled studies with oral ribavirin in doses of 1000 to 1200 mg/day for four to six months have been performed. Serum aminotransferase levels decreased 60% to 70% from pretreatment values and normalized in 30% of treated patients. Unfortunately, the response was short-lived with most patients relapsing shortly after discontinuation of therapy.[135,136]

Treatment of Chronic Hepatitis D

29. What treatments are effective in the management of CAH in patients with coexisting chronic hepatitis B and hepatitis D infection?

Therapeutic trials in the management of chronic HDV infection have been disappointing. Treatment with either prednisone or azathioprine is ineffective.[137] The use of α-interferon in the treatment of chronic delta hepatitis has been reviewed using meta-analysis of five small, randomized, controlled trials. Patients treated with α-interferon (5 million units/day or 9 million units three times weekly) for 12 months experienced a 30% incidence of complete disease remission (normalization of ALT values) compared to 1% observed in untreated controls.[138] In the largest trial published to date, patients with chronic hepatitis D were randomized to either interferon α-2b, 5 million units three times weekly for four months then 3 million units three times weekly for an additional eight months or placebo. Serum ALT reductions of greater than 50% from baseline were observed in 42% of α-interferon treated patients at four months compared to 7% of untreated controls. However, the treatment effect was not sustained as only 26% of treated patients maintained reductions in ALT levels at 12 months. Relapses after discontinuation of therapy were common and histologic improvement was not statistically different from controls.[139] A more recent trial using α-interferon (9 million units three times weekly) demonstrated both virologic and histologic improvement after 48 weeks of therapy. As in the previous trials, the treatment effect was not sustained and relapse was common after drug discontinuation.[140]

Treatment of Autoimmune Chronic Hepatitis

30. What treatments are effective in the management of CAH in patients with negative viral hepatitis markers?

Symptomatic patients with idiopathic autoimmune chronic active hepatitis with severe histological disease negative for HBV and HCV markers require long-term treatment with corticosteroids. The goal of corticosteroid therapy in CAH is the reduction of inflammation and aminotransferase levels with the minimal doses necessary to maintain symptomatic improvement. Corticosteroids are ineffective against fibrosis and do not always prevent cirrhosis or improve its prognosis.

The usual initial regimen to treat autoimmune CAH consists of prednisone or prednisolone 20 to 60 mg/day. Because prednisone is metabolized to prednisolone in the liver, prednisolone is the theoretical drug of choice in patients with impaired liver function. Despite this concern, adequate serum concentrations of prednisolone have been achieved when prednisone was administered to patients with chronic active liver disease.[141]

In patients unable to tolerate side effects from corticosteroids, lower doses of prednisone or prednisolone (10 mg/day) in combination with azathioprine (50 to 100 mg/day) can be used. The combination regimen appears to minimize adverse effects from corticosteroids while maximizing the therapeutic response.[142,143] Patients not responding to combination therapy generally have advanced disease (cirrhosis, markedly elevated ALT and PT values).[142] Azathioprine alone will not induce remission but may prevent relapse. In patients with chronic active hepatitis who had been in complete remission while receiving combination prednisolone and azathioprine therapy, 32% of the patients relapsed when azathioprine was withdrawn as compared to only 6% of patients in the control group who continued to receive combination therapy.[144]

Untreated patients with symptomatic CAH have a five-year survival of less than 50% and a ten-year survival of less than 30%. Patients treated with corticosteroids have a five- and ten-year survival of 85% to 90% and 60% to 70%, respectively.[145,146]

Criteria for discontinuation of immunosuppressive therapy are arbitrary. With treatment, symptoms generally are controlled within three months, liver function is improved within three to six months, and histologic findings resolve within two years. Withdrawal of treatment may be considered when clinical symptoms subside, serum aminotransferase stabilizes at levels less than two times normal, and active hepatic cell necrosis is absent on liver biopsy.[142] Drug therapy should be tapered slowly over 6 to 12 months. Unfortunately, up to 50% of patients relapse within three to six months of cessation of therapy.[147] If the liver biopsy shows normal histologic findings and complete resolution of inflammation before discontinuation of drug therapy, relapse is less common.[148] Treatment frequently is required for at least three to five years. Patients relapsing after discontinuation of therapy usually respond after reinitiation of therapy.[144] Patients refractory to medical therapy with signs of advanced hepatic failure or cirrhosis should be considered for liver transplantation.

References

1   **Centers for Disease Control.** Hepatitis Surveillance. Report No. 54. Atlanta: Centers for Disease Control; 1992:22.

2   **Corey L, Holmes KK.** Sexual transmission of hepatitis A in homosexual men: incidence and mechanism. N Engl J Med. 1980;302:435.

3   **Gingrich GA et al.** Serological investigation of an outbreak of hepatitis A in rural day-care center. Am J Public Health. 1983;73:1190.

4   **Sherertz RJ et al.** Transmission of hepatitis A by transfusion of blood products. Arch Intern Med. 1984;144:1579.

5   **Lemon SM.** Type A viral hepatitis. New developments in an old disease. N Engl J Med. 1985;313:1059.

6   **Scott RM et al.** Experimental transmission of hepatitis B virus by semen and saliva. J Infect Dis. 1980;142:67.

7   **Kryger P et al.** Acute type B hepatitis among HBsAg negative patients detected by anti-HBc IgM. Hepatology. 1982;2:50.

8   **Stevens CE et al.** Epidemiology of hepatitis C virus. A preliminary study in volunteer blood donors. JAMA. 1990;263:49.

9   **Alter MJ et al.** Risk factors for acute non-A, non-B hepatitis in the United States and association with hepatitis C virus infection. JAMA. 1990;264:2231.

10 **Akahane Y et al.** Hepatitis C virus infection in spouses of patients with type C chronic liver disease. Ann Int Med. 1994;120:748.

11 **Ohto H et al.** Transmission of hepatitis C virus from mothers to infants. N Engl J Med. 1994;330:744.

12 **Aach RD, Kahn RA.** Post-transfusion hepatitis: current perspectives. Ann Int Med. 1980;92:539.

13 **Donahue JG et al.** The declining risk of post-transfusion hepatitis C virus infection. N Engl J Med. 1992;327:369.

14 **Hoofnagle JH.** Type D (delta) hepatitis. JAMA. 1989;261:1321.

15 **Ramalingaswami V, Purcell RH.** Waterborne non-A, non-B hepatitis. Lancet. 1988;1:571.

16 **Repsher LH, Freebern RK.** Effects of early and vigorous exercise on recovery from infectious hepatitis. N Engl J Med. 1969;281:1393.

17 **Chalmers TC et al.** The treatment of acute infectious hepatitis. Controlled studies of the effects of diet, rest, and reconditioning on the acute course of the disease and on the incidence of relapse and residual abnormalities. J Clin Invest. 1955;34:1163.

18 **Evans AS et al.** Adrenal hormone therapy in viral hepatitis. II. The effect of cortisone in the acute disease. Ann Intern Med. 1953;38:1134.

19 **Blum AL et al.** A fortuitously controlled study of steroid therapy in acute viral hepatitis. Am J Med. 1969;47:82.

20 **Ware AJ et al.** A controlled trial of steroid therapy in massive hepatic necrosis. Am J Gastroenterol. 1974;62:130.

21 **Gregory PB et al.** Steroid therapy in severe viral hepatitis. A double blind, randomized trial of methyl-prednisolone versus placebo. N Engl J Med. 1976;294:681.

22 **European Association for the Study of the Liver (EASL).** Randomized trial of steroid therapy in acute liver failure. Gut. 1979;20:620.

23 **Acute Hepatic Failure Study Group.**

Failure of specific immunotherapy in fulminant type B hepatitis. Ann Int Med. 1977;86:272.

24 **Sanchez-Tapias JM et al.** Recombinant α2c-interferon therapy in fulminant viral hepatitis. J Hepatol. 1987;5:205.

25 **Schweitzer IL et al.** Oral contraceptives in acute viral hepatitis. JAMA. 1975;233:979.

26 **Jorup-Ronstrom C et al.** Reduction of paracetamol and aspirin metabolism during viral hepatitis. Clin Pharmacokinet. 1986;11:250.

27 **Roberts RK et al.** Effect of age and parenchymal liver disease on the disposition and elimination of chlordiazepoxide (Librium). Gastroenterology. 1978;75:479.

28 **Narang APS et al.** Pharmacokinetic study of chloramphenicol in patients with liver disease. Eur J Clin Pharmacol. 1981;20:479.

29 **Gugler R et al.** Clofibrate disposition in renal failure and acute and chronic liver disease. Eur J Clin Pharmacol. 1979;15:341.

30 **Klotz U et al.** The effects of age and liver disease on the disposition and elimination of diazepam in adult man. J Clin Invest. 1975;55:347.

31 **Williams RL et al.** Influence of viral hepatitis on the disposition of two compounds with high hepatic clearance: lidocaine and indocyanine green. Clin Pharmacol Ther. 1976;20:290.

32 **Kraus JW et al.** Effects of aging and liver disease on disposition of lorazepam. Clin Pharmacol Ther. 1978;24:411.

33 **McHorse TS et al.** Effect of acute viral hepatitis in man on the disposition and

elimination of meperidine. Gastroenterology. 1975;68:775.

34 **Dylewicz P et al.** Bioavailability and elimination of nitrendipine in liver disease. Eur J Clin Pharmacol. 1987;32:563.

35 **Eandi M et al.** Pharmacokinetics of norfloxacin in healthy volunteers and patients with renal and hepatic damage. Eur J Clin Microbiol. 1983;2:253.

36 **Shull HJ et al.** Normal disposition of oxazepam in acute viral hepatitis and cirrhosis. Ann Int Med. 1976;84:420.

37 **Alvin J et al.** The effect of liver disease in man on the disposition of phenobarbital. J Pharmacol Exp Ther. 1975;192:224.

38 **Blaschke TF et al.** Influence of acute viral hepatitis on phenytoin kinetics and protein binding. Clin Pharmacol Ther. 1975;17:685.

39 **Karbwang J et al.** The pharmacokinetics of quinine in patients with hepatitis. Br J Clin Pharmacol. 1993;35:444.

40 **Holdiness MR.** Clinical pharmacokinetics of the antitubercular drugs. Clin Pharmacokinet. 1984;9:511.

41 **Staib AH et al.** Pharmacokinetics and metabolism of theophylline and patients with liver disease. Int J Clin Pharmacol Ther Toxicol. 1980;18:500.

42 **Williams RL et al.** Influence of acute viral hepatitis on disposition and plasma binding of tolbutamide. Clin Pharmacol Ther. 1977;21:301.

43 **Williams RL et al.** Influence of acute viral hepatitis on disposition and pharmacologic effect of warfarin. Clin Pharmacol Ther. 1976;20:90.

44 **Hadler SC et al.** An outbreak of hep-

atitis B in a dental practice. Ann Intern Med. 1981;95:133.

45 **Reingold AL et al.** Transmission of hepatitis B by an oral surgeon. J Infect Dis. 1982;145:262.

46 **Centers for Disease Control.** Recommendations for preventing transmission of human immunodeficiency virus and hepatitis B virus to patients during exposure-prone invasive procedures. MMWR. 1991;40(No. RR-8):1–9.

47 **Centers for Disease Control.** Recommendations of the immunization practices advisory committee (ACIP). Protection against viral hepatitis. MMWR. 1990;39:1.

48 **Werzberger A et al.** A controlled trial of formalin inactivated hepatitis A vaccine in healthy children. N Engl J Med. 1992;327:453.

49 **Westblom TU et al.** Safety and immunogenicity of an inactivated hepatitis A vaccine: effect of dose and vaccination schedule. J Infect Dis. 1994; 169:996.

50 **Innis BL et al.** Protection against hepatitis A by an inactivated vaccine. JAMA. 1994;271:1328.

51 **West DJ.** Clinical experience with hepatitis B vaccines. Am J Infect Control. 1989;17:172.

52 **Ellis RW et al.** Plasma-derived and yeast-derived hepatitis B vaccines. Am J Infect Control. 1989;17:181.

53 **Centers for Disease Control.** Suboptimal response to hepatitis B vaccine given by injection into the buttock. MMWR. 1985;34:105.

54 **Ukena T et al.** Site of injection and response to hepatitis B vaccine. N Engl J Med. 1985;313:579. Letter.

55 **Krugman S et al.** Immunogenic effect of inactivated hepatitis B vaccine: comparison of 20 μg and 40 μg doses. J Med Virol. 1981;8:119.

56 **Szmuness W et al.** The immune response of healthy adults to a reduced dose of hepatitis B vaccine. J Med Virol. 1981;8:123.

57 **Szmuness W et al.** Hepatitis B vaccine in medical staff of hemodialysis units. Efficacy and subtype cross-protection. N Engl J Med. 1982;307:1481.

58 **Szmuness W et al.** Hepatitis B vaccine. Demonstration of efficacy in a controlled clinical trial in a high-risk population in the United States. N Engl J Med. 1980;303:833.

59 **Francis DP et al.** The prevention of hepatitis B with vaccine. Report of the CDC multi-center efficacy trial among homosexual men. Ann Int Med. 1982; 97:362.

60 **Coutinho RA et al.** Efficacy of a heat inactivated hepatitis B vaccine in male homosexuals: outcome of a placebo controlled double blind trial. Br Med J. 1983;286:1305.

61 **Szmuness W et al.** A controlled clinical trial of the efficacy of the hepatitis B vaccine (Heptavax B): a final report. Hepatology. 1981;1:377.

62 **Barin F et al.** Immune response in neonates to hepatitis B vaccine. Lancet. 1982;1:251.

63 **Wainwright RB et al.** Duration of immunogenicity and efficacy of hepatitis B vaccine in a Yupik eskimo population. JAMA. 1989;261:2362.

64 **Dentico P et al.** Long-term immunogenicity safety and efficacy of a recombinant hepatitis B vaccine in healthy adults. Eur J Epidemiol. 1992;8:650.

65 **Hadler SC et al.** Long-term immunogenicity and efficacy of hepatitis B vaccine in homosexual men. N Engl J Med. 1986;315:209.

66 **Hollinger FB et al.** Response to hepatitis B vaccine in a young adult population. In: Szmuness W et al., eds. Viral Hepatitis: 1981 International symposium. Philadelphia: Franklin Institute Press; 1982:451.

67 **Stevens CE et al.** Hepatitis B vaccine in patients receiving hemodialysis. Immunogenicity and efficacy. N Engl J Med. 1984;311:496.

68 **Collier AC et al.** Antibody to human immunodeficiency virus (HIV) and suboptimal response to hepatitis B vaccination. Ann Int Med. 1988;109:101.

69 **Wood RC et al.** Risk factors for lack of detectable antibody following hepatitis B vaccination of Minnesota health care workers. JAMA. 1993;270: 2935.

70 **Roome AJ et al.** Hepatitis B vaccine responsiveness in Connecticut public safety personnel. JAMA. 1993;270: 2931.

71 **Jilg W et al.** Immune response to hepatitis B revaccination. J Med Virol. 1988;24:377.

72 **Weissman JY et al.** Lack of response to recombinant hepatitis B vaccine in nonresponders to the plasma vaccine. JAMA. 1988;260:1734.

73 **Bush LM et al.** Evaluation of initiating a hepatitis B vaccination schedule with one vaccine and completing it with another. Vaccine. 1991;9:807.

74 **Chan CY et al.** Booster response to recombinant yeast-derived hepatitis B vaccine in vaccinees whose anti-HBs response were initially elicited by a plasma-derived vaccine. Vaccine. 1991;9:765.

75 **Centers for Disease Control.** Recommendations of the immunization practices advisory committee (ACIP). Hepatitis B virus: a comprehensive strategy for eliminating transmission in the United States through universal childhood vaccination. MMWR. 1991; volume 40;(No.RR-13):1–25.

76 **Tabor E et al.** Nine-year follow-up study of a plasma-derived hepatitis B vaccine in a rural African setting. J Med Virol. 1993;40:204.

77 **Milne A et al.** Hepatitis B vaccination in children: five year booster study. NZ Med J. 1992;105:336.

78 **Krahn M et al.** Should Canada and the United States universally vaccinate infants against hepatitis B? A cost-effective analysis. Med Decis Making. 1993;13:4.

79 **Bloom BS et al.** A reappraisal of hepatitis B virus vaccination strategies using cost-effective analysis. Ann Intern Med. 1993;118:298.

80 **Seeff LB et al.** Type B hepatitis after needle-stick exposure: prevention with hepatitis B immune globulin. Ann Intern Med. 1978;88:285.

81 **Szmuness W et al.** Passive-active immunization against hepatitis B: immunogenicity studies in adult Americans. Lancet. 1981;1:575.

82 **Redeker AG et al.** Hepatitis B immune globulin as a prophylactic measure for spouses exposed to acute type B hepatitis. N Engl J Med. 1975;293: 1055.

83 **Centers for Disease Control.** 1993 Sexually transmitted diseases treatment guidelines. MMWR. 1993;42:91.

84 **Xu ZY et al.** Prevention of perinatal acquisition of hepatitis B virus carriage using vaccine: preliminary report of a randomized, double-blind placebo-controlled and comparative trial. Pediatrics. 1985;76:713.

85 **Beasley RP et al.** Prevention of perinatally transmitted hepatitis B virus infections with hepatitis B immune globulin and hepatitis B vaccine. Lancet. 1983;2:1099.

86 **Beasley RP et al.** Efficacy of hepatitis B immune globulin for prevention of perinatal transmission of the hepatitis B virus carrier state: final report of a randomized double-blind, placebo-controlled trial. Hepatology. 1983;3:135.

87 **Wong VCW et al.** Prevention of the HBsAg carrier state in newborn infants of mothers who are chronic carriers of HBsAg and HBeAg by administration of hepatitis B vaccine and hepatitis B immunoglobulin: double-blind randomized placebo-controlled study. Lancet. 1984;1:921.

88 **Beasley RP et al.** Hepatocellular carcinoma and hepatitis B virus: a prospective study of 22,707 men in Taiwan. Lancet. 1981;2:1129.

89 **Beasley RP.** Hepatitis B virus as the etiologic agent in hepatocellular carcinoma—epidemiologic considerations. Hepatology. 1982;2(Suppl.):21.

90 **Stevens CE et al.** Yeast-recombinant hepatitis B vaccine. Efficacy with hepatitis B immune globulin in prevention of perinatal hepatitis B virus transmission. JAMA. 1987;257:2612.

91 **Stevens CE et al.** Perinatal hepatitis B virus transmission in the United States. Prevention by passive-active immunization. JAMA. 1985;253:1740.

92 **Krugman S et al.** Infectious hepatitis. Studies on the effect of gamma globulin and on the incidence of inapparent infection. JAMA. 1960;174:823.

93 **Landrigan PJ et al.** The protective efficacy of immune serum globulin in hepatitis A. A statistical approach. JAMA. 1973;223:74.

94 **Krugman S.** Effect of human immune serum globulin on infectivity of hepatitis A virus. J Infect Dis. 1976;134:70.

95 **Maddrey WC, Boitnott JK.** Severe hepatitis from methyldopa. Gastroenterology. 1975;68:351.

96 **Black M et al.** Nitrofurantoin-induced chronic active hepatitis. Ann Intern Med. 1980;92:62.

97 **Maddrey WC, Boitnott JK.** Isoniazid hepatitis. Ann Intern Med. 1973;79:1.

98 **Tonder M et al.** Sulfonamide-induced chronic liver disease. Scand J Gastroenterol. 1974;9:93.

99 **Weiss M et al.** Propylthiouracil-induced hepatic damage. Arch Intern Med. 1980;140:1184.

100 **Hoofnagle JH et al.** Randomized, controlled trial of recombinant human α-interferon in patients with chronic hepatitis B. Gastroenterology. 1988;95: 1318.

101 **Perrillo RP et al.** Prednisone withdrawal followed by recombinant alpha interferon in the treatment of chronic type B hepatitis. A randomized, controlled trial. Ann Intern Med. 1988; 109:95.

102 **Perez V et al.** Recombinant interferon alfa-2b following prednisone withdrawal in the treatment of chronic type B hepatitis. J Hepatol. 1990;11:S113.

103 **Perrillo RP et al.** A randomized, controlled trial of interferon alfa-2b alone and after prednisone withdrawal for the treatment of chronic hepatitis B. N Engl J Med. 1990;323:295.

104 **Perez V et al.** A controlled trial of high dose interferon, alone and after prednisone withdrawal, in the treatment of chronic hepatitis B: long term follow up. Gut. 1993;33(Suppl.):S91.

105 **Korenman J et al.** Long-term remission of chronic hepatitis B after alpha-interferon therapy. Ann Intern Med. 1991;114:629.

106 **Brook MG et al.** Which patients with chronic hepatitis B virus infection will respond to α-interferon therapy? A statistical analysis of predictive factors. Hepatology. 1989;10:761.

107 **Renault PF, Hoofnagle JH.** Side effects of alpha interferon. Semin Liver Dis. 1989;9:273.

108 **Perrillo RP.** The management of chronic hepatitis B. Am J Med. 1994; 96(Suppl. 1A):34S.

109 **Schering Corporation.** Intron-A package insert. Kenilworth, NJ: 1992 May.

110 **Schalm SW et al.** Contrasting features and responses to treatment of severe chronic active liver disease with and without hepatitis Bs antigen. Gut. 1976;17:781.

111 **Lam KC et al.** Deleterious effect of prednisolone in HBsAg-positive chronic active hepatitis. N Engl J Med. 1981;304:380.

112 **Hoofnagle JH et al.** A short course of prednisolone in chronic type B hepatitis. Ann Intern Med. 1986;104:12.

113 **Scullard GH et al.** Effects of immunosuppressive therapy on viral markers in chronic active hepatitis B. Gastroenterology. 1981;81:987.

114 **Lok AS et al.** A controlled trial of interferon with or without prednisone priming for chronic hepatitis B. Gastroenterology. 1992;102:2091.

115 **Bassendine MF et al.** Adenine arabinoside therapy in HBsAg positive chronic liver disease: a controlled study. Gastroenterology. 1981;80:1016.

116 **Weller IVD et al.** Randomized controlled trial of adenine arabinoside 5′-monophosphate (ARA-AMP) in chronic hepatitis B virus infection. Gut. 1985;26:745.

117 **Hoofnagle JH et al.** Randomized controlled trial of adenine arabinoside monophosphate for chronic type B hepatitis. Gastroenterology. 1984;86: 150.

118 **Perrillo RP et al.** Comparative efficacy of adenine arabinoside 5′ monophosphate and prednisone withdrawal followed by adenine arabinoside 5′ monophosphate in the treatment of chronic active hepatitis type B. Gastroenterology. 1985;88:780.

119 **Garcia G et al.** Adenine arabinoside monophosphate (vidarabine phosphate) in combination with human leukocyte interferon in the treatment of chronic hepatitis B. A randomized, double-blinded, placebo-controlled trial. Ann Intern Med. 1987;107:278.

120 **Janssen HLA et al.** Interferon-α and zidovudine combination therapy for chronic hepatitis B: results of a randomized placebo-controlled trial. Hepatology. 1993;17:383.

121 **Bruch HR et al.** Treatment of chronic hepatitis B with interferon α-2b and interleukin-2. J Hepatol. 1993;17(Suppl. 3):S52.

122 **Ruiz-Moreno M et al.** Levamisole and interferon in children with chronic hepatitis B. Hepatology. 1993;18:264.

123 **Berk L et al.** Failure of acyclovir to enhance the antiviral effect of α lymphoblastoid interferon on HBe-seroconversion in chronic hepatitis B. A multi-centre randomized controlled trial. J Hepatol. 1992;14:305.

124 **Mutchnick MG et al.** Thymosin treatment of chronic hepatitis B: a placebo-controlled pilot trial. Hepatology. 1991;14:409.

125 **Martin J et al.** Pilot study of recombinant human granulocyte-macrophage colony-stimulating factor in the treatment of chronic hepatitis B. Hepatology. 1993;18:775.

126 **Stokes P et al.** Effects of short-term corticosteroid therapy in patients with chronic non-A, non-B hepatitis. Gastroenterology. 1987;92:1783.

127 **Pappas SC et al.** Treatment of chronic non-A, non-B hepatitis with acyclovir: pilot study. J Med Virol. 1985;15:1.

128 **Davis GL et al.** Treatment of chronic hepatitis C with recombinant interferon alpha. A multicenter randomized, controlled trial. N Engl J Med. 1989;321:1501.

129 **Di Bisceglie AM et al.** Recombinant interferon alfa therapy for chronic hepatitis C. A randomized, double-blind, placebo-controlled trial. N Engl J Med. 1989;321:1506.

130 **Causse X et al.** Comparison of 1 or 3 MU of interferon alfa-2b and placebo in patients with chronic non-A, non-B hepatitis. Gastroenterology. 1991;101:497.

131 **Marcellin P et al.** Recombinant human α-interferon in patients with chronic non-A, non-B hepatitis: a multicenter randomized controlled trial from France. Hepatology. 1991;13:393.

132 **Iino S et al.** Treatment of chronic hepatitis C with high-dose interferon α-2b: a multicenter study. Dig Dis Sci. 1993;38:612.

133 **Picciotto A et al.** Interferon therapy in chronic hepatitis C. Evaluation of a low dose maintenance schedule in responder patients. J Hepatol. 1993;17:359.

134 **Liaw Y-F et al.** Effects of prednisolone pretreatment in interferon alfa therapy for patients with chronic non-A, non-B (C) hepatitis. Liver. 1993;13:46.

135 **Di Bisceglie AM et al.** A pilot study of ribavirin therapy for chronic hepatitis C. Hepatology. 1992;16:649.

136 **Reichard O et al.** Ribavirin treatment for chronic hepatitis C. Lancet. 1991;337:1058.

137 **Rizzetto M et al.** Chronic hepatitis in carriers of hepatitis B surface antigen, with intrahepatic expression of the delta antigen. Ann Intern Med. 1983;98:437.

138 **Hadziyannis SJ.** Use of α-interferon in the treatment of chronic delta hepatitis. J Hepatol. 1991;13:S21.

139 **Rosina F et al.** A randomized controlled trial of a 12-month course of recombinant human interferon-α in chronic delta (type D) hepatitis: a multicenter Italian study. Hepatology. 1991;13:1052.

140 **Farci P et al.** Treatment of chronic hepatitis D with interferon alfa-2a. N Engl J Med. 1994;330:88.

141 **Uribe M et al.** Oral prednisone for chronic active liver disease: dose responses and bioavailability studies. Gut. 1978;19:1131.

142 **Soloway RD et al.** Clinical, biochemical and histological remission of severe chronic active liver disease: a controlled study of treatments and early prognosis. Gastroenterology. 1972;63:820.

143 **Summerskill WHJ et al.** Prednisone for chronic active liver disease: dose titration, standard dose, and combination with azathioprine compared. Gut. 1975;16:876.

144 **Stellon AJ et al.** Randomized controlled trial of azathioprine withdrawal in autoimmune chronic active hepatitis. Lancet. 1985;1:668.

145 **Cook GC et al.** Controlled prospective trial of corticosteroid therapy in active chronic hepatitis. Q J Med. 1971;40:159.

146 **Kirk AP et al.** Late results of the Royal Free Hospital prospective controlled trial of prednisolone therapy in hepatitis B surface antigen negative chronic active hepatitis. Gut. 1980;21:78.

147 **Czaja AJ et al.** Clinical features and prognosis of severe chronic active liver disease (CALD) after corticosteroid-induced remission. Gastroenterology. 1980;78:518.

148 **Czaja AJ et al.** Complete resolution of inflammatory activity following corticosteroid treatment of HBsAg-negative chronic active hepatitis. Hepatology. 1984;4:622.

Urinary Tract Infections

Jan Sahai

Definitions 63-1
Epidemiology 63-2
Etiology 63-2
   Community-acquired infections (See Table 63.1) .. 63-2
   Hospital-acquired infections 63-2
Pathogenesis 63-2
Predisposing Factors 63-2
Clinical Presentation 63-3
Laboratory Diagnosis 63-3
Lower Urinary Tract Infection (UTI) 63-4
   Initiation of Therapy (See Table 63.2) 63-4
   Duration of Therapy 63-4
   Single-Dose Therapy 63-4
   Trimethoprim-Sulfamethoxazole (TMP-SMX) 63-4
   Interpretation of Culture and Sensitivity 63-6
   Fluoroquinolone Therapy 63-6
     Drug interactions 63-6
Hospital-Acquired Acute UTI 63-7
Acute Pyelonephritis 63-7
   Signs and Symptoms 63-7
   Treatment 63-8
     Triage for hospitalization 63-8
     Antimicrobial choice 63-8
     Serum versus urine concentrations 63-8
     Oral therapy 63-9
Symptomatic Abacteriuria 63-9
   Clinical Presentation 63-9
   Antibiotic Treatment 63-9
   Phenazopyridine 63-9
     Adverse effects 63-9
Asymptomatic Bacteriuria 63-9
   Antibiotic Treatment 63-9

In Pregnancy and the Elderly 63-10
Recurrent UTI 63-10
   Relapse versus Reinfection 63-10
   Oral Contraceptives as a Risk Factor 63-10
   Treatment for Reinfection 63-10
   Evaluation Procedures (Localization) 63-11
   Treatment of Relapse 63-11
     Trimethoprim-sulfamethoxazole (TMP-SMX) 63-11
     Trimethoprim 63-11
   Chronic Prophylaxis (See Table 63.4) 63-11
Special Cases 63-12
   Prostatitis 63-12
     Acute bacterial 63-12
     Chronic bacterial 63-12
     Treatment 63-12
   UTI and Sexual Intercourse 63-13
   UTI and Pregnancy 63-13
     Teratogenicity 63-14
   Urinary Catheters 63-14
   Renal Failure 63-15
Adverse Drug Reactions and Drug Interactions ... 63-15
   Sulfonamides 63-15
     Hemolytic anemia 63-15
     Rash and drug fever 63-16
     Sulfonamide-sulfonylurea interaction 63-16
   Trimethoprim-Sulfamethoxazole 63-16
     TMP-SMX folate deficiency 63-16
     TMP-SMX warfarin interaction 63-16
   Nitrofurantoin 63-16
     Gastrointestinal (GI) disturbance 63-16
     Pneumonitis 63-17
     Neurotoxicity 63-17
   Ciprofloxacin-Cyclosporine 63-17

This chapter begins with a brief review of urinary tract infections (UTIs), but focuses on the management of patients with UTIs. For a more detailed discussion of the etiology, pathophysiology, and diagnosis of urinary tract infections, the reader is referred to some excellent texts and review articles.[1–6]

Definitions

Acute pyelonephritis: Inflammation of the kidney, with flank pain and tenderness, bacteriuria (often bacteremia), pyuria, and fever.

Bacteriuria. Bacteria cultured from urine when it is obtained by either suprapubic aspiration, catheterization, or from a freshly voided specimen. Asymptomatic bacteriuria exists if colony counts exceed 10^5/mL in a patient without UTI symptoms. Clinically significant bacteriuria probably exists if colony counts are $\geq 10^2$/mL in patients with UTI symptoms.

Chronic Pyelonephritis. A chronic, inflammatory condition of the kidney with associated calyceal dilatation and overlying cortical scarring. A nonspecific pathologic appearance of the kidney seen with many disease entities, only one of which is bacterial infection of the kidney.

Cystitis. An inflammation of the bladder and urethra, with dysuria, frequency, urgency, pyuria, clinically significant bacteriuria, and suprapubic tenderness on examination.

Prostatitis. An inflammatory condition affecting the prostate. It may be acute or chronic. Frequently, specific bacterial organisms cannot be detected.

Pyuria. White blood cells (WBCs) in the urine. A WBC count of ≥ 8/mm^3 of uncentrifuged urine or 2 to 5/high powered field (HPF) in centrifuged urine sediment is consistent with a UTI.

Subclinical Pyelonephritis. A kidney infection, but with lower UTI signs and symptoms only.

Urethritis. An inflammation of the urethra with dysuria. The etiologic organisms most commonly implicated are *Neisseria gonorrhoeae*, *Ureaplasma urealyticum*, *Chlamydia trachomatis*, and Herpes simplex virus.

Urinary Tract Infection. The presence of micro-organisms (bacteria, fungi, viruses) in the urinary tract, including the bladder, prostate, kidneys, and collecting duct. Although fungi and viruses are occasional etiological agents, urinary tract infections are predominantly caused by bacteria.

Vaginitis. Inflammation of the vagina, with dysuria, vaginal discharge, and vaginal odor. Common etiologic agents include *Candida albicans*, *Gardnerella vaginalis*, and trichomonads.

Urinary tract infections encompass a spectrum of clinical entities ranging in severity from asymptomatic infection to acute pyelonephritis with sepsis.[1,2]

Epidemiology

Infections of the urinary tract occur frequently in both community and hospital environments and are the most common bacterial infections in humans.[1] After one year of age and until about age 50, UTI is predominantly a disease of females. From ages 5 through 14, the incidence of bacteriuria is 1.2% among girls and 0.03% among boys. One to three percent of women between the ages of 15 and 24 have bacteriuria, the incidence increasing 1% to 2% for each ensuing decade of life, up to a rate of approximately 10% by the sixth decade.[1] Approximately 10% to 20% of women in the general population will experience a urinary tract infection during their lifetime.[5] Women have more UTIs than men probably because of anatomical and physiological differences. The female urethra is relatively short, which allows bacteria easy access to the bladder. In contrast, males are partly protected because the urethra is longer and antimicrobial substances are secreted by the prostate.[1,6]

The incidence of urinary tract infections in neonates is about 1%, and most neonatal cases of UTI occur in males.[7] Many of these patients prove to have congenital structural abnormalities. The mortality rate among newborns with UTIs is about 10% to 11%.[7]

Urinary tract infections again become a problem for males after the age of 50, when prostatic obstruction, urethral instrumentation, and surgery influence the infection rate. Infection at an earlier age in a male is rare and requires careful evaluation for the presence of urinary tract pathology.[6]

In general, 10% to 20% of the elderly living at home have bacteriuria. This increases to 20% to 25% in extended care facilities, 30% in hospitals, and 35% to 40% in long-stay hospitals.[8,9] The frequency of infection also tends to rise with increasing age for those ≥65 years of age. Most of the UTIs in these patients are asymptomatic, but they are still important because they often result in symptomatic infection.[10] In addition, bacteriuria in old age may be associated with a decreased survival.[11] The reasons for higher UTI rates in elderly people include the high prevalence of prostatitis in males, poor bladder emptying, and fecal incontinence in very old patients.[10,12]

Etiology

Community-Acquired Infections. Most UTIs are caused by gram-negative aerobic bacilli from the intestinal tract (see Table 63.1). *Escherichia coli* (serotypes 01, 02, 04, 06, 07, 075) cause 80% to 90% of noninstitutionally acquired, uncomplicated urinary tract infections.[1,2] Other Enterobacteriaceae (*Proteus mirabilis*, *Klebsiella*) and *Enterococcus faecalis* also are common pathogens.[1,2] Coagulase-negative staphylococci (i.e., *Staphylococcus saprophyticus*) were considered contaminants at one time, but now are recognized as common causative organisms.[13,180]

Hospital-Acquired Infections. Hospital-acquired urinary tract infections and those associated with urinary tract pathological abnormalities are termed complicated infections. *E. coli* is still the most prevalent etiologic organism, but *Pseudomonas aeruginosa*, indole-positive proteus, *Enterobacter*, *Serratia*, and *Acinetobacter* are encountered more often than with community-acquired infections. Multiple organisms can be cultured from the urine in the

Table 63.1	Urinary Tract Infections[a]
Organisms Commonly Found	Antibacterial of Choice
Uncomplicated UTI	
Escherichia coli	TMP-SMX
Proteus mirabilis	TMP-SMX
Klebsiella pneumoniae	TMP-SMX
Enterococcus faecalis	Amoxicillin
Staphylococcus saprophyticus	1st-generation cephalosporin or TMP-SMX
Complicated UTI[b]	
Escherichia coli	1st-, 2nd-, or 3rd-generation cephalosporin
Proteus mirabilis	1st-, 2nd-, or 3rd-generation cephalosporin
Klebsiella pneumoniae	1st-generation cephalosporin
Enterococcus faecalis	Ampicillin or vancomycin + aminoglycoside
Pseudomonas aeruginosa	Antipseudomonal penicillin + aminoglycoside; ceftazidime; fluoroquinolone
Enterobacter	Fluoroquinolone; TMP-SMX; imipenem
Indole-positive *Proteus*	3rd-generation cephalosporin
Serratia	3rd-generation cephalosporin
Acinetobacter	Imipenem; TMP-SMX
Staphylococcus aureus	Penicillinase-resistant penicillin or vancomycin

[a] TMP-SMX = Trimethoprim-sulfamethoxazole; UTI = Urinary tract infection.
[b] Oral therapy when appropriate.

presence of structural abnormalities.[1] UTIs due to *Staphylococcus aureus* usually are the result of hematogenous spread.[1]

Pathogenesis

The most common pathway for the spread of bacteria to the urinary tract is the ascending route. A urinary tract infection usually begins with heavy and persistent colonization of the vaginal vestibule with intestinal bacteria, especially in women with recurrent UTIs. Once introital colonization has occurred, colonization of the urethra leads to retrograde infection of the bladder.[4,14]

Even with urethral colonization, the bladder has certain defense mechanisms which prevent further spread of the infection. Micturition washes bacteria out of the bladder and is effective if urine can flow freely and the bladder is emptied completely. Elements in the urine, including organic acids (which contribute to a low pH) and urea (which contributes to a high osmolality) are antibacterial. The bladder mucosa also has antibacterial properties.[1,3]

Focal renal involvement may result from the spread of bacteria via the ureters and may be facilitated by the presence of vesicoureteral reflux or decreased urethral peristalsis. Reflux can be produced by cystitis alone or by anatomic defects. Urethral peristalsis is decreased by pregnancy, urethral obstruction, or gram-negative bacterial endotoxins.[1]

Predisposing Factors

Extremes of age, female gender, pregnancy, instrumentation, urinary tract obstruction, neurologic dysfunction, renal disease, and expression of A, B, and H blood group oligosaccharides on the surface of epithelial cells are predisposing factors for the development of UTIs.[15]

The incidence of bacteriuria in pregnant women is 4% to 10%, which is at least twice that of similarly-aged nonpregnant women.[1] The incidence of acute symptomatic pyelonephritis in pregnant women with untreated bacteriuria also is high. Factors that render the pregnant female more susceptible to symptomatic disease are not known, although hormones and anatomical changes are implicated.[16]

Instrumentation of the urinary tract (i.e., urethral and ureteral catheterization) is an important predisposing factor for hospital-acquired urinary tract infections in particular. As many as 67% of nosocomial UTIs are preceded by urinary tract instrumentation.[17] Other urologic procedures, such as cystoscopy, transurethral surgery, prostate biopsy, and upper urinary tract endoscopy are much less likely to result in infection, unless there is pre-existing bacteriuria or other contaminated sites (e.g., prostate, stones).

Any obstruction to the free flow of urine (e.g., urethral stenosis, stones, tumor) or mechanical difficulty in evacuating the bladder (e.g., prostatic hypertrophy, urethral stricture) predisposes patients to UTIs. Furthermore, infections associated with urethral or renal pelvic obstruction can lead to rapid destruction of the kidney and sepsis.[1]

Renal disease increases the susceptibility of the kidney to infection.[1] Kidney transplant patients demonstrate a high incidence of asymptomatic bacteriuria.[18]

Patients with spinal cord injuries, stroke, atherosclerosis, or diabetes may have neurological dysfunctions which can result in UTIs. The neurological dysfunction may cause urinary retention which can lead to catheterization. Furthermore, prolonged immobilization facilitates hypercalciuria and stone formation in some of these patients.[1]

Other factors which have been said to increase the risk of UTIs are now in question. For example, diabetes mellitus has been associated with urinary tract infections, but studies in adult diabetics have yielded conflicting results.[19,20] Furthermore, the prevalence of UTIs in juvenile diabetics is similar to that of the general population of school-age children.[19,20] Some studies have tended to support an association between sexual intercourse and UTIs.[21,22]

Clinical Presentation

Symptoms commonly associated with lower urinary tract infections (e.g., cystitis) include burning on urination (dysuria), frequent urination, and suprapubic pain. Patients with acute pyelonephritis also may present with loin pain, costovertebral angle (CVA) tenderness, fever, chills, nausea, vomiting, and blood in the urine (hematuria).[1]

These signs and symptoms correlate poorly with the extent of the infection. For example, symptoms common in lower UTIs often are the only positive findings in upper UTIs (i.e., subclinical pyelonephritis).[1,23] They also correlate poorly with the actual presence of urinary tract infection. However, certain factors enhance the probability of true infection in these patients; namely, a history of previous UTI, back pain, pyuria, hematuria, and bacteriuria. If four or five of these findings exist together in a patient, there is an 86% probability that the patient has an actual urinary tract infection.[24] Many elderly patients with UTI are asymptomatic without pyuria. Additionally, since many patients have frequency and dysuria, it is difficult to distinguish between noninfectious and infectious causes based upon symptoms.[1] Nonspecific symptoms such as failure to thrive and fever may be the only manifestations of UTI in neonates and children less than two years.[1]

Laboratory Diagnosis

The *urinalysis* (UA) is a series of laboratory tests commonly performed in individuals suspected of having a urinary tract infection. First, there is a macroscopic analysis in which a technician describes the color of the urine, measures its specific gravity, and estimates the pH and the glucose, protein, ketone, blood, and bilirubin content by a rapid "dipstick" method. Then the urine sediment, obtained by centrifugation, is examined under a microscope for the presence and quantity of leukocytes, erythrocytes, epithelial cells, crystals, casts, and bacteria.[23]

Microscopic examination of the urine sediment in patients with documented UTIs reveals the presence of many bacteria (usually >20/HPF). A Gram's stain of the unspun urine will show at least one organism per immersion oil field and usually will correlate with a positive urine culture. Pyuria (i.e., 8 WBC/mm^3 of unspun urine or 2 to 5 WBC/HPF of centrifuged urine), frequently is seen in patients with UTIs. White blood cell casts in the urine strongly suggest acute pyelonephritis.[1,2]

A rapid diagnostic "dipstick" test for the detection of bacteriuria, the nitrite test, detects nitrite formation from the reduction of nitrates by bacteria. This test is both widely available and easily performed; however, at least 10^5 bacteria/mL are necessary to form enough nitrite for the reaction to occur.[25] Although a positive nitrite reading on reagent stick examination is useful, false negatives occur. The leukocyte esterase test detects the esterase activity of leukocytes in the urine. A positive test correlates well with the presence of significant pyuria;[26] however, both false-negative and false-positive findings can occur with the leukocyte esterase panel.

The major criterion used for the diagnosis of a UTI is the *urine culture*. Proper interpretation of these cultures depends upon appropriate urine collection techniques. Urinating into a sterile collection cup is the most practical method of urine collection. This method of urine specimen collection is especially useful for males but is less useful in female patients because contamination is extremely difficult to avoid.[1] The external urethral area first must be thoroughly cleaned and rinsed before collecting the urine specimen after initiation of the urine stream (hence "midstream").

Suprapubic bladder aspiration, although unpleasant from a patient's point of view, generally is not painful and is very reliable. It is not practical for routine office or clinic practice, but may be especially useful when voided urine samples repeatedly yield questionable results, or when patients have voiding problems. Since contamination is negligible, any number of bacteria found by this method reflects infection.[1]

Urinary catheterization for a urine culture sample yields fairly reliable results if performed carefully. Infections may result from the procedure itself because organisms may be introduced into the bladder at the time of catheterization.[25]

Urine must be plated on culture media within 20 minutes of collection to avoid erroneously high colony counts from bacterial growth in urine at room temperature. Otherwise, it should be refrigerated promptly until it can be cultured. Colony counts also can be affected by the concentration of bladder urine. For example, bacterial counts are higher in first-voided morning urines than those obtained in the same patient later that day.[27]

Urine cultures in the bacteriology laboratory usually are evaluated by the pour-plate or streak-plate method. Greater than 10^5 colonies of bacteria/mL cultured from a midstream urine specimen confirms the presence of a UTI. A single, carefully collected urine specimen provides 80% reliability, and two consecutive cultures of the same organism are virtually diagnostic.[3]

Simplified culture methods such as the filter-paper method (e.g., Testuria-R), dip-slide method (e.g., Uricult), and pad-culture method (Microstix) are as reliable as the traditional laboratory methods for bacterial identification and quantification. The filter-paper method is relatively inexpensive, but it does not differentiate between gram-positive and gram-negative organisms. The dip-slide and pad-culture methods are accurate, differentiate between gram-positive and gram-negative organisms, and are similar in cost. The dip-slide method has the added advantages of ease in storage and a nitrite indicator pad.

Lower Urinary Tract Infection (UTI)

Initiation of Therapy

1. V.Q., a 20-year-old female (married, no children) with no previous history of UTI, complains of burning on urination, frequent urination of a small amount, and bladder pain. She has no fever or CVA tenderness. A clean-catch midstream urine sample shows gram-negative rods on Gram's stain. A culture and sensitivity (C&S) test is ordered, and the results of a STAT UA are as follows: appearance: straw-colored; specific gravity 1.015; pH 8.0; protein, glucose, ketones, bilirubin, and blood negative; WBC 10–15 cells/mm^3; RBC 0–1 cells/mm^3; bacteria: many; epithelial cells 3–5 cells/mm^3. Based upon these findings, V.Q. is thought to have a lower UTI. What should be the treatment plan at this time?

Drug treatment of a lower UTI often is started before culture and sensitivity results are known because the most probable infecting organism and its sensitivity to antibiotics can be predicted. As noted earlier, about 90% of community-acquired infections are caused by the Enterobacteriaceae (especially *E. coli*). Although these organisms may be sensitive to ampicillin, amoxicillin, the tetracyclines, and the sulfonamides, increased resistance to these agents is becoming prevalent.[1] Another relatively common organism is *S. saprophyticus*. Most strains are susceptible to sulfonamides, trimethoprim-sulfamethoxazole (TMP-SMX), and cephalosporins, but not to penicillins or tetracyclines.[13] Alternative medications and doses can be found in Table 63.2.

Duration of Therapy

2. What treatment duration options are available for V.Q.?

Outpatients with acute, uncomplicated, initial UTIs can be treated successfully with a 7- to 14-day course of oral medications;[1] a three-day course of therapy; or by single-dose therapy. A urine culture and sensitivity may be obtained before antibacterial therapy and repeated two to three weeks after the completion of therapy,[3,6] although this practice is seldom necessary in young adult females with a lower urinary tract infection.

The duration of therapy for urinary tract infections has been shortened considerably. The traditional 7- to 14-day course of antibiotic therapy now is considered to be excessive for patients with uncomplicated infections. A three-day antibiotic treatment regimen is just as effective as a ten-day regimen in eradicating urinary tract organisms.[32–34] TMP-SMX, amoxicillin-clavulanic acid (Augmentin), and the fluoroquinolones (e.g., norfloxacin) are recommended. Due to the relatively high incidence of *E. coli* resistance to sulfonamides, ampicillin, or amoxicillin, some experts do not recommend using these agents.[2,3] The choice of a specific agent should be based upon geographical sensitivities.

Even a single dose of an antibiotic may be effective. Bacteria disappear from the urine within hours after antibacterial therapy has been initiated.[35] This, coupled with the urinary bladder's ability to defend itself through micturition, acidification, and inherent antibacterial activity, give theoretical support to the clinical evidence that a large dose of an antibiotic can eradicate a UTI.

Single-Dose Therapy

3. Would a 3-day course of therapy or single-dose therapy be preferred for V.Q.?

A single antibiotic dose is reasonably effective in treating acute, lower urinary tract infections in young, adult females.[36–40] Commonly used regimens are TMP-SMX (2 or 3 double strength tablets), trimethoprim 400 mg, amoxicillin-clavulanate 500 mg, amoxicillin 3 gm, ampicillin 3.5 gm, sulfisoxazole 2 gm, nitrofurantoin 200 mg, ciprofloxacin 500 mg, and norfloxacin 400 mg.[1,2] Again, choice of a specific agent should be based upon local sensitivity patterns. Female patients with systemic manifestations of infection, renal disease, anatomical abnormalities of the urinary tract, diabetes mellitus, pregnancy, a history of antibiotic resistance, or a history of relapse on single-dose therapy should not receive single-dose therapy. Neither should males with UTIs. Since Q.V. does not have any of these contraindications, she could receive single-dose therapy with an appropriate agent.

The advantages of single-dose treatment of urinary tract infections include: improved compliance, cost savings, proven efficacy in a defined population of patients (i.e., young women with acute, lower UTIs), minimal side effects, and a potentially decreased incidence of bacterial resistance associated with antibiotic overuse. Furthermore, failure to eradicate the organism with a single dose of an antibiotic may help to identify patients who have subclinical pyelonephritis and require more intensive investigation of their urinary tract.

There also are some concerns about single-dose therapy.[41–46] First, sample sizes in most of the comparative studies to date have been relatively small. Consequently, it is difficult to determine whether differences in effectiveness or in incidence of side effects between single-dose and multiple-dose therapy are clinically significant. In a study of a relatively large sample size,[43] a ten-day course of trimethoprim-sulfamethoxazole was more effective than single-dose treatment with the same drug. Although side effects with the longer course of therapy were more common, they were mild and well tolerated. A multicentered Canadian study suggested that a three-day course of norfloxacin (400 mg BID) was significantly more efficacious than a single 800 mg dose (91% versus 79%).[47] There were no differences in adverse drug reactions between the two groups. A three-day course of therapy is recommended for simple cystitis.

A second area of concern relates to recurrences in patients treated with single-dose therapy. Do these recurrences represent a relapse due to seeding from a deep-seated kidney infection or a reinfection due to seeding from coliform organisms that colonize the vagina? The answer is unclear; however, if it is assumed that patients who receive single-dose therapy are selected properly, then reinfection is a more likely explanation.

Finally, the safety of single-dose therapy in patients with subclinical pyelonephritis needs further evaluation. Will these patients develop more deeply seated infection, bacteremia, or renal impairment? Based upon the above information, a three-day antibiotic course is reasonable in V.Q.

Trimethoprim-Sulfamethoxazole (TMP-SMX)

4. TMP-SMX, 1 double strength tablet BID for 3 days was prescribed for V.Q. Is this appropriate therapy?

Yes. TMP-SMX (Bactrim, Septra) has been shown to be effective for single- and multiple-dose therapy for uncomplicated cystitis. Gram-positive and gram-negative organisms, with the notable exception of *P. aeruginosa* and anaerobes, generally are susceptible to TMP-SMX.[48] The efficacy of this drug combination largely depends upon the sensitivity of the organism to trimethoprim, although *Neisseria gonorrhoeae* is relatively more susceptible to the sulfonamide component. Individually, trimethoprim and sulfamethoxazole are bacteriostatic, but in combination, they are bac-

Table 63.2	Commonly Used Oral Antimicrobial Agents for Acute Urinary Tract Infections[1,3,28–31]				
	Usual Dose				
Drug	**Adult**	**Pediatric**	**Pregnancy[a]**	**Breast Milk[a]**	**Comments[b]**
Amoxicillin	250 mg Q 8 hr or 3 gm single dose	20–40 mg/kg/day in 3 doses	Crosses placenta (*cord*) = 30% (maternal)[c]	Small amount present	Watch for resistant organisms
Amoxicillin + potassium clavulanate	250 + 125 mg Q 8 hr	20 mg/kg/day (amoxicillin content) in 3 doses	Unknown	Unknown	
Ampicillin	250–500 mg Q 6 hr	50–100 mg/kg/day in 4 doses	Crosses placenta	Variable amount (*milk*) = 1%–30% (serum)[c]	Watch for resistant organisms. Should be taken on an empty stomach
Cefadroxil	0.5–1 gm Q 12 hr	15–30 mg/kg/day in 4 doses	Crosses placenta		Alternate choices for patients allergic to penicillins, although cross-hypersensitivity can occur. May be associated with high failure rates
Cephalexin	250–500 mg Q 6 hr	15–30 mg/kg/day in 4 doses	Crosses placenta	Enters breast milk	
Cephradine	250–500 mg Q 6 hr	15–30 mg/kg/day in 4 doses	Crosses placenta (cord) = 10% (maternal)[c]	(*milk*) = 20% (serum)[c]	
Norfloxacin	400 mg Q 12 hr		Arthropathy in immature animals	Unknown	Useful for Pseudomonal infection. *Avoid antacids and di-trivalent cations. May cause dizziness*
Ciprofloxacin	250 mg Q 12 hr		Arthropathy in immature animals	Unknown	Useful for Pseudomonal infection. *Avoid antacids and di-trivalent cations. May cause dizziness*
Ofloxacin	200 mg Q 12 hr		Arthropathy in immature animals	Unknown	Useful for Pseudomonal infection. *Avoid antacids and di-trivalent cations. May cause dizziness*
Nitrofurantoin	50–100 mg Q 6 hr	5–7 mg/kg/day in 4 doses	Hemolytic anemia in newborn	Variable amounts; not detectable to 30%; may cause hemolysis in G6PD deficient baby	Alternate choice. *To be taken with food or milk. May cause brown or rust-yellow discoloration of urine.* See Questions 49–51
Doxycycline	100 mg Q 12 hr		Congenital limb abnormalities; cataracts; tooth discoloration and dysplasia; inhibition of bone growth in fetus; hepatic toxicity and azotemia with IV use in pregnant patients with renal dysfunction or with overdosage	(milk) = 30%–40% (serum)[c]

Risk may be less because of binding to milk calcium, but best to avoid | Effective for urethritis. Avoid in children <8 yr. Alters bowel flora to favor resistant organisms. *To be taken 1 hr before or 2 hr after meals (doxycycline may be taken with food or milk). Avoid simultaneous ingestion of dairy products, antacids, laxatives, iron products. May cause photosensitivity* |
Tetracycline	250–500 mg Q 6 hr			(milk) = 20%–140% (serum)[c]	
Sulfisoxazole	0.5–1 gm Q 6 hr	50–100 mg/kg/day in 4 doses	Crosses placenta; hemolysis in newborn with G6PD deficiency; displacement of bilirubin may lead to hyper-bilirubinemia and kernicterus; teratogenic in some animal studies	Enters breast milk; displacement of bilirubin may lead to neonatal jaundice; may cause hemolysis in G6PD deficient baby	Alters bowel flora to favor resistant organisms. *To be taken on an empty stomach with a full glass of water. Photosensitivity may occur*
Sulfamethoxazole (SMX)	1 gm Q 12 hr	60 mg/kg/day in 2 doses			
Trimethoprim (TMP)	100 mg Q 12 hr		Crosses placenta (cord) = 60%; (maternal) folate antagonism; teratogenic in rats	(*milk*) >1 (serum)[c]	Alternate choice
TMP-SMX	160 + 800 mg Q 12 hr or 0.48 + 2.4 gm single dose		Crosses placenta (cord) = 60%; (maternal) folate antagonism; teratogenic in rats	(*milk*) >1 (serum)[c]	*To be taken on an empty stomach with a full glass of water. Photosensitivity may occur.* Monitor HIV infected patients very closely for development of adverse reactions

[a] Includes unique patient consultation information in italics.
[b] Also see Chapter 45: Teratogenicity and Drugs in Breast Milk.
[c] Denotes drug concentration.

tericidal against most urinary pathogens.[48] Furthermore, this combination is almost uniformly successful in the treatment of uncomplicated UTIs, even against organisms that originally were resistant to either agent alone. In one study, 78% of patients with recurrent, persistent infections unresponsive to treatment with sulfamethoxazole and trimethoprim separately responded to the combination.[49] However, since the rate of trimethoprim resistance is low, trimethoprim alone would be effective in managing most simple urinary tract infections.

The ratio of trimethoprim to sulfamethoxazole in the available products is 1:5 (e.g., 80 mg trimethoprim/400 mg sulfamethoxazole) in the tablet. This has been chosen to achieve a peak serum concentration of the two drugs that approximates 1:20. This ratio is optimal for synergistic activity against most micro-organisms.[48] However, since trimethoprim has a much larger volume of distribution than sulfamethoxazole, the concentration ratios achieved in other tissues and fluids (e.g., urine) vary. Nevertheless, the drugs remain synergistic and bactericidal in ratios ranging from 1:5 to 1:40 *in vitro*.[50] The urine concentrations of trimethoprim and sulfamethoxazole far exceed the minimum inhibitory concentrations (MICs) for most susceptible urinary pathogens, accounting for the combination's effectiveness in the management of UTIs.[51] Therefore, the *in vitro* activity, excellent clinical success, and low cost make TMP-SMX a good choice in V.Q.

Interpretation of Culture and Sensitivity

5. C&S studies in V.Q. show a few *Klebsiella* and >10⁵ bacteria/mL *P. mirabilis* which are sensitive to ampicillin, cephalosporins, trimethoprim, TMP-SMX, and gentamicin. The *Proteus* is intermediately sensitive to sulfonamides, carbenicillin, and nalidixic acid, and resistant to tetracycline. Based upon V.Q.'s clinical presentation and recent culture reports, did she have a true UTI?

Yes. Most women with lower urinary tract infection have greater than 100,000 bacterial colonies/mL of urine. A major revision in the diagnostic criteria for symptomatic UTI has been the abandonment of the requirement for growth of at least 10^5 bacterial colonies/mL of urine. In one group of patients, the criterion of ≥100 bacteria/mL provided optimal sensitivity and specificity for the purpose of correctly diagnosing and treating most women with symptomatic coliform infection.[52] This same criterion can be applied to lower UTIs when the isolated organism is *S. saprophyticus*[13] because *S. saprophyticus* urinary tract infections usually are associated with low urine bacterial colony counts, suboptimal growth on commonly used media, and negative findings on nitrite screening.

The presence of mixed flora (≥2 organisms) is rare except in severely debilitated individuals. Thus, presence of mixed flora frequently suggests contamination, and a repeat specimen should be obtained.

6. What is the correlation between sensitivity of the organism to a particular drug and treatment outcome in acute cystitis?

Bacterial susceptibility to different antimicrobial drugs usually is tested by placing discs impregnated with antibacterial agents on an agar surface which has been seeded with the infecting organism. Bacterial sensitivity or susceptibility is indicated by a zone of inhibited growth around the disc containing the drug. Most discs are impregnated with a quantity of drug which correlates with achievable serum concentrations. However, drugs useful in the treatment of UTIs are excreted primarily by the kidney, and urine concentrations of these drugs may be 20 to 100 times greater than the serum concentration. Therefore, an organism which is only intermediately sensitive, or even "resistant" to the concentration of

antibacterial drug in the testing disc might be very sensitive to the high concentration of drug present in the urine.[53]

When antimicrobial therapy is chosen empirically without the benefit of culture and sensitivity testing results, the patient is in essence serving as her own "sensitivity study." If the infecting organism is sensitive, the urine will be sterile in 24 to 48 hours. If a urine specimen collected 48 hours after initiation of therapy is not sterile and the patient has been taking the medication properly, the antibiotic probably is inappropriate or the focus of infection is deeper (e.g., pyelonephritis, abscess, obstruction). If the urine specimen in the patient is sterile and the patient is symptomatically better, the appropriate antimicrobial is being used (regardless of sensitivity studies), and the full course of therapy should be completed.

7. Was it necessary to order a pretreatment urine C&S for V.Q.?

Some investigators question the value of pretreatment urine cultures.[5,43] Women with a lower UTI usually have pyuria on urinalysis and respond rapidly to antimicrobial treatment. Pyuria appears to be a better predictor of treatable infection than the colony count obtained on urine culture. Furthermore, the urine culture accounts for a large portion of the cost of managing a patient with a urinary tract infection. Consequently, in patients with uncomplicated, acute, lower UTI, it is more cost-effective to order a urinalysis and, if pyuria is present, to forego a urine culture. Instead, the patient should be empirically treated with a conventional three- to seven-day course of antibiotic therapy. If she remains symptomatic 48 hours later, a culture and sensitivity test can be ordered.

Fluoroquinolone Therapy

8. I.B., a 48-year-old female, presents with a community-acquired UTI. She has experienced a rash with TMP-SMX and has a Type I hypersensitivity reaction to penicillins. What is the role of fluoroquinolones in the treatment of I.B.'s community-acquired UTI?

The fluoroquinolones are derivatives of nalidixic acid and include norfloxacin, ciprofloxacin, enoxacin, lomefloxacin and ofloxacin. Several other agents are being investigated. The fluoroquinolones are administered orally and have excellent *in vitro* activity against most gram-negative organisms, including *P. aeruginosa*.[54] They are also active *in vitro* against many gram-positive organisms including *S. saprophyticus*.[54] Resistance to the fluoroquinolones occurs less frequently than nalidixic acid. Although the activity of many fluoroquinolones *in vitro* is antagonized by the presence of urine (acidic pH, divalent cations), this is unlikely to be of clinical significance.[55] This is due to the high concentration achieved in the urine, which is several hundredfold greater than serum levels.[56] Although the fluoroquinolones are equally effective as trimethoprim-sulfamethoxazole in the treatment of uncomplicated UTIs[57] these agents are not recommended as first-line therapy since they are more expensive and probably no more effective than conventional drugs. The agents do represent alternatives for patients unable to receive a drug of choice or for patients with multiple resistant organisms, such as *P. aeruginosa*. In addition, the fluoroquinolones have been effective in treating patients with structural or functional abnormalities of the urinary tract.[58]

A fluoroquinolone would be appropriate for I.B. because it would be effective and because she has experienced previous adverse reactions to penicillins and sulfas.

Drug Interactions

9. I.B. also is taking Maalox for a duodenal ulcer. What is the likelihood that this antacid will affect the action of the fluoroquinolones?

It is imperative that the clinician questions I.B. regarding other medications (both prescription and nonprescription) that she may be taking. Products containing di- and trivalent cations (Mg^{++}, Ca^{++}, Zn^{++}, Al^{++}, Fe^{++}) significantly decrease the absorption of fluoroquinolones, and this may result in therapeutic failures.[59–61] Although the administration of these medicines probably can be timed to avoid the interaction, this is complicated and inconvenient for the patient.[62] Patients simply should avoid these products when ingesting fluoroquinolones. An H_2-receptor antagonist such as ranitidine can be used for those patients with gastrointestinal ulcers.[62]

Quinolones also interfere with theophylline metabolism, especially enoxacin [60% increase in area under the concentration curve (AUC)] and ciprofloxacin (30% increase in AUC).[63] Norfloxacin increases the theophylline AUC by about 15%.[64] Therefore, theophylline levels should be monitored closely in those patients receiving theophylline and quinolones together. The newer fluoroquinolones, ofloxacin, lomefloxacin, and fleroxacin, do not significantly alter methylxanthine metabolism.[65,66] While ciprofloxacin interferes with the metabolism of caffeine, newer agents such as lomefloxacin do not.[68] Although the clinical significance of the interaction between fluoroquinolones and caffeine is unclear, patients should be monitored carefully for signs and symptoms of caffeine toxicity. This is especially important for patients ingesting large quantities of caffeine and in the elderly.

There have been isolated reports of a clinical interaction between quinolones and warfarin,[69–72] although there seems to be no pharmacokinetic interaction.[73] There also have been cases of increased toxicity with coadministration of quinolones and nonsteroidal anti-inflammatory drugs (NSAIDs),[74] and cyclosporine (see Question 52).

Hospital-Acquired Acute UTI

10. P.M., an alert, 70-year-old female with chest pain, was hospitalized to rule out acute myocardial infarction. This is her third hospitalization for chest pain in the last 6 months. Two days after admission, she complained of burning on urination and bladder pain. TMP-SMX double strength, 1 tablet BID was ordered after microscopic examination of the urine indicated the presence of a UTI. Why was this empiric therapy appropriate?

Hospital-acquired (or nosocomial) urinary tract infections occur in approximately half a million patients per year; most are associated with the use of indwelling bladder catheters. Not only can these infections result in complications like bacteremia and sepsis, but they may ultimately result in death.[75] They also are costly. Nosocomial UTIs prolong hospitalization by an average of 2.5 days. This, plus the drugs themselves, adds substantially to the cost of care.[76] Prevention is the best way to manage nosocomial UTIs, but in hospitalized patients who develop urinary tract infection symptoms, antibiotic treatment usually is initiated.

The sensitivity of community-acquired pathogenic bacteria to antimicrobial agents differs from hospital-acquired bacteria, and this antibacterial susceptibility frequently varies from one hospital to another. Therefore, the microbiology department of a particular hospital should be consulted to determine current trends in the antibiotic susceptibility of bacteria acquired in that setting. In general, *E. coli* still is the predominant urinary tract pathogen, but there is an increase of infections caused by other gram-negative bacteria such as *Proteus* and *Pseudomonas*.

Repeated courses of antibiotic therapy, anatomic defects of the urinary tract, old age, and repetitive exposure to the hospital environment are associated with a higher incidence of infection with antibiotic-resistant organisms. In particular, *Pseudomonas*, *Proteus*, *Providencia*, *Morganella*, *Klebsiella*, *Enterobacter*, *Acinetobacter*, and *Serratia* are difficult to eradicate because they usually are less susceptible to commonly used antimicrobial agents.

P.M. is elderly, hospitalized, and has been repeatedly exposed to potentially resistant organisms during her multiple hospitalizations. However, since prompt treatment is deemed necessary, oral TMP-SMX is a reasonable first choice because *E. coli* still is the most likely causative agent and P.M. is only mildly ill with signs and symptoms of lower UTI. Once culture and sensitivity tests are known, therapy can be changed accordingly.

11. If P.M. had additional symptoms of fever, chills, flank pain, and vomiting, how would her treatment differ?

In seriously ill patients with possible sepsis, broad spectrum parenteral antibiotics usually are preferred. (See Table 63.3.) The advent of third-generation cephalosporins with antipseudomonal activity (e.g., ceftazidime), extended-spectrum penicillins (e.g., ticarcillin-clavulanate), a carbapenem antibiotic (imipenem-cilastatin), and a monobactam (aztreonam) makes the choice of antibiotic(s) a difficult one. The newer antibiotics appear to be at least as effective as the aminoglycosides, and lack the ototoxic and nephrotoxic potential of the older drugs. On the other hand, newer agents are more costly and may be associated with the emergence of resistant organisms. For example, superinfection with *enterococcus* and enterobactor can occur when cephalosporins are used.

In general, the newer beta-lactam antibiotics remain the drugs of choice for nosocomial urologic sepsis. The combination of a beta-lactam and an aminoglycoside may be advantageous in neutropenic individuals. Once the susceptibility pattern of the infecting organism is known, therapy should be altered to less expensive, single-agent therapy. The role of intravenous (IV) fluoroquinolones remains to be determined[78] in light of their cost and acquired resistance to these agents.

Acute Pyelonephritis
Signs and Symptoms

12. L.B., a 45-year-old female diabetic, comes to the emergency room (ER) complaining of frequent urination, fever, shaking chills, and flank pain. She takes 20 units of NPH insulin SQ every morning. Positive physical findings include a temperature of 103 °F, a pulse of 110 beats/min, blood pressure (BP) of 90/60 mm Hg, and CVA tenderness. A Gram's stain of L.B.'s urine reveals gram-negative rods, and a STAT UA demonstrates glucosuria, macroscopic hematuria, 20–25 WBCs/mm³, numerous bacteria, and the presence of WBC casts. She also has a blood sugar of 400 mg/dL. L.B. is admitted to the hospital with a diagnosis of acute bacterial pyelonephritis, and routine laboratory tests including an SMA, a complete blood count (CBC) with differential, and specimens of urine and blood for C&S are ordered. L.B. is started on an IV of normal saline, 1 gm of ampicillin IV Q 6 hr, and a sliding-scale schedule of regular insulin based upon Q 6 hr blood sugars. Which signs and symptoms in L.B. are consistent with a kidney infection? [SI units: blood sugar 22.20 mmol/L]

It is not always possible to differentiate clinically between upper and lower urinary tract infections. Symptoms common in lower UTIs often are the only positive findings in upper UTIs (i.e., subclinical pyelonephritis).[1,23] However, L.B. does manifest signs and symptoms consistent with acute bacterial pyelonephritis, including fever, shaking chills, flank pain, CVA tenderness, hematuria, and WBC casts. In addition, her diabetes may predispose her to renal infections, possibly because diabetics have altered antibacterial defense mechanisms.[79]

Table 63.3		Parenteral Antimicrobial Agents Commonly Used in the Treatment of Urinary Tract Infections			
		Average Adult Daily Dose		Usual Dosage Interval[a]	
Class	Drug	UTI	Sepsis		Comments
Ampicillins	Ampicillin	2–4 gm	8 gm	Q 4–6 hr	Use should be based upon local susceptibility patterns
Extended-spectrum penicillin	Ticarcillin	12 gm	18 gm	Q 4–6 hr	
	Ticarcillin/ clavulanate	9 gm	18 gm	Q 4–6 hr	
	Piperacillin	12 gm	18 gm	Q 4–6 hr	
	Mezlocillin	12 gm	18 gm	Q 4–6 hr	
1st-generation cephalosporins	Cefazolin	3 gm	6 gm	Q 8–12 hr	More effective than 2nd- or 3rd-generation cephalosporins against gram-positive organisms
2nd-generation cephalosporins	Cefonicid	1 gm	2 gm	Q 24 hr	Intermediate between 1st- and 3rd-generation cephalosporins against gram-negative organisms
	Ceforanide	1 gm	2 gm	Q 12 hr	
	Cefamandole	3 gm	8 gm	Q 4–8 hr	
	Cefoxitin	3 gm	8 gm	Q 4–8 hr	
	Cefuroxime	2.25 gm	4.5 gm	Q 8 hr	
	Cefotetan	1–4 gm	6 gm	Q 12 hr	
3rd-generation cephalosporins	Cefotaxime	3 gm	8 gm	Q 6–8 hr	Better coverage than 1st- and 2nd-generation cephalosporins against gram-negative organisms. Ceftazidime is most effective against *Pseudomonas*. All generations of cephalosporins are ineffective against *Enterococcus faecalis* and methicillin-resistant Staphylococci
	Ceftizoxime	3 gm	8 gm	Q 8–12 hr	
	Ceftriaxone	1 gm	2 gm	Q 12–24 hr	
	Cefoperazone	2 gm	8 gm	Q 6–12 hr	
	Ceftazidime	2 gm	6 gm	Q 8–12 hr	
Carbapenem	Imipenem/cilastatin	1 gm	2 gm	Q 6 hr	The most broad-spectrum coverage of any antibiotic listed. Resistance may develop especially with *Pseudomonas*. Toxic in some pregnant animals
Monobactam	Aztreonam	1–2 gm	2 gm	Q 8–12 hr	Active against gram-negative aerobic pathogens, including *Pseudomonas sp.*
Aminoglycosides	Gentamicin	3 mg/kg	5 mg/kg	Q 8 hr	Potent against gram-negative bacteria including *Pseudomonas*. Associated with possible 8th nerve toxicity in the fetus. Amikacin should be reserved for multi-resistant bacteria
	Tobramycin	3 mg/kg	5 mg/kg	Q 8 hr	
	Amikacin	7.5 mg/kg	15 mg/kg	Q 12 hr	
Quinolones	Ciprofloxacin	400–800 mg	800 mg	Q 12 hr	Use for resistant organisms. Change to oral therapy where indicated
	Ofloxacin	400–800 mg	800 mg	Q 12 hr	

[a] Assuming normal renal function.

Treatment

Triage for Hospitalization

13. Why was L.B. hospitalized?

Since the majority of patients with clinical pyelonephritis can be managed as outpatients, the need for hospitalization often is determined by the social situation as well as the ability of the individual to maintain an adequate fluid intake and tolerate oral medications. Patients like L.B. with evidence of bacteremia (e.g., fever, shaking chills) or endotoxemia (e.g., hypotension) should be hospitalized and treated with parenteral antibiotics. It also is prudent to hospitalize L.B. because her acute pyelonephritis can predispose her to diabetic ketoacidosis.

Antimicrobial Choice

14. Was ampicillin appropriate treatment for L.B.?

Ampicillin is not an appropriate choice for L.B. because diabetics (as well as patients treated with corticosteroids) are prone to colonization with unusual organisms. Since L.B. is acutely ill and has gram-negative organisms in her urine, she should be treated with an antibiotic that has a better spectrum of activity against gram-negative organisms. Therefore, she should be treated with a parenteral, third-generation cephalosporin, aminoglycoside, or aztreonam. Since most hospital laboratories will be able to report culture and sensitivity within 48 hours, these antibiotics can be replaced with more specific ones if appropriate.

Serum versus Urine Concentrations

15. Is it more appropriate to achieve bactericidal concentrations in the urine or in the serum for L.B.? How long should she be treated? How should therapeutic success be determined?

When the renal parenchyma is infected (e.g., pyelonephritis as opposed to uncomplicated cystitis), adequate tissue concentrations of the antimicrobial agents are needed. Therefore, antibiotics which achieve bactericidal serum concentrations should be selected. Patients requiring hospitalization should be treated with parenteral antibiotics until fluids can be taken orally, the patient is symptomatically improved, and is afebrile for 24 to 48 hours. This should be followed with a course of oral antibiotics for at least 10 to 14 days. Specimens for culture and sensitivity should be obtained on the second day of therapy (to rule out treatment failure), two to three weeks after the completion of therapy, and again at three months.[1]

For patients who have relapsed after 14 days, retreatment for six weeks usually is curative. There have been reports of successful therapy with five days of treatment;[80] however, one week of therapy is not as efficacious as three weeks.[81]

Oral Therapy

16. When would you recommend oral therapy for the initial treatment of acute pyelonephritis?

Patients with mild, acute pyelonephritis (absence of nausea, vomiting, signs of sepsis) can be managed with oral antibiotics such as trimethoprim-sulfamethoxazole for 14 days.[82] This regimen is as effective as six weeks of TMP-SMX and significantly better than six weeks of ampicillin. The fluoroquinolones may be useful for the management of patients infected with resistant organisms, due to their excellent *in vitro* activity against gram-negative organisms and high kidney tissue concentrations (2- to 10-fold greater than serum).[56,57] Agents such as amoxicillin-clavulanic acid, cefixime, cefuroxime, or oral monobactams also can be used in this setting; however, their high costs should be taken into account before prescribing them.

Symptomatic Abacteriuria

Clinical Presentation

17. R.D., a 22-year-old female, complains of urinary frequency and painful urination which have developed over the past 4–5 days. UA reveals 10–15 WBCs/mm³, but no bacteria are seen on a Gram's stain of the urine. Phenazopyridine (Pyridium) 200 mg TID is prescribed. What is a reasonable assessment of R.D.'s clinical presentation?

The absence of an organism on Gram's stain may mean that the urine specimen is sterile or that the concentration of the organism in the urine sample is small. Patients with these findings still may have a UTI even though the voided urine is sterile or contains less than 10^5 micro-organisms/mL. In a study of 59 patients with the acute urethral syndrome,[83] 27 had ''bladder bacteriuria,'' which was confirmed by pure isolates from suprapubic aspiration. The causative organisms and the pathogenesis of infection in these cases are the same as for lower UTIs. Of the remaining 32 patients with sterile urine, 11 had evidence of recent or active Chlamydial infection in the urethra and cervix. Other organisms that may cause urethritis in this setting are *N. gonorrhoeae* and *Trichomonas vaginalis*.[84]

Most cases of urinary tract infection with low bacterial counts are associated with bacteriuria or *Chlamydia*, and also demonstrate pyuria (>8 WBCs/mm³).[83] Conversely, pathogens are seldom present in patients with the acute urethral syndrome when pyuria is absent. Since R.D. is symptomatic, has 10 to 15 WBCs/mm³ in her urine, and no bacteria on Gram's stain, a Chlamydial infection is likely.

Antibiotic Treatment

18. Should R.D. be treated with antibiotics?

Yes. A double-blind, placebo-controlled study evaluated the use of doxycycline 100 mg twice daily in patients with UTI and low bacterial counts. Clinical cure of bacteriuria and pyuria was significantly greater in the doxycycline-treated group, but doxycycline did not alter symptoms in patients without pyuria. *E. coli*, other coliforms, and *Chlamydia trachomatis* are the usual causes of acute urethral syndrome. Therefore, an antibiotic like doxycycline with activity against *Chlamydia* is reasonable initial treatment for patients like R.D. presenting with urinary tract symptoms (without bacteriuria) if pyuria also is present. All tetracyclines and sulfonamides, with or without trimethoprim, also are likely to be effective in such patients, but only doxycycline has been studied to date. Of the fluoroquinolones, norfloxacin[86] and ciprofloxacin[87] cannot be recommended as first-line therapy at this time due to the high failure rates. However, newer agents such as ofloxacin[88] and fleroxacin[89] offer some promise as alternatives to doxycycline.

Azithromycin as a single dose may have a major role for treating chlamydial infections (see Chapter 64: Sexually Transmitted Diseases).

Prolonged therapy, lasting for two to four weeks, and treatment of sexual partners may be required to prevent reinfection through intercourse. Prolonged therapy is appropriate if the patient has a history consistent with Chlamydial urethritis; a sexual partner with recent urethritis; a recent new sexual partner; a gradual rather than abrupt onset of symptoms which has occurred over a period of days (as in R.D.); and absence of hematuria.[83] However, patients without such a history can be managed with a short course of antibiotics like any other patient with a lower urinary tract infection.

Phenazopyridine

19. Why is phenazopyridine inappropriate for R.D.?

Phenazopyridine, a urinary tract analgesic, often is prescribed alone or concurrently with an antibacterial agent for the symptomatic relief of dysuria. Although 200 mg three times a day may relieve dysuria,[90] it is ineffective in the management of true urinary tract infections. Therefore, the drug is not likely to be of value in R.D. who probably is infected. Phenazopyridine plus an antibiotic is not any better than an antibiotic alone.

Adverse Effects

20. What adverse effects have been associated with phenazopyridine?

Phenazopyridine is an azo dye and may discolor the urine to an orange-red, orange-brown, or red color which can stain clothes. Other adverse effects of phenazopyridine occur following an acute overdose or as a result of accumulation in elderly patients[90] or patients with decreased renal function taking the drug chronically. *In vivo*, about 50% of phenazopyridine is metabolized to aniline, which can cause methemoglobinemia and hemolytic anemia.[91] The hemolytic anemia associated with phenazopyridine occurs primarily in patients with glucose-6-phosphate-dehydrogenase (G6PD) deficiency.

Rare cases of acute renal failure have occurred and may be more pronounced in the presence of other nephrotoxic agents.[92] The acute renal failure occurred within days of initiating therapy and reversed one to two weeks after the drug was discontinued.

Cases of allergic hepatitis have been rare following brief exposure to phenazopyridine. A fever spike with nausea and abdominal pain was a common initial symptom; re-exposure to phenazopyridine resulted in recurrence of symptoms within 24 hours.[93]

Asymptomatic Bacteriuria

Antibiotic Treatment

21. A.K., an asymptomatic 6-year-old school girl, is found to have significant bacteriuria on routine screening. Should she be treated with an antimicrobial agent?

The management of patients with asymptomatic bacteriuria depends upon the clinical setting in which it is found. Asymptomatic bacteriuria occurs in a heterogeneous group of patients with different prognoses and risks. Some patients will have significant bacteriuria (>10^5 bacteria/mL of urine) without pyuria. Others may have pyuria without significant bacteriuria. The patients in this latter group probably have self-limiting infections and do not require treatment if they are asymptomatic. However, since asymptomatic patients with significant bacteriuria and pyuria may develop overt pyelonephritis, therapy is probably warranted if significant bacteriuria is confirmed on successive cultures.[1]

Although the management of asymptomatic bacteriuria is inconsistent, the potential for long-term complications from urinary tract infections must be considered. UTIs in infants and preschool children (predominantly girls) occasionally are associated with renal tissue damage during the growth phase of this organ.[94] Asymptomatic bacteriuria of childhood also is important because it may be a manifestation of an anatomical or mechanical defect in the urinary tract. Therefore, it should be fully evaluated. In conclusion, screening for bacteriuria in young females and treating those with positive cultures, regardless of their clinical presentation, seems reasonable.[94,95] Furthermore, treatment of A.K. is important, because renal damage resulting from asymptomatic bacteriuria generally occurs during childhood.

In Pregnancy and the Elderly

22. The decision to treat the asymptomatic bacteriuria of A.K. was based primarily upon the increased probability of renal damage during childhood. What other population groups should be tested for asymptomatic bacteriuria?

In the absence of urinary tract obstruction, UTIs in adults rarely lead to progressive renal damage.[1] Therefore, asymptomatic bacteriuria does not require treatment in adult patients who have no evidence of mechanical obstruction or renal insufficiency. However, aggressive antimicrobial therapy is appropriate during pregnancy because as many as 40% of pregnant women with asymptomatic bacteriuria later develop symptomatic urinary tract infections, particularly pyelonephritis. In addition, infants with lower birth weights have been born to mothers with asymptomatic bacteriuria.[96]

Treatment can be based upon *in vitro* susceptibility testing or by selecting the least expensive, least toxic agent. Tetracyclines should be avoided because they may stain and weaken the forming dentition of the unborn child. Sulfonamides should be avoided in late pregnancy because they can contribute to kernicterus in the neonate. (See Questions 37 and 38.) Fluoroquinolones should be avoided during pregnancy.

Bacteriuria in the elderly is common and has been associated with excess mortality in a relatively select population of elderly patients.[97] Nevertheless, therapy of asymptomatic bacteriuria in the elderly is by no means mandatory in the absence of obstruction.[2] The UTI can be cured in these patients, but frequent relapse and reinfection require continual retreatment or chronic suppressive therapy. As a result, some practitioners have opted to withhold therapy in the asymptomatic older patient when the expense, side effects, and potential complications of drug therapy appear to outweigh the theoretical benefits.[98,99]

Recurrent UTI

Relapse versus Reinfection

23. T.W., a 28-year-old female with a history of recurrent infections, recently was treated for an *E. coli* UTI with TMP-SMX for 10 days. A repeat UA was scheduled, but she canceled her appointment because she "felt fine." Eight weeks later, she returned to the clinic with signs and symptoms of another UTI. The only other medication she has taken is an oral contraceptive. Why would C&S testing of a urine sample be especially useful at this time?

Repeat culture and sensitivity data should aid in the determination of whether this infection represents a relapse or a reinfection. *Relapse* refers to a recurrence of bacteriuria caused by the same micro-organism that was present before the initiation of therapy. Most relapses occur within one to two weeks after the completion of therapy and are assumed to be due to the persistence of the organism in the urinary tract.

Reinfection implies recurrence of bacteriuria with a different micro-organism. Reinfections may occur at any time during or after the completion of treatment, but most appear several weeks to several months later. Approximately 80% of recurrences are due to reinfection.[1] Reinfections generally are due to introital colonization with Enterobacteriaceae from the lower intestinal tract;[1] of these, *E. coli* is the most common. Certain *E. coli* strains have been shown to adhere to vaginal epithelial cells and in women with recurrent UTI, there is an increased receptivity of epithelial cells for these organisms.[14,100] That T.W. was symptom free for eight weeks suggests that this is a reinfection.

Oral Contraceptives as a Risk Factor

24. Is there an association between T.W.'s use of oral contraceptives and her risk of contracting a UTI?

The available literature on the association between oral contraceptive use and urinary tract infections is controversial. The prevalence of bacteriuria in 12,000 healthy women taking oral contraceptives was 2.4%, compared to a 1.6% prevalence among those who had never taken oral contraceptives.[101] Although greater sexual activity among the oral contraceptive users might partially account for these findings, there was a positive correlation between the dose of estrogen and the frequency of bacteriuria. However, the overall incidence of bacteriuria in this study population was low compared to that expected for the general population (2% to 10%). In a community-based study of women below the age of 50, the incidence of bacteriuria was 5.6% in oral contraceptive users and 4% in nonusers.[102] These two studies contrast with others in which no association between oral contraceptive use and bacteriuria was found to exist.[22] The reason for the conflicting results may be related to the definition of bacteriuria and failure to control for confounding factors and biases. In the studies showing a positive association, the culture criteria for determining significant bacteriuria were less stringent.

The association between diaphragm use and urinary tract infection appears to be stronger. In one study, diaphragm users were 2 to 2.5 times more likely to develop a UTI than women using other contraceptive methods. Possible explanations include urethral obstruction by the diaphragm and increased vaginal colonization with coliform organisms.[103]

Treatment for Reinfection

25. Pending the C&S results, what therapy should be instituted in T.W.?

T.W. has a history of recurrent infections and now probably has a reinfection. Therefore, TMP-SMX may be a reasonable choice once again. The probability that a resistant organism will be responsible for the infection increases when the interval between infectious episodes is short. If several months elapse between each episode of antimicrobial therapy, normal fecal bacterial flora become reestablished.

The alteration of fecal flora caused by the sulfonamides and tetracyclines makes these drugs poor choices for repeated use in cases of frequent reinfection, especially when culture and sensitivity results are unknown. The development of bacterial resistance also may limit the usefulness of these agents for chronic antimicrobial therapy.[104]

26. If T.W. developed an adverse reaction to TMP-SMX, what are some other therapeutic alternatives?

Nitrofurantoin (Furadantin) is effective against 80% to 90% of *E. coli* strains. It does not significantly alter the fecal or introital flora, and the development of resistance in previously sensitive strains does not occur. Therefore, it generally is a useful agent for the treatment of recurrent *E. coli* infections. *P. mirabilis* and *Klebsiella*, on the other hand, tend to be somewhat resistant to this drug.

Nitrofurantoin is absorbed orally. Food substantially decreases the rate of absorption, but increases the total bioavailability of nitrofurantoin from both the macrocrystalline capsules and the microcrystalline tablets by about 40%. This effect lengthens the duration of therapeutic urine concentrations by about two hours.[105] This drug barely reaches detectable levels in the plasma because it is eliminated rapidly (half-life: 20 minutes) and almost exclusively in the urine and bile; urine levels are 50 to 250 mg/L.[105] Consequently, nitrofurantoin is used exclusively for urinary tract infections. While the Kirby-Bauer disc sensitivity test measures the sensitivity of an organism to the expected serum levels of most antibiotics, in the case of nitrofurantoin, the test measures urinary levels.[53]

The fluoroquinolones also are useful in this setting.[106,107] However, their widespread use should not be encouraged in light of their high cost and selection of resistant organisms.

Evaluation Procedures (Localization)

27. Greater than 10^5 bacteria/mL *P. mirabilis*, sensitive to ampicillin, are cultured in T.W.'s urine. One week after completing her second course of ampicillin therapy, signs and symptoms of a UTI again appeared. How should T.W. be assessed at this time?

One should first attempt to rule out common causes for relapse. Inadequate therapy resulting from patient noncompliance with the prescribed treatment, inappropriate antibiotic selection, or bacterial resistance to the prescribed agent should be considered if significant bacteriuria persists despite treatment. Next, one must consider renal infections, which cause the great majority of relapsing UTIs.[1,3] Finally, if these common causes are not present, radiologic tests to rule out surgically correctable structural abnormalities of the urinary tract should be performed (e.g., intravenous pyelogram). Infected kidney stones and unilateral atrophic kidneys are common but correctable abnormalities in females. Since *P. mirabilis* is the most common organism found in infected stones, repeated *Proteus* infections, as in T.W., should raise the index of suspicion for an infected stone which is "seeding" the bladder.[108]

Radiologic tests are indicated when urinary tract infections start to occur in children; males younger than 50 years of age; and patients with UTIs in association with bacteremia, ureteral colic, or passage of stones. These populations are most likely to have surgically correctable lesions. In contrast, these procedures rarely are necessary in adult women and elderly males until the common causes of relapse in these populations have been eliminated.[109,110] Chronic bacterial prostatitis, a frequent cause of recurrent infections in males, need not be considered in this case.

Treatment of Relapse

Trimethoprim-Sulfamethoxazole (TMP-SMX)

28. Pending C&S results, TMP-SMX is prescribed. Why is this a reasonable medication for T.W. at this time?

TMP-SMX is a systemic bactericidal agent that is active against most urinary pathogens and demonstrates a low order of bacterial resistance. The possibility of renal involvement and the frequency of urinary tract infections in T.W. call for an antibacterial agent with these characteristics.

29. How long should this therapy be continued?

The duration of therapy for relapsing infections usually is 14 days. In patients who relapse after a second two-week course of therapy, treatment for six weeks should be instituted.[1] If relapse occurs after a six-week course, some authors recommend longer courses of six months to one year.[1] These prolonged courses should

be reserved for children, adults who have continuous symptoms, or adults who are at high risk for developing progressive renal damage. Asymptomatic adults without evidence of obstruction should not receive these longer courses. T.W. should be treated for at least two weeks and perhaps as long as six weeks.

Trimethoprim

30. T.W. was previously treated with TMP-SMX and experienced nausea and vomiting after taking the medication. Why is trimethoprim alone an appropriate substitute?

Trimethoprim alone and in combination with sulfamethoxazole is active *in vitro* against many of the Enterobacteriaceae associated with urinary tract infections, and is an effective alternative to TMP-SMX in the management of both chronic and acute UTIs.[111] It would be especially appropriate for T.W. because gastrointestinal intolerance to TMP-SMX is most commonly attributed to the sulfamethoxazole component, and trimethoprim is associated with a lower incidence of adverse effects. There is some concern for the potential development of resistant organisms,[112] but studies using trimethoprim alone have failed to demonstrate a significant increase in bacterial resistance.[113,114]

Trimethoprim is used for the treatment of acute, uncomplicated UTIs in a dosage of 200 mg/day.

Chronic Prophylaxis

31. T.W. was treated successfully with trimethoprim for 6 weeks. Is prophylactic antimicrobial therapy indicated for her? If so, how long should it be continued?

Chronic urinary tract infections may be managed by treating each recurrent infection with an appropriate antibacterial. A single dose or longer course may be used. More commonly, chronic urinary tract infections are managed by administering chronic, low-dose prophylactic therapy. The frequency of urinary infections probably is the main determinant of whether chronic suppressive therapy should be used, since data suggest that repeated treatment of recurrent infections eventually will result in a decreased incidence of subsequent infections.[1] According to the U.S. Public Health Service Cooperative Study, the prevalence of recurrent infections was significantly less (40%) in males taking chronic antimicrobials than in males taking placebos (71%) over one year, although the differences became insignificant after two years.[115]

The direct costs (composed of clinic visit, drug, laboratory, and x-ray charges) of one year of urinary prophylaxis in a patient approximate those of treating one episode of cystitis.[116] This did not include any indirect costs, such as time lost from work, which also may be incurred during an episode of cystitis. Thus, from a pure cost-effectiveness standpoint, women having more than one episode of cystitis per year benefited from antimicrobial prophylaxis. For women with three or more episodes of cystitis per year, prophylaxis clearly was more cost effective than treatment of individual infections. Therefore, chronic antimicrobial prophylaxis should be considered in any patient with two or more episodes of UTI per year.

The duration of prophylactic therapy also is determined by the frequency of infection. Women with three or more urinary tract infections in the 12 months before a six-month course of antimicrobial prophylaxis have a significantly higher recurrence rate (75%) in the six months following prophylaxis than women who had two infections in the 12 months before prophylaxis (26%).[117] Therefore, prophylaxis should be continued for six months in patients with less than three UTIs per year and for at least 12 months in patients with three or more UTIs per year.

Before chronic antimicrobial suppressive therapy is initiated, active infections must be completely eradicated with an appropriate course of antibiotic therapy. The low doses of antimicrobials used for chronic prophylaxis suppress bacterial growth but do not eliminate active infection. Furthermore, surgically correctable anatomical deformities which predispose the patient to recurrent infections (e.g., obstruction, stones) and renal infections should be ruled out. Patients with urologic abnormalities respond poorly to prophylactic therapy.[113] Age also should be considered when contemplating chronic antimicrobial therapy. An asymptomatic, elderly patient taking many other medications is not a candidate for chronic prophylactic treatment,[118] but suppressive therapy is indicated in the young patient.[116]

Since T.W., a 28-year-old female, has had at least three UTIs in the past few months, has undergone extensive evaluation, and has just been successfully treated with trimethoprim, a 12-month course of antimicrobial prophylaxis would seem reasonable. She also should be evaluated at regular intervals for recurrent urinary tract infections and for the development of resistant organisms.[1–3]

32. What drugs can be used for long-term suppressive therapy?

Although numerous drugs are used for prophylaxis, TMP-SMX may be the drug of choice for chronic antimicrobial therapy. In a crossover study of 40 females comparing TMP-SMX, one-half tablet daily, to methenamine mandelate 500 mg four times a day, sulfamethoxazole 500 mg/day, and placebo, the incidence of recurrence was significantly less in those patients treated with TMP-SMX compared to those patients treated with the other regimens over a one-year period.[119] In another study, one-half tablet of TMP-SMX daily for six months in women with histories of recurrent UTI yielded a lower incidence of positive vaginal and fecal cultures during therapy than a 100 mg/day regimen of nitrofurantoin for a similar time period. This was associated with a lower order of bacterial resistance to both anti-infectives.[120] Furthermore, thrice-weekly TMP-SMX is an effective, well-tolerated prophylactic regimen.[121,122]

Successful prophylaxis, however, is significantly decreased in patients with urological abnormalities or renal dysfunction.[123] Also, infections which are not eradicated by a short-term therapeutic trial of TMP-SMX are not likely to respond to a long-term regimen.[123] Finally enterococci may colonize introitally in patients on chronic TMP-SMX.[117,119] A double-blind, placebo-controlled trial indicated that norfloxacin (200 mg/day PO) was effective in preventing relapses without significant adverse reactions or the development of resistance.[107] However, further studies addressing the minimum effective dose are needed. Fluoroquinolones should be used only when antimicrobial resistance exists or if the patient is intolerant to other recommended drugs.

When selecting a drug for chronic antimicrobial therapy, one must consider efficacy, the likelihood that resistant organisms will develop, long-term toxicity, and convenience to the patient. The most commonly used agents are listed in Table 63.4.

Based upon the available information, it appears that T.W. could be switched to TMP-SMX. Although she has a history of gastrointestinal distress due to this drug, this may not be a problem with the lower doses used for prophylaxis. If it is, trimethoprim alone or a fluoroquinolone also should be effective.

Special Cases

Prostatitis

Prostatitis is a common but poorly understood entity. Many clinicians group all prostatic diseases into one category; but in fact, there are many types and causes of prostatitis. The most prevalent

Table 63.4	Antimicrobial Agents Commonly Used for Chronic Prophylaxis Against Recurrent UTIs[3]	
Agent	Adult Dose	Comments[a]
Nitrofurantoin	50–100 mg nightly	Contraindicated under 1 month of age. *To be taken with food or milk. May cause brown or rust-yellow discoloration of urine*
Trimethoprim	100 mg nightly	Not recommended in children <12 yr
Trimethoprim 80 mg + Sulfamethoxazole 400 mg	0.5–1 tab nightly or 3 × week	Not recommended for use in infants <2 months. *To be taken on an empty stomach with a full glass of water. Photosensitivity may occur*
Norfloxacin	200 mg/day	Avoid antacids; monitor theophylline levels
Cephalexin	125–250 mg/day	
Sulfamethoxazole	500 mg/day	

[a] Includes unique patient consultation information in italics.

forms include acute and chronic bacterial prostatitis, chronic calculus prostatitis, nonbacterial prostatitis, and prostatodynia.[124]

Acute bacterial prostatitis is characterized by the sudden onset of chills and fever; perineal and low back pain; urinary urgency and frequency; nocturia, dysuria, and generalized malaise; and prostration. Patients also may complain of myalgias, arthralgias, and symptoms of bladder outlet obstruction. Rectal examination usually discloses an exquisitely tender, swollen prostate that is firm and warm to the touch. The pathogens generally can be identified by culture of the voided urine and usually are similar to those causing UTIs in women (see Table 63.1). In patients with acute bacterial prostatitis, prostatic massage should be avoided because of patient discomfort and the risk of bacteremia.[125]

Chronic bacterial prostatitis is one of the most common causes of recurrent urinary tract infections in men. Except in males with spinal cord injuries, infectious stones, or obstructive abnormalities of the urinary tract, recurrent infections are almost assuredly relapses due to persistence of bacteria in the prostate. Normally, males secrete a prostatic antibacterial factor; however, this substance is absent in men with chronic prostatitis.[125] Simple UTIs will often eventually involve the prostate gland, where bacteria are difficult to eradicate.

The clinical manifestations of chronic bacterial prostatitis are highly variable. In fact, many patients are asymptomatic. The disease usually is suspected when a male is treated for UTI relapses. The diagnosis is confirmed by examination of expressed prostatic secretions.[125] To ensure accurate localization (i.e., to distinguish prostatic from urethral bacteria), segmented urine samples are taken. The first 10 mL of voided urine represents the urethral sample, the midstream urine collected represents the bladder sample, and the first 10 mL voided immediately after prostatic massage represents the prostate sample. When the bladder sample is sterile or nearly so, bacterial prostatitis is diagnosed if the bacterial count in the prostate sample is at least one logarithm greater than that in the urethral sample. The bacterial pathogens responsible for chronic prostatitis often are similar to those of acute prostatitis and UTIs in general (see Table 63.1).[125]

33. Treatment. D.G., a 60-year-old male, experienced his first UTI at age 40, with symptoms of frequency, dysuria, nocturia, perineal pain, chills, and fever, but no flank pain. Acute prostatitis was diagnosed. *E. coli* was cultured from the urine, and

treatment with a sulfonamide was successful. After 12 asymptomatic years, acute prostatitis due to *E. coli* recurred and again responded to sulfonamide therapy. Two more *E. coli* infections occurred over the next 8 years which responded to sulfonamide therapy. Why were sulfonamides appropriate treatment for D.G.'s acute episodes of bacterial prostatitis?

Any appropriate antibacterial drug, including sulfonamides, can be used for the treatment of acute bacterial prostatitis because the diffuse, intense inflammation of the prostate gland allows many drugs to readily penetrate into the prostatic fluid.[125] Antimicrobial therapy, however, should be continued for about a month to prevent the development of chronic prostatitis.[125]

In retrospect, sulfonamides were appropriate for D.G. because they were effective in the treatment of his infections.

34. Many antibiotics are available on the market. Taking into account the pathophysiology of prostatitis, outline your choice of therapy for D.G.

Since inflammation is minimal in patients with chronic prostatitis, most antibiotics which are acidic do not readily cross the prostatic epithelium into the alkaline prostatic fluid. Trimethoprim, clindamycin, erythromycin, oleandomycin, and rosamicin are the only antibiotics that achieve high prostatic concentrations in dog experiments.[126] However, the pH of normal human prostatic fluid is higher than that of the dog, and even higher in the presence of chronic bacterial prostatitis.[127]

Theoretically, this increased alkalinity should impair the diffusion of trimethoprim and enhance the diffusion of the tetracyclines, certain sulfonamides, and the macrolide antibiotics such as erythromycin. Nevertheless, TMP-SMX has the best documented cure rates in the treatment of chronic bacterial prostatitis. Long-term therapy for 4 to 16 weeks with TMP-SMX is associated with a cure rate of 32% to 71%, which significantly exceeds the cure rate associated with short-term therapy of two weeks or less.[127]

The fluoroquinolones now are becoming the agents of choice for the management of prostatitis.[128] In a comparative trial, treatment with norfloxacin for four to six weeks eliminated pathogens in 92% of patients, while trimethoprim-sulfamethoxazole eliminated organisms in 67%. However, this study was seriously flawed due to the short follow-up (1 month). In studies with ciprofloxacin administered for one to three months, infecting organisms were eliminated in 67% and 77% of patients, respectively.[129,130] Similar studies with ofloxacin indicate that bacteriologic cure may be achieved in 80% to 90% of patients treated for six weeks.[131] Although these studies seem promising, further comparative studies are needed before the use of fluoroquinolones can be recommended as initial therapy. However, in patients who are unresponsive or intolerant to conventional therapy, or in those infected with resistant organisms, a trial of a fluoroquinolone chronic suppressive therapy (one-half normal doses) may be warranted in a patient who relapses after conventional treatment.[1]

Although limited, some studies have reported success with erythromycin and carbenicillin indanyl sodium in the treatment of chronic bacterial prostatitis.[132] In addition, one investigator has experimented with direct perineal injections of antibiotics into prostatic lobes.[133] More experience with these therapies is needed. Based upon the studies to date, D.G. should be treated with TMP-SMX for six weeks.

In the event that D.G. continues to develop recurrent infections, chronic low-dose therapy with TMP-SMX, fluoroquinolones, nitrofurantoin, or acidifying agents can alleviate the symptoms of episodic bladder infection associated with chronic bacterial prostatitis. Infections eventually recur with greater frequency in most of these patients, although some become asymptomatic, even in the presence of chronic bacteriuria. Chronic, low-dose antibacterial

therapy sterilizes the bladder, alleviates symptoms, confines bacteria to the prostate, and prevents infection of and damage to the rest of the urinary tract. Chronic bacterial prostatitis is one of the few indications for continuous antibiotic therapy.

UTI and Sexual Intercourse

35. On routine screening, asymptomatic bacteriuria is noted in W.W., a 30-year-old pregnant female in her first trimester. Five years ago, during her first pregnancy, she developed acute bacterial pyelonephritis which required hospitalization and treatment with parenteral antibiotics. Since that time, she has had recurrent UTIs, apparently related to sexual intercourse. These subsided when she began taking a single dose of nitrofurantoin after coitus, but she discontinued the practice before this pregnancy because she was afraid of the potential effects of this drug on the fetus. What is the association between sexual intercourse and the occurrence of UTIs?

Although studies tend to support an association between sexual intercourse and symptomatic UTIs,[21,22] a causal relationship has not been adequately established. Studies do indicate that introital (vaginal vestibule and urethral mucosa) bacterial colonization by fecal bacteria has a definite role in recurrent infection. There is an increase in the number of introital enterobacteria immediately before urinary tract infection, and they are identical serotypically to the infecting bacteria cultured from the urinary tract. It appears that there is a high risk of UTI after sexual intercourse only if the appropriate organisms, primarily Enterobacteriaceae, are present in the region beforehand.

Since UTIs are uncommon in males, transmission of an infection from male to the female is unlikely. Occasionally, bacteria harbored under the foreskin of an uncircumcised male may be transmitted to his partner in intercourse.[4]

36. Was it rational to manage these infections with a single dose of an antibiotic after intercourse?

Postcoital antibiotic prophylaxis often is recommended when a UTI is thought to result from sexual intercourse. Theoretically, a single dose of an antimicrobial agent produces bactericidal activity in the urine before bacteria have a chance to multiply. The patient should be instructed to empty her bladder just after intercourse and before taking the medication to minimize the number of bacteria present in the bladder and to eliminate unnecessary dilution of the drug in the urine. Since most drugs effective in UTIs are rapidly excreted by the kidney and reach high urinary concentrations, this regimen appears reasonable and does lower the incidence of postcoital infections. However, it has the same drawbacks as any other type of antibiotic prophylaxis, and is not recommended in patients with structural abnormalities of the urinary tract or decreased renal function. It also is important to treat symptomatic infection, before beginning prophylaxis.

Depending upon the frequency of intercourse, postcoital prophylaxis may result in less antibiotic consumption. TMP-SMX probably is the drug of choice; however, other agents such as nitrofurantoin, fluoroquinolones, and cephalexin may be used.[134]

UTI and Pregnancy

37. Since W.W.'s UTI is asymptomatic at this time, should treatment be withheld because of her pregnancy?

No. Acute symptomatic pyelonephritis may develop in pregnant women with untreated bacteriuria. In addition, there is evidence that maternal urinary tract infections during pregnancy are associated with an increase in perinatal mortality rates and more frequent preterm deliveries.[135] Although a cause and effect relationship has not been established, this is an important consideration and strengthens the argument for treating maternal UTIs.

Screening pregnant women for bacteriuria is appropriate because it is so common. The high frequency of bacteriuria early in pregnancy and its rarity late in pregnancy suggests that screening should be done early in pregnancy, particularly during the 16th gestational week.[136] Therefore, treatment with an appropriate antimicrobial agent is recommended for all pregnant patients with significant bacteriuria.[137]

38. Teratogenicity. **Which antimicrobial agents are contraindicated in W.W.?**

The use of antibiotics in pregnancy has been reviewed thoroughly in reference 29. As indicated in Table 63.2, tetracyclines are contraindicated in pregnant women and in nursing mothers because they can cause permanent yellow, grayish-brown, or brown discoloration of the teeth in the fetus or nursing infant. In addition, tetracyclines have been associated with the development of fatty liver and nephropathy in the pregnant female. Thus, tetracyclines should always be avoided in pregnant and nursing mothers.

Sulfonamides and sulfonamide combinations (e.g., TMP-SMX) can cause kernicterus in neonates if given to mothers during the third trimester of pregnancy or to lactating women. The sulfonamides displace unconjugated bilirubin from plasma albumin, thereby allowing bilirubin to enter the brain; this induces encephalopathy in the newborn. Sulfonamides in breast milk can cause hemolytic anemia in infants with G6PD deficiency.

Teratogenicity attributed to TMP-SMX has not been reported to date, although the total number of females who have taken this drug during the first trimester (when the fetus is most susceptible to teratogenic effects) is too small to make any conclusion about its safety.[138,139] Fetal malformations have been associated with other folic acid antagonists, so it may be best to avoid the use of TMP-SMX and trimethoprim during pregnancy or the nursing period.

Since teratogenic effects of nitrofurantoin have not been observed clinically, it is recommended by several investigators. However, *in vitro* investigations suggest a slight mutagenic potential. Nitrofurantoin also could cause hemolytic anemia in a G6PD-deficient nursing infant; however, only very small amounts have been detected in breast milk.[138]

Adverse genetic effects from nalidixic acid in humans have not been reported, but it increases the rate of gene mutation in insects. It is advisable to avoid nalidixic acid during the first month of pregnancy. It, too, can cause hemolytic anemia in a G6PD-deficient infant.[138] The fluoroquinolones are contraindicated in pregnancy due to the arthropathy observed in immature animals.[140]

The penicillins, cephalosporins, and aminoglycosides appear to be relatively safe for use during pregnancy, although caution with the aminoglycosides is warranted because of possible eighth nerve toxicity in the fetus. These drugs, along with the others listed in Tables 63.2 and 63.3, cross the placental barrier; thus, the risk of toxicity or teratogenicity to the fetus always must be considered before deciding to treat a pregnant patient with a UTI.

In this case, ampicillin or sulfisoxazole could be prescribed for treatment of W.W.'s UTI. W.W. was correct in discontinuing her nitrofurantoin before pregnancy, since the risk to the fetus, though small, tends to offset the advantage of antimicrobial prophylaxis. However, W.W. must receive proper follow-up care. (Also see Chapter 45: Teratogenicity and Drugs in Breast Milk.)

39. How long should W.W. be treated?

There are few studies comparing single-dose and three days to conventional therapy for seven days in pregnant patients. However, initial trials demonstrated that cure rates of single-dose therapy were lower compared with seven- to ten-day therapy.[141] Although more recent trials have shown that single-dose therapy effectively eradicates bacteriuria in pregnancy these studies were conducted in a small number of patients.[16] Therefore, it is recommended that these patients receive a seven- to ten-day course of therapy.

Irrespective of the duration of therapy, clinicians must document elimination of pathogens one to two weeks after therapy. Patients should be followed at monthly intervals for the remainder of gestation. If bacteriuria recurs, therapy should be given for relapse or reinfection and the patient evaluated radiologically for structural abnormalities.[1]

Urinary Catheters

Catheter-induced urinary tract infections are the most common type of hospital-acquired infection. Catheterization and other forms of urologic instrumentation are involved in 75% of all hospital-acquired UTIs, and catheter-associated UTI is said to account for 30% of all nosocomial infections. These UTIs also are the major cause of gram-negative bacteremia.

Catheter infection may occur by bacterial entry from several routes. The urethral meatus and the distal third of the urethra normally are colonized by bacteria; therefore, initial catheter insertion can introduce bacteria into the bladder. Migration of bacteria contaminating catheter junctions and the urine collection bag through the catheter lumen to the bladder can initiate infection.[142] The extraluminal space in the urethra also has been considered a potential route of contamination.[143] In fact, one study suggests that periurethral colonization actually precedes the development of catheter-associated bacteriuria, especially in women.[144] The risk of infection is directly related to catheter insertion technique, care of the catheter, duration of catheterization, and the susceptibility of the patient. A diagnostic or single, short-term catheterization is associated with a much lower risk of infection than indwelling, long-term catheterization. Despite careful technique, there always is the risk of contaminating a sterile bladder with urethral bacteria. The incidence of infection following a single catheterization is 1% in healthy young women and 20% in debilitated patients.[145] Each reinsertion of the catheter introduces a risk of infection.

Infections have been reduced dramatically by the closed, sterile drainage system, the most common type of catheter currently in use. With this system, the drainage tube leads from the catheter directly to a closed plastic collection bag. The overall incidence of infection from the closed system with careful insertion and maintenance is about 20%; the risk increases to 50% after 14 days of catheterization. If the system is disconnected or contaminated accidentally, the infection rate is similar to that of an open system.[142]

Condom catheters appear to be associated with a lower incidence of bacteriuria than indwelling urethral catheters. However, although these avoid problems of a tube directly into the urinary tract, urine within the catheters may have high concentrations of organisms and therefore colonization of the urethra and subsequent cystitis may develop.[142]

To prevent bacterial contamination of the bladder with meatal and urethral flora when the catheter is inserted, the periurethral area should be cleansed carefully with soap and water followed by some type of antiseptic solution. An iodophor solution often is recommended. Once the catheter is in place, maintenance of the closed system is imperative for decreasing the incidence of infections. To this end, caregivers must be trained in the techniques of obtaining urine samples from closed systems. The catheter should be removed as quickly as possible. Studies addressing application of antibacterial substances to the collection bag and also to the catheter-urethral interface have failed to demonstrate consistent benefit.[146,147]

40. J.W., an 18-year-old male, was hospitalized following a diving accident which resulted in a spinal cord injury with paralysis. Included among a number of initial interventions was insertion of a Foley catheter with a closed drainage system because of bladder incontinence. Two weeks after admission to the hospital, J.W. was noted to have an asymptomatic UTI. How should this be treated?

A systemic antibiotic selected specifically for the infecting organism will result in a sterile urine. However, reinfection, often by a resistant organism, occurs in one-third to one-half of these cases if closed drainage catheterization is continued during therapy.[1] For this reason, it generally is recommended that systemic antimicrobial therapy be initiated after or just before catheter removal.[1] Since bacteriuria is an inevitable consequence of long-term catheterization, Kunin suggests that asymptomatic patients (like J.W.) be left untreated to avoid the complications of recolonization and potential bacteremia with highly resistant organisms.[1] However, if fever, flank pain, or other symptoms indicative of UTI develop, therapy must be started.[1] The strictest adherence to good catheter care is the primary concern in the chronically catheterized patient. Recatheterization with a new, sterile unit is necessary whenever catheter contamination is suspected.

41. Is systemic antimicrobial prophylaxis useful for J.W.?

The benefits of systemic antibiotics in preventing catheter-induced UTIs have not been clarified. Studies using closed drainage systems with diligent catheter care indicate that systemic antibiotics decrease the daily and overall incidence of infection in patients with sterile urines before catheterization.[149,150] The preventive effect of the antimicrobial agents is greatest for short-term catheterizations or during the first four to seven days of catheterization.[149,150] Thereafter, the rate of infection increases. Although the overall infection rate remains lower than that of the untreated patients, the emergence of resistant organisms is significant. Therefore, in deciding to use systemic antimicrobials, one must consider the patient's underlying diseases or risk factors, duration of catheterization, and the potential complications of drug toxicity or resistant organisms which may result from the chronic use of antimicrobial agents. Since long-term catheterization for J.W. was anticipated, antimicrobial prophylaxis for J.W. is not recommended.

42. C.A., a 60-year-old female admitted for coronary bypass, is catheterized for urinary incontinence. Two days after removal of the catheter, she still has asymptomatic bacteriuria. How should she be treated?

Catheter-acquired bacteriuria that persists 48 hours after catheter removal should be treated even if the patient is asymptomatic.[148] Either a large single-dose or a three-day regimen of TMP-SMX may be used. Older women (>65 years) probably should be treated with a ten-day course. However, the optimal duration in this age group is unknown. Whether these treatment regimens can be used in males requires further study.

Renal Failure

43. K.M., a 55-year-old male with a history of hypertension and chronic renal failure, develops a UTI. His creatinine clearance (Cl_{Cr}), determined from a recent 24-hour urine collection, is 20 mL/min. What antimicrobial agent should be prescribed?
[SI unit: SrCr 0.33 mL/sec]

The major problem encountered in selecting an antimicrobial agent for the treatment of a urinary tract infection in a patient with renal failure is achievement of adequate urine concentrations of the drug without causing systemic toxicity. The ideal drug would be a) inherently nontoxic, even at high serum concentrations, making dosage adjustments unnecessary; b) excreted unchanged in the urine (i.e., not metabolized); and c) eliminated by renal tubular

secretion. The latter remains active in all but the most severe cases of renal failure, resulting in adequate levels of antibiotic in the urine. Unfortunately, no such ideal drug exists.

Nitrofurantoin, doxycycline, and many of the sulfonamides are substantially metabolized by the liver. Such drugs usually are not recovered in high concentrations in the urine and generally produce low levels in the urine of uremic patients. Tetracycline and the aminoglycosides are eliminated almost exclusively by the kidneys. The dose reductions necessary to avoid toxicity in uremic patients also will result in inadequate urine concentrations. The penicillins, the cephalosporins, trimethoprim, and the fluoroquinolones, are metabolized partly by the liver, but also eliminated by the kidney to a significant extent. These agents most closely meet the criteria for an ideal drug as described above.

Adverse Drug Reactions and Drug Interactions
Sulfonamides

Hemolytic Anemia

44. G.R., a 45-year-old black male with an 8-year history of congestive heart failure, was admitted to the hospital with increasing shortness of breath. His hematocrit (Hct) was stable at 39%–43% and his total serum bilirubin was reported to be 0.8 mg/dL. Sixteen days after admission, a UTI due to *E. coli* was discovered, and G.R. was treated with sulfisoxazole, 4 gm/day. Twenty days after admission, the Hct suddenly dropped to 25% and the hemoglobin (Hgb) to 8.4 gm/dL. There were no signs of bleeding, but his sclerae became icteric. Twenty-three days after admission, the Hct was still 25%, but the reticulocyte count had risen to 6.6% and the total serum bilirubin was 3.0 mg/dL. Sulfisoxazole was discontinued, and over a period of 2 weeks the Hct steadily rose to 40%. What mechanism might explain G.R.'s sulfonamide-induced hemolytic anemia? Is his presentation typical? Are there any other drugs used to treat UTIs which can cause a similar reaction?
[SI units: Hct 0.39–0.43, 0.25, and 0.40, respectively; bilirubin 1.4 and 51.3 μmol/L, respectively; Hgb 84 gm/L; reticulocyte count 0.066]

Hemolytic anemia is associated with sulfonamide administration and can be mediated by a number of mechanisms including: abnormally high blood levels; acquired hypersensitivity as reflected by the development of a positive Coombs' test; genetically determined abnormalities of red blood cell metabolism (e.g., deficiency of G6PD); or the presence of an "unstable" hemoglobin in the red blood cell (e.g., Hgb Zurich, Hgb Towns, Hgb H).[151]

In this case, hemolytic anemia due to G6PD deficiency could be confirmed by measuring red blood cell levels of this enzyme. (See Chapter 89: Drug-Induced Blood Disorders for a discussion of G6PD deficiency.) Although the defect appears to be most common and severe in Mediterranean males, one variant affects as many as 11% of American black males.[152,153]

The acute hemolytic anemia induced by sulfonamides in G6PD-deficient individuals does not appear to be a dose-related phenomenon. It usually is abrupt in onset and occurs within the first week of therapy. Typical symptoms include nausea, fever, vertigo, jaundice, hepatosplenomegaly, and occasionally, hypotension. Hematocrit and hemoglobin values may fall precipitously and may be reduced to 30% to 50% of the normal values, as illustrated by G.R.; leukocytosis and reticulocytosis are common; and acute renal failure may result from the hypotension and hemoglobinuria. A mild hemolytic episode is characterized by reticulocytosis without a significant fall in hemoglobin or hematocrit.[153] Several other urinary tract antimicrobials such as nalidixic acid, nitrofurantoin, and TMP-SMX also induce G6PD-deficiency hemolysis.[153]

Clinical illness, as well as drug administration, may precipitate hemolysis in patients with G6PD deficiency. Patients with chronic bacterial infections of the urinary or upper respiratory tract who receive chronic or repetitive courses of certain drugs are particularly predisposed to hemolysis.[153]

Individuals with enzyme deficiencies [especially those enzymes associated with the pentose-phosphate shunt (as is G6PD)] can develop hemolytic reactions when taking drugs commonly used to treat UTIs. Future use of sulfonamides, nitrofurantoin, or nalidixic acid should be avoided in G.R.

Rash and Drug Fever

45. J.P., a 63-year-old diabetic female taking tolbutamide (Orinase) 2 gm/day, developed an acute UTI for which sulfisoxazole 500 mg QID for 10 days was prescribed. Seven days later she appeared in the ER with a pruritic maculopapular rash and fever. She also complained of nausea and lightheadedness. Are the rash and fever in J.P. typical of that caused by the sulfonamides?

Yes. Rash is one of the more common adverse effects noted after sulfonamide administration; it occurs in about 2% of patients treated with sulfisoxazole. A variety of hypersensitivity skin and mucous membrane reactions have been reported including morbilliform, scarlatinal, urticarial, erysipeloid, pemphigoid, purpuric, and petechial rashes. Erythema nodosum, exfoliative dermatitis, photosensitivity reactions, and the Stevens-Johnson Syndrome also are associated with sulfonamides. Skin eruptions usually appear after one week of treatment, although more rapid onset may occur in a sensitized person.[48]

Sulfonamide-Sulfonylurea Interaction

46. Why might the nausea and lightheadedness in J.P. be drug related?

J.P.'s subjective complaints may represent symptoms of hypoglycemia induced by the interaction of sulfisoxazole and tolbutamide. A three- to fourfold prolongation of sulfonylurea hypoglycemic activity has been reported in patients receiving sulfisoxazole or other antibacterial sulfonamides concurrently.[154] It has been suggested that the increased and prolonged hypoglycemia is due either to protein displacement or to a decreased rate of metabolism of the sulfonylurea.[154]

The hypersensitivity reactions and possible tolbutamide interaction that occurred in J.P. signify that she should avoid sulfonamides. An alternate drug should be used to treat future urinary tract infections.

Trimethoprim-Sulfamethoxazole

TMP-SMX Folate Deficiency

47. D.M., a 50-year-old epileptic female, has been taking TMP-SMX nightly for 3 months for chronic recurrent UTI prophylaxis. She takes phenytoin (Dilantin) 300 mg/day with effective control of her seizures. Further history reveals that she also takes diazepam (Valium) 2 mg TID, smokes 1 pack of cigarettes/day, and drinks 1 pint of gin/day. Routine CBC after a clinic visit shows an Hgb of 9 gm/dL, an Hct of 30%, a mean corpuscular volume (MCV) of 105 μm³, and a mean corpuscular hemoglobin concentration (MCHC) of 32%. How could TMP-SMX account for D.M.'s megaloblastic anemia? [SI units: Hgb 90 gm/L; Hct 0.30; MCV 105 fL; MCHC 0.32]

On rare occasions, folate-deficiency megaloblastic anemia has been associated with the use of TMP-SMX.[154] The ability of the sulfonamides to inhibit folic acid synthesis in the bacterial cell does not affect the human cell to a significant degree. Although trimethoprim also has a greater affinity for the bacterial and protozoal cell, it also may affect folic acid utilization in humans when given in high doses.[35] It is especially a problem in patients with known or questionably deficient folic acid stores, such as pregnant women,

the elderly, patients with malabsorption or malnutrition, alcoholics, patients receiving anticonvulsants, or those with chronic hemolysis (such as sickle-cell disease). Concomitant administration of folic acid will reverse these effects without interfering with antimicrobial activity.[49] It is doubtful that significant folate deficiency would occur following short-term therapy or in patients without the above risk factors.

In D.M., both phenytoin and alcohol undoubtedly contributed to folate deficiency anemia. Whether or not TMP-SMX was a significant factor may be questioned, but an alternate antibacterial may be preferable in a patient already at risk for folate deficiency.

TMP-SMX Warfarin Interaction

48. R.S., a 50-year-old female asthmatic, was admitted to the hospital for acute asthma which had progressively worsened over the previous 2 weeks. She was placed on IV aminophylline and metaproterenol (Alupent) by nebulization. Other medications included warfarin (Coumadin) for deep vein thrombophlebitis that occurred 3 months ago and hydrochlorothiazide for mild hypertension. During her hospitalization, she developed an acute UTI, and TMP-SMX BID was ordered pending C&S results. Three days later, the C&S reports showed *E. coli* sensitive to ampicillin, tetracycline, nitrofurantoin, TMP-SMX, carbenicillin, and gentamicin. At this time, a prolongation of the prothrombin time (PT) to 38 seconds (control: 12) was noted. Because a TMP-SMX-warfarin interaction was suspected, warfarin was withheld for 2 days and ampicillin 500 mg QID was given instead of the TMP-SMX. Subsequently, the PT was maintained at 22 seconds during the remainder of the hospitalization. Why was this problem attributed to a drug interaction?

TMP-SMX can potentiate the anticoagulant effects of racemic warfarin (the form administered to humans).[153] There is recent evidence that TMP-SMX has a stereoselective interaction with warfarin, causing a greater increase in serum levels of the more potent levorotatory warfarin enantiomorph and a decrease in the less potent dextrorotatory enantiomorph.[156] The net effect is no change in the total warfarin level, but a higher concentration of the potent enantiomorph and an increase in the prothrombin time. Although a few cases of sulfonamide-induced hypoprothrombinemia have been reported, current evidence does not rule out the possibility that trimethoprim may play a role in the reports of TMP-SMX-induced hypoprothrombinemia.[157]

Nitrofurantoin

Gastrointestinal (GI) Disturbance

49. J.R., a 45-year-old, 110 pound female, is placed on nitrofurantoin 100 mg QID for 14 days for an acute UTI. She complains of nausea and GI upset after the ingestion of each dose of nitrofurantoin. How can this effect be minimized?

Nausea is a fairly frequent complication of nitrofurantoin therapy, and the patient's compliance with the prescribed regimen may be severely affected by this common side effect. It is not fully known whether the mechanism by which nitrofurantoin produces nausea is central or local, but a central component may be present because nausea occurs after parenteral administration. Several approaches can be used to decrease nitrofurantoin-induced nausea:

Take Each Dose with Food. All manufacturers of nitrofurantoin recommend that the drug be taken with food or milk. If the nausea is a locally-mediated effect, the food may serve as a buffer; if the nausea is centrally-mediated, then food may be helpful by slowing the rate of absorption and lowering the peak serum concentration of the drug. Interestingly, however, food may increase the bioavailability of nitrofurantoin. This slowing of absorption has the benefit of decreasing the incidence of nausea and vomiting associated with the smaller, microcrystalline product.[158,159]

Change to a Macrocrystalline Product. A study of the incidence of nitrofurantoin adverse effects demonstrated significantly fewer adverse effects with the use of the macrocrystalline preparation (17% versus 39%).[159] The cure rate did not differ significantly. The larger particle size of the macrocrystalline preparation results in a slower rate of dissolution and absorption and lower serum levels. This may decrease the nausea and vomiting associated with the smaller, microcrystalline product.[160] A disadvantage of the macrocrystalline form is the cost, which may be two to ten times that of the microcrystalline form, depending upon the product source.

Lower the Dose. Nausea and vomiting appear to be dose related and occur more frequently in small persons.[161] The minimum effective dose of nitrofurantoin generally is stated to be 5 mg/kg/day and the average dose is usually 7 mg/kg/day. At daily doses above 7 mg/kg, the incidence of nausea appears to increase markedly, so the dose in this 110 pound (50 kg) patient could be decreased.

Pneumonitis

50. J.R. tolerated the macrocrystalline form taken with meals and continued her regimen. However, 10 days later she presented with dyspnea, tachypnea, coughing, and wheezing. Examination revealed a temperature of 38.4 °C, pulse of 115 beats/min, and soft inspiratory and expiratory rhonchi with a few bibasilar rales. Nitrofurantoin was stopped, and IV aminophylline and steroids were administered. Symptoms gradually disappeared after a few days; however, rechallenge with a single 50 mg dose of nitrofurantoin caused a recurrence of the respiratory distress. What is the nature of the apparent nitrofurantoin-induced respiratory reaction which occurred in J.R.?

Several hundred cases of nitrofurantoin-induced pulmonary reactions have been reported.[162–164] Acute, subacute, and chronic reactions have been described. The acute form illustrated by J.R. often manifests within several days of initiating the drug with a sudden flu-like syndrome consisting of fever, dyspnea, and cough. The subacute form tends to occur after at least a month of exposure; symptoms include fever and dyspnea. The chronic form tends to be more insidious with milder dyspnea and low-grade fever. In all forms, rales are commonly heard and pulmonary infiltrates can be demonstrated on chest x-ray. Although eosinophilia frequently occurs with the acute form, it may be absent with the subacute and chronic forms. Antinuclear antibodies are elevated in the latter two forms. Discontinuation of nitrofurantoin results in complete symptomatic recovery after several weeks; however, permanent fibrotic changes may persist with the chronic pulmonary reaction. Although steroids are frequently administered when the adverse reaction is diagnosed, their efficacy has not been demonstrated. Rechallenge with oral nitrofurantoin results in rapid reappearance of pulmonary symptoms in those who have suffered an acute reaction.

Neurotoxicity

51. G.T., a 55-year-old female, has been taking nitrofurantoin 100 mg QID for an acute UTI. Pertinent history includes hypertension and moderate renal failure. Medications include methyldopa (Aldomet), hydrochlorothiazide (Oretic), and allopurinol (Zyloprim). On the 10th day of therapy, she complains that both her hands and feet feel numb and weak. Physical examination shows marked sensory loss to the hands and feet, as well as absent ankle reflexes, although knee and arm reflexes are present. What are the characteristics of the neuropathy which is associated with nitrofurantoin therapy?

Peripheral neuropathy usually is characterized by symmetrical dysesthesia and paresthesia in the distal extremities which progress in a central and ascending fashion. It usually occurs within the first 63 days of treatment, although neuropathy can be recognized up to 42 days after discontinuation of therapy in 16%. Symptom severity is unrelated to the total nitrofurantoin dose. Reversibility is related to severity and, in some cases, occurs months after drug withdrawal. A small number of patients may have permanent neuropathy. Also, renal failure is a risk factor but neuropathy has been reported in patients with normal renal function as well.[158]

Nitrofurantoin excretion is impaired in renal failure; however, serum levels do not rise proportionately, suggesting that the drug might be sequestered in an extravascular space. It has been postulated that neurotoxicity is due to accumulation of nitrofurantoin in neural tissue,[158] or that toxic metabolites are involved.[158] In view of the inability to achieve adequate urinary concentrations of nitrofurantoin even in mild renal failure, G.T. should not be given this drug.

Ciprofloxacin-Cyclosporine Interaction

52. Y.B., a 53-year-old female, is receiving maintenance cyclosporine for a renal transplant performed 1 year ago. Two days before this admission, she experienced dysuria and polyuria. Because she has a sulfa allergy, her physician wishes to use ciprofloxacin. Is there a drug interaction between ciprofloxacin and cyclosporine?

Two case reports suggest that the addition of ciprofloxacin to cyclosporine therapy may result in acute renal failure.[165,166] However, several studies revealed no significant alterations in cyclosporine pharmacokinetics or renal function in transplant patients who received cyclosporine and ciprofloxacin concurrently.[167–169] It is recommended that while quinolones are not contraindicated, renal function and cyclosporine concentrations be followed closely in those patients receiving both agents concomitantly.

References

1 **Sobel JD, Kaye D.** Urinary tract infections. In: Mandell GL et al., eds. Principles and Practice of Infectious Diseases. New York: Churchill Livingstone; 1995:662–90.
2 **Stamm WE, Hooton TM.** Management of urinary tract infections in adults. N Engl J Med. 1993;329:1328–334.
3 **Johnson JR, Stamm WE.** Urinary tract infections in women: diagnosis and treatment. Ann Intern Med. 1989; 111:906–17.
4 **Sobel JD.** Pathogenesis of urinary tract infections: host defenses. Infect Dis Clin North Am. 1987;1:751–72.

5 **Komaroff AL.** Acute dysuria in women. N Engl J Med. 1984;310:368–74.
6 **Lipsky BA.** Urinary tract infections in men: epidemiology, pathophysiology, diagnosis and treatment. Ann Intern Med. 1989;110:138–50.
7 **Jodal U.** The natural history of bacteriuria in childhood. Infect Dis Clin North Am. 1987;1:713–29.
8 **Boscia JA et al.** Epidemiology of bacteriuria in an elderly ambulatory population. Am J Med. 1986;80:208–14.
9 **Boscia JA, Kaye D.** Asymptomatic bacteriuria in the elderly. Infect Dis Clin North Am. 1987;1:893–905.

10 **Kaye D.** Urinary tract infections in the elderly. Bull N Y Acad Med. 1980;56: 209.
11 **Dontas AS et al.** Bacteriuria and survival in old age. N Engl J Med. 1981; 304:939.
12 **Resnick NM et al.** The pathophysiology of urinary incontinence among institutionalized elderly persons. N Engl J Med. 1989;320:1–7.
13 **Latham RH et al.** Urinary tract infections in young adult women caused by Staphylococcus saprophyticus. JAMA. 1983;250:3063.
14 **Schoolnik GK.** How Escherichia coli

infect the urinary tract. N Engl J Med. 1989;320:804–5.
15 **Shleinfeld J et al.** Association of Lewis blood group phenotype with recurrent tract infections in women. N Engl J Med. 1989;307:773–77.
16 **Patterson TF, Andriole VT.** Bacteriuria in pregnancy. Infect Dis Clin North Am. 1987;1:807–12.
17 **Warren JW.** The catheter and urinary tract infection. Med Clin North Am. 1991;75:481–93.
18 **Prat V et al.** Urinary tract infection in renal transplant patients. Infection. 1985;13:207.

19 Wheat LJ. Infection in diabetes. Diabetes Care. 1980;3:187.

20 Korzeniowski OM. Urinary tract infection in the impaired host. Med Clin North Am. 1991;75:391–404.

21 Nicolle LE et al. The association of urinary tract infection with sexual intercourse. J Infect Dis. 1982;146:579.

22 Strom BL et al. Sexual activity, contraceptive use and other risk factors for symptomatic and asymptomatic bacteriuria. Ann Intern Med. 1987;107:816–23.

23 Kamaroff AL. Urinalysis and urine culture in women with dysuria. Ann Intern Med. 1986;104:212.

24 Wigton RS et al. Use of clinical findings in the diagnosis of urinary tract infection in women. Arch Intern Med. 1985;145:2222.

25 Schaeffer AJ. Office laboratory. Urol Clin North Am. 1980;7(Feb):29.

26 Shaw ST et al. Routine urinalysis: is the dipstick enough? JAMA. 1985;253:1596.

27 Roberts AP et al. Some factors affecting bacterial colony counts in urinary infection. Br Med J. 1967;1:400.

28 Anon. The choice of antimicrobial drugs. Med Lett Drugs Ther. 1986;28:33.

29 Chow AW, Jewesson PJ. Pharmacokinetics and safety of antimicrobial agents during pregnancy. Rev Infect Dis. 1985;7:287–313.

30 Briggs GG et al. Drugs in Pregnancy and Lactation. 2nd ed. Baltimore: Williams & Wilkins; 1986.

31 Anon. Safety of antimicrobial drugs in pregnancy. Med Lett Drugs Ther. 1985;27:93.

32 Norrby SR. Short-term treatment of uncomplicated lower urinary tract infections in women. Rev Infect Dis. 1990;12:458.

33 Greenberg RN et al. Randomized study of single-dose, three-day, and seven-day treatment of cystitis in women. J Infect Dis. 1986;153:277.

34 Fair WR et al. Three-day treatment of urinary tract infections. J Urol. 1980;123:717.

35 Gould JC et al. Dosage of antibiotics relation between the in vitro and in vivo concentrations effective in urinary tract infections. Lancet. 1953;1:361.

36 Hooton TM, Stamm WE. Management of acute uncomplicated urinary tract infection in adults. Med Clin North Am. 1991;75:339–57.

37 Norrby SR. Short-term treatment of uncomplicated lower urinary tract infections in women. Rev Infect Dis. 1990;12:458.

38 Savard-Fenton M et al. Single-dose amoxicillin therapy with follow-up urine culture: effective initial management for acute uncomplicated urinary tract infections. Am J Med. 1982;3:808.

39 Hooton TM et al. Single-dose therapy for cystitis in women: a comparison of trimethoprim-sulfamethoxazole, amoxicillin, and cyclacillin. JAMA. 1985;253:387.

40 Buckwold FJ et al. Therapy for acute cystitis in adult women: randomized comparison of single-dose sulfisoxazole versus trimethoprim-sulfamethoxazole. JAMA. 1982;247:1839.

41 Stamm WE. Single-dose treatment of cystitis. JAMA. 1980;244:591. Editorial.

42 Kunin CM. Use of antimicrobial agents in treating urinary tract infection. Adv Intern Med. 1984;29:39.

43 Schultz HJ et al. Acute cystitis: a prospective study of laboratory tests and duration of therapy. Mayo Clin Proc. 1984;59:391.

44 Carlson KJ, Mulley AG. Management of acute dysuria: a decision-analysis model of alternative strategies. Ann Intern Med. 1985;102:244.

45 Gleckman RA. Treatment duration for urinary tract infection in adults. Antimicrob Agents Chemother. 1987;31:1–5.

46 Philbrick JT et al. Single-dose antibiotic treatment for uncomplicated urinary infections. Less for less? Arch Intern Med. 1985;145:1672–678.

47 Saginur R et al. Single dose compared with 3 days norfloxacin for treatment of uncomplicated urinary infection in women. Arch Intern Med. 1992;152:1233–237.

48 Cockerill FR, Edson RS. Trimethoprim-sulfamethoxazole. Mayo Clin Proc. 1991;66:1260–269.

49 Cox CE et al. Combined trimethoprim-sulfamethoxazole therapy of urinary tract infection. Postgrad Med J. 1969;45(Suppl.):65.

50 Rubin RH et al. Trimethoprim-sulfamethoxazole. N Engl J Med. 1980;303:426.

51 Patel RB et al. Clinical pharmacokinetics of co-trimoxazole (trimethoprim-sulfamethoxazole). Clin Pharmacokinet. 1980;5:405.

52 Stamm WE et al. Diagnosis of coliform infection in acutely dysuric women. N Engl J Med. 1982;307:463.

53 Fair WR, Fair WR III. Clinical value of sensitivity determination in treating urinary tract infections. Urology. 1982;19:565.

54 Wolfson JS et al. The fluoroquinolones: structures, mechanisms of action and resistance, and spectra of activity in vitro. Antimicrob Agents Chemother. 1985;28:581–86.

55 Wolfson JS et al. Fluoroquinolone antimicrobial agents. Clin Microbiol Rev. 1989;2:328.

56 Hooper DC et al. The fluoroquinolones: pharmacology, clinical uses and toxicity in humans. Antimicrob Agents Chemother. 1985;28:716–21.

57 Wolfson JS et al. Treatment of genitourinary tract infections with fluoroquinolones: in vitro, pharmacokinetics, and clinical efficacy in urinary tract infections and prostatitis. Antimicrob Agents Chemother. 1989;33:1655–661.

58 Allais JM et al. Randomized double-blind comparison of ciprofloxacin and trimethoprim-sulfamethoxazole for complicated urinary tract infections. Antimicrob Agents Chemother. 1988;32:1327–330.

59 Polk RE. Drug-drug interactions with ciprofloxacin and other fluoroquinolones. Am J Med. 1989;87 (Suppl. 5A):765–815.

60 Gillum G et al. Pharmacokinetic drug interactions with antimicrobial agents. Clin Pharmacokinet. 1993;25:450–82.

61 Noyes M, Polk RE. Norfloxacin and absorption of magnesium-aluminum. Ann Intern Med. 1988;109:168–69.

62 Nix DE et al. Effects of aluminum and magnesium antacids and ranitidine on the absorption of ciprofloxacin. Clin Pharmacol Ther. 1989;46:700–5.

63 Edwards DJ et al. Inhibition of drug metabolism by quinolone antibiotics. Clin Pharmacokinet. 1988;15:194–204.

64 Ho G et al. Evaluation of the effect of norfloxacin on the pharmacokinetics of theophylline. Clin Pharmacol Ther. 1988;44:35–8.

65 LeBel M et al. Influence of lomefloxacin on the pharmacokinetics of theophylline. Antimicrob Agents Chemother. 1990;34:1254–256.

66 Parent M et al. Safety of fleroxacin coadministered with theophylline to young and elderly volunteers. Antimicrob Agents Chemother. 1990;34:1249–253.

67 Healy DP et al. Interaction between oral ciprofloxacin and caffeine in normal volunteers. Antimicrob Agents Chemother. 1989;33:474–78.

68 Healy DP et al. Lack of interaction between lomefloxacin caffeine in normal volunteers. Antimicrob Agents Chemother. 1991;35:660–64.

69 Leor J et al. Ofloxacin and warfarin. Ann Intern Med. 1988;109:761.

70 Linville T et al. Norfloxacin and warfarin. Ann Intern Med. 1989;110:751–52.

71 Kamada AK. Possible interaction between ciprofloxacin and warfarin. DICP, Ann Pharmacother. 1990;24:27–8.

72 Mott FE et al. Ciprofloxacin and warfarin. Ann Intern Med. 1989;111:542–43.

73 Toon S et al. Enoxacin-warfarin interaction: pharmacokinetic and stereochemical aspects. Clin Pharmacol Ther. 1987;42:33–41.

74 Morikawa K et al. Unusual CNS toxic action of new quinolones. In: Proceedings of the 27th Interscience Conference on Antimicrobial Agents and Chemotherapy. Oct 1987; Abstract 255.

75 Platt R et al. Mortality associated with nosocomial urinary-tract infection. N Engl J Med. 1982;307:637.

76 Rutledge KA, McDonald HP. Costs and strategies for managing nosocomial urinary tract infections. Drug Intell Clin Pharm. 1986;20:587.

77 File TM, Tan JS. Empiric antimicrobial therapy of serious urinary tract infections. Urology. 1986;27:80.

78 Cox CE. Brief report: sequential intravenous and oral ciprofloxacin versus intravenous ceftazidime in the treatment of complicated urinary tract infections. Am J Med. 1989;87(Suppl. 5A):1575–590.

79 Meyrier A, Guibert J. Diagnosis and drug treatment of acute pyelonephritis. Drugs. 1992;44:356–67.

80 Bailey RR et al. Treatment of acute urinary tract infection in women. Ann Intern Med. 1987;107:430.

81 Jernelius H et al. One- or three-week treatment of acute pyelonephritis. A double-blind comparison using a fixed combination of pivampicillin plus pivmecillinam. Acta Med Scand. 1988;223:469–77.

82 Stamm WE et al. Acute renal infection in women: treatment with trimethoprim-sulfamethoxazole or ampicillin for two- or six-weeks. A randomized trial. Ann Intern Med. 1987;106:341–45.

83 Stamm WE et al. Causes of acute urethral syndrome in women. N Engl J Med. 1980;303:409.

84 Demetriou E et al. Dysuria in adolescent girls: urinary tract infection or vaginitis? Pediatrics. 1982;70:299.

85 Stamm WE et al. Treatment of acute urethral syndrome. N Engl J Med. 1981;304:956.

86 Bowie WR et al. Failure of norfloxacin to eradicate chlamydia trachomatis in nongonococcal urethritis. Antimicrob Agents Chemother. 1986;30:594–97.

87 Fong IW. Treatment of nongonococcal urethritis with ciprofloxacin. Am J Med. 1987;82(Suppl. 4A):331–36.

88 Weider W et al. Acute nongonococcal epididymitis. Aetiological and therapeutic aspects. Drugs. 1987;34(Suppl. 1):111–17.

89 Pust RA et al. Clinical efficacy and tolerance of fleroxacin in patients with urethritis caused by chlamydia trachomatis. J Antimicrob Chemother. 1988;22(Suppl. D):227–30.

90 American Hospital Formulary Service. American Society of Hospital Pharmacists. Bethesda, MD: 1995; 2457–458.

91 Fincher ME, Campbell HT. Methemoglobinemia and hemolytic anemia after Pyridium administration in end-stage renal disease. South Med J. 1989; 82:372–74.

92 Engle JE, Schoolwerth AC. Additive nephrotoxicity from roentgenographic contrast media: its occurrence in phenazopyridine-induced acute renal failure. Arch Intern Med. 1981;141:784–85.

93 Badley BWD. Phenazopyridine-induced hepatitis. Br Med J. 1976;2:850.

94 Sherbotie JR, Cornfeld D. Management of urinary tract infections in children. Med Clin North Am. 1991;75:327–38.

95 Marsson S et al. Untreated bacteriuria in asymptomatic girls with renal scarring. Pediatrics. 1989;84:964.

96 Andriole VT, Patterson TF. Epidemiology, natural history, and management of urinary tract infections in pregnancy. Med Clin North Am. 1991;75:359.

97 Dontas AS et al. Bacteriuria and survival in old age. N Engl J Med. 1981; 304:939.

98 Nicolle LE et al. Bacteriuria in elderly institutionalized men. N Engl J Med. 1983;309:1420.

99 Boscia JA et al. Asymptomatic bacteriuria in elderly persons: treat or do not treat. 1987;106:764–66.

100 Schaeffer AJ et al. Association of in vitro Escherichia coli adherence to vaginal and buccal epithelial cells with susceptibility of women to recurrent urinary-tract infections. N Engl J Med. 1981;304:1062.

101 Takahashi M et al. Bacteriuria and oral contraceptives. JAMA. 1974;227:762.

102 Evans DA et al. Oral contraceptive use and bacteriuria in a community-based study. N Engl J Med. 1978;299:536.

103 **Fihn SD et al.** Association between diaphragm use and urinary tract infection. JAMA. 1985;254:240.

104 **Smilack JD et al.** Tetracyclines, chloramphenicol, erythromycin, clindamycin, and metronidazole. Mayo Clin Proc. 1991;66:1270–280.

105 **Andriole VT.** Urinary tract agents: nitrofurantoin and methenamine. In: Mardell GL et al., eds. Principles and Practice of Infectious Diseases. New York: Churchill Livingstone; 1989: 1658–673.

106 **Sheehan GJ et al.** Double-blind, randomized comparison of 24 weeks of norfloxacin and 12 weeks of norfloxacin followed by 12 weeks of placebo in the therapy of complicated urinary tract infection. Antimicrob Agents Chemother. 1988;32:1292.

107 **Nicolle LE et al.** Prospective, randomized, placebo-controlled trial of norfloxacin for the prophylaxis of recurrent urinary tract infection in women. Antimicrob Agents Chemother. 1989; 33:1032–35.

108 **Eisenstein BI.** Enterobacteriaceae. In: Mandell GL et al., eds. Principles and Practice of Infectious Diseases. New York: Churchill Livingstone; 1989: 1658–673.

109 **Aascher AW.** Investigation and differential diagnosis. In: The Challenge of Urinary Tract Infections. New York: Grune & Stratton; 1980:83.

110 **Fowler JE, Pulaski ET.** Excretory urography, cystography, and cystoscopy in the evaluation of women with urinary-tract infection. N Engl J Med. 1981;304:462.

111 **Reeves D.** Sulphonamides and trimethoprim. Lancet. 1982;2:370–73.

112 **Bacterial resistance to trimethoprim.** Br Med J. 1980;281:571. Editorial.

113 **Trimethoprim.** Lancet. 1980;1:519. Editorial.

114 **Huovinen P et al.** Trimethoprim resistance in Finland after five years use of plain trimethoprim. Br Med J. 1980;1: 72.

115 **Freeman RB et al.** Long term therapy for chronic bacteriuria in men. Ann Intern Med. 1975;83:133.

116 **Stamm WE et al.** Is antimicrobial prophylaxis of urinary tract infections cost-effective? Ann Intern Med. 1981; 94:251.

117 **Stamm WE et al.** Antimicrobial prophylaxis of recurrent urinary tract infections. A double-blind, placebo-controlled trial. Ann Intern Med. 1980;92: 770.

118 **Baldassare JS et al.** Special problems of urinary tract infection in the elderly. Med Clin North Am. 1991;75:375–90.

119 **Harding GKM et al.** A controlled study of antimicrobial prophylaxis of recurrent urinary infection in women. N Engl J Med. 1974;291:597.

120 **Stamey TA et al.** Prophylactic efficacy of nitrofurantoin macrocrystals and trimethoprim-sulfamethoxazole in urinary infections. Biologic effects on the vaginal and rectal flora. N Engl J Med. 1977;296:780.

121 **Harding GKM et al.** Prophylaxis of recurrent urinary tract infection in female patients. Efficacy of low-dose, twice weekly therapy with trimethoprim-sulfamethoxazole. JAMA. 1979; 242:1975.

122 **Harding GKM et al.** Long-term antimicrobial prophylaxis for recurrent UTI in women. Rev Infect Dis. 1982; 4:438.

123 **O'Grady F et al.** Long-term treatment of persistent or recurrent urinary tract infection with trimethoprim-sulfamethoxazole. J Infect Dis. 1973;128 (Suppl.):S652.

124 **Meares EM.** Prostatitis and related diseases. DM. 1980;26:1.

125 **Meares EM.** Prostatitis. Med Clin North Am. 1991;75:405–24.

126 **Meares EM.** Prostatitis syndromes: new perspectives about old woes. J Urol. 1980;123:141.

127 **Fair WR et al.** A re-appraisal of treatment in chronic bacterial prostatitis. J Urol. 1979;121:437.

128 **Sabbaj J et al.** Norfloxacin versus co-trimoxazole in the treatment of recurring urinary tract infections in men. Scand J Infect Dis. 1986;48(Suppl.): 48–53.

129 **Guibert J et al.** Ciprofloxacin: clinical evaluation in urinary tract infections due to Pseudomonas aeruginosa. Chemoterapia. 1986;6(Suppl. 2):524–25.

130 **Guibert J et al.** Ciprofloxacin in the treatment of urinary tract infection due to enterobacteria. Eur J Clin Microbiol. 1986;2:247–48.

131 **Remy G et al.** Use of ofloxacin for prostatitis. Rev Infect Dis. 1988;10 (Suppl. 1):S173–174.

132 **Drach GW, Nolan PE.** Chronic bacterial prostatitis: problems in diagnosis and therapy. Urology. 1986;27 (Suppl.): 26.

133 **Baert L.** A re-appraisal of treatment in chronic bacterial prostatitis. J Urol. 1980; 123:606. Letter.

134 **Stapleton A et al.** Post-coital antimicrobial prophylaxis for recurrent urinary tract infection. JAMA. 1990;264: 703.

135 **Gilstrap LC et al.** Renal infection and pregnancy outcome. Am J Obstet Gynecol. 1981;141:709.

136 **Stenquist K et al.** Bacteriuria in pregnancy. Am J Epidemiol. 1989;129:372.

137 **Andriole VT, Patterson TF.** Epidemiology, natural history, and management of urinary tract infections in pregnancy. Med Clin North Am. 1991;75: 359–75.

138 **Dukes MNG et al.** Meyler's Side Effects of Drugs. Vol 8 & 9. New York: Excerpta Medica; 1975,1980.

139 **Pedler SJ et al.** Management of bacteriuria in pregnancy. Drugs. 1987;33: 413–21.

140 **Christ W et al.** Specific toxicology aspects of the quinolones. Rev Infect Dis. 1988;10(Suppl. 1):S141–146.

141 **Campbell-Brown M et al.** Bacteriuria in pregnancy treated with a single dose of cephalexin. Br J Obstet Gynaecol. 1983;90:1054.

142 **Warren JW.** The catheter and urinary tract infection. Med Clin North Am. 1991;75:481.

143 **Garibaldi RA et al.** Meatal colonization and catheter-associated bacteriuria. N Engl J Med. 1980;303:316.

144 **Daifuku R, Stamm WE.** Association of rectal and urethral colonization with urinary tract infection in patients with indwelling catheters. JAMA. 1984; 252:2028.

145 **Kunin CM.** Urinary tract infections. Surg Clin North Am. 1980;60:223.

146 **Burke J et al.** Evaluation of daily meatal care with polyantibiotic ointment in prevention of urinary-catheter associated bacteriuria. J Urol. 1983;129:331–34.

147 **Thompson RL et al.** Catheter-associated bacteriuria: failure to reduce attack rates using periodic installations of a disinfectant into urinary drainage systems. JAMA. 1984;257:747–51.

148 **Harding GKM et al.** How long should catheter-acquired urinary tract infection in women be treated? Ann Intern Med. 1991;144:713–19.

149 **Mountokalakis T et al.** Short-term versus prolonged systemic antibiotic prophylaxis in patients treated with indwelling catheters. J Urol. 1985;134: 506–8.

150 **Nyren P et al.** Prophylactic methenamine hippurate or nitrofurantoin in patients with an indwelling urinary catheter. Ann Clin Res. 1981;13:16–21.

151 **Dukes MN et al.** Meyler's Side Effects of Drugs. 12th ed. The Netherlands: Elsevier Publications; 1992:718.

152 **Davies DM, ed.** Textbook of Adverse Drug Reactions. 4th ed. Oxford: Oxford Medical Publications; 1991:32.

153 **Burka ET et al.** Clinical spectrum of hemolytic anemia associated with glucose-6-phosphate dehydrogenase deficiency. Ann Intern Med. 1966;64:817.

154 **Wing LMH et al.** Co-trimoxazole as an inhibitor of oxidative drug metabolism: effects of trimethoprim and sulfamethoxazole separately and combined on tolbutamide disposition. Br J Clin Pharmacol. 1985;20:482.

155 **Kaufman JM et al.** Potentiation of warfarin by trimethoprim-sulfamethoxazole. Urology. 1980;16:601.

156 **O'Reilly RA.** Stereoselective interaction of trimethoprim-sulfamethoxazole with the separated enantiomorphs of racemic warfarin in man. N Engl J Med. 1980;302:333.

157 **Hansten PD, Horn JR.** Drug Interactions & Updates Quarterly. Vancouver: Applied Therapeutics; 1995.

158 **D'Arcy PF.** Nitrofurantoin. Drug Intell Clin Pharm. 1985;19:540–47.

159 **Kalowski HA et al.** Crystalline and macrocrystalline nitrofurantoin in the treatment of urinary tract infections. N Engl J Med. 1974;290:385.

160 **Cuhna BA.** Nitrofurantoin—current concepts. Urology. 1988;32:67–71.

161 **Koch-Weser J et al.** Adverse reactions to sulfisoxazole, sulfamethoxazole and nitrofurantoin. Arch Intern Med. 1971; 128:399.

162 **Hawley HB et al.** Nitrofurantoin pneumonitis. Med Times. 1982;110:34–9.

163 **Holmberg L et al.** Pulmonary reactions to nitrofurantoin. 447 cases reported to the Swedish Adverse Drug Reaction Committee. 1966–1976. Eur J Resp Dis. 1981;62:180–89.

164 **Penn RG et al.** Adverse reactions to nitrofurantoin in the UK, Sweden and Holland. Br Med J. 1982;284:1440–442.

165 **Elston RA et al.** Possible interaction of ciprofloxacin and cyclosporin. J Antimicrob Chemother. 1988;22:679.

166 **Avent CK et al.** Synergistic nephrotoxicity due to ciprofloxacin and cyclosporin. Am J Med. 1988;85:452–53.

167 **Hooper TL et al.** Ciprofloxacin: a preferred treatment for Legionella infections in patients receiving cyclosporin A. J Antimicrob Chemother. 1988;22: 952–53.

168 **Lang J et al.** Cyclosporin A pharmacokinetics in renal transplant patients receiving ciprofloxacin. Am J Med. 1989;87(Suppl. 5A):825–95.

169 **Kruger HU et al.** Investigation of potential interaction of ciprofloxacin with cyclosporine in bone marrow transplant recipients. Antimicrob Agents Chemother. 1990;34:1048–52.

170 **Elder NC.** Acute urinary tract infection in women. Postgrad Med. 1992; 92:159.

Sexually Transmitted Diseases

Teresa A Tartaglione
Connie L Celum

Gonorrhea (See Figure 64.1) 64-2
  Uncomplicated Gonorrhea 64-2
    Transmission 64-2
    Signs and symptoms: Males 64-2
    Diagnosis: Males 64-2
    Signs and symptoms: Females 64-2
    Diagnosis: Females 64-3
    Treatment (See Table 64.1) 64-3
      Ceftriaxone 64-3
      Spectinomycin 64-4
      Quinolones 64-4
      Sexual partners 64-4
      Follow-up 64-4
      Antibiotic-resistant *Neisseria gonorrhoeae*
      (See Figure 64.2) 64-4
  Anorectal and Pharyngeal Gonorrhea 64-5
    Epidemiology 64-5
    Signs and symptoms 64-5
    Treatment 64-5
    Prevention 64-6
Pelvic Inflammatory Disease (PID) 64-6
  Etiology 64-6
  Signs and symptoms 64-6
  Clinical Sequelae 64-6
  Diagnosis and Treatment (See Table 64.2) ... 64-6
Complicated Gonorrhea 64-7
  Disseminated Gonococcal Infection (DGI) 64-7
    Signs and symptoms 64-7
    Treatment (See Table 64.3) 64-7
  Treatment of Gonococcal Endocarditis and
    Meningitis 64-8
  Ophthalmia Neonatorum 64-8
    Prophylaxis 64-8
      Silver nitrate: adverse effects 64-8
    Gonococcal ophthalmia neonatorum 64-8
      Signs and symptoms 64-8
      Treatment failures 64-8
      Management 64-8
  Neonatal disseminated gonococcal infection:
    treatment 64-8
***Chlamydia Trachomatis* (See Table 64.4)** 64-8
  Nongonococcal Urethritis (NGU) 64-9
    Etiology 64-9
    Signs and symptoms 64-9
    Treatment 64-9
      Recurrent infection 64-9
    Sexual partners 64-10
  Lymphogranuloma Venereum (LGV) 64-10

    Etiology and signs and symptoms 64-10
    Treatment 64-10
Syphilis 64-10
  Epidemiology (See Figure 64.3) 64-10
  Clinical Stages 64-10
    Primary 64-12
    Secondary 64-12
    Latent 64-12
    Tertiary 64-12
  Laboratory Tests 64-12
    Dark-field examination 64-12
    Serological tests (See Table 64.5) 64-12
    Nontreponemal tests 64-12
    Treponemal tests (See Table 64.6) 64-13
  Treatment (See Table 64.7) 64-13
    Neurosyphilis 64-13
    Follow-up 64-13
    Pregnancy 64-14
    Jarisch-Herxheimer reaction 64-14
    Neonatal 64-15
Chancroid 64-15
  Signs and Symptoms 64-15
  Treatment 64-15
Bacterial Vaginosis 64-15
  Signs and Symptoms and Diagnosis 64-15
  Treatment 64-15
Trichomoniasis 64-15
  Signs and Symptoms 64-15
  Treatment 64-16
    Metronidazole 64-16
      Adverse effects 64-16
    Pregnancy 64-16
      Treatment 64-16
Genital Herpes 64-16
  Etiology 64-16
  Epidemiology 64-16
  Signs and Symptoms (See Figure 64.4) 64-17
    Recurrence 64-17
  Transmission 64-17
  Diagnostic Tests 64-17
  Treatment 64-18
    Acyclovir (ACV) (See Table 64.8) 64-18
      Adverse effects 64-19
    Patient education and counseling 64-19
  Complications 64-20
    Neonatal 64-20
      Treatment 64-20
Genital Warts 64-21

Although descriptions of sexually transmitted diseases (STDs) can be discerned in the earliest of written records, only recently have the common STDs been differentiated from each other; unique STD syndromes continue to be described today. For example, of the common STDs, bacterial vaginosis was not described clearly as a syndrome (initially called *Haemophilis vaginalis* vag-

initis) until the 1950s; herpes simplex virus (HSV) type 2 (the usual cause of genital herpes) was not differentiated from HSV type 1 until the 1960s; the spectrum of genital chlamydial infections were not well worked out until the 1970s; and the newest sexually transmitted pathogen, the human immunodeficiency virus (HIV), was not recognized until the 1980s. As the medical aspects of STDs have become better understood, social attitudes toward the diagnosis and therapy for STDs have become more enlightened.

This chapter will review the older and the more recently defined STDs. Of special note, however, are the observations of an overall decrease in the prevalence of gonorrhea in the United States and Europe; although, higher rates are being reported in minority and adolescent groups. Additionally, a sharp increase in *Chlamydia trachomatis*, as well as viral STDs (HSV, human papillomavirus, and HIV), has been noted in the 1990s. Acquired immunodeficiency syndrome (AIDS) is discussed in Chapter 68. Treatment modalities, including prevention measures and public health concerns, will be emphasized.

Gonorrhea

Gonorrhea is caused by *Neisseria gonorrhoeae*, a gram-negative diplococcus. In 130 A.D., Galen coined the term gonorrhea (Greek for ''flow of seed'') for the syndrome associated with this infection because he believed the urethral exudate was semen.

Although the role of the gonococcus in causing urethral discharge in men has been known over 100 years, the manifestations of gonorrhea in women have not been studied as well until recently.

In the 1930s, sulfonamides became the first form of effective antimicrobial therapy for gonorrhea, but the penicillins and tetracyclines have been the mainstay of therapy until recently. Newer antimicrobials are required now in many areas of the world because high levels of resistance have been developing to these two antimicrobial classes.

In the U.S., the incidence of gonorrhea rose steadily (15% per year) from the early 1960s through 1975 and then fell steadily from 1976 throughout 1984. It has been estimated that equal numbers were diagnosed but were not reported during this period.[2] Surprisingly, despite the growing fear of AIDS and other viral STDs and aging of the baby boom generation, the incidence of gonorrhea in heterosexuals rose sharply in 1985 for the first time in a decade. Since 1985 it has declined, but this has been largely limited to whites and Asians. (See Figure 64.1.) The highest incidence of gonorrhea is in males aged 21 to 25 years and in females aged 18 to 21 years. Additional demographic risk factors for gonorrhea include low socioeconomic status, urban residence, unmarried marital status, illicit drug use, prostitution, and a previous history of gonorrhea.[3] The risk of gonorrhea has been much higher in homosexual men than in heterosexual men in the past, but the incidence of gonorrhea dropped rapidly in homosexual men during the AIDS era. Data suggest a reversal in this trend with an increase in cases of rectal gonorrhea in homosexual men.[4]

Uncomplicated Gonorrhea

Transmission

1. J.C., a 23-year-old male naval officer, recently stationed in the Philippines, complains of dysuria, meatal pain, and a profuse yellow urethral discharge for 2 days. He admits to extramarital sex with a prostitute over the past week. He is accompanied by his pregnant wife, B.C., who is asymptomatic. J.C. engages in vaginal sex but there is no history of oral or anal sex with either partner.

Assuming the prostitute has gonorrhea, what is the likelihood that J.C. and B.C. have been infected?

Following one or two episodes of vaginal intercourse with an infected prostitute, a man has approximately a 50% risk of acquiring a urethral infection; the risk increases with repeated exposures.[5] The prevalence of infection in women, such as B.C., who are secondary sex contacts of infected men has been reported to be as high as 80% to 90%.[6] Therefore, the likelihood that J.C. and B.C. are infected is high.

Signs and Symptoms: Males

2. What signs and symptoms in J.C. are consistent with the diagnosis of gonorrhea? Describe J.C.'s anticipated clinical course if he is untreated.

In males, gonorrhea usually becomes clinically apparent one to seven days after contact with an infected source. A purulent discharge associated with dysuria is the first sign of infection and both are exhibited by J.C. The discharge, which is presumably caused by chemotactic factors such as C5a that are released when antigonococcal antibody binds complement, may become more profuse and blood-tinged as the infection progresses. Some strains of gonorrhea have a propensity to cause asymptomatic or minimally symptomatic infection, perhaps because they do not generate chemotactic factors in as high a quantity as do others.[7]

The usual course of gonococcal urethritis, if untreated, is spontaneous resolution after several weeks; more than 95% of patients are asymptomatic within six months.[8] Patients with asymptomatic disease serve as reservoirs for the infection. At one time, only females were thought to have asymptomatic gonorrhea, but now it is known that men may be asymptomatic carriers as well.[9]

In the preantimicrobial era, gonococci occasionally spread to the epididymis, causing unilateral epididymitis; the prevalence was 5% or more of patients in some studies. Now epididymitis occurs in less than 1% of men with gonorrhea. Urethral stricture after repeated attacks and sterility after epididymitis are rare complications of gonococcal infection because antibiotics are so effective.

Diagnosis: Males

3. Intracellular gram-negative diplococci were seen on the Gram's stain of J.C.'s urethral exudate. Is any further diagnostic testing required?

Demonstration of intracellular gram-negative diplococci in the Gram's-stained exudate confirms the diagnosis. Until recently, it was recommended by some experts that cultures be reserved for those individuals with negative Gram's stain of urethral exudate. Today, however, cultures are recommended for all patients to permit isolation and testing of the bacteria for antibiotic susceptibility. Cultures usually are performed on Thayer-Martin (TM) medium, an enriched chocolate agar to which vancomycin, colistimethate, and nystatin have been added.[10] Cultures from the throat should be obtained if J.C. was exposed by cunnilingus to the prostitute. In J.C.'s case, a urethral culture is indicated.

Signs and Symptoms: Females

4. B.C. is asymptomatic. What symptoms would be consistent with gonorrhea in B.C.? Will the symptoms differ because she is pregnant? What is the natural course of gonorrhea in women if left untreated?

Since the endocervical canal is the primary site of urogenital gonococcal infection in women, the most common symptom is vaginal discharge due to mucopurulent cervicitis. Many women with gonorrhea have abnormalities of the cervix, including purulent or mucopurulent endocervical discharge, erythema, friability, and ectopy.[11] Urethral or rectal infection also is present in 70% or more of these individuals and may cause dysuria or rectal symptoms,[11] although in our local experience, the prevalence of rectal gonococcal infection in women is considerably lower. The incubation period for urogenital gonorrhea in women is variable, but those who develop local symptoms apparently do so within ten days of exposure.[12] Infection may ascend to the endometrium or fallopian tubes in 15% or more of women causing menorrhagia or lower abdominal pain and pelvic tenderness.[13,14] The assessment of signs and symptoms in women with gonorrhea often is confounded by a high prevalence of coexisting infection, especially with *C. trachomatis* or *Trichomonas vaginalis*.

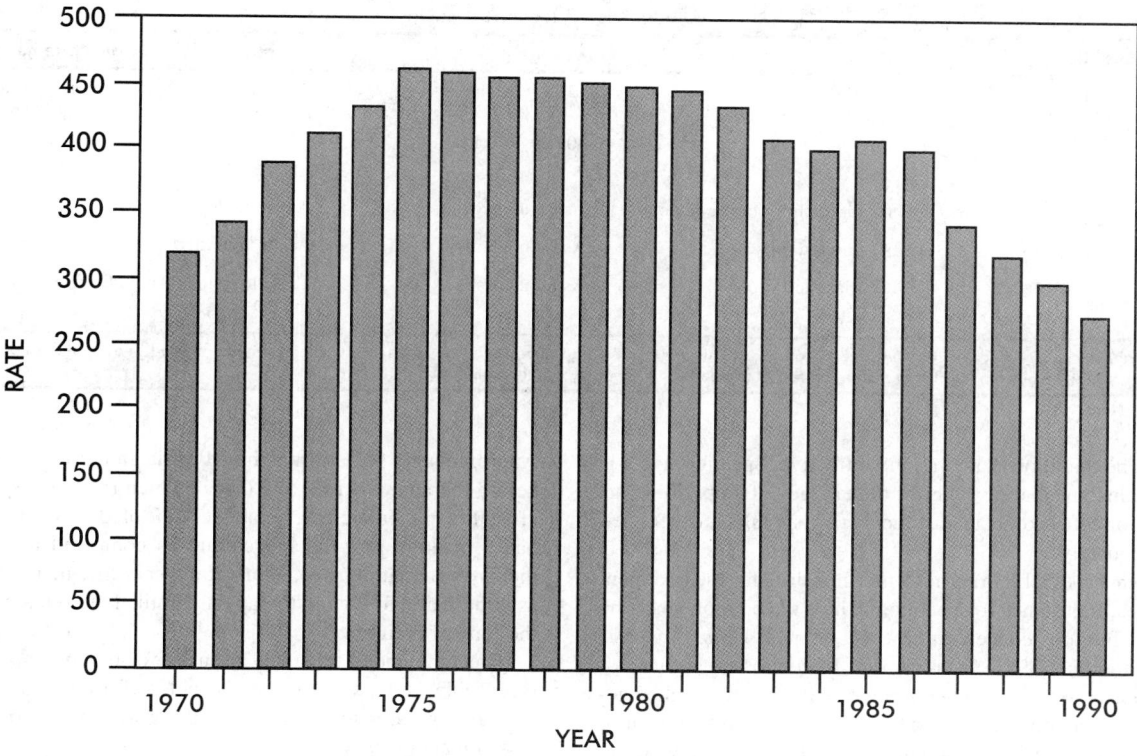

Fig 64.1   Rates of Gonorrhea per 100,000 Population: United States, 1970–1990   Centers for Disease Control Reports.

Although lower genital tract symptoms in women may disappear, they remain carriers of *N. gonorrhoeae* and should be treated. Complications of urogenital gonorrhea in pregnancy include spontaneous abortion,[15] premature rupture of the fetal membranes, premature delivery, and acute chorioamnionitis.[16] Other complications include gonococcal arthritis (see Question 16) and gonococcal conjunctivitis in the newborn (see Question 19). For these reasons, it is critical that B.C. be worked up thoroughly for gonorrhea.

Diagnosis: Females

5. How should gonorrhea be ruled out in B.C.?

B.C. should undergo an endocervical culture which is positive in 80% of women with gonorrhea.[17] This test should be a part of every pelvic examination of sexually active women. In B.C., anal cultures also could be performed since the rectum can serve as a reservoir for gonococci.

Treatment

6. Compare the various drug regimens used for uncomplicated gonorrhea.

Many antimicrobial regimens effectively treat uncomplicated gonorrhea; the recommendations of the Centers for Disease Control (CDC) are summarized in Table 64.1. Although many clinicians traditionally have used single-dose treatment strategies with a beta-lactam or spectinomycin, combination therapies with tetracycline eradicate coexisting chlamydial infections.

The 1985 CDC recommendations removed tetracycline as a therapy of choice because there had been an emergence of tetracycline-resistant *N. gonorrhoeae*. The 1987 guidelines removed aqueous procaine penicillin G as a treatment choice because of its unacceptable toxicity (pain upon injection, procaine reactions) and relatively high resistance rates. Amoxicillin combined with probenecid also no longer is recommended because of relatively high resistance rates. The 1993 CDC guidelines recommend ceftriaxone (Rocephin) as a single, small-volume injection in the deltoid or

cefixime (Suprax) as a single oral dose as therapy for gonorrhea due to the ever-growing problem of plasmid and chromosomally mediated resistance.[18]

Many strains of *N. gonorrhoeae* produce plasmids which inactivate penicillin [penicillinase-producing *N. gonorrhoeae* (PPNG) and/or tetracycline (TRNG)]. Additionally, significant levels of chromosomally mediated resistance to penicillin, tetracycline, and cefoxitin have been reported.[19] Ceftriaxone and cefixime are effective against all types of resistance to date. Since a high percentage of patients with gonorrhea also have coexisting *C. trachomatis* infections, we recommend a concurrent seven-day course of tetracycline or doxycycline (see Question 28). Acceptable alternative regimens are listed in Table 64.1. The final decision regarding the most appropriate therapy is patient specific.

Ceftriaxone is a third-generation cephalosporin that is highly effective against penicillin-susceptible and resistant strains of gonococci. It is given as a single, small-volume intramuscular (IM) injection (e.g., 125 or 250 mg diluted with 0.9 mL 1% lidocaine solution). Many studies have shown a dose of 125 mg to be as efficacious.[20] This feature is a significant advantage over the 10 cc volume required for injection of aqueous procaine penicillin G (APPG). Like APPG, ceftriaxone eradicates anal and pharyngeal gonorrhea. Pregnant women can be treated safely with ceftriaxone or cefixime. Other cephalosporins (notably ceftizoxime, cefuroxime, cefpodoxime) have been found to be as effective, although coverage for pharyngeal infections has not been studied as well. Cefixime appears to be effective against pharyngeal infection, but few patients with pharyngeal gonococcal infection have been studied. Ceftriaxone offers the advantage of being effective against incubating syphilis, whereas cefixime's activity against *Treponema pallidum* is unknown.

Spectinomycin is preferable to cephalosporins in patients with true penicillin allergy. Ceftriaxone and spectinomycin are ineffective against *C. trachomatis* and in the prevention of postgonococcal

Table 64.1	CDC Recommendations for Treatment of Uncomplicated Gonorrhea		
Stage/Presentation	Drugs of Choice	Dosage	Alternatives for Allergic Patients
Urethritis or cervicitis[a]	Ceftriaxone	125 mg IM once	Spectinomycin 2 gm IM once; ciprofloxacin 500 mg PO once; ofloxacin 400 mg PO once
	Cefixime	400 mg PO once	
Rectal			
Women	As for urethritis or cervicitis	As for urethritis	As for urethritis
Men	As for urethritis	As for urethritis	As for urethritis
Pharyngeal	Ceftriaxone	As for urethritis	Ciprofloxacin 500 mg PO once, ofloxacin 400 mg PO once

[a] Since a high percentage of patients with gonorrhea have coexisting Chlamydia trachomatis infections, many clinicians recommend treating all patients with gonorrhea with a 7-day course of doxycycline, as recommended for treatment of Chlamydia.

urethritis. The quinolones are variably effective. Spectinomycin is inactive against incubating syphilis; the efficacy of ampicillin plus probenecid or ceftriaxone against incubating syphilis has not been studied adequately.

Spectinomycin (Trobicin) is not a first-line drug for the treatment of gonorrhea. Resistance to spectinomycin is uncommon since the minimum inhibitory concentration (MIC) for *N. gonorrhoeae* is independent of that of the beta-lactams. In contrast, resistance of *N. gonorrhoeae* to various other antimicrobials often is linked genetically.[21] Spectinomycin should be reserved for the treatment of patients who have failed treatment with ceftriaxone or who are allergic to penicillin. Spectinomycin is not effective in the treatment of pharyngeal gonorrhea, incubating syphilis, or *C. trachomatis*.[22] It currently is recommended for pregnant, penicillin-allergic patients. (See Table 64.3.)

Quinolones. The quinolones also are available as a therapy for gonorrhea. A single oral dose of either ciprofloxacin, ofloxacin, or norfloxacin is effective against greater than 95% of strains.[23,24] The quinolones have variable activity against *C. trachomatis*. Quinolones lack activity against *T. pallidum*.

7. How should J.C.'s urethritis be treated? B.C. has a history of periorbital edema and urticaria secondary to penicillin. Since she is totally asymptomatic and the results of her cultures are pending, should she be treated empirically? If so, what drug(s) would you recommend?

Since J.C. has gonococcal infection limited to the urethra (uncomplicated), a number of treatment regimens are possible as outlined in Question 6. Ceftriaxone or cefixime is the preferred treatment. Because no single-dose therapy for gonorrhea is effective against chlamydia, additional concurrent therapy needs to be administered. Doxycycline or azithromycin are two effective therapies that B.C. could be given to adequately cover the potential of a chlamydia coinfection.

Sexual Partners. B.C. also should be treated even though she appears asymptomatic. Treatment of all sex partners recently (i.e., within four weeks) exposed to patients with gonorrhea is recommended. This is especially true when the partner is pregnant because gonorrhea during pregnancy is associated with chorioamnionitis and prematurity, as well as with neonatal infection. Pregnant women can be treated safely with cephalosporins. Since B.C. is penicillin-allergic, spectinomycin is the treatment of choice.

8. Follow-Up. How does one determine if the drug therapy of gonorrhea has been effective in J.C. and B.C.?

The absence of discharge and other symptoms following therapy is inadequate proof of cure in the female. A retrospective evaluation of 4897 males with gonorrhea revealed that 183 (3.7%) were treatment failures on days three through seven following therapy.[25]

Approximately 95% of men had dysuria and/or urethral discharge before therapy, whereas 582 (11.9%) men remained symptomatic after therapy. Interestingly, about 18% of the symptomatic men had a positive post-therapy culture as compared to only 2% in the asymptomatic group. Thus, it appears that men who become asymptomatic following therapy are unlikely to remain infected at the time of reculture.

If recommended therapies are used for treatment of gonorrhea (see Table 64.1), a test of cure is not performed routinely. However, test of cures still may be useful for pharyngeal gonorrhea and disseminated disease.[18]

For women, repeat cultures should be taken from the endocervical canal, rectum, and the pharynx if warranted by history. In women, 30% of treatment failures are detected by rectal culture only, regardless of whether anorectal infection was detected before therapy.[26]

9. Antibiotic-Resistant *Neisseria Gonorrhoeae*. J.C. states that he was treated with penicillin in the past for a gonococcal infection. Why are penicillins not prescribed routinely today?

Failure of penicillin to eradicate the gonococcus can be due to plasmid (PPNG) or chromosomally mediated (CMRNG) antibiotic resistance. PPNG contain plasmids which produce beta-lactamase, an enzyme that hydrolyzes the beta-lactam ring of penicillin G or ampicillin. Chromosomally mediated resistance does not involve beta-lactamase production and often is associated with increased resistance to other beta-lactams. The clinical significance of CMRNG is questionable since high serum levels of approved antibiotics can be achieved above the MIC, such that treatment failure is unlikely. However, to date, CMRNG remain largely susceptible to ceftriaxone. Chromosomally mediated resistance to spectinomycin has reached levels of up to 10% of strains in a few cities of Europe, the United Kingdom, the U.S., and Asia. High-level tetracycline resistance has been found; gonococci carry plasmid-encoded resistance to ≥16 µg/mL of tetracycline. These strains are known as TRNG. Although not of major concern in the U.S., development of resistance to alternative therapies is a continuing concern.[27]

The first cases of PPNG infection were reported in the U.S. in 1976.[28] PPNG are especially prevalent in Southeast Asia, the Far East, and West Africa where the prevalence often exceeds 50%. In the United States, PPNG strains account for an increasing percentage of gonococcal infections especially in New York City, Los Angeles, Southern Florida, and other selected cities. From 1982 to 1985, the number of PPNG cases rose from 4500 to 8800; the number of cases again doubled between 1984 and 1986 and the incidence continues to rise (see Figure 64.2). TRNG strains were first identified in 1985, but fortunately, most TRNG isolates still are sensitive to beta-lactam antibiotics. As of 1991, 17% of gonococcal isolates had PPNG and/or TRNG.

Due to the increasing frequency of PPNG within the U.S. today, one needs to consider these organisms in the initial management of uncomplicated genital gonorrhea patients who have traveled recently or whose sexual contacts have traveled recently to areas where PPNG is endemic. In endemic areas (areas where PPNG accounts for 3% of all gonococcal isolates), ceftriaxone IM or cefixime orally are the drugs of choice. Antibiotic susceptibility testing is recommended for all isolates associated with apparent treatment failure, all isolates from children, and all isolates from patients with complicated gonococcal disease. Ceftriaxone intramuscularly or cefixime orally also are the drugs of choice in hyperendemic areas (areas in which PPNG accounts for >3% of all gonococcal isolates).

If J.C. had been treated initially with ceftriaxone, he probably would have been free of gonococcal infection within three days. Patients whose test-of-cure culture yields strains of PPNG should be treated with single doses of ceftriaxone 125 mg IM or spectinomycin 2 gm IM. To date, ceftriaxone-resistant strains of *N. gonorrhoeae* have not been reported.

Anorectal and Pharyngeal Gonorrhea

Epidemiology

10. M.B. is a 24-year-old, sexually active homosexual male with a 2 month history of perianal itching, painful defecation, constipation, a bloody mucoid rectal discharge, and a sore throat. Sigmoidoscopy revealed rectal mucosal inflammation but no apparent ulcers or fissures. Stool examination for parasites was negative and a Venereal Disease Research Laboratory (VDRL) test was nonreactive. Rectal and pharyngeal cultures both revealed *N. gonorrhoeae*. How does gonorrhea in homosexual men compare to gonorrhea in heterosexual men?

The most prevalent bacterial STD among the homosexual male population is gonorrhea. Almost all cases of gonorrhea in the het-

erosexual male population are confined to the urethra (99.9%). In contrast, anorectal (46.8%) and pharyngeal (15%) gonococcal infections occur frequently in the male homosexual population.[29] Since 80% to 90% of all pharyngeal and 70% to 90% of all anorectal gonococcal infections are asymptomatic, there is a large reservoir of asymptomatic carriers in the homosexual male population.[30–33] Only 7% of all penile gonococcal infections are asymptomatic by comparison.

Signs and Symptoms

11. Are M.B.'s signs and symptoms consistent with gonorrhea?

Rectal gonorrhea produces the syndrome of proctitis with anorectal pain, mucopurulent anorectal discharge, constipation, tenesmus, and anorectal bleeding. The differential diagnosis of proctitis in the homosexual male includes rectal infection with *N. gonorrhoeae*, *C. trachomatis*, HSV, and syphilis. Proctitis, limited to the distal rectum, should be differentiated from proctocolitis often caused by *Shigella sp.*, *Campylobacter sp.*, or *Entamoeba histolytica* in homosexual men. Rectal symptoms should not be attributed to trauma until specific infections are excluded. The evidence of rectal infection in homosexual men declined because of changing sexual practices in the AIDS era, but may be on the rise once again.[4]

Treatment

12. How should M.B. be managed?

The treatment of choice for patients such as M.B. with anorectal and/or pharyngeal gonorrhea is ceftriaxone 125 to 250 mg IM as a single dose (see Table 64.1). A tetracycline should be given for one week to those with rectal gonorrhea to treat possible coexisting rectal chlamydial infection. Patients such as M.B. with either anorectal or pharyngeal gonorrhea should be advised to avoid further unprotected sexual activity and should be counseled and tested for infection with HIV. Homosexual men exposing themselves to gonorrhea are at exceptionally high risk of HIV infection.

Fig 64.2 Incidence of Plasmid-Mediated Resistance to *Neisseria gonorrhoeae* in the United States between 1987–1990 Centers for Disease Control.

13. What are alternative regimens for patients with isolated anal or pharyngeal gonorrhea?

Women with anorectal gonorrhea alone should be treated with ceftriaxone. Alternative regimens for isolated anorectal infection include spectinomycin or a quinolone. Patients with anorectal gonorrhea who are allergic to penicillin should be treated with 2 gm of spectinomycin hydrochloride IM, which is nearly 100% effective for anorectal gonorrhea. It lacks spirocheticidal activity, however, and is not effective for pharyngeal gonococcal infection.[32,34] Quinolones are effective for pharyngeal gonococcal infection.

Patients with pharyngeal gonorrhea who are truly allergic to penicillin could be treated with a quinolone or trimethoprim (80 mg) and sulfamethoxazole (400 mg) nine tablets daily for five days.[35]

Prevention

14. What measures have been used to prevent the sexual transmission of infection?

Condoms, when used properly, appear to provide a high degree of protection against the acquisition and/or transmission of STDs.[36] The effectiveness of the diaphragm used with a spermicide, or of a spermicide-impregnated cervical sponge, is uncertain. Topical bactericidal agents are ineffective;[37] similarly, urinating, washing, or douching after intercourse is of little value in preventing the transmission of STDs.[37]

The prophylactic administration of antibiotics immediately before or soon after sexual intercourse reduces the risk of infection,[38] but can result in selection and transmission of antibiotic-resistant strains of *N. gonorrhoeae*. Routine antibiotic prophylaxis after all casual sexual encounters is not cost effective and could cause more disease than is prevented. Development of an effective vaccine and public health measures, such as education, are the best hopes for prevention of gonorrhea.

Pelvic Inflammatory Disease (PID)

The term pelvic inflammatory disease commonly has been used for a variety of acute and chronic conditions caused by ascending, surgical, or trauma-related infections in the female genital tract. This term does not denote the primary infection site (the fallopian tubes) nor the causative micro-organisms. PID also has been used to connote an infection that occurs acutely when either vaginal or cervical micro-organisms traverse the sterile endometrium and ascend to the fallopian tubes. Acute salpingitis also may be used to describe an acute infection of the fallopian tubes. Therefore, the terms PID and salpingitis will be used interchangeably in the following discussion to denote an acute infection involving the fallopian tubes.

Approximately 85% of all cases of acute PID occur by sexual transmission in females of reproductive age with another 15% following procedures requiring instrumentation including intrauterine device insertion, abortion, or dilation and curettage.[39] Acute PID develops in an estimated 1% of sexually active young women annually and causes more morbidity in women (15 to 25 years of age) than all other serious infections combined.[39,40] "Silent" and atypical PID may be more common than acute PID and present challenges in reducing morbidity from PID. Worldwide PID is a leading cause of infertility and in the U.S. it is considered responsible for the upswing in ectopic pregnancy in the early 1980s.[41] In 1986 the cost of health care for PID and its sequelae was estimated to be four billion dollars annually.[42]

Etiology

The etiology of PID is polymicrobial, and the traditional classifications of gonococcal and nongonococcal disease can be misleading.[40,43,44] Sexually transmitted organisms that are thought to cause PID include *N. gonorrhoeae*, *C. trachomatis*,[45,46] *Mycoplasma hominis*,[47,48] and *Ureaplasma urealyticum*.[46-48] It generally is accepted that *N. gonorrhoeae* and *C. trachomatis* are the major pathogens responsible for sexually transmitted PID.[43] Facultative enteric gram-negative bacilli and a variety of anaerobic bacteria also have been implicated.

Signs and Symptoms

The onset of symptoms of abdominal pain attributable to PID due to either gonococci or chlamydia often occurs soon after the menstrual period. The onset of chlamydial PID is slower than gonococcal disease; the duration of pain is longer and the clinical manifestations are milder.[49,50] Symptoms of vaginal discharge, menorrhagia, and dysuria commonly are associated with PID. Signs include uterine and adnexal tenderness and a mucopurulent endocervical exudate. Since clinical diagnosis is predictive of PID only 65% of the time, laparoscopy is considered to be the definitive diagnostic tool.[49]

Clinical Sequelae

An abscess may form in the pelvic or abdominal cavity and in one or both of the fallopian tubes. Chronic abdominal pain developed in 18% of women with PID in our study and may be due to pelvic adhesions surrounding the tubes and ovaries.[39] Tubal occlusion and fibrosis secondary to fallopian tube inflammation (salpingitis) result in infertility in up to 13% of women following a single episode of PID and in up to 60% of women after three or more episodes of PID.[51] The risk of ectopic pregnancy is increased approximately eightfold after one or more episodes of PID.[39]

Diagnosis and Treatment

15. B.O., a 19-year-old, sexually active female, complains of mild dysuria, a purulent vaginal discharge, fever, and moderately severe, bilateral, lower abdominal pain of three days' duration. Examination confirms uterine and adnexal tenderness, a purulent cervical exudate, and a temperature of 38 °C. Laboratory examinations show a normal VDRL and urinalysis. A pregnancy test performed at this time was negative. The peripheral white blood cell (WBC) count was mildly elevated (11,000/mm³) with 70% polymorphonuclear leukocytes. Does B.O. have PID? How should she be treated? [SI unit: WBC count 11 × 10⁹/L]

Although fever and leukocytosis often are absent in mild or subacute PID, the presence of these findings in a woman with adnexal tenderness and cervical exudate increases the likelihood of acute PID. Treatment of PID varies with the severity of the infection and is based upon the assumption that the precise bacteriologic etiology often is unknown (see Table 64.2). The most recent CDC recommendations for ambulatory therapy include a single dose of cefoxitin (Mefoxin) or cefotetan (Cefotan) plus probenecid or ceftriaxone alone, followed by doxycycline for ten days. To improve anaerobic coverage in PID treatment, the 1993 CDC STD guidelines include ofloxacin 300 mg orally twice daily plus either metronidazole 500 orally twice daily or clindamycin 450 mg orally four times a day, both for 14 days, as an alternative to cefoxitin or ceftriaxone plus doxycycline. The cost of the ofloxacin regimen is considerably higher. Tetracyclines no longer are used for treatment of PID as monotherapy because they lack optimal activity against gram-negative aerobic and anaerobic organisms and against some strains of *N. gonorrhoeae*. However, a tetracycline or alternative drug active against *C. trachomatis* always should be included.

Patients such as B.O. with moderate to severe PID should be hospitalized and treated empirically with parenteral antibiotics af-

Table 64.2	Antimicrobial Regimens Recommended by the CDC for Treatment of Acute Pelvic Inflammatory Disease			
Treatment Setting, Drugs, Schedule	**Advantage**	**Disadvantage**	**Clinical Considerations**
Inpatient			
Cefoxitin or cefotetan plus doxycycline Administer cefoxitin (2 gm IV Q 6 hr) or cefotetan (2 gm IV Q 12 hr) plus doxycycline (100 mg IV Q 12 hr) for a total of at least 4 days and for at least 48 hr after defervescence. Continue doxycycline (100 mg PO, BID) after discharge to complete 10–14 days of therapy	Optimal coverage of *N. gonorrhoeae* (including resistant strains) and *C. trachomatis*	Possible suboptimal anaerobic coverage	Penicillin-allergic patients also may be allergic to cephalosporins. Tetracycline use in pregnant patients may cause discoloration of teeth and reversible inhibition of skeletal growth in the fetus
Clindamycin plus an aminoglycoside Administer clindamycin (900 mg IV Q 8 hr) plus gentamicin or tobramycin (1.5–2 mg/kg IV Q 8 hr) for a total of at least 4 days and for at least 48 hr after defervescence. Continue clindamycin (450 mg PO QID) after discharge to complete 10–14 days of therapy	Optimal coverage of anearobes and gram-negative enteric rods	Possible suboptimal coverage of *N. gonorrhoeae* and *C. trachomatis*	Patients with decreased renal function may not be good candidates for aminoglycoside treatment or may need a dose adjustment
Outpatient			
Cefoxitin or cefotetan plus probenecid or ceftriaxone and doxycycline Administer cefoxitin (2 gm IM once) or cefotetan (2 gm IV once) plus probenecid (1 gm PO once) or ceftriaxone (250 mg IM once). Concomitantly administer doxycycline (100 mg PO Q 12 hr) for a total of 10–14 days	Good to excellent coverage of *N. gonorrhoeae* and optimal coverage of *C. trachomatis*	Possible suboptimal anaerobic coverage	Considerations outlined above with regard to penicillin-allergic patients and tetracycline use in pregnant patients apply
Ofloxacin plus metronidazole or clindamycin Administer ofloxacin (400 mg PO BID) plus either metronidazole (500 mg PO BID) or clindamycin (450 mg PO QID) for a total of 10–14 days			

ter a cervical discharge has been obtained for Gram's stain and culture. Intravenous cefoxitin plus doxycycline are the CDC's first-line drugs of choice and should be given for at least four days and at least 48 hours beyond the first signs of improvement. Oral doxycycline should be continued to complete 10 to 14 days of total therapy. Clindamycin (Cleocin) plus an aminoglycoside can be used alternatively in penicillin-allergic and pregnant females.

Complicated Gonorrhea

Disseminated Gonococcal Infection (DGI)

Signs and Symptoms

16. S.P., a 28-year-old, sexually active female, was seen for stiffness and pain of the right wrist and left ankle and fever (38 °C). Upon physical examination, the knee and wrist joints were found to be hot, red, and swollen; papules and pustular lesions were observed on S.P.'s legs and forearms. A latex fixation test for rheumatoid factor was negative. A tap of the right knee yielded an effusion with a WBC count of 34,000/mm³ [80% polymorphonuclear (PMN) leukocytes]. Cultures of the skin lesions were negative; however, *N. gonorrhoeae* was isolated from the throat, cervix, blood, and synovial fluid. A chest radiograph, echocardiogram, and electrocardiogram all were normal, and no murmur could be appreciated. Assess S.P.'s clinical presentation. [SI unit: WBC count 34 × 10⁹/L]

S.P.'s signs, symptoms, and laboratory findings are consistent with gonococcal bacteremia which today occurs in less than 1% of women and men with gonorrhea. The most common manifestation of gonococcemia is the gonococcal arthritis-dermatitis syn-

drome or disseminated gonococcal infection exhibited by S.P. Symptoms include fever, occasional chills, a mild tenosynovitis of the small joints, and skin lesions involving primarily the distal extremities that are petechial, papular, pustular, and hemorrhagic in appearance.[52,53]

Diagnosis of DGI is made by Gram's stain and culture. Blood cultures are positive only in 25% of DGI cases, even when they are cultured early in the course of the infection.[54] The low positive yield from blood cultures may be due to the low inoculum and/or intermittent bacteremic period. Additionally, inhibitory substances in blood culture media, like sodium polyanethole-sulfonate may reduce the chance of recovering *N. gonorrhoeae*.[55] Routine culture of the urethra, cervix, pharynx, and rectum should be performed in any patient suspected of having DGI.

Treatment

17. How should S.P. be managed? How quickly will she respond to therapy?

Patients like S.P. with gonococcal arthritis and bacteremia should be hospitalized for treatment with ceftriaxone 1 gm IM or IV daily for three days (see Table 64.3). If the strain is proven to be sensitive to penicillin, therapy may then be changed to cefixime 400 mg orally twice daily or ciprofloxacin 500 mg orally twice daily for a total of seven days. Since patients with gonococcal arthritis caused by PPNG have been encountered, therapy should be initiated with ceftriaxone. An alternative therapy for the patient who is allergic to penicillin is spectinomycin 2 gm IM every 12 hours.

Table 64.3	Treatment of Disseminated Gonococcal Infection[a]	

No Penicillin Allergy
Parenteral
Ceftriaxone 1 gm IV or IM Q 24 hr *OR* Cefotaxime 1 gm IV 8 hr *and*
Doxycycline 100 mg PO BID[b] *OR* Erythromycin base 500 mg PO
QID[b] (if pregnant)
Oral
Amoxicillin 500 mg *and* clavulanic acid 125 mg PO TID *OR*
Ciprofloxacin 500 mg PO BID *OR* Cefixime 400 mg PO BID

Penicillin Allergy
Parenteral
Spectinomycin 2 gm IM Q 12 hr *and* Doxycycline 100 mg PO BID[b]
OR Erythromycin base 500 mg PO QID[b] (if pregnant)
Oral
Ciprofloxacin 500 mg PO BID

[a] Duration of treatment is 7 days.
[b] For possible concomitant Chlamydia infection; treat for 7 days.

Symptoms and signs of tenosynovitis should be improved markedly within 48 hours. Septic gonococcal arthritis with purulent synovial fluid may require repeated aspiration and will resolve more slowly.

Treatment of Gonococcal Endocarditis and Meningitis

18. How should gonococcal endocarditis and meningitis be treated?

Gonococcal endocarditis and meningitis require high-dose IV therapy such as ceftriaxone (2 gm IV every 24 hours) for ten or more days in the case of meningitis, and for three to four weeks in the case of endocarditis.

Ophthalmia Neonatorum

Prophylaxis

19. A.C., a female with no history of gonorrhea, has given birth by cesarean section to a full-term infant. Is prophylaxis for gonococcal ophthalmia indicated? If so, which agents are effective?

Prophylaxis for gonococcal ophthalmia neonatorum is recommended for all newborns in the U.S. Approximately one-third of infants born to infected mothers develop gonococcal ophthalmia. The CDC and the American Academy of Pediatrics recommend 1% silver nitrate solution from a single-dose ampule or single-use tubes of ophthalmic ointments containing 1% tetracycline or 0.5% erythromycin as effective and acceptable regimens for prophylaxis of gonococcal ophthalmia neonatorum.[56–58] Prophylaxis should be given within one hour of the birth. Erythromycin and tetracycline ophthalmic ointments may or may not be more effective than silver nitrate in preventing chlamydial conjunctivitis. If ocular prophylaxis is not administered immediately after delivery, but is delayed for several minutes, efficacy may be reduced.

Prevention of ophthalmia neonatorum is a principal goal of medical care of the newborn. The optimal method of achieving this goal is to prevent, identify, and treat gonorrhea in the mother so that exposure of the newborn is eliminated. Therefore, endocervical cultures for gonorrhea should be performed in the first trimester and repeated in the third trimester in women at high risk for gonorrhea. Women with gonorrhea early in pregnancy have a 30% incidence of recurrence during pregnancy.[59]

20. Silver Nitrate: Adverse Effects. A.C.'s full-term infant above received 1% silver nitrate. Two hours later, the nurse noted inflamed conjunctiva and swelling around the eyes. Was this caused by the silver nitrate? Can it be prevented?

Silver nitrate drops can produce a mild chemical conjunctivitis in as many as 90% of infants. The conjunctivitis usually appears within six hours of therapy and clears spontaneously. Use of single dose ampules minimizes the risk of severe chemical conjunctivitis.

Flushing the eyes with sodium chloride or sterile water after the instillation of these agents does not decrease the incidence of chemical conjunctivitis and, in fact, may decrease the efficacy of prophylactic therapy.[60] Therefore, the newborn's eyes should not be flushed following the instillation of any of the prophylactic medications.[56,58]

Gonococcal Ophthalmia Neonatorum

21. T.P. is a 2060 gm newborn whose mother had a documented gonococcal infection at term. What prophylactic therapy should T.P. receive for gonococcal ophthalmia?

Topical prophylaxis alone is insufficient for infants such as T.P. who are born to mothers with documented gonococcal infections. These infants should receive, in addition to prophylaxis, ceftriaxone intramuscularly in a single dose of 125 mg for full-term infants. T.P., who is a low birth weight infant, should receive 25 to 30 mg/kg.[56,58] Ceftriaxone has replaced aqueous penicillin G due to the increased prevalence of PPNG.

22. Signs and Symptoms. T.P. was treated with 1% silver nitrate drops at birth. Three days later he developed increasing inflammation and a profuse purulent discharge from the left eye. A Gram's stain of the discharge revealed gram-negative intra- and extracellular diplococci. A presumptive diagnosis of gonococcal ophthalmia was made. Is T.P.'s presentation consistent with gonococcal ophthalmia?

Yes. Gonococcal ophthalmia neonatorum characteristically develops one to three days after birth, but the onset ranges from 1 to 12 days following delivery.[61] Initially, a profuse purulent conjunctival discharge is seen; this is followed by the development of moderate to severe edema and hyperemia of the eyelids.[57] The newborn usually is afebrile and has no signs of systemic disease. The differential diagnosis includes conjunctivitis due to chlamydia, other bacteria, or HSV.

23. Treatment Failures. T.P. failed to respond to silver nitrate. What are the causes of prophylaxis failures?

Prophylaxis failure can occur when drugs are applied inappropriately and when eyes are flushed following instillation of the prophylactic agent. They also occur in infants with well-established infections at the time of delivery and infants born long after rupture of the membranes.

24. Management. How should T.P. be managed?

Gonococcal ophthalmia is highly contagious; therefore, all patients should be hospitalized and isolated for 24 hours after initiating therapy. Neonates with gonococcal ophthalmia should receive IV or IM ceftriaxone (25 to 50 mg/kg/day) for seven days. Saline irrigation of the eyes should be performed as needed. Topical antibiotic preparations are insufficient when used alone and not required when appropriate systemic antibiotic therapy is given.[56,58]

Neonatal Disseminated Gonococcal Infection: Treatment

25. How should neonatal DGI and meningitis be managed?

Neonatal DGI and meningitis should be treated with ceftriaxone (25 to 50 mg/kg every 24 hours) for at least 10 to 14 days.

Chlamydia Trachomatis

C. trachomatis was first isolated from patients with lymphogranuloma venereum (LGV). However, chlamydial genital infections were not studied extensively until improved procedures for culture isolation and serology were developed and applied during the 1960s and 1970s.[62] In the U.S., chlamydial genital infection has become recognized increasingly among adolescents and young adults. Asymptomatic infection is observed frequently among both men and women. Sequelae in women include PID, ectopic pregnancy, and infertility.

C. trachomatis, an intracellular obligate parasite, is a difficult organism to demonstrate in clinical specimens because this requires cell culture techniques that routinely are not available to the practitioner. Since some practitioners have access to facilities for isolation of *C. trachomatis*, most chlamydial infections are diagnosed and treated upon clinical impression alone. New nonculture diagnostic tests, such as immunofluorescence and polymerase chain reaction, are sensitive methods for detecting *C. trachomatis*. These newer tests can be used on urine, as well as genital swab specimens.

The variety of clinical syndromes that now are known to be caused by *C. trachomatis* are outlined in Table 64.4. Note that the infections closely resemble those caused by the gonococcus which is the reason why many patients presenting with these syndromes are treated with drugs effective against both organisms.

Serovars A, B, and C of *C. trachomatis* are responsible for hyperendemic blinding trachoma; serovars D, E, F, G, H, I, J, and K are responsible for nongonococcal urethritis (NGU), cervicitis, endometritis, salpingitis, and epididymitis. LGV is caused by serovars L[1], L[2], and L[3]. Serovars D through K can be transmitted to the newborn during delivery through an infected cervix, causing inclusion conjunctivitis or chlamydial pneumonia in the newborn.[64]

C. trachomatis is sensitive to the tetracyclines, erythromycin, azithromycin, and ofloxacin but is unresponsive to the penicillins, cephalosporins, aminoglycosides, clarithromycin, most fluoroquinolones (except ofloxacin), and metronidazole (Flagyl).[64–68] Sulfamethoxazole also is active against chlamydiae, although trimethoprim offers minimal, if any, synergy when used with sulfamethoxazole against this organism.[65,69] Little clinical data are available, however, on the use of sulfa drugs for chlamydia and they are not used commonly.

Nongonococcal Urethritis (NGU)

Etiology

26. T.K., a 26-year-old, sexually active male, complains of mild dysuria and a mucoid-like urethral discharge which started about 15 days after his last intercourse. There was no fever, lymphadenopathy, penile lesions, or hematuria. A Gram's stain smear of an anterior urethral specimen showed 20 PMNs per oil immersion (1000×) field and no intracellular gram-negative diplococci. What pathogens are associated with NGU?

C. trachomatis is responsible for 20% to 40% of all cases of NGU,[63,70] and *U. urealyticum* may cause 25% to 40% of NGU cases.[66,71] Together, *C. trachomatis* and *U. urealyticum* account for no more than 70% to 80% of all reported cases of NGU. Of the remaining 20% to 30% of cases, a small proportion are caused by *T. vaginalis* or HSV, and the rest are considered idiopathic.[64,70,72,73]

Signs and Symptoms

27. Describe the clinical presentation of NGU. Is T.K.'s presentation consistent with NGU? How does one differentiate between NGU and gonococcal urethritis?

T.K.'s presentation is typical. Compared to gonococcal urethritis, nongonococcal urethritis typically produces less severe and less frequent dysuria and less penile discharge. Chlamydial urethral infection is completely asymptomatic more often than gonococcal urethral infection. The incubation period for gonococcal urethritis is two to seven days, whereas the incubation period for NGU is typically two to three weeks.

Nonetheless, NGU and gonococcal urethritis cannot be differentiated reliably solely upon the basis of symptoms and signs. If there is objective evidence of a urethral discharge (expressed by milking the urethra) or ≥5 PMN/1000 × field in the urethral secretion, the diagnosis of NGU is made by excluding the presence of *N. gonorrhoeae* by Gram's stain and/or culture.

Treatment

28. How should T.K. be treated?

Doxycycline is the drug of choice for the treatment of NGU and is given in a dose of 100 mg two times a day for seven days.[64,66,72] Because doxycycline can be given twice a day and because it is available as a generic product, it is preferred over tetracycline and minocycline. Erythromycin, in a dosage equivalent to 500 mg of base or stearate orally every six hours, is an alternative CDC-approved regimen. Azithromycin 1 gm orally (single dose) is an accepted alternative for chlamydial infections, but limited data are available about its use for empiric treatment of urethritis and cervicitis. While azithromycin appears to have similar efficacy and toxicity to doxycycline,[68] doxycycline has several advantages including extensive use and lower cost. Azithromycin, however, has the advantage of single-dose administration which may lead to higher cure rates due to improved compliance.

Patient counseling should emphasize the need to avoid further sexual activity without protection by a condom until the prescribed course of therapy has been completed by the patient and his sexual partner(s).

29. Recurrent Infection. T.K. was treated with doxycycline 100 mg BID for 7 days. He remained asymptomatic for 14 days following completion of his therapy when he again noticed similar symptoms of dysuria and a mucoid-like urethral discharge. How should T.K.'s recurrent infection be treated?

The major problem encountered in the treatment of NGU is the high rate of recurrent infections. Approximately 15% to 30% of

Table 64.4	Clinical Parallels between Genital Infections Caused by *N. Gonorrhoeae* and *C. Trachomatis*[a]	
	Resulting Clinical Syndrome	
Site of Infection	*N. gonorrhoeae*	*C. trachomatis*
Men		
Urethra	Urethritis	Nongonococcal urethritis, postgonococcal urethritis
Epididymis	Epididymitis	Epididymitis
Rectum	Proctitis	Proctitis
Conjunctiva	Conjunctivitis	Conjunctivitis
Systemic	Disseminated gonococcal infection	Reiter's syndrome
Women		
Urethra	Acute urethral syndrome	Acute urethral syndrome
Bartholin's gland	Bartholinitis	Bartholinitis
Cervix	Cervicitis	Cervicitis
Fallopian tube	Salpingitis	Salpingitis
Conjunctiva	Conjunctivitis	Conjunctivitis
Systemic	Disseminated gonococcal infection	Arthritis-dermatitis (Reiter's syndrome)

[a] Reprinted with permission from reference 63.

patients will experience recurrent urethritis within six weeks after completing a course of tetracycline.[74] The rate of recurrence is highest in patients with idiopathic urethritis; that is, those not infected with *C. trachomatis* or *U. urealyticum*. Recurrence suggests reexposure to an untreated partner whereas persistent urethritis (without improvement during therapy) suggests the presence of tetracycline-resistant *U. urealyticum*, infection with either *T. vaginalis* or HSV, urethral stricture, or chronic prostatitis.[72,75] NGU which persists or recurs despite treatment of the female partner often responds to retreatment with doxycycline, erythromycin 500 mg four times daily for 14 to 21 days, or azithromycin 1 gm as a single dose.

Men with acute epididymitis often have chlamydial or gonococcal infection, particularly if they are less than 35 years of age or have a urethral discharge. Older men with epididymitis more often are infected with *Escherichia. coli* or other urinary pathogens. If testicular tenderness is present with urethritis, and the clinical impression is consistent with epididymitis, we recommend ceftriaxone 250 mg IM followed by doxycycline 100 mg orally twice a day or ofloxacin 300 mg orally twice a day for ten days.

Sexual Partners

30. A.C., T.K.'s girlfriend, comes into the clinic 3 weeks after T.K.'s last visit. She is worried that she may have a similar infection although she has no signs or symptoms. What clinical manifestations of chlamydial infections are seen in women? Should A.C. be treated for suspected chlamydial infection?

In the absence of cultures for chlamydia, empirical treatment of women who are sexual partners of men with NGU is recommended. Many partners will be asymptomatic, but from 30% to 70% are culture positive if tested. A.C. should be examined carefully for mucopurulent cervicitis and salpingitis. While many women with chlamydial infection of the cervix are asymptomatic, at least one-third will have evidence of mucopurulent discharge and hypertrophic ectopy.[76] Gram's stain of appropriately collected mucopurulent endocervical discharge from these patients shows many PMNs and an absence of gonococci.

Regardless of findings, treatment should be initiated with the same tetracycline regimen used for nongonococcal urethritis. If A.C. is pregnant, tetracyclines and fluoroquinolones should be avoided; erythromycin or amoxicillin (500 mg three times a day for seven to ten days) should be prescribed. Coinfection with chlamydia is common in heterosexual men and women with gonorrhea. Therefore, drug regimens effective against both organisms are recommended in patients with gonorrhea to prevent postgonococcal chlamydial morbidity (epididymitis, mucopurulent cervicitis, salpingitis) and to reduce the genital reservoir of *C. trachomatis*.

Lymphogranuloma Venereum (LGV)

Etiology and Signs and Symptoms

31. S.F., a 32-year-old male student who recently arrived from Uganda, presents to the STD clinic with a chief complaint of pain and swelling in the groin. He reports the appearance of a small ulcer on his penis about 2 weeks ago which resolved rapidly. Upon examination, he has a bubo (inflammatory swelling of one or more lymph nodes in the groin) with surrounding erythema on his right side. S.F. also has a fever (39 °C). Laboratory findings are remarkable for a mild leukocytosis (WBC 12,000 cells/mm³).

What organisms are responsible for LGV? Describe its clinical course. What subjective and objective manifestations in S.F. are consistent with LGV? [SI unit: WBC 12,000 × 10⁹/L]

Three stages of LGV infection are recognized in heterosexual men.[77] During Stage I, a small genital papule or vesicle appears from 3 to 12 days following exposure.[78] The patient usually is asymptomatic and the ulcer heals rapidly, leaving no scar.[77,78] This

primary lesion is consistent with the penile ulcer reported by S.F. Many patients with LGV recall no primary lesion.

Stage II is characterized by acute painful lymphadenitis with bubo formation (the inguinal syndrome); it often is accompanied by pain and fever as illustrated by S.F. Without treatment, the buboes may rupture, forming numerous sinus tracts that drain chronically. Healing occurs slowly and the majority of patients suffer no serious sequelae.[79] Patients in this stage also may present with an anogenitorectal syndrome which is accompanied by proctocolitis and hyperplasia of intestinal and perirectal lymphatic tissue. Late or tertiary manifestations include perirectal abscesses, rectovaginal fistulas (in women), rectal strictures, and genital elephantiasis.[80] Appropriate treatment of stage II LGV usually prevents these late complications.

An acute anorectal syndrome of LGV occurs in homosexual men who acquire the infection through rectal receptive intercourse. In these cases, a primary anal ulcer may be noted with associated inguinal adenopathy (anal lymphatics drain to inguinal nodes). Subsequently, acute hemorrhagic proctocolitis occurs with tenesmus, rectal pain, constipation, and a mucopurulent, bloody rectal discharge. Rectal biopsy may show granulomatous colitis, mimicking Crohn's disease. Perirectal pelvic adenopathy occurs.

Treatment

32. How should S.F. be managed?

Current CDC recommendations for lymphogranuloma venereum include treatment with oral doxycycline (100 mg every 12 hours) or erythromycin (500 mg every six hours) for 21 days. Surgical intervention may be needed for later forms of the disease.

Syphilis

Epidemiology

Syphilis, a disease caused by the spirochete *T. pallidum*, is an extremely common infection; an estimated 5% to 10% prevalence rate has been reported in various autopsy series.[81] The incidence of primary and secondary syphilis in the U.S. increased in the late 1980s related to crack/cocaine use. In general, it appears that the incidence of syphilis has increased in the heterosexual population whereas there has been a dramatic decline in homosexual males. Coincident with the increase in heterosexuals, rates of congenital syphilis have risen markedly (see Figure 64.3).

The clinical manifestations of syphilis have not changed appreciably since their first description. However, early diagnosis, treatment, and greater physician/patient awareness of the disease have reduced the incidence of its severe forms. Penicillin continues to be the mainstay of therapy. Vaccine development, although premature, hopefully will advance as more is learned about the biology of *T. pallidum*.

Clinical Stages

33. D.M., a 27-year-old homosexual male, presents to the STD clinic with complaints of malaise, headache, and fever of 4 days' duration. He also reveals that he had a sore on his penis about 8 weeks ago, but it resolved. Upon examination, he is afebrile and has a widespread maculopapular skin rash that also involves the soles of the feet; general lymphadenopathy also is appreciated. Past medical history is unremarkable except for one episode of gonorrhea 2 years ago which was treated with procaine penicillin. Laboratory findings include a normal peripheral WBC count, a negative serology for HIV antigen, and a positive Rapid Plasma Reagin (RPR) test and Fluorescent Treponemal Antibody Absorption (FTA-Abs) test. Describe the clinical course of syphilis. Are D.M.'s symptoms consistent with this infection?

Fig 64.3 Incidence of Syphilis (Primary and Secondary): By Sex and Congenital Syphilis (<1 Year), United States between 1970–1991
Centers for Disease Control. *The CDC changed their case definition of syphilis in 1990, thus, the distortion in this graph beginning in 1990.

Primary Stage

The average incubation period for syphilis is three weeks and ranges from 10 to 90 days.[82] During this incubation period, *T. pallidum* can be demonstrated in the lymph and blood. The primary chancre develops at the site of inoculation as a painless papule which becomes ulcerated and indurated. The ulcer is nontender and filled with spirochetes. The chancre usually involves the penis in the heterosexual male; the penis or anus in the homosexual male; and the vulva, perineum, or cervix of the female. Occasionally, the lip or tongue is involved. Regional lymph nodes are enlarged, firm, and nontender. Unfortunately, the typical chancre described above often is missed, particularly in women or homosexual men.[83] Without treatment, the primary chancre will resolve spontaneously, usually in two to six weeks. The differential diagnosis of genital ulcers includes chancroid and genital herpes. Like chancroid, genital herpes produces painful, superficial, noninduated ulcers with tender inguinal adenopathy. However, unlike chancroid, lesions of genital herpes characteristically proceed through a vesicular state and often are associated with urethritis, cervicitis, and constitutional symptoms, such as fever and chills.

Secondary Stage

Approximately six weeks after a chancre first appears, the untreated patient will begin to manifest signs and symptoms of the secondary stage of syphilis. This is illustrated by D.M.

Skin lesions of secondary syphilis may erupt in a variety of patterns and they usually are widespread in distribution. A macular syphilid often is the earliest manifestation in this stage. The lesion is round or oval, occurs primarily on the trunk, and is rose or pink in color. As lesions mature they become papular or nodular, with scaling (the so-called papulosquamous rash). The differential diagnosis of diffuse papulosquamous rashes includes psoriasis, pityriasis rosea, and lichen planus. In syphilis, the palms and soles are characteristically involved and oral lesions (''mucous patches'') may occur. Generalized lymphadenopathy usually is present and patching alopecia may be seen. The most infectious lesion of secondary syphilis is condyloma latum. Condylomata lata are characteristically wet, indurated lesions occurring in women in most intertriginous areas, such as the labia minora and the perianal area.

Laboratory studies sometimes reveal anemia, leukocytosis, or an increased erythrocyte sedimentation rate.[84] Up to 10% of patients have mild hepatitis.[85] Other manifestations of secondary syphilis include aseptic meningitis, neuropathies, and glomerulonephritis.[86]

Latent Stage

By definition, persons with serological evidence for syphilis who have not been treated but who have no clinical manifestations have latent syphilis.

The latent stage is divided into two phases: the early latent (less than one year's duration) and late latent (more than one year's duration). In the Oslo study of patients with untreated syphilis, 25% experienced secondary relapses, usually within the first year.[87] Patients who relapse to the secondary stage are infectious; those in the late latent stage are not infectious.

Tertiary Stage

Morbidity and mortality of syphilis in adults are due primarily to a variety of late manifestations involving the skin, bones, central nervous system (CNS), and cardiovascular system. Infectious granulomas (gumma), the characteristic lesions of tertiary syphilis, now are observed infrequently. Most gummas respond quickly to specific therapy, although if critical organs are involved (heart, brain, liver), they can be fatal.[88]

The most common manifestations of syphilitic cardiovascular disease are aortic insufficiency and aortitis, with aneurysm of the ascending aorta.

Late neurosyphilis may be asymptomatic or accompanied by a variety of manifestations; the most common syndromes are meningovascular syphilis, general paresis, tabes dorsalis (locomotor ataxia), and optic atrophy. In patients with asymptomatic neurosyphilis, examination of the cerebrospinal fluid (CSF) typically reveals mononuclear pleocytosis, an elevated protein concentration, and a positive VDRL reaction.

Patients with asymptomatic neurosyphilis are at increased risk for the development of clinical neurologic disease. Meningeal neurosyphilis typically begins abruptly with hemiparesis or hemiplegia, aphasia, or seizures.[89] General paresis is characterized by extensive parenchymal damage and includes abnormalities associated with the mnemonic paresis [personality, affect, reflexes (hyperactive), eye (Argyll Robertson pupil), sensorium (hallucination, delusions, illusions), intellect (decreased recent memory, calculations, judgment) and speech]. Tabes dorsalis occurs following demyelinization of the spinal cord. Symptoms observed include an ataxic, wide-based gait and foot slap; paresthesias; bladder irregularities; impotence; areflexia; and loss of position, deep pain, and temperature sensation. The Argyll Robertson pupil, seen in both paresis and tabes dorsalis, is a small, irregular pupil which reacts to accommodation but not to light.

Laboratory Tests

34. Evaluate D.M.'s laboratory findings.

Dark-Field Examination

Exudate expressed from the chancre or from condyloma latum is examined with a dark-field microscope. The diagnosis of syphilis is based upon demonstration of spirochetes with characteristic corkscrew morphology and mobility. Dark-field examination is reliable only when the microscopist is experienced in the diagnosis of syphilis. We perform three dark-field examinations on consecutive days before considering the test negative in suspected primary syphilis.

Serological Tests

Serological tests become reactive during the primary stage, but as shown in Table 64.5, they may be negative at the time of presentation with primary syphilis. When the history or examination suggest primary syphilis, a VDRL should be sent to the laboratory or an RPR should be performed in the clinic (see discussion on nontreponemal tests below). If initial serology and dark-field examinations are negative, the serology should be repeated in one to four weeks to exclude primary syphilis.

Serologic tests are essentially always positive during secondary syphilis. There are two types of tests used for the serodiagnosis of syphilis: nontreponemal tests, which measure serum concentrations of reagin (antibody to cardiolipin) and treponemal tests, which detect the presence of antibodies specific for *T. pallidum*.[90]

Nontreponemal Tests

Nontreponemal tests are not specific for *T. pallidum* but can be quantified. They are inexpensive and useful for screening large numbers of people. The most widely used nontreponemal tests are the VDRL test and the RPR Card test.

The result reported in the quantitative VDRL test is the most dilute serum concentration with a positive reaction. This test may be used to follow the decline in VDRL titer after effective therapy. (See Question 37.) When false-positive tests occur (Table 64.6), the titer usually is low (e.g., VDRL titer $\leq$1:8).[91]

Table 64.5	False Negative Results with VDRL and FTA-Abs Tests[a]	
	Percentage	
Stage of Syphilis	VDRL	FTA-Abs
Primary	24%	14%
Secondary	<0.1%	<0.1%
Early latent	5%	1%
Late latent	28%	5%

[a] VDRL = Venereal disease research laboratory; FTA-Abs = Fluorescent treponemal antibody absorption.

Treponemal Tests

Specific treponemal tests are most useful to confirm a positive nontreponemal test. The FTA-Abs test is the most commonly used treponemal test. Since the FTA-Abs test requires fluorescence microscopy, it is relatively difficult and expensive to perform.

The Treponema Pallidum Immobilization (TPI) test, the Microhemagglutination (MHA-TP) test, and the Hemagglutination test for syphilis (HATTS) are three other treponemal tests. The TPI test is used rarely because of its cost and complexity. The MHA-TP and HATTS tests are both easier to perform and less expensive than the FTA-Abs test, but are less sensitive in primary syphilis.

Treatment

35. How should D.M. be treated?

Penicillin G is the drug of choice for the treatment of all stages of syphilis (see Table 64.7).[86,92] Every effort should be made to rule out penicillin allergy before choosing other antimicrobials which have been studied much less extensively than penicillin in the treatment of syphilis. If penicillin is contraindicated, the alternative is tetracycline or doxycycline. If the patient is penicillin allergic, is not pregnant, and cannot tolerate tetracycline or doxycycline, erythromycin 500 mg orally four times a day for two weeks may be used. If compliance and follow-up cannot be ensured, the patient should be skin tested for hypersensitivity to penicillin and if truly allergic, be desensitized before treatment with that antibiotic. Although certain cephalosporins (e.g., ceftriaxone) may prove useful as alternatives for syphilis, there currently are insufficient data concerning *in vivo* efficacy. Since *T. pallidum* has not developed antimicrobial resistance, treatment regimens for syphilis have changed relatively little in recent years.

As shown in Table 64.7, recommended therapy for primary, secondary, or latent syphilis (with a negative CSF) of less than one year's duration is a single, intramuscular 2.4 MU dose of benzathine penicillin G. Doxycycline 100 mg orally twice a day for 15 days is the recommended alternative. Latent syphilis (more than one year's duration) and cardiovascular syphilis are treated with intramuscular benzathine penicillin G weekly (2.4 MU) for a total of three weeks. The alternative regimen is doxycycline 100 mg twice a day for 30 days. CSF examination is recommended if nonpenicillin therapy is being considered.

Neurosyphilis

36. Would D.M.'s treatment differ if his CSF had tested positive for syphilis?

When conventional IM doses of benzathine penicillin G are administered, no measurable levels of penicillin are obtained in the CSF.[93] It now is recognized that treatment failures, as well as late clinical progression to neurosyphilis, can occur following treatment with the recommended intramuscular regimen.[94,95] There-

fore, the CDC guidelines recommend treatment of neurosyphilis with aqueous penicillin G, 2 to 4 MU IV every four hours for 10 to 14 days. Neurosyphilis also can be treated with procaine penicillin (2.4 MU IM) plus probenecid (500 mg orally every six hours) for 10 to 14 days, although some experts add benzathine penicillin G after the completion of aqueous penicillin G or procaine penicillin in the hope of providing persistent treponemicidal blood/tissue/CSF levels. Alternatives to penicillin which can be considered include doxycycline and ceftriaxone. The dose and duration of therapy using these alternatives and the plan for monitoring response should be discussed with an expert consultant. Penicillin-allergic patients who cannot tolerate tetracycline should have their allergy confirmed.

Follow-Up

37. D.M. was treated with a single IM dose of benzathine penicillin (2.4 MU). How should his response to therapy be monitored?

Physical examinations and quantitative VDRL tests for early syphilis as well as congenital stages should be repeated at least 3, 6, and 12 months after therapy.[86] Patients who also are infected with HIV should have more frequent serologic testing (i.e., 1, 2, 3, 6, 9, and 12 months). Patients with syphilis of more than one year's duration should be retested six months after treatment. Close serologic monitoring is necessary if antibiotics other than penicillin are used; CSF examination should be performed in these patients at their last follow-up visit. Patients with neurosyphilis should be monitored serologically every six months; CSF examinations should be repeated at six month intervals until normal. If still abnormal at two years, retreatment should be considered. Return of lesions, a fourfold increase in titer, or a titer of ≥1:8 which does not fall at least fourfold within 12 months indicates the need for retreatment due to relapse or reinfection. Suspected treatment failures, especially if there is an abnormal CSF, should be treated as described for neurosyphilis. However, false-positive serologic results should be ruled out (see Table 64.6).

In two years, most patients with early syphilis become seronegative. However, if the disease is treated during the late stages, complete seroreversal may not occur. Patients treated with oral doxycycline or erythromycin are less likely to become seronegative.[90] Therapy is considered adequate in patients who never become seronegative if the titer decreases fourfold. While the disease process may be halted in patients with tertiary syphilis, existing damage to the cardiovascular system or nervous system cannot be reversed.

Table 64.6	Causes of False Positive VDRL and FTA-Abs Tests[a]
VDRL	**FTA-Abs**
Technical error	Technical error
Other spirochetal diseases (yaws, bejel, pinta)	Genital herpes
	Heroin addiction
Lupus erythematosus	Leprosy
Hashimoto's thyroiditis	Mononucleosis
Malaria	Collagen vascular disease
Mononucleosis	Pregnancy
Pregnancy	
Vaccinations	
Immunizations	
IV narcotic abuse	

[a] VDRL = Venereal Disease Research Laboratory; FTA-Abs = Fluorescent Treponemal Antibody Absorption.

Table 64.7	Treatment Guidelines for Syphilis[192]	
Stage of Syphilis	Patients without Penicillin Allergy	Patients with Penicillin Allergy
Primary, secondary, or early latent[a]	Benzathine penicillin G, 2.4 MU single dose IM (1.2 MU in each hip)	Doxycycline 100 mg BID x 15 days
Late latent or latent of uncertain duration	Lumbar puncture CSF *normal*: Benzathine penicillin G, 2.4 MU/week IM x 3 weeks. CSF *abnormal:* Treat as neurosyphilis	Lumbar puncture *CSF normal:* Treat as neurosyphilis *CSF abnormal:* Treat as neurosyphilis
Neurosyphilis[b] (asymptomatic or symptomatic)	Aqueous procaine penicillin G, 2.4 MU IM QD plus probenecid 500 mg QID x 30 both for 10 days followed by benzathine penicillin G 2.4 MU IM weekly x 3 weeks. *Or* aqueous penicillin G, 12–24 MU/day IV for at least 10 days	Doxycycline 100 mg BID x 30 days
Late cardiovascular or benign tertiary	Benzathine penicillin G, 2.4 MU/wk x 3 weeks	Treat as neurosyphilis
Congenital	Aqueous procaine penicillin G, 50,000 U/kg IM QD for at least 10 days *Or* aqueous crystalline penicillin G, 50,000 U/kg/day, IM or IV, in 2 divided daily doses for at least 10 days *Or only* if CSF *normal:* benzathine penicillin G, 50,000 U/kg IM in a single dose	Antibiotics other than penicillin should not be used[c]
Syphilis in pregnancy	According to stage	See text

a Some experts recommend multiple doses if benzathine penicillin G for HIV-infected patients with late syphilis.

b Benzathine penicillin G does not achieve treponemicidal levels in the cerebrospinal fluid and has given inferior results for treatment of neurosyphilis. For penicillin-allergic patients, doxycycline is recommended though there are no controlled studies to supports its efficacy. Doxycycline has theoretical efficacy for neurosyphilis because of doxcycline CSF penetration, but has not been examined carefully. Hospitalization and desensitization are recommended now for pregnant women who are penicillin-allergic.

c Failure of erythromycin to prevent congenital syphilis has been documented repeatedly in the literature. Penicillin allergy should be confirmed by skin test before alternative regimes are used. Some experts recommend hospitalization and desensitization of penicillin-allergic women in order to permit penicillin therapy. All infants born to women treated during pregnancy with erythromycin *must* be treated with penicillin at birth.

Pregnancy

38. N.W., a 27-year-old female in the 19th week of gestation, has a positive VDRL and FTA-Abs. How should N.W. be managed? How would management be altered in the face of penicillin allergy?

Although pregnancy has been a reported cause of false-positive nontreponemal[91] and even treponemal tests, the presence of both a positive treponemal test and a nontreponemal test virtually excludes a false-positive reaction.[95] The next step is to determine whether N.W. already has been treated adequately. If she previously has received adequate treatment and follow-up shows no evidence of persistence or recurrence of syphilis, she requires no further therapy, although the infant should be observed carefully. If N.W. has not been treated previously for syphilis, she should be treated with penicillin in the same doses recommended for nonpregnant women.

The goal of therapy should be to treat the mother with syphilis as soon as possible. Therapy initiated after 18 weeks of gestation will cure the fetal spirochetemia, but may not prevent the development of congenital syphilis. If the mother is left untreated, the fetus may be aborted, stillborn, or born with congenital syphilis (see Question 35).[96]

There is no completely satisfactory alternative for the pregnant woman allergic to penicillin. Tetracycline, as well as doxycycline, should be avoided during pregnancy, especially during the second or third trimester, because of tetracycline's known effects upon the fetus (tooth staining and damage to the long bones) and its association with maternal liver and kidney damage.[97,98]

Erythromycin has been used in the past for treatment of pregnant patients with syphilis. Fetal blood levels of erythromycin, however, are only 6% to 20% of those achieved in the maternal blood.[99] This may explain why some patients treated with erythromycin aborted or gave birth to stillborn infants. At least eight cases of syphilis in pregnancy treated with erythromycin have been reported; five delivered babies with congenital syphilis.[100,101] Therefore, erythromycin no longer is recommended as therapy for syphilis in the pregnant patient. A woman with a history of allergy to penicillin should be skin tested. If the allergy is confirmed, she should be desensitized and treated with penicillin.[102] It is possible that newer cephalosporins may ultimately prove to be more acceptable alternatives to penicillin G in the pregnant woman with syphilis who is allergic to penicillin, assuming that appropriate precautions are taken to minimize risks of cross-allergenicity.

During pregnancy, the patient should be followed with monthly quantitative VDRL titers to evaluate the effectiveness of therapy; thereafter, she should be followed as any other syphilitic patient.

Jarisch-Herxheimer Reaction

39. N.W. was treated with an IM injection of 2.4 MU of benzathine penicillin G. Six hours later she complained of diffuse myalgias, chills, headache, and an exacerbation of her rash. She was tachypneic, but normotensive. What has happened? How should N.W. be managed?

N.W. has developed the Jarisch-Herxheimer reaction, a benign, self-limited complication of treponemal antibiotic therapy which develops in a high proportion of patients within a few hours after treatment of early syphilis. The pathogenesis of the syndrome is uncertain. The reaction is *not* an allergic reaction to penicillin and normally subsides spontaneously in 18 to 24 hours even while antibiotics are continued.[103,104] Notably, the Jarisch-Herxheimer reaction can occur following the administration of many antimicrobials and is not exclusive to penicillins. The primary risk of this reaction has been noted in pregnant women who have suffered a miscarriage, premature labor, or fetal distress.[18] The reaction in most cases can be controlled with antipyretics; antibiotic therapy should not be discontinued. Pregnant women should seek medical attention if contractions or a change in fetal movements are noted.

Neonatal

40. How should N.W.'s baby be treated if a diagnosis of congenital syphilis is confirmed?

Infants born to mothers treated for syphilis during pregnancy should be carefully examined at birth, at one month, and every three months for 15 months and then every six months until the VDRL is negative or stable at a low titer. If the serologic test at three months is positive, the infant should be treated.[105] Aqueous penicillin G 50,000 U/kg IM or IV daily for ten days is recommended by the CDC. Procaine penicillin G 50,000 U/kg/day IM for at least ten days is an alternative regimen. Additionally, infants should be treated at birth, even if they are asymptomatic, when maternal treatment is unknown, inadequate, or if infant follow-up cannot be guaranteed. A CSF examination should be performed before treatment is begun in all infants with congenital syphilis to rule out neurosyphilis. Although benzathine penicillin (50,000 U/kg IM) as a single dose is recommended by some clinicians to treat infants who may not be followed, data on the efficacy of this treatment are lacking and benzathine penicillin is not recommended by the CDC.

Chancroid

Chancroid or soft chancre is a painful genital ulcer disease that often is associated with tender inguinal adenopathy. It is caused by *Haemophilus ducreyi*, a gram-negative bacillus.

Chancroid is endemic in developing countries and has been implicated as a cofactor for transmission of HIV. Microepidemics occur occasionally in the U.S. For example, the incidence of chancroid increased during the mid 1980s in New York, Los Angeles, Chicago, New Orleans, and Southern Florida.

Signs and Symptoms

41. E.J., a 31-year-old male, presents to the STD clinic with complaints of tender lesions on the penis and inguinal regions. He noticed the penile lesions on the external surface of the prepuce (foreskin) 2 days before his visit. The lesions were sharply demarcated but were not indurated; the base of the penile ulcer was covered by a yellow-gray purulent exudate. Right inguinal adenitis was present and extremely painful on palpation. A dark-field examination of the purulent exudate was negative. Gram's stain revealed a mixture of gram-positive and gram-negative flora. E.J. claims to have no drug allergies. What is the natural course of chancroid? Does E.J. have signs or symptoms consistent with chancroid? What diagnostic procedures are necessary?

Uncircumcised males are at increased risk of infection. The chancroid ulcer appears three to ten days after exposure and begins as a tender red papule which becomes pustular and ulcerates within two days. As illustrated by E.J., the ulcer may be covered by a grayish or yellow exudate. Multiple ulcers are seen in about 50% of cases.[106] Tender inguinal lymph nodes also are seen in up to 50% of patients, and these may become fluctuant. Aspiration of fluctuant nodes may be necessary to prevent rupture.

Treatment

42. How should E.J.'s chancroid be treated?

Most strains of *H. ducreyi* produce a TEM-type beta-lactamase, and many strains are resistant to the antimicrobials that traditionally were used to treat chancroid, such as sulfonamides[107,108] and tetracycline.[109] The drug of choice today is a single dose of ceftriaxone (260 mg IM); erythromycin (500 mg orally four times a day for seven days), or azithromycin (1 gm orally once) also are regimens recommended by the CDC. Alternative regimens recommended by the CDC include amoxicillin 500 mg plus clavulanic acid 125 mg orally three times daily for seven days or ciprofloxacin 500 mg orally

twice daily for three days.[18] Ciprofloxacin is contraindicated in pregnant and lactating women and children ≤17 years of age. Since E.J. has no history of penicillin hypersensitivity, ceftriaxone as a single dose is the preferred treatment. Single-dose therapy may not be effective if the patient is coinfected with HIV.

Bacterial Vaginosis

Bacterial vaginosis [formerly called nonspecific vaginitis[110] or *Gardnerella vaginalis* (formerly *Haemophilus vaginalis*)] is associated with an increased, malodorous vaginal discharge. The normal vaginal lactobacillus flora is overgrown by *Mobiluncus sp.*, *Bacteroides sp.*, *Peptococcus sp.*, and *M. hominis*, and increased numbers of *Gardnerella*.

Up to 50% of sexually active women are infected with *G. vaginalis* at any one time; yet only some of these are symptomatic or have signs of abnormal vaginal discharge.[111,112] It is unknown why some women colonized with these organisms develop vaginosis while others do not.[112] Occasionally *G. vaginalis* is found to colonize the urethras of men.[113]

Signs and Symptoms and Diagnosis

43. S.D. is a 19-year-old, sexually active female with a 1-week history of a moderate vaginal discharge that has a "fishy" odor, most notable following coitus. She has no complaints of vaginal pruritus or burning. On examination, the discharge appears gray, homogeneous, and it is notably malodorous. A wet mount of the vaginal secretion revealed few leukocytes and numerous "clue cells." The vaginal pH was 4.8, and a characteristic fishy odor was noted when the discharge was mixed with 10% KOH. Does S.D. have signs and symptoms consistent with bacterial vaginosis? What diagnostic tests are required?

S.D.'s symptoms and signs are typical of bacterial vaginosis. The clinical diagnosis can be confirmed by a vaginal Gram's stain that shows overgrowth of the vagina with *G. vaginalis* and other organisms noted above.

A small drop of 10% KOH mixed with vaginal secretion will yield a transient "fishy" odor due to the increased production of biogenic diamines (positive amine test).[114] A wet preparation of the specimen will reveal "clue cells": exfoliated vaginal epithelial cells with adherent coccobacillary pathogens.[110,111] If there are many white cells, other infections (e.g., *T. vaginalis*) should be suspected.

Treatment

46. How should S.D. be treated?

Oral metronidazole, 500 mg twice a day for seven days, is the most effective treatment of bacterial vaginosis. Nearly all women are clinically normal at the end of therapy, and 85% remain well six weeks after completion of therapy.[112,115] Ampicillin no longer is considered an alternative treatment, because 50% of women develop recurrent symptoms within six weeks.[115,116] Clindamycin, 300 mg orally, two times a day for seven days has been recommended as an alternative regimen by the CDC. Metronidazole 0.75% gel twice daily for five days and clindamycin 2% cream every night at bedtime for seven days are effective topical therapies.

In the absence of signs of bacterial vaginosis, isolation of flora from the vagina is not an indication for treatment. There so far is no proof that treatment of sex partners is beneficial.

Trichomoniasis
Signs and Symptoms

45. N.J. is a 32-year-old female with a recent history of profuse vaginal discharge with vaginal irritation. A wet mount

examination of vaginal secretions revealed numerous trichomonads. Examination confirms the presence of an increased, yellow vaginal discharge. What subjective and objective clinical data support a diagnosis of trichomoniasis?

Trichomoniasis is an STD caused by the protozoan *T. vaginalis.* Trichomoniasis in the female can be symptomatic or asymptomatic. Because trichomoniasis often is associated with other genital infections, it is necessary to exclude other cofactors in order to define the clinical manifestations of trichomoniasis. These manifestations include those symptoms and signs presented by N.J. Colposcopy shows red spots on the cervix (strawberry cervix) in 50% or more of those with positive wet mounts.[117]

In the male *T. vaginalis* presumably infects the urethra, although the site of infection (urethra versus prostate) is uncertain. Men with *T. vaginalis* infection usually are asymptomatic.

Diagnosis of trichomoniasis on clinical grounds alone is insufficient. Laboratory confirmation by observation of motile trichomonads on a fresh preparation of vaginal secretions mixed with saline in symptomatic patients with a yellow vaginal discharge is fairly sensitive. Culture is required to detect infections that are *not* associated with vaginal discharge.

Treatment

Metronidazole

46. How should N.J.'s trichomoniasis be treated?

The only drugs effective for the treatment of *T. vaginalis* are the nitroimidazoles. In the U.S. metronidazole is the only available nitroimidazole. Metronidazole has been used in a dose of 250 mg three times a day for seven days. Now the preferred dose for males or females is a single dose of 2 gm; sex partners should be treated simultaneously. Cure rates are at least 85% to 90%.[118–121] Treatment "failures" usually represent reinfection or noncompliance. However, occasional strains are encountered that are not inhibited by 6.4 µg/mL of metronidazole under aerobic conditions. These resistant strains usually can be eliminated by higher, more prolonged doses of metronidazole.[122] Because doses of 3 gm/day for longer than a few days can cause irreversible peripheral neuropathy, this treatment should be monitored closely by an expert.

47. Adverse Effects. M.J. was treated with metronidazole, 250 mg TID for 7 days. On the fourth day of therapy, while attending a party, N.J. developed a severe headache, followed by nausea, sweating, and dizziness. Could N.J.'s symptoms be caused by metronidazole?

Minor side effects associated with metronidazole therapy include nausea, vomiting (especially with single dose therapy), headache, skin rashes, and alcohol intolerance.[118] The alcohol intolerance is due to a metronidazole-induced inhibition of aldehyde dehydrogenase, which results in the build-up of high serum acetaldehyde levels. Severe "antabuse reactions" are uncommon; however, patients still should be warned about the possibility of nausea, vomiting, flushing, and respiratory distress following ethanol ingestion.[123,124]

48. S.G. also is concerned that metronidazole may inactivate oral contraceptives. What evidence supports this claim?

To date, there are no data that indicate that metronidazole "inactivates" oral contraceptives. Other antibiotics may alter the metabolism of contraceptives, most notably rifampin.[125]

Pregnancy

49. S.G., a 31-year-old female, is in her first trimester of pregnancy and has a history of recurrent trichomoniasis. She now complains of a frothy, yellow vaginal discharge. The preliminary diagnosis of trichomoniasis is confirmed by a wet mount examination of vaginal secretions which revealed numerous trichomonads. S.G. has read much of the lay press on

metronidazole and is concerned about her own safety as well as that of her fetus. Can metronidazole be used in S.G.?

Metronidazole is mutagenic in facultative bacteria and contains a nitro-reductase enzyme. Long-term, high-dose metronidazole in laboratory mice is associated with the development of pulmonary and hepatic tumors; however, treated rodents appear to live longer than untreated rodents.[126] The significance of these findings is uncertain, and no increased incidence of cancer in human patients treated with metronidazole has been documented yet.[127,128]

Human studies have not documented conclusively an increased risk of congenital defects in infants born to women using metronidazole during pregnancy.[129] Two small studies have failed to show increased teratogenicity.[130,131] However, insufficient numbers of women have been studied in a controlled fashion to rule out even a small risk. Presently, metronidazole is not administered during the first trimester of pregnancy and is avoided if possible during the second and third trimesters. If the pregnant patient is symptomatic, as in the case of S.G., local therapy should be tried.

50. Treatment. How should S.G. be treated?

Clotrimazole (Lotrimin) cream, 100 mg intravaginally at bedtime for seven days, can be used; however, this agent is not as effective as oral metronidazole.[132,133] A trial of vinegar (2 tablespoons per quart of water daily for seven days, then twice weekly) or other acidifying douches also can be used. She can be treated with metronidazole after the first trimester.

Genital Herpes

The word *Herpes* is of Greek origin and means "to creep." Herpes simplex virus is a DNA-containing virus. HSV consists of two antigenic distinct serotypes, HSV_1 and HSV_2. HSV_1 is the primary cause of herpes labialis (cold sores), herpes keratitis, and herpetic encephalitis. Genital herpes and neonatal herpes primarily are the result of HSV_2 infections. However, 10% to 15% of all reported cases of genital herpes are due to HSV_1 infections acquired through oral sex.[134–136]

Etiology

Most infants are exposed to HSV_1 within 18 months of birth as confirmed by antibody tests.[137] The infection often is asymptomatic and generally is acquired via primary infection of the respiratory tract. The initial, primary disease is a gingivostomatitis characterized by vesicles in the oral cavity and occasionally, an elevated temperature; life-threatening encephalitis or keratitis may appear during this interval. Usually after primary exposure, HSV_1 enters cells of the trigeminal ganglion where it may remain latent for the lifetime of the host.[138]

Initial HSV_2 infections usually follow puberty and coincide with the onset of sexual activity, although transfer to a neonate from an infected mother can occur. After primary infection, the virus enters a state of latency in the sacral dorsal root ganglia in many infected individuals; a high percentage of infected persons may never manifest the disease clinically.[138]

In both HSV_1 and HSV_2 infections, the latent virus can reactivate. Recurrent disease may occur even when circulating antibody and sensitized lymphocytes are present. Clinically, the lesions periodically erupt at the same location; the interval between episodes varies widely between individuals. Stress, sunshine, fever, and other nonspecific stimuli appear to be associated with reactivation of HSV.

Epidemiology

Although herpes was recognized several thousand years ago, genital herpes was not described formally until the eighteenth century. The prevalence of genital herpes appears to have increased dramatically in the U.S. over the last 20 years according to a national survey.[139] Genital HSV infection was diagnosed in approximately 5% of all individuals attending STD clinics in King County, Washington, in the early 1980s.[140] In the nonSTD clinic patient populations, HSV_2 has been isolated in 0.25% to 3.0% of patients.[141,142] The seroprevalence for HSV_2 antibody is approximately 25%.[143]

The prevalence of antibody to genital herpes is greater in non-Caucasian groups and increases with age.[144] Demographic characteristics obtained at the University of Washington indicate that the mean number of lifetime sexual partners before acquisition of the disease was 8.8 in women compared to 32.8 in men. The mean time from the last sexual exposure to the onset of disease was 5.8 days.[140]

Signs and Symptoms

51. B.J., a 28-year-old, sexually active male, complains of painful penile lesions and tender inguinal adenopathy. The lesions were vesicular and limited to the scrotum, glands, and shaft of the penis. The onset of the lesions was preceded by a 1-week period of fever, malaise, headache, and itching. Viral culture of the lesions was positive for HSV infection.
Describe the typical course and clinical presentation of herpes genitalis in men and women. What subjective and objective clinical data in B.J. are compatible with herpes genitalis?

Most initial episodes of genital herpes, especially in the male, are symptomatic. As illustrated by B.J., the symptoms usually start about one week after the initial exposure with prodromal signs of tingling, itching, paresthesia, and/or genital burning.[134] The prodromal stage, which can last from a few hours to several days, is followed by the appearance of numerous vesicles. The vesicles eventually erupt, resulting in painful genital ulcers. The pain and edema associated with genital herpetic lesions, especially if they are infected secondarily, can be severe enough to result in dysuria and urinary retention. Bilaterally distributed lesions of the external genitalia are characteristic. The lesions usually are limited to the glands, corona prepuce, and shaft of the penis in the male, and to the vulva and vagina in the female. However, lesions can occur on the buttocks, thighs, and urethra.[134,138] In addition, women with primary and nonprimary genital HSV_2 infections have concomitant HSV cervicitis at rates of 90% and 70%, respectively.[145,146] Rectal and perianal HSV_2 infections increasingly are being recognized. HSV proctitis usually is seen in homosexual men and heterosexual men who engage in anorectal intercourse. Symptoms include anorectal pain and discharge, tenesmus, and constipation.

Prior infections with HSV_1 appear to ameliorate the severity of first episodes of genital herpes. In primary infections, the local symptoms of pain, itching, and urethral or vaginal discharge last from 11 to 14 days, with a complete disappearance of lesions in three to six weeks.[134] The clinical course of primary herpes is presented in Figure 64.4. Of importance, however, is that only one-third of patients seropositive for HSV_2 recall signs or symptoms for herpes, indicating the importance of subclinical and asymptomatic disease.[147]

Recurrence

52. Is B.J.'s infection likely to recur?

Most patients (50% to 80%) will experience a recurrence of their initial infection.[134,135] The rate of repeat infections varies among individual patients; however, less than 10% of patients will have more than four such episodes per year for the first two years and some patients may never experience a recurrence.[138] The severity of the primary episode as well as the host's immune response to the disease appear to influence the subsequent recurrence rate.[148]

Recurrent infections usually appear at or near the site of the initial infection and prodromal symptoms are reported by about 50% of persons with recurrent infection. Males appear to have slightly more frequent recurrences. In contrast to primary infections, there are fewer lesions and they are often unilateral.[134,138] Constitutional symptoms such as lymphadenopathy, fever, and malaise generally are milder.[134,149] Recurrent infections are shorter in duration (average: one week); local symptoms such as pain and itching last four to five days and the lesions themselves last seven to ten days.[134,145,149] Overall, recurrent infections are less severe than primary infections and reappear less frequently with time.

Transmission

53. B.J. states that this is the first time he has had such lesions and that he has had only one sexual partner for the last 14 months. His sexually active female partner has no prior history of herpes genitalis or any other venereal disease. The couple is very curious as to how B.J. acquired his infection. How is HSV transmitted?

Transmission of HSV occurs by direct contact with active lesions or from a symptomatic or asymptomatic person shedding virus at a peripheral site, mucosal surface, or secretion.[150] Genital HSV_2 infections usually are acquired through sexual (vaginal or anorectal) intercourse, whereas genital HSV_1 infections are acquired via oral-genital sexual practices. Since HSV is inactivated readily by drying and exposure to room temperature, aerosol and formitic spread are unusual means of transmission.[151] Condoms may act as an effective barrier to viral transmission, although this method does not offer complete protection.[140]

A patient with genital herpes is contagious only when he or she is shedding the virus. The patient will begin to shed virus during the prodromal phase, which may be several hours to days before the actual lesions first appear.[150] Lesions are most contagious during the ulcerative phase. The median duration of viral shedding as defined from onset to the last positive culture is about 12 days.[140] The mean time from the onset of vesicles to the appearance of the crust stage ($\approx$10.5 days) correlates well with the duration of viral shedding. However, there is considerable overlap between the duration of viral shedding and the duration of crusting. Therefore, patients should be advised to refrain from sexual activity until the lesions have completely healed. Women appear to require a longer total lesion healing time than men, 19.5 and 16.5 days, respectively.[140] The mean duration of viral shedding from the cervix is 11.4 days.

A genital herpes infection may be acquired from an individual who has never had symptomatic genital lesions. States of "asymptomatic" viral shedding occur in the majority of women with recurrent genital herpes and probably are due to limited infections involving the cervix and/or vagina as well as unrecognized symptoms.[152] The source and frequency of shedding in asymptomatic males is uncertain.[153,154]

Diagnostic Tests

54. An HSV antibody test (Western blot) of B.J.'s serum taken on day 1 of the illness was negative. However, 20 days later the HSV_2 antibody was positive. Viral cultures of B.J.'s genital lesions grew HSV_2. A genital Pap smear and serologic antibody detection tests were negative in B.J.'s asymptomatic sexual partner. How are these laboratory tests to be interpreted?

The accuracy with which herpes genitalis can be diagnosed without the aid of laboratory tests generally is quite good, especially if the infection is recurrent in nature. However, due to the potentially severe psychological and physiological ramifications of such a diagnosis, either virological and/or serological confirmation of the diagnosis may be obtained.[150]

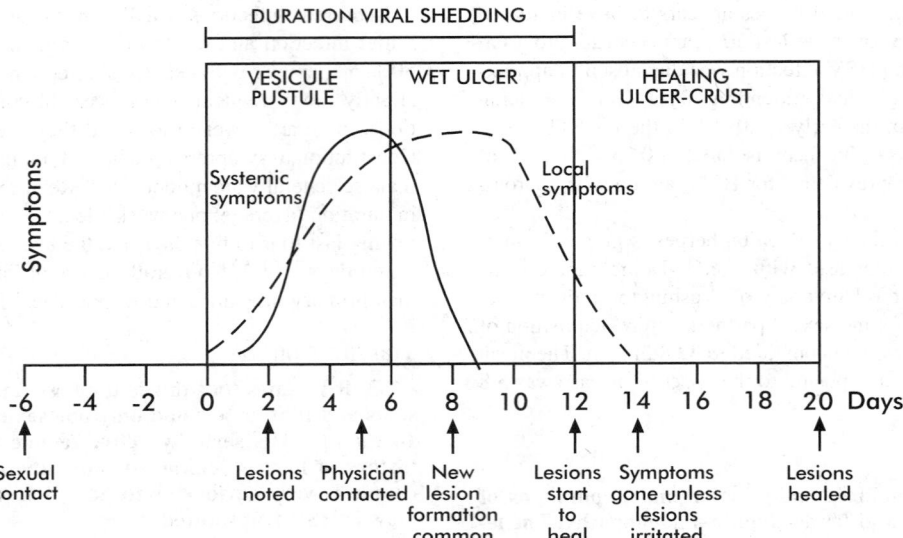

Fig 64.4   The Clinical Time Course of Primary Genital Herpes Infections   Reprinted with permission from reference 140.

The laboratory diagnosis of HSV_1 or HSV_2 infection depends upon isolation of virus from tissue culture; detection of viral particles by electron microscopy; visibility of giant cells or intranuclear inclusions by Papanicolaou or Giemsa staining (which are insensitive and nonspecific); or establishment of viral antigens by use of immunologic techniques. Tissue culture currently is the most sensitive method for detecting mucocutaneous herpes simplex infection. Tests which measure serologic response (as in B.J.'s partner), are valuable in documenting primary infection. It is possible to differentiate between antibody to HSV_1 and HSV_2 by means of the Western Blot Assay.[155]

Primary HSV infections are characterized by a fourfold or greater rise in the HSV antibody titer as seen in B.J.'s case. Neutralizing HSV antibodies can inactivate extracellular virus and interrupt the spread of HSV infection.[156] Less than 10% of patients with recurrent episodes of disease experience a serological rise in antibody titer between acute and convalescent sera.[148]

B.J.'s partner's results need to be interpreted cautiously. The negative Pap smear is not completely diagnostic. A nonreactive serology (absence of HSV antibodies) implies the absence of a primary infection, although false negative reactions have occurred. Absence of antibody to HSV_2 by Western blot would be good evidence against asymptomatic carriage.

Treatment

Acyclovir (ACV)

55. How should B.J.'s lesions be managed? Since the likelihood of recurrence of genital herpes is high, what treatment and prevention measures are recommended currently?

The great anxiety commonly associated with the diagnosis of genital herpes is because there is presently no effective treatment available for the condition.[134] Therapies ranging from antiviral agents to photoinactivation to vaccines have been tried. Currently, only ACV has promise for treatment of genital herpes.

The ideal antiHSV agent should: 1) prevent infection; 2) shorten the clinical course; 3) prevent the development of latency; 4) prevent recurrence in patients with established latency; 5) decrease transmission of disease; and 6) eradicate established latent infection. To date, no single agent has been successful in reducing signs and symptoms of HSV disease and in preventing infection.

Both acyclovir and vidarabine are efficacious for the short-term treatment of some HSV infections. In general, ACV appears to be more effective than vidarabine in the treatment of mucocutaneous and visceral HSV infections. Acyclovir, a nucleotide analog, is a substrate for HSV-specific thymidine kinase.[157] Through a series of phosphorylation steps, ACV is transformed to ACV-triphosphate, a competitive inhibitor of viral DNA polymerase.[157] Acyclovir has potent *in vitro* activity against both HSV_1 and HSV_2.[158]

In a study of severe, primary genital herpes, intravenous ACV (5 mg/kg every eight hours) significantly reduced the duration of viral shedding, decreased the duration of signs and symptoms of disease by a mean of five days, and hastened the time to healing of lesions by a mean of 12 days over placebo-treated patients.[159] Similar findings have been shown in the immunocompromised patient population.[160,161] Intravenous and oral acyclovir also prevent HSV reactivation in seropositive immunocompromised patients who are undergoing induction chemotherapy for acute leukemia or who have just undergone transplantation.[162,163] Currently, IV therapy is recommended only for patients with severe genital or disseminated infections who cannot take oral medication.

Topical therapy with ACV ointment (5% in polyethylene glycol) has minimal effect on the duration of viral shedding, symptoms, and lesion healing in first-episode primary genital herpes and has no effect on the recurrence rate.[164] Currently, topical ACV is not recommended as first-line therapy for primary genital herpes.

The introduction of an oral acyclovir product has replaced the use of the topical preparation and is indicated for B.J. Like IV therapy, oral ACV speeds the healing and resolution of symptoms of first and recurrent episodes of genital HSV_2 infections.[165–167] Yet, at currently recommended doses (200 mg orally five times a day for seven to ten days or at ''out of label'' regimens of 400 mg three times a day), ACV does not appear to influence the recurrence rate of genital herpes.[165] Also, the benefits of treating acute episodes of recurrent genital infection with oral ACV are limited; only severe episodes should be treated. Recurrent episodes of severe genital HSV_2 and rectal HSV_2 infection are treated at our clinics with oral ACV in doses of 200 mg and 400 mg five times a day, respectively.

Daily suppressive therapy with acyclovir is useful in reducing the frequency of reactivation episodes among patients with frequent (more than six episodes per year) genital herpes.[168] The number of recurrent episodes is diminished greatly, although breakthrough recurrences will still occur intermittently. Thus, the use of suppressive therapy does not eliminate totally viral transmission. The dose of acyclovir required for suppression varies. Initial doses of 400 mg orally twice a day or 200 mg orally four times a day are recommended but may be lowered with time. Immunocompromised patients may require higher doses for suppression. Increased frequency of resistant strains has been reported in immunocompromised hosts with long-term therapy.[169] B.J. is not yet a candidate for daily suppressive acyclovir therapy. A summary of the indications for ACV is outlined in Table 64.8. (See Chapter 68: Acquired Immunodeficiency Syndrome (AIDS) for information regarding acyclovir resistance.)

56. Adverse Effects. What adverse effects secondary to acyclovir should be anticipated?

Overall, all forms of ACV seem to be relatively free of adverse reactions. Intravenous and oral acyclovir are well tolerated.

Hematuria and an increase in blood urea nitrogen and serum creatinine may occur, primarily in patients with underlying renal disease or those receiving concomitant nephrotoxic agents. Interestingly, transient elevations in serum creatinine are associated more frequently with intravenous than oral administration; a prevalence of 4.7% has been associated with intravenous ACV.[170] When given intravenously in high doses, ACV has been shown to crystallize in the renal collecting tubules of animals and to cause transient renal insufficiency in ambulatory patients.[171,172] The renal complications appear to be related to high peak acyclovir plasma levels (possibly a rapid infusion rate) and may be attributable partially to dehydration.[172] If oral ACV is administered to produce plasma levels equivalent to intravenous doses, similar changes in renal function may be observed. Dose adjustment is necessary if patients are compromised renally.

High-dose IV acyclovir (1200 mg/m^2) has been associated with signs of neurotoxicity including tremors[173] and delirium.[162] Recently, one possible case of reversible neurotoxicity (increased fatigue, lethargy, irritability, and depression) was reported in a 57-year-old male with chronic lymphocytic leukemia receiving oral ACV (200 mg three times daily).[174]

Intravenous acyclovir occasionally has been associated with cutaneous irritation and phlebitis, reversible leukopenia,[161] and transient elevations of liver transaminases.[175] Oral ACV did not produce any clinical or laboratory side effects that were significantly different from placebo in clinical trials.[165–167] Patients receiving oral ACV may complain of nausea, dizziness, diarrhea, and headaches.

Topical acyclovir usually is well tolerated. Local reactions, including transient pain, burning, or rash, have been reported with the 5% ACV ointment, although discontinuation of therapy often was not necessary.[164] Similar reactions have been reported by placebo recipients.[164]

Patient Education and Counseling

57. What are the roles of education and counseling for patients with genital herpes? Are other forms of local or symptomatic care useful?

Most genital herpes infections are benign and will heal spontaneously unless the patient is immunocompromised or the lesions have become infected secondarily. The patient should be instructed to keep the involved areas clean and dry. To prevent autoinoculation, the patient should be told not to touch the lesions and to wash his hands immediately afterwards if he comes in contact inadvertently. Local anesthetics provide relief from the pain of genital lesions; however, they should be avoided if possible since they counteract efforts to keep the lesions dry. Local corticosteroid therapy is contraindicated because it may predispose the patient to secondary bacterial infections.[135]

Patient counseling is an important facet in the therapy of genital herpes and should include the source contact and any future partner. Health care practitioners should attempt to relieve patients' feelings of guilt and anxiety; discussion of long-term consequences should take place after the acute symptoms of the infection have resolved.

For individuals with frequent recurrences, efforts should be made to identify and avoid stimulatory factors such as sunlight, trauma, or emotional stress. The limitations of therapy and the decreased severity and frequency of recurrences with time should be explained to the patient. The periods of infectivity and the need

Table 64.8	Current Status of Antiviral Chemotherapy of Genital HSV$_2$ Infections[191]
Type of Infection	Treatment and Benefits
Mucocutaneous HSV Infections	
Immunocompromised Patients	
Acute symptomatic first or recurrent episodes	IV or oral acyclovir relieves pain and speeds healing; with localized external lesions, topical acyclovir may be beneficial
Suppression of reactivation of disease	IV or oral acyclovir taken daily prevents recurrences during high-risk period (e.g., immediately after transplantation)
Immunocompetent Patients	
First episodes of genital herpes	Oral acyclovir (200 mg 5 times a day for 7–10 days) is the treatment of choice. IV acyclovir may be used if severe disease or neurologic complications are present
Symptomatic recurrent genital herpes	Oral acyclovir (200 mg 5 times a day or 400 mg TID or 800 mg BID for 5 days) has some benefits in shortening lesions and viral shedding time if given within 2 days of onset of lesions. Acyclovir is recommended for severe, not routine, cases
Suppression of recurrent genital herpes	Daily oral acyclovir (400 mg BID) prevents reactivation of symptomatic recurrences; use should be re-evaluated at 1 year in patients with frequent recurrences
First episodes of oral-labial HSV	Oral acyclovir may be of benefit
Recurrent episodes of oral-labial HSV	Topical acyclovir is of no clinical benefit; oral acyclovir may be of benefit

to avoid sexual activity during these times also should be emphasized. Women with herpes genitalis should be scheduled for a routine Pap smear every year and should be instructed to discuss the problem with their physicians should they become pregnant.

Currently, there is no proven way to prevent the transmission of HSV_2 infection. Barrier forms of contraception, in particular condoms, may reduce the transmission of disease.[140] However, herpes still may be transmitted through a condom when active lesions are present. Nonoxynol-9, a spermicide which has in vitro HSV activity, is ineffective in the treatment of established genital HSV infection.[176] Its ability is ineffective in the treatment of established genital HSV infection[176] and its ability to decrease transmission of disease has not been established. Prophylaxis of HSV infections with vaccines currently is under study.

Complications

58. M.F. is a 23-year-old, sexually active female student with a history of frequent and severe recurrences of genital herpes since her initial infection 3 years ago. M.F. has tried numerous therapies including topical ether, small pox vaccinations, photoinactivation, and BCG vaccines. None of these therapies has provided M.F. with any relief of her symptoms, nor have they decreased the frequency of her recurrences. M.F. has read much in the lay press about herpes and is concerned about the possible complications of the disease, especially cervical cancer. What are the potential complications of herpes genitalis?

Previous research suggested that HSV_2 may be an oncogenic agent responsible for carcinoma of the cervix. The theoretical association between HSV_2 and carcinoma of the cervix primarily is based upon the following facts: females with carcinoma of the cervix show a higher frequency of HSV_2 antibodies than do cancer-free controls (37% and 7.1%, respectively);[177] females with a history of HSV_2 infection had a greater incidence of premalignant cervical changes than did women without a history of HSV_2 infection;[178] and some herpes viruses are known to be oncogenic in laboratory animals.[179] However, data from other excellent studies cast doubts upon these correlations,[180,181] and it currently is believed that human papillomavirus is more likely the responsible agent.

Neonatal

59. A.P., a 26-year-old female in her 32nd week of gestation, was hospitalized with complaints of painful genital lesions, headache, fever, increased vaginal discharge, and dysuria of 1 week's duration. Multiple ulcerative lesions consistent with genital herpes were present on the cervix, vulva, labia minora, and thighs. There is concern that A.P.'s infant is at risk for neonatal herpes. What are the consequences of this infection?

Neonatal herpes is a devastating systemic infection of the newborn, associated with high morbidity and mortality.[182] In Seattle, the incidence of neonatal herpes increased from two cases per 100,000 live births during 1966 to 1969 to 13.8 cases per 100,000 live births during 1978 to 1982.[183] Of untreated infants who acquire neonatal herpes, 65% will die and severe neurological toxicities and/or blindness will occur in up to 50% of those infants who survive.[135] The diagnosis of neonatal herpes often is missed since characteristic herpetic lesions, which are not limited to the genitals and may involve any external site including the eyes and oral cavity, appear in only 54% of infants with neonatal herpes.[182] Therefore, neonatal herpes should be ruled out in any severely ill newborn whose mother is known to have genital herpes. Neonatal herpes also must be considered if the mother's sexual partners have genital herpes.

HSV_2 causes approximately 75% of all neonatal herpes; HSV_1 accounts for the remaining 25% of cases.[140] HSV_2 usually is trans-

mitted to the newborn during passage through an infected birth canal, although ascending infections in newborns delivered by cesarean section six hours after the membranes have ruptured have been known to occur.[184] The risk of vertical transmission of HSV is greatest during primary HSV_2 infection (i.e., initial episode in a HSV_2 seronegative woman).

60. Treatment. How should A.P. be treated?

Herpes genitalis infections in pregnant females occur three times more frequently than in nonpregnant females, with 0.1% of all pregnant females experiencing an active genital herpes infection at or near term.[184] Unfortunately, a large percentage (36%) of those infections occurring during pregnancy are limited to the cervix and are totally asymptomatic.

Although the drug therapy for neonatal herpes has progressed rapidly over the last few years, the best therapy for neonatal herpes is prevention. Pregnant patients with a history of recurrent genital herpes should be examined carefully when they present in labor for evidence of active disease. Surveillance cultures should be performed from the cervix and vulva even if lesions are absent. The safety of systemic acylovir in pregnant women has not been established in controlled trials and therefore is not clearly indicated for A.P. Case reports do not reveal an increase in birth defects among those women receiving acyclovir during pregnancy.[18] Regardless, firm conclusions recommending the use of acyclovir in pregnancy cannot be made at this time. If the mother has an active herpes genitalis infection at the time of delivery (either active genital lesions or asymptomatic HSV_2 cervicitis), the baby should be delivered by cesarean section within four hours after the membranes have ruptured to prevent exposure of the neonate to the virus.[184,185] However, if no genital lesions are present at the time of delivery, vaginal delivery can be recommended.[186]

61. While in the emergency room, A.P.'s membranes ruptured and the child, C.P., was delivered by cesarean section 36 hours later. Cultures of the uterine fluid, cord blood, and placenta at the time of delivery were negative. However, cultures of the mother's lesions were positive for HSV_2.

C.P. presented as a normal 1600 gm infant whose hospital course was routine until the onset of fever and diarrhea on day 4. A lumbar puncture performed at this time was positive for HSV_2 and vesicles first appeared on the trunk and face on day 8. The baby continued to suffer from progressive liver enlargement and secondary convulsions and died at 12 weeks secondary to adrenal insufficiency. Autopsy revealed focal necrosis of the liver and adrenal glands as well as CNS involvement. How should C.P. have been treated?

Neonatal herpes first appears in the infant as a mild fever and diarrhea two to ten days after birth.[184] Herpetic lesions, if they are to appear, will do so one to three weeks after birth. This is followed rapidly by necrotic involvement of the liver, adrenal glands, lungs, and CNS that results in jaundice, convulsions, and respiratory and adrenal failure.

Infants born to mothers with documented herpes genitalis at term should be isolated and monitored closely for any signs of HSV infection. Antiviral chemotherapy has markedly reduced the mortality of neonatal herpes to 25%; however, the morbidity is still very high.[187]

Intravenous acyclovir has been shown to be more effective than vidarabine in reducing the morbidity and mortality of herpes encephalitis.[188] However, this study was completed in patients older than six months of age. New data suggest that ACV (10 mg/kg every eight hours) also reduces disease in neonates and was equivalent to vidarabine in outcome and toxicity.[189]

Genital Warts

62. S.L., a 19-year-old female, presents to the women's health clinic for her annual pelvic examination. One week later, her Pap smear is read as showing koilocytosis. A colposcopy is subsequently performed which shows changes consistent with cervical flat warts. What is the etiology of S.L.'s infection? How should she be managed?

Human papilloma viruses (HPV), primarily types 6 and 11, now are recognized as the cause of genital warts. These cause Pap smear changes, including koilocytosis and cervical dysplasia. In the female, visible warts occur on the labia, the introitus, and the vagina. Subclinical lesions also commonly occur on these sites and on the cervix as in S.L.'s case. They are visible only by colposcopy after applying acetic acid.

Currently, no treatment is entirely satisfactory. Podophyllin is used as a 10% or 25% solution in tincture of benzoin;[190] it is washed off after three to four hours and reapplied once or twice a week until the warts have disappeared. The rate of recurrence is extremely high, probably 50% or higher; it is associated with a high frequency of adverse events; and has limited efficacy when given intralesionally. Podophyllin is toxic if absorbed in large amounts and, therefore, should be applied in limited doses and should not be used in pregnancy. Purified podophyllotoxin (0.5%) is less variable in potency and can be applied by the patient. Cryotherapy by application of liquid nitrogen is more effective than podophyllin. Cryotherapy is easier to administer and is associated with little toxicity. TCA (80% to 90%) is used topically in the treatment of some genital warts, but efficacy is uncertain. To date, interferons are not recommended due to expense, high frequency of toxicity when given systemically, and limited efficacy for intravesimal administration. Cases refractory to topical drug therapy should be considered for surgical treatment.

Acknowledgment

We gratefully acknowledge King K Holmes and Jane R Schwebke whose work provided a foundation for this chapter.

References

1 **Rendtorff RC et al.** Economic consequences of gonorrhea in women: experience from an urban hospital. J Am Vener Dis Assoc. 1974;1:40.

2 **Handsfield HH.** Gonorrhea and uncomplicated gonococcal infection. In: Holmes KK et al., eds. Sexually Transmitted Diseases. New York: McGraw-Hill Books Co.; 1984:2.

3 **Handsfield HH et al.** Localized outbreak of penicillinase-producing *Neisseria gonorrhoeae*. JAMA. 1989;261:2357.

4 **Handsfield HH et al.** Trends in gonorrhea in homosexually active men—King County, Washington, 1989. MMWR. 1989;38:762.

5 **Holmes KK et al.** An estimate of the risk of men acquiring gonorrhea by sexual contact with infected females. Am J Epidemiol. 1970;91:170.

6 **Thin RNT et al.** Direct and delayed methods of immunofluorescent diagnosis of gonorrhea in women. Br J Vener Dis. 1970;47:27.

7 **Handsfield HH et al.** Asymptomatic gonorrhea in men: diagnosis, natural course, prevalence and significance. N Engl J Med. 1974;290:117.

8 **Pelouze PS.** Gonorrhea in the Male and Female. Philadelphia, PA: Saunders; 1941.

9 **Pariser H.** Asymptomatic gonorrhea. Med Clin North Am. 1972;56:1127.

10 **Thayer JD et al.** Improved medium selective for cultivation of *N. gonorrhoeae* and *N. meningitides*. Public Health Rep. 1966;81:559.

11 **Barlow D, Phillips I.** Gonorrhea in women: diagnostic, clinical, and laboratory aspects. Lancet. 1978;1:761.

12 **Pratt R, McCormack WM.** Pelvic inflammatory disease (PID): a common early complication of gonococcal infection, Abstract no. 669. Twentieth Interscience Conference of Antimicrobial Agents and Chemotherapy. New Orleans, LA: 1980 September 22–24.

13 **McCormack WM et al.** Clinical spectrum of gonococcal infection in women. Lancet. 1977;2:1182.

14 **Curran JW et al.** Female gonorrhea: its relation to abnormal uterine bleeding, urinary tract symptoms, and cervicitis. Obstet Gynecol. 1975;45:195.

15 **Sarrel PM, Pruett KA.** Symptomatic gonorrhea during pregnancy. Obstet Gynecol. 1968;32:670.

16 **Edwards LE et al.** Gonorrhea in pregnancy. Am J Obstet Gynecol. 1978;132:637.

17 **Rothenberg RB et al.** Efficacy of selected diagnostic tests for sexually transmitted diseases. JAMA. 1976;235:49.

18 **CDC.** 1993 Sexually Transmitted Diseases Treatment Guidelines. MMWR. 1993;42:1–102.

19 **Jones RN et al.** Disk diffusion antimicrobial susceptibility testing of *Neisseria gonorrhoeae*. MMWR. 1990;39:167.

20 **Judson FN.** Treatment of uncomplicated gonorrhea with ceftriaxone: a review. Sex Transm Dis. 1986;13:199.

21 **Sparling PF.** Antibiotic resistance in the gonococcus. In: Roberts RB, ed. The Gonococcus. New York: Wiley; 1978:111.

22 **McCormack WM.** Treatment of gonorrhea. Ann Intern Med. 1979;90:845.

23 **Crider SR et al.** Treatment of penicillin-resistant *Neisseria gonorrhoeae* with oral norfloxacin. N Engl J Med. 1984;311:137.

24 **Roddy RE et al.** Comparative trial of single-dose ciprofloxacin and ampicillin plus probenecid for treatment of gonococcal urethritis in men. Antimicrob Agents Chemother. 1986;30:267.

25 **Schmid GP et al.** Symptomatic response to therapy of men with gonococcal urethritis: do all need post-treatment cultures. Sex Transm Dis. 1987;14:37–40.

26 **Schroeter AL, Reynolds G.** The rectal culture as a test of cure of gonorrhea in the female. J Infect Dis. 1972;125:499.

27 **Boslego JWS et al.** Effect of spectinomycin use on the prevalence of spectinomycin-resistant and of penicillinase-producing *Neisseria gonorrhoeae*.

N Engl J Med. 1987;317:272–78.

28 **Siegal MS et al.** Penicillinase-producing *Neisseria gonorrhoeae*: results of surveillance in the United States. J Infect Dis. 1978;137:170.

29 **Judson FN et al.** Comparative prevalence rates of sexually transmitted diseases in heterosexual and homosexual men. Am J Epidemiol. 1980;112:836.

30 **Klein ES et al.** Anorectal gonorrhea. Ann Intern Med. 1977;86:340.

31 **Bro-Jorgensen A et al.** Gonococcal pharyngeal infections: report of 110 cases. Br J Vener Dis. 1973;49:491.

32 **Fluker JL et al.** Rectal gonorrhea in male homosexuals. Presentation and therapy. Br J Vener Dis. 1980;56:397.

33 **Wiesner PJ.** Gonococcal pharyngeal infections. Clin Obstet Gynecol. 1975;18:121.

34 **Sands M.** Treatment of anorectal gonorrhea infections in men. JAMA. 1980;243:1143.

35 **Anon.** Treatment of sexually transmitted diseases. Med Lett Drugs Ther. 1986;28:23.

36 **Barlow D.** The condom and gonorrhea. Lancet. 1977;2:811.

37 **Barrett-Connor E.** The prophylaxis of gonorrhea. J Am Med Sci. 1975;269:4.

38 **Harrison WO et al.** A trial of minocycline given after exposure to prevent gonorrhea. N Engl J Med. 1979;300:1074.

39 **Westrom L.** Incidence, prevalence, and trends of acute pelvic inflammatory disease and its consequences in industrialized countries. Am J Obstet Gynecol. 1980;138:880.

40 **Eschenbach DA.** New concepts of obstetric and gynecologic infection. Arch Intern Med. 1982;142:2039.

41 **Ory HW and the Women's Health Study.** Ectopic pregnancy and intrauterine contraceptive devices: new perspectives. Obstet Gynecol. 1981;57:137.

42 **Washington AE, Arno PS, Brooks MA.** The economic cost of pelvic inflammatory disease. JAMA. 1986;255:1735.

43 **Holmes KK et al.** Salpingitis: overview of etiology and epidemiology. Am J Obstet Gynecol. 1980;138:893.

44 **Eschenbach DA et al.** Polymicrobial etiology of acute pelvic inflammatory disease. N Engl J Med. 1975;293:166.

45 **Mardh PA et al.** *Chlamydia trachomatis* infection in patients with acute salpingitis. N Engl J Med. 1977;296:1377.

46 **Henry-Suchet J et al.** Microbiology of specimens obtained by laparoscopy from controls and from patients with pelvic inflammatory disease or infertility with tubal obstruction: *Chlamydia trachomatis* and *Ureaplasma urealyticum*. Am J Obstet Gynecol. 1980;138:1022.

47 **Cassell GH, Cole BC.** Mycoplasmas as agents of human disease. N Engl J Med. 1981;304:80.

48 **Mardh PA, Westrom L.** Tubal and cervical cultures in acute salpingitis with special reference to *Mycoplasma hominis* and T-strain mycoplasmas. Br J Vener Dis. 1970;46:179.

49 **Jacobsen L et al.** Objectivized diagnosis of acute pelvic inflammatory disease: diagnostic and prognostic value of routine laparoscopy. Am J Obstet Gynecol. 1969;105:1088.

50 **Svensson L et al.** Differences in some clinical and laboratory parameters in acute salpingitis related to culture and serologic findings. Am J Obstet Gynecol. 1980;138:1017.

51 **Westrom L.** Effect of acute pelvic inflammatory disease on fertility. Am J Obstet Gynecol. 1975;121:707.

52 **Kraus SJ.** Complications of gonococcal infection. Med Clin North Am. 1972;56:115.

53 **Bayer AS.** Gonococcal arthritis syndromes. An update on diagnosis and management. Postgrad Med. 1980;67:200.

54 **Holmes KK et al.** Disseminated gonococcal infection. Ann Intern Med. 1971;74:979.

55 **Eng J, Ireland H.** Inhibitory effect *in vitro* of sodium polyethanol sulfonate

on the growth of *Neisseria meningitidis*. J Clin Microbiol. 1975;1:444.

56 **Centers for Disease Control.** Gonorrhea: CDC-recommended treatment schedules, 1979. J Infect Dis. 1979; 139:496.

57 **Armstrong JH et al.** Ophthalmia neonatorum: a chart review. Pediatrics. 1976;57:884.

58 **American Academy of Pediatrics.** Prophylaxis and treatment of neonatal gonococcal infections. Pediatrics. 1980;65:1047.

59 **Jones DED et al.** Gonorrhea in obstetric patients. J Am Vener Dis Assoc. 1976;2:30.

60 **Nishida H et al.** Silver nitrate ophthalmic solution and chemical conjunctivitis. Pediatrics. 1975;56:358.

61 **Lossick JG.** Prevention and management of neonatal gonorrhea. Sex Transm Dis. 1979;6:192.

62 **Gordon FB, Quan AL.** Isolation of the trachoma agent in cell culture. Proc Soc Exp Biol Med. 1965;118:354.

63 **Schachter J.** Chlamydial infections. N Engl J Med. 1978;298:428,490,540.

64 **Felman YM et al.** Nongonococcal urethritis: a clinical review. JAMA. 1981; 245:381.

65 **Paavonen J et al.** Treatment of nongonococcal urethritis with trimethoprim-sulphadiazine and with placebo. A double-blind partner controlled study. Br J Vener Dis. 1980;56:101.

66 **Bowie WR et al.** Tetracycline in nongonococcal urethritis. Br J Vener Dis. 1980;56:332.

67 **Tartaglione TA, Horton TM.** The role of fluoroquinolones in sexually transmitted diseases. Pharmacotherapy. 1993;13:189–201.

68 **Martin DH et al.** A controlled trial of a single dose of azithromycin for the treatment of chlamydial urethritis and cervicitis. N Engl J Med. 1992;327: 921–25.

69 **Kuo CC et al.** Antimicrobial activity of several antibiotics and a sulfonamide against *Chlamydia trachomatis* organisms in cell culture. Antimicrob Agents Chemother. 1977;12:80.

70 **Holmes KK et al.** Etiology of nongonococcal urethritis. N Engl J Med. 1975; 292:1199.

71 **Loufalik ED et al.** Treatment of nongonococcal urethritis with rifampicin as a means of clearing the role of *Ureaplasma urealyticum*. Br J Vener Dis. 1979;55:36.

72 **Oriel JD.** Management of nongonococcal urethritis. Drugs. 1979;18:398.

73 **Furness G et al.** *Corynebacterium genitalium* (non-specific Corynebacterium): biologic reactions differentiating commensals of the urogenital tract from the pathogens responsible for urethritis. Invest Urol. 1977;15:23.

74 **Handsfield HH et al.** Differences in the therapeutic response of chlamydia-positive and chlamydia-negative forms of nongonococcal urethritis. J Am Vener Dis Assoc. 1976;2:5.

75 **Stimson JB et al.** Tetracycline-resistant *Ureaplasma urealyticum*: a cause of persistent nongonococcal urethritis. Ann Intern Med. 1981;94:192.

76 **Tait LA et al.** Chlamydial infection of the cervix in partners of men with NGU. Br J Vener Dis. 1980;56:37.

77 **Schachter J.** Lymphogranuloma veneered and other nonocular *Chlamydia trachomatis* infections. In: Hobson D, Holmes KK, eds. Nongonococcal Urethritis and Related Infections. Washington: American Society for Microbiology; 1977;91–7.

78 **Smith EB, Custer RP.** The histopathology of lymphogranuloma veneered. J Urol. 1950;63:546.

79 **Greaves AB et al.** Chemotherapy in bubonic lymphogranuloma venerium. Bull WHO. 1957;16:277.

80 **Annamuthodo H.** Rectal lymphogranuloma veneered in Jamaica. Ann R Coll Surg Engl. 1961;29:141.

81 **Rosahn PD.** Autopsy studies in syphilis. Journal of Venereal Disease Information, supplement no. 21, U.S. Public Health Service, Venereal Disease Division, 1947.

82 **Turner TB, Hollander DH.** Biology of the treponematosis. WHO Monogr. 1957;35:3.

83 **Chapel TA.** The variability of syphilitic chancres. Sex Transm Dis. 1978; 5:68.

84 **Fowler W.** The erythrocyte sedimentation rate in syphilis. Br J Vener Dis. 1976;52:309.

85 **Feher J et al.** Early syphilitic hepatitis. Lancet. 1975;2:896.

86 **Knox JM, Rudolph AH.** Acquired infectious syphilis. In: Holmes KK et al., eds. Sexually Transmitted Diseases. New York: McGraw-Hill Books Co.; 1984:305.

87 **Gjestland T.** The Oslo study of untreated syphilis: an epidemiologic investigation of the natural course of syphilitic infection based on a restudy of the Boeck-Bruusgaard material. Acta Derm Venereol (Stockh). 1955; 35(Suppl. 34):1.

88 **Sparling PF.** Natural history of syphilis. In: Holmes KK et al., eds. Sexually Transmitted Diseases. New York: McGraw-Hill Books Co.; 1990:213.

89 **Merritt HH et al.** Neurosyphilis. New York, NY: Oxford; 1946.

90 **Felman YM et al.** Syphilis serology today. Arch Dermatol. 1980;116:84.

91 **Tuffanelli DL et al.** Fluorescent treponemal-antibody absorption tests: studies of false-positive reactions to tests for syphilis. N Engl J Med. 1967;276: 258.

92 **Bulkley BH.** Cardiovascular syphilis. In: Holmes KK et al., eds. Sexually Transmitted Diseases. New York: McGraw-Hill Books Co.; 1984:334.

93 **Yoder FW.** Penicillin treatment of neurosyphilis: are recommended dosages sufficient? JAMA. 1975;232:270.

94 **Berry CD et al.** Neurologic relapse after benzathine penicillin therapy for secondary syphilis in a patient with HIV infection. N Engl J Med. 1987; 316:1587–589.

95 **Salo OP et al.** False-positive serological tests for syphilis in pregnancy. Acta Derm Venereol. 1969;49:332.

96 **Holdern WR et al.** Syphilis in pregnancy. Med Clin North Am. 1972;56: 1151.

97 **Kline AH et al.** Transplacental effect of tetracycline on teeth. JAMA. 1964; 188:178.

98 **Dowling HF et al.** Hepatic reactions to tetracycline. JAMA. 1964;188:307.

99 **South MA et al.** Failure of erythromycin estolate therapy in utero syphilis. JAMA. 1974;190:70.

100 **Thompson S.** Treatment of syphilis in pregnancy. J Am Vener Dis Assoc. 1976;3:159.

101 **Hashisaki P et al.** Erythromycin failure in the treatment of syphilis in a pregnant woman. J Am Vener Dis Assoc. 1983;10:36.

102 **Schulz F.** Congenital syphilis. In: Holmes KK et al. Sexually Transmitted Diseases. New York: McGraw-Hill Books Co.; 1990:821.

103 **Rudolph AH et al.** Penicillin reactions among patients in venereal disease clinics: a national survey. JAMA. 1973;223:499.

104 **Meislin HW et al.** Jarisch-Herxheimer reaction case report. JACEP. 1976;5: 779.

105 **Mamunes P et al.** Early diagnosis of neonatal syphilis. Am J Dis Child. 1970;120:17.

106 **Hammond GW et al.** Clinical, epidemiological, laboratory and therapeutic features of an urban outbreak of chancroid in North America. Rev Infect Dis. 1980;2:867.

107 **Combes FC et al.** Treatment of chancroid with sulfathiazole: investigation of the minimal effective dose. Am J Syph. 1943;27:700.

108 **Culp OS.** Treatment of chancroid with sulfanilamide. Am J Syph. 1940;24: 622.

109 **Kerber RE et al.** Treatment of chancroid. A comparison of tetracycline and sulfisoxazole. Arch Dermatol. 1969; 100:604.

110 **Gardner HL, Dukes CD.** *Haemophilus vaginalis* vaginitis. A newly defined specific infection previously classified "nonspecific" vaginitis. Am J Obstet Gynecol. 1955;69:962.

111 **Pheifer TA et al.** Nonspecific vaginitis: role of *Haemophilus vaginalis* and treatment with metronidazole. N Engl J Med. 1978;298:1429.

112 **Piot P, Vanderheyden J.** *Gardnerella vaginalis* and nonspecific vaginitis. In: Holmes KK et al, eds. Sexually Transmitted Diseases. New York: McGraw-Hill Books Co.; 1984:421.

113 **Bowie WR et al.** Bacteriology of the urethra in normal men and men with nongonococcal urethritis. J Clin Microbiol. 1977;6:482.

114 **Spiegel CA.** Curved anaerobic bacteria in bacterial (nonspecific) vaginosis and their response to antimicrobial therapy. J Infect Dis. 1983;148:817.

115 **Spiegel CA et al.** Anaerobic bacteria in nonspecific vaginitis. N Engl J Med. 1980;303:601.

116 **Rodgers HA et al.** *Haemophilus vaginalis (Corynebacterium vaginale)* vaginitis in women attending public health clinics: response to treatment with ampicillin. Sex Transm Dis. 1978; 5:18.

117 **Catterall RD.** Trichomonal infection of the genital tract. Med Clin North Am. 1972;56:1203.

118 **Hager WD et al.** Metronidazole for vaginal trichomoniasis. Seven-day vs single-dose regimens. JAMA. 1980; 244:1219.

119 **Pereyra AJ et al.** Urogenital trichomoniasis: treatment with metronidazole in 2,002 incarcerated women. Obstet Gynecol. 1964;24:499.

120 **Dykers JR.** Single-dose metronidazole for trichomonal vaginitis: patient and consort. N Engl J Med. 1975;293:23.

121 **Czonka GW.** Trichomonal vaginitis treated with one dose of metronidazole. Br J Vener Dis. 1971;47:456.

122 **Lussick JG et al.** *In vitro* drug susceptibility and doses of metronidazole required for cure in cases of refractory vaginal trichomoniasis. J Infect Dis. 1986;153:948–55.

123 **Penick SB.** Metronidazole in the treatment of alcoholism. Am J Psychiatry. 1969;125:1063.

124 **Gupta NK.** Effect of metronidazole on liver alcohol dehydrogenase. Biochem Pharmacol. 1970;19:2805.

125 **D'Arcy PF.** Drug interactions with oral contraceptives. Drug Intell Clin Pharm. 1986;353–62.

126 **Rustia M et al.** Experimental induction of hepatomas, mammary tumors, and other tumors with metronidazole in non-inbred sas.mrc(wi)Br rats. J Natl Cancer Inst. 1979;63:863.

127 **Beard CM et al.** Lack of evidence for cancer due to the use of metronidazole. N Engl J Med. 1979;301:519.

128 **Friedman CD.** Cancer after metronidazole. N Engl J Med. 1980;302:519.

129 **Peterson WF et al.** Metronidazole in pregnancy. Am J Obstet Gynecol. 1966;94:343.

130 **Morgan IFK.** Metronidazole treatment in pregnancy. In: Phillips I, Collier J, eds. Metronidazole. London: Academic Press; 1979;245–47.

131 **Rosenkranz HS, Speck WT.** Mutagenicity of metronidazole: activation by mammalian liver microsomes. Biochem Biophys Res Commun. 1975;66: 520–25.

132 **Schnell JD.** The incidence of vaginal candida and trichomonas infections and treatment of trichomonas vaginitis with clotrimazole. Postgrad Med J. 1974;50:579.

133 **Legal HP.** The treatment of trichomonas and candida vaginitis with clotrimazole vaginal tablets. Postgrad Med J. 1974;50:581.

134 **Davis LG et al.** Genital herpes simplex virus infections: clinical course and attempted therapy. Am J Hosp Pharm. 1981;38:825.

135 **Chang T et al.** Genital herpes. JAMA. 1974;229:544.

136 **Dowdle WR et al.** Association of antigenic type of herpes-virus hominis with site of viral recovery. J Immunol. 1967;99:974.

137 **Nahmias AJ, Roizman D.** Infection with herpes simplex virus 1 and 2. N Engl J Med. 1973;269:667,289:719, 781.

138 **Baringer JR, Swoveland P.** Recovery of herpes simplex virus from trigeminal ganglions. N Engl J Med. 1973;288:648.

139 **Centers for Disease Control.** Genital herpes infections. United States, 1966–1979. MMWR. 1982;31:137–39.

140 **Corey L.** Genital herpes. In: Holmes KK et al., eds. Sexually Transmitted Diseases. New York: McGraw-Hill Books Co.; 1984;449.

141 **Rauh JL et al.** Genital surveillance among sexually active adolescent girls. J Pediatr. 1977;90:844.

142 **Knox GE et al.** Comparative prevalence of subclinical cytomegalovirus and herpes simplex virus in the genital and urinary tracts of low-income urban women. J Infect Dis. 1979;140:419.

143 **Johnson R et al.** U.S. genital herpes trends during the first decade of AIDS:

prevalences increased in young whites and elevated in blacks. International Soc for STD Res; Helsinki, Finland, Aug 29–Sept 1, 1993. Abstract no. 22.

144 **Johnson RE et al.** A seroepidemiologic survey of the prevalence of herpes simplex virus type 2 infections in the United States. N Engl J Med. 1989;321:7.

145 **Adams HG et al.** Genital herpetic infection in men and women: clinical course and effect of topical application of adenine arabinoside. J Infect Dis. 1976;133:A151.

146 **Corey L et al.** Clinical course of genital herpes simplex virus infections in men and women. Ann Intern Med. 1983;48:973.

147 **Koutsky LA et al.** Underdiagnosis of genital herpes by current clinical and viral-isolation procedures. N Engl J Med. 1992;326:1533.

148 **Reeves WC et al.** Risk of recurrence after first episodes of genital herpes: relation to HSV type and antibody response. N Engl J Med. 1981;305:315.

149 **Rahray MC et al.** Recurrent genital herpes among women: symptomatic vs asymptomatic viral shedding. Br J Vener Dis. 1978;54:262.

150 **Hamilton R.** The Herpes Book. J.P. Tarchar, Inc.; 1980.

151 **Langenberg A et al.** Development of clinically recognizable genital lesions among women previously identified as having "asymptomatic" herpes simplex virus type 2 infection. Ann Intern Med. 1989;110:882.

152 **Kawana T et al.** Clinical and virological studies on genital herpes. Lancet. 1976;2:964.

153 **Centrifanto YM et al.** Herpes virus type 2 in the male genitourinary tract. Science. 1972;178:318.

154 **Jeansson S et al.** Genital herpes hominis infection: a venereal disease? Lancet. 1970;1:1064.

155 **Ashley RL et al.** Comparison of Western blot and gG-specific immunodot enzyme assay for detecting HSV-1 and HSV-2 antibodies in human sera. J Clin Microbiol. 1988;26:662.

156 **Notkins AL.** Immune mechanisms by which the spread of viral infections is stopped. Cell Immunol. 1974;11:478.

157 **Schaeffer JH et al.** 9-(2-Hydroxy-ethoxymethyl) guanine activity against viruses of the herpes group. Nature. 1978;272:583.

158 **Crumpacker CS et al.** Growth inhibition by acycloguanosine of herpes virus isolated from human infections. Antimicrob Agents Chemother. 1979; 15:642.

159 **Corey L et al.** Intravenous acyclovir for the treatment of primary genital herpes. Ann Intern Med. 1983;98:914.

160 **Shepp DH et al.** Oral acyclovir therapy for mucocutaneous herpes simplex virus infections in immunocompromised marrow transplant recipients. Ann Intern Med. 1985;102:783.

161 **Straus SE et al.** Acyclovir for chronic mucocutaneous herpes simplex virus infection in immunosuppressed patients. Ann Intern Med. 1982;96:270.

162 **Saral R et al.** Acyclovir prophylaxis of herpes-simplex-virus infection: a randomized, double-blind, controlled trial in bone-marrow-transplant recipients. N Engl J Med. 1981;305:63.

163 **Wade JC et al.** Oral acyclovir for prevention of herpes simplex virus reactivation after marrow transplantation. Ann Intern Med. 1984;100:823.

164 **Corey L et al.** Double-blind placebo-controlled trial of topical acyclovir in first and recurrent episodes of genital herpes simplex virus infection. N Engl J Med. 1982;206:1313.

165 **Mertz GJ et al.** Double-blind placebo-controlled trial of oral acyclovir in first-episode genital herpes simplex virus infection. JAMA. 1984;252:1147.

166 **Bryson YJ et al.** Treatment of first episodes of genital herpes simplex virus infection with oral acyclovir. N Engl J Med. 1983;398:916.

167 **Reichman RC et al.** Treatment of recurrent herpes simplex infections with oral acyclovir: a controlled trial. JAMA. 1984;251:2103.

168 **Gold D et al.** Acyclovir prophylaxis for herpes simplex virus infection.

Antimicrob Agents Chemother. 1987; 31:361.

169 **Erlich KS et al.** Foscarnet therapy for severe acyclovir-resistant herpes simplex virus type-2 infections in patients with acquired immunodeficiency syndrome (AIDS). Ann Intern Med. 1989; 110:710.

170 **Laskin OL.** Acyclovir: pharmacology and clinical experience. Arch Intern Med. 1984;144:1241.

171 **Keeney RE et al.** Acyclovir tolerance in humans. Ann J Med. 1982;73:176.

172 **Bean B, Aeppli D.** Adverse effects of high-dose intravenous acyclovir in ambulatory patients with acute herpes zoster. J Infect Dis. 1985;151:362.

173 **Wade JC et al.** Treatment of cytomegalovirus pneumonia with high-dose acyclovir. Paper presented to 21st Interscience Conference on Antimicrobial Agents and Chemotherapy. Chicago, IL: 1981 Nov 4.

174 **Krigel AL.** Reversible neurotoxicity due to oral acyclovir in a patient with chronic lymphocytic leukemia. J Infect Dis. 1986;154:184.

175 **Fife KH et al.** Double-blind placebo-controlled trial of intravenous acyclovir for severe primary genital herpes. Paper presented to the 21st Interscience Conference on Antimicrobial Agents and Chemotherapy. Chicago, IL: 1981 Nov 4.

176 **Vontver LA et al.** Clinical course and diagnosis of genital herpes simplex virus infection and evaluation of topical surfactant therapy. Am J Obstet Gynecol. 1979;133:548.

177 **Centifanto YM et al.** Relationship of herpes simplex genital infection and carcinoma of the cervix population studies. Am J Obstet Gynecol. 1971; 110:690.

178 **Naib ZM et al.** Cytology and histopathology of cervical herpes simplex infection. Cancer. 1973;19:1026.

179 **Purchase HG.** Role of herpes virus in Marek's disease, a malignant lymphoma of chickens. Ped Proc. 1972;31: 1634.

180 **Adams E et al.** Seroepidemiological studies of herpes-virus type 2 and carcinoma of the cervix. 1. Case-control matching. J Natl Cancer Inst. 1971;47: 941.

181 **Amstay MS et al.** Herpes virus cervicitis and neoplasia. Cancer. 1973;32: 1321.

182 **Nahmias AJ et al.** Infection of the newborn with Herpes-virus hominis. Adv Pediatr. 1970;17:185.

183 **Sullivan-Bolyai J et al.** Neonatal herpes simplex virus infection in King County, Washington: increasing incidence of epidemiologic correlates. JAMA. 1983;250:3059.

184 **Kibrick S.** Herpes simplex infection at term. What to do with mother, newborn and nursery personnel. JAMA. 1980; 243:157.

185 **Light IJ et al.** Neonatal herpes simplex infection following delivery by cesarean section. Obstet Gynecol. 1974;44: 496.

186 **Prober CG et al.** Low risk of herpes simplex virus infections in neonates exposed to the virus at the time of vaginal delivery to mothers with recurrent genital HSV infections. N Engl J Med. 1987;316:240.

187 **Corey L, Spear PG.** Infection with Herpes simplex viruses. N Engl J Med. 1986;314(Pt. 2):749.

188 **Whitley RJ et al.** Vidarabine versus acyclovir therapy in herpes simplex encephalitis. N Engl J Med. 1986;314: 144.

189 **Whitley RJ et al.** A controlled trial comparing vidarabine with acyclovir in neonatal herpes simplex infection. N Engl J Med. 1991;324:444.

190 **Oriel JD.** Genital Human Papillomavirus. In: Holmes KK et al., eds. Sexually Transmitted Diseases. New York: McGraw-Hill Books Co.; 1990:443.

191 **Correy L, Spear PG.** Infections with Herpes Simplex Virus (2). N Engl J Med. 1986;314:749.

192 **Braunwald E et al.,** eds. Harrison's Principles of Internal Medicine. New York: McGraw-Hill Books Co.; 1991; 11:122.

Osteomyelitis/Septic Arthritis

Ralph H Raasch

Bone Anatomy and Physiology (See Figure 65.1) 65-1
Hematogenous Osteomyelitis 65-1
Acute Osteomyelitis 65-2
Usual Clinical Presentation 65-2
Patient Work-Up 65-3
Treatment 65-3
   Empiric antibiotic therapy
    (See Tables 65.2 and 65.3) 65-3
   Antibiotic bone penetration and protein binding 65-3
   Duration of therapy 65-4
   Use of oral antibiotics and serum
    bactericidal titers (SBTs) 65-4
   Duration of follow-up for recurrent infection 65-5
Secondary Osteomyelitis 65-5
Osteomyelitis Secondary to a Contiguous
  Source of Infection 65-5
Osteomyelitis Associated with Vascular Insufficiency ... 65-6
Usual Clinical Presentation 65-6
Initial Treatment 65-6

Osteomyelitis Due to *Pseudomonas* 65-7
Chronic Osteomyelitis 65-7
Usual Clinical Presentation 65-7
Response to Oral Antibiotics 65-8
Intravenous (IV) Antibiotics 65-8
**Osteomyelitis Associated with Prosthetic
  Material** 65-8
Usual Clinical Presentation 65-8
Treatment 65-8
Septic Arthritis 65-9
Nongonococcal Arthritis 65-9
   Usual clinical presentation 65-10
   Initial antimicrobial therapy: treatment
    in beta-lactam allergic patient 65-10
   Duration of therapy 65-10
Gonococcal Arthritis 65-10
   Usual clinical presentation 65-10
   Patient work-up and treatment in the clinic 65-11
   Full course of therapy 65-11

Osteomyelitis is defined as an inflammation of the bone marrow and surrounding bone and is almost always caused by an infecting organism. It can occur in any bone of the body and often leads to serious morbidity even with early diagnosis and treatment. Despite the development of new diagnostic procedures (e.g., radionuclide imaging), advances in antimicrobial therapy, and the use of prophylactic antibiotics before orthopedic procedures, osteomyelitis continues to be a serious problem from both a diagnostic and therapeutic standpoint.

Previously, osteomyelitis was more common in children and the elderly and the causative micro-organisms were usually gram-positive cocci such as streptococci and staphylococci. Although *Staphylococcus aureus* remains the most common causative organism, the prevalence of infection due to gram-negative and anaerobic bacilli is increasing and can affect all age groups.[1,2]

Bone can be infected by three main routes: 1) hematogenous spread of bacteria from a distant infection site; 2) direct infection of bone from an adjacent or contiguous source of infection; and 3) infection of bone due to vascular insufficiency. Table 65.1 summarizes important characteristics of these types of osteomyelitis.[3] Patients with recurrent osteomyelitis are considered to have chronic osteomyelitis.

Bone Anatomy and Physiology

To properly understand the pathophysiology of osteomyelitis, a basic understanding of bone anatomy and physiology is essential. Figure 65.1 is a graphic representation of a long bone of the body. The bone is divided into three sections: 1) the epiphysis, located at the end of the bone, 2) the metaphysis, and 3) the diaphysis. The epiphysis and metaphysis are separated by the epiphyseal growth plate. This is the rapidly growing area of the bone and, therefore, a large number of blood vessels supply this area. Surrounding most of the bone is a fibrous and cellular envelope. The external portion of this envelope is called the periosteum, while the internal portion is referred to as the endosteum.

The blood vessels that supply bone tissue are located predominantly in the bone's epiphysis and metaphysis. The nutrient arteries enter the bone at the metaphyseal side of the epiphyseal growth plate and lead to capillaries that form harp loops within the growth plate. These capillaries lead to large sinusoidal veins that eventually exit the metaphysis of the bone through a nutrient vein. Within the sinusoidal veins, blood flow is slowed considerably and infection can begin if bacteria settle in this area.

Variations exist in the vasculature of bone for different age groups, and this leads to different forms of osteomyelitis. In the neonate and the adult, vascular communications are present between the epiphysis and metaphysis which may allow infection to spread from the metaphysis to the epiphysis and the adjacent joint. However, during childhood this area often is protected from infection because the epiphyseal plate separates the vascular supply for these two regions.

Hematogenous Osteomyelitis

Hematogenous osteomyelitis classically has been a disease of children, although the number of cases reported in adults is increasing rapidly. Osteomyelitis in children tends to be acute and hematogenous and often responsive to antibiotic therapy alone. In comparison, osteomyelitis in adults tends to be subacute or chronic and commonly results from trauma, prosthetic devices, or other insult. As a result, surgical debridement often is needed in addition to antibiotics when managing osteomyelitis in adults.

Infection in children develops primarily in the metaphysis of the rapidly growing long bones of the body, probably because the slow blood flow in these areas allows bacteria to settle and multiply. The acute infectious process (e.g., edema, inflammation) causes a rise in pressure within the bone that compromises blood flow and eventually leads to necrosis. Eventually, the elevated pressure and necrosis may cause devitalized bone to fragment from healthy bone (sequestra). With continued spread of the infection into outer layers of the bone and soft tissue, abscess and draining sinus tracts form.[4]

Table 65.1		Features of Osteomyelitis	
Feature	Hematogenous	Adjacent Site of Infection	Vascular Insufficiency
Usual age of onset (yr)	1–20; ≥50	≥50	≥50
Sites of infection	Long bones, vertebrae	Femur, tibia, skull, mandible	Feet
Risk factors	Bacteremia	Surgery, trauma, cellulitis	Diabetes, peripheral vascular disease
Common bacteria	*S. aureus*, gram-negative bacilli; usually 1 organism	*S. aureus*, gram-negative bacilli; anaerobic organisms; often mixed infection	*S. aureus*, coagulase-negative staphylococci, gram-negative and anaerobic organisms; usually mixed infection
Clinical findings			
Initial episode	Fever, local tenderness, swelling; limitation of motion	Fever, warmth, swelling	Pain, swelling, drainage, ulcer formation
Recurrent episode	Drainage	Drainage, sinus tract	As above

In children, hematogenous infection most commonly occurs in the long bones, especially the femur and tibia.[5] In adults, the vertebra are more commonly involved and infection usually occurs in the fifth and sixth decades of life.[6] In the neonate, hematogenous osteomyelitis is an especially serious disease that often involves multiple bones, especially the long bones. Rapid spread across the epiphyseal plate can involve the adjacent joint making immediate, aggressive treatment crucial.[7]

The most common organism causing hematogenous osteomyelitis is *Staphylococcus aureus* which accounts for 33% to 66% of cases in children.[5] This is due partly to the proclivity of this bacterial species to settle in skeletal sites. In adults, *S. aureus* is also the most common causative pathogen; however, gram-negative bacilli (*Escherichia coli*, *Klebsiella*, *Proteus*, *Salmonella*, and *Pseudomonas*) are responsible for an increasing number of cases of osteomyelitis. Intravenous (IV) drug abuse often leads to infection with *Pseudomonas aeruginosa*, while *Salmonella* species is a common cause in patients with hemoglobinopathies such as sickle cell anemia.[3]

The clinical features of hematogenous osteomyelitis vary depending upon the age of the patient and the site of infection. In children, infection usually is characterized by an abrupt onset of high fever and localized pain, tenderness, and swelling. Unfortunately, systemic symptoms often are absent in neonates, delaying the diagnosis. Therefore, a diagnosis must be made on the basis of localized symptoms such as edema and restricted limb move-

ment.[1,3,5] Systemic symptoms are also less common in adults. However, those suffering from vertebral osteomyelitis usually present with fever, back pain, and stiffness.[1,3,6]

Acute Osteomyelitis
Usual Clinical Presentation

1. A.R., a 7-year-old male, suddenly developed spiking high fevers for 1 week before admission to the hospital. His fever was treated with acetaminophen and ibuprofen. He also had right anterior tibial tenderness which was thought to be due to sports activity, but no trauma to the area was reported. Two days before admission, A.R. was seen by his pediatrician who noted mild distal tibial tenderness without right ankle joint effusion. White blood cell (WBC) count was 8500 cells/mm^3 (Normal: 5000–10,000) and an x-ray of the leg was normal, but the erythrocyte sedimentation rate (ESR) was 55 mm/hr (Normal: 0–15). A.R. was sent home with directions for bed rest and continued use of antipyretics. However, 2 days later, he was admitted to the hospital because of severe pain and tenderness in his right leg and a fever of 39.2 °C. Plain x-rays were again normal, but a bone scan was positive for inflammation in the right distal tibia. What findings in A.R. are consistent with hematogenous osteomyelitis? [SI units: WBC 8500 × 10^9/L (Normal: 5000–10,000); ESR 55 mm/hr (Normal: 0–15)]

A.R. displays most of the usual signs and symptoms of acute hematogenous osteomyelitis. Localized pain and tenderness of the right distal tibia, abrupt onset of high fever, and an elevated ESR are characteristic of bone infection. The plain x-ray of A.R.'s leg was normal on two occasions before hospitalization, however, plain x-rays of bone are usually normal over the first two weeks of infection. Bone scans usually are able to detect bone changes earlier in the course of disease and the bone scan of A.R. upon hospitalization detected inflammation in the right distal tibia.[26] As in many cases of osteomyelitis, the specific event that caused bacteremia in A.R., and allowed bacterial dissemination to bone, is unknown.

Although laboratory tests should be obtained in every child suspected of having osteomyelitis, no laboratory tests are specific for the diagnosis of osteomyelitis. The laboratory tests should be used to confirm the clinical diagnosis and should never be relied upon to make the diagnosis. A complete blood count (CBC) and an erythrocyte sedimentation rate should be obtained.

An increased WBC count is consistent with osteomyelitis; however, leukocytosis is absent in 40% to 75% of children with osteomyelitis at the time of initial examination.[8] Thus, the WBC count of 8500/mm^3 in A.R. is not unusual. In adults, leukocytosis does occur, but it is more commonly associated with an acute infection than recurrent disease. When leukocytosis is present, the white count rarely exceeds 16,000.[2,3]

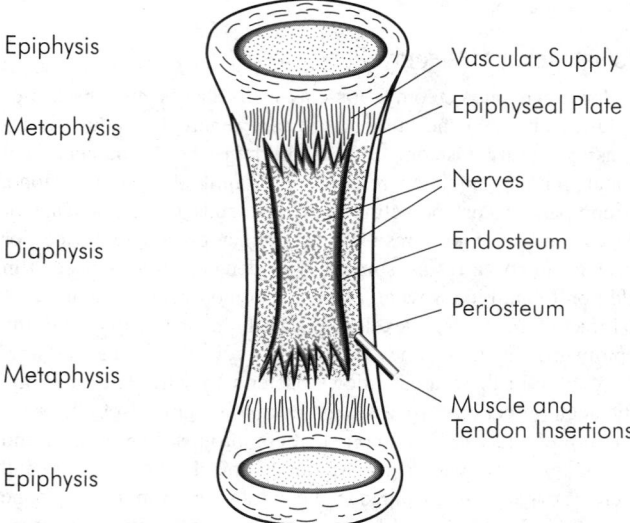

Epiphysis

Metaphysis

Diaphysis

Metaphysis

Epiphysis

Vascular Supply

Epiphyseal Plate

Nerves

Endosteum

Periosteum

Muscle and Tendon Insertions

Fig 65.1 Adapted from reference 84.

Although the ESR is relatively nonspecific, most patients with osteomyelitis have ESR values in excess of 20 mm/hour.[8,9] Therefore, the increased ESR of 55 mm/hour in A.R. also is consistent with osteomyelitis. Destructive changes of bone can be seen in plain x-rays, although these do not appear until at least 10 to 14 days after the onset of symptoms.[3,5] Bone scans can detect inflammation of bone more quickly than plain x-rays. Hence, a normal plain film does not rule out acute osteomyelitis if obtained within the first two weeks of infection. The bone scan in A.R. was extremely helpful because it detected acute osteomyelitis before the appearance of osteomyelitis on plain x-rays.

Predisposing factors for hematogenous osteomyelitis include any risk factors that promote bacteremia (e.g., indwelling catheters in the neonate, hemodialysis shunts, central venous catheters used for chemotherapy or hyperalimentation). A distant focus in the gastrointestinal or urinary tract can lead to bacteremia and predispose a patient to the development of osteomyelitis. Intravenous drug abuse leading to bacteremia can be a predisposing factor for osteomyelitis in young adults.[3,6,10] None of these factors seem to have predisposed A.R. to the development of osteomyelitis.

In children who have no history of fractures or penetrating injury, the most common cause for acute hematogenous osteomyelitis is *S. aureus*.

Patient Work-Up

2. What additional patient and diagnostic information should be obtained before A.R. receives his first dose of antibiotics?

Before A.R. receives a course of antibiotic therapy, an assessment of the possibility of drug allergy, especially penicillin allergy, should be undertaken. Patient interviews, discussions with his parents, and a compulsive review of his medical record are necessary activities, especially if a history of allergy is reported. Details of an allergic reaction, including symptoms, onset of the reaction, probable etiologic agent, treatment, and exposure to related compounds should be sought.

An attempt to obtain material for culture to identify a specific bacterial etiology for A.R.'s osteomyelitis also should be part of the initial work-up. Obtaining material for culture *after* the institution of antibiotics often renders cultures negative, thereby necessitating the use of broader-spectrum, empiric antibiotic therapy for several weeks, which increases cost and toxicity. Cultures of blood and bone aspirate material are the best methods to identify the bacterial etiology. These sites are culture positive 35% to 90% of the time.[5,8,9] Once material has been obtained for culture, then initial, empiric therapy should be started as soon as possible.

Treatment

Empiric Antibiotic Therapy

3. A.R. has no history of drug allergies. He has received penicillin in the past for episodes of strep throat. Blood and tibial aspirate are sent for culture. Gram's stain of aspirate material shows gram-positive cocci. What antibiotic treatment should be started? What is the relevance of bone concentrations or protein binding of antibiotics in the selection of therapy for osteomyelitis?

For initial antimicrobial treatment of hematogenous osteomyelitis, the agent chosen should be administered intravenously in high doses to achieve adequate levels in the infected bone. It is important to initiate treatment as soon as possible to improve the chances for complete eradication of infection and avoid the need for future surgery; empiric antibiotic therapy often is instituted before culture and sensitivity results are known.

Based upon the epidemiology of A.R.'s infection and the bone aspirate Gram's stain, the most likely etiologic agent is *S. aureus*. However, at this time, osteomyelitis due to streptococci cannot be ruled out. The initial treatment should be with an intravenous penicillinase-resistant penicillin, such as oxacillin or nafcillin, or with cefazolin. Because A.R. acquired his infection outside of the hospital, the possibility that methicillin-resistant *S. aureus* (MRSA) is responsible for his infection is very low. MRSA is resistant to all beta-lactam antibiotics. Other common causative organisms include *Staphylococcus epidermidis*, *Streptococcus pyogenes*, *Streptococcus pneumoniae*, *Haemophilus influenzae*, and *P. aeruginosa*. In the neonate with osteomyelitis, pathogens other than *S. aureus* are more commonly responsible and include *H. influenzae* type b and Group B streptococci.[5,9] Cultures of blood and infected bone material (bone aspirate) may reveal the causative organism, although half the time, these cultures are negative. Needle aspiration of the involved bone for culture is the diagnostic method of choice in order to confirm infection and to isolate the responsible pathogens, as was done in A.R.

The age of the child with acute osteomyelitis is important in the selection of appropriate empiric antibiotics. *H. influenzae* type b is more common in children less than three years old. Table 65.2 summarizes recommended drugs and dosages in children with acute osteomyelitis.[12,27,28] A.R. is placed on oxacillin therapy intravenously at 150 mg/kg/day given every six hours.

Antibiotic Bone Penetration and Protein Binding

Whether it is important to select an antibiotic which penetrates into bone when treating osteomyelitis is unclear. However, clinical experience suggests that successful therapy requires adequate penetration and high serum and tissue concentrations. Data are available on the bone-penetrating qualities of many antibiotics (see Table 65.3). In general, bone tissue concentrations for the antibiotics are several times greater than the minimum inhibitory concentration (MIC) values for the infecting pathogens being treated with these agents. However, the relationship between bone concentrations, measured as µg antibiotic/gm bone, and MIC values assessed *in vitro* as µg/mL, and outcome of therapy are not clear. There is no direct evidence that bone concentrations at some level above the MIC for an organism are necessary for effective treatment.[29-37]

Antibiotic penetration into bone varies from study to study and this may be due to the difficulties encountered assaying antibiotic concentrations in bone. A number of methods have been used. For example, antibiotic concentrations have been measured following elution of the drug from bony fragments using a buffer solution. This method may fail to measure the total amount of antibiotic present. Antimicrobial levels also have been determined by direct assay of the coarse bone specimens; however, this method may be inaccurate due to premature degradation of the drug.[33,34]

In addition to assay difficulties, there are other methodological limitations. Often, bone samples are collected during a surgical procedure when blood flow to the infected area may be impeded; this may decrease the amount of drug delivered to the tissue. Also, it is believed that antibiotic penetration into the better-perfused bone near the medullary cavity is more important than penetration into the bone's cortex. In most cases, however, bone samples are taken from the exterior cortical area.[30,38]

Other factors besides penetration of an antibiotic into normal bone may influence its effectiveness. For example, higher tissue concentrations may be achieved in infected bone that is highly vascularized than in normal bone. Finally, during the extraction procedure used to measure bone concentrations of antibiotics, bone is homogenized and there is no attempt to separate the bone's different components (i.e., vascular, interstitial, cellular, and crystalline). These parts may have different protein concentrations and binding affinities, factors that may influence antimicrobial pharmacological activity.[1,38]

How extensively an antibiotic is protein bound may theoretically influence the drug's clinical efficacy since it is believed that the free drug rather than the protein-bound drug diffuses from plasma into tissue. However, studies evaluating the penetration of highly protein-bound drugs, such as cefazolin (90% protein bound), suggest the contrary. High levels of cefazolin are achieved within bone following a single 1 gm IV dose which exceed those levels achieved with cephalothin, a drug with only 20% protein binding. In addition, cefazolin and ceftriaxone, two highly protein-bound drugs, usually are effective in treating osteomyelitis, provided high doses are given and the responsible pathogen is susceptible.[33,34]

Duration of Therapy

4. On the second day of A.R.'s hospitalization, the bone aspirate culture is growing S. aureus, resistant to penicillin, but sensitive to oxacillin and cefazolin. Should A.R. stay on oxacillin, or should his antibiotic be changed?

Continuing to treat A.R. with oxacillin given every six hours follows treatment recommendations for staphylococcal osteomyelitis. Antistaphylococcal penicillins achieve high levels in bone and usually provide effective therapy as long as the treatment regimen is followed with frequent doses for an adequate duration of treatment. Changing A.R. to cefazolin allows slightly less frequent dosing (every 8 hours) which may offer an advantage for home treatment or an easy transition to once-daily intravenous ceftriaxone given on an outpatient basis to decrease his length of hospital stay. While the logistics of outpatient therapy in A.R. are investigated, he should remain on oxacillin while in the hospital.

5. A.R.'s parents both work to support a family of 3 children. Their work schedules would prevent them from leaving their jobs to transport A.R. to an outpatient antibiotic treatment center. In addition, even with every 8 hour treatment with cefazolin, no one would be at home to help A.R. with an after-school antibiotic dose. Why is it necessary to continue the hospitalization of A.R.?

Outpatient IV antibiotic therapy for A.R. does not seem possible given his family situation. He should remain in the hospital for the first part of his treatment regimen with intravenous oxacillin. Assuming an adequate response to his antibiotic treatment, A.R.

should be treated for four weeks. Children with S. aureus osteomyelitis had a 19% recurrence rate if treated for less than three weeks, whereas treatment for three or more weeks reduced the recurrence rate to 2%.[39] When data from several treatment trials are combined, recurrent infection occurred in 12% of 227 patients treated for less than 36 days, whereas recurrence arose in 1.3% of 151 patients treated for ≥36 days.[27,39] Despite this clinical trial data, the final decision regarding the length of treatment for A.R. will be affected by actual duration and extent of infection, the necessity and adequacy of surgical debridement, the state of his host defenses, and his clinical response to therapy. For example, if he is still febrile with an ESR of 60 mm/hour after one week of therapy, then consideration should be given for further surgical evaluation. If further bone debridement is necessary, then the duration of subsequent antibiotic treatment after this operation should be at least four to six weeks.

Use of Oral Antibiotics and Serum Bactericidal Titers (SBTs)

6. After 1 week of IV oxacillin in the hospital, A.R. is afebrile, and the pain and tenderness in his right leg is markedly reduced. The ESR is now 40 mm/hr. Can A.R. be switched to oral antibiotics to complete a total of 4 weeks of treatment? If so, what is an appropriate dosing regimen and how often should he return to the clinic for evaluation? [SI unit: ESR 40 mm/hr]

Because intravenous therapy for several weeks in the hospital is inconvenient and expensive, the use of oral antibiotics to complete a course of therapy has been evaluated. Investigators have used serum bactericidal titers (SBTs) to monitor antimicrobial levels of drugs in the bloodstream since assays of beta-lactam antibiotics generally are unavailable. The SBT is the dilution of A.R.'s serum that exerts a bactericidal effect *in vitro* against the staphylococci cultured from his bone aspirate. Peak and trough SBTs can be ascertained depending upon whether the serum sample was obtained immediately after an antibiotic dose (peak SBT), or immediately before a dose (trough SBT).[40]

In the reports of oral therapy for staphylococcal osteomyelitis, children were treated with intravenous antibiotics until fever and local signs of infection (swelling, erythema, tenderness) resolved. The duration of intravenous therapy was usually 14 days. Oral therapy then was instituted in doses necessary to achieve at least

Table 65.2	Empiric Antibiotics for Acute Osteomyelitis in Children			
			Dosage	
Host	Likely Etiologies	Antibiotics	(mg/kg/day)	(dose/day)
Neonate	Group B streptococci	Nafcillin +	100	4
	Gram-negative bacilli	cefotaxime *or*	150	4
		Nafcillin +	100	4
		gentamicin	5–7.5	3
<3 yr	S. aureus	Cefuroxime *or*	100	4
	H. influenzae Type b	Ceftriaxone *or*	50	2
		Nafcillin +	150	4
		cefotaxime	100	4
≥3 yr	S. aureus	Nafcillin *or*	150	4
		Oxacillin *or*	150	4
		Cefazolin *or*	100	3
		Clindamycin	30–40	3
After puncture wound through shoe	P. aeruginosa	Ceftazidime	150	3
Child with sickle cell disease	Salmonella sp.	Nafcillin +	150	4
	S. aureus	cefotaxime	100	4

Table 65.3	Concentrations of Various Antibiotics in Bone and Serum (mg/L) versus Average MIC (mg/L) Determinations[a]				
Drug	Bone	Serum	S. aureus	E. coli	P. aeruginosa
Penicillins					
Penicillin[29]	Undetectable	0.5–9.4	R	R	R
Methicillin[29]	1.05–12.1	17.1–70	1.25–2.5	R	R
Dicloxacillin[72]	1.8–21	7.0–9.0	0.25–0.5	R	R
Cephalosporins					
Cefazolin[29]	2.1–43.3	10–70	0.2–0.8	0.8–100	R
Cephalothin[29]	0.0–3.9	12–15	0.2–0.8	1.6 to >200	R
Cephalexin[30]	2.2–2.8	15 (peak)	3.1–100	3.1–25	R
Cefamandole[73]	0.2–20.4	70 (peak)	0.2–1.0	<0.125–2.0	R
Cefoxitin[30]	4.8	70 (peak)	1.6–6.3	1–8	R
Cefuroxime[74]	0.3–12.7	100 (peak)	0.5	2.0–4.0	R
Cefotaxime[30]	0.7–8.4	50 (peak)	1.2–2.0	<0.1–8	2 to >128
Ceftazidime[75]	20.0	80 (peak)	<2 to >128	<0.1–8	0.5–32
Clindamycin[75–79]					
300 mg Q 8 hr IM	2.7	7.3	0.04–0.8	R	R
600 mg Q 8 hr IM	3.8	8.5			
300 mg Q 6 hr IV	1.3	6.5			
Aminoglycosides					
Gentamicin[29]	3.7	3.7–6	R	0.5–1.0	0.5–2.0
Tobramycin[30]	NA		R	0.5–1.0	0.5–1.0
Rifampin[79]	0.9	6.5	0.003–0.012	NA	NA
Ciprofloxacin					
750 mg PO (single dose)[80,82]	1–1.4	2.9	0.125–0.25	0.008–0.06	0.06–1.0
Aztreonam[83]	10–15	NA	R	0.2	12.5–25.0

[a] IM = Intramuscular; IV = Intravenous; MIC = Minimum inhibitory concentration; NA = Not available; R = Resistant.

a trough SBT of 1:2. Initial recommendations were that the peak SBT should be ≥1:16, but subsequent evaluation indicated that peak SBTs were not predictive of cure in acute osteomyelitis. In order to achieve a trough SBT of >1:2, oral doses of dicloxacillin or cephalexin given were at least 100 mg/kg/day. Probenecid given before these antibiotics increased trough SBT in some patients.[41–43]

On the basis of the above discussion, A.R. is a candidate for oral therapy. However, certain factors should be considered before conversion to oral therapy occurs. He has responded promptly to the IV therapy, that is, his fever and leg pain and tenderness have resolved after seven to ten days of therapy, and the ESR is reduced. Appropriate laboratory personnel should be able to reliably accomplish SBT assessment; however, this may be a major issue because of inconsistent results from a variety of laboratories.[40] Oral therapy only works if A.R. is compliant; therefore, assurances must be in place to guarantee oral doses will be taken. A.R.'s parents have made arrangements with his school's nurse to help him take his oral antibiotic during school time. However, in some cases, patients have stayed in the hospital for oral therapy to assure compliance. Initial oral therapy with a quinolone is not appropriate for A.R. because of emergence of resistance by staphylococci to ciprofloxacin, and due to the contraindication of quinolone use in children.

Since the above circumstances and assurances are met, A.R. can complete his four-week course of antibiotics with oral dosing of dicloxacillin. Doses should begin at 25 mg/kg every six hours, with probenecid 7 to 10 mg/kg every six hours if necessary, to achieve a trough SBT of at least 1:2. Doses should be increased empirically to achieve desired trough SBT. There is no evidence that a given dosage increase (or decrease) causes a proportional change in SBT. Close follow-up of A.R. is required under these circumstances to monitor for compliance and clinical response to therapy. Serum bactericidal titers should be monitored on a weekly basis with re-establishment of parenteral therapy if A.R.'s compliance is not perfect, the goal SBTs are not achieved, or symptoms (or increased ESR) recur.[3,27]

Duration of Follow-Up for Recurrent Infection

7. **A.R. has completed 4 weeks of treatment for his acute staphylococcal osteomyelitis. Clinical evidence for osteomyelitis completely resolved and the ESR was normal. How long should A.R. be followed closely for possible recurrence of his infection?**

Relapses of osteomyelitis can occur years after the initial acute episode.[1,2] In A.R.'s case of uncomplicated acute osteomyelitis, he should be followed closely for possible recurrence for at least two years. In evaluating the results of treatment trials for acute osteomyelitis, follow-up should be at least two years in order to increase assurance that recurrent episodes of infection are reported.

Secondary Osteomyelitis

Osteomyelitis Secondary to a Contiguous Source of Infection

Osteomyelitis secondary to a contiguous focus of infection can be caused by direct infection of bone from an exogenous source or can occur due to spread of an infection from adjacent tissue. A history of surgery for open reduction of a fracture is the most likely etiology for osteomyelitis. Any orthopedic procedure may potentially result in infection, but 80% of surgically-related osteomyelitis cases follow open reductions of fractures.[2] The bones most commonly involved are the hip, tibia, and femur.

Other factors that may precipitate the development of contiguous-spread osteomyelitis include any penetrating injury such as a gun-shot wound or stepping on a nail. Osteomyelitis of the mandible may develop in patients with a history of dental infections, oral surgery, and cancer radiation treatment to the oral cavity.[2,13] Osteomyelitis also can develop from soft tissue infections such as those involving the fingers and toes, or at sites of pressure sores.[14]

Unlike hematogenous osteomyelitis which occurs mostly in children, acute contiguous infection occurs more often in adults over the age of 50. This is explained by the higher incidence of precipitating factors within this age group, such as hip fractures, orthopedic procedures, oral cancers, sternotomy incisions for cardiac surgery, and craniotomies.[2,3,15]

Several organisms often are involved in contiguous-spread osteomyelitis, while hematogenous osteomyelitis usually involves only a single pathogen. Although *S. aureus* is the most common pathogen, it is often part of a mixed infection. Other organisms responsible for infection include *Pseudomonas, Proteus, Streptococcus, Klebsiella, E. coli, S. epidermidis,* and anaerobes. Most cases of osteomyelitis involving the mandible, pelvis, and small bones (e.g., those of the hands and feet) are caused by gram-negative organisms. *Pseudomonas* often is isolated from infections due to puncture wounds of the foot.[2,13]

Anaerobes also are associated with contiguous-spread osteomyelitis and often are found in association with other organisms. Possible predisposing factors include previous fractures or injuries due to human bites. Adjacent soft tissue infections also may lead to anaerobic infections of bone as in the case of sacral osteomyelitis which often results from severe decubitus ulcers. Periodontal infections and paranasal sinusitis have been known to cause anaerobic osteomyelitis involving the cranium and jaw. The organisms most commonly isolated in these cases are *Bacteroides fragilis* and *Bacteroides melaninogenicus.*[16]

Few systemic signs and symptoms that are consistent with acute osteomyelitis are seen in secondary osteomyelitis. The objective evidence usually present in hematogenous disease, such as fever, leukocytosis, and an elevated ESR, is absent. The most common finding for acute contiguous osteomyelitis is pain in the area of infection which often is accompanied by localized tenderness, swelling, and erythema. Since several weeks may pass before the patient becomes symptomatic, x-ray studies at the time of diagnosis may reveal abnormalities consistent with bone deterioration.[2,3]

Treatment for secondary osteomyelitis should be based upon cultures of bone biopsies, because cultures of adjacent wound or sinus tract material may not predict the organism actually infecting bone.[17] Depending upon the site of infection, initial empiric antibiotic therapy should be broad-spectrum, covering for gram-positive and gram-negative organisms, including anaerobes, especially if the sinuses or oral cavity are involved.

Osteomyelitis Associated with Vascular Insufficiency

Patients with impaired blood flow usually develop osteomyelitis in the toes or small bones of the feet. Often, infection first presents as cellulitis, which frequently progresses to deep ulcers. Finally, the infection spreads to the underlying bone. In many cases of osteomyelitis associated with vascular insufficiency, multiple pathogens can be cultured from surgical specimens or the wound. The most commonly isolated pathogens are staphylococci; however, gram-negative and anaerobic bacteria also are often recovered.

Systemic signs of infection such as fever and leukocytosis are lacking. This is common for patients who develop infection secondary to vascular insufficiency. Local symptoms such as pain, swelling, and erythema usually dominate the picture.[2,3]

The antibiotic treatment selected should be active against both gram-positive and gram-negative micro-organisms. An antistaphylococcal penicillin, plus an aminoglycoside for gram-negative coverage is the regimen most often used empirically. Therapy with a single agent such as cefotaxime, which provides good coverage against both gram-negative organisms and staphylococci also can be prescribed. If anaerobic bacteria are believed to be involved, clindamycin or metronidazole (Flagyl) should be added to the regimen.

Inadequate blood flow secondary to severe peripheral vascular disease makes treatment of osteomyelitis very difficult. Osteomyelitis of bone of the feet in patients with diabetes and vascular insufficiency is very difficult to treat. Antibiotic delivery to the site of infection may be compromised due to small vessel disease of the lower extremities. Despite surgical debridement of the infection followed by appropriate treatment with long-term IV antibiotic therapy, the reported cure rates are very low. Even "minor" amputations (1 or 2 toes) are unsuccessful in eradicating infection. Unfortunately, radical surgical approaches such as transmetatarsal, below-the-knee or above-the-knee amputations often are necessary to cure these infections.[2,3]

Usual Clinical Presentation

8. C.P., a 59-year-old male, suffered a severe fracture of his left distal tibia 2 weeks ago in an automobile accident. His fracture was set by open reduction and he had an unremarkable postoperative course. He had completed a 7-day course of cefazolin which was started on the day of surgery. However, 2 days ago he developed pain and swelling in his left calf. Evaluation for deep venous thrombosis was negative. On presentation, his left calf is tender, warm, swollen, and erythematous, and he is afebrile. Other physical findings are within normal limits. Laboratory data, including WBC count, ESR, serum creatinine and blood urea nitrogen, are normal. Plain bone films and bone scan, however, are consistent with left tibial inflammation, due either to bone healing or infection. What findings in C.P. are characteristic of secondary osteomyelitis?

C.P.'s case displays the usual findings in secondary osteomyelitis. Probable infection has arisen in his left calf at a site adjacent to the surgical repair of a fracture of his left distal tibia. Local symptoms (pain, tenderness, erythema) are seen most frequently while systemic signs of infection (fever, leukocytosis, elevated ESR) usually are not observed. C.P.'s development of localized symptoms two days ago and his absence of fever and leukocytosis is characteristic of secondary osteomyelitis. Secondary osteomyelitis often is polymicrobial, therefore, C.P. should undergo surgical re-evaluation and biopsy of involved bone at the probable site of infection.[1–3] The bone films and bone scan will help localize the possible infectious process in C.P. to direct the surgical biopsy.

Initial Treatment

9. C.P. returns to the operating room for surgical exploration and bone tissue is obtained for culture. He has no drug allergies. What antibiotics should be started postoperatively?

Mixed infections are more common in secondary osteomyelitis than in bone infection acquired hematogenously. *S. aureus* is still the most common pathogen, but other organisms, particularly gram-negative enteric bacilli, need to be considered, especially since C.P. has completed a course of antistaphylococcal therapy with cefazolin. The infecting organisms in C.P. could have been acquired by trauma at his automobile accident, or in the hospital during or after his surgery. Coverage for *S. aureus* and gram-negative bacilli is necessary. An antistaphylococcal penicillin (oxacillin or nafcillin, 2 gm Q 4 hr) plus a third-generation cephalosporin (cefotaxime, ceftriaxone, or ceftazidime) for gram-negative coverage should be started. Ceftazidime (2 gm Q 8 hr) is preferred because of its superior activity against *P. aeruginosa*. If there is a high rate of methicillin-resistant *S. aureus* (>25% of isolates) found locally, then vancomycin (1 gm Q 12 hr) should be substituted for oxacillin or nafcillin. Despite concerns of inferior tissue penetration of vancomycin compared to beta-lactams, vancomycin does penetrate into bone, usually at adequate levels for effective treatment. Third-generation cephalosporins should not be relied upon to treat serious staphylococcal infection, therefore, combined therapy is necessary.[3,11,37] Oxacillin and vancomycin have activity against gram-positive anaerobes, but not against an important gram-negative anaerobe, *B. fragilis*. If *B. fragilis* is cultured, additional therapy with clindamycin or metronidazole is indicated.

Osteomyelitis Due to *Pseudomonas*

10. The bone biopsy from C.P. grows *P. aeruginosa*, which is sensitive to piperacillin, ceftazidime, imipenem, gentamicin, tobramycin, and ciprofloxacin. His leg pain is no worse than it was 2 days ago; he is still afebrile. How should C.P. now be treated? Is he a candidate for oral therapy?

Standard therapy for C.P. would be to continue ceftazidime, add gentamicin, and delete oxacillin.[3] Therapeutic serum levels of gentamicin under circumstances of osteomyelitis have not been well studied. In other gram-negative infections where serum levels of aminoglycosides have been correlated with efficacy, treatment against the gram-negative pathogen was with the aminoglycoside alone.[44,45] Aggressive antipseudomonal therapy for C.P. would include a second agent active against the gram-negative organism, such as an extended-spectrum penicillin or third-generation cephalosporin. It may no longer be the case that "therapeutic" aminoglycoside levels defined previously are relevant to current therapy with two active agents. Nevertheless, C.P. should be continued on ceftazidime, 2 gm every eight hours, with gentamicin added, to complete a four-week course of therapy. In order to facilitate antibiotic therapy at home, C.P. is a candidate for once-a-day doses of gentamicin. Because he has normal renal function, a 5 mg/kg dose once daily can be administered. Although only a few patients with osteomyelitis have been reported, the bulk of evidence indicates that once-a-day therapy is as effective as multiple daily doses and possibly less toxic.[46–49] At home, C.P. should have trough gentamicin concentrations measured weekly, with desired levels being less than 1 μg/mL.

In order to avoid risks of aminoglycoside toxicity altogether, some investigators have administered cephalosporins or ciprofloxacin alone over four to six weeks in osteomyelitis due to *Pseudomonas*. These reports are small case series without control groups, or where follow-up was too short (≤6 months).[50–54] In order to provide the best chance of cure, C.P. should receive ceftazidime and gentamicin for the entire four-week course of therapy. C.P. should be followed closely thereafter for at least two years in order to detect recurrent infection. C.P.'s antibiotic therapy can be reasonably accomplished at home.

Chronic Osteomyelitis

Inadequate treatment of an acute episode of osteomyelitis can lead to sequestra formation and recurrent symptoms consistent with recurrent or chronic disease. Draining sinus tracts frequently develop from the bone to the skin in cases of chronic osteomyelitis. However, only those cultures from specimens obtained by deep aspiration of bone biopsy can provide a definitive diagnosis. Therefore, therapy should be based upon these culture results or the patient's previous culture results. Antibiotics should not be selected on the basis of organisms isolated from a draining sinus tract.[17]

Surgery plays a very important role in the treatment of osteomyelitis, especially in cases of chronic infection. Bone necrosis will progress if decompression and draining of the infected area is not carried out as soon as possible. When it appears impossible to excise all necrotic bone, all sequestra, devitalized tissue, and sinus tracts should be removed. Treatment should be continued with long-term antimicrobial therapy. Additional surgical procedures include microvascular techniques allowing transplantation of a muscle flap to areas of infected bone.[3,18]

Often, treatment with parenteral antibiotics is initiated before surgery and continued for at least four to six weeks. Unfortunately, the optimum duration of therapy for chronic osteomyelitis has not been determined. Despite prolonged IV therapy in conjunction with surgical debridement, chronic infection often is difficult to eradicate. It generally is recommended that parenteral therapy be followed by one to two months of treatment with oral antibiotics.[3]

Treatment of chronic osteomyelitis is often problematic because it is difficult to achieve adequate antibiotic concentrations in avascular, necrotic bone. Local irrigation of the affected area with antibacterial solutions following surgery has been used to improve therapeutic results. However, there are no controlled data supporting the use of this technique.

Antibiotic-impregnated polymethyl methacrylate bead implantation also is being used following surgical debridement of chronic osteomyelitis. Though data are few, some success has been reported with aminoglycoside-impregnated bone cement or beads.[3,19]

Usual Clinical Presentation

11. D.J., a 42-year-old man, had sustained a fracture of the left humerus in an automobile accident 10 years ago. Two years later, a draining sinus tract developed after bone grafting was done for malunion of the fracture. D.J. continued to have slight drainage from the sinus over the next 8 years. He took a variety of antibiotics intermittently over this time including dicloxacillin and ciprofloxacin, which he stopped taking ≈6 months ago. One month ago, he noted increased sinus drainage, pain, swelling, and erythema of his left upper arm. Ciprofloxacin was restarted, and cultures of sinus drainage grew *Proteus mirabilis*, coagulase-negative staphylococci, *Corynebacterium* species, *Peptostreptococcus micros*, and *Bacteroides* species. Fourteen days later, surgical debridement was done because of increased drainage and poor appearance of the wound. Bone cultures grew *P. mirabilis* and *B. fragilis*. The *Proteus* was resistant to ampicillin, cefazolin, and ticarcillin, but sensitive to cefotaxime, ceftriaxone, gentamicin, and ciprofloxacin. Sensitivities to the *Bacteroides* were not done. What aspects of D.J.'s case are characteristic of chronic osteomyelitis?

D.J. developed a chronic bone infection after injury. The persistence of sinus tract drainage in his left upper arm is indicative of an indolent infection of bone which was periodically suppressed, but not treated, by his courses of oral antibiotics. Cultures of sinus drainage now grow multiple organisms; and as seen in D.J., components of the topical normal bacterial flora usually are found. These cultures usually do not correlate with the organisms actually causing bone infection.[17] D.J.'s long course of bone involvement with drainage and local symptoms, and lack of any remarkable systemic symptoms, is classic for chronic osteomyelitis. In addition to further considerations for antibiotic therapy, D.J. should be evaluated by an orthopedic surgeon. He may require more extensive surgical treatment now because of continued bone destruction and necrosis, and bone sequestra formation. This infected material, as well as sinus tracts, could be surgically removed. Postoperatively, D.J. still would require long-term antibiotic therapy.

Response to Oral Antibiotics

12. D.J. had ciprofloxacin, 750 mg BID, restarted when his left arm became more painful and drainage increased. Did he have an unusually poor response to this therapy?

Oral antibiotic therapy in D.J. at this point would not be expected to be very effective. Without initial surgical removal of necrotic bone and other poorly vascularized, infected material, even intravenous antibiotics would be prone to failure. After adequate surgical treatment, then it is felt necessary to achieve high levels of antibiotics over a prolonged period of time.[3] However, the optimal duration of therapy for chronic osteomyelitis is not understood on the basis of clinical trials.

As the bone culture results are evaluated in D.J., it also should be recognized that his infection was caused, in part, by *B. fragilis*, an anaerobic bacteria resistant to ciprofloxacin. Therefore, D.J.'s response to oral ciprofloxacin therapy was poor because of the presence of avascular infected bone and infection by a resistant organism. Optimal treatment of chronic osteomyelitis should be based upon culture and sensitivity information obtained from specimens of infected bone material. Recurrent surgical treatment also may be necessary to finally eradicate chronically infected bone. Initial treatment with IV antibiotics for one to two months is indicated for D.J., with the final duration of therapy actually dependent upon the rate of healing.[3,11]

Intravenous (IV) Antibiotics

13. What would be reasonable antibiotic therapy for D.J.?

On the basis of the bone culture and sensitivity results, D.J. needs high dose intravenous therapy directed at *P. mirabilis* and *B. fragilis*. For purposes of convenience and future home therapy, ceftriaxone 2 gm IV every 24 hours should be started for coverage of *Proteus*. The anaerobic activity of ceftriaxone is inadequate for infections due to *Bacteroides*; therefore, metronidazole 500 mg IV every eight hours also should be started. Clindamycin could be used instead. Because of the excellent oral bioavailability of metronidazole, when D.J. goes home, his dose could be changed to 500 mg orally three times daily. He should be counseled about the "disulfiram-like" reaction between metronidazole and ethanol.[55,56]

The use of oral antibiotics, rather than parenteral agents, immediately after surgical treatment has been explored.[57–59] The results are somewhat positive using ofloxacin as the oral agent, although a 20% relapse rate occurred due to *S. aureus* and *P. aeruginosa*.[60] At this point, D.J. should receive at least four weeks of ceftriaxone and metronidazole as suggested above. After four weeks, then oral therapy with ciprofloxacin and metronidazole could be continued for another period of months. If his sinus tract has not healed, or his arm is still painful, then repeat surgical exploration and repeat bone culture would be necessary. There is little evidence that local irrigation of the site of infection with antibiotics, or use of antibiotic-impregnated beads, improves efficacy of intensive, prolonged systemic antibiotic therapy directed at organisms cultured from the infected bone.[3,61] D.J. should be counseled that curative therapy for his infection will require long-term antibiotics, and perhaps repetitive surgical evaluation and removal of infected bone.

Osteomyelitis Associated with Prosthetic Material

Joint replacement surgery has become a frequent orthopedic procedure for patients with significant joint destruction due to rheumatoid arthritis (RA) and other disabling diseases. Prosthetic knee, shoulder, elbow, or hip devices made of metallic alloys are cemented to adjacent bone to re-establish joint function. Infection of these foreign bodies can occur due to hematogenous dissemination of bacteria or by contiguous spread from a topical wound. Staphylococci are most frequently involved in prosthetic joint infections, followed by streptococci, gram-negative bacilli, and anaerobes. Bacteria infect bone adjacent to the joint prosthesis, including the bone-cement interface, which results in a loosened and less functional prosthesis.[69]

Usual Clinical Presentation

14. E.W., a 76-year-old male, underwent left total knee replacement 8 years ago for chronic osteoarthritis. He was seen in orthopedic clinic because of a 10-day history of worsening left leg pain and inability to bear weight. In clinic, his knee was noted to be swollen and warm, and he had a temperature of 38.3 °C. Aspiration of fluid from the knee revealed a total nucleated cell count of 71,000/mm^3 with 92% neutrophils. Gram's stain of this fluid showed 4+ polymorphonuclear leukocytes (PMNs) and 1+ gram-positive cocci. His peripheral WBC count was 9200 cells/mm^2. He was begun on antibiotic therapy with oxacillin and cefotaxime pending cultures, and he was scheduled for operative evaluation and possible removal of his prosthetic joint. Does E.W. have a prosthetic joint infection? [SI unit: WBC count 9200 × 10^9 cells/L]

The development of chronic pain, swelling, erythema, and tenderness over a prosthetic joint is typical of findings associated with prosthetic joint infection. E.W. has a relatively short duration of symptoms associated with his left knee which also could be due to joint loosening, but his concomitant fever is suggestive of joint infection. The predominance of neutrophils in his joint fluid and gram-positive cocci on Gram's stain are consistent with an infected prosthesis. He has no obvious source of infection on his skin or other site from which bacteria could disseminate which is not unusual. Occasionally, sources of infection with hematogenous dissemination to the prosthetic joint can be identified, such as dental infections, cellulitis, or urinary tract infections. Given the Gram's stain result, E.W. should be "covered" for staphylococci and streptococci with an antistaphylococcal penicillin. These are the most commonly isolated bacteria responsible for prosthetic infection. Because gram-negative bacteria also can infect these joints, it is not unreasonable to add gram-negative coverage to E.W.'s regimen until the results of joint fluid cultures are finalized.

Treatment

15. Does E.W. need surgery and antibiotics to cure his infection?

Yes. Surgery to remove E.W.'s knee prosthesis and chronic antibiotics for six weeks are the current recommendations for optimal eradication of prosthetic joint infection.[69] A "two-stage" orthopedic procedure is involved: removal of the infected prosthesis, joint immobilization and antibiotics for six weeks, then reinsertion of a new joint prosthesis. Since avascular bone cement and prosthetic material can become seeded with bacteria, the complete removal of this material is necessary to have the greatest chance of curing the infection. Six weeks of systemic antibiotic therapy in combination with orthopedic surgery results in superior joint function (97% success) compared to antibiotics for two weeks before joint reinsertion (35% success).[70,71]

16. Joint fluid cultures grow methicillin-susceptible *S. aureus*. How should E.W. be treated with antibiotics for the next 6 weeks?

As long as E.W. stays in the hospital, he should receive high-dose oxacillin (2 gm IV Q 4 hr) after prosthetic joint removal to eradicate bone infection in unremoved tissue. In his case, the duration of hospital stay will depend upon his postoperative course and the logistics of setting up outpatient intravenous therapy. E.W.

will need more permanent IV access (central line or peripherally inserted central catheter) for six weeks of outpatient therapy. His outpatient antibiotic therapy should be vancomycin for ease of once- or twice-daily administration.

17. F.A. is a 45-year-old man with hemophilia A and chronic right knee hemarthroses. Ten years ago he underwent a right total knee replacement which has been complicated by recurrent prosthetic joint infections. F.A. also has been human immunodeficiency virus (HIV)-seropositive for 8 years; his last CD4 count 2 months ago was 40 cells/mm^3 (Normal: >800 cells/mm^3). His current visit to hemophilia clinic is prompted by a 2-week history of right knee tenderness and warmth and decreased range of motion. He discontinued a 6-week course of oral ciprofloxacin 2 months ago which was given to treat the previous prosthetic joint infection due to P. mirabilis. He is not a surgical candidate at this time due to his severe hemophilia and overall prognosis. His other medications include fluconazole for oral thrush, zidovudine combined with didanosine, and trimethoprim-sulfamethoxazole [(TMP-SMX) 1 double-strength tablet daily]. Is F.A. a candidate for life-long suppressive therapy for recurrent joint infection?

Yes. F.A. should receive antibiotics to suppress recurrent osteomyelitis and prosthetic knee infections for the rest of his life. Suppressive therapy may reduce the frequency of symptoms of osteomyelitis and joint infection (tenderness, joint immobility), but also may decrease the risk of dissemination of infection and bacteremia. F.A. should have blood cultures obtained, and, if these are positive, be admitted to the hospital for initial intravenous antibiotics. After cultures are obtained, then reinstitution of oral ciprofloxacin, 750 mg orally twice daily, is reasonable. He should continue ciprofloxacin for the rest of his life. It is likely that the previous *Proteus* infection recurred clinically because the infected avascular prosthetic joint could not be totally eradicated of bacteria. In the absence of systemic antibiotics, viable bacteria are able to proliferate, eventually resulting in symptoms of recurrent, chronic osteomyelitis and prosthetic joint infection.

Septic Arthritis

Septic arthritis or infectious arthritis usually is acquired hematogenously. The highly vascular synovium of the joint allows for easy passage of bacteria from blood into the synovial space. Bacteremia, secondary to *Neisseria gonorrhoeae* or *S. aureus* in particular, often is associated with the development of joint infections. Septic arthritis also can develop secondary to the spread of osteomyelitis into the joint. This is especially a problem in children below the age of one year who still have capillaries perforating the epiphyseal growth plate.

Several factors predispose patients to the development of infectious arthritis. Trauma can directly inoculate the synovium or allow infecting organisms to penetrate the synovium more easily. Patients with certain systemic disorders such as diabetes mellitus, rheumatoid arthritis, osteoarthritis, chronic granulomatous disease, cancer, or chronic liver disease, are more susceptible to development of infection. Endocrine factors can predispose pregnant or menstruating women to the development of gonococcal arthritis. In the menstruating patient, this can be partially explained by the increased endocervical shedding of *N. gonorrhoeae*.[20–22]

Nongonococcal Arthritis

A single joint is involved in 90% of bacterial or suppurative arthritis cases. The joint most commonly involved is the knee. Other potential sites of infectious arthritis in adults include the hip, shoulder, sternoclavicular, and sacroiliac joints; the ankle and elbow are common sites of infection in children. The wrist and interphalangeal joints of the hand also may be involved, but in these cases, the infectious pathogens are most often *N. gonorrhoeae* and *Mycobacteria tuberculosis*.[20] The most common systemic indication of infectious arthritis is fever. Localized symptoms include pain, decreased mobility of the involved joint, and swelling.

Ninety percent of patients also have joint effusion on physical examination. When evaluating a patient who possibly may have a joint infection, any purulent joint effusion should be considered septic until a thorough work-up proves otherwise. On the other hand, a number of noninfectious conditions may present as single joint involvement with synovial effusions (e.g., acute RA, gout, chondrocalcinosis).[21]

Aspirated joint-fluid should be cultured, since isolation of bacteria is the only definitive diagnostic test for bacterial arthritis. The leukocyte count in the synovial fluid usually is markedly elevated, with counts ranging from 50,000 to 200,000 cells/mm^3. Leukocyte counts of less than 20,000 rarely are seen during infection, except in early cases of bacterial arthritis or in patients with disseminated gonococcal infection (DGI). Synovial fluid from an infected joint also may have a decreased glucose concentration, but this is seen in only about 50% of cases.[21,23]

Another laboratory finding consistent with infectious arthritis is the elevated erythrocyte sedimentation rate. Although this value is higher in the case of bacterial infection, viral or fungal arthritis also may be associated with this finding. Increased WBC counts in serum are common in the younger patient but rare in adults. Anemia also may be associated with infection, especially in patients with chronic involvement or in cases where predisposing factors such as rheumatoid arthritis are present.[20,21]

When attempting to determine the most likely pathogen, the patient's age must be taken into consideration. In the adult population and in children over the age of two years, *S. aureus* is the most common cause of bacterial arthritis. However, in adults under age 30, *N. gonorrhoeae* is more likely to be the etiologic agent. Bacterial arthritis in children under two years of age is most likely due to *H. influenzae* type b.[20,21,23] Streptococci, such as Group A beta-hemolytic streptococci, can cause infection in children and adults. Other organisms such as Group B streptococci, anaerobic streptococci, and gram-negative bacteria can cause infection. Gram-negative bacilli are responsible for approximately 15% of cases and often infect multiple joints. Infections with these organisms usually are associated with predisposing factors such as rheumatoid arthritis, osteoarthritis, or heroin use. The organism most commonly isolated from the patient with bacterial arthritis who has a history of intravenous drug abuse is *P. aeruginosa*.[10,20,22] Treatment of nongonococcal arthritis includes drainage of purulent joint fluid (by needle aspiration or surgery) and appropriate antibiotic therapy. Because *S. aureus* is most likely involved, initial, empiric therapy with a penicillinase-resistant penicillin, a cephalosporin, or vancomycin should be initiated.

Although few studies have been carried out to determine the optimum duration of therapy for bacterial arthritis, the current recommendation is to treat for two to three weeks; some investigators recommend that treatment be extended to four weeks for infectious arthritis due to *S. aureus* or gram-negative bacilli.[20–22]

Most joint fluid cultures become negative after seven days of treatment with intravenous antibiotics. Joint inflammation and other symptoms also should improve by this time. However, the duration of articular symptoms before antibiotic therapy has been shown to correlate with subsequent time required to sterilize the synovial fluid. Therefore, delay in initiating antibiotic treatment may necessitate a longer course of therapy. If the patient continues to improve clinically, oral antibiotics often are substituted for intravenous therapy late in the therapeutic course.[21,22,24]

Usual Clinical Presentation

18. A.W., a 44-year-old man, is referred to rheumatology clinic for right knee swelling. Four days ago, his right knee became painful and swollen, and he became unable to flex the joint. He also noted a temperature of 100.5–102 °F over at least 5 days. A joint effusion is present on physical examination, and joint fluid is aspirated for cell count, Gram's stain, and culture. His past medical history is unremarkable except for an episode of hives after receiving cephalexin for an episode of cellulitis 6 months ago. Laboratory data available includes WBC count 12,000 cells /mm³ and ESR 40 mm/hr. WBC count in the synovial fluid from his right knee contains 80,000 cells/mm³ with 90% neutrophils. Synovial fluid Gram's stain shows gram-positive cocci and fluid culture is pending. His temperature is 38.5 °C. What findings in A.W. are consistent with septic arthritis?
[SI units: WBC count 12,000 and 80,000 × 10⁹ cells/L, respectively; neutrophils 0.90; ESR 40 mm/hr]

A.W. has had the acute onset of monoarticular joint pain and swelling, with reduced range of motion and fever. These findings are classic for septic, nongonococcal arthritis. The tap of his joint effusion with a predominance of neutrophils in the joint fluid confirms the diagnosis. In these circumstances, A.W.'s knee has been infected hematogenously from a distant, usually unrecognized, source of infection. The knee is involved most commonly, and *S. aureus* is the usual causative organism. However, if A.W. had a urinary tract infection as well, then gram-negative bacilli would more commonly be responsible for joint infection. Occasionally, a predisposing factor may be present in the involved joint, such as pre-existing arthritis (i.e., RA) or trauma.[22,62]

Initial Antimicrobial Therapy:
Treatment in Beta-Lactam Allergic Patient

19. A.W. describes his reaction to cephalexin as the acute onset (over several hours) of intense pruritic skin lesions over his trunk and upper extremities. The reaction appeared after several doses of cephalexin. He did not experience wheezing or shortness of breath, and his reaction was treated symptomatically by stopping the cephalexin and administering diphenhydramine. He says he had received several types of oral antibiotics before this episode without difficulty, but has not taken antibiotics since then. How should A.W. be treated?

A.W.'s reaction to cephalexin is worrisome. Readministration of a penicillin or cephalosporin would likely cause allergic manifestations to reappear. Because this is a circumstance where alternative, effective nonbeta-lactam treatment is available, it is not necessary to rechallenge A.W. with a beta-lactam. A.W. has septic arthritis from gram-positive cocci, probably due to *S. aureus*, but streptococci also could be involved. Vancomycin (1 gm IV Q 12 hr) will cover both organisms and should be started as soon as possible. In the nonpenicillin-allergic patient, oxacillin and nafcillin (2 gm IV Q 4 hr) are recommended. Beta-lactams and vancomycin penetrate joint effusions in adequate concentration for gram-positive infections.[63] If A.W. acquired his infection in the hospital, then vancomycin also would be initially indicated because of the possibility that methicillin-resistant *S. aureus* is involved. Therapy then can be changed on the basis of sensitivity testing to oxacillin if the organism is susceptible.[22,62] Teicoplanin, another glycopeptide antibiotic for gram-positive infections similar to vancomycin, also may be a suitable beta-lactam alternative for treatment of septic arthritis. However, more experience with this agent must be accumulated before it can be recommended over vancomycin.[64]

Duration of Therapy

20. How long should A.W. be treated? How should the efficacy of treatment be monitored?

A.W. should be treated for at least three weeks.[20,43] His response to therapy should be monitored clinically (resolution of symptoms, fever, and falling ESR) as well as by periodic evaluation of joint fluid. Frequent aspirations of joint fluid, initially on a daily basis, should be done with evaluation of cell count and fluid culture. Effective therapy results in a diminishing WBC count in the joint fluid and negative cultures usually within three to four days of treatment. A poorer outcome (permanent joint dysfunction) can result if joint fluid cultures are still positive after six days of treatment for gram-positive infection. In the case of persistently positive fluid cultures, more aggressive surgical management is necessary in order to preserve joint function.[24,65,66]

Similar to the case with hematogenous osteomyelitis, oral antibiotics have been used in septic arthritis to complete a course of treatment where an adequate response initially has occurred with intravenous therapy. Case series with generally positive results are reported; adequately controlled, randomized clinical trials comparing intravenous and oral therapy are not available.[21,43,59,63] Because of A.W.'s allergy to cephalexin, the choice of adequate oral therapy to complete at least three weeks of treatment is difficult. Due to the continuing emergence of resistance among gram-positive organisms to ciprofloxacin, use of this agent should be discouraged. Clindamycin could be used, but published experience is primarily with pediatric patients.[67] If the *S. aureus* isolated from A.W. is sensitive to trimethoprim-sulfamethoxazole, then this agent may be an alternative to clindamycin for oral treatment. However, published experience with this mode of treatment also is lacking. A.W. should be advised that parenteral treatment with vancomycin, which can be accomplished at home, would be the most effective mode of treatment.

Gonococcal Arthritis

Arthritis in multiple joints is one of the most common features of disseminated infection due to *N. gonorrhoeae*. Unlike nongonococcal arthritis which is almost exclusively monoarticular, gonococcal arthritis involves multiple joints in approximately 50% of cases. Clinically, patients present initially with a migratory polyarthralgia and later with fever, dermatitis, and tenosynovitis. The skin lesions are an important clue in the diagnosis of disseminated gonococcal disease and often begin as tiny erythematous papules which later develop into larger vesicles. Other symptoms such as purulent and swollen joints, are present in only 30% to 40% of patients. As in hematogenously-acquired nongonococcal arthritis, the synovial fluid leukocyte count usually is elevated, but to a lesser degree. Unfortunately, *N. gonorrhoeae* is recovered in less than 50% of purulent joint effusions; however, blood cultures often are positive for this organism and with the patient's clinical presentation can be used to make a definitive diagnosis.[20,21,23] Because of possible penicillinase production by *N. gonorrhoeae*, recommended therapy is with ceftriaxone initially. If the organism can be cultured and is sensitive, oral treatment to complete a ten-day course with amoxicillin or doxycycline usually is effective.[20] When sensitivities are not available, oral therapy with cefixime or ciprofloxacin is recommended.[25]

Usual Clinical Presentation

21. A.S., a 19-year-old woman, is seen in the walk-in medicine clinic because of right knee and right shoulder pain, nausea, and vomiting. Upon physical examination, her right knee is swollen and she has decreased range of motion of her right shoulder. Several erythematous, papular skin lesions are noted on both hands. She also has a vaginal discharge. Her temperature is 38.2 °C, and her WBC count is 15,000 cells/mm³. She

gives a history of having 2 recent sexual partners. Cultures of blood, joint fluid, and vaginal discharge are obtained; joint fluid Gram's stain shows heavy PMNs, but no organisms are seen. Why is A.S. considered to have gonococcal arthritis? [SI unit: WBC count 15,000 × 10^9 cells/L]

Polyarticular arthritis in a young, sexually active adult is caused most commonly by *N. gonorrhoeae*. A.S. has systemic signs of infection, skin lesions, and multiple joint involvement which is classic for disseminated gonococcal infection. Her history of recent sexual activity and the presence of a vaginal discharge is consistent with gonococcal infection, although evidence or symptoms of mucosal infection with *N. gonorrhoeae* are not necessary for disseminated infection to occur.[3,22,68]

Patient Work-Up and Treatment in the Clinic

22. What additional work-up should be accomplished in A.S.? Can she be treated immediately in the clinic?

A.S. should be evaluated for other sexually-transmitted diseases, specifically syphilis and HIV infection. Serologic testing for syphilis [rapid plasma reagent (RPR) or venereal disease research laboratory (VDRL) testing] and for antibody to HIV should be obtained. In addition, A.S. should have a pregnancy test. Some of the antibiotics that may be used in A.S. are contraindicated during pregnancy, including doxycycline and ciprofloxacin.

A.S. should receive her first dose of antibiotics for disseminated gonococcal infection in the clinic. Many strains of *N. gonorrhoeae* now produce penicillinase, therefore, ceftriaxone 1 gm IV or IM should be administered.

Full Course of Therapy

23. Results of RPR and pregnancy testing in A.S. are negative. How should she complete her course of therapy?

Disseminated gonococcal infection should be treated for seven days. A.S. also should begin treatment with doxycycline (100 mg PO BID × 7 days) for the possibility of concomitant *Chlamydia* infection. A.S. can complete her course of treatment for DGI orally, although parenteral therapy is recommended until signs and symptoms resolve. This usually takes two to four days.[68] She will have to return to the clinic for daily ceftriaxone unless other arrangements for parenteral therapy can be made. Current recommendations from the Center for Disease Control are that oral treatment should be either ciprofloxacin 500 mg orally twice daily or cefixime 400 mg orally twice daily. Improvement in symptoms usually occurs within 48 hours.[25,68] Treatment guidelines for DGI are included in the gonorrhea section of Chapter 64: Sexually Transmitted Diseases.

Acknowledgment

We gratefully acknowledge Francesca T Aweeka whose work provided a foundation for this chapter.

References

1 **Waldwogel FA, Vasey H.** Osteomyelitis: the past decade. N Engl J Med. 1980;303:360.

2 **Waldwogel FA et al.** Osteomyelitis: review of clinical features, therapeutic considerations and unusual aspects. N Engl J Med. 1970;282:198.

3 **Norden CW.** Osteomyelitis. In: Mandell GL et al., eds. Principles and Practice of Infectious Diseases. 3rd ed. New York: Churchill Livingstone; 1990:922.

4 **Emslie KR, Nade S.** Pathogenesis and treatment of acute hematogenous osteomyelitis: evaluation of current views with reference to an animal model. Rev Infect Dis. 1986;8:841.

5 **Nelson JD.** Acute osteomyelitis in children. Infect Dis Clin North Am. 1990;4:513.

6 **Silverthorn KG, Gillespie WJ.** Pyogenic spinal osteomyelitis: a review of 61 cases. N Z Med J. 1986;99:62.

7 **Jackson MA et al.** Pyogenic arthritis associated with adjacent osteomyelitis: identification of the sequela-prone child. Pediatr Infect Dis J. 1992;11:9.

8 **Anderson JR et al.** The treatment of acute osteomyelitis in children: a 10-year experience. J Antimicrob Chemother. 1981;(Suppl. A):43.

9 **Vaughn PA et al.** Acute hematogenous osteomyelitis in children. J Pediatr Orthop. 1987;7:652.

10 **Chandrasekar PH, Narula AP.** Bone and joint infections in intravenous drug abusers. Rev Infect Dis. 1986;8:904.

11 **Gentry LO.** Antibiotic therapy for osteomyelitis. Infect Dis Clin North Am. 1990;4:485.

12 **Prober CG.** Current antibiotic therapy of community-acquired bacterial infections in hospitalized children: bone and joint infections. Pediatr Infect Dis J. 1992;11:156.

13 **Calhoun KH et al.** Osteomyelitis of the mandible. Arch Otolaryngol Head Neck Surg. 1988;114:1157.

14 **Sugerman B et al.** Osteomyelitis beneath pressure sores. Arch Intern Med. 1983;143:683.

15 **Johnson P et al.** Management of chronic sternal osteomyelitis. Ann Thorac Surg. 1985;40:69.

16 **Hall B et al.** Anaerobic osteomyelitis. J Bone Joint Surg (Am). 1983;65:30.

17 **Mackowiak P et al.** Diagnostic value of sinus-tract cultures in chronic osteomyelitis. JAMA. 1978;329:2772.

18 **Fitzgerald RH Jr et al.** Local muscle flaps in the treatment of chronic osteomyelitis. J Bone Joint Surg (Am). 1985;67:175.

19 **Keogh BS et al.** The effect of local antibiotics in treating chronic osseous staphylococcus aureus infection. J Oral Maxillofac Surg. 1989;47:940.

20 **Smith JW.** Infectious arthritis. In: Mandell GL et al., eds. Principles and Practice of Infectious Diseases. 3rd ed. New York: Churchill Livingstone; 1990:911.

21 **Goldenberg DL, Reed JI.** Bacterial arthritis. N Engl J Med. 1985;312:764.

22 **Smith JW.** Infectious arthritis. Infect Dis Clin North Am. 1990;4:523.

23 **O'Brien JP et al.** Disseminated gonococcal infection: a prospective analysis of 49 patients and a review of the pathophysiology and immune mechanisms. Medicine (Baltimore). 1983;62:395.

24 **Ho G, Su EY.** Therapy for septic arthritis. JAMA. 1982;247:797.

25 **Centers for Disease Control and Prevention.** 1993 sexually transmitted diseases treatment guidelines. MMWR. 1993;42:61.

26 **Schauwecker DS et al.** Diagnostic imaging of osteomyelitis. Infect Dis Clin North Am. 1990;4:441.

27 **Dagan R.** Management of acute hematogenous osteomyelitis and septic arthritis in the pediatric patient. Pediatr Infect Dis J. 1993;12:88.

28 **Fisher MC et al.** Sneakers as a source of *Pseudomonas aeruginosa* in children with osteomyelitis following puncture wounds. J Pediatr. 1985;106:607.

29 **Smilack JD et al.** Bone concentrations of antimicrobial agents after parenteral administration. Antimicrob Agents Chemother. 1976;9:169.

30 **Smith BR et al.** Bone penetration of antibiotics. Orthopedics. 1983;6:187.

31 **Schurman DJ et al.** Cefazolin concentrations in bone and synovial fluid. J Bone Joint Surg Am. 1978;60A:359.

32 **Dornbusch K et al.** Antibacterial activity of cefuroxime in human bone. Scand J Infect Dis. 1980;12:49.

33 **Neu HC.** Cephalosporin antibiotics as applied in surgery of bones and joints. Clin Orthop. 1984;190:50.

34 **Wilber RB.** Beta-lactam therapy of osteomyelitis and septic arthritis. Scand J Infect Dis. 1984;2:155.

35 **Fong IW et al.** Ciprofloxacin concentrations in bone and muscle after oral dosing. Antimicrob Agents Chemother. 1986;29:405.

36 **Adam D et al.** Concentrations of ticarcillin and clavulanic acid in human bone after prophylactic administration of 5.2 g of Timentin. Antimicrob Agents Chemother. 1987;31:935.

37 **Graziani AL et al.** Vancomycin concentrations in infected and non-infected human bone. Antimicrob Agents Chemother. 1988;32:1320.

38 **Fitzgerald RH Jr et al.** Pathophysiology of osteomyelitis and pharmacokinetics of antimicrobial agents in normal and osteomyelitic bone. In: Esterhai JL Jr et al., eds. Musculoskeletal Infection. Park Ridge: American Academy of Orthopaedic Surgeons; 1990:387.

39 **Dich VQ et al.** Osteomyelitis in infants and children. Am J Dis Child. 1975;129:1273.

40 **Wolfson JS, Swartz MN.** Serum bactericidal activity as a monitor of antibiotic therapy. N Engl J Med. 1985;312:968.

41 **Prober CG, Yeager AS.** Use of the serum bactericidal titer to assess the adequacy of oral antibiotic therapy in the treatment of acute hematogenous osteomyelitis. J Pediatr. 1979;95:131.

42 **Weinstein MP et al.** Multicenter collaborative evaluation of a standardized serum bactericidal test as a predictor of therapeutic efficacy in acute and chronic osteomyelitis. Am J Med. 1987;83:218.

43 **Syrogiannopoulos GA, Nelson JD.** Duration of antimicrobial therapy for acute suppurative osteoarticular infections. Lancet. 1988;1:37.

44 **Moore RD et al.** The association of aminoglycoside plasma levels with mortality in patients with gram-negative bacteremia. J Infect Dis. 1984;149:443.

45 **Moore RD et al.** Association of aminoglycoside plasma levels with therapeutic outcome in gram-negative pneumonia. Am J Med. 1984;77:657.

46 **Gilbert DN.** Once-daily aminoglycoside therapy. Antimicrob Agents Chemother. 1991;35:399.

47 **Nordstrom L et al.** Does administration of an aminoglycoside in a single

daily dose affect its efficacy and toxicity? J Antimicrob Chemother. 1990; 25:159.

48 Maller R et al. Efficacy and safety of amikacin in systemic infections when given as a single daily dose or in two divided doses. J Antimicrob Chemother. 1991;27(Suppl. C):121.

49 Prins JM et al. Once versus thrice daily gentamicin in patients with serious infections. Lancet. 1993;341:335.

50 Bach MC, Cocchetto DM. Ceftazidime as single-agent therapy for gram-negative aerobic bacillary osteomyelitis. Antimicrob Agents Chemother. 1987;31:1605.

51 Sheftel TG, Mader JT. Randomized evaluation of ceftazidime or ticarcillin and tobramycin for the treatment of osteomyelitis caused by gram-negative bacilli. Antimicrob Agents Chemother. 1986;29:112.

52 Norrby SR et al. Therapy of acute and chronic gram-negative osteomyelitis with ciprofloxacin. J Antimicrob Chemother. 1988;22:221.

53 Gentry LO, Rodriguez GG. Oral ciprofloxacin compared with parenteral antibiotics in the treatment of osteomyelitis. Antimicrob Agents Chemother. 1990;34:40.

54 Dan M et al. Oral ciprofloxacin treatment of Pseudomonas aeruginosa osteomyelitis. Antimicrob Agents Chemother. 1990;34:849.

55 Jensen JC, Gugler R. Single and multiple-dose metronidazole kinetics. Clin Pharmacol Ther. 1983;34:481.

56 Roe RJC. Metronidazole: review of uses and toxicity. J Antimicrob Chemother. 1977;3:205.

57 Ingram C et al. Antibiotic therapy of osteomyelitis in outpatients. Med Clin North Am. 1988;72:723.

58 Hoogkamp-Korstanje JAA et al. Treatment of chronic osteomyelitis with ciprofloxacin. J Antimicrob Chemother. 1989;23:427.

59 Black J et al. Oral antimicrobial therapy for adults with osteomyelitis or septic arthritis. J Infect Dis. 1987;155: 968.

60 Gentry LO, Rodriguez-Gomez G. Ofloxacin versus parenteral therapy for chronic osteomyelitis. Antimicrob Agents Chemother. 1991;35:538.

61 Dirschl DR, Almekinders LC. Osteomyelitis: common causes and treatment recommendations. Drugs. 1993; 45:29.

62 Mikhail IS, Alarcon GS. Nongonococcal bacterial arthritis. Rheum Dis Clin North Am. 1993;19:311.

63 Sattar MA et al. Concentrations of some antibiotics in synovial fluid after oral administration, with special reference to antistaphylococcal activity. Ann Rheum Dis. 1983;42:67.

64 Weinberg WG. Safety and efficacy of teicoplanin for bone and joint infections: results of a community-based trial. South Med J. 1993;86:891.

65 Broy SB et al. A comparison of medical drainage (needle aspiration) and surgical drainage (arthrotomy or arthroscopy) in the initial treatment of infected joints. Clin Rheum Dis. 1986; 12:501.

66 Ivey M, Clark R. Arthroscopic debridement of the knee for septic arthritis. Clin Orthop. 1985;199:201.

67 Jackson MA, Nelson JD. Etiology and medical management of acute suppurative bone and joint infections in pediatric patients. J Pediatr Orthop. 1982; 2:313.

68 Scopelitis E, Martinez-Osuna P. Gonococcal arthritis. Rheum Dis Clin North Am. 1993;19:363.

69 Brause BD. Infections with prostheses in bones and joints. In: Mandell GL et al., eds. Principles and Practice of Infectious Diseases. 3rd ed. New York: Churchill Livingstone; 1990:919.

70 Insall JN et al. Two-stage re-implantation for the salvage of infected total knee arthroplasty. J Bone Joint Surg Am. 1983;65:1087.

71 Rand JA, Bryan RS. Re-implantation for the salvage of an infected total knee arthroplasty. J Bone Joint Surg Am. 1983;65:1081.

72 Jacobs JC. Acute osteomyelitis medical management in children. N Y State J Med. 1978;78:910–12.

73 Tetzlaff TR et al. Antibiotic concentrations in pus and bone of children with osteomyelitis. J Pediatr. 1978;92: 135.

74 Bernstein BM, Fass RJ. Treatment of osteomyelitis and septic arthritis with cefamandole. Am J Med Sci. 1982; 284:2.

75 Nelson JB. Benefits and risks of sequential parenteral-oral cephalosporin therapy for suppurative bone and joint infections. J Pediatr Orthop. 1982;2: 255.

76 Adam D et al. Penetration of ceftazidime into human tissue in patients undergoing cardiac surgery. J Antimicrob Chemother. 1983;12(Suppl. A):269.

77 Nicholas P et al. Concentration of clindamycin in human bone. Antimicrob Agents Chemother. 1975;8:220.

78 Dornbusch K et al. Antibacterial activity of clindamycin and lincomycin in human bone. J Antimicrob Chemother. 1977;3:153.

79 Norden CW. Experimental osteomyelitis. IV. Therapeutic trials with rifampin alone and in combination with gentamicin, sisomicin, and cephalothin. J Infect Dis. 1975;132:493.

80 Eron LJ et al. Ciprofloxacin therapy of infections caused by Pseudomonas aeruginosa and other resistant bacteria. Antimicrob Agents Chemother. 1985; 27:308.

81 Gentry LO. Treatment of skin, skin structure, bone and joint infections with ceftazidime. Am J Med. 1985; 79(S2A):229.

82 Fong IW et al. Penetration of ciprofloxacin into bone and muscle tissue. Antimicrob Agents Chemother. 1986; 29:405.

83 Neu HC. Aztreonam activity, pharmacology and clinical uses. Am J Med. 1990;88(S3C):3C–3S.

84 Triffitt JT. Organic matrix of bone tissue. In: Urist MR, ed. Fundamental and Clinical Bone Physiology. Philadelphia: JB Lippincott; 1980:46.

Traumatic Skin and Soft Tissue Infections

James P McCormack
Glen Brown

Organisms (See Table 66.1) 66-2
Antibiotics (See Table 66.2) 66-3
Cellulitis 66-1
  Definition and Causative Organisms 66-1
  Empiric Antibiotic Therapy for Moderate Cellulitis 66-2
  Treatment for the Penicillin Allergic Patient
    (Also see Question 8) 66-2
  Doses of Antibiotics 66-2
  Treatment Duration 66-2
  Evaluation of Therapy 66-4
  Role of Topical Antibiotics 66-4
  Empiric Antibiotic Therapy for Moderate to Severe
    Cellulitis 66-4
  Penicillin Allergy (Also see Question 2) 66-4
  Culture and Sensitivity Results 66-4
  Intravenous (IV) Drug Abuser 66-4
    Causative organisms 66-5
    Empiric antibiotic therapy 66-5
Soft Tissue Infections in Diabetics 66-5
  Predisposing Factors 66-5
  Causative Organisms 66-5

Empiric Antibiotic Therapy 66-6
Postamputation Antibiotic Treatment 66-6
Prevention 66-6
Necrotizing Soft Tissue Infections 66-6
  Definitions, Terminology, and Causative Organisms 66-6
  Causative Organisms 66-7
  Empiric Antibiotic Therapy 66-7
Erysipelas 66-7
  Signs, Symptoms, and Causative Organisms 66-7
  Causative Organisms 66-7
  Empiric Antibiotic Therapy 66-7
Acute Traumatic Wounds 66-8
Animal Bite Wounds 66-8
  Evaluation of Dog and Cat Bites 66-8
  Causative Organisms and Empiric Antibiotic Therapy .. 66-8
Human Bite Wounds 66-9
  Evaluation of Human Bites 66-9
  Empiric Antibiotic Therapy and Causative Organisms .. 66-9
Tetanus Prophylaxis 66-9

Skin and soft tissue infections refer to those infections involving any or all layers of the skin (epidermis, dermis), subcutaneous fat, fascia, or muscle. Many terms or classifications are used to describe various skin and soft tissue infections, and these often are based upon the site of infection and causative organism(s). However, these terms or classifications add little to the understanding and treatment of these infections. In fact, confusion in terminology may be detrimental if treatment is delayed until a causative organism is identified.[1,2]

While mild skin and soft tissue infections often are self-limiting, moderate to severe infections can, if not treated appropriately, progress to complicated infections such as septic arthritis, osteomyelitis, or systemic infections (bacteremia). Soft tissue infections in diabetic patients can lead to gangrene and loss of limb while necrotizing soft tissue infections, even with appropriate treatment, can be fatal in 30% to 50% of patients.[1-3]

This chapter will focus on skin and soft tissue infections that are primarily due to a break in the skin following an abrasion, skin puncture, ulceration, surgical wound, intentional or unintentional insertion of a foreign body, or following a blunt soft-tissue contusion. Superficial skin infections such as impetigo, infections that originate within the hair follicle (e.g., folliculitis, furuncles, carbuncles) or sweat pores, styes, acne, diaper rash, and skin infestations will not be presented.

The treatment of traumatic skin and soft tissue infections often is empiric and based upon the severity and site of infection, the underlying immunocompetence of the patient, and the triggering event (e.g., abrasion, bite, insertion of a foreign object), because attempts to isolate the causative organism often are futile.[4,5] The potential organisms that should be considered when empirically treating patients presenting with a traumatic skin and soft tissue infection are outlined in Table 66.1. Some of the more common antibiotics used in skin and soft tissue infections and their spectrum of activity are outlined in Table 66.2.

Cellulitis

Definition and Causative Organisms

1. T.E., a 25-year-old female, presents to her family doctor with a 2–3 day history of worsening pain, redness, and swelling on her left leg following a scrape which occurred sliding into second base during a softball tournament. The area is warm to the touch with a defined erythematous border. Over the last 24–36 hours the leg has become increasingly painful and "tight." Mild lymphadenopathy is present and T.E. has a temperature of 38.2 °C. The presumptive diagnosis is a moderate cellulitis and cloxacillin (Tegopen, Cloxapen) is prescribed. Why is cloxacillin appropriate empiric treatment for T.E.?

Cellulitis is an acute inflammation of the skin and subcutaneous fat and is characterized by symptoms of local tenderness, pain, swelling, warmth, and erythema with or without a definite entry point. Cellulitis is usually secondary to trauma or an underlying skin lesion which allows bacterial penetration into the skin and underlying tissues. Local treatment (i.e., cleaning/irrigation of the site with soap and water) is all that is required for mild cellulitis in patients with no evidence of a systemic infection. In T.E., however, the elevated temperature, increasing pain, and lymphadenopathy suggest a more serious infection. Antibiotics, in addition to local wound care, should be prescribed for T.E. Cellulitis most often is caused by group A beta-hemolytic streptococci (*Streptococcus pyogenes*) and less often, *Staphylococcus aureus* (see Table 66.1).[4-6] However, wound cultures often are negative and fail to identify the causative organism.[4,5] Other organisms (*Escherichia coli*, *Pseudomonas aeruginosa*, *Klebsiella pneumoniae*) also can cause cellulitis, but only should be suspected in patients who are

Table 66.1	Potential Organisms Causing Skin and Soft Tissue Infections[a]							
	Gram-Positive		Gram-Negative		Anaerobes			
	Staphylococcal	Streptococcal	E coli, Klebsiella, Proteus	Pasteurella multocida	Eikenella corrodens	Oral Anaerobes	Clostridium sp	Bacteroides fragilis
Cellulitis	X	X						
Diabetic soft tissue	X	X	X					X
Necrotizing infections	X	X	X			X	X	X
Erysipelas		X						
Animal bites	X	X		X		X		
Human bites	X	X	X		X	X		

[a] X = These organisms should be covered empirically with appropriate antibiotic therapy.

immunocompromised or in patients who fail treatment with antibiotics that have activity limited to gram-positive organisms.

Empiric Antibiotic Therapy for Moderate Cellulitis

Oral cloxacillin (Tegopen, Cloxapen) is appropriate empiric therapy for cellulitis in an otherwise healthy individual such as T.E. Cloxacillin has good activity against staphylococcal and streptococcal organisms and is better tolerated than erythromycin (E-Mycin) or clindamycin (Cleocin). Dicloxacillin (Dynapen), another antistaphylococcal penicillin, produces slightly higher total serum concentrations than cloxacillin, but is more highly protein bound, resulting in slightly lower free serum concentrations.[7] Flucloxacillin [(Floxapen) not available in the U.S.] provides similar total serum concentrations to dicloxacillin (Dynapen), but is less protein bound and produces higher free concentrations than either cloxacillin or dicloxacillin.[7] These small differences in pharmacokinetics do not affect clinical outcome and the choice between these agents should be based upon cost. If the cellulitis is well demarcated and there are no pockets of pus or evidence of vein thrombosis, penicillin (V-Cillin K, Pen-Vee K) alone can be appropriate because the causative organism is likely to be streptococcal. Many other available antibiotics that have activity against staphylococcal and streptococcal organisms have been evaluated for effectiveness in skin and soft tissue infections (see Table 66.2). While many of these antibiotics are effective for the treatment of cellulitis, none are more effective than cloxacillin or dicloxacillin for the treatment of cellulitis. Cephalexin (Keflex) is probably as effective and as well tolerated as cloxacillin or dicloxacillin and comparable in cost. Cephalexin has been shown to be just as effective as more expensive agents (ofloxacin).[8] The gram-negative activity of cephalexin (not seen with cloxacillin or dicloxacillin) is not required for most cases of cellulitis in otherwise healthy patients. In many emergency rooms (ERs), a single dose of a long-acting parenterally-administered cephalosporin (e.g., ceftriaxone), followed by oral therapy with one of the above agents is often the preferred treatment regimen. This regimen is not more effective than oral therapy alone, and ceftriaxone (Rocephin) significantly adds to the cost of treatment. A single dose of ceftriaxone is as, if not more expensive, than a ten-day course of appropriate oral therapy.

In the above case, antibiotic treatment is required, and T.E. should receive the least expensive of either cloxacillin, dicloxacillin, or cephalexin. In addition to systemic therapy, T.E. should be instructed to keep the area clean with soap and water (if an open wound is present) and protect the area.

Treatment for the Penicillin Allergic Patient

2. What agents could be chosen if T.E. was penicillin allergic?

Oral erythromycin (E-mycin) or clindamycin (Cleocin) could be chosen in patients with a documented history of penicillin or cephalosporin allergy. Erythromycin causes nausea, vomiting, diarrhea, and cramps in 30% to 40% of patients but this can be decreased by taking it with food. Clindamycin causes diarrhea in 20% of patients and can cause serious toxicity secondary to pseudomembranous colitis. Erythromycin is much less expensive than clindamycin and unless a patient has documented gastrointestinal (GI) intolerance to erythromycin it is preferred over clindamycin. In addition, trimethoprim-sulfamethoxazole (Bactrim, Septra) has very good activity against gram-positive organisms and while it has not been significantly evaluated or compared against other antibiotics for soft tissue infections, it would be a useful inexpensive alternative in a patient with an allergy to penicillin.

Doses of Antibiotics

3. What dose should be prescribed for T.E.?

The recommended doses in the literature for cloxacillin (Tegopen, Cloxapen) and dicloxacillin (Dynapen) are 250 mg to 500 mg orally every six hours and 125 to 250 mg orally every six hours, respectively.[9] Although lower doses of dicloxacillin can be used, cloxacillin and dicloxacillin produce relatively similar free serum concentrations and should be prescribed in similar doses.[10] The dose for mild to moderate infections should be 250 mg orally every six hours, and for moderate to severe infections 500 mg orally every six hours. Doses up to 1000 mg orally every six hours have been used, but GI intolerance (usually diarrhea) may occur. The above doses also apply to cephalexin and erythromycin. The dose for Pen-V is 250 to 500 mg orally every six hours, and 150 to 450 mg orally every six hours for oral clindamycin. As cloxacillin is the drug chosen for T.E., a dose of 250 mg orally every six hours should be sufficient. However, if she was more severely ill, the higher dose 500 mg orally every six hours could be chosen.

Treatment Duration

4. How long should T.E. be treated?

The usual duration of therapy for cellulitis is ten days or four to five days after the patient has become afebrile and has improved clinically. T.E. should be counseled to expect a response within one to two days after therapy initiation (erythema may persist longer) and that if the condition does not improve or worsens over the next couple of days, she should return for re-evaluation.

Table 66.2

Spectrum of Activity for Antibiotics Useful in the Treatment of Skin and Soft Tissue Infections

Antibiotics	Spectrum of Activity								
	Gram-Positive			Gram-Negative			Anaerobes		
	Streptococci Other Than Enterococcus	Enterococci	Staphylococci	E. coli, Klebsiella, Proteus	Pasteurella multocida	Eikenella corrodens	Oral Anaerobes	Clostridium sp	Bacteroides fragilis
Penicillin	++++	++++	+	−	++++	++++	++++	++++	−
Cloxacillin, Nafcillin, Flucloxacillin, Dicloxacillin	+++	−	++++	−	+	−	+++	++++	−
Amoxicillin/clavulanate, Ampicillin/sulbactam	+++	++++	++++	+++	++++	++++	++++	++++	+++
Piperacillin	++	++++	+	+++	++	++	+++	++++	+++
Piperacillin/tazobactam	+++	++++	+++	++++	++	++	+++	++++	+++
Ticarcillin/clavulanate	+++	−	+++	++++	++	++	+++	++++	+++
Cephalexin, Cefazolin	+++	−	++++	++	−	−	++++	+	−
Cefoxitin, Ceftizoxime, Cefotetan, Cefmetazole	++	−	+++	+++	++	++	+++	+	+++
Cefotaxime, Ceftriaxone	++	−	+++	++++	++	++	+++	+	−
Clindamycin	++++	−	+++	−	−	−	++++	+++	++++
Metronidazole	−	−	−	−	−	−	+++	++++	++++
Vancomycin	++++	++++	++++	−	−	−	+++	+++	−
Erythromycin	+++	−	+++	−	+	+	++	+++	−
Gentamicin	+	++	+++	+++	−	+	−	−	−
Trimethoprim/sulfamethoxazole (Co-trimoxazole)	+++	+	+++	+	++	+	−	−	−
Tetracycline Doxycycline	++	−	+++		++	++	−	+++	−
Ciprofloxacin	+	++	+++	+++	+++	+++	++	−	−

Evaluation of Therapy

5. What further diagnostic evaluation should be undertaken for T.E.?

In otherwise healthy individuals, identification of the causative organism in cases of cellulitis is unnecessary. Needle aspiration, fine-needle aspiration biopsy, and punch biopsy have isolated the causative organism in only about 15% to 25% of patients.[4-6] Appropriate empiric treatment is effective in the vast majority of patients and an attempt to isolate the organism does not contribute to the success of treatment and adds significantly to the cost of care. Although organisms often are not cultured, attempts at identification of the organism are recommended if initial treatment fails and when treating immunocompromised patients, patients with potential joint or tendon damage, and patients with life-threatening infections requiring hospitalization. In these cases, a swab of the primary wound and a needle aspiration or punch biopsy of the leading edge of the cellulitis should be obtained for Gram's stain and culture before initiating antimicrobial therapy. Blood for cultures should be drawn in addition to wound cultures in these patients. Anaerobic cultures need only be drawn when the wound contains necrotic tissue, is foul smelling, or crepitus is present. Despite obtaining wound and blood cultures, many infections will be culture negative (74%).[4] Culture information, when used in conjunction with clinical course, can be used to modify subsequent treatment. As T.E. only has a moderate cellulitis, cultures are not required and therapy can be given empirically.

Role of Topical Antibiotics

6. What role do topical antibiotics play in the treatment of T.E.'s cellulitis?

The value of topical antibiotics in the prevention or treatment of skin infections is questionable. Most topical antibiotics have not been evaluated in appropriately designed trials. Although mupirocin produces positive bacteriologic results over placebo in the treatment of some types of wound infections,[11,12] most of the studies show no important clinical differences.[12] Mupirocin has been compared favorably to erythromycin and cloxacillin in the treatment of patients with impetigo, minor wound infections, and mild cellulitis; however, most cases of mild cellulitis will improve with only local wound care (e.g., cleansing or irrigation of the area). In patients with moderate to severe infections, mupirocin or any topical antibiotics (neomycin, bacitracin, polymyxin B) should not be used to replace or augment systemic antibiotics. Topical antibiotics likely do little but add to the cost of therapy and occasionally are responsible for the development of a contact dermatitis.[12] T.E., therefore, should not be treated with topical antibiotics because her moderately severe cellulitis should be managed adequately by her systemic antimicrobial therapy.

Empiric Antibiotic Therapy
for Moderate to Severe Cellulitis

7. J.M., a 34-year-old male, presents to the ER with a 3–4 day history of increasing pain around his left hip secondary to an injury he received falling off the sidewalk while trying out his new Rollerblades. In addition, he has a fever and symptoms of weakness, lethargy, and nausea. An examination reveals a very swollen, warm, and extremely tender hip. J.M. has a temperature of 39.8 °C and appears quite ill. A diagnosis of moderate to severe cellulitis is made and J.M. is hospitalized because of the severity of the infection. J.M. has no other underlying medical problems. What empirical antibiotic regimen would be reasonable for J.M.?

In moderate to severely ill patients, when hospitalization is required, antibiotics should be administered parenterally. The par-

enteral agent of choice is nafcillin (Nafcil, cloxacillin in Canada). Some clinicians add penicillin G (2 MU Q 6 hr) to nafcillin to ensure adequate coverage against streptococcal organisms because the minimum inhibitory concentrations for penicillin against streptococci are lower than those with nafcillin;[10] however, this "double coverage" is unnecessary if high dose nafcillin (2 gm IV Q 6 hr) is used. Cefazolin (2 gm IV Q 8 hr) would be an appropriate alternative if it is less expensive than nafcillin. Second- and third-generation cephalosporins [cefuroxime (Zinacef), cefoxitin (Mefoxin), ceftriaxone (Rocephin), cefotaxime (Claforan)] and some quinolones are potentially as effective as nafcillin but provide no clinical advantages and are more expensive. Therefore, J.M. should receive the least expensive of nafcillin or cefazolin. Wound site needle aspiration and blood samples should be taken for culture and sensitivity (C&S) testing. Initial empiric therapy should be continued for 48 hours, and further therapy should be based upon the assessment of clinical improvement and culture and sensitivity results. Once J.M. has become afebrile and has clinically improved for two days, the parenteral antibiotic should be discontinued and appropriate oral therapy (cloxacillin) initiated to complete at least a ten-day course (treat for 2 weeks if patient responds slowly).

Penicillin Allergy

8. Two days after starting therapy J.M. develops a maculopapular skin rash. What alternative therapy should be chosen?

Regardless of when during the course of therapy a drug rash occurred (early or late), the precipitant drug should be discontinued because there is a chance, although small, that the reaction could worsen. In patients who develop a penicillin allergy and who still require parenteral therapy, clindamycin, erythromycin, or vancomycin (Vancocin) could be chosen. As all of these agents are equally effective, the decision of which drug to be used in J.M. should be based upon cost and dosing convenience (clindamycin 600 mg IV Q 8 hr, erythromycin 500 mg IV Q 6 hr, and vancomycin 1000 mg IV Q 12 hr). The administration of intravenous erythromycin is not convenient because of its significant local irritative properties, and either vancomycin or clindamycin would be preferred for J.M.

Culture and Sensitivity Results

9. After 48 hours of therapy, C&S results are available. What changes, if any, should be made in J.M.'s treatment?

If cultures show only streptococcal organisms, in a nonpenicillin allergic patient, therapy should be switched to penicillin G since it is effective, well tolerated, and less expensive than nafcillin (Nafcil). If cultures show staphylococcal species (*S. aureus, S. epidermidis*) that are methicillin sensitive, continue with the initial empiric therapy. If the organisms are methicillin-resistant, switch therapy to vancomycin using a dose of 15 mg/kg/dose intravenously every 12 hours. Since J.M. has developed a presumed penicillin allergy, he should continue with his existing therapy of either clindamycin or vancomycin.

Intravenous (IV) Drug Abuser

10. M.C., a 22-year-old female, presents to the ER with a 3–4 day history of pain in her left forearm. On examination, a swollen and erythematous area approximately 8 × 12 cm in the antecubital fossa of the left arm is seen. The area is warm and tender to the touch. M.C. has a temperature of 39.2 °C. She admits to injecting heroin daily and track marks can be seen on both arms. She states that she uses "filtered tap water" as a diluent for her narcotics. M.C. states that "the arm has only been hurting for the last 3 days." There are no signs of

lymphangitis or thrombophlebitis. What tests need to be obtained to confirm the diagnosis?

M.C. has all the cardinal signs of cellulitis (i.e., induration, edema, erythema, and tenderness to touch). Given her history of an injury (injection), her presentation is compatible with cellulitis. No additional tests are required unless on clinical examination, there is a suspicion of additional injury beyond the injection site or of a deeper infection (e.g., osteomyelitis). Obtaining a specimen from the infection site (by aspiration) to identify the organism(s) is unnecessary unless the patient has a concurrent condition that could impair her immunological response.[5] The sensitivity of needle aspiration at the edge of the wound or site of greatest inflammation in identifying the infecting organism is only about 10%;[13] therefore, aspiration of the wound is not warranted. The sensitivity of needle aspiration increases to 25% in patients with underlying immunological dysfunction (e.g., diabetes, malignancy, poor peripheral circulation) and may be beneficial in identifying the infecting organism(s) in these patients.[5] Since M.C. gives no history of any disease which could impair her host defenses, needle aspiration is unnecessary. For patients, such as M.C., with signs and symptoms (e.g., fever) where the injury is a significant risk for bacteremia and potentially for endocarditis, blood cultures are warranted. Blood cultures should be drawn before antibiotics are started to assess the presence of bacteria. If the blood cultures return positive, further assessment for potential endocarditis is warranted.

Causative Organisms

11. Are the suspected organisms in this patient population similar to those found in other patients with cellulitis?

A wide range of organisms can cause cellulitis in an IV drug abuser because of the potential for direct inoculation of any organism via the drug of abuse. Despite the efforts of an IV drug abuser to make as sterile an intravenous "product" as possible, the IV drug abuser frequently is injecting a contaminated solution. Despite the potential for inoculation of almost any organism, the infecting bacteria causing cellulitis in an IV drug abuser are similar to those found in normal hosts. Beta-hemolytic group A streptococci and staphylococci, particularly *S. aureus*, are the most common infecting organisms.[14-16] *Staphylococcus epidermidis* and gram-negative organisms, including *P. aeruginosa*, are rarely the causative organisms unless the drug abuser has taken oral cephalexin concurrent with her injections, which is a common undertaking of IV drug abusers.[14] If the patient lives in an area of known high prevalence of methicillin-resistant *S. aureus*, a similar resistance pattern may be seen in an IV drug abuser with cellulitis.[17]

Empiric Antibiotic Therapy

Antibiotic therapy directed at eradicating all possible infecting organisms is not required. Since streptococci and staphylococci account for the majority (>94%) of all infecting organisms in IV drug abusers with soft tissue infections,[14] therapy need only cover the sensitivity patterns of these organisms in the treatment area. Cloxacillin, dicloxacillin, or nafcillin would be appropriate therapy (see Question 1). Oral therapy is appropriate for mild cases of cellulitis. Infections that involve a large area or are associated with lymphangitis should be treated with parenteral antibiotics. Likewise infections involving the hand also should be treated parenterally.[18] If methicillin-resistant *S. aureus* is prevalent in the treatment area, antibiotic coverage should address this sensitivity pattern. Since there is no evidence to suggest that M.C. comes from an area with high methicillin-resistant *S. aureus* and since she has not taken cephalexin prophylactically, treatment with cloxacillin, dicloxacillin, or nafcillin would be appropriate. If treatment does

not result in some resolution of inflammation within 48 hours, antimicrobial coverage should be expanded to cover gram-negative organisms.

For patients not responding to initial therapy and for patients with signs or symptoms of a systemic response (e.g., rigors, hypotension), parenteral nafcillin 2 gm IV every six hours with gentamicin (Garamycin) 2 mg/kg/dose every eight hours or 6 mg/kg/dose IV every 24 hours (assuming normal renal function) is appropriate empiric therapy. The combination of nafcillin with gentamicin provides coverage against the other common organisms causing cellulitis (i.e., *S. aureus*, *E. coli*, and *Klebsiella pneumoniae*). While some clinicians would suggest that a third-generation cephalosporin or a quinolone should be chosen over an aminoglycoside because of concerns about toxicity, an aminoglycoside is effective, safe, and inexpensive when used for a short period of time (5 to 7 days).[19] However, in patients with poor renal function (estimated creatinine clearance <60 mL/minute or 1 mL/second), the aminoglycoside should be replaced with either ciprofloxacin (Cipro) 500 mg orally every 12 hours (400 mg IV Q 12 hr if parenteral therapy required) for moderate infections, or 750 mg orally every 12 hours (400 mg IV Q 12 hr if parenteral therapy is required) for severe infections, or a third-generation cephalosporin such as cefotaxime (Claforan) 1 gm IV every eight hours (2 gm IV Q 8 hr if severe) or ceftriaxone (Rocephin) 1 gm IV every 24 hours (2 gm IV Q 24 hr if severe), whichever is the least expensive. The degree of dosage reduction or interval extension would be based upon the degree of renal impairment.

Treatment of cellulitis in an IV drug abuser should include rest, immobilization and elevation of the infected arm, antibiotics, and surgical drainage or débridement as required. If there is any sign of pus collection in the wound, the wound must be surgically explored and drained. If no area of pus collection can be seen or palpated, immobilization and elevation, combined with systemic antibiotic therapy is appropriate treatment. The wound should be assessed daily for signs of local tenderness, pain, erythema, swelling, ulceration, necrosis, and wound drainage until the wound shows signs of resolution to insure that subsequent surgical treatment is not required.[18]

Soft Tissue Infections in Diabetics

Skin and soft tissue infections are very common in patients with diabetes mellitus. Approximately 25% of diabetic patients report a history of skin and soft tissue infections[20] and as many as 5% to 15% of diabetic patients may undergo limb amputation at some time.[21] In addition to the cost associated with treating skin and soft tissue infections, functional disability can occur, which can significantly decrease the quality of life.

Predisposing Factors

Diabetic patients are at particular risk for foot problems, primarily due to the neuropathies and peripheral vascular diseases associated with long-standing diabetes. The decreased pain sensation allows the patient to continue to bear weight in the presence of skin damage, thereby promoting the formation of an ulcer. In addition, minor trauma (e.g., cuts, foreign body insertion) may go unnoticed and when left untreated can become infected and extensive. While these infections are common, preventative measures can reduce the frequency of amputations.[21]

Causative Organisms

12. P.U., a 67-year-old male diabetic, presents to his general practitioner for a routine checkup and has no specific complaints. P.U. has a 15-year history of poorly controlled nonin-

sulin-dependent diabetes and a 3-year history of recurrent foot ulcers. Today, on examination, the physician sees that one of the ulcers from the underside of the foot that had previously healed over is now open and inflamed, and purulent fluid can be expressed from the wound. P.U. reports no pain around the area and was unaware that the ulcer had worsened. His temperature is normal and there are no other signs of a systemic infection. Does P.U. have an active infection and is antibiotic therapy required?

All open wounds, in diabetic or nondiabetic patients, will become colonized with bacteria, but only infected wounds should be treated with antibiotic therapy.[22]

It often is difficult to determine if an open wound is infected, but signs and symptoms such as purulent drainage, erythema, pain, and swelling around the area are suggestive of infection. Based upon his symptoms, P.U. should be considered to have an infection that requires treatment.

Empiric Antibiotic Therapy

13. What treatment should P.U. receive?

Mild infections can be treated empirically in a similar fashion to other soft tissue infections[22] as these are commonly caused by aerobic gram-positive cocci. A penicillinase-resistant penicillin (e.g., cloxacillin, nafcillin) will be effective in most cases, however, a culture of either the drainage or the infected site should be obtained to help guide future treatment. In addition, for all diabetic patients with soft tissue infections, potential osteomyelitis must be ruled out. In patients with significant vascular compromise, crepitus, or gangrene, an x-ray should be taken to identify any bone involvement.

In more severe infections, antibiotic coverage should be expanded due to the potential for multiple organisms being responsible for the infection. An average of two to six organisms are cultured from foot ulcers in patients with diabetes.[22–24] The following organisms (in no particular order) are found in greater than 20% of wounds in patients with diabetes: *S. aureus*, *S. epidermidis*, *Enterococcus faecalis*, other *Streptococcus*, *Proteus sp.*, *E. coli*, *Klebsiella sp.*, *Peptococcus sp.*, *Peptostreptococcus species*, and *Bacteroides sp.*[22–25] While these infections are often polymicrobic, effective treatment can be achieved even if all cultured pathogens are not covered.[22,23]

While antibiotics are important, drainage and surgical débridement to remove all the infected or necrotic tissue are essential components to the treatment and are considered by some to be the mainstay of treatment.[22,23]

Cultures of the affected areas may not be that useful[23] unless bone involvement is suspected. Although anaerobic organisms often are difficult to culture, anaerobic organisms must be considered if an abscess or devitalized, necrotic, foul-smelling tissue is present or the wound is a result of abdominal surgery. Empiric coverage for *E. faecalis* is only required for severe (necrotizing) infections.[22] Even if enterococcus is found in the wound, enterococcal coverage probably is needed only if it is the predominant organism.

There are no "best regimens" for the treatment of diabetic soft tissue infections. Clindamycin 600 mg IV every eight hours with gentamicin 2 mg/kg every eight hours or 6 mg/kg IV every 24 hours (assuming normal renal function) is a very effective combination which will provide coverage against most potential pathogens (gram-positive, gram-negative, and anaerobes) with the exception of *E. faecalis*.

However, clindamycin can cause *C. difficile*, and the parenteral formulation is expensive. Aminoglycosides are associated with serious toxicity if used for an extended period of time, and should likely be avoided in patients with pre-existing renal impairment.

A quinolone or a third-generation cephalosporin could be used in place of the aminoglycoside in patients with poor renal function; however, the cost of these agents combined with clindamycin is high and provides similar coverage to cefoxitin (Mefoxin), ceftizoxime (Cefizox), cefotetan (Cefotan), and cefmetazole (Zefazone). Although cefoxitin, cefotetan, ceftizoxime, and cefmetazole cover a similar spectrum of organisms as that covered by the combination of clindamycin and gentamicin, their activity is not as good against gram-negative and anaerobic organisms as the combination of clindamycin and gentamicin. Cefoxitin should be dosed 1 gm IV every six hours (2 gm IV Q 6 hr if severe), cefotetan is dosed 1 gm IV every 12 hours (2 gm IV Q 12 hr if severe), and ceftizoxime or cefmetazole is dosed 1 gm IV every eight hours (2 gm IV Q 8 hr if severe). Piperacillin (Pipracil) not only provides similar coverage to that seen with cefoxitin, cefotetan, ceftizoxime, and cefmetazole, but also adds useful coverage against *Enterococcus* and could be chosen over these agents if it is less expensive. However, piperacillin usually is dosed at more frequent intervals (1 gm IV Q 6 hr if moderate, 2 gm IV Q 4 hr if severe) than these other antibiotics and these additional doses must be included in the cost analysis. Cefazolin plus metronidazole (Flagyl) is likely as effective as cefoxitin, ceftizoxime, cefotetan, and cefmetazole and could be chosen over these agents if this combination is less expensive.[26] In many cases, diabetic foot infections are difficult to treat, but aggressive treatment can prevent extension of the infection, development of osteomyelitis, and on occasion, loss of limb. Treatment should be continued for three to four days after all signs of infection are absent. Oral therapy should be considered once the infection has begun to improve. As P.U. is an elderly diabetic patient and does not appear to be severely ill, aminoglycosides should and can be avoided. Therefore, the least expensive of piperacillin, cefoxitin, cefotetan, ceftizoxime, or cefmetazole should be chosen as empiric therapy for P.U. In addition, ampicillin/sulbactam (Unasyn), ticarcillin/clavulanate (Timentin), or piperacillin/tazobactam (Zosyn) could be chosen if they are less expensive than the above agents, or if local sensitivity patterns suggest that organisms typically found in these types of infections are routinely resistant to the other less expensive agents.

Postamputation Antibiotic Treatment

14. Unfortunately, despite aggressive antibiotic therapy and débridement, P.U.'s infection spreads and an amputation is required. How long should antibiotics be prescribed following surgery in P.U.?

The best option for uncontrollable life-threatening infections often is amputation to remove the infected area. Once the infected area has been removed, antibiotic therapy is no longer required. However, if it was not possible to remove all of the infected tissue, treatment should be continued as above.

Prevention

15. What could have been done to prevent this complication in P.U.?

Many of the foot problems associated with the diabetic patient can be prevented if proper foot care (see Table 66.3) is maintained[21] and these preventative measures must be stressed. Diabetic patients with neuropathies or those who are elderly should take care of their feet regularly (every 1 to 2 days).

Necrotizing Soft Tissue Infections
Definitions, Terminology, and Causative Organisms

Skin and soft tissue infections are described as necrotizing when the inflammation is rapidly progressing and necrosis of the skin or

Table 66.3	Foot Care for the Diabetic Patient

- Inspect feet daily for the presence of cuts, blisters, or scratches. Pay particular attention to the area between the toes and use a mirror to examine the bottom of the foot
- Wash feet daily in tepid water and dry thoroughly
- Apply lotion to feet to prevent calluses and cracking
- Ensure shoes fit properly (not too tight or too loose) and inspect them daily
- Trim nails regularly making sure to cut straight across the nail
- Do not use chemical agents to remove corns or calluses

underlying tissue is present. The following clinical signs are associated with necrotizing infections but not with simple cellulitis: edema beyond the area of erythema, skin blisters or bullae, localized pallor or discoloration, gas in the subcutaneous tissues (crepitus), and the absence of lymphangitis and lymphadenitis. Necrotizing soft tissue infections may progress rapidly to cause additional local effects (i.e., necrosis and loss of skin sensation) and severe systemic effects (e.g., hypotension and shock).

Group A beta-hemolytic strep, *Pseudomonas*, other gram-negative organisms, *Clostridium perfringens*, *Peptostreptococcus*, and *B. fragilis* can cause necrotizing infections.[1-3]

Necrotizing cellulitis involves the skin and subcutaneous tissues. *Necrotizing fasciitis* involves both superficial and deep fascia; and necrotizing infections involving the muscle are termed *myonecrosis* can be used to describe all three of these processes. Gas gangrene is myonecrosis caused by a *Clostridium* subspecies, most commonly *C. perfringens* (70%).[2] The finding of gas in a wound by either palpation or x-ray is not necessarily indicative of gas gangrene caused by *C. perfringens*. Gas in a wound also can be produced by gram-negative organisms (e.g., *E. coli*, *Proteus*, *Klebsiella*), or anaerobic streptococci. Air also could have been introduced at the time of the injury. Gas gangrene is characterized by acute onset of worsening pain which is usually out of proportion to the degree of injury.[27]

Clostridial myonecrosis (true "gas gangrene"), *streptococcal gangrene* (caused by Group A hemolytic streptococci), and *synergistic bacterial gangrene* (caused by anaerobic and aerobic bacteria, usually gram-negative) are other terms used to describe necrotizing skin and soft tissue infections. *Fournier's gangrene* (a type of synergistic bacterial gangrene of the scrotum), *nonclostridial crepitant gangrene* (nonclostridial gas gangrene), and *necrotizing fasciitis* (all necrotizing soft tissue infections other than clostridial myonecrosis or sometimes just streptococcal gangrene) are other commonly used terms.[2,28]

Empiric Antibiotic Therapy

16. M.T., a 45-year-old alcoholic male who lives on the streets of the city, presents to the ER with a broken nose and facial lacerations which he received following a fight outside one of the local taverns. On examination, in addition to the facial wounds, an area of severe inflammation, erythema and necrosis is found on his left calf. The area is very painful, crepitation is felt over the area and a purulent discharge is present. M.T. states this is secondary to a knife wound obtained approximately 1 week ago. What treatment should be provided?

In addition to setting the broken nose and suturing the facial laceration, the infection on M.T.'s calf should be evaluated. A Gram's stain and culture of the purulent discharge should be done before initiating antimicrobial therapy. Because crepitus is present, the area should be incised and a specimen of the infected tissue should be obtained for Gram's staining and culture.[2]

The primary treatment for necrotizing soft tissue infections involves extensive debridement of the area to remove all necrotic tissue and drain the area. Thus, a surgical consultation will be required for M.T. In addition, intravenous antibiotics are required. In this case, one must remember that gas in the tissues can be caused by many potential organisms and empiric antibiotic therapy should be broad spectrum and should include coverage against gram-positive organisms, the Enterobacteriaceae and *B. fragilis*. Clindamycin plus gentamicin would be appropriate empiric therapy for M.T. If aminoglycosides were contraindicated, cefoxitin, ceftizoxime, cefotetan, or cefmetazole would likely suffice in the mild to moderately ill patient. In the severely ill patient, penicillin G (3 MU Q 4 hr) should be added to this regimen to allow for additional coverage against *Clostridium perfringens*. If the Gram's stain of the discharge shows only gram-positive rods (which would likely be clostridial subspecies), the therapy could be streamlined to just high-dose penicillin. Further changes to therapy should be on the basis of clinical response and culture results.

Erysipelas
Signs, Symptoms, and Causative Organisms

17. D.D., a 70-year-old male, presents to the ER with a red swollen face. He describes the area as "a swollen, red spot" that has appeared over the last 2 days. He also describes feeling unwell for the previous 3 days and having a fever. On examination, D.D. has a bright red, shiny, edematous lesion on his right cheek that is ≈4 cm in diameter. It is a continuous lesion with a clearly demarcated border. What signs and symptoms support the diagnosis of erysipelas in D.D.?

Erysipelas is a superficial skin infection caused by streptococci, predominantly Group A, although group C or G and group B in children also may cause the infection.[29] Erysipelas is diagnosed based upon characteristics of the skin lesion and concurrent systemic symptoms.[29,30] Patients with erysipelas have associated systemic symptoms of high fever, chills, frequent history of rigors, and general malaise. This constellation of systemic symptoms differentiates erysipelas from other local skin disorders. The lesion is a continuous, indurated, edematous area, and the most common site of infection is the face. Early in the course, the lesion is bright red, but may turn to brown as the lesion ages or grows in size. The lesion spreads peripherally with no islands of unaffected tissue. The initial lesion results from a small break in the skin that becomes infected, although signs of the initial wound often are not evident. The streptococci may originate from a prodromal respiratory infection, although culture of the respiratory tract at the time of the lesion eruption will rarely produce positive cultures.[29]

D.D. has the classic signs and symptoms of erysipelas: a well-demarcated, edematous, red lesion with associated systemic signs. No further diagnostic tests are required since aspiration of the lesion or a superficial swab are not useful in detecting the offending organism.

Empiric Antibiotic Therapy

18. What antibiotic therapy should be initiated for D.D.?

Erysipelas will respond promptly to antibiotics with activity against group A streptococci.[30] Oral penicillin V 250–300 mg (depending on available dosage form) orally every six hours or parenteral penicillin G (1 million units Q 6 hr IV) should reduce the systemic symptoms (e.g., fever, malaise) within 24 to 48 hours.[29] It will take several more days for the skin lesion to resolve. If D.D. does not feel better within 72 hours following initiation of antibiotics, he should be instructed to return for reassessment. If D.D. had an allergy to penicillins, a macrolide such as erythromycin also would be effective. Antibiotic therapy should be continued for ten days even if signs and symptoms resolve quickly to avoid a relapse which could lead to chronic infection or scarring.[30]

Acute Traumatic Wounds

19. J.K., a 25-year-old male construction worker, presents to the ER with a deep cut on his left forearm secondary to accidentally putting his hand through a plate glass window. Fourteen stitches are required to close the wound. Is antibiotic therapy required for J.K.?

While almost all traumatic wounds are contaminated with bacteria,[31] routine antibiotic therapy is not indicated unless there is evidence of an infection. Contaminated wounds do become infected more often than noncontaminated wounds, however, prophylactic antibiotic therapy does not appear to decrease the chance of infection.[31] For all traumatic wounds, aggressive wound care (e.g., irrigation, removal of foreign objects) is required. A course of antibiotic therapy should be given only to immunocompromised patients (e.g., diabetes mellitus, peripheral vascular disease, acquired immunodeficiency syndrome, chronic corticosteroid use, leukopenia). Antibiotic therapy would be similar to that given to patients with cellulitis (see Question 1). Patients with risk factors for the development of infective endocarditis (i.e., mitral valve prolapse with regurgitation, an indwelling nonnative cardiac valve, a previous history of endocarditis, a history of congenital heart malformations, surgically constructed systemic-pulmonary shunts, and cardiomyopathy) should receive prophylactic amoxicillin (Amoxil) 3 gm orally followed by 1.5 gm in six hours or erythromycin 1000 mg orally followed by 500 mg orally in six hours if patient is penicillin allergic.[32] As J.K. has no risk factors, all that is required is removal of any glass fragments, irrigation, and suturing of the area.

Animal Bite Wounds

Evaluation of Dog and Cat Bites

20. P.J., a 14-year-old male, presents to the ER ≈3 hours following a wound to the leg. While visiting his neighbor, he was attacked by the neighbor's dog and has a laceration, 14 cm long, on his medial calf. Four distinct puncture marks, suggestive of teeth marks, also are present on the calf. There is no suggestion of bone injury. P.J. was healthy before the attack and has no chronic illness. Should P.J. receive any treatment other than suturing of his laceration?

Any wound caused by an animal that results in the skin being cut or punctured should be examined to ensure no underlying tissue damage has occurred. This is especially true in patients with bites of the hand or around other joints. Washing the wound with clean water should be initiated as soon as possible after the bite.[33] Irrigation of the wound, including puncture sites, should be extensive to reduce the risk of subsequent infection. Obtaining specimens for cultures is not required and wound irrigation should begin as soon as possible.[33]

P.J.'s wound should be evaluated for deep tissue injury, devascularization of any tissue, and potential bone injury.[33] Loose suturing or closure with adhesive strips is appropriate for lacerations following irrigation.[33] Although the safety of closure of bite wounds has been debated, good therapeutic response has been obtained following the closure of wounds.[34] P.J. should be instructed to keep his leg elevated and immobilized until signs of any infection have resolved.[35]

The need for antibiotics is controversial and guided by wound characteristics. The patient should receive a course of antibiotics[36] if the wound involves the hand or is near joints;[33] involves deep punctures; is difficult to irrigate; the patient is immunocompromised (e.g., diabetes, splenectomy); or if the wound is not well perfused. Antibiotics are not required for dog bites in which no deep tissue injury is present and the wound can be well irrigated, particularly if the wound is on the lower extremities in healthy adults or children.[37]

Prophylaxis for rabies is required only if the animal is from an area with endemic rabies or if the bite was the result of an unprovoked attack by a wild animal.[33,35,38] Contact with the local health board will determine the recent rabies risk within the area. If P.J. has not received a tetanus toxoid booster within the last five years, a booster should be administered. If P.J. has never been immunized for tetanus, tetanus immune globulin should be administered in addition to the tetanus toxoid (see Question 24).[38]

Causative Organisms and Empiric Antibiotic Therapy

21. Since P.J. has several punctures that were difficult to irrigate, he is a candidate for antibiotic therapy. Which antibiotic(s) should he receive?

The selection of the appropriate antibiotic is based upon the most likely pathogens from the specific animal bite. Animals have different oral flora which alters the potential pathogens associated with bites. The most common pathogens in dog bites are alpha-hemolytic streptococci, *Staphylococcus aureus*, *Pasteurella multocida*, anaerobic bacteria (particularly *Bacteroides* species), and *Fusobacterium* species.[38] Although *Pasteurella multocida* frequently is considered the primary pathogen of dog bites, it only occurs in 25% of infections and antibiotic coverage also must address the other common pathogens.[38] A combination of penicillin V 500,000 IU orally every six hours with a penicillinase-resistant drug such as dicloxacillin or cloxacillin 500 mg orally every six hours will provide coverage for the predominant organisms in dog bites. The more expensive alternative of amoxicillin-clavulanate (Augmentin) has not been demonstrated superior to the combination of cloxacillin and penicillin V.[37] If the patient is penicillin-allergic, tetracycline or doxycycline provides adequate coverage.[34] Doxycycline is preferred over tetracycline because it is more convenient to administer (BID for doxycycline versus QID for tetracycline), can be used in patients with decreased renal function, may be taken with food, and the generic formulation is only a little more expensive than tetracycline.

If the penicillin-allergic patient cannot take a tetracycline, which is contraindicated in children and during pregnancy, erythromycin 500 mg orally four times a day can be used, despite poorer activity against *P. multocida*.[39] In all cases, but particularly in patients treated with erythromycin, patients should be instructed to watch for a positive response, and if the wound does not improve or worsens within 48 hours, they will need to be re-evaluated.

Antibiotic treatment should not extend beyond five days unless signs of an infection remain.[33] Appropriate therapy for P.J. would be penicillin V and a penicillinase-resistant penicillin (e.g., dicloxacillin or cloxacillin) orally.

For cat bites, the role of *P. multocida* appears more significant since this organism can be found in up to 75% of a cat's oral flora.[34] While for some dog bites antibiotic treatment is not required, reports of a greater than 50% incidence of infection following cat bites[35] suggest that all patients with cat bites should receive antibiotics.[34] Since *P. multocida* frequently is resistant to penicillinase-resistant penicillins and first-generation cephalosporins, the use of these agents in cat bites should be avoided.[34] Therefore, either the combination of penicillin plus a penicillinase-resis-

Table 66.4	Tetanus Prophylaxis in Routine Wound Management: Adults[44]			
History of Adsorbed Tetanus Toxoid	Clean, Minor Wounds[a]		All Other Wounds[a,b]	
	Td[c]	TIG	Td[c]	TIG
Unknown or <3 doses	Yes	No	Yes	Yes
≥ 3 doses	No[d]	No	Yes[e]	No

[a] Td = Tetanus and diphtheria toxoid; TIG = Tetanus immune globulin.

[b] Such as, but not limited to, wounds contaminated with dirt, feces, soil, and saliva; puncture wounds, avulsions; and wounds resulting from missiles, crushing, burns, frostbite.

[c] For children <7 years old, diphtheria-tetanus-pertussis (DTP) is preferred to tetanus toxoid alone. For persons ≥7 years, Td is preferred to tetanus toxoid alone.

[d] Yes, if >10 years since last dose.

[e] Yes, if >5 years since last dose. (More frequent boosters are not needed and can accentuate the side effects.)

tant penicillin or amoxicillin-clavulanate is appropriate for cat bites and the choice between these regimens should be based upon cost.

If the patient presents with an established infection, parenteral therapy is warranted if the infection is over a joint, has lymphatic spread, or involves the hand or head. If the patient has not responded to oral therapy, parenteral second-generation cephalosporins such as cefoxitin 1 gm IV every six hours, cefotetan 1 gm IV every 12 hours, or ceftizoxime or cefmetazole 1 gm IV every eight hours have activity against *P. multocida*, streptococci, staphylococci, and anaerobes.[35] The value of parenteral administration of clindamycin or erythromycin is limited by poor activity against *P. multocida*.[35] The poor activity of quinolones against anaerobes has limited their use, despite good activity against *P. multocida*.[40] Parenteral therapy should be continued until resolution of the wound is evident, and therapy should then be continued with oral antibiotics. Treatment should continue for at least seven days or until all clinical signs of the infection have resolved.

Human Bite Wounds

Evaluation of Human Bites

22. E.D., a 40-year-old male, presents with a sore arm 24 hours after receiving a bite to his left forearm by his neighbor in a "discussion over property boundaries." E.D. was previously healthy and has no chronic diseases. A 6 × 8 cm area of his left forearm is swollen, erythematous, and includes several distinct puncture marks consistent with a human bite. No joint deformity or bone abnormality is detected on clinical examination. How should E.D. be treated?

The treatment of a human bite is similar to any other laceration and would include cleansing, irrigation, exploration, debridement, drainage, excision, and suturing as required.[38] All human bites should be cleansed as soon as possible, and any lacerations or punctures irrigated copiously. Surgical exploration with debridement, drainage, or excision should be undertaken for any wound which suggests deeper tissues have been injured or where pus collection could have occurred. Exploration for damage to subcutaneous nerves, tendons, joints, or vascularity is particularly important in bites to the hand, especially knuckles, since subsequent infections could seriously affect hand function. Since E.D. presents 24 hours following the injury, thorough exploration and irrigation of all lacerations or punctures is required. If there is evidence of pus accumulation in his wound, the area should be explored and

drained. E.D. also should receive systemic antibiotic therapy to eradicate potential infecting organisms. Tetanus toxoid booster should be administered if E.D. has not received a booster within the last five years.

Empiric Antibiotic Therapy and Causative Organisms

23. Which antibiotic should be prescribed to E.D.?

If E.D. had been seen within 12 hours of the injury, the wound could likely have been treated adequately with simple irrigation. This is especially true if the human bite does not involve the hand.[37] If the hand has been bitten or the patient is immunocompromised, a course of antibiotics using oral agents is appropriate. If the wound is severe (i.e., involves subcutaneous tissues, a joint, or a large area) or if the patient is unlikely to be compliant with oral antibiotics, parenteral administration of antibiotics is required.[38] The most common pathogens in human bites are alphahemolytic streptococci, *S. aureus*, *Eikenella corrodens*, and *Corynebacterium* subspecies.[38,41,42] Anaerobic bacteria, including *Bacteroides* subspecies, also are frequently involved.[38] Treatment with a combination of penicillin G and a penicillinase-resistant penicillin is appropriate therapy.[38] Therapy with a penicillinase-resistant penicillin or a first-generation cephalosporin alone is not appropriate because *E. corrodens* commonly is resistant to these antibiotics.[35,40,43] If the anaerobic flora of the patient's community is frequently resistant to penicillin, alternative anaerobic coverage with amoxicillin-clavulanate may be required.[38] If parenteral therapy is required, a second-generation cephalosporin with antianaerobic activity (e.g., cefoxitin, cefotetan, ceftizoxime) would be appropriate.[38] Cefuroxime should not be used as single-agent therapy since it lacks activity against anaerobes and *E. corrodens*.[40,43] Third-generation cephalosporins and quinolones have good activity against *E. corrodens*, but cannot be recommended because of their inferior activity against anaerobic organisms.[35]

Tetanus Prophylaxis

24. G.T., a 48-year-old female, presents to the ER 1 hour after receiving a 2 cm laceration to her foot from stepping on a nail while walking around in her neighborhood. Examination of the wound found it to be clean, with no subcutaneous extension. The wound was closed with superficial sutures and no antibiotics, systemic or topical, were prescribed. Should G.T. receive tetanus prophylaxis?

Tetanus is a preventable disease through primary prophylaxis and appropriate wound management. Every child should receive primary prophylaxis of three separate doses of tetanus toxoid. This provides adequate coverage for at least ten years.[44] Tetanus can develop in patients who have not been immunized or who have not received a booster dose within the last ten years. If G.T. has received her primary tetanus immunization and had a booster dose within the previous ten years, no additional tetanus prophylaxis is required for her wound (see Table 66.4). If her primary immunization status is unknown or more than ten years has elapsed since her last dose, a single 0.5 mL subcutaneous tetanus toxoid dose should be administered. If primary immunization is unknown or incomplete, G.T. should receive the initial 0.5 mL dose immediately and be scheduled to complete the primary immunization over the next two months. For adults, the combination product of tetanus and diphtheria toxoid is the recommended treatment since this will enhance protection against diphtheria.

If G.T. presented with a dirty wound, defined as contaminated with dirt, feces, soil, or saliva, or if the wound resulted from a burn, frostbite, missile (bullet), crush, or avulsion, she should receive passive tetanus immunization with tetanus immune globulin in addition to the tetanus toxoid described above. A single 250 U intramuscular dose of tetanus immune globulin will provide passive immunization in addition to the active immunization produced from exposure to the tetanus toxoid (see Table 66.4).

Acknowledgment

The authors gratefully acknowledge Andrew Pattullo, M.D., for his thorough review of this chapter and his thoughtful comments.

References

1 **Freischlag JA et al.** Treatment of necrotizing soft tissue infections: the need for a new approach. Am J Surg. 1985; 149:751–55.

2 **Lewis RT.** Necrotizing soft-tissue infections. Infect Dis Clin North Am. 1992;6:693–703.

3 **Pessa ME, Howard RJ.** Necrotizing fasciitis. Surg Gynecol Obstet. 1985; 161:357–61.

4 **Hook EW et al.** Microbiologic evaluation of cutaneous cellulitis in adults. Arch Intern Med. 1986;146:295–97.

5 **Sachs MK.** The optimum use of needle aspiration in the bacteriologic diagnosis of cellulitis in adults. Arch Intern Med. 1990;150:1907–912.

6 **Lutomski DM et al.** Microbiology of adult cellulitis. J Fam Pract. 1988;26: 45–8.

7 **Sutherland R et al.** Flucloxacillin, a new isoxazolyl penicillin, compared with oxacillin, cloxacillin, and dicloxacillin. Br Med J. 1970;4:455–60.

8 **Powers RD.** Soft tissue infections in the emergency department: the case for the use of simple antibiotics. South Med J. 1991;84:1313–315.

9 **USP Dispensing Information.** Drug Information for the Health Care Professional. 13th ed. Rockville: Rand McNally;1993:2180–181.

10 **Neu HC.** Penicillins. In: Mandell GL et al., eds. Principles and Practice of Infectious Diseases. 3rd ed. New York: Churchill Livingstone; 1990: 230–46.

11 **Ward A, Campoli-Richards DM.** Mupirocin: a review of its antibacterial activity, pharmacokinetic properties and therapeutic use. Drugs. 1986;32: 425–44.

12 **Hirschmann JV.** Topical antibiotics in dermatology. Arch Dermatol. 1988; 124:1691–700.

13 **Sachs MK.** Cutaneous cellulitis. Arch Dermatol. 1991;127:493–96.

14 **Beaufoy A.** Infections in intravenous drug users: a two-year review. Can J Infect Control. 1993;8:7–9.

15 **Wallace JR et al.** Social, economic, and surgical anatomy of a drug-related abscess. Am Surg. 1986;52:398–401.

16 **Orangio GR et al.** Soft tissue infections in parenteral drug abusers. Ann Surg. 1984;199:97–100.

17 **Sheagren JN.** Treatment of skin and skin infections in the patient at risk. Am J Med. 1984;76(5B):180–86.

18 **Hausman MR, Lisser SP.** Hand infections. Orthop Clin North Am. 1992;23: 171–85.

19 **McCormack JP, Jewesson PJ.** A critical reevaluation of the ''therapeutic range'' of the aminoglycosides. Clin Infect Dis. 1992;14:320–39.

20 **LeFrock JL, Joseph WS.** Lower extremity infections in diabetics. Infect Surg. 1986;5:135–45.

21 **Most RS, Sinnock P.** The epidemiology of lower extremity infections in diabetic individuals. Diabetes Care. 1983;6:87–91.

22 **Lipsky BA et al.** The diabetic foot: soft tissue and bone infection. Infect Dis Clin North Am. 1990;4:409–32.

23 **Scher KS, Steele FJ.** The septic foot in patients with diabetes. Surgery. 1988;104:661–66.

24 **Louie TJ et al.** Aerobic and anaerobic bacteria in diabetic foot ulcers. Ann Intern Med. 1976;85:461–63.

25 **Fierer J et al.** The fetid foot: lower extremity infections in patients with diabetes mellitus. Rev Infect Dis. 1979; 1:210–17.

26 **Brown G, Clarke AM.** Therapeutic interchange of cefazolin with metronidazole for cefoxitin. Am J Hosp Pharm. 1992;49:1946–950.

27 **Hutson RH, Auerbach PS.** Skin and soft tissue infections. In: Harwood-Nuss A, ed. The Clinical Practice of Emergency Medicine. Philadelphia: J.B. Lippincott Company; 1991:1026–030.

28 **Swartz MN.** Subcutaneous tissue infections and abscesses. In: Mandell GL et al., Principles and Practice of Infectious Diseases. 3rd ed. New York: Churchill Livingstone;1990:808–12.

29 **Swartz MN, Weinberg AN.** Infections due to gram-positive bacteremia. In: Fitzpatrick TB et al., eds. Dermatology in General Medicine. 3rd ed. New York: McGraw-Hill;1987:2104–106.

30 **Arnold HL et al.** Erysipelas. In: Arnold HL et al., eds. Andrew's Diseases of the Skin. Philadelphia: WB Saunders;1990:277–78.

31 **Rodgers KG.** The rational use of antimicrobial agents in simple wounds. Emerg Med Clin North Am. 1992;10: 753–65.

32 **Dajani AS et al.** Prevention of bacterial endocarditis—recommendations by the American Heart Association. JAMA. 1990;264:2919–922.

33 **Anderson CR.** Animal bites. Guidelines to current management. Postgrad Med J. 1992;92(July):134–49.

34 **Goldstein EJ, Richwald GA.** Human and animal bite wounds. Am Fam Physician. 1987;36:101–09.

35 **Goldstein EJ.** Bite wounds and infection. Clin Infect Dis. 1992;14:633–40.

36 **Dire DJ.** Emergency management of dog and cat bite wounds. Emerg Med Clin North Am. 1992;10:719–36.

37 **Callaham M.** Controversies in antibiotic choices for bite wounds. Ann Emerg Med. 1988;17:1321–330.

38 **Brooks I.** Human and animal bite infections. J Fam Pract. 1989;28:713–18.

39 **Goldstein EJ et al.** Susceptibility of bite wound bacteria to seven oral antimicrobial agents, including RU-985, a new erythromycin: considerations in choosing empiric therapy. Antimicrob Agents Chemother. 1986;29:556–59.

40 **Goldstein EJ, Citron DM.** Comparative susceptibilities of 173 aerobic and anaerobic bite wound isolates to sparfloxacin, temafloxacin, clarithromycin, and older agents. Antimicrob Agents Chemother. 1993;37:1150–153.

41 **Legge M, Murphy MF.** Human bite wounds. J Emerg Nurs. 1990;16:145–48.

42 **Goldstein EJ et al.** Bacteriology of human and animal bite wounds. J Clin Microbiol. 1978;8:667–72.

43 **Goldstein EJ, Citron DM.** Comparative activities of cefuroxime, amoxicillin-clavulanic acid, ciprofloxacin, enoxacin, and ofloxacin against aerobic and anaerobic bacteria isolated from bite wounds. Antimicrob Agents Chemother. 1988;32:1143–148.

44 **Advisory Committee on Immunization Practices, CDC.** Diphtheria, tetanus, and pertussis: guidelines for vaccine use and other preventative measures. MMWR. 1991;40:(RR10).

Infections in Immunocompromised Hosts

Hilary D Mandler

**Therapeutic Considerations for Treatment
of Infections in Immunocompromised Patients** ... 67-1
  Risk Factors for Infection (See Table 67.1) 67-1
    Neutropenia (See Figure 67.1) 67-2
    Damage to physical barriers 67-2
    Alterations in the immune system 67-2
    Colonization 67-3
    Organ transplantation 67-3
  Infections in Neutropenic Cancer Patients 67-3
    Clinical signs and symptoms 67-3
    Confirmation of infection 67-3
    Infecting pathogens 67-4
    Colonization 67-4
  Empiric Antibiotic Therapy 67-4
    Rationale 67-4
    Bacterial coverage 67-4
    Factors influencing response to therapy 67-5
      Host factors 67-5
      Antibiotic susceptibility 67-5
    Antimicrobial combinations 67-5
      Synergy 67-5
      Prevention of resistant strains 67-5
    Serum bactericidal titers (SBTs) 67-6
Choice of Antibiotic Regimens (See Table 67.3) 67-6
  Aminoglycoside/Beta-Lactam Combinations 67-6
    Two-drug regimens 67-6
    Three-drug regimens 67-7
  Empiric Vancomycin 67-7
  Drug Dosing and Monitoring Considerations 67-7
    Intermittent versus continuous infusion
      of antibiotics 67-7
    Once-daily aminoglycoside dosing 67-7
    Aminoglycoside degradation 67-8
  Double Beta-Lactam Combinations 67-8
    Cephalosporins plus ureidopenicillins 67-8
    Hematologic abnormalities 67-8
      Coagulopathy 67-9
      Neutropenia 67-9
  Monotherapy 67-9
    Cephalosporins 67-9
    Carbapenems 67-10
  Alternative Regimens 67-10

    Monobactams 67-10
    Fluoroquinolones 67-10
      Summary 67-10
**Continuation of or Changes in Initial
  Antibiotic Therapy** 67-11
  Duration of Therapy (See Figure 67.2) 67-11
  Modifications of Therapy 67-11
    Pathogen-directed therapy 67-11
    Antimicrobial adjuvants 67-12
    Addition of antimicrobials (See Table 67.2) 67-12
    Antifungal therapy 67-12
      Significance of fungal infections 67-12
      Empiric amphotericin B therapy 67-12
Prophylaxis of Systemic Infections 67-13
  Myeloid Colony Stimulating Factors (CSFs) 67-13
  Antimicrobial Prophylaxis 67-13
    Nonabsorbable regimens 67-13
      Selective decontamination regimens 67-13
    Systemically absorbed agents 67-14
      Trimethoprim/sulfamethoxazole (TMP-SMX) 67-14
      Fluoroquinolones 67-14
    Antifungals 67-14
      Topical antifungals 67-14
      Systemic antifungals 67-14
Infections in Transplantation 67-15
  Risk Factors for Infection (See Table 67.1) 67-15
    Bone marrow transplantation (See Figure 67.3) 67-15
    Solid organ transplantation (see Figure 67.4) 67-16
  Viral Infections in Transplantation 67-16
    Herpes simplex virus (HSV) 67-17
    Varicella-zoster virus (VZV) 67-17
    Cytomegalovirus (CMV) 67-17
      Transmission 67-17
  Prophylaxis of CMV Infection 67-17
    Screened blood products 67-17
    Antivirals (See Table 67.3) 67-17
      Acyclovir 67-17
      Ganciclovir 67-17
    Immunoglobulins 67-17
      Intravenous immune globulin (IVIG) 67-17
      CMV hyperimmune globulin (CMVIG) 67-17

The lives of many patients have been prolonged through therapeutic advances in chemotherapy, immunotherapy, and transplantation. Despite these advances, infectious complications continue to be a major cause of morbidity and mortality in these patients.[1–4] Although broad-spectrum antimicrobial agents and chemotherapeutic agents (e.g., azathioprine, cyclosporine) have altered the frequency and types of infectious complications in patients with both solid and hematologic malignancies[5] and in transplant recipients,[4] the management of infections in immunocompromised hosts remains a major challenge to health care professionals. Infectious complications have become frequent causes of morbidity and mortality in these patients, often replacing the primary disease as the leading cause of death.[34]

Therapeutic Considerations for Treatment of Infections in Immunocompromised Patients
Risk Factors for Infection

Patients are rendered ''immunocompromised'' when there is a disruption or deficiency of one of the host defenses, either caused by the underlying disease or induced by its treatment. These risk factors include neutropenia, iatrogenic damage to skin and mucosal barriers, and impaired humoral (antibody and complement) and cell-mediated immune defenses.[1,5,6] Bacteria, fungi, viruses, and protozoa may infect various sites depending upon the specific immunodeficiency (see Table 67.1).

This chapter will focus on the management of infectious complications in patients with cancer as well as those undergoing bone marrow or solid organ transplantation. Infectious complications associated with human immunodeficiency virus (HIV) are presented in Chapter 68: Human Immunodeficiency Virus (HIV) Infection.

Neutropenia

Granulocytes, or granular leukocytes, represent an important defense against bacterial and fungal infections.[7,8] Neutropenia or granulocytopenia, defined as a reduction in the number of circulating granulocytes or neutrophils, predisposes the host to infections. The terms granulocytopenia and neutropenia often are used interchangeably. The degree of neutropenia is expressed by the absolute neutrophil count (ANC). The ANC is defined as the total number of granulocytes (polymorphonuclear leukocytes and band forms) present in the circulating pool of white blood cells (WBCs). In general, the risk of infection is low when the ANC exceeds 1000/µL; however, as the ANC drops below 500/µL, the risk of infection rapidly increases (see Figure 67.1). The risk of developing bacteremia is further increased as the ANC drops below 100/µL.[9,10] Febrile patients with short durations of neutropenia (<1 week) generally respond promptly to empiric antibiotics and rarely develop serious infections. On the other hand, patients that are rendered neutropenic for longer periods, such as those receiving more intensive chemotherapy regimens, are more vulnerable to serious infection.

Damage to Physical Barriers

The intact skin and mucosal surfaces of the body constitute the host's primary physical defense against microbial invasion.[5] The integrity of this physical barrier may be disrupted by tumor (e.g., obstruction), treatment (e.g., surgery, irradiation), or a number of medical procedures [e.g., placement of intravenous (IV) or urinary catheters, venipuncture, measurement of rectal temperature].[9,13] Device-related infections, including those caused by tunneled Hickman catheters, are commonly caused by migration of skin flora (e.g., coagulase-negative staphylococci) through the cutaneous insertion site. Infections resulting from damaged mucosal lining of the gastrointestinal (GI) tract usually are caused by the Enterobacteriaceae and Pseudomonas aeruginosa.[156]

Alterations in the Immune System

Patients with immunoglobulin deficiencies such as those with hypogammaglobulinemia, chronic lymphocytic leukemia, or splenectomy are at increased risk for infections with encapsulated bacteria such as Neisseria meningitidis, Haemophilus influenzae, and Streptococcus pneumoniae: these bacteria must undergo antibody opsonization for efficient phagocytosis. Hodgkin's disease, organ transplantation, and HIV disease can disrupt the cellular immune system, thus increasing the risk for infections with obligate and facultative intracellular organisms, such as mycobacteria, Listeria, Toxoplasma, viruses, and fungi.[6,7]

Some chemotherapeutic regimens have profound effects on both cellular and humoral defenses.[5] Corticosteroids exert their immunosuppressive effects on the cellular immune system, particularly at the T-lymphocyte and macrophage level. Patients receiving corticosteroids have a depressed resistance to infections with viral, bacterial, protozoal, and fungal organisms. Infectious complications associated with glucocorticoid use appear to be dose dependent; the risk of infection increases with daily doses in excess of 10 mg or cumulative doses greater than 700 mg of prednisone or its equivalent.[16]

Table 67.1		Infections in Immunocompromised Patients[a]			
Immunologic Defect	Underlying Condition(s)	Bacteria	Fungi	Parasites	Viruses
Neutropenia	Chemotherapy; acute leukemia	S. aureus, S. epidermidis, enterococci, E. coli, K. pneumoniae, P. aeruginosa	Candida, Aspergillus, Fusarium		
T-helper lymphocyte (cell-mediated immunity)	Immunosuppressive therapy; Hodgkin's disease; transplantation	Listeria monocytogenes, Nocardia asteroides, Legionella, Salmonella, mycobacteria	C. neoformans, Aspergillus, Candida, H. capsulatum, Mucoraceae	P. carinii, T. gondii	Herpes simplex, varicella-zoster, cytomegalovirus
Gamma-globulin (humoral immunity)	Splenectomy; chronic lymphocytic leukemia; hypogammaglobulinemia; bone marrow transplantation	S. pneumoniae, H. influenzae, N. meningitidis		P. carinii, Babesia sp.	
Damage to physical barriers	Surgical procedures	S. aureus; S. epidermis, S. pyogenes; Enterobacteriaceae; P. aeruginosa, Bacteroides	Candida		
	Indwelling catheters; venipuncture	S. aureus, coagulase-negative staphylococci, Corynebacterium	Candida		
	Chemotherapy; endoscopy; radiation	S. aureus, coagulase-negative staphylococci, streptococci, Enterobacteriaceae, P. aeruginosa, Bacteroides	Candida		Herpes simplex
Microbial colonization	Chemotherapy; antibiotics; hospitalization	S. aureus, S. epidermis, Enterobacteriaceae, P. aeruginosa, Legionella	Candida, Aspergillus		
Transplantation	Bone marrow; solid organ		Candida	T. gondii	Cytomegalovirus; hepatitis B and C; Epstein-Barr virus

[a] Adapted from reference 6.

Fig 67.1   Risk of Infection According to Granulocyte Count   Risk of infection increases as the granulocyte count falls below 500/mm³. Adapted from reference 9.

Cyclosporine and tacrolimus (formerly known as FK506) effects on both humoral and cellular immunity are the result of decreased T-cell, interleukin-2, interferon, and natural killer cell activation.[44] Although an increase in the frequency of infections would be expected in patients receiving cyclosporine, this is not the case. In fact, fewer bacterial and viral infections have been documented in patients receiving cyclosporine and prednisone compared with patients receiving an azathioprine and prednisone combination. Perhaps this difference is due to the lower doses of prednisone required in those patients receiving cyclosporine.[17] For this reason, the clinician should be aware that patients receiving corticosteroids for prolonged periods are at high risk for a wide spectrum of infections due to bacteria, fungi, and opportunistic pathogens.[18]

Colonization

Microbial colonization is an important prerequisite to infection in patients with granulocytopenia. Colonization may be defined as the recovery of an organism from any particular site (e.g., stool, nasopharynx) in the absence of clinical signs of infection.[24] Most infections in neutropenic patients are caused by the host's endogenous microflora or hospital-acquired pathogens that have colonized the alimentary tract, upper respiratory tract, and skin.[28]

Organ Transplantation

Transplantation of bone marrow and solid organs predisposes patients to the development of opportunistic infections. These infections may be acquired from the donor organ, blood products, or reactivation of latent host infection. A more detailed explanation of the types of infections are detailed later in this chapter. (Also see Chapters 33: Solid Organ Transplantation and 94: Bone Marrow Transplantation.)

Infections in Neutropenic Cancer Patients

Clinical Signs and Symptoms

1. B.C., a 41-year-old female, was admitted to the cancer center for placement of a Hickman catheter for chemotherapy of acute nonlymphocytic leukemia in relapse. She was diagnosed 2 years ago and was treated with cytarabine plus daunorubicin which resulted in a complete remission for 33 months. This admission, she was treated with high dose cytar- abine plus etoposide for reinduction. Seven days after completing chemotherapy, B.C. developed a fever of 102 °F. Vital signs were as follows: blood pressure (BP) 109/70 mm Hg, pulse rate 102 beats/min, and respirations 25/min. Physical examination demonstrated a clear throat without exudates or plaques. Chest and cardiac examination were normal. The exit site for the Hickman catheter was clean and nontender. There were no signs of erythema or induration. The perineum and rectum were nontender and no masses were noted.

Laboratory data were as follows: hematocrit (Hct) 20% (Normal: 33–43), hemoglobin (Hgb) 7 gm/dL (Normal: 14–18), WBC count 1400/μL (Normal: 3200–9800) with 3% polymorphonuclear leukocytes (PMNs) (Normal: 54–62), 1% band forms (Normal: 3–5), 70% lymphocytes (Normal: 25–33), and 22% monocytes (Normal: 3–7). Platelet count was 17,000/μL (Normal: 130,000–400,000). Blood glucose was 160 mg/dL (Normal: 70–110). Serum creatinine (SrCr) and blood urea nitrogen (BUN) were 1.1 mg/dL (Normal: 0.6–1.2) and 24 mg/dL (Normal: 8–18), respectively. What are the signs and symptoms of infection in B.C.? What are the most common sites and sources of infection in patients like B.C.? [SI units: Hct 0.2 (Normal: 0.33–0.43); Hgb 70 gm/L (Normal: 140–180); WBC count 1.4 × 10⁹/L (Normal: 3.2–9.8) with 0.03 PMNs (Normal: 0.54–0.62), 0.01 band forms (Normal: 0.03–0.05), 0.7 lymphocytes (Normal: 0.25–0.33), and 0.22 monocytes (Normal: 0.03–0.07); platelets 17 × 10⁹/L (Normal: 130–400); glucose 8.88 mmol/L (Normal: 3.89–6.11); SrCr 97.24 μmol/L (Normal: 53.04–106.08); BUN 8.57 mmol/L urea (Normal: 2.86–6.43)]

As illustrated by B.C., fever is the earliest and often the only sign of infection in the neutropenic patient.[19,20] Although the lung is the most frequent site of serious infection in neutropenic cancer patients, fever and a dry cough are often the only presenting signs and symptoms of pneumonia. The impaired inflammatory response in these patients often makes sputum production scant, and Gram's stains often contain few polymorphonuclear cells. Radiological evidence of a pulmonary infection is minimal or absent, and the chest examination is frequently nondiagnostic. Pneumonia has a mortality rate approaching 80% in neutropenic patients, especially if it occurs in conjunction with bacteremia.[21]

Invasive procedures such as venipuncture, IV catheter placement (e.g., Hickman catheter), and skin biopsies can produce cellulitis and systemic infections. However, detection of skin and soft tissue infections is also difficult because the typical signs and symptoms of infection (e.g., pain, heat, erythema, swelling) often are absent.[6,22] This is primarily due to the lack of adequate numbers of granulocytes as well as the suppression or absence of other components of the inflammatory response.[9,22] Ulceration of the oral and gastrointestinal mucosa also is a frequent complication of cytotoxic therapy (e.g., cyclophosphamide, methotrexate).[23] Colonization of these lesions may result in local infection and systemic dissemination of bacteria and fungi. Bacteremia occurs primarily from entry of bacteria through unrecognized ulcerations in the gastrointestinal and perirectal areas.[5,21,24]

Confirmation of Infection

2. How can the existence of an infection be confirmed in patients such as B.C.?

The frequent lack of physical signs and symptoms of infection makes it imperative that the clinician obtain an accurate history and conduct a careful physical examination at the first sign of fever. Special attention should be placed on the oropharynx, axillae, groin, and perianal areas. Before antibiotics are initiated, specimens of the blood, urine, and other suspected sites of infection should be obtained for culture. Any indwelling urinary or intravenous catheter should be considered as a potential focus of infection and, if possible, removed and cultured.[13]

Despite comprehensive laboratory evaluation, an infectious etiology for fever can be documented in only 60% of neutropenic cancer patients.[19,25] Forty percent of these febrile episodes have a documented microbiological etiology; the remaining 20% are attributed to infection based upon clinical findings alone. Immunological methods which detect the presence of bacterial, fungal, and viral antibodies or antigens may improve the clinician's ability to establish an infectious etiology of fever.[26]

Infecting Pathogens

3. What are the most likely pathogens causing fever in B.C.?

Bacteria are the primary pathogens associated with infection in the febrile neutropenic patient. Enteric gram-negative bacilli are the most frequently isolated organisms from cancer patients with infection;[28] however, over the past decade the proportion of gram-negative infections has decreased with a proportional increase in gram-positive infections, especially the *Staphylococcus* species (see Table 67.1). The re-emergence of staphylococci (particularly *S. epidermidis*) as an important pathogen in neutropenic patients is due in part to the frequent use of permanent intravascular catheters, use of more intensive chemotherapy regimens, and the widespread use of prophylactic and therapeutic antibiotic administration.[34] All of the above factors can contribute to the development of infection in patients like B.C.[34]

Most bacterial infections in neutropenic cancer patients are caused by *Pseudomonas aeruginosa, Escherichia coli, Klebsiella pneumoniae,* and *Staphylococcus aureus.*[18,19,25,28,32,33] In addition to the common bacterial pathogens, neutropenic patients are susceptible to infections with uncommon organisms as well as those with limited pathogenicity. Methicillin-resistant *S. aureus* and *Staphylococcus epidermidis*, streptococci, and *Corynebacterium jeikeium* have become important pathogens in some cancer centers.[18] Moreover, enterococcal and fungal infections are increasing in frequency due to routine use of certain antibiotic regimens. Meningitis caused by the intracellular organism, *Listeria monocytogenes*, is observed in patients with defective cellular immunity due to disease or prolonged corticosteroid use. In general, anaerobic bacteria are an infrequent cause of infection in granulocytopenic patients with hematologic malignancies; they may occur more frequently in patients with GI malignancies.[21,35]

Colonization

4. Cultures of swabs taken from B.C.'s axillae and nasopharynx and a stool specimen grew the following: *C. jeikeium* (axillae), *S. aureus* (axillae and nasopharynx), and *P. aeruginosa* (nasopharynx and stool). What is the significance of these culture results? Should routine, serial cultures be performed in patients such as B.C.?

Several factors influence the colonization and subsequent infection by micro-organisms in cancer patients such as B.C.[36] During the early 1970s, Schimpff et al.[28] found that about 85% of the organisms isolated from infected patients were previously cultured in endogenous flora; almost one-half of these infecting organisms were acquired during hospitalization. The sources and factors contributing to colonization are numerous and include: staff-to-staff and patient-to-patient transmission (e.g., lack of frequent and adequate handwashing techniques); direct transmission from the environment (e.g., inadequately disinfected bathtubs, sinks, toilet bowls); food-borne sources (e.g., raw fruits and vegetables); inhalation from contaminated fomites (e.g., respirators, air-ventilating systems); and parenteral therapy.[38]

In addition to immunosuppression, the underlying malignancy and chemotherapy have other effects which diminish the cancer patient's resistance to colonization and infection.[24,28] For example, chemotherapy induces changes in the microbial binding receptors on epithelial cells in the oropharynx. This allows gram-negative bacilli to adhere to these surfaces and change the composition of the oropharyngeal flora from a mixture of gram-positive aerobes and anaerobes to gram-negative aerobic bacteria.[36] Colonization with resistant organisms also is enhanced by antibiotic administration which may suppress the growth of anaerobic flora in the GI tract. This anaerobic suppression may allow overgrowth of resistant micro-organisms.[14,39] For example, neither *P. aeruginosa* or *K. pneumoniae* are commonly found in the stool of normal healthy adults, but frequently are recovered from the stools of hospitalized cancer patients.[24,36]

Organisms that colonize cancer patients differ in their invasiveness and propensity to cause infection.[23,28] Colonization with *P. aeruginosa* is more likely to result in infection than is colonization with less virulent organisms such as *E. coli* or *S. epidermidis*.[32] However, if the degree of host impairment is sufficiently profound, virtually any organism has the capacity to become a serious pathogen.

The acquisition of, and subsequent colonization by, pathogenic microbes can be monitored by serial cultures of specimens obtained from various body sites.[40] Specimens obtained from the nasopharynx, axilla, urine, and rectum are cultured on admission and at least twice weekly during hospitalization. These surveillance cultures may reveal changes in the normal distribution of organisms and may lead to early recognition of colonization (and subsequent infection) by noteworthy pathogens such as *P. aeruginosa*. Information gained from surveillance cultures also may aid the clinician in selecting appropriate antibiotics should the clinical signs of infection develop.[40] Although surveillance cultures have provided useful information on the dynamic changes in microflora during hospitalization, they are not a cost-effective method for predicting or identifying the etiologic pathogen from the vast array of organisms recovered.[36,41]

In summary, B.C.'s surveillance culture results indicate that she is colonized with several pathogens associated with infection in the immunocompromised host. These results may be useful in selecting empiric antibiotics for B.C.'s fever.

Empiric Antibiotic Therapy

Rationale

5. Should B.C. be started on antibiotic therapy immediately? Is this rational in view of the fact that neither the source of her fever nor pathogen has been established?

All febrile patients with an ANC of less than 500 cells/μL or between 500 to 1000 cells/μL and dropping should be considered to have a potentially life-threatening bacterial infection and promptly started on broad-spectrum antibiotics.[9,41,42] Early studies documented the poor prognosis of neutropenic patients whose gram-negative infections were untreated during the first 24 to 48 hours following the onset of fever.[42] Mortality secondary to *P. aeruginosa* bacteremia was the greatest; 50% of patients died within 72 hours of the first positive blood culture. Ultimately 91% of patients died from infection.[32,42] These observations emphasized the need for prompt empiric institution of antibiotic therapy to prevent early morbidity and mortality due to bacterial infection.

Bacterial Coverage

6. What antimicrobials should be initiated as empiric therapy in B.C.? Do all possible pathogenic organisms need to be covered?

Empiric antibiotic regimens should provide maximum coverage against those organisms most commonly isolated from neutropenic cancer patients: *E. coli, K. pneumoniae, P. aeruginosa,* and staphylococci. Combination antibiotic regimens have been largely used in empiric therapy and may consist of two or more of the following antibiotics: an aminoglycoside such as gentamicin, tobramycin, or amikacin (Amikin); a cephalosporin such as cefoperazone (Cefobid) or ceftazidime (Fortaz); an antipseudomonal penicillin, such as ticarcillin alone (Ticar) or combined with clavulanic acid (Timentin), mezlocillin (Mezlin), or piperacillin (Pipracil),[45-47] and vancomycin.[48,49] Many organisms, including those recovered from surveillance cultures, may be pathogens in B.C. Those associated with a high mortality rate during the first 48 hours should be optimally treated pending receipt of culture and sensitivity results. Therefore, a combination regimen with optimum activity against gram-negative bacilli should be employed in B.C.

Factors Influencing Response to Therapy

7. Host Factors. B.C. is started on piperacillin and tobramycin. One day later, blood cultures collected before initiation of antibiotic therapy grow _P. aeruginosa_. Three days later, B.C. is afebrile and her WBC count is 3000/μL with 15% PMNs, 5% bands, 65% lymphocytes, and 10% monocytes. What factors may have influenced B.C.'s clinical response to antimicrobial therapy? [SI units WBC count 3 × 10⁹/L with 0.15 PMNs, 0.05 bands, 0.65 lymphocytes, and 0.1 monocytes]

The most important determinant of a favorable outcome in patients such as B.C. with neutropenia and gram-negative bacteremia is the recovery of the granulocyte count.[25,50] Patients with profound, persistent neutropenia (PPN), defined as the presence of less than 100/μL granulocytes which do not rise during therapy or an initial ANC of 100 to 500/μL which declines during therapy, tend to respond less favorably to antibiotics than patients whose bone marrow recovers.[3,25,45,51,52] The initial granulocyte count is less important than the trend towards granulocyte recovery in influencing the patient's overall response to therapy. The site of infection also influences outcome: septic shock and pneumonia are associated with high mortality in bacteremic neutropenic patients.[2,3] The increase in B.C.'s ANC from 56/μL to 600/μL (20% × 3000/μL) was the most important determinant of her favorable response to therapy.

8. Antibiotic Susceptibility. The organism, _P. aeruginosa_, cultured from B.C.'s blood is susceptible to tobramycin, but resistant to gentamicin and piperacillin. Is her antimicrobial therapy optimal? How does drug resistance affect response to antimicrobial therapy?

A number of antibiotic-related factors also can influence the prognosis of infection in neutropenic patients. The susceptibility of the infecting pathogen to antibiotics correlates with clinical response. If the pathogen is sensitive to at least one antibiotic in the initial regimen, the response usually is greater than 60%; however, if the pathogen is resistant, the response rarely exceeds 30%.[3,52]

In patients with profound persistent neutropenia and bacteremia, the susceptibility of the organism to the antibiotics used in early treatment may influence the response to therapy. Love et al.[52] retrospectively evaluated the prognostic determinants of recovery in neutropenic cancer patients with bacteremia due to gram-negative rods who were treated with combination antibiotic regimens. Outcome of the infection was directly related to the _in vitro_ susceptibility of the infecting organism. Resolution of the infection was noted in 75% of patients with persistent profound neutropenia treated with two active antibiotics, whereas only 44% of patients responded when treated with only one active antibiotic. A favorable response was obtained in most patients with evidence of marrow recovery regardless of the organism's susceptibility to one or both antibiotics in the regimen. Todeschini et al.[3] also found a significant difference in response rates between patients with bacteremia due to antibiotic-resistant or antibiotic-sensitive organisms. _In vitro_ susceptibility to two or more antibiotics resulted in a 65%

response rate, whereas susceptibility to only one antibiotic used in a combination regimen was associated with a 47% response rate (p <0.01).

The correlation between clinical response and _in vitro_ susceptibility enables one to compare the clinical efficacy of various antimicrobial regimens in neutropenic cancer patients.[50,54,55] In bacteremic patients whose infecting organism was susceptible only to the aminoglycoside in a beta-lactam/aminoglycoside regimen, Sculier and Klastersky[56] found the rate of failure to be high; three of nine patients with adequate granulocyte counts and six of nine patients with neutropenia failed to respond to antibiotic therapy. In other studies, susceptibility of the infectious pathogen to the beta-lactam antibiotic used in combination empiric therapy was an important determinant of response to infection.[54,57]

Based upon these data, it appears that B.C.'s antibiotic regimen is suboptimal. Since the _P. aeruginosa_ isolated is susceptible to tobramycin but resistant to piperacillin, a different beta-lactam should be substituted based upon _in vitro_ susceptibility of the isolate.

Antimicrobial Combinations

9. Synergy. What is the rationale behind the use of antimicrobial combinations in patients like B.C.? How does antimicrobial synergy influence the clinical response of neutropenic patients with infection?

Combination antibiotic regimens have been favored due to their broad spectrum of activity and the additive or synergistic effects which may occur when two or more agents are used in combination.[59,60] Synergy is defined as an interaction between antimicrobial agents in which the effect produced by the combination is greater than the sum of each of their individual effects.[60] Antimicrobial synergy may be demonstrated in the laboratory by a number of methods using either bacteriostatic or bactericidal endpoints. However, the results of these tests often vary according to the methodology used. Moreover, the pharmacokinetic profiles of each antibiotic under study are not considered. Although these tests are very useful for testing antimicrobial combinations in the research laboratory, their clinical utility in individual patients appears to be limited.

The use of synergistic antibiotic combinations can enhance clinical response and increase the likelihood of a favorable outcome in infected neutropenic patients like B.C.[25,60,64,65] Patients treated with synergistic antibiotic combinations have a better response to therapy than patients treated with nonsynergistic combinations (79% versus 46%; p <0.05).[64-66] De Jongh et al.[50] compared the efficacy of synergistic and nonsynergistic antibiotic combinations in cancer patients with bacteremia and profound persistent neutropenia. All bacterial isolates were susceptible to both antibiotics individually. In 18 patients whose regimen demonstrated synergism or partial synergism against the infecting pathogen, eight improved. In contrast, none of 13 patients receiving nonsynergistic antibiotic regimens responded; this difference was statistically significant (p = 0.005). In another study, imipenem and ceftazidime were administered, each alone and in combination with amikacin in 19 febrile neutropenic patients with documented _P. aeruginosa_ infections. Sixty-three percent of patients responded to single agent therapy whereas 100% of patients responded to the amikacin containing regimen.[134] Therefore, it is important to maintain B.C. on a synergistic combination of antibiotics, such as a beta-lactam plus an aminoglycoside, in order to maximize antimicrobial therapy against _P. aeruginosa_.

10. Prevention of Resistant Strains. Why would the use of antibiotic combinations be expected to decrease the emergence of resistant bacterial strains?

Resistant bacterial strains can emerge with single agent therapy despite the availability of more potent agents. For example, trials of monotherapy with ceftazidime,[67] piperacillin,[68] and imipenem (Primaxin)[69] indicate that the incidence of resistant *P. aeruginosa* emerging during therapy is 5% to 33%. The addition of a beta-lactam antibiotic to an aminoglycoside can limit the emergence of resistance.[70]

To determine whether the combined use of a beta-lactam antibiotic (piperacillin) with an aminoglycoside prevented the emergence of resistant bacteria during therapy, Gribble et al.[71] randomized patients to receive either piperacillin alone or carbenicillin plus an aminoglycoside. Forty-two percent of patients receiving piperacillin alone developed superinfection with resistant organisms compared to 17% of patients receiving the carbenicillin-aminoglycoside regimen (p <0.05). The emergence of resistant organisms accounted for five of the nine treatment failures in the group treated with piperacillin alone. In the group treated with the combination, infection with resistant organisms accounted for two out of ten treatment failures. Therefore, an aminoglycoside should be added to beta-lactam regimens to prevent the emergence of resistant pathogens.

Serum Bactericidal Titers (SBTs)

11. B.C. is continued on the initial antibiotic regimen of tobramycin plus piperacillin. Blood samples are collected when the antibiotics are expected to exhibit peak activity, and the serum inhibitory and bactericidal titers against the *P. aeruginosa* recovered from B.C.'s blood are determined. The inhibitory and bactericidal titers are 1:16 and 1:8, respectively. Why are bactericidal antibiotics necessary for treating infections in neutropenic patients? What is the meaning and significance of these tests and their results?

In addition to broad-spectrum activity, antibiotic regimens should have potent, bactericidal activity against the infecting pathogen. This is based upon the supposition that when defense mechanisms are impaired (e.g., neutropenia) antibiotic agents which kill rather than inhibit the organism's growth must be used. However, there are no comparative trials of bacteriostatic versus bactericidal antibiotics in humans. The need for bactericidal activity has been based upon studies relating the bactericidal activity of patients' serum during antibiotic therapy to their clinical response.[25,60]

Determination of the serum bactericidal titer is a direct method for measuring the inhibitory and bactericidal activity of a patient's serum during antimicrobial therapy against the specific micro-organism causing infection. The SBT integrates the activity [i.e., the minimum inhibitory (MIC) and minimum bactericidal (MBC) concentrations] of an antibiotic with serum concentrations of the drug in the patient. However, as with the MIC and MBC tests, there are many factors which influence the results and, therefore, limit the clinical utility of this test.[72]

High serum bactericidal activity may improve the prognosis of cancer patients with bacterial infection. In the setting of gram-negative bacteremia, peak serum bactericidal titers ≥1:8 are predictive of outcome in non-neutropenic patients,[64,73] whereas titers ≥1:16 are predictive of a favorable outcome in patients with neutropenia.[56] (Also see Chapter 57: Endocarditis for further explanation of serum bactericidal titers.)

The SBT has been utilized in the clinical evaluation of antibiotic synergy. In patients receiving two antibiotics, high serum bactericidal titers with antibiotic combinations compared with either drug alone may suggest the presence of antimicrobial synergism. In two clinical studies,[64,65] synergistic antibiotic combinations administered to cancer patients with gram-negative bacillary infections were associated with significantly higher peak SBTs (median:

1:16) compared to those achieved in patients receiving nonsynergistic combinations (median: 1:4).

The serum bactericidal titer of 1:8 measured in B.C. is consistent with the *in vitro* susceptibility pattern for B.C.'s pathogen (tobramycin-susceptible and piperacillin-resistant). Although B.C. has responded appropriately to the empiric regimen, one might choose to utilize a different beta-lactam with greater activity (lower MICs) against the *P. aeruginosa* isolated from her blood. For example, imipenem, cefoperazone, or ceftazidime may be substituted. This change would be expected to increase the serum bactericidal titer against B.C.'s *Pseudomonas* isolate.

Choice of Antibiotic Regimens

A variety of regimens containing one to four antibacterial agents have been studied for the empiric management of febrile, neutropenic patients. The most commonly studied regimens include: an aminoglycoside plus a beta-lactam; the combination of two beta-lactams; monotherapy with a beta-lactam; and the addition of vancomycin to the above regimens. Each regimen has its own inherent advantages and disadvantages and there is no well documented evidence that one is superior to another. The comparability of end points for each study varies significantly based upon the definitions of neutropenia, the incidence of documented infections, and statistical methodology.[31,108] The development of specific guidelines for evaluating new agents in this population should aid in minimizing these problems in the future.[26]

Aminoglycoside/Beta-Lactam Combinations

Two-Drug Regimens

12. B.L., a 13-year-old male, presented with a 3-week history of "always being tired" and a persistent sore throat. Initial evaluation revealed anemia, thrombocytopenia, and a WBC count of 130,000/μL (Normal: 3200–9800/μL) with a predominance of immature lymphoblasts. Further evaluation demonstrated that B.L. had "high-risk" acute lymphocytic leukemia. Remission induction treatment was initiated with teniposide plus cytarabine followed by prednisone, vincristine, and L-asparaginase. Seven days after induction chemotherapy, B.L. developed a fever (102 °F) and chills. The ANC was 200/μL. SrCr and BUN were 1.0 mg/dL (Normal: 0.6–1.2 mg/dL) and 15 mg/dL (Normal: 8–18 mg/dL), respectively. What aminoglycoside combination regimen could be used to treat B.L.'s suspected infection? Are there any differences in efficacy between these combinations? [SI units: SrCr 88.4 μmol/L (Normal: 53.04–106.08); BUN 5.36 mmol/L urea (2.86–6.43)]

Up until the past decade, most febrile neutropenic patients were treated with a two- or three-drug regimen which contained an aminoglycoside plus one or two beta-lactam antibiotics, such as an antipseudomonal penicillin and/or a cephalosporin.[51,74,75] Although most studies have not demonstrated any difference in the overall response rates between these combinations, these regimens differ in their activity against certain pathogens. For example, an antipseudomonal penicillin plus tobramycin would be expected to be more active against *P. aeruginosa* than the combination of cefazolin plus tobramycin.[25,76–78] In contrast, an aminoglycoside-cephalosporin regimen, such as cefazolin plus gentamicin may be advantageous for infections due to *K. pneumoniae* or *S. aureus*.[9]

Aminoglycosides are commonly used in combination with other antibiotics to provide additive or synergistic action and to minimize the development of resistance. Of concern, however, is an increase in gentamicin-resistant *P. aeruginosa* to the aminoglycosides. In one institution, gentamicin resistance to *P. aeruginosa* ranged from 14% to 30% when gentamicin was the formulary aminoglycoside. When replaced with amikacin, the incidence of gentamicin resistance decreased about 16%.[99] However, even in gentamicin-susceptible strains, there often is a twofold difference in minimum inhibitory concentrations between gentamicin and tobramycin, 1.0 µg/mL versus 0.5 µg/mL, respectively.[116] This difference in MICs warrants using tobramycin over gentamicin for the management of documented *P. aeruginosa* infections or for empiric therapy in high-risk patients such as B.L. In summary, a combination of an aminoglycoside plus an antipseudomonal beta-lactam such as piperacillin or ceftazidime can be used to treat B.L. empirically. Tobramycin would be the most appropriate aminoglycoside to use in B.L. given the higher MICs and increased incidence of *P. aeruginosa* resistant to gentamicin.

Three-Drug Regimens

13. B.L. is begun on a 3-drug regimen of piperacillin, tobramycin, and cefazolin. What is the rationale for using a three-drug regimen as empiric therapy? Are these regimens more effective than the 2-drug regimens?

In the 1970s and early 1980s, three-drug regimens combining an aminoglycoside, an antipseudomonal penicillin, and a cephalosporin were utilized because many beta-lactam-aminoglycoside combinations have "gaps" in optimal activity against key pathogens. Despite the theoretical benefit of providing coverage for the most likely pathogens (e.g., *Klebsiella* species, *E. coli*), these three-drug regimens are not superior to their two-drug counterparts.[51,81] The additional antistaphylococcal activity provided by the addition of a cephalosporin to an aminoglycoside/antipseudomonal penicillin regimen may not have been observed in these studies because of the unreliable activity of these agents against coagulase-negative staphylococci.[82]

Empiric Vancomycin

Since many cephalosporins have poor and often only bacteriostatic activity against coagulase-negative staphylococci, vancomycin has been added to empiric regimens. Febrile neutropenic patients with cancer had a more rapid resolution of fever, fewer days of bacteremia, and a lower frequency of treatment failure with the addition of vancomycin to an initial regimen of aminoglycoside plus an antipseudomonal penicillin, than those who did not receive vancomycin initially.[48,84] Similarly, the addition of vancomycin to ceftazidime improved results over those observed with ceftazidime alone or with the three-drug combination of a first-generation cephalosporin, gentamicin, and an antipseudomonal penicillin.[43]

In other studies, mortality was not increased when vancomycin therapy was delayed.[49,79,80] This may be because the mortality from staphylococcal infections is low (<4%) during the first 48 hours following the onset of fever. In addition, the activity of both the aminoglycosides and certain beta-lactams against gram-positive organisms, albeit low, may be adequate until the results of blood cultures are available. Therefore, there is time to modify therapy, if needed, to provide optimal antibiotic coverage for staphylococci after culture and sensitivity results are received.

The routine use of vancomycin presents concerns because of the increasing incidence of vancomycin-resistant enterococci as well as infections caused by inherently resistant organisms such as *Leuconostoc* species. However, in patients or institutions with an increased incidence of infections caused by coagulase-negative staphylococci, methicillin-resistant *S. aureus*, *Corynebacterium* species, or alpha-hemolytic streptococci, vancomycin should probably be included in the initial empiric regimen in patients with obvious evidence of infection at the exit or tunnel sites of central venous catheters. In other patients, careful monitoring of blood cultures and other symptoms allows for the timely addition of vancomycin to empiric therapy regimens such as the aminoglycoside/beta-lactam regimen recommended in Question 12.

Drug Dosing and Monitoring Considerations

Intermittent versus Continuous Infusion of Antibiotics

14. Should B.L.'s antibiotics be given intermittently (i.e., divided doses) or as a continuous infusion?

One of the more controversial aspects regarding the use of antibiotics in patients with cancer is whether these drugs should be administered by continuous or intermittent infusions. Studies with beta-lactam antibiotics in animal and *in vitro* models of infection suggest that prolonged exposure of bacteria to drug concentrations above a therapeutic level (e.g., the MIC) may be linked to improved bacterial killing and survival.[89] In patients with early "breakthrough" bacteremia (i.e., recurrence of bacteremia while receiving appropriate antibiotic therapy), the antibiotic concentrations were below the infecting organism's MIC in the majority of patients and failure to maintain drug concentrations above inhibitory concentrations for the antibiotics may have been the reason for the relapses.[85]

Based upon these observations and the poor prognosis of neutropenic cancer patients with bacteremia, several trials were conducted to evaluate continuous versus intermittent administration of aminoglycosides in the treatment of suspected infection in cancer patients. In several studies, the response of patients treated with an aminoglycoside was greater when the aminoglycoside was administered by continuous rather than intermittent infusion.[86] However, these reports are difficult to evaluate since many of the patients were entered into the studies after "failing" previous antibiotic regimens. Patients often differed markedly in their immune status (e.g., differences in incidence of neutropenia between study groups, uncontrolled use of granulocyte transfusions), and the total *daily* dose of the aminoglycoside was often higher in the continuous infusion group. The claim that continuous infusion therapy is superior to intermittent infusion is based upon the combined results of several small studies, each of which used different aminoglycosides. In the only randomized, prospective study conducted to date, there was no statistical difference between the two modes of administration.[86]

The most convincing argument against the continuous infusion of aminoglycosides relates to the incidence of toxicity. Studies in established animal models of aminoglycoside-induced nephrotoxicity show that the uptake of aminoglycosides into renal cortical tissue increased and glomerular function decreased more when the dose was infused continuously rather than given as single or divided doses.[87] Studies in humans have confirmed less drug accumulation with single daily dosing.[92]

Neutropenic patients with gram-negative bacillary infections have been effectively managed with continuous infusion of beta-lactam antibiotics.[109] Bodey et al.[94] randomized patients to receive carbenicillin plus tobramycin or carbenicillin plus cefamandole by continuous or intermittent infusion. The regimen of carbenicillin plus cefamandole was significantly more effective when given by continuous infusion than by intermittent administration in patients with profound, persistent neutropenia. There were no differences in toxicity.

In conclusion, the maintenance of beta-lactam antibiotic concentrations above certain critical levels (as might be provided by continuous infusion) appears rational; however, data demonstrating improved effects with newer, more potent agents in patients with cancer are unavailable.

Once-Daily Aminoglycoside Dosing

15. What is the role of once-daily aminoglycoside dosing in febrile neutropenic patients such as B.L.?

Several studies in animals,[87,89] in humans,[88,93] and in *in vitro*[90,91] models of infection in a neutropenic patient have compared the efficacy of different modes of aminoglycoside administration. Powell et al.[87] compared once daily bolus dosing versus continuous infusion of the same total dose in several animal models of infection and concluded that there was no difference in efficacy. Studies in an *in vitro* model of infection suggest that once daily dosing of an aminoglycoside alone or in combination with a beta-lactam antibiotic is similar or even superior to the bactericidal effects observed with traditional or continuous infusion regimens.[90,91]

A study in 13 children with fever and granulocytopenia undergoing bone marrow transplantation evaluated the safety and pharmacokinetics of single daily dosing of amikacin (20 mg/kg) plus ceftazidime.[93] Thirty-minute postinfusion concentrations of amikacin on the first day of therapy were 72.3 ± 11.6 mg/L [mean ± standard deviation (SD)]; trough amikacin concentrations were less than 3 mg/L by six hours in most patients and in all trough samples. A significant increase in serum creatinine during therapy for 7 to 15 days was observed in only one patient receiving cyclosporine; no change in auditory function was detected. All patients survived, with modification of the initial regimen in response to recovery of other pathogens and clinical response.

In a European Organization for Research in the Treatment of Cancer (EORTC) study, single daily doses of amikacin and ceftriaxone were as effective and no more toxic than conventional therapy with ceftazidime plus multiple daily doses of amikacin in febrile neutropenic patients.[88]

In summary, once-daily dosing of aminoglycosides appears safe and effective in both immunocompetent and immunocompromised patients;[83] however, additional clinical studies need to be conducted in febrile neutropenic patients before its use is widely accepted.[109]

Aminoglycoside Degradation

16. Peak and trough tobramycin levels are collected following the 3rd dose late Friday afternoon for B.L. Assay results of these samples, available Monday afternoon, showed no detectable tobramycin in either sample. Additional levels are collected and assayed stat the following morning; these results show peak and trough levels within the therapeutic range. What is the likely explanation for these results?

Aminoglycoside antibiotics are inactivated by certain ureidopenicillin and carboxypenicillin derivatives.[95] These drugs interact readily *in vitro* and should not be admixed in the same intravenous solution. Aminoglycosides also can be inactivated by some penicillins *in vivo* in patients with renal failure.[95,96] The extent of aminoglycoside degradation is dependent upon the concentration of the penicillin in the sample, storage time, and temperature. Inactivation following 24 hours of incubation at 27 °C is significant when penicillin concentrations exceed 250 mg/L.[96] Inactivation proceeds more rapidly at higher temperatures.[97] There are no significant differences between antipseudomonal penicillins in their inactivating potential; however, amikacin and netilmicin are less susceptible to inactivation compared to gentamicin and tobramycin.[96] Therefore, serum specimens containing aminoglycoside-penicillin combinations should be assayed for aminoglycoside immediately; if this is impossible, the specimen should be frozen or treated with beta-lactamase. Although freezing of the specimen may significantly slow the degradation of the aminoglycoside by the penicillins, the addition of small amounts of concentrated beta-lactamase to the serum specimen to degrade the penicillin is the most reliable method of preventing artifactually low aminoglycoside levels resulting from *in vitro* laboratory inactivation.[97]

The discrepancies between B.L.'s tobramycin levels drawn Friday and Monday are possibly due to *in vitro* degradation of tobramycin by piperacillin. Since the samples were drawn on late Friday

afternoon, it is possible that the serum was incorrectly processed or improperly stored over the weekend before it was assayed, thus hastening *in vitro* degradation of tobramycin.

Double Beta-Lactam Combinations

17. Seven days into therapy, despite rehydration, B.L.'s SrCr and BUN rose to 2.0 mg/dL and 45 mg/dL, respectively. Since B.L. has developed nephrotoxicity, what other nonaminoglycoside combination regimens could be used? Are these regimens as effective as aminoglycoside-containing regimens?
[SI units: SrCr 176.8 μmol/L; BUN 16.07 mmol/L urea]

Aminoglycoside nephrotoxicity and the development of more potent beta-lactams have sparked an interest in the use of combination antibiotic regimens which exclude aminoglycosides. For example, many double beta-lactam antibiotic combinations consisting of a cephalosporin plus an antipseudomonal penicillin have been studied. These so-called "double-beta" regimens provide a broad-spectrum of activity against the most common pathogens and may have synergistic activity against some strains of *P. aeruginosa* and other gram-negative bacteria.[103] However, combinations of strong inducers of Bush Group 1 beta-lactamases (e.g., imipenem, cefoxitin) with weak inducers (e.g., piperacillin) may result in antagonism *in vitro* and *in vivo*.[102,105]

Cephalosporins plus Ureidopenicillins

The overall response rate of patients treated with a third-generation cephalosporin (e.g., ceftazidime) plus a ureidopenicillin (e.g., piperacillin) is not significantly different than that of patients treated with aminoglycoside/beta-lactam regimens.[76–78,106] Experience with double beta-lactam combinations in patients with neutropenia or patients with documented infections due to *P. aeruginosa* is limited, and available results are somewhat disturbing. Winston et al.[107] observed a lower response in profound persistent neutropenic patients treated with moxalactam plus piperacillin (48%) compared to those treated with moxalactam plus amikacin (77%). Since the number of patients studied was small, these differences only approached statistical significance (p = 0.08). A poorer response in patients with infection due to *P. aeruginosa* was observed: one out of five patients treated with moxalactam plus piperacillin versus seven out of nine patients treated with moxalactam plus amikacin responded (p < 0.06). Two patients with bacteremia due to *P. aeruginosa* that was initially susceptible to the double beta-lactam regimen relapsed with isolates resistant to multiple beta-lactam antibiotics. These results are compatible with the selection of bacteria producing high amounts of the Bush Group 1 beta-lactamase which is capable of inactivating third-generation cephalosporins as well as other less stable beta-lactams.[105]

In summary, given the limited experience with these regimens in patients with profound persistent neutropenia or infections due to *P. aeruginosa*, empiric therapy with double beta-lactam regimens should be reserved for patients who are at high risk of developing aminoglycoside-related nephrotoxicity and those in whom the likelihood of infection due to bacteria carrying Group 1 beta-lactamase (e.g., *P. aeruginosa, Enterobacter* species) is low.[76,103,110] In light of B.L.'s aminoglycoside-induced nephrotoxicity, negative blood cultures, and afebrile state, a double beta-lactam regimen may be an appropriate alternative; however, he should be monitored carefully for signs of recurring infection.

Hematologic Abnormalities

18. B.L. is changed to a combination of piperacillin plus cefoperazone. Seven days later, persistent epistaxis is noted. Relevant laboratory values were as follows: Hgb 13.1 gm/dL; Hct 38%; WBC count 1100/μL (30% polys, 60% lymphocytes);

prothrombin time 20 seconds (control: 12); platelet count 280,000/μL; no fibrin split products. What are the possible drug-induced causes of B.L.'s hematologic problems? [SI units: Hgb 131 gm/L; Hct 0.38; WBC count 1.1×10^9/L with 0.3 polys, 0.6 lymphocytes]

Coagulopathy. Coagulopathy due to hypoprothrombinemia or platelet dysfunction has been associated with the use of certain cephalosporin and penicillin antibiotics. Hypoprothrombinemia has been associated with the following cephalosporins: moxalactam, cefoperazone, cefotetan, and cefamandole. Although coagulopathy usually presents as a prolonged prothrombin time only, severe bleeding episodes have been reported.[111–113,122]

Two mechanisms for the hypoprothrombinemia have been proposed. One hypothesis is that the significant biliary excretion of some compounds suppresses intestinal bacteria (e.g., *B. fragilis*) which produce vitamin K, a necessary cofactor in the synthesis of four clotting factors.[114] Critics of this hypothesis argue that there is only meager evidence that menaquinone, the vitamin K_2 synthesized by certain intestinal bacteria, is absorbed and utilized in humans.[115]

The methylthiotetrazole (MTT) moiety located at the 3-position of the cephem or oxa-cephem nucleus of some beta-lactams has been proposed as the cause of hypoprothrombinemia.[104] *In vitro* studies have shown that the MTT group can inhibit gamma-carboxylation of glutamic acid, the vitamin K-dependent step in the synthesis of clotting factors.

The prevalence of coagulopathy, however, may be greater in high-risk patients regardless of the antibiotic(s) administered.[118] The combination of acute and chronic deficiency in vitamin K activity leads to increased frequency of hypothrombinemia.[119] Patients at high risk for coagulopathy disorders include the elderly, malnourished patients, surgical patients, patients with renal disease, and patients with hematologic malignancy, such as B.L. Coagulopathy can be minimized in these patients by administering vitamin K prophylactically, 10 mg/week, to avoid the consequences of vitamin K deficiency.

Penicillins also may induce platelet dysfunction, resulting in a prolongation of bleeding time. These drugs bind to the platelet surface and inhibit serotonin release and platelet aggregation. Several penicillins, including carbenicillin, ticarcillin, piperacillin, and nafcillin (Nafcil), impair platelet function *in vitro* and *in vivo*. Of the ureidopenicillins, mezlocillin appears to be the least potent inhibitor.[120,121] Cephalosporins do not appear to inhibit platelet aggregation at concentrations achieved in man; however, moxalactam is an exception.[112]

The antiplatelet effects of antipseudomonal penicillins differ from one another. *In vitro*, the antiplatelet effect of piperacillin and mezlocillin appears to be less than that of ticarcillin and carbenicillin.[121] A prospective study of bleeding associated with ticarcillin, mezlocillin, piperacillin, and cefotaxime (the latter agent included as a negative control) showed that elevations in bleeding time and bleeding episodes were more frequently associated with ticarcillin, followed by piperacillin, and then mezlocillin. However, receipt of cancer chemotherapy was the most significant factor predisposing patients to clinical bleeding or elevated bleeding times. No significant differences between drugs could be demonstrated in this subset of patients, but the statistical power of the study was low.[113]

Neutropenia. The beta-lactams also can increase the duration and severity of neutropenia in granulocytopenic patients.[120,123] Neutropenia associated with the cephalosporins and penicillins results from an antigen-antibody reaction characterized by rapid destruction of peripheral neutrophils.[123] Since prolonged neutropenia is associated with a poor response to antibiotic therapy and an

increased susceptibility to superinfection, B.L. also may be subjected to prolonged myelosuppression if the two beta-lactam agents are combined for prolonged periods.[103] This may further limit the utility of double beta-lactam regimens in patients like B.L. with profound, persistent neutropenia.

In summary, B.L.'s antibiotic regimen (piperacillin plus cefoperazone) is a possible cause of his hematologic problems. The additive effects of these two drugs could have predisposed B.L. to bleeding episodes. The hypoprothrombinemia induced by cefoperazone is best treated with administration of vitamin K. Fresh frozen plasma can be given in patients who exhibit severe hemorrhage. Alternative antibiotics which do not contain a methylthiotetrazole group and have less potent antiplatelet effects should be substituted if antibiotic therapy is to continue,[111] and 10 mg vitamin K should be administered weekly during the course of antibiotic therapy.[118] Coagulopathy from other than drug-induced causes also needs to be evaluated.

Monotherapy

19. Can any of the more potent, extended-spectrum beta-lactams be used as monotherapy in febrile neutropenic patients?

Until recently, only synergistic combinations of antibiotics were capable of providing broad-spectrum and high bactericidal activity against pathogens associated with infection in febrile neutropenic patients. Many of the newer beta-lactams have more potent activity against likely pathogens and produce serum bactericidal activity comparable to that observed with synergistic combinations of other agents.

Cephalosporins

Third-generation cephalosporins have potent broad-spectrum activity against many gram-negative and gram-positive pathogens associated with infection in cancer patients. Peak serum concentrations exceeded the MIC for most pathogens by several-fold; serum bactericidal activity (SBA) is comparable and may even exceed that obtained with standard synergistic antibiotic combinations.[129] Of the currently available agents, ceftazidime, and cefoperazone have the best activity against *P. aeruginosa*. Ceftazidime has less activity against *Staphylococcus* species compared to other available agents in its class (e.g., cefepime). Thus, as a class, the third-generation cephalosporins possess a number of unique attributes which would enable them to be used as single-agents for the treatment of infection in immunocompromised patients. Of the currently available third-generation cephalosporins, only ceftazidime and cefoperazone have been widely studied as monotherapy for infection in immunocompromised patients.

When cefoperazone alone (12 gm/day) was compared to cefoperazone (4 gm/day) in combination with amikacin in 154 cancer patients (49 were neutropenic upon entry into the study) the response rate was similar between the two regimens.[129] Serum bactericidal titers were high (range: 1:4 to 1:2048) and similar for both regimens. However, the dose of cefoperazone (12 gm/day) was far in excess of that currently recommended, and only six documented infections were due to *P. aeruginosa*. Antibiotic failure occurred in the amikacin-cefoperazone group in a single patient with profound granulocytopenia and infection with an amikacin-resistant *P. aeruginosa*.

Several trials have evaluated ceftazidime as monotherapy for presumed infection in febrile cancer patients. While overall response rates appear comparable to that observed with combination antimicrobial regimens, the efficacy in patients with documented staphylococcal infections was suboptimal.[131,132] Subsequent trials have included the addition of an antistaphylococcal agent (e.g., vancomycin).[79,108]

A National Cancer Institute (NCI) study of 550 cancer patients with fever and neutropenia compared ceftazidime (6 gm/day) to a three-drug regimen consisting of cephalothin, carbenicillin, and gentamicin. Overall, ceftazidime was as effective as the standard regimen in patients with documented infections and unexplained fever.[132] An EORTC trial evaluated the effectiveness of ceftazidime plus either a full or a short, three-day course of amikacin in febrile neutropenic cancer patients.[33] Patients with gram-negative bacteremia responded better to the full course of both ceftazidime and amikacin than to the regimen of six doses of amikacin combined with a full course of ceftazidime or to a full course of azlocillin plus amikacin (controlled regimen). These data confirm the superiority of combined therapy with ceftazidime plus an aminoglycoside in gram-negative bacteremia.

Cefepime (Maxipime) is a fourth-generation cephalosporin with broad-spectrum activity against gram-positive and gram-negative bacteria. Cefepime, 6 gm/day, has been compared with ceftazidime and to piperacillin plus gentamicin.[98] There was no significant difference between cefepime and the other regimens with regard to clinical or microbiologic response. When cefepime was administered in another uncontrolled trial as monotherapy in 91 neutropenic patients, the overall survival rate was 96%.[162] Additional well-controlled cefepime studies need to be performed before its role in the management of febrile, neutropenic patients can be defined.

Carbapenems

The carbapenems are a unique class of beta-lactam antibiotics with broad-spectrum activity against numerous gram-positive and gram-negative bacteria, including anaerobes. Imipenem, in combination with the dehydropeptidase inhibitor, cilastatin (Primaxin), was the first in this class to become available, and meropenem (Merrem) is awaiting FDA approval.[100]

Imipenem has been studied alone as empiric therapy in febrile neutropenic patients and results have been comparable with beta-lactam plus aminoglycoside[134,135] and double beta-lactam regimens.[133] When imipenem was compared to ceftazidime as initial monotherapy in febrile neutropenic patients, patient response was significantly better with the imipenem regimen.[163] This was probably because of ceftazidime's poor activity against gram-positive bacteria and a possible increase in gram-positive infections in the ceftazidime-treated patients. Studies evaluating the role of meropenem in febrile neutropenic patients are ongoing.

In summary, these studies suggest that monotherapy with certain beta-lactam antibiotics may be a suitable alternative to combination antimicrobial therapy in selected febrile neutropenic patients. However, one has to be cautious in applying these data to all immunocompromised patients. Only a few patients with bacteremic infections due to P. aeruginosa have been treated in these studies.[129,132,135] Neutropenia often was absent or of short duration in some trials[132] and experience in patients with profound persistent neutropenia (who have the poorest prognosis for response to infection) is limited. Careful monitoring and appropriate modifications of the empiric antibiotic regimen are necessary during the first 72 hours of therapy to ensure a successful outcome.[177]

Alternative Regimens

Both the monobactams and the fluoroquinolones have a role in the therapeutic management of febrile neutropenic patients, especially as empirical alternatives in patients with beta-lactam allergies.

Monobactams

Aztreonam (Azactam), the only monobactam currently available in the U.S., is active only against gram-negative aerobic bacilli at clinically achievable concentrations. Its potency is similar to that of the third-generation cephalosporins. Aztreonam has no appreciable activity against gram-positive bacteria or anaerobes.

Aztreonam (6 gm/day) was compared to ceftazidime (6 gm/day) as empiric therapy for suspected gram-negative septicemia in immunocompromised patients.[127] Overall, there was no difference in efficacy between the two regimens; however, P. aeruginosa was not isolated from any of these patients. There was an increased frequency and severity of superinfections due to gram-positive bacteria in the aztreonam group (28%). Until more studies are completed, aztreonam should be combined with other antimicrobial agents to provide optimal activity against gram-negative bacteria, particularly P. aeruginosa, and to prevent the development of superinfection.

Fluoroquinolones

The fluoroquinolones offer a new approach to the empiric management of febrile neutropenic patients. Agents in this class are rapidly bactericidal against most gram-negative bacilli, including P. aeruginosa. Of the currently available quinolones, ciprofloxacin (Cipro) is the most active against P. aeruginosa. The availability of oral formulations can reduce the need for intravenous antibiotics and hospitalization in this patient population.

The fluoroquinolones have been studied in both monotherapy and combination therapy regimens in febrile neutropenic patients.[164] Monotherapy with these agents has met with mixed success. A EORTC trial comparing ciprofloxacin 400 to 600 mg/day versus piperacillin plus amikacin was terminated prematurely due to significantly poorer response rates in the ciprofloxacin treated patients (65%) compared to the combination group (91%), (p = 0.002).[165] This may be due in part to the low ciprofloxacin dosage utilized as well as the impact of fluoroquinolone prophylaxis on the institution's nosocomial flora. Two additional studies demonstrated better results with ciprofloxacin used as monotherapy.[166,167] However, until the newer fluoroquinolones, such as sparfloxacin, with improved activity against gram-positive organisms, are approved, the fluoroquinolones should be combined with additional antibiotics in order to provide better coverage against gram-positive and some gram-negative organisms.[170,171]

Combination therapy of a fluoroquinolone plus either an aminoglycoside or a beta-lactam has been more favorable. The response rate in patients treated with the combination of ciprofloxacin plus azlocillin was similar to those treated with ceftazidime plus amikacin, although a high number of gram-positive breakthrough bacteremias occurred after conversion to oral monotherapy with ciprofloxacin.[168] In another study,[169] the combination of ciprofloxacin plus netilmicin was as effective as piperacillin plus netilmicin, however, the ciprofloxacin-treated group developed an outbreak of infections caused by ciprofloxacin-resistant S. epidermidis.

Summary. In conclusion, the diversity of organisms causing infection in immunocompromised patients makes it difficult to recommend a single best regimen for empiric use in all institutions. Since there are institutional differences in prevailing pathogens, antibiotic selection should be based upon the experience and susceptibility patterns within each institution. Patient-related factors also play a role, depending upon presumed site of infection as well as patient allergies. Published studies provide useful information on drug selection, but may not be applicable to all institutions.

Continuation of or Changes in Initial Antibiotic Therapy

Duration of Therapy

20. M.H., a 24-year-old female with a recent diagnosis of ovarian cancer, developed neutropenia following chemotherapy. Five days after becoming neutropenic, she developed a fever of 101 °F and was begun on an empiric antibiotic regimen of ceftazidime 2 gm Q 8 hr. M.H. rapidly became afebrile; the results of initial cultures remained negative at 48 hours. How long should antibiotic therapy be continued in M.H.? How do the culture results influence this decision?

The management of febrile neutropenic cancer patients whose initial evaluation after 48 to 72 hours fails to demonstrate an infectious etiology remains a diagnostic and therapeutic dilemma.[108,137] (See Figure 67.2.) After empiric antibiotic administration for 72 hours in febrile neutropenic patients, the patient may become afebrile or the fever may persist. In general, all of these patients should continue to receive their antibiotic regimen for at least one week.[18] Continuation of empiric antibiotics for more than a week may increase the risk of drug toxicity or superinfection with yeast and/or resistant bacteria. Conversely, premature withdrawal of antibiotics may predispose these patients to recrudescence of bacterial infection and increase the risk of infection-related morbidity and mortality.[13]

Two prospective studies have contributed to the development of guidelines for the duration of antimicrobial therapy in febrile neutropenic patients who become afebrile following antibiotic initiation. When 26 neutropenic cancer patients were afebrile for four days after responding to empiric treatment with carbenicillin plus cephalothin, none of the 26 patients who continued therapy died; in contrast, three of 30 patients whose antibiotics were stopped after four days died of infection.[138] Two of these patients' infections were due to bacteria susceptible to the initial empiric antibiotic regimen. This study concluded that those patients who promptly respond to empiric antibiotics (as evidenced by defervescence) can have antibiotics stopped after seven to ten afebrile days.

When 142 cancer patients with unexplained fever who became afebrile following empiric antibiotics were randomized to continue or discontinue antibiotic therapy after seven days, the patients whose neutropenia resolved had no infectious sequelae regardless of whether antibiotics were continued or discontinued.[139] However, the outcome in the persistently neutropenic patients was different. Of these, 94% of patients randomized to continue antibiotics until their ANC was greater than 500/μL remained afebrile without infectious complications; however, fever recurred in 41% of patients randomized to discontinue antibiotics. These observations suggest that patients who respond to initial antimicrobial therapy, but remain neutropenic, benefit from continuation of antimicrobial therapy for at least seven days or until their ANC rises above 500/μL. Response to empiric therapy in these patients is most likely due to effective therapy of a clinically unrecognized or microbiologically undocumented bacterial infection.

M.H.'s rapid response to antibiotic therapy suggests that the empiric choice of ceftazidime has been effective. If cultures remain negative, M.H. should be treated with ceftazidime for a minimum of seven days or until her neutropenia resolves.

Modifications of Therapy

Pathogen-Directed Therapy

21. On day 3, M.H. spikes a fever to 102 °C and subsequent blood cultures grow S. aureus resistant to ceftazidime, susceptible to vancomycin. Her ANC is 170/μL. How should therapy be modified in M.H.?

In contrast to neutropenic patients, *non-neutropenic* patients (ANC >500/μL) with documented gram-positive infections may be treated with a single, pathogen-specific antibiotic for 10 to 14 days. Pizzo et al.[140] treated 78 neutropenic cancer patients with documented gram-positive bacteremias with a single drug (e.g., oxacillin, nafcillin) or a broad-spectrum combination regimen (carbenicillin plus cephalothin plus gentamicin). Seven of the fifteen patients treated with a single drug who remained neutropenic for more than seven days developed a second infection. In contrast,

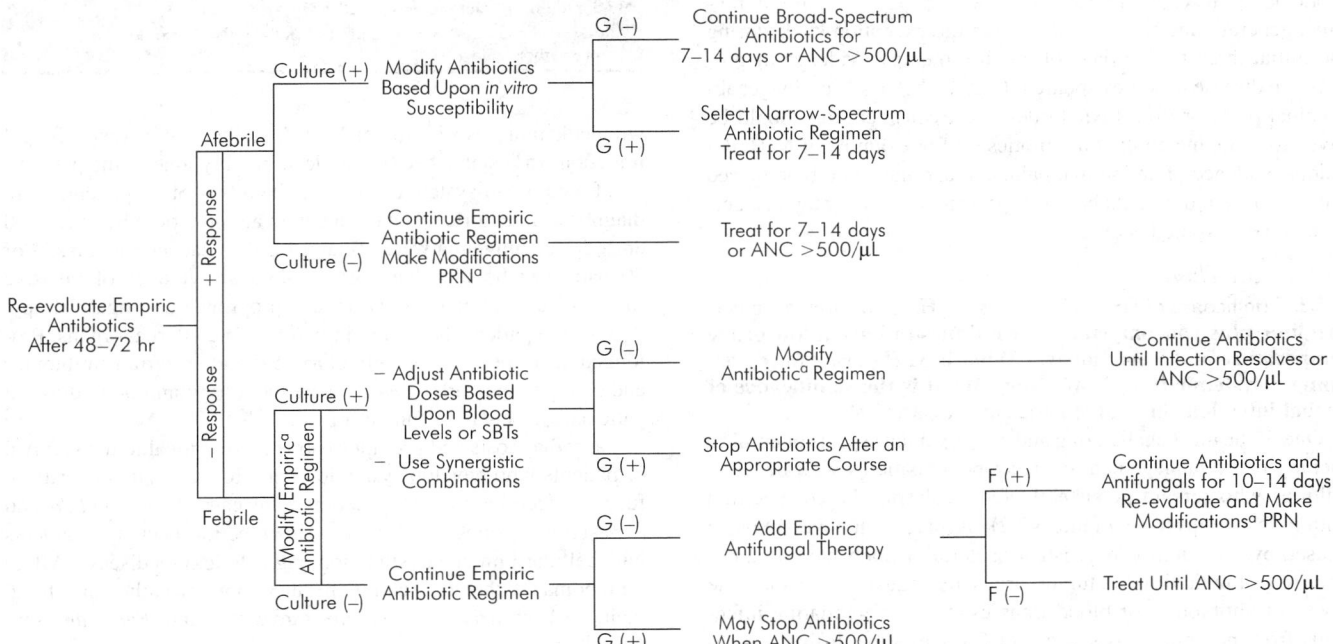

Fig 67.2 Approach to Management of Febrile Neutropenic Patients a = See Table 67.3; G(+) = ANC >500/μL; G(−) = ANC <500/μL; SBT = Serum bactericidal titer; F(+) = Temperature >38 °C; F(−) = Afebrile; ANC = Absolute neutrophil count.

none of the 24 patients who continued to receive the broad-spectrum combination regimen developed secondary infections.

Based upon these findings, broad-spectrum antibiotics (with activity against the infecting organism) should be continued in persistently neutropenic patients. If the patient's neutropenia resolves, broad-spectrum antimicrobials may be discontinued and a narrow-spectrum regimen, directed against the infecting pathogen, should be continued for an appropriate duration. Given that M.H. remains neutropenic, an antistaphylococcal agent, such as vancomycin, should be added to her empiric regimen.

Antimicrobial Adjuvants

The duration of neutropenia is the single, most important factor which affects outcome in these patients.

Granulocyte transfusions have been used adjunctively in patients with persistent neutropenia and documented infections who, despite appropriate antibiotics, fail to respond after 24 to 48 hours.[52,142] However, the high cost, risk of blood-born viral infections, and questionable efficacy of granulocyte transfusions in these patients has resulted in a decreased use of this therapeutic strategy.[18] The role of cytokines, such as the colony-stimulating factors (CSFs), as adjuvants to antimicrobial therapy is being studied and these agents probably will have an increasingly important role in the therapy and prevention of infectious diseases (see Prophylaxis of Systemic Infections: Myeloid Colony Stimulating Factors).[125,173]

Addition of Antimicrobials

Within 48 to 72 hours of instituting empiric antibiotics, the patient's clinical response should be assessed and adjustments made accordingly. Within the first few days after initiation of empiric antibiotics, the lack of fever resolution or the reappearance of fever, as with M.H., necessitates therapeutic modifications (see Figure 67.2 and Table 67.2).[132]

When the pathogen is known, antibiotic dosage adjustments (based upon serum levels or SBTs) or additional antimicrobials may be required.[141] Therapy is commonly modified by the addition of an aminoglycoside, an antifungal agent, clindamycin, or vancomycin. In patients with protracted periods of neutropenia, antibiotic additions or modifications of the empiric antimicrobial regimen generally are the rule rather than the exception.[141] If during the initial three to five days of empiric therapy evidence of progressive disease becomes apparent (e.g., catheter-site drainage, abdominal pain) or drug toxicity develops, consideration should be given to changing empiric antibiotics.[108] For example, if M.H. develops evidence of abdominal pain, ceftazidime could be replaced with imipenem due to its broader spectrum of activity against aerobic and anaerobic bacteria.

Antifungal Therapy

22. Significance of Fungal Infections. M.H. is continued on ceftazidime plus vancomycin. She continues to have a low grade temperature and feels "lousy." What is M.H.'s risk for developing a systemic fungal infection? What is the significance of fungal infections in neutropenic cancer patients?

One of the most challenging and controversial aspects of empiric therapy is the management of neutropenic patients with negative cultures who remain persistently febrile despite broad-spectrum antibiotic therapy (see Figure 67.2). A persistent fever may be caused by infection with resistant bacteria or nonbacterial pathogens (e.g., fungi, viruses), tumor, drugs, inadequate serum or tissue levels of antibiotics, or blood transfusions. Differentiating infectious from noninfectious sources of fever may be difficult, especially in granulocytopenic patients. In one retrospective review,[146] the incidence of documented invasive fungal infections in patients

Table 67.2	Therapeutic Modifications in Patients with Neutropenia and Fever[a,b]
Clinical Condition	**Suspected Pathogen(s) and Type of Modification(s)**
Fever (Persistent or Recurrent)	Undetected fungal infection: add empiric amphotericin B
Positive Blood Cultures	
Before antibiotic initiation	*Gm(+)*: Add vancomycin, pending further identification
	Gm(−): If *P. aeruginosa* or *Enterobacter*, add aminoglycoside
Isolated while on empiric antibiotics	*Gm(+)*: Add vancomycin
	Gm(−): If *P. aeruginosa* or *Enterobacter*, add aminoglycoside
Head, Eyes, Ears, Nose, Throat	
Necrotizing gingivitis	*Anaerobes*: Add clindamycin or metronidazole
Vesicular or ulcerative lesions	*Herpes Simplex* virus: Add acyclovir
Oral mucositis	*Candida*: Add oral clotrimazole, nystatin, ketoconazole, or fluconazole
Sinus tenderness	*Aspergillus* or *Mucormycosis*: Add amphotericin B
Gastrointestinal Tract	
Esophagitis	*Candida* and/or *Herpes Simplex*: Add antifungal agent; if no response, add acyclovir
Acute abdominal pain/perianal tenderness	*Anaerobes*: Add clindamycin or metronidazole to empiric regimen or switch to imipenem/cilastatin
Respiratory Tract	
Interstitial pneumonitis	*Pneumocystis carinii*: Institute trial of TMP-SMX[b] or pentamidine
	Legionella: Add erythromycin
	Cytomegalovirus: Add ganciclovir + IVIG
Focal lesion on chest x-ray	*Aspergillus*: Administer high dose amphotericin B (1.0–1.5 mg/kg/day) or itraconazole
Central Venous Catheter Tunnel Infection	Remove catheter; treat appropriately based upon culture and susceptibility

[a] Adapted from references 141 and 171.
[b] IVIG = Intravenous immune globulin; TMP-SMX = Trimethoprim-sulfamethoxazole.

with leukemia was 27% (32 of 119). A diagnosis of invasive fungal infection was established before death in only nine of the patients, all of whom had systemic candidiasis. Only 4 of 17 patients were diagnosed antemortem and treated with amphotericin B. When 200 episodes of fungemia were reviewed in 188 cancer patients, 32 of 50 patients who died had microbiological evidence of invasive fungal disease at autopsy. Despite appropriate antifungal therapy, 81% of the patients had fungi in two or more internal organs. Prolonged neutropenia, fever refractory to broad-spectrum antibiotics, and colonization with *Candida* were the most common findings in patients with invasive fungal infection.[145]

Early diagnosis and prompt treatment are critical to the survival of patients who develop systemic fungal disease. The majority of fungal infections in cancer patients are caused by *Candida* and *Aspergillus* species.[151] Cryptococcal infection occurs in patients with cellular immune dysfunction (e.g., Hodgkin's disease, AIDS, lymphoma). Other less common but important pathogenic fungi include *Alternaria* species, Phycomycetes, and *Fusarium* species.[146,147]

23. Empiric Amphotericin B Therapy. **Why should amphotericin B therapy be initiated in M.H.?**

Early institution of empiric antifungal agents in patients with protracted fever and granulocytopenia is essential.[137,146,153,154] After seven days of empiric broad-spectrum antibiotics, 50 patients with unexplained fever, prolonged granulocytopenia, and evidence of GI tract colonization with *Candida* species were randomized to one of three groups.[153] Patients in group I continued to receive broad-spectrum antibiotics, those in group II had their antibiotics discontinued, and those in group III had amphotericin B added empirically to their antibiotic regimen. Infectious complications (e.g., bacterial or fungal infection, shock) developed in 9 of 16 patients (56%) in group II within three days of stopping antibiotics. Of the 16 patients in group I who continued to receive antibiotics until neutropenia resolved, an infectious complication developed in six (38%), five of which were due to fungal infections. In the 18 patients randomized to receive amphotericin B, only two patients developed infectious complications. Notably, one of these infections in the latter group was due to an amphotericin B-resistant organism (*Petriellidium boydii*).

These observations support empiric institution of amphotericin B for the treatment of M.H.'s persistent fever (despite broad-spectrum antibacterial therapy). Although overall patient mortality is not altered, available data suggest that empiric antifungal therapy decreases deaths due to fungal infections.[146,155] However, empiric antifungal regimens may result in a shift in pathogens to those that are resistant to the empiric regimens.[145,147,153]

Prophylaxis of Systemic Infections

24. Three months later, M.H. is readmitted for her 2nd course of chemotherapy. Since M.H. was neutropenic for more than 15 days from her 1st course of chemotherapy, should a CSF be administered to her before her 2nd course of chemotherapy?

Numerous methods to boost the host's defense against infection have been investigated. Studies have focused on the prophylactic and therapeutic impact of immunomodulating agents,[213] active/passive immunizations,[214–216] monoclonal antibodies,[178] and granulocyte transfusions.[142] Although granulocyte transfusions have been studied most extensively, their usefulness in immunocompromised patients has waned with the availability of recombinant colony-stimulating factors.[178,218]

Myeloid Colony Stimulating Factors (CSFs)

Hematopoiesis is regulated by a variety of different cytokines and hormones. During the past few years, several of these cytokines, or growth factors, have been developed and studied. Four colony-stimulating factors influence the survival, proliferation, differentiation, and functional activity of myeloid hematopoiesis: granulocyte-CSF (G-CSF), macrophage-CSF (M-CSF), granulocyte-macrophage CSF (GM-CSF), and interleukin-3 (formerly known as multi-CSF).[218] Colony-stimulating factors act on various stages of cell proliferation and differentiation in the bone marrow and are separated into two major groups: multilineage and lineage specific. GM-CSF is a multilineage factor which is essential for the growth of the granulocyte and macrophage cell lines. G-CSF, on the other hand, is lineage specific and acts on the latter steps of cell proliferation and differentiation to neutrophils.[125,126]

Only recombinant human G-CSF (filgrastim) and recombinant human GM-CSF (sargramostim) have been approved for use in the U.S. for treatment of chemotherapy-related neutropenia in bone marrow transplantation and standard-dose chemotherapy, respectively.[199] In neutropenic cancer patients, cytokines can accelerate the recovery of phagocytic cells and may have a beneficial role in both the prevention and the early treatment of infections in these patients.[157] The CSFs primarily have been studied in patients with

chemotherapy-induced neutropenia, bone marrow transplantation, and myelodysplastic disorders. Patients with AIDS, aplastic anemia, and other rare disorders also have been treated with these agents.[181,200]

The impact of CSFs on febrile morbidity (i.e., number of febrile days, incidence of infection, antibiotic usage) has been well documented. In two studies, patients with small-cell lung cancer who were treated with G-CSF, the incidence of febrile neutropenic events, infections, hospitalizations, antibiotic usage, and duration of antibiotic therapy were all significantly reduced.[158,159]

In a placebo-controlled trial, Devereaux et al.[201] studied GM-CSF in 31 patients receiving chemotherapy and autologous bone marrow transplantation. The infection rates were 58% and 68% for the GM-CSF treated and control groups, respectively. Nemunaitis et al.[209] studied the effects of GM-CSF in patients undergoing bone marrow transplantation for lymphoid cancer. Documented infection developed in 17% of patients receiving GM-CSF compared to 30% in the placebo arm. While the trend toward reduction in infection was promising, it did not achieve statistical significance. Patients receiving GM-CSF received significantly fewer days of antibiotics (24 days) compared to the control group (27 days) and required six fewer days of hospitalization compared to controls (p = 0.01). No difference in survival was observed between the two groups at day 100. Conversely, Biesma et al.[180] treated 35 patients with chemotherapy-related fever and neutropenia and noted no decrease in the number of antibiotic days in those patients receiving GM-CSF.

Uncontrolled trials have suggested that GM-CSF may be associated with more toxicities than G-CSF. However, no controlled comparative studies are available at this time. Rash, bone pain, headache, fever, and myalgias, and other constitutional symptoms have been reported for both agents. Dose-limiting toxicities, including pericarditis[191] and pericardial effusions,[161] have been associated with doses of GM-CSF of greater than 20 µg/kg/day. These reactions have not been observed with G-CSF.

In conclusion, the colony stimulating factors represent an important advance in the management of neutropenic patients. Both G-CSF and GM-CSF can decrease the duration of neutropenia and the number of documented infections in patients receiving chemotherapy. The impact of these agents on duration of hospitalization and antimicrobial use could enhance the cost-effectiveness of these agents. However, the role of these agents in improving the outcome and overall survival of cancer patients needs to be further established.

Administration of one of the CSFs, such as G-CSF, may have a beneficial role in reducing the duration of M.H.'s chemotherapy-induced neutropenia. G-CSF should be initiated one day after her last dose of chemotherapy and should be stopped when the neutrophil count rises between 5000 to 7000 cells/µL, to avoid rapid rebound leukocytosis. Since the duration of neutropenia generally increases with each cycle of chemotherapy, prophylactic G-CSF may be needed for longer periods in the later cycles of M.H.'s chemotherapy.[218]

Antimicrobial Prophylaxis

25. What is the role of oral antimicrobial prophylaxis during the neutropenic period?

Nonabsorbable Regimens

As discussed in Question 4, microbial colonization is a prerequisite to the development of infection in neutropenic patients. During the last two decades, preventive strategies have focused primarily on methods which suppress or eliminate endogenous microflora or prevent the acquisition of new micro-organisms.

Exogenous contamination is prevented by strict protective isolation of patients in specially designed rooms which maintain a sterile environment. These laminar air flow rooms (LAFRs) are ventilated with air that is passed through a HEPA (high-efficiency particulate air) filter which removes over 99% of all particles larger than three microns in size. Total protective isolation is accomplished by strict isolation in conjunction with the administration of sterile food and water; local skin care; use of nonabsorbable antibiotics [i.e., gentamicin, vancomycin, nystatin (GVN)]; and intensive microbial surveillance.[197,224] However, total body decontamination using this regimen is burdensome to the patient and nursing staff, difficult to accomplish and maintain, and expensive; thus, it has been utilized in only a few treatment centers.[220]

Since the alimentary tract is recognized as an important reservoir of potential pathogens, total gut decontamination with and without total protective isolation has been investigated. Oral, nonabsorbable antibiotic regimens (e.g., GVN) have been used to suppress both alimentary tract colonization and infection during the neutropenic period.[14] These agents, when administered orally, undergo minimal systemic absorption, thereby reducing intestinal colonization without systemic toxicity. When the liquid formulation of each antibiotic is used, the microbial flora of the entire alimentary tract are affected. However, when these agents are administered as capsules or tablets, only the intestinal flora are affected.

Oral, nonabsorbable antibiotic regimens, when used alone, substantially reduced infection rates in two prospective, controlled trials;[197,223] however, one study failed to demonstrate any benefit.[224] A major problem with most nonabsorbable antibiotic regimens has been poor patient compliance, usually due to unpleasant taste. Lack of compliance in one study was associated with an increased frequency of infection due to gram-negative bacilli in neutropenic patients.[197] An additional concern is that total alimentary suppression may promote emergence of antibiotic-resistant bacteria acquired from the hospital environment.[223] Frequent monitoring of the fecal flora in patients receiving nonabsorbable antibiotic regimens can be used to detect the emergence of antibiotic resistance.

Systemically Absorbed Agents

In view of the difficulties associated with total gut sterilization, selective antimicrobial modulation (SAM) or selective decontamination regimens have been developed. In animals, van der Waaij and colleagues demonstrated that selective elimination of aerobic GI flora, with maintenance of the anaerobic flora prevented colonization with potentially pathogenic aerobic gram-negative bacteria.[39,221] The development and maintenance of this "colonization resistance" has been the rationale behind the use of various nonabsorbable regimens, such as the combination of oral polymyxin B, neomycin, and amphotericin B.[220] This principle also underlies systemic antibiotic selection and the use of newer agents such as ceftazidime and imipenem, which preserve the anaerobic gut flora when used in the empiric treatment of infection.[192,222]

The overall effectiveness of oral, nonabsorbable antibiotic regimens, particularly with protective isolation, in preventing infection in immunocompromised patients is well documented.[197,223,224] These measures appear to be particularly useful in patients in whom profound, persistent neutropenia exceeding 20 days is likely (e.g., patients receiving intensive chemotherapy regimens or undergoing bone marrow transplantation).

Trimethoprim/Sulfamethoxazole (TMP-SMX). Preservation of colonization resistance with systemically absorbed antibiotics, such as trimethoprim/sulfamethoxazole, was first demonstrated during a study of *Pneumocystis carinii* pneumonia (PCP) prophylaxis in leukemic children.[58] In this study, children receiving TMP-SMX had significantly fewer bacterial infections. These observations prompted several studies examining the benefits of TMP-SMX prophylaxis compared to placebo,[61,203] nalidixic acid,[62] and gentamicin plus nystatin.[196] While the results of these trials confirm the utility of TMP-SMX prophylaxis for prevention of infection in neutropenic patients, variations in study design, the types of patients being treated, and the concomitant use of other preventative measures confound the true benefits of prophylaxis. The potential benefits of TMP-SMX prophylaxis must be carefully balanced against the potential for prolonged neutropenia,[62] hypersensitivity reactions,[160] the emergence of TMP-SMX-resistant organisms, and development of superinfections (especially those due to *P. aeruginosa* and *C. albicans*).[61,203] TMP-SMX has substantially reduced the incidence of PCP pneumonia [see Chapter 68: Human Immunodeficiency Virus (HIV) Infection].

Fluoroquinolones. The fluoroquinolones, ciprofloxacin, norfloxacin (Noroxin), and ofloxacin (Floxin), have all been evaluated for infection prophylaxis in neutropenic patients. Since these agents do not substantially affect the anaerobic colonic flora, thus maintaining colonization resistance, the fluoroquinolones appear to be suitable oral prophylactic agents.[174,198] Clinical experience with these agents has demonstrated a reduction in the incidence of gram-negative infections; yet there appears to be an increased incidence of gram-positive infections with staphylococci and streptococci. The benefits of fluoroquinolone prophylaxis may soon be offset by the emergence of resistant organisms if these agents are overused.[175,192]

Antifungals

26. Since M.H. required empiric amphotericin B during her last neutropenic episode, is there a role for antifungal prophylaxis in neutropenic patients?

Invasive fungal infections are a major cause of morbidity and mortality among neutropenic cancer patients and patients undergoing bone marrow transplantation.[101] Antifungal prophylaxis can prevent the development of superficial, oropharyngeal candidiasis and deep-seated fungal infections in these patient populations.

Topical Antifungals. A variety of topical antifungal agents have been successful in preventing local and disseminated candidiasis. Topical agents, such as oral nystatin[196,197] and clotrimazole,[204] and oral amphotericin B[202,203] can reduce the likelihood of the development of oropharyngeal candidiasis in neutropenic patients; however, only oral amphotericin B has significantly reduced the incidence of disseminated candidiasis compared to fluconazole.[207]

Nystatin suspension (2 million international units/day) did not prevent oropharyngeal and disseminated candidiasis in leukemic patients.[206] Higher doses (20 to 30 million international units/day) were not any more efficacious.[196,197] In fact, the compliance of these high dose regimens has been poor, perhaps contributing to suboptimal results with many of these studies. Oral administration of amphotericin B tablets (200 mg/day) has significantly reduced the incidence of disseminated candidiasis compared to placebo.[217] However, more recent results comparing amphotericin suspension (1500 mg/day) with placebo were disappointing.[208] Clotrimazole troches, 10 mg five times daily, have been used successfully to prevent oral and esophageal candidiasis in patients receiving immunosuppressive chemotherapy; lower doses (30 mg/day) were effective in renal transplant patients, but not in patients with leukemia.[204]

Systemic Antifungals. The imidazoles, miconazole (Monistat) and ketoconazole (Nizoral), have been used for fungal prophylaxis, but each have met with inherent problems. The adverse effects associated with intravenous administration of miconazole have limited its clinical utility.[184] Ketoconazole, at doses of 400 to 600 mg/day, has not been universally effective in preventing fungal dissemination.[210,211] The erratic bioavailability of ketoconazole caused by achlorhydria or the use of antacids or H_2-receptor blocking agents may account for the variability in response.[176] (See Table 67.3.)

The availability of the newer triazoles, fluconazole (Diflucan) and itraconazole (Sporanox), has increased the antifungal armamentarium.[183,194] Itraconazole is indicated for the treatment of *Aspergillosis* in patients refractory to amphotericin B. Fluconazole has been well studied for the prevention of invasive candidiasis in neutropenic patients and bone marrow transplant recipients.

When fluconazole 400 mg/day was compared to placebo for fungal prophylaxis in bone marrow transplant recipients, fluconazole significantly reduced the incidence of invasive candidiasis and delayed the initiation of empiric amphotericin B from day 17 to day 21.[205] Infections caused by *C. krusei* were not significantly different between both the fluconazole and placebo study arms. Another study in acute leukemics undergoing chemotherapy, fluconazole prophylaxis did not prevent development of invasive fungal infections or reduce the use of empiric amphotericin B when compared to placebo.[212] Disparities between these studies possibly may be explained by the different frequencies of invasive fungal infections in acute leukemic patients versus patients undergoing bone marrow transplantation, most likely due to different durations of neutropenia between the two groups.

In summary, prophylaxis with oral antimicrobials remains an unresolved issue. Use of these agents does not always reduce the need for empiric, systemic antimicrobials. Also, the impact of these agents on the selection of multiresistant bacteria (i.e., vancomycin-resistant enterococci, quinolone-resistant coagulase-negative staphylococci) and fungi (azole-resistant *C. albicans*) remains a major therapeutic dilemma. Caution must be exercised with the widespread use of antifungal prophylaxis, since prolonged use can potentially select for resistant molds and yeast.[172] The cytokines, such as G-CSF and GM-CSF, by ameliorating neutropenia, may become the most effective agents for prophylaxis of bacterial and invasive fungal infections in immunocompromised patients.[157,177]

Patients receiving cytotoxic chemotherapy for solid tumors, such as M.H., have lower rates of invasive fungal infections compared to patients receiving therapy for hematologic malignancies. For this reason, antifungal prophylaxis may not be cost beneficial in patients like M.H. She can be managed with empiric antifungal therapy, such as amphotericin B, in the event of persistent fever and neutropenia (see Question 23).[176]

Infections in Transplantation

The introduction of alternative forms of immunosuppression, such as cyclosporine, has significantly improved the survival rates for most transplant recipients.[11] Over the past decade, the types and numbers of organ transplants have markedly increased (see Chapters 33: Solid Organ Transplantation and 94: Bone Marrow Transplantation). Infections, however, continue to remain a major consequence of all transplants due to the antirejection therapy given in solid-organ transplants and the marrow-ablative therapy in bone marrow transplant recipients (see Table 67.1).[4,12,15]

Risks Factors for Infection

Bone Marrow Transplantation (BMT)

Bone marrow transplantation involves ablation of the patient's hematopoietic and immune systems followed by replacement with those of the marrow donor. Normal bone marrow may be derived

Table 67.3	Antimicrobial Therapy in Immunocompromised Patients[a]
Agent	**Advantage/Disadvantages**
Antibiotics	
Aminoglycosides	Broad-spectrum activity. Must be used in combination with beta-lactams or fluoroquinolones. May cause nephrotoxicity
Antipseudomonal penicillins	Broad-spectrum gram-negative activity. Emergence of resistance if not combined with an aminoglycoside. Should not be used as monotherapy in neutropenic patients
3rd-generation cephalosporins	Excellent gram-negative,[b] suboptimal gram-positive activity.[c] Superinfections and coagulopathies[d] may occur with some agents. Emergence of resistant *P. aeruginosa* if not combined with an aminoglycoside
Carbapenems	Very broad-spectrum. Emergence of resistant *P. aeruginosa* if not combined with an aminoglycoside
Monobactams	Alternative in beta-lactam allergic patients. Combine with vancomycin for empiric therapy. Add aminoglycoside to minimize development of resistance. Do not use as monotherapy
Fluoroquinolones	Broad-spectrum gram-negative activity.[e] Alternative in beta-lactam allergic patients. Emergence of resistance can occur if used routinely for prophylaxis
Glycopeptides[f]	Excellent gram-positive activity. Empiric use common in centers with high incidence of methicillin-resistant staphylococci. Emergence of vancomycin-resistant enterococci is of increasing concern
Antivirals	
Acyclovir	Oral and parenteral (IV) therapy for herpes simplex. Parenteral therapy only recommended for varicella-zoster infections in severely immunocompromised patients and for cytomegalovirus prophylaxis in bone-marrow transplant recipients
Ganciclovir	For treatment and prevention of cytomegalovirus infection. Combine with immunoglobulin for cytomegalovirus pneumonitis. Can cause neutropenia
Antifungals	
Amphotericin B	Agent of choice for empiric use and treatment of documented fungal infections. High incidence of adverse reactions, especially nephrotoxicity, fever/chills, and phlebitis
Ketoconazole	Effective treatment of candidal thrush and esophagitis. No IV formulation. Tablets require an acidic environment for oral absorption. Multiple drug interactions exist
Fluconazole	Effective for management of thrush and candidal esophagitis. Prophylactic use in some centers has resulted in emergence of resistant candidal infections (e.g., *C. krusei*)
Itraconazole	Effective against *Aspergillus*. Disadvantages similar to ketoconazole

[a] Adapted from reference 177.
[b] Ceftazidime, cefoperazone, and cefepime have the best antipseudomonal activity in this class.
[c] e.g., ceftazidime.
[d] e.g., cefoperazone.
[e] Ciprofloxacin has the best antipseudomonal activity in this class.
[f] Includes vancomycin and teicoplanin (investigational).

from a complete or partially immunologically compatible donor, whether related or unrelated (allogeneic transplant); from the patient's own, previously stored, marrow (autologous transplant), or from an identical twin (syngeneic transplant). Allogenic transplant patients become profoundly immunosuppressed in the post-transplant period due to administration of antirejection immunosuppressive therapy. This therapy is administered for over 100 days post-transplant in order to minimize development of graft-versus-host disease (GVHD).[15] BMT recipients have varying alterations in host defenses during the pre- and post-transplant period; as a consequence, different types of infections are encountered during these periods (see Figure 67.3).

Pretransplant conditioning with ablative chemotherapy plus or minus total body irradiation is done to suppress the recipient's immune system in order to prevent graft rejection.[124] Conditioning causes a breakdown of mucosal barriers and results in profound, persistent neutropenia for three to four weeks depending upon the regimen utilized.

Bone marrow transplant recipients remain at high risk for infectious complications for several months post-transplant because defects in neutrophil function and humoral and cellular immunity persist. GVHD, both in the acute and chronic forms, increases the risk of infections as a result of the immunosuppressive regimens utilized to minimize graft rejection. Most BMT patients eventually will develop normal immunity if graft-versus-host disease can be prevented.[15]

Around the time of bone marrow transplantation, chemotherapy-induced neutropenia predisposes patients to bacterial and fungal infections, similar to those which develop in neutropenic cancer patients. Infections caused by *Candida* species occur earlier in the post-transplant period than do those caused by *Aspergillus* species.[101] Therapeutic management of bacterial and fungal infections in BMT patients is similar to that of the febrile neutropenic patient.

Solid Organ Transplantation

Liver, heart, heart-lung, and pancreas-kidney transplants have become as commonplace as kidney transplants. Most infections related to these transplants occur within four to six months of transplantation. The types, frequencies, and severity of infections vary considerably with each type of transplant. Bacterial and fungal infections occur most commonly and usually develop within the first month; viral infections, especially cytomegalovirus (CMV), usually develop during the second month; and protozoal infections, such as PCP, occur within the first six months post-transplantation. In one transplant center, renal transplant recipients had the lowest infection rate and death per patient, followed by heart, liver, and heart-lung transplant recipients.[11]

Viral Infections in Transplantation

27. D.R., a 45-year-old male, underwent cadaveric renal transplantation for chronic glomerulonephritis. D.R. was CMV seronegative before transplant yet the donor kidney was CMV seropositive. He was begun on an immunosuppressive regimen consisting of cyclosporine, azathioprine, and prednisone. Pertinent laboratory tests performed 10 days post-transplant were: Hgb 9.2 gm/dL, Hct 31%, WBC 8500/μL, platelet count 120,000/μL, BUN 48 mg/dL, and SrCr 1.8 mg/dL. D.R. was doing well and was discharged. Six weeks later, during a routine follow-up visit, D.R. complained of anorexia, malaise, and weakness. He denied any nausea or vomiting, shortness of breath, or diarrhea. His vital signs were: temperature 102.3 °F; pulse 110 beats/min; BP 160/90 mm Hg; and respirations 16/min. A chest radiograph was normal. Laboratory findings were: Hgb 9 gm/dL, Hct 30%, WBC 1600/μL with a differential of 35 polys, 58 lymphocytes, 4 monocytes, 3 basophils, platelets 117,000/μL, BUN 55 mg/dL, SrCr 2.2 mg/dL. Cyclosporine levels were within normal limits. CMV culture of the urine was positive. What are the risk factors for viral infection, such as CMV, following transplantation? Is the incidence of

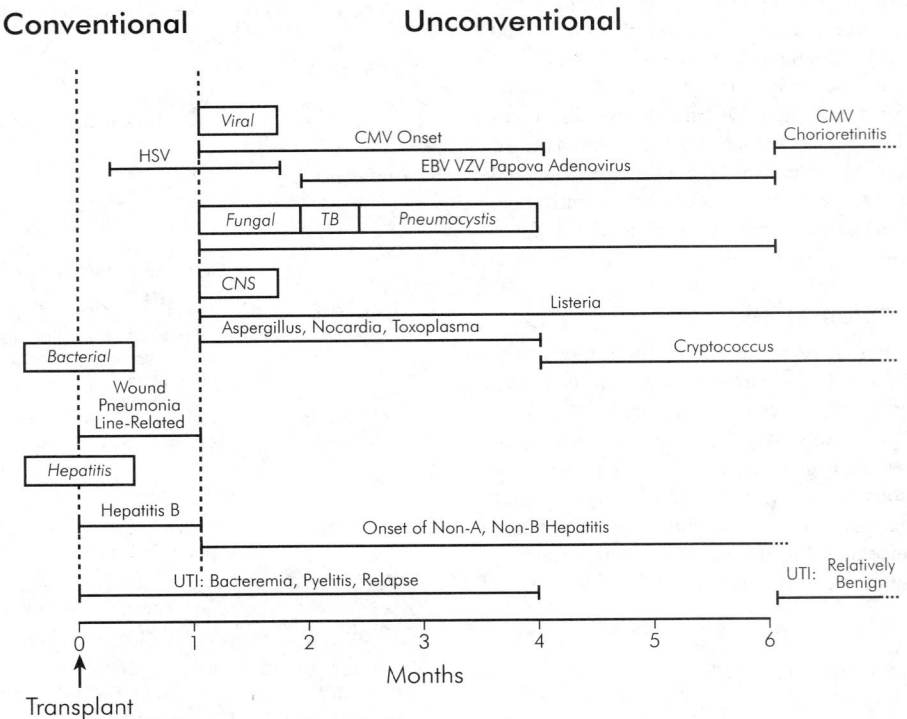

Fig 67.3 **Timetable for the Occurrence of Infection in Renal Transport Recipients** CMV = Cytomegalovirus; HSV = Herpes simplex virus; EBV = Epstein-Barr virus; VZV = Varicella-zoster virus; CNS = Central nervous system; UTI = Urinary tract infection. Reprinted with permission from Rubin RH.

these infections different between BMT and solid organ transplant recipients? [SI units: Hgb 92 and 90 gm/L, respectively; Hct 0.31 and 0.30, respectively; WBC count 8.5 and 1.6 × 10⁹/L, respectively; platelets 120 × 10⁹/L; BUN 17.14 and 19.64 mmol/L urea, respectively; SrCr 159.12 and 194.48 μmol/L, respectively]

Viral infections, most often due to herpes viruses, commonly develop in transplant recipients as early as the first month to one year post-transplantation.[11,27,30] Viral infections in transplant recipients usually result from reactivation of latent, endogenous virus in patients receiving immunosuppressive therapy to prevent graft rejection or in patients experiencing active allograft rejection.[37]

Herpes Simplex Virus (HSV)

Immunosuppressive patients with defects in cell-mediated immunity (CMI) experience more frequent, severe and extensive HSV infections than those with deficits in humoral immunity.[30] HSV infections usually develop during the first month following transplantation. Gingivostomatitis and pharyngitis, often causing severe pain and the inability to eat or drink, may spread from direct extension of the lesions. Direct extension can cause HSV esophagitis and focal pneumonitis, whereas hematogenous spread of the virus usually causes interstitial pneumonia.[136]

Varicella-Zoster Virus (VZV)

VZV infections can occur between 3 to 12 months post-transplantation. The incidence of VZV is among the highest in BMT recipients; however, VZV may occur in solid organ transplant recipients, but to a lesser extent.[143] (See Chapter 70: Viral Infections for a more extensive discussion of VZV.)

Cytomegalovirus (CMV)

CMV usually develops within the first four months post-transplantation. Infections are usually asymptomatic in immunocompetent individuals; however, symptomatic CMV infection is common in immunosuppressed transplant patients. Infection usually manifests as a nonspecific viral illness, similar to D.R.'s complaints of fever, anorexia, and malaise. More severe forms of CMV disease, such as pneumonia, hepatitis, nephritis, and gastroenteritis also may develop. The risk of developing CMV pneumonia is higher in BMT patients with graft-versus-host disease and in patients undergoing solid organ rejection, especially those receiving antithymocyte globulin, high-dose corticosteroids, and OKT3.[37,53,63] Severe CMV disease can lead to allograft rejection, graft loss, and death. (Also see Chapters 33: Solid Organ Transplantation, 68: Human Immunodeficiency Virus (HIV) Infection, 70: Viral Infections.)

28. CMV Transmission. How did D.R. acquire CMV infection? How do donor and recipient CMV status impact on the development of CMV infection?

In transplant patients, three major epidemiologic patterns of CMV infection are found: primary infection, reactivation, and superinfection. Occasionally, however, a seronegative individual can develop primary CMV infection months after transplantation through sexual contact or blood transfusions.[37] Primary CMV infection occurs when a CMV-seronegative recipient acquires the virus from a seropositive donor, either through the transplanted organ or through blood products. Donor seropositivity is a significant risk factor for developing CMV disease. Since D.R. was seronegative before transplant and received a seropositive kidney, this is probably the mode in which he acquired CMV.

The other two epidemiologic patterns of CMV infection are reactivation and superinfection. Reactivation of CMV occurs when latent, endogenous virus reactivates in the host during profound immunosuppression. CMV reactivation develops in 70% to 80% of recipients who are seropositive before transplantation.[27] The third pattern of CMV infection is superinfection, in which a seropositive individual receives an allograft from a seropositive donor and the virus strain that is activated is of donor rather than recipient origin. As many as 50% of kidney transplant recipients who are seropositive before transplantation and receive a seropositive kidney activate the donor virus rather than their own endogenous virus.[37]

Prophylaxis of CMV Infection

29. What therapeutic strategies can be employed to prevent or minimize the development of CMV infection in transplant recipients like D.R.?

Several strategies have been employed in attempt to prevent the morbidity and mortality associated with CMV infection in transplant recipients. Since CMV-positive organs are the most important source of primary CMV disease, CMV-seronegative patients should not receive these organs, if possible. Screening of blood products and prophylactic antiviral and immunoglobulin regimens have been utilized to prevent CMV reactivation and pneumonia in transplant patients (see Chapter 33: Solid Organ Transplantation).

Screened Blood Products

Reducing the risk of transfusion-associated CMV can be accomplished by administering CMV-antibody negative blood products or by utilizing blood transfusion filters on CMV-seronegative patients.[117,130] There is probably no benefit for using screened blood products in CMV-seropositive patients.

Antivirals

Acyclovir. Antiviral prophylaxis with high-dose acyclovir (Zovirax), administered orally to renal transplant recipients (800 mg Q 6 hr) and intravenously to BMT recipients (500 mg/m² Q 8 hr) significantly reduced CMV reactivation and decreased patient mortality.[144,193] An additional benefit of these regimens is their ability to prevent or attenuate HSV and Epstein-Barr virus-mediated disease.[195] Foscarnet (Foscavir) may play a role in preventing CMV, but further studies are needed.[148]

Ganciclovir. Ganciclovir (Cytovene), which is more active against CMV than acyclovir,[149] has been studied in BMT[150,152] and solid organ transplant recipients.[179] In bone marrow transplantation, ganciclovir prophylaxis effectively reduced the incidence of CMV infection in seropositive recipients but was not overtly associated with beneficial outcomes.[150,152] In fact, ganciclovir, which is toxic to the bone marrow, caused many neutropenia-associated complications.[150] When used in heart-lung recipients, ganciclovir significantly reduced the morbidity associated with CMV infection in recipients of seropositive heart transplants, yet had no effect on CMV-seronegative heart recipients.[179] Therefore, the toxicities associated with prophylactic ganciclovir administration should limit its widespread use in this setting. On the other hand, administration of ganciclovir pre-emptively, based upon detection of CMV before disease occurrence, has met with some success in a few studies.[182,185]

Immunoglobulins

Passive immunization with intravenous immune globulin (IVIG) or CMV-hyperimmune globulin (CMVIG) has been studied in both BMT and solid organ transplant recipients.

Intravenous Immune Globulin (IVIG). Pooled plasma IVIG has been demonstrated to have a beneficial effect on reducing the development of CMV pneumonia and graft-versus-host disease in bone marrow transplant patients.[53,186] On the basis of these findings, IVIG is used prophylactically in many centers in allogeneic BMT recipients.[117]

CMV hyperimmune globulin (CMVIG) is a CMV-antibody enriched gamma globulin product. CMVIG (CytoGam) is currently approved by the Food and Drug Administration for use in CMV-seronegative recipients of seropositive renal allografts, such as D.R.

A review of seven CMVIG prophylactic trials in BMT found that CMVIG reduced the incidence of CMV viremia and overall infection, but there was no difference in the incidence of CMV pneumonia or enteritis in these studies.[117] Snydman et al.[187] demonstrated that CMVIG prophylaxis reduced the incidence of CMV pneumonia and fungal infections in liver transplant recipients. However, in the CMV-donor positive, recipient-negative liver transplant recipients, there was no beneficial effect of CMVIG prophylaxis. In renal transplant recipients, Snydman et al.[188] demonstrated that CMVIG prophylaxis reduced the incidence of CMV-associated fever and leukopenia and the incidence of fungal infections and PCP pneumonia in CMV-seronegative recipients receiving seropositive kidneys. However, there was significantly less efficacy when antilymphocyte antibody therapies or OKT3 were added to the immunosuppressive regimens.

A number of unanswered questions remain. What is the optimal prophylactic dosing regimen for CMVIG? Are the commercially prepared IVIGs equivalent, less effective, or better than CMVIG? Since the cost of CMVIG per patient course is significantly higher ($8000) than for IVIG ($1000), further investigation into these questions is imperative.[189]

D.R.'s CMV infection may have been prevented with prophylactic administration of CMVIG[188] or high-dose oral acyclovir,[144] 800 to 3200 mg/day for 12 weeks post-transplantation. The dosing schedule for CMVIG in renal transplant recipients, like D.R., who are seronegative before transplant yet receive a seropositive kidney is: 150 mg/kg within 72 hours of transplant followed by 100 mg/kg biweekly on weeks two, four, six, and eight, then 50 mg/kg on weeks 12 and 16 post-transplant.[225] Patients receiving CMVIG should be monitored closely for adverse reactions such as flushing, chills, muscle cramps, back pain, fever, nausea, vomiting, and wheezing. If anaphylaxis or hypotension should occur, the infusion should be discontinued and an antidote such as diphenhydramine or adrenaline should be administered.[225]

In summary, the prevention of CMV disease in seropositive allograft recipients appears to be possible with any of the above regimens. In solid organ transplant recipients, all regimens are beneficial as long as antilymphocyte antibody therapies are not used concurrently for rejection episodes. Preventing CMV-reactivation in BMT patients, can best be accomplished with either prophylactic IVIG or acyclovir, or with pre-emptive use of ganciclovir therapy. The combination of an antiviral plus an immunoglobulin for CMV prophylaxis awaits further study.[190]

References

1 Ketchel SJ, Rodriguez V. Acute infections in cancer patients. Semin Oncol. 1978;5:167.

2 Sculier JP et al. Causes of death in febrile granulocytopenic cancer patients receiving empiric antibiotic therapy. Eur J Clin Oncol. 1984;20:55.

3 Todeschini G et al. Gram-negative septicemia in patients with hematologic malignancies. Eur J Cancer Clin Oncol. 1984;20:327.

4 Sweny P. Infection in solid organ transplantation. Curr Opin Infect Dis. 1993;6:412–16.

5 Bodey GP. Infections in cancer patients: a continuing association. Am J Med. 1986;81(1A):11.

6 Armstrong D. History of opportunistic infection in the immunocompromised host. Clin Infect Dis. 1993;17(Suppl. 2):S318–21.

7 Peterson PK. Host defense abnormalities predisposing the patient to infection. Am J Med. 1984;76(5A):2.

8 Lehrer RI, moderator. Neutrophils and host defense. Ann Intern Med. 1988;109:107.

9 Schimpff SC. Therapy of infection in patients with granulocytopenia. Med Clin North Am. 1977;61:1101.

10 Bodey GP et al. Quantitative relationships between circulating leukocytes and infection in patients with acute leukemia. Ann Intern Med. 1966;64:328.

11 Ho M et al. Infections in solid organ transplant recipient. In: Mandell GL et al., eds. Principles and Practices of Infectious Diseases, 3rd ed. New York: Churchill Livingstone; 1990;2294.

12 Brayman KL et al. Analysis of infectious complications occurring after solid organ transplantation. Arch Surg. 1992;127:38–48.

13 Pizzo PA. Infectious complications in the child with cancer. I. Pathophysiology of the compromised host and the initial evaluation and management of the febrile cancer patient. J Pediatr. 1981;98:341.

14 Bodey GP et al. Protected environment for cancer patients: effect of a prophylactic antibiotic regimen on the microbial flora of patients undergoing cancer chemotherapy. Arch Intern Med. 1968;122:23.

15 Meyers JD. Infection in marrow transplant recipients. In: Mandell GL et al., eds. Principles and Practices of Infectious Diseases, 3rd ed. New York: Churchill Livingstone; 1990;2291.

16 Stuck AE. Risk of infectious complications in patients taking glucocorticoids. Rev Infect Dis. 1989;11:954.

17 Kim JH, Perfect JR. Infection and cyclosporine. Rev Infect Dis. 1989;11:677.

18 Hughes WT et al. Guidelines for the use of antimicrobial agents in neutropenic patients with unexplained fever. J Infect Dis. 1990;161:381.

19 Gurwith MJ et al. Granulocytopenia in hospitalized patients. I. Prognostic factors and etiology of fever. Am J Med. 1978;64:121.

20 Gill FA et al. The relationship of fever, granulocytopenia and antibiotic therapy to bacteremia in cancer patients. Cancer. 1977;39:1704.

21 Elting LS et al. Polymicrobial septicemia in the cancer patient. Medicine (Baltimore). 1986;65:218.

22 Sickles EA et al. Clinical presentation of infection in granulocytopenic patients. Arch Intern Med. 1975;135:715.

23 Kurrle E et al. Risk factors for infection of the oropharynx and respiratory tract in patients with acute leukemia. J Infect Dis. 1981;144:128.

24 Johanson WG et al. Changing pharyngeal bacterial flora of hospitalized patients. Emergence of gram-negative bacilli. N Engl J Med. 1969;281:1137.

25 EORTC International Antimicrobial Therapy Project Group. Three antibiotic regimens in the treatment of infection in febrile granulocytopenic patients with cancer. J Infect Dis. 1978;137:14.

26 Hughes WT et al. Evaluation of new anti-infective drugs for the treatment of febrile episodes in neutropenic patients. Clin Infect Dis. 1992;15(Suppl. 1):S206–15.

27 Meyers JD et al. Risk factors for cytomegalovirus infection after human marrow transplantation. J Infect Dis. 1986;153:478–88.

28 Schimpff SC et al. Origin of infection in acute nonlymphocytic leukemia: significance of hospital acquisition of potential pathogens. Ann Intern Med. 1972;77:707.

29 Rubin RH. Infections in the organ transplant recipient. In: Rubin RH, Young LS, eds. Clinical Approach to Infection in the Compromised Host. 3rd ed. New York: Plenum Publishing; 1994:629.

30 Meyers JD et al. Infection with herpes simplex virus and cell-mediated immunity after marrow transplantation. J Infect Dis. 1980;142:338.

31 Wade JC. Antibiotic therapy for the febrile granulocytopenic cancer patient: combination therapy versus monotherapy. Rev Infect Dis. 1989;11(Suppl. 7):S1572.

32 Schimpff SC et al. Significance of Pseudomonas aeruginosa in the patient with leukemia or lymphoma. J Infect Dis. 1974;30:S24.

33 Calandra T et al. Empiric antibiotic therapy for gram-negative rod bacteremia in granulocytopenic patients: a prospective randomized study of ceftazidime plus short- or full-course amikacin. N Engl J Med. 1987;317:1692.

34 Koll BS, Brown AE. The changing epidemiology of infections at cancer hospitals. Clin Infect Dis. 1993;17(Suppl. 2):S322.

35 Bodey GP et al. Pseudomonas bacteremia: retrospective analysis of 410 episodes. Arch Intern Med. 1985;145:1621.

36 Fainstein V et al. Patterns of oropharyngeal and fecal flora in patients with acute leukemia. J Infect Dis. 1981;144:10.

37 Rubin RH. Impact of cytomegalovirus infection on organ transplant recipients. Rev Infect Dis. 1990;12(Suppl. 7):S754–66.

38 Newman KA, Schimpff SC. Hospital hotel services as risk factors for infection among immunocompromised patients. Rev Infect Dis. 1987;9:206.

39 van der Waaij D, Berghuis JM. Determination of the colonization resistance of the digestive tract of individual mice. J Hyg (Camb). 1974;72:379.

40 Schimpff SC. Surveillance cultures. J Infect Dis. 1981;144:81.

41 Pizzo PA et al. Approaching the controversies in antibacterial management of cancer patients. Am J Med. 1984;76:436.

42 Whitecar JP et al. Pseudomonas bacteremia in cancer patients. Am J Med Sci. 1970;260:216.

43 Kramer BS et al. Randomized comparison between two ceftazidime-containing regimens and cephalothin-gentamicin-carbenicillin in febrile granulocytopenic cancer patients. Antimicrob Agents Chemother. 1986;30:64.

44 **Suthanthiran M, Strom TB.** Renal transplantation. N Engl J Med. 1994; 331:365.

45 **Schimpff SC.** Empiric antibiotic therapy for granulocytopenic cancer patients. Am J Med. 1986;80(Suppl. 5C): 13.

46 **Pizzo PA et al.** New beta-lactam antibiotics in granulocytopenic patients: new options and new questions. Am J Med. 1985;79(Suppl. 2A):75.

47 **Klastersky J.** Treatment of severe infections in patients with cancer: the role of the new acyl-penicillins. Arch Intern Med. 1982;142:1984.

48 **Karp JE et al.** Empiric use of vancomycin during prolonged treatment-induced granulocytopenia. Randomized double-blind, placebo-controlled trial in patients with acute leukemia. Am J Med. 1986;81:237.

49 **Rubin M et al.** Gram-positive infections and the use of vancomycin in 550 episodes of fever and neutropenia. Ann Intern Med. 1988;108:30–50.

50 **De Jongh CA et al.** Antibiotic synergism and response in gram-negative bacteremia in granulocytopenic cancer patients. Am J Med. 1986;80(5C):96.

51 **EORTC International Antimicrobial Therapy Project Group.** Combination of amikacin and carbenicillin with or without cefazolin as empirical treatment of febrile neutropenic patients. J Clin Oncol. 1983;1:597.

52 **Love LJ et al.** Improved prognosis for granulocytopenic patients with gram-negative bacteremia. Am J Med. 1980; 68:643.

53 **Winston DJ et al.** Cytomegalovirus infections after allogeneic bone marrow transplantation. Rev Infect Dis. 1990; 12(Suppl. 7):S776–92.

54 **EORTC Antimicrobial Therapy Project Group.** Prospective randomized comparison of three antibiotic regimens for empirical therapy of suspected bacteremic infection in febrile granulocytopenic patients. Antimicrob Agents Chemother. 1986;29:263.

55 **Klastersky J et al.** Empiric therapy for cancer patients: comparative study of ticarcillin-tobramycin, ticarcillin-cephalothin, and cephalothin-tobramycin. Antimicrob Agents Chemother. 1975;7:640.

56 **Sculier JP, Klastersky J.** Significance of serum bactericidal activity in gram-negative bacillary bacteremia in patients with and without granulocytopenia. Am J Med. 1984;76:429.

57 **Bodey GP et al.** Beta-lactam antibiotics alone or in combination with gentamicin for therapy of gram-negative bacillary infections in neutropenic patients. Am J Med Sci. 1976;271:179.

58 **Hughes WT et al.** Successful chemoprophylaxis for Pneumocystis carinii pneumonia. N Engl J Med. 1977;297: 1419.

59 **Michea-Hamzehpour M et al.** Combination therapy: a way to limit emergence of resistance. Am J Med. 1986; 80(6B):138.

60 **Klastersky J, Zinner SH.** Synergistic combinations of antibiotics in gram-negative bacillary infections. Rev Infect Dis. 1982;4:294.

61 **EORTC International Antimicrobial Therapy Project Group.** Trimetho-

prim-sulfamethoxazole in prevention of infection in neutropenic patients. J Infect Dis. 1984;150:372.

62 **Wade J et al.** Selective antimicrobial modulation as prophylaxis against infection during granulocytopenia: trimethoprim-sulfamethoxazole vs nalidixic acid. J Infect Dis. 1983;147:624.

63 **Stratta RJ.** Clinical patterns and treatment of cytomegalovirus infection after solid-organ transplantation. Transplant Proc. 1993;25(Suppl. 4):15.

64 **Klastersky J et al.** Significance of antimicrobial synergism for outcome of gram-negative sepsis. Am J Med Sci. 1977;273:157.

65 **Klastersky J et al.** Clinical significance of in vitro synergism between antibiotics in gram-negative infection. Antimicrob Agents Chemother. 1972; 2:470.

66 **Anderson LT et al.** Antimicrobial synergism in the therapy of gram-negative rod bacteremias. Chemotherapy. 1978; 24:45.

67 **Bergin CJ et al.** Treatment of Pseudomonas and Serratia infections with ceftazidime. J Antimicrob Chemother. 1985;15:613.

68 **Simon GL et al.** Clinical trial of piperacillin with acquisition of resistance by Pseudomonas and clinical relapse. Antimicrob Agents Chemother. 1980; 18:167.

69 **Winston DJ et al.** Imipenem therapy of Pseudomonas aeruginosa and other serious bacterial infections. Antimicrob Agents Chemother. 1984;26:673.

70 **Young LS.** Use of aminoglycosides in immunocompromised patients. Am J Med. 1985;79(1A):21.

71 **Gribble MJ et al.** Prospective randomized trial of piperacillin monotherapy versus carboxypenicillin-aminoglycoside combination regimens in the empirical treatment of serious bacterial infections. Antimicrob Agents Chemother. 1983;24:388.

72 **Wolfson JS, Swartz MN.** Serum bactericidal activity as a monitor of antibiotic therapy. N Engl J Med. 1985; 312:968.

73 **Klastersky J et al.** Antibacterial activity in serum and urine as a therapeutic guide in bacterial infections. J Infect Dis. 1974;129:187.

74 **DeJongh CA et al.** Empiric antibiotic therapy for suspected infection in granulocytopenic cancer patients: a comparison between the combination of moxalactam plus amikacin and ticarcillin plus amikacin. Am J Med. 1982; 73:89.

75 **Wade JC et al.** Piperacillin or ticarcillin plus amikacin: a double-blind prospective comparison of empiric antibiotic therapy for febrile granulocytopenic cancer patients. Am J Med. 1981; 71:983.

76 **DeJace P, Klastersky J.** Comparative review of combination therapy: two beta-lactams versus beta-lactam plus aminoglycoside. Am J Med. 1986;80 (6B):29.

77 **Feld R et al.** A multicenter comparative trial of tobramycin and ticarcillin vs moxalactam and ticarcillin in febrile neutropenic patients. Arch Intern Med. 1985;145:1083.

78 **Fainstein V et al.** Moxalactam plus ticarcillin or tobramycin for treatment of

febrile episodes in neutropenic cancer patients. Arch Intern Med. 1984;144: 1766.

79 **European Organization for Research in the Treatment of Cancer (EORTC) International Antimicrobial Therapy Cooperative Group, National Cancer Institute of Canada-Clinical Trials Group.** Vancomycin added to empirical combination antibiotic therapy for fever in granulocytopenic cancer patients. J Infect Dis. 1991;163:951.

80 **Granowetten L et al.** Ceftazidime with or without vancomycin vs cephalothin, carbenicillin and gentamicin as initial therapy of the febrile neutropenic pediatric cancer patient. Pediatr Infect Dis. 1988;7:165–70.

81 **Lawson RD et al.** Randomized study of tobramycin plus ticarcillin, tobramycin plus cephalothin, and ticarcillin, or tobramycin plus mezlocillin in the treatment of infections in neutropenic patients with malignancies. Am J Med Sci. 1984;287:16.

82 **Davies AJ, Stone JW.** Current problems of chemotherapy of infections with coagulase-negative staphylococci. Eur J Clin Microbiol. 1986;5:277.

83 **Gilbert DN.** Once-daily aminoglycoside therapy. Antimicrob Agent Chemother. 1991;35:399.

84 **Shenep J et al.** Vancomycin, ticarcillin and amikacin compared with ticarcillin-clavulanate and amikacin in the empirical treatment of febrile, neutropenic children with cancer. N Engl J Med. 1988;319:1053–58.

85 **Anderson ET et al.** Simultaneous antibiotic levels in "breakthrough" gram-negative rod bacteremia. Am J Med. 1976;61:493.

86 **Bodey GP et al.** The role of schedule in antibiotic therapy of the neutropenic patient. Infection. 1980;8(Suppl. I): S75.

87 **Powell SH et al.** Once-daily vs. continuous aminoglycoside dosing: efficacy and toxicity in animal and clinical studies of gentamicin, netilmicin, and tobramycin. J Infect Dis. 1983;147: 918.

88 **The International Antimicrobial Therapy Cooperative Group of the European Organization for Research in the Treatment of Cancer (EORTC-IATCG).** Efficacy and toxicity of single daily doses of amikacin and ceftriaxone versus multiple daily doses of amikacin and ceftazidime for infection in patients with cancer and granulocytopenia. Ann Intern Med. 1993;119:584.

89 **Drusano GL.** Role of pharmacokinetics in the outcome of infections. Antimicrob Agents Chemother. 1988;32: 289–97.

90 **Zinner SH et al.** In vitro models for the study of combination antibiotic therapy in neutropenic patients. Am J Med. 1986;80(6B):156.

91 **Blaser J et al.** Efficacy of intermittent versus continuous administration of netilmicin in a two-compartment in vitro model. Antimicrob Agents Chemother. 1985;27:343.

92 **Verpooten GA et al.** Once-daily dosing decreases renal accumulation of gentamicin and netilmicin. Clin Pharmacol Ther. 1989;45:22.

93 **Viscoli C et al.** Serum concentrations and safety of single daily dosing of amikacin in children undergoing bone marrow transplantation. J Antimicrob Chemother. 1991;27(Suppl. C):113–20.

94 **Bodey GP et al.** A randomized study of carbenicillin plus cefamandole or tobramycin in the treatment of febrile episodes in cancer patients. Am J Med. 1979;67:608–16.

95 **Thompson MIB et al.** Gentamicin inactivation by piperacillin or carbenicillin in patients with end-stage renal disease. Antimicrob Agents Chemother. 1982;21:268.

96 **Pickering LK, Gearhart P.** Effect of time and concentration upon interactions between gentamicin, tobramycin, netilmicin, or amikacin and carbenicillin or ticarcillin. Antimicrob Agents Chemother. 1979;15:592.

97 **Ebert SC et al.** Comparative assessment of in vitro inactivation of gentamicin in the presence of carbenicillin by three different gentamicin assay methods. J Clin Microbiol. 1984;20: 701.

98 **Ramphal R et al.** Clinical experience with cefepime as empiric therapy for fever and neutropenia. Am J Med. 1993;95(Suppl. 4A):48.

99 **Gerding DN et al.** Aminoglycoside resistance and aminoglycoside usage: ten years of experience in one hospital. Antimicrob Agents Chemother. 1991; 35:1284.

100 **Moellering RC et al.** The carbapenems: new broad spectrum β-lactam antibiotics. J Antimicrob Chemother. 1989;24:(Suppl. A):1.

101 **Morrison VA et al.** Non-Candida fungal infections after bone marrow transplantation: risk factors and outcome. Am J Med. 1994;96:497.

102 **Livermore DM.** Clinical significance of beta-lactamase induction and stable derepression in gram-negative rods. Eur J Clin Microbiol. 1987;6:439–45.

103 **Barriere SL.** Therapeutic considerations in using combinations of newer beta-lactam antibiotics. Clin Pharm. 1986;5:24.

104 **Lipsky JJ et al.** Production of hypoprothrombinemia by moxalactam and 1-methyl 5-thiotetrazole in rats. Antimicrob Agent Chemother. 1984;25:380.

105 **Bush K.** Classification of β-lactamases: Groups 1, 2a, 2b, and 2b¹. Antimicrob Agent Chemother. 1989;33: 264.

106 **De Jongh CA et al.** A double beta-lactam combination versus an aminoglycoside-containing regimen as empiric antibiotic therapy for febrile granulocytopenic cancer patients. Am J Med. 1986;80(5C):101.

107 **Winston DJ et al.** Moxalactam plus piperacillin versus moxalactam plus amikacin in febrile granulocytopenic patients. Am J Med. 1984;77:442.

108 **Bodey GP.** Empirical antibiotic therapy for fever in neutropenic patients. Clin Infect Dis. 1993;17(Suppl. 2): S378.

109 **Craig WA, Ebert SC.** Continuous infusion of β-lactam antibiotics. Antimicrob Agent Chemother. 1992;36: 2577–583.

110 **Moore RD et al.** Risk factors for nephrotoxicity in patients treated with

aminoglycosides. Ann Intern Med. 1984;100:352.

111 **Fainstein V et al.** Coagulation abnormalities induced by β-lactam antibiotics in cancer patients. J Infect Dis. 1983;148:745.

112 **Bang NU et al.** Effects of moxalactam on blood coagulation and platelet function. Rev Infect Dis. 1982;4(Suppl.): S546.

113 **Fass RJ et al.** Platelet-mediated bleeding caused by broad-spectrum penicillins. J Infect Dis. 1987;155:1242.

114 **Conly JM et al.** Hypoprothrombinemia in febrile, neutropenic patients with cancer: association with antimicrobial suppression of intestinal microflora. J Infect Dis. 1984;150:202.

115 **Smith CR, Lipsky JJ.** Hypoprothrombinemia and platelet dysfunction caused by cephalosporin and oxalactam antibiotics. J Antimicrob Chemother. 1983;11:496.

116 **Murphy JE.** Aminoglycosides: another look at current and future roles in antimicrobial therapy. Pharmacother. 1990;10:217.

117 **Zaia JA.** Prevention and treatment of cytomegalovirus pneumonia in transplant recipients. Clin Infect Dis. 1993; 17(Suppl. 2):S392.

118 **Grasela TH et al.** Prospective surveillance of antibiotic-associated coagulopathy in 970 patients. Pharmacotherapy. 1989;9:158.

119 **Schentag JJ et al.** Determinants of antibiotic-associated hypothrombinemia. Pharmacotherapy. 1987;7:80.

120 **Neftel KA et al.** Inhibition of granulopoiesis *in vivo* by beta-lactam antibiotics. J Infect Dis. 1985;152:90.

121 **Babiak LM, Rybak MJ.** Hematological effects associated with beta-lactam use. Drug Intell Clin Pharm. 1986;20: 833.

122 **Holt J.** Hypoprothrombinemia and bleeding diatheses associated with cefotetan therapy in surgical patients. Arch Surg. 1988;123:523.

123 **Kirkwood CF et al.** Neutropenia associated with beta-lactam antibiotics. Clin Pharm. 1983;2:569.

124 **Yee GC, McGuire TR.** Allogeneic bone marrow transplantation in the treatment of hematologic diseases. Clin Pharm. 1985;4:149.

125 **Roilides E, Pizzo PA.** Perspectives on the use of cytokines in the management of infectious complications of cancer. Clin Infect Dis. 1993;17(Suppl. 2): S385.

126 **Smith SP, Yee GC.** Hematopoiesis. Pharmacother. 1992;12(2 Pt. 2):11S.

127 **Lagast H et al.** Empiric antimicrobial therapy with aztreonam or ceftazidime in gram-negative septicemia. Am J Med. 1986;80(5C):79.

128 **Jones P et al.** Aztreonam plus vancomycin (plus amikacin) versus moxalactam plus ticarcillin for the empiric treatment of febrile episodes in neutropenic cancer patients. Rev Infect Dis. 1985;7:S741.

129 **Piccart M et al.** Single-drug versus combination empirical therapy for gram-negative bacillary infections in febrile cancer patients with and without granulocytopenia. Antimicrob Agents Chemother. 1984;26:870.

130 **Sayers MH et al.** Reducing the risk for transfusion transmitted cytomegalovi-

rus infection. Ann Intern Med. 1992; 116:55.

131 **Verhagen S et al.** Randomized prospective study of ceftazidime versus ceftazidime plus cephalothin in empiric treatment of febrile episodes in severely neutropenic patients. Antimicrob Agents Chemother. 1987;31: 191.

132 **Pizzo PA et al.** A randomized trial comparing ceftazidime alone with combination antibiotic therapy in cancer patients with fever and neutropenia. N Engl J Med. 1986;315:552.

133 **Winston DJ et al.** Beta-lactam antibiotic therapy in febrile granulocytopenic patients. Ann Intern Med. 1991;115: 849.

134 **Rolston KVI et al.** A comparison of imipenem to ceftazidime with or without amikacin as empiric therapy in febrile neutropenic patients. Arch Intern Med. 1992;152:283.

135 **Mortimer J et al.** Comparison of cefoperazone and mezlocillin with imipenem and empiric therapy in febrile neutropenic cancer patients. Am J Med. 1988;85(Suppl. 1A):17–20.

136 **Corey L, Spear PG.** Infection with *Herpes Simplex* viruses (Parts 1 & 2). N Engl J Med. 1986;314:686–91, 749–57.

137 **Joshi JH et al.** Can antibacterial therapy be discontinued in persistently febrile granulocytopenic cancer patients? Am J Med. 1984;76:450.

138 **Rodriguez V et al.** Management of fever of unknown origin in patients with neoplasms and neutropenia. Cancer. 1973;32:1007.

139 **Pizzo PA et al.** Duration of empiric antibiotic therapy in granulocytopenic patients with cancer. Am J Med. 1979; 67:194.

140 **Pizzo PA et al.** Treatment of gram-positive septicemia in cancer patients. Cancer. 1980;45:206.

141 **Pizzo PA.** After empiric therapy: what to do until the granulocyte comes back. Rev Infect Dis. 1987;9:214.

142 **Young LS.** The role of granulocyte transfusions in treating and preventing infection. Cancer Treat Rep. 1983;67: 109.

143 **Straus SE et al.** Varicella-Zoster virus infections: biology, natural history, and prevention. Ann Intern Med. 1988;108: 221.

144 **Balfour et al.** A randomized, placebo-controlled trial of oral acyclovir for the prevention of cytomegalovirus disease recipients of renal allografts. N Engl J Med. 1989;320:1381.

145 **Horn R et al.** Fungemia in a cancer hospital. Changing frequency, earlier onset, and results of therapy. Rev Infect Dis. 1985;7:646.

146 **DeGregorio MW et al.** Fungal infections in patients with acute leukemia. Am J Med. 1982;73:543.

147 **Vartivarian SE et al.** Emerging fungal pathogens in immunocompromised patients: classification, diagnosis, and management. Clin Infect Dis. 1993; 17(Suppl. 2):S487.

148 **Reusser P et al.** Phase I-II trial of foscarnet for prevention of cytomegalovirus infection in autologous and allogeneic marrow transplant recipients. J Infect Dis. 1992;166:473.

149 **Cole NL, Balfour HH Jr.** In vitro sus-

ceptibility of cytomegalovirus isolates for immunocompromised patients to acyclovir and ganciclovir. Diagn Microbiol Infect Dis. 1987;6:255.

150 **Goodrich JM et al.** Ganciclovir prophylaxis to prevent cytomegalovirus disease after allogeneic marrow transplantation. Ann Intern Med. 1993;118: 173.

151 **Bodey GP.** Fungal infection and fever of unknown origin in neutropenic patients. Am J Med. 1986;80(5C):112.

152 **Winston DJ et al.** Ganciclovir prophylaxis of cytomegalovirus infection and disease in allogeneic bone marrow transplant recipients: results of a placebo-controlled double-blind trial. Ann Intern Med. 1993;118:179.

153 **Pizzo PA et al.** Empiric antibiotic and antifungal therapy for cancer patients with prolonged fever and granulocytopenia. Am J Med. 1982;72:101.

154 **Stein RS et al.** Clinical value of empirical amphotericin B in patients with acute myelogenous leukemia. Cancer. 1982;50:2247.

155 **Holleran WM et al.** Empiric amphotericin B therapy in patients with acute leukemia. Rev Infect Dis. 1985;7:619.

156 **Groeger JS et al.** Infectious morbidity associated with long-term use of venous access devices in patients with cancer. Ann Intern Med. 1993;119: 1168.

157 **Rose RM.** The role of colony-stimulating factors in infectious disease: current status, future challenges. Semin Oncol. 1992;19:415–21.

158 **Trillet-Lenoir V et al.** Recombinant granulocyte colony stimulating factor reduces the infectious complications of cytotoxic chemotherapy. Eur J Cancer. 1993;29A:319.

159 **Crawford J et al.** Reduction by granulocyte colony-stimulating factor of fever and neutropenia induced by chemotherapy in patients with small-cell lung cancer. N Engl J Med. 1991;324: 1773.

160 **Young LS.** Antimicrobial prophylaxis against infection in neutropenic patients. J Infect Dis. 1983;147:611.

161 **Brandt SJ et al.** Effect of recombinant human granulocyte-macrophage colony stimulating factor on hematopoietic reconstitution after high dose chemotherapy and autologous bone marrow transplantation. N Engl J Med. 1988;318:869.

162 **Eggimann P et al.** Cefepime monotherapy for the empirical treatment of fever in granulocytopenic cancer patients. J Antimicrob Chemother. 1993; 32(Suppl. B):151.

163 **Liang R et al.** Ceftazidime versus imipenem-cilastatin as initial monotherapy for febrile neutropenic patients. Antimicrob Agent Chemother. 1990; 34:1336.

164 **Van der Auwere P, Gerain J.** Use of the quinolones in the prophylaxis and treatment of granulocytopenic immunocompromised cancer patients. Drugs. 1993;45(Suppl. 3):81.

165 **Meunier F et al.** Prospective randomized evaluation of ciprofloxacin versus piperacillin plus amikacin for empiric antibiotic therapy in febrile granulocytopenic cancer patients with lymphoma and solid tumors. The European Organization for Research in the Treat-

ment of Cancer, International Antimicrobial Therapy Cooperative Group. Antimicrob Agent Chemother. 1991; 35:873.

166 **Johnson PRE et al.** A randomized trial of high-dose ciprofloxacin versus azlocillin and netilmicin in the empirical therapy of febrile neutropenic patients. J Antimicrob Chemother. 1992;30:203.

167 **Malik IA et al.** Randomized comparison of oral ofloxacin alone with combination of parenteral antibiotics in neutropenic febrile patients. Lancet. 1992;339:1092.

168 **Flaherty JP et al.** Multicenter randomized trial of ciprofloxacin plus azlocillin versus ceftazidime plus amikacin for empiric treatment of febrile neutropenic patients. Am J Med. 1989; 87(Suppl. 5A);278S.

169 **Chan CC et al.** Randomized trial comparing ciprofloxacin plus netilmicin versus piperacillin plus netilmicin for empiric treatment of fever in neutropenic patients. Antimicrob Agent Chemother. 1989;33:87.

170 **Kelsey SM et al.** Teicoplanin plus ciprofloxacin versus gentamicin plus piperacillin in the treatment of febrile neutropenic patients. Eur J Clin Microbiol Infect Dis. 1992;11:509.

171 **Piddock LJV.** Newer fluoroquinolones and gram-positive bacteria. ASM News. 1993;59:603.

172 **Perfect JR.** Antifungal prophylaxis: to prevent or not. Am J Med. 1993;94: 233–34.

173 **Murray HW.** Cytokines as antimicrobial therapy for the T-cell deficient patient: prospects for treatment of non-viral opportunistic infections. Clin Infect Dis. 1993;17(Suppl. 2):S407.

174 **Maschmeyer G.** Use of the quinolones for the prophylaxis and therapy of infections in immunocompromised hosts. Drugs. 1993;45(Suppl. 3):73.

175 **Truckis M et al.** Emerging resistance to fluoroquinolones in staphylococci: an alert. Ann Intern Med. 1991;114: 424.

176 **Walsh TJ, Lee JW.** Prevention of invasive fungal infections in patients with neoplastic diseases. Clin Infect Dis. 1993;17(Suppl. 2):S468.

177 **Pizzo PA.** Management of fever in patients with cancer and treatment-induced neutropenia. N Engl J Med. 1993;328:1323.

178 **Groopman JE et al.** Hematopoietic growth factors—biology and clinical applications. N Engl J Med. 1989;321: 1449.

179 **Merigan TC et al.** A controlled trial of ganciclovir to prevent cytomegalovirus disease after heart transplantation. N Engl J Med. 1992;326:1182.

180 **Biesma B et al.** Efficacy and tolerability of recombinant human granulocyte-macrophage colony stimulating factor in patients with chemotherapy related leukopenia and fever. Eur J Cancer. 1990;26:932.

181 **Gabrilove J.** The development of granulocyte colony-stimulating factor in its various clinical applications. Blood. 1992;80:1382.

182 **Schmidt GM et al.** A randomized controlled trial of prophylactic ganciclovir for cytomegalovirus pulmonary infection in recipients of allogeneic bone marrow transplants. The City of Hope-

Stanford-Syntex CMV Study Group. N Engl J Med. 1991;324:1005.

183 **Cleary JD et al.** Imidazoles and triazoles in antifungal therapy. DICP. 1990;24:148.

184 **Heel RC et al.** Miconazole: a preliminary review of its therapeutic efficacy in systemic fungal infections. Drugs. 1980;19:7.

185 **Goodrich JM et al.** Early treatment with ganciclovir to prevent cytomegalovirus disease after allogeneic bone marrow transplantation. N Engl J Med. 1991;325:1601.

186 **Sullivan KM et al.** Immunomodulatory and antimicrobial efficacy of intravenous immunoglobulin in bone marrow transplantation. N Engl J Med. 1990;323:705.

187 **Snydman DR et al.** Cytomegalovirus immune globulin prophylaxis in liver transplantation. Ann Intern Med. 1993; 119:984.

188 **Snydman DR et al.** Use of cytomegalovirus immune globulin to prevent cytomegalovirus disease in renal transplant recipients. N Engl J Med. 1987; 317:1049.

189 **Adler SP.** Cytomegalovirus hyperimmune globulin: who needs it? Pediatr Infect Dis. 1992;11:266.

190 **Rubin RH, Tolkoff-Rubin NE.** Antimicrobial strategies in the care of organ transplant recipients. Antimicrob Agent Chemother. 1993;27:619.

191 **Antman KS et al.** Effect of recombinant human granulocyte-macrophage colony stimulating factor on chemotherapy-induced myelosuppression. N Engl J Med. 1988;319:593.

192 **Verhoef J.** Prevention of infections in the neutropenic patient. Clin Infect Dis. 1993;17(Suppl. 2):S359.

193 **Meyers JD et al.** Acyclovir for prevention of cytomegalovirus infection and disease after allogenic marrow transplantation. N Engl J Med. 1988; 318:70.

194 **Dismukes WE.** Azole antifungal drugs: old and new. Ann Intern Med. 1988;109:177.

195 **Gold D, Corey L.** Acyclovir prophylaxis for *Herpes Simplex* virus infection. Antimicrob Agents Chemother. 1987;31:361.

196 **Wade JC et al.** A comparison of trimethoprim-sulfamethoxazole plus nystatin with gentamicin plus nystatin in prevention of infection in acute leukemia. N Engl J Med. 1981;304:1057.

197 **Schimpff SC et al.** Infection prevention in acute nonlymphocytic leukemia: laminar air flow versus reverse isolation with oral, nonabsorbable antibiotic prophylaxis. Ann Intern Med. 1975;82:351.

198 **Young LS.** The new fluorinated quinolones for infection prevention in acute leukemia. Ann Intern Med. 1987;106: 144.

199 **Louie SG, Jung B.** Clinical effects of biologic response modifiers. Am J Hosp Pharm. 1993;50(Suppl. 3):S10.

200 **Blackwell A, Crawford J.** Colony-stimulating factors: clinical applications. Pharmacotherapy. 1992;12(Pt. 2):20S.

201 **Devereaux S et al.** GM-CSF accelerates neutrophil recovery after autologous bone marrow transplantation for Hodgkin's disease. Bone Marrow Transplant. 1988;4:49.

202 **De Vries-Hosper HG et al.** The effect of amphotericin B lozenges on the presence and number of *Candida* cells in the oropharynx of neutropenic leukopenic patients. Infection. 1982;10: 71.

203 **Dekker AW et al.** Prevention of infection by trimethoprim-sulfamethoxazole plus amphotericin B in patients with acute nonlymphocytic leukemia. Ann Intern Med. 1981;95:555.

204 **Owens NJ et al.** Prophylaxis of oral candidiasis with clotrimazole troches. Arch Intern Med. 1984;144:290.

205 **Goodman JL et al.** A controlled trial of fluconazole to prevent fungal infections in patients undergoing bone marrow transplantation. N Engl J Med. 1992;326:845.

206 **DeGregorio MW et al.** *Candida* infections in patients with acute leukemia: ineffectiveness of nystatin prophylaxis and relationship between oropharyngeal and systemic candidiasis. Cancer. 1982;50:2780.

207 **Menichetti F et al.** Preventing fungal infections in neutropenic patients with acute leukemia: fluconazole compared with oral amphotericin B. Ann Intern Med. 1994;120:913.

208 **Meunier F.** Prevention of mycoses in immunosuppressed patients. Rev Infect Dis. 1987;9:408.

209 **Nemunaitis J et al.** Recombinant granulocyte-macrophage colony-stimulating factor after autologous bone marrow transplantation for lymphoid cancer. N Engl J Med. 1991;324:1773.

210 **Hann IM et al.** Ketoconazole vs. nystatin plus amphotericin B for fungal prophylaxis in severely immunocompromised patients. Lancet. 1982;1:826.

211 **Donnelly JP et al.** Oral ketoconazole and amphotericin B for the prevention of yeast colonization in patients with acute leukemia. J Hosp Infect. 1984; 5:83.

212 **Winston DJ et al.** Fluconazole prophylaxis of fungal infections in patients with acute leukemia. Ann Intern Med. 1993;118:495.

213 **Fauchi AS et al.** NIH conference. Immunomodulators in clinical medicine. Ann Intern Med. 1987;106:421.

214 **Pizzo PA.** Empirical therapy and prevention of infection in the immunocompromised host. In: Mandell GL et al., eds. Principles and Practice of Infectious Diseases. New York: Churchill Livingstone, Inc.; 1990:2303.

215 **Zeigler EJ et al.** Treatment of gram-negative bacteremic shock with human antiserum to a mutant *E. coli*. N Engl J Med. 1982;307:1225.

216 **Pennington JE et al.** Passive immunotherapy for experimental *Pseudomonas aeruginosa* pneumonia in the neutropenic host. J Infect Dis. 1987; 155:973.

217 **Ezdinli EZ et al.** Oral amphotericin for candidiasis in patients with hematologic neoplasms: an autopsy study. JAMA. 1979;242:258.

218 **Lieschke GJ, Burgess AW.** Granulocyte colony-stimulating factor and granulocyte-macrophage colony-stimulating factor. Parts I and II. N Engl J Med. 1992;327:28,99.

219 **MedImmune, Inc.** Cytogam package insert. Gaithersburg; 1993 March.

220 **Guiot HFL et al.** Selective antimicrobial modulation of the intestinal flora of patients with acute non-lymphocytic leukemia: a double-blind placebo-controlled study. J Infect Dis. 1983;147: 615.

221 **van der Waajj D et al.** Colonization resistance of the digestive tract of mice during systemic antibiotic treatment. J Hyg (Camb). 1972;70:605.

222 **Vollaard EJ et al.** Effect on colonization resistance: an important criterion in selecting antibiotics. DICP. 1990;24: 60.

223 **Klastersky J et al.** Use of oral antibiotics in protected unit environments: clinical effectiveness and role on the emergence of antibiotic-resistant strains. Pathol Biol. 1974;22:5.

224 **Levine AS et al.** Protected environments and prophylactic antibiotics: a prospective controlled study of their utility in the therapy of acute leukemia. N Engl J Med. 1973;288:477.

Human Immunodeficiency Virus (HIV) Infection

Gene D Morse
Mark J Shelton
Alice M O'Donnell

Background 68-2
Pathophysiology 68-2
   Central role of the CD4+ lymphocyte in immune
   regulation and the impact of HIV infection 68-2
   The life cycle of HIV and the demise
   of the CD4+ lymphocyte 68-2
   Multiorgan nature of HIV disease 68-3
Diagnosis 68-4
   Adults 68-4
   Neonates 68-4
Epidemiology 68-5
Prognosis 68-5
Therapeutic Goals 68-6
   Surrogate markers 68-6
Pharmacotherapy of HIV Infection 68-6
Viral Binding to Cell Surface Receptors 68-6
Reverse Transcriptase (RT) Inhibitors 68-7, 68-11
   Nucleoside analogs (Also see Question 73) 68-7
      Zidovudine (ZDV) (Also see Questions 2 to 4) 68-7
      Didanosine (ddI) 68-8
      Zalcitabine (ddC) 68-8
      Stavudine (D4T) 68-9
      Lamivudine (3-Thiacytidine or 3TC) 68-9
   Current considerations for antiretroviral trials
   (See Figure 68.3) 68-9
   Nonnucleoside reverse transcriptionase (RT)
   inhibitors (NNRTIs) 68-9
   Combination therapy 68-11
      Nucleoside analog/nucleoside analog 68-11
      Nucleoside analog/non-nucleoside analog 68-11
   Resistance to reverse transcriptase inhibitors 68-11
   Nucleoside analog RT Inhibitor toxicity 68-12
Protease Inhibitors 68-10
Gene Regulating Compounds 68-11
Immunotherapies 68-12
Monitoring Therapy 68-12
The Use of CD4+ Counts to Stratify Treatment
and Therapeutic Endpoints 68-13
Zidovudine 68-13
   Initiation 68-13
   Monitoring parameters 68-14
   Considerations for declining CD4+ count
   (See Table 68.4) 68-14
   In pregnancy (See Question 67) 68-34
Didanosine 68-14
   Gastrointestinal (GI) intolerance 68-14
Pneumocystis carinii **Pneumonia (PCP)** 68-14
Clinical Presentation 68-15
Antimicrobial Selection (See Table 68.5) 68-15
   Trimethoprim-sulfamethoxazole (TMP-SMX) 68-15
   Alternatives to TMP-SMX 68-16
Initiation of Corticosteroids 68-17
Prophylaxis (See Table 68.6) 68-17
HIV-Wasting 68-18
Cytomegalovirus (CMV) Retinitis 68-18
   Diagnosis 68-18

Goal of Therapy 68-18
Drug Therapy 68-18
   Ganciclovir (Also see Questions 21 and 22) 68-19
   Foscarnet 68-19
      Nephrotoxicity 68-19
      Adverse effects 68-19
      Dosage adjustments 68-19
   Alternatives (See Question 20) 68-20
Suppression Therapy 68-19
Relapse 68-20
Oral Ganciclovir 68-20
Varicella Zoster Virus (VZV) 68-20
Acyclovir 68-20
   Dosing 68-20
   Adverse effects 68-21
   Prophylaxis 68-21
   Resistance 68-21
Cryptococcal Meningitis 68-21
Clinical Presentation and Prognosis 68-21
Treatment 68-21
   Amphotericin B 68-21
      Intrathecal (IT) 68-22
      Adverse effects and administration 68-22
   Fluconazole 68-22
   Itraconazole 68-23
   Duration of therapy 68-23
   Investigational therapies 68-23
   Maintenance therapy 68-23
Primary Prophylaxis 68-23
Toxoplasma **Encephalitis** 68-24
Clinical Presentation 68-24
Diagnosis 68-24
Prophylaxis 68-24
Treatment 68-24
   Sulfadiazine/pyrimethamine 68-24
   Suppressive therapy 68-25
   Alternative therapies 68-25
Mycobacterium tuberculosis 68-25
Clinical Presentation 68-25
Treatment (See Table 68.7) 68-26
Prophylaxis 68-26
   HIV− individuals: multidrug-resistant
   tuberculosis 68-26
   HIV+ individuals: drug-sensitive tuberculosis 68-26
Mycobacterium avium **Complex (MAC) Infection** .. 68-27
Clinical Presentation 68-27
Treatment 68-27
   Initiation 68-27
Drug susceptibility as a basis for treatment 68-27
Drug therapy (See Table 68.8) 68-28
   Monitoring therapy 68-28
   Drug interactions 68-29
Prophylaxis 68-29
Enteric Infections 68-29

(Continued)

HIV-Associated Malignancies 68-31
    Kaposi Sarcoma (KS) 68-31
    NonHodgkin's Lymphoma (NHL) 68-31
Postexposure Chemoprophylaxis 68-32
Women and HIV Disease 68-32
    Clinical Presentation 68-32
    Antiretroviral Therapy 68-32
    Cervical Intraepithelial Neoplasia 68-33
        Pharmacologic intervention 68-33
    Pregnancy and Vertical Transmission Risk 68-33

Zidovudine in Pregnancy 68-34
Pediatric HIV Disease 68-34
    Clinical Presentation 68-34
    Lymphoid Interstitial Pneumonitis (LIP) 68-35
    Vaccination in HIV-Infected Children 68-35
    PCP Prophylaxis (See Table 68.9) 68-35
    Antiretroviral Therapy (See Table 68.10) 68-36
        Nucleoside analogue therapy 68-36
    Intravenous Immune Globulin (IVIG) Therapy 68-37
Summary 68-38

Background

Human immunodeficiency virus (HIV) infection is an intracellular infection (primarily invading CD4+ T lymphocytes) caused by a member of the family of *Retroviridae*. The infectious virion of the *Retroviridae* possesses nucleic acid composed of RNA. Replication of the virus involves creation of a proviral DNA genome, integration into the host cell DNA, and subsequent transcription back to RNA as new HIV progeny (see Figure 68.1). HIV cannot continue its life cycle out of the host's cells and virus-containing body fluids or infected host cells must be transmitted between individuals for the virus to be spread to others. The most common routes of HIV transmission have been through sexual contact, sharing unclean intravenous (IV) needles, contaminated blood products, and maternal-fetal transfer.

Symptomatic HIV infection was first recognized in 1981 as an acquired immunodeficiency syndrome (AIDS).[1-3] At the time, the etiologic agent for AIDS was unknown; however, researchers were previously aware of lymphocytotropic viruses which caused a similar syndrome in animals [i.e., simian immunodeficiency virus (SIV)].[4,5] The initial series of AIDS cases described the occurrence of Kaposi sarcoma (an unusual malignancy in nonimmunocompromised individuals) and opportunistic infections (primarily *Pneumocystis carinii*) among homosexual men.[1-3] These uncommon cases were then followed by numerous other reports from across the U.S. and an increasing number of cases from around the world. A few years later, the causative organism was identified as the human T-cell lymphotropic virus (HTLV).[6-8] Later renamed HIV, this retrovirus is acknowledged by most researchers to be the causative organism of the current global HIV epidemic.

Pathophysiology

Central Role of the CD4+ Lymphocyte in Immune Regulation and the Impact of HIV Infection

Knowledge of the immune system has increased exponentially since the beginning of the AIDS epidemic, primarily due to significant advances in molecular biology and biotechnology. Whereas the immune system was previously described as two discrete arms, the humoral and cellular components, a greater appreciation of the integration between the two has led to an expanded picture of how the body responds to foreign antigens (see Figure 68.2). The complex mechanism of communication among the affector and effector components of the immune system is now more clearly defined with the recognition of soluble protein mediators [i.e., cytokines, lymphokines, colony stimulating factors (CSFs), interferons]. These mediators are synthesized in some immune and nonimmune cells and released locally and into the systemic circulation to elicit the immune response. Within the grand scheme of the immune system, the CD4+ lymphocyte functions as a "helper" which modulates the actions of the other key cellular components of the immune system. The eventual loss of CD4+ lymphocytes is the underlying pathophysiologic problem which leads to AIDS. The reader is referred to comprehensive immunology texts for a more detailed explanation of immune function and inflammation during HIV infection.[9,10]

The Life Cycle of HIV and the Demise of the CD4+ Lymphocyte

With an understanding of both the central role of the CD4+ lymphocyte in orchestrating the immune response to foreign antigen and of the immune surveillance of self-antigens, the devastating effect of HIV infection can be appreciated. Following the binding of the HIV surface glycoprotein (gp120) to the CD4+ molecule of some human lymphocytes, the virus undergoes fusion, cell entry, and subsequent uncoating with the release of virion contents into the host cell cytoplasm.

HIV is a single-stranded RNA virus which contains a virally encoded DNA polymerase enzyme, reverse transcriptase (RT). The HIV RT is the enzyme responsible for transcribing viral RNA into DNA, a cytoplasmic event (see Figure 68.1). Following reverse transcription, the HIV DNA enters the cell nucleus and, through the action of another viral enzyme (integrase), is incorporated into the host cell genome. It is this event, the incorporation into host DNA, which makes HIV infection a chronic, lifelong disease, since each time the lymphocyte is activated and the DNA transcribed and translated, new HIV virions are created and released. *Thus, HIV is able to invade human lymphocytes, establish chronic infection, and utilize the normal host cellular transcription and translation events to complete its life cycle.*[11]

In some cells, HIV DNA is retained in the cytoplasm as a circular double-stranded DNA molecule: in other cells, the proviral DNA is integrated into host DNA.[12] The reason for this differential integration process is unknown. The infected CD4+ lymphocyte is able to function normally for a period of time, but often develops cellular dysfunction as manifested by an abnormal response to soluble mitogens.[13-15] It is this cellular functional deficit, compounded by the eventual decline in the absolute number of CD4+ lymphocytes, which leads to the occurrence of opportunistic infections and malignancies. HIV strains which are able to induce syncytia formation *in vitro* (i.e., SI phenotype) also have been identified and associated with an accelerated decline in CD4+ lymphocytes.[16-20] Given the tropism of HIV for CD4+ lymphocytes and the clinical manifestations of a decline in, or depletion of, CD4+ cells, CD4+ lymphocytes are the primary clinical surrogate marker of immune suppression and antiretroviral activity.[18]

The pathophysiology of HIV infection is a complicated process, but the end result is CD4+ lymphocyte depletion and the progression of the underlying immunosuppressed state heralded by the occurrence of opportunistic infections, the onset of malignancies, or neurologic dysfunction. The severity of the opportunistic infections may range from relatively minor events, such as oral candidiasis or oral hairy leukoplakia, to sight-threatening episodes of cytomegalovirus (CMV) retinitis or life-threatening *Pneumo-*

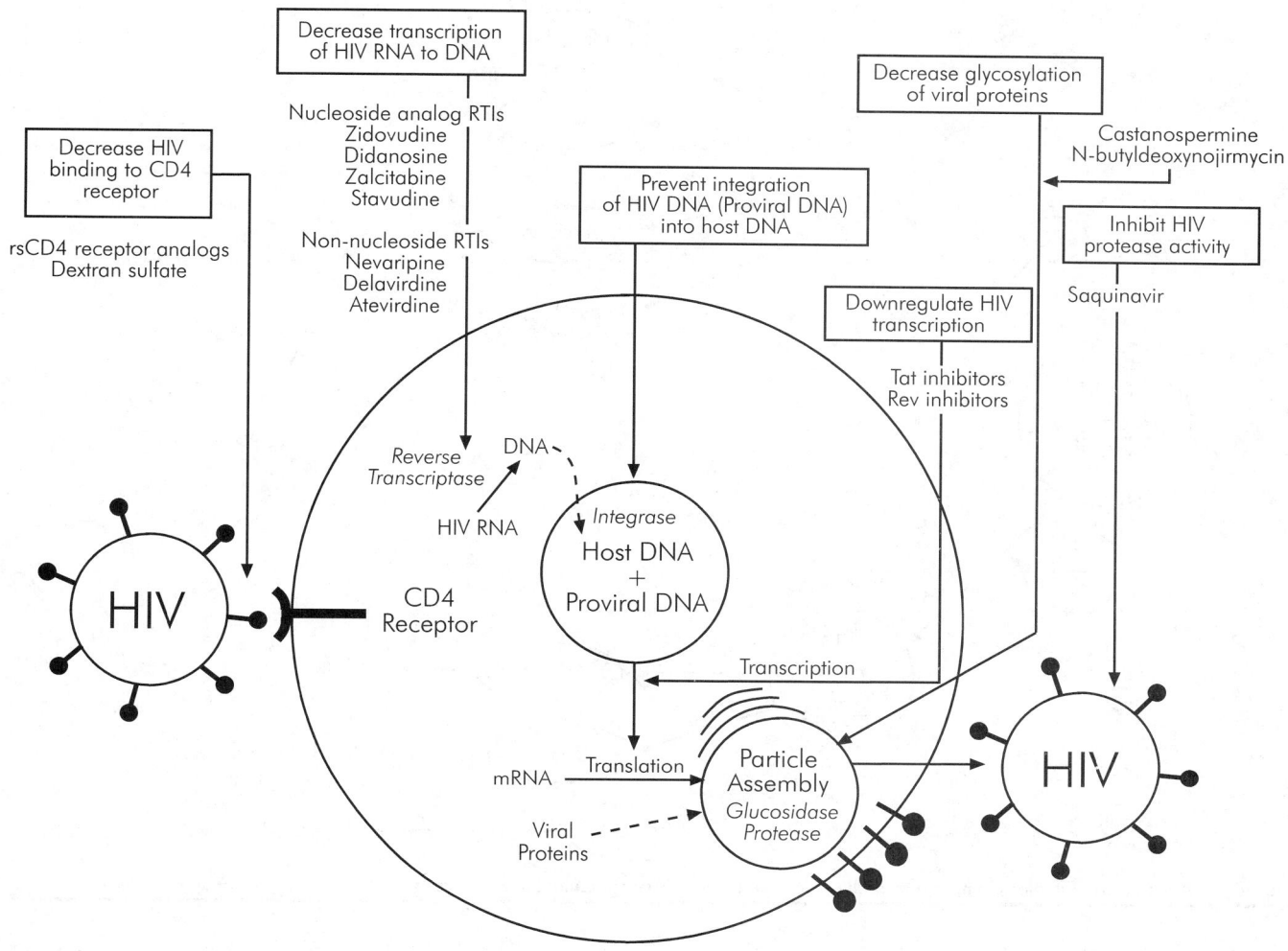

Fig 68.1   HIV Life Cycle Illustrating the Key Stages of Replication Which Are Also the Focus of Antiretroviral Drug Development

cystis carinii pneumonia (PCP). Some opportunistic infections will require life-long prophylaxis or suppressive treatment (e.g., ganciclovir or foscarnet for CMV; fluconazole or amphotericin B for cryptococcal meningitis; sulfadiazine/pyrimethamine for toxoplasmosis; trimethoprim-sulfamethoxazole, pentamidine, or dapsone for PCP). Other acute, intermittent opportunistic infections such as protozoal or bacterial gastrointestinal infections, fungal infections, or viral infections may require prolonged treatment periods as well.

Kaposi sarcoma and nonHodgkin's lymphoma are the malignancies most often noted among HIV-infected male patients. In addition, an increasing incidence of invasive cervical cancer has been recognized in female patients with HIV infection. These malignancies may be treated with chemotherapy, with or without immunotherapy, or radiation during which time it is often difficult to continue antiretroviral treatment because of additive toxicities. For example, the myelosuppressive effects of some regimens may make it difficult to continue zidovudine treatment. However, more recent protocols have included the administration of colony stimulating factors in an attempt to offset the marrow suppression and allow for continued antiretroviral therapy. Similarly, chemotherapy regimens which include drugs with neurotoxic effects (e.g., vincristine) may make it difficult to continue didanosine or zalcitabine treatment (see below).

Multiorgan Nature of HIV Disease

While advanced HIV disease often follows the pattern described above, many patients at earlier stages of disease present with other

symptoms (e.g., neurologic involvement). In addition, the now routine use of prophylaxis for P. carinii pneumonia has necessitated the revision of the Centers for Disease Control (CDC) classification system for HIV infection and expansion of the surveillance case definition for AIDS (see Table 68.1). The revised classification system now includes a stratification for the CD4+ lymphocyte count as well as a subgrouping by clinical categories. As a result, the case definition for AIDS has been modified from the original case definition which required specific AIDS-defining opportunistic infections or malignancies to include all symptomatic (see Table 68.2) and all asymptomatic patients with a CD4+ cell count less than 200 cells/mm^3 (patients with a clinical condition not previously used as an AIDS-defining diagnosis).[22]

While many individuals think of HIV infection solely as a state of immunodeficiency, the progression of HIV disease eventually involves many vital organs. The central nervous system (CNS), kidneys, liver, gastrointestinal (GI) tract, skin, bone marrow, and endocrine system may be affected to varying extents in different patients.[23,24] The multiorgan nature of HIV disease also has many implications for the success of chronic antiretroviral therapy. For example, when antiretroviral therapy is initiated, patients may develop achlorhydria or diarrhea which may, depending upon the characteristics of the drug, decrease the bioavailability of the antiviral and other concurrent drug therapy. Furthermore, some patients may develop hepatitis or renal dysfunction that could alter the clearance of prescribed drugs.[25] There are no guidelines for

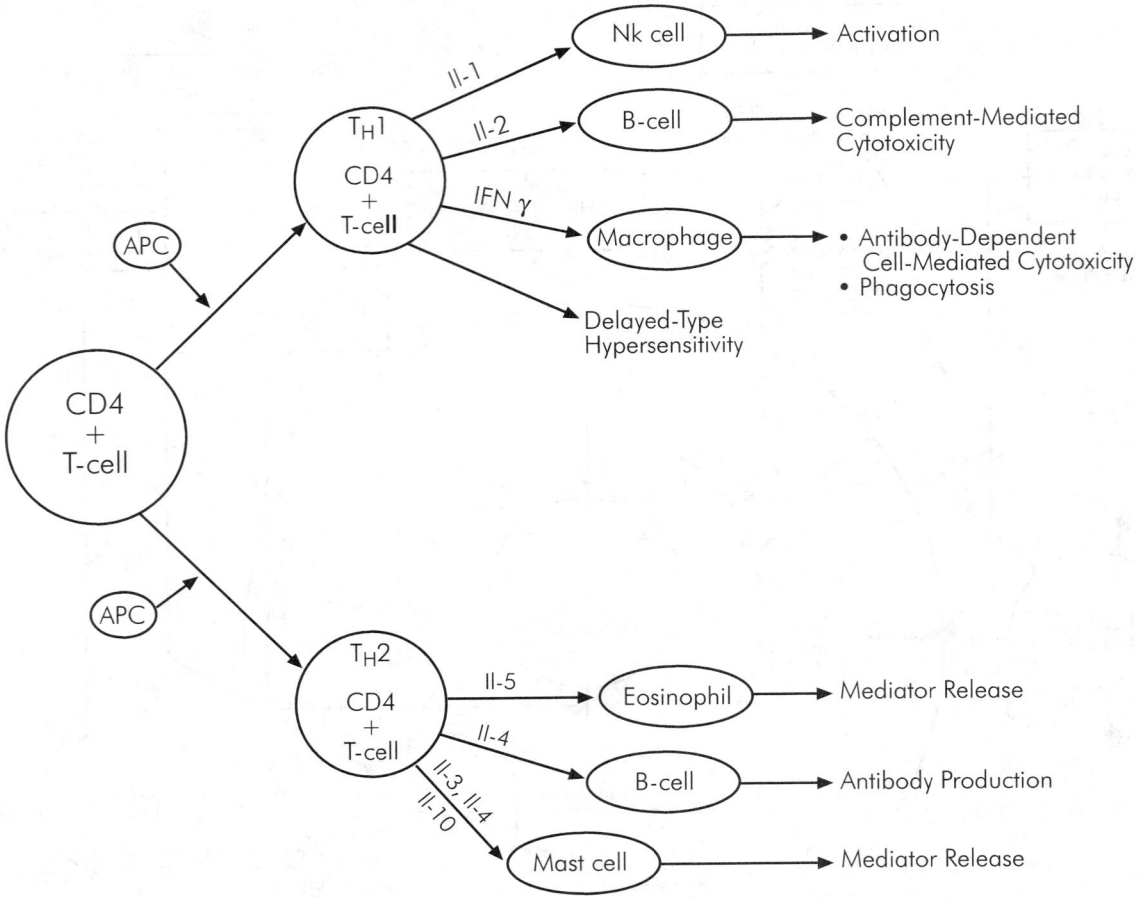

Fig 68.2   Affector and Effector Components of the Adaptive (Antigen-Recognizing) Immune System   APC = Antigen-presenting cell; Il = Interleukin.

dosage adjustments of antiretrovirals based upon plasma concentrations, and it is unknown whether individualization of antiretroviral dosing based upon pharmacokinetic parameters will have any impact on patient outcomes. In clinical practice, dose reductions or drug discontinuation are based upon the development of toxicity. Thus, the long-term management of the HIV-infected patient is based upon the chronic suppression of HIV replication and the management of intermittent episodes of infection and/or malignancy with drugs which may interact on a pharmacokinetic or a pharmacodynamic basis with the primary therapy for HIV.

Diagnosis

Adults

The initial or screening tests for the detection of anti-HIV antibodies in plasma in most clinical laboratories are enzyme-linked immunosorbent assays (ELISA). All specimens found reactive with ELISA screening techniques for HIV are then confirmed by another more specific test. The Western blot has been recognized as the most sensitive and specific test for detection of HIV-1 antibody. Therefore, HIV is diagnosed in adults by the detection in the plasma of antibody to the HIV virus and confirmed by a Western blot antibody test, viral culture, or plasma HIV RNA. HIV should be considered when susceptible individuals present with opportunistic infections, malignancies, or a change in mental status. A serum p24 antigen concentration and a CD4+ lymphocyte count also are useful diagnostic tests. In addition, more specific and sensitive polymerase chain reaction (PCR)-based tests are being developed for detecting small amounts of viral RNA in

plasma. *Although tests may confirm infection with HIV, a diagnosis of HIV infection is not synonymous with a diagnosis of AIDS.* The diagnosis of AIDS, is reserved for patients who are HIV-positive *and* have a CD4+ cell count less than 200/mm^3 or an AIDS-indicating condition (see Tables 68.1 and 68.2).

Neonates

Because infants can harbor maternal IgG antibodies (reflective of HIV infection) for as long as 15 months, the use of ELISA and

Table 68.1	1993 Revised Classification System for HIV Infection and the Expanded CDC Surveillance Case Definition for AIDS in Adults and Adolescents^a		
	Clinical Categories		
CD4+ T-Cell Categories	(A) Asymptomatic, Acute (Primary) HIV or PGL	(B) Symptomatic, Not (A) or (C) Conditions	(C) AIDS-Indicator Conditions
1) >500/mm^3	A1	B1	C1
2) 200–499/mm^3	A2	B2	C2
3) <200/mm^3 (AIDS indicator T-cell count)	A3	B3	C3

^{a} The modifications to the prior 1986 Surveillance Case Definition, which have been included in the 1993 revision, include the use of CD4 cell count (<200 cells/mm^3) or *CD4 cell percent* (<14%) and the additional AIDS-indicating conditions of pulmonary tuberculosis, recurrent pneumonia, and invasive cervical cancer (see Table 68.2).

Western blot tests is not helpful in the early diagnosis of HIV disease in the infant born to an infected mother.[568] The serum p24 antigen assay also is not a very useful diagnostic tool in newborns because not all infants may be p24-positive at birth.[569] Viral culture, although labor-intensive, is both a sensitive and specific technique which may be used in the diagnosis of perinatally-acquired HIV infection.[568] A recently developed HIV-specific IgA antibody assay may aid in the diagnosis of HIV infection in infants since IgA antibodies do not readily cross from the HIV mother to the infant through the placenta.[570] The highly sensitive and specific polymerase chain reaction tests correlate well with viral cultures. Although PCR assays are only about 50% sensitive at birth and HIV culture is also negative in some infants with infection, a combination of these tests may be used to diagnose perinatally acquired HIV infection during routine postpartum follow-up.

A key aspect of neonatal diagnosis is the suspicion that the newborn is at high-risk (i.e., the history of the mother is suggestive that transmission is likely). HIV testing should be offered to all pregnant women at risk for HIV infection; and viral culture and a polymerase chain reaction test should be obtained as soon as possible after birth. If these tests results are positive for HIV, then tests should be repeated. If test results are negative in the newborn at high risk, the test should be repeated at one month and again at two to three months. If these tests for HIV are still negative three months after birth, the high-risk newborn should be monitored at 12 and 18 months postpartum with measurements of anti-HIV IgG.

Epidemiology

In individuals 25 to 44 years old, HIV infection was the leading cause of death among men, and the fourth among women in 1992. 339,250 cases of AIDS and 201,775 AIDS-related deaths were reported from 1981 to 1993. More than 50% of the AIDS cases have been associated with male homosexual transmission and 24% with contaminated intravenous drug abuse (IVDA) equipment. The early spread of HIV disease in the U.S. occurred predominantly among homosexual men, IV drug users, and patients receiving contaminated blood products. While these modes of transmission still contribute significantly (except for blood products) to the spread of HIV, intensive community awareness programs promoting monogamous sexual activity, the use of condoms, and needle exchange programs have decreased the number of new cases of HIV infection. A decrease in the number of reported AIDS cases over the last three years has been attributed to decreases in the number of cases among gay men and IV drug abusers, and to increased heterosexual transmission of HIV (but not AIDS) to females and infants. While the number of cases due to heterosexual transmission has steadily increased in all regions of the U.S., the most dramatic increases from 1988 to 1992 have occurred in the South. The major source of HIV infection for women has been sexual contact with a male IV drug abuser; and in many cases, the women have had multiple sexual partners. As of October 1993, 4906 pediatric AIDS cases and 2615 AIDS-related deaths among children less than 13 years old were reported. Most of these cases have been attributed to perinatal transmission. The epidemiology among children is similar to that in women, and occurs 15 and 5 times more often among black and Hispanic children respectively, compared to white children. AIDS among blacks and Hispanics is about three to four times greater than among whites. For both black and Hispanic men, the more common method of HIV exposure is through homosexual contact (42% to 45% of cases) with IV drug abusers accounting for 36% and 38%, respectively.

The earlier identification of HIV-infected individuals along with earlier use of antiretroviral therapy and antibiotic prophylaxis for

Table 68.2	Conditions Included in the 1993 Surveillance Case Definition

Category A
Asymptomatic HIV Infection
Persistent generalized lymphadenopathy
Acute HIV Infection with accompanying illness or history of HIV infection

Category B
Bacillary angiomatosis
Candidiasis, oropharyngeal (thrush)
Candidiasis, vulvovaginal; persistent, frequent, or poorly responsive to treatment
Cervical dysplasia/carcinoma *in situ*
Constitutional symptoms, such as fever >38 °C or diarrhea >1 month
Hairy leukoplakia
Herpes zoster (shingles), involving at least 2 distinct episodes or more than 1 dermatome
Idiopathic thrombocytopenia purpura
Listeriosis
Pelvic inflammatory disease, particularly if complicated by tubo-ovarian abscess
Peripheral neuropathy

Category C
Candidiasis of bronchi, trachea, or lungs
Candidiasis, esophageal
Cervical cancer, invasive
Coccidioidomycosis, disseminated or extrapulmonary
Cryptococcosis, extrapulmonary
Cryptosporidiosis, chronic intestinal (>1 month)
Cytomegalovirus disease (other than liver, spleen, or nodes)
Cytomegalovirus retinitis (with loss of vision)
Encephalopathy, HIV-related
Herpes simplex: chronic ulcer(s) (>1 month); or bronchitis, pneumonitis, or esophagitis
Histoplasmosis, disseminated or extrapulmonary
Isosporiasis, chronic intestinal (>1 month duration)
Kaposi sarcoma
Lymphoid interstitial pneumonia and/or pulmonary lymphoid hyperplasia[a]
Lymphoma, Burkitt's (or equivalent term)
Lymphoma, immunoblastic (or equivalent term)
Lymphoma, primary, of brain
Mycobacterium avium-intracellulare complex or *M. kansasii*, disseminated or extrapulmonary
Mycobacterium tuberculosis, any site (pulmonary[b] or extrapulmonary)
Mycobacterium, other species or unidentified species, disseminated or extrapulmonary
Pneumocystis carinii pneumonia
Pneumonia, recurrent[b]
Progressive multifocal leukoencephalopathy
Salmonella septicemia, recurrent
Toxoplasmosis of brain
Wasting syndrome due to HIV

[a] Children <13 yr old.
[b] Added in the 1993 expansions of the AIDS surveillance case definition for adolescents and adults.

PCP also has contributed to the decline in the number of AIDS cases. However, without continued public education on prevention of HIV transmission, the incidence of newly diagnosed cases of HIV infection could again increase.

Prognosis

The prognosis of HIV disease is most appropriately described by considering the stage of disease at the time of presentation, the presence of cofactors that accelerate disease progression, the nutritional status of patients, and the compliance behavior of a patient when antiretroviral therapy is prescribed. Some patients can remain in a relatively stable state for an undefined period of time. The disease course generally is characterized by intermittent episodes of acute opportunistic infection, sometimes requiring hospitalization. Outpatient and home-based therapies for PCP prophylaxis and treatment, as well as the use of indwelling catheters for the outpatient administration of other antivirals (e.g., ganciclovir, foscarnet), parenteral nutrition, and chemotherapy also have impacted on the changing nature of long-term HIV management. While some patients live longer as a result of antiretroviral therapy and antibiotic prophylaxis for opportunistic infections, the disease is generally fatal. Once the CD4+ cell count declines and opportunistic infections or malignancy begin to occur, the fatality rate accelerates.

Therapeutic Goals

The integration of proviral DNA into human DNA and the resultant chronic intracellular infection establish the need for lifelong treatment of HIV disease. The major therapeutic goal of antiretroviral treatment is the suppression of viral replication to an extent which will slow the eventual decline in the total number of CD4+ lymphocytes. In addition, the development of opportunistic infection or malignancy requires that therapeutic goals be modified throughout the course of treatment based upon the changing clinical status of the patient.[34–37]

Surrogate Markers

The effectiveness of zidovudine in patients with HIV infection was first demonstrated in patients who were at more advanced stages of disease [i.e., those with AIDS or AIDS-related complex (ARC)]. The primary endpoints of this study were progression of ARC to AIDS and mortality.[38] Since mortality is no longer a feasible endpoint for drug studies, surrogate markers of antiretroviral activity have been adopted as a means of evaluating new therapies. The acceptance of surrogate markers of anti-HIV activity as therapeutic endpoints is based upon the assumption that drugs which elicit favorable surrogate marker changes will decrease mortality from HIV disease.[21,39] While this issue remains controversial, surrogate markers continue to be used for both investigational and clinical decision making.[40–46] Data from the Concorde study, however, suggest that drug-induced short-term increases in CD4+ lymphocyte count in asymptomatic patients may not translate into a long-term clinical benefit.[47]

The primary surrogate marker that has been used is the *CD4+ lymphocyte count.* The CD4+ cell count is obtained by determining the percentage of lymphocytes counted in the differential of a total leukocyte count which are CD4+ (determined by flow cytometry). A limitation of the CD4+ cell count is the considerable interlaboratory variability (although within the same laboratory, the results are often reliable). There is also a diurnal variation which leads to changes in the count within a patient if sampled at different times of the day. Furthermore, the measurement of trends in the CD4+ cell count represents the later stages of the process of HIV replication, after HIV has spread to noninfected CD4+ lymphocytes, and their ultimate removal from the circulation has occurred. With regard to evaluating new antiretrovirals, the use of the CD4+ cell count has been highly criticized, but it remains a standard measurement for all new investigational drug protocols. Some investigators have suggested that a beneficial increment in the CD4+ cell count can be used as a pharmacodynamic marker with which drug exposure may be correlated.[48]

In contrast, another surrogate marker, the serum concentration of p24 antigen (an HIV core protein), also has been used routinely in both *in vitro* and clinical research protocols as a measure of viral replication. Since p24 is a viral core protein, circulating p24 is thought to be proportional to HIV replication (i.e., increased p24 concentrations reflect higher levels of replication). Likewise, re-

ductions in p24 concentrations following antiretroviral therapy are considered a marker of anti-HIV activity. The prevalence of p24 antigenemia is related to the stage of HIV disease. For example, as few as 20% to 30% of patients may have detectable p24 before the initiation of zidovudine therapy at a CD4+ count of less than 500 cells/mm³. Furthermore, the clinical significance of p24 antigenemia is questionable because no correlation could be found between p24 antigenemia and survival in several studies. This test is still not approved for routine use on a clinical basis, despite the fact that many Phase I/II studies have used it as a primary surrogate marker endpoint of antiviral activity.[49–52] Since p24 may circulate as antigen-antibody complexes, a modification of the p24 antigen test includes a dissociation step. While antibody dissociation appears to increase the sensitivity of the assay, further investigation is needed to document the role for this test.[53,54]

Other antiretroviral surrogate markers such as weight loss, Karnofsky score (a rating system which quantitates well being), β₂ microglobulin serum concentration (a marker of immune activation), and neopterin (a product of macrophage metabolism) have been utilized. While none of these markers alone has been studied extensively enough to provide a basis for selecting one marker over another, it is plausible that a combination of markers may be better than any one alone.[55–62] More recent progress in the area of markers of antiviral activity during antiretroviral therapy includes assays that use the polymerase chain reaction (PCR) to detect HIV RNA in plasma or HIV DNA in circulating lymphocytes.[63–66] Also quantitative microculture techniques are being evaluated as a measure of viral burden within an individual.[58–61,67–69]

In summary, the use of surrogate markers for antiretroviral activity has been an evolutionary process with considerable overlap between clinical and research application of the different tests. Unfortunately, the inclusion of numerous surrogate marker tests in any given clinical protocol becomes very expensive, thus limiting the ability of researchers to compare the markers at different stages of disease.

Pharmacotherapy of HIV Infection

The classification of antiretroviral agents for HIV infection is primarily based upon the stage of the life cycle which is interrupted by the therapeutic intervention (see Figure 68.1). As can be seen in Figure 68.1, the primary steps in the life cycle include: 1) viral binding to cell surface receptors; 2) viral entry and uncoating; 3) transcription to DNA via the action of viral reverse transcriptase; 4) integration into the host DNA via the action of viral integrase; 5) transcription of the proviral DNA to mRNA and viral RNA and the translation of other viral proteins; 6) glycosylation of viral proteins; 7) viral assembly; and 8) budding of new viral particles through the host cell membrane (a time during which the action of HIV protease is evident). Each of these stages is currently under investigation in order to examine the potential value at each point of interference with HIV replication.[37]

Viral Binding to Cell Surface Receptors

Although not thought to be the exclusive mechanism, the binding of the HIV membrane glycoprotein (gp120) to cells expressing the CD4+ molecule is thought to be a primary mechanism of viral entry. Interference with this binding interaction has been exploited as a means of decreasing viral attachment to cells, and thus decreasing the spread of CD4+ cell infection.[70,71] The recombinant DNA technology needed to produce CD4+ receptor analogs was developed rapidly and a pharmaceutical preparation for clinical evaluation was produced quickly. However, the lack of beneficial effect following the intravenous administration of the recombinant soluble CD4+ (rsCD4+) molecule, as judged by a lack of sur-rogate marker response, was disappointing enough to slow the clin-ical research effort with this family of antiretrovirals.[72–74] Struc-tural modifications were made to the rsCD4+ molecule in order to establish a more favorable pharmacokinetic profile [i.e., longer plasma half-life ($t^{1/2}$)] and continuous intravenous infusions also were evaluated.[75] In addition, cellular toxins have been linked to rsCD4+ molecules in an attempt to target HIV-infected cells. The products which remain under clinical investigation are primarily CD4+ analogs with a linked cellular toxin for which the goal is to target HIV-infected cells expressing viral gp120. The CD4+ analogs bind to the HIV-infected cell, enter these cells and release the accompanying cellular toxin. Clinical studies of this approach are underway. rsCD4+ is synergistic with nucleoside analog RT inhibitors *in vitro*[76,77] and as a result clinical trials are planned which will investigate combined treatment with RT inhibitors. Un-fortunately, one study of rsCD4+ and didanosine found little anti-viral activity as judged by surrogate marker responses.[75]

Reverse Transcriptase (RT) Inhibitors

Nucleoside Analogs

Zidovudine (ZDV). The primary target of antiretroviral therapy has been and remains the administration of drugs that inhibit the HIV reverse transcriptase enzyme which is responsible for cata-lyzing the transcription of viral RNA to DNA.[37,78–80] The unique nature of the RT and relative selectivity of these compounds for HIV RT compared to human polymerase enzymes, has made this enzyme an attractive target for antiretroviral drug development.[81] The first RT inhibitor approved for the treatment of HIV infection was zidovudine [(ZDV) formerly azidothymidine, (AZT)], a thy-midine analog which acts as a chain terminator and/or a compe-titive antagonist. Zidovudine is available orally and following administration undergoes extensive and variable first-pass metabo-lism.[82] Zidovudine, which reaches the systemic circulation, is ap-proximately 30% bound to plasma proteins.[83] Unbound zidovudine distributes throughout body tissues with a volume of distribution of 1 to 1.5 L/kg. The serum to cerebrospinal fluid (CSF) ratio is approximately 0.2. Upon entry into cells zidovudine interacts with cellular kinases which catalyze its phosphorylation to the mono-, di-, and tri-phosphate form. While it is the zidovudine-triphosphate which is the active antiretroviral compound (intracellular half-life of ≈3 to 4 hours), the rate-limiting step is the conversion of the mono- to di-phosphate form.[84] This step also may play a role in the myelosuppressive effects of zidovudine, since the accumulation of the monophosphate may decrease the *de novo* synthesis of thy-midine triphosphate as well, resulting in reduced host DNA syn-thesis.[84]

Hepatic glucuronidation is the primary metabolic pathway for zidovudine, with a minor amount of zidovudine metabolized via oxidative metabolism to aminothymidine.[82,85,86] Up to 30% of a dose may be recovered in the urine as unchanged zidovudine. The plasma half-life of zidovudine is one to two hours. However, longer half-life values have been noted with prolonged sampling periods and the use of a more sensitive assay method (radioim-munoassay).[87] The disposition of zidovudine has been studied in patients undergoing hemodialysis and peritoneal dialysis. In gen-eral, the zidovudine half-life is not influenced by either dialysis method. However, the plasma half-life of zidovudine glucuronide (an inactive metabolite) is markedly prolonged.[88–91] The phar-macokinetics of zidovudine also have been evaluated using pop-ulation-based methods which employ nonlinear mixed-effect mod-eling (NONMEM). Using this technique, Gitterman et al. were able to derive a population clearance from their cohort of patients which was similar to clearance values obtained from traditional phar-macokinetic studies.[92]

The initial clinical use of zidovudine was primarily in patients with more advanced disease, ARC and AIDS. The significant de-crease in mortality among patients treated with zidovudine prompted the switching of placebo-treated patients to zidovu-

Table 68.3		Currently Approved Nucleoside Analog Reverse Transcriptase Inhibitors				
Drug	Active Form	Dosage[a]	Dosage Formulation[a]	Adverse Effects[a]	Pharmacokinetic Characteristics[a]	Resistance
Zidovudine	ZDV-triphosphate	*Adult*: 100 mg Q 4 hr *Pediatric*: 180 mg/m² PO Q 6 hr	10 mg cap, 50 mg/mL syrup (for pediatric use)	Anemia, neutropenia, myopathy (uncommon), hepatitis (uncommon), nail pigmentation	Variable bioavailability (mean: ≈65%), low protein binding, hepatic glucuronidation (major), aminothymidine (minor), 10%–30% unchanged in urine, CSF/plasma ≈0.2	Noted after prolonged dosing, up to 100 × ↓ in susceptibility
Didanosine	Dideoxy-adenosine triphosphate	*Adult*: 200 mg Q 12 hr if >60 kg; 125 mg Q 12 hr if <60 kg *Pediatric*: 100 mg/m² PO Q 12 hr	25, 50, 100, 150 mg tab; powder for PO 10 mg/mL solution (for pediatric use)	Pancreatitis, peripheral neuropathy, GI discomfort, hyperuricemia	Variable bioavailability (mean: ≈40%), metabolized to hypoxanthine→uric acid, 10%–20% unchanged in urine, mineral protein binding, CSF/plasma ≈0.2	Noted in patients after prolonged use, however zidovudine susceptibility returns
Zalcitabine	Zalcitabine triphosphate	*Adult*: 0.75 mg Q 8 hr *Pediatric*: 0.005–0.01 mg/kg PO Q 8 hr	0.375, 0.75 mg tab; 0.1 mg/mL syrup (for pediatric use)	Peripheral neuropathy, oral ulcers, pancreatitis (rarely)	Good bioavailability (mean: ≈85%), primarily excreted in urine unchanged, CSF/plasma ≈0.2	Primarily noted *in vitro*
Stavudine	D4T-triphosphate	*Adult*: 40 mg BID if >60 kg; 30 mg BID if <60 kg; Cl$_{Cr}$: 26–50 mL/min 20 mg BID (15 mg BID if <60 kg); Cl$_{Cr}$: 10–25 mL/min 20 mg BID (15 mg BID if <60 kg) *Pediatric*: Data not available	15, 20, 30, 40 mg cap	Peripheral neuropathy	Good bioavailability (mean: ≈86%), ≈40% unchanged in urine	Data not available

[a] cap = Capsule; Cl$_{Cr}$ = Creatinine clearance; CSF = Cerebrospinal fluid; GI = Gastrointestinal; tab = Tablet.

dine.[93,94] Subsequent studies have sought to evaluate the role of zidovudine among patients with less advanced disease and also to examine the efficacy of reduced daily dosages (500 to 600 mg/day versus 1200 mg/day) which yielded similar surrogate marker changes.[95-99] Despite the encouraging findings from these important clinical trials, the Concorde study did not support the beneficial effects of zidovudine in patients with early HIV disease[47] and the AIDS in Europe study group found that the beneficial effect on mortality was not evident after two years of zidovudine in patients with AIDS even though they had a higher CD4+ cell count.[100] As a result of these often confusing developments, guidelines adopted by the Agency for Health Care Policy and Research provide an overview of consideration for the management of early HIV infection.[101]

The evaluation of lower daily doses of zidovudine was prompted by intolerable hematologic toxicity (anemia, neutropenia) which was noted among many patients receiving higher doses,[102] and less toxicity at the lower daily doses.[99,103,104,104] Other adverse effects of zidovudine include headache, nausea, nail pigmentation, and myopathy. While the myopathy is relatively uncommon, it is an important clinical symptom to monitor for since reversal requires discontinuation of zidovudine. Serum concentrations of creatine kinase often are elevated before the onset of clinical manifestations of the myopathy, and have been attributed to zidovudine's affinity for enzymes within skeletal muscle.[105,106] Interestingly, HIV also may play a role in inducing an underlying autoimmune event resembling myositis, which may contribute to the myotoxic effects of zidovudine. Lastly, cardiomyopathy also has been reported.[107-109]

As monotherapy with "low-dose" zidovudine became the accepted initial drug therapy for most HIV-infected patients with a CD4+ cell count less than 500 cells/mm^3, an increasing awareness that clinical deterioration may occur among certain patients with more advanced disease while on zidovudine for longer than 12 to 18 months arose. In addition, the identification of resistant HIV isolates among patients receiving chronic zidovudine was observed. These findings have prompted researchers to intensify their efforts to identify alternative antiretrovirals (see below).

Didanosine (ddI). The second agent which gained a qualified FDA approval was didanosine (ddI, originally dideoxyinosine).[110,111] Didanosine is a purine nucleoside analog RT inhibitor, which is active intracellularly as dideoxyadenosine triphosphate (ddATP). The intracellular half-life of ddATP is approximately 12 to 24 hours, in contrast to zidovudine triphosphate which is three to four hours. Thus, didanosine has been dosed on a less frequent schedule despite the fact that it has a similar plasma half-life (1 to 1.5 hours) to zidovudine.[112,113] Didanosine is also less potent than zidovudine with an IC$_{50}$ of 2.5 to 10 μM (compared to <1 μM for zidovudine)[114] and demonstrates synergy with other nucleoside analogs and non-nucleoside reverse transcriptase inhibitors.

The CSF/plasma ratio of didanosine is 0.1, and animal studies suggest that CNS uptake may be dose dependent and increased by probenecid.[115,116] Didanosine is primarily metabolized to uric acid with up to 50% excreted renally as parent drug.[117,118] Didanosine has been measured in fetal body fluids during times when the mother was receiving didanosine.[119] Didanosine is acid-labile and requires a buffered formulation to ensure sufficient bioavailability. Interestingly, no influence on bioavailability was noted when combined with ranitidine.[120] A number of different formulations have been studied.[121] The tablet formulation is a buffered tablet which provides either 25 or 100 mg/tablet. The buffered formulations are associated with gastrointestinal intolerance and may decrease the absorption of other drugs which require an acidic gastric milieu such as dapsone, atevirdine, and delavirdine.[122-124] Didanosine

therapy is associated with anti-HIV activity as documented by a decline in serum p24 antigen and an increase in CD4+ cell counts.[43,52,125-127] Didanosine is a viable alternative for patients who previously were on zidovudine.[128,129] However, didanosine has a markedly different toxicity profile from zidovudine, with *pancreatitis* and *peripheral neuropathy* among the more severe adverse effects which require close monitoring during chronic therapy.[130-133] Other adverse effects include retinal toxicity,[134,135] nephrotoxicity,[136] heart failure,[137] hepatic failure,[138] and Stevens-Johnson syndrome.[139] Didanosine should be prescribed according to the patient's weight (tablet formulation: 125 mg Q 12 hr <60 kg; 200 mg Q 12 hr >60 kg) and this agent should be used cautiously in patients with renal impairment, prior hepatitis, pancreatitis, or peripheral neuropathy. The concurrent administration of didanosine with oral ganciclovir results in a significant enhancement of didanosine effect even when didanosine is administered two hours before ganciclovir.[641] Patients receiving didanosine and oral ganciclovir may be at higher risk of toxicity. Patients receiving didanosine should be monitored every two to four weeks during the initial three months of didanosine therapy by measuring serum concentrations of amylase, lipase, liver enzymes, and uric acid. Pancreatitis and neuropathy are related more to cumulative dose and systemic exposure of didanosine.[140] Therefore, as patients enter into prolonged therapy they should be educated to contact their provider if any signs of neuropathy or abdominal pain develop. The variable bioavailability which is characteristic of didanosine makes it difficult to predict which patients are at greatest risk for pancreatitis or neuropathy since therapeutic monitoring is not done in the clinical setting.[48,141,142] Patients should receive a thorough physical examination at each clinic visit closely assessing peripheral extremities for paresthesias or pain and the abdomen for pain and discomfort. Didanosine should be discontinued at the first sign of peripheral neuropathy or pancreatitis until resolved. In certain patients who have resolved their neuropathy or pancreatitis, the drug can be restarted at one half the dose (or lower) and the patient followed closely. Peripheral neuropathy and pancreatitis also may be a manifestation solely of HIV disease.[143]

Zalcitabine (ddC). The third nucleoside analog RT inhibitor to gain conditional approval for HIV infection was zalcitabine (ddC, dideoxycytidine).[36,144] Zalcitabine is the most potent *in vitro* inhibitor of the approved nucleoside analog RT inhibitors. It is approved for use in combination with zidovudine in patients with a CD4+ cell count less than 300 cells/mm^3 and also is available as monotherapy through an expanded access program. The reason for this type of indication is that the value of zalcitabine as a single agent remains to be clarified. When zidovudine, zalcitabine, and the combination of zidovudine and zalcitabine were administered to zidovudine "naive" patients, beneficial effects of zalcitabine monotherapy were not evident.[145] In another study, zalcitabine was as effective as didanosine as monotherapy in patients who were previously treated with zidovudine. The patient outcomes in both groups were suboptimal, with considerable patient withdrawal during long-term therapy primarily due to drug toxicity.[146] Thus, the exact role for zalcitabine monotherapy remains to be clarified.

Zalcitabine is the most well absorbed of the three nucleoside analog RT inhibitors, with approximately 90% bioavailability after oral dosing.[147] Zalcitabine also requires intracellular phosphorylation and the intracellular half-life of ddCTP (≈1 to 2 hours) is similar to zidovudine. Zalcitabine is one of the most potent *in vitro* inhibitors of HIV replication.[148,149] While early studies which were hampered by the development of severe peripheral neuropathy utilized relatively high doses of zalcitabine, more recent studies have indicated that an initial dose of zalcitabine of 0.75 mg every eight hours generally is well tolerated. Zalcitabine is predominantly renally excreted in unchanged form and, therefore, must be used cautiously in patients with renal impairment. There is no information describing the influence of dialysis on zalcitabine clearance, primarily because of assay limitations which preclude measurement of zalcitabine at very low concentrations in dialysate. Zalcitabine also is associated with peripheral neuropathy and to a lesser extent pancreatitis, rashes, oral aphthous ulcers, esophageal ulceration, and ototoxicity.[150–154] Patients developing any of these toxicities should have the drug discontinued until resolution, and be restarted at one half the daily dose (or lower) with close clinical monitoring or be given another agent. *In vitro* resistance has been observed to zalcitabine with a mutation noted which confers cross resistance to didanosine.[155]

Stavudine (D4T) was synthesized in an attempt to provide a thymidine analog (similar to zidovudine) which was less myelosuppressive. Stavudine (Zerit) is less toxic to some cell culture lines *in vitro*, and only minimal hematologic suppression has occurred during clinical trials. However, stavudine is neurotoxic and peripheral neuropathy occurs when doses are greater than 2.0 mg/kg/day. Stavudine is relatively well absorbed with approximately 30% to 40% excreted renally as the parent compound: the plasma half-life is 1 to 1.6 hours.

Stavudine has been approved for patients who experienced toxicity or disease progression with other therapies, and for patients with contraindications to other therapies. In a phase 3, multicenter, double-blind trial, patients who were previously receiving zidovudine for at least 24 weeks were randomized to receive either continued zidovudine (200 mg TID) or stavudine 40 mg twice a day if greater than 60 kg (30 mg BID if <60 kg). Among 359 patients the mean change in CD4+ count from baseline at 12 weeks was +22 cells/mm^3 (range: −185 to +375) for the stavudine group and −22 cells/mm^3 (range: −215 to +430) for the patients continued on zidovudine. In a randomized double-blind parallel track program, stavudine 20 mg twice daily was compared to 40 mg twice daily for patients weighing more than 60 kg. These doses were weight-adjusted to 15 or 30 mg twice daily if body weight was 40 to 60 kg and to 10 or 20 mg twice daily for patients less than 40 kg. All of these patients had a CD4+ count less than 300 cells/mm^3 and had failed, were intolerant of, or had contraindications to zidovudine or didanosine. The patient population was predominantly white males who had received prolonged treatment with zidovudine (99% for a median duration of 91 weeks) or didanosine (98% for a median duration of 22 weeks). An interim analysis in approximately 9000 patients who had received stavudine for a median duration of 18 weeks indicated that the 40 week survival rates were similar among both groups. Combination studies of stavudine with other RT inhibitors and agents which act at other sites in HIV life cycle are in progress.

Lamivudine [3-Thiacytidine (3-TC)], an investigational cytidine analog RT inhibitor, appears to be well tolerated, and the combination of 3-TC with zidovudine has beneficial effects on CD4+ count and viral burden.

Current Considerations for Antiretroviral Trials

As mentioned above, clinical research with zidovudine has continued and led to studies which support the use of lower daily doses, and up until the release of the Concorde study results, also its use in patients who are still relatively asymptomatic (i.e., CD4+ cell count <500/mm^3). The identification of HIV isolates with decreased susceptibility to zidovudine, and the data from the Concorde study, have forced clinical researchers to rethink the timing of initiation of zidovudine therapy. For example, if zidovudine

resistance develops after prolonged administration, should treatment be withheld until later stages of the disease? This is balanced by the more recent findings that HIV may be replicating in lymph nodes during early stages of disease when the CD4+ cell count is still elevated and stable. Lastly, the evaluation of new antiretrovirals must now occur within the setting of patients who are ''zidovudine-naive'' or ''zidovudine-experienced.'' This aspect of prior exposure to zidovudine is important when evaluating both susceptibility changes and surrogate marker responses to investigational RT inhibitors. For example, in one study, zalcitabine was compared to zidovudine in patients who had previously been on zidovudine. While seemingly beneficial effects were noted among the patients switched to zalcitabine compared to those who continued on zidovudine, statistically significant differences were not observed (possibly due to the small sample size).[145] Two studies compared a switch to didanosine or continued zidovudine among patients either receiving greater than 16 weeks of zidovudine or with documented clinical deterioration while on zidovudine in patients with advanced HIV disease.[128,156] In patients switched from zidovudine to 500 mg/day of didanosine, the rate of disease progression was slower.[128] Thus, consideration of prior antiretroviral therapy is now an established criterion for the development of new protocols evaluating RT inhibitors. An algorithm for approaching antiretroviral therapy in HIV-infected patients is presented in Figure 68.3.

Nonnucleoside Reverse Transcriptionase (RT) Inhibitors (NNRTIs)

Compounds which inhibit RT activity but are not nucleoside analogs are referred to as non-nucleoside RT inhibitors.[160,161] These compounds are chemically diverse yet have in common the ability to act as allosteric inhibitors of RT. Some examples of NNRTIs are tetrahydroimidazole-benzodiazepin (TIBO) compounds, pyridinone derivatives (L-697,661), a dipyridodiazepinone (nevirapine), and bisheteroarylpiperazines (atevirdine and delavirdine).[160,162,163] The initial enthusiasm for NNRTIs was due to their relatively broad *in vitro* therapeutic range.[164,165] That is, the concentration of NNRTI which decreased HIV replication by 50% (i.e., the IC_{50}) was much lower than the concentration which was toxic to the cell line into which the virus was infected. Phase I studies of these agents given as monotherapy yielded positive results with regard to surrogate marker changes over a four week period. However, after four weeks of NNRTI alone, the beneficial surrogate marker changes subsided and returned toward baseline values.[166] These changes also were associated with changes in drug susceptibility, thus providing intriguing data which indicate the importance of decreasing HIV susceptibility during antiretroviral therapy. These discouraging results led certain manufacturers to abandon the development of some non-nucleoside reverse transcriptionase inhibitors. On the other hand, an incentive for continued development is that NNRTIs appear to be well tolerated with the major therapy-limiting toxicity being the development of rash with or without hepatic enzyme elevation.[167,168] Another interesting aspect of the NNRTIs is that their pharmacokinetics are much more complex than the nucleoside analogs. While NNRTIs do not require intracellular phosphorylation to be active, they tend to be highly protein bound, have capacity-limited metabolism, and may induce their own metabolism.[87,169]

Continued interest in this area has prompted renewed research of NNRTIs, specifically, when combined with nucleoside analog RT inhibitors. Nevirapine, atevirdine, and delavirdine are examples of NNRTIs which are currently in Phase II/III evaluation (see below).

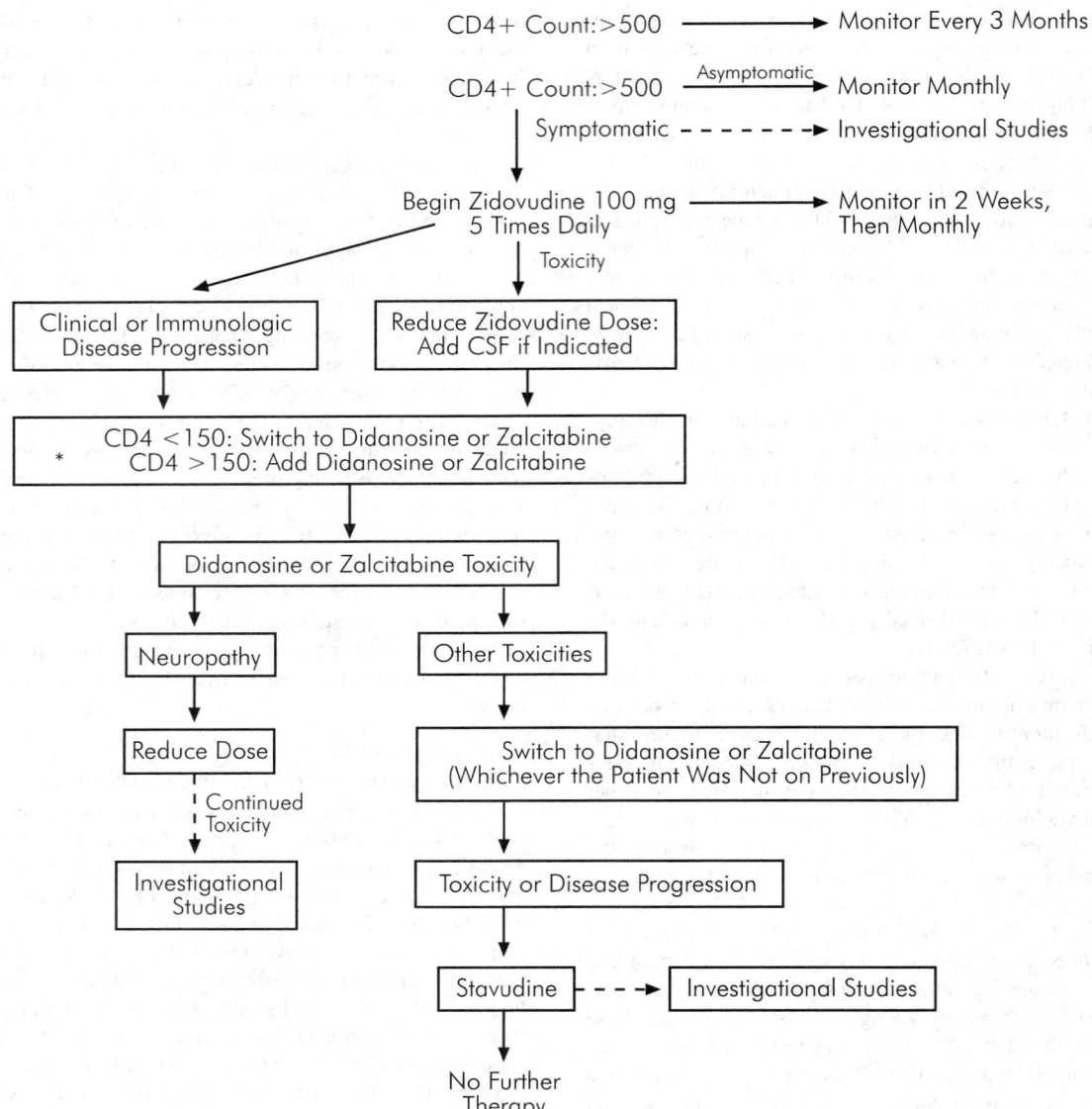

Fig 68.3   Algorithm For Antiretroviral Therapy with the Currently Approved Therapies   The decision to switch or add these agents depends upon the individual patient situation and concurrent clinical considerations.

Protease Inhibitors

The HIV protease (an aspartyl protease) is crucial to the successful life cycle of HIV. The *gag* and *pol* regions of the HIV genome are translated into larger polyproteins which are later cleaved at specific enzymatic sites to yield the virion core structural proteins (p17, p24, p15, p9, and p6) and the *pol* enzymatic proteins characteristic of the mature virion. For example, the polyprotein, Pr160*gag-pol* contains the gag structural proteins, followed by RT/ribonuclease H, and the integrase enzyme. For each of these proteins to become available to perform their biologic function, the protease enzyme must first cleave each of the proteins into its mature and active form. Therefore, inhibition of this protease enzyme would be expected to be useful in combating HIV.

Protease inhibitors (at nM concentrations) have demonstrated *in vitro* additive or synergistic activity with zidovudine, zalcitabine, and interferon-alpha. Studies of combination therapy with protease inhibitors and nucleoside analogs are ongoing; however, the bioavailability of oral formulations of these protease inhibitors has been a problem.

European studies of *saquinavir* 25 to 600 mg three times daily in patients with, and without, prior zidovudine exposure and CD4+ counts of either less than 500 cells/mm^3 or lower (50 to 250 cells/mm^3) observed the greatest increases in CD4+ counts in patients who received the higher doses (600 mg). As a result of the positive findings in the European trials, the first U.S. trial (ACTG 229) compared a triple drug regimen of saquinavir (600 mg TID), zalcitabine (0.75 mg TID), and zidovudine (200 mg TID) to saquinavir 600 mg three times daily plus zidovudine and zidovudine plus zalcitabine in patients with extensive prior zidovudine treatment. The clinical outcomes of the study were based upon immunologic (CD4+ count) and virologic (quantitative microculture to assess viral load) parameters. Both the double drug groups had similar, favorable responses, but the triple drug group had even better improvements in CD4+ count, time to return to baseline CD4+ count, and quantitative viral studies. Further study of saquinavir, as well as protease inhibitors by other pharmaceutical companies, is currently underway.

Gene Regulating Compounds

Research into the molecular biology of the stages of proviral transcription and translation have identified the mechanisms for synthesis of both regulatory proteins and structural proteins. The *Tat* gene product is intimately involved in many steps which control virus gene expression.[172] In addition to gene expression, Tat plays a role in regulating certain cellular processes, and enhances the growth of Kaposi's sarcoma-derived tissue by acting as a growth factor or cytokine.[173] For these reasons, and other possible roles for *Tat*, attempts have been made to identify compounds which act as Tat antagonists. The second important regulatory protein is the regulator of gene expression.[649] The primary role of *Rev* is thought to be in mediating the export of viral mRNA from the nucleus to the cytoplasm. These intracellular observations have led researchers to pursue the development of compounds which inhibit these events and to date at least one *Tat* antagonist has entered initial clinical testing.[174] It is hoped that a better understanding of the nuclear events involved in HIV replication will lead to novel drugs which can interrupt the retroviral life cycle.

Drugs acting at other stages of the life cycle with enzymatic activity such as glycosylation of viral surface glycoproteins (i.e., glycosidase) and integration of viral DNA into host DNA (i.e., integrase) also are being studied.[175] Glycosylation of the HIV envelope protein is required in order for the virus to be able to bind its receptor, the CD4+ protein. Mutations which result in decreased glycosylation or viruses exposed to glycosylation inhibitors yield viral particles with deficient fusogenic activity and reduced specific infectivity.[176] The first glycosylation inhibitor to enter clinical trial was castanospermine, an agent which proved to have excessive toxicity. Another glycosidase inhibitor, N-butyl deoxynojirimycin, has less cytotoxicity and is currently under clinical investigation.

Reverse Transcriptase (RT) Inhibitors

Combination Therapy

Nucleoside Analog/Nucleoside Analog. One new approach to HIV therapy with nucleoside analog RT inhibitors has been to pursue the use of combination regimens.[97] The rationale for combining two nucleoside analogs is based upon the following: 1) combinations of nucleoside analogs often demonstrate synergistic antiretroviral activity *in vitro*;[177,178] 2) different nucleoside analogs have nonoverlapping toxicities; 3) nucleoside analogs have different intracellular metabolic profiles (i.e., phosphorylation); 4) patients may be infected with different strains of HIV with varying susceptibilities; and 5) isolates from patients receiving long-term zidovudine who are switched to didanosine have their resistant genotype revert back to zidovudine-sensitive suggesting that combination therapy may suppress resistant strains.[179] Initial studies of zidovudine and zalcitabine in combination or in alternating regimens were inspired by the clinical intolerance of higher doses of zalcitabine and the initial hematologic toxicity when higher doses of zidovudine were prescribed (i.e., >1200 mg/day). In general, studies of combined zidovudine and zalcitabine in lower doses than prescribed for each drug alone found that beneficial surrogate marker responses can be attained with reduced drug toxicity.[180,181] However, the combination of zidovudine and zalcitabine has only been approved with the currently recommended zidovudine dose of 100 mg every four hours.

The combination of ZDV and ddI also has been evaluated in two large clinical trials with encouraging results obtained with regard to surrogate marker responses and reduced drug toxicity.[182–184] However, except for the zidovudine/zalcitabine regimen that has been approved, the efficacy of other combination nucleoside analog treatments remains to be further investigated.

Nucleoside Analog/Nonnucleoside Analog. Emerging *in vitro* data have indicated that the NNRTIs are synergistic with nucleoside analog RT inhibitors.[185] As a result of the data on synergy, interest in NNRTIs has been rekindled and many clinical studies have been undertaken to evaluate the antiretroviral activity attained from this combination of antivirals. In addition, *in vitro* findings suggest that the use of three drug combinations may enhance the likelihood that nonreplicating mutations of HIV emerge over time.[186] This observation has led to the design of triple drug protocols which are currently underway. These studies are investigating zidovudine, didanosine, and nevirapine; zidovudine, didanosine, and atevirdine; and zidovudine, didanosine, and delavirdine.

Resistance to Reverse Transcriptase Inhibitors

Recently, it has been suggested that clinical deterioration after prolonged zidovudine may be contributed to the development of decreased antiviral susceptibility. While multiple factors may contribute to a decrease in antiretroviral effect (see Table 68.3), the exact contribution of HIV resistance remains to be clarified. With regard to RT inhibitors, the development of decreased HIV susceptibility during monotherapy has emerged as a possible factor.[187–189] A majority of the experience with resistant HIV isolates has been with patients receiving long-term zidovudine. Although there also have been reports of patients with primary HIV infection due to zidovudine resistant isolates.[190–192] Information obtained from patients taking zidovudine as well as from *in vitro* studies employing site-directed mutagenesis indicates that mutations which result in alterations in amino acid residues at different sites in the RT gene can result in up to a 100-fold decrease in HIV susceptibility to zidovudine.

The primary codons noted for zidovudine resistance are 67, 70, 215, 219, and 41.[189,193] The use of site-directed mutagenesis to introduce these mutations one at a time results in a stepwise reduction in zidovudine susceptibility with each additional mutation. Individual patients may develop various combinations of these mutations which may lead to additive, synergistic, or antagonistic effects with regard to decreased antiviral susceptibility. Boucher et al. found in patients receiving zidovudine that an increasing number of point mutations at the locus for RT leads to a decreasing susceptibility to zidovudine *in vitro*.[194] Interestingly, the stage of HIV disease seems to play a role in the development of zidovudine-resistant strains. For example in one study, 89% of patients with late-stage disease developed zidovudine-resistance, compared to 31% of asymptomatic patients.[192] Other data suggest that the dose of zidovudine also may contribute in that patients receiving 1200 to 1500 mg/day developed resistance sooner than patients on 500 to 600 mg/day. Furthermore, resistance has been noted among asymptomatic patients on zidovudine during the third year of therapy.[192] The resistance subsides when patients are discontinued from zidovudine. Little cross-resistance has been found for these mutations with other nucleoside analogs (i.e., ddI, ddC). Mutations at residues 74, 135, and 184 have been noted to confer resistance to didanosine and at residue 69 for decreased susceptibility to zalcitabine.

The issue of combination reverse transcriptase inhibitors and the different mutations induced by different nucleoside analogs has become an important clinical and research question. Some data have accumulated which address the issue of HIV resistance patterns among patients who are switched from zidovudine to didanosine. The studies tend to support the following: 1) HIV susceptibility to didanosine decreases somewhat during the course of didanosine therapy; 2) during didanosine treatment, HIV susceptibility to zidovudine returns suggesting that combination therapy with zidovudine and didanosine may prevent the emergence of resistant strains;[195,196] 3) mutations at 184 tend to decrease susceptibility to both didanosine and zalcitabine;[155,197] 4) alternating zidovudine and zalcitabine does not prevent the development of zidovudine resistance; 5) some data suggest that primary infection with HIV resistant to zidovudine may occur; and 6) data are emerging upon which detection of HIV resistance can be correlated with a poorer clinical outcome.

Interestingly, resistance to NNRTIs is commonly associated with a mutation at the 181 site.[198] However, HIV strains obtained from patients receiving both zidovudine and one NNRTI, atevirdine, do not appear to develop the zidovudine resistance mutations at the same rate as in patients taking pyridinone or nevaripine.[168,199] In addition, resistance to delavirdine, which often occurs at 236, appears to enhance the activity of other NNRTIs.[161] Thus, based upon *in vitro* and *in vivo* findings, some data exist which provide a rationale for combining nucleoside analogs as well as nucleoside analogs with an NNRTI.

Lastly, Chow et al. have examined triple drug activity *in vitro* and noted that the combination of zidovudine, didanosine, and an NNRTI leads to the emergence of nonreplicating strains of HIV.[186] These data, along with the synergy data mentioned above, have led to the design of clinical trials which are evaluating triple drug regimens of zidovudine, didanosine, and either atevirdine, delavirdine, or nevirapine.

Nucleoside Analog RT Inhibitor Toxicity

A therapy-limiting aspect of nucleoside analog RT inhibitors is the affinity of these drugs for human DNA polymerase enzymes. For example, zidovudine may elicit bone marrow suppression, myopathy, hepatotoxicity, and esophageal ulceration,[200] while didanosine and zalcitabine induce peripheral neuropathy as a result of DNA polymerase γ-inhibition. An important consideration in evaluating the potential for drug toxicity is the impact of HIV disease progression itself. As the CD4+ cell count declines, patients often develop anemia and neutropenia.[201] HIV disease also is associated with a number of central and peripheral neuropathies.[202] The addition of a nucleoside analog in a patient already manifesting one of these potential adverse effects would seem to be a potential factor for eventual clinical intolerance. For this reason certain investigators advocate prescribing nucleoside analogs early in HIV infection when they are most tolerated. The other side of the issue relates to whether early use elicits resistance and, therefore, early use may decrease the duration of time therapy will be effective. Clearly additional drugs are needed to overcome these problems.

Immunotherapies

Interleukin-2 (Il-2) has been investigated as an agent which may augment the faltering immune system.[203–207] As monotherapy, Il-2 did not result in beneficial effects on CD4+ counts or p24 antigen levels. However, Il-2 has now been studied at higher doses during continuous infusion and in combination with zidovudine and the results appear more promising.[208] However, further studies are needed to examine the role for Il-2. Other immune modulators such as ampligen have appeared promising but have not yielded convincing clinical results.[209]

Interferons, primarily interferon alpha, have been investigated extensively in patients with HIV infection, predominantly among individuals with Kaposi sarcoma (KS). Interferon alpha has demonstrated *in vitro* activity against HIV and is synergistic with zidovudine *in vitro*. Clinical studies have noted that certain patients may attain a partial to complete remission of KS, and demonstrate a beneficial effect on their CD4+ cell count and p24 serum concentration as well. However, the need for parenteral injection, neurologic toxicity, and the additive myelosuppression when combined with zidovudine have made interferon alpha an end-stage therapeutic alternative, except among patients with KS.[210] (See HIV-Associated Malignancies.)

Both granulocyte colony stimulating factors (G-CSF) and granulocyte-macrophage CSF (GM-CSF) have been investigated in HIV-infected patients.[211,212] Both colony stimulating factors are able to increase the granulocyte count in HIV infected patients with primary granulocytopenia from HIV or zidovudine-induced granulocytopenia.[213–215] GM-CSF, secondary to its effects on monocytes/macrophages, may be associated with more adverse effects, probably due to enhanced cytokine release from macrophages. Also, conflicting *in vitro* data indicate that GM-CSF may increase HIV replication in macrophages.[216,217] Therefore, patients receiving GM-CSF also should be receiving an RT inhibitor. Both of these colony stimulating factors can be used to support a patient's bone marrow through periods of concurrent myelosuppressive drug therapy. For example, the use of ganciclovir for cytomegalovirus (CMV) infection often necessitates that zidovudine be discontinued to avoid excessive neutropenia. With the concurrent use of G-CSF or GM-CSF patients may be able to continue their zidovudine along with ganciclovir, thus avoiding the need for entirely stopping antiretroviral therapy.[218] Alternatively, CMV may be treated with foscarnet which also is active against HIV, avoiding the use of two myelosuppressive drugs. Newer CSFs, such as stem cell factor, are being evaluated in HIV-infected patients.[219] Colony stimulating factors also may be able to enhance defective granulocyte function.[220]

Zidovudine is now prescribed at lower daily doses compared to the doses which were used during its initial clinical testing. When higher doses were still being used in patients, the observation that anemia occurred frequently and often was associated with the need for blood transfusion, prompted the evaluation of recombinant erythropoietin for alleviation of zidovudine-induced anemia.[221] Erythropoietin doses of 25 to 50 units/kg subcutaneously (SQ) were effective at increasing the hemoglobin (Hgb) and hematocrit (Hct) among AIDS patients with endogenous erythropoietin plasma concentrations which were less than 500 units/L. The drug was notably less effective when the endogenous levels were greater than 500 units/L. While the incidence of anemia has decreased with the lower doses of zidovudine which are now prescribed, certain patients still may develop anemia and for these patients erythropoietin is a valuable adjunct to therapy which may allow the patient to continue zidovudine.

Monitoring Therapy

Monitoring for efficacy of HIV therapy in patients with early disease is primarily related to routine physical examination of the patient for early signs or symptoms of HIV progression such as lymphadenopathy, oral candidiasis, malignancy, changing neurologic status, or other signs and symptoms of deteriorating immune function. The CD4+ cell count also should be measured at routine clinic visits every four to six months among patients with initial counts of 400 to 500/mm³. Many patients receiving a nucleoside analog RT inhibitor will experience a mild rise in their CD4+ count over the first one to five months of treatment. If patients are taking zidovudine, the mean corpuscular volume (MCV) will increase; this finding has been suggested as a means of assessing compliance with zidovudine therapy. In phase I studies where p24 antigen concentrations are measured concurrently, patients experiencing an increase in CD4+ count often will have a decrease in their p24 level. However, measurement of the p24 antigen serum concentration has not yet become a routine parameter in clinical care. In patients who present with altered mental status, monitoring for efficacy will include the routine assessment of mental status with objective measurements used to evaluate changes in CNS function. Patients with more advanced disease should be monitored for efficacy by noting the time between opportunistic infections and/or the recurrence rate of malignancies.

The role of therapeutic drug monitoring has been a controversial issue almost as long as zidovudine has been available. During Phase I trials zidovudine, didanosine, and zalcitabine were routinely measured in plasma for the purpose of evaluating their pharmacokinetic characteristics. The assays used for these drugs in Phase I testing were primarily high performance liquid chromatography, a technique that is highly specific but often lacking in sensitivity (often unreliable below $\approx$50 ng/mL). On the other hand a commercial radioimmunoassay for zidovudine and the reagents to prepare a radioimmunoassay for didanosine and zalcitabine are currently available and studies attempting to correlate plasma concentrations are ongoing. In addition, the use of drug levels to evaluate patient compliance has been addressed.[222] Some data do exist which describe the relationship between nucleoside analog plasma concentrations and surrogate marker responses. For example, didanosine response has been related to daily area under the concentration-time curve.[48,223] In addition, neutropenia has been correlated with steady-state zidovudine plasma concentrations.[224] Furthermore, the application of population pharmacokinetics has been demonstrated to be a reasonable alternative to traditional pharmacokinetics and may provide a simplified means of evaluating a patient's daily antiretroviral exposure.[92,225] The correlation of daily drug exposure with pharmacodynamic outcomes, in order to develop a therapeutic window, is currently under evaluation.

Another controversial issue in the area of therapeutic monitoring is related to the appropriate compound and biologic matrix to be studied. While the plasma is the usual biomatrix that is studied, the nucleoside analogs are only active after they have been sequentially phosphorylated to their triphosphate form. Herein lies a dilemma which has yet to be clarified. The intracellular phosphorylated metabolites are present in very low concentration in patients taking these drugs on a chronic basis.[226–228] The analytical methods for measuring these phosphorylated species have not been well established and thus the designs of clinical studies to investigate this issue have lagged behind the development of sensitive assays of intracellular metabolites.[229] Studies indicate a differential pattern of phosphorylation between zidovudine, didanosine, and zalcitabine, suggesting the need to examine the intracellular/extracellular relationship for each approved agent.[230] Certainly, more research is needed in this area to clarify the relationship between extracellular and intracellular antiretroviral concentrations.

The Use of CD4+ Counts to Stratify Treatment and Therapeutic Endpoints

1. J.R., a 35-year-old white male, has been known to be HIV+ for 3 years. He has been followed at the immunodeficiency clinic where his CD4+ lymphocyte count has been monitored every 6 months. His CD4+ cell count 18 months ago was 650 cells/mm³; 580 cells/mm³ 12 months ago; 540 cells/mm³ 6 months ago; and 460 cells/mm³ at this visit. How can the treatment of HIV be stratified based upon a patient's CD4+ cell count upon diagnosis, and what are the therapeutic endpoints?

Patients with a CD4+ cell count greater than 500 cells/mm³ should not be started on antiretroviral therapy.

Patients with a CD4+ cell count of 200 to 500 cells/mm³ can be advised to delay starting antiretroviral therapy until symptoms of advancing immunosuppression develop. Alternatively, these pa-

tients can be treated with zidovudine (Retrovir) 100 mg every four hours with the primary goal of preventing further decline in the CD4+ cell count and, thereby, delaying the onset of a clinical event such as an opportunistic infection or malignancy. It is presumed that delay in the appearance of these morbid events would prolong the duration of life and improve the quality of life for these individuals. The overall health status of these patients, therefore, should be considered before starting zidovudine therapy. Although drug toxicity is encountered less frequently by patients in earlier stages of the disease, toxic endpoints may be reached during the course of zidovudine treatment. Monitoring the hematological status of the patient may reveal anemia or neutropenia which often requires temporary discontinuation of zidovudine until the myelosuppressive effects resolve. Some patients also may experience myopathy (noted clinically as muscle weakness and associated with an increased serum concentration of creatine kinase) or hepatitis (noted by increased serum concentrations of hepatic enzymes).[232]

Patients with CD4+ cell count less than 200 cells/mm³ often experience their first episode of *Pneumocystis carinii* pneumonia (PCP) or CMV retinitis as the first evidence of HIV infection. In these patients, the therapeutic endpoints are similar to those for patients with higher CD4+ cell counts, but these end-points may be more difficult to attain. In many cases the endpoint may be prevention of a second episode of PCP, relapse of retinitis, or the onset of other opportunistic infections (e.g., cryptococcal meningitis, toxoplasmic encephalitis, atypical mycobacterium disease). The hematologic toxicity of zidovudine is often more prevalent among patients with more advanced HIV disease. In addition, sicker patients will require concurrent treatment for opportunistic infections with drugs which often potentiate the myelosuppressive effects of zidovudine. For example, the use of intravenous trimethoprim-sulfamethoxazole (TMP-SMX) for acute PCP or intravenous ganciclovir for CMV infection often necessitates the temporary discontinuation of zidovudine to avoid neutropenia. These situations may be approached with the coadministration of the costly colony stimulating factors such as granulocyte colony stimulating factor or granulocyte-macrophage colony stimulating factor. In these cases, the therapeutic endpoints of zidovudine remain virtually the same but the clinical scenario becomes more complicated requiring vigilant attention to laboratory tests and individual patient dose requirements. Patients who become intolerant to zidovudine may receive didanosine, zalcitabine, or stavudine.

Zidovudine

Initiation

2. J.R. is currently asymptomatic and has not lost any weight over the past 6 months. Why should (or should not) zidovudine be initiated in J.R.?

According to current guidelines, a patient with a CD4+ count of less than 500 cells/mm³ is eligible for zidovudine therapy;[101] therefore, J.R. is a candidate for antiretroviral treatment based upon his last CD4+ count of 460 cells/mm³. A number of studies have indicated a beneficial short-term effect for patients with early HIV disease, but the initiation of early zidovudine is controversial. While patients may tolerate zidovudine better earlier in the disease process, others may experience a decrease in zidovudine efficacy over time; resistant HIV isolates may develop within a patient; and the benefit of early intervention has been questioned by the initial results of the Concorde study.[47]

J.R. should be made aware of these conflicting data and be allowed to participate in the decision to receive drug treatment. If therapy is to be started, zidovudine 100 mg every four hours while awake should be prescribed and he should be monitored every two weeks for the first one to two months or until he tolerates the daily prescribed dose. Some patients may develop nausea or headaches upon initiation of zidovudine. These patients can be managed with reduction in the zidovudine dose or these symptoms can be treated with medication. Patients also may benefit by taking zidovudine with food to decrease the nausea. While concurrent food intake may lower the peak zidovudine plasma concentration, food does not decrease the overall bioavailability of this drug.[231] Patients should, however, be instructed to take zidovudine in a consistent manner during chronic therapy. A 200 mg every eight hour dosing regimen might facilitate the ease of use of zidovudine and is being investigated.

Monitoring Parameters

3. J.R. was started on zidovudine (Retrovir) and asked to return to the clinic within 2 weeks and to schedule monthly visits for the next 6 months. What monitoring parameters or clinical endpoints should be followed during zidovudine therapy and how reliable are they for assessing the progression of J.R.'s HIV disease?

The initial study of zidovudine in patients with ARC and AIDS was interrupted because the placebo group was experiencing a higher rate of mortality and a greater rate of progression from ARC to AIDS. Since mortality is not a reasonable endpoint for monitoring the ongoing effectiveness of treatment, the use of surrogate markers has become the mainstay of monitoring antiretroviral therapy. When available, the p24 serum antigen concentration may be used, however, the primary monitoring parameters include the CD4+ cell count, weight, well-being (i.e., Karnofsky score), and the development of opportunistic infections, malignancy, or neurologic changes. Nevertheless, the CD4+ cell count merely is reflective of the later stages of HIV replication (i.e., after considerable replication and spread to other CD4+ lymphocytes). Therefore, the CD4+ cell count would not logically be a good marker for total viral burden, and this logic is supported by polymerase chain reaction evaluation of plasma RNA, branched chain DNA, and lymph node studies. The use of the CD4+ cell count is analogous to following the serum creatinine in a renal transplant patient because the serum creatinine rises only after inflammatory changes have already occurred within the allograft. Nevertheless, the serum creatinine concentration is monitored in renal transplant patients and CD4+ counts are monitored in HIV patients in the absence of more optimal markers. In addition, a complete blood count (CBC) should be ordered for J.R. at each clinic visit to monitor for anemia and neutropenia.

Considerations for Declining CD4+ Count

4. J.R. has done well on zidovudine for 18 months at which time his CD4+ cell count was noted to have declined to 380 cells/mm³. His CD4+ cell count over the next 4 months has continued to decline and is now 240 cells/mm³. What are possible explanations for the continued decline in J.R.'s CD4+ cell count and how could his treatment be modified?

In a patient who begins to experience a decline in CD4+ cell count, the potential causes (see Table 68.4) need to be evaluated. First of all, J.R.'s compliance to his prescribed zidovudine regimen should be determined. Patients with HIV infection are similar to other patients with chronic disease in that periods of well being may prompt noncompliance. Thereafter, decreased zidovudine absorption (e.g., malabsorption) or enhanced zidovudine clearance (e.g., hepatic enzyme induction) should be evaluated. If these potentialities are not applicable, clinicians are left with the dilemma of whether to increase the zidovudine dose. Unfortunately, no guidelines exist for increasing zidovudine dosage when a decline

in CD4+ cell count is noted. Other possible causes for a declining CD4+ cell count can be attributed to increased HIV replication (measured by p24 serum antigen concentration and other viral burden tests), development of syncytia-inducing (SI) phenotype, decreased phosphorylation of intracellular zidovudine, and decreased susceptibility of HIV to zidovudine. Many of these considerations are still under clinical investigation and, therefore, alternative methods for optimizing and individualizing zidovudine therapy remain speculative.

The emergence of HIV strains with decreased susceptibility to zidovudine has been noted *in vitro* and in patients who have received this drug for more than 12 to 18 months. While the decreased responsiveness to zidovudine has not been directly correlated with greater HIV replication, patients receiving zidovudine therapy for more than 12 to 18 months often experience a decrease in CD4+ cell count and occurrence of opportunistic infection or malignancy. J.R. has done well on his zidovudine for about 18 months, but appears to be experiencing a decline in responsiveness to zidovudine.

Treatment options at this time consist primarily of entering an investigational protocol or switching to didanosine therapy. J.R. has not experienced prior pancreatitis or peripheral neuropathy and has good renal function. Didanosine has antiretroviral activity, however, it is currently indicated only for patients who are intolerant to zidovudine or who clinically deteriorate while on zidovudine. Data from AIDS Clinical Trial Group 116B/117 indicate that patients who have been on zidovudine and are switched to didanosine may do better than patients who are continued on zidovudine.[156] "Zidovudine-experienced" patients who are switched to didanosine may revert back to having zidovudine susceptible HIV strains.[232] In "zidovudine naive" patients, the addition of zalcitabine does not appear to be as effective as switching to didanosine.[128,145,156]

Didanosine

Gastrointestinal (GI) Intolerance

5. J.R. was switched to didanosine (Videx) 200 mg Q 12 hr and his CD4+ cell count was stable at about 340 CD4+ cells/mm³ for the next 6 months. However after this time, J.R. became noncompliant because of GI intolerance associated with didanosine and his CD4+ cell count decreased to 280 cells/mm³. How should this problem be managed for J.R.?

A new didanosine formulation which may be better tolerated is expected to be released, however, it is not available at this time. Meanwhile, J.R. can be treated with zidovudine in combination with zalcitabine (Hivid). While zalcitabine has demonstrated beneficial surrogate marker activity as monotherapy, its effects have not been sufficient to merit approval as single agent antiretroviral treatment. Rather, zalcitabine is indicated for patients with a CD4+ cell count which is less than 300 cells/mm³ when given in combination with zidovudine. Nevertheless, some clinicians prescribe zalcitabine as monotherapy. J.R. should be monitored at each visit for signs of peripheral neuropathy (burning feet, paresthesias) and for any change in renal function (zalcitabine, also known as ddC, is primarily excreted renally).

Pneumocystis carinii Pneumonia (PCP)

As an indication of the relative obscurity of this organism, a comprehensive text on *Pneumocystis carinii* was not available until 1983.[233] The taxonomy of this organism remains unclear, and it is still undecided whether it is a fungus or a protozoan. Its morphologic resemblance to a protozoan has led to its life cycle being described as a *cyst* form, with up to eight *sporozoites* per cyst. The

Table 68.4	Possible Consideration for a Declining CD4+ Cell Count in a Patient Receiving Zidovudine Therapy	
Consideration	Possible Actions	Current Status
1) Noncompliance	Detailed patient medication history. Measure zidovudine plasma concentration	Routine practice; investigational
2) ↓ ZDV bioavailability	Obtain medication history for addition of drugs which may ↓ ZDV absorption or ↑ ZDV metabolism. Measure ZDV plasma concentrations	Routine practice; investigational
3) ↑ HIV replication	Measure p24 antigen serum concentration or markers of ↑ viral burden	Investigational (some centers may measure p24)
4) Development of Syncytia inducing (SI) phenotype	Perform MT2 SI assay	Investigational
5) Development of HIV resistance to ZDV	Perform in vitro susceptibility tests	Investigational
6) ↓ intracellular phosphorylation to ZDVTP	Measure intracellular ZDV and phosphorylated ZDV	Investigational

extracystic form is called a *trophozoite* and has different staining characteristics (does not stain with toluidine-blue O or Grocott-Gomori stains) compared to the cyst or sporozoites.

Clinical Presentation

6. J.R. had developed a mild, nonproductive cough for the last 4 weeks. He has had a low grade fever, but no spiking temperatures, chills, or pleuritic chest pain. His chest radiograph demonstrated a diffuse, symmetric interstitial infiltrate. Following hypertonic saline nebulization for sputum induction and subsequent bronchoalveolar lavage, examination of the specimens with the modified Giemsa stain revealed both intracystic bodies and extracystic trophozoites. How is the clinical presentation of J.R. consistent with *Pneumocystis carinii* pneumonia?

Earlier in this century, an outbreak of PCP occurred among malnourished infants in Europe characterized by an interstitial plasma cell pneumonitis. The clinical features of PCP in AIDS patients differ from non-AIDS patients in that a more subtle onset with mild fever, a cough, tachypnea, and dyspnea is typically seen in HIV patients.[234] J.R.'s low grade fever and mild, nonproductive cough of four weeks duration are consistent with this description of PCP. His history of HIV infection and the finding of trophozoites on Giemsa stain further support a diagnosis of PCP. The presence of diffuse infiltrates on J.R.'s chest x-ray also is classic for PCP. Generally, most individuals experience asymptomatic infection with *Pneumocystis carinii* and the organism persists in a latent state unless the immune system of the host becomes impaired. PCP has become a hallmark complication of progressive HIV infection and has now evolved into a widely researched area which has led to significant advances in diagnosis, treatment, and prevention.

Antimicrobial Selection

7. A diagnosis of PCP was made and J.R. needs to be treated. What patient factors are important for the selection of an antimicrobial? What would be a reasonable drug to select for J.R. and how might his course of PCP be monitored?

The treatment of acute PCP is determined by the clinical severity upon presentation. The arterial oxygen status upon presentation is an important indicator of overall outcome. In one study, surviving patients had a mean PaO_2 of 70 torr while the mean of the non-survivors was 55 torr.[235,236] Key factors to consider when initiating therapy for PCP are: the arterial blood gases; initial or repeat episode of PCP; need for parenteral therapy; and the prior history of drug reactions.

Patients with PCP often can be classified into mild, moderate, and severe disease based upon their oxygenation. Patients with mild PCP often have a room air $PA-aO_2$ gradient of less than 35; patients with moderate disease have a $PA-aO_2$ of 36 to 45; and severe cases have a gradient greater than 45. With the advent of corticosteroid use for moderate to severe cases of PCP, it is useful to calculate the $PA-aO_2$ gradient. A number of other clinical tests have been used to identify and monitor PCP. The lactate dehydrogenase (LD) concentration in plasma or bronchoalveolar lavage fluid has been utilized to diagnose, monitor therapy, and predict outcome during PCP. However, the overlap among patients is too great for LD to be used alone. The chest radiograph also is variable. The most common picture is one of bilateral diffuse interstitial pneumonitis, but atypical patterns, such as pleural effusion, cavities, pneumatoceles, and nodules may occur as well. A normal chest x-ray is associated with a better clinical outcome.

The natural course of PCP among untreated HIV-infected patients is progressive dyspnea and hypoxemia. The increased experience with treatment of PCP in AIDS patients (compared to non-HIV infected patients) indicates that a longer duration of therapy is needed. Despite the greater appreciation of PCP in AIDS patients, up to 50% of cases may not respond to therapy. Many patients experience worsening hypoxemia during the first three to five days after treatment is started. This period of clinical worsening is least tolerated by those patients with moderate to severe PCP at the outset. In the sicker patients, this period may lead to respiratory failure and the need for intubation with continued critical care. While many would associate the need for intensive care unit admission as a poor prognostic factor, many patients do well despite the need for mechanical ventilation and intravenous antibiotics. Especially in light of the now appreciated role of corticosteroids, patients with PCP and respiratory failure may be viewed as manageable and treated aggressively.

Trimethoprim-Sulfamethoxazole (TMP-SMX)

Patients with reasonably good gas exchange (i.e., pO_2 >70 mm Hg), but with signs of clinical deterioration, most often are admitted to the hospital, given oxygen by nasal cannula, and started on an agent which interferes with microbial folate metabolism, usually intravenous trimethoprim-sulfamethoxazole (15 to 20 mg/kg/day TMP; 75 to 100 mg/kg/day SMX PO or IV for 14 to 21 days). A good response may be expected in 60% to 90% of patients receiving TMP-SMX. However, more than 50% of patients receiving TMP-SMX may develop a hypersensitivity response which may include rash, fever, leukopenia, hepatitis, and thrombocytopenia. The role of excessive doses, plasma concentration monitoring or metabolic capability (i.e., rapid or slow acetylation) in the development of hypersensitivity reactions is still under study.[237,238] Most patients who develop a hypersensitivity reaction can be restarted on TMP-SMX after the rash resolves. However, patients displaying prior severe adverse reactions to TMP-SMX (urticarial rash) should be switched to another antipneumocystis agent, rather than being rechallenged with this drug. Since J.R. appears to have a moderate case of PCP, has not previously experienced an episode of PCP, and has no history of adverse effects to TMP-SMX, a course of TMP-SMX would be reasonable. Patients who present with mild PCP without evidence of clinical deterioration can be managed as outpatients. In this setting, TMP-SMX often is prescribed because of its availability as an oral formulation. The decision to hospitalize J.R. will be based upon the assessment of the severity of his illness.

Alternatives to TMP-SMX

8. If J.R. experienced a significant adverse effect to TMP-SMX, what other drugs could be prescribed for treatment of his PCP?

Some patients tolerate TMP-SMX well, but others may require an alternative treatment[239] such as parenteral pentamidine, oral dapsone, or oral TMP/dapsone (see Table 68.5). Some clinicians may favor intravenous *pentamidine* (Pentam) to treat acute PCP; however, the toxicity profile of pentamidine prompts many clinicians to initially try a course of TMP-SMX.[240,241] Responses to pentamidine are also good, however, the toxicities from pentamidine are more extensive than those to TMP-SMX and can be dose limiting. Serious toxicities noted during pentamidine include: azotemia, pancreatitis, dysglycemia, hypocalcemia, and leukopenia. Other reported, but less common, toxicities are: thrombocytopenia, orthostatic hypotension, ventricular tachycardia, nausea, and vomiting.[242] Patients receiving pentamidine should be monitored closely and serum concentrations of glucose, creatinine, amylase, and lipase obtained daily during treatment.[243] The occurrence of renal toxicity often responds to a reduction in the dose of pentam-

idine; however, the drug should be discontinued in patients who develop signs and symptoms of pancreatitis. Risk factors for pentamidine-induced pancreatitis include prior episodes of pancreatitis and concurrent therapy with other drugs known to cause pancreatitis. While the prior use of didanosine may be a risk factor for pancreatitis during pentamidine therapy, only one case has been reported.[244] The daily pentamidine dose of 4 mg/kg is based more upon clinical tolerance rather than target plasma concentrations. The exact mechanisms for elimination of pentamidine are not well understood. The drug is not excreted by renal mechanisms and no metabolites have been identified.[245,246] The half-life of pentamidine tends to increase during multiple dosing and may increase to 12 days after the last dose in a regimen.[240] Further work is needed to clarify the optimal method of dosing pentamidine.

Other drugs that have been investigated for their antipneumocystis activity include: dapsone, TMP/dapsone, trimetrexate, atovaquone, clindamycin/primaquine, and eflornithine.[249–255] These agents remain second-line choices due to their lower success rates and toxicities.[256] *Trimetrexate*, a highly potent inhibitor of dihydrofolate reductase, was first studied as salvage therapy in patients failing available drugs. The ability of trimetrexate to enhance survival in these often fatal situations gave hope to the future of this treatment. However, subsequent studies have not provided as promising results. Nonetheless, trimetrexate has been approved for mild to moderate cases of PCP. Patients receiving trimetrexate should be monitored for myelosuppression with daily CBCs. Patients who receive dapsone or primaquine must be tested for glucose-6-phosphate dehydrogenase (G6PD) deficiency to avoid hemolytic anemia. *Atovaquone* (Mepron) is another recent addition to the agents available for treatment of pneumocystosis.[234,257–260] The mechanism of action of atovaquone remains unclear, however, atovaquone demonstrates activity *in vitro* and in animal models. In addition, atovaquone is active against *Toxoplasma gondii*, another common pathogen in AIDS patients. Thus, this compound

Table 68.5		Treatment of *Pneumocystis carinii* Pneumonia[a]	
Regimen	Dose	Route	Adverse Effects
Approved			
TMP-SMX	5 mg/kg TMP + 25 mg/kg SMX Q 6–8 hr × 14–21 days	IV, PO	Hypersensitivity, rash, fever, neutropenia ↑ LFTs, nephrotoxicity
Pentamidine isethionate	4 mg/kg IV daily over 60–90 min × 14–21 days	IV	Pancreatitis, hypotension, hypoglycemia, hyperglycemia, nephrotoxicity
Trimetrexate +	45 mg/m² Q 6 hr × 21 days	IV	Hematologic, gastrointestinal, CNS, rash
Leucovorin	20 mg/m² Q 6 hr × 21 days	PO	
with or without sulfadiazine	1 gm Q 6 hr × 21 days	PO	
Atovaquone	750 mg Q 8 hr × 21 days	PO	Headache, nausea, diarrhea, rash, fever, ↑ LFTs
Investigational			
Trimethoprim +	5 mg/kg Q 6 hr	PO	
Dapsone	100 mg/day × 14–21 days	PO	Methemoglobinemia, hemolytic anemia (contraindicated in G6PD deficiency)
Clindamycin +	450–900 mg Q 6–8 hr	PO or IV	Rash, diarrhea
Primaquine	15–30 mg (base) daily × 14–21 days	PO	Methemoglobinemia, hemolytic anemia (contraindicated in G6PD deficiency)
Difluoromethylornithine (DFMO, eflornithine)	400 mg/kg daily by continuous infusion or in 4 divided doses × 41–21 days, followed by 4–6 weeks oral therapy	IV	Myelosuppression, gastrointestinal toxicity

[a] CNS = Central nervous system; G6PD = Glucose-6 phosphate dehydrogenase; IV = Intravenous; LFTs = Liver function tests; PO = Oral; TMP-SMX = Trimethoprim-sulfamethoxazole.

may have benefit for patients with more than one opportunistic infection. The bioavailability of atovaquone is low, and is increased by co-administration of a high-fat meal.[234] Adverse effects include rash, fever, increased hepatic enzymes, and emesis.

Dapsone, an agent previously used for leprosy, also has been studied in patients with PCP. While monotherapy (200 mg/day) with dapsone has proved to be ineffective, the addition of TMP (20 mg/kg/day) to dapsone (100 mg/day) seems to provide an effective alternative regimen.[253] Interestingly, when dapsone is co-administered with trimethoprim the resulting plasma concentrations for both drugs are higher then when either drug is taken alone.[249] In a comparative trial of *TMP/dapsone* versus TMP-SMX, response rates of 93% and 90% were observed, respectively.[250] Lastly, the combination of *clindamycin* and *primaquine* has activity *in vitro* and in animal models against *P. carinii*. A number of small trials have reported success rates of 70% to 100% with clindamycin 3600 mg/day IV or 1800 mg/day orally when given in conjunction with 30 mg/day of primaquine base. Although skin rashes were common with this combination, they often subsided with continued therapy. Some patients experienced toxicities requiring discontinuation which included fever, rash, granulocytopenia, and methemoglobinemia. As with dapsone, patients should be screened for G6PD deficiency before starting primaquine.

Initiation of Corticosteroids

9. When should corticosteroids be initiated and what would be a reasonable regimen for patients with PCP?

Corticosteroids have an important role in the management of patients with acute PCP who are clinically ill and have a low PaO$_2$.[261–265] Many patients who are started on anti-PCP therapy develop an acute period of clinical deterioration which may be associated with the rapid killing of *Pneumocystis* organisms. Particularly among patients with moderate to severe PCP at the initiation of therapy, the use of prednisone within the first 72 hours of treatment may prevent acute deterioration which may be fatal in some patients. The recommended dose of prednisone is 40 mg twice daily for five days, then 40 mg/day for five days, then 20 mg/day for 11 days for a total of 21 days. Patients requiring IV corticosteroids may receive methylprednisolone at 75% of the prednisone dose. The impact of this period on further immunosuppression has not been clearly defined, however, the risk versus benefit estimation in this situation indicates that corticosteroids have a beneficial role as adjunctive therapy.[236]

Prophylaxis

10. J.R. was hospitalized and responded well to treatment. What regimens are available for the prophylaxis of PCP and which would be a good choice for J.R. when discharged from the hospital?

The recognition of the efficacy of TMP-SMX prophylaxis among AIDS patients with Kaposi's sarcoma[38] led to the eventual widespread application of prophylaxis and the development of guidelines for PCP prophylaxis[267] (see Table 68.6). A clear relationship between the CD4+ cell count and the occurrence of PCP led researchers to conclude that a majority of the initial episodes of PCP could be prevented or delayed by instituting prophylaxis. Studies which examined HIV-infected patients who were not receiving antiretrovirals or prophylaxis indicated that an incidence of 8.4%, 18.4%, and 33.3% of patients with a CD4+ cell count less than 200 cells/mm^3 developed PCP at 6, 12, and 36 months, respectively.[268] These data have formed the basis upon which patients receive these PCP prophylaxis regimens. In addition to patients with CD4+ cell counts less than 200 cells/mm^3, other pa-

Table 68.6	Antibiotic Regimens for Prophylaxis of *Pneumocystis Carinii* Pneumonia	
Regimen	Dose	Route
Approved		
TMP-SMX	160 mg TMP + 800 mg SMX daily, BID or 3 × week (see text)	PO
Pentamidine isethionate	300 mg every month	by Respirgard II nebulizer
Investigational		
Pentamidine isethionate	2 week induction (5 doses), then 60 mg 2 × week	Fisoneb nebulizer
Pentamidine isethionate	4 mg/kg 2 × week[a]	IV
Dapsone	50, 100, 200 mg 1–2 × week or QD–BID	PO
Dapsone + Pyrimethamine	50–100 mg/day 25–50 mg/day, or 1–2 × week	PO PO
Pyrimethamine + Sulfadoxine (Fansidar)	150 mg/day 500 mg 1–2 × week or 3 × month	PO PO
Clindamycin + Primaquine	150 mg QID 15 mg primaquine base daily	PO PO
Atovaquone	Under investigation	PO

a Range is once a month to twice a week.

tients at risk for PCP include those with persistent unexplained fevers, oral thrush, disseminated *Mycobacterium avium* complex, end-organ CMV disease, or AIDS-related complex. Prophylaxis for PCP can be further subdivided into patients without prior PCP (primary prophylaxis) or those who have already had PCP (secondary prophylaxis).

The agents primarily used for prophylaxis are TMP-SMX, aerosolized pentamidine, dapsone, TMP/dapsone, and clindamycin/primaquine (see Table 68.6). Many patients may be intolerant of TMP-SMX and, therefore, close monitoring is needed and an eventual switch to alternative prophylactic regimens must be expected. The clinical benefit realized from TMP-SMX and aerosolized pentamidine is relatively good, however, the increased incidence of intolerance to TMP-SMX offsets the benefit of its enhanced effectiveness.[269] The development of aerosolized pentamidine and its eventual comparison to TMP-SMX has provided a reasonable alternative for PCP prophylaxis.[270]

About 50 cases of extrapulmonary (e.g., lymph nodes, spleen, liver, bone marrow, adrenal gland, GI tract) *P. carinii* have been noted in patients receiving inhaled pentamidine prophylaxis.[247,248] Aerosolized pentamidine for PCP prophylaxis, therefore, may not prevent the development of extrapulmonary infection. In addition, aerosolized pentamidine administration may decrease the likelihood that patients with acute PCP will present with the classic chest x-ray consisting of diffuse infiltrates. Upper lobe infiltrates, cystic lesions, pneumothoraces, cavitary lesions with nodular infiltrates, and pleural effusions have been described during pentamidine prophylaxis.

Prophylaxis following an acute episode of PCP might be more appropriately called chronic suppression. In any event, the same agents are available for secondary prophylaxis and the expected relapse rates among patients taking zidovudine are 31% and 66% at 6 and 12 months of follow-up after the initial episode of PCP, respectively.[271] The management of patients who have already experienced PCP is more complicated because when the CD4+ cell count declines, the development of other opportunistic infections may further immunosuppress the patient and override the benefits of prophylaxis. Despite this decreased immune status, the response rates for first, second, and third episodes of PCP are similar.[272] Since J.R. responded well to TMP-SMX in the hospital, this drug can be administered to him for PCP prophylaxis.

The prophylaxis of PCP in children is still in need of further clinical research. The use of 200 CD4+ cells/mm³ is not as reliable in infants because they have higher normal values for lymphocyte counts. The current recommendations are to give PCP prophylaxis to children in the following age groups: 1 to 11 months when the CD4+ count is less than 1500 cells/mm³, 12 to 23 months when the CD4+ count is less than 750 cells/mm³, 24 months to 5 years old when the CD4+ count is less than 500 cells/mm³, and to children more than 6 years of age when the CD4+ count is less than 200 cells/mm³. The recommended regimen is TMP-SMX (75 mg TMP, 375 mg SMX/m²) twice daily.[242]

HIV-Wasting

11. J.R. has been followed in the HIV clinic for several years. His last CD4+ cell count was 90 cells/mm³ 2 months ago and his history of PCP began 5 years ago. His chronic oral candidiasis is managed with intermittent fluconazole. Over the last 2 visits, J.R.'s weight has dropped from a baseline weight of 140 pounds to 115 pounds. He reports occasional, but not chronic diarrhea. What could be the cause of J.R.'s weight loss and how can it be managed?

Significant weight loss in HIV-infected patients is associated with more rapid disease progression. In many cases, weight loss may be a clinical sign of an opportunistic infection (e.g., enteric infection, PCP, or *Mycobacterium avium* complex). Therefore, patients with weight loss should be evaluated to rule out infectious or treatable causes. Nevertheless, HIV patients may demonstrate weight loss in the absence of these conditions. HIV-related weight loss may be a multifactorial problem, resulting from decreased nutrient intake, decreased nutrient absorption, or accelerated nutrient metabolism (or a combination of these factors). Various cytokines, such as tumor necrosis factor (TNF), interleukin-1 (Il-1), or interferon alpha, may play a role in the wasting syndrome.

Several agents have recently received Food and Drug Administration (FDA)-approval for the treatment of HIV-related wasting. *Megestrol acetate* suspension is approved for HIV-infected patients who have lost at least 10% of their ideal body weight. Once-daily megestrol dosing has been associated with weight gains of approximately 5 to 10 kg.[636,637] Dronabinol (Marinol) 2.5 mg one hour before lunch and one hour before dinner has been approved for AIDS-related anorexia associated with weight loss. The dronabinol significantly increased appetite as determined by a visual analog scale,[638] and appeared to improve body weight and mood. Euphoria, dizziness, confusion, and somnolence occurred in 18% of dronabinol-treated patients. A reduction in the dose of dronabinol to 2.5 mg one hour before supper or bedtime may reduce adverse events. Due to its potential for misuse, dronabinol should be used with caution in patients with a history of substance abuse. Patients should be counseled to avoid driving, operating machinery, or other potentially hazardous activities until it is established that the patient can safely perform these activities. Furthermore, concurrent administration of alcohol or other CNS depressants may result in additive central nervous system depression. An investigational new drug application for *human growth hormone* has been approved in the U.S. for the treatment of HIV-associated weight loss (i.e., 10% of ideal body weight) in patients who are refractory

to, or intolerant of, megestrol acetate or dronabinol. Subcutaneous growth hormone injections of 0.1 mg/kg/day have been associated with increases in lean body mass and functional performance.[639]

Cytomegalovirus (CMV) Retinitis
Diagnosis

12. P.Z., a 39-year-old, homosexual, male with AIDS comes to the clinic complaining of floating spots in his vision and difficulty reading road signs when he drives. His most recent blood urea nitrogen (BUN) and serum creatinine (SrCr) are 17 and 0.8 mg/dL, respectively. His last CD4+ cell count was 40 cells/mm³ ≈3 months ago. His current weight is 63 kg. His medications include zalcitabine 0.75 mg Q 8 hr, acyclovir 200 mg Q 8 hr, rifabutin 300 mg/day, and atovaquone 750 mg/day. P.Z. has a history of hematologic intolerance to zidovudine and TMP-SMX. A CBC taken in clinic shows a white blood cell (WBC) count of 1.2 × 10³/mm³ with 63% segs and 6% bands. P.Z. is known to have a positive CMV antibody titer. Funduscopic examination reveals the presence of alternating areas of hemorrhaging and scar tissue (a "pizza pie" appearance) in the proximity of the retina in his left eye. What is the likely cause of P.Z.'s visual problems? [SI units: BUN 6.07 mmol/L; SrCr 70.72 μmol/L; WBC count 1.2 × 10⁹/L with 0.63 segs and 0.06 bands]

Cytomegalovirus is the most likely pathogen causing P.Z.'s retinitis. Many HIV patients have been previously infected with CMV, but reactivation disease typically occurs when CD4+ cell counts are less than 100 cells/mm³. While CMV can cause colitis, pneumonitis, and hepatitis, retinitis is the most common manifestation of CMV infection in HIV patients. Diagnosis is usually presumptive, since biopsy is difficult given the inaccessibility of the retina. Serology is indicative of previous CMV infection, but not active disease. Cultures (serum, urine, and/or saliva), may be useful for monitoring therapy since patients frequently have disseminated CMV disease. Thus, patients with positive cultures for CMV while on therapy, may be at higher risk of relapse.[273] Typically the diagnosis of CMV is established with funduscopic examination and serology.

Goal of Therapy

13. What is the goal of treating CMV retinitis in HIV patients?

CMV retinitis therapy may be categorized into primary prophylaxis; treatment of active disease or induction therapy; and secondary prophylaxis or suppressive therapy. Suppressive therapy is necessary because most patients relapse without such therapy. While no agents are currently recommended for primary prophylaxis of CMV disease, ganciclovir and foscarnet have been approved by the FDA for the treatment of active CMV retinitis in AIDS patients. Once CMV disease has stabilized, secondary prophylaxis or suppressive therapy significantly delays disease progression.

While the visual changes induced by the inflammation associated with CMV retinitis may improve with ganciclovir therapy, the visual loss which has occurred is, for the most part, irreversible. The goal of therapy is to delay disease progression, since disease progression is commonplace despite maintenance therapy. Funduscopic examinations are monitored throughout CMV therapy to assess patient response. Treatment of active CMV retinitis typically requires two to three weeks of therapy.

Drug Therapy

14. What are two treatment options for P.Z.'s acute CMV retinitis and which one would be preferred for P.Z.?

While both ganciclovir (Cytovene) and foscarnet (Foscavir) appear to have similar efficacy in the treatment of CMV retinitis, the choice of agents typically depends upon the toxicity profile of each drug. *Ganciclovir* is an acyclic nucleoside with enhanced *in vitro* activity against CMV relative to acyclovir.[274,275] Like other nucleosides, ganciclovir must be taken into cells and subjected to a series of three phosphorylation reactions before it can compete with endogenous nucleotides for binding to viral enzymes.[276] Ganciclovir pharmacokinetics are characterized by low oral bioavailability (F ≈5% to 9%), biexponential disposition following intravenous administration (terminal t½ ≈2.5 hours), and total body clearance which is highly dependent upon renal filtration and tubular secretion.[277]

Ganciclovir

Ganciclovir, dosed at 5 mg/kg every 12 hours IV, is approximately 80% effective in delaying the progression of CMV retinitis.[278-281] The primary dose-limiting adverse event with ganciclovir is bone marrow suppression, resulting in neutropenia in approximately 50% of patients. Absolute neutrophil counts (ANCs) should be monitored frequently during ganciclovir therapy. If the ANC falls to less than 1000 cells/mm³, ganciclovir dosage should be reduced or alternatives should be considered. If the absolute neutrophil count falls to less than 500 cells/mm³, ganciclovir should be discontinued and foscarnet initiated (see below). Given the high prevalence of neutropenia during ganciclovir therapy, full-dose zidovudine (500 to 600 mg/day) should not be given to patients during treatment of active CMV retinitis.[282] If continued treatment of HIV infection is desired, didanosine or zalcitabine may be used,[283] especially if the patient has a long history of zidovudine use prior to CMV therapy.

Foscarnet

Foscarnet is a pyrophosphate analog which acts by selectively inhibiting viral DNA polymerases and reverse transcriptase. At currently recommended doses for induction therapy (60 mg/kg Q 8 hr IV), peak foscarnet concentrations of 100 to 300 μM are attained which inhibit CMV *in vitro*.[284] As primary therapy, foscarnet and ganciclovir are about equally effective:[285,287] both drugs can successfully delay the progression of CMV retinitis by two to three months.[288] In contrast to ganciclovir, the dose-limiting toxicity with foscarnet is nephrotoxicity, which probably results from its crystallization in nephrons[289] because of its low solubility in water.

Patients (with normal renal function) receiving foscarnet survived approximately four months longer than the patients receiving ganciclovir (12.6 versus 8.5 months, respectively).[286] However, foscarnet-treated patients with a creatinine clearance of less than 1.2 mL/minute/kg had a worse survival rate. Whether the difference in survival in the patients with better renal function was due to the anti-HIV activity of foscarnet[285,288,290,291] or the ability of foscarnet-treated patients to continue receiving zidovudine is unknown and remains a subject of controversy. Since P.Z. already has a low absolute neutrophil count of about 828 (i.e., 69% of 1200 WBCs), the bone marrow suppressive effects of ganciclovir would be of concern. Foscarnet probably would be preferred for P.Z. because he has good renal function (SrCr 0.8 mg/dL) and foscarnet might be more effective in patients with normal renal function.

15. Nephrotoxicity. Foscarnet 60 mg/kg IV is to be infused over 2 hours for P.Z. at 8 hour intervals. How can the risk of nephrotoxicity from foscarnet be minimized?

Adequate hydration during foscarnet therapy is important in the prevention of nephrotoxicity. Dilution of foscarnet in 1 to 2 L of IV fluid before administration is a simple way to ensure that pa-

tients receive adequate fluids. Careful dosage titration based upon P.Z.'s estimated creatinine clearance also may help to minimize nephrotoxicity. Serum creatinine concentrations should be measured at least twice weekly during foscarnet treatment of CMV retinitis. Drugs with nephrotoxic potential, such as amphotericin B or aminoglycosides, should be avoided if possible. CMV infection has been associated with acute interstitial nephritis, which also may lead to an acute increase in the serum creatinine. The two-hour infusion period and concomitant fluid infusions may be inconvenient for patients. Several European investigators report similar efficacy with a foscarnet regimen of 100 mg/kg given every 12 hours, although their study designs were not prospective.[292,293] If this twice daily foscarnet regimen proves to be as effective as the 60 mg/kg every eight hour regimen, it would be preferred.

16. Adverse Effects. What toxicities, other than nephrotoxicity, have been associated with foscarnet therapy?

Foscarnet, a pyrophosphate analog, binds to unbound calcium *in vivo* and should be infused over one to two hours to avoid high foscarnet plasma concentrations which have been associated with hypocalcemia.[291] Unbound calcium concentrations should be monitored during foscarnet therapy, ideally at the time of peak foscarnet concentration. Fatal hypocalcemia in an AIDS patient receiving both foscarnet and parenteral pentamidine has been reported; thus coadministration of these two drugs should be avoided. Penile ulceration from foscarnet has been problematic, especially in uncircumcised male patients. Characterized as a fixed drug eruption, careful attention to genital hygiene may minimize the potential for penile ulceration. Other adverse events associated with foscarnet include seizures, hypomagnesemia, anemia, nausea, fever, and rash. Dosage adjustment based upon renal function also may help reduce the incidence of adverse events. The subjective tolerance of patients to foscarnet is probably less relative to ganciclovir: 36% of patients randomized to foscarnet were switched to ganciclovir in the only comparative study.[286]

17. Dosage Adjustments. After 14 days of foscarnet therapy, P.Z.'s SrCr has increased from 0.8 mg/dL to 1.2 mg/dL despite the coadministration of 2 L of normal saline daily. What dosage adjustment should be made for the remainder of the foscarnet treatment period? [SI units: SrCr 70.72 and 106.08 μmol/L, respectively]

Since both ganciclovir and foscarnet are highly dependent upon renal elimination, dosages (or dosing intervals) should be adjusted at a relatively low threshold for renal dysfunction. For example, the creatinine clearance threshold for dosage reduction for ganciclovir is below 80 mL/1.73 m²/minute and 1.6 mL/minute/kg for foscarnet. In contrast, the renal threshold for acyclovir and many other drugs is a creatinine clearance of 50 mL/minute. Therefore, careful monitoring of renal function is important throughout CMV therapy. AIDS patients may be at high risk for renal dysfunction due to their HIV infection, nephrotoxic medications, and/or various infectious or metabolic complications. P.Z.'s estimated creatinine clearance is 1.2 mL/minute/kg; therefore, his foscarnet dosage should be adjusted to 46 mg/kg IV every eight hours.

Suppression Therapy

18. P.Z. has now completed 21 days of foscarnet induction therapy. How can his CMV retinitis be suppressed in the future?

Since almost all patients relapse without continued anti-CMV therapy, maintenance therapy is indicated for the remainder of P.Z.'s life. Ganciclovir (5 mg/kg/day IV × 7 days/week or 6 mg/kg/day × 5 days/week) and foscarnet (90 to 120 mg/kg/day IV) prolong the time between recurrences of CMV retinitis.[294] Uncontrolled reports indicate that intermittent (3 times weekly) ganciclovir at 10 mg/kg may be effective as maintenance therapy, but the relative safety and efficacy of this regimen awaits a controlled clinical trial.[273,278,295]

Relapse

19. After 5 months of maintenance therapy with foscarnet, a routine funduscopic examination reveals retinal CMV disease progression. How should P.Z.'s retinitis be managed?

As patients with CMV disease live longer,[296,297] they may relapse despite maintenance therapy with either ganciclovir or foscarnet. However, repeat induction therapy with the same drug may be beneficial in these patients. Since P.Z. has tolerated foscarnet therapy thus far, repeat induction therapy with foscarnet is indicated. While ganciclovir- and foscarnet-resistant strains of CMV have been reported in patients, their precise role in the clinical failure of these regimens remains to be determined.[258] Due to the different mechanisms of action of ganciclovir and foscarnet, viral strains resistant to one drug may retain sensitivity to the other.[299]

To take advantage of their distinct mechanisms of action and toxicity profiles, ganciclovir in combination with foscarnet (at approximately one-half their usual doses) has been evaluated; however, the utility of this combination is still under evaluation. There have been several case reports of patients responding to combination ganciclovir/foscarnet therapy.[300-304] In the largest of these series, neutropenia and thrombocytopenia were noted with similar frequency during ganciclovir monotherapy and combination therapy; however, the incidence of anemia was significantly greater during combination therapy.[300]

Drug Therapy

Alternatives

20. What alternatives (other than foscarnet) are available to patients who are intolerant of ganciclovir's myelosuppression?

Several options exist for patients with ganciclovir-induced bone marrow suppression. G-CSF (filgramostim) or GM-CSF (sargramostim)[305,306] have been used with success. While neither of these agents has an FDA approval for this indication, use of the CSFs may allow a patient to complete sight-saving or life-prolonging therapy. That GM-CSF may stimulate HIV replication in macrophage cell lines is a potential limitation to its use,[216,307] and it is recommended that patients receiving GM-CSF be on an antiretroviral as well.

Intra-vitreal administration of ganciclovir is a method of selectively providing ganciclovir to the site of infection.[308-314] Doses of 200 to 400 μg two to three times a week for active disease, followed by weekly injections for maintenance therapy have been used. Potential complications of intravitreal injections are bacterial endophthalmitis, vitreous hemorrhage, and retinal detachment. Furthermore, only experienced ophthalmologists may be comfortable with the injection techniques. A surgically implantable delivery device also has been developed which is capable of delivering ganciclovir into the vitreous humor over a four to five month period.[315,316] While local administration of anti-CMV therapy to the retina avoids systemic toxicity, a serious limitation is the potential development of CMV disease in other areas, such as unaffected eyes or the gastrointestinal tract. CMV viremia would not be reduced by intra-vitreal ganciclovir.[313,317]

Oral Ganciclovir

21. Would P.Z. be a candidate for oral ganciclovir (Cytovene) therapy?

Despite its low bioavailability, oral ganciclovir is available in the U.S. for the suppressive treatment of CMV retinitis in AIDS patients. Taken with food, ganciclovir oral doses of 1000 mg appear to provide about 75% of the exposure to intravenous doses of 5 mg/kg: peak concentrations with oral dosing are substantially lower. The bioavailability of oral ganciclovir is increased by 22% when administered with food. Patients, therefore, should be counseled to take all doses with food to maximize their exposure.[640] Although oral ganciclovir is a viable alternative to intravenous ganciclovir, the time to relapse may be sooner with the oral formulation. The intravenous and oral ganciclovir formulations are both associated with neutropenia or anemia in approximately 40% to 60% of patients; however, the risk might be lower with oral dosing.[641] While oral ganciclovir may eliminate the need for intravenous access, P.Z. would still be at risk for developing neutropenia, and the previously discussed strategies would still apply.

22. What is the present role of oral ganciclovir?

At present, oral ganciclovir appears to offer an oral agent which is effective in the suppression of CMV disease; however, the time interval before progression of CMV infection from oral, relative to intravenous suppressive therapy, may be shorter. Since the placement of an intravenous catheter is still required for induction therapy, it would seem prudent to continue an intravenous suppressive regimen until problems arise, such as inaccessibility to home care or line-related complications. Preliminary data from a placebo-controlled trial for the prevention of CMV disease in HIV-infected patients with positive CMV serology indicate that oral ganciclovir may be helpful in the primary prevention of CMV disease in patients with CD4+ lymphocyte counts of ≤50 cells/mm^3,[641] although further study will be required before routine use of oral ganciclovir in this setting can be recommended.

The expense of oral ganciclovir is likely to stir controversy, although it must be kept in mind that cost comparisons must include the intravenous catheter-associated costs, as well as the additional cost of catheter-associated complications, such as sepsis. Furthermore, quality of life issues may weigh in favor of oral ganciclovir. While the exact role of oral ganciclovir remains to be elucidated, its recent FDA-approval will provide access to this agent for many HIV-infected patients.

Varicella Zoster Virus (VZV)

Acyclovir

Dosing

23. G.T., a 43-year-old black male, presented to his local medical doctor complaining of blisters on his back. G.T.'s medical history is significant for syphilis 5 years earlier, which was treated with penicillin. Upon examination, localized "cobblestone-like" blisters consistent with varicella-zoster virus were seen just above G.T.'s left hip. Acyclovir (Zovirax) 200 mg Q 4 hr (5 times daily) was prescribed. G.T. is suspected of being at risk for HIV infection and HIV testing is initiated. Three weeks later, G.T.'s results come back positive by both ELISA and Western blot techniques. CD4+ lymphocyte measurement via flow cytometry indicates an absolute count of 530 cells/mm^3. Why is the acyclovir dose prescribed for G.T. inappropriate?

Herpes zoster usually represents a reactivation of varicella zoster, which is common in HIV-infected patients. For some patients, such as G.T., Herpes zoster may be the first indication of immunosuppression. While VZV is related to herpes simplex virus (HSV), higher concentrations are required to inhibit VZV in vitro. Given the low and variable bioavailability of acyclovir, the 200 mg dose prescribed will not result in sufficient in vivo serum concentrations to inhibit VZV. Therefore G.T.'s dose should be increased to 800 mg every four hours (5 times/day). Since G.T.'s zoster appears to be localized to the hip area, oral acyclovir therapy is appropriate. While immunocompromised patients are at higher risk for complications of VZV, G.T. is otherwise healthy.

Adverse Effects

24. What are two likely adverse effects of high dose acyclovir that could be experienced by G.T.?

High dose acyclovir generally is well tolerated, although gastrointestinal side effects may be problematic. The limited water solubility of acyclovir is likely responsible for the nephrotoxicity seen with intravenous acyclovir, due to crystallization in the nephron. Thus, nephrotoxicity is a potential problem with high-dose oral acyclovir as well. G.T.'s renal function should be monitored and G.T. should be instructed to take adequate fluids.

Prophylaxis

25. G.T. is instructed to complete a 10-day course of acyclovir (Zovirax) and to notify his physician if the lesions continue to progress or any respiratory or CNS symptoms (headache, vomiting, lethargy, ataxia, tremors, and dizziness) occur. G.T. returns to the clinic after 10 days of acyclovir. Physical examination reveals a crusted area just above the left hip, but G.T. has no other complaints. Does G.T. need to continue acyclovir as prophylaxis for VZV infection?

Patients with recurrent herpes infections may benefit from acyclovir prophylaxis. G.T., however, only has experienced one episode of Herpes zoster, and acyclovir should not be continued. Furthermore, acyclovir-resistant strains of VZV and HSV have been reported in patients with HIV or AIDS. Acyclovir should be reserved unless G.T. encounters other episodes of zoster.

Resistance

26. What treatment options are available for acyclovir-resistant herpes infections?

Chronic problems with herpes infections, such as oral-labial lesions, genital lesions, and ano-rectal lesions are typically encountered. While prolonged treatment with acyclovir may reduce the frequency and severity of these lesions, acyclovir-resistant herpes can emerge. *Foscarnet* is effective in the treatment of acyclovir-resistant isolates. In a comparative trial with vidarabine (adenine arabinoside), foscarnet was significantly more effective.[642]

Famciclovir (Famvir) also is effective for the treatment of acute varicella zoster infection in immunocompetent patients. Famciclovir, a prodrug of penciclovir, is a relatively nontoxic agent with good bioavailability ($\approx 77\%$). When compared to acyclovir in immunocompetent patients, oral famciclovir at 500 mg three times daily demonstrated similar efficacy, although the rates of headache and nausea appeared to be higher with famciclovir. At present there is little information regarding the use of famciclovir in HIV-infected populations or its use in the setting of acyclovir-resistant strains of varicella.[643-645]

Cryptococcal Meningitis
Clinical Presentation and Prognosis

27. A.S. is a 28-year-old, HIV +, 48 kg female. Her boyfriend who was a known IV drug user died of AIDS 2 years ago. She presents with a fever of 103 °F and for the past week has experienced "splitting headaches." Laboratory tests include: Hgb 11.2 mg/dL, peripheral WBC count 4100/mm^3, platelets 73,000/mm^3, SrCr 0.9 mg/dL, and CD4+ lymphocyte count 92 cells/mm^3. Physical examination reveals no nuchal rigidity. With the exception of moderate lethargy, her neurologic examination is unremarkable. Chest x-ray is negative as well as 3 sets of blood cultures for bacteria and fungi. Skin testing demonstrates anergy. A CT scan is nondiagnostic. Lumbar puncture reveals the following: glucose 72 mg/dL; protein 45 mg/dL; WBC count 10 cells/mm^3; and a cryptococcal antigen titer of 1:2048. A CSF India-ink stain is positive for cryptococcus. Five days later a CSF culture grows *Cryptococcus neoformans*. How is A.S.'s clinical presentation typical for a patient with AIDS and cryptococcal meningitis? What is her likely prognosis? [SI units: Hgb 112 gm/L; WBC count 4.1 × 10^9/L; platelets 73 × 10^9/L; SrCr 79.56 μmol/L; glucose 4 mmol/L; protein 0.45 gm/L]

Cryptococcosis develops in approximately 9% to 13% of AIDS patients and meningitis is the most common clinical presentation.[319,320] A.S. is HIV positive. After HIV encephalopathy and toxoplasmosis, cryptococcosis is the most common CNS infection associated with AIDS.[321] The lungs are presumed to be the initial portal of entry where the organism is normally contained by an intact cell-mediated immune system. Cryptococcal disease typically develops in patients with profound defects in cell-mediated immunity, usually with a CD4+ count less than 100 cells/mm^3.[321] (A.S.'s CD4+ count is 92 cells/mm^3.) Unlike bacterial meningitis, cryptococcal CNS infection has a much more insidious onset, with the most common symptoms being fever and headache. (A.S. has a temperature of 103 °F and has experienced splitting headaches for about a week.) Other signs and symptoms which may be observed less frequently are nausea and vomiting, meningismus, photophobia, and altered mental status. (With the exception of moderate lethargy, A.S. does not present with these other symptoms.) Focal neurologic deficits and seizures are unusual, being observed in less than 10% of patients.[322] CSF glucose and protein are frequently within the normal range; however, CSF India-ink preparations, CSF cryptococcal antigen titer, and CSF culture are frequently positive and, along with the clinical presentation, form the basis for diagnosis. (A.S.'s CSF culture, India-ink stain, and 1:2048 cryptococcal antigen titer are indicative of cryptococcosis.) Overall outcome is poor with a mean survival of five months.[323] Relapse within six months may occur in 50% of patients without follow-up prophylaxis.[319] Altered mental status at baseline, a CSF WBC count of less than 20 cells/mm^3, and a high CSF cryptococcal antigen titer ($>1:1000$) have all been associated with a poor prognosis.[322,324,325] In conclusion, A.S.'s clinical presentation is typical for an AIDS patient with cryptococcal meningitis, and her cerebrospinal fluid WBC count of 10 cells/mm^3 and high cryptococcal antigen titer would suggest a poor prognosis.

Treatment
Amphotericin B

28. What therapy should be initiated to treat A.S.'s cryptococcal meningitis?

Amphotericin B, 0.3 to 0.7 mg/kg day intravenously, is still considered the therapeutic standard. It is believed to act by binding to sterols in the fungal cell membrane, causing leakage of cytoplasmic contents.[326] Although *in vitro* data have demonstrated synergy between amphotericin B and flucytosine, the addition of the latter agent remains controversial, particularly in AIDS patients because of the potential for bone marrow toxicity.[321,327] Flucytosine, a purine analog, is converted intracellularly to 5-fluorouracil, an antimetabolite. A classic, prospective study conducted in HIV- patients favored the use of the combination.[328] The protocol randomized patients to receive either amphotericin B monotherapy (0.4 mg/kg/day × 6 weeks followed by 0.8 mg/kg/day QOD for 4 weeks) for ten weeks or amphotericin B plus flucytosine (150 mg/kg/day divided Q 6 hr) for six weeks. Fewer failures or relapses (3 versus 11), more rapid CSF sterilization (p <0.0001), and less nephrotoxicity (p <0.05) occurred in the combination group: mortality was similar for both groups. Nine of thirty-four patients (27%) assigned to the combination developed leukopenia, thrombocytopenia, or both. In a retrospective review of 89 AIDS patients with cryptococcal meningitis confirmed by CSF culture, there was no survival difference between those who received only amphotericin B monotherapy and those who also were treated with the combination.[322] Bone marrow suppression, which may be enhanced by renal dysfunction induced by amphotericin B, was the reason for discontinuation of flucytosine in over half of the patients. Neutropenia, thrombocytopenia, and diarrhea, have been associated with sustained blood levels greater than 100 mg/dL; however, not all patients with high blood concentrations experienced adverse effects which suggests variable patient responses or possibly a toxic metabolite. If flucytosine is chosen as adjunctive therapy, renal function and complete blood counts should be monitored closely. However, even if doses are reduced due to azotemia or cytopenia, ongoing toxicity might not reverse.[328] Whether prospective evaluation of flucytosine or 5-fluorouracil blood levels would reduce the incidence of toxicity is unknown. AIDS patients may already have reduced bone marrow reserves because of HIV disease and concomitant myelotoxic therapies (i.e., zidovudine). The addition of flucytosine to the therapeutic regimen in these patients warrants extremely careful monitoring.

29. Intrathecal (IT) Amphotericin B. Should A.S. also receive intrathecal Amphotericin B?

Although amphotericin B does not penetrate into CSF very well, intravenous therapy for cryptococcal meningitis generally is adequate. The use of intrathecal amphotericin B in AIDS patients has not been adequately studied. One small retrospective review of 13 patients with a first episode of cryptococcal meningitis and underlying malignancy (11/13) favored insertion of an Ommaya reservoir.[329] Six patients received intraventricular amphotericin B (0.5 mg/day after gradually increasing increments). Both groups of patients received 1 mg/kg/day amphotericin B intravenously and 100 mg/kg/day flucytosine orally as tolerated. Although there were fewer deaths and more patients with sterile CSF and declining CSF cryptococcal antigen titers in the Ommaya reservoir group, the two groups of patients in this small, retrospective study were not equally matched. Complications from use of an Ommaya reservoir occurred in 30% of these patients (e.g., chemical ventriculitis, bacterial infection, headache, fever, and tinnitus). Intravenous amphotericin B should be sufficient for the initial management of A.S.'s infection.

30. Adverse Effects and Administration. How should A.S.'s amphotericin B be administered and what laboratory tests should be monitored?

Adverse effects related to amphotericin B therapy can be categorized into two groups: 1) those that are acutely related to IV infusion; and 2) those that are associated with chronic, organ-related toxicity. After a 1 mg test dose, titration up to full dose should be done as rapidly as patient tolerance permits, particularly in severely ill patients. The dose of amphotericin B generally is diluted to a concentration of no more than 0.1 mg/mL in 5% dextrose and infused over four to six hours to minimize patient discomfort.[330] Fever, headache, chills, nausea and vomiting, myalgias, arthralgias, hypotension, and thrombophlebitis are commonly observed during the period of infusion. These signs and symptoms may be alleviated by premedicating the patient with acetaminophen, diphenhydramine, and antiemetics. Hydrocortisone (25 mg/day) significantly decreases the incidence of fever, chills, nausea, and vomiting; however, no additional benefit is gained by increasing the dose to 50 mg.[331] In another report, 4 patients on amphotericin B and 25 to 40 mg/day of hydrocortisone developed cardiomegaly and congestive heart failure.[332] These two adverse effects were attributed to hypokalemia-induced arrhythmias and circulatory overload from corticosteroid-induced sodium and water retention. After the hydrocortisone was discontinued and potassium supplements were given, both the cardiac enlargement and the congestive

heart failure resolved. Corticosteroids should only be used as an amphotericin premedicant if absolutely necessary. Fluid and electrolyte balance, as well as cardiac function, warrant close monitoring. Thrombophlebitis may improve with the addition of 500 to 1000 units of heparin to the infusion although this has not been studied in a controlled fashion. Rotation of the infusion site beginning with distal veins, and the use of in-line filters and pediatric scalp-vein needles also may minimize the discomfort of the amphotericin B intravenous infusions in A.S.[330]

Amphotericin B can reduce glomerular filtration rate, cause renal tubular acidosis, and decrease renal concentrating ability. Amphotericin B binds to sterols in the cell membrane causing an increase in passive permeability to sodium, potassium, hydrogen ion, water, and low molecular weight solutes such as urea. Although there is no clear relationship to dose, irreversible renal damage is more commonly associated when the total dose of amphotericin is ≥ 4 gm.[333,334] Hypokalemia is the most common electrolyte imbalance associated with amphotericin B therapy and appears in conjunction with renal tubular acidosis. Alkaline urinary pH and increased potassium in the urine are indicators of distal tubular damage.[330] Serum magnesium also may decrease during amphotericin B therapy. Electrolyte disturbances, particularly potassium, may trigger cardiac arrhythmias. While receiving amphotericin B, A.S. should be kept well hydrated. Serum electrolytes, BUN, and serum creatinine should be monitored daily especially during the acute phase of therapy. If her serum creatinine reaches 2.5 to 3.0 mg/dL, the dose should be held for 24 to 48 hours to allow renal function to stabilize. The dose may then be restarted at half the original dose and increased to maximum tolerance.[330] Potassium supplementation is frequently necessary; often the requirement exceeds what can be given orally without gastrointestinal upset. No more than 60 mEq of K^+ should be added per liter of IV fluid at an infusion rate not to exceed 10 mEq/hour.[330] Most patients develop a normocytic, normochromic anemia which is believed to be a direct inhibition of red cell production.[335] Blood transfusion is rarely necessary unless the hematocrit falls below 25%. Erythropoietin therapy may be required particularly if the patient is concurrently taking zidovudine. Leukopenia and thrombocytopenia also may complicate amphotericin B therapy. Complete blood counts with differential should be performed routinely throughout a therapeutic course of amphotericin B. (Also see Chapter 69: Fungal Infections.) In conclusion, A.S. should be monitored for amphotericin B infusion reactions; and her fluid and electrolyte balance, renal function, urine pH and urine potassium, and hematological status should be monitored as well.

Fluconazole

31. Could A.S. be treated with fluconazole instead of amphotericin B?

Fluconazole, one of the triazole antifungal agents, is believed to inhibit a fungal cytochrome P450 enzyme which is necessary for the conversion of lanosterol to ergosterol. Without ergosterol, the fungal cell membrane becomes defective and loses its selective permeability properties.[336] Fluconazole is well absorbed, even in the presence of an elevated gastric pH (unlike ketoconazole), has excellent CNS penetration, and a very good toxicity profile.[336] However, the role of fluconazole as initial therapy for the treatment of acute cryptococcal meningitis remains controversial. In a prospective, randomized, multicenter trial, the National Institute of Allergy and Infectious Diseases (NIAID) Mycoses Study Group and AIDS Clinical Trials Group (ACTG) compared amphotericin B with 200 mg/day of fluconazole (after a 400 mg load) for ten weeks in 194 patients.[337] The dose of amphotericin B (mean dose: 0.4 to 0.5 mg/kg/day) and the use of flucytosine were left to the discretion of the individual investigators. Although the overall mortality was similar (14% for amphotericin B versus 18% for fluconazole), and treatment success as defined by two consecutive negative CSF cultures within the ten-week treatment period was similar (40% for amphotericin B versus 34% for fluconazole), more patients in the fluconazole group died during the first two weeks (15% versus 8% for amphotericin B). Furthermore, the median time to the first negative CSF culture in the successfully treated patients was less in the amphotericin B group than in the fluconazole group (16 versus 30 days). In a small, prospective, randomized trial of 20 male patients with AIDS, oral fluconazole (400 mg/day) for ten weeks was compared with amphotericin B (0.7 mg/kg/day for 1 week, followed by the same dose thrice weekly for 9 weeks) combined with flucytosine (150 mg/kg/day).[338] There were four deaths in the fluconazole group and none in the amphotericin B group (p = 0.27). Eight of fourteen patients in the fluconazole group were treatment failures whereas none of the amphotericin B patients failed (p = 0.04). The mean duration of positive CSF cultures was 41 days in the fluconazole group and 16 days in the amphotericin B group (p = 0.02). These results, in conjunction with those of the large AIDS Clinical Trial Group trial, have led most clinicians to avoid choosing fluconazole as initial treatment for severe cryptococcal meningitis, at least at doses of 200 to 400 mg/day. Therefore, A.S. should be treated with amphotericin B rather than fluconazole.

Itraconazole

32. What is the role of itraconazole (Sporanox) in the treatment of cryptococcal meningitis?

Although CSF penetration of itraconazole, a new oral triazole, appears to be poor, efficacy has been demonstrated in an animal model of cryptococcal meningitis.[339,340] In an uncontrolled trial, all symptoms resolved and cultures were negative, in 71% (10/14) of AIDS patients with cryptococcal meningitis who were treated with itraconazole (200 mg BID) as monotherapy.[341] These patients continued to receive itraconazole for one year and were monitored for an additional year after the itraconazole was discontinued. The median survival of these patients exceeded 10.5 months. In a controlled trial, 42% (5 of 12) itraconazole-treated patients (200 mg BID PO) responded completely compared to 100% (10 of 10) of patients who received amphotericin B (0.3 mg/kg/day IV) plus flucytosine (150 mg/kg/day) for six weeks (p = 0.009).[342] In both studies, itraconazole generally was well tolerated; however, its role as initial therapy for acute cryptococcal meningitis remains to be clarified.

Duration of Therapy

33. How long should treatment for A.S. continue?

Treatment for cryptococcal meningitis in AIDS patients should continue for six to ten weeks.[337,338,342] Because serious toxicities are encountered with both amphotericin B and flucytosine, and since both fluconazole and itraconazole have shown promise in the treatment of cryptococcal meningitis in AIDS patients, an ongoing, multicenter AIDS Clinical Trial Group trial is randomizing patients to receive either 400 mg/day of fluconazole or 200 mg twice a day of itraconazole for eight weeks after patients have completed two weeks of therapy with amphotericin B (0.7 mg/kg/day) and flucytosine (100 mg/kg/day). Results of this trial are currently in preliminary stages of analysis at the time of this writing. Some clinicians now switch to either fluconazole or itraconazole after two to three weeks of amphotericin B plus or minus flucytosine, particularly if CSF sterilization has occurred, although documentation in support of this regimen is limited.[321]

Investigational Therapies

34. What other therapies are currently under investigation?

The combination of fluconazole plus flucytosine appears to be superior to fluconazole alone. High-dose fluconazole alone (800 to 1600 mg/day for up to 6 months) was compared to high-dose fluconazole and flucytosine (150 mg/kg/day for 4 weeks) in 36 AIDS patients.[343] Nine of twelve (75%) patients in the combination group survived and became CSF culture negative whereas only 7 of 24 (29%) patients on fluconazole monotherapy showed similar results (p = 0.03). Liposomal amphotericin B also shows some promise. AIDS patients (n = 23) with cryptococcosis were treated for a minimum of 42 days with liposomal amphotericin B (3 mg/kg/day).[344] Eighteen of twenty-three patients showed a complete or partial clinical response and, of these, 12 of 18 had negative CSF cultures after a median of 11 days.

Maintenance Therapy

35. Should A.S. receive maintenance therapy following successful treatment?

After cryptococcal meningitis treatment, A.S. and all AIDS patients should receive maintenance therapy indefinitely.[321] A higher relapse rate, as well as a shorter life expectancy, have been observed in patients who did not receive chronic secondary prophylaxis.[319,322] Fluconazole has emerged as the suppressive treatment of choice. In a randomized, placebo-controlled trial of 61 AIDS patients, four recurrent cases of meningitis developed in the placebo group and none in the fluconazole group (p = 0.03) after a median duration of 164 days of follow-up.[345] A multicenter, comparison trial randomized patients to receive either weekly amphotericin B (1 mg/kg/day) intravenously or 200 mg/day of fluconazole orally.[346] Of 189 patients after a median follow-up of 286 days, 18% relapsed in the amphotericin B group compared to 2% in the fluconazole group (p <0.001). Serious toxicity, as well as bacterial infections, were more frequent in the amphotericin B group. Preliminary data for itraconazole also are encouraging. Four of five patients maintained on itraconazole (200 to 400 mg/day) for 3 to 12 months after acute treatment showed three- to sixfold declining CSF cryptococcal antigen titers.[347] The fifth patient refused repeat lumbar puncture. A randomized, comparative trial of fluconazole (200 mg/day) versus itraconazole (200 mg/day) also is underway sponsored by the NIAID Mycoses Study Group.

Primary Prophylaxis

36. What is the role for primary prophylaxis of cryptococcal meningitis?

Primary prophylaxis against cryptococcal disease in HIV+ patients has only been studied in a few clinical trials. In an open-label study, 329 HIV+ patients were given 100 mg fluconazole daily after their CD4+ count dropped to 68 cells/mm^3 and the results compared with 337 historical controls.[348] Maximum follow-up time was one year. Sixteen cases of cryptococcal meningitis occurred in the historical controls (4.8%) and only one case in the fluconazole group (0.3%). In a prospective, randomized AIDS Clinical Trial Group (ACTG) study, fluconazole 200 mg/day was compared to clotrimazole troches (10 mg five times a day) for the prevention of fungal infections in 428 patients with advanced HIV disease (CD4+ counts of <200 cells/mm^3). After a median follow-up of 35 months, 32 cases of invasive fungal infection were confirmed. Of these, the majority (17/32) were cryptococcosis: 2 cases in the fluconazole group and 15 cases in the clotrimazole group. The greatest benefit derived from fluconazole was observed in those patients with less than 50 CD4+ cells/mm^3.[646] No effect on survival was noted. In the fluconazole group, 11% of patients had at least one episode of candidiasis during the study; fluconazole resistance, as previously reported in HIV+ patients receiving long-term fluconazole[349] is a concern. The costs of daily fluconazole therapy for large numbers of patients also must be weighed against the costs of careful monitoring of the individual patient. Despite the current controversies surrounding primary prophylaxis against cryptococcal infection, it may be a reasonable option in those HIV+ patients with less than 50 CD4+ cells/mm^3.

Toxoplasma Encephalitis
Clinical Presentation

37. W.O. is a 40-year-old black male, discovered to be HIV-positive during admission to a detoxification program for alcohol and heroin dependency. W.O. presented to the AIDS clinic in July 1994 with esophageal candidiasis, a CD4+ cell count of 60 cells/mm^3, and a toxoplasma IgG titer of 1:256. W.O. remained well until January 1995 when he presented to the emergency room (ER) reporting 2 seizures in the past 24 hours. His medications at that time included: didanosine 200 mg Q 12 hr, rifabutin 300 mg/day, acyclovir 200 mg TID, and inhaled pentamidine 300 mg monthly. W.O. had a temperature of 100.1 °F and had difficulty walking. MRI of the head revealed several ring-shaped lesions in the brainstem. Toxoplasma encephalitis was presumptively diagnosed. Should W.O. be isolated from other patients and health care workers to prevent the spread of this organism?

Toxoplasma gondii is a parasitic protozoan which can infect a variable number of persons worldwide, depending upon environmental factors, such as contact with cats or consumption of raw or undercooked meats. Immunocompetent persons may have mild, ''mono-type'' symptoms when they are first infected with *T. gondii*, but these symptoms generally are transient and do not cause problems (except in women who acquire primary infection during pregnancy). Recrudescent disease from *T. gondii* becomes problematic, however, in patients with suppression of the cellular immune system, such as those infected with HIV or those receiving antineoplastic or immunosuppressive medications. Any HIV patient infected with *T. gondii* is at risk for the development of disease, especially when CD4+ cell counts fall to ≤100 cells/mm^3, or when the HIV is symptomatic.[350] In HIV patients, the most frequent manifestation of *T. gondii* is encephalitis, an inflammation of the brain or brainstem. The clinical signs and symptoms of Toxoplasma encephalitis can be either focal (indicating a specific region of the brain which is infected/inflamed) or generalized (indicating diffuse inflammation of the brain). The prevalence of *Toxoplasma* encephalitis among HIV patients is variable, depending upon the prevalence of infection with *T. gondii* among the general population in the geographical region of interest. For example, in European countries where uncooked meat is more commonly eaten, more persons are infected, and *Toxoplasma* encephalitis may develop in as many as 25% to 50% of AIDS patients. In the U.S., only 3% to 10% of AIDS patients develop encephalitis. W.O. need not be isolated from other patients and health care workers.

Diagnosis

38. Is there sufficient clinical evidence to establish a diagnosis of *Toxoplasma* encephalitis in W.O.?

Diagnosis of *Toxoplasma* encephalitis usually is presumptive, since demonstration of cysts or trophozoites in brain tissue is required for a definitive diagnosis. Serum titers of antibodies against *T. gondii* typically reflect past infection with the organism, but generally are not considered indicative of active infection. Most patients with encephalitis have single or multiple lesions demonstrated on computerized axial tomography or magnetic resonance

imaging of the head. At present, most practitioners reserve brain biopsy for patients with symptoms of encephalitis who are seronegative, those who do not respond to presumptive antitoxoplasmosis therapy after one or two weeks,[351,352] or perhaps those receiving systemic prophylactic therapy for PCP.[350] Due to the nonspecific diagnosis of *Toxoplasma* encephalitis, a high index of suspicion for other causes of encephalitis (e.g., CNS lymphoma or tuberculosis) should be maintained throughout the treatment period for presumed *Toxoplasma* encephalitis.[353] Although W.O. is HIV positive, has a *Toxoplasma* titer of 1:256, and has ring-shaped lesions in the brainstem on MRI, his diagnosis of *Toxoplasma* encephalitis is still only presumptive.

Prophylaxis

39. Should W.O. have been receiving prophylaxis for *T. gondii*?

Like many of the other opportunistic infections associated with HIV, therapy for toxoplasmosis can be categorized into primary prophylaxis, treatment of acute disease, and secondary prophylaxis or maintenance therapy. While primary prophylaxis is not currently recommended, many of the agents used to prevent *Pneumocystis carinii* pneumonia have activity against *T. gondii*, and may afford some protection. For example, preliminary data indicate that intermittent therapy with TMP-SMX or dapsone/pyrimethamine may be effective as primary prophylaxis of *T. gondii*.[354–356] Intermittent pyrimethamine monotherapy (50 mg thrice weekly with leucovorin 15 mg), did not influence the rate of *Toxoplasma* encephalitis, nor did it affect survival in a placebo-controlled trial of 554 patients.[357] Another placebo-controlled trial of pyrimethamine was halted after finding a higher mortality rate and a higher rate of *Toxoplasma* encephalitis in the pyrimethamine group.[358] Therefore, pyrimethamine monotherapy generally is not recommended for primary prophylaxis of *T. gondii* infection. Due to the localized delivery of inhaled pentamidine, W.O. is not receiving any agent with antitoxoplasmosis activity.

Treatment
Sulfadiazine/Pyrimethamine

40. What is the recommended treatment of Toxoplasmic encephalitis?

Approximately 80% of patients with acute *Toxoplasma* encephalitis, can be treated successfully with a combination of sulfadiazine (4 to 6 gm/day in 3 to 4 daily divided doses) and pyrimethamine (a single 100 to 200 mg loading dose, followed by 50 to 75 mg/day as a single dose).[362,363] Toxicity (especially bone marrow suppression or rash) to these agents may limit the completion of a full course of therapy in as many as 40% of patients.[361] The clinical and radiological response of the patient should be monitored closely especially since the diagnosis of *Toxoplasma* encephalitis is only presumptive without a definitive finding on a brain biopsy.

41. W.O. is treated with sulfadiazine/pyrimethamine. What are the limitations to the use of this combination for the treatment of *Toxoplasma* encephalitis?

As with other sulfa-drugs in HIV patients, rashes are common with sulfadiazine therapy. Various desensitization regimens have been published;[362,363] however, it may be easier to use alternative therapies in such patients. Patients with increases in serum creatinine, blood in urine, or decreased urine output, may have crystalluria secondary to sulfadiazine. The water solubility of sulfadiazine is less than that of other sulfa-drugs; therefore hydration (2 to 3 L/day) is needed to prevent crystalline nephropathy. Renal function should be monitored throughout therapy,[364–368] and prophylactic alkalization of the urine with sodium bicarbonate has been advocated.[368] Aggressive hydration and alkalinization should rapidly reverse urine sulfadiazine crystal formation. Although many manufactures no longer market sulfadiazine, this drug is available from the Centers for Disease Control.[369,370] Triple sulfa combination therapy may be less likely than sulfadiazine to crystallize in the urine, because the water solubilities of each sulfa are independent of one another and the antimicrobial activity is at least additive.

42. Why is the pyrimethamine component not likely to cause problems for W.O.?

Pyrimethamine can suppress bone marrow function; thus, concomitant therapy with other medications which also suppress marrow function (e.g., zidovudine or ganciclovir), may be intolerable. Folinic acid (5 to 10 mg/day) usually is given in conjunction with pyrimethamine to maintain bone marrow function, although it is not always successful. Folic acid should be avoided, because it also can be utilized by protozoal organisms and may antagonize pyrimethamine/sulfadiazine activity.[371–373] It may be prudent to discontinue vitamin preparations containing large quantities of folic acid (some contain as much as 600 mg of folic acid). Pyrimethamine may inhibit renal tubular secretion of creatinine accounting for an approximately 27% decrease in estimated creatinine clearance, with no associated change in inulin clearance.[374] W.O. is not presently taking medications that would make him particularly susceptible to the myelosuppressive effects of pyrimethamine and is not presently anemic. If, however, drugs such as zidovudine or ganciclovir are initiated, he would be more vulnerable to myelosuppression if his pyrimethamine is continued.

Suppressive Therapy

43. Once W.O. has completed acute therapy of his *Toxoplasma* encephalitis, should he receive suppressive therapy?

Most antiprotozoal agents are incapable of eradicating the cyst form of *T. gondii* and since HIV patients are not expected to regain normal immune function, lifelong suppression is indicated. Most patients with a history of toxoplasmic encephalitis relapse even with continued therapy. While the optimal agent(s)/regimens have not been determined, suppressive therapy, at approximately half of the treatment doses of sulfadiazine/pyrimethamine generally are recommended. A retrospective chart review of 35 patients receiving maintenance therapy for *Toxoplasmosis* suggested that sulfadiazine/pyrimethamine may be more effective than clindamycin/pyrimethamine or pyrimethamine alone.[375] Low-dose intermittent pyrimethamine monotherapy has been used,[381] but at least one trial of pyrimethamine monotherapy as secondary prophylaxis was halted due to an unacceptably high rate of mortality in the pyrimethamine group.

Alternative Therapies

44. What treatment options exist for patients who are intolerant of sulfadiazine and do not wish to undergo desensitization?

An alternative to sulfadiazine, especially for intolerant patients, is clindamycin 600 mg four times daily.[350,375–380] However, poor tolerance also may limit the use of clindamycin/pyrimethamine therapy.

Although atovaquone (Mepron) has been approved only for pneumocystosis, it also has *in vitro* activity against the cyst form of *T. gondii* and is effective in an animal model.[259,383,384] In several small studies, atovaquone seemed promising for treating toxoplasmic encephalitis in HIV patients who failed or were intolerant of other therapies.[267,385,386] Doxycycline is effective although clinical experience with this agent is limited,[387] and minocycline has been successful in several patients.[388] Clarithromycin has *in vitro* activity[388] and an azithromycin/pyrimethamine combination is currently under investigation for treatment of cerebral toxoplasmosis.

Mycobacterium tuberculosis
Clinical Presentation

45. C.J., a 45-year-old, heterosexual male with AIDS, is a prison inmate. He presents with fever, cough, and occasional night sweats. A tuberculin purified protein derivative skin test is negative, but C.J. appears to be anergic based upon his response to other skin test antigens. Several acid-fast bacilli (AFB) sputum smears are also negative. Chest x-ray reveals hilar adenopathy with a questionable right middle lobe localized infiltrate. No cavitary lesions are seen. Why is infection with *M. tuberculosis* a possibility in C.J.?

Although the majority of AIDS patients do not have tuberculosis, the incidence of tuberculosis associated with AIDS has been increasing in recent years.[389,390] The incidence of tuberculosis in the U.S. had been steadily declining, however, approximately 40,000 more cases of tuberculosis were reported to the Centers for Disease Control from 1985 through 1991 than was expected.[391] HIV disease is believed to be a major factor contributing to this increase in the number of tuberculosis cases and to the recent emergence of multidrug-resistant tuberculosis. *M. tuberculosis* resistant to isoniazid and rifampin, with or without resistance to other agents, has become a major public health concern.[391–393] In 1991 in New York City, 33% of *M. tuberculosis* were resistant to at least one drug and 19% were resistant to both isoniazid and rifampin.[394] These drug resistant strains have been found primarily in large urban areas, coastal or border communities, and institutional settings.[391,392] Nine outbreaks of multidrug-resistant tuberculosis in hospital and prison settings in New York and Florida were investigated by the CDC in 1990.[395–397] A high prevalence of HIV infection (range: 20% to 100%), a high mortality rate (72% to 89%), and a short median survival (range: 4 to 16 weeks) were common to these outbreaks. These multidrug resistant strains have been transmitted to health care workers and prison staff and at least 17 cases of active multidrug-resistant tuberculosis have been documented in these individuals.[391]

C.J. presents with fever, cough, night sweats, and a right middle lobe infiltrate with hilar adenopathy on chest x-ray. These clinical features are consistent with tuberculosis and his HIV status in combination with his incarceration within a prison increase the probability of infection with multidrug-resistant tuberculi.

46. Sputum cultures from C.J. have subsequently grown *M. tuberculosis* that is resistant to both isoniazid and rifampin. Why are the negative tuberculin skin test, negative sputum smears for acid-fast bacilli, and lack of cavitary lesions in C.J. still consistent with *M. tuberculosis* infection?

The clinical presentation of tuberculosis is somewhat different for patients with an HIV infection. For example, as many as one-half to two-thirds of AIDS patients with tuberculosis have extrapulmonary sites of infection.[389,390,398] These extrapulmonary sites include lymph nodes, bone marrow, spleen, liver, cerebrospinal fluid, and blood.[398] *M. tuberculosis* was rarely found in blood before the AIDS era, but tuberculosis bacteremia has now been documented in several reports.[399,400] HIV-infected patients with tuberculosis infection also may be at increased risk for developing meningitis.[401] Chest radiography in HIV-infected patients may reveal hilar or mediastinal adenopathy, or localized infiltrates in the middle or lower lung fields; and it is unusual to see typical apical infiltrates or cavitation observed in HIV-infected patients.[398] Furthermore, concomitant *P. carinii* pneumonia may confuse interpretation of chest x-rays. In addition, AFB smears of sputum in HIV-infected patients may be falsely negative, as in C.J.'s case.[402] Finally, anergy is extremely common in HIV disease. Only 10% to 40% of HIV-infected patients with tuberculosis have a positive tuberculin skin test.[389,403] Definitive diagnosis rests on positive cultures from sputum, or other tissue and body fluid specimens. (See Chapter 59: Tuberculosis.)

Treatment

47. How should A.J. be treated and monitored?

The natural occurrence of resistant *M. tuberculosis* through random genetic mutation is fairly low: $1/10^8$ for rifampin, $1/10^6$ for isoniazid and streptomycin, and $1/10^4$ for ethambutol.[391] However, administration of a single antitubercular drug often results in the rapid development of a resistant bacterial population. Therefore, effective regimens against *M. tuberculosis* must contain multiple drugs to which the organism is sensitive, particularly when treating multidrug-resistant tuberculosis. Since it is frequently necessary to begin treatment empirically before culture results are known, it may be difficult to select a combination of two drugs to which the tubercle bacillus is sensitive. Improper selection of drugs initially may lead to further development of bacterial resistance. For this reason, a four-drug empiric regimen consisting of isoniazid, rifampin, pyrazinamide, and ethambutol or streptomycin (available from CDC) is now recommended by the CDC Advisory Council for the Elimination of Tuberculosis (ACET) for the initial treatment of tuberculosis. This regimen applies to all patients unless the likelihood of resistance to isoniazid or rifampin is very low.[391] When *in vitro* susceptibility results are available, the regimen should be altered appropriately. If the organism is sensitive to both isoniazid and rifampin, then the third and fourth drug may be discontinued after two months. When treating an institutional outbreak of multidrug-resistant tuberculosis or an individual patient with a prior history of antituberculous therapy, initial therapy may need to include five or six drugs.[391] In C.J.'s case, if his organism is resistant to both isoniazid and rifampin, those two agents should be discontinued, and at least three more drugs should be added to his regimen. The dosing regimens for HIV patients and for non-HIV patients are the same, but a longer duration of treatment is necessary for the patients with concurrent HIV infection. Treatment should continue for a total of nine months for HIV-infected patients and for six months after sputum cultures become negative.[404]

The optimal duration of treatment for multidrug-resistant tuberculosis has not been established. The National Jewish Center for Immunology and Respiratory Medicine treats patients with resistant organisms for 24 months with oral medications after sputum cultures become negative. Parenteral medication is continued for four to six months if toxicity remains manageable.[392] Intermittent therapy (administered 2 or 3 times/week) is allowable as long as it is directly observed.[391] The mortality rate was higher (9% versus 1%, p <0.005) during therapy in 176 HIV-infected patients receiving directly observed, thrice weekly treatment for six months for nonmultidrug-resistant tuberculosis, compared to 247 HIV-infected patients receiving daily therapy.[405] All patients with organisms resistant to either isoniazid or rifampin should have their ingestion of antitubercular medications directly observed. Although directly-observed drug regimens are labor intensive, these regimens are cost effective.[392] Whenever organisms resistant to either isoniazid or rifampin are isolated, a medical expert should be consulted. Since patient intolerance (particularly gastrointestinal) is common on antituberculous regimens, the National Jewish Center recommends that initial therapy begin in the hospital in order to monitor toxicity before a patient becomes totally averse to taking medication.[392] This Center also initiates therapy with small doses of each agent followed by gradual escalation to the target dose over three to ten days.[392] C.J. should be monitored for a decrease in the frequency of his fevers and night sweats, as well as improvement in his cough. Sputum cultures should be followed routinely. These results are the major marker of response and may determine the duration of treatment. Chest radiography may be the last parameter to improve.[392]

Prophylaxis

HIV− Individuals: Multidrug-Resistant Tuberculosis

48. A nurse inadvertently entered C.J.'s room without taking adequate precautions and suctioned respiratory secretions. Four weeks later her tuberculin skin test converted to positive. What prophylactic regimen should be initiated for this nurse?

Currently, there is no known prophylactic regimen with proven efficacy against multidrug-resistant tuberculosis.[392,407] Several multidrug prophylactic regimens have been recommended: pyrazinamide (25 to 30 mg/kg/day) combined with ethambutol (15 to 25 mg/kg/day); pyrazinamide with ofloxacin (400 mg BID); and pyrazinamide combined with ciprofloxacin (750 mg BID).[411,412] Sparfloxacin also has demonstrated good *in vitro* activity and may prove to be useful clinically.[413] If the exposed person is HIV-infected, or otherwise immunosuppressed, multidrug prophylaxis should continue for 12 months; otherwise six months of therapy is recommended by the CDC.[407]

HIV+ Individuals: Drug-Sensitive Tuberculosis

49. K.D., a 26-year-old HIV+ male, comes in for a routine clinic visit. It is discovered that he is a household contact of a person known to have active, untreated, drug-sensitive tuberculosis. His CD4+ count is 350 cells/mm³. A tuberculin skin test [5 tuberculin units (TU) of purified protein derivative (PPD)] and 2 other skin test antigens are administered and he is instructed to return to the clinic in 48 hours. His PPD has been negative in the past and he has demonstrated delayed hypersensitivity responsiveness. How would the results of K.D.'s skin tests be interpreted and should he receive prophylaxis?

The CDC and the American Thoracic Society currently recommend one year of isoniazid prophylaxis (300 mg/day) for all HIV-infected persons who have a ≥5 mm induration reaction to PPD, unless otherwise contraindicated and regardless of Bacillus-Calmette-Guerin vaccination status.[404] This is in contrast to a

Table 68.7	Second-Line Agents in the Treatment of *Mycobacterium tuberculosis* Infection[a]	
Drug	**Dosage[4]**	**Major Dose-Limiting Toxicity**
Ofloxacin[b]	400 mg PO BID	Rare CNS: Nightmares, hallucinations, seizures
Ciprofloxacin[b]	750 mg PO BID	Rare CNS: Nightmares, hallucinations, seizures
p-Aminosalicylic Acid	3 gm PO QID	GI: Nausea, vomiting, abdominal pain, diarrhea
Cycloserine	250 mg PO BID or TID	CNS: Seizures, psychotic reactions
Amikacin[b]	15 mg/kg/day IV or IM	Oto- and nephrotoxicity
Kanamycin[b]	15 mg/kg/day IV or IM	Oto- and nephrotoxicity
Capreomycin	15 mg/kg/day deep IM	Oto- and nephrotoxicity
Ethionamide	250 mg BID or TID	GI: Nausea, vomiting, abdominal pain, diarrhea, bitter metallic taste, anorexia

[a] See also Chapter 59: Tuberculosis.
[b] Not FDA-approved for the treatment of tuberculosis.

≥ 10 mm induration cutoff for HIV-negative individuals.[414] Few failures of isoniazid prophylaxis have been reported, although this has not been systematically studied. An inverse relationship has been discovered between the presence of cutaneous anergy and a CD4+ count of less than 500 cells/mm[3].[415] If K.D. proves to be anergic, he should still be considered to be in need of isoniazid prophylaxis since he is a close contact of an infectious person.[397] Prophylaxis also should be considered for anergic, HIV+ persons who are members of groups known to have a $\geq 10\%$ prevalence of tuberculosis infection. In the U.S., these groups include IV drug users, prison inmates, residents of homeless shelters, and persons born in Latin American, Asian, or African countries with high rates of tuberculosis.[416] Before any prophylactic regimen is begun, the presence of active disease needs to be ruled out.

Mycobacterium avium Complex (MAC) Infection
Clinical Presentation

50. M.E., an HIV+ 38-year-old female with a history of IV drug use, presents with fevers, drenching night sweats, poor appetite, and a 20-pound weight loss (>15% of baseline) over the last 4 months. M.E. has not received any antiretroviral therapy for the past year due to intolerance to zidovudine (Retrovir), didanosine (Videx), and zalcitabine (Hivid). She has had no opportunistic infections to date. Physical examination reveals a cachectic female with mild hepatosplenomegaly. Pertinent laboratory test results include: Hct 23%, WBC count 3500 cells/mm[3] with 68% neutrophils, 2% bands, 22% lymphocytes, and 8% monocytes. Absolute CD4+ lymphocyte count is 55 cells/mm[3] and p24 antigenemia is present at 956 pg/dL. Hepatic transaminases and alkaline phosphatase are elevated: AST 135 IU/L (Normal: 0–35); ALT 95 IU/L (Normal: 0–35); and alkaline phosphatase 186 IU/L (Normal: 30–120). Skin testing reveals anergy. Chest radiography is normal. A presumptive diagnosis of *Mycobacterium avium* complex (MAC) infection is made. After blood cultures are drawn, M.E. is begun on a 4-drug regimen immediately. Why is M.E.'s clinical presentation consistent with MAC infection? [SI units: Hct 0.23; WBC count 3.5 × 10⁹/L with 0.68 neutrophils, 0.02 bands, 0.22 lymphocytes, 0.08 monocytes; AST 135 U/L (Normal: 0–35); ALT 95 U/L (Normal: 0–35), alkaline phosphatase 186 U/L (Normal: 30–120)]

Disseminated MAC infection may be an inevitable outcome in end-stage AIDS patients who have not succumbed to other opportunistic infections.[417] It has been found in approximately half of AIDS patients at autopsy.[418] (M.E. has AIDS and has not experienced opportunistic infections to date.) Until recently, it was uncertain if the presence of disseminated MAC infection had an impact on survival; however, several large-scale studies have now clearly demonstrated increased mortality in AIDS patients with disseminated MAC infection, compared to AIDS patients without disseminated MAC.[299,419–422] The predominant organism in HIV-positive patients is *Mycobacterium avium* (97% of typeable isolates), followed by *Mycobacterium intracellulare* (3%).[423] The risk of developing disseminated MAC infection has been strongly associated with declining CD4+ lymphocyte counts of less than 100 cells/mm[3].[417,419] When 1006 HIV+ patients were monitored for the development of MAC bacteremia over a three-year period, 93% of 191 patients who developed positive MAC blood cultures had CD4+ lymphocyte counts of less than 100 cells/mm[3]. Furthermore, the risk of developing MAC bacteremia was inversely proportional to the CD4+ count, once the CD4+ count fell below 100 cells/mm[3].[417] (M.E.'s CD4+ count is 55 cells/mm[3].) Differences in age, gender, or race have not been associated with increased risk of disseminated MAC infection.[417,422] Overall prognosis was poor, with a mean survival of three to seven months.[420,421,424] Prior opportunistic infection, severe anemia, zi-

dovudine dose interruption, and low total lymphocyte count all have been identified as poor prognostic indicators.[422,425] (M.E. is severely anemic with a Hct of 23% and she has discontinued her zidovudine therapy.)

M. avium is ubiquitous in nature, being found in food, water, soil, and house dust.[426] The most likely portal of entry is either the gastrointestinal or respiratory tract.[398] Therefore, sputum and stool samples frequently are colonized with MAC. The significance of MAC colonization remains controversial. Common presenting symptoms of MAC infection are fever, night sweats, anorexia, malaise, profound weight loss (>10% body weight), lymphadenopathy, and diarrhea.[427] (M.E. presents with fevers, drenching night sweats, poor appetite, a 20-pound weight loss, and mild hepatosplenomegaly.)

Treatment
Initiation

51. Why is it appropriate to initiate M.E.'s drug therapy before blood culture results are known?

Disseminated MAC is best diagnosed by peripheral blood cultures.[427] The finding of acid-fast bacilli on a blood smear also can be diagnostic, but the results of these are variable.[428] Conventional culture methods using solid media may have a turnaround time of as long as eight weeks; however, newer radiometric broth systems which detect the release of C[14]-labeled CO_2 from mycobacteria, may detect bacterial growth in as little as seven to ten days.[428] Organism identification (*M. tuberculosis* versus *M. avium* or other strains) by conventional biochemical methods also may take several weeks to months. Newer techniques, such as DNA probes, make this possible within several hours.[428] Quantitative blood cultures which measure colony-forming units (CFU)/mL have been useful in clinical trials in order to monitor the effects of drug therapy, but may not be practical on a routine clinical basis. Radiometric broth methods also may determine *in vitro* drug susceptibility in another seven to ten days. Even if all of the newer laboratory tests are available at a given institution, test results generally are not available for two to three weeks. In view of this lag time, it is in the patient's best interest to initiate empiric therapy as quickly as possible. Although MAC is typically isolated from blood, it may be more rapidly demonstrated on acid-fast smears of lymph node, liver, or bone marrow biopsies. Because these organs are rich in monocyte/macrophages, the target cell for MAC infection, the organism load may be very high (up to 10[10] CFU/gm). Granuloma formation or inflammation may not be evident due to profound suppression of cell-mediated immunity in end-stage AIDS patients.[429] On autopsy, MAC organisms also have been observed in the lungs, spleen, colon, adrenals, kidneys, brain, and skin.[424]

52. What is the relevance of M.E.'s discontinued antiretroviral therapy to her development of *Mycobacterium avium* complex infection?

The impact of antiretroviral therapy on the development of disseminated MAC infection is difficult to assess, although HIV also is known to infect monocyte/macrophages. In *in vitro* macrophage culture studies, the intracellular growth rate of *M. avium* was greatly enhanced in those cells which also were infected with HIV.[430] Conversely, if macrophages taken from HIV-infected patients were infected with *M. avium*, latent HIV virus began to replicate in some of these cultures.[430] Clinically, the two organisms may act synergistically, leading to a hastened deterioration of the host.[421]

Drug Susceptibility as a Basis for Treatment
53. Should M.E.'s therapy be based upon *in vitro* drug susceptibility results?

Correlation between *in vitro* drug susceptibility results and clinical efficacy has not been clearly established. This may be true for a number of reasons. First, results are method dependent: MAC isolates appear to be more sensitive if broth is used rather than agar.[428,431] Second, current *in vitro* methods are cell-free which does not take into account the intracellular nature of MAC infection. Thus, drugs which have excellent cellular penetration may perform well clinically despite the absence of supporting *in vitro* mean inhibitory concentration (MIC) data. Conversely, drugs which have good MIC data, may not be very effective clinically if they do not reach the intracellular environment.[431] Investigations incorporating murine macrophages into an *in vitro* drug susceptibility testing system are in progress.[431] If this type of system becomes standardized in the future, it may be a better predictor of clinical outcome. Drug susceptibility studies also correlate poorly with clinical efficacy because *in vitro* results for individually tested drugs may show resistance, but combinations often provide additive or synergistic effects.[427] Finally, some antimycobacterial agents exhibit large differences between MIC and mean bactericidal concentration (MBC) data which may reflect the difficulty of eradicating this organism, particularly in a severely immunocompromised host.[432] Despite these limitations, many clinicians still choose to use *in vitro* drug susceptibility data as a guide to therapy. Beige mouse animal model data also may be useful. Only until recently have any large-scale, randomized, comparison clinical trials been undertaken. Until results of these trials are forthcoming, the need to rely on *in vitro* drug susceptibility data, animal model data, and the results of small, uncontrolled trials will continue.

Drug Therapy

54. What drug regimens could be selected for M.E.'s treatment?

Until recently, it was controversial whether patients with disseminated MAC infection should be treated at all. Results of early, uncontrolled trials were disappointing with poor microbiologic response rates, little improvement in clinical symptoms, and a high incidence of adverse drug reactions. Only 2/26 (8%) patients in one study (mean follow-up: 6 weeks) cleared their bacteremia after treatment with rifabutin, clofazimine, and either ethambutol or ethionamide.[424] Only 1/13 patients in another study where the primary treatment was rifabutin, clofazimine, and amikacin had symptomatic improvement associated with conversion to a negative blood culture.[433] More recent clinical trials have been more promising, showing a decrease or eradication of MAC bacteremia and improvement or resolution of clinical symptoms. The reasons for better results with more recent trials are not clear, but probably include earlier diagnosis, longer follow-up, availability of antiretroviral therapy, and newer anti-MAC agents with greater intracellular penetration.[427] In a small, retrospective review, survival was improved in 16 disseminated MAC patients who received treatment (median: 8 months) versus matched controls who did not (4 months).[434] In one of the few placebo-controlled trials, four of nine patients treated for eight weeks with rifampin, ethambutol, and ciprofloxacin had greater than 1 log decreases in CFU/mL versus zero of ten placebo patients (p = 0.006). However, 9/12 treated patients experienced dose-limiting toxicity versus 1/12 placebo patients (p = 0.005). In another placebo-controlled trial, seven of eight patients who received 2 gm/day of clarithromycin monotherapy eradicated *M. avium* from their blood cultures after four weeks. In contrast, all five placebo patients showed increases in CFU/mL (21). The California Collaborative Treatment Group, in an uncontrolled trial, treated 31 disseminated MAC patients with rifampin, ethambutol, clofazimine, and ciprofloxacin. Thirteen patients (42%) became culture-negative after an average of ten weeks

of treatment. The frequency of fevers and night sweats also decreased significantly compared to baseline.[435] Nineteen patients (46%) required withdrawal of one or more drugs because of adverse events. In an uncontrolled, monotherapy trial of azithromycin (500 mg/day), 21 patients treated for 20 or 30 days, showed a mean decrease from 2028 CFU/mL to 136 CFU/mL. Resolution of fevers and night sweats occurred in 71% and 67% of patients, respectively.[436] However, bacteriologic relapse occurred after treatment was discontinued, even in ten patients who elected to continue azithromycin suppressive therapy of 250 mg/day which suggests the emergence of resistance. Similar results have been observed with clarithromycin monotherapy.[437,438]

The U.S. Public Health Service Task Force on Prophylaxis and Therapy for *Mycobacterium avium* Complex infection has made three recommendations regarding treatment.

- Treatment regimens outside of a clinical trial should include at least two agents.[391] Clinical trials with clarithromycin and azithromycin have shown that monotherapy eventually will lead to breakthrough bacteremia and resistance.[436–438] In one study, all isolates were initially susceptible to clarithromycin, but after 12 weeks of clarithromycin monotherapy (1 to 4 gm/day), *in vitro* resistance developed in 16/72 (22%) patients.[439]

- All regimens should contain either clarithromycin or azithromycin.[391] Both of these new macrolides demonstrate excellent intracellular penetration and have prolonged half-lives.[440–443] One *in vitro* clarithromycin study, using a murine macrophage cell-line infected with *M. avium*, reported an intracellular:extracellular concentration ratio of 17:1.[441] Both drugs have *in vitro* and *in vivo* activity against *M. avium*.[435–444] Gastrointestinal toxicity (e.g., nausea, vomiting, diarrhea, abdominal pain, and anorexia) is the most frequent adverse effect encountered with either agent.[436,439] Adverse GI effects are apparently dose related. Patients receiving 4 gm/day of clarithromycin are more likely to have their therapy discontinued because of GI upset than patients receiving lower doses.[445] Many experts prefer ethambutol as the second agent. One or more of the following drugs are then added as the third or fourth drug: rifabutin, rifampin, ciprofloxacin, and clofazimine, with or without amikacin.[391] The role of amikacin should become more clear when the results of an ongoing AIDS Clinical Trial Group trial are analyzed. The protocol will compare two groups of patients randomly assigned to receive rifampin, ethambutol, ciprofloxacin, and clofazimine with or without amikacin. Isoniazid and pyrazinamide are not effective agents for the treatment of MAC infection.[391,431,438,446] A summary of the most commonly used drugs in disseminated MAC disease with dosages and toxicities is shown in Table 68.8.

- Finally, if microbiologic and clinical improvement are observed, therapy should continue for the lifetime of the patient.[391] Relapse is not uncommon even if uninterrupted multidrug therapy continues; however, it will occur sooner if treatment is discontinued altogether, or if only monotherapy is implemented.[433,436–438]

Conventional interpretation of *in vitro* susceptibility results should not be applied to disseminated MAC infection. *In vitro* results may demonstrate resistance for individually tested agents, but combinations may be synergistic.[427,431,447]

55. Monitoring Therapy. How should M.E. be monitored?

M.E. should be monitored for signs of symptomatic relief as well as microbiologic response. M.E.'s temperature and frequency

Table 68.8	Drugs Commonly Used in the Treatment of *Mycobacterium avium* Complex Infection[a,20–25,27,33,44,45]	
Agent	Dose	Toxicities
Clarithromycin	500–2000 mg PO BID[b]	Nausea, vomiting, diarrhea, abdominal pain, serum transferase elevations, bitter taste
Azithromycin	500 mg/day PO	Nausea, vomiting, diarrhea, abdominal pain, serum transferase elevations
Ethambutol	15–25 mg/kg/day PO	Optic neuritis[c]
Rifabutin	450–600 mg/day PO	Nausea, vomiting, diarrhea, serum transferase elevations, hepatitis, neutropenia, thrombocytopenia, rash, orange discoloration of body fluids
Rifampin	600 mg/day PO	Nausea, vomiting, diarrhea, serum transferase elevations, hepatitis, neutropenia, thrombocytopenia, rash, orange discoloration of body fluids, ↑ clearance of other drugs due to hepatic microsomal enzyme induction[d]
Ciprofloxacin	750 mg PO BID	Nausea, vomiting, diarrhea, abdominal pain, headache, rare insomnia, hallucinations, seizures
Clofazimine	100–300 mg/day PO[e]	Dusty, gray-lack discoloration of skin,[f] ichthyosis, rash, nausea, vomiting, diarrhea, abdominal pain, rare ↓ visual acuity
Amikacin	7.5–15 mg/kg/day IV or IM	Nephrotoxicity, ototoxicity

[a] See also Chapter 59: Tuberculosis.
[b] GI adverse effects are more common at 4 gm/day.
[c] Visual testing should be done monthly in patients receiving >15 mg/kg/day.
[d] Similar types of drug interactions should be considered with rifabutin until more data available.
[e] Skin discoloration and GI intolerance are more frequent at doses >100 mg/day.
[f] Usually disappears within 6–12 months after discontinuation of therapy.

of night sweats should be followed carefully. Oral nutritional supplementation should be encouraged to induce weight gain. Clinical improvement may be observed as early as two to four weeks, whereas eradication of bacteremia frequently takes longer (4 to 12 weeks).[447] M.E. also should be followed for development of toxicities related to drug therapy.

56. Drug Interactions. What drugs can interact with anti-MAC regimens?

Rifampin is a hepatic microsomal enzyme inducer, and, therefore, increases the metabolism of many drugs. Serum concentrations of fluconazole and ketoconazole are decreased by 25% and 80%, respectively.[448,449] Dapsone levels may be lowered by as much as 90%.[450] Rifampin may induce acute withdrawal when given with methadone.[451] The activity of oral contraceptives and warfarin anticoagulants also may be inhibited. Rifampin also lowers serum concentrations of theophylline, anticonvulsants, corticosteroids, sulfonylureas, and digoxin.[427] Drug interactions with rifabutin, a new rifamycin derivative similar to rifampin, have not been well characterized; however, in rodent studies, rifabutin, in contrast to rifampin, did not induce hepatic microsomal enzymes at doses greater than 60 mg/kg/day.[452] Until more information is available in humans, however, the potential for rifampin-like drug interactions should be considered. At least one study has documented a decreased area under the concentration-time curve for zidovudine if rifabutin is given concurrently, although the clinical significance of this is unknown.[453] Ciprofloxacin may significantly reduce theophylline clearance.[427] Clarithromycin may induce increased serum concentrations of theophylline, carbamazepine, and terfenadine.[454–456] Theophylline and carbamazepine serum concentrations should be monitored closely, whereas the combination of clarithromycin and terfenadine probably should be avoided.

Prophylaxis

57. How should patients be prophylaxed against MAC infection?

Two large-scale clinical trials have shown that, in patients with low CD4+ counts, the risk of developing disseminated MAC infection may be reduced by approximately 50% by daily administration of 300 mg of rifabutin.[457] Therefore, the Public Health Task Force on Prophylaxis and Treatment of Disseminated *Mycobacterium avium* Complex has recommended that all patients receive 300 mg/day of rifabutin, once their CD4+ count has dropped below 100 cells/mm³. If patients break through their rifabutin prophylaxis, their disseminated MAC should not be treated any differently. There is no evidence which suggests that these isolates have different susceptibility patterns compared to those recovered from patients not receiving prophylaxis.[446] Even though other agents have demonstrated *in vivo* activity against disseminated MAC, there are no large, prospective, placebo-controlled studies to confirm their valid use as prophylactic agents. A large prophylaxis trial (AIDS Clinical Trial Group 196) is underway which will compare the efficacy of rifabutin, clarithromycin, or the combination. All patients should be assessed for the presence of active MAC infection, including blood cultures, before prophylaxis is begun. The presence of *M. tuberculosis* infection also should be ruled out before initiation of prophylaxis. If a patient develops symptoms of *M. tuberculosis* infection while receiving rifabutin prophylaxis, the possibility of tuberculosis resistant to both rifabutin and rifampin must be considered.[446]

Enteric Infections

58. A.B., a 38-year-old male with a four year history of HIV infection and a CD4+ count of 160 cells/mm³ has developed an increasing number of unformed bowel movements over the last month. What gastrointestinal pathogens need to be considered in the differential diagnosis among HIV-infected patients who develop diarrhea?

Enteric infections caused by bacterial, viral, fungal, or protozoan pathogens are common among HIV-infected patients. In general, clinical manifestations secondary to gastrointestinal infections tend to appear as the CD4+ cell count declines, with a majority of patients presenting with a change in bowel habits, predominantly diarrhea. A number of gastrointestinal complications, other than enteric infections, also occur in patients due to primary HIV disease (e.g., gastric achlorhydria, pancreatitis, cholangitis, hepatitis, proctitis, Kaposi sarcoma, lymphoma, carcinoma, and HIV enteropathy).[458]

Fungal infections tend to appear commonly in the oropharynx and esophagus, predominantly due to *Candida* species, primarily *Candida albicans*. Up to 75% of AIDS patients develop oral candidiasis, as a result of their failing immune system and the frequent colonization of the oropharynx with fungi. Patients presenting with localized white plaques within the oral cavity most likely have developed oral candidiasis (thrush) and should be started on antifungal therapy. Initially, patients may be treated with local antifungal therapy (e.g., ''swishing and swallowing'' nystatin suspension 3 million units 4 to 5 times daily or sucking on miconazole troches 4 to 5 times daily). If no response is noted or symptoms of esophageal involvement develop (e.g., dysphagia or odynophagia), esophagitis (see below) can be assumed and systemic antifungal therapy initiated with oral ketoconazole (Nizoral) or fluconazole (Diflucan), or parenteral amphotericin B (if the oral route is not indicated).

Esophagitis due to *C. albicans* is also common as HIV disease progresses. Not all patients with thrush will have esophagitis; however, among patients with thrush who experience concurrent esophageal symptoms, almost all will have esophagitis. Endoscopy often yields multiple white or gray plaques which may be discrete or appear as continuous exudates.[459] Therapy for esophageal candidiasis will likely require intravenous amphotericin and long-term suppressive therapy with an oral agent such as fluconazole.

Other fungal infections in AIDS patients do not commonly effect the GI tract. However, patients with disseminated histoplasmosis may develop diarrhea.

Viruses that infect the gastrointestinal tract of AIDS patients are not the usual viruses (i.e., rotaviruses, enteric adenoviruses, Norwalk agent, coronavirus, and cosackieviruses) known to cause diarrhea in non-HIV patients. More common among HIV patients are *Cytomegalovirus* or *Herpes simplex* infections. Disseminated CMV infection is common in HIV-infected patients with advanced disease and CMV retinitis is the most common problem (see Questions 12 to 22). Up to 2% of patients have gastrointestinal involvement with CMV.[398] Although CMV can occur throughout the GI tract, when it presents as esophagitis, the primarily symptom is odynophagia. The optimal test for CMV esophagitis is to obtain a biopsy and examine the specimen for large cells with intranuclear or paranuclear inclusions.[460] CMV also may involve the colon, and in this case the common presentation is diarrhea. Once again, the use of biopsied tissue for histologic examination is preferred for a definitive diagnosis. CMV infection of the pancreas, liver, gall bladder, and biliary tree also have been described.[461] Patients with CMV esophagitis have a poor prognosis. The treatment of CMV esophagitis requires either ganciclovir or foscarnet therapy (see Questions 14 to 22 and Chapter 67: Infections in Immunocompromised Hosts).

The other common cause of viral GI disease is *Herpes simplex*, which presents in a similar clinical fashion to disseminated CMV, but can be differentiated from CMV by site of infection and biopsy findings. HSV type 1 primarily is associated with ulcerated esophageal lesions. In contrast, HSV type 2 is often the cause of proctitis. While not usually associated with diarrhea, proctitis may result in bloody stools with mucous present. Lastly, HSV also can cause perianal lesions which are often large and painful. Treatment for *Herpes simplex* gastrointestinal lesions usually consists of acyclovir or if herpes-resistant virus is suspected, foscarnet.

Bacteria such as *Salmonella*, *Shigella*, and *Campylobacter* also are important pathogens causing gastrointestinal disease among HIV patients and generally are more virulent in the setting of HIV disease. For example, *Salmonella* may persist despite appropriate antibiotics; bacteremia may be more frequent compared to non-HIV patients; and the bacteremia may be recurrent in spite of antibiotic therapy. In addition, lifelong treatment may be required.[462] *Campylobacter* infections also are associated with poor responses to antibiotics;[463] and *Shigella* infections are associated with an increased frequency of bacteremia and the need for a prolonged course of therapy.[464] Disseminated MAC disease, *Mycobacterium tuberculosis*, *Helicobacter pylori*, and *Clostridium difficile* also can cause diarrhea in HIV-infected patients.[458]

As a group, *Protozoal* infections are the most common cause of diarrhea among HIV-infected patients. Opportunistic protozoans such as *Cryptosporidium*, *Isospora belli*, and microsporidia have become well known GI pathogens since the HIV epidemic has progressed. Other nonopportunistic protozoans such as *Giardia lamblia*, *Entameba histolytica*, and the helminth, *Strongyloides stercoralis* have been identified in patients with gastrointestinal manifestations.[458]

Cryptosporidium, a coccidian protozoan with a life cycle which occurs entirely within a single host, can be transmitted to humans from animals by fecal contamination of water or person-to-person (fecal-oral) spread.[465] While prevalence rates of 3% to 16% have been noted among AIDS patients in the U.S., up to 41% have been noted in other countries (e.g., Haiti).[466] In contrast to the explosive onset that occurs in non-HIV patients, acute cryptosporidiosis in AIDS patients is more insidious and progresses in severity as the degree of immunosuppression heightens.[467] Intestinal cryptosporidiosis may be complicated by concurrent biliary involvement leading to jaundice and hepatosplenomegaly. While the diagnosis of cryptosporidiosis was at one time dependent upon intestinal tissue biopsy, newer techniques such as staining techniques for detecting oocytes (modified acid-fast methods) and fluorescent antibody assays have been developed. The treatment of cryptosporidiosis remains investigational and studies have progressed slowly. Supportive care including fluid and electrolytes, parenteral hyperalimentation, and antidiarrheal agents often are required due to the voluminous amounts of diarrhea. The long-acting somatostatin analog, octreotide acetate also has been used with benefit in some patients. Trials of alpha-difluoromethylornithine (DFMO), paromomycin, and oral spiramycin have yielded inconsistent results. Other drugs such as intravenous spiramycin, letrazuril, and hyperimmune bovine colostrum and transfer factor (a dialyzable leukocyte extract obtained from cow lymph nodes) also are currently under investigation.[465]

Isospora belli, a coccidian protozoan with a similar life cycle to cryptosporidium, is associated with a relatively low incidence (<0.2%) of enteric infections among AIDS patients in the U.S.; but it is considerably more common in Haitian patients with AIDS.[468] Clinically, these patients develop diarrhea, steatorrhea, cramping, and weight loss. In AIDS patients, and infants or children without AIDS, the normally self-limited enteritis may progress to a protracted illness.[469] The diagnosis of isosporiasis is made with acid-fast techniques, as used for cryptosporidium, except *Isospora* oocysts are larger and morphologically distinct.[465] Importantly, and in contrast to cryptosporidiosis, isosporiasis can be treated with TMP-SMX (160 mg/day and 800 mg/day, respectively). Chronic suppressive therapy often is needed and can be accomplished with lower doses of TMP-SMX or pyrimethamine/sulfadoxine.[470]

Microsporidium (ubiquitous, obligate intracellular protozoan parasites) is the genus which is used to classify the four genera (out of hundreds) of microsporidia known to cause human disease.

Microsporidiosis primarily affects immunocompromised individuals. Among AIDS patients, the cornea, liver, peritoneum, and small intestine have been reported to be infected with microsporidium.[471] The species of microsporidium noted to infect AIDS patients has been designated as a new genus, *Enterocytozoon bienusi*. *Enterocytozoon bienusi* can be identified in intestinal biopsy specimens using electron microscopy, hematoxylin and eosin-stained paraffin-embedded sections, as well as other staining techniques. Although no effective treatment is currently available, some successful cases have been described with pyrimethamine, metronidazole, TMP-SMX, and albendazole.[465]

Gastrointestinal manifestations of progressive HIV infection assume an important aspect of the clinical care for these patients, especially at later stages of disease. As a result, A.B. should be evaluated for a possibly treatable enteric infection. Furthermore, consideration of GI malignancy, HIV enteropathy, nutritional support (oral or parenteral) for wasting disease, as well as appetite stimulants (i.e., megestrol acetate) should be part of the overall therapeutic plan.

HIV-Associated Malignancies

59. Despite an extensive microbiologic work-up, no organism was identified and other considerations for A.B.'s change in bowel habits were evaluated. What neoplastic conditions could be contributing to A.B.'s GI status?

In addition to the opportunistic infections described above, a number of malignancies have been noted among patients with HIV infection which have the gastrointestinal tract as a common site for involvement. As the CD4+ cell count declines and HIV disease progresses, patients may develop Kaposi sarcoma (see below), lymphoma, and invasive cervical cancer (see Questions 61 to 65). The mechanism for the increased occurrence of malignancy is unknown but may be related to the decrease in number and function of CD4+ lymphocytes with a resulting impaired immune surveillance. In addition, the development of prophylaxis regimens for opportunistic infections has allowed patients to live longer, thus increasing the likelihood of a malignancy being detected.[472]

Kaposi Sarcoma (KS)

Kaposi sarcoma in non-HIV infected patients was a previously well described clinical entity with a fairly uneventful prognosis. As a result, limited studies were conducted comparing innovative chemotherapy regimens. In contrast, the KS in HIV-infected patients has been observed predominantly in young homosexual men, may be more invasive, and associated with increased morbidity and mortality.[473] The pathogenesis of Kaposi sarcoma in HIV patients is thought to be related to the existence of cells with the potential to become KS lesions. Following HIV infection, the release of certain cytokines from activated immune cells may stimulate the proliferation of KS precursor cells at a time when the immune surveillance for such cells is becoming progressively impaired (i.e., HIV disease progression). Furthermore, some cells may produce a growth factor for KS cells (i.e., angiogenic factors);[473] and the expression of a *tat* gene may produce growth factors that induce vascular KS-like tumors.[474]

Kaposi sarcoma often presents with three types of lesions: flat, raised, and nodular. The lesions occur primarily on the skin, oral mucosa, gastrointestinal tract, and lungs. KS lesions may be asymptomatic, painful, and in the case of intestinal or pulmonary lesions, they may be associated with significant clinical symptoms such as dyspnea or the diarrhea being experienced by A.B. Cutaneous lesions often appear first as small, flat lesions which progress to reddish or purple nodules.[473] They are generally asymptomatic

and follow a pattern of cutaneous lymphatic drainage. Progression of KS leads to the recognition of lesions in the oral cavity (in ≈⅓ of cases).[475]

Therapy for KS in AIDS patients has included administration of immune-based therapy such as interferons or tumor necrosis factor. The use of interferon-alpha for KS in patients with AIDS has been well studied, alone and combined with antiretroviral therapy.[476-478] Early dose-escalation studies of interferon-alpha noted that AIDS patients developed neutropenia and neurological toxicity at high doses.[98] Nonresponders tend to have high circulating levels of endogenous interferon.[479] Subsequently, *in vitro* data indicated that interferon-alpha was synergistic with zidovudine against HIV. As a result of this observation and the antiproliferative activity of interferon versus KS, trials were conducted which studied dose-escalation, beginning at lower doses of interferon, in combination with an antiretroviral agent (zidovudine).[98,480] Unfortunately, increasing doses of both interferon-alpha and zidovudine yielded additive toxicity manifested as neutropenia, hepatitis, and neurologic toxicity. Responses among patients who could tolerate the combination were encouraging with partial or complete remissions noted among many patients receiving interferon-alpha and zidovudine. In addition, antiretroviral effects, as measured by decreasing p24 antigen plasma concentrations and increasing CD4+ cell counts were encouraging. The continued occurrence of hematologic toxicity has prompted researchers to evaluate interferon, zidovudine, and colony stimulating factors (CSFs) such as G-CSF, GM-CSF. Preliminary results indicated that CSFs offset the hematologic toxicity.[481-483] While interferon may be helpful for certain patients with KS, the overall lack of tolerance of the combination requires that alternative therapy be pursued. For this reason drugs which inhibit the effects of angiogenic factors are of interest for future treatment options for Kaposi sarcoma patients.

NonHodgkin's Lymphoma (NHL)

The incidence of nonHodgkin's lymphoma (primarily B-cell type) is increased in patients with HIV infection, especially in patients with low CD4+ cell counts.[484] High-grade nonHodgkin's lymphomas account for approximately 3% of initial AIDS-defining illnesses in adults and adolescents.[485] The reason for the increased incidence is unknown, however, antiretroviral therapy and prophylaxis of opportunistic infection leading to increased patient survival may play a role.[472] In addition, the possible contributing role of nucleoside analog therapy needs to be considered.

HIV patients often have disseminated disease at the time of recognition. In fact, many patients (87% to 95%) with systemic nonHodgkin's lymphoma have extranodal disease. Patients also may present with gastrointestinal involvement with sites such as the oral cavity, esophagus, small bowel, large bowel, appendix, and anorectum being involved. Still other areas such as subcutaneous and soft tissue masses, the epidural space, and cardiac and pericardial lymphoma have been reported. The diagnosis of nonHodgkin's lymphoma may be complicated by the presentation of central neurologic changes which could be interpreted as cerebral toxoplasmosis or HIV dementia.

The treatment of nonHodgkin's lymphoma is dependent upon the organs involved. Patients with evidence of CNS involvement often require local radiation or intrathecal chemotherapy. On the other hand, a number of combination regimens have been evaluated for systemic chemotherapy.[486] Regimens have included: cyclophosphamide with doxorubicin, vincristine, prednisone (CHOP); cyclophosphamide with methyl GAG, bleomycin, prednisone, doxorubicin, vincristine (NHL-7); cyclophosphamide combined with vincristine, intrathecal methotrexate, doxorubicin, and prednisone (L-17); and methotrexate, bleomycin, doxorubicin, cyclophosphamide, and dexamethasone (m-BACOD). Of these regimens m-BACOD is considered to be the standard therapy with a response rate of approximately 50%.[487] Patients developing nonHodgkin's lymphoma tend to have more advanced HIV disease which often is accompanied by reduced bone marrow reserves. As a result, these patients do not tolerate the full doses of these chemotherapy regimens very well and often develop leukopenia. More recently, protocols employing the traditional regimens at full doses (or lower doses) along with a CSF (GM-CSF, G-CSF) have demonstrated that patients may be able to receive more extensive chemotherapy as well as remain on antiretroviral treatment.[488]

Lastly, invasive cervical cancer has been increasingly noted among HIV-infected women and has been added to the CDC list of AIDS defining diagnoses. (See Questions 61 to 67.)

Postexposure Chemoprophylaxis

60. D.T. is 26-year-old female nurse who works in the HIV unit at the medical center. One day after drawing a blood sample from an HIV-infected patient, she inadvertently stuck herself with the blood drawing needle. Should D.T. be given zidovudine to decrease her risk of acute HIV infection?

The use of zidovudine as a chemoprophylactic agent following occupational exposure to HIV is a controversial issue. Given the low estimated risk of infection following a needlestick injury from an infected source (1/300), very large numbers of patients would be needed to demonstrate the efficacy of any drug regimen in a placebo-controlled study. Such a study was attempted, but terminated after enrolling only 84 patients. The reluctance of health care workers to accept the possibility of receiving a placebo was considered to be a barrier to enrollment. Thus, clinical data, at present, consist only of case-reports.

Various *in vitro* studies and animal models of acute HIV infection indicate that zidovudine may be beneficial despite its virostatic nature; however, the short time interval between viral exposure and zidovudine probably increased the likelihood of a benefit. Several factors may determine the potential for HIV transmission after exposure to contaminated fluid or tissue (e.g., type of fluid/tissue, stage of HIV of the index patient, exposure site, and degree of injury). There have been several reports of zidovudine failure,[489-491] despite its expeditious use.[492] In contrast to a potential, but unproven, benefit of zidovudine prophylaxis, disadvantages to its use include mild toxicity (nausea, vomiting, headache), an unknown potential for teratogenicity and mutagenicity, a potentially delayed antibody seroconversion, and cost. Furthermore, since the transmission of zidovudine-resistant strains of HIV has been documented,[493] the choice of zidovudine as a prophylactic agent in the face of wide-spread use of zidovudine in the health care setting may be questionable. Thus, the decision regarding the use of zidovudine (or other agents that are now available) is one which should be made on an individual basis, incorporating the expertise of an infectious diseases specialist, institutional policies and procedures, and the wishes of a well-informed patient.[494]

Women and HIV Disease

Clinical Presentation

61. L.P., a 38-year-old female, was heterosexually infected with HIV. She also has a history of human papilloma virus (HPV) infection. During a routine HIV clinic visit, a cheesy, vaginal discharge with mild itching is noted. Physical examination is unremarkable except for the vaginal discharge. A potassium hydroxide stain of vaginal secretions is positive for hyphae indicating a yeast infection. A CBC includes: Hgb 13.3 gm/dL; WBC count 5500 cells/mm³, and platelets 95,000/mm³.

Her CD4+ lymphocyte count for the first time has declined to 435 cells/mm³. She has received no prior antiretroviral therapy. Is L.P.'s presentation typical of a woman with relatively early HIV disease? [SI units: Hgb 130 gm/L; WBC count 5.5 × 10⁹/L; platelets 95 × 10⁹/L]

Because the great majority of AIDS cases in the U.S. throughout the 1980s was seen in males, issues concerning women and HIV disease have not been investigated as extensively. As of December, 1991, more than 20,000 cases of AIDS in women had been reported to the CDC which represented approximately 10% of all cumulative cases of AIDS in the U.S. at the time.[495] Fifty-seven percent of women with AIDS in the U.S. report IV drug use which is similar to European statistics.[495,496] Epidemiologists predict increases in the incidence of AIDS in heterosexuals, particularly among minority women.[497,498] Heterosexual transmission poses a greater risk for women because the virus is more efficiently transmitted from men to women than vice versa.[499] The female:male ratio among heterosexually-transmitted cases of AIDS in the U.S. is 3:1.[499] The question of whether or not women survive for a shorter period of time after initial HIV infection remains unanswered. In early studies women were noted to have a significantly shorter survival after AIDS diagnosis than men.[500,501] However, since manifestations of HIV disease progression may be different in women compared to men, women may have been diagnosed at a later stage of disease. Other variables which confound interpretation of gender survival comparisons include institutional differences in scope of clinical care and loss of patient follow-up, patient socioeconomic status, and differential access to the health care system.[502,503] Also, since the majority of women with AIDS in the U.S. are IV drug users, this variable also needs to be controlled for in a carefully-designed study. Several survival studies which controlled for important variables such as age, initial AIDS-indicator condition, and zidovudine therapy have found no significant gender differences in survival.[504-508] Although PCP is also a common opportunistic infection seen in HIV+ women, especially with CD4+ counts of less than 200 cells/mm³, HIV wasting syndrome and candidal esophagitis have been associated more frequently with an AIDS diagnosis in women than men.[509,510] Pre-AIDS defining conditions commonly observed in HIV-infected women include candidal infection of oral and genital mucous membranes, genital herpes, human papillomavirus infection, and cervical dysplasia.[511-514] L.P.'s presentation is very typical. Her vaginal yeast infection should be treated with an antifungal agent such as fluconazole (100 mg/day) for at least seven days. She should be followed closely to ensure that her infection clears because HIV+ patients frequently may not respond to the standard duration of therapy.

Antiretroviral Therapy

62. Why should L.P. be started on antiretroviral therapy?

Most clinicians in the U.S. begin patients on antiretroviral therapy once their CD4+ counts have dropped below 500 cells/mm³. There are no data at this time to suggest that the optimal time to initiate antiretroviral therapy is any different for women. Zidovudine is the agent of choice unless the patient is anemic or neutropenic. There are scant data comparing nucleoside analog pharmacokinetic gender differences, although at least one study compared pharmacokinetic parameters over three phases of the menstrual cycle in six women on chronic ZDV. Mean interphase variability in pharmacokinetic parameters was not impressive, although there was great interindividual variability.[515] Since L.P.'s CBC results are normal, she should be started on 500 mg/day of zidovudine, given in divided doses. She should be counseled about adverse effects, both acute and long-term, and she should be followed in clinic every month, initially, in order to monitor her tolerance and compliance.

Cervical Intraepithelial Neoplasia

63. L.P. comes back to clinic in a week and her vaginal infection has cleared nicely. A routine Pap smear is done on this visit which shows cellular changes consistent with a low-grade squamous intraepithelial lesion. Should any therapeutic intervention follow this abnormal Pap smear report?

Women at increased risk of precancerous cervical cytology include those who have HIV infection, HPV infection, and cigarette smokers.[516-518] HPV infection which is more prevalent among HIV+ women than HIV− women, has been causally implicated in the development of pre-invasive and invasive cervical neoplasms.[519-522] Furthermore, the greater the degree of immunosuppression, the higher the risk of development of cervical intraepithelial neoplasia.[522] Rapidly progressive cervical malignancy and death have been reported in HIV-infected women.[516,523,524] As of January 1, 1993, the CDC has added invasive cervical cancer to the list of AIDS-defining illnesses.[22] In HIV-infected women, approximately 15% of low-grade squamous intraepithelial lesions progress to high-grade lesions which includes moderate to severe dysplasia, or carcinoma *in situ*.[525,526] Since the risk of progression may be greater in HIV+ women, many gynecologists would recommend that L.P. undergo subsequent colposcopic examination (microscopic inspection of the entire cervical area) with directed biopsy.[526] Once the biopsy report confirms the presence of precancerous cellular changes, one of a number of surgical procedures may be performed, aimed at destruction or removal of the dysplastic tissue.[526] After surgery, L.P. should have follow-up Pap smears performed every three months for at least one year.[527] It is unknown at this time if the relapse rate following successful surgical treatment is higher in HIV+ women.

Pharmacologic Intervention

64. Has any pharmacologic intervention proven successful in the treatment of cervical intraepithelial neoplasia?

Surgical treatment for cervical intraepithelial neoplasia requires the use of surgical expertise and expensive equipment. Postsurgical complications may develop including prolonged bleeding or impairment of fertility due to cervical stenosis.[528,529] Since interferons have antiviral as well as antimitotic and immunomodulatory properties, it seems reasonable to investigate the use of these agents in the treatment of cervical intraepithelial neoplasia.[530] Many such studies have been done; however, most of them have been conducted with small numbers of women and many of them are uncontrolled. The best results have been seen with systemic therapy although the majority of patients experience adverse effects.[530] When 15 women were treated with interferon beta, 2 million international units/day, intramuscularly, for ten days, and were compared to 15 women treated with saline,[531] 14 of 15 (93%) of the treated women had a complete response compared to 6 of 15 (40%) placebo patients after more than six months of follow-up.[531] In a placebo-controlled trial in 16 women using the same dosage regimen,[532] women with earlier stage cervical intraepithelial neoplasia disease had an excellent response, but women with more advanced disease responded poorly. The most common toxicity has been a "flu-like syndrome" consisting of fever, chills, headache, malaise, arthralgia, and myalgia, although these symptoms tend to better tolerated with continued treatment.[530] Studies investigating the use of topical interferon alpha have reported a lower incidence of adverse effects; but this route of administration also resulted in lower efficacy.[533,534] Intralesional interferon injections also have been tried, although the efficacy has been inferior to the systemic route

and again, the use of expert personnel is required.[535,536] The exact role of interferons in the treatment of cervical intraepithelial neoplasia, particularly in the arena of HIV disease, remains to be clarified by large-scale studies.

Pregnancy and Vertical Transmission Risk

65. L.P.'s abnormal cervical tissue is ultimately excised surgically. Three months later she comes back for routine follow-up care. She has not had a menstrual period since her surgery. A human chorionic gonadotropin screening test reveals that she is pregnant. Her CD4+ count is 400 cells/mm³. How will her pregnancy affect her HIV disease and vice versa?

CD4+ cell counts naturally decline during pregnancy, reaching a nadir at seven months, before returning to the prepregnancy baseline.[537] This decrease may be 10% to 20% greater among HIV+ women compared to HIV− controls.[537] Despite this decrease in cell-mediated immune function, however, several investigators have not found that HIV disease progression occurs more rapidly in pregnant women.[538-541] Early reports of HIV disease acceleration in pregnant women may have been biased since many of these women were already in advanced stages of illness.[538,542] If an HIV+ woman becomes pregnant with less than 200 CD4+ cells/mm³, however, she is much more likely to develop opportunistic infections and disease progression. The effect of HIV disease on pregnancy outcome also has been studied. One retrospective review suggested that HIV-infected women were more likely to have complications such as prematurity or low birth weight.[538] However, since then several investigators who prospectively followed asymptomatic HIV+ women and HIV− matched controls have not found any association between HIV infection and pregnancy outcome.[543,544] At least one study, however, has reported a higher infant mortality rate in symptomatic HIV+ mothers compared to asymptomatic HIV+ controls and HIV− mothers.[545]

66. What is the risk of HIV transmission to L.P.'s baby?

Eighty percent of women with AIDS are of reproductive age.[546] Vertical HIV transmission can occur by one of three vectors: *in utero*, intrapartum, and postpartum through breast-feeding. *Perinatal HIV transmission* in the U.S. accounts for more than 80% of all cases of pediatric AIDS.[496] As the number of children infected from HIV-infected blood or blood products has decreased dramatically since 1985 when blood screening procedures were instituted, this proportion can only be expected to approach 100%. *Intrauterine HIV infection* has been documented by viral culture of neonatal cord blood, amniotic fluid, and placental and fetal tissue samples at 15 to 34 weeks gestation.[547-552] *Intrapartum transmission* also occurs, due to infant exposure to maternal blood, either during vaginal delivery or Cesarean section.[553,554] Finally, although rare, case reports have described HIV *transmission through breast-feeding* in women who received HIV+ blood transfusions in the immediate postpartum period.[555-558] Current vertical transmission risk estimates in the U.S. and Europe range from approximately 20% to 35%.[538,559-562] Earlier reports of maternal-infant transmission rates as high as 50% or greater have been criticized for flaws in study design.[554,563,564] The rate of HIV transmission probably is related to stage of maternal disease. Risk factors associated with vertical transmission were assessed by the European Collaborative Study which followed more than 700 children at least 18 months after birth. This group found an increased risk of HIV transmission associated with lower CD4+ counts, the presence of p24 antigenemia, and delivery before 34 weeks gestation.[565] The French Prospective Multicenter Cohort Study correlated disease progression in HIV-infected infants with stage of maternal disease at delivery. Fifty percent of HIV-infected infants born to mothers with AIDS had encephalopathy or opportunistic infections by 18 months of age versus 14% of children born to mothers with earlier stages of disease.[566] The risk of infant mortality at 18 months also was associated with the following maternal factors: disease stage, p24 antigenemia, and CD4+ count less than 400 cells/mm^3.[566] Timing of transmission also has been correlated to onset of disease in the infected infant. When 74 mother-infant pairs were prospectively monitored, 22 (28%) transmitted the virus. Positive viral cultures at birth were found in 11 of 22 (50%) infants which is evidence of *in utero* infection.[567] Positive viral cultures eventually were obtained in the remaining 11 infants, but initially, cultures at birth and during the neonatal period were negative, indicative of intrapartum transmission. Median time to onset of symptoms was significantly earlier in the *in utero* group (6 weeks) versus the intrapartum group (86 weeks; p = 0.02).[567]

Zidovudine in Pregnancy

67. Should L.P. continue taking her ZDV?

The use of ZDV during pregnancy is based upon the premise that the therapeutic benefits to the mother and the baby may outweigh the risks. Theoretically, ZDV may preserve the health of the mother while possibly affording some protection from infection to the infant. Preliminary data regarding teratogenic effects of ZDV are promising. A survey of 45 infants born to 43 HIV+ mothers who took ZDV for varying periods throughout their pregnancies revealed no pattern of fetal malformations or premature births.[573] Seven infants were anemic at birth which could have been partially attributable to zidovudine. Two cases of intrauterine growth retardation occurred, but both of these women had been exposed to other drugs during pregnancy. No birth defects were observed in the ten infants whose mothers began taking zidovudine in the first trimester and remained on therapy throughout the remainder of the pregnancy. A placebo-controlled AIDS Clinical Trial Group trial was designed to look at whether the use of ZDV during pregnancy could decrease or eliminate the rate of vertical transmission. This study was interrupted because preliminary data analysis on 363 infants showed that the vertical transmission rate in the ZDV group was only 8% compared to 26% in the placebo group.[648] In addition to receiving 500 mg/day during pregnancy, a continuous IV infusion was given intrapartum (2 mg/kg/hour followed by 1 mg/kg/hour), and the newborn received oral ZDV for six weeks (2 mg/kg Q 6 hr). Women enrolled in the study had to have at least 200 CD4+ cells/mm^3 and began taking ZDV after the 14th week of gestation. The ZDV-treated infants had lower hemoglobin values (1 gm/dL) compared to placebo infants, but this was correctable. Even though these data are encouraging, the decision to begin ZDV during pregnancy should be one that is made jointly between the health care professional and the patient, after all relevant benefits and risks have been weighed.

Pediatric HIV Disease

Clinical Presentation

68. L.P. also has a 2-year-old son at home, A.P., who had been previously healthy. For the past several weeks, however, he has been having a dry, nonproductive cough and some shortness of breath. Generalized lymphadenopathy is noted on physical examination. His temperature is within normal limits. A CBC with differential is unremarkable. CD4+ lymphocyte count is 472 cells/mm^3; p24 antigenemia is undetectable. An HIV test (ELISA) is positive. A second ELISA test, followed by a Western blot, confirm that A.P. is also HIV infected. A chest x-ray reveals bilateral diffuse interstitial infiltrates. Sputum cultures are negative for bacteria. A bronchoalveolar lavage specimen is negative for *P. carinii*. An arterial blood gas is as follows: pH 7.44 mm Hg; pCO$_2$ 41 mm Hg; pO$_2$ 65 mm Hg; and serum HCO$_3$ 25 mEq/L. How is A.P.'s clinical presentation typical of a child with HIV infection? [SI units: pCO$_2$ 5.47 kPa; pO$_2$ 9.2 kPa]

The first cases of AIDS in infants and children were recognized between 1979 and 1983.[574] Since then, the number of newly-diagnosed pediatric AIDS cases has continued to increase at an alarming rate. Although some children have been infected by contaminated blood or blood products especially before 1985 (when screening began), the vast majority of pediatric AIDS cases in the U.S. have been perinatally acquired.[574] Most infants are asymptomatic at birth; however, it is clear that HIV infection progresses faster in children than adults.[574–577] In one prospective study, 80% of HIV-infected infants developed clinical disease within the first 24 months of life.[578] The highest incidence of AIDS occurs during the first year of life, although this incidence is higher among children born to infected mothers than to children who received infected blood transfusions as neonates.[579] This is indirect evidence that timing of transmission may be a factor in onset of symptoms. Early *in utero* infection may result in a more rapid onset of symptoms. No matter when transmission occurs in the infant's development, HIV is a major infectious insult to an immature immune system. No doubt both of these factors contribute to the more rapid progression of HIV disease in the pediatric population.[580] In a retrospective analysis, Scott et al. found a median survival of 38 months in a cohort of 172 HIV-infected children born between June 1979 and December 1987 with the highest mortality during the first year of life.[581] However, most of these children were diagnosed only after they became symptomatic; in addition, a minority received antiretroviral therapy or prophylaxis for *Pneumocystis carinii* pneumonia. In a later study, Tovo et al. evaluated 573 perinatally HIV-infected children in Italy and found a median survival of approximately eight years.[582]

Both studies calculated survival from time of diagnosis of HIV infection, but the latter study also included asymptomatic children who were diagnosed earlier. Timing of transmission also may play a role in survival. Byers et al. in an active surveillance project found evidence of two distinct populations of perinatally HIV-infected children: one group had a high probability of death (99%) before four years of age whereas in contrast, 88% of the second group were surviving beyond four years of age.[583] The investigators could find no differences between the two groups controlling for antiretroviral therapy, PCP prophylaxis, birth weight, or the presence of AIDS-defining and nonspecific conditions. These authors speculated that the observed survival differences might be explained by timing of transmission, with children infected early in gestation following a more rapid disease progression compared to those infected later in gestation or during delivery. In summary, the natural history of HIV infection in children continues to change with time as new diagnostic techniques become available which allow for earlier diagnosis and treatment. In addition, the availability of antiretroviral therapy and PCP prophylaxis also may affect the course of disease progression.

Children with HIV infection can present clinically in a number of ways. PCP is very common, particularly in the first year of life.[581,584,585] Nonspecific presentation may include any or several of the following: failure to thrive, poor appetite, weight loss, unexplained fevers or diarrhea, oral candidiasis or monilial diaper rash, generalized lymphadenopathy, hepatosplenomegaly, or chronic eczematoid dermatitis.[575,576,586–591]

More than 90% of pediatric AIDS patients fail to thrive and nearly 40% have chronic debilitating diarrhea.[586] When an infant has HIV infection, unlike an adult, the individual has not yet been exposed to many common bacterial pathogens and, therefore, does not have memory cells to make antibodies quickly. As a result, children often present with recurrent bacterial infections such as otitis media, sinusitis, pneumonia, bacteremia, osteomyelitis, urinary tract infections, cellulitis, and meningitis.[574,576,587–591]

Common infecting organisms include *Staphylococcus aureus*, *Streptococcus pneumoniae*, *Haemophilus influenzae*, and *Salmonella* species.[592,593] Hospitalized patients or those treated with antibiotics are more likely to harbor gram-negative *Enterobacteriaceae* and *Pseudomonas* species.[592] These infections usually predate opportunistic infections and are commonly seen in the first three years of life.[574] Children also may present with varying degrees of HIV encephalopathy. Clinical signs may include developmental delay, a steady decline in intellectual and cognitive abilities, deteriorating motor skills, and behavioral abnormalities.[575,576,594] The majority of HIV-infected children experience some degree of neurologic impairment.[594]

A unique feature of HIV infection in pediatrics is lymphoid interstitial pneumonitis (LIP). This disease usually is seen in children older than one year and carries a better prognosis than PCP or other opportunistic infections. Median survival has been estimated at 91 months in contrast to PCP with a median survival of 14 months.[595] LIP is characterized by chronic lymphoid hyperplasia with interstitial infiltrates on radiography, sometimes accompanied by hilar or mediastinal adenopathy.[586] Definitive diagnosis is made by lung biopsy, but if clinical and radiographic findings are typical, a presumptive diagnosis may be made.[586] Symptomatic hypoxemia may be observed, as in A.P.'s case. Children with LIP tend to have high Epstein-Barr virus (EBV) titers. Both EBV DNA and HIV RNA have been isolated in lung specimens from affected children.[586,596–598] The pathogenesis of LIP is poorly understood, but may involve an interaction between HIV pulmonary infection and EBV-infected B cells in lung tissue, resulting in lymphoid proliferation.

Lymphoid Interstitial Pneumonitis (LIP)

69. A.P. is presumptively diagnosed with lymphoid interstitial pneumonitis. Describe appropriate treatment and monitoring for A.P.

Management of the HIV-infected child with LIP is largely supportive. In addition to supplemental oxygen for symptomatic hypoxemia, several investigators have recommended a tapering 4 to 12 week course of prednisone for children with a PaO$_2$ less than 65 mm Hg.[599,600] A.P. also should be monitored closely for the development of secondary bacterial pulmonary infection. Administration of influenza, pneumococcal, and *Haemophilus influenzae* vaccines also should be considered.[575]

Vaccination in HIV-Infected Children

70. L.P. has kept her son's vaccination schedule up-to-date; however, now that she knows he is HIV-infected, she is concerned about how he will react to any vaccination. What vaccines are contraindicated in HIV-infected children?

Recommendations regarding pediatric vaccination in HIV-infected children have been controversial. The major factor in favor of vaccination is the risk of developing childhood infection. Opposing factors include the use of live viral vaccines in an immunocompromised population, the possibility of an inadequate protective antibody response, and the theoretical possibility of antigenic stimulation leading to increased HIV replication.[576] In general, the Immunization Practices Advisory Committee recommends that HIV-infected children should follow the same vaccination schedule as healthy children with a few exceptions. Originally, this committee recommended that live measles, mumps, and rubella vaccines not be given to symptomatic HIV-infected chil-

dren, but because of serious and fatal reports of measles in HIV-infected children and the lack of any adverse reactions in HIV-infected children who have received the vaccine, this recommendation has been changed.[601–603] All HIV-infected children should receive diphtheria and tetanus toxoids, pertussis vaccine, and *Haemophilus influenzae* Type b vaccine. In addition, these children should receive (or at least be considered for) measles, mumps, and rubella vaccines like other children.[603] Inactivated poliovirus vaccine should be used in HIV-infected children rather than oral, attenuated poliovirus vaccine.[603] In addition, symptomatic children with HIV infection should be considered for both pneumococcal and influenza immunization.[603]

PCP Prophylaxis

71. Should A.P. receive PCP prophylaxis?

Although PCP can develop at any age, in the pediatric population it most commonly appears between three and six months of age, with a median survival of only one to four months after the first episode.[577,581,604–606] To be most effective, PCP prophylaxis needs to be instituted during the first few months of life, often before true HIV infection is definitively diagnosed, even with the availability of more rapid diagnostic techniques. Strong correlates of PCP infection include age less than one year, HIV-associated symptoms, and declining CD4+ lymphocyte counts.[607–609] Normal CD4+ lymphocyte counts are much higher in children than adults, peaking during the first year of life at approximately 3000 cells/mm^3 and gradually declining thereafter to adult values by six years of age.[610] More than 50% of all episodes of pediatric PCP for which CD4+ cell count data are available occur during the first year of life.[604] Ninety percent of these children have CD4+ cell counts of less than 1500 cells/mm^3.[591,606,608,611,612] Based upon available mean age-adjusted normative CD4+ lymphocyte data and depressed CD4+ cell count data correlated with the development of PCP, the Working Group on PCP Prophylaxis in Children in 1991 created guidelines for the initiation of PCP prophylaxis.[604] (See Table 68.9.) Because PCP rarely occurs in neonates and also to avoid possible drug-related toxicity, primary prophylaxis should begin only after the first month of life.

A.P. is two years old and has less than 500 CD4+ cells/mm^3; therefore, he should be started on PCP prophylaxis. Since these guidelines have been published, a review of pediatric PCP cases from January of 1991 to June of 1993 has shown that only one-fourth of these patients were receiving prophylaxis at the time they developed PCP. Of the patients not receiving prophylaxis, more than half had not yet been identified as HIV-infected.[613] For these reasons, some clinicians believe that frequent monitoring of CD4+ cell counts in infants is not enough. In some infants, rapid falls in CD4+ cell counts occur during the first few months of life when the risk of developing PCP is the greatest.[614] This report raises the feasibility of initiating PCP prophylaxis in all infants of HIV-infected mothers after one month of life and discontinuing therapy in uninfected infants at six months of age. Prophylaxis also could be interrupted in infected, asymptomatic infants with CD4+ cell counts above the recommended thresholds after one

Table 68.9	Initiation of *Pneumocystis carinii* Pneumonia Prophylaxis in Children
Age	CD4+ Cell Count
1–11 months	<1500
12–23 months	<750
24 months to 5 yr	<500
≥6 yr	<200

year of life.[613,614] This maneuver would put many patients on unnecessary prophylaxis, but it also would protect more infants at risk. Oral or intermittent (3 days/week) administration of trimethoprim-sulfamethoxazole can be effective chemoprophylaxis for immunocompromised children with cancer.[615,616] The current recommendation of the Working Group on PCP Prophylaxis in Children is 150 mg TMP/m^2/day with 750 mg SMX/m^2/day given orally in divided doses twice a day on three consecutive days per week.[604] Acceptable alternative schedules include the following: same regimen only given as a single daily dose rather than divided twice daily; same regimen only given on three alternate days per week instead of consecutive days; and same regimen only given seven days per week instead of three days per week.

Due to the possibility of bilirubin displacement and subsequent development of kernicterus, the use of TMP-SMX should be avoided in the first month of life. Dermatological and hematological disorders are the most common adverse events associated with TMP-SMX. Among children with leukemia receiving TMP-SMX three days/week for PCP prophylaxis, mild cutaneous reactions (primarily an erythematous, maculopapular rash) were observed in 16%.[616] Exfoliative dermatitis and Stevens-Johnson syndrome are rare occurrences ($\approx$1 of 200,000 cases).[617,618] The incidence of hematologic adverse events during prophylaxis is minimal but may be as high as 34% on treatment regimens.[619,620] Because young children are not able to use a nebulizer correctly, aerosolized pentamidine is used infrequently. It is an alternative for those children who cannot tolerate TMP-SMX and are $\geq$5 years old. No data are available on the use of dapsone for PCP prophylaxis in children. Dapsone has been used in pediatrics for the treatment of Hansen's disease at 1 to 2 mg/kg/day. The most common drug-related toxicity is dose-dependent hemolysis which has been observed in individuals with and without G6PD deficiency.[604] The suggested dose for PCP prophylaxis is 1 mg/kg/day given orally, not to exceed 100 mg/day.[604] The tablets (25 or 100 mg) may be crushed and given with food. Complete blood counts with differential should be performed monthly in children receiving either TMP-SMX or dapsone for PCP prophylaxis to detect any adverse hematologic effects.[604]

Antiretroviral Therapy

72. Should A.P. be started on antiretroviral therapy?

Antiretroviral therapy should be instituted in all pediatric patients who are definitely HIV-infected and have either 1) HIV-associated symptoms or 2) significant signs of immunodeficiency.[621] Not enough data have accumulated to advocate routine use of antiretroviral therapy in asymptomatic, HIV-infected children with intact immune status. Children with a singular finding of lymphadenopathy, hepatomegaly, or hypergammaglobulinemia are not considered to be "symptomatic." In June of 1993, the recommendations of an expert panel, The Working Group on Antiretroviral Therapy from The National Pediatric HIV Resource Center, were published including when to initiate antiretroviral therapy in the pediatric population. According to the panel consensus, any of the following clinical criteria justifies initiation of antiretroviral drug therapy in children regardless of CD4+ lymphocyte count: failure to thrive despite aggressive oral nutrition, progressive HIV encephalopathy, AIDS-defining opportunistic infection, HIV-associated malignancy, recurrent septicemia or meningitis, thrombocytopenia (<75,000/mm^3), or hypogammaglobulinemia.[622] In addition to these, the individual health care provider may elect to start antiretroviral therapy in a given child who develops other symptoms not listed above, depending upon overall clinical presentation. The Working Group also suggested guidelines for the

initiation of antiretroviral therapy in asymptomatic children based upon age-adjusted CD4+ lymphocyte counts. These are listed in the Table 68.10.

Since A.P. is two years old and his CD4+ count is only 472 cells/mm^3, he should be started on antiretroviral therapy.

Nucleoside Analogue Therapy

73. What therapeutic choices are available regarding pediatric nucleoside analogue therapy for A.P. and what important parameters should be monitored?

Until 1995, studies showed that zidovudine alone was effective in symptomatic HIV-infected children.[623–625] In one study, all 13 HIV-infected children who had signs of HIV encephalopathy improved neurologically on a continuous intravenous infusion of ZVD.[623] IQ scores, after three and six months of therapy, rose in these 13 patients, as well as five other patients who had no signs of encephalopathy at study entry.[623] In addition, coordination, language skills, social interactions, appetite, weight, CD4+ counts, lymphadenopathy, hepatosplenomegaly, and positron emission and computed tomographies all were improved.[623] In some patients neurologic improvement was the only positive response to ZDV therapy. Many of these early findings have been corroborated in a multicenter trial of 61 HIV-infected children who improved clinically and demonstrated positive surrogate marker responses.[625] As in other pediatric and adult ZDV trials, anemia and neutropenia were the major drug-related toxicities encountered, occurring in 26% and 48% of patients, respectively.[625] Dosage recommendations for ZDV by age group are as follows: 2 mg/kg/dose every six hours for zero to two weeks of age; 3 mg/kg/dose every six hours for two to four weeks of age; and 180 mg/m^2/dose every six hours for 4 weeks to 13 years.

Adolescents with signs of HIV encephalopathy may require higher doses.[622] If dosage must be reduced because of adverse effects, the minimum recommended dose is 75 mg/m^2/dose for children older than one month.[622] For children with pretherapy anemia or neutropenia, ZDV may be initiated at 120 mg/m^2/dose and gradually increased if no progression of abnormal hematologic indices is noted.[623]

Zidovudine monotherapy (180 mg/m^2 Q 6 hr), didanosine monotherapy (120 mg/m^2 Q 12 hr), and a combination of zidovudine (120 mg/m^2 Q 6 hr) with didanosine (90 mg/m^2 Q 12 hr) were evaluated in a prospective, blinded AIDS Clinical Trial Group study of 839 children ranging in age from 3 months to 18 years. Only patients with little or no prior antiretroviral therapy were eligible. An independent monitoring committee, during the course of an interim data analysis, discovered that the zidovudine monotherapy arm was proving to be the least effective and most toxic of the three study groups. Children assigned to zidovudine monotherapy had a higher rate of growth failure, neurologic deterioration, new opportunistic infections, and death. The greatest proportion of anemia and neutropenia also occurred in this zidovudine monotherapy arm.[647] For these reasons, the trial was interrupted and the zidovudine monotherapy arm was stopped. These results were unanticipated since in similar adult trials, zidovudine monotherapy proved to be equal, or superior, to combination therapy or

Table 68.10	Initiation of Antiretroviral Therapy
Age	CD4+ Count (cells/mm^3)
<1 yr	<1750
1–2 yr	<1000
2–6 yr	<750
>6 yr	<500

other single antiretroviral agents. Despite this development, if an individual patient is tolerating zidovudine and is not experiencing disease progression, continued zidovudine therapy may be warranted. The results of this interim trial analysis, however, provide justification for initiating antiretroviral therapy with ddI alone or ZDV/ddI combination therapy.

While the interim results of this ACTG study showed that zidovudine is the least effective of the three selected regimens, it is not known whether didanosine monotherapy or the combination of zidovudine and didanosine is the better choice. Further information to guide the selection of initial therapy in children with AIDS must await the completion of this ACTG study and data analysis later in 1995.

If patients fail to respond or begin to clinically deteriorate after an initial response to ZDV, alternative antiretroviral treatment should be initiated. The main indications of a loss of therapeutic response to ZDV in pediatrics are growth failure and worsening of CNS symptoms.[623] If the patient develops symptomatic cardiomyopathy, nephrotic syndrome, or elevated hepatic transaminases (>fivefold above normal values) and other causes are ruled out (not HIV-related), or an AIDS-defining opportunistic infection, antiretroviral therapy should be strongly considered. If a patient becomes intolerant of ZDV, a change in nucleoside analogue therapy also is warranted.

Didanosine is the only FDA-approved agent as second-line therapy in pediatric HIV disease. Didanosine is advantageous from the perspective of sparing the bone marrow, although it has other serious adverse effects. When 43 symptomatic children with HIV infection received 60 to 540 mg/m^2/day of didanosine orally, the median CD4+ cell count rose from 218 to 327 cells/mm^3 after 20 to 24 weeks of therapy and the median p24 antigen concentration fell from 272 pg/mL to 77 pg/mL.[627] Two patients (5%) developed pancreatitis. In another study, 34 children with AIDS received either 120 or 270 mg/m^2/day of didanosine orally in two divided doses for at least six months: a significant reduction in p24 antigenemia and quantitative cellular viremia compared to baseline was observed.[628] No pancreatic or neurologic toxicity was seen.[628] The recommended pediatric dose of didanosine is 90 to 135 mg/m^2/day given every 12 hours orally on an empty stomach.[622] In addition to pancreatitis (especially at doses >270 mg/m^2/day), peripheral retinal depigmentation developed in approximately 5% of pediatric patients taking didanosine, however, this condition thus far has not been associated with loss of vision.[622] Serum amylase and lipase, as well as hepatic transaminases should be monitored routinely in all patients treated with didanosine.

There are no approved therapies for those pediatric patients who fail to respond to didanosine or who develop unacceptable toxicity. If these patients cannot be enrolled in clinical trials, they may be eligible for investigational agents via FDA-approved expanded access programs. Although zalcitabine (ddC) is commercially available for use in combination therapy with ZDV in adults and adolescents (0.01 mg/kg PO Q 8 hr), pediatric data are limited. In a pilot study of 15 symptomatic, HIV-infected children who were treated with oral ddC (0.015 to 0.04 mg/kg/dose Q 6 hr), CD4+ counts increased in eight and p24 antigenemia had decreased in six during eight weeks of ddC monotherapy. No anemia or neutropenia occurred, however, three developed a rash and nine experienced oral ulcerations.[629]

In children whose HIV disease progresses while on ZDV, ZDV/ddI or ZDV/ddC regimens also may be tried since these combinations do not have overlapping toxicities.[622] Another option, particularly in the case of ZDV intolerance, is to alternate two agents allowing the patient to recover from the toxicity of one

agent while receiving the other.[622,630] In a ZDV/ddI salvage therapy trial of 15 HIV-infected children with rapidly declining CD4+ counts (<100 cells/mm^3) and p24 antigenemia, patients who had failed either ZDV or ddI monotherapy were switched to continuous, combination therapy. After six months of this regimen, even though the mean CD4+ response was not significant, some individual children had marked increases in their CD4+ counts. Six patients became p24 antigen-negative.[631]

74. What other nucleoside analogues are under investigation for pediatric HIV disease?

Phase I clinical trials are underway evaluating the therapeutic role of *stavudine* (d4T). Kline et al. have enrolled 18 children, most of whom are symptomatic with a prior history of ZDV therapy, in a dose-escalating trial of dideoxydidehydrothymidine (d4T) (0.125 to 2 mg/kg/day in 2 divided doses). After a median 47 weeks of treatment, no peripheral neuropathy has been observed.[632] During the first 12 weeks of therapy, CD4+ count increases were seen in those patients who were initially assigned to 1 to 2 mg/kg/day doses. No increases were observed in patients assigned to lower doses. In most patients, serum p24 concentrations have either not changed or decreased.[632]

Lamivudine (3TC) is another investigational nucleoside analogue. Sixty-nine children have been enrolled in a Phase I/II, dose-escalating trial (1 to 20 mg/kg/day in 2 divided doses) of 2-deoxy-3-thiacytidine (3TC) in one of two arms, depending upon whether or not they have received prior antiretroviral therapy. During the initial 24-week study period, CD4+ counts did not change, although decreases were observed in p24 antigenemia and quantitative viremia in those patients who were assigned to receive at least 4 mg/kg/day.[633]

Intravenous Immune Globulin (IVIG) Therapy

75. With supportive care, A.P. recovers uneventfully from his lymphoid interstitial pneumonitis. He is discharged on PCP prophylaxis and ZDV therapy. He does relatively well for the next 12 months, with the exception of 2 bouts of pneumococcal sepsis (despite his pneumococcal vaccination), requiring hospitalization and IV antibiotics. His present CD4+ lymphocyte count is 356 cells/mm^3. His pediatrician, an HIV specialist, is now considering intermittent intravenous immune globulin (IVIG) therapy for him. What are the pros and cons of this approach?

Serious, recurrent bacterial infection is a primary underlying cause of morbidity and mortality in pediatric HIV disease. Since IVIG therapy prevents recurrent bacterial infection in primary immunodeficiency, a double-blind, placebo-controlled trial which enrolled 372 children with vertically transmitted HIV infection, was undertaken to determine if the same results would be found in acquired immunodeficiency. Study patients, all of whom had clinical or immunologic evidence of HIV infection, were randomly assigned to receive either intravenous immune globulin (400 mg/kg) or placebo every 28 days. Median follow-up time was 17 months. For children who had baseline CD4+ counts of ≥200 cells/mm^3, the interval free of serious bacterial infection was greater in those children who received IVIG (p = 0.01).[634] No benefits were observed in those children who had CD4+ counts of less than 200 cells/mm^3 at study entry. The beneficial effects of IVIG therapy were seen primarily in the prevention of invasive pneumococcal infection and clinically diagnosed acute pneumonia.[634] Despite these positive effects, no survival differences between treatment groups were demonstrated. The investigators cautioned against extrapolation of the results to all HIV-infected children. The study design excluded hemophiliacs and any children infected by HIV+ blood or blood products. The majority of children were less than five years of age (78%) and only those were included who were symptomatic or had clear signs of immunodeficiency. Despite these limitations and the relative expense of IVIG, the group proposed that HIV-infected infants and children with signs of humoral deficiency including hypogammaglobulinemia, poor response to vaccine therapy, or significant recurrent bacterial infections despite treatment with appropriate antibiotics, are candidates for routine IVIG prophylaxis.[622,634] A follow-up study of 148 patients from the original trial (67 placebo and 81 IVIG) assigned all patients to open label IVIG at the same dose and frequency. The serious bacterial infection rate did not change for those patients originally assigned to receive IVIG; in contrast, the patients who had originally been assigned to placebo showed a significant reduction in this index (similar to the patients who had received IVIG in the original study).[635] The reduction in serious bacterial infection rate was observed regardless of whether or not patients were receiving PCP prophylaxis or ZDV therapy.[635] Since A.P. has ≥200 CD4+ cells/mm^3, and has had two episodes of pneumococcal sepsis within one year, he is a candidate for routine IVIG prophylaxis (400 mg/kg/day every 28 days).

Summary

76. W.W. is admitted through the ER for an episode of acute PCP. She is receiving zalcitabine and zidovudine for antiretroviral therapy and chronic foscarnet for CMV retinitis. The admission orders call for IV pentamidine for 21 days. What factors should be prospectively evaluated during W.W.'s course of therapy?

This chapter has attempted to provide a summary of the disease-related events which impact on an individual's life following HIV infection. Clearly, the progression of HIV disease leads to a number of conditions which require pharmacotherapy. The developments of HIV resistance and the emerging trend toward combination antiviral therapy requires that a continuum be established so that a given patient's care includes consideration of prior antiretroviral chemoprophylaxis regimens and intermittent treatment for opportunistic infections, malignancies, nutritional status, and pain management and other medical components of HIV disease which require drug therapy. The now well-accepted multidrug approach to HIV-infected patients requires persistent attention to drug-drug interactions, pharmacokinetic considerations (i.e., decline of renal and hepatic function, malabsorption), compliance behavior, and certain aspects of home-based therapies. The current system of providing treatment to HIV-infected patents may be fragmented and discontinuous. In W.W.'s case, adverse drug effects (e.g., pentamidine-induced renal dysfunction) which could impact on zalcitabine and foscarnet dosing requirements should be anticipated.

References

1 Kaposi's sarcoma and *Pneumocystis* pneumonia among homosexual men—New York City and California. MMWR. 1981A;30:305–8.

2 *Pneumocystis* pneumonia—Los Angeles. MMWR. 1981B;30:250–52.

3 **Curran JW.** AIDS—Two years later. N Engl J Med. 1983;309:609–11. Editorial.

4 **Clavel F et al.** Molecular cloning and polymorphism of the human immune deficiency virus type 2. Nature. 1986;324:691–95.

5 **Letvin N et al.** Induction of AIDS-like disease in macaque monkeys with T-cell tropic retrovirus STLV-III. Science. 1985;230:71–3.

6 **Barre-Sirouss F.** Isolation of a T-lymphotropic retrovirus from a patient at risk for acquired immune deficiency syndrome (AIDS). Science. 1983;220:868–71.

7 **Gallo RC et al.** Frequent detection and isolation of cytopathic retroviruses (HTLV-III) from patients with AIDS and at risk for AIDS. Science. 1984;224:500–03.

8 **Levy JA et al.** Isolation of lymphocytopathic retroviruses from San Francisco patients with AIDS. Science. 1984;225:840–42.

9 **Hamburg MA et al.** Immunology of AIDS and HIV infection. In: Mandell GL et al., eds. Principles and Practice of Infectious Diseases. 3rd ed. New York: Churchill Livingstone; 1990:1046–059.

10 **Paul WE.** Fundamental Immunology. New York, NY: Raven Press; 1993.

11 **O'Brien WA et al.** Molecular pathogenesis of HIV-1. AIDS. 1990;4(Suppl. 1):S41-8.

12 **Rabson AB.** The molecular biology of HIV infection: clues for possible therapy. In: Levy JA, ed. AIDS Pathogenesis and Treatment. New York: Marcel Dekker; 1988.

13 **Lane HC et al.** Qualitative analysis of immune function in patients with the acquired immunodeficiency syndrome. N Engl J Med. 1985;313:79–84.

14 **Smolen JS et al.** Deficiency of the autologous mixed lymphocyte reaction in patients with classic hemophilia treated with commercial factor VIII concentrate. J Clin Invest. 1985;75:1828–834.

15 **Gupta S et al.** Autologous mixed lymphocyte reaction in man. XIV. Deficiency of the autologous mixed lymphocyte reaction in acquired immune deficiency syndrome (AIDS) and AIDS related complex (ARC). In vitro effect of purified interleukin-1 and interleukin-2. Clin Exp Immunol. 1984;58:395–401.

16 **Sodrowski J et al.** Role of the HTLV-III/LAV envelope in syncytium formation and cytopathicity. Nature. 1986;322:470–74.

17 **Lifson JD et al.** Induction of CD4-dependent cell fusion by the HTLV-III/LAV envelope glycoprotein. Nature. 1986;323:725–28.

18 **Lifson JD et al.** AIDS retrovirus induced cytopathology: giant cell formation and involvement of CD4 antigen. Science. 1986;232:1123–127.

19 **Yoffe B et al.** Fusion as a mediator of cytolysis in mixtures of uninfected CD4+ lymphocytes and cells infected by human immunodeficiency virus. Proc Natl Acad Sci U S A. 1987;84:1429–433.

20 **St Clair MH et al.** Zidovudine resistance, syncytium-inducing phenotype, and HIV disease progression in a case-control study. The VA Cooperative Study Group. J Acquir Immune Defic Syndr. 1993;6(8):891–97.

21 **Yarchoan R et al.** CD4 count and the risk for death in patients infected with HIV receiving antiretroviral therapy. Ann Intern Med. 1991;115(3):184–89.

22 1993 revised classification system for HIV infection and expanded surveillance case definition for AIDS among adolescents and adults. MMWR. 1992;41(RR–17):1.

23 **Michel C et al.** Nephropathy associated with infection by human immunodeficiency virus: a report on 11 cases including 6 treated with zidovudine. Nephron. 1992;62(4):434–40.

24 **Chaisson RE, Volberding PA.** Clinical manifestations of HIV infection. In: Mandell GL et al., eds. Principles and Practice of Infectious Diseases. 3rd ed. New York: Churchill Livingstone; 1990:1059.

25 **Rao TK.** Clinical features of human immunodeficiency virus associated nephropathy. Kidney Int Suppl. 1991 Dec;35:S13–8.

26 **Cornblath DR et al.** Inflammatory demyelinating peripheral neuropathies associated with human T-cell lymphotrophic virus type III infection. Ann Neurol. 1987;21:32–40.

27 **Lipkin WI et al.** Inflammatory neuropathy in homosexual men with lymphadenopathy. Neurology. 1985;35:1479–483.

28 **Levy RM et al.** Neurological manifestations of the acquired immunodeficiency syndrome (AIDS): experience at UCSF and review of the literature. J Neurosurg. 1985;62:475.

29 **McArthur JC.** Neurologic manifestations of AIDS. Medicine. 1987;66:407–37.

30 **Cello JP.** Gastrointestinal manifestations of HIV infection. Infect Dis Clin North Am. 1988;2:387–96.

31 **Schleupner CJ.** Detection of HIV-1 infection. In: Mandell GL et al., eds. Principles and Practice of Infectious Diseases. 3rd ed. New York: Churchill Livingstone; 1990.

32 **Chamberland ME, Curran JW.** Epidemiology and Prevention of AIDS and HIV infection. In: Mandell GL et al., eds. Principles and Practice of Infectious Diseases. 3rd ed. New York: Churchill Livingstone; 1990:1029.

33 **Berkley S.** AIDS in the developing world: an epidemiologic overview. Clin Infect Dis. 1993;17(Suppl. 2):S329–36.

34 **Eron JJ Jr et al.** New anti-HIV-1 therapies and combinations: current data and prospects. AIDS. 1990;4(Suppl. 1):S193–200.

35 **McLeod GX et al.** Zidovudine: five years later. Ann Intern Med. 1992;117(6):487–501.

36 **Shelton MJ et al.** Zalcitabine. Ann Pharmacother. 1993;27(4):480–89.

37 **Hirsch MS et al.** Therapy for human immunodeficiency virus infection. N Engl J Med. 1993;328(23):1686–695.

38 **Fischl MA et al.** Safety and efficacy of sulfamethoxazole and trimethoprim chemoprophylaxis for *Pneumocystis carinii* pneumonia in AIDS. JAMA. 1988;259:1185–189.

39 **Masur H et al.** CD4 counts as predictors of opportunistic pneumonias in human immunodeficiency virus (HIV) infection. Ann Intern Med. 1989;111:223–31.

40 **Choi S et al.** CD4+ lymphocytes are an incomplete surrogate marker for clinical progression in persons with asymptomatic HIV infection taking zidovudine. Ann Intern Med. 1993 May;118(9):674–80.

41 **DeGruttola V et al.** Modeling the relationship between survival and CD4 lymphocytes in patients with AIDS and

AIDS-related complex. J Acquir Immune Defic Syndr. 1993;6(4):359–65.

42 **Lin DY et al.** Evaluating the role of CD-4-lymphocyte counts as surrogate endpoints in human immunodeficiency virus clinical trials. Stat Med. 1993 May;12(9):835–42.

43 **Reddy MM et al.** Evaluation of HIV P24 antigen, beta 2-microglobulin, neopterin, soluble CD4, soluble CD8, and soluble interleukin-2 receptor levels in patients with AIDS or AIDS-related complex treated with 2′,3′-dideoxyinosine (ddI). J Clin Lab Anal. 1991;5(6):396–98.

44 **Reddy MM et al.** An improved method for monitoring efficacy of antiretroviral therapy in HIV-infected individuals: a highly sensitive HIV p24 antigen assay. J Clin Lab Anal. 1992; 6(3):125–29.

45 **Nightingale SD et al.** Logarithmic relationship of the CD4 count to survival in patients with human immunodeficiency virus infection. Arch Intern Med. 1993;153(11):1313–318.

46 **Bogner JR et al.** Lymphocyte subsets as surrogate markers in antiretroviral therapy. Infection. 1991;19(Suppl. 2):S103–S108.

47 **Seligmann M et al.** Concorde: MRC/ANRS randomized double-blind controlled trial of immediate and deferred zidovudine in symptom-free HIV infection. Lancet. 1994;343:871–81.

48 **Drusano GL et al.** Relationship between dideoxyinosine exposure, CD4 counts, and p24 antigen levels in human immunodeficiency virus infection. A phase I trial. Ann Intern Med. 1992; 116(7):562–66.

49 **Zamora L et al.** Influence on survival of p24 antigen levels in patients with AIDS or advanced AIDS related complex treated with zidovudine. Eur J Clin Microbiol Infect Dis. 1992;11 (12):1181–185.

50 **Edlin BR et al.** Zidovudine-interferon-alpha combination therapy in patients with advanced human immunodeficiency virus type 1 infection: biphasic response of p24 antigen and quantitative polymerase chain reaction. J Infect Dis. 1992;165(5):793–98.

51 **Merigan TC et al.** Circulating p24 antigen levels and responses to dideoxycytidine in human immunodeficiency virus (HIV) infections. A phase I and II study. Ann Intern Med. 1989;110(3):189–94.

52 **Lambert JS et al.** 2′,3′-dideoxyinosine (ddI) in patients with the acquired immunodeficiency syndrome or AIDS-related complex. A phase I trial. N Engl J Med. 1990;322(19):1333–340.

53 **Ascher DP et al.** Acidification modified p24 antigen capture assay in HIV seropositives. J Acquir Immune Defic Syndr. 1992;5(11):1080–83.

54 **Bollinger RC Jr et al.** Acid dissociation increases the sensitivity of p24 antigen detection for the evaluation of antiviral therapy and disease progression in asymptomatic human immunodeficiency virus-infected persons. J Infect Dis. 1992;165(5):913–16.

55 **Siller L et al.** Serum levels of soluble CD8, neopterin, beta 2-microglobulin and p24 antigen as indicators of disease progression in children with AIDS on

zidovudine therapy. AIDS. 1993;7(3):369–73.

56 **Bacchetti P et al.** Early predictors of survival in symptomatic HIV-infected persons treated with high-dose zidovudine. J Acquir Immune Defic Syndr. 1992;5(7):732–36.

57 **Bass HZ et al.** The effect of zidovudine treatment on serum neopterin and β 2-microglobulin levels in mildly symptomatic, HIV type 1 seropositive individuals. J Acquir Immune Defic Syndr. 1992;5(3):215–21.

58 **Winters MA et al.** Quantitative RNA and DNA gene amplification can rapidly monitor HIV infection and antiviral activity in cell cultures. PCR Methods Appl. 1992 May;1(4):257–62.

59 **Brew BJ et al.** Cerebrospinal fluid beta 2-microglobulin in patients with AIDS dementia complex: an expanded series including response to zidovudine treatment. AIDS. 1992;6(5):461–65.

60 **Katzenstein DA et al.** Plasma viremia in human immunodeficiency virus infection: relationship to stage of disease and antiviral treatment. J Acquir Immune Defic Syndr. 1992;5(2):107–12.

61 **Mildvan D et al.** Endogenous interferon and triglyceride concentrations to assess response to zidovudine in AIDS and advanced AIDS-related complex. Lancet. 1992 Feb;339(8791):453–56.

62 **Jacobson MA et al.** Surrogate markers for survival in patients with AIDS and AIDS related complex treated with zidovudine. Br Med J. 1991;302(6768):73–8.

63 **Piatak M Jr et al.** High levels of HIV-1 in plasma during all stages of infection determined by competitive PCR. Science. 1993 Mar;259(5102):1749–754.

64 **Spector SA et al.** Virologic markers of human immunodeficiency virus type 1 in cerebrospinal fluid. The HIV Neurobehavioral Research Center Group. J Infect Dis. 1993;168(1):68–74.

65 **Holodniy M et al.** Measurement of HIV virus load and genotypic resistance by gene amplification in asymptomatic subjects treated with combination therapy. J Acquir Immune Defic Syndr. 1993;6(4):366–69.

66 **Shepp DH et al.** Effect of didanosine on human immunodeficiency virus viremia and antigenemia in patients with advanced disease: correlation with clinical response. J Infect Dis. 1993;167(1):30–5.

67 **Escaich S et al.** HIV detection in culture of peripheral blood mononuclear cells: a relevant in vitro correlate of the antiviral effect of ZDV in vivo. J Acquir Immune Defic Syndr. 1992;5(8):829–34.

68 **Saag MS et al.** High-level viremia in adults and children infected with human immunodeficiency virus: relation to disease stage and CD4+ lymphocyte levels. J Infect Dis. 1991;164(1):72–80.

69 **Srugo I et al.** Virus burden in human immunodeficiency virus type 1-infected children: relationship to disease status and effect of antiviral therapy. Pediatrics. 1991;87(6):921–25.

70 **Hussey R et al.** A soluble CD4 protein selectively inhibits HIV replication and

syncytium formation. Nature. 1988;331:78–81.

71 **Fisher R et al.** HIV infection is blocked in vitro by recombinant soluble CD4. Nature. 1988;331:76–8.

72 **Schooley R et al.** Recombinant soluble CD4 therapy in patients with the acquired immunodeficiency syndrome (AIDS) and AIDS-related complex. Ann Intern Med. 1990;112:247–53.

73 **Husson RN et al.** Phase I study of continuous-infusion soluble CD4 as a single agent and in combination with oral dideoxyinosine therapy in children with symptomatic human immunodeficiency virus infection. J Pediatr. 1992;121(4):627–33.

74 **Kahn J et al.** The safety and pharmacokinetics of recombinant soluble CD4 (sCD4) in subjects with the acquired immunodeficiency syndrome (AIDS) and AIDS-related complex. Ann Intern Med. 1990;112:254–61.

75 **Husson RN et al.** The use of nucleoside analogues in the treatment of HIV-infected children. AIDS Res Hum Retroviruses. 1992;8(6):1059–64.

76 **Johnson VA et al.** Synergistic inhibition of human immunodeficiency virus type 1 (HIV-1) replication in vitro by recombinant soluble CD4 and 3′-azido-3′-deoxythymidine. J Infect Dis. 1989 May;159(5):837–44.

77 **Johnson VA et al.** Three-drug synergistic inhibition of HIV-1 replication in vitro by zidovudine, recombinant soluble CD4, and recombinant interferon-alpha A. J Infect Dis. 1990 Jun;161(6):1059–67.

78 **Matthews SJ et al.** Zidovudine and other reverse transcriptase inhibitors in the management of human immunodeficiency virus-related disease. Pharmacotherapy. 1991;11(6):419–49.

79 **Morse GD et al.** Zidovudine update: 1990. DICP. 1990;24(7–8):754–60.

80 **Sommadossi JP.** Nucleoside analogs: similarities and differences. Clin Infect Dis. 1993;16(Suppl. 1):S7–15.

81 **Darby G.** Reverse transcriptase of HIV as a target for anti-viral drugs. Biochemical Soc Trans. 1992;20(2):505–08.

82 **Blum MR et al.** Pharmacokinetics and bioavailability of zidovudine in humans. Am J Med. 1988;85(Suppl. 2a):189–94.

83 **Luzier A et al.** Intravascular distribution of zidovudine: role of plasma proteins and whole blood components. Antiviral Res. 1993;21:267–80.

84 **Furman PA et al.** Phosphorylation of 3′-azido-3′-deoxythymidine and selective interaction of the 5′-triphosphate with human immunodeficiency virus reverse transcriptase. Proc Natl Acad Sci U S A. 1986;83:8333–337.

85 **Morse GD et al.** Pharmacokinetics of orally administered zidovudine among patients with hemophilia and asymptomatic human immunodeficiency virus infection. Antiviral Res. 1989;11:57–66.

86 **Stagg MP et al.** Clinical pharmacokinetics of 3′-azido-3′-deoxythymidine (zidovudine) and catabolites with formation of a toxic catabolite, 3′-amino-3′-deoxythymidine. Clin Pharmacol Ther. 1992;51(6):668–76.

87 **Morse GD et al.** Comparative pharmacokinetics of antiviral nucleoside

analogues. Clin Pharmacokinet. 1993;2:101–23.

88 **Gallicano KD et al.** Pharmacokinetics of single and chronic dose zidovudine in two HIV positive patients undergoing continuous ambulatory peritoneal dialysis (CAPD). J Acquir Immune Defic Syndr. 1992;5(3):242–50.

89 **Kremer D et al.** Zidovudine pharmacokinetics in five HIV seronegative patients undergoing continuous ambulatory peritoneal dialysis. Pharmacotherapy. 1992;12(1):56–60.

90 **Garraffo R et al.** Influence of hemodialysis on zidovudine (AZT) and its glucuronide (GAZT) pharmacokinetics: two case reports. Int J Clin Pharmacol Ther Toxicol. 1989;27(11):535–39.

91 **Singlas E et al.** Comparative pharmacokinetics of zidovudine (AZT) and its metabolite (GAZT) in healthy subjects and HIV seropositive patients. Eur J Clin Pharmacol. 1989;36(6):639–40.

92 **Gitterman SR et al.** Population pharmacokinetics of zidovudine. The Veterans Administration Cooperative Studies Group. Clin Pharmacol Ther. 1990;48(2):161–67.

93 **Fischl MA et al.** The efficacy of azidothymidine (AZT) in the treatment of patients with AIDS and AIDS-related complex: a double-blind, placebo-controlled trial. N Engl J Med. 1987;317:185–91.

94 **Fischl MA et al.** Prolonged zidovudine therapy in patients with AIDS and advanced AIDS-related complex. AZT Collaborative Working Group. JAMA. 1989;262(17):2405–410.

95 **Gelber RD et al.** Quality-of-life evaluation in a clinical trial of zidovudine therapy in patients with mildly symptomatic HIV infection. The AIDS Clinical Trials Group. Ann Intern Med. 1992;116:961–66.

96 **Hamilton JD et al.** A controlled trial of early versus late treatment with zidovudine in symptomatic human immunodeficiency virus infection. Results of the Veterans Affairs Cooperative Study. N Engl J Med. 1992;326(7):437–43.

97 **Merigan TC et al.** Placebo-controlled trial to evaluate zidovudine in treatment of human immunodeficiency virus infection in asymptomatic patients with hemophilia. NHF-ACTG 036 Study Group. Blood. 1991;78(4):900–6.

98 **Fischl MA.** Antiretroviral therapy in combination with interferon for AIDS-related Kaposi's sarcoma. Am J Med. 1991;90(4A):2S–7S.

99 **Volberding PA et al.** Zidovudine in asymptomatic human immunodeficiency virus infection. A controlled trial in persons with fewer than 500 CD4-positive cells per cubic millimeter. The AIDS Clinical Trials Group of the National Institute of Allergy and Infectious Diseases. N Engl J Med. 1990; 322(14):941–49.

100 **Lundgren JD et al.** Comparison of long-term prognosis of patients with AIDS treated and not treated with zidovudine. JAMA. 1994;271(14):1088–092.

101 **Agency for Health Care Policy and Research.** Early HIV Infection Guideline Panel. Clinical Practice Guideline

#7: evaluation and management of early HIV infection. 1994;94–0572.

102 **Richman DD et al.** The toxicity of azidothymidine (AZT) in the treatment of patients with AIDS and AIDS-related complex. A double-blind, placebo-controlled trial. N Engl J Med. 1987;317: 192–97.

103 **Collier AC et al.** A pilot study of low-dose zidovudine in human immunodeficiency virus infection. N Engl J Med. 1990;323(15):1015–021.

104 **Fischl MA et al.** The safety and efficacy of zidovudine (AZT) in the treatment of subjects with mildly symptomatic human immunodeficiency virus type 1 (HIV) infection. A double-blind, placebo-controlled trial. The AIDS Clinical Trials Group. Ann Intern Med. 1990;112(10):727–37.

105 **Chariot P et al.** Partial cytochrome c oxidase deficiency and cytoplasmic bodies in patients with zidovudine myopathy. Neuromuscul Disord. 1991; 1(5):357–63.

106 **Chen SC et al.** Concurrent zidovudine-induced myopathy and hepatotoxicity in patients treated for human immunodeficiency virus (HIV) infection. Pathology. 1992;24(2):109–11.

107 **Herskowitz A et al.** Cardiomyopathy associated with antiretroviral therapy in patients with HIV infection: a report of six cases. Ann Intern Med. 1992; 116(4):311–13.

108 **Herzberg NH et al.** Major growth reduction and minor decrease in mitochondrial enzyme activity in cultured human muscle cells after exposure to zidovudine. Muscle Nerve. 1992;15 (6):706–10.

109 **Mhiri C et al.** Zidovudine myopathy: a distinctive disorder associated with mitochondrial dysfunction. Ann Neurol. 1991 Jun;29(6):606–14.

110 **Shelton MJ et al.** Didanosine. Ann Pharmacother. 1992;26(5):660–70.

111 **Faulds D et al.** Didanosine. A review of its antiviral activity, pharmacokinetic properties and therapeutic potential in human immunodeficiency virus infection. Drugs. 1992 Jul;44(1):94–116.

112 **Cooley TP et al.** Once-daily administration of 2′,3′-dideoxyinosine (ddI) in patients with the acquired immunodeficiency syndrome or AIDS-related complex. Results of a phase I trial. N Engl J Med. 1990A;322(19):1340–345.

113 **Liebman HA et al.** Didanosine in the treatment of AIDS and AIDS-related complex: a critical appraisal of the dose and frequency of administration. Clin Infect Dis. 1993 Feb;16(Suppl. 1): S52–8.

114 **Hitchcock MJ.** In vitro antiviral activity of didanosine compared with that of other dideoxynucleoside analogs against laboratory strains and clinical isolates of human immunodeficiency virus. Clin Infect Dis. 1993;16(Suppl. 1):S16–21.

115 **Hoesterey BL et al.** Dose dependence in the plasma pharmacokinetics and uptake kinetics of 2′,3′-dideoxyinosine into brain and cerebrospinal fluid of rats. Drug Metab Dispos Biol Fate Chem. 1991;19(5):907–12.

116 **Galinsky RE et al.** Probenecid enhances central nervous system uptake

of 2′,3′-dideoxyinosine by inhibiting cerebrospinal fluid efflux. J Pharmacol Exp Ther. 1991;257(3):972–78.

117 **Knupp CA et al.** Pharmacokinetics of didanosine in patients with acquired immunodeficiency syndrome or acquired immunodeficiency syndrome-related complex. Clin Pharmacol Ther. 1991;49(5):523–35.

118 **Hartman NR et al.** Pharmacokinetics of 2′,3′-dideoxyadenosine and 2′,3′-dideoxyinosine in patients with severe human immunodeficiency virus infection. Clin Pharmacol Ther. 1990;47(5): 647–54.

119 **Pons JC et al.** Fetoplacental passage of 2′,3′-dideoxyinosine. Lancet. 1991; 337(8743):732. Letter.

120 **Knupp CA et al.** Pharmacokinetic-interaction study of didanosine and ranitidine in patients seropositive for human immunodeficiency virus. Antimicrob Agents Chemother. 1992;36 (10):2075–79.

121 **Hartman NR et al.** Pharmacokinetics of 2′,3′-dideoxyinosine in patients with severe human immunodeficiency infection. II. The effects of different oral formulations and the presence of other medications. Clin Pharmacol Ther. 1991;50(3):278–85.

122 **Metroka CE et al.** Failure of prophylaxis with dapsone in patients taking dideoxyinosine. N Engl J Med. 1991 Sep;325(10):737. Letter.

123 **Morse GD et al.** Effect of didanosine (ddI) on the single-dose pharmacokinetics (PK) of delavirdine (DLV) in HIV+ patients. Paper presented to the 34th International Conference on Antimicrobial Agents and Chemotherapy. Orlando, FL: 1994.

124 **Shelton MJ et al.** Gastric hypoacidity (GH) among HIV-infected outpatients. Paper presented to the 34th International Conference on Antimicrobial Agents and Chemotherapy. Orlando, FL: 1994.

125 **Connolly KJ et al.** Phase I study of 2′-3′-dideoxyinosine administered orally twice daily to patients with AIDS or AIDS-related complex and hematologic intolerance to zidovudine. Am J Med. 1991;91(5):471–78.

126 **Cooley TP et al.** Treatment of AIDS and AIDS-related complex with 2′,3′-dideoxyinosine given once daily. Rev Infect Dis. 1990;12(Suppl. 5):S552–60.

127 **Dolin R et al.** 2′,3′-Dideoxyinosine in patients with AIDS or AIDS-related complex. Rev Infect Dis. 1990;12 (Suppl. 5):S540–51.

128 **Kahn JO et al.** A controlled trial comparing continued zidovudine with didanosine in human immunodeficiency virus infection. The NIAID AIDS Clinical Trials Group. N Engl J Med. 1992; 327(9):581–87.

129 **McLaren C et al.** Longitudinal analysis of responses to oral didanosine therapy following zidovudine therapy in advanced infection with human immunodeficiency virus. Clin Infect Dis. 1993;16(Suppl. 1):S32–9.

130 **Yarchoan R et al.** The National Cancer Institute phase I study of 2′,3′-dideoxyinosine administration in adults with AIDS or AIDS-related complex: analysis of activity and toxicity profiles. Rev Infect Dis. 1990;12(Suppl. 5):S522–33.

131 **Yarchoan R et al.** Long-term toxicity/activity profile of 2′,3′-dideoxyinosine in AIDS or AIDS-related complex. Lancet. 1990;336(8714):526–29.

132 **Daniels M.** Pancreatitis in AIDS patients treated with didanosine. Am J Gastroenterol. 1993;88:459–60. Letter.

133 **Seidlin M et al.** Pancreatitis and pancreatic dysfunction in patients taking dideoxyinosine. AIDS. 1992;6(8):831–35.

134 **Lafeuillade A et al.** Optic neuritis associated with dideoxyinosine. Lancet. 1991;337(8741):615–16. Letter.

135 **Whitcup SM et al.** Retinal toxicity in human immunodeficiency virus-infected children treated with 2′,3′-dideoxyinosine. Am J Ophthalmol. 1992; 113(1):1–7.

136 **Crowther MA et al.** Dideoxyinosine-associated nephrotoxicity. AIDS. 1993 Jan;7(1):131–32.

137 **deJong MD et al.** Didanosine and heart failure. Lancet. 1992;339(8796): 806–7. Letter.

138 **Lai KK et al.** Fulminant hepatic failure associated with 2′,3′-dideoxyinosine (ddI). Ann Intern Med. 1991;115(4): 283–84.

139 **Parneix-Spake A et al.** Didanosine as probable cause of Stevens-Johnson syndrome. Lancet. 1992;340(8823): 857–58.

140 **Allan JD et al.** Long-term follow-up of didanosine administered orally twice daily to patients with advanced human immunodeficiency virus infection and hematologic intolerance of zidovudine. Clin Infect Dis. 1993;16(Suppl. 1): S46–51.

141 **Lambert JS et al.** Didanosine: long-term follow-up of patients in a phase 1 study. Clin Infect Dis. 1993;16(Suppl. 1):S40–5.

142 **Balis FM et al.** Clinical pharmacology of 2′,3′-dideoxyinosine in human immunodeficiency virus-infected children. J Infect Dis. 1992;165(1):99–104.

143 **Kieburtz KD et al.** Extended follow-up of peripheral neuropathy in patients with AIDS and AIDS-related complex treated with dideoxyinosine. J Acquir Immune Defic Syndr. 1992;5(1):60–4.

144 **Broder S et al.** Dideoxycytidine: current clinical experience and future prospects. A summary. Am J Med. 1990;88(5B):31S–33S.

145 **Fischl MA et al.** Zalcitabine compared with zidovudine in patients with advanced HIV-1 infection who received previous zidovudine therapy. Ann Intern Med. 1993;118(10):762–69.

146 **Abrams DI et al.** A comparative trial of didanosine or zalcitabine after treatment with zidovudine in patients with human immunodeficiency virus infection. N Engl J Med. 1994;330(10): 657–62.

147 **Gustavson LE et al.** A pilot study of the bioavailability and pharmacokinetics of 2′,3′-dideoxycytidine in patients with AIDS or AIDS-related complex. J Acquir Immune Defic Syndr. 1990; 3(1):28–31.

148 **Balzarini J et al.** The in vitro and in vivo anti-retrovirus activity, and intracellular metabolism of 3′-azido-2′,3′-dideoxythymidine and 2′,3′-dideoxycytidine are highly dependent on the

cell species. Biochem Pharmacol. 1988;37:897–903.

149 **Mitsuya H et al.** Inhibition of the in vitro infectivity and cytopathic effect of T-lymphotrophic virus type III/lymphadenopathy-associated virus (HTLV-III/LAV) by 2′,3′-dideoxynucleosides. Proc Natl Acad Sci USA. 1986;82: 7096–100.

150 **Indorf AS et al.** Esophageal ulceration related to zalcitabine (ddC). Ann Intern Med. 1992 Jul;117(2):133–34.

151 **Berger AR et al.** 2′,3′-dideoxycytidine (ddC) toxic neuropathy: a study of 52 patients. Neurology. 1993;43(2): 358–62.

152 **Dubinsky RM et al.** Reversible axonal neuropathy from the treatment of AIDS and related disorders with 2′,3′-dideoxycytidine (ddC). Muscle Nerve. 1989;12(10):856–60.

153 **Lewis LD et al.** Ultrastructural changes associated with reduced mitochondrial DNA and impaired mitochondrial function in the presence of 2′,3′-dideoxycytidine. Antimicrob Agents Chemother. 1992;36(9):2061–065.

154 **Powderly WG et al.** Ototoxicity associated with dideoxycytidine. Lancet. 1990 May;335(8697):1106. Letter.

155 **Gu Z et al.** Novel mutation in the human immunodeficiency virus type 1 reverse transcriptase gene that encodes cross-resistance to 2′,3′-dideoxyinosine and 2′,3′-dideoxycytidine. J Virol. 1992 Dec;66(12):7128–131.

156 **Spruance SL et al.** Didanosine compared with continuation of zidovudine in HIV-infected patients with signs of clinical deterioration while receiving zidovudine. Ann Intern Med. 1994; 120:360–68.

157 **Ho HT et al.** Cellular pharmacology of 2′,3′-dideoxy-2′,3′-didehydrothymidine, a nucleoside analog active against human immunodeficiency virus. Antimicrob Agents Chemother. 1989;33: 844–49.

158 **Browne MJ et al.** 2′,3′-didehydro-3′-deoxythymidine (d4T) in patients with AIDS or AIDS-related complex: a phase I trial. J Infect Dis. 1993;167(1): 21–9.

159 **Dudley MN et al.** Pharmacokinetics of stavudine in patients with AIDS or AIDS-related complex. J Infect Dis. 1992;166:480–85.

160 **Romero DL et al.** Nonnucleoside reverse transcriptase inhibitors that potently and specifically block human immunodeficiency virus type 1 replication. Proc Natl Acad Sci USA. 1991; 88:8806–810.

161 **Dueweke TJ et al.** A mutation in reverse transcriptase of bis(heteroaryl) piperazine-resistant human immunodeficiency virus type 1 that confers increased sensitivity to other nonnucleoside inhibitors. Proc Natl Acad Sci USA. 1993;90:4713–717.

162 **Pauwels R et al.** Potent and selective inhibition of HIV-1 replication in vitro by a novel series of TIBO derivatives. Nature. 1990;343(6257):470–74.

163 **Richman D et al.** BI-RG-587 is active against zidovudine-resistant human immunodeficiency virus type 1 and synergistic with zidovudine. Antimicrob Agents Chemother. 1991;35(2):305–08.

164 **Merluzzi VJ et al.** Inhibition of HIV-

1 replication by a nonnucleoside reverse transcriptase inhibitor. Science. 1990;250:1411–413.

165 Grob PM et al. Nonnucleoside inhibitors of HIV-1 reverse transcriptase: nevirapine as a prototype drug. AIDS Res Hum Retroviruses. 1992;8(2):145–52.

166 Richman DD. Loss of nevirapine activity associated with the emergence of resistance in clinical trials. Paper presented to the VIII International Conference on AIDS/III STD World Congress. Amsterdam, The Netherlands: 1992.

167 Saag MS et al. A short-term clinical evaluation of L-697,661, a nonnucleoside inhibitor of HIV-1 reverse transcriptase. N Engl J Med. 1993;329:1065–72.

168 Reichman RC et al. Phase I study of atevirdine, a non-nucleoside reverse transcriptase inhibitor, given in combination with zidovudine. J Infect Dis. 1995;171:297–304.

169 Cheeseman SH et al. Pharmacokinetics of nevirapine: initial single-rising-dose study in humans. Antimicrob Agents Chemother. 1993;37(2):178–82.

170 Debouck C. The HIV-1 protease as a therapeutic target for AIDS. AIDS Res Hum Retroviruses. 1992;8(2):153–64.

171 Johnson VA et al. Human immunodeficiency virus type 1 (HIV-1) inhibitory interactions between protease inhibitor Ro 31-8959 and zidovudine, 2′,3′-dideoxycytidine, or recombinant interferon-alpha A against zidovudine-sensitive or -resistant HIV-1 in vitro. J Infect Dis. 1992;166(5):1143–146.

172 Rosen CA. HIV regulatory proteins: potential targets for therapeutic intervention. AIDS Res Hum Retroviruses. 1992;8(2):1992.

173 Ensoli B et al. Tat protein of HIV-1 stimulates growth of cells derived from Kaposi's sarcoma lesions of AIDS patients. Nature. 1990;345:84–6.

174 Hsu M et al. Inhibition of HIV replication in acute and chronic infection in vitro by Tat antagonist. Science. 1991;254:1799–802.

175 Ratner L et al. Mechanism of action of N-butyl deoxynojirimycin in inhibiting HIV-1 infection and activity in combination with nucleoside analogs. AIDS Res Hum Retroviruses. 1993;9(4):291–97.

176 Ratner L. Glucosidase inhibitors for treatment of HIV-1 infection. AIDS Res Hum Retroviruses. 1992;8(2):165–73.

177 Dornsife RE et al. Anti-human immunodeficiency virus synergism by zidovudine (3′-azidothymidine) and didanosine (dideoxyinosine) contrasts with their additive inhibition of normal human marrow progenitor cells. Antimicrob Agents Chemother. 35(2):322–28.

178 Johnson VA et al. Two-drug combinations of zidovudine, didanosine, and recombinant interferon-alpha A inhibit replication of zidovudine-resistant human immunodeficiency virus type 1 synergistically in vitro. J Infect Dis. 1991;164(4):646–55.

179 Eron JJ Jr et al. Synergistic inhibition of replication of human immunodeficiency virus type 1, including that of a zidovudine-resistant isolate, by zidovudine and 2′,3′-dideoxycytidine in vitro. Antimicrob Agents Chemother. 1992;36:1559–562.

180 Meng TC et al. Combination therapy with zidovudine and dideoxycytidine in patients with advanced human immunodeficiency virus infection. A phase I/II study. Ann Intern Med. 1992;116:13–20.

181 Meng TC et al. AIDS Clinical Trials Group: phase I/II study of combination 2′,3′-dideoxycytidine and zidovudine in patients with acquired immunodeficiency syndrome (AIDS) and advanced AIDS-related complex. Am J Med. 1990;88:27S–30S.

182 Ragni MV et al. Combination zidovudine and dideoxyinosine in asymptomatic HIV(+) patients. Paper presented to the VIII International Conference on AIDS. Amsterdam, The Netherlands: 1992.

183 Collier AC et al. Combination therapy with zidovudine and didanosine compared with zidovudine alone in HIV-1 infection. Ann Intern Med. 1993;119:786–93.

184 Yarchoan R et al. A randomized pilot study of alternating or simultaneous zidovudine and didanosine therapy in patients with symptomatic human immunodeficiency virus infection. J Infect Dis. 1994;169:9–17.

185 Campbell TB et al. Inhibition of human immunodeficiency virus type 1 replication in vitro by the bisheteroarylpiperazine atevirdine (U-87201E) in combination with zidovudine or didanosine. J Infect Dis. 1993;168:318–26.

186 Chow YK et al. Use of evolutionary limitations of HIV-1 multidrug resistance to optimize therapy. Nature. 1993;361(6413):650–54.

187 Mayers DL et al. Characterization of HIV isolates arising after prolonged zidovudine therapy. J Acquir Immune Defic Syndr. 1992;5:749–59.

188 McLeod GX et al. Didanosine and zidovudine resistance patterns in clinical isolates of human immunodeficiency virus type 1 as determined by a replication endpoint concentration assay. Antimicrob Agents Chemother. 1992;36(5):920–25.

189 Larder BA et al. Multiple mutations in HIV-1 reverse transcriptase confer high-level resistance to zidovudine (AZT). Science. 1989;246:1155–158.

190 Larder BA et al. Infectious potential of human immunodeficiency virus type 1 reverse transcriptase mutants with altered inhibitor sensitivity. Proc Natl Acad Sci U S A. 1989;86(13):4803–807.

191 Richman DD. Antiviral therapy of HIV infection. Annu Rev Med. 1991;42:69–90.

192 Richman DD. HIV drug resistance. AIDS Res Hum Retroviruses. 1992;8(6):1065–71.

193 Kellam P et al. Fifth mutation in human immunodeficiency virus type 1 reverse transcriptase contributes to the development of high-level resistance to zidovudine. Proc Natl Acad Sci U S A. 1992;89:1934–938.

194 Boucher CA et al. Ordered appearance of zidovudine resistance mutations during treatment of 18 human immunodeficiency virus-positive subjects. J Infect Dis. 1992;165(1):105–10.

195 St Clair MH et al. Resistance to ddI and sensitivity to AZT induced by a mutation in HIV-1 reverse transcriptase. Science. 1991;253(5027):1557–559.

196 Reichman RC et al. Didanosine (ddI) and zidovudine (ZDV) susceptibilities of human immunodeficiency virus (HIV) isolates from long-term recipients of ddI. Antiviral Res. 1993;20:267–77.

197 Martin JL et al. Mechanism of resistance of human immunodeficiency virus type 1 to 2′,3′-dideoxyinosine. Proc Natl Acad Sci U S A. 1993;90:6135–139.

198 deVreese K et al. Resistance of human immunodeficiency virus type 1 reverse transcriptase to TIBO derivatives induced by site-directed mutagenesis. Virology. 1992;188:900–04.

199 Richman DD. HIV drug resistance. Annu Rev Pharmacol Toxicol. 1993;33:149–64.

200 Edwards P et al. Esophageal ulceration induced by zidovudine. Ann Intern Med. 1990;112:65–6.

201 Caron D et al. Hematologic findings in HIV infection. In: Wormser GP, ed. AIDS and Other Manifestations of HIV Infection. 2nd ed. New York: Raven Press; 1992.

202 Koppel BS. Neurological complications of AIDS and HIV infection. In: Wormser GP, ed. AIDS and Other Manifestations of HIV Infection. 2nd ed. New York: Raven Press; 1992: 315–48.

203 Teppler H et al. Efficacy of low doses of the polyethylene glycol derivative of interleukin-2 in modulating the immune response of patients with human immunodeficiency virus type 1 infection. J Infect Dis. 1993;167:291–98.

204 Wood R et al. Safety and efficacy of polyethylene glycol-modified interleukin-2 and zidovudine in human immunodeficiency virus type 1 infection: a phase I/II study. J Infect Dis. 1993;167:519–25.

205 Clark AG et al. Decrease in HIV provirus in peripheral blood mononuclear cells during zidovudine and human rIL-2 administration. J Acquir Immune Defic Syndr. 1992;5:52–9.

206 Mazza P et al. Recombinant interleukin-2 (rIL-2) in acquired immune deficiency syndrome (AIDS): preliminary report in patients with lymphoma associated with HIV infection. Eur J Haematol. 1992;49:1–6.

207 Schwartz EL et al. Pharmacokinetic interactions of zidovudine and methadone in intravenous drug-using patients with HIV infection. J Acquir Immune Defic Syndr. 1992;5:619–26.

208 Lane HC et al. Zidovudine in patients with human immunodeficiency virus (HIV) infection and Kaposi sarcoma. A phase II randomized, placebo-controlled trial. Ann Intern Med. 1989;111:41–50.

209 O'Marro SD et al. The effect of combinations of ampligen and zidovudine or dideoxyinosine against human immunodeficiency viruses in vitro. Antiviral Res. 1992;17:169–77.

210 Davey RT Jr et al. A phase I/II trial of zidovudine, interferon-alpha, and jects. J Infect Dis. 1992;165(1):105–10.

211 Miles SA. Hematopoietic growth factors as adjuncts to antiretroviral therapy. AIDS Res Hum Retroviruses. 1992;8:1073–080.

212 Kimura S et al. Efficacy of recombinant human granulocyte colony-stimulating factor on neutropenia in patients with AIDS. AIDS. 1990;4:1251–255.

213 Levine JD et al. Recombinant human granulocyte-macrophage colony-stimulating factor ameliorates zidovudine-induced neutropenia in patients with acquired immunodeficiency syndrome (AIDS)/AIDS-related complex. Blood. 1991;78:3148–154.

214 Pluda JM et al. Subcutaneous recombinant granulocyte-macrophage colony-stimulating factor used as a single agent and in an alternating regimen with azidothymidine in leukopenic patients with severe human immunodeficiency virus infection. Blood. 1990;76:463–72.

215 Hewitt RG et al. Pharmacokinetics and pharmacodynamics of granulocyte-macrophage colony-stimulating factor and zidovudine in patients with AIDS and severe AIDS-related complex. Antimicrob Agents Chemother. 1993;37:512–22.

216 Perno CF et al. Effects of bone marrow stimulatory cytokines on human immunodeficiency virus replication and the antiviral activity of dideoxynucleosides in cultures of monocyte/macrophages. Blood. 1992;80:995–1003.

217 Perno CF et al. Replication of human immunodeficiency virus in monocytes. Granulocyte/macrophage colony-stimulating factor (GM-CSF) potentiates viral production yet enhances the antiviral effect mediated by 3′-azido-2′3′-dideoxythymidine (AZT) and other dideoxynucleoside congeners of thymidine. J Exp Med. 1989;169:933–51.

218 Hewitt RG et al. Granulocyte-macrophage colony-stimulating factor and zidovudine in the treatment of neutropenia and human immunodeficiency virus infection. Pharmacotherapy. 1992;12:455–61.

219 Miles SA et al. Potential use of human stem cell factor as adjunctive therapy for human immunodeficiency virus-related cytopenias. Blood. 1991;78:3200–208.

220 Pos O et al. Impaired phagocytosis of Staphylococcus aureus by granulocytes and monocytes of AIDS patients. Clin Exp Immunol. 1992;88:23–8.

221 Fischl M et al. Recombinant human erythropoietin for patients with AIDS treated with zidovudine. N Engl J Med. 1990;322:1488–493.

222 Lim LL. Estimating compliance to study medication from serum drug levels: application to an AIDS clinical trial of zidovudine. Biometrics. 1992;48:619–30.

223 Beltangady M et al. Relation between plasma concentrations of didanosine and markers of antiviral efficacy in adults with AIDS or AIDS-related complex. Clin Infect Dis. 1993;16 (Suppl. 1):S26–31.

224 **Balis FM et al.** The pharmacokinetics of zidovudine administered by continuous infusion in children. Ann Intern Med. 1989;110:279–85.

225 **Pai SM et al.** Population pharmacokinetic analysis of didanosine (2',3'-dideoxyinosine) plasma concentrations obtained in phase I clinical trials in patients with AIDS or AIDS-related complex. J Clin Pharmacol. 1992;32:242–47.

226 **Stretcher BN et al.** Concentrations of phosphorylated zidovudine (ZDV) in patient leukocytes do not correlate with ZDV dose or plasma concentrations. Ther Drug Monit. 1991;13:325–31.

227 **Stretcher BN et al.** Pharmacokinetics of zidovudine phosphorylation in patients infected with the human immunodeficiency virus. Ther Drug Monit. 1992;14:281–85.

228 **Slusher JT et al.** Intracellular zidovudine (ZDV) and ZDV phosphates as measured by a validated combined high-pressure liquid chromatography-radioimmunoassay procedure. Antimicrob Agents Chemother. 1992;36:2473–477.

229 **Kuster H et al.** A method for the quantification of intracellular zidovudine nucleotides. J Infect Dis. 1991;164:773–76.

230 **Gao WY et al.** Differential phosphorylation of azidothymidine, dideoxycytidine, and dideoxyinosine in resting and activated peripheral blood mononuclear cells. J Clin Invest. 1993;91:2326–333.

231 **Shelton MJ et al.** Prolonged, but not diminished, zidovudine absorption induced by a high-fat breakfast. Pharmacotherapy. 1994;14(6):671–677.

232 **Wu AW et al.** Functional status and well-being in a placebo-controlled trial of zidovudine in early symptomatic HIV infection. J Acquir Immune Defic Syndr. 1993;6:452–58.

233 **Young LS.** Pneumocystis Carinii pneumonia. In: Walzer PD, ed. Pneumocystis Carinii Pneumonia. 2nd ed. New York: Marcel Dekker; 1984.

234 **Hughes WT et al.** Safety and pharmacokinetics of 566C80, a hydroxy-naphthoquinone with anti-pneumocystis carinii activity: a phase I study in human immunodeficiency virus (HIV)-infected men. J Infect Dis. 1991;163:843–48.

235 **Montgomery AB.** Pneumocystis carinii pneumonia in patients with the acquired immunodeficiency syndrome. Pathophysiology and therapy. AIDS Clin Rev. 1991;127–43.

236 **Sattler FR et al.** New developments in the treatment of Pneumocystis carinii pneumonia. Chest. 1992;101:451–57.

237 **Sattler FR, Jelliffe RW.** Pharmacokinetic and pharmacodynamic considerations for drug dosing in the treatment of Pneumocystis carinii pneumonia. In: Walzer PD, ed. Pneumocystis Carinii Pneumonia. 2nd ed. New York: Marcel Dekker, Inc.; 467–85.

238 **Lee BL et al.** Altered patterns of drug metabolism in patients with acquired immunodeficiency syndrome. Clin Pharmacol Ther. 1993;53:529–35.

239 **Davey RT Jr et al.** Recent advances in the diagnosis, treatment, and prevention of Pneumocystis carinii pneumonia. Antimicrob Agents Chemother. 1990;34:499–504.

240 **Conte JE Jr et al.** Intravenous or inhaled pentamidine for treating Pneumocystis carinii pneumonia in AIDS. A randomized trial. Ann Intern Med. 1990;113:203–09.

241 **SooHoo GW et al.** Inhaled or intravenous pentamidine therapy for Pneumocystis carinii pneumonia in AIDS. A randomized trial. Ann Intern Med. 1990;113:195–202.

242 **Walker RE, Masur H.** Current regimens of therapy and prophylaxis. Walzer PD, ed. Pneumocystis Carinii Pneumonia. 2nd ed. New York: Marcel Dekker, Inc.; 439–66.

243 **Antoniskis D et al.** Acute, rapidly progressive renal failure with simultaneous use of amphotericin B and pentamidine. Antimicrob Agents Chemother. 1990;34:470–72.

244 **Foisey M et al.** Pancreatitis during intravenous pentamidine therapy in an AIDS patient with prior exposure to didanosine. Ann Pharmacother. 1994;28:1025–028.

245 **Comtois R et al.** High pentamidine levels associated with hypoglycemia and azotemia in a patient with Pneumocystis carinii pneumonia. Diagn Microbiol Infect Dis. 1992;15:523–26.

246 **Comtois R et al.** Higher pentamidine levels in AIDS patients with hypoglycemia and azotemia during treatment of Pneumocystis carinii pneumonia. Am Rev Respir Dis. 1992;146:740–44.

247 **Telzak EE, Armstrong D.** Extrapulmonary infection and other unusual manifestations of Pneumocystis carinii. In: Walzer PD, ed. Pneumocystis Carinii Pneumonia. 2nd ed. New York: Marcel Dekker, Inc.; 361–78.

248 **Noskin GA et al.** Extrapulmonary infection with Pneumocystis carinii in patients receiving aerosolized pentamidine. Rev Infect Dis. 1991;13:525.

249 **Lee BL et al.** Dapsone, trimethoprim, and sulfamethoxazole plasma levels during treatment of pneumocystis pneumonia in patients with the acquired immunodeficiency syndrome (AIDS). Ann Intern Med. 1989;110:606–11.

250 **Medina I et al.** Oral therapy for Pneumocystis carinii pneumonia in the acquired immunodeficiency syndrome. A controlled trial of trimethoprim-sulfamethoxazole versus trimethoprim-dapsone. N Engl J Med. 1990;323:776–82.

251 **Noskin GA et al.** Salvage therapy with clindamycin/primaquine for Pneumocystis carinii pneumonia. Clin Infect Dis. 1992;14:183–88.

252 **Paulson YJ et al.** Eflornithine treatment of refractory Pneumocystis carinii pneumonia in patients with acquired immunodeficiency syndrome. Chest. 1992;101:67–74.

253 **Safrin S et al.** Dapsone as a single agent is suboptimal therapy for Pneumocystis carinii pneumonia. J Acquir Immune Defic Syndr. 1991;4:244–49.

254 **Sahai J et al.** Eflornithine for the treatment of Pneumocystis carinii pneumonia in patients with the acquired immunodeficiency syndrome: a preliminary review. Pharmacotherapy. 1989;9:29–33.

255 **Sattler FR et al.** Trimetrexate-leucovorin dosage evaluation study for treatment of Pneumocystis carinii pneumonia. J Infect Dis. 1990;161:91–6.

256 **Amsden GW et al.** Trimetrexate for Pneumocystis carinii pneumonia in patients with AIDS. Ann Pharmacother. 1992;26:218–26.

257 **Dohn MN et al.** Open-label efficacy and safety trial of 42 days of 566C80 for Pneumocystis carinii pneumonia in AIDS patients. J Protozool. 1991;38:220S–221S.

258 **Falloon J et al.** A preliminary evaluation of 566C80 for the treatment of Pneumocystis pneumonia in patients with the acquired immunodeficiency syndrome. N Engl J Med. 1991;325:1534–538.

259 **Gutteridge WE.** 566C80, an antimalarial hydroxynaphthoquinone with broad spectrum: experimental activity against opportunistic parasitic infections of AIDS patients. J Protozool. 1991;38:141S–143S.

260 **Hughes W et al.** Comparison of atovaquone (566C80) with trimethoprim-sulfamethoxazole to treat Pneumocystis carinii pneumonia in patients with AIDS. N Engl J Med. 1993;328:1521–527.

261 **Bozzette SA et al.** A controlled trial of early adjunctive treatment with corticosteroids for Pneumocystis carinii pneumonia in the acquired immunodeficiency syndrome. California Collaborative Treatment Group. N Engl J Med. 1990;323:1451–457.

262 **Bozzette SA et al.** Salvage therapy for zidovudine-intolerant HIV-infected patients with alternating and intermittent regimens of zidovudine and dideoxycytidine. Am J Med. 1990;88:24S–26S.

263 **Gagnon S et al.** Corticosteroids as adjunctive therapy for severe Pneumocystis carinii pneumonia in the acquired immunodeficiency syndrome. A double-blind, placebo-controlled trial. N Engl J Med. 1990;323:1444–450.

264 **Montaner JS et al.** Corticosteroids prevent early deterioration in patients with moderately severe Pneumocystis carinii pneumonia and the acquired immunodeficiency syndrome (AIDS). J Acquir Immune Defic Syndr. 1990;113:14–20.

265 **Nielsen TL et al.** Adjunctive corticosteroid therapy for Pneumocystis carinii pneumonia in AIDS: a randomized European multicenter open label study. J Acquir Immune Defic Syndr. 1992;5:726–31.

266 **Connor E et al.** Clinical and laboratory correlates of Pneumocystis carinii pneumonia in children infected with HIV. JAMA. 1991;265:1693–697.

267 **Kovacs JA et al.** Prophylaxis for Pneumocystis carinii pneumonia in patients infected with human immunodeficiency virus. Clin Infect Dis. 1992;14:1005–009.

268 **Phair J et al.** The risk of Pneumocystis carinii pneumonia among men infected with human immunodeficiency virus type 1. N Engl J Med. 1990;322:161–65.

269 **Golden JA et al.** Prevention of Pneumocystis carinii pneumonia by inhaled pentamidine. Lancet. 1989;1(8639):654–57.

270 **Leoung GS et al.** Aerosolized pentamidine for prophylaxis against Pneumocystis carinii pneumonia. The San Francisco community prophylaxis trial. N Engl J Med. 1990;323:769–75.

271 **Fischl MA et al.** A randomized controlled trial of a reduced daily dose of zidovudine in patients with the acquired immunodeficiency syndrome. The AIDS Clinical Trials Group. N Engl J Med. 1991;323:1009–014.

272 **Dohn MN, Frame PT.** Clinical manifestations in adults. In: Walzer PD, ed. Pneumocystis carinii Pneumonia. 2nd ed. New York: Marcel Dekker, Inc.; 1994:331–59.

273 **Jennens ID et al.** Cytomegalovirus cultures during maintenance DHPG therapy for cytomegalovirus (CMV) retinitis in acquired immunodeficiency syndrome (AIDS). J Med Virol. 1990;30:42–4.

274 **Mar E et al.** Effect of 9-(1,3-dihydroxy-2-propoxymethyl)guanine on human cytomegalovirus replication in vitro. Antimicrob Agents Chemother. 1983;24:518–21.

275 **Smee DF et al.** Anti-herpesvirus activity of the acyclic nucleoside 9-(1,3-dihydroxy-2-propoxymethyl)guanine. Antimicrob Agents Chemother. 1983;23:676–82.

276 **Biron KK et al.** A human cytomegalovirus mutant resistant to the nucleoside analog 9-{(2-hydroxy-1-(hydroxymethyl)ethoxy)methyl}guanine (BW B759U) induces reduced levels of BW B759U triphosphate. Proc Natl Acad Sci U S A. 1986;83:8769–773.

277 **Fletcher CV et al.** Evaluation of ganciclovir for cytomegalovirus disease. DICP. 1989;23:5–12.

278 **Peters BS et al.** Cytomegalovirus infection in AIDS. Patterns of disease, response to therapy and trends in survival. J Infect. 1991;23:129–37.

279 **Laskin OL et al.** Ganciclovir for the treatment of suppression of serious infections caused by cytomegalovirus. Am J Med. 1987;83:201–07.

280 **Weisenthal RW et al.** Long-term outpatient treatment of CMV retinitis with ganciclovir in AIDS patients. Br J Ophthalmol. 1989;73:996–1001.

281 **Jabs DA et al.** Cytomegalovirus retinitis and acquired immunodeficiency syndrome. Arch Ophthalmol. 1989;107:75–80.

282 **Hochster H et al.** Toxicity of combined ganciclovir and zidovudine for cytomegalovirus disease associated with AIDS. An AIDS Clinical Trials Group Study. Ann Intern Med. 1990;113:111–17.

283 **Jacobson MA et al.** A dose-ranging study of daily maintenance intravenous foscarnet therapy for cytomegalovirus retinitis in AIDS. J Infect Dis. 1993;168:444–48.

284 **Aweeka F et al.** Pharmacokinetics of intermittently administered intravenous foscarnet in the treatment of acquired immunodeficiency syndrome patients with serious cytomegalovirus retinitis. Antimicrob Agents Chemother. 1989;33:742–45.

285 **Jacobson MA et al.** Foscarnet treatment of cytomegalovirus retinitis in patients with the acquired immunodeficiency syndrome. Antimicrob Agents Chemother. 1989;33:736–41.

286 **SOCA.** Mortality in patients with the acquired immunodeficiency syndrome treated with either foscarnet or ganci-

clovir for cytomegalovirus retinitis. Studies of Ocular Complications of AIDS Research Group, in collaboration with the AIDS Clinical Trials Group. N Engl J Med. 1992;326:213–20.

287 Moyle G et al. Foscarnet and ganciclovir in the treatment of CMV retinitis in AIDS patients: a randomized comparison. J Infect. 1992;25:21–7.

288 Palestine AG et al. A randomized, controlled trial of foscarnet in the treatment of cytomegalovirus retinitis in patients with AIDS. Ann Intern Med. 1991;115:665–73.

289 Deray G et al. Foscarnet nephrotoxicity: mechanism, incidence and prevention. Am J Nephrol. 1989;9:316–21.

290 Sandstrom EG et al. Inhibition of human T-cell lymphotropic virus type III in vitro by phosphonoformate. Lancet. 1985;1480–482.

291 Jacobson MA et al. Foscarnet therapy for ganciclovir-resistant cytomegalovirus retinitis in patients with AIDS. J Infect Dis. 1991;163:1348–351.

292 Katlama C et al. Foscarnet induction therapy for cytomegalovirus retinitis in AIDS: comparison of twice-daily and three-times-daily regimens. J Acquir Immune Defic Syndr. 1992;5(Suppl. 1):S18–24.

293 Taburet AM et al. Pharmacokinetics of foscarnet after twice-daily administrations for treatment of cytomegalovirus disease in AIDS patients. Antimicrob Agents Chemother. 1992;36:1821–824.

294 Jacobson MA et al. Randomized, placebo-controlled trial of rifampin, ethambutol, and ciprofloxacin for AIDS patients with disseminated mycobacterium avium complex infection. J Infect Dis. 1993;168:112.

295 Hall AJ et al. Low frequency maintenance ganciclovir for cytomegalovirus retinitis. Scand J Infect Dis. 1991;23:43–6.

296 Holland GN et al. Survival of patients with the acquired immune deficiency syndrome after development of cytomegalovirus retinopathy. UCLA CMV Retinopathy Study Group. Ophthalmology. 1990;97:204–11.

297 Harb GE et al. Survival of patients with AIDS and cytomegalovirus disease treated with ganciclovir or foscarnet. AIDS. 1991;5:959–65.

298 Drew WL et al. Prevalence of resistance in patients receiving ganciclovir for serious cytomegalovirus infection. J Infect Dis. 1991;163:716–19.

299 Jacobson MA et al. In vivo additive antiretroviral effect of combined zidovudine and foscarnet therapy for human immunodeficiency virus infection (ACTG Protocol 053). J Infect Dis. 1991;163:1219–222.

300 Dieterich DT et al. Concurrent use of ganciclovir and foscarnet to treat cytomegalovirus infection in AIDS patients. J Infect Dis. 1993;167:1184–188.

301 Butler KM et al. Treatment of aggressive cytomegalovirus retinitis with ganciclovir in combination with foscarnet in a child infected with human immunodeficiency virus. J Pediatr. 1992;120:483–86.

302 Coker RJ et al. Treatment of cytomegalovirus retinitis with ganciclovir and foscarnet. Lancet. 1991;338 (8766):574–75.

303 Peters M et al. Combined and alternating ganciclovir and foscarnet in acute and maintenance therapy of human immunodeficiency virus-related cytomegalovirus encephalitis refractory to ganciclovir alone. A case report and review of the literature. Clin Invest. 1992;70:456–58.

304 Nelson MR et al. Salmonella, Campylobacter and Shigella in HIV-seropositive patients. AIDS. 1992;6:1495–498.

305 Jacobson MA et al. Ganciclovir with recombinant methionyl human granulocyte colony-stimulating factor for treatment of cytomegalovirus disease in AIDS patients. AIDS. 1992;6:515–17.

306 Hardy WD. Combined ganciclovir and recombinant human granulocyte-macrophage colony-stimulating factor in the treatment of cytomegalovirus retinitis in AIDS patients. J Acquir Immune Defic Syndr. 1991;4:S22–8.

307 Koyanagi Y et al. Cytokines alter production of HIV-1 from primary mononuclear phagocytes. Science. 1988;241:1673–675.

308 Cochereau-Massin I et al. Efficacy and tolerance of intravitreal ganciclovir in cytomegalovirus retinitis in acquired immune deficiency syndrome. Ophthalmology. 1991;98:1348–355.

309 Harris ML et al. Intravitreal ganciclovir in CMV retinitis: case report. Br J Ophthalmol. 1989;73:382–84.

310 Henry K et al. Use of intravitreal ganciclovir (dihydroxy propoxymethyl guanine) for cytomegalovirus retinitis in a patient with AIDS. Am J Ophthalmol. 1987;103:17–23.

311 Ussery FM III, et al. Intravitreal ganciclovir in the treatment of AIDS-associated cytomegalovirus retinitis. Ophthalmology. 1988;95:640–48.

312 Cantrill HL et al. Treatment of cytomegalovirus retinitis with intravitreal ganciclovir. Long-term results. Ophthalmology. 1989;96:367–74.

313 Heinemann MH. Long-term intravitreal ganciclovir therapy for cytomegalovirus retinopathy. Arch Ophthalmol. 1989;107:1767–772.

314 Young SH et al. High dose intravitreal ganciclovir in the treatment of cytomegalovirus retinitis. Med J Aust. 1992;157:370–373.

315 Sanborn GE et al. Sustained-release ganciclovir therapy for treatment of cytomegalovirus retinitis. Use of an intravitreal device. Arch Ophthalmol. 1992;110:188–95.

316 Anand R et al. Control of cytomegalovirus retinitis using sustained release of intraocular ganciclovir. Arch Ophthalmol. 1993;111:223–27.

317 Freeman WR. Intraocular antiviral therapy. Arch Ophthalmol. 1989;107:1737–739.

318 Jacobson MA et al. Human pharmacokinetics and tolerance of oral ganciclovir. Antimicrob Agents Chemother. 1987;31:1251–254.

319 Zuger A et al. Cryptococcal disease in patients with the Acquired Immunodeficiency Syndrome. Ann Intern Med. 1986;104:234.

320 Eng RHK et al. Cryptococcal infections in patients with acquired immune deficiency syndrome. Am J Med. 1986;81:19.

321 Powderly WG. AIDS commentary: cryptococcal meningitis and AIDS. Clin Infect Dis. 1993;17:837.

322 Chuck SL et al. Infections with Cryptococcal meningitis and AIDS. N Engl J Med. 1989;321:794.

323 Grant IH et al. Medical Management of AIDS: fungal infections in AIDS. Infect Dis Clin North Am. 1988;2:457.

324 Saag MS et al. Comparison of amphotericin B with fluconazole in the treatment of acute AIDS-associated cryptococcal meningitis. N Engl J Med. 1992;326:83.

325 Dismukes WE et al. Treatment of cryptococcal meningitis with combination amphotericin B and flucytosine for four as compared with six weeks. N Engl J Med. 1987;317:334.

326 Goodman L, Gilman A, eds. The Pharmacological Basis of Therapeutics. 5th ed. New York, NY: Macmillan; 1975:1236.

327 Shadomy S et al. In vitro studies with combination 5-fluorocytosine and amphotericin B. Antimicrob Agents Chemother. 1975;8:117.

328 Bennett JE et al. A comparison of amphotericin B alone and combined with flucytosine in the treatment of cryptococcal meningitis. N Engl J Med. 1979;301:126.

329 Polsky B et al. Intraventricular therapy of cryptococcal meningitis via a subcutaneous reservoir. Am J Med. 1986;81:24.

330 Maddux MS et al. A review of complications of amphotericin-B therapy: recommendations for prevention and management. Drug Intell Clin Pharm. 1980;14:177.

331 Tynes BS et al. Reducing amphotericin B reactions. Am Rev Respir Dis. 1963;87:264.

332 Chung D et al. Reversible cardiac enlargement during treatment with amphotericin B and hydrocortisone. Am Rev Respir Dis. 1971;103:831.

333 Butler W et al. Nephrotoxicity of amphotericin B: early and late effects in 81 patients. Ann Intern Med. 1964;61:175.

334 Winn W. Coccidioidomycoses and amphotericin B. Med Clin North Am. 1963;47:1131.

335 Brandriss MW et al. Anemia induced by amphotericin B. JAMA. 1964;189:663.

336 Grant SM et al. Fluconazole: a review of its pharmacodynamic and pharmacokinetic properties, and therapeutic potential in superficial and systemic mycoses. Drugs. 1990;39:877.

337 Saag MS et al. Comparison of amphotericin B with fluconazole in the treatment of acute AIDS-associated cryptococcal meningitis. The NIAID Mycoses Study Group and the AIDS Clinical Trials Group. N Engl J Med. 1992;326:83–89.

338 Larsen RA et al. Fluconazole compared with amphotericin B plus flucytosine for cryptococcal meningitis in AIDS. Ann Intern Med. 1990;113:183.

339 Perfect JR et al. Comparison of itraconazole and fluconazole in treatment of cryptococcal meningitis and candida

pyelonephritis in rabbits. Antimicrob Agent Chemother. 1986;29:579.

340 Perfect JR et al. Penetration of imidazoles and triazoles into cerebrospinal fluid of rabbits. J Antimicrob Chemother. 1985;16:81.

341 Denning DW et al. Itraconazole therapy for cryptococcal meningitis and cryptococcosis. Arch Intern Med. 1989;149:2301.

342 deGans J et al. Itraconazole compared with amphotericin B plus flucytosine in AIDS patients with cryptococcal meningitis. AIDS. 1992;6:185–90.

343 Milefchik E et al. High dose fluconazole with and without flucytosine for AIDS associated cryptococcal meningitis. Paper presented to the IX International Conference on AIDS. Berlin, Germany: 1993.

344 Coker R et al. Treatment of cryptococcosis with liposomal amphotericin B (Ambisome) in 23 patients with AIDS. AIDS. 1993;7:829.

345 Bozzette SA et al. Peripheral nerve function in persons with asymptomatic or minimally symptomatic HIV disease: absence of zidovudine neurotoxicity. J Acquir Immune Defic Syndr. 1991;4:851–55.

346 Powderly WG et al. A controlled trial of fluconazole or amphotericin B to prevent relapse of cryptococcal meningitis in patients with the acquired immunodeficiency syndrome. The NIAID AIDS Clinical Trials Group and Mycoses Study Group. N Engl J Med. 1992;326:793–98.

347 deGans J et al. Itraconazole as maintenance treatment for cryptococcal meningitis in the acquired immune deficiency syndrome. Br Med J. 1988;296:339.

348 Nightingale SD et al. Primary prophylaxis with fluconazole against systemic fungal infections in HIV-positive patients. AIDS. 1992;6:191.

349 Leen CLS et al. Fluconazole resistant candidiasis in patients with AIDS. Paper presented to the VII International Conference on AIDS. Florence, Italy: 1991.

350 Luft BJ M.D. et al. Toxoplasmic encephalitis in patients with the acquired immunodeficiency syndrome. N Engl J Med. 1993;329:995–1000.

351 Cohn JA et al. Evaluation of the policy of empiric treatment of suspected Toxoplasma encephalitis in patients with the acquired immunodeficiency syndrome. Am J Med. 1989;86:521–27.

352 Luft BJ et al. Toxoplasmic encephalitis. AIDS. 1990;4(6):593–95.

353 Harrison PB et al. Focal brain lesions on computed tomography in patients with acquired immune deficiency syndrome. Can Assoc Radiol J. 1990;41:83–6.

354 Girard PM et al. Dapsone-pyrimethamine compared with aerosolized pentamidine as primary prophylaxis against Pneumocystis carinii pneumonia and toxoplasmosis in HIV infection. The PRIO Study Group. N Engl J Med. 1993;328:1514–520.

355 Hardy WD et al. A controlled trial of trimethoprim-sulfamethoxazole or aerosolized pentamidine for secondary prophylaxis of Pneumocystis carinii pneumonia in patients with the acquired immunodeficiency syndrome.

AIDS Clinical Trials Group Protocol 021. N Engl J Med. 1992;327:1842–848.

356 Carr A et al. Roundtable discussion: management issues in didanosine therapy. J Acquir Immune Defic Syndr. 1993;6(Suppl. 1):S51–55.

357 Leport C et al. An open study of the pyrimethamine-clindamycin combination in AIDS patients with brain toxoplasmosis. J Infect Dis. 1989;160: 557–58.

358 Anon. Burroughs Wellcome's Daraprim May Accelerate HIV Progression. Health News Daily. 1992;2.

359 Navia BA et al. Cerebral toxoplasmosis complicating the acquired immune deficiency syndrome: clinical and neuropathological findings. Ann Neurol. 1986;19:224–38.

360 Wanke C et al. *Toxoplasma* encephalitis in patients with acquired immune deficiency syndrome: diagnosis and response to therapy. Am J Trop Med Hyg. 1987;36:509–16.

361 Haverkos HW. Assessment of therapy for toxoplasma encephalitis. Am J Med. 1987;82:907–14.

362 Tenant-Flowers M et al. Sulfadiazine desensitization in patients with AIDS and cerebral toxoplasmosis. AIDS. 1991;5:311–15.

363 delaHozCaballer B et al. Management of sulfadiazine allergy in patients with acquired immunodeficiency syndrome. J Allergy Clin Immunol. 1991; 88:137–38.

364 Molina JM et al. Sulfadiazine-induced crystalluria in AIDS patients with toxoplasma encephalitis. AIDS. 1991;5: 587–89.

365 Oster S et al. Resolution of acute renal failure in toxoplasmic encephalitis despite continuance of sulfadiazine. Rev Infect Dis. 1990;12:618–20.

366 Christin S et al. Acute renal failure due to sulfadiazine in patients with AIDS. Nephron. 1990;55:233–34.

367 Ventura MG et al. Sulfadiazine revisited. J Infect Dis. 1989;160:556–57.

368 Simon DI et al. Sulfadiazine crystalluria revisited. The treatment of Toxoplasma encephalitis in patients with acquired immunodeficiency syndrome. Arch Intern Med. 1990;150:2379–384.

369 Remington J. Availability of sulfadiazine—United States. JAMA. 1993; 269:461.

370 Skolnick PR. Treatment of CMV retinitis. N Engl J Med. 1992;326(25): 1701.

371 Holliman RE. Folate supplements and the treatment of cerebral toxoplasmosis. Scand J Infect Dis. 1989;21:475–76.

372 Frenkel JK et al. Relative reversal by vitamins (*p*-aminobenzoic, folic, and folinic acids) of the effects of sulfadiazine and pyrimethamine on toxoplasma, mouse and man. Antibiot Chemother. 1957;VII(12):630–38.

373 Eyles DE et al. The effect of metabolites on the antitoxoplasmic action of pyrimethamine and sulfadiazine. 1960; 277–83.

374 Opravil M et al. Pyrimethamine inhibits renal secretion of creatinine. Antimicrob Agents Chemother. 1993;37: 1056–060.

375 Leport C et al. Long-term follow-up of patients with AIDS on maintenance therapy for toxoplasmosis. Eur J Clin Microbiol Infect Dis. 1991;10:191–93.

376 Rolston KV. Treatment of acute toxoplasmosis with oral clindamycin. Eur J Clin Microbiol Infect Dis. 1991;10: 181–83.

377 Dannemann BR et al. Treatment of acute toxoplasmosis with intravenous clindamycin. The California Collaborative Treatment Group. Eur J Clin Microbiol Infect Dis. 1991;10:193–95.

378 Katlama C. Evaluation of the efficacy and safety of clindamycin plus pyrimethamine for induction and maintenance therapy of toxoplasmic encephalitis in AIDS. Eur J Clin Microbiol Infect Dis. 1991;10:189–91.

379 Foppa CU et al. A retrospective study of primary and maintenance therapy of toxoplasmic encephalitis with oral clindamycin and pyrimethamine. Eur J Clin Microbiol Infect Dis. 1991;10: 187–89.

380 Ruf B et al. Role of clindamycin in the treatment of acute toxoplasmosis of the central nervous system. Eur J Clin Microbiol Infect Dis. 1991;10:183–86.

381 Bhatti N et al. Low-dose alternate-day pyrimethamine for maintenance therapy in cerebral toxoplasmosis complicating AIDS. J Infect. 1990;21:119–20.

382 Pedrol E et al. Central nervous system toxoplasmosis in AIDS patients: efficacy of an intermittent maintenance therapy. AIDS. 1990;4:511–17.

383 Araujo FG et al. In vitro and in vivo activities of the hydroxynaphthoquinone 566C80 against the cyst form of *toxoplasma gondii*. Antimicrob Agents Chemother. 1991;36:326–30.

384 Araujo FG et al. Remarkable in vitro and in vivo activities of the hydroxynaphthoquinone 566C80 against tachyzoites and tissue cysts of Toxoplasma gondii. Antimicrob Agents Chemother. 1991;35:293–99.

385 Gianotti N et al. Efficacy and safety of atovaquone (566C80) in the treatment of cerebral toxoplasmosis (CT) and *Pneumocystis carinii* pneumonia (PCP) in HIV infected patients. Paper presented to the IXth International Conference on AIDS in affiliation with the IVth STD World Congress. Berlin, Germany: 1993.

386 White A et al. Comparison to natural history data of survival of toxoplasmic encephalitis patients treated with atovaquone. Paper presented to the IXth International Conference on AIDS in affiliation with the IVth STD World Congress. Berlin, Germany: 1993.

387 Chang HR et al. In vitro and in vivo effects of doxycycline on Toxoplasma gondii. Antimicrob Agents Chemother. 1990;34:775–80.

388 Alder J et al. Treatment of experimental *Toxoplasma gondii* infection by clarithromycin based combination therapies. Paper presented to the 1st National Conference on Human Retroviruses. Washington, DC: 1993.

389 Chaisson RE et al. Tuberculosis in patients with the Acquired Immunodeficiency Syndrome. Am Rev Respir Dis. 1987;136:570.

390 Handwerger S et al. Tuberculosis and the Acquired Immunodeficiency Syndrome at a New York City hospital: 1978–1985. Chest. 1987;91:176.

391 Initial therapy for tuberculosis in the era of multidrug resistance: recommendations of the advisory council for the elimination of tuberculosis. MMWR. 1993;42(RR-7):1.

392 Iseman MD. Treatment of multidrug-resistant tuberculosis. N Engl J Med. 1993;329:784.

393 Goble M et al. Treatment of 171 patients with pulmonary tuberculosis resistant to isoniazid and rifampin. N Engl J Med. 1993;328:527.

394 Frieden TR et al. The emergence of drug-resistant tuberculosis in New York City. N Engl J Med. 1993;328: 521.

395 Nosocomial transmission of multidrug-resistant TB to health-care workers and HIV-infected patients in an urban hospital—Florida. MMWR. 1990;39:718.

396 Nosocomial transmission of multidrug-resistant TB among HIV-infected persons—Florida and New York, 1988–1991. MMWR. 1991;40:585.

397 Purified protein derivative (PPD)-tuberculin anergy and HIV infection: guidelines for anergy testing and management of anergic persons at risk of tuberculosis. MMWR. 1991;40(RR-5): 27.

398 Jacobson MA et al. Retinal and gastrointestinal disease due to cytomegalovirus in patients with the acquired immune deficiency syndrome: prevalence, natural history, and response to ganciclovir therapy. Q J Med. 1988;67: 473–86.

399 Saltzman BR et al. Mycobacterium tuberculosis bacteremia in the Acquired Immunodeficiency Syndrome. JAMA. 1986;256:390.

400 Barber TW et al. Bacteremia due to mycobacterium tuberculosis in patients with human immunodeficiency virus infection. Medicine (Baltimore). 1990; 69:375.

401 Berenguer J et al. Tuberculous meningitis in patients infected with the Human Immunodeficiency Virus. N Engl J Med. 1992;326:668.

402 Louie E et al. Tuberculosis in non-Haitian patients with Acquired Immunodeficiency Syndrome. Chest. 1986; 190:542.

403 Pitchenik AE et al. Tuberculosis, atypical mycobacteriosis, and the Acquired Immunodeficiency Syndrome among Haitian and Non-Haitian patients in South Florida. Ann Intern Med. 1984;1011:641.

404 TB and human immunodeficiency virus infection: recommendations of the Advisory Committee for the Elimination of TB (ACET). MMWR. 1989B; 38:236,243.

405 Holt E et al. Efficacy of supervised, intermittent, short course therapy of tuberculosis in HIV infection. Paper presented to the IX International Conference on AIDS. Berlin, Germany: 1993.

406 Chen CH et al. Minimal inhibitory concentrations of rifabutin, ciprofloxacin and ofloxacin against mycobacterium tuberculosis isolated before treatment of patients in Taiwan. Am Rev Respir. 1989;140:987.

407 Management of persons exposed to multidrug-resistant tuberculosis. MMWR. 1992;41(RR-11):1.

408 Tsukamura M. Antituberculosis activity of ofloxacin (DL 8280) on experimental tuberculosis in mice. Am Rev Respir Dis. 1985;132:915.

409 Tsukamura M et al. Therapeutic effect of new antibacterial substance ofloxacin (DL 8280) on pulmonary tuberculosis. Am Rev Respir Dis. 1985; 131:353.

410 Hong Kong Chest Service/British Medical Research Council. A controlled study of rifabutin and an uncontrolled study of ofloxacin in the retreatment of patients with pulmonary tuberculosis resistant to isoniazid, streptomycin and rifampicin. Tuber Lung Dis. 1992;73:59.

411 American Thoracic Society. Treatment of tuberculosis and tuberculosis infection in adults and children. Am Rev Respir Dis. 1986;134:355.

412 Gorzynski EA et al. Comparative antimycobacterial activities of difloxacin, temafloxacin, enoxacin, pefloxacin, reference fluoroquinolones and a new macrolide, clarithromycin. Antimicrob Agents Chemother. 1989;33:591.

413 Rastogi N et al. In vitro activity of the new difluorinated quinolone sparfloxacin (AT-4140) against mycobacterium tuberculosis compared with activities of ofloxacin and ciprofloxacin. Antimicrob Agents Chemother. 1991;35: 1933.

414 Hecht FM et al. TB and HIV: preventive care. AIDS Clin Care. 1992;4:1.

415 Brix D et al. Correlation of in vivo cellular immunity with CD4 number and disease progression in HIV seropositive patients. Paper presented to the Fifth International Conference on AIDS. Montreal, Canada: 1989.

416 Rieder HL et al. Tuberculosis in the United States. JAMA. 1989;262:385.

417 Nightingale SD et al. Incidence of mycobacterium avium-intracellulare complex bacteremia in human immunodeficiency virus-positive patients. J Infect Dis. 1992;165:1082.

418 Walker JM et al. Mycobacterium avium complex infection in patients with the acquired immunodeficiency syndrome. Chest. 1988;93:926.

419 Chaisson RE et al. Incidence and natural history of mycobacterium avium-complex infections in patients with advanced human immunodeficiency virus disease treated with zidovudine. Am Rev Respir Dis. 1992;146:285–89.

420 Chaisson RE et al. Mycobacteria and AIDS mortality. Am Rev Respir Dis. 1989;139:1.

421 Horsburgh CR et al. The epidemiology of disseminated non-tuberculosis mycobacterial infection in the acquired immunodeficiency syndrome (AIDS). Am Rev Respir Dis. 1989;139:4.

422 Sathe SS et al. Severe anemia is an important negative predictor for survival with disseminated mycobacterium avium-intracellulare in acquired immunodeficiency syndrome. Am Rev Respir Dis. 1990;142:1306.

423 Yakrus MA et al. Geographic distribution, frequency and specimen source of mycobacterium avium complex serotypes isolated from patients with acquired immunodeficiency syndrome. J Clin Microbiol. 1990;28:926.

424 Hawkins CC et al. Mycobacterium avium complex infections in patients with the acquired immunodeficiency syndrome. Ann Intern Med. 1986;105:184.

425 **Chaisson RE et al.** Pneumocystis prophylaxis and survival in patients with advanced human immunodeficiency virus infection treated with zidovudine. The Zidovudine Epidemiology Group. Arch Intern Med. 1992;152:2009-013.

426 **Good RC, Bean RE.** Seroagglutination. In: Kubica GP, Wayne L, eds. The Mycobacteria: A Source Book. New York: Marcel Dekker; 1984:15:105.

427 **Ellner JJ et al.** Mycobacterium avium infection and AIDS: a therapeutic dilemma in rapid evolution. J Infect Dis. 1991;163:1326-335.

428 **Woods GL.** Management of mycobacterium avium complex (MAC) in patients with HIV infection: diagnosis and susceptibility testing. Paper presented to the IX International Conference on AIDS. Berlin, Germany: 1993.

429 **Wong B et al.** Continuous high-grade mycobacterium avium-intracellulare bacteremia in patients with the acquired immune deficiency syndrome. Am J Med. 1985;78:35.

430 **Hoffner SE et al.** Control of disease progress in mycobacterium avium-infected AIDS patients. Res Microbiol. 1992;143:391.

431 **Yajko DM.** In vitro activity of antimicrobial agents against the mycobacterium avium complex inside macrophages from HIV-1-infected individuals: the link to clinical response to treatment? Res Microbiol. 1992;143:411.

432 **Yajko DM et al.** Therapeutic implications of inhibition versus killing of mycobacterium avium complex by antimicrobial agents. Antimicrob Agents Chemother. 1987;31:117.

433 **Masur H.** Effect of combined clofazimine and ansamycin therapy on mycobacterium avium-mycobacterium intracellulare bacteremia in patients with AIDS. J Infect Dis. 1987;155:127.

434 **Horsburgh CR et al.** Survival of patients with acquired immune deficiency syndrome and disseminated mycobacterium avium complex infection with and without antimycobacterial chemotherapy. Am Rev Respir Dis. 1991;144:557.

435 **Kemper CA et al.** Treatment of mycobacterium avium complex bacteremia in AIDS with a four-drug oral regimen: rifampin, ethambutol, clofazimine, and ciprofloxacin. Ann Intern Med. 1992;116:466.

436 **Young LS et al.** Azithromycin for treatment of mycobacterium avium-intracellulare complex infection in patients with AIDS. Lancet. 1991;338:1107.

437 **Heifets LB et al.** Clarithromycin minimal inhibitory and bactericidal concentrations against Mycobacterium avium. Am Rev Respir Dis. 1992;145:856-58.

438 **Heifets LB et al.** Individualized therapy versus standard regimens in the treatment of mycobacterium avium infections. Am Rev Respir Dis. 1991;144:1.

439 **Chaisson RE et al.** Clarithromycin therapy for disseminated mycobacterium avium-complex (MAC) in AIDS. Paper presented to the Thirty-Second Interscience Conference on Antimicrobial Agents and Chemotherapy. Anaheim, CA: 1992.

440 **Ishiguro M et al.** Penetration of macrolides into human polymorphonuclear leukocytes. J Antimicrob Chemother. 1989;24:719.

441 **Mor N et al.** Accumulation of clarithromycin in macrophages infected with mycobacterium avium. Pharmacotherapy. 1994;14:100.

442 **Girard AE et al.** Pharmacokinetic and in vivo studies with azithromycin (CP-62,993), a new macrolide with an extended half-life and excellent tissue distribution. Antimicrob Agents Chemother. 1987;31:1948.

443 **Gladue RP et al.** Intracellular accumulation of azithromycin by cultured human fibroblasts. Antimicrob Agents Chemother. 1990;34:1056.

444 **Dautzenberg B et al.** Activity of clarithromycin against Mycobacterium avium infection in patients with the acquired immune deficiency syndrome. A controlled clinical trial. Am Rev Respir Dis. 1991;144:564-69.

445 **Barradel LB et al.** Clarithromycin: a review of its pharmacological properties and therapeutic use in mycobacterium avium-intracellulare complex infections in patients with acquired immune deficiency syndrome. Drugs. 1993;46:289.

446 **Masur H.** Recommendations on prophylaxis and therapy for disseminated mycobacterium avium complex disease in patients infected with the human immunodeficiency virus. N Engl J Med. 1993;329:898.

447 **Masur H et al.** Recommendations on prophylaxis and therapy for disseminated mycobacterium avium complex for adults and adolescents infected with human immunodeficiency virus. MMWR. 1993A;42:14.

448 **Englehard D et al.** Interaction of ketoconazole with rifampin and isoniazid. N Engl J Med. 1984;311:1681.

449 **Lazar JD et al.** Drug interactions with fluconazole. Rev Infect Dis. 1990;12(3):327.

450 **Pieters FA et al.** Influence of once-monthly rifampicin and daily clofazimine on the pharmacokinetics of dapsone in leprosy patients in Nigeria. J Clin Pharmacol. 1988;34:73.

451 **Holmes VF.** Rifampin-induced methadone withdrawal in AIDS. J Clin Psychopharmacol. 1990;10:443.

452 **Fanfani A et al.** Rifabutin: LM427 Ansamycin. Milan, Italy: Farmitalia Carlo Erba; 1985.

453 **Narang P et al.** Does rifabutin affect zidovudine disposition in HIV(+) patients? Paper presented to the VIII International Conference on AIDS. Amsterdam, The Netherlands: 1992.

454 **Peters DH et al.** Clarithromycin. A review of its antimicrobial activity, pharmacokinetic properties and therapeutic potential. Drugs. 1992;44:117.

455 **Albani F et al.** Clarithromycin-carbamazepine interaction. Case report. Epilepsia. 1993;34:161.

456 **Honig P et al.** Effect of erythromycin, clarithromycin and azithromycin on the pharmacokinetics of terfenadine. Clin Pharmacol Ther. 1993;53:161.

457 **Nightingale SD et al.** Two controlled trials of rifabutin prophylaxis against mycobacterium avium complex infection in AIDS. N Engl J Med. 1993;329:828.

458 **Dworkin BM.** Gastrointestinal manifestations of AIDS. In: Wormser GP, ed. AIDS and Other Manifestations of HIV Infection. 2nd ed. New York: Raven Press; 1992:419-32.

459 **Blackstone MO.** Endoscopic Interpretation. New York: Raven Press; 1984:19-33.

460 **Wu GD et al.** A comparison of routine light microscopy, immunohistochemistry, and in situ hybridization for the detection of cytomegalovirus in gastrointestinal biopsies. 1989;84:1517-520.

461 **Connolly GM et al.** Fixed drug eruption due to foscarnet. Genitourin Med. 1990;66(2):97-8.

462 **Profeta S et al.** Salmonella infections in patients with acquired immunodeficiency syndrome. Arch Intern Med. 1985;145:670-72.

463 **Bernard E et al.** Diarrhea and *Campylobacter* infections in patients infected with the human immunodeficiency virus. J Infect Dis. 1989;159:143-44.

464 **Blaser MJ et al.** Recurrent shigellosis complicating human immunodeficiency virus infection: failure of pre-existing antibodies to confer protection. Am J Med. 1989;86:105-07.

465 **Naficy AB, Soave R.** Cryptosporidiosis, isosporiasis, and microsporidiosis in AIDS. In: Wormser GP, ed. AIDS and Other Manifestations of HIV Infection. 2nd ed. New York: Raven Press; 1992:433-41.

466 **Laughon BE et al.** Prevalence of enteric pathogens in homosexual men with and without acquired immunodeficiency syndrome. Gastroenterology. 1988;94:984-93.

467 **Soave R et al.** Cryptosporidiosis in homosexual men. Ann Intern Med. 1984;110:504-11.

468 **DeHovitz JA et al.** Clinical manifestations and therapy of *Isospora belli* infection in patients with acquired immunodeficiency syndrome. N Engl J Med. 1986;315:87-90.

469 **Forthal DN et al.** *Isospora belli* enteritis in three homosexual men. Am J Trop Med Hyg. 1984;33:1060-064.

470 **Pape JW et al.** Treatment and prophylaxis of *Isospora belli* infection in patients with the acquired immunodeficiency syndrome. N Engl J Med. 1989;320:1044-047.

471 **Bryan RT et al.** Microsporidia: opportunistic pathogens in patients with AIDS. In: Sun T, ed. Progress in Clinical Parasitology. Philadelphia: Field and Wood; 1990:1-26.

472 **Pluda JM et al.** Parameters affecting the development of non-Hodgkin's lymphoma in patients with severe human immunodeficiency virus infection receiving antiretroviral therapy. J Clin Oncol. 1993;11:1099-107.

473 **Levine AM et al.** Neoplastic complications of HIV infection. In: Wormser GP, ed. AIDS and Other Manifestations of HIV Infection. 2nd ed. New York: Raven Press; 1992:443-54.

474 **Vogel J et al.** The HIV tat gene induces dermal lesions resembling Kaposi's sarcoma in transgenic mice. Nature. 1988;335:606-11.

475 **Friedman-Kien AE et al.** Disseminated Kaposi's sarcoma in homosexual men. Ann Intern Med. 1982;96:693-700.

476 **Krown SE et al.** Medical management of AIDS patients. Kaposi's sarcoma. Med Clin North Am. 1992;76(1):235-52.

477 **Lane HC.** The role of alpha-interferon in patients with human immunodeficiency virus infection. Semin Oncol. 1991;18(5 Suppl. 7):46-52.

478 **Pluda JM et al.** Therapy of AIDS and AIDS-associated neoplasms. Cancer Chemother Biol Response Modif. 1992;13:404-39.

479 **Sawyer LA et al.** Effects of interferon-alpha in patients with AIDS-associated Kaposi's sarcoma are related to blood interferon levels and dose. Cytokine. 1990;2:247-52.

480 **Kovacs JA et al.** Combined zidovudine and interferon-alpha therapy in patients with Kaposi sarcoma and the acquired immunodeficiency syndrome (AIDS). Ann Intern Med. 1989;111:280-87.

481 **Krown SE et al.** Interferon-alpha, zidovudine, and granulocyte-macrophage colony-stimulating factor: a phase I AIDS Clinical Trials Group study in patients with Kaposi's sarcoma associated with AIDS. J Clin Oncol. 1992;10:1344-351.

482 **Miles SA et al.** Combined therapy with recombinant granulocyte colony-stimulating factor and erythropoietin decreases hematologic toxicity from zidovudine. Blood. 1991;77:2109-117.

483 **Scadden DT et al.** Granulocyte-macrophage colony-stimulating factor mitigates the neutropenia of combined interferon alfa and zidovudine treatment of acquired immune deficiency syndrome-associated Kaposi's. J Clin Oncol. 1991;9:802-08.

484 **Moore RD et al.** Non-Hodgkin's lymphoma in patients with advanced HIV infection treated with zidovudine. JAMA. 1991;265:2208-211.

485 **Pluda JM et al.** Development of non-Hodgkin lymphoma in a cohort of patients with severe human immunodeficiency virus (HIV) infection on long-term antiretroviral therapy. Ann Intern Med. 1990;113:276-82.

486 **Tirelli U et al.** Prospective study with combined low-dose chemotherapy and zidovudine in 37 patients with poor-prognosis AIDS-related non-Hodgkin's lymphoma. French-Italian Cooperative Study Group. Ann Oncol. 1992;3:843-47.

487 **Levine AM.** Therapeutic approaches to neoplasms in AIDS. Rev Infect Dis. 1990;12:938-43.

488 **Pluda JM et al.** Hematologic effects of AIDS therapies. Hematol Oncol Clin North Am. 1991;5:229-48.

489 **Jeffries DJ.** Zidovudine after occupation exposure to HIV. Br Med J. 1991;302:1349-351.

490 **Looke DFM et al.** Failed prophylactic zidovudine after needlestick injury. Lancet. 1990;335:1280.

491 **Lange JMA et al.** Failure of zidovudine prophylaxis after accidental exposure to HIV 1. N Engl J Med. 1990;322:1375-377.

492 **Anon.** HIV seroconversion after occupational exposure despite early prophylactic zidovudine therapy. Lancet. 1993;341:1077-078.

493 **Erice A et al.** Brief report: primary infection with zidovudine-resistant hu-

man immunodeficiency virus type 1. N Engl J Med. 1993;328:1163–165.

494 **Tokars JI et al.** Surveillance of HIV infection and zidovudine use among health care workers after occupational exposure to HIV-infected blood. The CDC Cooperative Needlestick Surveillance Group. Ann Intern Med. 1993; 118:913–19.

495 **Centers for Disease Control.** HIV/AIDS surveillance report, 1991.

496 **Centers for Disease Control.** Monthly HIV/AIDS surveillance report, 1990.

497 **Brookmeyer R.** Reconstruction and future trends of the AIDS epidemic in the United States. Science. 1991;253: 37.

498 **Rosenberg PS et al.** National AIDS incidence trends and the extent of zidovudine therapy in selected demographic and transmission groups. J Acquir Immune Defic Syndr. 1991;4:392–401.

499 **Jones L et al.** Women and HIV disease. Br J Hosp Med. 1989;41:526.

500 **Kloser P et al.** Women with AIDS: a continuing study 1988. Paper presented to the V International Conference on AIDS. Montreal, Canada: 1989.

501 **Parker R et al.** Survival with the acquired immunodeficiency syndrome. N Engl J Med. 1987;317:1297.

502 **Bacchetti P et al.** Survival with AIDS in New York. N Engl J Med. 1988;318: 1464.

503 **White BM et al.** Survival in patients with acquired immunodeficiency syndrome in Australia. Med J Aust. 1989; 150:358.

504 **Moore RD et al.** Zidovudine and the natural history of the acquired immunodeficiency syndrome. N Engl J Med. 1991;324:1412–416.

505 **Turner BJ et al.** Survival patterns of women and men with AIDS: impact of health care use prior to AIDS. Paper presented to the VII International Conference on AIDS. Florence, Italy: 1991.

506 **Araneta MR et al.** Survival trends among women with AIDS in San Francisco. Paper presented to the VII International Conference on AIDS. Florence, Italy: 1991.

507 **Horsburgh CR et al.** Predictors of survival in HIV infection include CD4+ cell count, AIDS-defining condition and therapy but not sex, age, race, or risk activity. Paper presented to the VII International Conference on AIDS. Florence, Italy: 1991.

508 **Lemp GF et al.** Survival trends for patients with AIDS. JAMA. 1990;263: 402.

509 **Nahlen F et al.** HIV wasting syndrome in the U.S. Paper presented to the VII International Conference on AIDS. Florence, Italy: 1991.

510 **Fleming PL et al.** Sex-specific differences in the prevalence of reported AIDS-indicative diagnoses, United States, 1988–1989. Paper presented to the VII International Conference on AIDS. Florence, Italy: 1991.

511 **Hankins CA et al.** HIV disease and AIDS in women: current knowledge and a research agenda. J Acquir Immune Defic Syndr. 1992;5:957.

512 **Iman N et al.** Hierarchical pattern of mucosal candida infections in HIV-seropositive women. Am J Med. 1990;89: 142.

513 **Wolfgang F et al.** Increased frequency of cervical dysplasia/neoplasia in HIV-infected women is related to the extent of immunosuppression. Paper presented to the VI International Conference on AIDS. San Francisco, CA: 1990.

514 **Anderson J et al.** Gynecologic infection in women with HIV infection. Paper presented to the VI International Conference on AIDS. San Francisco, CA: 1990.

515 **Cordaro JA et al.** Zidovudine pharmacokinetics in HIV-positive women during different phases of the menstrual cycle. Pharmacotherapy. 1993; 13:369.

516 **Maiman M et al.** Human immunodeficiency virus infection and cervical neoplasia. Gynecol Oncol. 1990;38: 377.

517 **Schiffman MH.** Recent progress in defining the epidemiology of human papillomavirus infection and cervical neoplasia. J Natl Cancer Inst. 1992;84:394.

518 **Winklestein W.** Smoking and cervical cancer—current status: a review. Am J Epidemiol. 1990;131:945.

519 **Zur HH.** Human papillomavirus and their possible role in squamous cell carcinomas. Curr Top Microbiol Immunol. 1977;78:1.

520 **Ambros RA et al.** Current concepts in the relationship of human papillomavirus infection to the pathogenesis and classification of precancerous squamous lesions of the uterine cervix. Semin Diagn Pathol. 1990;7:158.

521 **Henry MJ et al.** Association of human immunodeficiency virus-induced immunosuppression with human papillomavirus infection and cervical intraepithelial neoplasia. Am J Obstet Gynecol. 1989;160:352.

522 **Vermund SH et al.** Risk of human papillomavirus and cervical squamous intraepithelial lesions highest among women with advanced HIV disease. Paper presented to the VI International Conferences on AIDS. San Francisco, CA: 1990.

523 **Rellihan MA et al.** Rapidly progressing cervical cancer in a patient with human immunodeficiency virus infection. Gynecol Oncol. 1990;36:435.

524 **Monfardini S et al.** Unusual malignant tumors in 49 patients with HIV infection. AIDS. 1989;3:449.

525 **Nasiell K et al.** Behavior of mild cervical dysplasia during long-term follow up. Obstet Gynecol. 1986;67:665.

526 **American College of Obstetricians and Gynecologists.** Cervical cytology: evaluation and management of abnormalities. ACOG Technical Bulletin. 1993;183.

527 **Ferenczy A, Winkler B.** Cervical intraepithelial neoplasia and condyloma. In: Kurman RJ, ed. Blaustein's Pathology of the Female Genital Tract. 3rd ed. New York: Springer Verlag; 1987: 177.

528 **Berget A et al.** Cervical intraepithelial neoplasia. Examinations, treatment and follow-up. Obstet Gynecol Surv. 1985; 40:545.

529 **Wetchler SJ.** Treatment of cervical intraepithelial neoplasia with the CO2 laser: laser versus cryotherapy. A review of effectiveness and cost. Obstet Gynecol Surv. 1984;39:469.

530 **Bornstein J et al.** Treatment of cervical intraepithelial neoplasia and invasive squamous cell carcinoma by interferon. Obstet Gynecol Surv. 1993;48: 251.

531 **Miliffi L et al.** Moderate cervical dysplasia treated by intramuscular injection of interferon-alpha. Paper presented to the Second European Winter Conference: Gynecology & Obstetrics. Madonna Di Campiglis, Italy: 1989.

532 **Costa S et al.** Intramuscular β-interferon treatment of human papillomavirus lesions in the lower female genital tract. Cervix LFGT. 1988;6:203.

533 **Byrne MA et al.** The effect of interferon on human papillomaviruses associated with cervical intraepithelial neoplasia. Br J Obstet Gynaecol. 1986; 93:1136.

534 **Ylikoski M et al.** Topical treatment with human leukocyte interferon of HPV 16 infections associated with cervical and vaginal intraepithelial neoplasias. Gynecol Oncol. 1990;36:353.

535 **Puligheddu P et al.** Activity of interferon β in condylomata with dysplastic lesion of the uterine cervix. Eur J Gynecol Oncol. 1988;9:161.

536 **Frost L et al.** No effect of intralesional injection of interferon on moderate cervical intraepithelial neoplasia. Br J Obstet Gynaecol. 1990;97:626.

537 **Bigger RJ et al.** Helper and suppressor lymphocyte changes in HIV: infected mothers and their infants. Paper presented to the IV International Conference on AIDS. Stockholm, Sweden: 1988.

538 **Minkoff HL.** AIDS in pregnancy. Curr Probl Obstet Gynecol Fertil. 1989:206.

539 **Schaefer A et al.** The effect of pregnancy on the natural course of HIV disease. Paper presented to the IV International Conference on AIDS. Stockholm, Sweden: 1988.

540 **MacCallum LR et al.** The effects of pregnancy on the natural course of HIV disease. Paper presented to the IV International Conference on AIDS. Stockholm, Sweden: 1988.

541 **Berrebi A et al.** The influence of pregnancy on the evolution of HIV infection. Paper presented to the IV International Conference on AIDS. Stockholm, Sweden: 1988.

542 **Minkoff H et al.** Pneumocystis carinii pneumonia associated with acquired immunodeficiency syndrome in pregnancy: a report of three maternal deaths. Obstet Gynecol. 1986;67:284.

543 **Semperini AE et al.** HIV infection and AIDS in newborn babies of mothers positive for HIV antibody. Br Med J. 1987;294:610.

544 **Johnstone FD et al.** Does HIV infection affect the outcome of pregnancy? Br Med J. 1988;296:467.

545 **Mok JQ et al.** Infants born to mothers seropositive for human immunodeficiency virus: preliminary findings from a multicentre European study. Lancet. 1987;1:1164.

546 **Gloeb DJ et al.** Human immunodeficiency virus infection in women. JAMA. 1988;259:756.

547 **Joviasis E et al.** Vertical transmission in a 20-week fetus. Lancet. 1986;2:288.

548 **Sprecher S et al.** Vertical transmission in a 15-week fetus. Lancet. 1986;2: 288.

549 **Rubinstein A et al.** The epidemiology of pediatric acquired immunodeficiency syndrome. Clin Immunol Immunopathol. 1986;40:115.

550 **Lapointe N et al.** Transplacental transmission of HTLV-III virus. N Engl J Med. 1985;312:1325.

551 **Ryder R et al.** Perinatal transmission of the human immunodeficiency virus Type 1 to infants of seropositive women in Zaire. N Engl J Med. 1989; 320:1637.

552 **diMaria H et al.** Transplacental transmission of human immunodeficiency virus. Lancet. 1986;2:215.

553 **Minkoff H et al.** Pregnancies resulting in infants with acquired immunodeficiency syndrome or AIDS related complex. Obstet Gynecol. 1987;69:285.

554 **Scott GB et al.** Mothers of infants with the acquired immunodeficiency syndrome: evidence for both symptomatic and asymptomatic carriers. JAMA. 1985;253:363.

555 **Lepage P et al.** Postnatal transmission of HIV mother to child. Lancet. 1987; 2:400.

556 **Thiry L et al.** Isolation of AIDS virus from cell free breast milk of three healthy virus carriers. Lancet. 1985;2: 892.

557 **Weinbreck P et al.** Postnatal transmission of HIV infection. Lancet. 1988;1: 482.

558 **Zeigler JB et al.** Postnatal transmission of AIDS associated retrovirus from mother to infant. Lancet. 1984;1: 896.

559 **Giaquinto C et al.** Natural history of pediatric HIV infection. Paper presented to the IV International Conference on AIDS. Stockholm, Sweden: 1988.

560 **Terrangana A et al.** Perinatal HIV infection: evaluation of the risk for the mother and child. Paper presented to the IV International Conference on AIDS. Stockholm, Sweden: 1988.

561 **Peckham CS et al.** Mother to child transmission of HIV infection. Lancet. 1988;2:1039.

562 **Tovo PA et al.** Epidemiology, clinical features and prognostic factors of pediatric HIV infection. Lancet. 1988;2: 1043.

563 **Ciraru-Vigneron N et al.** Prospective study for HIV infection among highrisk pregnant women. Paper presented to the IV International Conference on AIDS. Stockholm, Sweden: 1988.

564 **Ryder RW et al.** Perinatal HIV transmission in two African hospitals: one year follow-up. Paper presented to the IV International Conference on AIDS. Stockholm, Sweden: 1988.

565 **European Collaborative Study.** Risk factors for mother-to-child transmission of HIV-1. Lancet. 1992;339:1007.

566 **Blanche S et al.** Relation of the course of HIV infection in children to the severity of the disease in their mothers at delivery. N Engl J Med. 1994;330:308.

567 **Bryson Y et al.** The role of timing of HIV maternal-fetal transmission (in utero vs. intrapartum) and HIV phenotype on onset of symptoms in vertically-infected infants. Paper presented to the IX International Conference on AIDS. Berlin, Germany: 1993.

568 **MacGregor SN.** Human immunodefi-

ciency virus infection in pregnancy. Clin Perinatol. 1991;18:33.

569 **Andiman WA et al.** Prospective studies of a cohort of 50 infants born to human immunodeficiency virus (HIV) seropositive mothers. Pediatr Res. 1988;23:363A.

570 **Lyons SF et al.** Identification of HIV-infected infants by HIV-specific IgA or p24 antigen detection. Paper presented to the IX International Conference on AIDS. Berlin, Germany: 1993.

571 **Rios O et al.** Markers of HIV infection in children born to HIV-1 infected mothers. Paper presented to the IX International Conference on AIDS. Berlin, Germany: 1993.

572 **Butcher A et al.** Rapid detection of HIV-1 DNA in pediatric specimens from a microsample of blood. Paper presented to the IX International Conference on AIDS. Berlin, Germany: 1993.

573 **Sperling RS et al.** A survey of zidovudine use in pregnant women with human immunodeficiency virus infection. N Engl J Med. 1992;326:857–61.

574 **Dowe DA et al.** Human immunodeficiency virus infection in children. Clin Imaging. 1992;16:145.

575 **Quinn TC et al.** HIV infection and AIDS in children. Annu Rev Public Health. 1992;13:1.

576 **Falloon J et al.** Human immunodeficiency virus infection in children. J Pediatr. 1989;114:1.

577 **Oxtoby MJ.** Perinatally acquired human immunodeficiency virus infection. Pediatr Infect Dis J. 1990;9:609.

578 **Hutto C et al.** A hospital-based prospective study of perinatal infection with human immunodeficiency virus type 1. J Pediatr. 1991;119:327.

579 **Jones DJ et al.** The epidemiology of transfusion-associated AIDS in children in the United States, 1981–1988. Paper presented to the V International Conference on AIDS. Montreal, Canada: 1989.

580 **Ammann A.** Immunopathogenesis of pediatric acquired immunodeficiency syndrome. J Perinatol. 1988;8:154.

581 **Scott GB et al.** Survival in children with perinatally acquired human immunodeficiency virus type I infection. N Engl J Med. 1989;321:1791.

582 **Tovo PA et al.** Prognostic factors and survival in children with perinatal HIV-1 infection. Lancet. 1992;339:1249.

583 **Beyers B et al.** Survival of children with perinatal HIV-infection: evidence for two distinct populations. Paper presented to the IX International Conference on AIDS. Berlin, Germany: 1993.

584 **Lampert R et al.** Life table analysis of children with acquired immunodeficiency syndrome. Pediatr Infect Dis J. 1986;5:374.

585 **Rogers MF.** AIDS in children: a review of the clinical, epidemiologic and public health aspects. Pediatr Infect Dis J. 1985;4:230.

586 **Rubenstein A.** Pediatric AIDS. Curr Probl Pediatr. 1986;16:361.

587 **Pahwa S et al.** Spectrum of human T-cell lymphotropic virus type III infection in children: recognition of symptomatic, asymptomatic and seronegative patients. JAMA. 1986;255:2299.

588 **CDC.** Unexplained immunodeficiency and opportunistic infections in infants—New York, New Jersey, California. MMWR. 1982;31:665.

589 **Oleske J et al.** Immune deficiency syndrome in children. JAMA. 1983;249:2345.

590 **Rubenstein A et al.** Acquired immunodeficiency with reversed T4/T8 ratios in infants born to promiscuous and drug-addicted mothers. JAMA. 1983;249:2350.

591 **Scott GB et al.** Acquired immunodeficiency in infants. N Engl J Med. 1984;310:76.

592 **Bernstein LJ et al.** Bacterial infection in the acquired immunodeficiency syndrome of children. Pediatr Infect Dis. 1985;4:472.

593 **Shannon KM et al.** Acquired immune deficiency syndrome in childhood. J Pediatr. 1985;106:332.

594 **Brouwers P et al.** Central nervous system involvement: manifestations and evaluation. In: Pizzo PA et al., eds. Pediatric AIDS: The Challenge of HIV Infection in Infants, Children and Adolescents. 1st ed. Baltimore: Williams & Wilkins; 1990.

595 **Thomas PA et al.** Survival analysis of children reported with AIDS in New York City, 1982–1986. Paper presented to the III International Conference on AIDS. Washington, DC: 1987.

596 **Rubenstein A et al.** Pulmonary disease in children with acquired immune deficiency syndrome and AIDS-related complex. J Pediatr. 1986;108:498.

597 **Andiman WA et al.** Opportunistic lymphoproliferations associated with Epstein-Barr viral DNA in infants and children with AIDS. Lancet. 1985;2:1390.

598 **Chayt KJ et al.** Detection of HTLV-III RNA in lungs of patients with AIDS and pulmonary involvement. JAMA. 1986;256:2356.

599 **Connor EM et al.** Lymphoid interstitial pneumonitis. In: Pizzo PA et al., eds. Pediatric AIDS: The Challenge of HIV Infection in Infants, Children, and Adolescents. 1st ed. Baltimore: Williams & Wilkins; 1990.

600 **Oleske JM et al.** Treatment of HIV infected infants and children. Ann Pediatr (Paris). 1988;17:332.

601 **CDC.** Immunization of children infected with human T-lymphotropic virus type III/lymphadenopathy-associated virus. MMWR. 1986;35:595.

602 **CDC.** Immunization of children infected with human immunodeficiency virus: supplementary ACIP statement. MMWR. 1988;37:181.

603 **CDC.** Measles in HIV-infected children—United States. MMWR. 1988; 37:183.

604 **CDC.** Working group on PCP prophylaxis in children: guidelines for prophylaxis against pneumocystis carinii pneumonia for children infected with human immunodeficiency virus. MMWR. 1991;40:1.

605 **Blanche S et al.** Longitudinal study of 94 symptomatic infants with perinatally acquired human immunodeficiency virus infection: evidence for a bimodal expression of clinical and biological symptoms. Am J Dis Child. 1990;144:1210.

606 **Bernstein LJ et al.** Prognostic factors and life expectancy in children with acquired immunodeficiency syndrome and pneumocystis carinii pneumonia. Am J Dis Child. 1989;143:775.

607 **Krasinski K et al.** Prognosis of human immunodeficiency virus infection in children and adolescents. Pediatr Infect Dis J. 1989;8:216.

608 **Kovacs A et al.** CD4 T-lymphocyte counts and pneumocystis carinii pneumonia in pediatric HIV infection. JAMA. 1991;265:1698.

609 **Roilides E et al.** Helper T-cell responses in children infected with human immunodeficiency virus type 1. J Pediatr. 1991;118:724.

610 **Denny TN et al.** Age related changes of lymphocyte phenotypes in healthy children. Pediatr Res. 1990;27:155A.

611 **Connor E et al.** Clinical and laboratory correlates of pneumocystis carinii pneumonia in children infected with HIV. JAMA. 1991A;265:1693.

612 **Leibovitz E et al.** Pneumocystis carinii pneumonia in infants infected with the human immunodeficiency virus with more than 450 CD4 T lymphocytes per cubic millimeter. N Engl J Med. 1990; 323:531.

613 **Simonds RJ et al.** Pneumocystis carinii pneumonia among U.S. children with perinatally acquired HIV infection. JAMA. 1993;270:470.

614 **Pitt J.** Rethinking PCP prophylaxis guidelines for infants. AIDS Clin Care. 1994;6:32.

615 **Hughes WT et al.** Successful chemoprophylaxis for pneumocystis carinii pneumonitis. N Engl J Med. 1977;297:1419.

616 **Hughes WT et al.** Successful intermittent chemoprophylaxis for pneumocystis carinii pneumonitis. N Engl J Med. 1987;316:1627.

617 **Gutman LT.** The use of trimethoprim-sulfamethoxazole in children: a review of adverse reactions and indications. Pediatr Infect Dis J. 1984;3:349.

618 **Girdwood RH.** The nature of possible adverse reactions to co-trimoxazole. Scand J Infect Dis. 1976;(Suppl. 8):10.

619 **Lawson DH et al.** Adverse reactions to trimethoprim-sulfamethoxazole. Rev Infect Dis. 1982;4:429.

620 **Jick H.** Adverse reactions to trimethoprim-sulfamethoxazole. Rev Infect Dis. 1982;4:426.

621 **Connor E et al.** Antiretroviral treatment of human immunodeficiency virus infection in children. Semin Pediatr Infect Dis. 1991B;2:285.

622 **Pizzo PA et al.** Antiretroviral therapy and medical management of the human immunodeficiency virus-infected child. Pediatr Infect Dis J. 1993;12:513.

623 **Pizzo PA et al.** Effect of continuous intravenous infusion of zidovudine (AZT) in children with symptomatic HIV infection. N Engl J Med. 1988; 319:889.

624 **McKinney RE et al.** Safety and tolerance of intermittent intravenous and oral zidovudine therapy in human immunodeficiency virus-infected pediatric patients. J Pediatr. 1990;116:640.

625 **McKinney RE et al.** A multicenter trial of oral zidovudine in children with advanced human immunodeficiency virus disease. N Engl J Med. 1991;324:1018.

626 **Henry DH et al.** Recombinant human erythropoietin in the treatment of anemia associated with human immuno-

deficiency virus (HIV) infection and zidovudine therapy: overview of four clinical trials. Ann Intern Med. 1992; 117:739.

627 **Butler KM et al.** Dideoxyinosine in children with symptomatic human immunodeficiency virus infection. N Engl J Med. 1991;324:137.

628 **Blanche S et al.** Randomized study of two doses of didanosine in children infected with human immunodeficiency virus. J Pediatr. 1993;122:966.

629 **Pizzo PA et al.** Dideoxycytidine alone and in an alternation schedule with zidovudine in children with symptomatic human immunodeficiency virus infection. J Pediatr. 1990;117:799.

630 **Pizzo PA.** Treatment of human immunodeficiency virus-infected infants and young children with dideoxynucleosides. Am J Med. 1990;88(Suppl. 5B):16S.

631 **Beach RS et al.** AZT/ddI salvage therapy in pediatric HIV-infected patients. Paper presented to the IX International Conference on AIDS. Berlin, Germany: 1993.

632 **Kline MW et al.** Phase I evaluation of stavudine (d4T) in infants and children with vertically acquired HIV infection. Paper presented to the First National Conference on Human Retroviruses and Related Infections. Washington, DC: 1993.

633 **Lewis L et al.** Phase I evaluation of stavudine (d4T) in infants and children with vertically acquired HIV infection. Paper presented to the First National Conference on Human Retroviruses and Related Infections. Washington, DC: 1993.

634 **Mofenson LM et al.** Intravenous immune globulin for the prevention of bacterial infections in children with symptomatic human immunodeficiency virus infection. N Engl J Med. 1991;325:73.

635 **Mofenson LM et al.** Crossover of placebo patients to intravenous immunoglobulin confirms efficacy of immunoglobulin for prevention of serious bacterial infections. Paper presented to the First National Conference on Human Retroviruses and Related Infections. Washington, DC: 1993.

636 **Von Roenn JH et al.** Megestrol acetate in patients with AIDS-related cachexia. Ann Intern Med. 1994;121: 393–99.

637 **Oster MH et al.** Megestrol acetate in patients with AIDS and cachexia. Ann Intern Med. 1994;121:400–08.

638 **Roxane Labs, Inc.** Marinol (dronabinol) package insert. Columbus, OH: 1993.

639 **Schambelan M et al.** Recombinant human growth hormone (rhGH) increases lean body mass (LBM) and improves functional performance in patients with HIV-associated wasting. Program and abstracts of the Second National Conference on Human Retroviruses and Related Infections. January 28–February 2, 1995. Washington, DC: American Society for Microbiology.

640 **Syntex.** Cytovene (ganciclovir) package insert. Palo Alto, CA: 1994.

641 **Spector SA et al.** A randomized, double-blind study of the efficacy and safety or oral ganciclovir for the prevention of cytomegalovirus disease in

HIV-infected persons. Program and abstracts of the Second National Conference on Human Retroviruses and Related Infections. January 28–Febrary 2, 1995. Washington, DC: American Society for Microbiology.

642 **Safrin S et al.** Adjunctive folinic acid with trimethoprim-sulfamethoxazole for Pneumocystis carinii pneumonia in AIDS patients is associated with an increased risk of therapeutic failure and death. J Infect Dis. 1994;170(4):912–17.

643 **Smith Kline Beecham.** Famvir (famciclovir) package insert. Philadelphia, PA: 1994.

644 **Degreed H.** Famciclovir Herpes Zoster Clinical Study Group. Famciclovir, a new oral antiherpes drug: results of the first controlled clinical study demonstrating its efficacy and safety in the treatment of uncomplicated herpes zoster in immunocompetent patients. International Journal of Antimicrobial Agents. 1994;4:241–46.

645 **Saltzman R et al.** Safety of famciclovir in patients with herpes zoster and genital herpes. Antimicrob Agents Chemother. 1994;38:2454–457.

646 **Powderly WG et al.** A randomized trial comparing fluconazole with clotrimazole troches for the prevention of fungal infections in patients with advanced human immunodeficiency virus infection. N Engl J Med. 1995;332:700.

647 **Anon.** Questions and answers about ACTG Protocol 152. National Institute of Allergy and Infectious Diseases Bulletin. February 15, 1995.

648 **Connor EM et al.** Reduction of maternal-infant transmission of Human Immunodeficiency Virus Type 1 with zidovudine treatment. N Engl J Med. 1994;331:1173.

649 **Hammarskjold ML et al.** Human immunodeficiency virus env expression becomes Rev-independent if the env region is not defined as an intron. J Virol (KCV). 1994;68(2):951–8.

Chapter 69

Fungal Infections

John D Cleary
Stanley W Chapman
Alice Clark
Helen Lucia

Mycology 69-1
Morphology 69-1
Classification 69-2
Organism (see Table 69.1) 69-2
Clinical (see Table 69.2) 69-2
Pathogenesis of Infection 69-2
Endogenous 69-2
Exogenous 69-2
Host Defenses 69-2
Antimycotics 69-3
Approved Antifungal Agents (See Table 69.3) 69-3
Mechanisms of Action 69-3
Antifungal Spectrum 69-4
New Frontiers for Antifungal Therapy 69-4
Superficial and Cutaneous Mycoses 69-4
Tinea Pedis: Treatment 69-4
Tinea Unguium (Onychomycosis): Treatment 69-5
Vaginal Candidiasis 69-5
Treatment 69-5
Topical 69-5
Systemic 69-6
Candida hypersensitivity 69-6
Sporotrichosis 69-6
Treatment options 69-6
Heat 69-6
Potassium iodide 69-6
Itraconazole 69-6
Dosing 69-7
Systemic Mycoses 69-7
Candida Infection 69-7
Epidemiology 69-7
Characteristics 69-7
Risk factors 69-7
Diagnostic tests 69-7

Direct examination 69-7
Culture 69-9
Antigen detection 69-9
Antibody detection 69-9
Skin testing 69-9
Necessity of treatment 69-9
Treatment options 69-10
Pharmacokinetic properties (see Table 69.5) 69-11
Amphotericin 69-10
Dosing 69-10
Premedication 69-10
Infusion reactions 69-10
Infusion protocol (see Table 69.6) 69-12
Nephrotoxicity 69-11
Antifungal drug interactions (see Table 69.4) 69-8
Antimycotic prophylaxis 69-12
Costs and regimens (see Table 69.7) 69-13
Candiduria 69-13
Treatment 69-13
Table of options for therapy (see Table 69.8) 69-13
Blastomycosis 69-13
Etiology 69-13
Treatment 69-14
Antifungals in pregnancy 69-15
Histoplasmosis 69-15
Treatment (See Table 69.9) 69-15
Azole adverse effects 69-16
Azole drug interactions 69-16
Coccidioidomycosis 69-17
Serological tests 69-17
Antifungal central nervous system (CNS)
penetration 69-17
Intrathecal amphotericin 69-17
Aspergillosis: Treatment (See Table 69.10) 69-17
Cryptococcosis 69-19

Mycotic (fungal) infections, once observed only occasionally, are now the fourth most commonly encountered nosocomial infection. This increase in occurrence of fungal infections can, in part, be attributed to the growing numbers of immunocompromised hosts that have resulted from organ transplants, cancer chemotherapy, and the acquired immunodeficiency syndrome (AIDS) epidemic. Practitioners must be abreast of current concepts in medical mycology that affect the treatment and monitoring of patients with fungal infections. The mycology, diagnosis, antimycotics, and therapeutics for common mycotic infections are reviewed in this chapter. For a more in-depth presentation of the basic biology of fungi, as well as the epidemiology, pathogenesis, immunology, diagnosis, and monitoring of mycotic infections, the reader is referred to the text of Kwon-Chung and Bennett.[1] In addition, other chapters in this book address specific areas of antifungal therapy and should be reviewed by the reader. These topics include the treatment of fungal meningitis (see Chapter 56: Central Nervous

System Infections), endocarditis (see Chapter 57: Endocarditis), intra-abdominal and hepatosplenic infections (see Chapter 61: Intra-Abdominal Infections), bone and joint infections (see Chapters 65: Osteomyelitis/Septic Arthritis and 66: Traumatic Skin and Soft Tissue Infections), and infections in immunocompromised patients with and without human immunodeficiency virus (HIV) infections (see Chapters 67: Infections in Immunocompromised Hosts and 68: HIV Infection). The treatment of uncommon fungal infections (e.g., paracoccidioidomycosis, mucormycosis, and pseudallescheriasis) will not be presented.

Mycology
Morphology

The pathogenic fungi that infect humans are nonmotile eucaryotes that reproduce by sporulation and exist in two forms: filamentous molds and unicellular yeasts. These forms are not mutually exclusive and, depending upon the growth conditions, a fungus

Table 69.1	Organism Classification

Hyphae

Hyalohyphomycetes
Aspergillus species, *Pseudallescheria boydii*
Dermatophytes: *Epidermophyton floccosum*, *Trichophyton* species, *Microsporum* species

Phaeohyphomycetes
Alternaria species, *Anthopsis deltoidea*, *Bipolaris hawaiiensis*, *Cladosporium* species, *Curvularia geniculata*, *Exophiala* species, *Fonsecaea pedrosoi*, *Phialophora* species

Zygomycetes
Absidia corymbiera, *Mucor indicus*, *Rhizomucor pusillus*

Dimorphic fungi

Blastomycosis species, *Coccidioidomycosis* species, *Paracoccidioidomycosis* species, *Histoplasma* species, *Sporotrichosis* species

Yeast

Candida species, *Cryptococcus neoformans*

may exist in one or even both of these forms (see Table 69.1). The dimorphic fungi (e.g., *Histoplasma capsulatum* and *Blastomyces dermatitidis*) grow as a mold in nature (27 °C), but quickly convert to the parasitic yeast form after infecting the host (37 °C). This mycelium-to-yeast conversion is an important factor in the pathogenesis of disease caused by these organisms. Other pathogenic fungi, such as *Aspergillus* species, grow only as a mold form, while *Cryptococcus neoformans* always grows as a yeast form. *Candida* species grow with a modified form of budding whereby newly budded cells remain attached to the parent cells and form pseudohyphae. Fungi are aerobic and are easily grown on routine culture media similar to that used to grow bacteria. Most fungi grow best at 25 to 35 °C. Fungi that cause only cutaneous and subcutaneous disease grow poorly at temperatures above 37 °C. This temperature selective growth explains, at least in part, why these organisms rarely disseminate from a primary focus in the skin or subcutaneous tissues.

Classification

Fungal infections are best classified by the area of the body infected (see Table 69.2). *Superficial mycoses* involve only the outermost keratinized layers of the skin (stratum corneum) and hair. The *cutaneous mycoses* extend deeper into the epidermis and also may infect the nails. The *subcutaneous mycoses* infect the dermis and subcutaneous tissues: entry into these sites is by inoculation or implantation of dirt or vegetative matter. The *systemic mycoses* cause disease of the internal organs of the body. The respiratory tract is the most frequent primary portal of entry into the patient and infection in the lungs may be symptomatic or asymptomatic. Systemic infection with *Candida* usually results from a primary focus in the gastrointestinal (GI) tract or skin. In each case, the organism may spread hematogenously from the primary focus throughout the body and result in disseminated disease. The *opportunistic mycoses* occur primarily in the immunocompromised host and require more aggressive treatment. The list of fungi causing opportunistic infection is rapidly expanding, especially with the AIDS epidemic.[2] The *nonopportunistic* fungi (primary pathogens) usually cause disease in the immunologically normal host. Some primary pathogens, however, result in unique clinical syndromes when infection occurs in the compromised host, such as histoplasmosis in AIDS.[1]

Pathogenesis of Infection

Endogenous. Fungal infection may be acquired from both exogenous and endogenous sources. The only fungi known to be normal flora (commensals) in humans are *Pityrosporum obiculare*, which causes the noninflammatory superficial condition of tinea versicolor, and *Candida* species. Infections with these yeast organisms primarily develop from the patient's own normal flora (endogenous infection). These endogenous fungal infections of the skin or mucous membranes occur when host resistance is lowered and the organism proliferates in high numbers. Excess heat and humidity, oral contraceptives, pregnancy, diabetes, malnutrition, and immunosuppression facilitate endogenous local infection by both *Pityrosporum* and *Candida*. Systemic candidal infections occur in the immunocompromised host when the organism colonizing the patient's skin or GI tract is hematogenously disseminated throughout the body.

Exogenous occurs when the fungus is acquired from an environmental source. In the case of dermatophytes (ringworm fungi), the organism may be acquired from dirt, animals, or another infected individual. The subcutaneous mycoses result from direct inoculation of infected material, often a thorn or other vegetable matter, through the skin. Infections of the skin and subcutaneous tissues by *Aspergillus* and the agents causing mucormycosis (e.g., *Rhizopus*, *Absidia*, *Mucor*) have resulted from contaminated wound dressings and cast materials.[3] Exogenous fungi colonized or carried on the hands of health care workers can infect patients; therefore, health care workers, especially in intensive care units, should wash their hands to prevent cross infection between patients.[4] Other than candidal infections, the systemic mycoses are primarily the result of inhalation of dust contaminated by the infectious spores, with a primary focus of infection in the lungs. If local or systemic host defenses are unable to control the primary infection, the organism may be spread hematogenously to other organs. Some of the systemic mycoses have defined geographic (endemic) areas in which the fungus is more frequently encountered in the environment. For example, histoplasmosis and blastomycosis occur most often in the regions of the Mississippi and Ohio river valleys, while coccidioidomycosis is endemic in the southwestern U.S. and the Central Valley of California.

Host Defenses

Host defenses against fungal infection involve both nonimmune (also known as nonspecific or natural resistance) and immune (also known as specific or acquired resistance) mechanisms. Nonimmune resistance plays a primary role in preventing colonization and invasion of a susceptible tissue. The normal bacterial flora of the skin and mucous membranes prevent colonization (coloniza-

Table 69.2	Clinical Classification of Mycoses	
Classification	Site Infected	Example
Superficial	Outermost skin and hair	Malasseziasis (Tinea versicolor)
Cutaneous	Deep epidermis and nails	Dermatophytosis
Subcutaneous	Dermis and subcutaneous tissue	Sporotrichosis
Systemic	Disease of ≥1 internal organs	
Opportunistic		Candidiasis, cryptococcosis, aspergillosis, mucormycosis
Nonopportunistic		Histoplasmosis, blastomycosis, coccidioidomycosis

tion resistance) by more pathogenic bacteria and fungi. Patients treated with broad-spectrum antibiotics are at greater risk for colonization and infection by fungi because of the alteration in their bacterial flora. The barrier function of the intact skin and mucous membranes is also an important defense against fungal infection. Skin defects, whether the result of intravenous (IV) catheters, burns, surgery, or trauma predispose individuals to local invasion and fungemia, especially with *Candida* species. When these physical barriers are breached, the polymorphonuclear leukocyte (neutrophil) is the cell involved earliest in host defense against fungi. The antifungal activity of neutrophils involves phagocytosis and intracellular killing, but also may include extracellular killing by secreted lysosomal enzymes. Neutropenia is the most common neutrophil defect predisposing to fungal infection, but functional defects of neutrophils, such as those occurring in patients with chronic granulomatous disease of childhood and myeloperoxidase deficiency, also have been associated with an increased frequency of fungal infections, especially with *Candida* and *Aspergillus*.

Antibody and complement may have some role in resistance to certain fungal infections, but they are not the primary effectors of acquired resistance. Cellular immunity, mediated by antigen-specific T lymphocytes, cytokines, and activated macrophages, is the primary acquired (immune) host defense against fungi. Patients with defective cellular immunity, such as immunosuppressed organ transplant recipients, patients with lymphomas and AIDS, and those treated with corticosteroids or cytotoxic agents are at greatest risk for fungal infection. The immunodeficiency noted in these patients is also the primary reason for the poor therapeutic outcome despite appropriate antifungal therapy. An additional factor associated with an increased risk for fungal infection is the use of total parenteral nutrition.[1]

Antimycotics

Mechanisms of Action

Listed in Table 69.3 are the Food and Drug Administration (FDA) approved topical and systemic antimycotics for the treatment of fungal infections. Griseofulvin and potassium iodide have limited clinical utility and are not utilized to treat systemic fungal infections. Griseofulvin inhibits growth by inhibiting fungal cell mitosis due to polymerization of cell microtubules, thereby disrupting mitotic spindle formation. It has activity only against the dermatophyte fungi. The antifungal mechanism of potassium iodide is unclear. It is only effective for the treatment of lymphocutaneous sporotrichosis.

The six antifungal drugs utilized for systemic disease fall into three structural classes that act by three mutually exclusive mechanisms. *Amphotericin B*, a polyene macrolide, acts principally by binding to ergosterol in the fungal cell membrane, effectively creating pores in the cell membrane, leading to depolarization of the membrane and cell leakage.[16] Amphotericin B binds with greater affinity to ergosterol than to cholesterol.[17] This phenomenon is believed to be mediated through both hydrophilic hydrogen bonding and hydrophobic, nonspecific van der Waals forces. Investigations using[31] P nuclear magnetic resonance spectroscopy to study the interactions of polyene macrolides with sterols documented that the presence of the double bond in the side chain of ergosterol (not present in cholesterol) accounts for the greater affinity of amphotericin B for ergosterol.[16] Unfortunately, amphotericin B also binds to sterols of mammalian cells (i.e., cholesterol), a fact that is believed to account for most of the toxic effects of amphotericin B. Alteration in the lipid content of the cell membrane may play a role in the development of resistance,[18] although, this alone is apparently not sufficient to affect that development.[19]

Table 69.3	Antifungal Agents Approved For Use
Agent (Brand Name)	Route of Administration
Systemic Agents	
Amphotericin B (Fungizone)	IV
Fluconazole (Diflucan)	IV, tablet
Fluorocytosine [Flucytosine] (Ancobon)	Capsule
Itraconazole (Sporanox)	Capsule
Ketoconazole (Nizoral)	Tablet
Miconazole (Monistat)	IV, vaginal tablet, cream
Griseofulvin	Tablet
Potassium iodide	Solution
Primary Topicals, Class I: Nonprescription	
Amphotericin B	Cream, lotion, ointment
Clioquinol (Vioform)	Cream, ointment
Clotrimazole	Cream, lotion, lozenge, pessary, solution, tablet
Miconazole	Aerosol, cream, lotion, pessary, spray, suppository
Naftifine (Naftin)	Cream, gel
Nystatin	Cream, lozenge, ointment, powder, suspension, tablet
Tolnaftate	Cream, gel, powder, solution, spray
Undecylenic acid	Cream, foam, ointment, powder, soap
Topicals, Class I: Prescription Only	
Butoconazole (Femstat)	Ointment
Ciclopirox (Loprox)	Cream, lotion
Econazole (Spectazole)	Cream
Haloprogin (Halotex)	Cream, solution
Ketoconazole (Nizoral)	Cream
Naftifine (Naftin)	Cream, gel
Oxiconazole (Oxistat)	Cream, lotion
Sulconazole (Exelderm)	Cream, solution
Terbinafine (Lamisil)	Cream
Terconazole (Terazol 7)	Cream
Tioconazole (Vagistat)	Ointment
Triacetin (Fungoid)	Cream, solution, spray

However, the lethal antifungal effects of amphotericin B are due not only to cell leakage resulting from ergosterol binding, but also to oxygen-dependent killing.[17,20]

5-Flucytosine (5-FC), a fluorinated cytosine analog, is believed to act principally by inhibition of nucleic acid synthesis through active transportation into susceptible cells by the enzyme cytosine permease, where it is metabolically transformed by deamination to the toxic metabolite, 5-fluorouracil. Fluorouracil, when converted to 5-fluorouridine triphosphate, functions as an antimetabolite and is substituted for uracil in the incorporation into fungal RNA, thus disrupting protein synthesis.[21,22] 5-Fluorouracil also may be converted to fluorodeoxyuridine monophosphate, which inhibits thymidylate synthase and thus disrupts DNA synthesis.[22,23]

The *azole antifungals* all appear to act by the same principal mechanism: inhibition of sterol biosynthesis by interference with cytochrome P450-dependent lanosterol C14 demethylase, a critical enzyme in the biosynthesis of ergosterol.[24–26] The improved affinity of the triazoles (fluconazole, itraconazole) for fungal versus mammalian enzyme, as compared to the imidazoles (ketoconazole, miconazole) generally is believed to account for the reduced toxicity and improved efficacy of the triazoles.[26] The consequence of sterol biosynthesis inhibition is a faulty cell membrane with altered permeability. In general, the azoles are viewed as fungistatic in their action. The clinical relevance of *in vitro* fungicidal versus fungistatic action is an issue open to considerable debate. Nevertheless, it seems logical that fungicidal action, if it can also be achieved *in vivo*, might be preferable in immunosuppressed hosts.

Antifungal Spectrum

The evaluation of *in vitro* antifungal activity has long challenged investigators. Results are influenced substantially by a variety of factors, including selection of culture medium, pH, inoculum size, incubation period, and other factors. Attempts to use *in vitro* assay results for the evaluation of the susceptibility of clinical isolates to approved agents, for monitoring therapeutic progress, and for comparisons between existing agents and new drug candidates have, therefore, led to frustration. Based upon the known incidence of variability in assay results, a wide variety of minimum inhibitory concentrations have not surprisingly been reported for each of the clinically available agents.

In 1993, the National Committee for Clinical Laboratory Standards (NCCLS) recommended a standardized method for determination of *in vitro* antifungal susceptibilities for yeasts.[27] In addition, a new method for *in vitro* evaluation is said to be free of variation due to inoculum size, pH, temperature, and time of incubation.[28] An E-Test (AB Biodisk; Piscataway, NJ) to evaluate yeast susceptibilities to the systemic antimycotics also is being studied and appears promising. There are no approved testing methods to evaluate the susceptibilities of molds. Despite these recent advances, the determination of *in vitro* susceptibilities or resistance in clinical practice is of limited utility and not readily available.

Despite these limitations, certain generalities should be emphasized. First, amphotericin B has broad *in vitro* activity and clinical efficacy against the yeasts and filamentous molds. The azole antifungals *generally* have clinically significant activity only against the yeasts and most dimorphic fungi. A caveat to this generalization is itraconazole, which in preliminary studies has demonstrated both *in vitro* and clinical efficacy against *Aspergillus* species.

New Frontiers for Antifungal Therapy

Various efforts have been directed at both enhancing efficacy and reducing the toxicity of antifungal drugs, including biochemical modifications of the agent, improved delivery systems, and combination therapy. For example, efforts to improve the delivery system for amphotericin B have included formulating it as lipid complexes, liposomes, and colloidal dispersions.[29] Aerosolization of amphotericin B for delivery to the lungs also has been employed.[30] Of particular interest are the ongoing studies and case reports in which Intralipid 20% is combined with amphotericin B (1 to 2 mg/mL) and doses of ≥1 mg/kg/day are administered.[31] Presently, this latter practice cannot be recommended until randomized, controlled trials document efficacy and reduced toxicity of these Intralipid-amphotericin B formulations as compared to amphotericin B alone.

Even more challenging are the attempts to discover or design new prototype antifungal compounds. Substantial hurdles exist since both mammalian cells and fungal cells are eukaryotes and share many similar biochemical processes, unlike bacterial cells which are prokaryotes. Essentially, the drug discovery process depends upon the ability to detect compounds (either natural products or synthetic compounds) that selectively inhibit or destroy fungal cells. This process is accomplished by one or both of two approaches: 1) the evaluation of existing compounds (natural or synthetic) for potentially useful antifungal activity; and 2) the design and synthesis of new compounds that selectively block fungal tar-

gets. The former approach relies on a supply of compounds with structural diversity and a reliable biological assay to detect antifungal activity. The latter depends upon a knowledge of the basic biology of the pathogen that can be exploited in drug design and synthesis. Unfortunately, knowledge of the basic biology of these pathogens is limited in comparison to other more common pathogens (e.g., bacteria). This, coupled with the intrinsic similarities of fungal and mammalian cells, means that the rational design of new antifungal drugs is in its infancy. Thus, at this time, the discovery of totally new compounds (lead compounds) that differ structurally from existing compounds remains the principal means by which new antifungal drugs are identified. Prototype compounds serve two important and critical functions in the drug discovery process: as lead compounds for development of a novel class of clinically useful agents, or as molecular "probes" to identify previously unknown targets that exist in the pathogen. Natural products historically have provided a vast array of compounds with novel structural diversity and therapeutically useful biological activity. In fact, many of the drugs in clinical use today had their beginnings as natural products. In the future, the rational design and synthesis of compounds that interact with specific molecular targets in the fungal cell will develop as more information about the basic biology of the pathogens becomes available.

Superficial and Cutaneous Mycoses
Tinea Pedis: Treatment

1. C.W., a 28-year-old male construction worker, is evaluated for a chronic case of "athlete's foot." He wears boots all day at work and notes intense itching of both feet throughout the day. He has been using tolnaftate powder (Tinactin) with no real therapeutic benefit. On examination the web spaces between all the toes are white, macerated, and cracked. A few vesicles also are present over the dorsum of the foot at the base of the toes. Scrapings of the lesions examined as a potassium hydroxide preparation reveal branching, filamentous hyphae compatible with a dermatophyte infection. The diagnosis is "athlete's foot." What therapeutic options are available for C.W.?

Selection of antifungal therapy should be based upon the extent and type of infection. Superficial or cutaneous infections should initially be approached topically. Any follicular, nail, or widespread [>20% of body surface area (BSA)] infection should be treated systemically under medical supervision owing to poor penetration of topical applications. Topical antifungals have been reviewed as a class by the FDA advisory review panel on over-the-counter (OTC) antimicrobial drug products[32] and on an individual basis as newer products have been released. In order to receive a Class I recommendation, each agent (or combination) must have been tested in well-designed clinical trials and found to be microbiologically and clinically effective against dermatophytosis or candidiasis and have insignificant toxicity (irritation). Class I agents are listed in Table 69.3. Class II agents (camphor, candicidin, coal tar, menthol, phenolates, resorcinol, tannic acid, thymol, tolindate) are considered to have higher risk-benefit ratios associated with their pharmacotherapy. Class III agents (benzoic acid, borates, caprylic acid, oxyquinolines, iodines, propionic acid, salicylates, triacetin, gentian violet) lack adequate scientific data to determine efficacy. Topical therapy with any Class I agent applied twice daily to the affected area for two to six weeks should be adequate. Therapy should be titrated to response.

Since C.W. has not responded to tolnaftate powder, another antifungal cream or lotion (e.g., miconazole) should be applied to the web spaces between all his affected toes twice daily. C.W. also should be careful to use nonocclusive footwear (e.g., cotton rather than synthetic fiber socks, and leather rather than vinyl boots). Application of an absorbant or antifungal powder to his feet and footwear also would be helpful. (See Chapter 36: Dermatotherapy for a further discussion of tinea pedis.)

Tinea Unguium (Onychomycosis): Treatment

2. If C.W. also suffered from an infection of the toenail (on-ychomycosis), what additional therapy could be offered to him?

Griseofulvin (microsized or ultramicrosized) administered orally at 10 mg/kg/day (≈750 mg/day) and titrated to response should be effective against most dermatophytes causing onychomycosis (Tinea unguium). The successful treatment of tinea unguium requires three to six months of therapy for fingernails and 6 to 12 months for toenails. Owing to the large doses given for prolonged periods, C.W. should be monitored closely at each prescription refill for signs and symptoms of hypersensitivity (urticaria, angioedema, Type II hypersensitivity reactions), photosensitive dermatitis, gastrointestinal distress, and neurological complications (headache, paresthesias, altered sensorium). *Candida* species and other hyphal fungi also can cause nail and paronychial infections and do not respond to griseofulvin therapy.[33] Therefore, nail scrapings and cultures will be helpful in planning initial treatment for C.W. Once cultures are known, griseofulvin or an oral azole can be selected. All oral azole antifungals are effective against *Candida* species and dermatophytes causing onychomycosis. Due to their relative safety and once daily dosage, they are quickly becoming the drug-of-choice for many clinicians. The length of therapy is similar to that with griseofulvin.

Removal of the toenail as the sole therapy is not recommended because of the high relapse rate without concomitant systemic therapy. Likewise, intravenous antifungals are not indicated.

3. Describe the role of corticosteroids, antibacterials, or other additives to the antimycotic regimen in C.W.

Many patients with superficial, cutaneous or nail infections will suffer more morbidity associated with local inflammation and secondary bacterial infections. Inflammation is primarily caused by a Type IV hypersensitivity reaction. Topical corticosteroids in conjunction with antifungals often will relieve itching and erythema secondary to inflammation. Bacterial (*Proteus* or *Pseudomonas* species) superinfection also can occur in these inflamed or macerated areas and may require concomitant topical antibacterial therapy. Pharmaceutical manufacturers of OTC preparations often combine a drying agent or astringent (e.g., alcohol, starch, talc, camphor) to their preparations in order to increase desquamation of the stratum corneum. Hyperhidrosis also can be relieved by these pharmaceutical additions. Such combination treatments should not be routinely used since they increase the risk of toxicity and have not been proven to increase efficacy. If required for symptomatic relief, they should only be used for the initial days of treatment.

The affected web spaces between C.W.'s toes are macerated and cracked and vesicles are present at the base of his toes. A topical corticosteroid cream probably would facilitate the healing process and make him more comfortable during the first few days of antifungal therapy. The selection of topical corticosteroid formulations is presented in Chapter 36: Dermatotherapy.

Vaginal Candidiasis

Treatment

4. Topical. T.T., a 32-year-old female, presents to her gynecologist with a 2 day history of perineal pruritus and a nonmalodorous vaginal discharge. She has been taking birth control pills for 5 years and doxycycline was prescribed 4 days ago for the treatment of presumed bacterial sinusitis. On physical examination erythema and excoriations of the vulva are noted. Speculum examination of the vagina reveals a thick, white, cheesy discharge with a vaginal pH of 3.5. A wet preparation of vaginal secretions using a 10% potassium hydroxide (KOH) solution shows budding yeast and pseudohyphae compatible with *Candida* (see Figure 69.1). What therapies may be used for T.T.?

The first line of therapy involves identification and removal of risk factors for mucocutaneous candidiasis. Possible risk factors include: corticosteroid therapy, broad-spectrum antibiotic use, diabetes, and immunosuppression. Additionally, oral contraceptives, pregnancy, and tight fitting clothing have been associated with an increased risk of vulvovaginal candidiasis. Topical mycotics are recommended as the initial therapy of most patients with mucocutaneous candidiasis (e.g., vaginitis, stomatitis, intertrigo). Both miconazole and clotrimazole are equally safe and effective; and either would be appropriate for T.T. Agent selection should, therefore be based upon patient preference and cost. Intravaginal applications (cream or insert) are best administered at bedtime for at least seven days. Symptoms of vulvar pruritus and vaginal discharge usually improve in three days and resolve completely in a week.[34-36] Douching has no added therapeutic benefit and is not recommended.

The more costly prescription-only vaginal products are not more beneficial topicals, however, some are FDA-approved for single-day or three-day regimens (e.g., butoconazole, terconazole). Therapy with a single 150 mg oral dose of fluconazole received FDA

Fig 69.1 Candida on Wet Preparation

approval in 1994 after demonstrating efficacy rates of greater than 85%.[37,38] However, the expense of a physician visit and higher drug fluconazole cost currently outweighs the cost of a nonprescription topical antifungal such as miconazole or clotrimazole.

T.T.'s broad-spectrum antibiotic (doxycycline) and birth control pills probably increased her risk for the development of this episode of vaginal candidiasis. Since her diagnosis is based both upon the assessment of her gynecologist and upon the finding of budding yeasts and pseudohyphae from her vaginal secretions, a prescription vaginal cream should be prescribed. Future vaginal candidiasis infections can be treated with nonprescription antifungal preparations as described in Chapter 46: Gynecological Disorders and Question 13 of Chapter 1: Assessment of Therapy and Pharmaceutical Care.

5. Systemic. Which patients with vaginal candidiasis should be treated with systemic antifungals?

More intensive topical therapy or a switch to systemic therapy is warranted for patients with chronic or recurrent vaginal candidiasis. Systemic therapy is often the most appropriate choice due to compliance problems with topical therapy. Chronic or recurrent vaginal candidiasis is defined as more than three episodes per year. The reasons for recurrent disease are elusive and may include an antigen specific host defect against *Candida*. Mycotic resistance to antifungal agents does not appear to be a factor. Failures to treat sexual partners may contribute to reinfection and recurrent disease. Control of risks factors is also critical in these patients. Persistent colonization of the bowel with *Candida* has been speculated as a source of reinfection, but bowel decontamination with an oral polyene has shown no benefit.[36]

Acute symptomatic exacerbations have been successfully managed with either ketoconazole (200 mg/day) or fluconazole (200 mg loading dose followed by 100 mg/day) given for 7 to 14 days.[36,38,39] In a few patients recurrent disease may be so frequent and debilitating as to warrant chronic suppressive therapy over months to years to microbiologically suppress *Candida albicans*.[36,40] Ketoconazole (100 mg/day) is effective in reducing the frequency of symptomatic vaginal candidiasis when compared to both placebo and topical applications.[36,41–44] Antifungals also are effective in disease suppression in a variety of regimens, including once weekly and once monthly regimens.[42–44] Fluconazole appears to be better tolerated and have fewer drug interactions as compared to ketoconazole. Therefore, fluconazole is the preferred agent for patients needing long-term suppressive therapy.

Candida Hypersensitivity

6. What subjective or objective data in T.T.'s history would support a diagnosis of *Candida* Hypersensitivity syndrome?

Candida infection or colonization has been associated with a hypersensitivity "disease" termed candidiasis hypersensitivity syndrome, chronic candidiasis, or *Candida*-related complex.[45,46] This "disease" was sensationalized by a book entitled, "The Yeast Connection: A Medical Break Through," and is hypothesized to be secondary to *Candida* overgrowth and subsequent allergic response.[45] Patients present with chronic *Candida* vaginitis, chronic gastrointestinal dysfunction, chronic central nervous system manifestations (depression, fatigue, loss of memory and mentation, and anxiety), menstrual irregularities, and other constitutional symptoms. No scientific data exist defining and correlating these symptom complexes with *Candida* and both topical and systemic treatment of presumed disease has no impact on presenting symptoms or disease progression.[47] T.T probably does not have *Candida* hypersensitivity syndrome because she does not have chronic candidiasis, gastrointestinal dysfunction, chronic central nervous system manifestations, or other constitutional symptoms.

Furthermore, the candida hypersensitivity syndrome needs to be more clearly defined and objectively evaluated before this somewhat dubious diagnosis is established for a patient.

Sporotrichosis

Treatment Options

7. O.M., a 62-year-old male, has had a painless, slowly enlarging ulcer on his left hand for the last 4 months. He is an avid gardener but can identify no antecedent local trauma. The primary lesion began as a red papule which slowly enlarged and then ulcerated. At the same time the ulcer developed, O.M. also noted painless, red nodules which spread proximally up his arm. He denies any chills, fever, weight loss, or cough. The ulcer has slowly enlarged despite daily application of a povidone-iodine ointment and 2 weeks of cephalexin treatment. On physical examination O.M. is afebrile. A 1.5 cm ulcer is present on the dorsum of the left hand. Extending proximal from the ulcer is a palpable cord and multiple nontender, erythematous nodules distributed linearly up the forearm, elbow, arm, and axilla. A culture of this ulcer obtained 4 weeks ago is now growing *Sporothrix schenckii*. What is the recommended therapy for O.M.?

Heat Treatment. *Sporothrix schenckii* infection most frequently causes lymphocutaneous disease as evident in O.M. Rarely, extracutaneous disease may occur and can involve the lungs, bones, or joints. In the 1930s and 1940s local heat was applied to very mild plaque or lymphocutaneous disease.[48] Germination rates of this dimorphic fungus actually can be decreased by increased temperature, and heat therapy one hour/day for three months is effective in 90% of patients with plaques (very mild disease).[49] Heat treatment could be particularly useful in pregnant patients when pharmacotherapy is contraindicated.

Potassium Iodide. The cornerstone of pharmacotherapy for lymphocutaneous disease has been potassium iodide saturated solution (SSKI 1 g/mL) 1.0 mL administered three times a day in a beverage. This dose can be increased gradually by about 0.33 mL/day to a total daily dose of 8 to 12 gm or until symptoms of toxicity limit further dose escalation. Therapy usually is continued until the lesions have been resolved or for at least four to six weeks.[50] SSKI is associated with a high incidence of adverse effects (e.g., cutaneous pustule formation, GI intolerance, excessive lacrimation and salivation, swelling of salivary glands, thyrotoxicosis) and is not effective for the treatment of extracutaneous disease.

Itraconazole. Itraconazole is more active *in vitro* against *S. schenckii* than other imidazoles or SSKI and has dramatically improved the therapy of sporotrichosis. Cure rates for sporotrichosis cutaneous and lymphocutaneous disease are greater than 90% with itraconazole 100 to 200 mg/day for three to six months. For extracutaneous disease, higher doses of itraconazole (200 mg BID) for one to two years achieve response rates of 81%, but relapse occurs frequently (27%) after stopping therapy.[51–53] The toxicity and safety profile for itraconazole also appears very favorable in these patients. Patients with extracutaneous disease who are unable to tolerate the higher itraconazole doses or whose disease continues to progress need to be treated with amphotericin B. An amphotericin B total dose of 2.0 to 2.5 gm is most frequently recommended. Neither ketoconazole or fluconazole are effective in the treatment of sporotrichosis.[50]

Therefore, in O.M. with lymphocutaneous disease, itraconazole 100 mg/day for a minimum of three months is the treatment of choice. If significant improvement is not observed in the first six weeks, the itraconazole dose should be increased to 200 mg/day and continued for six months. Most patients will respond to this dose, but an occasional patient may need doses of 300 or 400 mg/day. Treatment should be continued until both the ulcer and lymphangitis have resolved.

8. *Itraconazole Dosing*. What instructions should O.M. be receiving for taking his itraconazole dose?

The peak serum concentrations of itraconazole are ninefold higher when the drug is taken with food (i.e., 0.18 μg/mL with food and 0.02 μg/mL in fasting subjects).[54] The influence of food on absorption appears to be somewhat dependent upon the nature of the food. High-carbohydrate meals decrease the absorption of itraconazole, and high-lipid content meals appear to increase itraconazole absorption.[55,56] Patients who have difficulty eating (e.g., AIDS patients, cancer patients on antineoplastic therapy) may not absorb itraconazole well enough to achieve therapeutic plasma concentrations following a typical oral dose.[57] Although itraconazole manifests nonlinear serum pharmacokinetics (i.e., administering the total dose in 2 divided doses is associated with higher peak serum concentrations than a single larger dose), no clinical benefit of splitting the dose has been demonstrated. Therefore, T.T. should be instructed to take his itraconazole dose with his highest fat content meal of the day.

9. How would instructions for taking the itraconazole dose be modified if T.T. was achlorhydric due to medications or AIDS gastropathy?

Itraconazole, like ketoconazole, requires an acidic environment for dissolution and absorption. Thus, patients who are achlorhydric, either due to medications, surgery, or underlying disease (e.g., AIDS gastropathy) may not absorb itraconazole adequately.[57] Use of ketoconazole in achlorhydric patients historically required concomitant administration of 4 mL, 0.2N hydrochloric acid aqueous solution.[39] Etching of tooth enamel by the acid concerned many clinicians and other alternatives have been explored. The administration of ketoconazole and itraconazole with a low pH liquid (e.g., 8 to 16 fluid ounce of a Coca-Cola or orange juice) improves absorption to 65.2% of normal[58,59] in patients who are achlorhydric or on histamine₂-blockers (see Table 69.4).

Serum ketoconazole or itraconazole concentrations less than 0.25 μg/mL have been associated with treatment failures. Therapeutic drug monitoring is, therefore, justified in patients failing therapy.[60] Serum antimycotic concentrations may be more easily monitored in the future as assays become available and correlations between concentration and efficacy are more clearly established.

Systemic Mycoses
Candida Infection

10. L.K., a 21-year-old, 5′8″, 170 pound male with acute myeloblastic leukemia in remission, was admitted to the hospital 16 days ago for intensification chemotherapy. Previous induction therapy was complicated by prolonged neutropenia and *Escherichia coli* bacteremia. He completed consolidation therapy 3 months ago without incident. Daunorubicin, cytarabine, and thioguanine were given during the 1st week. Five days after completion of chemotherapy, his absolute neutrophil count (ANC) was 210 cells/mm³, and he had a fever of 39.1 °C, chills, and a blood pressure (BP) of 100/70 mm Hg. Vancomycin and ceftazidime were promptly begun after obtaining cultures. Despite 4 days of antibiotics he is still having daily fever. His physical examination reveals a Hickman catheter in the right subclavian that is functioning normally and there are no inflammatory changes evident at the exit site. A single erythematous nodule about 0.5 cm in diameter is noted near the left wrist. The funduscopic examination of both eyes is normal. The ANC is currently 95 cells/mm³. A chest radiograph is normal. What subjective and objective data in this case are sufficiently suspicious of a possible *Candida* infection to warrant further diagnostic evaluations in L.K.?

Epidemiology

Although L.K. might be infected with bacterial pathogens that are not susceptible to vancomycin and ceftazidime, the possibility of a candidal infection in L.K. should be considered. In epidemiologic studies, *Candida* species are the most common nosocomial fungal pathogens. *Candida* species were responsible for 72.2% of mycoses in hospitalized cases and *Candida albicans* accounted for 55% of these cases in the Centers for Disease Control, National Nosocomial Infections Surveillance System. These statistics may well be an underestimate of the true occurrence because systemic candidiasis is difficult to diagnose. For example, autopsy-based studies indicate that 30% to 50% of patients with systemic candidal infection are diagnosed only at postmortem in neutropenic patients with hematologic malignancies.[64] Therefore, the morbidity for systemic candidiasis may even be higher due to the limited number of autopsies actually performed.

Characteristics

The diagnosis of systemic candidal infection is difficult because the characteristics of systemic candidal infection are subtle. Salient clinical features include constitutional symptoms (e.g., fever, chills, hypotension, prostration) and evidence of end-organ dissemination such as nodular skin lesions that are usually erythematous, endophthalmitis, liver abscess, and spleen abscess. In addition, only about 50% of patients, or less, will have a positive candida blood culture.

Risk Factors

Risk factors for candidemia in patients include central venous catheters, broad-spectrum antibiotic use, extensive surgical procedures, *Candida* colonization, hyperalimentation, neutropenia or neutrophil dysfunction, and immunosuppression (e.g., premature infants, burn patients, AIDS patients).[61–63]

In this case, L.K. has chills, a temperature of 39.1 °C, and is hypotensive. He is probably immunosuppressed due to his chemotherapy and his ANC of 95 cells/mm³ substantially increases his risk of infection. His Hickman catheter could serve as a possible portal of entry for an infectious agent and his broad-spectrum antibiotic therapy with vancomycin and ceftazidime would be expected to be adequate for most of the likely bacterial pathogens. Since L.K. still has manifestations of an infection despite four days of antibiotics, additional diagnostic studies seem warranted.

Diagnostic Tests

11. What diagnostic tests could be ordered for L.K. to evaluate a possible fungal infection?

The diagnosis of fungal infection may be made with varying levels of certainty. Sometimes the diagnosis is absolutely certain, for example, the isolation and identification of a pathogenic fungus from a clinical specimen provides convincing evidence for infection. This is referred to as a definitive or microbiologically confirmed diagnosis. At other times, the physician can only determine that there is a high probability of infection. This is designated as a presumptive diagnosis. To illustrate, a patient with a chest radiograph showing nodular lesions, and a high complement fixation antibody against *Histoplasma capsulatum* would have a presumptive diagnosis of histoplasmosis. This may be as certain a diagnosis as is possible without performing a more invasive procedure to obtain lung tissue. In this event, a trial of drug therapy may be undertaken on the presumptive diagnosis alone. A diverse spectrum of tests are available for clinicians to diagnose and monitor therapeutic responses.

Direct examination of the specimen often is useful in diagnosing fungal infection. Traditionally, the specimen is treated with 10%

Table 69.4 Significant Drug Interactions[a]

Interacting Agent	Antifungal	Class[b]	Onset[c]	Manifestation
Gastrointestinals				
Antacids[38,182]	KTZ, FCZ, ITZ	2	R	Poor dissolution of dosage form, therefore ↓ azole availability. Specifically, KTZ and ITZ should be administered 2 hr postantacid dose. Be sure to note drugs like didanosine also contain buffers like antacids
Histamine$_2$-blockers[d,182]	KTZ, FCZ, ITZ	2	R	Antifungal should not be administered with H$_2$-blocker due to ↓ in antifungal absorption
Sucralfate[182]	KTZ	2	R	A 20% ↓ in KTZ absorption
Omeprazole	KTZ	2	R	Theoretical, no data currently. Agents should not be administered together
Anticholinergics[182]	KTZ	2	R	Antifungal should not be administered with H$_2$-blocker due to ↓ in antifungal absorption
Anticoagulants				
Warfarin[182,183]	MIC, KTZ, FCZ, ITZ, griseofulvin	1	D	Poorly documented mechanism. Antifungals hypothesized to ↓ warfarin protein binding and hydroxylation by liver, ↑ the risk of bleeding
Anticonvulsants[182,184]				
Carbamazepine, phenytoin, mephenytoin	MIC, KTZ, FCZ, ITZ	2	D	A significant ↑ in phenytoin serum concentrations appears possible with concomitant FCZ therapy. ITZ serum concentrations have been reduced and therapeutic failures have occurred. Data extrapolated for KTZ and MIC
Antituberculars				
Isoniazid[182]	KTZ	2	D	Combination can lead to a significant ↓ in serum antifungal concentrations potentially leading to treatment failure
Rifampin[d,182,185]	KTZ, FCZ, ITZ	2	D	Combination can lead to a significant ↓ in serum antifungal concentrations potentially leading to treatment failure
Histamine$_1$-Blockers				
Terfenadine[d,38,134,135]	KTZ, ITZ	1	D	↓ clearance of terfenadine and cardiovascular adverse effects with KTZ. Data on ITZ and FCZ extrapolated from KTZ. However, these agents are currently contraindicated with terfenadine or astemizole
Chemotherapeutic Agents[186]				
Doxorubicin, carmustine, cyclophosphamide, fluorouracil	AmphoB	2	D	Enhanced pharmacologic effect of chemotherapeutic agent, secondary to ↑ cellular uptake
Miscellaneous Products				
Corticosteroids[d,182]	KTZ	2	D	A 2-fold ↑ in serum methylprednisolone was observed with concomitant KTZ. A similar reaction with prednisone has been observed
ACE inhibitors[182]	KI	2	D	Hyperkalemia
Cyclosporine[d,182,186]	KTZ, ITZ, FCZ	2	D	A significant ↑ in serum cyclosporine concentrations can result in ↑ toxicity[182,186]
	AmphoB	1	D	Enhanced nephrotoxicity
Didanosine[182]	KTZ, ITZ	2	R	Acid neutralizing agents in didanosine will prevent ITZ absorption. KTZ extrapolated
Digoxin[182]	AmphoB	2	D	AmphoB-induced hypokalemia can lead to ↑ digoxin toxicity
Lithium[182]	KI	2	D	Hypothyroidism
NSAIDs	AmphoB	2	R	Combination has additive/synergistic nephrotoxicity
Oral contraceptives[38,182]	FCZ, griseofulvin			↓ oral contraceptive efficacy
Pentamidine[187]	AmphoB	2	D	Combination has additive/synergistic nephrotoxicity
Potassium sparing diuretics[182]	KI	2	D	Hyperkalemia
Quinidine[188]	KTZ	2	D	↑ quinidine serum concentrations have been observed
Sulfonylureas[182,189]	MIC, KTZ, FCZ, ITZ	2	D	Antifungal therapy significantly ↑ sulfonylurea concentrations
Theobromines[38,182]	FCZ, KTZ	2	R	Antifungal therapy can inhibit theophylline absorption
Sedative Hypnotics[182]				
Benzodiazepines, ethanol, barbiturates	ITZ, KTZ, griseofulvin	3	D	A 20% ↓ in chlordiazepoxide clearance has been demonstrated with KTZ. An ↑ in griseofulvin clearance also has been observed with concomitant barbiturate or ethanol consumption
Transfusions				
Leukocyte[190,191]	AmphoB	1	R	Severe pulmonary leukostasis is observed with potential for respiratory failure

[a] ACE = Angiotensin-converting enzyme; AmphoB = Amphotericin B; FCZ = Fluconazole; ITZ = Itraconazole; KI = Potassium iodide; KTZ = Ketoconazole; MIC = Miconazole; NSAIDs = Nonsteroidal anti-inflammatory drugs.
[b] Classification: 1 = Major; 2 = Moderate; 3 = Minor.
[c] R = Rapid; D = Delayed.
[d] Clinically significant interaction which the authors recommend the reader should focus upon.

potassium hydroxide (KOH) to digest the cells and debris, resulting in clear visualization of the hyphae or yeast. Treatment of cerebrospinal fluid (CSF) specimens with KOH is not necessary because this fluid is naturally clear. India ink can be added to CSF to increase contrast and outline the organisms. Calcofluor white, a fluorescent fabric brightener that binds to fungi and fluoresces brilliantly when viewed under the ultraviolet microscope, also can be used to assist in recognition of fungal elements.

Histologic examination of biopsy specimens is an important tool for diagnosing and monitoring the presence of fungal infection, but, identification of the precise species of fungus involved may be difficult. This is because only the tissue phase can be observed, and the fungal organisms in the specimen may be few. Recognition of the presence of fungus on hematoxylin- or eosin-stained sections may be difficult, and a number of special stains have been developed to assist in this.[5] Periodic acid-schiff staining capitalizes on the presence of linked sugar groups in the fungal cell wall. Material with these sugar groups is stained intensely magenta, thus increasing the contrast and making visualization of the fungal form easier. Likewise, several silver precipitation stains, such as Gomori methenamine silver (sometimes also called Grocott's Method), have been developed. These rely on the presence of a charge on the surface of the fungus to reduce oxidized silver to metallic silver. This process coats the fungus with a black layer, again outlining the form.[6] The pathologist then examines the slide, and determines whether the fungus is growing as a yeast or a mold. Sometimes this is all that can be determined. The size of the organism, manner of budding, and the presence or absence of septae can all help narrow the possibilities. The Mucicarmine stain imparts a deep red color to complex polysaccharides, such as mucin. It also will stain the thick capsule of *Cryptococcus neoformans*. Because no other yeast has a positive mucicarmine stain, the definitive diagnosis of cryptococcosis can be made.[7]

Culture. The most definitive method for diagnosing or monitoring a fungal infection is by culture. Sputum, bronchial lavage specimens, transbronchial biopsies, fine needle aspirates, biopsy tissue specimens, CSF, bone marrow, urine, or blood specimens should be inoculated on several different types of fungal media, some of which contain antibiotics to inhibit bacterial overgrowth. Swab specimens have a very low yield, especially for hyphal fungi and should be avoided in follow-up cultures. Yeast may grow rapidly and be isolated within 24 to 48 hours, but many fungi grow slowly and four to six weeks incubation may be necessary for isolation and identification of the organism. When the fungus has grown, it may be identified by a variety of methods. Yeast usually are recognized by their patterns of metabolic activity on a variety of substrates while mycelial organisms may produce characteristic spores and fruiting bodies that are used for identification. Occasionally, a mycelial organism will be slow in producing recognizable spores, and immunologic testing for a characteristic isoantigen may be used for identification.

Antigen Detection. Fungi synthesize polysaccharides that cannot be broken down by human enzymatic systems. These polysaccharides may accumulate within the body and be excreted in the urine. These fungal antigens can be detected by using monoclonal antibodies that specifically recognize a particular species of fungus, thereby providing a diagnosis. The most commonly used antigen detection test is a latex agglutination test for cryptococcal antigen. This assay can be performed on serum or cerebrospinal fluid. Antigenemia is present in 80% to 100% of patients with culture-proven cryptococcal meningitis. This test also can be used to monitor patient response to therapy by determining the end-point dilution for the positive reaction and following this end-point over time as the patient is treated. If treatment is successful, the titer will decline.[8,9]

Tests for other fungal antigens are not as well established. Latex particle agglutination tests to detect candidal antigens are available, but their utility has not been clearly demonstrated. Several studies have reported only 25% to 49% sensitivities of the commercially available tests for candidal antigens, with specificities of 43% to 98%.[10–13] Assays for detecting *Histoplasma capsulatum* antigen in serum and urine have been reported.[14] Antigen can be detected in the blood of 50% and the urine of 80% to 90% of patients with systemic histoplasmosis. This test is available through a single reference laboratory; the reagents for this test are not yet marketed commercially.

Antibody Detection. Detection of antibody can be useful for some fungal diseases but not for others. Serologic diagnosis of systemic candidiasis is complicated because most people have anti-*Candida* antibodies. A rising titer is not specific for infection, and may indicate colonization only. Furthermore, dissemination of *Candida* is most likely in people who are immunocompromised and, therefore, may not respond by producing antibody.[10] On the other hand, seropositivity can be demonstrated in greater than 90% of patients with symptomatic histoplasmosis.[15] The most important serologic tests use the complement fixation, immunodiffusion, and enzyme immunoassay (EIA) techniques. Appropriate evolution of serologic results requires an understanding of the sensitivity, specificity, and predictive value of each methodology. In general, serologic tests only allow a presumptive diagnosis of mycotic infections.

Skin Testing. Antigens to be used for skin tests for delayed hypersensitivity have been developed for the dimorphic fungi. However, these are most useful as epidemiologic tools to define the geographic foci of infection. A large percentage of people living in the endemic areas for these organisms will have had asymptomatic, self-limited infection with these agents, making the skin tests less useful in diagnosing clinical illness. Furthermore, patients with severe disease with any of the dimorphic fungi may develop a state of immunologic anergy in which all skin tests are negative. In general, skin testing can only help narrow the diagnostic probabilities and cannot be used to monitor therapy or diagnose infection.

While any of the above tests could be ordered for L.K., a direct examination of his blood and urine specimens is a reasonable first step and could show possible budding yeasts or hyphae because *Candida* is a likely pathogen. A blood and urine specimen from L.K. also should be cultured on different fungal media. Since a candidal infection is suspected, the culture could isolate *Candida* within 24 to 48 hours. The other fungal tests described above need not be ordered immediately and should await the results from direct examination and culture.

Necessity of Treatment

12. The urinalysis (UA) from L.K. showed many budding yeasts and the clinical laboratory reports that a single blood culture obtained from 2 days ago is growing *Candida* species. Why is therapy necessary in L.K. with only a single positive blood culture?

In the past, most experts withheld antifungal therapy unless a patient had sustained candidemia or had evidence of end organ-disease. However, more recent studies of candidemia noted a 85.6% mortality in the untreated patients compared to a 41.8% mortality when patients were treated early.[61,62] Isolation of *Candida* from the blood stream of patients is now viewed very seriously and therapy should be initiated immediately. Removal of risk factors may improve the clinical outcome of candidemia and removal of central venous catheters is believed to improve morbidity.[61] However, removal of centrally-inserted catheters may make pharmacotherapy difficult, and L.K.'s other risk factors (e.g., neutropenia and broad-spectrum antibiotics) are perhaps of even more importance.

Treatment Options

13. What therapeutic options are available for the treatment of candidemia? What option would be best for L.K.?

Therapeutic options are individualized and based upon the competence of a patient's host defenses. In immunocompetent patients, amphotericin B and fluconazole decrease morbidity and mortality associated with this disease.[65] In the only well-controlled comparative trial, 206 non-neutropenic patients were randomized to amphotericin B 0.5 to 0.6 mg/kg/day or fluconazole 400 mg/day for 14 days. Mortality was less than 9% in both groups with no significant difference in successful outcomes (amphotericin B 80%, fluconazole 72%); however, less toxicity was noted in the fluconazole group.[66] Therefore, fluconazole 400 mg/day is equally effective as amphotericin B 0.5 mg/kg/day for non-neutropenic patients with candidemia. Higher doses of fluconazole (800 to 1000 mg/day) are being evaluated as is a regimen consisting of initial amphotericin B therapy with step-down therapy to fluconazole.[67] In febrile neutropenic patients, amphotericin B remains the first line of therapy. The most effective dose of amphotericin B for treatment of candidemia still needs to be established. In one uncontrolled trial, a 68.7% mortality occurred in patients treated with less than 500 mg amphotericin B as compared to a 10% mortality in patients treated with more than 500 mg.[61]

Since L.K. is neutropenic, he should be treated with amphotericin B. The total dose should be based upon clinical response and resolution of neutropenia (see Question 15). The efficacy of this therapy should be monitored by assessing the patient-specific signs and symptoms of candidemia previously identified. Although delayed type hypersensitivity skin testing with *Candida* antigens is available, it has no role in the diagnosis or monitoring of disease.

14. This fungal species has now been identified as *Candida kruseii*. How does this affect the therapeutic options for T.K.?

Antimycotic resistance, especially to the azoles, is rapidly becoming an important clinical issue in pharmacotherapy. Isolation of *C. kruseii* pre-empts the use of fluconazole in L.K. since *C. kruseii* is intrinsically resistant to the azoles and treatment failures would be expected. This scenario has been replayed for each new anti-infective: new release, increased use, development of acquired resistance with therapeutic failures, re-evaluation, and finally identification of optimal indication(s). The use of fluconazole for prophylaxis of *Candida* infections in bone marrow transplant recipients and other high risk immunocompromised patients has now led to an increased incidence of acquired resistance.[69] *C. albicans*, *C. tropicalis*, and *Torulopsis (Candida) glabrata* have acquired fluconazole drug resistance probably associated with altered fungal cell membrane permeability and/or changes in the cytochrome P450 enzyme.[70] The true rate of acquired resistance to azoles is unknown and vigilant reassessments of the optimal indications for the use of azoles for treatment and prophylaxis are ongoing. Fluconazole resistance up to 9% has now been observed in cancer centers that utilize fluconazole as prophylaxis in patients experiencing prolonged neutropenia.[70]

Amphotericin

15. Dosing. How should amphotericin B be dosed and administered to L.K.?

The amphotericin B dose and duration of therapy should be individualized based upon the severity of infection and immunocompetence of the patient. Candidemic (or other mycotic infections discussed in this chapter) patients who are clinically stable and

have no evidence of deep seated infection should have therapy initiated with amphotericin B 0.3 mg/kg/day for at least seven days then switched to 0.6 mg/kg every other day. Patients who are unstable or have deep-seated (organ involvement) infections, should be treated with 0.5 to 0.6 mg/kg/day for at least seven days then switched to 1.2 mg/kg every other day. In general, the every other day regimen should not exceed 50 mg/dose. If the patient develops concomitant septic shock they should receive a minimum daily amphotericin B dose of 1.0 mg/kg. In some centers this daily dose is administered in a twice daily divided dose schedule and/or flucytosine is added to the initial few days of treatment. Once the patient is stable, therapy should be changed to one of the applicable regimens discussed above.

Amphotericin B should be dosed on lean body mass. Tissues that contain large numbers of macrophages sequester significant amounts of amphotericin B (liver 17.5% to 40.3%, spleen 0.7% to 15.6%, kidney 0.6% to 4.1%, lung 0.4% to 13%), and amphotericin B does not distribute well into adipose tissue (<1.0%).[71,72] Since L.K. is 5'8" tall and not obese, his lean body weight should be about 70 kg (LBW = 50 kg + 2.3 × height in inches >5 ft). Therefore, amphotericin B 35 mg/day (0.5 mg/kg) should be initiated because L.K. is not clinically stable, is significantly neutropenic, and is likely to need the higher dose regimen. One-half the full dose should be given on the first two days of therapy and the full dose given on subsequent days. In more seriously ill patients, the full first day's dose of amphotericin B could be initiated immediately. Although the optimal dosing regimen for the initiation of amphotericin B is not well established most clinicians gradually titrate the dose upward over two or three days to minimize infusion-related reactions.

Peak amphotericin B serum concentrations achieved following parenteral administration are a function of dose, frequency of dosing, and rate of infusion. When the amphotericin B total dose is less than 50 mg, the serum concentration is directly proportional to the dose; doses greater than 50 mg show a plateau in serum concentrations.[73] After administration, amphotericin B undergoes a biphasic elimination: peak serum concentrations drop rapidly [initial half-life ($t\frac{1}{2}$: 24 to 48 hours)] and low concentrations (0.5 to 1.0 µg/mL) are detectable for up to two weeks (terminal $t\frac{1}{2}$: ≈15 days)[73] (see Table 69.5). The long terminal-elimination half-life has been used as a justification for the common practice of every other day amphotericin B dosing, whereby twice the daily dose is given every other day. This dose usually does not exceed 50 mg/day. Every-other-day regimens have not been scientifically evaluated but are rationalized based upon the potential for reduced nephrotoxicity. Administration of 0.5 mg/kg/day or 1.0 mg/kg/every other day results in trough amphotericin B concentrations with sufficient postdose antifungal effects that inhibit the common pathogenic fungi.[74] Once L.K.'s clinical status has improved, the potential for renal toxicity could outweigh the concerns of potential reduced efficacy, and implementation of amphotericin B every-other-day therapy needs to be reconsidered.

Premedication for prevention of amphotericin B infusion-related reactions and a test dose of amphotericin B are not needed for L.K. Most practices of premedicating and administering test doses are performed out of ritual rather than scientific study and acute allergic reactions are extremely rare.[75] Until clinical trials clarify the risk/benefit ratio of premedications, concomitant therapy should be restricted to acetaminophen for fever or headache and heparin for thrombophlebitis prevention when possible.

16. Infusion Reactions. L.K. has no complaints except for fevers and shaking chills during his 6–8 hour amphotericin B administration for the last 3 days. He has been receiving acetaminophen 650 mg administered 30 minutes before amphoter-

Table 69.5			Pharmacokinetic Properties of Systemically Active Antifungals[177–181]			
	Imidazoles		Triazoles			
Characteristic[a]	Miconazole[b]	Ketoconazole[b]	Itraconazole[b]	Fluconazole[b]	Amphotericin	Flucytosine
Absorption						
Relative bioavailability	<10	75[c]	99.8 (40)[c]	(85–92)[c]	<10	75–90[c]
C_{max} (µg/mL)	1.90	3.29	0.63	1.4	1.0–2.0	70–80
T_{max} (hr)	1.0	2.6	4.0	1.0–4.0	NA	<2
AUC[c] (µg/hr/mL)	ND	12.9 (13.6)	1.9 (0.7)	42	ND	ND
Distribution						
Protein binding (%)	91–93	99	99.8	11	90–95	2–4
CSF/serum concentration (%)	<10	<10	<10	>60	<10	>60
Excretion						
Beta t½ (hr)	2.1	8.1[d]	17[d]	23–45	1–15 days	2.5–6.0
Active drug in urine (%)	1	2	<10	60–80	40	80

[a] AUC = Area under the concentration-time curve; C_{max} = Maximum concentration; CSF = Cerebrospinal fluid; ND = No data; T_{max} = Time of maximum concentration; t½ = Half-life.

[b] Above parameters are estimated from the administration of currently recommended doses. Miconazole 7.4–14.2 mg/kg/day (500–1000 mg) parenterally, ketoconazole 2.8 mg/kg/day orally (200 mg), itraconazole 1.4–2.8 mg/kg/day orally (100–200 mg), fluconazole 0.7–1.4 mg/kg/day orally, amphotericin 0.3–0.6 mg/kg/day parenterally, and flucytosine 150 mg/kg/day parenterally.

[c] With meals (fasting), absorption altered by gastric acidity.

[d] Dose and/or infusion dependent.

icin B infusion, but he has refused today's amphotericin B dose. What measures can be taken to minimize these infusion-related reactions?

Adverse reactions are common with amphotericin B administration and are best classified as acute infusion-related, dose-related, or idiosyncratic reactions. Infusion-related reactions include an acute symptom complex of fever, chills, nausea, vomiting, headache, hypotension, and thrombophlebitis. Dose-related reactions also may be acute (e.g., cardiac arrhythmias) or chronic (e.g., renal dysfunction with secondary electrolyte imbalances and anemia).

Many infusion-related reactions appear to be mediated by amphotericin B-induced cytokine (interleukin-1, tumor necrosis factor, prostaglandin E_2) expression by mononuclear cells.[76,77] Hydrocortisone is extremely effective in suppressing cytokine expression[76] and also blunting the fever and chills associated with amphotericin B administration.[78] Hydrocortisone, however, does not reduce the frequency of dose-related toxicity such as renal insufficiency, and corticosteroid-induced immunosuppression could decrease amphotericin B fungicidal activity.[79] Nonsteroidal anti-inflammatory drugs (NSAIDs) also appear effective in preventing fever, most likely by the suppression of prostaglandin E_2 expression.[80] However, NSAIDs cannot be recommended for routine use because of the potential for additive nephrotoxicity when used concomitantly with amphotericin B.

The mild to moderate elevations in temperature and the other infusion-related symptoms usually subside when the infusion is completed and tolerance to these effects develops over three to five days. L.K. initially should be counseled that these reactions will abate over the next couple of days without intervention. If assessment of the reactions suggests the need for more aggressive premedication, a short course of hydrocortisone should be initiated as outlined in Table 69.6. A dose of meperidine 25 to 50 mg by rapid IV infusion reduces amphotericin B-induced rigors, and can be repeated every 15 minutes as required while monitoring for signs and symptoms of opiate toxicity. Administration of an average meperidine dose of 45 mg has been found to resolve chills three times faster than placebo.[81] The mechanism of this pharmacologic effect is currently under investigation.

Faster amphotericin B infusion rates (<4 to 6 hours) are associated with the earlier onset of infusion-related reactions, but not with more severe reactions.[82–85] Many patients prefer rapid infusions (1 to 2 hours) since the infusion-related reactions abate quickly upon completion of the amphotericin B infusion. Rapid infusions, however, are not safe in all patients. Amphotericin B-induced cardiac arrhythmias[86,87] appear to be dose and infusion rate related.[82] Too rapid an infusion can increase serum concentrations of amphotericin B and precipitate severe cardiac adverse events. Arrhythmias have been reported most frequently in patients who are anuric or have previous cardiac disease.[88–90] Electrocardiographic evaluations of one hour infusions indicate that this rate of amphotericin infusion is safe at currently recommended doses in patients without renal or heart disease.[91]

17. Nephrotoxicity. On day 4 of therapy with amphotericin B L.K.'s serum creatinine (SrCr) and blood urea nitrogen (BUN) are 2.3 mg/dL and 42 mg/dL, respectively. How could amphotericin B exacerbate L.K.'s renal dysfunction and how could it be prevented from worsening? [SI units; SrCr 203.32 µmol/L; BUN 14.99 mmol/L urea]

Amphotericin B directly damages renal tubules and, due to electrolyte wasting, disrupts the tubuloglomerular feedback mechanism. When amphotericin B therapy had to be prematurely discontinued or when the amphotericin B dose had to be adjusted because of toxicity, in 80% of these cases, the amphotericin B therapy was modified because of renal dysfunction. The clinical manifestations of amphotericin B-induced renal damage include azotemia, renal tubular acidosis, hypokalemia, and hypomagnesemia.[26,75] Generally, amphotericin B-related renal toxicity is reversible within two weeks of cessation of therapy. Administration of normal saline (250 mL) immediately before amphotericin B administration can decrease amphotericin B-induced nephrotoxicity in man[92–94] and should be initiated before L.K.'s next dose. However, it is critical to emphasize, amphotericin B should not be admixed with normal saline because sodium causes amphotericin B to precipitate into an inactive particulate in intravenous admixture formulations.[95] The amphotericin daily dose and total treatment dose should be kept low, other nephrotoxins should be avoided (especially diuretics; see Table 69.4), and already compromised renal function should be monitored closely.[96] Hypokalemia and hypomagnesemia also need to be monitored closely and replacement therapy should be initiated promptly upon detection of a de-

Table 69.6	Amphotericin B Infusion Protocol

A. Dilute amphotericin in D$_5$W; the final concentration should not exceed 0.1 mg/mL. Initial dosing (0.25 mg/kg based upon lean body mass) should not exceed 30 mg. Infuse the dose over 0.75–4 hr immediately after a meal. Record temperature, pulse rate, and blood pressure every 30 min for 4 hr. If patient develops significant chills, fever, respiratory distress, or hypotension, administer adjunctive medication before the next infusion. If initial dose is tolerated, advance to maximum dose by the 3rd–5th day. Consult an **infectious diseases clinician** for any questions concerning maximum daily dose, total dose, and duration of therapy

B. Adjunctive Medications

1) **Heparin 1000 units** may diminish thrombophlebitis for peripheral lines. Observe the contraindications to the use of heparin (e.g., thrombocytopenia, ↑ risk of hemorrhage, concomitant anticoagulation)

2) Administration of **250 mL of normal saline** before amphotericin B may help ↓ renal dysfunction

3) Acetaminophen administered 30 min before amphotericin B infusion may ameliorate the fever

4) **Hydrocortisone 0.7 mg/kg** (Solu-Cortef) can be added to the amphotericin infusion. Hydrocortisone is given to ↓ infusion-related reactions. It only should be used for significant fever (>2.0 °F elevation from baseline) and chills during infusions and should be discontinued as soon as possible (3–5 days). It is not necessary to add hydrocortisone if the patient is receiving supraphysiologic doses of adrenal corticosteroids

5) Meperidine hydrochloride 25–50 mg parenterally in adults may be used to ameliorate chills

C. Laboratory[a]

1) At least twice weekly for first 4 weeks, then weekly: Hct, reticulocyte count, magnesium, potassium, BUN, creatinine, bicarbonate, and UA. The GFR may fall 40% before stabilizing in these patients. **Discontinue for 2–5 days if renal function continues to deteriorate and reinstate after improvement**. Hct frequently falls 22%–35% of the initial level

2) Monitor closely for hypokalemia and hypomagnesemia

D. Caveats

1) **Electrolytes.** Addition of an electrolyte to an amphotericin solution causes the colloid to aggregate and probably results in suboptimal therapeutic effect. This includes IV piggyback medications containing electrolytes or preservatives

2) **Filtering.** The colloidal solution is partially retained by the 0.22 micron pore membrane filter: do not use filters if possible

3) The infusion bottle need not by light-shielded

E. Patients Needing Closer Monitoring

1) Addisonian patients tolerate infusion poorly. Treatment with corticosteroids improves patient tolerance

2) Patients should receive neither granulocyte transfusion nor Indium scanning

3) Patients with anuria or previous cardiac history may have an ↑ risk of arrhythmias and slower infusions are recommended

[a] BUN = Blood urea nitrogen; GFR = Glomerular filtration rate; Hct = Hematocrit; IV = Intravenous; UA = Urinalysis.

creasing potassium or magnesium trend. Anemia, associated with decreased renal production of erythropoietin, should resolve after amphotericin B discontinuation and need not be treated.[97] These measures for prevention of further renal deterioration need to be implemented and the amphotericin B therapy continued cautiously in this immunosuppressed patient with systemic candidiasis.

18. L.K. has developed significant renal failure due to acute tubular necrosis. How should his dose of systemic antifungal drugs be altered?

Renal elimination characteristics of the antimycotics vary tremendously. For systemically administered amphotericin B, only 5% to 10% of unchanged drug is eliminated in urine and bile during the first 24 hours[75] and there is no evidence supporting significant metabolism of amphotericin B. Significant accumulation during renal dysfunction does not occur. Therefore, no substantial dosage adjustment is required for patients with renal or hepatic dysfunction. Although many clinicians will withhold amphotericin B doses if renal failure develops during therapy, concerns of drug-induced-nephrotoxicity in L.K. must be balanced against the likelihood of mortality being as high as 85% in untreated immunocompromised patients with deep-seated infections.[61,62] Alternative systemic antifungal therapy also needs consideration.

Ketoconazole and itraconazole undergo first pass metabolism and have a biphasic dose-dependent elimination.[26,54,55] These agents are extensively metabolized with primary biliary excretion. Small amounts of unchanged drug are excreted in the urine. Therefore, there is no requirement for dosage adjustment in patients with renal dysfunction or patients undergoing dialysis.[119] Fluconazole, unlike ketoconazole and itraconazole, is not extensively metabolized. More than 90% of a fluconazole dose is excreted in urine, with about 80% as unchanged drug and about 20% as metabolites.[120] Since fluconazole is excreted primarily unchanged in the urine, doses should be adjusted in patients with renal insufficiency. Therefore, if fluconazole is used in L.K., the dose must be adjusted based upon published nomograms.[121]

Antimycotic Prophylaxis

19. What measures could have been undertaken to prevent invasive fungal infections in L.K.?

Selective gastrointestinal decontamination or systemic antimycotic pharmacotherapy can be used in high-risk, immunocompromised patients to prevent the development of fungal infections and could have been used for L.K. Selective gastrointestinal decontamination in high risk patients would ideally include the use of a nonabsorbable antifungal such as amphotericin B or nystatin. Oral amphotericin B decreases systemic candidal infections from 15% to 24% to 3% to 5% in high risk patients;[99,100] however, oral amphotericin B is not commercially available in the U.S. Therefore, the parenteral product can be used to formulate an oral solution in a concentration of 0.1 mg/mL and the patient instructed to swish about 15 mL of the solution in the mouth and swallow the solution four times a day.[101] Nystatin is available in an oral solution, tastes better, is less expensive, and also decreases *Candida* colonization in the GI tract.[102]

The problems of availability of amphotericin B oral formulations, questionable nystatin stool concentrations,[103,104] and poor compliance have led to imidazole (clotrimazole, miconazole, ketoconazole) use. However, this could increase adverse effects and potential drug interactions due to systemic azole absorption. The trade off can be improved patient compliance in regimens using an azole.[98] Imidazoles are more effective in preventing oral pharyngeal candidiasis (OPC) than placebo.[105,106] However, only small studies[98,107,108] with inadequate sample sizes have evaluated the clinical efficacy of imidazoles compared to polyene antifungals (e.g., amphotericin B) for prevention of either oropharyngeal or systemic candidiasis. Reduced rates for oropharyngeal and systemic candidiasis have been noted in noncomparative studies using fluconazole[100,109,110] and itraconazole.[111] Rates of superficial and systemic fungal infections appear equivalent for amphotericin B or fluconazole prophylaxis.[100]

Although antifungal prophylaxis is controversial, selective gastrointestinal decontamination with 12 million units/day of nystatin to ensure adequate fecal concentrations would be our preference over amphotericin B or systemic azoles.[104] Once prophylaxis is begun, it should be continued until either L.K. develops a systemic

Table 69.7		Antimycotic Prophylaxis Regimens and Costs		
Agent	Dose/Day	Formulation	Recommended Regimen	Cost[a]
Selective Gastrointestinal Decontamination				
Amphotericin B	6 mg	Topical	Swish and swallow QID	29.21
Nystatin	12 million units	Topical	Swish and swallow QID	4.50
Systemic				
Clotrimazole	30–80 mg	Topical	TID–QID	7.85–22.25
Ketoconazole	400 mg	Oral	QD	2.70
Itraconazole	400 mg	Oral	QD	5.39
Fluconazole	50–400 mg	Oral	QD	4.38–27.52

[a] From 1995 Red Book AWP Price.

infection, chemotherapy or immunosuppression ends, or he recovers from neutropenia. If discharged from the hospital and treated as an outpatient, a systemic azole (imidazole or triazole) is preferable over a polyene due to compliance, however, systemic therapy increases the risk of resistance, adverse effects, drug interactions (see Table 69.4), and cost (see Table 69.7).

Candiduria

Treatment

20. M.Y., a 24-year-old male, has been hospitalized in the surgical intensive care unit for the treatment of multiple trauma resulting from a motor vehicle accident. Shortly after admission he required exploratory laparotomy for a ruptured spleen and lacerated liver. He subsequently suffered respiratory and renal failure. M.Y. currently is intubated and on mechanical ventilation. Since admission he has been nutritionally supported with central hyperalimentation, has had a Foley catheter, and has been on broad-spectrum antibiotics (gentamicin, ampicillin, and metronidazole). Two recent UAs show budding yeast and cultures were positive for >100,000 colony forming units of C. albicans. He is currently afebrile, his funduscopic exam is normal, and there are no macronodular skin lesions present. The white blood cell (WBC) count is 8900 cells/mm³ and 3 sets of blood culture drawn over the last 2 days are negative. M.Y. has a Candida species in his urine. How should M.Y.'s candiduria be treated? [SI unit: 8.9 × 10⁹/L]

Eradication of fungi in the urine (specifically *C. albicans*) should begin with removal of both indwelling urinary catheters and risk factors for fungal disease. If catheter removal does not clear the urine within 48 hours or removal of candidemic risk factors are not possible, therapy should be considered (see Table 69.8). If M.Y. was scheduled for a genitourinary procedure he should receive systemic therapy due to the high rate of candidemia (3.6% to 10.8%) postsurgery.[112] In addition, any patient at high risk for dissemination (e.g., patients with diabetes, genitourinary abnormalities, renal insufficiency, or immunosuppression) into the blood should be treated.[112]

Bladder irrigation with amphotericin B has been commonly used and concentrations of ≥150 µg/mL are effective in killing 5 × 10⁶ *C. albicans* in the urine within two hours.[113] However, the clinical studies evaluating the efficacy of continuous amphotericin B irrigations are limited and often have had serious design flaws. Likewise, systemic antifungal therapy with flucytosine,[114] ketoconazole,[115,116] and flucoconazole[117] also has been used. None of these studies using systemic treatment regimens are comparative or randomized. Therefore, the optimal treatment option has not been established.

Caution must be used when selecting pharmacotherapy for M.Y. with funguria. It is difficult to differentiate between cystitis, urethritis, or systemic infection with clearance of fungi in the urine. Similarly it is difficult to differentiate colonization from infection

since candiduric patients are usually asymptomatic. The diagnosis of funguria lacks specific criteria for the determination of location or severity of invasion. Diligent monitoring for signs and symptoms of systemic disease should be continued until a diagnosis of colonization, cystitis, or urethritis is confirmed and risk of dissemination is excluded. Therefore, treatment of M.Y.'s candiduria should await a definitive diagnosis.

Blastomycosis

Etiology

21. C.P., a 17-year-old female, is admitted to the hospital with a chronic pneumonia that has not responded to antibiotics. Three months ago she had the insidious onset of a cough which eventually became productive of purulent sputum. She also noted intermittent blood streaking in her sputum. Two months ago she developed "boils" on her lower extremities and back which spontaneously drained. She was hospitalized at another hospital but failed to respond to amoxicillin and erythromycin. C.P. denies fever, chills, or night sweats and has lost 11 pounds. When admitted to the hospital her temperature is 38.2 °C. There is a 2 by 2 cm subcutaneous, fluctuant, tender mass over the right mandible and a second fluctuant mass about 4 cm in diameter on the lower back. There are also several 0.5 to 1 cm ulcers with heaped-up, hyperkeratotic margins on the lower extremities (see Figure 69.2). Rales are heard at the right lung base. C.P.'s leukocyte count is slightly elevated

Table 69.8	Therapeutic Options for Resolution of Candiduria

Step 1
Removal of indwelling urinary catheter
Removal of risk factors

Step 2
If cultures continue to be positive without evidence of systemic disease, assume local infection or colonization. Treat with:
  Topical Therapy
  Intermittent amphotericin B irrigations 15–30 mg in 100 mL sterile water retained for 1 hr daily for 3–7 days
    or
  Continuous amphotericin B irrigations 50 mg in 1000 mL for 3–7 days

  Systemic Therapy
  Fluconazole 0.6–1.4 mg/kg PO/IV × 7 days
    or
  Amphotericin B 0.3 mg/kg IV single dose
    or
  Flucytosine 100–150 mg/kg/day PO/IV × 7 days
    or
  Adjust dose based upon renal function

Step 3
Assume systemic infection if there is:
  1) Relapse in symptoms
  2) Recurrence of positive culture

at 13,500 cells/mm³. A chest radiograph shows a mass-like infiltrate in the right mid-lung field (see Figure 69.3). Wet preparation of ulcer scrapings and material aspirated from a subcutaneous abscess reveal numerous broad-based, budding yeast forms with refractile cell walls and multiple nuclei which are typical of *Blastomyces dermatitidis*. Cultures of sputum, skin scrapings, and abscess material eventually confirmed the diagnosis. What was the likely portal of entry for C.P.'s disseminated blastomycosis? Why should it be treated? [SI unit: 13.5 × 10⁹/L]

Typical of the other endemic mycoses, the primary portal of entry for *B. dermatitidis* is the lungs. A pulmonary origin for C.P.'s infection also is likely because her insidious onset of cough, purulent sputum, and blood-streaked sputum were evident about a month before her cutaneous lesions appeared on her legs and back. An acute pulmonary infection is most often asymptomatic and when symptomatic usually requires only observation. Chronic pulmonary or extrapulmonary blastomycoses will develop in an unknown number of these patients. C.P.'s rales at the base of her right lung and chronic pneumonia process that is unresponsive to antibiotics indicate that her acute pulmonary infection has developed into a chronic pulmonary disease over these past three months. Chronic pulmonary disease often presents with radiographic studies which can be mistaken for tuberculosis or lung cancer; and the mass-like infiltrate in her right lung on chest x-ray also is consistent with chronic pulmonary disease. Extrapulmonary infections present with cutaneous (verrucous or ulcerative skin lesions), skeletal, genitourinary (prostatitis, epididymo-orchitis), or

Fig 69.3 Chest Radiograph of Pulmonary *Blastomyces dermatitidis*

central nervous system (meningitis or brain abscess) manifestations. If untreated, these chronic or extrapulmonary infections will be fatal in 21% to 100% of patients.[122] Since C.P. presents with pulmonary and cutaneous evidence of blastomycosis, she should be treated.

Treatment

22. What specific therapy should be initiated for C.P.?

Until recently, amphotericin B was considered the treatment of choice for blastomycosis and total doses of greater than 2 gm were associated with 97% cure rates and low relapse rates. However, toxicity was observed in 70% of patients.[123] Ketoconazole and itraconazole currently are advocated as safe and effective preferences to amphotericin B in patients with nonlife-threatening, non-central nervous system infections. The NIAID-Mycoses Study Group confirmed the effectiveness of azoles for the treatment of chronic pulmonary and extrapulmonary disease caused by the endemic mycoses, blastomycosis, and histoplasmosis. In uncontrolled evaluations of chronic pulmonary and extrapulmonary infections (excluding life-threatening or central nervous system), ketoconazole at doses of 400 to 800 mg/day resulted in cure rates of about 89%, failure rates of about 6%, and relapses of about 5%.[124] In similar studies, itraconazole 200 to 400 mg/day for a median of 6.2 months resulted in cure rates of 88% to 95%.[125] Fluconazole was ineffective at doses less than 400 mg/day;[122] however, higher doses are being evaluated. Although these trials are neither comparative nor controlled, itraconazole appears to be less toxic than ketoconazole. Therefore, itraconazole appears to have the best benefit (efficacy) to risk (toxicity) ratio.

In C.P. with mild to moderate disease, an initial itraconazole dose of 200 mg/day should be started. If there is no clinical improvement or if the disease progresses despite therapy, the dose of

Fig 69.2 Disseminated *Blastomyces dermatitidis* Skin Ulcers

itraconazole can be titrated upwards in 100 mg increments to a maximum dose of 400 mg/day. Treatment should be continued for at least six months. If C.P. develops severe or meningeal disease, itraconazole should be discontinued and amphotericin B 0.3 to 0.5 mg/kg/day should be initiated to provide a total dose of 1.5 gm. C.P. should be followed up for 12 months because of the possible risk of relapse. Unlike histoplasmosis, skin and serologic testing are not sensitive enough to diagnose blastomycosis or evaluate the effectiveness of treatment.[125,126] Rather, patients should be closely evaluated for resolution of symptom (constitutional, pulmonary), negative microbiologic samples, and improvement in radiographic studies.

Antifungals in Pregnancy

23. C.P. reports she has not menstruated in 3 months and a urine pregnancy test is positive. How does this information change the therapeutic options for her?

The data on the safety of antimycotics for treating patients who are pregnant or lactating are limited but comprehensively reviewed according to FDA categories of the teratogenic risks of drugs (see Chapter 45: Teratogenicity and Drugs in Breast Milk).[127,128] The systemic azoles are contraindicated in pregnant or lactating women who are breast-feeding due to their potential endocrine toxicity in the fetus or newborn. Like griseofulvin and flucytosine, the azoles have been classified as risk factor C. This suggests that there are animal studies, but no human studies, demonstrating significant adverse effects (embryotoxicity and teratogenicity). These agents should not be used in C.P. since the risk clearly outweighs the therapeutic benefit. There are little or no data on the secretion of these agents in breast milk. Therefore, breast-feeding should be discouraged in women receiving these antifungal agents.

Amphotericin B is classified as risk factor B. Therapeutic agents in this category have no fetal risk based upon animal studies, or when risk has been found in animals, controlled human studies have not confirmed the results. Further, considerable clinical ex-

perience with amphotericin B in pregnant women has documented successful treatment of systemic mycoses with no excess toxicity to either the mother or fetus. Thus, amphotericin B has been the mainstay of antifungal therapy in pregnancy.

Histoplasmosis

Treatment

24. J.N., a 47-year-old male with severe rheumatoid arthritis, has been maintained on daily prednisone for the past 6 years; his current dose being 20 mg/day. For the past 4 weeks he has experienced daily fevers to 38.4 °C, drenching night sweats, anorexia, and an 8.2 kg weight loss. His prednisone dosage was increased to 40 mg/day with little clinical effect. On admission to the hospital J.N. appears chronically ill and has many of the stigmata of chronic steroid therapy. His temperature is 37.8 °C with an associated rapid heart rate of 105 beats/min. A shallow mouth ulcer is present on the hard pallet. The liver is enlarged to a total span of 18 cm and the spleen is palpable 3 cm below the left costal margin. Stool is positive for occult blood. A chest radiograph shows bilateral interstitial infiltrate (see Figure 69.4A). He is pancytopenic, with a hematocrit (Hct) of 29%, a WBC count of 3500 cells/mm³, and the platelet count is 78,000 cells/mm³. The bilirubin is normal but the aminotransferases are elevated to about 1.5 times over normal. A UA reveals 8–10 white blood cells/high powered field. The SrCr is 1.9 mg/dL and BUN is 42 mg/dL. A bone marrow aspirate and biopsy of the mouth ulcer reveal multiple, small intracellular yeast forms compatible with _H. capsulatum_ in macrophages and polymorphonuclear leukocytes (see Figure 69.4B). Culture of blood, urine, bone marrow aspirate, and mouth ulcer biopsy grew _H. capsulatum_. What should be the primary antifungal therapy in this case of systemic _H. capsulatum_? What clinical parameters should be monitored to assess the efficacy and toxicity of J.N.'s therapy? [SI units: Hct 0.29; WBC count 3.5 ×10⁹/L; SrCr 167.96 μmol/L; BUN 14.99 mmol/L urea]

The treatment benefits of antifungal therapy in systemic histoplasmosis have not been well studied; however, the treatment op-

A.

B.

Fig 69.4 Histoplasmosis Infection A) Chest radiograph showing bilateral interstitial infiltrate. B) A gram-stain of peripheral blood showing leukocytes with intercellular organisms.

Table 69.9   Treatment of Histoplasmosis[a]

Disease	Primary	Secondary
Acute Pulmonary	Resolves spontaneously	Not applicable
Prolonged symptomatology (>2 weeks)	ITZ 50–100 mg/day (3–6 months)	AmphoB 0.3–0.5 mg/kg/day[b]
Immunocompromised	AmphoB 0.3–0.5 mg/kg/day	ITZ 1.5–2.8 mg/kg/day (≥6 months)
Respiratory distress (PaO$_2$ <70 mm Hg)	AmphoB 0.5–1.0 mg/kg/day (TD 250–500 mg) ± corticosteroids	ITZ (has not been investigated in life-threatening situations)
Chronic Pulmonary		
Active	ITZ 1.5–2.8 mg/kg/day (≥9 months)[b]	AmphoB 0.5 mg/kg/day[b] *or* KTZ 400 mg/day (≥6 months)
Inactive		
Histoplasmoma	No treatment	Not applicable
Mediastinal fibrosis	Surgery[c]	Not applicable
Systemic disease	AmphoB (*total dose recommended:* 35 mg/kg) or ITZ 2.8 mg/kg/day	KTZ

[a] AmphoB = Amphotericin B; ITZ = Itraconazole; KTZ = Ketoconazole.
[b] Treatment should be continued until the patient is symptom free and culture negative for 3 months. The recommendations for duration of therapy or total doses should only be used as guides for initial therapy.
[c] Only indicated for serious symptoms (i.e., hemoptysis).

tions for histoplasmosis are outlined in Table 69.9.[129] Accordingly, J.N. should be treated with amphotericin B 0.3 to 0.5 mg/kg/day and his course of therapy monitored both for efficacy and toxicity.

Blood and urine cultures, pancytopenia (except anemia in amphotericin B treated patients), constitutional symptoms, and hepatosplenomegaly are excellent measures for evaluating outcome to amphotericin B therapy of J.N.'s histoplasmosis. Anemia and chest radiographs are poor measures of treatment response. Chest radiographs usually reflect calcified granulomas with scarring which rarely resolve even with extensive therapy. Evaluation of deterioration but not improvement is possible due to this pathological process. In addition, amphotericin-induced renal disease with secondary anemia can confuse evaluation of disease resolution. Anemia must be excluded as a prognostic indicator in patients receiving amphotericin B for durations of ≥3 weeks regardless of the dose.[97]

Diligent follow-up of patients is required because relapses occur in 5% to 15% of amphotericin B treated patients within three years. Relapses occurred in patients who received less than a 30 mg/kg total dose of amphotericin B, or had concomitant untreated Addison's Disease, immunosuppression, vascular infections (endocarditis, grafts, aneurysms), or meningeal infections.[129,130] More than 90% of HIV-positive patients experienced a relapse of histoplasmosis subsequent to adequate amphotericin B. Even the initiation of subsequent immunosuppressive therapy is of particular concern because of the potential for reactivation (relapse) and dissemination of histoplasmosis from a dormant foci especially in patients with residual granulomas.

Potential adverse effects to amphotericin B also need to be monitored in J.N. (e.g., infusion-related reactions, nephrotoxicity, anemia, hypokalemia, neurotoxicity, thrombophlebitis). Additionally, J.N.'s adrenal status should be monitored closely because of his long-term corticosteroid therapy and his histoplasmosis. Patients who are Addisonian secondary to histoplasmosis infections appear to experience more episodes of acute hypotension.

Azole Adverse Effects

25. After treatment with a total amphotericin B dose of 750 mg, clinical improvement of J.N.'s histoplasmosis is subjectively and objectively documented. Therefore, ketoconazole at 400 mg/day is substituted for his amphotericin B regimen. Six

weeks later, J.N. complains of impotence and wonders if this could be due to his medication. What is the likelihood that ketoconazole is the cause of J.N.'s impotence?

In comparison to miconazole, itraconazole, and fluconazole, ketoconazole has been associated with more adverse reactions and greater potential for drug interactions. Fortunately, the most common side effects of ketoconazole are nausea and vomiting. Gastrointestinal distress appears to be dose related, since a substantially smaller percentage of patients experience these effects when receiving 400 mg/day ketoconazole doses as compared to 800 mg/day doses.[132] The most significant ketoconazole toxicities requiring monitoring are endocrinologic and hepatic. Dose-related endocrinologic toxicities (hypoadrenalism, oligospermia, and diminished libido in males) have been observed during ketoconazole therapy.[26,132] These endocrine-related effects usually resolve with drug discontinuation. Therefore, J.N.'s complaints of impotence might well be attributed to his ketoconazole. Liver enzymes also should be monitored because of about a 10% risk of serious hepatitis and hepatic failure.[26,133]

The triazoles, itraconazole and fluconazole, are much better tolerated and require less monitoring than ketoconazole therapy. This has been attributed to the greater affinity of the triazoles for fungal demethylase and less interference with mammalian enzymes.[133] Neither itraconazole nor fluconazole exhibit any substantial hepatotoxicity or antiandrogenic effects, and nausea and vomiting occurs in substantially fewer patients (<5%) receiving the triazoles as compared to imidazoles. J.N. should be given a trial of itraconazole.

Azole Drug Interactions

26. J.N. chose to continue with his ketoconazole therapy. He now returns with an upper respiratory tract infection and has been prescribed terfenadine (Seldane). What potential serious problem could this antihistamine cause for J.N.?

Drug interactions with systemic azoles and polyenes can lead to mild inconveniences or life-threatening events (see Table 69.4). The interaction between azoles and nonsedating H$_1$-selective antihistamines can be life-threatening and this combination should be avoided. Electrocardiographic changes (QT prolongation and serious ventricular arrhythmias) have been associated with the concurrent use of either ketoconazole or itraconazole with terfenadine. Serum terfenadine concentrations increase within 19 hours of coadministration of itraconazole and terfenadine and remain elevated for more than 60 hours. All nonsedating H_1-selective antihistamines (e.g., terfenadine, astemizole) should be avoided in patients taking any of the systemic azoles.[134,135] This drug interaction has been attributed to ketoconazole and itraconazole inhibition of the cytochrome P450 enzymes that metabolize terfenadine and astemizole.

Coccidioidomycosis

Serological Tests

27. F.W., 32-year-old Filipino female and a life long resident of the Central Valley in California, is admitted to the hospital with a 3rd recurrence of coccidioidal meningitis. Approximately 4 years ago she was treated with a total amphotericin B dose of 2.2 gm which resulted in a good clinical response. Nine months later she relapsed and received a 2nd course of amphotericin B to a total of 1.6 gm. She did well over the next 18 months and was able to return to work as a secretary. Over the past 4 months, however, F.W. has noted chronic headaches, has been unable to concentrate at work and is reported by family members to have a very labile personality. A CT scan of the brain reveals mild hydrocephalus. An opening pressure of 19 mm Hg was documented at lumbar puncture. Analysis of the CSF showed 110 white blood cells/mm³, a glucose of 18 mg/dL, and a protein of 190 mg/dL. Complement fixation antibodies were positive in the CSF at a titer of 1:32. How should serological tests for coccidioidomycosis be interpreted?

The most important serological tests for fungal infections use the complement fixation (CF), immunodiffusion, and enzyme-linked immunoassay (EIA) techniques. Tests for complement fixing antibodies (i.e., *complement fixation*) to the dimorphic fungi (see Table 69.1) are well established and a variety of antigens have been used. Coccidioidin is the mycelial phase antigen for *Coccidioides immitis*. Of patients with coccidioidomycosis, 61% will have coccidioidin CF titers of at least 1:32 and 41% will have titers of 1:64. Rising titers are a bad prognostic sign, but falling titers indicate clinical improvement. Therefore, F.W.'s CSF complement fixation titer of 1:32 is consistent with active coccidioidomycosis. *Immunodiffusion* testing for coccidioidomycosis using coccidioidin reveals that seropositive results appear one to three weeks after onset of primary infection in 75% of patients and this positivity usually disappears within four months if the infection resolves.[192] IgG and IgM specific *enzyme-linked immunoassays* (EIA) using a combination of antigens for *C. immitis* have been developed. These tests offer sensitivities of greater than 92% and specificities of 98% for serum and CSF. EIA reactivity appears earlier than CF reactivity.[193,194]

Antifungal Central Nervous System (CNS) Penetration

28. What is a pharmacokinetic explanation for the treatment failure of F.W.? How might this problem be overcome?

F.W. has received prolonged parenteral amphotericin B administration and the cerebrospinal fluid still contains fungal organisms. Treatment failures in this case may be due, in part, to the limited penetration of amphotericin B into the CSF[136] (see Table 69.5). Amphotericin B is highly lipid-bound (91% to 95%) with CSF concentrations, at best, only 2% to 4% of the serum concentration:[75,133] peritoneal, synovial, and pleural fluid concentrations are slightly less than 50% of the serum concentrations. Due to the problem with antifungal penetration in the cerebrospinal fluid, the addition of local injections (intraventricular or intrathecal) to systemic antifungal administration may improve outcome by maximizing therapy.[140–143] Intrathecal amphotericin B doses in adults normally range from 0.25 to 0.5 mg diluted in 5 mL of 5% glucose.[140,141,144] A few studies suggest that doses greater than 0.7 mg improve the cure rate and decrease relapse.[145] Cisternal or intraventricular administration are recommended as the routes of choice due to flow characteristics of CSF from the ventricles to the

spinal cord.[136,144–147] When lumbar administration is necessary, amphotericin B is administered in a hypertonic solution of 10% glucose and the patient is placed in a Trendelenburg position in an attempt to improve distribution of the drug to the basilar meninges and ventricles and reduce local toxicity.[145]

Flucytosine and the systemic azoles might be alternatives to amphotericin B. Flucytosine is not significantly protein bound and penetrates the CSF, vitreous, and peritoneal fluids: its volume of distribution approximates that of total body water.[137] Flucytosine concentration in the CSF is 74% of the serum concentration, resulting in its extensive use in treatment of central nervous system mycoses. Unfortunately, flucytosine has no activity in coccidioidomycosis and, therefore, cannot be used in F.W. The volume of distribution of fluconazole approaches that of total body water,[138,139] and concentrations of fluconazole in CSF are about 60% of simultaneous serum concentrations. Ketoconazole has only about 1% of the dose present as free drug because ketoconazole is highly bound to plasma proteins (>80%) and to erythrocytes (15%). Ketoconazole, therefore, penetrates poorly into the CSF except with doses of ≥1200 mg/day. Itraconazole is similar to ketoconazole in that it is more than 99% protein bound; however, itraconazole concentrates intracellularly in host alveolar macrophages and that may account for its efficacy against fungal central nervous system infection in spite of its inability to penetrate into the CSF.[138] Therefore, fluconazole and itraconazole might be alternatives to CNS instillation of amphotericin B based only upon pharmacokinetic considerations.

Preliminary studies with fluconazole, investigated at doses ≥400 mg/day, are promising for control of disease in patients with coccidioidomycosis meningitis. However, relapse rates are high once fluconazole therapy is stopped.[148] Early reports with itraconazole appear promising.[149,150] Ketoconazole, which must be given at very high doses and results in significant toxicity, should only be utilized if other therapies are contraindicated.[132,151,152]

Intrathecal Amphotericin

29. What adverse events might be observed with the intrathecal administration of an antifungal in F.W.?

Cisternal antifungal administration has been associated with headaches, nausea, vomiting, cranial nerve paresis, and cisternal hemorrhage due to needle trauma.[144,145,153,154] An Ommaya reservoir often is utilized to facilitate intraventricular administration of amphotericin B. Frequent complications of these devices include shunt occlusion, bacterial colonization or bacterial meningitis, Parkinsonian symptoms, and seizures.[136,155,156] Lumbar administration has been used due to its simplicity but often has to be discontinued due to chemical arachnoiditis,[157] headache, transient radiculitis, paresthesia, nerve pulses, difficulty voiding, impaired vision, vertigo, and tinnitus.[158] Acute toxic delirium,[159] demyelinating peripheral neuropathy,[160] and spinal cord injury[161] also have been reported. Regardless of the substantial and serious adverse effects, intrathecal administration may be effective in treating patients with meningitis who have severe disease or who are pharmacologic nonresponders.

Aspergillosis: Treatment

30. M.Z., an otherwise healthy 29-year-old male, presented for allogeneic bone marrow transplantation (BMT) 12 days ago. He has had no serious complications associated with his chloroquine-induced aplastic anemia during his 7 month wait for BMT. On BMT days −5 to −2 the induction therapy was initiated with cyclophosphamide (50 mg/kg) and total body irradiation, then bone marrow from his HLA compatible brother was infused on day 0. The onset of neutropenia was

noted on day 3 and the WBC count on day 16 is 50 cells/mm^3. M.Z. has only complained of stomatitis and diarrhea before today. This morning he is complaining of fever, chest pain, and headache. On physical examination his temperature is 37 °C and chest auscultation reveals right sided rales with a friction rub. Chest radiograph shows a nodular infiltrate in the right middle lobe. Fiberoptic bronchoscopy was immediately performed finding eroded bronchioles with necrotic tissue. Biopsy and methenamine silver nitrate stain of the sample revealed fragmented, closely septated hyphal bodies and conidiophores. The hyphae branched at 45° angles. The samples were sent to microbiology for cultures. All previous blood and sputum cultures have been negative except an *Aspergillus niger* from sputum before admission which was classified as a ''contaminate.'' The diagnosis at this time is probable Aspergillosis. What steps should be taken when considering treatment of Aspergillosis?

Drug therapy needs to be approached by first determining whether the infection is likely to be invasive or noninvasive disease (see Figure 69.5). Most patients inhale *Aspergillus* species and never become symptomatic or only have mild hypersensitivity pneumonitis. Invasive infections are more likely to occur in immunocompromised patients, especially those with prolonged neutropenia associated with bone marrow transplantation. The subjective and objective data in this case clearly represent invasive symptomatic disease and the need for aggressive treatment.

Aspergillosis is a model for invasive mold infections which have a propensity to invade blood vessels and tissue. Antimycotic pharmacotherapy needs to be initiated rapidly and aggressively (see Table 69.10) in conjunction with removal or reversal of immunosuppression if possible. Empiric therapy with high dose amphotericin B is recommended for patients suspected of having invasive aspergillosis which is associated with high mortality.[63,162,163] In spite of early and intensive amphotericin B therapy, mortality from invasive aspergillosis can be higher than 50%.[164]

Patients with mild to moderate *Aspergillus* can be treated with an azole as an alternative to amphotericin B. Itraconazole *in vitro* appears the most promising azole currently available for the treatment of *Aspergillus* infections. Clinical and microbiologic cure rates of 50% to 71% have been reported in itraconazole treated patients with invasive aspergillosis. Further studies are necessary to define the optimal dose and duration of itraconazole in invasive forms of aspergillosis. In itraconazole unresponsive patients, amphotericin B in combination therapy with either flucytosine, rifampin, or itraconazole can be considered.

New amphotericin B formulations also have been available for compassionate use while clinical trials are underway. A case series with liposomal amphotericin B found the agent 71% effective (clinical and microbiologic cure) in patients unresponsive or intolerant to amphotericin B.[165]

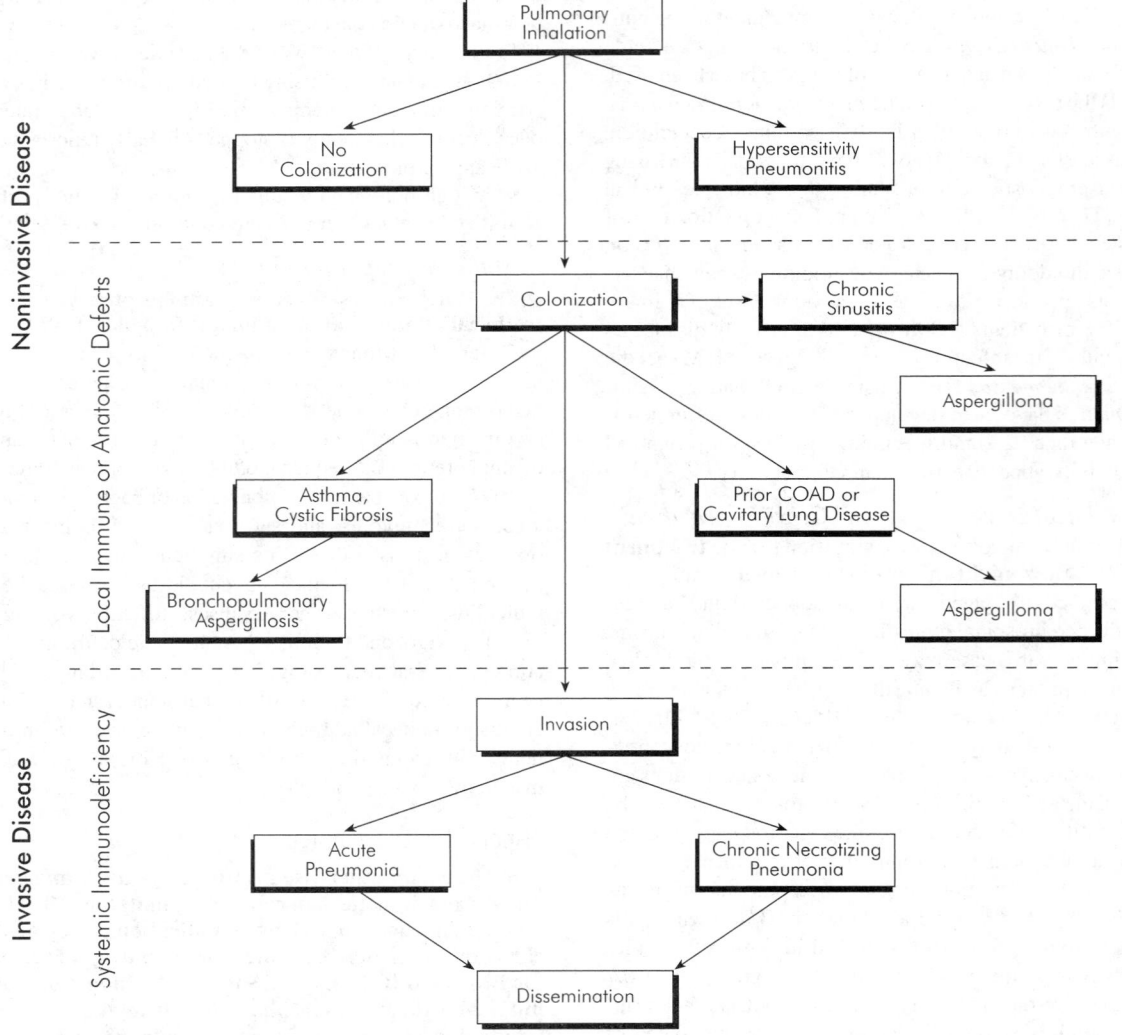

Fig 69.5   Classification of Aspergillosis Infections

Table 69.10	Therapeutic Options for Treatment of Aspergillosis[a]	
Disease	Primary	Secondary
Hyalohyphomycetes		
Aspergillosis		
Allergic bronchopulmonary	Prednisone 1 mg/kg/day followed by 0.5 mg/kg/day or QOD × 3–6 months. No antifungal therapy	ITZ 200 mg BID × 4 months[b]
Aspergilloma	Observation	Surgery[c]
Systemic (invasive)		
Serious	AmphoB 1.0–1.5 mg/kg/day	—
Mild/moderate	AmphoB 0.5–0.6 mg/kg/day	ITZ 200 mg TID loading dose × 3 days then 200 mg BID with meals (6 month minimum)

[a] AmphoB = Amphotericin B; ITZ = Itraconazole.
[b] Treatment should be continued until the patient is symptom free and culture negative for 3 months. Noted durations or total doses should only be used as a compass to help guide therapy.
[c] Only indicated for serious symptoms (e.g., hemoptysis).

Cryptococcosis

31. D.W., a 48-year-old male, was hospitalized with fever and severe headache. His past history was significant for Hodgkin's lymphoma, which is in remission. Lumbar puncture revealed 50 leukocytes/mm³, a positive India-ink preparation, and a cryptococcal antigen titer of 1:4096. Serology for HIV infection was negative. Culture of the CSF eventually grew *Cryptococcus neoformans*. The presumptive diagnosis is cryptococcal meningitis. What are the treatment options for D.W. with cryptococcal meningitis?

There are currently only two therapeutic options for meningeal cryptococcal disease: amphotericin B with or without flucytosine and fluconazole. Flucytosine cannot be utilized alone for therapy or prophylaxis due to the rapid development of resistance. Patients not infected with HIV have improved treatment outcomes when the combination of amphotericin B and flucytosine is used.[166,167] Further, when flucytosine is used in combination therapy, the dose of amphotericin B may be reduced to 0.3 to 0.6 mg/day which decreases the frequency of dose-related amphotericin B toxicity. In patients not able to be treated with flucytosine, the dose of amphotericin B must be increased to greater than 0.6 mg/kg/day. Patients with cryptococcal meningitis should be treated with the combination of amphotericin B and flucytosine (100 to 150 mg/kg/day divided into four daily doses).

Fluconazole is an alternative to amphotericin B in HIV-infected patients with cryptococcal meningitis with selected caveats. Sterilization of the cerebrospinal fluid is more rapid and mortality during the first two weeks of therapy was lower in patients treated with amphotericin B as compared to fluconazole treated patients.[168,169] Early mortality was especially high in those fluconazole treated patients who presented with altered mental status.[169] Thus, initial therapy of cryptococcus should be initiated with amphotericin B for at least two weeks or until the patient has clinically stabilized. At this point, fluconazole may be substituted at an initial dose 400 mg/day. The dose may be titrated upwards to a dose of 800 mg/day depending upon clinical response. After completing a ten week course of therapy, the dose of fluconazole is reduced to a maintenance dose of 200 mg/day for life.

In D.W., initial treatment should focus on elimination of all identified immunosuppression. Antifungal therapy should then be initiated immediately with amphotericin B 0.3 to 0.6 mg/kg/day plus flucytosine 100 to 150 mg/kg/day. A minimum of six weeks is required to optimize the chance of a cure,[167] especially in transplant patients.[170]

32. What parameters should be monitored while D.W. is treated with flucytosine?

The most common side effect of flucytosine is gastrointestinal distress (e.g., nausea, vomiting, and diarrhea). Although flucytosine is not metabolized *per se* by mammalian cells, gut flora may be responsible for metabolism of flucytosine to fluorouracil. This toxic metabolite has been speculated to account, in part, for the gastrointestinal distress associated with flucytosine therapy.[21,28,171] Other flucytosine adverse effects include leukopenia, thrombocytopenia, and hepatotoxicity. Dose-dependent bone marrow suppression, which can be fatal, generally is seen in patients whose serum concentration of flucytosine exceeds 100 μg/mL. Thus, it is important to monitor blood concentrations and maintain concentrations below this level.[172–174] If assays for flucytosine serum concentrations are unavailable, signs and symptoms of bone marrow suppression or worsening renal function should result in a dosage reduction or discontinuation of the drug.

Flucytosine is eliminated by glomerular filtration, with 80% to 95% of the dose excreted unchanged in the urine. Renal excretion of flucytosine is directly related to creatinine clearance and doses should be adjusted based upon creatinine clearance to prevent accumulation to toxic concentrations in patients with renal impairment.[119,137] Patients with creatinine clearances of 10 and 40 mL/minute should have the dose of flucytosine reduced by 50% (usual dose: 37.5 mg/kg Q 12 hr). For patients with creatinine clearance less than 10 mL/minute, dosing should be initiated at 37.5 mg/kg every 24 hours with frequent monitoring of flucytosine serum concentrations. Dosage adjustment and close monitoring also are required for patients on hemodialysis and it is recommended that the dose be given postdialysis.

33. Why would combination therapy be useful for D.W.?

In vitro results of antifungal combinations against many common mycotic pathogens have been variable. Combination antifungals have been found to be synergistic, additive, antagonistic, or to have no effect. These *in vitro* evaluations involved the concomitant administration of amphotericin B with flucytosine, rifampin, or azoles, and azoles concomitantly administered with flucytosine, rifampin, sulfamethoxazole, and nikkomycins. These inconsistent findings have been attributed to variable incubation times, variable concentrations of antifungal, and variable sequence of antifungal addition.[175] As a result, clinical decisions about combination therapy should be based upon *in vivo* evaluations. Due to the limited clinical data, combination antifungal therapy should be initiated cautiously. Except for the treatment of cryptococcal meningitis, combination therapy should be reserved for cases of treatment failure without other established pharmacologic options for therapy.

References

1 **Kwon-Chung KJ, Bennett JE, eds.** Medical Mycology. Malvern, PA: Lea and Febiger; 1992.

2 **Rinaldi MG.** Systemic fungal infections: diagnosis and treatment II— emerging opportunists. Infect Dis Clinic North Am. 1989;3:65–76.

3 **Khardori N et al.** Cutaneous Rhizopus and Aspergillus infections in five patients with cancer. Arch Dermatol. 1989;125:952–56.

4 **Wingard JR.** Importance of *Candida* species other than *C. albicans* as pathogens in oncolgy patients. Clin Infect Dis. 1995;20:115–25.

5 **Myerowitz R.** The Pathology of Opportunistic Infections; with Pathogenetic, Diagnostic, and Clinical Correlations. New York, NY: Raven Press; 1983.

6 **Arrington JB.** Bacteria, fungi, and other microorganisms. In: Prophet EB et al., eds. Laboratory methods. In: Histotechnology, Armed Forces Institute of Pathology. Washington, D.C.; Am Reg of Path, Washington, D.C.; 1992: 203–13.

7 **Woods GL, Gutierrez Y.** Diagnostic Pathology of Infectious Diseases. Philadelphia, PA: Lea & Febiger; 1993.

8 **Coovadia YJ, Solwa Z.** Sensitivity and specificity of a latex agglutination test for detection of cryptococcal antigen in meningitis. S Afr Med J. 1987; 71:510–12.

9 **Loshi G et al.** Coagglutination (CoA) test for the rapid diagnosis of cryptococcal meningitis. J Med Microbiol. 1989;29:189–94.

10 **Crislip MA, Edwards JE.** Candidiasis, in systemic fungal infections: diagnosis and treatment II. Infect Dis Clin North Am. 1989;2:103–33.

11 **De Repentigne L, Reiss E.** Current trends in the immunodiagnosis of candidiasis and aspergillosis. Rev Infect Dis. 1983;6:301.

12 **Herent P et al.** Retrospective evaluation of two latex agglutination tests for detection of circulating antigens during invasive candidosis. J Clin Microbiol. 1992;30:2158–164.

13 **Phillips P et al.** Nonvalue of antigen detection immunoassays for diagnosis of candidemia. J Clin Microbiol. 1990; 28:2320–326.

14 **Wheat LJ et al.** Diagnosis of disseminated histoplasmosis by detection of *H. capsulatum* antigen in serum and urine specimens. N Engl J Med. 1986; 314:83–8.

15 **Wheat LJ.** Histoplasmosis in systemic fungal infections; diagnosis and treatment I. Infect Dis Clin North Am. 1988;2:841–59.

16 **Brajtburg J et al.** Amphotericin B: current understanding of mechanisms of action. Antimicrob Agents Chemother. 1990;34:183.

17 **Gruda I et al.** Application of different spectra in the UV-visible region to study the formation of amphotericin B complexes. Biochem Biophys Acta. 1980;602:260.

18 **Hitchcock CA et al.** The lipid composition and permeability to azole of an azole- and polyene-resistant mutant of *Candida albicans.* J Med Vet Mycol. 1987;25:29.

19 **Pierce AM et al.** Lipid composition and polyene antibiotic resistance of *Candida albicans.* Can J Biochem. 1978;56:135.

20 **Brajtburg J et al.** Stimulatory, permeabilizing, and toxic effects of amphotericin B on L cells. Antimicrob Agents Chemother. 1984;26:892.

21 **Diasio RB et al.** Mode of action of 5-fluorocytosine. Biochem Pharmacol. 1978;27:703.

22 **Chouini-Lalanne N et al.** Study of the metabolism of flucytosine in *Aspergillus* specis by ^{19}F nuclear magnetic resonance spectroscopy. Antimicrob Agents Chemother. 1989;33:1939.

23 **Polak A, Scholer HJ.** Mode of action of 5-fluorocytosine and mechanisms of resistance. Chemotherapy. 1975;21:113.

24 **van den Bossche H et al.** Hypothesis on the molecular basis of the antifungal activation of N-substituted imidazoles and triazoles. Biochem Soc Trans. 1983;11:665.

25 **van den Bossche H.** Biochemical targets for antifungal azole derivatives: hypothesis of the mode of action. In: McGinnis M, ed. Current Topics in Medical Mycology. New York: Springer-Verlag; 1985:313–51.

26 **Bodey GP.** Azole antifungal agents. Clin Infect Dis. 1992;14(Suppl. 1): S161.

27 **Galgiani JN et al.** Reference method for broth dilution antifungal susceptibility testing of yeasts; proposed standard. NCCLS Document M27-P. 1992; 12(25):1–22.

28 **Anaissie E et al.** Fluconazole susceptibility testing of *Candida albicans*: microtiter method that is independent of inoculum size, temperature and time of reading. Antimicrob Agents Chemother. 1991;35(8):1641–646.

29 **Cleary JD, Ziska DS.** Lipid-associated amphotericin B. Florida J Hosp Pharm. 1994;14:19–22.

30 **Gilbert BE et al.** Aerosolized liposomal amphotericin B for treatment of pulmonary and systemic *Cryptococcus neoformans* infections in mice. Antimicrob Agents Chemother. 1992;36: 1466.

31 **Chavanet PY et al.** Trial of glucose versus fat emulsion in preparation of amphotericin for use in HIV infected patients with candidiasis. Br Med J. 1992;305:921–25.

32 **Federal Register.** 1982;47:12480.

33 **Schering-Plough Healthcare Products.** Fulvicin package insert. Liberty Corner, NJ: 1994 January.

34 **Miles Pharmaceuticals.** Mycelex-7 package insert. New Haven, CT: 1994 January.

35 **Ortho Pharmaceuticals.** Monistat-7 package insert. Raritan, NJ: 1994 January.

36 **Sobel JD.** Pathogenesis and treatment of recurrent vulvovaginal candidiasis. Clin Infect Dis. 1992;14:S148–53.

37 **International Multicenter Trial.** A comparison of single-dose oral fluconazole with 3-day intravaginal clotrimazole in the treatment of vaginal candidiasis. Br J Obstet Gynaecol. 1989; 96:226–32.

38 **Pfizer Laboratory Division.** Fluconazole package insert. New York, NY: 1994 January.

39 **Janssen Pharmaceuticals.** Nizoral package insert. Piscataway, NJ: 1994 January.

40 **Edwards JE.** *Candida* species. In: Mandell GL et al., eds. Principles and Practice of Infectious Diseases. 3rd ed. New York: Churchill Livingstone; 1990:1943–958.

41 **Sobel JD.** Recurrent vulvovaginal candidiasis: a prospective study of the efficacy of maintenance ketoconazole therapy. N Engl J Med. 1986;315: 1455–458.

42 **Janssen Pharmaceuticals.** Itraconazole package insert. Piscataway, NJ: 1994 January.

43 **Osser S et al.** Treatment of candidal vaginitis. A prospective randomized investigator-blind multicenter study comparing topically applied econazole with oral fluconazole. Acta Obstet Gynecol Scand. 1991;70:73–8.

44 **Stein GE, Mummaw NL.** Prevention of recurrent vulvovaginal candidiasis with weekly terconazole cream. Paper presented to 34th Interscience Conference on Antimicrobial Agents and Chemotherapy. Orlando, FL: 1994 Oct 4.

45 **Crook WG.** The Yeast Connection: A Medical Breakthrough. Jackson, TN: Professional Books; 1983.

46 **Executive Committee of the American Academy of Allergy and Immunology.** Candidiasis hypersensitivity syndrome. J Allergy Clin Immunol. 1986;78:271–73.

47 **Dismukes WE et al.** A randomized, double-blind trial of nystatin therapy for the candidiasis hypersensitivity syndrome. N Engl J Med. 1990;323: 1717–723.

48 **Vanderveen EE et al.** Sporotrichosis in pregnancy. Curtis. 1982;30:761–63.

49 **Kauffman CA.** Old and new therapies for sportotrichosis. Paper presented to 31st Annual Infectious Diseases Society of American Meeting. New Orleans, LA: 1993 Oct 3.

50 **Bennett JE.** *Sporothrix schenckii.* In: Mandell GL et al., eds. Principles and Practice of Infectious Diseases. 3rd ed. New York: Churchill Livingstone; 1990:1972–977.

51 **Restrepo A et al.** Itraconazole therapy in lymphangitic and cutaneous sporotrichosis. Arch Dermatol. 1986;122: 413–17.

52 **Breeling JL, Weinstein L.** Pulmonary sporotrichosis treated with itraconazole. Chest. 1993;103(1):313–14.

53 **Kan VL, Bennett J.** Efficacies of four antifungal agents in experimental murine sporotrichosis. Antimicrob Agents Chemother. 1988;32:1619–623.

54 **Wishart JM.** The influence of food on the pharmacokinetics of itraconazole in patients with superficial fungal infection. Amer Acad Dermatol. 1987:220.

55 **Barone JA.** Food interaction and steady-state pharmacokinetics of itraconazole capsules in healthy male vol-unteers. Antimicrob Agents Chemother. 1993;37:778.

56 **Lelawongs P et al.** Effect of food and gastric acidity on absorption of orally administered ketoconazole. Clin Pharm. 1988;7:228.

57 **Smith D et al.** The pharmacokinetics of oral itraconazole in AIDS patients. J Pharm Pharmacol. 1992;44:618.

58 **Chin TWF et al.** Effects of Coca-Cola on the oral absorption of ketoconazole in the presence of achlorhydria. Paper presented to 33rd Interscience Conference on Antimicrobial Agents and Chemotherapy. New Orleans, LA: 1993 Oct 17.

59 **Hardin J et al.** The effects of cola beverage on the bioavailability of itraconazole in the presence of H2 blockers. Paper presented to 34th Interscience Conference on Antimicrobial Agents and Chemotherapy. Orlando, FL: 1994 Oct 4.

60 **Brincker H.** Prevention of mycosis in granulocytopenic leukemia patients with prophylactic ketoconazole treatment. Paper presented to 21st Interscience Conference on Antimicrobial Agents and Chemotherapy. Chicago, IL: 1982 Oct 7.

61 **Edwards JE, Filler SG.** Current strategies for treating invasive candidiasis: emphasis on infections in nonneutropenic patients. Clin Infect Dis. 1992; 14:S106–13.

62 **Harvey RL, Myers JP.** Nosocomial fungemia in a large community teaching hospital. Arch Intern Med. 1987; 147:2117–120.

63 **National Nosocomial Infection Surveillance System.** Nosocomial fungal infections in U.S. hospitals 1980– 1990. Paper presented to 30th Interscience Conference on Antimicrob Agents and Chemother. Atlanta, GA: 1990 Oct 21.

64 **Meunier-Carpentier F et al.** Fungemia in the immunocompromised host: changing paters, antigenemia, high mortality. Am J Med. 1981;71:363–70.

65 **Meunier F et al.** Candidemia in immunocompromised patients. Clin Infect Dis. 1992;14:S120–25.

66 **Rex JH et al.** A randomized trial comparing fluconazole with amphotericin B for the treatment of candidemia in patients without neutropenia. N Engl J Med. 1994;331:1325–330.

67 **Roerig Pfizer Protocol 1995.**

68 **Millon L et al.** Fluconazole-resistant recurrent oral candidiasis in human immunodeficiency virus-positive patients: persistence of *Candida albicans* strains with the same genotype. J Clin Microbiol. 1994;32:1115–118.

69 **Wingard JR et al.** Increase in *Candida krusei* infection among patients with bone marrow transplantation and neutropenia treated prophylactically with fluconazole. N Engl J Med. 1991;325: 1274–277.

70 **Wingard JR.** Infections due to resistant Candida species in patients with cancer who are receiving chromotherapy. Clin Infect Dis. 1994;19(Suppl. 1):S49–53.

71 **Christiansen KJ et al.** Distribution

and activity of amphotericin in humans. J Infect Dis. 1985;152(5):1037–43.

72 **Collette N et al.** Tissue concentrations and bioactivity of amphotericin B in cancer patients treated with amphotericin B-deoxycholate. Antimicrob Agents Chemother. 1989;33(3):362–68.

73 **Daneshmend TK, Warnock DW.** Clinical pharmacokinetics of systemic antifungal drugs. Clin Pharmacokinet. 1983;8:17–42.

74 **Carver P.** Effect of pH, concentration and time of exposure on the postantibiotic effect (PAE) of combinations of antifungal agents. Paper presented to 33rd Interscience Conference on Antimicrobial Agents and Chemotherapy. New Orleans, LA: 1993 Oct 17.

75 **Gallis HA et al.** Amphotericin B: 30 years of clinicial experience. Rev Infect Dis. 1990;12:308.

76 **Cleary JD et al.** Inhibition of interleukin 1 release from endotoxin or amphotericin B stimulated monocytes. Antimicrob Agents Chemother. 1992; 36(5):977–81.

77 **Cleary JD, Chapman SW.** Pharmacologic modulation of prostaglandin E2 (PGE2) production by bacterial endotoxin (LPS) or amphotericin B (AB) stimulated mononuclear cells (MNCs). Antimicrob Agents Chemother. 1993. (Manuscript under revision.)

78 **Tynes BS et al.** Reducing amphotericin B reactions. Am Rev Respir Dis. 1963;87:264–68.

79 **Hoeprich PD.** Clinical use of amphotericin B and deriviative: lore, mystique, and fact. Clin Infect Dis. 1992; 14:S114–19.

80 **Gigliotti F et al.** Induction of prostaglandin synthesis as the mechanism responsible for the chills and fever produced by infusing amphotericin B. J Infect Dis. 1987;156:784–89.

81 **Burks LC et al.** Meperidine for the treatment of shaking chills and fever. Arch Intern Med. 1980;140:483–84.

82 **Fields BT et al.** Effect of rapid intravenous infusion of serum concentrations of amphotericin B. Appl Microbiol. 1971;22(4):615–17.

83 **Cleary JD et al.** Effect of infusion rate on amphotericin B-associated febrile reactions. Drug Intell Clin Pharm. 1988;22:769–72.

84 **Oldfield EC III et al.** Randomized, double-blind trial of 1- versus 4-hour amphotericin B infusion durations. Antimicrob Agents Chemother. 1990; 34(7):1402–406.

85 **Cruz JM et al.** Rapid intravenous infusion of amphotericin B: a pilot study. Am J Med. 1992;93:123–30.

86 **Butler WT et al.** Electrocardiographic and electrolyte abnormalities caused by amphotericin B in dog and man. Proc Soc Exp Biol Med. 1964;116:857–63.

87 **Cleary JD et al.** Amphotericin B overdose in pediatric patients with associated cardiac arrest. Ann Pharmacother. 1993;27:715–18.

88 **Craven PC, Gremillion DH.** Risk factors of ventricular fibrillation during rapid amphotericin B infusion. Antimicrob Agents Chemother. 1985;27 (5):868–71.

89 **DeMonaco HJ, McGovern B.** Transient asystole associated with amphotericin B infusion. Drug Intell Clin Pharm. 1983;17:547–48.

90 **Brent J et al.** Amphotericin B overdoses in infants: is there a role for exchange transfusion? Vet Hum Toxicol. 1990;32(2):124.

91 **Bowler WA et al.** The safety of a one-hour infusion of amphotericin B documented by continuous electrocardiographic monitoring. Paper presented to 1990 Interscience Conference on Antimicrobial Agents and Chemotherapy. Atlanta, GA: 1990 Oct 21.

92 **Feely J et al.** Sodium depletion enhances nephrotoxicity of amphotericin B. Lancet. 1981;8235:1422–423.

93 **Heidemann HTH et al.** Amphotericin B nephrotoxicity in humans decreased by salt repletion. Am J Med. 1983;75: 476–81.

94 **Branch RA.** Prevention of amphotericin B-induced renal impairment: a review on the use of sodium supplementation. Arch Intern Med. 1988;148: 2389–394.

95 **Jurgens RW et al.** Compatibility of amphotericin B with certain large-volume parenterals. Am J Hosp Pharm. 1981;38:377–78.

96 **Fisher MA et al.** Risk factors for amphotericin B-associated nephrotoxicity. Am J Med. 1989;87:547–52.

97 **Lin AC et al.** Amphotericin B blunts erythropoietin response to anemia. J Infect Dis. 1990;161:348–51.

98 **Shepp DH et al.** Comparative trial of ketoconazole and nystatin for prevention of fungal infection in neutropenic patients treated in a protective environment. J Infect Dis. 1985;152(6):1257–263.

99 **Ezdinli EZ et al.** Oral amphotericin for Candidiases in patients with hematologic neoplasms. J Am Med Assoc. 1979;242:258–60.

100 **Menichetti F et al.** Fluconazole vs. oral amphotericin B for antifungal prophylaxis in neutropenic patients. Paper presented to 32nd Interscience Conference on Antimicrobial Agents and Chemotherapy. Anaheim, CA: 1992 Oct 11.

101 **Brandell R et al.** Treatment of oral candidiasis with amphotericin B solution. Clin Pharm. 1988;7:70–2.

102 **Wiesne RH.** The incidence of gram-negative bacterial and fungal infections in liver transplant patients treated with selective decontamination. Infection. 1990;18(Suppl. 1):519–21.

103 **Degregorio MW et al.** Candida infections in patients with acute leukemia: ineffectiveness of nystatin prophylaxis and relationship between oropharyngeal and systemic candidiasis. Cancer. 1982;50:2780–784.

104 **Hofstra W et al.** Concentrations of nystatin in faeces after oral administration of various doses of nystatin. Infection. 1979;7:166–70.

105 **Cuttner J et al.** Clotrimazole treatment for prevention of oral candidiasis in patients with acute leukemia undergoing chemotherapy. Am J Med. 1986; 81:771–74.

106 **Yeo E et al.** Prophylaxis of oropharyngeal candidiasis with clotrimazole. J Clin Oncol. 1985;3:1668–671.

107 **Owens NJ et al.** Prophylaxis of oral candidiasis with clotrimazole troches. Arch Intern Med. 1984;290–93.

108 **Slotman GJ, Burchard KW.** Ketoconazole prevents candida sepsis in critically ill surgical patients. Arch Surg. 1987;122:147–51.

109 **Samonia G et al.** Prophylaxis of oropharyngeal candidiasis with fluconazole. Rev Infect Dis. 1990;12:5369–373.

110 **Graybill JR.** Therapeutic agents. Infect Dis Clin North Am. 1988;2:805–26.

111 **Tricot G et al.** Ketoconazole vs itraconazole for antifungal prophylaxis in patients with severe granulocytopenia: preliminary results of two nonrandomized studies. Rev Infect Dis. 1987;9: S94–9.

112 **Ang BSP et al.** Candidemia from a urinary tract source: microbiological aspects and clinical significance. Clin Infect Dis. 1993;17:662.

113 **Fong IW et al.** The fungicidal effect of amphotericin B in urine to assess the feasability of bladder washout for localization of site of candiduria. Paper presented to 30th Interscience Conference on Antimicrobial Agents and Chemotherapy. Houston, TX: 1989 Sept 17.

114 **Fujihior S et al.** Flucytosine in the treatment of urinary fungal infections. Clinical efficacy and background factors. Jpn J Antibiot. 1991;44:14–21.

115 **Graybill JR et al.** Ketoconazole therapy for fungal urinary tract infections. J Urol. 1983;29:68–70.

116 **Symoens J et al.** An evaluation of two years of clinical experience with ketoconazole. Rev Infect Dis. 1980;2:674–87.

117 **Ikemoto H.** A clinical study of fluconazole for the treatment of deep mycoses. Diag Microbiol Infect Dis. 1989; 12(Suppl. 4):239S–47S.

118 **Walsh JJ, Pizzo PA.** Treatment of systemic fungal infections. Recent progress and current problems. Eur J Clin Microbiol Infect Dis. 1988;7:460.

119 **Bennett WM et al.** Drug prescribing in renal failure: dosing guidelines for adults. Am J Kidney Dis. 1983;3:155–93.

120 **Grant SM, Clissold SP.** Fluconazole: a review of its pharmacodynamic and pharmacokinetic properties and therapeutic potential in superficial and systemic mycoses. Drugs. 1990;39:877.

121 **Graybill JR.** New antifungal agents. Eur J Clin Microbiol Infect Dis. 1989; 8:402.

122 **Bradsher RW.** Blastomycosis. Clin Infect Dis. 1992;14:582–90.

123 **Parker JD et al.** A decade of experience with blastomycosis and its treatment with amphotericin B. Am Rev Respir Dis. 1969;99:895–902.

124 **National Institute of Allergy and Infectious Diseases Mycoses Study Group: Treatment of blastomycosis and histoplasmosis with ketoconazole: results of a prospective, randomized clinical trial.** Ann Intern Med. 1985;103:861–72.

125 **Bradsher RW.** Blastomycosis. In: Systemic fungal infections; diagnosis and treatment I. Infect Dis Clin North Am. 1988;2:877–98.

126 **Chapman SW.** *Blastomyces dermatitis.* In: Mandell GL et al., eds. Principles and Practice of Infectious Diseases. New York: Churchill Livingstone; 1990;1999–2008.

127 **Briggs GG et al.** Drugs in Pregnancy and Lacatation: A Reference Guide to Fetal and Neonatal Risk. Baltimore, MD: Williams & Wilkins; 1994.

128 **Federal Register.** 1980;44:37434-67.

129 **Wheat LJ.** Histoplasmosis in systemic fungal infections; diagnosis and treatment I. Infect Dis Clin North Am. 1988;2:841–59.

130 **Sutliff WD et al.** Histoplasmosis cooperative study. Am Rev Respir Dis. 1964;89:641–50.

131 **Sugar AM et al.** Pharmacology and toxicity of high dose ketoconazole. Antimicrob Agents Chemother. 1987; 31:1874–878.

132 **Pont A et al.** Ketoconazole blocks adrenal steroid synthesis. Ann Intern Med. 1982;97:370–72.

133 **Lyman CA, Walsh TJ.** Systemically administered antifungal agents. Drugs. 1992;44:9.

134 **Pohjola-Sintonen S et al.** Itraconazole prevents terfinadine metabolism and increases risk of torsades de pointes ventricular tachycardia. Eur J Clin Pharmacol. 1993;45:191–93.

135 **Honig PK et al.** Terfinadine-ketoconazole interactions: pharmacokinetic and electrocardiographic consequences. JAMA. 1993;269:1513–518.

136 **Ratcheson RA, Ommaya AK.** Experience with the subcutaneous cerebrospinal fluid reservoir: a preliminary report of 60 cases. N Engl J Med. 1968; 279(19):1-25-1031.

137 **Fujihior S et al.** Flucytosine in the treatment of urinary fungal infections. Clinical efficacy and background factors. Jpn J Antibiot. 1991;44:14–21.

138 **Brammer KW, Tarbit MH.** A review of the pharmacokinetics of fluconazole (UK-49,858) in laboratory animals and man. In: Fromtling RA ed. Recent Trends in the Discovery, Development and Evaluation of Antifungal Agents. Barcelona: JR Prous Science Publishers; 1987:141–49.

139 **Brammer KW et al.** Pharmacokinetics and tissue penetration of fluconazole in humans. Rev Infect Dis. 1990; 12(Suppl. 3):S318.

140 **Salaki JS.** Fungal and yeast infections of the central nervous system: a clinical review. Medicine. 1984;63:108–32.

141 **Oldfield EC et al.** Prediction of relapse after treatment for coccidioidomycosis. Paper presented to 33rd Interscience Conference on Antimicrobial Agents and Chemotherapy. New Orleans, LA: 1993 Oct 17–20;812.

142 **Shehab ZM et al.** Imidazole therapy of coccidioidal meningitis in children. Pediatr Infect Dis J. 1988;7:40–4.

143 **Galgiani JN et al.** Fluconazole therapy for coccidioidal meningitis. Ann Intern Med. 1993;119:28–35.

144 **Winn WA.** The treatment of coccidioidal meningitis. Cal Med. 1964; 101(2):78–89.

145 **Labadie EL, Hamilton RH.** Survival improvement in Coccidioidal meningitis by high dose intrathecal amphotericin B. Arch Intern Med. 1986;146: 2013–18.

146 **Butler WT et al.** Diagnostic and prognostic value of clinical and laboratory findings in cryptococcal meningitis. N Engl J Med. 1964;207:59–67.

147 **Winn WA.** Coccidioidomycosis and Amphotericin B. Med Clin North Am. 1963;47:1131–148.

148 **Knoper SR, Galgiani JN.** Coccidioidomycosis. Infect Dis Clin North Am. 1988;2:861–76.

149 **Phillips P et al.** Tolerance to and efficacy of itraconazole in treatment of systemic mycoses: preliminary results. Rev Infect Dis. 1987;9(Suppl. 1):S87–S93.

150 **Ganer A et al.** Initial experience in therapy for progressive mycoses with itraconazole, the first clinically studied triazole. Rev Infect Dis. 1987;9(Suppl. 1):S77–S86.

151 **Galgiani JN et al.** Ketoconazole therapy of progressive coccidioidomycoses: comparison of 400 and 800 mg doses and observations at higher doses. Am J Med. 1988;84:603–10.

152 **Craven PC et al.** High-dose ketoconazole for treatment of fungal infections of the central nervous system. Ann Intern Med. 1983;98:160–67.

153 **Witorsch P et al.** Intraventricular administration of amphotericin B. J Am Med Assoc. 1965;194(7):109–12.

154 **Sung JP et al.** Intravenous and intrathecal miconazole therapy for systemic mycoses. West J Med. 1977;126:5–13.

155 **Harrison HR et al.** Amphotericin B and imidazole therapy for coccidioidal meningitis in children. Pediatr Infect Dis. 1983;2(3):216–21.

156 **Fisher JF, Dewald J.** Parkinsonism associated with intraventricular amphotericin B. J Antimicrob Chemother. 1983;12:97–9.

157 **Littman ML et al.** Coccidioidomycosis and its treatment with amphotericin B. Am J Med. 1958;568–92.

158 **Utz JP et al.** Amphotericin B toxicity. Ann Intern Med. 1964;61:334–54.

159 **Winn RE et al.** Acute toxic delirium: neurotoxicity of intrathecal administration of amphotericin B. Arch Intern Med. 1979;139:706–7.

160 **Haber RW, Joseph MJ.** Neurologic manifestations after amphotericin B therapy. Br Med J. 1962;1:230–31.

161 **Carnevale NT et al.** Amphotericin-induced myelopathy. Neurology. 1977;359.

162 **Denning DW et al.** Pulmonary aspergillosis in the acquired immunodeficiency syndrome. N Engl J Med. 1991;324:654–62.

163 **Rinaldi MJ.** Invasive Aspergillosis. Rev Infect Dis. 1983;5:1061–77.

164 **Armstrong D.** Problems in management of opportunistic fungal diseases. Rev Infect Dis. 1989;11:1591–599.

165 **Weber RS, Lopez-Berestein G.** Treatment of invasive Aspergillus sinusitis with liposomal-Amphotericin B. Laryngoscope. 1987;97:937–41.

166 **Larsen RA et al.** Fluconazole compared with amphotericin B plus flucytosine for cryptococcal meningitis in AIDS: a randomized trial. Ann Intern Med. 1990;113:183–87.

167 **Bennett JE et al.** A comparison of amphotericin B alone and combined with flucytosine in the treatment of cryptococcal meningitis. N Engl J Med. 1979;301:126–30.

168 **Saag MS et al.** Comparison of amphotericin B with fluconzole in the treatment of acute AIDS associated cryptococcal meningitis. N Engl J Med. 1992;326:83–90.

169 **Dismukes WE et al.** Treatment of cryptococcal meningitis with combination amphotericin B and flucytosine for four as compared with six weeks. N Engl J Med. 1987;317:334–41.

170 **Hibberd PL, Rubin RH.** Clinical aspects of fungal infection in organ transplant recipients. Clin Infect Dis. 1994;19:S33–S40.

171 **Kauffman CA, Framd PT.** Bone marrow toxicity associated with 5-fluorocytosine therapy. Antimicrob Agents Chemother. 1977;11(2):244–47.

172 **Schroter GPJ et al.** Fungus infections after liver transplantation. Ann Surg. 1977;186(1):115–22.

173 **Diasio RB et al.** Evidence for conversion of 5-fluorocytosine to 5-fluorouracil in humans: possible factor in 5-fluorocytosine clinical toxicity. Antimicrob Agents Chemother. 1978;14(6):903–8.

174 **Stamm AM et al.** Toxicity of amphotericin B plus flucytosine in 194 patients with cyptococcal meningitis. Am J Med. 1987;83:236–42.

175 **Craven PC, Graybill JR.** Combination of oral flucytosine and ketoconazole as therapy for experimental cryptococcal meningitis. J Infect Dis. 1984;149:584–90.

176 **Finley R et al.** Fluconazole penetration into the human prostate. Antimicrob Agents Chemother. 1995;39(2):553–55.

177 **Daneshmend TK, Warnock DW.** Clinical pharmacokinetics of systemic antifungal drugs. Clin Pharmacokinet. 1983;8:17–42.

178 **Daneshmend TK, Warnock DW.** Clinical pharmacokinetics of ketoconazole. Clin Pharmacokinet. 1988;14:13–34.

179 **Louria DB.** Some aspects of the absorption, distribution and excretion of amphotericin B in man. Antibiot Med Clin Therapy. 1958;5(5):295–301.

180 **VanCauteren H et al.** Itraconazole pharmacologic studies in animals and humans. Rev Infect Dis. 1987;9(Suppl. 1):S43–S46.

181 **Hardin TC et al.** Pharmacokinetics of itraconazole following oral administration to normal volunteers. Antimicrob Agents Chemother. 1988;32:1310–313.

182 **Tatro DS, ed.** Drug Interaction Facts. St. Louis, MO. Facts and Comparisons, 1994.

183 **Dupont Pharmaceuticals.** Coumadin package insert. Wilmington, DE: 1994 January.

184 **Tucker RM et al.** Interaction of azoles with rifampin, phenytoin, and carbamazepine: *in vitro* and clinical observations. Clin Infect Dis. 1992;14:165–74.

185 **Grant SM, Glissold SP.** Itraconazole. Drugs. 1989;37:310–44.

186 **Present CA.** Amphotericin B induction of sensitivity to adriamycin, BCNU plus cyclophosphamide in human neoplasia. Ann Intern Med. 1977;86:47–9.

187 **Antoniskis D, Larsen RA.** Acute, rapidly progressive renal failure with simultaneous use of amphotericin B and pentamidine. Antimicrob Agents Chemother. 1990;34:470–72.

188 **McNalty RM et al.** Transient increase in plasma quinidine concentrations during ketoconazole-quinidine therapy. Clin Pharm. 1989;8:222–25.

189 **Personal communication: Pfizer Pharmaceuticals.**

190 **Wright DG et al.** Lethal pulmonary reactions associated with the combination use of amphotericin B and leukocyte transfusions. N Engl J Med. 1981;304:1185–189.

191 **Dutcher JP et al.** Granulocyte transfusion therapy and amphotericin B adverse reactions? Am J Hematol. 1989;31:102–8.

192 **Stevens DA.** *Coccidioides immitis.* In: Mandell GL et al., eds. Principles and Practice of Infectious Diseases. New York: Churchill Livingstone; 1990:1989–999.

193 **Peter JB.** Use and Interpretation of Tests in Medical Microbiology. 3rd ed. Santa Monica, CA: Specialty Laboratories; 1992.

194 **Galgiani JN et al.** New serologic tests for early detection of coccidioidomycosis. J Infect Dis. 1991;163:671–74.

Viral Infections

Milap C Nahata

Herpes Simplex Virus (HSV) Infections 70-1
  Herpes Encephalitis 70-1
    Clinical presentation 70-2
    Treatment: acyclovir 70-2
      Versus vidarabine 70-2
      Pharmacokinetics (See Tables 70.1 to 70.3) 70-2
      Adverse effects 70-3
      Conversion to oral therapy 70-3
  Neonatal Herpes 70-4
    Risk factors 70-4
    Treatment: vidarabine 70-4
      Administration 70-5
      Adverse effects 70-5
  Oral-Facial Herpes 70-5
    Indications for antiviral treatment 70-5
    Acyclovir 70-5
      Treatment 70-5
      Resistance 70-6
  Herpes Keratitis 70-6
    Drug of choice 70-6
Varicella Zoster Infections 70-6
  Chickenpox 70-6
    Clinical presentation 70-6
    Antiviral treatment 70-6

    Supportive treatment 70-7
  Shingles 70-7
    Antiviral therapy in immunocompromised patients .. 70-7
      Acyclovir toxicity 70-7
Cytomegalovirus (CMV) Infections 70-7
  Treatment 70-7
    Ganciclovir 70-7
      Combination therapy with immunoglobulin 70-8
    Prophylaxis 70-8
Influenza 70-8
  Clinical Presentation 70-9
    Amantadine therapy 70-9
      Adverse effects 70-9
  Prevention 70-9
    Influenza vaccines (Also see Table 70.4) 70-10
    Amantadine 70-10
    Rimantadine 70-10
    Emergence of resistance 70-10
Respiratory Syncytial Virus (RSV) Infections 70-10
  Clinical Presentation and Ribavirin Therapy 70-10
    Administration 70-10
    Adverse effects 70-11
Hantavirus Infections 70-11

Viral infections are common causes of human disease. It has been estimated that 60% of illnesses in developed countries occur due to viruses, compared to only 15% resulting from bacteria. These may include the common cold, chicken pox, measles, mumps, influenza, bronchitis, gastroenteritis, hepatitis, poliomyelitis, rabies, and numerous diseases due to the herpes virus. Up to 90% of the U.S. population is affected each year by an upper respiratory tract infection, the common cold, or influenza.[1] Over 60 million patients visit physicians each year with symptoms of upper respiratory tract infection.[2] Although a vast majority of these patients have a self-limiting illness, influenza can cause significant mortality, particularly in the elderly. For example, in the 1918 to 1919 world-wide epidemic, 500 million people became infected and 20 million died from influenza.[3]

Influenza vaccines can reduce the impact of this illness in susceptible populations. However, there are no available vaccines to prevent a variety of other potentially severe viral infections including herpes encephalitis, neonatal herpes, disseminated varicella-zoster, and respiratory syncytial virus bronchiolitis. Hence, the need for safe and effective antiviral agents is obvious.

Substantial progress has been made in antiviral chemotherapy as a result of advances in our knowledge of molecular virology and genetic engineering. New antiviral agents can be designed to inhibit functions specific to viruses; this maximizes their therapeutic benefits while minimizing adverse effects to the host cell.

Current technology also permits rapid diagnosis of viral diseases. It is now possible to make a specific diagnosis of several viral illnesses within hours to a few days; previously, specific diagnosis took days to months. This has made it possible to select an appropriate antiviral drug early for the treatment of acute viral infection.

The primary objective of this chapter is to describe the etiology, pathogenesis, and treatment of common viral infections. Specific case presentations will illustrate the optimal use of antiviral drugs in patients with viral infections.

Herpes Simplex Virus (HSV) Infections

Herpes virus is an extremely important pathogen in man. It causes a variety of illnesses including herpes encephalitis and neonatal herpes which are associated with significant mortality and sequelae and genital herpes which causes substantial pain and emotional suffering. Fortunately, antiviral drugs can decrease morbidity, mortality, and duration of symptoms in most cases.

Herpes Encephalitis

HSV encephalitis is the most common sporadic viral infection of the central nervous system (CNS). The estimated incidence is about 2.3 cases per million population per year, although this may be an underestimate because of the difficulty in diagnosing this disease. It can occur at any age and is characterized by acute onset of fever, headache, decreased consciousness, and seizures. Any pediatric patient with fever and altered behavior should be evaluated carefully. This is a devastating infection because without treatment, the mortality approaches 70%; only 10% of patients recover enough to lead normal lives.[4,5]

HSV_1 is the etiologic agent in most patients with herpes encephalitis, but HSV_2 is more common in newborn infants. The infection may be localized to the brain or involve cutaneous and mucous membranes. Although any area of the brain can be involved, the orbital region of the frontal lobes and portions of the temporal lobes are affected frequently.

Herpes encephalitis often is difficult to diagnose and is always a very serious disease. A computerized tomography (CT) scan usually is indicated to rule out other conditions including brain abscess or other space-occupying lesions which may produce similar symptoms. The CT or radionucleotide scans may be unremarkable early in the course of the disease.

Cerebrospinal fluid (CSF) examination usually reveals pleocytosis (predominately lymphocytes) with 50 to 2000 white blood cells (WBCs)/mm³; polymorphonuclear leukocytosis and red blood cells (RBCs) also may be seen. Many patients have an elevated protein level in the CSF (median: 80 mg/dL). The presence of antibody to HSV_1 is useful in making the diagnosis.

The electroencephalogram (EEG) is the most sensitive but least specific test. There usually are CT or brain scan abnormalities, but these may take a day or two longer to appear. The EEG, CT, and brain scan findings compatible with HSV encephalitis can be mimicked by other conditions, and a brain biopsy is required to clearly establish the diagnosis. Rapid diagnosis of herpes encephalitis by a polymerase chain-reaction assay of HSV DNA in the cerebrospinal fluid is available at certain medical centers. This is a highly sensitive, specific, and rapid method for the diagnosis of herpes encephalitis.[124]

Clinical Presentation

1. R.F., a 7-year-old boy, was seen in the emergency room (ER) following a seizure. Over the previous 3 days, R.F. had a decreased appetite, headache, fever (101–102 °F) and was lethargic and disoriented. The leukocyte count was 13,000/mm³ with a shift to the left. Ceftriaxone (50 mg/kg IV Q 12 hr) and dexamethasone (0.15 mg/kg IV Q 6 hr) were initiated for presumed bacterial meningitis. Phenobarbital (100 mg/day IV) was given for seizure control. Examination of the CSF was normal and no bacteria could be identified. Over the next 2 days, R.F. became increasingly less responsive and lapsed into a coma. A CT scan of the brain revealed decreased density in a localized area of the left temporal lobe. Because of a high suspicion of herpes encephalitis, a brain biopsy was performed. Acyclovir 10 mg/kg (200 mg) IV Q 8 hr was started immediately after the procedure. HSV_1 was isolated from the biopsy specimen 24 hours later.

What findings in R.F. are consistent with the diagnosis of herpes encephalitis? Why was a brain biopsy performed? [SI units: leukocytes 13 × 10⁻⁹]

Low-grade fever, headache, lethargy, and disorientation are common features of herpes encephalitis. As illustrated by R.F., CSF examination can be normal in some patients. The CT scan showing decreased density in the left temporal lobe is suggestive of herpes encephalitis. Finally, a negative CSF culture also suggests the absence of a bacterial infection. These findings, however, cannot establish the diagnosis of herpes encephalitis.

Brain biopsy is the most definitive diagnostic procedure for herpes encephalitis. Biopsy is particularly important because other treatable conditions, including cryptococcosis and aspergillosis, can be missed by other diagnostic procedures. The morbidity (bleeding) due to brain biopsy is low (1%) in medical centers with extensive experience. As expected, a specific pathogen (HSV_1) was isolated from the biopsy specimen in R.F.

Treatment: Acyclovir

2. Acyclovir versus Vidarabine. Is acyclovir the treatment of choice for herpes encephalitis?

Two recent studies comparing acyclovir and vidarabine have demonstrated that intravenous acyclovir, 10 mg/kg every eight hours for ten days, clearly is the treatment of choice in patients with herpes encephalitis.[6,7] The mortality was 19% to 28% in the acyclovir-treated group and 50% to 54% in the vidarabine-treated group. Of great importance was the fact that nearly one-half of the acyclovir-treated patients returned to normal life compared to only 13% to 15% of those treated with vidarabine.[6,7]

Acyclovir-resistant herpes is not an important consideration in the management of herpes encephalitis in most patients; however, it can be important in Acquired Immunodeficiency Syndrome (AIDS) patients who receive multiple repeated courses of acyclovir [see Chapter 68: Human Immunodeficiency Virus Infection (HIV)].

3. Acyclovir Pharmacokinetics. Is the acyclovir dosage regimen appropriate based upon the serum concentrations required for the inhibition of viral replication? How should the effect of acyclovir be monitored in R.F.?

In adults receiving single IV doses of acyclovir, 2.5 to 5 mg/kg, a peak plasma concentration of 3.4 to 6.8 µg/mL has been reported.[8,9] The mean peak and trough plasma concentrations were 9.9 and 0.7 µg/mL following multiple doses of 5 mg/kg every eight hours.[10] At larger IV doses of 10 to 15 mg/kg, the peak plasma concentrations of acyclovir have ranged from 10 to 30 µg/mL.[11]

Limited data are available on acyclovir pharmacokinetics in pediatric patients, particularly premature infants. Acyclovir pharmacokinetics for children over one year of age are similar to those of adults.[12] In neonates receiving acyclovir, 5 to 15 mg/kg IV every

Table 70.1		Pharmacokinetic Properties of Antiviral Drugs		
	Dose Used in Study	Peak Serum Concentration (µg/mL)	% Recovered Unchanged in Urine	Elimination Half-life (hr)
Acyclovir[11,22,23,93–95]	5 mg/kg IV	9.8	52–82	1.8–3.1
Vidarabine[a,29,96,97]	10–20 mg/kg IV	0.2–0.4	60	3.3
Ganciclovir[b,93,97,98,107]	2.5–5 mg/kg IV	4.8–12.4	91–99	1.8–4.7
Foscarnet[154]	90 mg/kg IV	297–1775	80–90	2–8
Amantadine[c,62,63,99–102]	100–300 mg/day	0.2–0.6	52–88	15–20
Rimantadine[d,148–151]	100–200 mg/day	0.11–0.42	8	24–37
Ribavirin[103]	0.82 mg/kg x 20 hr	1–3	—	6.5–11

a Peak concentration of its less active metabolite ranged from 3–6 µg/mL.
b CSF concentration ranged from 24%–67% of plasma concentration.
c Tracheal concentration 1 µg/mL; CSF concentration about 60% of plasma concentration.
d Serum concentration tenfold lower and nasal wash concentration 1000-fold higher after administration of aerosolized rimantadine, 20 µg/L of air than oral rimantadine, 200 mg.[149]

Table 70.2		Clinical Pharmacokinetics of Antiviral Drugs			
Drug	Type of Patients	Total Clearance	Volume of Distribution	Elimination Half-life (hr)	Comments
Acyclovir[a,9,12,14,22,104,105]	Adults	307 mL/min/1.73 m^2	50 L/1.73 m^2	2.5–3.0	Use 100% of recommended dose but extend dosage interval to 12 and 24 hr if Cl_{Cr} ranges from 25–50 and 10–25 mL/min/1.73 m^2, respectively; use 50% of recommended dose Q 24 hr if Cl_{Cr} ranges from 0–10 mL/min/1.73 m^2
	Neonates	98–122 mL/min/1.73 m^2	24–30 L/1.73 m^2	3.2–4.1	
Amantadine[a,63,106]	Adults	2.5–10.5 L/hr	1.5–6.1 L/kg	22.6–37.7	Adjust doses in renal failure: 200 mg on Day 1 and then 100 mg/day if Cl_{Cr} 30–50; 200 mg on Day 1 and then 100 mg QOD if Cl_{Cr} 15–29; 200 mg Q 7 days if Cl_{Cr} <15 mL/min/1.73 m^2
Ganciclovir[107,108]	Adults	117–363 mL/min/1.73 m^2	29–45 L/1.73 m^2	1.8–4.7	Adjust doses in renal failure: 5 mg/kg/12 hr if Cl_{Cr} ≥80; 2.5 mg/kg/12 hr if Cl_{Cr} 50–79; 2.5 mg/kg/24 hr if Cl_{Cr} 25–49; 1.25 mg/kg/24 hr if Cl_{Cr} <25 mL/min/1.73 m^2
	Neonates	63–350 mL/hr/kg	0.39–1.3 L/kg	1.6–7.1	
Foscarnet[153]	Adults	0.11–0.2 L/hr/kg	0.3–0.6 L/kg	1.3–3.4	Use dosing guide available with the product literature to adjust foscarnet dose based upon Cl_{Cr}
Rimantadine[148,151]	Adults	20–48 L/hr	25 L/kg	29–37	Since undergoes extensive metabolism, dose may have to be adjusted in patients with severe liver disease. Dose adjustment may also be necessary in elderly and in those with severe renal failure (Cl_{Cr} ≤10 mL/min). Manufacturer recommends 50% reduction in dose in such cases

[a] Bioavailability for oral acyclovir ranges from 0.15–0.30 and for amantadine from 0.86–0.90.

eight hours, the peak and trough serum concentrations have ranged from 3.1 to 38 µg/mL and 0.23 to 30 µg/mL, respectively.[13,14] Acyclovir distributes into all tissues with the highest concentrations occurring in the kidney (ten times the plasma concentration) and the lowest concentrations in the CSF (25% to 70% of plasma concentration).[11] (See Tables 70.1 and 70.2.) For R.F. the regimen is appropriate. Although the pharmacokinetics in children over 1 year old are similar to adults, higher doses are needed in view of its relatively poor distribution into CSF. (See Table 70.3.)

Although the relationship between the *in vitro* susceptibility of herpes simplex virus to antiviral drugs and clinical response has not been established, these serum levels are adequate to inhibit viral replication. HSV_1 clinical isolates have a mean ID_{50} of 0.46 µg/mL,[15] the concentration which produces 50% inhibition of the viral cytopathic effect. The clinical status of patients is monitored for efficacy of acyclovir. Most patients begin to improve within 48 hours after starting treatment.

4. Adverse Effects. **What type of adverse effects can occur due to IV acyclovir therapy in R.F.? How should these be monitored and how can they be minimized?**

Acyclovir is a relatively safe drug. Renal toxicity associated with IV acyclovir, however, should be considered. Blood urea nitrogen (BUN) and serum creatinine (SrCr) can increase in about 10% of patients.[16] These changes appear to be reversible. Acyclovir is relatively insoluble: maximum urine solubility at 37 °C is 1.3 mg/mL. Therefore, a transient crystal nephropathy may occur at high acyclovir concentrations.[16,17] Since dehydration predisposes patients to high urinary concentrations, it has been recommended

that 1 L of fluid be administered with each gram of IV acyclovir over one hour to prevent its crystallization or deposition in the renal collecting tubules in adults.[18]

Nausea, lightheadedness, and thirst have been observed in patients receiving IV acyclovir for acute herpes zoster,[19] although some of these side effects may have been related to dehydration. In one child with chickenpox, both nausea and vomiting have been associated with intravenous acyclovir therapy.[20] Lethargy, agitation, tremor, and disorientation have been reported in bone marrow transplant patients receiving multiple drugs, including intrathecal methotrexate.[21] The neurologic side effects appear to be uncommon and reversible.[18] Transient elevation of liver enzymes may occur.[6] Finally, intravenous acyclovir can cause phlebitis and pain at the site of injection.[16] This can be minimized by administering acyclovir at a concentration of about 5 mg/mL (maximum: 7 mg/mL).

5. Conversion to Oral Therapy. **After 7 days of IV acyclovir, R.F. is alert, responsive, actively moving about, and eating a normal diet. The intern suggests switching him to oral acyclovir and discontinuing IV therapy. Is this appropriate?**

Oral therapy is inappropriate for R.F. for one reason. Based upon studies in adults, the absorption of acyclovir after oral administration is variable, slow, and incomplete. The bioavailability of acyclovir is low (F = 0.15 to 0.30) and decreases with increasing doses.[22] The mean peak plasma concentration, occurring at 1.5 to 2 hours, has ranged from only 0.15 to 1.3 µg/mL following multiple acyclovir doses of 200 to 600 mg every four hours.[22,23] Thus, the concentrations of acyclovir in the cerebrospinal fluid may be inadequate for R.F.

Table 70.3		Recommended Drugs for Various Viral Infections		
Disease	Drug	Dose (Age Group)	Route	Duration
Herpes encephalitis	Acyclovir (Zovirax)	*Adults:* 10 mg/kg/8 hr *6 months–12 years:* 500 mg/m²/8 hr	IV	10 days
Neonatal herpes	Acyclovir (Zovirax)	10 mg/kg/8 hr	IV	10–21 days
Mucocutaneous herpes (Immunocompromised patients)	Acyclovir (Zovirax)	*Adults:* 5 mg/kg/8 hr *<12 years:* 250 mg/m²/8 hr	IV	7 days
Varicella zoster (Immunocompromised patients)	Acyclovir (Zovirax)	*Adults:* 10 mg/kg/8 hr *Children:* 500 mg/m²/8 hr	IV IV	7 days
Herpes zoster (Normal host)	Acyclovir (Zovirax)	800 mg five times/day	PO	7–10 days
Varicella (Chickenpox)	Acyclovir (Zovirax)	*Adults and Children >2 years:* 20 mg/kg (≤800 mg) QID	PO	5 days
Herpes keratitis	Trifluridine 1% ophthalmic solution (Viroptic)	1 drop Q 2 hr; then 1 drop Q 4 hr	Topical	Until corneal ulcer re-epithelialized; 7 days
Cytomegalovirus retinitis (Immunocompromised patients)	Ganciclovir (Cytovene)	5 mg/kg/12 hr; then 5 mg/kg/day or 6 mg/kg, 5 days/week	IV	14–21 days for induction; maintenance
Influenza A	Amantadine[a] (Symmetrel)	*Adults and Children >9 years:* 100 mg BID *Children 1–9 years:* 4.4–8.8 mg/kg/day but less than 150 mg/day	PO	10 days (treatment), 14–21 days (protection with vaccine), 90 days (protection without vaccine)
	Rimantadine (Flumadine)	*Adults and Children ≥10 years:* 100 mg BID *Children 1–10 years:* 5 mg/kg/day (<150 mg/day)	PO	7 days (treatment), up to 6 weeks for prophylaxis (not approved for treatment in children)
Respiratory syncytial virus	Ribavirin (Virazole)	6 gm in 300 mL over 12–18 hr/day	Inhalation	3–7 days

[a] Foscarnet, 40 mg/kg IV Q 8 hr is recommended for acyclovir-resistant herpes simplex virus or varicella-zoster virus; and 60 mg/kg IV Q 8 hr for cytomegalovirus retinitis as an alternative to ganciclovir.

Neonatal Herpes

Most neonates acquire herpes from the infected genital secretions of the mother at the time of delivery. The incidence ranges from one in 3500 to 5000 deliveries per year in the U.S. The infection can present in one of three forms: localized to the skin, eye, and mouth (45%); encephalitis (35%); or disseminated disease (25%). The mortality has ranged from 15% in those with CNS involvement to 50% in those with disseminated disease.[125] Neonatal HSV_1 infections also may be acquired after birth through contact with immediate family members with symptomatic or asymptomatic oral-labial HSV_1 infection or from nosocomial transmission. When the virus is transmitted by the mother, clinical evidence of infection in the neonate usually is present 5 to 17 days after birth. Although skin vesicles are the hallmark of infection, at least 20% of neonates never have skin lesions.[25] In 70% of patients, the disease may progress from isolated skin lesions to involve other organs, including the lungs, liver, spleen, central nervous system, and eyes.

Diagnosis of this infection can be made by direct fluorescent antibody examination of epithelial cells from the infant or the mother. Examination of the base of a vesicular lesion may show giant cells and intranuclear inclusions, which are characteristic of HSV infections. Serologic test results also are helpful in making a specific diagnosis of neonatal herpes.

Risk Factors

6. S.P., an 18-year-old female, was admitted to labor and delivery with premature rupture of the membranes. Four hours later, S.P. vaginally delivered a 2.5 kg baby boy, R.P., who had an estimated gestational age of 33 weeks. Twenty-four hours after delivery, S.P. reported the onset of vesicles in the genital area; she had a history of previous episodes of genital herpes. The last infection was during her first trimester of pregnancy. Is R.P. at risk of developing herpes infection?

R.P. is at risk of acquiring herpes infection because the mother had genital herpes during the first trimester and because he was delivered vaginally rather than by cesarean section. The risk of newborn acquisition from infected mothers with primary disease is about 35%; that from mothers with reactivation is 3%.

Treatment: Vidarabine

7. Ten days after birth, R.P. developed poor feeding patterns, irritability, and respiratory distress. Three days later, skin lesions appeared. What is a Food and Drug Administration (FDA)-approved drug that could be used for R.P.?

At this time, vidarabine is the only antiviral drug approved by the FDA for the management of neonatal herpes. R.P. could receive intravenous vidarabine (15 mg/kg/day) because it has reduced the mortality of this infection from about 74% to 38%.[26] However, in another study, the progression of severe disease occurred in 24% of patients after the administration of the FDA-approved dose of 15 mg/kg/day, and in 4% of those receiving 30 mg/kg/day.[125]

Vidarabine (adenine arabinoside; Ara-A; Vira-A) was the first useful antiviral drug for the treatment of systemic herpes infections. Its spectrum of activity is similar to that of acyclovir. Although the exact mechanism of action of vidarabine is unclear, it inhibits viral DNA synthesis at concentrations much lower than those required to inhibit DNA synthesis in the host cell.[27,28]

Preliminary results of studies comparing vidarabine and acyclovir indicate that both are equally effective and safe.[123] Although more studies are needed to determine the relative efficacy and safety of these drugs, most clinicians prefer to use acyclovir because it is equally efficacious and easier to administer.

8. Administration. The intern has prescribed vidarabine for R.P. What precautions should be taken for drug preparation and administration?

Vidarabine should be administered intravenously over 12 hours each day for about ten days. Intramuscular and subcutaneous administration are unsuitable because the drug's poor solubility results in pain at the site of injection and inadequate absorption. One of the major problems associated with the intravenous use of this drug is its poor solubility. One liter of IV fluid is required to solubilize 450 mg of vidarabine, which means 2 to 2.5 L of fluid may be necessary each day to administer an average dose (15 mg/kg/day). This can pose serious problems in patients with CNS infections and cerebral edema. Warming the diluent to 35 to 40 °C may facilitate the dissolution of vidarabine. A final in-line filter is recommended for drug administration.[29]

9. Adverse Effects. What adverse effects may occur due to vidarabine therapy?

Vidarabine is relatively nontoxic during a typical ten-day course of therapy, particularly in neonates; the side effects may include nausea and vomiting. Other adverse effects include tremors, myoclonus, dizziness, jitteriness, hallucinations, and ataxia. These usually occur in older patients receiving doses higher than 15 to 20 mg/kg/day of vidarabine or in patients with renal insufficiency.[29–33] Theophylline and allopurinol can inhibit the xanthine oxidase metabolism of the major metabolite of vidarabine, arabinosyl hypoxanthine. Because this metabolite also is active, patients receiving theophylline concomitantly may be at increased risk for neurotoxicity.[34,35]

Oral-Facial Herpes

Both primary and recurrent oral-facial HSV_1 infections can be asymptomatic. Gingivostomatitis and pharyngitis are the most frequent clinical manifestations of a first episode of HSV_1 infection, and recurrent herpes labialis is most commonly due to reactivated HSV infection. Clinical features include fever, malaise, myalgias, inability to eat, and irritability. It should be noted that immunocompromised patients with oral-facial herpes have severe pain, extensive lesions, and prolonged viral shedding; thus, they are considered candidates for antiviral therapy.

Herpes labialis (cold sores) is the most common oral-facial HSV infection. Clinical features include pain or paresthesia and erythematous or papular lesions followed by vesiculation and swelling. These lesions usually crust and heal in the next few days. Viral cultures often are positive within two or three days. Rapid diagnosis can be made by visualizing viral particles in vesicular fluid with electron microscopy or fluorescent antibody staining of cells from vesicles.

Indications for Antiviral Treatment

10. M.K., a 26-year-old male, developed pain and erythematous skin lesions on his face and around his mouth over a 2-day period following contact with another patient with active lesions. Over the next 2 days, significant swelling was noted. M.K. had no previous history of cold sores or any other illnesses; should he be treated with antiviral drugs?

Most patients with herpes labialis have a self-limiting benign course. Antiviral drugs (e.g., acyclovir) are indicated only when the patients have primary infection, underlying illnesses, or a compromised immune system which may lead to prolonged illness or dissemination.

Table 70.4	Adverse Effects of Approved Antiviral Drugs
Drug	**Adverse Effects**[a]
Acyclovir	Local irritation and phlebitis (9%); ↑ SrCr and BUN (5%–10%); N/V (7%); itching and rash (2%); ↑ liver transaminases (1%–2%); CNS toxicity (1%)
Amantadine	Nausea, dizziness (lightheadedness), and insomnia (5%–10%); depression, anxiety, irritability, hallucination, confusion, dry mouth, constipation, ataxia, headache, peripheral edema, and orthostatic hypotension (1%–5%)
Ganciclovir	Neutropenia (40%); thrombocytopenia (20%); CNS toxicity (5%); anemia, fever, rash, ↑ liver transaminases (each 2%); phlebitis, N/V, ↑ SrCr or BUN
Foscarnet	Fever (65%), nausea (47%), anemia (33%), diarrhea (30%), abnormal renal function (27%), vomiting (26%), headache (26%), and seizure (10%)
Ribavirin[b]	Worsening of respiratory status, bacterial pneumonia, pneumothorax, apnea, ventilator dependence; cardiac arrest, hypotension; rash and conjunctivitis
Rimantadine	CNS (insomnia, dizziness, headache, nervousness, fatigue) and GI (N/V, anorexia, dry mouth, abdominal pain) (each 1%–3%)
Trifluridine	Burning or stinging upon instillation (4.6%); palpebral edema (2.8%); keratopathy, hypersensitivity reaction, stromal edema, hyperemia, ↑ intraocular pressure
Vidarabine[b]	Anorexia, N/V, diarrhea; ↓ in Hgb, Hct, WBC count, and platelet count; CNS toxicity; ↑ liver transaminases; rash, pruritus, and irritation at injection site

[a] SrCr = Serum Creatinine; BUN = Blood urea nitrogen; CNS = Central nervous system; GI = Gastrointestinal; Hgb = Hemoglobin; Hct = Hematocrit; N/V = Nausea and vomiting; WBC = White blood cell.
[b] Incidence unknown.

Although ice, ether, lysine, silver nitrate, and smallpox vaccine have been used to treat cold sores, no data support their efficacy. Aspirin and acetaminophen sometimes are suggested for symptomatic relief.

11. P.L., a 16-year-old male diagnosed with acute lymphocytic leukemia 8 months ago, now is admitted for a bone marrow transplant. Admission laboratory tests reveal that he has antibodies against HSV_1 and that 4 months ago during a course of chemotherapy he developed an oral-facial herpes infection. What is the significance of these findings for P.L. who is about to undergo a bone marrow transplant?

Immunosuppressed patients have more frequent and severe mucocutaneous HSV infections. Therefore, IV acyclovir should be considered to suppress the reactivation of oral-facial HSV infections.[36,37]

Acyclovir

12. Treatment. P.L. did not receive antiviral therapy. Two weeks later, he developed oral-mucosal and skin lesions on his face which were painful and associated with malaise. HSV was identified from the lesion by an immunofluorescence technique. What is the treatment of choice for P.L.?

At our institution, we use IV acyclovir 5 mg/kg every eight hours for two to three weeks until lesions are healed, and then oral acyclovir 200 mg three times daily for about six months. In patients with marrow transplants and culture-proven recurrent mucocutaneous herpes simplex, oral acyclovir (400 mg five times daily for ten days) is significantly more effective than placebo in reducing pain, virus shedding, new lesion formation, and lesion healing time.[38] Furthermore, oral acyclovir is as effective as, or more effective than, IV acyclovir in marrow recipients[7] or topical acyclovir in immunosuppressed patients.[39] The latter group includes patients receiving corticosteroids, leukemic patients, and renal allograft patients.[39]

13. N.B., a 43-year-old female, experiences 8–10 cold sores/year. These typically are preceded by "colds" or sun exposure. She requests a prescription for acyclovir to "prevent" cold sores when she feels one coming on. What is the role of acyclovir in immunocompetent patients with recurrent herpes labialis?

Acyclovir is not approved for use in such cases. However, limited studies indicate that it may be effective in certain situations. Oral acyclovir, 400 mg five times daily for five days, was found to be more effective than placebo in reducing mean duration of pain and healing time (loss of crust) in immunocompetent patients with a history of one to five episodes of herpes labialis per year.[126] In another study of immunocompetent patients with six or more episodes of herpes labialis, oral acyclovir, 400 mg twice daily for four months, was more effective than placebo in decreasing the number of recurrences.[127] Topical acyclovir (ointment or cream) was no more effective than placebo.[128,129]

14. Resistance. How should an acyclovir-resistant HSV infection be treated?

Foscarnet, 40 mg/kg IV every eight hours, was found to be more effective and less toxic than vidarabine, 15 mg/kg/day IV, in patients with AIDS and mucocutaneous herpetic lesions unresponsive to IV acyclovir. HSV isolates resistant to acyclovir *in vitro*, however, were sensitive to both foscarnet and vidarabine.[130]

Herpes Keratitis

Drug of Choice

15. Z.F., a 20-year-old male, complained of acute pain, blurred vision, swelling of the conjunctival tissue around the cornea (chemosis), and vesicles on the eyelids. The conjunctivitis and characteristic dendritic lesions of the cornea were consistent with the diagnosis of herpes keratitis. What is the antiviral drug of choice?

HSV infections of the eye are the most frequent cause of corneal blindness in the U.S. HSV_1 is the common pathogen in adults and children beyond the neonatal period. Z.F. should be treated with a topical antiviral drug because drug therapy has been shown to enhance healing.[40,41] There are three approved drugs available to treat this condition: trifluridine, idoxuridine, and vidarabine.

Trifluridine is at least as effective as vidarabine[42,43] and superior to idoxuridine.[44,45] Trifluridine is considered the drug of choice because it is thought to be more effective than vidarabine when ameboid ulcers are present[43] and idoxuridine is associated with more local adverse effects than vidarabine.[46] Acyclovir ointment (5%) has been shown to be as effective as vidarabine ointment (3%),[47] but the ophthalmic acyclovir ointment is unavailable in the U.S.

Varicella Zoster Infections

Chickenpox

Chickenpox is a common childhood infection. Approximately 3.5 million cases occur per year in the U.S. and 60% of cases occur in children between five and nine years of age; 80% occur in those under ten. Although it is a benign disease in most patients, complications and mortality (7/10,000 cases) can occur in patients under 5 and over 20 years of age, and in immunocompromised patients.

This is a highly contagious disease. Children are considered infectious from two days before the onset of rash until all vesicles have crusted (usually four to six days after onset of rash). After household exposure, over 90% of susceptible individuals become infected. Thus, history can assist in making a diagnosis. A smear of cells scraped from the lesions will show multinucleated giant cells. Viruses also can be identified in vesicular lesions by electron microscopy or antigen can be detected by counter-current immunoelectrophoresis. Chickenpox is a primary varicella zoster infection, whereas herpes zoster (shingles) is caused by the reactivation of the varicella zoster virus (VZV). (See Chapter 95: Pediatric Considerations for chickenpox vaccination.)

Clinical Presentation

16. A.V., a 10-year-old boy, was admitted to the hospital for treatment and evaluation of possible recurrent chickenpox with progressive lesions. According to both his mother and private physician, he had a mild case of chickenpox at age 4 years. At the time of admission, A.V. had a 10-day history of progressive vesicular and pustular lesions, which began on the neck and spread to the back, trunk, extremities, and face. Although he had been febrile (up to 40.5 °C orally) over the past 3 days, temperature on admission was 37 °C. A.V. had episodes of vomiting during the 4 days before admission.

On admission, he was alert, cooperative, and well-oriented, but had overt ataxia with abnormal cerebellar signs. Lesions classic VZV infection were extensive and confluent over the face, neck, chest, and back. Stages of lesions varied from tiny thin-walled vesicles with an erythematous base to umbilicated vesicles. Few crusted lesions were present. Blood analysis revealed a BUN of 9 mg/dL, SrCr of 0.2 mg/dL, and slightly elevated serum transaminase levels (AST 65 IU/L and ALT 122 IU/L). Due to the possibility of cerebellar involvement with varicella zoster infection and possible underlying immunodeficiency, therapy with acyclovir 550 mg IV Q 8 hr (1500 mg/m²/day) was instituted. Diphenhydramine also was prescribed for itching, but A.V. required only 2 doses on the first hospital day.

New lesions were noted on the second day of acyclovir therapy, but by the third day no new lesions appeared and previous lesions were healing. The ataxia improved daily. He was discharged on day 7 with no further complaints of nausea and vomiting. Follow-up serologic evaluation demonstrated a fourfold rise in the optical density for the VZV enzyme-linked immunosorbent assay (ELISA) from day 20 to day 60 after the onset of infection. These results suggested primary VZV infection. Is the use of acyclovir in A.V. appropriate? [SI units: BUN 3.213 mmol/L; SrCr 15.25 μmol/L; AST 1.084 μkat/L; ALT 2.034 μkat/L]

Antiviral Treatment

Neonates, adults, immunocompromised hosts, patients with progressive varicella, and those with extracutaneous complications can benefit from specific antiviral therapy. Acyclovir and vidarabine are the two available agents. One study compared IV acyclovir (500 mg/m² every eight hours) and vidarabine (10 mg/kg/day) in severely immunocompromised patients with varicella. Acyclovir was more effective than vidarabine in preventing dissemination of VZV infection, accelerating cutaneous healing, and decreasing fever and pain.[48] Thus, the use of IV acyclovir was appropriate in A.V.

17. C.J., an 8-year-old boy, developed a case of chickenpox and was kept home from school. Four days later, his 15-year-old brother, K.J., began to exhibit similar symptoms. What is the role of acyclovir in immunocompetent patients with chickenpox? Should C.J. or K.J. be treated with acyclovir?

Two studies in children (2 to 12 years of age) have shown that oral acyclovir, 20 mg/kg (when initiated within 24 hours of disease onset) four times daily for five days, was more effective than placebo in accelerating healing and decreasing the formation of new lesions, fever, and itching. However, acyclovir produced only modest benefits (usually healing one day sooner than placebo) and was not effective in reducing the complications of varicella.[131,132] Thus, acyclovir is not indicated for C.J.

Adolescents and adults are more likely to develop complications (e.g., pneumonia, encephalitis) than children. Acyclovir, 800 mg orally four times daily for five days in adolescents and 800 mg orally five times daily for five days in adults (initiated within 24 hours of disease onset), was more effective than placebo in decreasing the number of lesions, time for healing, fever, and itching. The effect of acyclovir on complications could not be assessed.[133,134] Thus, acyclovir therapy should be considered in those at increased risk of severe chickenpox, for example, those like K.J. older than 14 years of age or those with chronic respiratory or skin disease.[135]

Supportive Treatment

18. What is the role of supportive treatment in A.V. and C.J.?

Cool baths and application of calamine or other topical antipruritic agents may decrease itching. In severe cases, a systemic antipruritic/antihistamine preparation may be useful since some degree of sedation may be desired. In A.V., aspirin should not be used because Reye's syndrome has been associated with the use of salicylates in chickenpox or flu-like illness. (See Chapter 95: Pediatric Considerations.)

Shingles

Antiviral Therapy in Immunocompromised Patients

19. R.F. is a 68-year-old woman seen in the ER with a chief complaint of vesicles on her face associated with severe pain. She has a past medical history of polymyalgia rheumatica and possible temporal arteritis causing headaches that generally are responsive to steroids. She had been having increasing headaches on the right side of her forehead 5 days before admission. Two days before admission, her family physician increased the dose of prednisone from 30 mg/day to 60 mg/day. Vesicles developed on her face 1 day before admission. She was admitted for pain control and diagnosed with herpes zoster infection. Six hours after admission, R.F. began having visual hallucinations, hearing noises, and talking to herself. A lumbar puncture was performed with the following results: 3 WBCs (2 lymphocytes and 1 monocyte); 3 RBCs; protein 84 mg/dL; and glucose 86 mg/dL. Herpes zoster was isolated from the CSF. IV acyclovir was started at a dose of 10 mg/kg Q 8 hr. Is antiviral therapy indicated in R.F.? Should her prednisone be continued or discontinued?

Antiviral therapy is indicated for R.F. Acyclovir may halt the progression of acute herpes zoster infection in immunocompromised hosts, such as R.F. who has been taking large doses of corticosteroids.[49] Similarly, vidarabine has been shown to decrease pain, distal cutaneous dissemination, and postherpetic neuralgia.[50]

In a comparative study of acyclovir, 500 mg/m^2 IV every eight hours for seven days, versus vidarabine, 10 mg/kg IV given over a 12-hour infusion every day for seven days in severely immunocompromised patients with VZV infection, acyclovir was more effective. Cutaneous dissemination of infection occurred in none of ten acyclovir recipients and five of ten vidarabine recipients. Acyclovir also was more effective than vidarabine in reducing fever and pain and in promoting healing of the lesions.[109] Another study compared acyclovir, 10 mg/kg given IV every eight hours daily, and vidarabine, 10 mg/kg administered by continuous IV infusion over 12 hours daily, each for 7 days. Although the efficacy and adverse effects were similar, patients receiving acyclovir were discharged from the hospital earlier than those on vidarabine. This led to an estimated savings of $2464 per patient in the acyclovir group.[136]

The incidence of herpes zoster infection rises in immunologically normal hosts with advancing age. In patients like R.F., over 55 to 60 years of age, the pain may persist as postherpetic neuralgia for months after the disappearance of cutaneous lesions.[51] Although IV acyclovir has shortened the duration of acute pain and promoted healing, the incidence of postherpetic neuralgia is unaffected.[52] Oral acyclovir, 800 mg five times daily given for seven to ten days, has been found to be effective in decreasing symptoms of acute infection and postherpetic neuralgia. However, routine use of acyclovir in immunocompetent patients is not well established.

Systemic corticosteroids are of unproven usefulness and may slow healing of lesions.[53] Therefore, if possible, R.F.'s prednisone should be slowly tapered.

20. Acyclovir Toxicity. On the fourth day of acyclovir therapy, R.F. developed severe nausea and vomited three times. The laboratory data showed a BUN of 45 mg/dL and SrCr of 3.2 mg/dL (baseline BUN 10 mg/dL and SrCr 1.0 mg/dL). Is alteration in the acyclovir dose necessary for R.F.? [SI units: BUN 16.07 and 3.57 mmol/L, respectively; SrCr 282.88 and 88.40 µmol/L, respectively]

Nausea and vomiting have been reported with the use of acyclovir in patients with herpes zoster infections.[20] Similarly, elevation of serum creatinine and BUN can occur in association with acyclovir therapy. This may be secondary to acyclovir crystallization in the renal tubules, particularly when fluid intake is inadequate.[19] Because the creatinine clearance in R.F. falls between 10 and 25 mL/min/1.73 m^2, the acyclovir dosage interval should be extended to 24 hours. Every effort should be made to maintain adequate hydration for the duration of acyclovir therapy. (See Table 70.2 and Chapter 2: Clinical Pharmacokinetics for creatinine clearance calculation.)

Cytomegalovirus (CMV) Infections

Cytomegalovirus infections are very common throughout the world. The incidence in adults over 35 years of age is about 40%. Although most of these patients are asymptomatic, infections occurring *in utero* and in patients with compromised immune systems can be extremely serious.

Intrauterine infection may be caused by primary acquisition or reactivation of a latent virus in the mother. One to three percent of all newborn infants have CMV isolated from the urine at birth. Although they may appear normal, the risk of subsequent deficiency in intelligence and hearing loss is substantial. Of infected infants, 10% to 15% have classic findings including chorioretinitis, microcephaly, intracerebral calcification, jaundice, hepatosplenomegaly, thrombocytopenia with petechiae, and subsequent mental retardation.

Most adults with CMV infections are asymptomatic. Immunocompromised patients are at increased risk of infection with CMV acquired from blood, granulocyte transfusions, organ transplants, other persons, or from activation of latent virus. Treatment with immunosuppressive agents can activate cytomegalovirus. Disseminated disease often is associated with liver and lung involvement and fatal outcome. Interstitial pneumonia is the major cause of death in patients with CMV after otherwise-successful bone marrow transplantation.

Cytomegalovirus can be recovered from tissues and body fluids (e.g., urine, saliva, blood, semen, cervicovaginal secretions, intraocular fluid, pharyngeal secretion, breast milk). In patients with presumed CMV interstitial pneumonia, a lung biopsy to determine whether inclusion bodies are present may be required for diagnosis. The diagnostic value of antibody titers is controversial.

Treatment

Ganciclovir

21. S.N., a 41-year-old male, presented with fever, sore throat, decreased vision, diarrhea, and weight loss 10 days fol-

lowing a bone marrow transplantation. CMV was isolated from the urine and he was placed on ganciclovir, 5 mg/kg IV infused over 1 hr Q 8 hr. After 14 days of therapy, the symptoms resolved and the viral titers decreased from 163 to 5 plaque-forming U/mL at the end of treatment. However, serum transaminase levels were elevated (AST 560 U) and the absolute neutrophil count was 1100/mm³ (Normal: 3500–7000). What is the role of ganciclovir in the treatment of CMV? Could the abnormal values be related to drug therapy? Is it equally effective in CMV infections affecting various organs? [SI units: AST 9.335 μkat/L]

In a collaborative study of 26 immunodeficient patients (including 22 with AIDS) with severe life- or sight-threatening CMV infection, treatment with ganciclovir [9-(1,3-dihydroxy-2-propoxymethyl) guanine, Cytovene], resulted in clinical and virological improvement. A dose of 5 mg/kg was administered intravenously over one hour every 8 to 12 hours for 14 days. Patients with extrapulmonary sites of involvement responded particularly well; 84% of patients with retinal involvement and 62% of those with gastrointestinal (GI) involvement also were clinically improved. However, 57% of patients with CMV pneumonia died before completing a 14-day course of ganciclovir. Further, in many patients, the benefit was transient; clinical and virologic relapses occurred in 11 of 14 patients who were followed after ganciclovir was discontinued.[54] Two additional studies, however, have reported improved efficacy of ganciclovir CMV pneumonia in patients with bone marrow transplants.[111,112]

Ganciclovir, 5 mg/kg every 12 hours IV, was effective in the treatment of CMV infections in the recipients of bone marrow transplants and other immunocompromised patients. Clinical improvement occurred in 17 of 18 patients with viremia, fever, wasting, hepatitis, retinitis, or colitis compared with 11 of 21 patients with pneumonia.[110] Ganciclovir doses of 7.5 to 15 mg/kg/day have been used to treat CMV pneumonia in bone marrow, renal, liver, heart, and heart-lung transplant patients.[137]

Combination Therapy with Immunoglobulin. One of these studies used ganciclovir, 2.5 mg/kg every eight hours for 20 days plus IV immune globulin [IVIG (Gammagard)], 500 mg/kg every other day for ten doses. Patients were then given ganciclovir, 5 mg/kg/day three to five times a week, for 20 or more doses and IVIG, 500 mg/kg twice a week, for eight more doses.[111] In the second study, ganciclovir, 2.5 mg/kg every eight hours for 14 days, was given with CMV immunoglobulin (CMV IVIG), 400 mg/kg on days one, two, and seven, and 200 mg/kg on day 14. Patients who showed improvement but were still symptomatic on day 14 were given maintenance therapy with ganciclovir 5 mg/kg/day for an additional 14 days and CMV IVIG, 200 mg/kg on day 21.[112] Several other regimens of ganciclovir and CMV IVIG have been described.[137] Although CMV IVIG contains higher anti-CMV specific antibody than IVIG, the clinical significance of this difference is unclear.

Neutropenia and elevation of liver transaminases were the most common adverse effects of ganciclovir, each occurring in six patients.[54] Thus, ganciclovir can be very useful in certain immunosuppressed patients with CMV infections such as S.N., but patients should be monitored closely for hematologic and hepatic toxicities during treatment. Further studies are needed to characterize ganciclovir's pharmacokinetics so that optimal dosage guidelines can be developed.

Prophylaxis

22. How can CMV infection be prevented in patients with bone marrow transplantation?

First, all donors to seronegative patients should be screened for CMV. Although there are limited data, prophylaxis with IV acyclovir has improved the survival and decreased the risk of both CMV infection and disease in seropositive patients after allogeneic bone marrow transplantation.[113] Acyclovir, 500 mg/m² (≈10 mg/kg) every eight hours was given intravenously from five days before transplantation to 30 days afterward or until discharge from the hospital if discharge occurred before 30 days.[113] Although acyclovir may prevent CMV infection in seropositive patients, it may not be effective in seronegative patients receiving seronegative bone marrow.[137] Further, it may not be effective in preventing infection in the recipients of solid organ transplants.[138]

Ganciclovir 5 mg/kg, IV twice daily for five days, followed by once daily until day 100 after allogeneic bone marrow transplant, was effective in suppressing CMV infection and disease. Neutropenia occurred in 30% of patients.[139] Finally, ganciclovir, 5 mg/kg twice daily for two weeks and then five times weekly until day 120, was found to be effective in preventing CMV pneumonia in bone marrow transplant patients with asymptomatic infection.[140]

Influenza

Influenza is an acute infection caused by the virus of the Orthomyxoviridae family. Epidemics of influenza usually are caused by the type A virus; type B virus generally is associated with sporadic infection. Infection is transmitted by the inhalation of virus-containing droplets ejected from the respiratory tract of a person with influenza. It can be spread by direct contact, large droplets, or articles recently contaminated by nasopharyngeal secretions.

Influenza A viruses are classified into subtypes of hemagglutinin (H) and neuraminidase (N) surface antigens. Three subtypes of hemagglutinin (H_1, H_2, H_3) and two subtypes of neuraminidase (N_1, N_2) have caused influenza in humans. Infection with a virus of one subtype may confer little or no protection from viruses of other subtypes. In addition, significant antigenic variation (antigenic drift) within a subtype may occur over time. Thus, infection or vaccination with one strain may not protect against a distantly related strain of the same subtype. This is why major epidemics of influenza continue to occur and influenza vaccines are reformulated each year with current viral strains to maximize immunity.

Although influenza can occur at any age, the persons at highest risk are the elderly (≥65 years of age); residents of nursing homes and other chronic care facilities housing persons of any age with chronic medical conditions; adults and children with chronic disorders of the pulmonary or cardiovascular systems, including children with asthma; adults and children who have required regular medical follow-up or hospitalization during the preceding year because of chronic metabolic diseases (e.g., diabetes mellitus), renal dysfunction, hemoglobinopathies, or immunosuppression; and children and teenagers (6 months to 18 years of age) receiving long term aspirin therapy who may be at risk for Reye's syndrome after influenza. Each year's vaccine contains three virus strains (generally two type A and one type B) which are likely to circulate in the community for the upcoming season. If there is a good match with the circulating viruses, the vaccine can prevent illness in about 70% of healthy adults and children. It appears to be effective in preventing hospitalization and pneumonia in 70% of elderly living in the community and in 50% to 60% of elderly residing in nursing homes. However, the efficacy of vaccine in preventing illness often may be 30% to 40% among the frail elderly.

Individuals who can transmit influenza to persons at high risk include physicians, nurses, and other personnel in both hospital and ambulatory settings; employees of nursing homes and chronic care facilities; providers of home care services; and household members, including children.

Persons at high risk and those who may transmit the virus to those at high risk should be vaccinated annually. Table 70.5 de-

Table 70.5	Influenza Vaccines[141]			
Age	Type of Vaccine[a]	Dosage	Number of Doses	Route[c]
>12 years including adults	Whole or split virus	0.5 mL	1	IM
9–12 years	Split virus only[b]	0.5 mL	1	IM
3–8 years	Split virus only	0.5 mL	1 or 2[d]	IM
6–35 months	Split virus only	0.5 mL	1 or 2[d]	IM

[a] The 1993–94 available vaccines contained 15 µg each of A/Texas/36/91-like (H1N1), A/Beijing/32/92-like (H3N2), and B/Panama/45/90-like hemagglutinin antigens in each 0.5 mL. The products are Fluzone whole or split virus vaccine; Flu-immune purified surface antigen vaccine; Fluogen split virus vaccine; and Flu-Shield split vaccine.

[b] Only split virus vaccines should be used in children because it causes less febrile reactions; adverse effects of whole-virus and split-virus vaccines are similar in adults.

[c] The recommended site is deltoid muscle for adults and older children, and the anterolateral aspect of the thigh in infants and young children.

[d] Two doses given at least one month apart for children <9 years who are receiving the vaccine for the first time.

scribes the four types of vaccines, dosage, number of doses, and route of administration for four age groups. The optimal time for vaccine administration is between midOctober and midNovember because the influenza activity peaks between late December and early March in the U.S.

Because influenza vaccine contains no infectious viruses, it cannot cause influenza. The most common adverse effect is soreness (in less than one-third of recipients) at the administration site lasting for up to two days. Fever, malaise, myalgia, and other systemic reactions occur infrequently; these may develop within 6 to 12 hours after vaccine dose and persist for one to two days. Immediate hypersensitivity to egg protein (hives, angioedema, allergic asthma, or systemic anaphylaxis) occurs rarely. Persons with anaphylactic hypersensitivity and those with acute febrile illness should not be given the vaccine. However, minor illnesses with or without fever are not contraindications for influenza vaccine, particularly in children with mild upper respiratory tract infection or allergic rhinitis. When the vaccine is contraindicated, an antiviral drug (amantadine or rimantadine) should be used for prophylaxis.[141]

Clinically, it is impossible to differentiate between influenza A and B. This is important because current antiviral therapy is effective only against influenza A. Definitive diagnosis can be made by the isolation of the virus from throat washings or sputum and a significant increase in antibody titers during the convalescent period.

Clinical Presentation

23. J.T., a 74-year-old man, is brought to the ER from a nursing home with chief complaints of fever 103 °F, shaking chills, headache, malaise, anorexia, and photophobia. On physical examination, he appeared flushed, his skin was hot and moist, and he was working hard to breathe. Vital signs were as follows: blood pressure 150/90 mm Hg, pulse 108 beats/min, respiratory rate 22 breaths/min, temperature 103 °F. Rales were audible on auscultation of both lungs. A chest roentgenogram showed bilateral infiltrates but no consolidation. Blood gas studies showed marked hypoxia with a PaO_2 of 50 mm Hg and $PaCO_2$ of 50 mm Hg. Past medical history was significant for chronic bronchitis and a stroke 16 months ago.

Blood, sputum, and urine cultures were obtained, and J.T. was started on antibiotics [gentamicin 140 mg loading dose, then 90 mg Q 12 hr IV piggy back (IVPB) and clindamycin

900 mg Q 8 hr IVPB]. Gram's stain of the sputum sample showed many WBCs, but no bacteria. He was started on oxygen therapy at 4 L/min via nasal cannula.

Twenty-four hours later, respiratory symptoms became worse and arterial blood gases deteriorated slightly (PaO_2 40 mm Hg, $PaCO_2$ 55 mm Hg). J.T. was intubated and a sputum sample was obtained and sent to the virology lab. He was started on amantadine 200 mg administered via the nasogastric (NG) tube then 100 mg Q 12 hr administered via the NG tube pending culture results. Three days later, influenza A virus was isolated from the sputum. Blood, urine, and sputum cultures were all negative for bacterial pathogens.

Is this presentation consistent with influenza infection? Was amantadine indicated? [SI units: PaO_2 6.665 and 5.332 kPa, respectively; $PaCO_2$ 6.665 and 7.332 kPa, respectively]

Yes. Most patients with influenza A have an abrupt onset of fever, chills, and headache. In elderly patients like J.T. and those with underlying diseases, the course of influenza can worsen quickly.

Amantadine Therapy

Amantadine (1-adamantanamine hydrochloride; Symmetrel) was marketed in 1966 for the prophylaxis of infections due to influenza A viruses and subsequently was approved for therapy of influenza A in 1976. Amantadine prevents penetration of the host cell by influenza A viruses by preventing uncoating of the virus once it is attached to the cell membrane.[55,56]

Several studies have demonstrated that oral amantadine, 200 mg/day for five to ten days, is more effective than placebo for the treatment of influenza A infection;[57,58] one study reported 100 mg/day for five days was therapeutically equivalent to 200 mg/day.[59] Although benefit from amantadine therapy in patients with complicated or serious influenza has not been examined fully, its use in J.T. seems appropriate.

24. Adverse Effects. Six days after starting amantadine therapy, clinical improvement was noted, but J.T. complained of nausea, anorexia, and dizziness. Could these be related to amantadine therapy?

A limitation of amantadine therapy is its toxicity, which has occurred in 2% to 33% of recipients in various studies. The most common adverse effects are anorexia and nausea; 5% to 10% of otherwise healthy adults taking amantadine have reported insomnia, lightheadedness, irritability, and difficulty concentrating.[60] In one study using amantadine, 200 mg/day, the drug had to be discontinued in a number of adult volunteers who complained of dizziness, nervousness, and insomnia.[61] Central nervous system toxicity appears to be related to high plasma concentrations of amantadine; oral doses exceeding 300 mg/day and plasma concentrations over 0.6 µg/mL have been associated with adverse effects.[62–64] Nasal irritation, rhinorrhea, and dysgeusia (decreased taste) have been noted with the use of amantadine aerosol.[65,66] The aerosol (unavailable in the U.S.) should be used with caution in patients with pre-existing airway hyperreactivity since cough and wheezing have been reported in these patients.[65,66]

It seems clear that the adverse effects can be minimized by administering lower doses of amantadine. In a study utilizing amantadine, 100 mg/day, there was 78% protection from influenza A and no adverse effects in healthy adult volunteers.[114] Thus, a dose of 100 mg/day may be attempted in those unable to tolerate the recommended dose of 200 mg/day.

Prevention

25. Over the next 3 weeks, two other nursing home patients developed influenza A infections. What measures should be taken to prevent further outbreak of influenza among other residents?

Influenza Vaccines

The nursing home residents and staff should receive influenza vaccine plus amantadine therapy. The Centers for Disease Control (CDC) recommends immunization of all high-risk groups.[60] The top priority groups include: adults and children with chronic cardiovascular or pulmonary disease severe enough to warrant regular medical care during the preceding year; residents of nursing homes and other chronic care facilities; and physicians, nurses, and other personnel who have extensive contact with high-risk patients. Second in priority are otherwise-healthy adults over 65 years of age and children with chronic metabolic diseases severe enough to warrant regular follow-up during the preceding year. However, the efficacy of influenza vaccine is incomplete (70%).[60] Therefore, the CDC recommends the use of amantadine in high-risk individuals to supplement the protection by vaccine.

Amantadine

Investigators who have studied prophylactic amantadine therapy have reported protection rates of about 50% in experimentally-induced influenza A[67,68] and 28% to 100% during naturally-acquired influenza A outbreaks.[60-73] The CDC reports that amantadine is 70% to 90% effective in preventing illness caused by influenza A.[60] The recommended dose of amantadine is 200 mg/day (100 mg twice daily) to prevent influenza A infections. Treatment should begin *as soon as* possible and continue for 14 to 21 days if given with vaccine and 90 days if vaccine is not given.

Rimantadine

26. Is there any other drug that can be used in patients unable to tolerate amantadine for prophylaxis?

Rimantadine (Flumadine) is a structural analog of amantadine and is more active than amantadine *in vitro* against influenza A viruses.[74,75] Rimantadine appears to be less toxic than amantadine[57,64,76] and this may be related to the higher serum concentration produced by amantadine relative to rimantadine following equivalent doses.[62]

Rimantadine is marketed in the U.S. for the prophylaxis and treatment of illness caused by various strains of influenza A in adults, and for prophylaxis against influenza A virus in children. The recommended oral dose is 100 mg twice daily in adults and children ten or more years of age, and 5 mg/kg (not to exceed 150 mg) daily in children younger than ten years of age. For the treatment of influenza A, the therapy should be initiated as soon as possible (preferably within 48 hours) and continued for seven days after onset of symptoms. Rimantadine, 100 mg/day for six weeks after the onset of influenza season, also has been found to be more effective than placebo in the prevention of influenza A illness in healthy adults.[142]

In a prophylaxis study which compared amantadine, rimantadine, and placebo in adults during an influenza outbreak, both drugs had similar protective efficacy rates (91% for amantadine and 85% for rimantadine). However, those receiving rimantadine experienced fewer side effects.[76] Another comparative study also demonstrated that the therapeutic efficacy of amantadine and rimantadine was comparable.[77]

Emergence of Resistance

27. What can be done to minimize emergence of resistance and transmission of influenza A virus to close contacts and family members?

Although amantadine and rimantadine are effective in the prevention and treatment of influenza A, resistant strains have been isolated from treated patients as well as close contacts.[115,116] The clinical significance of this resistance, however, is unknown.[143,144]

The emergence of resistance may be minimized by limiting the treatment to those who are likely to have severe disease or who might develop complications. The close contacts to be protected, however, can receive the prophylaxis with amantadine or rimantadine.

Respiratory Syncytial Virus (RSV) Infections

Respiratory syncytial virus is an important pathogen causing bronchiolitis and bronchopneumonia. Bronchiolitis is a lower respiratory tract viral infection characterized by the acute onset of wheezing which affects 6% to 10% of all children less than two years of age.[78] Nearly 50% of hospitalized patients may have lung function abnormalities 12 months after the acute illness.[79]

Respiratory syncytial virus infections usually occur in the winter months. The chest x-ray and blood gases often are abnormal and the virus can be isolated in the nasopharyngeal secretions. Virus isolation, serologic tests during illness, and increased antibody titers during convalescence can establish the diagnosis of RSV infections.

Clinical Presentation and Ribavirin Therapy

28. J.R., a 6-month-old infant who is lethargic, tachypneic, and cyanotic, is brought to the ER. He has a fever (102 °F) and his breathing is labored; wheezing is audible on expiration. The chest roentgenograms show a flattened diaphragm and hyperinflated lung parenchyma. Because of hypoxemia and hypercarbia, J.R. is placed on ambient oxygen to maintain the alveolar oxygen pressure at >60 mm Hg. RSV is present in the respiratory secretions. Is antiviral therapy indicated for the treatment of J.R., who has underlying immunodeficiency?

Ribavirin (1-β-D-ribofuranosyl-1,2,4-triazole-3-carboxamide; Virazole), an antiviral agent which possesses unique inhibitory activity against a large number of both DNA and RNA viruses,[73] is indicated for the treatment of infections due to respiratory syncytial virus. The virus is inhibited at serum concentrations of 3 to 16 μg/mL.[80,81] Two studies evaluating the efficacy of ribavirin aerosol in the treatment of infants hospitalized with bronchiolitis indicate that the drug has beneficial effects.[82,83] Ribavirin aerosol also has been shown to be effective in infants with underlying diseases who are at high-risk for severe and fatal RSV infection.[81,84,85] These studies have reported clinical recovery and improvement in patients' arterial oxygenation. Whether ribavirin decreases long-term sequelae and the severity of illness in high-risk groups (including premature infants, patients with bronchopulmonary dysplasia, congenital heart disease, cystic fibrosis, and immunodeficiency) has not been determined. Although ribavirin is indicated for J.R., its routine use in previously healthy infants and children has not been clearly established.[117] A recent study, however, found ribavirin to be ineffective in patients with a variety of risk factors.[145]

Administration

29. How is ribavirin administered and what precautions should be taken during drug administration in J.R.?

Ribavirin is administered as an aerosol through a collision generator which generates particles small enough (1 to 2 μm diameter) to reach the lower respiratory tract. This assures that high concentrations of ribavirin penetrate respiratory secretions at the site of viral replication while minimizing systemic absorption. The concentration of the ribavirin solution in the reservoir is 20 mg/mL. The administered dose has been estimated to be 0.8 mg/kg/hr,[86,87] although the actual dose delivered may depend upon the patient's ventilation and lung pathology.[88]

The FDA has not approved the use of ribavirin in patients requiring mechanical ventilation. This is based upon the premise that ribavirin is hygroscopic and that aerosol particles can deposit in the tubing and around the expiratory valve of a ventilator. The precipitated drug can obstruct the expiratory valve and alter the peak end-expiratory pressure.[89] However, since patients requiring ventilation also may require ribavirin, close monitoring of respiratory therapy is advised to avoid this problem. In addition to the inspection of tubing, modifications of standard ventilatory circuits have been suggested.

Adverse Effects

30. What are the important adverse effects of ribavirin?

In clinical studies using aerosol for the treatment of bronchiolitis, no major adverse effects have been reported due to ribavirin. The effect of ribavirin on the young and developing lung, however, is unknown and a long-term follow-up evaluation is needed.[117]

Ribavirin is contraindicated in women or girls who are or may become pregnant during exposure to the drug. Although there are no human data, ribavirin has been found to be teratogenic and/or embryolethal in nearly all animal species in which it has been tested. Teratogenesis was evident after a single oral dose of 2.5 mg/kg in the hamster and following daily oral doses of 10 mg/kg in the rat. Malformation of the skull, palate, eye, jaw, skeleton, and GI tract were noted in animals. Ribavirin has reduced the survival of fetuses and offspring of animals tested. It is lethal to the rabbit embryo in daily oral doses as low as 1 mg/kg. There are no studies which address teratogenicity in humans, but female nurses or other hospital personnel who are pregnant or may be pregnant should avoid exposure to this drug.[117]

It is important to consider the environmental effects of ribavirin on the personnel involved with its administration. One study found no detectable plasma or urine concentrations of ribavirin in 19 nurses,[118] while another reported its presence in red blood cells of a nurse caring for a patient who received ribavirin via oxygen tent.[119] The ribavirin concentration in the air was highest when it was administered via oxygen tent followed by mist mask and lowest after administration via endotracheal tubes of mechanically ventilated patients.[119] This has led to several recommendations: 1) ribavirin aerosol should be administered solely via endotracheal tube of mechanically ventilated patients in a closed filtered system;[117] 2) children receiving ribavirin should be placed in a containment chamber equipped with a high-efficiency particulate air filter exhaust in an isolation room with negative air pressure;[120] 3) disposable full body coverings and either a powdered air-purifying respirator or disposable particulate respirator should be made available to all health care personnel;[120] and 4) men and women planning to have children should not care for patients receiving ribavirin via oxygen tents.[119] ICN Pharmaceuticals is marketing an aerosol delivery system for oxygen and ribavirin that decreases the liberation of ribavirin into the environment.[121] Although this may reduce the exposure, the small size of the vacuum exhaust hood limits its use to children weighing <5 kg.[122] Thus, ribavirin should not be used routinely in patients with RSV infections until its benefits in reducing treatment duration, hospital days, need for supportive care, long-term complications, and mortality are further substantiated.

Hantavirus Infections

31. K.C., a previously healthy 55-year-old female, was seen with abrupt onset of fever, myalgia, and shortness of breath. K.C. lived in eastern Texas and had not traveled out of state during the last 6 months. Diagnostic evaluation including complete blood count with differential, blood and sputum cultures, was negative. On day 3, K.C. remained febrile, and had vomiting, hypotension, hypoxemia, and bilateral diffuse infiltrates on the chest radiograph.

K.C. suddenly developed adult respiratory distress syndrome and expired. The hantavirus immunoglobulin M enzyme-linked immunosorbent assay titer, performed from the K.C.'s serum specimen at the CDC, was elevated. What is hantavirus infection?

Rodents are the primary reservoir hosts of hantaviruses, and the deer mouse (*Peromyscus maniculatus*) is the main reservoir in the U.S. These viruses apparently do not cause illness in the reservoir hosts; however, infection in humans occurs when infected saliva, urine, and feces are inhaled as aerosols produced by the animal. Person-to-person transmission has not been documented.

The earlier cases in 1993 occurred in Arizona, Colorado, New Mexico, and Utah. As of April 5, 1994, nearly 100 cases from 21 states have been reported in the U.S., with a mortality rate of 51%. The clinical features in most patients include fever, myalgia, headache, and cough. Abdominal pain, nausea, and/or vomiting also may be present. The physical examination has been unreliable. The laboratory abnormalities may include leukocytosis, thrombocytopenia, and hypoalbuminemia. The chest radiographs may be normal initially, and can progress rapidly to bilateral infiltrates. Because of the nonspecific signs and symptoms, some patients may be misdiagnosed as having influenza.

Four serotypes of hantavirus have been identified. The case definition used by the CDC includes clinical evidence of a) febrile illness characterized by unexplained adult respiratory distress syndrome or acute bilateral pulmonary interstitial infiltrates; b) an autopsy finding of noncardiogenic pulmonary edema resulting from an unexplained respiratory illness [laboratory evidence consists of a positive serology (i.e., presence of hantavirus-specific immunoglobulin M or rising titers of immunoglobulin G)]; c) positive immunohistochemistry for hantavirus antigen in a tissue specimen; or d) positive polymerase chain reaction for hantavirus RNA in a tissue specimen.[146]

32. Can this infection be treated with an antiviral drug?

There is no FDA-approved drug to treat hantavirus infections. Based upon one study in 242 patients, IV ribavirin was more effective than placebo in reducing the mortality and the morbidity (oliguria and hemorrhage) in China. Ribavirin was given intravenously as a loading dose of 33 mg/kg followed by 16 mg/kg every six hours for four days, and 8 mg/kg every eight hours for the next three days. Each dose was infused over 30 minutes. The reversible anemia was the main adverse effect of ribavirin.[147] Additional studies are needed to confirm these observations. Intravenous ribavirin, however, is available as an investigational agent through a CDC-supported open label study.

References

1 **Gordon M et al.** A review of approaches to viral chemotherapy. J Med. 1981;12:289–382.

2 **Davis DJ.** Measurements of the prevalence of viral infections. J Infect Dis. 1976;133:A3–A5.

3 **Robins RK.** Synthetic antiviral agents. Chem Eng News. 1986;64:28–40.

4 **Whitley RJ et al.** Adenine arabinoside therapy of biopsy-proved herpes simplex encephalitis. N Engl J Med. 1977; 297:289–94.

5 **Jones BR et al.** Efficacy of acycloguanosine (Wellcome 2486) against herpes-simplex corneal ulcers. Lancet. 1979;1:243–44.

6 **Skoldenberg B et al.** Acyclovir versus vidarabine in herpes simplex encepha-

litis. Lancet. 1984;2:707–11.

7 **Whitley RJ et al.** Vidarabine versus acyclovir therapy in herpes simplex encephalitis. N Engl J Med. 1986;314: 144–49.

8 **Whitley RJ et al.** Pharmacokinetics of

acyclovir in humans following intravenous administration. Am J Med. 1982; 73(1A):165–71.

9 de Miranda P et al. Acyclovir kinetics after intravenous infusion. Clin Pharmacol Ther. 1979;26:718–28.

10 Fiddian AP, Brigden D. Acyclovir: an update of the clinical applications of this antiherpes agent. Antiviral Res. 1984;4:99–117.

11 Laskin OL et al. Pharmacokinetics and tolerance of acyclovir, a new antiherpes virus agent, in humans. Antimicrob Agents Chemother. 1982;21: 393–98.

12 Blum MR et al. Overview of acyclovir pharmacokinetic disposition in adults and children. Am J Med. 1982;73(1A): 186–92.

13 Yeager AS. Use of acyclovir in premature and term neonates. Am J Med. 1982;73(1A):205–09.

14 Hintz M et al. Neonatal acyclovir pharmacokinetics in patients with herpes virus infection. Am J Med. 1982; 73(1A):210–14.

15 Collins P et al. Sensitivity of herpes, virus isolates from acyclovir clinical trials. Am J Med. 1982;73(1A):380–82.

16 Keeney RE et al. Acyclovir tolerance in humans. Am J Med. 1982;73(1A): 176–81.

17 Brigden D et al. Renal function after acyclovir intravenous injection. Am J Med. 1982;73(1A):182–85.

18 Balfour HH Jr. Acyclovir. In: Peterson PK, Verhoef J, eds. Antimicrobial Agents Annual. New York: Elsevier; 1985:324–34.

19 Bean B, Aeppli D. Adverse effects of high-dose intravenous acyclovir in ambulatory patients with acute herpes zoster. Infect Dis. 1985;151:362–65.

20 Lisby S et al. Nausea and vomiting possibly associated with intravenous acyclovir. Drug Intell Clin Pharm. 1986;20:371–73.

21 Wade JC, Meyers JD. Neurologic symptoms associated with parenteral acyclovir treatment after marrow transplantation. Ann Intern Med. 1983;98: 921–25.

22 Laskin OL. Acyclovir: pharmacology and clinical experience. Arch Intern Med. 1984;144:1241–246.

23 Bryson YJ et al. Treatment of first episodes of genital herpes simplex virus infection with oral acyclovir. N Engl J Med. 1983;308:916–21.

24 Corey L, Spear PG. Infections with herpes simplex viruses. N Engl J Med. 1986;314:749–57.

25 Stagno S, Whitley RJ. Herpesvirus infections of pregnancy: herpes simplex virus and varicella-zoster as virus infections. N Engl J Med. 1985;313: 1327–330.

26 Whitley RJ et al. Vidarabine therapy of neonatal herpes simplex virus infection. Pediatrics. 1980;66:495–501.

27 Muller WEG et al. Inhibition of herpesvirus DNA synthesis by 9-D-Arabinofuranosyladenine in vitro and in vivo. Ann NY Acad Sci. 1977;284:34–48.

28 Brink JJ, LePage GA. Metabolic effects of 9-D-arabinosylpurines in ascites tumor cells. Cancer Res. 1964;24: 312–18.

29 Whitley RJ et al. Vidarabine: a preliminary review of its pharmacological

30 Ross AH et al. Toxicity of adenine arabinoside in humans. J Infect Dis. 1976;133(Suppl.):192–98.

31 Sacks SL et al. Toxicity of vidarabine. JAMA. 1979;241:28–9. Letter.

32 Bassedine MF et al. Adenine arabinoside therapy in HB$_s$Ag-positive chronic liver-disease—a controlled study. Gastroenterology. 1981;80:1016–022.

33 Lauter CB et al. Microbiologic assays and neurological toxicity during use of adenine arabinoside in humans. J Infect Dis. 1976;134:75–9.

34 Friedman HM, Grasela T. Adenine arabinoside and allopurinol—possible adverse drug interaction. N Engl J Med. 1981;304:423. Letter.

35 Cannon R et al. Possible interaction between vidarabine and theophylline. Ann Intern Med. 1984;101:148–49.

36 Saral R et al. Acyclovir prophylaxis of herpes simplex virus infections: a randomized, double-blind, controlled trial in bone marrow transplant recipients. N Engl J Med. 1981;305:63–7.

37 Gluckman E et al. Prophylaxis of herpes infections after bone marrow transplantation by oral acyclovir. Lancet. 1983;2:706–08.

38 Shepp DH et al. Oral acyclovir therapy for mucocutaneous herpes simplex virus infections in immunocompromised marrow transplant patients. Ann Intern Med. 1985;102:783–85.

39 Whitley RJ et al. Infections caused by herpes simplex virus in the immunocompromised host: natural history and topical acyclovir therapy. J Infect Dis. 1984;150:323–29.

40 Kaufman HE. Herpetic keratitis: proctor lecture. Invest Ophthalmol Vis Sci. 1978;17:941–57.

41 Pavan Langston D. Ocular viral diagnosis. In: Galasso GJ et al., eds. Antiviral Agents and Viral Diseases of Man. 2nd ed. New York: Raven Press. 1984:207–46.

42 McKinnon JR et al. A coded clinical evaluation of adenine arabinoside and trifluorothymidine in the treatment of herpetic keratitis. In: Pavan Langston D et al., eds. Adenine Arabinoside: An Antiviral Agent. New York: Raven Press; 1975:401–10.

43 Coster DJ et al. Clinical evaluation of adenine arabinoside and trifluorothymidine in the treatment of corneal ulcers caused by herpes simplex virus. J Infect Dis. 1976;133(Suppl.):A173–77.

44 Wellings PC et al. Clinical evaluation of trifluorothymidine in the treatment of herpes simplex corneal ulcers. Am J Ophthalmol. 1972;73:932–42.

45 Pavan Langston D, Foster CS. Trifluorothymidine and idoxuridine therapy of ocular herpes. Am J Ophthalmol. 1977;84:818–25.

46 Vidarabine (Vira-A). Med Lett Drugs Ther. 1977;19:42–3.

47 O'Brien WJ, Taylor JL. Chemotherapy of herpetic keratitis induced by acyclovir-resistant strains of herpes simplex virus type 1. Am J Med. 1982; 73(1A):294–99.

48 Shepp DH et al. Treatment of varicella-zoster virus infection in severely immunocompromised patients. N Engl J Med. 1986;314:208–12.

49 Balfour HH Jr et al. Acyclovir halts

50 Whitley RJ et al. Early vidarabine therapy to control the complications of herpes zoster in immunosuppressed patients. N Engl J Med. 1982;307:971–75.

51 Hirsch MS, Schooley RT. Treatment of herpes virus infections. N Engl J Med. 1983;309:963–70.

52 Bean B et al. Acyclovir therapy for acute herpes zoster. Lancet. 1982;2: 118–21.

53 Whitley RJ et al. Vidarabine for herpes zoster. N Engl J Med. 1983;308: 526–27.

54 Collaborative DHPG Treatment Study Group. Treatment of serious cytomegalovirus infections with 9-(1,3-dihydroxy-2-propoxymethyl) guanine in patients with AIDS and other immunodeficiencies. N Engl J. Med. 1986;314:801–05.

55 Kato N, Eggers HJ. Inhibition of uncoating of fowl plague by 1-adamantanamine hydrochloride. Virology. 1969; 37:632–41.

56 Skebel J et al. On the mechanism of inhibition of influenza virus replication by amantadine hydrochloride. J Gen Virol. 1977;38:91–110.

57 Van Voris LP et al. Successful treatment of naturally occurring influenza A/USSR/77 H1N1. JAMA. 1981;245: 1128–131.

58 Van Voris LP. Antiviral chemotherapy. In: Belshe RB, ed. Textbook of Human Virology. Littleton: PSG Publishing Co.; 1984:193–229.

59 Youkin SW et al. Reduction in fever and symptoms in young adults with influenza A/Brazil/78 N$_1$N$_1$ infection after treatment with aspirin or amantadine. Antimicrob Agents Chemother. 1983;23:577–82.

60 Prevention and control of influenza. MMWR. 1985;24:261–68,273–74.

61 Bryson YJ et al. A prospective double-blind study of side effects associated with the administration of amantadine for influenza A virus prophylaxis. J Infect Dis. 1980;141:543–47.

62 Hayden FG et al. Differences in amantadine hydrochloride and rimantadine hydrochloride side effects relate to differences in pharmacokinetics. Antimicrob Agents Chemother. 1983; 23:564–64.

63 Horadam VW et al. Pharmacokinetics of amantadine hydrochloride in subjects with normal and impaired renal function. Ann Intern Med. 1981;94: 454–58.

64 Hayden FG et al. Comparative toxicity of amantadine hydrochloride and rimantadine hydrochloride in healthy adults. Antimicrob Agents Chemother. 1981;19:226–33.

65 Hayden FG et al. Amantadine aerosols in normal volunteers: pharmacology and safety testing. Antimicrob Agents Chemother. 1979;16:644–50.

66 Knight V et al. Amantadine aerosol in humans. Antimicrob Agents Chemother. 1979;16:572–78.

67 Smorodintsev AA et al. Evaluation of amantadine in artificially-induced A2 and B influenza. JAMA. 1970;213: 1148–151.

68 Jackson GG et al. Serological evi-

dence for prevention of influenzal infection in volunteers by an anti-influenzal drug adamantanamine hydrochloride. In: Sylvester JC, ed. Antimicrob Agents Chemother. Ann Arbor: American Society of Microbiologists; 1964: 703–07.

69 Dolin R et al. A controlled trial of amantadine and rimantadine in the prophylaxis of influenza A infection. N Engl J Med. 1982;307:580–84.

70 Petterson RF et al. Evaluation of amantadine in the prophylaxis of influenza A (H$_1$N$_1$) virus infection: a controlled field trial among young adults and high-risk patients. J Infect Dis. 1980;142:377–83.

71 Monto AS et al. Prevention of Russian influenza by amantadine. JAMA. 1979; 241:1003–007.

72 Smorodintsev AA et al. The prophylactic effectiveness of amantadine hydrochloride in an epidemic of Hong Kong influenza in Leningrad in 1969. Bull WHO. 1970;42:865–72.

73 Nafia I et al. Administration of amantadine for the prevention of Hong Kong influenza. Bull WHO. 1970;42:423–27.

74 Hayden FG et al. Plaque inhibition assay for drug susceptibility testing of influenza viruses. Antimicrob Agents Chemother. 1980;17:865–70.

75 Burlington DB et al. Anti-influenza A virus activity of amantadine hydrochloride and rimantadine hydrochloride in ferret tracheal ciliated epithelium. Antimicrob Agents Chemother. 1982;21: 794–99.

76 Dolin R et al. A controlled trial of amantadine and rimantadine in the prophylaxis of influenza A infection. N Engl J Med. 1982;307:580–84.

77 Wingfield WL et al. Therapeutic efficacy of amantadine HCl and rimantadine HCl in naturally occurring influenza A2 respiratory illness in man. N Engl J Med. 1969;281:579–84.

78 Nahata MC et al. DA: management of bronchitis. Clin Pharm. 1985;4:297–303.

79 Stokes GM et al. Lung function abnormalities after acute bronchiolitis. J Pediatr. 1981;93:871–74.

80 Hruska JF et al. Effects of ribavirin on respiratory syncytial virus in vitro. Antimicrob Agents Chemother. 1980; 17:770–75.

81 Hall CB et al. Ribavirin treatment of respiratory syncytial viral infection in infants with underlying cardiopulmonary disease. JAMA. 1985;254:3047–051.

82 Hall CB et al. Aerosolized ribavirin treatment of infants with respiratory syncytial viral infection. A randomized double-blind study. N Engl J Med. 1983;308:1443–447.

83 Taber LH et al. Ribavirin aerosol treatment of bronchiolitis due to respiratory syncytial virus infection in infants. Pediatrics. 1983;72:613–18.

84 Rodriguez WJ et al. Short-course aerosolized ribavirin for respiratory syncytial virus infection. Pediatr Res. 1985;19:115. Abstract.

85 McIntosh K et al. Treatment of respiratory viral infection in an immunodeficient infant with ribavirin aerosol. Am J Dis Child. 1984;138:305–08.

86 Knight V et al. Ribavirin small-particle aerosol treatment of influenza. Lancet. 1981;3:945–49.

87 **McClung HW et al.** Ribavirin aerosol treatment of influenza B virus infection. JAMA. 1983;249:2671–674.

88 **Hall CB.** Ribavirin beginning the blitz on respiratory viruses? Pediatr Infect Dis. 1985;4:668–71.

89 **Hall CB.** Ribavirin and respiratory syncytial virus. Am J Dis Child. 1986;140:331–32.

90 **Gwaltney JM Jr.** Rhinoviruses. In: Evans AS, ed. Viral Infections of Humans: Epidemiology and Control. New York: Plenum Press; 1982:491–517.

91 **Hayden FG et al.** Prevention of natural colds by contact prophylaxis with intranasal alpha$_2$ interferon. N Engl J Med. 1986;314:71–5.

92 **Douglas RM et al.** Prophylactic efficacy of intranasal alpha$_2$ interferon against rhinovirus infections in the family setting. N Engl J Med. 1986; 314:65–70.

93 **Deeter RG, Khanderia U.** Recent advances in antiviral therapy. Clin Pharm. 1986;5:961–76.

94 **Van Dyke RB et al.** Pharmacokinetics of orally-administered acyclovir in patients with herpes progenitalis. Am J Med. 1982;73(1A):172–75.

95 **Straus SE et al.** Acyclovir for chronic mucocutaneous herpes simplex virus infection in immunosuppressed patients. Ann Intern Med. 1982;96:270–77.

96 **Arnoff GR et al.** Hypoxanthine-arabinoside pharmacokinetics after adenine arabinoside administration to a patient with renal failure. Antimicrob Agents Chemother. 1980;18:212–14.

97 **Shepp DH et al.** Activity of 9-[2-hydroxy-1-(hydroxymethyl) ethoxymethyl] guanine in the treatment of cytomegalovirus pneumonia. Ann Intern Med. 1985;103:368–73.

98 **Felsenstein D et al.** Treatment of cytomegalovirus retinitis with 9-[2-hydroxy-1-(hydroxy-methyl)-ethoxymethyl] guanine. Ann Intern Med. 1985;103: 377–80.

99 **Van Voris LP et al.** Comparative pharmacokinetics of rimantadine HCl and amantadine HCl. Program and Abstracts of the 23rd ICAAC. American Society for Microbiology Meeting. Las Vegas, NV; 1983 Oct 24–26.

100 **Endo Laboratories Inc.** Symmetrel: amantadine hydrochloride and influenza A. Physician's monograph. Garden City, NY: E.I. Du Pont de Nemours and Co.; 1977.

101 **Bleidner WE et al.** Absorption, distribution, and excretion of amantadine hydrochloride. J Pharmacol Exp Ther. 1965;150:484–90.

102 **Aoki FY et al.** Amantadine kinetics in healthy young subjects after long-term dosing. Clin Pharmacol Ther. 1979;26: 729–36.

103 **Connor JD et al.** Ribavirin pharmacokinetics in children and adults during therapeutic trials. In: Smith RA et al., eds. Clinical Applications of Ribavirin. New York: Academic Press, Inc.; 1984:107–23.

104 **de Miranda P et al.** Disposition of intravenous radioactive acyclovir. Clin Pharmacol Ther. 1981;30:662–72.

105 **Laskin OL.** Clinical pharmacokinetics of acyclovir. Clin Pharmacol. 1983;8: 187–201.

106 **Aoki FY, Sitar DS.** Amantadine kinetics in healthy elderly men: implications for influenza. Clin Pharmacol Ther. 1985;37:137–44.

107 **Fletcher C et al.** Human pharmacokinetics of the antiviral drug DHPG. Clin Pharmacol Ther. 1986;40:281–86.

108 **Syntex Laboratories.** Ganciclovir sodium. Product monograph. Palo Alto, CA; 1989.

109 **Shepp DH et al.** Treatment of varicella-zoster virus infection in severely immunocompromised patients. A randomized comparison of acyclovir and vidarabine. N Engl J Med. 1986;314: 208–12.

110 **Winston DJ et al.** Ganciclovir therapy for cytomegalovirus infections in recipients of bone marrow transplants and other immunosuppressed patients. Rev Infect Dis. 1988;10:S547–14.

111 **Emanuel D et al.** Cytomegalovirus pneumonia after bone marrow transplantation successfully treated with the combination of ganciclovir and high-dose intravenous immune globulin. Ann Intern Med. 1988;109:777–82.

112 **Reed EC et al.** Treatment of cytomegalovirus pneumonia with ganciclovir and intravenous cytomegalovirus immunoglobulin in patients with bone marrow transplants. Ann Intern Med. 1988;109:783–88.

113 **Meyers JD et al.** Acyclovir for prevention of cytomegalovirus infection and disease after allogeneic marrow transplantation. N Engl J Med. 1988; 318:70–5.

114 **Sears SD, Clements ML.** Protective efficacy of low-dose amantadine in adults challenged with wild-type influenza A virus. Antimicrob Agents Chemother. 1987;31:1470–73.

115 **Hayden FG et al.** Emergence and apparent transmission of rimantadine-resistant influenza A virus in families. N Engl J Med. 1989;321:1696–702.

116 **Hall CB et al.** Children with influenza A infection: treatment with rimantadine. Pediatrics. 1987;80:275–82.

117 **Lugo RA, Nahata MC.** Pathogenesis and treatment of bronchiolitis. Clin Pharm. 1993;12:95–116.

118 **Rodriguez WJ et al.** Environmental exposure of primary care personnel to ribavirin aerosol when supervising treatment of infants with respiratory syncytial virus infections. Antimicrob Agents Chemother. 1987;31:1143–146.

119 **Harrison R et al.** Assessing exposure of health-care personnel to aerosols of ribavirin—California. MMWR. 1988; 37:560–63.

120 **Fackler JC et al.** Precautions in the use of ribavirin at the Children's Hospital. N Engl J Med. 1990;322:634.

121 **ICN Pharmaceuticals.** Product information. Aerosol Delivery Hood. Costa Mesa, CA: ICN Pharmaceuticals, Nov 1988.

122 **Bradley JS et al.** Exposure of health-care workers to ribavirin during therapy for respiratory syncytial virus infections. Antimicrob Agents Chemother. 1990;34:668–70.

123 **Whitley R et al.** A controlled trial comparing vidarabine with acyclovir in neonatal herpes simplex virus infection. N Engl J Med. 1991;324(7): 444–49.

124 **Aurelius E et al.** Rapid diagnosis of herpes simplex encephalitis by nested polymerase chain reaction assay of cerebrospinal fluid. Lancet. 1991;337: 189–92.

125 **Whitley RJ.** Neonatal herpes simplex virus infections: pathogenesis and therapy. Pathol Biol. 1992;40:729–34.

126 **Spruance SL et al.** Treatment of recurrent herpes simplex labialis with oral acyclovir. J Infect Dis. 1990;161: 185–90.

127 **Rooney JF et al.** Oral acyclovir to suppress frequently recurrent herpes labialis: a double-blind, placebo-controlled trial. Ann Intern Med. 1993;118:268–72.

128 **Raborn GW et al.** Herpes labialis treatment with acyclovir 5% ointment. Sci J. 1989;55:135–37.

129 **Raborn GW et al.** Herpes labialis treatment with acyclovir 5% modified aqueous cream: a double-blind, randomized trial. Oral Surg Oral Med Oral Pathol. 1989;67:676–79.

130 **Safrin S et al.** A controlled trial comparing foscarnet with vidarabine for acyclovir resistant mucocutaneous herpes simplex in the acquired immunodeficiency syndrome. N Engl J Med. 1991;325:551–55.

131 **Dunkle LM et al.** A controlled trial of acyclovir for chickenpox in normal children. N Engl J Med. 1991;325: 1539–544.

132 **Balfour HH.** Acyclovir treatment of varicella in otherwise healthy children. J Pediatr. 1990;116:633–39.

133 **Whitley RJ.** Therapeutic approaches to varicella-zoster virus infections. J Infect Dis. 1992;166(Suppl. 1):S51-7.

134 **Wallace MR et al.** Treatment of adult varicella with oral acyclovir: a randomized placebo-controlled trial. Ann Intern Med. 1992;117:358–63.

135 **Report of the Committee on Infectious Diseases.** Varicella-zoster infection. American Academy of Pediatrics. Elk Grove Village, IL: 1994:510–17.

136 **Whitley RJ et al.** Disseminated herpes zoster in the immunocompromised host: a comparative trial of acyclovir and vidarabine. J Infect Dis. 1992;165: 450–55.

137 **Levinson ML, Jacobson PA.** Treatment and prophylaxis of cytomegalovirus disease. Pharmacotherapy. 1992; 12:300–18.

138 **Bailey TC et al.** Failure of high-dose oral acyclovir with or without immune globulin to prevent primary cytomegalovirus disease in recipients of solid organ transplants. Am J Med. 1993;95: 273–78.

139 **Goodrich JM et al.** Ganciclovir prophylaxis to prevent cytomegalovirus disease after allogeneic marrow transplant. Ann Intern Med. 1993;118:173–78.

140 **Schmidt GM et al.** A randomized, controlled trial of prophylactic ganciclovir for cytomegalovirus pulmonary infection in recipients of allogeneic bone marrow transplants. N Engl J Med. 1991;324:1005–011.

141 **CDC.** Prevention and control of influenza: Part 1, Vaccines. MMWR. 1993; 42:1–14.

142 **Brady MT et al.** Safety and prophylactic efficacy of low-dose rimantadine in adults during an influenza A epidemic. Antimicrob Agents Chemother. 1990;34:1633–636.

143 **Monto AS, Arden NH.** Implications of viral resistance to amantadine in control of influenza A. Clin Infect Dis. 1992;15:362–67.

144 **Hayden FG et al.** Recovery of drug-resistant influenza A virus during therapeutic use of rimantadine. Antimicrob Agents Chemother. 1991;35: 1741–747.

145 **Wheeler JG et al.** Historical cohort evaluation of ribavirin efficacy in respiratory syncytial virus infection. Ped Infect Dis J. 1993;12:209–13.

146 **CDC.** Update: Hantavirus pulmonary syndrome — United States, 1993. MMWR. 1993;42:816–20.

147 **Huggins JW et al.** Prospective, double-blind, concurrent, placebo-controlled clinical trial of intravenous ribavirin therapy of hemorrhagic fever with renal syndrome. J Infect Dis. 1991;164:119–27.

148 **Wills RJ et al.** Pharmacokinetics of rimantadine hydrochloride in patients with chronic liver disease. Clin Pharmacol Ther. 1987;42:449–54.

149 **Atmar RL et al.** Safety and pharmacokinetics of rimantadine small-particle aerosol. Antimicrob Agents Chemother. 1990;34:2228–233.

150 **Wills RJ et al.** Rimantadine pharmacokinetics after single and multiple doses. Antimicrob Agents Chemother. 1987;31:826–28.

151 **Hayden FG et al.** Comparative single-dose pharmacokinetics of amantadine hydrochloride and rimantadine hydrochloride in young and elderly adults. Antimicrob Agents Chemother. 1985; 28:216–21.

152 **Trang JM et al.** Linear single dose pharmacokinetics of ganciclovir in newborns with congenital CMV infections. Clin Pharmacol Ther. 1993;53: 15–21.

153 **Aweeka FT et al.** Pharmacokinetics of concomitantly administered foscarnet and zidovudine. Antimicrob Agents Chemother. 1992;36:1821–824.

154 **Hengge UR et al.** Foscarnet penetrates the blood brain barrier: rationale for therapy of CMV encephalitis. Antimicrob Agents Chemother. 1993;37: 1010–014.

Parasitic Infections

JV Anandan

Malaria 71-1
  Overview 71-1
    Distribution and mortality 71-1
    Life cycle 71-1
    Epidemiology 71-2
    Drug resistance 71-2
  Acute Malaria 71-2
    Signs and symptoms 71-2
    Treatment 71-2
      Quinidine and quinine 71-2
      Pyrimethamine-sulfadoxine 71-2
    Chemoprophylaxis and pregnancy and malaria 71-3
      Chloroquine and primaquine phosphate 71-3
      Mefloquine 71-3
    Malaria vaccine 71-3
    Chloroquine-resistant *Plasmodium falciparum*
      (CRPF) malaria 71-3
    Side effects of antimalarials 71-4
    Glucose-6-phosphate dehydrogenase (G6PD)
      deficiency 71-4

Amebiasis 71-4
  Overview 71-4
    Prevalence and mortality 71-4
    Life cycle 71-4
  Amebic Dysentery 71-6
    Diagnosis 71-6
    Drugs 71-7
    Amebic cyst passer 71-7

Giardiasis 71-8
  Overview 71-8
    Prevalence and transmission 71-8
    Life cycle 71-8
  Diagnosis 71-8
    Signs and symptoms 71-8
    Treatment 71-8
      Metronidazole 71-8
      Quinacrine 71-9
      Furazolidone 71-9

Enterobiasis 71-9
  Overview 71-9
    Prevalence 71-9
    Life cycle 71-9
  Signs and Symptoms 71-9
  Treatment 71-9
    Pyrantel pamoate, mebendazole, and albendazole ..71-9
    Household contacts 71-9

Cestodiasis 71-9
  Overview 71-9
    Description 71-9
    Life cycle 71-10
    Epidemiology 71-10
  Taenia saginata and *Taenia solium* 71-10
    Signs and symptoms 71-10
    Diagnosis 71-10
    Treatment 71-10
      Niclosamide 71-10
        Side effects (See Question 24) 71-11
      Praziquantel 71-10
        Side effects (See Question 24) 71-11
  Diphyllobothrium latum and *Hymenolepsis nana* 71-10
    Complications 71-11

Pediculosis 71-11
  Overview 71-11
    Prevalence 71-11
    Life cycle 71-11
    Epidemiology 71-11
  Signs and Symptoms 71-11
  Treatment 71-11
    Pyrethrin, lindane, and malathion 71-11
    Physostigmine ointment 71-11
    Decontamination measures 71-11
    Toxicity 71-11

Scabies 71-12
  Treatment 71-12
    Lindane, permethrin, and crotamiton 71-12

Malaria

Distribution and Mortality. Malaria remains endemic in more than 100 countries including those of Africa, Asia, Oceania (Irian Jaya, Papua New Guinea, and Solomon Islands), Latin America, the Caribbean Islands, and Turkey. The population exposed to malaria exceeds 1.5 billion and the prevalence of the disease worldwide is estimated to be between 200 to 300 million cases.[1-3]

Life Cycle. Malarial infection is transmitted by the female mosquito of the genus *Anopheles* which injects the asexual forms or sporozoites into the human host during a blood meal. Following a lapse of about 9 to 16 days and an asexual multiplication stage in the liver called *exoerythrocytic schizogony*, daughter cells or merozoites are released into the blood to infect red blood cells. The merozoites develop into the characteristic ring or trophozoite forms in red blood cells and then go through another asexual reproductive stage called *erythrocytic schizogony* to produce more merozoites.

When the infected red blood cells rupture, the merozoites then invade new blood cells and repeat the erythrocyte cycle. In one or two weeks, a subpopulation of merozoites differentiates into the sexual forms resulting in male and female gametocytes. If the gametocytes in the host blood are ingested by a female *Anopheles* mosquito during a blood meal, fertilization and an asexual division in the mosquito midgut will propagate the infective sporozoites to complete the cycle.

The characteristic malarial paroxysms of chills and fever in patients usually coincide with the periodic release of merozoites and other pyrogens in the blood. In *Plasmodium falciparum* infections, this periodicity may not always be apparent; however, intervals of 48 hours between paroxysms are reported for *Plasmodium vivax*, *Plasmodium ovale,* and *Plasmodium falciparum* (tertian periodicity) and 72 hours for *Plasmodium malariae* (quartan periodicity). Unlike infections due to *P. falciparum* and *P. malariae*, infections with *P. vivax* and *P. ovale* have a latent form of the exoerythrocytic phase which can persist in the host liver for months and years; this latent form can produce relapses of erythrocytic infection.

Epidemiology. Although malaria is endemic to the tropics, approximately 1000 cases were diagnosed in the U.S. in 1988.[4] The majority of these cases were in immigrants from endemic areas; however, 30% of these were in U.S. citizens who had been infected while traveling abroad. In the U.S., the incidence of malaria transmission from blood transfusions has been reported as 0.25 cases per million donor units.[5] Transfusion malaria frequently is due to *P. malariae* which can persist in the blood without producing symptoms for extended periods of time.[6] Malaria also can be transmitted congenitally and through contaminated needles.[3,7]

Drug Resistance. Chloroquine-resistant *P. falciparum* (CRPF) is increasing in frequency in Africa, South America, and Asia.[1,2,8-11] Prophylactic drug regimens for individuals traveling to endemic areas are problematic (see Question 5).[12-15]

Acute Malaria

Signs and Symptoms

1. A.R., a 26-year-old male student, presents in the emergency room (ER) with complaints of malaise, myalgia, headache, and fever of 4 days' duration. A.R., a native of Kenya, West Africa, recently visited his parents and returned to the U.S. 3 weeks ago. Two days before admission, he had an abrupt onset of coldness and chills which were followed 1 hour later by a high fever, headache, nausea, and vomiting. The episode of chills and fever lasted about 24 hours, after which he became asymptomatic. On the afternoon of admission, he again had a bout of chills which preceded a fever of 40 °C.

Physical examination revealed a slender black male who was acutely ill and complaining of severe abdominal pain. Abdominal examination revealed a soft, tender spleen that was slightly enlarged. Blood pressure (BP) was 110/70 mm Hg; pulse was 120 beats/min; respiration rate was 32/min; and temperature was 40 °C. Laboratory findings included the following: hemoglobin (Hgb) 11 gm/dL (Normal: 12–16); hematocrit (Hct) 34% (Normal: 36–47); white blood cell count (WBC) 3300 cells/mm³ (Normal: 4000–11,000) with 76% neutrophils (Normal: 45–65), lymphocytes 23% (Normal: 15–35) and 1% monocytes (Normal: 1–6); platelets 83 × 10³/mm³ (Normal: 150–450) and bilirubin 1.0 mg/dL (Normal: 0.1–1). Urinalysis revealed trace amounts of albumin and the presence of urobilinogen. Thick and thin films of A.R.'s blood were prepared. A Giemsa stain of the thin film demonstrated *P. falciparum* gametocytes. Why is the presentation of A.R. consistent with *P. falciparum* malaria? [SI units: Hgb 110 gm/L (Normal: 120–160); Hct 0.34 (0.36–0.47); WBC 3.3 × 10⁹/L (Normal: 4–11) with 0.76 neutrophils (Normal: 0.45–0.65), 0.23 lymphocytes (Normal: 0.15–0.35), 0.01 monocytes (Normal: 0.01–0.06); platelets 83 × 10⁹/L (Normal: 150–450); bilirubin 18 µmol/L (Normal: 2–18)]

A.R. recently visited Kenya in West Africa where *P. falciparum* is endemic.[2] *P. vivax* malaria accounts for about 60% of all cases of malaria reported in the U.S.; however, the prevalence of *P. falciparum* malaria has been increasing and accounts for about 33% of all malarial cases.[4] The incubation period for *P. falciparum* is between 8 to 12 days and infected subjects usually experience prodromal symptoms (primarily headache, muscular aches and pains, malaise, nausea, and vomiting) the second week after exposure.[16] This time frame is consistent with A.R.'s onset of symptoms. However, the incubation period and the onset of primary symptoms for *P. falciparum* malaria can be delayed for months.[10,16] History of travel to an endemic area, the typical paroxysmal episode of chills and fever, thrombocytopenia and jaundice, and the positive identification of *P. falciparum* gametocytes in A.R.'s blood confirm the diagnosis of malaria.

Treatment

2. How should the *P. falciparum* malaria in A.R. be treated? How would A.R.'s treatment differ from that used for other species of *Plasmodia*?

P. falciparum malaria is the most severe form of malaria and has the highest mortality.[8,10,17] The fever spikes, unlike those associated with *P. vivax* and *P. ovale* malaria, normally are very high (40 to 41 °C), and complications (including confusion, vomiting, diarrhea, severe abdominal pain, hypoglycemia, renal failure, and encephalopathy) are frequent.[3,6,8,10]

Quinidine and Quinine. A.R. is very ill and may be unable to tolerate oral medications due to nausea and vomiting. He should be admitted to an acute care unit and started on intravenous (IV) quinidine gluconate.[18-21] Intravenous quinine dihydrochloride, which was used instead of quinidine gluconate, no longer is available from the Centers for Disease Control (CDC).[20] A loading dose of 10 mg/kg of quinidine gluconate (6.2 mg quinidine base) diluted in 250 mL normal saline should be administered slowly over a two-hour period. This should be followed by a continuous infusion of 0.02 mg/kg/minute of quinidine gluconate (0.012 mg quinidine base) for 72 hours.[3,11,21] While on the intravenous quinidine, A.R.'s electrocardiogram and blood pressure should be monitored closely.[18-21] Supportive care including fluid and electrolyte management, dialysis, blood transfusion, and mechanical assisted ventilation are important adjunctive therapy in seriously ill patients. The serum concentration of quinidine should be determined once daily during the continuous infusion. Quinidine levels should remain between 6.1 to 18.5 µmol/dL. The quinidine infusion should be slowed or stopped if the QRS complex exceeds 50% of baseline, or hypotension is unresponsive to fluid challenge, or the quinidine serum concentration is greater than 18.5 µmol/dL. When A.R. can be switched to oral therapy, he should receive oral quinine sulfate 650 mg every eight hours to complete three days of therapy.[11,18-21] The quinine is administered for seven days if *P. falciparum* is acquired in Thailand.[11,18]

Pyrimethamine-Sulfadoxine. Since A.R. is from an endemic area for chloroquine-resistant *P. falciparum*, mefloquine is not recommended. Treatment of CRPF should overlap adjunctive therapy with either the quinidine or quinine and the addition of mefloquine would increase the potential for additive cardiotoxicity.[18] If A.R. does not respond (i.e., failure to reduce parasitemia to <1% and fever continues over this period) within 48 to 72 hours to the quinidine or quinine regimen, other adjunctive therapy must be considered.[11,18] One of the recommended drugs for CRPF infection is the combination of pyrimethamine 25 mg and sulfadoxine 500 mg (Fansidar) as a single dose on the third day of quinine regimen; quinine would be discontinued on the third day. Other alternatives that are added to quinine therapy include tetracycline 250 mg four times daily for seven days (tetracycline should overlap the quinine for 2 to 3 days before the latter is discontinued),[18] or clindamycin 900 mg four times a day for three days.[11] If a patient is unable to tolerate oral tetracycline, intravenous doxycycline 100 mg every 12 hours can be substituted.[21] Halofantrine (Halfan), an agent pending approved by the Food and Drug Administration (FDA) in 1992 may be another alternative therapy in CRFP.[9,11]

A patient infected with one of the other species of *Plasmodia* (*P. vivax*, *P. ovale*, or *P. malariae*) should receive oral chloroquine phosphate (Aralen). The initial dose is 1 gm (600 mg base) followed by 500 mg (300 mg base) six hours later; subsequently, 500 mg (300 mg base) is administered daily for two days.[11] Patients with *P. ovale* and *P. vivax* also should be given primaquine to prevent relapses from the latent exoerythrocytic stages in the liver. The adult dose of primaquine is 26.3 mg/day (15 mg base) for 14 days; this should follow the chloroquine regimen.[11]

Chemoprophylaxis and Pregnancy and Malaria

3. R.P., a male medical resident from Colombia, is planning to visit his seriously ill mother. He will be accompanied by his 16-week pregnant wife, J.P., and their 4-year-old daughter. What prophylactic medications for malaria should be administered to each member of the family?

All travelers to endemic areas should receive chemoprophylaxis for malaria. In Latin America, including Colombia, all four types of malaria are present.[11] R.P. and his family may have to take prophylactic therapy for all malarial species, including a regimen which will protect them against chloroquine-resistant *P. falciparum* infections. To verify if a country is included in the chloroquine-resistant *P. falciparum* list or to obtain other relevant information on malaria prophylaxis, R.P. should call the CDC, which provides a touch tone-activated, computer-assisted service: (404) 332–4555.[9] Pregnant women are at greater risk for malaria infection and its complications (especially severe hemolytic anemia and splenomegaly) and should be advised not to travel to areas endemic for malaria, if possible.[9,22–24] (Current publications that provide updated information on parasitic diseases and immunization requirements include the following: Medical Letter, Morbidity and Mortality Weekly Reports, and Health Information for International Travel.)

Chloroquine and Primaquine Phosphate. Chloroquine phosphate is an effective chemoprophylactic agent against all species of *Plasmodia* except drug-resistant *P. falciparum*. The adult dose of chloroquine phosphate is 500 mg (300 mg base) once weekly beginning one week before departure and continuing for four weeks after last exposure. The pediatric dose of chloroquine is 5 mg/kg base (8.3 mg chloroquine phosphate) once weekly beginning one week before departure and continuing for four weeks after exposure. A suspension of chloroquine in chocolate syrup can be prepared for pediatric patients (5 mg/mL). Chloroquine prophylaxis is safe during pregnancy and the benefits outweigh the risk of malaria and the drug's possible side effects.[3,6,24–26]

By taking the chloroquine one week before travel, one can achieve adequate antimalarial chloroquine levels in the blood by the second week. Potential side effects also can be detected early. A weekly dose of 0.5 gm of chloroquine phosphate produces average plasma concentrations of chloroquine between 0.47 to 0.78 μmol/L. Most strains of *P. vivax* and *P. falciparum* are susceptible to plasma levels between 0.046 to 0.093 μmol/L, respectively.[27,28] Mefloquine (Lariam) 250 mg (salt) once weekly beginning one week before departure and for four weeks after leaving a malarious area is an alternative regimen to chloroquine.[11] However, mefloquine is not recommended during pregnancy or in children weighing less than 15 kg because the safety of this agent has not been established in this population.[9] Chloroquine suppresses the asexual erythrocytic forms of the malaria parasite and has no action against the exoerythrocytic phase of *P. vivax* and *P. ovale*.[29] *Primaquine phosphate*, however, prevents relapses of *P. vivax* and *P. ovale* by inhibiting the exoerythrocytic stage; it also has a marked gametocytocidal effect against all species.[9,30,31] To prevent an attack after departure from an area where *P. vivax* and *P. ovale* are present, primaquine phosphate 26.3 mg/day (15 mg base) for 14 days, to coincide with the last two weeks of chloroquine regimen, should be prescribed. Primaquine should not be administered to pregnant subjects.[6] The major toxicity of concern, aside from the teratogenic risk, is hemolytic anemia in subjects with red blood cell glucose-6-phosphate dehydrogenase (G6PD) deficiency.[32–34]

Mefloquine. Prophylaxis for chloroquine-resistant *P. falciparum* also can be achieved by taking mefloquine in the doses indicated above instead of the chloroquine regimen.[9,11] An alternative to mefloquine is doxycycline 100 mg/day beginning one day before

travel and continuing for the duration of the stay and for four weeks after leaving the malarial area. Travelers such as R.P. should be advised to take measures to reduce contact with infected mosquitoes by wearing long-sleeved shirts and trousers, applying insect repellent containing 31% to 33% N,N-diethyl-m-toluamide (DEET) (e.g., Cutter Evergreen Scent repellent or Ultrathon Insect Repellent), sleeping in a screened room, or using netting impregnated with permethrin.[9] If chloroquine is selected as the prophylactic drug, the combination of pyrimethamine-sulfadoxine (Fansidar) must be added in CRPF areas. Because pyrimethamine-sulfadoxine has caused serious cutaneous reactions, the CDC has modified its guidelines for the use of this preparation in the prophylaxis of CRPF infections.[12] Currently, travelers who are in the endemic area for less than three weeks should withhold taking Fansidar prophylactically. However, three tablets should be taken at the first onset of fever. Pediatric patients between the ages of four and eight years should receive one-half the adult dose.[11,12] Both prophylaxis and treatment of CRPF pose special problems in pregnancy. Pyrimethamine has teratogenic effects while quinine, mefloquine, and sulfonamides are contraindicated in pregnancy.[9,11,25] In conclusion, R.P. and J.P. should reconsider their decision to travel together because of the lack of good CRPF prophylaxis during pregnancy. Chloroquine, however, can be used by all family members and should be effective against all but chloroquine-resistant *P. falciparum*. Physical barriers (e.g., clothes, mosquito nets), insect repellent, and a short stay in the endemic area also should be helpful.

Malaria Vaccine

4. Why can J.P. not be vaccinated as an alternative to prophylaxis with 8-aminoquinolines such as chloroquine?

Currently, there is no vaccination available. However, as the result of successful *in vitro P. falciparum* cultivation and advances in genetic engineering and monoclonal antibody research, the development of a vaccine for malaria seems imminent.[35–38] The malaria plasmodium undergoes many transformations during its development and each stage expresses a different plasmodial genome that generates a large number of antigens. The development of a malaria vaccine relies upon the identification and characterization of these antigens and the subsequent production of monoclonal antibodies.[37]

At present, three types of vaccines against *P. falciparum* are under study: a merozoite vaccine which would induce immunity against the erythrocytic forms of plasmodia in the blood; a sporozoite vaccine which would protect against the exoerythrocytic or liver phase; and a gamete vaccine which would prevent transmission of malaria in epidemic areas.[2,38] When a vaccine for malaria is available, it is expected to provide an immune response for at least one year. Furthermore, the safety of these vaccines to the fetus and mother during pregnancy also will need evaluation.

Chloroquine-Resistant Plasmodium falciparum (CRPF) Malaria

5. T.S., a permanent U.S. resident of Cambodian origin, is planning to travel to the Thai-Kampuchean refugee camp. What antimalarial agents should he use for chemoprophylaxis?

T.S. is traveling to the Thai-Burma border which is epidemic for falciparum malaria. Chemoprophylaxis against malaria in this region of southeast Asia has become progressively difficult due to the appearance of *P. falciparum* strains resistant to chloroquine, pyrimethamine-sulfadoxine, quinine, and even mefloquine.[9,11,39–44] The combination of quinine and tetracycline which is indicated for the multidrug-resistant strain of *P. falciparum* must be administered three times a day for a total of seven to ten days to achieve a cure, and therefore, is not suitable for prophylaxis.[39]

T.S. will have to take chemoprophylaxis against both *P. vivax* and multidrug-resistant *P. falciparum*. He should take mefloquine (Lariam), a new antimalarial drug approved by the FDA for prevention and treatment of *P. falciparum*.[40,44] For prophylaxis, the recommended dose is 250 mg of mefloquine once weekly starting one week before travel and continuing weekly for duration of stay and for four weeks after leaving Thailand.[41] Upon return from his visit, T.S. should take primaquine phosphate to prevent an attack of *P. vivax* because mefloquine has no effect on the exoerythrocytic phase of *P. vivax* (see Question 3 for doses of primaquine).[11] An alternative regimen to mefloquine is chloroquine phosphate 500 mg (300 mg base) orally once weekly. A single dose (3 tablets) of pyrimethamine-sulfadoxine (Fansidar) should be carried and taken if a febrile illness occurs.[11,12] Since pyrimethamine-sulfadoxine has been associated with serious adverse effects, this combination should be used cautiously.[12,45-50] A safer alternative to Fansidar for prophylaxis against *P. falciparum* malaria for T.S. would be doxycycline 100 mg taken once daily beginning one to two days before departure, and continuing for four weeks after he returns from Thailand.[11,43,44]

A new drug, ginghaosu, is undergoing field trials and may prove to be useful for resistant *P. falciparum*. Ginghaosu, a plant extract (artemisinin compounds), has been used for many centuries in China for fever and malaria.[45] The antimalarial agent, halofantrine (Halfan), may be another alternative to mefloquine.[9,11]

Side Effects of Antimalarials

6. A.K., a 36-year old Malaysian male, is seen in the ER of a local hospital with 2-day complaints of fever, chills, and bouts of diarrhea following his return from West Malaysia where he was visiting his parents for 3 weeks. A.K. indicated that he had not taken any prophylaxis for malaria. A blood smear stained with Giemsa solution demonstrated *P. vivax* and A.K. was placed on chloroquine 1 gm (600 mg base) initially, to be followed by 500 mg (300 mg base) 6 hours later and 500 mg at 24 and 48 hours. Upon completion of the chloroquine regimen, A.K. was instructed to take primaquine 26.5 mg/day (15 mg base) for 14 days. However, A.K. was seen again in the ER a day later with complaints of abdominal pain, severe headache, vomiting, and "bitter taste" in the mouth. What subjective evidence does A.K. exhibit that is compatible with the toxicity of antimalarials?

The major side effects of chloroquine (e.g., nausea, abdominal pain, pruritus, vertigo, headache, and visual disturbances)[27,46,47] usually are associated with large doses such as those that are needed for therapy of A.K. The gastrointestinal (GI) complaints and severe headache experienced by A.K. are consistent with chloroquine therapy and the bitter taste he described is experienced consistently by all subjects who are placed on chloroquine or other 8-aminoquinoline preparations. Since A.K. also will be taking primaquine after the course of chloroquine, he should be told that he probably will experience some GI upset with this drug as well. Abdominal cramps associated with primaquine may be relieved by antacids or by taking the drug after meals. The severe nausea and vomiting may have dehydrated A.K. and he should be encouraged to replenish his fluids. Table 71.1 lists the adverse effects of antimalarials.

Glucose-6-Phosphate Dehydrogenase (G6PD) Deficiency

7. Why is A.K. at risk for primaquine sensitivity?

Primaquine sensitivity or G6PD deficiency is an inherited error of metabolism transmitted by a gene of partial dominance located on the X-chromosome. Patients with this enzyme deficiency are

sensitive to the 8-aminoquinolines, sulfonamides, para-aminosalicylates, nitrofurantoin, sulfone, aspirin, quinine, quinidine, nalidixic acid, and methylene blue.[32] G6PD in red blood cells preserves glutathione in the reduced form (see Figure 89.2 in Chapter 89: Drug-Induced Blood Disorders) by regenerating nicotinamide adenine dinucleotide phosphate (NADPH). Reduced glutathione protects red blood cell membranes from increased oxidant stress. Patients with low levels of glutathione and impaired regeneration of NADPH, as seen with G6PD deficiency, are susceptible to the oxidizing effect of drugs.[32-34] If these patients are exposed inadvertently to oxidizing drugs (e.g., primaquine), red blood cell hemolysis, methemoglobinemia, and Heinz body formation will result. The amount of hemolysis is dependent upon the dose of the drug and age of the erythrocyte population. Older red blood cells which have lower levels of G6PD hemolyze first, while the younger cells may be more resistant.[33] Hemolysis reportedly occurs on the third day of drug ingestion and usually is manifested as abdominal discomfort, anemia, and hemoglobinuria.[33]

The incidence of G6PD deficiency in the Southeast Asian refugee population is approximately 5.2%.[51] Since A.K. is a native of Malaysia and may have G6PD deficiency, he may be at risk of hemolysis if primaquine is ingested. Therefore, he should be screened for G6PD deficiency before being treated with this drug. Although a number of simple and satisfactory screening tests for G6PD deficiency are available, the fluorescent Spot test is the simplest, most reliable, and sensitive.[32] The Spot test is based upon the addition of a reagent containing NADP to a hemolysate of the patient's red cells. After an incubation period, the mixture is spotted on filter paper and examined under long-wave ultralight. Fluorescence of the mixture on the filter paper will indicate the presence of NADPH generated by G6PD. In patients who have G6PD deficiency, it will fluoresce only weakly or no fluorescence will be detected. There are large variants among those with the mutant gene and if A.K. has a variant with relatively mild episodic clinical manifestations (variant A, with 10% to 60% residual enzyme activity), he may be treated with primaquine at 45 mg/week for eight weeks.[18]

Amebiasis

Prevalence and Mortality. Amebiasis, which is caused by a small protozoan parasite, *Entamoeba histolytica*, results in amebic dysentery and hepatic abscess.[52-54] Approximately 10% of the world population (predominantly in Latin America, Africa, and Asia) are infected, and about 75,000 die annually from this infection.[52,54] In the U.S., amebiasis is considered endemic in homosexual males because 20% to 30% of this population are infected with *E. histolytica*.[53-58] Amebiasis can be asymptomatic or it can present as colitis or dysentery. Extraintestinal lesions, primarily abscesses in the liver, also can be characteristic.[58-65]

Life Cycle. The amebic parasite or trophozoite lives in the lumen of the colon and the colonic mucosa. Trophozoites do not survive outside the host body, and if ingested accidentally, will be destroyed by gastric juice. In contrast, the encysted trophozoites can survive drying and freezing: they are killed only by temperatures in excess of 55 °C or by hyperchlorination of water.[53,54,66,67] Infection occurs by ingestion of cysts present in contaminated water or food. Once ingested by the host, each cyst dissolves in the alkaline media of the small intestine and undergoes asexual division to produce eight trophozoites.[53,54] The trophozoites, which represent the invasive form of *E. histolytica*, then move to the large bowel, invade the mucosal crypts, and produce ulcerations.[53,54] Ulcerations of the bowel wall may result in amebic dysentery, inflammatory lesions in the bowel (amebomas), amebic appendicitis,

Table 71.1	Drug Therapy of Parasitic Infection[a,9,11,27,70–72,101,147]	
Drug of Choice	**Dosage**	**Adverse Effects**
Amebiasis (Including Cyst Passers)		
Asymptomatic		
Iodoquinol	*Adult:* 650 mg PO TID x 20 days	Rash, acne, thyroid enlargement
OR	*Pediatric:* 30–40 mg/kg/day PO TID x 20 days	
Diloxanide furoate	*Adult:* 500 mg PO TID x 10 days	
OR	*Pediatric:* 20 mg/kg/day PO TID x 10 days	
Paromomycin	*Adult:* 25–30 mg/kg/day PO TID x 7 days	Nausea, vomiting
	Pediatric: Same as adult	
Mild to Moderate GI Disease		
Metronidazole	*Adult:* 750 mg PO TID x 10 days	Nausea, headache, metallic taste, disulfiram reaction
FOLLOWED BY	*Pediatric:* 35–50 mg/kg/day PO TID x 10 days	with alcohol, paresthesia
Iodoquinol	*Adult:* 650 mg PO TID x 20 days	Rash, acne, thyroid enlargement
	Pediatric: 30–40 mg/kg/day PO TID x 20 days	
Severe GI Disease		
Metronidazole	*Adult:* 750 mg PO TID x 10 days	Nausea, headache, metallic taste, disulfiram reaction
FOLLOWED BY	*Pediatric:* 35–50 mg/kg/day PO TID x 10 days	with alcohol, paresthesia
Iodoquinol	*Adult:* 650 mg PO TID x 20 days	Rash, acne, thyroid enlargement
	Pediatric: 30–40 mg/kg/day PO TID x 20 days	
Alternatives		
Dehydroemetine	*Adult:* 1–1.5 mg/kg/day IM x 5 days (*max:* 90 mg/day)	Arrhythmias, hypotension, ECG: PR, QT, QRS
FOLLOWED BY	*Pediatric:* Same as adult	prolongation and ST depression
Iodoquinol	*Adult:* 650 mg PO TID x 20 days	Rash, acne, thyroid enlargement
	Pediatric: 30–40 mg/kg/day PO TID x 20 days	
Amebic Liver Abscess		
Metronidazole	*Adult:* 750 mg TID x 10 days	Nausea, headache, metallic taste, disulfiram reaction
FOLLOWED BY	*Pediatric:* 35–50 mg/kg/day PO TID x 10 days	with alcohol, paresthesia
Iodoquinol	*Adult:* 650 mg PO TID x 20 days	Rash, acne, thyroid enlargement
OR	*Pediatric:* 30–40 mg/kg/day PO TID x 20 days	
Alternatives		
Dehydroemetine	*Adult:* 1–1.5 mg/kg/day IM x 5 days (*max:* 90 mg/day)	Arrhythmias, hypotension, ECG: PR, QT, QRS
FOLLOWED BY	*Pediatric:* Same as adult	prolongation and ST depression
Chloroquine phosphate	*Adult:* 600 mg base/day x 2 days, then 300 mg base/day x 2–3 weeks	
PLUS	*Pediatric:* 10 mg/kg/day (*max:* 300 mg base/day) x 2–3 weeks	
Iodoquinol	*Adult:* 650 mg PO TID x 20 days	Rash, acne, thyroid enlargement
	Pediatric: 30–40 mg/kg/day PO TID x 20 days	
Ascariasis (Roundworm)		
Mebendazole	*Adult/Pediatric:* 100 mg BID PO x 3 days	Diarrhea, abdominal pain
Enterobiasis (Pinworm)		
Pyrantel pamoate	*Adult/Pediatric:* 11 mg/kg PO once (*max:* 1 gm), repeat in 2 weeks	
Filariasis		
Diethylcarbamazine	*Adult:* Day 1 50 mg PC; Day 2 50 mg TID; Day 3 100 mg TID; Days 4–21 6 mg/kg/day in 3 doses	Severe allergic/febrile reactions, GI disturbance, rarely encephalopathy
	Pediatric: Day 1 25–50 mg; day 2 25–50 mg TID; Day 3 50–100 mg TID; Days 4–21 6 mg/kg/day in 3 doses	
Flukes (Trematodes)[b]		
Praziquantel	*Adult/Pediatric:* 75 mg/kg/day in 3 doses x 1 day (*Exceptions: C. sinensis* and *P. westermani* x 2 days)	Malaise, headache, dizziness, sedation, fever, eosinophilia
Giardiasis		
Metronidazole[c]	*Adult:* 250 mg PO TID with meals x 5 days	Nausea, headache, metallic taste, disulfiram reaction
	Pediatric: 15 mg/kg/day PO TID x 5 days	with alcohol, paresthesia
Hookworm		
Mebendazole	*Adult/Pediatric:* 100 mg PO BID x 3 days	Diarrhea, abdominal pain
Lice		
1% Permethrin (Nix)	Topical administration	Occasional allergic reaction, mild stinging, erythema
Malaria		
All Plasmodia except Chloroquine-Resistant		
Parental Therapy		
Quinidine gluconate	*Adult:* Loading dose 10 mg/kg of salt (6.2 mg base) diluted in 250 mL normal saline and infused IV over 2 hr, followed	ECG findings: QT and QRS prolongation; hypotension, syncope, arrhythmias; cinchonism

Continued

Table 71.1	Drug Therapy of Parasitic Infection[a,9,11,27,70–72,101,147] (Continued)	
Drug of Choice	**Dosage**	**Adverse Effects**
	by a continuous IV infusion of 0.02 mg/kg/min (0.012 mg base) for 72 hr. Should be switched to oral quinine 650 mg Q 8 hr as soon as possible *Pediatric:* Same as adult	
Oral Therapy		
Quinine sulfate	*Adult:* 650 PO TID x 3 days	Cinchonism
PLUS	*Pediatric:* 25 mg/kg/day PO TID x 3 days	
Pyrimethamine-Sulfadoxine (Fansidar)	*Adult:* 3 tab at once (withhold until febrile episode) *Pediatric:* ¼–2 tab (dependent upon age)[d]	GI, erythema multiforme, Stevens-Johnson syndrome, toxic epidermal necrolysis
OR		
Mefloquine	*Adult:* 1250 mg once *Pediatric:* 25 mg/kg once (>45 kg)	Dose-related: vertigo, nausea, dizziness, light-headedness, headache, visual disturbances, toxic psychosis seizures
Prevention of Relapses: (P. vivax and P. ovale)		
Primaquine phosphate	*Adult:* 26.3 mg/day (15 mg base) for 14 days. This follows chloroquine or mefloquine regimen	Abdominal cramps, nausea, hemolytic anemia in G6PD
Scabies		
5% Permethrin (Elimite cream)	Topical administration	Rash, edema, erythema
Alternatives		
Lindane (Kwell)	Apply topically once	Not recommended in pregnant women, infants, and in people with massive excoriated skin
Crotamiton 10% (Eurax)	Topically	Local skin irritation
Tapeworm[e]		
Praziquantel	*Adult/Pediatric:* 25 mg/kg PO x 1 dose	Malaise, headache, dizziness, sedation, eosinophilia, fever
Hydatid cysts[f]		
Albendazole	*Adult:* 400 mg BID x 28 days, repeat if necessary *Pediatric:* 15 mg/kg/day x 28 days, repeat if necessary (surgical resection may precede drug therapy)	Diarrhea, abdominal pain, rarely hepatotoxicity, leukopenia
Trichomoniasis		
Metronidazole	*Adult:* 2 gm PO x 1 day or 250 mg PO TID x 7 days *Pediatric:* 15 mg/kg/day PO TID x 7 days	Nausea, headache, metallic taste, disulfiram reaction with alcohol, paresthesia

[a] CNS = Central nervous system; ECG = Electrocardiograph; G6PD = Glucose-6-phosphate dehydrogenase; GI = Gastrointestinal; IM = Intramuscular; IV = Intravenous; tab = Tablets.

[b] *Schistosoma haematobium, Schistosoma mansoni, Schistosoma japonicum, Clonorchis sinensis, Paragonimus westermani.*

[c] Quinacrine no longer is available in the U.S. or any other country at this time.

[d] <1 year: ¼ tablet; 1–3 years: ½ tablet; 4–8 years: 1 tablet; 9–14 years: 2 tablets.

[e] *Diphyllobothrium latum* (fish), *Taenia saginata* (beet), *Taenia solium* (pork), *Dipylidium caninum* (dog), *Hymenolepsis nana.*

[f] *Echinococcus granulosus, Echinococcus multicularis.* Albendazole is an investigational drug in the U.S.

and perforation of the colon or intestine.[53,54] The amebae also can enter into the portal vein, which transports them to the liver where they can initiate multiply abscesses.[53–55,61–68]

Amebic Dysentery

Diagnosis

8. M.B., a 35-year-old homosexual male, presented to the ER with a 10-day history of abdominal pain and multiple, loose watery stools with occasional streaks of blood. Upon physical examination, he is a thin man with abdominal distress. His vital signs were: temperature 38 °C, pulse 88 beats/min, and BP 120/80 mm Hg. He had no skin lesions, jaundice, or lymphadenopathy. The examination was remarkable for slight abdominal distension with some right lower quadrant tenderness. Rectal examination revealed some tenderness and brown liquid stool positive for occult blood. Proctosigmoidoscopy demonstrated colonic mucosa which was diffusely edematous and friable. A biopsy specimen could not be obtained because M.B. was uncooperative and combative. Initial laboratory findings were as follows: Hgb 13.04 gm/dL; Hct 40%; leukocyte count 13,800 cells/mm³ with 68% neutrophils, 14% bands, 5% lymphocytes, and 13% monocytes; albumin was 3.1 gm/dL (Normal: 3.5–5). A liver scan and liver function tests were normal. On ultrasound examination, a tender mass palpable in the lower right quadrant proved to be a 3 cm collection of fluid consistent with abdominal abscess. During an exploratory operation, 100 mL of a brownish-yellow material was drained. Smears of the drained material were positive for *E. histolytica* trophozoites and culture of the material was negative for bacteria. Fresh stool examination was positive for *E. histolytica* and the indirect hemagglutination antibody (IHA) test was positive at 1:512. How was amebic colitis differentiated from ulcerative colitis in M.B.? What is the significance of obtaining serology in M.B.? [SI units: Hgb 130.4 gm/L; Hct 0.40; leukocyte count 13.8 × 10⁹/L with 0.68 neutrophils, 0.14 bands, 0.05 lymphocytes, and 0.13 monocytes; albumin 31 gm/L (Normal: 35–50)]

M.B.'s abdominal symptoms, elevated temperature, right lower quadrant tenderness, occult blood in the stool examination, together with the proctosigmoidoscopic findings, strongly suggest either a bacterial or a protozoan infection.[53,54,67–69] Stool examination confirms that M.B. has amebiasis while the presence of *E. histolytica* from the abdominal abscess and bloody stools confirm the diagnosis of amebic colitis. Serological tests are useful, especially when the parasite is absent from the stool or abscess material, and are considered highly sensitive (>90%).[61] The IHA which detects specific antibody to the amebae is helpful for the differential diagnosis between ulcerative colitis and amebic colitis, although in M.B., positive *E. histolytica* from the stool and smear from the abdominal abscess were diagnostic. When appropriate stool samples are not available, endoscopic or colonoscopic specimens may be critical for diagnosis and positive serology will affirm the diagnosis of amebiasis.[54,70] A titer of 1:512 or higher is detected in more than 85% of patients with invasive amebic colitis; the absence of serum antibodies to E. histolytica after seven days of symptoms is evidence against a diagnosis of invasive amebiasis.[70] M.B.'s indirect hemagglutination titer of 1:512 and the finding of this parasite in his stool and in an abdominal abscess confirm his diagnosis of amebiasis.

Drugs

9. What are the major drugs that can be used to treat M.B.? What regimen might be preferred in M.B.?

The two classes of drugs that can be used to treat M.B.'s amebiasis are the luminal-acting drugs, which act only in the bowel lumen, and the tissue amebicides, which have activity in the bowel wall, liver, and other extraintestinal tissues.[71,72] Luminal-acting drugs achieve high concentrations in the bowel but only minimal systemic absorption takes place. These drugs include diiodohydroxyquin of iodoquinol (Yodoxin), diloxanide furoate (Furamide), and paromomycin (Humatin). Tetracycline should be considered a secondary bowel amebicide for M.B. because tetracycline is not active against liver amebae.[73] Tetracycline modifies the enteric bowel flora and reduces amebic colonization; it usually is combined with another luminal-acting agent when it is used for intestinal amebiasis.[73]

M.B. needs to be treated with a tissue amebicide in combination with a luminal agent because he has positive serology which indicates tissue invasion by E. histolytica. Tissue amebicides are well absorbed and attain adequate systemic levels to treat extraintestinal amebiasis.[53,54,71–74] Since their concentrations in the bowel may be insufficient to eradicate E. histolytica, they must be combined with a luminal-acting agent to treat both serious intestinal amebiasis and extraintestinal amebic lesions.[54,73] The tissue amebicides include metronidazole (Flagyl), chloroquine phosphate (Aralen), emetine, and dehydroemetine. Chloroquine is effective only as a liver amebicide.[71,72] Neither diloxanide nor dehydroemetine is commercially available, but both can be obtained from the CDC.[11]

M.B.'s acute amebic dysentery should be treated with a combination of metronidazole and a luminal agent like iodoquinol or diloxanide furoate. Metronidazole should be administered in a dose of 750 mg three times daily for ten days. If M.B. is too ill to tolerate the oral tablets, a loading dose of 15 mg/kg of metronidazole can be administered intravenously over one hour followed by a maintenance dose of 7.5 mg/kg every six hours.[73,74] Intramuscular emetine, 1 mg/kg (maximum: 65 mg/day) or dehydroemetine 1 to 1.5 mg/kg (maximum: 90 mg/day) can be used instead of metronidazole.[11,53,54,73] Dehydroemetine is as effective as emetine and less toxic;[11] however, both are highly toxic compared to other available agents such as metronidazole and iodoquinol and should be avoided if possible.[70] The regimen of metronidazole in M.B. should be followed by a luminal agent such as iodoquinol, 650 mg three times daily for 20 days, or diloxanide furoate, 500 mg three times daily for ten days.[11,70] M.B. needs to be monitored and his stool should be examined over the ensuing three months. A colonoscopy could document cure. Relapse rate of amebic colitis is around 10%.[11,70]

Amebic Cyst Passer

10. P.C., a 47-year-old male whose stool was found to be positive for E. histolytica cysts on routine examination, was completely asymptomatic. Would you treat P.C.? What are other drug regimens for amebiasis?

P.C. is an asymptomatic cyst passer and the infection may be chronic. Invasive amebiasis and extraintestinal disease are a potential threat to P.C. and he also is a source of infection to others.[61] For these reasons, he should be treated with a full course of a luminal amebicide (diloxanide or iodoquinol).[11,70,73,76] To verify the eradication of the infection, P.C.'s stool should be examined monthly for three months.[54] (For other treatment regimens for amebiasis, see Table 71.1).

11. If P.C. is not treated, what complications might be encountered?

Amebic liver abscess is one of the most frequent complications of amebiasis, with the right lobe of the liver being involved in 90% of all cases.[61,66] Patients usually present with fever, tenderness over an enlarged liver, leukocytosis, elevated sedimentation rate, and anemia.[61,66] Liver scans (utilizing radioactive isotope with either ^{99}technetium or sulfur colloid), ultrasonography, and serology (IHA >1:256) usually confirm the presence of an abscess.[60,63,73,77,78] Liver abscesses can extend to the lungs through fistulas and cause empyemas and lung abscesses.[69,73] Amebic peritonitis also may result from liver abscesses.[61,66] Other complications include amebic pericarditis, brain abscess, amebic strictures secondary to dysentery, and cutaneous amebiasis.[61,63,77,78] Management of these complications include exploratory operations to drain the abscesses, needle aspiration directed by radiologic monitoring, appropriate cultures of aspirate fluid, and drug therapy with metronidazole combined with a luminal agent like iodoquinol.[54] Lesions may take from two to ten months to resolve; healing can be monitored through periodic radiologic studies.[61,77] The consequence of not treating P.C. can be serious and lead to some significant medical problems.

12. C.R., a 24-year old pregnant female, upon returning from Thailand, presented with a 5-day history of watery stools, bloody mucus, and fever. She is 22 weeks pregnant. Her past medical history includes rheumatic fever at age 5 and heart murmurs. She initially was treated with ampicillin to which she did not respond. She is referred to the University Medical Center for evaluation by her physician. Upon physical examination, C.R.'s temperature was 38.2 °C, and her abdomen was soft but nontender; she complained of severe cramps. Examination of fresh stools showed blood by hemoccult and the wet mount demonstrated trophozoites with ingested red cells. A trichrome stain showed E. histolytica trophozoites. Bacterial culture was negative for pathogenic bacteria. An abdominal computed tomography scan was negative for abdominal or liver amebiasis and anti-amebic antibody was negative. A diagnosis of intestinal amebiasis was made. How would you treat C.R.? If C.R. subsequently develops amebic colitis, how would you treat her and what are some toxicities of concern with the selected regimens?

C.R. needs to receive a luminal amebicide to treat her intestinal amebiasis. However, since she is 22 weeks pregnant and has an underlying cardiovascular problem, therapeutic options are rather limited. Metronidazole, iodoquinol, and emetine are not preferred regimens for C.R. because of potential adverse effects to mother or fetus. A drug that has minimal systemic effects would be optimal so as not to jeopardize her fetus. Paromomycin, a nonabsorbable aminoglycoside, is effective and has been used in pregnant patients.[70] C.R. should receive paromomycin 30 mg/kg/day in three divided doses for seven days. The most common side effect of paromomycin is gastrointestinal upset manifested as increased frequency of stools.[11,70] C.R. should be instructed to bring her stools at the end of the course of therapy and this should be tested to verify a cure. A serology for serum amebic antibodies also should be evaluated. If serology is positive, C.R. must be considered for a full course of metronidazole followed by a luminal agent, either iodoquinol or diloxanide furoate.[69,70] C.R. would be in the third trimester of pregnancy during this period if and when she develops amebic colitis or hepatic amebiasis.

Used concomitantly with a luminal amebicide, metronidazole still remains the drug of choice for all patients with severe amebic colitis, hepatic abscess, and extraintestinal amebiasis.[54,70-73] The most common side effects include nausea, diarrhea, furry tongue, and glossitis.[71,72] Metronidazole causes disulfiram-like effects if alcohol is consumed while the patient is on the drug.[72] Of major concern are the reports of carcinogenicity in rodents and mutagenic activity of metronidazole in bacteria.[72,79] The clinical significance of carcinogenicity in the human population has not been fully assessed because a cause-and-effect relationship between use of the drug and malignancy has not been documented adequately.[11,72] Although metronidazole is considered safe to be used in C.R. who now is in her third trimester, it should be avoided, if possible, during the first trimester of pregnancy.[70,72]

If amebic colitis or hepatic amebiasis has developed, C.R. needs to receive either iodoquinol or diloxanide furoate to follow her metronidazole regimen. If iodoquinol is selected, the side effects associated with usual doses include nausea and vomiting, abdominal discomfort, diarrhea, headache, and occasionally, enlargement of the thyroid gland.[71,72] Serious neurologic side effects, specifically subacute myelo-optic neuropathy (SMON), have been associated with another analog, iodochlorhydroxyquin (Clioquinol, Entero-Vioform), which has been withdrawn from the U.S. market.[71,72] SMON is a syndrome that manifests as abdominal discomfort, peripheral polyneuritis, weakness of the lower limbs, optic atrophy, and vision disturbances.[71,72] Controversy as to whether SMON is caused by the drug or a viral infection remains unresolved.[72]

If diloxanide furoate is selected instead of iodoquinol, this agent is essentially free of side effects with the exception of some minor GI symptoms that include flatulence (belching and abdominal distension) and stomach cramps.[71,72] This may be preferable to iodoquinol for C.R.; however, this drug needs to be obtained from the CDC.[11]

C.R. should not receive either emetine or dehydroemetine because of her history of rheumatic disease and heart murmurs and the potential for these two drugs to cause serious cardiovascular toxicity, such as arrhythmias, hypotension, and precordial pain.[54,71,72] Electrocardiographic changes associated with emetine and dehydroemetine include Q-T, P-R, and QRS prolongation and S-T segment depression.[71]

Giardiasis

Prevalence and Transmission. Giardiasis, manifested as nausea, abdominal cramping, and diarrhea is caused by a protozoan, *Giardia lamblia*.[80,81] The disease is endemic in large areas of the world, especially where sanitation and sanitary habits are poor.[81] Although the prevalence is low in most developed countries, a number of outbreaks of giardiasis have been reported in Russia, Eastern Europe, and the U.S.[82-89] *G. lamblia* is the most frequently reported pathogen in infectious diarrhea among Americans.[87,88] Water-borne outbreaks of giardiasis occur more frequently than food-borne outbreaks.[81,83] Giardia seems more prevalent in children, older debilitated individuals, subjects with dysgammaglobulinemias (specifically those with a deficiency of IgA), and the homosexual population.[89-92]

Life Cycle. *G. lamblia* exists in two forms: the trophozoite and the cyst. The cyst is excreted in the stool, and if it is ingested accidentally in contaminated water or food, will excyst in the stomach to produce trophozoites.[88] The trophozoites migrate to the small intestine and produce the GI symptoms characteristic of giardiasis. Symptoms appear 5 to 15 days after ingestion of the cyst.[88]

Diagnosis

Signs and Symptoms

13. J.T., a 23-year-old female student, has just returned from Mexico after spending a month there with a local church group. Two days before returning to the U.S., J.T. had a bout of diarrhea with "offensive yellow stools." She now complains of nausea, abdominal discomfort, and occasional foul-smelling diarrhea alternating with constipation. J.T. indicates that she has lost about 10 pounds over the previous 2 weeks. Three stool samples were examined for ova and parasites and a stool culture also was ordered. Two of the three stool samples were positive for *G. lamblia* cysts, and the culture was negative for bacterial pathogens. Why is this a typical presentation of giardiasis?

The symptoms of giardiasis are variable. Some patients present with profuse watery stools, abdominal distension, and cramping for several weeks while others complain only of mild abdominal discomfort, flatulence, and occasional loose stools.[87,88] J.T.'s symptoms are typical and consistent with the description of giardiasis. Symptoms usually begin about two weeks following transmission of the infection and include anorexia, nausea, and diarrhea with bulky foul-smelling stools.[87,88] The acute phase of giardiasis can be followed by a period of chronic intermittent diarrhea alternating with constipation.[81-86] During this period, anorexia and malabsorption will cause weight loss. Malabsorption from severe or chronic giardiasis can result in deficiencies in vitamin B_{12} and cause carbohydrate depletion.[93] *G. lamblia* cysts usually are found in the stool, although there may be periods when cysts are difficult to detect due to a low count.[88,89,94] The onset of symptoms, foul-smelling stools, and weight loss are consistent with symptomatic giardiasis in J.T.

14. If the stool examination had been negative for *G. lamblia*, what alternative steps would have been necessary to obtain a diagnosis in J.T.?

Bacterial infection caused by *Salmonella*, *Shigella*, or *Campylobacter* was ruled out by a negative stool culture in J.T.[95,96] The next step would be to use the Entero-test in an attempt to obtain a diagnosis for giardiasis.[97] The Entero-test consists of a gelatinous capsule attached to a string. The patient swallows the capsule and the other end of the string is secured to the face with tape. Following a lapse of four to six hours, the string is pulled up, and the bile-stained end is examined under a microscope. The Entero-test sample obtained from the duodenum will demonstrate the trophozoite rather than the cyst and reportedly has a better yield than a stool examination.[97]

Several other tests to detect *Giardia* antigen in the stool have become commercially available.[101] These tests have sensitivity of 85% to 98% and specificity of 90% to 100%.[101] An immunofluorescence assay using monoclonal antibody against *Giardia* cysts is available from Diagnostics, Inc. Some clinicians may prefer to use these newer tests rather than the Entero-test. However, if the Entero-test is negative, most clinicians would initiate a therapeutic trial rather than subject a patient to other invasive diagnostic procedures.[87,88] As a last resort, aspiration of duodenal fluid or biopsy by gastroscopy may be attempted.[87]

Treatment

15. How would you treat J.T.?

Metronidazole is the drug of choice for giardiasis in J.T.[11] Metronidazole, 250 mg three times daily for seven days, is equally effective as quinacrine in the treatment of giardiasis.[73,101] Although metronidazole was reported to be mutagenic in bacteria and carcinogenic in high doses in animals, there is no evidence that it represents a risk in the human population at this time.[79]

Quinacrine (Atabrine) administered as 100 mg three times daily for five days with cure rates of 90% to 95% and once considered the drug of choice for giardiasis, no longer is available in the U.S. or any other country at this time.[11,81,86–88,101]

Furazolidone (Furoxone) is an alternative to metronidazole and available in the U.S. as a tablet and suspension for treatment of giardiasis.[73,98,99] Furazolidone has cure rates of 80% to 90% and the adult dose is 100 mg four times daily for seven days.[98,99] Furazolidone, which is available as a suspension, is preferred by some clinicians for pediatric patients; however, metronidazole should be considered the drug of choice for giardiasis in both adults and pediatric patients. Tinidazole, an analog of metronidazole which is not available in the U.S., also is highly effective for giardiasis.[100,101]

Following therapy, diarrhea usually subsides within a day or two and completely resolves in about ten days.[88] Cyst excretion is disrupted two days after initiation of therapy.[73,88] Complete normalization of intestinal functions, especially recovery from malabsorption, in J.T. may require four to eight weeks.[88] If J.T. does not respond to one course of therapy, she may need to receive a second course of metronidazole.[73,88]

Enterobiasis

Prevalence. Enterobiasis is an intestinal infection caused by the pinworm, *Enterobius vermicularis*. Pinworm is the most common helminthic infection in the U.S. and has an estimated incidence of 42 million.[102] A study of elementary school children documented a 15% to 20% prevalence rate of pinworm infection.[103] Enterobiasis is a cosmopolitan disease that usually affects all members of a family when one member is infected. Therefore, all household residents must be treated simultaneously. Institutionalized patients, preschool children in day care centers, and homosexual males may be at greater risk for acquiring enterobiasis.[103–105]

Life Cycle. Infection is initiated with the ingestion of pinworm eggs which reach the mouth on soiled hands or contaminated food and drink. Following ingestion, the eggs hatch in the intestine, releasing the larvae which attach to the jejunum or upper ileum.[16] After copulation, the female worm migrates to the lower bowel and produces eggs. Under the stimulus of air or change in temperature, the female releases eggs in the perianal skin.[16] Cutaneous irritation in the perianal region produced by migrating females and the presence of eggs can cause severe pruritus.

Signs and Symptoms

16. L.C., a 6-year-old male, is brought in by his mother, K.C., to see the family physician. K.C. indicates that L.C. was sent home from school because of inattention and disruptive behavior. She has noticed that he has been very irritable. L.C. has complained of abdominal discomfort and perianal pain on 2 occasions the previous week. A cellophane tape swab placed over the perianal skin demonstrated translucent eggs of E. vermicularis. Explain the symptoms observed in L.C. What pathologic changes are associated with enterobiasis?

Pinworm infection may be asymptomatic; however, the most common symptom is intense pruritus ani caused by the presence of the sticky pinworm eggs in the perianal skin. Pruritus can cause constant scratching and may result in dermatitis and secondary bacterial infections.[104–117] A heavy load of worms can cause anorexia, restlessness, and insomnia, resulting in behavioral changes as illustrated by L.C.[115]

Generally, pinworms do not cause any serious intestinal pathology.[104,109] Rarely, *E. vermicularis* ectopic lesions can be

caused by a gravid worm which has migrated from the perianal region into the vagina, uterus, or fallopian tubes. The adult worm may travel through the fallopian tubes to the peritoneal cavity.[110,111] The association between cystitis in young females and enterobiasis presumably results when the female worm enters the urethra and makes its way into the bladder carrying enteric bacteria.[112]

Treatment

Pyrantel Pamoate, Mebendazole, and Albendazole
17. How should L.C. be treated?

Three different preparations are available to treat pinworm infection in L.C.: pyrantel pamoate (Antiminth), mebendazole (Vermox), and albendazole (Zentel).[11,16,104,105,113–117] The drug of choice is pyrantel pamoate which is available as a suspension of 50 mg base/mL. L.C. should receive a single dose of 11 mg/kg (maximum: 1 gm) of pyrantel pamoate followed by a second dose in two weeks.[11,104] Some patients will experience mild GI upset, headache, and fever from this therapy.[113]

Mebendazole is as effective as pyrantel for enterobiasis.[11,104,113–117] Mebendazole, a broad-spectrum antihelmintic agent, also is given as a single dose (100 mg) which is repeated in two weeks.[11] Since mebendazole is poorly absorbed, there are no systemic side effects associated with its use.[117] Albendazole, another broad-spectrum antihelmintic, recently available, is administered as 400 mg once and repeated in two weeks.[11]

Household Contacts
18. What suggestions and advice should be given to K.C.?

Pinworm infection can recur as a result of reinfection within families.[104] Therefore, all members of L.C.'s family need to be treated simultaneously. Pinworm infection's cycle of transmission can be interrupted by encouraging careful hand washing and fingernail scrubbing after toilet use and before meals.[104] In spite of meticulous precautions, it still may be difficult to eradicate the infection because of contact with nonfamily members outside the home. It may be necessary to repeat treatment for some members of the family at a later date.[104,113] K.C. needs to be reassured that pinworm infection in the home does not represent substandard hygiene.[16,113]

Cestodiasis

Description. Cestodiasis (tapeworm infection) is caused by members of the phylum Platyhelminths (flat worms) which include, among others, *Taenia solium* (pork tapeworm), *Taenia saginata* (beef tapeworm), *Diphyllobothrium latum* (broad fish tapeworm), and *Hymenolepis nana* (dwarf tapeworm).[16,119,120]

The tapeworm body is made up of an anterior attachment organ called a scolex, accompanied by a chain of segments or proglottids, called a strobila. The strobila grows throughout the life of the tapeworm with the extension taking place just posterior to the scolex.[16,119] At the end of the strobila, mature or gravid segments contain eggs enclosed in the uterus which, because of its characteristic shape and size, may be used for identifying tapeworm species.[16]

Tapeworms remain attached to the mucosal wall of the upper jejunum by the scolex, which contains two to four muscular cup-shaped suckers. The parasite lacks an alimentary canal and obtains nutrients directly from the host's intestine. A protrusible structure called a rostellum is located in the center of the scolex and may contain hooks in some species.[16,119,120] The scolex is very specific for each species and is used for definitive diagnosis.[16]

Tapeworms cause disease in humans by existing in either the adult or larval stage. The symptoms in the host primarily are gastrointestinal when the adult form is present. Larvae or cysticerci become encysted in various visceral organs causing a disease called cysticercosis.[119,120]

Life Cycle. Pork tapeworm (*T. solium*) and beef tapeworm (*T. saginata*) infections are caused by ingestion of poorly cooked meat. The larva or cysticercus is released from the contaminated meat by bile salts and matures in the host jejunum in about two months.[119] The pork tapeworm has been reported to reach a length of 10 to 20 feet, while adult beef tapeworms can measure up to 30 feet. Gravid proglottids, which contain the eggs, are passed in the host's feces and are the source of infection in animals. When ingested by animals, the embryos are released from the eggs; these migrate through the lymphatics and blood, developing into cysticerci (encysted larvae) in various muscles.[16,119,120]

Epidemiology. The pork tapeworm occurs worldwide and is prevalent in Mexico, Latin America, Slavic countries, Africa, Southeast Asia, India, and China.[120] The beef tapeworm is cosmopolitan but is found predominantly in Ethiopia, Europe, Japan, the Philippines, Latin America, and the Middle East.[120] Both occur in the U.S. although the prevalence is low.[120]

Diphyllobothrium latum (broad fish tapeworm) inhabits the ileum in the human host and infection is acquired by ingesting raw or inadequately cooked fresh water fish.[120] *D. latum* also infects other fish-eating animals including fox, mink, bear, walrus, and seal. These animals can serve as reservoirs.

Broad tapeworm disease or diphyllobothriasis is common in Finland, Scandinavia, Russia, the lake regions of North Italy, Switzerland, and France.[120] In North America, the highest incidence of infection has been reported in Alaska and Canada.[120]

Hymenolepis nana (dwarf tapeworm) is cosmopolitan in distribution with a high incidence in children in the tropics and subtropics.[120] It is the most common human tapeworm in the U.S., particularly in the southeastern section. The infection is passed primarily from person to person by contaminated hands or formites.

Taenia saginata and Taenia solium

Signs and Symptoms

19. B.R., a 10-year-old male student from Mexico, has moved to the U.S. with his parents. He was seen on several occasions by the school nurse when he complained of vague abdominal discomfort and pain. Upon questioning, B.R. reports seeing "white noodle-like" objects in his stools. B.R. is seen in the clinic. A cellophane impression of the perianal region and 3 stool samples over several days demonstrated infection with *T. saginata*. The immunoglobulin E (IgE) level and eosinophil count were within normal limits. Explain the presenting symptoms in B.R.

Patients having tapeworm infections (either *T. saginata*, as in B.R., or *T. solium*) present with symptoms ranging from mild epigastric or abdominal pain to burning sensation, general weakness, weight loss, headache, constipation, and diarrhea.[16,120] Since the adult worm is weakly immunogenic, some patients can present with moderate eosinophilia and elevated levels of IgE.[120] However, B.R. did not. He reported worm segments ("white noodle-like" objects) in the stool; this frequently is the way diagnosis is made. Segments are sometimes found in underclothing.

Diagnosis

20. How can one differentiate *T. saginata* infection from *T. solium* in B.R.?

Eggs of *T. saginata* and *T. solium* are identical and, when found in the stool, will not aid in diagnosis. The presence of gravid proglottids or a scolex in the stool is necessary to determine the species.[16,119,120]

Placing gravid proglottids obtained from the stool of B.R. between two slides and injecting India ink into the central uterine system will demonstrate the characteristic anatomical differences.[16,119,120]

An intact scolex recovered from B.R.'s stool after treatment, also will confirm the species. The scolex of *T. saginata* has no hooklets ("unarmed"), while that of *T. solium* contains a double row of hooklets ("armed").[16]

Treatment

21. How should B.R. be treated? Indicate how you would evaluate therapy in B.R.

Niclosamide. The drug of choice for both *T. saginata* and *T. solium* is the same: niclosamide (Niclocide).[11,121,122] The single dose in adults is 2 gm (4 tablets of 0.5 gm). Children weighing more than 34 kg should receive 1.5 gm (3 tablets), while those weighing between 11 to 34 kg should receive two tablets.[11] B.R. should receive between two to three tablets, depending upon his weight. These should be chewed thoroughly and swallowed with water in the morning on an empty stomach. A suspension of the vanilla-flavored tablet can be made for children by crushing the tablets and mixing with water. B.R. should abstain from eating for two hours after niclosamide administration. Niclosamide kills both the segments and scolex of tapeworm but does not destroy the eggs.[119,120]

The potential for eggs to be released when gravid segments of *T. solium* disintegrate after treatment should be noted because the release of embryos from the eggs can cause cysticercosis. To minimize this possibility, a purgative (magnesium sulfate 15 to 30 gm) should be given two hours after administration of niclosamide when *T. solium* infection is suspected.[16,119,120]

Praziquantel. The alternative drug for *T. saginata* and *T. solium* infection is praziquantel (Biltricide).[121] The dose of praziquantel is 25 mg/kg as a single dose.[11,121] When treating *T. solium* infection, a purgative should be administered two hours after praziquantel therapy, since it also has no effect on released eggs.[121]

Follow-up treatment in B.R. should include biweekly examination of stools for three to four months.[120] B.R. should be told that segments of the tapeworm will be passed for several days following treatment.

Diphyllobothrium latum and Hymenolepis nana

22. Could B.R. have *D. latum* or *H. nana* infection? How are these treated?

Infection with *D. latum* is highly unlikely in B.R., as diphyllobothriasis is almost exclusively found among raw fish-eating populations of the Baltic countries, Alaska, and Canada;[120] B.R. is from Mexico. In addition, neither the characteristic operculate eggs or distinctive almond-shaped scolex of *D. latum* were found during stool examination.

H. nana (dwarf tapeworm) infection is worldwide and is a possibility in B.R. It is unusual to find proglottids of *H. nana* because they usually disintegrate before passage.[120] Instead, identification is made by the presence of the characteristic eggs.

Treatment of *D. latum* is identical to that of *T. saginata* except that a purgative is not necessary after therapy. *H. nana* infections are treated with praziquantel 25 mg/kg as a single dose. If niclosamide is used, four tablets (2 gm) must be administered daily for seven days.[11,121–123]

Complications

23. Could B.R. develop cysticercosis? If B.R. had *D. latum* instead of *T. saginata*, what would be some subjective and objective findings?

It is unlikely that B.R. can develop cysticercosis. Cysticercosis is caused by the release of eggs of *T. solium* in the GI tract resulting from treatment or autoinfection due to retrograde peristalsis.[120,124-126] B.R. is infected with *T. saginata* and infection with the larva of *T. saginata* never occurs.[120,126] B.R. could develop other complications from the beef tapeworm including appendicitis, obstruction of pancreatic ducts, and intestinal obstruction.[120]

If B.R. had been infected with *D. latum* instead of *T. saginata*, he may complain of being tired and possibly sleepy, which may be manifestations of anemia. *D. latum* can cause a megaloblastic anemia because the tapeworm competes with the host for dietary vitamin B_{12}.[127] Although 40% of patients with *D. latum* infection have reduced levels of vitamin B_{12}, less than 2% actually develop anemia from this deficiency.[120] Decreased levels of other nutritional elements have included ascorbic acid, folic acid, and riboflavin.[120] In those who do develop deficiency in vitamin B_{12} from *D. latum* infection, manifestations may include glossitis, tachycardia, and neurological symptoms such as weakness, paresthesia, and motor coordination disturbances.[120]

24. Niclosamide and Praziquantel: Side Effects. Would the side effect profile of niclosamide make it a more preferable choice over praziquantel in B.R.?

Since niclosamide is not absorbed in the GI tract, it has minimal systemic effects and the only reported side effects are nausea and vomiting. This may be the preferred agent in B.R.[11] Praziquantel, which is equally effective as niclosamide for *T. saginata*, is associated with headache, dizziness, drowsiness, nausea, abdominal pain, myalgia, and uticaria.[11,120,121] The side effects usually appear about two hours after administration and dissipate within 48 hours.

Pediculosis

Prevalence. Pediculosis (lice infections) may be caused by the following: head lice (*Pediculus humanus capitis*), body lice (*P. humanus*), or crab lice (*Phthirus pubis*). Lice infections may be present in all socioeconomic groups but are seen more frequently among the poor because of the crowded living conditions and infrequent washing.[128-133]

Life Cycle. Head and body lice have similar life cycles, though habitat preference characterizes the two varieties.[130] The adult fertilized female lays eggs which remain glued to hair or seams of clothing. The oval-shaped eggs (nits) hatch in seven to ten days and produce nymphs, which go through a number of molts to evolve into mature adults.[128-132] Both larvae and adults feed on the host's blood. The lice penetrate the host skin by use of stylets within their head and attach themselves by a circlet of teeth on their proboscis.[128] Crab lice usually are found in pubic hair although at times these organisms may be found on eyebrows, eyelashes, and axillary hairs.[128-133]

Epidemiology. The highest incidence of head lice is seen among school children.[128,129] The incidence of all types of lice infestation in the U.S. has been estimated to be six million cases.[129] Head and body lice are transferred between hosts by personal and clothing contact, while crab lice are transmitted by sexual contact.[130,131] Human lice have been important vectors in a number of diseases that have resulted in large epidemics and high mortality.[131] Diseases transmitted by lice include typhus, trench fever, and relapsing fever.[16,131,137]

Signs and Symptoms

25. M.L., a 54-year-old male occupant of the city shelter for destitute citizens, is brought into the clinic by his welfare worker. M.L. has excoriations and numerous pustular lesions all over his body. The welfare worker indicates that M.L. has "lice all over his body." Why are the symptoms in M.L. consistent with lice infection?

The most common complaint of patients with head and body lice is pruritus of the scalp, ears, neck, and other body parts. However, with severe infestations as seen in M.L., intractable itching and scratching can result in folliculitis, hemorrhagic macules or papules, postinflammatory skin thickening, and pigmentation. This condition often is called "Vagabond's Disease."[130,131]

In contrast, schoolchildren who are exposed frequently to head lice may only have minor pruritus affecting the scalp, ears, and neck.[130]

Treatment

26. How should M.L. be treated for lice infection of the head, body, and genital areas?

Concurrent treatment for the pustular bacterial lesions and lice infestations should be initiated in M.L. Head lice can be treated with pyrethrin 0.3% plus 3% piperonyl butoxide (RID). Both pyrethrin preparations and malathion 0.5% (Prioderm) are as effective as gamma benzene hexachloride or lindane 1% (Kwell).[131-133,134-137] The eradication rate for lindane is only 88% as compared to over 99% with a new synthetic derivative of pyrethrin, Permethrin (NIX).[135]

Pyrethrin, Lindane, and Malathion. Pyrethrin, which contains extracts of chrysanthemum flowers, acts by blocking the transmission of nerve impulses in lice and kills them in a few minutes.[131] About 30 to 50 mL of the pyrethrin lotion should be massaged into M.L.'s scalp, left for about ten minutes, then rinsed out. The treatment should be followed by a plain shampoo. A fine-tooth comb should be used to remove nits from the hair. The whole course of treatment should be repeated within seven to ten days to eradicate the organisms hatched after initial therapy.[130,131,134-136] Subjects who have a history of ragweed allergy occasionally can react to pyrethrin preparations.[131] If M.L. has an allergy to pyrethrin, lindane shampoo 1% or malathion lotion 0.5% may be alternatives.[136] Lindane is left on the scalp for ten minutes, while malathion should be left on for 12 to 24 hours.

For body and pubic lice in M.L., either pyrethrin combinations or lindane lotions should be applied. It may be necessary to leave the lotion on for four to six hours to eradicate crab lice.[131,136,137] The applications should be followed by a warm bath. The treatment should be repeated in seven to ten days.

Physostigmine Ointment. To remove pubic lice from eyelids or eyelashes in M.L., plain petrolatum or physostigmine ointment can be used.[130,131] Petrolatum is applied to eyelashes and lid margins with cotton swabs three to four times daily. This regimen will either suffocate the lice or physically remove them.[133,141]

Decontamination Measures. Treatment for pediculosis should include thorough decontamination to avoid reinfection. All personal articles of clothing should be boiled or dry cleaned. Hair brushes, combs, or other plastic articles can be decontaminated by soaking in rubbing alcohol.[131,137] In institutions and schools where lice infestations are a problem, outer clothing (coats, hats, scarves) of individuals should be isolated in separate plastic bags at the beginning of the day. This measure will reduce reinfection significantly.

27. Toxicity. What are the toxicities of the common pediculicides?

Lindane can cause neurological symptoms including tremors, ataxia, insomnia, and seizures in subjects who are exposed to it over extended periods.[138,139] It also is reported to cause aplastic anemia.[11] However, when it is applied for ten minutes to treat head or body lice, it is considered safe and effective.[131] Malathion, an organophosphate cholinesterase inhibitor, is degraded rapidly by hepatic enzymes in humans, and occasionally can cause some local irritation.[11,130,134] These agents are not contraindicated during pregnancy and may be used for treatment.[130]

Scabies

Scabies is caused by *Sarcoptes scabiei var. horminis*.[140,141] The female mite burrows into the skin of the host and lays eggs which hatch into a larvae after 72 to 84 hours. Following a number of molts, the adult mites mate and the male dies. The female gravid mite continues to burrow into new areas of skin, primarily in interdigital web spaces between the fingers, wrists, elbows, periumbilical skin, and buttocks.[140] The hallmark of scabies is intense itching with erythematous papules and excoriations. In infants, scabies may be vesicular or bullous; it is not uncommon to have secondary pyoderma. Transmission is by intimate contact and institutional epidemics have been reported.[137,140,141,144]

Treatment

28. T.R., a 4-year-old female, has pruritic rash with excoriations in the interdigital areas of both hands. The mother volunteers that T.R.'s 7-year-old brother, G.R., has a similar rash affecting his hands, groin, and feet. The lesions are scraped and microscopic examination reveals mites and ova of *Sarcoptes scabiei*. How should T.R. and G.R. be treated? Indicate special instructions and precautions that should accompany therapy.

Lindane, Permethrin, and Crotamiton. The agents available for treatment of scabies include lindane 1% (Kwell), crotamiton 10% (Eurax), Permethrin 5% cream (Elimite), and sulfur 5% in petro-

latum.[11,137,142] The agent that has been used most extensively is lindane; however, lindane's safety still remains a point of contention.[138,139] When lindane is left on the skin too long (especially excoriated skin), percutaneous absorption can cause neurotoxicity.[138,139] Crotamiton 10% and sulfur 5% in petrolatum presumably are safe in infants and pregnant subjects; however, definitive data do not exist.[140] A single application of Permethrin 5% cream is more effective than crotamiton or lindane.[106,142,143]

T.R. and G.R. should have their nails trimmed to minimize further excoriation. They then should be bathed using a soft scrub wash cloth to remove loose crusts. Thereafter, permethrin cream should be massaged into the skin from head (including the scalp) to the soles of the feet.[132,141–144] The cream should be left on for 8 to 14 hours before they are bathed again. If crotamiton is selected, it should be applied to the entire body (including the scalp) and left on for 24 hours after the initial bath. A second 24-hour application is recommended before the children are bathed again. When lindane is used, it is applied to the entire body (avoiding the eyes and mucous membranes) and the application is left on the body for approximately six hours.[11,140] After six hours, a cool bath should be taken. Pruritus from scabies may be treated symptomatically with an oral antihistamine such as hydroxyzine (Vistaril) or diphenhydramine (Benadryl), or with a low potency topical steroid.[141]

Clothes and all linen belonging to T.R. and G.R. should be freshly laundered and they should be re-examined after a week. If there is evidence of active infestation (positive microscopic findings), a second treatment course may be initiated in these patients. They should be informed that pruritus may persist for more than ten days. Pruritus usually results from retained parts of the scabietic mites.

References

1 **Wyler DJ.** Malaria—resurgence, resistance and research. (First of two parts). N Engl J Med. 1983;308:875.

2 **Bruce-Chwatt LJ.** Recent trends of chemotherapy and vaccination against malaria: new lamps for old. Br Med J. 1985;291:1072.

3 **Wyler DJ.** Plasmodium and Babesia. In: Gorbach SL et al., eds. Infectious Diseases. Philadelphia: WB Saunders; 1992:1967.

4 **Centers for Disease Control.** Summary of notifiable diseases, United States. MMWR. 1989;37:(54).

5 **Guerrero IC et al.** Transfusion malaria in the United States, 1972–1981. Ann Intern Med. 1983;99:221.

6 **Krogstad DJ.** Plasmodium species (malaria). In: Mandell GL et al., eds. Principles and Practice of Infectious Diseases. New York: Churchill Livingstone; 1995:2415.

7 **Friedmann CT et al.** A malaria epidemic among heroin users. Am J Trop Med Hyg. 1973;22:302.

8 **Peters W, Hall AP.** The treatment of severe falciparum malaria. Br Med J. 1985;291:1146.

9 **Wyler DJ.** Malaria chemoprophylaxis for the traveller. N Engl J Med. 1993; 329:31.

10 **Greenberg AE, Lobel HD.** Mortality from *Plasmodium falciparum* malaria in travellers from the United States, 1959 to 1987. Ann Intern Med. 1990; 113:326.

11 **Anon.** Drugs for parasitic infections. Med Lett Drugs Ther. 1993;35:111.

12 **Centers for Disease Control.** Adverse reactions to Fansidar and updated recommendations for its use in the prevention of malaria. MMWR. 1985;33: 713.

13 **Hatton CSR et al.** Frequency of severe neutropenia associated with amodiaquine prophylaxis against malaria. Lancet. 1986;1:411.

14 **Center for Disease Control.** Agranulocytosis associated with use of amodiaquine for malaria prophylaxis. MMWR. 1986;35:165.

15 **Larrey D et al.** Amodiaquine-induced hepatitis. Ann Intern Med. 1986;104: 801.

16 **Markell EK et al.** Medical Parasitology. Philadelphia: WB Saunders; 1992:102, 226.

17 **Marik PE.** Severe Falciparum malaria: survival without exchange transfusion. Am J Trop Med Hyg. 1989;41:627.

18 **Zucker JR, Campbell CC.** Malaria. Principles of prevention and treatment. Infect Dis Clin North Am. 1993;7:547.

19 **Phillips RE et al.** Intravenous quinidine for the treatment of severe falciparum malaria. N Engl J Med. 1985; 312:1273.

20 **Center for Disease Control.** Treatment with quinidine gluconate for persons with severe *Plasmodium falciparum* infection. Discontinuation of parenteral quinine from CDC Drug

Service. MMWR. 1991;40:(RR-4):21.

21 **Miller KD et al.** Treatment of severe malaria in the United States with a continuous infusion of quinidine gluconate and exchange transfusion. N Engl J Med. 1989;321:65.

22 **Currier JS, Maguire JH.** Problems in the management of Falciparum malaria. Rev Infect Dis. 1989;11:988.

23 **Parke A.** Antimalarial drugs and pregnancy. Am J Med. 1985;76(Suppl. 4A):30.

24 **Wolfe MS, Cordero JF.** Safety of chloroquine in suppression of malaria during pregnancy. Br Med J. 1985;290: 1466.

25 **Main EK et al.** Treatment of chloroquine-resistant malaria during pregnancy. JAMA. 1983;249:3207.

26 **Looareesuwan S et al.** Quinine and severe falciparum malaria in late pregnancy. Lancet. 1985;2:4.

27 **Webster LT Jr.** Drugs used in the chemotherapy of protozoal infections. Malaria. In: Gilman AG et al., eds. The Pharmacological Basis of Therapeutics. New York: Pergamon Press; 1990: 978.

28 **White NJ.** Clinical pharmacokinetics of antimalarial drugs. Clin Pharmacokinet. 1985;10:187.

29 **Howells PE.** The antimalarial action of chloroquine and mechanism of resistance. Ann Trop Med Parasitol. 1987; 81:629.

30 **Krongstad DJ et al.** Antimalarial

agents: specific treatment regimens. Antimicrob Agents Chemother. 1988; 32:957.

31 **Strickland GT et al.** Effects of chloroquine, amodiaquine and pyrethamine-sulfadoxine on *Plasmodium falciparum* gametocytemia. Am J Trop Med Hyg. 1986;35:259.

32 **Valentine WN et al.** Hemolytic anemias and erythrocyte enzymopathies. Ann Intern Med. 1985;103:245.

33 **Mina S, Fujii H.** Molecular aspects of erythro-enzymopathies associated with hereditary hemolytic anemias. Am J Hematol. 1985;19:293.

34 **Beuller E.** Glucose-6-phosphate dehydrogenase deficiency. New Engl J Med. 1991;324:169.

35 **Moreno A, Patarroyo ME.** Development of an asexual blood stage malaria vaccine. Blood. 1989;74:537.

36 **Egan JE et al.** Humoral immune response in volunteers immunized with irradiated *Plasmodium falciparum* sporozoites. Am J Trop Med Hyg. 1993; 49:166.

37 **Godson GN.** Molecular approaches to malaria vaccines. Sci Am. 1985; 252(May):52.

38 **Ballou WR et al.** Safety and efficacy of a recombinant DNA *Plasmodium falciparum* sporozoite vaccine. Lancet. 1987;1:1277.

39 **Meek SR et al.** Treatment of falciparum malaria with quinine and tetracycline or combined mefloquine/sulfa-

doxine/pyrimethamine on the Thai-Kampuchean border. Am J Trop Med Hyg. 1986;35:246.

40 **Anon.** Mefloquine for malaria. Med Lett Drugs Ther. 1990;31:13.

41 **Anon.** Advice for travellers. Med Lett Drugs Ther. 1992;34:41.

42 **Nosten F et al.** Mefloquine-resistant falciparum malaria on the Thai Burmese border. Lancet. 1991;337:1140.

43 **Pang LW et al.** Doxycycline prophylaxis for falciparum malaria. Lancet. 1987;1:1161.

44 **Centers for Disease Control.** Recommendations for the prevention of malaria among travellers. MMWR. 1990;39:1.

45 **Looareesuwan S et al.** Treatment of patients with recrudescent falciparum malaria with sequential combination of artesunate and mefloquine. Am J Trop Med Hyg. 1993;47:794.

46 **Osifo N.** Chloroquine-induced pruritus among patients with malaria. Arch Dermatol. 1984;120:80.

47 **Salako LA.** Toxicity and side effects of antimalarials in Africa: a critical review. Bull World Health Organ. 1984; 62:63.

48 **Hornstein OP, Ruprech KW.** Fansidar-induced Stevens-Johnson syndrome. N Engl J Med. 1982;307:1529.

49 **Olsen VV et al.** Serious reaction during prophylaxis with pyrimethamine-sulfadoxine. Lancet. 1982;2:994.

50 **Miller KD et al.** Severe cutaneous reactions among American travelers using pyrimethamine-sulfadoxine (Fansidar) for malaria prophylaxis. Am J Trop Med Hyg. 1986;35:451.

51 **Schwartz IK et al.** Glucose-6-phosphate dehydrogenase deficiency in southeastern Asian refugees entering the United States. Am J Trop Med Hyg. 1984;33:182.

52 **Walsh JA.** Problems in recognition and diagnosis of amebiasis: estimation of the global magnitude of morbidity and mortality. Rev Infect Dis. 1986;8: 228.

53 **Ravdin JI, Petri WA.** *Entamoeba histolytica* (Amebiasis). In: Mandell GL et al., eds. Principles and Practice of Infectious Diseases. New York: Churchill Livingstone; 1995:2395.

54 **Schain D, Ravdin J.** *Entamoeba histolytica* and other intestinal amoebae. In: Gorbach SL et al., eds. Infectious Diseases. Philadelphia: WB Saunders; 1992:1953.

55 **Markell EK et al.** Intestinal protozoa in homosexual men of the San Francisco Bay area: prevalence and correlates of infection. Am J Trop Med Hyg. 1984;33:239.

56 **Baker RW, Peppercorn MA.** Gastrointestinal ailments of homosexual men. Medicine. 1982;61:390.

57 **Philips SC et al.** Sexual transmission of enteric protozoa and helminths in a venereal disease clinic population. N Engl J Med. 1981;305:603.

58 **Pomerantz MB et al.** Amebiasis in New York City 1950–1978; identification of the male homosexual high risk population. Bull N Y Acad Med. 1980;56:232.

59 **Abuabara SF et al.** Amebic liver abscess. Arch Surg. 1982;117:239.

60 **Ylvisakey JT, McDonald GB.** Sexually acquired amebic colitis and liver abscess. West J Med. 1980;132:153.

61 **Ravdin JI.** Intestinal disease caused by Entamoeba histolytica. In: Ravdin JI, ed. Amebiasis: Human infection by *Entamoeba histolytica*. New York: Churchill Livingstone; 1988;495.

62 **Kubitschek KR et al.** Amebiasis presenting as pleuropulmonary disease. West J Med. 1985;142:203.

63 **Greenstein AJ et al.** Amebic liver abscess: a study of 11 cases compared with a series of 38 patients with pyogenic liver abscess. Am J Gastroenterol. 1985;80:472.

64 **Eggleston FC et al.** Amebic peritonitis secondary to amebic liver abscess. Surgery. 1982;91:46.

65 **Saltzberg DM, Hall-Craggs M.** Fulminant amebic colitis in a homosexual man. Am J Gastroenterol. 1986;81:209.

66 **Monroe LS.** Gastrointestinal parasites. In: Berke JE, ed. Gastroenterology. Vol. 7. Philadelphia: WB Saunders; 1985:4250.

67 **Krogstad DJ.** Isoenzyme patterns and pathogenicity in amebic infection. N Engl J Med. 1986;315:390.

68 **Thompson JE Jr et al.** Amebic liver abscess: a therapeutic approach. Rev Infect Dis. 1985;7:171.

69 **Ravdin JI.** Pathogenesis of disease caused by Entamoeba histolytica: studies of adherence, secreted toxins, and contact-dependent cytolysis. Rev Infect Dis. 1986;8:247.

70 **Aucott JN, Ravdin JL.** Amebiasis and ''nonpathogenic'' intestinal protozoa. Infect Dis Clin North Am. 1993;7:467.

71 **Goldsmith RS.** Antiprotozoal drugs. In: Katzung BG, ed. Basic and Clinical Pharmacology. Los Altos: Appleton & Lange; 1989:645.

72 **Webster LT Jr.** Drugs used in the chemotherapy of protozoal infections: amebiasis, giardiasis and trichomoniasis. In: Gilman AG et al., eds. The Pharmacological Basis of Therapeutics. New York: Pergamon Press; 1990:999.

73 **Wolf MS.** The treatment of intestinal protozoan infections. Med Clin North Am. 1982;66:707.

74 **Kovaleski T et al.** Treatment of an amebic liver abscess with intravenous metronidazole. Arch Intern Med. 1981; 141:132.

75 **Cushing AH et al.** Metronidazole concentrations in a hepatic abscess. Pediatr Infect Dis. 1985;4:697.

76 **Spillman R et al.** Double-blind test of metronidazole and tinidazole in the treatment of asymptomatic *Entamoeba histolytica* and *Entamoeba hartmanni* carriers. Am J Trop Med Hyg. 1976; 25:549.

77 **Couter RL et al.** Differentiation of pyogenic from amebic hepatic abscesses. Surg Gynecol Obstet. 1986;162:114.

78 **Filice C et al.** Outcome of hepatic amebic abscesses managed with three different therapeutic strategies. Dig Dis Sci. 1992;37:240.

79 **Beard CM et al.** Cancer after exposure to metronidazole. Mayo Clin Proc. 1988;63:147.

80 **Pickering LK et al.** Occurrence of *Giardia lamblia* in children in day care centers. J Pediatr. 1984;104:522.

81 **Farthing MJG.** *Giardia lamblia*. In: Gorbach SL et al., eds. Infectious Diseases. Philadelphia: WB Saunders; 1992:1959.

82 **Craun GF.** Waterborne giardiasis in the United States 1965–1984. Lancet. 1986;2:513.

83 **Mintz ED et al.** Foodborne giardiasis in a corporate office setting. J Infect Dis. 1993;167:250.

84 **Center for Disease Control.** Waterborne giardiasis—California, Colorado, Oregon, Pennsylvania. MMWR. 1980;29:121.

85 **Dykes AC et al.** Municipal waterborne giardiasis: an epidemiologic investigation. Beavers implicated as a possible reservoir. Ann Intern Med. 1980;92: 165.

86 **Quick R et al.** Restaurant-associated outbreak of giardiasis. J Infect Dis. 1992;166:673.

87 **Gorski ED.** Management of giardiasis. Am Fam Physician. 1985;32:157.

88 **Hill DR.** *Giardia lamblia*. In: Mandell GL et al., eds. Principles and Practice of Infectious Diseases. New York: Churchill Livingstone; 1995:2487.

89 **White KE et al.** An outbreak of giardiasis in a nursing home with evidence for multiple modes of transmission. J Infect Dis. 1989;160:298.

90 **LoGalbo PR et al.** Symptomatic giardiasis in three patients with X-linked agammaglobulinemia. J Pediatr. 1982; 101:78.

91 **Keystone JS et al.** Intestinal parasitic infections in homosexual men. Prevalence, symptoms and factors in transmission. Can Med Assoc J. 1980;123: 512.

92 **Baker RW, Peppercorn MA.** Gastrointestinal ailments of homosexual men. Medicine. 1982;61:390.

93 **Solomons NW.** Giardiasis: nutritional implications. Rev Infect Dis. 1982;4: 859.

94 **Danziger M, Lopez M.** Numbers of giardia in feces of infected children. Am J Trop Med Hyg. 1975;24:237.

95 **Blaser MJ, Reller LB.** Campylobacter enteritis. N Engl J Med. 1981;305: 1444.

96 **Rubin RH.** Human salmonellosis: epidemiology, pathogenesis and clinical symptoms. Infect Dis Pract. 1982;6:1.

97 **Rosenthal P, Liebman WM.** Comparative studies of stool examination, duodenal aspiration and pediatric Entero-Test for giardiasis in children. J Pediatr. 1980;96:278.

98 **Quiros-Buelna E.** Furazolidone and metronidazole for treatment of giardiasis in children. Scand J Gastroenterol. 1988;169(Suppl.):65.

99 **Craft JC et al.** Furazolidone and quinacrine comparative study of therapy for giardiasis in children. Am J Dis Child. 1981;135:164.

100 **Jokipii L, Jokippi AMM.** Single-dose metronidazole and tinidazole as therapy for giardiasis: success rates, side effects, and drug absorption and elimination. J Infect Dis. 1979;140:984.

101 **Hill DR.** Giardiasis. Issues in diagnosis and management. Infect Dis Clin North Am. 1993;7:503.

102 **Blumenthal DS.** Intestinal nematodes in the United States. N Engl J Med. 1977;297:1437.

103 **Wagner ED, Eby W.** Pinworm prevalence in California elementary school children, and diagnostic methods. Am J Trop Med Hyg. 1983;32:998.

104 **Cline BL.** Current drug regimens for the treatment of intestinal helminth infections. Med Clin North Am. 1982;66: 721.

105 **Baker RW, Peppercorn MA.** Enteric diseases in homosexual men. Pharmacotherapy. 1982;2:32.

106 **Talpin D et al.** A comparative trial of three treatment schedules for eradication of scabies. J Am Acad Dermatol. 1983;9:550.

107 **Abadi K.** Single dose mebendazole therapy for soil-transmitted nematodes. Am J Trop Med Hyg. 1985;34:129.

108 **Stephenson LS et al.** Treatment with a single dose albendazole improves growth of Kenya school children with hookworm, *Trichuris trichuris* and *Ascaris lumbricoides* infections. Am J Trop Med Hyg. 1989;41:78.

109 **Freedman DO.** Intestinal nematodes. In: Gorbach SL et al., eds. Infectious Diseases. Philadelphia: WB Saunders; 1992:2003.

110 **Pearson RD et al.** Chronic pelvic peritonitis due to the pinworm *Enterobius vermicularis*. JAMA. 1981;245:1340.

111 **Reyes CV et al.** Omental oxyuriasis: case report. Mil Med. 1984;149:682.

112 **Simon RD.** Pinworm infestation and urinary tract infection in young girls. Am J Dis Child. 1974;128:211.

113 **Goldsmith RS.** Anthelmintic drugs. In: Katzung BG, ed. Basic and Clinical Pharmacology. Los Altos: Appleton & Lange; 1989:666.

114 **Keystone JS, Murdock JK.** Mebendazole. Ann Intern Med. 1979;9:582.

115 **Muttalib MA et al.** Single-dose regimen of mebendazole in the treatment of polyparasitism in children. Am J Trop Med Hyg. 1981;84:159.

116 **Sinniah B, Sinniah D.** The anthelmintic effects of pyrantel pamoate, oxantel-pyrantel pamoate, levamisole and mebendazole in the treatment of intestinal nematodes. Ann Trop Med Parasitol. 1981;75:315.

117 **Webster LT.** Drugs used in the chemotherapy of helminthiasis. In: Gilman AG et al., eds. The Pharmacological Basis of Therapeutics. New York: Pergamon Press; 1990:959.

118 **Ottesen EA et al.** A controlled trial of Ivermectin and Diethylcarbamazine in lymphatic filariasis. N Engl J Med. 1990;322:1113.

119 **Liu LX, Weller PF.** Strongyloidiasis and other intestinal nematode infections. Infect Dis Clin N Am. 1993;7: 655.

120 **Willms K.** Cestodes (tapeworms). In: Gorbach SL et al., eds. Infectious Diseases. Philadelphia: WB Saunders; 1992:2021.

121 **Pearson RD, Hewlett EL.** Niclosamide therapy for tapeworm infections. Ann Intern Med. 1985;102:550.

122 **Pearson RD, Guerrant RL.** Praziquantel: a major advance in anthelminthic therapy. Ann Intern Med. 1983;99: 195.

123 **Gupta S, Katiyar JC.** Comparative activity of anticestode drugs—praziquantel, niclosamide and compound 77-6, against *Hymenolepis nana*. J Helminthol. 1983;57:31.

124 **Wilson JF, Rusch RL.** Alveolar hydatid disease. A review of clinical features of 33 indigenous cases of *Echinococcus multilocularis*: infection in

Alaskan Eskimos. Am J Trop Med Hyg. 1980;29:1340.

125 **Schantz PM et al.** Neurocysticercosis in an orthodox Jewish community in New York City. N Engl J Med. 1992; 327:692.

126 **Botero D et al.** Taeniasis and cysticercosis. Infect Dis Clin North Am. 1993; 7:683.

127 **Pathogenesis of the tapeworm anaemia.** Br Med J. 1976;2:1028. Editorial.

128 **Slonka GF et al.** An epidemic of pediculosis capitis. Clin Pediatr. 1978;17: 318.

129 **Billstein S, Loane P.** Demographic study of head lice infestations in Sacramento county school children. Int J Dermatol. 1979;18:301.

130 **Rasmussen JE.** Advances in the treatment of head and pubic lice. Drug Therapy. 1983;13:185.

131 **Pritcham R.** Pediculosis. Can Pharm J. 1984;117:416.

132 **Wilson BB.** Lice (Pediculosis). In: Mandell GL et al., eds. Principles and Practice of Infectious Diseases. New York: Churchill Livingstone; 1995: 2558.

133 **Spielman A, Wachtel M.** Insects and mites. In: Gorbach SL et al., eds. Infectious Diseases. Philadelphia: WB Saunders; 1992;2037.

134 **Meinking TA et al.** Comparative efficacy of treatments for Pediculosis capitis infestations. Arch Dermatol. 1986; 22:267.

135 **Deinard AS et al.** 1% Permethrin cream rinse vs. 1% Lindane shampoo in treating Pediculosis capitis. Am J Dis Child. 1986;140:894.

136 **Talpin D et al.** Malathion for treatment of *Pediculus humanus var capitis* infestations. JAMA. 1982;247:3103.

137 **Kolar KA, Rapini RP.** Crusted (Norwegian) scabies. Am Fam Physician. 1991;44:1317.

138 **Ramachander V et al.** Lindane toxicity in an infant. West Indian Med J. 1991;40:41.

139 **Friedman SJ.** Lindane neurotoxic reaction in nonbullous ichthyosiform erythroderma. Arch Dermatol. 1987; 123:1056.

140 **Wilson BB.** Scabies. In: Mandell GI et al., eds. Principles and Practice of Infectious Diseases. New York: Churchill Livingstone; 1995:2560.

141 **Arlian LG et al.** Prevalence of *Sarcoptes scabiei* in the homes and nursing homes of scabietic patients. J Am Acad Dermatol. 1988;19:806.

142 **Schultz MW et al.** Comparative study of 5% Permethrin cream and 1% Lindane lotion for the treatment of scabies. Arch Dermatol. 1990;126:167.

143 **Permethrin for scabies.** Med Lett Drugs Ther. 1990;32:21.

144 **Parish LC et al.** Scabies in extended care facility. Revisited. Int J Dermatol. 1991;30:703.

145 **Gurevich AW.** Scabies and lice. Pediatr Clin North Am. 1985;32:987.

Lyme Disease

Tom Christian

Spirochete Identification and Pathology 72-1
Tick Vector 72-1
   Spirochetal behavior 72-1
   Tick identification 72-1
   Host identification 72-1
Stages and Laboratory Testing of Lyme Borreliosis
  (Also see Table 72.1 and Question 1) 72-2
Treatment 72-2
Erythema Migrans (EM) 72-3

Signs, Symptoms, and Disease Course 72-3
Serologic Testing 72-4
Clinical Approach 72-4
Lyme Borreliosis Treatment 72-4
Antibiotics 72-4
Chronic Lyme Arthritis 72-5
Intravenous (IV) Antibiotics 72-5
Laboratory Testing of Lyme Borreliosis 72-5
Lyme Prevention 72-6

Lyme disease, or more accurately, Lyme borreliosis, is a multisystem spirochetal disease transmitted by the bite of a tick.[1-9] Although the responsible spirochete, *Borrelia burgdorferi*, was not identified until the 1980s, late manifestations of a dermatitis produced by a *Borrelia* species had been described in Europe more than a century ago.[10]

Spirochete Identification and Pathology

There are three genomic subgroups of *B. burgdorferi* worldwide which probably account for the clinical variations observed in the disease. North American strains identified to date belong to the *B. burgdorferi sensu stricto* group. Although all three groups have been found in Europe, most isolates are *B.garinii* or *B. afzelli*.

Lyme disease is multisystem in that it may affect the skin, eyes, joints, and cardiovascular system, as well as the central and peripheral nervous systems. The gastrointestinal (GI) and reticuloendothelial systems are involved less commonly. The ailment is named for the villages of "Lyme" and "Old Lyme," Connecticut, where arthritic complications of this disease were first recognized. Lyme disease accounts for at least 90% of vector-borne illness in the U.S.[2-5]

Tick Vector

Spirochetal Behavior. The tick acquires the *B. burgdorferi* spirochete from feeding on an infected host. The spirochete remains dormant in the tick's midgut until the tick feeds again. When the tick begins another blood feast, the spirochete penetrates the midgut wall and invades the salivary glands and other tissues of the tick. The spirochete then passes through the salivary ducts of the tick and is injected through the skin of the new host with the tick bite. Therefore, few spirochetes are transmitted from the tick to its host during the first 24 to 36 hours of attachment of the tick to its host; however, an infected nymphal tick invariably transfers spirochetes when attached to its host for more than 72 hours.[11,14,15]

Tick Identification. The tick is small, less than 3 mm, the size of a freckle or printed comma (,). Therefore, the tick frequently is unnoticed and less than half of patients with Lyme disease recall having been bitten by a tick.[2] The tick feeds on small, medium, or large-sized mammals, lizards, or birds during its larval and nymphal (immature) stages. Adult ticks parasitize only medium or large-sized mammals; they do not feed on small mammals, birds, or lizards.[11] Man is an inadvertent host of any stage of the tick.[12] While the tick can feed on many different animals, each tick species has preferred hosts. For example, the immature *Ixodes scap-*

ularis prefers to be hosted by the white-footed mouse, while the mature tick prefers the white-tailed deer. Collectively, these tick species, *I. scapularis* (formerly *dammini*),[2] *I. ricinus, I. persulcatus*, and *I. pacificus* have been referred to as the *Ixodes ricinus complex*. In the Northeastern and Midwestern U.S., *I. scapularis* is the primary vector whereas *I. pacificus* is the primary vector for the western U.S. In Europe, *I. ricinus* is the vector while *I. persulcatus* is the primary vector for Asia.[1,11,14,15] The discovery of *B. burgdorferi*-like organisms from *I. ovatus* in Japan and *Haemaphysalis longicornis* in China, both of which parasitize domestic animals and humans, demonstrates greater diversity of endemic vectors and cycles in Asia. The geographical distribution of Lyme disease, therefore, matches the geographical range of the specific *Ixodes* species.

Host Identification. Host type and the host's ability to harbor and transmit the spirochete to the tick (i.e., "reservoir competency") are important considerations in understanding the epidemiology and prevalence of Lyme disease. The reservoir-competent white-footed mouse and the reservoir-incompetent (i.e., incapable of harboring and transmitting the spirochete) white-tailed deer are the preferred hosts for the immature and adult forms of *I. scapularis* in the Northeastern U.S., respectively[1,2,7,11,12] Subadult *I. pacificus* preferentially feed on Western fence lizards, which are reservoir-incompetent, and deer are not important hosts for mature *I. pacificus*.[1,12,13] Similarly, in the Southern U.S., immature *I. scapularis* feed primarily on lizards.[12] In Europe, various reservoir-competent mice and vole species are reported hosts for *I. ricinus*.[11,12]

How then is Lyme borreliosis transmitted to humans in the Western U.S. if the preferred hosts are not reservoir-competent? It is suggested that the dusky-footed wood rat and kangaroo rat, which can support *B. burgdorferi*, are the hosts of the spirochete for the few immature *I. pacificus* which incidentally feed on the rats. Thus, an estimated 1% to 3% of *I. pacificus* are spirochete-infected contrasting with infection rates for *I. scapularis* in the Northeastern U.S. of 20% to 50%.[1] In Europe *I. ricinus* infection rates vary from 4% to 40%. Additionally, bird parasitism by ticks enables the ticks to be carried long distances even intercontinentally during spring and fall migrations. Birds can bring ticks into new areas and also serve as maintenance hosts like mammals.[11]

Thus, the complex interplay of spirochete, host, and vector in a particular area influence the risk of Lyme disease after a tick bite. *Borrelia* also have been detected in soft-bodied ticks, mosquitoes, and horse and deer flies, and erythema migrans (EM) has developed after deer fly bites.[11]

Stages and Laboratory Testing of Lyme Borreliosis

The clinical features of Lyme borreliosis by tradition are divided into three stages: *early localized* (*Stage 1*), *early disseminated* (*Stage 2*), and *chronic, persistent,* or *late disease* (*Stage 3*).[10,14–17] (See Table 72.1.) However, the stages may overlap and not all stages appear sequentially. Patients may not have symptoms of any of the disease stages and may suffer no sequelae. Although Lyme disease may be debilitating, it is not a life-threatening disease.

The most specific marker of Lyme borreliosis is a characteristic skin rash called erythema migrans (EM). This solitary skin lesion occurs in 50% to 70% of patients with the disease.[14–18] No other physical finding of Lyme borreliosis is diagnostic. Except for direct isolation and culture of *B. burgdorferi* from body sites (a costly, low-yield, and time-consuming endeavor) no laboratory "gold standard" exists to date. Laboratory diagnosis of Lyme borreliosis is problematic due to the lack of sufficiently sensitive and specific tests. Deficiencies in laboratory standardization confound the is-

Table 72.1	Lyme Borreliosis Stages[a,1,14,17,32–35]

Early localized infection (Stage 1): Usually Days After Tick Bite
EM skin rash
Myalgia, arthralgia, headache, stiff neck, fatigue, lethargy
Viral-like syndrome

Early Disseminated Disease (Stage 2): Days to Months After Bite
Musculoskeletal: Fibromyalgia, Arthralgia
 Migratory arthritis
 Large or small joint swelling, especially the temporomandibular joint
 Painful, unilateral hand/finger swelling in Europe
Heart (8% of Untreated Patients in the U.S.)
 Cardiomyopathy, CHF, myo- or pericarditis
 Conduction defects, varying degrees of AV or bundle branch block, but permanent pacing not indicated
 Arrhythmias
Nervous System (Neuroborreliosis)
 Cranial nerve (Bell's) palsy
 Meningitis, lymphocytic
 Radiculoneuritis, myelitis
 Sensory or motor peripheral neuropathy
 Ataxia
 Encephalomyelitis
Eye
 Iritis, conjunctivitis, choroiditis, uveitis, optic neuritis, retinal vasculitis, panophthalmitis
Lymph
 Generalized or localized lymphadenopathy
Skin
 Multiple secondary EM lesions in 50% with primary EM.
 Lymphocytoma (lymphadenosis benigna cutis) rare in the U.S., but 1% in Europe
Liver
 Hepatitis, recurrent; Abnormal LFTs
Lung
 Acute respiratory distress syndrome
Kidney
 Microscopic hematuria or proteinuria
Testicle
 Orchitis

Chronic or Persistent Disease (Stage 3): Months to Years After Bite
Musculoskeletal (62% in the U.S., less common in Europe)
 Chronic (10% of untreated in the U.S.) or intermittent arthritis of ≥1 large joints, especially the knee
Skin (10% in Europe, rare in the U.S.)
 Acrodermatitis chronica atrophicans (unique to Lyme borreliosis)
Fibromyalgia
Late Neurological
 Peripheral neuropathy, subacute encephalopathy (memory impairment, sleep disturbance, dementia) and in Europe, progressive encephalomyelitis

[a] AV = Atrioventricular; CHF = Congestive heart failure; EM = Erythema migrans; LFTs = Liver function tests.

sue.[8] Thus, the diagnosis of Lyme borreliosis is based upon the presence of clinical findings combined with a thorough history. Positive results of blood tests for an antibody response to the spirochete only support a diagnosis of Lyme borreliosis because the test is not sufficiently sensitive and specific. The immunoglobulin M (IgM) antibody response develops two to four weeks after infection, peaks at six to eight weeks, and declines to the normal range after four to six months. In some patients IgM levels may remain high or reappear. The immunoglobulin G (IgG) antibody response begins six to eight weeks after disease onset, peaks at four to six months, and may remain elevated indefinitely.[9] In the absence of erythema migrans, serologic tests for antibody response often are used to help confirm the diagnosis of Lyme borreliosis. However, overuse of serologic testing and overreliance on the results of serologic tests have resulted in excessive and inaccurate diagnoses of Lyme borreliosis.[13,19–22] For example, clinicians at a Lyme borreliosis referral center in British Columbia, Canada, an area not endemic for Lyme borreliosis, determined that only two of the first 65 patients referred to them had probable Lyme borreliosis. Alternate diagnoses were established for 59 of the remaining 63 patients. Before that time the Provincial Health Laboratory performed only immunofluorescent antibody serologic testing and high titers were considered as diagnostic for Lyme borreliosis. Overdiagnosis of Lyme borreliosis also occurs due to its resemblance to other diseases.[1,6,13,23–28]

Treatment

The stage of Lyme borreliosis disease and the extent of infection should govern the treatment strategy of this disease.[14–17,29–32] However, the optimal drug, dose, and duration of therapy for Lyme borreliosis are not established.[31] Treatment failures occur with all regimens and despite treatment for early erythema migrans, 5% to 10% of patients are treated unsuccessfully.[14,18] Poor patient compliance, use of ineffective antibiotic regimens, intra-articular corticosteroid injections before or during antibiotic treatment for arthritic complications, and ongoing immune responses imitating active infection can affect the success rate of therapy. *B. burgdorferi* can invade fibroblasts (abundant in the skin) and other cells and elude destruction by potent antibiotics such as ceftriaxone.[14] However, in order to effect a cure, it is not necessary to continue antibiotic treatment until all symptoms have resolved.[31] There is a growing tendency to use longer treatment periods of months or even years, especially in the U.S. There are, however, no scientific investigations supporting such prolonged treatment regimens.[29] (See Table 72.2.) Finally, it is important to distinguish fibromyalgia and chronic fatigue from active Lyme borreliosis since the symptoms of fibromyalgia do not respond to antibiotic therapy. This is true whether or not Lyme borreliosis originally triggered the fibromyalgia.[14] Fibromyalgia does respond well to other therapies.[3]

1. J.S., a 38-year-old male, reports to his local physician with symptoms of low-grade fever and muscle aches 3 days after deer hunting in Washington state. After hunting deer for ≈6 hours, he noticed a small tick on his thigh and immediately destroyed it. A little, itchy spot that he felt at the site of the tick bite is no longer a problem. The temporal relationship of the tick bite with his symptoms of fever and myalgias prompts his physician to collect blood samples for Lyme borreliosis antibody testing. Antibiotic therapy also is initiated. Why is the blood test not likely to be of value? Why is empirical antibiotic therapy not appropriate for J.S.?

The antibody response to *B. burgdorferi* is not detectable for the first two to four weeks after a tick bite.[14] Therefore, the blood tests for antibodies to *B. burgdorferi* are not likely to be positive because J.S.'s tick bite occurred only three days ago.

Table 72.2	Suggested Treatment Recommendation for Lyme Borreliosis[14–17,29–33]

Erythema Migrans, Early, Uncomplicated

Adult: Doxycycline (Vibramycin 100 mg PO BID x 10–21 days (or 200 mg QD x 10–21 days)
or
Amoxicillin (Polymox) 500 mg PO TID x 10–21 days
or
Cefuroxime axetil (Ceftin) 500 mg PO BID x 21 days
Child (<8 yr): Amoxicillin 40 mg/kg/day PO in 3 divided doses x 10 days. (Doxycycline contraindicated)

Erythema Migrans with Signs of Dissemination
Carditis
Adult: Ceftriaxone (Rocephin) 2 gm IV QD x 14 days
or
Cefotaxime (Claforan) 2 gm IV TID x 14 days
or
Penicillin G (Pfizerpen) 20 MU, divided QID x 14 days
or
For mild cardiac involvement only: Doxycycline or amoxicillin in doses as noted above x 21 days
Child: Ceftriaxone IV 100 mg/kg/day, divided BID x 14 days
or
Cefotaxime IV 180 mg/kg/day, divided TID x 14 days
or
Penicillin G IV 300,000 U/kg/day, divided Q 6 hr x 14 days

Neurologic Disease
Facial nerve paralysis as an isolated early finding: In doses as noted above for early EM x 21 days
Meningitis, radiculitis, or encephalitis: IV drugs in doses as noted above for carditis x 21–30 days *or* doxycycline 100 mg IV BID x 21–30 days

Chronic Disease
Acrodermatitis: Oral regimens for 30 days
Arthritis
Adult: Doxycycline 200 mg/day PO x 30 days
or
Amoxicillin 500 mg + probenecid (Benemid) 500 mg PO TID x 30 days
or
Ceftriaxone or cefotaxime in doses as noted above x 14–21 days
Child: Amoxicillin 40 mg/kg + probenecid 30 mg/kg PO, divided TID x 21 days (Note: probenecid not for children <2 yr)
or
Ceftriaxone or cefotaxime (pediatric dosing) x 14–21 days

Pregnant/Breastfeeding
Amoxicillin 500 mg PO TID x 21 days. If evidence of dissemination: penicillin G IV 20 MU/day x 14–21 days. (Doxycycline contraindicated)

The risk of developing Lyme borreliosis can be affected by: transmission rates of the spirochete from infected ticks to humans; the length of time before the tick is removed during its bite; the prevalence of spirochete infestation of ticks in an area, which varies with the tick species; and the reservoir-competency of host animals in the region.

While transmission rates of Lyme borreliosis from an infected tick bite are estimated at approximately 10%,[30] the risk is reduced dramatically if the tick is removed within 24 hours of attachment, such as in J.S.'s case. The small, itchy spot experienced by J.S. probably represented a hypersensitivity reaction to the bite.

Empirical antibiotic treatment for J.S. is warranted if he was hunting in an area highly endemic for Lyme borreliosis. Specifically, if the probability of *B. burgdorferi* infection after a tick bite is 3.6% or higher, then empirical prophylactic therapy is indicated. If the probability of infection ranges from 1% to 3.5%, then immediate treatment may be preferred to awaiting the development of signs and symptoms of Lyme borreliosis. However, empirical therapy is not warranted if the probability of infection is less than 1%. If these criteria are met, doxycycline (Vibramycin) 100 mg orally twice a day for 14 days initiated immediately is cost-effective.[4] The goal of empirical treatment in this setting is the prevention of the rheumatological, neurological, and cardiac sequelae that may arise with attendant increased costs of diagnosis and treatment. Since J.S. was hunting in Washington state which is not highly endemic for Lyme borreliosis and because he removed the tick within six hours of the tick attachment to his thigh, empirical antibiotic therapy for J.S. probably is not warranted. If the physician has encountered recent cases of Lyme borreliosis and if J.S. is unduly alarmed, perhaps a 14-day course of doxycycline might be cost justified.

Erythema Migrans (EM)
Signs, Symptoms, and Disease Course

2. K.T., a 34-year-old female, presents with right knee pain and multiple, large, discrete skin rashes which she has had for the last 10 days. Three months ago in July, she visited friends in Massachusetts and spent much of her time engaged in outdoor activities (e.g., hiking, biking, swimming). Two months ago, her husband noticed a circular area ≈9 cm in size of intense redness in her left armpit. The rash grew considerably larger over the next 2 weeks and had a red outer border. K.T. attributed the expansion of the rash to scratching the mildly itchy area. The rash gradually disappeared. In late August, K.T. experienced fatigue, nausea, and headache for a week and thought it was "summer flu." In early September, she experienced right knee pain which she treated with ibuprofen (Advil) and gained some relief. Upon examination she was afebrile and had mild soft tissue swelling of the right knee. Her white blood cell (WBC) count was normal. Erythrocyte sedimentation rate (ESR) was elevated at 45 mm/hr. Electrocardiogram (ECG) was normal. Serum samples contained antibody titers to *B. burgdorferi* of 1:60 and 1:400 for IgM and IgG, respectively. A venereal disease research laboratory test for syphilis was negative.

K.T. is started on a 4-week course of doxycycline 100 mg PO BID and told to continue ibuprofen for symptomatic relief of her knee pain. What characteristics of K.T.'s skin rash are consistent with the EM of Lyme borreliosis? [SI unit: ESR 45 mm/hr]

The erythema migrans of Lyme borreliosis usually develops within 30 days (median: 7 days) of a (usually asymptomatic) tick bite at the site of inoculation of the spirochete. The erythema migrans rash begins as an erythematous (red) macule or papule typically in the groin, axilla, or thigh. It expands outward within a few days to a diameter of 5 to 60 cm (mean: 15 cm) generally with some central clearing. The classic annular or ring-like patch may have complex concentric inner erythematous circles rendering a bulls-eye or target-like total appearance. The rash may be warm to touch and is usually painless, but there may be mild burning or itching in some patients.[14,16–18] In contrast, the commonly intense pruritic hypersensitivity reactions to insect bites occur within 24 hours.[18] One half or more of patients with erythema migrans have multiple secondary erythema migrans lesions that most likely represent blood-borne spread of the spirochete to other skin sites rather than multiple tick bites.[16] When the erythema migrans is untreated, it generally fades within several weeks. If the erythema migrans is treated, it usually resolves in several days.

Low-grade fever and other nonspecific symptoms such as fatigue, malaise, lethargy, headache, stiff neck, myalgia, arthralgia, and regional or generalized lymphadenopathy may accompany erythema migrans. Up to 40% of patients with Lyme borreliosis either do not notice or display erythema migrans. Some may not have the other early symptoms of the disease. Some clinicians prefer abandoning the term "flu-like illness" in favor of "viral-like syndromes" to describe the nonspecific symptoms of early Lyme disease because cough and coryza usually do not occur.[16] Others have documented the existence of a "flu-like illness" without erythema migrans in early Lyme borreliosis.[36]

Serologic Testing

3. What might have been the rationale for the laboratory tests that were undertaken in K.T. and what would be reasonable interpretations of laboratory tests in patients with Lyme disease?

An antibody titer measured by enzyme-linked immunoabsorbent assay (ELISA) is considered positive for IgM when it is ≥100 and for IgG when ≥130. K.T.'s results are supportive of a Lyme borreliosis diagnosis since the IgM has fallen naturally by this time. Syphilis and other known biologic causes (periodontal spirochetes) of false-positive serologic testing should be excluded.[9] An ECG might have shown atrioventricular (AV) nodal block as Lyme carditis can occur within days or as long as nine months after the onset of erythema migrans in 8% of untreated U.S. patients.[16] Elevated ESR is a nonspecific indicator of inflammation that occurs in 50% of erythema migrans patients; however, rheumatoid factor or antinuclear antibody tests usually are negative in Lyme borreliosis. These tests help differentiate rheumatoid arthritis or systemic lupus erythematosus from Lyme borreliosis. Mild liver function test abnormalities occur in one-fifth of erythema migrans patients.[17] WBC count is normal or mildly elevated in Lyme borreliosis. Most interesting in K.T. is the presence of secondary erythema migrans lesions which develop in 50% to 70% of untreated patients in the U.S. and represent disseminated infection. Lyme borreliosis as the etiology of arthritis always should be ruled out before corticosteroids are injected into a joint because intra-articular corticosteroids before antibiotic therapy in Lyme borreliosis arthritis predispose the patient to treatment failure. Steroid injections were appropriately not used in K.T. but could provide temporary symptomatic relief after the completion of antibiotic therapy.[32]

The expression of erythema migrans as an early indicator of Lyme borreliosis grants physicians the best opportunity for diagnosis and treatment. Early treatment can prevent the devastating sequelae of disseminated disease.[18]

Clinical Approach

4. Since the finding of erythema migrans offers the best opportunity for the early diagnosis of Lyme borreliosis, how might the physician evaluate erythema migrans in a patient, particularly when found in an area in which Lyme borreliosis is not prevalent?

The best approach for many clinicians might be to request that the patient save the live tick for further identification and spirochete testing. The urine and blood obtained from the patient during the initial office visit should be frozen and saved for future testing. The erythema migrans rash should be documented by recording the dimensions of the rash and photographing the erythema migrans rash. A skin culture of the erythema migrans rash also should be obtained if possible.

Lyme Borreliosis Treatment

Antibiotics

5. Considering the *in vitro* data presented in Table 72.3, why was doxycycline (Vibramycin) chosen to treat K.T.?

Table 72.3	*In Vitro* Susceptibility of Different Isolates of *B. burgdorferi* to Selected Antimicrobial Agents[29,49-53]	
Antibiotic	MIC[a] (μg/mL)	MBC[a] (μg/mL)
Penicillin G	0.06–3.0	6.4–25.0
Amoxicillin	0.03–0.06	0.03–2.0
Cefuroxime	0.06–0.18	1.0
Ceftizoxime	0.06–0.5	0.25–1.0
Cefotaxime	0.03–0.12	0.03–0.25
Ceftriaxone	0.02–0.06	0.03–0.16
Erythromycin	0.03–0.25	0.06–0.5
Clarithromycin	0.03–0.06	0.06–0.25
Azithromycin	—	0.04
Tetracycline	—	1.6–3.2
Doxycycline	0.125–2.0	0.25–6.4

[a] MIC = Minimum inhibitory concentration; MBC = Minimum bactericidal concentration.

As previously mentioned, the optimal therapy for Lyme borreliosis has not been firmly established and treatment failures occur with all regimens studied to date. Treatment failure should be considered if minor symptoms of continued infection such as fatigue, headache, or arthralgias persist after several weeks following initial treatment or if progression to neurological disease ensues.

B. burgdorferi is susceptible to the action of macrolides, amoxicillin, tetracyclines, and some second- and third-generation cephalosporins based upon *in vitro* data. It is only moderately sensitive to penicillin G (Pfizerpen) and is resistant to rifampin (Rimactane), co-trimoxazole (Bactrim), aminoglycosides, chloramphenicol (Chloromycetin), and the fluoroquinolones.

Penicillin, tetracycline, and erythromycin historically were drugs of choice for the treatment of Lyme borreliosis because they are given orally, are relatively inexpensive, and appeared to have good *in vitro* activity. Unfortunately, disappointing *in vivo* results were realized with all these agents except penicillin. In Europe, in particular, penicillin still is used with continued success.[29] Amoxicillin (Polymox) has better absorption and a longer serum half-life than penicillin V (Veetids) and continues to be effective in treating Lyme disease.

Compared to the third-generation cephalosporins, the second-generation drug, cefuroxime axetil (Ceftin), is available in an oral dosage form and has good *in vitro* activity as well as *in vivo* performance. Of the third-generation cephalosporins, ceftriaxone (Rocephin) has the strongest *in vitro* activity. The long half-life of ceftriaxone allows the convenience of once-daily dosing in an outpatient program. However, ceftriaxone is expensive and has a higher incidence of diarrhea than other beta-lactams, probably due to partial biliary excretion. Cefotaxime (Claforan) is an alternative to ceftriaxone and comparable in cost, but must be dosed more frequently.

The macrolides, clarithromycin (Biaxin) and azithromycin (Zithromax) have excellent *in vitro* activity, rivaling ceftriaxone. However, like erythromycin, treatment failures are documented for azithromycin and roxithromycin (not available in the U.S.).[29] Azithromycin does have better tissue penetration than ceftriaxone and has been used for treatment failures of the latter, but a potential disadvantage of azithromycin is its limited ability to cross the blood-brain barrier which may be important in preventing central nervous system (CNS) infection by the spirochete.[15]

Doxycycline is well absorbed orally and is less expensive than third-generation cephalosporins which must be administered parenterally. Doxycycline also has a long serum half-life of 18 to 22 hours and may be dosed once daily.[29] Additionally, doxycycline is lipid soluble compared to the water-soluble beta-lactams, accumulates intracellularly, and penetrates into the cerebrospinal fluid (CSF) at concentrations of at least 10% of serum levels even in the absence of meningeal inflammation.[29] Doxycycline can complex with di- or trivalent cations in the gut, and absorption can be decreased as a result. In comparison to other tetracyclines, doxycycline has the least affinity for divalent calcium cations and oral absorption is reduced by only 20% if given with milk. The major side effect of doxycycline is phototoxicity which is of concern since Lyme borreliosis usually occurs during sunny times of the year. Despite less *in vitro* activity compared to some beta-lactam antibiotics, *B. burgdorferi* is sufficiently susceptible to doxycycline and clinical experience with doxycycline has been favorable.[15]

In conclusion, doxycycline was a suitable choice for K.T. and the four-week duration of therapy matches the recommendation for adult arthritis treatment outlined in Table 72.2.

Chronic Lyme Arthritis

6. K.T. continues to have knee inflammation for 1 year despite treatment and now is considered to have chronic Lyme arthritis. Why should antibiotic therapy be repeated (or not repeated) for K.T.'s arthritis?

The chronic Lyme arthritis which develops in about 10% of untreated U.S. patients (see Table 72.1) has been associated with an increased frequency of the class II major histocompatibility complex alleles, HLA-DR4 and HLA-DR2 human leukocyte antigens (see Chapter 41: Rheumatic Disorders). Patients with these markers may be predestined for the development of chronic arthritis despite antibiotic therapy.[31] Destructive changes in the involved joint may occur with the synovium showing vascular proliferation, villous hypertrophy, and a lymphoplasma cellular infiltrate similar to other inflammatory arthritis.[14] Thus, in some patients, chronic Lyme arthritis may not be due to the persistence of active infection by the spirochete in a protected site. Such patients often respond well to synovectomy, again suggesting that the presence of synovitis may not be due to the persistence of infection.[14,32]

A sensible approach for K.T. would be to follow the initial oral therapy, if it failed, immediately with a two- to four-week course of intravenous (IV) ceftriaxone.[31] If K.T. is HLA-DR4 positive and has antibody reactivity to the outer surface proteins, OspA or OspB of *B. burgdorferi*, she will likely be treatment resistant and synovectomy may be offered instead of repeated antibiotic treatment.[14]

Intravenous (IV) Antibiotics

7. E.C., a 54-year-old man, presents with symptoms of Lyme borreliosis meningitis with concurrent Bell's palsy (Banwarth's syndrome). Physical examination and serologic and CSF analyses confirm the diagnosis. Why should E.C. be treated with antibiotics and for how long?

Although the acute neurologic manifestations of Lyme borreliosis can remit spontaneously, intravenous antibiotic therapy hastens the resolution of symptoms and prevents the more chronic sequelae (e.g., mild cognitive dysfunction or low-grade peripheral neuropathies) of persistent CNS infection. The development of these other syndromes in E.C. may be evidence of irreversible neurologic damage; therefore, the approach to diagnosis and treatment should be aggressive. IV antibiotic therapy is indicated (see Table 72.2).[31] The mean duration of meningeal symptoms in antibiotic-treated patients is only one week, as compared to 29 weeks in untreated patients.[29]

As for other stages of Lyme borreliosis, the optimal duration of therapy has not been firmly established. Most authorities recommend a minimum of two to four weeks.[15,29,30–32]

Other candidates for intensive IV regimens of antibiotic therapy include patients with high degree AV block or other signs of disseminated disease that have not responded to oral therapy.[15]

All patients with Lyme borreliosis should be treated with antibiotics because the majority of cases can be managed effectively with appropriately chosen antibiotics. Recommendations are based upon the disease stage present and the extent of the infection.[31] In conclusion, E.C. should be treated aggressively with a parenteral third-generation cephalosporin such as ceftriaxone 2 gm IV daily for three to four weeks.

Laboratory Testing of Lyme Borreliosis

8. P.S., a 35-year-old, asymptomatic male with a history of a tick bite from a nonendemic Lyme borreliosis area, just tested positive on ELISA. He was tested because he expressed a "fear" of Lyme borreliosis. Why is this positive result alone sufficient (or insufficient) to begin treatment for Lyme borreliosis? What other tests could be considered to help confirm the diagnosis?

Problems of standardization, sensitivity, and specificity have caused marked inter- and intralaboratory variations in test results in the serodiagnosis of Lyme borreliosis.[8–10,18–23,37,38] Serologic testing for an antibody response to the spirochete is incapable of distinguishing between active infection and prior exposure.[40–42,46] However, demonstration of local cerebrospinal fluid antibody production and comparison to serum concentrations is highly useful in the diagnosis of neuroborreliosis.[8] Despite these problems detection of the antibody response to *B. burgdorferi* is the most commonly used laboratory procedure for the diagnosis of Lyme borreliosis.

Immunofluorescent assay (IFA) detection of antibody response was the first tool used in the diagnosis of Lyme borreliosis. This test, however, is labor intensive, subjective in the interpretation of the results, and has been replaced by ELISA analysis. Even with ELISA, 5% to 7% of test results may be false-positive. The Western Blot (immunoblotting) test has been advocated by some to increase the specificity of ELISA results, but its utility in early Lyme borreliosis is equivocal.[8,41,46]

Detection of *B. burgdorferi* antigens in the urine of Lyme borreliosis patients has been accomplished using monoclonal antibody and antigen capture techniques.[8] Still in the developmental stages are detection of immune complexes and spirochetal antigens in the cerebrospinal fluid.

The polymerase chain reaction (PCR) test can detect as few as one to ten chromosomal genomes of *B. burgdorferi* by gene amplification. Unfortunately, it is so sophisticated and sensitive that it is subject to false-positives by the accidental contamination of a sample with small quantities of the target DNA. Thus, it requires meticulous laboratory standards and quality assurance.[46] It also is unable to differentiate between actively infecting spirochetes and dead ones as it searches only for DNA. In patients with acute Lyme borreliosis, spirochetes or spirochetal DNA circulate in the blood only intermittently or at such low levels that PCR serologic testing is unlikely to prove generally useful.[42]

If sera from actively infected Lyme borreliosis patients were to be incubated *in vitro* with live *Borrelia* spirochetes, *B. burgdorferi* organisms should die when complement is added. When this has been done, 36% to 99% more spirochetes died after 72 hours than with sera from normal individuals. Additionally, sera from patients with relapsing fever (another *Borrelia*), syphilis, Rocky Mountain spotted fever, mononucleosis, or rheumatoid factor failed to kill the Lyme borreliosis spirochete.[47] Whether this method of laboratory testing for Lyme borreliosis will become practical or widely useful remains to be established.

Direct cultivation of *B. burgdorferi* from patient tissue or fluid is the irrefutable diagnostic procedure for Lyme borreliosis. Direct biopsy of erythema migrans lesions or techniques of cutaneous lavage of the margin of erythema migrans sometimes are successful.[18] Isolation of the organism from the blood is difficult and generally not likely to be useful in the diagnosis of those patients without erythema migrans.[42]

In summary, P.S. should not be treated for active Lyme borreliosis based solely upon a positive ELISA test. Although the Western Blot might help establish the diagnosis, only a careful history and physical examination in combination with the serologic testing will accurately diagnose Lyme borreliosis. The erythema migrans rash is key to early diagnosis.

Lyme Prevention

9. P.S. is alarmed that his family members may contract Lyme borreliosis as he may have. How do you advise him?

Most vector-borne diseases are prevented through vector control. This has proven difficult for tick-borne diseases due to lack of efficacy or environmental concerns. Methods tried include habitat destruction by fire, chemical spraying, eradication of host deer, or protection of mice from tick infestation.[1]

The prevention of Lyme borreliosis has been limited thus far to personal protection efforts. Tick repellents may be applied to the skin or clothing. N,N-diethyl-*m*-toluamide (DEET) skin repellents (Repel Sportsman) combined with a permethrin (Permanone) clothing repellent offer the best overall protection.[7]

DEET has been tested against ixodid ticks for repellency and found to be more effective than dibutyl phthalate, dimethyl phthalate, pyrethrum, and two combination products. Against three species of ixodid ticks at larval, nymphal, and adult stages, DEET (concentrations not specified) was 99%, 81.6%, and 95.5% respectively repellent.[7] Although DEET historically was considered safe, studies suggest that up to 50% of an applied dose may be absorbed through the skin; distributed to fat, liver, and muscle tissue; and most of it excreted in the urine within 24 hours. However, since DEET is lipid soluble, it can accumulate in fatty tissue and the brain.

Adverse DEET effects reported in adults include tingling, dryness, and some desquamation around the nasal area after repeated application of a 50% DEET solution to the face and arms. Two days after discontinuation of the solution these side effects usually resolve.[7] More severe adverse reactions in adults include acute hypersensitivity reactions with permanent scarring developing due to hemorrhagic blistering as well as anaphylaxis and an episode of acute manic psychosis. In children, on the other hand, serious reactions including hypersensitivity, toxic encephalopathy, and a death have been documented.[7] Prolonged or excessive application is not recommended. The use of a 100% DEET repellent is unnecessary and should be avoided in small children. In theory, the final concentration of DEET on the skin after application of any percentage DEET-containing product can increase due to evaporation of the solvent vehicle.[7]

Physical barriers to ticks such as protective garments, tucking pants into boots, and closed-toed shoes should be helpful in preventing infection. Regularly checking the body for the presence of ticks and promptly removing any that are found, or avoiding tick habitats entirely, also would minimize the potential for infection.[7]

Vaccinations for Lyme borreliosis, already available for pets, are undergoing human trials.[1] Questions about vaccination development include whether there will be adequate cross coverage between *Borrelia* strains, the risks of adverse reactions, and who should be vaccinated.[14]

References

1 **Steere AC.** Lyme disease: a growing threat to urban populations. Proc Natl Acad Sci U S A. 1994;91:2378.

2 **Spach DH et al.** Tick-born-diseases in the United States. N Engl J Med. 1993; 329:936.

3 **Coyle PK.** Neurologic complications of lyme disease. Rheum Dis Clin North Am. 1993;19:993.

4 **Magid D et al.** Prevention of lyme disease after tick bites. N Engl J Med. 1992;327:534.

5 **Horowitz HW et al.** Dermatomyositis associated with lyme disease: case report and review of lyme myositis. Clin Infect Dis. 1994;18:166.

6 **Steere AC et al.** The overdiagnosis of lyme disease. JAMA. 1993;269:1812.

7 **Couch P, Johnson CE.** Prevention of lyme disease. Am J Hosp Pharm. 1992; 49:1164.

8 **Berger BW.** Laboratory tests for lyme disease. Dermatol Clin. 1994;12:19.

9 **Rahn DW, Malawista SE.** Lyme disease: recommendations for diagnosis and treatment. Ann Intern Med. 1991; 114:472.

10 **Pfister HW et al.** Lyme borreliosis: basic science and clinical aspects. Lancet. 1994;343:1013.

11 **Anderson JF, Magnarelli LA.** Epizootiology of lyme disease-causing borreliae. Clin Dermatol. 1993;11:339.

12 **Barbour AG, Fish D.** The biological and social phenomenon of lyme disease. Science. 1993;260:1610.

13 **Burdge DR, O'Hanlon DP.** Experience at a referral center for patients with suspected lyme disease in an area of nonendemicity: first 65 patients. Clin Infect Dis. 1993;16:558.

14 **Kalish R.** Lyme disease. Rheum Dis Clin North Am. 1993;19:399.

15 **Berger BW.** Lyme disease. Semin Dermatol. 1993;12:357.

16 **Sigal LH.** Lyme disease: testing and treatment. Rheum Dis Clin North Am. 1993;19:79.

17 **Sigal LH.** Current recommendations for the treatment of lyme disease. Drugs. 1992;43:683.

18 **Masters EJ.** Erythema migrans. Postgrad Med. 1993;94:133.

19 **Ley C et al.** The use of serologic tests for lyme disease in a prepaid health plan in California. JAMA. 1994;271:460.

20 **Luger SW, Krause E.** Serologic tests for lyme disease. Arch Intern Med. 1990;150:761.

21 **Miralles D et al.** Not everything that glitters is lyme disease. Am J Med. 1992;93:352. Editorial.

22 **Corpuz M et al.** Problems in the use of serologic tests for the diagnosis of lyme disease. Arch Intern Med. 1991; 151:1837.

23 **Sood SK et al.** Positive serology for lyme borreliosis in patients with juvenile rheumatoid arthritis in a lyme borreliosis endemic area: analysis by immunoblot. J Rheumatol. 1993;20:739.

24 **Sigal LH, Patella SJ.** Lyme arthritis as the incorrect diagnosis in pediatric and adolescent fibromyalgia. Pediatrics. 1992;90:523.

25 **Hsu VM et al.** ''Chronic lyme disease'' as the incorrect diagnosis in patients with fibromyalgia. Arthritis Rheum. 1993;36:1493.

26 **Coyle PK et al.** Significance of reactive lyme serology in multiple sclerosis. Ann Neurol. 1993;34:745.

27 **Zoschke DC.** Is it lyme disease? Postgrad Med. 1992;91:46.

28 **Schned ES, Williams DN.** Special concerns in lyme disease. Postgrad Med. 1992;91:65.

29 **Stiernstedt G.** Therapeutic aspects of lyme borreliosis. Clin Dermatol. 1993; 11:423.

30 **Sanford JP et al.** Guide to Antimicrobial Therapy. Dallas, TX: Antimicrobial Therapy; 1994.

31 **Rahn DW.** Antibiotic treatment of lyme disease. Postgrad Med. 1992;91:57.

32 **Weber K, Pfister HW.** Clinical management of lyme borreliosis. Lancet. 1994;343:1017.

33 **Finkel MJ, Halperin JJ.** Nervous system lyme borreliosis—revisited. Arch Neurol. 1992;49:102.

34 **Hammers-Berggren S et al.** Screening for neuroborreliosis in patients with stroke. Stroke. 1993;24:1393.

35 **Cox J, Krajden M.** Cardiovascular manifestations of lyme disease. Am Heart J. 1991;122:1449.

36 **Feder HM et al.** Early lyme disease: a flu-like illness without erythema migrans. Pediatrics. 1993;91:456.

37 **Aguero-Rosenfeld ME et al.** Serodiagnosis in early lyme disease. J Clin Microbiol. 1993;31:3090.

38 **Pachner AR, Ricalton NS.** Western blotting in evaluating lyme seropositivity and the utility of a gel densitometric approach. Neurology. 1992;42:2185.

39 **Sigal LH.** Immunopathogenesis of lyme borreliosis. Clin Dermatol. 1993; 11:415.

40 **Sigal LH.** The polymerase chain reaction assay for Borrelia burgdorferi in the diagnosis of lyme disease. Ann Intern Med. 1994;120:520.

41 **Dressler F et al.** Western blotting in the serodiagnosis of lyme disease. J Infect Dis. 1993;167:392.

42 **Wallach FR et al.** Circulating Borrelia burgdorferi in patients with acute lyme disease: results of blood cultures and serum DNA analysis. J Infect Dis. 1993;168:1541.

43 **Scully RE et al.** Case records of the Massachusetts general hospital. N Engl J Med. 1993;329:194.

44 **Kaslow RA.** Current perspective on lyme borreliosis. JAMA. 1992;267: 1381.

45 **Sigal LH.** Persisting complaints attributed to chronic lyme disease: possible mechanisms and implications for management. Am J Med. 1994;96:365.

46 **Finkel MF.** The progressive paralytic disorders associated with lyme disease. Semin Neurol. 1993;13:299.

47 **Callister SM et al.** Characterization of the borreliacidal antibody response to Borrelia burgdorferi in humans: a sero-diagnostic test. J Infect Dis. 1993;167: 158.

48 **Burmester GR.** Lessons from lyme arthritis. Clin Exp Rheumatol. 1993;11 (Suppl. 8):S23.

49 **Levin JM et al.** In vitro susceptibility of *Borrelia burgdorferi* to 11 anti-microbial agents. Antimicrob Agents Chemother. 1993;37(7):1444.

50 **Agger WA et al.** In vitro susceptibility of *Borrelia burgdorferi* to five oral cephalosporins and ceftriaxone. Antimicrob Agents Chemother. 1992;36: 1788.

51 **Johnson RC et al.** In-vitro and in-vivo susceptibility of *Borrelia burgdorferi* to azithromycin. J Antimicrob Chemother. 1990;25(Suppl. A):33.

52 **Johnson RC et al.** Comparative in vitro and in vivo susceptibilities of the lyme disease spirochete *Borrelia burgdorferi* to cefuroxime and other anti-microbial agents. Antimicrob Agents Chemother. 1990;34(11):2133.

53 **Dever LL et al.** In vitro antimicrobial susceptibility testing of *Borrelia burgdorferi*: a microdilution MIC method and time-kill studies. J Clin Microbiol. 1992;30(10):2692.

Anxiety Disorders

Sara R Grimsley

Overview 73-1
  Prevalence and Significance of Anxiety Disorders 73-2
  Classification and Diagnosis of Anxiety Disorders 73-2
  Clinical Assessment and Differential Diagnosis
    of Anxiety 73-2
    Diagnostic decision tree for anxiety disorders
      (See Figure 73.1) 73-3
    Secondary causes of anxiety (See Table 73.1) 73-2
    Comorbidity with other psychiatric disorders 73-4
Generalized Anxiety Disorder (GAD) 73-4
  Epidemiology 73-4
  Diagnostic Criteria (See Table 73.2) 73-4
  Etiology and Pathophysiology 73-5
    GABA-benzodiazepine receptor complex
      (See Figure 73.2) 73-5
    Noradrenergic systems 73-5
    Serotonergic systems 73-5
  Treatment of Generalized Anxiety Disorder 73-6
    Nonpharmacological treatments 73-6
    Benzodiazepines 73-6
      Mechanism of action 73-6
      Clinical comparison of benzodiazepines
        (See Table 73.3) 73-7
    Buspirone 73-7
    Antidepressants 73-7
    Beta blockers 73-7
    Clonidine 73-8
    Antihistamines 73-8
  Clinical Presentation and Assessment 73-8
  Indications for and Goals of Treatment 73-8
  Selection of Treatment 73-8
  Benzodiazepine Treatment 73-9
    Factors influencing benzodiazepine selection 73-9
      Pharmacokinetics and metabolic pathways
        (See Tables 73.4 and 73.6 and Figure 73.3) 73-9
    Adverse effects and patient counseling 73-10
    Abuse and dependence 73-11
      Benzodiazepine withdrawal symptoms
        (See Table 73.5) 73-11
      Minimization of abuse and dependence and
        patient counseling 73-12
    Duration of treatment 73-13
    Treatment and management of withdrawal 73-13
    Physiologic variables influencing benzodiazepines
      (See Table 73.6) 73-13
    Benzodiazepine drug interactions
      (See Table 73.7) 73-14
    Teratogenicity 73-14
    Benzodiazepine overdose 73-16
      Flumazenil 73-16
  Buspirone Therapy 73-16
    Clinical comparison with benzodiazepines 73-17
    Adverse effects 73-17

    Antidepressant effects 73-17
    Conversion from benzodiazepine to
      buspirone therapy 73-17
    Drug interactions 73-17
Panic Disorder 73-17
  Diagnostic Criteria (See Table 73.8) 73-17
  Epidemiology 73-18
  Etiology and Pathophysiology 73-18
  Treatments of Panic Disorder 73-18
  Clinical Presentation and Differential Diagnosis 73-19
  Alprazolam Treatment 73-20
    Comparison with antidepressants 73-20
    Dosing guidelines and goals of treatment 73-20
    Duration of treatment 73-20
    Treatment discontinuation 73-20
  Antidepressant Treatment 73-20
    Adverse effects 73-20
    Dosing guidelines 73-21
Phobic Disorders 73-21
  Diagnostic Criteria (See Table 73.9) 73-21
  Specific Phobias 73-21
  Social Phobias 73-21
    Epidemiology 73-21
    Comorbidity and clinical significance 73-22
    Treatment 73-22
  Clinical Presentation of Social Phobia 73-22
  Treatment Selection for Social Phobia 73-22
Obsessive-Compulsive Disorder (OCD) 73-22
  Diagnostic Criteria (See Table 73.10) 73-22
  Epidemiology 73-22
  Comorbidity with Other Psychiatric Disorders 73-23
  Etiology and Pathophysiology 73-23
  Treatment of Obsessive-Compulsive Disorder
    (See Figure 73.4) 73-24
  Clinical Presentation and Assessment 73-25
  Clomipramine Treatment 73-25
    Comparison with other tricyclic antidepressants ...73-25
    Dosing and monitoring guidelines 73-26
    Adjunctive behavioral therapy 73-26
    Adverse effects and patient counseling 73-26
    Drug interactions 73-26
  Duration of Treatment and Selective Serotonin
    Reuptake Inhibitor (SSRI) Treatment 73-26
**Posttraumatic Stress Disorder (PTSD) and
Acute Stress Disorder** 73-27
  Diagnostic Criteria (See Table 73.11) 73-27
  Epidemiology 73-27
  Etiology and Pathophysiology 73-27
  Treatment 73-27
  Clinical Presentation and Assessment of PTSD 73-28
  Treatment Selection in PTSD 73-28

Anxiety can be described as an uncomfortable feeling of vague fear or apprehension accompanied by characteristic physical sensations. It is a *normal and often beneficial response* to situations that we as human beings perceive as threatening, frightful, or otherwise disturbing. Anxiety serves the therapeutic purpose of alerting us to take appropriate measures for dealing with such stressful circumstances. Thus, unlike other mental disorders such as schizophrenia or depression, anxiety can be both a normal emotion and a psychiatric illness.[1] Anxiety usually involves two basic components: *mental* features (e.g., worry, fear, difficulty concentrating) and *physical* symptoms [e.g., racing heart, shortness of breath (SOB), trembling, pacing].

Sometimes the anxiety experienced by a person is excessive for the situation (in intensity or duration) or very distressing, to the point that it can interfere with daily functioning. It is these cases, when the harmful effects of the anxiety outweigh the beneficial, which constitute pathological anxiety or anxiety disorders. Pathological anxiety can be differentiated according to whether it occurs: 1) as a primary anxiety disorder; 2) as a secondary anxiety disorder due to medical causes or substances; 3) in response to acute stress (e.g., loss of a loved one, marital or family problems); or 4) as a symptom in association with other psychiatric disorders. This differentiation often is difficult but is important because it dictates optimal management approaches.

Prevalence and Significance of Anxiety Disorders

As a group, the anxiety disorders represent the most common of psychiatric illnesses, with a one-year prevalence of 4% to 10%.[7,8] Anxiety disorders affect approximately 15% of people, more often females, at some time in their life; however, less than one-third of those who suffer from pathological anxiety seek treatment.[6,8] Reasons for this are unclear but probably include issues such as shame, absence of social support to do so, limited finances, and lack of understanding about potential effectiveness of treatments. Another reason may be as a direct result of the illness, as in the case of a house-bound agoraphobic patient with panic disorder who cannot leave her house to go to work or the grocery store, much less to seek medical treatment. Because anxiety is a feeling with which everyone is familiar, there is a tendency to trivialize the impact that it can have upon a sufferer's functional abilities and quality of life. Yet, during the past decade, a major research emphasis on anxiety has markedly increased our understanding of its nature and management. Most anxiety disorders are effectively treatable with medications, cognitive or behavioral therapies, or combinations thereof. Treatment of chronic anxiety disorders is not curative but can provide substantial symptomatic relief and optimize overall functioning. An increased understanding about pathological anxiety is needed in society in general and health care professionals in particular so that sufferers seek and receive the needed treatment. Practitioners must be knowledgeable about the clinical characteristics and treatment options for various anxiety disorders, and be able to share this information with patients and other health care professionals alike. Patients need to make the best use of their anxiolytic medications, which can result in decreased disability associated with the illness and improve the overall quality of life.

Classification and Diagnosis of Anxiety Disorders

The fourth edition of the Diagnostic and Statistical Manual of Mental Disorders (DSM-IV) classifies primary anxiety disorders into six types: generalized anxiety disorder (GAD), panic disorder, phobic disorders, obsessive-compulsive disorder (OCD), posttraumatic stress disorder (PTSD), and acute stress disorder.[2] The additional category of anxiety disorder not otherwise specified is used to indicate cases not meeting the diagnostic criteria for any of these six types, or when it cannot be determined whether the anxiety disorder is primary or secondary. Each disorder involves pathological anxiety, but the characteristic type and severity of symptoms, as well as courses of illness, vary from one disorder to

another. Efficacy of drug and nondrug treatments also varies between disorders, indicating probable underlying biological differences.[1] The DSM-IV secondary anxiety disorders include anxiety disorder due to a general medical condition and substance-induced anxiety disorder.[2]

Clinical Assessment and Differential Diagnosis of Anxiety

1. J.K., a 66-year-old male, complains to his physician of having trouble sleeping and of feeling nervous and worrying too much. J.K.'s wife passed away 1 year ago and he recently retired from his job as an accountant. Since that time, he has become very involved in his hobbies of gardening and writing short stories but claims that he often cannot concentrate enough to write. J.K. suffered a myocardial infarction (MI) 2 years ago and his currently prescribed medications include: enalapril 10 mg BID; nitroglycerin SL PRN; lovastatin 20 mg/day; and sucralfate 1 gm QID. He also takes over-the-counter (OTC) diphenhydramine and pseudoephedrine for allergies, naproxen for back pain, and docusate sodium PRN for constipation. J.K. states that he drinks several cups of coffee each morning, and drinks 1 or 2 glasses of beer several nights per week to help him calm down when he has had a stressful day. He denies any history of psychiatric illness but states that he has always been a "high-strung" individual. What factors should be considered in the clinical assessment and differential diagnosis of J.K.'s symptoms of anxiety?

Secondary Causes of Anxiety

A diagnostic decision tree such as that in Figure 73.1 can be used to assist the clinician in differentiating among various causes of anxiety and between the different anxiety disorders. According to DSM-IV criteria for primary anxiety disorders, the symptoms are not secondary to any medical (drug or disease) causes. As illustrated in Table 73.1, the potential "organic" or secondary sources for anxiety symptoms are numerous. A diagnosis of anxiety disorder due to a general medical condition is warranted when symptoms are believed to be the direct physiological consequence of a medical condition. In patients like J.K. who have a number of medical conditions, all of these illnesses must be considered as possible underlying precipitants of anxiety. A complete physical and laboratory work-up, with a thorough medical and psychiatric history, also are needed to exclude other, possibly reversible, causes before a primary anxiety disorder diagnosis is considered. Hypoglycemia, hyperthyroidism, electrolyte abnormalities, and angina pectoris notably are associated with anxiety symptoms.[3] Persons with chronic medical conditions such as chronic obstructive pulmonary disease, Parkinson's disease, cardiomyopathy, postmyocardial infarction, Grave's disease, and primary biliary cirrhosis have prevalences of anxiety that are markedly increased compared to healthy controls.[3] Medical illness in general, and especially in older patients such as J.K., is associated with higher rates of both anxiety and depression as compared to the general population.[3] In some cases, the anxiety is physically induced by the medical condition, but reactional anxiety also may occur in response to being faced with a medical illness, especially those which are serious. In either case, the presence of anxiety may complicate the medical picture and have a negative impact on the course of illness. Successful management of the medical condition often will relieve anxiety in such cases, but short-term use of anxiolytic medications or nondrug therapies (biofeedback, psychotherapy) also can be very helpful.

When evaluating for possible etiologies of secondary anxiety, it also is important to consider all medications a person is taking, including OTC drugs such as cough and cold preparations. A diagnosis of substance-induced anxiety disorder is warranted when

Fig 73.1   Diagnostic Decision Tree for Anxiety Disorders

Table 73.1	Secondary Causes of Anxiety[a]

Medical Illnesses

Endocrine and metabolic disorders: Hyperthyroidism, hypoglycemia, Addison's disease, Cushing's disease, pheochromocytoma, PMS, electrolyte abnormalities, acute intermittent porphyria

Neurologic: Seizure disorders, multiple sclerosis, chronic pain syndromes, traumatic brain injury, CNS neoplasm, migraines, myasthenia gravis, Parkinson's disease

Cardiovascular: Mitral valve prolapse, CHF, arrhythmias, postMI, hyperdynamic β-adrenergic state, hypertension, angina pectoris, postcerebral infarction

GI: PUD, Crohn's disease, ulcerative colitis, irritable bowel syndrome

Respiratory: COAD, asthma, pneumonia, pulmonary edema

Psychiatric

Depression, mania, schizophrenia, adjustment disorder, personality disorders, delirium, dementia

Drugs

CNS stimulants: Amphetamines, caffeine, cocaine, diethylpropion, ephedrine, MDMA (Ecstasy), methylphenidate, PCP, phenylephrine, phenylpropanolamine, pseudoephedrine

CNS depressant withdrawal: Barbiturates, benzodiazepines, ethanol, opiates

Psychotropics: Antipsychotics, bupropion, buspirone, fluoxetine, isocarboxazid, TCAs

Cardiovascular: Captopril, enalapril, digitalis, disopyramide, hydralazine, reserpine

Others: Albuterol, aminophylline, baclofen, bromocriptine, cycloserine, dapsone, dronabinol, interferon alfa, isoniazid, isoproterenol, levodopa, mefloquine, metoclopramide, monosodium glutamate, NSAIDs, norfloxacin, pergolide, quinacrine, steroids, theophylline, thyroid hormone

[a] CHF = Congestive heart failure; CNS = Central nervous system; COAD = Chronic obstructive airways disease; GI = Gastrointestinal; MI = Myocardial infarction; NSAID = Nonsteroidal anti-inflammatory drug; PCP = Phencyclidine; PMS = Premenstrual syndrome; PUD = Peptic ulcer disease; TCA = Tricyclic antidepressant.

anxiety symptoms occur in relation to substance intoxication or withdrawal, or when medication use is etiologically related to the symptoms. Among the medications that J.K. is taking, pseudoephedrine might be contributing to his anxiety. Other medications which have been reported to induce anxiety are listed in Table 73.1. Antipsychotic medications, metoclopramide, and prochlorperazine all can produce akathisia, a type of extrapyramidal symptom characterized by anxiety. Psychoactive substance abuse, withdrawal from central nervous system (CNS) depressants (e.g., alcohol, barbiturates, benzodiazepines), and excess caffeine intake also may be unrecognized as underlying precipitants of anxiety. In some cases, use of substances such as alcohol may begin in an attempt to self-medicate for anxiety but can continue to produce a cycle of dependency during which withdrawal efforts can worsen the anxiety.[4] J.K.'s current pattern of alcohol use, although not excessive at present, may represent an early stage of this cycle if his anxiety continues.

Other factors that should be considered in J.K. are the recent changes in his life (retiring, losing his spouse). Stressful or traumatic life events may be anxiety-provoking for anyone. Consider, for example, the couple going through a divorce, a family provider becoming unemployed, or a student threatened with failing at college. The anxiety experienced in such cases may be severe and functionally limiting but could be considered appropriate for the circumstances. Usually the anxiety is self-limiting and brief, subsiding over days to weeks as the person adapts to the new situation. Nevertheless, for some there may be serious difficulty in adjusting,

with prolonged, excessive, or debilitating symptoms that proceed into a primary and sometimes chronic disorder. If there is no past history of an anxiety disorder and the symptoms last only a few months, a diagnosis of adjustment disorder with anxious mood may be appropriate. If the symptoms are severe enough and continue for a prolonged period, a primary anxiety disorder may be present. The initial onset of a chronic anxiety disorder often is noted to occur during a stressful time period in the person's life. Short-term therapy with anxiolytic medication or counseling can be extremely beneficial in helping persons cope during acute stress. In contrast, management of primary anxiety disorders usually requires more extended treatment.

Comorbidity with Other Psychiatric Disorders

Anxiety symptoms also can accompany almost any other psychiatric illness. Depression, in particular, is associated notably with symptoms of anxiety, and there are marked degrees of comorbidity and symptom overlap between anxiety and depression. For example, J.K.'s symptoms of having trouble sleeping, difficulty concentrating, and worrying too much may be major target symptoms of either anxiety or depression, or possibly both. A proposed new diagnostic category known as mixed anxiety-depression is included in the DSM-IV appendix of criteria sets. Recovery of patients with coexistent major depression and generalized anxiety takes significantly longer than those who suffer from depression alone.[5] Certain anxiety disorders, such as obsessive-compulsive disorder and panic disorder, have marked degrees of comorbid depression.[6] Effective treatment of these anxiety disorders often (but not always) is accompanied by resolution of the depression. Other major psychiatric illnesses such as bipolar disorder and schizophrenia often are marked by symptoms of anxiety. In these cases, the anxiety may be alleviated with successful management of the primary disorder. However, benzodiazepine or other anxiolytics often are used as adjunctive therapy.

In summary, the factors present in J.K.'s case which warrant further investigation before a primary anxiety disorder diagnosis can be made include his medical illnesses (angina, postMI), his use of pseudoephedrine and caffeine, possible depression, and his adjustment to the recent changes in his life. These factors need to be addressed, and treated or corrected if possible, before an anxiety disorder diagnosis can be made and appropriate antianxiety management strategies begin.

Generalized Anxiety Disorder (GAD)

Epidemiology

Generalized anxiety disorder is the most common anxiety disorder, with a prevalence of 2.5% to 6.4%.[7] The onset of GAD usually is gradual and the typical course is chronic but fluctuating, with periods of relative remissions and relapse. GAD is equally common in both males and females and usually begins when the patients are in their 20s, although it may occur at any time when precipitated by psychological stressors.[9] Degrees of impairment in role functioning and quality of life can range from mild to severe.[10]

Diagnostic Criteria

The DSM-IV criteria for generalized anxiety disorder are presented in Table 73.2. Generalized anxiety disorder is characterized by unrealistic or excessive anxiety or worry about life issues for a duration of six months or longer.[2] The patient usually has great difficulty in controlling the worry, which is accompanied by at least three of the associated symptoms listed in Table 73.2. Although the types of physical symptoms are similar between GAD and other anxiety disorders such as panic disorder and obsessive-compulsive

Table 73.2	Diagnostic Criteria for GAD[a],[b]

A. Unrealistic or excessive anxiety and worry about life circumstances for a period of ≥6 months, during which the person has been bothered more days than not by these concerns

B. The person has difficulty controlling the anxiety and worry

C. The anxiety and worry are associated with at least 3 of the following symptoms:
 1) Restlessness or feeling keyed up or on edge
 2) Being easily fatigued
 3) Difficulty concentrating or mind going blank
 4) Irritability
 5) Muscle tension
 6) Sleep disturbances

D. If another psychiatric disorder is present, the focus of the anxiety and worry is unrelated to it

E. The anxiety, worry, or physical symptoms cause significant distress or impairment in social, occupational, or some other important aspect of functioning

F. The disturbance is not due to the direct effects of a substance, medication, or general medical condition, and does not occur only during the course of a mood disorder, a psychotic disorder, or a pervasive developmental disorder

[a] Adapted from reference 2.
[b] GAD = Generalized anxiety disorder.

disorder, the course of the symptoms in GAD is of relatively constant level compared to the sudden and episodic attacks of severe anxiety seen in panic disorder. If the anxiety is related to issues consistent with another anxiety disorder (e.g., obsession with germs, fear of being in social situations) then a GAD diagnosis is superseded. However, the majority of people with GAD also suffer from at least one other anxiety or depressive disorder at some point during their lifetime.[6,10] Reported rates of comorbidity in GAD patients have ranged from 3% to 47% for panic disorder, 23% to 27% for social phobia, 16% to 21% for simple phobia, 24% for obsessive-compulsive disorder, and 42% to 46% for major depression.[6,10]

Etiology and Pathophysiology

Genetic factors play a modest, but significant, role in the etiology of generalized anxiety disorder and may be the same as those involved in the hereditary development of major depression.[11] Theories for biological mechanisms underlying anxiety have focused on dysregulation of gamma-aminobutyric acid (GABA), benzodiazepine receptor, noradrenergic, and serotonergic functioning, but the particular type of dysfunction is believed to differ from one anxiety disorder to another.[1] Most of the evidence for these biological processes has come from research on drugs that are either used to treat anxiety or that induce anxiety. Discovery of the anxiolytic effects of benzodiazepines in the early 1960s marked the beginning of this era of research. However, the anxiety-reducing properties of alcohol and barbiturates were recognized long before.

GABA-Benzodiazepine Receptor Complex

Benzodiazepines work by facilitating the neurotransmitter gamma-aminobutyric acid. The primary role of GABA is to serve as an inhibitory regulator for other neurotransmitters such as norepinephrine, serotonin, and dopamine. Benzodiazepines bind to specific receptors in the CNS that are functionally linked to GABA-A receptors and the chloride (Cl) ionophore channel, (see the benzodiazepine-GABA-C1 receptor complex depicted in Figure 73.2). Benzodiazepines are agonists and bind to the benzodi-

azepine receptor, enhancing GABA-receptor binding. GABA promotes the direct opening of the chloride ion channel, allowing an increased influx of chloride ions into the neuron. This inward shift of chloride ions hyperpolarizes and stabilizes the membrane, resulting in a net inhibitory effect on neuronal firing.[12] Benzodiazepines alone have little effect on chloride ion channel permeability and depend upon the presence of GABA for their actions. Whereas benzodiazepines are full receptor agonists, a new class of compounds which are partial agonists at benzodiazepine receptors are being investigated for their anxiolytic potential. These agents may be associated with less sedation, tolerance, withdrawal, CNS impairment, and abuse potential than presently available benzodiazepines and include drugs such as bretazenil, abecarnil, pazinaclone, and imidazenil.

The discovery of benzodiazepine receptors led to the search for endogenous compound(s) which might interact with these receptors to possibly increase or decrease anxiety. A brain peptide known as diazepam-binding inhibitor (DBI) has been identified and localized on the human chromosome.[1] DBI is an inverse benzodiazepine-receptor agonist with opposite effects to that of the benzodiazepines, blocking GABA-mediated responses. The DBI peptide may be an endogenous anxiogenic substance.[12] Other benzodiazepine-receptor inverse agonists (also known as benzodiazepine antagonists with intrinsic activity) are esters of beta-carboline-3-carboxylic acid (beta-CC) and induce anxiety behaviors in both animals and humans.[12] An endogenous agonist for the benzodiazepine receptor has not been identified yet. Dysfunction of central benzodiazepine receptor function, such as a shift in the receptor ''set-point'' to the inverse agonist direction similar to that in benzodiazepine withdrawal, also has been proposed as a potential mechanism underlying anxiety.[1]

Noradrenergic Systems

The locus ceruleus area in the brain is the major source of norepinephrine, and its stimulation produces arousal and symptoms of anxiety. Increased levels of norepinephrine have been speculated to underlie some cases of anxiety, and elevated concentrations of norepinephrine and its major metabolite, 3-methoxy-4-hydroxy phenylglycol (MHPG), have been found in the plasma and cerebrospinal fluid of anxious patients.[1] Administration of yohimbine, an antagonist of the presynaptic α_2-adrenergic autoreceptor, increases norepinephrine release in the locus ceruleus and produces anxiety in humans.[1] Drugs that decrease noradrenergic function should possess anxiolytic effects. Clonidine, a presynaptic α-adrenergic agonist which decreases noradrenergic activity, reduces anxiety and also has been effective in the treatment of alcohol and opiate withdrawal syndromes characterized by symptoms of anxiety.[1] Facilitation of GABA by benzodiazepines also reduces noradrenergic activity.[12]

Serotonergic Systems

The serotonergic system may play a pivotal role in the pathophysiology of anxiety. Agents which reduce serotonin activity such as the benzodiazepines and buspirone (Buspar) are effective anxiolytics, and it has been suggested that anxiety may represent a state of relative serotonin excess.[13] Inhibition of the firing of dorsal raphe neurons, which is the primary origin of serotonergic pathways in the brain, may be a universal mechanism for anxiolytic effects produced by different treatments. However, neurotransmitters do not function in isolation, and interactions of neurotransmitter systems with secondary messengers are complex. The anxiolytic effects of drugs probably extend well beyond our present understanding of their primary apparent mechanisms of action.[14] Drugs with diverse mechanisms of action, for example, can have

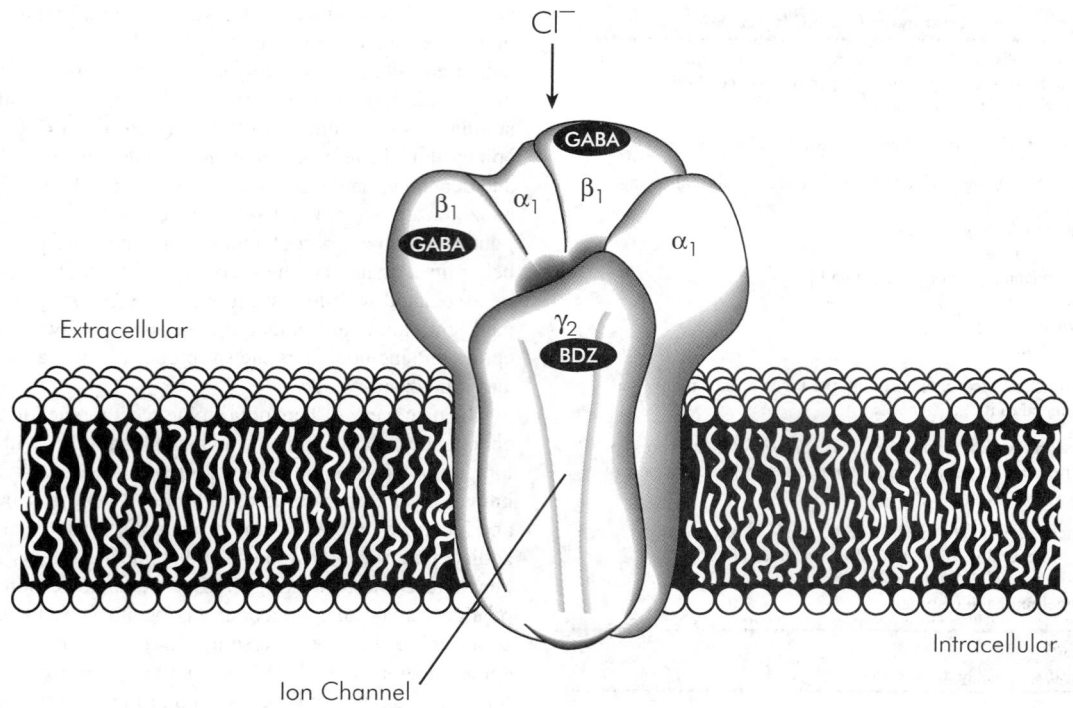

Fig 73.2   Model of the GABA-Benzodiazepine Receptor Complex   Current data suggest a pentameric protein composed of α-, β-, and γ-subunits: the proposed arrangement of subunits is arbitrary. There are two sites for GABA binding (on the β-subunits) and a single site for benzodiazepine binding (depicted on the γ₂-subunit). Homology between the GABA$_A$ receptor and the nicotinic acetylcholine receptor suggests that the chloride ion channel is formed by contributions from each subunit. Reprinted from reference 12.

similar anxiolytic efficacies. Substances such as dopamine, endogenous opioids, corticotropin-releasing factor, and cholecystokinin also may play important, but as yet undefined, roles in the pathophysiology of anxiety.[1]

Treatment of Generalized Anxiety Disorder

Nonpharmacological Treatments

Management of generalized anxiety disorder can involve non-pharmacologic and pharmacologic therapies. Nondrug treatments such as supportive psychotherapy, cognitive therapy, relaxation training, and biofeedback exercises often are helpful in relieving anxiety and improving coping skills. Cognitive therapy in particular, which is aimed at identifying negative thought patterns which may provoke or worsen anxiety and changing them to be more positive, has been associated with significant reductions in anxiety which are maintained over six months.[15] A small number of controlled comparisons of cognitive therapies and benzodiazepine treatment have reported comparable efficacies in GAD.[15] Unfortunately, the availability of these types of services often is limited due to lack of trained specialists or lack of affordability. However, optimal management of many anxiety disorders often involves the combination of medication with psychological or behavioral therapies.

Benzodiazepines

Benzodiazepines are the most widely prescribed anxiolytic agents today because their efficacy in the treatment of GAD and other anxiety disorders has been well established.[7,16,17] Nevertheless, some controlled studies have found these agents only comparable to placebo.[17] The benzodiazepines offer distinct clinical advantages over barbiturates, meprobamate, paraldehyde, and alcohol. These include lower fatality rates from acute toxicity and overdose, more favorable side effect profiles, lower potential for abuse, and less potential interactions with other drugs.[18] Currently,

use of these older nonbenzodiazepine agents as anxiolytics rarely is considered appropriate due to the advantages of benzodiazepines and other agents such as buspirone (Buspar).

Mechanism of Action. In humans, benzodiazepines have four distinct effects: anxiolytic, anticonvulsant, muscle relaxant, and sedative-hypnotic.[17] These agents are used to treat a wide variety of medical and psychiatric conditions including muscle spasms, seizures, anxiety disorders, agitation, and insomnia, and for the induction of conscious sedation. Two subtypes of central benzodiazepine receptors have been identified: BZ-1 and BZ-2 receptors. BZ-1 receptors are most abundant in the cerebellum and are thought to mediate sedative and anxiolytic effects. BZ-2 receptors are found in the hippocampus and basal ganglia and may be linked to effects such as muscle relaxation and cognitive impairment.[14,19] A third benzodiazepine receptor (BZ-p) is located predominately in the periphery and is not coupled to GABA receptors.[19] The BZ-1, BZ-2, and BZ-p receptors also sometimes are referred to as omega-1, omega-2, and omega-3 receptors, respectively.[19] Currently available benzodiazepine *anxiolytics* do not have a predilection for any of these receptor subtypes. Present research is aimed at developing new anxiolytic compounds with specific receptor subtype affinities, which have fewer side effects such as sedation. Zolpidem (Ambien) and quazepam (Doral) are examples of agents which have been introduced as selective benzodiazepine *hypnotics*. Quazepam, however, has a nonselective metabolite which can accumulate with chronic use.[14]

As previously explained, the benzodiazepines work by enhancing the inhibitory effects of GABA. Subtypes of GABA receptors also have been reported (GABA-A and GABA-B).[12] Evidence has linked both BZ-1 and BZ-2 receptors to the GABA-A receptor subtype.[12] In addition to benzodiazepine receptors, the GABA-A receptor complex also includes binding sites for barbiturates, ethanol, and anesthetic steroids, which all can influence response to GABA.[12] This correlation explains the cross tolerance observed between the benzodiazepines, barbiturates, and ethanol. The functional significance of the GABA-B receptor subtype is under investigation, but some researchers have alluded to the possibility of antidepressant activity with GABA-B compounds.

Clinical Comparison of Benzodiazepines. Of the 15 benzodiazepines commercially available in the U.S., eight are marketed as antianxiety agents, and five as oral sedative-hypnotics. These indications reflect the manufacturers' labeling decisions, as the anxiolytics can be effective sedatives and vice versa. In addition, midazolam (Versed), a short-acting, water-soluble benzodiazepine which is available only in parenteral formulation, is indicated for induction of sedation before surgery or for short diagnostic or endoscopic procedures. Clonazepam (Klonopin) is approved for the treatment of seizure disorders but also has a variety of unlabeled psychiatric applications, including its use as adjunctive therapy in the treatment of severe agitation associated with psychosis and mania, and efficacy in the treatment of GAD and other anxiety disorders.[20] Table 73.3 lists the comparable clinical profiles of marketed oral benzodiazepines.

Buspirone

Buspirone (Buspar) was marketed in the U.S. in 1986 as the first of a nonbenzodiazepine class of anxiolytics, the azapirones.[208] This class differs pharmacologically and clinically from the benzodiazepines and also contains several other investigational anxiolytics such as gepirone and ipsapirone.[28] Buspirone does not interact with the BZP-GABA-Cl complex and works as a partial agonist of the serotonin type 1A (5-hydroxytryptamine, 5-HT$_{1A}$) receptor (i.e., it binds to the receptor but exerts less of an effect than a full agonist).[18] This partial agonist activity results in a reduction of serotonergic neurotransmission. In addition, buspirone enhances noradrenergic and dopaminergic neurotransmission. Buspirone has comparable efficacy to the benzodiazepines in the treatment of GAD but is considered more "anxioselective" because it lacks general CNS depressant effects.[29] Also, the azapirones are considered to be relatively free of the potential for abuse and dependence.[29] In addition to its anxiolytic activity, buspirone possesses antidepressant efficacy comparable to standard antidepressants.[30] Buspirone often is considered preferable to benzodiazepines in certain patient types, such as those with a history of substance abuse or dependence, those with mixed anxiety-depression, and patients who are elderly or medically ill.[29]

Antidepressants

Although antidepressants such as the tricyclic antidepressants (TCAs), selective serotonin reuptake inhibitors (SSRIs), and monoamine oxidase inhibitors (MAOIs) are effective in the treatment of other anxiety disorders such as panic disorder and obsessive-compulsive disorder, information on their use for generalized anxiety disorder is more limited. However, well-controlled studies have found antidepressants such as imipramine (Tofranil), amitriptyline (Elavil), and trazodone (Desyrel) to have comparable or even superior efficacy to benzodiazepines in the treatment of GAD.[5,17,31] Most patients in these studies had substantial depressive symptoms in addition to GAD, but in light of the high comorbidity of depression with anxiety, this seems representative of the GAD population. Antidepressant-treated patients in these trials generally had a later onset of anxiolytic effects and experienced more side effects as compared to benzodiazepine-treated patients. Also, some TCA-treated patients may experience an increase in somatic symptoms of anxiety during the first weeks of treatment. The SSRIs and TCAs also have been significantly effective in reducing concurrent symptoms of anxiety in patients with primary depressive disorders.[207] Antidepressants may become a more widely used treatment option for generalized anxiety disorder in the future.

Beta Blockers

In a summary of 15 controlled trials involving over 500 patients, propranolol (Inderal) and other β-adrenergic receptor blocking

Table 73.3	Clinical Comparison of Benzodiazepine Agents				
Drug (Trade Name, Generic)	FDA-Approved Indications	Usual Dose Range ≤65 Years of Age	Maximum Recommended Dose ≥65 Years of Age	Year Introduced
Chlordiazepoxide (Librium, generic)	Anxiety, preoperative sedation, alcohol withdrawal, status epilepticus	15–100 mg/day	40 mg/day	1960
Diazepam (Valium, Valrelease, generic)	Anxiety, muscle spasms, alcohol withdrawal, preoperative sedation, status epilepticus	2–40 mg/day	20 mg/day	1963
Oxazepam (Serax, generic)	Anxiety, alcohol withdrawal	30–120 mg/day	60 mg/day	1965
Flurazepam (Dalmane, generic)	Sedative/hypnotic	15–30 mg HS	15 mg HS	1970
Clorazepate (Tranxene, Tranxene-SD, generic)	Anxiety, alcohol withdrawal, anticonvulsant	15–60 mg/day	30 mg/day	1972
Clonazepam (Klonopin)	Anticonvulsant	0.5–12.0 mg/day	3 mg/day	1975
Lorazepam (Ativan, generic)	Anxiety, anxiety/depression	2–6 mg/day	3 mg/day	1977
Prazepam (Centrax, generic)	Anxiety	20–60 mg/day	30 mg/day	1977
Alprazolam (Xanax, generic)	Anxiety, anxiety/depression, panic disorder	0.5–6.0 mg/day (up to 10 mg/day for panic disorder)	2 mg/day	1981
Halazepam (Paxipam)	Anxiety	60–160 mg/day	80 mg/day	1981
Temazepam (Restoril, generic)	Sedative/hypnotic	15–30 mg HS	15 mg HS	1981
Triazolam (Halcion)	Sedative/hypnotic	0.125–0.5 mg HS	0.125 mg HS	1983
Quazepam (Doral)	Sedative/hypnotic	7.5–15 mg HS	7.5 mg HS	1990
Estazolam (Prosom)	Sedative/hypnotic	1–2 mg HS	1 mg HS	1991

agents were effective in reducing symptoms of anxiety.[32] Beta blockers, however, are not as effective as benzodiazepines in the treatment of anxiety.[17,32] The ''fight or flight'' response activates the sympathetic nervous system. This response is regulated by β-adrenergic receptors and the peripheral effects can be reversed by beta blockers. These agents are especially effective in preventing performance anxiety or ''stage fright'' by suppressing sympathetic nervous system activity and autonomic symptoms (e.g., palpitations, tremor), but are ineffective in preventing the mental symptoms of anxiety.[33] Beta blockers are not recommended as a primary treatment option for GAD.

Clonidine

Clonidine (Catapres) may reduce symptoms of anxiety by decreasing the firing rate of the locus ceruleus and noradrenergic activity. Clinical trials of clonidine in the treatment of anxiety are lacking, but one study has reported superior efficacy over placebo in the treatment of a small number of GAD patients.[34] Frequently reported side effects with clonidine include dry mouth, drowsiness, dizziness, nausea, and hypotension. Clonidine has demonstrated efficacy for the treatment of opioid withdrawal and Tourette's syndrome, but more studies are needed before it can be considered a viable treatment option in anxiety disorders.

Antihistamines

Histamine (H_1)-receptor blocking agents such as hydroxyzine (Vistaril) and diphenhydramine (Benadryl) have been used for years in the treatment of anxiety and insomnia. Due to their potent sedative effects, these antihistamines generally are used on an as-needed basis for insomnia or for their calming effects in a variety of patient types.[35] There is no evidence for their efficacy in the treatment of primary anxiety disorders. Although these drugs are considered to be quite benign and diphenhydramine is available over the counter, they do possess significant anticholinergic effects which can produce problems such as confusion, cognitive impairment, nausea, and constipation.[36] Elderly patients, especially those who are medically ill or have dementia, are particularly vulnerable to these side effects.[36]

Clinical Presentation and Assessment

2. B.A., a 27-year-old female, has been employed as a bank clerk for the past 5 years. She had an excellent work record until 6 months ago when excessive absences and a tendency to become easily upset at customers and coworkers became noticeable. Upon clinical assessment, B.A. complains of being tired and tense with frequent stomach problems and diarrhea. She has no previous history of mental illness; however, she admits to often becoming stressed out and worrying too much about ''just little things,'' which she cannot seem to control no matter how hard she tries. B.A. denies experiencing episodic ''attacks'' of severe anxiety (which might be indicative of panic disorder), or of having obsessive-compulsive thoughts or behaviors.

Physical examination was unremarkable and she states there is no history of mental illness in her family, although her mother was a ''nervous person.'' B.A. denies any past or present use of any illicit substances or alcohol. B.A.'s mental status examination focused on her appearance and behavior, mood, sensorium, and thought. *Appearance and behavior*: B.A. is neatly groomed and dressed, speaks coherently, but constantly fidgets and taps her right foot. She states that she often has difficulty falling asleep, but generally remains asleep through the night. *Mood*: B.A. is anxious and worried about the clinician's evaluation and admits to occasionally feeling sad. *Sensorium*: B.A. is oriented to person, place, and time. *Thoughts*: B.A. denies any auditory or visual hallucinations. She states

that at times she has difficulty speaking, is unable to relax, and startles easily. She realizes that work has been difficult for her lately and fears that her job is in immediate jeopardy unless she improves her performance. B.A. states that she just wants to be able to relax and enjoy life. Insight and judgment are good, and she is motivated to obtain treatment. She denies suicidal ideation. *Provisional Diagnosis*: Generalized Anxiety Disorder (DSM-IV criteria). What clinical features of generalized anxiety are present in B.A., and how can her symptoms be assessed objectively?**

B.A. exhibits the following target symptoms associated with generalized anxiety disorder: excessive worry which is difficult to control; irritability; tension and inability to relax; fatigue; and sleep disturbances. Other typical symptoms of anxiety present in B.A. include gastrointestinal problems (upset stomach and diarrhea), being startled easily, difficulty speaking, and fidgeting. These target symptoms are not necessarily diagnostic of any particular mental illness, but other factors in association with these symptoms are consistent with probable generalized anxiety disorder. The absence of physical or other psychiatric illnesses, as well as use of any illicit substances or alcohol, excludes possible secondary causes of anxiety. The six-month duration of symptoms is consistent with a diagnosis of GAD, and B.A. is at a common age for onset of GAD. More importantly, the symptoms are causing significant occupational impairment for B.A. and interfering with her ability to enjoy life; therefore, a diagnosis of generalized anxiety disorder is appropriate in B.A.

The Hamilton Anxiety Rating Scale (HAM-A) is a useful assessment tool in the evaluation of clinical anxiety, although one limitation is its focus on somatic symptoms. The HAM-A is considered a standard instrument used in GAD trials, and a score of ≥18 generally is considered indicative of clinical anxiety. The HAM-A can be used to assess baseline symptoms of anxiety in patients like B.A. and to monitor response throughout treatment.

Indication For and Goals of Treatment

3. Based upon the information presented in B.A.'s case, how can it be determined whether or not treatment is indicated? What are the goals of treatment?

B.A. meets the diagnostic criteria for GAD and is suffering significant disability from her anxiety disorder. In addition, she has insight into her illness and desires treatment to be able to improve her job performance and quality of life. Appropriate treatment of GAD can help achieve these goals and, therefore, is indicated for patients like B.A. Desired outcomes of treatment include reductions in B.A.'s cognitive (worrying, irritability) and somatic (GI symptoms, fatigue, insomnia) symptoms of anxiety, improved performance at work, and increased ability to relax and ''enjoy life.''

Selection of Treatment

4. What factors should be considered in the process of selection of the most appropriate treatment option for B.A.?

As discussed, treatment options for GAD may include both pharmacological and nondrug therapies. Psychological treatments such as cognitive therapy can be effective in the treatment of generalized anxiety disorder, but use of these therapies alone generally is reserved for patients with mild to moderate symptoms, those in whom anxiety is related to stressful life events, or when immediate symptom relief is not necessary. As mentioned, the availability of trained therapists often is limited, and these psychological treatments can be expensive as well as time-consuming. In B.A.'s case, there is a need for prompt treatment because she feels that her job is in immediate jeopardy due to impairments associated with her anxiety. Therefore, pharmacotherapy, in combination with psychological therapy, if available, is indicated in B.A. Among potential drug treatments, the benzodiazepines and buspirone are the primary options for management of GAD. Benzodiazepines may be preferred over buspirone in B.A. because of their rapid onset of anxiolytic effects, as compared to the delayed onset of therapeutic effects with buspirone. B.A. is young, healthy, and has no past or present history of substance or alcohol use which might make use of benzodiazepines unsuitable.

Factors Influencing Benzodiazepine Selection

5. The physician decides that B.A. is a good candidate for benzodiazepine treatment. What factors are important in the selection of a benzodiazepine agent for B.A.?

Of the available benzodiazepines, none has demonstrated clear superior efficacy in the treatment of anxiety. Certain agents, however, have been used much more extensively than others. For example, since its introduction in 1981, alprazolam (Xanax) has replaced diazepam (Valium) as the most frequently prescribed benzodiazepine anxiolytic.[16] Alprazolam also is distinctive in that it is the only drug approved for the treatment of panic disorder, and it may be unique among benzodiazepines in its efficacy for some forms of depression.[16]

Pharmacokinetics and Metabolic Pathways. The primary differences among the benzodiazepines are in their pharmacokinetic properties, and these often are among the main factors considered in drug selection. (See Table 73.4.) Benzodiazepines can be classified *pharmacokinetically* according to their elimination half-life (t½) or their metabolism to active and inactive moieties (see Figure 73.3 and Table 73.4). Diazepam, halazepam (Paxipam), and chlordiazepoxide (Librium) have half-lives between 10 to 40 hours but are metabolized by hepatic oxidative pathways to an active metabolite, desmethyldiazepam, which has a half-life of at least 100 hours.[101] The prodrugs, prazepam (Centrax), quazepam (Doral), and clorazepate (Tranxene) also are metabolized to desmethyldiazepam. When benzodiazepines or their active metabolites have very long elimination half-lives, these drugs can accumulate with chronic dosing and produce prolonged effects, especially in the elderly, those with liver disease, or persons taking other drugs that compete for hepatic oxidation (see Table 73.6). Although their long durations of action make once-daily dosing possible, low divided daily doses most often are used clinically to minimize side effects. Clonazepam undergoes various routes of hepatic metabolism, including oxidative hydroxylation, reduction, and acetylation.[102] At least five metabolites have been identified, but their pharmacological activity is uncertain. The elimination half-life of clonazepam ranges from 20 to 80 hours; this marked variability may be due, in part, to its acetylation metabolic pathway in which the metabolism rate is influenced by phenotypic status of the patient.[102] For example, rapid acetylators are likely to require higher doses and more frequent drug administration than slow acetylators.

Alprazolam (Xanax) and lorazepam (Ativan) have intermediate half-lives of 10 to 20 hours. Alprazolam is a triazolobenzodiazepine which is metabolized to an active metabolite, α-hydroxy alprazolam, that has a short half-life of approximately two hours.[101] A sustained-release preparation of alprazolam and approval for once-a-day dosing are awaiting Food and Drug Administration (FDA) action. The currently available formulation of alprazolam usually requires three times daily administration.[103] Oxazepam (Serax) has a short to intermediate half-life of 5 to 14 hours. Lorazepam, temazepam (Restoril), and oxazepam undergo hepatic glucuronide conjugation and are free of active metabolites. As a result, they are unlikely to accumulate with chronic administration and require multiple daily dosing for sustained effects. These agents often are preferred in patients with liver disease and in the elderly.

Benzodiazepines are absorbed readily within two to three hours following oral administration, with the exception of prazepam, which can take 12 hours to reach peak plasma concentrations.[101] They are widely distributed in the body and accumulate preferentially in lipid-rich areas such as the central nervous system and adipose tissue. Lipid solubility varies between the agents, resulting in differences in rates of absorption and speed of onset of clinical effects (see Table 73.4). Diazepam and clorazepate have the highest lipid solubilities and the quickest onsets of action, which can be desirable when rapid anxiolysis is needed but also can produce an unpleasant "drugged" or "high" effect in some patients. A

Table 73.4		Pharmacokinetic Comparison of Benzodiazepine Agents[a]		
Drug	Elimination t½ (hr)	Active Metabolites	Pathway of Metabolism	Rate of Onset after PO Administration
Chlordiazepoxide	>100	Desmethyldiazepam	Oxidation	Intermediate
Diazepam	>100	Desmethyldiazepam	Oxidation	Very fast
Oxazepam	5–14	None	Conjugation	Slow
Flurazepam	>100	Desalkylflurazepam, hydroxyethylflurazepam	Oxidation	Fast
Clorazepate	>100	Desmethyldiazepam	Oxidation	Fast
Lorazepam	10–20	None	Conjugation	Intermediate
Prazepam	>100	Desmethyldiazepam	Oxidation	Very slow
Alprazolam	12–15	Insignificant	Oxidation	Intermediate
Halazepam	>100	Desmethyldiazepam	Oxidation	Slow
Temazepam	10–20	Insignificant	Conjugation	Intermediate
Triazolam	1.5–5	Insignificant	Oxidation	Intermediate
Quazepam	>5	2-oxoquazepam, desalkyloxoquazepam	Oxidation	Fast
Estazolam	8–31	Insignificant	Oxidation	Intermediate
Clonazepam	20–80	Insignificant	Oxidation	Fast
Midazolam	1–4	None	Oxidation	NA

[a] NA = Not applicable; t½ = Half-life.

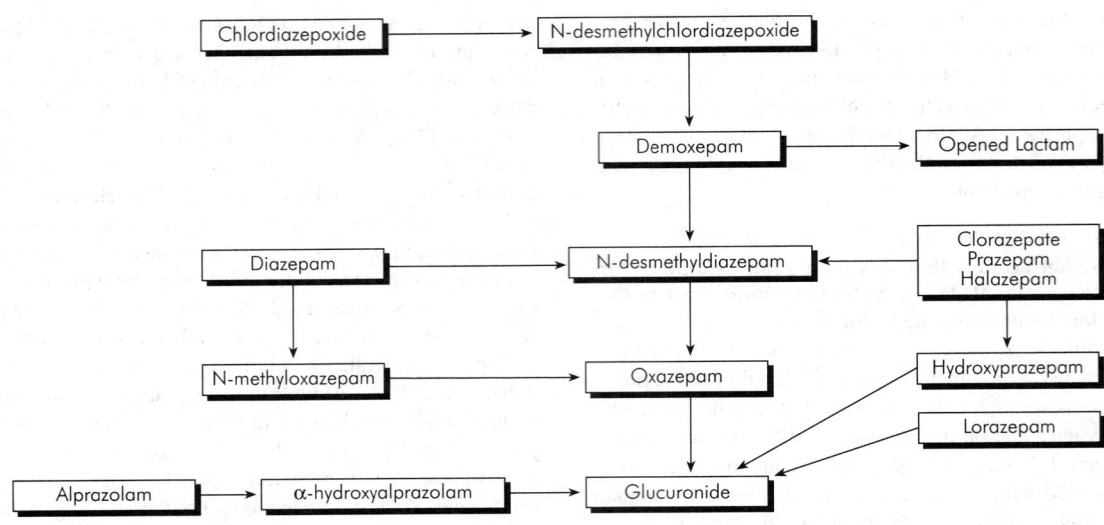

Fig 73.3   Metabolic Pathways of Benzodiazepines

controlled-release diazepam preparation (Valrelease) is available which is absorbed more slowly than diazepam tablets. Diazepam, lorazepam, and chlordiazepoxide also are available for parenteral [intravenous (IV) and intramuscular (IM)] administration. Parenteral formulations usually are reserved for treatment of severe agitation or seizures, or for induction of preoperative sedation and anxiolysis. Intramuscular diazepam should be injected into the deltoid muscle, as administration into other sites can result in erratic and unpredictable absorption.[104] Intramuscular chlordiazepoxide is absorbed slowly, resulting in lower peak plasma levels compared to oral or IV administration and limiting its usefulness.[104] Intramuscular injection of both chlordiazepoxide and diazepam can be very painful.[104] Lorazepam is absorbed rapidly and completely after IM injection with peak levels occurring at 1.15 ± 0.3 hours; it most often is the preferred agent when parenteral dosing is needed for quick control of anxiety or agitation.[104] The absorption of sublingual lorazepam, alprazolam, and triazolam (Halcion) is comparable or slightly faster than the oral absorption.[101] Oral administration of the selected agent is considered the standard route of administration for generalized anxiety disorder.

Cost is another important factor in benzodiazepine selection. Benzodiazepines are expensive medications, but less costly generic formulations are available for most agents. (See Table 73.3.) Potential drug interactions also should be considered in the selection of an agent, as they can result in alterations in pharmacokinetics and clinical effects. (See Table 73.7.)

Because B.A. is young and healthy and not taking any other medications, treatment with benzodiazepines should not be accompanied by pharmacokinetic impairments. Nevertheless, many clinicians still prefer to use shorter-acting agents such as lorazepam or alprazolam for patients such as B.A. Appropriate starting doses would be lorazepam, 0.5 to 1 mg three times daily, or alprazolam, 0.25 to 0.5 mg three times daily. Doses can be increased every three to four days, guided by side effects and reductions in anxiety, within the dosage ranges indicated in Table 73.3. B.A. should notice a decrease in her anxiety symptoms within the first few days of treatment. Prescription of generic formulations can reduce costs associated with treatment.

Adverse Effects and Patient Counseling

6. Lorazepam, 0.5 mg TID, is prescribed for B.A. What side effects may occur with benzodiazepine treatment and how should B.A. be counseled regarding benzodiazepine therapy?

Sedation and feelings of tiredness are the most common side effects of the benzodiazepines, but sedation also can be beneficial in alleviating the insomnia which often accompanies anxiety. These effects usually subside after one to two weeks of continued treatment. *Tolerance* to a drug implies that a decrease in response occurs as a result of continued use, and a larger dose is required to achieve the original effect.[105] This tolerance to the sedative effects of benzodiazepines probably is due to functional changes in benzodiazepine receptors with chronic administration. Specifically, a ''down regulation'' of benzodiazepine receptor sensitivity, but not number, has been reported within seven days of benzodiazepine administration.[24] These changes are an example of *functional tolerance*, which indicates that an organ system becomes altered during long-term drug use, and are the basis underlying the recommendation that hypnotic use of benzodiazepines be limited to 14 consecutive days. This is in contrast to the *metabolic tolerance* that can occur with some drugs, in which the agent ceases to produce the same effect during long-term use due to pharmacokinetic changes. An example of metabolic tolerance is the autoinduction of carbamazepine metabolism, which results in decreasing serum drug levels over the first several weeks of therapy. Fortunately, development of tolerance to the anxiolytic and muscle relaxant effects of the benzodiazepines has not been reported.[24,105]

In addition to sedation, patients taking benzodiazepines may report cognitive impairment such as difficulty concentrating or slowing of thought processes, or problems with balance and incoordination.[24,26,106] It is imperative that patients such as B.A. be advised about the possibility of these psychomotor effects, especially when starting benzodiazepine therapy. Ingestion of benzodiazepines when operating a motorized vehicle has been associated with a fivefold increased risk of being in a serious car accident.[7] Anterograde amnesia is another reported adverse effect of the benzodi-

Table 73.5	Symptoms of Benzodiazepine Withdrawal	
Frequent	**Common**	**Rare**
Anxiety	Nausea	Confusion
Insomnia	Depression	Delirium
Irritability	Ataxia	Psychosis
Muscle aches/weakness	Hyperreflexia	Seizures
	Blurred vision	
	Fatigue	

azepines. This typically involves impaired ability to acquire or store information or to recall acts performed after drug administration.[107] These effects are temporary and reversible and have been associated most often with lorazepam and triazolam.[24,107] Several cases of transient global amnesia have been reported with the use of triazolam to prevent jet lag during traveling, but most involved concurrent use of alcohol.[107,108] Diazepam, clorazepate, and prazepam may be less likely to produce memory or psychomotor impairment.[107]

Paradoxical effects of benzodiazepines, such as agitation, increased anger, and hostility, have been reported in a small number of patients.[26,109] Most of these cases have involved patients with pre-existing psychiatric disorders such as bipolar disorder, schizophrenia, or personality disorders.[109] The reported incidence of this paradoxical response is extremely small, and most of the literature consists of anecdotal reports. Nevertheless, media attention has focused on such cases reportedly leading to aggressive or self-destructive acts, and has resulted in the removal of triazolam from some markets outside the U.S. (United Kingdom and Finland).[110] These effects may reflect an expression of underlying anger or psychopathology which is facilitated by reduction in anxiety rather than a direct effect of the benzodiazepines.[26] There is minimal evidence that benzodiazepines are causally related to violent or suicidal behaviors.[26,110]

Benzodiazepines also have been associated with causing clinical depression, although evidence to support this relationship is very limited.[111,112] This belief may result from confusion regarding statements that benzodiazepines are *CNS depressants*.[111] In fact, benzodiazepines, notably alprazolam, are effective in treating depression, both with and without symptoms of anxiety.[17,112]

Respiratory depression is another potential adverse effect of benzodiazepines, but usually is only of clinical significance in those with severe respiratory disease or in overdose situations. (See Question 13.) Long-acting benzodiazepines probably should be avoided in patients with sleep apnea.[36] Respiratory complications are encountered most frequently when benzodiazepines are administered intravenously. Midazolam IV has been associated with a number of deaths due to cardiorespiratory arrest during use for conscious sedation, most often in patients premedicated with narcotics or with chronic obstructive airways disease.[113] Severe respiratory depression also has been reported with the concurrent use of lorazepam with either loxapine (Loxitane) or clozapine (Clozaril).[24,114]

In short, B.A. should be told that she may experience sedation and possibly difficulties in concentrating during the first week or so of therapy, but that these side effects should resolve once her body gets used to the drug. She should be extremely careful while driving or performing other tasks that require psychomotor skill, especially during the first week. It also is imperative that B.A. be counseled against the use of alcohol while she is taking benzodiazepines.

Abuse and Dependence

7. One month later B.A. returns to the clinic. She reports that the lorazepam has been extremely effective in relieving her anxiety, and she currently is taking 1 mg TID as directed by her physician. However, some friends have told her that she will become addicted to lorazepam, and she expresses a desire to stop taking the drug because of this concern. What potential for abuse and dependence is associated with benzodiazepines? How should B.A. be counseled regarding "becoming addicted" to lorazepam?

An important issue in the clinical use of benzodiazepines is that of abuse and dependence. Benzodiazepines are classified as schedule IV controlled substances, reflecting a relatively limited abuse

and dependence liability.[22] There appear to be differences within the class regarding abuse potential. Diazepam, alprazolam, and lorazepam are reported to be more likely to be abused than are oxazepam, halazepam, and chlordiazepoxide.[23] This difference in abuse potential is related to the quicker onset of effects for drugs such as diazepam, which produces a more distinct peak that may be associated with a subjective euphoric sensation.[24]

Abuse is related to use outside the therapeutic setting and is characterized by recreational use, continued use despite negative consequences, dose escalation, and loss of control over use.[23] Patients without a history of substance abuse who take benzodiazepines for therapeutic purposes are unlikely to escalate doses or use them in ways characteristic of abuse.[25-27] Misuse and abuse of benzodiazepines is limited largely to those with a current or past history of abusing other substances, including alcohol.[23,115] Despite this fact, concern over these issues has led to negative attitudes about benzodiazepines among both health professionals and patients.[22,105] As a result, patients may be deprived of generally safe and effective treatment options for anxiety. A prime example was the Triplicate Prescription Program enacted in New York State in 1989.[22] This regulation involved mandatory prescription of benzodiazepines on a triplicate prescription form, of which one copy was forwarded to regulatory agencies and the other two were retained by the prescribing physician and dispensing pharmacist. The purpose of this program was to reduce diversion, abuse, and inappropriate prescribing of benzodiazepines, and it placed them under the same regulatory control as opiates, barbiturates, and amphetamines.[22] The result was a reduction in prescription of benzodiazepine anxiolytics and hypnotics by 48% and 50%, respectively. However, there was a concurrent increase in prescriptions for barbiturates, meprobamate, and nonbenzodiazepine hypnotics (chloral hydrate, ethchlorvynol, glutethimide, methaqualone) by 27%, 129%, and 87%, respectively. These older agents are considered less effective and much more dangerous than benzodiazepines, and this program was criticized harshly for depriving New York State residents of safe and effective treatments for anxiety and insomnia, and for promoting "unnecessary human suffering and risk."[22] Clinicians can play an important role in resolving some of the misunderstandings which surround benzodiazepine use and abuse. One important component is the differentiation between addiction, physical dependence, and benzodiazepine discontinuation syndromes.

Benzodiazepine Withdrawal Symptoms. Although the term addiction historically has been used loosely to describe a variety of drug abuse patterns, a currently accepted definition of *addiction* refers to "a behavioral pattern of *drug abuse*, characterized by overwhelming involvement with the use of a drug, the securing of its supply, and a high tendency to relapse after discontinuation."[116] The inclusion of a pattern of drug abuse in this definition implies drug administration outside the therapeutic setting or in an unacceptable or unsafe manner. *Physical dependence* refers to the need to continue using a drug to relieve or avoid physical withdrawal symptoms, and may or may not be associated with abuse.[105] Three types of benzodiazepine discontinuation syndromes have been described: relapse, rebound, and withdrawal.[7,115] *Relapse* indicates a recurrence of the original symptoms of the underlying anxiety following discontinuation of treatment. Since benzodiazepines do not cure anxiety disorders, this type of syndrome may be expected in those with chronic illness. The time frame for onset of relapse may vary from weeks to months after drug discontinuation, and may be misinterpreted by the patient as symptoms of withdrawal. The *rebound* syndrome also is similar to the original anxiety, but symptoms are more intense. It usually occurs within hours to days after the drug is discontinued and lasts for only a few days, after which symptoms may lessen to that of relapse (the original anxiety). Rebound is not associated with physical dependence. The benzodiazepine *withdrawal* syndrome implies some degree of physical dependence, and its onset, duration, and severity can vary according to dose, duration of treatment, speed of withdrawal, and elimination half-life of the agent used. Withdrawal symptoms following discontinuation of agents with short half-lives usually appear within one to two days and may be more short-lived but more intense than after discontinuation of benzodiazepines with long half-lives. Withdrawal symptoms usually appear five to ten days after discontinuation of agents with long elimination half-lives. Symptoms of benzodiazepine withdrawal, which are listed in Table 73.5, generally are mild when the drug is tapered gradually during discontinuation.[117] Increased risk of withdrawal and severity of symptoms is associated with abrupt discontinuation, use of high doses, long-term (>3 to 4 months) treatment, and use of high-potency agents.[7,118,119] Rarely, serious symptoms such as seizures

or psychosis may occur.[24] Factors which may predispose to the development of benzodiazepine withdrawal seizures include head injury, alcoholism, electroencephalogram abnormalities, and use of other drugs which lower the seizure threshold.[24] Although the withdrawal symptoms usually subside within one to two weeks, a persistent benzodiazepine discontinuation syndrome lasting months to years has been described.[23] This syndrome actually may represent the underlying disorder of chronic anxiety.[26]

Minimization of Abuse and Dependence and Patient Counseling. Clinically, the potential problems with benzodiazepine abuse and dependence can be avoided or minimized several ways. First is the identification of patients who are susceptible to abuse and the use of alternative treatments in such cases. Patients considered to be at high risk for benzodiazepine abuse include alcoholics and those with a history of other substance abuse.[23] Second, patients should be counseled about duration of drug use, the possibility of withdrawal symptoms, and the importance of gradual drug tapering when therapy is to be discontinued. The distinction between "ad-

Table 73.6		Physiological Factors That Can Influence Benzodiazepine Pharmacokinetics	
Factor	Drug	Pharmacokinetic Effect[a]	Comments
Age	Chlordiazepoxide[125]	Slower absorption ↑ t½β (↑ Vd, ↓ Cl)	Dose adjustments. Caution with prolonged use
	Clorazepate[126]	↑ t½β (↓ Cl)	Noted to occur only in elderly males
	Prazepam[124]	↑ t½β (↑ Cl, ↓ Vd); slight ↓ protein binding	Noted to occur only in elderly males
	Diazepam[127]	↑ t½β (↑ Vd); ↓ protein binding	Accentuated effect seen in elderly
	Alprazolam[128]	↑ t½β (↓ Cl); slight ↓ protein binding	Noted to occur only in elderly males
	Lorazepam[129]	No significant effect on t½β (slight ↑ Vd and ↓ Cl); ↓ protein binding	None reported
	Oxazepam[130]	No significant effect; ↓ protein binding	None reported
Gender	Clorazepate[126]	See age effects	See age effects
	Prazepam[124]	See age effects	See age effects
	Diazepam[130,131]	↑ t½β (↓ Cl)	Only in elderly males
		↑ t½β (↓ Cl, ↑ Vd)	Only in elderly females
	Alprazolam[128]	↑ absorption t½	Only in elderly females
	Lorazepam[129]	↓ protein binding	Only in elderly males
	Temazepam[130]	↑ t½β (↓ Cl)	Only in females
	Oxazepam[130]	↑ t½β (↓ Cl)	Only in females
Obesity	Clorazepate[132]	↑ t½β (↑ Vd)	Dose adjustment needed. Prolonged time to steady state
	Alprazolam[133]	↑ t½β (↑ Vd, ↓ Cl)	Same as clorazepate
	Lorazepam[134]	No significant changes in t½β (↑ Cl, ↑ Vd)	None reported
	Oxazepam[134]	Same as lorazepam	None reported
Hepatic disease	Chlordiazepoxide[137]	↑ t½β (↓ Cl) in cirrhosis	↓ dosage needed or change drug. Possible accumulation with prolonged use
	Diazepam[131]	↑ t½β (↓ Cl, ↓ protein binding) in cirrhosis, acute viral hepatitis, chronic active hepatitis	See chlordiazepoxide. Upon recovery from acute viral hepatitis, ↑ t½β comparable to normals
	Alprazolam[135]	Slower absorption. ↑ t½β (↓ Cl) in alcoholic liver disease	Dosage adjustments needed
	Lorazepam[136]	↑ t½β (↑ Vd) in cirrhosis but no change in acute hepatitis	Dosage adjustments only in cirrhosis
	Oxazepam[137]	No significant changes	No dose adjustments needed
	Triazolam[138]	No significant changes in cirrhosis	No dose adjustments needed
Renal function	Clorazepate[139]	↑ t½β (↓ Vd); ↓ protein binding	Dosage adjustments needed. Disease alters protein binding
	Diazepam[139]	↓ protein binding for parent drug and desmethyl metabolite	See clorazepate
	Lorazepam[140]	↑ t½β (↑ Vd); slight ↓ Cl. Multidose studies reported impaired elimination	Dosage adjustments can be required with long-term use
	Oxazepam[141]	↑ t½β (↑ Vd); no changes in Cl, ↓ protein binding. Minimal dialyzability	None reported
Ethnicity	Diazepam[142]	↑ t½β (↓ Cl) in Asians	Clinical significance unknown

[a] Cl = Clearance; t½ = Half-life; Vd = Volume of distribution.

diction'' and appropriate therapeutic use, which may be accompanied by some degree of physical dependence, also should be emphasized. Discussion about these issues should occur at the onset of therapy. One survey found that approximately one-half of 312 patients on long-term alprazolam received no information from their physicians about drug discontinuation.[27] These patients frequently tried to stop the drug use on their own and experienced withdrawal symptoms, leading to perceptions of addiction. Patients in this survey apparently were not asked about other sources of drug information (e.g., from their pharmacist). These findings are a prime example of how patient education could have a potentially vital impact on helping patients make the best use of their medication.

B.A. should be advised that as long as the medication is helping her anxiety and she is taking it according to her physician's instructions, her use of lorazepam does not constitute addiction. However, her body may become accustomed to the drug so that if she stops taking it abruptly she could experience symptoms of increased anxiety. When the decision is made to discontinue treatment, the drug dosage will be decreased gradually over several weeks so that minimal withdrawal symptoms should occur.

Duration of Treatment

8. After 2 more months of lorazepam treatment, B.A. still is doing well. How long should benzodiazepine therapy continue?

Generalized anxiety disorder is a chronic disorder which can fluctuate in severity and often requires long-term treatment. Relapse following discontinuation of benzodiazepines in generalized anxiety disorder patients occurs in about 60% to 80% of the patients.[33] However, some cases actually may be benzodiazepine withdrawal, which can confound the assessment of relapse. Long-term use of benzodiazepines generally is safe and effective, although controversial.[23,105] Due to the potential for physical dependence and withdrawal syndromes, it is desirable to limit treatment duration to the shortest time period necessary. The distinction should be made between a biological anxiety disorder versus intermittent environmental or personal factors which can cause anxiety over extended time periods. Initial benzodiazepine treatment for generalized anxiety disorder should last for a period of two to four months, after which a trial of discontinuation should begin.[9] Since B.A. has been receiving lorazepam for a total of three months, it now may be desirable to initiate a gradual discontinuation of this medication, and several months may be required to completely withdraw the medication. A drug-free period of several weeks is necessary to differentiate between symptoms of benzodiazepine withdrawal versus relapse of anxiety. Chronic generalized anxiety disorder can be accompanied by substantial distress and disability, and continued treatment with a benzodiazepine or alternative agent is warranted if relapse occurs.[9] The need for continued treatment should be reassessed on a regular basis during long-term treatment, but the benefits of effective control of GAD (or other anxiety disorders) often outweigh the potential risks.

Treatment and Management of Withdrawal

9. R.T., a 32-year-old male, has been taking diazepam 40 mg/day for 6 months for its muscle relaxant effects after sustaining a dislocated shoulder and other injuries while playing soccer. R.T. denies the use of tobacco, alcohol, or other drugs of abuse. Four days before hospitalization, R.T. was unable to refill his prescription for financial reasons. A brief mental status examination reveals mild confusion and irritability. Physically, R.T. is trembling and complains of overall body aching and an upset stomach. Past medical history indicates no current medical problems or psychiatric illnesses. How should R.T. be treated?

Since R.T. has not taken his prescribed diazepam for four days, it is possible that he is experiencing a withdrawal syndrome from long-term benzodiazepine use. His mental and physical symptoms are consistent with benzodiazepine withdrawal. Diazepam, 10 to 20 mg orally, should be administered and repeated within one to two hours if needed. Reinstitution of his previous dose of 40 mg/day of diazepam should effectively treat his withdrawal symptoms. Since his acute injury occurred six months ago, it may be desirable to begin discontinuation of the benzodiazepine.

Various time periods and dosage reduction schedules for benzodiazepine discontinuation have been proposed. Even when managing the withdrawal of patients from low-dose benzodiazepine use, doses should be reduced slowly over 4 to 16 weeks.[23,26] The rapidity of the drug discontinuation should always be monitored closely and individualized to the patient, but a general recommendation is a 10% to 25% decrease in the dosage every one to two weeks. Withdrawal symptoms often are more apparent during the last half of the dosage taper. In R.T.'s case, the discontinuation period may take several months. An example of a withdrawal schedule for R.T. is as follows:

Week	Dose (mg/day)	Week	Dose (mg/day)
1	35	8	10
2	30	9	8
3	26	10	6
4	22	11	4
5	19	12	2
6	16	13	1
7	13	14	withdrawn from diazepam

In general, the same benzodiazepine the patient has been taking should be used during withdrawal. However, since severity of withdrawal symptoms is more severe during discontinuation of agents with short elimination half-lives, substitution of a long-acting agent at an equivalent dose during the taper can lessen severity of the withdrawal.

In difficult cases, adjunctive medications have been used to ease tolerability of the gradual withdrawal. Carbamazepine (Tegretol) has been effective in attenuating the symptoms of withdrawal from benzodiazepines as well as alcohol.[63] Flumazenil (Romazicon) also has been used successfully in providing relief from benzodiazepine withdrawal.[23] Propranolol decreases benzodiazepine withdrawal symptoms by ameliorating the increased sympathetic release during abstinence; however, the anxiety is not treated effectively and the risk of seizures is not addressed.[120] Limited reports indicate that trazodone and valproate (Depakene, Depakote) also may be useful in reducing the severity of symptoms during benzodiazepine withdrawal.[63,121] Clonidine and buspirone are ineffective in the treatment of benzodiazepine withdrawal.[122,123]

Physiologic Variables Influencing Benzodiazepines

10. B.G., a 78-year-old male, is 5′8″ tall and weighs 195 pounds. Two weeks ago he started to volunteer 3 days a week in the renal dialysis unit where he also is a patient. After he began volunteering, he was prescribed diazepam 10 mg BID. One day as he was assisting a nurse with a patient, he was accidentally punctured by a needle. Since the other patient had chronic active hepatitis, B.G. was given an injection of hepatitis immune globulin. Six weeks later, the dialysis nurse noticed

that B.G. was drowsy, mildly confused, and unsteady as he walked. B.G. also is taking cimetidine (Tagamet), 300 mg QID for peptic ulcer disease (PUD). What factors could be influencing diazepam's disposition in B.G.?

Benzodiazepine pharmacokinetics can be affected by various physiologic factors including age, gender, obesity, hepatic and renal disease, and ethnicity. (See Table 73.6.)

Increased age can decrease the ability to metabolize drugs by oxidative hepatic pathways, resulting in two- to threefold prolongations in the elimination half-lives of long-acting benzodiazepines and alprazolam.[124-128] The conjugation pathways are affected minimally with age, so no such effect is seen with lorazepam or oxazepam.[129,130] Normal aging is accompanied by decreased hepatic blood flow and increased volumes of distribution of lipid-soluble compounds (due to decreased muscle mass and increased fat). These factors also can contribute to increased elimination half-lives of all benzodiazepines in the elderly.[35] Increased pharmacodynamic responses to benzodiazepines also are observed in the elderly, possibly due to changes in benzodiazepine and GABA-A receptor binding.[211] This effect increases the sensitivity of older patients to CNS effects such as sedation and psychomotor impairment. An increased risk of hip fractures due to falls in the elderly has been associated with the use of long-acting, but not short-acting, benzodiazepines.[24] Due to these combined factors, the recommended benzodiazepine doses for patients over the age of 65 generally are one-third to one-half of those used in healthy adults (see Table 73.3).

Gender also may influence benzodiazepine clearance.[124,126,128–131] The studies which have examined gender effects have yielded mixed results, probably due to wide interindividual differences.[130] In elderly patients, some investigators have found lower clearances of clorazepate, diazepam, and alprazolam in men as compared to women.[126,128,130] In contrast, the conjugated benzodiazepines temazepam and oxazepam have had lower clearance rates among females in several studies.[130]

Obesity increases the volume of distribution of benzodiazepines, and dose adjustments have been suggested for clorazepate and alprazolam.[132,133] Since both the clearance and volume of distribution of lorazepam and oxazepam are increased in obese patients, significant changes in the elimination half-lives are not observed.[134] As expected, liver dysfunction can reduce the elimination rate and prolong the half-life of benzodiazepines, resulting in decreased dosage requirements.[131,135] The elimination half-lives of diazepam and lorazepam usually return to normal upon recovery from acute viral hepatitis.[131,136] No significant changes have occurred with oxazepam or triazolam in liver disease.[137,138] Decreased protein binding is the most prominent change in benzodiazepine kinetics observed in patients with renal insufficiency, and increased free fractions of clorazepate and diazepam have been reported.[139] However, no significant changes in clearance or volume of distribution have been noted. Lorazepam elimination was impaired in two patients with renal dysfunction, but the elimination half-life of conjugated benzodiazepines generally is not altered significantly in renal disease.[139-141] Regarding ethnicity, slower metabolism and decreased clearance of diazepam have been reported in Asian subjects as compared to Caucasians.[142]

In summary, the physiologic factors that can alter benzodiazepine disposition in B.G. are his age, obesity, male gender, and concurrent renal disease. Changes in the disposition of diazepam probably account for B.G.'s behavior. In addition to these factors, cimetidine can decrease the clearance of diazepam significantly, resulting in increased side effects (see Table 73.7).[143] If continued benzodiazepine therapy is deemed necessary for B.G., a switch to lorazepam or oxazepam would be appropriate because these agents would be least affected by the influencing factors present in B.G. Dosage conversions among benzodiazepines are based upon relative potencies, and suggested equivalent doses for the various agents are as follows: diazepam 5 mg = chlordiazepoxide 10 mg = prazepam 10 mg = oxazepam 15 mg = clorazepate 7.5 mg = lorazepam 1 mg = alprazolam 0.5 mg = clonazepam 0.25 mg. However, these equivalences are only guidelines and dosing conversions should take patient variables and usual dosage ranges into consideration. For example, even though B.G. had been maintained on 20 mg/day of diazepam, the calculated equivalent dose of lorazepam (4 mg/day) exceeds the recommended dosage range for an elderly individual. He should be started on a lower dosage, such as 2 mg/day, and monitored carefully for adverse effects or symptoms of withdrawal with the lower dose.

Benzodiazepine Drug Interactions

11. R.G., a 24-year-old female college student, has been diagnosed with GAD. She has no medical illnesses but reports feeling anxious most of the day, which often interferes with her ability to study. R.G. also takes a low-dose oral contraceptive, Ortho-Novum 1/35, smokes 2 packs of cigarettes per day, and drinks up to 6 cups of coffee per day. Diazepam 5 mg TID is prescribed. What potential drug interactions should be discussed with R.G.?

Table 73.7 summarizes the reported drug interactions with the benzodiazepines.[143-167] The most significant drug interactions involve other CNS depressants, such as alcohol or barbiturates, or medications which compete for hepatic metabolism. Although pharmacokinetic interactions can cause statistically significant changes in benzodiazepine serum concentrations, the clinical consequences of these interactions often are unpredictable. Carefully designed studies are needed to assess the clinical significance of many benzodiazepine drug interactions.

R.G. should be encouraged to decrease her coffee consumption because *caffeine* can increase anxiety and precipitate panic attacks as well as possibly decrease diazepam concentrations.[49,154] Pharmacodynamically, caffeine's anxiogenic effect may result from its competitive inhibition with diazepam binding at the BZ receptor. The most likely mechanism of action for caffeine's anxiogenic activity, however, probably results from its antagonism of central adenosine receptors.[154] Adenosine and other purines can serve as neuromodulators that regulate several neurotransmitter systems, including GABA.

Low-dose oral contraceptives can decrease the clearance of oxidized benzodiazepines such as diazepam, potentially resulting in increased CNS effects.[156] A dose reduction may be indicated if R.G. experiences oversedation or other side effects. In contrast, the clearance of conjugated benzodiazepines such as lorazepam, oxazepam, and temazepam can be accelerated by low-dose contraceptives; however, this interaction is thought to be clinically insignificant.[156]

Cigarette smoking may increase clearance of benzodiazepines in some patients. However, some studies have found smoking to have no effects on benzodiazepine kinetics.[131,164-166] Therefore, the effect of smoking is unpredictable and only careful monitoring of R.G.'s clinical status can determine if dosage adjustments are needed. R.G. should be urged to quit smoking due to general health reasons as well as the substantial risks for serious cardiovascular events in heavy smokers taking oral contraceptives.

Teratogenicity

12. At her clinic visit 2 months after starting treatment with diazepam, R.G. states that she and her husband have decided to start a family. She has discontinued her oral contraceptives and plans to become pregnant soon. What is the teratogenic potential of diazepam? What alternative treatment is available for the management of R.G.'s anxiety?

Table 73.7	Drug Interactions With Benzodiazepines[a]	
Drug	**Pharmacokinetic Effect**	**Comments**
Alcohol	Conflicting reports with single-dose studies; undetermined in long-term studies.[144] No significant effect on single-dose of diazepam or buspirone[145]	↑ CNS and respiratory depression. Impaired psychomotor skills noted with diazepam and lorazepam with acute ingestion and single dose. No significant effects in performance noted with buspirone[145]
Antacids	Delayed peak Cp and absorption with single dose of clorazepate and diazepam. No significant changes in steady-state clorazepate Cp[146]	Delayed clinical response with only single doses. No dosage adjustments needed with long-term therapy
Anticholinergics	↓ absorption from ↓ motility[147]	Clinical significance unknown
Anticonvulsants	Carbamazepine reported to ↓ Cp of clonazepam and alprazolam.[148]	Clinical significance unknown. Other anticonvulsants (phenytoin, phenobarbitol) may have same effect
	↑ phenytoin levels reported after diazepam[149]	Phenytoin toxicity noted in case reports with choreoathetoid movements
Antidepressants	Alprazolam reported to ↓ imipramine and desipramine Cl.[150] Lorazepam reported to ↑ desipramine levels.[151]	No ↑ in side effects noted
	Fluoxetine reported to ↓ alprazolam Cl[152]	Possible ↑ in benzodiazepine side effects
	Nefazodone[224] markedly ↑ Cp of triazolam and alprazolam	50% to 75% reduction in benzodiazepine dosage required if nefazodone added
Antipsychotics	Alprazolam reported to ↑ Cp of fluphenazine and haloperidol[114]	Possible ↑ antipsychotic adverse effects. Neurotoxicity/respiratory arrest reported with clozapine-benzodiazepine combination[114]
Antitubercular drugs	INH reported to ↓ diazepam Cl, rifampin shown to ↑ diazepam Cl[153]	Dosage adjustments needed with diazepam
Caffeine	↓ diazepam Cp[154]	Antagonism at benzodiazepine receptor. Slight improvement in selected performances. Impaired cognitive effects unrelieved by caffeine[154]
Cimetidine	↓ Cl reported for all benzodiazepines except lorazepam, oxazepam, and temazepam[143]	Dosage adjustment needed with long-acting benzodiazepines. Possible to change to ranitidine[155]
Contraceptives (low-dose estrogens)	↓ Cl diazepam, slight changes in alprazolam, lorazepam, and temazepam. No changes in triazolam[156]	Dosage adjustments needed for long-acting benzodiazepines or switch to oxazepam or lorazepam
Digoxin	Alprazolam and diazepam reported to ↓ digoxin Cl, resulting in toxicity.[209] Alprazolam also reported not to interfere with digoxin[157]	Careful digoxin monitoring suggested; effect may be ↑ in elderly or at higher benzodiazepine doses
Disulfiram	↓ Cl of diazepam and chlordiazepoxide noted; no change in oxazepam reported[158]	See contraceptives
Erythromycin	↓ Cl of triazolam by 50%[210]	Potential ↑ triazolam side effects; dose reduction may be required
Heparin	↑ ff of diazepam noted to occur in 15 min. ↑ ff diazepam, chlordiazepoxide, and oxazepam. No effect on lorazepam[159]	Transient ↑ in ff occurs within 90 min and returns to baseline
Naproxen	Delayed Cp and absorption of naproxen with single diazepam dose.[160] No change in bioavailability	Possible delayed onset of naproxen effects
Omeprazole	↓ Cl (↑ Cp) of diazepam[161]	Possible ↑ diazepam adverse effects
Propoxyphene	Significant ↓ alprazolam Cl, slight ↓ diazepam Cl (NS), no change in lorazepam[162]	Impairment mainly by aliphatic hydroxylation
Propranolol	↓ Cl diazepam, no effect on alprazolam or lorazepam[163]	Dosage adjustment needed with long-acting benzodiazepines
Tobacco smoke	↑ Cl reported for diazepam,[131] clorazepate,[164] chlordiazepoxide, and alprazolam.[165] No changes reported with diazepam, lorazepam, chlordiazepoxide, and midazolam[166]	↑ sedation noted among nonsmokers
Warfarin	No significant effect observed with diazepam, chlordiazepoxide, and flurazepam. Possible stereochemical interaction with lorazepam[167]	Careful patient monitoring needed

[a] Cl = Clearance; Cp = Peak concentration; ff = Free fraction; INH = Isoniazid, NS = Not significant.

Early reports implicated diazepam in causing several birth deformities, including cleft lip and/or cleft palate and limb and digit malformations.[168] However, more recent studies have failed to support an association between benzodiazepine exposure during pregnancy and fetal abnormalities.[168,169] Lack of proven teratogenicity of a compound does not imply absolute safety, and no psychotropic drug is FDA-approved for use during pregnancy. It always is desirable to avoid drug use during pregnancy whenever possible, especially in the first trimester. In patients such as R.G., the benzodiazepine should be tapered and discontinued before she becomes pregnant. Nondrug treatments for her generalized anxiety disorder such as relaxation therapy, meditation, and biofeedback or cognitive therapy may be helpful. If necessary, single doses or repeated low doses of benzodiazepines during the second and third trimesters are unlikely to have important adverse effects on a healthy fetus. Prolonged or high doses, especially of long-acting agents, should be avoided because they may lead to drug accumulation in the fetus due to limited metabolic capacity.[170] Fetal dependence and neonatal withdrawal symptoms after delivery have been reported in babies whose mothers regularly took diazepam during pregnancy.[170]

Pregnancies sometimes are unplanned, and the clinical situation of unexpected pregnancy in a woman maintained on benzodiazepines also can arise. The general course of action in such cases often is to discontinue all medications. In a patient who is receiving chronic benzodiazepine treatment for a severe anxiety disorder, it is unwise to abruptly stop treatment, as the resultant withdrawal syndromes can be detrimental to both mother and child.[168] Benzodiazepine doses should be tapered to the lowest dose necessary and discontinued if possible. It is necessary to weigh the risks of untreated anxiety against the apparently low risks of teratogenicity. Benzodiazepines are excreted readily in breast milk and should not be used by nursing mothers.[170] (Also see Chapter 45: Teratogenicity and Drugs in Breast Milk.)

Benzodiazepine Overdose

13. C.G., a 40-year-old male, presents to the emergency room (ER) in an unconscious state with respiratory depression. His roommate states that C.G. had been drinking vodka and presents an empty prescription vial of clorazepate 7.5 mg (#60), with directions to take 1 tablet BID. The roommate thinks that C.G. may have overdosed. The roommate indicates the medication was prescribed by C.G.'s physician about 1 month ago for "nervousness and depression." How should C.G. be treated?

Flumazenil (brand name Romazicon, formerly known as Mazicon) is the first benzodiazepine antagonist approved for clinical use in the U.S.[203] Before its availability, physostigmine (Antilirium) and naloxone (Narcan) had been used to reverse benzodiazepine-induced sedation, but with mixed results.[21] Flumazenil is effective in reversing the sedation associated with benzodiazepine intoxication.[21] Its effects on respiratory depression are inconsistent, but improved breathing may occur secondarily to increased consciousness.[171] Flumazenil works by specific competitive interaction at the central benzodiazepine receptor within the GABA-A complex, and does not antagonize the effects of alcohol, barbiturates, or general anesthetics. It is indicated for the management of benzodiazepine overdose as well as for the reversal of benzodiazepine-induced sedation following anesthesia or diagnostic procedures.[171] Other potential uses for which flumazenil has been investigated include reversal of coma of unknown origin and management of hepatic encephalopathy.[21]

Flumazenil should not be used in cases of suspected heterocyclic antidepressant overdose, as manifested by symptoms such as motor twitching or rigidity, cardiac dysrhythmias or collapse, and anticholinergic signs, because of the increased potential for seizures in such situations.[171] An electrocardiogram (ECG) should be obtained before flumazenil administration to exclude the presence of cardiac arrhythmias.[203] It also should not be used in patients physically dependent upon benzodiazepines or those maintained on benzodiazepines for control of potentially life-threatening situations (e.g., seizure disorders or intracranial pressure) because it can precipitate withdrawal and seizures.[171] Other risk factors for seizures with flumazenil include underlying medical causes for seizures and severe head injury. Administration of flumazenil should occur only in settings prepared for seizure management. The most common side effects from flumazenil include agitation, dizziness, nausea, general discomfort, tearfulness, anxiety, and sensation of coldness.[21] The use of flumazenil in patients with panic disorder can induce panic attacks.[23] Rapid or excessive infusion has been associated with tachycardia and hypertension.[21]

Flumazenil is available as a 0.1 mg/mL intravenous injection, although an oral formulation is under investigation. The elimination half-life following IV administration is 41 to 79 minutes and it undergoes extensive hepatic metabolism to inactive metabolites.[21] Dosage reductions are recommended in patients with liver dysfunction, but flumazenil pharmacokinetics are not altered significantly by gender, increased age, or renal impairment.

Flumazenil is indicated for treatment of C.G.'s suspected benzodiazepine overdose. There is no evidence for ingestion of cyclic antidepressants or other risk factors for seizures. Although C.G. has been taking clorazepate for about a month, the likelihood of significant physical dependence is minimal with the low dose prescribed (15 mg/day) and relatively short duration of use. The clinical utility of flumazenil for mixed benzodiazepine-ethanol intoxication is controversial, although some studies have reported beneficial effects in such cases.[21] Other supportive measures, such as gastric lavage and administration of activated charcoal, are indicated only in cases when large benzodiazepine doses have been ingested within the past one to two hours, or when overdose of other, more toxic drugs is suspected.[203]

The recommended initial dose of flumazenil for the treatment of benzodiazepine overdose is 0.2 mg IV, preferably administered through a free-running IV infusion to minimize injection site pain.[171] All doses should be injected slowly over 30 seconds. A second dose of 0.3 mg may be administered one minute later if the desired level of consciousness has not been obtained. Thereafter, additional 0.5 mg doses may be given at one-minute intervals as needed up to a maximum total dose of 3 mg. Improved consciousness in C.G. could be expected within the first several minutes of flumazenil administration, but ventilatory support may be required for his respiratory depression. Dosing guidelines for reversal of sedation following anesthesia or diagnostic procedures involve lower initial and repeated doses (0.2 mg) than those for benzodiazepine overdose.[171]

Because the duration of effects of clorazepate and other long-acting benzodiazepines exceeds that of flumazenil, C.G. should be monitored for resedation which can occur within one to two hours. Repeated doses of 0.2 mg every 20 minutes may be administered if resedation does occur. Alternatively, a continuous IV infusion, at a rate of 0.5 mg/hour, may be used.[203] Flumazenil is compatible and stable when admixed with 5% dextrose injection, lactated Ringer's injection, 0.9% sodium chloride, aminophylline, heparin sodium, famotidine, and the hydrochloride forms of dobutamine, dopamine, cimetidine, ranitidine, lidocaine, and procainamide.[205] Upon successful recovery (at least 3 to 4 hours of stable alertness) and before discharge, C.G. should be advised that the effects of the benzodiazepines may recur and to avoid driving or performing other potentially hazardous activities for 24 hours. Also, he should not take any alcohol or OTC medications during this time period. Most importantly, these instructions should be provided to C.G. in writing or to a responsible care giver because flumazenil does not consistently reverse benzodiazepine-associated amnesia and he may not remember the discharge instructions.

Buspirone Therapy

14. Following successful recovery of his overdose, C.G. is re-evaluated by his psychiatrist. C.G. admits that the clorazepate had helped his anxiety somewhat but he had been severely stressed out over financial and work problems. He reports that although he is an alcoholic, he had been abstinent for over 1 year when the stress and depression just got to him and led to his relapse to drinking and overdose. C.G. states that "it was the wrong thing to do" and denies current suicidal ideation. C.G.'s psychiatrist decides to switch him to buspirone. How does the clinical profile of buspirone compare to that of the benzodiazepines? What factors in C.G.'s case make buspirone a good choice?

Clinical Comparison with Benzodiazepines

Buspirone was the first agent marketed as an anxiolytic which lacks CNS depressant effects. In contrast to the benzodiazepines, it produces no significant sedation, cognitive or psychomotor impairment, or respiratory depression.[29,172] Buspirone also lacks the muscle relaxant and anticonvulsant effects characteristic of the benzodiazepines. Buspirone lacks reinforcing properties or potential for abuse, and it is not classified as a controlled substance.[116] It does not produce physical dependence or withdrawal syndromes upon discontinuation, even after long-term therapy.[116,173] Buspirone also does not interact with alcohol or other CNS depressants, and is relatively safe in overdose situations.[208]

Buspirone is equally as effective as benzodiazepines such as alprazolam, oxazepam, lorazepam, diazepam, and clorazepate in the treatment of generalized anxiety disorder.[17,174] Its superiority over placebo also is well established.[173,175] However, buspirone has a delayed onset of anxiolytic effects of one to two weeks as compared to the almost immediate onset with benzodiazepines. Regular dosing is required for therapeutic efficacy of buspirone and it is not appropriate for use on an as-needed basis.[208] Benzodiazepines are preferred in cases when immediate anxiety relief is necessary or in transient anxiety when only occasional or intermittent medication use is required. Patients starting buspirone therapy should be advised that it is important to take the drug regularly as scheduled and that it may take one to two weeks before they notice beneficial results. Otherwise, they may believe that the medication is ineffective. In particular, patients who have been treated previously with benzodiazepines and are accustomed to their rapid anxiolytic effects may perceive that buspirone does not alleviate their anxiety during the onset of treatment. Buspirone may be slightly less effective in benzodiazepine-pretreated patients than those who have never taken benzodiazepines.[29]

Adverse Effects

The most common side effects from buspirone therapy are nausea, dizziness, headache, and nervousness.[208] Some patients may experience mild drowsiness or fatigue upon initiation of therapy. Rare events such as hypomania, mania, abnormal movements, oral dyskinesias, generalized myoclonus, and psychosis have been reported in isolated cases.[176] Buspirone's adverse effect profile overall is very favorable and probably better tolerated than the benzodiazepines.[18,174] Buspirone's lack of cognitive, sedative, and respiratory depressant effects make it particularly useful in older patients, and it is safe, effective, and well tolerated in elderly anxious patients with a variety of chronic medical conditions.[35,176] No buspirone dosage adjustments are required in the elderly.

Antidepressant Effects

Numerous studies provide evidence for buspirone's antidepressant efficacy.[30,177,178] This antidepressant effect has been observed in patients with generalized anxiety disorder accompanied by substantial depressive symptoms as well as patients suffering from primary major depression. Effective antidepressant doses of buspirone generally are higher (40 to 60 mg/day) than those required for sole anxiolytic effects (15 to 30 mg/day). Buspirone also has been used effectively for the control of agitation and aggression in patients with a variety of organic mental syndromes including dementia, mental retardation, traumatic brain injury, attention deficit hyperactivity disorder, and autism.[28,179,180] Open studies indicate possible efficacy of buspirone in the treatment of various other disorders such as premenstrual dysphoric disorder (premenstrual syndrome), social phobia, posttraumatic stress disorder, nicotine dependence, sleep apnea, migraine headaches, and tardive dyskinesia.[208]

In summary, the factors which make buspirone a good choice for anxiolytic therapy in C.G. include its lack of potential for abuse, dependence, or interaction with alcohol (he is a recovering alcoholic); its potential antidepressant efficacy (he has prominent depressive features); and its relative safety in overdose situations (of which he has a history). Buspirone also has been reported to reduce alcohol consumption and craving, so this may provide additional benefit since C.G. is recovering from alcoholism.[28,181]

Conversion from Benzodiazepine to Buspirone Therapy

15. How should patients be switched from benzodiazepine to buspirone therapy?

Since buspirone has no CNS depressant effects and is not cross-tolerant with the benzodiazepines, it is not effective in preventing or treating benzodiazepine withdrawal. Thus, when patients are being converted from benzodiazepine to buspirone therapy, the guidelines for gradual benzodiazepine discontinuation must be followed. Since it takes one to two weeks before the therapeutic effects of buspirone are realized, it should be initiated two to four weeks before the benzodiazepine taper begins to allow time for the onset of buspirone's effects so that antianxiety coverage will be provided during the withdrawal period.[29,182] The usual recommended starting dose of buspirone is 5 mg three times a day. Daily dosage can be increased in 5 mg/day increments every three to four days. Optimal doses are usually in the range of 20 to 30 mg/day, with 60 mg/day being the manufacturer's recommended maximum. Because buspirone's half-life is in the range of 2 to 11 hours it should be taken on a three times daily basis.

Drug Interactions

16. What are important drug interactions with buspirone?

Coadministration of buspirone has no significant effect on plasma concentrations of alprazolam, diazepam, or amitriptyline. However, buspirone may increase levels of desmethyldiazepam and haloperidol and potentially lead to toxicity.[7,114,183] There have been reports of elevated blood pressure with the concurrent use of buspirone and MAOIs, suggesting that this combination should be avoided. As discussed, there are no synergistic CNS depressant effects between buspirone and CNS depressants such as alcohol.

Panic Disorder

Diagnostic Criteria

The DSM-IV criteria for panic disorder are presented in Table 73.8.[2] The hallmark characteristic of panic disorder is the occurrence of sudden and distinct panic attacks, which are marked by a tremendous wave of symptoms and feelings (e.g., racing heart rate, dizziness, shortness of breath, and fear of dying or losing control). Three characteristic types of panic attacks have been defined with regard to the context in which they occur: *unexpected or uncued* panic attacks (the onset of the attacks is not associated with a situational trigger); *situationally bound* panic attacks (the attacks invariably occur upon exposure to a situational trigger); and *situationally predisposed* panic attacks (the attacks are more likely to, but do not invariably, occur upon exposure to a situational trigger).[2] The DSM-IV criteria for panic disorder require the occurrence of at least two unexpected or uncued attacks which are followed by persistent worry or concern about having another panic attack, or a significant change in behavior related to the attacks. Situationally bound panic attacks generally are characteristic of phobic disorders rather than panic disorder, and situationally predisposed panic attacks may occur in either panic or phobic disorders. Panic attacks also may occur during the course of other anxiety disorders.

Table 73.8	Diagnostic Criteria for Panic Disorder[a,b]

A. The presence of ≥2 unexpected panic attacks, characterized by at least 4 of the following symptoms, which develop abruptly and reach a peak within 10 min:
  1) Palpitations, pounding heart, or accelerated heart rate
  2) Sweating
  3) Trembling or shaking
  4) Sensations of SOB or smothering
  5) Feeling of choking
  6) Chest pain or discomfort
  7) Nausea or abdominal distress
  8) Feeling dizzy, unsteady, lightheaded, or faint
  9) Derealization or depersonalization
  10) Fear of losing control or going crazy
  11) Fear of dying
  12) Numbness or tingling sensations
  13) Chills or hot flushes

B. At least 1 of the attacks has been followed by at least 1 of the following symptoms for a duration of ≥1 month:
  1) Persistent concern about having another attack
  2) Worry about the implications or consequences of the attack
  3) A significant change in behavior because of the attack

C. The symptoms are not due to the direct effects of a medication, substance, or general medical condition

D. The panic attacks are not better accounted for by another psychiatric or anxiety disorder (e.g., phobias, OCD)

E. May occur with or without agoraphobia (see text)

[a] Adapted from reference 2.
[b] OCD = Obsessive-compulsive disorder; SOB = Shortness of breath.

Because panic attacks occur unpredictably, they often lead to a generalized anxiety or constant anticipatory fear of sudden attacks.[37] Two subtypes of panic disorder have been identified: without agoraphobia or with agoraphobia. *Agoraphobia* refers to a fear of being in places or situations from which escape might be difficult or embarrassing, or help might be unavailable, in the event of a panic attack. Although agoraphobia previously was classified as a type of phobic disorder, more recent evidence reveals that it usually occurs in the context of panic disorder and that other apparent cases actually represent social phobia (see Phobic Disorders).[48] Mild to moderate agoraphobia often is characterized by selective avoidance of certain places or situations such as shopping malls, theaters, grocery stores, elevators, and driving alone.[37] In severe cases of agoraphobia, the sufferer may become completely housebound, unable even to step outside his front door. Such cases significantly impair occupational and social functioning.

Epidemiology

About 10% to 15% of the general population experiences a single isolated panic attack at some time in their life.[37] Approximately 3.6% of persons experience recurrent panic attacks which are not often or severe enough to meet the diagnostic criteria for panic disorder; however, these persons still can suffer substantial morbidity.[38] Full-fledged panic disorder is estimated to affect at least 1.6% of the American population at some time in their life.[39] Women suffer from panic disorder two to three times more often than men. The onset of panic disorder may occur at any time, including childhood and late life, but most commonly is in the late teens to early adulthood. Most persons report onset of the disorder at some particularly stressful time in their life. Panic disorder can be very disabling and is accompanied by marked degrees of co-morbid depression, alcohol abuse, and impairments in quality of life.[10] It also is associated with a substantial risk of suicide at-tempts, comparable or possibly greater than that with major depression, especially in cases complicated by depression, personality disorders, or substance abuse.[40]

Etiology and Pathophysiology

Panic disorder probably is biologically based. The exact mechanisms which underlie panic disorder are not known, but it is believed that acute panic attacks are caused by dysregulated firing in the locus ceruleus as described earlier (see Etiology and Pathophysiology of GAD). Since the activity of the locus ceruleus is regulated by various neuronal systems, including the α_2-adrenergic autoreceptor, benzodiazepine receptors, GABA, serotonin, norepinephrine, and acetylcholine, research has focused on identifying possible dysregulations in these systems which may underlie panic disorder. An interesting component to panic disorder research is that administration of certain substances almost consistently will induce panic attacks in persons with panic disorder, but not in normal healthy subjects, unless much higher doses are given.[1] These substances include caffeine, isoproterenol, sodium lactate, yohimbine, flumazenil, and cholecystokinin tetrapeptide (CCK-4). Also, administration of effective medication treatments for panic disorder blocks the effects of these panic-inducing substances. Based upon this research, there is evidence for dysregulations in both noradrenergic and serotonergic function, as well as reduced benzodiazepine receptor sensitivity in panic disorder.[41-44] Animal studies indicating that CCK-4 is an anxiogenic neuropeptide have led to the hypothesis of an endogenous anomaly of the CCK-4 system in panic disorder.[45] In addition, chronic respiratory disturbances, in which there is carbon dioxide hypersensitivity predisposing to hyperventilation, may be a key element in the illness.[46] Family, twin, and adoption studies support the presence of a genetic influence in its development.[47] In addition to these pathophysiological findings, cognitive factors also are known to contribute to panic attacks. Persons with panic disorder have been described as having "catastrophic cognitions" in which harmless normal somatic stimuli are misinterpreted as being dangerous and cause for fear.[1] These negative cognitive patterns, although often occurring unconsciously, may be integral in potentiating recurrent panic attacks in a biologically predisposed individual. In support, cognitive-behavioral therapy can be very effective in the treatment of panic disorder. Obviously, no one biological defect can explain panic disorder, and further research will be needed to define the complex interplay of the various pathophysiological and cognitive findings in this illness.

Treatment of Panic Disorder

Approximately 70% to 90% of panic disorder patients can experience substantial relief with currently available treatments, which include both pharmacological and cognitive-behavioral therapies.[37] Three classes of medications primarily are considered effective in the treatment of panic disorder: benzodiazepines; TCAs; and MAOIs. Among the benzodiazepines, the high-potency triazolobenzodiazepine alprazolam has been the most extensively studied and currently is the only agent FDA-approved in the treatment of panic disorder.[16,52,53] Clonazepam and lorazepam are comparably as effective as alprazolam.[16] Low-potency benzodiazepines such as diazepam and chlordiazepoxide initially were thought to be ineffective for panic disorder, but more recent evidence suggests that in high enough doses (40 to 50 mg/day of diazepam), they can be effective.[17] However, many patients cannot tolerate the adverse effects of these increased doses of low-potency benzodiazepines, which are more pronounced than with effective doses of alprazolam or clonazepam.

Imipramine and clomipramine (Anafranil) have been the most widely studied TCAs in the treatment of panic disorder, and appear comparably effective to alprazolam, although less well tolerated.[16,54,55] Superiority of clomipramine over imipramine has been reported in one controlled study.[33] Only one controlled trial with desipramine (Norpramin) has been conducted in panic disorder, which found that it markedly and significantly improved symptoms, but was not significantly different from placebo.[56] Well-conducted investigations involving other TCAs are lacking. Among the MAOIs, phenelzine (Nardil) has been the most commonly used in the treatment of panic disorder.[37] In one study, phenelzine was more effective than imipramine, but the imipramine doses may have been subtherapeutic.[33] Phenelzine seems especially useful in treating the phobic component of panic disorder and for treatment-resistant cases.[37] Reversible inhibitors of monoamine oxidase A (RIMA) such as moclobemide and brofaromine also reportedly are effective for panic disorder, but are currently unavailable in the U.S.[1,57]

The selective serotonin reuptake inhibitors fluvoxamine (Luvox), fluoxetine (Prozac), paroxetine (Paxil), and citalopram (not marketed in the U.S.) also are effective for panic disorder.[57–61] Sertraline (Zoloft) also would be expected to be effective, although no controlled studies in panic disorder have been published. These agents may become established treatment options for panic disorder because of their advantages over TCAs and benzodiazepines. (See Chapter 76: Mood Disorders I: Major Depressive Disorders.) Persons with panic and other anxiety disorders seem to be especially sensitive to the adverse effects (anxiety and nervousness) of fluoxetine in particular. Use of low initial fluoxetine doses (5 mg/day) with gradual upward titration is well tolerated and effective in the treatment of panic disorder.[59] The combination of fluoxetine with a TCA has been effective in several panic disorder patients who were partially responsive to treatment with either agent alone.[213] This type of augmentation strategy may be useful in difficult to treat patients, keeping in mind the important drug interaction between fluoxetine and TCAs (which may lead to TCA toxicity). Bupropion (Wellbutrin) and trazodone are ineffective for panic disorder; and buspirone was effective in one study, but ineffective in others.[16,33] Trials of propranolol have yielded mixed, but largely negative, results.[33] Clonidine has been beneficial in relieving symptoms of panic-associated anxiety, but overall is not considered an effective treatment option in panic disorder.[223] The anticonvulsants, carbamazepine and valproate, and the investigational anxiolytic, gepirone, have been used successfully in a small number of patients with panic disorder.[62,63,212]

Cognitive and behavioral therapies, including exposure treatment and relaxation training, also are established as being effective in panic disorder.[15,64] Medication appears to be most effective in reducing the frequency and severity of panic attacks, whereas nonpharmacological treatments are most beneficial for treating associated phobic behaviors and modifying negative cognitions.[64] Cognitive-behavioral treatments reportedly result in benefits which are maintained long after therapy is stopped, and also have been effective in making benzodiazepine discontinuation easier.[64]

Clinical Presentation and Differential Diagnosis

17. S.K., a 24-year-old female graduate student, presents to the ER complaining of chest pain, difficulty breathing, dizziness, and extreme nausea. She describes feeling ''as if my head is going off in space and I am outside my body.'' She states that she has been under extreme stress lately with examinations, working too much, and recently breaking up with her boyfriend. S.K. fears that she has had a heart attack or stroke brought on by her stressful life. S.K. recently visited her family physician for the same symptoms but a complete physical examination and laboratory workup yielded no abnormalities, and she was advised to try to relax. She states that her first ''attack'' occurred out of the blue about 5 months ago while she was studying in the library and that she can never predict when they will happen. Since that time her symptoms have become more severe and frequent, and she started skipping classes for fear they would return. S.K. denies any drug or alcohol use or history of past psychiatric illness. An ECG is performed and found to be normal. Provisional diagnosis: Panic disorder with mild agoraphobia. What clinical features of panic disorder does S.K. display, and what are the important factors in the differential diagnosis of panic disorder?

S.K. exhibits many typical characteristics of panic disorder. As illustrated in this case, the first panic attack typically occurs without warning while the person is involved in a normal everyday activity and lasts several seconds to minutes. Panic attacks are extremely terrifying and usually leave the sufferer feeling anxious and convinced that something is medically wrong with her body. As with S.K., it is not uncommon for persons to make emergency room visits following or during panic attacks believing they have had a heart attack or other serious event. Unfortunately, panic disorder often is not recognized in primary care settings, and no medical cause can be identified for their symptoms.[37] In the face of findings that they apparently are healthy, persons may make repeated emergency room visits and consult different doctors and specialists in an attempt to uncover a physical explanation for their frightening symptoms.[37]

S.K. exhibits the following target symptoms of panic disorder: chest pain, shortness of breath, dizziness, abdominal distress, and depersonalization (''my head is going off in space, I am outside my body''). Mild agoraphobia is present because she has started limiting class attendance due to her panic attacks. Other factors consistent with a diagnosis of panic disorder include her young age, female gender, lack of abnormal physical findings, and absence of possible precipitating substances. This case also illustrates the association between onset of panic disorder and stressful life events as well as the frequent lack of recognition of panic disorder in primary care practice.

Because different substances or medical conditions can cause severe anxiety and panic, it is necessary to rule out these potential etiologies in the person presenting with panic disorder symptoms (see Table 73.1).[49] The substances most notably implicated in triggering panic attacks include caffeine, alcohol, nicotine, nonprescription cold preparations, cannabis, and cocaine.[49] Persons also can be affected with both panic disorder and a medical illness in which the anxiety can worsen the physical condition. Panic disorder is associated with higher than expected comorbidities with hypertension, mitral valve prolapse, coronary artery disease, respiratory disease, peptic ulcer disease, and irritable bowel syndrome.[37,46,50,51]

Panic attacks also can occur during the course of other anxiety disorders, notably specific phobias, social phobia, obsessive-compulsive disorder, and posttraumatic stress disorder. However, in these other anxiety disorders, the panic attacks usually are situationally bound or situationally predisposed and occur upon exposure to a feared object or situation (in phobic disorders), an object of obsession (in obsessive-compulsive disorder), or a stimuli associated with a traumatic stressor (in posttraumatic stress disorder). S.K. reports that her panic attacks occur unexpectedly, and situationally bound or predisposed attacks are not evident; therefore, the features are consistent with panic disorder.

Alprazolam Treatment

Comparison with Antidepressants

18. S.K. is referred to a psychiatrist who decides to initiate treatment with alprazolam (Xanax). What advantages does alprazolam offer over other treatments for panic disorder?

Overall, no one agent has demonstrated superior efficacy in the treatment of panic disorder. Selection of an appropriate medication for a particular patient involves consideration of various risks and benefits of the different treatment options. One primary advantage of benzodiazepines as compared to antidepressants in the treatment of panic disorder is their relatively quick onset of action within days, whereas the TCAs and MAOIs require several weeks before onset of therapeutic effects.[184] Benzodiazepines have the added benefit of reducing anticipatory anxiety which accompanies panic disorder, and benzodiazepines are better tolerated overall than TCAs in persons with panic disorder.[37] Prominent adverse effects of the TCAs include anticholinergic effects, orthostatic hypotension, sexual dysfunction, weight gain, and initial increases in anxiety. Benzodiazepines also are relatively safe in overdose situations, in contrast to the TCAs or MAOIs, in the event of a suicide attempt. They also are considered safer in patients with certain medical illnesses. Disadvantages of the MAOIs include the necessary dietary restrictions to avoid hypertensive crisis and other prominent adverse effects (see Chapter 76: Mood Disorders I: Major Depressive Disorders). The drawbacks of benzodiazepine treatment include sedative and cognitive side effects, the need for multiple daily dosing, and the potential for physical dependence.[185] Alternatives to benzodiazepines are preferred in patients with a current or past history of substance or alcohol abuse. Discontinuation of drug therapy in panic disorder is more difficult with the benzodiazepines than with antidepressants.[186] In patients with comorbid major depression, the antidepressants often are used over the benzodiazepines, even though alprazolam has documented antidepressant efficacy.[37] When considering the costs of various treatments, generic formulations are available for most of the TCAs, phenelzine, and benzodiazepines, but not for clomipramine or the selective serotonin reuptake inhibitors.

Dosing Guidelines and Goals of Treatment

19. What are the clinical guidelines for use of alprazolam in panic disorder and what are the goals of treatment?

Appropriate dosing is an important issue in the optimal use of alprazolam for panic disorder. Higher doses than those used in generalized anxiety disorder, in the range of 4 to 6 mg/day, often are required for the most beneficial results. Some patients may require and tolerate up to 10 mg/day of alprazolam in the treatment of panic disorder. However, treatment should begin with usual low initiation doses of 0.5 mg two or three times a day, with gradual dose increases every three to four days guided by efficacy and toleration of side effects. Treatment with alprazolam and lorazepam has been associated with "breakthrough anxiety" between doses, and these agents should be administered on a three or four times a day basis to minimize this effect. A switch to long-acting clonazepam is an alternative for patients who experience this problem despite four times a day alprazolam dosing. A sustained-release preparation of alprazolam which allows once-daily dosing is awaiting FDA approval and will be targeted for the treatment of panic disorder.[103] Although therapeutic drug monitoring of benzodiazepine plasma concentrations historically has not been considered useful, a serum concentration of 20 to 39 ng/mL may be optimal for alprazolam in the treatment of panic disorder.[187]

The treatment goals in panic disorder are first to block panic attacks, then to reduce anticipatory anxiety, followed by reversing phobic avoidance.[184] This should be accomplished by using the lowest *effective* doses of whatever treatment is employed to minimize adverse drug effects. Cognitive-behavioral therapies used in conjunction with medications can maximize treatment benefits.[64] Secondary desired outcomes of treatment involve improved overall functioning and quality of life.

20. Over the subsequent weeks, as S.K.'s alprazolam dose is increased to 6 mg/day, her panic attacks cease. Six months later at her clinic appointment, she reveals that her life has improved dramatically. She is going to class, making good grades, and has a new boyfriend. S.K. is experiencing no drug adverse effects, but complains that Xanax is expensive and wonders how long she should continue taking it since she is doing so well. What is the recommended duration of treatment for panic disorder?

Duration of Treatment

Long-term medication trials conducted in the treatment of panic disorder support the recommendation that treatment should continue for an additional 6 to 12 months following acute stabilization in patients with panic disorder.[186] Patients maintained on therapy for this time period experienced superior treatment benefits than those treated for shorter periods of two months. This maintenance period of treatment gives patients time to resume normal lifestyles and re-establish daily activities following acute cessation of panic attacks.[186] Effective maintenance doses of both TCAs and benzodiazepines may be lower than those used during initial treatment.[188,189] Following successful maintenance treatment, a trial of medication discontinuation is desirable to determine if continued pharmacotherapy is necessary. Withdrawal of medication should proceed gradually with all treatments: tricyclic antidepressants, selective serotonin reuptake inhibitors, and monoamine oxidase inhibitors may be withdrawn over a period of one to three months, but benzodiazepines may require a much longer time for discontinuation.[26,221] Because panic disorder generally runs a chronic but fluctuating course, an estimated 20% to 80% of patients relapse after medications are discontinued.[189] Due to the devastating impact that panic disorder can have, reinstitution of drug treatment is indicated in persons who experience significant return of symptoms. Long-term (1.5 to 2.9 years) treatment with alprazolam, clonazepam, and imipramine has resulted in maintained treatment benefits without deleterious effects or dosage escalations.[190,191] In fact, panic disorder has been recommended by the American Psychiatric Association as an appropriate indication for long-term benzodiazepine use.[115]

Treatment Discontinuation

At this point, a trial of gradual medication discontinuation is indicated for S.K. She should be counseled about the possibility of benzodiazepine withdrawal symptoms and monitored for them as well as for recurrence of panic attacks. Regarding her financial concerns about Xanax, a switch to generic alprazolam would be less expensive. As with brand to generic switches with other medications, the potential for differences in bioequivalence or efficacy exists. Previously controlled patients have experienced return of panic attacks upon conversion from Xanax to generic alprazolam.

Antidepressant Treatment

Adverse Effects

21. M.W., a 32-year-old male, is started on imipramine 25 mg TID for the treatment of panic disorder. He also is clinically depressed. During the 1st week of treatment, M.W. feels more anxious and nervous and wonders if this is the right drug for him. What is the reason for these symptoms and how can they be managed?

Patients with panic disorder commonly complain of increased anxiety during the first week or two of treatment with tricyclic antidepressants. This phenomenon could be related to the fact that TCAs initially block the reuptake of catecholamines, causing a temporary "surge" in noradrenergic flow. With chronic TCA therapy, secondary receptor down-regulation occurs, leading to reduced locus ceruleus adrenergic outflow and the delayed clinical benefit. M.W. should be counseled that his increased "nervousness" is temporary and will dissipate within a couple of weeks of continued medication use. Also, some clinicians recommend starting TCAs at lower doses of 10 mg/day with increases every three to four days, but some patients find even these doses intolerable.[37] A dosage reduction from M.W.'s current 75 mg/day should lessen this effect. Temporary use of benzodiazepines during the first week of TCA therapy has been advocated by some to decrease the TCA-associated anxiety. This cotreatment strategy has resulted in quicker improvements in panic disorder as compared to imipramine alone, but is not recommended because a substantial number of patients then have difficulty being withdrawn from the benzodiazepine.[192] Alprazolam also may increase serum imipramine concentrations.[150]

Dosing Guidelines

22. Six weeks later, M.W. states that he is still having panic attacks, although not as frequently as before. However, he still is depressed and feels anxious much of the time. M.W.'s imipramine dose has been increased to 125 mg/day. He refuses to take higher doses because of side effects that he is tolerating with much difficulty, including constipation, blurred vision, and dry mouth. Why is this treatment apparently not effective for M.W.?

Effective TCA doses for treatment of panic disorder are similar to those required for depression, in the range of 150 to 300 mg/day.[33] M.W.'s current dose of 125 mg/day probably is subtherapeutic for the treatment of either his panic disorder or depression. Therapeutic plasma concentrations of imipramine in the treatment of panic disorder usually are in the range of 100 to 150 ng/mL (imipramine + desipramine).[54] Yet, because of the intolerable side effects that M.W. still is experiencing after six weeks of imipramine treatment, further dosage increases may not be possible and a switch to another medication probably is indicated. Since he also is depressed, appropriate options may include alprazolam, phenelzine, or an SSRI. SSRIs in particular are used increasingly in panic disorder. Fluoxetine, paroxetine, and fluvoxamine offer distinct advantages over benzodiazepines or MAOIs, and one of these might be the preferred agent for M.W. The presence of concurrent depression, as in M.W., generally is associated with greater severity of panic disorder and poorer response to treatment than in panic disorder alone.[33]

Phobic Disorders

Diagnostic Criteria

Phobic disorders are among the most common of all psychiatric illnesses but have been relatively ignored until recent years.[65,200] Phobic disorders involve fears that are excessive or unreasonable and lead to avoidance behavior to minimize anxiety. Phobic disorders can be broadly classified into two types: specific phobia and social phobia. In either type, the phobia should not be related to having a panic attack or another primary anxiety disorder. Also, both types involve significant interference with some aspect of functioning due to the phobia. Phobic disorders are characterized by an early onset in life, most commonly between the ages of 5 and 13.[200] The DSM-IV criteria for phobic disorders are presented in Table 73.9.[2]

Table 73.9	Diagnostic Criteria for Phobic Disorders[a,b]

Simple Phobia
1) A marked and persistent fear of a specific object or situation, which is excessive or unreasonable
2) Exposure to the stimulus provokes an immediate anxiety response
3) The person realizes the fear is excessive or unreasonable (not required in children)
4) The situation is avoided or endured with intense anxiety or distress
5) The fear or avoidance significantly interferes with the person's normal routine or activities, or causes marked distress
6) In individuals <18 years of age, the duration of the fear is at least 6 months
7) The anxiety or phobic avoidance are not better accounted for by another psychiatric disorder (e.g., fear of having a panic attack, obsessions which accompany OCD, or trauma related to PTSD)

Social Phobia
1) A marked and constant fear of one or more social situations where the person is exposed to unfamiliar people or possible scrutiny by others and the person fears humiliation or embarrassment
2) Other criteria (2–7) which are listed above for simple phobia

[a] Adapted from reference 2.
[b] OCD = Obsessive-compulsive disorder; PTSD = Posttraumatic stress disorder.

Specific Phobias

Specific phobia (formerly called simple phobia) refers to a persistent fear of a specific object or situation. Specific phobias are classified into five subtypes: animal type (snakes, dogs, spiders); natural environment type (heights, water); blood-injection type (blood, injury, medical procedures); situational type (flying, bridges, tunnels); and other.[2] Exposure to the feared circumstance produces intense anxiety, sometimes to the degree of panic attacks, and avoidance of the stimuli is common and may interfere with functioning. For example, about 10% of the population has a phobia of airplane travel to the extent that they do not fly at all. In this jet-set age, the missed opportunities (occupational, recreational) from avoidance of flying are likely to be substantial. Management of specific phobias traditionally has involved mere avoidance of the stimuli. Medications generally are not considered beneficial, but cognitive-behavioral therapies involving repeated exposure to the feared situation and systemic desensitization are very effective.[37]

Social Phobias

Epidemiology

Social phobia has a lifetime prevalence of approximately 13% in the U.S. and is two and one-half times more common in women than men.[200] The clinical course is that of a chronic and unremitting disorder.[65] It is characterized by an intense irrational fear of scrutiny or evaluation by others in social situations due to anticipation of humiliation or being made to appear ridiculous.[65] The generalized type of social phobia refers to cases in which fears relate to most social situations (e.g., fear of general social interactions, speaking to people, attending social functions, dating); whereas the nongeneralized type involves more specific or discrete phobias (e.g., speaking in public or to strangers, eating in public, using public restrooms). Social phobia is differentiated from agoraphobia by involving the fear of humiliation and social scrutiny rather than fear of panic attacks or losing control, or concerns over being unable to escape.[200] Symptoms most frequently experienced by social phobics involve blushing, muscle twitching, and stuttering, in addition to other typical symptoms of anxiety.[47,200] Panic attacks also may occur during the course of social phobia.

Comorbidity and Clinical Significance

Social phobia often has been thought of as a benign personality trait such as mere shyness. The disability associated with social phobia, however, can be severe, including preventing attainment of educational and vocational potential, financial dependence, high use of social support assistance, and never marrying.[66,200] Social phobia is accompanied by excessive alcohol abuse in 23% of sufferers and major depression in approximately 16%.[65] It is thought to be a familial disease but the relative influences of genetic versus environmental etiological factors have not been differentiated.[202] Early factors which may predispose to the development of social phobia include childhood behavioral inhibition, anxious behavior modeling in parents, and parental overprotection.[202] Biological studies suggest the presence of possible noradrenergic, serotonergic, or adenosinergic dysfunction, or abnormalities of growth hormone function, in the pathophysiology of social phobia.[67,201] However, no consistent findings are apparent which provide a neurobiological explanation for social phobia.

Treatment

Pharmacotherapy traditionally has not been considered a primary treatment option in social phobias. Yet, due to the increased recognition of the serious and devastating impact that this disorder can have, use of medications is increasing. Classes of drugs that offer potential efficacy for social phobia include the MAOIs, benzodiazepines, β-adrenergic blockers, and SSRIs.[65,203] Open and controlled studies have demonstrated the efficacy of phenelzine and suggest that it is superior to alprazolam and atenolol in generalized social phobia.[68,69,203] The reversible inhibitor of monoamine oxidase A, moclobemide, is comparably as effective as phenelzine and better tolerated, but currently is unavailable in the U.S.[70] Tranylcypromine (Marplan), fluoxetine, and buspirone also may be effective for social phobia.[70–72,203] Among the benzodiazepines, alprazolam is moderately effective, but less so than phenelzine.[68] Three open studies and one placebo-controlled trial have demonstrated substantial improvements in social phobics treated with clonazepam.[65,73] Trials of the beta blockers, atenolol (Tenormin) and propranolol, have yielded mixed results, and these agents currently are considered most appropriate for the treatment of those who suffer from specific social phobias such as public speaking and performance anxiety.[70] Use of monoamine oxidase inhibitors or other medications usually is reserved for the treatment of more generalized social phobias.[65,70] Psychological treatments such as cognitive-behavioral treatments, exposure therapy, and social skills training also have been very effective in treating social phobias.[67]

Clinical Presentation of Social Phobia

23. S.H., a 19-year-old male, is brought for psychiatric consultation by his mother who complains that her son is extremely shy. S.H. was referred to the psychiatrist by his family practice physician who reports that S.H. is physically healthy. S.H.'s mother states that he is a very bright young man who made straight As in high school despite frequent absenteeism, but has no friends and has never been on a date. S.H.'s mother says that during high school S.H. never attended any school social functions and only stayed in his room working on his computer. Upon graduation from high school he received a full scholarship to a community college but refused to go. When questioned by the psychiatrist, S.H.'s face turns bright red and his voice shakes when he speaks. S.H. admits that his behavior is not normal, but says that he is afraid that he might do something stupid when he is around people and becomes extremely embarrassed when he has to talk to anyone. He fantasizes about someday dating, but the thought of asking a girl out is

horrifying. The psychiatrist's diagnosis is social phobia. What clinical features of social phobia are present in S.H.?

S.H. exhibits many characteristic features of social phobia, generalized type. S.H. admits that he does not like being around people for fear of embarrassment and he generally avoids social situations, which are classic traits of social phobia. The symptoms of blushing and quivering voice when addressed in conversation also are common in individuals with social phobia, as well as other typical anxiety symptoms such as palpitations, trembling, sweating, tense muscles, dry throat, hot/cold sensations, and a sinking feeling in the stomach. S.H. also realizes that his behavior and fears are unreasonable. His young age also is consistent with social phobia, as the usual age of onset is during childhood or adolescence.

S.H.'s case illustrates the substantial disability that can result from social phobia. S.H.'s anxiety disorder has deprived him of normal social development, acquisition of friends, participating in social functions and dating, and pursuing higher education. Future impairments throughout S.H.'s life are likely to be significant unless his anxiety is treated successfully.

Treatment Selection for Social Phobia

24. What treatment options would be appropriate for S.H.?

Because S.H.'s disorder involves generalized social phobia which is severely impacting his life, medication treatment is indicated. Phenelzine currently is the medication most often used as a first-line treatment for cases such as S.H.[65] It can be started at a dose of 15 mg every morning and increased by 15 mg/day every three to seven days up to a range of 45 to 90 mg/day. S.H. should be counseled about the necessary food and drug restrictions during MAOI treatment and about possible side effects including sedation and anticholinergic-like effects (see Chapter 76: Mood Disorders I: Major Depressive Disorders). Social skills training or other cognitive-behavioral therapies also may be beneficial for S.H. Desired outcomes of treatment include reduction of fear associated with social situations, and secondarily, enabling S.H. to comfortably interact socially and attend college.

Obsessive-Compulsive Disorder (OCD)
Diagnostic Criteria

The DSM-IV criteria for OCD are presented in Table 73.10.[2] Obsessive-compulsive disorder is characterized by the presence of recurrent obsessions or compulsions, which are severe enough to be distressing, consume at least one hour a day, or significantly interfere with some aspect of functioning.[74] An *obsession* is defined as an intrusive or recurrent thought, image, or impulse that is anxiety-provoking to the person, and that cannot be ignored or suppressed voluntarily. The most common obsessions include contamination, pathological doubt, somatic concerns, need for symmetry, and aggressive or sexual thoughts.[75] A *compulsion* is a behavior or ritual that is performed in a repetitive or stereotypic way which is designed to reduce anxiety associated with obsessions or prevent some future event or situation. However, the compulsions are not actually connected to the obsessions in any realistic way. Frequent compulsions include checking, washing, cleaning, counting, needing to ask questions or confess, arranging symmetrically, and hoarding.[75] The obsessions and compulsions are disturbing to the sufferer, who usually realizes that they are senseless and excessive.

Epidemiology

Obsessive-compulsive disorder once was thought to be a rare disorder, but between 2% and 3% of the worldwide population, or up to six million people in the U.S., suffer from obsessive-com-

Table 73.10	Diagnostic Criteria for OCD[a,b]

A. The presence of either obsessions or compulsions:

Obsessions:
1) Recurrent and persistent ideas or thoughts that are experienced, at some time during the disturbance, as intrusive and senseless
2) The thoughts, impulses, or images are not simply excessive worries about real-life problems
3) The person attempts to ignore or neutralize the ideas or thoughts with some other thought or action
4) The person realizes the obsessions are the product of his own mind

Compulsions:
1) Repetitive and intentional behaviors or mental acts performed in response to the obsession or according to rigid rules
2) The behavior is designed to prevent or reduce distress or to prevent some dreaded event; however, the activity clearly is excessive and unrealistic to neutralize the situation

B. At some point during the disturbance, the person realizes that the obsessions and compulsions are excessive or unreasonable

C. The obsessions or compulsions cause marked distress, are time-consuming (>1 hr/day), or significantly interfere with some aspect of daily functioning

D. The content of the symptoms are not related to another psychiatric disorder, and the disturbance is not due to the direct effects of a substance, medication, or general medical illness

[a] Adapted from reference 2.
[b] OCD = Obsessive-compulsive disorder.

pulsive disorder at some point in their lifetime.[75,214] Males and females seem to be affected at comparable rates, but males have an earlier onset of the disorder.[75] The average age of onset is ages 19 to 20, but an estimated one-third to one-half of patients have onset during childhood or adolescence.[75] Less than 10% of cases have onset after the age of 35.[74] The course and severity of obsessive-compulsive disorder is highly variable and unpredictable, with some persons only mildly or intermittently affected and others suffering severely and constantly throughout their lifetime. The majority of those with obsessive-compulsive disorder have chronic, but fluctuating, symptoms and are mildly to moderately impaired in their functioning. Like with most psychiatric disorders, the severity of illness worsens during stressful life periods.[74]

Comorbidity with Other Psychiatric Disorders

As with other anxiety disorders, obsessive-compulsive disorder often is accompanied by psychiatric comorbidity.[75] Two-thirds of those with obsessive-compulsive disorder will develop major depression during their lifetime.[75] There is a higher than expected overlap of obsessive-compulsive disorder with disorders such as specific and social phobias, generalized anxiety disorder, and eating disorders. Sixty percent of obsessive-compulsive disorder patients experience panic attacks in relation to their obsessive fears, and 12% actually meet criteria for panic disorder at some point in their life.[75] An estimated 14% to 16% of obsessive-compulsive disorder patients become dependent upon alcohol.[75] Identification of comorbid conditions with obsessive-compulsive disorder is important as it can influence choice of treatments.[75]

Health care professionals and providers can help increase awareness about obsessive-compulsive disorder and its potential treatability, and need to be knowledgeable about the illness to do so. Most obsessive-compulsive disorder patients do not seek treatment until the disorder is seriously affecting their lives. One study found that OCD patients waited an average of seven and one-half years after the onset of obsessive-compulsive disorder before seeking medical evaluation for their disorder.[74] This may be because most obsessive-compulsive disorder patients realize that their symptoms are senseless, so they attempt to hide their disorder due to embarrassment. Indeed, obsessive-compulsive disorder patients often are very successful at concealing their symptoms from friends, co-workers, and even family members, secretly carrying out their rituals. Increased recognition that obsessive-compulsive disorder is a biological disorder affecting millions of people, and for which effective treatments are available, is needed among the general public as well as health care professionals. In one group of patients who consulted a dermatologist due to nonspecific dermatitis, 36% were found to actually have obsessive-compulsive disorder, but none had told the dermatologist about their compulsive hand-washing.[198] At some point in their illness, some of these patients probably consulted their pharmacist or other health care provider for creams or lotions to treat their dermatitis.

Three simple questions are recommended for screening for potential obsessive-compulsive disorders:[198] Do you have to wash your hands over and over? Do you have to check things repeatedly? Do you have thoughts that distress you that you cannot get rid of? Only physicians are qualified to make a diagnosis of obsessive-compulsive disorder, but it is within the duty of other health care providers to let suspected obsessive-compulsive disorder patients know that they may have an anxiety disorder that can be treated successfully, and to make appropriate treatment referrals.

Etiology and Pathophysiology

There has been a wealth of research attempting to identify a specific biological foundation for obsessive-compulsive disorder. A leading hypothesis has been that of serotonergic dysfunction, due to the finding that all effective medication treatments for obsessive-compulsive disorder primarily influence serotonergic transmission.[76] However, the multitude of studies involving serotonergic challenges and other methods for assessing central serotonergic function in obsessive-compulsive disorder have resulted in inconsistent or nonconclusive findings, leading to more questions than answers.[76] It is reasonable to speculate that serotonin dysfunction is involved in the pathophysiology of obsessive-compulsive disorder, due to its preferential treatment response to serotonergic agents, but the exact role for serotonin underlying obsessive-compulsive disorder still has not been determined. It is interesting that naturally occurring animal models of obsessive-compulsive disorder have been observed in dogs (canine acral lick) and birds (feather-picking disorder), and these conditions have been treated successfully with serotonin reuptake inhibitors.[222]

More promising areas of current research into obsessive-compulsive disorder involve functional brain imaging techniques such as positron emission tomography and single-photon emission computed tomography.[77] These techniques are used to assess regional metabolic activity in different areas of the brain. Studies in OCD patients have resulted in fairly consistent findings of abnormal hyperactivity (as compared to normal controls) in certain frontal lobe and basal ganglia regions, specifically the orbital frontal cortex, cingulate cortex, and head of the caudate nucleus.[76,219] Within individuals, the abnormal activation in these brain areas is increased significantly during provocation of obsessive-compulsive disorder symptoms, as compared to nonprovoked or resting states.[219] Interestingly, these regional brain metabolic abnormalities normalize following successful treatment of obsessive-compulsive disorder, with either medications or behavioral therapy.[76,78] These findings have led to the current prevailing hypothesis that obsessive-compulsive disorder is a neurological disorder characterized by a hyperfunctioning circuit involving the aforementioned brain regions.[77] In support, neurosurgical techniques which interrupt this circuit are often effective in the treatment of obsessive-compulsive disorder. A quantitative electroencephalographic study has found that obsessive-compulsive disorder patients can be divided into two subtypes based upon neurometric abnormality patterns, and that one group responds to medications while the other does not.[79] This technique may prove valuable in the future in guiding treatment selection for OCD patients.

In addition to biological factors, twin and family studies provide evidence that genetic factors also are important in the etiology of obsessive-compulsive disorder.[80] Chronic motor tics and Tourette's syndrome occur at a substantially increased prevalence in patients with obsessive-compulsive disorder, and these disorders may represent different phenotypic expressions of the same underlying gene.[80]

Treatment of Obsessive-Compulsive Disorder

Both medications and behavioral therapies are effective in the treatment of obsessive-compulsive disorder. Behavioral therapy probably is considered to be more important for obsessive-compulsive disorder than in any other psychiatric disorder, and most believe the combination of drugs plus behavioral therapy provides optimal treatment. As indicated, all of the medications consistently effective in the treatment of OCD are potent inhibitors of serotonin reuptake.[82] These include clomipramine, which is a tricyclic antidepressant, and the selective serotonin reuptake inhibitors fluvoxamine, fluoxetine, and sertraline. Clomipramine, fluoxetine, and fluvoxamine currently are the only agents FDA-approved for the treatment of obsessive-compulsive disorder. The largest controlled trial with clomipramine, the Clomipramine Collaborative Study Group, involved over 500 patients and confirmed findings of previous studies that clomipramine treatment is far superior to placebo and significantly improves OCD symptoms in approximately 60% to 70% of patients.[83] However, most clinical trials in OCD define a "clinical response" as a 35% to 50% reduction in Yale-Brown Obsessive-Compulsive Symptom Checklist (Y-BOCS) scores (see Question 25). Therefore, even those considered to be responders may be left with 50% to 65% of their original symptoms and, depending upon the initial degree of severity, this may or may not result in significant improvements in functioning or quality of life.

In double-blind placebo-controlled studies, fluvoxamine, fluoxetine, and sertraline are effective in the treatment of obsessive-compulsive disorder, with the largest number of trials involving fluvoxamine.[80,84,85,218] Large-scale studies comparing these three agents to clomipramine are underway, and published studies to date have reported both fluoxetine and fluvoxamine to be comparably as effective as clomipramine.[84,216] One crossover study found no overall difference in efficacy between clomipramine and fluoxetine, but clomipramine was less well tolerated.[84] Since a crossover design was used, all patients received a trial of both fluoxetine and clomipramine, and interestingly, some patients showed preferential response to one or the other medication. Clomipramine may be *slightly* more effective than the SSRIs in the treatment of obsessive-compulsive disorder, but has a less favorable side effect profile.[82] However, any differences in efficacy can be confirmed only after results from comparative studies are available. In depression trials, patients treated with tricyclic antidepressants are more likely to discontinue drug therapy due to side effects, as compared to SSRI-treated patients who are more likely to continue medication treatment and derive therapeutic benefits. This observation also may be applicable to treatment of obsessive-compulsive disorder, and the selective serotonin reuptake inhibitors may be preferable to clomipramine for many patients for this reason. Paroxetine (Paxil) also may be effective in the treatment of obsessive-compulsive disorder. As compared to other TCAs [including desipramine, nortriptyline (Pamelor), imipramine, and amitriptyline], the serotonergic agents clomipramine and fluvoxamine are superior in the treatment of obsessive-compulsive disorder.[80,83]

Numerous other medications also have been studied in obsessive-compulsive disorder.[80] Phenelzine was as effective as clomipramine in one controlled study and is considered especially useful in obsessive-compulsive disorder accompanied by panic disorder or social phobia.[80,82] Several reports have described successful use of buspirone in obsessive-compulsive disorder; however, just as many report no benefit from this drug.[80] Likewise, use of buspirone, as an adjunct to ongoing clomipramine or SSRI therapy, has been effective in one report and ineffective in three.[80] Overall, the efficacy of buspirone in obsessive-compulsive disorder has not been established. There does appear to be a subgroup of patients who may benefit from the drug, especially as an adjunctive agent.[80] Lithium has augmented the effects of chronic clomipramine and fluoxetine therapy in case reports, but two controlled studies showed no benefit from lithium augmentation.[80] Benzodiazepines have been helpful in reducing generalized anxiety in obsessive-compulsive disorder patients but are considered to have little effect on obsessions or compulsions.[86] One exception appears to be clonazepam, which is thought to be different from other benzodiazepines in its serotonergic properties. An interesting double-blind comparative study of clonazepam, clomipramine, clonidine, and diphenhydramine (used as a control instead of placebo due to its sedative and anticholinergic effects similar to the comparison agents) found both clonazepam and clomipramine to be comparably and significantly effective in the treatment of obsessive-compulsive disorder.[87] The required clonazepam doses (mean = 6.8 mg/day) were relatively high and clomipramine was much better tolerated. Clonidine was ineffective but, surprisingly, diphenhydramine treatment resulted in a clinically significant response in some patients. Antipsychotics alone are not effective for obsessive-compulsive disorder, but patients with comorbid chronic tics or Tourette's syndrome may benefit from addition of an antipsychotic (e.g., haloperidol) to ongoing clomipramine or SSRI therapy.[88,217] Trazodone appears to be largely ineffective for OCD but, again, there are mixed results and some patients have been reported to improve with trazodone.[88]

The overall conclusion of the multitude of drug treatment trials in OCD is that clomipramine, fluvoxamine, fluoxetine, and sertraline are significantly effective. Beyond this, no other medications have shown consistent beneficial results, but the potential options for patients who do not respond satisfactorily to initial treatment are numerous.[88,215] Approximately 20% of treated patients with obsessive-compulsive disorder fall into this category and will require additional trials with second-line strategies.[215] Figure 73.4 displays a proposed algorithm for the biological treatment of OCD which has been recommended by leading clinicians.[88] This decision tree does not include the behavioral therapies which are considered an integral component of obsessive-compulsive disorder treatment. Electroconvulsive therapy and neurosurgery are considered options of last resort in treatment-refractory patients. Indications for neurosurgical treatment of obsessive-compulsive disorder include patients who are severely disabled from their obsessive-compulsive disorder, and who have failed on various treatments (drugs and behavioral therapies) that have been tried systematically for at least five years.[89] Success rates of neurosurgery in obsessive-compulsive disorder range from 50% to 90% and complications, including potential infections, personality changes, cognitive impairment, and epilepsy, are infrequent.[89]

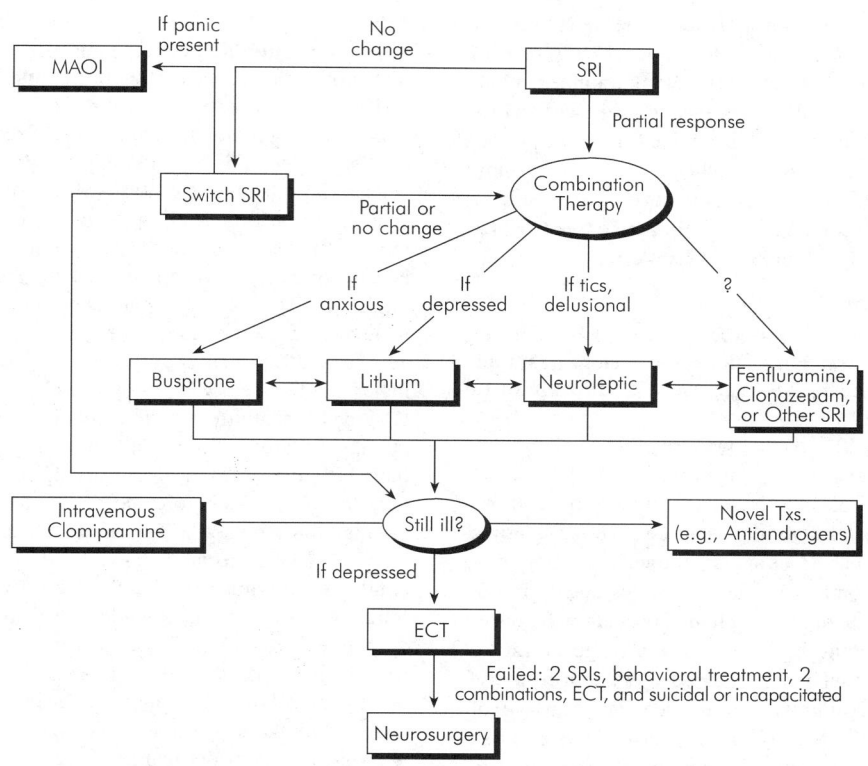

Fig 73.4   Proposed Algorithm for Biological Treatment of Obsessive-Compulsive Disorder   For the purposes of this illustration, the SRI-behavioral therapy combination has not been included. See text for discussion. ECT = Electroconvulsive therapy; MAOI = Monoamine oxidase inhibitor; SRI = Potent serotonin reuptake inhibitor (clomipramine, fluoxetine, fluvoxamine, paroxetine, sertraline), Tx = Treatment. Reprinted with permission from reference 88.

Clinical Presentation and Assessment

25. R.G. is a 25-year-old Asian female whose husband complains that she spends 1.5 hours a day cleaning the stove and takes 4 showers each day. The unusual behavior began about 1 year ago following the birth of their son, but has continued to get worse, and R.G.'s husband states that he cannot deal with her "odd habits" anymore. R.G. recently lost her job as a secretary because of tardiness (it took her 3 hours to get ready for work) and spending too much time away from her desk in the ladies' room. R.G. admits that it is silly, but she has irresistible urges to make sure that both she and her surroundings are completely free of germs so that her child will not get sick. She also confines herself to 1 floor of their 3-level house because she is afraid that she will fall down the stairs while carrying her son. R.G. also states that she constantly has "what if" thoughts about horrible things happening to her family which are very disturbing. The physician's diagnosis is OCD. What clinical features of OCD does R.G. display, and how can her symptoms be objectively evaluated?

R.G. displays many characteristic symptoms of obsessive-compulsive disorder. The most commonly encountered clinical presentation of OCD involves patients with excessive fear of contamination with dirt, germs, or toxins, and who repeatedly wash their hands or clean objects or their surroundings. These persons also typically avoid touching possibly dirty objects (e.g., doorknobs, money) or shaking hands with people. Another common clinical presentation is the OCD patient with pathological doubt who constantly is worried that something bad will happen due to her negligence. These persons are afraid that they have failed to lock the door, turn off the stove, shut the refrigerator door, or secure the medicine cabinet from children. As a result, they continuously check and recheck their actions.

Consistent with these common clinical presentations of OCD, R.G. displays obsessions of contamination and pathological doubt,

and compulsions of excessive cleaning and washing. In addition, these symptoms are time-consuming, cause significant distress, and have led to her unemployment and marital difficulties. As seen in this case, most persons present with a mixture of various obsessions and compulsions, and predominant symptoms can change over the course of the illness. R.G. also realizes that her thoughts and behaviors are "silly," which most often is the case in OCD. This case also illustrates the onset of OCD during times of stressful or significant life events. Pregnancy, death of a relative, and marital discord have been identified as precipitating factors in the onset of obsessive-compulsive disorder.[74]

The Yale-Brown Obsessive-Compulsive Symptom Checklist (Y-BOCS) is a useful tool in the initial assessment of persons presenting with symptoms of obsessive-compulsive disorder, and may be used in the objective assessment of R.G.'s symptoms. The Y-BOCS is a ten-item scale with a maximum possible score of 40; a score of more than 15 generally is considered to represent clinically significant obsessive-compulsive symptoms.[215] This scale is considered a standard for evaluating antiobsessional drug efficacy in clinical trials and often is used in clinical practice to assess changes in response to treatments.[81] Other commonly used assessment instruments include the National Institute of Mental Health Obsessive-Compulsive Scale and the self-rated Maudsley Obsessional-Compulsive Inventory.[81]

Clomipramine Treatment

26. The physician decides to treat R.G. with a TCA. He considers using nortriptyline because of its lower sedative, cardiovascular, and anticholinergic effects as compared to clomipramine. Why is this treatment inappropriate?

Comparison with Other Tricyclic Antidepressants

Clomipramine is the only TCA that is effective for the treatment of obsessive-compulsive disorder. Although it differs structurally from imipramine only by the presence of a chlorine substitution at the C-3 position, it has much more potent effects on serotonin reuptake inhibition than other TCAs.[193] But clomipramine is not a *selective* serotonin reuptake inhibitor because its major active metabolite, desmethylclomipramine, also is a potent inhibitor of noradrenergic reuptake. Clomipramine also blocks adrenergic, histaminergic, and cholinergic receptors similarly to other TCAs resulting in an adverse effect profile comparable to imipramine (see Chapter 76: Mood Disorders I: Major Depressive Disorders).[194]

Dosing and Monitoring Guidelines

27. Upon realizing that nortriptyline is not a good choice to treat R.G.'s OCD, her physician decides to use clomipramine. What are the clinical guidelines for the use of clomipramine in OCD?

Clomipramine can be initiated at a low dose of 25 to 50 mg/day in the treatment of obsessive-compulsive disorder. Divided daily doses administered with meals are preferred initially to minimize adverse effects, but the total daily dose can be given at bedtime after dose titration. The pharmacokinetic parameters of clomipramine are comparable to other tricyclic antidepressants, with an average elimination half-life of 36 to 39 hours, thus allowing once-daily dosing.[194] Doses should be increased to a range of 150 to 250 mg/day over two to four weeks, guided by patient response and tolerability. The maximum recommended daily dosage of clomipramine is 250 mg/day because of the sharply increased risk of seizures (2.1% to 3.4%) with higher doses as compared to the seizure risk with doses less than 250 mg/day (0.24% to 0.48%).[193,194] Longer duration of clomipramine therapy also may increase the risk of seizures.[193] Clomipramine should be used with caution in persons with a history of seizures or head injury. No therapeutic range for plasma drug concentrations has been firmly established for clomipramine in obsessive-compulsive disorder, but therapeutic drug monitoring may be clinically useful in certain patients to avoid drug toxicity.[193] For example, plasma levels of clomipramine and its metabolites should be monitored in Asian patients such as R.G. due to the especially large intraindividual variations in metabolic capacities in this ethnic population.[195] Elevations in liver enzymes have been observed frequently during the first three months of clomipramine treatment, and baseline liver function tests should be obtained before starting treatment. The liver enzyme elevations are reversible upon discontinuation of drug therapy.

Adjunctive Behavioral Treatment

28. In addition to clomipramine treatment, R.G.'s physician refers her to a behavioral therapist to receive "exposure and response prevention" therapy. Why is behavioral therapy needed at this time?

The decision to include behavioral therapy in R.G.'s treatment plan is highly appropriate. The overall efficacy of these nonpharmacologic treatments is estimated to be 50% to 70% when used alone, and their use to complement pharmacotherapy is considered vital.[196] The behavioral technique most often used is "exposure and response prevention," in which the person is exposed to a feared object or situation but prevented from responding in her usual compulsive manner. For example, with R.G., the procedure might involve covering her hands with mud and not allowing her to wash them. These behavioral techniques cause extreme anxiety and discomfort which often lead to dropout from therapy or non-compliance with "homework assignments" (which involve continuation of the therapy principles outside the clinical setting), but are highly effective if the patient complies with treatment.

Adverse Effects and Patient Counseling

29. How should R.G. be counseled about potential side effects and other aspects of clomipramine treatment?

The side effects that R.G most likely will experience upon initiation of clomipramine therapy include sedation (54%), dry mouth (84%), dizziness (54%), and tremor (54%).[194] Constipation (47%), nausea (33%), blurred vision (18%), insomnia (25%), and headache (52%) also are quite possible. R.G. should be advised that these are not serious effects, and they usually subside with continued treatment. Many patients receiving long-term clomipramine (and other TCA) therapy gain substantial amounts of weight. In males, ejaculation abnormalities and impotence occur at a rate of 42% and 20%, respectively.[194] Anorgasmia occurred in 8% of males and females. R.G. also should be advised about the additive CNS depressant effects with alcohol and to be cautious about the possible sedative effects while driving or performing other potentially hazardous activities. R.G. also should be informed that it may take several weeks before she notices any beneficial effects from clomipramine therapy. The onset of clomipramine's therapeutic activity in OCD usually is evident by week four but gradually continues up until week 12. Extreme patience is required during initial weeks of treatment while the person suffers adverse effects with little obvious benefit. Because of this response pattern, at least four to six weeks of *no improvement* should elapse before a treatment is discontinued for ineffectiveness. If partial response is realized at six weeks, treatment should continue for four to six more weeks to allow for optimal response.

Drug Interactions

30. What are the important drug interactions with clomipramine?

As indicated in Figure 73.4, combination medication treatments may be indicated in patients who do not respond to drug monotherapy. The most potentially serious drug interaction with clomipramine is with monoamine oxidase inhibitors. Although other tricyclic antidepressants can be used with caution in combination with MAOIs, the concurrent use of clomipramine with an MAOI is strictly contraindicated.[193] In addition, it is vital that at least two weeks be allowed between use of clomipramine and an MAOI. Pharmacokinetic interactions can result in increases in plasma clomipramine concentrations and potential toxicity when administered with methylphenidate, haloperidol, fluoxetine, paroxetine, or enalapril.[152,193,197] This should be kept in mind when combination SSRI-clomipramine therapies are used, and clomipramine dosage reductions usually will be indicated in such cases. Hepatic enzyme inducers such as carbamazepine, phenytoin, or phenobarbital may decrease clomipramine levels.[152] Medications with marked sedative or anticholinergic effects cause increases in these effects when administered with clomipramine.

Duration of Treatment and Selective Serotonin Reuptake Inhibitor (SSRI) Treatment

31. After 3 months of treatment with clomipramine and behavioral therapy, R.G. is improved substantially with regard to her OCD symptoms. She still feels the urge to wash and clean but no longer carries out the compulsions excessively. R.G. is using the stairs in her home with only mild discomfort, and reports that her marriage has improved. Her current clomipramine dose is 175 mg/day; however, she continues to complain of dry mouth and more importantly, she has gained 20 pounds. R.G. requests stopping clomipramine treatment or being switched to another drug because of her side effects and weight gain. Why is continued drug treatment necessary for R.G. despite her significant improvements? What other medications would be appropriate?

As previously mentioned, the course of obsessive-compulsive disorder is highly unpredictable. Estimates of relapse following discontinuation of successful drug treatment are between 23% and 90%.[82,86] No consensus has been accepted by clinicians as to the most appropriate duration of continued treatment following response, but in light of the potentially high relapse rate, maintenance therapy should continue for at least one year before trying to discontinue the medication.[86] Therefore, continued drug treatment for several more months probably is indicated for R.G.

Because of the significant adverse effects that R.G. is experiencing from clomipramine, a change to an alternative medication is indicated. The goals of treatment cannot be accomplished if medication side effects substantially interfere with functioning or quality of life. Due to the weight gain from clomipramine, R.G. could be switched to either fluoxetine, fluvoxamine, or sertraline, which should not cause weight gain and may promote weight loss. It should be kept in mind that some OCD patients respond preferentially to one serotonergic agent or another, and R.G. should be monitored for evidence of worsening of OCD when converted to another drug. All three of these selective serotonin reuptake inhibitors offer substantial advantages over clomipramine because of better adverse effect profiles and safety in overdose. The primary differences between the SSRIs focus on their pharmacokinetic properties and potential for drug interactions. (See Chapter 76: Mood Disorders I: Major Depressive Disorders.)

Fluoxetine treatment previously was believed to require doses in the range of 60 to 80 mg/day for efficacy in OCD. A more recent study has revealed no differences in efficacy between doses of 20, 40, and 60 mg/day; however, the patients taking the higher daily doses experienced more adverse effects.[220] Thus, lower doses of 20 to 40 mg/day may be comparably effective and better tolerated in OCD patients. Since individuals with anxiety disorders are more sensitive to the side effects of fluoxetine, therapy probably should begin with 10 mg/day to maximize tolerability. Therapy with fluvoxamine or sertraline is initiated at 50 mg/day and titrated to a usual range of 100 to 200 mg/day.

Posttraumatic Stress Disorder (PTSD) and Acute Stress Disorder

Diagnostic Criteria

Posttraumatic stress disorder occurs following the experience of a severely distressing event and is characterized by symptoms of intrusive re-experiencing, avoidance features, and symptoms of autonomic hyperarousal.[90] PTSD has been recognized most commonly in war veterans and was referred to as "shell shock" following World War I, but also occurs in persons exposed to events such as natural disasters, violent crimes, rape, physical or sexual abuse, and political victimization (refugees, concentration camp survivors, hostages).[91] The most common types of trauma experienced in one PTSD population were childhood physical or sexual abuse (57%), adult rape (56%), war (45%), and witnessing violence during childhood (33%).[92]

The DSM-IV criteria for PTSD are presented in Table 73.11. Posttraumatic stress disorder can be classified as having an acute or delayed (after 6 months) onset in relation to the trauma, and symptoms must persist for a minimum of one month. *Acute stress disorder* is a new diagnostic category in the DSM-IV and involves the same clinical features as in PTSD, except that the duration of symptoms is from two days to four weeks. In both PTSD and acute stress disorder, the symptoms must be sufficiently severe to interfere with some aspect of functioning. The majority of PTSD patients presenting for treatment also suffer from other disorders at

Table 73.11	Diagnostic Criteria for PTSD[a,b]

A. The person has experienced a traumatic event in which the individual witnessed, experienced, or was confronted with actual or threatened death, or serious injury to self or others, and to which the person responded with intense fear, helplessness, or horror

B. The traumatic event is re-experienced persistently in some way (e.g., dreams, nightmares, flashbacks, recurrent thoughts or images), or intense distress is experienced upon exposure to stimuli associated with the traumatic event

C. Persistent avoidance of stimuli associated with the event or numbing of general responsiveness (e.g., avoidance of thoughts, people, or places associated with the event, impaired recall of the event, anhedonia, feelings of detachment, restricted affect)

D. Persistent symptoms of increased arousal (not present before the event) that includes at least 2 of the following:
1) Sleep disturbances
2) Irritability or anger outbursts
3) Difficulty concentrating
4) Hypervigilance
5) Exaggerated startle response

E. Duration of the disturbance (B, C, and D) of at least 1 month

F. The disturbance causes significant impairment in some aspect of daily functioning

[a] Adapted from reference 2.
[b] PTSD = Posttraumatic stress disorder.

some point in their lifetime, including major depression (59% to 68%), generalized anxiety disorder (47% to 53%), panic disorder (30% to 55%), and alcohol or other substance dependence (32% to 59%).[98] In one study, PTSD had a severe negative impact on virtually all aspects of quality of life.[99]

Epidemiology

The estimated lifetime prevalence of PTSD in the general U.S. population is 1%.[93] The prevalence in those exposed to traumatic events is markedly increased, occurring in approximately 40% of Israeli civilian evacuees during the Persian Gulf War, 15% to 50% of Southeast Asian refugees, 15% to 22% of combat-exposed Vietnam War Veterans, and 85% of Nazi concentration camp survivors.[91,94–96] The duration and severity of the stressor are the most critical factors affecting development of PTSD.

Etiology and Pathophysiology

Biological studies have led to various findings in PTSD, although a precise abnormality has not been identified. Evidence of altered noradrenergic, serotonergic, and dopaminergic functioning has been found in PTSD.[90,97] Stress-induced hyperactivity of central dopamine and noradrenergic systems are thought to lead to the generalized anxiety and autonomic hyperarousal associated with PTSD.[97] The similarity of PTSD symptoms to opioid withdrawal led to studies of endogenous opiate function, which indicate a possible role for this system in the pathophysiology of PTSD.[97] Alterations in hypothalamic-pituitary-adrenal function are demonstrated by blunted corticotropin-releasing factor response to adrenocorticotropic hormone and increased suppression of cortisol upon dexamethasone challenge.[90] In addition, a sensitization of brain limbic structures due to "kindling" (repeated subthreshold stimulation) has been proposed in some persons with PTSD who are subject to repeated exposure to chronic trauma.[90]

Treatment

When evaluating the treatment options for PTSD, there is a striking paucity of published controlled medication trials.[100] Only six

Table 73.12	Comparative Medication Treatment Options for Anxiety Disorders		
Disorder[a]	Agents with Established Efficacy	Agents with Probable Efficacy	Agents with Possible Efficacy
GAD	Benzodiazepines, buspirone	Amitriptyline, doxepin, imipramine, paroxetine, trazodone	Fluoxetine
Panic disorder	Alprazolam, clomipramine, clonazepam, imipramine, phenelzine	Chlordiazepoxide, desipramine, diazepam, fluoxetine, fluvoxamine, paroxetine, sertraline	Propranolol,[b] buspirone[b]
Social phobia	Clonazepam, phenelzine	Alprazolam, atenolol,[c] propranolol,[c] tranylcypromine, fluoxetine	Buspirone, sertraline, paroxetine
OCD	Clomipramine, fluoxetine, fluvoxamine, sertraline	Clonazepam, phenelzine, paroxetine	Buspirone,[d] lithium,[d] trazodone[d]
PTSD	None	Amitriptyline, fluoxetine, imipramine, phenelzine	Alprazolam, buspirone, carbamazepine, clonazepam, lithium, propranolol, valproate

[a] GAD = Generalized anxiety disorder; OCD = Obsessive-compulsive disorder; PTSD = Posttraumatic stress disorder.
[b] Studies yield very mixed results.
[c] For discrete social phobias such as performance anxiety.
[d] As adjunctive therapy.

double-blind studies have been conducted and three of these lasted only four to five weeks, which is considered too short. Effective drug treatment in PTSD may require eight to ten weeks or longer for optimal benefit.[100] The three controlled trials lasting at least eight weeks found amitriptyline, phenelzine, imipramine, and fluoxetine to be modestly superior to placebo in reducing symptoms of PTSD.[90,100] Phenelzine was more effective than imipramine in the comparative trial of these agents.[100] In the other three shorter controlled studies, phenelzine, alprazolam, and desipramine were no more effective than placebo for PTSD symptoms, but alprazolam was beneficial for generalized anxiety.[100] Phenelzine, amitriptyline, imipramine, and fluoxetine have been effective in several other open studies lasting up to six months.[90] In most of these PTSD studies, patients experienced relief from intrusive re-experiencing symptoms much more so than avoidant symptoms, although amitriptyline and fluoxetine also were effective in reducing avoidance.[90]

Many other medications have been studied for PTSD in open trials. Three reports have revealed carbamazepine's usefulness in treating PTSD symptoms such as impulsivity, hyperarousal, flashbacks, and nightmares.[63] Propranolol also has been used successfully for the same types of symptoms.[90] PTSD patients treated with valproate have shown significant improvements, especially for hyperarousal and hyperactivity symptoms.[63] Positive results also have been observed with alprazolam and clonazepam, although their use in PTSD patients with substance abuse problems should be limited.[90] Benzodiazepines primarily are considered useful for generalized anxiety rather than for core PTSD symptoms. Lithium improves impulsivity, anxiety, mood, nightmares, and insomnia in PTSD.[90] In addition to pharmacotherapy, various cognitive and behavioral therapies have been effective in treating PTSD.[100]

Clinical Presentation and Assessment

32. D.D., a 42-year-old female, served as an army nurse in the Persian Gulf War in 1991. She presents to her physician complaining that she cannot sleep and that she feels jumpy and irritable. When questioned, she reveals that her symptoms started about 9 months after her return from the war. She states that at that time she began to experience nightmares of Scud missile attacks and would wake up sweating. D.D. is irritated easily by minor incidents at the hospital and jumps whenever the phone rings or someone approaches her unexpectedly. D.D. avoids thinking about the war and refuses to see her old friends with whom she served in Desert Storm. She is particularly bothered by recurrent memories of an ambush in which an explosion killed a fellow nurse. This behavior has made it difficult for her to maintain steady employment and has strained her marriage. What clinical features of PTSD does D.D. display?

Persons with posttraumatic stress disorder often present with nonspecific complaints indicative of a generalized anxiety, depressive, or substance use disorder. They often may not realize an association between their symptoms and the trauma that they have experienced. Careful evaluation by the clinician is required to elicit a pattern suggestive of PTSD. D.D. displays many target symptoms of PTSD, including re-experiencing (nightmares, recurrent memories), avoidance of people who remind her of the war, irritability, and exaggerated startle response. In addition, she is experiencing distress, marital problems, and impairment in occupational functioning as a result of her symptoms. The disturbance first occurred nine months after the experience and, therefore, would be classified as delayed-onset PTSD.

Treatment Selection

33. What factors are important in the selection of a treatment for D.D.?

Because of the many different symptoms that can be displayed in PTSD, treatment selection for a particular patient should depend upon which symptoms predominate. From the limited evidence available from drug trials, it appears that phenelzine, imipramine, amitriptyline, and fluoxetine are most beneficial for intrusive re-experiencing symptoms and depression, with the latter two also possibly being useful for avoidance symptoms.[90,91,199] Impulsivity or aggression seem to respond best to carbamazepine, valproate, or lithium.[63] In consideration of D.D.'s primary symptoms, fluoxetine or amitriptyline might be the best choices. Fluoxetine may be the preferred agent because of its more favorable side effect profile. (See Chapter 76: Mood Disorders I: Major Depressive Disorders.) Substantial improvements may not occur until after six to eight weeks of treatment, and high doses (60 to 80 mg/day) of fluoxetine may be required.[199] The goals of treatment are a reduction in her target symptoms, with resultant improvements in the areas of functioning which are being negatively affected by her anxiety disorder.

For a comparison of the different treatment options available for the five classifications of anxiety disorders, see Table 73.12.

References

1 **Nutt DJ.** The pharmacology of human anxiety. Pharmacol Ther. 1990;47:233.

2 **American Psychiatric Association.** Diagnostic and Statistical Manual of Mental Disorders. 4th ed. Washington, DC: American Psychiatric Association; 1994.

3 **Wise MG, Rieck SO.** Diagnostic considerations and treatment approaches to underlying anxiety in the medically ill. J Clin Psychiatry. 1993;54(Suppl. 5):22.

4 **Kushner MG et al.** The relation between alcohol problems and the anxiety disorders. Am J Psychiatry. 1990;147:685.

5 **Rickels K, Schweizer E.** The treatment of generalized anxiety disorder in patients with depressive symptomatology. J Clin Psychiatry. 1993;54(Suppl. 1):20.

6 **Brown TA, Barlow DH.** Comorbidity among anxiety disorders: implications for treatment and DSM-IV. J Consult Clin Psychol. 1992;60:835.

7 **Dubovsky SL.** Generalized anxiety disorder: new concepts and psychopharmacologic therapies. J Clin Psychiatry. 1990;5(Suppl. 1):3.

8 **Regier DA et al.** The de facto US mental and addictive disorders service system. Epidemiologic catchment area prospective 1-year prevalence rates of disorders and services. Arch Gen Psychiatry. 1993;50:85.

9 **Gorman JM, Papp LA.** Chronic anxiety: deciding the length of treatment. J Clin Psychiatry. 1990;5(Suppl. 1):11.

10 **Massion AO et al.** Quality of life and psychiatric morbidity in panic disorder and generalized anxiety disorder. Am J Psychiatry. 1993;150:600.

11 **Kendler KS et al.** Major depression and generalized anxiety disorder: same genes, (partly) different environments? Arch Gen Psychiatry. 1992;49:716.

12 **Zorumski CF, Isenberg KE.** Insights into the structure and function of GABA-benzodiazepine receptors: ion channels and psychiatry. Am J Psychiatry. 1991;148:162.

13 **Eison MS.** Serotonin: a common neurobiologic substrate in anxiety and depression. J Clin Psychopharmacol. 1990;10(Suppl. 3):26.

14 **Dubovsky SL.** Approaches to developing new anxiolytics and antidepressants. J Clin Psychiatry. 1993;54 (Suppl. 5):75.

15 **Chambless DL, Gillis MM.** Cognitive therapy of anxiety disorders. J Consult Clin Psychol. 1993;61:248.

16 **Jonas JM, Cohon MS.** A comparison of the safety and efficacy of alprazolam versus other agents in the treatment of anxiety, panic, and depression: a review of the literature. J Clin Psychiatry. 1993;54(Suppl. 10):25.

17 **Hollister LO et al.** Clinical uses of benzodiazepines. J Clin Psychopharmacol. 1993;13(Suppl. 6):1.

18 **Petracca A et al.** Treatment of generalized anxiety disorder: preliminary clinical experience with buspirone. J Clin Psychiatry. 1990;51(Suppl. 9):31.

19 **Cutler SJ.** Advances in anxiolytic research. Am J Pharm Educ. 1993;57:172.

20 **Cohen LS, Rosenbaum JF.** Clonazepam: new uses and potential problems. J Clin Psychiatry. 1987;48(Suppl. 10):50.

21 **Hoffman EJ, Warren EW.** Flumazenil: a benzodiazepine antagonist. Clin Pharm. 1993;12:641.

22 **Shader RI et al.** Appropriate use and regulatory control of benzodiazepines. J Clin Pharmacol. 1991;31:781.

23 **Sussman N.** Treating anxiety while minimizing abuse and dependence. J Clin Psychiatry. 1993;54(Suppl. 5):44.

24 **Teboul E, Chouinard G.** A guide to benzodiazepine selection. Part II: clinical aspects. Can J Psychiatry. 1991;36:62.

25 **Garvey MJ, Tollefson GD.** Prevalence of misuse of prescribed benzodiazepines in patients with primary anxiety disorder or major depression. Am J Psychiatry. 1986;143:1601.

26 **Shader RI, Greenblatt DJ.** Use of benzodiazepines in anxiety disorders. N Eng J Med. 1993;328:1398.

27 **Romach MK et al.** Characteristics of long-term alprazolam users in the community. J Clin Psychopharmacol. 1992;12:316.

28 **Glitz DA, Pohl R.** 5-HT$_{1A}$ partial agonists. What is their future? Drugs. 1991;41:11.

29 **Rickels K.** Buspirone in clinical practice. J Clin Psychiatry. 1990;51(Suppl. 9):51.

30 **Robinson DS et al.** Clinical effects of the 5-HT$_{1A}$ partial agonists in depression: a composite analysis of buspirone in the treatment of depression. J Clin Psychopharmacol. 1990;10(Suppl. 3):67.

31 **Rickels K et al.** Antidepressants for the treatment of generalized anxiety disorder. A placebo-controlled comparison of imipramine, trazodone, and diazepam. Arch Gen Psychiatry. 1993;50:884.

32 **Noyes R.** β-adrenergic blocking drugs in anxiety and stress. Psychiatr Clin North Am. 1985;44:38.

33 **Roy-Byrne P et al.** Psychopharmacologic treatment of panic, generalized anxiety disorder, and social phobia. Psychiatr Clin North Am. 1993;16:719.

34 **Hoehn-Saric R et al.** Effect of clonidine on anxiety disorders. Arch Gen Psychiatry. 1981;38:1278.

35 **Markovitz PJ.** Treatment of anxiety in the elderly. J Clin Psychiatry. 1993;54(Suppl. 5):64.

36 **Stoudemire A, Moran MG.** Psychopharmacologic treatment of anxiety in the medically ill elderly patient: special considerations. J Clin Psychiatry. 1993;54(Suppl. 5):27.

37 **National Institute of Mental Health.** Panic disorder in the medical setting, by Katon,W. Washington, DC: Supt. of Docs., U.S. Govt. Printing Office, 1993; NIH publication no. 93-3482.

38 **Klerman GL et al.** Panic attacks in the community. Social morbidity and health care utilization. JAMA. 1991;265:742.

39 **Katerndahl DA, Realini JP.** Lifetime prevalence of panic states. Am J Psychiatry. 1993;150:246.

40 **Clark DC, Kerkhof JFM.** Panic disorders and suicidal behavior. Crisis. 1993;14:2.

41 **Butler J et al.** The Galway study of panic disorder II: changes in some peripheral markers of noradrenergic and serotonergic function in DSM-III-R panic disorder. J Affect Disord. 1992;26:89.

42 **Charney DS et al.** Noradrenergic neuronal dysregulation in panic disorder: the effects of intravenous yohimbine and clonidine in panic disorder patients. Acta Psychiatr Scand. 1992;86:273.

43 **Nutt DJ et al.** Flumazenil provocation of panic attacks. Evidence for altered benzodiazepine receptor sensitivity in panic disorder. Arch Gen Psychiatry. 1990;47:917.

44 **Roy-Byrne PR et al.** Reduced benzodiazepine sensitivity in panic disorder. Arch Gen Psychiatry. 1990;47:534.

45 **Bradwejn J.** Neurobiological investigations into the role of cholecystokinin in panic disorder. J Psychiatr Neurosci. 1993;18:178.

46 **Papp LA et al.** Carbon dioxide hypersensitivity, hyperventilation, and panic disorder. Am J Psychiatry. 1993;150:1149.

47 **Taylor L, Gorman J.** Theoretical and therapeutic considerations for the anxiety disorders. Psychiatr Quart. 1992;63:319.

48 **Horwath E et al.** Agoraphobia without panic: clinical reappraisal of an epidemiologic finding. Am J Psychiatry. 1993;150:1496.

49 **Roy-Byrne PR, Uhde TW.** Exogenous factors in panic disorder: clinical and research implications. J Clin Psychiatry. 1988;49:56.

50 **Katerndahl DA.** Panic and prolapse. Meta-analysis. J Nerv Ment Dis. 1993;181:539.

51 **Lydiard RB et al.** Panic disorder and gastrointestinal symptoms: findings from the NIMH epidemiologic catchment area project. Am J Psychiatry. 1994;151:64.

52 **Ballenger JC et al.** Alprazolam in panic disorder and agoraphobia: results from a multicenter trial. I. Efficacy in short-term treatment. Arch Gen Psychiatry. 1988;45:413.

53 **Noyes R et al.** Alprazolam in panic disorder and agoraphobia: results from a multicenter trial. II. Patient acceptance, side effects, and safety. Arch Gen Psychiatry. 1988;45:423.

54 **Schweizer E et al.** Maintenance drug treatment of panic disorder. I. Results of a prospective, placebo-controlled comparison of alprazolam and imipramine. Arch Gen Psychiatry. 1993;50:51.

55 **Wilkinson G et al.** Meta-analysis of double-blind placebo-controlled trials of antidepressants and benzodiazepines for patients with panic disorders. Psychological Med. 1991;21:991.

56 **Lydiard RB et al.** Preliminary report: placebo-controlled, double-blind study of the clinical and metabolic effects of desipramine in panic disorder. Psychopharmacol Bull. 1993;29:183.

57 **Humble H, Wistedt B.** Serotonin, panic disorder and agoraphobia: short-term and long-term efficacy of citalopram in panic disorders. Int Clin Psychopharmacol. 1992;6(Suppl. 5):21.

58 **Hoen-Saric R et al.** Effect of fluvoxamine on panic disorder. J Clin Psychopharmacol. 1993;13:321.

59 **Louie AK et al.** Use of low-dose fluoxetine in major depression and panic disorder. J Clin Psychiatry. 1993;54:435.

60 **Judge R et al.** Paroxetine in the treatment of panic disorder. Eur Neuropsychopharmacol. 1993;3:374.

61 **Black DW et al.** A comparison of fluvoxamine, cognitive therapy, and placebo in the treatment of panic disorder. Arch Gen Psychiatry. 1993;50:44.

62 **Pecknold JC et al.** Geipirone and the treatment of panic disorder: an open study. J Clin Psychopharmacol. 1993;13:145.

63 **Keck PE et al.** Valproate and carbamazepine in the treatment of panic and posttraumatic stress disorders, withdrawal states, and behavioral dyscontrol syndromes. J Clin Psychopharmacol. 1992;12(Suppl. 1):36.

64 **Otto MW et al.** Discontinuation of benzodiazepine treatment: efficacy of cognitive-behavioral therapy for patients with panic disorder. Am J Psychiatry. 1993;150:1485.

65 **Marshall JR et al.** Medication therapy for social phobia. J Clin Psychiatry. 1994;55(Suppl. 6):33.

66 **Schneier FR et al.** Social phobia: comorbidity and morbidity in an epidemiologic sample. Arch Gen Psychiatry. 1992;49:282.

67 **Uhde TW et al.** Phenomenology and neurobiology of social phobia: comparison with panic disorder. J Clin Psychiatry. 1991;52(Suppl. 11):31.

68 **Gelernter CS et al.** Cognitive-behavioral and pharmacological treatments of social phobia. A controlled study. Arch Gen Psychiatry. 1991;48:938.

69 **Liebowitz MR et al.** Phenelzine versus atenolol in social phobia. A placebo-controlled comparison. Arch Gen Psychiatry. 1992;49:290.

70 **Liebowitz MR et al.** Treatment of social phobia with drugs other than benzodiazepines. J Clin Psychiatry. 1991;52(Suppl. 11):10.

71 **Schneier FR et al.** Buspirone in social phobia. J Clin Psychopharmacol. 1993;13:251.

72 **Ameringen MV et al.** Fluoxetine in social phobia. J Clin Psychiatry. 1993;54:27.

73 **Davidson JRT et al.** Treatment of social phobia with clonazepam and placebo. J Clin Psychopharmacol. 1993;13:423.

74 **Zetin M, Kramer MA.** Obsessive-compulsive disorder. Hosp Community Psychiatry. 1992;43:689.

75 **Rasmussen SA, Eisen JL.** The epidemiology and clinical features of obsessive compulsive disorder. Psychiatr Clin North Am. 1992;15:743.

76 **Insel TR, Winslow JT.** Neurobiology

of obsessive compulsive disorder. Psychiatr Clin North Am. 1992;15:813.

77 **Insel TR.** Toward a neuroanatomy of obsessive-compulsive disorder. Arch Gen Psychiatry. 1992;49:739.

78 **Baxter LR et al.** Caudate glucose metabolic rate changes with both drug and behavior therapy for obsessive-compulsive disorder. Arch Gen Psychiatry. 1992;49:681.

79 **Prichep LS et al.** Quantitative electroencephalographic subtyping of obsessive-compulsive disorder. Psychiatry Res: Neuroimaging. 1993;50:25.

80 **McDougle CJ et al.** The psychopharmacology of obsessive compulsive disorder. Psychiatry Clin North Am. 1993;16:749.

81 **Goodman WK, Price LH.** Assessment of severity and change in obsessive compulsive disorder. Psychiatr Clin North Am. 1992;15:861.

82 **Rasmussen SA et al.** Current issues in the pharmacologic management of obsessive-compulsive disorder. J Clin Psychiatry. 1993;54(Suppl. 6):4.

83 **The Clomipramine Collaborative Study Group.** Clomipramine in the treatment of patients with obsessive-compulsive disorder. Arch Gen Psychiatry. 1991;48:730.

84 **Pigott TA et al.** Controlled comparison of clomipramine and fluoxetine in the treatment of obsessive-compulsive disorder. Arch Gen Psychiatry. 1990; 47:926.

85 **Dominguez RA.** Serotonergic antidepressants and their efficacy in obsessive-compulsive disorder. J Clin Psychiatry. 1992;53(Suppl. 10):56.

86 **Jenike MA.** Pharmacologic treatment of obsessive compulsive disorders. Psychiatr Clin North Am. 1992;15:895.

87 **Hewlett WA et al.** Clomipramine, clonazepam, and clonidine treatment of obsessive compulsive disorder. J Clin Psychopharmacol. 1992;12:420.

88 **Goodman WK et al.** Biological approaches to treatment-resistant obsessive compulsive disorder. J Clin Psychiatry. 1993;54(Suppl. 6):16.

89 **Mindus P, Jenike MA.** Neurosurgical treatment of malignant obsessive compulsive disorder. Psychiatr Clin North Am. 1992;15:921.

90 **Vargas MA, Davidson J.** Post-traumatic stress disorder. Psychiatr Clin North Am. 1993;16:737.

91 **Choy T, de Bosset F.** Post-traumatic stress disorder: an overview. Can J Psychiatry. 1992;37:578.

92 **Fierman EJ et al.** Trauma and posttraumatic stress disorder in subjects with anxiety disorders. Am J Psychiatry. 1993;150:1872.

93 **Silver JM et al.** New approaches in the pharmacotherapy of posttraumatic stress disorder. J Clin Psychiatry. 1990; 51(Suppl. 10):33.

94 **True WR et al.** A twin study of genetic and environmental contributions to liability for posttraumatic stress symptoms. Arch Gen Psychiatry. 1993;50: 257.

95 **Soloman Z et al.** The psychological impact of the gulf war: a study of acute stress in Israeli evacuees. Arch Gen Psychiatry. 1993;50:320. Letter.

96 **Mollica RF et al.** The effect of trauma and confinement on functional health and mental health status of Cambodi-

ans living in Thailand-Cambodia border camps. JAMA. 1993;270:581.

97 **Charney DS et al.** Psychobiologic mechanisms of posttraumatic stress disorder. Arch Gen Psychiatry. 1993; 50:294.

98 **Mellman TA et al.** Phenomenology and course of psychiatric disorders associated with combat-related posttraumatic stress disorder. Am J Psychiatry. 1992;149:1568.

99 **Warshaw MG et al.** Quality of life and dissociation in anxiety disorder patients with histories of trauma or PTSD. Am J Psychiatry. 1993;150:1512.

100 **Soloman SD et al.** Efficacy of treatments for posttraumatic stress disorder. An empirical review. JAMA. 1992; 268:633.

101 **Teboul EA, Chouinard G.** Principles of benzodiazepine selection. Part I: pharmacological aspects. Can J Psychiatry. 1990;35:700.

102 **DeVane CL et al.** Pharmacokinetics, pharmacodynamics, and treatment issues of benzodiazepines: alprazolam, adinazolam, and clonazepam. Psychopharmacol Bull. 1991;27:463.

103 **Schweizer E et al.** Double-blind, placebo-controlled study of a once-a-day sustained-release preparation of alprazolam for the treatment of panic disorder. Am J Psychiatry. 1993;150: 1210.

104 **Erstad BL, Meeks ML.** Influence of injection site and route on medication absorption. Hosp Pharm. 1993;28:853.

105 **Sellers EM et al.** Alprazolam and benzodiazepine dependence. J Clin Psychiatry. 1993;54(Suppl. 10):64.

106 **Lucki I et al.** Chronic use of benzodiazepines and psychomotor and cognitive test performance. Psychopharmacology. 1986;88:426.

107 **Barbee JG.** Memory, benzodiazepines, and anxiety: integration of theoretical and clinical perspectives. J Clin Psychiatry. 1993;54(Suppl. 10):86.

108 **Kushner MJ.** You don't have to be a neuroscientist to forget everything with triazolam—but it helps. JAMA. 1988; 259:350. Letter.

109 **Cole JO, Kando JC.** Adverse behavioral events reported in patients taking alprazolam and other benzodiazepines. J Clin Psychiatry. 1993;54(Suppl. 10): 49.

110 **Vuori E, Klaukka T.** Triazolam and violent deaths. Lancet. 1992;339:676.

111 **Tiller JWG, Schweitzer I.** Benzodiazepines. Depressants or antidepressants? Drugs. 1992;44:165.

112 **Kravitz HM et al.** Alprazolam and depression: a review of risks and benefits. J Clin Psychopharmacol. 1993;54(Suppl. 10): 78.

113 **Lavezo LA.** Adverse effects of benzodiazepines. US Pharmacist. 1993;9:72.

114 **Goff DC, Baldessarini RJ.** Drug interactions with antipsychotic agents. J Clin Psychopharmacol. 1993;13:57.

115 **American Psychiatric Association.** Benzodiazepine dependence, toxicity, and abuse: a task force report of the American Psychiatric Association. Washington, DC: American Psychiatric Association; 1990.

116 **Lader M.** Can buspirone induce rebound, dependence or abuse? Br J Psychiatry. 1991;159(Suppl. 12):45.

117 **Schweizer E et al.** Long-term thera-

peutic use of benzodiazepines. II. Effects of gradual taper. Arch Gen Psychiatry. 1990;47:908.

118 **Rickels K et al.** Long-term therapeutic use of benzodiazepines. I. Effects of abrupt discontinuation. Arch Gen Psychiatry. 1990;47:899.

119 **Wolf B, Griffiths RR.** Physical dependence on benzodiazepines: differences within the class. Drug Alcohol Depend. 1991;29:153.

120 **Abernethy DR et al.** Treatment of diazepam withdrawal syndrome with propranolol. Ann Intern Med. 1981;94: 354.

121 **Ansseau M, De Roeck J.** Trazodone in benzodiazepine dependence. J Clin Psychiatry. 1993;54:189.

122 **Goodman WK et al.** Ineffectiveness of clonidine in the treatment of the benzodiazepine withdrawal syndrome: report of three cases. Am J Psychiatry. 1986;143:1590.

123 **Schweitzer E, Rickels E.** Failure of buspirone to manage benzodiazepine withdrawal. Am J Psychiatry. 1986; 143:1590.

124 **Allen MD et al.** Desmethyldiazepam kinetics in the elderly after oral prazepam. Clin Pharmacol Ther. 1980;28: 196.

125 **Shader RI et al.** Absorption and disposition of chlordiazepoxide in young and elderly male volunteers. J Clin Pharmacol. 1977;17:709.

126 **Shader RI et al.** Effect of age and sex on disposition of desmethyldiazepam formed from its precursor clorazepate. Psychopharmacology. 1981;75:193.

127 **Swift CG et al.** Responsiveness to oral diazepam in the elderly: relationship to total and free plasma concentrations. Br J Clin Pharmacol. 1985;20:111.

128 **Greenblatt DJ et al.** Alprazolam kinetics in the elderly. Arch Gen Psychiatry. 1983;40:287.

129 **Divoll M et al.** Effect of age and sex on lorazepam protein binding. J Pharm Pharmacol. 1982;34:122.

130 **Yonkers KA et al.** Gender differences in pharmacokinetics and pharmacodynamics of psychotropic medication. Am J Psychiatry. 1992;149:587.

131 **Greenblatt DJ et al.** Diazepam disposition determinants. Clin Pharmacol Ther. 1980;27:301.

132 **Abernethy DR et al.** Prolongation of drug half-life due to obesity: studies of desmethyldiazepam (Clorazepate). J Pharm Sci. 1982;71:942.

133 **Abernethy DR et al.** The influence of obesity on the pharmacokinetics of oral alprazolam and triazolam. Clin Pharmacokinet. 1984;9:177.

134 **Abernethy DR et al.** Enhanced glucuronide conjugation of drugs in obesity; studies of lorazepam, oxazepam and acetaminophen. J Lab Clin Med. 1983;101:873.

135 **Juhl RP et al.** Alprazolam pharmacokinetics in alcoholic liver disease. J Clin Pharmacol. 1984;24:113.

136 **Kraus JW et al.** Effects of aging and liver disease on disposition of lorazepam. Clin Pharmacol Ther. 1978;24: 411.

137 **Sellers EM et al.** Chlordiazepoxide and oxazepam disposition in cirrhosis. Clin Pharmacol Ther. 1979;26:240.

138 **Robin DW et al.** Triazolam in cirrhosis: pharmacokinetics and pharmaco-

dynamics. Clin Pharmacol Ther. 1993; 54:630.

139 **Ochs HR et al.** Clorazepate dipotassium and diazepam in renal insufficiency; serum concentrations and protein binding in diazepam and desmethyldiazepam. Nephron. 1984;37: 100.

140 **Morrison G et al.** Effect of renal impairment and hemodialysis on lorazepam kinetics. Clin Pharmacol Ther. 1984;35:646.

141 **Greenblatt DJ et al.** Multiple-dose and dialyzability of oxazepam in renal insufficiency. Nephron. 1983;34:234.

142 **Lin KM et al.** Pharmacokinetic and other related factors affecting psychotropic responses in Asians. Psychopharmacol Bull. 1991;27:427.

143 **Powell HR, Donn KH.** Histamine H2-antagonist drug interactions in perspective: mechanistic concept and clinical implications. Am J Med. 1984;77(5B): 57.

144 **Lane EA et al.** Effects of ethanol on drug and metabolite pharmacokinetics. Clin Pharmacokinet. 1985;10:228.

145 **Erwin CW et al.** Effects of buspirone and diazepam, alone and in combination with alcohol, on skilled performance and evoked potentials. J Clin Psychopharmacol. 1986;6:199.

146 **Shader RI et al.** Steady-state plasma desmethyldiazepam during long-term clorazepate use: effect of antacids. Clin Pharmacol Ther. 1982;31:180.

147 **Schuckit MA.** Drug interactions in anticholinergics. Fam Pract Recertification. 1984;10(Suppl.):23.

148 **Schweizer E et al.** Carbamazepine treatment in patients discontinuing long-term benzodiazepine therapy. Effects on withdrawal severity and outcome. Arch Gen Psychiatry. 1991;48: 448.

149 **Rogers HJ et al.** Phenytoin intoxication during concurrent diazepam therapy. J Neurol Neurosurg Psychiatry. 1977;40:890.

150 **Antal EJ et al.** Multicenter evaluation of the kinetic and clinical interaction of alprazolam and imipramine. Clin Pharmacol Ther. 1986;39:178.

151 **Rosenblatt JE.** Lorazepam and desipramine serum concentrations. Am J Psychiatry. 1982;139:536.

152 **Preskorn SH.** Pharmacokinetics of antidepressants: why and how they are relevant to treatment. J Clin Psychiatry. 1993;54(Suppl. 9):4.

153 **Ochs HR et al.** Diazepam interactions with anti-tuberculosis drugs. Clin Pharmacol Ther. 1981;29:671.

154 **Ghoneim MM et al.** Pharmacokinetic and pharmacodynamic interactions between caffeine and diazepam. J Clin Psychopharmacol. 1986;5:75.

155 **Abernethy DR et al.** Ranitidine does not impair oxidative or conjugative metabolism: noninteraction with antipyrine, diazepam and lorazepam. Clin Pharmacol Ther. 1984;35:188.

156 **Stoehr GP et al.** Effect of oral contraceptives on triazolam, temazepam, alprazolam and lorazepam kinetics. Clin Pharmacol Ther. 1984;36:683.

157 **Ochs HR et al.** Effect of alprazolam on digoxin kinetics and creatinine clearance. Clin Pharmacol Ther. 1985; 38:628.

158 **MacLeod SM et al.** Interaction of di-

sulfiram with benzodiazepines. Clin Pharmacol Ther. 1978;5:583.

159 Desmond PV et al. Effect of heparin administration on plasma binding of benzodiazepines. Br J Clin Pharmacol. 1980;9:171.

160 Rao BR, Rambhau D. Influence of diazepam on the pharmacokinetic properties of orally administered naproxen. Drug Invest. 1992;4:416.

161 Marti-Masso JF et al. Ataxia following gastric bleeding due to omeprazole-benzodiazepine interaction. Ann Pharmacother. 1992;26:429.

162 Abernethy DR et al. Interaction of propoxyphene with diazepam, alprazolam and lorazepam. Br J Clin Pharmacol. 1985;19:51.

163 Ochs HR et al. Propanolol interactions with diazepam, lorazepam and alprazolam. Clin Pharmacol Ther. 1984;36:451.

164 Norman TR et al. Pharmacokinetics of N-desmethyldiazepam after a single oral dose of clorazepate: the effect of smoking. Eur J Clin Pharmacol. 1981;21:229.

165 Smith RB et al. Single and multiple-dose pharmacokinetics of oral alprazolam in healthy smoking and non-smoking men. Clin Pharm. 1983;2:139.

166 Ochs HR et al. Kinetics of diazepam, midazolam and lorazepam in cigarette smokers. Chest. 1985;87:233.

167 Fitos I et al. Stereoselective binding of 3-acetoxy, and 3-hydroxy-1, 4-benzodiazepine-2-ones to human serum albumin. Biochem Pharmacol. 1986;35:263.

168 Cohen LS et al. Treatment guidelines for psychotropic drug use in pregnancy. Psychosomatics. 1989;30:25.

169 Bergman U et al. Effects of exposure to benzodiazepine during fetal life. Lancet. 1992;340:694.

170 Loudon JB. Prescribing in pregnancy. Psychotropic drugs. Br Med J. 1987;294:167.

171 Shepherd MF. Criteria for use of flumazenil in adult inpatients and outpatients. Clin Pharm. 1993;12:536.

172 van Laar MW et al. Therapeutic effects and effects on actual driving performance of chronically administered buspirone and diazepam in anxious outpatients. J Clin Psychopharmacol. 1992;12:86.

173 Gammans RE et al. Use of buspirone in patients with generalized anxiety disorder and coexisting depressive symptoms. A meta-analysis of eight randomized, controlled studies. Pharmacopsychiatry. 1992;25:193.

174 Dimitriou EC et al. Buspirone versus alprazolam: a double-blind comparative study of their efficacy, adverse effects and withdrawal symptoms. Drug Invest. 1992;4:316.

175 Feighner JP, Cohn JB. Analysis of individual symptoms in generalized anxiety—a pooled, multistudy, double-blind evaluation of buspirone. Neuropsychobiology. 1989;21:124.

176 Manfredi RL et al. Buspirone: sedative or stimulant effect? Am J Psychiatry. 1991;148:1213.

177 Rickels K et al. Buspirone in major depression: a controlled study. J Clin Psychiatry. 1991;52:34.

178 Fabre LF. Buspirone in the management of major depression: a placebo-controlled comparison. J Clin Psychiatry. 1990;5(Suppl. 9):55.

179 Gualtieri CT. Buspirone for the behavior problems of patients with organic brain disorders. J Clin Psychopharmacol. 1991;11:280.

180 Ratey J et al. Buspirone treatment of aggression and anxiety in mentally retarded patients: a multiple-baseline, placebo lead-in study. J Clin Psychiatry. 1991;52:159.

181 Tollefson GD et al. Treatment of comorbid generalized anxiety in a recently detoxified alcoholic population with a selective serotonergic drug (buspirone). J Clin Psychopharmacol. 1992;12:19.

182 Udelman HD, Udelman DL. Concurrent use of buspirone in anxious patients during withdrawal from alprazolam therapy. J Clin Psychiatry. 1990;51(Suppl. 9):46.

183 Buch AB et al. A study of pharmacokinetic interaction between buspirone and alprazolam at steady state. J Clin Pharmacol. 1993;33:1104.

184 Bradwejn J. Benzodiazepines for the treatment of panic disorder and generalized anxiety disorder: clinical issues and future directions. Can J Psychiatry. 1993;38(Suppl. 4):109.

185 Schatzberg AF, Ballenger JC. Decisions for the clinician in the treatment of panic disorder: when to treat, which treatment to use, and how long to treat. J Clin Psychiatry. 1991;52(Suppl. 2):26.

186 Ballenger JC et al. Medication discontinuation in panic disorder. J Clin Psychiatry. 1993;54(Suppl. 10):15.

187 Greenblatt DJ et al. Plasma alprazolam concentrations. Relation to efficacy and side effects in the treatment of panic disorder. Arch Gen Psychiatry. 1993;50:715.

188 Mavissakalian M, Perel JM. Clinical experiments in maintenance and discontinuation of imipramine therapy in panic disorder with agoraphobia. Arch Gen Psychiatry. 1992;49:318.

189 Rickels K et al. Maintenance drug treatment for panic disorder. II. Short- and long-term outcome after drug taper. Arch Gen Psychiatry. 1993;50:61.

190 Pollack MH et al. Long-term outcome after acute treatment with alprazolam or clonazepam for panic disorder. J Clin Psychopharmacol. 1993;13:257.

191 Nagy LM et al. Long-term outcome of panic disorder after short-term imipramine and behavioral group treatment: 2.9-year naturalistic follow-up study. J Clin Psychopharmacol. 1993;13:16.

192 Woods SW et al. Controlled trial of alprazolam supplementation during imipramine treatment of panic disorder. J Clin Psychopharmacol. 1992;12:32.

193 Jemain DM, Crismon ML. Pharmacotherapy of obsessive-compulsive disorder. Pharmacotherapy. 1990;10:175.

194 Peters MD et al. Clomipramine: an antiobsessional tricyclic antidepressant. Clin Pharm. 1990;9:165.

195 Shimoda et al. Interindividual variations of desmethylation and hydroxylation of clomipramine in an Oriental psychiatric population. J Clin Psychopharmacol. 1993;13:181.

196 Dar R, Greist JH. Behavior therapy for obsessive-compulsive disorder. Psychiatr Clin North Am. 1992;15:885.

197 Toutoungi M. Potential effect of enalapril on clomipramine metabolism. Hum Psychopharmacol. 1992;7:147.

198 Rasmussen SA, Eisen JL. The epidemiology and differential diagnosis of obsessive compulsive disorder. J Clin Psychiatry. 1992;53(Suppl. 4):4.

199 Nagy LM et al. Open prospective trial of fluoxetine for posttraumatic stress disorder. J Clin Psychopharmacol. 1993;13:107.

200 Judd LJ. Social phobia: a clinical overview. J Clin Psychiatry. 1994;55(Suppl. 6):5.

201 Udhe TW. Anxiety and growth disturbance: is there a connection? A review of biological studies in social phobia. J Clin Psychiatry. 1994;55(Suppl. 6):17.

202 Rosenbaum JF et al. The etiology of social phobia. J Clin Psychiatry. 1994;55(Suppl. 6):10.

203 Hojer J. Management of benzodiazepine overdose. CNS Drugs. 1994;2:7.

204 Davidson JR et al. Treatment of social phobia with benzodiazepines. J Clin Psychiatry. 1994;55(Suppl. 6):28.

205 Olsen KM et al. Stability of flumazenil with selected drugs in 5% dextrose injection. Am J Hosp Pharm. 1993;50:1907.

206 Potokar, Nutt DJ. Anxiolytic potential of benzodiazepine receptor partial agonists. CNS Drugs. 1994;1:305.

207 Tollefson GD et al. Fluoxetine, placebo, and tricyclic antidepressants in major depression with and without anxious features. J Clin Psychiatry. 1994;55:50.

208 Gelenberg AJ. Buspirone: seven-year update. J Clin Psychiatry. 1994;55:222.

209 Guven H et al. Age-related digoxin-alprazolam interaction. Clin Pharmacol Ther. 1993;54:42–4.

210 Phillips JP et al. A pharmacokinetic interaction between erythromycin and triazolam. J Clin Psychopharmacol. 1986;6:297.

211 Marazziti D et al. Age-related changes in peripheral benzodiazepine receptors of human platelets. J Psychiatr Neurosci. 1994;19:136.

212 Woodman CL, Noyes R. Panic disorder: treatment with valproate. J Clin Psychiatry. 1994;55:134.

213 Tiffon L et al. Augmentation strategies with tricyclic or fluoxetine treatment in seven partially responsive panic disorder patients. J Clin Psychiatry. 1994;55:66.

214 Weissman MM et al. The cross national epidemiology of obsessive compulsive disorder. The Cross National Collaborative Group. J Clin Psychiatry. 1994;55(Suppl. 3):5.

215 Jenike MA, Rauch SL. Managing the patient with treatment-resistant obsessive-compulsive disorder: current strategies. J Clin Psychiatry. 1994;55(Suppl. 3):11.

216 Freeman CPL et al. Fluvoxamine versus clomipramine in the treatment of obsessive compulsive disorder: a multicenter, randomized, double-blind, parallel group comparison. J Clin Psychiatry. 1994;55:301.

217 McDougle CJ et al. Haloperidol addition in fluvoxamine-refractory obsessive-compulsive disorder. A double-blind, placebo-controlled study in patients with and without tics. Arch Gen Psychiatry. 1994;51:302.

218 Wood A et al. Pharmacotherapy of obsessive-compulsive disorder—experience with fluoxetine. Int Clin Psychopharmacol. 1993;8:301.

219 Rauch SL et al. Regional cerebral blood flow measured during symptom provocation in obsessive-compulsive disorder using oxygen 15-labeled carbon dioxide and positron emission tomography. Arch Gen Psychiatry. 1994;51:62.

220 Tollefson GD et al. A multicenter investigation of fixed-dose fluoxetine in the treatment of obsessive-compulsive disorder. Arch Gen Psychiatry. 1994;51:559.

221 Dilsaver SC. Withdrawal phenomena associated with antidepressant and antipsychotic agents. Drug Saf. 1994;10:103.

222 Rapoport JL et al. Drug treatment of canine acral lick. An animal model of obsessive-compulsive disorder. Arch Gen Psychiatry. 1992;49:517–21.

223 Puzantian T, Hart LH. Clonidine in panic disorder. Ann Pharmacother. 1993;27;1351–352.

224 Devane CL. Pharmacokinetics of newer antidepressants: clinical relevance. Am J Med. 1994;97:6.

Sleep Disorders

Julie A Dopheide

Societal Impact 74-1
Epidemiology 74-2
    Sleep disorders (See Table 74.1) 74-2
    Hypnotic use 74-2
The Sleep Stages (Figure 74.1) 74-2
    Normal sleep cycle 74-2
    Nonrapid eye movement (NREM) sleep 74-2
    Rapid eye movement (REM) sleep 74-2
    Abnormal sleep cycle 74-3
Neurochemistry of Sleep/Wake Cycle 74-3
    Wakefulness- and sleep-promoting
      neurochemicals 74-3
    Drug-induced effects on neurochemicals 74-3
Patient Assessment 74-4
    Questions to ask patients 74-4
    Classification of sleep disorders (See Table 74.2) 74-4
    Nonpharmacological treatment (See Table 74.3) ... 74-4
    Pharmacological treatment 74-4
Dyssomnias 74-5
    In a Normally Healthy Patient 74-5
    Patient assessment 74-5
    Nonprescription sleep aids 74-5
    Time-zone shift (jet-lag) 74-5
    Patient education 74-6
    Short-acting hypnotics 74-6
      Triazolam 74-6
      Zolpidem 74-6
    In a Medically Ill Patient 74-7
    Insomnia and effect on sleep stages 74-7
    Drug/disease etiologies (See Table 74.4) 74-7
    Comparing available hypnotics (See Table 74.6) ... 74-8

Dependence and tolerance 74-9
In Psychiatric Disorders 74-10
    Stepwise approach to selecting a hypnotic
      (See Table 74.7) 74-10
    Sleep disturbance of depression 74-10
    Causes: psychiatric and substance abuse 74-10
    Treatment 74-11
      Hypnotics 74-12
      Antidepressants 74-12
In the Elderly 74-12
    Patient assessment 74-12
    Age-related effects on sleep 74-12
    Age-related effects on hypnotic disposition 74-13
      Pharmacokinetic and pharmacodynamic
        differences 74-13
      Other drugs used as hypnotics 74-13
    Rebound insomnia and withdrawal symptoms 74-13
Sleep Apnea 74-13
    Clinical Presentation 74-13
    Drug Treatment Considerations 74-14
Narcolepsy 74-14
    Comparing Treatments 74-14
      Methylphenidate versus imipramine 74-14
      Naps and other behavioral interventions 74-15
      Other agents 74-15
**Periodic Limb Movements During Sleep
  (PLMS)** 74-15
    Treatment 74-15
Pediatric Insomnia 74-16
Formulary Management of Hypnotics 74-16

''I wake to sleep, and take my waking slow. I learn by going where I have to go.''

The Waking—Theodore Roethke

The human drive to sleep is strong and enduring. Most healthy individuals spend one-third of their lives asleep. Such a major part of life deserves full exploration and study. This chapter will start by reviewing the impact, epidemiology, and classification of disorders of the sleep/wake cycle. An overview of normal sleep physiology and neurochemistry will follow.

Societal Impact

Knowledge in sleep disorders has expanded rapidly over the past decade and global questions have been raised about the impact of sleep disorders on overall health, accidents, productivity, and quality of life. Insomnia is as powerful a predictor of early death as obesity; insomnia or excessive daytime sleepiness can be warning signs of untreated disorders.[1] For example, 57% of those reporting insomnia may have a psychiatric condition or may develop one within a year,[2] and excessive daytime sleepiness has been associated with sleep apnea, fibromyalgia, and chronic fatigue.[3] Myocardial ischemia and increased risk for cardiac problems have been linked to abnormal events during sleep. Sudden infant death syndrome predominantly occurs at night and is thought to be related to pathophysiological mechanisms of sleep.[1]

Similar to the association between sleep disorders and disease, a relationship between traffic accidents and sleep disturbances is becoming well established. For example, one-third of heavy trucking accidents that resulted in fatalities have been attributed to fatigue and 20% of all drivers reportedly have fallen asleep at least once while driving.[1] Motor vehicle accidents also tend to peak during the early-morning and midafternoon hours when sleep tendency is high.[1] Certain sleep disorders may carry a greater risk. A two- to sevenfold increase in road traffic accidents has been noted in patients with sleep apnea. In one study, 25% of sleep apnea patients fell asleep at least once a week while driving.[4] Patients with narcolepsy can fall asleep without warning, grossly impairing their functional ability.

When sleep is disrupted, productivity decreases and morbidity increases. Excessive sleepiness constitutes a public health hazard in firefighters, police, emergency utility workers, and health care workers as night shift work is associated with a particularly high risk of impaired performance. For example, physicians and nurses who experience disrupted sleep due to work schedules have decreased reaction time and increased error rate.[5,6] About 40% of high school and college students are estimated to be seriously sleep-deprived, and laboratory studies have documented performance impairment.[7,8]

Epidemiology

Sleep Disorders

One in seven Americans has a long-standing sleep/wake disorder.[1] During a year, about 30% of the population will experience insomnia, and about one-third of this population considers the problem severe.[9] The term insomnia is used when it takes an individual longer than 30 minutes to fall asleep, when individuals awaken throughout the night and cannot immediately return to sleep, when individuals experience early-morning awakening, or when total sleep time is decreased to ≤6 hours. Insomnia is the most common sleep complaint, but the resulting daytime sleepiness, fatigue, or hypersomnia becomes the most troubling aftereffect. Insomnia may be categorized into three general types, *transient* (lasting a few days), *short-term* (lasting up to 3 weeks), or *chronic* (persisting for >3 weeks).[1,9]

Major sleep disorders in order of decreasing prevalence are listed in Table 74.1. Nightmares, nocturnal leg cramps, and snoring are other sleep disorders that tend to be more benign. Nightmares occur in 10% to 50% of children aged three to five years of age and about 50% of adults have occasional nightmares, with 1% experiencing nightmares more than once a week. Primary snoring often can contribute to less restful sleep and can be a problem in 40% to 50% of men and women over 65 years of age.[1]

Hypnotic Use

Even though the problem of sleep disorders is widespread, only one in five patients seeks treatment.[9] Treatments range from behavioral interventions to drug therapy. Benzodiazepines are the class of drugs most widely used as hypnotics. In 1992 six of the top 200 drugs dispensed from pharmacies were benzodiazepines.[10] With aging, sleep typically changes in quality and quantity[11] and the elderly consume the most hypnotics: 10% of elderly men and 15% of elderly women use hypnotics.[11,12] This is two to three times more frequently than the general population uses hypnotics.[9]

Sleep problems often are treated with hypnotics without careful evaluation of patients. In an analysis of the diagnosis and treatment of insomnia in both young adults and the elderly, only 12% of patients seen by internists and surgeons had sleep assessments documented in charts before being prescribed a hypnotic. The same study found 30% of patients were prescribed inappropriately large quantities of hypnotic medication.[13] Furthermore, elderly individuals who took a variety of nonprescription medications to facilitate sleep were two and one-half times more likely to die than those who did not use medication to help them sleep.[14]

The Sleep Stages

Normal Sleep Cycle

Each sleep stage serves a physiological function and each stage can be measured in sleep laboratories by polysomnography. Polysomnography is the term used to describe three electrophysiologic measures: the electroencephalogram (EEG), the electromyogram (EMG), and the electro-oculogram (EOG). The patterning of these measures (brain waves, muscle tone, and eye movements) divides sleep into broad categories of REM (rapid eye movement) sleep and NREM (nonrapid eye movement) sleep.[15,16]

Nonrapid Eye Movement (NREM) Sleep is divided further into four stages with different quantities of time spent in each stage. Stage 1 is a transition between sleep and wakefulness known as "relaxed wakefulness" and generally comprises about 2% to 5% of sleep. Approximately 50% of total sleep time is spent in stage

2 which is rapid-wave (alpha) or lighter sleep. Stages 3 and 4 are slow-wave (delta) or deep sleep. Stage 3 occupies an average of 5% of sleep time, while stage 4 comprises 10% to 15% of sleep time in young, healthy adults. At sleep onset, the brain quickly passes through stage 1 and moves to stage 2. Muscle activity shuts down and brain waves become less active. After a brief REM period, the brain moves into slow-wave sleep (NREM stages 3 and 4) approximately one to three hours after falling asleep. The body continually moves through all of the sleep stages over the course of the night (see Figure 74.1). REM periods become longer and deep sleep lessens over the last half of the night.[16,17]

NREM sleep stages differ qualitatively as well as quantitatively. The function of stage 1 is to initiate sleep. Stage 2 provides rest for the muscles and brain through muscle atonia and low-voltage brain wave activity. Arousability from sleep is highest during stages 1 and 2. In contrast, it is quite difficult to awaken someone during stages 3 and 4 or delta sleep. Delta sleep, also known as restorative sleep, is enhanced by serotonin, adenosine, cholecystokinin, and interleukin-1. The ability of interleukin-1 to promote slow-wave sleep supports a widely held theory linking deep sleep to the augmentation of immune function. Some hormones (e.g., somatostatin, growth hormone) are released mainly during slow-wave sleep. Deep sleep is most abundant in infants and children and tends to level off at approximately four hours a night during adolescence.[16,17] At age 65 deep sleep accounts for only 10% of sleep and at age 75 it often is nonexistent.[16-18]

Rapid Eye Movement (REM) Sleep. While NREM sleep is necessary for rest and rejuvenation, the purpose of REM sleep remains a mystery. REM sleep also is called paradoxic sleep because it has aspects of both deep sleep and light sleep. Body and brain-stem functions appear to be in a deep sleep state as muscle and sympathetic tone drop dramatically. In contrast, neurochemical processes and higher cortical brain function appear active. Dreaming is associated closely with REM sleep, and when a person is awakened from REM, alertness returns relatively quickly.

Numerous physiological functions are altered during REM. Breathing is irregular, consisting of sudden changes in both respiratory amplitude and frequency corresponding to bursts of rapid eye movement. Temperature control is lost and the body temperature typically lowers. REM sleep brings on variability in heart rate, blood pressure (BP), cerebral blood flow, and metabolism. Cardiac output and urine volume decrease. Blood may become thicker as a result of autonomic instability and temperature changes.[16,17]

REM periods cycle approximately every 90 minutes throughout the night. Duration of REM increases in the last half of the night, becoming longer and more intense just after the minimum body temperature, around 5:00 a.m. Despite the mystery as to why REM is important, it is clear the human body needs REM. When de-

Table 74.1	Incidence of Major Sleep Disorders
Sleep Disorder	Incidence
Insomnia	30%–35%
Transient	Few days
Short-term	up to 3 weeks
Chronic	>3 weeks
PLMS[a] (nocturnal myoclonus)	5%–20%
Sleep apnea	2%
Narcolepsy	0.15%
Primary snoring	45%

[a] PLMS = Periodic limb movements during sleep.

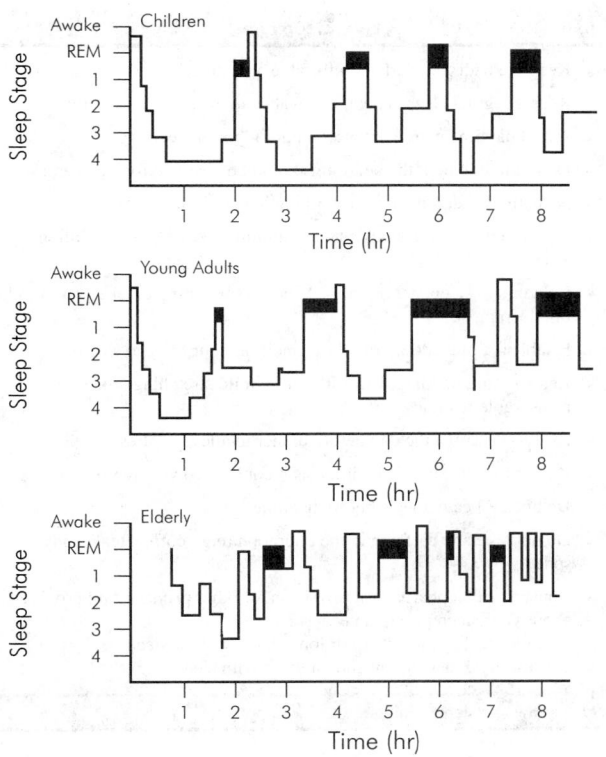

Fig 74.1   Normal Sleep Cycles

prived of REM, whether through poor sleep, drugs, or disease states, the brain and body try to catch up. REM rebound occurs, which may result in vivid dreams or overall less restful sleep.[16,17]

Abnormal Sleep Cycle

Primary insomnia (difficulty sleeping not related to any drug, psychiatric, or medical condition) can resemble a normal sleep pattern, but may be associated with increased time to sleep, multiple awakenings, or decreased total sleep time. Polysomnographic readings evaluating insomnia secondary to psychiatric disorders can be markedly different. In depressive disorders, decreased REM latency (i.e., the time from sleep onset to the appearance of REM) is a classic finding. Acute psychotic disorders feature prolonged global sleeplessness, with sleep onset latency, fragmented sleep, and decreased slow-wave sleep. Medical disorders can be associated with significantly altered sleep stage patterning (e.g., arthritis, cancer, infections). Uncontrolled pain can result in frequent awakenings, decreasing total sleep time; and patients with cystic fibrosis spend more time in stage 1 and less time in both stage 2 and REM sleep. Oxygen desaturation is worst during REM sleep; therefore, less time in REM may be advantageous for patients with cystic fibrosis and other breathing disorders.[3,19,20]

Primary sleep disorders, including periodic limb movement during sleep [PLMS (synonymous with nocturnal myoclonus)] may cause intermittent partial arousals out of stage 2 sleep and can impair ability to progress to slow-wave sleep. This may disrupt the quality of sleep and contribute to daytime impairment. Sleep apnea syndrome signals the brain to initiate multiple miniarousals in response to breathing cessation during sleep, and decreases the quality of sleep. Patients with narcolepsy may have the most unique pattern of sleep disruption as they fall almost immediately into REM sleep (instead of the usual 90 minute latency) and may experience an increased number of REM episodes.[16]

While polysomnographic readings from sleep laboratories are interesting and can be useful diagnostic and assessment tools, they are neither routinely available nor paid for by insurance companies. A thorough history of sleep problems obtained through patient interview, along with both physical and psychiatric evaluations, are the most widely used methods of patient assessment. While acknowledging the usefulness of clinical assessment, it is clear certain patients should have sleep laboratory evaluations which are useful in identifying serious problems such as sleep apnea, narcolepsy, or excessive daytime impairment.

Neurochemistry of Sleep/Wake Cycle

Wakefulness- and Sleep-Promoting Neurochemicals

A basic understanding of brain neurochemistry is essential in understanding sleep disorders and the clinical use of hypnotics. Hypnotics exert their effects by modulating brain neurotransmitters and neuropeptides such as serotonin, norepinephrine, acetylcholine, histamine, adenosine, and gamma-amino-butyric-acid (GABA). The neuronal systems where neurotransmitters and neuropeptides act to control the sleep/wake cycle lie in the brainstem, hypothalamus, and basal forebrain, with connections in the thalamus and cortex. Noradrenergic, histaminic, and acetylcholine-containing neurons promote wakefulness as they modulate cortical and subcortical neurons. Excitatory amino acids like glutamate and stimulating neuropeptides (e.g., substance P, thyrotropin-releasing factor, corticotrophin-releasing factor) also promote wakefulness.[16,21]

Wakefulness and sleep are antagonistic states competing for control of brain activity. Sleep takes over as the wakefulness-maintaining neurons and neurotransmitters weaken and sleep-promoting neurons become active. Serotonin-containing neurons of the brainstem raphe dampen sensory input and inhibit motor activity promoting the emergence of slow-wave sleep.[16,21] Opiate peptides (e.g., enkephalin, endorphin) and GABA, an inhibitory neurotransmitter, also promote sleep.[21,22]

Drug-Induced Effects on Neurochemicals

The neurochemistry of sleep also can be understood by considering the effect of hypnotic drugs on specific neurotransmitters. GABA is facilitated when a benzodiazepine compound attaches to the benzodiazepine-chloride-ionophore complex and causes chloride channels to open and overexcited areas of the brain to be inhibited or calmed. GABA-facilitating hypnotics such as benzodiazepines induce sleep and decrease arousals between stages providing more continuous stage 2 sleep. Unfortunately, benzodiazepines also may decrease stage 4 slow-wave sleep and suppress REM, leading to REM rebound upon abrupt discontinuation.[15,16,22] Some antihistamines promote sleep by blocking histamine-containing neurons involved in maintaining wakefulness. The excitatory effects of caffeine and other methylxanthines are attributed to their antagonism of adenosine receptors. Adenosine is a sleep promoting neurotransmitter/neuromodulator.[21]

Neurotransmitter alteration may or may not affect REM sleep. Drug-induced noradrenergic and serotonergic modulation usually decrease REM sleep.[23] An increase in dopaminergic neurotransmission can increase wakefulness but has no direct effect on REM sleep.[24] By contrast, increased cholinergic neurotransmission triggers REM sleep.[25,26] Cortisol decreases REM sleep and increases slow-wave sleep.[27,28] It is useful to think of the brain centers and neurochemicals involved as an interactive network regulating our sleep/wake cycle. Certainly, drugs or disease states which alter neurochemistry can have significant impact on the sleep/wake cycle. Sensory input (visual and acoustic) works with the internal network and signals brain centers to either wake or sleep. Thus, when it gets dark outside, the visual cue may prepare the brain for sleep. Similarly, bright light serves to prepare the brain for wakefulness.[16]

Patient Assessment

Questions to Ask Patients

The first step in patient assessment is determining whether the sleep problem is difficulty falling asleep, difficulty maintaining sleep, early morning awakening, poor quality sleep, or excessive daytime sleepiness. This step in the assessment of a patient's sleep disorder can be assisted greatly by specific questions (e.g., ''how long does it take you to fall asleep and how many hours do you sleep?''). Answers should be compared to the patient's normal sleep pattern to determine how it varies. Not all patients need the same amount of sleep. Questions (e.g., ''How do you feel during the day: well rested, sleepy, or something else?'') also can help assess functional impairment. About six to nine hours of sleep is optimal for most people: too much sleep can be as problematic as not enough.[29] The International Classification of Sleep Disorders and the Diagnostic and Statistic Manual of Mental Disorders, fourth edition (DSM-IV) have categorized sleep disorders largely based upon pathophysiology and presumed etiology.[30,31] Four main categories of sleep disorders are useful for clinical assessment (see Table 74.2).

The next step in patient assessment involves investigating the possible causes of the sleep disorder. All medical, psychiatric, drug, environmental, and social causes must be considered and treated. The degree of functional impairment should be assessed to evaluate the severity of the disorder. After ruling out drug and disease causes for insomnia, treatment should begin with behavioral methods of improving sleep (see Table 74.3).

Nonpharmacological Treatment

The sleep environment should be dark and comfortable, free from noise or distractions, not too warm or too cold. Along with

Table 74.2	Classification of Sleep Disorders[a]

Dyssomnias[b]

Intrinsic: Idiopathic insomnia, narcolepsy, sleep apnea, periodic limb movements of sleep

Extrinsic: Inadequate sleep fitness, substance-induced sleep disorder

Circadian Rhythm Sleep Disorders: Jet lag, shift work, delayed sleep phase syndrome

Parasomnias[c]

Arousal: Confusional arousals, sleep walking, sleep terrors

Sleep/Wake Transition Disorders: Sleep talking, nocturnal leg cramps

Associated with REM: Nightmares, sleep paralysis, impaired sleep-related penile erections

Other: Primary snoring, sudden infant death syndrome, sleep bruxism

Medical/Psychiatric/Substance-Induced Sleep Disorders

Associated with Mental Disorders: Mood disorders, anxiety disorders, psychotic disorders

Associated with Neurologic Disorders: Parkinson's disease, Huntington's disease, dementia

Associated with Other Medical Disorders: Heart disease, renal insufficiency, pulmonary disease

Associated with a Substance: Medication/substance abuse (e.g., phenylpropanolamine, cocaine)

Proposed Sleep Disorders

Menstrual-associated sleep disorder, pregnancy-associated sleep disorder, short or long sleeper

[a] Adapted with permission from references 30 and 31.
[b] Any sleep pattern which is abnormal (e.g., insomnia or excessive sleepiness).
[c] Any unusual behavior which emerges during sleep.

Table 74.3	Sleep Fitness Guide[a]

- Keep the bedroom dark, comfortable, and quiet
- Keep a regular sleep schedule. Awaken at the same time daily
- Avoid daytime naps even after a poor night of sleep
- Do not live in bed: the bedroom should be reserved for sleep and sex
- No eating, watching TV, or working in bed; it increases stress
- Turn the face of the clock aside to minimize anxiety about falling asleep
- If unable to sleep, get out of bed and do something to take your mind off sleeping
- Establish a prebedtime ritual to condition your body to sleep
- Relax before bedtime with soft music, mild stretching, yoga, or pleasurable reading
- Exercise early in the day before dinner to alleviate stress
- Do not exercise before bedtime as it could keep you awake
- Do not eat heavy meals before bedtime
- Do not take any caffeine in the afternoon (e.g., coffee, tea, candy, soda)
- Consult with a pharmacist, physician, or other primary care provider about your sleep problem because:
  A physical or mental condition can cause poor sleep
  Prescribed medication can interfere with sleep

[a] Also known as sleep hygiene.

creating a sleep-friendly setting, establishing regular sleep hours, particularly a regular wake time, is necessary to condition the body to sleep. Even after a poor night's sleep, it is important for healthy sleepers to avoid daytime naps and stay awake until the regular sleep time. In some cases, brief (e.g., 20 minute) naps may be refreshing without disrupting nocturnal sleep. Phototherapy, bright light exposure for one hour upon awakening in the morning, is an additional tool which can help set the circadian rhythm for regular sleep/wake cycles.[16,32] Healthy sleep often can be facilitated by avoiding activities in the bedroom such as problem-solving exercises (e.g., finances, crossword puzzles), strenuous physical exercise, thereby reserving the area for sleep and sex. Exercise early in the day can improve sleep fitness. Exercise should be completed before dinner time, so the body has a few hours to relax before it is time to sleep. Relaxation is the key to healthy sleep. If a sleeper finds himself tossing or turning, it is time to get out of bed, stretch, read, or listen to soft music in order to relax. Guided imagery and biofeedback have been described as helpful, but systematic studies are lacking. Health care practitioners should remind patients to avoid large meals at bedtime because the digestion of heavy meals can impair sleep. Lastly, chemicals which can disrupt sleep like alcohol, caffeine, or other stimulants should be eliminated when possible.[20,33]

Pharmacological Treatment

When insomnia is severe and persists, nondrug therapeutic interventions may not be sufficient, and a hypnotic medication may be needed to treat transient or short-term insomnia. The most commonly prescribed hypnotics are benzodiazepines because of their effectiveness and relative safety. Barbiturates are prescribed less commonly for management of insomnia because of the risk of excessive central nervous system (CNS) depression.[34,35]

Some patients may need pharmacologic treatment for chronic insomnia, although the indications are less clear. Despite the availability of treatment, few insomniacs seek help from their physicians. Although only one in five insomnia sufferers receives a prescription for a hypnotic medication to treat insomnia,[9] alcohol and over-the-counter (OTC) sleep aids containing antihistamines are widely used to self-medicate insomnia.[20,34]

The ideal hypnotic has a rapid onset of effect (within 20 minutes, the natural time to fall asleep), helps the patient sleep throughout the night, does not cause daytime impairment, and has no abuse potential. Currently, there are no ideal hypnotics. Hypnotics which act at benzodiazepine receptors come the closest to ideal.[35-37] Available agents vary in onset, duration, and potential for daytime impairment mostly because of their individual pharmacokinetic profiles.[34] The selection of the appropriate hypnotic should consider the type of insomnia to be treated and the physiological characteristics of the patient. For example, if someone cannot fall asleep but has no trouble staying asleep and wants no carry-over effect into the next day, a rapid-acting hypnotic with a short half-life and no active metabolites may be desirable.[36]

Less common sleep disorders are treated with a variety of medications as well as some nondrug therapies. Periodic limb movements during sleep can be improved with benzodiazepines such as clonazepam.[38] Narcolepsy is treated with stimulants, dopamine agonists, and some antidepressants.[39] Both sleep apnea and primary snoring can be worsened with central nervous system depressants but usually improve with nondrug therapies such as continuous positive airway pressure (CPAP).[40,41] Sleep disturbances associated with medical and psychiatric diagnoses require special attention because a hypnotic can improve or worsen the problem.[20]

Dyssomnias

In a Normally Healthy Patient

Patient Assessment

1. E.P., a 31-year-old female, is requesting a medication for treatment of her insomnia. She just returned to California from Hong Kong 2 days ago and now is having difficulty getting to sleep. When she arrived in Hong Kong, she reports that she went to sleep immediately even though it was only 4 p.m. and then awoke at 3 a.m. with nothing to do. Her sleep pattern adjusted during her 6-week visit in Hong Kong, but upon her return to California, it takes her hours to fall asleep. She then has difficulty awaking in the morning and, as a result, sleeps past the noon hour. She needs to be alert during the day to fulfill her obligations as a schoolteacher. What information provided by E.P. is important in the assessment of her insomnia? What additional information should be obtained from E.P. to assist in the assessment of her sleep disturbance?

E.P. describes a time-zone shift or disruption in circadian rhythm which is a common cause of transient insomnia. Her major complaint is difficulty falling asleep, as she reports no trouble staying asleep or awakening too early. It is important for E.P. not to be sedated during the day because she is a teacher. Additional information needed from E.P. includes: duration of insomnia, methods already tried to relieve insomnia/efficacy, concurrent medications, coexisting medical or psychiatric problems, alcohol use, caffeine use, and current life stresses. E.P. should be advised that assessing all of the above is necessary in treating her sleep problem.

2. In response to your additional questions, you learn that E.P. saw her family physician last month and was given a clean bill of health. However, she did catch a cold while traveling and has been taking pseudoephedrine at night for nasal stuffiness. She takes no prescription medication. She denies drinking alcoholic beverages and coffee but admits to recently increasing her tea intake to try and stay awake during the day. She denies a long history of insomnia but adds, "I have not been able to sleep as well in my new apartment; I don't know why." What factors could be contributing to E.P.'s insomnia?

There are several factors contributing to E.P.'s type of insomnia which can be classified as circadian rhythm sleep disorder related to jet lag. Her circadian rhythm has been disrupted, due to travel, but she also takes a stimulating decongestant (i.e., pseudoephedrine) and drinks a caffeine-containing beverage (i.e., tea). In addition, she sleeps in new surroundings which can take some time for adjustment. All these factors can make it difficult to fall asleep. Circadian rhythm sleep disorder results from a mismatch between the sleep/wake schedule required by a person's environment and her circadian sleep/wake pattern.

Nonprescription Sleep Aids

3. E.P. would like to purchase a nonprescription sleep medication. What would you recommend?

An individual risk-versus-benefit assessment is essential before recommending any medication, even OTC products. Most nonprescription sleep aids contain antihistamines such as diphenhydramine (Benadryl). The antihistamines can cause drowsiness and can help patients fall asleep. When single doses of either diphenhydramine 50 mg, triazolam 0.25 mg, ethanol 0.6 gm/kg (2 to 4 drinks) or placebo were administered over two nights to volunteers, both diphenhydramine and triazolam (Halcion) produced comparable levels of sedation which differed from the nonsedative effects of ethanol and placebo.[42] The ability to cause sedation does not necessarily impart hypnotic efficacy. Some patients do not feel well rested the next day after taking an antihistamine,[43,44] and daytime residual effects are experienced by about 50% of patients. The "hangover effect" (i.e., residual sedation in the subsequent morning) can be significant and may be related to the lipid solubility and central histaminic (H_1) blockade of the antihistamine. Antihistamines with low lipid-solubility (e.g., terfenadine) do not cross the blood brain barrier readily and do not cause sedation.[45] Although diphenhydramine is the most common antihistamine found in nonprescription sleep medications, some preparations contain the antihistamines doxylamine and hydroxyzine. Tolerance may develop to the sedative effects of antihistamines after one to two weeks of continued use. Due to a high incidence of daytime sedation, antihistamines probably are a poor choice for E.P. who is a teacher and must stay alert throughout the day. Therefore, E.P.'s insomnia probably should be managed with behavioral interventions to promote sleep fitness before initiating drug therapy with a diphenhydramine-containing nonprescription medication.

Time-Zone Shift

4. Why is E.P. especially susceptible to the effects of time-zone shift (i.e., "jet lag") and how might she avoid this problem in future travels?

Time-zone shift disrupts the natural circadian rhythm which helps regulate sleep. E.P. traveled east, then west through multiple time zones. The severity of jet lag is related to the direction traveled and the number of time zones crossed. Older individuals more than 50 years of age and those traveling eastward will have more difficulty in adjusting their circadian rhythm to time-zone changes. Travelers should be made aware of the problem and should take steps to help their systems adjust. Upon arrival in the new time zone, travelers like E.P. should reset their watches and participate in activities corresponding to the new time. Staying active until the new time-zone bedtime and avoiding naps and stimulants can be helpful.

Short- to intermediate-acting hypnotics may be used to induce and regulate sleep if the stay will be relatively short (<5 days) and if critical activities must be accomplished during the first 48 hours after arrival at the destination.[33] Long-acting hypnotics such as flurazepam (Dalmane) may prevent the traveler from awakening in the morning and should be avoided. Some hypnotic medications, especially the short half-life drug triazolam, can cause anterograde amnesia that is sufficiently severe to make the traveler unable to remember new information learned on the trip. If the traveler is on vacation and not bound by a demanding schedule, it usually is best to shift to the local time gradually by adjusting daily activities an hour or two each day.[46]

Patient Education

5. What information should be provided to E.P. about her sleep problem?

E.P. should be informed about the likely causes of her insomnia (i.e., jet lag, tea, pseudoephedrine, new surroundings). She also should understand that it may take one to three weeks for her system to readjust after traveling.[46] The importance of sleep fitness (see Table 74.3) should be emphasized. For E.P., it is necessary to pay particular attention to regulating her sleep cycle by making herself awaken at the same time each day and resisting daytime naps even after a poor night of sleep. This process, called "chronotherapy," regulates the internal time-clock. In addition, an hour of bright light in the morning can serve as an environmental stimulus, normalizing circadian rhythm.[32] If E.P.'s insomnia persists despite adhering to the sleep fitness guidelines for several days, a prescription hypnotic may be necessary.

Short-Acting Hypnotics

6. Triazolam. **Two weeks have passed and E.P. has questions about her new prescription for triazolam (Halcion) 0.25 mg Q HS PRN for sleep. She reports she was able to sleep better after reregulating her sleep cycle as previously recommended; however, new stresses at work prompted her to get a prescription to help her fall asleep on those occasional nights when it is difficult. Once she is asleep, she has no trouble staying asleep. What subjective and objective data in E.P.'s history make triazolam an appropriate selection for treatment of her insomnia?**

E.P.'s insomnia seems to have changed from transient to short term (i.e., more than a few days but <3 weeks). Although the previously recommended sleep fitness guidelines were somewhat beneficial, her initial insomnia persists and seems to be aggravated by increased stress at work. Triazolam seems appropriate for E.P.'s specific type of insomnia (i.e., occasional difficulty in falling asleep). It induces sleep rapidly because it reaches peak plasma concentrations in 30 minutes, and its ultrashort elimination half-life of two to five hours minimizes its ability to cause residual daytime sedation.[35,48] This is particularly important for E.P. who is a teacher and must be alert. Short-acting hypnotics, such as triazolam, may be used safely on an as-needed basis.

7. Subsequently, E.P. reported that the triazolam worked well for about a week but she then noticed significant nervousness and even worse insomnia when she tried to discontinue its nightly use. Why is it possible that triazolam may be causing E.P.'s worsening symptoms?

E.P.'s increased nervousness and enhanced difficulty falling asleep when she discontinued her use of triazolam represent the phenomenon known as rebound insomnia. Rebound insomnia can occur after discontinuing the use of any benzodiazepine hypnotic, but it is particularly likely with triazolam due to its pharmacodynamic and pharmacokinetic properties.[47] Pharmacodynamically, triazolam has a high-binding affinity to the benzodiazepine GABA-chloride/ionophore receptor complex which may be responsible for both hypnotic intensity and withdrawal difficulties.[49,50] Pharmacokinetically, triazolam's short half-life and rapid decrease in blood levels create the potential for the withdrawal symptoms of anxiety and insomnia. Triazolam is highly effective in inducing sleep when used on an as-needed basis. When used on consecutive

days or nights, routinely, the risk of adverse effects may increase, including rebound insomnia upon drug discontinuation.[51]

8. What is E.P.'s risk of developing other CNS adverse effects from triazolam, and is this risk greater with triazolam than with other benzodiazepines?

Central nervous system depression (drowsiness, dizziness, fatigue, or impaired coordination) was the most common adverse effect occurring in 14.2% of patients taking triazolam 0.25 mg.[51] Triazolam also can cause new memory impairment (also known as anterograde amnesia), confusion, hyperexcitability states, suspiciousness, depression, and even reports of violent behavior and psychotic reactions.[52,53] The elderly, those taking doses ≥ 0.5 mg, those with underlying psychiatric disorders, and those who take alcohol with triazolam may be at increased risk for adverse effects.[48] Alcohol does alter the area under the concentration-time curve of triazolam. When volunteers took triazolam 0.25 mg and ethanol 0.9 gm/kg (3 to 6 drinks) together, they experienced markedly increased psychomotor impairment.[54] E.P. is 31 years old, a nondrinker, with no underlying psychiatric disorder taking no more than 0.25 mg of triazolam per dose; therefore, while she may experience additional adverse effects, she is not at high risk.

Considering all clinical data, triazolam has an increased incidence of CNS reactions when compared to other available benzodiazepine hypnotics and the effects may be related to dose and duration of use.[52,55] The Upjohn Company in 1991 responded to the Food and Drug Administration's and the public's concerns over the safety of triazolam by changing the dosing, packaging, and usage guidelines for its triazolam product, Halcion. This drug now is available in dose packs of ten along with strong recommendations for short-term treatment (7 to 10 days) with the lowest possible dose (0.125 or 0.25 mg). Patients should not receive more than 30 tablets at a time and the package insert warns of CNS reactions.[56] Since 1988, when it was the most prescribed hypnotic, Halcion use has decreased substantially largely due to concerns over possible adverse effects. Despite these concerns, triazolam still offers effective sleep induction with a low to moderate risk of CNS adverse effects when used as recommended.

9. Zolpidem. **What are alternatives to triazolam for E.P. which offer the same rapid onset and low risk of residual daytime sedation but without rebound nervousness and insomnia?**

Zolpidem (Ambien) is an alternative to triazolam with similar pharmacokinetic parameters and corresponding clinical activity. Zolpidem is absorbed rapidly, reaches peak serum levels in one to two hours and is eliminated rapidly with an average half-life of approximately two and one-half hours. Zolpidem has no active metabolites and, like triazolam, it has a low risk of residual daytime sedation in recommended doses.[37,58] As stated earlier, E.P. must be alert during the day.

Zolpidem is an imidazopyridine compound, structurally different from benzodiazepines. Despite its structural difference, zolpidem binds to the benzodiazepine-receptor complex much like medications with the chemical "benzodiazepine" structure.[57] What sets zolpidem apart is its selectivity for the benzodiazepine (ω_1) receptor. All benzodiazepine compounds affect all three known benzodiazepine receptors and have varying degrees of anxiolytic, sedative, muscle relaxant, and anticonvulsant effects. Zolpidem's benzodiazepine$_1$-receptor selectivity seems to impart hypnotic efficacy with only minimal anticonvulsant, anxiolytic, or muscle relaxant activity.[58,61] Mild rebound insomnia upon abrupt discontinuation has been reported to the manufacturer; however, tolerance and withdrawal effects have not been reported during clinical trials with patients taking 10 to 20 mg/night.[37,58,59] Tolerance and withdrawal reactions have been described in case reports. One patient increased her zolpidem dose to 40 to 50 mg over a two-month period, then experienced a daytime withdrawal reaction very similar to benzodiazepine withdrawal (tremor, tachycardia, sweating, and severe anxiety).[62] At doses greater than 20 mg, zolpidem may lose benzodiazepine-receptor selectivity, increasing the risk of withdrawal reactions. In summary, rebound nervousness seems to be less likely with zolpidem than with triazolam, particularly at recommended zolpidem doses of 5 to 10 mg/day. Therefore, zolpidem could be an alternative to triazolam for E.P.

10. What are other differences between triazolam and zolpidem which may be of clinical relevance to E.P.? Considering the differences between drugs and E.P.'s individual characteristics, what is an optimal dose of zolpidem for E.P.?

Unlike triazolam, zolpidem's possible adverse effects include nausea and diarrhea. Zolpidem has been associated with CNS adverse effects (e.g., dizziness, somnolence, headache, confusion, memory problems) which appear to be dose related. The incidences of all adverse effects are significantly higher with doses ≥20 mg.[63] It is difficult to compare the risk of psychiatric adverse effects between triazolam and zolpidem, although to date there are fewer reports with zolpidem. Case reports of nonviolent, brief psychotic reactions have been reported in three young women prescribed zolpidem 10 mg for insomnia. One woman was anorexic with below-normal body weight; therefore, she may have had higher-than-usual plasma levels.[64,65] Unlike benzodiazepines, zolpidem does not appear to alter sleep stages at usual doses (5 to 10 mg); at higher doses (≥20 mg) sleep stages are affected.[54] The clinical significance of altered sleep stages requires further clarification. Zolpidem 10 to 20 mg has helped patients fall asleep faster and increased total sleep time.[58–60] The 5 mg dose of zolpidem may be no better than placebo in either inducing or maintaining sleep in a young, healthy population.[58,61] In contrast, therapy should be started in the elderly with 5 mg doses because they are at greater risk of CNS adverse reactions. Confusion and falls have occurred in elderly patients taking 10 mg of zolpidem. The highest percentage of falls occurred at doses ≥20 mg.[58,59,63] Since E.P. is a 31-year-old, otherwise healthy individual, she should receive a zolpidem dose of 10 mg to be taken on an as needed basis for insomnia.

11. How should E.P. be counseled in order to experience maximum benefit from zolpidem with low risk of adverse effects?

Patient counseling is most effective when it is interactive. Interactive means both patient and practitioner are actively listening to each other while exchanging information. The practitioner asks questions to verify patient understanding and addresses specific patient concerns. In this interaction with E.P., the importance of consistently adhering to sleep fitness guidelines even though a prescription for zolpidem is available should be emphasized. The practitioner explains the directions and the rationale for selecting zolpidem (similar rapid onset and minimal daytime sedation with a lower risk of rebound anxiety and insomnia than triazolam). The practitioner recalls E.P.'s history of taking triazolam every night and emphasizes that zolpidem should be used occasionally, short-term, for a maximum of seven to ten days in the treatment of situational insomnia like hers. The possible adverse effects of zolpidem (nausea, dizziness, sleepiness, and headache) should be explained, and E.P. should be encouraged to report both effectiveness and all adverse effects. E.P. should be instructed not to increase her dose on her own and to consult her health care practitioner before mixing zolpidem with any new medication. Alcohol should be avoided due to the potential for an intensified sedative effect. The practitioner should conclude the patient counseling by advising E.P. to call if she has any questions or concerns.

In a Medically Ill Patient

Insomnia and Effect on Sleep Stages

12. A.T., a 42-year-old female with a 5-year history of hypothyroidism and a 3-month history of rheumatoid arthritis (RA), was just transferred out of the intensive care unit (ICU) into a medical unit. Her cardiac status is considered "stable" 10 days postmyocardial infarction (MI). She is 5′ 9″ tall and weighs 72 kg. She is receiving aspirin (enteric-coated), levothyroxine, and nifedipine during this hospitalization. Her main complaint is insomnia, difficulty falling asleep, difficulty maintaining sleep, and early morning awakenings. A.T. reports insomnia before admission which only worsened during the hospitalization. What type of insomnia does A.T. have and how might the insomnia affect her sleep cycle?

A.T. has a severe type of insomnia involving difficulty falling asleep, maintaining sleep, and early morning awakening. She has short-term to chronic insomnia because symptoms have been present for at least ten days during the hospitalization. The insomnia may be chronic if she experienced difficulty sleeping before admission. Since the normal sleep cycle moves through all the stages of NREM and REM sleep in a continuous cycle, a patient deprived of continuous sleep may not receive enough time in each sleep cycle. If stage 3 and 4 sleep are eliminated, the healing process can be disrupted. If REM sleep is deprived, neurotransmitter function may be altered and physiologic homeostatic processes may be disrupted. Research on sleep problems and myocardial infarction showed that an increase in insomnia predictably increased the risk of MI two weeks later.[3]

Drug/Disease Etiologies

13. What individual drug/disease state factors will you assess in A.T. before developing a treatment plan?

Numerous medical disorders are associated with difficulty falling asleep and maintaining sleep (see Table 74.4).[3,19] First of all, A.T. has rheumatoid arthritis and about 25% of these patients report restless nights three to four times a week. The insomnia may be related to the disorder itself or poor pain management.[3] In one rheumatology clinic, 29% of 127 patients were taking benzodiazepines for night pain and insomnia.[70] A.T.'s pain management should be assessed for optimal efficacy. Secondly, A.T. just came out of the intensive care unit. There is an alarmingly high rate of sleep deprivation in ICUs (20% to 60%) attributed to the continuous lighting, noise throughout day and night, and constant interventions.[3] Sleep deprivation may prolong or worsen a disease process by preventing healing which occurs during stages 3 and 4 of NREM sleep.[16,19,20] The irregular sleep in an ICU along with the recent trauma of a myocardial infarction may have disrupted A.T.'s natural sleep patterns, leading to persistent insomnia.

Medications also can be contributing to A.T.'s insomnia (see Table 74.4). Levothyroxine can overstimulate the central nervous system if given in excessive doses;[68,69] therefore, A.T.'s thyroid status should be re-evaluated to make sure the thyroid dose is appropriate, especially in the light of her postMI status. Nifedipine also has been associated with occasional sleep disturbances; therefore, it too should be ruled out as a contributing factor.[69] An interview with A.T. confirms chronic insomnia (i.e., insomnia present for >3 weeks) which often is related to multiple causes and can be resistant to treatment. Another clue to a possible cause of A.T.'s sleep problem is her description of early-morning awakening which could be related to hospital activity during these hours or to the presence of a major depressive disorder. A.T. will require psychiatric evaluation to rule out depression which occurs in 33% to 88% of postMI patients.[71] In general, patients with chronic illnesses are at increased risk of developing major depression. For

Table 74.4   Potential Causes of Chronic Sleep Disorders[a,68,69]

Psychiatric Disorders

Anxiety disorders	Depressive disorders
Bipolar disorder	Psychotic disorders
Personality disorders	Somatoform disorders
Organic mental disorder	Substance abuse

Medical/Neurological Disorders

Angina pectoris	Cancer
Bronchitis	Dementia
Chronic fatigue	PUD
Cystic fibrosis	Hyper- and hypothyroidism
Huntington's disease	Asthma
Parkinson's disease	COAD
Hypertension	Epilepsy
Arthritis	Gastroesophageal reflux
Cardiac disease	Renal insufficiency
Chronic pain	Connective tissue disease

Sleep Disorders

PLMS (nocturnal myoclonus)	Sleep apnea (obstructive or
Circadian Rhythm Sleep Disorder	central)
(jet lag, shift workers, delayed	Primary snoring
sleep phase)	

Drugs Associated with Sleep Disturbance

Insomnia	*Hypersomnia*
Alcohol	Alcohol
Bupropion	Benzodiazepines
Fluoxetine	Antihypertensives
Sertraline	Clonidine
MAOIs	α-adrenergic blockers
TCAs	ACE inhibitors
Thyroid supplements	Beta blockers
Calcium channel blockers	Anticonvulsants
Decongestants	Analgesics
Appetite suppressants	Chloral hydrate
Theophylline	Antipsychotics
Corticosteroids	Antihistamines
Dopamine agonists	Opioids

[a] ACE = Angiotensin-converting enzyme; COAD = Chronic obstructive airways disease; MAOIs = Monoamine oxidase inhibitors; PLMS = Periodic limb movements during sleep; PUD = Peptic ulcer disease; TCAs = Tricyclic antidepressants.

example, Parkinson's disease is associated with a 40% incidence of depression and a high prevalence of sleep disturbance even in those not suffering from depression.[3,19,72]

Comparing Available Hypnotics

14. An increase in A.T.'s aspirin dose has provided better pain control; her levothyroxine dose is determined to be appropriate and nifedipine-induced sleep disturbance has been ruled out. A psychiatric evaluation finds that A.T. does not have major depression but she is mildly anxious about "life after a heart attack." She continues to have trouble falling asleep and staying asleep. She will be discharged in 2 days. The pain management team suggests a benzodiazepine hypnotic because benzodiazepines are useful as adjuncts for better pain control.[73] Which hypnotic is best for A.T. considering her individual clinical characteristics?

The ideal hypnotic for A.T. should act quickly and continue working throughout the night to provide her with uninterrupted sleep. A hypnotic that is not metabolized in the liver would have a lower potential for drug interactions and lessen the opportunity for systemic accumulation. However, if daytime drug concentrations are needed to calm anxiety or aid in pain control, a hypnotic with slowly eliminated active metabolites may be desirable. The comparable doses of the hypnotic medications are listed in Table 74.5. When considering available hypnotic medications, differences in pharmacodynamic and pharmacokinetic properties (see Table 74.6) should be considered.

Onset of effect is related to lipophilicity, receptor-binding affinity, and time to maximum concentration.[35] Of the available benzodiazepines, midazolam (Versed) is the most lipophilic, reaching peak plasma concentrations within 45 minutes after intramuscular injection. It has the most rapid onset (5 to 15 minutes) and a short duration of action of about two hours (range: 1 to 6 hours). Midazolam's pharmacokinetic profile is optimal for rapidly inducing mild anesthesia with accompanying anterograde amnesia. For these reasons it is used parenterally as a premedication for surgical procedures.[74] As a hypnotic, midazolam would be expected to induce sleep quickly but not maintain sleep throughout the night, possibly resulting in rebound insomnia. Contrary to expectations, a comparative trial of midazolam 15 mg versus flurazepam 15 mg, flurazepam 30 mg, and placebo for 14 days in chronic insomniacs showed no difference in sleep maintenance throughout the night and no rebound insomnia.[75] The possible lower risk of rebound insomnia with midazolam when compared to triazolam may be related to triazolam's stronger binding affinity to the benzodiazepine-receptor complex.[49,50,76] Midazolam is not marketed or used as a hypnotic in the U.S. because it is available only parenterally. Therefore, it is not an option for A.T.

The pharmacodynamic and pharmacokinetic properties of triazolam (Halcion) and zolpidem (Ambien) have already been presented. They both have a rapid onset, an advantage for A.T.; however, the duration of action of both would not be long enough to help A.T. stay asleep. In addition, neither should be used for longer than seven to ten days due to the greater potential for adverse effects with prolonged use and the possibility of significant rebound insomnia upon withdrawal. Zolpidem appears to have a lower risk of rebound insomnia at this point, although tolerance and withdrawal problems have been reported after prolonged use over one to two months.[62] A.T. may require a hypnotic for a longer period of time.

Flurazepam (Dalmane) induces sleep within 15 to 45 minutes during chronic dosing. On the first night of use, however, flurazepam does not seem to induce sleep as well as triazolam, zolpidem, or midazolam. It has intermediate fat solubility but is dependent upon plasma concentrations of its metabolite, desalkylflurazepam, for most of its activity.[76] Desalkylflurazepam concentrations take approximately 24 hours to accumulate and induce sleep. Studies show flurazepam maintains efficacy in sleep induction for at least 30 days. Desalkylflurazepam has weak receptor binding affinity and a long half-life, resulting in gradual elimination from the system and little chance for rebound insomnia.[35,76] Desalkylflurazepam may accumulate during chronic dosing and can affect daytime cognition in some patients or compete for hepatic metabolism resulting in altered levels of other hepatically metabolized medications.[35,75-77] Accumulation and daytime sedation can be therapeutic for some patients with daytime anxiety. A.T. has difficulty moving around during the day because of her rheumatoid arthritis

Table 74.5   Hypnotic Dosing Comparison

Drug	Dose (mg)	Range (mg)
Midazolam (Versed)	15	10–30
Zolpidem (Ambien)	10	5–20
Triazolam (Halcion)	0.25	0.125–0.25
Temazepam (Restoril)	15	7.5–30
Estazolam (ProSom)	1	1–2
Flurazepam (Dalmane)	15	15–30
Quazepam (Doral)	15	7.5–30

Table 74.6			Pharmacokinetic Properties of Hypnotics Acting at Benzodiazepine Receptors[a]		
Active Substance	Lipid Solubility	T_{max} (hr)	Onset (min)	t$\frac{1}{2}$ (hr)	Duration (hr)[b]
Zolpidem	Low	1–2	30	2.5	2–4
Triazolam	Moderate	1	15–30	2–5	2–4
Temazepam	Moderate	1.5–2.0	60–120	10–20	8–12
Estazolam	Low	2	60–120	10–20	10–15
Flurazepam					
Hydroxyethyl-	Low	1	—	2–3	—
Aldehyde-	Low	1	—	1	—
N-desalkyl-	Moderate	10	30–60	50–100	10–30
Quazepam	High	2	30	20–40	10–30
2-oxo	High	2	30	20–40	—
N-desalkyl-flurazepam	Moderate	10	30–60	50–100	—

[a] T_{max}= Time of maximum concentration; t$\frac{1}{2}$ = Half-life.
[b] Time the patient feels the effects after a single dose; usually approximates t$\frac{1}{2}$ with multiple doses; interindividual variability exists; and tolerance may develop with continued use, lessening the duration.

and oversedation from accumulation may impair her daytime functioning. While flurazepam is a viable alternative, it is useful to explore other options.

Quazepam (Doral) is quite similar to flurazepam: both are hepatically metabolized to the same active metabolite, desalkylflurazepam. They have similar half-lives (30 to 100 hours) and can both accumulate under multiple dosing conditions, especially in the elderly or in those with hepatic or renal impairment. Neither are associated with REM rebound upon discontinuation.[35,77,78] However, quazepam and its minor active metabolite, 2-oxoquazepam, have considerably greater lipid solubility, thus a more rapid onset of effect (25 to 30 minutes) during the first night of use.[35,78] On subsequent nights, the difference in onset is insignificant. In addition, the specificity of quazepam and 2-oxoquazepam for the benzodiazepine-ω_1 receptor is distinctive.[79] Quazepam and 2-oxoquazepam remain in the system for a significant time period (t$\frac{1}{2}$ = 20 to 40 hours), yet their relative contributions to the clinical effects of quazepam are not established clearly.[34] One study in both young and elderly patient populations noted less daytime drowsiness and psychomotor impairment in patients taking quazepam when compared to those on flurazepam.[80] More studies are needed to confirm these findings and to clarify the possible clinical significance of benzodiazepine-ω_1 specificity. Quazepam is another consideration for A.T. due to its rapid onset and continued duration throughout the night.

Temazepam (Restoril) takes one to two hours to induce sleep. It has moderate fat solubility, similar to desalkylflurazepam, but it has a longer dissolution time. Temazepam takes one and one-half to two hours to reach peak plasma concentrations. Temazepam's longer dissolution time is due to its large drug particle size in a gelatin capsule. The European product formulation consisting of a solution in a wax matrix induces sleep in 30 minutes.[35,76] A potential advantage for using temazepam in A.T.'s case is its lack of hepatic metabolism and intermediate duration of action of 8 to 12 hours. It does not interfere with the metabolism of other hepatically metabolized drugs and it does not accumulate, minimizing the potential for daytime impairment.[81,82] The long onset of effectiveness may be of concern, although A.T. could take it one to two hours before bedtime to give it a chance to work.

Estazolam (ProSom) is similar to alprazolam (Xanax) and triazolam (Halcion) in chemical structure, as all are triazolobenzodiazepine derivatives. Pharmacokinetically, estazolam is more similar to temazepam. Estazolam reaches peak plasma concentration one and one-half to two hours after ingestion and is somewhat less fat soluble than temazepam. Like temazepam, it induces sleep in

one to two hours. Estazolam has an elimination half-life of 10 to 20 hours, also comparable to temazepam.[35] The difference is that estazolam is metabolized oxidatively in the liver and can accumulate in the elderly or in those with hepatic or renal impairment. Abrupt discontinuation can lead to transient rebound insomnia.[83] Estazolam has been studied mainly in patients with insomnia over a seven-day period. Efficacy and safety in chronic insomniacs are unknown.[84,85] Estazolam probably would not be a good choice for A.T. who suffers from chronic insomnia and may need a hypnotic for longer periods of time.

For A.T., the two most appropriate choices are temazepam and quazepam. Temazepam's advantages are intermediate activity keeping her asleep throughout the night and low risk of daytime impairment due to no known active metabolites. Quazepam's advantages are rapid onset of sleep induction and slow elimination, providing some daytime carryover which may be useful adjunctively to alleviate A.T.'s pain. A study examined the feasibility of an every-other-night regimen of quazepam designed to take advantage of carryover effects. On nights when quazepam was not taken, a decrease in time to sleep was noted. The 20 insomniacs taking quazepam did not experience daytime impairment. While further study of every-other-night regimens is needed, this strategy may prove useful for some patients.[86] Upon further discussion with A.T. and the pain management service, quazepam is selected. It is to be taken by A.T. for insomnia on an as-needed basis. The clinical team agrees upon the importance of her falling asleep quickly in order to avoid lying awake in pain. She has good hepatic function, so excessive buildup is not expected during intermittent use. A.T. will be monitored regularly as an outpatient.

Dependence and Tolerance

15. As A.T. is preparing to leave the hospital, her daughter B.T. expresses her concerns about the potential of physical dependence to quazepam and the risk of A.T. becoming an addict. How would you respond to her concerns?

Fear of dependence and addiction to medications is a current concern among the general public which, as a whole, is becoming more health conscious. It seems that every television station has a "medical expert," every popular magazine has a "health section," and every famous person who has ever had a drug problem has his story told on the evening news. Such publicity may increase the potential for confusion, erroneous impressions, and misinformation. For health care practitioners, it becomes even more crucial to provide sound drug information in common, easy to understand terms.

An example of the practitioner's response may be, "I'm glad you have expressed a concern; it gives us a chance to discuss quazepam therapy before your mother leaves the hospital. Quazepam has been prescribed for a medical reason, to improve your mother's sleep and to aid in her healing process. The therapeutic benefits of quazepam include its rapid onset, so your mother won't have to toss and turn trying to sleep as in the past. She will be able to sleep throughout the night so that she is well rested during the day. It also may decrease her anxiety over not sleeping and that puts less stress on her heart. The pain control specialists have recommended using this hypnotic because other hypnotics of the same type have helped with control of your mother's type of arthritis pain.''

''The possible side effects of quazepam include sedation, unsteadiness, and dizziness. She should let her doctor know if she experiences any adverse effects. Right now, it is unclear how long your mother will be taking quazepam. Duration of therapy will need to be assessed on an ongoing basis. If your mother takes quazepam every night for more than four weeks, two things could happen. One, she may develop a tolerance and it may not help her sleep anymore. Two, her system may develop a dependence where she may have worse insomnia if she does not take it. These two scenarios do not always occur and are not likely since your mother will be taking it on an as-needed basis. If one or the other does happen, some other intervention may be tried to help with her sleep or the quazepam can be tapered off slowly, preventing withdrawal problems. It is important to advise your mother to take the medication only as directed (no more or less), avoid alcohol, and report any decrease in effectiveness or adverse effects to her health care practitioner. Your mother, with no substance abuse history, is not likely to become an addict. Dependence is something to pay attention to, but what matters is the functional ability of the individual on and off the hypnotic.''

After discussing the information with B.T., the practitioner reviews the literature on benzodiazepine dependence and withdrawal. Epidemiologic data indicate that benzodiazepines are widely used by Americans primarily for brief periods of time, but are taken by a smaller number on a more chronic basis. Dependence can occur after continued use over a two- to four-month period.[83] Daily users for more than one year tend to be older, medically ill, chronically dysphoric, have panic disorder, or chronic insomnia. Most, but not all, chronic use appears to be medically appropriate and does not lead to dose escalation or abuse. Among chronic dysphoric patients, the indications are less clear, and dose escalation is noted sometimes without notable therapeutic benefit. Benzodiazepines rarely are taken alone for pleasure, and in general are not likely to be abused. Among substance abusers, however, they frequently are taken as part of a polysubstance abuse pattern by alcoholics, narcotics and methadone users, and cocaine users. In these groups, abuse is highly prevalent. Benzodiazepines are used to augment euphoria (narcotics and methadone users), decrease anxiety and withdrawal symptoms (alcoholics), and to ease the ''crash'' from stimulant-induced euphoria.[34,87]

Physiologic dependence, resulting in a withdrawal and abstinence syndrome, develops to benzodiazepines usually after two to four months of daily use of the longer half-life benzodiazepines. There is some evidence that shorter half-life benzodiazepine use can result in physiologic dependence earlier (days to weeks) and may be associated with more withdrawal problems.[47,49,88–90] (See Table 74.6 for a comparison of pharmacokinetic properties of hypnotics.)

In Psychiatric Disorders

Stepwise Approach to Selecting a Hypnotic

16. P.H., a 35-year-old male, is hospitalized after a suicide attempt with an amphetamine and alcohol overdose 1 week ago. Before the overdose attempt, P.H. had been ''clean'' (i.e., abstinent) and sober for 2 years. He is diagnosed with major depression and organic mood disorder secondary to psychoactive substance abuse. His target symptoms include a 20-pound weight loss, low energy, social withdrawal, depressed mood, hopelessness, inability to experience pleasure, trouble falling asleep, and early morning awakening. His medications include, fluoxetine (Prozac) 20 mg QD, ranitidine (Zantac) 150 mg BID, and a multivitamin QD, all started 5 days ago. After completing your interview with P.H., you learn that he was doing well until 2 months ago when his significant other left him and he became increasingly depressed. He began to attend Alcoholics Anonymous groups more regularly but his depression worsened. Two weeks before admission, he went on a drinking binge which led to the suicide attempt. P.H. reports feeling restless and sleeping only 3–4 hours a night. What could be one general approach to solving sleep problems such as that of P.H.?

Use Table 74.7 to compare the clinically significant differences of available hypnotics and to demonstrate how such information can be used to develop patient-specific treatment plans.

This stepped process serves as a useful guide for applying the information to an individual patient. Once the type of insomnia is known (DFA, DMS, EMA), possible causes must be identified and treated. Before a hypnotic is prescribed, behavioral interventions ''sleep fitness'' should be implemented. At step three, if significant insomnia persists despite sleep fitness, a medication can be considered.

Step four lists factors to consider in the drug selection process. For example, agents with long-acting metabolites (flurazepam, quazepam) may accumulate or cause daytime hangover and therefore if a person is elderly, in general, it is best to avoid flurazepam and quazepam. If the hypnotic has no hepatic metabolism, it will not be subject to drug interactions with other agents which are hepatically metabolized. If insomnia is chronic and resistant to hypnotic treatment, or if low to no potential for abuse is desired (e.g., person with existing addictive disorder), trazodone or a tricyclic antidepressant (TCA) may be selected.

Sleep Disturbance of Depression

17. What type of insomnia does P.H. have and how is it different from other types of insomnia?

P.H. has trouble falling asleep, early morning awakening, and decreased sleep time to three or four hours a night. He is diagnosed with major depression and sleep difficulty is part of the disorder. The typical type of insomnia that is associated with depression generally is initial insomnia and early-morning awakening. P.H. has both.

The insomnia of depression probably is related to a dysregulation of neurotransmitters such as serotonin, norepinephrine, or even dopamine. All are involved in regulating the sleep/wake cycle.[16,21] Neurotransmitter activity is modified by the effects of antidepressants on REM sleep. Most effective antidepressants suppress REM, causing increased REM latency and decreased total REM time.[91] Indeed, REM sleep deprivation can elevate mood.[92] Depressed patients deliberately deprived of REM sleep have shown improvement in depressive symptoms. In addition to effects on REM, antidepressants redistribute slow-wave sleep to more physiologically natural patterns, with increased intensity in the first half of the night.[91]

Causes: Psychiatric and Substance Abuse

18. What other factors may be contributing to insomnia in P.H.? How can his sleep problem be solved?

P.H. has been prescribed fluoxetine to treat his depression. Fluoxetine can cause insomnia in 10% to 20% of patients[93] and should

Table 74.7		Stepwise Approach to Selecting a Hypnotic for Insomnia[a]		
	Step 1. Determine type of insomnia: DFA, DMS, EMA, duration			
	Step 2. Consider possible etiologies: medical, psychiatric, drug; treat causes			
	Step 3. Sleep fitness ineffective or only partially effective, significant insomnia persists			
	Step 4. Assess type of patient: age, size, diagnosis, organ function, drug interactions, abuse potential			

	Type of Insomnia		
Treatment Options	DFA	DMS	EMA
Antidepressants	*Duration of Therapy:* Chronic use in depressive diagnosis *Onset and Duration of Effects:* Intermediate to long onset *Pharmacokinetic Considerations:* See individual antidepressant *Clinical Considerations:* Substance abuse; treatment-resistant insomnia		*Duration of Therapy:* Chronic use in depressive diagnosis *Onset and Duration of Effects:* Intermediate to long onset *Pharmacokinetic Considerations:* See individual antidepressant *Clinical Considerations:* Substance abuse; treatment-resistant insomnia
Chloral Hydrate	*Duration of Therapy:* Short-term use, 2–7 days *Onset and Duration of Effects:* Rapid onset; intermediate duration *Pharmacokinetic Considerations:* Major metabolite, trichloroethanol, is active *Clinical Considerations:* GI side effects; rapid tolerance; no EEG effects; drug interactions		
Estazolam		*Duration of Therapy:* Short-term and chronic *Onset and Duration of Effects:* Long onset; moderate duration *Clinical Considerations:* Hepatic metabolism	
Flurazepam or Quazepam	*Duration of Therapy:* Short-term and chronic *Onset and Duration of Effects:* Rapid onset; long duration *Pharmacokinetic Considerations:* Active metabolite *Clinical Considerations:* Efficacy long-term	*Duration of Therapy:* Short-term and chronic *Onset and Duration of Effects:* Rapid onset; long duration *Pharmacokinetic Considerations:* Active metabolite *Clinical Considerations:* Efficacy long-term	
Temazepam		*Duration of Therapy:* Short-term and chronic *Onset and Duration of Effects:* Long onset; moderate duration *Pharmacokinetic Considerations:* No hepatic metabolism	
Zolpidem or Triazolam	*Duration of Therapy:* Short-term use, 7–10 days *Onset and Duration of Effects:* Rapid onset; short duration *Pharmacokinetic Considerations:* Short half-life *Clinical Considerations:* Rebound insomnia; CNS side effects		

[a] CNS = Central nervous system; DFA = Difficulty falling asleep; DMS = Difficulty maintaining sleep; EEG = Electroencephalogram; EMA = Early morning awakening; GI = Gastrointestinal.

be dosed in the morning for this reason. P.H. also was abusing alcohol and stimulants before admission. Drug withdrawal and the lingering ''abstinence syndromes'' frequently are associated with insomnia, although sometimes hypersomnia is the predominant symptom.[87,94]

Treatment

The treatment of P.H.'s insomnia should begin with patient education. P.H. should be informed that almost all depressed patients have trouble sleeping, either too little or too much, and his sleep should improve after the depression clears (over 2 to 6 weeks). Sleep fitness counseling may be appropriate when P.H.'s depression begins to clear and P.H. is more motivated to help himself sleep better. In the meantime, the potential contribution of fluoxetine to his restlessness or insomnia should be assessed by confirming that the drug is being dosed in the early morning to minimize this effect.

Hypnotics. Prescribing a hypnotic usually is inappropriate for depressed patients because improvement in insomnia is a useful clinical marker to assess antidepressant response. Even with less sedating, more activating antidepressants like fluoxetine, sleep will improve as the depression lifts. Furthermore, the addition of a benzodiazepine hypnotic to a sedating antidepressant may cause additive CNS depression and lead to excessive side effects.[95]

Another reason why a benzodiazepine hypnotic is not a good choice for P.H. is his drug abuse history. Benzodiazepines can have a euphoriant effect, are cross-tolerant with alcohol, and are likely to be abused in patients with substance abuse problems.[87,94] If the clinician determines P.H.'s insomnia is worse because of fluoxetine treatment, trazodone may be added. When trazodone 25 to 75 mg is added to a monoamine oxidase inhibitor, fluoxetine, bupropion, or other antidepressants, time to sleep is decreased and patients sleep better through the night. The addition of trazodone to other antidepressants caused intolerable grogginess in a high percentage of fluoxetine-treated patients. Tolerance did not develop to the sedative effects of trazodone.[96,97]

Trazodone's sedative effects have been evaluated in other patient subtypes. In one trial evaluating depressed insomniacs on no other medication, trazodone improved both sleep and mood.[98] Another study found trazodone was effective for treating insomnia and depression in ten benzodiazepine-dependent patients.[99] The serotonin antagonist properties of trazodone at low dosages and its α-adrenergic blocking effects provide the probable rationale for its efficacy as a sedating agent. When compared to the tricyclic antidepressant trimipramine over five days in a sleep laboratory, trazodone (50 to 200 mg) significantly increased the percentage of time spent in slow-wave or deep sleep in healthy volunteers not suffering from insomnia.[100] Although more controlled studies are needed to assess the overall hypnotic efficacy of trazodone in the treatment of depressed patients with chronic insomnia, trazodone would be preferred over a benzodiazepine as treatment for P.H.'s sleep disorder.

19. Antidepressants. What antidepressants other than trazodone are effective in the treatment of insomnia? Discuss the pros and cons of using other sedating antidepressants for the treatment of insomnia in P.H.

Tricyclic antidepressants (e.g., amitriptyline, doxepin) are used routinely to treat primary insomnia despite the lack of controlled clinical trials testing their efficacy in a nondepressed insomniac population. Case reports describe the effectiveness of amitriptyline, for example, in doses ranging from 10 to 75 mg, in treating primary chronic insomnia.[101,102] The main objection to using tricyclics in the treatment of insomnia is based upon the exploitation of an unevaluated side effect, sedation, to treat a symptom of an unknown condition. Tricyclic antidepressants increase the risk of cardiovascular problems and anticholinergic side effects (see Chapter 76: Mood Disorders I: Major Depressive Disorders). In addition, there are no data indicating tricyclic antidepressants are as effective and safe as benzodiazepine hypnotics. Nevertheless, experts in the treatment of primary insomnia have recommended trying low doses of tricyclic antidepressants when primary insomnia has been resistant to other therapies.[102]

For P.H., tricyclic antidepressants raise additional safety concerns. P.H. has a history of substance abuse and prior suicide attempts. Both are risk factors for future suicide attempts. Tricyclic antidepressants are more toxic upon overdose when compared to trazodone and there are multiple reports of tricyclic antidepressant plasma levels increasing to toxic levels when administered in combination with fluoxetine (see Chapter 76: Mood Disorders I: Major Depressive Disorders).

In the Elderly
Patient Assessment

20. S.B., a 76-year-old female, just moved to a skilled nursing facility from her daughter's home because her family could not take care of her. She was unable to sleep at night and paced the house. Six weeks ago, she fell and broke a hip. She had a total hip replacement and uses a walker now. S.B. takes the following medications: salsalate 750 mg BID, lorazepam 0.5 mg TID, hydrochlorothiazide 12.5 mg Q PM, K-DUR 20 mEq QD, hydroxyzine 50 mg Q AM, and Senokot 1 tablet Q AM and Q HS. Flurazepam 15 mg Q HS has just been prescribed to treat insomnia, first dose to start tonight. What additional information is needed in order to evaluate S.B.'s sleep problem?

So far, it is unclear what type of insomnia S.B. suffers from: difficulty falling asleep, staying asleep, early morning awakening, or just overall less restful sleep. Learning the type of insomnia will help solve the problem. Next, as discussed in previous cases, there are many possible causes of sleep problems (e.g., disease states, medications, psychosocial factors, poor sleeping habits). The usual thorough evaluation is needed to understand the etiology of S.B.'s sleep disorder, after which her medication regimen can be optimized.

21. S.B. typifies the nursing home patient, struggling with medical problems and adjusting psychologically to new life situations. Upon review of the progress notes in the medical record, the consultant discovers S.B.'s type of insomnia is described as difficulty falling asleep and maintaining sleep. S.B. is charted as "stable" medically with satisfactory pain control and no major psychiatric diagnosis. The progress notes do mention situational anxiety secondary to her move to the nursing home. Lorazepam (Ativan) was prescribed 3 days ago to treat the anxiety. No side effects had been documented in the chart (i.e., the medical record) but the nursing notes describe S.B. taking 2-hour naps 2–3 times a day and awakening nightly 2–3 times to urinate. What should be considerations for treating insomnia in an elderly patient like S.B.?

Age-Related Effects on Sleep

S.B.'s age is an important consideration because sleep is qualitatively and even quantitatively different in the elderly. There are fewer cycles into slow-wave sleep, more frequent awakenings, and increased reports of early morning awakenings.[11,16] A survey of 430 elderly (ages 65–84) noted that difficulty in maintaining sleep was the most common type of insomnia experienced by 37% of the men and 30% of the women.[12] The most common reasons given for the difficulty maintaining sleep were breathing difficulties (75%), pain (67%), and muscle cramps (63%). Higher incidences of sleep-related respiratory disturbances and *periodic leg movements* in the elderly have been documented in other studies.[103–105] These two conditions are so prevalent that they may be solely responsible for the "lighter sleep" and increased awakenings experienced by older individuals. The proportion of sleep time spent in REM does not appear to change significantly with aging, although there are some reports of increased time in the first cycle of REM with overall decrease in REM time.[11]

Elderly individuals with chronic illness or social isolation report significantly more problems with sleep than those who are actively involved (e.g., club membership, religion, work) or have a close friend.[1,3,11,14] Anxiety and depression often are associated with insomnia, and the elderly tend to be more susceptible to anxieties and depression as they cope with bereavement, retirement, financial security, and social losses. All of the above factors can contribute to poor sleep in the elderly. The elderly also are more likely to experience illness than younger individuals and illnesses can worsen sleep problems.[3,19,20] An often overlooked problem in the elderly is an alarmingly high rate of alcohol and drug abuse.[106] Alcohol ingestion is associated with more fragmented, poor-quality sleep.[94]

Age-Related Effects on Hypnotic Disposition

Pharmacokinetic and Pharmacodynamic Differences. Insomnia is not an easy problem to solve for most elderly patients due to the complex causes and potential risks of drug treatment. Risks can be minimized by consideration of the pharmacodynamic and pharmacokinetic differences in the way aged bodies respond to drugs. Pharmacodynamically, small amounts of drug can elicit pronounced pharmacological effects in the elderly, and pharmacokinetic differences greatly affect the amount of drug available at the receptor site.[82,107] Absorption of benzodiazepines can be decreased by diminished gastric acidity and decreased gut motility. The volume of distribution of a hypnotic drug can be affected because the elderly may have increased or decreased plasma proteins depending upon whether they have inflammatory disease or poor nutrition. Excessive fat stores can increase the volume of tissue available for the drug to redistribute.[82,107] Oxidative metabolism might be compromised in the elderly; however, results from several studies show no age-related change in oxidative metabolism.[108] Hypnotic drugs that undergo oxidative biotransformation (e.g., flurazepam, quazepam) probably accumulate more as a result of competition for hepatic metabolism and a decline in renal function than to changes in oxidative metabolism. Elderly patients typically are on multiple drugs competing for metabolism in the liver. Excretion of more hydrophilic active metabolites can be slowed in the elderly secondary to a well-documented age-related decline in renal function.[82,108]

22. Other Drugs Used as Hypnotics. **What are the potential problems with S.B.'s current medication regimen and what changes are needed?**

S.B. is receiving lorazepam three times daily and hydroxyzine every morning. The hydroxyzine can exert intense, long-lasting sedation in the elderly and, when combined with multiple daily doses of lorazepam, probably is capable of inducing her frequent daytime naps.[109] One short nap during the day often is the norm for elderly people and usually does not impair nocturnal sleep, but multiple naps during the day could prevent S.B. from sleeping through the night.[11] Although lorazepam is not marketed as a hypnotic, it possesses sedative effects like all benzodiazepine compounds. Lorazepam does not undergo oxidative hepatic metabolism and interacts only with a few drugs. It has an intermediate elimination half-life of 10 to 20 hours which could help S.B. maintain sleep, and it has no active metabolites to accumulate.[82] Since S.B. currently is taking lorazepam for anxiety, a change in her dosing schedule from 0.5 mg three times daily to 0.5 mg every morning and 1 mg every night may be useful in shifting daytime sedation more towards bedtime to help S.B. initiate sleep and maintain sleep throughout the night. The risk versus benefit of hydroxyzine should be assessed and subsequently discontinued if at all possible, because hydroxyzine can impair cognition as a result of central anticholinergic activity in addition to its contribution to excessive daytime sedation.

Flurazepam has been prescribed for S.B. Long-acting benzodiazepines such as flurazepam can accumulate and have been implicated in causing falls in geriatric patients.[110] Some investigators found no association between benzodiazepines and falls,[111,112] and one study of 280 women with hip fractures noted that "fallers" were more likely to be taking a diuretic than other medications.[112] Nevertheless, flurazepam probably is a bad choice for S.B. who cannot take the chance of daytime loss of coordination while recovering from her total hip replacement surgery. Her flurazepam should be discontinued because her increased evening dose of lorazepam may be sufficient to resolve her sleeping difficulties when combined with these other interventions.

S.B. also takes her thiazide diuretic in the evening which may be exacerbating her nocturia. Since nocturia is a prevalent cause of sleep disruption in the elderly,[11] her hydrochlorothiazide dose should be changed to morning administration.

Rebound Insomnia and Withdrawal Symptoms

23. An attendant at a skilled nursing facility seeks assistance for 1 of his patients by presenting the following problem: "L.R. really has been complaining since his sleeping medication was changed. He is agitated, irritable, sweaty, and tosses and turns all night barely sleeping. I have even noticed some blood pressure and pulse fluctuations. He was taking flurazepam 15 mg Q PM for many years and about a week ago his new doctor discontinued the flurazepam and started zolpidem 5 mg. Do you think it could be due to the medication change?" What is causing L.R.'s symptoms?

L.R. is experiencing symptoms of benzodiazepine withdrawal. He took flurazepam every night for years and apparently developed a physical dependence. Withdrawal reactions are more common with short half-life benzodiazepines such as triazolam, but long half-life drugs such as flurazepam also can elicit withdrawal responses.[88,89,113] With long half-life drugs, the withdrawal symptoms typically occur later, one to two weeks after drug discontinuation. The lag time is due to the slow elimination of flurazepam. Zolpidem is cross-tolerant with benzodiazepines, including flurazepam. However, it could not prevent the withdrawal reaction because it was given in a significantly lower relative dose. In addition, zolpidem is metabolized and eliminated rapidly.

24. What therapeutic interventions should be initiated to manage L.R.'s withdrawal symptoms and rebound insomnia?

A slow, gradual dosage reduction is better tolerated by patients than immediate benzodiazepine discontinuation. Since L.R. is experiencing withdrawal symptoms, his nightly flurazepam should be restarted. Once the withdrawal symptoms (e.g., agitation, irritability, autonomic fluctuations, insomnia) are gone and L.R. is comfortable, his physician can discuss the gradual dosage reduction process with him. The gradual discontinuation of flurazepam in L.R. should begin by administering the flurazepam every other night. Subsequently, the flurazepam should be administered every few nights until L.R. no longer needs the medication. The withdrawal process may require several weeks. Unfortunately, the physical withdrawal he experienced may contribute to his becoming psychologically dependent upon the flurazepam. L.R. needs reassurance, and he should be taught sleep fitness guidelines.[87]

Sleep Apnea
Clinical Presentation

25. O.R., a 58-year-old male, presents to an ambulatory care clinic complaining of chronic fatigue, low energy, excessive snoring, and overall less restful sleep. He describes his sleep: "It feels like I'm just skimming the surface of sleep, I'm tired all day, and my wife says my snoring keeps her awake." His symptoms have worsened over the past year and a half since mandatory retirement, and he has gained some weight since then. O.R.'s vital signs are normal; however, his BP reading is borderline high 140/90 mm Hg. O.R. currently is taking TheoDur 300 mg BID and uses Ventolin inhaler PRN for wheezing. He is on a 3 gm sodium diet to control mild essential hypertension. What are the possible causes of O.R.'s sleep disorder and why is it important for O.R. to have his problem evaluated in a sleep laboratory?

O.R. reports diminished sleep quality, excessive snoring, and weight gain. While a number of causes could be responsible for

O.R.'s symptoms, one of the most serious is sleep apnea. Sleep apnea is a neurological disorder characterized by mini-episodes of cessation of breathing which may occur 10 to 200 times an hour. The brain responds to these episodes with "miniarousals," waking the patient up to stimulate breathing.[16,40] These frequent mini-arousals prevent the patient from obtaining quality sleep by not allowing sufficient time in deep, slow-wave sleep or REM. If sleep apnea is not the cause, it could be an anatomical problem made worse by weight gain. The extra weight places pressure on the throat and uvula narrowing the space into which air must travel; this results in the difficulty in breathing and excessive snoring. Another issue is O.R.'s airway disease and whether his obstructive airway disease allows enough air to get into his lungs to allow him to sleep undisturbed. His airway disease, therefore, should be evaluated.

O.R.'s hypertension may be a factor contributing to his problem, particularly if it is poorly controlled. Several studies show an increased risk of sleep apnea in hypertensive patients. Although sleep apnea occurs in approximately 2% of the general population, it occurs in up to 30% of patients with hypertension.[40,114] A study of several patient groups with sleep apnea showed that the hypertensive patients whose blood pressures were within the desired range had significantly less apneic episodes than those whose blood pressure remained high.[115] The same study found that the patients with controlled hypertension and fewer apneic episodes also had fewer penile erectile episodes. Several characteristics (e.g., aging, obesity, male gender, erectile episodes) are common to both sleep apnea and hypertension. O.R.'s hypertension should be evaluated and his sleep should be monitored by polysomnography (i.e., EEG, EOG, EMG) overnight in a sleep laboratory to record the sleep stages and episodes of breathing cessation which can be life-threatening in some cases.

Drug Treatment Considerations

26. O.R.'s airway disease was evaluated and found to be stable and well controlled by medication. His last BP readings were 150/100, 160/95, and 150/95 mm Hg, and an antihypertensive medication is being considered. Results from the sleep laboratory study clearly document O.R.'s problem as obstructive sleep apnea. He experiences apneic episode on the average of 56/hr. O.R.'s weight gain and inactivity probably contribute to the problem. Another, less common type of apnea is central sleep apnea. Central sleep apnea patients lack respiratory effort and frequently gasp for air during the night. Central sleep apnea frequently occurs along with obstructive sleep apnea. Both are serious, potentially life-threatening conditions. Why should O.R.'s sleeping difficulties not be treated with a hypnotic medication?

Hypnotics, alcohol, or any CNS depressant can be deadly for sleep apnea patients and should not be prescribed for O.R. CNS depressants interfere with the "miniarousals" required to stimulate breathing once it has stopped. In this case, the $1500 to $2000 sleep laboratory study may have saved O.R. from a potential life-threatening breathing disorder that could have been precipitated by a CNS depressant.

Obstructive sleep apnea can be treated by tracheostomy, nasal surgery, tonsillectomy, uvulopalatoplasty, and by continuous positive airway pressure.[40] Currently, CPAP therapy is in vogue: the patient wears a light-weight mask to bed each night and a constant flow of air is provided mechanically to prevent breathing cessation and allow for more restful sleep.[116] Although CPAP is very effective, the results are short-lived and apneic episodes typically reappear when continuous positive airway pressure therapy is stopped. Weight loss could be beneficial for O.R.'s hypertension and sleep apnea, and the combination of weight loss and CPAP can produce lasting antiapneic results.[117]

27. If weight loss, surgery, and CPAP all are ineffective or impractical, what drug treatments are potentially effective for O.R.'s sleep apnea?

Protriptyline, medroxyprogesterone, theophylline, and acetazolamide have been used successfully in the treatment of sleep apnea.[38] Protriptyline 10 to 30 mg/day, decreases apneic episodes by decreasing REM sleep caused by oxygen desaturation. Unfortunately, the protriptyline-mediated decrease in apneic episodes is statistically significant, but not clinically significant for most patients.[118] Medroxyprogesterone and theophylline can increase respiratory drive; however, the results usually are not clinically significant.[40] O.R. experienced apneic episodes while taking theophylline (TheoDur); therefore, nondrug therapy is more promising for O.R. than drug therapy.

Narcolepsy

Narcolepsy is a disorder characterized by two main features: irrepressible sleep attacks and cataplexy. REM sleep episodes, known as "sleep attacks," can intrude at any time upon the narcoleptic's waking state. Cataplexy is the loss of muscle tone in the face or limb muscles and often is induced by emotions or laughter. Cataplexy can be subtle where the patient is limp and not moving, or dramatic where the narcoleptic collapses to the floor.[39] Hypnagogic hallucinations and sleep paralysis are other secondary symptoms not present in all narcoleptics. Hypnagogic hallucinations are perceptual disturbances (i.e., auditory, visual, tactile) which occur while experiencing a "sleep attack." The patient may see objects, hear sounds, or feel sensations that are not occurring in reality. Sleep paralysis is a terrifying experience that may occur upon falling asleep or upon awakening. Patients are unable to move their limbs, to speak, or even breathe deeply. Fortunately, narcoleptics learn that sleep paralysis episodes are benign and brief (lasting <10 minutes).[120]

Symptoms of narcolepsy often begin at puberty, but usually patients are not diagnosed until years later in their late teens or early twenties. Early symptoms consist of excessive daytime sleepiness and poor sleep quality. The narcoleptic's sleep cycle becomes progressively more erratic with frequent bursts of REM and decreased regularity of deep or slow-wave sleep. Narcolepsy is thought to stem from genetic or early developmental abnormalities in catecholamine regulation within the brain.[39,120]

Comparing Treatments

Methylphenidate (Ritalin) and dextroamphetamine (Dexedrine) were the first drugs used to treat narcolepsy and still are considered the most effective by many patients who notice an alerting effect within hours after taking a dose. Pemoline (Cylert) also is used, but it is less effective and therapeutic effects can be delayed for a few weeks. These stimulant drugs decrease the number of sleep attacks, improve task performance, and increase the time to fall asleep, but cannot eliminate sleep attacks altogether. Cataplexy does not respond to stimulants but can be treated effectively with low doses of antidepressants. Imipramine and clomipramine were the first antidepressants used, but protriptyline, desipramine, and even newer agents like fluoxetine also are effective. The effectiveness of antidepressants for treatment of cataplexy is due to their noradrenergic reuptake blocking effects and REM suppressant effects. Unfortunately, antidepressants are not effective in decreasing sleep attacks.[39,120]

Methylphenidate versus Imipramine

28. G.B., a 23-year-old narcoleptic male, is receiving methylphenidate extended-release (Ritalin SR) 20 mg BID and imipramine 75 mg Q HS to treat his narcolepsy and cataplexy.

What are the potential risks of using both methylphenidate and imipramine to treat G.B.?

Anorexia, stomach pain, nervousness, irritability, and headaches are common side effects of stimulant drugs.[39] Psychotic reactions also can occur in narcoleptic patients taking stimulants; however, these symptoms resolve when the stimulant is discontinued. Hypertension and abnormal liver function are more serious complications of long-term stimulant use. Stimulants, even at high doses (e.g., 80 mg methylphenidate), usually do not bring a narcoleptic to a normal level of alertness, and sometimes nocturnal sleep is disrupted. To prevent stimulant-induced insomnia, doses should be taken before 3:00 p.m. The extended-release preparations should be taken eight hours apart to prevent excessive accumulation of drug.[121] Unfortunately, tolerance may develop to the therapeutic effects of stimulants in some patients with narcolepsy.[120] Drug holidays sometimes can allow the patient to recapture therapeutic benefit. Nevertheless, it can be troubling for the patient when the drug stops working.

Imipramine, like all tricyclic antidepressants, can cause orthostatic hypotension, anticholinergic side effects, sedation, cardiac conduction changes, and periodic limb movements. In addition, G.B.'s imipramine therapy will be more complex because methylphenidate can inhibit the metabolism of imipramine, resulting in higher levels of imipramine.[121] G.B. should be monitored closely during the initiation of imipramine therapy and imipramine plasma levels should be assessed to minimize side effects and prevent toxicity. The optimal therapeutic plasma concentration of imipramine for treatment of cataplexy has not been established, but clearly, low doses are effective and risk of toxicity from imipramine increases when serum imipramine concentrations are greater than 300 ng/mL.

Naps and Other Behavioral Interventions

29. The benefits, possible risks, and importance of regular physician assessment have been explained to G.B. and he agrees to report efficacy and adverse effects to his primary care provider regularly. G.B.'s last imipramine level 2 weeks ago on the lower methylphenidate dose was 115 ng/mL and G.B. is reminded to take the medicine at regular intervals along with daytime naps. Why are naps helpful in the treatment of G.B. and what other behavioral interventions are useful in treating narcolepsy?

Strategically timed 15- to 20-minute naps taken at lunch and then again at 5:30 p.m. can be refreshing for narcoleptics and increase their time between "sleep attacks." Narcolepsy support groups are available and may help G.B. better cope with such a life-changing chronic illness. It also is important for G.B. to avoid alcohol and regulate his bedtime and wake-up time in attempt to normalize his sleep habits.[120]

Other Agents

30. What other treatments are being investigated for narcolepsy?

Methamphetamine, a longer-acting, more potent dextroamphetamine analog is effective for narcolepsy and it may be taken once or twice a day. Unfortunately, methamphetamine has the same potential problems of adverse effects, tolerance, and abuse as the currently used stimulants.[122] Gamma-hydroxybutyrate, a shortchain fatty acid used as an anesthetic in Europe, is effective for both narcolepsy and cataplexy but is not approved for use in the U.S.[123] Another investigational agent not available in the U.S. is modafinil. Modafinil, an investigational α-adrenergic agonist is effective in increasing wakefulness.[120] L-dopa may improve daytime alertness but it does not alter sleep structure or objective measures of alertness.[124] Bromocriptine has mixed results in improving narcolepsy but may be effective for periodic leg movements in sleep or restless legs syndrome (RLS).[125]

31. Ever since G.B.'s imipramine dose was increased about a month ago, he has been awakened by occasional leg cramps. What is the relationship of G.B.'s new symptom to his disorders?

Narcolepsy is associated with a higher incidence of periodic limb movements during sleep. Also, imipramine and other medications in the same family can cause leg movements during sleep. Sometimes a dose adjustment downward will alleviate the problem.

Periodic Limb Movements of Sleep (PLMS)

Patients with restless legs syndrome have paresthesias occurring at rest that induce an irresistible urge to move. RLS occurs during wakefulness but often occurs with periodic limb movements during sleep. PLMS, also known as nocturnal myoclonus, are repetitive, stereotypic flexions of the hips, knees, and ankles that recur at regular intervals of 5 to 90 seconds.[36] The severity of these symptoms can wax and wane over a lifetime. Sudden remissions, which may last for months or even years, are as difficult to explain as relapses, which appear without any apparent reason. RLS and PLMS can occur in any age group but may be most common in the elderly.[99] PLMS results in frequent awakenings and less restful sleep. Sufferers report daytime sleepiness and impaired functioning.

Treatment

There are three categories of drug treatment options for RLS and PLMS symptoms: benzodiazepines, dopaminergic agents, and opioids. Benzodiazepines, particularly clonazepam (Klonopin), are considered first-line therapy for most patients with PLMS who need drug treatment;[16,36] however, small studies (6 patients) suggest clonazepam may not be better than placebo. In most clinical trials, both clonazepam and temazepam (Restoril) increased the total sleep time and reduced the number of arousals and awakenings associated with leg jerks more than the number of leg movements. While any benzodiazepine may improve RLS, clonazepam has been studied most extensively. About 55% of RLS patients report initial satisfactory therapeutic response to clonazepam at doses of 0.5 to 1.0 mg/day. The most common adverse effects to clonazepam were excessive daytime somnolence and decreased libido.[38] There is some evidence to suggest that short half-life (≥5 hours) benzodiazepines may contribute to confusional states and nocturnal wandering in RLS patients. If benzodiazepines are used to treat RLS and PLMS, intermediate to long half-life medications such as clonazepam should be used.[126]

Dopaminergic agents such as levodopa with carbidopa (Sinemet) and bromocriptine can decrease the number of restless and jerky movements of RLS and PLMS. Unfortunately, the effects are short-lived and patients exhibit rebound symptoms during the last third of the night unless a middle-of-the-night dose is given.[127] Patients also may complain of insomnia when treated with levodopa. Dopaminergic agonists frequently have an alerting or stimulating effect. Currently, selegiline (Eldepryl), a monoamine oxidase type B inhibitor, has demonstrated some efficacy in small numbers of patients with RLS and PLMS. Selegiline interferes with the breakdown of dopamine and also can produce an alerting effect. Dopaminergic agonists are not effective for patients with Parkinson's disease and PLMS, possibly due to the more profound dopaminergic dysfunction associated with Parkinson's.[38,128]

Propoxyphene and other opioids have been used in small numbers of patients with mixed results. There appears to be a subgroup of patients who respond well to opioids. However, the risk for abuse and addiction may limit their clinical utility. If opioids are used, low doses (e.g., 100 to 300 mg/night of propoxyphene) should be used with frequent monitoring to detect adverse effects, tolerance, and potential for abuse. Adverse affects may include constipation, sedation, or nausea.[128]

Pediatric Insomnia

Chloral hydrate has been used extensively for many years in both children and adults for its sedative effect, with relatively low associated toxicity. There are several reasons for its widespread use: rapid onset, moderate duration, and lack of significant effects on the EEG. Chloral hydrate induces sedation and allows brain wave assessment without drug interference.[129]

Some concern has been raised over the risk of carcinogenicity of choral hydrate. The concern stems from the assumption that chloral hydrate is a metabolite of trichloroethylene. Although trichloroethylene, an industrial solvent, has been linked to liver tumors in mice when given in high doses over a two-year period, chloral hydrate-associated carcinogenicity in humans has not been established. In addition, multiple epidemiologic studies in humans have failed to document an increase in cancer incidence associated with trichloroethylene exposure, although the ability of these studies to detect small increases in risk of cancer is limited.[130]

Therapeutic effects and known potential toxicities from chloral hydrate are associated with its two active metabolites, trichloroethanol and trichloroacetic acid. A single dose of trichloroethanol, the metabolite responsible for sedation, induces sedation within 30 minutes and has a usual duration of action of four to eight hours, similar to its half-life of 8 to 11 hours in adults. The half-life can be longer, 9 to 40 hours in children depending upon the age and maturity of the patient. Trichloroacetic acid is a minor metabolite which does not achieve significant levels in most patients after a single dose. Upon multiple dosing, trichloroacetic acid can displace bilirubin or warfarin from albumin binding sites, potentially resulting in hyperbilirubinemia or hypoprothrombinemia.[130,131] The half-life of trichloroacetic acid is much longer (2 to 6 days) and this metabolite can accumulate under multiple dosing conditions.

The most common adverse effects of chloral hydrate administration are nausea, vomiting, or diarrhea which can be minimized by giving the drug diluted or with food. Tolerance to the sedative effects develops rapidly over a 5- to 14-day period of continued use.[129] Chloral hydrate generally is void of cardiac toxicity but has been linked to arrhythmias in four children undergoing complex cardiac surgery. Therefore, it should not be used, or only with extreme caution, in these patients.[130] Chloral hydrate usually does not depress respiratory function significantly, but there are two case reports of respiratory failure linked to chloral hydrate use in children with suspected obstructive sleep apnea.[133] The risk of respiratory problems increases with prolonged use.

32. Why is chloral hydrate used so much in children compared to other sedatives?

When considering the best sedative for a child, it is useful to compare the advantages and disadvantages of available agents. Barbiturates (e.g., phenobarbital, pentobarbital) are sedating but can have a higher incidence of cardiac, respiratory, and CNS depression than chloral hydrate or benzodiazepines.[133] There are some reports of increased risk of brain tumors in children exposed to barbiturates as well. Benzodiazepines (diazepam, lorazepam) have not been studied systematically in children, but there are some reports of paradoxical excitatory reactions, psychomotor impairment, and excessive sedation in young age groups.[134] Respiratory depression and altered EEG patterns can occur secondary to benzodiazepine therapy. Benzodiazepines in high doses over long periods also have been associated with cancer in lab animals. Chloral hydrate has been studied extensively in children and the carcinogenicity risk has not been established clearly.

The American Academy of Pediatrics considers chloral hydrate to be an effective sedative with a low incidence of acute toxicity when administered orally in the recommended dosage of 10 to 50 mg/kg (depending upon the indication; see Chapter 95: Pediatric Considerations). Single or intermittent dosing is considered safe. Repetitive dosing is of concern because of the accumulation of the metabolites. Data are not available to establish the superiority of other sedatives with respect to safety and efficacy in children.[130] It comes down to the risk versus benefit of using a sedative, and each case should be considered on an individual basis. Any sedative should be used for the shortest period of time possible, with careful monitoring of respiratory, cardiac, and CNS function.

Formulary Management of Hypnotics

33. A large number of medications are marketed and it is impractical for a pharmacy department to have every single pharmaceutical product immediately available to the practitioners affiliated with the facility. As a result, the medical staffs of health care facilities usually seek input from their fellow clinicians, especially from those who would be most likely to be impacted, for a consensus decision on the medications that should be made available to them from the pharmacy department. The medical staff has determined that 4 hypnotics should be able to meet the needs of all patients of all ages within their facility. What thought processes should be involved in the selection of these hypnotics?

There are many factors to consider before deciding upon four hypnotics and the decision should be supported by a solid base of scientific knowledge. Therapeutic efficacy and versatility, of course, should be foremost in the decision-making process. The selected hypnotics also should be the safest hypnotics available and known adverse effects should be manageable. The third increasingly important factor is cost. Balancing high-quality care with economic common sense is the challenge facing all health care providers. Lastly, needs of the organization must be matched with the available drugs.

When balancing the clinical therapeutics against the economic realities of the available hypnotics, it is useful to think of the hypnotics as differing in four ways: onset, duration of effect, metabolism, and cost. (See Table 74.5 to review pharmacokinetic profiles.) A hypnotic with a rapid onset and short duration with no accumulation of active metabolites is advantageous for patients who only have difficulty falling asleep because there is low to no risk of daytime impairment. Zolpidem (Ambien) and triazolam (Halcion) fit this clinical profile. Zolpidem may be associated with fewer adverse reactions upon withdrawal and does not appear to affect sleep stages at recommended doses. Neither zolpidem or triazolam has been studied in children. Both drugs are more expensive, relative to other hypnotic drugs, because they are not available in generic form.

Chloral hydrate has a rapid onset and short to intermediate duration of action with no daytime hangover in patients with good hepatic function. Chloral hydrate has clinical usefulness in all age groups and unlike other hypnotics, it is available in liquid, capsule, and suppository forms which are priced inexpensively. Chloral hydrate has been studied in all age groups. Potential disadvantages of chloral hydrate are its gastrointestinal irritation and protein-binding interactions.

Estazolam (ProSom) and temazepam (Restoril) have long onsets of action (1 to 2 hours) and intermediate duration (10 hours) of action. Temazepam offers several advantages over estazolam, however. It is not oxidized in the liver and will not compete for metabolism with other hepatically metabolized drugs or accumulate with chronic use. Temazepam is significantly less expensive than estazolam because it is available in generic form. In addition, temazepam has been studied in both young age groups as a premedication and in older age groups as a hypnotic.

Flurazepam (Dalmane) and quazepam (Doral) both are hepatically metabolized with long-acting active metabolites. Each is able to keep the patient asleep throughout the night and provide residual daytime sedation if needed for agitation or anxiety. They both maintain hypnotic efficacy over at least 30 days of continuous use. Quazepam has a faster onset the first night of use, but the difference is insignificant on subsequent nights. When considering economic

common sense, flurazepam has the advantage. It is available in a relatively inexpensive generic form.

In consideration of the available clinical and cost data, chloral hydrate, temazepam, and flurazepam would be reasonable choices for inclusion in the formulary. Zolpidem could be added to the formulary with restrictions: available upon request if an ultra short duration of effect is required or chloral hydrate is ineffective or intolerable. Despite zolpidem's ω_1 selectivity and lack of effects on sleep stages at recommended doses, the clinical usefulness of this pharmacodynamic characteristic has not been established. A review of this formulary decision should be conducted in six months to determine if these selections need to be changed based upon new information.

References

1 **Shapiro CM, Dement WC.** Impact and epidemiology of sleep disorders. Br Med J. 1993;306:1604.

2 **Ford DB, Kramerow DB.** Epidemiological study of sleep disturbances and psychiatric disorders. JAMA. 1989;262:1479.

3 **Shapiro CM et al.** Sleep problems in patients with medical illness. Br Med J. 1993;306:1532.

4 **Aldrich MS.** Automobile accidents in patients with sleep disorders. Sleep. 1989;12(6):487.

5 **Lurie N et al.** How do house officers spend their nights? N Engl J Med. 1989;320:1673.

6 **Gold DR et al.** Rotating shift work, sleep, and accidents related to sleepiness in hospital nurses. Am J Public Health. 1992;82(7):1011.

7 **Mitlerr MM et al.** Sleep medicine, public policy and public health. In: Kryger MH eds. Principles of Sleep Medicine. Philadelphia: WB Saunders; 1994:453.

8 **Carskadon MA, Dement WC.** Cumulative effects of sleep restriction on daytime sleepiness. Psychophysiology. 1981;18(2):107.

9 **The Gallup Organization.** Sleep in America: a national survey of U.S. adults. (Commissioned by the National Sleep Foundation) Princeton, NJ; 1991.

10 **Top 200 drugs of 1992.** American Druggist. Feb 1993:49.

11 **Bliwise DL.** Sleep in normal aging and dementia. Sleep. 1993;16(1):40.

12 **Gislason T et al.** Sleep habits and sleep disturbances among the elderly—an epidemiological survey. J Intern Med. 1993;234:31.

13 **Shorr RI, Bauwens SF.** Diagnosis and treatment of outpatient insomnia by psychiatric and nonpsychiatric physicians. Am J Med. 1992;93:78.

14 **Rumble R, Morgan K.** Hypnotics, sleep and mortality in elderly people. J Am Geriatr Soc. 1992;40:787.

15 **Dahl RE.** The pharmacologic treatment of sleep disorders. Psychiatr Clin North Am. 1992;15(1):161.

16 **Culebras A.** Update on disorders of sleep and the sleep-wake cycle. Psychiatr Clin North Am. 1992;15(2):467.

17 **Carskadon MA, Dement WC.** Normal human sleep: an overview. In: Kryger MG et al., eds. Principles of Sleep Medicine. Philadelphia: WB Saunders; 1994:16.

18 **Bliwise DL.** Normal aging. In: Kryger MH et al., eds. Principles of Sleep Medicine. Philadelphia: WB Saunders; 1994:26.

19 **Wooten V.** Medical causes of insomnia. In: Kryger MH et al., eds. Principles of Sleep Medicine. Philadelphia: WB Saunders; 1994:26.

20 **Barthlen GM, Stacy C.** Dyssomnias, parasomnias, and sleep disorders, associated with medical and psychiatric diseases. Mt Sinai J Med. 1994;61(2):139–60.

21 **Jones B.** Basic mechanisms of sleep-wake states. In: Kryger MH, et al., eds. Principles of Sleep Medicine. Philadelphia: WB Saunders; 1994:26.

22 **Mendelson WB.** Mechanism of action of benzodiazepine hypnotics. Clin Neuropharmacol. 1992;15(Suppl. 1, Pt. A):357A.

23 **Jones BE.** Paradoxical sleep and its chemical/structural substrates in the brain. Neuroscience. 1991;40(3):637.

24 **Nicholson AN, Pascoe PA.** Dopaminergic transmission and the sleep-wakefulness continuum in man. Neuropharmacology. 1990;29(4):411.

25 **Velaszquez-Moctezuma JV et al.** Acetylcholine and acetylcholine receptor subtypes in REM sleep generation. Prog Brain Res. 1990;84:407.

26 **Hobson JA.** Sleep and dreaming: induction and mediation of REM sleep by cholinergic mechanisms. Curr Opin Neurobiol. 1992;2:759.

27 **Holsboer F et al.** Effects of corticosteroids and neurosteroids on sleep EEG. Clin Neuropharmacol. 1992;15 (Suppl. 1, Pt. A):588A.

28 **Follenius M et al.** Nocturnal cortisol release in relation to sleep structure. Sleep. 1991;15(1):21.

29 **Hauri PJ, Esther MS.** Insomnia. Mayo Clin Proc. 1990;65:869.

30 **Thorpy MJ.** Classification of sleep disorders. In: Kryger MH et al., eds. Principles of Sleep Medicine. Philadelphia: WB Saunders; 1994:426.

31 **The Diagnostic and Statistics Manual Fourth Edition.** Washington, DC: American Psychiatric Association; 1994.

32 **Terman M.** Light treatment. In: Kryger MH et al., eds. Principles of Sleep Medicine. Philadelphia: WB Saunders; 1994:426.

33 **Gillin JC, Byerley WF.** The diagnosis and management of insomnia. N Engl J Med. 1990;322:239.

34 **Dement WC.** Overview of the efficacy and safety of benzodiazepine hypnotics using objective methods. J Clin Psychiatry. 1991;52(Suppl.):27.

35 **Greenblatt DJ.** Benzodiazepine hypnotics: sorting the pharmacokinetic facts. J Clin Psychiatry. 1991;52 (Suppl. 9):42.

36 **Mendels J.** Criteria for selection of appropriate benzodiazepine hypnotic therapy. J Clin Psychiatry. 1991;52 (Suppl. 9):42.

37 **Scharf MB et al.** A multicenter, placebo-controlled study evaluating zolpidem in the treatment of chronic insomnia. J Clin Psychiatry. 1994;55(5):192.

38 **Montplaisir J et al.** The treatment of the restless leg syndrome with or without periodic leg movements in sleep. Sleep. 1992;15(5):391.

39 **Krieger J.** Pharmacological treatment of narcolepsy. Clin Neuropharmacol. 1992;15(Suppl. 1; Pt. A):362A.

40 **Kryger MH.** Management of Obstructive Sleep Apnea: Overview. In: Kryger MH et al., eds. Principles of Sleep Medicine. Philadelphia: WB Saunders; 1994:736.

41 **Series F, Marc I.** Changes in snoring characteristics after 30 days of nasal continuous positive airway pressure in patients with non-apneic snoring: a controlled trial. Thorax. 1994;49:562.

42 **Roehrs T et al.** Sedative effects and plasma concentrations following single doses of triazolam, diphenhydramine, ethanol and placebo. Sleep. 1993;16 (4):301.

43 **Rickels K et al.** Diphenhydramine in insomniac family practice patients. J Clin Pharmacol. 1983;23:235.

44 **Rickels K et al.** Doxylamine succinate in insomniac family practice patients: a double blind study. Curr Ther Res Clin Exp. 1984;35:532.

45 **Roehrs TA et al.** Daytime sleepiness and antihistamines. Sleep. 1984;7(2):137.

46 **Graeber RC.** Jet lag and sleep disruption. In: Kryger MH et al., eds. Principles of Sleep Medicine. Philadelphia: WB Saunders; 1994:463.

47 **Lader M.** Rebound insomnia and newer hypnotics. Psychopharmacology. 1992;108(3):248.

48 **Friedman H et al.** Population study of triazolam pharmacokinetics. Br J Clin Pharmacol. 1986;22:639.

49 **Greenblatt DJ et al.** Effect of gradual withdrawal on the rebound sleep disorder after discontinuation of triazolam. N Engl J Med. 1987;317:722.

50 **Greenblatt DJ et al.** Neurochemical and pharmacokinetic correlates of the clinical action of benzodiazepine hypnotics. Am J Med. 1990;88(Suppl. 3A):18S.

51 **Greenblatt DJ et al.** Adverse reactions to triazolam, flurazepam, and placebo in controlled clinical trials. J Clin Psychiatry. 1984;45:192.

52 **Wysowski DK, Barash D.** Adverse behavioral reactions attributed to triazolam in the Food and Drug Administration's spontaneous reporting system. Arch Intern Med. 1991;151:2003.

53 **Weingartner HJ et al.** Selective effects of triazolam on memory. Psychopharmacology. 1992;106:341.

54 **Dorian P et al.** Triazolam and ethanol interaction: kinetic and dynamic consequences. Clin Pharmacol Ther. 1985;37:558.

55 **Jonas JM et al.** Comparative clinical profiles of triazolam versus other shorter-acting hypnotics. J. Clin Psychiatry. 1992;53(Suppl.):49.

56 **Upjohn Laboratories.** Halcion package insert. Kalamazoo, MI: 1991 Dec.

57 **Arbilla S et al.** High affinity [3H] zolpidem binding in the rat brain: an imidazopyridine with agonist properties at central benzodiazepine receptors. Eur J Pharmacol. 1986;130:257–63.

58 **Langtry HD, Benfield P.** Zolpidem: a review of its pharmacodynamic and pharmacokinetic properties and therapeutic potential. Drugs. 1990;40:291.

59 **Roger M, Attali P.** Multicenter, double-blind controlled comparison of zolpidem and triazolam in elderly patients with insomnia. Clin Ther. 1993;15(1):127.

60 **Merlotti L et al.** A controlled trial of zolpidem versus placebo. J Clin Psychopharmacol. 1989;9:9.

61 **Balkin TJ et al.** Comparison of the daytime sleep and performance effects of zolpidem versus triazolam. Psychopharmacology. 1992;107:83.

62 **Cavallaro R et al.** Tolerance and withdrawal with zolpidem. Lancet. 1993;342:374.

63 **Scharf et al.** Dose response effects of zolpidem in normal geriatric subjects. J Clin Psychiatry. 1991;52(2):77.

64 **Ansseau M et al.** Psychotic reactions to zolpidem. Lancet. 1992;339:809. Letter.

65 Iruela LM et al. Zolpidem induced macropsia in anorexic woman. Lancet. 1993;342:443. Letter.

66 Evans SM et al. Zolpidem and triazolam in humans: behavioral and subjective effects and abuse liability. J Pharmacol Exp Ther. 1990;256(3):1246-255.

67 Schlich D et al. Long-term treatment of insomnia with zolpidem: a multicentre general practitioner study of 107 patients. J Int Med Res. 1991;19:271.

68 Berlin RM. Management of insomnia in hospitalized patients. Ann Intern Med. 1984;100:398.

69 Drugs that cause psychiatric symptoms. Med Lett Drugs Ther. 1993;35 (901):65.

70 Hardo PG, Kennedy TD. Night sedation and arthritic pain. J Royal Soc Med. 1991;84:73.

71 Roose SP et al. Death, depression, and heart disease. J Clin Psychiatry. 1991; 52(Suppl. 6):34.

72 Cummings JL. Depression and Parkinson's disease: a review. Am J Psychiatry. 1992;149(4):443.

73 Clavier N et al. Benzodiazepines and pain: effects of midazolam on the activities of nociceptive non-specific dorsal horn neurons in the rat spinal cord. Pain. 1992;48:61.

74 Vercellino CE. Preoperative medications and techniques of induction and maintenance. In: Barash PG, ed. Handbook of Clinical Anesthesia. 2nd ed. Philadelphia: Lippincott; 1993;233.

75 Kripke DF et al. Sleep evaluation in chronic insomniacs during 14-day use of flurazepam and midazolam. J Clin Psychopharmacol. 1990;10:32S.

76 Greenblatt DJ et al. Pharmacokinetic determinants of dynamic differences among three benzodiazepine hypnotics. Arch Gen Psychiatry. 1989;46:326.

77 Kales A et al. Quazepam and flurazepam: long-term use and extended withdrawal. Clin Pharmacol Ther. 1982;32:781.

78 Hilbert JM, Battista D. Quazepam and flurazepam: differential pharmacokinetic and 5 pharmacodynamic characteristics. J Clin Psychiatry. 52 (Suppl. 9):21.

79 Walmsley JK, Hunt MA. Relative affinity of quazepam for type-1 benzodiazepine receptors in brain. J Clin Psychiatry. 1991;52(Suppl. 9):15.

80 Dement WC. Objective measurements of daytime sleepiness and performance comparing quazepam with flurazepam in two adult populations using the multiple sleep latency test. J Clin Psychiatry. 1991;52(Suppl. 9):31.

81 McElnay JC et al. Temazepam: new drug evaluation. Drug Intell Clin Pharm. 1981;16:650.

82 Greenblatt DJ et al. Clinical pharmacokinetics of anxiolytics and hypnotics in the elderly. Clin Pharmacokinet. 1991;21(3):165.

83 Estazolam—a new benzodiazepine hypnotic. Med Lett Drugs Ther. 1991; 33(854):91.

84 Scharf MB et al. Estazolam and flurazepam: a multicenter, placebo-controlled comparative study in outpatients with insomnia. J Clin Pharmacol. 1990;30:461.

85 Cohn JB et al. Hypnotic efficacy of estazolam compared with flurazepam in outpatients with insomnia. J Clin Pharmacol. 1991;31:747.

86 Scharf MB. Feasibility of an every-other-night regimen in insomniac patients: subjective hypnotic effectiveness of quazepam, triazolam, and placebo. J Clin Psychiatry. 1993;54(1):33.

87 Salzman C. Benzodiazepine dependency: summary of the APA task force on benzodiazepines. Psychopharmacol Bull. 1990;26:61.

88 Rickels K et al. Benzodiazepine dependence: management of discontinuation. Psychopharmacol Bull. 1990:26:63.

89 Busto U et al. Withdrawal reaction after long-term therapeutic use of benzodiazepines. N Eng J Med. 1986;315:854.

90 Saletu B et al. Insomnia in generalized anxiety disorder: polysomnographic, psychometric and clinical investigations before, during and after therapy with a long- versus a short-half-life benzodiazepine (quazepam versus triazolam). Pharmacopsychiatry. 1994;29:69.

91 Kupfer DJ et al. Antidepressants and sleep disorders in affective illness. Clin Neuropharmacol. 1992;15(Suppl. 1; Pt. A):360A.

92 Vogel GW et al. Drug effects on REM sleep and on endogenous depression. In: Neuroscience and Biobehavioral Review. Pergamon Press; 1990;14:49.

93 Stark P, Hardison CD. A review of multicenter controlled studies of fluoxetine versus imipramine and placebo in outpatients with major depressive disorder. J Clin Psychiatry. 1985;46(3):53.

94 Christian-Gillin J. Sleep and psychoactive drugs of abuse and dependence. In: Kryger MH et al., eds. Principles of Sleep Medicine. Philadelphia: WB Saunders; 1994:934.

95 Nierenberg A, Roose SP. Treatment of depression. J Clin Psychiatry. 1992; 53(Suppl. 9):16.

96 Jacobsen FM. Low-dose trazodone as a hypnotic in patients treated with MAOIs and other psychotropics: a pilot study. J Clin Psychiatry. 1990; 51(7):298.

97 Nierenberg AA et al. Trazodone for antidepressant-associated insomnia. Am J Psychiatry. 1994;151(7):1069.

98 Scharf MB, Sachais BA. Sleep laboratory evaluation of the effects and efficacy of trazodone in depressed insomniac patients. J Clin Psychiatry. 1990;51(Suppl. 9):13.

99 Ansseau M, De Roeck J. Trazodone in benzodiazepine dependence. J Clin Psychiatry. 1993;54(5):189.

100 Catesby-Ware J, Pittard JT. Increased deep sleep after trazodone use: a double-blind placebo-controlled study in healthy young adults. J Clin Psychiatry. 1990;51(Suppl. 9):18.

101 Catesby-Ware J. Tricyclic antidepressants in the treatment of insomnia. J Clin Psychiatry. 1983;44(Suppl. 9; Sec. 2):25.

102 Hauri P. Primary insomnia. In: Kryger MH et al., eds. Principles of Sleep Medicine. Philadelphia: WB Saunders; 1994:494.

103 Mosko SS et al. Sleep apnea and sleep-related periodic leg movements in community resident seniors. J Am Geriatr Soc. 1988;36:502.

104 Berry DTR et al. Sleep-disordered breathing in healthy aged persons: one year follow-up of daytime sequelae. Sleep. 1989;12:211.

105 Ancoli-Israel et al. Periodic limb movements in sleep in community dwelling elderly. Sleep. 1991;14:486.

106 Miller NS et al. Alcohol and drug dependence among the elderly: epidemiology, diagnosis, and treatment. Compr Psychiatry. 1991;32(2):153.

107 Wengel SP et al. Use of benzodiazepines in the elderly. Psychiatric Annals. 1993;23(6):325.

108 Rudorfer MV. Pharmacokinetics of psychotropic drugs in special populations. J Clin Psychiatry. 1993;54 (Suppl. 9):50.

109 Simons KJ et al. Pharmacokinetic and pharmacodynamic studies of the H_1-receptor antagonist hydroxyzine in the elderly. Clin Pharmacol Ther. 1989;45:9.

110 Ray WA et al. Benzodiazepines of long and short elimination half-life and the risk of hip fracture. JAMA. 1989; 262:3307.

111 Grisso JA et al. Risk factors for falls as a cause of hip fracture in women. N Engl J Med. 1991;324:1326.

112 Taggert H McA. Do drugs affect the risk of hip fracture in elderly women? J Am Geriatr Soc. 1988;36:1006.

113 Roth T, Roehrs, TA. A review of the safety profiles of benzodiazepine hypnotics. J Clin Psychiatry. 1991;52 (Suppl. 9):38.

114 Fletcher EC et al. Undiagnosed sleep apnea in patients with essential hypertension. Ann Intern Med. 1985;103:190.

115 Hirshkowitz M et al. Hypertension, erectile dysfunction, and occult sleep apnea. Sleep. 1989;12(3):223.

116 Wilcox I et al. Effect of nasal continuous positive airway pressure during sleep on 24-hour blood pressure in obstructive sleep apnea. Sleep. 1993; 16(6):539.

117 Aubert-Tulkens G et al. Cure of sleep apnea syndrome after long-term nasal continuous positive airway pressure therapy and weight loss. Sleep. 1989: 12(3):216.

118 Brownell LG et al. Protriptyline in obstructive sleep apnea: a double-blind trial. N Engl J Med. 1982;307:1037.

119 Strakowski SM et al. Four cases of obstructive sleep apnea associated with treatment-resistant mania. J Clin Psychiatry. 1991;52(4):156.

120 Guilleminault G. Narcolepsy Syndrome. In: Kryger MH et al., eds. In: Principles of Sleep Medicine. Philadelphia: WB Saunders; 1994:549.

121 Ciba-Geigy Laboratories. Ritalin SR package insert. Triangle Park, NJ: 1990 Dec.

122 Mitler M et al. Treatment of narcolepsy with methamphetamine. Sleep. 1993;16(4):306.

123 Lammers GJ et al. Gammahydroxybutyrate and narcolepsy: a double-blind placebo-controlled study. Sleep. 1993;16(3):216.

124 Boivin DB, Montplaisir J. The effects of L-dopa on excessive daytime sleepiness in narcolepsy. Neurology. 1991; 41:1267.

125 Boivin DB et al. Effects of bromocriptine in human narcolepsy. Clinical Neuropharmacology. 1993;16(2):120.

126 Lauerma H. Nocturnal wandering caused by restless legs and short-acting benzodiazepines. Acta Psychiatr Scand. 1991;83:492.

127 Kaplan PW et al. A double-blind, placebo-controlled study of the treatment of periodic limb movements in sleep using carbidopa/levodopa and propoxyphene. Sleep. 1993;16(8):717.

128 Walters AS et al. Successful treatment of the idiopathic restless legs syndrome in a randomized double-blind trial of oxycodone versus placebo. Sleep. 1993;16(4):327.

129 Kales A. Comparative effectiveness of nine hypnotic drugs: sleep laboratory studies. JAMA. 1979;241:1692.

130 Kauffman RE et al. The use of chloral hydrate for sedation in children. Pediatrics. 1993;92(3):471.

131 Onks DL et al. The effect of chloral hydrate and its metabolites, trichloroethanol and trichloroacetic acid, on bilirubin-albumin binding. Pharmacol Toxicol. 1992;71:196.

132 Hirsch IA, Zauder HL. Chloral hydrate: a potential cause of arrhythmias. Anesth Analg. 1986;65:691.

133 Bibin P et al. Adverse effect of chloral hydrate in two young children with obstructive sleep apnea. Pediatrics. 1993; 92(3):461.

134 Coffey B. Review and update: benzodiazepines in childhood and adolescence. Psychiatric Annals. 1993;23(6):332.

Schizophrenia

Patricia A Marken
Steven W Stanislav

Epidemiology 75-1
Pathophysiology 75-1
Mechanism of Drug Action (See Table 75.1) 75-2
Diagnosis and Clinical Features (See Table 75.2) 75-3
Clinical Course and Long-Term Prognosis
  (See Table 75.3) 75-3
Differential Diagnosis (See Table 75.4) 75-4
Substance Abuse and Schizophrenia 75-4
Clinical Presentation 75-5
Target Symptoms (See Table 75.5) 75-5
Diagnosis and Outcome 75-6
Treatment 75-6
Goals of Treatment 75-6
Role of Nondrug Therapy 75-6
Efficacy of Pharmacotherapy and Predictors of
  Medication Response 75-6
Acute Treatment/Rapid Tranquilization 75-6
Antipsychotic Selection (See Tables 75.6 and 75.7) 75-7
Onset of Antipsychotic Action 75-8
Duration of Therapy and Goal of Maintenance
  Treatment 75-8
Long-Term Dosing Strategies 75-9
Depot Antipsychotic Therapy 75-9
  Indications 75-9
  Depot products 75-9
  Conversion from oral to depot therapy 75-10
    Fluphenazine decanoate conversion 75-10
    Haloperidol decanoate conversion 75-10
Partial Response 75-10
  Lithium 75-10
  Benzodiazepines 75-10
  Propranolol 75-10
  Carbamazepine 75-11

Clozapine 75-11
  Indications 75-11
  Initiation of therapy (See Table 75.8) 75-11
  Serum Concentration Monitoring 75-12
Antipsychotic-Induced Adverse Effects and
** Their Treatment** 75-13
  Pseudoparkinsonism (See Table 75.9) 75-13
    Clinical presentation 75-13
    Treatment (See Table 75.10 and Figure 75.1) 75-13
      Risks of long-term treatment 75-13
    Prevention 75-15
  Acute Dystonia 75-15
  Akathisia 75-16
  Tardive Dyskinesia (TD) 75-16
    Clinical presentation and assessment
      (See Figure 75.2) 75-17
    Management (See Figure 75.3 and
      Tables 75.11 and 75.12) 75-17
  Neuroleptic Malignant Syndrome (NMS) 75-19
  Hematological Adverse Effects 75-19
  Amenorrhea and Galactorrhea 75-20
  Hepatic Dysfunction 75-21
  Temperature Dysregulation and Dermatological
    Effects 75-21
  Ocular Effects 75-21
  Psychogenic Polydipsia 75-21
  Sexual Dysfunction 75-22
  Seizures 75-22
  Considerations in Pregnancy 75-22
  Weight Gain 75-23
Polytherapy 75-23
Drug Selection in the Elderly 75-23

Psychotic disorders are marked by deterioration in social functioning, loss of reality testing and perceptual deficits (including hallucinations and delusions), and affective or mood instability. Of the various psychotic disorders, schizophrenia is the most common and most misunderstood. Its chronic nature drains health care and social service resources in our society. In 1985, the total economic cost of schizophrenia in the U.S. was estimated at $22.7 billion, with direct treatment costs accounting for almost half of this figure. Schizophrenia uses about 2.5% of our total annual health care costs and afflicted persons represent about 10% of this country's disabled population.[1]

This chapter, by focusing on the pathophysiology, assessment, clinical course, and treatment, provides a framework for the clinician to develop skills in schizophrenia management. Therapy is best evaluated by combining objective and subjective information obtained directly from interviews of the patient with data from previous medical records and family, or caregiver, interviews. Structured mental status evaluations are important to assist in evaluating clinical response to pharmacotherapy. Although this chapter uses terminology based upon mental status assessments, the reader is referred elsewhere for reviews on specific interviewing techniques.[2]

Epidemiology

The lifetime prevalence of schizophrenic disorders is between 0.5% and 2.0%, depending upon the diagnostic criteria used. Schizophrenia typically has its onset during late adolescence or early adulthood, with men probably experiencing an earlier onset than women. Schizophrenia is distributed equally between sexes and, after adjusting for differences in diagnostic criteria, has similar prevalence rates across cultures.[3,4]

Pathophysiology

Schizophrenia is a complex disorder likely to have multiple etiologies based upon biological, psychosocial, and environmental influences. Traditional biological theories of schizophrenia attribute psychotic symptoms to an overactive dopaminergic system. These theories are supported by studies that show symptomatic improvement when dopamine (DA) receptors are blocked by antipsychotic medications; findings that correlate DA_2-receptor-binding affinity to clinical potency of antipsychotics; and observations that agents which increase presynaptic DA release (amphetamine, levodopa, methylphenidate) can cause or exacerbate psychotic symptoms.[5–7] However, the overactive dopaminergic theory is unable to explain cases of schizophrenia where residual or "negative" symptoms predominate. The "hypofrontality" theory suggests that decreased dopaminergic functioning in the frontal cortex of patients with chronic schizophrenia may cause the negative symptoms.[8]

The dysregulation theory of schizophrenia, one modification of the dopamine theory, is based upon the defective regulation of mechanisms responsible for neurotransmitter synthesis, release, reuptake, metabolism, and receptor activity. For example, a problem may exist with the presynaptic DA autoreceptor, resulting in ineffective feedback mechanisms and postsynaptic DA receptor hypersensitivity. The goal of drug therapy, therefore, would be to normalize these autoregulatory mechanisms either directly by receptor stimulation or inhibition, or indirectly through a neuromodulating process. The dysregulation theory could explain why pharmacologic agents with different mechanisms of action are effective against similar symptoms of schizophrenia.[9]

The involvement of the excitatory amino acids, or the glutamatergic system, in the pathogenesis of schizophrenia only recently has been suggested.[10–12] Decreased activation of N-methyl-D-aspartic acid (NMDA) or glutamate receptors may increase cortical dopamine release, and produce a syndrome resembling schizophrenia. This theory is supported by the ability of phencyclidine, an NMDA antagonist, to produce clinically florid psychosis. Gamma aminobutyric acid (GABA), a major inhibitory amino acid, also may act as a third link between the neuromodulation of glutamate and dopamine receptors.

In addition to a biological basis for schizophrenia, individuals with a family history of psychiatric illness may have a greater vulnerability to developing schizophrenia. First-degree biological relatives of individuals with schizophrenia are more likely to have this disorder than the general population. In addition, nine major studies of twins strongly implicate the role of a genetic predisposition in schizophrenia. A concordance rate of developing schizophrenia in dizygotic and monozygotic twins may be as high as 14% and 48%, respectively.[3]

Mechanism of Drug Action

Multiple central dopamine receptors (D_1, D_2, D_3, D_4, D_5) have been identified. D_1- and D_2-receptors correlate with antipsychotic efficacy. D_2-receptors are involved in the pathogenesis of antipsychotic-induced movement disorders and D_1-receptors probably modulate their intensity.[13] With the development of newer, "atypical" antipsychotic drugs with mechanisms of action other than dopamine receptor blockade, researchers are gaining more insight into the pathogenesis of schizophrenia. Clozapine (Clozaril), approved in 1990, is the first "atypical" antipsychotic marketed in the U.S. Clozapine decreases positive and negative symptoms, whereas traditional or "typical" agents such as chlorpromazine (Thorazine) and haloperidol (Haldol) have poor efficacy against negative symptoms of schizophrenia (see Diagnosis and Clinical Features). Clozapine is only minimally associated with adverse effects normally associated with central dopamine blockade [i.e., extrapyramidal side effects (EPSEs), tardive dyskinesia (TD), hyperprolactinemia].[14] Atypical agents seem to primarily affect dopaminergic receptors in the limbic system (the area of the brain responsible for emotion) more than the basal ganglia (the area responsible for movement). This preference for the limbic system may explain the relative lack of movement disorders associated with atypical agents. Also, unlike "typical" antipsychotics, clozapine does not upregulate postsynaptic D_2-receptors, and appears to be more specific to D_1- and D_4-receptors.[15]

Dopamine antagonism does not solely explain antipsychotic mechanism of action because central dopamine concentrations in subgroups of schizophrenic patients can be low or normal.[12,16–18] Neuroimaging studies suggest that dysfunction in other neurotransmitter systems, particularly the serotonergic system, contributes to the pathophysiology of schizophrenia. Classical antipsychotics affect dopamine, histamine₁, α-adrenergic, and muscarinic receptors, whereas atypical antipsychotics have greater affinity for the $5HT_2$ and lower affinities for dopamine. Risperidone, a potent $5HT_2$ and D_2 antagonist, has probable dose-related affinities for postsynaptic serotonergic receptors.[19] Lower affinity for the serotonergic receptor may explain the loss of efficacy against negative symptoms and a greater incidence of extrapyramidal side effects at higher doses. Although direct neurochemical evidence of the role of serotonin in schizophrenia is lacking, serotonergic receptors are distributed in brain areas believed to influence behavior, and elevated serotonin concentrations have been found in patients with chronic schizophrenia.[20] Investigators also suggest an inhibitory effect of serotonin on dopaminergic receptors or dopamine release. Clozapine and risperidone's greater efficacy against negative symptoms, and lower incidence of causing EPSEs, may be due in part to both augmentation of striatal and limbic dopaminergic function via serotonergic antagonism, and lower D_2-receptor occupancy.[21,22]

Table 75.1	Neurochemical/Pharmacological Profiles of Haloperidol, Clozapine, and Risperidone[d,23]		
Effect	Haloperidol[a]	Clozapine[b]	Risperidone[c]
Block of DA-stimulated adenylate cyclase	+	+	NA
Block of cAMP formation induced by apomorphine	+	+	NA
Displacement of (^{3}H)-DA binding	+	+	+
↑ DA turnover	+	±[e]	+
↑ prolactin plasma levels	+	−	+
Block of apomorphine-induced stereotypy	+	−	+[f]
Block of amphetamine-induced hyperactivity	+	−	+[f]
Catalepsy[g]	+	−	+[f]
Block of apomorphine-induced emesis	+	−	+[f]

[a] Haloperidol: Typical antipsychotic.
[b] Clozapine: Atypical antipsychotic with D_1 and serotonin type 2 receptor effects.
[c] Risperidone: Atypical antipsychotic with D_2 and serotonin type 2 receptor effects.
[d] DA = Dopamine; cAMP = Cyclic adenosine monophosphate; (^{3}H)-DA = Radio-labeled haloperidol.
[e] Turnover increased only at high doses.
[f] Dose-related effects.
[g] Catalepsy = Rigidity of muscles so that the patient tends to remain in any position in which he is placed.

Other agents that preferentially block the D_2-receptor, have little affinity for the D_1-receptor, and function as agonists or antagonists at the sigma receptor, also are under investigation in the U.S. Table 75.1 compares animal and *in vitro* responses for typical and atypical antipsychotic medications in standard models used to screen drugs for antipsychotic and extrapyramidal effects.[23]

Diagnosis and Clinical Features

Schizophrenia is a heterogeneous disorder, and is comprised of a cluster of signs and symptoms that includes thought disorder, perceptual and cognitive deficits, speech and language problems, poor judgment and insight, and behavioral disturbances. Each patient follows a different clinical course and will demonstrate some or all of the symptoms of schizophrenia. Schizophrenia was first described by Kraepelin around the turn of the century as "dementia praecox" (a syndrome of cognitive and behavioral deficits which tend to appear early in life). Kraepelin emphasized that dementia praecox largely followed a chronic course and patients usually did not recover. Bleuler concurred with Kraepelin's initial description of schizophrenia, although he suggested that some patients did recover and subsequently could lead productive lives. Bleuler described the "4-As" of schizophrenia which include *autism* (preoccupation with internal stimuli), *inappropriate affect* (external manifestations of mood), *loose associations* (illogical or fragmented thought processes), and *ambivalence* (simultaneous, contradictory thinking). Schneider later described "first-rank" symptoms of schizophrenia that assisted the clinician in diagnosing schizophrenia. "First-rank" symptoms include delusions, auditory hallucinations, thought withdrawal, thought insertion, thought broadcasting, and experiencing feelings or actions under someone else's control. Schneider's "first-rank" symptoms provided the framework for the systematic diagnostic criteria used today in psychiatry.[24]

More recently, investigators have attempted to categorize schizophrenia into two types: Type 1 and Type 2.[25] Type 1 schizophrenia is characterized by predominately "positive" symptoms of hallucinations, delusions, thought disorder, combativeness, and hostility, while Type 2 schizophrenia consists of "negative" symptoms such as social and emotional withdrawal, apathy, blunted affect, and poor insight and judgment. Although it is possible that Type 1 and Type 2 schizophrenia are two distinct diagnostic entities with different underlying pathophysiologies, most patients will exhibit both positive and negative symptoms. Early in the course of schizophrenia, positive symptoms tend to predominate; however, once the illness becomes more chronic, negative symptoms usually are more apparent.

The Diagnostic and Statistical Manual of the American Psychiatric Association, fourth edition (DSM-IV) is the latest edition of the guide for diagnosing and classifying schizophrenia and other psychiatric disorders. A diagnosis of schizophrenia should be made only if the DSM-IV criteria are met. Changes in DSM-IV from DSM-III-R, the previous edition, include a greater emphasis on negative symptoms and residual deficits, and increased attention is given to social and occupational dysfunction associated with schizophrenia. Overall, DSM-IV more concisely describes schizophrenia (see Table 75.2) without changing the epidemiologic base rate of the disorder.[24]

Clinical Course and Long-Term Prognosis

Kraepelin initially described schizophrenia as a chronic illness with intermittent, acute psychotic episodes, which follow a progressively downhill clinical course. Numerous studies have examined symptom progression in schizophrenia, however, they have

Table 75.2 — **DSM-IV Criteria for Schizophrenia[a]**

A. Characteristic Symptoms
At least two of the following, each present for a significant portion of time during a 1-month period (or less if successfully treated):
1. delusions
2. hallucinations
3. disorganized speech (e.g., frequent derailment or incoherence)
4. grossly disorganized or catatonic behavior
5. negative symptoms (i.e., affective flattening, alogia, or avolition)

Note: Only one "A symptom" is required if delusions are bizarre or hallucinations consist of a voice keeping up a running commentary on the person's behavior or thought, two or more conversations with each other.

B. Social/Occupation Dysfunction
For a significant portion of the time since the onset of the disturbance, one or more major areas of functioning, such as work, interpersonal relationships, or self-care is markedly below the level achieved before the onset.

C. Duration
Continuous signs of the disturbance persist for at least 6 months. This 6-month period must include at least 1 month of symptoms (or less if successfully treated) that meet criterion A (i.e., active phase symptoms), and may include prodromal and/or residual periods when the "A criterion" is not fully met. During these periods, signs of the disturbance may be manifested by negative symptoms or two or more symptoms listed in "criterion A" present in an attenuated form (e.g., blunted affect, unusual perceptual disturbances).

D. Schizoaffective Disorder and Mood Disorder Exclusion
Schizoaffective disorder and mood disorder with psychotic features have been ruled out because either (1) no major depressive, manic, or mixed manic episodes have occurred concurrently with the active phase symptoms; or (2) if mood episodes have occurred during active phase symptoms, their total duration has been brief relative to the duration of the active and residual periods.

E. Substance/General Medical Condition Exclusion
The disturbance is not due to direct physiological effects of a substance (drug of abuse or medication) or a general medical condition.

F. Relationship to a Pervasive Development Disorder
If there is a history of autistic disorder or another pervasive development disorder, the additional diagnosis schizophrenia is made only if prominent delusions or hallucinations also are present for at least a month (or less if successfully treated).

[a] Adapted with permission from reference 24.

varied in methodologies and patient populations, especially with regard to duration of illness.[26-29] For example, over-representation of chronically ill patients with a history of multiple admissions, versus first-time admissions, in outcome studies may skew the results toward a more negative clinical course. Some studies that describe a more favorable course for schizophrenia also are limited methodologically as they differed in length of time for monitoring clinical outcome or utilized different diagnostic instruments.[30,31] More recent findings suggest a poor long-term outcome for schizophrenia even in first-episode patients, with a relapse and recurrence rate as high as 60% in the two-year period immediately after the first hospitalization.[27] A 12-year follow-up study of first-episode schizophrenic patients showed 78% with deterioration in functioning, 38% attempting suicide, and almost 25% experiencing a major affective illness after the initial psychotic episode.[26] *Relapse* refers to the reappearance of symptoms during the same psychotic episode, and usually is secondary to insufficient treatment of the primary episode, noncompliance, or poor transition of the patient from inpatient to outpatient life. A *recurrent episode* generally refers to a new psychotic episode. Remission is sustained in only a very small group of schizophrenic patients. As patients with schizophrenia age, the frequency and severity of acute episodes may decrease, however, psychosocial functioning remains poor.

Table 75.3	Prognosticators of Outcome for Schizophrenia Treated with Antipsychotics[a,23]	
Feature	Good Prognosis	Poor Prognosis
Premorbid functioning	High	Low
Precipitating factors	Present	Absent
Age at onset	Older than average	Younger than average
Onset of symptoms	Sudden	Insidious
Family history	Positive for affective illness and negative for schizophrenia	Positive for schizophrenia
Interpersonal relationships	Married/stable home environment	Single
Affective symptoms	Present	Blunted affect
Behavioral features	Positive symptoms predominate	Negative symptoms predominate
CNS morphology by CT or MRI scan	Normal	Ventricular enlargement, cortical atrophy
Dopamine system	Hyperactive in limbic system	Hypoactive in frontal cortex
Response to typical neuroleptics	Good	Fair to poor

[a] CNS = Central nervous system; CT = Computed tomography; MRI = Magnetic resonance imaging.

A more sudden onset of schizophrenia, fewer psychotic episodes before first hospitalization, higher premorbid functioning, being married, having a stable family environment, being floridly psychotic on admission, being older at the time of first episode, and medication compliance are all associated with a more positive clinical outcome.[32] Other predictors of favorable outcome may include female gender, shorter duration of initial episode, negative family history for schizophrenia, a positive family history for affective disorders, and presence of affective symptoms (see Table 75.3).[23]

Differential Diagnosis

Psychoses have a multitude of causes and all must be excluded before the diagnosis of schizophrenia is made. Common differential diagnoses are listed in Table 75.4. Clinicians often can misdiagnose psychotic patients when their diagnosis is based upon presenting symptoms alone, without an examination of the longitudinal clinical course. An accurate diagnosis is important because treatments vary for psychoses with different origins.[33]

Other psychotic illnesses to be considered in the differential of schizophrenia are listed in Table 75.4. *Schizophreniform disorder* is similar to schizophrenia except its duration is greater than two weeks, but less than six months. *Brief reactive psychosis* is diagnosed when psychosis is present for more than a few hours, but less than one month. After the episode subsides, premorbid functioning usually returns. Various personality disorders including *schizotypal*, *schizoid*, and *paranoid* types also can resemble schizophrenia; however, these disorders lack the chronic thought disturbances seen in schizophrenia. Bipolar affective disorder, manic or depressive phase, and major depression can have psychotic features which usually are mood-congruent. Negative symptoms of schizophrenia such as anergy, apathy, and social withdrawal may resemble depression, but do not respond to antidepressant therapy.

Drug-induced psychosis is an important differential diagnosis when evaluating patients with schizophrenia. Illicit drugs may cause psychotic symptoms in any individual, but do not cause schizophrenia in persons without a predisposition to mental illness or an underlying psychiatric disorder. Drugs causing acute psychotic symptoms include amphetamines, cocaine, cannabis, phencyclidine (PCP or "angel dust"), and lysergic acid diethylamide (LSD). In addition, anticholinergic delirium can occur if excessive doses or combinations of therapeutic agents with anticholinergic properties are prescribed. A urine toxicology screen can help evaluate the contribution of substance abuse to psychosis, but because of the risk of false negative results, the quality and progression of the presenting symptoms and physical findings also must be considered in order to make an accurate diagnosis. A particularly difficult problem is evaluating the cause of psychosis in a patient with schizophrenia and concurrent drug or alcohol abuse. Distinguishing between the two may not be possible until the patient becomes drug-free and residual symptoms are assessed. There are some differences in the presentation of drug-induced psychosis and schizophrenia. For example, chronic stimulant abuse usually does not present with a formal thought disorder. Cannabis psychosis may be differentiated from acute paranoid schizophrenia since patients with the former usually experience a subjective feeling of panic and retain insight into their problem.[34] Acute PCP ingestion can cause psychotic symptoms such as paranoia and acute catatonia, but other concomitant symptoms such as ataxia, hyperreflexia, nystagmus, and hypertension are not found in schizophrenia. (See Chapters 81 to 86 for further discussion on the presentation of drug-induced psychosis and its treatment.)

Substance Abuse and Schizophrenia

Substance abuse is a common comorbid illness in individuals with schizophrenia. Schizophrenia is second only to antisocial personality disorder in occurring concurrently with substance abuse, and may occur in as many as 50% of chemical substance abusers.[35] The risk of having a substance abuse disorder is four to five times greater in persons with schizophrenia than among the general public.[36,37] It is unclear why schizophrenic patients abuse drugs; however, several theories have been proposed. Schizophrenic patients may use illicit drugs to "self-medicate" either against untreated or residual symptoms of schizophrenia, or to reduce bothersome medication-induced side effects such as akathisia. Some investi-

Table 75.4	Differential Diagnosis for Schizophrenia (DSM IV)

Drug-Induced Psychoses
 Amphetamine
 Cocaine
 Cannabis (marijuana)
 Phencyclidine (PCP)
 Lysergic acid diethylamide (LSD)
 Anticholinergics

Primary Psychiatric Disorders
 Brief reactive psychosis
 Schizophreniform disorder
 Bipolar affective disorder, manic type
 Mood disorder with psychotic features

Personality Disorders
 Schizotypal
 Schizoid
 Paranoid

gators believe that the type of substances abused by schizophrenic patients are predetermined and not random. For example, schizophrenic patients may preferentially select stimulants or hallucinogens to self-treat negative symptoms.[38] Another important contributor to the high incidence of substance abuse in schizophrenia may be environment, as many live in areas that are economically disadvantaged and substances of abuse are readily available.[39]

Substance abuse impacts clinical outcome in persons with schizophrenia. Chronic schizophrenic patients living in the community have difficulties maintaining stable housing, managing finances, and complying with medication regimens when substance abuse also is present.[40] Schizophrenic patients who abuse cocaine also may have a significantly greater risk for recurrence and rehospitalization than substance abusers without a psychiatric disorder.[41] Alcohol use was associated with rehospitalization in a subgroup of schizophrenic patients.[42]

Coexisting substance abuse and schizophrenia must be treated concurrently. Treating one disorder while ignoring the other likely will result in negative outcome and rehospitalization.[43] In addition, schizophrenic patients with dual diagnoses may be at greater risk for relapse within the first year following their initial episode. Therefore, it is imperative that adequate social networks are identified before hospital discharge.[41]

Clinical Presentation

Target Symptoms

1. R.S., a 28-year-old single, unemployed male, was brought into the emergency room (ER) of the mental health hospital by the police after he was found running barefooted downtown dodging cars in subzero weather. In the ER, R.S. was extremely frightened, and stated "they won't let me go."

History of Present Illness. **R.S. is not a good historian. He is agitated easily and threatens the interviewer when asked questions regarding his illness. R.S. said he came to this city 8 years ago "to spread the word of jazz music." He did not complete high school, has lost touch with his family, and has been living at the Salvation Army for the past 3 years. He has no close friends, and does not trust most people. He states that he often experiences voices from "dead people" telling him he is worthless and that he "will be killed." He also complains of insomnia. Past records indicate he experienced similar auditory hallucinations during a hospitalization 7 years ago. He also reports strange experiences such as "the newscasters on the television are reading my mind and telling everyone my personal secrets."**

Past Medical History. **Records indicate that over the past 7 years R.S. has been hospitalized 4 times for acute psychotic episodes marked by extreme agitation, and bizarre, paranoid behavior. He has received thioridazine (Mellaril) in doses up to 800 mg/day, and chlorpromazine (Thorazine) 1200 mg/day. R.S. states that these drugs "spaced me out." During his last hospitalization, he was discharged on trifluoperazine (Stelazine) 60 mg/day; however, he stopped taking the trifluoperazine "because it made me so stiff I couldn't play the guitar or sing," and he stated "I don't want that stuff again!"**

Psychosocial History. **R.S.'s mother frequently was hospitalized with schizoid personality and adjustment disorder with psychotic features, and his father was "never around." He admitted to being somewhat of a "rebel" as a child, and had such a bad temper that he physically abused the neighbor's cats. He did not finish high school, has not held steady employment, and relies on Social Security income and money from strangers to survive.**

Physical Examination/Laboratory Test. **R.S. was given a noncontributory physical examination. All of his laboratory tests, including complete blood count with differential (CBC with diff), SMA-28 laboratory panel, thyroid, and liver function tests (LFTs) were within normal limits. Urine drug screen was negative.**

Mental Status Exam. *Appearance and behavior*: **R.S. is a thin, disheveled-looking man with very poor hygiene. He appears much older than his stated age. He is extremely suspicious of the interviewer and his surroundings, and he continually asks, "Where am I, who are you, and what do you want?" He also is agitated easily.** *Mood*: **Very anxious and worried, concerned that the "dead people" are going to track him down and "bury me alive." His affect is blunted, with minimal range of reactivity to his emotions.** *Memory*: **Remote memory appears intact, although his immediate and short-term memory are difficult to assess as he is uncooperative.** *Sensorium:* **He is oriented to person, place, and time.** *Insight and Judgment*: **Both are poor as evidenced by R.S.'s denial of his mental illness and need for treatment, and his behavior precipitating admission.** *Thought Process*: **R.S. is very suspicious, and exhibits loose associations such as "What are you doing to me? Don't you like my socks? Jazz musicians will save the world. You are with the FBI!" He appears to be responding to internal stimuli (auditory hallucinations) since he is mumbling to himself throughout the interview.**

Provisional Diagnosis. **Schizophrenia, paranoid type, chronic course with an acute exacerbation. What target symptoms of schizophrenia are present in R.S.? How are target symptoms utilized in treatment?**

R.S. exhibits many of the classic "first-rank" symptoms of schizophrenia, including auditory hallucinations (hearing voices from "dead people" telling him that he will be killed), delusions ("Jazz musicians will save the world. You are with the FBI. They will bury me alive"), and thought broadcasting ("The newscasters on the television are reading my mind"). Other target symptoms include agitation, suspiciousness, loose associations, poor grooming and hygiene, impaired sleep, decreased social skills, and impaired insight and judgment.

Target symptoms are critical monitoring parameters that are used to assess change in clinical status and response to medications. Specific target symptoms are not diagnostic for single psychiatric disorders and often are seen across multiple disorders. Target symptoms must be clearly identified and documented before and during the course of treatment. In addition, the treatment goals and baseline level of functioning should be established at the onset of drug therapy. Common target symptoms seen in schizophrenia and their relative responsiveness to drugs are listed in Table 75.5.[23]

Table 75.5	Relative Responsiveness of Target Symptoms to Drug Therapy[a,23]
Combativeness and hostility	
Tension and hyperactivity	
Hallucinations	
Sleep	
Appetite	
Dress	
Delusions	
Social skills	
Affect	
Amotivation	
Diminished speech, content of speech	
Social inadequacy	
Realistic planning	
Judgment	
Insight	

[a] Symptoms are listed in order from most responsive to least responsive from top to bottom, respectively.

Diagnosis and Outcome

2. What other factors in R.S.'s past history are consistent with the diagnosis of schizophrenia, and what is his prognosis?

Other factors that are consistent with schizophrenia in R.S. include onset of illness in early adulthood (typical age of onset is late adolescence to early 30s), a positive family history of psychiatric illness, inability to maintain steady employment and establish interpersonal relationships with others, and the chronicity of the illness over the past seven years.[44] His acute exacerbations of psychosis with intermittent hospitalization also are characteristic of chronic schizophrenia. Because R.S. was young at the time of his first psychotic episode, has a positive family history for thought disorder, an unstable home environment, and a low premorbid level of functioning, his long-term prognosis is not good.

Treatment

Goals of Treatment

3. What are the overall goals of treatment in schizophrenia?

The ideal outcome from treating schizophrenia is induction of remission, prevention of recurrence, and restoration to baseline level of functioning. Since schizophrenia is not curable, most patients will experience residual symptoms for most of their lives. Realistically, treatment is aimed at decreasing the severity of those target symptoms that most interfere with functioning. The ultimate goal is to restore behavioral, cognitive, and psychosocial processes and skills to as near baseline levels as possible so the patient reintegrates into the community. The initial goals of antipsychotics are to both calm the agitated patient who may be a physical threat to himself or others and to begin treatment of psychosis and thought disorder.

4. What are the specific treatment goals in R.S.?

The initial treatment goal in R.S. is to reduce his agitation since he may be a physical threat to himself and others. Intermediate goals are to attenuate, or eliminate, if possible, symptoms of psychoses and thought disorder. Long-term goals should include assisting R.S. in developing a psychosocial support system (e.g., mental health workers, peer groups) which will enhance medication compliance, and enable him to obtain semi-independent living and possible part-time employment.

Role of Nondrug Therapy

5. What is the role of nondrug therapy for treating schizophrenia?

Both drug and nondrug therapies are critical in the maintenance treatment of schizophrenia. Nonpharmacologic interventions such as individual psychotherapy to improve insight into the illness and to assist the patient in coping with stress; group therapy to enhance socialization skills; behavioral or cognitive therapy; and vocational training are of benefit to patients such as R.S. In addition, schizophrenic patients living independently must maintain a close contact with mental health workers to discuss psychosocial problems and minimize stress. Because relapses and recurrences are often insidious in nature, careful observation with rapid intervention is the key in preventing rehospitalization. Patients living independently or in group homes also are encouraged to attend weekly medication management classes to increase personal awareness of their drug regimens, and understand why life-long pharmacotherapy may be essential in schizophrenia. Long-term outcome is improved in patients with an integrated drug and nondrug treatment approach.[45]

Efficacy of Pharmacotherapy and Predictors of Medication Response

6. How effective is pharmacotherapy in the treatment of schizophrenia? What are predictors of response to antipsychotic agents in persons with schizophrenia? Which of R.S.'s symptoms are more likely to respond to drug therapy?

Antipsychotic agents are more effective than placebo in treating schizophrenia and all antipsychotics, with the exception of clozapine and risperidone (Risperdal), are equally effective when used in equipotent doses. Clozapine and risperidone are more effective than typical antipsychotic medications against negative symptoms. Long-term pharmacotherapy reduces the risk of recurrence in schizophrenic patients, and also may reduce the risk of environmental and stress-induced relapse compared to chronic patients not receiving drug therapy.[46-48] However, patients do not respond equally to pharmacotherapy and up to 20% receive no benefit at all.

Attempts are underway to identify predictors of antipsychotic responders, although consensus is lacking.[32,49] A more favorable treatment response with typical antipsychotics may occur when: a) baseline symptoms are severe and mainly positive in nature; b) significant improvement in symptoms occurs within the first several days of treatment; c) patients experience a nondysphoric response to an antipsychotic test dose; d) plasma homovanillic acid (major dopamine metabolite) concentrations decrease within the first several weeks after antipsychotic administration; and e) computerized tomography (CT) scans show minimal brain atrophy (e.g., lower ventricle to brain ratio, normal size of lateral brain ventricles) compared to normal controls.[50,51] Others argue that an absence of these predictors indicates a need for atypical agents. Clearly, predictive parameters must be better validated before they can be applied to direct patient care problems.

Positive symptoms of agitation, insomnia, auditory hallucinations, thought broadcasting, suspiciousness, loose associations, and poor hygiene and dress are most likely to respond to drug therapy in R.S. His impaired judgment, poor insight into his illness, blunted affect, and poor socialization skills are less likely to respond to typical antipsychotics compared to atypical agents.[52] Delusions, especially long-standing ones, often continue after other target symptoms resolve, although patients may not act on them. Since R.S. has experienced persecutory/threatening delusions for over six years, they may not be completely ameliorated with treatment.

Acute Treatment/Rapid Tranquilization

7. How is pharmacotherapy used to treat acute schizophrenia and what pharmacotherapeutic regimen should be prescribed initially for R.S.?

The first goal of pharmacotherapy in an acutely ill schizophrenic patient is to decrease the risk of harm to self and/or others. Pharmacotherapy should be started with the scheduled antipsychotic dose likely to be needed for maintenance therapy. Additionally, antipsychotics and/or benzodiazepines should be available to be given every four to six hours "as needed" for agitation and combativeness. By combining benzodiazepines and antipsychotics, during the acute phase of treatment, the total antipsychotic dose is decreased, lessening the risk of adverse effects, especially in patients needing large antipsychotic doses and in those more prone to developing acute EPSEs.[53] Lorazepam (Ativan) is the preferred benzodiazepine because it is available orally and as an injectable. Medication is administered either in the oral (tablet or concentrate) or intramuscular (IM) form, depending upon the patient's willingness to take medication and the risk of imminent harm. If the patient requires frequent "as needed" doses, then the scheduled antipsychotic dose should be increased, or scheduled benzodiazepines added until agitation and combativeness subsides.

Some clinicians prefer giving low potency antipsychotics early in treatment since they are more sedating than the high potency agents, but the difference in their ability to calm the patient may not be clinically significant. Additionally, there is more dose flexibility with high potency agents, because more chlorpromazine equivalents can be given with less risk of anticholinergic and cardiovascular complications.

Another method to control extremely agitated and dangerous patients is "rapid tranquilization." Rapid tranquilization can be achieved when repeated IM injections of high potency antipsychotics or benzodiazepines are given every hour until either the patient is adequately calmed, a maximum recommended daily dose is reached, or dose-limiting adverse effects such as acute dystonia (antipsychotics) or ataxia and slurred speech (benzodiazepines) occur. Rapid tranquilization is neither intended for, nor more effective for, quickly controlling thought disorder, hallucinations, or delusions. Vital signs should be obtained before each injection and the dose held if clinically significant adverse effects occur.[54,55]

Fluphenazine (Prolixin) 5 mg IM three times a day should be prescribed on admission in the emergency room since it is a high potency agent, has a rapid onset of action, and because R.S. is uncooperative and likely to refuse oral medication. (See Question 8 for a discussion of factors influencing drug selection.) If additional pharmacotherapy is needed to reduce acute agitation and aggression, lorazepam 1 to 2 mg orally or IM every four to six hours as needed may be given with fluphenazine. Lorazepam may be more appropriate than fluphenazine as an "as needed" agent considering R.S.'s past history of EPSEs. "As needed" medication should be available until R.S. demonstrates no aggressive behavior for a few days.

Antipsychotic Selection

8. What factors should be considered when selecting an antipsychotic for inducing remission and what type of workup is necessary before treatment? Scheduled fluphenazine 5 mg PO BID is started after one IM injection resolved R.S.'s agitation. Why is this a reasonable choice?

Once the patient is no longer dangerous, the next priority is to control the thought disorder and induce a remission of the psy-

chotic episode. A complete medical, medication, and psychiatric history, physical exam, laboratory panel [electrolytes, liver, renal, and thyroid function tests, CBC with differential, urinalysis, urine toxicology screen], and electrocardiogram should be obtained as soon as possible after admission to rule out other causes of psychosis and give guidance for selecting an antipsychotic.

One of the best predictors of current response to an individual antipsychotic is the patient's, or their first-degree relative's, previous response to that same agent. If a patient experienced a poor response to a particular antipsychotic, another agent from a different chemical class should be prescribed. If a patient is on multiple medications, the antipsychotic with the least potential to cause drug-drug or drug-disease interactions should be selected. Consideration also should be given to the risk of specific antipsychotic-induced adverse effects when selecting a medication for an individual patient (see Tables 75.6 and 75.7).[23,56] An empiric approach is used in newly diagnosed, medically healthy patients, or in those without past medication histories.

The optimal dose for scheduled antipsychotics needed to induce remission is controversial, although some suggest that low doses are sufficient for most patients (see Question 11). Because higher doses used for initial behavioral control often are excessive for long-term treatment, it is important to re-evaluate both the antipsychotic dose and the need for continued benzodiazepines before discharge.

The last hospital discharge summary suggested that R.S. responded to trifluoperazine. Past experience with antipsychotics also is important in predicting therapeutic success. R.S. may not be compliant with trifluoperazine since it caused undesirable side effects resulting in noncompliance. Even though the "stiffness" that R.S. experienced could have been treated with appropriate antiparkinsonian therapy (see Question 21), his dissatisfaction with trifluoperazine may impair future compliance. Also, R.S. probably would not take thioridazine or chlorpromazine again because they made him feel "spaced out." Therefore, a high potency agent from a similar pharmacologic class to trifluoperazine, such as fluphenazine, would be a reasonable selection. Fluphenazine 5 mg twice a day is a common starting dose for inducing remission when the optimal dose for an individual patient is unknown. R.S.'s antipsychotic dose on previous hospital discharge (trifluoperazine 60 mg/day) should not be assumed to be optimal since many patients

Table 75.6	Relative Incidence of Antipsychotic Drug Adverse Effects[23]			
	Sedation	EPSE[a]	Anticholinergic	Cardiovascular
Low Potency Agents				
Chlorpromazine (Thorazine)	High	Moderate	Moderate	High[b]
Thioridazine (Mellaril)	High	Low	High	High[b]
High Potency Agents				
Trifluoperazine (Stelazine)	Low	High	Low	Low
Fluphenazine (Prolixin)	Low	Very High	Low	Low
Thiothixene (Navane)	Low	High	Low	Low
Haloperidol (Haldol)	Very Low	Very High	Very Low	Very Low
Loxapine (Loxitane)	Moderate	High	Low	Moderate[c]
Molindone (Moban)	Very Low	High	Low	Low
Atypical Agents				
Clozapine (Clozaril)	High	Very Low	High	High[b]
Risperidone (Risperdal)	High	Very Low[d]	Low	Moderate[e]

[a] EPSE = Extrapyramidal side effects.
[b] Orthostatic hypotension; arrhythmias can occur in overdose.
[c] Orthostatic hypotension; not arrhythmogenic in overdose.
[d] Very low at doses <8 mg/day.
[e] Orthostatic hypotension, tachycardia; arrhythmogenic in overdose (1 case).

Table 75.7	Antipsychotic Drug Dosage and Relative Potency by Chemical Class[a]					
	Relative Potency[b]			Traditional Equivalence	Acute Dose (mg/day)	Maintenance Dose (mg/day)
Chemical Class (Drug)	Acute	Chronic	Range			
Phenothiazines						
Aliphatic Type						
Chlorpromazine (Thorazine)	100	100	100	100	300–1500[c]	150–1000
Piperidine Type						
Thioridazine (Mellaril)	107	96	72–116	100	300–800[d]	150–800[d]
Piperazine Type						
Perphenazine (Trilafon)	8.5	9	7.7–10	10	32–96[c]	8–48
Trifluoperazine (Stelazine)	2.8	3.4	2.1–6.2	5	10–100	5–40
Fluphenazine (Prolixin)	1.2	1.4	1–1.5	2	5–80	2.5–40
Nonphenothiazines						
Thioxanthene						
Thiothixene (Navane)	3.4	3.1	1.3–5.4	4	5–100[c]	4–40
Butyrophenone						
Haloperidol (Haldol)	2.8	2.3	0.3–3.5	2	5–100	2–40
Dibenzoxazepine						
Loxapine (Loxitane)	10	8.8	7.5–10	10	50–250[c]	25–100
Dibenzazepine						
Clozapine (Clozaril)	50	50	—	50	150–900	50–400
Dihydroindolone						
Molindone (Moban)	7.6	4.4	3.1–10	10	25–400	25–100
Diphenylbutylpiperidone						
Pimozide (Orap)	—	1.2	0.7–1.6	1	10–30	4–10
Benzisoxazole						
Risperidone (Risperdal)	NA	NA	NA	NA	4–8	—[e]

[a] Adapted from reference 23.
[b] Acute, chronic, and range of antipsychotic potencies.[56]
[c] Dosages can be exceeded with caution, but high dose therapy rarely is needed.
[d] Maximum dose not to be exceeded due to risk for toxic retinopathy.
[e] Insufficient data to determine.

have short hospitalizations and are discharged on acute doses not appropriate for chronic schizophrenia. Concurrent antiparkinsonian therapy also should be considered.

Onset of Antipsychotic Action

9. When should R.S.'s target symptoms start to respond to fluphenazine?

During the first week, often known as the *medicated cooperation stage*, R.S. should respond to the calming properties of the antipsychotic, and his symptoms of hostility, agitation, and insomnia should improve. During the next two to six weeks, the *improved socialization stage*, R.S. should begin to obey hospital rules, attend ward meetings, and generally become more social. Severely ill schizophrenic patients with chronic disease may never reach this stage. The *elimination of thought disorder stage* can occur within any time frame, but usually takes at least two to three weeks and up to several months to occur. During this stage, the core symptoms of schizophrenia, such as delusions, hallucinations, and thought disturbance improve. During the final stage, or the *maintenance therapy stage*, the patient achieves his baseline level of functioning. Rapid dose escalation and rapid tranquilization will not reduce the antipsychotic response time. Patients, their families, and the treatment team must be educated to give antipsychotics an adequate chance to work before unnecessarily escalating the dose and increasing the risk of adverse effects. If no improvement of core symptoms is observed after three weeks, then the dose can be increased slowly and the patient observed for another three weeks.

Duration of Therapy and Goal of Maintenance Treatment

10. R.S. wants to know when he can stop the medication. What evidence suggests the need for long-term treatment in R.S.?

The goal of maintenance treatment in schizophrenia is to prevent relapse of the current psychotic episode and recurrence of future episodes. Placebo-controlled trials evaluating the efficacy of antipsychotics in relapse prevention found a mean one-year relapse rate of 74% of placebo subjects versus 16% for those on antipsychotic medication.[57] In practice, antipsychotic efficacy is much lower, with up to 50% of schizophrenics relapsing in the first year.[58] The long-term efficacy of antipsychotics in preventing recurrence is uncertain because of insufficient numbers of long-term studies (i.e., >5 years).

The following guidelines for maintenance therapy should be followed as there are no reliable predictors of relapse and recurrence for an individual patient. All schizophrenic patients should receive maintenance therapy, unless antipsychotics are not tolerated, or the diagnosis is uncertain. Treatment should continue for one to two years after an initial episode and for at least five years after multiple episodes. Life-long treatment is indicated in patients who present significant risk to themselves or others when unmedicated or for patients with a history of multiple recurrent episodes.[59,60] Since R.S. experienced his first episode of schizophrenia seven years ago, and also has a history of multiple hospitalizations, it is likely he will need life-long treatment.

Long-Term Dosing Strategies

11. What dose should be used in long-term management of patients?

During the 1960s and 1970s, high-dose antipsychotic therapy for the chronic treatment of schizophrenia was used because high-dose regimens were thought to shorten the length of hospitalization, decrease costs, and improve patient outcome. More recent studies, however, have shown no difference in response rates in schizophrenic patients receiving high- versus low-dose therapy (haloperidol 10 mg/day versus 30 mg/day versus 80 mg/day; haloperidol 11.6 mg/day versus 3.4 mg/day).[61,62] However, most of these trials have evaluated response in the acute, short-term treatment of schizophrenia only.

When developing a long-term strategy for prevention of recurrence, both total daily antipsychotic dose and the dosing schedule must be considered. The higher doses used initially for behavioral control do not serve as the basis for determining a maintenance dose. After remission of acute symptoms, maintenance medication should continue at the same total daily dose that produced the remission for an additional three to six months. Then dose reductions aimed at finding the minimum effective dose should be undertaken. Because of the long lag time between dose changes and onset of symptoms, and because patients are most likely to experience a recurrence within the first year after dose reduction, a conservative decrease of 20% every three to six months is recommended.[60,63] The rate of dose reduction may be more aggressive after an initial episode so that antipsychotics are discontinued within one to two years.

The minimum effective dose varies for individual patients, however, analysis of several trials suggests that doses as low as 2.5 mg/day of oral fluphenazine, 6.5 to 12.5 mg every two weeks of fluphenazine decanoate (Prolixin-D), or 50 to 200 mg of haloperidol decanoate (Haldol-D) every four weeks can prevent recurrence.[60,64–66] Administration of the lowest effective dose improves quality of life and social functioning, and reduces the incidence of pseudoparkinsonism, akathisia, and tardive dyskinesia.

Very low doses of fluphenazine decanoate (1.25 to 5 mg Q 2 weeks) have been compared to standard doses (12.5 to 50 mg Q 2 weeks). More recurrences were reported in the very low dose group, however, they usually did not result in rehospitalization, caused little social disruption, and responded to temporary dose increases. Patients on lower doses had better social functioning and perhaps a lower risk for tardive dyskinesia.[67]

Intermittent therapy also has been used to minimize antipsychotic exposure. With intermittent therapy, antipsychotics are tapered slowly and discontinued, then the patient is evaluated regularly and restarted on antipsychotics at the first sign of decompensation. This strategy has merit because patients with schizophrenia usually do not experience abrupt recurrences. However, the patient and caregiver must be able to accurately detect prodromal symptoms and immediately restart medication in order to abort a full-blown psychotic episode. In addition, data suggest that patients receiving intermittent therapy have more psychotic episodes and rehospitalizations than patients receiving continual treatment.[68,69] Research that better describes the risks and benefits of intermittent antipsychotic therapy is needed.

Once R.S. has been stabilized for about six months on fluphenazine, then the dose can be reduced by 20% every three to six months. If he exhibits recurrent target symptoms of schizophrenia or decompensation, then the dose should be increased to the previous effective dose. Since it is likely R.S. will require life-long antipsychotics, it is important to find the minimal effective dose to prevent recurrence.

Depot Antipsychotic Therapy

Indications

12. M.S., a 24-year-old male, was brought to the ER by the police because voices told him to strike his mother. His medical workup and urine drug screen were negative. M.S. has a diagnosis of schizophrenia, undifferentiated type, and has been rehospitalized 4 times in the last 2 years secondary to medication noncompliance. He has had the same presentation on all previous hospitalizations. During his last hospitalization, M.S. was stabilized on thiothixene (Navane) 20 mg HS without any signs of adverse effects. How can depot therapy with an IM formulation decrease readmissions, and how do we determine if M.S. is a good candidate for IM depot therapy?

Noncompliance rates with antipsychotic therapy are high, with estimates that only 40% to 50% of patients who require maintenance therapy follow through with treatment.[70] Clearly, noncompliance is a cause of early relapse and recurrence. Administration of intramuscular long-acting fluphenazine decanoate or haloperidol decanoate at weekly to monthly intervals ensures consistent medication delivery. A study comparing two-year rehospitalization rates in outpatients with schizophrenia who received either no medication, oral, depot, or combined therapy (oral and depot) found significantly fewer rehospitalizations with the depot group and the most with the combined group. Both oral and depot patients were noncompliant, but the problem was greater with the oral group.[71]

Despite the relative advantages of intramuscular depot therapy, some physicians are reluctant to use it. Estimates indicate that 10% to 20% of American patients receive depot therapy, compared to 50% in the United Kingdom. Underutilization may be based upon concerns over increased adverse effects, poor acceptance of injections, or medicolegal reasons. A comparison of complications from oral and intramuscular depot therapy found no evidence of an increased risk of neuroleptic malignant syndrome (NMS), extrapyramidal side effects, or tardive dyskinesia specifically related to the depot dosage form. Patients have varied reactions to receiving medication by injection; thus, individual discussions are needed to evaluate potential compliance. Finally, there are no data to demonstrate greater liability for physicians using one antipsychotic dosage form over another.[72]

Good candidates for depot therapy include patients who are noncompliant with oral medication and in need of long-term maintenance antipsychotics. Patients who respond to the oral formulation of an antipsychotic medication that also is available for depot administration, and who are able to tolerate high-potency antipsychotics, currently are stabilized, and express willingness to receive injections also serve as excellent candidates for depot therapy. Intramuscular depot therapy also is indicated if there is evidence of poor absorption of the oral dosage form.

M.S. is a good candidate for depot therapy because he requires maintenance therapy as evidenced by multiple recurrences secondary to noncompliance. He should be able to tolerate higher potency antipsychotics because he has minimal adverse effects from a good size dose of thiothixene. Further evaluation is needed to determine whether he will respond to haloperidol or fluphenazine, or be willing to take injections.

Depot Products

13. What intramuscular depot preparations are available and what are the differences between them?

Fluphenazine is available in the decanoate ester and enanthate forms. The decanoate form is preferred because it has a longer duration of action and fewer adverse effects.[73] Haloperidol is available only in the decanoate form. Fluphenazine and haloperidol decanoate are both high potency antipsychotics with adverse effects similar to their oral counterparts. The major difference between the decanoate products is the frequency of administration, as fluphenazine usually is given every one to three weeks, while haloperidol is given every two to four weeks. These products should never be given intravenously (IV).

Conversion from Oral to Depot Therapy

14. How could M.S. be converted from oral therapy to depot therapy?

A trial lasting several days to weeks of the oral dosage formulation should be given before converting to the depot product. This trial is necessary to ensure that high potency antipsychotics can be tolerated, the patient is responsive to the medication and, when possible, to determine the minimum effective oral dose. Caution is needed during the conversion to prevent administration of unnecessarily high doses. A study compared medical records of 20 randomly identified schizophrenic patients receiving fluphenazine decanoate to 20 randomly identified schizophrenic patients taking oral medications. The decanoate group had a significantly higher mean chlorpromazine-equivalent dose than the oral group. The two groups did not differ on any other variables such as age, education, race, sex, socioeconomic status, or mean age at first admission.[74]

Various formulas to convert oral to decanoate have been proposed, with no single method clinically superior to another. Goals of depot therapy also should include using the longest dosing interval between injections and minimizing the duration of combination oral and depot therapy. Since no one method of conversion is superior, careful evaluation of both tolerance and response is required for several months after initiation of depot therapy.

Fluphenazine Decanoate Conversion. After stabilizing the patient on oral fluphenazine, multiply the total daily fluphenazine oral dose by 1.2 and administer as fluphenazine decanoate IM every one to two weeks.[75] The decanoate dosing interval may be increased to every three weeks after four to six weeks of therapy because of fluphenazine accumulation.[23]

Alternatively, 12.5 mg of fluphenazine decanoate can be administered intramuscularly every one to two weeks for every 10 mg (rounding to the nearest 10 mg increment) of oral fluphenazine a day (e.g., 25 mg/day PO rounded to 30 mg/day and given as 37.5 mg of decanoate).[76] There are no specific guidelines for the continuation of oral therapy after initiating the depot formulation, however, combination oral and intramuscular therapy should be limited to the initiation period or during times of decompensation.

Haloperidol Decanoate Conversion. Initial guidelines for converting to haloperidol decanoate described a slow titration upward of the decanoate with continuation of oral therapy for up to three months. This method often resulted in slow stabilization over several months, a problem generally resolved by newer recommendations. Current recommendations are as follows: Elderly patients or those stabilized on less than 10 mg of oral haloperidol per day should receive haloperidol decanoate in an intramuscular dose that is 10 to 15 times the oral dose every four weeks. If higher oral doses are needed for stabilization, then the first decanoate dose should be 15 to 20 times the oral daily dose to a maximum of 450 mg.[77] The first injection of haloperidol decanoate should not exceed 100 mg, and if more is required, the balance of the dose can be given in an additional one to two injections (providing there are no EPSEs) over three to seven days. Due to haloperidol accumulation, the monthly decanoate dose should be decreased by 25% a month until a minimum effective dose is achieved. The average maintenance dose appears to be about 200 mg every four weeks. Guidelines for concomitant oral therapy remain unclear and should be based upon response and adverse effects, with the goal of depot alone by three to four months of treatment.[64,66,67]

M.S. should be started on 10 mg of oral haloperidol a day, based upon the conversion from thiothixene 20 mg (see Table 75.7). The oral haloperidol should be continued alone for one week or longer until M.S. is stabilized. Then, haloperidol decanoate 100 mg IM can be given, followed with 50 mg IM given three days later (if no adverse effects are noted after first injection) for a total of 150 mg every four weeks (15 times the oral dose). No oral medication would be given at this time unless M.S. shows signs of decompensation. M.S. should be monitored carefully for EPSEs and response. M.S. will receive haloperidol decanoate 150 mg IM every four weeks with the dose adjusted according to response and tolerance. The decanoate dose should be decreased after three to four months because of accumulation.

Partial Response

15. M.C., a 33-year-old male, was diagnosed with chronic paranoid schizophrenia at age 21 and has been hospitalized 15 times since his diagnosis. He always presents in a paranoid and hostile state complaining of auditory hallucinations and paranoid delusions where the police and the people in his apartment building are trying to kill him. He has been treated with haloperidol, chlorpromazine, thiothixene, and loxitane. M.C. has had only a partial response to each medication and remains symptomatic, despite adequate trials. After each discharge, he stays out of the hospital for about 6 months, then relapses. He currently is taking haloperidol 15 mg HS. Can adjunctive medications be added to improve response to the antipsychotic?

Lithium. Forty-seven subjects were evaluated in three studies to determine the efficacy of adding *lithium* to antipsychotics in nonresponsive patients with schizophrenia or schizoaffective disorder.[78-80] About 50% of subjects had improvement in mood, psychosis, and "psychotic excitement." Affective symptoms are not a prerequisite for response to lithium.[78,79] From the limited data, a one-month trial of lithium in doses to provide serum concentrations of 0.9 to 1.2 mEq/L can be tried in nonresponsive patients. Reports of increased neurotoxicity from combining lithium and antipsychotics are inconclusive, and the risk may be no different than with either medication alone. The best study compared 69 subjects receiving lithium and antipsychotics to 60 patients on antipsychotics alone and found no cases of neurotoxicity.[81]

Benzodiazepines can improve schizophrenia-related insomnia and anxiety. The trials evaluating the effect of benzodiazepines on the core features of schizophrenia are equivocal, with some showing no improvement and others finding a reduction in psychotic symptoms.[82] Alprazolam (Xanax) in doses up to 5 mg a day for four weeks improved hallucinations, paranoia, and thought disorder in about half of the patients.[83] It is impossible at this point to predict who may respond to adjunctive alprazolam, and any potential benefit must be balanced with the risk of benzodiazepine abuse and withdrawal if the patient is noncompliant. A two- to four-week trial may be tried in nonresponders without a history of substance abuse or personality disorders.[82,84]

Propranolol (Inderal), in combination with antipsychotics, has been evaluated in nonresponders, with variable results. Potential explanations for the enhanced efficacy include a drug interaction leading to higher antipsychotic serum concentration, relief of akathisia, or a primary improvement in psychosis. Additionally, propranolol may be useful in managing chronic aggression sometimes found in patients with schizophrenia.[85] Some patients respond to the addition of propranolol despite poorly defined dosing guidelines; however, high doses generally are well tolerated. Propranolol should be started at 40 to 80 mg twice a day and increased every other day until intolerable adverse effects occur (systolic BP of <90 mm Hg or a heart rate <50 beats/minute). Doses as low as

160 mg and as high as 1920 mg have been effective; however, a reasonable trial usually is considered to be at least 240 mg/day for two months.[46,85,86]

Carbamazepine (Tegretol) has been evaluated in several clinical trials with conflicting results. A review by Neppe summarized that patients with nonresponsive psychosis and agitation, aggression, or "interpersonal difficulties" may benefit from a trial of carbamazepine.[87] A later trial comparing 162 nonresponders receiving carbamazepine or placebo in addition to chlorpromazine for four weeks found carbamazepine (mean dose: 586 mg/day) to be superior to placebo for "excitement" and psychosis. However, the differences had limited clinical significance.[88] Because of the lack of consensus, carbamazepine should be considered only after trials of lithium, benzodiazepines, and possibly propranolol have failed, or for patients with significant affective lability or concurrent mania.[84]

Since M.C. has no precautions or contraindications to adjunctive medications, he is a candidate for a one-month lithium trial or a two-week alprazolam trial along with haloperidol therapy.

Clozapine

Indications

16. M.C. has continued to deteriorate and become less responsive to antipsychotic therapy. He also has become more socially withdrawn and has not stayed out of the hospital for more than 1 month over the past 6 months. M.C. was just readmitted. He has no other medical conditions, and currently is medication-free except for lorazepam 1-2 mg Q 4-6 hr PRN. Because of his refractory illness, M.C. is being considered for clozapine therapy. What makes M.C. a good candidate for clozapine therapy?

Clozapine is approved by the Food and Drug Administration (FDA) for treatment of resistant schizophrenia or when adverse effects such as tardive dyskinesia and extrapyramidal side effects preclude use of other antipsychotics. Resistant schizophrenia is defined as at least moderate degrees of positive or negative symptoms accompanied by declining social functioning after adequate trials of three or more antipsychotics in two or more pharmacological classes.[89] In the pivotal study demonstrating clozapine's benefit in refractory schizophrenia, 33% of clozapine patients responded, while only 4% of chlorpromazine subjects responded. In addition to improvement in positive symptoms, clozapine patients also had significant improvement in Brief Psychiatric Rating Scale (BPRS) negative symptom subscales for emotional withdrawal, affective blunting, and psychomotor retardation. Even though one-third of subjects improved, many remained moderately ill.[90] Because of M.C.'s progressive decline in social functioning and inadequate response to haloperidol, chlorpromazine, thiothixene, and loxitane, clozapine should be considered. In addition, the long-term financial burden of M.C.'s illness may be decreased since clozapine can significantly reduce costs by reducing the frequency and duration of hospitalizations in chronically ill patients.[91]

Clozapine is contraindicated in patients with a history of myeloproliferative disorders, bone marrow suppression, or clozapine-induced agranulocytosis. There is debate whether to use clozapine in patients with a history of medication-induced agranulocytosis; however, previous carbamazepine-induced bone marrow suppression does not appear to increase the risk for agranulocytosis from clozapine. Clozapine also should be used with caution in patients intolerant to anticholinergic effects, those at risk for drug-induced orthostasis, or in patients with significant renal or hepatic disease.[89,92] M.C. is a good candidate for clozapine because he has no medical contraindications and he had a poor response despite adequate trials to four antipsychotics in four chemical classes.

Initiation of Therapy

17. How should clozapine be initiated in M.C.?

Whenever possible, clozapine should be initiated when a patient is medication free. If the patient is too ill to be off antipsychotics before adding clozapine, the first antipsychotic can be discontinued after a therapeutic clozapine dose has been achieved. Alternatively, clozapine may be initiated while the first antipsychotic is slowly tapered. When necessary, high potency antipsychotics should be used during initiation of clozapine to minimize additive adverse effects such as sedation, anticholinergic side effects, or orthostasis. Benzodiazepines can be used cautiously as "PRNs" for behavioral and anxiety control early in treatment, but large doses should be avoided because of the potential for respiratory failure.[53,89]

Due to the risk for agranulocytosis, baseline and repeated weekly complete blood counts are required during treatment. Although current guidelines mandate weekly CBCs, arguments for obtaining biweekly CBCs have been made since most patients who develop agranulocytosis typically have a slow prodromal duration of neutrophil decline. Noncompliance with scheduled appointments for blood work necessitates discontinuation of clozapine. Clozapine can be started in an outpatient setting if there is careful monitoring of vital signs. The starting dose is usually 12.5 to 25 mg once a day with increases of 25 mg every other day until the dose is 100 mg/day. Subsequently, the dose can be increased by 50 mg every other day until reaching 300 to 450 mg/day. These doses are increased gradually to avoid oversedation and orthostasis. Clozapine also should be given in divided doses. Initially, the dose should not exceed 600 mg/day because of a dose-related seizure risk, but can be increased to a maximum of 900 mg/day in poor responders. Response should be based upon improvement of individual target symptoms and can be measured by an instrument such as the BPRS. Additionally, the overall ability of a patient to function and care for himself during clozapine therapy also should be considered.[93]

About 30% of patients will have an initial response after six weeks. An adequate trial is 4 to 12 months in duration, as more patients continue to respond and those who responded earlier can have continued improvement.[94] As with all antipsychotics, informed consent should be documented in the patient records. Adverse effects of clozapine versus traditional antipsychotics are described in Table 75.8.[92,95]

If baseline laboratory work is within normal limits and an informed consent is obtained, clozapine 25 mg at bedtime can be started in M.C. His clozapine dose should be increased by 25 mg every other day until the dose is 100 mg/day. Subsequently, the clozapine should be increased incrementally according to the guidelines described above. If M.C. has no response to 300 mg after a few weeks (based upon a reduction in BPRS scores and global improvement), then the dose can be increased to 450 mg. If response still is inadequate, then the dose can be increased slowly to a maximum of 900 mg/day. Careful monitoring for orthostasis and over sedation is needed, especially during early titration.

18. Four weeks after starting clozapine, M.C.'s white blood cell (WBC) count drops to 4000/mm³. Two weeks later, he has a WBC count of 3100/mm³ and an absolute neutrophil count (ANC) of 1000/mm³. What action, if any, should be taken? [SI units: WBC count 4.0 and 3.1 × 10⁹/L, respectively]

The hematological profile for clozapine is very different than with other antipsychotics. The incidence of clozapine-induced agranulocytosis is about 1%, at least 10 to 20 times greater than the incidence with typical antipsychotics.[89] Analysis of data from 11,555 patients followed by the Clozaril Patient Management System found agranulocytosis in 73 patients and two related deaths.

Table 75.8	Most Frequently Reported Adverse Reactions in Percent of Patients Reporting[a],[92],[95]				
Adverse Reaction	Clozapine (n=634)	Chlorpromazine (n=204)	Haloperidol (n=67)	Chlorpromazine + Benztropine (n=142)	Haloperidol + Benztropine (n=305)
Central Nervous System					
Drowsiness	44	46	39	13	6
Dizziness	22	14	12	17	3
Tremor	7	12	25	1	4
Syncope	7	2	4	1	0
Headache	7	8	6	10	9
Insomnia	6	22	36	3	4
Restlessness	5	18	24	0	0
Hypokinesia	5	10	16	0	0
Rigidity	5	6	30	1	5
Akathisia	4	7	28	1	7
Agitation	4	10	24	4	5
Confusion	4	5	4	1	0.3
Hyperkinesia	2	0.5	12	0	0
Convulsions	2	0.5	0	1	1
Speech difficulty	1	1	0	3	0
Appetite loss	1	0.5	0	0	1
Lethargy	1	0	0	0	0.3
Weakness	1	1	1	0	0.3
Autonomic					
Salivation	32	11	16	1	0.3
Sweating	8	9	15	0	0
Dry mouth	7	23	16	20	16
Cardiovascular					
Tachycardia	10	2	1	11	1
Hypotension	7	2	1	38	7
Hypertension	3	0	1	5	1
Gastrointestinal					
Constipation	14	11	6	12	11
Nausea/vomiting	11	7	12	20	8
Abdominal discomfort	3	0	0	11	6
Integumentary					
Rash	1	2	1	1	1
Hematologic					
Leukopenia/white blood cells	2	0	0	4	0
Miscellaneous					
Fever[a]	4	1	1	4	2
Weight gain	3	0	0	0	0

[a] Underestimated due to study design.

Sixty-one of the seventy-three patients developed agranulocytosis within the first three months of treatment. The incidence increased with age and was higher among women.[96] There are occasional cases of agranulocytosis reported up to five years after clozapine initiation.[53],[89] Trends in the weekly CBCs showing a continual decline in WBC count, even if it remains above 3000/mm^3, require careful attention. A total WBC count below 3000/mm^3, or an absolute neutrophil count below 1500/mm^3 necessitates immediate clozapine discontinuation. Clozapine should be discontinued immediately in M.C., and hospitalization and management with a hematologist and/or infectious disease specialist is indicated. Clozapine rechallenge in a patient who developed agranulocytosis is contraindicated.[97] If clozapine is discontinued when the WBC count is between 2000 to 3500/mm^3, rechallenge can be tried after the WBC count normalizes. More frequent WBC counts and very careful clinical monitoring may be indicated because of increased risk for developing agranulocytosis.[89] Clozapine probably should not be retried in M.C. due to the very low ANC.

Serum Concentration Monitoring

19. E.H., a 68-year-old female, was diagnosed with chronic undifferentiated schizophrenia over 30 years ago and continues to need maintenance antipsychotics because she relapsed when her dose was decreased to 10 mg/day. She has been taking haloperidol 15 mg at bedtime for 6 weeks with no response, despite compliance. She has moderate pseudoparkinsonism controlled by benztropine 1 mg BID. Why should a serum concentration of haloperidol be obtained before increasing E.H.'s dose of this drug?

Antipsychotic serum concentrations are not part of routine clinical care, but can be considered under the following circumstances:[98],[99]

- Poor response to moderate doses after an adequate trial (dose and duration).
- Serious or unexpected adverse effects at moderate doses.
- Deterioration in a compliant and previously stable patient.
- Using higher than usual doses.

- Evaluating whether the lowest effective dose is used in maintenance therapy.
- Children, elderly, and medically-compromised patients with potentially-altered pharmacokinetics.

It is unnecessary and not cost effective to obtain serum concentrations for antipsychotics without defined therapeutic ranges. Most studies describe haloperidol's therapeutic range to be between 5 to 15 ng/mL.[100-102] One study found the therapeutic range to be 15 to 40 ng/mL for patients with chronic illness.[103] The recommended ranges for fluphenazine and thiothixene are 0.2 to 2.8 ng/mL and 2 to 15 ng/mL, respectively.[104-107] In one study, 64% of subjects responded to clozapine greater than 350 ng/mL, while 22% responded to concentrations less than 350 ng/mL.[108] Further evaluation of the data in this study and newer work suggest the optimal concentration for clozapine to be between 400 to 500 ng/mL.[109] Samples should be collected five to seven days after a fixed dose and 10 to 12 hours after the last dose for oral preparations. Two to three months should elapse before samples are collected in patients taking depot preparations.[98]

E.H. has received an adequate trial of haloperidol and has moderate pseudoparkinsonism. In order to prevent exposure to higher than necessary doses, a serum haloperidol concentration is warranted before increasing the dose. The target serum concentration should be between 5 to 15 ng/mL.

Antipsychotic-Induced Adverse Effects and Their Treatment

Pseudoparkinsonism

Pseudoparkinsonism is one of a group of antipsychotic-induced adverse effects collectively called the extrapyramidal side effects (EPSEs). Pseudoparkinsonism has many features of idiopathic Parkinson's disease, except that symptoms [e.g., resting tremor, lead pipe or cogwheeling (ratchet-like) rigidity in the limbs, akinesia (reduction in spontaneous activity), reduced arm swing, drooling, and mask-like facies] are reversible. Tremors and rigidity may be unilateral or bilateral.[53,110] A perioral lip tremor called "rabbit syndrome" is a rare complication. Symptoms can occur at any time, but usually develop within four weeks after antipsychotic initiation or a dose increase. The incidence of pseudoparkinsonism varies with age; and women, especially older women, are more susceptible. The incidence increases with total daily dose and potency of the antipsychotic. Akinesia can be easily confused with depression or negative schizophrenia, and both must be considered as part of the differential diagnosis. The Modified Simpson Angus Rating Scale commonly is used to assess the presence and severity of EPSEs (see Table 75.9).[111]

Pseudoparkinsonism is thought to be secondary to postsynaptic dopamine receptor blockade in the nigrostriatal system, leading to an imbalance between the dopaminergic and cholinergic systems. Reasons for the delay in onset between receptor blockade, which occurs within hours after initiating an antipsychotic, and development of symptoms are not well understood.[110]

Clinical Presentation

20. S.B., a 31-year-old male, has a diagnosis of chronic undifferentiated schizophrenia and was treated with loxapine 50 mg TID with inadequate response. The dose cannot be increased because he becomes oversedated. Because of the incomplete response, S.B. was switched to haloperidol 5 mg Q AM and 10 mg HS. One week after the switch, S.B. returns to clinic complaining of feeling "real slow." He has a bilateral hand tremor that improved when he picked up his coffee cup. Physical examination detected cogwheel rigidity in both arms,
worse on the right side. S.B. wants to be taken off this "bad" medication. What evidence suggests that S.B. has pseudoparkinsonism?

The onset of symptoms within one week of starting a new, high potency antipsychotic is the first clue to the presence of extrapyramidal effects. The "slow feeling" perhaps is indicative of akinesia and S.B.'s bilateral tremor and cogwheel rigidity also are features of pseudoparkinsonism.

Treatment

21. What antiparkinsonian drug could be selected for S.B., if any?

The initial treatment of pseudoparkinsonism is to reduce the dose of the antipsychotic, or add an antiparkinsonian medication (see Figure 75.1 and Table 75.10).[112] All antiparkinsonian agents are equally effective, although there are differences in adverse effects and duration of action. Trihexyphenidyl is the least sedating, while diphenhydramine is the most sedating. Benztropine has the longest duration and can be used once or twice a day if needed, while the others have to be used three to four times a day.[113] Benztropine 2 mg twice a day could be initiated for S.B. because he probably is too psychiatrically unstable to tolerate a reduction in haloperidol dose. The tremor, rigidity, and akinesia should improve greatly over the next few days of treatment and anticholinergic side effects should not be apparent.

22. How long should benztropine be continued in S.B. now that his EPSEs are resolved?

Some patients develop tolerance to the symptoms of pseudoparkinsonism, while others have only partial resolution of symptoms and need long-term treatment. As many as 30% of patients chronically treated with antipsychotics will continue to have symptoms of pseudoparkinsonism.[53] Antiparkinsonian treatment for S.B. should be continued for three months. If S.B. is asymptomatic at the end of three months, the dose of the antiparkinsonian drug should be decreased and then discontinued. If symptoms of pseudoparkinsonism recur after the discontinuation of benztropine, reinstitute it for an additional three months before attempting to discontinue it again. If symptoms still recur then re-evaluation can be extended to every 6 to 12 months. Extended antiparkinsonian treatment is only indicated for patients with chronic pseudoparkinsonism. Antiparkinsonian therapy should always be re-evaluated after any change in antipsychotic therapy.

23. Risks of Long-Term Treatment. What risks are associated with long-term anticholinergic treatment and would S.B. be particularly susceptible to these risks?

Some patients will abuse anticholinergic medications for mood elevating and hallucinogenic effects. Factors such as fear of discontinuation because of EPSEs or inadequate treatment of EPSEs should be considered before affixing a diagnosis of anticholinergic drug abuse and stopping treatment. A study to identify factors associated with anticholinergic abuse found that the abusers had significantly more subjective effects (e.g., euphoria or a "buzz") from the anticholinergic drugs than did the control group. The abusers had ingested significantly more drugs in the past and had taken antipsychotics and anticholinergics longer than did the control group.[114] Long-term anticholinergic therapy in patients with concurrent substance abuse should be monitored carefully for excessive use. The relationship between long-term anticholinergic usage and tardive dyskinesia will be presented later in the chapter. S.B. does not have a history of substance abuse and should be continued on benztropine as long as needed to control his EPSEs.

24. One week after the benztropine was started, S.B.'s psychiatric symptoms began to respond to the haloperidol, but he developed acute urinary retention. Reduction of the benztropine dose to 2 mg/day did not improve his urinary retention.

Table 75.9		Modified Simpson Angus Scale for Evaluating Extrapyramidal Symptoms[a,b]	
Gait	The patient is examined as he walks into the examining room. His gait, the swing of his arms, his general posture, all form the basis for an overall score.	0 - Normal 1 - Diminution in swing 2 - Marked diminution in swing 3 - Stiff—loss of swing 4 - Shuffling	
Arm dropping	The patient and the examiner both raise their arms to shoulder height and let them fall to their sides. In a normal subject, a stout slap is heard as the arms hit the sides. In the patient with extreme Parkinson's syndrome, the arms fall very slowly.	0 - Normal 1 - Less audible contact 2 - No rebound 3 - No slap 4 - As though against resistance	
Shoulder shaking	The subject's arms are taken one at a time by the examiner who grasps one hand and also clasps the other around the patient's elbow, bending the arm at a right angle at the elbow. The subject's upper arm is pushed to and fro and the humerus is externally rotated. The degree of resistance from normal to extreme rigidity is scored.	0 - Normal 1 - Slight rigidity 2 - Moderate rigidity 3 - Marked rigidity 4 - Extreme rigidity	
Elbow rigidity	The elbow joints are separately bent at right angles and passively extended and flexed, with the subject's biceps observed and simultaneously palpated. The resistance to this procedure is rated.	0 - Normal 1 - Slight rigidity 2 - Moderate rigidity 3 - Marked rigidity 4 - Extreme rigidity	
Wrist rigidity (fixation of position)	The wrist is held in one hand and the fingers held by the examiner's other hand, with the wrist moved to extension flexion and both ulnar and radial deviation. The resistance to this procedure is rated.	0 - Normal 1 - Slight rigidity 2 - Moderate rigidity 3 - Marked rigidity 4 - Extreme rigidity	
Glabella tap	The subject is told to open his eyes wide and not to blink. The glabella region is tapped at a steady, rapid speed. The number of times patient blinks in succession is rated.	0 - 0–5 blinks 1 - 6–10 blinks 2 - 11–15 blinks 3 - 16–20 blinks 4 - 21 or more blinks	
Tremor	Patient is observed walking into examining room and then is re-examined for tremor.	0 - Normal 1 - Mild finger tremor 2 - Spasmodic tremor of limb 3 - Persistent tremor of limb(s) 4 - Body tremor	
Salivation	Patient is observed while talking and then asked to open his mouth and elevate his tongue.	0 - Normal 1 - Pooling in mouth 2 - Occasional difficulty in speaking 3 - Consistent difficulty in speaking 4 - Drooling	
Akathisia	Motor restlessness seen as increased body activity during interview including inability to sit still or inappropriate pacing. Feelings of inner restlessness ("I want to jump out of my skin") also qualify.	0 - Normal 1 - Slight increase in motor rate or inner tension 2 - Moderate increase in motor rate or inner tension 3 - Marked increase in motor rate or inner tension 4 - Extreme: Cannot sit still, walks around	
Akinesia	The patient's entrance and exit are noted for evidence of reduced rate of motor activity. In parkinsonism, there may be an obviously reduced rate of spontaneous motor activity of which the patient may or may not be aware. This symptom may masquerade as apathy or autism.	0 - Absent 1 - Mild: Loss of energy, apathetic 2 - Moderate: Some slowed movements and loss of muscle tone 3 - Severe: Definite motor slowing and loss of facial expression 4 - Extreme: Patient sits most of time, moves with great effort	
Cogwheel rigidity	The examiner "shakes hands" with the patient placing his free hand on the patient's elbow. The patient's forearm is passively driven by the examiner in a circular, front and back motion resembling the drive shaft on the wheels of a steam locomotive. The quality of movement of the forearm is rated. In Parkinsonism, the movement is not smooth, with alternating phases of increased and decreased resistance.	0 - Normal 1 - Mild hints of sporadic, increased resistance 2 - Obvious evidence of cogwheel rigidity 3 - Marked evidence of cogwheel rigidity 4 - Arm moves only with great resistance	

[a] Reprinted with permission from reference 111.
[b] Head drop rating removed in modified scale.

What alternative treatments are available to manage S.B.'s pseudoparkinsonian symptoms that are without anticholinergic effects?

S.B. is just beginning to gain benefit from his haloperidol; therefore, the haloperidol dose should not be reduced. Amantadine (Symmetrel), an antiparkinsonian medication that directly stimulates postsynaptic dopamine receptors and restores the cholinergic and dopaminergic balance in the nigrostriatium, would be a reasonable alternative to benztropine in S.B. Amantadine is an option for patients intolerant or poorly responsive to anticholinergics and often is preferred in the elderly because of the lower incidence of cognitive impairment. The parkinsonian symptoms usually respond within 24 hours.

Amantadine 100 mg twice a day should be started in S.B., provided that the cost is not prohibitive, as amantadine costs about five times more than anticholinergic therapy. Benztropine also should be discontinued. He should be monitored to determine whether EPSEs reappear and whether his urinary retention problem is corrected. He also should be monitored for the appearance of amantadine-associated, dose-related adverse effects such as tremor, slurred speech, ataxia, depression, hallucinations, rash, orthostatic hypotension, and insomnia. If S.B. cannot tolerate amantadine, or if amantadine does not control his EPSEs, benztropine can be restarted with the addition of bethanechol 25 mg three times a day. Bethanechol is a cholinergic agonist used to treat urinary retention from a multitude of causes.

Prevention

25. Could pseudoparkinsonism have been prevented in S.B.?

The decision of when to use prophylactic antiparkinsonian medications remains controversial. Anticholinergic drugs such as benztropine can prevent uncomfortable, subtle, and poorly recognized adverse effects which can lead to noncompliance of antipsychotic medications; however, routine prophylaxis can expose patients to unnecessary anticholinergic adverse effects. Candidates for prophylactic antiparkinsonian therapy include patients with a history of EPSEs, significant risk factors, or compliance risks if symptoms develop. If a clear decision cannot be made, ''as needed'' antiparkinsonian agents accompanied with conversion to scheduled medication if symptoms develop can be considered. Follow-up for prophylaxis is the same as with active treatment (see Figure 75.1).

S.B. previously was treated with loxapine, a medium potency antipsychotic without experiencing difficulties, but because of inadequate response was converted to an equivalent dose of haloperidol, a high-potency agent. He is at some risk for EPSEs because he is young and is now taking a more potent antipsychotic. Either an ''as needed'' or prophylactic antiparkinsonian agent for about two weeks with re-evaluation might have prevented pseudoparkinsonism in S.B.

Acute Dystonia

Acute dystonia has the earliest onset of all the EPSEs, as most cases occur within the first few days after an increase in the dose or after initiation of antipsychotic medication. Acute dystonia presents with a sudden onset of brief or sustained abnormal postures, including tongue protrusion, oculogyric crisis (eyes rolling back into head), trismus (spasm of the jaw), torticollis (torsion of the neck), and unusual positions in the trunk, limbs, and toes. Differential diagnoses include malingering, hysteria, and seizures. Young patients, especially males and those receiving high potency antipsychotics, are at greatest risk to experience dystonia.[53,110]

The exact pathophysiology of acute dystonia is uncertain. Conflicting theories describe either a hypodopaminergic or hyperdopaminergic state after an antipsychotic-induced blockade of post-

Fig 75.1 An algorithm for managing acute extrapyramidal syndromes (EPS) Reprinted with permission from reference 11. ªEPSE = Extrapyramidal side effect.

synaptic dopamine receptors. Rising or falling antipsychotic concentrations early in treatment also may play a role. Acute dystonia likely is caused by dysregulation of the dopamine system and imbalance between neurotransmitter systems after acute antipsychotic administration.[110]

26. J.P., a 19-year-old male, was brought to the psychiatric ER because of assaultive behavior toward his mother. J.P. struck her because the devil told him to do it. Trifluoperazine 5 mg IM Q 4-6 hr PRN was started to control his assaultive behavior. He received four IM injections over 24 hours and was converted to 15 mg HS. On day 2 of the admission he complained of a stiff neck and protruding tongue. J.P. became very upset and wanted to leave the hospital and never take these medications again. No other medical conditions were noted. What evidence suggests that J.P. is experiencing an acute dystonia reaction?

The sudden appearance of a stiff neck and a protruding tongue in J.P. is consistent with acute dystonia. Additionally, J.P.'s young age, male gender, and use of a high potency antipsychotic also place him at high risk for experiencing dystonia.

27. How should acute dystonia be treated in J.P.?

Acute dystonia requires immediate treatment, even though it is self-limiting, because of the distress it creates for the patient and the paranoia that may be directed at both the antipsychotic medication and caregivers. The initial goal of treatment is to relieve symptoms as soon as possible. J.P. can be given either benztropine 1 to 2 mg or diphenhydramine 25 to 50 mg by IM injection. There are no specific advantages of either medication. Even though the

Table 75.10	Agents to Treat Pseudoparkinsonism and Akathisia	
Medication	Equivalent Dose (mg)	Dose/day (mg)
Anticholinergics		
Benztropine (Cogentin)[a]	0.5	2–8
Biperiden (Akineton)[a]	0.5	2–8
Diphenhydramine (Benadryl)[a]	25	50–250
Procyclidine (Kemadrin)	1.5	10–20
Trihexyphenidyl (Artane)	1	2–15
Dopaminergic		
Amantadine	—	100–300
Gabaminergic		
Diazepam (Valium)	10	5–40
Clonazepam (Klonopin)	2	1–3
Lorazepam (Ativan)[a]	2	1–3
Noradrenergic Blockers		
Propranolol (Inderal)	—	30–120

[a] PO or IM can be used.

IV route has a faster onset of action, it is not needed in J.P. because his reaction is not severe. If symptoms do not resolve within 15 to 30 minutes, then the dose should be repeated. Lorazepam 1 to 2 mg IM could be used if J.P. had a contraindication to anticholinergics. J.P. also must be reassured that this is a temporary condition that can be prevented and treated. Finally, further dystonic reactions can be prevented by oral anticholinergic therapy for two weeks after this dystonic reaction in doses commonly used for pseudoparkinsonism.[110] Therefore, anticholinergic prophylaxis probably should be given to J.P. because he is being treated with a high potency antipsychotic and because he has just experienced a dystonic reaction.[115]

Akathisia

Akathisia is a syndrome consisting of subjective feelings of anxiety and restlessness, and objective signs of pacing, rocking, and inability to sit or stand in one place for extended periods of time. Akathisia can increase aggression, is a frequent cause of noncompliance, and often is difficult to distinguish from psychomotor agitation and decompensation. It usually develops within days to weeks after initiating antipsychotic therapy.

Akathisia is the least understood of the neurologic antipsychotic-induced adverse effects. The adrenergic system may be involved because beta blockers are an effective treatment. Dopaminergic-cholinergic imbalance may not be directly involved because of the poor response to antiparkinsonian medications.[110]

28. J.P. was diagnosed with paranoid schizophrenia, acute episode and improved with trifluoperazine 15 mg HS with no other dystonic reactions. Two weeks later he became increasingly agitated, began pacing the floor, was unable to sit or lie down for more than 10 minutes at a time, and subjectively described a feeling like "I have ants in my pants." J.P. is observed rocking back and forth from one foot to the other while standing in line for his dinner. He has no symptoms of pseudoparkinsonism. Why are J.P.'s symptoms probably not an indication of a need to increase his dose of antipsychotics?

J.P.'s symptoms of rocking, pacing, agitation and the inability to sit still are consistent with akathisia. Because his psychiatric symptoms have improved with antipsychotics and the new symptoms developed within two weeks after the initiation of trifluoperazine, a diagnosis of akathisia is more probable. The trifluoperazine dose, therefore, should not be increased because it can worsen the akathisia.

29. How should J.P.'s akathisia be managed?

First-line treatment for J.P.'s akathisia should be a 5 mg/day dose reduction of trifluoperazine. If symptoms of his psychosis return, or the akathisia persists, then a beta blocker, an anticholinergic, or low-dose lorazepam or clonazepam can be considered. Lipophilic beta blockers such as propranolol (30 to 120 mg/day) are the agents of choice because they are most consistently effective. Anticholinergics should be used if pseudoparkinsonism is present concurrently with his akathisia. Replacement of J.P.'s trifluoperazine with a lower potency antipsychotic also can relieve his akathisia.

J.P. should be started on propranolol 20 mg three times a day increasing by 20 mg every other day to a maximum of 120 mg if his symptoms do not improve in response to a dosage reduction of his trifluoperazine within a week.[116] He has no contraindications to beta blocker therapy and does not have pseudoparkinsonism; therefore, antiparkinsonian agents (see Table 75.10 for doses) would not be preferred over propranolol. Benzodiazepines should be tried if the akathisia persists despite propranolol 120 mg/day therapy for one week.

Tardive Dyskinesia (TD)

Tardive dyskinesia is a syndrome of persistent and involuntary hyperkinetic abnormal movements that occur in individuals taking long-term antipsychotics. Symptoms of tardive dyskinesia commonly involve the face (tics, blinking, grimacing), tongue (chewing, protrusion, tremor, writhing), lips (smacking, pursing, puckering), neck and trunk (torsion and torticollis), and limbs (toe tapping, pill rolling, and writhing). Irregular breathing, grunting, and belching because of respiratory muscle involvement also can occur as part of the presentation. The severity of symptoms of tardive dyskinesia can fluctuate daily and symptoms often will remit during sleep.[110,117]

The prevalence of tardive dyskinesia ranges from 0.5% to 70%, but probably occurs in about 15% to 20% of patients. The yearly incidence is about 5%, with the greatest risk being in the first five years of treatment with antipsychotic medications. However, new cases can occur at any time.[110,118] Tardive dyskinesia is reversible in some cases and is not always progressive. About 60% to 70% of cases are mild and only 3% are severe enough to cause trouble breathing, swallowing, or speaking, or cosmetic disfigurement.[119] Both the prevalence of tardive dyskinesia and risk for irreversible symptoms increase with age, as TD occurs in as many as 70% of elderly taking antipsychotics.[119,120] Noncaucasians are more susceptible than Caucasians to the development of tardive dyskinesia, and women are twice as likely as men to experience this adverse effect of antipsychotic medications. Large doses of neuroleptic drugs and long duration of therapy also increase the likelihood of development of tardive dyskinesia.[118,120–122] All antipsychotics, with the exception of clozapine, can induce tardive dyskinesia.[53,110] It is unclear whether a specific psychiatric disorder or concurrent anticholinergic use increases the risk of developing tardive dyskinesia.[110,118]

The exact cause of TD is unknown. Biochemical and brain imaging studies note inconsistent associations of dopamine receptor activity or of the presence of brain lesions in patients with tardive dyskinesia. According to the dopamine receptor hypersensitivity theory, postsynaptic dopamine receptor concentrations increase in the nigrostriatal area after prolonged antipsychotic therapy, resulting in hyperdopaminergic functioning in the area of the brain that controls movement. Postmortem studies, however, do not support overactive dopamine functioning as a cause. An increase in antipsychotic dose can clinically mask the symptoms of tardive dyskinesia and a decrease in dose can unmask tardive dyskinesia symptoms; therefore, dopamine probably has at least a partial role in the etiology of tardive dyskinesia.

In all likelihood, the cause of tardive dyskinesia probably is multifactorial involving more than a single neurotransmitter dysfunction. In the animal model, a role is described for dopamine hypersensitivity and for GABA concentrations.[123] Noradrenergic dysfunction also might be involved because dopamine β-hydroxylase and norepinephrine concentrations are higher in patients with tardive dyskinesia.[124]

Clinical Presentation and Assessment

30. C.M., a 31-year-old female, was diagnosed with chronic paranoid schizophrenia 9 years ago. She responds to antipsychotics, but has been rehospitalized 6 times because of noncompliance. She has taken loxapine, haloperidol, and fluphenazine in the past. C.M. currently is being treated in an outpatient program and is taking trifluoperazine 25 mg HS, decreased from 30 mg one month ago. She has been taking trihexyphenidyl 2 mg TID for the past 5 years. Involuntary movements including tongue protrusion, frequent blinking, and writhing movements of her legs were noted during a recent evaluation. What data in C.M.'s history are consistent with tardive dyskinesia?

The nine years of antipsychotic treatment and the symptoms of tongue protrusion, blinking, and writhing leg movements are consistent with features commonly associated with tardive dyskinesia. Long-term trihexyphenidyl treatment also may contribute to the development of C.M.'s abnormal movements. Further assessment (see Question 31) is required before a definitive diagnosis of TD can be made. The severity and reversibility of C.M.'s symptoms are unknown at this time.

31. C.M. was evaluated using the Dyskinesia Identification System: Condensed User System (DISCUS) and had a score of 7. She has no history of abnormal movements and currently has no EPSEs. What disorders or medications can produce symptoms similar to those of tardive dyskinesia? How should C.M.'s DISCUS score be interpreted?

Tourette's syndrome, dental problems, Huntington's or Sydenham's chorea, chorea of pregnancy, and systemic lupus erythematosus (SLE) are some of the disorders that have been associated with dyskinetic movements. Medications such as metoclopramide, amoxapine, bromocriptine, and levodopa/carbidopa also can cause TD. *Spontaneous* or *"senile" dyskinesia* resembles tardive dyskinesia but can occur in patients not previously exposed to antipsychotic medications;[110,119] and is 16 times more likely than tardive dyskinesia to occur in people less than 40 years of age. For patients more than 40 years of age, spontaneous dyskinesia (SD) and tardive dyskinesia occur in about equal frequency (i.e., 1 to 1.5:1 SD to TD). Therefore, a baseline dyskinesia rating is essential before treating elderly patients with antipsychotic medications to avoid the potential diagnostic dilemma of differentiating spontaneous or senile dyskinesia from tardive dyskinesia.[125]

Tardive dyskinesia varies in severity and presentation and can be reversible in many cases; therefore, rating scales are needed to standardize assessments and diagnoses. The Abnormal Involuntary Movement Scale (AIMS) rates dyskinetic movements from 0 to 4, is simple to use, and is widely recognized, but is not exclusively diagnostic for tardive dyskinesia. The DISCUS rates the presence and severity of abnormal movements and considers other variables when formulating a diagnosis (see Figure 75.2).[117] The DISCUS evaluation also specifically describes the type of tardive dyskinesia and allows diagnoses to change over time. For example, *masked TD* symptoms can be hidden by an increase in the dose of antipsychotic. *Withdrawal TD* appears after the dose of an antipsy-

chotic is reduced or when it is discontinued. Withdrawal TD disappears spontaneously in one to three months. *Persistent TD* occurs when symptoms continue for more than 3 to 12 months. *Remitted TD* occurs in patients with previously persistent TD, but these patients are now symptom free and have had no changes in antipsychotic therapy.

Patients taking long-term antipsychotics should be evaluated for dyskinesias by a well-trained clinician every three to six months using a standardized rating scale such as AIMS or DISCUS. Findings always should be documented in patient records, both to ensure continuity of care and medicolegal protection.

A DISCUS score of five or more is a "red flag" that alerts the rater to a high probability of some type of tardive dyskinesia.[117,119] C.M.'s DISCUS score of seven supports a diagnosis of tardive dyskinesia, but follow-up DISCUS ratings are needed to determine whether she has withdrawal dyskinesia from a recent trifluoperazine dose reduction or persistent TD. An interim diagnosis of probable or withdrawal TD would be reasonable for C.M. If her DISCUS subsequently increases despite continued therapy with trifluoperazine 25 mg/day, the diagnosis can be changed to persistent TD.

Management

32. How should C.M.'s tardive dyskinesia be managed?

The first consideration in the management of tardive dyskinesia should focus on prevention (i.e., reserving antipsychotics for conditions known to respond to treatment and by minimizing total dose and duration of treatment). Early diagnosis of tardive dyskinesia also is key to improving outcome because this disorder may be reversible in the early stages. Drug holidays will not reduce and may increase the risk of tardive dyskinesia.[124] Since tardive dyskinesia already has been diagnosed in C.M., evaluation of the risks and benefits of continued antipsychotic treatment must be discussed with C.M. and family and documented in the chart (see Figure 75.3).[112]

A rapid reduction in the dose of trifluoperazine in C.M. should be avoided to prevent severe withdrawal dyskinesias. Her trifluoperazine dose, however, should be reduced, if possible, to minimize her exposure to the antipsychotic.

Anticholinergics may both cause and aggravate tardive dyskinesia. The data, however, are conflicting[110] and pseudoparkinsonism can coexist in some patients with tardive dyskinesia. Therefore, C.M. should continue her trihexyphenidyl treatment. Anticholinergics also are useful for treating tardive dystonia. Whenever possible, anticholinergic antiparkinsonian medications should be discontinued over two to three weeks after TD is identified.

Overall, pharmacologic treatment for tardive dyskinesia is not very successful. Most studies are small and poorly done, with wide-ranging results. Table 75.11 compared single and double-blind studies completed before 1980 to those done in the 1980s to determine the percentages of patients improved with each treatment.[126] The most beneficial treatments are anticholinergic withdrawal, noradrenergic antagonists (clonidine, beta blockers), and benzodiazepines.[127–134] Antipsychotic dose increases are most effective; however, they simply mask symptoms and eventually will worsen TD.

Vitamin E has been used for prevention and treatment of TD because of its ability to reduce free radicals, but further evaluation is needed.[135–137] Calcium channel blockers, especially nifedipine, may be beneficial for elderly patients and for severe cases, but long-term studies are needed to assess tolerance and the impact of dopamine antagonist properties of calcium channel blockers.[138–141] Table 75.12 lists the doses used in studies of the most effective medications.[126–134,138–142] There is no consensus on the optimal

NAME   **I.D.**

_____
(facility)

Dyskinesia Identification System: Condensed User Scale (DISCUS)

CURRENT PSYCHOTROPICS/ANTI-CHOLINERGIC AND TOTAL MG/DAY

_____ _____ mg

_____ _____ mg

_____ _____ mg

_____ _____ mg

See Instructions On Other Side

EXAM TYPE (check one)
- 1. Baseline
- 2. Annual
- 3. Semi-Annual
- 4. D/C—1 Month
- 5. D/C—2 Month
- 6. D/C—3 Month
- 7. Admission
- 8. Other

COOPERATION (check one)
- 1. None
- 2. Partial
- 3. Full

SCORING

0 — **Not Present** (movements not observed or some movements observed but not considered abnormal)

1 — **Minimal** (abnormal movements are difficult to detect or movements are easy to detect but occur only once or twice in a short non-repetitive manner)

2 — **Mild** (abnormal movements occur infrequently and are easy to detect)

3 — **Moderate** (abnormal movements occur frequently and are easy to detect)

4 — **Severe** (abnormal movements occur almost continuously and are easy to detect)

NA — **Not Assessed** (an assessment for an item is not able to be made)

ASSESSMENT
DISCUS Item and Score (circle one score for each item)

FACE	1.	Tics	0	1	2	3	4	NA
	2.	Grimaces	0	1	2	3	4	NA
EYES	3.	Blinking	0	1	2	3	4	NA
ORAL	4.	Chewing/Lip Smacking	0	1	2	3	4	NA
	5.	Puckering/Sucking/Thrusting Lower Lip	0	1	2	3	4	NA
LINGUAL	6.	Tongue Thrusting Tongue in Cheek	0	1	2	3	4	NA
	7.	Tonic Tongue	0	1	2	3	4	NA
	8.	Tongue Tremor	0	1	2	3	4	NA
	9.	Athetoid/Myokymic/Lateral Tongue	0	1	2	3	4	NA
HEAD/NECK/TRUNK	10.	Retrocollis/Torticollis	0	1	2	3	4	NA
	11.	Shoulder/Hip Torsion	0	1	2	3	4	NA
UPPER LIMB	12.	Athetoid/Myokymic Finger-Wrist-Arm	0	1	2	3	4	NA
	13.	Pill Rolling	0	1	2	3	4	NA
LOWER LIMB	14.	Ankle Flexion/Foot Tapping	0	1	2	3	4	NA
	15.	Toe Movement	0	1	2	3	4	NA

COMMENTS/OTHER

_____

_____

_____

_____

TOTAL SCORE (items 1–15 only)

EXAM DATE

RATER SIGNATURE AND TITLE   NEXT EXAM DATE   PHYSICIAN SIGNATURE   DATE

EVALUATION (see other side)

1. Greater than 90 days neuroleptic exposure? : YES NO
2. Scoring/intensity level met? : YES NO
3. Other diagnostic conditions? : YES NO (if yes, specify)

_____
_____
_____

4. Last exam date: _____
Last total score: _____
Last conclusion: _____

Preparer signature and title for items 1–4 (if different from physician):

5. Conclusion (circle one):
- A. No TD (if scoring prerequisite met, list other diagnostic condition or explain in comments)
- B. Probable TD
- C. Masked TD
- D. Withdrawal TD
- E. Persistent TD
- F. Remitted TD
- G. Other (specify in comments)

6. Comments:

_____
_____
_____
_____
_____
_____
_____

Fig 75.2 Reprinted with permission. Sprague RL, Kalachnik JE (1981). Reliability, validity, and total score cutoff for the Dyskinesia Identification System Condensed User Scale (DISCUS) with mentally ill and mentally retarded populations. Psychopharmacol Bull. 27(1):51–58.

dose of these drugs; therefore, it would be prudent to begin therapy with low doses and to gradually increase the dose according to tolerance and response.

Since C.M. has had multiple psychotic episodes when noncompliant to antipsychotics, she is not a candidate for trifluoperazine discontinuation. As previously discussed, further trifluoperazine doses should be reduced (also see Question 10); and her trihexyphenidyl should be discontinued over two to three weeks, provided that she has no concurrent EPSEs. If C.M.'s tardive dyskinesia persists or if her psychosis worsens during the trifluoperazine taper, she can be switched to a low potency antipsychotic such as chlorpromazine. If she remains symptomatic with tardive dyskinesia despite these interventions, one-month trials of propranolol, clonidine, and lorazepam can be tried. Polypharmacy must be avoided; institution of a systemic approach of one-month trials with the most effective medications can be considered for moderate to severe cases. DISCUS ratings should be completed at monthly intervals to assess C.M.'s response to the adjunctive medication (see Figure 75.3).[143]

33. C.M.'s tardive dyskinesia is worse 1 year later, despite reducing the trifluoperazine dose to 20 mg/day, discontinuing the trihexyphenidyl, and 1-month trials of propranolol 20 mg BID and lorazepam 1 mg BID. Her DISCUS score is now 12. What else can be done to treat her TD while maintaining control of her psychosis?

Clozapine is indicated for patients with severe tardive dyskinesia because it has both a lower risk for causing tardive dyskinesia and may alleviate abnormal movements.[53] Due to the progressive nature of C.M.'s tardive dyskinesia and because antipsychotics cannot be discontinued without precipitating reappearance of psychotic symptoms, clozapine should be given under similar guidelines as for refractory psychosis.

Neuroleptic Malignant Syndrome (NMS)

34. C.B., a 25-year-old male, was hospitalized with the diagnosis of schizophrenia, paranoid type, and was started on loxapine 25 mg BID. After 2 days of therapy, C.B. became rigid, appeared confused at times, and had a fever of 41 °C. A diagnosis of NMS was made. What features of this syndrome does C.B. have and how should it be treated?

Neuroleptic malignant syndrome is a rare, but potentially lethal, adverse effect associated with antipsychotic therapy. Neuroleptic malignant syndrome can occur hours to months after the initial drug exposure and the morbidity rate is reported to be as high as 20%.[144] The cardinal features of NMS include muscular rigidity, hyperthermia, autonomic dysfunction, and altered consciousness. Extrapyramidal dysfunction (e.g., rigidity) and akinesia usually develop initially or concomitantly with a temperature elevation as high as 41 °C. Autonomic dysfunction includes tachycardia, labile blood pressure, profuse diaphoresis, dyspnea, and urinary incontinence. The patient's level of consciousness may vary from alert to mutism, stupor, and coma. Other neurologic findings include sialorrhea, dyskinesia, and dysphagia. Symptoms usually develop rapidly over 24 to 72 hours. The WBC count, creatine kinase (CK), and liver function tests are not diagnostic for NMS, but usually are increased. C.B.'s fever of 41 °C, rigidity, and confusion are consistent with neuroleptic malignant syndrome.

C.B.'s loxapine should be discontinued and supportive measures initiated to treat hyperthermia and prevent dehydration. Secondary complications such as pneumonia and renal failure should be managed as they develop. Due to his muscular rigidity, parenteral anticholinergics could be considered, but a review of 60 NMS cases showed that anticholinergic agents did not lessen the severity of symptoms or decrease the morbidity.[144,145] Dantrolene (Dantrium), a direct skeletal muscle relaxant, is a better choice for C.B.'s muscular rigidity and 100 to 300 mg/day can be given in divided oral doses or 1.25 to 1.5 mg/kg intravenously as a single dose.[146–148]

Neuroleptic malignant syndrome has been attributed to dopamine depletion caused by neuroleptic drug blockade of dopamine pathways in the basal ganglia and hypothalamus. Therefore, dopamine agonists such as amantadine 100 to 200 mg two to three times daily and bromocriptine (Parlodel) 2.5 to 15 mg three times daily sometimes are beneficial.[149–153] C.B. should be started on dantrolene 50 mg four times daily and either bromocriptine 2.5 mg

Fig 75.3 An Algorithm for Managing Tardive Dyskinesia (TD)
Reprinted with permission from reference 143.

three times daily or amantadine 100 mg three times daily to achieve the most rapid resolution of his NMS.[154] If he is unable to take oral medications, IV dantrolene should be used. The primary focus of his treatment, however, must be on supportive measures, especially the cooling of his body temperature and discontinuation of his loxapine.

Neuroleptic malignant syndrome is self-limiting and usually lasts five to ten days after the oral antipsychotic is discontinued or two to three times longer after discontinuation of depot medications. C.B.'s response to therapy can be assessed by frequent monitoring of his vital signs and daily CK measurements. Significant improvement should be noted within 24 to 72 hours after initiation of treatment. Reduction of confusion and mutism and normalization of the vital signs usually are noted within 24 to 96 hours after the start of treatment. Symptoms of extrapyramidal rigidity usually will resolve within one week.[155]

Hematological Adverse Effects

35. B.V., a 25-year-old male, recently was diagnosed with chronic undifferentiated schizophrenia and started on fluphenazine 20 mg HS. The subsequent development of EPSEs that were unresponsive to reductions in the dose of fluphenazine or pharmacological interventions, necessitated a switch to thio-

Table 75.11	Comparison of Studies of Treatment for TD in the 1980s with Those in Previous Decades[a–d]					
	Before 1980 Results		1980 Results		Total	
Treatment	No.	Improved (%)	No.	Improved (%)	No.	Improved (%)
Neuroleptic withdrawal	1005	36	42	55	1047	37
Neuroleptics	501	67	34	44	535	66
Noradrenergic antagonists	85	61	54	65	139	63
Other catecholamine antagonists	255	43	124	39	379	42
Catecholaminergic drugs	146	25	43	28	189	25
GABAergic drugs	204	54	89	35	293	48
Cholinergic drugs	379	39	52	21	424	38
Anticholinergic drugs	177	7	10	20	187	7
Anticholinergic withdrawal	—	—	15	60	15	60
Miscellaneous	347	39	52	21	399	37
Total	3099	44	515	38	3614	43

[a] Reprinted with permission from reference 126.
[b] TD = Tardive dyskinesia.
[c] Not all studies could be included because it was not always possible to determine the number of patients with >50% improvement.
[d] Jeste and Wyatt (1982). This review included 1980 studies.

ridazine 300 mg HS. B.V.'s baseline CBC with differential was within normal limits, but 2 weeks after the conversion to thioridazine his WBC count was 3500 mm³. B.V. has no fever or chills and feels well. Should the thioridazine be discontinued?
[SI unit: 3.5 × 10⁹/L]

The WBC count transiently decreases in about 0.8% of patients receiving antipsychotics.[156] Neuroleptic-induced agranulocytosis has been reported rarely and usually develops within the first month of therapy, with the WBC count recovering within two weeks after the antipsychotic is discontinued. Routine monitoring of the CBC is not helpful in detecting the initial stages of antipsychotic-induced agranulocytosis, because the WBC count usually decreases too quickly to be detected by routine blood monitoring. Rather, attention to the signs and symptoms of leukopenia and agranulocytosis, followed by aggressive intervention when problems develop is recommended for monitoring early antipsychotic treatment.[156]

Because B.V.'s white blood cell count is 3500 mm³, not dangerously low, and he feels well, thioridazine should be continued. Laboratory tests should be repeated only if signs and symptoms of infection develop. The thioridazine should be discontinued if the total WBC count falls below 3000 mm³ or if the neutrophil count is less than 1500 mm³. Hematological effects of clozapine are discussed in Question 16.

Amenorrhea and Galactorrhea

36. G.M., a 26-year-old female, has taken haloperidol 15 mg HS for 7 months to treat chronic paranoid schizophrenia. She is medication compliant and her illness is well controlled. At her outpatient clinic visit, G.M. complains of amenorrhea of 2-months duration and of a white discharge from her breasts

Table 75.12	Doses of Medications Used to Treat Tardive Dyskinesia[126–134,138–142]
Medication	Range of Doses in Studies (mg/day)
Clonidine	0.15–0.9
Clonazepam	1–10
Diazepam	15–40
Nifedipine	20–80
Propranolol	20–800

during the past month. A home pregnancy test was negative. How might G.M.'s amenorrhea and galactorrhea be attributed to her haloperidol?

Prolactin is responsible for milk production and is synthesized and released by the anterior pituitary gland. Prolactin follows a circadian rhythm with concentrations increasing during sleep, peaking in the early morning, and declining upon awakening. Basal concentrations will vary, but usually range between 5 to 25 ng/mL in men and nonpregnant, nonlactating women.[157] Dopamine acts as the prolactin inhibitory factor, blocking release of prolactin in the lactotrophs of the anterior pituitary gland. Shortly after initiation of antipsychotics, prolactin concentrations usually will increase, then level off before normalizing after a week. When prolactin serum concentrations remain elevated, galactorrhea, amenorrhea, and anovulation can occur in women, and azoospermia, impotence, and gynecomastia can develop in men.[158]

Even though there are no specific long-term consequences of hyperprolactinemia, amenorrhea is a problem for G.M. who is concerned about a possible pregnancy. G.M. may have other causes of hyperprolactinemia that must be ruled out. Her serum concentration of prolactin should be evaluated and if it is greater than 100 ng/mL, or if G.M. complains of headache or visual disturbances, a pituitary adenoma should be considered.[159] Since G.M.'s prolactin serum concentration is only 75 ng/mL and she has no neurological symptoms, haloperidol is the likely cause for her galactorrhea and amenorrhea.

An attempt should be made to reduce G.M.'s haloperidol dose. If schizophrenic symptoms return, her previous haloperidol dose can be reinstituted and a dopamine agonist such as bromocriptine or amantadine can be added. Bromocriptine has been evaluated in doses ranging from 5 to 15 mg, either alone or with antipsychotics.[161–163] Symptoms usually improve after 15 days, but may take up to nine weeks for complete resolution.[161,163] Amantadine is effective in doses of 200 to 300 mg/day.[164,165] Even though tolerance does not appear to develop to the prolactin-reducing effects of bromocriptine, long-term efficacy and safety studies are lacking. Short courses of a dopamine agonist when symptoms are problematic may be the best approach.[160] G.M. should use nonhormonal contraceptive methods during bromocriptine treatment as ovulation may be restored.[166] Clozapine has not been associated with galactorrhea or amenorrhea and can be tried if the symptoms continue despite dose reductions and dopamine agonists.[167]

Hepatic Dysfunction

37. A.S., a 19-year-old female, is brought to the hospital because of unusual behavior and violence toward her mother. The presumptive diagnosis for A.S. is psychosis, not otherwise specified. Chlorpromazine 100 mg TID has been initiated for A.S. until the exact cause of her symptoms is more precisely determined. Her baseline laboratory tests (i.e., CBC with differential, a chemistry profile that included LFTs and serum electrolytes) were within normal limits. The same tests were repeated 10 days later during further evaluation of her psychosis. The aspartate aminotransferase (AST) and alanine aminotransferase (ALT) are now 1.5 times normal. She has no gastrointestinal complaints or medical problems. Should chlorpromazine be discontinued at this time?

Benign elevations in liver function tests (i.e., increases in AST or ALT <2 to 3 times normal) have been encountered early in the course of antipsychotic therapy and are not problematic. Of greater significance, chlorpromazine causes cholestatic jaundice in about 1% to 2% of patients. Most antipsychotics also cause cholestatic jaundice, although less frequently. About 80% to 90% of antipsychotic-induced cholestatic jaundice develops within the first month of therapy.[168] The jaundice usually is preceded by prodromal symptoms of fevers, chills, nausea, upper gastric pain, malaise, and pruritus. Discontinuation of the antipsychotic and symptomatic care are the primary modalities of treatment because the cholestatic jaundice usually is self-limiting and usually resolves within two to eight weeks. Occasionally, a more chronic course may develop. Once the signs and symptoms have resolved, an alternate class of antipsychotic, preferably a nonphenothiazine, should be prescribed.

The liver function tests in A.S. are only modestly abnormal and she is not experiencing symptoms of hepatotoxicity or cholestatic jaundice. Therefore, A.S.'s chlorpromazine should be continued. Routine laboratory monitoring of liver function tests is not beneficial in preventing drug-induced cholestatic jaundice, thus no follow-up laboratory tests are required unless symptoms of jaundice develop. Awareness and evaluation of prodromal symptoms is the most appropriate action for A.S. at this time.[169]

Temperature Dysregulation and Dermatological Effects

38. N.M., a 27-year-old male, recently was diagnosed with undifferentiated schizophrenia and was stabilized with chlorpromazine 400 mg HS during a 3-month stay on an inpatient unit. N.M. has continued chlorpromazine 400 mg HS as an outpatient and has done so well that he is ready to return to work as a laborer at a construction site. Because N.M. is taking antipsychotics, what precautions should he take when working outside?

N.M. should be advised to wear a hat when working outside, drink lots of fluids, stay in the shade as much as possible, and seek a cooler environment if he feels hot because antipsychotics can cause temperature dysregulation, probably by inhibiting hypothalamic temperature regulation. The net result is poikilothermia (i.e., the normal body temperature cannot respond to heat or cold and patients become hypo- or hyperthermic depending upon the surrounding temperature).[170] Additionally, the strong anticholinergic effects of N.M.'s chlorpromazine can impair cutaneous heat elimination and further exacerbate the problem.

N.M. should use a sunscreen with maximum block along with protective clothing because he works outdoors at a construction site and sun exposure can cause an exaggerated sunburn because of chlorpromazine-induced photosensitivity. The tricyclic structure of some antipsychotics absorbs ultraviolet rays, producing free radicals that damage skin. Chlorpromazine is the most common cause of photosensitivity, but it can occur with all phenothiazines and with thiothixene.[170]

Another reason for N.M. to use sunscreen is to prevent problems with abnormal pigmentation of the skin. Long-term antipsychotic administration, especially high doses of low potency agents, can discolor skin from tan to a blue-black color. Discoloration usually is worse in sun-exposed areas, and may fade after antipsychotics are discontinued. Abnormal pigmentation is less common today because lower doses of antipsychotic agents are used and high potency agents, which have a lower risk for causing dermatological changes, are more commonly prescribed.

Other dermatologic reactions can occur with antipsychotics and N.M. should be advised to report any of the following to his physician: Dermatitis, presenting with a maculopapular rash on the face, neck, and upper chest occurs in about 5% of patients shortly after starting chlorpromazine. Localized or generalized urticaria also can develop. Antihistamines usually provide adequate relief, but the medication may have to be discontinued in severe cases. The rash rarely reappears after resumption of treatment.

Ocular Effects

39. Can photosensitivity and pigmentary changes in the skin indicate discoloration in other parts of the body?

The likelihood of corneal and lens pigmentation is high if skin discoloration is present or severe photosensitivity develops. Whitish or brown pigmentation can deposit on the interior subcapsular area of the eye but generally does not affect lens transparency or vision. The conjunctiva can be discolored with brown pigment. If N.M. has pigmentary changes or photosensitivity while being treated with high doses of chlorpromazine, his eyes should be examined routinely.

Psychogenic Polydipsia

40. R.J., a 37-year-old female with chronic paranoid schizophrenia, was taken to the ER from her boarding home because she experienced a seizure. Upon evaluation, her serum sodium was 121 mEq/L and morning urine specific gravity was 1.010. She has been stabilized on depot fluphenazine 25 mg Q 2 weeks for 5 years and benztropine 2 mg BID. R.J. was given lorazepam 2 mg IV stat and the seizure stopped. R.J. smokes 2 packs of cigarettes per day, but is otherwise in good health. What is the likely cause of her seizure? [SI unit: 121 mmol/L]

About 6% to 17% of the chronically mentally ill, especially those with schizophrenia, experience polydipsia and hyponatremia.[171,172] The polydipsia often is psychogenic in origin and involves self-induced water intoxication and compulsive drinking of water. Many patients remain asymptomatic, but some develop headaches, weakness, tremor, cramps, seizures, coma, and death. Chronic water intoxication also can exacerbate congestive heart failure and bowel and bladder problems.[173] The exact mechanism remains unclear, but altered antidiuretic hormone release secondary to stress, psychotropics, nicotine, or the illness itself all have been implicated. Anticholinergics may exacerbate the problem, but are unlikely to be the primary cause. Excess water consumption often increases as psychosis worsens.[174]

Psychogenic polydipsia is a diagnosis of exclusion, but R.J. does not seem to be afflicted by other disorders (e.g., pituitary tumors or metastatic lung cancer). Her seizures can be treated with lorazepam or phenytoin. Once the seizure is controlled, her fluids should be restricted to restore her sodium balance. R.J. should be encouraged to discontinue her cigarette smoking and anticholinergic medications to minimize exacerbation of this problem. Fluid restriction should be continued although she may resist or hide her water consumption. Demeclocycline 600 mg twice a day is the most promising pharmacologic intervention, and should be reserved for R.J. if she is unresponsive to nonpharmacologic measures.[175]

Sexual Dysfunction

41. K.J., a 24-year-old male with chronic paranoid schizophrenia, was rehospitalized secondary to noncompliance to thioridazine 400 mg HS. During the medication history it is discovered that he stopped taking thioridazine because he has lost his interest in sex. When he tries to have intercourse, he experiences delayed ejaculation. About a week after stopping the thioridazine he is able to have a normal ejaculation. How does thioridazine contribute to K.J.'s sexual dysfunction and what other symptoms might he also develop?

Thioridazine is the most common cause of antipsychotic-induced sexual dysfunction, as evidenced by a study finding a 60% incidence in the thioridazine group versus 25% in the nonthioridazine group.[176] Ejaculatory dysfunction is the most common type of sexual dysfunction caused by antipsychotics.[177] Decreased libido, anorgasmia, impotence, and priapism also have been reported. The causes of antipsychotic-induced sexual dysfunction are multifactorial and include α-adrenergic and calcium channel blockade as well as anticholinergic, endocrine, and sedative effects.[177,178] Schizophrenia also can affect sexual desire, making an accurate diagnosis difficult. K.J.'s sexual dysfunction likely is related to the thioridazine because the symptoms resolved after stopping the medication. Either a dose reduction to 300 mg or conversion to a high potency antipsychotic, such as haloperidol, may relieve his symptoms.[177]

Seizures

42. R.A., a 26-year-old female, is brought to the hospital after assaulting a neighbor. She presents in an acute psychotic state and has not calmed down since entering the hospital. She struck two staff members on the psychiatric unit. R.A. has had generalized tonic-clonic seizures since age 14 and currently is taking carbamazepine 300 mg TID (serum concentration on admission 8.2 µg/mL). R.A. has been seizure free for a year. She needs acute treatment with an antipsychotic because of her dangerous behavior. What is the best choice of antipsychotic in light of her seizure disorder?

Antipsychotics can lower the seizure threshold, producing seizures in patients who previously were seizure free. Risk factors for antipsychotic-induced seizures include: history of epilepsy or drug-induced seizures, history of perinatal problems, abnormal electroencephalogram, acute head trauma, polytherapy, rapid titration to high doses, and low potency antipsychotics.[179] Chlorpromazine is associated with the highest incidence of seizures (0.3% to 5%) but higher doses administered during the 1950s and 1960s may be partially responsible for the high incidence.[179,180] Trifluoperazine and perphenazine have a moderate risk for seizures, while thioridazine, molindone, fluphenazine, and haloperidol have the least epileptogenic potential.[179] Clozapine also causes seizures, although epilepsy is not an absolute contraindication to therapy. Clozapine-induced seizures generally are dose related with a prevalence of less than 2% with doses below 300 mg/day versus 4% to 6% with doses more than 600 mg/day.[181]

Antipsychotics should be used in R.A. if benefits outweigh the risks. R.A. is a danger to herself and to others and needs short-term management with antipsychotics until the cause of her dangerous behavior can be determined. Haloperidol, an agent at low risk for causing seizures, should be selected; however, large doses and rapid adjustments of dose should be avoided. Haloperidol 5 mg orally or 2.5 mg intramuscularly stat should be given. Scheduled haloperidol at doses of ≤15 mg/day can be continued until the psychosis resolves or she is no longer dangerous. Supplemental benzodiazepines may be used in order to avoid high doses of haloperidol.

A carbamazepine serum concentration should be obtained before initiation of an antipsychotic and should be repeated three days after initiating the haloperidol. Doses should be adjusted to maintain the serum concentration of carbamazepine at about 8 µg/mL.

Considerations in Pregnancy

43. D.M., a 26-year-old female, has a 6-year history of chronic undifferentiated schizophrenia and comes to her outpatient clinic taking thioridazine 400 mg HS. D.M. currently is psychiatrically stable and was last hospitalized 2 years ago. When D.M. decompensates, she isolates herself, is unable to care for herself, does not eat properly, and does not maintain her grooming and hygiene. She just found out that she is 8 weeks pregnant. Should her thioridazine be continued and what are the risks if the medication is continued?

Antipsychotics are not contraindicated in pregnancy and are FDA category C medications. (Also see Chapter 45: Teratogenicity and Drugs in Breast Milk.) There are no consistently reported teratogenic changes with any of the antipsychotics. Most studies are case reports or are trials not specific to schizophrenia. A prospective study of 12,764 patients at a prenatal clinic (315 took phenothiazines) found a significant increase in heart, genital, central nervous system, and lip malformations in women taking phenothiazines with an aliphatic side chain when compared to unexposed infants. Of the drugs in this group, only chlorpromazine is available in the U.S.[182] Other reasons to avoid low potency antipsychotics during pregnancy are unrelated to teratogenic effects. Low potency agents can worsen constipation and cause orthostatic hypotension and uteroplacental insufficiency. Overall, the teratogenic risk from antipsychotics is low, but exposure during the sixth to tenth weeks should be avoided unless the patient is dangerous, because the fetus is most susceptible to teratogenic risks during this time.[183] Whenever possible, antipsychotics should be discontinued about one week before delivery to minimize neonatal complications, such as dystonia, withdrawal dyskinesias, temperature dysregulation, and irritability.

The relationship between long-term behavioral changes, behavioral teratogenicity, and *in utero* antipsychotic exposure has been poorly studied. One small study found no change in IQ scores in four-year-olds exposed to antipsychotics when compared to unexposed controls.[184] Breast-feeding is not contraindicated during antipsychotic therapy, although the infant should be monitored for adverse effects.[185]

D.M.'s schizophrenia has been stable for two years. Her thioridazine, therefore, can be discontinued because she is in the first trimester of her pregnancy and it is a low potency antipsychotic. Because she historically presents a danger to herself when ill, it is critical that treatment be initiated at the first evidence of decompensation. D.M. should be seen every other week by her clinician and more often by a family member or case worker who can observe for such symptoms. Treatment should be restarted with haloperidol or fluphenazine 2 to 5 mg at night, as most patients who need antipsychotics during pregnancy are started on the smallest possible dose of a nonphenothiazine high potency agent. If she does not respond to low dose haloperidol, or develops intolerable EPSEs, then a lower potency antipsychotic can be selected. D.M.'s chart should include the following documentation: specific behaviors that necessitate treatment (danger to self, fetus, or others); goals of therapy (acute control of dangerous behavior or remission); dose, route of administration, schedule, and projected duration of treatment; obstetrical history and other medications used during pregnancy; alcohol or illegal drug use; regular progress notes on response and need for continued treatment; and informed consent from the patient or guardian.

Weight Gain

44. L.A., a 29-year-old female, recently was diagnosed with schizophrenia and has been treated with thiothixene 20 mg at night. Before initiation of thiothixene, 4 months ago, L.A. was 5'4" and weighed 132 pounds. She has responded well to the thiothixene; however, she now weighs 141 pounds. Why can L.A.'s weight gain be attributed to her thiothixene?

Weight gain of three to nine pounds commonly accompanies antipsychotic therapy and is especially significant during the first 12 weeks of therapy. All antipsychotics, including clozapine and molindone cause significant weight gain.[186,187] The cause of antipsychotic-induced weight gain is multifactorial and may include a primary effect of the drug, change in food preferences, increased food intake, carbohydrate craving, or a lack of activity.

L.A.'s weight gain should be taken seriously because of increased morbidity from weight gain, and because she is at risk for noncompliance. L.A. should be evaluated for akinesia, in case it is causing inactivity, and asked whether she is pregnant and whether she lost weight during her last psychotic episode. The assessment also should address L.A.'s exercise habits and normal weight fluctuations. The only effective treatment for antipsychotic-induced weight gain is exercise and dietary restriction, thus a program of weight reduction can be recommended based upon the findings of her evaluation.

Polytherapy

45. P.D., a 52-year-old man with chronic undifferentiated schizophrenia, presents to the outpatient medication clinic for his first visit. P.D. was discharged from the hospital 2 weeks ago after receiving treatment for an acute psychotic episode. Referral records indicate he previously was hospitalized for schizophrenia 5 times in another state. During his clinic visit, P.D. was very confused, could not remember his name, and had difficulty answering questions because he kept falling asleep. His stated mood was "good" and he denied feeling sad, except during the first few days of his last hospitalization. There is no documented history of major depression in P.D. or any first-degree relative. P.D. denied auditory or visual hallucinations, but complained of dry mouth and constipation. Vital signs were stable, and physical examination was noncontributory, with the exception of extremely dry mucous membranes. No abnormal movements or extrapyramidal side effects were noted. Current medications include chlorpromazine 600 mg PO a.m. and 200 mg HS (initiated during last hospitalization), haloperidol 5 mg PO BID (initiated 2 years ago), trihexyphenidyl 5 mg BID, amitriptyline (Elavil) 100 mg PO BID, diphenhydramine 25 mg PO BID seasonal allergies, and clonazepam 0.5 mg TID. How could P.D.'s drug regimen be contributing to his clinical presentation and how can it be optimized?

P.D. is receiving what commonly is referred to as polytherapy or polypharmacy. Polytherapy often is seen in patients with a long history of schizophrenia and multiple hospitalizations. During polytherapy, additional drugs are started before existing regimens are optimized, or agents are continued long after they are needed. Polytherapy almost always results in increased side effects and noncompliance. Also, the irrational use of multiple drugs makes differentiating between drug-induced side effects and disease-related signs and symptoms difficult.

P.D. is receiving multiple drugs for no clear indications and it is likely that the sedation and confusion are directly related to his drug regimen. Often, the combined use of agents with high sedative and anticholinergic properties can impair cognition (impair short-term memory, decrease concentration and attention) and cause confusion, disorientation, and akinesia; and thereby, mimic negative schizophrenia or depression.[188] Two antipsychotics are not more effective than a single agent.[189] Chlorpromazine was added during his last hospitalization, even though he was already on haloperidol. The haloperidol should have been optimized or discontinued instead of adding chlorpromazine. Trihexyphenidyl probably is not needed because he currently is not experiencing EPSEs and it can contribute to negative cognitive effects. Amitriptyline was initiated during P.D.'s last hospitalization for subjective complaints of feeling sad. P.D. currently is not depressed, nor does he have a history of major depression; thus, maintenance antidepressants are not warranted. Amitriptyline is both highly sedating and anticholinergic, which probably contributes to P.D.'s sedation, dry mucous membranes, constipation, and confusion. The diphenhydramine only should be used as needed for seasonal allergies. If chronic antihistamines are needed, then a less sedating agent (e.g., terfenadine) should be considered. Finally, it is unclear why clonazepam was prescribed. Long-term use of benzodiazepines in the absence of a clearly defined anxiety disorder or tardive dyskinesia is unwarranted and could further impair cognition.[190] P.D.'s current pharmacologic regimen must be prioritized and a therapeutic plan developed to discontinue those agents first which are most likely causing his current problems. Abrupt withdrawal of any agent could destabilize P.D. or cause cholinergic rebound. As unnecessary agents are withdrawn, an improvement in clinical status is likely.

Drug Selection in the Elderly

46. F.P., a 69-year-old man with a 35-year history of schizoaffective disorder, recently has been very noncompliant to his medication regimen. He says it makes him feel "tired all the time." Upon presentation to the hospital, his chief complaint is hearing voices telling him to "end his life." Mental status examination reveals a disheveled-looking elderly man with a sad affect and significant psychomotor retardation. In addition to hearing voices, his speech is slowed and somewhat loose in associations. F.P. also complains of extreme sedation and "feeling lightheaded" a lot. Medical history is significant for a 20-year history of essential hypertension, currently stable with enalapril (Vasotec) 10 mg Q AM, and periodic exertional angina relieved with sublingual nitroglycerin. He was switched from fluphenazine decanoate 12.5 mg Q 3 weeks 6 months ago because "it made me stiff," to his present regimen of thioridazine 300 mg PO BID. F.P. was maintained on fluphenazine decanoate for 10 years and was hospitalized only once during that period. Should F.P. have been switched to thioridazine?

Special considerations must be given to elderly patients when choosing pharmacotherapy. Due to normal age-related physiologic decline in organ function, altered protein binding, changes in fat and water body composition, and unpredictable drug disposition, lower starting and maintenance doses are recommended in the elderly.[191] The elderly also are more susceptible to confusion and cognitive impairment from low potency agents because of sedation and anticholinergic effects.[192] Additionally, many elderly have cardiovascular disease and, therefore, may be more prone to orthostasis and falls resulting in hip fractures from low potency agents. Drugs or doses that cause minimal orthostasis and other cardiovascular changes are preferred in the elderly.

Thioridazine 600 mg/day is too high a dose for F.P. He is noncompliant to his current regimen probably because of the excessive sedation, confusion, and "lightheadedness." In addition, F.P.'s history of cardiovascular disease makes him a less than ideal candidate for thioridazine. Fluphenazine previously was effective for F.P. since he was hospitalized only once in ten years while treated with this agent. Chronic dosing of long-acting decanoate preparations can lead to drug accumulation, especially in the elderly, because of an increase in the fat-to-water ratio with highly lipid drugs such as antipsychotics. His stiffness may have resolved with a lower fluphenazine decanoate dose or addition of an antiparkinsonian agent. The thioridazine should be tapered over one week while slowly titrating oral fluphenazine to the lowest effective dose. Fluphenazine 2 mg twice a day should be initiated in F.P. and doses should not be increased sooner than every two to three weeks if response is inadequate. Once F.P. is stable, conversion to fluphenazine decanoate may be considered.

References

1 **Rupp A, Keith SJ.** The costs of schizophrenia. Assessing the burden. Psychiatr Clin North Am. 1993;16:413.

2 **Freeman AM et al.** Mental status exam. In: Freeman AM et al., eds. Modern Synopsis of Psychiatry, II. Baltimore: Williams and Wilkins; 1976: 347.

3 **Kendler KS, Diehl SR.** The genetics of schizophrenia: a current genetic-epidemiologic perspective. Schizophr Bull. 1993;19:261.

4 **Babigian HM.** Schizophrenia: epidemiology. In: Kaplan HI, Sadock BJ, eds. Comprehensive Textbook of Psychiatry. Baltimore: Williams and Wilkins; 1985;643.

5 **Seeman P et al.** Brain receptors for dopamine and neuroleptics. Adv Chem Psychopharmacol. 1978;19:167.

6 **Seeman P et al.** Antipsychotic drug doses and neuroleptic/dopamine receptors. Nature. 1976;261:717.

7 **Snyder SH.** Amphetamine psychosis: a model of schizophrenia mediated by catecholamines. Am J Psychiatry. 1973; 120:61.

8 **Tandon R, Greden JF.** Cholinergic hyperactivity and negative schizophrenic symptoms. Arch Gen Psychiatry. 1989;46:745.

9 **Heritch AJ.** Evidence for reduced and dysregulated turnover of dopamine in schizophrenia. Schizophr Bull. 1990; 16:605.

10 **Deutsch SJ et al.** A glutamatergic hypothesis of schizophrenia: rationale for pharmacotherapy with glycine. Clin Neuropharmacol. 1989;12:1.

11 **Carlsson M, Carlsson A.** Schizophrenia: a subcortical neurotransmitter imbalance syndrome. Schizophr Bull. 1990;16:425.

12 **Carlsson A.** Antipsychotic drugs, neurotransmitters and schizophrenia. Am J Psychiatry. 1978;135:164.

13 **Ereshefsky L et al.** Pathophysiologic basis for schizophrenia and the efficacy of antipsychotics. Clin Pharm. 1990;9: 682.

14 **Jann MW.** Clozapine. Pharmacotherapy. 1991;11(3):179-95.

15 **Van Tol HM et al.** Cloning of the gene for a human dopamine D4 receptor with high affinity for the antipsychotic clozapine. Nature. 1991;350:610.

16 **Ortiz A et al.** The future of neuroleptic psychopharmacology. J Clin Psychiatry. 1986;47(Suppl.):3.

17 **Berger PA.** Biochemistry and the schizophrenias: old concepts and new hypotheses. J Nerv Ment Dis. 1981; 169.

18 **Lieberman JA, Koreen AR.** Neurochemistry and neuroendocrinology of schizophrenia: a selective review. Schizophr Bull. 1993;19:371.

19 **Meltzer H.** New drugs for the treatment of schizophrenia. Psychiatr Clin North Am. 1993;16:365.

20 **Bleich A et al.** The role of serotonin in schizophrenia. Schizophr Bull. 1988; 14:297.

21 **Ceulemans DLS et al.** Effect of serotonin antagonism in schizophrenia: a pilot study with setoperone. Psychopharmacol. 1985;329.

22 **Jenner P et al.** Noradrenaline and 5-hydroxytryptamine modulation of brain dopamine function: implications for the treatment of Parkinson's disease. Br J Clin Pharmacol. 1983; 15(Suppl.):2779.

23 **Ereshefsky L, Richards AL.** Psychoses. In: Koda-Kimble MA, Young LY, eds. Applied Therapeutics: The Clinical Use of Drugs. Vancouver: Applied Therapeutics, Inc; 1992:56-1.

24 **American Psychiatric Association.** Diagnostic and Statistical Manual of Mental Disorders, 4th ed. (DSM-IV); Washington DC: American Psychiatric Press; 1994.

25 **Crow TJ.** Molecular pathology of schizophrenia: more than one disease process? Br Med J. 1980;280:66.

26 **Breier A et al.** National Institute of Mental Health longitudinal study of chronic schizophrenia. Arch Gen Psychiatry. 1991;48:239.

27 **Ram R et al.** The natural course of schizophrenia: a review of first-admission studies. Schizophr Bull. 1992;18: 185.

28 **McGlashan TH.** A selective review of recent North American long-term follow-up studies of schizophrenia. Schizophr Bull. 1988;14:515.

29 **Tsuang MT et al.** Stability of psychiatric diagnosis: schizophrenia and the affective disorders followed up over a 30- to 40-year period. Arch Gen Psychiatry. 1988;38:535.

30 **Harding CM et al.** The Vermont longitudinal study of persons with severe mental illness, II: long-term outcome of subjects who retrospectively met DSM-III criteria for schizophrenia. Am J Psychiatry. 1987;144:727.

31 **Bland RC et al.** Prognosis in schizophrenia: a ten-year followup of first admissions. Arch Gen Psychiatry. 1976; 33:949.

32 **Stern RG et al.** Predictors of response to neuroleptic treatment in schizophrenia. Psychiatr Clin North Am. 1993;16: 313.

33 **Smith GN et al.** Diagnostic confusion in treatment-refractory psychotic patients. J Clin Psychiatry. 1992;53:197.

34 **Thacore VR, Shukla SRP.** Cannabis psychosis and paranoid schizophrenia. Arch Gen Psychiatry. 1976;33:383.

35 **Reigier DA et al.** Comorbidity of mental disorders with alcohol and other drug abuse: results from the epidemiological catchment area study. JAMA. 1990;264:2511.

36 **Mueser K et al.** Prevalence of substance abuse in schizophrenia: demographic and clinical correlates. Schizophr Bull. 1990;16:31.

37 **Caton CLM et al.** Young chronic patients and substance abuse. Hosp Community Psychiatry. 1989;40:1037.

38 **Schneier FR, Siris SG.** A review of psychoactive substance use and abuse in schizophrenia—patterns of drug choice. J Nerv Ment Dis. 1987;175: 641.

39 **Selzer JA, Lieberman JA.** Schizophrenia and substance abuse. Psychiatr Clin North Am. 1993;16:401.

40 **Drake RE, Wallach MA.** Substance abuse among the chronically mentally ill. Hosp Community Psychiatry. 1989; 40:1041.

41 **Stanislav SW et al.** A longitudinal analysis of factors associated with morbidity in cocaine abusers with psychiatric illness. Pharmacotherapy. 1992; 12:114.

42 **Drake RE, Osher FC.** Alcohol use and abuse in schizophrenia, a prospective community study. J Nerv Ment Dis. 1989;177:408.

43 **Kofoed L, Kania J et al.** Outpatient treatment of patients with substance abuse and coexisting psychiatric disorders. Am J Psychiatry. 1986;143: 867.

44 **Kolb LC.** Modern Clinical Psychiatry. Philadelphia, PA: WB Saunders; 1973: 308.

45 **Liberman RP.** The effects of social skills training on personality with schizophrenia. Relapse. 1993;3:9.

46 **Rifkin A.** Pharmacologic strategies in the treatment of schizophrenia. Psychiatr Clin North Am. 1993;16:351-63.

47 **Davis JM.** Overview, maintenance therapy in psychiatry. I. Schizophrenia. Am J Psychiatry. 1975;132:1237.

48 **Bartko G, Maylath E.** Comparative study of schizophrenic patients relapsed on and off medication. Psychiatry Res. 1987;22:221.

49 **Lydiard RB, Laird LA.** Prediction of response to antipsychotics. J Clin Psychopharmacol. 1988;8:3.

50 **Luchins DJ et al.** Lateral ventricular size in the psychoses: relation to psychopathology and therapeutic and adverse response to medication. Psychopharmacol Bull. 1983;19:518.

51 **Weinberger DR et al.** Cerebral ventricular enlargement in chronic schizophrenia: an association with poor response to treatment. Arch Gen Psychiatry. 1980;37:11.

52 **Andreasen NC et al.** Positive and negative symptoms in schizophrenia. Arch Gen Psychiatry. 1990;47:615.

53 **Marder SR et al.** Schizophrenia. Psychiatr Clin North Am. 1993;16:567.

54 **Zavodnick S.** A pharmacological and theoretical comparison of high and low potency neuroleptics. J Clin Psychiatry. 1978;39(4):332.

55 **Dubin WR.** Rapid tranquilization: antipsychotics or benzodiazepines? J Clin Psychiatry. 1988;49(Suppl.):5.

56 **Wyatt RJ.** Biochemistry and schizophrenia. The neuroleptics. Psychopharmacol Bull. 1976;12(Pt. IV):5.

57 **Davis JM et al.** Important issues in the drug treatment of schizophrenia. Schizophr Bull. 1980;6:70.

58 **Gaebel W, Dietzcker A.** One-year outcome of schizophrenia patients—the interaction of chronicity and neuroleptic treatment. Pharmacopsychiatry. 1985;18:235.

59 **Kissling W.** The current unsatisfactory state of relapse prevention in schizophrenic psychoses—suggestions for improvement. Clin Neuropharmacol. 1991;14(Suppl. 2):533.

60 **Kissling W, ed.** Guidelines for neuroleptic relapse prevention in schizophrenia. Berlin: Springer-Vorlag; 1991.

61 **Rifkin A et al.** Dosage for haloperidol for schizophrenia. Arch Gen Psychiatry. 1991;48:166.

62 **McEvoy JP et al.** Optimal dose of neuroleptic in acute schizophrenia. Arch Gen Psychiatry. 1991;48:739.

63 **Faraone SV et al.** Neuroleptic dose reduction for schizophrenic patients: a three-year follow-up study. Hosp Community Psychiatry. 1988;39:1207.

64 **Kane JM.** Neuroleptics: dosage, relapse and quality of life. Relapse. 1993; 3:3.

65 **Marder SR et al.** Low- and conventional-dose maintenance therapy with fluphenazine decanoate. Arch Gen Psychiatry. 1987;44:518.

66 **Ereshefsky L et al.** A loading dose strategy for converting from oral to depot haloperidol. Hosp Community Psychiatry. 1993;44:1155.

67 **Kane JM et al.** Low dose neuroleptic treatment of outpatient schizophrenia: I. Preliminary results for relapse rates. Arch Gen Psychiatry. 1983;40:893.

68 **Carpenter WT et al.** A comparative trial of pharmacologic strategies in schizophrenia. Am J Psychiatry. 1987; 11:1466.

69 **Herz MI et al.** Intermittent versus maintenance medication in schizophrenia. Two-year results. Arch Gen Psychiatry. 1991;48:333.

70 **Kane JM.** Compliance issues in outpatient treatment. J Clin Psychopharmacol. 1985;5:22.

71 **Babiker IE.** Comparative efficacy of long-acting depot and oral neuroleptic medications in preventing schizophrenic recidivism. J Clin Psychiatry. 1987;48:94.

72 **Glazer WM, Kane JM.** Depot neuroleptic therapy: an underdeveloped treatment option. J Clin Psychiatry. 1992;53:426.

73 **Van Pragg HM, Dols LCW.** Fluphenazine enanthate and decanoate: a comparison of their duration of action and motor side effects. Am J Psychiatry. 1973;130:801.

74 **Inderbitzin LB et al.** Fluphenazine de-

canoate: a clinical problem? Am J Psychiatry. 1989;146:88.

75 Ereshefsky L et al. Future of depot neuroleptic therapy: pharmacokinetic and pharmacodynamic approaches. J Clin Psychiatry. 1984;45:50.

76 McEvoy GK, ed. American Hospital Formulary System Drug Information. Bethesda: American Society of Hospital Pharmacists; 1993:1338.

77 McNeil Pharmaceutical. Haldol Decanoate package insert. Raritan, NJ: 1993 July.

78 Small J et al. A placebo-controlled study of lithium combined with neuroleptics in chronic schizophrenic patients. Am J Psychiatry. 1975;132:1315.

79 Carmen JS et al. Lithium combined with neuroleptics in chronic schizophrenic and schizoaffective patients. J Clin Psychiatry. 1981;42:124.

80 Growe GA et al. Lithium in chronic schizophrenia. Am J Psychiatry. 1979;136:454.

81 Goldney RD, Spence ND. Safety of the combination of lithium and neuroleptic drugs. Am J Psychiatry. 1986;143:882.

82 Hollister LE et al. Clinical use of benzodiazepines. J Clin Psychopharmacol. 1993;13(Suppl. 1):1.

83 Wolkowitz OM et al. Alprazolam augmentation of the antipsychotic effects of fluphenazine in schizophrenic patients. Preliminary results. Arch Gen Psychiatry. 1988;45:655.

84 Christinson GW et al. When symptoms persist: choosing among alternative somatic treatments for schizophrenia. Schizophr Bull. 1991;17:217.

85 Sorgi PJ et al. Beta-adrenergic blockers for the control of aggressive behaviors in patients with chronic schizophrenia. Am J Psychiatry. 1986;143:775.

86 Lindstrom L, Persson E. Propranolol in chronic schizophrenia: a controlled study in neuroleptic treated patients. Br J Psychiatry. 1980;137:126.

87 Neppe VM. Carbamazepine in nonresponsive psychosis. J Clin Psychiatry. 1988;49(Suppl. 4):22.

88 Okuma T et al. A double-blind study of adjunctive carbamazepine versus placebo in excited states of schizophrenia and schizoaffective disorders. Acta Psychiatr Scand. 1989;80:250.

89 Meltzer HY. New drugs for the treatment of schizophrenia. Psychiatr Clin North Am. 1993;16:365.

90 Kane J et al. Clozapine for the treatment-resistant schizophrenic: a double-blind comparison with clozapine. Arch Gen Psychiatry. 1988;45:789.

91 Meltzer HY et al. Cost effectiveness of clozapine in neuroleptic-resistant schizophrenia. Am J Psychiatry. 1993;150:1630.

92 Ereshefsky L et al. Clozapine: an atypical antipsychotic agent. Clin Pharm. 1989;8:691.

93 Breier A et al. Clozapine treatment of outpatients: outcome and long-term response patterns. Hosp Community Psychiatry. 1993;44:1145.

94 Meltzer HY. Duration of a clozapine trial in neuroleptic-resistant schizophrenia. Arch Gen Psychiatry. 1989;46:672.

95 Sandoz Inc. Clozaril, a new drug application. Volumes 28–31, 36, 39, 48, 50, 52, 84, 98, 99, 100, 103. East Hanover, NJ: 1987 Aug 10.

96 Alvir JMJ et al. Clozapine-induced agranulocytosis: incidence and risk factors in the United States. N Engl J Med. 1993;329:162.

97 Safferman AZ et al. Rechallenge in clozapine-induced agranulocytosis. Lancet. 1992;2: 1296.

98 Preskorn SH et al. Therapeutic drug monitoring: principles and practice. Psychiatr Clin North Am. 1993;16:611.

99 Kane J, Marder SR. Psychopharmacologic treatment of schizophrenia. Schizophr Bull. 1993;19:287.

100 Perry PS et al. The relationship of haloperidol concentrations to therapeutic response. J Clin Psychopharmacol. 1988;8:38.

101 Kirch DG et al. Serum haloperidol concentrations and clinical response in schizophrenia. Schizophr Bull. 1988;14:283.

102 Smith RC. Plasma haloperidol levels and clinical response. Arch Gen Psychiatry. 1987;44:1110.

103 Santos JL et al. Clinical response and plasma haloperidol in chronic and subchronic schizophrenia. Biol Psychiatry. 1989;26:381.

104 Dysken MW et al. Fluphenazine pharmacokinetics and therapeutic response. Psychopharmacology. 1981;73:205.

105 Marder SR et al. Fluphenazine plasma levels and clinical response. Psychopharmacol Bull. 1990;26:256.

106 Mavroides M et al. Clinical relevance of thiothixene plasma levels. J Clin Psychopharmacol. 1984;4:155.

107 Yesavage J et al. Correlation of initial thiothixene serum levels and clinical response. Arch Gen Psychiatry. 1983;40:301.

108 Perry PJ et al. Clozapine and norclozapine plasma concentration and clinical response of treatment-refractory schizophrenic patients. Am J Psychiatry. 1991;148:231.

109 Hasegawa M et al. Relationship between clinical efficacy and clozapine plasma levels in schizophrenia: effect of smoking. J Clin Psychopharmacol. 1993;13:383.

110 Casey DE. Neuroleptic-induced acute extrapyramidal syndromes and tardive dyskinesia. Psychiatr Clin North Am. 1993;16:589.

111 Simpson G, Angus JWS. A rating scale for extrapyramidal side effects. Acta Psychiatr Scand. 1970;46(Suppl 221):11.

112 Casey DE, Keepers GA. Neuroleptic side effects: acute extrapyramidal syndromes and tardive dyskinesia. In: Casey DE, Christensen AV, eds. Psychopharmacology: Current Trends. Berlin: Springer-Verlag; 1988:80.

113 Hoffman BF. The diagnosis and treatment of neuroleptic-induced parkinsonism. Hosp Community Psychiatry. 1981;32:110.

114 Wells BG et al. Characterizing anticholinergic abuse in community mental health. J Clin Psychopharmacol. 1989;9:431.

115 Boyer WF et al. Anticholinergic prophylaxis of acute haloperidol-induced dystonic reactions. J Clin Psychopharmacol. 1989;7:164.

116 Fleischhacker WW et al. The pharmacological treatment of neuroleptic-induced akathisia. J Clin Psychopharmacol. 1990;10:12.

117 Sprague RL, Kalachnik JE. Reliability, validity and a total score cutoff for the Dyskinesia Identification System: Condensed User Scale (DISCUS) with mentally ill and mentally retarded populations. Psychopharmacol Bull. 1991;27:51.

118 Morgenstern H, Glazer WM. Identifying risk factors for tardive dyskinesia among long-term outpatients maintained with neuroleptic medications. Results of the Yale tardive dyskinesia study. Arch Gen Psychiatry. 1993;50:723.

119 Kalachnik JE et al. Tardive dyskinesia monitoring and the Dyskinesia Identification System: Condensed User Scale (DISCUS). Training and Quality Assurance Manual. Sandoz: 1991.

120 Smith JM, Baldessarini RJ. Changes in prevalence, severity and recovery in tardive dyskinesia with age. Arch Gen Psychiatry. 1980;37:1368.

121 Kane JM et al. Incidence of tardive dyskinesia: five-year data from a prospective study. Psychopharmacol Bull. 1984;20:39.

122 Kane JM et al. Tardive dyskinesia: a task force report to the American Psychiatric Association. Washington, DC: American Psychiatric Association; 1992.

123 Nguyen JA et al. Gamma-aminobutyric acid (GABA) pathways in tardive dyskinesia. Psychiatric Annals. 1989; 19:302.

124 Jeste DV et al. Tardive dyskinesia—reversible and irreversible. Arch Gen Psychiatry. 1979;36:585.

125 Khot V, Wyatt RJ. Not all that moves is tardive dyskinesia. Am J Psychiatry. 1991;148:661.

126 Jeste DV et al. Pharmacologic treatments of tardive dyskinesia in the 1980s. J Clin Psychopharmacol. 1988; 8(Suppl.):388.

127 Bacher NM, Lewis HA. Low dose propranolol in tardive dyskinesia. Am J Psychiatry. 1980;137:495.

128 Novac A. Improvement in tardive dyskinesia and MMPI scores with propranolol. J Clin Psychiatry. 1986;47:218.

129 Schrodt GR et al. Treatment of tardive dyskinesia with propranolol. J Clin Psychiatry. 1982;43:328.

130 Freedman R et al. Clonidine treatment of schizophrenia. Double-blind comparison to placebo and neuroleptic drugs. Acta Psychiatr Scand. 1982;65:35.

131 Thaker GK et al. Clonazepam treatment of tardive dyskinesia: a practical GABA mimetic strategy. Am J Psychiatry. 1990;147:445.

132 Bobruff A et al. Clonazepam and phenobarbital in tardive dyskinesia. Am J Psychiatry. 1981;138:189.

133 Singh MM et al. Diazepam-induced changes in tardive dyskinesia: suggestions for a new conceptual model. Biol Psychiatry. 1982;17:729.

134 Weber SS et al. Diazepam in tardive dyskinesia. Drug Intell Clin Pharm. 1983;17:523.

135 Egan MF et al. Treatment of tardive dyskinesia with Vitamin E. Am J Psychiatry. 1992;149:773.

136 Shriqui CL et al. Vitamin E in the treatment of tardive dyskinesia. A double-blind, placebo-controlled study. Am J Psychiatry. 1992;149:391.

137 Adler LA et al. Vitamin E treatment of tardive dyskinesia. Am J Psychiatry. 1993;150:1405.

138 Kushner SL, Rodner JT. Calcium channel blockers for tardive dyskinesia in geriatric psychiatric patients. Am J Psychiatry. 1989;146:1218.

139 Duncan E et al. Nifedipine is the treatment of tardive dyskinesia. J Clin Psychopharmacol. 1990;10:414.

140 Stedman TJ et al. Effects of nifedipine on psychosis and tardive dyskinesia. J Clin Psychopharmacol. 1991;11:43.

141 Cates M et al. Are calcium channel blockers effective in the treatment of tardive dyskinesia? Ann Pharmacother. 1993;27:191.

142 Nishikawa T et al. Tardive dyskinesia treatment with clonidine. Kurume Med J. 1980;27:209.

143 Casey DE. Tardive dyskinesia. West J Med. 1990;153:538.

144 Caroff SM. The neuroleptic malignant syndrome. J Clin Psychiatry. 1980;41:79.

145 Pearlman CA. Neuroleptic malignant syndrome: a review of the literature. J Clin Psychopharmacol. 1986;6:257.

146 Goekoop JG et al. Treatment of neuroleptic malignant syndrome. Am J Psychiatry. 1983;139:944.

147 Bismuth C et al. Dantrolene—a new therapeutic approach to neuroleptic malignant syndrome. Acta Neurol Scand. 1984;70(Suppl. 100):193.

148 Khan A et al. Resolution of resolution neuroleptic malignant syndrome with dantrolene sodium: case report. J Clin Psychiatry. 1987;48:69.

149 McCarron MM et al. A case of neuroleptic malignant syndrome successfully treated with amantadine. J Clin Psychiatry. 1982;43:381.

150 Amdurski S et al. A therapeutic trial of amantadine in haloperidol-induced neuroleptic malignant syndrome. Curr Ther Res. 1983;33:225.

151 Gangadhar BN et al. Amantadine in the neuroleptic malignant syndrome. J Clin Psychiatry. 1984;45:526.

152 Mueller PS et al. Neuroleptic malignant syndrome—successful treatment with bromocriptine. JAMA. 1983;249:386.

153 Verhoeven WMA et al. Neuroleptic malignant syndrome: successful treatment with bromocriptine. Biol Psychiatry. 1985;20:680.

154 Lazarus A. Therapy of neuroleptic malignant syndrome. Psychiatr Dev. 1986;4:19.

155 Dhib-Jalbut S et al. Bromocriptine treatment of neuroleptic malignant syndrome. J Clin Psychiatry. 1987;48:69.

156 Litvak R et al. Agranulocytosis, leukopenia and psychotropic drugs. Arch Gen Psychiatry. 1971;24:265.

157 Horrbin DF et al. Prolactin in mental illness. Postgrad Med J. 1976;52:79.

158 Martin JB, Reichlin S. Clinical Neuroendocrinology. 2nd ed. Contemporary Neurology Series. Philadelphia; FA Davis: 1987.

159 Tolis G et al. Prolactin secretion in 65 patients with galactorrhea. Am J Obstet Gynecol. 1974;118:91.

160 Marken PA et al. Management of psy-

chotropic-induced hyperprolactinemia. Clin Pharm. 1992;11:851.

161 **Beaumont P et al.** Bromoergocryptine in treatment of phenothiazine-induced galactorrhea. Br J Psychiatry. 1975; 126:285.

162 **Matsuoka I et al.** Effects of bromocriptine on neuroleptic-induced amenorrhea, galactorrhea and impotency. Jpn J Psychiatry Neurol. 1986;40:639.

163 **Varia IM et al.** Bromocriptine in treatment of haloperidol-induced galactorrhea. N C Med J. 1982;43:769.

164 **Corea N et al.** Amantadine in the treatment of neuroendocrine side effects of neuroleptics. J Clin Psychopharmacol. 1987;7:91.

165 **Siever LJ.** The effects of amantadine on prolactin levels and galactorrhea in neuroleptic-treated patients. J Clin Psychopharmacol. 1981;1:2.

166 **McEvoy GK, ed.** American Hospital Formulary System Drug Information. Bethesda: American Society of Hospital Pharmacists; 1993:2329.

167 **Kane JM et al.** Clozapine: plasma levels and prolactin response. Psychopharmacology. 1991;73:184.

168 **Sherlock S.** Progress report: hepatic

reactions to drugs. Gut. 1979;20:634.

169 **Regal RE et al.** Phenothiazine-induced cholestatic jaundice. Clin Pharm. 1987; 6:787.

170 **Simpson CM et al.** Adverse effects of antipsychotic drugs. Drugs. 1981;21: 138.

171 **Jos CJ et al.** Self-induced water intoxication: a comparison of 34 cases with matched controls. Am J Psychiatry. 1979;136:221.

172 **Blum A et al.** Somatic findings in patients with psychogenic polydipsia. J Clin Psychiatry. 1983;44:55.

173 **Illowsky BP, Kirch DG.** Polydipsia and hyponatremia in psychiatric patients. Am J Psychiatry. 1988;145:675.

174 **Dubovsky SL et al.** Syndrome of inappropriate antidiuretic hormone with exacerbated psychosis. Ann Intern Med. 1973;79:551.

175 **Nixon RA et al.** Demeclocycline in prophylaxis of self-induced water intoxication. Am J Psychiatry. 1982;139: 828.

176 **Kotin J et al.** Thioridazine and sexual dysfunction. Am J Psychiatry. 1976; 133:82.

177 **Smith PJ, Talbert RL.** Sexual dys-

function with antihypertensives and antipsychotics. Clin Pharm. 1986;5:373.

178 **Gould RJ et al.** Calcium channel blockade: possible explanation for thioridazine's peripheral side effects. Am J Psychiatry. 1984;141:352.

179 **Cold JA et al.** Seizure activity associated with antipsychotic therapy. DICP Ann Pharmacother. 1990;24:601.

180 **Logothetis JL.** Spontaneous epileptic seizures and electroencephalographic changes in the course of phenothiazine therapy. Neurology. 1967;17:869.

181 **Devinsky O et al.** Clozapine-related seizures. Neurology. 1991;41:369.

182 **Rumeau-Rouuquette C et al.** Possible teratogenic effects of phenothiazines in human beings. Teratology. 1977;15:57.

183 **Sitland-Marken PA et al.** Pharmacologic management of acute mania in pregnancy. J Clin Psychopharmacol. 1989;9:78.

184 **Sloane D et al.** Antenatal exposure to phenothiazines in relation to congenital malformations, perinatal mortality rate, birth weight and intelligence quotient score. Am J Obstet Gynecol. 1977;128: 468.

185 **Mortola JF.** The use of psychotropic

agents in pregnancy and lactation. Psychiatr Clin North Am. 1989;12:69.

186 **Leadbetter R et al.** Clozapine-induced weight gain: prevalence and clinical significance. Am J Psychiatry. 1992; 149:68.

187 **Parent MM et al.** Effect of molindone on weight change in hospitalized schizophrenic patients. Drug Intell Clin Pharm. 1986;20:873.

188 **Tune LE et al.** Serum levels of anticholinergic drugs and impaired recent memory in chronic schizophrenic patients. Am J Psychiatry. 1982;139: 1460.

189 **Merlis S et al.** Polypharmacy in psychiatry: patterns of differential treatment. Am J Psychiatry. 1970;126: 1647.

190 **Ghoneim MM, Mewaldt SP.** Benzodiazepines and human memory: a review. Anesthesiology. 1990;72:926.

191 **Miller SW et al.** Drug product selection: implications for the geriatric patient. Consult Pharm. 1990;5:30.

192 **Rovner BW et al.** Self-care capacity and anticholinergic drug levels in nursing home patients. Am J Psychiatry. 1988;45:107.

Mood Disorders I: Major Depressive Disorders

Lyle Knight Laird
William H Benefield, Jr

Overview 76-1
  Epidemiology 76-2
  Diagnosis and Classification (See Table 76.1) 76-2
    Clinical presentation (See Table 76.2) 76-2
    Classification 76-3
  Differential Diagnosis (See Tables 76.3 and 76.4) 76-3
    Disease- and drug-induced depression 76-3
  Pathophysiology 76-3
    Early theories 76-3
    Dysregulation hypothesis 76-4
    Neuroendocrine findings 76-4
    Imaging studies 76-5
  Patient Assessment Tools 76-5
    Mental status examination (See Table 76.5) 76-5
    Behavioral rating scales (Also see Table 76.6) 76-5
    Biological markers 76-6
  Nondrug Therapies for Depression 76-6
    Psychotherapy 76-6
    Light therapy 76-6
    Electroconvulsive therapy (ECT) 76-6
Major Depressive Disorder 76-8
  Diagnosis (See Table 76.7) 76-8
  Suicide Assessment 76-8
Drug Management 76-9
  Drug Selection: General Considerations
    (Also see Tables 76.8, 76.9, and 76.10) 76-9
  Response Rate of Target Symptoms 76-9
  Tricyclic Antidepressants (TCAs) 76-9
    Adverse effects 76-9
    Dosage titration 76-10
  Use in Pregnancy 76-10
  Duration of Therapy 76-11
    In single episode 76-11
    In recurrent depression 76-11
  Plasma Concentration Monitoring 76-11
  Special Populations 76-12
    Cardiac disease 76-12
    Orthostatic hypotension 76-12

    Antidepressants and left ventricular function 76-13
    Antidepressants and arrhythmias 76-13
    Antidepressants and conduction
      (See Table 76.11) 76-14
    Drug selection 76-14
  Epilepsy (See Tables 76.12 and 76.13) 76-14
    Seizure risk 76-14
    Drug selection 76-14
  Acquired Immunodeficiency Syndrome (AIDS) ...76-15
    Clinical presentation 76-15
    Drug selection 76-15
  The elderly 76-15
    Clinical presentation 76-15
    Drug selection 76-16
    Trazodone 76-16
  Selective Serotonin Reuptake Inhibitors (SSRIs) 76-16
    Use in elderly 76-16
    Pharmacokinetics (Also see Table 76.14) 76-16
    Adverse effects 76-17
    Drug interactions 76-18
  Depression with Atypical Features
    (Atypical Depression) 76-19
    Monoamine oxidase inhibitors (MAOIs)
      (See Table 76.15) 76-19
      Adverse effects 76-19
      Drug-food interactions (See Table 76.16) 76-20
      Drug-drug interactions (Also see Table 76.17) 76-20
  Depression with Psychotic Features
    (Psychotic Depression) 76-21
    Antidepressant plus antipsychotic 76-21
    Amoxapine 76-22
    Length of therapy 76-22
  Refractory Depression 76-22
    Stepped-care approach 76-23
    Other treatments 76-23
    Augmentation strategies 76-23
      Lithium and thyroid 76-23
    ECT 76-24

Depression has been a common part of the human experience for as long as recorded history. The ancient Egyptians wrote about depression over 3000 years ago. The First Book of Samuel, dating back to the eighth century B.C., probably describes the oldest written account of the illness. Saul, the King of Israel, is overcome by an "evil spirit" which causes him to feel incapacitated, guilt-ridden, and hopeless.[1]

Cultures throughout history have speculated on the origin of depression. The ancient Greeks thought depression was due to an excess of bile. Hippocrates thoroughly described the condition as a somatic illness and is believed to have coined the term *melancholia* which literally translates as "black bile." During the Middle Ages, depression, along with other psychiatric illnesses, was considered a punishment or an affliction from a vengeful God rather than an actual illness. At that time, the church and society believed it to be a result of being weak-minded or sinful. Even today in our

modern society, many people in a depressive episode carry the stigma of "having a nervous breakdown" and medications are viewed as a "crutch" to help cope with daily life. Diagnosed individuals usually can remain productive members of society with proper treatment. Depression has affected the lives of such famous people as Abraham Lincoln, Ludwig Van Beethoven, Sylvia Plath, and Ernest Hemingway.[1]

Although many individuals experience the day-to-day "down in the dumps," the term *depression* is reserved in psychiatry to describe a specific entity having biologic and pharmacologic implications. Depressive disorders are a growing health concern. Studies show that the physical and social dysfunction produced by depression outweigh most chronic medical conditions. For example, the Medical Outcomes Study demonstrated that the degree of impairment in depressed patients is comparable only to patients with chronic heart disease.[2] In turn, the cost of care for depression produces a tremendous burden upon society. The annual estimated cost of depression in the U.S. in 1990 was $43.7 billion.[3]

This chapter will discuss the pathophysiology, target symptoms, and treatment of major depressive disorder in adults. (See Chapter 78: Psychiatric Disorders in Children, Adolescents, and People with Developmental Disabilities for the treatment of depression in special populations such as children, adolescents, and the developmentally disabled.)

Epidemiology

Since World War II, rates of depression have increased persistently.[4] Today, symptoms of depression may occur in 13% to 20% of the population, making it the most common psychiatric disorder in adults.[5] The National Institute of Mental Health Epidemiologic Catchment Area study estimated major depression to have a lifetime prevalence of 5.8% in individuals ≥18 years old within the U.S.[6] Other studies from Europe and the U.S. estimate a lifetime prevalence of 5% to 12% in males and 9% to 26% in females.[7] The average age of onset of depression is in the late twenties, although depression may occur at any age. The observed peak onset for unipolar depression in females is from 35 to 45 years, whereas in males, it usually occurs after age 55. The prevalence of depression might be as high as 10% in persons over 65 years of age, reaching up to 20% at ages ≥80 years.[8]

Genetic factors may play an important role in the etiology of depression. A genetic predisposition often is unmasked by a stressful life event, demonstrating the importance of psychosocial and biological interplay. First-degree relatives (children, siblings, parents) of depressed individuals are one and one-half to three times more likely to have depression when compared to the general population. Concordance rates for monozygotic (identical) twins range from 54% to 65% whereas dizygotic (fraternal) twins range from 14% to 24%.[9] Adoption studies suggest a higher rate of depression and suicide in adopted children whose natural parents were depressed compared to children raised by adoptive parents who are depressed.[10] Genetic factors also may be more contributory in patients who have their first depressive episode at an earlier age (<30) than in older subjects.[11] Finally, there does not seem to be any scientific evidence to suggest that any particular race, ethnicity, or socio-economic class places an individual at a higher risk for depressive episode.

Diagnosis and Classification

The diagnosis and classification of depression has undergone many transformations since Emil Kraeplin's biological model of

Table 76.1	Classification of Mood Disorders[a]
Depressive Disorders	
Major Depressive Disorder, Single Episode	
Major Depressive Disorder, Recurrent	
Dysthymic Disorder	
Depressive Disorder Not Otherwise Specified	
Bipolar Disorders	
Bipolar I Disorder	
Bipolar II Disorder	
Cyclothymic Disorder	
Bipolar Disorder Not Otherwise Specified	
Secondary Mood Disorder Due to a General Medical Condition	
Substance-Induced Mood Disorder	
Mood Disorder Not Otherwise Specified	

[a] Adapted with permission from reference 13.

Table 76.2	Target Symptoms of Major Depressive Disorder	
Emotional	**Psychotic**	
Worthlessness, guilt, or shame	Bizarre behavior	
Hopelessness, helplessness	Hallucinations	
Thoughts of death and suicide	Delusions	
Self-deprecation	**Physical**	
Sadness	Anhedonia	
Pessimism	Somatic complaints	
Irritability	Fatigue	
Anhedonia	Weight change	
Cognitive	Sleep disturbance	
↓ ability to concentrate	Slowed movement	
Indecisiveness	↓ libido	
Poor memory	↓ hygiene	
	Crying spells	

the late 19th century. Kraeplin separated the functional psychoses into two groups: manic-depressive insanity and dementia praecox. Kraeplin's detailed descriptions of these two mental illnesses has laid the foundation for modern psychiatry.[12] In 1994 the American Psychiatric Association published standardized criteria for diagnosing depressive disorders in the new Diagnostic and Statistical Manual of Mental Disorders, Fourth Edition (DSM-IV).[13] Depressive Disorders are classified under Mood Disorders along with Bipolar Disorders (see Chapter 77: Mood Disorders II: Bipolar Affective Disorders). Depressive Disorders, according to DSM-IV, comprise the following: Major Depressive Disorder, single episode or recurrent (formerly known as Major Depressive Episode and Major Depression in DSM-III-R), Dysthymic Disorder, and Depressive Disorder Not Otherwise Specified.[13] See Table 76.1 for the classification of mood disorders.

As stated above, a *major depressive disorder* may occur as either a single or recurrent event. Single episodes may occur in 30% to 50% of depressed individuals, whereas the remainder will have recurrent episodes.[7] Recurrent depression varies with some people having episodes separated by many years, whereas others have many episodes on a frequently occurring basis. Seasonal patterns of depression are characterized by a regular cycle between the episode and a particular period of the year.

Clinical Presentation

In order for a diagnosis of major depressive disorder to be made, symptoms must be present for at least two weeks. Individuals must have at least five of the following symptoms, with at least one being depressed mood or loss of interest or pleasure (anhedonia): disturbances in appetite or weight, sleep or psychomotor activity, decreased energy, decreased libido, feelings of guilt or worthlessness, decreased ability to concentrate or think, or suicidal ideation. The mood disturbance also must cause marked distress or a clinically significant impairment in social or occupational functioning.[13] Table 76.2 lists the target symptoms of major depressive disorder.

Individuals who have depressive symptoms may report sadness, hopelessness, or a withdrawal from usual activities. Some report extreme guilt about something (usually trivial) they have done in the past. Additionally, sleep and appetite typically are affected, either of which may be increased or decreased. Some individuals may present with somatic complaints (headache, dizziness, constipation) and irritability. Psychomotor agitation may be seen with wringing of hands, pacing, or shouting. Others may have psychomotor retardation, with slowed speech, slowed body movements, and muteness. On occasion, psychotic symptoms may occur such as auditory hallucinations, persecutory delusions, or somatic delusions of serious illnesses. The elderly usually present with the same symptoms of depression as younger adults. However, they may be less likely to report feelings of worthlessness or guilt and more likely to experience weight loss and somatic complaints.[8]

Classification

Depressive disorders may be subclassified using cross-sectional symptom features or specifiers according to DSM-IV. For example, the term ''with melancholic features'' is used when patients experience depression in the morning, usually accompanied by early morning waking. Other symptoms suggestive of melancholia include marked psychomotor retardation or agitation, significant anorexia or weight loss, and excessive or inappropriate guilt. The term ''with atypical features'' is used when depressive symptoms include significant weight gain or increase in appetite, hypersomnia, or leaden paralysis. On occasion, symptoms such as auditory hallucinations, persecutory delusions, or somatic delusions of serious illnesses may occur in which case the term ''with severe psychotic features'' is used.[13] Other diagnostic specifiers utilized in DSM-IV include ''with catatonic features'' and ''with postpartum onset.''

Dysthymic disorder is a chronic mood disturbance involving depressed mood with less severity than major depressive disorder. Symptoms must be present for at least two years whereas major depressive disorder has one or more specific depressive episodes. Oftentimes, however, dysthymic disorder is difficult to differentiate from major depressive disorder. Dysthymic disorder usually is less responsive to somatic therapies including medication. Some patients may have dysthymic disorder superimposed upon major depressive disorder. This is known as ''double depression'' which is even less responsive to therapy. In addition, dysthymic patients have a greater risk of having a recurrence of major depression than patients without dysthymia.[14]

Depressive Disorder Not Otherwise Specified is used when the depressive symptoms do not meet the criteria for any specific mood disorder.[13]

The DSM-IV, like previous editions, uses a multiaxial system (Axes I–V) for organizing diagnoses and psychosocial assessments. Axes I and II comprise mental disorders with Depressive Disorders being on Axis I along with other mental illnesses such as schizophrenia and bipolar disorders. Mental retardation and personality disorders are examples of disorders that are coded under Axis II. Axis III includes concomitant physical disorders and conditions (e.g., hypertension, diabetes, seizures), whereas Axes IV and V represent a patient's list of psychosocial stressors and global assessment of functioning, respectively.[13]

Differential Diagnosis

Disease- or Drug-Induced Depression

Psychosocial stressors such as a death of a loved one, loss of job, marital separation, distress over one's sexual orientation, or the ending of an important relationship may precipitate a depressive episode. Symptoms of depression also may appear as a result of numerous medical conditions, such as certain neoplasms and infections. Other central nervous system (CNS), endocrine, cardiovascular, and degenerative disorders also can precipitate depressive symptoms.[15] See Table 76.3 for a partial listing of medical conditions that may mimic signs and symptoms of depression. Substance abuse such as alcohol or cocaine also may cause a depressive episode. See Table 76.4 for some commonly prescribed medications which may produce depressive symptoms or precipitate a major depressive episode in a predisposed individual.

Table 76.3	Selected Medical Conditions Which May Mimic Depression[a],[b]
CNS	**Endocrine**
Alzheimer's disease	Acromegaly
Amyotrophic lateral sclerosis	Addison's disease
Brain tumors	Cushing's disease
Cerebrovascular accident	Diabetes mellitus
Creutzfeldt-Jacob disease	Hyperparathyroidism
HIV-associated dementia complex	Hypothyroidism
Huntington's disease	Apathetic hyperthyroidism
Multiple sclerosis	Insulinoma
Myasthenia gravis	Pheochromocytoma
Normal pressure hydrocephalus	**Malignancies**
Trauma (postconcussion)	Breast
Wernicke's encephalopathy	GI
Parkinson's disease	Lung
Pulmonary	Pancreas
Chronic bronchitis	Prostate
Emphysema	**Metabolic abnormalities**
Cardiovascular	Electrolyte imbalance
Cerebral arteriosclerosis	Hepatic encephalopathy
CHF	Pick's disease
MI	Uremia
Paroxysmal dysrhythmias	Wilson's disease
Autoimmune	**Others**
RA	Malnutrition
System lupus erythematosus	Pancreatic disease
Infectious diseases	Pernicious anemias
Pneumonia	Pellagra
Encephalitis	Chronic pain syndrome
Meningitis	
Neurosyphilis	
TB	

[a] Adapted from reference 245.
[b] CHF = Congestive heart failure; CNS = Central nervous system; GI = Gastrointestinal; HIV = Human immunodeficiency virus; MI = Myocardial infarction; RA = Rheumatoid arthritis; TB = Tuberculosis.

Pathophysiology

Early Theories

The biological basis for depressive disorders has come a long way since Hippocrates first identified bile as a possible cause. Since the 1960s, modern theories as to the origin of depression have evolved and focused upon the various neurotransmitter systems within the brain [e.g., serotonin (5-HT), dopamine (DA), and norepinephrine (NE)]. As our understanding of the mechanisms of action of the antidepressants continues to improve, the neurotransmitter theories of depression undoubtedly will continue to evolve.

In the past, the *monoamine hypothesis* proposed that either decreased synaptic concentrations of serotonin or norepinephrine caused depression. The norepinephrine depletion theory originally was based upon the observation that reserpine, which causes a depletion of brain norepinephrine, also causes depression in some individuals.[16],[17] This theory eventually evolved into the *permissive hypothesis* which emphasized a greater role for serotonin. In this hypothesis, a low concentration of serotonin, combined with a decrease in catecholamines, produces depression, whereas decreased levels of serotonin, combined with elevated levels of norepinephrine, produce mania. Antidepressants, therefore, were believed to treat depression by inhibiting the uptake of norepinephrine and/or serotonin from the synapse back into the neuron.[18]

Table 76.4	Medications That May Precipitate Depression[a]

Anti-inflammatory and analgesic agents
  Indomethacin
  Phenacetin
  Phenylbutazone
  Pentazocine

Antimicrobial agents
  Sulfonamides
  Ethambutol
  Cycloserine
  Selected gram-negative antibiotics

Cardiovascular/antihypertensive agents
  Digitalis
  Clonidine
  Guanethidine
  Methyldopa
  Reserpine
  Hydralazine
  Propranolol
  Reserpine
  Indapamide
  Prazosin
  Procainamide

CNS[b] agents
  Amantadine
  L-dopa
  Barbiturates
  Chloral hydrate
  Carbamazepine
  Succinimide derivatives
  Diazepam and other benzodiazepines
  Phenothiazines
  Alcohol
  Amphetamines

Hormonal agents
  Corticosteroids
  Estrogen
  Progesterone

Others
  Disulfiram
  Physostigmine
  Antineoplastic agents
  Organic pesticides

[a] Adapted from reference 245.
[b] CNS = Central nervous system.

Although these earlier theories were useful in our initial understanding of how antidepressants worked, they tend to be overly simplistic in their "teeter-totter" view of depression today. First of all, the rapid effect of the antidepressants to block the reuptake of neurotransmitters does not coincide with the delayed onset of action (i.e., up to 8 weeks). Secondly, synaptic concentrations of biogenic amines are not decreased in most patients with depression. Paradoxically, concentrations may be greater than, equal to, or less than those in normal controls.[19,20] Thirdly, differences in efficacy when switching between agents are not explained. Lastly, antidepressants in development can work via other mechanisms of action which do not inhibit reuptake of the biogenic amines significantly.

Dysregulation Hypothesis

The most recent theory considers depression, as well as other psychiatric disorders, to be the result of a dysregulated neurotransmitter system. Specific criteria for a system to be dysregulated have been proposed as follows: 1) an impairment in the regulatory or homeostatic mechanisms; 2) an erratic basal output of the neurotransmitter system; 3) a disruption in the normal periodicities (circadian rhythm); 4) a less selective response to environmental stimuli; 5) a perturbation in the system resulting in a slower return to baseline; and 6) a restoration to an efficient regulation via pharmacologic agents.[20]

Regardless of the antidepressant mechanism of action, changes in the pre- and postsynaptic receptor number (density) or sensitivity have been described as being *downregulated*.[21] Changes include a decrease in postsynaptic beta-adrenergic-receptor sensitivity, along with alterations in the sensitivities of the alpha-adrenergic- and serotonin-receptor subtypes, 5-HT$_{1A}$ and 5-HT$_2$. Newer, highly selective serotonin reuptake inhibiting drugs such as flu-

oxetine (Prozac), paroxetine (Paxil), and sertraline (Zoloft) increase the efficiency of serotonergic neurotransmission. After a lag period, these agents cause increased release of 5-HT secondary to presynaptic autoreceptor downregulation (5-HT$_{1A}$). Of the many 5-HT receptor subtypes that have been identified today, 5-HT$_{1A}$ and 5-HT$_2$ are believed to be involved in human depression.[22,23]

The dysregulation hypothesis, therefore, incorporates the diversity of antidepressant mechanisms with the changes that occur over a period of weeks in receptor sensitivities leading to downregulation. The theory in its simplest form suggests that antidepressants virtually "kick" the neurotransmitter system, similar to "tripping a thermostat" or restarting a computer when it "hangs." This allows a compensatory homeostatic change to occur in neuronal regulation by altering the sensitivity of norepinephrine and serotonin receptors. A more efficient "signal to noise" ratio of neurotransmission ultimately results, thereby ameliorating depressive target symptoms.

Greater emphasis now is being placed upon the serotonergic system in regulating depressive target symptoms. Appetite, energy, sleep, mood, libido, motor function, anxiety, aggression, and cognitive function all are regulated to some extent by 5-HT. Decreased levels of brain serotonin also can produce a relapse in stable, previously depressed patients.[24] The cerebrospinal fluid (CSF) concentration of serotonin's metabolite, 5-hydroxyindoleacetic acid (5-HIAA), is decreased in some depressed patients as well. However, other studies show no correlation between CSF-5-HIAA and the severity of the depressive episode.[24] Serotonin seems to have a role in suicide and other violent acts. Low CSF 5-HIAA concentrations have been found in subjects who have attempted suicide.[25] Other biochemical abnormalities associated with serotonin's role in depression include alterations in plasma tryptophan and blood platelet serotonin.[24] However, these findings have not been elucidated clearly at this time.

Neuroendocrine Findings

Along with dysregulated neurotransmitter systems, neuroendocrine abnormalities may contribute to the etiology of depression. Depressed patients often have abnormal thyroid function tests, particularly low triiodothyronine (T$_3$) and/or thyroxine (T$_4$) levels.[26] The release of thyroid-stimulating hormone (TSH) from the pituitary is under the regulation of the hypothalamic thyrotropin-releasing hormone (TRH). Approximately 25% to 35% of depressed patients with normal baseline thyroid function test exhibit a blunted TSH response to TRH. Approximately 15% of depressed patients exhibit an exaggerated TSH response to TRH[27,28] and CSF concentrations of TRH in depressed patients are threefold higher than in normal controls.[29] However, the role of the thyroid axis in depression is unclear and further research is needed.

The hypothalamic-pituitary-adrenal (HPA) axis also may contribute in the pathogenesis of depression. Corticosteroids modulate serotonin synthesis, metabolism, and reuptake, and may exert regulatory effects at the level of serotonin receptors, G-proteins, and effector units.[30,31] Furthermore, depressed patients may have elevated 24-hour integrated cortisol and corticotropin levels, and blunted HPA responses to both corticotropin-releasing hormone (CRH) and arginine vasopressin.[32–34] These findings suggest increased HPA activity exists in depression secondary to an elevation of CRH. CRH plays an important role in the vegetative symptoms of depression such as psychomotor retardation, decreased libido, and anorexia.[35] Serotonin also activates postsynaptic serotonin receptors in certain areas of the hypothalamic paraventricular nucleus causing a serotonergic-mediated stimulatory action in CRH-secreting neurons.[30] Other neuroendocrine abnormalities such as decreased concentrations of somatostatin (which plays a role in memory in animals) and increased levels of growth hormone also have been found in depressed individuals.[36,37]

Imaging Studies

Imaging studies including computed tomography, magnetic resonance imaging, positron emission tomography, and single photon emission computed tomography suggest patients with depression have regional brain dysfunction. Alterations in cerebral blood flow and/or metabolism in the frontal-temporal cortex and caudate nucleus are associated with common depressive symptoms such as anhedonia, dysphoria, hopelessness, and flat affect (sad facies).[38,39]

The biological basis of depression continues to be a complex interaction between dysregulated neurotransmitter and neuroendocrine systems. Refer to Figure 76.1 for a proposed schematic of how these systems may interact.

Patient Assessment Tools

Mental Status Examination

Pharmaceutical care in the depressed patient requires specialized knowledge and skills. In order to obtain specific target symptoms of depression and to assess a particular drug's therapeutic and adverse effects, personal communication with the patient is vital. The structured mental status examination or "AMSIT" report is a systematic way of assessing a patient's psychiatric target symptoms (see Table 76.5). There are five major headings in a mental status examination. Through this structured interview, the clinician has

an observational basis for evaluating a patient's appearance, behavior, speech; mood and affect; sensorium; current intellectual function, and several aspects of the patient's thoughts. The reader is referred to other sources for a more detailed discussion on the mental status examination and interview technique.[40,41]

Behavioral Rating Scales

Behavioral rating scales are used routinely in efficacy drug studies evaluating various psychiatric disorders including depression. Rating scales are useful in selecting research subjects, assessing the severity of a psychiatric illness, measuring changes in target symptoms over time, and determining treatment efficacy. Rating scales vary in type and may be assessed by the patient, a trained interviewer, the ward, or someone who has close contact with the patient such as a family member. Numerous depression scales have been developed over the past four decades including the Beck Depression Inventory, Depression Status Inventory, Depression Adjective Checklists, Minnesota Multiphasic Personality Inventory-Depression Scale, and the Hamilton Rating Scale for Depression (HAM-D). The HAM-D is the most commonly used instrument for rating depressive target symptoms in clinical drug trials. In addition, it is the "gold standard" when validating other depression rating scales (see Table 76.6). The 17-item HAM-D is the most commonly used version. Other versions of the scale have been developed to include such symptoms as anxiety-somatization, cognitive disturbance, diurnal variation, psychomotor retardation, and sleep disturbance. Although usually reserved for clinical efficacy studies, rating scales such as the HAM-D can be a useful tool

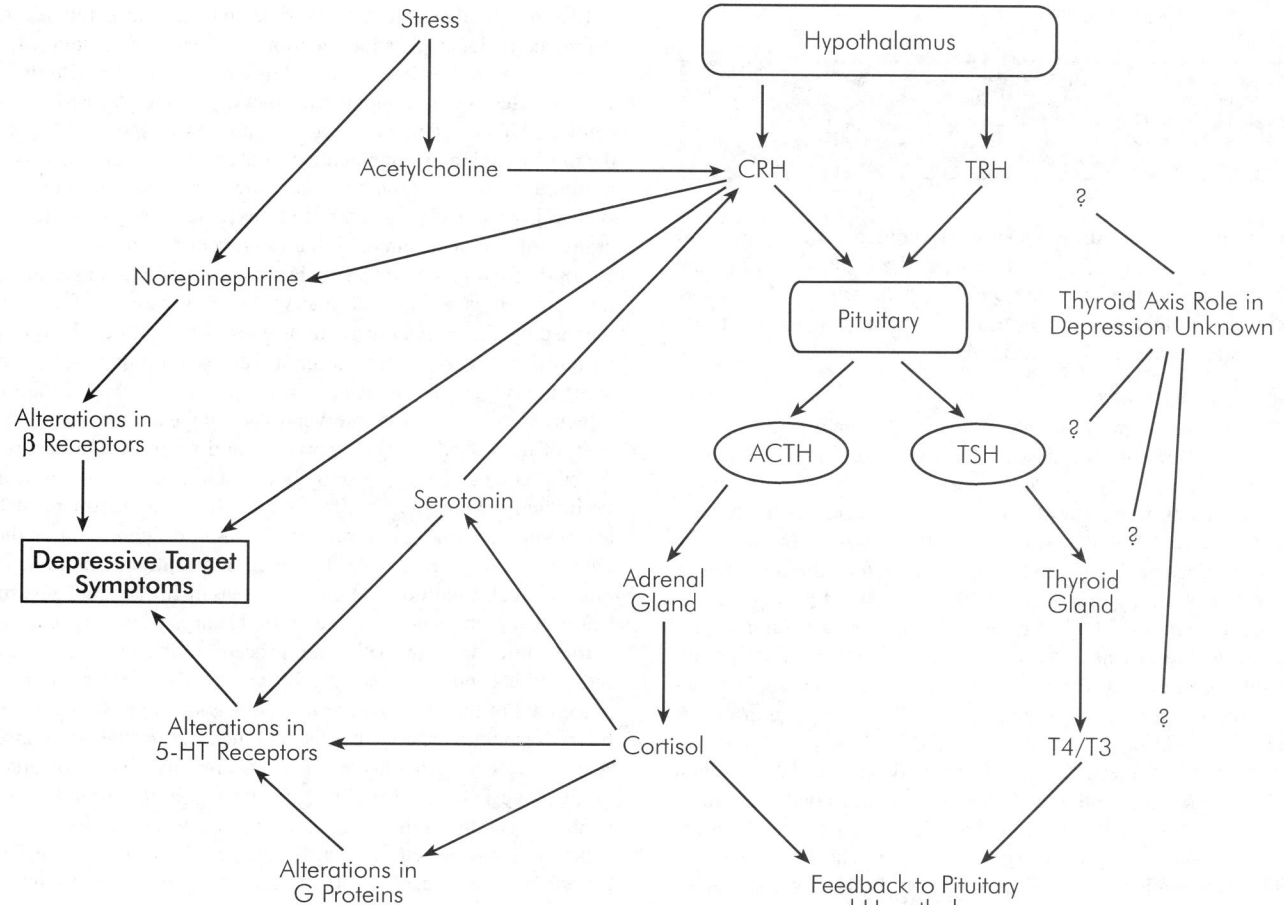

Fig 76.1 Proposed Schematic of the Neurotransmitter and the Neuroendocrine Interactions and Depressive Target Symptoms   ACTH = Adrenocorticotrophic hormone; CRH = Corticotropin-releasing hormone; TRH = Thyrotropin-releasing hormone; TSH = Thyroid-stimulating hormone; T_4 = Thyroxine; T_3 = Triiodothyronine.

Table 76.5	Mental Status Examination (AMSIT)

General Appearance, Behavior, Speech
- Apparent age; appear ill or in distress?
- Dress
- General reaction to examination; negativism
- Posture and gait
- Unusual movements
- Facial expression
- Signs of anxiety
- General level of activity
- Repetitious activities (stereotypy, mannerisms, compulsions)
- Disturbances of attention: distractibility
- Speech: mute, word salad, echolalia, clang, neologisms[a]

Mood and Affect
- Quality of prevailing mood; intensity and depth
- Constancy of mood, patient stated mood
- Affect: range, appropriateness, lability, flatness

Sensorium
- Orientation for time, place, person, situation
- Memory: recent and remote, immediate recall

Level of Intellectual Functioning
- An estimate of current intellectual functioning, not an estimate of original intellectual potential
- General fund of information: presidents, oceans, governor, large cities, current events. Why does the moon appear larger than the stars?
- Vocabulary
- Serial 7 subtractions (also tests attention and sensorium)

Thought Processes
- Pattern of associations (tempo, rhythm, organization, distortions, excesses, deficiencies)
- False perceptions (hallucinations, illusions, delusions, distortions of body image, depersonalization)
- Thought content (what patient tells, main concerns, obsessive ideation)
- Abstracting ability (tests by similarities, proverbs)
- Judgment and insight

[a] Clang = Pathologic punning and/or rhyming of words in a nonsensical association; Echolalia = Pathologic repetition of the speech of another; Neologisms = A new word or phrase coined by a person that has no meaning to others; Word salad = A mixture of words or phrases that lack meaning or logical coherence.

in monitoring patient drug response to supplement findings from the mental status examination. However, the evaluation may take up to an hour and it requires an experienced interviewer. The reader is referred to other sources for a more detailed discussion on behavior rating scales in depression.[42,43]

Biological Markers

Currently, there are no clinically useful laboratory tests which can aid the clinician in assessing whether a patient is becoming less depressed while on an antidepressant. However, in multiple studies, one-half to two-thirds of depressed individuals fail to suppress their circulating cortisol levels following the administration of dexamethasone. The standard procedure for administrating a dexamethasone suppression test (DST) consists of giving the patient dexamethasone 1 mg orally at 11 p.m. Blood samples are obtained the following day at 4 and 11 p.m. to measure serum cortisol concentration. The results are considered abnormal or positive if either of the two samples of cortisol are ≥5 µg/mL. A number of studies demonstrate that the DST is more abnormal in older depressed subjects. The DST also may be affected by certain drugs or other concomitant medical/psychiatric conditions. In a meta-analysis, a baseline DST was predictive of a poorer outcome in patients who were positive posttreatment.[44] The American Psychiatric Association (APA) Task Force on the Use of Laboratory Tests in Psychiatry has outlined some of the uses and limitations of the DST.[45] The DST is not a routine screening test at this time for all depressed patients, but may be used in some clinical situa-

tions when the diagnosis of depression is questionable. A DST result should not replace good clinical judgment.

A thorough assessment of the patient's target symptoms, past medical and psychiatric history, psychological issues, life stressors, family history, and psychosocial and cultural environments all should be considered before selecting treatment.

Nondrug Therapies for Depression

Psychotherapy and Light Therapy

Therapy for depression does not always include only pharmacotherapy. Psychotherapy is an important component of the overall treatment of the depressed patient. In ambulatory patients, interpersonal psychotherapy is equally comparable to antidepressant therapy, and the combination is superior to either alone.[46] During maintenance therapy, antidepressants decrease relapse rates while psychotherapy improves social functioning.[47] Since these treatment modalities are complementary, both should be used whenever possible. Somatic therapies for depression include electroconvulsive therapy (ECT), sleep deprivation, and bright light therapy. The diversity of these interventions underscores the complexity of the environment-brain interaction. Sleep deprivation and phototherapy are experimental interventions which modify intrinsic biological rhythms resulting in changes in brain chemistry. Phototherapy traditionally has been administered to patients with seasonal affective disorder in the morning hours; however, light therapy can be effective when given at other times during the day.[48] This intervention has been reviewed elsewhere.[49]

Electroconvulsive Therapy (ECT)

Electroconvulsive therapy may be indicated in some severely depressed patients. This intervention has been subject to a waxing in popularity in the 1940s with a subsequent waning with the advent of effective psychopharmacotherapy in the 1950s. More recently, ECT has gained popularity again. As it is used today, with the modern adjunctive medications that prevent adverse effects and morbidity (e.g., methohexital for anesthesia, an antimuscarinic such as glycopyrrolate to dry secretions in the airways and decrease bradycardia, and succinylcholine to prevent fractures that can occur during the procedure secondary to tonic-clonic muscular contractions), it is a low-risk intervention. However, ECT still is plagued by a negative image in the eyes of the public which is due partially to its early history when it was used routinely for a broad spectrum of psychiatric disorders. Presently, it is one of the most effective antidepressant interventions with estimates of 70% to 90% of depressed patients showing good response.[50] Because of the stigma attached to its use by both clinicians and the public and its limited availability, it often is thought of as treatment of last resort and used mostly in refractory cases of depression or those who are acutely suicidal. ECT is a relative contraindication in certain medical conditions, such as increased intracranial pressure, space-occupying lesions in the brain, aneurysms, and recent myocardial infarction (MI).[51] The procedure involves electrically inducing a generalized seizure by either a bilateral or unilateral placement of the electrode. Some medications (e.g., lithium, some benzodiazepines) should be discontinued before the procedure.[51] Adverse effects generally are few and mainly consist of anterograde amnesia (i.e., difficulty remembering things around the time of the procedure), retrograde amnesia as well as confusion, headaches, and muscle aches.[51] Cardiovascular effects (e.g., ventricular arrhythmias, MI, cardiac arrest) are the most ominous adverse events but virtually never occur during the procedure (i.e., has not occurred once in any of 22,210 consecutive ECT treatments).[52] The modern ECT procedure is well presented by Kellner.[53]

Table 76.6	Hamilton Depression Scale[a,b]

For each item, check the box next to the response that best characterizes the patient

1. Depressed mood (sad, hopeless, helpless, worthless)	0 ❑ Absent 1 ❑ These feeling states indicated only on questioning 2 ❑ These feeling states spontaneously reported verbally 3 ❑ Communicates feeling states nonverbally (i.e., through facial expression, posture, voice, and tendency to weep) 4 ❑ Patient reports VIRTUALLY ONLY those feeling states in his spontaneous verbal and nonverbal communication
2. Feelings of guilt	0 ❑ Absent 1 ❑ Self-reproach, feels he has let people down 2 ❑ Ideas of guilt or rumination over past errors or sinful deeds 3 ❑ Presents illness as a punishment. Delusions of guilt 4 ❑ Hears accusatory or denunciatory voices and/or experiences threatening visual hallucinations
3. Suicide	0 ❑ Absent 1 ❑ Feeling life is not worth living 2 ❑ Wishes he were dead or any thoughts of possible death itself 3 ❑ Suicide ideas or gesture 4 ❑ Attempts at suicide (only serious attempts rate 4)
4. Insomnia early	0 ❑ No difficulty 1 ❑ Complains of occasional difficulty falling asleep (i.e., >½ hr) 2 ❑ Complains of nightly difficulty falling asleep
5. Insomnia middle	0 ❑ No difficulty 1 ❑ Patient complains of being restless and disturbed during the night 2 ❑ Waking during the night (any getting out of bed rates 2, except for purposes of voiding)
6. Insomnia late	0 ❑ No difficulty 1 ❑ Waking in early hours of the morning but goes back to sleep 2 ❑ Unable to fall asleep again if gets out of bed
7. Work and activities	0 ❑ No difficulty 1 ❑ Thoughts and feeling of incapacity, fatigue, or weakness related to activities, work, or hobbies 2 ❑ Loss of interest in activity; hobbies, or work; either directly reported by patients, or indirect in listlessness, indecision, and vacillation (feels he has to push self to work or activities) 3 ❑ ↓ in actual time spent in activities or decrease in productivity; in hospital, rates 3 if patient does not spend at least 3 hours a day in activities (hospital job or hobbies), exclusive of ward chores 4 ❑ Stopped working because of present illness; in hospital, rate 4 if patients engaged in no activities except ward chores, or if patient fails to perform ward chores unassisted
8. Retardation (slowness of thought and speech; impaired ability to concentrate; ↓ motor activity)	0 ❑ Normal speech and thought 1 ❑ Slight retardation at interview 2 ❑ Obvious retardation at interview 3 ❑ Interview difficult 4 ❑ Complete stupor
9. Agitation	0 ❑ None 1 ❑ "Playing with" hands, hair, etc. 2 ❑ Hand-wringing, nail-biting, hair-pulling, biting of lips
10. Anxiety psychic	0 ❑ No difficulty 1 ❑ Slight retardation at interview 2 ❑ Obvious retardation at interview 3 ❑ Interview difficult 4 ❑ Complete stupor
11. Anxiety somatic	0 ❑ Absent Physiological concomitants of anxiety, such as: 1 ❑ Mild GI—dry mouth, wind, indigestion, diarrhea, cramps, belching 2 ❑ Moderate Cardiovascular—palpitations, headaches 3 ❑ Severe Respiratory—hyperventilation, sighing 4 ❑ Incapacitating Sweating
12. Somatic symptoms GI[b]	0 ❑ None 1 ❑ Loss of appetite but eating without staff encouragement. Heavy feelings in abdomen 2 ❑ Difficulty eating without staff urging. Requests or requires laxatives or medication for bowels or medication for GI symptoms
13. Somatic symptoms General	0 ❑ None 1 ❑ Heaviness in limbs, back, or head. Backaches, headache, muscle aches. Loss of energy or fatiguability 2 ❑ Any clear-cut symptoms rates 2
14. Genital Symptoms	0 ❑ None Symptoms such as: Loss of libido 1 ❑ Mild Menstrual disturbances 2 ❑ Severe
15. Hypochondriasis	0 ❑ Not present 1 ❑ Self-absorption (bodily) 2 ❑ Preoccupation with health 3 ❑ Frequent complaints, requests for help, etc. 4 ❑ Hypochondriacal delusions
16. Loss of weight (Answer only A or B)	**A. When rating by history:** 0 ❑ No weight loss

Continued

Table 76.6	Hamilton Depression Scale[a],[b] (Continued)

For each item, check the box next to the response that best characterizes the patient

	1 ☐ Probably weight loss associated with present illness
	2 ☐ Definite (according to patient) weight loss
	B. On weekly ratings by ward psychiatrist, when actual weight changes are measured:
	0 ☐ <1 lb/week weight loss
	1 ☐ >1 lb/week weight loss
	2 ☐ >2 lb/week weight loss
17. Insight	0 ☐ Acknowledges being depressed and ill
	1 ☐ Acknowledges illness but attributes cause to bad food, climate, overwork, virus, need for rest, etc.
	2 ☐ Denies being ill at all

Investigator's signature:

[a] Reprinted from reference 246.
[b] GI = Gastrointestinal.

Major Depressive Disorder

Diagnosis

1. A.R., a 25-year-old female, presents to the student health clinic for a routine annual examination. During her visit, A.R. has the chief complaint: "I have been feeling depressed and sometimes I think about hurting myself." Her physical exam is unremarkable and all laboratory tests (complete blood count with differential, chemistry panel, and thyroid functions studies) are within normal limits. A beta human chorionic gonadotropin is negative. She takes no medication other than an oral contraceptive. She is referred to a psychiatrist for a further evaluation.

A.R. states that over the past few months she has had increasing periods of depressed mood with frequent crying episodes. She reports that she has no interest in most of her usual activities (playing the piano, bicycling, gardening). She is engaged to be married in a few months but feels she does not deserve to be a wife. Over the last 2 months, her appetite has decreased and she reports a 15-pound weight loss. She reports feeling hopeless about all of the plans that need to be done before the wedding. Apparently, she also has difficulty in sleeping as she reports waking up in the early morning and cannot get back to sleep. Consequently, she has had no energy lately and has difficulty concentrating. This is a major concern since she is a graduate student at a local university. She also reports an older sister who has had depression and currently is maintained on desipramine (Norpramin).

A.R. is appropriately dressed with clean clothes. She is alert, coherent, and logical. She cries easily to the point of sobbing. Affect is constricted, apprehensive, and sad. Mood is depressed and she admits having suicidal ideation but no specific plan. She is oriented to person, place, and time but shows some recent memory deficits. Her intelligence is estimated to be above average. Concentration and abstractions (e.g., "Don't cry over spilled milk" or "Rolling stones gather no moss") are satisfactory. She denies hearing voices or other hallucinations. She has good insight and judgment into her illness. **What signs and symptoms does A.R. have which would support the diagnosis of major depressive disorder?**

A.R.'s target symptoms of depression may be recalled easily by the helpful mnemonic *D:SIG-E-CAPS*[244] (see Table 76.7). Based upon A.R.'s history, she describes a dysphoric mood as well as anhedonia (e.g., lack of interest in playing the piano, bicycling). In addition, she demonstrates frequent episodes of crying, decreased appetite (with a 15-pound weight loss), poor concentration, fatigue, suicidal ideation, hopelessness, and inappropriate guilt ("doesn't deserve to be a wife"). Her mental status examination is consistent with these target symptoms revealing a constricted, sad affect (facial expression) and frequent crying episodes during the interview.

Based upon DSM-IV, A.R. easily meets the criteria for major depressive disorder. This is based upon the numerous target symptoms that she is experiencing for at least two weeks without evidence of psychosis, other medical disorders, or uncomplicated bereavement. Based upon her target symptoms of anhedonia and vegetative signs (early morning waking, decreased appetite, weight loss), A.R. also meets the DSM-IV criteria for melancholia. Since this is A.R.'s first episode of depression, she is classified as having major depression, single episode.

Suicide Assessment

2. What is the risk of A.R. hurting herself? How should suicidal ideation be assessed?

Patients with major depressive disorder always should be assessed for the presence of suicidal thoughts with the question, "Are you thinking about hurting or killing yourself?" Suicide is viewed by the depressed patient as a remedy to their insurmountable problems when all other options appear closed. Comments made by patients alluding to suicide (e.g., "Life is not worth living anymore" or "I am leaving and may never see you again") should be taken seriously. Misunderstandings surrounding suicidal ideation by the general public include the following myths: that a person is more likely to commit suicide if asked about it; a person is just looking for attention when threatening suicide; and a person attempts suicide because of a sudden traumatic event.

Several factors may place a person at greater risk for a suicide attempt. First of all, a more detailed plan indicates a strong intent and a higher risk for suicide. The clinician should be concerned if a change in A.R.'s personality is noticed (e.g., A.R. giving away possessions or making a will, or A.R. recently has purchased a gun or is asking about the lethal dose of a drug in her possession). Other risks for suicide that have been identified include people living alone, physical illness, unemployment, age greater than 40,

Table 76.7	Depressive Disorder Target Symptom Mnemonic[a]
D	**D**epressed mood
SIG	**S**leep (insomnia or hypersomnia); **I**nterest (loss of, including libido); **G**uilt
E	**E**nergy loss
CAPS	**C**oncentration (loss); **A**ppetite (loss or gain); **P**sychomotor (agitation or retardation); **S**uicide (ideation)

[a] Reprinted with permission from reference 244.

history of alcohol/drug abuse, family history for suicide, distress over one's sexual orientation, a lack of a support system, or a history of previous attempts at suicide.[25,54–56] Women attempt suicide two to three times more often than men; however, men are three times more likely to succeed. Partially filling a prescription for a medication of high-potential toxicity, calling the treating physician and family, or taking the time to counsel the patient directly may be beneficial life-saving interventions. One also should have an emergency resource "hot line" phone number readily available.

A.R. is at some risk for suicide, although she does not have any detailed plan. Her risk for suicide may increase during the first few weeks of antidepressant therapy, as she develops more energy and a capacity to act on any self-destructive plans. She should be monitored closely during the first few weeks of therapy by friends or family members. If her suicidal ideation becomes severe, A.R. should be admitted to a facility during the recovery period for her own safety. Unfortunately, it is not possible to predict whether A.R. will attempt to kill herself. Even with the best precautions, a small percentage of depressed individuals succeed in their suicide attempts.

Drug Management

Drug Selection: General Considerations

3. A.R. is diagnosed AXIS I: Major Depressive Disorder, single episode, with melancholic features; AXIS II: None; AXIS III: None. What drug treatment options are available for A.R.'s depressive target symptoms? What considerations should be made when selecting antidepressant therapy?

First episodes of depression, uncomplicated by concomitant medical illness or special features (atypical, psychotic), may be treated with any marketed antidepressant. Antidepressant medications can be classified into four categories: tricyclic antidepressants (TCAs), selective serotonin reuptake inhibitors (SSRIs), other novel cyclic antidepressants (bupropion, nefazodone), and the monoamine oxidase inhibitors (MAOIs). Refer to Table 76.8 for the standard doses and pharmacology for various antidepressants currently marketed in the U.S. The TCAs are the oldest antidepressants. They can be subdivided further into the tertiary amines [amitriptyline (Elavil), imipramine (Tofranil), doxepin (Sinequan), and trimipramine (Surmontil)] and the secondary amines [nortriptyline (Pamelor), desipramine (Norpramin), and protriptyline (Vivactil)]. Newer agents such as the SSRIs are replacing older therapies due to their more attractive side effect profile. Agents which recently have come to market include venlafaxine (Effexor) and nefazodone (Serzone).

Since similar rates of response occur with all antidepressants, other factors should be used in the selection of an antidepressant for A.R. The selection of an antidepressant should be based upon family and patient history if available. A medication that A.R. (or another family member) has responded to in the past with minimal side effects likely will induce a good response when selected.

The side effect profile for each of the antidepressants also should be considered when individualizing treatment for A.R. (See Tables 76.9 and 76.10.) For example, if a sedating drug is desired for insomnia or anxiety, then agents such a trazodone (Desyrel), doxepin, or imipramine should be used. Since A.R. is a student, a less sedating antidepressant such as an SSRI, protriptyline, or desipramine really should be considered. If A.R. had been elderly and more sensitive to anticholinergic side effects, trazodone, an SSRI, or desipramine would have been a reasonable choice. Likewise, to avoid cardiovascular adverse effects such as orthostatic hypotension, an SSRI, bupropion (Wellbutrin), or nortriptyline might be preferable (see Table 76.10).

Since A.R. is a healthy young person, any agent may be used for initial treatment. However, desipramine may be a reasonable choice given the history of her sister's positive response and its relatively nonsedating properties.

Response Rate of Target Symptoms

4. A.R. is placed on desipramine 25 mg TID and asked to return in 2 weeks for follow-up. How fast should A.R.'s depressive target symptoms be expected to respond to antidepressant therapy?

Target symptoms respond differently during the course of antidepressant therapy. Within the first week, symptoms such as anxiety, insomnia, and decreased appetite usually begin to improve. During the next two to three weeks, increases in energy and libido are seen. A.R. may be at higher risk for suicide during this time. With time, however, the day-to-day functioning should return with sadness and pessimism being the last target symptoms to respond to therapy.

A.R. should be counseled concerning the two- to four-week delay in full response with her new medication. In some instances, it may take up to eight weeks before the full effects of the medication are seen. A.R. should be encouraged to continue to take her medication as prescribed over this time frame.

Tricyclic Antidepressants (TCAs)

Adverse Effects

5. Since A.R. is going to be placed on a TCA, what are the major adverse effects and toxicities of the TCAs?

The most common adverse reactions of the tricyclic antidepressants are listed in Table 76.9. Common antimuscarinic or anticholinergic adverse effects of the TCAs include dry mouth, blurred vision, constipation, and urinary retention.[57] Although A.R. may develop tolerance to these side effects over time, they may never disappear completely. Of the CNS side effects, sedation is the most common. In adults, this can be minimized by single daily dosing at bedtime.

The most potentially dangerous adverse effect of the TCAs is their quinidine-like effect (Type IA) on prolonging cardiac conduction through the His-Purkinje system. This, in conjunction with positive chronotropic and adrenergic-stimulating properties of the TCAs, can lead to re-entry arrhythmias (e.g., Torsade de Pointes and other ventricular arrhythmias). In patients with pre-existing conduction defects and in overdose, there is a greater risk for cardiac arrhythmias.[58] Therefore, A.R. should receive a baseline electrocardiogram (ECG) before therapy.

Postural hypotension also may occur early in therapy. A.R. should be cautioned to rise slowly from bed and not to rapidly change her posture. If A.R. experiences dizziness, she should be instructed to lie or sit down and place her head between her knees. Of all of the tricyclic antidepressants, nortriptyline is the least likely to produce orthostasis.[59]

Tricyclic antidepressants, and most other classes of antidepressants can cause sexual dysfunction. This dysfunction usually manifests as decreased libido, erectile failure, or decreased sensation of ejaculation/orgasm. Sexual dysfunction may affect as many as 28% of men and women treated with imipramine. Estimations of sexual dysfunction caused by antidepressants may be underdiagnosed as many patients may be reluctant to discuss this matter with their clinician. Management of these adverse effects includes changing to an alternative antidepressant or coadministration of medication to treat the dysfunction. Case reports have described the beneficial effects of bethanecol (Urecholine) 10 to 30 mg one

Table 76.8			Antidepressant Medications: Neurotransmitter Uptake, Dosage, and Plasma Drug Concentrations[a]				
Drug	Serotonin	Norepinephrine	Dopamine	Starting Dose[b] (mg)	Dosage Range[c] (mg/day)	Therapeutic Plasma Concentration Range (ng/mL)
Amitriptyline (Elavil)	++++	++++	0	25 TID	50–300	60–200[d]
Amoxapine (Asendin)	+++	+++	0	50 TID	100–600	180–600[d]
Bupropion (Wellbutrin)	0/+	+	+	100 BID	300–450	50–100[d]
Desipramine (Norpramin)	+	++++	0/+	25 TID	50–300	125–250[e]
Doxepin (Sinequan)	+++	+	0	25 TID	75–300	110–250
Fluoxetine (Prozac)	+++++	0	0	10–20 Q AM	10–80	—
Fluvoxamine[f] (Luvox)	+++++	0	0	—	100–300	—
Imipramine (Tofranil)	+++	++	0/+	25 TID	50–300	180[d,e]
Lithium (Various)	++/0[g]	0	0	8 mEq TID	24–60 mEq	0.6–1.2[e]
Maprotiline (Ludiomil)	0	++++	0	25 TID	50–300	200–400[d]
Nefazodone (Serzone)	+++[h]	0/+	0	50 BID	100–600	—
Nortriptyline (Pamelor)	++	+++	0	25 TID	50–200	50–150[e]
Paroxetine (Paxil)	+++++	0	0	20 QD	10–50	—
Protriptyline (Vivactyl)	+	++++	0	5 TID	15–60	100–200
Sertraline (Zoloft)	+++++	0	0	50 QD	50–200	—
Trazodone (Desyrel)	++[h]	0	0	50 TID	50–600	800–1600
Trimipramine (Surmontil)	++	++	0	25 TID	15–90	—
Venlafaxine (Effexor)	++++	++++	0	25 TID/37.5 BID	75–375	—

[a] ++++ = High; +++ = Moderate; ++ = Low; + = Very low; 0 = None.
[b] In geriatric patients, use ⅓–½ starting dose.
[c] The specific product package insert should be consulted to confirm FDA-approved dosing.
[d] Parent and metabolite.
[e] Therapeutic plasma level established.
[f] Approved for obsessive-compulsive disorder.
[g] Acutely ↑; chronically stabilizes.
[h] Very low-dose antagonist; higher-dose antagonist without uptake blockade as principle effect.

to two hours before coitus to treat erectile dysfunction and decreased sensation of ejaculation/orgasm.[60]

Other adverse effects of the TCAs include weight gain, changes in blood glucose concentrations, rash, photosensitivity reactions,[61] blood dyscrasias,[62] and allergic hepatitis.[63]

Dosage Titration

6. Two weeks later, A.R. returns for her follow-up visit. She reports she is sleeping better. However, she still reports a loss in pleasure of her usual activities and a saddened mood. She has not experienced any major side effects except for a slightly dry mouth early in therapy. How should A.R.'s therapy be managed at this point?

A.R. has experienced some initial response to desipramine with regard to improvement in her sleeping pattern. One could argue that no change in desipramine therapy should be made at this time until another two weeks have elapsed since A.R. could continue to respond at this lower dosage. In addition, A.R. also is on an oral contraceptive. Lower dosages of TCAs may be required since oral contraceptives can inhibit hepatic enzymes. However, based upon her existing target symptoms, she may have a better response with a higher daily dose.

The usual therapeutic dose of desipramine for an acutely depressed patient is 75 to 300 mg/day. Since A.R. is at the lower end of the dosage range, an increase to 150 mg/day would be a reasonable change at this time. The daily dose of desipramine may be consolidated now for easier administration. A.R. should continue to be monitored for any side effects at this dosage and for any further response in her target symptoms on a weekly basis. Weekly increments of 50 mg then may be tried if she continues to be unresponsive. If, after four weeks at the upper dosage and therapeutic

range (based on plasma levels), she has not fully responded, an alternative drug should be considered.

Use in Pregnancy

7. Three months later, A.R. is doing well while being maintained on desipramine 150 mg/day. She is going to be married within the next month. How should she and her fiancé be counseled with regard to starting a family?

Ideally, A.R. and her fiancé should plan a pregnancy in consultation with a clinician so that A.R.'s antidepressant may be tapered over several weeks before conception. Once her antidepressant has been tapered and she appears stable, her oral contraceptive then may be discontinued. In the event that A.R. becomes pregnant while on maintenance therapy (despite taking an oral contraceptive), the decision to continue antidepressant therapy during pregnancy should be weighed against the possible risk of drug toxicity to the fetus. TCAs have been administered during the first trimester of pregnancy without harmful fetal effects; however, irritability, hyperhidrosis, tachycardia, tachypnea, and cyanosis have been reported in neonates born to TCA-treated mothers.[15,64] If A.R. is stable at the time of pregnancy, a taper of antidepressant medication for at least the first trimester is warranted.

Many women find that affective illness is stabilized during the gestational period, thus allowing minimal use of medication. However, A.R. should be told that childbirth may precipitate a major depressive episode postpartum. She also should be counseled about her greater risk for developing a recurrence of a depressive episode postpartum and about having her antidepressant restored after delivery for this reason. Postpartum depressive illness should be treated according to the same principles as any other depressive episode. However, it is quite normal for a transient, seven- to ten-day depressive episode known as "postpartum blues" to occur.

This condition usually is mild, does not meet the criteria for major depressive disorder, and does not require medication.[14]

The decision to breast-feed following birth is another major issue that needs to be addressed. TCAs, as well as other antidepressants, are excreted in breast milk. The clinical effects of this exposure are not known.[15,64] A.R. should not breast-feed her infant if she is restored on antidepressant therapy (also see Chapter 45: Teratogenicity and Drugs in Breast Milk).

Duration of Therapy

In Single Episode

8. How long should A.R. stay on the antidepressant once she has responded to therapy?

If A.R. exhibits a satisfactory response to desipramine, therapy should continue for a minimum of four to six months after achieving full remission. The first eight weeks of symptom resolution is when a patient is more vulnerable for relapse.[65] Since A.R. has no history of recurrent depression, a slow taper of the antidepressant dosage over several weeks may be warranted in the future. Tapering of an antidepressant may vary with each patient and within each antidepressant class. In general, TCA should be tapered (25% per week) to avoid cholinergic rebound (hypersalivation, diarrhea), whereas an SSRI may be stopped abruptly. Tapering may be faster if the patient is experiencing intolerable side effects. A decision to taper an antidepressant should be discussed with the patient and the risk versus benefit thoroughly explained. When desipramine is discontinued, A.R. should be monitored during the taper as well as after discontinuation to ensure stabilization.

In Recurrent Depression

9. T.M., a 36-year-old female, has an AXIS I diagnosis of major depressive disorder, recurrent. Over the past 3 years, T.M. has experienced 2 depressive episodes (1 with suicide attempt) while off antidepressant medication. Since her last depressive episode 6 months ago, she has been maintained on sertraline 50 mg/day without the return of any target symptoms. Should T.M. continue her antidepressant indefinitely? How long should a recurrent depression be treated?

Depression tends to be a recurrent disorder in 50% to 85% of patients. Patients with multiple episodes of depression should be considered for maintenance medication treatment. Factors increasing the risk of recurrence include a prior history of a chronic, general medical disorder, prior history of multiple episodes of depression, persistence of dysthymic symptoms after recovery from a depressive episode, and the presence of a nonaffective psychiatric diagnosis.[66] A future episode of depression also may increase in severity in patients with a history of serious suicide attempts, psychotic features, or severe functional impairment.[14] The decision to continue therapy in T.M. should be based upon the severity of her previous episodes and her attitude towards compliance with her medication.

Data evaluating long-term antidepressant treatment are limited. When imipramine was used at normal doses as maintenance therapy in unipolar depression, benefit at the end of three and five years was significant. Patients whose depressive episodes occur less than 30 months apart should be considered for prophylactic maintenance for at least five years.[67,68] Other studies looking at one-year follow-up with the SSRIs (fluoxetine, sertraline, paroxetine) also have found prophylactic effectiveness.[69] In addition, psychotherapy helps to extend the period between acute depressive episode for those patients who are unable to receive, or who refuse, medication. Whether lower doses of antidepressant during the maintenance phase are as effective as the full dose is not known. Therefore, patients should be continued at the full dose used to achieve the initial therapeutic effect. Some patients with frequent episodes

Table 76.9	Selected Adverse Effects of the Heterocyclic Antidepressants[a,b]			
Medication	Anticholinergic	Sedation	Seizures[c]	GI-Nausea
Tricyclics				
Imipramine (Tofranil)	+++	++	++	+
Amitriptyline (Elavil)	++++	++++	+++	+
Doxepin (Sinequan)	+++	++++	++	+
Desipramine (Norpramin)	++	++	++	+
Nortriptyline (Pamelor)	+++	+++	++	+
Protriptyline (Vivactil)	+++	+	++	+
Trimipramine (Surmontil)	++++	++++	++	+
Clomipramine (Anafranil)	++++	++++	++	+
2nd Generation				
Amoxapine (Asendin)	++++	+++	+++	+
Maprotiline (Ludiomil)	+++	+++	+++	+
Trazodone (Desyrel)	–	+++	+	+
Bupropion (Wellbutrin)	+	–	++++	+
SSRIs				
Fluoxetine (Prozac)	–	–/+	–/+	+++
Sertraline (Zoloft)	–	–	–	+++
Paroxetine (Paxil)	+	++	–	+++
Fluvoxamine (Luvox)	+	++	–	++++
Newer Agents				
Venlafaxine (Effexor)	+	+/++	+	++
Nefazodone (Serzone)	+	++	–	++

[a] GI = Gastrointestinal; SSRI = Selective serotonin reuptake inhibitor.
[b] ++++ = High; +++ = Moderate; ++ = Low; + = Very low; – = None.
[c] Although ranked, "high risk" for seizure is still <2%.

may require medication indefinitely. When stopping the antidepressant medication, a careful and gradual tapering is recommended.[14] Further study is needed to develop better recommendations for clinical practice.

Plasma Concentration Monitoring

10. T.M. returns for a follow-up appointment and a blood sample obtained for evaluation of sertraline concentration and other routine tests. Are sertraline plasma concentrations clinically useful in monitoring T.M.'s therapy? When should antidepressant plasma concentrations be obtained?

The usefulness of measuring serum concentrations of the antidepressants varies with the clinical situation and the particular drug (see Table 76.8).[70–72] Serum concentrations of the SSRIs, like the second-generation agents, do not correlate with antidepressant efficacy; therefore, routine sertraline levels are not recommended in T.M.

Table 76.10			Cardiovascular Effects for Antidepressant Medications[a,b,c]				
Medication[d]	↑ BP	Orthostatic Hypotension	HR Effects	Proarrhythmic Effects (Healthy/Cardiac Patient)	Antiarrhythmic Effects	Conduction Effects (Healthy/Cardiac Patient)	Contractility Effects
Tricyclics							
Imipramine (Tofranil)	+[e]	++++	+++	++/++++	+++	+/+++	0
Amitriptyline (Elavil)	+[e]	++++	++++	++/++++	+++	+/+++	0
Doxepin (Sinequan)	+[e]	+++	+++	++/+++	+++	+/+++	0
Desipramine (Norpramin)	+[e]	+++	++	++/+++	++	+/+++	0
Nortriptyline (Pamelor)	+[e]	++	++	++/+++	++	+/+++	0
Protriptyline (Vivactil)	+[e]	+++	++	++/++++	++	+/+++	0
Trimipramine (Surmontil)	+[e]	++++	++++	++/++++	+++	+/+++	0
Clomipramine (Anafranil)	+[e]	++++	++++	++/++++	+++	+/+++	0
2nd Generation							
Amoxapine (Asendin)	0	+	+++	++/+++	0?	+/+	?
Maprotiline (Ludiomil)	?	+	+++	++/+++	+	+/?	0?[f]
Trazodone (Desyrel)	0	+++[g]	0	+/++	0	0/+	0[f]
Bupropion (Wellbutrin)	0	0	0	0/0	+	0/+	0[f]
MAOIs (A+ B)	+++[h]	+++	–	?[f]	?[f]	0/+	+/–
SSRIs							
Fluoxetine (Prozac)	0	0	–	0/?	0?	0?	0?
Sertraline (Zoloft)	0	0	–	0/?	?	0/?	0/?
Paroxetine (Paxil)	0[f]	0	0?	0/?	0?	0/?[e]	0?[f]
Fluvoxamine (Luvox)	0	0	–	0/?	0?	0/?	0?[f]
Newer Agents							
Venlafaxine (Effexor)	++	+	+	0/+	0?	0/+	0?
Nefazodone (Serzone)	0	+	0	0/+	0	0/?	0/?

[a] Compiled from references 106, 113, 116, and 247.
[b] ++++ = High; +++ = Moderate; ++ = Low; + = Very low; 0 = None; – = ↓.
[c] BP = Blood pressure; HR = Heart rate; MAOI = Monoamine oxidase inhibitor; SSRI = Selective serotonin reuptake inhibitor.
[d] Assume therapeutic doses in noncardiac patients, unless otherwise indicated.
[e] Low doses.
[f] Demonstrated in animal models.
[g] Peak effect (4–6 hours), worse on empty stomach.
[h] Interaction with tyramine in foods/indirect sympathomimetic.

In contrast to the newer agents, the serum concentration of some tricyclic antidepressants does correlate with clinical response. Nortriptyline exhibits a curvilinear effect,[73] whereas imipramine demonstrates a sigmoidal relationship between serum levels and clinical response. Maximum benefit of imipramine usually is associated with serum levels of imipramine plus its demethylated metabolite, desipramine of greater than 200 ng/mL.[74,75] The relationship between plasma concentration of desipramine and clinical response is less clear, but it appears that a linear relationship is likely.[76,77] The most controversy surrounds amitriptyline; studies have shown a linear relationship,[78–80] a curvilinear relationship,[81–83] and no relationship between serum concentration and outcome.[84,85]

The APA Task Force on the Use of Laboratory Tests in Psychiatry recommends plasma concentration monitoring when patients are elderly, not responding to therapy, noncompliant, experiencing adverse effects, or on multiple medications that may result in a possible drug interaction.[86] Among the TCAs, the therapeutic plasma concentration of imipramine, nortriptyline, and desipramine has been established most firmly. Plasma concentrations of imipramine, nortriptyline, and desipramine should be obtained after at least one week of a constant dosage when steady state has been achieved and samples should be drawn at 12 hours after the last dose has been administered. Therapeutic blood monitoring of other antidepressants is not recommended because information

concerning their usefulness is limited; however, serum levels may be useful on a nonroutine basis for evaluating compliance in some patients.

Special Populations

Cardiac Disease

11. Orthostatic Hypotension. B.H., a 52-year-old obese male suffering from major depressive disorder, first episode, with melancholia, has been a tobacco smoker for the past 30 years. He has an 8-year history of congestive heart failure (CHF) [New York Heart Association (NYHA) functional class II] with an ejection fraction of 35% and atrial fibrillation; he currently is taking digoxin (Lanoxin) 0.25 mg PO Q AM and enalapril (Vasotec) 10 mg PO BID. The CHF has been well controlled on these medication regimens and B.H. remains asymptomatic with regard to the CHF. His atrial fibrillation occurs about once every several months. All laboratory parameters are within normal limits. His psychiatrist wishes to choose an antidepressant medication, but is concerned about exacerbating B.H.'s cardiac status. What is the most bothersome of the adverse cardiac effects potentially associated with using an antidepressant such as a TCA in B.H.?

Orthostatic hypotension is the most troublesome cardiovascular effect of the TCAs and MAOIs[87] and can result in significant morbidity and mortality.[88] Major clinical consequences of orthostatic hypotension include falls leading to bone fractures, lacerations, and even myocardial infarction.[89] Patients with CHF, such as B.H., are at greatest risk for developing orthostatic hypotension.[90,91] Operational definitions for orthostatic hypotension vary. Some clinicians define it as at least a 20 mm Hg decrease in systolic pressure one to two minutes after the patient moves from the supine to the standing position.[92] Others define it as a 50-point drop in systolic pressure on three separate days and/or symptoms of dizziness that prevent the patient from standing.[93] The diastolic pressure also may fall. These various definitions for orthostatic hypotension account for some of the variability in the reported incidence of this adverse effect. Orthostatic hypotension occurs in about 5% to 10% of depressed patients without pre-existing cardiovascular disease[94] and in as many as 50% of patients with CHF.[90] Patients with NYHA grades of disease 3 or 4 seem to be more vulnerable to orthostatic hypotension than those with lower grades of the disease. Furthermore, medical disorders that lower blood pressure [BP (e.g., CHF)] increase the chances of developing orthostatic hypotension when TCAs are used.[91] Over several weeks, the orthostatic hypotension associated with the TCAs appears to subjectively wane while, objectively, it still is present.[95] Hence, one should not assume that when the subjective feelings of lightheadedness and dizziness no longer are reported by the patient that monitoring for orthostatic hypotension can be discontinued.

12. Which TCAs are most likely to cause orthostatic hypotension? When does it occur and is it dose-related? Are there predictors for this adverse effect?

Imipramine and nortriptyline have been studied best with respect to their association with orthostatic hypotension:[89,94,96,97] amitriptyline,[98] desipramine,[99] doxepin,[100] and clomipramine (Anafranil)[101] also are capable of producing it to varying degrees. Although systematic comparisons of the propensity of the TCAs to cause orthostatic hypotension generally are lacking, the tertiary amines (e.g., imipramine) may cause more severe orthostatic hypotension than the secondary amines (e.g., nortriptyline).[58] Table 76.10 depicts relative propensity of the various antidepressants for causing orthostatic hypotension. Nortriptyline currently is the only TCA with a recognized and well-documented reduced risk for causing orthostatic hypotension.[102,103] In 15 patients free of any underlying cardiovascular disease, nortriptyline decreased the systolic blood pressure by 13 mm Hg, while imipramine decreased the systolic blood pressure by an average of 46 mm Hg.[97] Imipramine patients who could not tolerate the orthostatic hypotension were switched to nortriptyline and symptoms associated with orthostasis resolved. This use of patients as their own control demonstrates that nortriptyline is less likely to cause orthostatic hypotension than imipramine.[93] The fall in blood pressure does not appear to be dose-related and often occurs before therapeutic dosages or steady-state serum concentrations are achieved. Since orthostatic hypotension can occur soon after the first dose of TCA, a reduction in the dose is unlikely to decrease the probability of orthostatic hypotension or the severity of orthostasis when it does occur. Some investigators have used a 10 to 15 mm Hg difference between pretreatment supine and standing systolic blood pressure readings to predict those patients at greatest risk for developing orthostatic hypotension secondary to TCA medication.[58,94]

13. What can be done to minimize orthostatic hypotension in B.H. or other patients treated with antidepressants and are there therapeutic options?

Pharmacologically, nortriptyline is the TCA of choice because it minimizes orthostasis and also has the advantage of serum concentrations that correlate with efficacy.[73] The nonselective MAOIs [phenelzine (Nardil), tranylcypromine (Parnate), and isocarboxazid (Marplan)] readily cause orthostatic hypotension.[104] Trazodone is well known to cause orthostatic hypotension that appears to be

correlated to its peak serum concentration approximately four to six hours after a dose and appears to be worse on an empty stomach.[105] While the second-generation drugs maprotiline (Ludiomil) and amoxapine (Asendin) may have fewer cardiovascular effects when used in therapeutic dosages, they share many of the other adverse effects with the TCAs, and are highly toxic in overdose. Additionally, amoxapine has the additional adverse effects of extrapyramidal side effects associated with its dopamine-receptor-blocking activity. Antidepressants that apparently do not cause orthostatic hypotension include the SSRIs, bupropion, and venlafaxine (see Table 76.10).

Nonpharmacologic measures to minimize orthostatic hypotension include cautioning the patient to avoid rising from a lying or sitting position too quickly (i.e., arising slowly over at least a minute), maintaining adequate ambulation, hydration, and salt intake [unless contraindicated by cardiovascular disease (e.g., CHF)], and wearing support hose.[106]

14. What types of patients are at greatest risk from orthostatic hypotension induced by cyclic antidepressants? Are males or geriatric patients more prone to developing orthostatic hypotension?

Gender differences appear to have little to no predictive value for orthostatic hypotension.[58] The actual degree to which patients experience orthostatic hypotension does not vary directly with age, yet elderly patients clearly are at greatest risk for suffering from morbidity associated with orthostatic hypotension. For example, more than 4% of 148 consecutive imipramine-treated patients averaging 60 years of age experienced physical injury including fractures and lacerations requiring sutures.[107]

15. Antidepressants and Left Ventricular Function (LVF). If TCAs are used in B.H., would the CHF in B.H. be exacerbated by worsening LVF?

Until the 1980s, left ventricular function often was measured by the Systolic Time Interval (STI) method which used a ratio of pre-ejection phase to left ventricular ejection phase, a ratio that reflects QRS duration. Thus, when the test showed an apparent decrease in LVF, in actuality it was reflecting the fact that TCAs decrease conduction through the A-V node. STI since has been largely replaced in monitoring CHF by radionuclide angiography. Studies with this method have shown that there is no evidence of TCA-impaired LVF in depressed cardiac patients.[90,100,108] CHF patients, however, are at great risk for developing orthostatic hypotension.

16. Antidepressants and Arrhythmias. Will the choice of antidepressant affect B.H.'s arrhythmia?

Tricyclic antidepressants increase heart rate probably via intrinsic anticholinergic properties that increase sinus node activity. Clinically, this effect generally is not significant, especially in medically healthy, depressed patients.[107] However, it may be important in those with underlying conduction disease, coronary artery disease, or CHF. TCAs, when used in antidepressant dosages, decrease premature atrial and ventricular contractions in both depressed and nondepressed patients.[109,110] Antidepressants with Class 1A antiarrhythmic activity (i.e., TCAs) also may have arrhythmogenic activity and, thus, increase the chances of ventricular arrhythmias and sometimes, of sudden death. This effect on rhythm and conduction is believed to be related to the inhibitory effects on the fast sodium channels and a decrease in Purkinje fiber action potential amplitude, membrane responsiveness, and slowed conduction.[111] The nonselective MAOIs do not seem to affect rhythm significantly, although they generally do slow heart rate.[112] The second generation medications (i.e., amoxapine, maprotiline, and trazodone) do affect rhythm and can be arrhythmogenic.[113] Bupropion apparently is devoid of this activity, even in depressed cardiac patients.[114] The SSRIs and venlafaxine apparently do not ap-

Table 76.11	Interactions on TCA Serum Concentration at Steady-State Conditions[a],[b]	
Lower		
Acid pH (ammonium chloride)	Chloral hydrate	Primidone
	Doxycycline	Smoking
	Glutethimide	Trihexyphenidyl
Barbiturates	Phenytoin	
Carbamazepine		
Raise		
Alprazolam	Disulfiram	Levomepromazine
Basic pH (NaHCO₃)	Erythromycin	Methylphenidate
Beta blockers	Estrogens	Norethindrone
Chloramphenicol	Fenfluramine	Perphenazine
Chloramphenicol	Fluoxetine	Sertraline
Chlorpromazine	Fluvoxamine	Thioridazine
Chlorprothixene	Haloperidol	
Cimetidine	Isoniazid	

[a] Modified with permission from reference 249.
[b] TCA = Tricyclic antidepressant.

pear to cause clinically significant effects on rhythm in noncardiac patients with depression. Although the SSRIs can cause a clinically insignificant decrease in heart rate in noncardiac patients[92,115,116] that could be problematic in some cardiac patients with conduction abnormalities, they should not be considered as entirely safe in this population at present because of inadequate experience with these agents.

17. Antidepressants and Conduction. What are the effects of antidepressants in patients with conduction abnormalities?

Because the TCAs decrease conduction through the A-V node, they should be used with caution in any patient with conduction disease. They are contraindicated specifically in patients with second- or third-degree block or bundle-branch disease. They are relatively safe in this respect in noncardiac, depressed patients. Attention should be paid to other medications that might increase serum TCA concentrations (see Table 76.11 on drugs that might increase TCA serum levels such as erythromycin or one of the SSRIs). Conduction abnormalities are in direct proportion to TCA dosage and serum concentrations.[117,118] The other antidepressants are relatively safe in what we know about their effects on conduction, although most experience is with patients without cardiovascular disorders (see Table 76.10).

18. Drug Selection. What are the choices for the pharmacotherapy of B.H.'s depression?

The use of TCAs may be indicated; one must use extreme caution after making this choice and use careful periodic follow-up by a cardiologist. The choice of nortriptyline or one of the SSRIs, bupropion, or venlafaxine would decrease the chances of orthostatic hypotension in B.H. The other TCAs, the nonselective MAOIs, and trazodone all could result in orthostatic hypotension. TCAs, MAOIs, and the newer drugs either have been shown to be relatively safe with respect to exacerbation of LVF or little is known. The MAOIs, trazodone, maprotiline, amoxapine, the SSRIs, and venlafaxine either have not been studied adequately in CHF cases or there is an overall dearth of experience with these medications in these patients. Thus, all antidepressant medications should be used with caution in patients with compromised LVF. One should avoid combining an antidepressant with Class IA antiarrhythmic activity with other medications sharing this property [e.g., quinidine (Quinidex) or procainamide (Pronestyl)]. A TCA may be of benefit in B.H. due to its intrinsic antiarrhythmic properties; however, adequate follow-up by a cardiologist is recommended. The SSRIs, bupropion, and venlafaxine are potential al-

ternatives to nortriptyline in B.H. To help avoid toxic situations when using TCAs and the potential array of cardiac effects associated with them, one should obtain baseline and then follow-up periodic serum concentrations and avoid other medications that can increase the TCA serum concentration (see Table 76.11).

Epilepsy

19. C.B., a 20-year-old female, has major depressive disorder, single episode. Since the age of 8, she has had the diagnosis of partial complex seizures. Her seizures have been difficult to control in the past (>6 per month) while on numerous agents. However, her seizures presently are under good control (seizure-free for 8 months) with carbamazepine (Tegretol) plus gabapentin (Neurontin). Are there any special considerations with regard to antidepressant selection in this patient?

Seizure Risk. While seizures as an adverse effect of antidepressant medications are uncommon events, they are serious when they occur. The incidence of antidepressant-related seizures ranges from about 0.1% to 4%.[119] Table 76.12 enumerates situations that may place an individual on antidepressants at greater risk for suffering a seizure. Antidepressant-related seizures most often occur after acute overdose of the drug, and primarily with the TCAs. For TCA overdoses, the seizure incidence ranges from 3.5% to 41%[120] and seizures in these situations correlate to TCA peak levels (i.e., levels >1000 ng/mL are more predictive of a seizure than those <1000 ng/mL).[121] Temporally, most TCA overdose seizures occur within six hours of the overdose.[122] The specific antidepressant taken in overdose seems to be of some importance in terms of the likelihood of developing a seizure: amoxapine was more likely associated with seizures, then maprotiline, followed by the TCAs, and finally trazodone.[123]

Drug Selection. When evaluating the association of seizure activity with therapeutic doses of antidepressants, a dose-dependent relationship[119] is apparent and serves as the primary reason for dose limitations for bupropion (450 mg/day), maprotiline (225 mg/day), and clomipramine (250 mg/day). The great interpatient variability in serum concentrations achieved with a given dose (i.e., at least a 40-fold variation in TCA blood levels between 2 individuals on the same dose) tends to compound the dose-dependent relationship.[124] Therefore, someone on an apparently benign dosage may exhibit a disproportionately high serum level and be at risk for a seizure. For this reason, serum drug concentrations of TCAs are measured periodically. Case reports suggest that seizures are more likely in the first week of therapy or immediately after an increase in the dose.[119] Table 76.13 presents the relative risk for seizures in relationship to several available antidepressant medications. Since there is less experience with the SSRIs and seizures, less is known about their propensity to cause seizures. As a class, they are not devoid of epileptogenic potential as fluoxetine has been associated with seizures.[125]

Table 76.12	Relationship of Antidepressants in Seizures[a]

More likely in individuals with predisposition to seizures (personal or family history of seizures, status post-head injury)

Possible dose-dependent relationship

Possible serum concentration relationship

Seizure incidence possibly highest immediately after a dose ↑

Unknown if seizure incidence changes with time during prolonged treatment

Possible relationship to other disorders: bulimia nervosa, OCD[b]

[a] Adapted with permission from reference 119.
[b] OCD = Obsessive-compulsive behavior.

Table 76.13	Relative Risk for Seizures[a,b]
Lower Risk	**Intermediate Risk[c]**
Fluoxetine	TCAs
Sertraline	Bupropion
Trazodone/Nafazodone	Maprotiline
Nonselective MAOIs	Amoxapine
Vimafaxine	

[a] Adapted with permission from reference 119.
[b] MAOI = Monoamine oxidase inhibitor; TCA = Tricyclic antidepressant.
[c] At recommended doses, seizure rates of 4–6/1000.

Because of C.B.'s seizure history, choosing a medication from the list of medication with a "lower" associated seizure risk would be clinically prudent. Because she also is receiving carbamazepine, the potential of a drug-drug interaction (i.e., may tend to lower the antidepressant level) is increased when an antidepressant medication is used. This interaction could result in undertreatment of the depressive episode and would argue for using an antidepressant for which serum concentrations have been well correlated with clinical efficacy such as nortriptyline or imipramine.[73–75]

Acquired Immunodeficiency Syndrome (AIDS)

20. Clinical Presentation. K.H., a 33-year-old, human immunodeficiency virus (HIV)-positive female, has been reasonably healthy over the past 2 years, but recently developed AIDS after an episode of oral candidiasis. Over the past few months, she has noticed difficulty in concentrating (she has to read a sentence several times before she can comprehend its meaning) accompanied with loss of interest, decreased energy, and fatigue. She also reports a depressed mood but denies suicidal ideation. Her only medications at the present time are zidovudine (Retrovir) and oral clotrimazole troche (Mycelex). After a thorough medical work-up, other opportunistic infections have been ruled out. She is referred to psychiatry services for further evaluation. What precipitating factors may be contributing to K.H.'s current symptoms of depression?

Patients with terminal illnesses such as HIV/AIDS or certain cancers are faced with an extreme psychosocial stressor that can precipitate a depressive episode. Studies evaluating the severity of emotional distress in persons with HIV have shown elevated anxiety, depression, social isolation, and suicidal ideation.[126,127] K.H. currently is, or will be, confronted with a number of psychological issues including chronic somatic preoccupations, fear of developing an opportunistic infection, debilitation, death at a young age, anger, anxiety, and depression.[128,129]

Although K.H.'s depressive target symptoms (fatigue, decreased concentration, depressed mood) may represent a depressive episode secondary to psychosocial stressors, her differential diagnosis also includes HIV-1-associated cognitive/motor complex or dementia due to HIV disease (formally known as AIDS dementia complex).[130] HIV-associated dementia closely resembles the symptoms of a depressive disorder and is part of the Center for Disease Control classification system for HIV infection (Category C).[131] Neoplasms and opportunistic infections of the central nervous system secondary to AIDS also can alter mental status; however, a thorough medical work-up ruled out opportunistic infection in K.H.

21. Drug Selection. Based upon K.H.'s target symptoms, is she a candidate for antidepressant therapy? What considerations should be made when selecting antidepressant therapy for K.H.?

K.H. would benefit from antidepressant therapy to help ameliorate her target symptoms of decreased energy, lack of concentra-

tion, decreased energy, and depressed mood regardless of whether it is a major depressive episode or direct HIV involvement within the central nervous system. However, several considerations should be made when selecting antidepressant medication in an HIV/AIDS patient. Limited studies show that patients with AIDS generally respond to lower doses of antidepressants in much the same way as geriatric patients. Likewise, patients may be at increased risk for severe anticholinergic adverse effects.[132,133] Therefore, antidepressants such as SSRIs, trazodone, venlafaxine (Effexor), or alprazolam (Xanax) may be the best choices when used in one-half to one-third the usual dose.

The psychostimulants [e.g., methylphenidate (Ritalin), dextro-amphetamine (Dexedrine)] in low dosages also have improved cognitive function and depressive symptoms in patients with AIDS.[133] ECT also has been administered safely to patients with AIDS.[134]

The Elderly

22. Clinical Presentation. R.M., a 71-year-old male, is brought for psychiatric evaluation by his daughter, C.M., with whom he has been living for the past 3 years. C.M. reports that R.M. had been in good health until 3 months ago when he was noted to keep to himself and began showing little interest in his usual activities. She reports that he used to be a happy, very outgoing person. He has lost weight over the past 4 months, has been noted to be irritable, anxious, and has trouble falling asleep. He also frequently becomes agitated over insignificant things. He has appeared on occasion to be confused and slow in understanding concepts. His recent physical examination is normal except for benign prostatic hypertrophy (BPH). Laboratory examinations are within normal limits except for a subnormal serum creatinine. He currently is on no medication except for a daily stool softener and a bulk laxative.

Mental status examination reveals a thin, nervous, sad-appearing man. His responses to questions are slow. Affect is sad. He shows no signs of delusions or hallucinations. He shows mild impairments in his ability to think through problems and mathematical exercises. He denies suicidal ideation but feels hopeless at the present time. How does a depressive episode in late life, such as that in R.M., differ from a depressive episode earlier in life?

Depression in late life typically is more difficult to recognize when compared to younger adults. Clinicians and patients may attribute, inappropriately, depressive target symptoms to the "aging" process. In addition, lower functional expectations during retirement often make evaluating the degree of impairment difficult. Depression in the elderly commonly accompanies chronic diseases such as cancer, cardiovascular disorders, arthritis, and sensory loss. These other medical conditions in the elderly patient can make an underlying depression.[135]

In general, the elderly usually present with the same depressive target symptoms as younger patients. However, they may be less likely to report feelings of worthlessness or guilt and more likely to experience weight loss, irritability, and somatic complaints. In the elderly, psychomotor activity also may be decreased, with slowed speech and slowed body movements. On occasion, however, patients may become agitated with wringing of the hands and pacing.

23. What is R.M.'s differential diagnosis? Should R.M. be placed on antidepressant therapy?

In assessing nonspecific behavioral and cognitive target symptoms in R.M., a careful differential diagnosis between medical and other psychiatric disorders is essential because numerous medical illnesses can mimic depressive symptoms. However, R.M.'s recent physical examination and laboratory work-up essentially are normal. Since R.M. could be developing primary degenerative dementia (PDD), a thorough work-up for dementia is needed. Dementia usually presents with a lack of spontaneous interaction, retardation, and loss of memory and ability to concentrate; therefore, depressed individuals with secondary cognitive disturbances can be indistinguishable from those with true dementias. In the past, the term "pseudodementia" was used to describe this syndrome; however, the term "dementia syndrome of depression" replaced "pseudodementia."[136]

The frequency of depression from cross-sectional studies in Alzheimer's disease ranges from 0% to 88%. One reason for this wide range is the differing application of the diagnostic criteria for depression. If the mood component of Alzheimer's (e.g., sadness and depression) is interpreted to allow anhedonia and loss in interest in activities to satisfy the mood criterion, then most Alzheimer's patients will fulfill the diagnostic criteria for depression.

Drug Selection. A therapeutic trial of an antidepressant in the depressed patient with cognitive impairment may reverse the symptoms of the illness and restore the individual's functional capacity. Moreover, since primary degenerative dementia is a diagnosis of exclusion, a trial of antidepressants is indicated in patients demonstrating target symptoms consistent with depression, or in those with a positive family or personal history for mood disorders. Patients with PDD also might benefit from antidepressant therapy even if they do not present with a mood disorder.[69,136] Overlapping pathophysiology and neuroanatomic dysfunction in these two disorders might explain the efficacy of antidepressants for selected symptoms of degenerative dementia. Although R.M.'s diagnosis is uncertain at this point, a therapeutic trial of an antidepressant is warranted based upon his current depressive target symptoms.

24. Trazodone. The decision is made to treat R.M. with trazodone. What advantages and disadvantages does trazodone offer that make it a reasonable choice for R.M.?

Trazodone can be a suitable choice in treating depression in older adults because its pharmacokinetics appear to not be altered by age or concomitant disease states. One of trazodone's most common adverse effects, sedation, can be therapeutic in R.M. since he is experiencing insomnia and anxiety.[137] Trazodone's low anticholinergic activity relative to TCAs is advantageous because R.M. suffers from benign prostatic hypertrophy and constipation. Trazodone also produces less cardiac conduction delay than tricyclic antidepressants, although it is not entirely without cardiac toxicity and may exacerbate ventricular arrhythmias.[138] These cardiovascular adverse effects, however, should not be a problem in R.M. based upon his medical history.

Although R.M. currently is not suicidal, the elderly are at increased risk for suicide. Suicide is ranked among the top ten causes of death in individuals older than 65 years of age.[139] Trazodone is a safe drug in overdose due to both its low anticholinergic and cardiotoxic effects. To date, there are no reported fatalities with trazodone overdose when taken by itself.[140] In contrast, TCAs, maprotiline, and amoxapine are extremely toxic in overdose situations.

Trazodone, however, is not without adverse effects. It can produce gastrointestinal (GI) upset, which may be relieved by the coadministration of food. Trazodone also is a potent alpha-adrenergic blocker producing a significant amount of orthostasis.[141] Postural hypotension occurs early in therapy and the elderly are more susceptible to this effect.[142] Additionally, injury following a fall (e.g., hip fracture) is a significant risk factor in the elderly. R.M. should be warned to rise slowly from bed and not to rapidly change his posture. If R.M. experiences dizziness, he should be instructed to lie or sit down and place his head between his knees.

Another adverse reaction of trazodone in males is priapism (i.e., a persistent abnormal erection of the penis). This adverse effect also has been reported in females (manifested as clitoral priapism). It is rare, however, with only a 0.016% incidence. Nevertheless, R.M. also should be counseled regarding this side effect.

Based upon trazodone's pharmacologic profile and safety record, it is an excellent choice in R.M. since he is experiencing depression and accompanying anxiety, agitation, and insomnia. Orthostatic hypotension, however, may be a concern due to his age. Although typical doses for young adults range from 200 to 600 mg/day, R.M. probably will require doses of 150 mg to 450 mg/day.

Selective Serotonin Reuptake Inhibitors (SSRIs)

Use in the Elderly

25. R.M. began trazodone 50 mg TID. Several days later he experienced lightheadedness upon standing. Tachycardia and a mean systolic BP change of 20 mm Hg between sitting and standing positions were noted. R.M.'s psychiatrist is considering replacing trazodone with 1 of the SSRIs. How do the SSRIs efficacy compare to the older agents in treating depression in the elderly?

Since the report of the National Institutes of Health Consensus Development Conference on Diagnosis and Treatment of Depression in Late Life, research effort to study the effects of antidepressants in the elderly has increased. Thus far, few studies have been published which specifically target this population in evaluating the efficacy and tolerability of the SSRIs. As is the case for most efficacy studies,[143-146] elderly populations studied were free of significant medical illness and were not taking concomitant drug therapy. Although it is necessary to attempt to evaluate as homogeneous a population as possible, these studies may not reflect the average geriatric patient having multiple medical problems and taking multiple prescription and nonprescription medications.

Most studies used the Hamilton Depression Rating scale to assess the efficacy of a particular SSRI in comparison to a standard drug (in most cases, a tertiary tricyclic antidepressant). Studies did not show any difference in efficacy between the SSRI and TCA in decreasing symptoms of depression as measured on the HAM-D. Some differences, however, did exist in geriatric tolerability of an SSRI versus a TCA. Significantly more patients complained of adverse drug effects while on a TCA compared to an SSRI, resulting in increased dropout rates in the former groups. The side effects elicited were typical of this class of drugs including anticholinergic, cardiovascular, and somnolence. Elderly patients generally tolerated the SSRIs but did complain of headache, nausea, and nervousness. Clearly, more studies are needed in the depressed geriatric patient. Questions that remain unanswered are duration of therapeutic effect, appropriate dose/response in this population, and different efficacy or tolerability between SSRIs.

Pharmacokinetics

26. How do the SSRIs differ from each other in their pharmacokinetics? What pharmacokinetic alterations of the SSRIs should be expected in R.M.?

The pharmacokinetic parameters of the SSRIs are given in Table 76.14. Paroxetine, fluoxetine, and fluvoxamine are nearly completely absorbed. Administration with food does not alter the mean area under the concentration-time curve (AUC) of fluvoxamine or paroxetine, but does decrease the rate (not extent) of fluoxetine absorption.[147] Administration of sertraline with food increases the AUC by 39% and the postdose maximum serum concentration by 25% to 32%.[147,148] The plasma protein binding of fluoxetine, paroxetine, and sertraline is greater than 95% compared to 77% for fluvoxamine. Fluoxetine and sertraline are bound to albumin and α_1-acid glycoprotein.[148,149] Due to their extensive protein binding,

Table 76.14			Pharmacokinetics of the Heterocyclic Antidepressants		
Medication	Availability Oral (%)	Bound in Plasma (%)	Vd (L/kg)	Parent t½ (hr)	Active Metabolite(s)
Tricyclics					
Imipramine (Tofranil)	19–35	95	15–31	11–25	2-Hydroxyimipramine Desipramine 2-Hydroxydesipramine
Amitriptyline (Elavil)	37–49	95	12–16	10-22	Nortriptyline 10-Hydroxynortriptyline
Doxepin (Sinequan)	17–37	68–85	12–28	11–23	Desmethyldoxepin
Desipramine (Norpramin)	51	90	26–42	12–24	2-Hydroxydesipramine
Nortriptyline (Pamelor)	46–56	92	14–22	18–44	10-Hydroxynortriptyline
Protriptyline (Vivactil)	77–93	92	21–23	18–44	None
Trimipramine (Surmontil)	18-63	93–97	26.4–34.4	7–40	None
Clomipramine (Anafranil)	36–62	96.5	9–25	35	Desmethylclomipramine
2nd Generation					
Amoxapine (Asendin)	18–54	92	65.7	8–30	8-Hydroxyamoxapine
Maprotiline (Ludiomil)	37	88	23	27–57	Desmethylmaprotiline
Trazodone (Desyrel)	—	92	—	10–12	meta-Chloro-phenylpiperazine
Bupropion (Wellbutrin)	>90	85	19–21	11/14	Erythro-, threo-amino alcohols Erythro-amino diol; Morpholinol
SSRIs[b]					
Fluoxetine (Prozac)	80	95	20–42	24–72	Norfluoxetine[a]
Sertraline (Zoloft)	64	95	17	10–16	Desmethylsertraline
Paroxetine (Paxil)	44	99	25	26	None
Fluvoxamine (Luvox)	94	77	>5	5	None
Newer Agents					
Venlafaxine (Effexor)	92	25–29	7.5	3–7	O-desmethylvenlafaxine
Nefazodone (Serzone)	15–23	99	—	2.6–7.4	Hydroxynefazodone Desethylnefazodone

[a] t½ = 168 hours.
[b] SSRI = Selective serotonin reuptake inhibitor.

paroxetine, sertraline, and fluoxetine may be involved in drug displacement interactions (see Question 29).

Because the half-lives of paroxetine and sertraline are approximately 20 hours, steady state can be achieved within one to two weeks. The elimination half-lives of fluoxetine (2 days) and its metabolite, norfluoxetine (7 days), result in a time to steady-state concentration of longer than four weeks. Multiple dosing decreases the elimination rates of paroxetine and fluoxetine and increases their half-lives to 21 hours and 5.7 days, respectively. The mean plasma AUC of these drugs also increases with multiple dosing. These findings suggest that these drugs inhibit their own metabolism.[148] Paroxetine, for example, partially saturates one of its metabolic pathways (oxidation) and may exhibit nonlinear pharmacokinetics in some patients.[150] The long half-lives of fluoxetine and norfluoxetine and the potential autoinhibition of metabolism of fluoxetine and paroxetine indicate that these drugs will not be eliminated from the body for weeks after the discontinuation of therapy. This fact should be kept in mind when initiating MAOI or TCA therapy (see Question 29), or evaluating adverse effects of a patient.

The SSRIs are metabolized extensively by the liver. Fluoxetine is demethylated to its active metabolite, norfluoxetine. The renal excretion of unchanged parent compound and active metabolite is small, 2.5% and 10%, respectively. The remaining are excreted as conjugated metabolites.[150] Paroxetine (Paxil) is metabolized oxidatively to an unstable catechol intermediate which is conjugated to a glucuronide or sulfate and renally excreted.[147,149] Sertraline (Zoloft) is N-demethylated to its primary metabolite, desmethylsertraline. Desmethylsertraline is metabolized further to the ketone form, hydroxylated, conjugated, and eliminated in the urine and bile. Less than 0.2% of a sertraline dose is recovered in urine as unchanged parent drug.[148,149] Thus far, investigators have isolated eleven metabolites of fluvoxamine, none being pharmacologically active.[149]

Because of their favorable side effect profile, SSRIs are being used increasingly in patients such as R.M. The pharmacokinetics of sertraline do not appear to be altered in elderly versus young healthy subjects. However, paroxetine and fluoxetine's metabolism is impaired in the elderly. Elderly patients develop higher plasma levels of fluoxetine (and its metabolite) or paroxetine when given comparable doses as young adults. The steady-state concentration and half-life of paroxetine in the elderly may increase twofold compared to younger subjects.[151] If R.M. is started on paroxetine or fluoxetine, doses should be reduced, especially since R.M. could be sensitive to the adverse effects.

Adverse Effects

27. Trazodone is discontinued and R.M. is placed on fluoxetine 20 mg Q PM. During the following week he is noted to have nausea, vomiting, and trouble sleeping at night. How should R.M. be managed?

R.M. is experiencing typical side effects that have been reported with fluoxetine. The adverse effects of the SSRIs predominantly are GI (nausea, vomiting, diarrhea), CNS (insomnia, headache, confusion, dizziness, sedation), and sexual dysfunction.[149] The incidence of these side effects increases with higher doses of fluoxetine. Patients experience significantly more adverse effects without additional improvement in depressive symptoms at fluoxetine doses exceeding 20 mg/day.[152] The elderly may have increased side effects at even 20 mg; thus, lower initial doses of 10 mg should be used.

The majority of the adverse effects that R.M. is experiencing have been deemed "nuisance side effects." It could be bothersome to R.M., however, and lead to discontinuation of therapy. Administration of the SSRI with food may decrease some of the GI side effects, since only sertraline absorption is affected appreciably by food. Since R.M. complains of insomnia, his dose may need to be decreased and administered in the morning. Although some clinicians have treated SSRI-associated insomnia with low-dose trazodone (25 to 50 mg Q HS), current literature has not evaluated the efficacy of this strategy fully.[153] One could choose another antidepressant for R.M. or perhaps manage this adverse effect with a short-term hypnotic agent. If R.M. benefits from the antidepressant effects of fluoxetine, an alternative consideration may be the more sedating SSRI, paroxetine.

28. What are other adverse effects of the SSRIs that R.M. may experience during therapy?

Treatment with SSRIs also can be associated with anxiety, tremor, and akathisia.[151,154] Although not understood completely, the mechanism of SSRI-induced akathisia and tremor is hypothesized to involve the inhibitory effect of serotonin on dopaminergic neurons in the ventral tegmental area and substantia nigra.[154,155] SSRIs may cause weight loss in contrast to weight gain typically associated with TCA therapy. The average weight loss for patients on fluoxetine is approximately three pounds.[149] Although the weight loss usually is mild, this may be a concern in treating elderly patients who may have difficulty maintaining their weight.[156] Weight change, as a function of drug effect, is difficult to interpret because depressive symptoms themselves may cause significant changes in weight (either increase or decrease).

Selective serotonin reuptake inhibitors do not bind appreciably to adrenergic, histaminic, or muscarinic receptors. The incidence of orthostatic hypotension, sedation, and anticholinergic side effects is significantly less than the TCAs. Additionally, SSRIs appear to lack the quinidine-like cardiovascular effects of the TCAs, thus the mortality and morbidity associated with overdose are much less.[118] Although the SSRIs lack the quinidine-like effects of the TCAs, cardiovascular side effects are associated with this class of drugs. Some studies have described mild bradycardia with fluoxetine and fluvoxamine. Case reports have described severe slowing of the SA node with fluoxetine therapy. Paroxetine and sertraline do not alter ECGs in otherwise healthy individuals; however, the effects of SSRIs in patients with cardiovascular disease have not been evaluated.[118]

As with other classes of antidepressants, sexual dysfunction among the SSRIs has been described, and the incidence may be higher with this class of drugs. It is difficult to compare the incidence of this adverse effect among classes of antidepressants and among the SSRIs because many of the antidepressant trials did not assess this potential adverse effect adequately. Many patients will not report this side effect spontaneously and clinicians must ask direct questions to adequately assess this adverse effect. The incidence of sexual dysfunction among fluoxetine-treated men and women is approximately 10%. The incidence of sexual dysfunction appears to be higher for sertraline and seems to affect 9% to 21% of men. Sertraline most often is associated with ejaculatory disturbances. A small percentage of women report orgasmic difficulties. Management of sexual dysfunction includes waiting for resolution with continued therapy, decreasing the SSRI dose, changing

antidepressants, or coadministration of drug therapy such as cyproheptadine (Periactin) and bethanechol as previously described.[60] Very little data are available for paroxetine and fluvoxamine, for which further evaluation is necessary.

Drug Interactions

29. Given his age, R.M. may develop other medical illnesses which may require medication management. What are significant drug interactions with fluoxetine that should be considered in R.M.?

The SSRIs, like most psychotropics, are metabolized oxidatively by the cytochrome P450 enzyme system. This enzyme system is comprised of many distinct isoenzymes. The best studied of these isoenzymes is CYP2D6. Genetic polymorphism of this isoenzyme is observed. Ninety to ninety-five percent of European and African-Americans have this isoenzyme and are termed extensive metabolizers (EMs). The remaining 5% to 10% have either complete or almost complete absence of this enzyme and are termed poor metabolizers (PMs).[157]

Drugs that have been studied and identified as substrate for the CYP2D6 isoenzyme include SSRIs, TCAs, antipsychotics [haloperidol (Haldol), perphenazine (Trilafon), or thioridazine (Mellaril)], antiarrhythmics [flecainide (Tambocor), encainide (Encaid)], and beta blockers.[157] As substrate, these drugs compete for the same metabolic pathway. The drug having the higher affinity for this isoenzyme may inhibit the metabolism of the other. This type of drug interaction is clinically relevant for those CYP2D6-dependent drugs which have a low therapeutic index, require this isoenzyme for conversion to therapeutically active metabolites, or cannot be eliminated via other routes. However, not all inhibitors of CYP2D6 are substrates for this isoenzyme. Quinidine is a potent inhibitor of CYP2D6 but is metabolized by another isoenzyme (CYP3A4).[158]

R.M. is at greatest clinical risk for a drug interaction if he experiences a change in metabolic status (e.g., extensive metabolizers being converted to poor metabolizers as the result of a drug addition to a therapeutic regimen). As a poor metabolizer, he would not be able to metabolize the CYP2D6-dependent drug and may suffer adverse drug reactions. The clinical relevance of the drug interaction is dependent upon factors such as the extent of isoenzyme inhibition and the capability of other isoenzymes/pathways to metabolize the drug.

The SSRIs and TCAs inhibit CYP2D6 and have the potential to cause clinically significant drug interactions when coadministered with drugs eliminated via this pathway. The most well-characterized and widely reported interactions of this type are between SSRIs and TCAs. Fluoxetine and its metabolite, norfluoxetine, are potent inhibitors of CYP2D6[59] and, when coadministered with desipramine, decrease desipramine clearance by up to tenfold.[160] However, R.M. (or any patient) probably would not be treated with an SSRI and a TCA concomitantly.

Grimsley et al. found that fluoxetine increased the AUC of carbamazepine and its 10,11 epoxide by 30%;[161] however, other investigators have not found such a drug interaction.[162] Clearly, more research is needed to fully characterize the effect of the SSRIs on serum concentrations of carbamazepine and its metabolite. Fluoxetine also decreases the clearance of the oxidatively metabolized benzodiazepines, diazepam,[163] and alprazolam.[164]

A pharmacodynamic interaction occurs with SSRIs and other serotonergic drugs. This interaction has been well characterized for SSRIs and MAOIs and is termed the serotonin syndrome. The clinical signs and symptoms of this interaction is change in mental status, restlessness, hyperreflexia, diaphoresis, and tremor.[165] These symptoms usually resolve once the serotonergic agent is discontinued and supportive care instituted. Although lithium has been used concomitantly with fluoxetine in the treatment of depression without adverse sequelae,[166] some cases of neurotoxicity have been associated with this combination of psychotropics.[167,168]

Depression with Atypical Features (Atypical Depression)

Monoamine Oxidase Inhibitors (MAOIs)

30. G.R., a 38-year-old, 73 kg female, presents at the university outpatient psychiatric clinic with a chief complaint of extreme lethargy and depressed mood more days than not for the past 1.5 months. During this period, she has had trouble both with sleeping too much and overeating (she says she has gained at least 10 pounds in the past 6 weeks). On interview, she also reports an intense fear of heights and consequently will not travel if it means driving over a bridge or flying in an airplane. She reports that this episode seems to have started around the time of the break-up with her boyfriend and she becomes extremely anxious and tearful in revealing this piece of her history. Her past psychiatric history is consistent with at least 2 other similar depressive episodes, the first when she was 18 years of age and the second occurring around age 25. She currently weighs 73 kg and her physical examination and laboratory assessments are within normal limits. Past pharmacotherapy response history shows poor responses to trials of imipramine or nortriptyline (both to adequate dosages, serum concentrations and for up to periods of 6 weeks). On her last episode, she is noted to have responded to phenelzine 60 mg/day.

G.R.'s depressive illness manifests differently from that expected in most cases of depression. How is this depression of G.R. different from melancholic depression?

G.R. suffers from hysteroid dysphoria, more commonly known as atypical depression.[170] DSM-IV now refers to it as depression with atypical features. Clinically, atypical depression generally has been regarded as a fairly heterogenous group of depressive symptoms that represent a form of depressive illness. The term atypical depression first was used to describe patients with some symptoms of depression and who experienced worsening of mood in the evening, lethargy, phobic and somatic anxiety, and emotional overreactivity to environmental events. These patients typically responded well to treatment with iproniazid, the MAOI.[169] Atypical depression also describes patients with phobic anxiety who may not have concurrent depression, those with a reversal of endogenous vegetative shifts in sleep, appetite, and diurnal variation in mood (i.e., hypersomnia, hyperphagia, and a mood that is good in the morning and progressively worsens through the day), and those with depression but without endogenous symptoms.[171] In studying this disorder, its validity and response to medication, one group of investigators has identified a set of explicit operational criteria (the "Columbia" criteria) based upon the literature and their own clinical experience that describe atypical depression.[172] Briefly, the criteria are as follows: patients must meet criteria for DSM depressive disorder; they are excluded, however, if they have pervasive anhedonia (i.e., they have a "mood reactivity" or enjoy some activities or daily experiences), and must have at least two of the following: 1) hypersomnia; 2) leaden paralysis (intense lethargy); 3) hyperphagia; 4) pathologic sensitivity to interpersonal rejection (rejection sensitivity). The features of atypical depression and melancholia are compared in Table 76.15.

By report, G.R. is depressed; she also reports extreme lethargy, phobic avoidance of bridges or high places and a recent problem with hypersomnia and hyperphagia with subsequent weight gain. She also seems to have a prominent rejection sensitivity regarding the relationship with her boyfriend.

31. What medication would you recommend for G.R.? Outline a dosage titration and treatment plan.

Table 76.15	A Comparison of Features of Atypical Depression and Melancholia[a]	
Feature	Atypical Depression	Melancholia
Onset	Teens or younger	≥30 years
Course	Chronic	Episodic
Phenomenology		
Appetite/weight	↑	↓
Sleep	↑	↓
Energy	Leaden feelings	Low but without feeling leaden
Reaction to rejection/criticism	Devastation or rage	Indifference
Treatment response	MAOI > TCA	TCA = MAOI

[a] Adapted with permission from reference 172.
[b] MAOI = Monoamine oxidase inhibitor; TCA = Tricyclic antidepressant.

Although the MAOIs have been used in other countries for depressive disorders since the 1950s,[173] the MAOIs were not used more widely in the U.S. for depression and specifically, atypical depression until the 1970s. Amitriptyline may be more effective than phenelzine for patients with melancholic depression (especially those with early morning awakening and weight loss); however, phenelzine may be more effective in those with symptoms of difficulty falling asleep, lack of insomnia, and lack of weight loss or weight gain.[174–176] MAOIs have been well studied and are used in the treatment of atypical depression. Melancholic patients and those with simple mood reactive depression seem to respond about equally well to TCAs and MAOIs.[172,177]

Because of G.R.'s past positive response to phenelzine, this choice of antidepressant/antiphobic medication would be reasonable at this point. TCAs are not as effective as MAOIs for the treatment of atypical depression,[172] and the newer antidepressants, including the "second-generation" agents and the SSRIs, have not yet been assessed for atypical depression. Phenelzine should be started for G.R. at 30 mg/day[178] (given as 15 mg PO in the morning and at noon). This dose then should be increased by 15 mg every week to a target dose of 60 mg/day by 14 days. Some investigators have recommended measuring platelet MAO activity and using this as an index of clinical outcome,[179] the idea being that good response is an MAO inhibition of at least 80%. The availability of this laboratory parameter may be limited at some institutions. G.R. should be carefully followed clinically for resolution of target symptoms over a six- to eight-week period. The use of a psychometric rating instrument such as the HAM-D at every follow-up visit is valuable in quantifying any signs of improvement in target symptoms over the treatment period. Adjustments in the dose of 15 mg/week to a maximum of 90 mg/day may be necessary to manage symptoms.

32. Adverse Effects. During this period of phenelzine therapy, G.R. should be monitored carefully for suicidal ideation, especially since the MAOIs potentially are lethal when taken in overdose. What adverse effects of the nonselective MAOIs should be looked for in G.R. while she is being treated with phenelzine?

Orthostatic hypotension, weight gain, edema, and sexual dysfunction are common during MAOI therapy.[180] As is the case with the TCAs, the nonselective MAOIs can cause clinically significant postural decreases in blood pressure; however, with the MAOIs, the mechanism is thought to be a direct sympatholytic effect[181] and both the lying and the standing systolic blood pressures are decreased.[182] Phenelzine seems to cause orthostatic hypotension more than tranylcypromine or isocarboxazid.[183] As the orthostatic hypotension appears to be dose-related,[184] a reduction in dose may be helpful. The orthostatic hypotension has been managed pharmacologically by the addition of 25 µg/day of triiodothyronine as well as the addition of 9-alpha-fluorohydrocortisone 0.025 mg to 0.05 mg once to twice a day.[185] Monitoring for blood pressure changes as well as edema and serum electrolyte changes (e.g., hypokalemia) is paramount if these pharmacological interventions are used. MAOI-induced weight gain may be managed by monitoring carbohydrate and fat intake. Edema can be treated by elevation of the affected limbs and/or use of a thiazide diuretic (e.g., hydrochlorothiazide 25–50 mg BID) with careful monitoring of other medications (e.g., serum lithium levels) for potential drug interactions.[185] Sexual dysfunction in up to 20% of patients on MAOIs[186] may diminish and disappear spontaneously over time[185] and possibly could be managed with bethanechol (Urecholine) in doses up to 50 mg/day in both men and women.[180]

A switch into mania has been reported in up to 10% in patients with a history of bipolar disorder;[180] therefore, the MAOIs should be avoided in patients with positive histories of bipolar disorders. Although the MAOIs are not known as antimuscarinic medications, some patients complain of anticholinergic-like side effects, including blurred near vision and urinary retention. Dosage reduction may be helpful but these effects may diminish over time. Paresthesias also have been reported with the MAOIs and can be treated with pyridoxine 50 to 150 mg/day.[187] The nonselective MAOIs are not associated with proarrhythmic, antiarrhythmic, or contractility effects when used in therapeutic dosages (see Table 76.10).

33. Drug-Food Interactions. G.R. states that what she most fears is the "cheese reaction." What steps can be taken to avoid it?

The "cheese reaction," also known as hypertensive crisis, is so named because it occurred in patients who were taking nonselective MAOIs and ingested foods high in tyramine such as aged cheese. When tyramine is ingested in the presence of an MAOI, the tyramine is not metabolized by the MAO. Tyramine then displaces norepinephrine from storage granules. This surge of norepinephrine, combined with the fact that the MAOI also is preventing the metabolism of the norepinephrine, can result in a precipitous increase in blood pressure.[188] Systolic blood pressures as high as 160 to 220 mm Hg and diastolics from 100 to 130 mm Hg can occur. The event is heralded by severe headache (occipital and temporal), a choking sensation, palpitations, diaphoresis, and nausea and vomiting.[189] This potentially life-threatening event can occur at any time after ingesting the tyramine-containing food and probably is not related to MAOI dosage or duration of therapy.[180] Because of the possible clinical consequences, including cerebral vascular accident and/or death, this food-drug interaction is feared widely and this fact could result in underuse of the nonselective MAOIs. Reports of hypertensive crisis are sporadic and, therefore, have been difficult to quantify. About 8% of phenelzine patients and 2% of tranylcypromine patients reported hypertensive reactions based upon a chart review of 198 patients taking MAOIs.[180] It is a relatively rare event, however, and certainly is found less often than MAOI-related hypotension.

Patients who are to receive nonselective MAOIs should be reliable individuals who are willing to comply with food and medication restrictions. This adverse event can be minimized with a low-tyramine diet that begins several days before starting the MAOI and continues for three to four weeks after stopping the MAOI. The severity of the "cheese reaction" is related to the amount of tyramine in any given food (i.e., 20 mg of tyramine can produce a severe hypertensive reaction)[190,191] and the amount of tyramine can vary greatly in "high-tyramine food items". Foods that ab-

solutely should not be consumed with nonselective MAOIs include aged cheeses, concentrated yeast extracts, fava beans, and sauerkraut.[192] Likewise, consumption of any food that has spoiled, is overripe, or has fermented even if it is not found in the restricted list, should be avoided. Foods that typically contain tyramine and, therefore, should be avoided or consumed with caution when taking a MAOI are listed in Table 76.16.

34. How can a hypertensive MAOI-induced crisis be managed in G.R.?

A hypertensive crisis should be considered a medical emergency, especially because of her phenelzine therapy. In a hospital setting, general supportive measures are employed with attention to respiratory, metabolic, and cardiovascular systems. The urine should be acidified (e.g., with vitamin C); phentolamine (Regitine) 5 mg intravenously (IV) followed by 0.25 to 0.50 mg IV every four to six hours or chlorpromazine (Thorazine) 100 mg intramuscularly (IM) followed by 25 mg IM every one to two hours, with careful attention to blood pressure. Some patients may be advised to carry chlorpromazine 50 mg tablets to be used if they have ingested a food that is on the high-tyramine list or if they have developed a headache.[185]

35. Drug-Drug Interactions. What common drug-drug interactions associated with the nonselective MAOIs should be avoided in G.R.?

Several potentially fatal drug-drug interactions occur with this group of antidepressants (see Table 76.17). Like the reaction with tyramine, the indirect sympathomimetics such as phenylpropanolomine and pseudoephedrine (common ingredients in over-the-counter cold preparations and diet pills) can cause a precipitous rise in blood pressure that can result in cerebrovascular accident. Likewise, several antihypertensives such as guanethidine (Ismelin) and methyldopa (Aldomet) can result in hypertension when combined with the MAOIs by rendering the antihypertensive inactive.[193] Meperidine (Demerol) can cause a life-threatening interaction with MAOIs. This reaction is manifested by agitation, hyperpyrexia, and circulatory collapse and is a result of the MAOI interfering with the degradation of the meperidine.[193] Other narcotic analgesics do not appear to have this effect when combined

Table 76.16	Foods Containing Tyramine[a]
High amounts of Tyramine[b]	
Smoked, aged, or pickled meat or fish	
Sauerkraut	
Aged cheeses (e.g., Swiss, cheddar)	
Yeast extracts	
Fava beans	
Moderate amounts of tyramine[c]	
Beer	
Avocados	
Meat extracts	
Red wines (e.g., Chianti)	
Low amounts of tyramine[d]	
Caffeine-containing beverages	
Distilled spirits	
Chocolate	
Soy sauce	
Cottage and cream cheese	
Yogurt and sour cream	

[a] Adapted from reference 192.
[b] May not consume.
[c] May consume in moderation.
[d] May consume.

Table 76.17	Interaction Between MAOIs and Other Substances[a]			
Effect	Interacting Drug	Mechanism	Onset	Importance
↑ BP, possible hypertensive crisis	Sympathomimetics (amphetamines, phenylpropanolamine, ephedrine, phenylephrine, pseudoephedrine)	Liberation of catecholamine stores	Fast	Major
Hypertensive reaction	Antihypertensives (guanethidine, reserpine, methyldopa)	Release of accumulated catecholamines	Slow	Moderate
Agitation, hyperpyrexia, circulatory collapse	Meperidine	Interference with meperidine degradation	Fast	Major
Hypotension; CNS depression	Anesthetics	Potentiation	Fast	Moderate
Hypoglycemia	Hypoglycemics (insulin, sulfonylureas)	Potentiation	Fast	Moderate
↑ therapeutic and toxic effects	TCAs	Additive side effects at receptor level	Fast	Major
	Levodopa, dopamine		Fast	Major
	SSRIs, tryptophan	MAO inhibition	Fast	Major
		Possible stimulation of serotonergic system		

[a] BP = Blood pressure; CNS = Central nervous system; MAO = Monoamine oxidase; MAOI = Monoamine oxidase inhibitor; SSRI = Selective serotonin reuptake inhibitor; TCA = Tricyclic antidepressant.

with the MAOIs. The potential for serious drug-drug interaction between SSRIs and the MAOIs has been realized. The additive effects of these two types of antidepressant can precipitate a "serotonin syndrome" consisting of tremor, hyperreflexia, diarrhea, and altered mental status.[165] Caution should be exercised to avoid starting an SSRI too soon after stopping the MAOI (i.e., at least 14 days postMAOI).

Depression with Psychotic Features
(Psychotic Depression)

36. R.S., a 41-year-old male, is brought to the Crisis Stabilization Unit (CSU) by the police because of extreme agitated behavior. His wife had called the police because R.S. was on the roof of their home with a gun shooting into the shingles. R.S. had worried for some time that the mortgage balance on the house was too large; now he was yelling that the house was "killing his spirit" and that he could not handle it any longer. He had told his wife that he was "inadequate as a provider" for her and their 2 children. In your interview with him at the CSU, he tells you that for the past week he has been hearing the voice of his deceased father telling him to kill himself after destroying the house. This has distressed him greatly. It also is noted that he recently was terminated from his place of employment as the manager of a local grocery store. His sleep is reported by both his wife and him to have been poor over the past month with difficulties falling asleep and with waking up during the night and not getting back to sleep. His mood is depressed and he has lost 15 pounds in the past 2 weeks due to decreased appetite. His psychiatric history is positive for 2 past episodes of depression, 1 at age 22 and the other at age 35. Both episodes resolved after 8-week courses of imipramine to 250 mg/day. He is diagnosed with major depressive disorder, recurrent severe with psychotic features and admitted to the adjacent hospital for treatment. What features of psychotic depression are manifested by R.S.?

Psychotic depression, also known as delusional depression or depression with psychotic features, is a type of depressive illness (either unipolar or bipolar) in which the depressed individual manifests not only the typical mood symptoms found in depression, but also demonstrates psychotic features such as delusions (fixed, false beliefs) and/or hallucinations (generally auditory).[13] The delusions and hallucinations generally are classified as being mood-

congruent or mood-incongruent. *Mood congruent psychotic features* imply that the psychosis is consistent with the depressive illness. In depression, mood-congruent delusions might include self-deprecatory thoughts, extreme feelings of guilt, sinfulness, or nihilistic ideation. R.S. described mood-congruent hallucinations when he spoke of his dead father commanding him to kill himself. His ideas of being inadequate and not a good provider also are consistent with a mood-congruent delusion. *Mood-incongruent psychotic features* imply that the psychotic content is not consistent with the overall mood, but rather, is bizarre, much like that seen in schizophrenia. Psychotic depression has been estimated conservatively to be at least 5% of the depression admissions to acute care hospitals in the U.S.[194]

37. Why is it critical to resolve R.S.'s psychotic depression promptly? Why would ECT be preferred over pharmacotherapy for R.S.?

Psychotic depression is reported to carry a higher risk of suicide than other types of depressive illness[195] (and this factor currently is a major concern in R.S.'s case because he has reported suicidal ideation). Psychotic depression also is fairly refractory to normal single-drug pharmacotherapy.[196] Because of these two points, electroconvulsive therapy is a first-line treatment for the disorder.[197] ECT has a success rate of 80% to 85% in this otherwise refractory form of depression[198] and is the treatment of choice for R.S.

Antidepressant Plus Antipsychotic

38. If ECT is contraindicated in R.S., should he be treated with an antipsychotic or an antidepressant?

If pharmacotherapy is used in R.S., he should be given an antipsychotic medication in addition to the antidepressant medication since he demonstrates psychotic symptoms as well as depressive ones. The combination of an antipsychotic and an antidepressant is superior to either component alone in psychotic depression.[194] Several combination products are available on the market that contain both an antipsychotic and an antidepressant (usually a phenothiazine and a TCA). Although these combination products probably work as well as the individual components, they are fixed-dose combinations and the dosage is more difficult to titrate than the dosages of the individual components. In psychotic depression, as the psychosis lifts, it is reasonable to taper and discontinue the antipsychotic while maintaining the antidepressant medication until the depression is resolved. Having an antipsychotic drug on board after the psychosis has lifted places the patient at greater risk for adverse effects from the antipsychotic (e.g., pseudoparkinsonism, tardive dyskinesia). Therefore, using two separate medications provides for more flexible dosing and possibly is more cost effective in the long-run, as many antipsychotics and antidepressants now are available as generics.

Amoxapine

Another option is using amoxapine. This metabolite of the antipsychotic, loxapine (Loxitane), retains some of the dopamine blocking activity of the parent compound. It also is an effective antidepressant medication. Some clinicians prefer amoxapine in psychotic depression because it is effective[199] and facilitates compliance, being a single agent. In a sense, it also is like a fixed-dose preparation and thus, has the inflexibility of not being able to taper the antipsychotic component without stopping the medication altogether. Like the fixed-dose combination products, amoxapine also would place the patient at some risk for developing adverse effects associated with antipsychotic medications (e.g., dystonia, pseudoparkinsonism, akathisia, neuroleptic malignant syndrome, galactorrhea, and tardive dyskinesia).[200-202]

Length of Therapy

39. R.S. is started on amitriptyline and perphenazine. Daily dosages of these 2 medications are titrated to 200 mg amitriptyline and 16 mg perphenazine. Within 3 weeks, R.S. reports that he no longer hears his father's voice and feels that his mood has improved substantially. He still feels badly about losing his job but now recognizes that there is some hope of continuing in his career. His sleep is normalized now and his appetite is coming back. He no longer reports suicidal thoughts. He is scheduled for discharge from the hospital; follow-up care will be in the outpatient clinic. How long should R.S. be continued on his current regimens and what should the plan be concerning future pharmacotherapy?

As R.S. continues to show signs of his depression, he should be continued on his present antidepressant medication and dosage. Psychotic symptoms are noted to have resolved. The plan at this point should be to insure that he is stable with respect to the resolution of his psychosis. A prudent plan would be to discharge him on his current regimen of perphenazine with the plan to discontinue it at around six weeks after resolution of the psychosis. To avoid potential withdrawal effects, the perphenazine should be tapered and stopped over a seven-day period. The antidepressant medication should be continued at the 200 mg dosage. It remains controversial as to whether an antidepressant should be continued at its peak dosage versus tapering to a ''maintenance'' dosage. It also is controversial whether the antidepressant should be stopped at all. There are only a few long-term studies of maintenance treatment, but the available data clearly support the viewpoint that the dosage of antidepressant should be reduced to a maintenance level once euthymia is achieved. Most patients are at greater risks for recurrence of depression if the medication is stopped.[203] Some individuals may require a lifetime maintenance antidepressant.

The risk for repeat depressive episodes increases as the number of past episodes increases[204] and, with each new episode, the length between episodes becomes shorter.[205] One decision tree to follow in determining who may require lifetime maintenance therapy at acute treatment dosage levels would be those individuals who: 1) are at least 50 years old at the time of the first episode; 2) are at least 40 years old at the time of the first episode and who have had at least two episodes of depression; or 3) have had at least three episodes regardless of current age.[203] If this rationale is applied to the current case, R.S. would need lifetime maintenance

antidepressant therapy of amitriptyline 200 mg/day. Because of his current antidepressant's known side effect profile, he needs careful follow-up care including patient education regarding how to manage adverse effects. If unexpected side effects emerge that are unbearable, patient compliance will be affected. Alternative antidepressant therapy (e.g., an SSRI or venlafaxine) should be considered for R.S. if this occurs and the new medication should be started as the old one is tapered and stopped to avoid any medication-free periods.

Refractory Depression

40. A.B., a 55-year-old female presenting for the first time to the outpatient clinic, has reportedly suffered multiple depressive episodes since the age of 30. She denies a history of alcohol or illicit drug use. By report, she has been hospitalized for depression on at least 5 occasions. Her history is sketchy; however, she believes her past medication trials included imipramine 100 mg/day, amitriptyline 150 mg/day, nortriptyline 75 mg/day, alprazolam 3 mg/day, and up until 8 weeks ago, fluoxetine 20 mg/day. She is not sure how long she took any of these medications; it is notable that she does not prefer amitriptyline as it reportedly made her ''dizzy'' and left a ''strange taste'' in her mouth. Her alprazolam was tapered and discontinued because she felt even ''more depressed'' while taking it. Currently, she feels despondent and helpless over her situation. Her laboratory parameters have not been evaluated recently. What is a reasonable next step with A.B.'s treatment/antidepressant pharmacotherapy?

If possible, A.B.'s complete medication history and better insight into her medication compliance, as well as laboratory reports, should be obtained. This information is important to better determine if her diagnosis of depression is a correct one as well as to determine if she has received ''adequate'' trials of any given medication(s). An incorrect diagnosis or a concomitant medical illness can complicate or even foil an otherwise appropriate treatment regimen. For example, patients who are clinically hypothyroid as well as depressed have a poor response to antidepressants, especially TCAs.[206] Concomitant medications also may contribute to the depression and its response. Various antihypertensives including reserpine (Reserpine), methyldopa, and possibly propranolol (Inderal) have been associated with depression. With most variables controlled for, a clear 20% to 30% of depressive patients nevertheless will fail pharmacotherapy.[207] An adequate trial of a given medication should consist of a therapeutic dosage and/or therapeutic serum concentration, if applicable, for a reasonable period of time. Presently, this period of time should be at least six to eight weeks before concluding that the patient is not responsive.[208] Further, some clinicians believe that a patient should receive at least two successive adequate trials of medication before considering the patient as treatment refractory.[14] A.B. is an outpatient with an apparent long history of taking antidepressant medications; therefore, several different trials of medication may not be possible before she becomes disillusioned and is lost to follow-up.

After a careful interview, it is determined that A.B. probably does suffer from major depression. Her past records are not available and she is not an adequate historian. A prudent next step would be to obtain a medical work-up including laboratory assessments such as a chemistry panel (including renal function indices and hepatic enzymes), ECG, and a thyroid function panel. These clinical objective assessments will give more insight into her overall medical condition and provide baseline information which may help in choosing an antidepressant. For example, renal impairment carries a risk of drug accumulation and may be a crucial index when selecting a TCA.[209] Knowledge of hepatic function is important because TCA use in cirrhosis can result in encephalopathy,[209] and knowledge of cardiac function can be important in medication choice as well (see Question 11). Evaluation of thyroid status also is important because thyroid abnormalities may exist in 25% of depressed patients.[210] These assessments were obtained for A.B. and all are reported as being within normal limits. A reasonable next step would be to start a careful, adequate, and documented therapeutic trial of a TCA such as imipramine. This medication is effective in depression; its side effects are well known; it is inexpensive and can be monitored with serum concentrations. In patients described as treatment refractory, careful monotherapy with a standard TCA, MAOI, or ECT can result in a remission rate of up to 70%.[211] A.B. is started on imipramine and the dosage is titrated gradually to 300 mg/day.

Stepped-Care Approach

41. A.B. experiences no intolerable imipramine side effects, although she initially was very sedated. Her serum imipramine level on 300 mg is 250 ng/mL (total imipramine plus desipramine) and after 5 weeks on this regimen she shows little improvement and her HAM-D score shows no significant change. What is a reasonable intervention at this point?

Since A.B. has not responded to a well-documented, adequate trial of imipramine, another TCA with a different pharmacological profile could be ordered for six to eight weeks, followed by a trial of an MAOI if the second TCA is ineffective, and finally a course of ECT.[212] This common pharmacotherapeutic approach has been challenged because there is no sound pharmacological rationale for the use of two different TCAs.[207] Depression no longer is conceptualized widely as a simple deficiency of neurotransmitters, but rather is seen as a dysregulation of homeostasis.[20] Therefore, if patients are diagnosed rigorously and treated carefully in a systematic fashion, only a small fraction then will need combinations of antidepressants or augmentation therapy strategies. Nevertheless, many clinicians still prefer to use some form of stepped-care approach.

A.B. has not shown any significant response to the 300 mg dosage of imipramine and her serum concentration of 250 ng/mL is within the "therapeutic" threshold for this TCA.[74] Had she shown a partial response at this point, some investigators[104] would have followed by carefully raising the dosage to 350 to 450 mg/day, adding d-amphetamine (5–20 mg/day) or methylphenidate 10 mg/day for at least ten days, followed by triiodothyronine 25 µg/day for a similar period. At such high TCA dosages, close monitoring of the ECG and the serum imipramine concentrations would be recommended highly. Klein has recommended going directly to ECT in cases of no response.[104]

A stepped-care approach using an SSRI would be a reasonable next line of treatment for A.B. because she has failed imipramine, and at least by history, has failed other TCAs. Furthermore, A.B. has a history of taking fluoxetine at 20 mg/day. It is controversial whether increasing the dose of fluoxetine to a maximum of 80 mg/day is any more effective than a 20 mg dose.[213] Doses as high as 80 mg/day have been used in some of the earlier clinical studies; however, higher doses of this SSRI also increase adverse effects without increasing efficacy.[214] If side effects (e.g., gastric complaints, headache) at 20 mg still are bothersome, it can be given every second or even third day to A.B. without decreasing its effectiveness because of this drug's long serum half-life.[213] This method may help to minimize adverse effects and increase compliance.

Other Treatments

42. After 5 weeks of fluoxetine 20 mg/day, A.B. subjectively reports little improvement in the depression. Her HAM-D score remains unchanged. What new pharmacological therapy should be instituted now to manage A.B.'s refractory depression?

There are several other less used strategies for refractory depression. An MAOI plus a TCA has long been considered a dangerous combination. These two different types of antidepressants may be used concomitantly under the following rigid conditions. First, these drugs must be initiated at the same time (i.e., at least 2 weeks after stopping the MAOI monotherapy or 5 to 10 days after stopping the TCA). Secondly, tranylcypromine plus imipramine or desipramine should not be used together in any combination.[215] Finally, vital signs must be monitored routinely and the patient must be instructed to contact her physician upon notice of signs of hypertensive crisis or the serotonin syndrome (hypomania, tremor, hyperreflexia, hypertension, diarrhea, and altered mental status).[216] The maximum dosage of the TCA should not exceed 150 mg equivalents of amitriptyline and 45 mg equivalents of phenelzine per day.[104] Unfortunately, the MAOI-TCA combination approach has not yielded overwhelmingly positive results.[217] In A.B.'s case, since she has been on fluoxetine, the fluoxetine should be washed out for at least five weeks before starting an MAOI to avoid the possibility of the serotonin syndrome. Several other medication combinations include TCA or MAOI plus stimulant, TCA plus reserpine, TCAs plus bromocriptine (Parlodel), TCAs plus L-Dopa, and lithium plus carbamazepine (Tegretol).[218–223] For the most part, these drug combination regimens have not been well studied and probably should be reserved until the time that more studies have been performed to better assess their efficacy and safety. These unproven interventions and the poor results from MAOI-TCA combinations seem to support another therapeutic approach for A.B.'s refractory depression.

Augmentation Strategies

Lithium and Thyroid. A.B. has been highly compliant for an outpatient who has not received significant improvement on at least two adequate trials of different antidepressants. A reasonable next step would be to augment her current fluoxetine regimen with another medication such as lithium or thyroid. Lithium augmentation in refractory depression has been well documented. In one report,[224] all eight nonresponsive patients in a group of 35 unipolar, depressed patients who had been treated for three weeks with various therapeutic doses of a TCA, responded to lithium augmentation within two days. Six of the eight patients subsequently were reported to have maintained the improvement. The short trial of the TCA in this study, however, weakens its validity because the apparent response to the lithium simply may be a reflection of the antidepressant finally starting to work. Nevertheless, other reports of successful lithium augmentation of various antidepressants in refractory depression have been reported[225–227] including augmentation of fluoxetine[228,229] or MAOI.[230] After supplementation with lithium, clinical improvement was noted after several days[224] or in some instances after one to six weeks.[227] The lithium dosage generally is within the range used to treat bipolar disorder. In one report,[228] when the lithium serum concentration dropped to 0.3 mEq/L, the depression relapsed and improved again when the dose of lithium was increased to achieve a serum level between 0.8 and 1.2 mEq/L. As with the use of lithium therapy in bipolar disorder, all appropriate clinical monitoring parameters should be followed carefully (see Chapter 77: Mood Disorders II: Bipolar Affective Disorders). Because both lithium and fluoxetine are serotonergic, the patient should be monitored for symptoms of the serotonin syndrome. Predictors of response to lithium augmentation has been studied. An immediate and marked response to lithium is considered as being predictive of a good outcome.[231] Age, gender, number of prior antidepressant trials, type of preceding antidepressant, or mean serum lithium concentration did not predict outcome to lithium augmentation.[232]

An alternative to adding lithium to the fluoxetine would be to augment the fluoxetine with thyroid hormone such as triiodothyronine or l-thyroxine. This option probably should be attempted after a trial of lithium, as a later controlled study has indicated that thyroid is no more effective than an additional four weeks of TCA.[233] Nevertheless, the theory behind the use of thyroid involves evidence supporting a role for a thyroid dysfunction in refractory depression (e.g., there is increased or decreased thyroid hormone levels that are associated with increased or decreased beta-adrenergic receptors in various animal models).[234] Beta receptors already have been implicated in the pathogenesis of depression. Although A.B.'s thyroid function tests are within normal limits, it is possible that she suffers from a subtle form of thyroid dysfunction such as a subclinical hypothyroidism since depressed patients are more likely to have such conditions as compared to nondepressives.[235] Triiodothyronine (Cytomel) at a dose of 25 µg/day can accelerate response to imipramine as measured by the HAM-D in both psychomotorically retarded[236] and nonpsychomotorically retarded depressives.[237] Other studies have demonstrated clearly the efficacy of thyroid hormone augmentation of TCA therapy in converting nonresponders to responders.[238] Thyroxine in a dose of 0.1 mg/day added to the antidepressant is another option.[239] The response to the thyroid supplementation should be notable within three weeks, much like that found when lithium is used to augment therapy.[239] Whether T_3 is superior to T_4 is not resolved yet. One study has seemed to indicate that more patients respond to the former than to the latter.[240] Whether lithium or thyroid augmentation is superior remains to be resolved. In a randomized, double-blind, placebo-controlled study of two weeks' duration, 50 nonpsychotically depressed outpatients who had failed to respond to TCA therapy responded equally well to both lithium or T_3 augmentation in contrast to their nonresponse to placebo.[241]

ECT

43. A.B. does not respond adequately to any of the treatment strategies tried with her. Would she be a candidate for ECT?

Electroconvulsive therapy should be reserved for those individuals who have not responded adequately to pharmacologic intervention. As an antidepressant intervention, it has the highest rate of response of any antidepressant treatment regimen and may be safer than many of the combination regimens described above. Up to 50% of patients not responding to pharmacotherapy will respond satisfactorily to ECT[242] and medication-resistant patients who have been given adequate pharmacotherapeutic trials preECT have a lower response to the procedure than those who have not received adequate medication trials preECT. Once response is achieved with ECT, relapse may be as high as 50% and seems to be clustered in the first four months after clinical response. A patient who has failed a given medication trial (e.g., a TCA), but who responds to ECT, does better if the postECT maintenance medication is of a different type, such as a MAOI or an SSRI.[50] If maintenance medication cannot be given, maintenance (monthly) ECT has been used successfully,[243] if however rare.

Update

Venlafaxine

Onset of Antidepressant Effects

U1. What is the validity to the claim that venlafaxine has a more rapid onset of effectiveness than other antidepressants?

It has been suggested in some studies[254,255] but not in others[256] that the response to venlafaxine (Effexor) is earlier than that found with other antidepressants (i.e., within the first 1 to 2 weeks versus the more recognized 2 to 6 weeks). It is theorized that a quicker onset of action may be related to a more rapid induction of noradrenergic subsensitivity[252] and that the effect may be dose related;[256] however, it should be noted that desensitization of the adrenergic system is not necessarily the mechanism of action for all antidepressants and has not even been clearly linked to antidepressant response.[253] Further studies and experience with venlafaxine are necessary before it can be said that venlafaxine has a quicker onset of action than other antidepressants.

Treatment of Refractory Depression

U2. What data support the contention that venlafaxine can treat depressed patients who have failed other antidepressive therapy?

There is limited evidence that venlafaxine may be useful in the treatment of refractory depression. An open-label study divided between two study sites followed 82 refractory depressed patients for at least six months. Approximately 40% of these patients showed a clinically significant response to venlafaxine doses as high as 450 mg/day.[250] It remains to be seen whether the individuals who improved will be able to sustain the improvement over time. Well-controlled studies are needed before venlafaxine can be confirmed as an important intervention in the treatment of refractory depression.

Nefazodone: Drug-Drug Interactions

U3. Why does nefazodone affect the dosing of some antihistamines, benzodiazepines, and MAOIs?

The new phenylpiperazine antidepressant, nefazodone (Serzone), is chemically related to trazodone (Desyrel). Nefazodone, like many of the newer antidepressant medications, is an inhibitor of the hepatic cytochrome P450 mixed oxidase system. Specifically, nefazodone is an inhibitor of the cytochrome P450 IIIA4 isoenzyme. This isoenzyme is important in the metabolism of drugs such as terfenadine and astemizole, two frequently utilized antihistamine medications. Because the inhibition of this isoenzyme may result in increased plasma concentrations of these two drugs with resultant cardiac toxicity, the co-administration of terfenadine and astemizole with nefazodone is contraindicated.[251,257] Furthermore, the combination of nefazodone with either of the two triazolobenzodiazepines, triazolam or alprazolam (both of which also are metabolized by cytochrome P450 IIIA4) can result in clinically important increases in plasma concentrations of these benzodiazepines. Thus, if nefazodone must be combined with either triazolam (Halcion) or alprazolam (Xanax), the dose of triazolam should be reduced by 75% and alprazolam by 50%. No dosage adjustment is necessary for nefazodone.[251,257] Other benzodiazepines that are not metabolized by the cytochrome P450 IIIA4 isoenzyme but are handled through the cytochrome P450 IID6 or by glucuronidation are not likely to interact with nefazodone. Thus lorazepam (Ativan) does not interact pharmacokinetically or pharmacodynamically with nefazodone and no dosage adjustments are required of either medication if they are co-administered. Because of the danger of serious, sometimes fatal reactions, nefazodone should not be combined with an MAOI, or within 14 days of discontinuing treatment with an MAOI. Additionally, at least one week should be allowed after stopping nefazodone before starting an MAOI.[251]

References

1 **Andreasen NC.** The Broken Brain: The Biological Revolution in Psychiatry. New York, NY: Harper & Row; 1984:36.

2 **Wells KB et al.** The functioning and well-being of depressed patients. JAMA. 1989;262:914.

3 **Greenberg PE et al.** The economic burden of depression in 1990. J Clin Psychiatry. 1993;54:405.

4 **The Cross-National Collaborative Group.** The changing rate of major depression. JAMA. 1992;268:3098.

5 **Winokur G.** Unipolar depression. In: Winokur G, Clayton P, eds. Medical Basis of Psychiatry. Philadelphia: WB Saunders; 1986:60.

6 **Regier DA et al.** One-month prevalence of mental disorders in the United States: based on five epidemiologic catchment area sites. Arch Gen Psychiatry. 1988;45:977.

7 **Hirschfeld RMA, Cross CK.** Epidemiology of affective disorders. Arch Gen Psychiatry. 1982;29:35.

8 **Blazer D.** Depression in the elderly. N Engl J Med. 1989;320:164.

9 **McGuffin P, Katz R.** The genetics of depression and manic-depressive disorder. Br J Psychiatry. 1989;155:294.

10 **Blehar MC et al.** Family and genetic studies of affective disorders. Arch Gen Psychiatry. 1988;45:289.

11 **Weissman MM et al.** Understanding the clinical heterogeneity of major depression using family data. Arch Gen Psychiatry. 1986;430.

12 **Kraepelin E.** Manic Depressive Insanity and Paranoia. Edinburgh: ES Livingstone; 1921.

13 **American Psychiatric Association.** Diagnostic and Statistical Manual of Mental Disorders. 4th ed. (DSM-IV). Washington, DC: American Psychiatric Association; 1994.

14 **Practice Guideline for Major Depressive Disorder in Adults.** Am J Psychiatry. 1993;150(4):1.

15 **Bryant SG, Brown CS.** Current concepts in clinical therapeutics: major affective disorders: Part 1. Clin Pharm. 1986;5:304.

16 **Schildkraut JJ.** Neuropsychopharmacology and the affective disorders. N Engl J Med. 1969;281:302.

17 **Maas JW.** Biogenic amines and depression. Arch Gen Psychiatry. 1975; 32:1357.

18 **Prange A.** L-tryptophan in mania: contribution to a permissive hypothesis of affective disorders. Arch Gen Psychiatry. 1974;30:56.

19 **Schatzberg A, Rosenbaum A.** Studies on MHPG levels as predictors of antidepressant response. McLean Hosp J. 1980;6:138.

20 **Siever LJ, Davis KL.** Overview: toward a dysregulation hypothesis of depression. Am J Psychiatry. 1985;142:1017.

21 **Charney DS et al.** Receptor sensitivity and the mechanisms of action of antidepressant treatment. Arch Gen Psychiatry. 1981;381:1160.

22 **Bonate PL.** Serotonin receptor subtypes: functional, physiological, and clinical correlates. Clin Neuropharmacol. 1991;14:1.

23 **Palacios JM et al.** Distribution of serotonin receptors. Ann N Y Acad Sci. 1990;600:36.

24 **Meltzer HY.** Role of serotonin in depression. Ann N Y Acad Sci. 1990; 600:486.

25 **Mann JJ et al.** Serotonin and suicidal behavior. In: Witaker-Azmitia PM, Peroutka SJ, eds. The Neuropharmacology of Serotonin. New York: Annals of the New York Academy of Sciences; 1990:476.

26 **Morely JE, Shafer RB.** Thyroid function screening in new psychiatric admissions. Arch Intern Med. 1982;42:591.

27 **Nemeroff CB.** Clinical significance of psychoneuroendocrinology in psychiatry: focus on the thyroid and adrenal. J Clin Psychiatry. 1989;50:13.

28 **Nemeroff CB, Evans DL.** Thyrotropin-releasing hormone (TRH), the thyroid axis, and affective disorder. Ann N Y Acad Sci. 1989;553:304.

29 **Banki CM et al.** Elevation of immunoreactive CSF TRH in depressed patients. Am J Psychiatry. 1988;145:1526.

30 **Cowen PJ et al.** Endocrinological responses to 5-HT. Ann N Y Acad Sci. 1990; 600:250.

31 **Rothchild AJ et al.** Hypothalamic-pituitary-adrenal axis activity and 1-year outcome in depression. Biol Psychiatry. 1993;34:392.

32 **Stokes PE, Sikes CR.** Hypothalamic-pituitary-adrenal axis in affective disorder. In: Meltzer HY, ed. Psychopharmacology: The Third Generation of Progress. New York: Raven Press; 1987:589.

33 **Gold PW et al.** Abnormal hypothalamic-pituitary-adrenal function in anorexia nervosa. N Engl J Med. 1986; 314:1335.

34 **Krahn DD et al.** Cortisol response to vasopressin in depression. Biol Psychiatry. 1985;20:918.

35 **Gold PN, Rubinow DR.** Neuropeptide function in affective illness: corticotrophin-releasing hormone and somatostatin as model systems. In: Meltzer HY, ed. Psychopharmacology: The Third Generation of Progress. New York: Raven Press; 1987:617.

36 **Mendlewicz J et al.** Diurnal hypersecretion of growth hormone in depression. J Clin Endocrinol Metab. 1985; 60:505.

37 **Garner RM, Yamada T.** Altered neuropeptide concentrations in cerebrospinal fluid of psychiatric patients. Brain Res. 1982;328:298.

38 **Cummings JL.** The neuroanatomy of depression. J Clin Psychiatry. 1993;54: 11(Suppl.):14.

39 **George MS et al.** SPECT and PET imaging in mood disorders. J Clin Psychiatry. 1993;54:6.

40 **Detre TP et al.** The assessment of the patient and examination, disposition and management. In: Detre TP et al., eds. Modern Psychiatric Treatment. New York: Lippincott; 1971:15.

41 **Freedman AM et al.** Mental status exam. In: Freedman AM et al., eds. Modern Synopsis of Psychiatry. II.

Baltimore: Williams and Wilkins; 1976: 347.

42 **Fankhauser MP, German ML.** Understanding the use of behavioral rating scales in studies evaluating the efficacy of antianxiety and antidepressant drugs. Am J Hosp Pharm. 1987;44:2087.

43 **Lyerly SB.** Handbook of Psychiatric Rating Scales. New York: Research and Education Association; 1981.

44 **Ribeiro SCM et al.** The DST as a predictor of outcome in depression: a meta analysis. Am J Psychiatry. 1993; 150(11):1618.

45 **American Psychiatric Association Task Force on the Use of Laboratory Tests in Psychiatry.** The dexamethasone suppression test: an overview of its current status in psychiatry. Am J Psychiatry. 1987;144:1253.

46 **Weissman MM et al.** The efficacy of drugs and psychotherapy in the treatment of acute depressive episodes. Am J Psychiatry. 1979;136:555.

47 **Tachibana H et al.** Effects of aging on cerebral blood flow in dementia. J Am Geriatr Soc. 1984;32:114.

48 **Wirz-Justice A et al.** Light therapy in seasonal affective disorder is independent of time of day or circadian phase. Arch Gen Psychiatry. 1993;50:929.

49 **Wehr TA.** Manipulations of sleep and phototherapy: nonpharmacological alternatives in the treatment of depression. Clin Neuropharmacol. 1990;13: S54.

50 **Devanand DP et al.** Electroconvulsive therapy in the treatment-resistant patient. Psychiatr Clin North Am. 1991; 14:905.

51 **Persad E.** Electroconvulsive therapy in depression. Can J Psychiatry. 1990; 35:175.

52 **Abrams R.** Electroconvulsive therapy in the medically compromised patient. Psychiatr Clin North Am. 1991;14:871.

53 **Kellner CH, ed.** Electroconvulsive therapy. Psychiatr Clin North Am. 1991;14.

54 **Vaillant GE, Blumenthal SJ.** Suicide over the life cycle: risk factors and life span development. In: Blumenthal SJ, Kupfer DJ, eds. Suicide Over the Life Cycle: Risk Factors, Assessment, and Treatment of Suicidal Patients. Washington, DC: American Psychiatric Press; 1990.

55 **Report of the Secretaries Task Force on Youth Suicide.** U.S. Department of Health and Human Services; 1989.

56 **Zweig RA, Hinrichsen GA.** Factors associated with suicide attempts by depressed older adults: a prospective study. Am J Psychiatry. 1993;150:1687.

57 **Snyder SH.** Antidepressants and the muscarinic acetylcholine receptor. Arch Gen Psychiatry. 1977;34:236.

58 **Cassem N.** Cardiovascular effects of antidepressants. J Clin Psychiatry. 1982; 43:22.

59 **Thayssen P et al.** Cardiovascular effects of imipramine and nortriptyline in elderly patients. Psychopharmacology. 1981;74:3600.

60 **Segraves RT.** Overview of sexual dysfunction complicating the treatment of

depression. J Clin Psychiatry. (Monograph Series). 1992;10:4.

61 **Boston Collaborative Drug Surveillance Program Report.** Adverse reactions to tricyclic antidepressant drugs. Lancet. 1972;1:529.

62 **Goodman HL.** Agranulocytosis associated with Tofranil. Ann Intern Med. 1961;55:321.

63 **Morgan DH.** Jaundice associated with amitriptyline. Br J Psychiatry. 1969;15:105.

64 **Bryant SG, Brown CS.** Current concepts in clinical therapeutics: major affective disorders: Part 2. Clin Pharm. 1986;5:385.

65 **Prien RF, Kupfer DJ.** Continuation drug therapy for major depressive episodes: how long should it be maintained? Am J Psychiatry. 1986;143:18.

66 **Mood Disorders: Pharmacologic Prevention of Recurrences.** Natl Inst Health Consensus Dev Conf Consensus Statement. 1984:5(4).

67 **Frank E et al.** Three year outcomes for maintenance therapies in recurrent depression. Arch Gen Psychiatry. 1990; 47:1093.

68 **Kupfer DJ et al.** Five year outcome for maintenance therapies in recurrent depression. Arch Gen Psychiatry. 1992; 49:769.

69 **Stokes PE.** Current issues in the treatment of major depression. J Clin Psychopharmacol. 1993;13:2.

70 **Boyer WF, Friedel RO.** Antidepressant and antipsychotic plasma levels. Psychiatr Clin North Am. 1984;7:603.

71 **Friedel RO.** The relationship of therapeutic response to antidepressant plasma levels: an update. J Clin Psychiatry. 1982;43:37.

72 **Risch SC et al.** Plasma levels of tricyclic antidepressants and clinical efficacy: review of the literature. J Clin Psychiatry. 1979;40:58.

73 **Åsberg M et al.** Relationship between plasma level and therapeutic effect of nortriptyline. Br Med J. 1971;3:331.

74 **Glassman AH et al.** Clinical implications of imipramine plasma levels for depressive illness. Arch Gen Psychiatry. 1977;34:197.

75 **Reisby N et al.** Imipramine clinical effects and pharmacokinetic variability. Psychopharmacology. 1977;54:263.

76 **Khalid R et al.** Desipramine plasma levels and therapeutic response. Psychopharmacol Bull. 1978;14:43.

77 **Nelson JC et al.** Desipramine plasma concentrations and antidepressant response. Arch Gen Psychiatry. 1982;39:1419.

78 **Braithwaite RA et al.** Plasma concentration of amitriptyline and clinical response. Lancet. 1972;1:1297.

79 **Ziegler VE et al.** Amitriptyline plasma levels and therapeutic response. Clin Pharmacol Ther. 1976;19:795.

80 **Kupfer DJ et al.** Amitriptyline plasma levels and clinical response in primary depression. Clin Pharmacol Ther. 1977;22:904.

81 **Montgomery SA et al.** Amitriptyline plasma concentration and clinical response. Br Med J. 1979;1:230.

82 **Vandel S et al.** Clinical response and

plasma concentration of amitriptyline. Eur J Clin Pharmacol. 1978;14:185.

83 Moyes ICA et al. Plasma levels and clinical improvement—a comparative study of clomipramine and amitriptyline in depression. Postgrad Med J. 1980;56:127.

84 Coppen A et al. Amitriptyline plasma concentration and clinical effect: a World Health Organization collaborative study. Lancet. 1978;1:63.

85 Robinson DS et al. Plasma tricyclic drug levels in amitriptyline-treated depressed patients. Psychopharmacology. 1979;63:223.

86 American Psychiatric Association Task Force. The use of laboratory tests in psychiatry: tricyclic antidepressants—blood level measurements and clinical outcome. An APA Task Force Report. Am J Psychiatry. 1985;142:155.

87 Rabkin JG et al. Adverse reactions to monoamine oxidase inhibitors: II. Treatment correlates and clinical management. J Clin Psychopharmacol. 1985;5:2.

88 Glassman AH. Cardiovascular effects of tricyclic antidepressants. Ann Rev Med. 1984;35:503.

89 Muller OF et al. The hypotensive effect of imipramine hydrochloride in patients with cardiovascular disease. Clin Pharmacol Ther. 1961;2:300.

90 Glassman AH et al. The use of imipramine in depressed patients with congestive heart failure. JAMA. 1983;250:1997.

91 Tesar GE et al. Orthostatic hypotension and antidepressant pharmacotherapy. Psychopharmacol Bull. 1987;23:182.

92 Laird LK et al. Cardiovascular effects of imipramine, fluvoxamine, and placebo in depressed outpatients. J Clin Psychiatry. 1993;54:224.

93 Roose SP et al. Tricyclic antidepressants in depressed patients with cardiac conduction disease. Arch Gen Psychiatry. 1987;44:273.

94 Glassman AH et al. Clinical characteristics of imipramine-induced orthostatic hypotension. Lancet. 1979;1:468.

95 Bigger JT Jr et al. Cardiovascular effects of tricyclic antidepressants. In: Lipton MA et al., eds. Psychopharmacology: A Generation of Progress. New York: Raven Press; 1978:1033.

96 Kantor SJ et al. The cardiac effects of therapeutic plasma concentrations of imipramine. Am J Psychiatry. 1978;135:534.

97 Roose SP et al. Comparison of imipramine- and nortriptyline-induced orthostatic hypotension: a meaningful difference. J Clin Psychopharamacol. 1981;1:316.

98 Kopera H. Anticholinergic and blood pressure effects of mianserin, amitriptyline, and placebo. Br J Clin Pharmacol. 1978;5:29.

99 Nelson JC et al. Major adverse reactions during desipramine treatment: relationship to plasma drug concentrations, concomitant antipsychotic treatment, and patient characteristics. Arch Gen Psychiatry. 1982;39:1055.

100 Veith RC et al. Cardiovascular effects of tricyclic antidepressants in depressed patients with chronic heart disease. N Engl J Med. 1982;306:954.

101 DeWilde JE et al. Clinical trials of flu-

voxamine vs chlorimipramine with single and three times daily dosing. Br J Clin Pharamcol. 1983;15(Suppl.):427.

102 Freyschuss U et al. Circulatory effects in man of nortriptyline, a tricyclic antidepressant drug. Pharmacologia Clinica. 1970;2:68.

103 Vohra J et al. Assessment of cardiovascular side effects of therapeutic doses of tricyclic antidepressant drugs. Aust N Z J Med. 1975;5:7.

104 Klein DF et al. Diagnosis and Drug Treatment of Psychiatric Disorders: Adults and Children. 2nd ed. Baltimore, MD: Williams and Wilkins; 1980.

105 Cole JO, Bodkin JA. Antidepressant drug side effects. J Clin Psychiatry. 1990;51(Suppl. 1):21.

106 Jefferson JW. Cardiovascular effects and toxicity of anxiolytics and antidepressants. J Clin Psychiatry. 1989;50:368.

107 Glassman AH, Bigger JT Jr. Cardiovascular effects of therapeutic doses of tricyclic antidepressants: a review. Arch Gen Psychiatry. 1981;38:815.

108 Roose SP et al. Nortriptyline in depressed patients with left ventricular impairment. JAMA. 1986;256:3253.

109 Bigger JT Jr et al. Cardiac antiarrhythmic effect of imipramine hydrochloride. N Engl J Med. 1977;296:206.

110 Giardina EGV, Bigger JT Jr. Antiarrhythmic effect of imipramine hydrochloride inpatients with ventricular premature complexes with psychological depression. Am J Cardiol. 1982;50:172.

111 Muir WW et al. Effects of tricyclic antidepressant drugs on the electrophysiological properties of dog Purkinje fibers. J Cardiovasc Pharmacol. 1982;4:82.

112 Davidson J, Turnbull CD. The effects of isocarboxazid on blood pressure and pulse. J Clin Psychopharmacol. 1986;6:139.

113 Warrington SJ et al. The cardiovascular effects of antidepressants. Psychol Med Monograph Suppl. 1989;16(Suppl.):1.

114 Roose SP et al. Cardiovascular effects of bupropion in depressed patients with heart disease. Am J Psychiatry. 1991;148:512.

115 Fisch C. Effect of fluoxetine on the electrocardiogram. J Clin Psychiatry. 1985;46:42.

116 Cohn CK et al. Double-blind, multicenter comparison of sertraline and amitriptyline in elderly depressed patients. J Clin Psychiatry. 1990;51(Suppl. 12):28.

117 Preskorn SH, Irwin HA. Toxicity of tricyclic antidepressants: kinetics, mechanisms, intervention: a review. J Clin Psychiatry. 1982;43:151.

118 Glassman AH, Preud'homme XA. Review of the cardiovascular effects of heterocyclic antidepressants. J Clin Psychiatry. 1993;54(Suppl. 2):16.

119 Rosenstein DL et al. Seizures associated with antidepressants: a review. J Clin Psychiatry. 1993;54:289.

120 Frommer DA et al. Tricyclic antidepressant overdose: a review. JAMA. 1987;257:521.

121 Bigger JT Jr et al. Tricyclic antidepressant overdose: incidence of symptoms. JAMA. 1977;238:135.

122 Boehnert MT, Lovejoy FM. Value of

the QRS duration versus the serum drug level in predicting seizures and ventricular arrhythmias after an acute overdose of tricyclic antidepressants. N Engl J Med. 1985;313:474.

123 Wedin GP et al. Relative toxicity of cyclic antidepressants. Ann Emerg Med. 1986;15:7.

124 Nelson JC et al. Clinical implications of tricyclic kinetics. In: Dahl SG, Gram LF, eds. Clinical Pharmacology in Psychiatry. New York: Springer-Verlag; 1989:219.

125 Henry JA, Martin AJ. The risk-benefit assessment of antidepressant drugs. Med Toxicol. 1987;2:445.

126 Atkinson JH Jr et al. Prevalence of psychiatric disorders among men infected with human immunodeficiency virus infection: a controlled study. Arch Gen Psychiatry. 1988;45:859.

127 Tross S et al. Determinants of current psychiatric disorders in AIDS-spectrum patients. In: Abstracts, III International Conference on AIDS. Washington, DC: 1987.

128 Beckett A, Rutan JS. Treating persons with ARCH and AIDS in group psychotherapy. Int J Group Psychother. 1990;40:19.

129 Faulstich ME. Psychiatric aspects of AIDS. Am J Psychiatry. 1987;144:551.

130 Perry AW. Organic mental disorders caused by HIV: update on early diagnosis and treatment. Am J Psychiatry. 1990;147:696.

131 Revised Classification System for HIV infection. MMWR. 1992;41:1.

132 Busch KA. AIDS and Psychiatry. Curr Clin Briefs. 1987;8:3.

133 Ostrow D et al. Assessment and Management of the AIDS patient with neuropsychiatric disturbances. J Clin Psychiatry. 1988;49:14.

134 Schaerf FW et al. ECT for major depression in four patients infected with human immunodeficiency virus. Am J Psychiatry. 1989;146:782.

135 Diagnosis and treatment of depression in late life: the NIH consensus development conference statement. Psychopharmacol Bull. 1993;29:87.

136 Cummings JL. Dementia and depression: an evolving enigma. J Neuropsych. 1989;1:236.

137 Karniol IG et al. Comparative psychotropic effects of trazodone, imipramine, and diazepam in normal subjects. Curr Ther Res. 1976;20:337.

138 Janowsky D et al. Ventricular arrhythmias possibly aggravated by trazodone. Am J Psychiatry. 1983;140:796.

139 Blazer DG et al. Suicide in late life: review and commentary. J Am Geriatr Soc. 1986;34:519.

140 Henry JA et al. Acute trazodone poisoning: clinical signs and plasma concentrations. Psychopathology. 1984;17:77.

141 Van Zweiten P. Inhibition of the central hypotensive effect of clonidine by trazodone, a novel antidepressant. Pharmacology. 1977;15:331.

142 Kanter SJ et al. The cardiac effects of therapeutic plasma concentration of imipramine. Am J Psychiatry. 1978;135:534.

143 Guillibert E et al. A double-blind, multicentre study of paroxetine versus clomipramine in depressed elderly patients. Acta Psychiatr Scand. 1989;80(Suppl. 350):132.

144 Dunner DL et al. Two combined, multicenter double-blind studies of paroxetine and doxepin in geriatric patients with major depression. J Clin Psychiatry. 1992;53(Suppl. 2):57.

145 Wakelin JS. Fluvoxamine in the treatment of the older depressed patient: double-blind, placebo-controlled data. Int Clin Psychopharmacol. 1986;1:221.

146 Phanjoo AL et al. A double-blind comparative multicentre study of fluvoxamine and mianserin in the treatment of major depressive episode in elderly people. Acta Psychiatr Scand. 1991;83:476.

147 Devane CL. Pharmacokinetics of the selective serotonin reuptake inhibitors. J Clin Psychiatry. 1992;53(Suppl. 2):13.

148 Van Harten J. Clinical pharmacokinetics of selective serotonin reuptake inhibitors. Clin Pharmacokinet. 1993;24:203.

149 Grimsley SR, Jann MW. Paroxetine, sertraline, and fluvoxamine: new selective serotonin reuptake inhibitors. Clin Pharm. 1992;11:930.

150 Sommi RW et al. Fluoxetine: a serotonin-specific, second-generation antidepressant. Pharmacotherapy. 1987;7:1.

151 Preskorn SH. Recent Pharmacologic advances in antidepressant therapy for the elderly. Am J Med. 1993;94(Suppl. 5A):2s–12s.

152 Beasley CM et al. Fluoxetine: relationship among dose, response, adverse events, and plasma concentrations in the treatment of depression. Psychopharmacol Bull. 1990;26:18.

153 Nierenberg AA et al. Possible trazodone potentiation of fluoxetine: a case series. J Clin Psychiatry. 1992;53:83.

154 Lipinski JF et al. Fluoxetine-induced akathisia: clinical and theoretical implications. J Clin Psychiatry. 1989;50:339.

155 Hamilton MS, Opler LA. Akathisia, suicidality, and fluoxetine. J Clin Psychiatry. 1992;53:401.

156 Brymer C, Winograd CH. Fluoxetine in elderly patients: is there cause for concern? J Am Geriatr Soc. 1992;40:902.

157 Brosen K. Recent developments in hepatic drug oxidation: implications for clinical pharmacokinetics. Clin Pharmacokinet. 1990;18:220.

158 Schellens JHM et al. Differential effects of quinidine on the disposition of nifedipine, sparteine, and mephenytoin in humans. Clin Pharmacol Ther. 1991;50:520.

159 Otton SV et al. Inhibition by fluoxetine of cytochrome P450 2D6 activity. Clin Pharmacol Ther. 1993;53:401.

160 Bergstrom RF et al. Quantification and mechanism of the fluoxetine and tricyclic antidepressant interaction. Clin Pharmacol Ther. 1992;51:239.

161 Grimsley SR et al. Increased carbamazepine plasma concentrations after fluoxetine coadministration. Clin Pharmacol Ther. 1991;50:10.

162 Spina E et al. Carbamazepine coadministration with fluoxetine or fluvoxamine. Ther Drug Monit. 1993;15:247.

163 Ciraulo DA, Shader RI. Fluoxetine drug-drug interactions. II. J Clin Psychopharmacol. 1990;10:213.

164 Greenblatt DJ et al. Fluoxetine impairs clearance of alprazolam but not

of clonazepam. Clin Pharmacol Ther. 1992;52:479.

165 **Sternbach H.** The serotonin syndrome. Am J Psychiatry. 1991;148: 705.

166 **Fontaine R et al.** Lithium carbonate augmentation of desipramine and fluoxetine in refractory depression. Biol Psychiatry. 1991;29:946.

167 **Noveske FG et al.** Possible toxicity of combined fluoxetine and lithium. Am J Psychiatry. 1989;146:1515. Letter.

168 **Austin LS et al.** Toxicity resulting from lithium augmentation of antidepressant treatment in elderly patients. J Clin Psychiatry. 1990;51:344.

169 **West ED, Dally PJ.** Effect of iproniazid in depressive syndromes. Br Med J. 1959;1:1491.

170 **Klein DF, Davis J.** Diagnosis and Drug Treatment of Psychiatric Disorders. 1st ed. Baltimore: Williams & Wilkins; 1968.

171 **Paykel ES et al.** Response to phenelzine and amitriptyline in sub-types of outpatient depression. Arch Gen Psychiatry. 1982;39:1041.

172 **Stewart JW et al.** Atypical depression: a valid clinical entity? Psychiatr Clin North Am. 1993;16:479.

173 **Zisook S.** A clinical overview of monoamine oxidase inhibitors. Psychosomatics. 1985;26:240.

174 **Ravaris CL et al.** A multiple-dose, controlled study of phenelzine in depression—anxiety states. Arch Gen Psychiatry. 1976;33:347.

175 **Ravaris CL et al.** Phenelzine and amitriptyline in the treatment of depression: a comparison of present and past studies. Arch Gen Psychiatry. 1980;37: 1075.

176 **Robinson DS et al.** The monoamine oxidase inhibitor, phenelzine in the treatment of depressive-anxiety. Arch Gen Psychiatry. 1973;29:407.

177 **Quitkin FM et al.** Phenelzine and imipramine in mood reactive depressives: further delineation of the syndrome of atypical depression. Arch Gen Psychiatry. 1989;46:787.

178 **Moreines E, Gold MS.** MAO inhibitors: predicting response/maximizing efficacy. In: Gold MS et al., eds. Advances in Psychopharmacology and Improving Treatment Response. Boca Raton: CRC Press, Inc; 1984:157.

179 **Robinson DS et al.** Phenelzine and amitriptyline in the treatment of depression. Arch Gen Psychiatry. 1978; 35:629.

180 **Rabkin JG et al.** Adverse reactions to monoamine oxidase inhibitors. Part II. Treatment correlates and clinical management. J Clin Psychopharmacol. 1985;5:2.

181 **Murphy DL et al.** Monoamine oxidase-inhibiting antidepressants: a clinical update. Psychiatr Clin North Am. 1984;7:549.

182 **Kronig MH et al.** Blood pressure effects of phenelzine. J Clin Psychopharmacol. 1983;3:307.

183 **Salzman C.** Clinical guidelines for the use of antidepressant drugs in geriatric patients. J Clin Psychiatry. 1985;46:38.

184 **Mallinger AG et al.** Pharmacokinetics of tranylcypromine in patients who are depressed: relationship to cardiovascular effects. Clin Pharmacol Ther. 1986;40:444.

185 **Pollack MH, Rosenbaum JF.** Management of antidepressant-induced side effects: a practical guide for the clinician. J Clin Psychiatry. 1987;48:3.

186 **Mitchell JE, Popkin MK.** Antidepressant drug therapy and sexual dysfunction in men: a review. J Clin Psychopharmacol. 1983;3:76.

187 **Stewart JW et al.** Phenelzine-induced pyridoxine deficiency. J Clin Psychopharmacol. 1984;4:225.

188 **Haefely W et al.** Biochemistry and pharmacology of moclobemide, a prototype RIMA. Psychopharmacology. 1992;106:S6.

189 **Davidson J et al.** Practical aspects of MAO inhibitor therapy. J Clin Psychiatry. 1984;45:81.

190 **Sheehan DV et al.** Monoamine oxidase inhibitors: prescription and patient management. Int J Psychiatry Med. 1980;10:99.

191 **Blackwell B et al.** Hypertensive interactions between monoamine oxidase inhibitors and foodstuffs. Br J Psychiatry. 1967;113:349.

192 **Shulman KI et al.** Dietary restriction, tyramine, and the use of monoamine oxidase inhibitors. J Clin Psychopharmacol. 1989;9:397.

193 **Hansten PD, Horn JR.** Drug Interactions & Updates Quarterly. Vancouver, WA: Applied Therapeutics, Inc.; 1995.

194 **Spiker DG et al.** The pharmacological treatment of delusional depression. Am J Psychiatry. 1985;142:430.

195 **Glassman AH, Roose SP.** Delusional depression. Arch Gen Psychiatry. 1981;38:424.

196 **Chan CH et al.** Response of psychotic and nonpsychotic depressed patients to tricyclic antidepressants. J Clin Psychiatry. 1987;48:197.

197 **Kantor SJ, Glassman AH.** Delusional depression: natural history and response to treatment. Br J Psychiatry. 1977;131:351.

198 **Avery D, Winokur G.** The efficacy of electroconvulsive therapy and antidepressants in depression. Biol Psychiatry. 1977;12:507.

199 **Anton RF Jr et al.** Amoxapine versus amitriptyline combined with perphenazine in the treatment of psychotic depression. Am J Psychiatry. 1990;147: 1203.

200 **Ayd F.** Amoxapine side effects: an update. Int Drug Ther Newsl. 1984;19:21.

201 **Cooper DJ et al.** The effects of amoxapine and imipramine on serum prolactin levels. Arch Intern Med. 1981;141: 1023.

202 **Madakasira S.** Amoxapine-induced neuroleptic malignant syndrome. Drug Intell Clin Pharm. 1989;23:50.

203 **Greden JF.** Antidepressant maintenance medications: when to discontinue and how to stop. J Clin Psychiatry. 1993;54(Suppl. 8):39.

204 **Thase ME.** Relapse and recurrence in unipolar major depression: short-term and long-term approaches. J Clin Psychiatry. 1990;51(Suppl. 6):51.

205 **Roy-Byrne P et al.** The longitudinal course of recurrent affective illness: life chart data from research patients at the NIMH. Acta Psychiatr Scand. 1985;71(Suppl. 317):5.

206 **Nemeroff CB.** Augmentation regimens for depression. J Clin Psychiatry. 1991;52(Suppl. 5):21.

207 **Guscott R, Grof P.** The clinical meaning of refractory depression: a review for the clinician. Am J Psychiatry. 1991;148:695.

208 **Quitkin FM et al.** Duration of antidepressant drug treatment: what is an adequate trial? Arch Gen Psychiatry. 1984;41:238.

209 **Hale SH.** New antidepressants: use in high-risk patients. J Clin Psychiatry. 1993;54(Suppl. 8):61.

210 **Gewirtz G et al.** Occult thyroid dysfunction in patients with refractory depression. Am J Psychiatry. 1988;145: 1012.

211 **MacEwan GW, Remick RA.** Treatment resistant depression: a clinical perspective. Can J Psychiatry. 1988;33: 788.

212 **Shaw DM.** The practical management of affective disorders. Br J Psychiatry. 1977;130:432.

213 **Kasper S et al.** Comparative efficacy of antidepressants. Drugs. 1992;43 (Suppl. 2):11.

214 **Altamura AC et al.** Efficacy and tolerability of fluoxetine in the elderly: a double-blind study versus amitriptyline. Int Clin Psychopharmacol. 1989; 4 (Suppl. 1):103.

215 **White K, Simpson G.** Combined MAOI-tricyclic antidepressant treatment: a reevaluation. J Clin Psychopharmacol. 1981;1:264.

216 **Feighner JP et al.** Adverse consequences of fluoxetine-MAOI combination therapy. J Clin Psychiatry. 1990; 51:222.

217 **Davidson J et al.** A comparison of electroconvulsive therapy and combined phenelzine-amitriptyline in refractory depression. Arch Gen Psychiatry. 1978;35:639.

218 **Feighner JP et al.** Combined MAOI, TCA, and direct stimulant therapy of treatment-resistant depression. J Clin Psychiatry. 1985;46:206.

219 **Fawcett J et al.** CNS stimulant potentiation of monoamine oxidase inhibitors in treatment-refractory depression. J Clin Psychopharmacol. 1991;11:127.

220 **Hopkinson G, Kenny F.** Treatment with reserpine of patients resistant to tricyclic antidepressants. Psychiatr Clin. 1975;8:109.

221 **Akiskal HS.** A proposed clinical approach to chronic and resistant depressions: Evaluation and treatment. J Clin Psychiatry. 1985;46:32.

222 **Gerner RH.** Systematic treatment approach to depression and treatment-resistant depression. Psychiatr Ann. 1983;13:40.

223 **Kramlinger KG, Post RM.** The addition of lithium to carbamazepine: Antidepressant efficacy in treatment-resistant depression. Arch Gen Psychiatry. 1989;46:794.

224 **de Montigny C.** Lithium induces rapid relief of depression in tricyclic antidepressant drug nonresponders. Br J Psychiatry. 1981;138:252.

225 **de Montigny C et al.** Lithium carbonate addition in tricyclic antidepressant-resistant unipolar depression. Arch Gen Psychiatry. 1983;40:1327.

226 **Charney DS et al.** Desipramine-yohimbine combination treatment of refractory depression. Arch Gen Psychiatry. 1986;43:1155.

227 **Thase ME et al.** Treatment of imipramine-resistant recurrent depression: II. An open clinical trial of lithium augmentation. J Clin Psychiatry. 1989;50: 413.

228 **Pope HG et al.** Possible synergism between fluoxetine and lithium in refractory depression. Am J Psychiatry. 1988;145:1292.

229 **Howland RH.** Lithium augmentation of fluoxetine in the treatment of OCD and major depression: a case report. Can J Psychiatry. 1991;36:154.

230 **Price LH et al.** Efficacy of lithium-tranylcypromine treatment in refractory depression. Am J Psychiatry. 1985;142:619.

231 **Nierenberg AA et al.** After lithium augmentation: a retrospective follow-up of patients with antidepressant-refractory depression. J Affective Disord. 1990;18:167.

232 **Rybakowski J, Matkowski K.** Adding lithium to antidepressant therapy: factors related to therapeutic potentiation. Eur Neuropsychopharmacol. 1992;2: 161.

233 **Gitlin MJ et al.** Failure of T3 to potentiate tricyclic antidepressant response. J Affective Disord. 1987;13: 267.

234 **Bilezikian JP, Loeb JN.** The influence of hyperthyroidism and hypothyroidism on alpha- and beta-adrenergic receptor systems and adrenergic responsiveness. Endocr Rev. 1983;4:378.

235 **Nemeroff CB et al.** Antithyroid antibodies in depressed patients. Am J Psychiatry. 1985;142:840.

236 **Prange AJ et al.** Enhancement of imipramine antidepressant activity by thyroid hormone. Am J Psychiatry. 1969;126:457.

237 **Wilson IC et al.** Thyroid hormone enhancement of imipramine in non-retarded depression. N Engl J Med. 1970; 282:1063.

238 **Goodwin FK et al.** L-triiodothyronine converts tricyclic antidepressant nonresponders to responders. Am J Psychiatry. 1982;139:37.

239 **Stein D, Avni J.** Thyroid hormones in the treatment of affective disorders. Acta Psychiatr Scand. 1988;77:623.

240 **Joffe RT, Singer W.** A comparison of triiodothyronine and thyroxine in the potentiation of tricyclic antidepressants. Psychiatry Res. 1990;32:241.

241 **Joffe RT et al.** A placebo-controlled comparison of lithium and triiodothyronine augmentation of tricyclic antidepressants in unipolar refractory depression. Arch Gen Psychiatry. 1993; 50:387.

242 **Crowe R.** Electroconvulsive therapy—a current perspective. N Engl J Med. 1984;311:163.

243 **Monroe RR Jr.** Maintenance electroconvulsive therapy. Psychiatr Clin N Am. 1991;14:947.

244 **Gross CC, M.D.**, Clinical Psychopharmacology Unit, Massachussetts General Hospital. Personal communication.

245 **Schoonover SC.** Depression. In: Bassuk EL et al., eds. The Practitioner's Guide to Psychoactive Drugs. 2nd ed. New York: Plenum Medical Book Co.; 1983:19.

246 **Hamilton M.** Development of a rating scale of primary depressive illness. Br J Soc Clin Psychol. 1967;2:278.

247 **Edwards JG et al.** Effect of paroxetine

on the electrocardiogram. Psychopharmacology (Berlin). 1989;97(1):96–8.

248 **De La Fuente JM.** Carbamazepine-induced low plasma levels of tricyclic antidepressants. J Clin Psychopharmacol. 1991;12:67.

249 **Razavi D, Mendlewicz J.** Tricyclic antidepressant plasma levels: the state of the art and clinical prospects. Neuropsychobiology. 1982;8:73–85.

250 **Feighner JP.** The role of venlafaxine in rational antidepressant therapy. J Clin Psychiatry. 1994;55(9 Suppl A): 62–8.

251 **Anon.** Serzone product labeling information. Bristol-Meyers Squibb Company, Princeton, NJ, 1995.

252 **Zajecka JM et al.** Coexisting major depression and obsessive-compulsive disorder treated with venlafaxine. J Clin Psychopharmacol. 1990;10:152–53.

253 **Cantu TG et al.** Focus on venlafaxine. A new option for the treatment of depression. Hosp Formul. 1994;29:25–33.

254 **Khan A et at.** Venlafaxine in depressed outpatients. Psychopharmacol Bull. 1991;27:141–44.

255 **Schweizer E et al.** Placebo-controlled trial of venlafaxine for the treatment of major depression. J Clin Psychopharmacol. 1991;11:233–36.

256 **Schweizer E et al.** Comparison of venlafaxine and imipramine in the acute treatment of major depression in outpatients. J Clin Psychiatry. 1994;55: 104–8.

257 **Anon.** Nefazodone for depression. Med Lett Drugs Ther. 1995;37:33.

Mood Disorders II: Bipolar Affective Disorders

Raymond C Love
Dale R Grothe

Classification 77-1
Epidemiology 77-1
Clinical Signs and Symptoms (Also see Table 77.1) 77-1
Course of Illness 77-2
Complications of Bipolar Illness 77-2
Clinical Assessment 77-2
Clinical Presentation and Diagnosis 77-2
Precipitating Factors (Also see Table 77.2) 77-3
Treatment of Acute Mania 77-4
Lithium 77-4
Prelithium work-up (Also see Table 77.3) 77-4
Antipsychotics and lithium 77-4
Side effects (Also see Table 77.4) 77-5
Drug interactions (Also see Table 77.5) 77-5
Patient education 77-6
Maintenance therapy 77-6
Psychotherapy 77-7
Hypothyroidism 77-7
Lithium toxicity 77-7
Lithium in pregnancy 77-8
Lithium refractoriness 77-8
Carbamazepine and valproate 77-9
Alternative therapies 77-9

Bipolar mood disorder is a chronic and progressive illness which produces significant morbidity and mortality for those afflicted. Based upon a 1993 report prepared by the National Institute of Mental Health Advisory Council on the Cost and Treatment of Severe Mental Illness, bipolar patients typically spend one-fourth of their adult lives in the hospital and one-half of their lives disabled.[1]

Classification

Mood disorders are diagnosed by using criteria established in the Diagnostic and Statistical Manual of Mental Disorders, fourth edition (DSM-IV).[2] The clinician first examines and characterizes discreet episodes of mood disturbances which the patient has experienced. These are determined to be *major depressive episodes*, *manic episodes* (episodes of elevated mood), *mixed episodes* (with features of both depression and mania), or *hypomanic episodes*. Hypomanic episodes are characterized as states of elevated mood which are less severe than mania and which are not severe enough to impair functioning, complicate a medical condition, or result in psychotic features.[2] A history of a manic, mixed, or hypomanic episode precludes the diagnosis of major depressive disorder.

Once the nature of past and current discreet episodes has been determined, an individual can be diagnosed as having a mood disorder. An individual who has experienced one or more episodes of depression, without past episodes of mania, is diagnosed as having a major depressive disorder. An individual who has experienced one or more manic or mixed (mania and depression) episodes is diagnosed as having *Bipolar I Disorder*. An individual who has experienced one or more episodes of both hypomania and depression (without a history of manic or mixed episodes) is diagnosed as having *Bipolar II Disorder*.[2]

Bipolar disorder also is known as manic-depressive disease, a term originally coined by Kraepelin.[3] The diagnosis of a cyclothymic disorder is used for an individual who has experienced at least two years of cycling mood characterized by numerous periods with hypomanic symptoms and separate periods with depressive symptoms which do not meet the criteria for a major depressive episode. Bipolar disorder, not otherwise specified refers to disorders with features of mania or hypomania which do not meet the criteria for a specific bipolar disorder.[2]

The DSM-IV also uses a series of descriptors called "specifiers" to further characterize the course of illness and the most recent type of episode experienced by the individual. Recent episodes are first classified as manic, mixed, or major depressive episode. They may be described further with regards to severity (mild, moderate, severe); the presence of psychotic features (in partial or full remission); with or without catatonic features; or with onset during the postpartum period. Other specifiers convey information regarding the pattern of illness. For example, some individuals experience major depressive episodes at a characteristic time of the year (usually the winter) or switch from depression to mania during a particular season. The specifier "with seasonal pattern" only applies to the pattern of major depressive episodes. Other specifiers describe whether full recovery between episodes (i.e., with or without full interepisode recovery) occurs and whether individuals experience rapid cycling ($\geq$4 episodes/year).[2]

Epidemiology

According to the National Institute of Mental Health (NIMH) Epidemiological Catchment Area study,[4,5] the prevalence rate for bipolar disorder is approximately 1.2% of the adult population. While there are no apparent gender differences in the occurrence of bipolar disorder, there are differences in presentation. Male bipolar patients have more manic episodes than female bipolar patients, and female bipolar patients have more depressive episodes than male bipolar patients.[6,7] This is in marked contrast to unipolar disorder (major depression) where the gender ratios of females to males are about 2:1.[5]

The familial nature of bipolar disorder has been well established. The concordance rate among monozygotic twin probands with bipolar disorder is approximately 75%. This contrasts with a rate of 27% in unipolar depression.[5]

Clinical Signs and Symptoms

A typical manic episode usually begins with a change in sleep patterns along with euphoria. Target symptoms typically include increased talkativeness, staying awake all night, and bursts of energy during which projects are begun but rarely completed. Mania is characterized frequently by thought disturbances. Patients may exhibit "flight of ideas," rapid speech which switches among multiple ideas or topics. They often may demonstrate delusions of grandeur. The behavior of manic patients is characterized as being intrusive, loud, intense, irritable, suspicious, and challenging. They frequently exercise poor judgment. They may spend large sums of money in business deals which ultimately fail, become sexually promiscuous, take excessive risks, or fail to obey laws.

These symptoms usually develop gradually over several days to more than a week in three stages. *Stage I* is characterized by euphoria, labile affect, grandiosity, overconfidence, racing thoughts, increased psychomotor activity, and an increase in the rate and amount of speech. This stage corresponds to an episode of hypomania. *Stage II* features increasing irritability, dysphoria, hostility, anger, delusions, and cognitive disorganization. Many patients progress no further than this stage. Others may proceed to stage III, in which the manic episode progresses to an undifferentiated psychotic state. Individuals in this *stage III* experience terror and panic. Their behavior is bizarre and psychomotor activity is frenzied. They may experience hallucinations. They progress from disorganized thought patterns to incoherence and disorientation. Just as the manic episode gradually builds, it declines in a gradual manner. Psychotic symptoms usually resolve first, while irritability, paranoia, and excessive behavior continue. Gradually, remaining symptoms like hyperverbosity, seductiveness, and dysphoria decrease.[158]

Course of Illness

In general, the first attack of bipolar disorder begins before the age of 33 and begins as a manic episode.[8] While the bipolar disorder can occur in either adolescence or in later life, it is unusual to find adult bipolar patients with a history of onset occurring before the age of 15.[9] The median age of onset is approximately 30 years of age with a significant decrease in first onset after 50 years of age.[4,10]

An untreated episode of bipolar disorder may last for several months. Single episode attacks are known to occur but are rare. Most individuals with this disorder have multiple episodes of mania, hypomania, or depression separated by periods of euthymia throughout the course of their lives. In a 25-year follow-up study of 66 bipolar patients, only 8% had a single episode, while the great majority had numerous attacks; several had ≥20 in their lifetimes.[8]

The course of illness for a given individual is characterized by episode length, length of euthymic intervals, frequency of relapse, severity of episode, and predominant syndrome (mania, hypomania, or depression). These factors do not remain fixed throughout an individual's illness. For instance, individuals may experience episodes of dysphoria and depression before ever experiencing hypomania or mania. Often the euthymic interval and cycle length decreases with additional episodes. Bipolar individuals can develop a course of alternating manic and depressive episodes without intervening euthymic episodes.

One group of individuals who experience shorter cycle lengths and suffer from four or more episodes of depression, hypomania, or mania in a year are identified as "rapid cyclers."[11] Rapid cyclers account for 5% to 15% of bipolar individuals[2] and women comprise 80% to 95% of patients with rapid cycling bipolar disorder.[11,12] Individuals with rapid cycling bipolar disorder frequently are refractory to conventional treatment and suffer significant morbidity and mortality due to their rapid changes in mood. They may have little or no euthymic period between manic and depressive episodes. This can have drastic family, social, and occupational consequences. The literature indicates that rapid cycling patients may be more likely than other bipolar patients to have

hypothyroidism, and that thyroid supplementation may exert a beneficial effect in this group.[13,14]

Complications of Bipolar Illness

Studies of patients with bipolar illness have demonstrated excess mortality due to both natural and unnatural causes. The excess natural mortality has been due largely to cardiovascular causes.[15] Suicide and excessive risk-taking behaviors during manic or hypomanic episodes also account for a high mortality rate in this group. Bipolar patients are especially prone to substance abuse. In one study, a 61% incidence of substance abuse and alcoholism was noted in bipolar patients.[16]

Clinical Assessment

Clinical Presentation and Diagnosis

1. H.M., a 27-year-old male, is accompanied to the clinic by his wife, A.M. A.M. had called the clinic before bringing in H.M. and reported much of the following information.

A.M. says that H.M. was doing well until ≈3 weeks ago when his niece was killed in an automobile accident. After the funeral, H.M. borrowed some "nerve pills" from his cousin. Since then, he has been acting increasingly "wild." He has been staying up later and later at night. He frequently bursts into the bedroom at 2 or 3 a.m. and loudly awakens his wife. Sometimes he presents her with expensive gifts which they cannot afford. Frequently he jumps on the bed and starts singing her love songs in a loud voice. A.M. notes that H.M. then almost always demands sex. After sex, he sleeps for a few hours and then loudly gets up and leaves the house.

A.M. also reports that H.M. recently has experienced problems at work. Over the last several weeks, H.M., a snack delivery truck driver, was noted to be loading his truck in a rapid and reckless manner. His boss received several reports that he was driving in an unsafe manner and at high speed. Store owners called to complain that he was giving away free cases of snacks to customers in the stores he called upon. He often did not complete his deliveries to the stores at the end of his route.

Last week, when A.M. told him that his boss had called to express concern over his behavior, H.M. told her he was quitting his job. He wrote an illegible resignation note which was at least 10 pages long. He called an overnight air delivery service to deliver the note to his employer, whose address is located only 3 miles from his home, then left before the driver arrived to pick it up. He showed up again several hours later driving a brand new foreign car and wearing an expensive new suit, red cowboy boots, and a bright green hat with a large feather. He told A.M. that he had a new job which was going to make him a millionaire.

Last night, she found a large sum of money in his pants pocket when emptying the clothes hamper. He did not come home at all, but he called her at 4 a.m. to tell her to pack for Dallas where he was going to become the new head coach of the Dallas Cowboys.

Upon arriving at the clinic, H.M. insists, "I don't need no doc. I am supercalifragilistic!" He then bursts into song. He is dressed flamboyantly but needs a shave and shower. He gives the examiner (a stranger) a bear hug. He has trouble sitting still, listening, or allowing others to talk. His speech is pressured and loud; he often fails to complete sentences or communicate entire ideas. He is rhyming and punning. His mood obviously is elevated. He becomes increasingly irritable throughout the examination. He insists he must get to Texas to sing the national anthem at a football game before the CIA can stop him. He then breaks down in tears. Within moments he is again smiling and talking of money-making schemes. He is oriented to person and place but thinks it is tomorrow. Intelligence seems average. When asked to interpret a proverb,

H.M. becomes angry, throws a chair across the room, and yells, "Enough of this bull! Air Force One is waiting for me!" He then storms out of the office. How is H.M.'s presentation consistent with the diagnosis of a manic episode?

The hallmarks of a manic episode are changes in mood, behavior, and thought (see Table 77.1).[17] H.M. first demonstrates an elevated mood. He is exuberant and notes how great he feels. However, manic patients often demonstrate lability in their mood. They may become irritable and easily frustrated, especially when challenged. H.M. becomes irritable and resentful when questioned by the examiner. His quick displays of sadness and anger further demonstrate the volatility of his mood.

H.M. displays behaviors typical of a manic patient. He demonstrates a reduced need for sleep, reckless behavior, and overactivity. H.M.'s speech is typical of that of a manic patient. It is pressured, loud, and full of rhymes and puns. The speech of manics may skip from topic to topic in a "flight of ideas." He sings to express his emotion. The behavior of manics often is characterized as being excessive and expansive. H.M. dresses flamboyantly, hugs his examiner, writes an unnecessarily lengthy letter of resignation, seeks an overnight courier service for local delivery, presents his wife with lavish gifts, and distributes merchandise to strangers.

Manic patients often are delusional. The delusions often are of a grandiose nature and deal with inflated abilities, self-importance, wealth, or special missions in life. H.M. makes grandiose comments about his money-making schemes, his singing ability, his

Table 77.1	DSM-IV Criteria for a Manic Episode[a,b,2]

1) A distinct period of abnormally and persistently elevated, expansive or irritable mood, lasting at least 1 week (or of any duration if hospitalization is necessary)

2) During the period of mood disturbance, ≥3 of the following symptoms have persisted (4 if the mood is only irritable) and have been present to a significant degree:

- Inflated self-esteem or grandiosity
- Decreased need for sleep (e.g., feels rested after only 3 hours of sleep)
- More talkative than usual or pressure to keep talking
- Flight of ideas or subjective experience that thoughts are racing
- Distractibility (i.e., attention too easily drawn to unimportant or irrelevant external stimuli)
- Increase in goal-directed activity (either social, at work or at school, or sexually) or psychomotor agitation
- Excessive involvement in pleasurable activities which have a high potential for painful consequences (e.g., the person engages in unrestrained buying sprees, sexual indiscretions, or foolish business investing)

3) The symptoms do not meet the criteria for a Mixed Episode

4) The mood disturbance is sufficiently severe to cause marked impairment in occupational functioning or in usual social activities or relationships with others, or to necessitate hospitalization to prevent harm to self or others, or there are psychotic features

5) The symptoms are not due to the direct physiological effects of a substance (e.g., a drug of abuse, a medication, or other treatment) or a general medical condition (e.g., hyperthyroidism)

[a] DSM-IV = The Diagnostic and Statistical Manual of Mental Disorders, Fourth Edition.
[b] A "Manic Syndrome" is defined as including criteria 1, 2, and 3. A "Hypomanic Syndrome" is defined as including criteria 1 and 2, but not 3 (i.e., no marked impairment). Manic-like episodes that are clearly caused by somatic antidepressant treatment (e.g., medication, electroconvulsive therapy, light therapy) should not count towards a diagnosis of Bipolar I Disorder.

Table 77.2	Drugs Reported to Induce Mania	
Antidepressants		**Stimulants**
Monoamine oxidase inhibitors[165]		Cocaine[164]
Tricyclic antidepressants[124–126]		Methylphenidate[169]
Bupropion[127,128]		
Fluoxetine[128–130]		**Endocrine**
Fluvoxamine[132,133]		Corticosteroids[171]
Sertraline[134]		Thyroid[164]
		Androgens[170]
Anxiolytics/Hypnotics		
Buspirone[135,136]		**Miscellaneous**
Alprazolam[137,138]		Levodopa[164]
Triazolam[139]		Amantadine[173]
		Cimetidine[172]
		Tolmetin[174]
		Folate[175]

position as the coach of a professional football team, and his intended use of the presidential plane. Manic patients also may have delusions of a persecutory nature such as H.M.'s fear that the CIA is going to stop him.

Manic patients frequently are disorganized and do not complete tasks. They tend to skip from idea to idea and scheme to scheme. H.M. neglects his hygiene, fails to complete his deliveries, and neglects sending out his resignation letter. His speech reflects this disorganization.

2. What differentiates H.M.'s signs and symptoms from those of schizophrenia?

Many of H.M.'s signs and symptoms are consistent with schizophrenia. The distinction between a manic episode and a schizophrenic episode is difficult. Most often mania is differentiated from schizophrenia based upon clinical course, premorbid history, and previous episodes. H.M. apparently has functioned well for most of his life. He has been able to sustain a relationship (i.e., his marriage) and hold down a job. Most importantly, he has not displayed psychotic symptoms for more than a month or had a sustained (6-month) period in which he displayed psychiatric symptoms and experienced social or occupational dysfunction as required for a diagnosis of schizophrenia.[160,161]

Precipitating Factors

3. What factors make H.M. vulnerable to the occurrence of a manic episode at this time?

The median age of onset for bipolar disorder is 29 years of age in men and 34.5 years of age in women.[17] Thus, H.M. is at the age where his disorder would be likely to first manifest itself. In addition, manic episodes frequently are precipitated by various psychosocial stressors.[2,18] The death of H.M.'s niece may have served as a predisposing factor for the development of a manic episode.

A variety of medications and clinical states can induce or precipitate manic episodes (see Table 77.2). The most frequent drug causes of mania involve medications which affect monoamine neurotransmitters[19] such as antidepressants and stimulants. Corticosteroids, anabolic steroids, isoniazid, levodopa, caffeine, and over-the-counter (OTC) stimulants can induce or aggravate mania.[20] Sleep loss also can be a significant cause of mania.[21] A reduction in sleep following the death of his niece could have helped contribute to the development of H.M.'s manic episode.

4. If the "nerve pills" borrowed by H.M. were antidepressants, could they have contributed to the development of his manic episode?

While it is not known whether an increase in norepinephrine activity actually causes manic episodes, enhanced adrenergic activity frequently is associated with manic episodes.[126] Monoamine oxidase inhibitors were one of the first antidepressant classes to be studied as precipitants of mania and "switches" from depression to mania. While tricyclic antidepressants are associated with a switch into mania 7 to 28 days after their initiation, this could reflect an increase in the speed of the depression-mania cycle rather than a push into mania.[161] The effects of the newer selective serotonin reuptake inhibitor (SSRI) antidepressants on bipolar disorder are much less clear. While their lack of associated norepinephrine activity might indicate that they are safe, there are reports of SSRI antidepressants inducing mania.[128–130,133] Thus, antidepressant agents may have helped precipitate a manic episode in H.M. or switched H.M. into an episode of mania from a pre-existing state of depression or normal mood.

Treatment of Acute Mania

5. Why does H.M. require treatment?

Manic episodes have a number of severe complications. Left untreated, severe mania can result in confusion, fever, exhaustion, and even death.[22] The impairment in judgment, the excesses, and the risk-taking which occur during manic episodes may devastate relationships, careers, and finances and lead to physical harm and loss of life. Manic individuals may engage in illegal activities or behave in a manner which results in a violation of the law. H.M. drives recklessly. He may have lost his job. He spends excessive amounts of money on gifts, clothing, and an automobile. He has plans to participate in a variety of money-making schemes. He has acquired a great deal of cash suddenly, perhaps from withdrawing all of his family's savings or from some type of illegal enterprise.

Manic patients also may engage in risky sexual encounters, leading to infection with sexually transmitted diseases or human immunodeficiency virus. Abuse of alcohol and drugs is frequent among these patients. Irritability, such as that demonstrated by H.M., can lead to episodes of violence, resulting in potential harm to the patient or to others.

Lithium

6. What is the appropriate treatment for H.M.'s acute manic episode?

A variety of agents are available for the treatment of H.M.'s mania. Lithium, valproic acid, and carbamazepine all have been used as specific antimanic agents. If H.M. had a history of rapid cycling or dysphoric bipolar disorder or had a contraindication to the use of lithium, valproic acid or carbamazepine would be preferred.[23–29] However, in a case of typical mania like H.M. is experiencing, there is little rationale for the choice of one of these agents over another.[20] Due to its long track record of efficacy, lithium remains the most widely used drug for the management of bipolar patients.[28] While one could employ any of the various strategies for calculating lithium dosage requirements,[30] it is simpler to begin H.M. at a dose of 300 mg three times a day. This is an average starting dose for a healthy adult patient. Since lithium does not work immediately, H.M.'s level then can be adjusted with the use of twice-weekly serum levels. Since patients experiencing an acute manic episode require higher lithium levels than those receiving maintenance lithium therapy, the goal for the acute management of H.M. is a serum level between 0.7 and 1.2 mEq/L.[20] As H.M. recovers and enters a maintenance phase of treatment, both his lithium dose and target lithium levels will require re-evaluation.

Lithium has a slow onset of action, taking as long as one to two weeks to fully exert its therapeutic effects.[27,31] Therefore, it is appropriate to use an adjunctive medication to help reduce H.M.'s acute symptoms. Both benzodiazepines and antipsychotics have been used in this manner.[20,31,32] Antipsychotics may be warranted as adjunctive therapy in acute mania when patients have halluci-

nations or mood incongruent delusions.[20,22,23,31,33] Either benzodiazepines or antipsychotics are useful in treating agitation, hyperactivity, and sleep disorders. Antipsychotics have the disadvantage of causing extrapyramidal side effects, neuroleptic malignant syndrome, tardive dyskinesia, and anticholinergic side effects. On a longer-term basis, individuals with affective disorders like bipolar disorder who receive antipsychotics may be at a higher risk for the development of tardive dyskinesia.[131] Because of these potential toxic effects, benzodiazepines generally are preferable to antipsychotics in the acute treatment of mania. The main concerns regarding benzodiazepines are sedation and potential for abuse and/or addiction. Since adjunctive therapy is administered in most cases on an inpatient basis for a short period of time, abuse and addiction are unlikely to be important considerations.

H.M. does not demonstrate hallucinations and his delusions are congruent with his mood. He is not extremely agitated or hyperactive. Therefore, H.M. should be started on lorazepam 2 mg with repeat doses being administered every two to eight hours as needed to relieve his symptoms of insomnia, impulsivity, and restlessness.[20,32] Lorazepam has the added advantage of being available as an intramuscular preparation should H.M.'s symptoms escalate and require rapid sedation. The lorazepam should be tapered as H.M. begins to respond to lithium. If H.M. requires frequent and/or large doses of lorazepam, it is advisable to taper the benzodiazepine to avoid rebound agitation or irritability in the individual who is still in stage I or II of mania.

In addition to being used as adjuncts to lithium, benzodiazepines have been used to allow reductions in the dose of concomitantly administered antipsychotic agents[32,34] and as the primary agent for treatment of acute manic episodes.[35–37] While there is little doubt that they can reduce the dosage of antipsychotic required to calm a manic patient, there is some controversy as to whether benzodiazepines (clonazepam or lorazepam) are effective as the sole mode of therapy in a substantial portion of manic patients.[23]

7. Prelithium Work-Up. What laboratory tests are required before initiating lithium therapy for H.M.?

Lithium can affect numerous organ systems. Therefore, it is necessary to establish baseline laboratory values before initiating lithium. These will serve to determine whether future abnormal values are lithium related. Furthermore, various physiologic states may affect lithium's excretion or predispose one to lithium toxicity. In these cases, baseline laboratory tests are useful in determining the presence of factors which contraindicate lithium or cause an adjustment in dosage. As a young, healthy male, H.M.'s prescreening laboratory battery should include electrolytes, blood urea nitrogen, creatinine, urine specific gravity, thyroid-stimulating hormone (TSH), thyroxine (T_4), and a white blood cell count (see Table 77.3).

8. Antipsychotics and Lithium. H.M. starts experiencing hallucinations and increasing paranoia. Why should antipsychotics be added to the regular dose of lithium which H.M. is receiving?

The appearance of hallucinations is an indication for the addition of antipsychotic medications to H.M.'s regimen. Complications resulting from the combined use of antipsychotics and lithium have been reported.[50,51] These complications usually have included severe neuromuscular symptoms, hyperthermia, and alterations in level of consciousness. More systematic reviews of manic patients treated with lithium and antipsychotics revealed no increase in toxicity when the lithium-antipsychotic combination was compared to lithium therapy alone.[52,53] Thus, the addition to H.M.'s regimen of haloperidol (or another antipsychotic in equivalent doses) in doses of 10 to 20 mg/day should be sufficient to help control his hallucinations and delusions.[20,31,34,54]

Table 77.3	Prelithium Workup
Baseline Determination[a,38,39,40]	**Rationale**
SrCr, BUN	Lithium is excreted renally
Urine specific gravity	Lithium may cause polyuria
Electrolytes	Hyponatremia and dehydration lead to ↑ renal reabsorption of lithium and subsequent lithium toxicity; hypokalemia may ↑ the risk of lithium-induced cardiac toxicity
ECG[b,41,42]	Lithium may worsen severe cardiac disease
CBC with differential	Lithium may cause a 15%–45% ↑ in the numbers of all WBC lines except basophils; lithium also may cause an ↑ in platelet counts [43,44]
T_4, TSH	Lithium may induce hypothyroidism[45]
Glucose	Lithium may induce weight gain and complicate the presentation of diabetes mellitus[46]
Weight	Lithium may induce weight gain[47]
Lithium level	Manic patients may at times be poor historians
Pregnancy test	Lithium is a potential teratogen[48,49]

[a] BUN = Blood urea nitrogen; CBC = Complete blood count; ECG = Electrocardiograph; SrCr = Serum creatinine; TSH= Thyroid-stimulating hormone; WBC = White blood cell.
[b] In those patients with a history or at risk for cardiac disease.

9. How long should H.M. be maintained on antipsychotics along with the lithium?

H.M. should continue to receive antipsychotics only until the mania starts to resolve.[26,55] As the manic symptoms start to subside, H.M. should experience a return towards his baseline behavior, a more normal sleep pattern, less irritability and extremes of mood, and a reduction in his grandiosity, hallucinations, and delusions. Though patients vary in their requirements for adjunctive antipsychotic therapy, one usually can begin to taper the antipsychotic within two weeks. Most patients can be maintained on lithium alone within three weeks.[163]

10. Side Effects. After 10 days of therapy, H.M. is demonstrating significant improvement in his sleep, impulsivity, delusions, and activity level. His lithium level remains at 0.8 mEq/L. Today, he arrives for his appointment complaining that the benztropine he is taking is not working on his hands. Soon after he sits down, he asks to be excused so that he can go to the bathroom. How might H.M.'s presentation be related to his medication? [SI unit: lithium 0.8 mmol/L]

When considering side effect management early in lithium therapy, it becomes important to monitor lithium levels closely. When patients start to recover from acute mania, the rate of lithium clearance may decrease[30] and patients may demonstrate an increase in lithium levels and worsening side effects. (See Table 77.4.) This does not seem to be the case in H.M.

H.M. is complaining of a problem with his hands which he felt should have been addressed by benztropine. He should be interviewed and examined to determine the origin of this complaint. In this case, likely medication-related causes for the complaint would include parkinsonian side effects from haloperidol or tremor secondary to lithium. The fact that an antiparkinsonian agent was not helpful points toward lithium being the cause.

Tremor occurs in more than 15% of those treated with lithium.[56] The tremor is characterized by being rapid, regular, and fine in

amplitude. This is quite different from the resting, coarse, slow (4 to 7 cycles/second) tremor at rest frequently seen in patients receiving antipsychotics. Often, this tremor occurs early in therapy and spontaneously resolves as therapy continues. Caffeine, anxiety, antidepressants, and adrenergic agents may worsen lithium-induced tremor.[57] The tremor is more frequent in patients with higher serum levels and may be worse at times of peak serum levels.[56,58] If H.M. is not bothered by the tremor and suffers no impairment, treatment is not necessary. If the tremor becomes problematic, the lithium dosage may be reduced or β-adrenergic-blocking agents can be added. Since H.M. is fairly early in treatment and has only a moderate lithium level, it would be prudent to add propranolol 10 mg three times a day rather than reduce the lithium dose if an intervention is required. Propranolol usually is effective in doses less than 160 mg/day.[59] H.M. also should be educated about his tremor and instructed to reduce his caffeine consumption.

H.M. also should be asked about his trip to the bathroom during this clinic visit. Lithium may cause both diarrhea and polyuria. Its most prominent renal effect is interference with the action of antidiuretic hormone in the distal tubule of the kidney resulting in nephrogenic diabetes insipidus.[60] With the lower serum levels of lithium commonly employed today, the actual increase in urine volume may be as low as 20%.[61] Thus, a decrease in H.M.'s lithium dosage may help reduce his polyuria. Urine output also has been correlated with troughs in lithium levels.[58] While once-daily administration of lithium is not universally accepted, switching a stabilized patient to this schedule with its lower trough levels also may help reduce urine volume.[62] If H.M. were to fail to respond to either of these interventions, either potassium supplementation[60,63] or amiloride could be employed concurrently.[60,64] Amiloride appears to antagonize lithium's effects on free water clearance by reducing the entry of the ion into renal epithelial cells.[65]

If H.M.'s trip to the bathroom was due to diarrhea, lithium should be evaluated as a possible cause. Up to 20% of patients started on lithium experience diarrhea, epigastric bloating, and sometimes pain.[72] Diarrhea from lithium is associated with high serum levels, once-daily dosing, and rapidly absorbed preparations. Institution of divided doses may help alleviate the problem if H.M. is suffering from lithium-associated diarrhea. Use of lower doses and switching to sustained-release preparations are alternative strategies which could be used. The use of sustained-release preparations has the potential to lead to reduced lithium levels if rapid gastrointestinal (GI) motility results in delayed lithium release in the distal portions of the intestinal tract.

If H.M. has either diarrhea or polyuria, his fluid status and lithium levels should be monitored carefully. Dehydration leads to increased lithium reabsorption in the proximal tubule and could result in accumulation to toxic levels.

11. Drug Interactions. H.M. has had a stable lithium level around 0.80 mEq/L for several weeks. His last 2 levels have dropped to 0.65 and 0.61 mEq/L. There has been no change in H.M.'s drug therapy. He insists that he is taking his medication as prescribed. The nursing staff feels he is compliant with his medication but notes that he is spending more time off the ward and in the canteen. What factors could contribute to a decrease in H.M.'s lithium levels? [SI units: lithium 0.80, 0.65, and 0.61 mmol/L, respectively]

Drug interactions are a frequent cause for changes in lithium levels, but there have been no changes in H.M.'s regimen. Changes in formulation or brand may sometimes have an impact on lithium levels. However, lithium is relatively well absorbed and has a long elimination half-life, so this usually does not result in great changes

| Table 77.4 | | Side Effects of Lithium |
Lithium Side Effect	Occurrence	Treatment Strategy
Cognitive effects	9%[69]	Insure that patient not depressed; consider supportive therapy;[66] differentiate from manic hyperacuity;[67] lower dosage[68,69]
Fine tremor	15% but ↓ with time[69]	May resolve with time; lower dosage; reduce caffeine intake; avoid tricyclic antidepressants, sympathomimetics; consider β-adrenergic-blocking agents such as propranolol 40–160 mg/day[57,59,70]
GI upset[a]	33% in first 2 weeks[71]	May resolve or improve with time; may be related to speed of rise of serum levels; consider divided doses or sustained-release preparations[72]
Diarrhea	6%–20%[69]	May be related to serum levels;[69] reduce dosage
Hypothyroidism	5%–8%[45]	Discontinue lithium or treat with levothyroxine[73]
Polyuria, polydipsia	36%[74]	May be related to serum levels;[74] reduce dosage; consider reducing frequency of administration;[60,62] consider amiloride[60,64]
Weight gain[42]	50%–75%; average ↑ of 4 kg[69]	Try to avoid polyuria and polydipsia and discourage use of high-calorie drinks;[47] regular exercise; dietary consultation
Worsening of dermatologic conditions[75]	Follicular eruptions 33%	Consider reduction in dosage or discontinuation depending upon severity of reaction; symptomatic treatment

[a] GI = Gastrointestinal.

in the 12-hour postdose lithium level. Occasionally, patients switched from lithium citrate to solid dosage forms will experience small changes in lithium levels. (See Table 77.5)

In H.M.'s case, one should consider the ramifications of his visits to the canteen. Diet can have a major influence on lithium excretion. If H.M. is consuming large amounts of caffeinated coffee or soft drinks or salty snacks in the canteen, these could be responsible for reductions in lithium levels. Both increases in dietary sodium[81] and the ingestion of methylxanthines (e.g., caffeine and theophylline)[82,83] can result in increases in lithium clearance.

Finally, acute mania can increase lithium clearance.[30] If H.M. were showing signs of a relapse, his decrease in lithium levels might be attributable to his return to a manic state.

12. Patient Education. What does H.M. need to know about lithium before he is discharged?

As with all drugs, H.M. should be instructed to disclose the medications he is taking to all health care professionals who provide care for him. He should be informed that dehydration, fever, vomiting, crash diets, or sodium-restricted diets could lead to increases in his lithium level.[81] Therefore, he needs to drink plenty of fluids and eat a diet consistent in its levels of sodium. H.M. should be instructed to contact his physician if he starts to experience worsening tremor, slurred speech, muscle weakness or twitches, or difficulty walking.[98]

H.M. also should be told to use caution in selecting OTC medications. Specifically, he should be warned to avoid preparations containing ibuprofen (Motrin) or naproxen (Naprosyn) which can increase lithium levels.[85] H.M. should know that caffeine sometimes can be troublesome in patients taking lithium. On a short-term basis, caffeine can worsen lithium tremor; on a longer-term basis, it may lower lithium levels.[99] With regards to serum level monitoring, H.M. needs to know that lithium levels usually are drawn approximately 12 hours after a dose of lithium.[30] If he is taking lithium in the evening and the morning, he should take his evening dose and then report for a blood sample to be drawn in the morning before taking his next dose.

13. What should H.M. be told regarding potential renal damage from lithium?

H.M. should be informed that lithium can cause renal side effects. However, cases of irreversible kidney damage are relatively rare and have occurred only when patients have had pre-existing

renal disease, episodes of lithium intoxication, or after many years of lithium therapy.[100] H.M. needs to understand that communication with his physician regarding situations which increase the risk of lithium toxicity and cooperation with regular lithium and renal function monitoring can reduce the risk of renal disease secondary to lithium therapy vastly.[40] Finally, he must be informed that polyuria is not related to any of the more serious renal side effects.[74]

14. Maintenance Therapy. After several weeks of therapy with lithium, H.M. no longer is overtly manic. However, his physician determines that H.M. may have had past episodes of depression and hypomania. Therefore, he decides to institute prophylactic (maintenance) lithium therapy. What are the goals of maintenance lithium therapy for H.M.? How should H.M. be monitored during this maintenance phase? How long should H.M. be maintained on lithium?

Lithium therapy is not 100% effective in preventing recurrences of mania and depression. Appropriate goals for maintenance therapy include an increase in the interval between episodes, a decrease in the frequency of episodes, and a reduction in the duration and severity of single episodes.[76] In H.M.'s case, the goal is to prevent future manic episodes. The target lithium level for H.M. should be in the range of 0.5 to 0.8 mEq/L.[77,78] However, at least one group has found that patients with lithium levels in the range of 0.4 to 0.6 mEq/L had relapse rates 2.6 times higher than patients having levels in the 0.8 to 1.0 mEq/L range. While these higher levels reduced the number of relapses, they also resulted in a higher incidence of side effects.[79]

In addition to determining appropriate maintenance lithium levels for H.M., this is an opportune time to consider whether potential gains in compliance and side effects can be made by employing once- or twice-a-day administration of lithium. During periods of dosage readjustment, H.M. will need to have regular monitoring of his lithium serum level. Once stabilized, the monitoring frequency can be reduced to monthly. Eventually, the interval for lithium serum level testing can be extended to as long as once every three months.[78] If H.M. were to exhibit any of the risk factors that could predispose him to lithium toxicity (see Question 10) or if other medication changes were to occur, more frequent monitoring should be reinstituted temporarily.

While continuing on lithium, H.M. should be monitored periodically for thyroid function in order to detect lithium-related hypothyroidism. Renal function should be measured regularly to detect the development of conditions which might require an alteration in lithium dose and to insure that any lithium effects on the kidney are detected early should they occur. These tests should be repeated approximately every 6 to 12 months.[68,78,80]

The decision to institute maintenance lithium therapy usually is made because of the severity of affective episodes and the belief that they will recur in the future. A period of successful maintenance therapy means that the individual is controlled, not cured. Most patients who are withdrawn from lithium will relapse eventually. With each recurrent manic episode, the risk of experiencing subsequent and more frequent manic episodes increases. Furthermore, as individuals experience successive episodes, they tend to recover less completely and function at a diminished level between occurrences.[165] H.M. had a serious manic episode which disrupted his employment, his finances, and perhaps his marriage. Since the goal is to avoid the trauma of repeated episodes and the deterioration that may accompany them, H.M. may well require lithium for the remainder of his life.[166]

Psychotherapy

15. Should H.M. undergo psychotherapy in addition to his pharmacotherapy?

While medication is the mainstay of treatment for bipolar disorder, psychotherapy is helpful in selected cases. It is hypothesized that early affective episodes are precipitated by stressful life events. If bipolar individuals and their families can learn to avoid or better cope with such stresses, future episodes may be avoided. Evidence suggests that later in the course of the illness, stress does not play a major role in precipitating individual episodes.[165]

Family therapy may be helpful in dealing with the emotion and stress that results from the disruption of a manic or depressive episode. Infidelity, unemployment, excessive bills, violent outbursts, reckless endangerment, lack of discretion, embarrassment, and fear concerning future episodes are among the issues with which a family must come to terms. Compliance with medication is another frequent issue in therapy sessions. The issue of medication frequently can turn into a struggle over who is in control. In addition, some patients must accept untoward effects or the fact that they will no longer experience their pleasant ''highs.''

Hypothyroidism

16. After receiving lithium for 1 year, H.M. returns complaining that the lithium is slowing him down. He says that he is tired and has gained weight in recent weeks. He thinks he is getting depressed. He complains that the examining room is too cold. What is the most likely cause of H.M.'s complaints? What treatment should be instituted?

H.M.'s symptoms are consistent with those of hypothyroidism. Lithium affects the incorporation of iodine into thyroid hormone, interferes with secretion of thyroid hormones, and may interfere with the peripheral degradation of T_4 to T_3.[157] Depending upon the criteria employed, rates of lithium-induced hypothyroidism have been estimated at between 3% and 42%.[45,158] The higher rates occurred in longitudinal studies which examined patients for as long as 20 years.[158] In one study, 7.8% of patients receiving lithium had clinical manifestations of hypothyroidism requiring treatment.[45] Subclinical hypothyroidism with elevated levels of thyroid-stimulating hormone may be present in an even larger number of lithium patients.[147,165–167] While it tends to occur early in the course of long-term lithium treatment, hypothyroidism can develop after many years of therapy. High doses of lithium and pre-existing thyroid disease may be predisposing factors for lithium-induced hypothyroidism. Hypothyroidism also tends to occur more frequently in females as do other forms of hypothyroidism.

If H.M. is found to be hypothyroid, he should receive levothyroxine in doses which normalize his thyroid function tests. Even if H.M. has an elevated TSH with normal levels of T_3 and T_4, treatment may help stabilize his course of illness, resolve his symptoms, and prevent breakthrough depressive symptoms.[165]

Lithium Toxicity

17. One day A.M. calls, concerned about H.M. He has been having nausea, vomiting, and diarrhea for several days. She says he has taken in very little orally except his medications. Over the past few hours, H.M. has developed confusion, a coarse tremor, and slurry speech. It has been 4 months since H.M. has had a lithium level. What action should be taken?

There is a strong possibility that H.M. is suffering from lithium toxicity. Lithium toxicity may occur acutely from an overdose or insidiously with a reduction in excretion. *Mild toxicity* usually in-

Table 77.5	Lithium Drug Interactions of Clinical Significance[a]

Drugs That May ↑ Lithium Levels

NSAIDs[85]
Many NSAIDs have been reported to ↑ lithium levels as much as 50%–60%. This probably is due to an enhanced reabsorption of sodium and lithium secondary to inhibition of prostaglandin synthesis[86]

Diuretics
All diuretics can contribute to sodium depletion. Sodium depletion can result in an ↑ proximal tubular reabsorption of sodium and lithium. Thiazide-like diuretics cause the greatest ↑ in lithium levels while loop diuretics[87] and potassium-sparing diuretics appear somewhat safer[64]

ACE Inhibitors
ACE inhibitors and lithium both result in volume depletion and a reduction in glomerular filtration rate. This results in reduced lithium excretion[88,89,90]

Drugs That May ↓ Lithium Levels

Theophylline, Caffeine
Theophylline[82] and caffeine may ↑ renal clearance of lithium and result in a ↓ in levels in the range of 20%[83]

Acetazolamide
Acetazolamide may impair proximal tubular reabsorption of lithium ions[91]

Sodium
High dietary sodium intake promotes the renal clearance of lithium[81]

Drugs That ↑ Lithium Toxicity

Methyldopa
Cases of sedation, dysphoria, and confusion due to the combined use of lithium and methyldopa[92] have been reported

Carbamazepine
Cases of neurotoxicity involving the combined use of lithium and carbamazepine have been reported in patients with normal lithium levels[93]

Calcium Channel Antagonists
Cases of neurotoxicity involving the combined use of lithium and the calcium channel blockers verapamil and diltiazem have been reported. Lithium does interfere with calcium transport across cells[94]

Antipsychotics
Cases of neurotoxicity (encephalopathic syndrome, extrapyramidal effects, cerebellar effect, EEG abnormalities) have been reported due to the combined use of lithium and various antipsychotics.[23,50] The interaction may be related to ↑ in phenothiazine levels, changes in tissue uptake of lithium and/or dopamine blocking effects of lithium. Studies attempting to demonstrate this effect have yielded differing results[51–53]

Serotonin Specific Re-Uptake Inhibitors
Fluoxetine has been reported to result in an ↑ of toxicity when added to lithium.[95,96] Sertraline has been reported to ↑ nausea and tremor in lithium recipients[97]

[a] ACE = Angiotensin-converting enzyme; EEG = Electroencephalogram; NSAIDs = Nonsteroidal anti-inflammatory drugs.

cludes feelings of apathy, lethargy, and muscle weakness accompanied by nausea and irritability. With *moderate toxicity*, symptoms progress to coarse tremor, slurred speech, unsteady gait, drowsiness, confusion, muscle twitches, and blurred vision. *Severe toxicity* can result in seizures, stupor, coma, and cardiovascular collapse. H.M. appears to be experiencing a moderate degree of lithium toxicity. He should be taken to the emergency room immediately for assessment and treatment. "Stat" laboratory tests for lithium level, electrolytes, and renal function tests should be ordered. Intravenous solutions should be started to assure that H.M. is hydrated adequately and electrolyte abnormalities should be corrected promptly. Depending upon the results of physical examination and laboratory tests, cardiac monitoring should be instituted.[165,168]

Lithium levels must be interpreted with caution if they were drawn within 12 hours of lithium ingestion. Levels drawn sooner than 12 hours may appear falsely high. If an individual ingested a large quantity of a sustained-release lithium formulation, levels which were drawn too soon may appear to be falsely low. Generally, lithium levels in excess of 3 mEq/L indicate a severe episode of lithium intoxication. Twelve-hour serum lithium levels greater than 2.5 mEq/L, coma, shock, further deterioration, or failure to improve with conservative management are indications for dialysis. Though peritoneal dialysis has been instituted in cases of lithium intoxication, hemodialysis is preferred.[165,170]

Lithium in Pregnancy

18. A.J., a 36-year-old female, has been maintained successfully on lithium therapy for 5 years for bipolar disorder. She asks whether she should stay on lithium since she plans on becoming pregnant in the near future.

Lithium has been associated with a variety of congenital malformations, including the rare cardiac malformation, Ebstein's anomaly.[49,101] However, there is considerable disagreement about the importance of lithium as a teratogen. Some studies report an overall risk of congenital malformations of approximately 11% in those taking lithium.[48] The risk for Ebstein's anomaly has been reported to be as high as 2.7%.[102] Others have not found data to support the teratogenic reputation of lithium or have tended to minimize the risk of lithium use during pregnancy.[103–105] Since malformations of this type are most likely to occur in the first trimester of pregnancy, it is advisable for patients to discontinue lithium therapy when possible before conception and especially during the first trimester.[48,106]

In addition to cardiac malformations, infants exposed to lithium often are heavier than those not exposed regardless of gestational age.[107] While the ramifications of increased weight for gestational age are unknown, this fetal macrosomia is thought to be due to effects of lithium on carbohydrate metabolism. At least one study argues against fetal macrosomia in infants exposed to lithium *in utero*.[108] Lithium administration during pregnancy increases the risk of premature delivery and its inherent complications by a factor of two to three.[108] Thus, A.J. and her physician should discuss the individual risks involved in her case. In addition to the risks of teratogenicity, they must consider the harm which could result from the possible recurrence of episodes of mania or depression and the risks inherent in discontinuing lithium or switching to another antimanic agent.

If A.J. and her physician decide that she is to remain on lithium, her levels must be monitored closely and her dosage adjusted periodically. Glomerular filtration rate and lithium clearance both are elevated markedly in the second and third trimesters of pregnancy, resulting in a reduction in lithium levels and the possibility of breakthrough manic episodes.[48] Approximately 16 weeks after

conception, screening tests and fetal echocardiography can be employed to determine if cardiac defects have developed.[107] If possible, A.J.'s physician should discontinue her lithium several days before delivery to minimize lithium levels in the newborn and to offset the reduction in lithium excretion that occurs following delivery. In deciding when to discontinue lithium before delivery, A.J. and her physician should consider the increased risk of premature delivery due to the use of lithium.

If A.J. and her physician decide that she is to discontinue lithium, they must be prepared to deal with the risks of lithium discontinuation. Several cases of what are thought to be rebound manic episodes have resulted from the abrupt cessation of lithium therapy. Instead, A.J. should be instructed to gradually reduce her lithium dose over four weeks.

19. A.J. was maintained throughout her pregnancy without using lithium. Following delivery, A.J. and her physician decide that she should be restarted on lithium. How soon can this take place?

Lithium can be restarted as soon as A.J. demonstrates urine output and a return to normal hydration. However, this decision also may be affected by whether or not A.J. chooses to breast-feed her child. Lithium does pass into the milk and is present in concentrations up to 50% of that found in the maternal blood.[48] Risks to the fetus include hypothyroidism and lithium toxicity during infantile illnesses. Thus, A.J. and her physician must discuss the advantages of breast-feeding versus the risks of exposing the newborn to lithium or withholding lithium during the postpartum period. A.J. should be informed that approximately 27% to 60% of bipolar women experience affective episodes following delivery.[109]

If A.J. chooses to breast-feed while taking lithium, she should consider using infant formula when the child becomes ill. Febrile illness, vomiting, or diarrhea all can increase the risk of lithium toxicity. She also should be instructed to contact her pediatrician should the infant experience diarrhea, vomiting, hypotonia, poor sucking, muscle twitches, restlessness, or other unexplained changes in behavior or status.[110]

Lithium Refractoriness

20. P.B., a 42-year-old female, has 5 previous hospitalizations for manic and/or depressive episodes. She has experienced approximately 6 severe mood swings in the past year including episodes of depression and hypomania. Despite adequate plasma levels, she has not responded to a regimen which includes desipramine and lithium. The addition of thioridazine (Mellaril) 100 mg HS resulted in no further improvement. She now presents as depressed, with expressions of suicidal hopelessness about her condition, sleep disturbances, and poor appetite. Why is P.B. failing to respond to lithium?

There are several potential reasons for P.B.'s poor response. Poor compliance always must be considered as a potential reason for lithium failure. However, P.B. has demonstrated adequate drug levels of both antidepressants and lithium. If P.B. had been intermittently compliant in the past or if her therapy had been stopped, she might have developed a syndrome called "lithium discontinuation-induced refractoriness."[111,112] This phenomenon occurs in patients who once responded to lithium and then had their lithium discontinued. When an affective episode recurs, they fail to fully respond to lithium reintroduction. If P.B. had been having more and more breakthrough affective episodes gradually, she simply could have become tolerant to lithium. This breakthrough pattern is exhibited in the estimated 25% to 44% of bipolar patients who eventually develop lithium tolerance.[111,112] Thus, a careful review of P.B.'s history of compliance and the pattern of her affective episodes is necessary.

P.B. has another potential reason for nonresponse. She has had at least six affective episodes in the past year. Therefore, she is a rapid cycler. Approximately 70% to 80% of rapid cyclers have a poor response to lithium.[113]

Carbamazepine and Valproate

21. Given that she suffers from a rapid cycling bipolar disorder, how should P.B. be treated? What monitoring is required for the new treatment regimen?

Carbamazepine and valproate are effective in a large number of lithium-resistant bipolar patients.[111,114] Numerous placebo-controlled trials have supported the antimanic efficacy of carbamazepine. Valproate's efficacy is supported by a fewer number of controlled trials and a large number of open-label studies. Anticonvulsants especially may be useful as alternatives for patients such as P.B. who have lithium-resistant rapid cycling bipolar disease. Rather than discontinuing lithium and then beginning an anticonvulsant, valproate or carbamazepine should be added to lithium.[111,115] In this manner, one can avoid the potential exacerbation of the disorder which might result from lithium withdrawal. If combined therapy is effective, an attempt can be made later to gradually taper the lithium over three to four weeks.

The choice between carbamazepine and valproate is based largely upon toxicity, drug interactions, one's evaluation of the literature, and personal preference. While the literature supporting carbamazepine includes a greater number of controlled trials, it has the disadvantage of being involved in a number of drug interactions due to induction of the hepatic microsomal system or inhibition of its own metabolism by competing agents. Carbamazepine also is associated with leukopenia, lowered platelet counts, hyponatremia, sedation, tremor, and ataxia. Valproate has few clinically important drug interactions. The dosage of valproate may be limited by the occurrence of GI upset. Sedation and minor elevations in liver transaminase also are frequent with valproate.[140,141]

While continuing lithium, P.B. should be started on carbamazepine 200 mg twice daily or valproate at a dose of 250 mg three times a day. If carbamazepine is chosen, her dosage should be increased by 200 mg every three to four days until adequate serum levels have been reached.[26] Though no correlation between carbamazepine serum levels and response in bipolar disorder has been established, one should strive to reach serum levels in the range of 8 to 12 µg/mL.

If valproate is chosen, the dose is then increased by 250 mg every two days. Mean dosage requirements usually are about 1250 to 1500 mg/day.[26] If the need for control is acute, an oral loading regimen for valproic acid of 20 mg/kg/day in divided doses for five days can be initiated to rapidly attain serum valproate concentrations of greater than 50 mg/L.[118,119]

Before receiving carbamazepine, P.B. should undergo baseline laboratory testing including a complete blood count with differential and platelets, electrolytes, and liver function tests. If P.B. had a history of AV conduction abnormalities, a baseline electrocardiogram also should be performed.[140] It is advisable to record baseline neurologic status, blood pressure, and the presence of skin rashes before starting carbamazepine to exclude the possibility that existing conditions are attributed later to carbamazepine toxicity. Baseline pregnancy testing is in order for females of child-bearing age. Special attention should be paid to medications which may be affected by carbamazepine or which may affect carbamazepine. In particular, oral contraceptives, warfarin, theophylline, haloperidol, valproate, and tricyclic antidepressants may have their levels and therapeutic effects reduced by the addition of carbamazepine. The presence of erythromycin, cimetidine, fluoxetine, or calcium channel blockers may lead to increased levels of carbamazepine and

unanticipated toxicity. Carbamazepine should be monitored with complete blood counts and liver enzymes every three weeks during the first three months of treatment and every six months thereafter (also see Chapter 52: Seizure Disorders).[140] Monitoring should include attention to abnormal bleeding or petechiae which might indicate thrombocytopenia, rashes, and signs and symptoms of infection which might indicate leukopenia. The monitoring of mental status may result in detection of hyponatremia.

If P.B. is to receive valproate, baseline laboratory tests should include a complete blood count with differential and platelets and liver function tests. P.B.'s baseline weight and neurologic status should be recorded. Since P.B. is premenopausal and has not undergone surgical sterilization, a baseline pregnancy test is warranted. As with carbamazepine, attention should be given to any medications which will be administered concurrently with valproate. Interactions with aspirin, phenytoin, phenobarbital, and carbamazepine are cited frequently. Once valproate is begun, liver function tests should be monitored at least monthly for the first three months and every six months thereafter.[140,141]

22. While on a dose of valproic acid capsules of 500 mg TID, P.B. complains of extreme nausea. Her last dose increase was 5 days ago. Her trough valproate level is 58 µg/mL. Her alanine aminotransferase (ALT) is 89 U/L (Normal: 7–56) and her aspartate aminotransferase (AST) is 59 U/L (Normal: 5–35). All other physical and laboratory findings are normal. What intervention should be undertaken? [SI units: ALT 1.48 µkat/L (Normal: 0.1–0.9); AST 0.98 µkat/L (Normal: 0.08–0.58)]

Valproate frequently causes nausea. While the nausea often is transient and resolves with continued use, it does seem to correlate with rapid increases in serum levels. When the nausea is severe, dosage reduction or change of formulation is appropriate. P.B. is at the lower end of the postulated therapeutic range for valproate. Therefore, a dosage reduction might reduce the chance of gaining a full therapeutic effect from the drug. In this case, P.B. could be switched to either divalproex sodium delayed-release tablets or to the divalproex "sprinkle" formulation administered with food. Either of these interventions will slow absorption without significant alteration of total bioavailability. This delay in absorption should result in a reduction of nausea. If this is not fully effective, some anecdotal reports suggest that concomitant administration of histamine$_2$-receptor antagonists may be helpful.[140,141]

Transient elevations in liver enzymes occur frequently in patients receiving valproate. P.B. should continue to have her enzyme levels monitored, but there is no need to discontinue medication unless there are other indications of hepatic dysfunction or her enzyme levels exceed twice the upper limit of the normal range (also see Chapter 52: Seizure Disorders). Even if discontinuation is necessary, P.B. can be rechallenged once her hepatic enzymes normalize.[141] While valproate has been associated with fatal hepatotoxicity, this has occurred primarily in patients under the age of ten years or in patients receiving multiple anticonvulsants.[142]

Alternative Therapies

23. Over several months, P.B. received trials of lithium plus valproate, valproate alone, lithium plus carbamazepine, and carbamazepine alone. She currently is on carbamazepine alone with a level of 10 µg/mL. Despite these efforts, she has continued to experience affective episodes. What additional options are available for the treatment of P.B.'s bipolar disorder?

A number of alternative strategies exist for the treatment of both acute manic episodes and for prophylaxis against recurrent episodes. Patients who have tolerated trials of individual anticonvulsants can be tried on a combination valproate and carbamazepine.[111,120,121]

Verapamil has been used for both acute manic episodes and prophylaxis in doses of up to 480 mg/day.[123] While some suggest it is as effective in acute mania as lithium, criticisms regarding verapamil have included a lack of controlled studies, use of only moderately manic patients in studies, and requirements for greater doses of adjunctive benzodiazepines and antipsychotics in subjects in the verapamil groups.[145,146] Reports have differed with regard to the efficacy of verapamil versus lithium in prophylaxis of recurrent episodes.[122,144] In individuals with depressive episodes, it generally is not considered useful.[113] At this point, verapamil would seem to be an alternative for lithium in those who cannot take lithium and who have only a mild degree of mood elevation.[143] While reports on the use of calcium channel blockers in rapid cycling disorder in particular are lacking, investigations are underway into the use of the L-type calcium channel blocker nimodipine for patients with extremely rapid fluctuations in mood.[114]

P.B.'s rapid cycling disorder would make her a candidate for the use of adjunctive thyroid treatment. A number of individuals with rapid cycling disorder have elevated levels of thyroid-stimulating hormone and evidence of clinical or subclinical hypothyroidism.[147–149] On this basis, rapid cyclers have been medicated successfully with levothyroxine at doses of 0.15 to 0.4 mg/day in order to achieve a free T_4 index above normal.[150] One hypothesis behind this strategy is that low levels of T_4 may predispose one to rapid cycling. Another hypothesis is that brain conversion of T_4 to T_3 is impaired somehow.[150] Thus, P.B. should be examined for physical and laboratory evidence of hypothyroidism. Even if no evidence is found, she could undergo a trial of levothyroxine supplementation.

If P.B.'s main problem concerned major depressive episodes, antidepressants could be used with lithium or anticonvulsants. Antidepressant augmentation of other mood stabilizing agents seems safest in those with Bipolar II Disorder and most risky in those with rapid cycling disorder.[162] While bupropion has been advanced as an antidepressant which is less likely to induce manic episodes, more recent reports generate doubt as to whether it has any significant advantages in bipolar disorder.[152–154]

One nonpharmacologic therapy that should not be overlooked is electroconvulsive therapy. It has proven effective in manic episodes, depressive episodes, and prophylaxis.[155,162]

References

1   **National Institutes of Mental Health.** Key facts about mental illness. Rockville, MD: 1993.

2   **American Psychiatric Association.** Mood disorders. In: Diagnostic and Statistical Manual of Mental Disorders. 4th ed. Washington: American Psychiatric Association; 1994:317–91.

3   **Silverstone T, Hunt N.** Symptoms and assessment of mania. In: Paykel ES, ed. Handbook of Affective Disorders. 2nd ed. New York: Churchill Livingstone; 1992:15–25.

4   **Regier DA et al.** The NIMH epidemiologic catchment area program: historical context, major objectives, and study population characteristics. Arch Gen Psychiatry. 1984;41:934–41.

5   **Weissman MM, Smith AL.** Epidemiology. In: Paykel ES, ed. Handbook of Affective Disorders. 2nd ed. New York: Churchill Livingstone; 1992: 111–29.

6   **Angst J.** The course of affective disorders II. Topology of bipolar manic-depressive illness. Arch Psychiatr Nervenkr. 1978;226:65–73.

7   **Roy-Byrne P et al.** The longitudinal course of recurrent affective illness: life chart data from research patients at NIMH. Acta Psychiatr Scand Suppl. 1985;71:5–32.

8   **Coryell W, Winokur G.** Course and outcome. In: Paykel ES, ed. Handbook of Affective Disorders. 2nd ed. New York: Churchill Livingstone; 1992: 15–25.

9   **Joyce PR.** Age of onset in bipolar affective disorder and misdiagnosis as schizophrenia. Psychol Med. 1984;14: 145–49.

10 **Cutler NR, Post RM.** Life course of illness in untreated manic-depressive patients. Compr Psychiatry. 1982;23: 101–05.

11 **Dunner D et al.** Rapid-cycling manic-depressive patients. Compr Psychiatry. 1974;18:561–66.

12 **Coryell W et al.** Rapid cycling affective disorder: demographics, diagnosis, family history, and course. Arch Gen Psychiatry. 1992;49:26–131.

13 **Cowdry R et al.** Thyroid abnormalities associated with rapid cycling bipolar illness. Arch Gen Psychiatry. 1983;40: 414–20.

14 **Stancer H, Persod E.** Treatment of intractable rapid cycling manic depressive disorder with levothyroxine: clinical observations. Arch Gen Psychiatry. 1982;39:311–12.

15 **Goodwin FK, Jamison KR.** The natural course of manic-depressive illness. In: Post RM, Ballenger JC, eds. The Neurobiology of Mood Disorders. Baltimore: William and Wilkins; 1984; 20–37.

16 **Reiger DA et al.** Comorbidity of mental disorders with alcohol and other drug abuse. JAMA. 1990;264(19): 2511–518.

17 **Hamilton M.** Mood disorders: clinical features. In: Kaplan HI, Sadock BJ, eds. Comprehensive Textbook of Psychiatry. V. Baltimore: Williams and Wilkins; 1989:892–913.

18 **Ambelas A.** Life effects and mania. A special relationship. Br J Psychiatry. 1987;150:235–40.

19 **Sultzer DL, Cummings JL.** Drug-induced mania-causative agents, clinical characteristics and management. A retrospective analysis of the literature. Medical Toxicology and Adverse Drug Experience. 1989;4(2):127–43.

20 **Gerner RH.** Treatment of acute mania. Psychiatr Clin North Am. 1993;16: 443–60.

21 **Wehr TA.** Sleep loss: a preventable cause of mania and other excited states. J Clin Psychiatry. 1989;50(Suppl. 12): 8–16.

22 **Dunner DL, Clayton PJ.** Drug treatment of bipolar disorder. In: Meltzer HM, ed. Psychopharmacology: The Third Generation of Progress. New York: Raven Press; 1987:1077–83.

23 **Chou J.** Recent advances in treatment of acute mania. J Clin Psychopharmacol. 1991;11:3–21.

24 **Calabrese JR et al.** Predictors of valproate response in bipolar rapid cycling. J Clin Psychopharmacol. 1993; 13:280–83.

25 **Clothier J et al.** Dysphoric mania. J Clin Psychopharmacol. 1992;12 (Suppl.): 13s–16s.

26 **Gerner RH, Stanton A.** Algorithm for patient management of acute manic states: lithium, valproate, or carbamazepine. J Clin Psychopharmacol. 1992; 12(Suppl.):57s–63s.

27 **Prein RF, Potter WZ.** NIMH workshop report on treatment of bipolar disorder. Psychopharmacol Bull. 1990;26: 409–27.

28 **Jefferson JW.** Lithium the present and the future. J Clin Psychiatry. 1990; 51(Suppl. 8):4–8.

29 **Post RM et al.** Treatment of rapid cycling bipolar illness. Psychopharmacol Bull. 1990;26:37–47.

30 **Perry PJ, Alexander B.** Dosage and serum levels. In: Johnson FN, ed. Depression and Mania: Modern Lithium Therapy. Oxford: IRL Press; 1987:67–73.

31 **Kane JM.** The role of neuroleptics in manic-depressive illness. J Clin Psychiatry. 1988;49(Suppl. 11):12–13.

32 **Lenox RH et al.** Adjunctive treatment of manic agitation with lorazepam versus haloperidol: a double-blind study. J Clin Psychiatry. 1992;53:47–52.

33 **Prien RF et al.** Comparison of lithium carbonate and chlorpromazine in the treatment of mania. Arch Gen Psychiatry. 1972;26:146–53.

34 **Busch FN et al.** A comparison of two adjunctive treatment strategies in acute mania. J Clin Psychiatry. 1989;50: 453–55.

35 **Chouinard G et al.** Antimanic effects of clonazepam. Biol Psychiatry. 1983; 18:451–66.

36 **Chouinard G.** The use of benzodiazepines in the treatment of manic-depressive illness. J Clin Psychiatry. 1988;49(Suppl. 11):15–19.

37 **Bradwejn J et al.** Double-blind comparison of the effects of clonazepam and lorazepam in acute mania. J Clin Psychopharmacol. 1990;10:403–8.

38 **Hullin R.** Preliminary tests. In: Johnson FN, ed. Depression and Mania: Modern Lithium Therapy. Oxford: IRL Press; 1987:59–63.

39 **Jefferson JW.** Current and potential uses of lithium. J Clin Psychiatry. 1990;51:392–99.

40 **Peet M, Pratt JP.** Lithium: current status in psychiatric disorders. Drugs. 1993;46(1):7–17.

41 **Martin CA et al.** Heart and blood vessels. In: Johnson FN, ed. Depression and Mania: Modern Lithium Therapy. Oxford: IRL Press; 1987:213–18.

42 **Jefferson JW.** Panel discussion I: recent advances in bipolar and obsessive compulsive disorders. J Clin Psychiatry. 1990;51(Suppl. 8):17–19.

43 **Prakash R.** Blood. In: Johnson FN, ed. Depression and Mania: Modern Lithium Therapy. Oxford: IRL Press; 1987: 218–20.

44 **Prakash R.** A review of the hematologic side effects of lithium. Hosp Community Psychiatry. 1985;36:127–28.

45 **Yassa R et al.** Lithium-induced thyroid disorders: a prevalence study. J Clin Psychiatry. 1988;49:14–16.

46 **Jefferson JW et al.** Lithium Encyclopedia for Clinical Practice. 2nd ed. Washington: American Psychiatric Press, Inc.; 1987:218–22.

47 **Storlien LH, Smythe GA.** Body Weight. In: Johnson FN, ed. Depression and Mania: Modern Lithium Therapy. Washington: IRL Press; 1987: 195–96.

48 **Schou M.** Lithium treatment during pregnancy, delivery, and lactation: an update. J Clin Psychiatry. 1990;51: 410–13.

49 **Warkany J.** Teratogen update: lithium. Teratology. 1988;38:593–96.

50 **Cohen WJ, Cohen NH.** Lithium carbonate, haloperidol and irreversible brain damage. JAMA. 1974;230:1283–287.

51 **Miller F, Menninger J.** Lithium-neuroleptic neurotoxicity is dose dependent. J Clin Psychopharmacol. 1987;7:89–91.

52 **Goldney RD, Spence ND.** Safety of the combination of lithium and neuroleptic drugs. Am J Psychiatry. 1986;143:882–84.

53 **Baastrup PC et al.** Adverse reactions in treatment with lithium carbonate and haloperidol. JAMA. 1976;236:2645–646.

54 **Janicak PG et al.** A comparison of thiothixene with chlorpromazine in the treatment of mania. J Clin Psychopharmacol. 1988;8:33–7.

55 **Rosenbaum JF.** Mania: important new findings. Summary. J Clin Psychiatry. 1989;50:45–47.

56 **Vestergaard P et al.** Prospective studies on a lithium cohort: tremor, weight gain, diarrhea, psychological complaints. Acta Psychiatr Scand. 1988;78:434–41.

57 **Carroll JA et al.** Treating tremor induced by lithium. Hosp Community Psychiatry. 1987;38:1280,1288.

58 **Mellerup ET.** The side effects of lithium. Biol Psychiatry. 1990;28:464–66.

59 **Jefferson JW et al.** Lithium Encyclopedia for Clinical Practice. 2nd ed. Washington: American Psychiatric Press, Inc.; 1987:656–61.

60 **Martin A.** Clinical management of lithium-induced polyuria. Hosp Community Psychiatry. 1993;44:427–28.

61 **Vestergaard P et al.** Prospective studies on a lithium cohort: renal function, water and electrolyte metabolism. Acta Psychiatr Scand. 1988;78:427–33.

62 **Mellerup ET et al.** Serum lithium minimum and diuresis. Psychiatry Res. 1985;14:309–13.

63 **Klemfuss H.** Diminishing toxic effects of lithium administration. Am J Psychiatry. 1992;149:846.

64 **Batle DC et al.** Amelioration of polyuria by amiloride in patients receiving long-term lithium therapy. N Engl J Med. 1985;312;408–14.

65 **Hays RM.** Agents affecting the renal conservation of water. In: Goodman AG et al., eds. The Pharmacological Basis of Therapeutics. 8th ed. New York: Pergamon Press; 1990:732–42.

66 **Jamison KR.** Psychological aspects of treatment. In: Johnson FN, ed. Depression and Mania: Modern Lithium Therapy. Oxford: IRL Press; 1987:121–24.

67 **Schou M.** Lithium treatment: a refresher course. Br J Psychiatry. 1986;149:541–47.

68 **Schou M.** Lithium prophylaxis: myths and realities. Am J Psychiatry. 1989;146:573–76.

69 **Vestergaard P et al.** Prospective studies on a lithium cohort: tremor, weight gain, diarrhea, psychological complaints. Acta Psychiatr Scand. 1988;78:434–41.

70 **Zubenko GS et al.** Comparison of metoprolol and propranolol in the treatment of lithium tremor. Psychiatry Res. 1984;11:163–64.

71 **Jefferson JW et al.** Lithium Encyclopedia for Clinical Practice. 2nd ed. Washington: American Psychiatric Press, Inc.; 1987:307–13.

72 **Kersten L.** The gastrointestinal system. In: Johnson FN, ed. Depression and Mania: Modern Lithium Therapy.

Oxford: IRL Press; 1987:196–202.

73 **Jefferson JW et al.** Lithium Encyclopedia for Clinical Practice. 2nd ed. Washington: American Psychiatric Press, Inc.; 1987:356–60.

74 **Vestergaard P et al.** Prospective studies on a lithium cohort: renal function, water and electrolyte metabolism. Acta Psychiatr Scand. 1988;78:427–33.

75 **Deadrea D et al.** Dermatological reactions to lithium: a critical review of the literature. J Clin Psychopharmacol. 1982;2:199–204.

76 **Jefferson JW et al.** Lithium Encyclopedia for Clinical Practice. 2nd ed. Washington: American Psychiatric Press, Inc.; 1987:1–32.

77 **Schou M.** Serum lithium monitoring of prophylactic treatment: critical review and updated recommendations. Clin Pharmacokinet. 1988;15:283–86.

78 **Consensus Development Panel.** Mood disorders: pharmacologic prevention of recurrences. Am J Psychiatry. 1985;142:469–76.

79 **Gelenberg AJ et al.** Comparison of standard and low serum levels of lithium for maintenance treatment of bipolar disorder. N Engl J Med. 1989; 321:1489–493.

80 **Gitlin MJ.** Lithium-induced renal insufficiency. J Clin Psychopharmacol. 1993;13:276–79.

81 **Atherton JC et al.** Lithium clearance in man: effects of dietary salt intake, acute changes in extracellular fluid volume, amiloride and frusemide. Clin Sci. 1987;73;645–51.

82 **Cook BL et al.** Theophylline-lithium interaction. J Clin Psychiatry. 1985;46:278–79.

83 **Anton RF.** The social drugs. In: Johnson FN, ed. Depression and Mania: Modern Lithium Therapy. Washington: IRL Press; 1987:186–90.

84 **Callahan AM et al.** Drug interactions in psychopharmacology. Psychiatr Clin North Am. 1993;16:647–71.

85 **Ragheb M.** The clinical significance of lithium-nonsteroidal anti-inflammatory drug interactions. J Clin Psychopharmacol. 1990;10:350–54.

86 **Boer WH et al.** Lithium clearance in renal physiology, pharmacology and pathophysiology. In: Christensen S, ed. Lithium and the Kidney. New York: Karger; 1990:62–74.

87 **Shalmi M et al.** Effect of chronic oral furosemide administration on the 24-hour cycle of lithium clearance and electrolyte excretion in humans. Eur J Clin Pharmacol. 1990;38:275–80.

88 **Correa FJ and Eiser AR.** Angiotensin-converting enzyme inhibitors and lithium toxicity. Am J Med. 1992;93:108–9.

89 **Baldwin CM, Safferman AZ.** A case of lisinopril-induced lithium toxicity. DICP. 1990;24:946–47.

90 **Gelenberg AJ.** ACE inhibitors and lithium toxicity. Biol Ther Psychiatry. 1988;11:43.

91 **Thomsen K.** Excretion. In: Johnson FN, ed. Depression and Mania: Modern Lithium Therapy. Washington: IRL Press; 1987:75–78.

92 **Jefferson JW et al.** Antihypertensive drugs. In: Jefferson JW et al., eds. Lithium Encyclopedia for Clinical Practice. Washington: American Psychiatric Press; 1987:94–100.

93 **Shukla et al.** Lithium-carbamazepine neurotoxicity and risk factors. Am J Psychiatry. 1984;141:1604–606.

94 **Hansten PD, Horn JR.** Drug Interactions & Updates Quarterly. Vancouver: Applied Therapeutics; 1993:468.

95 **Salama AA, Shafey M.** A case of severe lithium toxicity induced by combined fluoxetine and lithium carbonate. Am J Psychiatry. 1989;146:278.

96 **Noveske PG et al.** Possible toxicity of combined fluoxetine and lithium. Am J Psychiatry. 1989;146:1515.

97 **Apseloff G et al.** Sertraline does not alter steady-state concentrations or renal clearance of lithium in healthy volunteers. J Clin Pharmacol. 1992;32:643–46.

98 **Schou M.** Lithium Treatment of Manic-Depressive Illness: A Practical Guide. 5th ed. Basel, Switzerland: Karger; 1993:42–5.

99 **Jefferson JW.** Lithium tremor and caffeine intake: two cases of drinking less and shaking more. J Clin Psychiatry. 1988;49:72–3.

100 **Hetmar O et al.** Lithium: long-term effects on the kidney. A prospective follow-up study ten years after kidney biopsy. Br J Psychiatry. 1991;158:53–8.

101 **Zalzstein E et al.** A case-control study on the association between first trimester exposure to lithium and Ebstein's Anomaly. Am J Cardiol. 1990;65:817–18.

102 **Jefferson JW et al.** Lithium Encyclopedia for Clinical Practice. 2nd ed. Washington: American Psychiatric Press, Inc.; 1987:640–45.

103 **Jacobson SJ et al.** Prospective multi-centre study of pregnancy outcome after lithium exposure during first trimester. Lancet. 1992;339:530–33.

104 **Kallen B.** Comments on teratogen update: lithium. Teratology. 1990;42:205.

105 **Cunniff CM et al.** Pregnancy outcome in women treated with lithium. Teratology. 1989;39:447–48.

106 **Pajer KA.** Psychotropic drugs and teratogenicity. In: Keshavan MS, Kennedy JS, eds. Drug-Induced Dysfunction in Psychiatry. New York: Hemisphere Publishing; 1992:49–74.

107 **Jacobson SJ et al.** Prospective multi-centre study of pregnancy outcome after lithium exposure during first trimester. Lancet. 1992;339:530–33.

108 **Troyer WA et al.** Association of maternal lithium exposure and premature delivery. J Perinatol. 1993;13:123–27.

109 **van Gent EM, Verhoeven WM.** Bipolar illness, lithium prophylaxis, and pregnancy. Pharmacopsychiatry. 1992;25:187–92.

110 **Jefferson JW et al.** Lithium Encyclopedia for Clinical Practice. 2nd ed. Washington: American Psychiatric Press, Inc.;1987:518–25.

111 **Post RM.** Issues in the long-term management of bipolar affective illness. Psychiatric Annals. 1993;23:86–93.

112 **Maj M et al.** Long-term outcome of lithium prophylaxis in patients initially classified as complete responders. Psychopharmacology (Berl). 1989;98:535–38.

113 **Post RM.** Non-lithium treatment for bipolar disorder. J Clin Psychiatry. 1990;51(Suppl. 8):9–16.

114 **Post RM et al.** New developments in the use of anticonvulsants as mood

stabilizers. Neuropsychobiology. 1993;27:132–37.

115 **Sharma V et al.** Treatment of rapid cycling bipolar disorder with combination therapy of valproate and lithium. Can J Psychiatry. 1993;38:137–39.

116 **Calabrese JR et al.** Rapid cycling bipolar disorder and its treatment with valproate. Can J Psychiatry. 1993;38 (Suppl. 2):S57–S61.

117 **Clothier J et al.** Dysphoric mania. J Clin Psychopharmacol. 1992;12:13S–16S.

118 **Keck PE et al.** Valproate oral loading in the treatment of acute mania. J Clin Psychiatry. 1993;54:305–08.

119 **McElroy SL et al.** Valproate as a loading treatment in acute mania. Neuropsychobiology. 1993;27:146–49.

120 **Ketter TA et al.** Synergy of carbamazepine and valproic acid in affective illness: case report and review of literature. J Clin Psychopharmacol. 1992; 12:276–81.

121 **Keck PE et al.** Combined valproate and carbamazepine treatment of bipolar disorder. J Neuropsychiatry Clin Neurosci. 1992;4:319–22.

122 **Hoschl C.** Do calcium antagonists have a place in the treatment of mood disorders? Drugs. 1991;42(5):721–29.

123 **Dubovsky SL et al.** Calcium antagonists in mania: a double-blind study of verapamil. Psychiatry Res. 1986;18:309–20.

124 **Wehr TA, Goodwin FK.** Do antidepressants cause mania? Psychopharmacol Bull. 1987;23:61–5.

125 **Angst J.** Switch from depression to mania, or from mania to depression: role of psychotropic drugs. Psychopharmacol Bull. 1987;23:66–67.

126 **Pickar D et al.** Mania and hypomania during antidepressant pharmacotherapy: clinical and research implications. In: Post RM, Ballenger JC, eds. The Neurobiology of Mood Disorders. Baltimore: Williams and Wilkins; 1984; 836–45.

127 **Masand P, Stern TA.** Bupropion and secondary mania. Is there a relationship? Ann Clin Psychiatry. 1993;5:271–74.

128 **Berthier ML, Kulvisevsky J.** Fluoxetine-induced mania in a patient with post-stroke depression. Brit J Psychiatry. 1993;163:698–99.

129 **Turner SM et al.** A second case of mania associated with fluoxetine. Am J Psychiatry. 1985;142:274–75.

130 **Feder R.** Fluoxetine-induced mania. J Clin Psychiatry. 1990;51:524–25.

131 **Kane JM et al.** Tardive dyskinesia: prevalence, incidence, and risk factors. J Clin Psychopharmacol. 1988;52S–56S.

132 **Jefferson JW et al.** Fluvoxamine-associated mania/hypomania in patients with obsessive-compulsive disorder. J Clin Psychopharmacol. 1991;11:391–92.

133 **Dorevitch A et al.** Fluvoxamine-associated manic behavior—a case series. Ann Pharmacother. 1993;27:1455–457.

134 **Ghaziuddin M.** Mania induced by sertraline in a prebubertal child. Am J Psychiatry. 1994;151:944.

135 **Price WA, prepubertal M.** Buspirone-induced mania. J Clin Psychopharmacol. 1989;9:150–51.

136 **Lieggio NE, Yeragani VK.** Buspi-

rone-induced hypomania. J Clin Psychopharmacol. 1988;8:226–27.

137 **France RD, Krishnan KRR.** Alprazolam-induced manic reaction. Am J Psychiatry. 1984;141:1127–128.

138 **Pecknold JC, Fleury D.** Alprazolam-induced manic episode in two patients with panic disorder. Am J Psychiatry. 1986;143:652–53.

139 **Weilburg JB et al.** Triazolam-induced brief episodes of secondary mania in a depressed patient. J Clin Psychiatry. 1987;48:492–93.

140 **Zajecka J.** Pharmacology, pharmacokinetics, and safety issues of mood-stabilizing agents. Psychiatric Annals. 1993;23:79–85.

141 **McElroy SL et al.** Valproate in the treatment of bipolar disorder: literature review and clinical guidelines. J Clin Psychopharmacol. 1992;12:42S–52S.

142 **Dreifuss FE et al.** Valproic acid hepatic fatalities: II. US experience since 1984. Neurology. 1989;39:201–7.

143 **Sachs GS.** Adjuncts and alternatives to lithium therapy for bipolar affective disorder. J Clin Psychiatry. 1989; 50(12, Suppl.):31–39.

144 **Gianni AJ et al.** Verapamil and lithium maintenance therapy of manic patients. J Clin Pharmacol. 1987;27: 980–82.

145 **Warner JP.** Verapamil in mania. Am J Psychiatry. 1993;150:529–30.

146 **Garza-Trevino ES et al.** Verapamil versus lithium in acute mania. Am J Psychiatry. 1992;149:121–22.

147 **Bommer M, Naber D.** Subclinical hypothyroidism in recurrent mania. Biol Psychiatry. 1992;31:729–34.

148 **Ananth J et al.** Rapid cycling patients: conceptual and etiological factors. Neuropsychobiology. 1993;27:193–98.

149 **Bauer MS et al.** Rapid cycling bipolar disorder. I. Association with grade I hypothyroidism. Arch Gen Psychiatry. 1990;47–432.

150 **Bauer MS, Whybrow PC.** Rapid cycling bipolar disorder. II. Treatment of refractory rapid cycling with high-dose levothyroxine; a preliminary study. Arch Gen Psychiatry. 1990;435–40.

151 **Haykal RF, Akiskal HS.** Bupropion as a promising approach to rapid cycling bipolar II patients. J Clin Psychiatry. 1990;51:450–55.

152 **Masand P, Stern TA.** Bupropion and secondary mania. Is there a relationship? Ann Clin Psychiatry. 1993;5: 271–74.

153 **Fogelson D et al.** Bupropion in the treatment of bipolar disorders: the same old story? J Clin Psychiatry. 1992;53: 443–46.

154 **Fichtner C, Braun BG.** Bupropion-associated mania in a patient with HIV infection. J Clin Psychopharmacol. 1992;12:366–67. Letter.

155 **Small JG et al.** Electroconvulsive treatment compared with lithium in the management of manic states. Arch Gen Psychiatry. 1988;45:727–32.

156 **Lazarus JH.** Endocrine and Metabolic Effects of Lithium. New York: Plenum Publishing Corp.; 1986:99–124.

157 **Stancer HC, Forbath N.** Hyperparathyroidism, hypothyroidism, and impaired renal function after 10 to 20 years of lithium treatment. Arch Int Med. 1989;149:1042–45.

158 **Goodwin FK, Jamison KR.** The manic-depressive spectrum. In: Manic-Depressive Illness. New York: Oxford University Press; 1990:74–84.

159 **American Psychiatric Association.** Schizophrenia and Other Psychotic Disorders. In: Diagnostic and Statistical Manual of Mental Disorders. 4th ed. Washington: American Psychiatric Association; 1994:273–315.

160 **Goodwin FK, Jamison KR.** Diagnosis. In: Manic-Depressive Illness. New York: Oxford University Press; 1990: 85–123.

161 **Goodwin FK, Jamison KR.** Pathophysiology: Critical Evaluation, Integration, and Future Directions. In: Manic-Depressive Illness. New York: Oxford University Press; 1990:575–95.

162 **Goodwin FK, Jamison KR.** Medical Treatment of Acute Bipolar Depression. In: Manic-Depressive Illness. New York: Oxford University Press; 1990:630–64.

163 **Goodwin FK, Jamison KR.** Medical Treatment of Manic Episodes. In: Manic-Depressive Illness. New York: Oxford University Press; 1990:603–29.

164 **Goodwin FK, Jamison KR.** Course and Outcome 127–156. In: Manic-Depressive Illness. New York: Oxford University Press; 1990:603–29.

165 **Goodwin FK, Jamison KR.** Maintenance Medical Treatment. In: Manic-Depressive Illness. New York: Oxford University Press; 1990:665–724.

166 **Lombardi G et al.** Effects of lithium treatment on hypothalamic-pituitary-thyroid axis: a longitudinal study. J Endocrinol Invest. 1993;16:259–63.

167 **Bocetta A et al.** The course of thyroid abnormalities during lithium treatment: a two-year follow-up study. Acta Psychiatr Scand. 1992;86:38–41.

168 **Simard M et al.** Lithium carbonate intoxication, a case report and review of the literature. Arch Intern Med. 1989; 149:36–42.

169 **Koehler-Troy C et al.** Methylphenidate-induced mania in a prepubertal child. J Clin Psychiatry. 1986;47:566–67.

170 **Pope HG, Katz DL.** Affective and psychotic symptoms associated with anabolic steroid use. Am J Psychiatry. 1988;145:487–90.

171 **Viswanathan R, Glickman L.** Clonazepam in the treatment of steroid-induced mania in a patient after renal transplantation. N Engl J Med. 1989; 320:319–20.

172 **Hubain PP et al.** Cimetidine-induced mania. Neuropsychobiology. 1982;8: 223–24.

173 **Rego MD, Giller EL.** Mania secondary to amantadine treatment of neuroleptic-induced hyperprolactinemia. J Clin Psychiatry. 1989;50:143–44.

174 **Sotsky SM, Tossell JW.** Tolmetin induction of mania. Psychosomatics. 1984;25:626–28.

175 **Carney MWP et al.** Swithc and s-adenosylmethionine. Ala J Med Sci. 1989;25:316–19.

Psychiatric Disorders in Children, Adolescents, and People with Developmental Disabilities

Judith J Saklad
Judy L Curtis

Attention-Deficit Hyperactivity

Disorder (ADHD) 78-2
  Childhood 78-2
    Signs and symptoms 78-2
    Treatment 78-2
      Methylphenidate 78-2
        Side effects 78-2
      Other stimulants 78-3
      Diet therapy 78-3
  Adulthood 78-3
  ADHD with Concurrent Depressive Symptoms 78-3

Depressive Disorder 78-4
  Signs, Symptoms, and Risk Factors 78-4
  Treatment: Antidepressants 78-4

Bipolar Disorder 78-5
  Signs and Symptoms 78-5
  Treatment 78-5

Anxiety Disorders 78-5
  Separation Anxiety Disorder (SAD) 78-6
    Signs and symptoms 78-6
    Treatment 78-6
  Obsessive-Compulsive Disorder (OCD) 78-6
    Signs and symptoms 78-6
    Treatment 78-6

Schizophrenia 78-7
  Very Early Onset Schizophrenia (VEOS) 78-7

  Target symptoms 78-7
  Treatment 78-8
    Adverse effects of antipsychotics 78-8
  Patient education 78-8
  Withdrawal dyskinesia and re-emergence
    of psychosis 78-8

Tourette's Syndrome 78-9
  Diagnosis 78-9
  Treatment 78-9

Autistic Disorder (Autism)

(Also see Question 43) 78-10
  Signs and Symptoms 78-10
  Treatment 78-10

Disorders in People with

Developmental Disabilities 78-11
  Schizophrenia 78-12
    Signs and symptoms 78-12
    Treatment and target symptoms 78-12
  Depression 78-13
    Treatment 78-13
  Self-Injurious Behavior and Aggression 78-13
    Self-injurious behavior 78-14
      Evaluation 78-14
      Interventions 78-14
    Aggression 78-15
      Treatment 78-15

The recognition and management of psychiatric disorders in the specialized populations of children, adolescents, and people with developmental disabilities are complicated by a number of issues. These include symptom interpretation, diagnostic issues, research limitations, environmental influences such as family dysfunction, and societal attitudes regarding psychiatric illness and medication usage in these groups. For people with developmental disabilities, this also is complicated by a history of significant medication misuse, which has resulted in a climate that discourages the use of psychotropic medications and accreditation standards which impose strict rules on their use.

Symptoms must be assessed in light of the developmental level of the patient. The magical thinking and temper tantrums that are developmentally normal for a three-year-old may represent significant symptomatology in a ten-year-old. Elicitation of some psychiatric symptoms, such as reports of hallucinations or depressive mood, are dependent upon verbal communication skills, which also vary with developmental level. The presentation of a psychiatric illness, therefore, will vary with age, the developmental stage, psychosocial factors, and any cognitive delays or disabilities.

Unlike other areas of psychiatry, research in psychopharmacology of pediatrics and people with developmental disabilities has lagged. It is only recently that well-controlled medication studies in these groups have been published. Before this, most of the literature has been filled with anecdotal case reports and open trials, and one author's work in people with developmental disabilities has been retracted due to academic dishonesty.[1] Research has been hampered by a number of challenges. Diagnosis in these two groups is not as reliable as that for adult psychiatric patients, due to variability of presentation as discussed above. This leads to treatment groups which may have significant heterogeneity, making interpretation of study results difficult.

Additionally, environmental factors can influence the expression and severity of the psychiatric illness greatly. A dysfunctional family system may contribute significantly to the difficulties a child experiences. While the child may be the identified patient, it often is as important to treat the entire family as it is to treat the child. Family therapy can be an integral component of the multimodal approach to treatment. Similarly, for people with developmental disabilities, the structure and consistency of their environment and care givers significantly impact their behavior.

Behavioral therapies often are used as components of the overall treatment plan. Behavioral treatment strategies may include training of adaptive behavior by using reinforcement to increase appropriate responses. Token economy systems (providing tokens such as poker chips for adaptive behavior which are exchanged later to ''buy'' a desired item or activity) and checklists may be used to evaluate treatment and reward appropriate behavior.

The Diagnostic and Statistical Manual, fourth edition (DSM-IV)[2] diagnostic classifications will be used throughout this chapter, with the DSM-III-R[3] classification in parenthesis if there is a significant change in diagnostic criteria between editions. The reader is referred to the specific chapters of this text (e.g., Chapters 73: Anxiety Disorders; 74: Sleep Disorders; 75: Schizophrenia; 76: Mood Disorders I: Major Depressive Disorders; and 77: Mood Disorders II: Bipolar Affective Disorders) for pathophysiology, usual presentation in a psychiatric population, and general drug therapy. Only those aspects of presentation and therapy for children, adolescents, and people with developmental disabilities which differ from those seen in the usual adult psychiatric population will be discussed here.

Attention-Deficit Hyperactivity Disorder (ADHD)

The criteria for attention-deficit hyperactivity disorder (formerly known as attention deficit disorder) include a developmentally inappropriate inability to maintain attention and hyperactivity-impulsivity. These must have persisted for at least six months, with onset before age seven, and cause significant distress or impairments in social or academic function.[2] The DSM-IV has included wording regarding workplace as well as academic functioning to facilitate diagnosis of ADHD in adults; ADHD has been subdivided into Combined Type, Predominantly Inattentive Type, and Predominantly Hyperactive-Impulsive Type.

Childhood

ADHD is the most common psychiatric disorder in children. The age of onset usually is around three, although the child may not be brought in for treatment until entering school. It has a prevalence rate of 1.2% to 20% and a male to female ratio of 4 to 8:1,[4] although it may be underdiagnosed in girls.[5] ADHD is a familial disorder, with 20% to 30% of children having a parent or other family member with ADHD during childhood. Twin and adoption studies also suggest a genetic component.[6]

Dysregulation of monoamine neurotransmitter systems appears to be involved in the pathogenesis of ADHD.[7] The noradrenergic,[8] dopaminergic,[9] and serotonergic[10] systems all have been implicated in attention-deficit hyperactivity disorder. The mechanism of action of the stimulants, through one or a combination of these neurotransmitter systems, is to decrease motor activity and increase coordination and learning due to an increase in efficiency and attentiveness.

Signs and Symptoms

1. J.L., a physically healthy 5-year-old male, is brought to his pediatrician by his exhausted mother, T.L., after a conference with his kindergarten teacher. T.L. reports that J.L. frequently acts before thinking and has run into the street several times. He is unable to wait his turn in group activities and never seems to complete any activity before moving on to the next one. T.L. says that J.L. has not slowed down since he started to walk. During the course of the examination, J.L. is distracted easily by voices in another room, a truck passing by the window, and various objects in the room, which he picks up, then puts down almost immediately. Despite multiple attempts by both the examiner and T.L. to redirect his attention, J.L. is unable to focus on the examination or to sit in the chair for more than a minute at a time. What symptoms of ADHD are present in J.L.?

J.L. exhibits the classic symptoms of ADHD, including impulsivity (acts before thinking, runs into the street, unable to wait his turn), hyperactivity (unable to sit in the chair), and inattention

(never completes activities, distracted by noises outside the office). His behavior has been long-standing, is severe enough to concern his teacher, and is inappropriate for his developmental level.

Treatment

2. How should J.L. be treated?

In contrast to other areas of child psychiatry, the literature on ADHD is quite extensive and well controlled.[11,12] Stimulants have remained the drug of choice since benzedrine was first tried in 1937 for hyperactive children.[13] Methylphenidate (Ritalin) is the stimulant most commonly prescribed.[14]

Methylphenidate is absorbed rapidly but incompletely, with a bioavailability of 10.5% to 52.5%.[15] The plasma concentration peaks one hour after an oral dose.[16] The rate of gastrointestinal (GI) absorption of methylphenidate is increased with food,[15] but there is no difference in response.[17] There is no significant difference in efficacy between the sustained-release product (Ritalin SR) and the regular methylphenidate[18] in studies. In some individuals, however, there may be less efficacy seen with the sustained-release product. The serum half-life of methylphenidate is 2.5 to 3.5 hours, but serum levels do not correlate with response, and there is a large interindividual variation in serum levels on the same dose.[16]

Methylphenidate doses of 0.3 mg/kg/day improve performance on measures of cognitive function[19] and task persistence.[20] There appears to be little additional benefit in cognitive function at 0.6 mg/kg/day, although there may be additional behavioral improvement.[21] A decrease in cognitive performance has been noted at 1 mg/kg/day.[22]

Methylphenidate significantly improves attention and ability to learn in the classroom[23] and can produce long-lasting improvements in academic performance.[24] Methylphenidate normalizes classroom behavior,[25] improves peer interactions,[26] and improves self-esteem and sense of control during therapy.[27]

The usual starting dose is 5 mg of methylphenidate in the morning. An additional dose may be added at noon if necessary. Response should be rapid and may be seen within hours of the first dose although usual practice is to wait at least three to four days to assess the dose. The dosage is titrated up to achieve a maximum therapeutic response, up to 1 mg/kg, or a total of 60 mg/day. Some children require a third dose at 4 p.m. if their behavior is unmanageable at home. To avoid the stigma of receiving medication during the school day, the sustained-release product may be used. Many children feel that methylphenidate helps them and are willing to continue therapy despite minor side effects.[28] Children on the sustained-release product were more likely to have a positive attitude toward their medication.

As with any other psychiatric disorder in children, multiple therapeutic strategies, including family therapy, parent training, educational programming, behavioral therapy, and medication are used simultaneously.[29] In J.L.'s case, a checklist will be used at home to keep him on task, and he is referred to a preschool with a more structured setting. Additionally, methylphenidate 5 mg in the morning should be prescribed for J.L.

3. Side Effects. What potential side effects should be reviewed with T.L.?

The most common side effects with methylphenidate are insomnia and anorexia. Other side effects include nausea and abdominal pain, which can be managed by administering the medication on a full stomach, and transient unprovoked crying. However, the side effects reported with methylphenidate are the same as for placebo, and many are similar to symptoms of ADHD.[30] There is a potential for growth suppression in children taking the stimulants such as methylphenidate, but provision of "drug holidays" on the weekends and in the summer allow for catch-up growth for those children in whom careful monitoring of height indicates growth suppression.[31] There is no effect on growth in early adolescence.[32] Tics may be precipitated by the use of stimulants, especially in those patients with a family history of tic disorders such as Gilles de la Tourette's Syndrome. Because of its dopamine agonist properties, methylphenidate may worsen a pre-existing psychosis.[33]

4. Other Stimulants. What other stimulants are effective in ADHD?

Dextroamphetamine (Dexedrine) is as effective as methylphenidate in attention-deficit hyperactivity disorder.[34] The peak therapeutic effect is seen within one to two hours of dosing.[22] The usual starting dose is 2.5 mg at 8 a.m., with the addition of a dose at noon if necessary. Dextroamphetamine also is available as a sustained-release product. The adverse effects are identical to those seen with methylphenidate.

Pemoline (Cylert) is equivalent to methylphenidate for the treatment of ADHD.[35] It has a longer duration of action and a slower onset of action than methylphenidate or dextroamphetamine and it may take up to two weeks to see maximal effect from a dosage change. The half-life in children is seven hours.[36] It has the advantage of long duration, which allows for single daily dosing in the morning. The usual dosage range is from 18.75 to 112.5 mg/day, with similar adverse effects to the other stimulants. Pemoline may cause hepatotoxicity and liver function tests should be monitored routinely.[37]

5. T.L. asks whether J.L. will "grow out" of his ADHD. What is the likelihood pediatric patients will outgrow ADHD?

The conventional wisdom is that children outgrow their ADHD as they enter puberty and that stimulant medications should be stopped at that time. However, a number of studies which have looked at long-term outcome do not support this assumption.[38] In one prospective study, symptoms persisted into adolescence (age 13 to 15) in 68% of patients.[39] Persistence into adulthood will be discussed below.

6. Diet Therapy. J.L. has responded well to the combination of methylphenidate and the behavior checklist. T.L. sends him off for his annual summer visit to his father, S.L., and stepmother, G.L., with his methylphenidate, 30 copies of his daily behavioral checklist to be completed by S.L., and written instructions. One month later, J.L. returns with the full bottle of methylphenidate, 12 daily checklists in varying stages of completion, and reports that "they didn't let me eat any good stuff" as he bounces around the room. In a terse telephone discussion, G.L. reports that she couldn't give J.L. "that poison" when proper management of his diet could improve his behavior. What is the role of diet therapy in ADHD?

Scientific evidence does not support the hypothesis that a food additive-free diet, such as the Feingold diet, improves behavior in most hyperactive children.[40] Controlled trials show no worsening of ADHD symptoms with sugar.[41,42] Some children may worsen with a specific food or additive.[43] These may represent a true food allergy but should be tested in a blinded fashion with the child. However, many parents are convinced that diet affects their child's behavior, and much has been written in the lay press about dietary treatment for the ADHD child. While a diet restricting sugar and food additives probably will not improve the child's behavior, such a diet may not be harmful, provided that the dietary restrictions are not severe and do not produce major conflicts between the parent and child. It should be remembered that food is a very powerful reinforcement of behavior, and restriction of desired foods (e.g., "junk" food, chocolate) because of undesired behavior may have significant impact on behavior.

Adulthood

7. J.L.'s therapist arranges a meeting with T.L. (mother), S.L. (father), and G.L. (stepmother) to review J.L.'s progress and to coordinate treatment to provide consistency in both settings. During the course of the therapy session, T.L. reports that S.L. has "never taken responsibility for anything in his life" and is unable to hold a job for longer than 6 months. He dropped out of 9th grade because he was "always in detention." Both T.L. and G.L. report that S.L. often seems to act on impulse without thought to the consequences, is unreliable, loses things easily, and never seems to complete anything. T.L. says that he is "just like a child, exactly like J.L." and that his behavior was a major reason for their divorce. G.L. admits that these things also are a problem within their relationship. What is the likelihood S.L. also has an ADHD?

Attention-deficit hyperactivity disorder can persist into adulthood. In one follow-up study, 31% of young adults diagnosed as ADHD in childhood still had the full syndrome, and 9% had two of the three symptoms of ADHD (attention deficit, impulsivity, hyperactivity). Twenty percent were diagnosed as antisocial disorder, and 12% had substance abuse disorder. Those who still had ADHD were most likely to manifest other symptoms.[39] Another study estimated that 66% of adults with a history of ADHD still had some residual symptoms at a 15-year follow-up.[44] Adults with ADHD have a higher rate of substance abuse, antisocial personality disorder, depression, and anxiety than controls, and the cognitive deficits may persist even in uncomplicated cases.[45] There is some evidence that children with ADHD who are treated with stimulants have a better outcome as adults.[46]

Adults responded to methylphenidate in a placebo-controlled trial with an improvement in attention, and decreased affective lability, impulsivity and motor overactivity.[47] Bupropion also was effective in one open trial in adults.[48] Propranolol has been used to treat the temper outburst often seen in adult ADHD.[49]

ADHD with Concurrent Depressive Symptoms

8. R.J., a 9-year-old male with ADHD, also has appeared depressed, with episodes of withdrawal and crying spells over the past year. A trial of methylphenidate worsened his crying spells, although it did improve his ADHD somewhat. What alternative treatments are available?

The antidepressants may be preferable to the stimulants for those children who have depressive or anxious symptoms.[50] Up to 15% to 20% of patients will not respond adequately to stimulants and should be considered for antidepressant therapy.[51] Imipramine (Tofranil)[51] and desipramine (Norpramin)[52] are superior to placebo but less effective than stimulants for ADHD. Desipramine is effective in doses up to 5 mg/kg/day[53,54] and is equally effective for children with uncomplicated ADHD and those with comorbid conduct disorder, depression, or anxiety.[55] There appears to be no relationship between antidepressant serum levels and response.[56] Unlike the stimulants, desipramine does not appear to suppress growth.[57] There has been concern regarding potential cardiac toxicity of desipramine following several case reports of sudden death in children. Review of the cases and available literature, however, has questioned the causality of this association.[58] Ambulatory 24-hour electrocardiogram (ECG) monitoring in 71 children and adolescents on desipramine showed no significant difference from normal controls.[59] Nevertheless, a baseline ECG is recommended before initiation of imipramine or desipramine. The ECG should be repeated during the dosage titration to ensure that the PR interval remains below 0.21 msec and the QRS is less than 130% of baseline.[60]

The monoamine-oxidase inhibitors clorgyline (no longer marketed) and tranylcypromine (Parnate) are equivalent in efficacy to dextroamphetamine;[10] however, dietary restrictions may be difficult in children and adolescents. Bupropion (Wellbutrin) in doses up to 6 mg/kg/day, is superior to placebo.[61]

Clonidine (Catapres) 0.05 mg to 0.2 mg/day has been used in ADHD. Sedation seems to be the major side effect of clonidine in these patients.[62] Clonidine, therefore, represents a good alternative for the child with concurrent ADHD and Tourette's Syndrome (see Question 30). However, it would be relatively contraindicated in a child with depressive symptoms, as these may be worsened.

Depressive Disorder

Depression is one of the more common psychiatric illnesses in children and adolescents affecting about 2% of children in the general population[63] and 60% of children in psychiatric settings.[64] Children with first-degree relatives who are depressed[65] or alcoholic[66] are at higher risk for developing depression. Depression in childhood and adolescence often is chronic[67] and commonly is associated with other disorders, especially conduct or oppositional disorders, anxiety, and to a lesser extent, attention-deficit hyperactivity disorder.[68]

The symptoms of depression vary depending upon the age of the child.[69] In infancy, depression can be related to disruptions in the primary care giver-infant interaction and manifests as feeding problems, lack of growth, sleep disruption, lethargy, irritability, and social withdrawal or apathy. This may be known as failure to thrive or psychosocial dwarfism.

In early childhood (ages 3 to 4), language skills may not have developed adequately to express mood. Symptoms in this age group include abnormal motor or "acting-out" behavior, such as hyperactivity, aggression, and being in opposition to everything. Social withdrawal, separation problems, and eating or sleeping difficulties also can be seen.

In middle childhood (ages 5 to 8), depression can become more recognizable as low self-esteem issues, sadness, self-blame and feelings of guilt, social withdrawal, accident-proneness, somatic symptoms, lying, stealing, or being contrary, and aggression. School problems may present as underachievement.

In late childhood (ages 9 to 12), symptoms include sadness, apathy, a sense of helplessness, anhedonia (lack of pleasure in normally enjoyable activities), anxiety, irritability, somatic symptoms, school problems, and inability to concentrate. At this age, suicidal ideation and attempts may appear.

By adolescence, depression appears to be similar to that seen in adults. Symptoms include sleep and appetite disturbance, anhedonia, somatic symptoms, social withdrawal, antisocial behavior, and drug or alcohol abuse. Because adolescents tend to view the world in an all-or-none manner, with the feeling that things will never change, the risk of suicide is higher in this age group. Table 78.1 lists some of the risk factors associated with adolescent suicide attempts.[70]

Signs, Symptoms, and Risk Factors

9. C.M., an 11-year-old female, is referred to the outpatient clinic because of crying spells and school failure. She had been a friendly, well-behaved child who was active in gymnastics and was making good grades until about 1 year ago. At that time, she became withdrawn and irritable and began having crying spells. Her grades began to drop and she dropped out of gymnastics. Over the past few months, her appetite has decreased, and she has lost 5 pounds. C.M.'s mother also reports that she finds C.M. wandering around the house at night because she is unable to sleep. C.M.'s maternal aunt has had episodes of depression, including 1 suicide attempt. No significant psychosocial stressors (e.g., parental separation) are present. During the interview, C.M. tells the examiner that she is being evaluated "because I'm stupid," and that she wishes she

Table 78.1	Risk Factors for Adolescent Suicide[70]
Psychiatric Diagnosis	**Genetic Predisposition**
Mood disorders	Family history of mood disorders
Schizophrenia	Family history of suicide attempts
Conduct disorders	Family history of alcohol abuse
Substance abuse	
Personality disorders (especially borderline and antisocial)	**Other Factors**
Personality Traits	Biological factors (serotonin and dopamine)
Aggression	"Contagion" effect (suicide clusters)
Impulsiveness	Dysphoria regarding sexual orientation
Hopelessness	
Psychosocial stressors	
Family dysfunction	
Parental loss	
Medical illness	
Lack of social supports	

could "go to sleep and never wake up." What symptoms and risk factors for depression are present in C.M.?

Symptoms of depression shown by C.M. include low self-esteem ("I'm stupid"), decreased school performance, decreased appetite, sleep disturbance, irritability, crying spells, and suicidal ideation. The family history of depression places C.M. at higher risk for depression.

Treatment: Antidepressants

10. What antidepressant medications are effective in treating depression in children and adolescents?

Of the antidepressants, imipramine has been the best studied in children despite methodologic problems with many of the studies. These studies are complicated further by a high placebo response rate (as high as 60%) that is transient and lasts for several weeks.[71,72] The total plasma level (imipramine plus the active metabolite desipramine) seems to correlate with response to medication when in a therapeutic range of 125 to 225 ng/mL.[71,73] Serum concentrations greater than 225 ng/mL have been associated with an increased risk of tachycardia and slowing of cardiac conduction. The serum concentration of imipramine and metabolites do not correlate with side effects, such as dry mouth, drowsiness, blurred vision, or tremors.[74] Controlled trials with nortriptyline in preadolescents[75] and adolescents[72] show no difference between active drug and placebo. Nortriptyline serum concentrations were maintained in the range of 60 to 100 ng/mL (therapeutic range in adults: 50 to 150 ng/mL). Subjects in these studies had a long history of chronic, unremitting depression of several years duration. Children with concurrent diagnoses such as conduct disorder do not respond as well to antidepressant therapy as those with major depression alone.[76] Response may be seen within four weeks as in adults[77] or may take up to ten weeks.[78]

Although antidepressants may not be proven superior to placebo, some children still might benefit from their use. If a child is unresponsive to nonpharmacologic measures and continues to display significant functional impairment at school or home, a trial of an antidepressant should be considered.[60]

11. C.M.'s symptoms suggest she will respond to an antidepressant. How should therapy be initiated and what monitoring parameters should be followed?

Before starting antidepressant therapy, an ECG should be obtained. Therapy can begin with 1 to 2 mg/kg/day in two or more divided doses for imipramine and desipramine, and 1 mg/kg/day for nortriptyline. Doses can be increased gradually to obtain the desired therapeutic response. Symptom response pattern is similar to that seen in adults, with improvement in appetite and sleep seen before an improvement in mood. Full response may take four to ten weeks. The usual daily dose for imipramine and desipramine is 2 to 5 mg/kg/day, and for nortriptyline, 1 to 3 mg/kg/day. Data on the use of any of the newer antidepressant agents in children and adolescents are limited.

C.M.'s pulse and blood pressure should be monitored routinely. The ECG should be repeated if the pulse exceeds 130 beats/minute, if the pulse is irregular, and at 2.5 mg/kg/day and 5 mg/kg/day of imipramine or desipramine. The dosage should be decreased or discontinued if the ECG shows a PR interval greater than 0.16 second or a QRS interval more than 30% greater than baseline.[79]

In children, the half-life of imipramine is 6 to 15 hours. Therefore, preadolescent children should receive their imipramine in two or more divided daily doses to avoid peak-related side effects such as tachycardia. At steady state, plasma concentrations in younger children show a higher percentage of desipramine relative to imipramine than adults.[80] Older adolescents can receive their antidepressant in a single daily dose once they are at steady state. Imipramine is less protein-bound in children than adults; therefore, more free drug is available to bind to receptor sites.[81] In addition, children have proportionally more lean body mass than adults; therefore, less drug distributes into fatty tissue. This may explain the lower plasma concentrations tolerated in children.

Adverse effects of tricyclic antidepressants in children are similar to those seen in adults. The potential for cardiotoxicity with the tricyclic antidepressants can be minimized by adhering to the recommendations presented in Question 8. Children and adolescents tend to act impulsively; therefore, the possibility of intentional overdoses should not be disregarded. The smallest fatal dose recorded in the literature is 8 mg/kg.[82]

Bipolar Disorder
Signs and Symptoms

12. V.L., a 15-year-old male, is in his 3rd psychiatric hospitalization. He has a long history of depressive symptoms (crying, sleep disturbance, depressed mood), conduct disorder symptoms (runaway, truancy, fighting), and alcohol abuse. Previous psychosocial interventions have failed, primarily due to V.L.'s chaotic home environment. During his second hospitalization, he was treated with fluoxetine, to which he responded with a significant reduction in depressive symptoms. He was discharged to a therapeutic group home, where he continued to do well until 3 weeks before this admission. At that time, he began staying up all night, became more irritable, hyperactive and grandiose, and developed pressured speech. A diagnosis of bipolar disorder is made. What symptoms does V.L. display which are consistent with this diagnosis?

Symptoms of bipolar disorder in children and adolescents include silly, excited, hyperactive, irritable, paranoid, withdrawn, angry, or explosive behavior[83] and affective lability.[84] Symptoms also can be very similar to those of adult bipolar disorder.[85,86] The adolescent may experience several depressive episodes before his first manic episode. The symptoms displayed by V.L. (i.e., irritability, hyperactivity, grandiosity, pressured speech, staying up all night) are consistent with those commonly associated with bipolar disorder.

Bipolar mood disorder rarely is reported in preadolescent children.[87,88] It appears to be more common in adolescents,[89,90] with up to 20% of adult bipolar patients reporting onset of symptoms during adolescence.[91] It can be misdiagnosed as ADHD or schizophrenia. Children with a family history of affective disorders, especially bipolar disorder, are at higher risk for developing bipolar disorder.[85,92]

Treatment
13. How should V.L. be treated?

A switch from depression to mania can be precipitated by tricyclics[93] and fluoxetine.[94] As a result, the conversion of V.L.'s symptoms of depression to mania may represent a drug-induced mania. The first step would be to discontinue fluoxetine. If this is not effective, lithium may be started. If V.L. responds to discontinuation of fluoxetine, future depressive episodes should be treated with lithium or a combination of lithium and an antidepressant to prevent the switch to mania.

Lithium is effective in children and adolescents with major affective disorders, including bipolar disorder and cyclothymic disorder.[95,96] Preliminary results from one study also suggest that lithium is effective in adolescents with both bipolar disorder and substance abuse by reducing craving;[97] therefore, lithium may be especially appropriate for V.L. who also has a history of alcohol abuse.

Lithium carbonate 30 mg/kg/day (0.8 mEq/kg/day) in three divided doses should be initiated in V.L. if he fails to respond to the discontinuation of fluoxetine. The dose can be increased to obtain a serum concentration within the therapeutic range (0.6 to 1.2 mEq/L).[98] Administration with food will decrease gastrointestinal upset that commonly accompanies lithium therapy.

Overall, adverse effects with lithium therapy are less common in children than adults.[99] Children appear to be more resistant to lithium-induced nephrotoxicity, perhaps because they tend to have better underlying renal function. No change in renal function was noted in one long-term study which followed four children for three to five years.[100] However, proteinuria, polyuria, polydipsia, and a diabetes-insipidus-like syndrome also have been reported in children.[101] Therefore, urinalysis and serum creatinine concentrations should be monitored in children and adults alike. Additionally, children receiving lithium should be monitored closely in the summer to prevent dehydration, which increases the risk of lithium-induced renal damage.

Since V.L. is to be treated with lithium if the discontinuation of fluoxetine fails to reverse his symptoms of mania, his thyroid function should be monitored because lithium impairs thyroid function.[102] Maintenance of adequate thyroid function is especially important in children to maintain adequate growth. Additionally, lithium potentially can increase parathyroid hormone levels, and cause hypercalcemia, hypophosphatemia,[103] and a decrease in calcium deposition in bone. Lithium itself can deposit in bone, especially in immature bone,[104] and it only redistributes out of bone very slowly after the discontinuation of the drug. These effects of lithium on bone and on parathyroid hormone, calcium, and phosphate may be associated with its inhibitory effect on bone size in growing rats.[105] Although lithium's effect on bone growth in humans has not been studied adequately, accurate growth charts should be maintained for pediatric patients such as V.L. and height and weight should be evaluated every three months.

Anxiety Disorders

Anxiety disorders in children are very similar to those in adults. The diagnostic criteria are the same in all age groups for generalized anxiety disorder, panic disorder, obsessive-compulsive disorder (OCD), agoraphobia, social phobia, specific phobia, posttraumatic stress disorder, and anxiety disorder not otherwise specified. One anxiety disorder, however, is specific to children: separation anxiety disorder (SAD).[2]

Diagnosis of anxiety disorders is confounded by the developmental level of the child and difficulty in obtaining accurate information from the parent or care giver.[106] Furthermore, many of the disorders coexist with other psychiatric disorders, such as depression, attention-deficit hyperactivity disorder, and conduct disorder.[106-108]

Separation Anxiety Disorder (SAD)

Separation anxiety disorder is characterized by excessive anxiety about separation from parents or important attachment figures. The child's developmental level must be taken into account for both avoidant disorder and separation anxiety, because anxiety about strangers and separation is normal in preschool children.[106,109]

Signs and Symptoms

14. F.M., a 7-year-old male, is brought to the clinic by his parents. F.M. has refused to go to school for the last 3 weeks and refuses to leave his mother. His mother complains of not being able to leave the house without her son. He constantly hangs onto her and follows her. During the examination, he sits on her lap. When she attempts to leave, he throws a temper tantrum and wraps himself around her legs, refusing to let go. He states he is afraid his mother will be killed and wants her in sight at all times. The diagnosis of SAD is made. What symptoms differentiate separation anxiety disorder from generalized anxiety disorder in F.M.?

Separation anxiety disorder is more likely to present in a 7-year-old child than generalized anxiety disorder (overanxious disorder). Refusal to go to school is common to both separation anxiety disorder and generalized anxiety disorder. Children with separation anxiety disorder, however, are more likely to manifest marked self-consciousness, worry of future events, worry of competence, and require frequent reassurance. Children with generalized anxiety disorder usually are older and do not cling to a parent or care giver. F.M. exhibits four of the seven criteria as defined in the DSM-IV: school avoidance, fear of harm to the care giver, excessive anxiety when his mother attempts to leave, and clinging behavior. A diagnosis of depression is ruled out as F.M. does not have a sleep disturbance and enjoys activities with family and friends.

Treatment

15. What is the most appropriate treatment approach to F.M.'s problem?

The treatment approach to a child or adolescent with an anxiety disorder should be multimodal and targeted to the individual patient.[110] Initial intervention usually involves behavioral treatment techniques in a child with separation anxiety disorder. Behavioral techniques that are used include relaxation therapy/systemic desensitization, setting goals and limits, appropriate praise, and family therapy.[112] Alternative techniques include modeling, differential reinforcement of other behavior, and contracting.[106] Behavioral intervention requires the care giver and child to participate in a behavioral treatment plan.[106,111,112] Initial behavioral treatment for F.M. and his family should include desensitization and relaxation, where each day F.M. is taken closer to his classroom and taught to relax when the first signs of anxiety occur. His mother should progressively distance herself from F.M. after he successfully can enter his classroom.

16. F.M.'s parents ask if there is a drug that can be used to treat his separation anxiety. What pharmacologic options are available for F.M.?

Both benzodiazepines and tricyclic antidepressants are used to treat separation anxiety and school refusal. The use of these drugs is based upon sparse literature and few controlled studies. There are four double-blind, controlled studies using imipramine or clomipramine to treat separation anxiety and school refusal. Only one of these studies (performed in 1971) found imipramine superior to placebo in increasing school attendance.[112-114] More recent studies performed with more adequate protocols have not shown superiority of the tricyclic antidepressants to placebo. The common use of tricyclic antidepressant medications for separation anxiety and school refusal is questionable.[112] Both chlordiazepoxide and clonazepam have been used in small open trials. More adequately controlled trials of benzodiazepine derivatives, antidepressant medications, and buspirone are needed to ascertain their effectiveness.[112] F.M.'s problem is treated best with the recommended behavioral therapy. Currently, there is not adequate literature support to use pharmacologic interventions.

17. What is the expected course of response to behavior treatment?

Children such as F.M. begin to respond to behavioral treatment in three weeks and are able to attend school regularly shortly thereafter.

Obsessive Compulsive Disorder (OCD)

Signs and Symptoms

18. R.D., a 10-year-old female, is brought to the clinic by her parents. Her parents report that R.D. constantly is washing her hands at home. She also spends at least 2 hours preparing for bed and must complete specific routines every night before going to sleep. She brushes her teeth at least 10 times and her belongings all must be in the same place every night. She checks them repeatedly before she can lie down. The parents report that her teacher is very worried about her as she cannot complete school assignments. R.D. continually rewrites her school work even if it appears perfect to her teacher. R.D.'s routines and insistence on perfection are interfering greatly with normal functioning. She is late for school, cannot complete tasks, and has no friends. Her parents report that they noticed routines about 2 years ago, but they have become much worse over the last 6 months. The mental status exam reveals a well-developed child of average height and weight (72 pounds). Her hands are chapped and rough. R.D. appears very anxious and asks to go to the bathroom where she starts to wash her hands. The psychiatrist's diagnosis is OCD. What symptoms does R.D. display which are consistent with a diagnosis of OCD?

R.D. displays symptoms commonly seen in people with obsessive-compulsive disorder. Most common target symptoms found by Swedo et al. are excessive washing, bathing, or grooming (85%), repeating rituals (51%), excessive checking (46%), and rituals to remove contact with contaminants (23%).[115] R.D. displays excessive washing, repeating rituals (bedtime activities), and excessive checking (redoing school work and checking her belongings).

Treatment

19. What pharmacological interventions should be initiated for R.D.?

Clomipramine (Anafranil) and fluoxetine (Prozac) are the only drugs currently approved by the Food and Drug Administration (FDA) for use in obsessive compulsive disorder. Clomipramine is more effective in adults, children, and adolescents than either placebo or desipramine for this disorder.[115-118] Although clomipramine use in children less than ten years old has not been established and specific recommendations for children below age ten are unavailable from the manufacturer, the usual dose of clomipramine for children is 25 mg/day. The dose should be increased gradually to a maximum of 3 mg/kg or 100 mg/day, whichever is less during the first two weeks.[119] R.D. should be started, therefore, on clomipramine 25 mg at bedtime and the dose slowly increased to 100 mg/day in divided doses. Divided doses are recommended initially to decrease the occurrence of side effects.

20. R.D.'s parents are very concerned about "drugging" R.D. They specifically are concerned about side effects. What should they be told about clomipramine?

It is very important that the parents are informed completely about the drug and its risks and benefits, as they are responsible for giving consent for the use of the drug and assuring R.D.'s compliance with therapy. Both the patient and care givers need to be informed about the side effects, course of therapy, and expected outcomes. Clomipramine is a tricyclic antidepressant and has all the side effects and warnings associated with that group of drugs. The most common side effects include somnolence, tremor, headache, dry mouth, constipation, anorexia, and fatigue.[119] Generally, clomipramine is well tolerated by children.[115] The parents and the patient also should be aware that a full therapeutic effect may not be seen for six to ten weeks and that they should see a gradual response to the drug. They also should know that complete remission does not always occur, and that R.D. may continue to exhibit some obsessive-compulsive symptoms.[120] R.D. also may need to take the drug for an undetermined length of time as the disorder may be chronic and require continued treatment.[120]

21. In 2 months, R.D. and her parents return to the clinic. Though many of her OCD symptoms have disappeared, R.D. is more irritable and becoming involved in fights in school. This is very unusual behavior for R.D. and her parents are concerned. Could this behavior be a side effect of clomipramine?

Aggression and paranoid behavior have been associated with clomipramine use.[121] This presents a problem because R.D. is responding to the drug. The dose of clomipramine should be decreased to 75 mg at bedtime in an effort to decrease the irritability and combativeness of R.D.

22. R.D. returns to the clinic 1 month later. Her parents report that the previously reported behavioral symptoms have resolved and her OCD symptoms still are controlled. If the dose reduction of clomipramine had not been successful, what other treatment options are available for children and adolescents with OCD?

Fluoxetine has been used in patients with obsessive-compulsive disorder. Riddle et al. showed fluoxetine to be superior to placebo in a study of 75 children and adolescents.[122] A small pilot study by Kurlan et al. showed a trend for improvement, but not statistical significance in patients with both OCD and Tourette's Syndrome.[123] Six children with OCD who were unresponsive to single-agent therapy benefited from the combination of clomipramine and fluoxetine.[124] Behavior therapy using exposure and response prevention techniques have been successful with some patients; however, experience in children and adolescents is limited to single-case and small sample reports. This technique exposes the individual to their fears and then prevents their engagement in ritualistic behavior. Imaginal exposure, a variant of the exposure and response prevention technique also is employed. Patients are instructed to imagine being exposed to their fears (e.g., dirt) and then coping with them without their rituals. When anticipated consequences do not occur, their symptoms disappear. A multimodal approach to treatment may be the most appropriate, including supportive family therapy and social skills training.[3,115]

Schizophrenia

Schizophrenia in children and adolescents is rare and difficult to diagnose. The lifetime prevalence rate for schizophrenia is between 0.2% to 1%. The prevalence of schizophrenia in patients younger than 18 years of age is less than that of autism (0.04%). The DSM-IV defines childhood onset as below age 12 and adolescent onset between the ages of 12 and 18.[3,125] Werry defines *Early-Onset Schizophrenia (EOS)* as occurring between the ages of 13 and 18 years, and defines *Very Early-Onset Schizophrenia (VEOS)* as occurring before 13 years of age.[126] EOS and VEOS terminology will be used in this discussion. The diagnoses of EOS and VEOS are based upon the same criteria that are used for adults with schizophrenia.[3] The difficulty in diagnosis lies in the developmental level of the child and differentiation from autism and mood disorders.[127]

Diagnosis of schizophrenia is particularly difficult in children because symptoms (e.g., hallucinations) cannot be discerned until the child can communicate effectively. This may make diagnosis in a very young child or one who is severely developmentally delayed very difficult. Positive cognitive symptoms can be detected as early as five years of age, but below that age, their determination is questionable. Family history is an important risk factor in the development of schizophrenia. The incidence of schizophrenia in first-degree relatives of people with schizophrenia is 10% to 15%.[127] Careful consideration must be given to the diagnosis of schizophrenia. It is a serious disorder and carries with it considerable social stigma. Other disorders such as autism, mood disorders (especially bipolar disorder), schizoaffective disorder, and organic disorders must be ruled out.[126]

There are clinical features of schizophrenia in children and adolescents that are reported consistently in the literature. For example, EOS and VEOS occur predominantly in boys (2:1). Although a three-year-old and another at 5.7 years of age have been diagnosed as being schizophrenic, there does not appear to be enough information to specify a lower age limit on the diagnosis of schizophrenia. Onset of the illness usually is insidious in individuals with VEOS and with EOS. Between 50% to 94% of patients with EOS and VEOS have premorbid abnormalities. These abnormalities include social withdrawal, odd personality, and delays in cognitive, motor, sensory, and social functioning. There are few studies that have looked at outcome of the disease in children. VEOS presumably follows a more chronic course; however, EOS is not always associated with a poor prognosis. The course of schizophrenia of any age of onset is chronic.[126] The course is variable with some individuals displaying exacerbations and remissions, while others remain chronically ill. Some individuals have a relatively stable course, while others show progressive worsening.

Very Early Onset Schizophrenia (VEOS)

Target Symptoms

23. K.S., an 8-year-old male, is admitted to an inpatient unit. He was brought by his adopted parents. He was adopted as a baby and there is no family history information about his biological parents. Over the last several months before this hospitalization, K.S. has become progressively difficult to handle. His parents report that he is being very disruptive in school. His teacher reports that he gives nonsensical answers to questions and talks to unseen people. Occasionally he cries out "Stop hitting me!" and strikes out at the air. His parents state he talks to himself in his room. He also talks about being afraid of "bad people" who are trying to hurt him. As a toddler, he frequently was withdrawn and was described as odd by care givers.

Admission mental status reveals a somewhat unkempt child of normal weight (52 pounds) and height. His speech is loose and tangential and centers around the "bad people" that he says will hurt him. When asked who the bad people are he states, "Well, you know, the guys on TV and at school, the food in the cafeteria is great, and my teacher is really happy." He makes good eye contact with the examiner, his mood is euthymic, and affect is appropriate to the situation but mildly constricted. He is oriented to person and knows he is in a hospital. Intellect was not assessed formally but appears to be av-

erage for his age. **What target symptoms of schizophrenia does K.S. display? What differentiates a diagnosis of schizophrenia from other psychiatric disorders in K.S.?**

K.S. displays several target symptoms that are consistent with a diagnosis of schizophrenia. These include a mildly constricted affect (reduction in range and intensity of emotional expression), auditory and tactile hallucinations, and loose and tangential (disorganized switching to unrelated or peripherally related topics) speech. Autism is less likely because K.S. has good speech development and maintained good eye contact with the examiner. It is more difficult to rule out mood disorders. The symptoms of early-onset bipolar disorder overlap considerably with schizophrenia; and patients with bipolar disorder have been misdiagnosed with schizophrenia.[126–128] K.S.'s premorbid personality [personality characteristics before onset of illness (i.e., withdrawal and odd behavior)] is consistent with schizophrenia.[126] As with all children and adolescents with psychosis, organic causes must be ruled out.[126] Because diagnosis is not clear-cut, K.S. will require follow-up for many years to confirm this diagnosis.

Treatment

24. How should K.S. be treated?

Psychosis in a child or adolescent is treated in the same way as in an adult. Treatment should involve a multimodal program aimed at treating K.S.'s specific symptoms and providing psychological and social support for the family.[126] The only specific treatment in schizophrenia is antipsychotic medication. The effectiveness of antipsychotic medications is well established in adults, but the effectiveness of these medications in psychotic children and adolescents is not well studied.[129] Nevertheless, evidence of efficacy in the treatment of documented psychosis in children is sufficient to warrant the use of antipsychotic medications. Although no antipsychotic medication is superior to any other, side effect profiles are different and must be considered when a drug is selected. Currently, only three antipsychotic medications have been approved by the FDA for use in young children (haloperidol for children >3 years; chlorpromazine, >6 months; thioridazine >2 years). For older children, thiothixene has been approved for use over the age of 12 and trifluoperazine for children older than six years of age.[130] There are no recommendations regarding the use of other antipsychotic medications in children. K.S. should be treated with an antipsychotic medication.

25. What medication should be used to treat K.S., who weighs 52 pounds?

Haloperidol, thiothixene, fluphenazine, thioridazine, and loxapine have been studied in children with psychotic disorders.[129] However, there is no evidence to suggest that any one antipsychotic medication is more effective than any other. A drug should be chosen based upon the side effect profile, history of efficacy in the patient or family members, and cost.[126]

The high-potency antipsychotics (e.g., haloperidol, fluphenazine) cause a higher incidence of extrapyramidal symptoms (EPS), while lower-potency agents have higher anticholinergic and sedating effects. At least a six-week trial with adequate doses is necessary to gauge effectiveness of a drug.[126] However, it may be necessary to change medications earlier, if the patient cannot tolerate the medication. Recommendations for baseline assessment are listed in Table 78.2.[128]

Haloperidol should be started at a dose of 0.05 to 0.15 mg/kg/day for children more than three years old. This translates to a starting dose of 1 to 3 mg/day for K.S. who weighs about 24 kg. Therefore, he should be started on 1 mg tablet orally two times a day.[130] The dose may be increased slowly, no more than 1 mg/day once or twice a week, until an initial response is seen. As

Table 78.2	Recommended Baseline Assessment for Antipsychotic Medications[a]
Medical history (including seizures, liver and cardiac disease)	
Weight, height, BP, pulse rate	
Sleep and eating patterns	
CBC, LFTs	
ECG (for pimozide)	
Abnormal movement assessment (using an established rating scale)	

[a] BP = Blood pressure; CBC = Complete blood count; ECG = Electrocardiogram; LFTs = Liver function tests.

with adults, it may take four to six weeks to see the full therapeutic effect of the antipsychotic.[129]

Patient Education

26. K.S.'s parents are very concerned about giving him such a "strong" drug. What do they need to know about K.S.'s disease and the prescribed medication?

It is essential that the parents be fully informed about K.S.'s disease and treatment. As with all treatment for a child, informed consent must be obtained. The parents and child should be aware of the potential risks and benefits of taking a neuroleptic medication.[129] Potential side effects need to be addressed, including the long-term side effects of tardive dyskinesia. The parents should look for and report certain side effects such as tremor, stiffness, restlessness, and sedation.

27. Adverse Effects of Antipsychotics. Seven hours after his first dose, K.S. comes to the nurse's station crying, with his head tilted to his left side. He states that it hurts and he obviously is in distress. What is the likely cause of this new problem being experienced by K.S. How should K.S. be treated?

K.S. is experiencing an acute dystonic reaction. These reactions are involuntary tonic muscle contractions that usually occur during the first few days after starting treatment, increasing the dose, or switching to a higher-potency antipsychotic medication. These reactions may be very frightening to the patient but they rarely are serious. These reactions occasionally may present as laryngospasm and require prompt treatment to avoid interference with respiration. Risk factors for dystonic reactions include male gender and use of high-potency antipsychotics.[129] Dystonias are treated with diphenhydramine 1 mg/kg or benztropine 0.5 to 2 mg. Oral or intramuscular (IM) route of administration may be used depending upon the severity of the reaction. K.S. should be given diphenhydramine 25 mg intramuscularly to treat the dystonic reaction. The IM route is chosen because the onset of action is faster than oral administration and K.S. is in pain and very distressed. Diphenhydramine has sedative properties and will help K.S. to relax. Alternatively, oral benztropine could have been started with the haloperidol for the first week of therapy to prevent the occurrence of a dystonia.

Withdrawal Dyskinesia and Re-Emergence of Psychosis

28. K.S.'s behavior stabilizes after 6 weeks of haloperidol therapy and he is discharged to his parents. He is scheduled to be seen monthly by the clinic psychiatrist. After about 1 year, his parents call and tell the psychiatrist that K.S. is doing so well that they have stopped giving him his medication and do not intend to bring him again. Three weeks later, the family returns to the clinic. Some of K.S.'s disruptive behavior and paranoia have returned and he also is exhibiting repetitive movements of his tongue and lips. What has happened to K.S.?

It appears that K.S. is experiencing a withdrawal dyskinesia and re-emergence of his psychosis. Withdrawal dyskinesias usually present about 14 days after withdrawal of the drugs and may last up to 32 weeks. They must be distinguished from the re-emergence of stereotypies (persistent, inappropriate, mechanical repetition of movements) and mannerisms that may be present in psychotic, autistic, and mentally retarded children. A re-emergence of the psychosis may occur within one week.[129] Rebound behavioral problems also may occur. These problems may present as irritability and aggression occurring within two weeks of the discontinuation of the drug. Rebound autonomic symptoms also may occur, including insomnia, nightmares, sleep disturbances, and GI distress. K.S. has withdrawal dyskinesias as the movements have appeared only after his antipsychotic was discontinued. Stereotypic behavior is ruled out since K.S. did not exhibit these movements before or during drug treatment and the movements in his tongue and lips are consistent with antipsychotic-induced dyskinesias. It also appears that he is becoming psychotic again. The use of neuroleptics in K.S. must be evaluated carefully and the risk of irreversible involuntary movements taken into consideration. K.S. has a chronic disease that will become progressively worse without treatment. He should be maintained on the lowest possible dose of haloperidol and monitored regularly for the emergence of drug-induced involuntary movements.

Tourette's Syndrome

Tourette's Syndrome is a chronic familial disorder characterized by motor and phonic tics and behavioral and emotional problems.[131] It was first described in a single patient by Itard in 1825 and then in nine patients by Gille de la Tourette in 1885.[132] The syndrome once was thought to be rare but now is estimated to occur in 1 in 1000 males and 1 in 10,000 females. The age of onset for the syndrome is from 2 to 15 years old, with a mean of seven years for the motor tics and 11 for the vocal tics.[133] Onset usually is gradual with one or several transient episodes followed by more persistent motor and phonic tics.[131] Simple motor tics are seen in about 93% of individuals with Tourette's Syndrome. Simple phonic or vocal tics such as grunts also are reported frequently (98%), with coprolalia (foul language) reported about 30% of the time.[133]

Tourette's Syndrome is characterized by tics which are sudden, involuntary movements or sounds. The tics can be suppressed voluntarily with difficulty. Tics may be present during sleep and may wax and wane over time. Psychological stress tends to increase the intensity and frequency of tics.[132]

Behavioral symptomatology also is seen in Tourette's Syndrome. Between 55% to 74% of individuals experience symptoms of obsessive-compulsive disorder.[132,134] Approximately 50% of Tourette's patients also meet criteria for attention-deficit hyperactivity disorder.

Tourette's Syndrome is considered to be a genetically determined neurologic disorder with an autosomal dominant pattern of inheritance.[132] Tourette's Syndrome and OCD may represent different expressions of the same gene.[135] Although the exact pathophysiology is unknown, neuropathological changes have been identified in some affected individuals. Brain imaging studies show changes in the basal ganglia, thalamus, and cortex.[131] Excessive dopamine also may play a role in the pathophysiology of Tourette's Syndrome.[132]

Diagnosis

29. R.N., a 6-year-old male, is referred to the Tourette's clinic by his pediatrician. R.N. has facial and phonic tics that have been evident for a few years but recently have become much worse. Upon interview, R.N. demonstrates numerous tics characterized by blinking, eyebrow raising, and grimacing. Although unnoticed by previous examiners, he also shrugs his shoulders and shakes his head. He also demonstrates phonic tics with grunts and throat clearing. He states that he is unable to stop moving and grunting and that he feels relieved when he moves. When asked to suppress the movements, he can, but only for a few minutes. A report from his teachers indicates that he frequently is disruptive in school, lacks focus, and does not appear to be able to pay attention for any length of time. His parents report that R.N.'s uncle and cousin also have similar movements. A diagnosis of Tourette's Syndrome is made. What differentiates Tourette's Syndrome from other movement disorders in R.N.?

Involuntary movements occur with other disorders such as dystonias, choreas, athetoid movements, and myoclonus. Dystonic movements are slow, twisting movements that occur with prolonged states of muscular tension. Choreiform movements are random, dancing, irregular, and nonrepetitive. Myoclonic movements are brief muscle contractions. Athetoid movements are slow, writhing movements most frequently seen in fingers and toes.[2] The diagnosis of Tourette's Syndrome is made based upon the presence of both motor and vocal tics.[2] Tourette's Syndrome also can be differentiated from these by the ability of the patient to suppress the tics and increasing urge to perform the tic followed by a sense of relief.[132] R.N.'s movements and vocalizations are tics. They are rapid, recurrent, and sudden. He can suppress them, though only for a few minutes. R.N. also displays behavior that is consistent with ADHD which commonly is seen in individuals with Tourette's Syndrome. He is disruptive, lacks focus, and has trouble paying attention. His tics, behavior, and family history are consistent with the diagnosis of Tourette's Syndrome.

Treatment

30. What pharmacologic treatments are available for R.N.?

Haloperidol (Haldol) and pimozide (Orap) have been the mainstay of treatment of Tourette's Syndrome.[132,134] However, these drugs also cause serious side effects that result in medication discontinuation in up to 14% of patients.[134] Both of these medications suppress tics on a long-term basis. Relatively low doses are employed to treat patients with Tourette's Syndrome, using haloperidol 2 to 6 mg/day or pimozide 0.5 to 9 mg/day.[132,134] Side effects associated with haloperidol include all the extrapyramidal effects described with antipsychotic treatment. Pimozide additionally may cause cardiac complications, so periodic ECG monitoring is recommended.[132]

Clonidine, a centrally acting alpha-agonist, has been used to treat tics, attention deficits, and obsessive-compulsive symptoms seen in patients with Tourette's Syndrome.[132,133,135,136] It appears to be effective in 40% to 60% of patients with Tourette's Syndrome.[132] Clonidine usually is well tolerated, with the most frequently reported side effect being sedation.[136]

Antidepressants also have been used to treat Tourette's Syndrome. Two retrospective studies show response of ADHD and tics in children treated with nortriptyline and desipramine.[137,138] Clomipramine, imipramine, fluvoxamine, and fluoxetine have been used with equivocal results.[134,137] Other drugs that have been employed with varying results include lithium, calcium channel blockers, naltrexone, and clonazepam.[133]

31. It is decided to start R.N. on clonidine. R.N. weighs 51 pounds. Why was clonidine selected for R.N.? What is the appropriate starting dose for him? What is the expected time course of therapeutic response?

Clonidine is an effective treatment for children with Tourette's Syndrome and ADHD.[136] Clonidine is well tolerated and has fewer side effects than haloperidol or pimozide. Haloperidol can cause tardive dyskinesia and other permanent involuntary movements. It also can cause pseudoparkinsonism and akathisia. Pimozide causes the same side effects as the antipsychotic medications, as well as possible cardiac toxicity.[132] The antipsychotics have minimal efficacy in treating ADHD symptoms. The usual starting dose of clonidine in children with Tourette's Syndrome is 0.05 mg once or twice a day, administering the initial dose at bedtime to minimize daytime sedation. If the initial dose is tolerated, it may be increased by 0.05 mg every three days until sedation or dizziness is noted. Improvement in symptoms may take up to several weeks. The usual tolerated dose is 5.5 µg/kg/day.[139] R.N. should be started on clonidine 0.05 mg/day due to his age and size and the dose should be increased gradually to 0.15 mg/day as needed.

32. R.N. also is diagnosed with mild ADHD. His parents are concerned about using stimulants for him because of his Tourette's Syndrome. Can stimulants be used for children with both disorders?

The use of stimulants in children with coexisting ADHD and Tourette's Syndrome is controversial. There are reports of stimulants provoking or exacerbating tics in children with or without a pre-existing tic disorder. Clonidine is a logical choice for initial treatment as it is reported to be effective in treating both disorders. If it is not effective and hyperactivity is the prominent problem, stimulants may be used employing the lowest effective dose and careful monitoring.[133]

Autistic Disorder (Autism)

Autistic disorder is a developmental disorder characterized by qualitative impairment in social interaction, verbal and nonverbal communication skills, and a restricted set of activities and interests.[140,141]

Approximately 75% of individuals with the diagnosis of autism are developmentally delayed and about 25% have a seizure disorder.[140] Autism usually is diagnosed before children are 36 months of age; however, in some cases, the disorder was undetected for five to six years.[3] Autism may be detectable as early as 18 months of age.[142] The prevalence rate of autism is approximately four to five out of every 10,000 children. Autism reportedly is three or four times more common among males than females; however, some studies report both are affected equally.[3] Contrary to previous reports, autism is not linked to the upper socioeconomic class.[3,141]

The cause of autism is unknown; however studies of twins support a genetic component. Autism also is associated with medical disorders, such as the Fragile X syndrome, tuberous sclerosis, and herpes encephalitis.[140,141,143,144] Neurochemical changes are evident in many people with autism. For example, serum concentrations of blood serotonin are increased in approximately 33% of autistic people. Dopamine metabolism may be altered in autism.[141] People with autism also may have neuroanatomical abnormalities. Most notable are changes in the limbic system, amygdala, frontal lobe, cerebellum, hippocampus, and ventricles size. However, autism is a heterogenous disorder and these changes are nonspecific. There still is no known single anatomical abnormality associated specifically with autism.[141] Functionally, people with autism appear unable to integrate pieces of information into a coherent whole.[145]

The diagnosis of autistic disorder is made when criteria in each of three areas are met: impairment in social interaction, impairment in verbal and nonverbal communication, and a restricted pattern of activities and interests.[2] The major change from DSM-III-R criteria to DSM-IV criteria is a streamlining of the criteria, the addition of an age of onset below three, and the movement from an Axis II to Axis I diagnosis.

The impairments in social interaction in autistic disorder are described as nonreciprocal. Autistic people do make eye contact; however, it appears that they do not "connect" in a give-and-take manner. They have a markedly impaired awareness of others, especially the feelings of others (or even an awareness that others have feelings) and fail to develop peer relationships appropriate to their developmental level. They may fail to seek comfort from care givers when distressed.[141]

Impairments in nonverbal communication include an inability to use facial expressions or gestures to modulate communication, and an inability to interpret facial expressions and body language of others. If speech develops, it may be abnormal in pitch, intonation, rate and rhythm, and language may be stereotyped or idiosyncratic (i.e., repetitive use of a phrase, an odd use of a word). They do not appear to understand that language is a tool for communication. Many of these people can use words and phrases, yet do not use these for communication with other people.[141]

Individuals with autism display a restricted pattern of activities and interests. They may engage in stereotypic movements such as hand flapping. They may insist on sameness in the environment, exhibiting significant distress over small changes, such as moving their place at the dinner table. They may become preoccupied with a narrow interest, such as twirling a top. Imaginative play may be absent or markedly impaired.[141]

Signs and Symptoms

33. C.N., a 28-year-old male, lives in a group home and attends a local day program for adults with developmental disabilities. C.N. does not interact much with his coworkers or roommate. He prefers tasks that allow him to be alone and will hit his head on walls, furniture, or the floor if the room is too noisy or when he wants to be alone. C.N. engages in a bizarre ritual of self-restraint. He uses shoe strings and pieces of material to tie his hands together. As a child, he was described as distant and would not participate in family activities. He was diagnosed as autistic at age 3. C.N. can use words and phrases and can communicate needs and desires. He also has good receptive skills for verbal information. C.N. hesitates to speak when spoken to and repeats what was said to him before responding. He has never been seen having a casual conversation and rarely initiates conversation. C.N.'s preferred activities include looking at magazines and doing math puzzles and problems. Although he has superior ability in mathematics, C.N. tests in the moderate range of mental retardation. C.N. is otherwise healthy and has no medical problems. He requires assistance with his activities of daily living and cannot live alone. What characteristics of autistic disorder does C.N. have?

C.N. meets all three criteria. He is not involved with his coworkers or roommate. Although he can verbally communicate, his ability to carry on or initiate a conversation is limited. C.N. has very few preferred activities. He prefers to be alone, read magazines, and work his puzzles. He also displays other features often seen in people with autism, such as hypersensitivity to noise and self-injurious behavior (hitting his head on floors and walls).

Treatment

34. What is the preferred method of treatment for C.N.'s autism?

There is no cure or specific treatment for the symptoms of autism. Treatment should be individualized due to the wide variability of impairment. Typically, treatment for autism involves an integrated approach including pharmacological interventions, behavioral therapy, and special education. Behavioral approaches have proved the most successful, especially when integrated with appropriate educational programs.[146,147] In C.N.'s case, his self-injurious behavior is his way of telling his care givers that he wishes to be alone or the environment is noisy. His treatment program should teach him an appropriate way to communicate his need for a break.

Ideally, he should not be allowed to escape his environment when he engages in self-injurious behavior. His attempts to hit his head should be blocked with a soft pillow or blanket. Since he has verbal skills, C.N. should be trained to state that he wants a break and be allowed to leave his environment when he appropriately communicates without injuring himself.

35. What psychopharmacological intervention should be considered for C.N.?

Antipsychotic medications have been used widely in people with autism. Of these, haloperidol has been studied most extensively. Low-dose haloperidol (0.25 to 4.0 mg/day) appears to be effective in reducing stereotypies (abnormal repetitive movements) and withdrawal in autistic children in placebo-controlled trials.[148,149] Stimulant medications may cause a worsening of withdrawal, stereotypies, and other repetitive behaviors, but may help in those individuals that display target symptoms of inattentiveness, distractibility, hyperactivity, and impulsivity.[141] Both oral[150] and transdermal[151] clonidine have shown effectiveness in small double-blind, placebo-controlled studies, producing a reduction in irritability, stereotypy, hyperactivity, and inappropriate speech, and improvement in social relationships. Fenfluramine has been used to treat social adjustment, repetitive behaviors, hyperactivity, and distractibility; however, concerns about its central nervous system (CNS) toxicity and an inability to replicate some of the original findings have limited its use.[152,153]

People with autism may exhibit symptoms of other psychiatric disorders and require treatment. Self-injurious behavior may be seen in autism and is discussed below. C.N. does not engage in stereotypical movements or display hyperactivity. Therefore, antipsychotic medications, stimulants or clonidine are not indicated. C.N.'s bizarre rituals of self-restraint, however, may be symptomatic of obsessive-compulsive disorder. These rituals are interfering with his ability to carry out his usual daily activities and he appears driven to continue his self-restraint at all times. Clomipramine is effective in reducing stereotypies, anger, and compulsive ritualized behaviors.[154] It also is indicated for use in people with OCD. Though C.N. does not express obsessional thoughts, his ritualistic behavior may be indicative of compulsions.

The team treating C.N. decides to use clomipramine to treat C.N.'s self-restraint rituals. The staff is instructed to collect data on how much time C.N. spends in self-restraint. This will be used as baseline data to determine the effectiveness of the clomipramine. C.N. is a healthy adult male and should be started on clomipramine 25 mg nightly. The dose should be increased every three to four days until he reaches a dose of 100 mg nightly.[119] The staff at his day program and in his residence will collect data on how frequently he self-restrains. They may see an initial response in about two to three weeks, although full response may take much longer. Success of the pharmacologic intervention will be determined based upon how much time he spends in restraints. If a good response is seen (e.g., ≥75% decrease in time spent in restraints) he should remain on the current dose. If a less robust response is seen, the dose may be increased gradually up to a maximum of 250 mg nightly. As with any individual treated for OCD, C.N.'s compulsive symptoms may not disappear completely. The therapeutic objective for C.N. is to reduce his self-restraining rituals so that they no longer are interfering significantly with his activities of daily living.

Disorders in People with Developmental Disabilities

Mental retardation is defined as subaverage general intellectual functioning (IQ <70 on a standardized, individually administered intelligence test) with impairments of adaptive functioning, having onset before age 18. This is accompanied by significant limitations in two or more of the following skill areas: communication, self-care, home living, social/interpersonal skills, use of community resources, self-direction, functional academic skills, work, leisure, health, and safety.[2]

Individuals with developmental disabilities suffer from the same psychiatric disorders as those in the general population. This group may constitute the single most underserved population in the country.[155] A number of studies have estimated the prevalence of mental illness in people with developmental disabilities. Singh et al. summarized the findings of these studies.[155] About 50% to 60% of adults with developmental disabilities in institutions are likely to have at least one identifiable psychiatric disorder, and in 8% to 10%, the illness is severe and requires treatment. About 20% to 30% of children with developmental disabilities in both community and residential settings have mental illness.

There are many problems in diagnosing mental illness in these individuals. Many of these problems mirror those seen in nonretarded children. The developmental level of the individual must be taken into consideration. For example, communication skills and the ability to articulate are important in helping to make a diagnosis of psychosis. It often is difficult to know what symptoms are displayed by persons with severe or profound mental retardation when they are anxious, depressed, or psychotic. Our knowledge of signs and symptoms of mental illness in this population is incomplete.[155]

In general, persons with developmental disabilities do not refer themselves for treatment. Usually, a family member or care giver will initiate evaluations because of a problem behavior. The most common reason for referral is aggressive, self-abusive or self-injurious behavior, or self-stimulatory behaviors.[156] Psychiatric disorders may manifest differently in people with developmental disabilities. It is crucial to rule out environmental causes of the problem behaviors and treat them accordingly. These behavioral problems may be associated with medication side effects, medical illness, mental illness, need for attention, task avoidance, or inability to express needs.[156] A well-designed functional analysis performed by a qualified professional will assist in determining environmental influences. A functional analysis is an assessment process that determines the cause of the targeted behavior by observing events before, during, and after the targeted behavior.

A multimodal, multidisciplinary assessment best facilitates a valid analysis of a given disorder or problem behavior. Assessment techniques may include, but are not limited to, observation, rating scales, checklists, patient and care giver interview, and identification of antecedent and consequent events.[155]

Certain syndromes that result in developmental disabilities also may predispose the individual to psychiatric and behavioral disorders. These are listed in Table 78.3 with their associated disorders.[157–160,162]

There are special considerations when utilizing medication in people with developmental disabilities. Pharmacologic intervention is a very important and valuable tool to treat psychiatric illness and behavioral abnormalities in people with developmental disabilities. However, medications should be used to treat a specific psychiatric illness or well-defined target symptoms that respond to drug therapy.[162] There is a need for follow-up studies that look at the long-term effects of psychotropic medications in this population. Many individuals may receive psychotropic medications unnecessarily on a long-term basis.[163] If the original reason for use of the drugs no longer is valid, it is important to discontinue the medication. Withdrawal of the medication should be gradual with each dose reduction no greater than 20% to 25% of the total dose.

Table 78.3	Developmental Syndromes and Associated Behavioral and Psychiatric Disorders
Developmental Syndrome	**Associated Behavioral Disorder**
Down's syndrome	Alzheimer's dementia
Fragile X syndrome	Autism, hyperactivity, inattention, temper tantrums, anxiety
Prader-Willi syndrome	Compulsive eating, hoarding
Lesch-Nyhan syndrome	Severe self-injury (self-biting)
Cornelia de Lange syndrome	Self-injury
Rett's syndrome	Stereotypic hand movements (hand clasping, washing)
Fetal alcohol syndrome	Hyperactivity

Fewer withdrawal side effects should occur if the drug is discontinued slowly. Withdrawal effects may be either physical, such as nausea or dyskinesia, or behavioral, such as insomnia, hyperkinesis, aggression, destructiveness, screaming, irritability, and agitation.[164]

People with developmental disabilities may be acutely sensitive to side effects of psychotropic medications. Anticholinergic reactions, dizziness, ataxia, and constipation are a few of the adverse reactions that may be exacerbated. This is compounded further by the developmental level of the person. Many people with developmental disabilities lack functional communication skills and cannot express discomfort. The use of anticonvulsants and other medications also complicates detection of side effects. In general, use of low starting doses, slow and careful titration of the dosage, and implementation of a gradual taper when discontinuing medications will help minimize the occurrence of adverse reactions.

Schizophrenia

Signs and Symptoms

36. D. L., a 38-year-old moderately retarded female, is admitted to an institution for the developmentally disabled. Before admission, she lived in a group home with several other individuals with developmental disabilities. She was admitted due to increasing problems with her counselors and peers. D.L. had been taking chlorpromazine for many years, but it was discontinued recently by her primary physician due to lethargy, sedation, and constipation. Her care givers noticed increasing agitation and loud verbalizations over the last 3 or 4 weeks. D.L. has some long-standing difficult behaviors including aggression and dropping to the floor and acting like she was giving birth. She would appear to do this only when she was asked to do a task she did not like. Since her medication was discontinued, the staff noticed that she did not engage in these behaviors as much but would scream that she was being bitten by bugs. They also state that D.L. usually is concerned about her appearance and goes to work willingly. Lately, she has been refusing to go to work and has stopped taking baths. She spends most of her time in her room, refusing to come out. She disrobes and grabs at herself to get the bugs off of her. She states that they were biting her breasts and legs. This behavior occurs in all settings and at any time. Sometimes the staff is able to reassure her that no bugs are on her and that she is fine; at other times she cannot be consoled and requires restraint to keep her from hurting herself. Mental status examination upon admission reveals an attractive, well-developed female who appears very agitated. She is very distressed by the bugs she claims are crawling on her but calms down briefly when the interviewer reaches over and brushes the "bugs" off of her face and arm. She states that the bugs are trying to kill her and that the staff is helping the bugs to find her. She looks fearful and constantly looks over her shoulder. When asked about why she is doing this, she states that she is watching out for people bringing bugs into the room. Although she is fearful and agitated, she displays a constricted (limited range of expression) affect. D.L. has been institutionalized 3 times before, each resulting in a diagnosis of schizophrenia and institution of an antipsychotic medication. D.L. has a family history of mental illness. Her mother was institutionalized for most of her life with schizophrenia and has a maternal aunt who has bipolar disorder. **What are the signs and symptoms that support a diagnosis of schizophrenia in D.L.?**

A number of psychiatric disorders may be potentially confused with schizophrenia. It is very important to rule out environmental causes and other disorders. Individuals who function in the severe or profound range of mental retardation or are nonverbal may engage in strange behaviors that may look like catatonia but in fact may be merely stereotypical (e.g., persistent, inappropriate, mechanical, repetitive) in nature. People with mental retardation may engage in ritualistic behaviors that may mimic psychotic symptoms but really are indicative of an obsessive-compulsive disorder.[165] In this case the diagnosis of schizophrenia is fairly obvious. D.L. displays paranoia (bugs trying to kill her, people putting the bugs on her or helping them find her), and tactile and visual hallucinations (bugs crawling on her and biting her). Her history indicates that she responds to antipsychotic medication. She demonstrates marked deterioration in her activities of daily living and self-care skills. A diagnosis of schizophrenia may be made using DSM-IV criteria in individuals with mild or moderate retardation.[166] However, the diagnosis may not be possible in those who are nonverbal, and they may be given a diagnosis of psychosis NOS (Not Otherwise Specified). Some investigators suggest that a diagnosis of schizophrenia may be made in nonverbal retarded individuals based upon family history and behavior that correlates with schizophrenia (e.g., deteriorative changes in functioning, persistent withdrawal, and blunted affect which had not been previously present).[155,165]

Treatment and Target Symptoms

37. How should D. L. be treated, and what target symptoms should be monitored?

D.L. shows a positive response to antipsychotic medication by history. She had been taking chlorpromazine 600 mg orally daily. The decision to use psychotropic medication in developmental disability settings usually is made by a multidisciplinary team comprised of qualified individuals. The team, consisting of a psychiatrist, primary physician, pharmacist, psychologist, nurse, case worker, and direct care staff, decides to use haloperidol. Haloperidol was selected as D.L. is sensitive to the sedative and anticholinergic side effects of chlorpromazine. Haloperidol is a high-potency antipsychotic that causes less sedation and has few anticholinergic effects. The target symptoms are her verbal reports of bugs trying to hurt her, grabbing at her body to remove them, verbalizations of fear, and thinking that people are bringing bugs to her. Her mental status will be monitored by appropriate team members (psychiatrist, psychologist, and pharmacist). The residential staff that takes care of D.L. is trained by the pharmacist to look for side effects of the haloperidol such as akathisia or extrapyramidal symptoms and report any changes to the medical staff. The treatment plan is formulated and sent to the appropriate agency committees for approval.

38. What are the current regulations regarding the treatment of a person with developmental disabilities with psychotropic medication?

All agencies serving developmentally disabled individuals that receive funding from the federal government are subject to regulations as determined by the Health Care Financing Administration (sometimes referred to as Medicare or ICF-MR standards).[167] These regulations require a review of treatment plans for all individuals receiving psychotropic medications by qualified professionals. Each agency must have a specially constituted committee or committees to review, approve, and monitor individual programs designed to manage inappropriate behavior. Different states have additional regulations that also impact on behavior treatment. Behavior management plans may contain only behavior treatment techniques or psychotropic medications or a combination of the two. Informed consent is obtained from the individual, if he is competent, or from a legal guardian. In this case, D.L. is considered competent and has given consent for treatment. The committee's members give their approval and the treatment plan may be implemented.

39. Haloperidol 5 mg PO BID is started. After 2 weeks of therapy, D.L. is much calmer. She has stopped reporting any bugs hurting her and no longer is afraid that people are bringing in the bugs. Mental status examination reveals that she still is seeing the bugs but they no longer are biting her. She is taking better care of herself and has resumed working on a limited basis. A few weeks later, the residential staff report that D.L. is aggressive at times (she turned over chairs and hit a peer) and has dropped to the ground and acted like she is giving birth twice in the last week. What might be an explanation for these new behaviors in D.L.?

These symptoms may be a re-emergence of psychotic symptoms, but it is difficult to determine this without proper behavioral analysis. The psychologist is asked to perform a functional analysis. The results of the functional analysis reveal that the behaviors serve as a means for D.L. to avoid doing things that she does not want to do. Many behaviors may mimic psychiatric symptoms. In this case, D.L. has a psychiatric disorder and behavioral problems that are not necessarily related to her schizophrenia. The best treatment for the new behaviors is a behavior treatment plan that teaches her appropriate ways to communicate her need for a break and does not allow her to escape necessary duties. A new behavior treatment plan is formulated that integrates the use of psychotropic medication for her schizophrenia and a training plan to teach her appropriate behavior.

Depression

40. S.B., a 28-year-old severely retarded male, currently is residing in a group home with 3 other individuals with developmental disabilities. His care givers have brought him into a psychiatric clinic for the developmentally disabled due to a marked change in his behavior over the last several months. S.B. is nonverbal. He can dress, feed, and toilet himself and can make most needs known with gestures. He is described as a friendly, cooperative individual and is liked by his care givers. They are concerned because he appears to be withdrawn, is not sleeping well, and has lost 15 pounds in the last 2 months. He recently also has started hitting his head against a wall. He has required stitches due to the severity of his self-injurious behavior. They report that his appetite used to be very good and he particularly liked pizza. Now they cannot get him to eat even that. The care givers also report that his sister, who was very involved with him, recently moved away and does not visit him as much as she used to. Mental status examination reveals a very thin, young-looking man. He does not speak or meet the eyes of the interviewer. He responds to verbal direction, though slowly. S.B. does not receive any medication except for a multivitamin and he is reported to be otherwise healthy. The treatment team decides that S.B. may be depressed and that a trial of an antidepressant is warranted. What supports the diagnosis of depression in S.B. and how should he be treated?

The diagnosis of depression is based upon S.B.'s refusal to eat, withdrawal, and change in sleep patterns. As S.B. is nonverbal, symptoms of worthlessness, guilt, and thoughts of death cannot be determined.[155] S.B. should be given a thorough medical examination to rule out any potential medical causes. His sister's recent move also may be a factor in S.B's depression. Pharmacologic treatment of depression in people with developmental disabilities is the same as for the general population. The choice of drug should be based upon the patient and the side effect profile of the antidepressant. The clinician may choose from the traditional tricyclic antidepressants or the newer selective serotonin reuptake inhibitors. Controlled studies looking at the treatment of depression in the mentally retarded are limited at best.[165] However, there is a report of two cases of mentally retarded depressed adults with associated self-injurious behavior that were treated successfully with a selective serotonin reuptake inhibitor.[166] The tricyclic antidepressants are much less expensive; however, they carry with them unpleasant anticholinergic side effects (e.g., dry mouth, constipation). Since S.B. cannot communicate discomfort verbally, it is wise to try and minimize side effects as much as possible. Based upon the side effect profile of the selective serotonin reuptake inhibitors and the recent report of successful treatment of similar cases, the team decides that a selective serotonin reuptake inhibitor should be used to treat S.B.

41. Paroxetine (Paxil) was initiated in S.B. at 10 mg/day and is increased to 20 mg in a week. What is the time course of response to treatment and how will S.B. be monitored for response to paroxetine?

S.B. should respond to paroxetine in the same time course expected in the general population. Improvement of his withdrawal and an increase in activity level should be seen in four to six weeks, with sleep and appetite returning in two to four weeks. It is important to monitor specific target symptoms and assess the success of the antidepressant on changes in those symptoms. For S.B., the specific target symptoms are how much he eats and increase in weight. This should be monitored by having the staff record how much he eats for each meal and weekly weights. A sleep chart should be started and maintained for the duration of his treatment. The staff will maintain an hourly sleep chart. This will assist the psychiatric team in determining when and how much he is sleeping. Frequency data on his self-injurious behavior also will be maintained. The psychiatric team will determine effectiveness of the medication based upon improved sleep, increase in weight, and a decrease in the frequency of self-injurious behavior. If he does not respond, a second trial on a different antidepressant may be warranted.

Self-Injurious Behavior and Aggression

Self-injurious behavior in people with developmental disabilities is defined as "any chronic, repetitive behavior causing external trauma on a mechanical basis, occurring in a cognitively impaired patient."[168] Prevalence estimates vary, but most suggest 7% to 9% of developmentally disabled adults display self-injurious behavior.[169] Severe self-injurious behavior may be seen in people with Lesch-Nyhan syndrome and Cornelia de Lange syndrome and may be extremely refractory to psychopharmacologic treatment in those individuals.[170] Self-directed aggression also is seen in other disorders, such as borderline personality disorder and severe psychosis. These are beyond the scope of this chapter and will not be discussed further.

As noted above, self-injurious or aggressive behaviors often are the precipitant for referral of a person with developmental disabilities to a psychiatry clinic. Aggressive and self-injurious behaviors often occur together in the same individual or may occur singly. It is imperative that a thorough evaluation be performed to establish the underlying cause, if any, of the self-injurious or aggressive behavior before consideration of pharmacotherapy.[171] It also is important to have a reliable means of measuring the frequency and severity of these behaviors to obtain a baseline and to follow the effects of any interventions.

Self-injurious or aggressive behavior may serve as a means of communication, indicating a desire to escape a task, discomfort due to a noisy and chaotic environment, physical needs such as hunger, or to obtain attention from care takers. A good functional analysis as described above should help with this differentiation. A thorough medical review and examination also should be performed to rule out any source of physical discomfort that the individual is trying to communicate. A dental abscess, dysmenorrhea, or otitis media may produce a significant increase in aggressive or self-injurious behavior. These behaviors also may represent side effects of other medications. The medications most commonly implicated are phenobarbital, primidone, phenytoin, xanthines such as caffeine, and the high potency antipsychotics (due to akathisia).[171] Aggression and self-injurious behavior also are seen commonly as a major target symptom in other psychiatric disorders in the developmentally disabled. If any of these are determined to contribute to the individual's self-injurious or aggressive behavior, they should be addressed. A new behavior program, a trip to the dentist, or an adjustment in anticonvulsant therapy may preclude the need for additional pharmacotherapy.

If none of the above interventions are successful, pharmacotherapy may be indicated. Animal and human studies have implicated the dopaminergic, opioid, and serotonergic systems in self-injurious behavior.[170] Animal and human studies[172] in aggression indicate the involvement of dopaminergic, noradrenergic, GABA-ergic, and serotonergic systems. The precise pathophysiology of these disorders has not been worked out, and a more in-depth discussion of current theories is beyond the scope of this chapter. Current pharmacotherapy involves manipulation of one or more of the implicated neurotransmitter systems.

Self-Injurious Behavior

42. Evaluation. **T.J., a 26-year-old male with autistic disorder, functions in the moderately retarded range. He was transferred recently to a long-term care facility for the developmentally disabled from another facility, where he had resided since age 6. He has very limited verbal skills but is able to communicate basic needs with a combination of gestures and the use of a book of simple pictures prepared for him by the speech therapist. He understands basic verbal instructions. Recent physical examination and laboratory tests taken upon admission indicate he is in good physical health and he currently is receiving a multivitamin only. He is referred to the psychiatry clinic on an emergency basis by the treatment team due to his self-injurious behavior. The staff reports that he picks at the skin on his arms and legs, and has just completed a course of antibiotics for cellulitis secondary to his skin picking. He also becomes very agitated at times and bangs his head against the wall. He has required stitches to his forehead twice since his transfer. What are the first steps in evaluating T.J.'s self-injurious behavior?**

The first step is to obtain a good baseline functional analysis to determine what environmental influences, if any, affect his behavior. Records from T.J.'s previous placement should be obtained to determine if there were previous patterns of behavior and response to various interventions. The physical examination and laboratory tests were normal upon admission. Had there been any abnormalities, these should be followed up. A review of his medications indicates that he currently is on only a multivitamin, which should not influence his behavior. A psychiatric evaluation also should be obtained.

43. T.J. is seen in psychiatry clinic, where the diagnosis of autistic disorder is confirmed. How might this influence his self-injurious behavior?

Individuals with autistic disorder are very resistant to change and may become very distressed over minor changes in their environment. Being transferred to a new facility from the one where he had spent the past 20 years represents a major change in T.J.'s environment. The impact of these changes may be lessened somewhat by preparing the individual in advance with a visit to the new facility, if possible. The individual also should be permitted to take all of his personal belongings and any favorite objects.

T.J. also has limited communication skills, which are consistent with his autistic disorder. He is able to express basic needs through the use of his communication book. However, he may still experience frustration in trying to communicate.

44. Interventions. **Records from T.J.'s previous placement indicate that the skin picking is a long-standing behavioral problem that has failed to respond to several previous behavioral programs, although these programs were not always applied consistently. He has not received a trial of medication. The functional analysis reveals a significant increase in head banging when the living area is crowded and noisy. Skin picking occurs daily in all settings. What interventions should be implemented first?**

The treatment team should meet and review the results of the record review and the functional analysis. A behavioral plan should be developed to decrease T.J.'s self-injurious behavior.

In T.J.'s case, the team notes that the more severe self-injurious behavior, the head banging, increases when the living area is noisy and chaotic, such as just before dinner. This also appears to be a new behavior and is not in his records from the previous placement. The team also notes that previous behavior programs were not applied consistently, making an assessment of their efficacy difficult. A behavioral program is developed to teach alternative adaptive skills such as leaving the area that allow him to escape the noisy environment. His program also includes reinforcement of work and leisure tasks which keep his hands occupied to prevent picking. The team forwards the behavior program to the appropriate committees for emergency approval.

45. Three months later, T.J. is seen again in psychiatry clinic. His behavior program has been implemented consistently, and T.J. seems to have settled into the new environment. He has had no incidents of head banging in the past 2 months. His rate of skin picking has decreased by 30% to 40%, but he continues to have fresh sores several times a week, and is currently receiving an antibiotic for cellulitis of the forearm. What pharmacologic interventions can be used for the management of T.J.'s self-injurious behavior?

Most reports of medication efficacy in self-injurious behavior are case reports, retrospective record reviews, or small, often open trials.[173] Comparative trials have not been performed, so relative efficacy of the different agents is unknown. Medication choice may be made on the basis of the side effect profile of the drug, drug interactions to avoid, or consideration of other underlying medical or psychiatric problems. Medications will be discussed according to the neurotransmitter system which is thought to be the site of action in this disorder.

Dopamine. The antipsychotic agents have been the most commonly used agents in practice for the management of self-injurious behavior.[168] Thioridazine, haloperidol, and fluphenazine are the ones which have been used most frequently. It is unclear whether the benefits are due to specific D_1-blockade or nonspecific sedative effects.[168,174] Due to the long-term risk of tardive dyskinesia, antipsychotics should be reserved for those people who do not respond to other agents.

Opioid. The opiate antagonist naltrexone has been used to decrease self-injurious behavior in a number of case reports and small trials.[173] Response usually is rapid and is seen within days to a week with doses of 50 to 100 mg/day.[175,176] Mild nausea may be a dose-limiting side effect in some individuals.

Serotonin. These medications include propranolol, lithium, buspirone, and the serotonergic antidepressants, fluoxetine and clomipramine.

Case reports and open trials suggest that propranolol (Inderal) decreases self-injurious behavior.[177] Response may be seen with an average dose of 120 mg/day and may be immediate or gradual over several weeks.[179] The main dose-limiting effects are asymptomatic bradycardia and hypotension.

Several reports[179] and a double-blind study[180] suggest that lithium is effective in individuals with both aggressive and self-injurious behavior. In the double-blind trial, response was seen in two to eight weeks with a lithium serum concentration of 0.7 to 1.0 mEq/L.

There is one open trial of buspirone (BuSpar) in 14 developmentally disabled individuals with aggressive and self-injurious behaviors with anxiety.[181] Nine of the fourteen responded to doses of 20 to 45 mg/day, with maximal response seen more than three weeks later.

Several open trials of fluoxetine show it to be effective in reducing self-injurious behavior.[182] Response was seen with doses of 20 to 40 mg/day of fluoxetine when assessed at the end of a three-month trial.[183]

One open trial of clomipramine reports a reduction in stereotypic and self-injurious behaviors in 10 of 11 individuals.[184] Clomipramine did not provoke seizures in the six subjects with a history of seizures.

In T.J.'s case, the team thoroughly discusses the medication options presented by the pharmacist and psychiatrist. The decision is made to initiate naltrexone, due to its rapid onset and minimal side effect profile. The other medications listed will take two to eight weeks to take effect, while naltrexone should be effective within a week. Naltrexone will be started at 50 mg/day, and self-injurious behavior rates will be followed. The dosage will be increased to 100 mg/day if no response is seen within two weeks. The team will reconvene in one month to assess T.J.'s response. If he fails to respond to naltrexone, fluoxetine or buspirone will be considered. T.J. becomes very agitated with procedures such as venipunctures and blood pressure monitoring, making lithium and propranolol less desirable choices.

Aggression

46. M.S., a 24-year-old moderately retarded male, had lived at home until age 16, when his mother could no longer manage his severe aggressive outbursts. Retardation is thought to be secondary to hypoxia at birth, although he also sustained a head injury at age 2 which was thought to be secondary to abuse. After 7 years at a facility for people with developmental disabilities, he was placed successfully in a group home in the community. He is brought to psychiatry clinic by a member of the group home staff due to significant increases in property destruction and unprovoked aggression toward other residents. The severity of his aggression threatens his current placement. He has been on haloperidol for several years to manage his aggression. Over the past few months, his haloperidol dosage has been increased steadily to his current dose of 30 mg/day to try to manage his aggression. After careful review of the behavior data and medication dosing history, the team notes an increase in aggressive behavior after each dosage increase, rather than a reduction. What might account for the increase in aggressive behavior, rather than an improvement with increasing doses of haloperidol?

Antipsychotics, especially the higher-potency agents, may produce significant akathisia. Akathisia generally is described as a subjective sense of restlessness and the urge to move. It may be accompanied by objective signs, such as pacing and an inability to sit still. In many individuals, akathisia manifests as an increase in agitation and aggression.[171]

47. Treatment. How should M.S. be treated?

There are two approaches which could be taken. The first would be to decrease the dose of haloperidol to reduce the akathisia. The second would be to treat the akathisia with propranolol[185] or lorazepam.[186] Since propranolol also is useful to decrease aggression,[177,178] while benzodiazepines may produce paradoxical agitation,[187] propranolol would be a better choice to treat the akathisia. Case reports and open trials indicate that aggression is reduced with doses of 80 to 280 mg/day, and that response may be immediate or may take several weeks.[177,178]

In M.S.'s case, the team decides to implement a taper of his haloperidol dosage to its lowest effective dose and begin propranolol 20 mg three times a day for akathisia and aggression. While the team would prefer to implement one change at a time to fully assess the effect of each, M.S.'s severe aggressive behavior threatens his community placement and should be dealt with rapidly.

49. M.S. returns to psychiatry clinic 3 months later. He currently is on propranolol 60 mg TID, and his haloperidol dosage has been tapered to 10 mg/day. He has had no episodes of aggression toward others in 6 weeks, and incidents of property destruction (usually his own) are down to 2 a month. The team decides to continue his haloperidol taper and see if his long-standing aggressive behavior continues to be controlled by propranolol alone. If he had not responded to propranolol, what other medications could be used to treat aggression?

There are a number of other medications which have been used to treat aggression, both in developmentally disabled and nondisabled populations, but none are approved by the FDA for this indication.[188] There are several characteristics that distinguish aggressive episodes which are thought to be biologically mediated and, therefore, potentially amenable to medication therapy.[188] These include evidence of CNS dysfunction (e.g., history of head trauma, abnormal neurologic exam), sudden, unprovoked, and rapidly accelerating aggression, and rapid calming and remorse after the event. In M.S.'s case, his aggression is described as unprovoked, and he has a history of both hypoxic and traumatic brain injury.

Antipsychotics have been the most commonly used agents for aggression.[189] They are effective for management of aggression which is secondary to psychosis.[190] Their effect in nonpsychotic aggressive patients most likely is due to a nonspecific sedation, and they should be avoided in the nonpsychotic individual.

Benzodiazepines also have been used commonly to manage aggression. Intramuscular lorazepam is rapid and effective in calming the acutely agitated patient.[190] However, long-term use of benzodiazepines is not recommended for management of aggression. Additionally, individuals with developmental disabilities may disinhibit (develop paradoxical excitement) with the benzodiazepines.

Lithium has been shown in a number of case reports, open trials, and double-blind, placebo-controlled trials to reduce aggressive behavior in people with developmental disabilities.[179] Response appears to be greatest for those with the highest baseline rates of aggression and hyperactivity, and with serum lithium concentrations of 1.0 mEq/L.[192]

Buspirone has been used successfully in several case reports, an open trial[181] and a small placebo-controlled trial[192] to reduce aggressive behavior and anxiety in the developmentally disabled. The reduction in aggression may be secondary to reduction in anxiety or it may be due to a direct effect of buspirone on the serotonin system.

Carbamazepine is effective in managing aggression in adult psychiatric patients,[193] patients with dementia,[194] and children.[195] There are no studies showing its efficacy in the developmentally disabled. Response usually is seen with a serum concentration of 8 to 12 µg/mL. Valproic acid (Depakote, Depakene) also has been used to manage aggression in the developmentally disabled[196] and organic patients.[197] Anticonvulsants may be useful in the individual with a seizure disorder, allowing the use of one medication to handle two problems.

Update

Selective Serotonin Reuptake Inhibitors (SSRIs) in Children and Adolescents

U1. What is the role of the selective serotonin reuptake inhibitors, such as fluoxetine, paroxetine, sertraline and fluvoxamine, in children and adolescents?

The selective serotonin reuptake inhibitors (SSRIs) are being used in children and adolescents more frequently, primarily for obsessive-compulsive disorder. In an open label trial, fluvoxamine 100 to 300 mg/day was effective in treating adolescent inpatients with obsessive-compulsive disorder.[198] In a retrospective review, fluoxetine 1 mg/kg/day was noted to be effective in the treatment of children and adolescents with obsessive-compulsive disorder. Although neither of these two studies were designed to be blinded-controlled studies, both fluvoxamine and fluoxetine may prove to be a good alternative in patients who cannot tolerate clomipramine.

Fluoxetine also was reported to effectively treat obsessive-compulsive symptoms in people with Tourette's syndrome in open label trials.[200]

Fluoxetine also has been tried in several childhood anxiety disorders. In one open trial, 17 of 21 children with overanxious disorder, social phobia, or separation anxiety moderately or markedly improved at a mean fluoxetine dose of 25 mg/day.[201] In another report, five preadolescent children with anxiety disorders improved when treated with fluoxetine.[202] Fluoxetine in a double-blind, placebo-controlled trial for elective mutism (a type of social phobia in which the child refuses to talk in one or more major social situations, such as school), improved the response of children better than placebo according to parent ratings, but not teacher or clinician ratings.[203]

There is still very little published regarding the use of the SSRIs for depression in children and adolescents. Six adolescent inpatients with depression improved on fluvoxamine in one open trial.[198] The only other published reports involve adverse effects. Fluoxetine reportedly induced memory impairment in one adolescent child[204] and sertraline induced mania in a prepubertal child.[205]

The serotonin reuptake inhibitors may be useful in treating people with autism. Although the tricyclic antidepressant, clomipramine, reportedly improved social relatedness, obsessive-compulsive symptoms, aggression, and impulsive behavior in four of five autistic adults,[206] mixed results were seen with fluoxetine in an open trial in individuals with autism and mental retardation.[207] In conclusion, the SSRIs may be beneficial in treating obsessive-compulsive symptoms, aggression, and impulsivity in children and adolescents with these disorders.

References

1 **Holden C.** NIMH finds a case of "serious misconduct." Science. 1987;235:1566.

2 **American Psychiatric Association.** Diagnostic and Statistical Manual of Mental Disorders. 4th ed. Washington, DC: American Psychiatric Association; 1994.

3 **American Psychiatric Association.** Diagnostic and Statistical Manual of Mental Disorders. 3rd ed., revised. Washington, DC: American Psychiatric Association; 1987.

4 **Bosco JJ et al.** Hyperkinesis: prevalence and treatment. In: Whalen CK, Henker B, eds. Hyperactive Children: The Social Ecology of Identification and Treatment. New York: Academic Press; 1980:173.

5 **Berry C et al.** Girls with attention deficit disorder: a silent minority? A report on behavioral and cognitive characteristics. Pediatrics. 1985;76:801.

6 **Shaywitz SE et al.** Monoaminergic mechanisms in hyperactivity. In: Rutter M, ed. Developmental Neuropsychiatry. New York: The Guilford Press; 1983:330.

7 **Shenker A.** The mechanism of action of drugs used to treat attention-deficit hyperactivity disorder: focus on catecholamine receptor pharmacology. Adv Pediatr. 1992;39:337.

8 **Zametkin AJ.** Noradrenergic hypothesis of attention deficit disorder with hyperactivity: a critical review. In: Meltzer HY, ed. Psychopharmacology: The Third Generation of Progress. New York: Raven Press; 1987:837.

9 **Sokol MS et al.** Attention deficit disorder with hyperactivity and the dopamine hypothesis: case presentations with theoretical background. J Am Acad Child Adolesc Psychiatry. 1987;26:428.

10 **Zametkin AJ et al.** Treatment of hyperactive children with monoamine oxidase inhibitors. I. Clinical efficacy. Arch Gen Psychiatry. 1985;42:969.

11 **Laird LK et al.** Attention-deficit hyperactivity disorder. J Pharm Pract. 1990;3:241.

12 **Greenhill LL.** Pharmacologic treatment of attention deficit hyperactivity disorder. Psychiatr Clin North Am. 1992;15:1.

13 **Bradley C.** The behavior of children receiving benzedrine. Am J Psychiatry. 1937;94:577.

14 **Safer DJ et al.** Trends in medication treatment of hyperactive school children. Clin Pediatr. 1983;22:500.

15 **Chan YPM et al.** Methylphenidate hydrochloride given with or before breakfast: II. Effects on plasma concentration of methylphenidate and ritalinic acid. Pediatrics. 1983;72:56.

16 **Gualtieri CT et al.** Clinical studies of methylphenidate serum levels in children and adults. J Am Acad Child Psychiatry. 1982;21:19.

17 **Swanson JM et al.** Methylphenidate hydrochloride given with or before breakfast: I. Behavioral, cognitive and electrophysiologic effects. Pediatrics. 1983;72:49.

18 **Fitzpatrick PA et al.** Effects of sustained-release and standard preparations of methylphenidate on attention deficit disorder. J Am Acad Child Adolesc Psychiatry. 1992;31:226.

19 **Balthazor MJ et al.** The specificity of the effects of stimulant medication on classroom learning-related measures of cognitive processing for attention deficit disorder children. J Abnorm Child Psychol. 1991;19:35.

20 **Milich R et al.** Effects of methylphenidate on the persistence of ADHD boys following failure experiences. J Abnorm Child Psychol. 1991;19:519.

21 **Pelham WE et al.** Methylphenidate and children with attention deficit disorder. Arch Gen Psychiatry. 1985;42:948.

22 **Brown RT et al.** Methylphenidate in hyperkinetic children: differences in dose effects on impulsive behavior. Pediatrics. 1979;64:408.

23 **DuPaul GJ et al.** Does methylphenidate normalize the classroom performance of children with attention deficit disorder? J Am Acad Child Adolesc Psychiatry. 1993;32:190.

24 **Hartley L.** Hyperactivity, drugs and attention to features in a story. Br J Clin Psychol. 1991;30:210.

25 **Abikoff H et al.** The normalizing effects of methylphenidate on the classroom behavior of ADDH children. J Abnorm Child Psychol. 1985;13:33.

26 **Whalen CK et al.** Peer perceptions of hyperactivity and medication effects. Child Dev. 1987;58:816.

27 **Cohen NJ et al.** Perception and attitudes of hyperactive children and their mothers regarding treatment with methylphenidate. Can J Psychiatry. 1982;27:40.

28 **Bowen J et al.** Stimulant medication and attention deficit-hyperactivity disorder. The child's perspective. Am J Dis Child. 1991;145:291.

29 **Anastopoulos AD et al.** Stimulant medication and parent training therapies for attention deficit-hyperactivity disorder. J Learn Disabil. 1991;24:210.

30 **Fine S et al.** Drug and placebo side effects in methylphenidate-placebo trial for attention deficit hyperactivity disorder. Child Psychiatry Hum Dev. 1993;24:25.

31 **Mattes JA et al.** Growth of hyperactive children on maintenance regimen of methylphenidate. Arch Gen Psychiatry. 1983;40:317.

32 **Vincent J et al.** Effects of methylphenidate on early adolescent growth. Am J Psychiatry. 1990;147:501.

33 **Bloom AS et al.** Methylphenidate-induced delusional disorder in a child with attention deficit disorder with hyperactivity. J Am Acad Child Adolesc Psychiatry. 1988;27:88.

34 **Elia J et al.** Classroom academic performance: improvement with both methylphenidate and dextroamphetamine in ADHD boys. J Child Psychol Psychiatry. 1993;34:785.

35 **Conners CK et al.** Pemoline, methylphenidate and placebo in children with minimal brain dysfunction. Arch Gen Psychiatry. 1980;37:922.

36 **Collier CP et al.** Pemoline pharmacokinetics and long term therapy in children with attention deficit disorder and

hyperactivity. Clin Pharmacokinet. 1985;10:269.

37 **Pratt DS et al.** Hepatotoxicity due to pemoline (Cylert): a report of two cases. J Pediatr Gastroenterol Nutr. 1990;10:239.

38 **Hechtman L.** Long-term outcome in attention-deficit hyperactivity disorder. Child Adolesc Psychiatry Clin NA. 1992;1:553.

39 **Gittleman R et al.** Hyperactive boys almost grown up. Arch Gen Psychiatry. 1985;42:937.

40 **Wender EH.** The food additive-free diet in the treatment of behavior disorders: A review. Dev Behav Pediatr. 1986;7:35.

41 **Gans DA.** Sucrose and delinquent behavior: Coincidence or consequence? Crit Rev Food Sci Nutr. 1991;30:23.

42 **Wender EH et al.** Effects of sugar on aggressive and inattentive behavior in children with attention deficit disorder with hyperactivity and normal children. Pediatrics. 1991;88:960.

43 **Carter CM et al.** Effects of a few food diet in attention deficit disorder. Arch Dis Child. 1993;69:564.

44 **Weiss G.** Follow-up studies on outcome of hyperactive children. Psychopharmacol Bull. 1985;21:169.

45 **Biederman J et al.** Patterns of psychiatric comorbidity, cognition, and psychosocial functioning in adults with attention deficit hyperactivity disorder. Am J Psychiatry. 1993;150:1792.

46 **Hechtman L et al.** Young adult outcome of hyperactive children who received long-term stimulant treatment. J Am Acad Child Psychiatry. 1984;23:261.

47 **Wender PH et al.** A controlled study of methylphenidate in the treatment of attention deficit disorder, residual type, in adults. Am J Psychiatry. 1985;142:547.

48 **Wender PH et al.** Bupropion treatment of attention-deficit hyperactivity disorder in adults. Am J Psychiatry. 1990;147:1018.

49 **Mattes JA.** Propranolol for adults with temper outbursts and residual attention deficit disorder. J Clin Psychopharmacol. 1986;6:299.

50 **Plizka SR.** Tricyclic antidepressants in the treatment of children with attention deficit disorder. J Am Acad Child Adolesc Psychiatry. 1987;26:127.

51 **Rapoport JL et al.** New drug trials in attention deficit disorder. Psychopharmacol Bull. 1985;21:232.

52 **Garfinkel BD et al.** Tricyclic antidepressant and methylphenidate treatment of attention deficit disorder in children. J Am Acad Child Psychiatry. 1983;22:343.

53 **Biederman J et al.** A double-blind placebo controlled study of desipramine in the treatment of ADD: I. Efficacy. J Am Acad Child Psychiatry. 1989;28:777.

54 **Gualtieri CT et al.** Clinical and neuropsychological effects of desipramine in children with attention deficit hyperactivity disorder. J Clin Psychopharmacol. 1991;11:155.

55 **Biederman J et al.** A double-blind placebo controlled study of desipramine in the treatment of ADD: III. Lack of impact of comorbidity and family history factors on clinical response. J Am Acad

Child Adolesc Psychiatry. 1993b;32:199.

56 **Rapoport JL.** Antidepressants in childhood attention deficit disorder and obsessive-compulsive disorder. Psychosomatics. 1986;27(Suppl.):30.

57 **Spencer T et al.** Growth deficits in children treated with desipramine: a controlled study. J Am Acad Child Adolesc Psychiatry. 1992;31:235.

58 **Riddle MA et al.** Another sudden death in a child treated with desipramine. J Am Acad Child Adolesc Psychiatry. 1993;32:792.

59 **Biederman J et al.** A naturalistic study of 24 hour electrocardiographic recordings and echocardiographic findings in children and adolescents treated with desipramine. J Am Acad Child Adolesc Psychiatry. 1993a;32:805.

60 **Ambrosini PJ et al.** Antidepressant treatments in children and adolescents: I. Affective disorders. J Am Acad Child Adolesc Psychiatry. 1993;32:1.

61 **Casat CD et al.** Bupropion in children with Attention Deficit Disorder (ADDH), Presented at the NIMH New Clinical Drug Evaluation Unit Meeting. Key Biscaye, FL: 1988 June 2.

62 **Hart-Santora D et al.** Clonidine in attention deficit hyperactivity disorder. Ann Pharmacother. 1992;26(1):37.

63 **Kashani J et al.** Depression in a sample of 9-year-old children. Arch Gen Psychiatry. 1983;40:1217.

64 **Petti TA.** Depression in hospitalized child psychiatry patients: approaches to measuring depression. J Am Acad Child Psychiatry. 1978;17:49.

65 **Gershon ES et al.** A family study of schizoaffective, bipolar I, bipolar II, unipolar and normal probands. Arch Gen Psychiatry. 1982;39:1157.

66 **Strober M.** Familial aspects of depressive disorder in early adolescence. In: Weller EB, Weller RA, eds. Current Perspectives on Major Depressive Disorders in Children. Washington, DC: American Psychiatric Press; 1984:38.

67 **Harrington R et al.** Adult outcomes of childhood and adolescent depression. II. Links with antisocial disorders. J Am Acad Child Adolesc Psychiatry. 1991;30:434.

68 **Angold A et al.** Depressive comorbidity in children and adolescents: empirical, theoretical and methodological issues. Am J Psychiatry. 1993;150:1779.

69 **Aylward GP.** Understanding and treatment of childhood depression. J Pediatr. 1985;107:1.

70 **Kupfer DJ.** Summary of the national conference on risk factors for youth suicide. Final Report of the Secretary's Task Force Report on Youth Suicide, vol 2. Washington, DC: US Department of Health and Human Services, 1989; DHHS publication no. (ADM) 89-1622:9.

71 **Puig-Antich J et al.** Imipramine in prepubertal major depressive disorders. Arch Gen Psychiatry. 1987;44:81.

72 **Geller B et al.** Double-blind placebo-controlled study of nortriptyline in depressed adolescents using a "fixed plasma level" design. Psychopharmacol Bull. 1990;26:85.

73 **Weller EB et al.** Childhood depression: imipramine levels and response. Psychopharmacol Bull. 1983;19:59.

74 **Preskorn SH et al.** Plasma levels of

imipramine and adverse effects in children. Am J Psychiatry. 1983;140:1332.

75 **Geller B et al.** Pharmacokinetically designed double-blind placebo-controlled study of nortriptyline in 6- to 12-year-olds with major depressive disorder. J Am Acad Child Adolesc Psychiatry. 1992;31:34.

76 **Hughes CW et al.** The effect of a concomitant disorder in childhood depression in predicting response to treatment. Presented to NIMH New Clinical Drug Evaluation Unit Meeting. Key Biscayne, FL: 1989 June 1.

77 **Kaminer Y et al.** Observational measurement of symptoms responsive to treatment of major depressive disorder in children and adolescents. J Nerv Ment Dis. 1992;180:639–43.

78 **Ambrosini PJ et al.** Open nortriptyline treatment over 10 weeks in depressed adolescent outpatients. Proc Am Acad Child Adolesc Psychiatry. 1989;5:59.

79 **Puig-Antich J et al.** Plasma levels of imipramine and desmethylimipramine and clinical response in prepubertal major depressive disorder. J Am Acad Child Psychiatry. 1979;18:616.

80 **Weller EB et al.** Steady-state plasma imipramine levels in prepubertal depressed children. Am J Psychiatry. 1982;139:506.

81 **Winsberg B et al.** Imipramine fate and behavior in hyperactive children. Psychopharmacol Bull. 1973;9:45.

82 **Hayes TA et al.** Imipramine dosage in children: a comment on "Imipramine and electrocardiographic abnormalities in hyperactive children." Am J Psychiatry. 1975;132:546.

83 **Kymissis P et al.** The use of lithium in cyclical behavior disorders of adolescence: a case report. Mt Sinai J Med. 1979;46:141.

84 **Carlson GA.** Classification issues of bipolar disorders in childhood. Psychiatr Dev. 1984;4:273.

85 **Reiss AL.** Developmental manifestations in a boy with prepubertal bipolar disorder. J Clin Psychiatry. 1985;46:441.

86 **Potter RL.** Manic-depressive variant syndrome of childhood. Clin Pediatr. 1983;22:495.

87 **Poznanski EO et al.** Hypomania in a four-year-old. J Am Acad Child Psychiatry. 1984;23:105.

88 **Brumback RA et al.** Mania in childhood II. Therapeutic trial of lithium carbonate and further description of manic-depressive illness in children. Am J Dis Child. 1977;131:1122.

89 **Gammon GD et al.** Use of a structured diagnostic interview to identify bipolar disorder in adolescent inpatients: frequency and manifestations of the disorder. Am J Psychiatry. 1983;140:543.

90 **Strober M et al.** Bipolar illness in adolescents with major depression. Arch Gen Psychiatry. 1982;39:549.

91 **Loranger AW et al.** Age at onset of bipolar affective illness. Arch Gen Psychiatry. 1978;35:1345.

92 **Akiskal HS et al.** Affective disorders in referred children and younger siblings of manic-depressives. Arch Gen Psychiatry. 1985;42:996.

93 **Geller B et al.** Effect of tricyclic antidepressants on switching to mania and on the onset of bipolarity in depressed 6- to 12-year-olds. J Am Acad Child Adolesc Psychiatry. 1993;32:43.

94 **Venkataraman S et al.** Mania associ-

ated with fluoxetine treatment in adolescents. J Am Acad Child Adolesc Psychiatry. 1992;31:276.

95 **Sylvester CE et al.** Manic psychosis in childhood: report of two cases. J Nerv Ment Dis. 1984;172:12.

96 **Younes RP et al.** Manic-depressive illness in children: treatment with lithium carbonate. J Child Neurol. 1986;1:364–68.

97 **Geller B et al.** Early findings from a pharmacokinetically designed double-blind and placebo-controlled study of lithium for adolescents comorbid with bipolar and substance dependence disorders. Prog Neuropsychopharmacol Biol Psychiatry. 1992;16:281.

98 **Weller EB et al.** Lithium dosage guide for prepubertal children: a preliminary report. J Am Acad Child Psychiatry. 1986;25:92.

99 **Lena B.** Lithium in child and adolescent psychiatry. Arch Gen Psychiatry. 1979;36:854.

100 **Khandelwal SK et al.** Renal function in children receiving long-term lithium prophylaxis. Am J Psychiatry. 1984;141:278.

101 **Lena B et al.** The efficacy of lithium in the treatment of emotional disturbance in children and adolescents. In: Johnson FN et al. ed. Lithium in Medical Practice. Lancaster: MTP Press; 1978:79–83.

102 **Reisberg B et al.** Side effects associated with lithium therapy. Arch Gen Psychiatry. 1979;36:879.

103 **Davis BM et al.** Lithium's effect on parathyroid hormone. Am J Psychiatry. 1981;138:489.

104 **Birch NJ.** Lithium accumulation in bone after oral administration in rat and in man. Clin Sci Mol Med. 1974;46:409.

105 **Birch NJ.** Bone side-effects of lithium. In: Johnson FN, ed. Handbook of Lithium Therapy. Lancaster: MTP Press; 1980:365.

106 **Bernstein GA et al.** Anxiety disorders of childhood and adolescence: a critical review. J Am Acad Child Adolesc Psychiatry. 1990;30:519.

107 **Brady EU et al.** Comorbidity of anxiety and depression in children and adolescents. Psychol Bull. 1992;111:244.

108 **Zoccolillo M.** Co-occurrence of conduct disorder and its adult outcomes with depressive and anxiety disorders: a review. J Am Acad Child Adolesc Psychiatry. 1992;31:547.

109 **Kashani JH et al.** Current perspectives on anxiety disorders in children and adolescents: an overview. Compr Psychiatry. 1991;32:481.

110 **Biederman J.** The diagnosis and treatment of adolescent anxiety disorders. J Clin Psychiatry. 1990;51(Suppl. 5):2026.

111 **Kutcher SP et al.** The pharmacotherapy of anxiety disorders in children and adolescents. Psychiatr Clin North Am. 1992;15:41.

112 **Popper CW.** Psychopharmacologic treatment of anxiety disorders in adolescents and children. J Clin Psychiatry. 1993;54(Suppl. 5):52.

113 **Ambrosini PJ et al.** Antidepressant treatments in children and adolescents: II. Anxiety, physical, and behavioral disorders. J Am Acad Child Adolesc Psychiatry. 1993;32:483.

114 **Klein RG et al.** Imipramine treatment

of children with separation anxiety disorder. J Am Acad Child Adolesc Psychiatry. 1992;31:21.

115 **Swedo SE et al.** Obsessive-Compulsive disorder in children and adolescents. Arch Gen Psychiatry. 1989;46: 335.

116 **Leonard HL et al.** Treatment of obsessive-compulsive disorder with clomipramine and desipramine in children and adolescents. Arch Gen Psychiatry. 1989;46:1088.

117 **DeVeaugh-Geiss J et al.** Clomipramine hydrochloride in childhood and adolescent obsessive-compulsive disorder-a multicenter trial. J Am Acad Child Adolesc. 1992;31:45.

118 **Flament MF et al.** Clomipramine treatment of childhood obsessive compulsive disorder. Arch Gen Psychiatry. 1985;42:977.

119 **Basel Pharmaceuticals.** Anafranil package insert. Summit, NJ: 1992.

120 **Leonard HL et al.** A 2 to 7 year follow-up of 54 obsessive-compulsive children and adolescents. Arch Gen Psychiatry. 1993;50:429.

121 **Alarcon RD et al.** Paranoid and aggressive behavior in two obsessive-compulsive adolescents treated with clomipramine. J Am Acad Child Adolesc Psychiatry. 1991;30:999.

122 **Riddle MA et al.** Double-blind, crossover trial of fluoxetine and placebo in children and adolescents with obsessive-compulsive disorder. J Am Acad Child Adolesc Psychiatry. 1992;31: 1062.

123 **Kurlan R et al.** A pilot controlled study of fluoxetine for obsessive-compulsive symptoms in children with Tourette's syndrome. Clin Neuropharmacol. 1993;16:167.

124 **Simeon JG et al.** Treatment of adolescent obsessive-compulsive disorder with a clomipramine-fluoxetine combination. Psychopharmacol Bull. 1990; 26:285.

125 **Russel AT et al.** The phenomenology of schizophrenia occurring in childhood. J Am Acad Child Adolesc Psychiatry. 1989;28:399.

126 **McClellan JM et al.** Schizophrenia. Psychiatr Clin North Am. 1992;15:131.

127 **Werry JS.** Child and adolescent (early onset) schizophrenia: a review in light of DSM-III-R. J Autism Dev Disord. 1992;22:601.

128 **McClellan JM et al.** A follow-up study of early onset psychosis: comparison between outcome diagnoses of schizophrenia, mood disorders and personality disorders. J Autism Dev Disord. 1993;23:243.

129 **Whitaker A et al.** Neuroleptics in pediatric psychiatry. Psychiatr Clin North Am. 1992;15:243.

130 **Physicians' Desk Reference.** 47th ed. Montvale, NJ: Medical Economics Company, Inc; 1993:1422,2042,2107, 2319,2327.

131 **Cohen DJ.** Developmental psychopathology and neurobiology of Tourette's syndrome. J Am Acad Child Adolesc Psychiatry. 1994;33:2.

132 **Sandor P.** Gilles de la Tourette syndrome: a neuropsychiatric disorder. J Psychosom Res. 1993;37:211.

133 **Robertson MM et al.** Pharmacologic controversy of CNS stimulants in

Gilles de la Tourette's syndrome. Clin Neuropharmacol. 1992;15:408.

134 **Robertson MM.** The Gilles de la Tourette syndrome: the current status. Br J Psychiatry. 1989;154:147.

135 **Golden GS.** Tourette syndrome: recent advances. Pediatr Neurol. 1990;8:705.

136 **Steingard R et al.** Comparison of clonidine response in the treatment of attention-deficit hyperactivity disorder with and without comorbid tics. J Am Acad Child Adolesc Psychiatry. 1993; 32:350.

137 **Spencer T.** Nortriptyline treatment of children with attention-deficit hyperactivity disorder and tic disorder or Tourette's syndrome. J Am Acad Child Adolesc Psychiatry. 1993a;32:205.

138 **Spencer T.** Desipramine treatment of children with attention-deficit hyperactivity disorder and tic disorder or Tourette's syndrome. J Am Acad Child Adolesc Psychiatry. 1993b;32:354.

139 **Erenberg G.** Pharmacologic therapy of tics in childhood. Psychiatric Annals. 1988;18:399.

140 **Baily AJ.** The biology of autism. Psychol Med. 1993;23:7.

141 **Gillberg C.** Autism and related behaviors. J Intellect Disabil Res. 1993;37: 343.

142 **Baron-Cohen S et al.** Can autism be detected at 18 months? The needle, the haystack and the CHAT. Br J Psychiatry. 1992;161:839.

143 **LeCoureur A.** Autism: current understanding and management. Br J Hosp Med. 1990;43:448.

144 **Gillberg IC.** Autistic syndrome with onset at age 31 years: herpes encephalitis as a possible model for childhood autism. Dev Med Child Neurol. 1991; 33:912.

145 **Firth U.** Autism. Explaining the Enigma. Cambridge, MA: Blackwell; 1989.

146 **Kerbeshian J, Burd L.** A clinical pharmacological approach to the treatment of autism. The Habilitative Mental Healthcare Newsletter. 1991;10:33.

147 **Romanczyk RG et al.** Schizophrenia and autism. In: Matson JL, Barrett RP, eds. Psychopathology in the Mentally Retarded. 2nd ed. Needham Heights: Allyn & Bacon; 1993:149.

148 **Campbell M et al.** Autism and aggression. In: Simeon JH, Ferguson HB, eds. Treatment Strategies in Child and Adolescent Psychiatry. New York: Plenum Publishing Corp.; 1990:77.

149 **Anderson LT et al.** The effects of haloperidol on discrimination learning and behavioral symptoms in autistic children. J Autism Dev Disord. 1989; 19:227.

150 **Jaselskis CA et al.** Clonidine treatment of hyperactive and impulsive children with autistic disorder. J Clin Psychopharmacol. 1992;12:322.

151 **Fankhauser MP et al.** A double-blind, placebo-controlled study of the efficacy of transdermal clonidine in autism. J Clin Psychiatry. 1992;53:77.

152 **Aman MG et al.** Review of fenfluramine in the treatment of developmental disabilities. J Am Acad Child Adolesc Psychiatry. 1989;28:549.

153 **Campbell M et al.** Efficacy and safety of fenfluramine in autistic children. J Am Acad Child Adolesc Psychiatry. 1988;4:434.

154 **Gordon CT et al.** A double-blind comparison of clomipramine, desipramine, and placebo in the treatment of autistic disorder. Arch Gen Psychiatry. 1993; 50:441.

155 **Singh NN et al.** Assessment and diagnosis of mental illness in persons with mental retardation. Behav Modif. 1991;15:419.

156 **Lowry M et al.** The functional significance of problem behavior: a key to effective treatment. The Habilitative Mental Health Newsletter. 1991;10:59.

157 **Einfeld SL.** Clinical assessment of psychiatric symptoms in mentally retarded individuals. Aust N Z J Psychiatry. 1992;26:48.

158 **Simko A et al.** Fragile X syndrome: recognition in young children. Pediatrics. 1989;83:547.

159 **Bregman JD et al.** Fragile X syndrome: genetic predisposition to psychopathology. J Autism Dev Disord. 1988;18:343.

160 **Lovell RW et al.** Dual diagnosis: psychiatric disorders in developmental disabilities. Pediatr Clin North Am. 1993; 40:579.

161 **King BH.** Self-injury by people with mental retardation: a compulsive behavior hypothesis. Am J Ment Retard. 1993;98:93.

162 **Mercugliano M.** Psychopharmacology in children with developmental disabilities. Pediatr Clin North Am. 1993;40:593.

163 **Aman MG et al.** Pharmacological Intervention. In: Matson JL, Mulick JA, eds. Handbook of Mental Retardation. New York: Pergamon Press; 1991:347.

164 **Gualtieri CT et al.** Tardive dyskinesia and other clinical consequences of neuroleptic treatment in children and adolescents. Am J Psychiatry. 1984;141: 20.

165 **Myers BA et al.** Differentiating schizophrenia from other mental and behavioral problems in persons with developmental disabilities. The Habilitative Mental Healthcare Newsletter. 1993; 23:93.

166 **Sovner R et al.** Fluoxetine treatment of depression and associated self-injury in 2 adults with mental retardation. J Intellect Disabil Res. 1993;37:301.

167 **Federal Register.** Medicaid program: Conditions for Intermediate Care Facilities for the Mentally Retarded; Final Rule. Department of Health and Human Services, Health Care Financing Administration. Washington, DC: 1988;53:20448.

168 **Farber JM.** Psychopharmacology of self-injurious behavior in the mentally retarded. J Am Acad Child Adolesc Psychiatry. 1987;26:296.

169 **Baumeister AA et al.** Self-injurious behavior. In: Ellis NR, ed. International Review of Research in Mental Retardation, Vol 9. New York: Academic Press; 1976:1.

170 **Winchel RM et al.** Self-injurious behavior: a review of the behavior and biology of self-mutilation. Am J Psychiatry. 1991;148:306.

171 **Gualtieri CT.** The differential diagnosis of self-injurious behavior in mentally retarded people. Psychopharmacol Bull. 1989;25:358.

172 **Bhattacharya SK et al.** Aggressive

behaviour—basic and clinical frontiers. Indian J Med Res. 1989;90:387.

173 **Osman OT et al.** Self-injurious behavior in the developmentally disabled: pharmacologic treatment. Psychopharmacol Bull. 1992;28:439.

174 **Gualtieri CT et al.** Pharmacotherapy for self-injurious behavior: preliminary tests of the D_1 hypothesis. Psychopharmacol Bull. 1989;25:364.

175 **Sandman CA et al.** An orally administered opiate blocker, naltrexone, attenuates self-injurious behavior. Am J Ment Retard. 1990;95:93.

176 **Herman BH et al.** Naltrexone decreases self-injurious behavior. Ann Neurol. 1987;22:550.

177 **Ruedrich SL et al.** Beta adrenergic blocking medications for aggressive or self-injurious mentally retarded persons. Am J Ment Retard. 1990;95:110.

178 **Ratey JJ et al.** Beta-blockers in the severely and profoundly mentally retarded. J Clin Psychopharmacol. 1986; 6:103.

179 **Wickham EA et al.** Lithium for the control of aggressive and self-mutilating behavior. Int Clin Psychopharmacol. 1987;2:181.

180 **Craft M et al.** Lithium in the treatment of aggression in mentally handicapped patients: a double-blind trial. Br J Psychiatry. 1987;150:685.

181 **Ratey JJ et al.** Buspirone therapy for maladaptive behavior and anxiety in developmentally disabled persons. J Clin Psychiatry. 1989;50:382.

182 **Ricketts RW et al.** Fluoxetine treatment of severe self-injury in young adults with mental retardation. J Am Acad Child Adolesc Psychiatry. 1993; 32:865.

183 **Markowitz PI.** Effect of fluoxetine on self-injurious behavior in the developmentally disabled: a preliminary study. J Clin Psychopharmacol. 1992;1:27.

184 **Garber HJ et al.** Clomipramine treatment of stereotypic behaviors and self-injury in patients with developmental disabilities. J Am Acad Child Adolesc Psychiatry. 1992;31:1157.

185 **Adler L et al.** Efficacy of propranolol in neuroleptic-induced akathisia. J Clin Psychopharmacol. 1985;5:164.

186 **Bartels M et al.** Treatment of akathisia with lorazepam: An open clinical trial. Psychopharmacology. 1987;20:51.

187 **van der Bijl P et al.** Disinhibitory reactions to benzodiazepines: A review. J Oral Maxillofac Surg. 1991;49:519.

188 **Corrigan PW et al.** Pharmacological and behavioral treatments for aggressive psychiatric inpatients. Hosp Community Psychiatry. 1993;44:125.

189 **Yudofsky SC et al.** Pharmacologic treatment of aggression. Psychiatric Annals. 1987;17:397.

190 **Salzman C et al.** Parenteral lorazepam versus parenteral haloperidol for the control of psychotic disruptive behavior. J Clin Psychiatry. 1991;52:177.

191 **Spreat S et al.** Lithium carbonate for aggression in mentally retarded persons. Compr Psychiatry. 1989;30:505.

192 **Ratey JJ et al.** Buspirone treatment of aggression and anxiety in mentally retarded patients: a multiple-baseline, placebo lead-in study. J Clin Psychiatry. 1991;52:159.

193 **Mattes JA.** Comparative effectiveness of carbamazepine and propranolol for

rage outbursts. J Neuropsychiatry Clin Neurosci. 1990;2:159.

194 **Patterson JF.** A preliminary study of carbamazepine in the treatment of assaultive patients with dementia. J Geriatr Psychiatry Neurol. 1988;1:21.

195 **Kafantaris V et al.** Carbamazepine in hospitalized aggressive conduct disorder children: an open pilot study. Psychopharmacol Bull. 1992;8:193.

196 **Mattes JA.** Valproic acid for nonaffective aggression in the mentally retarded. J Nerv Ment Dis. 1992;180:601.

197 **Mazure CM et al.** Valproate treatment of older psychotic patients with organic

mental syndromes and behavioral dyscontrol. J Am Geriatric Soc. 1991;39:1110.

198 **Apter A et al.** Fluvoxamine open-label treatment of adolescent inpatients with obsessive-compulsive disorder or depression. J Am Acad Child Adolesc Psychiatry. 1994;33:342–8.

199 **Geller DA et al.** Similarities in response to fluoxetine in the treatment of children and adolescents with obsessive-compulsive disorder. J Am Acad Child Adolesc Psychiatry. 1995;34:36–44.

200 **Como PG, Lurlan R.** An open-label trial of fluoxetine for obsessive-com-

pulsive disorder in Gilles de la Tourette's syndrome. Neurology. 1991;41:872–4.

201 **Birmaher B et al.** Fluoxetine for childhood anxiety disorders. J Am Acad Child Adolesc Psychiatry. 1994;33:993–9.

202 **Manassis K, Bradley S.** Fluoxetine in anxiety disorders. J Am Acad Child Adolesc Psychiatry. 1994;33:761–2.

203 **Black B, Uhde T.** Treatment of elective mutism with fluoxetine: a double-blind, placebo-controlled study. J Am Acad Child Adolesc Psychiatry. 1994;33:1000–6.

204 **Bangs ME et al.** Fluoxetine-induced

memory impairment in an adolescent. J Am Acad Child Adolesc Psychiatry. 1994;33:1303–6.

205 **Ghaziuddin M.** Mania induced by sertraline in a prepubertal child. Am J Psychiatry. 1994;151:944.

206 **McDougle CJ et al.** Clomipramine in autism: preliminary evidence of efficacy. J Am Acad Child Adolesc Psychiatry. 1992;31:746–50.

207 **Cook EH et al.** Fluoxetine treatment of children and adults with autistic disorder and mental retardation. J Am Acad Child Adolesc Psychiatry. 1992;31:739–45.

Secondary Neuropsychiatric Disorders

Kevin M Furmaga
Mark D Watanabe

Diagnosis and Classification (See Table 79.1) 79-1
General Pharmacotherapeutic Issues and Limitations 79-1
Aggression and Disinhibition 79-2
Neurochemistry (See Figure 79.1) 79-2
Clinical Presentation 79-2
Diagnosis 79-2
Brain imaging techniques 79-2
Neuropsychological testing 79-3
Electroencephalogram (EEG) 79-3
Treatment (See Table 79.2) 79-3
Antipsychotics 79-3
Choice of agent 79-4

Anticonvulsants 79-4
Combination therapy 79-4
β-adrenergic antagonists 79-4
Serotonergic agonists 79-4
Benzodiazepines 79-5
Apathy 79-5
Differential Diagnosis 79-5
Treatment 79-5
Dopamine agonists 79-6
Bromocriptine 79-6
Methylphenidate 79-6

A neuropsychiatric disorder can be defined as any alteration in normal emotional, behavioral, or cognitive function that directly results from disease or trauma affecting the brain.[1] Clinical conditions which may induce such mental status changes include cerebral vascular disease, seizure disorders, direct traumatic brain injury, brain tumors, central nervous system (CNS) degenerative disorders (e.g., Alzheimer's disease and other dementias, infectious and inflammatory diseases of the CNS), chemically induced organic mental disorders, and developmental disorders which affect the brain.[2] Clearly, the first consideration in formulating a pharmacotherapeutic plan for these patients is to treat the primary medical conditions most likely to be the major etiology of behavior changes. Despite these interventions, however, psychiatric symptoms may persist. Clinical syndromes may include other features that exist at the interface between neurology and psychiatry (i.e., impairments in attention, alertness, perception, memory, language, and intelligence). Because the associations between psychopathology and brain lesions are not well defined, established paradigms for the pharmacotherapy of secondary neuropsychiatric disorders are lacking. The development of technologically advanced imaging techniques is broadening the knowledge base regarding where and how medications work in the brain. Until this knowledge can be adapted to widespread clinical application, clinicians rely upon the traditional "target symptom" psychiatric approach as well as extrapolation from animal model neuroscience data to select appropriate medications for treatment.

Diagnosis and Classification

Most neuropsychiatric disorders can be classified under the system established by the American Psychiatric Association in its Diagnostic and Statistical Manual for Mental Disorders, Fourth Edition (DSM-IV).[3] The general category is "Personality Change Due to a General Medical Condition," and the diagnostic criteria for this classification are listed in Table 79.1. The specific diagnosis is based upon 1) a clinically significant personality change and 2) the presence of a specific etiological general medical condition. The specific types of personality change include labile, disinhibited, aggressive, apathetic, and paranoid. If the personality change is not among those listed or if more than one feature predominates, the type of personality change is listed as "Other" or "Combined," respectively. Although the primary goal in managing a

neuropsychiatric disorder is to treat the underlying medical condition responsible for brain dysfunction, there are often cases where brain injury may not be reversible (e.g., closed-head injury) and mental status changes are more persistent. In such instances, chronic pharmacotherapeutic management of psychiatric symptoms may be indicated. This chapter will focus on acute pharmacologic management of three specific neuropsychiatric syndromes: apathy, disinhibition, and aggression, with brief comments addressing the issues surrounding long-term drug therapy.

Formulation of a diagnosis in neuropsychiatry routinely relies upon behavioral assessment techniques used in psychiatry to define and assess thought and mood dysfunction. In addition, tests and procedures commonly used in clinical neurology can help to identify the "organic" etiology of these disorders. The use of electroencephalograms (EEGs) to identify seizure disorders; magnetic resonance imaging (MRI) and computed tomography (CT) to identify tumors, cerebral vascular accidents, and other abnormalities in brain structure; and the use of imaging studies such as single photon emission computed tomography (SPECT) or positron emission tomography (PET) to identify regional abnormalities in cerebral blood flow and metabolism may give clues to the functional etiology of abnormal behavior.

General Pharmacotherapeutic Issues and Limitations

No medications are approved specifically for the treatment of neuropsychiatric disorders and, in fact, there are a limited number of widely accepted pharmacotherapeutic approaches. Neuropsychiatric pharmacotherapy is largely based upon empirical clinical experience and demonstrated efficacy in psychiatric populations with similar symptoms. There are a number of reasons for this. First, there are relatively few hospital units and clinics in the U.S. that specialize in treating patients with neuropsychiatric disorders. Also, of the neuropsychiatric facilities that do exist, many are small and often unable to generate the patient numbers necessary to conduct adequately controlled clinical trials. In addition, neuropsychiatric disorders are heterogeneous in that similar symptoms can result from a wide range of brain pathology. Finally, much of the technology necessary to clinically identify and diagnose the neurobiological basis of neuropsychiatric disorders, (e.g., *in vivo* brain imaging) has become available only recently. The knowledge base regarding secondary neuropsychiatric disorders is growing

Table 79.1	DSM-IV Diagnostic Criteria for Personality Change Due to a General Medical Condition[a,b]

- A persistent personality disturbance that represents a change from the individual's previous characteristic personality pattern. (In children, the disturbance involves a marked deviation from normal development or a significant change in the child's usual behavior patterns lasting at least 1 yr)
- There is evidence from the history, physical examination, or laboratory findings that the disturbance is the direct physiological consequence of a general medical condition
- The disturbance is not better accounted for by another mental disorder (including other mental disorders due to a general medical condition)
- The disturbance does not occur exclusively during the course of a delirium and does not meet criteria for a dementia
- The disturbance causes clinically significant distress or impairment in social, occupational, or other important areas of functioning

Specify Type

Labile Type: If the predominant feature is affective lability

Disinhibited Type: If the predominant feature is poor impulse control (e.g., sexual indiscretions)

Aggressive Type: If the predominant feature is aggressive behavior

Apathetic Type: If the predominant feature is marked apathy and indifference

Paranoid Type: If the predominant feature is suspiciousness or paranoid ideation

Other Type: If the predominant feature is not one of the above (e.g., personality change associated with a seizure disorder)

Combined Type: If more than 1 feature predominates in the clinical picture

Unspecified Type

[a] Adapted from reference 3.
[b] The name of the general medical condition always is included with the diagnosis.

rapidly, and more firmly established pharmacotherapeutic paradigms should arise as new information develops in the literature.

Aggression and Disinhibition

Neurochemistry

The concept that lesions affecting specific brain areas will result in predictable behavioral syndromes is easily grasped but oversimplified. Because of the complex interconnections between the cortical, subcortical, and brainstem regions, disinhibited and aggressive behavior in the brain-injured patient may result from damage to a variety of different brain areas. Various neurotransmitters [e.g., dopamine, norepinephrine, serotonin, gamma-aminobutyric acid (GABA)] mediate neuronal activity throughout the brain and, depending upon the function or dysfunction of the receptors involved, neurotransmitters can either increase or decrease neuronal firing at various brain regions. To illustrate the interactions between various brain regions and the neurotransmitters involved, Figure 79.1 schematically outlines neuropathways proposed in producing apathetic, disinhibited, or aggressive behavior.

Theoretically, pharmacologic management of aggressive or disinhibited behavior is based upon manipulation of central neurotransmitter concentrations with associated effects on receptors and ion channels. The response to medication, however, may be largely unpredictable, and even may result in a paradoxical worsening of aggression or disinhibition. However, one can use even a limited understanding of brain systems responsible for regulating impulsive behavior as a basis for therapeutic decisions.

Clinical Presentation

1. F.L., a 42-year-old, right-handed male, is admitted to the neuropsychiatry ward 18 months status post left frontal skull fracture. The chief complaints (per family members) include irritability, explosive and impulsive behavior, social inappropriateness, preoccupation with pornographic books and films, and decreased sexual interest in his wife of 20 years. F.L. has 2 children, ages 15 and 18 years. For the past 16 months, F.L. has become increasingly irritable, quick tempered, and at times physically abusive toward his wife and children. Before the trauma, F.L. was employed as a heavy equipment operator with the same company for 15 years, and was considered a competent employee. However, his job performance had deteriorated during the first 3 months following his return to work, and he was fired because of poor job performance. His wife states that they had been very active socially until the accident, yet because of F.L.'s profane public outbursts and frequent sexual and insulting comments at social gatherings, their circle of friends no longer associates with them. F.L. has no history of psychiatric or medical problems, and he is described by his family as having been a "kind and supportive individual" before his injury. Based upon F.L.'s history and presentation, what subjective evidence is there that his behavior represents neuropsychiatric disorder?

F.L.'s current behavior represents a persistent personality disturbance that is uncharacteristic. Before his trauma, F.L. appeared to be a responsible family man with a stable employment and social history. Irritability, verbal abuse, and physical violence were not part of his characteristic personality pattern. Also, F.L.'s inability to continue his job at which he worked for 15 years and alienation of close friends demonstrated behavioral changes not limited to interactions with immediate family.

Finally, the temporal relationship between F.L.'s trauma and deteriorated personality change suggests that his behavior is a direct physiological consequence of his head injury, and therefore considered to be a secondary neuropsychiatric disorder meeting the criteria of DSM-IV.

2. To more clearly diagnose F.L.'s neuropsychiatric disorder, a number of tests and procedures were ordered that included: neuropsychological testing, an EEG, an MRI, and a SPECT. What is the diagnostic value of these procedures, and how would they be used to guide drug therapy in F.L.?

As with pharmacotherapy in a psychiatric patient, the selection of pharmacological agents to treat the patient with a secondary neuropsychiatric disorder is determined largely by identification of target symptoms. However, because of the complexities of brain function, the etiology of a given target symptom may be multifactorial and variant, depending upon the specific disease or trauma affecting the brain. The value of neuropsychological testing, neuroimaging, EEG, and other procedures used in formulating a diagnosis is found in probing the clinical, anatomical, and neurobiological features of brain dysfunction. From a pharmacotherapeutic perspective, comprehensive evaluation and documentation of neuropsychiatric deficits often enable the clinician to select drug regimens that not only treat target symptoms, but also reveal features of their neurobiological cause. Equally important is that such assessment also provides a baseline by which response to therapy can be measured objectively.

Brain Imaging Techniques

Computerized axial tomography and magnetic resonance imaging in neuropsychiatry provide detailed images of brain anatomy that can suggest anatomical correlates to secondary cognitive, behavioral, and affective disorders. Although the data generated from these imaging technologies can be extremely helpful in formulat-

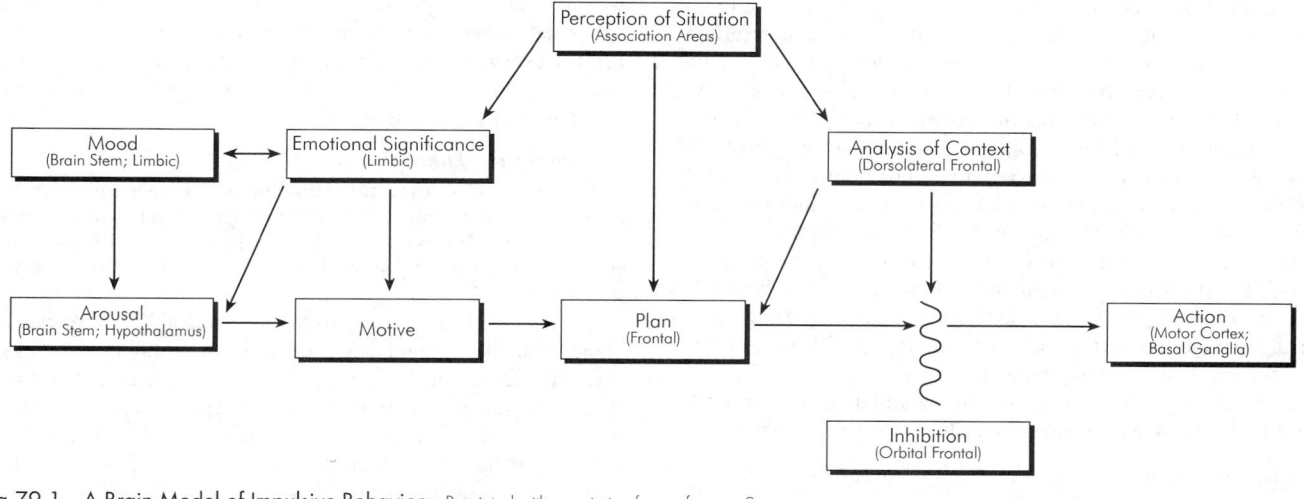

Fig 79.1   A Brain Model of Impulsive Behavior   Reprinted with permission from reference 2.

ing a diagnosis if positive findings are present, brain dysfunction often occurs at a level which is not reflected by visible damage on the scans. Positron emission tomography and single photon emission computed tomography are newer brain-imaging techniques which assess regional cerebral function based upon glucose utilization and blood perfusion studies, respectively. This information may be useful in F.L. as some of his inappropriate behavior may be secondary to lesions in the frontal lobe regions, and this may appear in a SPECT scan as hypoperfusion to these critical areas.

Neuropsychological Testing

Some assessment of F.L.'s neuropsychological capacity would be important. Although the chief complaints that prompted his neuropsychiatric admission were those reported by the family, they may not represent all of F.L.'s neuropsychological dysfunction. Disorders of behavior (e.g., impulse control, assaultiveness) and affect (e.g., depression, anxiety, irritability) pose the greatest burden on the patient's family or caregivers.[4–6] Effective treatment of these disorders can be anticipated to enhance the quality of long-term recovery. Conversely, neurological (e.g., sensory and motor impairment) and cognitive (i.e., deficits in memory, judgment, planning abilities, sequential processing) deficits may go unnoticed or be considered relatively unimportant by those caring for the patient. In addition, the nature and severity of their brain injury may leave patients either unaware of or unable to communicate their symptoms.

A wide variety of neuropsychological tests can be used to identify the nature and extent of F.L.'s deficits. They also can be useful in determining the specific areas of his brain that have been damaged. During an initial screen, a number of evaluations may assess orientation to time and place, language abilities (naming, repetition, comprehension), visual/spatial abilities, visual recognition (objects and faces), skilled motor movements (praxis), attention, and cognitive functioning (immediate, recent, and remote memory, judgment, planning abilities, sequential processing). Based upon these results, choices of medication may be constrained to those which are least likely to exacerbate any deficits (e.g., giving a highly sedating agent to F.L. if he has attention or cognitive impairments).

Electroencephalogram (EEG)

The use of the electroencephalogram to evaluate electrical activity in the brain is fairly standard. Often, impulsive and aggres-

sive behavior is a result of localized epileptogenic foci, particularly in the temporal lobe regions.[7,8] If F.L.'s EEG indicates that he may have a subclinical seizure disorder, the option of selecting an anticonvulsant known to be effective in behavioral outbursts in temporal lobe epilepsy (i.e., carbamazepine) should receive greater consideration.

Treatment

Antipsychotics

3. Upon admission to the neuropsychiatry unit, F.L.'s behavior becomes disruptive. He refuses to cooperate with the diagnostic procedures that have been scheduled. He attempts to enter a secured nursing area and the rooms of other patients without permission. Efforts to direct him to appropriate areas of the unit are met with verbal assaults that include threats of physical violence. Physical restraints are ordered for F.L. for his own protection. Haloperidol 5 mg intramuscularly (IM) is ordered for F.L. What are the therapeutic considerations concerning the use of an antipsychotic agent in F.L.?

Antipsychotic medications have been the traditional drugs of choice for the control of aggressive and violent patients, regardless of etiology. Until the diagnostic work-up of F.L.'s neuropsychiatric disorder is complete, the goal of antipsychotic therapy in F.L. should be control of his aggressive behavior without excessive sedation, if possible. Several antipsychotic regimens can be used in the acute management of F.L.'s behavior. A single 5 mg intramuscular dose of haloperidol (Haldol) often is effective in extremely agitated patients.[9] A single 2 to 4 mg dose of lorazepam (Ativan) given intramuscularly, in addition to the haloperidol, is very effective in calming disruptive patients who do not respond to antipsychotics alone.[10] An alternative approach is to titrate the haloperidol dose to the desired behavioral response. Haloperidol 2 mg IM may be administered every hour until control of aggression is achieved, followed by 1 to 2 mg IM every eight hours. Once F.L. is no longer agitated or violent for 48 hours, the daily haloperidol dose can be slowly tapered based upon the observed control of symptoms.[11]

While the sedative properties of antipsychotics make them highly effective in the acute management of disruptive behavior, their indication in chronic aggression due to a neuropsychiatric illness is limited. The use of these classical neuroleptics in this context generally should be reserved instead for patients in whom such behavior is clearly related to psychotic symptomatology (i.e., delusions or hallucinations). When these agents were commonly used in the past to control disruptive behavior regardless of diagnosis, their sedating effect probably was the basis for their effectiveness. The long term use of antipsychotics in nonpsychotic patients for behavioral control has a number of drawbacks. As discussed earlier, neuropsychiatric patients with aggressive symptoms often have cognitive dysfunction as well. Many agents in this class can worsen any existing cognitive impairments, thereby resulting in a slow or limited recovery. Also, the akathisia or restlessness often associated with antipsychotic use can increase patient agitation and irritability, making a patient's violent behavior worse. Tolerance can potentially develop with regard to the sedative effects of antipsychotics, rendering them ineffective over time. Finally, a major concern associated with the use of these agents is the inherent risk of extrapyramidal symptoms: acute dystonic reactions; pseudoparkinsonism; and the debilitating long-term adverse effect, tardive dyskinesia (see Chapter 75: Schizophrenia).

Choice of Agent

4. F.L. became less agitated and cooperative enough to complete the diagnostic procedures that were ordered after IM administration of 5 mg haloperidol. The MRI revealed abnormalities in the left frontal region consistent with his previous head injury. The SPECT scan showed hypoperfusion of the left frontal-orbital cerebral area. The EEG was unremarkable. Mental status and neuropsychological testing showed F.L.'s general intelligence to be within the high average range. Evidence of thought disorder, such as hallucinations or delusions, was not present, and there were no symptoms of depression. Significant findings on neuropsychological measures included mild weakness in his dominant (right) hand, and poor verbal fluency with speech described as slow and lacking emotion. F.L. also demonstrated impaired insight and social judgment, along with limited planning, sequencing, and organizational skills; he also had moderate difficulties with recent memory testing. Based upon the results of these diagnostic tests, how should selection of an appropriate drug regimen for F.L. be approached?

Based upon the history, clinical presentation, and results of neuropsychological testing, F.L.'s neuropsychological deficits are consistent with a diagnosis of orbitofrontal syndrome.[12] His symptoms of impulsive behavior, sexual disinhibition, and poor judgment and insight are characteristic of this diagnosis. There are extensive intercortical connections between this region of the brain and the limbic system that explain the emotional lability associated with this disorder. The frontal lobes are the center for the brain's executive functions, which include: scheduling, coordinating, innovating, censoring, disciplining, planning, and creativity. Damage to frontal brain regions also impairs decision-making abilities. The orbitofrontal area appears to be concerned with inhibition of behavior. Lesions affecting this region of the brain can result in disinhibition and present as impulsive behavior. Because of such extensive disability, F.L. is unable to respond to usual situations appropriately.

Since F.L. does not appear to have a thought disorder, long-term treatment with an antipsychotic would not be indicated. Drug therapy centered around mood stabilization, impulse control, and reduction of anxiety and irritability without cognitive impairment should be the initial goal of maintenance pharmacotherapy in F.L. once his acute symptoms have resolved.

Anticonvulsants

5. F.L. is started on carbamazepine for his behavior. What is the rationale for this selection?

Although it is widely used as an anticonvulsant, carbamazepine also possesses mood stabilizing properties (see Chapter 77: Mood Disorders II: Bipolar Affective Disorders). The mechanism by which it reduces impulsive behavior may be related to its abilities to regulate mood or to blunt electrical kindling which causes a localized seizure focus. When carbamazepine has been used in the treatment of mood disorders, efficacy correlated with serum concentrations of 8 to 12 μg/mL.[13,14]

Combination Therapy

6. Two weeks after initiation of carbamazepine, the frequency and duration of F.L.'s aggressive episodes are reduced significantly. However, he still has occasional episodes of impulse dyscontrol. Why should another agent be added to F.L.'s drug regimen?

Since F.L.'s behavior improved after the addition of carbamazepine, it should be continued. The decision to add a second agent is based upon clinical experience that demonstrates enhanced efficacy when using a polypharmacologic approach. Polypharmacy in the pharmacotherapeutic management of disease generally is discouraged due to the increased risk of adverse effects and often minimal increases in efficacy. However, multiple neurobiological systems are involved in the regulation of behavior, and may be affected by brain injury. Patients such as F.L. who demonstrate a partial response to a single medication may experience enhanced improvement from the addition of a second agent that affects a different neurobiological mechanism or system. Similarly, patients failing one pharmacotherapeutic approach can respond to a medication that modulates behavior by an alternative neuropharmacologic mechanism. The lack of a comprehensive model explaining the relationships among the central neuronal systems involved in behavior and incomplete knowledge on the exact mechanism of action of effective agents justifies the systematic substitution or addition of alternative medications. This approach requires close monitoring for response and adverse effects.

Other medications found to be effective in neuropsychiatric aggression include: 1) agents that decrease central noradrenergic tone, 2) agents that increase central serotonergic tone, 3) mood stabilizers, and 4) agents that increase central GABAergic tone.[15]

β-Adrenergic Antagonists

Based upon studies in animals and humans, elevation in central noradrenergic activity has been associated with aggressive behavior.[15] The role of β-adrenergic blockers in secondary aggressive disorders is supported by a number of clinical trials that report a decrease in the frequency and/or severity of violent episodes in the neuropsychiatric population.[16-19] The presumed mechanism of action is the antagonism of central postsynaptic noradrenergic receptors. Most studies suggest a lag time for response to beta-blockers of about two to six weeks. Propranolol (Inderal), metoprolol (Lopressor), nadolol (Corgard), and pindolol (Visken)[16-19] all are effective over a wide dosage range. Dosing guidelines are listed in Table 79.2. The use of a beta blocker should include consideration of the patient's other medical disorders (e.g., asthma, diabetes, cardiac disease) that may worsen with the use of these agents. Although some investigators recommend daily propranolol doses of as high as 800 mg, some patients may not tolerate large doses due to the cardiovascular side effects. Pindolol 20 to 60 mg/day is effective without the reduction in heart rate and blood pressure associated with propranolol.[19] This is probably a result of its intrinsic sympathomimetic properties. In addition, pindolol can be titrated much more rapidly than propranolol to a desired effective dose.

Serotonergic Agonists

A decrease in central serotonin activity also has been associated with increased aggressive behavior in a variety of populations.[15,20] Buspirone, which is a direct serotonin agonist, has been effective

Table 79.2	Agents Used in the Chronic Management of Aggressive and Disinhibited Behavior	
Drug	**Dose**	**Mechanism of Action**
Beta Blockers		
Propranolol (Inderal)	200–800 mg/day in divided doses	Beta-adrenergic blockade
Pindolol (Visken)	20–60 mg/day in divided doses	
Nadolol (Corgard)	80–320 mg/day in divided doses	
Metoprolol (Lopressor)	100–400 mg/day dose BID	
Serotonin Agonists		
Buspirone (BuSpar)	30–120 mg/day dose TID–QID	Direct serotonin agonist
Paroxetine (Paxil)	20–60 mg/day	SSRI
Fluoxetine (Prozac)	20–60 mg/day	SSRI
Mood Stabilizers/Anticonvulsants		
Carbamazepine (Tegretol)	600–1400 mg/day in 3 divided doses (8–12 µg/mL)	Anticonvulsant/mood stabilizer
Sodium divalproex (Depakote)	1000–3000 mg/day in 3 divided doses (50–100 mg/mL)	Mood stabilizer, anticonvulsant, GABA agonist
Lithium carbonate	600–1200 mg/day in 2–3 divided doses (0.6–1.2 mEq/L)	Mood stabilizer, serotonin agonist

ᵃ GABA = Gamma-aminobutyric acid; SSRI = Selective serotonin reuptake inhibitors.

in patients with aggression.[21,22] The ability of the serotonin-specific reuptake inhibitors to enhance central serotonergic tone should also theoretically be useful. (See Table 79.2 for a listing of serotonergic agents and doses used.) The advantage of these agents is that there appears to be relatively few side effects, limited drug/disease interactions, and an excellent safety profile.

In addition to carbamazepine, other mood stabilizers, such as valproic acid[23] and lithium,[24,25] may be used to treat aggression secondary to neuropsychiatric illness. It may be that specific effects of these agents on critical neurotransmitter systems also may be important. For example, carbamazepine and valproic acid have GABAergic activity, while lithium possesses serotonergic properties. Suppression of amygdala kindling or subclinical seizures that result in violent or disinhibited behavior in patients with brain injury also has been proposed as the mechanism by which carbamazepine and valproic acid control neuropsychiatric aggression.

Buspirone has been selected as the second agent to enhance F.L.'s response to carbamazepine. Its efficacy in treating the impulsive aggression seen in brain-injured patients, alternative mechanism of action, favorable side effect profile, and few reported drug interactions are the basis for selecting this agent. Buspirone is initiated at a starting dose of 5 mg orally three times daily, which can be increased by 15 mg/day increments, two to three times per week, until improvement is evident, side effects are intolerable, or a total daily dose of 120 mg is achieved.

Benzodiazepines

7. Why should a benzodiazepine sedative-hypnotic agent not be used?

While the benzodiazepines are effective in treating acute aggressive episodes, a number of reports describe delirium, disinhibition, and even an increase in violent behavior when they have been used.[26] Decreases in central neuronal activity via GABA-mediated inhibition and the resultant anti-anxiety effect appears to be the anti-aggression mechanism for benzodiazepines. However, in patients with neuropsychiatric disorders, disinhibition and further cognitive impairment also may occur. While benzodiazepines certainly may be useful in the acute management of aggressive behavior, their long-term use in the neuropsychiatric population (e.g., F.L.) should be limited and effects carefully monitored.

Apathy

Differential Diagnosis

8. C.R., a 45-year-old, right-handed male, was initially admitted to the University hospital with right-sided headache and left facial weakness. Past medical history was remarkable for childhood poliomyelitis and cocaine abuse. A CT scan revealed a right internal capsule infarction with compression of the frontal horn of the right lateral ventricle. C.R. had no previous psychiatric history. He was discharged with a diagnosis of cocaine-related stroke. Five months later, he was re-admitted when his family noticed that C.R. was "thinking and behaving differently." The family reported that he had now stopped walking with crutches, was neglecting his personal hygiene, and was refusing to leave the house. He became incontinent of urine and stool. The mental status examination revealed an affect that was indifferent and apathetic. C.R. denied any cocaine use since the stroke. He was initially re-admitted to a rehabilitation unit, where his behavior continued to deteriorate: in particular, there was evidence of inappropriate laughter and poor safety judgment. After transfer to the neuropsychiatric unit, he was noted to be uncooperative and unconcerned. There was an absence of delusions, hallucinations, and depressive mood. A routine neurological examination was unremarkable. Neuropsychological testing was positive for psychomotor slowing, poor spontaneous memory, and impaired planning and judgment. C.R.'s EEG showed mild slow waves in the left frontal and temporal areas. His MRI scan showed multiple subcortical infarcts. What subjective and objective evidence is there that C.R. may need to be specifically treated for apathy instead of another psychiatric disorder?

Apathy or lack of motivation can be confused with the "negative" or deficit symptoms of schizophrenia[27] or the withdrawal, anhedonia, and flattened affect of major depression.[28] In fact, there may be a co-existence of this syndrome with either of these psychiatric diagnoses. In C.R.'s case, there are no identifiable psychotic target symptoms that may be suggestive of schizophrenia (e.g., delusions or hallucinations). Also, as the epidemiology of schizophrenia is thought to have a familial component,[29] a negative family history of this disorder also might argue against the need for antipsychotic therapy. More commonly considered would be the initiation of an antidepressant, because apathy can be quite significant in a patient with major depression.[3] However, C.R.'s mental status examination clearly noted the absence of depressed mood, which is the *sine qua non* for this diagnosis.

The objective evidence provided by the imaging scans also supports the presence of a secondary, rather than primary, psychiatric disturbance as a result of C.R.'s stroke. The EEG may reflect regional brain dysfunction; in fact, patients with lesions of frontal cortex or subcortical regions projecting to frontal cortex are likely to present with apathy of a severity which impairs social adjustment and rehabilitation.[31,32]

Treatment

9. What are some initial pharmacotherapeutic considerations for C.R.?

First, a comprehensive medication history should be obtained from C.R. or a supportive caregiver. A review of his history must consider the potential contribution to the reduced motivation and diminished cognition from the side effects of current medications (e.g., antihypertensives, anticonvulsants). If this is a possibility, a risk-to-benefit assessment should be undertaken to determine the need to either continue or switch each of the medications in question.

Dopamine Agonists

Because apathy in C.R. appears to be independent of a major depressive disorder, he may be unlikely to respond to conventional antidepressant therapy. As previously mentioned, he also does not exhibit any psychotic features that would mark him as a candidate for antipsychotic medications. Dopamine agonists have been used successfully to treat apathetic syndromes in patients with anterior communicating artery aneurysm,[33] Wilson's disease,[34] and human immunodeficiency virus (HIV)-related dementia.[35] They also may be beneficial in patients who have experienced a cerebrovascular accident.[36] In general, stimulants may be preferable in C.R. to other psychotropic agents that may further impair global cognitive functioning, such as sedating tricyclic antidepressants. Assuming that C.R. has no other major physical or medical contraindications to this class of medications, a trial of dopaminergic agents such as bromocriptine or methylphenidate might be warranted. Some investigators have suggested that apathy without depression may be associated with dysregulated brain dopaminergic activity.[31]

10. Bromocriptine. C.R. was treated with bromocriptine 20 mg/day, and he began to show improvement in social behavior as well as an increased interest in ward activities. He was ultimately discharged on this dose of bromocriptine. However, after ≈2 months, his behavior deteriorated again, with a reemergence of apathy, incontinence, and neglect of personal hygiene. He was re-admitted to the neuropsychiatry unit 3 months after his last discharge. Urine toxicology screens for street drugs were negative, and serum prolactin levels were negligible. Was bromocriptine an appropriate choice?

Bromocriptine, a dopaminergic agonist, has been effective in the specific treatment of apathy and akinetic mutism (when a patient makes no effort to communicate while maintaining an empty, noncommunicative facial expression) in numerous case reports.[37-39] Much higher doses than those used in the treatment of Parkinson's disease were given, with daily doses ranging from 15 to 100 mg. Even at 20 mg/day, C.R. showed an initial therapeutic response which, unfortunately, did not persist. Hence, bromocriptine was not so much an "inappropriate" intervention as it was an ineffective agent as maintenance therapy for prophylaxis against symptom recurrence. Chronic bromocriptine administration in animal models has raised the possibility of tolerance or altered dopamine receptor sensitivity.[40,41] C.R.'s history of cocaine abuse, a substance which is known to cause dysregulation in central dopaminergic pathways,[42] also may have influenced the development of tolerance. It is clear from the negative urine toxicology screen and negligible serum prolactin concentrations (as dopamine inhibits prolactin secretion[43]) that neither street drug use nor noncompliance led to C.R.'s re-admission.

11. Methylphenidate. During C.R.'s second admission, a SPECT scan was obtained which showed bilateral hypoperfusion to the frontal lobe regions. Subsequent to these findings, his medication regimen was changed to methylphenidate 5 mg TID (at 9 a.m., 1 p.m., and 4 p.m.). How can this be rationalized?

As previously mentioned, the "frontal lobe syndrome" which can manifest as either aggression, apathy, or disinhibition also may be reflected in decreased regional blood flow to this area. The test results, therefore, corroborated the clinical presentation, strengthening the argument that a frontal lobe lesion is present. As with the primary psychiatric disorders, knowledge of prior responses to medication from a thorough medication history can be important in the selection of a particular pharmacotherapeutic agent. In this case, C.R. had at least a transient period of improvement while taking a dopaminergic stimulant, suggesting that a trial of an alternative agent in this class might be warranted.

Methylphenidate is another clinically effective psychostimulant with pharmacological and behavioral effects similar to *d*-amphetamine. Its mechanism of action also may be related to enhancement of central dopaminergic neurotransmission, either through presynaptic or postsynaptic mechanisms.[44] It has been specifically shown to be of benefit in the treatment of apathy in acquired immunodeficiency syndrome (AIDS)-related complex patients.[35] Because of C.R.'s history of a positive response to bromocriptine, he is deemed a likely candidate for a similar response to methylphenidate, an indirect dopaminergic agonist.

12. After 5 days of methylphenidate therapy, C.R.'s affect started to brighten, and he became more motivated to participate in unit activities. A second SPECT scan 2 days later revealed significantly increased cerebral blood perfusion to the frontal lobes. Episodes of incontinence were eliminated completely, and his hygiene improved dramatically. On discharge, C.R. received a prescription for methylphenidate 10 mg BID (at 9 a.m. and 1 p.m.). How should the effects of drug therapy be monitored?

One of the initial concerns for C.R. is that he would become tolerant to the methylphenidate as well, with recurrence of his behavioral and cognitive symptoms. The experience in treating children with attention deficit hyperactivity disorder suggests that tolerance to chronic methylphenidate is minimized when doses are adjusted appropriately for weight and age.[30,45] The caveat for the patient such as C.R. is that a previous history of cocaine abuse may have inherently dysregulated central dopaminergic pathways, and may have contributed to the unexpected tolerance. However, tachyphylaxis to bromocriptine does not necessarily predict an identical reaction to methylphenidate. Careful assessments taken during regular visits in the outpatient setting should detect the onset of new or recurrent symptoms. Unfortunately, there are no substantive studies that have directly examined the effects of long-term, maintenance methylphenidate therapy in patients with frontal lobe syndromes.

References

1 **Yudofsky SC, Hales RE.** The reemergence of neuropsychiatry: definition and direction. J Neuropsychiatry Clin Neurosci. 1989;1:1.

2 **Yudofsky SC, Hales RE.** The American Psychiatric Press Textbook of Neuropsychiatry. 2nd ed. Washington, DC: American Psychiatric Press; 1992: xx,338.

3 **American Psychiatric Association.** Diagnostic and Statistical Manual of Mental Disorders. 4th ed. (DSM-IV). Washington, DC: American Psychiatric Press; 1994:173,327.

4 **Levin HS, Grossman RG.** Behavioral sequelae of closed head injury. A quantitative study. Arch Neurol. 1978;35:720-27.

5 **Brooks N et al.** The five year outcome of severe blunt head injury: a relative's view. J Neurol Neurosurg Psychiatry. 1986;49:764-67.

6 **Oder W et al.** Behavioural and psychosocial sequelae of severe closed head injury and regional cerebral blood flow: a SPECT study. J Neurol Neurosurg Psychiatry. 1992;55:475-80.

7 **Tonkonogy J.** Violence and temporal lobe lesion: head CT and MRI data. J Neuropsychiatry Clin Neurosci. 1991; 3:189-96.

8 **Gedye A.** Episodic rage and aggression attributed to frontal lobe seizures. J Ment Defic Res. 1989;33:369-79.

9 **Marder SR et al.** Schizophrenia. Psychiatr Clin North Am. 1993;16:567.

10 **Dubin WR.** Rapid tranquilization: antipsychotics or benzodiazepines? J Clin Psychiatry. 1988;49(Suppl.):5.

11 **Yudofsky SC et al.** Pharmacologic management of aggression in the elderly. J Clin Psychiatry. 1990;5(Suppl. 10):22–8.

12 **Cummings JL.** Clinical Neuropsychiatry. Orlando, FL: Grune and Straton; 1985.

13 **Patterson JF.** A preliminary study of carbamazepine in the treatment of assaultive patients with organic brain disease. Psychosomatics. 1987;28:579–81.

14 **Gleason RP et al.** Carbamazepine treatment of agitation in Alzheimer's outpatients refractory to neuroleptics. J Clin Psychiatry. 1990;51:115–18.

15 **Eichelman B.** Neurochemical and psychopharmacologic aspects of aggressive behavior. In: Meltzer H, ed. Psychopharmacology: The Third Generation of Progress. New York: Raven; 1987.

16 **Greendyke RM et al.** Propranolol treatment of assaultive patients with organic brain disease. J Nerv Ment Dis. 1986;175:290.

17 **Mattes JA.** Metoprolol for intermittent explosive disorder. Am J Psychiatry. 1985;142:1108.

18 **Ratey JJ et al.** Nadolol to treat aggression and psychiatric symptomatology in chronic psychiatric inpatients: a double-blind, placebo controlled study. J Clin Psychiatry. 1992;53:41.

19 **Greendyke RM et al.** Therapeutic effects of pindolol on behavioral disturbances associated with organic brain disease: a double blind study. J Clin Psychiatry. 1986;47:423.

20 **Linnoila M et al.** Low cerebrospinal fluid 5-hydroxyindoleacetic acid concentration differentiates impulsive from non-impulsive violent behavior. Life Sci. 1983;33:2609.

21 **Ratey J et al.** Buspirone treatment of aggression and anxiety in mentally retarded patients: a multiple-baseline, placebo lead-in study. J Clin Psychiatry. 1991;42:159.

22 **Levine AM.** Buspirone and agitation in head injury. Brain Inj. 1988;2:165.

23 **Wilcox J.** Divalproex sodium in the treatment of aggressive behavior. Ann Clin Psychiatry. 1994;6:17.

24 **Craft M et al.** Lithium in the treatment of aggression in mentally handicapped patients. A double blind trial. Br J Psychiatry. 1987;150:685.

25 **Tyrer S et al.** Factors associated with a good response to lithium in aggressive mentally handicapped subjects. Prog Neuropsychopharmacol Biol Psychiatry. 1984;8:751.

26 **Dietch JT et al.** Aggressive dyscontrol in patients treated with benzodiazepines. J Clin Psychiatry. 1988;49:184.

27 **Andreasen NC.** Negative symptoms in schizophrenia. Arch Gen Psychiatry. 1982;39:784.

28 **Cassens G et al.** The neuropsychology of depressions. J Neuropsychiatry Clin Neurosci. 1990;2:202.

29 **Kendler KS, Diehl SR.** The genetics of schizophrenia: a current genetic-epidemiologic perspective. Schizophr Bull. 1993;19:261.

30 **Winsberg B et al.** Is there dose-dependent tolerance associated with chronic methylphenidate therapy in hyperactive children: oral dose and plasma considerations. Psychopharmacol Bull. 1987;23:107–10.

31 **Marin RS.** Apathy: a neuropsychiatric syndrome. J Neuropsychiatry Clin Neurosci. 1991;3:243.

32 **Cummings JL.** Frontal-subcortical circuits and human behavior. Arch Neurol. 1993;50:873.

33 **Parks RW et al.** Assessment of bromocriptine intervention for the treatment of frontal lobe syndrome: a case study. J Neuropsychiatry Clin Neurosci. 1992;4:109.

34 **Barrett K.** Treating organic abulia with bromocriptine and lisuride: four studies. J Neurol Neurosurg Psychiatry. 1991;54:718.

35 **Holmes VF et al.** Psychostimulant response in AIDS-related complex patients. J Clin Psychiatry. 1989;50:5.

36 **Watanabe MD et al.** Successful methylphenidate treatment of apathy after subcortical CVA: correlation with selective improvement of frontal-subcortical function. J Neuropsychiatry Clin Neurosci. In Press.

37 **Ross ED, Stewart RM.** Akinetic mutism from hypothalamic damage: successful treatment with a dopamine agonist. Neurology. 1981;31:1435.

38 **Catsman-Berrevoets CE, von Harskamp F.** Compulsive pre-sleep behavior and apathy due to bilateral thalamic stroke: response to bromocriptine. Neurology. 1988;38:647.

39 **Crismon ML et al.** The effect of bromocriptine on speech dysfunction in patients with diffuse brain injury (brain stem). Clin Neuropharmacol. 1988;11:462.

40 **Quik M, Iversen LL.** Subsensitivity of the rat striatal dopaminergic system after treatment with bromocriptine: effects on [^{3}H] spiperone binding and dopamine-stimulated cyclic AMP formation. Naunyn Schmiedebergs Arch Pharmacol. 1978;304:141.

41 **Smith RC et al.** Behavioral evidence for supersensitivity after chronic bromocriptine administration. Psychopharmacology (Berl). 1979;60:241.

42 **Post RM, Kopanda RT.** Cocaine, kindling, and psychosis. Am J Psychiatry. 1976;133:627–34.

43 **Ereshefsky L et al.** Pathophysiologic basis for schizophrenia and the efficacy of antipsychotics. Clin Pharm. 1990;9:682.

44 **Hoffman BB, Lefkowitz RJ.** Catecholamines and sympathomimetic drugs. In: Goodman and Gilman's. The Pharmacological Basis of Therapeutics. 8th ed. New York: Pergamon Press; 1990:187.

45 **Safter DJ, Allen RP.** Absence of tolerance to the behavioral effects of methylphenidate in hyperactive and inattentive children. J Pediatr. 1989;115:1003–8.

Eating Disorders

LaGenia Bailey

Overview 80-1
  Definitions 80-1
  Epidemiology 80-1
  Diagnostic Features 80-2
  Pathogenesis 80-2
  Pathophysiology 80-2
  Drug Treatment of Anorexia Nervosa 80-3
    Amitriptyline 80-4
    Lithium 80-4
    Clomipramine 80-4
    Selective serotonin reuptake inhibitors 80-4
  Drug Treatment of Bulimia Nervosa 80-4
    Antidepressants 80-4
    Desipramine 80-4
    Fenfluramine 80-5
    Trazodone 80-5
    Bupropion 80-5
    Phenelzine 80-5
    Amitriptyline 80-5
    Imipramine 80-5
    Fluoxetine 80-5
    Naltrexone 80-5
    Role relative to cognitive behavior therapy 80-5
Anorexia Nervosa 80-6
  Clinical Presentation 80-6
    Predisposing factors 80-6
    Comorbidity 80-6

  Diagnostic Criteria (see Table 80.1)
    and Medical Complications (See Table 80.2) 80-6
  Treatment 80-7
    Hospitalization 80-7
    Goals of treatment 80-7
    Psychotherapy 80-7
  Prognosis 80-8
Bulimia Nervosa 80-8
  Clinical Presentation 80-8
    Recognition 80-8
    Referral resources (See Table 80.3) 80-8
    Evaluation and hospitalization (See Table 80.4) 80-9
    Medical complications (See Table 80.5) 80-9
  Diagnostic Criteria 80-9
    DSM IV (See Table 80.6) 80-10
    Bingeing and vomiting 80-9
    Comparisons with anorexia 80-10
  Comorbidity 80-10
  Treatment 80-10
    Medications 80-10
    Monitoring for efficacy and toxicity 80-11
    Desipramine serum concentrations 80-11
    Precautions 80-11
    Adverse effects 80-11
    Alternative drugs 80-11
    Fluoxetine dosing 80-11
  Prognosis 80-12

Definitions

The social acceptability of various eating behaviors has differed throughout the ages. During the time of the Roman Empire, feasting on large meals followed by purging and continued eating were socially acceptable behaviors. Such behaviors are no longer acceptable and societies of industrialized countries have become increasingly focused on thinness. When this focus on weight and thinness becomes pathological and detrimental to a person's health, it is considered a disorder. Two of the eating disorders most recognized today are anorexia nervosa and bulimia nervosa.

Anorexia nervosa is characterized by the lack of willingness by an individual to maintain a minimally normal body weight and by excessive concern about gaining weight despite being underweight. Anorexia nervosa is further characterized according to two subtypes (i.e., restricting type and binge-eating/purging type). These subtypes delineate the presence or absence of binge-eating or purging during episodes of anorexia. *Bulimia nervosa* is characterized by binge eating followed by compensatory behaviors such as self-induced vomiting, fasting, excessive exercise, or misuse of laxatives. The presence or absence of regular use of purging methods as a means to compensate for binge eating account for the two subtypes of bulimia nervosa known as purging subtype and nonpurging subtype, respectively. Individuals with bulimia nervosa, unlike individuals with the diagnosis of anorexia nervosa with the binge-eating/purging subtype, are able to maintain body weight at or above a minimally normal level. An essential feature of both anorexia and bulimia is a disturbance in the perception of body shape and weight.[32]

Over the last 20 years, studies on the biological etiology of eating disorders have provided new insights and possibilities for the treatment of these diseases. Severe disturbances in eating behavior are multifaceted in nature and many approaches to treatment can be utilized. At times eating disorders are difficult to recognize in patients who may be reluctant to seek help. These patients often have little insight into their disease or understanding of the need for treatment due to the secrecy and denial inherent with the disease. Treatment and stabilization of the medical complications of the eating behavior need to be initiated before actual treatment of the eating disorder may begin. Eating misbehavior also could be merely the symptom of other problems or disorders such as depression, dysfunctional family problems, or drug and alcohol abuse. This chapter focuses on the current pathophysiology, recognition, and pharmacological treatment of anorexia and bulimia nervosa.

Epidemiology

Approximately 7.5 million Americans are affected by either bulimia or anorexia in addition to those with compulsive overeating disorders. Overall, eating disorders affect 10% to 15% of all females in the U.S. between 12 and 25 years of age. Females account for 95% of the eating disorder patients.[1,2] However, the prevalence for the development of eating disorders in homosexual men is higher than for heterosexual men (1/48 versus $\frac{1}{300}$).[3]

The onset of anorexia nervosa is bimodal with the peak ages of occurrence at 13 to 14 and 17 to 18 years of age. Bulimia nervosa affects about 4% to 10% of female high school, college, and graduate students.[1,2] The typical patient with an eating disorder is a female in adolescence or early adulthood.

Sociocultural mores may influence the acceptability of eating behaviors. Over the last 30 years, the American image of the perfect female has promoted thinness to the point of anorexia. Women's magazines commonly include articles on weight loss and perfecting the body figure. Fashions usually are modeled by thin women whose physical appearance is not within the norm for most women. Some groups of people, such as dancers and athletes, are at increased risk for the development of eating disorders because of rigorous weight control standards.[4-7]

Diagnostic Features

The presenting signs and symptoms of an eating disorder are vague and nonspecific. Amenorrhea, digestive problems, fatigue, and weight loss[4] are common initial symptoms in patients with eating disorders. These complaints should be taken seriously in individuals with demographic characteristics matching those of a typical eating disorder patient. A detailed history of lifestyle and dietary habits should be obtained in these patients.

Pathogenesis

Families of patients with eating disorders generally have the following four characteristics which may contribute to the problem: enmeshment, overprotectiveness, rigidity, and lack of conflict resolution. In families where one parent is an abuser of substances, the child may become the nonabusing parent's confidant and friend. As a result, the boundaries between the role of parent and child are absent and the home environment can become chaotic and unpredictable. These types of interactions discourage the development of the child's independence, autonomy, and decision making processes which result in a loss of self-identity of the child. An inability of the patient to develop an awareness of her identity and of her body and self leads to a feeling of being controlled by external forces and feelings of poor self-worth. The patient then attempts to gain a sense of control by manipulating the amount of weight gained or lost.[8]

One developmental theory on the etiology of eating disorders focuses on the parental failure to perceive and respond to infant and childhood needs. As a result, a feeling of helplessness is instilled within the child. The patient fails to learn how to differentiate between her needs and the needs of others. In an effort to gain control over her environment, to increase feelings of competence and effectiveness, and to gain relief from anxiety, the patient strives to become thin.[8]

Some sexual developmental theories postulate that anorexia represents a desire of the individual to avoid development of the adult female body and the sexual changes associated with puberty. Research into the sexual histories of these patients also reveal a high incidence of sexual abuse in this population. Eating behaviors, therefore, may merely reflect a feeling of a need to gain control over an uncontrollable environment.[9-11] The pathogenesis of eating disorders probably includes a mixture of sociocultural, developmental, familial, environmental, and biochemical influences.

Pathophysiology

Interactions between neurotransmitters, hormones, and peptides play an important role in the control of hunger, satiety, and eating behavior. Alterations in several of these chemicals have been observed in patients with eating disorders. These changes may play a part in the etiology of aberrant eating behavior.

Plasma concentrations of cortisol and adrenocorticotropin (ACTH) usually increase shortly after a midday meal and this increase is believed to assist in achieving a feeling of satiety after meals in most individuals. ACTH or cortisol plasma concentrations, however, were not increased in bulimic patients after a midday meal (see Figure 80.1). Furthermore, the mean plasma concentrations of cortisol over a 24-hour period were higher in bulimic patients than normal subjects ($p < 0.05$).[18] This lack of rise of ACTH and cortisol after a meal may result in the lack of a feeling of satiety after meals.

Several peptides are under investigation to determine their role in eating behavior. For example, neuropeptide Y and galanin in mammalian models cause hyperphagia or an increase in appetite,[19] and gastrointestinal (GI) peptides such as cholecystokinin, pancreatic glucagon, and bombesin decrease food ingestion. The role of these peptides in patients with eating disorders, however, has not been adequately studied. Nevertheless, these substances may be important in the future for the treatment of eating disorders.[20]

The calming effect after eating a meal has been attributed to increases in plasma concentrations of endogenous opiates in experimental animals, and this effect is antagonized by naloxone.[21] In humans, plasma concentrations of beta-endorphins are increased by stress, gastric stimulation, exercise, surgery, pregnancy, academic examinations, and chronic illness. Anorexia nervosa patients (see Figure 80.2) have higher basal plasma concentrations of beta-endorphins than normal subjects [75 + 6.1 pmoles/L versus 13 + 3.8 pmoles/L ($p < 0.001$)];[22] and bulimic patients also have markedly increased plasma concentrations of beta-endorphins after a standard glucose load compared to normal subjects.[20]

Serotonin plays an important role in the pathogenesis of mood disorders and eating disorders, and[24-28] increases in serotonin concentrations within the central nervous system (CNS) provide a satiating effect in humans. Decreases in CNS concentrations of serotonin have been associated with depression and impulsivity. Binge eating of high carbohydrate foods, therefore, might simply be a reflection of a need to self-treat depression secondary to hyposerotonergic functioning in the brain.[25] These neurochemical alterations perhaps could serve as the basis for the selection of a medication for the treatment of patients with both depression and an eating disorder. For example, use of the antidepressant agents that alter serotonergic concentrations may be beneficial in improving both mood and satiety.

Low-weight patients with anorexia nervosa have decreased cerebrospinal fluid concentrations of the serotonin metabolite 5-HIAA (5-hydroxyindoleacetic acid). After weight restoration, cerebrospinal fluid concentrations of 5-HIAA are higher in nonbingeing anorexic patients and lower in bingeing anorexics.[27]

Cerebrospinal concentrations of 5-HIAA are reduced in patients with a history of more frequent bingeing than in controls or patients with a lower binge frequency. In bulimic patients, serotonin uptake in platelets is decreased and ^{3}H-imipramine binding is reduced. Both of these tests reflect less serotonin efficiency in these patients indicating less serotonin utilization due to decreased serotonin concentrations and decreased binding of serotonin at the receptor site.[27]

Patients with anorexia nervosa appear to be deficient in zinc and this deficiency correlates with fasting and malnutrition.[29] Although other mineral deficiencies have not been noted in patients with anorexia nervosa, it would be reasonable to assume that severely anorectic patients probably are deficient in various vitamins, minerals, and other nutrients and that these deficiencies would reverse upon refeeding.

Fig 80.1   Cortisol and ACTH Concentrations in Bulimic Patients and Control Subjects Within a 24-Hour Period

In animal studies, norepinephrine stimulates the initiation of eating. Norepinephrine also plays an important role in the maintenance of normal mood and hemodynamic status. In patients with anorexia nervosa, serum concentrations of norepinephrine and its metabolite (MHPG) vary with the mood and nutritional status of the patient. The urinary excretion of MHPG is decreased in low-weight anorexic patients who are depressed but is not decreased in patients with equally low weight who are not depressed.[8,30] Therefore, the apparent norepinephrine deficiency seems to correlate more with depression than with the presence of anorexia. Norepinephrine plasma concentrations, however, normalize upon refeeding of these patients.

These variances in serum or CNS concentrations of norepinephrine, serotonin, endogenous opiates, neuropeptides, and minerals have led to multiple postulates on the pathogenesis of eating disorders as well as on the use of various drugs which attempt to correct the chemical imbalance in patients with eating disorders. Since the serum or CNS concentrations of these chemical substances are affected by various endogenous and exogenous stimuli, circadian rhythms, drugs, nutritional status, and medical stability of subjects, the precise role of these chemical imbalances in eating disorders is unclear.

Drug Treatment of Anorexia Nervosa

Several medications have been utilized in the treatment of anorexia nervosa. Agents that block serotonin (e.g., methysergide and cyproheptadine) can increase appetite and have been used with some success in treatment.[26] Medications which help to treat underlying major depressive disorders or anxiety disorders also can be helpful in the treatment of dysfunctional eating behavior, especially if the eating misbehavior represents a coping mechanism

for other concurrent psychiatric disorders. Unfortunately, no medication has been consistently effective in the treatment of this disease; thus, behavior modification remains the primary intervention in the treatment of anorexia nervosa. Some favorable results in the treatment of anorexia nervosa have been obtained with amitriptyline,[38,39] cyproheptadine,[39,40,41] lithium,[42] clomipramine,[43] clonidine,[44] fluoxetine,[45] and zinc.[46] Levodopa, naloxone, phenytoin, chlorpromazine, and pimozide have been used with less success.

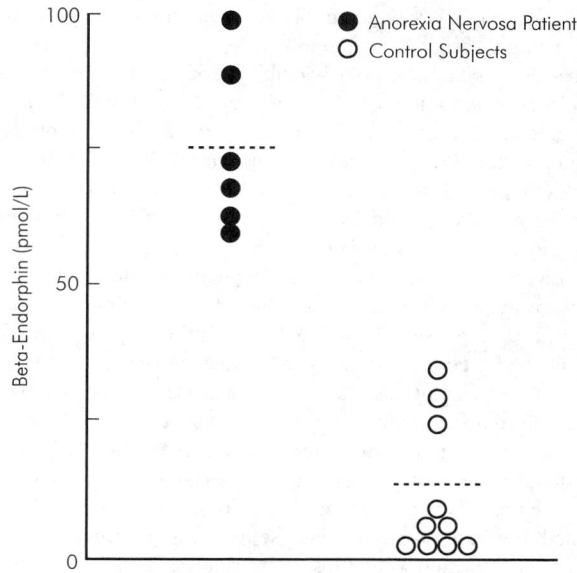

Fig 80.2   Beta-Endorphin Concentrations in Anorexia Nervosa Patients and Control Subjects

Amitriptyline (Elavil) sometimes can be effective in the treatment of patients with anorexia nervosa. In one trial, amitriptyline was not of benefit[38] when compared to placebo and psychosocial treatment. In this study, amitriptyline dosages were low, with a mean dose of 115 mg/day.[38] In another trial, amitriptyline (mean dose: 160 mg/day) was compared to cyproheptadine (mean: 32 mg/day) and placebo.[39] Cyproheptadine (Periactin) was better in producing weight gain than amitriptyline in patients who were restrictive anorexics (p <0.01), while amitriptyline fared better than cyproheptadine in patients who were bingeing anorexics (bulimic subtype). Although few side effects were noted with cyproheptadine, subjects taking amitriptyline experienced drowsiness, confusional states, tachycardia, dry mouth, and constipation. In patients with anorexia who already are focused on their body and body functions, amitriptyline's extensive side effect profile may preclude its use for the treatment of anorexia nervosa. In two other trials,[40,41] lower dosages of cyproheptadine (12 to 32 mg/day) were not effective.

Lithium. In one study,[42] lithium at therapeutic serum concentrations of 0.9 mEq/L to 1.4 mEq/L significantly improved the baseline weight of patients with anorexia when compared with placebo (p <0.05). The validity of this study, however, suffers from the lack of randomization of patients assigned to both groups, and the lithium-treated patients had a higher baseline food intake than the placebo group. Lithium may be a viable treatment for patients with anorexia nervosa, especially if the patient also has a concurrent bipolar mood disorder. Lithium is contraindicated in patients with abnormalities of cardiac, renal, electrolyte, or thyroid functions (see Chapter 77: Mood Disorders II: Bipolar Affective Disorders). Electrolyte disturbances, dehydration, cardiac abnormalities, renal problems, and stomach upset can occur with lithium, thus anorexic patients should be medically stabilized before initiation of lithium.

Clomipramine (Anafranil)[43] at a dosage of 50 mg/day, has modified eating misbehaviors and decreased the time to attain the desired target weight. Patients treated with clomipramine showed less denial and minimization of their illness and experienced fewer physical problems compared to a placebo group. Clomipramine is similar in structure to imipramine, a tricyclic antidepressant, and shares the anticholinergic, hypotensive, sedating, and arrhythmogenic side effects seen with the tricyclic antidepressants. Clomipramine is approved in the U.S. for the treatment of obsessive-compulsive disorder and may be a good choice for patients who show marked obsessive-compulsive symptoms associated with their eating disorder.

Selective Serotonin Reuptake Inhibitors (SSRIs). The selective serotonin reuptake inhibitors, such as fluoxetine (Prozac), can decrease depressive, obsessive-compulsive, and anxiety symptoms in patients with anorexia nervosa. In one trial,[45] fluoxetine 20 to 60 mg/day improved mood and increased weight in all six anorexic patients; however, mood can improve in anorexic patients upon refeeding alone. In another open trial,[46] 31 patients with anorexia nervosa and concurrent substantial problems with mood or refeeding were treated with fluoxetine. After three months, ten patients had a good response, 17 patients had a partial response, and four patients had a poor response. Three patients discontinued fluoxetine. One because of cost, the second because of discouragement, and the third because of irritability. Due to the design of these trials and the small number of patients, fluoxetine cannot be recommended for the treatment of anorexia nervosa unless a subset of anorexic patients who are more likely to respond to SSRIs can be defined. Furthermore, fluoxetine use has been associated with decreased appetite and weight loss. Nevertheless, a trial of fluoxetine might be warranted in some patients with treatment-resistant anorexia, or in those with concurrent depression and a history of

intolerance to tricyclic antidepressants. **Behavioral modification is the primary treatment for anorexia nervosa and medications seldom are used.** Pharmacotherapy can be initiated when patients are resistant to traditional treatment. If an individual with anorexia nervosa has a bingeing component to the anorexia, an antidepressant may be warranted even if the patient does not have concurrent depression. Restrictive anorexics (i.e., anorexia nervosa without a bingeing or purging subtype) might benefit from cyproheptadine which increases serotonin concentrations and aids in appetite stimulation. Antipsychotics, lithium, and clonidine are not recommended for treatment of anorexia nervosa because the adverse effects of these drugs are especially ominous in debilitated patients and the benefits are merely equivocal. More study of clomipramine is needed to determine if increased dosages may benefit patients with anorexia nervosa.

Drug Treatment of Bulimia Nervosa

Antidepressants are effective in decreasing bingeing behavior and mood symptoms in patients with bulimia nervosa.[51,56–62] Since serotonin has been postulated to play an important role in eating behavior, drugs that increase serotonin within the central nervous system could be of benefit in decreasing binge behavior and improving concurrent symptoms of depression. Serotonin concentrations may be increased within the central nervous system by administration of serotonin-precursor amino acids (tryptophan and 5-hydroxytryptophan), selective serotonin reuptake inhibitors (fluoxetine, sertraline, paroxetine, fluvoxamine), facilitators of serotonin release (cianopramine, femoxetine, zimelidine, dL-fenfluramine, dexfenfluramine), and postsynaptic agonists (MCPP, CM 57493). As these compounds increase serotonin within the central nervous system, they are potential therapeutic agents for decreasing bingeing behavior in bulimic patients.[14] Antidepressants often are used in the treatment of bulimia because of their effects on the neurotransmitters that regulate food intake, improve depression, allay anxiety, or subdue obsessive-compulsive symptoms. Antidepressants increase the synaptic concentration of neurotransmitters (e.g., norepinephrine, serotonin) by blocking their presynaptic reuptake. Fluoxetine (Prozac), sertraline (Zoloft), and paroxetine (Paxil) are SSRIs that are approved for the treatment of depression. The SSRI, fluvoxamine (Luvox), and the cyclic antidepressant, clomipramine (Anafranil), also are approved for the treatment of obsessive-compulsive disorder. No drug has been approved in the U.S. for the treatment of bulimia nervosa, but several drugs have benefited patients in controlled studies and open trials.

Desipramine. When desipramine (Norpramin) was given (mean dose: 200 mg/day) to ten patients (12 placebo; n = 22) for six weeks, 68% of desipramine-treated patients achieved remission.[63] All of the bulimia nervosa patients with abnormal dexamethasone-suppression tests (48% of the sample) achieved at least an 80% improvement in eating behavior. Patients with desipramine plasma concentrations of 125 to 275 ng/mL had the better response.

When desipramine (mean dose: 150 mg/day) was given to 47 patients for six weeks, 23 patients dropped out of the study: 13 patients due to personal reasons, eight due to side effects, one due to suicidal ideation, and one secondary to parotid gland swelling.[64] Desipramine was superior to placebo (p <0.01) in decreasing vomiting and bingeing behavior. One patient completely abstained from bingeing and vomiting behavior; three patients had a greater than 80% decrease; and 11 patients had greater than a 50% decrease in eating disorder behavior. In a third study,[65] bingeing decreased by 63% in 60% of nonpurging bulimics (an uncommon subgroup of bulimic patients) who received desipramine (mean dose: 188 mg/day) for 12 weeks.

Fenfluramine (Pondimin) 60 mg/day was better than desipramine 150 mg/day in inducing remission of bulimia (50% versus 20%, p <0.03). In this study, the mean daily dose of desipramine was less than the mean daily dose in other desipramine studies.

Trazodone (Desyrel) was minimally effective in inducing remission for bingeing and vomiting in two small double-blind, placebo-controlled studies at mean dosages of 355 and 410 mg/day, respectively.[69,84] Although trazodone has high specificity for blocking the reuptake of serotonin and has a low incidence of anticholinergic side effects, it cannot be recommended for treatment of bulimia nervosa because of the relative lack of substantive evidence of efficacy. Furthermore, three bulimic patients treated with trazodone developed visual hallucinations that resolved within 12 to 72 hours after decreases in dose or discontinuation of trazodone.[70]

Bupropion (Wellbutrin) decreased bingeing in 67% of 37 patients who completed an eight week course of therapy and induced complete remission in 30%.[71] Four patients (4%) experienced seizures during the trial with bupropion (usual incidence: 0.4%). Due to this relatively large percentage of patients experiencing a seizure, bupropion is not recommended for treatment of patients with eating disorders unless extreme caution is used with zealous monitoring.

Phenelzine (Nardil) induced remission (mean dose: 60 mg/day for 6 weeks) in 35% of bulimic patients compared to 4% of placebo-treated patients (p <0.01). Nine patients were unable to complete the trial due to side effects; three for orthostatic hypotension and two patients due to sedation. Since phenelzine is a monoamine oxidase inhibitor, a tyramine-free diet is essential to minimize the possibility of a hypertensive crisis. Although no patient in this study suffered such a reaction, caution must be exercised when prescribing this drug. Eating disorder patients characteristically have impulse control problems and this can be problematic when imposing dietary restrictions in people who have difficulties with food intake. The patient and the patient's family must receive rigorous dietary counseling that includes written information. When educating a patient about the use of a tyramine-free diet, obtain a good dietary history by questioning the use of specific foods, amounts ingested, and frequency of intake. Evaluate the probability of the patient's adherence to the diet based upon the degree of change necessary in his/her food habits, and not on intelligence or educational level of the patient. Be very specific about foods to be avoided and the consequences of noncompliance, and talk with people who prepare the patient's food. All health professionals involved in the patient's care should understand the dietary restrictions and be aware of the treatment plan. The diet and adherence to the treatment plan should be evaluated on a regular basis by asking specific questions of the patient. Patients must stay on the tyramine-free diet for at least two weeks after discontinuation of the monoamine oxidase inhibitor to prevent hypertensive crisis.

Amitriptyline (Elavil)[74] in a double-blind, placebo-controlled trial (mean dose: 150 mg/day) for eight weeks was not statistically better than placebo in decreasing the number of binges in bulimic patients. Dosages of amitriptyline, however, were low and plasma amitriptyline concentrations were not monitored. Imipramine (mean dose: 200 mg/day) for six weeks decreased binges in 44% of bulimic patients by at least 75% and in an additional 44% (4) of patients by at least 50% of baseline.

Imipramine. The efficacy of imipramine, placebo, imipramine with cognitive behavioral therapy, and placebo with cognitive behavioral therapy was evaluated in 171 patients with bulimia nervosa.[76] The patients who were in the cognitive behavioral treatment group experienced the most significant improvement in bulimic behavior and this improvement was even better in this group than in the group who received imipramine in combination with cognitive behavioral therapy. This study emphasizes that cognitive behavioral therapy should be utilized as a mainstay of treatment for patients with bulimia nervosa. Drug therapy should be reserved for the treatment of bulimia nervosa patients who fail to respond adequately to cognitive-behavioral therapy alone or have significant concurrent symptoms of anxiety or depression.

Fluoxetine. The efficacy of fluoxetine (20 and 60 mg) was evaluated against a placebo for eight weeks in 347 bulimic female outpatients enrolled in the Fluoxetine Bulimia Nervosa Collaborative Study Group.[77] Fluoxetine 60 mg was significantly better than placebo in decreasing self-induced vomiting and binge eating. Fluoxetine 20 mg decreased vomiting, but not binge eating behavior in these bulimic patients. Doses of fluoxetine to treat bulimia nervosa, therefore, apparently need to be higher than the doses needed to treat depression. Less than 5% of patients withdrew from the study because of adverse effects to fluoxetine. Insomnia, nausea, and tremor were the most commonly encountered adverse effects in this study.

Naltrexone. Since bingeing is thought to increase the plasma concentrations of beta- endorphins, naltrexone (Trexan) has been used to decrease the urge of continued bingeing by antagonizing the effects of endorphins. Naltrexone has been studied in three open label, two double-blind, placebo-controlled crossover trials, and one double-blind trial.[80] In the first open-label trial, naltrexone for six weeks (mean dose: 200 mg/day PO) did not reduce bingeing behavior. In the second open trial by the same investigators, naltrexone (up to 300 mg/day) for six weeks induced remission in three patients, reduced bingeing by 75% and 50% in four patients and one patient, respectively, and had no effect on bingeing in the two remaining patients. When 50 to 100 mg doses of naltrexone were compared to 200 to 300 mg doses, the higher doses were significantly more effective in reducing bulimic episodes. In the three remaining double-blind studies, naltrexone 100 to 150 mg/day was not more effective than placebo in reducing the number of bulimic episodes, however, naltrexone reduced the duration of bingeing episodes in one of the studies. Naltrexone is of limited usefulness due to the risk of hepatotoxicity at higher doses and the common side effects of nausea, headache, heart palpitations, diaphoresis, and racing thoughts. Naltrexone may be useful in severely afflicted bulimic patients who fail to respond to cognitive behavioral therapy or antidepressant agents. No other psychotropic drug therapies are recommended for the treatment of bulimia nervosa at this time.[81]

Drugs Relative to Cognitive Behavior Therapy. **Cognitive behavioral therapy continues to be the therapy of choice for the treatment of bulimia nervosa.** If further treatment is needed for eating disorder behaviors, or if significant anxiety, depression, or obsessive-compulsive symptoms are present, concomitant antidepressants may be prescribed for the treatment of bulimia nervosa. Several antidepressants have been tested with good results with better overall outcomes than with placebo. Imipramine, desipramine, and fluoxetine appear to be the most beneficial in the treatment of bulimia nervosa. Trazodone and bupropion are associated with adverse reactions which may contraindicate their use. If the patient fails to respond to a therapeutic trial of antidepressants, serum concentrations of these drugs can be measured to assess compliance or refractoriness of symptoms. The effectiveness of phenelzine is limited by dietary restrictions, especially in view of the increased risk of hypertensive crises if patients are noncompliant with these restrictions.

Generally, antidepressant treatment for bulimia nervosa is continued for six months to one year. After this period of time, a medication free trial should be considered and the patient assessed for continued recovery or relapse without medication. Cognitive behavioral therapy should be the mainstay of treatment and medications should be utilized only as adjunctive therapy for patients who are nonresponsive, lack optimal response to nonpharmacologic intervention, or who have marked symptoms of depression, obsessive-compulsive disorder, or anxiety.

Anorexia Nervosa

Clinical Presentation

Predisposing Factors

1. J.T., a 14-year-old female high school student, is known for her good grades, gymnastics, and wardrobe. She competes on the school gymnastics team and is required to weigh in every other day by her coach. She spends several hours per week reading magazines, clipping articles about the newest fashion, fad, and diet. She is often the life of the party, but if you ask her friends how she is actually feeling, most of them reply, "Okay, I guess, she usually doesn't talk about that stuff." Her father drinks significant amounts of alcohol and spends much of his time away from home. Her parents argue a lot and her father typically leaves the house in the middle of an argument. Her father's physician has suggested treatment for her father's alcoholism, but he vehemently denies there is a problem. Her mother worries about her father all the time and has little time to spend with the family. She constantly pressures J.T. to do well and to be careful. J.T. often feels that she never does anything right, and vows never to be angry like her father. What factors in this history could predispose J.T. to the development of an eating disorder?

J.T. has several factors that may predispose her to the development of an eating disorder. She matches the demographic profile of a person with an eating disorder by being 14 years of age and female. She appears to be interested in the societal image of femininity and seems to focus on physical appearance and fashion as evidenced by her clipping of articles from fashion magazines. Her participation on her gymnastics team requires her to weigh in every other day, and this undertaking again places an undue focus on the importance of body weight. The family system in which she is raised appears to be dysfunctional (e.g., her father's alcoholism and anger). J.T. does not feel she should express her emotions to her friends and vows never to express anger. Her father and mother argue and seem unable to resolve family conflicts. J.T.'s self-esteem may be decreased because she often feels that "she never does anything right." Her mother's pressure to do well and to be careful can be stifling to the emotional growth of an adolescent. The family characteristics of enmeshment, overprotectiveness, lack of conflict resolution, and rigidity might be contributing to J.T.'s need for control of her own personal environment through her manipulation of food intake.

Comorbidity

2. One year later, J.T. is referred to the school psychologist by one of her teachers. Her scholastic performance in her classes has fallen dramatically, her wardrobe consists of rumpled T-shirts and dirty jeans, and she often appears to be daydreaming in class. Collateral history given by her parents and friends confirm a lack of interest in many of the activities she used to enjoy, including "hanging out" with her friends, gymnastic events, shopping, difficulty sleeping, crying spells, and feeling "bummed out." The school psychologist refers her to a private psychiatrist for treatment of major depression. Why are J.T.'s symptoms of depression consistent with her eating disorder?

Many psychiatric disorders may occur simultaneously in patients with an eating disorder. Depression is believed to be associated in some manner with the pathogenesis of eating disorders and occurs in 50% of anorexic patients and 75% of patients with bulimia. Furthermore, the diagnosis of depression by the dexamethasone suppression test (DST) is positive in 47% of patients with eating disorders.[12] Eating disorder patients with a positive DST may be likely to respond well to antidepressant medication. Alexithymia (i.e., an inability to express and experience emotions and body sensations) is more common in eating disorder patients when compared to normal controls.[13] J.T.'s symptoms which include decreased school performance, poor hygiene and grooming, difficulty concentrating, anhedonia (lack of enjoyment), crying, and depressed mood indicate the possibility of a major depressive disorder that is concurrent with her eating disorder. Both problems need to be addressed concomitantly. In this case, antidepressant medication may help to treat both J.T.'s eating disorder and depression.

3. What psychiatric disorders (other than depression) commonly occur concurrently with eating disorders and which of J.T.'s symptoms are consistent with these disorders?

Obsessive-compulsive disorder is another psychiatric condition thought to contribute to the pathology of eating disorder patients.[14] Personality disorders, including borderline, self-defeating, dependent, avoidant, and histrionic disorders have been noted in 38% of bulimic patients.[15]

Eating disorder patients have an increased prevalence of impulsivity, psychiatric hospitalizations, drug use, and a history of more suicide attempts. Dysfunctional eating and psychological distress (e.g., depression, interpersonal sensitivity, obsessive compulsive behavior, hostility) even seem to be more common in patients with a history of stealing.[16]

Many eating disorder patients have an intense fear of obesity or a phobia for gaining weight. Both anorexic and bulimic patients have distorted perceptions of body image and body size when compared to normal controls.[17] As previously stated, J.T.'s symptoms are consistent with a diagnosis of major depression. She does not appear to have other psychiatric disorders.

Diagnostic Criteria and Medical Complications

4. T.R., a 20-year-old female, was brought to the eating disorders clinic by her friends. She is at 62% of her ideal body weight (IBW). Her best friend reports that they started on a diet program approximately 1 year ago. Thereafter, T.R. could not seem to stop dieting no matter what anyone told her about her appearance or how thin she was. She has experienced amenorrhea for the past 4 months. T.R. states that "I am fat

Table 80.1   DSM-IV Diagnostic Criteria for Anorexia Nervosa[32]
Refusal to maintain minimal normal weight for age and height (Weight ≤85% below expected weight)
Intense fear of gaining weight or becoming fat, even though underweight
Disturbance of body image or denial of the seriousness of the current low body weight
Amenorrhea for 3 consecutive menses
• Subtypes of anorexia nervosa
Binge-Eating or Purging Type: Regularly engages in binge-eating or self-induced vomiting (or misuse of laxatives, diuretics, or enemas) during the current episode
Nonpurging (i.e., Restrictive) Type: Person has used other inappropriate compensatory behaviors, such as fasting or excessive exercise, but has not self-induced vomiting or misused any medications to lose weight during the current episode

and need to lose weight.'' When asked would increasing her weight be a bad thing she states ''I'd rather die than gain weight.'' She continues to diet even though she currently weighs 84 pounds and is 5'7" in height. T.R. states on interview ''I diet because I am overweight.'' On physical examination she presents as a cachectic young female with thinning hair, rough and scaly skin, slowed movements, blood pressure (BP) 80/50 mm Hg, temperature 95 °F, and heart rate 45 beats/min. What subjective and objective data in T.R. are consistent with anorexia nervosa?

The diagnosis of anorexia nervosa is based upon criteria established by the American Psychiatric Association in the Diagnostic and Statistical Manual of Mental Disorders, fourth edition (DSM-IV).[32] T.R.'s symptoms of an intense fear of becoming fat, disturbed perception of body image (even though underweight) or denial of the seriousness of the current low body weight, an actual weight more than 15% below the expected weight, refusal to maintain minimal normal weight, and amenorrhea for four consecutive menses meet the criteria for anorexia nervosa (see Table 80.1).

T.R. is showing signs of severe anorexia (see Table 80.2) which include medical complications such as decreased scalp hair, weight loss, rough and scaly skin, decreased metabolic rate (heart rate 45, temperature 95 °F, BP 80/50), hypothermia, cardiac changes, weight of 62% IBW, lack of insight into her current condition, and amenorrhea. In some patients, dermatologic changes include not only decreased scalp hair but the presence of fine lanugo-like hair on face and trunk. Malnutrition and vitamin deficiencies lead to skin that is rough and scaly. Other changes that may be observed in patients with anorexia nervosa are variable but are compatible with signs and symptoms of severe malnutrition.

Treatment

Hospitalization

5. T.R. is hospitalized on an inpatient eating disorders unit to manage her anorexia nervosa. When should patients be hospitalized for treatment of anorexia? Why was T.R. hospitalized?

Patients should be hospitalized for treatment of eating disorders if any of the following criteria apply. The patient presents with a rapid weight loss of greater than 15% of body mass, persistent bradycardia of ≤50 beats/minute, hypotension with systolic blood pressure of less than 90 mm Hg, core body temperature of less than 97 °F, medical complications, suicidal ideation, sabotage of treatment or disruption of completion of outpatient treatment, or denial of the need for help.

T.R. was showing signs of weight loss of 38% of her ideal body weight, bradycardia of 45 beats/minute, blood pressure of 80/50 mm Hg, denial of the need for treatment, and core body temperature of 95 °F. These symptoms warrant inpatient stabilization and treatment.

Goals of Treatment

6. What goals should be achieved before T.R. is discharged from the hospital?

The goals that should be attained before T.R. is discharged from the hospital should include medical stabilization with correction of metabolic or other disturbances and nutritional stabilization with attainment of a target goal weight generally within 15% of her ideal body weight. Education is an important aspect of T.R.'s treatment and she should be taught the symptoms, complications, course, and outcome of anorexia nervosa both in a treated and untreated state. A nutritional meal plan and exercise plan should be developed with T.R. Her anorexic eating behavior should be resolved before she is discharged from the hospital and she should have better insight into her anorexia and understand the need for treatment of this disorder.

Table 80.2	Anorexia Nervosa Medical Complications[a,32–34]

Hair
  Scalp hair ↓
  Fine lanugo-like hair on face and trunk

Skin
  Rough, scaly

Starvation
  Slower metabolic rate
  ↓ heat loss
  Growth retardation

Cortical atrophy

ECG
  Heart rates <60 beats/min
  S-T segment depression, T wave changes
  Arrhythmias

Low blood pressure
  <100/50 mm Hg

Weight loss
  15% loss of ideal body weight

Osteopenia and osteoporosis

Early morning awakening and nocturia

Anemia, thrombocytopenia

Menses—absent
  ↓ LH secretion
  Low estradiol levels
  Nonmeasurable progesterone levels
  Lack of response to LHRH stimulation

Thyroid
  ↓ conversion of T_3 from T_4
  Symptoms of hypothyroidism

Cortisol
  ↑ plasma levels
  ↑ free or normal urinary cortisol levels

Mental
  Lability of mood
  Irritability
  Indecisiveness
  Poor grooming and hygiene
  Suicidal

[a] LH = Luteinizing hormone; LHRH = Luteinizing hormone releasing hormone; T_3 = Triiodothyronine; T_4 = Thyroxine.

Psychotherapy

7. A treatment plan consisting of group, family, and individual therapy has been devised for T.R. A behavior modification program also is instituted including attendance at Overeaters Anonymous meetings. Why were these treatments prescribed for T.R. in preference to drug therapy?

Individual, group, and family psychotherapy are essential for treatment success.[4] Individual therapy focuses on decreasing denial of the disorder while building self-confidence and self-esteem to decrease the risk of perpetuating the eating misbehavior. Group therapy reduces the shame, isolation, and secrecy of having an eating disorder; increases reality testing with peers; develops social skills; and enhances communication techniques. Family therapy provides support and education to the family. Treatment of other disturbances in the family support system can help the family to better cope with difficulties and to improve communication among family members.

Nutritional counseling is necessary to help the patient in food selection and in maintaining long-term abstinence from the disordered eating behavior. Refeeding plans must avoid excessive gastrointestinal discomfort or complications and eating plans should be supervised to assure compliance with dietary regimens.

Behavioral modification treatments help to reinforce positive outcomes for T.R. when she behaves appropriately. Rewards for good behavior may include removal of restrictions while hospitalized, increased privileges such as a day pass, unsupervised time alone, or retrieval of personal belongings as she improves.[61]

The compulsion to vomit or purge may require supervised use of the bathroom or restriction of bathroom privileges for a couple of hours after meals to prevent purging of ingested food. Suicide precautions and close observation may be necessary, especially in those patients with a history of impulsive behavior or with symptoms of depression.

Cognitive behavioral therapy focuses on identification of the thoughts and feelings that trigger the maladaptive eating behavior. Identification of these problems helps to challenge and evaluate the patient's attitudes about weight and eating; and helps the patient to formulate better coping strategies to deal with distressing thoughts and feelings. These better coping strategies and rejection of dysfunctional attitudes about weight and eating help to prevent the return to the disordered eating behavior.[61]

Self-help groups play an important part in on-going treatment for patients with all types of eating disorders (i.e., bulimia nervosa, anorexia nervosa, and compulsive overeating).[35] Food as an addiction often is discounted by the general population and considered less disabling an addiction when compared to alcohol or other drugs. Eating disorder patients are vulnerable to ''trigger'' foods each day (e.g., social activities often involve the ingestion of food). It is important to remember that for food abusers, it is impossible to abstain from all foods and that more willpower is not the answer. Continued support via self-help programs (e.g., Alcoholics Anonymous, Overeaters Anonymous) is crucial to therapeutic success both during and after treatment.[36,37] The principles of the 12-Step self-help programs usually are incorporated into treatment programs for patients with eating disorders. Overeaters Anonymous provides group support for the maintenance of nondisordered eating and is inclusive for all disordered eating behaviors. Although one might suspect that T.R. potentially could be adversely affected by participating in Overeaters Anonymous because she has difficulty in eating rather than ''overeating,'' patients with eating disorders actually do benefit from participating in Overeaters Anonymous which provides support for participants with various types of eating disorders.[37] These self-help groups offer an environment conducive to reduction of isolation, are free of charge, help to maintain long-term abstinence, and provide a place to vent feelings and frustrations without food as a coping mechanism. Many individuals attend two or more meetings per week indefinitely for maintenance of recovery. (See Chapter 81: Issues: Psychoactive Substance Use Disorders for a more detailed discussion of 12-Step programs.)

Prognosis

8. T.R. completed a 60-day treatment program. Her weight is now 100% of IBW. She is eating 3 meals a day, feels she can maintain her food intake, and is optimistic about her future. Her relationship with her family has improved and she attends an outpatient follow-up program and 2–3 group support meetings per week. What are the chances of T.R. maintaining her recovery at its current level?

Poor outcome predictors for anorexia nervosa include long duration of illness, poor motivation for treatment, social withdrawal, and poor family relations.[47] T.R.'s anorexia has not been longstanding as her behavior apparently began about a year ago when she first began dieting with a friend. She is reportedly eating three meals a day and she now weighs 100% of her ideal body weight. Her motivation for treatment, improvement in family relations, and

social involvement are good indications of continued success. Furthermore, she appears to be optimistic about her future.

Bulimia Nervosa
Clinical Presentation
Recognition

9. A.G., a 17-year-old female, has a prescription for furosemide (Lasix) 20 mg and also purchases several bottles of syrup of ipecac and 4 boxes of Ex-Lax. Why should A.G. be confronted?

The recognition of a patient with an eating disorder requires good observational skills because secrecy and denial are the hallmarks of the disease. A teenage or young adult female who frequently purchases laxatives, diet aids, or ipecac and receives prescriptions for a diuretic may be having difficulties with anorexia or bulimia. Other indicators of anorexia or bulimia may include evidence of bingeing, weight loss, vomiting, secrecy, vague medical complaints, impulse control difficulties, aloofness in socialization or lack of socialization, and strong emotional reactions to various food items.[34,48,49]

The frequent purchase of over-the-counter (OTC) and prescription medications to relieve bloating, to purge, or to decrease appetite should prompt suspicion of an eating disorder. About 60% of eating disorder patients abuse laxatives and about 20% use these drugs daily. The most commonly abused purging agents are fast-acting irritant laxatives. Some patients abuse laxatives multiple times each day (e.g., 15 to 20 times each day) and in one case, 300 to 600 laxatives doses were taken in one day. Nonprescription (OTC) appetite suppressant drugs are used in 50% of eating disorder patients, diuretics in 30%, and syrup of ipecac in 17%.[49,50]

Approaching a patient suspected of bulimia may be difficult due to their reluctance to acknowledge the need for treatment and denial. Providing medication education regarding the correct use of these products may help to open communication between the health care provider and the patient. Once this relationship is established, eating behavior may be explored and additional information provided (see Table 80.3) if necessary.

The A.G.'s primary care physician should be alerted to her use of medications and the possibility of an eating disorder. The phy-

Table 80.3	Resources for Eating Disorders

American Anorexia/Bulimia Association, Inc.
   133 Cedar Lane
   Teaneck, NJ 01616
   (201) 836-1800

National Association of Anorexia Nervosa and Associated Disorders
   P.O. Box 271
   Highland Park, IL
   (708) 831-3438

National Anorexic Aid Society, Inc.
   P.O. Box 29461
   Columbus, OH 43229
   (614) 846-2588

Overeaters Anonymous
   P.O. Box 92870
   Los Angeles, CA 90009
   1-800-589-OAOA

O-Anon General Services Office
   P.O. Box 4305
   San Pedro, CA 90731

Hazelden Education Materials
   Pleasant Valley Road
   Box 176
   Center City, MN 55012-0176
   1-800-328-9000

Table 80.4	Criteria for Inpatient Hospitalization for Patients with Eating Disorders[a,3,4]

- Rapid weight loss of >15% of body mass
- Persistent bradycardia of 50 beats/min
- Hypotension with systolic blood pressure of <90 mm Hg
- Core body temperature of <97 °F
- Medical complications
- Suicidal ideation
- Sabotage or disruption of outpatient treatment
- Denial of need for help

[a] When any one of these criteria is met.

sician may then be able to evaluate A.G. more thoroughly. Eating and purging behavior also can be the symptom of underlying depression or other psychiatric illness. Intervention may lead to an improvement in the patient's overall functioning and could help offset a lifetime of dysfunction.

Evaluation and Hospitalization

10. Two days later A.G. was rushed to the emergency room after collapsing during a track meet. She is alert and oriented to person, place, and time, her mood is depressed, and her affect is consistent with her mood. She expresses hopelessness with suicidal ideation and feelings of guilt. She states that she feels dizzy and restless. She further states that, "right after running the 50-yard dash, my heart was beating so hard it felt like it was going to jump out of my chest. Then my head started spinning, making it impossible to stand." Should A.G. be hospitalized to treat her current symptomatology?

On initial presentation, it is critical to medically stabilize A.G. and evaluate her clinical status. A physical examination, electrocardiogram (ECG), hematology profile, and the serum concentration of electrolytes should be evaluated. Liver function, thyroid function, serum amylase, pregnancy status, and a urine drug screen also should be assessed. Inpatient hospitalization for anorexia nervosa or bulimia nervosa is suggested if any one of the problems in Table 80.4 is identified. Although the results from the laboratory tests and physical examination findings are not yet available, A.G. should be hospitalized because of her current suicidal ideation.[3,4]

Medical Complications

11. A.G.'s laboratory evaluations show macrocytic anemia, serum potassium of 3.0 mEq/L, blood urea nitrogen/creatinine ratio >30. Her physical examination reveals scarring on the right dorsum of the hand, caries of the teeth, bloated facial features, and severe constipation. A detailed history reveals a 5-year-history of bingeing, vomiting, and purging episodes occurring from twice per week to 4 times a day. Her vital signs were as follows: BP 110/75 mm Hg supine and 90/70 mm Hg in the upright position; pulse 95 beats/min, temperature 98.2 °F, and respirations 20/min. What characteristics of A.G.'s clinical presentation are consistent with the medical complications associated with bulimia nervosa?

A.G.'s presentation has many features associated with bulimia nervosa. She is probably dehydrated base upon her BUN/creatinine ratio and orthostasis, and has evidence of hypokalemia. The decrease of systolic pressure of 20 mm Hg when A.G. moved from a supine to an upright position should alert the clinician to the possibility of volume depletion that perhaps can be attributable to vomiting. Two hallmark signs of bulimia nervosa are scarring on the dorsum of the hand and severe dental carries.[34] Her hand may have been traumatized by her teeth because of repeated self-in-

duced vomiting accomplished by insertion of her fingers into her mouth to initiate the gag reflex. The dental carries in A.G. could have occurred because of erosion of the enamel of the teeth caused by repeated exposure to gastric acid. Her bloated facial features may be secondary to salivary gland swelling that results from repeated vomiting. Since A.G. is volume depleted, her constipation could be the result of dehydration, laxative abuse, or repeated vomiting. The medical complications of bulimia can involve various organ systems (see Table 80.5).

Diagnostic Criteria

Bingeing and Vomiting

12. A.G. reports bingeing and vomiting several times per week and occasionally several times per day. This has recently worsened due to the pressure of applying to various colleges. How many calories are likely to be ingested during an episode of bingeing? How commonly is bingeing accompanied by vomiting?

Patients with either bulimia nervosa or anorexia nervosa may have episodes of bingeing behavior. The presence or absence of regular binge eating or purging during an episode of anorexia nervosa can further categorize an anorexic patient into the two subtypes (i.e., a restrictive-type or binge-eating/purging type). A bulimic patient "binge-eats" but may keep from gaining weight by either vomiting, purging, fasting, or exercising (see Table 80.6). A binge is considered to be a rapid consumption of high-caloric foods in a small amount of time. Generally, 4000 to 5000 calories are ingested during a single binge episode, however, the daily caloric intake ranges from 1000 to 20,000 calories. Binges most often occur in the early evening or late afternoon, a time when most eating disorder patients report a craving for food substances.[48] High carbohydrate and high caloric foods generally are ingested

Table 80.5	Bulimia Nervosa Medical Complications

Alkalosis
  Weakness
  Fatigue
  Kidney infection or damage
Electrolyte loss
  Weakness, fatigue, cardiac arrhythmias, hypernatremia, hypochloremia, hypokalemia, >5 vomiting episodes/day, phosphate may drop to ≤2.5 mEq/L
Dehydration
Gastrointestinal
  Erosion of teeth enamel
  Gum disease
  Swelling of salivary glands
  Heartburn (esophagitis)
  ↑ risk of cancer of the esophagus
  Esophagus perforation
  Gastric rupture
  Loss of elasticity of stomach wall
  Inhibition of gastric contractions
  "Lazy bowel syndrome" (intestinal distention, inadequate digestion, impaired absorption of nutrients)
Menstrual abnormalities
  Oligomenorrhea
  Dysmenorrhea
  Irregular menstruation
Decreased immunity
Vitamin deficiency
  Hair loss
  Blood clotting abnormalities
Cardiomyopathy
  Secondary to emetine toxicity
Bone decalcification

Table 80.6   DSM-IV Diagnostic Criteria for Bulimia Nervosa[32]

- Recurrent episodes of binge eating characterized by:
    1) Eating, in a discrete period of time, an amount of food which is considered larger than most people would eat during a similar period of time
    2) A sense of a lack of control over eating behavior

- Regular engagement of compensatory mechanisms to prevent weight gain such as self-induced vomiting, misuse of laxatives, diuretics, enemas or other medications, strict dieting or fasting, or vigorous exercise

- 2 binges/week for at least 3 months

- Self-evaluation that is unduly influenced by body weight and size

- Absence of anorexia nervosa

- Subtypes of bulimia nervosa
    Purging Type: Regularly engages in self-induced vomiting or misuse of laxatives, diuretics, or enemas
    Nonpurging Type: Does not purge but utilizes other compensatory behavior (e.g., fasting, excessive exercise)

during binge episodes, however, one study showed no difference in fat, protein, carbohydrate, or alcohol intake during binge versus nonbinge periods.[25] Frequency of vomiting in bulimic patients is variable, occurring several times per day to a few times a week. Vomiting usually correlates with bingeing activity 90% of the time.[34]

Comparisons with Anorexia

13. A.G. has been medically stabilized and is in the process of being admitted to an eating disorders treatment unit. Her family members have been notified and are involved in treatment. When A.G.'s family is interviewed, they deny that A.G. has a problem with weight or her eating, and that she looks perfectly healthy. Upon further discussion, it is discovered that A.G. is popular at school and maintains a high grade-point average. A.G. rarely has meals with her family, saying she has homework to do or that she will catch something to eat on her way to track practice. When she does eat, she generally eats healthy food and an occasional glass of wine. Her mother, however, has found bags of cookies in her closet and in A.G.'s desk which are confusing because she eats so healthy at other times. She weighs herself several times a day and is always worried about looking fat. How do the characteristics of patients with bulimia nervosa differ from those with anorexia nervosa?

Anorexic patients are generally more easily recognized by their marked decrease in weight than bulimic patients. Bulimic patients may be overweight, low, or normal weight, with the most common presentation being normal weight individuals. Body weight, however, can fluctuate 5 to 25 pounds per week in bulimics. Anorexic patients are generally ≥15% below their ideal body weight and have no recognition of the thinness of their own body.[34]

Patients with bulimia or anorexia nervosa can have food aversions as well as taste preferences. Anorexics have been found to have aversions to sugar, chocolate, apple pie, chewing gum, sweetened fruit juice, soft drinks, french fries, white bread, rice, lean meat, mayonnaise, and whole milk products.[52] Bulimic patients tend to have a higher preference for sweets compared to control subjects.[53]

Secrecy of the eating misbehavior is common to the eating disorder patient. Anorexic patients are generally more easily detected due to their loss of body weight and loss of social interactions. Bulimics are able to maintain social interactions, but tend to remain aloof to maintain the secrecy of their binge-purge behavior. Often, the bulimic patient will be the "ideal student or professional" with an extraordinary driving need for perfection. Underneath the facade often exists a person with suicidal ideation, low self-esteem,

depression, and anxiety. One fourth of these patients have made a suicidal gesture.[56] (See Tables 80.1 and 80.6 for the diagnostic criteria for both anorexia nervosa and bulimia nervosa.)

Comorbidity

14. A.G. has been in the eating disorders unit of the hospital for approximately 48 hours. She begins to develop tremors and hemodynamic instability. Her vital signs are as follows: temperature 100 °F, BP 140/100 mm Hg, and pulse 100 beats/min. She feels that bugs are crawling on her and that unit staff members are going to harm her. What is the possible etiology of these symptoms?

One third of bulimic patients have a history of problems with alcohol or other drugs.[54] In a survey of 364 college freshmen, 60% of women were currently on a diet with 29% using crash dieting or fasting; 20% reported use of diet pills at some time; and 13% reported present or past use of purgatives (i.e., emetics, laxatives, or diuretics). Women who were current purgative users were 4.1 times more likely to smoke cigarettes and 2.7 times more likely to use drugs as compared to nonpurgative users.[6] Chemical substance abusers experienced higher levels of anxiety and depression, but responded well to pharmacological treatment of bulimic symptoms.[55]

If A.G. had presented initially with alterations of her mental status such as hallucinations or paranoia, medical complications secondary to metabolic instability or drug intoxication would need to be considered. Due to the latency period for the onset of symptoms, the possibility that A.G. may be experiencing a drug withdrawal also needs to be considered. Further interview reveals alcohol use by A.G. consisting of 1 L/day of wine. The macrocytic anemia that was evident on initial laboratory assessment is consistent with possible alcohol use, but A.G.'s eating habits and possible vitamin deficiencies due to eating behavior alone would have been more reasonable explanations. Alcohol and drugs may be used by the bulimic patient to decrease abdominal pain, discomfort, and guilt associated with binge behavior. They also may be used as a way to self-medicate to avoid another binge or to suppress feelings during nonbingeing periods.[54] Alcohol and drug usage should always be considered during the initial evaluation of the patient and the possibility of chemical substance abuse supports the earlier recommendation for a urine drug screen as part of the work-up of a hospitalized patient (see Question 10). Clinicians should consider the possibility of a withdrawal reaction from alcohol or other chemical substances when hospitalized bulimic patients present with psychiatric symptoms. Again, medical stabilization of the patient is critical before initiation of treatment for the actual eating disorder.

Treatment

Medications

15. A.G. has been on the unit for approximately 1 week with no improvement in either her depressive symptoms or her bingeing or vomiting behavior. What medication should be prescribed?

An antidepressant medication is appropriate for A.G. because she apparently has not responded to cognitive behavioral therapy despite hospitalization and she continues to manifest concurrent symptoms of major depression. (See Drug Treatment of Bulimia Nervosa.) A.G.'s ECG is normal and the use of a tricyclic antidepressant or a selective serotonin reuptake inhibitor does not appear to be contraindicated. The efficacy of desipramine in the treatment of bulimia nervosa seems to be more clearly established than that for fluoxetine. Furthermore, the high cost of an SSRI probably would lead one to prescribe a tricyclic antidepressant for A.G. A dose of desipramine 50 mg orally at bedtime could be initiated and then increased by 50 mg at bedtime every one to two days until a target dosage of 150 to 200 mg/day is reached as long as A.G. tolerates the side effects.

Monitoring for Efficacy and Toxicity

16. What parameters should be monitored in A.G. after beginning treatment?

Desipramine (Norpramin) is a tricyclic antidepressant, a metabolite of imipramine, and a secondary amine. Secondary amine tricyclic antidepressants generally have fewer anticholinergic and cardiac side effects than tertiary amines, but these effects may still be problematic in many patients. Once desipramine is initiated in A.G., medication monitoring should focus on resolution of her target symptoms with respect to behavior and mood, and on the development of any adverse side effects. Specifically, any changes of eating behavior such as food cravings, frequency of vomiting or bingeing, and overall appetite should be noted. The symptoms classically associated with depression (e.g., disrupted amount and quality of sleep, poor concentration, lack of motivation, decreased socialization, diminished physical energy and motor activity, reduced pleasure in previously enjoyed activities, suicidal ideation) should be improved by the desipramine treatment. Certainly, the known potential adverse effects of desipramine (e.g., sedation, orthostatic hypotension, dry mouth, blurred vision, constipation) should be continually assessed.

When A.G. is discharged from the hospital she needs to be instructed to report any changes in her symptoms or discomfort with her medication to the health care team. She also should be advised to not become pregnant while taking this medication. Oral contraceptives may increase plasma antidepressant concentrations; a barrier method may be best used at this time unless A.G. discusses alternatives with her physician. An adjustment in medication dosage may be necessary if increased side effects appear or if oral contraceptives are begun.

Desipramine Serum Concentrations

17. A.G. has been on desipramine 200 mg Q HS for approximately 2 months. Her bingeing behavior has decreased by 80% during the first month of therapy. She states she has more energy and feels better than she has in the last year. Why should the serum concentration of desipramine continue to be monitored?

Generally, the serum concentrations of antidepressants are not monitored in patients who are responding well. They can be useful, however, to document the drug concentration at which the patient responds, or to evaluate the response of a patient with a history of recalcitrant symptoms, or in a patient with poor compliance. In one study of bulimic patients,[63] serum levels of desipramine adjusted to 125 to 275 µg/mL were associated with a better response. Antidepressant concentrations also may be useful to monitor patients who have compromised liver function, to guard against supratherapeutic levels in patients who overdose or otherwise experience toxicity, and to assess for adequate clearance of the drug. The desipramine serum concentration after one month of 150 mg/day of desipramine was 144 ng/mL (therapeutic range: 120 to 160 ng/mL).

Precautions

18. A.G. has completed her 30-day inpatient treatment program for an eating disorder. What precautions should be considered when prescribing desipramine for outpatient use?

When prescribing an antidepressant, several issues deserve consideration. If the patient is suicidal or has a history of impulsive actions, only one week's supply of a tricyclic antidepressant should be dispensed to reduce the risk of mortality if an overdose occurs. One gram of a tricyclic antidepressant is enough to cause death due to a cardiac arrhythmia.

A.G. and her family should be informed about potential side effects, which may affect compliance, and taught how to cope with these side effects if they become manifested. A.G. also should be instructed to notify her physician or pharmacist when side effects are intolerable to prevent noncompliance or adverse events.

Adverse Effects

19. Two months later, A.G. states that her bingeing has returned. She also describes a depressed mood with no suicidal ideation, hopelessness, helplessness, and a feeling of despair. Upon interview of A.G., it is found she is experiencing constipation and dry mouth. She has been taking 200 mg of desipramine every other night to try to decrease the side effects of the medication. She refuses to continue the medication despite a good response to desipramine. How should the treatment plan for A.G. be altered at this point in time?

A.G.'s knowledge about side effects and how to cope with side effects should be assessed. Drug interactions and possible additive anticholinergic adverse effects from other concomitant medications also should be taken into consideration. The serum concentration of desipramine should again be assessed to determine if A.G. is experiencing toxicity from the medication or from some change in the metabolic clearance of desipramine which could cause toxicity (see Chapter 76: Mood Disorders I: Major Depressive Disorders). Specifically, after assessing A.G.'s knowledge concerning potential adverse desipramine effects and the management of these effects, she may be advised to maintain fluid intake at eight to ten glasses of water per day and to increase consumption of fruits, vegetables, and other high-fiber foods in an effort to correct her constipation after consultation with her other care providers. In a patient with an eating disorder, laxatives and food can be abused and recommendations should not interfere with A.G.'s food plan that was instituted by her nutritionist or physician. Just as a health care provider would not recommend a drink to an alcoholic, diets should be adjusted with caution in patients with an eating disorder.

Alternative Drugs

20. A.G.'s serum concentration of desipramine was 80 ng/mL (range: 120–160 ng/mL). She has tried the alterations in diet recommended to relieve constipation for approximately 1 month with little success. What alternate therapy could be initiated for A.G.?

Desipramine has the least anticholinergic effects of all the tricyclic antidepressants, therefore, changing to another secondary or tertiary tricyclic antidepressant is not an option. Trazodone and bupropion have been used with some success; however, they are associated with delirium and a high incidence of seizures, respectively. An SSRI such as fluoxetine (Prozac) would be the next logical choice due to its relative lack of anticholinergic side effects and efficacy. In studies evaluating fluoxetine in the treatment of bulimia nervosa, fluoxetine dosages larger than those used for depression were necessary.[65] The initial fluoxetine dose of 20 mg once a day might need to be increased gradually over time. The desipramine should be discontinued gradually in A.G. over a two week period to prevent rebound anxiety caused by abrupt discontinuation of the antidepressant.

Fluoxetine Dosing

21. A.G. has been receiving fluoxetine 20 mg QD for 2 weeks. She states she was having some anxiety during the first week, but it improved over the second week. Her symptoms have improved, but not to the extent as they had on desipramine. She is sleeping well and eating 3 meals a day with a snack. She still has binges approximately 2 times a week, but the amount of food consumed and intensity of intake are decreased considerably. Should A.G.'s dose of fluoxetine be increased?

Several alternatives can improve A.G.'s clinical response to therapy. First, the dose of fluoxetine could be increased because she is not doing as well as she did on desipramine and higher doses of fluoxetine may be necessary for patients with bulimia. However, fluoxetine has a half-life of approximately three days and the active metabolite (norfluoxetine), a half-life of approximately 11 days. Since steady-state concentrations take four to six weeks to achieve, A.G. is probably not at a steady-state serum concentration of fluoxetine. Therefore, a better alternative would be to leave the daily fluoxetine dose at 20 mg and continue to monitor her for clinical improvement. The rationale for maintaining the fluoxetine dose the same should be discussed with the treatment team and A.G. Upon evaluation and discussion, A.G. feels relatively good about her current level of response and is willing to wait it out to see if further improvement occurs with her current dosage. She is continuing with her weekly sessions with her therapist and with her outpatient group therapy. She also attends a self-help, 12-step group two to three times per week on her own.

Prognosis

22. What factors influence the long-term outcome of patients with bulimia nervosa, and what are A.G.'s prospects for enhanced long-term clinical recovery?

Recovery from eating disorders involves treatment and a long-term commitment to the therapeutic interventions for most individuals. In one study involving bulimic patients, several factors were assessed during the follow-up period: length of history, age at onset, history of anorexia nervosa, self-esteem, neuroticism, extroversion, social adjustment, and depressive symptoms. These were assessed at the end of treatment and at 8 and 12 months after treatment. The only factor that correlated with continued recovery was a positive self-esteem. The higher the person's self-esteem, the greater the chances of a good response to treatment for patients with bulimia. This study suggests long-term therapeutic interventions which focus on improvement of self-esteem for patients with bulimia.[81] In this context, A.G. is afforded a good opportunity for long-term recovery. She already has stated her satisfaction and optimism about her current level of response and her chances for further improvement. More encouraging is her willing participation in weekly therapy, outpatient groups, and self-help 12-step programs. Such nonpharmacological interventions are better able to focus on issues of improving self-esteem beyond what may be treated by medication. In the pharmacotherapy of eating disorders, as is the case with much of psychiatry, the best prognosis for recovery may rest in using a combination of medication and some form of psychotherapy.

References

1 **Giannini A, Newman M.** Anorexia and bulimia. Am Fam Physician. 1990; 41(4):1169–176.

2 **Tolstoi L.** The role of pharmacotherapy in anorexia nervosa and bulimia. J Am Diet Assoc. 1989;89(11):1640–646.

3 **Yager J et al.** Behaviors and attitudes related to eating disorders in homosexual male college students. Am J Psychiatry. 1988;145(4):495–97.

4 **Price W.** Pharmacologic management of eating disorders. Am Fam Physician. 1988;37(5):157–62.

5 **Herzog D.** Antidepressant use in eating disorders. Psychosomatics. 1986;27 (11S):17–23.

6 **Frank R et al.** Weight loss and bulimic eating behavior: changing patterns within a population of young adult women. South Med J. 1991;84(4): 457–60.

7 **Green G et al.** Dietary intake and dieting practices of bulimic and non-bulimic female college students. J Am Diet Assoc. 1990;90(4):576–78.

8 **Palmer T.** Anorexia nervosa, bulimia nervosa: causal theories and treatment. Nurs Pract. 1990;15(4):12–21.

9 **Schwartz H.** Association of bulimia with sexual abuse. Am J Psychiatry. 1990;147(7):957.

10 **Hall RC et al.** Sexual abuse in patients with anorexia nervosa and bulimia. Psychosomatics. 1989;39:73–9.

11 **Oppenheimer R et al.** Adverse sexual experience in childhood and clinical eating disorders: a preliminary description. J Psychiatr Res. 1985;19:357–61.

12 **Hughes P et al.** The dexamethasone suppression test in bulimia before and after successful treatment with desipramine. J Clin Psychiatry. 1986;47:515–17.

13 **Schmidt U et al.** A controlled study of alexithymia in eating disorders. Compr Psychiatry. 1993;34(1):54–8.

14 **Hollander E et al.** Symptom relapse in bulimia nervosa and obsessive compulsive disorder after treatment with serotonin antagonists. J Clin Psychiatry. 1992;53(1):28.

15 **Ames-Frankel J et al.** Personality disorder diagnosis in patients with bulimia nervosa: clinical correlates and changes with treatment. J Clin Psychiatry. 1992; 53:90–6.

16 **Krahn D et al.** Stealing in eating disordered patients. J Clin Psychiatry. 1991;52:112–15.

17 **Horne R et al.** Disturbed body image in patients with eating disorders. Am J Psychiatry. 1991;148:211–15.

18 **Mortola et al.** J Clin Endocrinol Metab. 1989;68(3):1303–304.

19 **Helig M et al.** Effects of intracerebroventricular PP56, a proposed neuropeptide Y antagonist, on locomotor activity, food intake, central effects of NPY and MPY-receptor binding. Eur J Pharmacol. 1991;209:27–32.

20 **Smith G, Gibbs J.** Are gut peptides a new class of anorectic agents? Am J Nutr. 1992;55:283S–85S.

21 **Blass E et al.** Stress-reducing effects of ingesting milk, sugars, and fats: a development perspective. Ann NY Acad Sci. 1989;575:292–305.

22 **Melchoir J et al.** Negative allesthesia and decreased endogenous opiate system activity in anorexia nervosa. Pharmacol Biochem Behav. 1990;35:885–88.

23 **Fullerton D et al.** Plasma immunoreactive beta-endorphin in bulimics. Psychol Med. 1986;16:59–63.

24 **Samanin R, Garattini S.** Serotonin and the pharmacology of eating disorders. Ann N Y Acad Sci. 1989;575: 194–207.

25 **Jansen A et al.** Does bingeing restore bulimics alleged 5-HT-deficiency? Behav Res Ther. 1989;27(5):555–60.

26 **Nathan C, Rolland Y.** Pharmacological treatments that affect CNS activity: serotonin. Ann NY Acad Sci. 1987; 499:277–96.

27 **Jimerson D et al.** Serotonin in human eating disorders. Ann NY Acad Sci. 532–43.

28 **Kaye W et al.** Differences in brain serotonergic metabolism between nonbulimic and bulimic patients with anorexia nervosa. Am J Psychiatry. 1984; 141:1598–601.

29 **Lask B et al.** Zinc deficiency and childhood-onset anorexia nervosa. J Clin Psychiatry. 1993;54:63–6.

30 **Pirke K et al.** Noradrenaline, triiodothyronine, growth hormone and prolactin during weight gain in anorexia nervosa. Int J Eat Disord. 1985;4:449–509.

31 **Lesem M et al.** State-related changes in norepinephrine regulation in anorexia nervosa. Biol Psychiatry. 1989; 25:509–12.

32 **American Psychiatric Association.** Diagnostic and Statistical Manual of Mental Disorders. 4th ed. Washington, DC: American Psychiatric Association, 1994.

33 **Beumont P, Large M.** Hypophosphataemia, delirium and cardiac arrhythmia in anorexia nervosa. Med J Aust. 1991;155:519–22.

34 **Casper R.** The pathophysiology of anorexia nervosa and bulimia nervosa. Ann Rev Nutr. 1986;6:299–316.

35 **Flood M.** Addictive eating disorders. Nurs Clin North Am. 1989;24(1):45–53.

36 **Yeary J.** The use of overeaters anonymous in the treatment of eating disorders. J Psychoactive Drugs. 1987; 19(3):303–9.

37 **Chudley P.** An unhealthy obsession. Nurs Times. 1986;26:50–52.

38 **Biederman J et al.** Amitriptyline in the treatment of anorexia nervosa: a double-blind, placebo-controlled study. J Clin Psychopharmacol. 1985;5(1):10–16.

39 **Halmi K et al.** Anorexia nervosa: treatment efficacy of cyproheptadine and amitriptyline. Arch Gen Psychiatry. 1986;43:177–81.

40 **Vigersky RA, Loriaux DL.** The effect of cyproheptadine in anorexia nervosa: a double-blind trial. In: Vigersky RA, ed. Anorexia Nervosa. New York: Raven Press; 1977:349–56.

41 **Goldberg SG et al.** Cyproheptadine in anorexia nervosa. Br J Psychiatry. 1979;134:67–70.

42 **Gross HA et al.** A double-blind controlled trial of lithium carbonate in primary anorexia nervosa. J Clin Psychopharmacol. 1981;1:376–81.

43 **Lacey JH, Crisp AH.** Hunger, food intake and weight: the impact of clomipramine on a refeeding anorexia nervosa population. Postgrad Med J. 1980; 56:79–85.

44 **Casper R et al.** A placebo-controlled crossover study of oral clonidine in acute anorexia nervosa. Psychiatry Res. 1986;20:249–60.

45 **Gwirtsman HE et al.** Fluoxetine treatment of anorexia nervosa: an open clinical trial. J Clin Psychiatry. 1990;51: 378–82.

46 **Kaye W et al.** An open trial of fluoxetine in patients with anorexia nervosa. J Clin Psychiatry. 1991;52:464.

47 **Rosenvinge J, Mouland S.** Outcome and prognosis of anorexia nervosa: a retrospective study of 41 subjects. Br J Psychiatry. 1990;156:92–7.

48 **Camp G.** Recognize the bulimic (what educators need to know about the binge-purge syndrome). Nurs Success Today. 1986;3(9):18–22.

49 **Mitchell J et al.** Medical complications and medical management of bulimia. Ann Intern Med. 1987;107:71–7.

50 **Pomeroy C et al.** Prescription diuretic abuse in patients with bulimia nervosa. J Fam Pract. 1988;27(5):493–96.

51 **Pope H et al.** Antidepressant treatment of bulimia: preliminary experience and practical recommendations. J Clin Psychopharmacol. 1983;3(5):274–81.

52 **Van Binsbergen C et al.** Food preferences and aversions and dietary pattern in anorexia nervosa patients. Eur J Clin Nutr. 1988;42:671–78.

53 **Drewnowski A et al.** Taste and bulimia. Physiol Behav. 1987;41:621–26.

54 **Hoebel B et al.** Microdialysis studies in brain norepinephrine, serotonin, and dopamine release during ingestive behavior: theoretical and clinical implications. Ann N Y Acad Sci. 1989;575:171–93.

55 **Strasser T et al.** The impact of prior substance abuse on treatment outcome for bulimia nervosa. Addict Behav. 1992;17:387–95.

56 **Yates A.** Current perspectives on the eating disorders: treatment, outcome, and research directions. J Am Acad Child Adolesc Psychiatry. 1990;29(1):1–9.

57 **Kennedy S, Goldbloom D.** Current perspective on drug therapy for anorexia nervosa and bulimia nervosa. Drugs. 1991;41(3):367–77.

58 **Walsh T, Devlin M.** The pharmacologic treatment of eating disorders. Pediatr Psychopharmacol (New York). 1992;15(1):149–61.

59 **Walsh T.** Psychopharmacologic treatment of bulimia nervosa. J Clin Psychiatry. 1991;52(10S):34–8.

60 **Johnson C et al.** Psychopharmacological treatment of anorexia nervosa and bulimia: review and synthesis. J Nerv Ment Dis. 1983;171:524–34.

61 **Beumont P et al.** Treatment of anorexia nervosa. Lancet. 1993;341:1635–640.

62 **Herzog D et al.** The course and outcome of bulimia nervosa. J Clin Psychiatry. 1991;52(10S):4–8.

63 **Hughes P et al.** Treating bulimia with desipramine: a double-blind, placebo-controlled study. Arch Gen Psychiatry. 1986;43:182–86.

64 **Barlow J et al.** Treatment of bulimia with desipramine: a double-blind crossover study. Can J Psychiatry. 1988;33:129–33.

65 **McCann U, Agras S.** Successful treatment of nonpurging bulimia nervosa with desipramine: a double-blind, placebo-controlled study. Am J Psychiatry. 1990;147:1509–513.

66 **Walsh T et al.** Increased pulse and blood pressure associated with desipramine treatment of bulimia nervosa. J Clin Psychopharmacol. 1992;12:163–68.

67 **Blouin A et al.** Treatment of bulimia with fenfluramine and desipramine. J Clin Psychopharmacol. 1988;8(4):261–69.

68 **Jonas J, Gold M.** Treatment of antidepressant-resistant bulimia with naltrexone. Int J Psychiatry Med. 1987;26(4):305–8.

69 **Solyom L et al.** Trazodone treatment of bulimia nervosa. J Clin Psychopharmacol. 1989;9:287–90.

70 **Damlouji N, Ferguson J.** Trazodone-induced delirium in bulimic patients. Am J Psychiatry. 1984;141:434–35.

71 **Horne R et al.** Treatment of bulimia with bupropion: a multicenter controlled trial. J Clin Psychiatry. 1988;49(7):262–66.

72 **Walsh T et al.** Phenelzine vs placebo in 50 patients with bulimia. Arch Gen Psychiatry. 1988;45:471–75.

73 **Sabine E et al.** Bulimia nervosa: a placebo controlled, double-blind therapeutic trial of mianserin. Br J Clin Pharmacol. 1983;15:195S–202S.

74 **Michell J, Groat R.** A placebo-controlled, double-blind trial of amitriptyline in bulimia. 1984;4(4):186–93.

75 **Pope H et al.** Bulimia treated with imipramine: a placebo-controlled, double-blind study. Am J Psychiatry. 1983;140:554–58.

76 **Mitchell J et al.** A comparison study of antidepressants and structured intensive group psychotherapy in the treatment of bulimia nervosa. Arch Gen Psychiatry. 1990;47:149–57.

77 **Fluoxetine Bulimia Nervosa Collaborative Study Group.** Fluoxetine in the treatment of bulimia nervosa. Arch Gen Psychiatry. 1992;49:139–47.

78 **Tamai H et al.** The clinical efficacy of a 5-HT 1a agonist, SM-3997, in the treatment of bulimia. Int J Obes. 1990;14:289–92.

79 **Mitchell J et al.** Naloxone but not CCK-8 may attenuate binge-eating behavior in patients with the bulimia syndrome. Biol Psychiatry. 1986;21:1399–406.

80 **De Zwaan M, Mitchell J.** Opiate antagonists and eating behavior in humans: a review. J Clin Pharmacol. 1992;32:1060–72.

81 **Hsu L et al.** Treatment of bulimia nervosa with lithium carbonate: a controlled study. J Nerv Ment Dis. 1991;179:351–55.

82 **Marcus R, Katz J.** Inpatient care of substance abusing patient with a concomitant eating disorder. Hosp Community Psychiatry. 1990;41:59.

83 **Fairburn C et al.** Prognostic factors in bulimia nervosa. Br J Clin Psychol. 1987;26(3):223–24.

84 **Hudson J et al.** Treatment of bulimia nervosa with trazodone: short-term response and long-term follow-up. Clin Neuropharmacol. 1989;12:S38–S46.

Issues: Psychoactive Substance Use Disorders

Jeffrey N Baldwin

Marcus D Cook

Etiology 81-1	Fetuses and Neonates 81-8
Definitions 81-1	Adolescents 81-10
Diagnostic Classification 81-2	Women 81-10
Estimating Drug Abuse 81-2	The Elderly 81-10
Societal Impact 81-3	Ethnic and Cultural 81-11
Getting Help 81-4	Healthcare Professionals 81-11
Identification/Assessment 81-4	Dual Diagnosis 81-12
Treatment 81-5	**Societal Issues** 81-12
Recovery Support 81-6	Drugs in the Work Place 81-12
Populations at Risk 81-8	Drug Testing 81-13
	Confidentiality 81-14

Etiology

Although debate is ongoing, psychoactive substance use disorders are considered diseases both medically and legally. In 1785, Benjamin Rush suggested that drunkenness "... resembles certain hereditary, family and contagious diseases."[1] During the 1930s, physical differences were noted in alcoholics in addition to the previously identified psychological characteristics.[2] Alcoholism was defined as a disease by the American Medical Association in 1956. In 1990 alcoholism and other chemical dependencies were described by the American Society of Addiction Medicine (ASAM) as primary, chronic, relapsing diseases with genetic, psychosocial, and environmental factors influencing their development and manifestations.[3] A majority of treatment centers have adopted a "bio-psychosocial disease" model for alcoholism and other drug dependencies and use a multimodal approach to treatment. The reader might consider these diseases to be similar to diabetes mellitus or heart disease (i.e., chronic, progressive diseases which often can be managed through lifestyle changes and appropriate medical management).[4] Despite acceptance of alcoholism as an illness by 76%, and as treatable by 97% of respondents in a public survey, 47% of the participants considered alcoholics "morally weak."[5]

Definitions

Nomenclature related to psychoactive substance use has been confusing. The field of addiction treatment is relatively new. In 1952 the World Health Organization (WHO) addressed the problem of standardization of terminology as it tried to develop an international consensus on a definition of addiction. In 1957 WHO differentiated between the terms "addiction" and "habituation." However, these definitions resulted in confusion. In 1964 the WHO Expert Committee recommended substituting the term "drug dependence" for both "addiction" and "habituation." The following list of terms represents the current recommendations of the American Society of Addiction Medicine.[3]

Abstinence. Nonuse of a specific substance. In recovery, nonuse of any addictive psychoactive substance. May also denote cessation of addictive behavior (e.g., gambling, overeating).

Abuse. Harmful use of a specific psychoactive substance. The term also applies to one category of psychoactive substance use disorder (see DSM-IV criteria below). (ASAM recommends this term not be used because of its pejorative connotations.)

Addiction. A disease process characterized by the continued use of a specific psychoactive substance despite physical, psychological, or social harm.

Addictionist. A physician who specializes in addiction medicine.

Blackout. Acute antegrade amnesia with no formation of long-term memory, resulting from the ingestion of alcohol or other drugs (i.e., a period of memory loss for which there is no recall of activities).

Dependence. Used in three different ways:

- Physical dependence: a physiological state of adaptation to a specific psychoactive substance, characterized by the emergence of a withdrawal syndrome during abstinence, which may be relieved in total or in part by readministration of the substance.

- Psychological dependence: a subjective sense of need for a specific psychoactive substance, either for its positive effects or to avoid negative effects associated with its absence.

- One category of psychoactive substance use disorder.

Detoxification. A process of withdrawing a person from a specific psychoactive substance in a safe and effective manner.

Enabling. Any action by another person or an institution that intentionally or unintentionally has the effect of facilitating the continuation of an individual's addictive process.

Impairment. A dysfunctional state resulting from use of psychoactive substances.

Intervention. A planned intervention with an individual who may be dependent on one or more psychoactive substances, with the aim of making a full assessment, overcoming denial, interrupting drug-taking behavior, or inducing the individual to initiate treatment. The preferred technique is to present facts regarding psychoactive substance use in a caring, believable, and understandable manner.

Loss of Control. The inability to consistently limit the self-administration of psychoactive substances.

Misuse. Any use of a prescription drug that varies from accepted medical practice.

Problem Drinking. An informal term describing a pattern of drinking associated with life problems before establishing a definitive diagnosis of alcoholism. Also, an umbrella term for any harmful use of alcohol, including alcoholism. (ASAM recommends that the term not be used in this sense.)

Recovery. A process of overcoming both physical and psychological dependence on a psychoactive substance, with a commitment to sobriety.

Tolerance. State in which an increased dosage of a psychoactive substance is needed to produce a desired effect.

Withdrawal Syndrome. The onset of a predictable constellation of signs and symptoms following the abrupt discontinuation of, or rapid decrease in dosage of, a psychoactive substance.

Diagnostic Classification

The Diagnostic and Statistical Manual of Mental Disorders (DSM), published by the American Psychiatric Association (APA), lists the specific criteria for differentiating psychoactive use disorders. The fourth edition (DSM-IV) published in 1994 is currently used.[6] The DSM-IV divides substance related disorders into two large groups. These are the psychoactive *substance-induced disorders* and the *substance use disorders*.

The psychoactive substance use disorders define the specific patterns of behavior related to drug use. These are divided into psychoactive substance *abuse* (see Table 81.1) and psychoactive substance *dependence* (see Table 81.2). The diagnostic criteria for psychoactive substance abuse is more likely to be applicable to people who only recently have started taking psychoactive substances and is more likely to involve substances, such as cannabis, cocaine, and hallucinogens, that are less likely to be associated with marked physiologic signs of withdrawal and the need to take the substance to relieve or avoid withdrawal symptoms. The diagnostic criteria for psychoactive substance dependence are the same for each of the individual psychoactive drugs or drug classes. The diagnostic criteria for specifiers of psychoactive substance dependence are listed in Table 81.3.

Although many individuals affected by psychoactive substance dependence may have a "drug of choice" or a "drug of first choice," some do not. Factual drug histories may be very difficult to obtain where polysubstance dependence exists. For these individuals, the diagnosis of "polysubstance dependence" is based upon the following DSM-IV criteria: "This diagnosis is reserved for behavior during the same 12 month period in which the person has repeatedly used at least three categories of substances (not including nicotine and caffeine), but no single psychoactive sub-

Table 81.1	Diagnostic Criteria for Psychoactive Substance Abuse[a]

A) A maladaptive pattern of psychoactive substance use leading to clinically significant impairment or distress, as manifested by one or more of the following, occurring within a 12-month period

1) Recurrent substance use resulting in a failure to fulfill major role obligations at work, school, or home (e.g., repeated absences or poor work performance related to substance used; substance-related absences, suspensions, or expulsions from school; neglect of children or household)

2) Recurrent substance use in situations in which it is physically hazardous (e.g., driving an automobile or operating a machine when impaired by substance use)

3) Recurrent substance-related legal problems (e.g., arrests for substance-related disorderly conduct)

4) Continued substance use despite having persistent or recurrent social or interpersonal problems caused by or exacerbated by the effects of the substance (e.g., arguments with spouse about consequences of intoxication, physical fights)

B) The symptoms have never met the criteria for psychoactive Substance Dependence for this class of substance

[a] Reprinted with permission from reference 6.

Table 81.2	Diagnostic Criteria for Psychoactive Substance Dependence[a]

A maladaptive pattern of substance use, leading to clinically significant impairment or distress, as manifested by three (or more) of the following, occurring at any time in the same 12-month period:

1) Tolerance, as defined by either of the following:

   a) A need for markedly increased amounts of the substance to achieve intoxication or desired effect

   b) Markedly diminished effect with continued use of the same amount of the substance

2) Withdrawal, as manifested by either of the following:

   a) The characteristic withdrawal syndrome for the substance

   b) The same (or closely related) substance is taken to relieve or avoid withdrawal symptoms

3) The substance is often taken in larger amounts or over a longer period than was intended

4) There is persistent desire or unsuccessful efforts to cut down or control substance use

5) A great deal of time is spent in activities to obtain the substance (e.g., visiting multiple doctors or driving long distances), use the substance (e.g., chain smoking), or recover from its effects

6) Important social, occupational, or recreational activities are given up or reduced because of substance use

7) The substance use is continued despite knowledge of having a persistent or recurrent physical or psychological problem that is likely to have been caused or exacerbated by the substance (e.g., current cocaine use despite recognition of cocaine-induced depression, or continued drinking despite recognition that an ulcer was made worse by alcohol consumption)

[a] Reprinted with permission from reference 6.

stance predominated. Further, during this period, the dependence criteria were met for substances as a group, but not for any specific substance."[6]

For those disorders which cannot be classified according to any of the previous categories, or for use as an initial diagnosis in cases in which the specific substance is not yet known, "other (or unknown) substance dependence" and "other (or unknown) substance abuse" are residual DSM-IV categories which may be used.

Other (or Unknown) Substance-Related Disorders: "The other (or unknown) substance-related disorders category is for classifying substance-related disorders associated with substances not listed with their own category elsewhere in the DSM-IV. Examples of these substances, include anabolic steroids, nitrate inhalants ("poppers"), nitrous oxide, over the counter medications, and antihistamines. In addition, this category may be used when the specific substance is unknown (e.g., an intoxication after taking a bottle of pills)."[6]

Estimating Drug Abuse

Drugs of abuse tend to increase and decrease in popularity over time as each generation learns the adverse consequences of particular drugs or as new forms of drugs become available. The use of cocaine, which increased during the 1970s and accelerated further during the 1980s with the availability of "crack," has been decreasing. Increases in LSD usage are now being reported.

Reports of the number of alcoholics and other drug addicts are, at best, estimates. There is no clear definable point separating nonalcoholics from alcoholics. Abuse and addiction are similarly difficult to differentiate. A national household survey of drug abuse periodically is conducted and reported by the National Institute of Drug Abuse (NIDA) using personal interviews. The University of

Michigan Institute for Social Research conducts national surveys which track high school seniors throughout college and young adulthood. These surveys also are reported through NIDA. Although the validity and reliability of responses in surveys has been questioned, survey results have generally been shown to be truthful.[7,8]

Indirect methods may be used to estimate the total number of alcoholics or other drug addicts. Such methods may use death rates from cirrhosis of the liver or the incidence of hepatitis to predict total numbers of alcoholics or intravenous drug abusers. However, the death rates from alcoholism, typically reported at about 3% of deaths, are probably substantially underreported.[9] Seizures of drugs by enforcement agencies may reflect drug preferences, purity, and prices but do not accurately estimate the number of users. The Drug Abuse Warning Network (DAWN) publishes data semi-annually derived from hospital emergency rooms and other acute

Table 81.3	Specifiers[a]
Specify If	
With Physiologic Dependence	Evidence of tolerance or withdrawal
Without Physiologic Dependence	No evidence of tolerance of withdrawal
Course Specifiers	
Early Full Remission	This specifier is used if, for at least a month, but for less than 12 months, no criteria for Dependence or Abuse are met
Early Partial Remission	This specifier is used if, for at least a month, but less than 12 months, one or more criteria for Dependence or Abuse have been met (but the full criteria for Dependence have not been met)
Sustained Full Remission	This specifier is used if none of the criteria for Dependence or Abuse have been met at any time during a period of 12 months or longer
Sustained Partial Remission	This specifier is used if full criteria for Dependence have not been met for a period of 12 months or longer; however, one or more criteria for Dependence or Abuse have been met
On Agonist Therapy	This specifier is used if the individual is on prescribed agonist medication, and no criteria for Dependence or Abuse have been met for that class of medication for at least the past month (except tolerance to, or withdrawal from, the agonist). This category also applies to those being treated for Dependence using a partial agonist or an agonist/antagonist
In a Controlled Environment	This specifier is used if the individual is in an environment where access to alcohol or controlled substances is restricted, and no criteria for Dependence or Abuse have been met for at least the past month. Examples of these environments are closely supervised and substance-free jails, therapeutic communities, or locked hospital units

[a] Reprinted with permission from reference 6.

drug treatment facilities, crisis centers, medical examiners, and coroners. DAWN reports provide relatively current information on patterns of, and reasons for, drug use on a city-by-city basis. Ongoing prescription audits of physicians and pharmacies establish prescription patterns and trends and allow determination of the extent of illegal diversion of psychoactive prescription drugs.

Lifetime prevalences of tobacco, alcohol, marijuana, and cocaine use are all higher in men than women. Men more often obtain drugs through illicit sources; women are more likely to abuse prescription drugs obtained through medical sources. An incidence of alcoholism as high as 20% to 30% among the elderly may be hidden by other medical problems.[10] Heroin use among blacks declined during the 1970s, but was replaced by cocaine and, later, crack. Crack use peaked in about 1988. While black teenagers have lower rates of alcohol abuse than whites, heavy drinking increases beyond 20 years of age for blacks while tending to level off among whites. Blacks have a significantly higher cirrhosis mortality rate than whites.[11] A 1980 study found a lifetime prevalence rate for alcoholism of 19% for nonwhites and 5% for whites.[12] Mexican-Americans are less likely than blacks or whites to use stimulants or psychedelics, but more often have long histories of abuse, arrests, and incarceration and are later getting into treatment.[13] Native Americans have approximately the same proportion of alcohol users as the general population; however, a higher proportion are younger drinkers, and alcohol-related arrests and mortality are high.[14] Native American youth appear to use more inhalants and marijuana than do other young people. Acculturation stress and low social structure may contribute to higher rates of usage among some tribes. Low rates of alcohol problems among Jews may reflect intolerance of excessive drinking and moderate drinking norms.[15] As many as 30% of homeless people have alcohol problems, while up to 40% may have other drug problems. Since about two million Americans experience homelessness each year, this represents a significant societal problem.[16] About half of arrestees in 22 urban areas urine tested positive for at least one drug, with cocaine being most prevalent.[17] The more than doubling of the U.S. prison population since 1970 largely reflects drug-related convictions. About one-third of criminals were under the influence of a drug when committing their crimes. About two-thirds of patients treated for alcohol or other drug problems had other current psychiatric problems according to one report.[18]

Societal Impact

Alcohol is involved in 40% of all reported assaults and one-third of all forcible rape and child molestation cases.[19] Almost 50% of inmates reported being under the influence of alcohol, with or without other drugs, when committing their offense; fewer than 10% report being under the influence of other drugs alone.[20] When drug prices increase, property-related crimes increase. "When addicts were not dependent on heroin, their crime rate was 84% lower than when they were regularly using the drug."[21]

Trauma is the most common cause of death in young people, exceeding cancer and heart disease combined in potential years lost.[22] Drug use other than alcohol may occur in up to 40% of hospitalized trauma victims.[23] Alcohol is involved in more than half of all U.S. traffic fatalities and almost 80% of fatalities from crashes occurring between 8:00 p.m. and 4:00 a.m.[24] Alcohol was reportedly present in 63% of homicide victims, 49% of unintentional injury fatalities, 35% of suicide victims, and 14% of persons who died of natural causes in one rural state.[25] Chronic, but not acute, alcohol abuse increases the risk of complications following trauma.[26] Trauma patients should be screened routinely for alcohol and other drug abuse, and trauma centers should have chemical dependency intervention services available.[27,28]

Drunk drivers who are injured in motor vehicle crashes are less likely than drunk drivers without crash-related injuries to avoid prosecution, often because of failure to obtain a legal blood specimen or lack of legal follow-up.[29] Server liability laws have changed serving practices in a number of states, reducing the risk of drunk drivers.[30] Drunk driving is less likely in those who are aware of the consequences of being arrested for drunk driving (e.g., fines, incarceration, publication of names, criminal record) and those who feel that taking a taxi or calling a friend are reasonable alternatives to driving when intoxicated. Multimedia prevention messages addressing such topics should be undertaken.[31]

Increasing the legal drinking age to 21 years in the U.S. has resulted in lower usage of alcohol in high school seniors and young adults and has resulted in lowered involvement in alcohol-related fatalities in traffic crashes in those under 21.[32] Increased taxes on distilled spirits usually decrease sales and reduce traffic fatalities. Young drinkers, especially those who drink more than one drink per week, were less likely to consume beer when prices were raised. Increasing taxes on alcoholic beverages to help fund health insurance shifts some of the societal health-care burden of alcohol abuse to the user while reducing societal risk from the abuser.[33,34]

Health insurance coverage for chemical dependency generally has more limitations than for other illnesses. Total health care costs for treated alcoholics are significantly lower than for untreated alcoholics. The type and setting for treatment or individual patients should be matched to specific addictions.[35] Treatment is readily available to those who can afford it but often cannot be provided for those who cannot. Additional treatment facilities, especially for the indigent, are needed.

While drug abuse prevention efforts often are singularly unsuccessful, messages which are repeated through multiple media and demonstrate peer and social acceptance (e.g., athletes providing messages concerning drug abuse) appear to reduce use. Interruption of illegal drug movement will do little to reduce the societal burden of addiction as long as there exists a demand for the drug. Prevention of initiation of drug use and assistance for those who are addicted are more likely to be effective in reducing abuse of alcohol and other drugs.[36-39]

Getting Help
Identification/Assessment

1. K.M., a 68-year-old veteran, is admitted to the medical ward for complaints of severe gastrointestinal (GI) upset. He is a retired accountant who has been seen with increasing frequency for various GI complaints and minor trauma. During an interview, you smell alcohol on K.M.'s breath. His wife reports that K.M. "drinks a lot," has been increasingly hostile, and has withdrawn from many social activities. How probable is it that K.M. is alcoholic?

Primary care physicians fail to recognize about 50% to 90% of their ambulatory patients who are using alcohol or other drugs.[40-42] It is estimated that only 10% of patients are referred for treatment.[43] Specific patterns of behavior will be discussed in subsequent chapters. However, general patterns of behavior which are commonly observed across addictions include mood swings; changes in social behaviors and contacts, often with increasing isolation; family and financial problems; dishonesty; neglect of physical appearance and diet; uncharacteristic deterioration in health; traumatic injuries; and memory lapses. Some alcoholics and other addicts reach evaluation because of arrests or physical illness. Others are referred either because their families reach their limits of tolerating the addict's behavior or an employer becomes concerned about job performance or behavior. Initial contact outside of the institutional setting primarily occurs through referral to private counselors, employee assistance programs (EAPs), or addic-

tion treatment centers. Where necessary, these resources can assist the family, employer, or other concerned individuals to arrange a formal intervention to confront the suspected alcoholic or other drug addict with his behavior and demand that he seek an evaluation, and, if indicated, treatment.

K.M.'s history of gastrointestinal complaints, trauma, irritability, and social isolation and the presence of alcohol on the breath may all be suggestive of an alcohol problem, but are not diagnostic. Screening for alcohol and other psychoactive substance use disorders should be included routinely in patient evaluations.

2. When confronted with his wife's observations, K.M. denies having an alcohol problem, stating, "I'm no skid row bum, and besides, I don't drink as much as she does. She's the one with the problem. I can quit any time I want to; I just don't want to." Why is K.M. so judgmental about alcoholics? Is he really unaware that he may have a problem with alcohol?

There are many misconceptions about alcoholism and substance use dependence or addiction. Many people still think of alcoholism and addiction as moral weaknesses instead of disease processes.[5] Also, societal stereotyping of the alcoholic or addict as a "skid row bum," which is true in less than 10% of cases, frequently delays the identification of the alcoholic or addict in the rest of the population.[44] The most typical reaction of health profession students who attend an Alcoholics Anonymous (AA) meeting as a component of a course is, "There were all ages, even teenagers, and they were just like you and me."

Denial is a major impediment in diagnosing psychoactive substance use disorders. Alcoholics or other drug addicts usually have a delusional set of beliefs which protects them from reality. They often truly believe that they do not have a problem.

K.M.'s stereotypic identification of alcoholics as "bums" and failure to recognize problematic behaviors related to alcohol use characterize K.M.'s denial system. Until he is confronted with objective observations of specific alcohol-related behaviors or suffers major consequences of these behaviors, he will continue to truly believe that he does not have a problem.

3. What is a quick screening questionnaire which the clinician could use in assessing the probability that K.M. has alcoholism?

One of the most popular screening questionnaires for alcoholism is the "CAGE" questionnaire. This is a self-report questionnaire consisting of only four items which comprise the acronym, "CAGE" (see Table 81.4). These questions focus on the adverse consequences of the patient's alcohol use instead of the quantity or frequency of use. The CAGE questionnaire can be administered in less than one minute and has an 80% sensitivity and 85% specificity.[45-47]

In response to the "CAGE" questionnaire, K.M. admits that he has tried unsuccessfully to cut down his drinking on several occasions and he has an occasional "eye-opener" to take the edge off a hangover. According to Table 81.4, this suggests alcoholism. A positive screening test alone does not determine a psychoactive substance use disorder.

Table 81.4	CAGE Screening Questionnaire for Alcoholism[a]

C Have you ever felt the need to **C**ut down on your drinking?

A Have people ever **A**nnoyed you by criticism of your drinking?

G Have you ever felt **G**uilty about your drinking?

E Have you ever taken a morning **E**ye-opener to steady your nerves or get rid of a hangover?

A positive response to two questions suggests alcoholism. The likelihood of alcoholism increases with additional affirmative responses.

[a] Reprinted with permission from reference 45.

4. What additional testing is recommended before making a diagnosis of alcoholism for K.M.?

The Michigan Alcoholism Screening Test (MAST), consisting of 24 questions, is one of the oldest self-report measures of alcoholism.[48] This questionnaire demonstrates 90% sensitivity and 80% specificity.[49] A shorter version of the MAST, the Short Michigan Alcoholism Screening Test (SMAST) (see Table 81.5) demonstrates 70% sensitivity and 80% specificity.[50,51]

The Veterans Alcoholism Screening Test (VAST) utilizes the same 24 MAST questions but follows each original question with three additional questions to identify the specific time period to which an answer refers. Thus, the VAST distinguishes past alcohol use from current use.[52,53]

The Drug Abuse Screening Test (DAST) consists of 28 questions and takes about five minutes to administer. It is able to distinguish those patients with primarily drug-related problems from those with primarily alcohol or mixed alcohol and drug problems. The DAST has a sensitivity of 96% and specificity of 80%.[54–56]

Once he is medically stable, K.M. completes a SMAST. Four of his responses are indicative of alcoholism. Based upon these results and his medical history, K.M. is told that he has alcoholism.

5. K.M. continues to deny that he has alcoholism and insists on a second opinion. He is referred to an independent evaluator who reaches the same conclusion. Again, K.M. rejects the diagnosis. What other interventions might be attempted to break through K.M.'s denial?

A formal confrontation by family and friends, organized by a substance abuse counselor, sometimes is helpful in breaking through denial. In this particular case, K.M.'s wife, son, brother, and best friend all documented specific, problematic alcohol-related behaviors. They then presented this objective evidence to

Table 81.5	Short Michigan Alcoholism Screening Test (SMAST)[a]

1) Do you feel you are a normal drinker? (No)

2) Does your spouse, a parent, or other close relative ever worry or complain about your drinking? (Yes)

3) Do you ever feel guilty about your drinking? (Yes)

4) Do friends or relatives think you are a normal drinker? (No)

5) Are you able to stop drinking when you want to? (No)

6) Have you ever attended a meeting of Alcoholics Anonymous? (Yes)

7) Has drinking ever created problems between you and your spouse, a parent, or other close relative? (Yes)

8) Have you ever gotten into trouble at work because of your drinking? (Yes)

9) Have you ever neglected your obligations, your family, or your work for two or more days in a row because you were drinking? (Yes)

10) Have you ever gone to anyone for help about your drinking? (Yes)

11) Have you ever been in a hospital because of drinking? (Yes)

12) Have you ever been arrested for drunken driving, driving while intoxicated, or driving under the influence of alcoholic beverages? (Yes)

13) Have you ever been arrested, even for a few hours, because of other drunken behavior? (Yes)

Answers suggestive of alcoholism are shown in parentheses after each question. Three or more of these responses indicate a diagnosis of alcoholism; two indicate the possibility of alcoholism, one or less indicates that alcoholism is unlikely.

[a] Reprinted with permission from reference 51.

K.M. with the counselor present in a manner which expressed caring concern for K.M. Those participating in the intervention indicated that they wanted K.M. to enter treatment for alcoholism; if he refused, they stated that they would sever their contacts with him. Presented with so much evidence of the harm that alcohol was causing to himself and others, K.M. agreed to enter treatment. Because suicide risk is high following an intervention, he was not left alone and entered treatment that day.

Treatment

6. J.M., a 35-year-old male, has been receiving care from you for over 15 years. Over the past three years, he has been receiving lorazepam (Ativan) 2 mg tablets. He has gradually increased his usage from 60 to 240 tablets per month. He tells you that he is now taking his 8 lorazepam tablets per day and drinking more than 10 beers per day. He states, "I am tired of feeling this way. This has gotten out of hand. My life is out of control. I was pulled over by the police last night, but luckily they didn't give me a ticket. Boy, was I wasted! My wife is tired of this too. My children are scared of me. I don't know what to do." J.M.'s SMAST has nine responses indicative of alcoholism. J.M. agrees to enter treatment. What are the basic procedures and goals for treatment?

Alcoholic and drug-dependent patients have been hospitalized for their disease since the beginning of the 19th century. Treatment that focuses only on the symptoms of addictive disease, however, has little or no impact on the progression of the disease. With the formation of Alcoholics Anonymous (AA), a new approach to the disease of alcoholism revolutionized the way society and health care addressed this malady; consequently, successful treatments have been developed for the primary disease of alcoholism. There has been an evolution from treatment that withdrew the patient from alcohol and treated only continuing symptoms, to treatment that safely withdraws the patient, treats continuing symptoms, and provides continual recovery through education into the disease process and involvement with long-term self-help groups.[57]

Abstinence is the initial and primary goal of treatment. The remaining goals of recovery, in approximate sequence of consideration during treatment, are detoxification, medical evaluation, stabilization of life-threatening emotional issues, education, identification of barriers to recovery, readjustment of behavior toward recovery, and orientation and membership in a self-help or mutual-help 12-step program. Successful family contributions can make the difference between success or failure of treatment goals. Family members also may need to be treated; the physical, emotional, and spiritual effects of the addiction on family members can be more severe than on the chemically dependent person. The continuing care component of treatment maintains the link between the patient and the professional recovery community after discharge. Extended care allows for structured support of sobriety and often further progress through management of psychosocial issues identified during the initial treatment phase. A large variety of treatment options are available once the decision has been made to hospitalize the patient.[57]

The practitioner should identify inpatient and outpatient treatment programs (e.g., available in the Yellow Pages under "Alcoholism Information and Treatment" and "Drug Abuse Information and Treatment"). In this particular setting, J.M. selected a treatment program which was close to his home and which offered the recommended treatment services. The practitioner called the chosen treatment center to arrange an evaluation and possible admission. Transportation also was arranged since J.M. was very agitated. J.M.'s treatment started with a process that helped him to return to physical health via a detoxification regimen. The period of detoxification may last from hours to weeks depending upon the severity of drug usage. J.M.'s withdrawal resulted in minor agitation and some insomnia which lasted for several days. Inpatient detoxification programs may last from one to seven days. Once he was adequately withdrawn from medications and medically stable, J.M. progressed to a phase of mental rehabilitation, aimed at strengthening motivation for abstinence through continued participation in AA. A multidisciplinary treatment approach that incorporates a broad range of goals and methodologies often is used because of the complex problems of the alcoholic/addict.[58]

In this phase of treatment, J.M. learned about the disease process and the accompanying characteristics of denial, minimization, rationalization, and entitlement. Psychological testing for brain damage indicated depression, but no major cognitive deficits. J.M. participated in AA and Narcotics Anonymous meetings during treatment; attendance of at least three meetings per week and one counseling session was recommended as a component of his after-care plan. Patients who establish a strong support system before leaving treatment benefit greatly.

7. J.M.'s health insurance does not cover inpatient treatment beyond the 14 days. Is outpatient treatment appropriate for J.M.?

As with many other medical illnesses, the indications for inpatient or outpatient treatment are based upon the condition of the patient. Comparative effectiveness continues to be debated, but is difficult to quantify because of greater acuity of care needed for those who meet criteria for inpatient admission. Depending upon assessment of patient needs, some patients will need both inpatient and outpatient treatment, and others will need only one or the other.[59] Individualized treatment goals, continuity of care, and coordination of work and family involvement are now important determinants of the success of inpatient treatment.[57]

ASAM has published criteria for adults and adolescents[59] to facilitate assignment to one of the following four levels of care:

Level I	Outpatient treatment
Level II	Intensive outpatient treatment
Level III	Medically monitored intensive inpatient treatment
Level IV	Medically managed intensive inpatient treatment

Six dimensions are assessed to determine which level of care would be best for a patient such as J.M.

- Acute intoxication or withdrawal.
- Biomedical conditions and complications.
- Emotional and behavioral conditions and complications.
- Treatment acceptance and resistance.
- Relapse potential.
- Recovery environment.

Although the condition of the patient should be the major determinant for the decision of outpatient or inpatient treatment, the medical insurance coverage also is another variable to be considered. Insurance coverage for inpatient treatment has been progressively reduced; many insurers will provide only up to 14 days of inpatient care, where 30 to 40 day treatments were covered a decade ago. Cost containment, provider abuse of insurance coverage through inappropriately long stays, and improved outpatient treatment are all partially responsible. Although outpatient treatment is undeniably less expensive initially, appreciable long-term savings may not be realized because of the greater tendency for recidivism in the outpatient-treated group. Studies of treatment outcome and cost effectiveness support the view that contemporary alcoholism treatment should provide multiple levels of care, with appropriate matching of patients, depending upon severity and various demographic factors. This match may be difficult to realize in actual practice because of the wide variability among alcoholic patients.[60] Of particular concern is the limited availability of treatment for those who are uninsured or underinsured.

Inpatient treatment provides a safer environment than outpatient treatment for those who might go through a difficult withdrawal because medical support is more readily available. Inpatient treatment also allows the patient to begin recovery in an alcohol- and drug-free environment. The duration of inpatient treatment is usually 28 days, including approximately seven days of detoxification. The length of stay depends upon several factors, including the severity of the problem and the amount of insurance benefits available.

Outpatient treatment for alcoholism may be provided as "primary treatment" or as part of the continuum of care that may follow hospitalization. Primary outpatient treatment programs for carefully selected populations may reduce costs of treatment significantly. Unfortunately, they also may be the only treatment options available beyond detoxification to those who are uninsured or underinsured, regardless of addiction severity. The advantages of primary outpatient treatment include not only reduced cost but also, much less disruption of family and occupational life as a result of hospitalization.[60]

When choosing treatment for J.M., it appeared that J.M. might need medically intensive detoxification, and, therefore, inpatient evaluation and treatment were recommended. Following withdrawal, it was determined that J.M. could participate in outpatient treatment since he was willingly participating in the program; had good family, social, and job support; and was felt to have a low relapse risk. The use of a local treatment program facilitated visitation from family members and participation in a family evaluation and education program. Although J.M chose local treatment, some patients may elect to go to a distant treatment program, seeking more anonymity or because of the program's reputation, lower cost, or specialized services.

Recovery Support

8. J.D., a 42-year-old client who has been receiving care from you for several years, has just been discharged from an inpatient treatment program for alcoholism. He needs to attend three 12-step meetings each week as part of his recovery plan. What "12-step" meeting(s) should be recommended for J.D. and for how long should he attend them?

One of the goals of treatment is to familiarize patients with 12-step programs and hope that they become involved in these programs. Since the founding of AA in 1935, 148 twelve-step groups, each with a different recovery focus, have requested permission to use the 12 Steps. The 12-step programs have an estimated 2.6 million members in AA, Al-Anon Family Groups (Al-Anon or AFG), and Narcotics Anonymous (NA).[61] Of the U.S. adult population, 13.3% have been to an AA meeting at some time and 5.3% had attended in the prior year, according to a 1990 survey. This was up from the previous year when 4.9% had at some time attended an AA meeting, and 2.3% within the last year.[62]

The basic principles of recovery are based upon the 12 Steps originally developed by AA (see Table 81.6). Although words have been changed to accommodate different recovery programs (e.g., gambling, cocaine, overeaters), the basic principles remain the same. The reference to God in the 12 Steps may mislead the reader into believing that this is a religious organization; it is not. AA teaches the concept of spirituality; the terms "God," "Power greater than ourselves,'' and ''Higher Power'' are used often in AA. The primary belief is that there exists a power greater than the individual; each interprets this in relationship to his own beliefs. For some, this may represent an object, a person, or a group. A sense of purpose in life increases with continuing sobriety and with the practice of spiritual principles as outlined in the 12 Steps.[63] The Twelve Traditions (see Table 81.7) further define the role of these self-help groups in society and in the conduct of their programs.

Some groups, such as AA, will have offices and resource centers within each area; others will utilize a phone message or contact to provide meeting information. Local resources can be identified from the Yellow Pages as explained in Question 7. Meeting schedules for AA will list types of meetings. Open meetings may be attended by anyone, provided that the anonymity of individuals is preserved and the contents of the meeting are not disclosed. Closed AA meetings are only for those who ''have a desire to stop drinking''; most attendees will consider themselves AA members. Discussion meetings consider a specific topic or area, usually including open discussion, related to alcoholism or problems which might lead to drinking. Speaker meetings usually are open meetings where one or two speakers present their insights on their sobriety in detail; this may be followed by an open discussion. Step meetings involve an in-depth study of one of the 12 Steps or 12 Traditions; these are often closed meetings. Nonsmoking meetings are increasingly popular, although many meetings continue to allow smoking. Nicotine addiction remains a problem for many AA members. Some AA meetings have a specific target audience (e.g., women, gay/lesbian, men, certain professions); these enable participants to deal with is-

Table 81.6	Twelve Steps[a]

1) We admitted we were powerless over alcohol, that our lives had become unmanageable.

2) Came to believe that a Power greater than ourselves could restore us to sanity.

3) Made a decision to turn our will and our lives over to the care of God as we understood Him.

4) Made a searching and fearless moral inventory of ourselves.

5) Admitted to God, to ourselves, and to another human being the exact nature of our wrongs.

6) Were entirely ready to have God remove all these defects of character.

7) Humbly asked Him to remove our shortcomings.

8) Made a list of all persons we had harmed and became willing to make amends to them all.

9) Made direct amends to such people wherever possible, except when to do so would injure them or others.

10) Continued to take personal inventory, and when we were wrong promptly admitted it.

11) Sought through prayer and meditation to improve our conscious contact with God as we understood Him, praying only for knowledge of His will for us, and the power to carry that out.

12) Having had a spiritual awakening as the result of these steps, we tried to carry this message to alcoholics and to practice these principles in all our affairs.

a The Twelve Steps are reprinted with permission of Alcoholics Anonymous World Services, Inc. Permission to reprint this material does not mean that AA has reviewed or approved the contents of this publication, nor that AA agrees with the views expressed herein. AA is a program of recovery from alcoholism. Use of the Twelve Steps in connection with programs and activities patterned after AA but that address other problems does not imply otherwise.

Table 81.7	Twelve Traditions[a]

1) Our common welfare should come first; personal recovery depends on AA unity.

2) For our group purpose there is but one ultimate authority, a loving God as He may express Himself in our group conscience. Our leaders are but trusted servants; they do not govern.

3) The only requirement for AA membership is a desire to stop drinking.

4) Each group should be autonomous except in matters affecting other groups or AA as a whole.

5) Each group has but one primary purpose, to carry its message to the alcoholic who still suffers.

6) An AA group ought never endorse, finance, or lend the AA name to any related facility or outside enterprise, lest problems of money, property, and prestige divert us from our primary purpose.

7) Every AA group ought to be fully self-supporting, declining outside contributions.

8) AA should remain forever nonprofessional, but our service centers may employ special workers.

9) AA, as such, ought never be organized; but we may create service boards or committees directly responsible to those they serve.

10) AA has no opinion on outside issues; hence, the AA name ought never be drawn into public controversy.

11) Our public relations policy is based on attraction rather than promotion, we need always maintain personal anonymity at the level of press, radio, and films.

12) Anonymity is the spiritual foundation of all our Traditions, ever reminding us to place principles before personalities.

a The Twelve Traditions are reprinted with permission of Alcoholics Anonymous World Services, Inc. Permission to reprint this material does not mean that AA has reviewed or approved the contents of this publication, nor that AA agrees with the views expressed herein. AA is a program of recovery from alcoholism. Use of the Twelve Traditions in connection with programs and activities patterned after AA but that address other problems does not imply otherwise.

sues which may influence their recovery, yet might not be considered appropriate for a group with a more general focus. Usually, AA meetings do not restrict admittance for anyone who ''has a desire to stop drinking.''[64] The AA text, Alcoholics Anonymous, is central to the activities of most AA groups; it is often referred to as ''The Big Book.''[65] A sponsor is a specific person in AA, usually with at least one or two years of successful recovery who serves as a mentor and role model for a new member.

A number of other 12-step groups related to alcoholism and other drug dependencies [e.g., Narcotics Anonymous (NA) and Cocaine Anonymous (CA)] are for those desiring to stop other dependencies. International Pharmacists Anonymous (IPA) is for pharmacists and pharmacy students recovering from addictions/alcoholism in their own lives or in the lives of significant others. International Nurses Anonymous (INA) similarly serves the nursing profession. International Doctors in Alcoholics Anonymous (IDAA) membership includes both recovering and codependent professionals holding any health professional doctoral degrees. Adult Children of Alcoholics (ACOA) provides support for adults whose parents are or were alcoholics or other drug addicts. Similar programs exist for teens (Alateen) and younger children (Alatot) with alcoholic parents. Al-Anon is for those who are impacted by another's alcoholism. Nar-Anon is for those affected by another's drug addiction. Codependents Anonymous (CoDA) is for individuals dealing with problems associated with relationships. For more information about these and similar 12-step organizations, the national addresses and phone numbers (if available) are listed in Table 81.8.

Since alcohol is J.D.'s drug of abuse, AA was recommended. He could have additionally chosen to attend support groups for his profession or for any other problems he may have had, but these would not have replaced AA participation. Adult family members and his best friend began attending Al-Anon meetings, and his children attended Alateen. AA represents an inexpensive, effective source of support for J.D.'s recovery which is available essentially worldwide. Since alcoholism is an incurable disease, AA attendance is considered by most alcoholics to be a lifetime commitment.

9. While requesting a prescription for disulfiram (Antabuse), J.D. asks if there is an AA meeting nearby. What commonly available resources could you utilize to obtain this information?

It would be desirable for practitioners to keep a listing of local 12-step groups to provide information to patients. The practitioner might periodically contact groups such as AA and Al-Anon to obtain a schedule of meetings and periodically could visit resource centers at offices of 12-step programs to obtain information. J.D. should be referred at least to the local AA office which the practitioner could identify from the Yellow Pages of a telephone directory.

10. What issues should the practitioner consider in providing care for recovering addicts such as J.D.?

Although J.D.'s drug of abuse was alcohol, he is at risk for developing addictions to any other addicting drugs. In general, he should be advised to avoid any mood-altering substances (e.g., OTC antihistamines or decongestants, alcohol-containing products) unless he discusses their use in advance with a health professional (usually his physician) who understands addiction and J.D.'s recovery. Future use of any addicting substance should be supervised closely by a professional who understands addiction recovery. It is safest to assume that use of a mood-altering drug will cause J.D. to lose control of his ability to make decisions. Decisions regarding the use of drugs should be supervised. Treat-

ment generally should continue no longer than is usually required for the procedure or injury in question, and take-home medication should be avoided if possible or be controlled carefully.

Populations at Risk
Fetuses and Neonates

11. A.K., a 16-year-old female, delivers a 1300 gm male, R.K., who is small for his estimated gestational age of 32 weeks. No maternal prenatal care had been obtained. R.K. feeds poorly, is jittery, and is tremulous. A.K.'s social history is suggestive of polydrug abuse. What substances most often cause these problems?

Drug use during pregnancy results in many serious perinatal complications, such as stillbirths, premature rupture of the membranes, maternal hemorrhage (abruptio placentae or placenta previa), and fetal distress. Asphyxia, prematurity, low birth weight, infections, cerebral infarction, congenital malformations, and drug withdrawal complicate neonatal care. Long-term sequelae include delays in physical and mental development, sudden infant death syndrome (SIDS), and learning disabilities. Most abused drugs are excreted in breast milk in quantities sufficient to elicit pharmacologic effects in the infant.[66-70] (See Chapter 45: Drugs in Pregnancy and Lactation.)

During the late 1980s, it is estimated that intrauterine exposure to alcohol occurred for 73% of babies, marijuana 17%, cocaine 4.5%, and opiates 2% to 3%. Up to 739,000 infants were born annually with intrauterine exposure to illegal drugs (excluding alcohol or tobacco).[71]

Small, lipid soluble drug molecules readily diffuse across the placenta; placental blood flow is often the rate-limiting factor. Placental surface area and thickness, maternal and fetal pH, and plasma protein binding also influence transfer. Elimination of lipid-soluble drugs from the fetus is primarily through passive diffusion back to maternal circulation; fetal elimination half-lives for such drugs are similar to maternal values. With chronic use, steady-state

---

Table 81.8	Twelve Step Group Directory	

Adult Children of Alcoholics
PO Box 3216
2522 W. Sepulveda Boulevard, Suite 200
Torrance, California 90505
(213) 534-1815

Al-Anon (or Alateen)
Al-Anon Family Group Headquarters, Inc.
PO Box 862
Midtown Station, New York, New York 10018-0862
(212) 302-7240

Alcoholics Anonymous
PO Box 454
Grand Central Station
New York, New York 10017
(212) 686-1100

Cocaine Anonymous
World Service Office
3740 Overland Avenue, Suite G
Los Angeles, California 90034
(213) 559-5833
800-347-8998

Codependents Anonymous (CoDA)
PO Box 33577
Phoenix, Arizona 85067-3577
(602) 277-7991

Drugs Anonymous
PO Box 473
Ansonia Station
New York, New York 10023
(212) 874-0700

International Doctors in Alcoholics Anonymous
C. Richard McKinley, MD, Listkeeper
PO Box 199
Augusta, Missouri 63332
(314) 228-4548

International Nurses Anonymous
Pat Green, RN, MSW, Listkeeper
1020 Sunset Drive
Lawrence, Kansas 66044
(913) 749-2626 (work)
(913) 842-3893 (home)

International Pharmacists Anonymous
IPA Listkeeper
32 Cedar Grove Road
Annandale, New Jersey 08801-3358
(908) 735-2789 (answering machine)
(908) 730-9072

Marijuana Anonymous
1527 North Washington Avenue
Scranton, Pennsylvania 18509

Nar-Anon (Family Groups)
PO Box 2562
Palos Verdes, California 90274
(213) 547-5800

Narcotics Anonymous
PO Box 9999
Van Nuys, California 91409
(818) 780-3951

Pill Addicts Anonymous
PO Box 278
Reading, Pennsylvania 19603
(215) 372-1128

Smokers Anonymous
2118 Greenwich Street
San Francisco, California 94123

levels may be established in the fetus. Data from sheep suggest that fetal steady-state levels of all drugs studied, except alcohol, were lower than maternal levels. Lower protein binding, the presence of drug metabolizing enzymes in the fetal liver, and fetal renal clearance may be contributing factors. Fetal urine and diffusion across the chorioallantoic membrane are primary routes of accumulation of drugs and metabolites in the amniotic fluid: passive diffusion across the chorioallantoic membrane back to maternal circulation is the primary route of drug elimination from the amnionic fluid. Metabolites from the fetal liver which are excreted in bile and fetal swallowing of amniotic fluid may result in the accumulation of drugs and metabolites in fetal meconium. Since the meconium normally is not eliminated until after birth, it is a relatively noninvasive procedure for neonatal drug screening which may be more reflective than urine of intrauterine drug exposure. The presence of benzoyl ecgonine in neonatal hair indicates maternal cocaine use during the third trimester of pregnancy.[72-84]

Smoking during pregnancy increases, in dose-dependent fashion, the risk of spontaneous abortions, premature delivery, low birth weight infants, and perinatal mortality, as well as a greater risk later for SIDS. Approximately 4600 infants die each year in the U.S. because of maternal smoking during pregnancy. Carbon monoxide inactivation of hemoglobin, placental vasoconstriction by nicotine, reduced appetite and nutrition, and reduced plasma volume all may contribute. Pregnant women will more often quit smoking than nonpregnant women; counseling and support by caregivers are recommended.[85-89]

Fetal alcohol syndrome (FAS) is the most common known cause of mental retardation in Western countries. Children with FAS exhibit intrauterine and postnatal growth delays, neurologic abnormalities (e.g., learning and speech disabilities and behavioral problems), craniofacial abnormalities (e.g., microcephaly, small jaw, midface hypoplasia), cardiac abnormalities (e.g., atrial and ventricular septal defects), and genitourinary malformations. FAS may occur in up to 40% of newborns whose mothers are frank alcoholics. FAS usually is seen when more than three ounces of absolute alcohol per day has been ingested throughout pregnancy. Fetal alcohol effects (FAE) refers to occurrence of only some of these abnormalities and is associated with lower levels of drinking. Genetic, biologic, and environmental factors cause the threshold dose for FAS to vary. Many authorities consider total abstinence during pregnancy as the only safe approach to alcohol consumption.[88,90-96] (Also see Chapter 45: Drugs in Pregnancy and Lactation.)

There are few studies of the effects of marijuana on the fetus. Growth retardation and deficits in memory and verbal abilities may occur. Neonates may exhibit fine tremor and exaggerated startle reflexes. An additional concern is exposure to agents used to ''cut'' or enhance the effects of the marijuana.[97-100]

Both amphetamines and cocaine may cause maternal vasoconstriction and hypertension which may cause fetal hypoxia. Both may cause obstetric complications such as preterm birth, intrauterine growth retardation, abruptio placentae, spontaneous abortion, microcephaly, and SIDS. Intrauterine cocaine or amphetamine exposure may cause neonates to exhibit abnormal sleep patterns, tremors, poor feeding, hypotonia, fever, and vomiting. Although data are limited, cocaine-exposed infants may have a higher risk for genitourinary tract malformations, cardiac anomalies, and cerebral infarction. Developmental delays and long-term neurobehavioral deficits may occur with cocaine. Children of women who used cocaine only during the first trimester did not have an increased risk of anomalies: early prenatal care and screening for substance abuse are recommended.[101-103]

In utero exposure to opiates may cause prematurity, intrauterine growth retardation, and neonatal abstinence syndrome (irritability, sweating, nasal congestion, feeding difficulties, diarrhea, and vomiting). Methadone maintenance usually is recommended during pregnancy rather than exposing the mother and fetus to the stress of detoxification or the risks of overdosage, exposure to other toxic substances, or infection which complicate uncontrolled addiction. Benzodiazepines may be associated with neonatal lethargy and a withdrawal syndrome similar to narcotic abstinence; these manifestations may persist for weeks.[104-107]

Lysergic acid diethylamide (LSD) does not appear to have fetal adverse effects. Phencyclidine (PCP) has not been associated with fetal defects but can cause neonatal withdrawal characterized by irritability and jitteriness. The combination of pentazocine and tripelennamine (''Ts and Blues'') as a street drug may result in growth retardation and neonatal withdrawal symptoms.[88]

Polydrug use is common among illicit drug abusers. The abuse of multiple substances appears to increase the risk of fetal damage. Impurities and diluents such as cyanide, pesticides, strychnine, antihistamines, or warfarin also may be contained in street drugs and have adverse effects on the mother and fetus.[88]

Based upon incidence, smoking, alcohol use, or opiate use would be the most likely causes of R.K.'s problems; although marijuana, PCP, or ''Ts and Blues'' also are possible.

12. How could the prenatal use of these substances of abuse be confirmed?

Prenatal exposure to addicting drugs usually is ascertained by maternal interview or urine screening. The reliability of urine screening depends upon the pharmacokinetics, dose, and timing of exposure for the abused substance. Umbilical cord blood, amniotic fluid, and neonatal urine, meconium (first stool), and hair samples have all been used to assess drug exposure. While positive results are indicative of exposure, negative results must be interpreted with an understanding of pharmacokinetics of the drugs.

Because they are cleared rapidly, urine or blood from either A.K. or R.K. would be positive only if maternal use of nicotine, alcohol, or opiates occurred within about 24 hours of admission. Marijuana would test positive for up to six days after use. A screen of fetal meconium might reveal a profile of drugs used during pregnancy. R.K.'s urine was positive only for marijuana metabolites and benzodiazepines. Upon further interview, A.K. indicates that she smoked one pack of cigarettes and drank four to six beers per day throughout pregnancy and took ''about three nerve pills a day''; the ''nerve pills'' are determined to be diazepam (Valium).

13. How could the risk of fetal damage due to drug exposure have been reduced for A.K.?

The pregnant addict often has been raised in a household where chemical abuse occurred and has been sexually or physically assaulted. She is more susceptible to infections, including hepatitis B and human immunodeficiency virus (HIV), and is more likely to have nutritional deficiencies which will adversely affect the fetus. The lifestyle of a drug-dependent woman and fear of detection of addiction often delay seeking prenatal care. Such pregnancies are considered ''high risk'' and warrant specialized prenatal and perinatal care. Maternal care should include minimization of risk, preferably through a controlled detoxification and treatment program, education concerning parenting skills, and postnatal social and medical support.

A.K. had a ''high risk'' pregnancy and should have obtained early care. Fear of her parents' reaction to the revelation of her drug use and of possible prosecution discouraged her from getting prenatal care. The availability of a free, confidential prenatal clinic which was well publicized to, and trusted by, this at-risk population (teenagers) would have allowed A.K. to seek earlier help. Public health messages also may contribute to reduced alcohol and tobacco use during pregnancy.

14. A.K. asks you if she will be arrested for using alcohol during pregnancy since she is under the legal age for drinking. She has seen news reports indicating that some women have been prosecuted for child abuse because of drug use during pregnancy. What evidence supports the criminalization of drug use during pregnancy as a deterrent to use?

Several states have prosecuted women who used drugs during pregnancy for child abuse. It is probable that many such statutes may discourage prenatal care and may not survive constitutional challenge. Mandatory reporting of neonatal addiction may represent a more defensible course of action to alert social service agencies and protect the child.[108]

Programs which criminalize drug use during pregnancy discourage prenatal care. Early prenatal care and postnatal social and medical support are recommended to reduce risk to the fetus and child. A.K. was reassured that her alcohol use would not result in criminal charges. She received information about the effects of the drugs she was using, both on herself and her child. A.K. received referral through a social worker to an agency which provided free evaluation and treatment for her addictions and free child-care once R.K. was discharged from the hospital.

Adolescents

15. A.K. is 16 years old at the time of delivery. What factors predispose A.K. to addiction? What are the patterns of abuse in adolescents?

While thought becomes introspective during adolescence, it remains egocentric relative to adults. Sensation-seeking, risk-taking behaviors, and the need for immediate gratification combined with a sense of invulnerability place adolescents at risk for substance abuse. Adolescents develop substance abuse problems more quickly than adults. Substance abuse treatment programs for adolescents should provide academic services, social skills-training services, and coping skills training to compensate for developmental delays caused by the addiction.[109]

Alcohol remains the drug of choice for adolescents: use of alcohol during the past year was reported by 77% of high school seniors in a 1992 national survey.[111] Use of alcohol within the last 30 days was reported by 26% and 40% of eighth and tenth graders, respectively, and 51% of seniors. Binge drinking (five or more drinks at one sitting within the last two weeks) was reported by 13%, 21%, and 28% of the same age groups. Daily use of alcohol was reported by 3% of seniors. Cocaine use during the past year was reported by 3% of seniors. Use during the past year by seniors also had decreased from 1991 to 1992 for: any illicit drug (29% to 27%), marijuana (24% to 22%), and cocaine (4% to 3%). Use during the past year increased 0.2% (to 0.6%) for heroin and 0.4% (to 5.6%) for LSD from 1991 to 1992 for seniors.[110] Alcohol use under age 21 years is illegal throughout the U.S.; thus the predominant "illegal drug" is alcohol. A survey of high school seniors in 1988 found that for those who used drugs, the mean age of onset for alcohol use was 12.5 years, cigarette use 12.9 years, marijuana use 14.6 years, and cocaine use 15.9 years. For females, the use of cigarettes most often preceded marijuana use, while males tended to use alcohol, with or without cigarettes, before using marijuana. Earlier-than-average cigarette use was associated with increased risk of progression to cocaine use.[111] The need for drug-abuse education for preteens is evident, especially for alcohol and tobacco.

Approximately 15% of adolescents under age 18 have definable problems with alcohol or other drug use, usually involving habitual use.[112] Less than 1% of teenage drug or alcohol users are truly

chemically dependent.[113] Rejection of family-centered activities and placing greater value on peer-centered social activities rather than academic performance are predictors of increased risk for alcohol and other drug abuse.[114] Alcohol or other drug abuse within families of origin increases the risk of substance abuse.[115]

A.K. had been smoking since she was ten years old, drinking since she was 12, and began using marijuana at 13. The diazepam was prescribed by her physician for nervousness when she was 12. Although the risks of drug use had been presented in health class when she was 11, A.K. was already smoking by that time, and her smoking friends easily convinced her that those risks only occurred in other people. She became addicted by the time she was 14. Despite having an uncle and a mother who were recovering alcoholics and a grandfather who was an active alcoholic, A.K. had never been told that she was at greater risk for problems by her family or her physician. Earlier presentation of prevention messages, association with positive social and recreational influences, and early family discussion concerning expectations and risks might have prevented A.K.'s drug use.

Women

16. A.K. reports that she drank an average of 4 cans of beer a day throughout her pregnancy. She indicates that her boyfriend drinks about eight beers a day. If they both weighed the same, would A.K.'s risk of alcohol-related problems be about half the risk of her boyfriend?

Alcoholic women start drinking and abusing alcohol later than men, but generally appear in treatment at about the same age as male alcoholics. They drink less than men, but reach the same degree of impairment; differences in body size and composition, hormonal effects, and decreased levels of gastric alcohol dehydrogenase are contributing factors. They are more likely than men to have a chemically-dependent spouse; to exhibit psychiatric symptoms, especially depression; and to be suicidal. Alcoholic women often will have histories of other drug abuse, particularly tranquilizers, sedatives, and amphetamines by prescription but are less likely than men to abuse illicit drugs. There is often a history of physical or sexual abuse. Unfortunately, societal acceptance of chemically dependent women is less than of chemically dependent men. Childcare issues and pregnancy further complicate access to treatment. While about 33% of those suffering from alcoholism or other addictions are women, they represented only about 20% to 25% of the population receiving treatment in 1987. Treatment and recovery support programs need to recognize and accommodate gender differences and problems of societal labeling when caring for women.[116]

A.K. would probably exhibit a similar degree of impairment with four beers as would her boyfriend with eight, even corrected for body weight because of lower gastric alcohol dehydrogenase and hormonal differences. A.K.'s social worker identified a free treatment program where at least 40% of clients were female and found suitable childcare while A.K. was in treatment.

The Elderly

17. A.K. is referred for treatment of alcoholism. During her treatment, it is determined that her grandfather, L.K., is alcoholic as well. L.K. denies the diagnosis, insisting that he never drank until after he retired, and only has "three drinks" a day and "a few nerve pills." You determine that the "nerve pills" are alprazolam and that he has been taking them more frequently than prescribed. Is this consistent with a diagnosis of substance dependence?

The prevalence of alcoholism in community-based elderly may be as high as 15%, while it may be as high as 44% among elderly medical and psychiatric inpatients. While some elderly alcoholics have a lifelong pattern of drinking, others may become alcoholic for the first time late in life. Such individuals are less likely to have a family history and are generally more stable in psychosocial functioning. The elderly require less alcohol to become intoxicated because of changes in body composition, metabolizing ability, and neurologic sensitivity. Chronic alcohol use and, for males, age greater than 50 years reduces the activity of gastric alcohol dehydrogenase. The elderly comprise 12% of the population yet receive 25% of all prescriptions, about 25% of which are for psychoactive agents. Misuse of prescription medications and use with alcohol is common. Increasing physical illness and psychological distress increase the likelihood of substance abuse. Not all problems should be attributed to aging; the clinician must consider issues such as alcohol or drug abuse in the differential diagnosis of all problems affecting the elderly.[117-119]

L.K. has a known family history of alcoholism. He had strong values which prevented him from drinking during his working years, but he felt he could reward himself once he retired and had no perceived obligations. His retirement income and investments were inadequate to allow him to travel as he hoped he could in retirement, and his health began to deteriorate. He was given alprazolam for anxiety. Although L.K. reports drinking only three drinks per day, his wife reports that he finishes about two quarts of gin per week. Understatement of alcohol consumption is common in alcoholics. The combination of alcohol and alprazolam (in amounts greater than prescribed) with stress and genetic predisposition resulted in substance dependence. Once L.K. reached treatment, his withdrawal was longer than would be expected in adolescent or young adult males since his reduced ability to metabolize these substances resulted in elevated levels.

Ethnic and Cultural

18. A.K.'s best friend, D.M., is also chemically dependent. He is a homosexual black male. Would a mainstream treatment program be appropriate?

The incidence of chemical dependency in the gay and lesbian population is estimated to be about 30%. Addicted gay men and lesbians face not only recovery from chemical dependency but also societal homophobia. Gay-sensitive treatment and support is important, especially during early recovery.[120]

Most treatment models are based upon results obtained from treatment of a predominantly white population. Treatment of addicted members of minority groups in the U.S., new immigrants, and homeless persons needs to accommodate language, cultural, and social differences and needs to be optimally effective.[121-124]

Preferred treatment for D.M. is to be in a program which accommodates the treatment issues and needs of gay men and minorities. Since no such program was available near D.M.'s home, he obtained treatment in a treatment center in a larger urban area about 600 miles from his home. His parents and a sister participated in a week-long family program at the same center. Upon return home, D.M. began attending both gay/lesbian and mainstream AA meetings.

Healthcare Professionals

19. The physician who directs the treatment center, M.C., indicates to A.K. that he is a recovering alcoholic and addict. He indicates that he was an anesthesiologist before entering treatment. What are the patterns of drug abuse in healthcare professionals? What drugs would this physician, M.C., have been most likely to abuse?

Alcohol is the primary abused substance among healthcare professionals. Healthcare professionals over 40 years of age are more likely to abuse alcohol alone, while those under age 40 tend to use other drugs alone or in combination with alcohol. Illicit drug use among healthcare professionals is less than in the general population; prescription drugs, especially opioids and benzodiazepines, alcohol, and tobacco are abused most commonly. The incidence of chemical dependency among healthcare professionals probably is similar to the general population. The drug of choice and route of administration vary among professions. Those professions, such as nursing and medicine, which use injections in the course of their usual practice more often abuse injectable drugs. Pharmacists tend to abuse multiple oral drugs and are more likely than other healthcare professionals to abuse stimulants. Specific professions tend to abuse the most readily available drugs. Nitrous oxide addiction is problematic for dentists. Addiction to fentanyl (Sublimaze) or its analogs is common among anesthesiologists and nurse-anesthetists.

M.C. indicates that he began drinking when he was 16 years old and continued until he was 33. During college, he drank heavily on weekends, especially after examinations, but did not consider this a problem since all his friends did this as well. During his residency, the stress of long days and nights on call and of his practice lead to daily drinking whenever he could. Following a back injury at age 30, he received several doses of meperidine (Demerol) and a prescription for an oral product containing oxycodone. He now reports that when he took these opioids he felt "normal for the first time" in his life. Despite resolution of the back pain, he continued to obtain prescriptions for oral narcotics. When confronted about escalating use by his physician, he began seeing several other physicians and getting prescriptions filled at multiple pharmacies. While on duty one night, he realized that he had run out of medication in his locker, so he took fentanyl from stock and injected it. The experience was so positive that he switched his addiction to fentanyl, continuing use until age 33 when he was confronted about narcotic discrepancies during an intervention coordinated by the hospital's employee assistance program. Participants in the intervention included his supervisor, the hospital administrator, a colleague, his wife, and a representative of the state's physician recovery program. He agreed to seek help, entering a 28-day inpatient treatment program. Upon completion of the program, he expressed uncertainty about returning to his practice because of narcotic access and because his medical license had been suspended for six months. He became certified in addiction medicine and now directs the treatment center.

20. What assistance and prevention systems are there to protect the public from M.C.'s impairment and to support his recovery?

Concerns centered on societal and professional censure for being "an intelligent health professional who should know better" delay treatment for many addicted healthcare professionals. Fear of loss of licensure and professional and social status are powerful deterrents to getting help for an addicted professional, forming a very strong denial system. Most states now have programs designed to assist chemically impaired healthcare professionals and prefer to rehabilitate rather than prosecute addicted licensees. However, when the addiction has progressed to harming others or obvious violation of existing law, the addicted professional may face license suspension or revocation and even incarceration.

Although some professionals require the assistance of specialized healthcare professional treatment, most can be treated in mainstream programs. Any such treatment program needs to be able to deal with the "professional" personality and intellect which may complicate acceptance of the addiction and willingness to participate in, instead of trying to control, therapy. Similarly, many healthcare professionals may benefit from health professions recovery support groups in addition to attendance at mainstream 12-step meetings, such as AA or NA.

Too often the healthcare professional is inadequately educated concerning substance abuse recognition and treatment. Many physicians have difficulty recognizing alcoholism or other addictions, viewing alcoholics and other addicts in social stereotypic fashion. Healthcare professionals must be proactive in assuring that they receive education appropriate to their professional responsibilities, in providing appropriate prevention information to the public, in assisting clients and colleagues in obtaining early help, and in supporting recovery from addictions to reduce personal and societal harm.[125–127]

M.C. was successful for several years in obtaining narcotic prescriptions from practitioners. M.C.'s pattern of using multiple physicians and pharmacies for obtaining prescriptions is fairly common among those addicted to prescription medications. Diversion of fentanyl from hospital narcotic stock escalated to the point that M.C. became careless in hiding the diversion, and his mood changes while on duty were reported by operating room personnel. M.C. participated in a mainstream inpatient treatment program and participates in AA and NA meetings in his community. He also receives support from the state's physician assistance program, attends a local physician support group meeting weekly, and is a member of International Doctors in Alcoholics Anonymous (IDAA). Many healthcare professionals do return to positions which allow narcotic access under decreasing supervision as recovery progresses. M.C., with help from his treatment counselor, decided to change his career path since he did not feel that his impulse control would prevent use in the operating room environment. He now also lectures at local health profession colleges on addiction, serves as a consultant to those colleges on substance abuse curricular issues, and offers clerkship experiences to healthcare professional students at the treatment center.

Dual Diagnosis

21. A.K. has an uncle who fought in Vietnam who says he has "dual diagnosis." What is this, and what is the probability that A.K. has a coexisting psychiatric disorder?

"Dual diagnosis" refers to a patient who has a psychoactive substance use disorder and a coexisting psychiatric disorder requiring simultaneous treatment. There are two acronyms which often are used to describe this disorder: MICA (Mentally Ill Chemical Abusers) and PISA (Psychiatrically Impaired Substance Abusers).

Dual diagnosis may involve either a primarily psychiatric patient with a psychoactive substance use disorder or a patient with a primary psychoactive substance use disorder with a concurrent psychiatric illness. Psychiatric patients as a group are at significantly increased risk for developing or having a psychoactive substance use disorder.[128] Also, those patients with psychoactive substance use disorders are more likely to complain of psychiatric symptoms.[129]

Patients with a psychiatric disorder are at increased risk for having a psychoactive substance use disorder. Prevalence rates for alcohol and other psychoactive substance use disorders are about 7% in the general population.[130] Young, chronically mentally ill patients reported psychoactive substance use disorders at rates of about 50%.[131,132]

Among Vietnam veterans seeking treatment for post-traumatic stress disorder, 60% to 80% exhibit a concurrent psychoactive substance use disorder.[133–138] The Center for Disease Control's Vietnam Experience Study reported that 39% of veterans who met the criteria for post-traumatic stress disorder during the month before examination also met the criteria for a psychoactive substance use disorder.[139]

Psychiatric morbidity is more common among patients who seek treatment for chemical dependency. A lifetime prevalence rate of psychiatric disorder in addition to substance use disorder of 78% has been reported in one study. Approximately 65% had a current psychiatric disorder, most commonly antisocial personality disorder (36%), phobias (28%), generalized anxiety (26%), major depression (20%), panic disorder (1.5% to 8.5%), obsessive compulsive disorder (6.3%), schizophrenia (4.1%), and mania (1.5%).[140]

The prognosis in dual diagnosis is not as good as in single diagnosis cases. The dual stigma these patients experience often results in poorer social support, which is a very significant poor prognostic indicator for both their psychiatric and psychoactive substance use disorder. Patients with such "dual diagnoses" have poorer compliance with treatment and are at significantly increased risk of relapse to their drug of choice.[141]

Dually diagnosed persons represent a seriously distressed and disabled population that is growing in numbers and whose coexisting illnesses are difficult to treat. Conflicting treatment philosophies and fragmented service systems sometimes compound these problems. The use of the term dual diagnosis also attempts to signal others that these clients have special needs and require specialized treatment approaches.[142]

There was a significant chance that A.K. had other psychiatric diagnoses. Testing for these disorders was included in A.K.'s assessment during chemical dependency treatment. Major depression was identified, and a treatment plan was initiated. A.K. required antidepressant therapy in addition to counseling for the depression. A.K. was informed by her counselor and her physician that while the antidepressant had some mood-altering properties, it was not addicting. She also was advised that she may attend some 12-step meetings where the use of any medication is considered relapse; she was instructed that most health professionals and counselors support medical treatment of psychiatric illness when necessary and do not consider this relapse. A.K. was asked to inform the counselor or her physician if the mood alteration was causing increased difficulty in maintaining her recovery. A.K. completed treatment, is participating in ongoing counseling and her 12-step meetings, and has returned to school. R.K. is living at home with A.K. and her parents and is being cared for by the grandparents.

Societal Issues
Drugs in the Work Place

22. E.L., a 28-year-old male, works manufacturing automobile batteries. He drinks an average of 8 beers a day, sometimes during lunch breaks or while working, and regularly smokes "pot" (i.e., marijuana) and sometimes "Sherms" (i.e., marijuana with PCP), often during working hours. What influence does drug impairment have on E.L.'s job performance?

The economic impact of alcohol abuse and alcoholism in the U.S. was estimated to be $135 billion in 1990, mostly from lost productivity and employment. The economic impact of drug abuse other than alcohol was estimated at $60 billion for the same year.[143]

In a 1991 NIDA survey, illicit (i.e., marijuana or hashish, cocaine, inhalants, hallucinogens, heroin, or nonmedicinal use of psychotropics) drug use during the past year was reported by 13% of full-time and 14% of part-time employees over age 17. Of those age 18 to 25, 27% of full-time and 28% of part-time employees reported such illicit drug use. The most commonly used illicit drugs are marijuana and cocaine.[144] Substance-abusing employees have increased absenteeism and work site accidents; disciplinary problems; decreased productivity; increased medical benefit, disability, and workers' compensation claims; and increased employee turnover. Substance abuse especially reduces the ability to perform complex cognitive tasks, such as landing an airplane, and coping skills, such as reacting to a hazard on the road while driving and dealing with stress.

E.L. had been having his wife call in sick for him an average of three days a month because of hangovers. He was seen by his physician five times during the past four months for hypertension, gastritis, and traumatic injuries (i.e., extensive bruising and a knee injury which E.L. could not explain). His supervisor has noted declining job performance with an unacceptably high number of errors. E.L. told her this was because of his health problems and the stress of dealing with the death of his father. She attributed the problems to ''burn out'' until two other employees reported finding E.L. smoking a ''joint'' in the rest room. Upon discovery, E.L. became very hostile to the employees, threatening to ''get them'' if they reported him. The supervisor worked with the company's employee assistance program to arrange an intervention. E.L. accepted treatment, was retained in his employment, and is now one of the most reliable employees for the company. He has taken no sick days in the past three years.

23. What could the employer have done to reduce his risk from E.L.'s drug abuse?

Many employers, especially those with large numbers of employees, have increasingly responded to the challenge of substance abuse in the work force by developing policies and procedures for dealing with work place substance abuse, by responsible use of alcohol at company functions, and by promoting assistance and retention for chemically impaired employees. Employee assistance programs are now a benefit provided by many employers. These may either be based at the work site or contracted to another agency. Employee assistance programs can assist in providing chemical dependency intervention services for employees or family members and provide limited counseling and referral for any issue which may interfere with employee performance. Employee recovery contracts often are utilized as a means of supporting and directing the employee's recovery. These usually specify as conditions of continued employment attendance at support group meetings, care by specific physicians, prohibition of use of mood-altering substances without physician permission, and drug testing.[145]

E.L.'s company already had an EAP; he successfully completed a two-year recovery contract which was coordinated for the employer by their EAP. All urine screens during that period were negative for E.L. Furthermore, E.L. saw only his assigned physician, attended more support group meetings than were required, and his employee evaluations were excellent. If an EAP was not available, the company could have contracted with a chemical dependency counselor or treatment center for assistance with the intervention and referral for evaluation and treatment. Given E.L.'s history of behaviors suggestive of problems requiring employee assistance, the company reviewed and revised its substance abuse policy; distributed it to all employees and posted it throughout the work place; provided instruction to employees concerning recognition, referral, and recovery support mechanisms for substance abusing employees; and provided a clear statement from administration indicating support for chemical dependency treatment and recovery with job retention when possible.

Drug Testing

24. S.O. drives for a local grocery warehouse company; his employer does drug testing for all pre-employment physicals and following on-the-job accidents. S.O. crashes into a car stopped at a red light, injuring the driver; he claims that the truck slid on the rain-soaked pavement. He last smoked several joints (i.e., marijuana cigarettes) two days ago and drank 6 beers the night before. He also used cocaine for the past week. Can the employer legally require S.O. to provide a urine sample?

When drug testing is a stated condition of employment, the employer can test whenever the stated conditions are met. Federal and state laws additionally require testing of certain workers involved in critical public occupations, such as transportation. S.O.'s employer has not only a right but an obligation to test in this case.

25. S.O. has heard from friends that drug tests are not accurate and that he can probably successfully challenge the results. Is this information correct?

Pre-employment drug testing by urinalysis is increasingly being used by employers to screen potential employees; however, alcohol rarely is included in these testing programs despite being the most abused drug. Drug testing of employees may include random drug testing, often as a component of a chemical dependency recovery contract or of probation for an alcohol- or drug-related conviction; probable cause testing (e.g., following an on-the-job accident); or scheduled testing. Scheduled testing is probably the least effective, since substance abusers can stop drug use in anticipation of testing. Drug testing programs must consider the individual's right to privacy and due process and should be supported by written policies which have been legally reviewed and have been communicated to employees and supervisors. The urine samples should be collected in sites and ways which discourage sample adulteration or substitution, such as temperature check. When there is probable cause to believe that the employee is abusing drugs and is likely to attempt to tamper with the collection, the urine collection should be observed. Chain-of-custody procedures for the sample must be followed from obtaining the sample to the submission of the test report; a written record of all persons handling the sample should be maintained. The specimen should be retained in the original container for at least one year if a sample is positive. Initial screening tests use an immunoassay appropriate to the drugs being tested for (usually at least cocaine, amphetamines, marijuana, phencyclidine, and opiates). Positive samples must be confirmed with a more specific and accurate confirmatory test (e.g., gas chromatography-mass spectroscopy). Samples testing positive with both tests are then reviewed by a medical review officer (MRO) who obtains and considers information about medications and other potential confounding substances which the employee may have taken before testing. The distinction between legitimate use and nonmedical use is made by the MRO. The employee has the right to request that the retained sample be retested. Only after all these procedures are followed and the medical review indicates nonmedicinal use of a substance prohibited in the employer's written policy may sanctions be imposed upon the employee. Quality control procedures, including laboratory certification by NIDA, provide additional protection in this process.[146]

If requisite procedures are followed, very few false positives will occur. If an error is made, it is usually failure to detect substances present in low concentrations (false negatives). It would be unlikely that S.O. would be able to successfully challenge positive results. The retained sample could be analyzed to reverify the results.

26. What is the probability that S.O. will test positive?

The efficiency of utilizing drug testing to detect abuse is in part dependent upon the elimination characteristics of the drug and dose and chronicity of use. Marijuana metabolites may be detectable at cut-off concentrations for up to six days after a single use and up to 29 days with chronic use. Methaqualone, phencyclidine, and phenobarbital may test positive for up to six days. Methadone may be detected for up to three days and cocaine metabolites and benzodiazepines may be present for up to two days. Opioids, shorter-acting barbiturates, and amphetamines are positive for up to one day, and alcohol is detectable for less than one day. When testing individuals with known histories of substance abuse, the scheduling of random testing in part should be based upon these elimination characteristics, especially during early recovery.[147]

In S.O.'s case, it is likely that marijuana still will be present in the urine. Cocaine and metabolites probably will be present, and alcohol may be if it is included in the screening.

27. Is there any way that S.O. could reduce his risk of detection?

Various methods have been attempted to dilute drugs in the urine or to hasten excretion (e.g., exercise; hydration; use of diuretics or saunas; dilution of samples with water; or ingestion of vinegar, ammonium chloride, sodium bicarbonate, cranberry juice, or vitamin C to change urine pH in an effort to promote ion trapping and hasten excretion). Such efforts rarely are successful in preventing detection unless the drug is present in nearly undetectable quantities and often are detected by determination of urine pH or specific gravity. Enzyme immunoassays may produce false-negative results when adulterated with large amounts of vinegar, lemon juice, golden seal (*Hydrastis canadensis*) tea, drain cleaner (lye), or liquid soap, but these normally are detectable by initial test of urine pH, specific gravity, or shake tests for foaming. Benzalkonium chloride from eye drops such as Visine may cause false-negative enzyme immunoassays for marijuana and cocaine and usually can be detected only if specifically included in the assay. Substitution of a "clean" urine from someone else might avoid detection if it can be provided at body temperature and was not an observed-voided specimen.[147]

S.O. might avoid detection if he is able to substitute a "clean" urine from someone else, but it is probable that the employer will require an observed specimen following a crash. He might also escape detection by adding benzalkonium chloride eye drops to the specimen; this might produce a negative result on the initial assay, avoiding the confirmatory assay which would be positive. Adding the eye drops to an observed specimen would be difficult. Other methods of dilution or adulterants would likely either be detected by the laboratory or would not result in enough dilution to avoid detection of these drugs.

Confidentiality

28. S.O. is referred by his employer's EAP to treatment, but fails to complete it and is terminated. While intoxicated, he robs a convenience store, assaults the clerk, and causes a multicar crash while evading police pursuit. He is arrested and may potentially serve up to 10 years in prison. The attorney prosecuting S.O.'s case contacts the treatment center where S.O. originally had been referred by the employer, requesting a copy of S.O.'s treatment records; she also asks the employer's EAP for its records. What conditions must be met before these records can be released?

Most information pertinent to the treatment of an individual's alcoholism and other drug dependencies is protected by federal law. Disclosure of information from treatment providers or counselors usually can be made only with specific, written consent of the patient. Specific exceptions include mandatory reporting of child abuse or neglect, medical emergency, and court-ordered disclosures (which must meet specific, stringent criteria).[148] Unless S.O. signed a release or the attorney obtained a specific court order, the treatment center and EAP are legally obligated not to release the records.

29. If S.O. had discussed his history of drug use with a fellow employee, could that employee be required to divulge the information in court?

Individuals who are not specifically required by law to maintain the information in confidence may find that such information may be subject to disclosure in court. The employee would not be protected by confidentiality laws.

Some states have legislated that the records of health professional recovery programs are protected from such disclosure. Those working with these programs should be aware of relevant laws in their states.

30. S.O. also shared some information concerning his drug use when attending a 12-step meeting while still in treatment. Is this information subject to confidentiality laws?

Unfortunately, no. Although 12-step meetings stress anonymity and confidentiality, there are no laws preventing disclosure of information obtained from such meetings. The prosecuting attorney could seek testimony from any persons whom she could identify who attended the meeting.

Even in the absence of legal protection for confidentiality in 12-step meetings, anonymity is an important component of recovery. Specific information and identities of participants obtained at 12-step meetings should be maintained in confidence whenever possible. Failure to observe rules of anonymity in these programs may endanger the recovery and even life of program participants. Confidentiality of information obtained in the course of our professional activities must be maintained.

References

1 **Rush B.** An inquire into the effects of ardent spirits upon the human body and mind, with an account of the means of preventing and of the remedies for curing them. Q J Stud Alcohol. 1943;4:324.

2 **Silkworth WD.** Alcoholism is a manifestation of an allergy. Int Rec Med. 1937;145:249.

3 **Flavin D.** Nomenclature. In: Geller A. American Society of Addiction Medicine Review Course Syllabus. Washington DC: Wilford; 1990:27–30.

4 **O'Brien CP et al.** A learning model of addiction. In: O'Brien CP, Jaffe JH, eds. Addictive States. New York: Raven Press; 1992:157.

5 **Blum TC et al.** Public images of alcoholism: data from a Georgia survey. J Stud Alcohol. 1989;50:5.

6 **American Psychiatric Association.** Diagnostic and Statistical Manual of Mental Disorders. 4th ed. Washington, DC: American Psychiatric Association; 1994.

7 **Ball JC.** The reliability and validity of interview data obtained from 59 narcotic addicts. Am J Sociol. 1967;72:650.

8 **Bonito AJ, Nurco D.** Validity of addict self-report in social research. Int J Addict. 1976;11:719.

9 **Van Natta P et al.** The hidden influence of alcohol on mortality. Alcohol Health Res World. 1984–85;9:42.

10 **Hartford JT, Samojski T.** Alcoholism in the geriatric population. J Am Geriatr Soc. 1982;30:18.

11 **Nace EP.** Epidemiology of alcoholism and prospects for treatment. Annu Rev Med. 1984;35:293.

12 **Weissman MM et al.** Prevalence and psychiatric heterogeneity of alcoholism in the United States urban community. J Stud Alcohol. 1980;41:672.

13 **Desmond DP, Maddux JF.** Mexican-American heroin addicts. Am J Drug Alcohol Abuse. 1985;103:317.

14 **May PA.** Substance abuse and American Indians: prevalence and susceptibility. Int J Addict. 1982;17:1185.

15 **Glassner B, Berg B.** How Jews avoid alcohol problems. Am Sociol Rev. 1980;445:647.

16 **Ropers RH, Boyer R.** Homelessness as a health risk. Alcohol Health Res World. 1987;11:38.

17 **O'Neil JA.** The drug use forecasting (DUF) program reports 1989 results. NIJ Reports. 1990;221:10.

18 **Ross HE et al.** The prevalence of psychiatric disorders in patients with alcohol and other drug problems. Arch Gen Psychiatry. 2988;45:1023.

19 **Alcohol and Health: Fifth Special Report to the US Congress.** Washington, DC: US Government Printing Office, 1984; DHHS Pub No. (AMD)90-1291.

20 **Drugs and Crime Data Center.** Fact sheet: drug data summary. Washington, DC: US Department of Justice, 1991.

21 **Ball JC et al.** Cited in Study stresses link between heroin dependence and incidence of crime. New York Times. Mar 22, 1981:22.

22 **Committee on Trauma Research, Commission on Life Sciences, National Research Council and the Institute of Medicine.** Grossblatt N, ed.

Injury in America: A Continuing Public Health Problem. Washington, DC: National Academy Press; 1985.

23 **Kirby JM et al.** Comparability of alcohol and drug use in injured drivers. South Med J. 1992;85:800.

24 **Fell JC, Nash CE.** The nature of the alcohol problem in U.S. fatal crashes. Health Educ Q. 1989;16:335.

25 **Rutledge R, Messick WJ.** The association of trauma death and alcohol use in a rural state. J Trauma. 1992;33:737.

26 **Jurkovich GJ et al.** The effect of acute alcohol intoxication and chronic alcohol abuse on outcome from trauma. JAMA. 1993;270:51.

27 **Soderstrom CA et al.** Psychoactive substance dependence among trauma center patients. JAMA. 1992;267:2756.

28 **Rivara FP et al.** A descriptive study of trauma, alcohol, and alcoholism in young adults. J Adolesc Health. 1992; 13:663.

29 **McLaughlin JG et al.** Hospitalization and injure influence on the prosecution of drunk drivers. Am Surg. 1993;59: 484.

30 **Holder HD et al.** Alcoholic beverage server liability and the reduction of alcohol-involved problems. J Stud Alc. 1993;54:23.

31 **Turrisi R, Jaccard J.** Cognitive and attitudinal factors in the analysis of alternatives to drunk driving. J Stud Alc. 1992;53:405.

32 **O'Malley PM, Wagenaar AC.** Effects of minimum drinking age laws on alcohol use, related behaviors and traffic crash involvement among American youth: 1976–1987. J Stud Alc. 1991; 52:478.

33 **Cook PJ.** The effect of liquor taxes on drinking, cirrhosis, and auto accidents. In: Moore MH, Gerstein DR, eds. Alcohol and Public Policy: Beyond the Shadow of Prohibition. Washington, DC: National Academy of Sciences; 1981:255–85.

34 **Coate D, Grossman M.** Effects of alcoholic beverage prices and legal drinking ages on youth alcohol use. J Law Econ. 1988;31:145.

35 **National Institute on Alcohol Abuse and Alcoholism.** Alcohol research and public health policy. Rockville, MD: U.S. Department of Health and Human Services, 1993; Public Health Service publication no. PH 330 (Alcohol Alert; no. 20).

36 **Strasburger VC.** Prevention of adolescent drug abuse: why "Just Say No" won't work. J Pediatr. 1989;114:676.

37 **Jones RT.** Alternative strategies. Ciba Found Symp. 1991;166:224.

38 **American Medical Association Board of Trustees.** Drug abuse in the United States: strategies for prevention. JAMA. 1991;265:2102.

39 **Jonas S.** Public health approach to the prevention of substance abuse. In: Lowinson JH et al., eds. Substance Abuse A Comprehensive Textbook. 2nd ed. Baltimore: Williams and Wilkins; 1992:928–43.

40 **Coulehan JL et al.** Recognition of alcoholism and substance abuse in primary care patients. Arch Intern Med. 1987;147:349.

41 **Leckman AL et al.** Prevalence of alcoholism in a family practice center. J Fam Pract. 1984;18:867.

42 **Woodall HE.** Alcoholics remaining anonymous: resident diagnosis of alcoholism in a family practice center. J Fam Pract. 1988;26:293.

43 **Milhorn HT.** Chemical Dependence: Diagnosis, Treatment, and Prevention. New York, NY: Springer-Verlag; 1990: 2,27–30,36.

44 **Schuckit MA.** Overview: epidemiology of alcoholism. In: Schuckit MA, ed. Alcohol Patterns and Problems. New Brunswick: Rutgers University Press; 1985:1–42.

45 **Ewing JA.** Detecting alcoholism: the CAGE questionnaire. JAMA. 1984; 252:1905.

46 **King M.** At risk drinking among general practice attenders: validation of the CAGE questionnaire. Psychol Med. 1986;16:213.

47 **Wallace P, Haines A.** Use of a questionnaire in general practice to increase the recognition of patients with excessive alcohol consumption. Br Med J. 1985;290:1949.

48 **Selzer ML.** The Michigan Alcoholism Screening Test: the quest for a new diagnostic instrument. Am J Psychiatry. 1971;127:1653.

49 **Schuckit MA et al.** Diagnosis of alcoholism. Med Clin North Am. 1988; 72:1133.

50 **Zung BJ.** Psychometric properties of the MAST and two briefer versions. J Stud Alcohol. 1979;40:845.

51 **Selzer ML et al.** A self-administered Short Michigan Alcoholism Screening Test (SMAST). J Stud Alcohol. 1975; 36:117.

52 **Magruder-Habib K et al.** Validation of the Veterans Alcoholism Screening Test. J Stud Alcohol. 1982;43:910.

53 **Magruder-Habib K et al.** Relative performance of the MAST, VAST, and CAGE versus DSM-III-R criteria for alcohol dependence. J Clin Epidemiol. 1993;46:435.

54 **Skinner HA.** The drug abuse screening test. Addict Behav. 1982;7:363.

55 **Gavin DR et al.** Diagnostic validity of the Drug Abuse Screening Test in the assessment of DSM-III-R drug disorders. Br J Addict. 1989;84:301.

56 **Staley D, El-Guebaly N.** Psychometric properties of the Drug Abuse Screening Test in a psychiatric patient population. Addict Behav. 1990;15:257.

57 **Warner M, Mooney A.** The hospital treatment of alcoholism and drug addiction. Prim Care. 1993;20:95.

58 **Collins GB et al.** A multidisciplinary team approach to the treatment of drug and alcohol addiction. In: Miller NS, ed. Comprehensive Handbook of Drug and Alcohol Addiction. New York: Marcel-Dekker; 1991:981–99.

59 **Hoffman NG et al.** ASAM Patient Placement Criteria for the Treatment of Psychoactive Substance Use Disorders. Washington, DC: American Society of Addiction Medicine; 1991.

60 **Collins GM.** Contemporary issues in the treatment of alcohol dependence. Psychiatr Clin North Am. 1993;16:33.

61 **Resimann F.** Sources of the New Self Help Backlash. New York, NY: National Self Help Clearing House; 1990.

62 **Room R, Greenfield T.** Alcoholics anonymous, other 12 step movements and psychotherapy in the US population, 1990. Addiction. 1993;88:555.

63 **Carroll S.** Spirituality and purpose in life in alcoholism recovery. J Stud Alcohol. 1993;54:297.

64 **Marron J.** The twelve steps: a pathway to recovery. Prim Care. 1993;20: 107.

65 **Alcoholics Anonymous World Services, Inc.** Alcoholics Anonymous. 3rd ed. New York, NY: Alcoholics Anonymous World Services, Inc.; 1976.

66 **Ostrea EM, Cavus CS.** Perinatal problems (excluding neonatal withdrawal) in maternal drug addiction: a study of 830 cases. J Pediatr. 1979;94:292.

67 **Zelson C et al.** Neonatal narcotic addiction: 10 year observation. J Pediatr. 1971;48:178.

68 **Zuckerman B et al.** Effects of maternal marijuana and cocaine use on fetal growth. N Engl J Med. 1989;320:762.

69 **Cavus CJ et al.** Sudden infant death syndrome among infants of drug dependent mothers. J Pediatr. 1979;95:407.

70 **Wilson GS.** Clinical studies of infants and children exposed prenatally to heroin. Ann N Y Acad Sci. 1989;562:183.

71 **Gomby DS, Shiono PH.** Estimating the number of substance-exposed infants. The future of children. Center for the Future of Children. 1991;1:17.

72 **Szeto HH.** Kinetics of drug transfer to the fetus. Clin Obstet Gynecol. 1993; 36:246.

73 **Mihaly GW, Morgan DJ.** Placental drug transfer: effects of gestational age and species. Pharmacol Ther. 1984;23: 253.

74 **Reynolds F, Knott C.** Pharmacokinetics in pregnancy and placental drug transfer. Oxf Rev Reprod Biol. 1989; 11:389.

75 **Szeto HH et al.** Meperidine pharmacokinetics in the maternal-fetal unit. J Pharmacol Exp Ther. 1978;206:448.

76 **Brien JF et al.** Disposition of acute, multiple-dose ethanol in the near-term pregnant ewe. Am J Obstet Gynecol. 1987;157:204.

77 **Dvorchik BH et al.** Hydroxylation and glucuronidation of various xenobiotics in hepatic microsomes from the fetal lamb. Dev Pharmacol Ther. 1986;9:282.

78 **Szeto HH et al.** Urinary excretion of meperidine by the fetal lamb. J Pharmacol Exp Ther. 1979;209:244.

79 **Szeto HH et al.** Renal tubular secretion of meperidine by the fetal lamb. J Pharmacol Exp Ther. 1980;213:346.

80 **Clarke DW et al.** The role of fetal urinary excretion in the transfer of ethanol into amniotic fluid after maternal administration of ethanol to the near-term pregnant ewe. Can J Physiol Pharmacol. 1987;65:1120.

81 **Ostrea EM et al.** Drug screening of meconium in infants of drug-dependent mothers: an alternative to urine testing. J Pediatr. 1989;115:474.

82 **Ostrea EM et al.** Drug screening of newborns by meconium analysis: a large-scale, prospective, epidemiologic study. Pediatrics. 1992;89:107.

83 **Graham K et al.** Determination of gestational cocaine exposure by hair analysis. JAMA. 1989;262:3328.

84 **Forman R et al.** Accumulation of cocaine in maternal and fetal hair: the dose-response curve. Life Sci. 1992; 50:1333.

85 **Stillman RJ et al.** Smoking and reproduction. Fertil Steril. 1986;46:545.

86 **Centers for Disease Control.** Smoking-attributable mortality and years of potential life lost — United States, 1984. MMWR. 1987;36:693.

87 **Surgeon General.** The health consequences of smoking for women: a report of the surgeon general, 1983. US Dept of Health and Human Services, 1983; DHHS publication no. 410-889; 1284:191.

88 **Cunningham FG et al.** Prenatal care. In: Williams Obstetrics. Norwalk: Appleton & Lange; 1993:247–71, 959–80.

89 **Williamson DR et al.** Comparing the prevalence of smoking in pregnant and nonpregnant women, 1985 to 1986. JAMA. 1989;261:70.

90 **Sokol RJ, Clarren SK.** Guidelines for use of terminology describing the impact of prenatal alcohol on the offspring. Alcohol Clin Exp Res. 1989;13: 597.

91 **Jones KL et al.** Pattern of malformation in offspring of chronic alcoholic mothers. Lancet. 1973;1:1267.

92 **Mills JL, Granbard BI.** Is moderate drinking during pregnancy associated with an increased risk of malformations? Pediatrics. 1987;80:309.

93 **Abel EL, Sokol RF.** Incidence of fetal alcohol syndrome and economic impact of FAS-related anomalies. Drug Alcohol Depend. 1987;19:51.

94 **Day NL, Richardson GA.** Prenatal alcohol exposure: a continuum of effects. Semin Perinatol. 1991;15:271.

95 **Virji SK.** The relationship between alcohol consumption during pregnancy and infant birthweight. Acta Obstet Gynecol Scand. 1991;70:303.

96 **Royal College of Psychiatrists.** Alcohol and alcoholism. Ball R Coll Psychiatr. 1982;6:69.

97 **Zuckerman B et al.** Effects of maternal marijuana and cocaine use on fetal growth. N Engl J Med. 1989;320:762.

98 **Fried PA, Makin J.** Neonatal behavior correlates of prenatal exposure to marijuana, cigarettes and alcohol in a low risk population. Neurotoxicol Teratol. 1987;9:1.

99 **Fried PA et al.** Neonatal neurological status in a low-risk population after prenatal exposure to cigarettes, marijuana and alcohol. J Dev Behav Pediatr. 1987;8:318.

100 **Fried PA, Watkinson B.** 36- and 48-month neurobehavioral follow-up of children prenatally exposed to marijuana, cigarettes and alcohol. J Dev Behav Pediatr. 1990;11;49.

101 **Erickson M et al.** Amphetamine addiction and pregnancy. Acta Obstet Gynecol Scand. 1981;60:253.

102 **Oro AS, Dixon SD.** Perinatal cocaine and methamphetamine exposure: maternal and neonatal correlates. J Pediatr. 1987;111:571.

103 **Glantz JC, Woods JR.** Cocaine, heroin and phencyclidine: obstetric perspectives. Clin Obstet Gynecol. 1993; 36:279.

104 **Brown ER, Zuckerman B.** The infant of the drug-abusing mother. Pediatr Ann. 1991;20:555.

105 **Finnegan LP.** Neonatal abstinence syndrome. In: Nelson NM, ed. Current Therapy in Neonatal-Perinatal Medicine — 2. Philadelphia, BC Decker, 1990:314–20.

106 **Finnegan LP.** Perinatal substance abuse: comments and perspectives. Semin Perinatol. 1991;15:331.

107 **Inaba DS, Cohen WE.** Uppers, Downers, All Arounders. 2nd ed. Ashland, OR: CNS Productions; 1993:208.

108 **Connolly WB, Marshall AB.** Drug addiction, pregnancy and childbirth: legal issues for the medical and social services communities. Clin Perinatol. 1991;18:147.

109 **Dusenbury L et al.** Adolescent substance abuse: a sociodevelopmental perspective. In: Lowinson JH et al., eds. Substance Abuse A Comprehensive Textbook. 2nd ed. Baltimore: Williams and Wilkins; 1992:832-42.

110 **Johnston LD.** National Survey Results on Drug Use from Monitoring the Future Study, 1975-1992: Volume I Secondary School Students. Rockville, MD: National Institute on Drug Abuse; 1993. NIH publication no. 93-3597.

111 **Kandel D, Yamaguchi K.** From beer to crack: developmental patterns of drug involvement. Am J Pub Health. 1993;83:851.

112 **Miller JD.** Epidemiology of drug use among adolescents. In: Lettieri DJ, Ludford JP, eds. Drug Abuse and the American Adolescent. NIDA Research Monograph No. 38. Rockville, US Department of Health and Human Services (ADM), 1984:84.

113 **Farrow JA.** Adolescent chemical dependency. Med Clin North Amer. 1990;74:1265.

114 **Jessor R, Jessor SL.** Adolescent development and the onset of drinking. J Stud Alcohol. 1975;36:27.

115 **Gross J, McCaul ME.** A comparison of drug use and adjustment in urban adolescent children of substance abusers. Int J Addict. 1990-1991;25:495.

116 **Blume SB.** Alcohol and other drug problems in women. In: Lowinson JH et al., eds. Substance Abuse A Comprehensive Textbook. 2nd ed. Baltimore: Williams and Wilkins; 1992:794-807.

117 **Gambert SR.** Substance abuse in the elderly. In: Lowinson JH et al., eds. Substance Abuse A Comprehensive Textbook. 2nd ed. Baltimore: Williams and Wilkins; 1992:843-51.

118 **Haugland S.** Alcoholism and other drug dependencies. Prim Care. 1989; 16:411.

119 **Seitz HK et al.** Human gastric alcohol dehydrogenase activity: effect of age, sex, and alcoholism. Gut. 1993;34: 1433.

120 **Cabaj RP.** Substance abuse in the gay and lesbian community. In: Lowinson JH et al., eds. Substance Abuse A Comprehensive Textbook. 2nd ed. Baltimore: Williams and Wilkins; 1992: 852-60.

121 **Brown LS, Alterman AI.** African Americans. In: Lowinson JH et al., eds. Substance Abuse A Comprehensive Textbook. 2nd ed. Baltimore: Williams and Wilkins; 1992:861-67.

122 **Ruiz P, Langrod JG.** Substance abuse among Hispanic-Americans: current issues and future perspectives. In: Lowinson JH et al., eds. Substance Abuse A Comprehensive Textbook. 2nd ed. Baltimore: Williams and Wilkins; 1992: 868-74.

123 **Joseph H.** Substance abuse and homelessness within the inner cities. In: Lowinson JH et al., eds. Substance Abuse A Comprehensive Textbook. 2nd ed. Baltimore: Williams and Wilkins; 1992:875-89.

124 **Westermeyer J.** Cultural perspectives: native Americans, Asians, and new immigrants. In: Lowinson JH et al., eds. Substance Abuse A Comprehensive Textbook. 2nd ed. Baltimore: Williams and Wilkins; 1992:890-6.

125 **Hankes L, Bissell L.** Health professionals. In: Lowinson JH et al., eds. Substance Abuse A Comprehensive Textbook. 2nd ed. Baltimore: Williams and Wilkins; 1992:897-908.

126 **Chappel JN.** Attitudes toward the treatment of substance abusers. In: Lowinson JH et al., eds. Substance Abuse A Comprehensive Textbook. 2nd ed. Baltimore: Williams and Wilkins; 1992: 983-96.

127 **Davis AK et al.** Educational strategies for clinicians. Primary Care. 1993;20: 241.

128 **Ross HE et al.** The prevalence of psychiatric disorders in patients with alcohol and other drug problems. Arch Gen Psychiatry. 1988;45:1023.

129 **Hesselbrock MN et al.** Psychopathology in hospitalized alcoholics. Arch Gen Psychiatry. 1985;42:1050.

130 **Myers J et al.** Six month prevalence of psychiatric disorders in three communities. Arch Gen Psychiatry. 1984; 41:959.

131 **Bergman HC, Harris M.** Substance abuse among young adult chronic patients. Psychosocial Rehab J. 1985;9: 49.

132 **Safer D.** Substance abuse by young adult chronic patients. Hosp Community Psychiatry. 1987;38:511.

133 **Davidson RT et al.** Symptom and comorbidity patterns in World War II and Vietnam veterans with post traumatic stress disorder. Compr Psychiatry. 1990;31:162.

134 **Escobar JI et al.** Post traumatic stress disorder in Hispanic Vietnam veterans. Clinical phenomenology and sociocultural characteristics. J Nerv Ment Dis. 1983;171:585.

135 **Keane TM, Fairbank JA.** Survey analysis of combat-related stress disorders in Vietnam veterans. Am J Psychiatry. 1983;140:348.

136 **McFall ME et al.** Combat related PTSD and psychosocial adjustment problems among substance abusing veterans. J Nerv Ment Dis. 1991;179:33.

137 **Sierles FS et al.** Post traumatic stress disorder and concurrent psychiatric illness: a preliminary report. Am J Psychiatry. 1983;140:1177.

138 **Sierles FS et al.** Concurrent psychiatric illness in non-Hispanic outpatients diagnosed as having post traumatic stress disorder. J Nerv Ment Dis. 1986; 174:171.

139 **Center for Disease Control.** Health status of Vietnam veterans. Volume IV psychological and neuropsychological evaluation. Atlanta, GA: U.S. Department of Health and Human Services Public Health Service Center for Disease Control, 1989.

140 **Ross HE et al.** The prevalence of psychiatric disorders in patients with alcohol and other drug problems. Arch Gen Psychiatry. 1988;45:1023.

141 **Sheehan M.** Dual diagnosis. Psychiatr Q. 1993;64:107.

142 **Evans KE, Sullivan JM.** The nature of the disorder. In: Evans KE, Sullivan JM, eds. Dual Diagnosis: Counseling the Mentally Ill Substance Abuser. New York: Guilford Press; 1990:1-12.

143 **Burke TR.** The economic impact of alcohol abuse and alcoholism. Pub Health Rep. 1988;103:564.

144 **National Institute on Drug Abuse.** National Household Survey on Drug Abuse: Main Findings 1991. Rockville, MD: Substance Abuse and Mental Health Services Administration, 1993; DHHS publication no. (SMA) 93-1980.

145 **Engelhart P et al.** The workplace. In: Lowinson JH et al., eds. Substance Abuse A Comprehensive Textbook. 2nd ed. Baltimore: Williams and Wilkins; 1992:1034-48.

146 **DuPont RL.** Medicines and drug testing in the workplace. J Psychoact Drugs. 1990;22:451.

147 **Osterloh JD, Becker CE.** Chemical dependency and drug testing in the workplace. J Psychoact Drugs. 1990; 22:407.

148 **Brooks MK.** Ethical and legal aspects of confidentiality. In: Lowinson JH et al., eds. Substance Abuse A Comprehensive Textbook. 2nd ed. Baltimore: Williams and Wilkins; 1992:1049-66.

Alcohol Abuse

Paul W Jungnickel
David M Hunnicutt

Alcohol Content and Definitions 82-1
Consumption, Consequences, and Costs 82-1
Societal Response 82-2
Pharmacokinetics and Pharmacology 82-2
Acute Ethanol Intoxication 82-4
Clinical Presentation 82-4
Toxicology 82-4
Management of respiratory depression 82-4
Serum ethanol concentration 82-4
Calculating ethanol levels
(See Equations 82.1 and 82.2) 82-5
Acute Management 82-5
Hypotension 82-5
Hypoglycemia 82-5
Other Treatment Modalities 82-5
Gastrointestinal (GI) decontamination 82-5
Fructose 82-5
Hemodialysis 82-5
Alcohol Withdrawal 82-5
Signs and Symptoms 82-5
Therapy (Also see Table 82.1) 82-6

Chronic Alcoholism 82-6
Etiology 82-6
Diagnosis 82-7
Treatment Programs 82-7
Drug Therapy 82-7
Disulfiram Aversion Therapy 82-7
Patient selection 82-7
Physiological response 82-8
Dosage and precautions 82-8
Effects of Chronic Alcoholism 82-8
Hepatitis 82-8
Hematologic 82-9
Fetal Effects 82-9
Gastritis and Ulcer Disease 82-9
H_2-receptor antagonist interactions 82-10
Cancer 82-10
Pancreatitis 82-10
Wernicke-Korsakoff Syndrome 82-10
Cardiovascular 82-11
Endocrine 82-11
Myopathy 82-12

Alcohol Content and Definitions

Ethyl alcohol (ethanol) is one of the few intoxicating drugs which is widely available for legal human consumption throughout most countries in the world. Various beverages are available with a wide range of ethanol content. Available products include light beer (2% to 4% ethanol), beer (4% to 6% ethanol), ale and special beers (up to about 12% ethanol), wine (10% to 20% ethanol), and distilled beverages such as whiskey, rum, cognac, and liqueurs (most 35% to 55% ethanol, some as high as 95% ethanol). These products are prepared by fermentation or a combination of fermentation and distillation. Beer and wine are prepared by yeast fermentation which continues until the concentration of ethanol kills the yeast. The characteristic ethanol concentrations of the various beverages are determined by the type of yeast used in the fermentation. Beverages with higher concentrations of alcohol are prepared by distillation of wines and fermented grains, a process which concentrates the alcohol. Proof is another term used to refer to the alcohol content and typically is used when referring to distilled beverages. Proof is calculated by multiplying the ethanol concentration by two. Thus, 80 proof whiskey is 40% ethanol by volume; absolute (100%) ethanol is 200 proof. Several measures of alcohol are used commonly. A shot is 30 mL and a jigger is 45 mL. A fifth refers to one-fifth of a gallon which is 768 mL.

Denatured alcohol is ethanol which is rendered unsuitable for human consumption by addition of contaminants in the formulation which are specifically described by U.S. law.[1] Denatured alcohol is identified as SD Alcohol or SDA, which refers to "special denatured ethanols." For example, SD Alcohol 40 is a solution of ethanol with the addition of 0.125% v/w tert-butyl alcohol. Typical rubbing alcohols are 70% denatured alcohol or isopropanol. Colognes, perfumes, and after-shave lotions generally contain 70% to 90% ethanol, but are unsuitable for consumption due to other toxic ingredients.

The legal definition of drunkenness in most states in the U.S. is a 0.1% (100 mg/dL) blood alcohol concentration, although some states have lowered the legal limit to 0.08% (80 mg/dL). In the medical literature, ethanol usually is expressed in mg/dL although the Standard International (SI) units system which expresses concentrations in mmol/L is being used increasingly. The conversion used is (mg/dL) $\times$ (0.2171) = mmol/L. Thus a blood ethanol level of 100 mg/dL is expressed as 21.7 mmol/L.[2]

Consumption, Consequences, and Costs

Despite the fact that the overall use of alcohol has decreased in recent years, alcohol remains the most commonly used and socially accepted drug in the U.S.[3] In terms of prevalence, a household survey of persons 18 and older found that while 32% of adults in the U.S. abstain from using alcohol, approximately 68% reported consuming alcohol at least once in the past year.[4] In addition, men are more likely than women to be drinkers, and to be heavier drinkers. For the total population, whites are significantly more likely than blacks or Hispanics to have consumed alcohol in the past year.

In 1987, the per capita consumption of alcohol in the U.S. was 2.54 gallons of pure alcohol.[5] This is the amount of alcohol one would obtain from approximately 50 gallons of beer, 20 gallons of wine, or four gallons of distilled spirits.[6] However, it is important to understand that alcohol consumption is not evenly distributed across the population. Even though two-thirds of the adult population drink, approximately 5% to 10% of all drinkers (those who drink most heavily) drink half of all the alcohol consumed.[7]

Although the use of alcohol is illegal in all 50 states for anyone under the age of 21, its use remains widespread among young people.[8] In fact, 92% of high school students have tried alcohol and 64% of high-school seniors are current users (i.e., they have used it within the past month).[9] Approximately 35% of high school seniors have had five or more drinks in a row within the past two weeks.

Epidemiologic data indicate that alcohol consumption is far from a risk-free activity, and is widely associated with a variety of health concerns.[10] Annually, alcohol use contributes to nearly six million nonfatal injuries at home, at play, or in public places.[11] As many as 18 million Americans show signs of alcoholism or alcohol dependence.[10] Fetal alcohol syndrome (FAS) is one of the most common known causes of birth defects with accompanying mental retardation, and is entirely preventable.[12] High-risk alcohol use also is associated with liver cirrhosis, cardiovascular disease, and a variety of cancers, including mouth, throat, breast, and colorectal.[13–16] Several alcohol-related behaviors (e.g., dependence, abuse, and heavier drinking) are associated with significantly greater risk for human immunodeficiency virus (HIV) infection.[17]

Perhaps the most serious health consequence of alcohol abuse is death.[18] Alcohol is closely connected to the four leading causes of accidental deaths in the U.S.: auto crashes, falls, drownings, and burns.[19] Nearly half (45%) of all fatal highway crashes involve alcohol; 17,699 people died from such crashes in 1992.[20] In the workplace, up to 40% of industrial fatalities can be linked to alcohol consumption and alcoholism.[21]

As has been clearly demonstrated, alcohol is a major cause of premature death in the U.S. In fact, misuse of alcohol contributes to approximately 100,000 deaths annually.[10] On average, people who die from alcohol-related causes lose 26 years from their normal life expectancy.[7] Deaths, injuries, and other negative consequences related to alcohol consumption also represent serious health problems for today's young people, with adolescents and young adults having a particularly high rate of alcohol-related mortality and morbidity.[22,23] With respect to morbidity, alcohol is the major cause of all nonfatal crashes involving teen-aged drivers.[24] Moreover, the death rates in the U.S. for these age groups are dominated by causes associated with alcohol consumption. The number one killer of teens and young adults is the alcohol-related traffic crash.[25] Alcohol use also is associated with homicides, suicides, and drownings (the other three leading causes of death among youth).[26]

The expensive and devastating costs of alcohol abuse are a matter of national concern.[27] In 1990, the cost of alcohol abuse and dependence was estimated at $98.6 billion, an increase of $28.3 billion from the 1985 estimate of $70.3 billion.[28] Specifically, alcohol abuse and dependency are costly to the nation in reduced and lost productivity, medical resources used, treatment and rehabilitation, law enforcement, and motor vehicle crashes.[29]

For 1990, the direct costs of alcohol abuse amounted to $10.5 billion.[28] Morbidity costs (i.e., the value of reduced or lost productivity due to illness) amounted to $36.6 billion while mortality costs (i.e., the value of work years lost) amounted to $33.6 billion.[28] Other alcohol-related costs (e.g., crime, motor vehicle crashes, FAS) amounted to $15.8 billion.[28] In addition, alcohol abuse generated a large demand on the nation's health care system.[15] Problem drinkers average four times as many days in the hospital as nondrinkers, primarily because of alcohol-related injuries.[7] Further, research indicates that as many as 40% of all patients in general hospitals are there because of complications related to alcoholism.[7]

Societal Response

Because alcohol has been identified as the most widely used and abused drug in the U.S., and one which imposes enormous human and economic costs on our society, substantial attention has been focused on reducing and/or preventing the incidence and prevalence of high-risk alcohol use and related consequences.[29]

Perhaps the most common strategy for addressing high-risk alcohol use has been informational campaigns and educational programs outlining the dangers of drinking. Most of these programs are found within school systems, particularly at the elementary and secondary levels.[30] However, as a result of growing societal awareness of the human and economic costs attributable to alcohol abuse, and governmental mandates (e.g., the Drug-Free Workplace Act, the Drug-Free Schools and Communities Act), alcohol education programs now can be found in colleges, the workplace, and community settings.[31–33]

In addition, society has attempted to prevent alcohol-related problems by strengthening the social controls that regulate an individual's use or possession of alcoholic beverages.[33] These formal social controls have been expressed in the form of state and federal laws (e.g., minimum legal drinking age laws, open container laws) and institutional rules and sanctions (e.g., schools, colleges, worksites).[8]

Establishing rigorous physical and social controls regarding the availability of alcoholic beverages also has become a prevention priority and has received increased attention in recent years.[34] Physical availability is concerned with controlling the form and size of alcoholic beverage containers; the concentration of ethanol in beverages; the location, number, and density of retail outlets that sell alcoholic beverages; and the hours of the day or days of the week that beverages can be sold.[33] Social availability is concerned with controlling the promotion of alcoholic beverages at the point of purchase, within the community, and in the mass media.[35]

Researchers in the fields of injury prevention and traffic safety, as well as those interested in alcohol, have worked diligently to create safer physical environments through the adoption of passive countermeasures.[29] These are expected to reduce the incidence of alcohol-related casualties by making the environment more tolerant of the inept behavior that occurs due to the intoxicating effects of alcohol use. Examples of passive countermeasures include installing airbags in vehicles, enhancing driver perception by lighting more sections of the roadway at night, or by installing high-mounted brake lights in the center rear of the car. As a result of increased attention, prevention efforts in the U.S. are becoming more sophisticated. Ideally, the combined effects of primary prevention and educational efforts across a variety of settings (e.g., schools, worksites, the community at large) will, over time, have an increasingly positive impact on societal alcohol use behaviors. At present, however, alcohol abuse continues to present a significant challenge for health professionals, prevention specialists, and policymakers. As a result, clinicians can expect to routinely encounter patients with ethanol-related problems. By maintaining an accurate, current knowledge base concerning the issues surrounding alcohol use and abuse, health professionals will be equipped with the knowledge and skills necessary to address the issue should it arise within a professional situation. The remainder of the chapter will be devoted to clinical issues related to the management of various manifestations of alcohol abuse.

Pharmacokinetics and Pharmacology

When consumed in amounts typical of normal social drinking, the absorption of alcohol from the stomach, small intestine, and colon is complete; however, the rate is variable. Peak blood ethanol concentrations after oral doses in fasting subjects generally are reached in 30 to 75 minutes; however, a number of factors can influence the rate and extent of absorption.[36] The most rapidly absorbed formulations are carbonated beverages containing 10% to 30% ethanol. In contrast, very high concentrations of alcohol can produce vasoconstriction in the gastrointestinal (GI) mucosa which results in slowed or even incomplete absorption of ethanol. Absorption of ethanol from the small intestine appears to be more rapid than from any other part of the GI tract and is not dependent upon the presence or absence of food. Factors which control the rate of gastric emptying will significantly control the rate of absorption by controlling the rate at which ethanol is delivered to the small intestine. For example, beer or food in the stomach will slow the absorption of alcohol, probably by slowing gastric emptying.

The level of intoxication achieved is not solely related to the plasma concentration. For any particular plasma concentration, greater cognitive impairment is seen during times when the plasma level is rising than when ethanol is primarily being eliminated. The degree of intoxication also appears to be directly related to the rate at which pharmacologically active plasma concentrations are attained.[37]

Ethanol is distributed throughout the body with reported volumes of distribution of 0.58 to 0.70 L/kg; calculations typically use an average volume of distribution of 0.65 L/kg. The alcohol dehydrogenase pathway is the major enzyme system responsible for alcohol metabolism in humans. This pathway is found in Figure 82.1.

Alcohol dehydrogenase is found both in the gastric mucosa and liver. The pathway involves conversion of ethanol to acetaldehyde via alcohol dehydrogenase, resulting in the reduction of nicotine-adenine-dinucleotide (NAD+) to NADH. The second step is the conversion of acetaldehyde to acetate which also reduces NAD+ to NADH. These are the rate limiting steps in ethanol metabolism and this route becomes saturated when large amounts of ethanol deplete NAD+.[38] Acetate ultimately is converted to carbon dioxide and water.

In some situations, a portion of the absorbed dose of alcohol does not appear to enter the systemic circulation, suggesting first-pass metabolism. Alcohol dehydrogenase located in the gastric mucosa has been thought to account for this response, although this effect also has been attributed to hepatic alcohol dehydrogenase.[39-42] Although gastric alcohol dehydrogenase has a lower affinity for ethanol compared to hepatic alcohol dehydrogenase, it is thought to be capable of exerting significant metabolic effects at alcohol concentrations found in the stomach after a drink. The extent of first-pass extraction tends to be decreased as the dose of alcohol increases. This is likely due to saturation of alcohol dehydrogenase regardless of source. Lower first-pass metabolism also has been found in persons with alcoholism, women, the eld-

erly, and Japanese subjects.[39,41,43] Gastric alcohol dehydrogenase also may play a role in the effect of food in reducing ethanol bioavailability. Food, by delaying gastric emptying, will allow for more extensive gastric metabolism.

Ninety to ninety-eight percent of a dose of ethanol is oxidized in the liver, with the remaining drug excreted unchanged in the alveolar air and by the kidneys. As the plasma ethanol level increases, hepatic alcohol dehydrogenase becomes saturated, resulting in increased unchanged excretion of alcohol. This results in a more intense odor of alcohol on the breath as the plasma ethanol concentration increases.

Ethanol metabolism formerly was described by zero-order kinetics, however, Michaelis-Menten and other nonlinear, concentration-dependent models are more accurate.[44-46] When plasma ethanol levels are greater than 200 mg/dL, the alcohol dehydrogenase system tends to become saturated. The metabolism of alcohol then tends to become nonlinear due to stimulation of cytochrome P450 and the microsomal ethanol oxidizing system.[47]

The accepted average rate of ethanol oxidation commonly reported in the medical literature is 15 mg/dL/hour for men and 18 mg/dL/hour for women.[48] While this rate still is widely used for both legal and medical purposes, other data suggest wide variability among individuals with regard to ethanol metabolism. For example, wide differences in alcohol dehydrogenase activity have been demonstrated and attributed to heredity and other causes.[49,50] Chronic heavy drinkers frequently oxidize ethanol at twice the accepted rates, with their metabolic rates returning to baseline after a period of abstinence.[51] The rate of oxidation in chronic heavy drinkers also may increase with elevated blood ethanol levels.[52] In contrast, patients with end-stage liver disease may progress to the point where they have almost no metabolic capacity. Thus, serial determinations of plasma ethanol concentrations are needed to evaluate pharmacokinetic parameters in a particular patient.

Since the enzymatic oxidation of ethanol to acetaldehyde (see Figure 82.1) is accompanied by the reduction of NAD+ to NADH and H+, chronic ethanol use will result in a reduction of the available supply of NAD+ and an overproduction of NADH by the liver. To compensate for this, all the metabolic reactions in the liver will try to convert NADH back to NAD+. Several characteristic pathologic changes seen in persons with alcoholism are the direct result of this hepatic redox state. Pyruvate, rather than being converted to glucose via gluconeogenesis, is reduced preferentially to lactate in order to generate NAD+. This results in hypoglyce-

Fig 82.1 Pathway for Ethanol Metabolism

mia in the absence of plentiful ingestion of dietary carbohydrate, a scenario which is likely in malnourished persons with alcoholism. Hyperuricemia also occurs in chronic alcoholism, since uric acid excretion is inhibited by increased blood lactate levels.

A number of characteristic changes in the liver are found with chronic alcohol use. Hyperlipidemia and fat deposition in the liver occur due to shunting of the excess hydrogen into fatty acid synthesis and direct oxidation of ethanol for energy instead of body fat stores being used for energy. Fatty liver is the first step in a sequence of events that ultimately leads to alcoholic cirrhosis. Accumulated acetaldehyde has been implicated in playing a role in the hepatotoxic process: it interferes with mitochondrial function by shortening and thickening microtubules. The damaged microtubules then inhibit the secretory functions of the hepatocytes, which results in an increase in size and weight of the liver.[53] Although ethanol is widely recognized as a substance associated with significant hepatotoxic potential, the mechanisms have not been identified for its apparently damaging effects on the liver. It has been argued that ethanol is not a hepatotoxin *per se*, and that malnutrition is a co-existing requirement for the development of alcoholic liver disease.[54]

Ethanol ingestion can depress the central nervous system (CNS) through all the different stages of anesthesia. Tolerance to this effect occurs after chronic use such that a blood ethanol level of 150 mg/dL will not produce apparent behavioral or neurological dysfunction in individuals who drink a pint or more of 80 proof liquor (or its equivalent in another beverage) daily for several years.

Ethanol is an irritant to mucosal surfaces throughout the gastrointestinal tract and can produce nausea, vomiting, diarrhea, and bleeding, as well as motor dysfunction. Inflammation with edema and cellular destruction occurs to some degree after acute ingestion, especially of solutions with $\geq 40\%$ ethanol. Erosive gastritis is common in chronic drinkers.[55]

Acute Ethanol Intoxication

Clinical Presentation

Toxicology

1. S.L., a young female, is brought to the emergency room (ER). She is unresponsive, except to noxious stimuli. Her friends report an evening of heavy drinking on the occasion of her 21st birthday. Her respirations are 8 breaths/min and shallow. Blood pressure (BP) is 100/60 mm Hg, pulse is 100 beats/min, and temperature is 36 °C. "Stat" arterial blood gas determination reveals a pH of 7.29, pCO₂ of 52 mm Hg, and HCO₃ of 19 mEq/L. Why is S.L.'s respiratory status of concern? [SI units: pCO₂ 6.9 kPa; HCO₃ 19 mmol/L]

Ethanol can depress respirations by inhibiting the passive neuronal flux of sodium via a mechanism similar to that of general anesthetic agents.[56] The enzyme Na-K ATPase is inhibited, cyclic AMP concentrations are reduced, and gamma-aminobutyric acid (GABA) synthesis is impaired. Ethanol is clearly a central nervous system depressant and even the uninhibited behavior associated with it is due to preferential suppression of inhibitory neurons. More global neuronal inhibition is seen at high ethanol concentrations.

Death in ethanol-intoxicated patients most often is due to respiratory depression, often being accompanied by aspiration of vomitus. Respiratory depression also is responsible for the acid-base abnormality in S.L. which is primarily a respiratory acidosis. Even when blood ethanol levels are below those which cause medullary paralysis, a blunted respiratory response to hypercapnia and hypoxia will be seen.[57,58] This makes the assessment of respiratory status a primary concern in severely intoxicated patients such as S.L.

Management of Respiratory Depression

2. What therapy should be initiated to manage S.L.'s respiratory depression?

Immediate supportive care for S.L. includes endotracheal intubation for respiratory support. This should be sufficient to restore her acid-base balance to within normal limits, since her acidosis is primarily of respiratory origin (pH 7.29, pCO₂ 52 mm Hg). In cases where a metabolic acidosis is a significant component of the acid-base disturbance, it may be necessary to administer sodium bicarbonate. This should be done only in conjunction with appropriate respiratory support to prevent hypercapnia from developing. Analeptic agents such as doxapram (Dopram) and caffeine should not be used because they are ineffective and may cause seizures, arrhythmias, and hypertensive episodes.

S.L. appeared in the emergency room in a comatose state and it is unknown whether she has ingested other drugs. She should be given a 1 mg dose of naloxone (Narcan) because alcohol intoxication frequently is complicated by co-ingestion of other drugs and because naloxone does not have respiratory depressant agonist properties. This dose can be repeated at two to three minute intervals for up to ten doses depending upon patient response and the clinician's index of suspicion for ingestion of respiratory depressants other than alcohol. Naloxone has been used to reverse alcohol-induced coma, to reverse clonidine-induced coma, to treat septic or cardiogenic shock, and to treat acute respiratory failure.[65–69,165–170] While varying results have been seen with naloxone use for these indications that are not Food and Drug Administration (FDA) approved, its use in these conditions is based upon its postulated ability to reverse the effects of endogenous opiate-like agonists in the central nervous system. Use of naloxone generally would be safe in S.L. since, at her age, she probably has not experienced hypersensitivity reactions to naloxone and is not likely to have cardiovascular disease or other contraindications to naloxone use.

Serum Ethanol Concentration

3. Thirty minutes later the following laboratory results are reported: glucose 49 mg/dL; sodium (Na) 142 mEq/L; potassium (K) 3.5 mEq/L; chloride (Cl) 104 mEq/L; HCO₃ 20 mEq/L; blood urea nitrogen (BUN) 18 mg/dL; creatinine 0.9 mg/dL; osmolality 390 mOsm/L; and ethanol 475 mg/dL. Based upon the blood ethanol level, how severe is S.L.'s intoxication? [SI units: glucose 2.7 mmol/L; Na 142 mmol/L; K 3.5 mmol/L; Cl 104 mmol/L; HCO₃ 20 mmol/L; BUN 6.4 mmol/L of urea; creatinine 80 μmol/L; ethanol 103 mmol/L]

The blood ethanol concentration generally correlates with the clinical presentation of the patient, although tolerance varies among individuals. Impairment in motor function may become observable at levels of 50 mg/dL. Moderate motor impairment usually is seen at 80 mg/dL, and, as previously mentioned, the legal definition of intoxication in most states is 100 mg/dL. Respiratory depression may occur with ethanol concentrations greater than 450 mg/dL.[59] Therefore, the respiratory depression found in S.L. correlates well with the reported ethanol level of 475 mg/dL.

The accepted LD₅₀ for ethanol in humans is a blood concentration of 500 mg/dL, although fatalities have been reported with ethanol concentrations ranging from 295 to 699 mg/dL.[60,61] Factors which may be associated with fatalities at lower ethanol concentrations include ingestion of other drugs, heart disease, and pulmonary aspiration. For example, patients who died from combined ethanol and barbiturate ingestions had a mean ethanol concentration of only 359 mg/dL.[61] Therefore, a toxicological screening panel of S.L.'s urine should be obtained to rule out possible concurrent drug ingestion.

In S.L.'s case, both the blood ethanol concentration and respiratory depression are indicative of severe intoxication.

Calculating Ethanol Levels

4. If S.L. were admitted to a facility which could not perform a "stat" blood ethanol level, how could her ethanol level be calculated from other laboratory tests?

The blood ethanol concentration can be calculated from the osmolal (or osmol) gap. The serum osmolality is a measure of the solute which is dissolved in the serum. The major contributors to serum osmolality are sodium, potassium, chloride and bicarbonate ions, and glucose and urea. To simplify matters, only sodium, glucose, and urea are considered when calculating osmolality (see Equation 82.1). The osmol gap is the difference between the measured and calculated serum osmolality (see Equation 82.2).

$$\text{Calculated Osmolality (mOsm/kg)} = [2 \times \text{Na (mEq/dL)}] + \frac{\text{BUN (mg/dL)}}{2.8} + \frac{\text{Glucose (mg/dL)}}{18} \qquad Eq\ 82.1$$

$$\text{Osmol Gap} = \text{Measured Osmolality} - \text{Calculated Osmolality} \qquad Eq\ 82.2$$

An osmol gap is considered significant when the measured osmolality exceeds the calculated value by more than 10 mOsm/kg.[62] The most common sources of an elevated osmol gap are ethylene glycol and alcohols (e.g., ethanol, methanol, isopropanol). Drugs seldom are taken in quantities large enough to produce a significant osmol gap.

The osmol gap can be used to estimate a blood alcohol concentration if the gap is due to the presence of only one type of alcohol. In the case of ethanol, the estimated ethanol concentration in mg/dL is calculated by multiplying the osmol gap by a factor of 4.6. According to Equation 82.1, the calculated serum osmolality for S.L. is 294 mOsm/kg. This results in an osmol gap of 96 and an estimated blood alcohol concentration of 442 mg/dL (as calculated below) which corresponds fairly well with the measured blood ethanol level of 475 mg/dL.

$$\begin{aligned} \text{Osmol Gap} &= \text{Measured Osmolality} - \text{Calculated Osmolality} \\ &= 390\ \text{mOsm/kg} - 294\ \text{mOsm/kg} \\ &= 96\ \text{mOsm/kg} \end{aligned}$$

$$\begin{aligned} \text{Ethanol Serum Concentration} &= \text{Osmol Gap} \times 4.6 \\ &= 96\ \text{mOsm/kg} \times 4.6 \\ &= 442\ \text{mg/dL} \end{aligned}$$

Acute Management

5. After the respiratory support needs of S.L. are attended to, what other clinical conditions warrant attention in S.L.?

Hypotension. Volume depletion frequently occurs in ethanol intoxicated patients, resulting in hypotension. Hypothermia is also a complication of severe intoxication and can contribute to hypotension. S.L.'s blood pressure is not severely low and should normalize with fluid replacement and Trendelenburg bed positioning (i.e., lower portion elevated above upper portion of body).

Hypoglycemia. As previously discussed, hypoglycemia most often occurs in conjunction with reduced carbohydrate intake. This situation is common in malnourished persons with alcoholism but also might be particularly pronounced in S.L. if she were dieting. Since she is hypoglycemic, 50 mL of 50% glucose solution should be administered to her by intravenous (IV) push.

Other Treatment Modalities

6. What medical interventions can facilitate removal of ethanol from S.L.?

Gastrointestinal (GI) Decontamination. Gastric lavage may be useful if ingestion of other drugs is expected, or when a recent large ingestion of alcohol has occurred. Activated charcoal absorbs ethanol poorly and would be of little benefit to S.L., but should be administered when co-ingestion of other drugs is suspected.

Fructose has been advocated by some as a means to increase the metabolism of ethanol but may increase the risk of metabolic acidosis. Thus, it may be particularly hazardous in a patient such as S.L. who already has a respiratory acidosis.[60,63,64]

Hemodialysis rapidly removes ethanol from the body, but no clear guidelines exist as to when it should be used. In uncomplicated cases, it has been suggested that dialysis be initiated when the blood ethanol concentration exceeds 600 mg/dL.[60] However, ventilatory assistance and good supportive care usually are sufficient for most cases, since respiratory depression is the primary cause of death in ethanol intoxication. In the presence of good supportive care, dialysis would not be needed in a patient such as S.L. Dialysis may be considered in situations where the patient cannot be stabilized, or has other complicating factors such as co-existing disease states or ingestion of other drugs.

Alcohol Withdrawal

7. J.R., a 43-year-old male, is taken to the ER by ambulance after a single-car vehicle accident. Police officers at the scene of the accident noticed a heavy odor of alcohol both in the car and on J.R.'s breath. Physical examination upon admission revealed a probable fractured femur which was confirmed by x-ray. His medical record indicates 1 prior hospitalization for alcohol-related seizures. When contacted by telephone, his wife reported that J.R. had been drinking heavily for the past 3 weeks and had missed several days of work. She also reported that about a year ago he had participated for a few weeks in an outpatient alcohol treatment program. Blood ethanol level on admission was reported at 289 mg/dL. What are the immediate clinical concerns which deserve attention in J.R.? [SI unit: blood ethanol 63 mmol/L]

Numerous studies have shown a high incidence of intoxication and alcohol abuse in patients who are seen in emergency rooms and/or admitted to hospitals for both blunt or penetrating trauma, and alcohol-related trauma is seen in all age groups from adolescents to the elderly.[70–75] In cases where the involvement of alcohol is not as apparent as with J.R., patients seen in the emergency room or admitted to the hospital should be screened for alcohol abuse. Fortunately, in J.R.'s case, no innocent bystanders were injured.

J.R.'s fractured femur should be evaluated and properly managed. However, a more important concern in J.R. is the evaluation and treatment of alcohol withdrawal. This occurs when an individual who has been drinking for a long period of time either stops drinking or reduces the amount of ethanol consumed. While there is a great variation between individuals, those who maintain higher ethanol blood levels for longer periods of time will tend to have more severe withdrawal from alcohol.[76,77]

Signs and Symptoms

8. What signs and symptoms of alcohol withdrawal should be monitored in J.R.?

While the hangover syndrome which follows a drinking episode may involve some component of acute withdrawal, it is not considered one of the four stages of true alcohol withdrawal. *Stage one* typically begins within six to eight hours after the blood ethanol level begins to fall. Typical symptoms of stage one reflect a moderate autonomic hyperactivity and include tremulousness, anxiety, hyperreflexia, hypertension, tachycardia, diaphoresis, hyperthermia, nausea, vomiting, insomnia, and a craving for alcohol.

Stage two begins in about 24 hours and has a duration of one to three days. It is characterized by auditory and visual hallucinations, anxiety, tremor, and varying degrees of the autonomic hyperactivity that is seen in stage one. Most patients remain lucid and oriented during this period.

Approximately 4% of untreated patients will progress to *stage three* which involves grand mal seizures which occur from 7 to 48 hours after the drop in blood alcohol concentration. Several isolated seizures can be experienced within a day or two after the onset of withdrawal. This stage also is referred to as ''rum fits.''

Three to five days after the onset of withdrawal symptoms, about 5% of untreated patients will experience *stage four*, which is known as delirium tremens (DTs). Fever of ≥40 °C and untreated seizures during stage three are predictive for patients who will progress to DTs. Typical symptoms include confusion, illusions, hallucinations, agitation, tachycardia, diaphoresis, mydriasis, and fever. The estimated mortality associated with DTs is 5% to 15%, with mortality typically due to aspiration, shock, hyperthermia, cardiac arrhythmias, infection, and trauma.[78,79] Deficiencies in magnesium and potassium also have been implicated in DTs.[80]

Since J.R. has been drinking heavily for several weeks, and has had previously documented seizures, he is at risk for alcohol withdrawal which could be clinically serious. He should be monitored closely for symptoms of withdrawal and provided treatment to prevent withdrawal symptoms.

Therapy

9. What treatment should be provided to J.R. for alcohol withdrawal?

Therapy for ethanol withdrawal should include supportive measures including fluid and electrolyte management, thiamine, multiple vitamins, and magnesium.[81] Patients also should be provided benzodiazepine therapy in doses sufficient to prevent withdrawal symptoms.

Benzodiazepines are the drugs of choice for management of withdrawal due to their proven efficacy in managing withdrawal symptoms, and preventing agitation and seizures. Clinical experience with chlordiazepoxide (Librium), diazepam (Valium), and lorazepam (Ativan) is extensive. Most patients can be managed by high doses of oral benzodiazepine therapy, while parenteral therapy may be required in more acutely agitated and combative patients. For example, intravenous diazepam can be administered with an initial 10 mg IV dose, followed by an additional 5 mg dose every five minutes until the patient is calm. Comparable doses of chlordiazepoxide or lorazepam also may be used. For less severe cases, oral loading doses can be used. The dosage the patient receives can then be tapered in a manner similar to that shown in Table 82.1. Patients should be closely monitored with their benzodiazepine dosage carefully adjusted to provide effective anticonvulsant and sedative endpoints while preventing respiratory depression and hypotension which can result from excessive dosing.

It has been argued that lorazepam should be the benzodiazepine of choice for the management of alcohol withdrawal due to its shorter half-life (10–20 hours) and lack of active metabolites. In contrast, both chlordiazepoxide and diazepam are oxidatively metabolized with the resulting active metabolites having half-lives as long as 100 hours. Thus, a potential advantage of lorazepam may be that its shorter duration of action allows for easier dosage adjustment and prevention of excessive sedation, particularly in patients with significant liver disease. However, the longer-acting benzodiazepines also may have advantages in that their longer du-

Table 82.1	Summary of the Oral Dosing Considerations for Benzodiazepines in the Management of Acute Alcohol Withdrawal[82]	
Drug	Dose: Day 1	Dose: Taper
Diazepam[83]	20 mg, then 20 mg Q 2 hr until calm	Day 2: 10 mg, 5 mg, 10 mg Day 3: 5 mg TID Day 4: 5 mg BID
Chlordiazepoxide[84]	50–100 mg Q 6–8 hr until calm	Day 2: 50–100 mg Q 8 hr Day 3: 50–100 mg Q 12 hr Day 4: 50–100 mg HS
Lorazepam[85,86]	2 mg Q 6–8 hr until calm	Day 2: 2 mg Q 8 hr Day 3: 1 mg Q 8 hr Day 4: 1 mg Q 12 hr

ration of action allows for a smoother withdrawal from alcohol. Another potential advantage of lorazepam is its predictable absorption after intramuscular (IM) administration, while both chlordiazepoxide and diazepam are erratically absorbed via this route of administration especially when administered gluteally (see Chapter 73: Anxiety Disorders). In spite of these theoretical differences between the three agents, the results of limited comparative clinical trials have not been sufficient to establish the superiority of any agent.[79] Regardless of which agent is used, careful patient monitoring and dosage adjustment is of utmost importance.

Some other drugs have shown some utility in the management of withdrawal. Clonidine and beta blockers, particularly atenolol, may be used as ancillary therapy and work by countering adrenergic responses. Carbamazepine (Tegretol) is used widely in Scandinavia but infrequently in the U.S. Further investigation is needed to establish the efficacy of this agent.[82,87] Phenothiazines should not be used to sedate patients undergoing withdrawal because these drugs lower the seizure threshold, may cause hypotension and extrapyramidal effects, and could exacerbate hyperthermia. Antidepressant and other psychiatric medications may be useful in the rehabilitation of selected persons with alcoholism, but should not be used in withdrawal. Sufficient doses of benzodiazepines can control the symptoms of psychosis which occur during withdrawal. The routine prophylactic use of phenytoin (Dilantin) has not been supported by clinical trials and, in fact, may be of no benefit to the withdrawing person with alcoholism.[88] It may, however, be of use in patients with focal neurologic deficits, head trauma, status epilepticus, or underlying seizure disorders.[89,90] Of course, appropriate therapy should be provided to patients developing seizures during withdrawal.

As for J.R., he should be provided with supportive care and monitored for symptoms of alcohol withdrawal. Benzodiazepine therapy should be initiated with the dosage adjusted based upon his symptoms of withdrawal and response to therapy.

Chronic Alcoholism
Etiology

The etiology of chronic alcoholism has been attributed to genetic differences, psychosocial influences, and biochemical differences; however, the precise role of each is unknown. Alcoholism does not occur in everyone who drinks, but chronic drinking is required in order to become a person with alcoholism. Some investigators have attributed the sole cause of alcoholism to psychosocial conditioning and have termed this the ''nurture hypothesis.''[91] However, over the past 40 years, several epidemiologic population surveys and biochemical studies have noted a genetic predisposition to alcoholism, possibly including biochemical alterations in the metabolism of ethanol as well as neuropsychiatric differences in the behavioral response to ingestion of ethanol. This has been termed the "nature hypothesis."[92]

Several lines of evidence provide support for the role of genetic influences. For example, the sons of men with alcoholism have an incidence of alcoholism that is four times that of nonalcoholic men.[93] Several studies have identified similar genetic associations between alcoholism in offspring and parents of the same sex.[94] There also has been a suggestion that alcoholism is an X-linked recessive trait.[95] While possible biochemical markers for alcoholism have been sought, as yet there has been no reasonable screening test developed to identify increased susceptibility to alcoholism.[96]

Diagnosis

While most people seem to have an idea as to what constitutes a person with alcoholism, creating a strict diagnostic profile for this disease has not been easy. This difficulty is highlighted by the greater prevalence of both harmful use/abuse of and dependence on alcohol when the Diagnostic and Statistical Manual of Mental Disorders-Fourth Edition (DSM-IV) criteria are used for diagnosis as compared with the International Classification of Diseases-Tenth Revision (ICD-10).[97] Various questionnaires (CAGE, MAST, SMAST, VAST) which can be used to screen for the presence of alcoholism are discussed in Chapter 81: Issues: Psychoactive Substance Use Disorders, along with the DSM-IV criteria for substance dependence.[98] Thus, a variety of instruments could be used to assess the possibility of alcoholism in J.R. When using the DSM-IV, it is necessary for at least three of seven criteria to be met for a diagnosis of substance abuse. From the limited information available about J.R., it can be seen that he meets four of the DSM-IV criteria.

10. How can the diagnosis of alcoholism be discussed with J.R.?

Most persons with alcoholism will be reluctant to reveal their disease, and truly may believe that they do not have a problem. The majority will attempt to maintain the appearance of a normal and reasonably successful life. Even individuals such as J.R., who have been drinking continuously for several weeks, often will deny that they have a problem and will argue that they are able to control their alcohol consumption. Thus, when interviewing patients who deny that they have drinking problems, it is important to emphasize all objective data that support this diagnosis including medical complications related to drinking. Chronic drinkers may well consume the equivalent of one- to two-fifths of 80 proof liquor per day, but typically will underreport the amount consumed. However, consumption of much less than this may represent alcoholism. The common social belief that one must drink every day to be a person with alcoholism is also not accurate; weekend or binge drinkers also may have alcoholism. The issue is not necessarily how much one drinks, but rather, the loss of control once drinking starts and continued use despite clear evidence of adverse consequences. When questioning the patient about the amount consumed, the approach should be to start with large amounts and then work down. Many persons with alcoholism are great confabulators and will be able to counter each of the interviewer's subjective impressions. In confronting J.R., it is important to be firm in stressing the urgent need for treatment.

Treatment Programs

11. What treatment approach would be appropriate for J.R.?

After J.R. is successfully withdrawn from alcohol he should be referred to an alcohol treatment program. The various levels of treatment, ranging from outpatient treatment to intensive inpatient treatment, are discussed in Chapter 81: Issues: Psychoactive Sub-

stance Use Disorders. The selection of the type of program will depend not only upon the seriousness of J.R.'s disease, but also upon his ability to pay for treatment, either from his own finances or via insurance. Participation in an Alcoholics Anonymous (AA) group during and after treatment also is recommended. J.R.'s success in the treatment program will be positively influenced if he is willing to acknowledge his alcoholism and become an active participant in his treatment program and AA meetings.

The goal for J.R.'s successful recovery from alcoholism is complete abstinence from alcohol consumption. However, approximately 75% of recovering persons with alcoholism will relapse into periods of intoxication. Although there are reports of some persons with alcoholism being able to successfully resume limited consumption of alcohol, it cannot be recommended as few persons with alcoholism are able to evolve to stable moderate drinking.[99] It is also important to remember that many of the medical and psychiatric complications associated with years of heavy alcohol abuse can be exacerbated by resumption of alcohol use even in limited amounts.[100]

Drug Therapy

12. What drug therapy is available to assist J.R. in his recovery from alcoholism?

Drug therapy plays a secondary role in the management of alcoholism and should not be considered a substitute for participation in a treatment program and AA. Antidepressant, antipsychotic, and antimanic drugs are useful therapeutic adjuncts when specific untreated psychiatric conditions may be contributing to the patient's alcohol abuse. Benzodiazepines and other anxiolytic agents exhibit cross tolerance with ethanol. However, these CNS depressants do not appear to reduce chronic alcohol consumption and may replace ethanol as the drug of abuse.[101]

Future directions for the pharmacologic management of alcoholism may possibly include drugs with serotonergic effects. A number of studies have suggested that drugs such as fluvoxamine and zimelidine, which block serotonin reuptake, may attenuate alcohol consumption. In contrast, serotonin depletion promotes alcohol use.[102–105] Agents with mixed serotonin and norepinephrine reuptake blocking properties do not appear to be as effective.

In J.R.'s case, appropriate drug therapy should be provided based upon underlying disease states or as required for control of specific symptoms.

Disulfiram Aversion Therapy

Patient Selection

13. Why would disulfiram (Antabuse) therapy be appropriate for J.R.?

The rationale behind aversion therapy is that patients will not drink ethanol because they will fear the very unpleasant and potentially life-threatening effects which occur when ethanol is co-ingested with disulfiram. Although there are several drugs which can sensitize patients to ethanol, disulfiram is the only drug clinically used for this purpose in the U.S. Patients most likely to benefit from disulfiram are those who desire to remain abstinent, but have had periodic binge relapses. To be considered for disulfiram, patients must want to take the drug, be socially stable and not depressed, and have no medical contraindications to its use. Careful monitoring of compliance and adverse effects is essential in patients receiving disulfiram.[106] Since J.R. currently is just initiating treatment for his alcoholism, disulfiram would not be appropriate at the present time but could be considered should he have problems with binge relapses and be willing to take the drug to deter drinking episodes.

Physiological Response

14. J.R. successfully completes an outpatient treatment program, but has difficulty maintaining abstinence. After his third relapse in a 20-month period, he requests treatment with disulfiram. What would be the physiological response should J.R. consume ethanol while on disulfiram?

Disulfiram blocks the enzyme aldehyde dehydrogenase, and, as a result, blood acetaldehyde concentrations increase by fivefold to tenfold within 15 minutes after ethanol ingestion.[107] If he consumed alcohol, J.R. could expect the typical disulfiram-ethanol reaction (DER) which is characterized by peripheral vasodilation which is associated with flushing, tachycardia, dyspnea, palpitations, and a throbbing headache. These symptoms generally are followed by nausea, persistent vomiting, thirst, diaphoresis, chest pain, and postural hypotension. Transient changes of electrocardiographic (ECG) flattened T waves, ST segment depression, and QT prolongation might be seen. He typically would experience a period of weakness, dizziness, blurred vision, and confusion for a duration ranging from 30 minutes to several hours, followed by several hours of sleep and recovery.

Symptomatic care usually is sufficient to manage a DER, unless it is complicated by cardiac arrhythmias, myocardial infarction, acute congestive heart failure, seizures, cerebral edema, or intracranial hemorrhage. The severity of the reaction is directly related to the dose of ethanol or disulfiram, or both. However, there are anecdotal reports of DERs occurring from small exposures to unsuspected sources of alcohol including the topical use of shampoo that contains beer.[108,109]

Dosage and Precautions

15. What would be a reasonable dose of disulfiram for J.R., and what precautions should accompany the use of this drug?

The usual adult regimen for disulfiram consists of an initial dose of 500 mg/day for two weeks, followed by a daily dose ranging from 125 to 500 mg/day. In using disulfiram, clinicians should be aware of serious adverse effects associated with long-term use, including psychosis, peripheral neuropathy, hypercholesterolemia, hypertension, acetonemia, and hepatotoxicity.[110–113] Disulfiram may increase and prolong the effects of phenytoin (Dilantin), warfarin (Coumadin), and drugs metabolized by the mixed-function oxidase system.[114,115]

Thus, an appropriate dosage regimen for J.R. would be 500 mg/day for two weeks followed by 250 mg/day. J.R. should be warned to avoid all alcohol-containing products as well as occupational exposure to ethylene dibromide, and should be tested for sensitivity to rubber or other thiuram-containing products.[116,117] He should wear a medical alert bracelet which indicates that he is taking disulfiram. Before starting disulfiram, J.R. should have abstained from alcohol for at least 12 hours and should be advised that DERs can occur for up to 14 days after disulfiram is stopped, since it may take this long for aldehyde dehydrogenase stores to be replenished.[107]

Effects of Chronic Alcoholism

Hepatitis

16. D.T., a 33-year-old female, presents to the clinic with complaints of diminished appetite, weight loss, abdominal pain, and chills. She has an 8-year history of heavy drinking. She claims to have 5–6 drinks every evening with her husband and says that they binge drink on the weekends. Laboratory studies were done and the following results were obtained: hemoglobin (Hgb) 10.3 gm/dL (Normal: 11–15); hematocrit (Hct) 31% (Normal: 34–46); mean corpuscular hemoglobin concentration (MCHC) 30% (Normal: 34–36); mean corpuscular volume (MCV) 104 μm³ (Normal: 80–100); platelets 90 × 10³ (Nor-mal: 140–400); white blood cells (WBC) 2.8 × 10³ (Normal: 4–11); serum folate 3.8 ng/mL (Normal: 7–18); serum vitamin B$_{12}$ 230 pg/mL (Normal: >200); aspartate aminotransferase (AST) 235 IU/L (Normal: 0–56); alanine aminotransferase (ALT) 127 IU/L (Normal: 0–56); gamma glutamyl transpeptidase (GGT) 435 IU/L (Normal: 8–78); alkaline phosphatase 245 IU/L (Normal: 40–143); total bilirubin 3.4 mg/dL (Normal: ≤1.2); albumin 3.6 gm/dL (Normal: 3.5–5); BUN 6 mg/dL (Normal: 5–22); serum creatinine (SrCr) 0.6 mg/dL (Normal: 0.6–1.1). What is the likely cause of D.T.'s symptoms? [SI units: Hgb 103 gm/L (Normal: 110–150); Hct 0.31 (Normal: 0.34–0.46); MCHC 0.30 (Normal: 0.34–0.36); MCV 104 fl (Normal: 80–100); platelets 90 × 10⁹ (Normal: 140–400); WBC 2.8 × 10⁹ (Normal: 4–10); serum folate 8.6 nmol/L (Normal: 16–40); serum vitamin B$_{12}$ 169 pmol/L (Normal: >148); AST 235 U/L (Normal: 3.5–5); ALT 127 U/L (Normal: 0–56); GGT 435 U/L (Normal: 8–78); alkaline phosphatase 245 U/L (Normal: 40–143); total bilirubin 58 μmol/L (Normal: ≤21); albumin 36 gm/L (Normal: 35–50); BUN 2.1 mmol/L of urea (Normal: 1.8–7.9); SrCr 53 μmol/L (Normal: 53–97)]**

Hepatitis is part of a spectrum of liver disease which can occur in patients who consume large amounts of alcohol. Fatty liver, or alcoholic steatosis, is the first stage of hepatotoxicity and is probably present in nearly all individuals who consume ethanol in daily amounts of 20 to 40 gm. Alcoholic hepatitis develops in about 90% of persons with alcoholism with fatty livers if they continue to drink. Cirrhosis is the third and end-stage of alcohol-induced liver toxicity and develops in 8% to 20% of patients with chronic alcoholism. It may follow acute symptomatic hepatitis or develop in patients without previously documented clinical hepatitis.[118,119]

The clinical presentation of alcoholic hepatitis can vary from completely asymptomatic to fulminant.[120] The diminished appetite, weight loss, abdominal pain, and chills seen in D.T. are typical symptoms in a patient with alcoholic hepatitis. Other commonly seen symptoms include low grade and/or spiking fevers, vomiting, jaundice, and GI bleeding. More serious complications can include the development of esophageal varices, ascites, encephalopathy, splenomegaly, renal failure, and coagulopathies.[118,119] Patients with alcoholic hepatitis frequently exhibit anemia, leukocytosis or leukopenia, and thrombocytopenia. AST and ALT generally are elevated, although the AST is seldom more than five times the upper limit of normal and the ALT concentration is usually less than half the AST value. The GGT level generally is elevated but does not correlate with the severity of the disease. The alkaline phosphatase and bilirubin levels also generally are elevated, reflecting cholestasis which typically accompanies alcoholic hepatitis. In more severe cases, prothrombin time also may be elevated reflecting reduced production of clotting factors. Markedly reduced serum albumin may reflect reduced hepatic synthetic function or malnutrition.[120–122] (Also see Chapter 25: Alcoholic Cirrhosis.) D.T.'s symptoms and laboratory results are quite consistent with a diagnosis of alcoholic hepatitis.

17. How should D.T.'s hepatitis be managed, and what is her prognosis?

The cornerstone to the management of alcohol-induced liver disease is abstinence from alcohol. While abstinence is sufficient to produce resolution of fatty liver, it may not be sufficient to produce clinical recovery in patients with alcoholic hepatitis. This is particularly true in cases where alcoholic hepatitis is complicated by one or more of the previously discussed complications. In a Veterans Administration study of 358 patients with alcoholic hepatitis of varying degrees of severity, the 30-day mortality rate was 15% and the one-year mortality rate was 39.5%.[120] Thus, even complete abstinence from alcohol does not assure that a patient will survive an episode of alcoholic hepatitis.

General supportive care for patients with alcoholic hepatitis also should include bedrest, correction of dehydration, appropriate dietary intake of carbohydrate and protein, and replacement of severe vitamin and mineral deficiencies (e.g., bicarbonate, calcium, chloride, magnesium, potassium, phosphate, sodium, vitamin A, folic acid, thiamine, vitamin B_{12}, iron, zinc).[118,123,124]

Since D.T. does not have a large number of complicating factors, her prognosis may be fairly good if she abstains from alcohol and receives appropriate supportive care.

18. What specific drug therapy might be considered to treat D.T.'s alcoholic hepatitis?

Insulin and glucagon, propylthiouracil, penicillamine, and colchicine are drugs which have been studied in the management of alcoholic hepatitis, although further evaluation is needed before definitive conclusions can be drawn regarding their safety and efficacy.[53,119,125] The use of corticosteroids has been more widely studied, but varying results have resulted in controversy as to their appropriateness in alcoholic hepatitis, and the data to date have not been sufficient to establish optimum dosages. It is believed that corticosteroids may reduce short-term mortality only in alcoholic hepatitis accompanied by hepatic encephalopathy in patients without gastrointestinal bleeding. However, short-term benefit has not been found in other patients with alcoholic hepatitis. Data also are inconclusive regarding long-term benefits.[126] Thus, corticosteroid therapy is not indicated in D.T. since her alcoholic hepatitis is not accompanied by hepatic encephalopathy.

Hematologic

19. What is the explanation for D.T.'s abnormal hematological values?

Folate deficiency is the most common sign of malnutrition in chronic alcoholism with about 30% of patients with severe alcoholism developing a megaloblastic anemia.[127–129] A number of different etiologies account for folate deficiency in persons with alcoholism. Most common are, diets which are inadequate in sources of folate (i.e., green leafy vegetables, liver), impaired jejunal absorption of folate, decreased retention and storage of folate which accompanies severe liver disease, acute effects of ethanol on tissue affinity of circulating folate, probable alteration of enterohepatic cycling of folate, and excretion of larger amounts of folate secondary to hemolysis. People with chronic alcoholism also can experience derangements of iron metabolism which can produce both sideroblastic anemia and hemosiderosis. Sideroblastic anemia is a complex disorder which is due in part to deranged pyridoxine function and decreased enzyme activity involved with heme synthesis. Hemosiderosis is the accumulation of hemosiderin which is a by-product of phagocytic digestion of hematin containing up to 37% iron. Iron deficiency anemia also is common in alcoholism due to inadequate dietary intake and frequently occurring gastrointestinal blood loss. Hemolytic anemia also can result from liver damage. (Also see Chapter 88: Anemias.)

Several factors can make persons with alcoholism more prone to bleeding. Alcohol can prolong bleeding times by interfering with platelet function and produce thrombocytopenia by suppressing platelet formation. As mentioned above, alcohol-induced hepatotoxicity can result in diminished production of vitamin K-dependent clotting factors by the liver.

In D.T.'s case, the increased MCV, low serum folate level, and normal vitamin B_{12} level are characteristic of a folate-deficiency, megaloblastic anemia. The low platelet count may be due to the toxic effect of alcohol or related to D.T.'s alcoholic hepatitis.

20. How should D.T.'s anemia be managed?

D.T.'s stool should be tested for occult blood to ensure that GI blood loss is not contributing to the anemia. This will determine if an additional gastrointestinal work-up is necessary. D.T. should be

supplemented with an oral multiple vitamin with folic acid daily along with ferrous sulfate 325 mg/day. This supplementation should be continued until it can be reasonably assured that D.T. has stopped drinking and resumed an adequate dietary intake.

Fetal Effects

21. D.T. has no children but is interested in becoming pregnant. What effects could continued consumption of alcohol have on her fetus if she were to become pregnant?

The characteristics of fetal alcohol syndrome and fetal alcohol effects (FAE) are discussed in Chapter 45: Teratogenicity and Drugs in Breast Milk. The estimated incidence of FAS in the population as a whole ranges from one case per 700 to 2000 live births. All reported cases of FAS have been born to mothers with chronic alcoholism who drank heavily throughout pregnancy. Cases especially occurred when mothers drank at least 150 gm of ethanol per day. In prospective studies, fetal alcohol syndrome occurred in the offspring of alcohol-dependent women at rates ranging from 2.5% to 10%.[130,131] Both FAS and FAE have been observed in almost all ethnic groups and at various socioeconomic levels.

The most predictable consequence of prenatal exposure to alcohol is intrauterine growth retardation. The decrease in fetal growth is caused by alcohol itself and not by congeners present in alcoholic beverages. Alcohol appears to interfere with fetal growth by inducing hypoxia which interferes with cellular processes (e.g., placental transport, protein synthesis) which require oxygen. Although alcohol exerts its greatest impact on fetal growth when consumed during the third trimester, teratogenic effects also have been correlated with first trimester exposure to alcohol.[132] Thus, it is wise for women to avoid alcohol consumption throughout pregnancy.[132,133]

D.T. would be wise to not consider becoming pregnant until she has demonstrated a period of abstinence from alcohol. She should be provided with education as to the fetal hazards of alcohol consumption.

Gastritis and Ulcer Disease

22. R.K., a 45-year-old male, presents to his physician on a Monday morning with complaints of acute abdominal pain, nausea, vomiting, and diarrhea. He has been a heavy drinker for 15 years and particularly binges on weekends. He denies that his drinking is a problem, but entered an alcohol treatment program 4 years ago at the insistence of his wife and college-aged son. He resumed drinking within 2 weeks of completing the program. He has a 35 pack-year smoking history and currently smokes ≈1.5 packs/day. What is the likely cause of R.K.'s GI distress?

A wide variety of GI disturbances have been attributed to chronic ethanol ingestion. Diarrhea is a common symptom in binge drinkers, and may be related to alteration of intestinal cell morphology which results in interference with the absorption of water and nutrients (e.g., amino acids, glucose, thiamine, folic acid, vitamin B_{12}, potassium, magnesium, phosphate, zinc).[134–136] This also may partially account for the significant malnutrition seen in many persons with alcoholism.

Chronic alcohol ingestion can lead to chronic gastritis and atrophic gastritis with hypochlorhydria. This is assumed to be due to the injurious effects of alcohol on the gastrointestinal mucosa. Although predisposition to peptic ulcers has been attributed to ethanol consumption, a recent analysis found alcohol consumption to be associated with only a small increase in the risk of ulcer disease after controlling for cigarette smoking as well as other sociodemographic variables.[137] Alcohol also effects esophageal peristalsis and lowers esophageal sphincter pressure which can contribute to gastroesophageal reflux disease (GERD) and lead to esophageal bleeding and stricture formation. In some patients GERD, along with alcohol-induced impaired glottic reflexes, may result in aspiration and lung abscesses which typically occur during periods of alcoholic stupor.[138,139]

In R.K.'s case, alcohol-induced gastritis would seem to be a logical explanation for his symptoms although, peptic ulcer disease, alcoholic hepatitis, and/or pancreatitis (see Question 26) can present with similar symptoms.

23. A presumptive diagnosis of alcohol-induced gastritis is made. How should R.K. be treated for this?

Gastritis induced by alcohol consumption typically resolves within a few days after cessation of alcohol consumption. Antacids and H_2-receptor antagonists may speed healing and provide rapid pain relief, but generally are not required. R.K. should not receive any specific therapy at this time.

H_2-Receptor Antagonist Interactions

24. R.K.'s physician writes a prescription for famotidine 20 mg PO BID. What would be the consequences if R.K. continues to drink while taking this drug?

A number of studies have suggested that H_2-receptor antagonists may inhibit gastric alcohol dehydrogenase resulting in reduced first-pass metabolism, resultant higher blood alcohol concentrations after any particular ethanol dose, and increased chances of intoxication. This effect has been greatest with cimetidine (Tagamet); lesser effects have been seen with ranitidine (Zantac) and nizatidine (Axid), and no effect has been demonstrated with famotidine (Pepcid). Increases in blood alcohol concentrations have been greatest in studies where healthy young men consumed small doses of ethanol ($\approx$0.15 gm/kg) after a meal in the morning, but have not resulted in legal intoxication due to the small ethanol dosage. The effect appears to be less pronounced at higher ethanol doses, probably due to the saturation of gastric alcohol dehydrogenase which occurs with larger doses of ethanol. The FDA Advisory Committee on Gastrointestinal Drugs concluded that the available data do not support a clinically or socially significant ethanol interaction with H_2-receptor antagonists.[140] Since R.K. is taking famotidine, and is a chronic drinker, he is unlikely to have a significant drug interaction.

Cancer

25. R.K.'s wife has heard that heavy alcohol use increases the risk of certain cancers. She knows that R.K. already is at increased cancer risk due to his smoking. What is the role of alcohol in promoting cancer?

Excessive consumption of alcohol clearly results in an increased risk of developing cancer of the tongue, mouth, oropharynx, esophagus, and liver.[134] Alcohol is not a true carcinogen but may act as tumor "promoter" by chronically irritating membranes and possibly dissolving tobacco carcinogens, thus increasing their mucosal concentration in the mouth, pharynx, larynx, and esophagus.[134,135,141] This seems to explain the much higher incidence of these cancers in heavy drinkers who also smoke when compared to those who do not smoke.[134] Other evidence suggests that alcohol may act as an immunosuppressive which may be a cofactor in promoting cancer.[141]

R.K.'s drinking clearly increases his risk for cancer. If he stopped smoking but continued to drink, his cancer risk would be somewhat reduced.

Pancreatitis

26. R.K. presents to the ER 6 weeks later with more severe abdominal pain which radiates from the upper abdominal area through to both flanks. He also has experienced nausea and vomiting for the past 12 hours. His wife reports that he has been on an alcohol binge over the past 4 days. Physical examination reveals a tender and distended abdomen. Laboratory results include a plasma amylase of 675 IU/L (Normal: 0–130) and lipase of 1045 IU/L (Normal: 23–208). What would be the likely cause of R.K.'s clinical symptoms? [SI units: amylase 675 U/L (Normal: 0–130); lipase 1045 U/L (Normal: 23–208)]

Heavy alcohol consumption now is recognized as the second most common cause of acute pancreatitis, accounting for 35% of cases.[142] Acute exacerbations typically occur after binge drinking episodes. Many years of alcohol abuse generally are required before an acute episode of pancreatitis occurs. Other factors also must play a role in the development of this disorder, since only 5% of persons with alcoholism develop pancreatitis. In most patients, alcoholic pancreatitis presents as an acute episode which is superimposed on a chronic underlying pancreatic inflammation, while in a few patients acute pancreatitis probably develops in the absence of prior chronic disease. Hyperlipidemia, which frequently is present in patients with heavy alcohol consumption, also may contribute to the development of pancreatitis.[143]

Patients typically present with abdominal pain, often severe, which radiates from the upper abdomen through to the back or both flanks. The diagnosis generally is made by measuring serum amylase and lipase levels at the time patients present with abdominal pain. Lipase levels appear to be more sensitive and specific than amylase levels, since lipase levels may remain elevated for several days whereas amylase levels may quickly return to normal.[144] In addition, an elevated ratio of lipase to amylase has been reported to effectively differentiate pancreatitis induced by alcohol from other forms of acute pancreatitis.[145]

In R.K., the severe radiating abdominal pain, elevated amylase, lipase, and amylase:lipase ratio all are indicative of acute pancreatitis. Pancreatitis also may have been the cause of the symptoms he experienced six weeks earlier.

27. How should R.K. be treated?

The appropriate management for R.K. is supportive therapy. This includes eliminating all oral intake, providing sufficient parenteral analgesia, and instituting IV hydration or total parental nutrition if his nutritional status so dictates.[142] Since nasogastric suction has not been shown to promote pain relief or reduce hospital stays, it should not be employed in R.K. unless he develops ileus or severe vomiting. A variety of drugs, including cimetidine, have been studied in the hopes that they would reduce pancreatic stimulation. They generally should not be used in patients such as R.K. since their effectiveness has not been demonstrated.

Wernicke-Korsakoff Syndrome

28. T.W., a 58-year-old male, is brought to the ER in a comatose state, but responsive to pain. His family members report that he has been drinking heavily for the past few days. He has been drinking about a quart of bourbon daily for the past 11 years.

Vital signs upon admission include BP 100/70 mm Hg; pulse 120 beats/min; respiratory rate 20 breaths/min; and rectal temperature 101.5 °F. ECG reveals atrial fibrillation. An IV line is established with 5% dextrose infusion; T.W. receives IV doses of 0.8 mg of naloxone, 100 mg of thiamine, and 50 mL of 50% dextrose. What are the potential causes of T.W.'s comatose state?

Two potential causes of T.W.'s comatose state are acute ethanol intoxication and Wernicke's encephalopathy. Wernicke's encephalopathy is a neurologic disorder caused by thiamine deficiency and most commonly encountered in persons with severe alcoholism. This condition represents a medical emergency and carries an estimated 10% to 20% mortality rate. The classical presentation of Wernicke's encephalopathy is characterized by an abrupt onset and an evolving triad of symptoms which develop gradually over several days. However, classical Wernicke's encephalopathy is neither frequently nor consistently encountered in clinical practice. Typical symptoms include 1) CNS depression (e.g., mental sluggishness, restlessness, confusion, coma); 2) ambulatory difficulties (e.g., wide-based ataxic gait, vestibular paresis); and 3) ocular problems (e.g., horizontal nystagmus, conjugate-gaze palsies, pupillary abnormalities, retinal hemorrhages, papilledema). In addition to this triad of symptoms, patients also may experience hypothermia, hypotension, and polyneuropathy.[134,146,147]

Patients with chronic alcoholism, such as T.W., frequently are deficient in thiamine due to poor dietary intake. Since thiamine is a cofactor in glucose metabolism, thiamine deficiency, and consequently Wernicke's encephalopathy, can be precipitated by administration of a large glucose load. Therefore, parenteral thiamine (IM or slow IV push) should be administered before, or concurrently with, dextrose-containing intravenous fluids to known or suspected patients with alcoholism. Subsequently, oral thiamine should be administered in a dose of 50 to 100 mg/day to replenish thiamine stores.[146–148]

Korsakoff's psychosis will develop in about 80% of patients with Wernicke's encephalopathy who survive, but fail to recover in the first 48 to 72 hours. Characteristics of this condition include retrograde amnesia (inability to recall prior information) and anterograde amnesia (inability to assimilate new information). Confabulation (fabrication of stories) is typical in the early stages of this disease but frequently disappears during the later stages. About 25% to 50% of patients with Korsakoff's psychosis do not recover completely and may require long-term care.[147,148]

T.W.'s comatose condition could be caused by either acute ethanol intoxication or Wernicke's encephalopathy, and both possible diagnoses should be considered in developing his plan of care.

29. Was the therapy that T.W. received in the ER appropriate?

Naloxone should be administered to all comatose patients such as T.W. to reverse the effects of possible opiate overdose in individuals known to be substance abusers. For reasons described above, intravenous thiamine was appropriate since T.W. has a long history of alcohol consumption. The 50% dextrose was administered to manage potential hypoglycemia as previously discussed under acute ethanol intoxication.

Cardiovascular

30. What might be the most likely etiology for T.W.'s sudden development of atrial fibrillation?

A variety of beneficial and detrimental cardiovascular effects have been attributed to consumption of varying amounts of alcoholic beverages. Light to moderate alcohol consumption (up to 2 drinks/day) has been found in epidemiologic studies to be associated with reduced risk of myocardial infarction and cardiac death.[149] A potential mechanism for this beneficial effect appears to be the effect of alcohol on increasing high density lipoprotein-cholesterol, a factor which is inversely associated with coronary heart disease risk. Alcohol also may reduce cardiac risk though an antithrombotic action.[149,150]

Alcoholic cardiomyopathy is a frequently seen clinical entity in persons with chronic alcoholism and apparently is due to a number of alterations in contractile functions of the heart.[151] Among these individuals, about one-third have a depressed cardiac ejection fraction.[152] Alcoholic cardiomyopathy usually becomes clinically apparent between the ages of 30 and 60 years, and typically requires

at least ten years of excessive alcohol consumption. In terms of symptomatology, this disease reflects low-output cardiac failure and cannot be differentiated from other forms of low-output congestive heart failure.

A variety of studies have demonstrated an increased prevalence of hypertension in patients with alcoholism.[153] A daily alcohol consumption rate of three or more standard drinks seems to be the threshold for a consistent hypertensive response. Possible mechanisms by which alcohol consumption may increase blood pressure include 1) central nervous system imbalance, 2) impairment of the baroreceptors, 3) increased sympathetic activity, 4) stimulation of the renin-angiotensin-aldosterone system, 5) increased cortisol levels, 6) increased intracellular calcium with resultant increase in vascular reactivity, 7) stimulation of the endothelium to release endothelin or inhibition of endothelium-dependent nitric oxide production, and 8) chronic subclinical alcohol withdrawal.[154]

Heavy alcohol consumption has been associated with increased incidence of a variety of cardiac conduction disturbances.[153,155] Heavy binge drinkers may present with a sudden onset of paroxysmal arrhythmias including junctional tachycardia, premature ventricular or atrial contractions, atrial tachycardia, and ventricular tachycardia; however, atrial fibrillation and flutter are the two most commonly encountered arrhythmias.[156,157] These arrhythmias have been termed the ''holiday heart'' when they appear in persons free of overt cardiomyopathies who appear in emergency rooms following high alcohol consumption during holidays (e.g., New Year's Eve, St. Patrick's Day).[157] These arrhythmias have been attributed to a variety of factors including preclinical cardiomyopathy, electrolyte abnormalities (e.g., potassium, phosphate, magnesium), and conduction delays induced by alcohol and its metabolites. Renal tubular dysfunction frequently occurs during chronic alcohol abuse and produces electrolyte abnormalities which are reversible after four weeks of alcohol abstinence.[158] Obviously, such electrolyte disturbances may contribute to cardiac conduction defects.

In T.W.'s case, his recent heavy alcohol consumption may well be a factor which contributed to his development of atrial fibrillation.

31. How should T.W.'s atrial fibrillation be managed?

At present there are no good data on the management of alcohol-related cardiac arrhythmias. Since many of these arrhythmias terminate within 24 to 48 hours, it seems wise to withhold therapy or limit therapy to a short course of beta blockers. Either approach could be considered appropriate for T.W. His serum electrolytes should be measured and replenishment provided if deficiencies are found. Obviously, long-term treatment should be directed at managing his alcoholism.[159]

Endocrine

32. R.R., a 47-year-old male malnourished street person, comes to the medical clinic complaining of pain, weakness, and swelling of his leg muscles, especially in the calves. He also complains of recent loss of libido and sexual impotence. The findings on physical examination reveal a thin, unkempt male with loss of facial hair, gynecomastia, and testicular atrophy. He admits to drinking alcohol for the past 25 years. What signs and symptoms might suggest alterations of R.R.'s endocrine system due to alcohol abuse?

A variety of clinical features reflecting hypogonadism can occur in persons with alcoholism. Changes seen in women may include amenorrhea, anovulation, luteal phase dysfunction, hyperprolactinemia, and ovarian pathology. Subsequent reproductive consequences may range from infertility and increased risk of spontaneous abortion to impairment of fetal growth and development.[160]

In men, the hypogonadal features and changes that commonly are found are similar to those seen in R.R. They include loss of facial hair, gynecomastia, diminished muscle and bone mass, testicular atrophy, loss of libido, and sexual impotence. Alcohol may reduce testosterone by interfering with the testicular biosynthesis of testosterone as well as by induction of steroid reductases which results in increased hepatic metabolism of testosterone. It also is possible that alcohol may inhibit the pituitary release of luteinizing hormone which is involved in testosterone biosynthesis.[134,161] At present, there is no effective treatment for alcohol-induced hypogonadism, such as seen in R.R., other than complete cessation of alcohol consumption, which may result in improvement in some patients.

Myopathy

33. How could R.R.'s complaints of weakness, pain, and swelling of the calf muscles be attributed to alcohol abuse?

Alcoholic myopathy is a syndrome of muscle necrosis which can vary greatly in severity and occurs frequently in persons with alcoholism. Initial presentation can range from frank rhabdomyolysis with myoglobinuria to asymptomatic, transient elevations of the MM fraction of creatine kinase. Greater than 80% of cases have been reported in males between the ages of 40 to 60 years. When recurrent cases of myopathy occur, they almost always are associated with heavy drinking binges. When rhabdomyolysis occurs, it often is accompanied by acute tubular necrosis and subsequent renal failure which may be fatal if it is not rapidly detected and treated. Available evidence supports the contention that alcohol itself injures the skeletal muscle.[162,163] However, other factors such as crush injuries, seizures, or hypokalemia, may precipitate, or contribute to, rhabdomyolysis in patients with alcoholism. Recent data also suggest that cardiomyopathy frequently is present in patients presenting with skeletal muscular weakness.[164] R.R.'s symptoms and drinking history are consistent with alcohol-induced myopathy.

34. Since alcoholic myopathy is suspected in R.R., how should he be evaluated and managed?

Appropriate work-up for R.R. includes testing of the urine for myoglobin due to its toxic effects on the kidney. His serum creatine kinase concentration should be measured and his renal function and urine output should be assessed. Appropriate management for R.R. includes correction of any electrolyte abnormalities, particularly potassium and magnesium. Appropriate urine output should be established and maintained. In addition, if myoglobin is found in the urine, intravenous sodium bicarbonate should be adminis-

tered to maintain an alkaline urine which will prevent deposition of myoglobin in the renal tubules. Of course, attempts should be made to have R.R. participate in an appropriate alcohol treatment program.

Acknowledgment

We gratefully acknowledge James F Buchanan, Gerald Joe, and Howard E McKinney, Jr, whose work provided a foundation for this chapter.

Update
Naltrexone

U-1. Would naltrexone be useful as a suitable alternative to disulfiram for J.R. (the patient in Questions 7–15)?

Naltrexone (ReVia) has been approved by the Food and Drug Administration as an adjunct to psychosocial treatment for alcoholism.[171] In contrast to disulfiram which is used to produce aversion to alcohol consumption, naltrexone appears to reduce craving in patients who are abstinent and block the reinforcing effects of alcohol in patients who drink. The primary known pharmacological effect of naltrexone is that of a narcotic antagonist with minimal agonist effects, although the mechanism for its effects in managing alchoholism has not been established.[172] In two placebo-controlled trials, naltrexone, when used in conjunction with various psychosocial support measures, decreased craving for alcohol, reduced alcohol consumption, and increased abstinence rates.[173,174]

Naloxone should be prescribed only by experienced physicians and in the context of established alcohol treatment programs.[171] Before the initiation of therapy, patients should not have taken opioid drugs for at least seven days. Naltrexone is generally well tolerated with about a 10% prevalence of adverse reactions which are usually mild and well tolerated. Naltrexone can produce hepatocellular injury when given in excessive doses, and should not be given to patients with clinically evident liver disease. The recommended dose is 50 mg/day for up to 12 weeks. Treatment for more than 12 weeks has not been studied.

In J.R.'s case, naltrexone may be a beneficial adjunct to his alcohol treatment program. Naltrexone appears to have some advantages over disulfiram, particularly with regard to safety. However, additional studies will be needed to define its true place in the management of alcoholism, including its use on a long-term basis.

References

1 **Federal Register.** 2 June 1983;48 (107):24672.

2 **Lundberg GD et al.** Now read this: the SI units are here. JAMA. 1986;255: 2329.

3 **Department of Health and Human Services.** Healthy people 2000: national health promotion and disease prevention objectives. Washington, DC: U.S. Government Printing Office, 1991; DHHS publication no. (PHS)91-50212.

4 **National Institute on Drug Abuse.** National household survey on drug abuse: main findings 1991. Rockville, MD: Substance Abuse and Mental Health Services Administration, 1993; DHHS publication no. (SMA)93-1980.

5 **National Institute on Alcohol Abuse and Alcoholism.** Seventh special report to the U.S. Congress on alcohol

and health. Alexandria, VA: Editorial Experts, 1990; DHHS publication no. (ADM)90-1656.

6 **U.S. Department of Health and Human Services.** Sixth special report to the U.S. Congress on alcohol and health. Washington, DC: U.S. Government Printing Office, 1987; DHHS publication no. (ADM)87-1519.

7 **Institute for Health Policy, Brandeis University.** Substance Abuse: The Nation's Number One Health Problem. Princeton, NJ: The Robert Wood Johnson Foundation; 1993.

8 **Klitzner M et al.** Reducing underage drinking and its consequences. Alcohol Health Res World. 1993;17:12.

9 **National Institute on Drug Abuse.** Drug use, drinking and smoking: national survey results from high school,

college and young adult populations: 1975–1988. Washington, DC: U.S. Government Printing Office, 1989; DHHS publication no. (ADM)89-1638.

10 **McGinnis JM, Foege WH.** Actual causes of death in the United States. JAMA. 1993;270:32.

11 **National Council on Alcoholism and Drug Dependence.** NCADD Fact Sheet: Alcoholism and Alcohol-Related Problems. New York, NY: 1990.

12 **Day NL.** The effects of prenatal exposure to alcohol. Alcohol Health Res World. 1992;16:238.

13 **Smart RG, Mann RE.** Alcohol and the epidemiology of liver cirrhosis. Alcohol Health Res World. 1992;16:217.

14 **Arria AM, VanThiel DH.** The epidemiology of alcohol-related chronic dis-

ease. Alcohol Health Res World. 1992; 16:209.

15 **Center on Addiction and Substance Abuse.** The Cost of Substance Abuse to America's Health Care System, Report 1: Medicaid Hospital Costs. New York, NY: Columbia University; 1993.

16 **Longnecker MP.** Alcohol consumption in relation to risk of cancers of the breast and large bowel. Alcohol Health Res World. 1992;16:238.

17 **Stinson FS et al.** Association of alcohol problems with risk for AIDS in the 1988 National Health Interview Survey. Alcohol Health Res World. 1992; 16:245.

18 **Office for Substance Abuse Prevention.** Alcohol Practices, Policies and Potentials of American Colleges and Universities: A White Paper. Rock-

ville, MD: The National Clearinghouse for Alcohol and Drug Information; 1991.

19 **Cherpital CJ.** The epidemiology of alcohol-related trauma. Alcohol Health Res World. 1992;16:191.

20 **National Highway Traffic Safety Administration.** Traffic Safety Facts 1992: Alcohol. Washington, DC: National Center for Statistics & Analysis; 1993.

21 **Bernstein M, Mahoney JJ.** Management perspectives on alcoholism: the employer's stake in alcoholism treatment. Occup Med. 1989;4:223.

22 **Office for Substance Abuse Prevention.** Too Many Young People Drink and Know Too Little About the Consequences. Rockville, MD: National Clearinghouse for Alcohol and Drug Information; 1991.

23 **Roth RA.** The impact of liquor liability on colleges and universities. J Coll Univ Law. 1986;13:45.

24 **Centers for Disease Control.** Morbidity and mortality weekly report: results from the national adolescent student health survey. JAMA. 1989;261:2025.

25 **National Highway Traffic Safety Administration.** Fatal Accident Reporting System: 1987. Washington, DC: U.S. Department of Transportation; 1988.

26 **National Commission on Drug-Free Schools.** Toward a Drug-Free Generation: A Nation's Responsibility. Washington, DC: U.S. Department of Education; 1990.

27 **Jackson VM et al.** Measurement of social drinking: the need for specific guidelines. Health Values. 1990;14:25.

28 **Rice DP.** The economic cost of alcohol abuse and alcohol dependence: 1990. Alcohol Health Res World. 1993;17:10.

29 **Moskowitz J.** The primary prevention of alcohol problems: a critical review of the research literature. J Stud Alcohol. 1989;50:54.

30 **Hansen WB.** School-based alcohol prevention programs. Alcohol Health Res World. 1993;17:54.

31 **Anderson DS, Gadaleto AF.** Results of the 1991 College Alcohol Survey: Comparison with 1988 Results and Baseline Year. Fairfax, VA: George Mason University, Center for Health Promotion; 1991.

32 **Ames G.** Research and strategies for the primary prevention of workplace alcohol problems. Alcohol Health Res World. 1993;17:19.

33 **Giesbrecht N et al.** Community-based prevention research to reduce alcohol-related problems. Alcohol Health Res World. 1993;17:84.

34 **Gruenewald PJ et al.** Alcohol availability and the ecology of drinking behavior. Alcohol Health Res World. 1991;17:39.

35 **McKnight AJ.** Server intervention: accomplishments and needs. Alcohol Health Res World. 1993;17:76.

36 **David DJ, Spyker DA.** The acute toxicity of ethanol: dosage and kinetic nomograms. Vet Hum Toxicol. 1979; 21:272.

37 **Jones BM, Vega A.** Cognitive performance measured on the ascending and descending limb of the blood alcohol curve. Psychopharmacology (Berl). 1972;23:99.

38 **Hawkins RD, Kalant H.** The metabolism of ethanol and its metabolic effects. Pharmacol Rev. 1972;24:67.

39 **DiPadova C et al.** Effects of fasting and chronic alcohol consumption on the first pass metabolism of ethanol. Gastroenterology. 1987;92:1169.

40 **Caballaria J et al.** Gastric origin of the first-pass metabolism of ethanol in humans: effect of gastrectomy. Gastroenterology. 1989;97:1205.

41 **Caballaria J.** First pass metabolism of ethanol: its role as a determinant of blood alcohol levels after drinking. Hepatogastroenterology. 1992;39 (Suppl. 1):62.

42 **Levitt MD.** Review article: lack of clinical significance of the interaction between H_2-receptor antagonists and ethanol. Aliment Pharmacol Ther. 1993; 7:131.

43 **Seitz HK et al.** Human gastric alcohol dehydrogenase activity: effect of age, sex, and alcoholism. Gut. 1993;34: 1433.

44 **Wagner JG et al.** Elimination of alcohol from human blood. J Pharm Sci. 1976;65:152.

45 **Wilkinson PK et al.** Blood ethanol concentrations during and following constant-rate intravenous infusion of alcohol. Clin Pharmacol Ther. 1976; 19:213.

46 **Hammond KB et al.** Blood ethanol: a report of unusually high levels in a living patient. JAMA. 1973;226:63.

47 **Lieber CS et al.** Differences in hepatic and metabolic changes after acute and chronic alcohol consumption. Fed Proc. 1975;34:2060.

48 **Schumate RP et al.** A study of the metabolic rates of alcohol in the human body. J Forensic Med. 1967;14:83.

49 **Crabb DW et al.** Alcohol sensitivity, alcohol metabolism, risk of alcoholism, and the role of alcohol and aldehyde dehydrogenase. J Lab Clin Med. 1993; 122:234.

50 **Kopun M, Propping P.** The kinetics of ethanol absorption and elimination in twins and supplementary repetitive experiments in singleton subjects. Eur J Clin Pharmacol. 1977;11:337.

51 **Mendelson JH et al.** Effects of experimentally induced intoxication on metabolism of ethanol-1-C^{14} in alcoholic subjects. Metabolism. 1965;14:1255.

52 **Adachi J et al.** Comparative study on ethanol elimination and blood acetaldehyde between alcoholics and control subjects. Alcohol Clin Exp Res. 1989; 13:601.

53 **Lieber CS.** Alcohol and the liver: 1984 update. Hepatology. 1984;4:1243.

54 **Derr RF et al.** Is ethanol per se hepatotoxic? J Hepatol. 1990;10:381.

55 **Glass GBJ et al.** Biochemical and pathological derangement of the gastrointestinal tract following acute and chronic digestion of ethanol. In: Majchrowicz E, Nobel EP, eds. Biochemistry and Pharmacology of Ethanol. Vol. 1. New York: Plenum Press; 1979:511.

56 **Melgaard B.** The neurotoxicity of ethanol. Acta Neurol Scand. 1983;67:131.

57 **Kupari I et al.** Acute effects of alcohol, beta blockade and their combination on left ventricular function and hemodynamics in normal man. Eur Heart J. 1983;4:463.

58 **Michiels TM et al.** Naloxone reverses ethanol-induced depression of hypercapnic drive. Am Rev Respir Dis. 1983;128:823.

59 **O'Neill S et al.** Survival after high blood alcohol levels. Arch Intern Med. 1984;144:641.

60 **Sellers EM, Kalant H.** Alcohol intoxication and withdrawal. N Engl J Med. 1976;294:757.

61 **Poikolainen K.** Estimated lethal ethanol concentrations in relation to age, aspiration, and drugs. Alcohol Clin Exp Res. 1984;8:223.

62 **Enger E.** Acidosis, gaps and poisoning. Acta Med Scand. 1982;212:1.

63 **Brown SS et al.** A controlled trial of fructose in the treatment of acute alcoholic intoxication. Lancet. 1972;2: 898.

64 **Levy R et al.** Intravenous fructose treatment of acute alcohol intoxication. Arch Intern Med. 1977;137:1176.

65 **Barros SR, Rodriguez GJ.** Naloxone as an antagonist in alcohol intoxication. Anesthesiology. 1981;54:174.

66 **Jeffcoate WJ et al.** Prevention of effects of alcohol intoxication by naloxone. Lancet. 1979;2:1157.

67 **Banner W et al.** Failure of naloxone to reverse clonidine toxic effect. Am J Dis Child. 1983;137:1170.

68 **North DS et al.** Naloxone administration in clonidine overdosage. Ann Emerg Med. 1981;10:7.

69 **Tenenbein M.** Naloxone in clonidine toxicity. Am J Dis Child. 1984;138: 1084.

70 **Rivara FP et al.** The effects of alcohol abuse on readmission for trauma. JAMA. 1993;270:1962.

71 **Rivara FP et al.** The magnitude of acute and chronic abuse in trauma patients. Arch Surg. 1993;128:907.

72 **Rivara FP et al.** A descriptive study of trauma, alcohol, and alcoholism in young patients. J Adolesc Health. 1992;13:663.

73 **Rutledge R, Messick WJ.** The association of trauma death and alcohol use in a rural state. J Trauma. 1992;33:737.

74 **Jurkovich GJ et al.** The effect of acute alcohol intoxication and chronic alcohol abuse on outcome from trauma. JAMA. 1993;290:51.

75 **Adams WL.** Alcohol-related hospitalizations of elderly: prevalence and geographic variation in the United States. JAMA. 1993;270:1222.

76 **Isbell A et al.** An experimental study of the etiology of "rum fits" and delirium tremens. Q J Stud Alcohol. 1955;16:1.

77 **Victor M, Adams RD.** The effect of alcohol on the nervous system. Res Publ Assoc Res Nerv Ment Dis. 1953; 32:526.

78 **Holloway HC et al.** Recognition and treatment of acute alcohol withdrawal syndromes. Psychiatr Clin North Am. 1994;7:729.

79 **Bird RD, Makela EH.** Alcohol withdrawal: what is the benzodiazepine of choice? Ann Pharmacother. 1994;28: 67.

80 **Smith CM.** Pathophysiology of the alcohol withdrawal syndromes. Med Hypotheses. 1981;7:231.

81 **Thompson WL.** Management of alcohol withdrawal syndromes. Arch Intern Med. 1978;138:278.

82 **Guthrie SK.** The treatment of alcohol withdrawal. Pharmacother. 1989;9:131.

83 **Foy A.** The management of alcohol withdrawal. Med J Aust. 1986;145:24.

84 **O'Brien JE et al.** Double-blind comparison of lorazepam and diazepam in the treatment of acute alcohol abstinence syndrome. Curr Ther Res Clin Exp. 1983;34:825.

85 **Zilm DH et al.** Propranolol and chlordiazepoxide effects on cardiac arrhythmias during alcohol withdrawal. Alcohol Clin Exp Res. 1980;4:400.

86 **Koepke HH.** Double blind-comparison of lorazepam and chlordiazepoxide in the treatment of the acute abstinence syndrome. Clin Ther. 1983;6:520.

87 **Castaneda R, Cushman P.** Alcohol withdrawal: a review of clinical management. J Clin Psychiatry. 1989;50:278.

88 **Allredge BK et al.** Placebo-controlled trial of intravenous diphenylhydantoin for short-term treatment of alcohol withdrawal seizures. Am J Med. 1989; 87:645.

89 **Feussner JR et al.** Computed tomography brain scanning in alcohol withdrawal seizures: value of neurological examination. Ann Intern Med. 1981; 94(Pt. 1):519.

90 **Wilbur R, Kulik FA.** Anticonvulsant drugs in alcohol withdrawal: use of phenytoin, primidone, carbamazepine, valproic acid, and the sedative anticonvulsants. Am J Hosp Pharm. 1981;38: 1138.

91 **Roe A.** The adult adjustment of children of alcoholic parents raised in foster homes. Q J Stud Alcohol. 1944;5: 378.

92 **Amark C.** A study in alcoholism. Acta Psychiatr Neurol Scand. 1951;70 (Suppl.):256.

93 **Goodwin DW et al.** Drinking problems in adopted and non-adopted sons of alcoholics. Arch Gen Psychiatry. 1974;31:164.

94 **Mendelson JH, Mello NK.** Biologic concomitants of alcoholism. N Engl J Med. 1979;301:912.

95 **Spalt L.** Alcoholism: evidence of an X-linked recessive genetic characteristic. JAMA. 1979;241:2543.

96 **Rutstein DD, Veech RL.** 2,3-Butanediol: an unusual metabolite in serum of severely alcoholic men during acute intoxication. Lancet. 1983;2:534.

97 **Grant BF.** ICD-10 and proposed DSM-IV harmful use of alcohol/alcohol abuse and dependence. United States 1988: a nosological comparison. Alcohol Clin Exp Res. 1993;17:1093.

98 **American Psychiatric Association.** Diagnostic and Statistical Manual of Mental Disorders (DSM-IV). Washington, DC: American Psychiatric Association; 1994:181.

99 **Helzer JE et al.** The extent of long-term moderate drinking among alcoholics discharged from medical and psychiatric facilities. N Engl J Med. 1985;312:1678.

100 **Miller WR et al.** Abstinence and controlled drinking in the treatment of problem drinkers. J Stud Alcohol. 1977;38:986.

101 **Sellers EM, Kalant H.** Pharmacotherapy of acute and chronic alcoholism and alcohol withdrawal syndrome. In: Clarke NG, del Giudice J, eds. Prin-

ciples of Psychopharmacology. New York: Academic Press; 1978:721.

102 **Tollefson GD.** Serotonin and alcohol: interrelationships. Psychopathology. 1989;22(Suppl. 1):37.

103 **Gorelick DA.** Serotonin uptake blockers and the treatment of alcoholism. Recent Dev Alcohol. 1989;7:267.

104 **Naranjo CA, Sellers EM.** Serotonin uptake inhibitors attenuate intake in problem drinkers. Recent Dev Alcohol. 1989;7:255.

105 **Gill K, Amit Z.** Serotonin uptake blockers and voluntary alcohol consumption: a review of recent studies. Recent Dev Alcohol. 1989;7:225.

106 **Fuller RK, Roth HP.** Disulfiram for the treatment of alcoholism: an evaluation in 128 men. Ann Intern Med. 1979;90:901.

107 **Kitson TM.** The disulfiram-ethanol reaction. J Stud Alcohol. 1977;38:96.

108 **Stoll D, King LE.** Disulfiram-alcohol skin reaction to beer-containing shampoo. JAMA. 1980;244:2045.

109 **Kwentus J et al.** Disulfiram in the treatment of alcoholism. J Stud Alcohol. 1979;40:428.

110 **Peachey JE et al.** A comparative review of the pharmacological and toxicological properties of disulfiram and calcium carbimide. J Clin Psychopharmacol. 1981;1:21.

111 **Eneanya DI et al.** The actions and metabolic fate of disulfiram. Ann Rev Toxicol. 1981;21:575.

112 **Bartle WR et al.** Disulfiram-induced hepatitis: report of two cases and review of the literature. Dig Dis Sci. 1985;20:834.

113 **Bilbao JM et al.** Filamentous axonopathy in disulfiram neuropathy. Ultrastruct Pathol. 1984;7:295.

114 **O'Reilly RA.** Dynamic interaction between disulfiram and separated enantiomorphs of racemic warfarin. Clin Pharmacol Ther. 1981;29:332.

115 **Olesen OV.** The influence of disulfiram and calcium carbimide on the serum diphenylhydantoin: excretion of HPPH in the urine. Arch Neurol. 1967;16:642.

116 **Yodaiken RE.** Ethylene dibromide and disulfiram—a lethal combination. JAMA. 1978;239:2783.

117 **Webb PK et al.** Disulfiram hypersensitivity and rubber contact dermatitis. JAMA. 1979;241:2061.

118 **Mezey E.** Alcoholic liver disease: roles of alcohol and malnutrition. Am J Clin Nutr. 1980;33:2709.

119 **Pimstone NG, French SW.** Alcoholic liver disease. Med Clin North Am. 1984;68:39.

120 **Mendenhall CL.** Alcoholic hepatitis. In: Schiff L, Schiff ER, eds. Diseases of the Liver. 6th ed. Philadelphia: Lippincott; 1987:669.

121 **Maddrey WC.** Alcoholic hepatitis: clinicopathologic features and therapy. Semin Liver Dis. 1988;8:91.

122 **Maddrey WC.** Alcoholic hepatitis: pathogenesis and approaches to treatment. Scand J Gastroenterol. 1990;25 (Suppl. 175):118.

123 **Kaysen GK, Noth RH.** The effects of alcohol on blood pressure and electrolytes. Med Clin North Am. 1984;68:221.

124 **Russell RM.** Vitamin A and zinc metabolism in alcoholism. Am J Clin Nutr. 1980;33:2741.

125 **Mendenhall CL et al.** Short-term and long-term survival in patients with alcoholic hepatitis treated with oxandrolone and prednisolone. N Engl J Med. 1984;311:1464.

126 **Wrona SA, Tankanow RM.** Corticosteroids in the management of alcoholic hepatitis. Am J Hosp Pharm. 1994;51:347.

127 **Larkin EC, Watson-Williams EJ.** Alcohol and the blood. Med Clin North Am. 1984;68:105.

128 **Lindenbaum J, Roman MJ.** Nutritional anemia in alcoholism. Am J Clin Nutr. 1980;33:2727.

129 **Halstead CH.** Folate deficiency in alcoholism. Am J Clin Nutr. 1980;33:2736.

130 **Rosett HL, Weiner L.** Alcohol and pregnancy: a clinical perspective. Ann Rev Med. 1985;36:73.

131 **Turner TB et al.** Measurement of alcohol-related effects in man: chronic effects in relation to level of alcohol consumption. Johns Hopkins Med J. 1977;141(Pt. A):235.

132 **Day NL.** Prenatal exposure to alcohol: effect on infant growth and morphologic characteristics. Pediatrics. 1989;84:536.

133 **Burd L, Martsolf JT.** Fetal alcohol syndrome: diagnosis and syndromal variability. Physiol Behav. 1989;46:39.

134 **West LJ et al.** Alcoholism. Ann Intern Med. 1984;100:405.

135 **Burbige EJ et al.** Alcohol and the gastrointestinal tract. Med Clin North Am. 1984;68:77.

136 **Hyumpa AM Jr.** Mechanisms of thiamine deficiency in chronic alcoholism. Am J Clin Nutr. 1980;33:2750.

137 **Chou SP.** An examination of the alcohol consumption and peptic ulcer disease association—results of a national survey. Alcohol Clin Exp Res. 1994;18:149.

138 **Krumpe PE et al.** Alcohol and the respiratory tract. Med Clin North Am. 1984;68:201.

139 **Adams HG, Jordan C.** Infections in the alcoholic. Med Clin North Am. 1984;68:179.

140 **Marshall JM.** Interaction of histamine₂-receptor antagonists and ethanol. Ann Pharmacother. 1994;28:55.

141 **Mufti SI et al.** Alcohol, cancer and immunomodulation. Crit Rev Oncol Hematol. 1989;9:243.

142 **Steinberg W, Tenner S.** Acute pancreatitis. N Engl J Med. 1994;330:1198.

143 **Cameron JL et al.** Acute pancreatitis with hyperlipidemia: the incidence of lipid abnormalities in acute pancreatitis. Ann Surg. 1973;177:483.

144 **Gumaste V et al.** Serum lipase: a better test to diagnose acute alcoholic pancreatitis. Am J Med. 1993;92:239.

145 **Tenner SM, Steinberg W.** The admission serum lipase:amylase ratio differentiates alcoholic from nonalcoholic acute pancreatitis. Am J Gastroenterol. 1992;87:1755.

146 **Schenker S et al.** Hepatic and Wernicke's encephalopathies: current concepts of pathogenesis. Am J Clin Nutr. 1980;33:2719.

147 **Reuler JB et al.** Wernicke's encephalopathy. N Engl J Med. 1985;312:1035.

148 **Nakada T, Knight RT.** Alcohol and the central nervous system. Med Clin North Am. 1984;68:121.

149 **Klatsky AL.** Epidemiology of coronary heart disease—influence of alcohol. Alcohol Clin Exp Res. 1994;18:88.

150 **Rubin R, Rand ML.** Alcohol and platelet function. Alcohol Clin Exp Res. 1994;18:105.

151 **Thomas AP et al.** Effects of ethanol on the contractile function of the heart: a review. Alcohol Clin Exp Res. 1994;18:121.

152 **Rubin E, Urbano-Marquez A.** Alcoholic cardiomyopathy. Alcohol Clin Exp Res. 1994;18:111.

153 **Davidson DM.** Cardiovascular effects of alcohol. West J Med. 1989;151:430.

154 **Grogan JR, Kochar MS.** Alcohol and hypertension. Arch Fam Med. 1994;3:150.

155 **Segel LD et al.** Alcohol and the heart. Med Clin North Am. 1984;68:147.

156 **Rich EC et al.** Alcohol-related acute atrial fibrillation: a case-control study and review of 40 patients. Arch Intern Med. 1985;145:830.

157 **Ettinger PO et al.** Arrhythmias and the "holiday heart": alcohol-associated cardiac rhythm disorders. Am Heart J. 1978;95:555.

158 **De Marchi S et al.** Renal tubular dysfunction in chronic alcohol abuse—effects of abstinence. N Engl J Med. 1993;329:1927.

159 **Koskinen P, Kupari M.** Alcohol and cardiac arrhythmias. BMJ. 1992;304:1394.

160 **Mello NK, Mendelson JH.** Neuroendocrine consequences of alcohol abuse in women. Ann N Y Acad Sci. 1989;562:211.

161 **Noth RH, Walter RM Jr.** The effects of alcohol on the endocrine system. Med Clin North Am. 1984;68:133.

162 **Urbano-Marquez A.** The effects of alcoholism on skeletal and cardiac muscle. N Engl J Med. 1989;320:409.

163 **Haller RG, Knochel JP.** Skeletal muscle disease in alcoholism. Med Clin North Am. 1984;68:91.

164 **Fernandez-Sola J et al.** The relationship of alcoholic myopathy to cardiomyopathy. Arch Intern Med. 1994;120:529.

165 **DiPiro JT.** Pathophysiology and treatment of gram-negative sepsis. Am J Hosp Pharm. 1990;47(Suppl. 3):S6–S10.

166 **Hackshaw KV et al.** Naloxone in septic shock. Crit Care Med. 1990;18:47.

167 **Wright DJM et al.** Naloxone in shock. Lancet. 1980;2:1360.

168 **Higgins TL, Sivak ED.** Reversal of hypotension with naloxone. Cleve Clin Q. 1981;48:283.

169 **Reents SV, Beck CA.** Naloxone and naltrexone; application in COPD. Chest. 1988;92:217.

170 **Tobin MJ et al.** Effect of naloxone on breathing pattern in patients with chronic obstructive pulmonary disease with and without hypercapnia. Respiration. 1983;44:419.

171 **Anon.** Naltrexone for alcoholism. Amer Pharm. 1995;NS35(3):8.

172 **O'Mara NB, Wesley LC.** Naltrexone in the treatment of alcohol dependence. Ann Pharmacother. 1994;28:210.

173 **Volpicelli JR et al.** Naltrexone in the treatment of alcohol dependence. Arch Gen Psych. 1992;49:876.

174 **O'Malley SS et al.** Naltrexone and coping skills therapy for alcohol dependence: a controlled study. Arch Gen Psych. 1992;49:881.

Depressant and Inhalant Abuse

Jeffrey N Baldwin
Blaine Benson

Depressant Abuse 83-1
  Incidence 83-2
Opioids 83-2
  China White, Persian Brown, Mexican Tar, and
    Designer Drugs 83-2
  Heroin Addiction 83-3
    Opioid Withdrawal Symptoms 83-3
      Heroin 83-3
      Other opioids 83-3
  Iatrogenic Addiction 83-3
  Medical Complications 83-4
  Heroin Overdose 83-4
  Treatment of Opioid Dependence 83-5
  Methadone and Opioid Addictive Disease 83-5
    Methadone detoxification 83-6
    Methadone maintenance 83-6
    Pain management 83-7
    Methadone in pregnancy 83-7
      Neonatal addiction 83-7
      Withdrawal during pregnancy 83-7
      Breast-feeding 83-7
      Treatment of neonatal addiction 83-7
  Heroin Antagonist Treatments 83-8
  Therapeutic Communities 83-8
  Symptomatic Therapy of Opioid Withdrawal 83-8
    Musculoskeletal aches and pains 83-9

  Anxiety 83-9
  Insomnia 83-9
  Gastrointestinal hyperactivity 83-9
  Complications of Polydrug Abuse 83-9
Sedative-Hypnotics 83-10
  Onset of Sedative-Hypnotic Dependence 83-10
  Abstinence Syndromes 83-10
  Treatment of Sedative Withdrawal 83-10
  Acute Sedative Withdrawal 83-10
Inhalants 83-11
  Volatile Solvents (See Table 83.1) 83-11
    Acute intoxication 83-11
      Acute toxicity 83-11
      Clinical presentation 83-12
      Treatment 83-12
      Further evaluation (See Table 83.2) 83-12
      Rehabilitation 83-13
    Chronic abuse 83-13
      Complications (See Table 83.3) 83-14
      Treatment 83-15
      Rehabilitation 83-15
  Nitrous Oxide 83-15
  Volatile Nitrites 83-16
    Abuse 83-16
    Assessment 83-16
    Treatment 83-17

Depressant Abuse

Addicting substances which depress central nervous system (CNS) functioning include opiates (natural opium derivatives) and opioids (synthetic opiates), sedative-hypnotics, and alcohol (see Chapter 82: Alcohol Abuse). These cause progressive sedation, muscle relaxation, drowsiness, coma, and even death, usually in a dose-dependent fashion. The progression is very similar to that observed with general anesthetic agents.

Inhalants comprise a wide variety of compounds with varying pharmacologic effects: often their only commonalities are that they are gases and are abused by inhalation. They include *volatile solvents* such as trichloroethane and toluene, *nitrites* such as n-butyl and isobutyl nitrites, and *nitrous oxide*. Most authorities prefer to separate volatile solvents from nitrites and nitrous oxide because the latter two substance groups appeal to different user groups and because nitrites have quite distinct pharmacologic effects compared to volatile solvents and nitrous oxide.

Depressants affect a wide range of biochemical processes in the central nervous system. Three major classes of opioid receptors (hereafter, the term ''opioids'' will include both opiates and opioids) have been defined: mu, kappa, and delta. Pain modulation in the supraspinal system appears to primarily involve receptor subtypes μ_1, κ_3, and Δ_2, while μ_2, κ_1, and Δ_1 receptors appear to be the primary spinal receptors for pain. Endogenous opioid ligands include enkephalins, dynorphins, and beta-endorphin. Enkephalin appears to exert analgesic activity at delta receptors. The effect of dynorphins on kappa receptors is unknown. Beta-endorphin is a nonselective activator of all three receptors. Naloxone (Narcan) and naltrexone (ReVia) are antagonists of all these receptors. Morphine and other opioids act almost exclusively at the mu receptors. Pentazocine (Talwin) and butorphanol (Stadol) are agonist-antagonist agents which exert antagonist activities at mu receptors and some agonist activity at kappa receptors. Pentazocine and butorphanol may produce dysphoric reactions at higher doses which may decrease their abuse liability. Buprenorphine (Buprenex) is a partial mu-receptor agonist while exerting antagonist activities at kappa receptors. Major agonist effects mediated through mu-receptor activity include analgesia, respiratory depression, miosis, reduced gastrointestinal (GI) motility, nausea, vomiting, and euphoria. Chronic users of heroin and other mu-agonist opiates often will be constipated because little tolerance develops to the GI effects.[1–5] Benzodiazepines and barbiturates appear to independently interact with gamma-aminobutyric acid (GABA) recognition sites and chloride channels in the neuraxis to enhance the inhibitory effects of GABA. Additionally, barbiturates appear to enhance the effects of benzodiazepines at the receptor sites. Other sedative-hypnotic agents probably also are primarily involved in modulation of the activity of GABA.[6]

Although CNS mechanisms are unclear, volatile solvents produce effects that are similar to induction with anesthesia. Initially, there is central nervous system stimulation with euphoria, sneezing, coughing, and salivation. This is followed by CNS depression which begins with a sense of invulnerability, confusion, and disorientation and progresses with larger doses to ataxia, depression of reflexes, and finally, cardiorespiratory arrest.

Opiates, which are derived from the opium poppy, include drugs such as heroin, morphine, and codeine. Opioids are synthetic compounds with opiate-like activity: examples include fentanyl (Sublimaze), meperidine (Demerol), methadone (Dolophine), pentazocine, and propoxyphene (Darvon). Sedative-hypnotic agents include the various benzodiazepines [e.g., alprazolam (Xanax), diazepam (Valium), and lorazepam (Ativan)], the barbiturates [e.g., pentobarbital (Nembutal), secobarbital (Seconal), amobarbital (Amytal), and phenobarbital (Luminal)], and other drugs such as meprobamate, methaqualone (previously marketed as Quaalude), chloral hydrate (Noctec), and glutethimide. Although all of these drugs may be used illicitly for their euphoric effects and to avoid withdrawal for those who are physically dependent, the most commonly abused are those which have a rapid onset, preferably by routes, such as injection, which produce a bolus effect in the neuraxis. Heroin addicts often refer to this as a "flash" or "rush"; a heroin "high" may include nausea and vomiting, in addition to euphoria in addicts who do not have a high tolerance. Inhalants are used for euphoric effects but are not associated with withdrawal.

Incidence

In 1991 an estimated 5.1 million persons in the United States used an opiate analgesic for nonmedical purposes. Factors associated with higher-than-average use during the month preceding the survey were age less than 35 years, black race, living in an area of low population density, and living in the western United States.[7] Approximately 2.7 million persons in the United States report having used heroin, with approximately 500,000 being "heroin addicts" (i.e., multiple doses daily with tolerance, physical dependence, and drug-seeking behavior).[8] About 80% of heroin abusers are age 26 or older. New York has the largest population of heroin users, followed by Los Angeles.[9]

Lifetime use of barbiturate or other prescription sedatives for nonmedical purposes was estimated to occur in 4.3% of people in the United States. Factors associated with higher-than-average use during the month preceding the survey included female gender, age 18 to 25 years, black race, and either having not completed high school or being a college graduate.[7]

About 5% of all prescriptions and 37% of controlled substance prescriptions were for benzodiazepines during a recent year. Statistically, one benzodiazepine prescription was written for every two adults in the United States. Nearly two-thirds of benzodiazepine abusers are female.[9] An estimated 1.7% of the population used a prescription tranquilizer (primarily benzodiazepines) for a nonmedical purpose during 1991. Factors associated with higher-than-average use during the month preceding the survey included female gender, age 18 to 34 years, white race, residing in small cities, living in the north central United States, completion of a high school education or less, and being unemployed.[7] Benzodiazepine use for other than hypnotic purposes was estimated to occur in 11% of the population each year. Of the 11%, 80% report use for less than four months, 5% for 4 to 11 months, and 15% report being on the drug for 12 months or longer.[10,11] The older population tends to be overrepresented among users, and they tend to use benzodiazepines more chronically.[12] Among alcohol or opiate abusers, prevalences of benzodiazepine use as high as 75% and 80% are reported, respectively. Benzodiazepines are rarely the primary drugs of abuse, yet are commonly abused. While treatment for isolated benzodiazepine abuse was reported in only 12% of inpatient drug abusers, 80% reported abuse of benzodiazepines in addition to other drugs.[13,14]

Inhalants include substances such as gasoline, spray paints, aerosol sprays, glue, lacquer thinners, amyl nitrite, ether, nitrous oxide, and correction fluids. Lifetime use was reported by 7% of 12 to 17 year olds, 10.9% of 18 to 25 year olds, and 9.2% of 26 to 34 year olds. While amyl nitrite, nitrous oxide, and gasoline were the three most cited inhalants overall, those age 12 to 17 years most often used, in decreasing order of frequency, gasoline, glue, spray paint, and correction fluids.[7]

Opioids
China White, Persian Brown, Mexican Tar, and Designer Drugs

1. D.J., a 28-year-old male, has been "fixing" (intravenous injection) two to six "quarter bags" ($25 worth) of "junk" (heroin sold on the street) daily for about a month. This "run" (daily use) began when he met a new "connection" (drug supplier) at a party. D.J. describes a steady supply of "China White," "Persian Brown," and "Mexican Tar," all of which are "the big bad thing, real heavy stuff" (the drugs were potent and produced consistently profound effects when used). D.J. has heard about "designer drugs" and asks you if these are the same thing as "China White," "Persian Brown," and "Mexican Tar." Is there a difference?

Traditionally, heroin has been sold in balloons containing 250 to 400 mg of powder. This quantity of heroin is often called a "dime" ($10) or "quarter" ($25) "bag." Since about 1978, however, three highly potent opioids have been introduced to surprised addicts who were previously familiar only with street powders containing a maximum of 2% heroin. First, "Persian Brown," which is up to 92% heroin, was brought to the United States from Iran where heroin is mostly smoked. Heroin overdoses were epidemic when the supplies of this unusually potent drug were first spread throughout the drug distribution networks.[15]

The second group of potent "synthetic heroin" formulations to be introduced to the addict population in the 1980s was known collectively as "China White." The term "China White" was used initially in the 1800s to refer to highly refined, white heroin from China. Now, however, it most frequently refers to either the synthetic fentanyl derivatives or to any reasonably pure heroin.[16,17] These synthetic opioids, misrepresented as "China White" heroin for marketing purposes or sometimes sold as "synthetic heroin," were the first of the so-called "designer drugs." The term "designer drug" is misleading because there is no universal acceptance of its meaning.[18] Originally, the "designer drugs" were similar in pharmacological effect to other opioids but were not subject to controlled substance regulations. Since 1988, however, it has been illegal to manufacture or sell these drugs.[19]

The new "China White" consisted of a series of compounds based upon the commercial drug, fentanyl. The first in this series was identified in 1980 as "alpha methyl fentanyl." These compounds share many pharmacological properties with heroin, which they were intended to replace, except that they are considerably more potent and have longer durations of action (i.e., 10 or 12 hours in comparison to heroin's four- to six-hour duration of action). The substantial potency of these opioids makes it difficult to dilute the powder evenly in nonscientific settings. When these drugs are inadequately mixed with inactive powdered ingredients, one part of the powdered mixture may consist entirely of inactive diluent and another part may consist almost entirely of active drug. As a result, many overdose deaths have occurred. The new compounds, however, continue to be purchased widely by street addicts.[20-22]

"Persian" and "China White" are usually purchased in "quarter tenths" consisting of 25 mg of powder packaged in wax paper or aluminum foil folded into small envelopes called "bindles" or "cribbies." These sell for $25 to $30 apiece.

In 1982, patients began appearing with adverse effects from a "designer drug" known as "synthetic heroin," which turned out to be MPPP (1-methyl-4-phenyl-4-propionoxypiperidine), a meperidine analog. These patients presented with symptoms of Parkinson's disease that subsequently were attributed to selective destruction of dopaminergic cells of the nigrostriatal tract in the brain by MPTP (1-methyl-4-phenyl-1,2,3,6-tetrahydropyridine). MPTP is a by-product that was formed during the synthesis of MPPP.[23] The symptoms are progressive, permanent, and eventually lead to death.[24,25] A third new opioid appeared shortly after MPTP was identified as another cause of Parkinson's disease.

"Tar heroin" or "Mexican Tar" was merchandised in great quantity as an "organic heroin" that would not cause Parkinson's disease. "Mexican Tar" contains 40% to 80% pure heroin and looks and feels like sticky black roofing tar; hence, its descriptive name. The "tar heroin" is either sold "raw" as a sticky, 25 mg blob, or as "gum ball" which is placed in the bottom or corner of a twisted or folded piece of plastic wrap or cellophane. This "gum ball" is difficult for a dealer to discretely "cut" (i.e., dilute the desired drug with a cheap adulterant). Nevertheless, a version of "tar heroin" that has been diluted with lactose to a concentration of 3% to 4% heroin is being sold in bags, and resembles the old "Mexican brown" heroin which has been available since the mid1970s. "Tar heroin" also has been the cause of many overdose deaths because of its surprisingly high potency.[26,27]

Although there is no clear definition of "designer drugs," the "China White" that D.J. uses may be a synthetic "designer drug" rather than refined heroin.

Heroin Addiction

2. D.J.'s "Jones" (heroin habit) had become "bad" (tolerance developed and his daily requirement of drug to maintain euphoria had exceeded his ability to pay for it). He could not "hustle" (obtain by any means) any more cash on a daily basis. "Kicking" (withdrawal symptoms occurring after abrupt cessation of drug use) "cold turkey" (undergoing withdrawal without any therapy for symptoms) resulted in the "super flu" (descriptive of typical heroin withdrawal symptoms) which seemed unnecessarily unpleasant. Now he is "chipping" (occasional use only) because the drug supply is so good he does not want to simply "be clean" (complete abstinence) until he obtains more money. Is D.J. "hooked" (addicted)?

Nontolerant human volunteers given 18 to 30 mg of morphine per 70 kg as a single dose exhibit withdrawal signs when naloxone is given 6 to 24 hours later.[28] These symptoms of physical dependence are almost imperceptible (see Chapter 7: Pain). Noticeable physical dependence (demonstrated by the onset of an obvious withdrawal syndrome upon abstinence) is highly variable but usually is not apparent until after two to four weeks of daily doses of 60 mg or more of morphine.

Objective withdrawal signs, the involuntary manifestations of abstinence, are also known as "nonpurposive" symptoms. They are almost always accompanied by a cluster of "purposive" symptoms, which are subjective reports of discomforts reported by the patient for the purpose of obtaining opioids and other drugs or to generate sympathy and other self-serving manipulations. An attempt should be made to differentiate between "purposive" and "nonpurposive" symptoms of opioid abstinence syndromes.[29]

Abstinence precipitated a withdrawal syndrome in D.J.; therefore, he is, by definition, physically addicted to heroin. His ongoing desire to continue using heroin despite his inability to afford it and his all-day hustling constitute a psychological dependence on heroin.

Opioid Withdrawal

3. Heroin. D.J. arrives at the detoxification clinic ten hours after his last dose of heroin. He is sweating, shaking, and keeps yawning. Should he be treated for opioid withdrawal?

The character, severity, and time course of withdrawal symptoms that appear when an opioid drug is discontinued depend upon many factors, including the particular opioid, total daily dose, interval between doses, duration of use, the intent of drug use, and the health and personality of the user. Unlike the withdrawal symptoms from sedative-hypnotic drugs, seizures do not occur with opioid withdrawal, and the withdrawal rarely is fatal.[29]

Six to twelve hours after the last dose of morphine or heroin (diacetylmorphine), the addict will develop symptoms of anxiety, rhinorrhea, lacrimation, sweating, and yawning. As the syndrome progresses, mydriasis, restlessness, irritability, and anorexia occur. "Shaking" chills, profuse sweating, and pilomotor activity result in waves of "gooseflesh" of the skin (thus, the term "cold turkey"). Increasing irritability and insomnia, marked anorexia, nausea, vomiting, abdominal cramps, and diarrhea occur. Severe back pain may accompany muscle spasms that cause kicking movements; hence, the descriptive term "kicking the habit." These symptoms are most severe 48 to 72 hours after the last opioid dose. Elevations in heart rate and blood pressure and leukocytosis occur. Anorexia combined with fluid loss through vomiting, sweating, and diarrhea can result in weight loss, dehydration, ketosis, and acid-base imbalance. Cardiovascular collapse is an uncommon complication during the peak phase of opiate withdrawal. The more dramatic symptoms of heroin withdrawal subside after seven to ten days of abstinence even without treatment; however, a return to complete physiological equilibrium may require much longer. D.J. is exhibiting typical heroin withdrawal symptoms and some therapy would be appropriate.

4. Other Opioids. R.F. says he is addicted to methadone, but 18 hours after his last dose, he does not exhibit any signs of opioid withdrawal. Is this reasonable?

Physiological withdrawal symptoms from all opioid drugs are qualitatively similar but quantitatively different in the onset, duration, and severity.

Abstinence symptoms from meperidine appear within three hours of the last dose, peak within 8 to 12 hours, and persist for four to five days. Although mydriasis and GI symptoms appear less than those produced by morphine and heroin withdrawal, restlessness, nervousness, and muscular twitching often are more severe when the abstinence syndrome from meperidine is at its peak intensity.

Opioids with shorter durations of action tend to produce brief, intense abstinence syndromes, while those eliminated from the body at a much slower rate produce prolonged, but milder, withdrawal syndromes. The abstinence syndrome of methadone is consistent with that expected for a long-acting opioid. Methadone withdrawal symptoms do not become apparent until 24 to 48 hours after the last dose. Although the symptoms are qualitatively similar to those of morphine and heroin, they are less severe overall but are most intense around the fourth to sixth day of abstinence. The acute abstinence syndrome may not begin to subside until after several weeks and may be followed by a protracted period of hypochondriasis with feelings of inefficiency, tiredness, and weakness.[29] It is entirely possible that R.F. is methadone-addicted since his methadone withdrawal symptoms should not occur until one to two days after his last dose.

Iatrogenic Addiction

5. J.B., a 21-year-old male who underwent bowel surgery, required morphine 10 mg subcutaneously Q 4 hr for two weeks. Is J.B. physically addicted to morphine?

Mild symptoms of withdrawal, which may not even be recognized as such, will occur in patients who have received therapeutic doses of morphine several times daily for one or two weeks. When narcotic antagonists were administered to subjects who had received a single dose of morphine, withdrawal symptoms were precipitated.[28-30] Nevertheless, the percentage of patients who continue to seek opioids following the successful treatment of pain with narcotics is very small. The role of physical dependence in the development of compulsive heroin or morphine abuse is almost insignificant when one considers the extremely large number of patients who have received multiple daily doses of opiates during hospitalizations lasting more than two to three days. Therefore, it would be extremely unlikely that J.B. would be psychologically dependent upon opiates despite the fact that he most likely will experience mild withdrawal symptoms after terminating his morphine. These withdrawal symptoms are usually so mild that they seldom are attributed to opioid abstinence by the patient.

6. Some people feel that it is inappropriate for recovering addicts to receive any opioid therapy for pain. If J.B. were a recovering opioid addict, how would this affect his therapy?

Some members of 12-step programs such as Alcoholics Anonymous (AA) or Narcotics Anonymous (NA) maintain a belief that the use of any mood-altering drug constitutes relapse. However, the general consensus in the addiction treatment community is that use of mood-altering substances is appropriate in many circumstances, but that therapy should be directed by a health professional knowledgeable about addiction and relapse. If J.B. had any history of substance abuse or dependence, including alcohol, it is important to note this and anticipate that his narcotic requirements may be higher than usual. If he were a recovering addict, it might be necessary to titrate his dosage upward rapidly to a level affording adequate pain relief. It is also important to recognize that once the recovering addict is on the morphine, he may lose control of his ability to make rational decisions regarding narcotic dosing, requesting additional doses or therapy beyond the period of acute pain. This "controlled relapse" should be anticipated by caregivers; alternative nonopioid analgesics should be used if appropriate for the anticipated level of pain. If opioid use is indicated, adequate doses at appropriate times should be given, but J.B. should not be allowed to "con" the caregivers into shorter dosing intervals or into providing prescriptions for opioids beyond the period of acute pain. Many relapses occur because pain control in recovering addicts is mismanaged by well-intentioned health professionals who have received marginal education concerning substance abuse.

7. J.B. also has a family history of alcoholism and other drug addiction in an uncle, one grandfather, and his mother. If his sister, R.B., did not have a personal history of addiction, what precautions, if any, would be necessary should R.B. require therapy with mood-altering substances?

Histories of alcoholism or other drug addiction in immediate family members (e.g., parents, grandparents, siblings) appear to increase the liability for development of alcoholism or addictions. One study reported that 58% of alcoholics and 46% of other drug addicts reported having a parent who was alcoholic.[31] Another study of adult children of alcoholics revealed that 37% described themselves as alcoholics (versus 9.5% of controls).[32] R.B. would be considered at risk for addiction. She should be informed of the additional risk and be treated cautiously when mood-altering drugs must be given. Opioid therapy should be directed by the same principles outlined in Question 6.

Medical Complications

8. T.M., a 30-year-old female, is admitted to the emergency room (ER) with violent shaking chills. She admits that she is a heroin addict and was forced into "doing some cottons" because of an acute financial crisis. She now fears that she has "cotton fever." How should "cotton fever" be managed and what other medical complications of heroin addiction might be suspected?

When heroin is prepared for self-administration, cotton is used as a filter to trap adulterants; thus, some of the drug remains trapped in the cotton. These crude filters are saved, and when money or drug availability is poor, water or other solvents are added to the "old cottons" to extract any remaining drug for intravenous use. "Cotton fever" appears to be an allergic reaction, probably caused by tiny cotton fibers. The onset is within 30 minutes of injection, with shaking chills, diaphoresis, postural hypotension, tachycardia, and low-grade fever. These symptoms are initially suggestive of sepsis, but most of the symptoms resolve without treatment in two to four hours with complete recovery in one day. Nonetheless, these patients must be evaluated according to symptom presentation, and sepsis needs to be ruled out with blood cultures and other studies.

Bacterial endocarditis (usually acute rather than subacute; most commonly caused by *Staphylococcus aureus*), sepsis, pneumonia [*Streptococcus pneumoniae* most often; *Pneumocystis carinii* common in human immunodeficiency virus (HIV)-infected patients], osteomyelitis, septic arthritis, septic and aseptic abscesses, cellulitis, thrombophlebitis, and embolism also have resulted from both improper sterilization of injection apparatus and needles and poor injection techniques.[33]

The common practice of sharing "outfits" (needle and syringe) between friends has resulted in an estimated 60% or greater incidence of Acquired Immunodeficiency Syndrome (AIDS) among intravenous (IV) drug users.[34] Although only about 28% of AIDS cases in the United States were attributed to IV drug use, many other cases are attributable to risky behaviors related to drug and alcohol abuse, and many HIV-infected IV drug users die from complications which do not meet the surveillance definition of AIDS.[35] Other infectious diseases such as viral hepatitis, syphilis, tetanus, botulism, and malaria can be transmitted in a similar manner and should also be considered.[33]

T.M. had blood cultures drawn and was treated symptomatically in the ER; three hours later, her symptoms began to resolve. She was discharged from the emergency room with instructions to avoid "doing cottons," referral to a methadone maintenance program, and instructions to return should symptoms recur. T.M.'s blood cultures subsequently were determined to be negative for bacterial and viral disease (including HIV and hepatitis).

Heroin Overdose

9. T.F., a 21-year-old male, is unconscious after he allegedly "OD'd" (overdosed) on "junk" (heroin). He has a decreased respiratory rate (RR) of 4 breaths/min, cyanosis, symmetrically "pinned" (maximally miotic or pinpoint) pupils, and a slightly decreased blood pressure (BP). He has one "fresh track" (needle puncture wound) and several "old tracks" (healed scars from needle puncture wounds) in the antecubital fossa area. What is the immediate treatment of choice in T.F.?

Although naloxone is a specific pure opioid antagonist, it should not be viewed as the sole management of this situation. The first response should be to establish adequate ventilation through basic and advanced life support procedures, if indicated, while venous access is secured.

Initial IV administration of 0.4 to 2 mg naloxone (0.01 mg to 0.1 mg/kg for children <20 kg) should be slow and stopped if the patient responds. There is no need to precipitate opioid withdrawal symptoms; the endpoint of naloxone therapy is a relative stabilization of the patient's own vital signs. A naloxone-precipitated, sudden-onset withdrawal syndrome is more severe than the symptoms produced by abstinence alone. Nevertheless, if the first dose of naloxone does not revive the patient within two to three minutes, then additional 2 mg (up to 0.1 mg/kg for children <20 kg) bolus intravenous doses should be administered as needed for up to five or six additional doses. If the patient still has not responded once a total of 10 mg has been given, then another diagnosis should be considered. Severe pulmonary edema, which may occur with opioid overdosage, is countered with positive pressure respiratory support. Some drugs such as pentazocine, butorphanol, and nalbuphine (Nubain) will require higher naloxone doses. Buprenorphine may require as much as 10 gm (*grams, not milligrams*) of naloxone because it is so tightly bound to mu receptors.[1,36-38]

The duration of action of naloxone ranges from 20 to 60 minutes. Management of the methadone overdosed patient will require serial dosing of naloxone every 20 to 60 minutes since the toxic effects of this long-acting opiate recur. The patient must be carefully observed for about six hours following the termination of naloxone therapy to detect any reappearance of opioid intoxication. Continuous intravenous infusion of naloxone also may be used when high doses are needed, the patient has recurrent respiratory depression with intermittent doses, or when long-acting opioids are being antagonized. Naloxone has no agonist properties of its own and lacks the hallucinogenic, miotic, and subjective adverse effects reported when the partial agonists/antagonists are used. It does not produce tolerance or signs of physical dependence. Naloxone also has a very high therapeutic index; doses ten times the usual therapeutic dose may result only in slight drowsiness.[38]

Naltrexone is a longer-acting oral narcotic antagonist which may be used in maintenance therapy or following initial therapy with naloxone, but is rarely used in acute overdosage because it may precipitate severe withdrawal. Naloxone clearly is the best pharmacological antagonist in opioid overdoses.[36,38]

T.F. receives assisted ventilation while attaining venous access. He receives 2 mg of naloxone slowly without response. Two additional doses of 2 mg are given at about three and five minutes following the first dose; T.M. responds following the administration of a total of 6 mg of naloxone. Assisted ventilation is stopped, and he is observed overnight for further respiratory difficulty. Naloxone is readily available should additional doses be needed; none are required.

Treatment of Opioid Dependence

10. A.X. has been addicted to heroin for three years, is tired of the street scene, and wants to rehabilitate to steady employment. He is not sure he can stop using opioids but seems willing and determined to try anything. What treatments are available to him?

In a book published in 1868, H.B. Day wrote that there was no agreement among the medical profession as to the proper treatment of "opium disease" or "morphinism."[39] The statement still is applicable today: the treatment of heroin addiction is beset by legal, political, and medical controversy.

The ultimate goal of most detoxification programs is to transform the narcotic addict into a responsible, drug-free, emotionally stable, and productive member of society. Despite many claims, no program to date fulfills all of these goals. Furthermore, all programs either have a high recidivism rate or do not produce a drug-free state in the patient. Heroin addiction, or any other chronic compulsive form of drug abuse, is a symptom of a wide range of problems in the addictive disease patient.

Therefore, no single treatment modality can be applied universally to all patients. Medical management of the opioid addict

ranges from the opioid maintenance approach to the "cold turkey" approach of abrupt cessation of the opioid without any supportive therapy. Between these two extremes there are many therapeutic modalities aimed at management of acute opioid withdrawal and social rehabilitation of the opioid-addicted patient. There is a frustratingly high recidivism rate after acute detoxification from opiates in any detoxification program. Physiological and social influences, primarily mood lability and stress intolerance, are associated with the protracted abstinence syndrome often observed in recovering opioid addicts. However, drug-related stimuli, even in the absence of drugs, may cause conditioned withdrawal effects. Exposure of a recovering opioid addict to environmental cues or settings associated with previous drug use may precipitate these symptoms. This is especially problematic when the recovering addict is still in protracted withdrawal.[40] Avoidance of exposure to people, places, and objects associated with past drug abuse is, therefore, especially important during the first several years of recovery for opioid addicts.

With A.X.'s apparently strong psychological addiction to heroin (he does not know if he can live without opioids), it would seem appropriate to attempt gradual detoxification while aggressively pursuing occupational, psychiatric, and social counseling. If detoxification is unsuccessful, then A.X. might be a good candidate for long-term methadone maintenance therapy.

Methadone and Opioid Addictive Disease

11. A.X. read in a magazine article that methadone is a "cure" for heroin addiction. Will methadone "cure" his addiction?

Methadone plays a dual therapeutic role in the treatment of opioid addictive disease: that of *acute detoxification* (initial replacement of heroin with methadone to minimize withdrawal symptoms, followed by progressively decreasing doses until the patient is drug-free) and that of *maintenance* or long-term replacement therapy (the patient does not find it possible to live without opioids, so the illegal heroin is replaced by legally sanctioned methadone). Methadone is a synthetic, fully addictive, orally acting opiate with a prolonged duration of action of 12 to 24 hours. Pharmacologically, it is qualitatively identical to morphine and other opioid analgesics.[1] Pioneered by Dole and Nyswander, methadone substitution was considered the treatment of choice for opioid addiction by many researchers by 1970.[41,42] Although skepticism ran high, the clamor of "drug experts" and politicians for increased methadone maintenance treatment programs resulted in the hasty fabrication of many such projects throughout the United States. As might be expected, their effectiveness was not as good as the original reports indicated. Also, methadone emerged as a drug of abuse and many deaths resulted from its excessive use.[43,44] Methadone maintenance is used throughout the world for opioid addictions, especially heroin. Approximately 100,000 patients are receiving methadone maintenance in the United States: many recipients are those who are disenfranchised, prone to relapse, and at risk of HIV infection because of IV heroin use. With the availability of alternative therapies, such as naltrexone which became available in 1985, the methadone approach now is viewed more conservatively as one of the potential therapeutic modalities for the opioid addictive disease patient rather than as a panacea for opioid abuse.[45]

Acute detoxification with methadone might result in a drug-free state for A.X. Alcoholism and other drug addictions are chronic diseases; like diabetes mellitus, these diseases are incurable but may be placed in long-term, drug-free remission which requires long-term recovery support.

Methadone Detoxification

12. A.X. is being started on methadone detoxification at a drug detoxification center. He claims to have a $100/day "habit" of "junk." What is the recommended methadone dose for treatment of A.X.?

The quality of illicit heroin is highly variable, as affected by the variables of the illicit marketplace. Methadone treatment units, like most large drug detoxification centers, send drug samples from the street to their contract laboratory [often the Drug Enforcement Administration's (DEA's) or local police department's crime laboratory] for both qualitative and quantitative analysis. By this evaluation, the currently available supply (which may vary from 0.5% to about 95% purity) has an average of 10% heroin. Usually 1 mg of oral methadone is equivalent to parenteral doses of 20 mg of meperidine, 4 mg of morphine, or 2 mg of heroin. A 20% daily reduction in dose usually is well tolerated in hospitalized patients with little discomfort. In outpatients, it may be necessary to stabilize the patient for several days then gradually reduce the dose as dictated by the patient's withdrawal symptoms: withdrawal periods of up to 180 days are permitted under federal law. Because of methadone's pharmacokinetics, on about the third or fourth day of tapering, many patients will begin to experience modest withdrawal discomfort. The majority of patients can be withdrawn completely from opioids in less than ten days, although some mild abstinence symptoms may persist beyond the tapering period, and the protracted abstinence syndrome may persist (see Question 10). Some clinicians believe daily methadone doses in excess of 40 mg are unnecessary in most cases (e.g., health professionals on very high doses of pharmaceutical opioids may need higher doses).[29,36,46]

A.X. reportedly uses $100/day, or four "quarter bags" ($25) daily, each containing about 300 mg of powder, of which about 10% or 30 mg supposedly is heroin. Therefore, his total daily dose is about 120 mg heroin. A.X.'s use of 120 mg/day of heroin is comparable to approximately 60 mg/day of methadone, which is administered in divided doses. This initial methadone dose of 60 mg/day is decreased on subsequent days to daily doses of 48 mg, 38 mg, 30 mg, 24 mg, 19 mg, 15 mg, 12 mg, 10 mg, and 8 mg on the tenth day. Subsequently, the methadone can be discontinued. His clinicians will not discuss the dose of methadone with A.X. Objective evaluation of the appropriate dose of methadone for either detoxification or maintenance is best accomplished without the complication of patient bias concerning the "fairness" of a given dose. To facilitate administration of unrecognizable doses and to minimize diversion, the methadone dose is mixed into orange juice which the patient must drink in the presence of the clinician.

Methadone Maintenance

13. J.H. is director of the detoxification center; he is also interested in establishing a methadone maintenance component to its detoxification program. He is unsure if he has the staffing to administer daily doses of methadone. What should J.H. consider when making his decision?

Before anyone can legally administer methadone for treatment of heroin dependence for more than 180 days or operate a methadone clinic, the program must be approved by federal, state, and, in some cases, even local law enforcement and licensing agencies. The ultimate goal of methadone maintenance is controversial. By enabling addicts to escape from the illicit drug scene, review their present lifestyles, and reorient their goals, rehabilitation becomes possible and the inherent dangers of IV drug use can be avoided. Early enthusiasm for methadone maintenance has now been tarnished by its use in the same abuse patterns as other opioids. Methadone is now a desired substitute for heroin among the addict population, even though the "high" it provides generally is considered inferior to that of heroin, codeine, and other opioids.

During methadone maintenance, the addict is stabilized on a dose of methadone that will be sufficient to suppress heroin withdrawal symptoms for 12 to 24 hours without producing euphoria. The initial day's dose of 30 to 40 mg may be required, but no more. The dose can then be gradually increased in 10 mg increments every two to three days until the maintenance dose is reached. While tolerance to analgesic and sedative effects will develop at about four to six weeks of methadone therapy, tolerance to autonomic effects such as constipation and sweating develops more slowly. In the first phase of treatment during the initial three months, the drug usually is administered in one daily oral dose to maintain daily contact with the patient and reduce diversion for resale. The second phase of therapy may include vocational goals and take-home medication, depending upon the patient's progress. The third stage includes ongoing maintenance, often with weekly visits to obtain medications and submission of urine specimens for drug screening. Many patients will elect to withdraw from methadone after a successful period of maintenance. When patients are tapered off methadone, support services are required well beyond the date of total abstinence because of craving and protracted abstinence syndrome.[45,46]

The issue of whether or not successful rehabilitation occurs, or is even possible, is confused by the lack of clear and widely accepted goals of therapy. The addition of social objectives to the therapeutic medical goal of cessation of heroin self-administration further confuses the issue. For many, the elimination of heroin use must be accompanied by successful incorporation of the patient into the "straight" world to consider detoxification and rehabilitation successful. Additionally, some people believe the patient must remain completely drug-free for life (including methadone) to consider the treatment program a success. Others see opioid addictive disease as a disorder in which some opioid, methadone for example, always must be administered to the addict to correct the underlying biochemical pathology before any social rehabilitation can occur. J.H. should decide what his beliefs are on these matters, then set clear and individualized therapeutic goals for each patient.

Medical staffing problems and disruption of the patient's employment schedules brought about by the necessity for daily doses of methadone have stimulated the search for a longer-acting alternative to methadone. Levomethadyl acetate (ORLAAM), which has investigationally been known as "LAAM," is now available as an oral solution only to treatment programs approved by the DEA, Food and Drug Administration (FDA), and designated state authorities. These programs must follow federal guidelines for its use. This methadone homologue is a synthetic opioid which has analgesic effects similar to methadone while having a longer duration of action.

Levomethadyl is usually administered three times a week, either Monday, Wednesday, Friday or Tuesday, Thursday, Saturday. If withdrawal is a problem during the latter part of the 72-hour interval on the seventh day of the cycle, additional drug can be given on the dose before the 72-hour period or the patient may be placed on an every-other-day regimen. The initial dose for street addicts is 20 to 40 mg with 5 to 10 mg adjustments in subsequent dosages as needed to maintain consistent control. For those maintained on, and being switched from, methadone, the change is done abruptly, with substitution of levomethadyl at a dosage 1.2 to 1.3 times the maintenance methadone dose: initial maximum recommended levomethadyl dosage is 120 mg. Most patients will require chronic levomethadyl doses of 60 to 90 mg. The maximum recommended dosages of levomethadyl are: 140 mg three times a week or every other day; or, for patients who experience withdrawal during the 72-hour interval, 130 mg for the first two doses then 180 mg for the dose before the three-day interval.

Regulations prohibit take-home dosages of levomethadyl. Patients who are unable to come in for scheduled dosages, because of illness or hospitalization, personal crisis, or travel, are transferred temporarily to methadone therapy. The methadone should be started no sooner than 48 hours after the last levomethadyl dose, usually at a dosage of 80% of the levomethadyl dose. Detoxification with levomethadyl has been used occasionally, either by gradual reduction of 5% to 10% of the dose or through more abrupt withdrawal schedules.[47]

J.H should assess the local need for such services. When establishing a methadone maintenance program, J.H. must comply with federal, state, and local regulations which will entail significant record-keeping and control procedures. While some of his clients may become drug-free, many will require chronic maintenance services. His staff will need to be expanded to encompass the medical (including HIV infection and hepatitis), psychological, vocational, and social support required by his clients. He should evaluate levomethadyl as a potential component of his program.

Pain Management

14. T.A., a 44-year-old male maintained on 120 mg/day of methadone, is in severe pain due to fractures of his femur. What type and how much analgesic can be used safely in T.A.?

Because of tolerance to the analgesic effects of methadone, full therapeutic doses of analgesic opioids such as morphine, if indicated, should be used. In some cases, higher-than-usual doses and more frequent administration may be necessary. For T.A., an initial dose of 10 mg of morphine might be used. Opioid withdrawal should be strictly avoided in T.A. because it is associated with hypersensitivity to painful stimulus, followed by exaggerated catecholamine and anxiety responses. The usual maintenance dose of methadone should be continued. If necessary, intramuscular or subcutaneous methadone may be administered if the patient is unable to take it orally. The partial antagonist/agonist narcotics, buprenorphine, butorphanol, dezocine (Dalgan), nalbuphine, and pentazocine should be avoided because their narcotic antagonist properties may precipitate opioid withdrawal symptoms when used in the methadone-maintained patient. It is not unusual for patients receiving methadone to indicate that they are ''allergic'' to antagonists such as pentazocine.[33]

T.A.'s clinician at his methadone maintenance clinic should consult with the orthopedic surgeon to assure that these procedures are followed and should attempt to maintain contact with T.A. during the hospitalization to assure continuation of maintenance therapy and support throughout a period with high potential for relapse.

Methadone in Pregnancy

15. J.R., a 28-year-old female, has been maintained on 100 mg/day of methadone for the past year. She now is eight months pregnant. She denies IV drug use while on methadone. J.R. is negative for HIV and hepatitis. She wants to know if methadone or her past heroin use will cause her to have a ''monster baby.''

Although many babies born to methadone-maintained mothers are premature by weight, methadone does not appear to be teratogenic, nor does it appear to have an adverse effect on mental development. Methadone-maintained women frequently have regular menstrual periods, ovulate, conceive, and have normal pregnancies. Heroin-addicted mothers, however, generally experience more problematic pregnancies because their life-style often pre-

disposes them to a poor general state of health and precludes adequate prenatal medical care. Infants born to heroin-addicted mothers also may be exposed to other substances (e.g., alcohol, cocaine, tobacco). These infants tend to be smaller, of a lower body weight, and born prematurely more frequently than the children of nonopiate using mothers. Additionally, IV drug use is a major cause of HIV infection and hepatitis in infants. Regardless of the nature of drug abuse, women who obtained adequate prenatal care had a significantly lower infant mortality rate than those receiving inadequate care.[48-50]

J.R. has been taking only methadone throughout her pregnancy; she denies any IV drug use. She is negative for HIV and hepatitis. Her past drug use and current methadone maintenance, therefore, should not have an adverse effect on her child.

16. Neonatal Addiction. Since methadone crosses the placental barrier, will J.R.'s infant exhibit opioid withdrawal symptoms after birth?

Methadone crosses the placental barrier and can cause CNS and respiratory depression as well as opioid abstinence in the newborn. In one study, 50% of the infants born to methadone-maintained mothers exhibited withdrawal signs of twitching and irritability, and half of these required treatment. These withdrawal signs in the newborn of a methadone-maintained mother may be delayed for up to three days.[51]

J.R.'s infant will probably display some withdrawal symptoms such as irritability.

17. Withdrawal During Pregnancy. Why should methadone not be discontinued in J.R. despite its adverse effects on the fetus?

Since J.R. is in her eighth month of pregnancy, she probably should be maintained on methadone to avoid precipitating a withdrawal syndrome. A structured methadone maintenance program that provides access to counseling and medical care probably is at least as beneficial to the pregnancy as the pharmacologic prevention of withdrawal. Although some investigators suggest that in late pregnancy the daily methadone dose should be reduced to 20 mg or less to minimize the neonate's withdrawal symptoms, most evidence suggests that a dosage in the range of 35 to 80 mg of methadone be used daily during pregnancy to maintain maternal comfort.[48,51] Therefore, the dose of methadone should be titrated individually throughout the pregnancy. The neonate can be managed for either opioid depression or methadone withdrawal after delivery.

18. Breast-Feeding. Should J.R. be permitted to breast feed her infant, A.R., after delivery?

Methadone is excreted in the breast milk of methadone-maintained mothers. The quantities, though small, may be sufficient to cause some physical dependency in infants. J.R. should be encouraged to become drug-free if she wishes to breast-feed.[46]

19. Treatment of Neonatal Addiction. What opioid withdrawal symptoms are likely to be manifested by A.R. and how should they be managed?

Opioid withdrawal in the neonate manifests as a wide variety of nonspecific signs that might be compatible with numerous serious disorders of the newborn of a mother in poor health. In general, the most common withdrawal symptoms include restlessness, tremors, a high pitched cry, hypertonicity, hyperreflexia, regurgitation, tachypnea, diarrhea, yawning, mottling, fever, and sneezing. Seizures may also occur.

Not all infants born to opioid-dependent mothers develop abstinence syndromes; prophylactic therapy is not recommended. The infant should be observed for at least four days while in the hospital. Those who do develop an abstinence syndrome should be maintained in a calm, quiet, warm environment; handled as little as possible; and swaddled to reduce sensory stimulation. Because dehydration is probable due to poor feeding, vomiting, diarrhea, and increased insensible water loss through tachypnea and sweating, aggressive fluid, electrolyte, and caloric support is necessary. Mild withdrawal symptoms need no therapy; however, moderate to severe symptoms may require 14 or more days of treatment. Therapy of neonatal withdrawal should begin when observable symptoms occur.

Symptoms of physiological addiction are usually apparent within 48 hours of birth. At this time, treatment can be initiated. One of three medications currently is used to alleviate opioid withdrawal symptoms in the neonate, although dosage recommendations have not been well established. *Phenobarbital* is instituted in doses from 8 to 20 mg/kg in the first 24 hours, then tapered symptomatically, usually about 10% to 20% per day. Although paregoric (camphorated opium tincture) continues to be used widely, it is preferable to use *tincture of opium* (when diluted 1:25 with water, this is equivalent in opium concentration to paregoric) because paregoric contains camphor, which is a CNS stimulant, and benzoic acid, which may displace bilirubin and causes gasping and CNS depression. Diluted (i.e., 1:25) tincture of opium is given as three to six drops every three to six hours as needed, then is adjusted to control withdrawal symptoms. Alternatively, it can be given as 0.2 mL every three hours, then the dosage is increased by 0.05 mL every three hours until withdrawal symptoms are controlled. Paregoric, when used, would be given in the same dosage as diluted tincture of opium. After the patient has been stabilized for three to five days, the dosage is reduced gradually over two to four weeks. Doses of these drugs should be individualized so that neither withdrawal symptoms nor overdose occur. While therapy with tincture of opium is probably the most effective single intervention for alleviation of all neonatal withdrawal symptoms, tincture of opium is very easy to overdose and prolongs the withdrawal state. Therapy with phenobarbital is considered inferior to opium tincture for global symptom control. However, phenobarbital therapy may require fewer days than tincture of opium in some cases. Neonatal addiction is an area in need of much research.[52-54]

A.R., initially feeds poorly, requiring aggressive intravenous supplementation: he is kept in an isolette in a quiet corner of the nursery intensive care unit (ICU). At about two days of age, A.R. develops tremors and is extremely agitated and tachypneic. Tincture of opium diluted 1:25 is initiated, given as 0.2 mL every three hours; the dose is ultimately adjusted upward to 0.35 mL/dose to achieve adequate symptom control. This dose is administered for three days, then is tapered over two weeks.

Heroin Antagonist Treatments

20. A.J. is a surgeon seeking rehabilitation and reinstatement of his medical license following five years of meperidine abuse. Is the "antagonist" or "heroin blockade" approach to the treatment of opioid addiction appropriate for A.J.?

Purportedly, methadone (80 to 150 mg or more) blocks the euphoriant effects of other opioids without producing euphoria itself. This dose allegedly produces a high degree of crosstolerance to other opioids so that it is extremely difficult to "get off" (obtain euphoria) with IV injection of other opioids. However, the role of methadone has been questioned since addicts have been able to obtain euphoria from doses of 60 to 100 mg of methadone. Furthermore, at lower maintenance doses of methadone that do not produce euphoria, addicts have been able to reach euphoric states through the concomitant IV administration of other opioids. Methadone in high blocking doses has become a secondary drug of abuse.

If opioid addiction results from a process of classical and instrumental conditioning, and is positively reinforced by self-ad-

ministration and drug seeking behavior, then narcotic antagonists may break this addiction cycle. The narcotic antagonists naloxone and naltrexone can block the euphoriant effects of heroin and other opiates, prevent the development of physical dependence, and afford protection from opioid-overdose deaths.

Of these two antagonists, only naltrexone appears to have any practical utility. Naloxone is impractical because of its short duration of action and variable potency when taken orally. Naltrexone is orally active and provides a dose-related duration of opioid blockade. An oral dose of 100 mg of naltrexone will block opiate effects for two days, and 150 mg for three days. Thus, dosing on a Monday, Wednesday, Friday schedule is possible and convenient for the patient. There are few side effects, and abrupt withdrawal of naltrexone does not result in symptoms of abstinence. Patients selected for naltrexone therapy must be opioid-free to avoid precipitation of withdrawal. For heroin or morphine addicts, a four- to seven-day wait is recommended, while methadone addiction requires a 10- to 14-day wait. If there is doubt concerning the adequacy of the washout period or the addict's history of use, a naloxone challenge dose can be given and naltrexone initiated if withdrawal symptoms do not develop. Naloxone challenge involves IV administration of 0.5 mL of 0.4 mg/mL naloxone solution, waiting 30 seconds, then administering an additional 1.5 mL if there is no mydriasis, dysphoria, GI discomfort, or perspiration on the forehead. If no withdrawal symptoms occur within 20 minutes, naltrexone may be administered. When there is no venous access, 2 mL of the solution is given subcutaneously and the patient is observed for 45 minutes.

Health professionals and business executives who are motivated to abstain by their peer groups have been treated most successfully with this drug.[55-59] A.J. is a good candidate for naltrexone therapy because of his desire to rehabilitate and his need to remain drug-free despite continued access to opioids at work.

Therapeutic Communities

21. How might A.J. benefit from involvement in a "therapeutic community"?

A modality that has been successful in the total rehabilitation of a heroin addict is the therapeutic community or what is called the "third community" (the first community being the "straight world" in which an addict feels both different and alienated and the second being the "drug scene" which advocates the use of psychoactive drugs as a means of problem solving and escape). These long-term (i.e., 90 days to several years) therapeutic community programs appeal to relatively few addicts because of the live-in and total commitment aspects. They are most effective when there exists major leverage (criminal, licensure, job) to keep the addict in treatment, especially when there have been multiple relapses in the past.[58]

Other, short-term therapeutic communities (often called "halfway houses") emphasize returning the addict to society. Unfortunately, the same limitations and high recidivism rates of the full-time therapeutic communities also apply to these short-term facilities.

A.J. might benefit from such involvement if he has difficulty during treatment or with maintaining recovery, but less rigorous and time-consuming therapy is probably most appropriate initially.

Symptomatic Therapy of Opioid Withdrawal

22. What symptomatic management of the opioid withdrawal syndrome might be appropriate for A.J.?

As the heroin problem reached epidemic proportions in the late 1960s, outpatient treatment clinics integrated "street professionals'' (ex-addicts) with ''paper professionals'' (pharmacists, physicians, nurses, psychologists). These individuals serve a large percentage of the addict population and are reasonably successful.

Programs like the Haight-Ashbury Drug Detoxification and Aftercare Project in San Francisco use nonnarcotic drugs to treat heroin withdrawal symptoms and emphasize psychosocial counseling and social-vocational rehabilitation. The four primary symptoms of opioid withdrawal are musculoskeletal aches and pains, anxiety, insomnia, and gastrointestinal disorders. A formulary of medications to treat these symptoms is established by first determining which of the nonnarcotic drugs are acceptable to the patient population. Of these, only those drugs that afford the highest therapeutic index and lowest addiction liability are included. Medications are dispensed on a daily basis along with counseling and medical monitoring. After 20 years of use, the medications originally selected remain the best of the numerous alternatives now available.

Musculoskeletal Aches and Pains

Musculoskeletal aches and pains are managed individually. For bone or joint pain, a nonsteroidal anti-inflammatory drug (NSAID), such as ibuprofen (Motrin) 800 mg every eight hours with food, may be used. Muscle pain or cramps may be treated with a muscle relaxant such as chlorzoxazone (Parafon Forte) 500 mg or methocarbamol (Robaxin) 750 mg every six hours.

Anxiety

Anxiety can be treated with clonidine (Catapres) which has been used for opioid detoxification since 1978. Noradrenergic outflow from the locus ceruleus is increased during opiate withdrawal and is blocked by administration of mu agonist opioids. Symptoms of opioid withdrawal, therefore, are partly due to excessive sympathetic activity in the locus ceruleus. Clonidine, a central α_2-adrenergic agonist, acts on presynaptic autoreceptors to inhibit locus ceruleus noradrenergic outflow during mu agonist opioid withdrawal, thereby inhibiting some opioid abstinence symptoms, such as anxiety, nausea, vomiting, sweating, GI cramps, and diarrhea, while having little effect on muscle aches and back pain, insomnia, or opioid craving. Clonidine, therefore, is best used in a multidrug regimen. Contraindications to clonidine include diastolic blood pressure less than 70 mm Hg, concurrent dependence on sedative-hypnotics, and clonidine hypersensitivity or previous intolerance.

A sublingual or oral test dose of 0.1 mg (0.2 mg for patients >91 kg) of clonidine is given: if diastolic blood pressure remains above 70 mm Hg, additional doses may be instituted, usually as transdermal patches. Transdermal absorption of clonidine from patches (Catapres-TTS) avoids most of the problems encountered with oral therapy. The number of patches applied to a hairless area of the body (usually upper back or scapular area) depends upon lean body weight. Patients less than 50 kg receive clonidine 5 to 7.5 mg (two to three TTS-1 patches); 50 to 91 kg receive 10 mg (two TTS-2 patches or one TTS-2 and two TTS-1 patches); and patients more than 91 kg receive 10 to 15 mg (two to three TTS-2 patches) of clonidine. Patients less than 73 kg should use two of the TTS-1 patches and one TTS-2 patch to allow removal of one TTS-1 patch in the event of hypotensive complications. Patches are left on for seven days, are replaced with half the dosage during the second week, then are discontinued.

Because transdermal delivery of clonidine requires two days to reach therapeutic levels, propoxyphene, either as 65 mg capsules as the hydrochloride or 100 mg tablets as the napsylate, is given at a dose of two every eight hours for the first two days. Oral clonidine is not used during these initial two days because of hypotensive complications.

For patients who do not tolerate clonidine therapy, phenobarbital 30 mg or chlordiazepoxide 25 mg every four to six hours may be used for anxiety, propoxyphene (65 mg capsules or 100 mg tablets, two every eight hours) for pain, an NSAID for bone or joint pain, and a muscle relaxant for myalgias or cramps. Propoxyphene and antianxiety therapy are continued for 14 days then are tapered off every other day over one week.

Insomnia

Insomnia is treated with trazodone (Desyrel), 50 to 150 mg at bedtime. Alternatively, chloral hydrate 500 to 1500 mg, flurazepam (Dalmane) 30 to 90 mg, or doxepin (Sinequan) 50 to 100 mg can be used. Flurazepam should be avoided if the patient has concurrent benzodiazepine dependence; chloral hydrate should not be used for patients receiving disulfiram (Antabuse). Three weeks of therapy is usually required.

Gastrointestinal Hyperactivity

GI hyperactivity can be managed using belladonna alkaloids with phenobarbital, two tablets every eight hours. Dicyclomine (Bentyl) 20 mg every six hours is an alternative. For nausea, prochlorperazine (Compazine) 100 mg or trimethobenzamide (Tigan) every six hours is used. In addition to suppression of diarrhea and abdominal cramping, the anticholinergic effects of these drugs alleviate the rhinorrhea, sialorrhea, diaphoresis, and lacrimation present during opioid withdrawal.

These average daily doses are evaluated daily and adjusted to the particular needs of the individual patient. Polydrug abusers require individualized detoxification that may require additional therapy for alcohol, cocaine, or other drugs of abuse. The client is encouraged to participate in social-vocational programs while psychosocial counseling is actively continued.[36,60]

These therapeutic interventions have been effective for the population of heroin addicts treated at the Haight-Ashbury Clinic. For addict populations in different social, geographic, and cultural environments, modifications of these techniques will be required.

A.J. is evaluated for clonidine therapy. His diastolic blood pressure is 83 mm Hg, he denies sedative-hypnotic use, and has had no prior exposure to clonidine. A.J.'s diastolic blood pressure remains above 75 mm Hg following administration of a 0.1 mg oral test dose of clonidine. Since he weighs 70 kg, two of the Catapres-TTS-1 patches and one TTS-2 patch are placed upon his upper back. He also receives oral propoxyphene napsylate 200 mg every eight hours for the first two days of clonidine therapy. After seven days, the initial clonidine patches are removed and the dose is halved for the next week. Clonidine therapy is then discontinued. A.J. has not experienced hypotensive complications, and clonidine effectively suppressed most of his abstinence symptoms. Although he has some pain and insomnia, neither A.J. nor his physician feel that it is severe enough to require therapy.

Complications of Polydrug Abuse

23. K.R., a 34-year-old male, comes to a free medical clinic seeking treatment for opiate withdrawal symptoms. He reports a 0.25 gm/day habit with Mexican Tar heroin, occasional ''speedballing'' with cocaine, and sporadic use of six to eight tablet doses of ''codeine 4s'' (aspirin or acetaminophen with codeine 60 mg). When he is seen by the medical staff, he complains of nausea, diaphoresis, stomach cramps, myalgias, and anxiety. In addition to detoxification as outlined in Question 22, what additional treatments should be considered in K.R.?

''Speedballing'' refers to the simultaneous injection of heroin and cocaine which produces an enhanced euphoric effect. Combinations of morphine with amphetamine may increase analgesic and euphoric effects while reducing adverse effects of both drugs.

Mu-agonist opioids, cocaine, and amphetamines all increase dopamine release from the nucleus accumbens. It is proposed that this common pathway may be involved in the reinforcing actions of these drugs.[36,61]

K.R. may need treatment for cocaine as well as narcotic withdrawal (see Chapter 84: Central Nervous System Stimulant Abuse). K.R. should be evaluated for possible acetaminophen and salicylate toxicities because of his use of "codeine 4s" in supratherapeutic doses.

24. K.R. states that he used to do "Ts and blues" (tripelennamine and pentazocine) but no longer does since he got "the shakes" when he injected these drugs. Why did "the shakes" occur?

The combination of pentazocine with the antihistamine tripelennamine (PBZ), known as "Ts and blues," appears to be more euphorigenic than either drug alone. Although injection is the preferred route for "Ts and blues," the addition of naloxone to pentazocine tablets, which were ground and injected, has reduced use by this route, but oral use of the combination continues.[36,61] K.R.'s "shakes" were probably a symptom of narcotic withdrawal precipitated by naloxone administration with the pentazocine.

Sedative-Hypnotics
Onset of Sedative-Hypnotic Dependence

25. During a year of therapy for anxiety, B.J. increased his dose of diazepam to two 10 mg tablets QID. Now he wants to quit using sedative drugs. Will he experience withdrawal symptoms if he suddenly discontinues diazepam?

Withdrawal syndromes seen with sedative-hypnotics are similar to those seen with alcohol withdrawal. Those who have been on long-term courses of therapeutic doses of these drugs will often experience some withdrawal upon abrupt discontinuation of therapy, a factor which often leads to perpetuation of therapy beyond the period of therapeutic need.[29] Abrupt discontinuation will probably cause B.J. to experience withdrawal symptoms.

Abstinence Syndromes

26. B.J. agrees that he is addicted to diazepam, but is determined to be drug-free. He gives you the remainder of his tablets and proclaims, "Today, Friday, I have taken my last diazepam! By Monday I'll be a new man!" Should you encourage B.J. to pursue this course of action?

Abstinence signs and symptoms may include insomnia, anxiety, tremors of the upper extremities, nightmares, muscular weakness, anorexia, nausea, vomiting, and postural hypotension which usually appear early. Postural hypotension may be of value in differentiating the abstinence syndrome from ordinary anxiety states. Generalized tonic-clonic seizures may occur as isolated seizures or as status epilepticus. The psychoses that develop resemble the delirium tremens produced by alcohol withdrawal and are usually characterized by disorientation, agitation, delusions, and hallucinations. During the delirium, hyperthermia and agitation may lead to exhaustion, rhabdomyolysis, cardiovascular collapse, and death. The withdrawal syndrome for benzodiazepines is generally mild and self-limited, but seizures may occasionally occur.[29,62,63]

The time course depends upon the drug involved. Pentobarbital, secobarbital, and meprobamate withdrawal may begin 12 to 24 hours after the last dose and peak in intensity at one to three days in patients with normal liver function. Withdrawal from phenobarbital, diazepam, and chlordiazepoxide develops more slowly, peaking at five to seven days. With the exception of buspirone (BuSpar), severe withdrawal can occur when sedative-hypnotics have been taken at two or more times the normal maximum therapeutic dose for more than a month.[29,62]

B.J. has been taking twice the recommended upper limit for diazepam therapy. It is likely that he will experience withdrawal, possibly including seizures, if he were to abruptly discontinue the diazepam. He should be encouraged and applauded for his desire to be drug-free, but his withdrawal from this medication should be medically managed. Furthermore, the decision to begin detoxification therapy over a weekend when many clinics are closed is not wise. He should have an initial physical examination and plan to be absent from his place of employment for a week or more to begin detoxification.

Treatment of Sedative Withdrawal

27. Would it be appropriate to encourage B.J. to simply reduce his diazepam dose by 10% per day until he is drug-free?

Treatment of sedative-hypnotic dependence focuses on preventing major symptoms and minimizing minor symptoms. Patients could probably be stabilized on any sedative-hypnotic and tapered slowly.[62] While some clinicians may taper dosages of benzodiazepines with short half-lives by 25% each week, many prefer to taper the dosage over six weeks to four months.[63,64] With combined benzodiazepine and alcohol dependence, a longer-acting benzodiazepine may be substituted and tapered gradually. When there is polydrug abuse including benzodiazepines, some clinicians utilize a slow taper of phenobarbital.[65] Phenobarbital is preferred over shorter-acting barbiturates for substitution withdrawal of benzodiazepines, barbiturates, and other sedative-hypnotics because it has a wider safety margin, a longer duration of action, and is of low street value. Phenobarbital also is less likely to produce euphoria than the short-acting barbiturates because it attenuates peaks and troughs. Substitution of phenobarbital for the sedative-hypnotic drug of dependence generally is preferable.[62]

The patient is stabilized on oral or, if necessary, parenteral phenobarbital based upon the dosage of sedative-hypnotic being used. Phenobarbital 30 mg/day (maximum daily starting dosage: 500 mg), in three or four daily divided doses, will prevent serious withdrawal signs and symptoms when substituted for the following amounts of commonly abused sedative-hypnotics: alprazolam 1 mg; diazepam 10 mg; lorazepam 2 mg; amobarbital, butabarbital, butalbital, pentobarbital, or secobarbital 100 mg; chloral hydrate 500 mg; meprobamate 400 mg; and about 15 mL of pure ethanol. Where multiple sedative-hypnotics are being used, the totals for each drug and alcohol are summated. Before each dosage, the patient is checked for slurred speech, sustained horizontal nystagmus, or ataxia. If nystagmus is present, the next dose is withheld. If all three are present, two doses are withheld and subsequent dosages are reduced by 50%. If objective signs of withdrawal occur, the dosage is adjusted upward by 50% until a stable dosage is determined. After two days of stabilization, the dose is reduced 30 mg/day as long as withdrawal proceeds smoothly, or increased when withdrawal signs appear.[62]

Either benzodiazepine tapering or phenobarbital could be used to suppress B.J.'s withdrawal symptoms. Since B.J. has been receiving 80 mg/day of diazepam chronically, 240 mg/day of phenobarbital would be substituted if that therapy were chosen. However, since B.J.'s addiction involves only diazepam, a two-month diazepam-tapering regimen is chosen and is well tolerated.

Acute Sedative Withdrawal

28. K.C., an 18-year-old female, arrives at a free medical clinic in a state of extreme anxiety. She has a 12-month history of ingesting 200 mg of "reds" (secobarbital) and 10 mg of alprazolam daily. K.C.'s drug supply was depleted a week ago and she has become progressively more agitated. Friends brought her to the clinic today after she had a seizure at home.

K.C. is conscious but disoriented, agitated, thin, diaphoretic, and incontinent of urine. Her BP is 130/90 mm Hg; pulse is 100 beats/min; respirations are 15 breaths/min; and temperature is 37.5 °C. Her skin is warm and moist, and pupils are mildly dilated and reactive. What drug treatment program would be appropriate for K.C.?

K.C.'s presenting symptoms are typical of the sympathomimetic excess associated with sedative-hypnotic drug withdrawal combined with a post-ictal state. A daily withdrawal equivalence dosage of phenobarbital is 360 mg (i.e., 30 mg of phenobarbital × 10 mg of alprazolam + 30 mg of phenobarbital per 100 mg of secobarbital). She could be given 120 mg phenobarbital initially, followed by two additional 120 mg doses at eight-hour intervals. K.C.'s withdrawal symptoms should be controlled after a total dose of about 360 mg phenobarbital has been given, and mild intoxication can be expected after about 480 to 600 mg of phenobarbital. A stabilization dose of 120 mg three times a day is administered for five days, then the daily dose is tapered by 30 mg/day. No withdrawal symptoms are noted during detoxification and K.C. successfully completes the withdrawal process.

Inhalants

The first example of inhalant abuse may be in ancient Greek literature. Supposedly, the Oracle at Delphi could foretell the future by inhaling gases escaping from below the earth's surface via a natural rock vent. Abuse of nitrous oxide, chloroform, and diethyl ether flourished in the 1800s in England. In the United States, glue sniffing was first noted in California in 1950s. In the 1960s, abuse of inhalants spread from the west coast to the east coast. Since the 1950s, a variety of products have been abused by inhalation, including model airplane glue, antiperspirant, shoe polish, vegetable non-stick spray, acrylic spray paint, typewriter correction fluid, and refill canisters for pocket lighters.[66]

Today, volatile substance abuse appears to be increasing, particularly among adolescents. According to the National High School Senior Survey, use of volatile solvents during the past 12 months had increased from 3% in 1976 to 6.2% in 1992. This increase occurred despite a steady decline in drug use among this population in nearly all other substances being monitored. Seventeen percent of high school seniors admit to using volatile solvents within their lifetime; 2.3% admit to using volatile solvents within the last 30 days. The highest use exists among eighth graders, where, in 1992, 10% admitted to using volatile solvents within the last year. In this group, volatile solvents are used more than any other illicit substance. Their use is superseded only by alcohol and tobacco. This is the youngest group surveyed. It is likely that much inhalant abuse begins at an even younger age.[67]

Inhalants are popular among children and adolescents because of their low cost, ease of availability, convenient packaging, and low threat of legal intervention. Due to their high lipophilicity and route of administration, these substances produce a more rapid onset of effect than alcohol, making them easier to abuse while in school. In addition, they produce a euphoria that is qualitatively distinct from alcohol and marijuana. Some describe it as a "floaty high."[66]

Typically, inhalants are one of the first conscious-altering substances tried by children. Often they are introduced to the practice by friends in a group setting. As the child grows older he either abandons this substance group or he moves on to other drugs. About 10% of those who experiment with inhalants become habitual users.[68]

Volatile solvent abusers are most often 13 to 15 years old.[69–72] There is a slightly higher predominance of males to females (2:1). Often abusers come from unstable or dysfunctional families (e.g.,

alcoholism, drug addiction, family conflict, divorce, abandonment, unemployment), low socioeconomic status, and from populations experiencing acculturation stress (e.g., Native Americans).

Inhalant abuse results in a significant number of adolescent fatalities each year. The most complete mortality data come from Great Britain, where a formal volatile solvent death registry has been established and there is aggressive investigation of all possible solvent-related fatalities. In the United Kingdom, an average of two volatile solvent-related deaths occur each week. Seventy-two percent of the deaths involve individuals under 20 years of age with the most frequent victim age being 15 years.[69]

Volatile Solvents

Acute Intoxication

29. A.E., an 8-year-old male, is brought to the ER 15 minutes after collapsing while "huffing" spray paint with his friends. A.E. smells like airplane glue and answers questions slowly but appropriately. He has slowed deep tendon reflexes (DTRs). Vital signs are: BP 90/50 mm Hg; temperature 37.1 °C; pulse 50 beats/min; and respirations 10 breaths/min. What is "huffing"? What chemical most likely is responsible for A.E.'s symptoms?

A variety of techniques are used to abuse volatile solvents. In some cases, the user soaks a rag, handkerchief, or piece of clothing with the product to be abused and inhales from the soaked cloth. This is called "huffing." In other instances the product may be sprayed or poured into a plastic bag or rubber glove and then inhaled from the closure. This is referred to as "bagging." If the product is a liquid such as gasoline or typewriter correction fluid, it may be abused by inhaling directly from the container, a technique called "sniffing." There are reports of spraying the inside of a salad bowl or heating the solvent over a stove in order to enhance the high, presumably by increasing the concentration of solvent. Occasionally liquid solvents such as lighter fluid and fingernail polish remover are mixed into carbonated beverages and are drank or injected intravenously.[72]

The most likely chemical responsible for A.E.'s symptoms is toluene. This compound has aromatic, airplane-glue odor and is commonly found in spray paints. Table 83.1 lists the composition of commonly abused products and classifies products into more general chemical groups based upon their centrally active ingredient. The table may serve as a starting point when no other information is available. Other important sources of information which should be used to determine the active ingredient(s) include the product label, the local regional poison center, and the manufacturer. It should also be kept in mind that many of the products being abused are mixtures of compounds having multiple ingredients capable of affecting the CNS. One example is gasoline, which is comprised of saturated aliphatic hydrocarbons ranging in length from C5 to C12, unsaturated hydrocarbons (isoprene and butylene), and aromatic hydrocarbons (toluene, xylene).

30. Acute Toxicity. What other immediate effects might have occurred from A.E.'s volatile solvent abuse?

The greatest immediate danger associated with volatile solvent abuse is sudden and unexpected death due to direct toxicity of the solvent. This phenomenon has been called "sudden sniffing death syndrome" in the medical literature. Typically, the abuser inhales and then suddenly collapses and dies within minutes. Often, there is a short period of intense activity (running, dancing, yelling, sexual activity) or stress (hallucinogenic crisis, discovery by police or parents) immediately before the victim collapses. There are no premonitions before the event, and it may occur at any time, to either experienced or novice users. Postmortem examination is

Table 83.1   Commonly Abused Volatile Inhalants

Inhalant	Primary Active Constituent(s)	Chemical Group
Model airplane glue	Toluene	Aromatic hydrocarbons
Marker pen ink	Toluene, xylene	Aromatic hydrocarbons
Spray paint	Toluene, xylene	Aromatic hydrocarbons
Butane lighter/refill canister	Butane	Aliphatic hydrocarbons
Propane canister	Propane	Aliphatic hydrocarbons
Gasoline	C5–C8 aliphatic hydrocarbons, butylenes, isoprene	Aliphatic/aromatic hydrocarbons
Fabric protectant	Trichloroethane	Halogenated hydrocarbons
Paint/varnish remover	Methylene chloride	Halogenated hydrocarbons
Typewriter correction fluid	Trichloroethane, trichloroethylene	Halogenated hydrocarbons
Carburetor cleaner	Methylene chloride, toluene	Halogenated/aromatic hydrocarbons
Rubber cement	Toluene	Aromatic hydrocarbons
	Heptane, hexane	Aliphatic hydrocarbons
	Trichloroethane	Halogenated hydrocarbons
Paint/lacquer/varnish thinner	Toluene, xylene	Aromatic hydrocarbons
	Acetone, methyl ethyl ketone, methyl butyl ketone, methyl isobutyl ketone	Ketones

usually nonspecific, revealing only venous congestion and marked pulmonary edema.[69,73]

Sudden death from volatile solvents may result from a combination of anoxia, respiratory depression, vagal stimulation, and/or cardiac arrhythmias. All volatile solvents may sensitize the myocardium to normal physiologic concentrations of circulating catecholamines. With sudden exertion or stress there is a surge in endogenous catecholamines and a triggering of life-threatening ventricular arrhythmias. In addition, volatile solvents may cause CNS depression resulting in respiratory arrest. Anoxia may result if the respiratory arrest is prolonged, or if the patient aspirates vomit during the episode. Hypoxia exacerbates cardiac irritability and increases the risk of life-threatening arrhythmias. Prolonged vagal stimulation may result from cooling of the larynx when aerosolized products like butane are sprayed directly into the abuser's mouth. Vagal stimulation causes a slowing of the heart rate.[74]

Since volatile solvents tend to remain in lipophilic cell membranes such as the cardiac conduction system for extended periods of time, patients who abuse volatile solvents may be at risk for cardiac arrhythmias even hours after their original exposure.[74]

Direct toxicity is the most important cause of death during volatile solvent abuse accounting for over half of the fatalities in Great Britain. Other important causes of death include suffocation (16% of fatalities), aspiration of stomach contents (13% of fatalities), and trauma (12% of fatalities). Trauma often results from drowning, hanging, or head injury and is most often associated with inhalation of toluene-containing adhesives.[75]

A.E. is fortunate; he could have died from acute pulmonary or cardiovascular effects of the spray paint.

31. Clinical Presentation. What subjective and objective data are consistent with acute toxicity from volatile substance abuse in A.E.?

Volatile solvents produce clinical manifestations resembling ethanol intoxication. Patients develop euphoria, slurred speech, ataxia, diplopia, nystagmus, flushing, blurred vision, and varying degrees of central nervous system depression. Unlike ethanol intoxication, however, solvents often cause vivid hallucinations (visual) and disorientation to place and time. In addition, the symptoms usually subside more quickly than with ethanol (usually within 30 minutes); headaches are less frequent than with ethanol.[76] There may be a solvent odor on abuser's hair, clothing, and breath, as well as an eczematoid dermatitis around the patient's nose, mouth, face, and neck ("Glue sniffer's rash").[77]

Pertinent clinical findings consistent with acute intoxication from volatile solvents in A.E. include CNS depression, depressed reflexes, bradycardia, and bradypnea. His hypotension is most likely a result of the bradycardia.

Patients emerging from volatile substance inebriation often develop symptoms of central nervous system excitation (e.g., agitation, combativeness). The effects last 30 to 45 minutes; however, practiced abusers may maintain their high for up to 12 hours.[78]

32. Treatment. What treatments are indicated for A.E.?

The first priority for treating acute volatile solvent intoxication is to stabilize the patient's vital signs. If there are signs of poor ventilation (decreased respiratory rate, cyanosis, hypoxia, hypercarbia), mechanical ventilation and supplemental oxygen should be considered. Supplemental oxygen by itself should be used carefully in this setting since hypoxia may be the only factor stimulating the patient's respiratory drive (see Chapter 20: Chronic Obstructive Pulmonary Disease). Hypotension should be managed initially with fluid therapy and positioning. If possible, inotropes should be avoided because of the potential for precipitating ventricular arrhythmias, especially after intoxication from halogenated hydrocarbons. Cardiac arrhythmias should be managed with conventional therapies, making sure that electrolyte abnormalities have been corrected.[77,79] Hyperventilation has been proposed as a method to enhance pulmonary elimination of volatile solvents, although there are no data to support this recommendation.[76]

There are no antidotes for most volatile solvents. Exceptions are methylene chloride and leaded gasoline. Methylene chloride is slowly metabolized to carbon monoxide. Peak carboxyhemoglobin levels occurred as late as two hours postexposure in controlled occupational studies and may peak even later during inhalant abuse.[80] Oxygen (hyperbaric in some instances) is the antidote for this solvent when carbon monoxide poisoning is suspected.[81] Chronic abuse of leaded gasoline may produce lead poisoning; in this circumstance, conventional chelation therapy for lead is warranted.[82]

A.E.'s bradypnea is worrisome and should be monitored carefully. In this case, it worsens over five minutes (5 breaths/min) and requires mechanical ventilation by Ambu bag plus 100% humidified oxygen for 15 minutes. A.E.'s bradycardia is most likely responsible for his hypotension, so fluids and positioning are not used. Instead, 0.6 mg of atropine is administered and A.E.'s pulse increases to 123 beats/min. At the same time his blood pressure increases to 110/60 mm Hg.

33. Further Evaluation. What additional tests may be helpful in determining the severity of A.E.'s intoxication and the extent of neurologic injury?

A 12-lead electrocardiogram (ECG), serum electrolytes, and arterial blood gases (ABGs) would be helpful in completing the clinical evaluation of A.E. The electrocardiogram will show whether A.E. is having solvent-induced arrhythmias. Patients with cardiac arrhythmias usually are admitted and followed carefully in the intensive care unit. Electrolyte abnormalities (hypokalemia, hypophosphatemia) often are associated with aromatic hydrocarbon solvent exposure and may exacerbate cardiac arrhythmias. Arterial blood gases will determine whether A.E.'s ventilatory treatment was adequate.

Toxicologic analysis of blood and/or urine for specific solvents is of limited value since these tests are not routinely available, there is at best only a weak correlation between blood concentrations and clinical severity, and they do not affect management of the patient. Urinary analysis (UA) for metabolites of toluene (hippuric acid) or xylene (methyl hippuric acid) may be beneficial when monitoring abstinence from these solvents.[77]

A variety of tests are used to screen for specific acute and chronic complications associated with inhalant abuse (see Table 83.2). In this case, a serum creatinine and UA are ordered to determine whether there is evidence of toluene-induced renal damage (usually seen with chronic, heavy use). A serum creatinine phosphokinase is ordered to determine whether A.E.'s muscle weakness is due to acute toluene intoxication or rhabdomyolysis. All these tests are normal in A.E.

It would be helpful to know whether A.E. has been using volatile solvents long enough to cause neurologic injury. It is impossible to evaluate this risk based upon history alone since fear of self-incrimination and lack of recollection often diminish the accuracy of histories. Physical examination may reveal injury (allowing time for adequate detoxification) only late in the clinical course when little can be done to prevent further injury. Computerized tomography (CT) and magnetic resonance imaging (MRI) can identify structural abnormalities (cerebral atrophy, increased brain ventricles, loss of gray/white matter differentiation) associated with chronic volatile solvent abuse, but only after the patient develops overt neurologic abnormalities. In addition, the abnormalities are not specific for volatile solvents. Psychometric testing may be used to evaluate for subclinical functional abnormalities, but this method has been criticized for lack of valid, reproducible, controlled research to support the approach.[83]

A promising screening tool for subclinical neurologic injury is the use of evoked potentials. This test involves presenting visual, auditory, or somatosensory stimuli to a patient and measuring the electric response of the nervous system. Patients with overt neurologic damage have prolongation in response times to stimuli. Several studies have documented such prolongations in volatile solvent abuse patients having yet undeveloped neurologic abnormalities.[84-86]

A.E.'s physical examination reveals no evidence of neurologic deficits. Lacking such evidence, CT and MRI are not justifiable. A.E. refuses psychometric testing. It is probable that A.E. also would have refused evoked potential testing if this had been available locally.

34. Rehabilitation. What rehabilitative actions are appropriate for A.E.?

The extent of habituation determines the extent of intervention. Patients who experiment with volatile solvents rarely progress to habitual solvent abuse and require less extensive rehabilitation than habitual volatile solvent abusers.

Once A.E. is medically stable and no longer intoxicated, a more complete history should be obtained. The history should include an extensive drug history including age of onset of use, compounds used, where abuse takes place, methods of abuse, frequency of abuse, reasons for abuse, and indicators of severity of abuse (evidence of craving, school absenteeism, evidence of delinquency, importance of solvent abuse in life). A complete family history looking for evidence of dysfunction is indicated, as well as an emotional inventory looking specifically for suicidal ideation. Several standardized surveys are available to determine the degree of dependency present (e.g., McDonald questionnaire, Heilman questionnaire) and should be considered for routine evaluation.[87]

A.E. comes from a stable family. He experimented with solvents on several occasions, largely due to peer pressure. His dependency is assessed to be low from the McDonald questionnaire. An appointment is made with a substance abuse counselor and he is followed on an outpatient basis.

Chronic Abuse

35. M.S., a 23-year-old male, is brought to the ER by ambulance after his aunt found him unconscious in her apartment. Next to M.S. were several containers of a lacquer thinner (75% toluene). A rag soaked with the product was draped over his face. M.S. has been seen on several occasions in this ER over the last three years for complaints related to volatile solvent abuse (persistent nausea, muscle weakness). On physical examination M.S. is anorexic, lethargic, slowly answers ques-

Table 83.2		Evaluation of Inhalant Complications	
Inhalant	Test(s)[a]	Expected Result	Type of Complication (Acute vs. Chronic)
Aromatic hydrocarbons	Serum calcium	Low	Either
	Serum phosphate	Low	Either
	CPK	Elevated	Chronic
	UA	Hematuria, proteinuria, pyuria, glycosuria	Chronic
	SrCr	Elevated	Chronic
Gasoline (leaded)	Blood lead	Elevated	Chronic
Chlorinated hydrocarbons	Liver and renal function tests	Elevated	Chronic
Methylene chloride	Carboxyhemoglobin	Elevated	Acute
Nitrous oxide	CBC, peripheral blood smear, TIBC, serum iron, folate, and B_{12}	Megaloblastic anemia	Chronic
Nitrites	Methemoglobin	Elevated	Acute

[a] CBC = Complete blood count; CPK = Creatinine phosphokinase; SrCr = Serum creatinine; TIBC = Total iron binding capacity; UA = Urinalysis.

tions, and smells like airplane glue. He admits to inhaling for 8–10 hr/day over the last two weeks. Vital signs are: BP 150/60; temperature 37.1 °C; pulse 84 beats/min; and respirations 32 breaths/min. Multiple burns and bruises are noted on his arms and legs. Head, ears, eyes, nose, and throat (HEENT) examination reveals horizontal nystagmus and mydriatic pupils (8 mm), sluggishly reactive to light. Neurologic examination shows generalized muscle wasting and weakness. Admission lab work includes: Na 142 mEq/L; K 2.0 mEq/L; Cl 103 mEq/L; bicarbonate 7 mEq/L; lactate 0.6 mEq/L; blood urea nitrogen (BUN) 11 mg/dL; serum creatinine (SrCr) 1.3 mg/dL; urine pH 5.0; and no urinary ketones. ABGs drawn on admission while receiving oxygen by nasal cannula are: pH 7.15; pCO$_2$ 20; and pO$_2$ 110. What subjective and objective data are consistent with chronic volatile substance abuse in M.S.? [SI units: Na 142 mmol/L; K 2.0 mmol/L; Cl 1.3 mmol/L; BUN 3.95 mmol/L; SrCr 114.92 µmol/L]

Chronic abusers are usually older than experimenters (twenties instead of teens). They often abuse several times a day for years; frequently they use alone and have a history of unemployment and minor legal infractions. Their lives center around solvent abuse.[88,89]

Anorexia is a common, nonspecific finding among habitual solvent abusers. Muscle weakness has been associated with prolonged, intense toluene abuse. It has been described in patients abusing toluene for six to seven hours per day for 4 to 14 days. Many have two- to three-year histories of abuse.[90] Presumably, patients increase intensity of use after building a tolerance to toluene. In some cases, patients present to the emergency room with transient quadriparesis.[91]

In addition to muscle weakness, two other syndromes have been associated with chronic toluene abuse. A gastrointestinal syndrome characterized by abdominal pain, nausea, vomiting, and hematemesis is thought to result from systemic accumulation of benzoic acid. Benzoic acid is a metabolite of toluene and a known GI irritant. Varying degrees of headache, dizziness, ataxia, syncope, paresthesias, peripheral neuropathy, hallucinations, lethargy, or coma, on the other hand, comprise a neuropsychiatric syndrome. Altered mental status clears more rapidly than neuropathies and ataxia.[90]

Metabolic acidosis is common among all three of the toluene abuse syndromes just described, but is most prominent in patients suffering muscle weakness. The acidosis most likely results from depletion of bicarbonate as benzoic acid accumulates.[92] It is accompanied by hypokalemia, hypophosphatemia, and hypercalciuria. Urinary pH and serum chloride are normal.[93] In other instances the same patient may present with a distal type-I renal tubular acidosis, characterized by a nonanion gap metabolic acidosis, hypokalemia, hyperchloremia, urinary pH greater than 5.5, hypercalciuria, hypophosphatemia, and lack of azotemia.[90,91] Here, toluene may be blocking normal hydrogen secretion in the distal renal tubule. Recurrent urinary calculi often complicates distal type-I renal tubular acidosis.[94,95]

A number of treatable poisonings may produce metabolic acidosis with an elevated anion gap. Examples include methanol, ethylene glycol, salicylates, iron, paraldehyde, propylene glycol, isoniazid, iron, and various toxic gases. When the patient's solvent abuse history is unclear, these poisonings must be considered, and further toxicologic testing is indicated. Consultation with the regional poison center also is recommended.

Toluene's longevity in the brain is unknown. From the limited human data available, toluene's distribution appears to fit a two compartment model with a βt½ of 33.5 hours.[77] At least a 30-day detoxification period should elapse before testing for permanent cognitive dysfunction. Chronic toluene abuse has been associated with cognitive dysfunction that ranges from mild, transient impairment to permanent dementia. Cerebellar ataxia, corticospinal tract dysfunction, oculomotor abnormalities, tremor, deafness, and hyposmia also have been reported. The diffuse CNS impairment seen with toluene inhalation often manifests after a much longer period of use (usually five to ten years) and may resolve with abstinence.[89]

M.S.'s history of intense, chronic use (8 hours/day for several weeks) contrasts sharply with a solvent experimenter, such as A.E., and is consistent with the pattern seen in chronic abusers. He has a clear historical record of abuse over several years through the ER records. Often this may not be the case, since the patient may not visit the same hospital twice. Significant findings on M.S.'s physical examination include anorexia, muscle weakness, and muscle wasting. M.S.'s laboratory studies show metabolic acidosis with an elevated anion gap. His slowed mentation could be a permanent effect of chronic toluene abuse or could be secondary to acute intoxication. If this is a manifestation of chronic abuse, it may improve with abstinence. M.S.'s ocular findings are consistent with acute toluene intoxication. His tachypnea is secondary to metabolic acidosis. The scattered burns and bruises are nonspecific findings occasionally noted in solvent abusers. Self-mutilation is sometimes used to demonstrate invulnerability during solvent inebriation.[96]

36. Complications. Several of M.S.'s friends suggest that M.S. may have abused other volatile solvents in the past. They identify several products which contain chlorinated hydrocarbons or ketones. Could any of M.S.'s findings be caused by these other substances?

Table 83.3 summarizes complications associated with either long-term or intense short-term volatile solvent abuse. In reviewing these complications, several generalizations must be kept in mind. First, the exact incidence of each complication is unknown. Not enough high-risk solvent abuse patients have been followed longitudinally to establish how often a particular complication arises. Data from occupational exposure studies are of limited value because abusers subject themselves to doses that are several 10 to 1000 times higher than found in the industrial workplace. Second, the true toxicity of a product may not be reflected by its individual constituents. In some instances, this may be due to incomplete labelling by the manufacturer. N-hexane may be considered a "minor ingredient" and may not be listed on the product label. In other instances, there may be potentiation or diminution of toxicity by constituents. Methyl ethyl ketone, for example, is not neurotoxic; however, it is synergistic with n-hexane or methybutyl ketone. Third, there may be no relationship between the manifestations of acute and chronic toxicity since manifestations of chronic toxicity may be due to accumulation of a toxic metabolite. Such is the case with n-hexane, where the toxic metabolite, 2,5 hexadione, is responsible for peripheral neuropathy. Fourth, dose-response relationships are unclear. Studies which have examined the relationship of neurological complications to dose or duration of exposure have found either no correlation or a weak correlation. The relationship to nonneurologic complications is even less clear. In general, it would appear that several years of abuse are required for chronic complications to develop unless the individual uses solvents continuously at very high doses. Fifth, the onset and persistence of complications are variable. The sensorimotor polyneuropathy caused by methyl butyl ketone or n-hexane begins several months after chronic exposure and may continue to progress for three months after exposure stops. Mild to moderate residual effects persist for up to three years after the exposure.[89,97,98]

M.S. has no evidence of peripheral neuropathy which might be seen with chlorinated hydrocarbons or ketones. The chlorinated hydrocarbons may contribute to renal complications.

Table 83.3	Neurologic and Non-Neurologic Complications of Volatile Solvent Abuse[89,98-102]	
Volatile Solvent	Neurologic Complication[a]	Non-Neurologic Complication[a]
Aromatic hydrocarbons		
Toluene	Cognitive dysfunction, optic neuropathy, olfactory dysfunction, sensorineural hearing loss, diffuse CNS involvement, cerebellar ataxia, epilepsy, choreoathetosis	Type I distal tubular acidosis, glomerulonephritis, interstitial nephritis, hepatomegaly, hepatorenal failure, CHF, panacinar emphysema, embryopathy, anemia
Xylene	Cranial neuropathy, epilepsy	—
Chlorinated hydrocarbons		
Trichloroethane	—	CHF
Trichloroethylene	Trigeminal neuralgia, transverse myelopathy, CVA, peripheral neuropathy	Hepatic failure, renal tubular necrosis, cirrhosis, congestive heart failure, hepatocellular carcinoma
Tetrachloroethylene (perchloroethylene)	Peripheral neuropathy	—
Methylene chloride	—	Carbon monoxide poisoning, renal damage
Ketones		
Butanone	Peripheral neuropathy	—
Methyl n-butyl ketone	Peripheral neuropathy	—
Methyl n-butyl ketone + butanone or isobutyl ketone	Peripheral neuropathy	—
Aliphatic hydrocarbons		
n-Hexane	Peripheral neuropathy, cranial neuropathy, spasticity, autonomic dysfunction	Anemia

[a] CHF = Congestive heart failure; CVA = Cerebrovascular accident.

37. Treatment. Once M.S. is stabilized, what pharmacologic treatments are indicated, and how should these treatments be monitored?

The goals of treatment are to normalize gradually the acid-base and electrolyte abnormalities. Bicarbonate may worsen the patient's hypokalemia by driving potassium intracellularly, which in turn may result in terminal dysrhythmias. Bicarbonate also may worsen the patient's hypocalcemia causing tetany and cardiac arrest.[103]

Treatment should begin with gradual normalization of potassium using potassium chloride and potassium phosphate (see Chapter 28: Fluid and Electrolyte Disorders). Potassium phosphate is used since most chronic toluene abusers will be hypophosphatemia secondary to urinary calcium phosphate loss. Excessive supplementation may be prevented by continuously looking for signs of hyperkalemia on a cardiac monitor. Once the patient's serum potassium is at least 3 mEq/L, calcium supplementation should begin, followed by administration of bicarbonate.[95,104]

Hourly serum electrolytes including calcium, phosphate, and magnesium are indicated during supplementation therapy. Muscle weakness should resolve once normokalemia is restored.

Although it would be tempting to begin treating M.S. by administering sodium bicarbonate in order to correct his metabolic acidosis and to prevent a worsening of his rhabdomyolysis, this should not be the first step of therapy. Instead, potassium chloride and potassium phosphate are administered in IV fluids, and M.S. is placed on a cardiac monitor. After establishing a serum potassium of greater than 3 mEq/L, calcium gluconate is administered, then sodium bicarbonate therapy is initiated. Once electrolytes stabilize, the patient's weakness usually resolves.

38. Rehabilitation. What rehabilitative efforts are warranted for M.S.?

Without intervention, chronic volatile solvent abusers tend to drop out of school, lose their jobs, and develop criminal records.[88] Ideally, chronic solvent abusers would be admitted to an inpatient treatment program specifically designed for them. Unfortunately, few programs exist, so outpatient treatment through more generalized programs may be the only practical option available in most communities.

Treatment begins with prolonged detoxification. Since little is known about solvent longevity in the nervous tissue, it is unclear what an adequate time for detoxification should be. Periodic neurologic and psychometric tests should be conducted to monitor for improvement.

Once the patient has recovered sufficient cognitive and emotional skills, counselling may begin. Initial interviews should be short (20 to 30 minutes), nonconfrontational, and should center on abstinence and basic life skills. A comprehensive approach takes into account the patient's vocational, scholastic, economic, and social needs and includes the patient's family and peers. Behavior modification, suggestive techniques, hypnosis, and psychotherapy may be useful in supporting abstinence; however, the most important factors for success will be the patient's desire to abstain from volatile solvents and his willingness to accept help.

Family and peer support will be essential for successful rehabilitation. In situations where the family or peers have contributed to volatile solvent abuse, consideration must be given to family/peer intervention or complete removal of the patient from his environment and placement in foster care or a halfway house.

Treatment must also address vocational training, reintegration into the school, promotion of self-esteem, and restructuring of social relationships.[105]

Rehabilitation is urgently needed in M.S. A treatment program which deals with chronic volatile solvent abusers should be identified and utilized, if possible. Treatment should include detoxification, abstinence, education, social and vocational support, and societal reintegration.

Nitrous Oxide

39. R.C., an 18-year-old male, gets high by inhaling from whipped cream canisters in grocery stores. What agent is R.C. abusing, and what are the dangers associated with this practice?

The agent abused in this case is nitrous oxide or "laughing gas." Nitrous oxide is available in steel medical supply bottles, in 6.5 cm cylinders designed to charge whipped cream dispensers used by restaurants (referred to as "whippets") and in commercially available whipped cream canisters (e.g., Hunt's Reddi Whip, Rich's Whip Topping). Whipped cream canisters contain 3 to 3.5 L of 87% to 90% nitrous oxide as a propellant.[106] Nitrous oxide is used because it is bacteriostatic, imparts no taste, and is not explosive. Abusers may inhale directly from the container, being careful not to shake it, or may transfer the gas to a balloon first.[107]

Nitrous oxide produces an "exhilarating high" within 15 to 30 seconds after inhalation with peak effects lasting for two to three minutes. This euphoria is accompanied by giddiness, tingling of the face and head, and auditory illusions and hallucinations.[108] Nitrous oxide is both an analgesic and an anesthetic. Sedation occurs at concentrations of 25%, analgesia at 25% to 50%, and anesthesia at 70%. Euphoria and analgesia are likely due to its partial agonist effects on the mu-, kappa-, and sigma-opioid receptors. Nitrous oxide's addictive properties are thought to be mediated through the opioid system.[109]

Several dangers are associated with abuse of nitrous oxide. Acutely, abusers may die from anoxia. Since nitrous oxide's duration of action is very short, this situation arises most frequently when abusers are using continuous flow, high concentration nitrous oxide with a homemade mask or in a small confined area such as a car.[108,110] Interstitial emphysema and pneumomediastinum secondary to releasing a pressurized gas directly into the pulmonary tree have also been reported.[111]

Chronic abuse of nitrous oxide causes oxidization of the cobalt moiety in vitamin B_{12}, rendering it inactive. Vitamin B_{12} plays a key role in maintaining spinal cord integrity, ensuring proper functioning of nerve cells, and allowing normal development of bone marrow precursor cells. Depletion of "active" vitamin B_{12} causes varying degrees of bone marrow depression, megaloblastic anemia, combined sensorimotor neuropathy and spinal cord myelopathy, and toxic encephalopathy. Most often patients present with a stocking-glove distribution of numbness in their lower extremities. With continued abuse, clumsiness, loss of dexterity, leg muscle weakness, and loss of balance occurs. In severe poisoning, there is impotence, bladder spasticity, numbness of the trunk, inability to walk without assistance, and Lhermitte's sign (an electric sensation down the back with neck flexion). Encephalopathy may range from mild psychotic reactions (delusions, terrifying dreams, and persistent anxiety) to persistent toxic delirium (hallucinations, agitation, delusions, inappropriate behavior). Chronic toxicities generally resolve over a two- to three-month period without specific therapy.[112]

Abuse of nitrous oxide is especially prevalent among dental professionals.

Volatile Nitrites

Abuse

40. D.C., a 35-year-old male, presents to the ER with a headache, shortness of breath, and chest pain. He has been inhaling, ingesting, and administering "Rush" sublingually for the last seven hours in order to maintain a sexual high. He appears anxious and has generalized cyanosis. His vital signs are BP 70/palpable; pulse 126 beats/min; respirations 26 breaths/min; and temperature 36.6 °C. Are D.C.'s findings consistent with "Rush" abuse?

"Rush" is a foul-smelling liquid sold to the public as room odorizer. It contains greater than 90% isobutyl nitrite and is available through adult bookstores, discotheques, and mail-order catalogues. Rush is marketed as an orgasm enhancer and has been popular among male homosexuals because it relaxes the anal sphincter.[113]

This product belongs to the family of inhalants known as volatile nitrites, which includes amyl nitrite, butyl nitrite, and isobutyl ni-

trite. Amyl nitrite was the first of the group to be abused. In the 1960s, ampules of amyl nitrite became known as "poppers" or "snappers" because of the sound they made when they were crushed immediately before use. In 1969 amyl nitrite was moved from nonprescription to prescription drug status in an effort to curtail abuse. Immediately thereafter, isobutyl and butyl nitrite became available as legal replacements for amyl nitrite. They are sold under the trade names Rush, Locker Room, Bullet, Quick Silver, Thrust, Lightning Bolt, Hardware, and Climax. The volatile nitrites cause pronounced smooth muscle dilation, resulting in a pooling of blood in veins and relaxation of the smooth muscle of the rectum. Within 30 to 60 seconds of inhalation of amyl nitrite, there is a rapid fall in systolic blood pressure with the maximum effect occurring at one to three minutes after use.[114] It is this rapid pooling of blood in veins which produces the giddiness associated with nitrite abuse. Other effects noted by abusers include dizziness (100%), lightheadedness (100%), palpitations (67%), blurred vision (67%), pulsatile headache (34%), burning in nose (17%), and nausea (11%).[113]

There are three dangers associated with volatile nitrite abuse including: syncope, methemoglobinemia, and immunosuppression. Syncope is most likely in patients with underlying cardiac and/or atherosclerotic disease. These patients have more marked and more prolonged falls in diastolic blood pressure and may have prolonged syncopal spells.[114]

Methemoglobinemia is caused by the oxidation of ferrous hemoglobin to ferric methemoglobin by the volatile nitrite. Oxygen delivery to tissue is hampered because methemoglobin has a decreased oxygen carrying capacity and because remaining functional hemoglobin tends to cling to oxygen at the low oxygen tensions found at the tissue level (oxygen dissociation curve is shifted to the left). This condition is often life-threatening when greater than 70% of hemoglobin is oxidized to methemoglobin. The reduction back to oxyhemoglobin is normally catalyzed by NADH-methemoglobin reductase in the red blood cell. This is a relatively slow process ($t\frac{1}{2} = 15$ to 20 hours).

Patients with pre-existing anemia, cardiovascular or pulmonary compromise, and rare hereditary hemoglobin disorders (e.g., Hgb M, NADH-reductase deficiency) are more likely to develop significant toxicity after volatile nitrite inhalant abuse. Clinically significant methemoglobinemia has been reported from both inhalation and ingestion of isobutyl nitrite in patients without hereditary methemoglobinemias.[115,116]

Immunosuppression is of greatest concern in HIV-infected users. Nitrite inhalation may suppress immune function by decreasing peripheral lymphocyte counts and by reducing killer cell activity.[117,118] As a result, the HIV-infected patient who abuses nitrites may be at greater risk for developing Kaposi's sarcoma.

D.C.'s hypotension and reflex tachycardia most likely are due to the vasodilatory effects of isobutyl nitrite. His chest pain may be due to a combination of hypotension, poor oxygen delivery secondary to methemoglobinemia, or underlying cardiac disease.

Assessment

41. What additional tests would be helpful in determining the severity of D.C.'s poisoning?

A simple bedside screening test is to compare a drop of the patient's blood on filter paper with a drop of normal blood. Methemoglobin is a noticeable chocolate-brown color at hemoglobin concentrations of 15% or greater. In the early stages of poisoning, this darkly colored blood imparts a cyanotic look to the body even though oxygen delivery has not been significantly impaired.

The definitive lab test is to analyze the patient's blood for methemoglobin content. There is a good relationship between the percent of blood present as methemoglobin and symptoms. Patients may be cyanotic but asymptomatic with methemoglobin levels of 10% to 20%. At greater than 20%, fatigue, headache, syncope, dizziness, and weakness are common. Levels of greater than 50% are associated with tachypnea, dysrhythmias, hypoxia, acidosis, seizures, and coma. Death ensues at levels greater than 70%. Patients with low hemoglobin concentrations will be more symptomatic than patients with normal hemoglobin concentrations.[119]

Arterial blood gases also will be helpful in determining the severity of injury. The PaO_2 should be normal or elevated since this test reflects the amount of oxygen dissolved in plasma. Elevation may be due to hyperventilation. The oxygen saturation should be lowered since this test measures the degree of binding of oxygen to hemoglobin. Oxygen saturation must be measured by co-oximetry if methemoglobinemia is suspected. Oxygen saturations reported by blood gas analyzers and pulse oximeters will overestimate the oxygen saturation during methemoglobinemia.[120]

Since D.C. is having chest pain, an ECG and cardiac enzymes are obtained to determine whether there is evidence of myocardial infarction. D.C.'s blood is noticeably brown when it is being drawn for methemoglobin analysis. His ECG is normal as are his cardiac enzymes. His ABGs are: pO_2 126; pCO_2 27; pH 7.24; and O_2 saturation (calculated) 76%. His methemoglobin concentration is 54%.

These test results indicate that D.C. is suffering from significant methemoglobinemia. Impaired oxygen delivery has resulted in generation of lactic acid from anaerobic metabolism and development of a mild metabolic acidosis. Impairment is not severe enough to cause damage to the heart. The oxygen saturation reported overestimates the true oxygen saturation.

Treatment

42. What treatments are indicated for D.C.?
Supplemental oxygen should be administered until the level is reported. This treatment will optimize use of functioning hemoglobin.

Activated charcoal (1 gm/kg) and a cathartic should be administered orally to prevent further absorption of ingested isobutyl nitrite. Since nitrites are absorbed rapidly from the GI tract and because D.C. has inhaled this product more than an hour ago, this treatment will be of questionable benefit.

The antidote for treating methemoglobinemia is methylene blue (tetramethylthionine chloride). It is indicated in patients who are cyanotic and symptomatic or in asymptomatic patients with levels of greater than 30%. Methylene blue enhances conversion of methemoglobin to oxyhemoglobin via an enzyme system in the red blood cell known as NADPH-reductase. Under normal circumstances only 5% of reduction occurs through this pathway. In the presence of methylene blue, reduction occurs at a very fast rate ($t^{1/2}$ = 40 to 90 minutes) through NADPH-reductase allowing it to become the predominant conversion pathway.[121]

Methylene blue is administered intravenously at a dose of 1 to 2 mg/kg over five minutes. Its onset of action is rapid, with the majority of conversion occurring within an hour of administration. If cyanosis and signs of hypoxemia persist greater than an hour after methylene blue has been administered, another dose should be given. Methylene blue may color the skin and urine blue. High doses (>7 mg/kg total) are associated with precordial pain, dyspnea, restlessness, apprehension, tremor, and dysuria. Hemolysis may occur with doses greater than 15 mg/kg.[122]

Methylene blue should not be used in patients with glucose-6-phosphate dehydrogenase (G6PD) deficiency because they are at increased risk for developing hemolytic anemia, and the antidote does not work in these patients. G6PD is essential for generation of NADPH through the hexose monophosphate shunt. Patients who do not respond to methylene blue may be suffering from G6PD deficiency, NADPH-methemoglobin reductase deficiency (rare), or sulfhemoglobinemia.

D.C. is treated with supplemental oxygen by nasal cannula, 1 gm/kg of activated charcoal with sorbitol, and 1 mg/kg methylene blue. Immediately after the methylene blue is administered D.C.'s chest pain subsides and his color improves. His methemoglobin concentration one hour after methylene blue administration is 10%.

Acknowledgement

We gratefully acknowledge James F. Buchanan, Howard E. McKinney, Gregory N. Hayner, and Darryl S. Inaba, previous Applied Therapeutics Drug Abuse authors, whose work provided a foundation for this chapter.

References

1 **Jaffe JH, Martin WR.** Opioid analgesics and antagonists. In: Gilman AG et al., eds. The Pharmacological Basis of Therapeutics. New York: Pergamon Press; 1990:485–521.

2 **Terenium LT, O'Brien CP.** Receptors and endogenous ligands—implications for addiction. Res Publ Assoc Res Nerv Ment Dis. 1992;70:123.

3 **Pasternak GW.** Pharmacological mechanisms of opioid analgesics. Clin Neuropharmacol. 1993;16:1.

4 **Paul D et al.** Pharmacological characterization of nalorphine, a kappa₃ analgesic. J Pharmacol Exp Ther. 1991; 257:1.

5 **Clark JA et al.** Kappa opiate receptor multiplicity: evidence for two U50, 488-sensitive kappa₁ subtypes and a novel kappa₃ subtype. J Pharmacol Exp Ther. 1989;251:461.

6 **Rall TW.** Hypnotics and sedatives: ethanol. In: Gilman AG et al., eds. Goodman and Gilman's The Pharma-

cological Basis of Therapeutics. New York: Pergamon Press; 1990:345–82.

7 **Substance Abuse and Mental Health Services Administration.** National Household Survey on Drug Abuse: Main Findings 1991. Rockville, MD: Department of Health and Human Services, 1993; DHHS publication no. ADM 93–1980.

8 **Kreek MJ.** Multiple drug abuse patterns and medical consequences. In: Metzler HY, ed. Psychopharmacology: The Third Generation of Progress. New York: Raven Press; 1987;1597–604.

9 **Winick C.** Epidemiology of alcohol and drug abuse. In: Lowinson JH et al., eds. Substance Abuse A Comprehensive Textbook. 2nd ed. Baltimore: Williams and Wilkins; 1992:15–29.

10 **Balter MD et al.** A cross-national comparison of anti-anxiety/sedative drug use. Curr Med Res Opin. 1984;85:5.

11 **Mellinger GD et al.** Anti-anxiety agents: duration of use and character-

istics of users in the USA. Curr Med Res Opin. 1984;85:21.

12 **Lyndon RW, Russell JD.** Can overuse of psychotropic drugs by the elderly be prevented? Aust N Z J Psychiatry. 1990; 244:77.

13 **American Psychiatric Association.** Benzodiazepine Dependence, Toxicity, and Abuse: A Task Force Report of the American Psychiatric Association. Washington, DC: American Psychiatric Association; 1990.

14 **Wolf B et al.** Benzodiazepine abuse and dependence in psychiatric inpatients. Pharmacopsychiatry. 1989;22:54.

15 **Inaba DS et al.** Persian heroin in the San Francisco Bay Area: 1977–1980. Am J Drug Alcohol Abuse. 1981;8:123.

16 **Kram TC et al.** Behind the identification of China white. Anal Chem. 1981;53:1379a.

17 **Ayers WA et al.** The bogus drug: three methyl & alpha methyl fentanyl sold as

"China white." J Psychoactive Drugs. 1981;13:91.

18 **Beck J, Morgan PA.** Designer drug confusion: focus on MDMA. J Drug Educ. 1986;16(3):287.

19 **Ray O, Ksir C.** Drugs, Society, & Human Behavior. St. Louis, MO: Mosby; 1993:320–21.

20 **Ziporyn T.** A growing industry and menace: makeshift laboratory's designer drugs. JAMA. 1986;256(22):3061.

21 **Freishtat HW.** The Federal response to designer drugs: a new approach to a new problem. J Clin Psychopharmacol. 1985;5(6):350.

22 **LaBarbera M, Wolfe T.** Characteristics, attitudes and implications of fentanyl use based upon reports from self-identified fentanyl users. J Psychoactive Drugs. 1983;15(4):293.

23 **Langston JW et al.** Chronic parkinsonism due to a product of meperidine-analog synthesis. Science. 1983;219: 979.

24 **Bianchine JR, McGhee B.** MPTP and parkinsonism. Ration Drug Ther. 1985; 19(2):5.

25 **Snyder SH, D'Amato RJ.** MPTP: a neurotoxin relevant to the pathophysiology of Parkinson's disease. Neurology. 1986;36:250.

26 **Anon.** New fentanyl analog claims more lives in San Francisco Bay area. Pharm Chem Newsl. 1984;13(5):5.

27 **Pastan RS et al.** A musculoskeletal syndrome in intravenous heroin users: association with brown heroin. Ann Intern Med. 1977;87:22.

28 **Heishman SJ et al.** Acute opioid physical dependence in postaddict humans: naloxone dose effects after brief morphine exposure. J Pharmacol Exp Ther. 1989;248:127.

29 **Jaffe JH.** Drug addiction and drug abuse. In: Gilman AG et al., eds. The Pharmacological Basis of Therapeutics. New York: Pergamon Press; 1990:522–73.

30 **Bickel WK et al.** Buprenorphine: dose-related blockade of opioid challenge effects in opioid dependent subjects. J Pharmacol Exp Ther. 1988;247:47.

31 **Berenson D.** Alcohol and the family system. In: Guerin PF, ed. Family Therapy. New York: Gardner Press; 1976:284–97.

32 **Black C et al.** The interpersonal and emotional consequences of being an adult child of an alcoholic. Int J Addict. 1986;21:213.

33 **Novick DM.** The medically ill substance abuser. In: Lowinson JH et al., eds. Substance Abuse A Comprehensive Textbook. 2nd ed. Baltimore: Williams and Wilkins; 1992:657–74.

34 **Chaisson RE et al.** Human immunodeficiency virus infection in heterosexual intravenous drug users in San Francisco. Am J Public Health. 1987;77(2):169.

35 **DesJarlais DC et al.** HIV infection among intravenous drug users: epidemiology and emerging public health perspectives. In: Lowinson JH et al., eds. Substance Abuse A Comprehensive Textbook. 2nd ed. Baltimore: Williams and Wilkins; 1992:734–43.

36 **Jaffe JH.** Opiates: clinical aspects. In: Lowinson JH et al., eds. Substance Abuse A Comprehensive Textbook. 2nd ed. Baltimore: Williams and Wilkins; 1992:186–94.

37 **American Academy of Pediatrics Committee on Drugs.** Naloxone dosage and route of administration for infants and children: addendum to emergency drug doses for infants and children. Pediatrics. 1990;86:484.

38 **McEvoy GK et al., eds.** AHFS Drug Information 93. Bethesda, MD: American Society of Hospital Pharmacists; 1993:1258–259.

39 **Day HB.** The Opium Habit, with Suggestions as To Remedy. New York: Harper & Bros.; 1868.

40 **Greenstein RA et al.** Alternative pharmacotherapies for opiate addiction. In: Lowinson JH et al., eds. Substance Abuse A Comprehensive Textbook. 2nd ed. Baltimore: Williams and Wilkins; 1992:562–73.

41 **Dole VP et al.** A medical treatment for diacetylmorphine addiction. JAMA. 1965;193:646.

42 **Newman RG.** Methadone treatment: defining and evaluating success. N Engl J Med. 1987;317:447.

43 **Aronow R et al.** Childhood poisoning—an unfortunate consequence of methadone availability. JAMA. 1971; 219:321.

44 **Newmeyer IA et al.** Methadone for kicking and for kicks. Fourth National Conference on Methadone Treatment. San Francisco, 1972. National Assoc for the Prevention of Addiction to Narcotics. New York; 1972:461.

45 **Lowinson JH et al.** Methadone maintenance. In: Lowinson JH et al., eds. Substance Abuse A Comprehensive Textbook. 2nd ed. Baltimore: Williams and Wilkins; 1992:550–61.

46 **McEvoy GK et al., eds.** AHFS Drug Information 93. Bethesda, MD: American Society of Hospital Pharmacists; 1993:1222–224.

47 **Olin BR et al.** Facts and Comparisons. St Louis: Facts and Comparisons, Inc.; 1993:243m–n.

48 **Finnegan LP, Kandall SR.** Maternal and neonatal effects of alcohol and drugs. In: Lowinson JH et al., eds. Substance Abuse A Comprehensive Textbook. 2nd ed. Baltimore: Williams and Wilkins; 1992:628–56.

49 **Bashore RA et al.** Heroin addiction and pregnancy. West J Med. 1981;134:506.

50 **Little BB et al.** Maternal and fetal effects of heroin addiction during pregnancy. J Reprod Med. 1990;35:159.

51 **Ostrea EM et al.** A study of factors that influence the severity of neonatal narcotic withdrawal. J Pediatr. 1976; 88:642.

52 **Rosen TS.** Infants of addicted mothers. In: Farnoff AA, Martin RJ, eds. Neonatal-Perinatal Medicine. St. Louis: C.V. Mosby Co.; 1987:1114.

53 **Levy M, Spino M.** Neonatal withdrawal syndrome: associated drugs and pharmacologic management. Pharmacotherapy. 1993;13:202.

54 **McEvoy GK et al., eds.** AHFS Drug Information 93. Bethesda, MD: American Society of Hospital Pharmacists; 1993:1793–794.

55 **Kleber HD.** Naltrexone. J Subst Abuse Treat. 1985;2:117.

56 **Gray C et al.** Psychological factors on outcome in two opiate addiction treatments. J Clin Psychol. 1986;42(1):185.

57 **Preston KL, Bigelow GE.** Pharmacological advances in addiction treatment. Int J Addict. 1985;20(6 & 7): 845.

58 **Rawson RA, Ling W.** Opioid addiction treatment modalities and some guidelines to their optimal use. J Psychoactive Drugs. 1991;23:151.

59 **Galloway G, Hayner G.** Haight-Ashbury Free Clinics' drug detoxification protocols—part 2: opioid blockade. J Psychoactive Drugs. 1993;25:251.

60 **Galloway G, Hayner G.** Haight-Ashbury Free Clinics' drug detoxification protocols—part 1: opioids. J Psychoactive Drugs. 1993;25:157.

61 **Inaba DS, Cohen WE.** Uppers, Downers, All Arounders. Ashland, OR: CNS Publications; 1993:94–125.

62 **Wesson DR et al.** Sedative-hypnotics and tricyclics. In: Lowinson JH et al., eds. Substance Abuse A Comprehensive Textbook. 2nd ed. Baltimore: Williams and Wilkins; 1992:271–79.

63 **Shader RI, Greenblatt DJ.** Use of benzodiazepines in anxiety disorders. New Engl J Med. 1993;328:1398.

64 **Juergens SM.** Benzodiazepines and addiction. Psychiatric Clin N Amer. 1993;16:75.

65 **Smith DE, Landry MJ.** Benzodiazepine dependency discontinuation: focus on the chemical dependency detoxification setting and benzodiazepine poly-drug abuse. J Psychiatr Res. 1990; 24(Suppl. 2):145.

66 **McHugh MJ.** The abuse of volatile substances. Pediatr Clin North Am. 1987;34:333.

67 **Johnston LD et al.** National Survey Results on Drug Use from Monitoring the Future Study (Vol I). Rockville, MD: National Institute on Drug Abuse; 1993; NIH Pub. No. 93-3597.

68 **Morton HG.** Occurrence and treatment of solvent abuse in children and adolescents. Pharmacol Ther. 1987;33: 449.

69 **Ramsey J et al.** An introduction to the practice, prevalence and chemical toxicology of volatile substance abuse. Hum Toxicol. 1989;8:261.

70 **Billington AC.** Volatile substance abuse: The role of agencies in the community in prevention and counselling. Hum Toxicol. 1989;8:323.

71 **Newman IM.** Adolescent glue/inhalant aerosol use in Nebraska. Neb Jour. 1989;20:19.

72 **Barnes GE.** Solvent abuse: a review. Int J Addict. 1979;14:1.

73 **Bass M.** Sudden sniffing death. JAMA. 1970;212:2075.

74 **Shepard RT.** Mechanism of sudden death associated with volatile substance abuse. Hum Toxicol. 1989;8: 287.

75 **Johns A.** Volatile solvent abuse and 963 deaths. Br J Addic. 1991;86:1053. Editorial.

76 **Ellenhorn MJ, Barceloux DG.** Medical Toxicology—Diagnosis and Treatment of Human Poisonings. New York: Elsevier; 1988:840.

77 **Meredith TJ et al.** Diagnosis and treatment of acute poisoning with volatile substances. Hum Toxicol. 1989;8: 277.

78 **Wyse DG.** Deliberate inhalation of volatile hydrocarbons: a review. Can Med Assoc J. 1973;108:71.

79 **Poisindex Editorial Staff.** Trichloroethylene (management/treatment protocol). In: Rumack BH, Spoerke DG, eds. Poisindex Information System. Denver: Micromedex, Inc; (Edition expires 5/31/94).

80 **Monster AC.** Biological monitoring of chlorinated hydrocarbon solvents. J Occup Med. 1986;28:583.

81 **Poisindex Editorial Staff.** Methylene chloride (management/treatment protocol). In: Rumack BH, Spoerke DG, eds. Poisindex Information System. Denver: Micromedex, Inc.; (Edition expires 5/31/94).

82 **Fortenberry JD.** Gasoline sniffing. Am J Med. 1985;79:740.

83 **Tenenbein M.** Clinical/biophysiologic aspects of inhalant abuse. In: Sharp CW et al., eds. Inhalant Abuse: A Volatile Research Agenda. NIDA Research Monograph 129. Rockville: National Institute on Drug Abuse; 1992: 117–71. DHHS Pub. No. (ADM)93-3480.

84 **Cooper et al.** Neurophysiological signs of brain damage due to glue sniffing. Clin Electroencephalogr Neurophysiol. 1985;60:23.

85 **Rosenberg NL et al.** Central nervous system effects of chronic toluene abuse—clinical brainstem evoked response and magnetic resonance imaging studies. Neurotoxicol Teratol. 1988;10:489.

86 **Tenenbein M, Pilay N.** Sensory evoked potentials in inhalant (volatile solvent) abuse. J Paediatr Child Health. 1993;29:206.

87 **Richardson H.** Volatile substance abuse. Hum Toxicol. 1989;8:319.

88 **Oetting ER et al.** Psychosocial characteristics and their links with inhalants: a research agenda. In: Sharp CW et al., eds. Inhalant Abuse: A Volatile Research Agenda. NIDA Research Monograph 129. Rockville: National Institute on Drug Abuse; 1992:59–97. DHHS Pub. No. (ADM)93-3480.

89 **Rosenberg NL et al.** Solvent toxicity: a neurological focus. In: Sharp CW et al., eds. Inhalant Abuse: A Volatile Research Agenda. NIDA Research Monograph 129. Rockville: National Institute on Drug Abuse; 1992:117–71. DHHS Pub. No. (ADM)93-3480.

90 **Streicher HZ et al.** Syndromes of toluene sniffing in adults. Ann Int Med. 1981;94:758.

91 **Taher SM et al.** Renal tubular acidosis associated with toluene "sniffing". N Engl J Med. 1974;290:765.

92 **Jones CM et al.** An unusual case of toluene-induced metabolic acidosis. Clin Chem. 1988;34:2596.

93 **Fischman CM et al.** Toxic effects of toluene: a new cause of high anion gap metabolic acidosis. 1979;241:1713.

94 **Kaneko T et al.** Urinary calculi associated with solvent abuse. J Urol. 1992; 147:1365.

95 **Kroeger MR et al.** Recurrent urinary calculi associated with toluene sniffing. J Urol. 1980;123:89.

96 **Wyse G.** Deliberate inhalation of volatile hydrocarbons: a review. Can Med Assoc J. 1973;108:71.

97 **Ron M.** Volatile substance abuse: a review of possible long-term neurological, intellectual and psychiatric sequelae. Br J Psychiatry. 1986;148:235.

98 **Lolin Y.** Chronic neurological toxicity associated with exposure to volatile substances. Hum Toxicol. 1989;8:293.

99 **Marjot R et al.** Chronic non-neurological toxicity from volatile substance abuse. Hum Toxicol. 1989;8:301.

100 **Hayden et al.** The clinical toxicology of solvent abuse. Clin Toxicol. 1976;9: 169.

101 **Arnold et al.** Toluene embryopathy: clinical delineation and developmental follow-up. Pediatrics. 1994;93:216.

102 **Pearson MA et al.** Toluene embryopathy: delineation of the phenotype and comparison with fetal alcohol syndrome. Pediatrics. 1994;93:211.

103 **Lavoie FW et al.** Recurrent resuscitation and 'no code' orders in a 27-year-old spray paint abuser. Ann Intern Med. 1987;16:1266.

104 **Kirk et al.** Sudden death from toluene abuse. Ann Emer Med. 1984;13:120. Letter.

105 **Jumper-Thurman P et al.** Treatment of volatile solvent abusers. In: Sharp CW et al., eds. Inhalant Abuse: A Vol-

atile Research Agenda. NIDA Research Monograph 129. Rockville: National Institute on Drug Abuse; 1992: 203–13. DHHS Pub. No. (ADM) 93-3480.

106 **Murray MJ, Murray WJ.** Nitrous oxide availability. J Clin Pharmacol. 1980; 20:202.

107 **Block SH.** The grocery store high. Am J Psychiatry. 1978;135:126.

108 **Di Maio V, Garriott J.** Four deaths resulting from abuse of nitrous oxide. J Forensic Sci. 1978;23:169.

109 **Gillman MA.** Nitrous oxide, an opioid addictive agent. Am J Med. 1986;81:97.

110 **Brilliant L.** Nitrous oxide as a psyche-delic drug. N Engl J Med. 1970;283: 1522. Letter.

111 **LiPuma JP et al.** Nitrous oxide abuse: a new cause of pneumomediastinum. Radiology. 1982;145:602.

112 **Kunkle, DB.** Nitrous oxide: not a laughing matter anymore. Emerg Med. 1987;19:79.

113 **Schwartz RH.** Abuse of isobutyl nitrite inhalation (Rush). Clin Pediatr. 1986;25:308.

114 **Haley TJ.** Review of the physiological effects of amyl, butyl, and isobutyl nitrites. Clin Toxicol. 1980;16:317.

115 **Guss DA et al.** Clinically significant methemoglobinemia from inhalation of isobutyl nitrite. Am J Emerg Med. 1985;3:46.

116 **Wason S et al.** Isobutyl nitrite toxicity by ingestion. Ann Intern Med. 1980; 92:637.

117 **Dax EM et al.** Effects of nitrites on the immune system of humans. In: Haverkos HW, Dougherty JA, eds. Health Hazards of Nitrite Inhalants. NIDA Monograph. Rockville: National Institute on Drug Abuse; 1988:75–80. NTIS Pub #89-125496/AS.

118 **Lotzova E et al.** Depression of murine natural killer cell cytotoxicity by isobutyl nitrite. Cancer Immunol Immunother. 1984;17:130.

119 **Goldfrank LR et al.** Nitroglycerin (methemoglobinemia). In: Goldfrank LR et al., eds. Goldfrank's Toxicologic Emergencies. 4th ed. East Norwalk: Appleton & Lange; 1990:391–96.

120 **Watcha MF et al.** Pulse oximetry in methemoglobinemia. Am J Dis Child. 1989;143:845.

121 **Lovejoy FH.** Methemoglobinemia. Clin Tox Rev. 1984;6:1.

122 **Howland MA.** Antidotes in depth—methylene blue. In: Goldfrank LR et al., eds. Goldfrank's Toxicologic Emergencies. 4th ed. East Norwalk: Appleton & Lange; 1990:397–99.

Central Nervous System (CNS) Stimulant Abuse

David M Scott
Teri L Gabel

Amphetamines 84-1
  Medical Uses 84-2
    Narcolepsy 84-2
    Attention deficit hyperactivity disorder (ADHD) ... 84-2
    Short-term weight reduction 84-2
  Amphetamine Pseudonyms (See Table 84.1) 84-3
  Abuse and Hypertension 84-3
  Acute Effects of Amphetamine Abuse 84-3
  Chronic Abuse 84-3
  Pharmacokinetics 84-4
  Physical Dependence and Withdrawal 84-4
  Drug Interactions and Polydrug Use 84-4
  Toxicity 84-4
  Treatment 84-5
    Initial therapy 84-5
    Long-term therapy 84-5
  Pregnancy Complications 84-5

Phenylpropanolamine 84-6
  ''Look-Alike'' Drugs 84-6
  Eating Disorders 84-6
  Weight Control Strategies 84-6
  Smoking Cessation 84-7
  Adverse Effects 84-7
  Blood Pressure 84-7
  Contraindications 84-7

Cocaine 84-7
  History 84-7
  Prevalence 84-8
  Cocaine pseudonyms (See Table 84.2) 84-8
  Purity 84-8
  Legal sources 84-8
  Medical use 84-9
  Pharmacokinetics 84-9
  Routes of administration 84-9
    Snorting 84-9

    Intravenous 84-9
    Free-based cocaine 84-9
    Crack 84-9
  Pharmacology 84-9
  Acute intoxication 84-10
    Medical problems (See Table 84.4) 84-10
      Crack lung 84-11
    Treatment 84-11
  Toxicology 84-11
    Treating overdosage 84-11
    Cardiotoxicity (See Tables 84.5, 84.6,
      84.7, and 84.8) 84-12
    Respiratory toxicity 84-12
    Renal toxicity 84-12
    Hyperthermia 84-12
    Neurotoxicity (See Table 84.9) 84-12
  Body packing 84-13
  Chronic Use 84-13
    Depression 84-13
    Drug screening 84-13
    Psychiatric effects 84-13
    Pharmacotherapy 84-14
    Skin lesions 84-14
    Infectious complications 84-14
    Adverse effects in pregnancy 84-14
    Withdrawal 84-14
      Acute withdrawal: phase 1 84-14
      Craving: phase 2 84-15
      Extinction: phase 3 84-15
        Cue extinction 84-15
      Treatment 84-15
  Addiction liability 84-15
    Experimental use 84-16
    Compulsive use 84-16
    Dysfunctional use 84-16
  Treatment of addiction 84-16

Amphetamines

Almost three million Americans in 1992 used amphetamines for nonmedical reasons. Prescription-controlled stimulants have continued their long-term decline in use among 12th graders from 20% in 1982 to 7% in 1992. In college students, stimulants have dropped from 21% to 4% over the same period. According to this Monitoring the Future Study,[1] 11% of eighth graders reportedly had tried prescription-type stimulants and 3% had used them in the last 30 days.

The 1991 National Household Survey on Drug Abuse reported lifetime use of stimulants in the 12- to 17-year-old group was 3%, and use in the past month was 0.5%.[2] Although the use of central nervous system (CNS) stimulants such as amphetamines has decreased in recent years, with increasing pressure to decrease the use of cocaine in the U.S., amphetamine use may increase.

Central nervous system stimulants have been used both with and without social acceptance for thousands of years. Various plants such as the Chinese Ma-Huang plant (Ephedra vulgaris containing

ephedrine) and the Khat bush leaves (Catha edulis containing the alkaloid cathinone) contain stimulants.[3,4] Caffeine probably is the favorite CNS stimulant taken worldwide and is consumed commonly in coffee, tea, and various soft drinks. (See Chapter 85: Nicotine and Caffeine Abuse.)

Central nervous system stimulation first was reported from amphetamine in 1927,[5] and amphetamine, which is similar in chemical structure to ephedrine, was patented and introduced as an over-the-counter (OTC) product (Benzedrex inhaler) in 1932 for asthma. In 1937 psychology students at the University of Minnesota discovered that amphetamines allowed them to stay alert and were effective for ''cramming'' for exams. During World War II, amphetamines were used widely by soldiers in Germany, Japan, and Great Britain to stay alert for long periods of time. American soldiers used amphetamines during the Korean War. In the 1950s, amphetamines became very popular with truck drivers and other workers to keep them awake, often for ≥2 days.

Amphetamines have been used in sports dating back to the 1950s and are used as ''energy'' chemicals. Athletes trying to achieve the "competitive edge" may use amphetamines to increase their sports performances, especially in track and field, football, and swimming. The use of amphetamines and other CNS stimulants has been banned by the International Olympic Committee (IOC), the National Collegiate Athletic Association (NCAA) and most professional sport organizations. Amphetamine screening is included in athlete urine testing programs. (See Chapter 87: Drug Abuse in Athletics.)

Amphetamines were used for weight control beginning in 1939 when narcolepsy patients treated with amphetamines reported that they were not hungry after taking them. Amphetamine users discovered the need to take increasing quantities to lose weight; this discovery is indicative of the rapid development of tolerance. Although amphetamines were prescription drugs, it was relatively easy during the 1960s to obtain a prescription for amphetamines, sometimes in combination with thyroid supplements, for weight reduction.

The "speed scene" of the late 1960s became a focus of national concern and changed the way society viewed these drugs. The passage of the 1970 Controlled Substances Act placed amphetamines into the tightly controlled C-II classification for controlled substances. This discouraged the widespread prescribing and dispensing of amphetamines and established limits on the total amount of amphetamines that could be manufactured. With the legal market for prescription amphetamines largely curtailed, the illicit production of amphetamines increased substantially.[6]

Clandestine laboratories producing methamphetamine and other amphetamines have been a major source for illicit amphetamines since about 1970. The illicit production of methamphetamine ("speed") is relatively easy, so this drug continues to be readily available. Today, "speed labs" or "meth labs" frequently are raided by law enforcement agencies to reduce the availability of methamphetamine. While the use of CNS stimulants such as cocaine and other forms of amphetamines has declined recently, the use of methamphetamine has remained relatively constant and may be increasing.

Amphetamines are chemically similar to natural catecholamines such as epinephrine (adrenaline), norepinephrine (noradrenaline), and dopamine. Being similar in chemical structure, amphetamines easily occupy the catecholamine-receptor sites. They result in increased stimulation of norepinephrine and dopamine receptors and cause release of norepinephrine; therefore, they are classified as sympathomimetic agents.

Amphetamines cause leakage of catecholamines into synapses and block reuptake, thus increasing the intensity and duration of catecholamine effects. Amphetamine-stimulated release of catecholamine creates an artificial "fight-or-flight" response that is similar to one's normal reaction to an emergency situation.

Medical Uses

Approved medical uses of amphetamines are narcolepsy, attention deficit hyperactivity disorder (ADHD), and short-term weight reduction. Patient interview should identify the purpose of therapy.

Narcolepsy

The American Medical Association recognized amphetamines as an appropriate treatment for narcolepsy in 1935. Narcolepsy is a relatively rare disease where a person falls asleep without reason between 5 to 50 times a day. Symptoms include unexpected, inappropriate, and irresistible short spells of sleep. The idiopathic form usually occurs in young men and may be associated with cataplexy, sleep paralysis, and visual or auditory hallucinations. Narcolepsy also can occur secondary to head trauma, brain tumor, and/or cerebral vascular insufficiency.[7] Treatment usually is with

tricyclic antidepressants (TCAs), monoamine oxidase inhibitors (MAOIs), pemoline, amphetamines, or another CNS stimulant.[8] Low doses of amphetamines will help keep a narcoleptic person alert.

Attention Deficit Hyperactivity Disorder (ADHD)

Amphetamines also are used to treat ADHD. An estimated 1% to 2% of the school age (>600,000) children are affected. Most of the children treated are between six and ten years of age, although more recently there has been an increase in the use for teenagers with ADHD.[9] Children with ADHD commonly have academic difficulties and poor social skills development. Boys are more likely to be affected than girls, and these behavior problems usually impede learning. This condition affects mainly children into adolescence. The incidence is lower in adulthood, although adults may have a modified form.[10]

This syndrome is characterized by chronic difficulties in the area(s) of attention, impulsivity, and overactivity.[11] ADHD children have their greatest difficulty with sustaining attention to tasks, especially when they are required to pay attention to dull and repetitive tasks, such as schoolwork, homework, or chores. Impulsivity is a pattern of rapid inappropriate response to tasks. Children often respond quickly to a situation without waiting for adequate instructions and are commonly unnecessary risk-takers. The third characteristic of ADHD is overactivity; here, children with ADHD exhibit excessive or developmentally inappropriate levels of behavior, either vocally or by movement. These fidgeting movements often are irrelevant to the task. Children at school often are moving out of their seats or about the class without permission. Other characteristics include moving arms and legs, talking out of turn, making unusual vocal noises, and playing with objects not related to the task.[11]

Although children with behavioral problems benefit from dextroamphetamine (Dexedrine),[12] methylphenidate (Ritalin) has largely replaced amphetamines in ADHD treatment by capturing 90% of the stimulant medication market.[13] Although methylphenidate has been examined over short term in well-controlled studies, very few studies have looked at long-term effectiveness. Treatment with methylphenidate usually begins with a dose of 5 mg in the morning and at lunch, and subsequent doses are increased gradually based upon response, as noted by the physician in conjunction with input from parents and teachers. Since this drug has a short duration of action, most children require two or three daily doses or a 60 mg/day maximum dose.[14]

Short-Term Weight Reduction

Amphetamines and other related CNS stimulants also suppress appetite by depressing the appetite center in the hypothalamus, although the exact mechanism of action is unknown.[14] Since the implementation of federal controls on amphetamines in 1970, physicians have largely switched to CNS-related stimulants or nondrug weight control strategies. While having a different chemical structure than amphetamines, stimulants such as phentermine (Fastin), phenmetrazine (Preludin), diethylpropion (Tenuate), and pemoline (Cylert) have similar amphetamine-type effects.

Amphetamines are approved by the Food and Drug Administration (FDA) for short-term weight loss only (a few weeks) as an adjunct in a regimen of weight reduction based upon caloric restriction. Amphetamines have been more effective than a placebo in short-term (4 to 20 week), double-blind controlled studies. In most of these studies, amphetamines decreased weight more than placebos by up to 0.5 pounds per week. In other studies, the amphetamine effect waned after two to four weeks of treatment unless the dose was increased. Upon stopping the amphetamine, weight usually returns to, or above, initial weight.[15] Consequently, health care providers have changed their prescribing of these drugs drastically and favor behavioral modification programs, support groups, and counseling techniques as more effective therapies for weight control. The use of amphetamines without the help of a more comprehensive weight reduction program is not advocated.

Amphetamine Pseudonyms

Amphetamine and amphetamine-related drugs have a variety of different names. Some of the common names are listed in Table 84.1.

Abuse and Hypertension

1. P.J., a 28-year-old male, presents at the emergency room (ER) for bleeding from a laceration. P.J. is taking hydrochlorothiazide 25 mg/day for blood pressure (BP) control. He reports that he took some "speed," got in a fight, and was pushed through a window. P.J. reports taking "speed" for about a year, and most recently, about 6–10 "pills" a day with occasional "runs." Why would amphetamine abuse be expected to exacerbate P.J.'s hypertensive condition?

If the "speed" P.J. is using is an amphetamine, it probably is produced locally in a clandestine laboratory. Amphetamines in normotensive individuals may cause increases in heart rate, respiratory rate, blood pressure, and CNS stimulation. Hypertensive patients such as P.J. are at significant risk for hypertensive crisis and other problems associated with uncontrolled blood pressure. His blood pressure and vital signs should be taken immediately and the impact of blood pressure on the cardiovascular system and other organ systems should be assessed. Amphetamine abusers such as P.J. generally do not follow healthy lifestyle practices and should be assessed for metabolic abnormalities associated with thiazide use such as hypokalemia, hyperglycemia, and hyperuricemia. Medication noncompliance problems are paramount in drug users and also should be assessed. Amphetamine abuse is expected to exacerbate hypertensive conditions and P.J. should be managed if his blood pressure is elevated.

Acute Effects of Amphetamine Abuse

2. If the "speed" P.J. was using is amphetamine, what signs and symptoms are suggestive of acute amphetamine abuse?

If amphetamines were ingested, P.J.'s heart rate, respiratory rate, and blood pressure probably would be increased. He is likely to be agitated or excitable because small doses of amphetamines generally will produce an initial mild euphoria and a feeling of well-being. The user may feel confident, energetic, enthusiastic, talkative, and very ambitious. Generally, the desire for food is decreased

Table 84.1	Street Names of Methamphetamines and "Look-Alike" Products
Drug Name (Brand Name)	**Street Name**
Amphetamines (Synthetic)	
D.L. amphetamine (Benzedrine, Biphetamine)	Crosstops, black beauties, bennies
Methamphetamine (Methedrine, Desoxyn)	Crank, meth, crystal, speed
Dextroamphetamine (Dexedrine, Eskatrol)	Dexies
Dextromethamphetamine base Freebase methamphetamine	Ice, shabu
"Look-Alikes"	
Phenylpropanolamine (Dexadiet, Dexatrim)	Legal stimulants, legal speed

and the user cannot sleep. Users may go on "runs," staying up for three to ten days, by taking increasing amounts of amphetamines. This especially stresses the nervous and cardiovascular systems. Cardiovascular changes may include chills or perspiration, increased or decreased blood pressure, and bradycardia or tachycardia. Gastrointestinal (GI) symptoms may include nausea, vomiting, diarrhea, abdominal cramping, and dry mouth. Neurologic and psychiatric symptoms become more unpleasant as the "run" continues. Fear, irritability, suspiciousness, delusions, and hallucinations may occur. Repetitive behavior may occur (e.g., repeatedly cleans dishes or continually grooms hair). Amphetamines also will extenuate hostile, aggressive, and antisocial behavior. Progression to paranoia, panic states, violence, and even suicide may occur.[14] P.J. should be monitored for cardiovascular, gastrointestinal, neurologic, and psychiatric signs and symptoms commonly associated with amphetamine use.

While amphetamine use and aggressive behavior are associated in case reports, this relationship has not been studied extensively. "Speed kills" was a common street warning in the late 1960s and early 1970s due to amphetamine association with violent behavior. Amphetamine use leading to sudden violent offenses including murder has been reported. Self-reports of prison and jail inmates including juvenile offenders indicate that many have committed their crimes while intoxicated by amphetamines.[16] Ellinwood[17] concluded that CNS stimulants, more than any other drug class, are associated with violent behavior. Amphetamine association with violent behavior cannot be explained solely by pharmacological effects, but is a multifactorial problem that needs to be examined within the confines of previous experience, psychiatric history, and environmental influences.

Prolonged usage during a "run" eventually results in total exhaustion; the individual "crashes," which results in prolonged sleep lasting 24 to 48 hours. This may occur earlier if the supply of drug is exhausted or is discontinued for other reasons. Upon awakening, the individual is hungry, lethargic, and depressed. To negate these unpleasant effects, a user is inclined to take amphetamines again to begin a new cycle. The amphetamine user also may use other drugs including heroin, benzodiazepines, or sleeping pills to terminate an amphetamine "run."[18]

Chronic Abuse

3. P.J. has altered his pattern of amphetamine use and now uses amphetamines both orally and parenterally. He has lost 15 pounds over the last 14 days and is chronically tired. What other symptoms might be expected to be present in chronic amphetamine and methamphetamine abuse?

P.J.'s chronic exhaustion and weight loss probably are related to his chronic use of amphetamines. Of the most common psychiatric presenting complaints in 310 methamphetamine users seeking help at the Haight-Ashbury Medical Clinic[20] were, in descending order, acute anxiety reaction, "amphetamine psychosis," exhaustion syndrome, and withdrawal. Common medical presenting complaints (40% of the 310 patients) were primary somatic symptom or medical illnesses related to their methamphetamine use. Most often this was secondary illness due to general debility with malnutrition as a result of long-term "speed" use. The major medical problem was hepatitis which was endemic in this clinic's area. The primary etiologic factors were the use of contaminated needles (hepatitis B) and the crowded and unsanitary environment of the "speed freak" (hepatitis A). The advent of hepatitis A and hepatitis B vaccines should lower the frequency of these adverse effects. Long-term, high doses of methamphetamine also may have a direct effect upon the liver producing a chronic and relapsing form of hepatitis.[20] Amphetamines used in large doses over a long period of time may lead to substantial weight loss, liver disease, hypertensive disorders, kidney damage, stroke, heart attack, nonhealing ulcers, and sores in the skin.[18]

Pharmacokinetics

4. P.J. is readmitted to the ER after ingesting an unknown amount of amphetamine-containing "pills" and having "smoked" a free-base form of methamphetamine. Consider how pharmacokinetic parameters such as route, metabolism, and excretion are involved in P.J.'s situation. How long will P.J. be "high"?

P.J. has ingested an unknown amount of oral amphetamine and has complicated this situation further by smoking methamphetamine, creating a complex pharmacologic situation for the clinician. The abuse of amphetamines by combining the oral and inhalation routes of administration usually leads to a more intense effect and/or more toxic effect than if either was taken alone. The peak effects of orally administered amphetamines occur between two to three hours. Biological half-life is between 10 to 12 hours and the drug usually is eliminated in the urine within two days after the last oral dose. Amphetamine is a basic (pKa 9.90), highly lipid-soluble drug, which is mostly excreted unchanged in the urine. Renal excretion is enhanced by an acidic urine and approximately 99% of a dose is ionized by glomerular filtration and only the remaining nonionized portion of the drug is reabsorbed into the circulatory system.[16] The primary mode of amphetamine overdose treatment is to acidify the urine.[21]

Metabolic pathways for amphetamines include aromatic hydroxylation, beta-hydroxylation, and deamination.[16] The primary metabolic pathway involves oxidation of the nitrogen and its alpha-carbons by N-dealkylation and deamination, with the major metabolite excreted as benzoic acid.[22] If P.J. took the "speed" just orally, then the effects should begin to abate about three hours postingestion but may persist much longer.

In this situation, P.J. has taken amphetamine along with smoking of methamphetamine. Cook[23] studied the pharmacokinetics of methamphetamine in humans. A 21 mg dose of methamphetamine hydrochloride was smoked under carefully controlled laboratory procedures. Cook compared plasma levels after smoking methamphetamine and after smoking cocaine free-base. Cocaine levels after smoking rapidly peaked and then rapidly declined, with a half-life of 56 minutes. The initial plasma concentration of methamphetamine increased rapidly after smoking and maintained a plateau level for three to four hours, then declined slowly thereafter with an average elimination half-life of 11.5 hours.[23] This long plateau effect and the much longer half-life of methamphetamine versus cocaine suggests considerable dangers in repeated smoking of methamphetamine, since markedly higher plasma concentrations could be expected to occur if the dose is repeated, even at fairly long intervals.[23] P.J.'s smoking of methamphetamine and the resultant "high" may persist for 12 to 24 hours, which is determined partially by P.J.'s other drug use and sleep deprivation. This estimation of the duration of P.J.'s amphetamine "high" is based upon the assumptions that the "high" correlates with plasma concentrations of amphetamine, is linear with the plasma concentration, and correlates with plasma half-life.

Physical Dependence and Withdrawal

5. P.J. has a history of chronic "speed" use. What are the signs and symptoms of withdrawal ("crashing")?

The classic physical withdrawal symptoms seen after chronic administration of barbiturates and heroin do not occur with amphetamines. Until recently, amphetamines were not considered physically addicting. However, large doses of amphetamines taken over several days eventually will result in "crashing" and produce a consistent set of withdrawal symptoms. These withdrawal symptoms are depressed mood, low energy levels, and sleeping for ≥24 hours. Based upon criteria in the Diagnostic and Statistical Manual of Mental Disorders, Fourth Edition (DSM-IV), the essential feature of substance withdrawal is the development of a substance-specific syndrome due to the cessation of, or reduction in, amphetamine and related substance use that has been heavy and prolonged. Another diagnostic criterion for withdrawal is that the chronic amphetamine abuse causes clinically significant distress or impairment in social, occupational, or other important areas of functioning, and these symptoms are not due to a general medical condition and are not better accounted for by another mental disorder. Most individuals in withdrawal have a craving to readminister the substance to reduce the symptoms. Thus, the diagnosis of withdrawal by DSM-IV criteria is recognized for amphetamines and other related substances.[24]

A withdrawal state following cessation of chronic amphetamine use peaks in one to three days and may continue for a week. By ten days, oversleep, depression, sleep disturbances, headache, and GI upset usually resolve. However, associated psychiatric and emotional problems may persist and may require continued psychotherapy, medication, and supportive services.

Drug Interactions and Polydrug Use

6. P.J. states that he had taken other drugs to take the edge off when he "crashed" from a "speed run." What did P.J. most likely take and why?

Amphetamine and methamphetamine users often combine these drugs with other agents to increase the high, to take the edge off the crash, or to control the level of stimulation. Amphetamine users may combine amphetamine use with heavy use of alcohol, cigarette smoking, and marijuana. Alcohol will enhance the irritability from amphetamine usage. Other drugs that also are commonly used include the benzodiazepines, barbiturates, and heroin. Heroin sometimes is combined with amphetamines or cocaine ("speed balls").[18]

Concurrent use of amphetamines and monoamine oxidase inhibitors has resulted in hypertensive crisis, cerebral hemorrhage, and several deaths. This hypertensive reaction may occur several weeks after MAOIs are discontinued. Other cases of phenylpropanolamine-induced hypertension also have been reported.[26]

Toxicity

7. R.S., a 15-year-old male, arrives at a California ER with a complaint of insomnia and chest pain. R.S. states that he has taken "look alike" stimulants in the past, and a friend suggested that he try smoking "ice" instead. R.S. states that he had smoked "ice" about 4 hours ago and his chest pain began shortly after smoking and has become worse over the last few hours. Vital signs are pulse 150 beats/min, respiratory rate 23 breaths/min, and BP 165/105 mm Hg. Why should tests be obtained to confirm R.S.'s ingestion of "look-alike" stimulants and "ice"?

The ingestion of illicit substances of abuse may not produce predictable toxicological effects because the actual substance that was sold may not in actuality be what was represented to the purchaser. Emergency room clinicians should try to validate the identity of the ingested drug and to rule out the need to manage the patient for other drugs that may have been substituted for the "real thing" by an unscrupulous dealer or for other drugs that the patient may have ingested concurrently. A urine toxicology screen for illicit drugs could provide useful information, and other laboratory tests [e.g., electrocardiogram (ECG)] should be ordered to establish baselines that might be needed for treatment of complications. R.S.'s complaints of insomnia and chest pain, and the increases in his blood pressure, heart rate, and respirations are consistent with a possible cardiovascular morbid event, or these simply may reflect his reports of taking "look-alike" stimulant drugs and "ice."

The proliferation of "look-alikes" began in the 1970s when legal sanctions against widespread prescribing of amphetamines were instituted. These tablets and capsules are manufactured in clandestine laboratories to resemble the prescription amphetamines (hence, the name of "look-alikes"), but instead contain phenylpropanolamine, pseudoephedrine, ephedrine, caffeine, and other nonprescription "legal" stimulants. A thriving business in illicit production of methamphetamine powder also has provided more potent "look-alike" drugs to the marketplace. During the first half of 1987, California and the West Coast experienced a dramatic resurgence of methamphetamine-related hospital admissions, poison center calls, and law enforcement actions.

Historically, the illicit manufacture of methamphetamines has been dominated by motorcycle gangs. The "biker" gangs have been located primarily in three states, California, Texas, and Oregon, and accounted for about three-fourths of all methamphetamines seized in laboratories in 1988.[19] These laboratories were largely situated in remote areas where telltale fumes were vented easily without detection. Currently, groups are much more versatile in where they locate their laboratories. These laboratories have been located in private homes, rental homes, garages, campgrounds, moving vans, storage facilities, houseboats, and commercial establishments.[19] Former methamphetamine clandestine laboratories are environmental hazards and need to be decontaminated before these facilities can be used again safely.

8. What toxic effects of amphetamine and "ice" might be manifested by R.S.?

"Crystal meth" or "ice" is crystal methamphetamine and has been popular in Japan, Hawaii, and on the West Coast of the U.S. As with "crack" cocaine the "ice" crystals are heated and the vapor is inhaled. Absorption is fast and the "high" is rapid. The effect from smoking methamphetamine usually is achieved between 15 to 45 seconds after inhalation.

Acute toxic effects of amphetamines that are most likely to be seen in the emergency room occur in the inexperienced amphetamine user such as R.S., or the "speed" user who in fact has been receiving "look-alike" stimulants who unknowingly obtains an amphetamine product and continues the same dose as the "look-alikes." Signs and symptoms include dizziness, irritability, confusion, insomnia, tremor, and fever. Other effects include headaches, chills, flushing, palpitations, hypertension or hypotension, and possible circulatory collapse.[14] Fatal intoxication usually is preceded by hyperpyrexia, convulsions, and shock.[27] In dual diagnosis patients or those who also are mentally ill, amphetamine use may elicit psychotic effects and induce hostility, panic states, and homicidal or suicidal ideation.[14] R.S. probably was taking phenylpropanolamine, so problems related to switching unknowingly from phenylpropanolamine to methamphetamine-containing "speed" would not be expected. Potency differences might account for the aggressive behavior exhibited by R.S. while he was agitated.

9. What is the likelihood that R.S. took a toxic dose of amphetamine?

Since tolerance develops rapidly with amphetamine use, the acute toxic dose has a wide range. Doses as little as 2 mg, but more likely between 15 and 30 mg, may induce toxic effects. However, even doses of 400 to 500 mg are not uniformly fatal.[14]

An analysis of 310 cases of acute, high-dose methamphetamine toxicity in the Haight-Ashbury Medical Clinic of San Francisco in 1967 revealed that regular users of methamphetamine had used 500 to 1000 mg/day at a single injection without serious acute morbidity. There are other case reports of 1000 to 5000 mg/day of "black market" methamphetamine that have been used during a "speed binge."[20] R.S., however, does not appear to be a regular user of amphetamines and the amount he has taken is unknown.

Treatment

Initial Therapy

10. What initial treatment for amphetamine abuse should be considered for R.S.?

When drugs are used for the first time, a person may be "talked down" from an acute psychotic episode. This intervention is not appropriate for the long-term, heavy amphetamine-using "speed freak." This extremely agitated, paranoid state often requires the administration of haloperidol (Haldol) and lorazepam (Ativan), or droperidol (Inapsine) to the physically restrained patient. The combativeness and hallucinations typically will resolve within 15 to 30 minutes, although with the smokable form of methamphetamine ("ice"), this effect may persist much longer. When patients are not extremely agitated, benzodiazepines or haloperidol may be administered orally. Possible medical complications that R.S. may encounter include hypertension, seizures, cardiac complications, malnourishment, dehydration, and vomiting and should be treated using conventional therapy. Detoxification from excessive "ice" use usually takes several days longer than detoxifying from regular methamphetamine abuse.[25] R.S. should be monitored closely and his vital signs and chest pain should return to normal as the "ice" effect wears off.

Long-Term Therapy

11. What long-term treatment to encourage amphetamine abstinence should be considered for R.S.?

A pharmacological approach alone has not been effective in treating stimulant addiction. Currently, considerable research is being focused into the treatment of craving. Craving is the most difficult withdrawal symptom of amphetamine abuse and often leads to multiple relapse failures in recovery. Two major types of craving have been addressed: endogenous craving and environmentally triggered craving.[6] Endogenous craving is thought to be due to a depletion of dopamine in the nucleus acumbens of the limbic system. Various stimulators of dopamine in the nucleus acumbens have been used (i.e., amantadine, bromocriptine, and levodopa) that have diminished amphetamine craving.[6]

Environmentally triggered craving is more likely to lead to relapse than endogenous craving. Memory triggers such as peer pressure, family, money, drugs, paraphernalia, and familiar settings may lead to craving. Physiologic changes such as changes in body temperature, heart rate, and blood pressure may accompany craving. Intensive counseling, group sessions, and desensitization techniques are critical to successful treatment. Various techniques such as exercise, counseling, and cold showers have been used to bring the individual's responses back to normal. These techniques frequently are repeated as often as needed until the craving responses diminish.

While these techniques will help R.S. and other amphetamine-dependent individuals, the most important underlying theme is that "recovery is often a lifetime process."[6]

Pregnancy Complications

12. R.S.'s girlfriend, K.M., who is a long-term user of "speed," just received a positive pregnancy test result. What problems may arise for K.M. when amphetamines are taken during pregnancy?

Long-term amphetamine users are especially prone to malnutrition. Vitamin and mineral deficiencies and neglect of prenatal care all may complicate pregnancy and produce a small, malnourished infant.[28] This low birth weight could result from drug use in a number of ways: depression of the mother's appetite providing either too little or inadequate nutrition for the fetus, impairment of the fetus's ability to use available nutrients, or premature birth.[29] While amphetamine association with first trimester spontaneous abortions has been reported, the overall impact on fetal development and later child development is poorly documented.[27]

Cerebral malformations were more common in methamphetamine-exposed fetuses, probably secondary to the vasoconstrictive properties of amphetamines.[32] Illicit maternal amphetamine use may present significant risk to the fetus and newborn. These risks include intrauterine growth retardation; premature delivery; and the potential for increased maternal, fetal, and neonatal morbidity.[32] When amphetamines are used for genuine medical indications in FDA-recommended doses, teratogenic effects from the drug are not likely;[30,31] however, the legitimate medical indications for amphetamine use should be expected to provide significant benefits to justify the risks.

Amphetamine readily passes into and is concentrated in breast milk. Steiner[33] measured milk concentrations ranged from 55 to 138 ng/mL after receiving a daily dose of 20 mg of dextroamphetamine. The American Academy of Pediatrics considers amphetamines to be contraindicated during breast-feeding.[34]

K.M. most likely is pregnant and needs to be referred to a physician or public health clinic for confirmatory diagnosis. She should avoid amphetamine use during pregnancy because amphetamines would increase her chances for spontaneous abortion, premature delivery, and intrauterine growth retardation.

Phenylpropanolamine

"Look-Alike" Drugs

13. A.C. bought "speed" but is suspicious that what she was sold was "fake speed." How could A.C. tell if it was "fake speed"?

"Look-alike" drugs first were introduced between 1971 and 1976 into the U.S. when amphetamine production by clandestine laboratories failed to offset the dwindling prescription supply of amphetamines. "Look-alikes" include tablets and capsules whose appearance is almost identical to prescription amphetamines, and they often are misrepresented as such. The most popular amphetamine "look-alike" drugs contain a combination of caffeine, ephedrine, and phenylpropanolamine.[35] In one study of 11 patients in an emergency room with neurologic symptoms after taking "amphetamine" pills, the urine of each of these patients contained phenylpropanolamine and no evidence of amphetamines.

The FDA and other governmental bodies have attempted to limit or eliminate the use of legally manufactured "look-alike" drugs, but these efforts have met with limited success. Since many "look-alikes" can be either legal or illegal drugs and may be misrepresented to the buyer, obtaining honest and accurate use histories may be difficult for health care providers.

A.C. might be able to identify a legally manufactured product based upon the identification markings on solid dosage forms. Illegal "look-alike" dosage forms may resemble the legally manufactured amphetamine, so laboratory analysis may be the only way for A.C. to determine the content.

Eating Disorders

14. K.H., a 16-year-old, slightly overweight female, asks about the benefits of a product called Dietac (contains phen-ylpropanolamine), which a classmate told her is a great product to take weight off. What would you be concerned about? What would be your advice to her?**

Approximately 25% of the adolescent female population is estimated to suffer from an eating disorder such as bulimia or anorexia nervosa (see Chapter 80: Eating Disorders). Anorexia nervosa usually begins in early adolescence, chiefly affects females, and is characterized by self-imposed food restriction and starvation in an obsessive-compulsive effort to lose weight and achieve an unrealistic ideal of thinness. Those affected are preoccupied by diet and weight control and have a distorted perception of being fat, despite being at low normal or even below normal weight for age and height. This obsessive disorder may result in death (e.g., Karen Carpenter, the popular singer).

Bulimia nervosa usually starts in late teens; it is characterized by recurring episodes of binge eating and purging in an effort to avoid weight gain. Most people with this disorder have significant weight fluctuations and often may be overweight. Bingeing occurs when a large amount of food is eaten in a short period of time and one loses control over normal eating behavior. Purging occurs after a binge when the individual goes through extreme efforts such as vomiting, laxative abuse, severe dieting, and/or excessive exercise to compensate for the overeating.

In both anorexia nervosa and bulimia, affected individuals can suffer from low self-esteem, social withdrawal, fatigue, and other physical and psychological complications. Potential medical complications include loss of bone mass (osteoporosis), dental decay or acid erosion, severe gastrointestinal damage, abnormal cardiovascular activity, major depression, and suicide or sudden death. Nutrition counseling and support groups are needed once the psychological and physical problems are dealt with, depending upon the needs of the affected individual. This often is in an inpatient treatment setting not unlike the treatment of alcoholism and other drug dependencies.

K.H. has no evidence of an eating disorder and simply needs counseling on alternative weight reduction strategies (e.g., diet, exercise, counseling). The potential benefits of phenylpropanolamine are minor.

Weight Control Strategies

15. K.H. asks you how and why drugs such as Dietac work in losing weight.

Phenylpropanolamine is a sympathomimetic agent and causes vasoconstriction. It is structurally similar to amphetamine, differing only by a hydroxyl group on the beta carbon atom. Since it is widely available in OTC decongestants and diet pills, it has substantial potential to be abused, especially in those amphetamine-using individuals who on occasion may not have ready excess to amphetamines or methamphetamines. Phenylpropanolamine no longer is combined with caffeine in the U.S. Since cardiovascular and CNS effects are more pronounced when caffeine and phenylpropanolamine are used concurrently, caffeine has been withdrawn from diet products but may be ingested concurrently in beverages or food products.

Pharmacologic treatment of obesity is effective as an adjunctive measure used over a short period of time and must be used in conjunction with long-term weight control including caloric reduction and physical activity. The most important part of a weight reduction program is a reduced-calorie diet. To be effective, long-term eating habits also must change if weight loss is to be maintained. In addition to changing long-term eating patterns, an appropriate exercise program will assist in promoting weight loss. Weight loss products at best will provide only short-term assistance with weight loss.

Phenylpropanolamine is one of the most commonly used non-prescription drugs in the U.S. It is a sympathomimetic agent used as an appetite suppressant (maximum: 75 mg/day) or a decongestant (maximum: 150 mg/day). Its exact mechanism as a weight loss agent is unknown but is thought to be similar to that of amphetamines which affect the hypothalamus by depressing the satiety or appetite centers.[37] Phenylpropanolamine has been evaluated by the FDA Advisory Review Panel on Miscellaneous Internal Drug Products and was deemed generally safe and effective for short-term weight control.[38] For weight control, the maximum dose of phenylpropanolamine in immediate release products is 37.5 mg and for time-released preparations is 75 mg/dose. In the FDA's review in 1973 of 105 double-blind, placebo-controlled studies of anoretic agents, the drug treatment group lost 0.25 kg/week more than patients on placebo.[39] In a review of controlled clinical trials done before 1982, patients taking phenylpropanolamine plus caffeine lost an average of 0.22 kg/week more than placebo, but less than phenylpropanolamine as a single agent.[40] Greenway[41] conducted a meta-analysis of studies on a combined group of nearly 1100 patients on phenylpropanolamine or phenylpropanolamine plus caffeine and found that both groups lost 0.27 kg/week more than placebo. Since the weight loss was nearly equivalent when comparing phenylpropanolamine and prescription anorexics,[39] both are deemed equally effective in promoting weight loss.[41] In a 14-week study of 102 overweight subjects, 75 mg sustained-release capsules of phenylpropanolamine resulted in a weight loss of 0.78 pounds more than patients in the placebo group.[42] In another study, 75 mg/day of phenylpropanolamine induced a greater weight loss (group mean difference: 2 pounds) than those in the placebo group.[43] These studies collectively support the effectiveness of phenylpropanolamine, but the weight loss is minimal.

K.H. should be advised that phenylpropanolamine may help as an adjunctive measure to lose weight, but that she should use phenylpropanolamine-containing products for only a few weeks (4 to 6 weeks). A reduced-calorie diet and change in long-term eating habits are essential if weight loss is to be maintained, and these changes alone would be preferred to phenylpropanolamine product use.

Smoking Cessation

16. Because you have indicated your reluctance to recommend Dietac for long-term use, K.H. confides that she smokes and is trying to quit. She fears weight gain. She asks if phenylpropanolamine-containing products will prevent weight gain for her.

The 1988 Surgeon General's Report[44] reviewed 43 studies comparing weight status and smoking cessation over time: former smokers gained an average of about six pounds after cessation of smoking. For some individuals, the fear of weight gain may discourage smoking cessation. When the effects of phenylpropanolamine on dietary intake, physical activity, and body weight were evaluated after two weeks of abstinence from smoking, the patients using phenylpropanolamine gained less weight (mean: 0.09 pounds; standard deviation: 2.35) than patients using placebos (mean: 1.59 pounds; standard deviation: 2.29) or no treatment (mean: 1.94 pounds; standard deviation: 1.93). Thus, phenylpropanolamine may help to enhance short-term smoking cessation efforts and help to reduce weight gain.[45] Although these differences are statistically significant, the actual differences in weight of less than 1 pound really are inconsequential.

K.H. can be told that phenylpropanolamine may prevent weight gain for her if she quits smoking. She should be reminded that this is a short-term solution and that long-term change in eating habits is much more important in preventing weight gain.

Adverse Effects

17. K.H. decides to purchase Dietac. What adverse effects from phenylpropanolamine should K.H. be concerned about?

There are case reports of adverse reactions with phenylpropanolamine use including cerebral infarct, acute renal failure, arrhythmias, transient hypertension, and psychiatric disorders. Other commonly reported side effects include nausea, nervousness, insomnia, headache, dryness of the mouth, urinary retention, palpitation, and dysuria.[46] K.H. should be informed that phenylpropanolamine may cause adverse effects such as nervousness, insomnia, and mood changes. A health professional should monitor and counsel her accordingly.

Blood Pressure

18. K.H. begins taking Dietac. On her next physical examination, it is noted that her BP has increased from 115/80 mm Hg to 130/90 mm Hg. What is the likelihood that phenylpropanolamine is the cause?

The impact of phenylpropanolamine on blood pressure remains unclear. When 150 mg of phenylpropanolamine (2 diet aids), 75 mg of phenylpropanolamine in combination with 400 mg caffeine, and placebo were administered to normotensive subjects, the mean peak blood pressures were 173 mm Hg, 148 mm Hg, and 137 mm Hg, respectively. Maximal increases in supine diastolic blood pressure after all phenylpropanolamine-containing drugs were higher than that after placebo.[47] In another study, Lake found that greater increases in both systolic and diastolic blood pressures occurred after the combination (75 mg phenylpropanolamine and 400 mg caffeine) than after either drug alone.[48]

The elderly and patients who are hypertensive or at risk for stroke should avoid phenylpropanolamine-containing products. Patients who do not have a contraindicated condition should use phenylpropanolamine in the lowest therapeutic dose. At-risk patients who take phenylpropanolamine despite medical advice discouraging use should be monitored closely.

Since K.H. previously was normotensive, her increase in blood pressure may be the result of her phenylpropanolamine because of the temporal relationship. Several more blood pressure determinations should be assessed on subsequent visits, and other factors (e.g., stress, other medications) then should be considered as well (see Chapter 10: Essential Hypertension).

Contraindications

19. What are contraindications to the use of phenylpropanolamine? What drugs potentially might interact with K.H.'s phenylpropanolamine?

Phenylpropanolamine is contraindicated in patients with diabetes mellitus, heart disease, hyperthyroidism, and hypertension. Other contraindications include glaucoma, mental depression, MAOI use, hypersensitivity history, prostatic hypertrophy, and renal disease. Since phenylpropanolamine and MAOIs have resulted in hypertensive crises and intracranial hemorrhage, the phenylpropanolamine should not be administered within 14 days following MAOI therapy.[38]

Phenylpropanolamine safety during pregnancy and in lactating mothers has not been established. Avoid phenylpropanolamine use whenever possible because it can constrict uterine vessels and reduce uterine blood flow and cause fetal hypoxia.[38] K.H. must avoid concomitant use of phenylpropanolamine and MAOIs.

Cocaine
History

Cocaine is a naturally occurring alkaloid, found in the coca bush "Erythroxylum coca." Like many other naturally occurring products, it was long considered to be a safe "natural" stimulant. However, experience with cocaine has shown that cocaine in actuality is a highly addicting and potentially lethal substance.[49] Studies with animals demonstrate that cocaine is three times as lethal as heroin. Ninety percent of animals with free access to cocaine are dead in three months, while only 30% of those with free access to heroin are dead in the same amount of time.[50] Monkeys with unlimited access to cocaine will choose it over food until they starve.[51] Most cocaine addicts admit they cannot refuse cocaine if it is available; they continue to seek cocaine though their lives are being destroyed.[52]

Cocaine originally was cultivated by native South Americans for its ability to increase energy and decrease fatigue and hunger; chewing coca leaves enabled them to easily work high in the mountains. Cocaine was first isolated from the coca leaves in the mid1800s leading to its use in Europe. Through the early 1900s, cocaine was a common ingredient in many patent medicines and tonics. It was even a component in the original formulation of Coca-Cola and in vin Mariani, a wine endorsed by the Vatican. It was not until the Pure Food and Drug Act of 1906 that cocaine was removed from these various products. The Harrison Act of 1914 identified cocaine as a dangerous drug, labeling it a narcotic and prohibited its nonmedical uses. In 1970, as a result of the Drug Abuse Prevention and Control Act, cocaine became a schedule II controlled substance because of its extremely high abuse potential and low medicinal value.[53]

Prevalence

Cocaine epidemics are cyclical; the U.S. currently is in the latter phases of its "third cocaine epidemic."[54] Cocaine continues to be one of the most commonly abused substances, fourth only to alcohol, nicotine, and marijuana.[55]

Demographically, most addicts are male, under the age of 40, and use multiple drugs (75%). According to the Epidemiologic Catchment Area Study, 84% of persons diagnosed with cocaine dependence also met the criteria for alcohol dependence. A history of marijuana use was reported by 98% of cocaine addicts.[56] Barbiturates, benzodiazepines, and other drugs often are taken with or after cocaine. A potentially deadly combination is cocaine and heroin, called a "speed ball." It was this combination that allegedly killed actor John Belushi.[57] A newer phenomenon is the intentional combination of phencyclidine (PCP) and cocaine called "space base."[58]

In 1985 it was estimated that about four to five million Americans used cocaine regularly and about one million were addicted to it.[59] More recently, the National Household Survey in 1992 indicated that approximately 22.6 million people have tried cocaine, five million within the last year before the survey (down from 12 million in 1985 and 8 million in 1988), and 1.3 million used it at least once within the month before the survey.[60] Approximately two-thirds of users in this survey were male. Data indicate a positive general downward trend in the number of people who have used cocaine in the last 30 days from 5.8 million in 1985 and 1.6 million in 1990 to 1.3 million in 1992. The bad news is that the number of people using cocaine on a daily or weekly basis is rising. Of the current three million regular users, about 500,000 use crack (freebase cocaine).[57]

In 1978 an estimated 19 to 26 metric tons of cocaine entered the U.S., at an approximate market value of $12 to $16 billion.[61,62] In 1978 cocaine hydrochloride (HCl) was the form available and cocaine was expensive and primarily a drug abused by upper income groups. With the advent of "crack," cocaine has become an easily accessible, relatively inexpensive drug of abuse. Today, 1

gm of cocaine can cost $70 to $100, and crack can be purchased for $3 to $10 a dose (so inexpensive even children can afford it).[57,58] It is estimated that 80 tons of cocaine entered the U.S. in 1990.[56] At today's current street value, the probable value of 80 tons of cocaine is staggering. It is not surprising that crack has become the primary source of income of drug dealers and some of those living in poverty. Most dealers prefer to sell crack because of its high addiction potential, and the primary goal is to increase the number of users to increase profits.[63] The control cocaine can have over a person may be financial, psychological, and physical.

Cocaine Pseudonyms

Cocaine has many different names. Some of the most common names are: Snow, Flake, Blow, Lady, Happy Trails, Nose Candy, Toot, Crack, Readyrock, Teeth, Gold Dust, and Rock[58] (see Table 84.2).

Purity

Cocaine smuggled into the U.S. is relatively pure (80% to 95%). Once it reaches the dealers, the purity of cocaine HCl ranges anywhere from 10% to 85%, but when purchased it usually is less than 50% cocaine HCl. Cocaine typically is "cut" or "stepped on" with a variety of diluents. Substances such as mannitol, lactose, glucose, and cornstarch may be added to increase bulk. Amphetamines and caffeine as well as lidocaine (Xylocaine) or procaine (Novocaine) may be added to mimic the stimulating and numbing effects buyers expect to receive with cocaine. Substances such as strychnine, PCP, and other toxic agents also may be mixed in, often with malicious intent. Adulterants can have toxic consequences of their own as well as additive effects with the inherent toxicity of cocaine. Some adulterants cause particulate and septic embolization when injected. The National Institute of Drug Abuse, Drug Abuse Warning Network reports that emergency room episodes involving cocaine increased from 9000 in 1985 to 42,000 in 1989 but decreased in 1990 to 16,000.[64] While crack cocaine is relatively pure (95%), there is no guarantee; adulteration makes it impossible for a user, to tell how much cocaine they are truly using, or what the true risk of use is.

Legal Sources

Cocaine is not legally available except through pharmaceutical companies as a legend drug and then only through the use of special order forms. Some health food stores carry teas that contain "decocainized" tea leaves (i.e., "Health Inca Tea"). The amount remaining per bag may be approximately 4 to 6 mg.[48,49] Cocaine

Table 84.2	Street Names of Cocaine and Cocaine Combinations
Drug[a]	Street Name
Cocaine Alone	
Cocaine paste	Pasta, bazooka, buscuso
Cocaine HCl	"Yea-o," "C," snow, flake, blow, happy trails, girl, coke, nose candy, the lady, toot, gold dust
Freebase cocaine	Rock, crack, readyrock, teeth, french fries, gravel, cloud, dove, love, Roxanne, cookies
Cocaine Combinations	
Cocaine or crack and heroin	Speed ball
Cocaine or crack and PCP	Speed base

[a] PCP = Phencyclidine.

"look-alikes" are widely available and typically contain a stimulant and a local anesthetic to mimic the pharmacologic effects of cocaine.

Medical Use

Clinically, the use of cocaine is restricted to a small number of surgical procedures, such as nasal surgery. Applied as a topical solution, it is beneficial in these procedures for both its local anesthetic and vasoconstrictive properties. In all, its use is limited because of the number of other equally effective, relatively less toxic local anesthetics available without the complications of cocaine.

Pharmacokinetics

The form of cocaine and the route of administration affect the onset and duration of the pharmacologic effect achieved, but once in the blood stream, the pharmacokinetic profile of cocaine is constant. With all routes of administration, cocaine has a relatively rapid onset of action and a short duration of action. Cocaine has a half-life of about one hour and is highly metabolized by liver and serum cholinesterases to two primary (80%) inactive metabolites, ecgonine methyl ester and benzoylecgonine, which both are metabolized to ecgonine. These primary metabolites have half-lives longer than the parent compound ($\approx$5 and 8 hours, respectively). A small amount (10%) of cocaine is metabolized to a potentially toxic metabolite norcocaine. All metabolites then are excreted by the kidney, with less than 5% of cocaine being excreted unchanged.[69]

Routes of Administration

Cocaine abuse occurs via one of four routes of administration: buccal, snorting or intranasal, intravenous (IV), and smoking or inhalation.[70] The differences in the onset and duration of the euphoria experienced with each route are described in Table 84.3.

Chewing coca leaves still is common in parts of South America. The leaves are "chewed" like a plug of tobacco. Rolled coca leaves with a pinch of lime (limestone or seashell) to increase the extraction of the cocaine usually are placed between the gums and cheek.[71] This method results in the use of large doses, about 50 gm/day of cocaine. The buccal route results in the stimulating effects, but the slow absorption dramatically decreases the euphoria associated with cocaine use.

A paste form of cocaine commonly used in South America is called "bazooka," "buscuso," or "pasta." It is produced by combining dried coca leaves, alkaline bases, water, kerosene, and sulfuric acid.[72] This paste then is dried and smoked in mixture with tobacco or marijuana. Many negative physical and psychiatric consequences (dysphoria, hallucinosis, and psychosis) are experienced when coca paste is abused. Solvent residue in the paste is highly contributory to its toxic effects.

In the U.S., cocaine usually is found as the HCl salt or the base form. Cocaine HCl is a highly water soluble white powder and is snorted (intranasally) or taken intravenously. Since cocaine HCl melts at a very high temperature, it is not possible to smoke this form of cocaine. Free-based cocaine melts at much lower temperatures and can be smoked.

Snorting still is the most common route of cocaine abuse in the U.S. To snort cocaine, approximately 10 to 30 mg of cocaine HCl is placed on a flat surface (mirror or table) divided into lines or small piles with a razor blade or knife. These lines or piles then are inhaled into the nose by use of a straw or rolled paper, usually a dollar bill.[73] Many phrases are used to describe the behaviors associated with snorting cocaine. They include "taking a toot,"

Table 84.3	Pharmacokinetic Characteristics of Cocaine[57,70]	
Route	Onset of Euphoria (sec)	Duration of Euphoria (min)
Oral	600–800	45–90
Intranasal	120–180	30–45
Intravenous	30–45	10–20
Inhalation	8–10	5–10

"going to powder my nose," "snorting a line," or "doing a bullet." The euphoria experienced with snorting is achieved in several minutes and decreases over the next hour. The sustained lower level euphoria is due in part to the prolonged absorption of cocaine as a result of its vasoconstrictive actions on the blood vessels in the nasal mucosa.[74] The average amount of cocaine used per week via snorting will differ per user but can be $\geq$1 to 3 gm.

Intravenous cocaine use involves dissolving cocaine HCl in water and injecting it into a vein. Doses range from 30 mg to 1 gm per injection. Intravenous use results in a rapid euphoria that is faster than snorting but slower and of less intensity than the euphoria associated with smoking. With the high availability of crack cocaine and increased awareness and fear of disease from contaminated needles, probably less than 10% of abusers use the IV route.

Free-based cocaine is the base form of cocaine and is made by either of two methods. The first, using ether, results in the typical product associated with the term "freebase." The second method results in what is referred to as "crack" cocaine. Inhaled freebase results in an almost instantaneous and very intense euphoria that lasts only a short period of time after which the user craves another "hit."

Freebase cocaine is formed by dissolving cocaine HCl in ether, adding a base such as ammonia, and evaporating out the ether, leaving the freebase cocaine. Many of the adulterants are precipitated out during the process. About 500 mg of freebase is obtained from 1 gm of cocaine HCl. Usually, doses for a freebase session are 50 to 150 mg, but during a binge, $\geq$1 to 3 gm can be used in a day. Freebase is smoked using a glass pipe or "base pipe." When heated, the freebase vaporizes and is inhaled from the pipe. This freebase product is dangerous to make and to use. Ether may remain in the final product, which increases the risk of burns when smoked (e.g., allegedly associated with comedian Richard Pryor's accident).[72,75]

Crack on the other hand, is made cheaply, easily, and safely. To make crack, cocaine HCl is dissolved in water with baking soda and is heated. The freebase precipitates out and, when dried, forms the characteristic "rocks." Crack primarily is smoked in a glass or metal pipe and gets the name "crack" from the sound it makes when being heated. It also can be smoked in tobacco or marijuana cigarettes.[76] The amount of the smoked freebase that reaches the lungs can range from 6% to 32% depending upon whether it was smoked in a pipe or mixed into a cigarette.[61,77] In most states, drug paraphernalia is illegal, but there is a large black market for devices to use when using cocaine by any route. In 1980 sales of drug paraphernalia netted $50 million to $3 billion.[72] Many prefer smoking crack to snorting cocaine because of its much faster onset and more intense euphoria.

Pharmacology

Cocaine has both central and peripheral pharmacologic actions. Cocaine's peripheral activity causes vasoconstriction and blocks sodium channels in neurons. Sodium channel blockade prevents the initiation or conduction of nerve impulses by blocking permeability to sodium ions during depolarization, resulting in its local anesthetic effects. Cocaine blocks the peripheral and central reuptake of the neurotransmitters norepinephrine (NE), serotonin (5-HT), and dopamine (DA) into the presynaptic sympathetic neurons. This reuptake blockade increases the amount of neurotransmitter available in the synaptic cleft to stimulate postsynaptic receptors, resulting in increased adrenergic (sympathetic), serotonergic, and dopaminergic activity.[78]

Increased central sympathetic activity results in vasoconstriction, hypertension, tachycardia, mydriasis, increased muscle contractility, and hyperthermia (i.e., the fight or flight response). Increased dopaminergic activity yields the euphoria and psychotic symptoms associated with abuse. Dopamine is associated with the reward center in the brain, the limbic system. The limbic system is associated with mood and drive states such as hunger, sex, memory, and reward. Increased dopamine activity in the septal region of the brain results in euphoria. The serotonergic effects of cocaine use are not well understood.[79]

The euphoria and CNS stimulation resulting from acute cocaine use can give the impression that it increases abilities at sports. But cocaine does not have beneficial effects on sports performance.[80] Studies in rats demonstrate that cocaine decreases endurance performance and speeds the depletion of muscle glycogen.[81] Cocaine has a half-life much too short to provide long-lasting benefits in competition requiring sustained performance.[82] Cocaine impairs a person's ability to drive a car and likely also decreases abilities in other areas requiring concentration and coordination.[57] Physical activity coupled with the inherent strain cocaine places on the body can be devastating. Use of cocaine is illegal and outlawed in sports, and is dangerous as well.[83]

Acute Intoxication

20. Several of J.J.'s female friends entice him with tales of orgasmic euphoria, heightened sexual abilities, and other increased physical and intellectual abilities. Eventually J.J. gives in and tries the crack. A few seconds after use he experiences the intense rush his friends told him about. J.J. finds that he is more self-confident, and he thinks he could do just about anything. Are these feelings typical of cocaine use?

The powerful central nervous system stimulation associated with cocaine is the desired effect of those who abuse cocaine. Cocaine intoxication affects mood, cognition, drive states, and alertness or awareness.

Psychological symptoms associated with mild cocaine intoxication include euphoria, the perception of increased mental and physical abilities, increased self-confidence, talkativeness, increased concentration, heightened alertness, increased energy, general stimulation, enhanced libido, prolonged erection, and heightened orgasm. Also reported are decreased appetite, decreased short-term memory, and slight depersonalization (experiencing yourself as from a distance).

Physical symptoms associated with mild intoxication include mild tachycardia, increased respiratory rate, dilated pupils, and pallor. If cocaine is not used again, the initial symptoms are replaced by hunger, fatigue, mild depression, and the desire to sleep but being unable to.

The symptoms J.J. experienced are typical of cocaine intoxication. However, since J.J. used crack, these effects will decrease within minutes, so the effects are short-lived, leading to a depressed state and the desire to use again.

Medical Problems

21. C.R., a 34-year-old male, comes to the ER believing that he is having a heart attack. Highly agitated and irritable with the ER staff, C.R. admits to using about 1.5 gm of cocaine IV about 40 minutes before coming to the ER. He states he prefers to smoke crack but could only find "china white," so he "shot" up knowing that snorting would not give him the high he desired. After this use, he developed tachycardia, heart palpitations, and shortness of breath (SOB). Upon examination, C.R. is pale and sweaty and complains of a severe headache and a productive cough. He denies cigarette use. No infection is obvious at the injection site on C.R.'s arm. His ECG was positive for sinus tachycardia and an occasional premature ventricular contraction (PVC). His BP was 150/90 mm Hg; pulse 120 beats/min; respiratory rate 30 breaths/min; and temperature, 39.8 °C. A chest x-ray is remarkable for alveolar infiltrates in the right upper and middle lobes. How are C.R.'s problems consistent with his cocaine use pattern?

The medical consequences of cocaine abuse are numerous and can vary with route of administration (see Table 84.4). Cardiac complications can result from any form of cocaine abuse, possibly after even a single dose and in users with or without a history of cardiac problems. The severity of cocaine-induced cardiac complications can range from mild tachycardia to sudden death. Significant coronary artery constriction secondary to the increased sympathetic activity associated with cocaine abuse may result in ischemia or infarction. The dysrhythmogenic potential of cocaine can lead to supraventricular and ventricular dysrhythmias, such as sinus tachycardia, PVCs, ventricular tachycardia and fibrillation, and asystole.[84] Dysrhythmias also may be the result of ischemia, excessive catecholamine stimulation, seizures, hyperthermia, and acidosis. Hypertension, tachycardia, and other cardiac dysrhythmias generated by cocaine require immediate attention and treatment if cardiac function is affected.

Cocaine is known to cause cerebrovascular accidents. Sudden increases in blood pressure, adrenergic stimulation (vasoconstriction or vasospasm), and vasculitis or thrombosis secondary to cocaine-induced platelet aggregation can lead to many cerebrovascular complications, such as stroke, even in patients with no prior history.[85] Intracranial hemorrhage and subarachnoid hemorrhage can be a complication at all ages and have been reported in users and neonates born to abusing mothers.[86] While cocaine can precipitate seizures in users, children can develop seizures from passive inhalation of crack.[87,88]

C.R. has admitted that his preferred route of cocaine use is smoking crack and if his denial of cigarette use is factual, his res-

Table 84.4	Medical Consequences of Cocaine Abuse[a,50,70,71,83,84]	
Cardiac	**Respiratory**	**Dermatologic**
Hypertension	Bronchitis	Ulceration
Tachycardia	Pneumonia	Infection
MI	Pulmonary abscess	
Myocarditis	Sinus congestion	**Renal**
Dysrhythmias	Lung infection	Rhabdomyolysis
Vascular spasms	Sinusitis	
Coronary	Septal perforation	**Neurologic**
thrombosis	Pulmonary edema	Headache
Sudden death	Pulmonary	Seizures
	barotrauma	Stroke
Systemic	Pulmonary	Intracranial
Anorexia	hemorrhage	hemorrhage
Dehydration	Asthma	
↓ libido	Pneumonitis	**Psychiatric**
Hepatitis	Hypersensitivity	Anxiety
HIV		Depression
Septicemia	**GI**	Psychosis
Hyperprolactinemia	Ischemic bowel	Suicide
	disease	Delirium
	Colitis	

[a] GI = Gastrointestinal; HIV = Human immunodeficiency virus; MI = Myocardial infarction.

Table 84.5	Treatment of Acute Cocaine-Induced Dysrhythmias[a],[91–93]
Agent	Dose and Regimen
Propranolol	*Adults*: 0.5–3.0 mg IV repeated as necessary Q 5–10 min or 1 mg Q 1 min to max of 6 mg *Children*: 0.01–0.02 mg/kg IV to max of 1 mg/dose
Labetalol	*Adults*: 20 mg slow IV bolus over 2 min, may repeat with 40–80 mg at 10 min intervals to cumulative dose of 300 mg, or follow initial bolus by infusion of 2 mg/min adjust to effect or max dose of 300 mg *Children*: 0.25 mg/kg dose IV over 2 min
Esmolol	*Adults*: 500 µg/kg IV over 1 min (loading dose) then 50 µg/kg/min infusion titrated by 50 µg/kg/min at 5 min intervals as needed to max rate of 200 µg/min *Children*: NA
Phenytoin	*Adults*: 15–20 mg/kg IV (no faster than 50 mg/min) to max dose of 15 mg/kg *Children*: Rate 1 mg/kg/min

[a] IV = Intravenous; NA = Not applicable.

piratory symptoms could be secondary to "crack lung." The exact mechanism behind cocaine's effects on the lungs is not clear but may involve direct airway irritation, vasoconstriction, and damage to blood vessels in the tracheobronchial wall.

C.R.'s cardiovascular and neurologic signs and symptoms are consistent with cocaine's pharmacologic ability to increase sympathetic (noradrenergic) transmission and cause vasoconstriction, various dysrhythmias, and hypertension among other problems.

22. Crack Lung. Could smoking crack be an explanation for C.R.'s symptoms of cough and difficulty catching his breath?

A recent addition to the list of pulmonary problems due to crack is a phenomenon called "crack lung."[89,90] This condition presents with a productive cough, bronchospasm, severe chest pain, hemoptysis, difficulty breathing, and hyperthermia. A chest x-ray often is positive for alveolar infiltrates. Peripheral and bronchoalveolar eosinophilia and an increased serum level of IgE are other diagnostic findings in the majority of cases of "crack lung." Chest pain also may be suggestive of cardiac complications and requires careful evaluation.

In addition to his physical symptoms (productive cough, fever, SOB, and chest x-ray positive for alveolar infiltrates), bronchoalveolar lavage to rule out pulmonary infection and document pulmonary eosinophilia, laboratory documentation of his peripheral leukocyte count with eosinophil percentage, and a serum IgE would be helpful in determining if C.R.'s respiratory symptoms could be indicative of "crack lung."

Treatment

23. What treatment does C.R. require?

C.R. appears to have symptoms of acute cocaine intoxication. Because his tachycardia is mild, no immediate treatment is required beyond monitoring his cardiac status. C.R.'s symptoms may last only a few hours or persist longer, then fade.

In general, "crack lung" does not fully respond to antibiotics [cefazolin (Ancef), ampicillin (Amcill)] and bronchodilators [aminophylline (Amoline)], but most patients get some relief from anti-inflammatory agents (ibuprofen) and antihistamines [diphenhydramine (Benadryl), hydroxyzine (Vistaril)]. In many cases a short regimen of corticosteroids may be required. "Crack lung" can result in hypoxia, blood loss, and, in severe cases, death.

C.R.'s headache will be monitored for increasing severity or changes in vision. Unless these become severe, no treatment is required beyond pain relief.

Toxicology

24. D.D., a 29-year-old male, is brought to the ER by several friends. They tell the physician that D.D. came to their apartment acting very confused, nervous, and was shaking. They finally were able to get him to tell them he had been surprised by a knock on his apartment door and, believing it to be the police who followed him home from his latest cocaine buy, he swallowed his entire "stash" (supply) to avoid arrest. His friends tell the physician they had no idea how much cocaine he had ingested or exactly when this had occurred, so they decided to bring him in to the ER. Before leaving the apartment, D.D. became more confused and disoriented and had a tonic-clonic seizure; he was transported by ambulance. On the way to the ER, he became increasingly confused, had a BP of 190/110 mm Hg and a pulse of 190 beats/min, and experienced another tonic-clonic seizure. In the ER, he was comatose and unresponsive to painful stimuli. His respirations were shallow, systolic BP was 50 mm Hg, heart rate was 140 beats/min and regular, and rectal temperature was 39 °C. Physical examination revealed dilated and unresponsive pupils, hypoactive reflexes, and peripheral cyanosis. The ER resident said he had seen several cases of overdose due to ruptured condoms full of cocaine in "body packers" while doing his residency and proceeded to treat D.D. accordingly. Is D.D. in danger of dying?

Cocaine overdose is potentially life-threatening and should be considered a medical and psychiatric emergency. Careful monitoring and supportive measures are necessary because patient status can deteriorate rapidly. About one-third of overdose victims die within an hour of ingestion, and an additional third by the fifth hour. The first three hours after ingestion are the most critical, and survival past this three-hour mark seems to indicate an improved prognosis. Assuming D.D. did not wait too long to go to his neighbors for help, he might be within this three-hour threshold.

Treating Overdosage

25. How should D.D.'s cocaine overdose be treated?

Symptoms of cocaine overdose involve primarily the cardiovascular, autonomic, neurologic, and respiratory systems. Death usually is the result of cardiovascular and respiratory collapse.

Table 84.6	Treatment of Acute Cocaine-Induced Hypertension[a],[91–94]
Agent	Dose and Regimen
Nitroprusside	*Adults*: 3 µg/kg/min IV infusion titrated to effect (*max rate*: 10 µg/kg/min) *Children*: As above
Phentolamine	*Adults*: 1–5 mg IV bolus, may repeat at 5–10 min intervals to diastolic BP <100–110 mm Hg, can initiate constant infusion at 0.1–2.0 mg/min *Children*: 0.02–0.1 mg/kg bolus, may repeat as needed at 5–10 min intervals to diastolic BP <80 mm Hg. May initiate constant infusion at 0.1–0.2 mg/min
Labetalol	See Table 84.5 for doses
Beta blockers with vasodilators	See Table 84.5 for doses
Verapamil	*Adults*: 5–10 mg IV (or 75–150 µg/kg) slowly over 2 min, may repeat 10 mg (150 µg/kg) 30 min after initial dose *Children*: *<1 yr*: 100–200 µg/kg; *1–15 yr*: 100–300 µg/kg (not more than 5 mg). 30 min after initial dose: not more than 10 mg/single dose. Give all doses slowly over 2 min

[a] BP = Blood pressure; IV = Intravenous.

Table 84.7	Treatment of Cocaine-Induced Hypotension[a],[91–94]
Agent	Dose and Regimen
Norepinephrine	*Adults*: 4–8 µg/min IV infusion ↑ as needed Q 5 min, titrate maintenance 2–4 µg/min infusion to effect *Children*: 1–2 µg/min or 0.1 µg/kg/min IV infusion ↑ as needed to desired effect
Dopamine	*Adults*: Vasopressor effects: 5–10 µg/kg/min IV infusion, ↑ as needed Q 5–10 min up to max of 50 µg/kg/min *Children*: Same as adults

[a] IV = Intravenous.

Cardiotoxicity. Cardiac complications associated with cocaine overdose include hypertension or hypotension, variable pulse rates, skin pallor, and blood pressure and pulse increase proportionally to the severity of the overdosage.

Tachycardia, multiple PVCs, and other dysrhythmias precede acute left heart/circulatory failure and pulmonary edema. Hypoxia from seizures or respiratory failure can sensitize the heart to dysrhythmias, such as ventricular fibrillation. A direct cardiotoxic agent, cocaine has powerful inotropic and chronotropic effects on the heart: large doses can produce cardiac depression and arrest resulting in death. Sinus tachycardia at a rate significant enough to interfere with cardiac output can be treated with beta blockers such as propranolol (Inderal), labetalol (Trandate), esmolol (Brevibloc), or other α_1 selective agents.[91] Beta blockers also are used to treat other cocaine-induced dysrhythmias.[92]

Recommended agents and doses for the treatment of cocaine-induced cardiotoxicities are found in Tables 84.5 to 84.8.

Hypertension can be treated with vasodilators, such as phentolamine (Regitine) or nitroprusside (Nipride).[93] The beta blocker, propranolol, once thought to be cardioprotective in cocaine intoxication, may be problematic as a single agent, allowing for unrestricted α-adrenergic stimulation.[94,95] Although comparative trials have not been conducted, labetalol, with its alpha- and beta-blocking activities, currently is preferential to propranolol for hypertension.[96] Another treatment option are the calcium channel blockers, verapamil (Isoptin) and others, but their safety has been questioned by findings that these agents increased the toxicity of cocaine when used to treat cocaine toxic rats.[97–99]

Hypotension can be treated with norepinephrine (Levophed) or dopamine (Intropin) but may respond better to the direct action of supplemental norepinephrine because of the underlying neurotransmitter depletion (see Table 84.7). Intravenous administration of lactated Ringer's solution can be used to increase fluid volume and blood pressure.

Coronary spasm can be treated with verapamil in the same doses used for hypertension (see Table 84.6). Cardiac ischemia is treated with nitrates such as nitroglycerin (see Table 84.8). In these patients, propranolol and other β-adrenergic blocking agents should be avoided as they could potentiate coronary artery vasoconstriction.[100]

There is no ideal pharmacotherapy for cocaine-induced cardiotoxicity. Individualized, symptom-targeted treatment, electrolyte and acid-base stabilization, and other supportive care, as well as careful monitoring, are required.[101]

Respiratory Toxicity. Early stimulation of the respiratory center in the medulla results in an increased respiratory rate and depth. This may progress to cyanosis, dyspnea, and rapid gasping respiration, then to respiratory failure, cyanosis, and death. Respiratory assistance may be necessary in severe overdose.

Renal Toxicity. Rhabdomyolysis is another consequence of cocaine overdose, reflecting damage to muscle tissues. The mechanism for rhabdomyolysis is unclear but may be a result of vasoconstriction, increased activity, self-injury, seizures, or contamination from adulterants.[102] Levels of creatine kinase greater than five times normal indicate rhabdomyolysis. Myoglobinuria is another hallmark of rhabdomyolysis. Patients with rhabdomyolysis may go on to develop renal[103] or hepatic failure.[104] Treatment of rhabdomyolysis consists of adequate hydration and possible use of sodium bicarbonate to increase the solubility of myoglobin to prevent renal damage.

Hyperthermia. Malignant hyperthermia may contribute to a lethal outcome in cocaine overdose. Hyperthermia can result from increased muscle activity, vasoconstriction (decreased heat loss), and a direct central effect on the temperature regulating center of the brain in the hypothalamus. Aggressive cooling measures and antipyretic therapy are required to treat hyperthermia.

Neurotoxicity. Signs of neurologic overstimulation include apprehension, emotional lability, headache, coarse tremor, and facial and other muscle twitching. This may progress to increased deep tendon reflexes, a positive Babinski sign, grand mal seizures, and possible status epilepticus. Finally, coma, loss of reflexes, flaccid paralysis, loss of vital functions, and death may ensue.

Seizures are a common complication of cocaine use. These can be tonic-clonic, partial motor, or partial complex; single, recurrent, or status. Seizures can be a direct result of cocaine's ability to decrease the seizure threshold or be secondary to hyperthermia. Seizures associated with cocaine intoxication usually are not responsive to typical anticonvulsant medications; the current drugs of choice are the benzodiazepines, diazepam (Valium), and lorazepam (Ativan). If IV access is unavailable, use of intramuscular lorazepam is recommended. For refractory seizures, phenobarbital (Luminal) and phenytoin (Dilantin) are used. Table 84.9 reviews the dosages and regimens of these agents.

Treatment of D.D.'s overdose should be rigorous. Cardiac monitoring is required, and the necessary equipment for respiratory support available. Intravenous fluids are initiated to maintain venous access and adequate hydration. Blood samples should be obtained to evaluate D.D.'s electrolyte status and acid-base balance. Since oral ingestion of cocaine is involved in this case, total drug absorption may not have occurred (≤3 hours after overdose), attempts to empty the stomach are warranted. If D.D.'s overdose had occurred by one of the other routes of abuse, an attempt to prevent absorption would be less useful.[105]

Because of D.D.'s comatose status, an attempt to lavage will require insertion of a cuffed endotracheal tube to prevent aspiration. Then, approximately 60 to 100 mg of activated charcoal slurry is administered, followed by a 20 gm dose of sodium sulfate as a cathartic. Activated charcoal will adsorb cocaine in acidic and alkalotic environments.[106]

Table 84.8	Treatment of Acute Cocaine-Induced Cardiac Ischemia[a],[91–94]
Agent	Dose and Regimen
Nitroglycerin	*Adults*: Initial IV infusion: 5 µg/min, ↑ in increments of 5 µg/min at 3–5 min intervals to desired effect of rate of 20 µg/min. May ↑ by 10 µg at 3–5 min intervals if no effect seen at 20 µg/min *Children*: NA

[a] IV = Intravenous; NA = Not applicable.

Table 84.9	Treatment of Cocaine-Induced Seizures[a],[91–94]
Agent	Dose and Regimen
Diazepam	*Adults*: 5–10 mg IV over 2–3 min, may repeat Q 5–10 min to max dose of 30 mg. (*Max rate*: 5 mg/min) *Children*: 0.1–0.3 mg/kg IV ↑ to 5–10 mg over 2–3 min, repeated Q 10–15 min. [*Max dose*: 5 mg (30 days–5 yr); 10 mg (>5 yr). *Max rate*: 5 mg/min]
Lorazepam	*Adults*: 0.05 mg/kg (*max*: 4 mg) IV bolus given over 1–2 min. Rate no faster than 2 mg/min. Repeat if necessary after 10–15 min at 0.05 mg/kg dose *Children*: 0.05 mg/kg IV bolus. Rate no faster than 2 mg/min
Refractory Seizures	
Phenobarbital	*Adults*: Loading dose of 600–1200 mg IV at a rate of 25–50 mg/min. An additional 120–240 mg can be given IV Q 20 min as needed. (*Max rate*: <50 mg/min.) No max dose established. Monitor for respiratory depression. Desired blood levels: 15–20 µg/mL (up to 30 µg/mL in seizures) *Children*: Loading dose of 15–20 mg/kg at a rate of 25–50 mg/min, additional doses of 5–10 mg/kg can be given Q 20 min. (*Max rate*: <1 mg/kg/min.) No max dose established, monitor for respiratory depression (≥20 mg/kg). Desired blood levels: 15–25 mg/mL
Phenytoin	*Adults*: Load with 15–18 mg/kg IV at a rate no faster than 50 mg/min. Maintain dose at 100 mg Q 6–8 hr. Desired blood levels: 10–20 µg/mL *Children*: 15–20 mg/kg IV, at a rate no faster than 0.5–1.5 mg/kg/min. Repeat doses of 1.5 mg/kg Q 30 mg to max of 20 mg/day. Desired blood levels: 10–20 µg/mL. Monitor cardiac status
Resistant Seizures	Consider neuromuscular-blocking agents, general anesthetics

[a] IV = Intravenous.

Body Packing

26. M.E., a 25-year-old, smuggles cocaine by "body-packing." What complications could M.E. experience from "body packing"?

Body packers are smugglers who swallow latex-covered packets, latex condoms, or baggies filled with cocaine to evade customs agents. These packets then are retrieved from bowel movements. More than 100 packets may be swallowed at a time, each carrying up to 7 gm of cocaine. To speed up "removal" of these packets, stool softeners, mineral oil, or activated charcoal often are used.

M.E. risks having these packets rupture, causing rapid overdose and severe gastrointestinal complications such as intestinal ischemia and gangrene. Surgical intervention is required if toxicity develops.

Chronic Use

Depression

27. A.H. is admitted to the intensive care area of the psychiatric unit. She complains of long-standing depression associated with weight loss (30 pounds over the last year), no appetite, decreased interest in sex, decreased sleep, lack of energy, and a loss of interest in things that she used to enjoy doing (anhedonia). She denies illicit drug use and states she only drinks socially. Her admission physical examination is unremarkable except for reddened, irritated, scabby areas on her arms. Her physical complaints include chronic headaches, sinusitis, and rhinitis. Her vital signs were normal. A full standard laboratory panel, ECG, chest x-ray, pregnancy test, and a urine drug screen are ordered. The laboratory results are

pending. Her mental status exam reveals a 32-year-old female looking older than her stated age, sitting with her head down during the interview, and answering questions briefly. A.H. appears agitated and irritable, wringing her hands periodically, and glancing over her shoulder at the door throughout the interview. She is unkempt, thin, and pale. She is oriented to all spheres, denies delusions, or auditory and visual hallucinations. She is negative for loose associations and flight of ideas, but positive for paranoia of the hospital staff. She cannot do serial 7s but is able to complete serial 3s. She is able to recall 3 of 3 objects immediately but only 2 of 3 after several minutes. Her ability to abstract is intact, and insight and judgment appear poor to fair. The treatment team suspects that A.H. has major depression. What symptoms indicate that A.H. may be depressed?

A.H. has several of the neurovegetative signs and symptoms of depression that could indicate the need for antidepressant therapy: decreased sleep, decreased appetite and weight loss, psychomotor agitation, anhedonia, and decreased energy.[107] The team decides to wait for the results of her laboratory tests before selecting antidepressant therapy.

Drug Screening

28. A.H.'s chest x-ray and her ECG are negative. Her thyroid and renal tests are within normal limits, but her liver function tests are slightly elevated. Her complete blood count shows an elevated white count with a left shift. Her pregnancy test is negative but her urine drug screen is positive for cocaine. The team confronts A.H. with the results of her urine drug screen and lack of honesty with them. They ask her to tell them about her cocaine use. A.H. still denies using cocaine and tells the team that she had been to the dentist and the tests are picking up the shot of lidocaine she received. What is the validity to A.H.'s claim?

The screening test for cocaine and its metabolites usually is an enzyme-linked immunoassay for benzoylecgonine which is sensitive to 300 ng/mL. The time limit for detection after use on this screen is about two days. Confirmatory tests usually are gas chromatography/mass spectroscopy assay sensitive to 1 to 10 ng/mL. The time interval for detection with this test is about five to six days after use. High-dose, long-term use may be detected 10 to 22 days after last use. False-negative results are possible with the immunoassay test if drain cleaner, bleach, or table salt is added to the urine. Most official urines now are observed and verified, making such adulteration less likely. Most compounds similar to cocaine, such as lidocaine and other local anesthetics, and atropine do not cross-react on immunoassay tests. However, the local anesthetic prilocaine (Citanest) does cross-react.

Confronted with the facts, A.H. tells the team she has been snorting cocaine for the last five years and that her use has escalated over the last year to smoking crack. She denies ever using IV cocaine. A.H. also denies ever stealing to get crack but hesitantly admits to exchanging sex for crack. Because of the positive urine drug test for cocaine, her admission of use, and her history, the team orders a hepatitis screen and human immunodeficiency virus (HIV) test.

Psychiatric Effects

29. Are A.H.'s depression and paranoia a sign of an underlying psychiatric problem?

The symptoms of depression and the paranoia that A.H. is experiencing may be due to cocaine withdrawal, a symptom of her chronic use, or an actual underlying psychiatric diagnosis.[108] Paranoia, typically suspicion or belief that the police or others are after their cocaine, is seen quite commonly in cocaine abusers, both in acute toxicity, and in the later stages of abuse. With high doses and chronic use, euphoria may change to dysphoria, psychosis, or both.[109] Once this change has taken place, the threshold for the precipitation of psychosis is decreased: with continued cocaine use, psychosis develops sooner and with greater intensity.[110] The associated paranoia can be limited to the period of use or may persist long afterward.[111] In some patients, cocaine-induced psychosis (i.e., paranoia) becomes problematic.[112] This can be especially dangerous if the patient believes that her fears are real (substance-induced psychotic disorder) and acts on that belief to protect her drug supply.[10]

Hypervigilance, misperceptions of reality, loss of control, and the emergence of psychiatric symptoms may complicate use. It typically is the physical complications and psychiatric symptoms that bring the chronic user to the hospital. Chronic cocaine abusers look "burned out," tired, unkempt, and possibly malnourished (decreased vitamin B complex). Common physical complaints include seizures, rhinitis, bloody noses, perforated nasal septum, sinus problems, headaches, impotence, and chronic productive cough. Weight loss due to cocaine use is not uncommon. Because of cocaine's effect on the dopamine reward system, the urge to use cocaine replaces the urge to eat. Chronic abusers may have decreased cognitive functioning and, on the whole, are irritable, highly suspicious, and depressed. Self-destructive behavior such as suicide can be a common problem at this time. Increasing social dysfunction (e.g., increased family violence, legal problems) and occupational difficulties (e.g., lost jobs) also may be a motivation for seeking help.

Psychiatric symptoms secondary to the abuse of cocaine, such as "formication" and "snow lights," can be misidentified as symptoms of a primary psychiatric disorder (e.g., schizophrenia) if the proper diagnostic work-up is not done. The common tactile hallucination called formication, or "coke bugs," is described as the sensation of bugs crawling on the skin. "Snow lights" are flashing lights perceived in the peripheral vision; these occur less frequently than "coke bugs."[114] These can be readily mistaken for hallucinations associated with other psychotic disorders.

Another complication is pre-existing psychopathology. Depression and adult residual attention deficit disorder are most common, but anxiety and bipolar affective disorder are seen. Personality disorders also typically predate cocaine abuse. These pre-existing disorders can increase the severity of the patients response to cocaine.[68] Urine drug screens are an important part of the proper diagnostic workup, to rule in and out cocaine and other substances that contaminate the admission picture and complicate treatment.

A.H.'s depression and paranoia may be an indication of an underlying psychiatric problem. A prolonged period of abstinence is required before this can be accurately established.

Pharmacotherapy

30. Why should the medical staff treat (or not treat) A.H. with medication for her depression or her paranoia?

Because of the time required to accurately ascertain the true severity of A.H.'s depression,[115] A.H. should be referred to a substance abuse treatment center where the need for antidepressant therapy can be assessed as part of an overall individual treatment plan for her cocaine addiction and any co-existing primary depression. Antidepressants [e.g., desipramine (Norpramin), fluoxetine (Prozac)] are the drugs of choice in either case. Short-term symptomatic treatment with antipsychotics such as haloperidol (Haldol), could be useful for severe psychotic symptoms. Chronic psychiatric symptoms may persist in some patients, leaving residual psychiatric diagnosis which needs treatment. A thorough psychiatric evaluation is necessary to guide A.H.'s treatment.

Skin Lesions

31. What is the likely cause of A.H.'s irritated, reddened skin and scabs?

It is highly possible that A.H. picked at imaginary bugs crawling on her arms and then developed the sores which scabbed. If she denies this, a dermatologic consult may be necessary.

Infectious Complications

32. Since A.H. denies using cocaine IV, why are hepatitis screen and HIV tests ordered?

Current high levels of crack use have been associated with rises in the number of cases of sexually transmitted diseases such as syphilis, gonorrhea, hepatitis B and C, and acquired immunodeficiency syndrome (AIDS).[116] Inappropriate sexual activity secondary to cocaine use is one of the primary causes of increased cases of AIDS among the heterosexual population in the U.S.[70,117]

Early cocaine use causes an increased sexual arousal coupled with the lack of proper insight and judgment, leading to the failure to use condoms. Impotence and anorgasmia are more likely later in the cycle of chronic use and sex for drugs becomes the principle reason for unsafe sexual practices.

Although A.H. may not be injecting cocaine, her sexual exchanges for cocaine put her in a high-risk category. Many of her partners may inject cocaine and be HIV-positive, thus transmitting it to A.H.

Adverse Effects in Pregnancy

33. Why was a pregnancy test important for A.H.?

Cocaine can cause a variety of problems in pregnancy. Cocaine and its metabolites may last up to 120 hours after delivery in newborns and many go through cocaine withdrawal after delivery. Cocaine is excreted in breast milk and can cause symptoms of overstimulation and acute intoxication and the resulting cocaine withdrawal symptoms in the infant.[118]

Cocaine abuse during pregnancy increases the risk involved for both the mother and child. Pregnancy increases a woman's sensitivity to the cardiotoxicity of cocaine.[119] Cocaine abuse exposes the fetus to potential congenital urologic malformations, microencephaly, and other prenatal complications.[120] At birth, acute cocaine withdrawal symptoms and later neurobehavioral dysfunction can complicate the child's life.

If A.H. were pregnant, she and the baby would need to be monitored closely for sequelae from her cocaine abuse. A.H. would require extensive counseling on the effects of cocaine in pregnancy.

Withdrawal

34. Acute Withdrawal: Phase 1. T.N. is the new patient on your team; he is sleeping soundly when the team comes to see him. Earlier nursing reports indicate that T.N. had been very agitated, pacing, and slamming his hand against the wall. At that time, he received a single dose of lorazepam. He told the staff he wanted out of the hospital immediately: the staff believed he was craving cocaine although he denied needing cocaine. He refused breakfast and "crashed" in his room. A review of the admission record indicates that T.N. was picked up by the police secondary to belligerent behavior at a bar. On the way to jail he claimed to be suicidal and the police brought him to the hospital. He admitted on admission to the psychiatric unit that he had only claimed to be suicidal to avoid jail. He also admitted to snorting cocaine about 12 hours earlier. He could not remember how much but did say he had been using a lot of cocaine for the past few days. On awakening, T.N. is exhausted and ravenous. He tells the team he does not crave cocaine and is too tired to even think about it. Why is T.N.'s admission behavior typical of cocaine withdrawal?

Cocaine withdrawal has been described as a phenomenon which manifests in three phases with varying degrees of cocaine craving, and differing psychological, physiological, and behavioral symptoms.[121,122]

Phase 1 of cocaine withdrawal is described as the "crash," with symptoms appearing in nine hours to four days after last use. Initial symptoms include high cocaine craving, depression, agitation, irritability, anorexia, and anxiety; all of which increase for the first several hours. Later in phase 1, craving is replaced by exhaustion and an increased desire for sleep; depression continues. Hypersomnia, hyperphagia, and extreme fatigue without cocaine craving are the primary symptoms in the late stages of phase 1. Once the hypersomnia abates, mood normalizes. Recovery at this point is dependent upon sleep, diet, time, and abstinence for neurotransmitters to replenish.

T.N.'s behavior fits into this picture; his agitation was treated successfully with lorazepam and supportive care. A good nights sleep also contributed to his ability to behave more appropriately when he awoke.

35. Craving: Phase 2. T.N. agrees to enter drug rehabilitation and is transferred to the Substance Abuse Treatment Program. Although T.N. does quite well in treatment for the next week, he leaves the program against medical advice at the end of that week. His counselor reports T.N. was becoming increasingly irritable and anxious, and the substance abuse treatment program team believes he could not handle his cocaine craving any longer. Why is T.N.'s behavior a common occurrence in cocaine withdrawal?

Phase 2 of withdrawal is an enduring syndrome of decreased activity, apathy or a lack of motivation, intense boredom, and anhedonia. These symptoms develop slowly, are very subtle, and often go unnoticed by health care providers. This cluster of negative symptoms is in direct contrast to the vivid and exaggerated positive memory of the euphoric feelings associated with cocaine use; this contrast leads to a high level of cocaine craving.

Conditioned cues such as mood states, people, situations, white powder, money, mirrors, single-edged razors, and others worsen cocaine craving and may trigger relapse. At this stage, patients are encouraged to identify and avoid their cocaine cues.[122] The severity of symptoms and the duration of this second phase depend upon the degree of abuse before abstinence. Inability to tolerate these symptoms usually results in a return to cocaine use. If the user can abstain at this time, the symptoms usually resolve within two to ten weeks.

T.N. may have developed the severe cocaine craving and dysthymia of late phase 2 addiction and did not confide in his counselor for assistance. Had he sought help rather than reacting to the craving, he may have been able to make it to phase 3: extinction.

Extinction: Phase 3. At this point (phase 3), craving is periodic and lasts only hours. Depression and irritability may continue but generally are less severe than in phase 2. Conditioned cues continue to trigger cocaine craving. Treatment now includes "cue extinction" exposure to the specific cues without relapse.[123]

Cue extinction incorporates relaxation techniques and positive thinking patterns, which produce a calm outlook and positive thoughts about not needing cocaine. Once patients have learned these techniques, they are exposed cautiously to different places, persons, or things (cues) that trigger the desire to use cocaine.

The weakest cues are confronted first and the strongest last. Cue extinction usually begins with imagery and progresses to actual exposure to the cues. At each exposure, the patient is to use the relaxation techniques and positive thoughts to diminish the amount of craving experienced and the desire to use. The continued abstinence further decreases the duration of the episodes of craving that develop and this diminishes the power of the condition cues.

Periodic, short-lasting craving may be present in patients after years of abstinence. Patients learn to recognize craving, accept it as normal, and continue altering their environment and behavior to diminish the effect and control it has over them. A drug-free environment, healthy meals, talking it through [Cocaine Anonymous (CA) meeting or counselor], exercise, and meditation all are effective ways of diverting the thoughts about use.[123]

36. Treatment. What drug therapy could have been used to treat the symptoms of T.N.'s cocaine withdrawal?

Use of pharmacologic treatment for cocaine withdrawal depends upon the severity of the abuse and patient symptoms. Most often, simple cocaine withdrawal itself is not treated.

Severe anxiety and agitation associated with cocaine withdrawal are safely treated with the judicious short-term use of benzodiazepines. The preferred agents have a intermediate to slow onset of action and a medium to long half-life. Oxazepam (Serax), clonazepam (Klonopin), and lorazepam can be useful in treating agitation associated with acute cocaine withdrawal.

Insomnia can be treated acutely with benzodiazepines but preferably, diphenhydramine (Benadryl), chloral hydrate (Noctec), or a trial of zolpidem (Ambien) is attempted first.

Acute high-level cocaine craving, is believed to result from dopamine depletion, and, therefore, may be decreased by dopamine agonists like bromocriptine (Parlodel) and amantadine (Symmetrel). There are conflicting reports of the efficacy of these agents in decreasing cocaine withdrawal and craving.[124,125] However, results are encouraging enough to warrant medication trials in some patients experiencing cocaine craving.

Bromocriptine is initiated at a dose of 0.625 mg/day orally and titrated according to patient tolerance of side effects, severity of withdrawal symptoms, and craving. The average bromocriptine dose is 0.625 mg four times daily for several days. The dose then may be increased if necessary to a maximum of 2.5 mg twice daily. Another regimen maintains the bromocriptine dose at 0.625 mg four times daily for ≥ 1 month depending upon patient symptoms. In both regimens, the dose is tapered slowly over several days. Alternatively, amantadine is initiated at a dose of 100 mg orally twice daily for two to three weeks then increased to 200 mg twice daily for the next three weeks. Dose increases are determined by the patient's clinical status. Longer-term therapy may benefit many patients.

Amantadine may be better tolerated than bromocriptine and warrants a trial if the patient responds to bromocriptine but cannot tolerate the side effects (vertigo, nausea, fatigue, hypotension, headaches).[126]

T.N. may have benefited from pharmacotherapy for his reported symptoms of irritability, anxiety, and increased craving. Had T.N. talked with his counselor, both pharmacologic and psychologic treatments could have been initiated to help him through this period.

Addiction Liability

37. B.I. only snorts cocaine at parties when the coke is free and "everyone is doing it." Described as a wall flower, B.I. is shy and feels better in crowds after a "hit" or two. Why is B.I. in danger of becoming addicted to cocaine? What is the risk of addiction if B.I. only smokes crack when it is available?

Susceptibility to addiction, to a large degree, is dependent upon the route of cocaine administration. Other important factors include physiological and psychological changes resulting from drug use, the degree of change, the rate of onset and duration of change, and postdrug effects.[75] Substances or routes that result in a rapid, high-intensity, very short lasting euphoria are extremely reinforcing, promoting repeated use.

There is little difference between the ''recreational'' cocaine user and the ''addict.'' They are similar in income, marital status, and education. The primary difference between the two groups is duration of use. Most ''recreational'' users have been using cocaine for a shorter amount of time than the ''addict,'' who typically has been using cocaine for ≥5 years on average.[52] About 10% to 15% of people who try cocaine intranasally become abusers. Patients in treatment report an average of two to four years from initial exposure to cocaine to the onset of addiction.[127]

Smaller doses, lower plasma levels, use by a route that results in a slower onset, and a longer duration of action, as well as minimal or absent withdrawal effects, correlate with less addiction potential for cocaine. This pharmacokinetic profile is associated with chewing the leaves of the coca plant and possibly with small doses used intranasally. Only about 20% to 30% of a cocaine dose reaches the systemic circulation via these routes because of relatively poor absorption and the high rate of hepatic metabolism.[78,128] The rapid rise and fall of blood levels associated with smoking crack, promotes rapid repeated use (reinforcement).

Social use of cocaine is not uncommon; the majority of individuals who use cocaine avoid dependence. Many have described the different phases of developing cocaine dependence. Siegal breaks it into four escalating phases: experimental, social-recreational, circumstantial-situational, and intensified and compulsive.[129] Transition from phase to phase is an interaction of psychiatric and physiological characteristics of the user, drug availability, and route of ingestion.[130] All in all, cocaine abuse appears to progress through three basic stages: experimental use, compulsive use, and dysfunctional use before treatment and recovery.[131]

Experimental use includes social and recreational use with the rewards of use being the symptoms of mild intoxication: the perception of increased self-confidence, decreased anxiety, increased energy, enhanced communication skills, and intensification of emotions and sexual feelings. In this stage, most friends do not use and use occurs only when drug is offered. There is no impairment in functioning at work or home and no large loss of money.

Compulsive Use. If compulsive use begins, cocaine use intensifies and becomes isolative, the person buys for himself, and the goals of repeated use and higher doses primarily are to achieve euphoric effects and ward off depression and guilt. Negative personal, social, and occupational consequences begin; lifestyle changes occur, debts grow, work performance drops, and most friends now are users.

Dysfunctional Use. Later, dysfunctional use develops. In this stage, financial difficulties escalate and illegal activities often are necessary to obtain cocaine. All friends are users; divorce and job loss are common. Medical problems develop. Cocaine is used to feel normal rather than euphoric. The user is unable to stop using despite major physical and psychiatric adverse consequences. Binge use develops: once the binge is started, all available cocaine and money generally are used before the binge ends. Abusers may binge for 24 hours at a time, possibly several times a week. Some cocaine users change forms of abuse, evolving from snorting to IV use or smoking crack as their use escalates.

The more B.I. uses cocaine, or crack, the greater his risk of addiction. While all routes of abuse are addicting, clinical histories suggest that the incidence of addiction is highest with inhalation. Because crack is the most addicting form of cocaine and peer pressure can be a powerful force for continued use, B.I. stands a better chance of avoiding addiction if he only snorts cocaine. But his use to feel better about himself may encourage more frequent use and subsequent dependence. The chance that he would become dependent upon cocaine will increase if he smokes crack, even period-ically. For B.I., the only sure way not to become addicted is to abstain from cocaine altogether.

Treatment of Addiction

38. S.M. is addicted to cocaine. He had a great job, a beautiful house in the country, and a loving family. After getting into cocaine, he lost it all. Now he lives at the city shelter, works odd jobs, and attends Cocaine Anonymous. S.M. is lucky: he found help and new friends at a free community treatment center. How were S.M.'s cocaine abuse and addiction probably treated at the center?

Treatment of cocaine addiction is multifactorial with two primary goals: abstinence and relapse prevention. Many times successful treatment requires an inpatient program but outpatient programs can be successful for some abusers.

Inpatient treatment may be preferred in the presence of severe cocaine abuse or addiction (crack or IV use), severe medical or psychiatric complications, and polydrug abuse. Unwillingness to be treated, multiple failures in an outpatient setting, and lack of family and social support systems also are major factors for preferring inpatient treatment.[132]

Loss of self-control is a problem in cocaine addiction; the relearning of self-control is important in achieving abstinence. Early in treatment, external controls are placed upon the abuser while they relearn the necessary skills to control their own behaviors. Behavioral contracts (and inpatient programs) often are designed with this goal in mind; consequences of appropriate and inappropriate behavior and abstinence are predetermined by the patient and treatment team.[133] Urine drug screens may be built into these contracts to give a feedback measure of success to the patient and the program.

Multifactorial treatment of cocaine addiction uses pharmacological, psychological, and behavioral methods. Several steps are involved: the cycle of use must be broken, the anhedonic phase must be treated, cocaine craving cues extinguished, and the patient educated about the disease and its treatment.

Self-medication for an underlying psychiatric problem needs to be fully evaluated, analyzed, and addressed as part of complete treatment. Patients with an underlying affective disorder (depression or mania) may be better treated with a combination of a mood stabilizer, such as lithium (Eskalith), an antidepressant such as desipramine, or both. Patients with adult residual hyperactive disorder may respond well to the cautious use of methylphenidate (Ritalin) as part of their treatment plan.

Schizophrenics who abuse cocaine are very difficult to treat and antipsychotic medications are a necessary part of their treatment regimens. These ''dual-diagnosis'' patients are challenging to treat because both aspects of their illness must be addressed simultaneously for treatment to have a chance at being successful.

The underlying biological basis for cocaine craving and the changes that result with chronic use guide the pharmacotherapy of cocaine abuse. Neurochemically, chronic cocaine use leads to depletion of catecholamines and the development of receptor supersensitivity. Most therapies for cocaine addictions target these neurochemical deficiencies. The goal of pharmacotherapy is the reversal of the neurotransmitter depletion and down-regulating of supersensitive dopamine and adrenergic receptors, targeting the long-standing depression, irritability, anhedonia, and cocaine craving associated with late phase 2 of withdrawal. Treatment of this set of symptoms is an essential step in successful therapy.

Antidepressant agents currently are standard therapy for cocaine addiction. The tricyclic antidepressant desipramine is the most studied antidepressant agent used for cocaine abuse. In several studies, desipramine 150 to 200 mg/day in single or daily divided doses was effective in decreasing cocaine craving and increasing abstinence. Although no blood level range appears to predict response, antidepressant blood levels may be helpful in trying to correlate the craving as well as the dysphoria.

Bupropion (Wellbutrin) is an atypical antidepressant that increases dopamine and may be useful in cocaine withdrawal. In patients with cocaine and methadone abuse, bupropion 100 to 300 mg/day orally, was helpful in reducing cocaine craving. Imipramine (Tofranil) or other TCAs, as well as trazodone (Desyrel) and the serotonin reuptake inhibitors, such as fluoxetine (Prozac), may be effective.[134] The monoamine oxidase inhibitor phenelzine (Nardil) has demonstrated effectiveness in reducing cocaine craving, but concerns about concomitant MAOI and cocaine use leading to hypertensive crises limit their use except in special cases.[135]

Bromocriptine and amantadine may be useful in treatment of the craving for cocaine by increasing dopamine levels.[136] When started during phase 2 of withdrawal or continued over from phase 1, long-term therapy can be helpful in some patients.[137] A combination of desipramine and bromocriptine in the treatment of withdrawal was more effective than either drug alone. This combination targets two of the different mechanisms for cocaine craving: the dopamine and noradrenergic systems.[138]

Antipsychotics block dopamine receptors and may decrease the euphoria from cocaine and, therefore, decrease use; however, side effects limit their usefulness in nonschizophrenic abusers.[139] Newer atypical antipsychotic agents with milder side effect profiles have promise in the treatment of cocaine abuse.

Lithium and carbamazepine (Tegretol) also have been studied in the treatment of cocaine abuse. At one time, it was felt that lithium might decrease craving and antagonize the euphoric effects of cocaine. Some studies have demonstrated that lithium is effective in decreasing craving only in patients with associated affective disorders. Carbamazepine at doses of 400 to 1800 mg/day can decrease cocaine use and prevent cocaine kindling of seizure activity.[54,140,141]

Opioid antagonists, such as buprenorphine (Buprenex)[25] and naltrexone (Trexan),[113] and the novel anxiolytic buspirone (Buspar) with its ability to block dopamine autoreceptors, also are being studied for the treatment of cocaine addiction.

Once abstinence is obtained, increased efforts need to be made in changing several areas of daily living. These lifestyle changes include decreasing stress, drug-free socializing, making friends who do not abuse cocaine or other drugs, ongoing cue extinction, and predicting and preventing relapse upon exposure to cues that normally encourage use. Maintenance of abstinence is promoted by groups such as Cocaine Anonymous, Narcotics Anonymous, and Alcoholics Anonymous. Other self-help support groups are available and encouraged. Individual and group psychotherapy as well as family or couples therapy can be helpful. The behavioral programs developed early in treatment should become a routine part of recovery. As with all addictions, for many, abstinence and recovery from cocaine abuse is a lifelong process.

Acknowledgment

We gratefully acknowlege James F. Buchanan, Howard E. McKinney, Gregory N. Hayner, and Darryl S. Inaba whose work provided a foundation for this chapter.

References

1 **National Survey Results on Drug Use.** The Monitoring the Future Study 1975–1992 Volume II College Students and Young Adults. Rockville, MD: National Institute for Drug Abuse, 1993:22,99; DHHS publication no. (NIH)93-3598.

2 **National Household Survey on Drug Abuse: population estimates 1991.** Rockville, MD: National Institute for Drug Abuse, 1992; DDHS publication no. (ADM)92-1887.

3 **Chen K.** Ephedrine and related substances. Medicine (Baltimore). 1930; 9:1.

4 **Kalix P.** Khat: scientific knowledge and policy issues. Br J Addict. 1987; 82:47.

5 **Alles GA.** The comparative physiological actions of all phenylisopropylamines. J Pharmacol. 1927;32:121.

6 **Inaba DS, Cohen WE.** Uppers, Downers and All Arounders. 2nd ed. Ashland, OR: CNS Publications Inc.; 1993: 49–78.

7 **DeGowin EL, DeGowin RL.** Diagnostic findings in selected diseases. In: Bedside Diagnostic Examination. New York: Macmillan Publishing Co. Inc.; 1976:873.

8 **Zarcone P.** Narcolepsy. N Engl J Med. 1973;288:1156.

9 **Safer DJ, Krager JM.** Survey of medication treatment for hyperactive/inattentive students. JAMA. 1988;260: 2256.

10 **American Psychiatric Association.** Diagnostic and Statistical Manual of Mental Disorders, Fourth Edition.

Washington, DC: American Psychiatric Association; 1994:82.

11 **Barkley RA.** Primary symptoms and conceptualization. In: Barkley RA. Attention Deficit Hyperactivity Disorder: A Handbook for Diagnosis and Treatment. 1st ed. New York: The Guilford Press; 1990:39–73.

12 **Klein DF et al.** Diagnosis and drug treatment of childhood disorders. In: Diagnosis and Drug Treatment of Psychiatric Disorders: Adults and Children. 2nd ed. Baltimore: Williams & Wilkins; 1980:590–775.

13 **DuPaul GJ, Barkley RA.** Medication therapy. In: Barkley RA. Attention Deficit Hyperactivity Disorder: A Handbook for Diagnosis and Treatment. 1st ed. New York: The Guilford Press; 1990:573–612.

14 **Hoffman BB, Lefkowitz RJ.** Catecholamines and sympathomimetic drugs. In: Gilman AG et al., eds. Goodman and Gilman's: The Pharmacologic Basis of Therapeutics. 8th ed. New York: Pergamon Press; 1990:210–20.

15 **Craighead LW et al.** Behavior therapy and pharmacotherapy for obesity. Arch Gen Psychiatry. 1981;38(7):763–68.

16 **King GR, Ellinwood ER.** Amphetamines and other stimulants. In: Lowinson JH et al., eds. Substance Abuse: A Comprehensive Textbook. 2nd ed. Baltimore: Williams & Wilkins; 1992: 247–70.

17 **Ellinwood EH Jr.** Amphetamine psychosis: individuals, settings, and sequences. In: Ellinwood EH, Cohen S, eds. Current Concepts in Amphetamine

Abuse. Rockville: National Institute on Mental Health; 1972:143–57.

18 **Witters W et al.** Drugs in Society. Boston, MA: Jones and Bartlett Publishers; 1992:248–81.

19 **Irvine GD, Chin L.** The environmental impact and adverse health effects of the clandestine manufacture of methamphetamine. In: Miller MA, Kozel NJ, eds. Methamphetamine Abuse: Epidemiologic Issues and Implications. NIDA Research Monograph 115. Rockville: National Institute on Drug Abuse; 1991:33–46. DHHS publication no. (ADM)91-1836.

20 **Smith DS, Fischer CM.** An analysis of 310 cases of acute high-dose methamphetamine toxicity in Haight-Ashbury. Clin Toxicol. 1970;3(1):117.

21 **Vree TB, Henderson PT.** Pharmokinetics of amphetamines: in vivo and in vitro studies of factors governing their elimination. In: Caldwell J, ed. Amphetamines and Related Stimulants: Chemical, Biological, Clinical, and Sociological Aspects. Boca Raton: CRC Press Inc.; 1980:47–68.

22 **Caldwell J.** The metabolism of amphetamines and related stimulants in animals and man. In: Caldwell J, ed. Amphetamines and Related Stimulants: Chemical, Biological, Clinical, and Sociological Aspects. Boca Raton: CRC Press; 1980:29–46.

23 **Cook CE.** Pyrolytic characteristics, on pharmacokinetics, and bioavailability of smoked heroin, cocaine, phencyclidine, and methamphetamine. In: Miller MA, Kozel NJ, eds. Methamphetamine

Abuse: Epidemiologic Issues and Implications. NIDA Research Monograph 115. Rockville: National Institute on Drug Abuse; 1991:6–23. DHHS publication no. (ADM)91-1836.

24 **Ray O, Ksir C.** Drugs, Society and Human Behavior. 6th ed. St. Louis: Mosby; 1993:112–39.

25 **Kosten TR et al.** Buprenorphine for cocaine and opiate dependence. Psychopharm Bull. 1992;28:15.

26 **Tatro DS, ed.** Facts and Comparisons: Drug Interactions. St. Louis: Mediphor; 1994:33.

27 **Jaffe JH.** Drug addiction and drug abuse. In: Gilman AG et al., eds. Goodman and Gilman's: The Pharmacologic Basis of Therapeutics. 8th ed. New York: Pergamon Press; 1990:522–73.

28 **Little BB et al.** Methamphetamine abuse during pregnancy: outcome, and fetal effects. Obstet Gynecol. 1988;72: 541.

29 **Robins LN, Mills JL, eds.** Effects of in utero exposure to street drugs. Am J Public Health. 1993;83(Suppl.):15.

30 **Chernoff GF, Jones KL.** Fetal preventive medicine: tetratogens and the unborn baby. Pediatr Ann. 1981;10: 210.

31 **Kalter H, Warkany J.** Congenital malformations (second of two parts). N Engl J Med. 1983;308:491.

32 **Dixon SD, Bjar R.** Echoencephalographic findings in neonates associated with maternal cocaine and methamphetamine use: incidence and clinical correlates. J Pediatr. 1989;115:770.

33 **Steiner E et al.** Amphetamine secre-

tion in breast milk. Eur J Clin Pharmacol. 1984;27:123.

34 **Committee on Drugs, American Academy of Pediatrics.** Transfer of drugs and other chemicals into human milk. Pediatrics. 1989;84:924.

35 **Lake CR et al.** Transient hypertension after two phenylpropanolamine diet aids and the effects of caffeine: a placebo-controlled followup study. Am J Med. 1989;86:427.

36 **Mueller SM.** Neurologic complications of phenylpropanolamine use. Neurology. 1983;33:650.

37 **Lasagna L.** Phenylpropanolamine: A Review. New York: John Wiley and Sons; 1988:84–300.

38 **Williams DM.** Phenylpropanolamine hydrochloride. Am Pharm. 1990; NS30:47.

39 **Scoville BA.** Review of amphetamine like drugs by the Federal Drug Administration: clinical data and value judgements. In: George Bray, ed. Obesity in Perspective. Washington, DC: US Government Printing Office, 1973; DHEW publication no. (NIH)75-708.

40 **Weintraub M.** Phenylpropanolamine as an anorexiant in weight control: a review of published and unpublished studies. In: Morgan JP et al., eds. Phenylpropanolamine: Risks, Benefits, and Controversies. Philadelphia: Praeger Publishers; 1985:53–79.

41 **Greenway FL.** Clinical studies with phenylpropanolamine: a metanalysis. Am J Clin Nutr. 1992;55:203S.

42 **Greenway FL.** A double-blind clinical evaluation of the anoretic activity of phenylpropanolamine versus placebo. Clin Ther. 1989;11:584.

43 **Alger S et al.** Effect of phenylpropanolamine on energy expenditure and weight loss in overweight women. Am J Clin Nutr. 1993;57:120.

44 **U.S. Department of Health and Human Services:** The health consequences of smoking: nicotine addiction. A report of the Surgeon General. U.S. Department of Health and Human Services, Public Health Service, Centers for Disease Control, Center for Health Promotion and Education, Office on Smoking and Health, 1988; DHHS publication no. (CDC)88-8406.

45 **Klesges RC et al.** The effects of phenylpropanolamine on dietary intake, physical activity, and body weight after smoking cessation. Clin Pharmacol Ther. 1990;47:747.

46 **Appelt GD.** Weight control products. In: American Pharmaceutical Association, eds. The Handbook of Nonprescription Drugs. 9th ed. Washington, DC: APhA Publications; 1990:563–80.

47 **Lake CR et al.** Dose-dependent response to phenylpropanolamine: inhibition of orthostasis. J Clin Pharmacol. 1991;31:624.

48 **Lake CR et al.** Phenylpropanolamine increases plasma caffeine levels. Clin Pharmacol Ther. 1990;47:675.

49 **Kleber HD.** Cocaine abuse: historical, epidemiological, and psychological perspectives. J Clin Psychiatry. 1988; 49(Suppl. 2):3.

50 **Bozarth MA, Wise RA.** Toxicity associated with long-term intravenous heroin and cocaine self-administration in the rat. JAMA. 1985;254:81.

51 **Johanson CE et al.** Self-administration of psychostimulant drugs. The effects of unlimited access. Pharmacol Biochem Behav. 1976;4:45.

52 **Gold MS, Verebey K.** The psychopharmacology of cocaine. Psychiatr Ann. 1984;140:714.

53 **Gawin FH.** New uses of antidepressants in cocaine abuse. Psychosomatics. 1986;27(11S):24.

54 **Root RK.** Neurologic aspects of cocaine abuse. West J Med. 1988;149:442.

55 **Cohen S.** Recent developments in the abuse of cocaine. Bull Narc. 1984;36:3.

56 **Gold MS.** Crack abuse: it's implications and outcomes. Resid Staff Physician. 1987;33:45.

57 **Gold MS.** Cocaine (and crack): clinical aspects. In: Lowinson JH et al., eds. Substance Abuse A Comprehensive Textbook. 2nd ed. Baltimore: Williams & Wilkins; 1992:205.

58 **National Institute on Drug Abuse.** Cocaine/crack: the big lie. Rockville, MD: United States Department of Health and Human Services, Public Health Service. Alcohol, Drug Abuse and Mental Health Administration, 1991; DHHS publication no. (ADM) 91-1427.

59 **Miller GW.** The cocaine habit. Am Fam Physician. 1985;3:173.

60 **Substance Abuse and Mental Health Administration.** National household survey on drug abuse: Population estimates 1992. Rockville, MD: SAMHSA, Office of Applied Studies, 1993; DHHS publication no. (SMA)93-2053.

61 **Oderda GM, Klein-Schwartz W.** Cocaine. In: Skoutakis VA, ed. Toxicology of Drugs: Principles and Practice. Philadelphia: Lea and Febiger; 1982: 201.

62 **Wynne RD et al.** Community and legal responses to drug paraphernalia. NIDA Services Research Report. Rockville, MD: NIDA; 1980.

63 **Hannan DJ, Adler AG.** Crack abuse do you know enough about it? Postgrad Med. 1990;88:141.

64 **National Institute on Drug Abuse, Division of Epidemiology and Prevention Research.** Drug Abuse Warning Network (DAWN) Files. Rockville, MD: U.S. Department of Health and Human Services; 1990.

65 **Siegel RK et al.** Cocaine in herbal tea. JAMA. 1986;255:40. Letter.

66 **Floren AE, Small JW.** Mate de coca equals cocaine. J Occup Med. 1993;35:95. Letter.

67 **Rehrig M.** Cocaine look-alikes. Bulletin of the San Diego Regional Poison Control Center. 1982;6:6.

68 **Hisayasu GH et al.** Analysis of cocaine substitutes. J Psychoactive Drugs. 1982;14:351.

69 **Jatlow P.** Cocaine: Analysis, pharmacokinetics, and metabolic disposition. Yale J Biol Med. 1988;61:105.

70 **Manschreck TC.** The treatment of cocaine abuse. Psychiatr Q. 1993;64:183.

71 **Warner EA.** Cocaine abuse. Ann Intern Med. 1993;119:226.

72 **Siegel RK.** History of cocaine smoking. J Psychoactive Drugs. 1982;14:277.

73 **Fischman MW, Schuster CR.** Cocaine self-administration in humans. Fed Proc. 1982;41:241.

74 **Verebey K, Gold MS.** From coca leaves to crack: the effects of dose and routes of administration in abuse liability. Psychiatr Ann. 1988;18:513.

75 **Weinstein SP et al.** Cocaine users seen in medical practice. Am J Drug Alcohol Abuse. 1986;12:341.

76 **Siegel RK.** Cocaine smoking. N Engl J Med. 1979;300:373. Letter.

77 **Perez-Reyes M et al.** Free-base cocaine smoking. Clin Pharmacol Ther. 1982;32:459.

78 **Gold MS et al.** Cocaine (& crack): neurobiology. In: Lowinson JH et al., eds. Substance Abuse A Comprehensive Textbook. 2nd ed. Baltimore: Williams & Wilkins; 1992:222.

79 **Miller NS et al.** Cocaine. Am Fam Physician. 1989;39:115.

80 **Wagner JC.** Enhancement of athletic performance with drugs. An overview. Sports Med. 1991;12:250.

81 **Eichner ER.** Ergolytic drugs in medicine and sports. Am J Med. 1993;94:205.

82 **Smith DA, Perry PJ.** The efficacy of ergogenic agents in athletic competition, part II: other performance-enhancing agents. Ann Pharmacother. 1992;26:653.

83 **Cregler LL, Mark H.** Medical complications of cocaine abuse. N Engl J Med. 1986;315:1495.

84 **Gradman AH.** Cardiac effects of cocaine: a review. Yale J Biol Med. 1988; 61:137.

85 **Levine SR, Welch KM.** Cocaine and stroke. Stroke. 1988;19:1003.

86 **Chasnoff IJ et al.** Maternal cocaine use and perinatal cerebral infarction. J Pediatr. 1986;108:456.

87 **Bateman DA, Heagarty MC.** Passive freebase cocaine ("crack") inhalation by infants and toddlers. Am J Dis Child. 1989;143:25.

88 **Choy-Kwong M, Lipton RB.** Seizures in hospitalized cocaine users. Neurology. 1989a;39:425.

89 **Forrester JM et al.** Crack lung: an acute pulmonary syndrome with a spectrum of clinical and histopathologic findings. Am Rev Respir Dis. 1990;142:462.

90 **Kissner DG et al.** Crack lung: pulmonary disease caused by cocaine abuse. Am Rev Respir Dis. 1987;136:1250.

91 **Becker, Charles E.** Cocaine, toxicologic management. In: Poisindex, Micromedex Computerized Clinical Information System [database on CDROM]. Volume 80. Denver: Micromedex, Inc.; 1974–1994. (Updated 2/93).

92 **Benowitz NL.** Cocaine. In: Olsen KR, ed. Poisoning and Drug Overdose. Norwalk: Appleton & Lange; 1990:127.

93 **Therapeutic Drugs and Antidotes.** In: Olsen KR, ed. Poisoning and Drug Overdose. Norwalk: Appleton & Lange; 1990:57.

94 **Gay GR.** Clinical management of acute and chronic cocaine poisoning. Ann Emerg Med. 1982;11:562.

95 **Ramoska E, Sacchetti AD.** Propranolol-induced hypertension in treatment of cocaine intoxication. Ann Emerg Med. 1985;14:1112.

96 **Digregorio GJ.** Cocaine update: abuse and therapy. Am Fam Physician. 1990; 41(1):247.

97 **Loper KA.** Clinical toxicology of cocaine. Med Toxicol Adverse Drug Exp. 1989;4:174.

98 **Derlet RW, Albertson TE.** Potentiation of cocaine toxicity with calcium channel blockers. Am J Emerg Med. 1989;7:464.

99 **Morris DC.** Cocaine heart disease. Hosp Pract. 1991;15(9):83.

100 **Lange RA et al.** Potentiation of cocaine-induced coronary vasoconstriction by beta-adrenergic blockade. Ann Intern Med. 1990;112:897.

101 **Jonsson S et al.** Acute cocaine poisonings: importance of treating seizures and acidosis. Am J Med. 1983;75:1061.

102 **Lombard J et al.** Acute renal failure due to rhabdomyolysis associated with cocaine toxicity. West J Med. 1988; 148:466.

103 **Herzlich BC et al.** Rhabdomyolysis related to cocaine abuse. Ann Intern Med. 1988;15:335.

104 **Jandreski MA et al.** Rhabdomyolysis in a case of free-base cocaine ("crack") overdose. Clin Chem. 1989; 35:1547.

105 **Schwartz WK, Oderda GM.** Management of cocaine intoxications. Clin Tox Consultant. 1980;2:45.

106 **Tomaszewski C et al.** Cocaine adsorption to activated charcoal in vitro. J Emerg Med. 1992;10:59.

107 **Mohs ME et al.** Nutritional effects of marijuana, heroin, cocaine, and nicotine. J Am Diet Assoc. 1990;90:1261.

108 **Gawin FH, Ellinwood EH.** Cocaine dependence. Ann Rev Med. 1989;40:149.

109 **Snyder SH.** Amphetamine psychosis: a model of schizophrenia mediated by catecholamines. Am J Psychiatry. 1973; 130:61.

110 **Bell DS.** The experimental reproduction of amphetamine psychosis. Arch Gen Psychiatry. 1973;29:35.

111 **Satel SL et al.** Clinical features of cocaine-induced paranoia. Am J Psychiatry. 1991;148:495.

112 **Brady KT et al.** Cocaine-induced psychosis. J Clin Psychiatry. 1991;52:509.

113 **Kosten TR et al.** Role of opioid antagonists in treating intravenous cocaine abuse. Life Sci. 1989;44:887.

114 **Siegel RK.** Cocaine hallucinations. Am J Psychiatry. 1978;135:309.

115 **Gawin FH, Kleber HD.** Abstinence symptomatology and psychiatric diagnosis in cocaine abusers. Arch Gen Psychiatry. 1986;43:107.

116 **Lynn LA, Mackler SA.** Cocaine and the spread of AIDS. Hosp Pract. 1992; 3:105.

117 **Hannan DJ, Adler AG.** Crack abuse do you know enough about it? Postgrad Med. 1990;88:141.

118 **Farrar HC, Kearns GL.** Cocaine: clinical pharmacology and toxicology. J Pediatr. 1989;115:665.

119 **Woods JR, Plessinger MA.** Pregnancy increases cardiovascular toxicity to cocaine. Am J Obstet Gynecol. 1990;162:529.

120 **Volpe JJ.** Effect of cocaine use on the fetus. N Engl J Med. 1992;327:399.

121 **Gorski T.** Relapse-issues and answers. Addiction Recovery. 1991;5:22.

122 **Gawin FH, Kleber HD.** Abstinence symptomatology and psychiatric diag-

nosis in cocaine abusers. Arch Gen Psychiatry. 1986;43:107.

123 **Gawin FH, Ellinwood EH.** Cocaine and other stimulants: actions, abuse, and treatment. N Engl J Med. 1988; 318:1173.

124 **Dackis CA, Gold MS.** Pharmacologic approaches to cocaine addiction. J Subst Abuse Treat. 1985;2:139.

125 **Giannini AJ et al.** Bromocriptine therapy in cocaine withdrawal. J Clin Pharmacol. 1987;27:267.

126 **Giannini AJ et al.** Bromocriptine and amantadine in cocaine detoxification. Psychiatry Res. 1989;29:11.

127 **Gawin FH.** Cocaine addiction: psychology and neurophysiology. Science. 1991;251:001580.

128 **Jatlow PI.** Drug of abuse profile: co-

caine. Clin Chem. 1987;33(11 Suppl.): 66B.

129 **Siegal RK.** Cocaine: recreational use and intoxication. In: Petersen RC, Stillman RC, eds. Cocaine: 1977. NIDA Research Monograph 13. Rockville: US Department of Health and Human Services (ADM); 1977:119.

130 **Gawin FH.** New uses of antidepressants in cocaine abuse. 1986;27 (Suppl.):24.

131 **Smith DE.** Cocaine-alcohol abuse: epidemiological, diagnostic and treatment considerations. J Psychoactive Drugs. 1896;18:117.

132 **Pollack MH et al.** Cocaine abuse and treatment. Compr Psychiatry. 1989;30: 31.

133 **Anker Al, Crowley TJ.** Use of contingency contracts in specialty clinics for

cocaine abuse. In: Harris LS, ed. Problems in Drug Dependence, 1984. NIDA Research Monograph No. 41. Rockville: US Department of Health and Human Services (ADM); 1982: 452.

134 **Batki SL et al.** Fluoxetine for cocaine dependence in methadone maintenance: quantitative plasma and urine cocaine/benzoylecgonine concentrations. J Clin Psychopharmacol. 1993; 13:243.

135 **Golwyn DH.** Cocaine abuse treated with phenelzine. Int J Addict. 1988;23: 897.

136 **Teller DW, Devenyi P.** Bromocriptine in cocaine withdrawal—does it work? Int J Addict. 1988;23:1197.

137 **Tennant F, Berman ML.** Stepwise

detoxification from cocaine. Postgrad Med. 1988;84:225.

138 **Giannini AJ, Billet W.** Bromocriptine-desipramine protocol in treatment of cocaine addiction. J Clin Pharmacol. 1987;27:549.

139 **Gawin FH.** Neuroleptic reduction of cocaine-induced paranoia but not euphoria? Psychopharmacology. 1986; 90:142.

140 **Kuhn KL et al.** Carbamazepine treatment of cocaine dependence in methadone maintenance patients with dual opiate-cocaine addiction. NIDA Research Monograph. 95. Rockville: US Department of Health and Human Services (ADM); 1989:316.

141 **Halikas JA et al.** Treatment of crack cocaine use with carbamazepine. Am J Drug Alcohol Abuse. 1992;18:45.

Nicotine and Caffeine Abuse

Edward M DeSimone II

David M Scott

Nicotine 85-1
  Pharmacokinetics 85-1
    Absorption 85-2
    Distribution 85-2
    Metabolism 85-2
    Excretion 85-2
  Pharmacodynamics 85-2
    Central nervous system (CNS) 85-2
    Cardiovascular 85-2
    Other effects 85-2
    Tolerance 85-2
  Content 85-2
  Reproductive Effects 85-3
    Sperm production and motility 85-3
    Hormonal effects 85-3
    Hormonal effects and ovulation 85-3
    Fertility 85-3
    Menopause 85-3
  Prenatal and Neonatal Effects 85-3
    Spontaneous abortion 85-3
    Birth weight 85-3
    Congenital malformations 85-4
    Other disorders 85-4
  Breast-feeding 85-4
  Smoking and Cancer 85-4
  Cardiovascular Disease 85-4
    Cardiovascular effects 85-4
    Lipid effects 85-4
    Cerebrovascular effects 85-5
    Risk reduction 85-5
  Nicotine Dependence and Withdrawal 85-5
    Weaning 85-6

    Weight gain 85-6
  Pharmacologic Smoking Cessation Options 85-6
    Gum (Also see Question 17) 85-6
    Transdermal system 85-6
    Other methods 85-6
      Nicotine Inhaler 85-6
      Other nicotine cessation aids 85-6
      Citric acid inhaler 85-6
      Clonidine therapy 85-7
  Factors Affecting Smoking Cessation 85-7
    Cost of treatment 85-7
    Consideration for success 85-7
  Resources For Smokers 85-7
Caffeine 85-8
  Mechanism of Action 85-9
  Pharmacokinetics 85-9
  Caffeine Abuse 85-9
  Caffeine Self-Reports 85-10
  Drug Interactions 85-10
  Adverse Effects 85-10
    Central nervous system (CNS) effects 85-10
    Hemodynamic effects 85-11
    Effect on cholesterol and triglycerides 85-11
    Cerebrovascular effects 85-11
    Carcinogenic effects 85-11
  Overdosage 85-11
  Tolerance, Physical Dependence, and Withdrawal 85-11
    Physical dependence 85-12
    Tolerance 85-12
  Pregnancy 85-12
  Breast-Feeding 85-12
  Caffeine and Sports 85-13

Nicotine

Cigarettes are the major source for nicotine consumption. About 64 million Americans smoked cigarettes during 1992 (31.2% of the population: 33.8% male, 28.9% female).[1] Smoking is responsible for more than one out of every six deaths each year (>400,000 total deaths) and is considered to be the most preventable cause of illness and death in the U.S. This total includes 115,000 deaths from heart disease; 106,000 from lung cancer; 31,600 from other cancers; 57,000 from chronic obstructive airways disease (COAD); 27,500 from stroke; and 52,900 from other conditions.[2]

While nicotine is recognized as the primary cause for tobacco addiction, more than 4000 other compounds have been isolated from tobacco smoke.[3] A few of the major constituents of smoke include numerous tobacco alkaloids, carbon monoxide, acetaldehyde, benzene, hydrogen cyanide, and numerous phenolics and acids.[4] Some of the smoke constituents have biological activity and contribute to the hazards of smoking. Tar is the dry particulate matter in tobacco smoke without the nicotine. Smokers of low-tar cigarettes will take in more smoke to compensate for the low tar levels.[5] It is believed that tar constituents contribute to tobacco addiction through sensory stimulation, especially that of taste.

In addition to cigarettes, tobacco use in pipes and cigars was reported in 1990 by 8.7% of males and 0.3% of females.[6] A fourth source of nicotine is from smokeless tobacco in the form of oral snuff and chewing tobacco. In 1992, smokeless tobacco was used by 9.6% of males and 0.7% of females, with an estimated 17.4% of 18 to 25 year old males reporting use.[1]

Pharmacokinetics

Nicotine is a tertiary amine composed of a pyridine and a pyrrolidine ring. It is a weak base with a pKa of 8.5.

Absorption. Nicotine is carried into the mouth on tar droplets and in the smoke from tobacco (cigarettes, cigars, and pipes). The pH of American cigarette inhalants is acidic; therefore, the nicotine is almost completely ionized and poorly absorbed from the buccal membranes of the mouth.[12] However, the smoke of cigars and pipes, as well as some European cigarettes, is alkaline.[13] This produces mostly unionized nicotine which is absorbed readily from the mouth.[14] Nicotine also is absorbed rapidly from the alveoli of the lungs.

The manufacturers of chewing tobacco and snuff select tobaccos or use buffering agents which produce an alkaline pH in the mouth to enhance absorption of nicotine from the mouth. While the absorption of nicotine from cigarette smoke produces peaks levels at about the time the cigarette is finished (several minutes), oral snuff and chewing tobacco are slower in reaching peak concentrations of nicotine in the serum ($\approx$30 minutes). In addition, nicotine blood levels from smoking drop off sharply while levels from snuff and chewing tobacco can be twice as high as that from smoking for at least two hours.[15]

The bioavailability of swallowed nicotine is low. Although nicotine is absorbed from the alkaline environment of the small intestines, it undergoes a significant first-pass effect because of hepatic metabolism. Nicotine absorbed from the mouth and lungs circumvents first-pass metabolism.

Distribution. Nicotine has a steady-state volume of distribution of 180 L. Less than 5% of absorbed nicotine is bound to plasma proteins.[16] In animal studies, nicotine has a low affinity for adipose tissue at steady state, but a high affinity for the brain, liver, lungs, and spleen.[17] Nicotine, with a distribution half-life of nine minutes, moves swiftly from the blood to the brain.[18] Nicotine actually enters the brain more quickly after smoking than after intravenous injection.[19]

Metabolism. Nicotine is metabolized primarily in the liver (85% to 90%) although some is metabolized in the kidney and the lung.[20] The primary metabolites of nicotine are cotinine and nicotine-N'-oxide. Because it is cleared more slowly from the body, cotinine levels often are used as a measure of nicotine ingestion.

Excretion. Renal excretion of nicotine is pH dependent but generally is responsible for about 5% to 10% of total nicotine elimination. Decreasing urinary pH (to 4.4) can increase clearance as much as 600 mL/minute, and increasing urine pH to 7.0 can decrease clearance to as low as 17 mL/minute.[21] Total clearance is 1300 mL/minute with renal clearance accounting for 200 mL/minute.[22] Nicotine has an elimination half-life of two hours.

Pharmacodynamics

1. J.S., a 15-year-old, 5'9", 170 pound male, plays baseball in high school. Two weeks ago he succumbed to peer pressure and began using chewing tobacco since many of the older players consider it a "rite of passage" for ballplayers. He has suffered from chronic perennial asthma including exercise-induced asthma for the past 10 years. He takes 300 mg/day of controlled-release theophylline and uses an albuterol inhaler on an "as needed" basis. J.S. does not smoke and he is unconcerned about the nicotine content of chewing tobacco since he does not believe it would be as bad for him as cigarettes.

When he first tried the chewing tobacco, he experienced some nausea and vomiting and felt "out of sorts." During these past 2 weeks, he continued to experience some residual nausea but to a lesser degree. In addition, he does not feel as nervous when he pitches and he feels more "connected" to his teammates.

He visited his pediatrician with complaints of his heart racing followed by lightheadedness and dizziness. He also was concerned about some very minor shaking of his hand which does not really bother him except when he pitches. His asthma appeared to be under control during this time and he had no attacks.

Physical examination showed his temperature, pulse, and respirations to be within normal limits. His blood pressure also was normal. However, he appeared to have lost about 4 pounds. A very minor hand tremor also was confirmed. What signs and symptoms in J.S.'s clinical presentation might be caused by his use of chewing tobacco?

Central Nervous System (CNS). Nicotine is a potent CNS stimulant similar to cocaine and amphetamine.[23] In naive tobacco users, it produces nausea, vomiting, and dysphoria. With continued use, this is followed by a sense of well-being (pleasure), wake-

fulness, relief of anxiety, facilitation of memory, improved task performance, and anorexia.[24]

Cardiovascular. Nicotine increases heart rate and cardiac output as well as plasma catecholamine levels. There is an initial increase in blood pressure, coronary vasoconstriction, and tachycardia. Depending upon the amount of nicotine ingested, hypotension, dizziness, and bradycardia may follow. Nicotine also promotes platelet aggregation and hypercoagulability; and stimulates lipolysis to produce an increase in free fatty acids and an atherogenic lipid profile. All of these can contribute to the development and/or exacerbation of coronary heart disease.[25]

Other Effects. Nicotine produces a number of musculoskeletal effects including an increase in hand tremor, electroencephalographic (EEG) changes, skeletal muscle relaxation, and a decrease in deep tendon reflexes. Nicotine use also has been associated with a loss of body weight.[26]

Tolerance. Nicotine can produce acute tolerance or tachyphylaxis within minutes of smoking to some but not all of its effects.[17] For example, tolerance develops to dizziness, nausea, vomiting, headaches, and dysphoria,[27] but only incomplete tolerance develops to increases in heart rate, blood pressure, and hand tremor.[23] Tolerance does not appear to develop to skin temperature changes.[28]

Nicotine tolerance in humans has about a 35-minute half-life and after three half-lives (105 minutes), tolerance should be nearly gone.[29] Cigarette smokers, however, can feel the effects generated by the drop in serum and brain concentrations of nicotine and will smoke enough to maintain the necessary levels of nicotine in the body throughout the day to avoid withdrawal.[24] Tolerance does seem to be lost overnight,[24] and probably is the reason why the first cigarette of the day "feels best" to a smoker. After the first several years of smoking, nicotine levels and, therefore, tobacco consumption remain fairly constant.

Since a single cigarette delivers enough nicotine to produce physiological effects, it is logical to assume that both oral snuff and chewing tobacco would produce effects at least equal to those of cigarettes. The nausea, vomiting, and dysphoria ("out of sorts") which J.S. initially experienced often are encountered in novice nicotine users. When J.S. continued to use the tobacco, these initial effects subsided and he experienced a reduction in anxiety and a feeling of well-being ("connected" to his teammates). While his complaints of tachycardia, lightheadedness, and dizziness also can be attributed to nicotine, they should raise some concern since these generally only are encountered with high doses of nicotine. Since tolerance develops rapidly to nausea, the fact that he continues to experience some nausea despite continued use, also suggests possible excessive nicotine effects. The fine hand tremor and weight loss are consistent with nicotine use and can occur even in low dose users.

Content

2. What is the nicotine content of chewing tobacco relative to other tobacco products and would the quantity be sufficient to affect J.S.'s asthma or the drug therapy of his asthma?

The nicotine and tar contents of cigarettes, chewing tobacco, and oral snuff vary from manufacturer to manufacturer. However, the amount of nicotine in each cigarette or dose of tobacco used and the average daily consumption of nicotine have been reported: cigarettes 8.4 mg, 168 mg/20 cigarettes; oral snuff 14.5 mg, 157 mg/15 gm; and chewing tobacco 133 mg, 1176 mg/70 gm.[7-9] Nicotine content per cigarette can be as high as 13 mg.[10] Although the amount of nicotine can vary greatly, the amount of nicotine in oral snuff and chewing tobacco exceeds that of cigarettes. In addition to nicotine, tobacco contains many minor alkaloids including nornicotine, cotinine, anabasine, myosmine, nicotyrine, and anatabine, all of which have physiological and pharmacological effects similar to nicotine but are less potent.[11]

The pathogenesis and even some of the triggering events of asthma continue to produce significant discussion and debate (see Chapter 19: Asthma). Cigarette smoke is known to trigger asthmatic attacks; however, there is no evidence that nicotine plays a role in this event. Cigarette smoking also affects the action of a number of drugs (see Table 85.1). For example, hepatic enzyme induction, which is stimulated by polycyclic hydrocarbons in the tobacco smoke, increases the clearance of theophylline;[31] however, there is no evidence that nicotine is directly involved in any theophylline interactions.

While there is no evidence of any drug interactions or any relationship between his asthma and physical complaints, J.S. is exhibiting a number of effects that might be attributable to his theophylline (e.g., his nausea and vomiting, anorexia, dizziness, tachycardia, hypotension, and twitching of fingers and hands).[32] Since J.S. did not experience these effects before his use of the chewing tobacco, it would appear that they are related to it somehow. As noted above, each "dose" of chewing tobacco contains as much nicotine as 10 to 20 cigarettes. Since both nicotine and theophylline produce these effects and J.S. did not experience these symptoms with the theophylline alone, he is perhaps manifesting the additive effects of these two drugs. This conclusion is reinforced by the evidence that J.S. may be using higher than normal amounts of chewing tobacco, and, thereby, exceeding the rate of tolerance to some of these physiologic effects.

3. What actions should be recommended to J.S.?

The treatment plan for J.S. is simple: eliminate the tobacco and all of these problems should disappear. The hard part is for J.S. to "save face" with his peers. He has an advantage over other teenagers in one respect because he has a problem with the drug therapy of a medical condition: he *has* to stop chewing. Most teenagers have to resist their peers the hard way: by saying "No, it's not good for my health."

Table 85.1	Cigarette Smoking and Drug Effects[a]	
Drug/Class	**Action**	**Therapeutic Effect**
Antidepressants, tricyclic	↓ plasma levels	↓ efficacy
Benzodiazepines	↑ clearance	↓ sedative effect
Chlorpromazine	↓ side effects (e.g., drowsiness)	No effect
Heparin	↓ half-life; ↑ elimination rate	↓ thrombolytic effect
Insulin	↑ catecholamine release; ↑ steroid release; ↓ SQ insulin absorption	↓ hypoglycemic effect
Oral contraceptives	?	↑ cardiovascular adverse effects
Pentazocine	↑ hepatic metabolism	↓ efficacy
Propoxyphene	↑ hepatic metabolism	↓ efficacy
Propranolol	↓ serum concentration, ↑ clearance	↓ efficacy, especially in angina pectoris
Theophylline	↑ hepatic enzyme induction	↓ efficacy

[a] Adapted from reference 30.

Reproductive Effects

4. A.C. and R.C. are in their early 20s and would like to have children. They have been trying to conceive for the past 18 months without success. A.C. has been smoking about 15–20 cigarettes/day for the past 6 years, while R.C. has been smoking 25–30 cigarettes/day for 8 years. Neither of them has any medical condition or uses any medication. They have not observed any decrease in libido. What are the effects of cigarette smoking on infertility and could their difficulty in conceiving be correlated to their cigarette smoking?

The effect of nicotine on libido is not well-studied and the evidence is contradictory at best. Epidemiological data on nicotine and reproduction also are limited.

Sperm Production and Motility. Sperm motility in male cigarette smokers has been noted to be decreased as the amount of cigarette smoking is increased; and sperm motility increased after cessation of smoking.[33,34] The sperm of men at an infertility clinic were of lower quality and quantity in cigarette smokers compared to nonsmokers;[35] and sperm abnormalities were more common in cigarette smokers.[36] However, these findings were not noted in a follow-up study;[37] animal studies are inconclusive;[34,38] and semen characteristics and fertility were not altered in young adult males exposed to prenatal and early childhood maternal smoking.[36]

Hormonal Effects. Testosterone levels in male smokers were lower than in nonsmokers in two studies,[39,40] and were unchanged in two other studies.[36,41] Follicle stimulating hormone (FSH) and luteinizing hormone (LH) also were unaffected.[36]

Hormonal Effects and Ovulation. In animal studies, nicotine delayed the release of luteinizing hormone,[42,43] and inhibited ovulation.[44]

Fertility. Fertility is lower in female smokers than in nonsmokers.[45–47] Animal studies suggest that nicotine might alter the secretion of estrogens and progesterone, thereby adversely affecting successful implantation in the uterus.[48,49]

Menopause. Smokers experience an earlier onset of menopause than nonsmokers.[50–54] Another study on risk factors of myocardial infarction and menopause has confirmed this association.[55]

A.C. and R.C. should be informed that cigarette smoking could cause fertility problems and to stop smoking if they want to optimize their chances for successful conception. The inability to conceive in this couple, however, could be related to a variety of other causes.

Prenatal and Neonatal Effects

5. After 2 years, A.C. became pregnant. Although she initially tried to discontinue cigarette smoking, she relapsed within 3 weeks and continues to smoke ≈1 pack (20 cigarettes) a day. She now is concerned about the effects of her smoking on the fetus. What are the risks associated with smoking during A.C.'s pregnancy?

Nicotine rapidly enters fetal circulation to produce blood levels higher than those found in the maternal blood.[56]

Spontaneous Abortion. Numerous studies over the past 30 years have linked cigarette smoking to spontaneous abortion. The incidence of spontaneous abortion for smokers was 1.2 to 1.8 times higher than for nonsmokers.[57–59] The reason for this is not yet understood, although this may be due to an effect on the release of hormones necessary for successful implantation.[4]

Birth weight is a major indicator of prenatal development and maternal smoking is associated with low birth weight.[4] Low birth weight is associated with an increase in neonatal morbidity and mortality. In a review of 42 published studies involving almost 240,000 births, the average birth weight of babies born to smokers was seven ounces less than nonsmokers.[4] In the majority of these studies, smoking had little if any effect on the length of gestation, indicating that smoking itself, and not prematurity, was the critical factor. In addition, the birth weight of babies born to smokers, who did not smoke during pregnancy, was comparable to that of babies born to nonsmokers. The most significant time for cigarette smoke or nicotine to affect fetal growth and development seems to be in the third trimester. Although there is a definite association between smoking and low birth weight, a strong relationship between smoking and perinatal mortality has not yet been demonstrated.

Congenital Malformations. Fetal malformations often are associated with spontaneous abortions. Two studies were unable to demonstrate any stillborn deaths due to malformations from maternal smoking.[60,61] One study reported an increase in deaths from fetal malformations (especially anencephaly) when the mother smoked more than ten cigarettes daily, with an increased incidence as the number of cigarettes smoked per day increased.[62] Other reported problems with suggested association with maternal smoking include congenital heart disease, urogenital abnormalities, and cleft palate/lip.[58,63]

Other Disorders. An association between maternal cigarette smoking and both sudden infant death syndrome and respiratory disorders (e.g., pneumonia and bronchitis) has been reported.[64,65]

A.C. should be informed that cigarette smoking might increase the chance of spontaneous abortion, lower her child's birth weight, and increase the potential for other birth defects. She needs to be encouraged to stop smoking.

Breast-feeding

6. Although A.C. continued to smoke about 5–10 cigarettes/day throughout her pregnancy, she delivered a healthy 7 lb 2 oz boy within a week of her due date. She continues to smoke and would like to breast-feed him. What problems might A.C.'s son have if she decides to breast-feed him?

Nicotine is significantly secreted into breast milk.[66,67] The ratio of breast milk to plasma nicotine concentration is about 2.9. Nicotine can produce symptoms such as vomiting, diarrhea, restlessness, insomnia, and rapid pulse in the breast-fed infant. The immunological benefits of breast-feeding may be nullified by the hazards associated with smoking and breast-feeding, especially if the mother smokes more than 20 cigarettes/day.[4]

A.C.'s son may have gastrointestinal (GI) problems, be irritable, and sleep poorly if she breast-feeds him, with even more pronounced effects if she returns to her prepregnancy level of smoking.

Smoking and Cancer

7. L.R., a 62-year-old female, has just been diagnosed with cervical cancer. After a thorough history and physical, she has been told that cigarette smoking could be a contributing cause. She has been smoking 1 pack/day for over 40 years. She knows that lung cancer is caused by smoking but has never heard of other cancers being related to cigarettes. She says that she really would rather not quit smoking. What evidence should be presented to L.R. to encourage her to discontinue cigarette smoking?

Smoking is the primary known cause of cancer in the U.S. The risk is proportional to the number of cigarettes smoked and the number of years of smoking.[68] More than 39 tumorigenic substances have been identified in tobacco smoke.[2] Although cigar and pipe smokers have a somewhat lower incidence of cancer than cigarette smokers, probably due to less inhalation of the smoke, the risk of lung cancer, for example, is still seven times greater than in nonsmokers. With the rising number of female smokers over the past 20 years, the incidence of cancer in females also has increased significantly. Smoking-related cancers are divided

into those in which smoking is a major cause and those in which it is a contributing cause.[68]

Cancers for which smoking is considered a major cause include: the lung, oral cavity, larynx, and esophagus. Cigar and pipe smokers have a risk of oral, laryngeal, and esophageal cancer similar to cigarette smokers.[69] There is also an increased risk of oral cancer with the use of smokeless tobacco.[70] Heavy alcohol consumption increases the risk of oral, laryngeal, and esophageal cancers in tobacco users.[71] Smoking cessation can reduce the risk of lung cancer by 20% to 90%. As with lung cancer, the risk of all three other types of cancer declines after smoking cessation.[68]

For some types of cancer, smoking is not a major cause, but it does contribute to the overall incidence. That is, the incidence of cancer is higher in smokers than nonsmokers and there appears to be a dose-response relationship (although not as strong as with other cancers). Some of these cancers include the bladder, kidney, pancreas, stomach, and hematopoietic tissues. In some of these cases, tobacco smoke is believed to facilitate environmental causes of the cancer.[72]

Approximately 4000 new cases of cervical cancer (30% of total) are attributed to smoking.[73] Cigarette smoking is an independent risk factor for cervical cancer that is twice as high in smokers (especially >20 cigarettes/day or >40 years of smoking) than nonsmokers.[74] Tobacco smoke components in the cervical mucus of smokers are believed to be absorbed systemically.[75] The cessation of cigarette smoking reduces the risk of cervical cancer.[74]

Cardiovascular Disease

8. T. R., a 52-year-old male, complains of shortness of breath and substernal chest pain while playing golf. He was taken to the emergency room (ER) where an electrocardiogram (ECG) was unremarkable and cardiac enzymes were within normal limits. His chest pain had subsided by the time he arrived at the ER. A lipid profile showed a total cholesterol of 235 mg/dL, triglycerides of 100 mg/dL, low density lipoproteins (LDL) of 185 mg/dL, and high density lipoproteins (HDL) of 30 mg/dL. His body weight appears to be within normal limits for his age and height. He has smoked about 10 cigarettes/day for 30 years. He had a strong odor of tobacco smoke on his breath and clothes. His only aerobic exercise consists of 18 holes of golf once or twice each weekend. He has several alcoholic drinks on the weekend but rarely drinks during the week. He has had bronchitis 2 or 3 times during each of the past 3 years. He does not take any medication or vitamins. What is the relationship between smoking and T.R.'s vasospastic angina and hyperlipoproteinemia? [SI units: total cholesterol 6.08 mmol/L; triglycerides 1.13 mmol/L; LDL 4.78 mmol/L; HDL 0.78 mmol/L]

Cardiovascular Effects. The effect of nicotine on the development of atherosclerosis is well established. Atherosclerosis is a contributing factor to coronary artery vasoconstriction, and the incidence of vasospastic angina is 20 times higher in smokers than in nonsmokers.[76] Nicotine stimulates catecholamine release, induces arrhythmias, and increases myocardial oxygen demand. In addition, the carbon monoxide from cigarette smoking decreases the oxygen-carrying capacity of blood and increases the risk of sudden death from myocardial infarction.[77]

Lipid Effects. Nicotine increases free fatty acids as well as very low density lipoproteins (VLDL), and at the same time decreases the high density lipoprotein which protects against coronary heart disease (CHD).[78] As with cardiovascular effects, these atherogenic effects of nicotine are augmented by the additional effects of tobacco smoke on blood glycerol, glucose, cortisol, antidiuretic hormone, and peripheral blood lactate and pyruvate.[3] Cigarette smoke also appears to trigger vascular damage associated with an immune system response to smoke contaminants.

Cerebrovascular Effects. At least 50% of all strokes are estimated to be related to cigarette smoking and the relative risk of stroke for smokers compared to nonsmokers is threefold greater.[72] Women smokers appear to be especially at risk for the development of hemorrhagic stroke.[79]

T.R. has a number of problems related to cigarette smoking. His vasospastic angina can be triggered by nicotine stimulation of catecholamine release especially when he is exerting himself while walking on the golf course or even from the swinging of his golf clubs. His dyslipidemia should be a source of major concern because of its association with atherosclerosis and coronary heart disease. T.R. is at significant risk for exacerbation of his angina, and at increased risk of both myocardial infarction and stroke. At his age and with his condition, nicotine and the other constituents of cigarette smoke should be assumed to play a significant part.

9. Why is it important to know how much T.R. smokes?

Chronic obstructive airways disease, many types of cancer, and cardiovascular disease clearly are exacerbated by nicotine and cigarette smoking. However, the degree of smoking can affect the onset, duration, and severity of many manifestations of these diseases. Therefore, obtaining an accurate smoking history is important to the overall assessment of the patient. For example, as little as one cigarette can be responsible for reduced myocardial blood flow in a narrowed coronary artery.[80] The risk of stroke also directly correlates to the number of cigarettes smoked per day. Multiplying the number of packs of cigarettes smoked per day times the number of years of smoking provides the patient's pack-years of cigarette use. For T.R., 0.5 packs (10 cigarettes) times 30 years is 15 pack-years of smoking.

Generally, one has to assume that the information provided by the patient is true unless there are signs that the patient is being less than truthful. The number of cigarettes smoked often is understated by patients because of the social stigma that accompanies the continued abuse of a substance despite evidence of adverse health consequences. During discussions with their patients, clinicians should be observant of indications of possible excessive cigarette use. For example, brown stains on the teeth and fingers, significant wrinkling of the skin on the face, and a strong odor of smoke on clothing might suggest heavy cigarette use. The fact that T.R. has had bronchitis a number of times during the past three years also may be indicative of the development of long-term consequences of heavy smoking. In T.R.'s case, however, whether he has been smoking 10 or 40 cigarettes/day is no longer important because he has already begun to exhibit the smoking-induced problems of angina and hyperlipidemia, along with recurrent bronchitis.

10. Risk Reduction. What steps should T.R. undertake to minimize further progression of his cardiovascular disease?

T.R. should begin a low-fat diet to try and lower his LDL and VLDL cholesterol, and begin an aerobic exercise program approved by his physician in an effort to raise HDL levels (see Chapter 9: Dyslipidemias) and improve his cardiovascular fitness. Smoking cessation, however, is perhaps more important because it increases HDL-cholesterol,[81] decreases coronary artery disease in both men and women, and reduces stroke risk and stroke mortality.[82]

Nicotine Dependence and Withdrawal

11. R.B., a 42-year-old male, has been smoking 2 packs of cigarettes daily for 24 years. He is a sheet metal mechanic who works on high-rise building construction. Over the past year, he has experienced several "colds" with a strong productive cough which seems to linger for several weeks. Although he has not had any other medical problems, his total cholesterol was recently found to be 210 mg/dL. He has tried using a sta- tionary bicycle and a stair-step machine but cannot use either for more than 3–4 minutes without being totally out of breath. These problems, and the fact that his father died of emphysema when he was 69 years old, have prompted him to stop smoking. He has tried to quit smoking "many times" over the past 2 years. Every time he stops smoking, he becomes nervous and irritable, gets headaches, is unable to concentrate at work, has difficulty sleeping, and constantly craves a cigarette. It is especially bad the morning after he quits. Just seeing someone else smoking or smelling cigarette smoke causes him to "light up." His temperament gets so bad that neither his coworkers, wife, nor children want to be around him. What symptoms experienced by R.B., upon previous attempts to discontinue smoking, are consistent with physical dependence to nicotine?

Nicotine fits many of the criteria for psychoactive substance dependence as developed by American Psychiatric Association in its Diagnostic and Statistical Manual of Mental Disorders, 4th edition (DSM-IV).[30] When an individual is physically dependent upon a substance and then discontinues its use, withdrawal symptoms occur.[83,84] Nicotine is the causative agent for physical dependence upon tobacco, because administration of nicotine will reverse withdrawal symptoms. R.B.'s symptoms of anxiety, irritability, difficulty concentrating, and insomnia when he discontinued his cigarette smoking are symptoms that are associated with nicotine withdrawal. He has been smoking for more than several weeks (24 years); experienced four of the major withdrawal symptoms which begin within 24 hours of cessation; and his temperament during withdrawal adversely affects both his social and occupational relationships. All of these characteristics are consistent with the diagnostic criteria for nicotine withdrawal (see Table 85.2) as outlined by the American Psychiatric Association in DSM-IV.

There is some question whether smokers continue to smoke just to prevent withdrawal because only some withdrawal symptoms (e.g., craving and depression) are affected.[85] The withdrawal syndrome in smokeless tobacco users is the same as for cigarette smokers despite a less severe withdrawal in the smokeless group.[86] Many recovering alcoholics and those dependent upon other drugs are unable to stop smoking. The evidence is incontrovertible that nicotine is one of the most potent addictive substances available and that R.B. is, in fact, physically dependent upon nicotine. Even after complete physical withdrawal from the drug, the psychological dependence of cigarette smoking continues to exert a strong

Table 85.2	Diagnostic Criteria for Nicotine Withdrawal[a]

A. Daily use of nicotine for at least several weeks

B. Abrupt cessation of nicotine use, or reduction in the amount of nicotine used, followed within 24 hr by ≥4 of the following signs:
- Dysphoria or depressed mood
- Insomnia
- Irritability, frustration, or anger
- Anxiety
- Difficulty concentrating
- Restlessness
- ↓ heart rate
- ↑ appetite or weight gain

C. The symptoms in criterion B cause clinically significant distress or impairment in social, occupational, or other important areas of functioning

D. The symptoms are not due to a general medical condition and are not better accounted for by another mental disorder

[a] Reprinted with permission from reference 84.

influence on long-term users. The reinforcing effects of nicotine from years of use, particularly with the first cigarette of the day, after a meal, or with a cup of coffee, can significantly fortify psychological dependence. This is why R.B. cannot stand to see someone smoke or even to smell smoke. The craving for a cigarette may subside over a period of weeks or months. However, many former smokers claim that they must fight the craving for a cigarette even years after they have successfully conquered the physical dependence.

12. Weaning. Why cannot R.B. just smoke fewer cigarettes and wean himself off of nicotine?

Researchers have concluded that "smokers tend to smoke in ways that minimize the effect of attempted reductions in nicotine intake."[83] With low-nicotine cigarettes, or with low-tar cigarettes, smokers puff harder, longer, and more frequently in order to attain nicotine and/or tar levels normally achieved. There is no evidence that these compensatory behavioral adaptations in smoking are voluntary. The fact remains that nicotine is a powerful reinforcing drug with a strong propensity to produce and maintain addictive behavior. Even six months after cessation of cigarette smoking, 50% of individuals who have quit smoking report having a desire for a cigarette within the last 24 hours.[30]

13. Weight Gain. R.B. did not gain weight with previous attempts to discontinue smoking probably because he never quit smoking long enough as a result of his persistent craving for a cigarette. Since individuals commonly report weight gain when cigarette smoking is discontinued, what is the likelihood R.B. would be similarly affected?

A major factor affecting successful smoking cessation is weight gain. Weight increases an average of 2 to 3 kg over the first year after cessation of cigarette smoking and increased hunger and weight gain often persist for at least six months.[30] Debate has continued on whether weight gain is due to increased eating or metabolic changes. In a study involving twins, the effect of smoking on body weight was assessed.[26] Light smokers (1 to 19 cigarettes/day), moderate smokers (20 to 29 cigarettes), and heavy smokers (>29 cigarettes) were an average of 3.2, 2.4, and 4.0 kg lighter in weight, respectively, than nonsmokers when all other factors were taken into account. In addition, former smokers had a 1.8 times increased risk of clinically significant obesity when compared to active heavy smokers. Nicotine appears to exert a direct metabolic effect to reduce the weight of smokers. For most, a continuation of normal eating habits during smoking cessation will most likely produce weight gain. Regardless of the cause, weight gain needs to be addressed for all patients undergoing nicotine cessation.

Pharmacologic Smoking Cessation Options

14. What smoking cessation options are available to R.B. and what would be the best recommendation for him?

Gum. Nicotine polacrilex gum contains 2 or 4 mg of nicotine bound to an ion exchange resin which releases nicotine when chewed. The gum is buffered to an alkaline pH which facilitates the absorption of nicotine from the buccal mucosa. Peak plasma levels of nicotine are reached in 15 to 30 minutes as compared to one to two minutes from smoking a cigarette. Nicotine gum should not be used during the postmyocardial infarction period, in patients with life-threatening arrhythmias, severe angina, temporomandibular joint disease, and by pregnant women.

A recommended starting dose for a one-pack-per-day smoker is 12 to 15 pieces of the 2 mg nicotine gum. The number of pieces of nicotine gum/day should be slowly tapered over a period of three to six months. The 4 mg strength can be used if the 2 mg strength is insufficient to halt any of the signs or symptoms of withdrawal.

The most frequently reported side effects in decreasing order are: mouth or throat soreness, nausea and vomiting, jaw muscle ache, hiccoughs, nonspecific GI distress, and eructation.[87]

Nicotine gum is more effective than placebo gum in studies of less than six months duration. In long-term studies, the success rate has been only slightly better than that for placebo, ranging from 23% for the nicotine gum users compared to 13% for placebo.[88,89]

Transdermal System. Transdermal nicotine-containing patches utilize a controlled-release membrane which allows for the slow and steady absorption of nicotine through the skin. Three products deliver the nicotine over 24 hours while one uses a 16-hour system. Peak plasma levels are attained in eight to nine hours, with steady levels maintained thereafter with the 24-hour patches.

Patients over 100 pounds, those who smoke more than one-half pack per day, and those without cardiovascular disease should start with the 21 mg/22 mg per day patch (15 mg for the 16-hour patch). The patch should be removed daily and a new patch applied to an alternate skin site for 4 to 12 weeks. The patient should discontinue smoking cigarettes completely during this period. If the patient successfully has abstained from smoking, the dose should be decreased after each two to four weeks of treatment to the next lower strength patch. The lowest strength patch should be used for the last two to four weeks of treatment. The entire course of treatment should not be longer than 12 weeks in duration. If the patient is unable to discontinue smoking after four weeks, therapy should be stopped.

The most frequently reported side effects are local dermatological reactions such as erythema, pruritus, edema, and rash which often take several weeks to manifest themselves.[90] About a one-third to one-half of all patients can experience some local dermatological reaction. Gastrointestinal effects such as diarrhea or nausea also have been reported, but the incidence is much lower with the use of transdermal nicotine[91] than with other nicotine delivery systems.

After 12 weeks, 19.4% of nicotine patch users who smoked more than 24 cigarettes/day had confirmed smoking cessation compared to 11.7% of placebo patch users.[92] In another study of 600 smokers who smoked more than 15 cigarettes/day, the 16-hour nicotine patch was associated with cessation of smoking in 9.3% of the nicotine group which was much better than the 5.0% rate in the placebo-treated group.[93] Moderate or severe local irritation or itching at the patch site occurred in 15.8% and 16.4% in both studies, and was severe enough to cause withdrawal in one of the studies of 9.5% of subjects.

Other Methods: Nicotine Inhaler. A double-blind, placebo-controlled study measured the effectiveness of a nicotine inhaler in 286 subjects.[94] At the end of 52 weeks, 15% of subjects who used the nicotine inhaler abstained from smoking as compared to 5% in the placebo inhaler group. No serious adverse effects were reported. Other nicotine nasal aids currently being investigated for smoking cessation include nicotine nasal solution and nicotine nasal spray.

Other Nicotine Cessation Aids. Additional smoking cessation modalities being investigated include nicotine toothpicks, smoke-free cigarettes which contain nicotine, and "roll-on" tobacco extract.[95–97]

Citric Acid Inhaler. In a three-week study of 24 subjects who used a citric acid inhaler whenever the urge to smoke occurred, the citric acid inhaler helped to alleviate both the negative affect and craving for cigarettes induced by nicotine withdrawal.[98] Citric acid appears to simulate the tracheal sensations caused by cigarette smoke. While this holds some promise in smoking cessation, more long term studies are needed.

Clonidine Therapy. Clonidine has been used orally in doses ranging from 0.15 to 0.4 mg/day to prevent the withdrawal symptoms of nicotine. In one study with oral clonidine, a six-month follow-up with self-reported data showed an abstinence rate of 27% and 5% for clonidine and placebo-treated patients, respectively.[99] Clonidine may be helpful in facilitating smoking cessation when used in conjunction with behavior modification; however, more studies are needed.

R.B. should be advised that if he wants to quit smoking, he should stop smoking completely (''cold turkey'') and take medication to assist him in his smoking cessation effort. Although the success rates are not high, one in four individuals will be successful, at least initially. There are several considerations in selecting the best therapy for R.B. First, clonidine still needs more study to determine how it compares with the nicotine patch and gum. Because of the hazards associated with his employment (R.B. is a construction worker), the adverse CNS depression effects of clonidine (e.g., drowsiness) make it an unacceptable alternative to the nicotine-containing medications. The nicotine patch and nicotine gum appear to be equally effective in assisting patients in smoking cessation and would be preferred over clonidine for R.B. The patch is easy to apply and its once daily application facilitates compliance. On the average, it is also less expensive than nicotine gum. The nicotine patches can, however, produce skin irritation serious enough to require discontinuation of therapy. Nicotine gum, on the other hand, satisfies the need of some individuals to have something in the mouth. Although nicotine gum is more expensive than nicotine patch treatment, it also allows for greater flexibility of dosing.

Since R.B. is a heavy smoker, the greater flexibility in dosing of the gum may enhance his chances for success. Therefore, R.B. might be more successful with the 2 mg nicotine gum than the patch. Since both nicotine patch and nicotine gum are about equally effective, individual patient preferences should be considered. If the gum is selected, R.B. will most likely need to start with 25 to 30 pieces daily spaced out evenly over his waking hours because he is a heavy smoker. The improper use of the gum is probably the most common cause of failure.[100] The gum should be chewed on a regular schedule rather than waiting for the cigarette craving to occur. The gum should not be chewed continuously like regular gum but bitten intermittently and slowly (about six times) until tingling is felt. It should be placed between the cheek and the gum near the front of the mouth between chewing until the tingling effect subsides, at which time biting should be resumed.[101] Each piece should be chewed intermittently for about 30 minutes. This chewing procedure promotes the slow buccal absorption of the nicotine released from the gum. Chewing the gum too rapidly can release the nicotine too quickly and lead to nausea, hiccoughs, or throat irritation. Food and beverages can interfere with the buccal absorption of nicotine and should be avoided for about 15 minutes before and during chewing of nicotine gum. The number of gum doses should be gradually decreased over a period of not less than three months for R.B. He previously has failed in his attempts to discontinue smoking and another failure could be demoralizing; therefore, the gum doses should be decreased gradually.

Based upon the evidence to date, pharmacologic smoking cessation therapy appears to be much more effective if it is part of an overall program of behavioral therapy which includes education, counseling, and relapse prevention.[100] R.B. can enhance his chances for successful smoking cessation by participating in some sort of behavioral therapy program both during and *after* his pharmacologic therapy.

Factors Affecting Smoking Cessation

16. Even though R.B. wants to discontinue his smoking of cigarettes, he feels that it is just too hard. He also is concerned about the cost of drug treatment for smoking cessation. What should be recommended to R.B.?

Cost of Treatment. This is, perhaps, one of the least understood factors in smoking cessation. During the past 24 years, R.B. has spent approximately $20,000 on cigarettes. In today's dollars, he is spending just under $4 per day for cigarettes. The initial cost to R.B. for nicotine gum (2 mg, 30 pieces daily) or patch (21/22 mg) is $10 and $4 per day, respectively. In general, the cost of smoking cessation drug therapy for R.B. would be just slightly more than what he is currently spending on cigarettes. If money is a factor, the nicotine patch is less expensive than nicotine gum and would cost R.B. about what he is spending daily on cigarettes. When the cost of medical care related to future smoking-induced illnesses is taken into account, R.B. will actually save significant amounts of money in the long-term if he is successful.

Considerations for Success. The field of smoking cessation therapy is very new and much is still not known. While the interrelationship of factors affecting relapse is complex and unclear, craving for cigarettes seems to be a common cause for relapse.[102] R.B. is a typical example of these patients. In looking back at the long-term success rates for the various nicotine cessation therapeutic modalities (including nicotine patch and gum), the outlook is not optimistic. While there have been many successes, the long-term rate is marginally better than placebo in most cases. The fact that R.B. is highly motivated to quit cigarettes can enhance his chances of successfully completing his goal.

Since R.B. has previously expressed concern about weight gain, the addition of an aerobic exercise program (e.g., walking, light jogging, stationary bike) can compensate for any decreased metabolic changes. He should be encouraged to start exercising for short periods of time and slowly extend it as his physical conditioning improves. In addition, the exercise program can give R.B. a sense of well-being and accomplishment which also would increase his likelihood of success in his effort to cease cigarette smoking.

17. After almost 1 year of using nicotine gum, R.B. cannot seem to stop using it. What is the problem and what can be done?

One of the concerns that has arisen concerning nicotine gum is that it maintains the physical dependence upon nicotine even when the craving for cigarettes subsides. Nicotine gum appears to be comparable to methadone in that it transfers the form of the dependence, not the dependence itself. This seems to be the case with R.B. On the positive side, nicotine products reduce the medical problems associated with cigarette smoke and also eliminate the hazards of second-hand smoke. Some patients have remained on nicotine gum for years rather than tapering off. This may be the preferred situation in the short-term rather than have R.B. go back to smoking. It is incumbent upon R.B.'s physician to assist him in decreasing his reliance on the nicotine gum. R.B. needs to be reminded that the cardiovascular and other adverse effects of nicotine continue to occur as long as he uses the gum. Most importantly, success rates are extremely low without behavioral therapy. A patient like R.B. may be a good candidate for a 12-step smoking cessation group. These 12-step programs are patterned after the alcoholics anonymous program. R.B. would then be part of a self-help support group and could find a sponsor to help him taper off the gum.

Resources For Smokers

18. Where can smokers go to get information or help on smoking cessation?

A variety of resources are available. Table 85.3 lists organizations that provide educational material on smoking cessation and tobacco control.[103] For individuals who wish to quit smoking, their physicians may well be the best place to start. Physicians can assist patients directly or can refer patients to local smoking cessation programs. In addition, individuals can call their local office of the American Cancer Society, the American Heart Association, or the American Lung Association (which many feel has the strongest smoking cessation program). These organizations can assist individuals in finding self-help groups for smokers.

Caffeine

The world's most popular drug is probably caffeine. Approximately 90% of adults in North America regularly consume caffeine.[104] It occurs naturally in coffee, tea, cocoa, and chocolate, and is added to soft drinks and proprietary medicines (Table 85.4).[105] Most of the population begins consuming caffeine in childhood;[106] average adult consumption in the U.S. is estimated to be over 200 mg/day. Heavy tea and coffee consuming countries, such as the United Kingdom (444 mg) and Sweden (425 mg) have about double the caffeine consumption of the U.S.[104]

Caffeine has been used for at least the last 3000 years. An Arabian goat herder observed that sheep, after eating berries of the coffee plant (Coffea arabica), "bounced" around the hillside and moved about through the night instead of sleeping. Based upon these observations, the goat herder boiled the berries in water and drank possibly the first cup of coffee.[107]

Tea contains caffeine and small amounts of theophylline and theobromine. Tea is prepared from the leaves of *Thea sinensis*, a bush native to southern China and currently is cultivated in many other countries. In the United Kingdom about eight pounds of tea are consumed per capita compared to Americans consumption of less than one pound of tea per person per year. Some teas also contain varying quantities of tannins which, theoretically, could bind to caffeine and decrease the GI absorption of caffeine.

Chocolate comes from the seeds of *Theobroma cacao* which contains caffeine and theobromine. Chocolate also contains theobromine which is a xanthine having therapeutic actions similar to caffeine but is less potent in its central nervous system effects.

Table 85.3	Smoking Cessation and Tobacco Control Resources[a]
American Academy of Family Physicians 8880 Ward Parkway, Kansas City, MO 64114-3246 (800) 944-0000	**AAFP Stop Smoking Kit** An office-based cessation "kit" that includes waiting-room and patient handouts, office staff manual, self-help material, chart reminders/office record materials, and audio tape instructions to supplement physician/staff instruction. Charge
American Academy of Otolaryngology–Head and Neck Surgery One Prince Street, Alexandria, VA 22314 (703) 836-4444	**Through With Chew Kit** Brochures, posters, media materials, camera-ready art for office, community campaigns, and school-based presentations about smokeless tobacco. Free
American Cancer Society (Contact local offices)	**Tobacco-Free Young American Kit** Provides a wide array of posters, office staff/physician education materials, patient chart, and stickers. Free
American Lung Association (Contact local offices)	**A Healthy Beginning Counseling Kit** For family physicians/pediatricians, with information about passive smoking, poster, parent packet **Freedom from Smoking for You and Your Baby** Material specifically for pregnant patients
American Society of Addiction Medicine 5225 Wisconsin Avenue, NW, Suite 409, Washington, DC 20015 (202) 244-8948	Sponsors an annual clinical conference on nicotine dependence
Americans for Nonsmokers' Rights 2530 San Pablo Avenue, Suite J, Berkeley, CA 94702 (510) 841-3032	Information and activism concerning local tobacco control ordinances, environmental tobacco smoke issues, and related subjects. Newsletter
DOC—Doctors Ought to Care 5510 Greenbriar, Houston, TX 77005 (713) 798-7729	Posters, magazine, and kids' notebook stickers, slide presentations for use in schools, obituary cards, T-shirts, newsletter
National Center Institute Office of Cancer Communications, Building 31, Room 10A24 9000 Rockville Pike, Bethesda, MD 20892 (800) 4-CANCER	**How to Help Your Patients Stop Smoking: NCI Manual for Physicians** An excellent step-by-step manual describing a physician intervention, office strategy. Free **Clearing the Air** A brief intervention method for patients. Free; available in quantities
National Heart, Lung, and Blood Institute (202) 783-3238	**The Physician's Guide—** **How to Help Your Hypertensive Patients Stop Smoking** Minimum-contact approach. Free NIH Pub. No. 83-1271. 1983 **Clinical Opportunities for Smoking Intervention** Office-based strategy guide. NIH Pub. No. 86-2178. Free
Nicotine Anonymous World Service 218 Greenwich Street, San Francisco, CA 94123 (415) 922-8575	Newsletter, pamphlets, meetings list
Stop Teenage Addiction to Tobacco (STAT) 121 Lyman Street, Suite 210, Springfield, MA 01103 (413) 732-STAT	Newsletter, scripted slide set about tobacco use onset and prevention

[a] Reprinted with permission from reference 103.

The average cup of cocoa contains about 200 mg of theobromine and 4 mg of caffeine.[108]

Caffeinated soft drink beverages began with the advent of Coca Cola in 1886. Coca Cola contained caramel, fruit flavoring, phosphoric acid, caffeine, and a secret mixture called Merchandise #5. In 1903, the company admitted that small amounts of cocaine were contained in the beverage, but soon afterward removed it. In 1990, Coca Cola and Pepsi Company comprised nearly three-fourths of soft drinks shipments in the U.S.[108] While caffeine commonly is found in ''cola'' soft drinks, it also is found in many ''noncola'' beverages.

Caffeine is the only CNS stimulant ingredient recognized by the Food and Drug Administration (FDA) as safe and effective for nonprescription use.[109] Nonprescription caffeine-containing stimulants such as NoDoz and Vivarin commonly are used as an aid to staying awake and alert during long drives or studying for examinations.

Excedrin, Anacin, and Midol combine caffeine and analgesics to treat headache and other types of pain. Caffeine contained in over-the-counter (OTC) preparations is probably in subtherapeutic concentrations[110] when used for analgesia or to produce diuresis. In one study, 100 mg caffeine in combination with ibuprofen was significantly more effective in relieving pain following oral surgery than ibuprofen alone.[111] The mechanism(s) responsible for this observation remain unknown. Since analgesics and caffeinated beverages often are used together, concurrent use may result in substantial caffeine consumption.

Mechanism of Action

Caffeine is a methylxanthine that is closely related to theophylline and theobromine. These methylxanthines share common pharmacologic actions including CNS stimulation, diuresis, stimulation of cardiac muscle, and relaxation of bronchial smooth muscle.[110] Theophylline has the greatest, and caffeine the least, effect on the cardiovascular and respiratory systems. Caffeine has the greatest CNS effect; theobromine has basically no effect.

Usually 100 to 200 mg of caffeine will stimulate the cerebral cortex. This stimulation results in enhancement of alertness and diminishes the feeling of fatigue. Caffeine will stimulate formation of thought, the clear flow of thought, and increased capacity for sustained intellectual effort.[112] Caffeine also increases work output and physical endurance, and decreases reaction time.[112]

Caffeine's specific mechanism of action on the CNS has not been elucidated. One proposed mechanism is that caffeine inhibits the enzyme phosphodiesterase breakdown of 3',5'cyclic adenosine monophosphate (cyclic AMP). Increased levels of intracellular cyclic AMP probably mediate most of caffeine's pharmacologic actions.[113] Adenosine, a constituent of ATP and nucleic acids, is a neuromodulator that influences a number of metabolic functions in the central nervous system. Adenosine is thought to be inactivated at a uptake site believed to be distinct from the receptor site. Caffeine competes with adenosine for binding at the high-affinity adenosine receptor sites. Adenosine binding leads to a sedating or ''tranquilizing'' effect; however, when caffeine binds to the receptors instead, a ''stimulating'' or ''anxiogenic'' action occurs.[114] While more research is needed to further elucidate the mechanism of action, recent competitive antagonism of the adenosine receptor may account for many, though not all, of caffeine's behavioral effects.[114]

Pharmacokinetics

Caffeine is absorbed readily and maximal plasma concentrations are achievable within one hour. Caffeine is distributed to all body

Table 85.4	Approximate Caffeine Content in Foods and Beverages[a]
Item	Caffeine (mg)
Coffee (6 oz cup)	
Brewed drip method	72–216
Percolator brewed	48–204
Instant	36–144
Decaffeinated	
brewed	1–6
instant	1–6
Tea (6 oz cup)	
Brewed	
American	24–108
imported	30–132
Instant	30–60
Instant (12 oz)	22–76
Soft drinks (12 oz)	
Coca-Cola	45.6
Diet Coke	45.6
Pepsi-Cola	38.4
Pepsi Light	36.0
Diet Pepsi	36.0
Dr. Pepper	39.6
Mr. Pibb	40.8
Tab	46.8
Mountain Dew	54.0
Mello Yellow	52.8
Cocoa beverages (6 oz)	2–24
Chocolate	
Chocolate milk (8 oz)	2–7
Milk chocolate (1 oz)	1–15
Semi-sweet dark chocolate (1 oz)	5–35
Baking chocolate (1 oz)	26
Chocolate ice cream ($\frac{2}{3}$ cup)	4.5
Stimulants	
Caffedrine	200
NoDoz	100
Vivarin	200

[a] Reprinted with permission from Reference 105.

compartments and readily crosses the placental barrier and passes into breast milk. Caffeine's volume of distribution (Vd) is usually between 400 and 600 mL/kg; Vd is considerably higher in premature infants.[110]

Approximately 1% of caffeine is recovered unchanged in the urine. Caffeine and other methylxanthines are metabolized primarily in the liver; its principal metabolites are 1-methyluric acid, 1-methylxanthine, and an acetylated uracil derivative. Caffeine's plasma half-life is between three and seven hours.[115] The half-life of caffeine, however, may increase more than twofold in women during the later stages of pregnancy or with the chronic use of oral contraceptive steroids.[116] The rate of elimination of caffeine in premature infants is slow and its half-life is more than 50 hours.[110]

Caffeine Abuse

19. K.J., a 29-year-old female, complains of chronic headaches and difficulty sleeping. A review of her medical history notes she is taking Ortho-Novum 1/50 birth control pills and cimetidine (Tagamet) for a peptic ulcer. Medication history reveals that she has been alternating Anacin and Excedrin for chronic headaches that are most severe in the early morning hours. She has not had coffee for the last 6 months after suffering from headaches and no longer feels the need for caffeine.

Instead, she drinks imported tea (about 2–4 cups/day). She denies use of alcohol, tobacco, and other drugs. Upon further questioning, she tells you her only "vice" is an "occasional chocolate bar." She "only eats about 2 to 3 a day", but they are 16 oz in size. Her vital signs include a pulse of 75 beats/min and blood pressure of 130/80 mm Hg. What subjective and objective data should be monitored to establish whether K.J. has a caffeine-related problem?

When caffeine is used in excessive doses over long periods of time, one may develop physical dependence and suffer from withdrawal symptoms. Health providers need to inquire concerning the use of caffeine including coffee, tea, chocolate, soft drinks, and OTC medications (see Table 85.4). In this case, the health provider should inquire about the source of caffeine, as well as the daily consumption. It is also important to inquire about other drugs being consumed, medical, and psychiatric history. K.J. is taking caffeine from multiple sources (i.e., candy bars, imported tea, analgesics) and attempting relief with analgesic agents that also contain caffeine. One ounce of milk chocolate contains about 6 mg of caffeine and about 200 mg of theobromine.[108] K.J. easily could be ingesting more than 1 gm of caffeine daily. Health providers also need to inquire regarding potential caffeine related consequences such as insomnia, gastric distress, and increased blood pressure. Since K.J. is being treated for a peptic ulcer, caffeine may be aggravating this condition.

Caffeine Self-Reports

20. From her history, K.J. reported drinking 2–4 cups/day and based upon an interview with her spouse, you discover she is actually drinking 5–10 cups/day. Why are the symptoms manifested by K.J. in excess of what one could expect from 5–10 cups of tea a day. How accurate are self-reports?

James[117] employed bioanalytic methods for assessing the reliability of self-reported caffeine intake during a caffeine-fading regimen, and found that the self-report was an accurate measure of caffeine consumption. However, Kennedy investigated the validity of self-reports of caffeine use and found no significant differences between plasma levels of caffeine and metabolites for categories corresponding to low (<150 mg/day), intermediate, or high (>300 mg/day) caffeine use.[118] Kennedy concluded that self-reports of caffeine ingestion do not accurately reflect acute caffeine use.[118] K.J. uses caffeine as a social beverage and has other unrecognized medicinal and food sources. K.J. did not accurately report her caffeine use, so the health provider needs to probe and use other sources of information (e.g., spouse) to assess the level of use.

Drug Interactions

21. What drug interactions are involved in K.J.'s case, and what other significant interactions might occur with caffeine?

Cimetidine will decrease the clearance of caffeine thus increasing caffeine half-life, prolonging and enhancing its effects (see Table 85.5).[119] The impact of quinolone type antibiotics (e.g., ciprofloxacin, enoxacin) on caffeine's clearance is similar since these drugs are metabolized by hepatic microsomal enzymes.[120] Exaggerated or prolonged effects of caffeine may be expected in regular, heavy caffeine consumers. Similarly, the use of oral contraceptives will decrease the clearance of caffeine resulting in increased caffeine levels. If CNS adverse effects occur, reduction in caffeine consumption is warranted.[121]

Central nervous system stimulation and agitation may decrease the effectiveness of lithium in manic depressive illness. Two cases of worsening lithium tremor following coffee cessation from diets were attributed to a reduction in renal lithium clearance resulting in increased lithium levels.[122]

Table 85.5	Caffeine-Related Drug Interactions
Drug	Impact
Cimetidine	↓ caffeine clearance[119]
Quinolones	↓ caffeine clearance[120]
Ciprofloxacin	↓ caffeine clearance[120]
Enoxacin	↓ caffeine clearance[120]
Oral contraceptives	↓ caffeine clearance[121]
Lithium	Reduce lithium clearance[122]
Alcohol	Counteracts CNS stimulation, but no effect on motor coordination or judgment[112]

Caffeine also counteracts the depressant effects of alcohol by decreasing the desire for sleep, thus enabling a person who is out of control to remain agitated or belligerent for longer periods of time. While it counteracts the depressant effects, it does not improve motor coordination or judgment.[112]

Caffeine interferes with certain laboratory tests including the test to diagnose pheochromocytoma or neuroblastoma since it may slightly increase urinary vanilylmandelic acid (VMA) or catecholamine levels and may cause false-positive elevations of serum urate (Bittner method).[113]

The FDA ruled in 1989 that caffeine in OTC diet products is prohibited since the combination with phenylpropanolamine may lead to increased agitation, restlessness, tremor, and hallucinations. Lake found greater increases in systolic and diastolic pressure occurred after taking 75 mg PPA and 400 mg of caffeine together than after either drug alone.[123] While caffeine has been removed from diet products, this same combination can be achieved by caffeinated beverage or food intake and through the use of CNS stimulants containing caffeine. Many of the illicit "look-a-like" products sold on the streets to simulate amphetamines and other CNS stimulants often contain phenylpropanolamine and 100 to 200 mg of caffeine. The patient should be observed for signs and symptoms and caffeine intake adjusted accordingly.

Since drug users tend to take multiple drugs, amphetamine users may take caffeine in large amounts in addition to the amphetamine. The resultant effect may be prolonged stimulation, agitation, and hostility. Both cimetidine and oral contraceptive use may have increased K.J.'s caffeine levels which may aggravate gastrointestinal upset or peptic ulcer.

Adverse Effects

22. Central Nervous System (CNS) Effects. Why are K.J.'s headaches and sleeping difficulties likely to be caffeine related?

Caffeine increases the time to fall asleep and decreases sleep quality.[124] Caffeine when given in large doses may result in restlessness, insomnia, tremors, vomiting, and seizures. Signs of toxicity also may include headache, tachycardia, hypotension, and convulsions. Larger doses will stimulate the medullary, respiratory, vasomotor, and vagal centers of the brain. Toxic amounts will stimulate the entire brain and spinal cord and may result in convulsions.[125] K.J.'s headaches and insomnia probably are caused by excess caffeine consumption. Reports of deaths from caffeine overdose are rare. Caffeine plasma half-life is between three and seven hours,[105] and caffeine is metabolized primarily in the liver, so finding out when she took her last dose is important, especially if caffeine is causing sleep difficulties. K.J. should be advised to decrease her caffeine consumption and monitor her headaches, and sleeping difficulties should dissipate.

23. Hemodynamic Effects. Why is K.J. not at risk for cardiovascular complications of caffeine?

The impact of caffeine on blood pressure may be deceiving since it acts on a number of circulatory factors. Increases in blood pressure are more pronounced in older patients and in nonregular users than in chronic users of caffeine regardless of age.[126] Patients with and without borderline hypertension had initial increases in blood pressure, but these were not sustained over a seven-day trial period, probably because of tolerance development to caffeine effects.[127,128] However, other investigators report increased diastolic and systolic blood pressure after two to three cups of coffee over an eight day trial period.[129,130] Onrot[131] found that a 250 mg dose of caffeine raised blood pressure by 12 and 6 mm Hg for diastolic and systolic blood pressures, respectively. They concluded that caffeine is a pressor agent and will increase postprandial hypotension in autonomic failure. Caffeine's effects on blood pressure remain controversial.

The relationship between coffee consumption and coronary heart disease also remains controversial. La Croix[132] found that heavy coffee drinkers (≥5 cups/day) had a twofold increased risk of coronary heart disease. This study has been criticized because it enrolled a group of medical students who were followed for 35 years. Study limitations include inadequate data on serum cholesterol levels, and failed to assess levels of stress, influence of cigarette use, or dietary influences other than caffeine. Until there is a study that considers these potential confounding risk factors, the role of coffee in coronary heart disease will remain controversial. Caffeine avoidance or use in moderation is advisable for patients at risk for heart disease.

Caffeine's relationship in promoting arrhythmias and myocardial infarction is similarly unclear. Myers administered a 300 mg dose of caffeine in the recovery phase after an acute myocardial infarct and observed no relationship between caffeine and ventricular arrhythmia. While arrhythmias may be encountered in persons who use excessive amounts of caffeine, healthy individuals do not demonstrate significant changes in rhythm or heart rate.[133]

Since K.J. has no known cardiovascular risk factors and her vital signs are normal, she is probably not at risk for cardiovascular complications.

24. Effect on Cholesterol and Triglycerides. What impact might caffeine have on K.J.'s cholesterol and triglycerides?

Thelle[134] demonstrated a strong positive relationship between coffee consumption and serum total cholesterol and triglyceride concentrations in a Norwegian population. Ashton[106] suggests this impact may be due to the way Norwegians traditionally boil coffee, which may result in up to 500 mg of caffeine per cup, while other Europeans and Americans prefer percolated coffee (100 to 150 mg caffeine per cup). Bak and Grobbee found that serum cholesterol levels were affected by the method of preparation. Filtered coffee drinking did not affect serum lipid levels; however, boiled coffee increased serum cholesterol levels amounting to a mean net increase of 10% of the baseline level after nine weeks. Based upon this study, filtered coffee should be preferred to boiled coffee.[135] Since K.J. does not drink coffee and the effects of other caffeine sources have not been studied, it is possible but not yet proven, that K.J.'s high caffeine levels may elevate her cholesterol and triglyceride levels.

25. Cerebrovascular Effects. K.J. heard a recent report on the radio that caffeine reduces blood flow to the brain. What impact might caffeine have on reducing K.J.'s cerebrovascular blood flow?

Cerebrovascular constriction has been shown to occur with a relatively small dose of 250 mg of caffeine.[136,137] A 30% decrease in cerebral blood flow was noted by Cameron utilizing positron emission tomography (PET).[136]

Another study found no changes in cerebral blood flow in a low caffeine group, which was defined as consuming three cups or less of coffee per day over a three year period. However, the high caffeine group which was defined as consuming more than six cups of coffee daily for a minimum of three years was associated with a significant reduction in cerebral blood flow.[138] A reduction in cerebral blood flow after caffeine consumption is probably not severe enough to cause symptoms of cerebral ischemia in normal subjects. However, in high risk individuals (i.e., those who have had strokes, seizures, cerebral perfusion dementias, and cerebrovascular accidents), a reduction in cerebral blood flow could be problematic, and caffeine consumption should be discouraged.

K.J. has no personal or family history of cerebrovascular perfusion problems. Although caffeine may reduce blood flow somewhat, this is probably clinically insignificant for K.J.

26. Carcinogenic Effects. K.J. asks if she is at risk for cancer because of her caffeine consumption?

Nutritional guidelines established by the American Cancer Society in 1984 stated that there was no reason to consider caffeine a cancer risk factor. However, some researchers suggest that large quantities of caffeine consumption are correlated with cancers of the bladder, colon, kidneys, and ovaries. These studies have been questioned on the basis that coffee contains many different chemicals in addition to just the caffeine. In addition, they have not been substantiated by other studies, and have problems with design and controlling confounding variables.[112]

Some research reports have found an association between caffeine and fibrocystic breast disease, although this association has been questioned.[139] While fibrocystic breast disease involves benign cyst formation, the condition can be quite painful. While the results of these studies are inconclusive, many physicians advise patients with this condition to avoid or reduce their consumption of caffeine.

Current evidence does not suggest that K.J. is at increased risk for cancer. If K.J. had fibrocystic breast disease, the physician may advise caffeine moderation or avoidance.

Overdosage

27. K.J. asks if it is possible to overdose on caffeine?

"Caffeinism" is a syndrome associated with a high intake of caffeine (in excess of 1 gm/day). This syndrome is characterized by a variety of unpleasant symptoms including apprehension, restlessness, headache, irregular heartbeat, chest discomfort, diarrhea, and insomnia. Caffeinism has been confused with anxiety disorders.[140]

Reports of death from caffeine poisoning are extremely rare. It is estimated that between 5 and 10 gm (50 to 100 cups of coffee) in a short-term would be required to cause death from oral caffeine; although untoward reactions may be observed following ingestion of 1 gm (15 mg/kg or plasma concentrations >30 μg/mL).[110] Syed[141] reported one death from an intravenous injection of 3.2 gm of caffeine.

K.J. suffers from chronic headache; she may further aggravate this condition by self-medicating with an analgesic that also contains caffeine. Although K.J. may be chronically overdosing on caffeine, it is unlikely that her level of consumption would ever reach lethal amounts.

Tolerance, Physical Dependence, and Withdrawal

28. If K.J. stops all caffeine sources, would there be withdrawal? If so, what are the signs and symptoms?

Caffeine physical dependence, as evidenced by a withdrawal syndrome following cessation of chronic caffeine dosing, is well documented.[115] In their review of 37 clinical reports and experimental studies,[115] the most frequently reported withdrawal symptoms are headache and fatigue. Headache was reported in 19 of these reports, and two other reports described "fullness" and "pressure" in the head. In 15 of the clinical reports, the second most frequently cited symptom was fatigue.

Signs and symptoms of fatigue during caffeine withdrawal include mental depression, weakness, lethargy, apathy, drowsiness, disinclination to work, and decreased alertness. Another frequently cited symptom of caffeine withdrawal syndrome is anxiousness. Signs of anxiousness include nervousness and insomnia. While "craving" for coffee has been described, studies have not been done to document this as a coffee withdrawal symptom.

When caffeine withdrawal occurs, the severity of signs and symptoms can vary from mild to extreme. This may range from a slight "fullness" to a totally incapacitating headache. This withdrawal syndrome generally occurs between 12 and 24 hours after caffeine intake has been terminated. While substantial differences across subjects have been noted, the duration of caffeine withdrawal most often has been described to be about one week.[112]

Caffeine self-administration, withdrawal, and adverse effects also have been tested with double-blind studies.[115,142,143] Subjects first sampled caffeinated and decaffeinated coffees or capsules, then made choices of which coffee or capsule to use. In each study, most subjects repeatedly chose the coffee or capsule containing caffeine. Subjects with heavy coffee drinking histories were switched under double-blind conditions from caffeinated to decaffeinated coffee for ten days; the most reliable withdrawal symptom was headache, which occurred in all subjects and persisted through the third day.[115] Griffiths reported a withdrawal effect in all subjects when terminating low-dose chronic caffeine use (100 mg/day).[144] Silverman similarly found that persons who consumed low or moderate amounts of caffeine (mean: 235 mg/day) had a withdrawal syndrome upon cessation of daily caffeine consumption.[145] Hughes[146] assessed withdrawal and adverse effects of caffeine by daily alternation of decaffeinated and caffeinated coffee. Major adverse effects of caffeine were tremulousness, stomachaches, sweating, talkativeness, and tinnitus. Withdrawal symptoms during decaffeinated coffee days were headaches, drowsiness, and fatigue.[146] K.J. probably would suffer withdrawal effects such as headaches and fatigue if caffeine is stopped abruptly.

29. Physical Dependence. Would K.J.'s caffeine use meet DSM-IV criteria for substance dependence or abuse?

Caffeine as a form of drug dependence remains a controversial topic. Previous studies have not validated that coffee drinkers fulfilled previous DSM-IV criteria for psychoactive substance dependence or abuse.[147] Clinical indicators of dependence such as difficulty stopping use of caffeine despite harm have not been documented. Hughes[147] suggests that caffeine withdrawal but not caffeine abuse or dependence should be included as a diagnosis in DSM-IV and ICD-10. Hughes,[148] in a comparison of four prior studies, found that subjects who had withdrawal headaches and drowsiness were 2.3 to 2.6 times more likely to self-administer caffeinated coffee than decaffeinated coffee. Average caffeine intake did not predict caffeine self-administration or withdrawal.[148] However, coffee drinkers are less prone to unsuccessful efforts to cut down or control caffeine use, despite knowledge of having a problem or tolerance to the behavioral effects of caffeine.[146]

Although caffeine withdrawal symptoms frequently have been reported in studies, there are instances where individuals with histories of heavy caffeine use apparently experience no symptoms upon abrupt termination or restriction of caffeine.[151] Caffeine with-

drawal headaches usually are relieved by taking caffeine either in beverage sources or nonprescription analgesics that contain caffeine.

K.J. would not be considered substance dependent or substance abusing according to DSM-IV criteria.

30. Tolerance. What evidence is there that K.J. is tolerant?

Tolerance usually is associated with withdrawal. Colton[150] showed that coffee nondrinkers required more time than coffee drinkers to fall asleep after 150 mg of caffeine at bedtime, since tolerance develops to the sleep disturbing effects. Evans studied 32 healthy subjects who were stratified into either caffeine (300 mg TID) or placebo groups for 18 consecutive days and thereafter were exposed again to caffeine or placebo. Tolerance developed in the chronic caffeine group but not in the placebo group.[151] Tolerance to the CNS effects of caffeine may develop when taken in large doses over a long period of time.[113]

K.J. was inaccurate in self-reporting her caffeine use. She is taking possibly 1 gm of caffeine per day from multiple sources (i.e., candy bars, imported tea, analgesics) over a long period of time. Although K.J.'s headaches are most likely related to excessive consumption rather than withdrawal, her ability to sleep at all probably indicates some tolerance to this level of caffeine consumption.

Pregnancy

31. K.J. stops taking oral contraceptives but continues her caffeine consumption. She is getting a prescription filled for prenatal vitamins and asks if caffeine will harm her baby. What are the effects of caffeine during pregnancy and should caffeine use be discontinued during her pregnancy?

Mutagenic effects on micro-organisms, either alone or with other mutagens, have been shown with caffeine.[151] Chromosomal abnormalities in cultured mammalian cells and in plant cells also have been demonstrated. These effects seem to be associated with the inhibition of the DNA repair process and are observed when caffeine concentrations are in excess of those found in food and beverage sources.[110] Caffeine readily crosses the placental barrier. An FDA bulletin in 1980 issued a warning advising pregnant women to either avoid or use only small amounts of caffeine (FDA bulletin, 1980). Martin and Bracken[153] found an association between low birth weight and caffeine consumption during pregnancy. They found that caffeine slows the growth of the fetus so the baby may weigh less than normal at birth. In their study, the decreased birth weight observed was associated with slowed growth rather than premature birth. Some studies have found no association between malformation and low birth weight and caffeine consumption.[112,154]

Caffeine also has been implicated by increasing the chances of miscarriage.[155] In this prospective study, women who consumed more than 150 mg of caffeine per day were more likely to have late first or second trimester miscarriages than women who consumed smaller amounts of caffeine. However, confounding factors which are established risk factors for spontaneous abortions, such as smoking and alcohol consumption, were more common in caffeine users than nonusers. While more definitive research is needed, a pregnant woman such as K.J. should reduce or preferably avoid the use of caffeine.

Breast-Feeding

32. K.J. gave birth to a baby boy who was healthy until 3 days ago. Now the baby is having difficulty sleeping, is "whiny," "jittery," and "cranky" during the day. K.J.'s mother suggests that the baby has colic and K.J. should take the baby to see her physician about this condition. K.J. usually drinks a cup of tea just before she breast-feeds and drinks

another one while breast-feeding. Why is it likely (or unlikely) that K.J.'s infant is experiencing adverse effects from his mother's intake of caffeine?

Caffeine use during pregnancy and by breast-feeding women is very common. Caffeinated beverages resulted in appearance of caffeine in breast milk within 15 minutes, levels peaked at about one hour, and caffeine was detectable for up to 12 hours.[156] While no behavioral changes in the infants were noted with single doses, further research is needed to study the short- and long-term effects on infant's behavior. Because of reduced elimination, caffeine could accumulate in infants younger than four months; reduced caffeine intake or avoidance should be advocated by the health provider.

K.J. should be encouraged to avoid caffeine before and during breast-feeding, if possible, being sure that other caffeine sources (e.g., chocolate, tea, colas) are identified to her, or advocate at least moderation in caffeine use because her infant is irritable. She should, however, be told that if the child gets worse or does not improve she should contact a physician. This could represent a much more serious problem.

Caffeine and Sports

33. R.T., a 17-year-old male, runs on the high school track team and takes NoDoz and Vivarin to improve his perfor- mance. **What are the likely effects of caffeine on his athletic performance, and would the use of caffeine jeopardize his ability to obtain an athletic collegiate scholarship?**

Ingestion of caffeine increases a person's ability for muscular work. Bergland showed that 6 mg/kg of caffeine improved the racing performance of cross-country skiers.[157] Caffeine (4 to 8 mg/kg) elevates the concentration of free fatty acids in plasma, increases the basal metabolic rate, and reduces the need on muscle glycogen as a fuel source during exercise over a long period of time.

Athletes have taken caffeine in many forms as an ergogenic aid.[158] While endurance is prolonged, reaction time and fine motor coordination do not appear to be affected. Both the International Olympic Committee and National Collegiate Athletic Association banned the use of caffeine by athletes. About eight cups of strongly brewed coffee would need to be consumed to reach the banned caffeine levels.[159,160] (Also see Chapter 87: Drug Abuse in Athletics.)

While R.T.'s performance may be improved to a minimal extent with normal, moderate dietary intake, caffeine in excessive doses is banned. R.T.'s use of medicinal caffeine products for ergogenic purposes should be discouraged.

References

1 **National Institute on Drug Abuse.** National household survey on drug abuse: population estimates 1992. Rockville, MD: Substance Abuse and Mental Health Services Administration, 1993; DHHS publication no. (SMA) 93-2053.

2 **U.S. Department of Health and Human Services.** Reducing the health consequences of smoking: 25 years of progress. A report of the Surgeon General. Rockville, MD: U.S. Department of Health and Human Services, Public Health Service, Centers for Disease Control, Center for Chronic Disease Prevention and Health Promotion, Office on Smoking and Health, 1989; DHHS publication no. (CDC) 89-8411.

3 **U.S. Department of Health and Human Services.** The health consequences of smoking: cardiovascular disease. A report of the Surgeon General. Rockville, MD: U.S. Department of Health and Human Services, Public Health Service, Office on Smoking and Health, 1983; DHHS publication no. (PHS) 84-50204.

4 **Abel EL.** Marijuana, Tobacco, Alcohol, and Reproduction. Boca Raton, FL: CRC Press; 1983:55.

5 **Sutton SR et al.** Relationship between cigarette yields, puffing patterns, and smoke intake: evidence for tar compensation? Brit Med J (London). 1982; 285:600.

6 **Novotney TE et al.** Smokeless tobacco use in the United States: the adult use of tobacco surveys. In: Smokeless Tobacco Use in the United States—National Cancer Institute Monograph No. 8. Rockville, MD: National Institutes for Health, National Cancer Institute, Division of Cancer Prevention and Control, Smoking, Tobacco and Cancer Program, 1989; NIH publication no. 89-3055.

7 **Benowitz NL et al.** Smokers of low yield cigarettes do not consume less nicotine. N Engl J Med. 1983;309:139.

8 **Kozlowski LT et al.** The determinants of tobacco use: cigarette smoking in the context of other forms of tobacco use. Can J Public Health. 1982;73:236.

9 **Gritz ER et al.** Plasma nicotine and cotinine concentrations in habitual smokeless tobacco users. Clin Pharmacol Ther. 1981;30:201.

10 **Smolinske SC et al.** Cigarette and nicotine chewing gum toxicity in children. Hum Toxicol. 1988;7:27.

11 **Piade JJ, Hoffman D.** Chemical studies on tobacco smoke LXVII. Quantitative determination of alkaloids in tobacco by liquid chromatography. J Liquid Chromatography. 1980;3:1505.

12 **Gori GB et al.** Mouth versus deep airways absorption of nicotine in cigarette smokers. Pharmacol Biochem Behav. 1986;25:1181.

13 **Brunneman KD, Hoffman D.** The pH of tobacco smoke. Food Cosmet Toxicol. 1974;12:115.

14 **Russell MAH et al.** Clinical use of nicotine chewing gum. Brit Med J (London). 1980;280:1599.

15 **Benowitz NL et al.** Nicotine absorption and cardiovascular effects with smokeless tobacco use: comparison with cigarettes and nicotine gum. Clin Pharmacol Ther. 1988;44:23.

16 **Benowitz NL et al.** Circadian blood nicotine concentrations during cigarette smoking. Clin Pharmacol Ther. 1982;32:758.

17 **Benowitz NL.** Human pharmacology of nicotine. In: Cappell HD et al., eds. Research Advances in Alcohol and Drug Problems. Volume 9. New York: Plenum Press; 1986.

18 **Feyerabend C et al.** Nicotine pharmacokinetics and its application to intake from smoking. Br J Clin Pharmacol. 1985;19:239.

19 **Benowitz NE et al.** Nicotine dependence and tolerance in man: pharmacokinetic and pharmacodynamic investigations. In: Nordberg A et al., eds. Nicotine Receptors in the CNS. Their Role in Synaptic Transmission. Amsterdam: Elsevier;1989:279.

20 **Taylor P.** Agents acting at the neuromuscular junction and autonomic ganglia. In: Gilman AG et al., eds. The Pharmacological Basis of Therapeutics. 8th ed. Elmsford: Pergamon Press; 1990:166.

21 **Benowitz NL et al.** Cotinine disposition and effects. Clin Pharmacol Ther. 1983;309:139.

22 **Benowitz NL et al.** Interindividual variability in the metabolism and cardiovascular effects of nicotine in man. J Pharmacol Exp Ther. 1982;221:368.

23 **Jaffe JH.** Drug addiction and drug abuse. In: Gilman AG et al., eds. The Pharmacological Basis of Therapeutics. 8th ed. Elmsford: Pergamon Press; 1990:522.

24 **Benowitz NL.** Cigarette smoking and nicotine addiction. Med Clin North Am. 1992;76:415.

25 **Benowitz NL.** Clinical pharmacological of nicotine. Annu Rev Med. 1986; 37:21.

26 **Eisen SA et al.** The impact of cigarette and alcohol consumption on weight and obesity. Arch Intern Med. 1993; 153:2457.

27 **Gritz ER.** Smoking behavior and tobacco abuse. In: Mello NK, ed. Advances in Substance Abuse, Volume 1. Greenwich: JAI Press; 1980:91.

28 **Henningfield JE.** Behavioral pharmacology of cigarette smoking. In: Thompson T, Dews PB, eds. Advances in Behavioral Pharmacology, Volume 4. New York: Academic Press;1984: 131.

29 **Porchet HC et al.** Pharmacodynamic model of tolerance: application to nicotine. J Pharmacol Exp Ther. 1988; 244:231.

30 **Hansten PD, Horn JR.** Drug Interactions & Updates Quarterly. Vancouver: Applied Therapeutics; 1995.

31 **Jusko WJ.** Influence of cigarette smoking on drug metabolism in man. Drug Metab Rev. 1979;9:221.

32 **AHFS Drug Information.** McEvoy GK et al. eds. Bethesda: American Society of Hospital Pharmacists, Inc.; 1994:2380.

33 **Schirren C.** Die wirkung des nikotins auf die zeugungsfahigkeit des mannes. Rehabilitation. 1972;25:23.

34 **Viczian M.** The effect of cigarette smoke inhalation on spermatogenesis in rats. Experimentia. 1968;24:511.

35 **Evans HJ et al.** Sperm abnormalities and cigarette smoking. Lancet. 1981;1: 627.

36 **Ratcliffe JM et al.** Does early exposure to maternal smoking affect future fertility in adult males? Reprod Toxicol. 1992;6:297.

37 **Godfrey B.** Sperm morphology in smokers. Lancet. 1981;1:948.

38 **Dontewill W et al.** Experimental investigations of the effect of cigarette smoke on exposure on testicular function of Syrian golden hamsters. Toxicology. 1973;1:309.

39 **Briggs MH.** Cigarette smoking and infertility in men. Med J Aust. 1973;7: 616.

40 **Persky H et al.** The effect of alcohol and smoking on testicular function and aggression in chronic alcoholics. Am J Psychiatry. 1977;134:621.

41 **Winternitz WW and Quillen D.** Acute hormonal response to cigarette

smoking. J Clin Pharmacol. 1977;134: 621.

42 **Blake CA et al.** Nicotine delays the ovulatory surge of luteinizing hormone in the rat. Proc Soc Exp Biol Med. 1972;141:1014.

43 **McLean BK et al.** The differential effects of exposure to tobacco smoke on the secretion of luteinizing hormone and prolactin in the proestrous rat. Endocrinology. 1977;100:1566.

44 **Blake CA et al.** Effect of nicotine on the proestrous ovulatory surge of LH in the rat. Endocrinology. 1972;91: 1253.

45 **Tokauhata G.** Smoking in relation to infertility and fetal loss. Arch Environ Health. 1968;17:353.

46 **Pettersson F et al.** Epidemiology of secondary amenorrhea. I. Incidence and prevalence rates. Am J Obstet Gynecol. 1973;117:80.

47 **Vessey MP et al.** Fertility after stopping different methods of contraception. Brit Med J (London). 1978;1:265.

48 **Card JP and Mitchell JA.** The effects of nicotine administration on deciduoma induction in the rat. Biol Reprod. 1979;20:294.

49 **Yoshinaga K et al.** Effects of nicotine in early pregnancy in the rat. Biol Reprod. 1979;20:294.

50 **Jick H et al.** Relation between smoking and age of natural menopause. Report from the Boston Collaborative Drug Surveillance Program, Boston University Medical Center. Lancet. 1977;1:1354.

51 **Bailey A et al.** Smoking and age of natural menopause. Lancet. 1977;2:722.

52 **Daniell HW.** Smoking, obesity, and the menopause. Lancet. 1978;2:373.

53 **Lindquist O, Bengtsson C.** Menopausal age in relation to smoking. Acta Med Scand. 1979;205:73.

54 **Kaufman DW et al.** Cigarette smoking and age at natural menopause. Am J Public Health. 1980;70:420.

55 **Thorell B, Svardsudd K.** Myocardial risk factors and well-being among 50-year-old women before and after the menopause. Scand J Prim Health Care. 1993;11:141.

56 **Luck W et al.** Effect of nicotine and cotinine transfer to the human fetus, placenta and amniotic fluid of smoking mothers. Dev Pharmacol Ther. 1985;8: 384.

57 **Kline J et al.** Smoking as a risk factor for spontaneous abortion. N Engl J Med. 1977;297:793.

58 **Himmelberger DU et al.** Cigarette smoking during pregnancy and the occurrence of spontaneous abortion and congenital abnormality. Am J Epidemiol. 1978;108:470.

59 **Schramm W.** Smoking and pregnancy outcome. Mo Med. 1980;77:619.

60 **Andrews J, Mcgarry JM.** A community study of smoking in pregnancy. J Obstet Gynecol Br Commonw. 1972; 79:1057.

61 **Meyer MB, Tonascia JA.** Maternal smoking, pregnancy complications, and perinatal mortality. Am J Obstet Gynecol. 1977;128:494.

62 **Naeye RL.** Relationship of cigarette smoking to congenital anomalies and perinatal death. Am J Pathol. 1978;90: 289.

63 **Ericson A et al.** Cigarette smoking as

at etiological factor in cleft lip and palate. Am J Obstet Gynecol. 1979;135: 348.

64 **Lewak N et al.** Sudden infant death syndrome risk factors: prospective data review. Clin Pediatr. 1979;18:404.

65 **Nymand G.** Maternal smoking and immunity. Lancet. 1974;2:1379.

66 **Svensson CK.** Clinical pharmacokinetics of nicotine. Clin Pharmacokinet. 1987;12:30.

67 **Steldinger R et al.** Half-lives of nicotine in milk of smoking mothers: implications for nursing. J Perinat Med. 1988;16:261.82. Letter.

68 **Newcomb PA, Carbone PP.** The health consequences of smoking: cancer. Med Clin North Am. 1992;76:305.

69 **U.S. Department of Health and Human Services.** The health consequences of smoking: cancer. A report of the Surgeon General. Rockville, MD: U.S. Department of Health and Human Services, Public Health Service, Office of the Assistant Secretary for Health, Office on Smoking and Health, 1982; DHHS publication no. (PHS) 82-50179.

70 **U.S. Department of Health and Human Services.** The health consequences of using smokeless tobacco. A report of the Advisory Committee to the Surgeon General. Rockville, MD: U.S. Department of Health and Human Services, Public Health Service, National Institutes of Health, 1986; NIH publication no. 86-2874.

71 **Elwood JM et al.** Alcohol, smoking, social and occupational factors in the aetiology of cancer of the oral cavity, pharynx, larynx. Int J Cancer. 1984;34: 603.

72 **U.S. Public Health Services.** The health consequences of smoking: cancer and chronic lung disease in the workplace. A report of the Surgeon General. Washington, DC: U.S. Department of Health and Services, Public Health Service, Office on Smoking and Health, 1985; DHHS publication no. (PHS) 85-5027.

73 **Boring CC et al.** Cancer statistics, 1993. CA. 1993;43:7.

74 **U.S. Department of Health and Human Services.** The health benefits of smoking cessation. A Report of the Surgeon General. Rockville, MD: U.S. Department of Health and Human Services, Public Health Service, Centers for Disease Control, Center for Chronic Disease Prevention and Health Promotion, Office on Smoking and Health, 1990; DHHS publication no. (CDC) 90-8416.

75 **Sasson IM et al.** Cigarette smoking and cancer of the uterine cervix: smoke constituents in cervical mucus. N Engl J Med. 1985;312:315.

76 **Scholl JM et al.** Comparison of risk factors in vasospastic angina without significant fixed coronary narrowing to significant fixed coronary narrowing and no vasospastic angina. Am J Cardiol. 1986;57:199.

77 **U.S. Department of Education and Welfare.** The health consequences of smoking: cardiovascular disease. A report of the Surgeon General. Rockville, MD: U.S. Department of Health and Human Services, Public Health Service Office of Smoking and Health, 1983;

DHHS publication no. (PHS) 84-50204.

78 **Castelli WP et al.** Incidence of coronary heart disease and lipoprotein cholesterol levels. The Framingham study. JAMA. 1986;256:2835.

79 **Gill JS et al.** Cigarette smoking—a risk factor for hemorrhagic and nonhemorrhagic stroke. Arch Intern Med. 1989;149:2053.

80 **Deanfield JE et al.** Direct effects of smoking on the heart: silent ischemic disturbances of coronary flow. Am J Cardiol. 1986;57:1005.

81 **Stamford BA et al.** Effects of smoking cessation on weight gain, metabolic rate, caloric consumption, and blood lipids. Am J Clin Nutr. 1986;43:486.

82 **Wolf PA et al.** Cigarette smoking as a risk factor for stroke. The Framingham study. JAMA. 1988;259:1025.

83 **U.S. Department of Health and Human Services.** The health consequences of smoking: nicotine addiction. A report of the Surgeon General. Rockville, MD: U.S. Department of Health and Human Services, Public Health Service, Centers for Disease Control, Center for Health Promotion and Education, Office on Smoking and Health, 1988; DHHS publication no. (CDC) 88-8406.

84 **American Psychiatric Association.** Diagnostic and Statistical Manual of Mental Disorders. Fourth Edition. Washington, DC: American Psychiatric Association; 1994:244.

85 **Bock G, Marsh J.** eds. The Biology of Nicotine Dependence. West Sussex, England: John Wiley & Sons Ltd; 1990:240.

86 **Hatsukami DK et al.** Physiologic and subjective changes from smokeless tobacco withdrawal. Clin Pharmacol Ther. 1987;41:103.

87 **Anon.** Smoking deterrents. Facts and Comparisons. St. Louis: Facts and Comparisons; February 1992:736a.

88 **Lam W et al.** Meta-analysis of randomized controlled trials of nicotine chewing gum. Lancet. 1987;2:27.

89 **Hughes JR et al.** Long-term use of nicotine vs. placebo gum. Arch Int Med. 1991;151:1993.

90 **Rose JE et al.** Transdermal nicotine facilitates smoking cessation. Clin Pharmacol Ther. 1990;47:323.

91 **Rose JE et al.** Transdermal nicotine reduces cigarette craving and nicotine preference. Clin Pharmacol Ther. 1985;38: 450.

92 **Imperial Cancer Research Fund General Practice Research Group.** Effectiveness of a nicotine patch in helping people stop smoking: results of a randomized trial in general practice. Brit Med J. 1993;306:1304.

93 **Russell MA et al.** Targeting heavy smokers in general practice: randomized controlled trial of transdermal nicotine patches. Brit Med J. 1993;306: 1308.

94 **Tonnesen P et al.** A double-blind trial of a nicotine inhaler for smoking cessation. JAMA. 1993;269:1268.

95 **Hasenfratz M, Battig K.** Nicotine absorption and the subjective and physiologic effects of nicotine toothpicks. Clin Pharmacol Ther. 1991;50:456.

96 **Russell MAH et al.** Nicotine replacement in smoking cessation: absorption of nicotine vapor from smoke-free

cigarettes. JAMA. 1987;257:3262.

97 **Allen DW.** Transdermal tobacco extract reduces reported cigarette consumption. Med J Aust. 1988;149:342.

98 **Behm FM et al.** Clinical evaluation of a citric acid inhaler for smoking cessation. Drug Alcohol Depend. 1993; 31:131.

99 **Glassman AH et al.** Heavy smokers, smoking cessation, and clonidine: results of a double-blind, randomized trial. JAMA. 1988;259:2863.

100 **Hurt RD et al.** A comprehensive model for the treatment of nicotine dependence in a medical setting. Med Clin North Am. 1992;76:495.

101 **Merrill Dow Pharmaceuticals.** Nicorette package insert. Kansas City, MO: 1992 November.

102 **Hughes JR.** Risk-benefit assessment of nicotine preparations in smoking cessation. Drug Saf. 1993;8:49.

103 **American Medical Association.** How to Help Patients Stop Smoking: Guidelines for Diagnosis and Treatment of Nicotine Dependence. Chicago, IL: American Medical Assocation; 1994: AA41:93-668:275M:1/94.

104 **Gilbert RM.** Caffeine consumption. In: Spiller GA, ed. The Methylxanthine Beverages and Foods: Chemistry, Consumption, and Health Effects. New York: Liss;1984:213.

105 **Crismon ML, Jermain DM.** Sleep aids and stimulants. In: Covington TR, ed. Handbook of Nonprescription Drugs. 10th ed. Washington, DC: American Pharmaceutical Association; 1993:135.

106 **Ashton CH.** Caffeine and health. Brit Med J. 1987;295:1293.

107 **Compuzano U.** Brown Gold. New York, NY: Random House; 1954.

108 **Ray O, Ksir C.** Drugs, Society and Human Behavior. St. Louis, MO: Mosby-YearBook Inc. 1993:55–75.

109 **Federal Register.** 1988;53:6100.

110 **Rall TW.** Drugs used in the treatment of asthma: the methylxanthines, cromolyn, and other agents. In: Gilman AG et al., eds. Goodman and Gilman's: The Pharmacological Basis of Therapeutics. 8th ed. New York: Pergamon Press; 1990:618–37.

111 **Forbes JA et al.** Effect of caffeine on ibuprofen analgesia in postoperative oral surgery pain. Clin Pharmcol Ther. 1991;49:674.

112 **Curatolo PW, Robertson D.** The health consequences of caffeine. Ann of Intern Med. 1983;98:641.

113 **AHFS Drug Information.** McEvoy GK et al., eds. Bethesda:American Society of Hospital Pharmacists, Inc.; 1994:1472–473.

114 **Greden JF, Walters A.** Caffeine. In: Lowinson JH et al., eds. Substance Abuse: A Comprehensive Textbook. 2nd ed. Baltimore: Williams and Wilkins; 1992:357–70.

115 **Griffiths RR, Woodson PP.** Caffeine physical dependence: a review of human and laboratory animal studies. Psychopharmacology. 1988;94:437.

116 **Symposium (various authors).** Developmental pharmacology of the methylxanthines. In: Soyka LF, ed. Semin Perinatol. 1981;5:303–408.

117 **James JE et al.** Biochemical validation of self-reported caffeine consumption during caffeine fading. J Behav Med. 1988;11:15.

118 **Kennedy JS et al.** Validity of self-reports of caffeine use. J Clin Pharmacol. 1991;31:677.

119 **Tatro DS et al.**, eds. Drug Interaction Facts: Facts and Comparisons. St. Louis: Wolters Kluwer Co.; 1992:166.

120 **Tatro DS et al.**, eds. Drug Interaction Facts: Facts and Comparisons. St. Louis: Wolters Kluwer Co.; 1993:169.

121 **Tatro DS et al.**, eds. Drug Interaction Facts: Facts and Comparisons. St. Louis: Wolters Kluwer Co.; 1989:167.

122 **Jefferson JW.** Lithium tremor and caffeine intake: two cases of drinking less and shaking more. J Clin Psychiatry. 1988;49:72.

123 **Lake CR et al.** Phenylpropanolamine increases plasma caffeine levels. Clin Pharmacol Ther. 1990;47:675.

124 **Dorfman LJ, Jarvik ME.** Comparative stimulant and diuretic actions of caffeine and theobromine in man. Clin Pharmacol Ther. 1970;11:869.

125 **Wells SJ.** Caffeine: implications of recent research for clinical practice. Am J Pharm Ed. 1984;54:375.

126 **Izzo JL et al.** Age in prior caffeine use alter the cardiovascular and adrenomedullary responses to oral caffeine. Am J Cardiol. 1983;52:769.

127 **Robertson D et al.** Tolerance to the humoral and hemodynamic effects of caffeine in man. Gen Clin Invest. 1981; 67:1111.

128 **Robertson V et al.** Caffeine in hypertension. Am J Med. 1984;77:54.

129 **Pincomb GA et al.** Caffeine ability to alter blood pressure. Am J Cardiol. 1988; 61:798.

130 **Goldstein IB et al.** Blood pressure response to the ''second'' cup of coffee. Psychosom Med. 1990;52:337.

131 **Onrot J et al.** Hemodynamic and humoral effects of caffeine in autonomic failure: therapeutic implications for postprandial hypotension. N Engl J Med. 1985;313:549.

132 **LaCroix AZ et al.** Coffee consumption and the incidence of coronary heart disease. N Engl J Med. 1986;315:977.

133 **Myers MG et al.** Caffeine as a possible cause of ventricular arrthymias during the healing phase of acute MI. Am J Cardiol. 1987;59:1024.

134 **Thelle DS et al.** The Tromso heart study. N Engl J Med. 1983;308:1454.

135 **Bak AA, Grobbee DE.** The effect of serum cholesterol levels of coffee brewed by filtering or boiling. N Eng J Med. 1989;321:1432.

136 **Cameron OG et al.** Caffeine and human cerebral blood flow: a positron emission tomography study. Life Sci. 1990;47:1141.

137 **Mathew RJ, Wilson WH.** Substance abuse in cerebral blood flow. Am J Psychiatry. 1991;148:292.

138 **Mathew RJ, Wilson WH.** Caffeine consumption withdrawal in cerebral blood flow. Headache. 1985;25:305.

139 **Phelps HM, Phelps CE.** Caffeine ingestion and breast cancer. Cancer. 1988;61:1051.

140 **Caro JP, Dobrowski SR.** Sleep aid and stimulant products. In: American Pharmaceutical Association, eds. The Handbook on Nonprescription Drugs.

9th ed. Washington DC: APhA Publications; 1990:225–41.

141 **Syed IB.** The effects of caffeine. J Am Pharm Assoc. 1976;NS16:568.

142 **Griffiths RR et al.** Human coffee drinking: reinforcing and physical dependence producing effects of caffeine. J Pharmacol Ther. 1986;239:416.

143 **Stern KN et al.** Reinforcing and subjective effects of caffeine in normal human volunteers. Psychopharmacology. 1989;98:81.

144 **Griffiths RR et al.** Low-dose caffeine physical dependence in humans. J Pharmacol Exp Ther. 1990;255:1123.

145 **Silverman K et al.** Withdrawal syndrome after the double-blind cessation of caffeine consumption. N Engl J Med. 1992;327:1160.

146 **Hughes JR et al.** Caffeine self-administration, withdrawal, and adverse effects among coffee drinkers. Arch Gen Psychiatry. 1991;48:611.

147 **Hughes JR et al.** Should caffeine abuse, dependence, or withdrawal be added to DSM-IV and ICD-10. Am J Psychiatry. 1992;149:33.

148 **Hughes JR et al.** Caffeine self-administration and withdrawal: incidence, individual differences and interrelationships. Drug Alcohol Depend. 1993:32: 239.

149 **Reimann HA.** Caffeinism: a cause of long-continued, low-grade fever. JAMA. 1967;202:131.

150 **Colton T et al.** The tolerance of coffee drinkers to caffeine. Clin Pharmacol Ther. 1968;9:31.

151 **Evans SM, Griffiths RR.** Caffeine tolerance and choice in humans. Psychopharmacology. 1992;108;51.

152 **Timson J.** Caffeine. Mutata Res. 1977; 47:1.

153 **Martin TR, Bracken MB.** Association between low birth weight and caffeine consumption during pregnancy. Am J Epidemiol. 1987;126:813.

154 **Leviton A.** Caffeine consumption and the risk of reproductive hazards. J Reprod Med. 1988;88:175.

155 **Srisuphan W, Bracken MB.** Caffeine consumption during pregnancy and association with late spontaneous abortion. Am J Obstet Gynecol. 1986;154: 14.

156 **Berlin CM et al.** Disposition of dietary caffeine in milk, saliva, and plasma of lactating women. Pediatrics. 1984;73: 59.

157 **Berglund B, Hemmingsson P.** Effects of caffeine ingestion on exercise performance at low and high altitudes in cross-country skiers. Int J Sports Med. 1982;3:234–36.

158 **Delbeke FT, Debackere M.** Caffeine: use and abuse in sports. Int J Sports Med. 1984;5:179.

159 **van der Merwe PJ et al.** Caffeine in sport: urinary excretion of caffeine in healthy volunteers after intake of common caffeine-containing beverages. S Afr Med J. 1988;74:163.

160 **Wagner JC.** Enhancement of athletic performance with drugs. Sports Med. 1991;12:250.

Entactogen and Phencyclidine Abuse

Paul W Jungnickel

Classification and History 86-1
MDA, MDMA, MDEA 86-2
Entactogenic Effects 86-2
User Characteristics 86-3
Adverse Effects 86-3
Potential Therapeutic Uses 86-3
LSD 86-3
Entactogenic Effects 86-3
Management of Bad Trips 86-4
Reality therapy 86-4
Drug therapy 86-4
Physiological toxicities 86-4
Long-Term Adverse Effects 86-4
Flashbacks 86-4
Brain damage 86-4
Teratogenicity 86-5

Marijuana 86-5
Definitions and Products 86-5
Entactogenic Effects 86-5
Adverse Physical Effects 86-5
Other Potential Toxic Effects 86-5
Amotivational Syndrome 86-6
Tolerance and Addiction 86-6
Psychological Adverse Effects 86-6
Passive Inhalation 86-7
Fetal Risks 86-7
Phencyclidine (PCP) 86-7
Availability 86-7
Diagnostic Symptoms 86-7
Medical Complications 86-8
Medical Management of Intoxication 86-8
Psychological Adverse Effects 86-8

The term "entactogens" is used to refer to a variety of drugs with mind-altering properties. The term is derived from the Greek routes "en" meaning within and "gen" to produce, combined with the Latin "tactus" which means touch. Entactogens is an appropriate descriptive term, since these drugs promote a "touching within" which generally is regarded as a relaxed, meditative, introspective state, with the person having the sensation of attaining a singular vantage point to explore the inner working of their own psyche. At the same time, they maintain a clear sensorium and the ability to interact with their physical surroundings. The entactogenic effects generally are not dose related after a threshold dose has been reached. Entactogenic substances also produce dose-related sympathomimetic stimulation as well as illusions and hallucinations, so they sometimes are referred to as hallucinogens.

These drugs often are referred to as "psychedelic," meaning mind-infesting, and "psychotomimetic," meaning imitation of psychosis. Both terms are overused, not specifically defined, and imply that these drugs mimic psychosis. This is not generally true, although these drugs can produce perceptual distortions and bizarre reasoning that resemble some aspects of psychotic episodes. However, the facilitation of psychotherapy which has been described with some of these drugs is certainly not characteristic of psychotic behavior. Thus, entactogens is a term which best describes these drugs.

Use patterns of these drugs vary, with many individuals occasionally self-administering them for curiosity or to attain certain goals of self-analysis. In contrast, other individuals will use one or more of these drugs at frequent intervals and on a long-term basis. Habituation to these drugs is rare and they are not regarded as target drugs of addictive disease. A much greater concern with these agents is their propensity to produce toxicities requiring medical intervention.

Classification and History

While these drugs often are discussed as a single group, they can be classified into three groups based upon the neurotransmitters that they resemble.[1-3] *Group 1 compounds* are not structurally similar to any neurotransmitter and include the cannabis derivatives

(e.g., marijuana, hashish); these drugs are discussed in more detail later in the chapter. The drugs in groups 2 and 3 structurally resemble common neurotransmitters, however their pharmacologic effects appear to be produced by more complex mechanisms than the mere stimulation or blockage of a single neurotransmitter. It is important to note that increases and decreases in these neurotransmitters can be accomplished by administration of drugs that do not produce entactogenic, sympathomimetic, or hallucinogenic effects.[4] Table 86.1 provides a summary of the more common entactogenic agents.

Group 2 entactogens are phenylalkylamines structurally resembling the catecholamines and include mescaline, one of approximately 30 psychoactive ingredients found in the peyote cactus. Peyote has been used for centuries in the Americas, and by the year 1760 had been introduced into what is now the U.S.[5] The tops of the peyote cactus are eaten fresh or after they are dried into peyote or mescal buttons.[2] Approximately 8 to 20 buttons are required to produce entactogenic and hallucinogenic effects.

In the 1800s and early 1900s, the use of peyote spread to a number of Native American tribes. *Peyote* is regarded as a sacrament by the Native American Church, which combines elements of both Christianity and Native American religion. Anthropological study also has documented a role of peyote meetings as part of Native American health care.[6] Although the Native American Church has argued that the sacramental use of peyote is protected under religious liberty as provided for by the First Amendment, Supreme Court rulings have supported the rights of individual states to ban peyote use in this religious context.[7]

Mescaline and its derivatives have been referred to as "hallucinogenic amphetamines" since they share the same phenylethylamine structure as amphetamine and norepinephrine. Numerous congeners of mescaline have been produced in an attempt to develop entactogenic agents which do not produce hallucinations. TMA, the α-methyl homologue, was synthesized to produce a more potent mescaline-like drug with a longer duration of action. This drug does not produce entactogenic emotional effects, but instead anger, hostility and megalomanic thoughts, sensory hallucinosis, and moderate sympathetic stimulation when taken in an oral dose of 160 to 200 mg. By comparison, the effective dose of mescaline is 300 to 500 mg.[8,9] Modification of TMA by methylation of the catechol ring produced DOM (STP), a drug with potent mescaline-like effects lasting for about six hours after a 5 mg oral dose. Higher doses of up to 20 mg produce effects which last for up to three days.

The more recently available phenylethylamines are included among the compounds referred to as designer drugs (i.e., derivatives of legitimate pharmaceutical agents which have been "designed" or prepared to circumvent legal restrictions).[2,3,10] MDA, MDMA, and MDEA are the most commonly used agents and will be discussed in more detail. Drugs more recently introduced on the street include 2CB and U4EUH.

Group 3 compounds include agents such as lysergic acid diethylamide (LSD) which resemble serotonin. Besides LSD, other typical drugs in group 3 are plant derivatives: psilocybin, psilocin, ibogaine, harmine, harmaline, and DMT (dimethyltryptamine).

LSD ("acid"), the prototype of the group 3 compounds, was first synthesized by Albert Hoffman of Sandoz Laboratories in 1938.[5] He was working with a series of structural derivatives of lysergic acid, which is the nucleus common to the ergot alkaloids. LSD was the twenty-fifth compound of the series, and thus was given the abbreviation LSD-25. Developed as an analeptic agent, in animals it produced the uterine stimulation, characteristic of the ergot alkaloids, but also caused the animals to become excited and cataleptic. Five years later, after accidently ingesting some LSD-25, Dr. Hoffman experienced restlessness and, as a result, was forced to leave his laboratory and go home. Subsequently, he experienced two hours of intense visual hallucinations of kaleidoscopic images and colors as a result of his LSD ingestion.

Interest in LSD as an agent that could facilitate psychotherapy resulted in the publication of several hundred papers, with the first published reports appearing in 1947. Much of the work focused on the use of LSD as an agent useful in the management of addictive behavior. Soon after the appearance of the first published work, Sandoz provided free LSD-25 to investigators under the trade name Delysid. Two uses were listed. First, it was suggested that LSD could be used to "elicit release of repressed material and provide mental relaxation," particularly in anxiety states and obsessional neurosis. Second, it was suggested that a psychiatrist could take the drug, experience a model psychosis of short duration, and thereby "gain an insight into the world of ideas and sensations of mental patients."

Widespread self-experimentation with LSD, along with growing attention to adverse psychological reactions, resulted in Sandoz discontinuing production of LSD-25 (as well as psilocybin, psilocin, and related congeners) in August 1965. In the U.S., LSD was made a Schedule I controlled substance in 1970 after illicit suppliers had proliferated to meet the a large public demand for the drug.[11] LSD commonly is identified with the "hippie generation" of the 1960s. By the mid 1970s, interest in using the drug had declined substantially. However, since the mid 1980s, a resurgence in use of the drug has been seen particularly among individuals in their teens and twenties.[2] In a National Institute on Drug Abuse report, the percentage of high school seniors reporting LSD use in the previous year increased from 4.8% in 1988 to 5.6% in 1992.[12]

Psilocybin is perhaps the next most commonly used group 3 agent. It is found in three major genera of mushrooms ("shrooms"): Psilocybe, Panaelous, and Conocybe, and was first isolated by Dr. Hoffman in 1958.[13] These mushrooms also contain psilocin which is about half as potent as psilocybin. Both wild and cultivated mushrooms vary in potency, so one strong mushroom may contain as much of psilocin or psilocybin as ten weak ones.[2] Typical doses of two to four mushrooms have been reported in adolescents and young adults.[13]

MDA, MDMA, MDEA
Entactogenic Effects

1. P.S., a 35-year-old businessman, is seen by his physician for a routine physical examination. On questioning regarding drug use, he reports that he has used MDMA on several occasions recently to promote self-confidence in social situations. How is MDMA typically used, and what are the characteristic effects that P.S. might experience?

MDMA (Table 86.1) has become popular as an entactogenic agent which generally produces manageable and comfortable entactogenic effects with the person typically retaining a clear sensorium. It typically is taken in doses of 75 to 150 mg. After about 30 minutes, the user may experience an initial period of mild anxiety accompanied by a 10 to 15 mm Hg rise in systolic blood pressure, tachycardia, bruxism, jaw clenching, and increased motor activity. By one hour, these effects will be replaced by a period of quiet and relaxed euphoria. The intensity of the entactogenic effect fades after about two hours, so a "booster dose" of 50 to 75 mg often is taken which prolongs the effects for another two to three

Table 86.1		Classification of Entactogenic Agents	
Group	Drug Category	Neurotransmitters	Common Drugs
1	Cannabis derivatives	None	Marijuana Hashish
2	Phenylalkylamines	Catecholamines	3,4,5-trimethoxyphenylethylamine (Mescaline) 3,4,5-trimethoxyphenylisopropylamine (TMA) 2,5-dimethoxy-4-methylphenylisopropylamine (DOM, STP) 3,4-methylenedioxyamphetamine (MDA) 3,4-methylenedioxymethamphetamine (MDMA) 3,4-methylenedioxyethamphetamine (MDEA) 4-bromo-2,5-dimethoxyphenethylamine (2CB) 4-methylaminorex (U4EUH)
3	Lysergic acid diethylamide and various plant derivatives	Serotonin	Lysergic acid diethylamide (LSD-25, LSD-49) Psilocybin Psilocin Ibogaine Harmine Harmaline Diethyltryptamine (DMT)

hours. However, residual autonomic effects may occur for up to 24 hours, including fatigue, nausea, anorexia, and muscle twitching.

Autonomic effects also may be present. Following about 30 minutes of anxiety, jaw clenching, and hyperactivity, P.S. may experience feelings of empathy and closeness, along with a sense of insightfulness and inner contentment, euphoria, and enjoyable changes in time and visual perception.[14,15] He also may perceive increased ability to interact with, or be open with, others; decreased aggression, defensiveness, and fear; decreased separation and alienation from others; and increased awareness of emotions.

User Characteristics

2. How does P.S. compare to the typical MDMA user?

Such individuals frequently are affluent and well educated. MDMA also has been used by New Age seekers as an adjunct to spiritual pursuit.[16] A recent phenomenon, beginning around 1990, is the use of MDMA at dance (rave) clubs or parties, or by other recreational users.[14] These individuals seem to be more concerned about having "fun" rather than receiving insight and often combine MDMA with LSD or other hallucinogens. Patterns of use vary from those individuals who have used MDMA on one or several occasions to those individuals who use it on a routine basis. P.S. appears to be typical of the young professionals who use MDMA as a means to gain further self-insight.[15,17]

Adverse Effects

3. What serious adverse effects might P.S. be at risk for due to his MDMA use?

While the perception of many is that MDMA is a drug with little potential for toxicity, the user may be at risk for serious adverse effects. Deaths due to hyperthermia accompanied by coagulopathy and rhabdomyolysis have been reported, particularly in individuals using MDMA at rave clubs or parties where high levels of physical activity apparently increases the risk of hyperthermia accompanied by skeletal muscle damage.[18-21] Patients experiencing these adverse effects should be managed with supportive care, as there are no specific therapies to antagonize these MDMA effects.

Possible MDMA damage to brain serotonin neurons has been demonstrated in experimental animals.[22,23] Currently, there is little evidence to support the occurrence of this toxicity in humans, although MDMA users had a 26% reduction in cerebrospinal fluid 5-hydroxyindolacetic acid levels when compared to controls in one study.[24] Damage to serotonin neurons has been suggested as a possible mechanism for the reactions seen in some MDMA users, which have included severe anxiety and panic reactions, as well as chronic paranoid psychosis and psychosis with flashbacks.[25-30] However, these reactions frequently have occurred in individuals using high doses of MDMA on a frequent basis or in those with a history of psychiatric disease or polydrug abuse. Thus, it is difficult to evaluate the true role of MDMA in producing these effects.

P.S. risks possible hyperthermia or skeletal muscle damage; brain damage also could occur.

Potential Therapeutic Uses

4. One of P.S.'s reasons for experimenting with MDMA is that he has heard that it, and other similar drugs (e.g., MDA), are beneficial psychotherapeutic agents. What benefits could be anticipated?

MDA was first synthesized in 1910, but its entactogenic properties did not become known until the 1960s. Claudio Naranjio perhaps best described the use of MDA in psychotherapy, utilizing the state of mild euphoria, sense of detachment or out-of-body experience, and relaxed introspection to facilitate examination of

emotional issues.[31] Doses of 50 to 150 mg produce these effects for about eight hours, while at higher doses hallucinosis and moderate sympathetic activity are produced. MDA became a popular recreational drug, being given the street name "the love drug" due to its reputation as an aphrodisiac and facilitator of dancing and other gregarious party activities. Illegal production, unrestricted public use, and reports of toxicities and deaths led to MDA being classified as a Schedule I drug.

MDMA is produced by N-methylation of MDA, resulting in a drug with more comfortable and manageable entactogenic effects. A variety of names have been given to MDMA by the public including "Ecstasy," "XTC," "Adam," and "M&Ms." While MDMA was found to be useful as a facilitator of the psychotherapeutic interview, the media became aware of anecdotal reports of MDMA self-experimentation by both psychiatrists and other individuals.[32] In 1985, the Drug Enforcement Administration (DEA) classified MDMA as a Schedule I drug, and subsequently MDMA's popularity has soared with illicit supplies of the drug proliferating. Shortly thereafter, MDEA (Eve) became available as a nonscheduled substitute for MDMA.[33]

To date, MDEA and other related amphetamine derivatives have not been scheduled by the DEA. It should be pointed out to P.S. that the available data are insufficient to establish MDMA as a beneficial psychotherapeutic agent. Opinion remains divided. Advocates point to untapped therapeutic utility, while detractors express concern over potential central nervous system toxicity.[34,35]

Lysergic Acid Diethylamide (LSD)
Entactogenic Effects

5. S.W., a 17-year-old female high school student, regularly consumes alcohol and uses marijuana ≈1 time a week. She takes LSD while at a party with friends. Assuming this is her first LSD use, what effects is she likely to experience?

LSD is a very potent hallucinogen; it is active in doses ranging from 30 to 300 μg. At doses of 30 to 50 μg, the user will likely experience mild stimulatory effects along with mental changes such as spaciness, decreased perception of time, and mild euphoria. At doses of approximately 150 μg, the user's experience ("trip") typically would include mild to moderate sympathomimetic stimulation, profound visual hallucinosis, and sensations of disordered integration of sensory input. For example, sounds and music may be perceived as visual imagery, odors may be felt, and inanimate objects may assume life-like characteristics. Tolerance develops rapidly, so that with a few days of daily use most people can tolerate a 300 μg dose without major psychedelic effects. A more recently-available LSD derivative, called LSD-49, is sold on the street under the name "illusion" and appears to provide more intense visual effects than an equal dose of LSD-25.[2]

The onset of effects usually occurs within the first hour after oral ingestion of LSD and the peak intensity of effects occurs during the first two to three hours. The hallucinogenic and sympathomimetic effects wear off over the next five to ten hours, and during this time, the entactogenic effects predominate. A return to a normal psychological state occurs within 8 to 12 hours after LSD ingestion.

6. S.W. received ≈150 μg of LSD. She lost track of time and became euphoric, then experienced agitation and a strong sense that the furniture in the room was alive. Her hallucinations lasted about 6 hours. She felt normal the next morning. What differences in effects might S.W. experience if she were to use hallucinogenic agents other than LSD?

Mescaline and psilocybin are the next most commonly used hallucinogenic agents. While they are much less potent than LSD, the user often finds that their effects are quite similar when consumed in equipotent amounts. Cross tolerance occurs between the three agents. Much of what is sold on the street as mescaline and psilocybin actually contains LSD.[13,36] S.W. would experience effects similar to LSD with mescaline or psilocybin should she use them in equipotent amounts.

Management of Bad Trips

7. Reality Therapy. Several months later, S.W. was at a party with friends. The last few weeks had been particularly stressful in that she had not been doing well in school and was having frequent disagreements with her parents. A white powder in a glass jar labeled "Magic Powder" was brought to the party, dissolved in orange juice, and each person was given a small glass to drink. S.W. decided to join the group in the "trip" hoping that it might take her mind off her current difficulties. Within an hour she started to feel nervous and experienced mild nausea. After another hour, she became hysterical, crying and yelling about being crazy. Some of the others at the party attempted to talk to S.W., reassuring her that she was not crazy and that she had just taken a drug. She calmed down somewhat but then her anxiety and hysteria resumed despite further reassurance from her friends. About 3 hours after ingesting the "Magic Powder," she was very anxious, was sweating, her pupils were maximally dilated, and she was talking about being "out of control, out of her mind." Three friends who were at the party took S.W. to the hospital. What was the likely cause of this hysteria, and how should S.W. initially be managed?

The most frequently encountered adverse reaction associated with entactogenic drugs is a mental state of acute anxiety and fear which commonly is referred to as a "bad trip." Users may be able to calm themselves without outside intervention, and users who self-administer these drugs frequently use relaxation breathing exercises and other techniques to resolve inner stress while they are under their influence.[162]

The treatment of people experiencing "bad trips" has not changed in the past 30 years. The initial approach is called "reality therapy" and consists of "talking down" the fear and panic. This process also tends to reassure the person that she is in a safe physical environment and that the drug effects will subside in a few hours. Severe restraint should not be used because it may lead to rhabdomyolysis and renal failure.[163] Most of these "bummers" are resolved during the trip in which they arose, however, some may last for up to 24 to 48 hours. In general, these adverse psychological reactions occur in ≤1% of ingestions of these drugs.[37–40]

S.W. should be taken to a quiet, relaxed setting and should be assisted in focusing on explanations for the uncertainties that are causing her panic. While S.W. has previous experience using entactogenic agents, her current emotional state and the setting of a party likely increased her chances of having an unpleasant experience.

8. Drug Therapy. Despite reality therapy, S.W.'s fear and anxiety have not been alleviated. What drug treatments should be considered?

If the talk down approach is not successful in resolving the panic, drug therapy may be considered. Sedation with an oral benzodiazepine [e.g., diazepam (Valium) 5 to 20 mg] likely will be effective in alleviating panic. However, benzodiazepine administration will not stop a "bad trip," but will merely provide sedation.[41,42,163,164] Supportive talk down should be continued. Phenothiazines, and chlorpromazine (Thorazine) in particular, should not be used for acute management of "bad trips" because they may potentiate panic, cause orthostatic hypotension, and produce anticholinergic toxicity or mental depression.[43,44] If mild sedation does not stop the panic, or if the user requests that all entactogenic

and hallucinogenic effects be stopped, a large dose of an oral or intravenous benzodiazepine can be administered. This will permit the user to sleep through the duration of the entactogenic effects, which will last at most for 6 to 12 hours for the various entactogenic and hallucinogenic drugs.[45] Patients should be monitored closely during this period of benzodiazepine-induced sleep.

9. Physiological Toxicities. S.W. responded adequately to 10 mg of diazepam and verbal support, so no further therapy was necessary. What are the potential physiological toxicities that should be monitored for in S.W.?

After entactogenic drug use, a variety of physiological effects may occur that are severe enough to require therapy. A potentially fatal syndrome resembling malignant hyperthermia, similar to that seen with MDA and its derivatives, also has been seen with LSD ingestion.[46] In patients who manifest symptoms of muscular rigidity, diaphoresis, obtundation, mydriasis, nystagmus, and combative bizarre behavior, malignant hyperthermia should be suspected and rectal temperature should be monitored.

Since toxicities of entactogenic drugs can affect various organ systems, an electrocardiogram (ECG) should be performed, along with routine renal and liver function tests. Routine neurological monitoring also should be performed. Another important toxicity centers around ergot-like vascular spasm leading to arterial occlusion and focal neurological deficits.[47,48] The user should be examined for patent peripheral pulses, normal nail bed filling, temperature of extremities, and focal neurological signs.

Since the specific drug taken by S.W. has not been identified, the potential toxicities of the various entactogenic agents should be considered. S.W.'s rectal temperature is monitored, but remains below 38 °C. ECG, renal and liver function tests, and peripheral pulses and circulation are within normal limits. Neurological examination gradually returns to normal.

Long-Term Adverse Effects

10. What are the possible long-term effects might S.W. be at risk for were she to continue the use of entactogenic drugs on a prolonged basis?

Flashbacks are recurrences of part or all of the entactogenic drug experiences following a period of normal consciousness in a person who previously has used these drugs. The estimated prevalence of flashbacks has ranged from 15% to 77% of entactogenic drug users, although these estimates seem high considering that many people have taken ten or fewer trips and have never experienced a flashback. Flashbacks seem to occur more commonly in frequent users of entactogenic drugs and usually last a few hours, but may last from minutes to days to months. Flashbacks are treated like acute drug-induced events.[42,49,50,162]

Brain Damage. The possibility of "brain damage" resulting from the use of entactogenic agents has been difficult to establish since subtle changes in cognitive ability are difficult to document, and it is almost impossible to arrange matched pair controls for case control studies. A small percentage of persons who took many doses of entactogenic drugs (mostly LSD) during their late teens and early twenties have subsequently become "acid burnouts" or "acid casualties." These individuals have the clinical characteristics of chronic, undifferentiated schizophrenics.[42,162] While these individuals are socially disabled and treatment resistant, there is no evidence for a direct or singular drug etiology. Their psychological profile is the same as that of organic, chronic, undifferentiated schizophrenics. The low frequency with which these cases occur, and the similarity of the cases to organic schizophrenia, suggest that the entactogenic drug experiences may have merely unmasked underlying psychiatric conditions in these individuals.[51,52] Furthermore, those individuals who developed long-standing psychosis after LSD use appear to have a high incidence of preLSD psychopathology and familial mental illness.[53,54] Thus, it seems that these individuals may represent a singular personality type with a noncompetitive and eccentric nature which seems to seek out entactogenic experiences and enjoy the benefits, rather than a situation where the entactogenic drugs biochemically change a person into such a personality type.[55]

Teratogenicity. Concern over the potential teratogenicity of LSD arose after chromosomal damage was observed when LSD was added to a test tube containing a suspension of human white blood cells.[56] Case reports of birth defects have been reported, but it is difficult establish causal links due to the impurity of street drug supplies and the concomitant use of other drugs. For example, five mothers who took LSD during their pregnancies gave birth to children with defects but all five had used other drugs during their pregnancies.[57-61] In two other reports, one mother took LSD twice while another took LSD numerous times during pregnancy, yet both gave birth to normal infants.[62,63] Thus, studies published in the 1960s and early 1970s failed to provide compelling evidence to implicate LSD as a teratogenic agent when taken before or during pregnancy, and there has not been any recently published work on this issue.[165] Potential teratogenic effects of LSD when used by males before conception have not been studied.[64,65]

Thus, from the above information, it is apparent that S.W. may be at risk for a variety of long-term adverse effects, although the degree of risk for any specific effect is difficult to assess.

Marijuana

Definitions and Products

The entactogenic, euphoric, and psychoactive effects of various species of the Cannabis plant are due to the pharmacological effects of the cannabinoids, with Δ-9-tetrahydrocannabinol (THC) and cannabidiol (CBD) being the two most frequently studied as isolated compounds. However, there are many other chemical constituents of the Cannabis plant and the pharmacology of the crude plant extracts is similar to, but somewhat different than, the effects of the isolated chemical constituents.[66-69] *Cannabis sativa* can be grown in most parts of the world, and is the primary source of marijuana sold in the U.S.

In the U.S., the dried, chopped leaves and flowers of the Cannabis plant ("grass," "pot," "weed," "smoke," "boo," "mary jane") are smoked after being rolled into a cigarette paper ("joint," "reefer," "number," "doobie," "roach") or placed into a pipe. A typical joint weighs from 0.5 to 1 gm and has a tetrahydrocannabinol (THC) content which varies from 5 to 100 mg, depending upon the strength of the marijuana. A "bong" or "carburetor" refers to a tube which is fabricated from a cardboard cylinder, such as from a roll of toilet paper or paper towels, or a glass or wood device with both ends open. This device also contains a small hole along the surface to hold the pipe bowl or a rolled cigarette. The smoker uses the device by closing off the distal end of the cylinder with his or her hand and inhales only through the burning Cannabis which fills the chamber with smoke. After this, the smoker removes the hand from the distal end while maintaining inhalation, so that all the smoke in the chamber is delivered to the lungs in one dose ("hit," "blast").

Marijuana usually is sold in ounce ("lid," "can") or kilogram ("kilo," "brick") amounts. The potency (i.e., THC content) varies with the product being sold. The typical leaf contains about 3% THC, although lower quality products are available with THC content ranging from 0.5% to 1%. Sinsemilla consists of the dried material from the tops of female plants and, when carefully cultivated, can contain from 6% to 10% THC. Hashish ("hash," "tem-

ple balls") consists of the raw resin the Cannabis plant. It can be pressed into cakes, balls, or sticks which are eaten or smoked. Hashish may contain from 7% to 12% THC. The oils can be extracted from the plant by use of organic solvents to produce "hash oil," which may contain up to 60% THC.[5,70]

Entactogenic Effects

11. C.W., a 16-year-old male high school student, occasionally drinks alcohol but has never used other drugs. One evening, when he is out with some friends, he decides to join in with his friends who are smoking pot. What effects might C.W. experience?

The desired effects sought by must marijuana users include sedation, mental relaxation, euphoria, and mild entactogenic effects. Other effects which usually are perceived as pleasurable include silliness, subjective slowing of time, gregariousness, hunger, and mild perceptual changes of all the senses which engender an absorbing fascination with music, eating, and other sensual and sensory activities. The state of mind generated is referred to by numerous colloquial terms including "stoned," "high," "loaded," and "getting a buzz on." In the first three or four minutes, the user will likely experience numbness and tingling of the extremities, lightheadedness, loss of concentration, and a floating sensation. Some of these effects are thought to be due to hyperventilation which is associated with deep inhalation of the smoke and breath holding, both of which are done to allow maximum drug absorption in the lungs. Over the first 10 to 30 minutes, the user may experience tachycardia (with possible palpitations), mild diaphoresis, conjunctival injection, drying of the mouth, weakness, postural hypotension, periods of tremulousness, incoordination, and ataxia, as well as the mental effects described above. These effects usually resolve in one to three hours and are followed by a 30 to 60 minute period of sleepiness. After this, there is a return to normal consciousness. When taken orally, Cannabis products may have an onset of effects in 45 to 60 minutes and a duration of effects lasting for up to 24 hours.

C.W. initially experiences transient peripheral numbness and feels like he is floating, then he becomes very relaxed, giddy, and hungry. He notices that his heart is "pounding" and becomes dizzy when he stands up. Several hours later, he becomes sleepy. He finds that he feels normal once he awakens.

Adverse Physical Effects

12. The next night, C.W. and his friends smoke another joint, then decide to drive across town to their favorite "hang-out." Is it safe for them to do this?

Various studies have demonstrated that marijuana use can produce slowed psychomotor responses in chronic users as well as acutely intoxicated individuals.[71,72] Studies using aircraft simulators have demonstrated decrements in pilot performance lasting for up to 24 hours after marijuana use.[73-75] Thus, while the degree of psychomotor decrement does not appear to be as severe as that which occurs with alcohol, C.W. and his friends should not operate motor vehicles and other dangerous equipment for at least 24 hours.[76]

Other Potential Toxic Effects

13. What marijuana toxicities might C.W. be at risk for?

Several acute physiological complications have been associated with marijuana use. Included among these are an anaphylactic reaction to THC.[77] An outbreak of salmonellosis in 85 people resulted from marijuana to mouth transmission of the bacterium.[78] Marijuana samples purchased on the street have been found to be contaminated with *Aspergillus* and represent a potential infectious source.[79] Cannabis has been reported to induce seizures in some epileptic patients, although some Cannabis constituents may have antiepileptic properties.[80-82]

Serious morbidity has occurred with the use of various different cannabis products. The intravenous injection of a boiled broth of cannabis has produced myalgias, gastrointestinal upset, tachycardia, hypotension, fever, rhabdomyolysis, azotemia, and leukocytosis in the majority of reported patients.[83] Smoking ''AMP'' (marijuana soaked in formaldehyde) produced psychomotor retardation and immobility lasting for up to a week.[84] Marijuana mixed with insecticides, rodenticides, and other chemicals (''WAC'') has produced varying bizarre symptoms depending upon the particular chemical contaminant.[85] Phencyclidine should be suspected in patients reporting the use of ''superweed,'' and they should be managed as discussed below.

Potential pulmonary complications resulting from smoking marijuana are concerning, although acute oral and intravenous THC administration produces vasodilation and smoking or eating marijuana has been reported to relieve exercise-induced bronchospasm.[86] More recently it has been demonstrated that the bronchodilator properties of THC do not protect against the development of acute airway hyperactivity in cigarette smokers, and irritants in marijuana smoke actually may augment the effect of tobacco in increasing airway hyperactivity.[87] Impairment of pulmonary alveolar macrophage function and ciliary clearance of particulate matter from airways also has been seen as an acute effect of Cannabis smoking.[88] However, in contrast to the effects seen with short-term use, symptoms of airway obstruction have been documented in chronic marijuana users.[87,89,90] In addition, chronic cough, laryngitis, hoarseness, bronchitis, and cellular changes, typical of cigarette smokers, have been reported in chronic Cannabis smokers.[91-94]

Chronic marijuana users theoretically might be at increased risk for cancer since, when compared to cigarette smoke, smoke from marijuana joints contain higher concentrations of several key carcinogens.[95-97] Furthermore, case reports have implicated marijuana as a potential cause of cancer of the aerodigestive tract, including the mouth, upper jaw, throat, and larynx.[98-100] Evidence that marijuana adversely alters functioning of the immune system remains controversial. The *in vitro* work in this area suffers from methodological flaws and the work which more closely simulates clinical situations provides less than compelling evidence.[101]

From the above discussion, it is evident that C.W. and his friends may be at risk for a variety of toxic effects that have been associated with marijuana. However, the data are insufficient to allow precise quantification of the specific risks of various toxicities.

Amotivational Syndrome

14. C.W. found his experience with marijuana to be pleasurable and continues to use it over the next year. He now is to the point where he smokes it on a daily basis. He was previously an honor student but now his grades have dropped substantially. Could this be the result of his Cannabis use?

Both acute and chronic use of marijuana impair mental performance, and chronic use has been alleged to produce an amotivational syndrome.[102,103,166] Some investigators have even suggested that structural brain damage is associated with Cannabis use and that this could account for such a syndrome.[104-108] Other investigators have failed to find meaningful associations between Cannabis use and any amotivational syndrome.[109-114] Thus, the existence of such a syndrome remains controversial, and understanding of this issue is limited by the lack of published research during the past two decades. However, since C.W. is now using Cannabis

on a daily basis, both acute and chronic intoxication may be contributing to his decline in grades.

Tolerance and Addiction

15. Is C.W. addicted to marijuana?

The 1990s have produced different patterns of marijuana use in that many individuals smoke marijuana in a chronic and compulsive manner. The potency of currently available marijuana products also appears to be much greater than the products available in the 1960s.[2] These factors have cast new light on the issue of addiction.

Tolerance to the psychoactive effects of marijuana does develop, and, to obtain the full range of Cannabis effects, chronic users must either increase the dose or abstain for a period of days or weeks to regain initial sensitivity. Thus, tolerance develops to both the physiological and psychological effects of Cannabis.

Dependence, characterized by a physical withdrawal syndrome, occurs after chronic high-dose use, although the cumulative dose and duration of use needed to produce dependence have been quite variable. Typical withdrawal symptoms include irritability, restlessness, decreased appetite, sleep disturbances, sweating, tremor, nausea, vomiting, and diarrhea. The flu-like symptoms of dysphoria and malaise also may occur.[115-119] The increase in chronic high-dose Cannabis use has focused attention on treatment strategies for marijuana dependence.[120,121]

From the limited information we have about C.W., it is not possible to accurately determine if he is physically dependent upon Cannabis. However, he seems to be using marijuana in a compulsive manner on a daily basis, and has experienced a decline in school performance which has coincided with his increased use of the substance.

Psychological Adverse Effects

16. What other adverse psychological effects could occur in C.W. and his friends due to their Cannabis use?

A frequently occurring adverse effect of marijuana is a syndrome consisting of anxiety, paranoia, depersonalization, disorientation, and confusion which can lead to panic states and incapacitating fear. This condition is best managed by ''reality therapy'' as previously discussed, as well as avoidance of stimulant drugs (e.g., coffee, tea, cola, cocaine, amphetamines) or stressful stimuli. The dysphoria and anxiety generally resolve within a few hours of beginning such an approach. Oral benzodiazepines in doses equivalent to 5 to 10 mg of diazepam may be used to manage more severe panic reactions that do not respond to comforting reassurance, but this is rarely required. These adverse psychological reactions commonly occur with inexperienced cannabis users, high doses, concomitant use of other psychoactive drugs, and overly stressful situations. Flashbacks associated with marijuana are reported rarely and their etiology is unexplained.[122-129] There is also some evidence indicating that individuals who experience such psychotomimetic reactions have either pre-existing psychiatric disease or a family history of schizophrenia (suggesting a genetic predisposition).[130,131] However, a Swedish study has identified a risk of schizophrenia in high dose consumers of Cannabis (use on >50 occasions) that is six times higher than in nonusers.[132] This association persisted after adjustment to allow for social background as well as the persistence of other psychiatric illness. However, the authors correctly point out that statistical associations alone are not sufficient to establish cause and effect relationships.

With regard to C.W. and his friends, it is difficult to assess the precise risk of adverse psychological effects related to their Cannabis usage. From the above discussion, it is apparent that a wide variety of factors will influence this risk.

Passive Inhalation

17. One of C.W.'s friends does not use Cannabis, but frequents parties where marijuana is smoked. Could passive inhalation of the smoke from another persons's "joint" produce intoxication or a positive urine test?

Drug testing has become more prevalent as industry and society have responded to issues of workplace impairment and the provision of assistance to individuals abusing drugs.[167] Urine testing may be performed to periodically screen individuals in occupations where impairment could endanger public safety, to further evaluate individuals suspected of using drugs, or to confirm compliance of individuals in recovery programs. NIDA guidelines for testing of federal employees prescribe initial screening for marijuana using an immunoassay with a cutoff calibration of 100 ng/mL. Positive results obtained via immunoassay should be confirmed by gas chromatography-mass spectrometry (GC-MS) with a cutoff of 15 ng/mL.[168,169] The lower cutoff for the GC-MS assay is due to its greater specificity for 11-nor-Δ9-THC-9-carboxcyclic acid, the major urinary THC metabolite. In contrast, the immunoassays detect THC metabolites in general.[170]

Drug testing for Cannabis is influenced by the extensive fat storage of THC and its metabolites. Since these substances are released slowly from fat stores, urine samples may test positive for many days after an individual ceases the use of Cannabis. Using the NIDA recommended procedures, it commonly is believed that urine tests can remain positive for up to seven days after a single use of marijuana and for up to 30 days after the cessation of chronic use.[169] In chronic smokers, urine cannabinoid concentrations measured via immunoassay remained above 100 ng/mL for as long as 45 days after cessation of use and above 20 ng/mL for up to 77 days.[133]

It has been found that sufficient smoke can be inhaled to produce positive urine tests.[134,135] Intoxication from sidestream smoke can occur in environments with high levels of marijuana smoke. In one study, the intoxicating effects of sidestream smoke from 16 marijuana cigarettes was similar to the effects found after the smoking of one marijuana cigarette, and positive urine cannabinoid tests at the 100 ng/mL cutoff were found in two of five subjects.[134]

Thus, under extreme conditions, C.W.'s friend could be at risk for intoxication. His urine could test positive for up to several days after exposure to sidestream marijuana smoke.

Fetal Risks

18. Among C.W.'s group of friends are several high school girls who smoke marijuana. What are the risks to their offspring as a result of their Cannabis use?

The fetal risks of maternal marijuana use are largely unknown. Direct reproductive effects on the sperm and ova, as well as alterations in some of the hormonal systems that affect reproduction, have been demonstrated in various studies, although these effects appear to be reversible. Associations have been demonstrated between marijuana and other drug use by women during pregnancy and birth defects in offspring, although causal links to marijuana have yet to be established. Since THC crosses the placenta and also is concentrated in breast milk, marijuana use during pregnancy or lactation results in exposure of the fetus/infant to this substance.[136–140,171]

Marijuana users could have children with an increased risk of nonlymphoblastic leukemia should they smoke marijuana during or shortly before pregnancy. In this study, a tenfold increase in the risk of nonlymphoblastic leukemia was found in offspring of

mothers who smoked marijuana just before or during pregnancy. No other drug use (including tobacco, alcohol, or pain killers) was associated with such a risk. The children exposed to marijuana *in utero* also developed leukemia at an earlier age (19 months versus 93 months) compared to those who were not.[141]

C.W.'s friends should be aware that marijuana use might harm the fetus, can cause leukemia in their offspring, and should be avoided if breast-feeding.

Phencyclidine (PCP)
Availability

Phencyclidine [1-(1-phenylcyclohexyl)piperidine, arylcycloalkylamine, PCP] has sympathomimetic, hallucinogenic, and dissociative anesthetic properties. It was initially tested by Parke-Davis, under the trade name Sernyl, as an intravenous anesthetic.[142] Subsequent reports of postanesthetic dysphoric reactions caused the drug to be withdrawn from human use in 1965, but it was reintroduced in 1967 as Sernylan and was marked as a veterinary anesthetic until 1978. At that time the manufacture and sale of phencyclidine became illegal. Parke-Davis currently markets ketamine (Ketalar), a structurally similar anesthetic, which has caused adverse reactions similar to phencyclidine in some patients. Although abuse has decreased, Ketamine ("monkey morphine," "Vitamin K," "super K") continues to be available on the street and is used at rave parties and night clubs. Increased abuse by veterinarians, who have access to Ketamine through their practice setting, also has been reported.[2,143,144,172,173]

PCP first appeared on the street as the "PeaCe Pill" and "hog" in San Francisco and New York in 1966, and later as "angel dust," "dust," or "crystal."[145] The use of PCP was short-lived, presumably due to unexpected reactions encountered by users. Subsequently, it has reappeared as a substitute for substances such as LSD, mescaline, peyote, psilocybin, THC, MDA, amphetamine, and cocaine.

While oral, intranasal, and parenteral routes of administration are used by some, smoking PCP allows for more careful titration of dose and pharmacological effects. Currently, the most common route of PCP administration is smoking PCP that has been applied to parsley, marijuana ("dusted joint," "superweed," "sherm"), or tobacco cigarettes. The combination of cocaine and PCP in a freebase smoking mixture is called "SpaceBase."

Users of PCP products are at risk of encountering PCP analogs or other contaminants. When PCP is synthesized by clandestine laboratories, various analogs and intermediates rarely are removed from the finished product. Little is known about their pharmacological effects, potency, and drug interactions.[146–148] PCC, a synthetic intermediate, contains a labile cyano group which produces hydrogen cyanide upon heating.[149] Cyanide intoxication is a theoretical concern when smoking PCC contaminated products.

Diagnostic Symptoms

19. J.R., an 18-year-old male, was brought to the emergency department by police for violent, combative behavior. His friends said that he was smoking a "dusted joint." He appears agitated, diaphoretic, and disoriented. His vital signs include blood pressure of 160/100 mm Hg, pulse of 130 beats/min, respirations of 32/minute, and temperature of 101 °F. He has vertical and horizontal nystagmus. What drug is most likely to be responsible for J.R.'s presenting symptoms?

Combined horizontal and vertical nystagmus is quite specific for phencyclidine intoxication, while, in contrast, horizontal nystagmus can be seen during intoxication with a variety of drugs including phenytoin (Dilantin), diphenhydramine (Benadryl), ethanol, and most sedative-hypnotic drugs. Horizontal and vertical nystagmus are not consistently present throughout the course of phencyclidine intoxication but usually can be elicited during the first hour of observation.

The disorientation and combativeness seen in J.R. can occur following the use of most psychoactive drugs. Fever, tachycardia, and hyperthermia also are not particularly useful in the identification of the specific psychoactive agent. The most useful diagnostic symptom in J.R. is the horizontal and vertical nystagmus.

Medical Complications

20. What other symptoms of PCP intoxication should be anticipated in J.R?

A wide variety of pharmacological effects and symptoms of intoxication are seen with PCP use. These will vary with the PCP dose, route of administration, and serum concentration.[150,151] Smoking allows the user to titrate the dose of PCP to the desired degree of intoxication. Oral, intranasal, and intravenous use of PCP make dose titration more difficult and contribute to more serious toxic effects.

In low doses, PCP produces inebriation, ataxia, changes in body image, and a dissociative feeling. Horizontal and/or vertical nystagmus frequently are present. The anesthetic effect of phencyclidine raises the patient's pain threshold. Amnesia may occur following intoxication.

Increasing doses of PCP typically result in agitation, combativeness, and psychosis. The action of PCP on the autonomic nervous system becomes more prominent and is characterized by a confusing combination of adrenergic, cholinergic, and dopaminergic effects. Elevated blood pressure, tachycardia, tachypnea, and hyperthermia are symptoms which can be seen in moderately intoxicated patients.

Agitated and combative patients also may have feelings of great strength. This combined with the anesthetic effects of PCP may place patients at risk for serious injury. They may fail to stop injurious activity since they have no pain sensation. The anesthetic effect of phencyclidine also may make patient restraint difficult.

Large doses of PCP produce marked central nervous system depression to the point of unconsciousness. Nystagmus no longer may be present. Additional severe physiological effects that may compromise the patient's condition include respiratory depression, seizures, and acidosis. Rhabdomyolysis, potentially leading to renal failure, may particularly occur in the presence of acidemia.[152,153] Opisthotonic posturing and muscular rigidity occur frequently in the severely intoxicated patient.

J.R. should be observed for these various symptoms to enable proper assessment of the course of his intoxication; combative behavior is especially dangerous since he might injure himself or others.

Medical Management of Intoxication

21. How should J.R. be treated?

PCP-intoxicated patients should be placed in seclusion with environmental stimuli kept to a minimum. Attempts to "talk down" the user should be avoided since they may trigger a combative response. Chemical restraint frequently is needed to manage patient symptoms. Benzodiazepines are useful in managing anxious, agitated patients with mild to moderate phencyclidine intoxication. Patients who are combative and psychotic may present a danger to themselves or the health care professionals involved in their treatment. These symptoms may be controlled effectively with haloperidol (Haldol).[154] Chlorpromazine (Thorazine) is less effective and should be avoided due to the possibility of precipitating sei-

zures or hypotension. Control of extreme agitation, seizures, and hyperthermia are important to prevent rhabdomyolysis, as well as secondary myocardial, renal, or hepatic dysfunction. Anxiolytics, anticonvulsants, and cooling measures should be used as necessary. Diazepam (Valium) is a useful anticonvulsant for managing PCP-induced seizures. Supportive therapy should be used to manage other symptoms of phencyclidine intoxication.

J.R. should be secluded with minimal stimulation and given haloperidol if needed for psychosis and combativeness, and anxiolytics, anticonvulsants, or cooling as needed.

22. What treatment should be administered to J.R. in order to enhance the elimination of phencyclidine?

Harmonic mean elimination half-lives of 14 hours (IV administration), 24 hours (oral administration), and 17 hours (administration via smoking) have been reported in phencyclidine pharmacokinetic studies.[155,156] In the absence of aggressive measures to remove phencyclidine from the body, an elimination half-life of 12.5 hours was reported in a massively overdosed patient.[157] Thus, measures which promote removal of PCP from the body are useful in decreasing the period of intoxication.

Being a basic substance, PCP is secreted into the acidic milieu of the stomach and then reabsorbed in the alkaline environment of the duodenum.[158] This gastrointestinal recycling process may account for waxing and waning of phencyclidine intoxication symptoms. Activated charcoal adsorbs phencyclidine and may be effective in interrupting the enteric recycling process. Doses of 30 to 40 gm of charcoal administered orally or via nasogastric tube are recommended every six to eight hours. Continuous nasogastric suction also has been recommended as a means for removal of PCP.[150]

Intravenous administration of acidifying agents such as hydrochloric acid and ammonium chloride can greatly increase urinary excretion of PCP. However, given that only a small portion of drug is excreted renally, urinary acidification may not produce a clinically significant increase in drug elimination from the body. However, by lowering blood pH, these acidifying agents have been touted as useful due to their effects in shifting drug out of the central nervous system in patients requiring ventilatory assistance, experiencing convulsions or prolonged or deep coma, or who are deteriorating.[150]

Based upon the forgoing discussion, it appears that activated charcoal would be appropriate in J.R.'s case. Other measures to enhance PCP elimination would not appear to be warranted unless his condition deteriorates.

Psychological Adverse Effects

23. What adverse psychological effects, associated with the use of PCP, could occur in J.R.?

Phencyclidine can produce a variety of psychotic states, particularly in patients with underlying psychiatric pathology or a history of abusing multiple drugs.[144,145,159] Possible reactions include exacerbation of existing schizophrenia or precipitation of schizophreniform psychosis lasting for several days to months. Psychotic states (flashbacks) can recur over a 30 to 40 day period despite abstinence from phencyclidine use. These psychological disorders may be characterized by autistic and delusional thinking and global paranoia. The patient may experience delusions of superhuman strength and vulnerability or of persecution and grandiosity. Behavior may be extremely unpredictable, with the patient being cooperative one minute and violently assaultive the next. Higher rates of self-reported suspicion and assaultive behavior has been reported in prisoners with histories of PCP use when compared to nonusers. Among PCP users, those with histories of psychiatric hospitalizations reported higher levels of assault than those without psychiatric histories.[160]

Psychological dependence has been reported in chronic PCP users.[159] Long-term use has been associated with neurological impairment, characterized by memory lapses as well as speech and visual disturbances. Depression, anxiety, and confusion also have been described. Chronic users often complain of feeling "spaced" and may be irritable and antisocial. They may feel depersonalized and isolated from people. Prolonged depression may occur after phencyclidine use is stopped.[161]

J.R.'s risk for these various psychological effects likely will be determined by his psychological state and the extent of his past and future PCP use.

Acknowledgment

We gratefully acknowledge Darryl S Inaba, whose work provided a foundation for this chapter

References

1 **Beebe DK, Walley E.** Substance abuse: the designer drugs. Amer Fam Physician. 1991;43:1689.

2 **Inaba DS, Cohen WE.** Uppers, Downers, All Arounders: Physical and Mental Effects of Psychoactive Drugs. 2nd ed. Ashland, OR: CNS Productions; 1993.

3 **Sternbach GL, Varon J.** "Designer drugs": recognizing and managing their toxic effects. Postgrad Med. 1992; 91:169.

4 **Green JP et al.** Defining the histamine H2 receptor in man: the interaction with LSD. NIDA Research Monograph. 1978;22:38.

5 **Witters W et al.** Drugs and Society. 3rd ed. Boston, MA: Jones and Bartlett; 1992.

6 **Wiedman D.** Big and little moon peyotism as health care delivery systems. Med Anthropol. 1990;12:371.

7 **Bullis RK.** Swallowing the scroll: legal implications of the recent supreme court peyote cases. J Psychoactive Drugs. 1990;22:325.

8 **Peretz DI et al.** A new hallucinogen: 3,4,5-trimethoxyphenyl-beta-aminopropane (with notes on a stroboscopic phenomenon). J Ment Sci. 1955;101:317.

9 **Shulgin AT et al.** The psychotomimetic properties of 3,4,5-trimethoxyamphetamine. Nature. 1961;189:1011.

10 **Evanko D.** "Designer drugs": treating the damage caused by basement chemists. Postgrad Med. 1991;89:67.

11 **Grinspoon L, Bakalar JB, eds.** Psychedelic Reflections. New York: Human Science Press; 1983.

12 **National Institute on Drug Abuse.** National Survey Results on Drug Use from The Monitoring the Future Study, 1975–92: Volume 1: Secondary School Students Services, Rockville, MD: Department of Health and Human Services, 1993; NIH publication no. 93-3597.

13 **Schwartz RH, Smith DE.** Hallucinogenic mushrooms. Clin Ped. 1988; 27(2):70.

14 **Solowij N et al.** Recreational MDMA use in Sydney: a profile of 'Ecstasy' users and their experiences with the drug. Brit J Addict. 1992;87:1161.

15 **Liester MB et al.** Phenomenology and sequelae of 3,4-methylenedioxymethamphetamine use. J Nerv Ment Dis. 1992;180:1992.

16 **Watson L, Beck J.** New age seekers: MDMA use as an adjunct to spiritual pursuit. J Psychoactive Drugs. 1991; 23:261.

17 **Bost RO.** 3,4-methylenedioxymethamphetamine (MDMA) and other amphetamine derivatives. J Forensic Sci. 1988;33:576.

18 **Henry JA et al.** Toxicity and deaths from 3,4-methylenedioxymethamphetamine ("ecstasy"). Lancet. 1992;340:384.

19 **Chadwick IS et al.** Ecstasy, 3-4 methylenedioxymethamphetamine (MDMA), a fatality associated with coagulopathy and hyperthermia. JR Soc Med. 1991; 84:371.

20 **Screaton GR et al.** Hyperpyrexia and rhabdomyolysis after MDMA ("ecstasy") abuse. Lancet. 1992;339:677.

21 **Tehan B et al.** Hyperthermia associated with 3,4-methylenedioxyethamphetamine ('Eve'). Anaesthesia. 1993; 48:507.

22 **McCann UD, Ricaurte GA.** Reinforcing subjective effects of (±)3,4-methylenedioxymethamphetamine ("Ecstasy") may be separable from its neurotoxic actions: clinical evidence. J Clin Psychopharmacol. 1993;13:214.

23 **Rudnick G, Wall SC.** The molecular mechanism of "Ecstasy" [3,4-methylenedioxymethamphetamine (MDMA)]: serotonin transporters are targets for MDMA-induced serotonin release. Proc Nat Acad Sci. 1992;89:1817.

24 **Ricaurte GA et al.** Aminergic metabolites in cerebrospinal fluid of humans previously exposed to MDMA: preliminary observations. Ann N Y Acad Sci. 1990;600:699.

25 **McCann UD, Ricaurte GA.** Lasting neuropsychiatric sequelae of (±) methylenedioxymethamphetamine ("Ecstasy") in recreational drug users. J Clin Pyschopharmacol. 1991;11:302.

26 **Schifano F.** Chronic atypical psychosis associated with MDMA ("Ecstasy") abuse. Lancet. 1991;338:1335.

27 **McGuire P, Fahy T.** Chronic paranoid psychosis after misuse of MDMA ("Ecstasy"). Brit J Med. 1991;302:697.

28 **Creighton FJ et al.** "Ecstasy" psychosis and flashbacks. Brit J Psych. 1991;159:713.

29 **McGuire P, Fahy T.** Flashbacks following MDMA. Brit J Psych. 1992; 160:276.

30 **Winstock AR.** Chronic paranoid psychosis after misuse of MDMA. Brit Med J. 1991;302:1150.

31 **Naranjio C.** The Healing Journey: New Approaches to Consciousness. New York, NY: Pantheon; 1973.

32 **Shulgin AT.** The background and chemistry of MDMA. J Psychedelic Drugs. 1986;18:291.

33 **Dowling GP et al.** "Eve" and "Ecstasy": a report of five deaths associated with the use of MDEA and MDMA. JAMA. 1987;257:1615.

34 **Grob CS et al.** Commentary—the MDMA-neurotoxicity controversy: implications for clinical research with novel psychoactive drugs. J Nerv Ment Dis. 1992;180:355.

35 **Kosten TR, Price LH.** Commentary—phenomenology and sequelae of 3,4-methylenedioxymethamphetamine use. J Nerv Ment Dis. 1992;180:353.

36 **Schwartz RH.** Mescaline: a survey. Amer Fam Physician. 1988;37:122.

37 **Smart R et al.** Unfavorable reactions to LSD: a review and analysis of available case reports. Can Med Assn J. 1967;97:1214.

38 **Cohen S.** A classification of LSD complications. Psychomatics. 1966;7:182.

39 **McGlothlin WH et al.** LSD revisited: 10 year follow up of medical LSD users. Arch Gen Psychiatry. 1971;24:35.

40 **Ungerleider JT et al.** The dangers of LSD. An analysis of seven month's experience in a university hospital's psychiatric service. JAMA. 1966;197:389.

41 **Taylor RL et al.** Management of "bad trips" in an evolving drug scene. JAMA. 1970;213:422.

42 **Strassman RJ.** Adverse reactions to psychedelic drugs. J Nerv Ment Dis. 1984;172:577.

43 **Schwartz C.** Paradoxical responses to chlorpromazine after LSD. Psychosomatics. 1967;8:210.

44 **Solursh L, Clement W.** Use of diazepam in hallucinogenic drug crisis. JAMA. 1968;205:644.

45 **Hollister LE.** Drug-induced psychiatric disorders and their management. Med Toxicol. 1986;1:428.

46 **Klock JC et al.** Coma, hyperthermia, and bleeding associated with massive LSD overdose: a report of eight cases. Clin Toxicol. 1975;8:191.

47 **Sobel J et al.** Carotid artery obstruction following LSD capsule ingestion. Arch Intern Med. 1971;127:290.

48 **Lieberman AN et al.** Coronary artery occlusion following ingestion of LSD. Stroke. 1974;5:213.

49 **Schick J et al.** Analysis of the LSD flashback. J Psychedelic Drugs. 1970; 3:13.

50 **Blumenfield M.** Flashback phenomena in basic trainees who enter the U.S. Air Force. Milit Med. 1971;136:39.

51 **Glass G.** Psychedelic drugs, stress, and the ego. J Nerv Ment Dis. 1973;156:232.

52 **Glass G, Bowers M.** Chronic psychosis associated with long-term psychotomimetic drug abuse. Arch Gen Psychiatry. 1970;23:97.

53 **Anastasopoulas G, Photiades H.** Effects of LSD-25 on relatives of schizophrenic patients. J Ment Sci. 1962;108:95.

54 **Fink M et al.** Prolonged adverse reactions to LSD in psychotic subjects. Arch Gen Psychiatry. 1966;15:450.

55 **McWilliams S, Tuttle R.** Long term psychological effects of LSD. Psychol Bull. 1973;79:341.

56 **Dishotsky NI et al.** LSD and genetic damage. Science. 1971;172:431.

57 **Zellweger H et al.** Is lysergic acid diethylamide a teratogen? Lancet. 1967;2:1066.

58 **Hecht F et al.** Lysergide acid diethylamide and cannabis as possible teratogens in man. Lancet. 1968;2:1087.

59 **Carakushanski G et al.** Lysergide and cannabis as possible teratogens in man. Lancet. 1969;1:150.

60 **Assemany SR et al.** Deformities in a child whose mother took LSD. Lancet. 1970;1:1290.

61 **Eller JL et al.** Bizarre deformities in offspring of user of lysergide acid diethylamide. N Engl J Med. 1970;283:395.

62 **Sato H et al.** Lysergide a teratogen? Lancet. 1968;1:639.

63 **Warren RJ et al.** LSD exposure in utero. Pediatrics. 1968;45:466.

64 **McGlothlin WH et al.** Effect of LSD on human pregnancy. JAMA. 1970; 212:1483.

65 **Tijo JH et al.** LSD and chromosomes: a controlled experiment. JAMA. 1969; 210:849.

66 **Clark RC.** Marijuana Botany. Berkeley, CA: And/Or Press; 1981.

67 **Mechoulam R.** Marijuana chemistry. Science. 1970;168:1159.

68 **El-Feraly FS, Turner CE.** Alkaloids of Cannabis sativa leaves. Phytochemistry. 1975;14:2304.

69 **Turner CE.** Chemistry and metabolism. In: Petersen RC, ed. Marijuana Research Findings: 1980. Rockville. NIDA Research Monograph. 1980;31:81.

70 **Jones RT.** Human effects: an overview. In: Petersen RC, ed. Marijuana Research Findings: 1980. Rockville. NIDA Research Monograph. 1980;31:54.

71 **Heishman SJ.** Acute and residual effects of marijuana: profiles of plasma

THC levels, physiological, subjective, and performance measures. Pharmacol Biochem Behav. 1990;37:561.

72 **Chesher GB et al.** The effects of orally administered delta-9-tetrahydrocannabinol in man on mood and performance measures: a dose-response study. Pharmacol Biochem Behav. 1990;35:861.

73 **Yesavage JA et al.** Carry-over effects of marijuana intoxication on aircraft pilot performance: a preliminary report. Am J Psychiatry. 1985;142:1325.

74 **Leirer VO et al.** Marijuana, aging, and task difficulty effects on pilot performance. Aviat Space Environ. 1989;60:1145.

75 **Leirer VO et al.** Marijuana carry-over effects on aircraft pilot performance. Aviat Space Environ. 1991;62:221.

76 **Gieringer DH.** Marijuana, driving, and accident safety. J Psychoactive Drugs. 1988;20:93.

77 **Liskow B.** et al. Allergy to marijuana. Ann Intern Med. 1971;75:571.

78 **Taylor DM et al.** Salmonellosis associated with marijuana: a multistate outbreak traced by plasmid fingerprinting. N Eng J Med. 1982;306:1249.

79 **Kagan SL.** Aspergillus: an inhalable contaminant of marijuana. N Engl J Med. 1981;304:483.

80 **Keeler MH, Reifler CF.** Grand mal convulsions subsequent to marijuana use. Dis Nerv Sys. 1967;18:474.

81 **Perez-Reyes M, Wingfield M.** Cannabidiol and electroencephalographic epileptic survey. JAMA. 1974;230:1635.

82 **Cohen S.** Therapeutic aspects. In: Petersen RC, ed. Marijuana Research Findings: 1980. Rockville, MD: NIDA Research Monograph. 1980;31:199.

83 **Brandenburg D, Wernick R.** Intravenous marijuana syndrome. West J Med. 1986;145:94.

84 **Spector I.** AMP: a new form of marijuana. J Clin Psychiatry. 1985;46:498.

85 **Anon.** WAC'd out in Dallas: a dangerous new high. Newsweek. 1976;January 20:25.

86 **Lach E, Schachter EN.** Marijuana and exercise testing. N Engl J Med. 1979;301:438.

87 **Tashkin DP et al.** Effect of habitual smoking of marijuana alone and with tobacco on nonspecific airways hyperactivity. J Psychoactive Drugs. 1988;20:21.

88 **Huber GL et al.** Depressant effect of marijuana smoke on antibacterial activity of pulmonary alveolar macrophages. Chest. 1975;68:769.

89 **Tashkin DP et al.** Respiratory status of seventy-four habitual marijuana smokers. Chest. 1980;78:699.

90 **Gong H et al.** Acute and subacute bronchial effects of oral cannabinoids. Clin Pharmacol Ther. 1984;35:26.

91 **Henderson RL et al.** Respiratory manifestations of hashish smoking. Arch Otolaryngol. 1972;95:248.

92 **Abramson HA et al.** Respiratory disorders and marijuana use. J Asthma Res. 1974;11:97.

93 **Tennant FS et al.** Medical manifestations associated with hashish. JAMA. 1971;216:1965.

94 **Waldman MM.** Marijuana bronchitis. JAMA. 1970;211:501.

95 **Leuchtenberger C et al.** Cytological

and cytochemical effects of whole smoke and of the gas vapor phase from marijuana cigarettes on growth and DNA metabolism of cultured mammalian cells. In: Nahas GG, ed. Marijuana: Chemistry, Biochemistry, and Cellular Effects. New York: Springer-Verlag; 1976:243.

96 **Hoffman D et al.** On the carcinogenicity of marijuana smoke. Res Adv Phytochem. 1975;9:63.

97 **Novotny M et al.** A possible chemical basis for the higher mutagenicity of marijuana as compared to tobacco smoke. Experientia. 1976;32:280.

98 **Nahas G, Latour C.** The human toxicity of marijuana. Med J Aust. 1992;156:495.

99 **Caplan GA, Brigham BA.** Marijuana smoking and carcinoma of the tongue: is there an association? Cancer. 1990;66:1005.

100 **Taylor III FM.** Marijuana as a potential respiratory tract carcinogen: a retrospective analysis of a community hospital population. South Med J. 1988;81:1213.

101 **Hollister LE.** Marijuana and immunity. J Psychoactive Drugs. 1988;20:1.

102 **Leon-Carrion J.** Mental performance in long-term heavy cannabis use: a preliminary report. Psychol Rep. 1990;67:947.

103 **Block RI et al.** Acute effects of marijuana on cognition: relationship to chronic effects and smoking techniques. Pharmacol Biochem Behav. 1992;43:907.

104 **Kolansky H et al.** Effects of marijuana on adolescents and young adults. JAMA. 1971;216:486.

105 **Kolansky H, Moore WT.** Toxic effects of chronic marijuana use. JAMA. 1972;222:35.

106 **Campbell AMG et al.** Cerebral atrophy in young marijuana smokers. Lancet. 1971;2:1219.

107 **Jones RT.** Effects of marijuana on the mind. In: Tinklenberg JR, ed. Marijuana and Health Hazards. New York: Academic Press; 1975:115.

108 **Brill NQ, Christie RL.** Marijuana use and psychosocial adaptation. Arch Gen Psychiatry. 1974;31:713.

109 **Hannerz J, Hindmarsh T.** Neurological and neuroradiological examination of chronic cannabis smokers. Ann Neurol. 1983;13:207.

110 **Kuehnle J et al.** Computed tomographic examination of heavy marijuana smokers. JAMA. 1977;237:1231.

111 **Co BT et al.** Absence of cerebral atrophy in chronic cannabis users. JAMA. 1977;237:1229.

112 **Rubin V, Comitas L.** The clinical studies. In: Rubin V, Comitas L, eds. Ganja in Jamaica. The Hague: Mouton; 1975:81.

113 **Stefanis C et al.** Clinical and psychological effects of cannabis in long-term users. In: Braude MC, Szara S, eds. Pharmacology of Marijuana. New York: Raven Press; 1976:659.

114 **Coggins WJ et al.** Health status of chronic heavy cannabis users. Ann NY Acad Sci. 1976;282:148.

115 **Jones RT et al.** Clinical studies of cannabis tolerance and dependence. Ann NY Acad Sci. 1976;282:221.

116 **Fried PA.** Behavioral and electroencephalographic correlates of the

chronic use of marijuana review. Bull Narc. 1977;29(2):29.

117 **Nowlan R, Cohen S.** Tolerance to marijuana: heart rate and subjective "high." Clin Pharmacol Ther. 1977;22:550.

118 **Benowitz NL, Jones RT.** Cardiovascular effects of prolonged delta-9-tetrahydrocannabinol ingestion. Clin Pharmacol Ther. 1975;18:287.

119 **Benowitz NL, Jones RT.** Prolonged delta-9-tetrahydrocannabinol ingestion: effects of sympathomimetic amines and autonomic blockades. Clin Pharmacol Ther. 1977;21:336.

120 **Zweben JE, O'Connell K.** Strategies for breaking marijuana dependence. J Psychoactive Drugs. 1988;20:121.

121 **Roffman RA et al.** Treatment of marijuana dependence: preliminary results. J Psychoactive Drugs. 1988;20:129.

122 **Brown A, Stickgold A.** Marijuana flashback phenomenon. J Psychedelic Drugs. 1976;8:275.

123 **Weil AT.** Adverse reactions to marijuana. N Engl J Med. 1970;282:997.

124 **Smith DE, Mehl C.** An analysis of marijuana toxicity. Clin Toxicol. 1970;3:101.

125 **Weil AT et al.** Clinical and psychological effects of marijuana in man. Science. 1968;162:1243.

126 **Tart CT.** Marijuana: common experiences. Nature. 1970;226:701.

127 **Abruzzi W.** Drug-induced psychosis. Int J Addict. 1977;121:183.

128 **Tennant FS et al.** Psychiatric effects of hashish. Arch Gen Psychiatry. 1972;27:133.

129 **Weinberg D et al.** Intoxication from accidental marijuana ingestion. Pediatrics. 1983;71:848.

130 **Thacore VR, Shulka SRP.** Cannabis psychosis and paranoid schizophrenia. Arch Gen Psychiatry. 1976;33:383.

131 **Treffert DA.** Marijuana use in schizophrenia: a clear hazard. Am J Psychiatry. 1978;135:1213.

132 **Andreasson et al.** Cannabis and schizophrenia: a longitudinal study of Swedish conscripts. Lancet. 1987;2:1483.

133 **Ellis GM et al.** Excretion patterns of cannabinoid metabolites after last use in a group of chronic users. Clin Pharmacol Ther. 1985;38:572.

134 **Cone EJ, Johnson RE.** Contact highs and urinary cannabinoid excretion after passive exposure to marijuana smoke. Clin Pharmacol Ther. 1986;40:247.

135 **Moreland J et al.** Cannabinoids in blood and urine after passive inhalation of cannabis smoke. J Forensic Sci. 1985;30:997.

136 **Fried PA et al.** Marijuana use during pregnancy and perinatal risk factors. Am J Obstet Gynecol. 1983;146:992.

137 **Lind S et al.** The association of marijuana use with outcome of pregnancy. Am J Public Health. 1983;73:1161.

138 **Greenland S et al.** The effects of marijuana use during pregnancy. Am J Obstet Gynecol. 1982;143:408.

139 **Smith CG.** Effects of marijuana on neuroendocrine function. In: Petersen RC, ed. Marijuana Research Findings: 1980. Rockville: NIDA Research Monograph. 1980;31:120.

140 **Hacleode J.** The effect of marijuana on reproduction and development. In: Petersen RC, ed. Marijuana Research

Findings; 1980. Rockville: NIDA Research Monograph. 1980;31:137.

141 **Robson LL et al.** Maternal drug use and risk of childhood nonlymphoblastic leukemia among offspring: an epidemiologic investigation implicating marijuana (a report from the Children's Cancer Study Group). Cancer. 1989;63:1904.

142 **Domino EF.** History and pharmacology of PCP and PCP-related drugs. J Psychedelic Drugs. 1980;12:223.

143 **Siegel RK.** Phencyclidine and ketamine intoxication: a study of four populations of recreational users. In: Peterson RC, Stillman RC, eds. Phencyclidine (PCP) Abuse: An Appraisal. Rockville: NIDA Research Monograph. 1978;21:119.

144 **Lerner SE et al.** Phencyclidine use among youth: history, epidemiology and acute and chronic intoxication. In: Peterson RC, Stillman RC, eds. Phencyclidine (PCP) Abuse: An Appraisal. Rockville: NIDA Research Monograph. 1978;21:66.

145 **Reed A, Kane AW.** Phencyclidine (PCP): another illicit psychedelic drug. J Psychedelic Drugs. 1972;5:8.

146 **Shulgin AT, MacLean DE.** Illicit synthesis of phencyclidine (PCP) and several of its analogs. Clin Toxicol. 1976;9:533.

147 **Giannini AJ, Castellani S.** A case of phenylcyclohexylpyrrolidine (PHP) intoxication treated with physostigmine. J Toxicol Clin Toxicol. 1982;19:505.

148 **Giles HG et al.** Impurities in street phencyclidine. J Psychedelic Drugs. 1975;7:397.

149 **Soine WH et al.** Phencyclidine contaminant generates cyanide. N Engl J Med. 1979;301:438.

150 **Aronow R et al.** A therapeutic approach to the acutely overdosed PCP patient. J Psychedelic Drugs. 1980;12:259.

151 **McCarron MM et al.** Acute phencyclidine intoxication: incidence of clinical findings in 1000 cases. Ann Emerg Med. 1981;10:237.

152 **Barton CH et al.** Phencyclidine intoxication: clinical experience in 27 cases confirmed by urine assay. Ann Emerg Med. 1981;10:243.

153 **Patel R, Connor G.** A review of thirty cases of rhabdomyolysis associated renal failure among phencyclidine users. Clin Toxicol. 1986;23:547.

154 **Giannini AJ et al.** Comparison of haloperidol and chlorpromazine in the treatment of phencyclidine psychosis. J Clin Pharmacol. 1984;24:202.

155 **Cook CE et al.** Phencyclidine disposition after intravenous and oral doses. Clin Pharmacol Ther. 1982;31:625.

156 **Cook CE et al.** Phencyclidine and phenylcyclohexene disposition after smoking phencyclidine. Clin Pharmacol Ther. 1982;31:635.

157 **Jackson JE.** Phencyclidine pharmacokinetics after a massive overdose. Ann Intern Med. 1989;111:613.

156 **Done AK et al.** Pharmacokinetic bases for the diagnosis and treatment of acute PCP intoxication. J Psychedelic Drugs. 1980;12:253.

159 **Davis BL.** The PCP epidemic: a critical review. Int J Addict. 1982;17:1137.

160 **McCardle L, Fishbein DH.** The self-

reported effects of PCP on human aggression. Addict Behav. 1989;14:465.

161 **Smith DE et al.** The diagnosis and treatment of the PCP abuse syndrome. In: Peterson RC, Stillman RC, eds. Phencyclidine (PCP) Abuse: An Appraisal. Rockville: NIDA Research Monograph. 1978;21:229.

162 **Abraham HD, Aldridge AM.** Adverse consequences of lysergic acid diethylamide. Addiction. 1993;88:1327.

163 **Mercieca J, Brown EA.** Acute renal failure due to rhabdomyolysis associated with use of a straitjacket in lysergide intoxication. Br Med J. 1984;288:1949.

164 **Leiken JB et al.** Clinical features and management of intoxication due to hallucinogenic drugs. Med Toxicol Adverse Drug Exp. 1989;4:324.

165 **Lee CC, Chiang CN.** Maternal-fetal transfer of abused substances: pharmacokinetic and pharmacodynamic data. NIDA Res Monograph Series. 1985;60:110.

166 **Hollister LE.** Health aspects of Cannabis. Pharmacol Rev. 1986;38:1.

167 **Seymour RB, Smith DE.** Identifying and responding to drug abuse in the workplace: an overview. J Pyschoactive Drugs. 1990;22:383.

168 **NIDA.** Mandatory guidelines for federal workplace drug testing programs: final guidelines. Notice. Federal Register. 1988;53(69):11970.

169 **Osterloh JD, Becker CE.** Chemical dependency and drug testing in the workplace. J Psychoactive Drugs. 1990;22:407.

170 **Fretthold DW.** Drug-testing methods and reliability. J Psychoactive Drugs. 1990;22:419.

171 **Perez-Reves M, Wall ME.** Presence of delta-9-tetrahydrocannabinol in human milk. N Engl J Med. 1982;307:819.

172 **Jansen KLR.** Nonmedical use of Ketamine. Br Med J. 1993;306:600.

173 **Shomer RR.** Misuse of Ketamine. J Am Vet Med Assoc. 1992;200:256.

Drug Abuse in Athletics

Jon C Wagner
Warren A Narducci

Overview 87-1
   Historical Perspective 87-1
   Classification of Drug Use in Athletics 87-1
   Epidemiology 87-2
Anabolic Steroids 87-2
   Clinical Signs and Symptoms 87-2
   Hepatotoxicity 87-3
   Endocrine Effects 87-3
   Psychiatric Effects 87-4
   Dosing Patterns 87-4
Steroid Alternatives 87-5
   Gamma Hydroxybutyrate (GHB) 87-5

Clenbuterol 87-5
Chromium 87-5
Urine Drug Testing 87-5
   Detection of Anabolic Steroids 87-5
   Drug Use Control Programs in Athletics 87-6
   Masking Agents 87-6
Erythropoietin 87-6
   Effects on Performance 87-6
   Adverse Effects 87-7
   Limitations in Detecting Recombinant
     Erythropoietin Use 87-7
Exercise-Induced Asthma (EIA) 87-7

Historical Perspective

Drug use in athletics is not a new development. Although many of the drug-related incidents have been in the past two decades, abuse of drugs by athletes, particularly performance-enhancing drug use, can be traced back to the ancient Greek Olympics of the third century. Centuries later in the 1800s, cyclists in Europe often used substances in an attempt to increase endurance. Two popular concoctions were caffeine-based sugar cubes dipped into nitroglycerin (NTG) and *vin mariani*, a mixture of ground coca leaves and wine.[1]

By the 1950s, potent drugs had replaced these crude preparations. Stimulant use, most notably amphetamine, was first suspected at the 1952 Summer and Winter Olympics. The use of amphetamine was thought to be significant enough to prompt the American Medical Association (AMA) to convene a special committee to study the effects of amphetamine on athletic performance. Around this time, athletes from the former Soviet Union and the United States began experimenting with anabolic-androgenic steroids.

Despite the increased attention of sports officials and medical researchers, drug use continued among athletes. The deaths of two cyclists during competition, one at the 1960 Summer Olympics in Rome and the other during the 1967 Tour de France, were linked to the use of amphetamine.[1,2] In an attempt to reduce drug use, the International Olympic Committee (IOC) began drug testing athletes at the 1968 Olympic Games. The IOC defined performance-enhancing or *ergogenic* drug use as the administration of any substance foreign to the body or any physiological substance taken in abnormal quantity or taken by abnormal route of entry into the body with the sole intention of increasing in an artificial manner the athlete's performance in competition.[3] The broad nature of this definition includes the use of "physiological substances" such as testosterone, growth hormone, erythropoietin, and red blood cells; all have been reportedly used by athletes to improve athletic performance.

As drug detection methods became more sophisticated, the number of athletes testing positive for banned substances increased. At the 1983 Pan American Games in Caracas, Venezuela, 19 athletes were banned from competition following a positive drug test for a banned substance, primarily anabolic steroids. Many other athletes withdrew from competition rather than risk being tested.[1] The one single event that focused public attention on the use of drugs in athletics was the disqualification of Canadian sprinter Ben Johnson at the 1988 Summer Olympics in Seoul, South Korea. Following a decisive victory in the 100-meter dash, Johnson tested positive for the anabolic steroid, stanozolol.[4]

Not all drug use by athletes involved ergogenic substances. Several well-known athletes died from cocaine overdose or alcohol-related motor vehicle accidents, including Len Bias, Don Rogers, and Pelle Lindbergh.[4]

Classification of Drug Use in Athletics

Drugs used by athletes can be grouped into four categories: a) therapeutic drugs used to treat legitimate illness or injury, b) social drugs of abuse, c) ergogenic drugs, and d) drugs used to mask the presence of other drugs in the urine. Individual drugs often cross over into several categories. For example, a therapeutic drug such as a beta-agonist may be used by an athlete as a performance drug.

On occasion, athletes require drug treatment for illness or injury. For athletes competing in events where drug testing is conducted, drug products must be selected carefully. Health professionals who routinely care for athletes should become familiar with the lists of substances banned by athletic organizations. (See Tables 87.1 and 87.2.)[5,6]

Athletes may use alcohol and other drugs of abuse for all of the same reasons as non-athletes. Participation in sports does not impart immunity on athletes from the pressures to experiment with drugs of abuse.

In an attempt to improve performance, athletes may use ergogenic substances. Whether drugs can produce meaningful "on-field" improvements in performance is often debated. Performance in athletics is the result of diverse factors including skill level, opponent's skill level, playing conditions, and mental attitude.[7] Suggesting that taking an ergogenic substance results in a cause and effect relationship to improved performance is difficult. Ergogenic substances may potentially increase several physiological components associated with athletic performance such as muscle mass, strength, speed, and aerobic capacity. Changes in these variables would suggest that ergogenic drugs would have a greater effect on performance of one-dimensional sports such as running, throwing, and lifting events, and less of an effect on multi-dimensional team sports.

The newest drug use category in athletics is masking agents. As the use of urine drug testing at sporting events has increased, so have the attempts to avoid detection. Probenecid has been used by athletes to delay the renal elimination of performance drugs much in the same way it blocks excretion of penicillin. Probenecid was added to the IOC's and National Collegiate Athletic Association's (NCAA) lists of banned drugs in 1988 under the new classification of "masking agent."[8]

Epidemiology

Until the mid 1980s, most of what was known about drug use among athletes was anecdotal. In 1984, the NCAA commissioned a study of the substance abuse patterns of collegiate athletes. The study surveyed athletes participating in five men's and five women's sports representing all divisions of the NCAA. The results indicated that student athletes used a number of ergogenic and social drugs. With the exception of "psychedelics" and anabolic steroids, the majority of drug use began before entering college.[9] Follow-up surveys conducted in 1989 and 1993 showed little change in drug usage with the exception of dramatic increases in the use of smokeless tobacco.[10,11]

Studies involving high school athletes have exclusively investigated anabolic steroid use. The incidence of anabolic steroid use ranges from 6.5% to 11.1%.[12,13] Nearly 40% of the senior males who reported using anabolic steroids first used these drugs before the age of 15,[12] and anabolic steroid users also report using other drugs of abuse more frequently than nonanabolic steroid users.[14]

Anabolic Steroids
Clinical Signs and Symptoms

1. J.W., a 19-year-old male, is brought to the ER for treatment of traumatic injuries to his head and legs as a result of a motor vehicle accident after attempting to chase down a motorist who "cut him off" in traffic. He is agitated, hyperaggressive, and in a rage. He has been restrained by four security guards following an altercation with one of the ER nurses. Physical examination indicates excellent physical condition, other than the accident injuries, with hypertrophied muscles. He denies use of alcohol or other mood-altering drugs. The results of the routine drug screen are negative. What are the clinical indications that anabolic steroid use may have been involved in this case?

Table 87.1 Drugs Banned by the International Olympic Committee (IOC)—1993[a]

Stimulants		Anabolic Steroids	Diuretics
Amfepramone	Methylphenidate HCl	Bolasterone	Acetazolamide
Amfetaminil	Morazone	Boldenone	Amiloride
Amineptine	Nikethamide	Clenbuterol	Bendroflumethiazide
Amiphenazole	Pemoline	Clostebol	Benzthiazide
Amphetamine	Pentetrazol	Danazol-danocrine	Bumetanide
Bemigrade	Phendimetrazine	Dehydrochlormethyltestosterone	Canrenone
Benzphetamine	Phenmetrazine	Fluoxymesterone	Chlormerodrin
β_2-agonists[b]	Phentermine HCl	Growth hormone	Chlorthalidone
Caffeine[c]	Phenylephrine	Human chorionic gonadotropin	Diclofenamide
Cathine	Phenylpropanolamine	Mesterolone	Ethacrynic acid
Chlorphentermine	Propylhexedrine	Metandienone	Furosemide
Clobenzorex	Pseudoephedrine	Metenolone	Hydrochlorothiazide
Clorprenaline	Related compounds	Methandrostenolone	Mersalyl
Cocaine		Methyltestosterone	Spironolactone
Cropropamide	**Narcotic Analgesics**	Nandrolone	Triamterine
Crothetamide	Alphaprodine	Norethandrolone	Related compounds
Desoxyephedrine	Anileridine	Oxandrolone	
Diethylpropion HCl	Buprenorphine	Oxymesterone	**Peptide Hormones and**
Dimetamfetamine	Dextromoramide	Oxymetholone	**Analogues**
Ephedrine	Dextropropoxyphene	Stanozolol	Chorionic gonadotropin
Etafedrine	Diamorphine (heroin)	Testosterone[d]	Corticotrophin
Ethamivan	Dipipanone	Zeranol	Growth hormone
Etilamfetamine	Ethoheptazine	Related compounds	Erythropoietin
Fencamfamin	Ethylmorphine		
Fenetylline	Hydrocodone	**Beta Blockers[e]**	**Masking Agents**
Fenproporex	Hydromorphone	Acebutolol	Epitestosterone[d]
Furfenorex	Levorphanol	Alprenolol	Probenecid
Isoetharine HCl	Methadone HCl	Atenolol	Related compounds
Isoproterenol	Morphine	Labetalol	
Meclofenoxate	Nalbuphine	Metoprolol	
Mefenorex	Oxocodone	Nadolol	
Mesocarbe	Oxomorphine	Oxprenolol	
Metaproterenol	Pentazocine	Propranolol	
Methamphetamine	Pethidine	Sotalol	
Methoxyphenamine	Phenazocine	Related compounds	
Methylamphetamine	Tincture opium		
Methylephedrine	Trimeperidine		
	Related compounds		

[a] Reprinted with permission from reference 5.
[b] Salbutamol and terbutaline by aerosol or inhalant routes are permitted. The prescribing physician must give written notification to the IOC or the United States Olympic Committee (USOC).
[c] If urine concentration >12 µg/mL.
[d] If ratio of total urine concentration of testosterone to epitestosterone >6.
[e] Tests for beta blockers are performed at the request of International Federations and at the discretion of the IOC Medical Commission.

Table 87.2   Drugs Banned by the National Collegiate Athletic Association (NCAA): 1993–1994[6]

Stimulants
- Amiphenazole
- Amphetamine
- Bemegride
- Benzphetamine
- Caffeine[a]
- Chlorphentermine
- Cocaine
- Cropropamide
- Crotethamide
- Diethylpropion
- Dimethylamphetamine
- Doxapram
- Ethamivan
- Ethylamphetamine
- Fencamfamin
- Meclofenoxate
- Methamphetamine
- Methylphenidate
- Nikethamide
- Pemoline
- Pentetrazol
- Phendimetrazine
- Phenmetrazine
- Phentermine
- Picrotoxin
- Pipradol
- Prolintane
- Strychnine
- Related compounds

Anabolic Steroids
- Boldenone
- Clostebol
- Dehydrochlormethyltestosterone
- Dromostanolone
- Fluoxymesterone
- Mesterolone
- Methandienone
- Methenolone
- Methyltestosterone
- Nandrolone
- Norethandrolone
- Oxandrolone
- Oxymesterone
- Oxymetholone
- Stanozolol
- Testosterone[b]
- Related compounds

Substances Banned for Specific Sports

Rifle
- Alcohol
- Atenolol
- Metoprolol
- Nadolol
- Pindolol
- Propranolol
- Timolol
- Related compounds

Diuretics
- Acetazolamide
- Bendroflumethiazide
- Benzthiazide
- Bumetanide
- Chlorothiazide
- Chlorthalidone
- Ethacrynic acid
- Flumethiazide
- Furosemide
- Hydrochlorothiazide
- Hydroflumethiazide
- Methyclothiazide
- Metolazone
- Polythiazide
- Quinethazone
- Spironolactone
- Triamterene
- Trichlormethiazide
- Related compounds

Street Drugs
- Heroin
- Marijuana[c]
- THC[c,d]

Peptide Hormones and Analogues
- Chorionic gonadotropin
- Corticotrophin
- Erythropoietin
- Growth hormone
- All the respective releasing factors of the above-mentioned substances

Masking Agents
- Epitestosterone[b]
- Probenecid
- Related compounds

[a] If urine concentration >15 µg/mL.
[b] If ratio of total urine concentration of testosterone to epitestosterone >6.
[c] If urine concentration of the metabolite >25 ng/mL.
[d] THC = Tetrahydrocannabinol.

One of the hallmark symptoms of anabolic steroid use is rage or aggressive behavior in the apparent absence of other reasonable causes. Other subjective/objective symptoms can include headache, nausea, altered libido, euphoria, and an altered appetite.[15–18] In addition to the clinical interview and mental status examination, it is paramount to emphasize the importance of a good drug use history. Many times, steroid use is not identified because it is *not asked about*. Questions about the use of ergogenic aids (e.g., anabolic steroids, diet pills, amino acid supplements, nonprescription medications, other people's medications) should be included in each case when performing a history and physical examination in clinical situations such as that described above. Pertinent drug history information includes: a) types of anabolic steroids taken; b) dosage schedule, with special emphasis on maximum dosage in mg/wk and mg/cycle; c) identification of the cycle schedule which can be useful in understanding the pattern and/or extent of use; d) a written description of the client's *last* cycle of use; and e) an assessment of the use of other ergogenic aids in addition to the anabolic steroids.

Hepatotoxicity

2. The results of J.W.'s routine laboratory tests show an elevated LDL cholesterol level and abnormal liver function tests (LFTs). What anabolic steroids are more hepatotoxic than others?

A concern with current drug testing programs is that athletes may now be more inclined to take oral agents to avoid detection. In addition to being excreted from the body more quickly, these C-17-α-alkylated derivatives also have an increased potential for hepatotoxicity.[19–22] Thus, instead of discouraging anabolic steroid use, drug testing programs may be unintentionally encouraging use of potentially more toxic drugs. Examples of both oral and injectable anabolic agents are listed in Table 87.3.[23]

Liver complications caused by anabolic steroids include peliosis hepatis, hepatitis, hepatic tumors, and nonspecific elevations in liver function tests. Most of the reports of hepatotoxicity have been in patients receiving therapeutic doses of anabolic steroids for extended periods of time. Whether an individual taking supratherapeutic doses to enhance athletic performance is at similar risk for hepatic adverse effects is not known. For example, peliosis hepatis (i.e., a condition where blood-filled sacs form in the liver) has been seen in patients with aplastic anemia who are taking anabolic steroids, but not in athletes.[24] Hepatocellular carcinoma due to anabolic steroids has been reported with therapeutic and ergogenic doses.

Anabolic steroids can cause changes in LFTs. Intense resistance training alone can also increase liver enzymes that are also found in muscle. Liver function in steroid users is best monitored by following levels of alkaline phosphatase and the liver-specific isoenzyme of lactic dehydrogenase (LDH). Liver function tests typically return to baseline levels after anabolic steroids are discontinued.[25]

Endocrine Effects

3. What effects do anabolic steroids have on the reproductive and endocrine systems? Are these effects dose-related? What laboratory test profile might be expected in a chronic anabolic steroid user?

The toxicity of anabolic steroids on the reproductive system primarily results from the androgenic effects of these agents. In males, alopecia, gynecomastia, and testicular atrophy occur in about 10% of serious users. Reversible adverse effects include decreased spermatogenesis and decreased sperm motility. In females, irreversible virilization may occur, including hirsutism, male pattern baldness, coarsening and deepening of the voice, and clitoral hypertrophy.[26,27] Gonadotropin suppression [e.g., decreased LDH, follicle stimulating hormone (FSH), and sex hormone binding globulin] also has been reported.[28–30] Anabolic steroid effects on the endocrine system include alteration in skin lipids, resulting in acne; insulin resistance and glucose intolerance; and an altered thyroid profile,

Table 87.3	Androgenic-Anabolic Steroids[a-c]
Generic Name	Brand Name(s)

Oral Agents: 17-Alpha-Alkyl Derivatives of Testosterone

Ethylestrenol	Maxibolin
Fluoxymesterone	Halotestin, Android-F, Ora-Testryl
Methyltestosterone	Android, Metandren, Oreton, Testred, Virilon
Oxandrolone	Anavar
Oxymetholone	Anadrol, Anapolon 50[d]
Stanozolol	Winstrol

Injectable Agents: Testosterone, Testosterone Esters, and 19-Nortestosterone Esters (Nandrolone Products)

Nandrolone decanoate[e]	Anabolin LA-100, Androlone 50, Androlone-D, Deca-Durabolin, Hybolin Decanoate, Kabolin, Nandrobolic LA, Neo-Durabolic
Nandrolone phenpropionate[e]	Anabolin, Androlone, Durabolin, Hybolin-Improved, Nandrobolic
Testosterone (aqueous)	Andro 100, Andronaq-50, Histerone 50, Histerone 100, Malogen,[d] Testamone 100, Testaqua, Testoject-50
Testosterone cypionate[e]	Andro-Cyp, Andronaq-LA, Andronate, depAndro, Depotest, Depo-Testosterone, Depo-Testosterone Cypionate, Duratest, T-Cypionate, Testa-C, Testoject-LA, Testred Cypionate, Virilon IM
Testosterone enanthate[e]	Andro L.A. 200, Andropository 100, Andryl 200, Delatest, Delatestryl, Durathate-200, Everone, Malogex,[d] Testone L.A. 100, Testone LA 200, Testrin-P.A.
Testosterone propionate[e]	Malogen,[d] Testex

[a] Reprinted with permission from reference 23.
[b] Other anabolic steroids banned by the United States Olympic Committee (USOC) include: boldenone, clostebol, danazol, dehydrochlormethyltestosterone, mesterolone, methandienone, methenolone, norethandrolone, and oxymesterone.
[c] Some veterinary anabolic steroids with potential for human abuse include stanozolol (Winstrol-V) and boldenone undecylenate (Equipoise).
[d] Available in Canada only.
[e] Formulated in oil vehicle for sustained release from the injection site.

typically presenting as decreased triiodothyronine (T$_3$), thyroxine total (T$_4$), thyroid stimulating hormone (TSH), and thyroxine-binding globulin (TBG).[28,31-36] When comparing the incidence of adverse effects in individuals using anabolic steroids for legitimate medical purposes, it is apparent that these effects are dose-related; although there are no controlled studies that provide conclusive evidence. The laboratory profile for a chronic anabolic steroid user can be extremely complex, with elevations in low density lipoprotein (LDL) cholesterol, triglycerides, alkaline phosphatase, LDH, serum glucose, and hematocrit. The serum concentrations of high density lipoprotein (HDL) cholesterol, thyroid, and gonadotropins usually are decreased.[26-44] There are reports of cardiovascular toxicity from anabolic steroid abuse, including myocardial infarction (MI), left ventricular hypertrophy, and hypertension.[43,45-50] A comprehensive listing of reported adverse effects appears in Table 87.4.

Psychiatric Effects

4. Following overnight hospitalization, J.W. is referred by his junior college football team's physician to a psychiatrist for a mental health examination. He appears to be despondent, depressed, and expresses suicidal ideation during the interview. What are the psychological effects of anabolic steroid use?

A mental health examination may reveal any of the following psychological defects: a) increased aggression, hyperactivity, irritability; b) psychoses (auditory hallucinations, paranoid and grandiose delusions); c) manic episodes; d) panic disorders; and e) major depression and anxiety with or without suicidal ideation.[15,51] Often, the psychological effects are the first changes noticed by friends and family members. A withdrawal syndrome has also been described, indicating that anabolic steroids may have an addiction potential.[52-54] This syndrome is characterized by irritability, nervousness, and moodiness. Thus, adverse psychological effects may occur either during periods of use or nonuse, although rage and aggressive behavior are likely linked with cycles of use. The psychological and behavioral effects of anabolic steroids appear to be variable, transient upon discontinuation, and occur more frequently with orally ingested C-17-α-alkylated compounds.

Dosing Patterns

5. During subsequent meetings with the psychiatrist, J.W. describes a 15-month history of multiple anabolic steroid use, including "stacking" and "cycling" with both "oil-based" and "water-based" steroids. What are typical dosing regimens of anabolic steroids, and what do the above terms indicate about J.W.'s anabolic steroid use?

There are numerous published reports on the patterns of use and effects of anabolic steroids in athletes.[25,55-62] In general, serious users self-administer either oral (water-base) or injectable (oil-base) forms, or combinations of both (stacking), in cycles ranging from 12 to 18 weeks. Drug-free periods of four to six weeks between cycles are used to prevent/minimize testicular atrophy and other adverse effects. However, anecdotal evidence indicates that some users reduce dosages during their "off" cycles, but do not actually become drug free. Longer drug-free periods are used to avoid detection before competitions that require urine testing. Because urine testing is now required by a number of athletic organizations, many athletes are turning to oral agents, which have shorter biological half-lives than injectable agents, and avoidance of detection is thus more likely.

The drug doses ingested during each cycle of use may be as high as 10 to 200 times the approved dosages for legitimate medical indications. Large doses of steroids ingested during typical cycles of use will result in accumulation of body stores of drug, especially with the injectables formulated in oil. Detection of anabolic steroids following cessation of use is highly variable, and may be possible for up to three weeks for oral agents and up to six months for the oil injectables, which produce a slow-release depot effect from muscle tissue.

Steroid Alternatives

6. What steroid replacement and adjunct substances are currently being used either to optimize the ergogenic effects or minimize the adverse effects of anabolic steroids?

A number of substances may be used in combination with anabolic steroids. Although diverse in the mechanisms of action, these compounds are commonly referred to as "steroid alternatives." Steroid alternatives range from nutritional supplements to prescription drugs from foreign countries. Many of these substances are of unproven efficacy and are relatively nontoxic if taken in recommended doses. Several steroid alternatives can, however, result in serious medical consequences.

Gamma Hydroxybutyrate (GHB)

Gamma hydroxybutyrate is a naturally-occurring substance that has properties similar to neurotransmitters. GHB is a metabolic by-product of gamma aminobutyric acid (GABA). Since 1990, GHB

Table 87.4	Adverse Effects of Anabolic-Androgenic Steroids[a]
Reproductive	
Testicular atrophy	↓ spermatogenesis, altered sperm morphology, ↓ sperm motility
Gonadotropin suppression	↓ LH,[b] FSH,[b] and sex hormone binding globulin
Virilization (females)	Development of acne, hirsutism,[c] reduction in breast size, coarsening and deepening of the voice,[c] clitoral hypertrophy[c]
Feminization (males)	Gynecomastia
Musculoskeletal	
Connective tissue	↑ susceptibility to injury of ligaments/cartilage in weight-bearing joints
Bones	Premature epiphyseal closure[c] resulting in stunted growth in adolescent users
Cardiovascular and Cerebrovascular	
Sodium and water retention	Elevated blood pressure; edematous tissue
Lipid profile	↑ LDL[d] cholesterol and triglycerides
Heart, brain	MI,[b] stroke, left ventricular hypertrophy, atherosclerotic heart disease
Endocrine (other)	
Alteration in skin lipids	Acne
Altered glucose metabolism	Insulin resistance, glucose intolerance
Altered thyroid profile	↓ T_3,[e] T_4,[e] TSH,[e] and TBG[e]
Liver	
Hepatotoxicity	Peliosis hepatis,[c] hepatic carcinoma,[c] hepatoma, cholestatic jaundice

[a] Reprinted with permission from reference 23.
[b] LH = Luteinizing hormone; FSH = Follicle-stimulating hormone; MI = Myocardial infarction.
[c] Irreversible adverse effects.
[d] LDL = Low-density lipoprotein.
[e] T_3 = Triiodothyronine; T_4 = Thyroxine; TSH = Thyroid-stimulating hormone; TBG = Thyroxine-binding globulin.

has been marketed in health clubs and nutrition stores as a body-building supplement. The claims promote GHB as a powerful stimulant of growth hormone, although this has yet to be substantiated in human trials. GHB is available as a tablet or powder under several names including: sodium oxybutyrate, gamma hydroxide, gamma hydrate, and Somatomax PM. Adverse effects seen with GHB include headaches, nausea, vomiting, diarrhea, and central nervous system (CNS) depression. The effects on the CNS may range from sedation to coma, especially when combined with alcohol or other CNS depressants.[63,64] The serious nature of these CNS effects prompted the Food and Drug Administration (FDA) to recall the product from sale in the United States.

Clenbuterol

Another steroid alternative that is popular with athletes and bodybuilders is clenbuterol. Clenbuterol is a β_2-agonist available in countries other than the United States for the treatment of chronic obstructive airways disease under the proprietary names of Spiropent, Monores, and Clenasma. A more common use for clenbuterol, especially in Europe, is as a veterinary agent to increase lean weight in livestock and poultry.[65] Clenbuterol appears to be unique among β_2-agonists in possessing an anabolic effect. The sale of clenbuterol without a prescription is illegal in the United States.

Chromium

The trace mineral chromium is being marketed as a safe replacement for anabolic steroids. The proposed anabolic mechanism involves increased insulin activity which in turn stimulates intracellular uptake of amino acids. Chromium is most often sold as chromium picolinate through nutrition stores. Human performance data are limited to a few poorly-controlled studies involving small study populations. Although most people in the Unites States do not get enough chromium in their diet, taking chromium picolinate supplements in excess of the usual dose of 200 μg could potentially lead to anemia.[66]

Athletes and other anabolic steroid users have become extremely sophisticated in their knowledge of the pharmacology and toxicology of anabolic steroids, leading to their use of a number of other substances to either offset, minimize, or prevent adverse effects. These substances include human chorionic gonadotropin to reverse testicular atrophy, tamoxifen to prevent gynecomastia, and human growth hormone as either an adjunct or substitute anabolic agent.

Urine Drug Testing
Detection of Anabolic Steroids

7. J.W. agrees to undergo periodic, random urine drug testing to remain eligible for participation in athletics. What are the key components of a testing program for anabolic steroids?

Urine testing for anabolic steroid use before or during athletic competition is a complex process involving legal, ethical, and technical issues. Fortunately, many of these factors are of lesser importance in the diagnosis and treatment of the physical and affective toxicities of these agents by clinical toxicologists, emergency room physicians, and psychiatrists. Nevertheless, it is important for clinicians to be aware of the testing resources available to them, principally with regard to confirmation of steroid use in cases of patient denial.

Radioimmunoassay, thin-layer chromatography, gas-liquid chromatography, and high performance liquid chromatography methods have been used to detect anabolic steroids in urine. Although all of these methods have applications in screening and pharmacokinetic studies, none are appropriate for confirmation of steroid use, especially in situations involving legal or disciplinary outcomes, because they lack sensitivity and/or specificity.

The gas chromatography/mass spectrometry (GC/MS) method has become a widely accepted state-of-the-art analytical procedure used for urine analysis at major athletic events. GC/MS analysis is expensive, time-consuming, and technically complex, but provides unequivocal, extremely sensitive identification (1–10 ng/mL) of the anabolic steroid, as well as the known metabolites.[67] When combined with rigorous interpretation of the analytical data and adherence to chain of custody guidelines, there is virtually no possibility for the occurrence of false positive test results.

Persons who use anabolic steroids will normally have significantly depressed urine concentrations of testosterone, because of feedback inhibition on gonadotropins. Alternatively, individuals who administer exogenous testosterone will usually have high urine testosterone levels. Confirmation of exogenous testosterone use is made by evaluating the ratio of urine testosterone to epitestosterone, a normal testosterone metabolite. A ratio of 6:1 or greater is considered to be confirmatory of exogenous testosterone use.

In the relatively short time that anabolic steroid testing has been available, several concerns have surfaced. As with most drugs of abuse, a prime concern is the period of detectability. Anabolic steroids may be detected weeks after ingestion of oral agents or for several months after the use of oil-based injectables. Individuals taking anabolic steroids for ergogenic purposes are frequently aware of how long steroids may be detected. Some may even have serial urine samples assayed to determine their individual elimination patterns. Athletes participating in events where anabolic steroid testing is conducted may then abstain for the necessary amount of time to produce a negative sample.

As with other health care decisions, the expense of the test must also be considered. With the typical cost of an anabolic steroid screen at or above $200, a reasonable suspicion must exist of steroid-induced disease. Given the potential pitfalls and expense of testing for anabolic steroids described above, several guidelines can be suggested for the use of these assays in clinical practice: a) have reasonable physical and laboratory evidence of anabolic steroid-induced disease; b) conduct a thorough medication history; c) collect the urine specimen under direct observation; and d) screen for masking agents as well as for anabolic steroids.

Drug Use Control Programs in Athletics

8. What are the key components of a urine drug testing program administered by an athletic organization, such as the IOC or NCAA?

One of the earliest attempts at reducing nonmedical drug use among athletes has been urine drug testing. Testing policies and procedures vary widely between athletic organizations; however, all share common elements.[68] The majority of drug testing is conducted at athletic championships and football bowl games. Athletes selected for testing often are medal winners or, in the case of a team sport, a representative sampling of first team players. Once athletes are notified that they have been selected for testing, they must report to the drug testing center within a specific time period. Often, a drug testing official will remain with the athlete to prevent them from drinking beverages from unsecured containers, instilling drug-free urine into their bladder, or engaging in other activities to avoid detection.

Upon arriving at the drug testing center a medication history is conducted. The athlete is then asked to provide a urine specimen of approximately 75 mL. Voiding may be difficult, especially for endurance athletes who are dehydrated. Decaffeinated, nonalcoholic beverages are available to rehydrate the athlete and facilitate urination. The collection of the specimen must be done in the presence of a drug testing official. The specimen is usually divided into two samples. One sample is analyzed by the laboratory, the other sample is reserved for a repeat assay in the event the first sample is positive for a banned substance. Before being sent to the laboratory, the urine sample may be tested for temperature, pH, and specific gravity. Samples that fall outside of established limits are not analyzed and the athlete must provide an additional urine specimen.[8,69]

Many of the current drug testing protocols have been criticized for being ineffective. The primary limitation is that most drug testing occurs in an announced, predetermined format. Athletes can easily avoid detection, yet receive ergogenic benefits from performance drugs by discontinuing use shortly before an event where drug testing is conducted. The success of drug testing at predetermined events is debatable. For example, the NCAA announced that for the 1992–93 athletic season 4782 athletes were tested for drugs and only ten were ruled ineligible. Of those ten, four tested positive for anabolic steroids, three for marijuana, one for a masking agent, and two athletes became ineligible for failing to take a drug test. Using the self-reported figures from the 1993 NCAA-sponsored study, 2.5% of athletes reported taking anabolic steroids.[11] This would equate to potentially 120 steroid users, nearly 97% of whom were either not tested or avoided detection.

Aside from being easy to avoid, current drug testing programs have other limitations. Only a minority of athletes are actually drug tested. Those who are tested are often winners or athletes from successful teams. Drug testing at predetermined events has altered the way athletes use performance drugs, especially anabolic steroids. Oral anabolic steroids are used more frequently than in the past due to a shorter elimination time of several days to two weeks as compared to injectable agents that can remain detectable for 6 to 12 months. Drug testing, therefore, may be unintentionally "encouraging" the use of oral steroids with a potentially more serious adverse reaction profile. The final concern of current testing programs is financial. The expense of drug testing plus administrative costs make the expansion of drug testing to the high school level unlikely.

Masking Agents

9. A.N., a 23-year-old male world-class cyclist, complained of being "constantly tired and headachy." Despite rest and the use of a nonprescription analgesic, the condition continued. Several days later, A.N. went to see his physician when he began to experience jaw and joint pain. The physician prescribed amoxicillin and probenecid. After three weeks of therapy, A.N.'s condition improved. Several months later following a routine urine drug test at a sanctioned event, A.N. was notified that he had tested positive for probenecid, a banned substance, and would be banned from competition for two years. Why is probenecid considered a banned substance?

In 1987 at the Tenth Pan American Games in Indianapolis, the word among the athlete community was that probenecid could "mask" the presence of anabolic steroids in the urine. The mechanism was similar to the delay in renal excretion of penicillins. Although not a banned substance at the time, athletes selected for drug testing at the Pan Am Games were also screened for probenecid. An undisclosed number of samples contained the drug. The following year at the 1988 Winter Olympics in Calgary, probenecid was added to the banned substance list under a new category— "masking agents."[8]

Virtually all drugs on the banned substance lists of athletic organizations have legitimate therapeutic indications. On occasion, a drug taken for an illness or injury can result in a positive drug test. A more common example would be the athlete who takes a nonprescription cold preparation that contains phenylpropanolamine or ephedrine, which are banned by several sports associations as "stimulants." Athletes who are subject to drug testing should: a) make certain their physician and pharmacist know they are a competitive athlete and may have to submit to a drug test; b) provide drug testing personnel with a complete list of current drugs and those taken within the past 12 months; and c) if in doubt, check with the United States Olympic Committee Drug Hotline at 1–800–233–0393.

Erythropoietin

10. S.E., a male long-distance runner, complained of a tingling and numbing sensation on the left side of his face while training. Shortly thereafter, he collapsed, became unconscious, and was taken to a nearby ER where he was pronounced dead. The cause of death was listed as a severe stroke. Could any performance drugs have contributed to S.E.'s stroke?

Effects On Performance

Endurance athletes for some time have been known to use their own blood as an ergogenic aid. Blood doping is a technique where some of the athlete's blood is removed several weeks before a competition. Shortly before the competition, the red blood cells, which have been removed and stored, are infused back into the athlete. Blood doping increases the ability to carry oxygen to exercising muscles.[70] The latest method to artificially increase hematocrit in athletes is by injecting recombinant erythropoietin (rEPO, Epogen, Procrit).[70,71]

The extent that athletes have begun experimenting with recombinant erythropoietin is unknown, but reports suggest widespread use among amateur and professional endurance runners and cyclists. Unpublished studies conducted in Sweden showed an 8% rise in hematocrit when recombinant erythropoietin was given to highly-trained athletes. This has resulted in estimates of improving race times by 30 seconds for a runner competing in a 20 minute race. At the elite athlete level an ergogenic effect of that magnitude would be very significant.[72]

Adverse Effects

The potential for adverse reactions can be very significant as well. As blood viscosity increases so does the potential for hypertension, cardiac arrest, and stroke. Although never conclusively linked to recombinant erythropoietin, 18 world-class Dutch and Belgian cyclists have died of cardiac complications. One of those who died had finished twentieth in the Tour de France seven months earlier.

Limitations in Detecting Recombinant Erythropoietin Use

Use of recombinant erythropoietin (and blood doping) are banned by the IOC and NCAA. Detecting, and therefore deterring, users is difficult. First, recombinant erythropoietin is virtually indistinguishable from the naturally-occurring hormone. Secondly, the increase in erythropoietin is minute and lasts for 24 hours or less, even though the effect on red blood cell mass can last for several weeks. Rather than assay for erythropoietin, some have suggested establishing acceptable levels of hematocrit and disqualifying those with a level that is too high. The cut-off level chosen would have to take into consideration athletes with a normally elevated hematocrit, especially those that live or train in high altitudes. The fundamental limitation with any of these approaches to detecting recombinant erythropoietin use is that a blood specimen would be required. At present, the only biological fluid approved for drug testing in athletics is urine.[73]

Exercise-Induced Asthma (EIA)

11. P.K., an 18-year-old female high school senior, is the top-ranked tennis player in her state. During a recruiting visit to the state university, the head women's tennis coach learns that P.K. has exercise-induced asthma (EIA) and suffered a near fatal asthma attack as recently as six months ago. Despite her ranking, P.K. receives no scholarship offers from any major universities. Her father discovers that the coaches fear P.K.'s EIA will not only limit her ability to compete successfully at the collegiate level, but also will require the athletic department to provide additional medical care. Are coaches' concerns justified?

Exercise-induced asthma is a transient bronchospasm that usually occurs after 6 to 12 minutes of strenuous exercise. EIA occurs in 12% to 15% of the general population and is relatively common in athletes.[74] Of the 597 United States athletes that competed in the 1984 Summer Olympics in Los Angeles, 67 (11.2%) were asthmatic.[75] Similar surveys of high school and college athletes showed an incidence of EIA symptoms that ranged from 12% to 23%.[76–78]

Individuals with EIA do not always experience symptoms each time they exercise, making a definitive diagnosis difficult. Cardinal physical signs include wheezing, dyspnea, and tightness in the chest. More subtle clinical signs are cough, chest congestion, feeling of being "out of shape," lack of energy, inconsistent performance, frequent colds, intolerance of long periods of exercise, and symptoms that occur while running, but not while swimming.[79]

Athletes competing in sports requiring longer periods of exercise are at higher risk. Sports considered high risk include ice skating, cross-country skiing, basketball, football, middle to long-distance running, soccer, cycling, and rowing. Sports such as sprinting, gymnastics, baseball, and weight lifting present a low risk for EIA. Environmental conditions such as cold air, dry air, dusty air, pollen, smoke-filled air, and smog also can present a risk to the athlete.

Athletes with EIA do not need to limit their choice of sports to those that are low risk or are played in low-risk environments. With proper aerobic conditioning, P.K. can reduce the number and severity of bronchospasms. The following medication guidelines, done under the supervision of the athletic department medical staff, also can prevent EIA attacks during exercise or training:[80]

- 10 to 60 minutes before exercising, premedicate with an inhaled β-agonist and/or cromolyn.
- About 30 to 60 minutes before exercising, warm-up with 10 to 15 minutes of stretching exercises.
- Begin some form of aerobic exercise, such as jogging or running, to raise heart rate to 50% to 60% of maximum and sustain it for 5 to 10 minutes.
- Follow with a cool-down period of 10 to 30 minutes of gradually decreasing exercise.
- Repeat premedication described in Step 1 approximately 15 minutes before exercise.

The NCAA allows virtually all antiasthmatic drugs to be used by competing athletes. The IOC allows only inhaled albuterol and terbutaline. As previously mentioned, many athletes have heard that oral β-agonists, in particular clenbuterol, can produce anabolic effects. These drugs are banned by the IOC, but not the NCAA.[81–83] (For further discussion of exercise-induced asthma see Chapter 19: Asthma.)

Update

U1. What is the current status of drug distribution in athletics departments?

Until recently little more than anecdotal information was available about the distribution of drugs within athletics departments. A study funded by the NCAA explored this issue at a random sampling of NCAA Division I institutions.[84,85] The study's findings included:

- The majority of schools dispensed drugs from the training room.
- Only 10% of schools had pharmacists who were actively involved in drug distribution in the training rooms.
- At most schools, trainers and graduate assistant trainers were allowed to dispense prescription medications.
- Very few schools met state and federal packaging and labeling requirements.
- Every school had drug products in stock that were expired or had been recalled.
- None of the schools that dispensed Schedule II controlled drug products met the requirements of the Drug Enforcement Agency (DEA).
- The majority of schools allowed access to the locked drug cabinet by individuals other than the team physician.
- Few schools counseled athletes receiving a prescription medication when dispensed from the training room.

The implications from these findings for athletics departments are clear: Many current drug distribution practices are illegal and the health care of the athlete may be compromised. This was underscored in 1994 by a DEA investigation of the drug distribution practices at a major university athletics department.[86]

The opportunities for pharmacists should be equally clear. However, pharmacists interested in athletics medicine should recognize some unique aspects of athlete care. First, the health care needs of a competitive athlete are unique in that any condition that could limit participation, even if not medically critical, receives immediate treatment. This has led many athletic training rooms to provide their own ambulatory health services rather than accessing traditional sources of health care. These athletic training room/medicine clinics are in themselves unique in that physicians may be present for only brief periods of time when the training room is open. The one constant care giver is often the athletic trainer or, in some cases, a physical therapist.

Examples of successful collaborations between pharmacy and athletics departments do exist. One such program has been described in the literature.[87] This model university-based sports pharmacy program provides comprehensive services to the athletics department out of the student health center.

References

1   **Murray TH.** The coercive power of drugs in sports. Hastings Cent Rep. 1983;13:24.

2   **Thomason H.** Drugs and the athlete. In: Davies B et al., eds. Science and Sporting Performance: Management or Manipulation. Oxford: Oxford University Press; 1982.

3   **Anon.** Guide to banned medications. United States Olympic Committee. Sportsmediscope. 1988;7:1.

4   **Wadler GI, Hainline B.** Drugs and the Athlete. Philadelphia, PA: FA Davis; 1989:4.

5   **United States Olympic Committee.** USOC Drug Control Program Protocol, 1993. Colorado Springs, CO:U.S. Olympic House; 1993.

6   **Benson MT, ed.** The 1993–94 NCAA Drug-Testing Education Programs. Mission, KS: National Collegiate Athletic Association; 1993.

7   **Lombardo JA.** Drugs in sports. In: Krakauer LJ, ed. The 1986 Yearbook in Sports Medicine. Chicago: Yearbook Publisher; 1986.

8   **Wagner JC et al.** Pharmaceutical services at the Tenth Pan American Games. Am J Hosp Pharm. 1989;46:2023.

9   **Anderson WA et al.** The Substance Use and Abuse Habits of College Student-Athletes (Report No. 2). Mission, KS: National Collegiate Athletic Association; 1985.

10 **Anderson WA et al.** Replication of the National Study of the Substance Use and Abuse Habits of College Student-Athletes. Mission, KS: National Collegiate Athletic Association; 1989.

11 **Anderson WA et al.** Second Replication of a National Study of the Substance Use and Abuse Habits of College Student-Athletes. Mission, KS: National Collegiate Athletic Association; 1993.

12 **Buckley WE et al.** Estimated prevalence of anabolic steroid use among high school seniors. JAMA. 1988;260:3441.

13 **Johnson MD et al.** Anabolic steroid use by male adolescents. Pediatrics. 1989;83:921.

14 **DuRant RH et al.** Use of multiple drugs among adolescents who use anabolic steroids. N Engl J Med. 1993;328:922.

15 **Pope HG, Katz DL.** Affective and psychotic symptoms associated with anabolic steroid use. Am J Psychiatry. 1988;145:487.

16 **Lubell A.** Does steroid abuse cause—or excuse—violence? The Physician and Sports Medicine. 1989;17:176.

17 **Conacher GN, Workman DG.** Violent crime possibly associated with anabolic steroid use. Am J Psychiatry. 1989;146:679.

18 **Pope HG, Katz DL.** Homicide and near-homicide by anabolic steroid users. J Clin Psychiatry. 1989;51:28.

19 **Overly WL et al.** Androgens and hepatocellular carcinoma in an athlete. Ann Intern Med. 1984;100:158. Letter.

20 **Stang-Voss C, Appell HJ.** Structural alterations of liver parenchyma induced by anabolic steroids. Int J Sports Med. 1981;2:101.

21 **Goldman B.** Liver carcinoma in an athlete taking anabolic steroids. J Am Osteopath Assoc. 1985;85:56. Letter.

22 **Creagh TM et al.** Hepatic tumors induced by anabolic steroids in an athlete. J Clin Pathol. 1988;41:441.

23 **Narducci WA et al.** Anabolic steroids—a review of the clinical toxicology and diagnostic screening. Clin Toxicol. 1990;28:287.

24 **Cabasso A.** Peliosis hepatis in a young adult bodybuilder. Med Sci Sports Exerc. 1994;26:2.

25 **Haupt HA, Rovere GD.** Anabolic steroids: a review of the literature. Am J Sports Med. 1984;12:469.

26 **Hickson RC et al.** Adverse effects of anabolic steroids. Med Toxicol Adverse Drug Exp. 1989;4:254.

27 **Wilson JD.** Androgen abuse by athletes. Endocr Rev. 1988;9:181.

28 **Clerico A et al.** Effect of anabolic treatment on the serum levels of gonadotropins, testosterone, prolactin, thyroid hormones and myoglobin of male athletes under physical training. J Nucl Med Allied Sci. 1981;25:79.

29 **Ruokonen A et al.** Response of serum testosterone and its precursor steroids, SHBG and CBG to anabolic steroid and testosterone self-administration in man. J Steroid Biochem. 1985;23:33.

30 **Holma P, Adlercreutz H.** Effect of an anabolic steroid (metandienone) on plasma LH-FSH, and testosterone and on the response to intravenous administration of LRH. Acta Endocrinol. 1976;83:856.

31 **Kiraly CL et al.** Effect of androgenic and anabolic steroids on the sebaceous gland in power athletes. Acta Derm Venereol. 1987;67:36.

32 **Kiraly CL et al.** The effect of testosterone and anabolic steroids on the skin surface lipids and the population of Propionibacteria acnes in young postpubertal men. Acta Derm Venereol. 1988;68:21.

33 **Kiraly CL et al.** Effect of testosterone and anabolic steroids on the size of sebaceous glands in power athletes. Am J Dermatopathol. 1987;9:515.

34 **Scott MJ Jr, Scott MJ.** Dermatologist and anabolic-androgenic drug abuse. Cutis. 1989;44:30.

35 **Cohen JC, Hickman R.** Insulin resistance and diminished glucose tolerance in powerlifters ingesting anabolic steroids. J Clin Endocrinol Metab. 1987;64:960.

36 **Alen M et al.** Androgenic-anabolic steroid effects on serum thyroid, pituitary and steroid hormones in athletes. Am J Sports Med. 1987;15:357.

37 **Alen M, Rahkila P.** Reduced high-density-lipoprotein-cholesterol in power athletes: use of male sex hormone derivatives, an atherogenic factor. Int J Sports Med. 1984;5:341.

38 **Alen M et al.** Serum lipids in power athletes self-administering testosterone and anabolic steroids. Int J Sports Med. 1985;6:139.

39 **Lenders JW et al.** Deleterious effects of anabolic steroids on serum lipoproteins, blood pressure, and liver function in amateur body builders. Int J Sports Med. 1988;9:19.

40 **Hurley BF et al.** High-density-lipoprotein cholesterol in bodybuilders and powerlifters: negative effects of androgen use. JAMA. 1984;252:507.

41 **Webb OL et al.** Severe depression of high-density lipoprotein cholesterol levels in weight lifters and body builders by self-administration exogenous testosterone and anabolic-androgenic steroids. Metabolism. 1984;33:971.

42 **Alen M, Rahkila P.** Anabolic-androgenic steroid effects on endocrinology and lipid metabolism in athletes. Sports Med. 1988;6:327.

43 **Zuliani U et al.** Effects of anabolic steroids, testosterone, and HGH on blood lipids and echocardiographic parameters in body builders. Int J Sports Med. 1989;10:62.

44 **McKillop GM, Ballantyne D.** Lipoprotein analysis in bodybuilders. Int J Cardiol. 1987;17:281.

45 **Kleiner SM et al.** Dietary influences on cardiovascular disease risk in anabolic steroid-using and nonusing body-builders. J Am Coll Nutr. 1989;8:109.

46 **Bowman SJ et al.** Anabolic steroids and infarction. Br Med J. 1989;299:632.

47 **McNutt RA et al.** Acute myocardial infarction in a 22-year-old world class weight lifter using anabolic steroids. Am J Cardiol. 1988;62:164.

48 **Capezzuto A et al.** Myocardial infarction in a 21-year-old body builder. Am J Cardiol. 1989;63:1539.

49 **Frankle MA et al.** Anabolic androgenic steroids and a stroke in an athlete. Arch Phys Med Rehabil. 1988;69:632.

50 **Nagelberg SB et al.** Cerebrovascular accident associated with testosterone therapy in a 21-year-old hypogonadal man. N Engl J Med. 1986;314:649.

51 **Annitto WJ, Layman WA.** Anabolic steroids and acute schizophrenic episode. J Clin Psychiatry. 1980;41:143.

52 **Tennant F et al.** Anabolic steroid dependence with opioid-type features. N Eng J Med. 1988;319:578.

53 **Brower KF et al.** Anabolic-androgenic steroid dependence. J Clin Psychiatry. 1989;50:31.

54 **Kashkin KB, Kleber HD.** Hooked on hormones? An anabolic steroid addiction hypothesis. JAMA. 1989;262:3166.

55 **Lamb DR.** Anabolic steroids in athletes: how well do they work and how dangerous are they? Am J Sports Med. 1984;12:31.

56 **Alen M et al.** Changes in neuromuscular performance and muscle fiber characteristics of elite power athletes self-administering androgenic and anabolic steroids. Acta Physiol Scand. 1984;122:535.

57 **Crist DM et al.** Effects of androgenic-anabolic steroids on neuromuscular power and body composition. J Appl Physiol. 1983;54:366.

58 **Fahey TD, Brown CH.** The effects of an anabolic steroid on the strength, body composition, and endurance of college males when accompanied by a weight training program. Med Sci Sports. 1973;5:272.

59 **Hervey GR et al.** ''Anabolic'' effects of methadione in men undergoing athletic training. Lancet. 1976;2:699.

60 **Shepard RJ et al.** Responses to sustained use of anabolic steroids. Br J Sports Med. 1977;11:170.

61 **Windsor RE, Dumitru D.** Anabolic steroid use by athletes. Postgrad Med. 1988;84:37.

62 **Haupt HA.** Drugs in athletics. Clinics in Sports Medicine. 1989;8:561.

63 **Luby S.** GHB use in South Carolina. Am J Public Health. 1992;82:128. Letter.

64 **Mamelak M.** Gamma hydroxybutyrate: an endogenous regulator of energy metabolism. Neurosci Biobehav Rev. 1989;13:187.

65 **DiPasquale MG.** Clenbuterol: a new anabolic drug. Drugs in Sports. 1992;1:8.

66 **Wagner JC.** Use of chromium and cobamamide by athletes. Clin Pharm. 1989;8:832.

67 **Hatton CK, Catlin DH.** Detection of androgenic anabolic steroids in urine. Clinics in Laboratory Medicine. 1987; 7:655.

68 **Wagner JC.** Substance-abuse policies and guidelines in amateur and professional athletics. Am J Hosp Pharm. 1987;44:305.

69 **Davis A.** Drug testing procedures for athletics. In: Fuentes RJ et al, eds. Athletic Drug Reference '93. Durham: Clean Data; 1993:85.

70 **DiPasquale MG.** Blood doping and erythropoietin. Drugs in Sports. 1992; 1:7.

71 **Cowert VS.** Erythropoietin: a danger-ous new form of blood doping? Phys Sportsmed. 1989;17(Aug):115.

72 **Escher S, Maierhofer WJ.** Erythropoietin and endurance exercise: a recipe for disaster. Your Patient & Fitness. 1992;6(Sep/Oct):15.

73 **Gall SL.** Deterring rEPO use in athletes. Phys Sportsmed. 1991;19(Aug):17.

74 **McCarthy P.** Wheezing or breezing through exercise-induced asthma. Phys Sportsmed. 1989;17(Jul):125.

75 **Voy RO.** The U.S. Olympic Committee experience with exercise-induced bronchospasm. Med Sci Sports Exerc. 1984;18:328.

76 **Huftel MA et al.** Finding and managing asthma in competitive athletes. J Respir Dis. 1991;12:1110.

77 **Guill MF et al.** Unrecognized exercise-induced asthma in adolescent athletes. J Allergy Clin Immunol. 1991; 87:339. Abstract.

78 **Shield S, Wand-Dohlman A.** Incidence of exercise-induced bronchospasm in high school football players. J Allergy Clin Immunol. 1991;87:166. Abstract.

79 **Mellion MB et al.** Exercise-induced asthma. Am Fam Physician. 1992;45: 2671.

80 **Anderson SD.** EIA: new thinking and current management. J Respir Dis. 1986; 7:8.

81 **Katz RM.** Exercise-induced asthma in the Olympic athlete. J Asthma. 1992; 29:227.

82 **Morton AR, Fitch KD.** Asthmatic drugs and competitive sport. Sports Med. 1992;14:228.

83 **White J.** Doping at the Olympics: clenbuterol. Phys Sportsmed. 1992;20 (Aug):19.

84 **Laster-Bradley M, Berger BA.** Drug distribution in college athletics. Report to the National Collegiate Athletic Association. 1991.

85 **St. Jean AD.** Patient care compromised in college athletics programs. Am J Hosp Pharm. 1992;49:1590–601. News.

86 **Wagner JC, Narducci WA.** Drug therapy needs go beyond dispensing. NCAA News. 1994;31:4, 10. Editorial.

87 **Price KO et al.** University-based sports pharmacy program. Am J Health-Syst Pharm. 1995;52:302–9.

Anemias

Jim M Koeller
Carla Van Den Berg

Definition 88-1
Pathophysiology 88-1
Detection (See Figure 88.1) 88-2
   Signs and symptoms 88-2
   History 88-2
   Physical examination 88-2
   Laboratory evaluation
    (See Tables 88.2 and 88.3) 88-2
Iron Deficiency Anemia 88-3
   Causes (See Table 88.4) 88-5
   Predisposing Factors 88-4
   Signs, Symptoms, and Laboratory Tests 88-4
   Iron Therapy 88-5
    Oral iron dosing 88-5
    Product selection (See Tables 88.6 and 88.7) 88-5
     Product formulation 88-5
    Goals of therapy 88-6
    Patient information 88-6
    Parenteral iron therapy 88-7
     Indications 88-7
     Preferred route 88-7
     Dosage calculation 88-7
     Side effects 88-7
Megaloblastic Anemias 88-8
   Vitamin B_{12} Deficiency Anemia 88-8
   Vitamin B_{12} metabolism 88-8
   Pathogenesis and evaluation of
    vitamin B_{12} deficiency 88-8
   Laboratory evaluation 88-8
   Pernicious Anemia 88-9
    Signs, symptoms, and laboratory findings 88-9

Treatment 88-10
   Oral vitamin B_{12} 88-10
   Anemias after gastrectomy 88-10
Malabsorption of vitamin B_{12} 88-10
   Signs and symptoms 88-10
   Treatment 88-10
Folic Acid Deficiency Anemia 88-11
   Folic acid metabolism 88-11
   Predisposing factors 88-11
   Diagnosis and management 88-11
Sickle Cell Anemia (SSA) 88-12
   Pathogenesis 88-12
   Laboratory Evaluation 88-12
   Clinical Course and Management
    (Also see Question 20) 88-12
    Hemolytic anemia 88-12
    Infections 88-13
    Vascular occlusion episodes 88-13
    Neurologic complications 88-13
    Renal and genital complications 88-13
    Microinfarctions 88-13
    Future treatment 88-13
   Clinical Assessment 88-13
Anemia of Chronic Disease 88-13
   Human Recombinant Erythropoietin Therapy
    (See Table 88.8) 88-14
   Renal Insufficiency-Related Anemia 88-14
   Malignancy-Related Anemia 88-14
   Acquired Immunodeficiency Related
    (AIDS)-Related Anemia 88-15
Multifactorial Anemias 88-16

Definition

Anemia is defined as a reduction in red cell mass. It often is described as a decrease in the number of red blood cells per mm^3 or as a decrease in the hemoglobin concentration in blood to a level below the normal physiologic requirement that is necessary for adequate tissue oxygenation. The term ''anemia'' is not a diagnosis, but rather an objective sign of a disease. Diagnostic terminology for anemia requires the inclusion of the pathogenesis (e.g., megaloblastic anemia secondary to folate deficiency, microcytic anemia secondary to folate deficiency). An exact diagnosis is important to the understanding of the problem and implementation of specific therapy to correct the anemia.

Pathophysiology

Anemia is a symptom of many pathological conditions. It is associated with nutritional deficiencies, acute and chronic diseases, and may be drug induced. Anemia may be caused by decreased red cell production, increased red cell destruction, or increased red cell loss. If the anemia is due to decreased red cell production, it may be the result of disturbances in stem-cell proliferation or differentiation. Anemias due to increased red cell destruction may be secondary to hemolysis while increased red cell loss may be caused by acute or chronic bleeding. Anemias associated with acute blood loss, those that are iron-related, and those due to chronic disease comprise about 75% of all anemias.[2] Classifications of anemias according to pathophysiological and morphological characteristics are shown in Table 88.1.

Normally, RBC mass is maintained by feedback mechanisms that regulate levels of erythropoietin, a hormone which stimulates proliferation and differentiation of erythroid precursors in the bone marrow. Two types of erythroid precursors reside in the bone marrow, the BFUe (burst-forming unit, erythroid) and CFUe (colony-forming unit, erythroid). The BFUe is the earliest progenitor which eventually develops into a CFUe. BFUe is moderately sensitive to erythropoietin and is under the influence of other cytokines (e.g., IL-3, GM-CSF). CFUe is highly sensitive to erythropoietin and differentiates into erythroblasts and reticulocytes. Normal endogenous levels of erythropoietin range from 10 to 20 U/L.[97] Ninety percent of erythropoietin is produced in the kidney; liver synthesis accounts for the remaining 10%. Reduced oxygen-carrying capacity is sensed by renal peritubular cells and this stimulates release of erythropoietin into the blood stream. Patients with chronic anemia may have a blunted response for the degree of anemia present, or virtually no erythropoietin response because of renal insufficiency.

Table 88.1	Classifications of Anemia

Pathophysiologic (Classifies Anemias Based Upon Pathophysiologic Presentation)

Blood Loss
Acute: Trauma, ulcer, hemorrhoids
Chronic: Ulcer, vaginal bleeding, aspirin ingestion

Inadequate Red Blood Cell Production
Nutritional Deficiency: B_{12}, folic acid, iron
Erythroblast Deficiency: Bone marrow failure (aplastic anemia, irradiation, chemotherapy, folic acid antagonists) or bone marrow infiltration (leukemia, lymphoma, myeloma, metastatic solid tumors, myelofibrosis)
Endocrine Deficiency: Pituitary, adrenal, thyroid, testicular
Chronic Disease: Renal, liver, infection, granulomatous, collagen vascular

Excessive Red Blood Cell Destruction
Intrinsic Factors: Hereditary (G6PD), abnormal hemoglobin synthesis
Extrinsic Factors: Autoimmune reactions, drug reactions, infection (endotoxin)

Morphologic [Classifies Anemias by Red Blood Cell Size (Microcytic, Normocytic, Macrocytic) and Hemoglobin Content (Hypochromic, Normochromic, Hyperchromic)]

Macrocytic
Defective maturation with decreased production
Megaloblastic: Pernicious (B_{12} deficiency), folic acid deficiency

Normochromic, Normocytic
Recent blood loss
Hemolysis
Chronic disease
Renal failure
Autoimmune
Endocrine

Microcytic, Hyperchromic
Iron deficiency
Genetic Abnormalities: Sickle cell, thalassemia

ᵃ G6PD = Glucose 6-phosphate dehydrogenase.

Detection

Signs and Symptoms

Signs and symptoms of anemia vary with the degree of RBC reduction as well as with the time interval over which it developed. Anemic patients may experience tissue hypoxia because of the decreased oxygen-carrying capacity of the reduced red cell mass. As a result, perfusion to nonvital tissues (e.g., skin, mucous membranes, extremities) is decreased to sustain tissue perfusion of vital organs (e.g., brain, heart, kidneys). This compensatory mechanism accounts for the skin pallor that can be noted in cases of severe anemia [hemoglobin (Hgb) <8 mg/dL]. This is most easily observed in the conjunctiva, nail beds, and palmar creases of the hand. Uncorrected tissue hypoxia can lead to a number of complications in the central nervous, respiratory, and gastrointestinal (GI) systems. Changes in the blood hemoglobin concentration also lead to changes in the kidney tissue oxygen tension. The kidney responds to the hypoxemia by secreting erythropoietin, as discussed previously.[1–3]

In severe anemia, heart rate and stroke volume often increase in an attempt to improve the delivery of oxygen to tissues. These changes in heart rate and stroke volume may result in systolic murmurs, angina pectoris, high-output congestive heart failure, pulmonary congestion, ascites, and edema. Thus, anemia is generally not well tolerated in patients with cardiac disease.[4]

Anemia may be acute in onset or develop slowly. Slowly developing anemias may be asymptomatic initially or include symptoms such as slight exertional dyspnea, increased angina, fatigue, or malaise. The symptoms gradually increase as the anemia be-

comes more severe. Pallor of the skin and mucous membranes, jaundice, smooth or beefy tongue, cheilosis, and spoon-shaped nails (koilonychia) may be associated with severe anemia of different etiologies.

History

Due to the complexity of the pathological conditions associated with anemia, a thorough history and physical examination are essential. A timeline which begins with the onset symptoms (and surrounding events) and extends to current status is important. Long-standing anemias can indicate hereditary disorders; thus, a family history is important. Past hemoglobin or hematocrit (Hct) determinations, transfusion history, as well as occupational, environmental, and social histories may be valuable. Finally, a medication history can help eliminate drug reactions or interactions as the cause of the anemia.

Physical Examination

On physical examination of a patient with anemia, pallor is most easily observed in the conjunctiva, mucous membranes, nail beds, and palmar creases of the hand. In addition, postural hypotension and tachycardia can be seen when hypovolemia (acute blood loss) is the primary cause of anemia. Patients with B_{12} deficiency may exhibit neurological findings which include changes in deep tendon reflexes, ataxia, and loss of vibration and position sense. These are all consistent with nerve fiber demyelination. Patients with anemia due to hemolysis may be slightly jaundiced from bilirubin release. Manifestations of hemorrhage can include petechiae, ecchymoses, hematomas, epistaxis, bleeding gums, blood in the urine, or blood in the stool.

Laboratory Evaluation

Even though anemia may be suspected from the history and physical examination, a full laboratory evaluation is necessary to confirm the diagnosis, establish its severity, and determine its cause. A list of the routine laboratory evaluations used in the work up for anemia are found in Table 88.2. The cornerstone of this evaluation is the complete blood count (CBC). Normal hematologic values can be found in Table 88.3. Females reach adult levels of hematocrit by late childhood. At puberty, males have a higher hematocrit secondary to stimulation of erythropoiesis by androgen hormones. The hematocrit also is increased in individuals living at altitudes above 4000 feet in response to the diminished oxygen content of the atmosphere and blood.

Table 88.2	Routine Laboratory Evaluation for Anemia Work-Upᵃ

Complete blood count (CBC): Hgb, Hct, RBC count, red cell indices (MCV, MCH, MCHC), WBC count (and differential)

Platelet count

Red cell morphology

Reticulocyte count

Bilirubin and LD

Serum iron, TIBC, serum ferritin, transferrin saturation

Peripheral blood smear examination

Stool examination for occult blood

Bone marrow aspiration and biopsyᵇ

ᵃ Hct = Hematocrit; Hgb = Hemoglobin; LD = Lactic dehydrogenase; MCV = Mean corpuscular volume; MCH = Mean corpuscular hemoglobin; MCHC = Mean corpuscular hemoglobin concentration; RBC = Red blood cell; TIBC = Total iron binding capacity; WBC = White blood cell.
ᵇ Performed in patients with abnormal peripheral blood smears.

Table 88.3	Normal Hematology Values				
	Pediatric			Adult	
Laboratory Test[a]	1 week	6 months	1–15 years	Male	Female
RBC (mm^3)	5.3 ± 7	4.5 ± 6	4.7 ± 6	5.4 ± 0.7	4.8 ± 6
Hgb (gm/dL)	18 ± 4	12.5 ± 1.5	13 ± 2	16 ± 2	14 ± 2
Hct (%)	53 ± 9	37 ± 4	40 ± 5	47 ± 5	42 ± 2
MCV (μm^3)	101 ± 5	78 ± 5	80 ± 5	87 ± 7	90 ± 9
MCH (pg/cell)	37 ± 2	34 ± 2	33.5 ± 2	29 ± 2	34 ± 2
Reticulocyte count (%)	0.5–1.5	0.5–1.5	0.5–1.5	0.5–1.5	0.5–1.5
TIBC (μg/dL)	100–400	250–400	250–400	250–400	250–400
Fe (μg/dL)	100–250	100–400	50–120	50–160	40–150
Folate (ng/mL)	7–25	7–25	7–25	7–25	7–25
Vitamin B$_{12}$ (pg/mL)	>200	>200	>200	>200	>200
Ferritin (ng/mL)	25–200	50–200	7–140	15–200	12–150

[a] Fe = Iron; Hgb = Hemoglobin; Hct = Hematocrit; MCH = Mean corpuscular hemoglobin; MCV = Mean corpuscular volume; RBC = Red blood cell; TIBC = Total iron binding capacity.

The morphological appearance of the red blood cell (RBC) provides useful information about the nature of the anemia. Microscopic evaluation of the peripheral blood smear can detect the presence of macrocytic (large) red blood cells that usually are present when anemia is due to a vitamin B$_{12}$ or folic acid deficiency or microcytic (small) red blood cells that usually are associated with iron deficiency anemia. Acute blood loss generally is associated with normocytic cells.

Together with the information gained from the history and physical examination, the routine laboratory evaluation can provide enough information to distinguish between the most common forms of anemia (see Figure 88.1). If the etiology of the anemia is still not identified following routine evaluation, problems such as autoimmune disease, collagen vascular disease, chronic infection, endocrine disorders, or drug-induced destruction may be the cause. When uncertainty exists or an abnormal peripheral blood smear is noted, a bone marrow aspiration with biopsy is indicated.

There are many causes of anemia. This chapter will be limited to the most common anemias managed with drugs. Hemolytic anemias are covered in Chapter 89: Drug-Induced Blood Disorders. Before proceeding, the reader should review the basic hematologic laboratory tests used to evaluate and monitor anemia (see Chapter 4: Interpretation of Clinical Laboratory Tests).

Iron Deficiency Anemia

Iron deficiency is a state of negative iron balance in which the daily iron intake and stores are unable to meet the red blood cell and other body tissue needs.[5] The body contains approximately 3.5 gm of iron of which 2.5 gm are found in hemoglobin. A significant amount of iron is stored as ferritin or aggregated ferritin (hemosiderin) in the reticuloendothelial cells of the liver, spleen, and bone marrow and by hepatocytes. Men have iron stores of 600 to 1200 mg while women have stores between 100 to 400 mg. Only a small fraction of iron is found in plasma (100 to 150 μg/dL) and most is bound to transferrin, the transport protein.

Despite the continuing turnover of red blood cells, iron stores are well preserved because the iron is recovered and reutilized in new erythrocytes. Only about 0.5 to 1 mg/day of iron is lost from urine, sweat, and the sloughing of intestinal mucosal cells that contain ferritin. Another 0.5 to 1 mg of iron is lost daily during menstruation. Pregnancy and lactation are other common sources of iron loss.

Individuals with normal iron stores absorb roughly 10% of ingested dietary iron. The average American diet contains 6 mg of elemental iron/1000 KCal. Thus, the average daily intake ranges between 10 to 12 mg, enough to replace the 1 mg lost daily (based upon 10% absorption). However, for menstruating, pregnant, or lactating females, the daily iron intake requirement may be as high as 20 mg.

Iron is absorbed from the duodenum and upper jejunum by an active transport mechanism. Dietary iron, which is primarily in the ferric state, is converted to the more readily absorbed ferrous form in the acid environment of the stomach. It is the ferrous form that binds to transferrin for its journey to the bone marrow where it is incorporated into the hemoglobin of mature erythrocytes.

A portion of the iron is bound to another protein, ferritin, which is important in the storage of iron. Ferritin circulates at concentrations that reflect total iron body stores.

Gastrointestinal absorption of iron is increased from the usual 10% to as much as 20% to 30% in iron deficiency states or when erythropoiesis occurs at a more rapid rate. Animal sources of iron are better absorbed than plant sources. A gastrectomy or vagotomy may decrease the conversion of the ferric form of iron to the ferrous state, thereby diminishing iron absorption. Additionally, certain foods and drugs can complex with iron, decreasing its absorption.

Anemia due to iron deficiency is a common world-wide problem. Although there are many causes of iron deficiency anemia (see Table 88.4), blood loss is considered one of the more common. Each milliliter of whole blood contains 0.5 mg of iron, whereas each milliliter of packed red blood cells contains 1 mg of iron. Common causes of chronic blood loss include peptic ulcer disease, hemorrhoids, ingestion of gastrointestinal irritants, menstruation, multiple pregnancies, and multiple blood donations.

The increased amounts of iron required by pregnant or lactating women are hard to obtain through diet alone; thus, oral iron supplementation generally is necessary. (See Chapter 44: Obstetrics.) While maternal iron usually provides full-term infants with enough stored iron for the first six months, infants six months to three years of age experience rapid growth and a threefold increase in blood volume which can increase the risk of iron deficiency. Premature infants have reduced iron stores and thus require replacement therapy. Supplementation of 10 to 15 mg/day of iron may be required for up to the first year of life. Maintenance iron therapy for normal older infants and children is roughly 1 to 2 mg/kg/day (not to exceed 20 mg/day). If iron deficiency develops in the pediatric patient, 3 to 6 mg/kg/day of elemental iron should be administered in two to three divided doses.[7] Table 88.5 provides a listing of some available pediatric iron preparations.

Predisposing Factors

1. D.G., a 35-year-old female, is seen in the clinic. Her chief complaints include weakness, dizziness, and epigastric pain. She has a 5-year history of peptic ulcer disease, a 10-year history of heavy menstrual bleeding, and a 20-year history of chronic headaches. She has 4 children who are 1, 3, 5, and 7 years of age.

D.G. is currently taking tetracycline 250 mg BID for acne; aspirin 650 mg PRN headaches; and frequent doses of antacids for GI distress. Her review of systems is positive for decreased exercise tolerance. Physical examination reveals a pale, lethargic, white female appearing older than her stated age. Her vital signs are within normal limits; her heart rate is regular at 100 beats/min. Her examination is notable for pale nail beds and splenomegaly.

Significant laboratory results include: Hgb 8 gm/dL; Hct 27%; platelet count 800,000/mm^3; reticulocyte count 0.2%; mean corpuscular volume (MCV) 75 μm^3; mean corpuscular hemoglobin (MCH) 23 pg; mean corpuscular hemoglobin concentration (MCHC) 30%; serum iron 40 μg/dL; serum ferritin 9 ng/mL; total iron binding capacity (TIBC) 450 μg/dL; 4+ guaiac stools.

Iron deficiency is determined to be the cause of D.G.'s anemia. An upper GI series with a small bowel follow through are planned to evaluate her persistent epigastric pain. What factors predispose D.G. to iron deficiency anemia? [SI units: Hgb 80 gm/L; Hct 0.27; MCV 75 fL; MCH 23 pg; MCHC 0.3; iron 7.16 μmol/L; ferritin 9 μg/L; TIBC 80.87 μmol/L; platelets 800 × 10^9/L; reticulocyte 0.002]

Several factors predispose D.G. to iron deficiency anemia. Her history of heavy menstrual bleeding and the 4+ stool guaiac indicate menstrual and gastrointestinal sources of blood loss. The GI blood loss may be secondary to D.G.'s chronic use of salicylates and/or recurrent peptic ulcer disease.

Many women of childbearing age have a borderline iron deficiency that becomes more evident during pregnancy because of the increased iron requirements.[8–10] D.G. has given birth to four children. Therefore, her iron stores have been repeatedly taxed in recent years. Additionally, absorption of dietary iron may be compromised by her use of antacids and tetracycline (see Question 6).

Signs, Symptoms, and Laboratory Tests

2. What subjective or objective signs, symptoms, and laboratory tests are typical of iron deficiency in D.G.?

D.G.'s constitutional symptoms of weakness and dizziness could be a result of her severe anemia. Generally, until the anemia is severe, such symptoms occur with equal frequency in the non-anemic population. The most important signs and symptoms of iron deficiency anemia are related to the cardiovascular system and are a reflection of the imbalance between the ongoing demands for oxygen against a diminishing oxygen supply. D.G.'s increased heart rate, decreased exercise tolerance, and pale appearance are

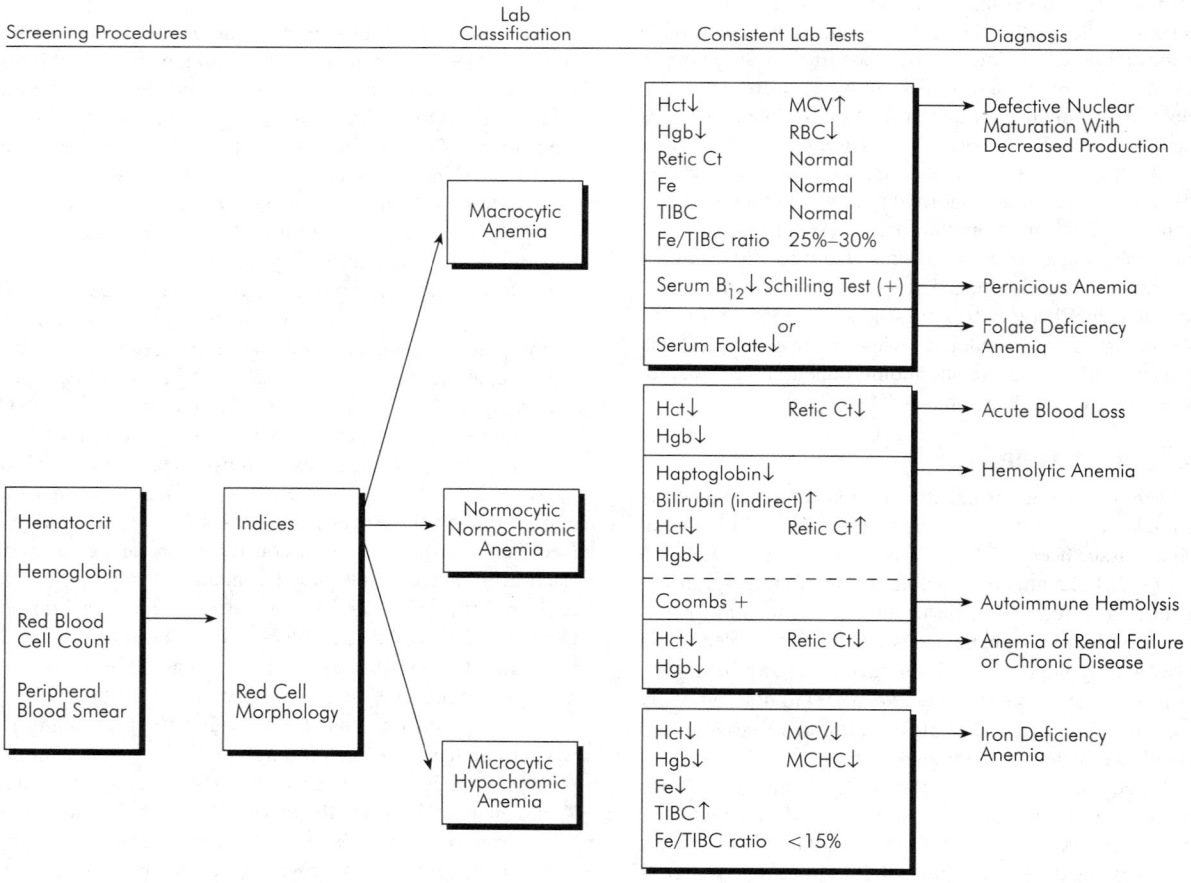

Fig 88.1   Laboratory Diagnosis of Anemia

Table 88.4	Iron Deficiency Anemia Causes

Blood Loss
Menstruation, gastrointestinal (e.g., peptic ulcer), trauma

Decreased Absorption
Medication (e.g., tetracycline), gastrectomy, regional enteritis

Increased Requirement
Infancy, pregnant/lactating females

Impaired Utilization
Hereditary, ↓ iron use

consistent with tissue anoxia and the cardiovascular response that may be seen in iron deficiency anemia.

D.G.'s iron deficiency has advanced to symptomatic anemia. However, in patients who are not yet symptomatic, depletion of iron stores can be detected by measuring ferritin, the iron storage compound. Although ferritin is primarily intracellular, serum concentrations of ferritin correlate closely with iron stores with only a few exceptions (e.g., liver disease and some malignancies).[11–14] A serum ferritin level less than 12 ng/mL is consistent with iron deficiency. An increased TIBC also can reflect depletion of storage iron, but it is less sensitive than serum ferritin. Thus, in iron deficiency, the serum ferritin concentration is low while the TIBC is usually high; both of these parameters can be detected before the clinical manifestations of anemia are apparent. These abnormalities persist and worsen as the patient progresses to anemia as illustrated by D.G.'s values. If the bone marrow is examined at this time, hemosiderin granules (which contain ≈25% to 30% of iron) would be absent. If the TIBC is low or normal rather than high, in association with a low serum ferritin, other causes of anemia such as abnormalities, infections, or inflammatory disorders should be considered. In these situations further documentation (e.g., bone marrow examination) is necessary to determine the cause of the anemia.[15–17]

D.G.'s low serum iron, low serum ferritin, and elevated TIBC are typical of the laboratory findings associated with iron deficiency anemia. In addition to examining the absolute values reported for serum iron and TIBC, the ratio of the serum iron concentration to the TIBC (or the transferrin saturation ratio) should be determined [$(S_{Fe}/TIBC) \times 100$]. In iron deficiency, the transferrin saturation ratio falls below 15%. D.G.'s calculated transferrin saturation ratio (i.e., $40/450 \times 100\%$) is 8.9% and is consistent with iron deficiency anemia.

After the iron in the storage compartment is depleted, heme and hemoglobin synthesis are decreased. In severe iron deficiency, the red blood cells become hypochromic (low MCHC) and microcytic (low MCV). Usually, the indices do not become abnormal until the hemoglobin concentration falls to less than 12 gm/dL in males or 10 gm/dL in females. D.G.'s corpuscular indices indicate that her anemia is hypochromic and microcytic.

About 10% of iron-deficient patients will experience neutropenia and either thrombocytopenia or thrombocytosis. Thrombocytosis can occur in 50% to 75% of patients with hypochromic anemia secondary to chronic blood loss. The thrombocytosis (e.g., 800,000 platelets) in D.G. will return to normal after adequate treatment with iron. The reticulocyte count provides an estimate of effective red cell production and is usually normal or low in iron deficiency anemia. D.G. has a reticulocyte count of 0.2% (normal: 0.5% to 1.5%) which also is compatible with iron deficiency anemia.

In the work-up of a microcytic, hypochromic anemia, the stool should be examined for occult blood. D.G. has a 4+ stool guaiac, which suggests blood loss via the gastrointestinal tract. Further

diagnostic evaluations (e.g., endoscopy, GI films) are necessary to determine the underlying problem.

In summary, D.G.'s signs, symptoms, and laboratory findings all support the diagnosis of an iron deficiency anemia.

Iron Therapy

Oral Iron Dosing

3. How should D.G.'s iron deficiency be managed? What dose of iron should be given to treat D.G.'s iron-deficiency anemia and for how long?

The primary treatment of D.G. should be directed toward control of the underlying causes of anemia, which in this case are many. D.G.'s iron stores are low because of gastrointestinal blood loss, multiple childbirths, heavy menstrual flow, and, perhaps, inadequate diet. Therefore, the cause of her gastrointestinal blood loss should be corrected, her dietary intake should be analyzed and modified, and supplemental iron should be prescribed to replenish her stores and correct the anemia.

The usual adult dose of ferrous sulfate is 325 mg (1 tablet) administered three times daily, between meals. Actually, if no iron is being lost through bleeding, the required daily dose of elemental iron can be calculated using a formula that assumes that 0.25 gm/dL/day is the maximal rate of hemoglobin regeneration.

$$\text{Elemental Iron} \atop (\text{mg/day}) = \left(\frac{0.25 \text{ gm Hgb}}{100 \text{ mL Blood/day}}\right)(5000 \text{ mL Blood})\left(\frac{3.4 \text{ mg Fe}}{1 \text{ gm Hgb}}\right)$$

$$= \frac{40 \text{ mg Fe/day}}{\substack{20\% \text{ Absorption} \\ (\text{approximate absorption rate in iron deficient states})}}$$

$$= 200 \text{ mg Fe/day}$$

$$= \substack{1000 \text{ mg Ferrous Sulfate/day (ferrous sulfate contains} \\ 20\% \text{ elemental iron})}$$

$$= 325 \text{ mg TID Ferrous Sulfate}$$

Product Selection

4. What are the differences between iron products? Which is the product of choice?

The ferrous form of iron is absorbed three times more readily than the ferric form. Although ferrous sulfate, ferrous gluconate, and ferrous fumarate are absorbed almost equally, each contains a different amount of elemental iron.[20,21] Table 88.6 compares the number of tablets of ferrous sulfate, gluconate, and fumarate required to provide a daily adult dose of 180 to 200 mg of elemental iron. If compliance is enhanced when the patient takes the smallest number of tablets, then ferrous sulfate or ferrous fumarate may be better choices.

Product formulation is of considerable importance in product selection. Some believe that the more expensive, sustained-release

Table 88.5	Iron Content of Liquid Iron Preparations[a–c]	
Preparation	Trade Name	Iron Content (mg Fe++/mL)
Ferrous Sulfate		
Elixir (44 mg/mL)	Feosol	8.8
Drops (125 mg/mL)	Fer-in-Sol	25.0
Syrup (18 mg/mL)	Fer-in-Sol	3.6
Ferrous Gluconate		
Elixir (60 mg/mL)	Fergon	7

[a] There are other iron preparations which may be equally efficacious, and generic equivalents may be available.
[b] The listed preparations are not being endorsed.
[c] Fe = Iron.

Table 88.6		Comparisons of Iron Preparations		
Preparation	Dose (mg)	Fe^{++} Content[b] (mg)	% Fe	AWP[a] ($/100)
Ferrous sulfate	325	65	20	0.85
Ferrous sulfate (enteric coated)	325	65	20	2.00
Ferrous fumarate	300	99	33	1.87
Ferrous gluconate	300	35	11	1.45
Feosol tablets	200	60	20	7.15
Fero-Gradumet (slow-release)	525	105	20	22.57

[a] AWP = Average wholesale price. This price does not include a prescription fee. Prescription fees will vary among pharmacies. AWP is based upon the 1994 Red Book.
[b] Fe = Iron.

(SR) iron preparations are inherently better. Sustained-release preparations fall into three groups: a) those claimed to increase gastrointestinal tolerance or decrease side effects; b) those formulated to increase bioavailability; and c) those with adjuvants claimed to enhance absorption. Because these products can be given once daily, increased compliance is an additional claim.

Anecdotal claims that SR iron preparations cause fewer gastrointestinal side effects have not been substantiated by controlled studies. In fact, these products transport iron past the duodenum and proximal jejunum, thereby reducing the absorption of iron.[22] Therefore, poor absorption and poor hematological responses may occur with ferrous sulfate sustained-release capsules. Ferro-Sequel, Vitron-C, Feosol Spansule, and enteric-coated ferrous sulfate all have a poor release of iron into the stomach and duodenum.[23]

Adjuvants are incorporated into many iron preparations in an attempt to enhance absorption or decrease side effects. Several products contain ascorbic acid (vitamin C) which maintains iron in the ferrous state; however, doses up to 1 gm increase iron absorption by only 10%. Lower doses of vitamin C (e.g., 100 mg) do not significantly alter iron absorption.[26] Table 88.7 lists a number of combination products that contain a stool softener (see below) or vitamin C. It is unlikely that the small amount of vitamin C added to these products significantly enhances absorption enough to justify the significant increase in cost.

Stool softeners are added to iron preparations to decrease the side effect of constipation. Generally, these combinations contain suboptimum doses of stool softener and are unwarranted. If constipation does develop, appropriate doses of stool softeners should be taken. It appears more rational to take iron supplements by themselves and to treat side effects as necessary.

In summary, D.G. should take the least expensive iron preparation containing ferrous sulfate, gluconate, or fumarate. Table 88.7 compares the relative costs of some of the various iron salts; generic preparations will provide the best value.

Goals of Therapy

5. What are the goals of iron therapy? How should D.G. be monitored?

The goal of iron therapy is to normalize the hemoglobin and hematocrit concentrations and to replete iron stores. Initially, if the doses of iron are adequate, the reticulocyte count will begin to increase by the third to fourth day, and peak by the seventh to tenth day of therapy. By the end of the second week of iron therapy, the reticulocyte count will fall back to normal.[28] The hemoglobin response is a convenient index to monitor in outpatients. Hemato-

logic response is usually seen in three weeks with a 2 gm/dL increase in hemoglobin and a 6% increase in the hematocrit. One can expect D.G.'s anemia to resolve in one to two months. However, iron therapy should be continued for three to six months after the hemoglobin is normalized to replete iron stores.[19,27,28] The duration of therapy is related to the absorption pattern of iron. During the first month of therapy, as much as 35 mg of elemental iron is absorbed from the daily dose. With time, the percentage of iron absorbed from the dose decreases, and by the third month of therapy, only 5 to 10 mg of elemental iron is absorbed.

Patient Information

6. What kind of information should be provided to D.G. upon dispensing oral iron? What can be done if she experiences intolerable GI symptoms (e.g., nausea, epigastric pain)?

Iron should be dispensed in a childproof container and D.G. should be told to store it in a safe place away from children. Accidental ingestion of even small amounts (3 to 4 tablets) of oral iron can cause serious consequences in small children.[29] (See Chapter 104: Clinical Toxicology.) D.G. should be told that oral iron therapy produces dark stools. She should try to take her iron on an empty stomach because food decreases the absorption by 40% to 50%.[25,30] Dairy products are the worst offenders (e.g., milk, eggs, cheese).

Gastric side effects occur in 5% to 20% of patients and include nausea, epigastric pain, constipation, abdominal cramps, and diarrhea. Constipation does not appear to be dose related, but side effects such as nausea and epigastric pain occur more frequently as the quantity of soluble elemental iron in contact with the stomach and duodenum increases.[27,31]

To minimize gastric intolerance, oral iron therapy can be initiated with a single tablet of ferrous sulfate 325 mg/day; the dose is increased by increments of one tablet per day every two to three days until the full therapeutic dose of ferrous sulfate, 325 mg three times daily, can be administered.[3,31]

Other causes of epigastric pain (e.g., recurrent peptic ulcer disease, other GI diseases) also should be investigated.

D.G. also should be educated about potential drug interactions that may occur with iron therapy. Currently, she is taking antacids for gastrointestinal distress. Historically, antacids have not been recommended in combination with iron therapy. Antacids are

Table 88.7			Combination Iron Products	
Drug	DOSS[a] (mg)	Vitamin C (mg)	Fe^{++} Content[a] (mg)	AWP[b] ($/100)
Ferrous Sulfate	0	0	65	0.85
Ferro-Grad 500 (filmtabs)	0	500	105	24.53
Ferancee (chew tabs)	0	150	64	13.02
Ferancee-HP	0	600	110	20.00
Mol-Iron w/C	0	75	39	7.86
Vitron C	0	125	66	8.40
Vitron C-Plus	0	250	132	16.8
Ferro DSS	100	0	50	14.56
Hemaspan (timed release)	20	200	110	22.87

[a] DOSS = Dioctyl sodium sulfosuccinate; docusate sodium; Fe = Iron.
[b] AWP = Average wholesale price. This price does not include a prescription fee. Prescription fees will vary among pharmacies. AWP is based upon the 1994 Red Book.

thought to inhibit serum iron absorption by increasing the pH of the stomach and decreasing the solubility of ferrous salts.[34,35] Certain anions in antacids (carbonate and hydroxide) also are thought to form insoluble complexes when combined with iron. A study evaluating the effect of antacids and iron absorption used patients with mild iron deficiency and found that when Mylanta II (5 mL) was given with 10 mg of iron, the increase in plasma iron seen two hours after the dose was not significantly different from the iron level seen two hours after a control dose.[50] However, in the same study, 1 gm of $NaHCO_3$ decreased the two-hour plasma ion concentration to 5% of the control level. $CaCO_3$ 500 mg also decreased the two-hour plasma levels, with serum iron levels attaining only one-third of the control dose. $CaCO_3$ did not appear to affect iron absorption when it was incorporated into a multivitamin containing iron.[50] Although the issue remains controversial, this study indicates that a therapeutic dose of liquid antacid containing aluminum hydroxide and magnesium hydroxide does not significantly alter absorption of iron in mildly deficient adults. Further documentation of the clinical significance of this potential iron-antacid interaction is needed. Therefore, initially, it is advisable to separate the doses of iron and antacid, and D.G. should be advised to take her iron at least one hour before or three hours after the antacid dose.

D.G. also is taking tetracycline for the treatment of acne. The absorptions of both iron and tetracycline are decreased when administered concomitantly. When both drugs are necessary, the iron should be taken three hours before or two hours after the tetracycline dose.[37] Antacids also may impair the absorption of tetracycline; therefore, tetracycline should be separated from antacids by one to two hours.

Parenteral Iron Therapy

7. Indications. Would parenteral iron therapy ever be indicated for D.G.?

There are several indications for parenteral iron administration. Failure to respond to oral iron therapy would prompt a re-evaluation of D.G. Causes of oral therapy failure can include noncompliance, misdiagnosis (e.g., inflammation), malabsorption (e.g., sprue, radiation enteritis, duodenal or upper small intestine resection), and continuing blood loss equal to or greater than the rate of RBC production. Malabsorption can be evaluated by measuring iron levels every 30 minutes for two hours after the administration of 50 mg of ferrous sulfate. If her plasma iron levels increase by more than 50%, absorption is adequate.

Besides failure to respond to oral therapy as one indication for parenteral iron administration, other reasons exist. Intolerance to oral therapy, required antacid therapy, or significant blood loss in patients refusing transfusion all can warrant injectable iron therapy.[38] In D.G.'s case, if it was documented that she had malabsorption or required continued high-dose antacid therapy for her gastritis, she would be a candidate for injectable iron.

8. Preferred Route. What is the preferred route of parenteral iron administration?

Iron can be given parenterally in the form of iron dextran for injection USP (Imferon). In this form, iron is a complex of ferric hydroxide and dextran and is packaged as a colloidal solution containing 50 mg/mL of iron. One formulation contains phenol 0.5% as a preservative and is intended for IM administration of smaller doses. If larger doses are to be given intravenously (e.g., >1 gm), ampules of Imferon are available without phenol. This product may be preferred because phenol has been associated with systemic reactions including respiratory insufficiency, CNS depression, and circulatory failure. However, only doses exceeding 8 gm have been associated with these reactions and the amount of phenol present

in a large dose of Imferon would not exceed a few hundred milligrams.[39] It can be administered undiluted IM or by very slow IV injection. Although not currently included in the labeling approved by the Food and Drug Administration (FDA), iron-dextran injection is commonly diluted in 0.9% NaCl and administered by IV infusion.

There are few instances in which IM dextran is the preferred treatment (e.g., patients with limited IV access). In these cases, undiluted drug should be administered using a Z-track technique to avoid staining the skin. (Pull the skin laterally before injection; inject; release the skin to avoid back leakage of dextran into the dermal layer.) Intramuscular dextran is absorbed in two phases. In the first 72 hours, 60% of the dose is absorbed, while the remaining drug is absorbed over weeks to months.[40]

Intravenous administration is preferred to IM administration in patients who have limited muscle mass available for an IM injection; situations of impaired absorption from the muscle (e.g., stasis, edema); patients at risk for uncontrolled bleeding (e.g., hemophilia, thrombocytopenia, anticoagulation therapy); and when large doses are indicated for therapy.

Intravenous iron dextran should not be administered at a rate exceeding 50 mg/minute. Iron dextran is FDA approved for bolus injection at a maximum dose of 100 mg/day but it is not approved for intravenous infusion. Although the data are limited, "total dose" iron dextran infusion is given in clinical practice[41-43] and has proven to be effective and convenient.[38] Infusions generally are given over two to six hours to minimize local pain and phlebitis.[27] The "total dose" method of administration may be associated with a higher prevalence of fever, malaise, flushing, and myalgias.

9. Dosage Calculation. How would you calculate a total dose of iron dextran for IV infusion that would be needed to achieve a normal Hgb for D.G. and replenish her iron stores. How quickly should she respond?

The total dose of iron dextran to be administered can be determined using the following equation:

$$\text{Iron (mg)} = \left[\text{Weight (pounds)} \times 0.3\right]\left[100 - \frac{100\,(\text{Hgb})}{14.8}\right]$$

Where Hgb is the patient's measured hemoglobin (gm/dL). The equation uses the individual's weight (in pounds) and assumes that a hemoglobin of 14.8 gm/dL is 100% of normal. Children weighing less than 30 pounds should be given 80% of the calculated dose, because the normal mean hemoglobin in this population is lower.

For patients with anemia due to blood loss such as hemorrhagic diatheses or patients on chronic dialysis, the iron requirement is based upon the estimate of iron contained in the blood lost. In this case, the following equation should be used:

$$\text{Iron (mg)} = \text{Blood Loss (mL)} \times \text{Hct (the patient's measured Hct}$$
$$\text{expressed as a decimal fraction)}$$

This formula assumes that 1 mL of normochromic blood contains 1 mg of iron.

Following parenteral administration, iron dextran is cleared by the reticuloendothelial cells and processed. The iron is then released back into the plasma and bone marrow. Because the rate of iron incorporation into hemoglobin does not exceed that achieved by oral iron therapy, the response time is similar to that of oral iron therapy, and one can expect the hemoglobin to increase at a rate of 1.5 to 2.2 gm/dL/week during the first two weeks and by 0.7 to 1.6 gm/dL/week thereafter until normal values are attained.

10. Side Effects. What side effects can be expected from parenteral iron therapy?

Anaphylactoid reactions can occur in less than 1% of patients treated.[27,41] It is unknown if this reaction is more frequent with IV or IM administration. Because of this, a 25 mg test dose is given intramuscularly or by intravenous infusion over five to ten minutes. If there are no complaints of headache, chest pain, anxiety, or signs of hypotension, the remainder of the dose can be given. However in 1% to 2% of patients, delayed reactions occurring 24 to 48 hours following large doses of IV iron dextran and lasting three to seven days have been reported. These reactions have included fever, urticaria, arthralgias, and lymphadenopathy.[44]

Megaloblastic Anemias

Megaloblastic anemia is a common disorder that may have several etiologies: 1) anemia associated with vitamin B_{12} deficiency; 2) anemia associated with folic acid deficiency; or 3) anemia due to metabolic or inherited defects resulting in the inability to utilize vitamin B_{12} or folic acid.[46-47]

Megaloblastosis results from impaired DNA synthesis in replicating cells and is recognized by a large immature nucleus. RNA and protein synthesis remain unaffected and the cytoplasm matures normally. Megaloblastic changes are observed hematologically as anemia but also may be observed in many proliferating cells, such as those observed in the cervix, skin, and GI tract.[46]

Although the clinical effects of vitamin B_{12} and folic acid deficiencies may be different in various organ systems, they are similar in their effects on the hematopoietic system. Typically, macrocytic anemia develops slowly and can be identified by large, oval, well hemoglobinized red cells; anisocytosis; and nuclear remnants. The reticulocyte count is low, and the bilirubin level will be elevated. Thrombocytopenia is present with the platelets large in appearance. Leukopenia occurs with hypersegmentation of polymorphonuclear leukocyte nuclei. If biopsied, the bone marrow will be markedly hypercellular. Nuclear immaturity will be present, but the megaloblasts will have normal maturation of the cytoplasm. Iron stores in the marrow are increased due to the intramedullary hemolysis. Symptoms include fatigue; exaggeration of pre-existing cardiovascular or pulmonary problems; a sore, pale, smooth tongue; diarrhea or constipation; and anorexia. Edema and urticaria also may be present.

Vitamin B_{12} Deficiency Anemia

Vitamin B_{12} Metabolism

Deficiency and poor utilization of vitamin B_{12} are two mechanisms for the development of megaloblastic anemia. Cobalamin (vitamin B_{12}) is naturally synthesized by micro-organisms, and since humans are incapable of synthesizing vitamin B_{12}, it must be provided nutritionally. Although micro-organisms found on roots and legumes of plants provide a source of vitamin B_{12} in vegetarian foods, animal protein is the primary dietary source of vitamin B_{12}. Meats richest in vitamin B_{12} include oysters, clams, liver, and kidney; moderate amounts of vitamin B_{12} are found in muscle meats, milk products, and egg yolks.[46]

The typical Western diet contains 5 to 15 µg/day of vitamin B_{12},[48,49] an amount sufficient to replace the 1 µg lost daily.[50] The total body stores of vitamin B_{12} range from 2000 to 5000 µg, much of which is stored in the liver.[57] Since body stores are extensive, three to four years are required before symptoms of vitamin B_{12} deficiency develop.

In the stomach, the vitamin B_{12} contained in food is released from protein complexes and bound to intrinsic factor which protects the B_{12} from degradation by gastrointestinal micro-organisms. Intrinsic factor is essential for the absorption of vitamin B_{12}. Specific mucosal receptors in the distal small ileum allow for attachment of the intrinsic factor: B_{12} complex. B_{12} is then transferred to the ileal cell and finally to portal vein blood. The intrinsic factor mechanism is saturated by 1.5 to 3 µg of B_{12}; however, passive diffusion can occur when B_{12} is present in large quantities.

After vitamin B_{12} is absorbed, it is bound to specific beta-globulin transport proteins, transcobalamin I, II, and III. Transcobalamin II is responsible for transporting B_{12} through cell membranes and delivering it to the liver and other organs. Fifty to ninety percent of the total body stores of B_{12} are found in the liver. All three of the transport proteins prevent loss of B_{12} in the urine, sweat, and other body secretions. In the liver, vitamin B_{12} is converted to coenzyme B_{12} which is essential for hematopoiesis, maintenance of myelin throughout the entire nervous system, and production of epithelial cells.[52,53]

Pathogenesis and Evaluation of Vitamin B_{12} Deficiency

Vitamin B_{12} deficiency may result from several etiologies: 1) decreased intake, absorption, transport, and utilization or 2) increased requirements, metabolic consumption, destruction, and excretion. Strict vegetarians most frequently present with signs and symptoms of vitamin B_{12} deficiency at age 13 to 80 years of age. Since this population also can be iron deficient because iron is poorly absorbed from plant sources, the microcytosis can mask the macrocytic appearance of RBCs. Other etiologies of vitamin B_{12} deficiency include inadequate proteolytic degradation of vitamin B_{12} from protein or congenital intrinsic factor deficiency. Additionally, the gastric mucosa may be unable to produce intrinsic factor under conditions such as partial gastrectomy, autoimmune destruction (e.g., addisonian or juvenile pernicious anemia), or destruction of the gastric mucosa from caustic agents such as lye ingestion.[46]

Pernicious anemia results from the inability to absorb vitamin B_{12}. It may be caused by inherited atrophic gastropathy accompanied by reduced intrinsic factor and hydrochloric acid secretion, or acquired from gastrectomy, pancreatic disease, or malnutrition. Pernicious anemia occurs frequently in patients with thyrotoxicosis, Hashimoto's thyroiditis, vitiligo, rheumatoid arthritis, or gastric cancer. Less frequently, anti-intrinsic factor antibodies have been observed in the serum or gastric juices of some patients with pernicious anemia.

The onset of the pernicious anemia is insidious. Patients usually have not been feeling well for the last 6 to 12 months and frequently complain of at least two of the following triad of symptoms: weakness, sore tongue, and symmetrical numbness or tingling in the extremities. The neurologic symptoms of vitamin B_{12} deficiency are associated with a defect in myelin synthesis and often are described as glove-stocking peripheral neuropathy or nonspecific complaints such as tinnitus, neuritis, vertigo, and headaches. Patients with neurologic symptoms have difficulty determining position and vibration sense and have an increase in deep tendon reflexes. These symptoms may progress to spastic ataxia, motor weakness, and paraparesis. However, no correlation exists between the extent of neurologic manifestations and severity of anemia. Mental changes (dementia) may occur in severe cases. Anorexia, pallor, and dyspnea on exertion are bothersome symptoms that may overshadow the diagnostic triad.

Laboratory Evaluation

In general, the *serum vitamin B_{12}* level reliably reflects vitamin B_{12} tissue stores. The microbiologic and radioisotope dilution assays have variable normal ranges. False low vitamin B_{12} concentrations may be observed in patients with folic acid deficiency or transcobalamin I deficiency, multiple myeloma, or in those taking megadoses of vitamin C. False elevated vitamin B_{12} concentrations

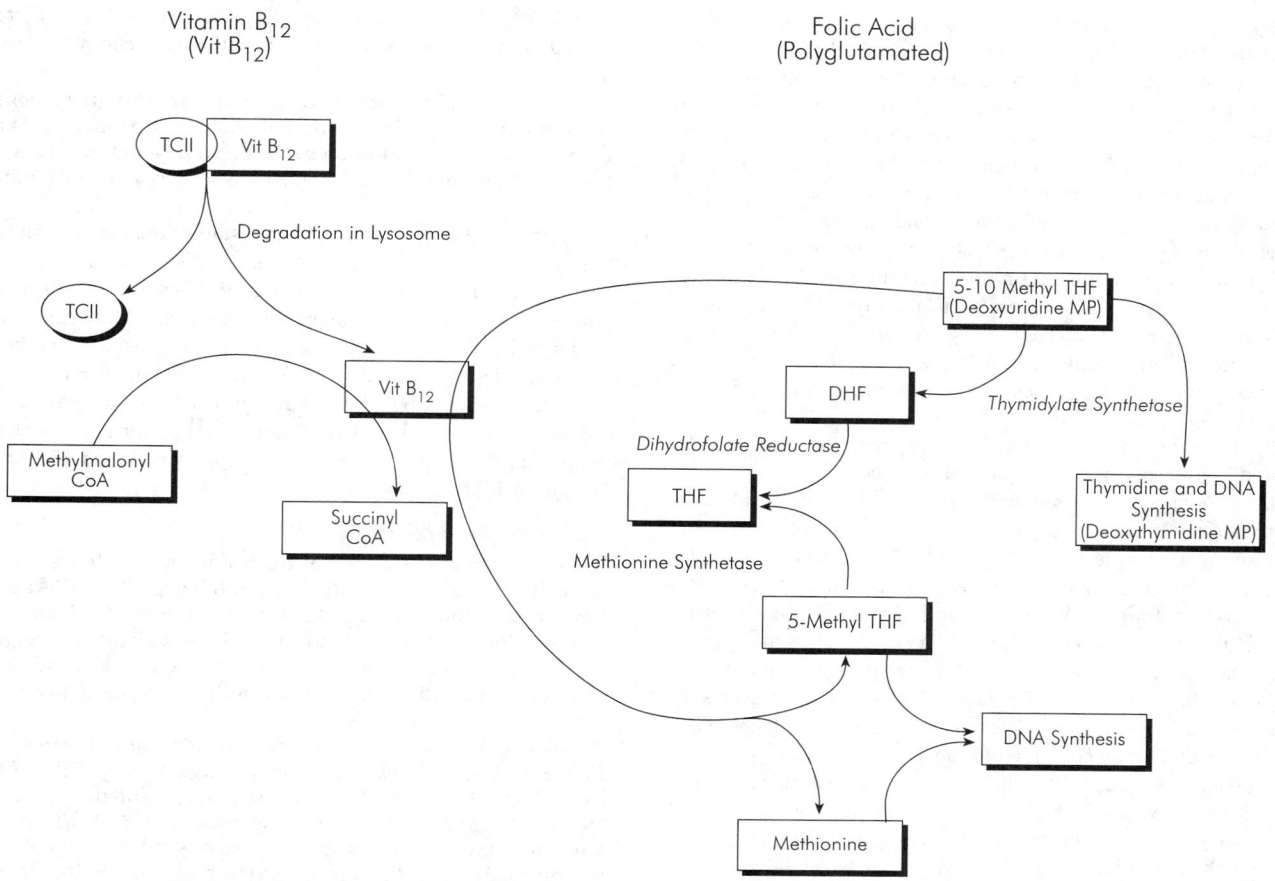

Fig 88.2 Intracellular Metabolic Pathways Vitamin B$_{12}$ and folic acid are both necessary for nucleic acid precursors used for DNA synthesis. DHF = Dihydrofolate; MP = monophosphate; TCII = Transcobalamine II; THF = Tetrahydrofolate.

may be observed in patients with myeloproliferative diseases, hepatomas, autoimmune diseases, monoblastic leukemias, and histiocytic lymphomas.[63] In active liver disease, vitamin B$_{12}$ liver stores can be released into the serum.[50] Thus, efflux of vitamin B$_{12}$ may be identified by measuring serum methylmalonic acid and homocysteine levels.[47] These tests may assist in differentiating between folate and vitamin B$_{12}$ deficiency. Once vitamin B$_{12}$ therapy has been instituted, serum levels of these chemicals decrease if true vitamin B$_{12}$ deficiency is present.[46]

The etiology of vitamin B$_{12}$ deficiency may be determined by the use of the *Schilling test*. Patients with pernicious anemia are not able to absorb vitamin B$_{12}$ because intrinsic factor is not available for binding. The Schilling test evaluates vitamin B$_{12}$ absorption in the following manner. A small tracer dose of radioactive vitamin B$_{12}$ (0.5 to 2 μg of CN-[^{57}Co] Cbl) is given orally. Two hours later, unlabeled vitamin B$_{12}$ (1 mg IM) is administered to saturate vitamin B$_{12}$ serum binding proteins. Urinary excretion of radioactive vitamin B$_{12}$ reveals the degree of absorption. Urinary excretion of less than 5% (normal: 15% to 50%) is consistent with pernicious anemia. Renal insufficiency, low urine output, or incomplete urine collection can result in a falsely low vitamin B$_{12}$ excretion.[64]

Some patients produce intrinsic factor but are still unable to absorb dietary vitamin B$_{12}$. Malabsorption can be caused by intestinal bacteria that usurp vitamin B$_{12}$, achlorhydria, pancreatic insufficiency, inadequate disassociation of vitamin B$_{12}$ from proteins, or lack of intrinsic factor receptors secondary to ileal loops, bypass, or surgical resection.[65] A "food Schilling test" in which

vitamin B$_{12}$ is administered as a protein-bound form, can determine whether the patient is able to disassociate proteins from vitamin B$_{12}$.[47,66]

Pernicious Anemia

11. Signs, Symptoms, and Laboratory Findings. C.L., a 60-year-old Scandinavian male, is seen by a private physician with a 1-year history of weakness and emotional instability. C.L. also complains of a painful tongue, alternating constipation and diarrhea, and a tingling sensation in both feet.

Pertinent findings on physical examination include: pallor, red tongue, loss of vibratory sense in the lower extremities, disorientation, muscle weakness, and ataxia.

Significant laboratory findings include: Hgb 9 gm/dL; Hct 29%; MCV 110 μm^3; MCH 38 pg; MCHC 34%; reticulocytes 0.4 %; poikilocytosis and anisocytosis on the blood smear; WBC count 4000/mm^3; platelets 105,000/mm^3 (Normal: 250,000–400,000); serum iron 80 μg/dL: TIBC 300 μg/dL; ferritin 150 ng/mL; RBC folate 300 ng/mL; serum vitamin B$_{12}$ 100 pg/mL; and <4% excretion on the Schilling test. What signs, symptoms, and laboratory findings are typical of pernicious anemia in C.L.? [SI units: Hgb 90 gm/L; Hct 0.29; MCV 110 fL; MCH 38 pg; MCHC 0.34; reticulocytes 0.004; WBC count 4 × 10^9/L; platelets 105 × 10^9/L (Normal: 250–400); iron 14.38 μmol/L; TIBC 53.91 μmol/L; ferritin 150 μg/L; RBC folate 679.8 nmol/L; vitamin B$_{12}$ 73.78 pmol/L]

C.L.'s signs and symptoms are classic for pernicious anemia. This disease occurs equally in both sexes (primarily in individuals of Northern European descent) with an average onset of 60 years. Pernicious anemia develops from a lack of gastric intrinsic factor production which causes vitamin B$_{12}$ malabsorption, and ultimately vitamin B_{12} deficiency. C.L.'s signs and symptoms of vitamin B_{12} deficiency include painful red tongue, loss of vibratory sense in lower extremities, vertigo, and emotional instability.

The elevated MCV suggests megaloblastic anemia. Folate and iron are two other factors that may affect the MCV and should be evaluated when working up a patient for anemia. In this case, C.L.'s folate and iron are normal, but his serum vitamin B_{12} level is low. The presence of poikilocytosis and anisocytosis observed in the blood smear represent ineffective erythropoiesis. Other cell lineages also may be affected in the bone marrow. Erythroid hypercellularity along with a decrease in the myeloid cells (leukocytes and platelets) increases the erythroid/myeloid ratio in C.L. The patient's low serum vitamin B_{12} levels and the low results obtained from the Schilling test are compatible with the diagnosis of pernicious anemia.

12. Treatment. **How should C.L.'s pernicious anemia be treated? How soon can a response be expected?**

C.L. should receive parenteral vitamin B_{12} in a dose sufficient to provide not only the daily requirement of approximately 2 µg, but also the amount needed to replenish tissue stores (about 2000 to 5000 µg; average 4000 µg). Initially, to replete the vitamin B_{12} stores, 30 to 100 µg of cyanocobalamin should be given IM daily for two to three weeks. Thereafter, 100 µg every two to four weeks should be given throughout C.L.'s life. Doses should not exceed 100 µg because rapid renal elimination can occur. IM or deep subcutaneous administration provides sustained release of vitamin B_{12} with better utilization compared to rapid IV infusion.

With adequate vitamin B_{12} therapy, one can expect the following response. Neurologic symptoms should improve within 24 hours. However, with long-standing vitamin B_{12} deficiency, several months may pass before some symptoms are relieved; other symptoms may never resolve. Hematologic parameters should begin to improve within the first few days. The bone marrow becomes normoblastic within 48 hours, the reticulocyte count should peak around day five of therapy, and the hematocrit should return to normal in one to two months. Because the rapid production of RBCs may increase potassium demand, serum potassium should be monitored and potassium supplementation provided as necessary. Peripheral blood counts should be obtained every three to six months to evaluate the adequacy of therapy. If maintenance therapy is discontinued, pernicious anemia will recur within five years.

13. Oral Vitamin B_{12}. **What factors affect the oral absorption of vitamin B_{12}? Compare the available oral products. Is oral vitamin B_{12} therapy an effective alternative to parenteral therapy?**

The amount of vitamin B_{12} that can be absorbed orally from a single dose or meal ranges from 1 to 5 µg. Approximately 5 µg of vitamin B_{12} is absorbed daily from the average American diet. The percent of vitamin B_{12} absorbed decreases with increasing doses. About 50% of a 1 to 2 µg dose of vitamin B_{12} is absorbed; whereas only about 5% of a 20 µg dose is absorbed.[74,81] Doses of $\geq$100 µg must be ingested to absorb 5 µg of vitamin B_{12}. Patients like C.L. with pernicious anemia treated with combination preparations containing vitamin B_{12} and intrinsic factor can become refractory to the therapy because of the formation of antibodies against intrinsic factor that is derived from hog mucosa.[82] Therefore, preparations containing hog mucosal intrinsic factor are not recommended. Although intrinsic factor is necessary for vitamin B_{12} absorption, oral therapy for pernicious anemia using high doses of oral cyanocobalamin (500 to 1000 µg) may be indicated in patients who refuse or cannot receive parenteral therapy (e.g., patients with severe bleeding disorders).[83] Overall, oral vitamin B_{12} therapy cannot be recommended routinely because noncompliance or lack of response places the patient at substantial risk of significant neu-

rological damage. Patients receiving oral vitamin B_{12} therapy should be monitored more frequently to ensure compliance with therapy.

14. *Anemias After Gastrectomy.* **F.M. has just undergone a total gastrectomy for recurrent nonhealing ulcers. What form(s) of anemia would be expected to develop in a postgastrectomy patient? Should F.M. receive prophylactic vitamin B_{12}?**

Partial or total gastrectomy often results in anemia, particularly pernicious anemia.[85] After a total gastrectomy, the source of intrinsic factor is lost, and oral vitamin B_{12} absorption will be impaired. The hematological and neurological abnormalities associated with B_{12} deficiency will not develop until existing vitamin B_{12} stores are depleted (about 2 to 3 years). Parenteral prophylactic vitamin B_{12} should be administered to this post-total gastrectomy patient. Since the vitamin B_{12} stores are not currently depleted, maintenance therapy, as discussed in Question 12, should be adequate for F.M.

Malabsorption of Vitamin B_{12}

15. Signs and Symptoms. **P.G., a 55-year-old female, complained of progressive confusion and lethargy 9 months ago. A CBC at that time only revealed mild leukocytosis. Today, she comes to the emergency room with a 4-week history of frequent (3–5/day) stools containing bright red blood. She reports continued lethargy, dizziness, ataxia, and parethesias in her hands and feet.**

Laboratory findings of interest include the following: Hgb 12.8 gm/dL, MCV 90 µm³, iron 150 µg/dL, iron/TIBC 11%, B_{12} 94 pg/mL, folate 21 ng/mL, hypersegmented PMNs, bilirubin 3.0 mg/dL, lactate dehydrogenase (LD) 520 U/L. A subsequent bone marrow aspirate demonstrates megaloblastic erythropoiesis, giant metamyelocytes, and a low stainable iron. A barium swallow and follow-through show numerous jejunal and duodenal diverticuli. Jejunal and duodenal aspirates reveal aerobic and anaerobic bacterial overgrowth. Radioactive vitamin B_{12} urinary excretion from the Schilling test is <4%. What signs, symptoms, and laboratory findings are typical for vitamin B_{12} deficiency in P.G.? [SI units: Hgb 120 gm/L; MCV 90 fL; iron 25.87 µmol/L; B_{12} 69.35 pmol/L; folate 47.59 nmol/L; 51.3 µmol/L; LD 520 U/L]

The signs and symptoms in P.G. that are consistent with B_{12} deficiency include confusion, dizziness, ataxia, and paresthesias. Other signs and symptoms may be due to other underlying conditions. For example, her lethargy may be due to prolonged blood loss secondary to diverticulitis.

Notably, P.G. initially presented with a mild leukocytosis. Evaluation nine months later shows a low Hgb, a low serum vitamin B_{12} level, and hypersegmented polymorphonucleocytes. The high LD and bilirubin reflect intramedullary hemolysis of megaloblastic RBCs consistent with vitamin B_{12} deficiency even though the MCV is within normal limits. The presence of megaloblastic erythropoiesis and giant metamyelocytes in the bone marrow also is consistent with vitamin B_{12} deficiency.

P.G.'s history of bloody stools and diverticuli suggests substantial long-term blood loss, which increased demand for iron and vitamin B_{12} to replace RBCs. Concurrent iron deficiency, may mask megaloblastic changes in red blood cells which explains the suspiciously normal MCV (dimorphic anemia). The serum folate concentration is also falsely normal. Even though the RBC folate level is likely to be low, serum folate concentrations are normal because monoglutamated folates leak from cells into the serum in vitamin B_{12} deficient states.

16. Treatment. **How should P.G.'s vitamin B_{12}-deficiency be treated?**

The etiology of vitamin B_{12} malabsorption must be corrected before P.G. is given oral vitamin B_{12} therapy. The presence of diverticuli is not the etiology of vitamin B_{12} malabsorption since diverticuli typically do not extend into the distal ileum. Instead, given P.G.'s medical history, the most likely cause of vitamin B_{12} malabsorption is bacterial usurpation of luminal vitamin B_{12}. P.G. should first be treated with a broad-spectrum antibiotic, such as tetracycline or a sulfonamide for seven to ten days. Thereafter, a repeat Schilling test should be normal and P.G. can begin daily oral vitamin B_{12} supplementation to replenish her body stores. In this case, normal levels of intrinsic factor permit oral therapy. The recommended daily dose of vitamin B_{12} is 25 to 250 μg. Following antibiotic therapy, P.G. also should begin to absorb vitamin B_{12} in her diet.

Folic Acid Deficiency Anemia

Folic Acid Metabolism

Folate is abundant in virtually all food sources, especially fresh green vegetables, fruits, yeast, and animal protein. The average American diet provides 50 to 2000 μg of folate per day; however, excessive or prolonged cooking (over 15 minutes) in large quantities of water destroys a high percentage of the folate that is contained in food.[55,56] Human requirements for folate vary with age and depend upon the rate of metabolism and cell turnover but are generally 3 μg/kg/day.[56] The minimum daily adult requirement of folate is 50 μg, but because absorption from food is incomplete, a daily intake of 200 μg is recommended. Folate requirements are increased in conditions in which the metabolic rate and rate of cellular division are increased (e.g., pregnancy, infancy, infection, malignancies, hemolytic anemia). The following are estimates of daily folate requirements based upon age and growth demands: children 3.3 μg/kg; infants 16 to 32 μg; pregnancy 3 μg/kg + 100 μg; lactating women 300 μg.[36,56]

Dietary folic acid (FA) is in the polyglutamate form and must be enzymatically deconjugated in the gastrointestinal tract to the monoglutamate form before it is absorbed. Once absorbed, the inactive dihydrofolate (FH_2) must be converted to active tetrahydrofolate (FH_4, folinic acid) by dihydrofolate reductase (DHFR).

In contrast to the large stores of vitamin B_{12}, the body's folate stores are relatively small (about 5 to 10 mg). Therefore, deficiency and subsequent megaloblastic anemia may occur within three to four months of decreased folate intake.

Predisposing Factors

There are several situations in which folate deficiency is most commonly observed including: alcoholism, rapid cell turnover, and dietary deficiency. In *alcoholics*, the daily intake of the folate contained in food may be restricted or absent. Additionally, enterohepatic recirculation of folate may be impaired by the toxic effect of alcohol on hepatic cells. Folate deficiency also may develop during the third trimester of *pregnancy* as a result of a marginal diet and the rapid metabolism of the fetus. Folate coenzymes are required for most metabolic pathways. Therefore, folate deficiency will develop in any condition of rapid cellular turnover (e.g., hemolytic anemias, hemoglobinopathies, sideroblastic anemia, leukemias, lymphomas, multiple myeloma) or a diet lacking in folate (e.g., food faddism or a slimming diet). Folate deficiency also may occur with chronic hemodialysis, diseases which impair absorption from the small intestine (e.g., sprue, regional enteritis), extensive jejunal resections, and from drugs that alter folate metabolism (e.g., trimethoprim, pyrimethamine, methotrexate, sulfasalazine, oral contraceptives, anticonvulsants).[46,58-60] Few patients have inborn errors of folate metabolism.[46,61]

The evaluation of megaloblastic anemia must be thorough because indiscriminate use of "shotgun" hematinic therapy may be dangerous. Large doses of folate can partially reverse hematolog-

ical abnormalities caused by vitamin B_{12} deficiency; however, folate cannot correct neurological damage caused by vitamin B_{12} deficiency. Therefore, folate deficiency absolutely must be differentiated from vitamin B_{12} deficiency before folate therapy is initiated. Otherwise the progression of the neurologic sequelae of vitamin B_{12} deficiency can occur.

17. T.J., a malnourished appearing female, is in her second trimester of pregnancy, presents to the local health clinic for her regular check-up. She is a multiparous, 22-year-old female who ran away from home when she was 16. T.J. has a 7-year history of excessive alcohol intake and has been using cocaine frequently for 3 years. She lives with her boyfriend and her 19-month-old daughter. During both pregnancies, T.J. lost 8–10 pounds during the first trimester secondary to nausea, vomiting, and anorexia. Her only complaints are dyspnea on exertion, palpitations, and diarrhea.

Pertinent laboratory values include: Hct 25.5%; MCV 112 μm³ (Normal: 76–100), MCH 34 pg (Normal: 27–33), RBC 1.1 × 10⁶/mm³ (Normal: 3.5–5.0), folate 30 ng/mL (Normal: in RBCs 140–960), serum vitamin B_{12} 250 pg/mL (Normal: 200–1000), reticulocytes 1%, platelets 75,000/mm³ (Normal: 130–400,000), WBC count 2000/mm³ with hypersegmented PMNs, LD 450 U/L (Normal: 50–150), bilirubin 1.5 mg/dL (Normal: 0.1–1). T.J. is not taking any prescription medications. What factors make T.J. at risk for folate deficiency? [SI units: Hct 0.255, MCV 112 fL (Normal: 76–100); MCH 34 pg (Normal: 27–33); RBC count 1.1 × 10¹²/L (Normal: 3.5–5); folate 67.98 nmol/L (Normal: 317–2175); vitamin B_{12}; folate 184.45 pmol/ (Normal: 150–750); reticulocytes 0.01; platelets 75 × 10⁹/L (Normal: 130–400); WBC 2 × 10⁹/L; LD 450 U/L (Normal: 50–150); bilirubin 25.65 μmol/L (Normal: 2–18)]

T.J. has a history of risk factors since she was 16. The diagnosis of folate deficiency is plausible, considering folate deficiency may develop in a matter of weeks to four months. Like most folate-deficient patients, T.J. has more than one risk factor for folate-deficiency. Cocaine and alcohol together with multiparity complicated by anorexia, nausea, and vomiting could lead to poor nutrition. Alcohol has toxic effects on the intestinal mucosa and interferes with folate use by the bone marrow.[68] T.J. should be asked specifically about her dietary habits and recent weight history. She may have a folate-poor diet for financial reasons or because she is overcooking her food. Alternatively, cocaine may be causing anorexia. The nutritional intake of alcohol and drug abusers is frequently poor.

Diagnosis and Management

18. Which laboratory values support the diagnosis of folate deficiency? How should T.J. be managed and monitored?

T.J.'s laboratory values reflect macrocytic anemia (Hct 25.5%, MCV 112 μm³) with pancytopenia (reduced number of RBC, WBC, and platelets). Serum vitamin B_{12} concentrations reflect normal vitamin B_{12} stores, but folate stores are inadequate as exemplified by the low RBC folate concentration, pancytopenia, and macrocytic anemia.

Serum folate concentrations generally reflect folate balance over the past three weeks, although one balanced meal can raise serum levels and "falsely elevate" body stores. Tissue folate stores are more accurately reflected by the RBC polyglutamated folate content, which is approximately 10 to 30 times the corresponding serum folate concentrations.[62] Hemolysis or vitamin B_{12} deficiency, causes leakage of monoglutamated folates from cell, thereby falsely elevating serum folate levels.[46,47]

T.J. should be counseled regarding her nutritional and social habits. Since the estimated total body folate store is only about 5 to 10 mg, 1 mg of folic acid given daily for two to three weeks should be more than adequate to replace her storage pool of folate. However, higher doses (up to 5 mg) may be needed if absorption is compromised by alcohol or other factors.[69] Once stores are replenished, T.J. should continue folate supplements throughout her pregnancy and lactation period. She should be reassessed after the course of therapy to determine response to therapy and if the cause of the folate deficiency has been corrected. Supplementation with folic acid 1 mg/day may be required as long as risk factors are present. T.J.'s fetus is unlikely to develop folate deficiency since maternal folate is preferentially delivered to the fetus.[59]

T.J.'s response to therapy may be monitored by use of several different parameters. Although routine bone marrow aspirates are not performed, the RBC morphology should begin to revert back to normal within 24 to 48 hours after therapy is initiated and hypersegmented neutrophils should disappear in the periphery in approximately one week. Serum chemistry and hemogram studies should begin to normalize within ten days. The reticulocyte count should increase by day two to three and peak by day ten. LD and bilirubin values should normalize in one to three weeks. Finally, the anemia should be corrected in one to two months. Once anemia is corrected, 0.1 mg of folate as a nutritional supplement should be adequate for maintenance treatment. If patients with underlying vitamin B_{12} deficiency are inappropriately treated with folate, neurologic sequela will persist and macrocytic anemia will improve but will not resolve completely.

Sickle Cell Anemia (SSA)

Pathogenesis

Sickle cell anemia is an inherited hemoglobin disorder characterized by a DNA substitution where the β-globin gene is located. Hemoglobin is a quarternary structure comprising two α-globin chains and two β-globin chains ($α_2β_2$) in adults. The β-globin gene locus encodes several globin gene products during the course of development. These products include the embryonic globin gene (ε), duplicated fetal genes (γ), and adult genes (δ and β). During fetal development the γ-globin is the primary β-globin expressed, forming fetal hemoglobin (Hb F or $α_2γ_2$). Normally, the period from birth to approximately three to six months of age is marked by the replacement of γ-globin with β-globin, giving rise to the adult form of hemoglobin (Hb A, $α_2β_2$). Low levels of γ-globin persist throughout life and Hb F, present in F cells, may account for approximately 1% of the total hemoglobin content.[70,71] F cell numbers may increase in response to erythropoietic stress.[70] B^S represents the inheritance of the sickle β-globin gene.[69,70]

Sickle cell anemia results from a DNA substitution of thymidine for adenine in the glutamic acid codon forming a B6 valine instead of glutamic acid.[70–72] The hemoglobin produced from such a substitution has a more negative charge than normal Hgb A and the deoxygenated state favors hemoglobin aggregation and polymerization which forms sickled RBCs.[71,72] Sickled RBCs are more rigid and may become "lodged" when passing through microvasculature resulting in vascular occlusions.

Additionally, the sickled RBC surface contains rearranged aminophospholipids and this alters the ability of the RBC to initiate coagulation, adhere to vascular endothelium, and activate complement. These abnormal interactions with other cell types produce several complications such as anemia, vaso-occlusive episodes, multiorgan damage, and increased susceptibility to polysaccharide-encapsulated organisms.[71] For these reasons, much effort has been focused on neonatal diagnosis to reduce morbidity and mortality in children under three years of age.[73]

There is more than one inheritance pattern that results in abnormal hemoglobin polymerization. Patients with SSA are homozygous and have inherited a sickle gene from each parent ($α_2β_{2S}$), whereas patients with sickle cell trait are heterozygous and have

inherited the sickle cell gene from one parent and the Hgb A gene from the other parent ($α_2β^Aβ^S$). Other inheritance patterns include patients with a sickle cell gene and a Hgb C gene [where glutamic acid is substituted for lysine B6, ($α_2β^Sβ^C$)]. Finally, patients may inherit the sickle cell gene and the B-thalassemic gene ($α_2β^Sβ^{Sthal}$), in which case the clinical course is less severe than with patients diagnosed with SSA. Hematologic abnormalities are more frequently observed in patients with SSA and less frequently in those with sickle cell hemoglobin C disease or sickle cell B_O-thalassemia.[70,71]

Laboratory Evaluation

Patients who have inherited the sickle cell gene can be diagnosed by electrophoretic procedures that separate different forms of hemoglobin. Fetal hemoglobin levels vary among patients. Frequently, an increase in the mean corpuscular hemoglobin concentration (MCHC) is used to predict the likelihood of polymer formation and vascular occlusion.

In the SSA patient hematologic studies are informative. The WBC and platelet counts frequently are elevated, but the WBC differential is normal.[71] The reticulocyte count (5% to 15%) and the MCV may be elevated. If MCV values are within the normal range, one must consider iron deficiency or B_O-thalassemia. Sickled cells may be observed in poorly oxygenated blood. In contrast, patients with the SS trait should have normal RBC morphology, and WBC, reticulocyte, and platelet counts. Sickled cells rarely are observed. In patients with sickle cell B_O-thalassemia, hematologic abnormalities vary depending upon the amount of hemoglobin A present. This form may be very difficult to distinguish from SSA; RBC microcytosis may be the only differentiating parameter.[71]

Clinical Course and Management

Patients carrying the SS trait experience milder symptoms than those with SSA. The kidney is the organ most frequently affected by micro-infarction which occurs in the renal medulla impairing the kidney's ability to concentrate urine. During pregnancy, there is an increased frequency of urinary tract infections and hematuria, but vaso-occlusive events are infrequent. If they do occur, they usually are caused by hypoxic conditions resulting from excessive exercise or high altitudes.

Sickle cell hemoglobin C disease usually is associated with few clinical complications. These patients may have a normal physical examination with only splenomegaly. Patients are at risk for bacterial infections and because of elevated hemoglobin levels, they may suffer from ocular, orthopedic, and pulmonary vaso-occlusive events.[71]

Unfortunately, the treatment of sickle cell anemia is largely directed toward prophylaxis against infections and supportive management of vaso-occlusive crises. The clinical course among patients with sickle cell disease is quite variable and difficult to predict. Some patients suffer from a multitude of health problems. Organs such as the kidneys, retina, spleen, and bones are frequent sites of vaso-occlusive events because these sites are characterized by a relatively low pH and hypoxic conditions. The health care professional frequently must manage complications such as pain, anemia, infections, and cardiac, pulmonary, neurologic, hepatobiliary, obstetric/gynecologic, ocular, dermatologic, and orthopedic complications. The management of these complications is organ-specific and aimed at supportive interventions.

Hemolytic anemia is caused by splenic sequestration of abnormal RBCs. Sequestration reduces the RBC lifespan from 120 days to 15 to 25 days and elevates the reticulocyte count. Erythropoietin response is typically blunted for the degree of anemia and may be a result of concurrent kidney dysfunction. Some patients may even experience aplastic anemia (bone marrow failure) when extensive hemolysis is accompanied by inadequate bone marrow response. However, it usually is self-limiting. Hemolytic anemia may also present in patients with glucose-6-phosphate dehydrogenase deficiency. Cardiac manifestations include high output failure secondary to anemia. Management of the underlying anemia may include splenectomy following the first splenic sequestration event. Alternatively, patients may be managed with transfusions and careful observation.[71,72]

Infections occur more frequently in patients with SSA because the complement pathway and granulocyte function may be altered along with B-cell immunity. Also, impaired splenic function increases the risk for infection from polysaccharide-encapsulated bacteria such as *Streptococcus pneumonia* and *Haemophilus influenzae*. Pneumonia may be caused by *S. pneumonia*, mycoplasma, or viruses. Pneumonia may worsen hypoxia and cause progression to vaso-occlusion and acute chest syndrome (chest pain in the presence of a local infiltrate on chest radiograph). Because of such complications, the prophylactic administration of penicillin has significantly reduced morbidity and mortality due to pneumonia in children less than three years of age. Pulmonary complications from pneumonia or vascular occlusion also can lead to right heart failure. Osteomyelitis from *Staphylococcus aureus* or *Salmonella typhymurium* or urinary tract infections due to *Escherichia coli* are frequent complications in SSA patients.[70-72] Because of the susceptibility of SSA patients to infections, antibiotic therapy should be instituted at the earliest sign of infection. Polyvalent pneumococcal vaccination of children between 6 and 12 months of age and a booster 6 to 12 months later has been recommended. Since SSA patients typically respond poorly, only 50% of patients will be protected by vaccination.

Vascular occlusion episodes or a "sickle cell crises" cause severe pain and organ damage. The pain typically lasts two to six days and should be managed with narcotic analgesics (morphine or morphine-derivatives). Narcotic addiction may occur over time but can be prevented by providing the patient with only a few days supply of analgesics following the crisis.[70,71]

Neurologic complications are age dependent. Stroke most frequently occurs in the first decade of life, whereas intracerebral hemorrhage is a complication associated with adulthood. Approximately 50% of patients experience recurrent strokes within three years unless they are managed by RBC transfusion therapy. Therapeutic goals are aimed at maintaining the hemoglobin S level below 30%.[71]

Renal and genital complications are common in sickle cell disease because the environment (hypoxic, acidotic, and hypertonic) predisposes the renal medulla or corpus cavernosum to infarction. Sequela include reduced potassium excretion, hyperuricemia, hematuria, hyposthenuria, and renal failure. Patients with renal disease may have inappropriately low levels of erythropoietin as well, and men experiencing occlusion of the corpus cavernosum can experience acute or chronic priapism. Conservative management includes intravenous fluid administration and pain control. Refractory cases may require transfusions or surgery.[71,72]

Microinfarctions frequently produce ophthalmic, hepatic, orthopedic, and obstetric/gynecologic complications as well. The reader is referred to other references addressing these topics in more detail.[71,72]

Future Treatment. Hemoglobin F has a protective effect against hemoglobin polymerization. Investigators have observed that patients with hemoglobin F levels exceeding 20% experience a relatively mild or benign course. Current research is aimed at methods that will increase hemoglobin F synthesis to 10% to 20%.[70,74] Clinical trials with hydroxyurea with or without erythropoietin have reduced the severity of disease in some SSA patients, although the optimal drug regimen has not yet been established.[75-79] Other areas of potential promise for the treatment of SSA include bone marrow transplantation and gene therapy.[70,80]

Clinical Assessment

19. J.T., a 28-year-old male with SSA, presented to the emergency room with the chief complaint of the rapid onset of abdominal pain and shortness of breath. Since infancy J.T. has been severely incapacitated by his disease. During early childhood he experienced several episodes of acute pain, swelling of the hands and feet, and jaundice. Three years before this admission, J.T. required a left hip replacement secondary to bony infarctions. Recently, frequent blood transfusions have reduced the frequency of sickling crisis.

On physical examination, J.T. is a thin black male in acute distress and scleral icterus. He has a pulse of 110/min, a respiratory rate 18/min, and his temperature is 98.6 °F. His lungs are clear and cardiac auscultation reveals a hyperdynamic pericardium and a systolic murmur at the left sternal edge. Splenomegaly is noted and a chest radiograph reveals only cardiomegaly.

A CBC is obtained. Notable results include: Hgb 5.5 gm/dL, Hct 25%, WBC count 5000/mm³, platelets 325,000/mm³, reticulocyte count 1%, bilirubin 5.8 mg/dL, serum creatinine (SrCr) 3.0 mg/dL, and blood urea nitrogen (BUN) 52 mg/dL. The peripheral blood smear shows target cells with an occasional sickled cell. What signs and symptoms are consistent with SSA? What is J.T.'s current complication? [SI units: Hgb 55 gm/L; Hct 0.25; WBC count 5 × 10⁹/L; platelets 325 × 10⁹/L; bilirubin 99.18 µmol/L; SrCr 265.2 µmol/L; BUN 18.56 mmol/L urea]

Based upon the presence of splenomegaly and anemia with target and sickled cells, J.T. currently is presenting with an acute splenic sequestration crisis. Splenomegaly rapidly evolves over several hours and is accompanied by progressive anemia. The low reticulocyte count is consistent with acute sequestration since a reticulocyte response would be expected if the anemia had developed in recent days. J.T.'s inadequate reticulocyte response may reflect rapid progression of the anemia or a blunted erythropoietin response secondary to compromised renal dysfunction. The hyperdynamic pericardium and systolic murmur are consistent with the high cardiac output required to deliver oxygen in an anemic state.

20. How should J.T. be managed?

J.T.'s signs and symptoms are serious enough to justify transfusion therapy. In addition, J.T. should be adequately hydrated, considering his elevated serum creatinine and BUN. SSA patients frequently lose the ability to concentrate urine and may easily become dehydrated which further contributes to sickling. Pain control also should be aggressively instituted for J.T.'s comfort and should be continued for a few days after hospital discharge. Splenectomy may be indicated in instances of severe splenomegaly, repeated infarction, or pain in adults, and is indicated when a crisis occurs in children. Those SSA patients who are bedridden should be placed on chronic heparin therapy to prevent vascular occlusions and deep vein thrombosis.

Anemia of Chronic Disease

Mild to moderate anemia can accompany diseases that last longer than one or two months. Diseases associated with anemia of chronic disease include chronic infections [e.g., subacute bacterial endocarditis, osteomyelitis, chronic urinary tract infections, tuberculosis, human immunodeficiency virus (HIV)], chronic inflammatory conditions (e.g., systemic lupus erythematosus, rheumatoid arthritis), malignancies, and treatment of malignancies with some chemotherapeutic agents. Patients with decreased renal, hepatic, or endocrine function also may develop anemia of chronic disease. Three factors are hypothesized to be responsible for the anemia of chronic disease: a) impaired release of iron from reticuloendothelial stores; b) decreased erythrocyte life span; and c) inadequate bone marrow response to a decreased erythrocyte life span.[81]

Since anemia accompanies many different diseases, symptoms are usually nonspecific and vary greatly. The signs and symptoms of anemia are usually less obvious than those of the underlying problem, and treatment usually focuses on the latter. Patients with severe anemia may require blood transfusions. Anemia of chronic disease is not usually progressive or life-threatening, although it generally affects a patient's quality of life. Unless a concurrent deficiency of vitamin B_{12}, folate, or iron exists, administration of vitamin supplements is not of value.

Human Recombinant Erythropoietin Therapy (rhEPO)

Human recombinant erythropoietin therapy (rhEPO) may be indicated in instances of chronic anemia, drug-induced anemia, or autologous blood transfusion for elective surgery. Previously, blood transfusions temporarily deterred symptomatic anemia of chronic disease; however, transfusion therapy is associated with risks such as hepatitis, viral infections, iron overload, and allergic reactions. Clinical trials with rhEPO have shown that response is not only dose dependent but also dependent upon the underlying etiology of anemia. rhEPO response has been evaluated by parameters such as increased serum ferritin, decreased transferrin saturation, increased corrected reticulocyte count, decreased transfusion requirements, and increased hemoglobin/hematocrit. Clinical trials have evaluated erythropoietin efficacy in several different populations (see Table 88.8).

Renal Insufficiency-Related Anemia

21. K.S., a 35-year-old male with a 25-year history of diabetes mellitus, is diagnosed with renal failure and placed on hemodialysis 3 times weekly. One year later, K.S. is noted to have become increasingly transfusion dependent for correction of his anemia. Significant laboratory values include: Hgb 7 gm/dL, Hct 26%, ferritin 360 ng/mL, and serum iron 98 µg/dL. Additionally, K.S. complains of constant fatigue, poor appetite, and a low level of energy. What treatments are available to correct K.S.'s anemia? [SI units: Hgb 70 gm/L; Hct 0.26; ferritin 1265.4 mmol/day; iron 17.55 µmol/L]

Unlike the anemia associated with most chronic diseases, the hematocrit of patients with chronic renal failure often is markedly reduced. The cause of the anemia is complex, but involves reduced erythropoietin production and a shortened red blood cell life span. In the past, these patients have been treated with transfusions and androgens.[82] Although effective, repeated transfusions cause complications such as iron overload, infections, reactions to leukocyte antigens, or the development of cytotoxic antibodies. Unfortunately only a limited number of patients respond to androgens and the response is dose dependent. Side effects, including liver dysfunction and hirsutism, often require discontinuation of therapy.

As discussed earlier, erythropoietin is secreted in the kidney in response to anoxia and is responsible for normal differentiation of RBCs from other stem cells. Recombinant human erythropoietin has been used to treat anemia in renal failure patients undergoing hemodialysis, and K.S. is a candidate for this therapy. A dose-dependent rise in hematocrit is observed in patients with end-stage renal disease at a dosage range of 50 to 100 units/kg three times weekly. Ninety percent of patients respond to doses of 150 to 500 units/kg. However, patients like K.S. with renal insufficiency appear to be predisposed to rhEPO-induced hypertension. Other adverse effects include functional iron deficiency preceded by an elevated reticulocyte count and a change in the rate of hematocrit rise.[108] Seizures also have been reported in approximately 5% of patients with end-stage renal disease.[109] (Also see Chapter 30: Chronic Renal Failure.)

Malignancy-Related Anemia

22. R.T., a 46-year-old female with a 3-year history of breast cancer that has metastasized to the bone, is being seen for her 5th cycle of chemotherapy. A CBC includes the following data: Hgb 9 gm/dL, Hct 27%, MCV 90 µm³ (90), MCHC 30%, serum erythropoietin 31 U/L (Normal: 10–20). The peripheral smear shows normochromic and normocytic RBCs. Her only complaints are weakness, decreased appetite, and exercise intolerance. Her only medication is ibuprofen 600 mg QID. What is the most likely cause of R.T.'s anemia? What is the appropriate treatment? [SI units: Hgb 90 gm/L; Hct 0.27; MCV 90 fL; MCHC 0.3]

From the data provided, R.T. appears to have anemia of chronic disease or chemotherapy-induced anemia. This anemia is generally normocytic, normochromic and develops when a disease has persisted for longer than one to two months. Generally, the anemia is mild with a limited number of distinguishing characteristics. As in R.T., the anemia is often asymptomatic or mildly symptomatic (weakness, decreased exercise tolerance). RBC hypochromia may or may not be present, and RBC size is generally normal. The reticulocyte count will usually be low or within normal limits. Both the serum iron and total iron binding capacity are decreased, and transferrin saturation is usually less than normal.[110] Serum ferritin is a reliable measurement of iron stores in patients with chronic disease. Serum ferritin usually is increased, but may be normal;

Table 88.8	Therapeutic Uses and Regimens for Recombinant Human Erythropoietin (rhEPO)[a]					
Anemia Pathogenesis[b,d]	Dose (units/kg)	Frequency	Maximum Dose Escalation[c]	Time to Respond (weeks)	Overall Response Rate (%)
AIDS	100	3 times/week	200	8–12	17–35
Chemotherapy-induced	150	3 times/week	300	2–8	32–61
MDS	40	3 times/week	570	4–6	20–30
Malignancy	150	3 times/week	150	4–5	47–85
Renal insufficiency	50	3 times/week	500	2–8	90–97

[a] 12–16 week course of rfEPO therapy.
[b] AIDS patients with endogenous erythropoietin levels <500 U/L.
[c] Moderate dose escalation is indicated if a partial response is observed after 4–8 weeks of therapy.
[d] AIDS = Acquired Immunodeficiency syndrome; MDS = Myelodysplastic Syndrome.

if the anemia is caused by iron deficiency, ferritin values will be decreased. A bone marrow aspirate would reveal an elevated hemosiderin content. Anemia of chronic disease does not respond to treatment with iron, vitamin B_{12}, or folic acid, unless there is an associated deficiency. Therapy is directed at treatment of the underlying disease, if possible.

Presently, the clinician may choose to delay R.T.'s course of chemotherapy. Alternatively, a transfusion may be given to relieve her symptoms and allow her to better tolerate chemotherapy. Human recombinant erythropoietin also should be considered. R.T.'s tumor has metastasized to the bone and tumor infiltration of the bone marrow is associated with anemia even when renal function and erythropoietin levels are normal. Erythropoietin increases hematocrit, hemoglobin, and decreases the need for blood transfusions. Patients undergoing erythropoietin therapy also report an improved quality of life. One trial reported a 75% increase in the platelet count,[105] and overall response rates ranged from 47.4% to 85%, usually occurring by week four or five after initiation of therapy. Patients with a significantly higher baseline erythropoietin level may be refractory to rhEPO or require higher doses.[100,105-107] There is no evidence that concurrent rhEPO administration adversely affects tumor burden or response to chemotherapy. Reported adverse drug reactions have been virtually absent in cancer patients.[106]

Initially, R.T. should be given rhEPO 150 units/kg subcutaneously or intravenously three times a week. A more aggressive regimen will provide a more rapid response in patients suffering from more severe symptoms. Response can be assessed initially by obtaining a reticulocyte count which should peak by day ten. A positive rhEPO response also can be predicted by the presence of an increased serum ferritin, decreased transferrin saturation, or serum erythropoietin levels less than 200 IU/L. After two to four weeks, hemoglobin and hematocrit values should increase with appropriate rhEPO therapy. If no response is seen at eight weeks, the dose may be increased to 300 international units. Once hemoglobin and hematocrit parameters have increased sufficiently to relieve symptoms, the rhEPO dose should be reduced every two to three weeks until the lowest dose required to maintain these levels has been reached.

Acquired Immunodeficiency Syndrome (AIDS)-Related Anemia

23. J.M., a 37-year-old male, is currently calling his primary physician with acute worsening of shortness of breath and pounding in his chest. J.M. has a known history of AIDS and has had recent episodes of *Pneumocystis carinii* pneumonia (PCP) and cytomegalovirus (CMV) esophagitis. J.M. also has complained of frequent diarrhea. Trimethoprim-sulfamethoxazole was given intravenously for treatment of PCP; however, J.M. complained of fever while on maintenance therapy. J.M. is currently on the following medications: dapsone 100 mg/day PO for PCP prophylaxis; ganciclovir 325 mg IV Monday through Friday for CMV prophylaxis; zidovudine 200 mg PO BID; fluconazole 100 mg/day PO PRN thrush; Imodium liquid 5 mL PRN diarrhea.

On physical examination the only remarkable findings include a respiratory rate of 24/min and a heart rate of 120 beats/min. A chest examination reveals that J.M. is tachypneic and has bilateral dry rales. The Hickman catheter in the left subclavian vein appears dry and clean. Further work-up of J.M.'s illness includes an unremarkable chest x-ray and negative cultures of the blood and sputum. The CBC includes normal WBC and platelet counts. Abnormal values include the RBC of 3300/mm³ (Normal: 4500–6200), Hgb 9.1 mg/dL, Hct 28% (Normal: 42–54). The morphology of the RBC was moderately anisocytic, hypochromic, and normocytic. What factors can

contribute to J.M.'s anemia? [SI units: RBC count 3.3 × 10¹²/L (Normal: 4.5–6.2); Hgb 91 gm/L; Hct 0.28 (Normal: 0.42–0.54)]

Like patients with renal insufficiency, anemia occurs eventually in 68% to 95% of AIDS patients and has been shown to correlate with the severity of the clinical syndrome.[83,84] Antibody responses against RBCs have been documented in AIDS patients,[85] although their role in the pathogenesis of AIDS has been challenged. Anemia occurs more frequently in patients with opportunistic infections (*Mycobacterium avium intracellulare*)[86] or neoplasms, and often occurs concurrently with granulocytopenia. The enhanced production of cytokines, such as tumor necrosis factor-α, also may be correlated with hematologic abnormalities.[87] Anemia may be a consequence of zidovudine, DDC (2′,3′-dideoxycytidine), DDA (2′,3′-dideoxyadenosine),[88-90] or other drugs frequently used to treat AIDS-associated illnesses (e.g., bone-marrow suppressive chemotherapy, trimethoprim-sulfamethoxazole, or dapsone).[58,91]

Iron stores in AIDS patients usually are adequate; yet, the characteristics of anemia are similar to those present in anemia of chronic disease: low serum iron and iron binding capacity and elevated serum ferritin. Vitamin B_{12} deficiency is a contributing cause to anemia in 16% to 25% of AIDS patients.[93-95] Vitamin B_{12} malabsorption may result from HIV-infected mononuclear cells within the lamina propia[94] or abnormal binding of vitamin B_{12} to transport proteins. Alterations in the utilization of vitamin B_{12} and folate[93,96] may place a patient at risk for hematologic toxicity of drugs such as zidovudine and trimethoprim. Also, zidovudine use is associated with an increased frequency of low vitamin B_{12} levels.[88]

As illustrated by J.M., HIV-associated anemia has a characteristic RBC morphology which is normochromic and normocytic.[86] Mild anisocytosis and poikilocytosis also may be observed. Zidovudine-associated anemia is typically macrocytic.[84,88]

Erythropoiesis is frequently defective in AIDS patients, as reflected by an inappropriately low reticulocyte count and an increased or blunted erythropoietic response for the degree of anemia.[84,92] An ineffective erythropoietin response may be observed in some patients on zidovudine therapy as well.[84]

J.M. has many risk factors for anemia of chronic disease including AIDS and its accompanying predisposition to malignancy and infection. He also is taking many medications (ganciclovir, zidovudine, dapsone) that can induce anemia.

24. J.M.'s physician determines that J.M.'s endogenous erythropoietin level is 737 units/liter (Normal: by RIA 3–30 unit/liter). Is J.M. a candidate for rhEPO? How can you best predict response to rhEPO? What would an appropriate dosing regimen be to start treating J.M.?

J.M.'s anemia is less likely to respond to rhEPO than patients who have endogenous erythropoietin levels less than 500 units/liter. However, an rhEPO trial of therapy may be initiated at 100 units/kg subcutaneously three times weekly. J.M. should be followed by evaluating his RBC indices in another six to eight weeks. If he responds appropriately, then the rhEPO dosage may be decreased to the lowest dose necessary to maintain RBC indices or to prevent symptoms or RBC transfusions. If J.M.'s response is marginal, then the dose should be increased up to 200 units/kg three times weekly and reassessed in another six to eight weeks. If he does not respond to 200 units/kg it is unlikely that he will benefit from further rhEPO therapy.

As previously discussed, several factors may contribute to longstanding anemia in patients with AIDS. Zidovudine may elicit an erythropoietin response, but it is usually inadequate to correct the anemia; rhEPO has been shown to correct anemia in AIDS patients.[98] Patients on zidovudine with baseline erythropoietin levels less than 500 IU/L experienced a significantly higher rate of increase in hematocrit compared to patients with high baseline erythropoietin levels.[89] Based upon erythropoietic studies, investigators have proposed two populations of AIDS patients undergoing zidovudine therapy. The first population develops macrocytic anemia with moderate erythropoietin response (<500 IU/L) and requires moderate transfusion support in response to zidovudine. The second group of AIDS patients develops normocytic anemia with a high erythropoietic response (>500 IU/L). This group has substantial transfusion requirements.[99] A significant reduction in transfusion requirements was observed in the first group given rhEPO 100 units/kg subcutaneously three times weekly. Other study groups have not found baseline erythropoietin levels to be predictive of response to rhEPO.

Multifactorial Anemias

25. P.W., a 33-year-old female in her 8th month of pregnancy, complains of extreme lethargy at a routine obstetric visit. Her CBC was reported as: Hct 28%, Hgb 9 gm/dL, MCV 90 μm³, reticulocytes 0.5%. Other laboratory results include: serum folate 4 ng/mL, serum vitamin B₁₂ 400 pg/mL, serum iron 40 μg/dL, ferritin 125 ng/mL, and TIBC 440 μg/dL. A peripheral smear demonstrates both microcytic and macrocytic erythrocytes, and hypochromia. P.W. admits that she has not been taking the prescribed iron and folate supplements regularly. Can the red cell indices be correlated with the peripheral smear? What other factors should be considered in the etiology of this mixed anemia? [SI units: Hct 0.28; Hgb 90 gm/L;

MCV 90 fL; folate 9.06 nmol/L; vitamin B₁₂ 295.12 pmol/L; iron 7.16 μmol/L; ferritin 125 μg/L; TIBC 78.8 μmol/L]

The combination of both macrocytic and microcytic RBCs offset each other to produce a normal MCV. The red cell indices reflect an average value and should only be considered as one of several diagnostic tools. Accordingly, a peripheral blood smear should be examined to ascertain RBC morphology and pathology. In this case, P.W. appears to have combined iron and folate deficiency anemia.

Many patients do not present with a single cause of anemia, and there are many examples of situations in which a mixed anemia will occur, including pregnancy. As previously discussed in this chapter, iron and folate requirements increase during pregnancy. Folate deficiency anemia may occur by the third trimester.[45] P.W. will require folic acid 1 mg/day and ferrous sulfate 325 mg three times daily to treat her anemia. Hematologic laboratory parameters should be evaluated at the next visit to insure compliance and appropriateness of therapy.

Mixed anemia also can occur in patients with large volume blood loss, chronic renal failure, cirrhosis, other liver diseases, and endocrine disorders.

Acknowledgment

We gratefully acknowledge Ann Bolinger for contributions to this chapter.

References

1 **Keitt AS.** Introduction to the anemias. In: Wyngaarden JB, Smith LH, eds. Cecil's Textbook of Medicine. 17th ed. Philadelphia: WB Saunders; 1985: 870–76.

2 **Bergin JJ.** Evaluation of anemia. Postgrad Med J. 1985;77:253–69.

3 **Dawson AA et al.** Evaluation of diagnostic significance of certain symptoms and physical signs in anaemic patients. Br Med J. 1969;4:436–40.

4 **Duke M, Abelmann WH.** The hemodynamic response to chronic anemia. Circulation. 1969;39:503–6.

5 **Finch CA, Huebers H.** Perspectives in iron metabolism. N Engl J Med. 1982; 306:1520–526.

6 **Levin R.** Iron deficiency anemia in the pediatric patient. Am Pharm Assoc J. 1971;NS11:670.

7 **Benitz WE, Tatro DS.** The Pediatric Drug Handbook. Chicago: Year Book Medical Publishers; 1981.

8 **Beal R.** Hematinics: pathophysiological and clinical aspects. Drugs. 1971;2: 190–207.

9 **Wintrobe MM.** Iron deficiency and iron deficiency anemia. In: Clinical Hematology. 8th ed. Philadelphia: Lea & Febiger; 1981:617–36.

10 **Bentley DP.** Iron metabolism and anemia in pregnancy. Clin Haematol. 1985;613–28.

11 **Lipschitz DA et al.** A clinical evaluation of serum ferritin as an index of iron stores. N Engl J Med. 1974;290:1213.

12 **Jacobs A et al.** Ferritin in serum: clinical and biochemical implications. N Engl J Med. 1975;292:951.

13 **Wheby MS.** Effect of iron on serum ferritin levels in iron deficiency anemia. Blood. 1980;55(1):138–40.

14 **Harju E, Parkarinen A.** The effect of iron treatment on serum ferritin concentrations and bone marrow stainable iron in iron deficient out-patients with gastritis, gastric ulcer and duodenal ulcer. J Int Med Res. 1984;12:56–61.

15 **Stojceski T et al.** Studies on the serum iron-binding capacity. J Clin Pathol. 1965;18:446.

16 **Fairbanks VF.** Iron deficiency: still a diagnostic challenge. Med Clin North Am. 1970;54:903.

17 **Beissner RS, Trowbridger AA.** Clinical assessment of anemia. Postgrad Med. 1986;80(6):83–95.

18 **Dallman PR.** Iron deficiency: diagnosis and treatment. West J Med. 1981; 134:496–505.

19 **Bentley DP, Jacobs A.** Accumulation of storage iron in patients treated for iron deficiency anemia. Br Med J. 1975; 2:64–6.

20 **Brise H et al.** Absorbability of different iron compounds. Acta Med Scand. 1962;171(Suppl. 376):23.

21 **Ekenved G.** Iron absorption studies: studies on oral iron preparations using serum iron and different radioiron isotope techniques. Scand J Haematol. 1976;28(Suppl.):7–97.

22 **Middletown E et al.** Studies on the absorption of orally administered iron from sustained-release preparations. N Engl J Med. 1966;274:136.

23 **Beutler E.** Iron deficiency. In: Williams W, ed. Hematology. New York: McGraw-Hill; 1983:308.

24 **Bairiel I.** Absorption of sustained release iron and the effects of ascorbic acid in normal subjects and after partial gastrectomy. Br Med J. 1974;4:505–8.

25 **Grebe G et al.** Effect of meals and ascorbic acid on the absorption of a therapeutic dose of iron as ferrous and ferric salts. Curr Ther Res. 1975;17: 382–97.

26 **Harju E, Lindberg H.** Ascorbic acid does not augment the restoration effect of iron treatment for empty iron stores in patients after gastrointestinal surgery. Am Surg. 1986;52(8):463–66.

27 **Dipetro-Heydorn J et al.** Antianemia drugs. In: McEvoy GK, McQuarrie GM, eds. American Hospital Formulary Service Drug Information 87. Bethesda: ASHP; 1987:640.

28 **Kellermeyer RW.** General principles of the evaluation and therapy of anemias. Med Clin North Am. 1984;68(3): 533.

29 **Saunders JR, Ferguson AW.** Ferrous sulfate: danger to children. Br Med J. 1977;1:57.

30 **Norrby A.** Iron absorption studies in iron deficiency. Scand J Haematol. 1974;20(Suppl.):5–125.

31 **Hillman RS.** Drugs effective in iron deficiency and other hypochromic anemias. In: Gilman AG et al., eds. Goodman and Gilman's: The Pharmacological Basis of Therapeutics. 8th ed. New York: Pergamon Press;1990:1282.

32 **Aronstam A et al.** Comparative trial of controlled release iron tablet preparation and ferrous fumarate tablets. Pharmatherapeutica. 1982;3(4):263–67.

33 **Beutler E.** Iron metabolism. In: Williams W, ed. Hematology. New York: McGraw-Hill; 1983:129.

34 **Ekenved G et al.** Influence of a liquid antacid on the absorption of different iron salts. Scand J Haematol. 1976; 28(Suppl.):65–77.

35 **Hall G et al.** Inhibition of iron absorption by magnesium trisilicate. Med J Aust. 1969;2:95.

36 **O'Neil-Cutting MA, Crosby WH.** The effect of antacids on the absorption of simultaneously ingested iron. JAMA. 1986;255(11):1468–470.

37 **Neuvonem P et al.** Interference of iron with the absorption of tetracyclines in man. Br Med J. 1970;4:532.

38 **Kumpf NJ, Holland EG.** Parenteral iron dextran therapy. DICP, Ann Pharmacother. 1990;24:162–66.

39 **Harvey SC.** Antiseptics and disinfectants: fungicides, ectoparasiticides. In: Gilman AG et al., eds. Goodman and Gilman's: The Pharmacological Basis of Therapeutics. 7th ed. New York: MacMillan; 1985:959–79.

40 **Will G.** The absorption, distribution and utilization of intramuscularly administered iron-dextran: a radioisotope study. Br J Haematol. 1968;14:395–406.

41 **Halpin TC et al.** Iron deficiency anemia in childhood inflammatory bowel disease: treatment with intravenous iron dextran. 1982;6(1):9–11.

42 **Reed MD.** Use of intravenous iron dextran injection in children receiving total parenteral nutrition. Am J Dis Child. 1981;135:829–31.

43 **Auerbach M et al.** Clinical use of the total dose intravenous infusion of iron dextran. J Lab Clin Med. 1988;111: 566–70.

44 **Wallerstein RO.** Intravenous iron dex-

tran complex. Blood. 1968;32:690–95.

45 **Strieff R.** Folic acid deficiency anemia. Semin Hematol. 1970;7:23.

46 **Antony AC.** Megaloblastic anemias. In: Hoffman R et al., eds. Hematology. Basic Principles and Practice. New York: Churchill Livingstone; 1991: 392–417.

47 **Beck WS.** Diagnosis of megaloblastic anemia. Annu Rev Med. 1991;42:311–22.

48 **Sullivan LW, Herbert V.** Studies on the minimum daily requirement for vitamin B_{12}. N Engl J Med. 1965;272: 340–46.

49 **Heyssel RM et al.** Vitamin B_{12} turnover in man: the assimilation of vitamin B_{12} from natural food stuff by man and estimates of minimal daily dietary requirements. Am J Clin Nutr. 1966; 18:176–84.

50 **Kanazawa S et al.** Removal of cobalamin analogue in bile by enterohepatic circulation of vitamin B_{12}. Lancet. 1983;1:707–8.

51 **Grasbeck R.** Calculations on vitamin B_{12} turnover in man. Scand J Clin Lab Invest. 1959;11:250–58.

52 **Hagedorn CH, Alpers DH.** Distribution of intrinsic factor-vitamin B_{12} receptors in human intestine. Gastroenterology. 1977;73:1019–22.

53 **Hooper DC et al.** Characterization of ileal vitamin B_{12} binding using homogeneous human and hog intrinsic factor. J Clin Invest. 1973;52:3074–83.

54 **Mathan VI et al.** Kinetics of the attachment of intrinsic factor-bound cobamides to ileal receptors. J Clin Invest. 1974;54:598–608.

55 **Butterworth CE.** The availability of food folate. Br J Haematol. 1968:14; 339–43.

56 **Herbert V.** Recommended dietary intakes (RDI) of folate in humans. Am J Clin Nutr. 1987;45:661–70.

57 **Carmel R.** Pernicious anemia. Arch Intern Med. 1988;148:1712–714.

58 **McKinsey DS et al.** Megaloblastic pancytopenia associated with dapsone and trimethoprim treatment of *O* pneumonia in the acquired immunodeficiency syndrome. Arch Intern Med. 1989;149:965.

59 **Kornberg A et al.** Folic acid deficiency, megaloblastic anemia and peripheral polyneuropathy due to oral contraceptives. Isr J Med Sci. 1989;25: 142–45.

60 **Baker SJ et al.** Vitamin-B_{12} deficiency in pregnancy and the puerperium. Br Med J. 1962;16:1658–661.

61 **Anon.** Hereditary dihydrofolate reductase deficiency with megaloblastic anemia. Nutr Rev. 1985;43:309–11.

62 **Chanarin I.** Megaloblastic anaemia, cobalamin, and folate. J Clin Pathol. 1987;40;978–84.

63 **Hsu JM et al.** Vitamin B_{12} concentra-

64 **Chanarin I, Waters DAW.** Failed Schilling tests. Scand J Haematol. 1974;12:245–48.

65 **Murphy MF et al.** Megaloblastic anaemia due to vitamin B_{12} deficiency caused by small intestinal bacterial overgrowth: possible role of vitamin B_{12} analogues. Br J Haematol. 1986; 62:7–12.

66 **Nilsson-Ehle H et al.** Low serum cobalamin levels in a population study of 70- and 75-year-old subjects. Dig Dis Sci. 1989;34:716–23.

67 **Hillman RS.** Vitamin B-12, folic acid, and the treatment of megaloblastic anemias. In: Gilman AG et al., eds. Goodman and Gilman's: The Pharmacologic Basis of Therapeutics. 8th ed. New York: Pergamon Press;1990:1294.

68 **Weskxler BB, Moore A.** Anemia. In: Andreoli TE et al., eds. Cecil Essentials of Medicine. 2nd ed. Philadelphia: WB Saunders; 1990:343–53.

69 **Vitamin B complex.** In: McEvoy GK et al., eds. American Hospital Formulary Service Drug Information ASHP 93. Bethesda: ASHP; 1993:2291–295.

70 **Stamatoyannopoulos JA.** Future prospectives for treatment of hemoglobinopathies. West J Med. 1992:157: 631–36.

71 **Lubin B, Vichinsky E.** Sickle cell disease. In: Hoffman R et al., eds. Hematology. Basic Principles and Practice. New York: Churchill Livingstone; 1991:450–71.

72 **Steingart R.** Management of patients with sickle cell disease. Med Clin North Am. 1992;76:669–82.

73 **John AB et al.** Prevention of pneumococcal infection in children with homozygous sickle cell disease. Br Med J. 1984;288:1567–570.

74 **Noguchi CT et al.** Levels of fetal hemoglobin necessary for treatment of sickle cell disease. N Engl J Med. 1988;318:96–9.

75 **Rodgers GP et al.** Augmentation by erythropoietin of the fetal-hemoglobin response to hydroxyurea in sickle cell disease. N Engl J Med. 1993;328:73–80.

76 **Charache S et al.** Hydroxyurea-induced augmentation of fetal hemoglobin production in patients with sickle cell anemia. Blood. 1987;69:109–16.

77 **Charache S.** Pharmacologic modification of hemoglobin F expression in sickle cell anemia: an update on hydroxyurea studies. Experientia. 1993; 49:126–32.

78 **Dover GJ, Charache S.** Hydroxyurea induction of fetal hemoglobin synthesis in sickle-cell disease. Semin Oncol. 1992;19:61–6.

79 **Goldberg MA et al.** Hydroxyurea and

erythropoietin therapy in sickle cell anemia. Semin Oncol. 1992;19:74–81.

80 **Bank A et al.** Gene transfer. A potential approach to gene therapy for sickle cell disease. Ann N Y Acad Sci. 1989; 565:37–43.

81 **Nichols CR, Akard LP.** Hematologic problems in patients with cancer and chronic inflammatory disorders. In: Hoffman R et al., eds. Hematology. Basic Principles and Practice. New York: Churchill Livingstone; 1991: 1733–746.

82 **Neff MS et al.** A comparison of androgens for anemia in patients on dialysis. N Engl J Med. 1981;304:871–75.

83 **Hoxie JA.** Hematologic manifestations of AIDS. In: Hoffman R et al., eds. Hematology. Basic Principles and Practice. New York: Churchill Livingstone; 1991:1759–780.

84 **Spivak JL et al.** Serum immunoreactive erythropoietin in HIV-infected patients. JAMA. 1989;261:3104–107.

85 **Donahue RE et al.** Suppression of in vivo haematopoiesis following immunodeficiency virus infection. Nature. 1987;326:200–3.

86 **Sathe SS et al.** Severe anemia is an important negative predictor for survival with disseminated *Mycobacterium avium-intracellulare* in acquired immunodeficiency syndrome. Am Rev Respir Dis. 1990;142:1306–312.

87 **Maury CPJ, Lahdevirta J.** Correlation of serum cytokine levels with haematological abnormalities in human immunodeficiency virus infection. J Intern Med. 1990;227:253–57.

88 **Richman DD et al.** The toxicity of azidothymidine (AZT) in the treatment of patients with AIDS and AIDS-related complex. N Engl J Med. 1987;317; 192–97.

89 **Fischl MA et al.** A randomized controlled trial of a reduced daily dose of zidovudine in patients with the acquired immunodeficiency syndrome. N Engl J Med. 1990;323:1009–14.

90 **Johnson M et al.** Inhibition of bone marrow myelopoiesis and erythropoiesis in vitro by anti-retroviral nucleoside derivatives. Br J Haematol. 1988; 70:137–41.

91 **McKinsey DS.** Editorial reply. Arch Intern Med. 1990;150:1141.

92 **Camacho J et al.** Serum erythropoietin levels in anaemic patients with advanced human immunodeficiency virus infection. Br J Haematol. 1992;82: 608–14.

93 **Beach RS et al.** Altered folate metabolism in early HIV infection. JAMA. 1988;259:519.

94 **Burkes RL et al.** Low serum cobalamin levels occur frequently in acquired immune deficiency syndrome and related disorders. Eur J Haematol. 1987; 38:141–47.

95 **Herert V.** Recommended dietary intake (RDI) of folate in humans. Am J Clin Nutr. 1987;45:661–70

96 **Tilkian SM et al.** Altered folate metabolism in early HIV infection. JAMA. 1988;259:3128.

97 **Erslev AJ.** The therapeutic role of recombinant erythropoietin in anemic patients with intact endogenous production of erythropoietin. Semin Oncol. 1992;19(Suppl. 8):14–8.

98 **Miles SA et al.** Potential use of human stem cell factor as adjunctive therapy for human immunodeficiency virus-related cytopenias. Blood. 1991;78: 3200–208.

99 **Fischl M et al.** Recombinant human erythropoietin for patients with AIDS treated with zidovudine. N Engl J Med. 1990;322:1488–493.

100 **Abels RI.** Use of recombinant human erythropoietin in the treatment of anemia in patients who have cancer. Semin Oncol. 1992;19(Suppl. 8):29–35.

101 **Vannucchi AM et al.** Stimulation of erythroid engraftment by recombinant human erythropoietin in ABO-compatible, HLA-identical, allogeneic bone marrow transplant patients. Leukemia. 1992;6:215–19.

102 **Laporte JPH et al.** Recombinant human erythropoietin at high dose is effective for the treatment of the anemia of myelodysplastic syndromes. Contrib Nephrol. 1991;88:271–72.

103 **Razzano M et al.** Therapy with recombinant erythropoietin in patients with myelodysplastic syndromes. Br J Haematol. 1992;81:98–104.

104 **Hirashima K et al.** Improvement in anemia by recombinant human erythropoietin in patients with myelodysplastic syndrome and aplastic anemia. Contrib Nephrol. 1991;88:254–65.

105 **Oster W et al.** Erythropoietin for the treatment of anemia of malignancy associated with neoplastic bone infiltration. J Clin Oncol. 1990;50:697–703.

106 **Ludwig H et al.** Erythropoietin treatment of anemia associated with multiple myeloma. N Engl J Med. 1990;322: 1693–699.

107 **Ludwig H et al.** Erythropoietin treatment of chronic anemia of malignancy. Blood. 1989;74(Suppl. 1):16a. Abstract.

108 **Eschbach JW et al.** Correction of the anemia of end-stage renal disease with recombinant human erythropoietin. N Engl J Med. 1987;316:73–8.

109 **Eschbach JW et al.** Recombinant human erythropoietin in anemic patients with end-stage renal disease. Ann Intern Med. 1989;111:992–1000.

110 **Dallman PR et al.** Prevalence and causes of anemias in the United States, 1976 to 1980. Am J Clin Nutr. 1984; 39(3):437–45.

Drug-Induced Blood Disorders

Carl W Peterson

Overview 89-1	Acute and chronic effects of alcohol 89-7
Definitions 89-1	Immune Destruction: Quinine/Quinidine 89-7
Epidemiology 89-1	Mechanisms and features 89-7
Drug-Induced Hemolytic Anemia	Management 89-8
(See Table 89.1) 89-2	Gold 89-8
Intravascular Hemolysis 89-2	Management 89-8
Extravascular Hemolysis 89-2	Heparin 89-8
Glucose-6-Phosphate Dehydrogenase (G6PD)	Mechanisms 89-8
Deficiency 89-2	Incidence 89-8
Etiology 89-2	Features (Also see Question 24) 89-9
Epidemiology 89-3	Thrombotic/embolic complications 89-9
Classification 89-3	Management 89-9
Features 89-4	**Drug-Induced Neutropenia** 89-9
Drugs (See Table 89.2) 89-4	Definitions 89-9
Management (Also see Question 2) 89-4	Epidemiology 89-10
Immune Hemolytic Anemia 89-4	Mechanisms 89-10
Coombs' test 89-4	Immune versus direct mechanisms: penicillins 89-10
Mechanisms (See Table 89.3) 89-5	Mechanisms 89-10
High affinity hapten-type reaction: penicillin 89-5	Management 89-10
Mechanisms 89-5	Idiosyncratic toxic effect: phenothiazines 89-10
Features 89-5	Mechanisms 89-10
Low affinity binding: quinidine 89-5	Features 89-11
Mechanisms 89-5	Management 89-11
Features 89-6	Colony stimulating factors (CSFs) 89-11
Management 89-6	Clozapine 89-11
Autoimmune reaction: methyldopa 89-6	Immune Peripheral Destruction: Aminopyrine 89-12
Mechanisms 89-6	**Drug-Induced Aplastic Anemia (See Table 89.4)** ..89-12
Features and Coombs' testing 89-6	Mechanisms 89-12
Management 89-6	Importance of a Careful History 89-13
Drug-Induced Thrombocytopenia 89-6	Features (See Table 89.4) 89-13
Suppressed Production: Thiazides 89-7	Management 89-14
Mechanisms 89-7	Bone marrow transplant 89-14
Amrinone 89-7	Immunosuppression 89-14
Features 89-7	Androgens 89-14
Management 89-7	Colony stimulating factors (CSFs) 89-14

Definitions

A drug-induced blood dyscrasia is simply a disease of the blood caused by a drug. The term blood dyscrasia in this chapter will refer to a reaction which usually is not predictable, is not a direct extension of a drug's pharmacologic effect, and occurs in only a small number of individuals exposed to the agent in question. Thus, the decrease in white blood cell (WBC) count that many patients experience during marrow suppressant cancer chemotherapy would not be considered a blood dyscrasia, whereas the same reaction in someone receiving phenytoin for a seizure disorder would. As always, exceptions exist and will be addressed. The four major types of drug-induced blood dyscrasias to be presented are hemolytic anemia, thrombocytopenia, agranulocytosis/neutropenia, and aplastic anemia. An international consensus meeting has proposed standardized definitions and general criteria to assess the cause of drug-induced blood dyscrasias.[1] These definitions will be discussed in the appropriate sections of the text. However, it should be noted that these definitions were published in 1991. Older reports have used similar, though not necessarily identical, criteria, and not all authors have adopted these standards since their publication.

Epidemiology

Although drug-induced blood dyscrasias are uncommon (i.e., 0.7 to 1.0 significant reactions per 100,000 patient-years),[2,3] they contribute significantly to overall drug-related morbidity and mortality. Blood dyscrasias accounted for about 5% of all adverse drug reactions[2] but 40% of fatal reactions[4] in Sweden over a ten year period from 1966 to 1975. The Australian Adverse Drug Reactions Advisory Committee reported figures of 2.6% and 14.4% respectively for the 1983 to 1985 period.[5] The Committee on Safety of Medicines in England noted that 18% of fatal drug reactions were caused by drugs.[6] Thrombocytopenia and agranulocytosis/neutropenia are about twice as common as hemolytic anemia, and aplastic anemia is, fortunately, least common. As is true for adverse drug reactions overall, older patients appear to be at increased risk.

Drug-Induced Hemolytic Anemia

Drug-induced hemolysis refers to an increased rate of red cell destruction that is caused, directly or indirectly, by a drug. The destruction can occur within the blood vessels (intravascular hemolysis) or outside the vascular space (extravascular hemolysis). Anemia occurs when the rate of hemolysis exceeds the rate at which the bone marrow is able to replace destroyed cells.

Table 89.1 lists the pathogenetic mechanisms by which drugs induce red cell destruction. The first is by a direct toxic effect on cells due to genetically determined enzymopathies or hemoglobinopathies. The red blood cells (RBCs) of patients with these inherited abnormalities are predisposed to lysis when exposed to certain drugs or chemicals that would otherwise not have any predictable toxic effect. Second, a number of drugs can induce an immune response that results in destruction of normal red blood cells; this occurs idiosyncratically (i.e., patients cannot be identified prospectively as being predisposed).

Intravascular Hemolysis

Many drug-induced hemolytic anemias related to hereditary red cell defects, as well as some of the immune-mediated variety, are caused by destruction of red blood cells within the vessels themselves. Free hemoglobin, a potentially nephrotoxic substance, is released into the bloodstream. The amount of hemoglobin released from erythrocytes during large scale hemolysis overwhelms the mechanisms that usually are capable of efficiently removing hemoglobin (Hgb) from the circulation. Free hemoglobin initially binds tightly to haptoglobin, a circulating alpha globulin. The resulting hemoglobin-haptoglobin complex is too large to be filtered at the glomerulus and is removed from the circulation by the fixed macrophages of the reticuloendothelial system. This occurs primarily in the liver, where the heme portion of the hemoglobin molecule is converted to bilirubin, iron is conserved, and serum levels of haptoglobin fall. Laboratory changes characteristic of hepatic hemoglobin and bilirubin metabolism after extravascular hemolysis, including hyperbilirubinemia and urobilinogenuria (see below), also are observed. If the hemoglobin-binding capacity of haptoglobin is exceeded either by an acute severe or brisk ongoing hemolysis, some hemoglobin will be renally filtered. The cells of the proximal tubule reabsorb hemoglobin, but as in the case of glucose there is a threshold concentration beyond which free hemoglobin will spill into the urine. The reabsorbed hemoglobin is degraded to bilirubin and the iron is converted to ferritin and hemosiderin. Bilirubin may appear in the urine and, as the hemoglobin-injured tubular cells slough, so will hemosiderin. Hemoglobin not bound to haptoglobin or filtered at the glomerulus is metabolized to methemoglobin, the hemin moiety of which may then dissociate and bind to the circulating beta globulin, hemopexin. In severe hemolysis, the hemin moiety of methemoglobin binds with circulating albumin to form methemalbumin; serum hemopexin levels will decrease and methemalbumin will be detectable in the serum. Hemin dissociates from albumin and binds to newly synthesized hemopexin as depleted hemopexin supplies are replaced. (See Figure 89.1.)

Table 89.1	Mechanisms of Drug-Induced Hemolytic Anemia
Hereditary RBC[a] Defects	**Immunologic Destruction**
G6PD[a] deficiency	Immune
Defects in glutathione metabolism	Autoimmune
Unstable hemoglobins	

a RBC = Red blood cell; G6PD = Glucose 6-phosphate dehydrogenase.

Extravascular Hemolysis

Most immune-mediated drug-induced red blood cell destruction occurs extravascularly. The RBCs are phagocytized by reticuloendothelial cells. The heme portion of hemoglobin is metabolized to unconjugated (indirect) bilirubin which complexes loosely with albumin in the bloodstream and is transported to the liver where it is conjugated with glucuronic acid. When the increased rate of bilirubin formation exceeds the ability of the liver to conjugate it, the serum concentration of indirect bilirubin increases and clinical jaundice can result. The conjugated (direct) bilirubin is passed from the liver to the intestine where it is metabolized to urobilinogen. Most urobilinogen is excreted in the feces, but part is reabsorbed and enterohepatically recycled with some urobilinogen appearing in the urine (also see Figure 4.1 in Chapter 4: Interpretation of Clinical Laboratory Tests).

Glucose-6-Phosphate Dehydrogenase (G6PD) Deficiency

1. F.S., a 55-year-old, Italian American male, noted suprapubic pain and burning upon urination. Laboratory data included Hgb 14.0 gm/dL (Normal: 12–16), Hematocrit (Hct) 43.6% (Normal: 38–48), WBC count 7500/mm³ (Normal: 4000–11,000), reticulocyte count 0.5% (Normal: 0.2–2.0), and normal serum electrolytes, bilirubin, prothrombin time (PT), and activated partial thromboplastin time (aPPT). Urinalysis (UA) was notable for 20–50 WBCs/high powered field (hpf) and moderate bacteria. A tentative diagnosis of cystitis related to benign prostatic hypertrophy was made, urine was sent for culture, and F.S. was given a prescription for co-trimoxazole (Bactrim, Septra) one double-strength tablet BID. Four days later, F.S. returned to the clinic noting that although his original symptoms had resolved, he had begun feeling very tired. He also noted that his urine had become dark. Hgb was now 9.9 gm/dL, Hct 32.5%, WBC count 9100/mm³, corrected reticulocyte count 11%, total bilirubin 3.8 mg/dL (Normal: <1.0), direct bilirubin 0.7 mg/dL (Normal: <1.0). UA now reveals 0–5 WBCs/hpf, no bacteria, and 4+ blood. The urine also was positive for bilirubin and urobilinogen. Physical examination was unremarkable except for scleral icterus and a mild tachycardia. What role, if any, might co-trimoxazole have in F.S.'s new onset anemia? [SI units: Hgb 140 gm/dL and 99 gm/dL, respectively (Normal: 120–160); Hct 0.436 1 and 0.325 1, respectively (Normal: 0.36–0.48); WBCs 7.5 × 10⁹ L and 9.1 × 10⁹ L, respectively (Normal: 4.0–11.0); reticulocytes .005 1 and .11 1, respectively (Normal: .002–.02); bilirubin 65 μmol/L (total), 12 (direct)]

Etiology

This clinical picture in a male of Mediterranean descent is strongly suspicious for sulfamethoxazole-induced hemolysis due to G6PD deficiency. Red blood cells deficient in this enzyme are susceptible to hemolysis when exposed to certain oxidant drugs.

The hexose monophosphate shunt in the red blood cell is responsible for maintaining glutathione in the reduced state. Glutathione is an antioxidant which prevents oxidation of hemoglobin to methemoglobin. NADPH is needed to keep glutathione in the reduced state and G6PD is needed to reduce NADP to NADPH (see Figure 89.2). When RBCs are deficient in G6PD, the amount of NADPH is inadequate to keep glutathione in the reduced state, free radicals accumulate intracellularly and the oxidation of hemoglobin to methemoglobin cannot be prevented. Heinz bodies (condensations of precipitated, denatured hemoglobin) appear in the red blood cells. The now fragile cells are removed from the circulation (lysed) prematurely, primarily while passing through the splenic pulp. It is unclear whether the presence of methemoglobin contributes to Heinz body formation or is merely a concomitant occurrence. The degree of hemolysis is related both to the oxidant potential of the drug and the dose.[7]

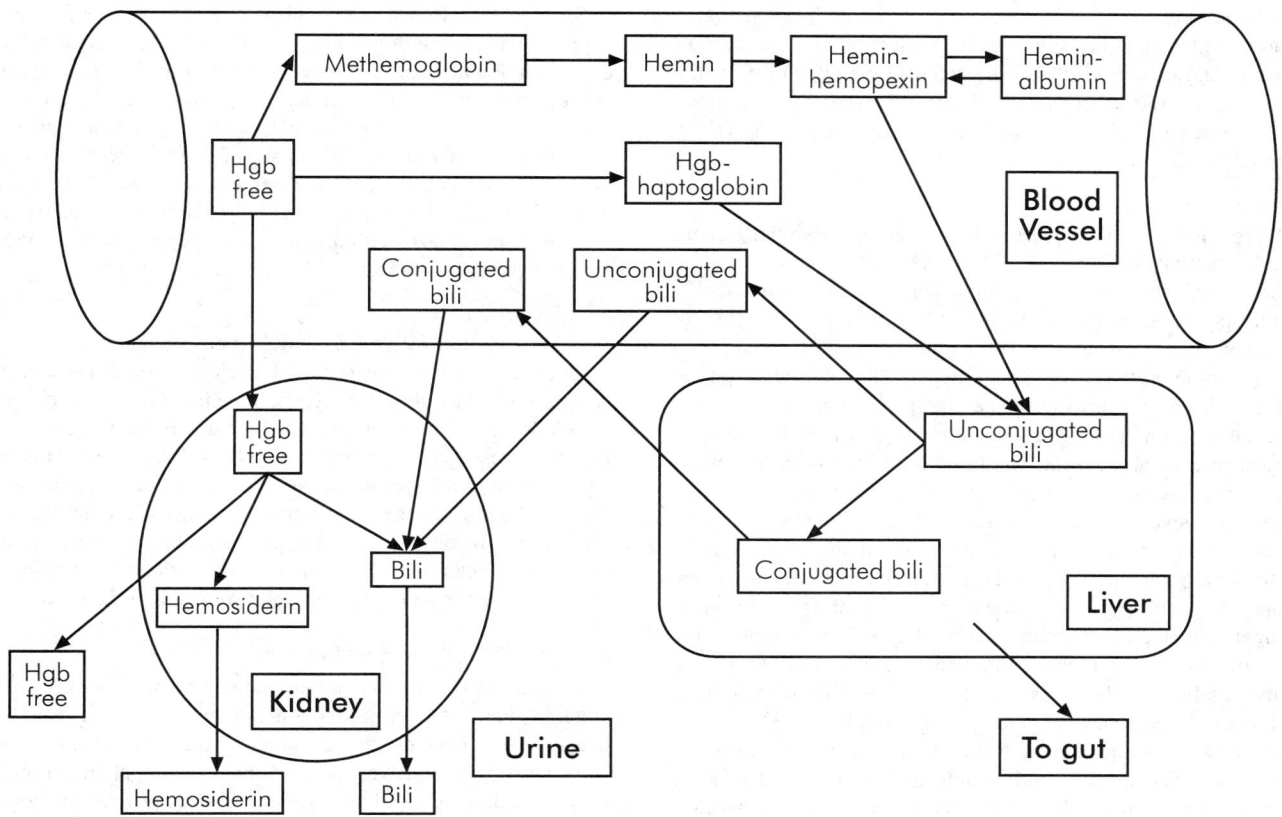

Fig 89.1   Intravascular Hemolysis   See Figure 4.1 in Chapter 4: Interpretation of Clinical Laboratory Tests for bilirubin metabolism after secretion into the gut.

Epidemiology

Over 100 million people carry the trait for hereditary G6PD deficiency.[8] The disorder is sex-linked with transmission from mother to son. While the defect will be fully expressed in males, female heterozygotes have a mix of both normal and deficient red blood cells and correspondingly less severe manifestations of disease. Over 150 variant forms of the enzyme have been identified,[9] but the two most common are the A- (African) and the Mediterranean types. The less severe A- variant affects about 10% of American blacks. Glucose-6-phosphate dehydrogenase activity in the A-type usually is 5% to 15% of normal. In this situation, individuals remain asymptomatic except for episodes of hemolysis precipitated by oxidant stress. Mediterranean-type deficiency is associated with very low levels of G6PD enzyme activity (e.g., in some patients <1% of normal). The RBCs are more susceptible to lysis in those with Mediterranean deficiency than those with A-type. The more severe forms of G6PD deficiency are most prevalent in people of Southern European ancestry, particularly Sardinian Italians, Greeks, and Kurdish Jews in whom the prevalence is approximately 50%. Other groups affected by G6PD variants include Sephardic Jews, Orientals, and American Indians. Cases have been reported rarely even in Western European and Scandinavian individuals.

Classification

Since the spectrum of G6PD deficiency is so broad, it may be more clinically meaningful to classify the disease by severity rather than by enzyme variant type.[10] Class I is the most severe form of deficiency and is marked by an ongoing hemolytic process even in the absence of identifiable oxidant stress. Class II deficiency is marked by G6PD activity less than 10% of normal but with severe episodic hemolysis rather than chronic hemolysis. Class III deficiency is characterized by occasional hemolytic episodes associated with identifiable precipitating factors. Class IV has normal G6PD activity, and enzyme activity in class V actually is increased. The degree of hemolysis in all classes is related both to the degree of enzyme deficiency and the strength of the precipitating stimulus. In the case of drugs, both the oxidant potential of the drug and the dose contribute to severity. Even topical administration of 1% silver sulfadiazine in a patient with extensive burns and 10% G6PD

Fig 89.2

activity has resulted in significant red blood cell destruction.[11] Nondrug inducers of hemolysis include infection, diabetic ketoacidosis, unknown factors during the neonatal period, and ingestion of fava beans. Also known as broad beans, fava beans are common fare in some parts of the world and can cause severe hemolysis in some G6PD deficient individuals.

Features

2. How is the clinical picture of F.S. compatible with drug-induced hemolysis due to G6PD deficiency?

F.S.'s clinical course to this point is typical of that seen in G6PD hemolysis due to drugs. Asymptomatic hemolysis begins one to three days after the drug is begun, with Heinz bodies appearing in the circulating erythrocytes. Serum hemoglobin concentration begins to fall and the urine becomes dark secondary to increased levels of urobilinogen. In severe cases, weakness and abdominal or back pain may occur and the urine may become nearly black (due to pyrollic substances produced from degradation of Heinz bodies). As levels of indirect bilirubin rise, the patient becomes icteric and a reticulocytosis develops as the body attempts to increase RBC production. In patients with class III deficiency, the hemoglobin will begin to rise toward normal in about one week as younger red blood cells with greater G6PD activity replace the older, lysed ones. Even with continued drug ingestion, symptoms, if any, resolve and the appearance of the urine becomes normal. With class II deficiency, even the younger red blood cells will be destroyed and significant hemolysis with anemia will continue unless the drug is stopped. A G6PD deficiency can be confirmed by assaying G6PD activity. In F.S.'s case, it is too early to determine with certainty the outcome if the drug were to be continued; the prudent course would be to discontinue the co-trimoxazole and substitute an appropriate nonoxidant agent. A cephalosporin or quinolone antibiotic are possible alternatives, but at this point culture results should be available and can be used to guide therapy.

3. Why did F.S.'s urine test positive for blood when no RBCs were present?

The urine tests for blood are based upon the ability to detect hemoglobin even after some or all of the red blood cells have disintegrated and are no longer visible microscopically on hpf. Therefore, the presence of hemoglobin in the urine will result in a positive urine test for blood. In this case, a positive test for hemoglobin in the absence of RBCs helps differentiate hemoglobinuria due to hemolysis from true hematuria.

Drugs

4. F.S. expresses surprise when he is informed of this reaction to co-trimoxazole, since he has taken sulfisoxazole (Gantrisin) in the past without difficulty. Do all sulfa drugs have the same potential for inducing hemolysis in patients with G6PD deficiency?

A large number of oxidant drugs have been reported to cause hemolysis in G6PD deficient individuals. In many cases, cause and effect has not been well established. Several drugs, particularly antipyretic and antibiotic agents, have been implicated as having caused hemolysis when, in fact, hemolysis may have been precipitated by the infections for which the drugs were being used. Other drugs have been implicated through the use of *in vitro* enzyme stability tests. The response of red blood cells in this enzyme stability test does not necessarily correlate with significant *in vivo* hemolysis, and this test also fails to measure the effect of drug metabolites. The most reliable method of testing for hemolytic potency is to administer the drug in question to normal volunteers who have been infused with ^{51}Cr-labeled G6PD deficient red blood cells.

Since laboratory tests and clinical case reports have not always been sufficiently rigorous, drug-induced hemolysis in G6PD deficient individuals can be somewhat confusing. Sulfamethoxazole (Gantanol), alone or in combination as co-trimoxazole, causes hemolysis in class II deficiency, but class III deficient individuals may be at low risk if the daily dose is 3.2 gm or less.[12] Sulfisoxazole does not cause significant hemolysis in usually-prescribed doses. Therefore, F.S.'s hemolytic response to sulfamethoxazole, but not to sulfisoxazole, is consistent with existing data. Table 89.2 lists other drugs associated with significant hemolysis.

Management

5. How should F.S.'s G6PD deficiency be treated?

Other than discontinuation and avoidance of drugs and substances known to cause hemolysis, there is no specific therapy for G6PD deficiency. If hemolysis is severe, red blood cell transfusion may be necessary. The patient should be well hydrated to maintain a good urine flow to prevent or attenuate renal toxicity from hemoglobin. Vitamin E has been tested as an antioxidant, but the slight reduction in hemolysis seen is statistically, but probably not clinically, significant.[13,14] F.S. should be cautioned regarding his G6PD deficiency and the deleterious effects of certain drugs.

Immune Hemolytic Anemia

Drug molecules are potentially antigenic, but generally are too small to elicit antibody production by themselves. They can, however, serve as haptens and be immunogenic when combined with some larger molecules (e.g., cell membranes, circulating proteins). Likewise, drug metabolites, particularly highly reactive metabolites, can act as haptens (e.g., penicillin and its penicilloyl by-product).[15,16]

Coombs' Test

6. R.L., a 53-year-old male, is admitted with gas gangrene of the left leg. His leg was amputated below the knee and he was started on gentamicin 120 mg Q 8 hr and penicillin G 4,000,000 units Q 4 hr along with aggressive local care. On the ninth hospital day, his Hct was noted to be 30%, decreased from 41% four days previously. No signs of bleeding were found. Further evaluation revealed a corrected reticulocyte count of 8% (no baseline drawn), elevated indirect bilirubin, and a positive direct Coombs' test. What is the significance of a positive direct Coombs' test in R.L.? [SI units: Hct 0.3 1 and 0.41 1 respectively; reticulocytes 0.08 1]

The development of a test which could detect antibodies directed against the red blood cell represented an important advance in the evaluation of patients such as R.L. with suspected immune hemolytic anemia, including the drug-induced variety. The Coombs', or antiglobulin, test can detect both antibody coating of RBCs and the presence of circulating immunoglobulins directed against RBCs. A positive Coombs' test supports, but does not prove, the presence of an immune-mediated hemolytic process.

To prepare the reagent, termed Coombs' serum, for the direct portion of the test, rabbits are injected with human gamma globulin

Table 89.2	Drugs Associated with Significant Hemolysis in G6PD[a] Deficiency[9,164]	
Acetanilid	Phenazopyridine	Sulfanilamide
Dapsone	Phenylhydrazine	Sulfapyridine
Methylene blue	Primaquine	Thiazolsulfone
Nalidixic acid	Sulfacetamide	Toluidine blue
Nitrofurantoin	Sulfamethoxazole	

[a] G6PD = Glucose 6-phosphate dehydrogenase.

causing them to form anti-human gamma globulin antibodies. Their serum is harvested and processed appropriately. The patient's red blood cells are washed to remove any loosely attached proteins and then incubated with Coombs' serum. If the cells are antibody-coated, the anti-human serum will bind to those antibodies, forming cross-links between red blood cells which will result in visible agglutination. Agglutination of red blood cells in Coombs' serum is termed a positive Coombs' test and indicates the presence of firmly bound antibodies on the surface of the cells. Bound components of complement, even in the absence of bound IgG, also may result in a positive test.[17] The direct Coombs' test does not tell whether hemolysis is occurring, and in fact, several drugs, including R.L.'s penicillin, are known to cause a positive test without significant red blood cell destruction.

The indirect Coombs' test is useful for determining the presence of antibodies in the serum rather than on RBC surfaces. In this case, normal donor RBCs are incubated with the patient's serum, washed, and suspended in Coombs' serum. Agglutination confirms that the patient's serum contained anti-red blood cell antibodies. A second form of the indirect Coombs' test utilizes animal serum containing known, specific antibodies to detect matching antigens attached to red blood cells.

Mechanisms

7. Can R.L.'s penicillin be causing his anemia, and if so, by what mechanism?

The three basic mechanisms by which drugs are thought to cause immunologic hemolytic anemia are: 1) a high-affinity hapten-type reaction; 2) a reaction precipitated by low-affinity binding to RBCs, either via a low-affinity hapten-type reaction or by circulating immune complex formation, also known as an "innocent bystander reaction"; and 3) an autoimmune reaction. (See Table 89.3.)

High-Affinity Hapten-Type Reaction: Penicillin. Penicillin is the prototype drug for the high-affinity hapten-type of immunologic hemolytic anemia. Penicillin and penicillin metabolites bind strongly to the red blood cell membrane in dose-related fashion and are detectable on the cells of nearly all patients receiving more than 10 MU/day[18] or whenever penicillin blood levels are high (e.g., secondary to probenecid or diminished renal function). About 3% of individuals receiving high-dose penicillin will produce IgG directed against the penicillin-membrane complex as detected by a positive Coombs' test.[19] Antibody-coated red blood cells in a small number of cases are then recognized and destroyed in significant numbers extravascularly by the macrophages of the reticuloendothelial system, primarily in the spleen.[20] Other drugs reported to produce high-affinity hapten-type hemolysis, though much less frequently than penicillin, are tetracycline and tolbutamide. Cephalosporins also have been implicated, but their binding to RBCs does not appear to be dose related.

8. *Features.* **Has R.L.'s clinical course been consistent with penicillin-induced hemolytic anemia, and how quickly will the problem resolve once the drug is discontinued?**

As in R.L.'s case, anemia is subacute in onset, usually developing after seven to ten days of high-dose therapy. In most, but not all, cases there are no other signs suggesting an allergic reaction, and other cell lines rarely are involved. R.L.'s laboratory findings are typical of those seen in extravascular hemolysis. The direct Coombs' test is strongly positive, and the indirect test is positive only for penicillin. Hemolysis of decreasing severity may continue for some time after the drug is discontinued, probably due to continued presence of cell-bound penicillin. The direct Coombs' test may remain positive for weeks or even several months.[21]

9. *Low Affinity Binding: Quinidine.* **H.J. is a 63-year-old female whose physician prescribed quinidine sulfate 200 mg QID yesterday for an "irregular heartbeat." She has taken quinidine for this problem in the past, but stopped taking it six months ago. She comes to the ER today with fever, chills, and shakes. H.J. is found to have a Hct of 24% and her urine tests positive for blood. What drug-induced problem is compatible with this picture?** [SI units: 0.24 1]

Mechanisms. The second mechanism by which drugs cause immune hemolysis is through a low-affinity binding process. The classic explanation for this type of hemolysis involves the binding of the offending drug or drug metabolite to circulating serum proteins to form a complete antigen. Antibodies, usually IgM, are produced and combine with this antigen to create a circulating immune complex. This immune complex, in turn, is adsorbed onto the surface of a red blood cell where it triggers activation of complement. The RBC is lysed and the immune complex, which has a low affinity for the cell membrane, dissociates and goes on to a second RBC to repeat the process. It is this "recycling" of the drug-antibody complex which explains the fact that only small doses of drug are needed to cause large scale hemolysis in previously sensitized individuals. Because antibodies are not directed against the cell itself, the red blood cell is destroyed as an innocent bystander and this immune complex-mediated cell destruction has been termed an "innocent bystander reaction." The direct Coombs' test is positive only against complement since washing will remove the immune complexes from the cells.

H.J.'s quinidine is the prototype drug for the immune-complex form of immunologic hemolytic anemia. However, the innocence

Table 89.3	Drug-Induced Immunologic Hemolytic Anemia		
Mechanism	Process[a]	Common Drugs[a]	Comment[a]
High-affinity hapten-type reaction	Drug binds tightly to RBC membrane surface; immunoglobulins then form against the drug-membrane complex	Cephalosporins, penicillin, tetracycline	Penicillin is the classic prototype of this dose-related reaction
Low-affinity hapten-type reaction or Immune complex formation	Drug binds to either a) low-affinity specific antigenic loci on the cell membrane or b) to circulating proteins to form an immune complex which adheres loosely to RBCs. Lysis via complement activation ensues	Acetominophen, ASA, chlorpromazine, chlorpropamide, hydrochlorothiazide, INH, PAS, phenacetin, probenecid, quinidine, quinine, rifampin, sulfonamides	Subsequent to hemolysis, the drug or immune complex dissociates from RBC fragments, adheres to another RBC, and repeats the process. Small doses can cause large scale hemolysis. Quinidine is the prototype drug
Autoimmune reaction	Drug stimulates production of anti-RBC antibodies. Autoantibodies coat RBCs and extravascular lysis occurs	Levodopa, mefenamic acid, methyldopa, procainamide	Methyldopa is the prototype drug for autoimmune hemolysis

[a] RBC = Red blood cell; ASA = Acetylsalicylic acid; INH = Isoniazid; PAS = Para-aminosalicylate sodium.

of the red blood cell in this reaction has recently been questioned.[22–26] An alternative explanation for findings in patients such as H.J. is the "low-affinity hapten." According to this hypothesis, the drug or a metabolite binds to a specific antigenic site on the cell membrane. It then forms a complete antigen or causes a conformational change in the membrane that reveals previously protected neoantigenic sites (sites that will not be recognized as "self" by the immune system). Antibodies directed against the new antigen are produced and bind to it, complement is activated, and cell lysis ensues. Since the drug has a relatively low affinity for its binding site, it is free to go on to another cell and repeat the process. Only cells with the particular drug-binding site would be able to form the drug-antigenic site-antibody complex needed to activate complement. The high degree of antigenic specificity inherent in this model applies to the immune destruction of white blood cells and platelets as well as red blood cells (see below) and helps explain why different drugs have a propensity to effect one cell line more frequently than others.[25,26]

10. Features. Why are H.J.'s symptoms more severe than those of R.L. with high-affinity hapten-type hemolysis?

The symptoms in hemolytic anemia are related to the degree of anemia produced (in relation to baseline blood count) and the severity or rapidity of hemolysis. Immune complex-mediated hemolysis frequently results in more rapid RBC destruction and more acute symptoms. Since the hemolysis is largely intravascular, large amounts of free hemoglobin may be released, resulting in hemoglobinuria and even acute renal failure due to hemoglobin renal toxicity.

11. Management. How should H.J. be managed at this point?

The suspected causative agent, quinidine in this case, should be discontinued and an alternative agent substituted if necessary. A good urine flow should be maintained with or without urinary alkalinization to prevent or attenuate renal failure. Red blood cell transfusion may be needed in symptomatic patients or in patients such as H.J. because of a significantly decreased Hct (e.g., 24%). Since immune complex hemolysis requires the presence of drug in the serum, it resolves soon after the drug is discontinued. An acute, severe red blood cell destruction can result from even a single dose of drug in a sensitized patient; therefore, this type of hemolysis should not be rechallenged. As always, patient education regarding the cause of this reaction and strict avoidance of quinidine are an important part of her therapy plan. (See Question 20 for a discussion of cross-sensitivity with quinine and Table 89.3 for other drugs associated with immune complex hemolysis.)

12. Autoimmune Reaction: Methyldopa. M.S., a 35-year-old female, was found to be mildly anemic during a hospital admission for another problem. She has been taking hydrochlorothiazide 50 mg/day for over 10 years and methyldopa 500 mg BID for about 2 years for hypertension. Work-up of her anemia is compatible with iron deficiency, but the direct Coombs' test is positive. Serum concentrations of bilirubin and haptoglobin as well as the UA are normal. Is there a drug-induced hemolytic component to M.S.'s anemia?

Mechanisms. The third mechanism by which drugs cause immune red blood cell destruction is by an autoimmune process. Methyldopa (Aldomet) is the most common cause of hemolysis via this mechanism. In some individuals, the use of methyldopa over a period of time results in the production of antibodies directed against the red blood cell in a manner almost identical to formation of antibodies against self in idiopathic autoimmune hemolytic anemia. The mechanism by which autoantibodies are induced is unknown. Evidence suggests interference with normal suppressor cell function,[27,28] and it has been suggested that drug may alter RBC membrane antigenicity early in the maturation process.[24] It is known, however, that while administering the drug may result in production of autoantibodies, its presence is not required for hemolysis to occur. Serum from a patient with this type of hemolysis will react with donor RBCs even in the absence of drug.

Features and Coombs' Testing. Because the cells are coated with anti-RBC antibody, the direct Coombs' test is positive in patients experiencing actual hemolysis. Approximately 15% of patients receiving methyldopa will develop a positive antiglobulin test; however, hemolysis occurs in less than 1%.[29] Without evidence of hemolysis and with an alternative explanation (i.e., iron deficiency) for her anemia, the presence of a positive Coombs' test in M.S. does not require discontinuation of methyldopa.

13. What are the characteristics of drug-induced autoimmune hemolysis (i.e., methyldopa type)?

The vast majority of drug-induced autoimmune hemolysis cases involve methyldopa. Levodopa (Larodopa), procainamide (Pronestyl),[30] and several of the nonsteroidal anti-inflammatory drugs[24] also have been reported to cause this problem. Methyldopa is, in fact, the most common cause of drug-induced hemolytic anemia. The direct Coombs' test becomes positive after three to six months of methyldopa therapy. This process appears to occur more frequently in individuals taking higher doses of the drug,[31,32] although actual hemolysis has not been shown to be dose related. The indirect antiglobulin test (i.e., indirect Coombs' test) also is positive in this group. The hemolysis itself usually is neither severe nor acute, and the destruction of the antibody-coated red blood cells takes place extravascularly, primarily in the spleen. Onset of symptoms is gradual and is related to the degree of anemia.

14. Management. How should M.S.'s methyldopa-induced autoimmune hemolysis be managed?

Treatment consists of drug discontinuation and red blood cell transfusion if anemia is severe. Hemolysis resolves gradually over the next several weeks to months, but the Coombs' test may remain positive for years. Despite the similarity of drug-induced autoimmune hemolytic anemia to the idiopathic variety, for which the role of corticosteroid therapy is well established, evidence supporting the use of steroids in patients with severe or life threatening drug-induced autoimmune hemolysis is anecdotal at best.[33–37]

15. How should M.S.'s methyldopa therapy be monitored now?

Some authors recommend Coombs' testing every six months or if anemia occurs during methyldopa therapy.[38,39] A positive direct test without hemolysis does not require drug discontinuation. However, a positive indirect Coombs' test can interfere with blood crossmatching; an alternative agent should be considered if it appears that blood transfusions may become necessary in the future. If Coombs' testing is financially or logistically unfeasible, the blood count could be monitored biannually. If anemia develops during treatment as it has in this case, appropriate diagnostic tests can be performed to determine the etiology.

There is no point in continuing to perform Coombs' tests on M.S. now that she is known to be positive without hemolysis. Therapy of her iron deficiency anemia should be monitored for an appropriate response.

Drug-Induced Thrombocytopenia

Thrombocytopenia is the most common of the drug-induced blood dyscrasias since virtually any drug can cause unexpected thrombocytopenia.[2,3,40] Thrombocytopenia is defined as a decrease in platelet count to less than 100,000/mm^3, although complications are uncommon at this level.[1] There are three primary mechanisms by which drugs cause thrombocytopenia: 1) immune-mediated suppression or destruction of platelets; 2) decreased production of platelets through direct suppression of thrombopoiesis; and 3), in the case of heparin, an apparently dose-related, nonimmune direct effect on circulating platelets.

Most drugs causing thrombocytopenia appear to do so through immune mechanisms, although it has proven difficult to distinguish between immune and toxic effects on thrombopoiesis. Well over 100 drugs have been implicated as causes of thrombocytopenia, most in the form of circumstantial case reports. It appears that immune platelet destruction occurs through reactions analogous to immunological red blood cell destruction.

Suppressed Production: Thiazides

Mechanisms

16. J.Y., a 56-year-old male with mild hypertension, was started on hydrochlorothiazide 50 mg/day. Routine blood work at this time showed an adequate platelet estimate (>150,000/mm^3). The platelet estimate after 2 weeks of therapy was likewise normal. At a one month follow-up visit, however, J.Y.'s complete blood count (CBC) revealed a decreased platelet estimate, and a subsequent platelet count was 78,000/mm^3. He reported no unusual bleeding, the physical examination was unremarkable, and the CBC was otherwise unchanged. Should the differential diagnosis include hydrochlorothiazide as a possible cause of J.Y.'s thrombocytopenia? [SI units: platelet counts >1.5 × 10^{11}/L and 0.78 × 10^{11}/L respectively]

Drugs should always be considered in evaluating blood dyscrasias. Thiazide diuretics as well as furosemide are known to be associated with thrombocytopenia. Drug-dependent antiplatelet antibodies have been identified in the serum of some patients with thrombocytopenia who also were taking thiazides,[41,42] suggesting an immune process. In most cases, however, antibodies are not demonstrable and marrow examination typically reveals decreased megakaryocytes, findings more consistent with suppression of platelet production. Thrombocytopenia recurs with rechallenge only after one to four weeks of drug administration, further supporting a nonimmune process. Although some cases of thiazide-induced thrombocytopenia may have an immunologic basis, the more common mechanism probably is one of direct marrow suppression.

Amrinone is another drug believed to cause thrombocytopenia through nonimmune, dose-related mechanisms. Evidence suggests that amrinone may affect platelet production in such a way that platelets in the periphery are larger and more prone to premature destruction than normal.[43,44] The incidence is reported to be 2.4% with short-term infusions,[45] but may be greater with longer infusions or higher doses.[46] One investigator demonstrated an association between thrombocytopenia and accumulation of the amrinone metabolite, N-acetylamrinone, prompting speculation that rapid acetylator phenotypes may be at increased risk.[46]

Features

17. A bone marrow examination reveals only decreased megakaryocytes, and the initial work-up fails to reveal other reasons for a low platelet count. Is J.Y.'s clinical picture compatible with thiazide-induced thrombocytopenia?

J.Y.'s course to this point has been typical of thrombocytopenia due to decreased thrombopoiesis. Onset is delayed, is gradual rather than sudden, and usually is not associated with fevers, rash, or other signs of immune reaction. The degree of platelet reduction frequently is mild, and in the absence of other risk factors, bleeding is relatively uncommon unless thrombocytopenia is severe.

Management

18. How should J.Y. be treated and monitored?

With discontinuation of hydrochlorothiazide, the platelet count would be expected to return to normal within about two weeks in J.Y. The drug should be discontinued and the platelet count should be monitored to verify resolution of the thrombocytopenia. J.Y. also should be monitored for signs of bleeding until recovery. For treatment of his hypertension, a suitable alternative agent should be prescribed. As always, J.Y. should be advised to avoid this drug in the future and to inform individuals involved in his future care of this reaction.

Acute and Chronic Effects of Alcohol

19. Should J.Y. be advised to avoid alcohol?

Alcohol has a general marrow suppressant effect. Chronic use of alcohol results in a decreased rate of platelet production as well as reduced platelet survival. Thrombocytopenia unrelated to splenic sequestration of platelets occurs in up to 26% of alcoholics hospitalized for alcohol-related reasons[47,48] and 3% of "well" alcoholics.[49] In addition, acute alcohol intoxication can result in deficient platelet function.[50] The combination of thrombocytopenia and platelet dysfunction can result in significant bleeding complications. This situation would be further exacerbated by concomitant coagulopathy due to alcoholic liver disease. In the patient with alcoholic thrombocytopenia, the platelet count begins to rise after several days of alcohol abstinence. By 5 to 21 days, the platelet count rises to well above baseline with one-third of patients overshooting to over 450,000/mm^3; in one to three additional weeks the platelet count returns to normal.[51]

There is no direct evidence that moderate alcohol intake would slow J.Y.'s recovery from hydrochlorothiazide-induced thrombocytopenia. Nevertheless, in view of the unfavorable effect of alcohol on platelet production, as well as the effect of acute ingestion on platelet function, it would seem prudent for him to abstain from excessive consumption of alcoholic beverages until platelet recovery is complete.

Immune Destruction: Quinine/Quinidine

Mechanisms and Features

20. K.B., a 65-year-old male, began taking quinine sulfate 300 mg HS for nocturnal leg cramps. He stopped taking the drug after 2 weeks when he read that stretching exercises might help. Three months later, with worsening cramps, he resumed taking the drug. The next morning he noted small, purple splotches on his skin which had not been present the evening before. This problem became worse throughout the day, particularly on his lower legs, causing him to seek medical help. Upon questioning, he recalled experiencing a hot, flushed sensation shortly after taking the quinine dose but thought little of it. How might quinine be responsible for these events?

Quinine and quinidine are well-studied causes of drug-induced immune thrombocytopenia. When patients have been sensitized through previous exposure to the drug in question, constitutional symptoms such as warmth, flushing, chills, and headache can occur soon after the first dose. The platelet count falls precipitously, often to very low levels, with bleeding (should it occur) commencing within hours or days of ingestion. Petechiae, purpura, and hemorrhagic oral bullae are frequent early signs, but patients can present with overt bleeding as the first indication of a drug reaction. Thrombocytopenia also can occur during initial exposure to drug, but this normally requires seven to ten days of therapy during which time antibodies are formed. Careful questioning of a patient with an acute reaction who denies having taken the drug before often will reveal previous drug use of which the patient was unaware. Exposure to the small amounts of quinine in tonic beverages is a typical example.[52,53] Thrombocytopenia caused by surreptitious use of quinidine (discovered through an assay for quinidine-dependent antiplatelet antibodies and serum quinidine levels) has been reported.[54]

The clinical and laboratory features are compatible with a low-affinity hapten-type reaction (see Immune Hemolytic Anemia). Specific platelet membrane glycoproteins against which antibodies in quinine/quinidine-induced thrombocytopenia are directed have been identified,[55-59] and it has been noted that in some patients, more than one antibody may be present.[60]

Management

21. How should K.B.'s acute reaction be treated?

Treatment consists of drug discontinuation and support. The platelet count usually begins to rise within three to four days and returns to normal in one to two weeks as the drug and its metabolites are cleared from the body and platelet destruction stops. Since transfused platelets are destroyed rapidly if given during the acute process, their use is reserved primarily for control of active bleeding. Although the use of corticosteroids has not been demonstrated to either reduce bleeding or alter the course of the reaction, some authors recommend their use.[61-63] Rechallenge with the suspected drug can result in a potentially fatal reaction and should not be attempted for either diagnostic or therapeutic reasons except under the most extreme conditions. In the case of quinine/quinidine, sensitivity to one does not absolutely preclude use of the other since the antibodies are isomerically specific. Cross-reactivity has been documented,[64,65] however, so it would be prudent to avoid either substance. The patient should be advised of his serious drug ''allergy'' and warned to avoid that agent. In this case, K.B. also should be warned against consuming beverages that contain quinine.

Gold

22. F.R. has been receiving gold injections weekly for the past 6 months, during which time her physician has been monitoring her platelet counts regularly. Believing that any problems should have appeared by now, she asks if she still needs these blood tests. What is a reasonable recommendation for F.R.?

Isolated thrombocytopenia is reported to occur in 1% to 3% of patients receiving gold therapy.[66] Most patients have been taking the drug for several months, and in some cases the platelet count has fallen after gold was discontinued. Although gold-induced thrombocytopenia usually is subacute in onset and can occur within one month of a normal platelet count, its occurrence can be more gradual.[67] The amount of gold administered, either in individual doses or total cumulative dose, does not seem to correlate with subsequent thrombocytopenia.[68] The presence of increased megakaryocytes in the marrow[69,70] and platelet-associated IgG[55,67] or gold-dependent antiplatelet antibodies[71] indicates a probable mechanism of immune-mediated peripheral destruction. Patients with HLA-DR3 appear to be at increased risk.[67] The ongoing risk of an adverse reaction should be explained to F.R. to enlist her continued cooperation with the drug monitoring regimen. Furthermore, F.R. should be monitored for other blood dyscrasias since gold salts can cause agranulocytosis and aplastic anemia, as well as thrombocytopenia.

Management

23. If F.R. develops thrombocytopenia from her gold therapy, how should this problem be managed?

Once gold has been discontinued, recovery from gold-induced thrombocytopenia is slow and frequently requires several months for complete resolution. This prolonged recovery period probably results from the persistence of gold within the body for long periods of time. For this reason, dimercaprol, a chelating agent, has been used to increase the rate of urinary gold elimination. Although dimercaprol may accelerate platelet recovery in some patients, clear proof of its efficacy is lacking. Corticosteroids in doses equivalent to about 60 mg/day of prednisone, with or without splenec-

tomy,[67] have been recommended. Immune globulin was used successfully in one patient.[72] Anecdotal reports of numerous other approaches to gold-induced thrombocytopenia have been published.[68] If F.R. develops thrombocytopenia, her gold treatments should be discontinued; the clinical situation will dictate whether dimercaprol and/or corticosteroids should be initiated.

Heparin

Mechanisms

24. M.U., a 65-year-old female with a painful, swollen left leg, was admitted to the hospital to rule out deep vein thrombosis (DVT). A heparin infusion was begun after an appropriate loading dose. The diagnosis of DVT was confirmed by noninvasive venous testing and warfarin was started on the fourth day; the plan was to discontinue heparin after several days of heparin/warfarin overlap. Pain and swelling had resolved by the fourth day with bed rest, leg elevation, and anticoagulation. In the evening of the seventh day, M.U. experienced a recurrence of her symptoms despite an aPPT within the desired range and an INR of 2.2. Her platelet count, which had been 225,000/mm³ on admission, was now 54,000/mm³. Is M.U.'s thrombocytopenia drug-induced? [SI units: 2.25 and 0.54 × 10¹¹/L respectively]

Heparin is the most common cause of drug-induced thrombocytopenia. There actually are two separate mechanisms by which heparin can affect platelet counts. Some patients experience a mild to moderate decrease in platelet count occurring early in therapy which may resolve despite continued drug administration.[73] This appears to be due to a direct platelet aggregating effect of heparin leading to reversible platelet clumping and undercounting by electronic counters which cannot distinguish between single platelets and platelet aggregates.[74] Counts rarely drop below 50,000/mm³ and complications are unlikely.

The second form of heparin-induced thrombocytopenia (HIT) is less common but more serious. Heparin binds to platelet membranes and forms a complete hapten with membrane components or causes a conformational change that exposes membrane neoantigens that normally are concealed.[75,76] In either case, IgG antibodies against the heparin-dependent antigen develop, bind to the platelet, and induce the platelet release reaction. This results in platelet clumping and a resultant decrease in the peripheral platelet count. It has been suggested that the propensity of heparin to initiate this sequence of events may depend upon its degree of sulfation.[77] If this is verified, it may help explain why low molecular weight heparins, which are less sulfated than standard heparin, are associated less often with HIT, and why the even less sulfated heparinoid, ORG 10172, is less reactive yet.

A platelet aggregation test can be performed. Heparin-dependent aggregation of donor platelets exposed to M.U.'s serum would confirm the diagnosis of HIT. This test, when performed properly (the concentration of heparin and the quality of donor platelets used is important), is highly specific with a low incidence of false-positive results.[78,79] However, the test is not highly sensitive; that is, a negative test does not rule out HIT.

Incidence

25. How common is heparin-induced thrombocytopenia?

Although rates as high as 24% to 31% were reported initially,[80-82] reviews of subsequent prospective studies using full doses of heparin and defining thrombocytopenia as a platelet count of less than 100,000/mm³ found a 2.9% to 5.4% incidence with bovine source heparin and 1.1% to 1.3% with porcine heparin.[83,84] The reason for the apparent difference between the two sources of heparin has not been clearly demonstrated but may be related to differences in charge, degree of sulfation, or average molecular weights.

Heparin-induced thrombocytopenia appears to be more common with full dose therapy, but it has been reported in all dose ranges. The incidence of thrombocytopenia with prophylactic heparin (5000 U Q 8 to 12 hr subcutaneously) is unknown but is much lower than with full dose heparin.[84] Thrombocytopenia has even been reported in association with heparin flushes (<500 U/day)[85] and heparin-coated pulmonary artery catheters.[86] Some institutions have moved to substitute saline flushes for heparin flushes whenever possible to minimize this problem.

Features

26. How is the onset of M.R.'s thrombocytopenia typical of thrombocytopenia induced by heparin?

The thrombocytopenia caused by heparin usually occurs after 6 to 12 days of therapy. However, thrombocytopenia can occur much earlier, particularly in previously sensitized patients.[87] Thrombocytopenia can be profound, but in some cases platelet count may remain above 100,000/mm^3 despite relatively large decreases in total count.[88,89] Once heparin is discontinued, platelets usually return to normal over the course of four to seven days although recovery can be delayed.

Thrombotic/Embolic Complications

27. What is the relationship between M.U.'s thrombocytopenia and the recurrence of her symptoms?

Heparin-induced thrombocytopenia can be complicated by the occurrence of embolic and thrombotic episodes.[74] Some patients with heparin-induced thrombocytopenia develop antibodies which deposit on vascular endothelial cells, creating a nidus for thrombus formation;[90] in others, the procoagulant properties of heparin-activated platelets may accelerate coagulation at sites of pre-existing thrombosis. The result is production/extension of thrombi in the venous or pulmonary circulation (i.e., "red clots"). Formation of large platelet aggregates (i.e., "white clots") in the arterial circulation results in stroke or arterial occlusion with or without secondary thrombus formation. There have been no prospective studies capable of defining the incidence of thromboembolic complications during heparin therapy. Thromboembolic phenomena associated with heparin-induced thrombocytopenia can be difficult to distinguish from treatment failure and disease recurrence, particularly if the platelet count has not been monitored to determine that thrombocytopenia has occurred. Recognition of heparin-associated thrombosis/embolism is important because it is associated with significant morbidity and mortality.[91,92] In addition, such a high degree of platelet activity can sometimes result in heparin resistance, probably caused by release of platelet factor 4 (anti-heparin factor). In M.U.'s case, it is likely that heparin has induced thrombocytopenia and a resultant recurrence of her left leg thrombosis.

Management

28. How should M.U. be managed at this point?

There is no advantage to delaying warfarin therapy once the diagnosis of thrombosis has been established;[93] early warfarin use would allow discontinuation of heparin before the usual onset of heparin-induced thrombocytopenia. Warfarin was delayed in M.U.'s case, but since she is almost fully anticoagulated on warfarin after four days of overlap, the best approach is simply to discontinue the heparin. She should be monitored carefully for signs of pulmonary embolism or further extension of her DVT and observed for signs of bleeding. Surprisingly, bleeding is uncommon in this setting.

Unlike M.U., patients often are not yet fully stabilized on warfarin and management decisions are not so easy. The full benefits of oral anticoagulants are delayed for several days, so they are not

suitable for immediate treatment. Antiplatelet agents as well as dextran-40 have been recommended in this setting,[75] but while antiplatelet drugs may attenuate or stop further platelet aggregation, they are ineffective in treating either heparin-induced or underlying thrombotic disease and may worsen the risk of bleeding. Iloprost, a prostacyclin analog with potent platelet inhibitory properties, also has been used.[94-97] Corticosteroids are not useful in this situation.

Low molecular weight heparins (LMWH) are associated with a lower incidence of heparin-induced thrombocytopenia than standard heparin. The manufacturer of enoxaparin (Lovenox) reports an incidence of 2% in preapproval trials as compared to 3% with standard heparin.[98] There have been numerous anecdotal reports of successful use of various LMWH preparations to anticoagulate patients with thrombocytopenia due to standard heparin. However, routine use of LMWH in patients with heparin-dependent antiplatelet antibodies is potentially hazardous. *In vitro* cross-reactivity[99] as well as unfavorable clinical outcomes after substitution, have been reported. The heparinoid, ORG 10172, cross-reacts with standard heparin-dependent antibodies 18% to 19.6% of the time as compared with 25.5% to 94% cross-reactivity of various low molecular weight heparins.[100,169]

Successful use of two investigational alternative anticoagulants has been reported. Ancrod, derived from the venom of the Malayan pit viper, is a defibrinogenating agent that reduces blood coagulability by degrading fibrinogen. It has produced favorable results in patients with heparin-induced thrombocytopenia when given in doses sufficient to decrease fibrinogen levels to 50 to 100 gm/dL (250 to 350).[101] Hirudin, a natural anticoagulant derived from leeches, and a recombinant analog inhibit coagulation by interfering with the activity of thrombin. A case report of the successful use of the recombinant product in a single patient with heparin-induced thrombocytopenia has been published.[102] Both agents currently are being evaluated for this indication under compassionate use protocols.

Thrombolytic agents have been used to simultaneously lyse heparin-induced venous and arterial thromboemboli while creating an anticoagulated state through fibrinogen degradation and production of fibrin/fibrinogen split products.[103-105] Thrombolytic therapy, however, is potentially dangerous in a severely thrombocytopenic patient and should be used only after careful consideration of both benefits and risks. Plasmapheresis[106,107] and plasma exchange[108] have each been used to remove heparin-associated IgG and hasten recovery.

Since transfused platelets meet the same fate as those of the patient, platelet transfusions are reserved for use in patients with active bleeding or at high risk for serious bleeding. Immune globulin 0.4 gm/kg IV daily for three days has been used in heparin-induced thrombocytopenia unresponsive to platelet transfusions.[109] Immune globulin resulted in improved response to platelet transfusions.

Drug-Induced Neutropenia
Definitions

Several terms are used to refer to abnormally low numbers of white blood cells. The broadest description, leukopenia simply describes a total WBC count of less than 3000/mm^3. Granulocytopenia describes a granulocyte count of less than 1500 granulocytes/mm^3 (including eosinophils and basophils), while neutropenia refers to a neutrophil count (segmented polymorphonucleocytes and band forms) of less than 1500/mm^3. Agranulocytosis is defined as a severe form of neutropenia with total granulocyte counts below 500/mm^3.[1] Unfortunately, there is variability in the definitions used by authors when reporting drug-induced white blood cell dyscrasias. The term agranulocytosis typically has been used to describe granulocyte counts ranging from less than 100 to less than 1000/mm³.

Epidemiology

The use of computerized information from Medicaid and managed care organization databases is a powerful tool for gaining epidemiologic health care information in the United States. Using this technique, Medicaid billing data from 1980 to 1984 in Minnesota, Michigan, and Florida was analyzed to identify patients with a hospital discharge diagnosis of agranulocytosis (the International Classification of Diseases or ICD9 code used also included neutropenia).[110] Medical charts of patients coded in this manner were then manually reviewed to exclude cases of recurrent or chronic neutropenia and those due to cytotoxic or immunosuppressive therapy. Defining neutropenia as any neutrophil count below normal and using standard criteria for agranulocytosis, the study found incidences of 35.7 and 7.2 per million, respectively. Not surprisingly, the incidence in Florida, a state with an older population and therefore greater drug use, was higher than in the other states. Men were found to be at slightly higher risk than women, and blacks were at higher risk than whites. Incidence was highest in the 50 to 59 year old age group. These incidence figures are considerably higher than the 2.4 to 2.5 per million reported through Sweden's national adverse drug reaction program,[2] a system likely to be less sensitive than the population-based method used in the United States.

Agranulocytosis is the most common fatal drug reaction, accounting for 26% of all drug-related deaths and 64% of deaths due to blood dyscrasias in one series.[4] The mortality rate was about 30% according to reports in the 1960s and 1970s.[2,111] A more recent report using a diagnosis by exclusion methodology (similar to, but less stringent than the above U.S. study) demonstrated 16% mortality from drug-induced agranulocytosis at six hospitals from 1970 to 1989.[112]

Mechanisms

There are two basic mechanisms by which drugs cause neutropenia. One is immunologically mediated, either through peripheral destruction of circulating neutrophils or immune suppression of marrow precursors. The second is through a direct, toxic effect on marrow precursors.

Immune versus Direct Mechanisms: Penicillins

29. Mechanisms. S.T. is a 54-year-old female admitted to the hospital with cellulitis. Nafcillin (Unipen) 2 gm Q 4 hr IV was begun. WBC count was 12,200/mm³ with 82% neutrophils, 3% band forms, 7% monocytes, and 8% lymphocytes. On the thirteenth day of therapy WBCs were found to be 2200/mm³ with 28% neutrophils and 5% bands. At this time, S.T. was experiencing no new symptoms and remained afebrile. Why might nafcillin be responsible for S.T.'s neutropenia?

Administration of penicillins, and to a lesser extent cephalosporins, in large doses for prolonged periods of time results in neutropenia in up to 15% of cases.[113] The problem occurs only rarely within the first week of therapy and is seen most often in patients receiving high doses of antibiotic for longer than two weeks.[114] Despite this apparent dose relationship, there is controversy regarding whether the neutropenia is immune-mediated or due to toxic suppression of granulocyte development in the marrow. Some investigators have found drug- or metabolite-dependent antigranulocyte antibodies in patients receiving penicillin[115,116] and cephalosporins.[117] Serum from a patient with ceftriaxone-associ-

ated agranulocytosis suppressed *in vitro* proliferation of CFU-GM, an early white blood cell precursor.[118] These findings are similar to findings in some cases of drug-induced agranulocytosis where effects do not appear dose related.[116,119] Others[113] have demonstrated dose-dependent inhibition of granulocyte colony growth *in vitro*, and therefore believe that beta-lactam-induced neutropenia is due to a direct toxic effect upon granulopoiesis. They suggest that antibodies frequently are present despite absence of identifiable granulocyte abnormalities. The common finding of apparent maturation arrest of granulocyte precursors on marrow examination is compatible with either toxic suppression or an immune effect on precursors. The presence of fever in 68%, rash in 41%, and eosinophilia in 32% of patients with penicillin-induced neutropenia[113] implies an immune process in many cases despite an apparent dose-relationship. Overall, it can be concluded that the mechanisms by which antibiotics cause neutropenia are heterogeneous, and that more information is necessary before a satisfactory understanding can be gained.[120] Few of the reports implicating over 100 drugs as having caused neutropenia provide enough evidence to draw conclusions as to mechanism.

30. Management. How should S.T. have been monitored while receiving high doses of a drug known to be associated with neutropenia?

First, the need for high doses of drug and long duration of therapy should be well established. In the case of antibiotics, many infections do not require maximum antibiotic dosage to achieve bacteriologic and clinical cure, and the incidence of neutropenia with short courses and more moderate amounts of drug is extremely low. One recommendation is to base drug dosage upon body size, as is done in pediatric patients, rather than following the common practice of using standardized dosing for all adults.[121] Of course, doses should always be altered appropriately for impaired renal or hepatic function. The WBC count should be monitored carefully, particularly after the second week of therapy, and the patient should be observed for unexplained fevers and rashes.

31. How should S.T. be managed at this point?

The suspected offending drug, nafcillin in this case, should be discontinued and replaced by a structurally dissimilar agent if continued therapy is indicated. The WBC count would be expected to return to normal within several days. Although the neutropenia may resolve after merely decreasing the drug dose, this approach should be considered only if an alternative is unavailable. The patient should be monitored for fever or other signs of new or recurrent infection until the neutropenia has resolved. The precise course of action will be determined by the clinical situation. In S.T.'s case, the nafcillin was discontinued with subsequent hematologic recovery and without recurrence of the original infection.

Idiosyncratic Toxic Effect: Phenothiazines

32. Mechanisms. J.K., a 34-year-old female with schizophrenia, was found on routine blood testing to be moderately neutropenic. She was started on chlorpromazine (Thorazine) 8 weeks ago when she began hearing voices warning her that she was being followed by the CIA and that her brain had been bugged. Her chlorpromazine dose was quickly titrated up to 400 mg/day which she has been taking for 6 weeks with a good clinical response. J.K. has no medical problems and takes no other medications. How likely is it that J.K.'s chlorpromazine is the cause of her neutropenia?

Phenothiazine derivatives are one of the most common causes of drug-induced neutropenia,[122] chlorpromazine being the model drug. The mechanism is one of toxic suppression of granulocyte production in the marrow of sensitive patients. Experiments utilizing cultured bone marrow from normal individuals as well as that of patients who had become neutropenic during chlorpromazine therapy have demonstrated an apparent drug effect on DNA synthesis resulting in defective granulocyte proliferation.[123] This appears to occur in at least one-half of individuals taking chlorpromazine, but the marrow of patients who do not become neutropenic is apparently able to compensate for this interference through proliferation of drug-resistant clones of committed stem cells. Patients who go on to develop neutropenia apparently do not have adequate compensatory mechanisms.

33. Features. Why is J.K.'s presentation typical of phenothiazine-induced neutropenia?

As in J.K.'s case, the most common presentation of phenothiazine-induced neutropenia would be that of decreased numbers of neutrophils. Patients usually remain asymptomatic unless they become infected. Phenothiazine-induced neutropenia rarely occurs in less than two weeks or later than ten weeks into therapy although latent periods of three months or more have been reported. J.K.'s six weeks of chlorpromazine therapy certainly falls within this usual time frame and her total dose of 10.8 gm also is representative of the doses usually associated with chlorpromazine-induced neutropenia. A total cumulative dose of 10 to 20 gm of chlorpromazine usually is required; neutropenia occurs only rarely in patients taking less than this amount of the drug. Patients who have developed neutropenia while taking high doses of chlorpromazine have subsequently been treated with reduced dosages uneventfully.[122] Rechallenge with high doses again results in a delayed-onset fall in the neutrophil count. In addition, approximately 10% of patients taking chlorpromazine will experience a transient leukopenia which resolves despite continuation of the drug.[124] Severe neutropenia is much less common; elderly females appear to be at increased risk. Most other phenothiazine derivatives, with the exception of promethazine (Phenergan), also have been reported to cause neutropenia, though none have been studied as extensively as chlorpromazine.

34. Management. How should J.K. be managed at this point?

Since J.K. is asymptomatic, no specific therapy is indicated at this time. Although it is possible that the neutropenia might resolve with a simple dose reduction of chlorpromazine, the most prudent course would be to withhold the drug completely until the WBC count returns to normal. Then, the patient could be restarted at a lower dose with close hematologic monitoring, or a neuroleptic agent with less propensity for marrow suppression could be substituted. Since the risk of agranulocytosis appears related to the absolute amount of phenothiazine given, a more potent agent or a nonphenothiazine neuroleptic should be chosen.

35. How quickly should J.K.'s WBC count return to normal once chlorpromazine has been stopped?

A peripheral hematologic response following the discontinuation of chlorpromazine will be delayed by four to six days but will then progress rapidly. In some cases, the increase in granulocytes may be preceded or accompanied by a monocyte increase, and myelocytes, metamyelocytes, and band forms may appear in relatively large numbers during the early recovery phase. The neutrophil and total WBC count then rapidly return toward normal, sometimes with a WBC count "overshoot" into the 15,000 to 20,000/mm^3 range. Recovery usually is complete within about two weeks.

36. Colony Stimulating Factors (CSFs). How can the rate of WBC recovery be hastened?

During the past decade, there has been an explosion of knowledge regarding mechanisms of hematopoiesis and the role of endogenous cytokines in this process. Many of the growth factors known to stimulate blood cell proliferation and maturation have been synthesized, and three of them, erythropoietin (Epoietin), granulocyte colony stimulating factor (GCSF, filgrastim, Neupo-

gen), and granulocyte-macrophage colony stimulating factor (GM-CSF, sargramostim, Leukine, Prokine) are available for clinical use. A fourth, interleukin-3 or multi-colony stimulating factor, is not yet on the market but is being extensively tested in a number of settings characterized by reduced marrow function. Our ability to modulate and stimulate hematopoiesis has increased greatly through the use of these agents.[125] However, the role of these agents in the treatment of drug-induced blood dyscrasias in general, and drug-induced agranulocytosis/neutropenia in particular, has not been well studied.

There are numerous anecdotal reports in which patients with agranulocytosis or neutropenia caused by various drugs have been treated with GCSF or GM-CSF. These cases are characterized by low to very low granulocyte counts despite discontinuation of the offending agent, often with fever, infection, or frank sepsis, at the time CSF therapy was begun. Granulocyte counts generally rise back into the normal range, sometimes with an overshoot, and remain normal when the CSF is discontinued. Patients usually recover completely. Cases in which patients do not respond to therapy either do not occur or are not reported.

It is difficult to determine the impact of intervention with CSFs on the clinical course or outcomes from case reports. Although one might expect that granulocyte recovery should be hastened by precursor stimulation, it cannot be assumed. Variability in time to recovery is great enough that increases occurring after CSFs are initiated could be due to the drug or they could represent the coincidental increases that would have been seen without any additional intervention. Likewise, it is difficult to determine whether patient outcomes would have been different had CSFs not been used.

However, anecdotal evidence providing support for clinical benefit does exist. In a case of methimazole-induced agranulocytosis, GM-CSF infusion led to a rapid increase in peripheral granulocyte counts and improvement in fever and laryngitis when neutropenia failed to resolve six days after drug discontinuation.[126] Two attempts to withdraw GM-CSF resulted in recurrent neutropenia which promptly resolved in each case when therapy was restarted. After 20 days, GM-CSF was discontinued and the granulocyte count remained above 3000/mm^3. In another case of methimazole-induced agranulocytosis, GM-CSF was initiated after three days of low granulocyte counts.[127] The neutrophil count rose to 2000/mm^3 over the next 12 days, GM-CSF was discontinued, and over the next three days the neutrophil count fell to 528/mm^3. GM-CSF was not restarted and the WBC count rose to normal in another seven days. In both cases, the rise in WBCs when CSF therapy was started was followed by a drop in WBCs when therapy was stopped. There was also a WBC count rise and fall with retreatment and withdrawal and resolution of infection in the first case. These observations provide strong evidence for a beneficial hematologic and clinical benefit of the CSF. Unfortunately, there have been no controlled clinical trials comparing CSF therapy with conservative management of patients with drug-induced agranulocytosis. The importance of the mechanism by which the dyscrasia was induced on the response to CSF is unknown. At present, the use of colony stimulating factors to hasten recovery is promising and is probably warranted in select cases where slow WBC recovery and/or severe symptoms justify going beyond customary supportive care.

Since J.K. presently is asymptomatic, there is no indication, at present, for use of colony stimulating factors.

Clozapine

37. The possibility of using clozapine (Clozaril) to treat J.K. is discussed. Having suffered chlorpromazine-induced neutropenia, is J.K. at increased risk for neutropenia due to clozapine?

Clozapine is a dibenzepine neuroleptic with good antipsychotic efficacy and what initially appeared to be a favorable side effect profile. However, in 1975 16 cases of clozapine-induced neutropenia were reported in Finland.[128] Eight fatalities resulted when discovery of the neutropenia was delayed and clozapine was not promptly discontinued. In 1989 clozapine was approved for use in the United States for severely ill schizophrenic patients who failed to respond adequately to standard antipsychotic drug treatment. Initially the manufacturer made the drug available to patients only through a controversial, privately contracted distribution system which included mandatory weekly white blood cell counts and criteria for intensified monitoring and discontinuation of therapy. The patient and blood count information collected before this system was discontinued in June 1991 provides what may be the most complete postmarketing database (in terms of blood dyscrasias) for any drug available for general use.

The incidence of agranulocytosis in the 11,555 patients treated was 0.8% at 1 year and 0.91% at 18 months.[129] This is lower than the previously estimated overall incidence of 1% to 2%[130] and may have been due, in part, to a scheme which required intense monitoring and intervention as soon as leukopenia occurred. The period of greatest risk is the first six months of therapy; only one case occurred after the first year and a half. There have been a total of seven deaths associated with agranulocytosis, two during the study period and five after.[129] The risk of agranulocytosis increased with age and was higher in women.

In most but not all patients, agranulocytosis is preceded by a steady decline in WBCs over a period of at least four weeks.[129] However, in 24% of cases leukopenia is not present within eight days of development of agranulocytosis. Once clozapine is discontinued, recovery usually occurs within two weeks.

The mechanism appears to be immune suppression of myeloid marrow precursors. There is no relationship between the dose and falling white blood cell count. Serum taken from patients during clozapine-induced agranulocytosis suppresses granulopoiesis and neutrophil function in vitro.[131] The presence of clozapine or metabolites is not required, and neither clozapine nor its metabolites have an effect on this test system when normal serum is used. Marrow examination in patients with agranulocytosis reveals decreased myeloid precursors. Rechallenge results in a more rapid white blood cell decline than in the initial episode.[132]

J.K. is not at increased risk for clozapine-induced hematologic toxicity since there does not appear to be cross-reactivity between clozapine and other psychotropic agents, including chlorpromazine.[130] Clozapine, however, is not indicated for J.K. because she is not refractory to more typical neuroleptic therapy.

Immune Peripheral Destruction: Aminopyrine

38. Are there drugs which cause acute onset agranulocytosis and how might this reaction become manifested?

A number of drugs have been associated with rapid onset, nondose-related destruction of circulating granulocytes. Aminopyrine, an analgesic agent no longer available in most countries, has been extensively studied. Occurrence of neutropenia caused by aminopyrine appears to be completely unrelated to dose. Initial sensitization typically requires seven to ten days, but a reaction may occur with the first dose if the drug has been taken previously. The neutrophil count drops precipitously. Chills and high fever, malaise, weakness, headache, tachycardia, and even mild shock may occur as the contents of destroyed white blood cells are released into the circulation. Necrotic lesions in the mouth and throat, oral abscesses, and bacteremia develop, and a fatal outcome can be expected if the drug is not discontinued. The granulocyte count returns toward normal within six to eight days if the causative agent is discontinued promptly.

If a volunteer is given serum from a patient who previously has experienced aminopyrine neutropenia, no reaction will occur. If the volunteer subsequently is given a dose of aminopyrine, the WBC count falls. Conversely, a volunteer taking aminopyrine without incident will experience a drop in WBC count when infused with serum from a previous reactor.[133] This information, along with in vitro demonstration of antineutrophil antibodies in individuals experiencing aminopyrine-induced agranulocytosis, supports an immune etiology for the reaction, probably of the low affinity binding type.

Other drugs associated with immediate, nondose-related granulocyte lysis include dipyrone (an aminopyrine derivative still available in many countries, sometimes called Mexican Aspirin),[134] several of the sulfa drugs, and antithyroid drugs.

Drug-Induced Aplastic Anemia

Aplastic anemia is defined as bicytopenia or pancytopenia with bone marrow trephine biopsy showing histological evidence of decreased cellularity and absence of infiltration and significant fibrosis. Pancytopenia is defined by the presence of anemia (Hgb <10 gm/dL), neutropenia, and thrombocytopenia. Bicytopenia is the presence of any two of these three abnormalities.[1] Diagnostic criteria also exist for cases of bi- or pancytopenia with less definitive bone marrow findings. Drugs and chemicals are implicated in approximately 50% of cases. Aplastic anemia is the rarest, least understood, and, with a mortality rate near 50% despite treatment,[135] the most serious of the drug-induced blood dyscrasias. Prognosis is worst for severely affected patients (severe bone marrow changes and meeting any two of the following three criteria: neutrophils <500/mm^3, corrected reticulocytes <1%, platelets <20/mm^3).

The underlying lesion is at the level of the pluripotent stem cell (PSC), before differentiation to committed stem cells. This is in contrast to reactions involving suppressed production of individual cell lines, in which drug mediated effects are expressed at points distal to the PSC. The result is decreased or absent circulating RBCs, WBCs, and platelets with marrow hypoplasia and fatty replacement.

Our current understanding of the pathophysiology of aplastic anemia, including the mechanisms by which drugs can cause it, remains poor despite recent advances in our understanding of hematopoiesis. A body of evidence points toward an immune mechanism (possibly with genetic predisposition) even in drug-induced cases where the primary insult to the PSC appears to be toxic in nature.[136,137] This view is supported by the efficacy of immunosuppressive therapy regardless of underlying cause and the similarity in clinical response between drug-induced and nondrug-related cases. Aplastic anemia caused by direct damage to the PSC and true immune-mediated marrow failure may be linked by the complex interactions between hematopoiesis and the lymphocyte/monocyte-produced cytokines that help modulate it.

Mechanisms

39. Why is chloramphenicol (Chloromycetin), an antibiotic with a broad spectrum of activity and excellent oral absorption, used so seldom?

Hundreds of cases of chloramphenicol-induced aplastic anemia have been reported since its introduction, with an estimated incidence of 1 in 20,000 to 30,000 patients. It is the only drug that has been well studied in this regard. The aplastic anemia is unpredictable and is not related to either dose or duration of use. The chemical structure of chloramphenicol contains a nitrobenzene ring whereas the closely related antibiotic thiamphenicol, a drug not clearly associated with aplastic anemia, does not. Unlike thiamphenicol, chloramphenicol inhibits DNA synthesis, and although conflicting information exists, cells from patients who have recovered from chloramphenicol-induced aplastic anemia may be more sensitive to this inhibition than normal.[138–142] Reduction of the nitrobenzene moiety produces a nitroso compound which affects DNA synthesis at very low concentrations, and in a manner which is not reversible. These data suggest that rare individuals whose marrow provides a milieu for reduction to the nitroso form may be predisposed, perhaps genetically, to chloramphenicol-induced aplasia.[143] It appears that this toxicity is confined primarily to the oral route of administration, suggesting a possible role for idiosyncratic aberrations in metabolism by the gut or perhaps by gut flora.[144] However, the intravenous[145,146] and ocular[147] routes also have been implicated.

In addition to aplastic anemia, chloramphenicol also can cause an anemia that is dose related, predictable, and reversible. This anemia results from chloramphenicol-induced inhibition of iron utilization and clinically appears with reticulocytopenia, maturation arrest of committed precursors in all cell lines, increased serum concentration of iron, and increased total iron-binding capacity (TIBC). Anemia due to inhibited iron utilization with reticulocytopenia and elevated serum iron is not uncommon in patients receiving large doses of chloramphenicol. Discontinuation of the drug results in complete recovery.

Importance of a Careful History

40. P.D., a 62-year-old male, notes gradually increasing tiredness and lack of energy over the past month. He seeks medical help after unsuccessful self-medication with stress formula vitamins. His only other medical problem is osteoarthritis for which he has been taking phenylbutazone (Butazolidin) 100 mg TID for the past 6 months as well as aspirin on a PRN basis, generally 4–6 regular strength tablets daily. Physical examination is unremarkable except for pallor, several bruises on various parts of the body, and findings typical of osteoarthritis. However, a blood count reveals a Hgb of 6.2 gm/dL, a corrected reticulocyte count of 0.5%, a WBC count of 1800/mm³ with 50% neutrophils, and a platelet count of 35,000/mm³. Diagnostic considerations include drug-induced aplastic anemia. What additional information is needed before one can conclude that P.D.'s anemia probably is drug-induced? [SI units: Hgb 62 gm/L; reticulocytes 0.005 1; WBCs 1.8 × 10⁹/L; platelets 0.35 × 10¹¹/L]

Drug-induced aplastic anemia certainly is a possibility, but at this point the data base is incomplete. Assuming this is indeed aplastic anemia, a more complete history would be necessary before one could implicate drugs as a causative factor. Many drugs and chemicals can cause marrow aplasia which first becomes apparent long after the last exposure. The family history should be examined for family members who have experienced ''blood problems'' or sensitivity to drugs or substances. Social history also is important. Information such as types of present and past employment or military service can provide important clues regarding exposure to chemicals of which the patient may not be aware. An employee in a paint factory, for instance, may be exposed to any of several industrial chemicals known to cause aplastic anemia. A farmer could come in contact with various marrow-toxic insecticides. Finally, an exhaustive drug history is mandatory. Use of all drugs past and present, prescription and nonprescription, legal or illegal, regardless of route of administration, should be elicited and documented. This is, of course, true whenever one suspects drug-induced disease, but in the case of drug-induced aplastic anemia the relationship between exposure to the causative agent and disease onset frequently is so inapparent that only careful detective work will reveal a possible association.

Features

41. A more complete history fails to reveal any additional pertinent information. Which of P.D.'s drugs is most likely to have caused this problem?

Phenylbutazone and its analog oxyphenbutazone are well-established causes of aplastic anemia. Estimates of incidence have ranged from 1 in 30,000 to 1 in 300,000. The International Agranulocytosis and Aplastic Anemia Study reported a rate of 6.6 per million or 1 in 150,000 exposures.[135] The risk for aplastic anemia is greater when phenylbutazone is taken regularly and for a sustained period by patients such as P.D. Aspirin has been implicated in case reports, but salicylates, despite widespread use, were not significantly associated with aplastic anemia in this particular international study. Phenylbutazone is the most likely culprit among P.D.'s drugs, although aspirin cannot be eliminated from the list of possible etiologies.

Despite the notoriety of the butazones as causing aplastic anemia, two other drugs in the analgesic group were more frequently associated with aplastic anemia. Indomethacin's (Indocin) risk was 10.1 per million and diclofenac's (Voltaren) was 6.8 per million. Other nonsteroidal anti-inflammatory agents were not associated with excess risk, but usage was low.

Drugs frequently associated with an increased risk of aplastic anemia are listed in Table 89.4. As one might expect in a disease where over 50% of cases are described as idiopathic, and for which no tests are available to determine etiology, a large number of other drugs have been pronounced guilty by association. Those less frequently associated with aplastic anemia are not listed in Table 89.4.

42. What symptoms and signs in P.D. are typical of an initial presentation of aplastic anemia?

The symptoms of aplastic anemia at initial presentation usually are nonspecific and are directly related to deficiencies within the suppressed cell lines. Thus, P.D.'s pallor, tiredness, and lack of energy are due to anemia and his easy bruisability is due to thrombocytopenia. His bruisability has been exacerbated by use of aspirin. Many patients present with more severe symptoms. With severe anemia, high-output congestive heart failure, angina pectoris, or intermittent claudication may occur. Thrombocytopenia can result in petechiae, purpura, nose bleeds, oozing blood from the gums, or frank hemorrhage. Oral lesions, fever, and/or infection secondary to leukopenia also may cause the patient to seek medical attention.

Table 89.4	Drugs Frequently Associated with Aplastic Anemia[2,135,153,165–168]
Drug	Incidence
Chloramphenicol	1/20,000–1/30,000
Diclofenac	1/160,000
Felbamate	1/5,000[a]
Furosemide	
Gold salts	
Hydantoins	
Indomethacin	1/100,000
Phenylbutazone/oxyphenbutazone	1/30,000–1/300,000
Potassium perchlorate	
Quinacrine	
Sulfas and derivatives	
Tolbutamide	

[a] Introduced in September, 1993. Estimate of incidence is based on a relatively small experience, 20 cases in about 100,000 patients.[170]

While white blood cell counts typically are low at initial presentation in aplastic anemia, the degree of abnormality varies. Anemia is normochromic and either normocytic or macrocytic. The hemoglobin level ranges from 12 to as low as 3 gm/dL. Because erythroid iron-consuming activity is low, serum iron and transferrin saturation usually are high, as are erythropoietin levels. Reticulocytes are low. The WBC count may be low normal or very low, but absolute neutropenia almost always is present. P.D.'s WBC count of 1800/mm^3 with 50% neutrophils (absolute neutrophil count = $1800 \times 50\% = 900$/mm^3) is compatible with this picture. Total lymphocyte count is affected least and may remain within normal limits until leukopenia becomes severe. Likewise, the platelet count may be near normal or, more commonly, severely depressed. The erythrocyte sedimentation rate (ESR) usually is elevated and, as previously noted, bone marrow is hypocellular with fatty replacement.

Management

43. Further evaluation, including bone marrow biopsy, confirms the diagnosis of aplastic anemia. No causes other than drugs are identified. How should P.D. be managed?

First and foremost, as is true in the management of most drug-induced problems, all suspected causative agents should be discontinued. In this case, both phenylbutazone and aspirin should be stopped. In addition, supportive measures should be initiated if needed.

The approach to treatment is based first upon severity of the disease. Patients with mild aplastic anemia have a relatively benign short-term prognosis and can be managed conservatively. There are two basic approaches to treating severe aplastic anemia; bone marrow transplant and immunosuppression.

Bone Marrow Transplantation[148,149]

The treatment of choice for patients younger than 40 to 45 years of age is bone marrow transplant from an HLA-identical sibling donor if available. Overall long term survival is achieved in 65% to 80% of cases treated in this way. Six year survival of 82% was reported in one study which separately analyzed results in drug-induced cases.[150] A higher incidence of graft versus host disease makes success less likely with this mode of treatment in older patients. Transplants from mismatched relatives and even unrelated donors have been successful,[151] but experience with such procedures remains limited.

Immunosuppression[148,149]

Immunosuppression is the alternative treatment for older patients and for young patients without suitable bone marrow donors. Antilymphocyte globulin (ALG) and antithymocyte globulin (ATG), cyclosporine A, and corticosteroids have all been used as single agents and in various combinations.[152,153] The mechanism by which benefit accrues is poorly understood, but it has been proposed that ATG and perhaps other types of immunosuppressive therapy may decrease the release of hematopoiesis-suppressing cytokines.[154,155] Although the optimum ATG regimen has not been determined, the manufacturer of the only ATG commercially available in the United States (Atgam) recommends a dose of 20 mg/kg/day for 8 to 14 days, followed by alternate-day therapy with the same dosage for up to another 14 days.[156] Symptoms of serum sickness are common and pre-existing thrombocytopenia may be exacerbated, requiring platelet transfusions to continue therapy. An intradermal skin test of 0.1 mL of a 1:1000 dilution of ATG along with a saline control is recommended before starting full dose therapy.

There are anecdotal reports of response to acyclovir (Zovirax),[157,158] but antiviral therapy is likely to benefit only virus-associated aplastic anemias.

Androgens

An alternative approach to treating aplastic anemia is to stimulate hematopoiesis. Considerable controversy exists regarding the use of androgenic steroids either alone or as an adjunct to ATG. While most trials have failed to demonstrate clear benefit, numerous questions regarding patient selection, timing and duration of therapy, choice of agent, and dosing, any of which may affect results, have been raised.[152,159–161]

Colony Stimulating Factors (CSFs)[125,162]

Infusions of human granulocyte-macrophage colony-stimulating factor in aplastic anemia have increased neutrophil counts significantly, but effects in most cases are transient, lasting only during the infusion period. In one report, GM-CSF increased neutrophil counts only if residual granulopoietic activity was present before treatment.[163] Platelets and red blood cells are not affected. It is not yet known whether factors acting at the level of the pluripotent stem cell, such as interleukin-3, will prove to be useful.

Since P.D.'s disease is not severe, discontinuing the drugs and transfusing red blood cells are the only treatments indicated at this time. It is not possible to predict whether his blood counts will improve once the causative agents are discontinued.

References

1 **Benichou C, Celigny PS.** Standardization of definitions and criteria for causality assessment of adverse drug reactions. Drug-induced blood cytopenias: report of an international consensus meeting. Nouv Rev Fr Hematol. 1991;33:257.

2 **Bottiger LE et al.** Drug-induced blood dyscrasias. A ten-year material from the Swedish Adverse Drug Reaction Committee. Acta Med Scand. 1979; 205:457.

3 **Danielson DA et al.** Drug-induced blood disorders. JAMA. 1984;252:3257.

4 **Bottiger LE et al.** Fatal reactions to drugs. A ten-year material from the Swedish Adverse Drug Reaction Committee. Acta Med Scand. 1979;205: 451.

5 **Roeser HP.** Drug-bone marrow interactions. Old and new issues in 1987. Med J Aust. 1987;146:145.

6 **CSM Update.** Blood dyscrasias. Br Med J. 1985;291:1269.

7 **Ballas SK.** The pathophysiology of hemolytic anemias. Trans Med Rev. 1990;4:236.

8 **Carson PE, Frischer H.** Glucose-6-phosphate dehydrogenase deficiency and related disorders of the pentose phosphate pathway. Am J Med. 1966; 41:744.

9 **Beutler E.** Erythrocyte disorders: anemias due to increased destruction of erythrocytes with enzyme deficiencies. In: Williams WJ et al, eds. Hematology, 4th ed. New York: McGraw-Hill; 1990:591.

10 **Valentine WN et al.** Hemolytic anemias and erythrocyte enzymopathies. Ann Intern Med. 1985;103:245.

11 **Eldad A et al.** Silver sulphadiazine-induced haemolytic anaemia in a glucose-6-phosphate dehydrogenase-deficient burn patient. Burns. 1991;17:430.

12 **Markowitz N, Saravolatz LD.** Use of trimethoprim-sulfamethoxazole in a glucose-6-phosphate dehydrogenase-deficient population. Rev Infect Dis. 1987;9(Suppl. 2):S218.

13 **Spielberg SP et al.** Improved erythrocyte survival with high dose vitamin E in chronic hemolyzing G6PD and glutathione synthetase deficiencies. Ann Intern Med. 1978;90:53.

14 **Corash L et al.** Reduced chronic hemolysis during high-dose vitamin E administration in Mediterranean-type glucose-6-phosphate dehydrogenase deficiency. N Engl J Med. 1980;303:416.

15 **Levine BB, Ovary Z.** Studies on the mechanism of the formation of the penicillin antigen. III. The N-(D-alpha-benzylpenicilloyl) group as an antigenic determinant responsible for hypersensitivity to penicillin. J Exp Med. 1961;114:875.

16 **Salama A et al.** Autoantibodies and drug- or metabolite-dependent antibodies in patients with diclofenac-induced immune hemolysis. Br J Haematol. 1991;77:546.

17 **Petz LD, Garratty GM.** Acquired Immune Hemolytic Anemias. New York, NY: Churchill Livingston; 1980:91.

18 **Levine BB, Redmond A.** Immuno-

chemical mechanisms of penicillin induced Coombs positivity and hemolytic anemia in man. Int Arch Allergy Appl Immunol. 1967;31:594.

19 **Petz LD, Garratty GM.** Acquired Immune Hemolytic Anemias. New York, NY: Churchill Livingston; 1980:279.

20 **Nesmith LW, Davis JW.** Hemolytic anemia caused by penicillin. JAMA. 1968;203:27.

21 **White JM et al.** Penicillin-induced haemolytic anaemia. Br Med J. 1968; 3:26.

22 **Habibi B.** Drug induced red blood cell autoantibodies co-developed with drug specific antibodies causing a hemolytic anemia. Br J Haematol. 1985;61:139.

23 **Salama A, Mueller-Eckhardt C.** On the mechanisms of sensitization and attachment of antibodies to RBC in drug-induced immune hemolytic anemia. Blood. 1987;69:1006.

24 **Packman CH, Leddy JP.** Drug-related immunologic injury of erythrocytes. In: Williams WJ et al, eds. Hematology, 4th ed. New York: McGraw-Hill; 1990:681.

25 **Mueller-Eckhardt C, Salama A.** Drug-induced immune cytopenias: a unifying pathogenetic concept with special emphasis on the role of drug metabolites. Trans Med Rev. 1990;4:69.

26 **Salama A, Mueller-Eckhardt C.** Immune-mediated blood cell dyscrasias related to drugs. Semin Hematol. 1992; 29:54.

27 **Kirtland HH et al.** Inhibition of suppressor T cell function by methyldopa. A proposed cause of autoimmune hemolytic anemia. Blood. 1978;52:151.

28 **Kirtland HH et al.** Methyldopa inhibition of suppressor-lymphocyte function. A proposed cause of autoimmune hemolytic anemia. N Engl J Med. 1980;302:825.

29 **Worsledge SM.** Immune drug-induced haemolytic anaemias. Semin Hematol. 1969;6:181.

30 **Kleinman S et al.** Positive direct antiglobulin tests and immune hemolytic anemia in patients receiving procainamide. N Engl J Med. 1984;311:809.

31 **Carstairs KC et al.** Incidence of a positive direct Coombs' test in patients on alpha-methyldopa. Lancet. 1966;2:133.

32 **Lo Buglio JF, Jandl JH.** The nature of alpha-methyldopa red cell antibody. N Engl J Med. 1967;276:658.

33 **Brandt NJ, Lund J.** Methyldopa and haemolytic anaemia. Lancet. 1966;1: 771.

34 **Buchanan JG et al.** Methyldopa and acquired haemolytic anaemia. Med J Aust. 1966;2:700.

35 **Hamilton M.** Some aspects of the long-term treatment of severe hypertension with methyldopa. Postgrad Med J. 1968;44:66.

36 **Murad F.** Immunohemolytic anemia during therapy with methyldopa. JAMA. 1968;203:149.

37 **Surveyor I et al.** Autoimmune haemolytic anaemia complicating methyldopa therapy. Postgrad Med J. 1968; 44:438.

38 **Petz LD, Garratty GM.** Acquired Immune Hemolytic Anemias. New York, NY: Churchill Livingston; 1980:295.

39 **Packman CH, Leddy JP.** Drug-related immunologic injury of erythrocytes. In: Williams WJ et al, eds. Hematology, 4th ed. New York: McGraw-Hill; 1990:681.

40 **Murphy WG, Kelton JG.** Idiosyncratic drug-induced thrombocytopenia. Curr Stud Hematol Blood Transf. 1988;54:71.

41 **Eisner EV, Crowell EB.** Hydrochlorothiazide-dependent thrombocytopenia due to an IgM antibody. JAMA. 1971; 215:480.

42 **Nordquist P et al.** Thrombocytopenia during chlorothiazide treatment. Lancet. 1959;1:271.

43 **Wilmhurst PT et al.** The effects of amrinone on platelet count, survival and function in patients with congestive cardiac failure. Br J Clin Pharmacol. 1984;17:317.

44 **Eason CT et al.** The relationship between the pharmacokinetics of amrinone in the marmoset and platelet effects. Eur J Drug Metab Pharmacokinet. 1988;13:129–33.

45 **Mattingly PM et al.** Pancytopenia secondary to short-term, high dose intravenous infusion of amrinone. DICP. 1990;24:1172.

46 **Ross MP et al.** Amrinone-associated thrombocytopenia: pharmacokinetic analysis. Clin Pharmacol Ther. 1993;53: 661.

47 **Eichner ER, Hillman RS.** The evolution of anemia in alcoholic patients. Am J Med. 1971;50:218.

48 **Cowan DH, Hines JD.** Thrombocytopenia of severe alcoholism. Ann Intern Med. 1971;74:37.

49 **Eichner ER et al.** Variations in the hematologic and medical status of alcoholics. Am J Med Sci. 1972;263:35.

50 **Haut MJ, Cowan DH.** The effect of ethanol on hemostatic properties of human blood platelets. Am J Med. 1974; 56:22.

51 **Cowan DH.** Effect of alcoholism on hemostasis. Semin Hematol. 1980;17: 137.

52 **Eisner EV, Korbitz BC.** Quinine-induced thrombocytopenic purpura due to an IgM and an IgG antibody. Transfusion. 1972;12:317.

53 **Belkin GA.** Cocktail purpura: an unusual cause of quinine sensitivity. Ann Intern Med. 1967;66:583.

54 **Reid DM, Shulman NR.** Drug purpura due to surreptitious quinidine intake. Ann Intern Med. 1988;108:206.

55 **Kelton JG et al.** Drug-induced thrombocytopenia is associated with increased binding of IgG to platelets both in vivo and in vitro. Blood. 1981;58: 524.

56 **Christie DJ, Aster RH.** Drug-antibody-platelet interaction in quinine- and quinidine-induced thrombocytopenia. J Clin Invest. 1982;70:989.

57 **Lerner W et al.** Drug-dependent and non-drug-dependent antiplatelet antibody in drug-induced immunologic thrombocytopenic purpura. Blood. 1985;66:306.

58 **Smith ME et al.** Binding of quinine- and quinidine-dependent drug antibodies to platelets is mediated by the Fab domain of the immunoglobulin GM and is not Fc dependent. J Clin Invest. 1987;79:912.

59 **Pfueller SL et al.** Heterogeneity of drug-dependent platelet antigens and their antibodies in quinine- and quinidine-induced thrombocytopenia: involvement of glycoproteins Ib, IIb, IIIa, and IX. Blood. 1988;72:1155.

60 **Visentin GP et al.** Characteristics of quinine- and quinidine-induced antibodies specific for platelet glycoproteins IIb and IIIa. Blood. 1991;77: 2668.

61 **De Gruchy GC.** Drug-induced Blood Disorders. Oxford: Blackwell Scientific; 1975.

62 **Moss RA.** Drug-induced immune thrombocytopenia. Am J Hematol. 1980;9:439.

63 **Aster RH, George JN.** Thrombocytopenia due to enhanced platelet destruction by immunologic mechanisms. In: Williams WJ et al, eds. Hematology, 4th ed. New York: McGraw-Hill; 1990:1370.

64 **Shulman NR.** Immunologic reactions to drugs. N Engl J Med. 1972;287:408.

65 **Christie DJ et al.** Structural features of the quinidine and quinine molecules necessary for binding of drug-induced antibodies to human platelets. J Lab Clin Med. 1984;104:730.

66 **Mettier SR et al.** Thrombocytopenic purpura complicating gold therapy for rheumatoid arthritis. Blood. 1948;3: 1105.

67 **Coblyn JS et al.** Gold-induced thrombocytopenia. A clinical and immunogenetic study of twenty-three patients. Ann Intern Med. 1981;95:178.

68 **Adachi JD et al.** Gold induced thrombocytopenia: 12 cases and a review of the literature. Semin Arthritis Rheum. 1987;16:287.

69 **Deren B et al.** Gold-associated thrombocytopenia: report of six cases. Arch Intern Med. 1974;134:1012.

70 **Levin HA et al.** Thrombocytopenia associated with gold therapy. Observations on the mechanism of platelet destruction. Am J Med. 1975;59:274.

71 **Kosty MP et al.** Thrombocytopenia associated with auranofin therapy: evidence for a gold-dependent immunologic mechanism. Am J Hematol. 1989; 30:236.

72 **Goldstein R et al.** Treatment of gold-induced thrombocytopenia by high-dose intravenous gamma globulin. Arthritis Rheum. 1986;29:426.

73 **Ansell J et al.** Heparin induced thrombocytopenia: a prospective study. Thromb Haemost. 1980;43:61.

74 **Bell WR.** Heparin-associated thrombocytopenia and thrombosis. J Lab Clin Med. 1988;11:600.

75 **Warkentin TE, Kelton JG.** Heparin-induced thrombocytopenia. Prog Hemost Thromb. 1991;10:1.

76 **Anderson GM.** Insights into heparin-induced thrombocytopenia. Br J Haematol. 1992;80:504.

77 **Greinacher A et al.** Heparin-associated thrombocytopenia: the antibody is not specific. Thromb Haemost. 1992; 67:545.

78 **Kelton JG et al.** Clinical usefulness of testing for a heparin-dependent platelet aggregating factor in patients with suspected heparin-associated thrombocytopenia. J Lab Clin Med. 1984;103: 606.

79 **Chong BH et al.** The clinical usefulness of the platelet aggregation test for the diagnosis of heparin-induced thrombocytopenia. Thromb Haemost. 1993; 69:344.

80 **Bell WR et al.** Thrombocytopenia occurring during the administration of heparin. Ann Intern Med. 1976;85:155.

81 **Nelson JC et al.** Heparin-induced thrombocytopenia. Arch Intern Med. 1978;138:548.

82 **Bell WR, Royall RM.** Heparin-associated thrombocytopenia: a comparison of three heparin preparations. N Engl J Med. 1980;303:902.

83 **Warkentin TE, Kelton JG.** Heparin-induced thrombocytopenia. Ann Rev Med. 1989;40:31.

84 **Schmitt BP, Adelman B.** Heparin-associated thrombocytopenia: a critical review and pooled analysis. Am J Med Sci. 1993;305:208.

85 **Heeger PS, Backstrom JT.** Heparin flushes and thrombocytopenia. Ann Intern Med. 1986;105:143.

86 **Laster JL et al.** Thrombocytopenia associated with heparin-coated catheters in patients with heparin-associated antiplatelet antibodies. Arch Intern Med. 1989;149:2285.

87 **Laster J et al.** Reexposure to heparin of patients with heparin-associated antibodies. J Vasc Surg. 1989;9:677.

88 **Phelan BK.** Heparin-associated thrombosis without thrombocytopenia. Ann Intern Med. 1983;99:637.

89 **Ramirez-Lassepas M et al.** Heparin-induced thrombocytopenia in patients with cerebrovascular ischemic disease. Neurology. 1984;34:736.

90 **Cines DB et al.** Immune endothelial-cell injury in heparin-associated thrombocytopenia. New Engl J Med. 1987; 316:581.

91 **Silver D et al.** Heparin-induced thrombocytopenia, thrombosis, and hemorrhage. Ann Surg. 1983;198:301.

92 **Laster J et al.** The heparin-induced thrombocytopenia syndrome: an update. Surgery. 1987;102:763.

93 **Hull RD et al.** Heparin for 5 days as compared with 10 days in the initial treatment of proximal venous thrombosis. New Engl J Med. 1990;322: 1260.

94 **Kappa JR et al.** Heparin-induced platelet activation in sixteen surgical patients: diagnosis and management. J Vasc Surg. 1987;5:101.

95 **Kraenzler EJ, Starr NJ.** Heparin-associated thrombocytopenia: management of patients for open heart surgery. Case reports describing the use of iloprost. Anesthesiology. 1988;69:964.

96 **Sobel M et al.** Surgical management of heparin-associated thrombocytopenia. Strategies in the treatment of venous and arterial thromboembolism. J Vasc Surg. 1988;8:395.

97 **Kappa JR et al.** Intraoperative management of patients with heparin-induced thrombocytopenia. Ann Thorac Surg. 1990;49:714.

98 **Rhone Poulenc.** Lovenox package insert. New Jersey: 1993.

99 **Gouault-Heilmann M et al.** Low molecular weight heparin fractions as an alternative therapy in heparin-induced thrombocytopenia. Haemostasis. 1987; 17:134.

100 **Chong BH et al.** Heparin-induced thrombocytopenia: studies with a new low molecular weight heparinoid, Org 10172. Blood. 1989;73:1592.

101 **Demers C et al.** Rapid anticoagulation

using ancrod for heparin-induced thrombocytopenia. Blood. 1991;78:2194.

102 **Nand S.** Hirudin therapy for heparin-associated thrombocytopenia and deep venous thrombosis. Am J Hematol. 1993;43:310.

103 **Krueger SK et al.** Thrombolysis in heparin induced thrombocytopenia with thrombosis. Ann Intern Med. 1985; 103:159.

104 **Clifton GD, Smith MD.** Thrombolytic therapy in heparin-associated thrombocytopenia with thrombosis. Clin Pharm. 1986;5:597.

105 **Mehta DP et al.** Heparin-induced thrombocytopenia and thrombosis: reversal with streptokinase a case report and review of literature. Am J Hematol. 1991;36:275.

106 **Nand S, Robinson JA.** Plasmapheresis in the management of heparin-associated thrombocytopenia with thrombosis. Am J Hematol. 1988;28:204.

107 **Brady J et al.** Plasmapheresis. A therapeutic option in the management of heparin-associated thrombocytopenia with thrombosis. Am J Clin Pathol. 1991;96:394.

108 **Bouvier JL et al.** Treatment of serious heparin-induced thrombocytopenia by plasma exchange: report of 4 cases. Thromb Res. 1988;51:335.

109 **Frame JN et al.** Correction of severe heparin-associated thrombocytopenia with intravenous immunoglobulin. Ann Intern Med. 1989;111:946.

110 **Strom BL et al.** Descriptive epidemiology of agranulocytosis. Arch Int Med. 1992;152:1475.

111 **Reizenstein P, Edgardh K.** Mortality in agranulocytosis. Lancet. 1974;2: 293.

112 **Julia A et al.** Drug-induced agranulocytosis: prognostic factors in a series of 168 episodes. Br J Haematol. 1991; 79:366.

113 **Neftel KA et al.** Inhibition of granulopoiesis in vivo and in vitro by B-lactam antibiotics. J Infect Dis. 1985;152: 90.

114 **Houmayouni H et al.** Leukopenia due to penicillin and cephalosporin homologues. Arch Intern Med. 1979;139: 827.

115 **Murphy MF et al.** Demonstration of an immune-mediated mechanism of penicillin-induced neutropenia and thrombocytopenia. Br J Haematol. 1983; 55:155.

116 **Salama A et al.** Immune-mediated agranulocytosis related to drugs and their metabolites: mode of sensitization and heterogeneity of antibodies. Br J Haematol. 1989;72:127.

117 **Murphy MF et al.** Cephalosporin-induced immune neutropenia. Br J Haematol. 1985;59:9.

118 **Rey D et al.** Ceftriaxone-induced granulopenia related to a peculiar mechanism of granulopoiesis inhibition. Am J Med. 1989;87:591.

119 **Levitt LJ.** Chlorpropamide-induced pure white cell aplasia. Blood. 1987; 69:394.

120 **Pisciotta AV.** Agranulocytosis during antibiotic therapy: drug sensitivity or sepsis? Am J Hematol. 1993;42:132.

121 **Antibiotic-induced neutropenia.** Lancet. 1985;2:814. Editorial.

122 **Pisciotta AV.** Immune and toxic mechanisms in drug-induced agranulocytosis. Semin Hematol. 1973;10:279.

123 **Pisciotta AV.** Drug-induced agranulocytosis. Drugs. 1978;15:132.

124 **Pisciotta AV.** Agranulocytosis induced by certain phenothiazine derivatives. JAMA. 1969;208:1862.

125 **Fleischman RA.** Clinical use of hematopoietic growth factors. Am J Med Sci. 1993;305:248.

126 **Heinrich B et al.** Methimazole-induced agranulocytosis and granulocyte-colony stimulating factor. Ann Intern Med. 1989;111:621.

127 **Yokoyama K et al.** Successful treatment of methimazole-induced agranulocytosis by granulocyte colony-stimulating factor. Am J Hematol. 1992;40: 76.

128 **Amsler HA et al.** Agranulocytosis in patients treated with clozapine. A study of the Finnish epidemic. Acta Psychiatr Scand. 1977;56:241.

129 **Alvir JMJ et al.** Clozapine-induced agranulocytosis. Incidence and risk factors in the United States. N Engl J Med. 1993;329:162.

130 **Lieberman JA et al.** Clozapine-induced agranulocytosis: non-cross-reactivity with other psychotropic drugs. J Clin Psychiatry. 1988;49:271.

131 **Pisciotta AV et al.** Cytotoxic activity in serum of patients with clozapine-induced agranulocytosis. J Lab Clin Med. 1992;119:254.

132 **Pisciotta AV et al.** On the possible mechanisms and predictability of clozapine-induced agranulocytosis. Drug Safety. 1992;7(Suppl. 1):33.

133 **Moeschlin S, Wagner K.** Agranulocytosis due to the occurrence of leukocyte agglutinins. Acta Haematol. 1952;8:29.

134 **Hargis JB et al.** Agranulocytosis associated with ''Mexican aspirin'' (dipyrone): evidence for an autoimmune mechanism affecting multipotential hematopoietic progenitors. Am J Hematol. 1989;31:213.

135 **International Agranulocytosis and Aplastic Anemia Study.** Risks of agranulocytosis and aplastic anemia. A first report of their relation to drug use with special reference to analgesics. JAMA. 1986;256:1749.

136 **Nissen C.** The pathophysiology of aplastic anemia. Semin Hematol. 1991; 28:313.

137 **Young NS.** The problem of clonality in aplastic anemia: Dr. Dameshek's riddle, restated. Blood. 1992;79:1385.

138 **Yunis AA et al.** Chloramphenicol toxicity: pathogenetic mechanisms and the role of the p-NO_2 in aplastic anemia. Clin Toxicol. 1980;17:359.

139 **Howell A et al.** Bone marrow cells resistant to chloramphenicol in chloramphenicol-induced aplastic anemia. Lancet. 1975;1:65.

140 **Kern P et al.** Bone-marrow cells resistant to chloramphenicol in chloramphenicol-induced aplastic anemia. Lancet. 1975;1:1190.

141 **Yunis AA et al.** DNA damage induced by chloramphenicol and its nitroso derivative: damage in intact cells. Am J Hematol. 1987;24:77.

142 **Jimenez JJ et al.** Chloramphenicol-induced bone marrow injury: possible role of bacterial metabolites of chloramphenicol. Blood. 1987;70:1180–185.

143 **Vincent PC.** In vitro evidence of drug action in aplastic anemia. Blut. 1984; 49:3.

144 **Yunis AA.** Chloramphenicol toxicity: 25 years of research. Am J Med. 1989; 87:44.

145 **Plaut ME, Best WR.** Aplastic anemia after parenteral chloramphenicol: a warning renewed. N Engl J Med. 1982; 306:1486.

146 **West BC et al.** Aplastic anemia associated with parenteral chloramphenicol: a review of 10 cases including the second case of possible increased risk with cimetidine. Rev Infect Dis. 1988; 10:1048.

147 **Fraunfelder FT, Bagby GC.** Ocular chloramphenicol and aplastic anemia. N Engl J Med. 1983;308:1536.

148 **Nissen C et al.** Management of aplastic anemia. Eur J Haematol. 1991;46:193.

149 **Gluckman E et al.** Recent treatments of aplastic anemia. Nouv Rev Fr Hematol. 1991;33:507.

150 **Bacigalupo A et al.** Bone marrow transplantation (BMT) versus immunosuppression for the treatment of severe aplastic anemia (SAA): a report of the EBMT SAA working party. Br J Haematol. 1988;70:177.

151 **Hows JM et al.** Histocompatible unrelated volunteer donors compared with HLA nonidentical family donors in marrow transplantation for aplastic anemia and leukemia. Blood. 1986;68: 1322.

152 **Katsanis E, Ramsay NKC.** Treatment of acquired severe aplastic anemia. Am J Ped Hematol Oncol. 1989;11:360.

153 **Adamson JW, Erslev AJ.** Aplastic anemia. In: Williams WJ et al, eds. Hematology, 4th ed. New York: McGraw-Hill; 1990:158.

154 **Gascon P et al.** Lymphokine abnormalities in aplastic anemia: implications for the mechanism of ATG. Blood. 1985;65:407.

155 **Gascon P, Scala GM.** Decreased interleukin-1 production in aplastic anemia. Am J Med. 1988;85:668.

156 **Upjohn Company.** Atgam package insert. Kalamazoo, MI: 1990 February.

157 **Bacigalupo A et al.** Acyclovir for the treatment of severe aplastic anemia. N Engl J Med. 1984;310:1606.

158 **Gomez-Almaguer D et al.** Acyclovir in the treatment of aplastic anemia. Am J Hematol. 1988;29:172.

159 **Gardner FH.** Anabolic steroids in aplastic anemia. Acta Endocrinol. 1985; 271(Suppl.):87.

160 **French Cooperative Group for the Study of Aplastic and Refractory Anemias.** Androgen therapy in aplastic anemia: a comparative study of high and low-doses and of 4 different androgens. Scand J Haematol. 1986;36:346.

161 **Seewald TR et al.** Successful treatment of severe refractory aplastic anemia with 3-B-etiocholanolone and nandrolone decanoate. Am J Hematol. 1989;31:216.

162 **Smith DH.** Use of hematopoietic growth factors for treatment of aplastic anemia. Am J Pediatr Hematol/Oncol. 1990;12:425.

163 **Antin JH et al.** Phase I/II study of recombinant human granulocyte-macrophage colony-stimulating factor in aplastic anemia of both acquired and myelodysplastic syndrome. Blood. 1988;72:705.

164 **Morse EE.** Toxic effects of drugs on erythrocytes. Ann Clin Lab Sci. 1988; 18:13.

165 **Gewirtz AM, Hoffman R.** Current considerations of the etiology of aplastic anemia. CRC Critical Rev Oncol Hematol. 1985;4:1.

166 **Vincent PC.** Drug-induced aplastic anemia and agranulocytosis. Incidence and mechanisms. Drugs. 1986;31:52.

167 **Lubran MM.** Hematologic side effects of drugs. Ann Clin Lab Sci. 1989;19: 114.

168 **Kelly JP et al.** Risks of agranulocytosis and aplastic anemia in relation to the use of cardiovascular drugs: the international agranulocytosis and aplastic anemia study. Clin Pharmacol Ther. 1991;49:330.

169 **Kikta MJ et al.** Can low molecular weight heparins and heparinoids be safely given to patients with heparin-induced thrombocytopenia syndrome? Surgery. 1993;114:705–10.

170 **Food and Drug Administration.** Recommendation for the immediate withdrawal of patients from treatment with Felbatol (felbamate). FDA Medical Bulletin. 1994;24(2):5.

Neoplastic Disorders and Their Treatment: General Principles

Rebecca S Finley
Cynthia L LaCivita
Celeste M Lindley

Introduction to Neoplastic Diseases 90-1
  Cancer Statistics (See Figure 90.1) 90-1
  Etiology (See Table 90.1) 90-1
  Prevention 90-2
    Chemoprevention (See Table 90.2) 90-2
    Diet 90-4
    Sun exposure (See Table 90.3) 90-4
  Tumors 90-5
    Growth (See Figure 90.2) 90-5
    Spread (See Table 90.4) 90-5
  Screening and Early Detection (See Table 90.5) 90-6
  Diagnosis and Staging (Also see Table 90.6) 90-6
  Clinical Presentation (See Tables 90.7 and 90.8) 90-7
  Complications of Malignancy 90-7
Treatment 90-8
  Surgery 90-8
  Irradiation (See Table 90.9) 90-8
  Chemotherapy 90-9
    Cytotoxic chemotherapy 90-9
    Mechanism of action
      (See Figure 90.3 and Table 90.10) 90-9
    Cell kill 90-9
    Factors which influence response to
      chemotherapy 90-9
    Dose intensity 90-10

    Schedule dependency 90-10
    Drug resistance (See Table 90.11) 90-10
    Tumor site 90-15
  Combination chemotherapy 90-15
    Choice of agents (See Table 90.12) 90-15
    Applications (See Table 90.13) 90-15
      Induction chemotherapy 90-15
      Adjuvant chemotherapy 90-15
      Primary/neoadjuvant chemotherapy 90-18
  Administration 90-18
    Systemic 90-18
    Regional (See Table 90.14) 90-19
  Assessing Response to Therapy
    (See Table 90.15) 90-19
    Tumor markers 90-19
  Hormonal Therapy 90-19
  Biologic Therapy 90-20
    Immunotherapy strategies (See Table 90.17) 90-20
    Interferon alfa 90-20
    Interleukin-2 (IL-2) 90-20
Handling of Cytotoxic Drugs 90-21
  Impact upon the Pharmacy 90-21
  Risks 90-21
  Policies and Procedures 90-22
  Necessary Equipment and Supplies 90-22

Introduction to Neoplastic Diseases

Cancer is not a single disease; rather, it is a group of diseases characterized by uncontrolled growth and spread of abnormal cells. Cancers may arise from any tissue in the body, and, if they are not controlled, most eventually will cause the death of the patient. The terms malignancy and neoplasm often are used synonymously with cancer. Other characteristics of cancers besides uncontrolled growth include the ability of these abnormal cells to invade adjacent normal tissues and break away from the primary tumor, travel through the blood or lymph, and establish a new tumor at a different site in the body. New tumors such as these are referred to as metastases. Cancer cells are also poorly differentiated and thus, unable to carry out the physiologic functions of their normal differentiated (mature) counterparts.

Cancer Statistics

The National Cancer Institute Surveillance, Epidemiology, and End Results Program has recently estimated that 44.8% and 39.3% of American men and women, respectively, will eventually have cancer, and that during 1995 about 1,252,000 new cases of cancer will be diagnosed.[1,2] The most common cancers and causes of cancer deaths in adult Americans are illustrated in Figure 90.1. In general, the incidence of cancer increases with age and both the incidence and mortality rates are higher among black Americans than among whites.[1] Other factors besides age and race that may increase an individual's risk of developing a cancer include immunosuppression and exposure to one or more of the potential carcinogens described in the following section.

Etiology

Cancers arise from the transformation of a single normal cell. Current theory suggests that some initial "event" causes damage or mutation to the cellular DNA.[3] These events include occupational, lifestyle, and environmental factors, as well as some medical therapies (e.g., cytotoxic chemotherapy, radiation) and hereditary factors. (See Table 90.1.)

Cigarette smoking is probably the most significant single factor which contributes to the development of cancers. The American Cancer Society estimates that cigarette smoking is responsible for about 85% of all lung cancer cases. In addition, smoking also has been implicated in cancers of the mouth, pharynx, larynx, esophagus, pancreas, uterine cervix, and bladder.

Specific genes within many cells also may be involved in the process of malignant transformation. When these genes, called oncogenes, are activated or altered by a DNA-damaging event the malignant transformation may occur.[12] Evidence supporting this theory is provided by studies which have shown that activated oncogenes are present in cell lines which have been transformed by chemical carcinogens.[13,14] In most cases, probably more than one oncogene within the cell must be activated before the malignant transformation can proceed.[12]

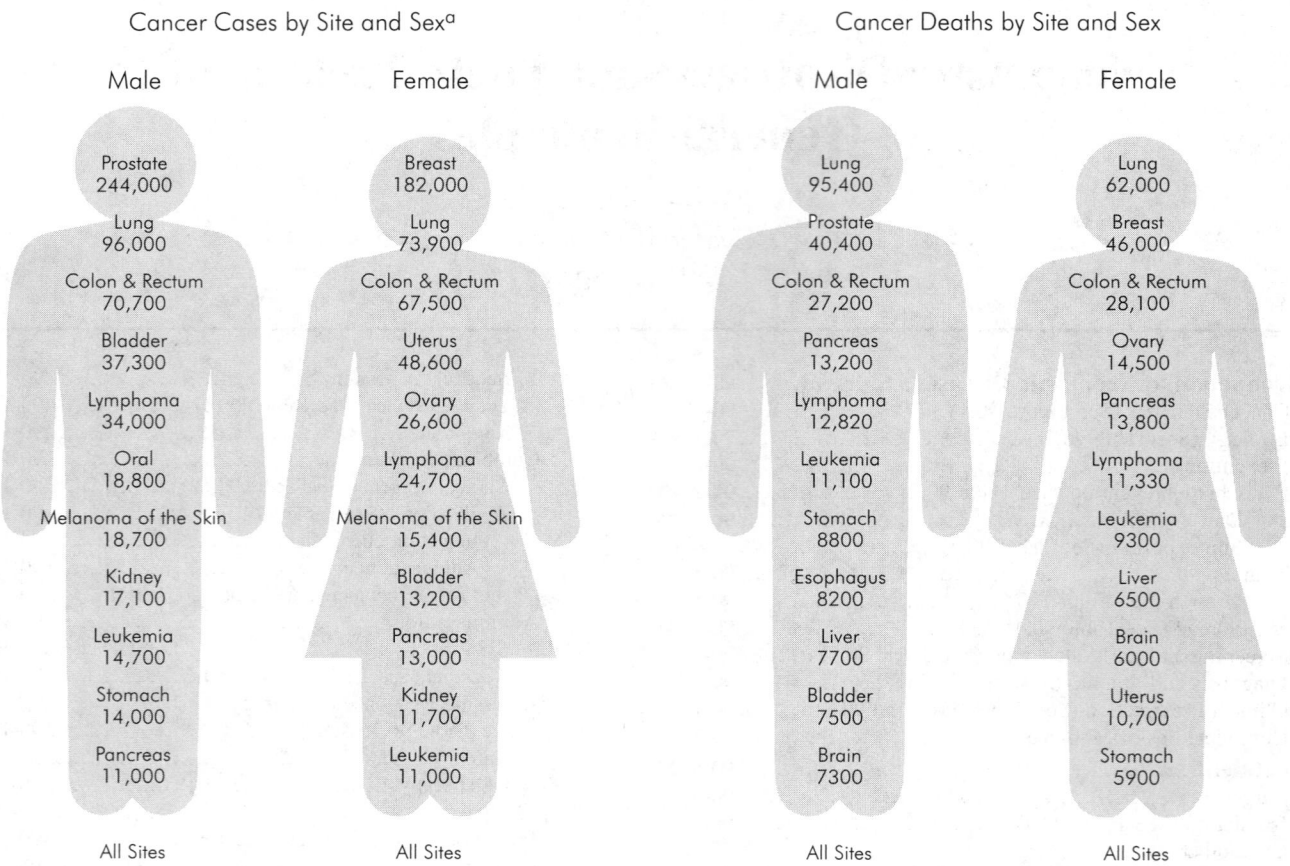

Cancer Cases by Site and Sex[a]

Male | Female

Male	Female
Prostate 244,000	Breast 182,000
Lung 96,000	Lung 73,900
Colon & Rectum 70,700	Colon & Rectum 67,500
Bladder 37,300	Uterus 48,600
Lymphoma 34,000	Ovary 26,600
Oral 18,800	Lymphoma 24,700
Melanoma of the Skin 18,700	Melanoma of the Skin 15,400
Kidney 17,100	Bladder 13,200
Leukemia 14,700	Pancreas 13,000
Stomach 14,000	Kidney 11,700
Pancreas 11,000	Leukemia 11,000
All Sites	All Sites

Cancer Deaths by Site and Sex

Male | Female

Male	Female
Lung 95,400	Lung 62,000
Prostate 40,400	Breast 46,000
Colon & Rectum 27,200	Colon & Rectum 28,100
Pancreas 13,200	Ovary 14,500
Lymphoma 12,820	Pancreas 13,800
Leukemia 11,100	Lymphoma 11,330
Stomach 8800	Leukemia 9300
Esophagus 8200	Liver 6500
Liver 7700	Brain 6000
Bladder 7500	Uterus 10,700
Brain 7300	Stomach 5900
All Sites	All Sites

Fig 90.1 Leading Sites of New Cancer Cases and Deaths—1995 Estimates   [a] Excluding basal and squamous cell skin cancer and carcinoma in adults.

Prevention

Chemoprevention

1. M.S., a regular patron of your community pharmacy asks about taking antioxidant vitamins to reduce her risk of cancer. She says that her mother died several years ago of colon cancer and she is fearful that she also will develop the disease. Does taking antioxidant vitamins alter the risk of cancer? What other measures might prevent cancer?

The majority of past efforts to prevent cancer have been aimed at removing the carcinogen or premalignant lesions. Cancer chemoprevention is focused on reversing carcinogenesis in the early phases and preventing new malignancies. Chemoprevention could include introduction of a natural (or fortified) or synthetic agent which exerts its protective effects by: 1) preventing the formation of carcinogens; 2) blocking the carcinogen from reacting with critical target sights; or 3) suppressing the promotion of an epidermal neoplasia.[15] Examples of chemoprotective agents currently in clinical trials are listed in Table 90.2.

Chemoprevention studies are designed to detect changes in cancer incidence as well as the rate of regression and progression of premalignant lesions. Additionally, biochemical parameters or cellular changes which occur with progression of the disease should be monitored.[17] If the agent is effective, life-long therapy probably will be necessary; therefore, ideal chemopreventive agents should be associated with minimal risk, low cost, and acceptable toxicity. Once daily dosing (or less) also is desirable to maximize compliance.

Antioxidant vitamins, including beta-carotene (and related forms of vitamin A), vitamin C, and vitamin E have been purported to reduce the incidence of various malignancies including lung,

Table 90.1	Carcinogens Associated with an Increased Risk of Malignancy in Humans[4–11]
Carcinogenic Risk Factor	**Associated Neoplasm(s)**
Environmental	
Ionizing radiation (Radon gas emitted from soil containing uranium deposits)	Leukemia, breast, thyroid, lung
Ultraviolet radiation	Skin, melanoma
Viruses[a]	Leukemia, lymphoma, nasopharyngeal
Occupational	
Asbestos	Lung, mesothelioma
Chromium, nickel	Lung
Vinyl chloride	Liver
Aniline dye	Bladder
Benzene	Leukemia
Lifestyle	
Alcohol	Esophagus, liver, stomach, oropharynx, larynx
Dietary factors	Colon, breast, gallbladder
Tobacco	Lung, oropharynx, pharynx, larynx, esophagus, bladder
Medical—Drugs	
Diethylstilbestrol	Vaginal in offspring
Alkylating agents	Leukemia, bladder
Azathioprine	Lymphoma

[a] Causal relationship credible but not firmly established.

Table 90.2

	Aspects of Chemoprevention[a]						
	Colorectal	Prostate	Lung	Breast	Bladder	Oral	Cervix
Agents classified by mechanism	Anti-inflammatories (e.g., sulindac, piroxicam, aspirin, ibuprofen)	Testosterone 5α-reductase inhibitors (e.g., finasteride)	Retinoids/carotenoids	Antiestrogens (e.g., tamoxifen, toremifene)	Anti-inflammatories (e.g., sulindac, piroxicam, aspirin, ibuprofen)	Retinoids/carotenoids	Retinoids
	Antiproliferatives (e.g., DFMO,[b] calcium)	Retinoids (e.g., 4-HPR)		Retinoids ras-farnesylation inhibitors (e.g., perillyl alcohol, d-limonene)	Antiproliferatives (e.g., DFMO[b])	Anti-inflammatories (e.g., carbenoxolone)	Antiproliferatives (e.g., DFMO[b])
		Antiproliferatives (e.g., DFMO[b])			Retinoids		Folic acid
Clinical cohorts	Patients with previous adenomas, patients with adenomas <1 cm in diameter; subjects at high risk	Patients with prostatic dysplasia without prostatic adenocarcinoma; patients scheduled for radical prostatectomy; patients with elevated serum PSA;[b] subjects ≥60 yr of age	Patients with recently resected Stage I lung or laryngeal cancer or previous lung, head or neck cancers; patients at high risk (exposure to asbestos or smokers)	Patients scheduled for breast cancer surgery or with previously treated breast cancer	Patients with previous superficial bladder cancer; subjects at high risk	Patients with dysplastic leukoplakia, previously treated head and neck cancers; those at high risk (e.g., smokers, tobacco chewers)	Patients with cervical dysplasia

[a] Adapted from reference 16.
[b] DFMO = Difluoromethylornithine; PSA = Prostate specific antigen.

oral, and colon cancer. An early chemoprevention trial used 13-cis-retinoic acid versus a placebo in patients with oral leukoplakia.[20] The treatment group had a dramatic reduction in premalignant lesions with an objective response rate of 67% versus 10% in the placebo group. Because of the impressive differences between the groups, the trial was terminated early. Unfortunately, more than 50% of the patients relapsed within three months after the 13-cis-retinoic acid was discontinued. As promising as this trial was, others have been equally disappointing. A trial in which randomized smokers received either vitamin E, beta-carotene, both, or placebo reported an unexpected increase in the incidence of lung cancer in those given beta-carotene.[21]

The mechanism of this protection is not clearly elucidated; however, it appears that the antioxidants stabilize oxygen-free radicals generated by many known carcinogens and protect the body from their damaging effects. Epidemiologic studies evaluating dietary intake of green and yellow vegetables and citrus fruits have led investigators to believe that these compounds contribute to the lower incidence of cancer in some populations.[22] This has led to chemoprevention studies in high-risk populations as well as public interest in dietary supplements.

Because the benefit of these dietary supplements is not clearly defined, their widespread use is controversial. However, when used in recommended antioxidant doses, they are relatively nontoxic and would not be contraindicated in M.S. It also would be reasonable to recommend that M.S. take one aspirin daily because it appears to reduce the risk of colon cancer in addition to its cardiovascular benefits.[23]

It would be very appropriate at this time to remind M.S. of other things she can do to reduce her overall risk of cancer. This would include maintaining a regular exercise program and a low-fat diet, avoiding tobacco and other known carcinogens, and drinking alcohol only in moderation.

Diet

Diet has been linked to the development of colon, breast, and prostate cancers. Epidemiologic studies show that colon cancer is the second most common cancer in the western world and a rare disease in the African countries.[24] Diets in underdeveloped countries generally tend to contain more fiber. The American Cancer Society (ACS) believes diet modifications which decrease fat and increase fiber consumption hold considerable potential for decreasing the risk of colon cancer. The impact of dietary interventions can be difficult to assess because multiple variables often are introduced as a result of a single dietary change. For example, if an individual increases natural sources of fiber in the diet, several other changes are likely to occur such as: 1) decreased fat consumption; 2) increased consumption of vitamins and minerals; and 3) weight loss.

The incidence of breast cancer is greatest in populations which have the highest fat consumption. Asian women have the lowest incidence of breast cancer; however, the offspring of women who have migrated to the U.S. have an incidence of breast cancer that approaches that of western populations.[25] Diet may not be the only variable in these studies. Other environmental or life-style factors are likely to play a role in the development of these diseases. For example, even moderate alcohol consumption also has been associated with an increased risk of breast cancer.[6]

Sun Exposure

Most of the risk factors for developing skin cancer with the exception of sun exposure are uncontrollable variables. A history of severe sunburn at any time in the individual's life increases the risk for skin cancer.[26] By the year 2000, it is projected that 1 of every 100 Caucasians will develop cutaneous malignant melanoma.[27] This epidemic is due to excessive, intermittent sun exposure and depletion of the ozone layer in the stratosphere. Prevention is simply based upon limiting sun exposure. Table 90.3 includes advice that should be provided to all light-skinned individuals (especially those in sun belts) along with recommendation for sun protectives as described below. The guidelines from the ACS recommend avoiding or limiting sun exposure during the hours of 10 a.m. and 2 p.m. when ultraviolet rays are the strongest. Protective clothing and sunscreens and/or sunblockers are advised to minimize exposure.

Products that provide protection from the sun are classified as sunblockers or sunscreens. Sunblockers physically reflect and scatter light. Zinc oxide, titanium oxide, iron oxide pigments, and talc are all considered sunblockers. Sunscreens are chemicals which absorb ultraviolet radiation (UVR); different agents absorb at slightly different ranges. Ideally, the skin should be protected from both UVB (290 to 320 nm) and UVA (321 to 440 nm) since both are implicated in photocarcinogenesis. Para-aminobenzoic acid (PABA), a UVB absorber, is used less frequently than it once was because it invokes photosensitivity and is difficult to incorporate

Table 90.3	A Guide to Protection from the Damaging Rays of the Sun[a]

- **Minimize sun exposure** during the hours of 10 a.m. to 2 p.m. when the sun is strongest. Try to plan your outdoor activities for the early morning or late afternoon
- **Wear a hat**, long-sleeved shirts, and long pants when out in the sun. Choose tightly woven materials for greater protection from the sun's rays
- **Apply a sunscreen** before every exposure to the sun, and reapply frequently and liberally at least Q 2 hr as long as you stay in the sun. The sunscreen always should be reapplied after swimming or perspiring heavily, since products differ in their degrees of water resistance. We recommend sunscreens with an SPF ≥15 printed on the label
- **Use a sunscreen** during high altitude activities such as mountain climbing and skiing. At high altitudes where there is less atmosphere to absorb the sun's rays, your risk of burning is greater. The sun also is stronger near the equator where the sun's rays strike the earth most directly
- **Do not forget to use your sunscreen** on overcast days. The sun's rays are as damaging to your skin on cloudy, hazy days as they are on sunny days
- **Individuals at high risk for skin cancer** (outdoor workers, fair-skinned individuals, and persons who have already had skin cancer) should apply sunscreens daily
- **Photosensitivity** (an increased sensitivity to the sun) is a possible side effect of certain medications, drugs, and cosmetics, and birth control pills. Consult your physician or pharmacist before going out in the sun if you are using such products. You may need to take extra precautions
- **If you develop an allergic reaction** to your sunscreen, change sunscreens. One of the many products on the market today should be right for you
- **Beware of reflective surfaces.** Sand, snow, concrete, and water can reflect more than half the sun's rays onto your skin. Sitting in the shade does not guarantee protection from sunburn
- **Avoid tanning parlors.** The UV light emitted by tanning booths causes sunburn and permanent aging, and increases your risk of developing skin cancer
- **Keep young infants out of the sun.** Begin using sunscreens on children at 6 months of age and then allow sun exposure with moderation
- **Teach children sun protection early.** Sun damage occurs with each unprotected sun exposure and accumulates over the course of a lifetime

[a] Also see Chapter 39: Photosensitivity and Burns for a listing and further discussion of sunscreens and sun protection.

Fig 90.2 The growth rate of a tumor is initially very rapid and eventually slows as it approaches 10^{11} cells. Two trillion (2×10^{12}) cells or 2 kg of tumor is lethal to the human. An effective chemotherapy treatment given at point A will decrease the tumor number to point B. Regrowth of the tumor will occur during the recovery period until further chemotherapy is given at point C.

into water-resistant formulations. Butyl methoxydibenzoylmethane (Parsol 1789), approved as a UVA absorber with an absorbance of 320 to 400 nm, used in combination with a UVB absorbing sunscreen (e.g., methyl anthranilite, oxybenzone) provides a broad spectrum of coverage against the damaging effects of the sun. For added protection a sunblocker can be applied.[28] (Also see Chapter 36: Dermatotherapy.)

Tumors

Growth

Proliferation of normal cells (or cell-renewal) is under fine control so that the loss of mature functional cells is balanced by production of new cells. Malignant transformation causes a defect of this self-renewal control and the tumor expands in a clonal fashion. Tumor cells tend to be genetically unstable, and are, therefore, subject to a high rate of random mutation during the clonal expansion.[29] The result is that individual cells within a tumor mass exhibit considerable heterogeneity in their morphology, biochemistry, metastatic behavior, and response to chemotherapeutic agents.[30–32] Some of the new subclones will exhibit a selective growth advantage and become dominant. As they continue to divide, the tumor progresses or expands.

The growth characteristics of tumors have been studied using techniques such as the thymidine labeling index and flow cytometry. Thymidine labeling measures the incorporation of a radio-labeled precursor of DNA (i.e., ^{3}H-thymidine) into a discrete population of cells. The proportion of labeled cells in a tissue at a specified time interval after injection is called the labeling index. It represents the proportion of cells that were undergoing DNA synthesis at the time of injection, and is a crude measure of the overall rate of cell proliferation in a tissue.[33] Flow cytometry stains cells with a fluorescent dye proportional to DNA content.[34] Analysis of the distribution of DNA content will then provide an estimate of the proportion of cells which are in each phase of the cell cycle.[33]

The rate at which a tumor expands is dependent upon many factors, including the length of time necessary for each cell to divide (i.e., the generation time), the percentage of cells within the tumor mass that are actively dividing (i.e., the growth fraction), and the rate at which tumor cells are dying. When the tumor is small the growth fraction is generally high and the tumor tends to grow rapidly. About 30 doublings of a single malignant cell are required before the tumor mass will be of sufficient size to be detected clinically (about 10^9 cells or a 1 gm mass); however, only ten further doublings would result in 10^{12} cells or a 1 kg mass, which is usually lethal. As the tumor expands, the growth decelerates due to a decrease in the growth fraction and an increase in the rate of cell death. This results from poor vascularity, hypoxia, and competition for nutrients.[33,35] (See Figure 90.2.) This decrease in the growth fraction with time produces a plateau in the tumor growth curve and is called Gompertzian kinetics.

Spread

2. D.J., a 14-year-old male, presented to the emergency room with a painful, swollen right leg. X-ray confirmed a fracture that appeared to be caused by a tumor mass in the bone. Biopsy confirmed osteogenic sarcoma. Routine chest x-ray showed 3 nodules which also were believed to be malignant tumors. Does D.J. also have lung cancer? Are the tumors in D.J.'s lungs related to the sarcoma in his leg?

The tumor nodules in D.J.'s lung are most likely metastases from the sarcoma in his leg. The ability of cancer cells to disseminate and form metastases represents their most malignant characteristic. Tumor metastases to distant sites generally have more impact on the rate of complications and the patient's quality of life than the primary tumor. (See Complications of Malignancy.) Metastases also are responsible for the majority of cancer deaths.[36] In all cases, documentation of metastatic spread confers a worse prognosis. The two major routes by which tumor cells travel throughout the body are the blood vessels and the lymphatics. Many tumors spread regionally via the lymphatics and also produce distant metastases via circulation in the blood. Although all neoplasms have the ability to metastasize, the incidence may be greater with some specific tumor types. Sites of metastatic tumor spread are largely determined by the blood and lymph drainage of the affected organ. (See Table 90.4.) Initially, the tumor tends to spread to the first capillary bed encountered by cells after their release from the primary tumor.[36,37] For tumors whose blood supply drains into the vena cava this bed would be located in the lung, and for tumors whose blood supply drains into the portal circulation the first bed would be located in the liver. If the cells do pass on through the

Table 90.4	Common Cancers and Sites of Metastases
Cancer	**Most Common Sites of Metastases[a]**
Breast	
Premenopausal	Lymph nodes, lung, liver, bone, brain, bone marrow
Postmenopausal	Lymph nodes, bone, soft tissue
Prostate	Lymph nodes, bone, liver, lungs
Lung	
Non-small cell	Lymph nodes, liver, bone, brain
Small cell	Lymph nodes, bone, liver, bone marrow, brain, adrenal glands
Colon	Lymph nodes, liver, serosal surface of peritoneum, brain
Lymphomas	
Hodgkin's disease	Liver, spleen, stomach, bone marrow, lung
Non-Hodgkin's	GI tract, bone marrow, liver, lung, CNS
Ovary	Peritoneum, lung, brain
Sarcomas	Lung

[a] CNS = Central nervous system; GI = Gastrointestinal.

capillary bed of the first organ encountered, they then can reach the arterial circulation and be distributed to other organs and tissues throughout the body.[37] Growth conditions (e.g., growth factors, physiologic conditions) within a tissue or organ also may influence the ability of specific tumor cells to actively grow at different sites.

Screening and Early Detection

Screening is the identification of unrecognized disease by physical examination, laboratory tests, or other procedures. Ideally, the screening method should be quick, simple, and not too costly. Screening should be included in routine care when it is likely to maximize disease detection in asymptomatic individuals. The economics of screening should balance effort and benefit.

The cancer screening tests or procedures recommended by the ACS meet four basic requirements: 1) there must be good evidence that it is effective in reducing morbidity or mortality (e.g., treatment must be available for the screened disease); 2) the benefits should outweigh the risks; 3) the costs must be reasonable for the benefits; and 4) the methods used must be practical and feasible for application in the existing health care setting.[38] Furthermore, it should be recognized that there is a difference between early detection and screening. Various professional organizations have suggested guidelines for cancer screening. (See Table 90.5.)

In 1980, the American Cancer Society Guidelines were made available to health care providers and the public. These guidelines were preliminary recommendations which were to be updated as new information became available. Initially, they were considered controversial and questions were raised about the value of these recommendations. Questions are still raised regarding the benefits of early intervention, specifically in diseases for which there is no standard therapy. The question that needs to be answered is: will screening alter the natural history of the disease or simply detect the disease earlier without changing patient morbidity? The National Cancer Institute (NCI) is conducting the Prostate, Lung, Colorectal and Ovary Cancer Screening Trial. This type of trial is very time consuming and labor intensive. It will take years to determine if early detection leads to any change in death rates. Despite introducing these guidelines over a decade ago, late diagnosis of cancer is still common, even in the case of potentially curable diseases.

Only minor changes have been made since the ACS guidelines were initially released because a newly discovered tumor marker or diagnostic procedure must be thoughtfully considered before it can be included in the guidelines. The addition of screening techniques could add substantial costs to an already stressed health care system without significant benefit to the patient.

The ACS guidelines were intended for the asymptomatic person at average risk. Modifications may be necessary for individuals who may be at increased risk due to genetics, environmental, or behavioral factors.[38]

Diagnosis and Staging

The histologic diagnosis is the most important determinant of the treatment of choice for a malignancy. This usually is accomplished by surgical biopsy or excision of the primary tumor followed by microscopic and biochemical evaluations by a pathologist. The histologic classification of a tumor influences its natural history, pattern of progression, and responsiveness to treatment.

3. J.S. is diagnosed with breast cancer after a large breast mass was biopsied. Chemotherapy, radiation, and surgery all play an important role in the management of breast cancer. How would clinicians decide which of these treatment modalities is most appropriate for J.S. at this time?

Staging is the process that determines the extent or spread of the disease. Once the histologic diagnosis has been confirmed, the stage of the disease is the most important factor in determining treatment and prognosis. Staging is crucial for J.S. because if the disease is limited to the breast, surgery followed by radiation and/or chemotherapy would be recommended. If the cancer has spread beyond the breast, surgery would probably be of no value and it would be important to consider systemic therapy (chemotherapy or hormones) immediately.

Staging schema have been developed for all major types of tumors.[40] For solid tumors, the most widely used and accepted staging classification is the TNM system which incorporates the size of the primary tumor (T), the extent of regional lymph node spread (N), and the presence or absence of metastatic spread to distant

Table 90.5	Guidelines for Early Detection of Cancer[39]		
	U.S. Preventative Task Force	American Cancer Society	National Cancer Institute
Self Examination			
Breast self-examination	Not recommended	≥20: Monthly	Not recommended
Testicular self-examination	Not recommended (unless high risk)	Not recommended	Periodic
Skin	High risk	Not recommended	Part of periodic exam
Clinician Examination			
Clinical breast examination	≥40:[a] Annual	20–40: 3 yr	20–40: 3 yr
			≥40: Annual
Digital rectal examination	Not recommended	≥40: Annual	≥40 men: Annual
Pelvic examination	Not recommended	20–40: 1–3 yr	Annual
		≥40: Annual	
Sigmoidoscopy	Not recommended	≥50: 3–5 yr	≥50: 3–5 yr
Laboratory Tests			
Stool guaiac	Not recommended	≥50: Annual	≥50: Annual
Prostate specific antigen	Not recommended	≥50: Annual	Not recommended
Pap smear	When sexually active: 1–3 yr	18 or sexually active:[b] Annual	18 or sexually active: Annual
Mammogram	40–49: Not recommended	40–49: 1–2 yr	40–49: 1–2 yr
	≥50: 1–2 yr	≥50: Annual	≥50: Annual

[a] For high risk women, start clinical breast examination at age 35.
[b] If pap normal for 3 consecutive years, then less frequently.

organs (M). Determining the stage of the disease, therefore, requires measuring the size of the primary tumor either physically or radiologically [e.g., using x-rays, computerized tomography (CT) scans, or magnetic resonance imaging (MRI) scans]; dissecting and pathologically examining regional lymph nodes; and assessing the patient for documentation of tumor spread. The latter involves assessing the most likely sites of tumor metastases (see Table 90.4) and evaluating any additional symptoms (e.g., pain) or signs (e.g., swelling, abnormal laboratory findings) which may indicate tumor involvement of an organ or tissue.

An example of the TNM classification for breast cancer is shown in Table 90.6. As also shown in Table 90.6, most solid tumor staging systems incorporate the TNM classification into broader groups which facilitate easier comparison between patient groups. For several tumors such as leukemias, lymphomas, and multiple myeloma, the TNM system is not practical and alternative staging strategies have been developed.

Cancers that arise from malignant transformation of a cell of hematopoietic origin are referred to as hematologic malignancies. Common hematologic malignancies include acute and chronic leukemia, myeloma, and the lymphomas. Since blood cells and lymphatic tissue are widely distributed throughout the body, the TNM staging system is not applicable. Separate and specific staging systems have been developed for the hematologic malignancies. Examples of widely accepted staging systems for hematologic malignancies include the RAI system for chronic lymphocytic leukemia, and the Ann Arbor staging classification for lymphomas. Like staging systems for solid tumors, those for hematologic malignancies define the extent of disease, guide selection of treatment, and provide prognostic information.

Staging systems for some tumors use other characteristics to further elucidate the stage and prognosis of the disease. These may include clinical signs or symptoms or biochemical characteristics of the tumor. An example is the inclusion of constitutional symptoms (i.e., fever, night sweats, weight loss) with the staging of Hodgkin's disease. Studies have indicated that the presence of these symptoms confers a poorer prognosis and, in some cases, may indicate the need for more intensive therapy.[42] The designation of subscript A along with the stage of the disease (e.g., stage II_A) indicates the patient has not experienced constitutional symptoms, whereas the subscript B indicates that the patient has experienced these symptoms.

Staging of the tumor is done at the time of initial diagnosis and periodically during treatment to assess the patient's response to therapy. Staging also must be repeated when a malignancy either progresses during treatment or recurs following therapy to establish the most appropriate second-line therapy and to enable measurement of response to that therapy.

Clinical Presentation

The initial signs and symptoms of malignant disease are varied and predominantly depend upon the histologic type and location of the tumor (including metastases), its size, and the underlying condition of the patient. Pain secondary to compression, obstruction, and destruction of adjacent tissues and organs is the most common presenting symptom. Table 90.7 lists many other common signs and symptoms of specific cancers. Other common initial symptoms reported by patients with cancer include anorexia, weight loss, and fatigue. Some cancers do not cause significant symptoms until the tumor is large. Symptoms also may be obscured by concomitant illness such as chronic lung disease in patients with lung cancer. In either circumstance, early diagnosis may be difficult and efforts to screen high-risk individuals may be useful.

Table 90.6	Staging of Breast Carcinoma[41]

TNM Classification[a]

Primary Tumor (T)

T1	Tumor ≤2 cm in greatest dimension
T2	Tumor >2 cm but not >5 cm in greatest dimension
T3	Tumor >5 cm in greatest dimension
T4	Tumor of any size with direct extension to chest wall or skin

Regional Lymph Nodes (N)

N0	No regional lymph node metastasis
N1	Metastasis to movable ipsilateral axillary lymph node(s)
N2	Metastasis to ipsilateral axillary lymph node(s) fixed to one another or other structures
N3	Metastasis to ipsilateral internal mammary lymph node(s)

Distant Metastasis (M)

M0	No distant metastasis
M1	Distant metastasis [includes metastasis to ipsilateral supraclavicular lymph node(s)]

Stage Grouping

Stage I	T1	N0	M0
Stage IIA	T0	N1	M0
	T1	N1	M0
	T2	N0	M0
Stage IIB	T2	N1	M0
	T3	N0	M0
Stage IIIA	T0	N2	M0
	T1	N2	M0
	T2	N2	M0
	T3	N1, N2	M0
Stage IIIB	T4	Any N	M0
	Any T	N3	M0
Stage IV	Any T	Any N	M1

[a] TNM = Tumor-node-metastasis. See text for full explanation of TNM system of classification.

4. G.D., a 68-year-old male presents with lethargy, weakness, and nausea. His wife states that he does not take any medications and only occasionally consumes alcohol. He has smoked 2 packs/day of cigarettes for the past 45 years. Routine laboratory tests revealed sodium (Na) 129 mEq/L. Chest x-ray showed a large mass in his right lung which was consistent with malignancy. Is the hyponatremia related to G.D.'s lung cancer? [SI unit: Na 129 mmol/L]

G.D.'s hyponatremia is likely to be due to the syndrome of inappropriate antidiuretic hormone (SIADH) caused by ectopic production of ADH (see Chapter 28: Fluid and Electrolyte Disorders) by his lung carcinoma. While most signs and symptoms can be directly correlated with the presence of a tumor at a specific site, clinical findings or symptoms which are distant from the site of the primary tumor or metastases occasionally are reported. These are referred to as paraneoplastic effects and are believed to be produced by substances that are secreted by the tumor. Table 90.8 lists some of the more common paraneoplastic effects.

Complications of Malignancy

Malignant disease can have a profound effect on the patient's quality of life and his or her ability to tolerate appropriate therapy. For example, malnutrition secondary to anorexia, mechanical obstruction, or pain may physically debilitate the patient. Also, tumor involvement of the liver, kidneys, or lungs may produce significant organ dysfunction and metabolic imbalances which may complicate cancer therapy as well as the management of other underlying

Table 90.7	Signs and Symptoms Associated with Common Cancers	
Cancer	Local	Distant[a,b]
Breast	Breast lumps; nipple discharge; skin changes; axillary lymphadenopathy	Bone pain; elevated LFTs
Prostate	Urinary hesitancy; nocturia; poor urine stream; dribbling; terminal hematuria	Bone pain; elevated acid phosphatase, PSA, and alkaline phosphatase
Lung	New cough; hoarseness; hemoptysis; dyspnea; unresolving pneumonias; chest wall pain	Anorexia; weight loss; elevated LFTs; hypercalcemia; hypertrophic osteoarthropathy (clubbing); SIADH; neurologic (brain metastases and neuromuscular disorders)
Colorectal	Alteration in bowel habits; ↓ in stool caliber; occult bleeding	Elevated LFTs, CEA, and alkaline phosphatase
Ovarian	Abdominal pain, discomfort or enlargement; postprandial flatulence; vaginal bleeding; abdominal mass	Peripheral neuropathies; hypercalcemia; pleural effusion; thrombophlebitis
Testicular	Painless enlargement; epididymitis; gynecomastia; back pain	Elevated HCG, α-fetoprotein, LD
Bladder	Hematuria; bladder irritability, urinary hesitancy or urgency; dysuria; flank or pelvic pain	Edema of lower extremities
Melanoma	Change in size, color or sensation, or surface characteristics of a pre-existing nevus	Lymphadenopathy; elevated LFTs
Lymphomas	Painless lymphadenopathy	Fever; night sweats; weight loss; bone or retroperitoneal pain; hepatomegaly; splenomegaly; abnormal CBC

[a] Local effects include those produced by the primary tumor, and distant effects include those associated with metastatic spread and paraneoplastic syndromes. Many cancers may not produce symptoms in the early stages and diagnosis at that time is dependent upon early detection and screening efforts.

[b] CBC = Complete blood count; CEA = Carcinoembryonic antigen; HCG = Beta human chorionic gonadotropin; LD = Lactate dehydrogenase; LFTs = Liver function tests; PSA = Prostate-specific antigen; SIADH = Syndrome of inappropriate antidiuretic hormone

diseases. Compression or obstruction by tumors also may produce a "mass effect" by impairing normal organ or tissue function and causing pain or other uncomfortable physical effects. Examples of these effects which may be life-threatening and require immediate intervention include obstruction of the superior vena cava, spinal cord compression, and brain metastases. Common complications of cancer are illustrated in Chapter 92: Hematological Malignancies and Chapter 93: Solid Tumors.

Treatment

5. T.J., a 40-year-old male with no significant medical history, presents to his physician with complaints of abdominal pain, nausea and vomiting, weakness, and weight loss. On physical examination, he is noted to be slightly icteric and the only significant laboratory abnormality is mild anemia [hemoglobin (Hgb) 11 gm/dL, hematocrit (Hct) 33%]. A CT scan of the abdomen revealed a mass present in the peri-pancreatic area that was suggestive of malignancy. T.J. is referred to a surgeon who explains that the first step in evaluating the mass is to obtain a tissue biopsy. T.J. asks the surgeon why he cannot remove all of the mass, instead of only part of it. He also wants to know whether this malignancy will be treated with surgery, radiation, chemotherapy, hormones, or immunotherapy. What is the basis for determining which cancer treatment modality is best suited for T.J.? [SI units: Hgb 110 gm/L; Hct 0.33]

The choice of specific therapy depends not only upon the histology and stage of the disease but also on the patient's probable tolerance of the side effects and complications of the various possible treatments.[35] The goal of therapy should always be to cure the patient. No matter what modality of therapy is under consideration, the likelihood of achieving this goal is highest when the tumor burden is lowest. In most circumstances either surgery or radiation therapy is the initial choice of therapy for tumors which are localized.

Surgery

Surgery is the oldest form of treatment for cancer and in recent decades, advances in surgical techniques and an improved understanding of the patterns of spread of various malignancies have allowed surgeons to perform successful resections for an increasing number of patients.[43] In addition to the treatment of cancer, surgery also is used to prevent cancer (e.g., removal of premalignant tissue such as colonic polyps or cervical dysplasia), diagnosis and staging (e.g., biopsy of tissues for histologic evaluation), and reconstruction. When surgery is used as a definitive (i.e., curative) therapy for a localized tumor, it is necessary to remove the tumor plus a margin of normal tissue surrounding the tumor.

Occasionally, surgery also is used to manage advanced cancers. Surgical reduction of large, localized tumors which cannot be completely removed may improve the likelihood that subsequent chemotherapy or radiation may succeed in eradicating the residual tumor. This type of cytoreductive surgery is useful only if there are effective therapies to treat the residual disease.[43,44] In addition, patients with limited metastatic disease (e.g., one or a few metastases at a single site) may benefit from surgical resection of the metastases if the primary tumor also can be controlled. Examples of this approach include resection of pulmonary metastases from sarcomas, hepatic metastases from colorectal carcinoma, and solitary brain metastases.[43] Palliative surgery also may be used to relieve pain or improve functional abnormalities caused by advanced tumors (e.g., gastrointestinal obstruction). The objective is to improve the patient's quality of life even though prolongation of survival is unlikely.

Irradiation

Irradiation also is used to eradicate a localized tumor mass. Not all cancers, however, are sensitive to the lethal effects of radiation (see Table 90.9). Therefore, this modality has limited application in the treatment of such diseases. Radiation has potential advantages over surgery in some circumstances. For instance, radiation may encompass a wider area around the tumor than surgery and may be used to treat regions of the body that cannot be surgically removed. It also can be used in cases where surgery would result in considerable disability or disfigurement. In addition, multiple metastatic sites may be treated simultaneously.[47] The usefulness of radiation can be limited by its toxic effects on normal tissues surrounding the tumor. Such toxicity may be exacerbated by concomitant administration of chemotherapy. In addition, administra-

Table 90.8	Paraneoplastic Syndromes Associated with Cancers
Syndrome	**Cancer**
Dermatologic	
Sweet's syndrome	Hematologic malignancies and various carcinomas
Endocrine	
Addison's syndrome[a]	Adrenal carcinoma, lymphomas
Cushing's syndrome[a]	Lung, thyroid, testicular, and adrenal cancers
Hypercalcemia (not associated with bone metastases)[a]	Lung
Syndrome of inappropriate antidiuretic hormone	Lung cancers
Hematologic/Coagulation	
Anemia[a]	Various cancers
Autoimmune hemolytic anemia[a]	Chronic lymphocytic leukemia, lymphomas, ovarian cancer
Disseminated intravascular coagulation[a]	Acute progranulocytic leukemia, lung, prostate, and pancreatic cancers
Thrombophlebitis	Lung, breast, ovarian, prostate cancers
Neuromuscular	
Dermatomyositis and polymyositis	Lung, gastric and ovarian cancers
Myasthenic syndrome (Eaton-Lambert syndrome)	Small cell lung, gastric, and ovarian cancers
Sensory neuropathies	Lung, gastrointestinal, and breast cancers

[a] This syndrome is discussed in more detail in other sections of this text. See the index.

tion of chemotherapy following completion of radiation therapy can produce a "recall" of local toxicity.

New techniques in radiation therapy, including intraoperative irradiation, three-dimensional imaging to minimize exposure of normal tissues, and the use of radiosensitizing drugs to enhance tumor responsiveness, continue to improve the clinical usefulness of this modality.

Not all cancers may be cured by surgery or radiation. In some cases, the tumor has already metastasized to distant sites of the body at the time of initial diagnosis, while in other patients the tumor may recur at some time following primary surgery or radiation. In either circumstance, it is evident that tumor cells have been released from the primary tumor mass and systemic treatment generally offers the only hope of rendering the patient free of disease. Systemic therapies used to treat cancer include cytotoxic chemotherapy, hormonal manipulations, and immunotherapy. Although chemotherapy was developed to treat advanced cancers, drugs now have clinical applications at many stages of malignant diseases. (See Applications of Cancer Chemotherapy.)

Chemotherapy

Cytotoxic Chemotherapy

The era of cytotoxic chemotherapy can be traced to World War II when an explosion of mustard gas produced bone marrow and lymphoid hypoplasia in seamen exposed to the gas.[48] This incident led to the use of alkylating agents (derivatives of mustard gas) in the treatment of Hodgkin's disease and other lymphomas.[49]

Mechanism of Action. Most cytotoxic chemotherapy kills cancer cells by damaging DNA or interfering with DNA synthesis or other steps during cellular division. Chemotherapeutic agents usually are classified by whether they exert their effects during a specific phase of the cell cycle or according to their mechanism of action at the cellular level. Drugs which only affect the cell during a specific phase often are referred to as cell-cycle specific, or more accurately, *phase specific agents*. In contrast, those that may cause damage during any phase of the cell cycle are called cell-cycle nonspecific or *phase-nonspecific agents*. (See Figure 90.3.)

Cancer cells, like all other mammalian cells, proceed through a specific and orderly set of events during cellular replication referred to as the cell cycle. (See Figure 90.3.) During the G_1 phase, enzymes necessary for DNA synthesis are produced. The actual replication of DNA, the cell's genetic material, occurs during the S-phase. RNA and other proteins are synthesized during the G_2 phase in preparation for actual cellular division which occurs during the M phase or mitosis. The cells which complete mitosis may then: 1) continue to proceed through the cell cycle and divide again; 2) differentiate or mature into specialized cells and eventually die; or 3) enter a resting phase (i.e., G_0). The specific mechanisms of many chemotherapeutic agents are described in Table 90.10. Because these agents act at some point during the cellular division process, their lethal effects are not realized until the cells proceed through division. Since cancer chemotherapy is most active on tumors which have a high growth fraction (see Tumors: Growth), cells in the G_0 phase are far less sensitive to the drugs.

Cell Kill. Rodent studies done during the 1960s demonstrated that when the growth fraction is 100% (i.e., all cells are dividing) and all cells are sensitive to a particular chemotherapeutic agent, the number of cells killed by the chemotherapy is proportional to the dose administered.[196,197] Thus, if a particular dose of chemotherapy reduces the tumor burden from 10^{10} to 10^8 cells, the same dose used when only 10^7 cells are present should reduce the tumor burden to 10^5 cells. This theory has become know as the cell kill or log-kill hypothesis. (See Figure 90.2.)

Factors Which Influence Response to Chemotherapy. Unfortunately, in the clinical setting, eradication of tumor masses is more complicated than this model, and tumors do not always decrease predictably with each successive course of chemotherapy. This is because: 1) the growth fraction of human tumors is not 100%; and 2) the cells within the tumor mass are heterogeneous and some may be resistant to the chemotherapy. Therefore, in patients with large tumors with a growth curve that has already plateaued, the fraction of cells killed is likely to be low. A third factor which also complicates this model is the ability of normal tissues to tolerate the toxic effects of chemotherapy. In most chemotherapy regimens, high doses are administered every three to four weeks to allow the normal tissues to recover from toxicity between doses. However, during this period, tumor cells also will recover and start to replicate again. Successful treatment, therefore, depends upon the administration of the next course of therapy before the tumor has regrown to its previous size, and the net effect is a further decrease in size with each successive course.

Table 90.9	Radiation Sensitivity of Common Tumors[45,46]	
Radiosensitive	**Intermediate**	**Radioresistant**
Acute lymphocytic leukemia	Squamous cell carcinoma of the head and neck	Gliomas
Seminoma		Melanomas
Neuroblastoma	Cervix cancer	Soft tissue sarcomas
Hodgkin's disease	Breast cancer	Thyroid cancer
Basal cell and squamous cell skin cancer	Ovarian cancer	
	Bladder cancer	

Fig 90.3   Effect of Cytotoxic Chemotherapeutic Drugs on the Cell Cycle

Dose Intensity. Unnecessary lengthening of the interval between courses or a decrease in the dose negatively affects treatment and has received much attention. It has been suggested that attenuation of doses is probably the main reason for treatment failure in patients with drug-sensitive tumors undergoing their first chemotherapy treatment.[198] Dose intensity has been defined as the amount of chemotherapy administered per unit of time.[199] In animal models, a reduction in the average dose intensity markedly decreases the cure rate before a significant reduction in the complete remission rate is noted.[200] This suggests that although the bulk of the tumor mass may be eradicated with lower doses, residual tumor cells are left behind which ultimately will be responsible for recurrence of the disease. A direct relationship between dose intensity and response rate also has been demonstrated in several human tumors including advanced ovarian, breast, and colon cancers, and the lymphomas.[199,201,202]

Bone marrow suppression is the major dose-related toxicity which limits the dose intensity for most chemotherapeutic regimens. Strategies to ameliorate this toxicity and allow for administration of higher doses have included the use of autologous bone marrow transplantations (see Chapter 94: **Bone Marrow Transplantation**), the use of hematopoietic growth factors (see Chapter 91: Adverse Effects of Chemotherapy), and alterations in the schedule of drug delivery.[203-206]

Schedule Dependency. The schedule of chemotherapy administration is also an important determinant of response. It influences dose intensity largely by affecting toxicity.[198] In some circumstances, changes in the administration schedule will reduce toxicity enough to allow for higher total doses to be administered or for courses to be given more frequently thus, increasing the dose intensity. The optimal schedule also is influenced by the pharmacokinetics of the drug. This is particularly important for phase-specific agents when antitumor activity is only possible during a definite portion of the cell cycle. If the agent has a short half-life and is given as a bolus injection, it is unlikely that a significant number of tumor cells will cycle through the vulnerable phase of the cell cycle during exposure to the drug. However, if the drug is given frequently or by prolonged infusion, then more cells may be exposed to the agent.

6. Drug Resistance. B.C. is a 39-year-old male with an aggressive nonHodgkin's lymphoma (NHL). At the time of diagnosis, B.C. had enlarged cervical lymph nodes, dyspnea, and a large mediastinal mass noted on chest x-ray. Chemotherapy was initiated with the CHOP regimen which consists of cyclophosphamide, doxorubicin, vincristine, and prednisone. After the first course of chemotherapy his lymphadenopathy was greatly reduced. Chest x-ray repeated after the second course of therapy showed marked improvement. When he returned for his fourth cycle of chemotherapy, recurrent lymphadenopathy was noted and chest x-ray confirmed enlargement of the mediastinal mass. Why is B.C.'s cancer growing despite continued chemotherapy and how should his treatment be altered?

It is most likely that B.C.'s cancer is now growing because it has become resistant to his chemotherapy; therefore, it would be unwise to continue the CHOP regimen. Biochemical resistance to chemotherapy is the major impediment to successful treatment with most neoplastic diseases.[198] Resistance occurs *de novo* in cancer cells or is developed during the process of replication, probably as a result of mutation.[207] In 1979, a mathematical model was proposed which predicted that tumor cells mutate to drug resistance at a rate related to the genetic instability of the tumor.[207] Thus, the probability that a tumor mass will contain resistant clones is related to both the rate of mutation and the size of the tumor. Many specific mechanisms now have been identified by which cancer cells resist the activity of cytotoxic agents. (See Table 90.11.)

Continued

Table 90.10

Clinical Pharmacology of Cytotoxic Chemotherapeutic Agents

Agents	Mechanism of Action	Pharmacokinetic Characteristics[a]	Dose Adjustment for Organ Dysfunction	Major Toxicities[a]
Altretamine (Hexalen)[50–53] Cap: 50 mg	Non-classic alkylating agent. Biochemical activation produces metabolites which bind to microsomal proteins and DNA	Bioavailability variable, probably due to extensive metabolism. $t\frac{1}{2}_\alpha = 30$ min; $t\frac{1}{2}_\beta = 4.7–13$ hr		Anorexia; nausea, vomiting; diarrhea; neurologic toxicity; myelosuppression
Asparaginase[54–56] (Elspar) Inj: 10,000 international units/vial	Depletion of essential amino acid, asparagine leads to inhibition of protein synthesis	$t\frac{1}{2} = 14–22$ hr; plasma clearance greatly accelerated in patients who develop hypersensitivity		Hypersensitivity; hypoalbuminemia; hyperglycemia; ↓ clotting factors (↑ PT, PTT, thromboplastin time; ↓ fibrinogen); cerebral dysfunction; pancreatitis; ↑ LFTs; nausea, vomiting; chills
Bleomycin[57–61] (Blenoxane) Inj: 15 mg/vial	Single- and double-strand breaks in DNA mediated by free radicals	$t\frac{1}{2}_\alpha = 24$ min; $t\frac{1}{2}_\beta = 2–4$ hr; longer $t\frac{1}{2}$ reported in patients with renal insufficiency; 45%–70% excreted in urine in 24 hr	↓ dose in proportion to ↓ in Cl_{Cr} for patients with clearance <25 mL/min/m²	Pulmonary toxicity; fever; cutaneous (erythema, induration, hyperkeratosis, hyperpigmentation, peeling, nail changes)
Busulfan (Myleran)[62–65] Tab: 2 mg	Alkylation of DNA	Well absorbed orally; metabolized extensively; no intact drug recovered in urine, but metabolites are excreted renally; 90% of dose cleared from plasma in 3 min		Myelosuppression; pulmonary fibrosis; hyperpigmentation; suppression of testicular, ovarian, and adrenal function
Carboplatin (Paraplatin)[66–70] Inj: 50, 150, 450 mg/vial	Binds to DNA, forms interstrand cross-links and intrastrand adducts	$t\frac{1}{2}_\alpha = 12–24$ min; $t\frac{1}{2}_\beta = 1.3–1.7$ hr; $t\frac{1}{2}_\gamma = 22–40$ hr; up to 90% excreted renally	↓ for Cl_{Cr} <60 mL/min or use methods described by Egorin or Calvert[70]	Myelosuppression, especially thrombocytopenia; nausea, vomiting
Carmustine (BiCNU)[71–73] Inj: 100 mg/vial	Metabolites alkylate with DNA	Renal excretion of metabolites is 30%; $t\frac{1}{2} = 5$ min; good CSF penetration	↓ dose may be necessary in patients with ↓ bone marrow reserve	Delayed myelosuppression; nausea, vomiting; pulmonary fibrosis; hepatotoxicity; renal toxicity
Chlorambucil (Leukeran)[74–77] Tab: 2 mg	Alkylation of DNA	Oral bioavailability 70%–80%, reduced by 10%–20% if ingested with food; rapidly metabolized to inactive metabolites and active phenylacetic acid mustard; $t\frac{1}{2} = 1.5–2$ hr (parent), 2.5 hr (active metabolite); <1% excreted unchanged in urine over 24 hr		Myelosuppression, pulmonary fibrosis
Cladribine (Leustatin) Inj: 10 mg/vial[78–80]	Following intracellular phosphorylation, accumulates, causing inhibition of enzymes and impairs DNA synthesis; also impairs DNA repair	$t\frac{1}{2}_\alpha = 35$ min; $t\frac{1}{2}_\beta = 6.7$ hr	Effect of renal or hepatic impairment is unknown	Myelosuppression; fever; immunosuppression (B- and T-cells); renal damage (acute tubular necrosis); neurotoxicity (paraparesis, quadriplegia); rash
Cisplatin (Platinol)[66,81–85] Inj: 10, 50 mg/vial	Binds to DNA, forms interstrand cross-links and intrastrand adducts	$t\frac{1}{2}_\alpha = 20–30$ min; $t\frac{1}{2}_\beta = 60$ min; $t\frac{1}{2}_\gamma = 24$ hr; 90% excreted by kidneys	↓ dose or hold for renal dysfunction	Nephrotoxicity; nausea, vomiting; peripheral neuropathies; ototoxicity; hypomagnesemia; visual disturbances (rare)
Cyclophosphamide (Cytoxan)[86–90] Inj: 100, 200, 500, 1000, 2000 mg/vial Tab: 25, 50 mg	Metabolite alkylates to DNA	Oral bioavailability ≈100%; must be activated in liver by microsomal enzymes to active compounds and toxic metabolites; renal elimination of 22% of parent drug and 60% of metabolites; $t\frac{1}{2} = 3–10$ hr (parent); 6.5 to ≥8 hr (alkylating activity)	None recommended; no difference in toxicity between patients with normal or impaired renal function	Myelosuppression; hemorrhagic cystitis; nausea, vomiting; alopecia; cardiomyopathy (rare); "allergic" interstitial pneumonitis; SIADH
Cytarabine (Cytosar)[91–94] Inj: 100, 500, 1000, 2000 mg/vial	Antimetabolite; incorporated into DNA; terminates DNA chain elongation and inhibits DNA polymerase	Metabolized by deamination primarily in liver; 8% of drug excreted unchanged in urine, 72% as metabolite; $t\frac{1}{2}_\alpha = 1.6$ to 20 min; $t\frac{1}{2}_\beta = 9–111$ min		Myelosuppression; nausea, vomiting; stomatitis; fever, rash; intrahepatic cholestasis, ↑ LFTs and bilirubin (rare)

Table 90.10 Clinical Pharmacology of Cytotoxic Chemotherapeutic Agents (Continued)

Agents	Mechanism of Action	Pharmacokinetic Characteristics[a]	Dose Adjustment for Organ Dysfunction	Major Toxicities[a]
Dacarbazine (DTIC-Dome)[101-13] Inj: 500 µg/vial	Alkylation of DNA	Extensively metabolized to active compound; ≈50% excreted in urine as parent drug, 9%–18% as major metabolite; some hepatobiliary excretion; $t\frac{1}{2}_\alpha = 3$ min; $t\frac{1}{2}_\beta = 41$ min	↓ dose may be required for moderate to severe hepatic or renal dysfunction	Myelosuppression; nausea, vomiting; myalgias, fever, malaise, headache; pain at injection site; photosensitivity; rare fatal hepatic vein occlusion
Dactinomycin (Cosmegen)[101-103] Inj: 500 µg/vial	Intercalation of DNA resulting in inhibition of RNA and protein synthesis	Urinary excretion 20%; fecal excretion 14%; $t\frac{1}{2}_\beta \geq 36$ hr		Myelosuppression; nausea, vomiting, diarrhea; mucositis; alopecia; hepatotoxicity; vesicant if extravasated
Daunorubicin (Cerubidine)[104-109] Inj: 20 mg/vial	Intercalation to DNA double helix; topoisomerase II mediated DNA damage; production of oxygen-free radicals which cause damage to DNA and cell membranes	Extensive binding to tissues; known routes of elimination only account for 50%–60% of dose; extensively metabolized by liver; $t\frac{1}{2}_\alpha = 40$ min; $t\frac{1}{2}_\beta = 45$–55 hr; biliary excretion accounts for 20%–30% of dose; 14%–23% excreted in urine as parent and metabolites	↓ dose only for very severe hepatic dysfunction (toxicity has not correlated with prolonged $t\frac{1}{2}$); dissociation from tissue binding limits elimination; severe renal impairment give 75% of dose	Myelosuppression; mucositis; alopecia; cumulative cardiac toxicity; dose-related acute ECG changes; severe tissue damage if extravasated
Doxorubicin (Adriamycin, Rubex)[110-112] Inj: 10, 20, 50, 100, 150, 200 mg/vial	Intercalation to DNA double helix; topoisomerase II mediated DNA damage; production of oxygen-free radicals which cause damage to DNA and cell membranes	Extensive binding to tissues; known routes of elimination only account for 50%–60% of dose; extensively metabolized by liver; $t\frac{1}{2}_\alpha = 40$ min; $t\frac{1}{2}_\beta = 45$–55 hr; biliary excretion accounts for 20%–30% of dose; 14%–23% excreted in urine as parent and metabolites	Recommend ↓ dose reduction for hepatic disease: bilirubin ≤1.2 give 100% of dose; 1.2–3.0 give 50% of dose; >3.0 give 25% of dose. ↑ toxicity not always seen with liver dysfunction	Myelosuppression; mucositis; nausea, vomiting; alopecia; cumulative cardiac toxicity; dose-related acute ECG changes; severe tissue damage if extravasated
Estramustine (Emcyt)[113-114] Cap: 140 mg	Probably impairs mitotic spindle formation	Milk ↓ absorption; readily dephosphorylated during absorption to estradiol and estrone congeners		Estrogenic effects; cardiovascular (edema, thrombophlebitis, pulmonary embolus); nausea, vomiting, diarrhea; gynecomastia; mild ↑ LFTs
Etoposide (VePesid)[115-121] Inj: 100 mg/5 mL Cap: 50 mg	Produces DNA strand breaks by inhibiting topoisomerase II; arrests cells in late S or early G_2 phase of the cell cycle	Oral bioavailability 37%–67% (average 50%); 30%–40% is excreted rapidly in the urine (70% of excreted drug is unchanged); terminal $t\frac{1}{2} = 6$–8 hr; about 6%–15% excreted in bile; <2% in feces	↓ dose in proportion to reductions in Cl_{Cr}; not required for hepatobiliary dysfunction	Myelosuppression; nausea, vomiting; alopecia; mucositis; hypotension (related to rapid infusion); hypersensitivity reactions; fever; bronchospasm
Floxuridine (FUDR)[122-124] Inj: 500 mg/vial	Antimetabolite; incorporation into RNA interferes with RNA function; inhibition of thymidylate synthase causing inhibition of DNA synthesis	$t\frac{1}{2} = 20$ min; >90% hepatically metabolized	Dosage adjustments are made depending upon clinical, hematological, and GI toxicity	Mucositis; myelosuppression; nausea, vomiting; diarrhea; dermatologic toxicity; neurotoxicity at high doses
Fludarabine (Fludara IV)[125-128] Inj: 50 mg/vial	Fluorinated adenine analog causes inhibition of DNA synthesis by inhibiting ribonucleotide reductase and DNA polymerase	Undergoes rapid dephosphorylation to F-ara-A; terminal $t\frac{1}{2}$ F-ara-A = 8 hr; terminal $t\frac{1}{2}$ F-ara-ATP = 15 hr		Myelosuppression; neurotoxicity; peripheral neuropathy; pulmonary toxicity; nausea, vomiting
Fluorouracil[122-125,129,130] Inj: 500 mg/vial	Antimetabolite; incorporation into RNA interferes with RNA function; inhibition of thymidylate synthase causing inhibition of DNA synthesis	$t\frac{1}{2} = 6$–20 min; ≥90% hepatically metabolized	Dosage adjustments are made depending upon clinical, hematological, and GI toxicity	Mucositis; myelosuppression; nausea, vomiting; diarrhea; dermatologic toxicity; neurotoxicity (high doses)
Idarubicin (Idamycin)[131-135] Inj: 5, 10 mg/vial	Intercalation to DNA double helix; topoisomerase II mediated DNA damage; production of oxygen-free radicals which cause damage to DNA and cell membranes	Terminal $t\frac{1}{2} = 15$–18 hr		Myelosuppression; mucositis; anorexia; nausea, vomiting, diarrhea; fever; alopecia

Drug	Mechanism	Pharmacokinetics	Dosage Adjustment	Toxicity
Ifosfamide (Ifex)[136-139] Inj: 1, 3 gm/vial	Metabolites cause alkylation of DNA	Renal excretion and t½ are dose and schedule dependent. 60%–80% recovered as unchanged drug or metabolite in urine within 72 hours after administration	Dosage or schedule adjustment may be necessary based upon clinical response in patients with severe renal impairment	Myelosuppression; hemorrhagic cystitis (should be administered with bladder protectant, MESNA); nephrotoxicity neurotoxicity; anorexia, nausea, vomiting; alopecia
Lomustine (CeeNu)[140-142] Cap: 10, 40, 100 mg	Metabolites cause alkylation of DNA	Well absorbed orally; t½ of metabolites =16–48 hr; 50% of metabolites excreted renally within 24 hr	↓ dosages may be required in patients with ↓ bone marrow reserves	Myelosuppression; nausea, vomiting; nephrotoxicity; pulmonary infiltrates/fibrosis; hepatotoxicity
Mechlorethamine (Mustargen)[143-145]	Alkylation of DNA	Rapid metabolism; <0.01% unchanged drug recovered in urine; 50% of metabolites found in urine within 24 hours		Myelosuppression; nausea, vomiting; sterility, menstrual irregularities; local irritant/vesicant if extravasated
Melphalan (Alkeran)[146-148] Tab: 2 mg Inj: 50 mg/vial	Alkylation of DNA	Oral absorption erratic and incomplete (≈30%); not actively metabolized but spontaneous chemical degradation; t½ = 90 minutes; 10%–15% of dose excreted in urine over 24 hr	t½ prolonged in patients with renal dysfunction; 50% dose reduction for BUN >30 mg/dL or creatinine >1.5 mg/dL	Myelosuppression; pulmonary fibrosis
Mercaptopurine (Purinethol)[149-150] Tab: 50 mg	Antimetabolite; inhibition of purine synthesis; incorporation into DNA or RNA	Oral absorption highly variable; t½ = 20–60 min; elimination primarily hepatic	Possible ↓ dose for patients with hepatic and/or renal dysfunction	Myelosuppression; anorexia, nausea, vomiting; hepatic toxicity (biliary stasis)
Methotrexate[122,151-156] Tab: 2.5 mg Inj: 25, 50, 100, 200, 250, 1000 mg/vial	Antifolate; inhibits dihydrofolate reductase resulting in depletion of reduced folates and inhibition of DNA synthesis	Oral absorption appears to be better with smaller doses; exhibits interpatient bioavailability; "third space" collections of fluid may provide a reservoir for drug accumulation; $t½_\alpha$ = 1.5–3.5 hr; $t½_\beta$ = 8–15 hr; 90% of administered dose recovered in urine within 24 hours	Monitor serum methotrexate levels especially with ↓ renal function and/or fluid accumulation. Dosage should be ↓ or withheld in patients with ↓ renal function	Myelosuppression; nephrotoxicity; hepatotoxicity; mucositis; pulmonary toxicity; neurotoxicity
Mitotane (Lysodren)[157-159] Tab: 500 mg	Causes suppression of adrenal corex, possibly alters the peripheral metabolism of steroids	≈40% absorbed orally; ≈10%–25% is recovered in urine as metabolite; 60% in feces		Anorexia, nausea, vomiting; dermatitis; adrenal insufficiency; lethargy, somnolence; vertigo
Mitoxantrone (Novatrone)[160-166] Inj: 20, 25, 30 mg/vial	Intercalation allows binding to nucleic acids inhibiting DNA and RNA synthesis and causing DNA strand breaks; inhibits topoisomerase II	$t½_\alpha$ =10 min; $t½_\beta$ = 6 hr; $t½_\gamma$ = 12 days; <10% of dose is recovered in the urine		Myelosuppression; cumulative cardiac toxicity has been reported at total doses >100 mg; risk may be (increased) with prior anthracycline therapy; nausea, vomiting, mild stomatitis
Paclitaxel (Taxol)[167-171] Inj: 30 mg/vial	Promotes microtubule assembly and arrests cell cycle in G_2 and M phases	<10% renal clearance; liver and biliary primary routes of elimination; $t½_\alpha$ = 0.3 hr; $t½_\beta$ = 1.3–8.6 hr	↓ doses recommended for severe neutropenia (following prior course), severe peripheral neuropathy, or hepatic dysfunction	Hypersensitivity reactions (premedication recommended); cardiac disturbances; sensory neuropathy; myalgia; arthralgia
Pentostatin (Nipent)[172-174] Inj: 10 mg/vial	Purine analog which inhibits adenosine deaminase and subsequent DNA and RNA synthesis	90% renal excretion; $t½_\alpha$ = 11–85 min; $t½_\beta$ = 5–15 hr (longer in patients with ↓ renal function)	↓ dose recommended for Cl_{Cr} <60 mL/min	Myelosuppression; immunosuppression; lethargy; seizures; conjunctivitis; rash; nausea, vomiting; rare renal dysfunction
Procarbazine (Matulane)[175-177] Cap: 50 mg	Prodrug. Metabolic activation produces several active species which bind covalently to DNA	Oral dose well absorbed; 70% recovered in urine as active metabolite	May alter activity of drugs which are microsomally activated; The converse is also true. ↓ dosage is recommended for SrCr >2.0 mg/dL or bilirubin >3.0 mg/dL	Myelosuppression; nausea, vomiting; neurotoxicity; sterility; pulmonary hypersensitivity; ↑ toxicity may occur with sympathomimetic drugs and tyramine-rich foods. Disulfiram reaction may occur with alcohol

Continued

Table 90.10

Clinical Pharmacology of Cytotoxic Chemotherapeutic Agents (Continued)

Agents	Mechanism of Action	Pharmacokinetic Characteristics[a]	Dose Adjustment for Organ Dysfunction	Major Toxicities[a]
Streptozocin (Zanosar)[178–180] Inj: 1000 mg/vial	Alkylation of DNA	$t\frac{1}{2}_\alpha = 5–15$ min; $t\frac{1}{2}_\beta = 35$ min; 60%–72% of drug eliminated renally within 4 hr	↓ dosage may be required in patients with renal dysfunction	Dose-related renal toxicity; nausea, vomiting; myelosuppression; abnormal glucose tolerance; hepatotoxicity
Teniposide (Vumon)[119,181–183] Inj: 50 mg/ampule	Similar to etoposide	4%–12% excreted in urine; terminal $t\frac{1}{2} = 6–10$ hr; ↑ hepatic enzymes correlate with ↓ clearance	Adjustments may be necessary for hepatic impairment	Myelosuppression; hypotension; nausea, vomiting; secondary leukemia
Thioguanine[149,184] Tab: 40 mg	Thiolated purine which acts as an antimetabolite. Interrupts purine synthesis ultimately resulting in inhibition of RNA and DNA synthesis	Oral absorption is incomplete and ↓ with food. Clearance is mainly hepatic with methylation of parent drug to inactive metabolites $t\frac{1}{2}_\alpha = 15$ min; $t\frac{1}{2}_\beta = 11$ hr	No adjustment necessary	Myelosuppression; stomatitis; hepatotoxicity with ↑ alkaline phosphatase and direct bilirubin; low incidence of nausea, vomiting
Thiotepa[63,74,185] Inj: 15 mg/vial	Alkylates DNA	Metabolized to TEPA; 15% of TEPA eliminated in urine during first 24 hours; $t\frac{1}{2}_\alpha = 7.5$ min; $t\frac{1}{2}_\beta = 109$ min	↓ dosage recommended for pre-existing bone marrow suppression	Myelosuppression; mild nausea, vomiting
Vinblastine (Velban)[63,119,186–189] Inj: 10 mg/vial	Reversible inhibition of mitosis. Binds to microtubule protein, tubulin, ultimately inhibiting formation of mitotic spindles	Primarily metabolized and excreted in bile. 10% excreted in feces. $t\frac{1}{2}_\alpha = 4.5$ min	↓ dose 50% or more may be required in hepatobiliary dysfunction (bilirubin >3 mg/dL)	Myelosuppression; rare neurotoxicity; vesicant if extravasated
Vincristine (Oncovin)[119,188–191] Inj: 1, 2, 5 mg/vial; 2 mg prefilled syringe	Reversible inhibition of mitosis. Binds to microtubule protein, tubulin, ultimately inhibiting formation of mitotic spindles	$t\frac{1}{2}_\alpha = <1$ min; $t\frac{1}{2}_\beta = 7.4$ min; $t\frac{1}{2}_\gamma = 164$ min		Neurotoxicity: primarily distal neuropathy affecting sensory and motor abilities; higher doses may cause autonomic neuropathies; SIADH; vesicant if extravasated
Vinorelbine (Navelbine)[192–195]	Reversible inhibition of mitosis. Binds to microtubule protein, tubulin, ultimately inhibiting formation of mitotic spindles	<20% renal excretion; $t\frac{1}{2}_\alpha = 2–6$ min; $t\frac{1}{2}_\beta = 1.9$ hr		Leukopenia; neurotoxicity ↓ DTRs; vesicant if extravasated

[a] BUN = Blood urea nitrogen; Cl$_{Cr}$ = Creatinine clearance; CSF = Cerebrospinal fluid; DTRs = Deep tendon reflexes; GI = Gastrointestinal; LFTs = Liver function tests; PT = Prothrombin time; PPT = Partial thromboplastin time; SIADH = Syndrome of inappropriate antidiuretic hormone secretions; SrCr = Serum creatinine; $t\frac{1}{2}_\alpha$ = Alpha half-life; $t\frac{1}{2}_\beta$ = Beta half-life; $t\frac{1}{2}_\gamma$ = Gamma half-life.

Table 90.11	Possible Mechanisms of Anticancer Drug Resistance
Mechanism	**Drugs**
Improved proficiency in repair of DNA	Cisplatin, cyclophosphamide, melphalan, mitomycin, mechlorethamine
↓ in drug activation	Cytarabine, doxorubicin, fluorouracil, mercaptopurine, methotrexate, thioguanine
↑ in drug inactivation	Cytarabine, mercaptopurine
↓ in cellular uptake of drug	Methotrexate, melphalan
↑ in efflux of drug (multidrug resistance)	Dactinomycin, doxorubicin, daunorubicin, etoposide, vincristine, vinblastine
Alternative biochemical pathways	Cytarabine, fluorouracil, methotrexate
Alterations in target enzymes	Fluorouracil, hydroxyurea, mercaptopurine, methotrexate, thioguanine

Some cell lines that become resistant to a single chemotherapeutic agent also have been found resistant to structurally unrelated cytotoxic compounds. This phenomenon is called pleiotropic drug resistance or multidrug resistance (MDR).[210] Cell lines that display this type of resistance generally are resistant to natural product cytotoxic agents such as the vinca alkaloids, the antitumor antibiotics, the epipodophyllotoxins, and taxanes.[198] The primary mechanism believed to be responsible for MDR is an increase in P-glycoprotein in the cell membrane which mediates efflux of drug and is associated with decreased drug accumulation within the cell (the site of drug activity).[211,212] A second type of multidrug resistance is mediated by altered binding to topoisomerase II, an enzyme believed to promote DNA strand breaks in the presence of anthracyclines and epipodophyllotoxins.[213,214] Because of the likelihood of MDR, B.C. should receive a chemotherapy regimen which does not include drugs inactivated by the MDR mechanism. An alternative regimen such as high-dose methotrexate with leucovorin rescue would be appropriate because it is effective against nonHodgkin's lymphoma and not affected by the MDR gene.

Various experimental systems have been developed to predict the sensitivity of specific tumors to individual drugs. The most widely studied is the human tumor colony-forming assay.[215] Although this technique allows for reliable culture of human ovarian cancers, renal cell carcinomas, malignant melanomas, soft tissue sarcomas, and multiple myeloma (and has apparent value for predicting sensitivity), many limitations have been reported.[35,216]

Tumor Site. The cytotoxic effects of chemotherapeutic agents are related to the time which the cancer cell is exposed to an effective concentration of the drug (i.e., concentration × time). This is influenced not only by the dose, rate, and route of administration, but also by the distributive characteristics of the drug and the size and site of the tumor. As tumors grow larger, the degree of vascularity lessens making it more difficult for drugs to penetrate throughout the tumor. In addition, some tumors are anatomically located in sites of the body where drug penetration is poor (e.g., the brain).

Combination Chemotherapy

7. **K.K. has advanced Hodgkin's disease and is to begin chemotherapy today with the ABVD (adriamycin, bleomycin, vinblastine, and dacarbazine) regimen. She is very reluctant because of her fear of side effects. She asks if rather than receiving all 4 drugs today, she could receive just one and if it does not work then try another one?**

Choice of Agents. Although early significant regressions of Hodgkin's disease, acute lymphocytic leukemia, and adult non-

Hodgkin's lymphomas were documented with single agent chemotherapy, most responses were only partial and of very short duration. Recognition that administration of single-agent chemotherapy rarely produced prolonged remission led to the combined use of chemotherapeutic agents. In Hodgkin's disease, the use of combination chemotherapy results in long-term, disease-free survival for greater than 60% of patients. If K.K. were to receive a single drug only, her chance of long-term survival would be almost zero. Therefore, combination chemotherapy is absolutely recommended. She should be reassured that appropriate measures, including prophylactic antiemetics, will be taken to reduce her chances of both acute and chronic toxicities.

Combination chemotherapy provides broader coverage against resistant cell lines within the heterogeneous tumor mass. Several principles provide the basis for selection of drugs to be included in a chemotherapy regimen:

- Only drugs which have demonstrated single agent activity against the specific type of tumor should be used.
- Drugs in the regimen should have different mechanisms of action.
- Drugs which do not have overlapping toxicities should be selected whenever possible.
- All drugs in the regimen should be used in their optimal dose and schedule.

Table 90.12 lists examples of commonly used regimens.

Applications. It has been estimated that over 500,000 patients are candidates for chemotherapy each year in the U.S. alone. Although effective chemotherapy regimens have not been reported for all cancers, many patients with advanced malignancies may benefit from this modality. Chemotherapy has been reported to cure a fraction of patients with each of the advanced tumors listed in Table 90.13. Chemotherapy also may prolong survival or provide symptomatic relief for many additional patients who cannot be cured. (See Figure 90.4.)

Induction Chemotherapy. Chemotherapy is used most often to treat patients with advanced malignancies. This includes patients who initially present with disseminated disease as well as patients who have recurrent disease at metastatic sites following other therapy. The term induction chemotherapy is used to describe the initial treatment for patients who present with advanced cancer for which no alternative treatment exists. Patients who fail after one drug treatment and require further chemotherapy pose a difficult treatment problem because their tumors often are advanced and resistant to available drugs. In addition, such patients often are debilitated due to their disease and prior therapy. Chemotherapy in these patients is referred to as salvage treatment.[218]

8. **F.R., a 36-year old female with no other medical problems, recently underwent a lumpectomy and radiation therapy for breast cancer. She has been told that the cancer is all gone; however, she also is told that she should now receive 6 months of chemotherapy. She knows that chemotherapy will cause her to vomit, lose her hair, and gain weight and will place her at risk for life-threatening infections. Why would chemotherapy be recommended now when she is disease-free?**

Adjuvant Chemotherapy. In some types of cancer, there is a high probability that the tumor will recur after primary treatment has removed all evidence of the disease. Systemic therapy given following initial curative surgery (or radiation) is referred to as adjuvant chemotherapy. The goal is to eradicate any undetectable residual disease. Because the tumor burden is lowest at this point, it is an optimal time to administer chemotherapy. The risk of recurrence must be high and there must be drugs available which are effective against the tumor if adjuvant therapy is to be beneficial.

Table 90.12		Commonly Used Chemotherapeutic Regimens[a]	
Acronym	Agents	Dose/Schedule[b]	Cycle
Breast Cancer			
CMF	Cyclophosphamide[217,218]	100 mg/m^2 PO days 1–14	Q 28 days
	Methotrexate	40–60 mg/m^2 IV days 1 and 8	
	Fluorouracil	600 mg/m^2 IV days 1 and 8	
CAF	Cyclophosphamide[218]	100 mg/m^2 PO days 1–14	Q 28 days
	Doxorubicin (Adriamycin)	30–50 mg/m^2 IV days 1 and 8	
	Fluorouracil	500 mg/m^2 IV days 1 and 8	
	or		
	Cyclophosphamide[219]	400 mg/m^2 IV day 1	Q 21 days
	Doxorubicin (Adriamycin)	40 mg/m^2 IV day 1	
	Fluorouracil	400 mg/m^2 IV day 1	
	or		
	Cyclophosphamide[220]	500 mg/m^2 IV day 1	Q 21 days
	Doxorubicin (Adriamycin)	50 mg/m^2 IV day 1	
	Fluorouracil	500 mg/m^2 IV day 1	
CMFVP	Cyclophosphamide[220]	60 mg/m^2/day PO × 1 year	
(Adjuvant)	Methotrexate	15 mg/m^2/week IV × 1 year	
	Fluorouracil	300 mg/m^2/week IV × 1 year	
	Vincristine	0.625 mg/m^2/week × 6 weeks	
	Prednisone	0.75 mg/kg/day × 10 days then taper	
	or		
	Cyclophosphamide[220]	400 mg/m^2 IV day 1	Q 28 days
	Methotrexate	30 mg/m^2 IV days 1 and 8	
	Fluorouracil	400 mg/m^2 IV days 1 and 8	
	Vincristine	1 mg/m^2 IV days 1 and 8	
	Prednisone	20 mg QID PO days 1–7	
Colorectal Cancer			
5-FU	Fluorouracil[221]	500 mg/m^2/day IVP days 1–5	Q 5 weeks
FU/Leucovorin	Fluorouracil[221]	370 mg/m^2/day IVP days 1–5	Q 28 days × 2 then Q 35 days
	Leucovorin	20 mg/m^2/day IVP days 1–5 immediately followed by FU	
	Fluorouracil[222]	600 mg/m^2 IVP at 1 hr into leucovorin infusion	Q week × 6
	Leucovorin	500 mg/m^2 IV over 2 hr	
	Fluorouracil[223]	435 mg/m^2 IVP days 1–5	Q 4–5 weeks
	Leucovorin	20 mg/m^2 IVP days 1–5	
FU/Levamisole	Fluorouracil[224]	450 mg/m^2/day IVP days 1–5; then beginning day 29, 450 mg/m^2 Q week for 1 yr	Q 4–5 weeks
(Adjuvant)	Levamisole	50 mg PO Q 8 hr × 3 days Q 2 weeks for 1 year	
Gastric Cancer			
FAM	Fluorouracil[225]	600 mg/m^2 IV days 1, 8, 29, and 36	Q 8 weeks
	Doxorubicin (Adriamycin)	30 mg/m^2 IV days 1 and 29	
	Mitomycin	10 mg/m^2 IV day 1	
EAP	Etoposide[226]	120 mg/m^2/day IV days 4, 5, and 6	Q 21–28 days
	Doxorubicin (Adriamycin)	20 mg/m^2 IV days 1 and 7	
	Cisplatin	40 mg/m^2 IV days 2 and 8	
Esophageal Cancer			
FCBM + RT	Fluorouracil[227]	1000 mg/m^2/day CIV days 1–4 and 29–32	
	Cisplatin	100 mg/m^2 IV over 2 hr days 1 and 29	
	Bleomycin	20 units/day CIV days 57–60 and 78–81	
	Mitomycin	10 mg/m^2 IV day 57	
	Radiation Therapy	200 cGy/day days 1–5, 8–12, 15–19, 99–103, and 106–110	
Pancreatic Cancer			
FAM	Fluorouracil[225]	600 mg/m^2 IV days 1, 8, 29 and 36	Q 8 weeks
	Doxorubicin (Adriamycin)	30 mg/m^2 IV days 1 and 29	
	Methotrexate	10 mg/m^2 IV day 1	
DDP + 5-FU	Fluorouracil[228]	300 mg/m^2 CIV for 10 weeks	Q 12 weeks
	Cisplatin (DDP)	20 mg/m^2 IV Q week for 10 weeks	

Continued

Table 90.12		Commonly Used Chemotherapeutic Regimens[a] (Continued)	
Acronym	Agents	Dose/Schedule[b]	Cycle
Ovarian Cancer			
CP	Cyclophosphamide[229]	1000 mg/m^2 IV day 1	Q 21 days
	Cisplatin	50 mg/m^2 IV day 1	
HEXA-CAF	Hexamethylmelamine[230]	150 mg/m^2 PO days 1–14	Q 28 days
	Cyclophosphamide	150 mg/m^2 PO days 1–14	
	Doxorubicin (Adriamycin)	40 mg/m^2 IV days 1, 8	
	Fluorouracil	600 mg/m^2 IV days 1, 8	
H-CAP	Hexamethylmelamine[231]	150 mg/m^2 PO days 1–14	Q 28 days
	Cyclophosphamide	350 mg/m^2 IV days 1 and 8	
	Adriamycin (Doxorubicin)	20 mg/m^2 IV days 1 and 8	
	Cisplatin (DDP)	60 mg/m^2 IV day 1	
Taxol/DDP	Paclitaxel (Taxol)[232]	135 mg/m^2 IV day 1	Q 21 days
	Cisplatin (DDP)	75 mg/m^2 IV day 1	
Testicular Cancer			
PVB	Cisplatin[233]	20 mg/m^2 IV days 1–5	Q 21 days
	Vinblastine	0.15 mg/kg IV days 1 and 2	
	Bleomycin	30 units IV days 2, 9, and 16	
BEP	Bleomycin[233]	30 units IV days 2, 9, and 16	Q 21 days
	Etoposide	100 mg/m^2 IV days 1–5	
	Cisplatin	20 mg/m^2 IV days 1–5	
VIP	Vinblastine[234]	0.11 mg/kg IV days 1 and 2	Q 21 days
	Ifosfamide	1.2 gm/m^2 IV days 1–5 (with MESNA bladder protection)	
	Cisplatin	20 mg/m^2 IV days 1–5	
	or		
	Etoposide (VP-16)[234]	75 mg/m^2 IV days 1–5	Q 21 days
	Ifosfamide	1.2 gm/m^2 IV days 1–5 (with MESNA bladder protection)	
	Cisplatin	20 mg/m^2 IV days 1–5	
Bladder Cancer			
M-VAC	Methotrexate[235]	30 mg/m^2 IV days 1, 15, and 22	Q 28 days
	Vinblastine	3 mg/m^2 IV days 2, 15, and 22	
	Adriamycin (Doxorubicin)	30 mg/m^2 IV day 2	
	Cisplatin	70 mg/m^2 over 1 hr IV day 2	
Small Cell Lung Cancer			
DDP + VP-16	Cisplatin (DDP)[236]	25 mg/m^2/day IV days 1–3	Q 21–28 days
	Etoposide (VP-16)	100 mg/m^2/day IV days 1–3 + radiation therapy	
PACE	Cisplatin[237]	20 mg/m^2/day IV days 1–5	Q 21–28 days
	Doxorubicin (Adriamycin)	45 mg/m^2 IV day 1	
	Cyclophosphamide	800 mg/m^2 IV day 1	
	Etoposide	50 mg/m^2/day IV days 1–5	
ACE or CAE	Doxorubicin (Adriamycin)[237]	45 mg/m^2 IV day 1	Q 21–28 days
	Cyclophosphamide	1000 mg/m^2 IV day 1	
	Etoposide	50 mg/m^2 IV days 1–5	
Non-Small Cell Lung Cancer			
DDP + VP-16	Cisplatin (DDP)[238]	100 mg/m^2 IV day 1	Q 21 days
	Etoposide (VP-16)	80 mg/m^2 IV days 1–3	
	Cisplatin[239]	60 mg/m^2 IV day 1	Q 21–28 days
	Etoposide	120 mg/m^2 IV days 4, 6, and 8	
MVP	Mitomycin[240]	10 mg/m^2 IV	Q 28 days
	Vinblastine	6 mg/m^2 IV	
	Cisplatin	40 mg/m^2 IV	
Head and Neck Cancer			
DDP/FU	Cisplatin (DDP)[241]	100 mg/m^2 IV day 1	Q 21 days
	Fluorouracil	1000 mg/m^2 CIV days 1–4	

Continued

Table 90.12		Commonly Used Chemotherapeutic Regimens[a] (Continued)	
Acronym	Agents	Dose/Schedule[b]	Cycle
Lymphomas			
Non-Hodgkin's Lymphomas			
CHOP	Cyclophosphamide[242]	750 mg/m^2 IV day 1	Q 21 days
	Doxorubicin (Hydroxyl-daunorubicin)	50 mg/m^2 IV day 1	
	Vincristine (**O**ncovin)	2 mg IV days 1 and 5	
	Prednisone	100 mg/m^2/day PO days 1–5	
m-BACOD	Methotrexate[243]	200 mg/m^2 IV with leucovorin rescue days 8 and 15	Q 21 days
	Bleomycin	4 mg/m^2 IV day 1	
	Doxorubicin (Adriamycin)	45 mg/m^2 IV day 1	
	Cyclophosphamide	600 mg/m^2 IV day 1	
	Vincristine (**O**ncovin)	1 mg/m^2 IV day 1	
	Dexamethasone	6 mg/m^2 PO days 1–5	
MACOP-B	Methotrexate[244]	400 mg/m^2 IV weeks 2, 6, and 10	Only 1 cycle is given
	Doxorubicin (Adriamycin)	50 mg/m^2 IV weeks 1, 3, 5, 7, 9, and 11	
	Cyclophosphamide	350 mg/m^2 IV weeks 1, 3, 5, 7, 9, and 11	
	Vincristine (**O**ncovin)	1.4 mg/m^2 IV weeks 2, 4, 6, 8, 10 and 12	
	Prednisone	75 mg/m^2 PO daily, tapered over last 15 days	
	Bleomycin	10 units/m^2 IV weeks 4, 8, and 12	
EVA	Etoposide[245]	100 mg/m^2 IV days 1–3	Q 28 days
	Vinblastine	6 mg/m^2 IV day 1	
	Doxorubicin (Adriamycin)	50 mg/m^2 IV day 1	
Hodgkin's Disease			
MOPP	Mechlorethamine[246]	6 mg/m^2 IV days 1 and 8	Q 28 day
	Vincristine (**O**ncovin)	1.4 mg/m^2 IV days 1 and 8	
	Prednisone	40 mg/m^2 PO days 1–14, cycles 1 and 4	
	Procarbazine	100 mg/m^2 PO days 1–14	
ABVD	Doxorubicin (Adriamycin)[247]	25 mg/m^2 IV days 1 and 15	Q 28 days
	Bleomycin	10 mg/m^2 IV days 1 and 15	
	Vinblastine	6 mg/m^2 IV days 1 and 15	
	Dacarbazine	375 mg/m^2 IV days 1 and 15	
Multiple Myeloma			
VAD	Vincristine[248]	0.4 mg/m^2/day CIV days 1–4	Q 28 days
	Doxorubicin (Adriamycin)	9 mg/m^2/day CIV days 1–4	
	Dexamethasone	40 mg/m^2 PO days 1–4, 9–12, 17–20	
MP	Melphalan[249]	0.25 mg/kg/day PO days 1–4	Q 42 days
	Prednisone	2 mg/kg/day PO days 1–4	
MP + IFN	Melphalan[250]	0.25 mg/kg/day PO days 1–4	Not specified
	Prednisone	2 mg/kg/day PO days 1–4	
	Interferon	after disease stabilization	

[a] Original citations should be consulted for dosage adjustments due to toxicity.
[b] CIV = Continuous intravenous infusion; IV = Intravenous; IVP = Intravenous push; PO = Oral.

Adjuvant therapy is commonly used to manage breast cancer but has benefited selected patients with colorectal cancer and some sarcomas.[251,252] (Also see Chapter 93: Solid Tumors.) The major dilemma of this approach is in determining who should receive it since it is impossible to predict which patients will eventually have a recurrence. Therefore, some patients who will not eventually relapse will be exposed to the risks of therapy in order to decrease the overall relapse rate.

Primary or Neoadjuvant Chemotherapy. The terms primary or neoadjuvant chemotherapy have been used to describe initial treatment for patients who present with locally advanced tumors (e.g., large tumors or those that are impinging on surrounding vital structures) that are unlikely to be cured with primary surgery or radiation. The potential advantage of this approach is that the che-

motherapy may reduce the tumor volume and increase the chance that it may be completely resected or eradicated with local surgery and/or radiation. The patient also may then require less radical surgery or radiation, thus preserving cosmetic appearances and functions of the surrounding normal tissues. The potential disadvantages of this approach are that the tumor may be resistant to the primary chemotherapy and continue to grow, making surgery even more difficult. Patients also may experience toxicities that delay surgery or impair healing following surgery.[198]

Administration

Systemic chemotherapy is most commonly administered by the intravenous (IV) route, although some chemotherapeutic agents are available in oral (PO) dosage forms. Occasionally, intramuscular

(IM) or subcutaneous (SQ) injections are used. Whichever route is selected, it is imperative that the individual administering the chemotherapy be proficient in the method of drug delivery and knowledgable of the acute and chronic toxicities of each drug. All aspects of drug administration should be discussed with the patient before chemotherapy is initiated, including what the patient should feel during the injection, how long it should take, and what to expect afterwards. Printed patient educational materials are recommended to supplement oral instructions.

Intravenous cancer therapy may be given via bolus injections (generally <15 minutes), short infusions (15 minutes to several hours), or continuous infusions lasting 24 hours to several weeks. Some of these drugs are potent vesicants or irritants if they are extravasated from the vein (see Chapter 91: Adverse Effects of Chemotherapy, Dermatologic Toxicities: Irritant and Vesicant Drugs). Many of these agents also may produce severe irritation and pain to peripheral veins which may result in sclerosis and thrombosis.[253] Other patients may have unsatisfactory venous access secondary to obesity, prior IV therapy with irritant drugs, or advanced age. Therefore, permanent central venous access devices are commonly used in patients receiving chemotherapy. Currently, tunneled central venous catheters (e.g., the Broviac, Hickman, or Groshong) or subcutaneous ports (e.g., Port-A-Cath or Infuse-A-Port) are the most widely used devices.

Regional. Although chemotherapy was initially developed for systemic use, techniques have been developed to administer drugs to specific sites of the body affected by the tumor. Tumors which are commonly managed by these special administration techniques are listed in Table 90.14. The rationale for regional or local chemotherapy is that high concentrations of drugs may be achieved at the site of the tumor while reducing systemic exposure and subsequent toxicity. On the other hand, if there are undetectable metastases at other sites in the body, they may not be exposed to the chemotherapy as they would be with systemic therapy.

Assessing Response to Therapy

A very important step in the process of treating a patient with chemotherapy is to assess their response to the treatment. This

Table 90.14	Local/Regional Routes of Administration of Cancer Chemotherapy
Route of Administration	Disease Used to Manage
Intrathecal/Intraventricular	Leukemia, lymphoma, breast cancer, lung cancer (meningeal metastases)
Intrapericardial	Malignant pericardial effusions
Intraperitoneal	Ovarian cancer, colorectal cancer (intra-abdominal metastases), mesothelioma, melanoma
Intrapleural	Malignant pleural effusions secondary to various cancers
Intra-Arterial	
Hepatic artery	Hepatomas, liver metastases of colon cancer
Limb perfusion	Sarcomas, melanomas
Carotid artery	Head and neck cancers, brain tumors
Intra-carotid	Head and neck tumors

includes not only the antitumor effects of the drugs but also the toxic effects, and the impact of these on the patient's overall quality of life and survival. Re-evaluation occurs at regularly scheduled intervals during the treatment process and includes physical examination, laboratory monitoring, and repeat diagnostic tests (radiologic or other tests such as bone marrow biopsy, bronchoscopy) which were used to define the extent of disease during the staging process. Usually, only tests which previously were positive for evidence of tumor are repeated unless new signs or symptoms suggest additional metastatic tumor involvement.

Several standard criteria are used to define the patient's response to treatment (see Table 90.15). The use of standardized criteria in clinical trials evaluating new therapies is especially important because it helps to define the potential utility of the new therapy compared to standard treatments. Criteria which assess the antitumor effects include direct measures of the change in tumor size, duration of response, and patient survival. Parameters to assess the toxic effects of a treatment regimen should include the incidence of specific toxicities and the relative severity of such effects. Standardized toxicity grading scales used to assess chemotherapy toxicity include those provided by the World Health Organization, the National Cancer Institute, and the Eastern Cooperative Oncology Group.[254,255]

Because the toxicities produced by many cytotoxic drugs are potentially severe, it is important to evaluate the risk of treatment in relationship to the potential benefit. The net effect of a cancer treatment regimen should outweigh its cost in patient suffering which includes how physical, mental, and social well-being are affected by the treatment. Several comprehensive quality of life assessment tools have been developed for this purpose.[256,257]

Tumor Markers. Tumor markers are biochemical indicators which usually are found in abnormally high concentrations in the presence of a neoplasm. The ideal tumor marker is produced and released primarily by cancer cells (or by other tissues in response to the tumor) at levels proportional to the mass of the tumor. Removal of the tumor or a therapeutic response to chemotherapy or radiation should result in a declining level of the marker. In addition, the ideal tumor marker should be detectable at very low levels so that tumors may be detected at sizes smaller than conventional diagnostic tests such as x-rays or CT scans permit.[258] Few tumor markers fulfill these criteria sufficiently to be clinically useful as sole screening or diagnostic tests. (See Table 90.15.) They are used primarily as confirmatory tests and as part of follow-up

Table 90.13	Tumors Which Respond To Chemotherapy

A Fraction of Patients With the Following Advanced Tumors Are Cured With Chemotherapy:

Choriocarcinoma	Wilm's tumor
Acute lymphocytic leukemia	Embryonal rhabdomyosarcoma
Testicular cancer	Peripheral neuroepithelioma
Acute myelogenous leukemia	Neuroblastoma
Hodgkin's disease	Small cell lung cancer
Non-Hodgkin's lymphoma (especially high grade lymphomas)	Ovarian cancer

Advanced Tumors in Which Chemotherapy May Prolong Survival But Not Produce Cures:

Bladder cancer	Endometrial cancer
Chronic myelogenous leukemia	Adrenocortical carcinoma
Hairy cell leukemia	Medulloblastoma
Multiple myeloma	Prostate cancer
Gastric carcinoma	Insulinoma
Cervical carcinoma	Breast cancer
Soft tissue sarcoma	Carcinoid tumors
Head and neck cancer	

Advanced Tumors Which Usually Do Not Respond to Chemotherapy:

Osteogenic sarcoma	Colorectal cancer
Pancreatic cancer	Non-small cell cancer
Renal cancer	Melanoma
Thyroid cancer	Hepatocellular carcinoma
Carcinoma of the vulva or penis	

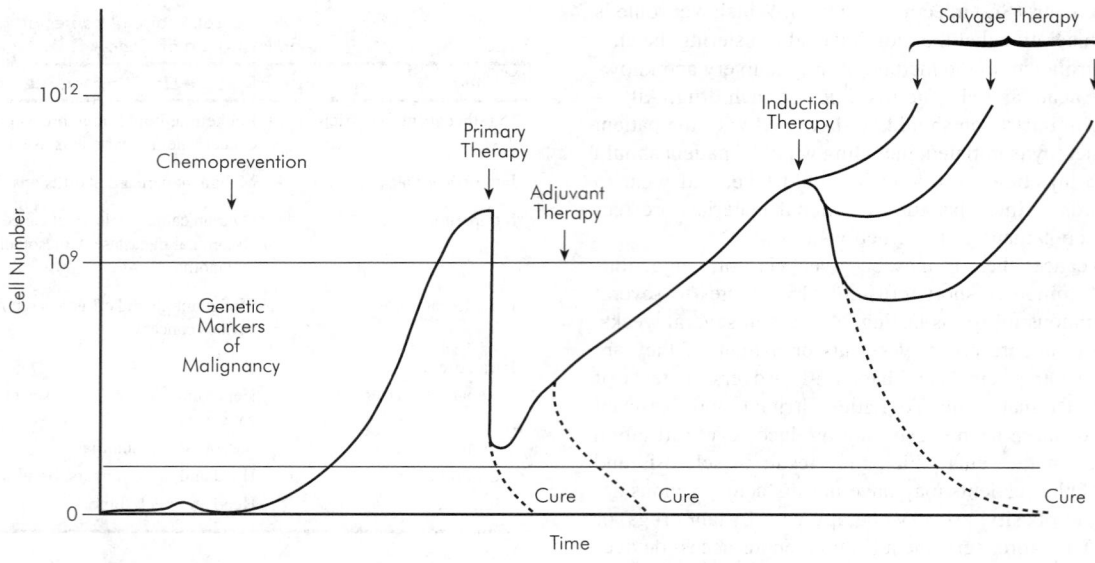

Fig 90.4   Chemotherapy During Various Phases of Malignancy

care to detect recurrent disease. In most cases the tumor markers lack specificity for the tumor and may be elevated in other disease states. Patients who had elevated levels of a particular marker at initial diagnosis are likely to have elevated levels when the disease recurs.

Hormonal Therapy

Hormones are used to treat several common tumors that arise from hormonally-mediated tissues including breast, prostate, and endometrial cancers. Hormones appear to interact with and bind to specific receptors located on the cell membrane or within the cytoplasm nucleus of the cell. Exogenous hormones which occupy receptors or interrupt the production or secretion of endogenous hormones that stimulate tumor growth can produce tumor regression. (*Note:* Interruption of hormonal secretion also can be achieved through surgical removal of hormonal producing organs.) Not all tumors arising from hormonally-mediated tissues respond to these manipulations. This is probably due to induction of cells

Table 90.15	Response Criteria Used For Evaluating Effects of Chemotherapy

Complete Response
Disappearance of all clinical evidence of active disease for at least 4 weeks. No new lesions may appear during this period

Partial Response
>50% reduction in the sum of the products of 2 perpendicular diameters of all measured tumors for at least 4 weeks. No tumor or metastasis may show progression and no new lesions may appear

Stable Disease
<50% reduction or 25% ↑ in the sum of the product of 2 perpendicular diameters of all measured lesions; no appearance of new lesions; and no deterioration of the performance status for a minimum of 4 weeks

Disease Progression
Reappearance of a lesion after complete response, appearance of any new lesions or an ↑ of ≥25% in the product of the 2 perpendicular diameters of any measurable lesion

Disease Free Survival
Time from documentation of complete response until disease relapse or death

Overall Survival
Time from treatment until time of death

which are not hormonally responsive or inadequate suppression of the endogenous hormones which stimulate tumor growth.[259]

Biologic Therapy

Biologic therapy includes agents which produce antitumor effects primarily through the action of natural host defense mechanisms.[260] Various cells making up the immune system and factors they secrete are believed to play a role in the host's response to human tumors. (See Table 90.16.) The intact immune system most likely protects the host against malignant cells as well as infectious pathogens. This is supported, for example, by the observation of a higher incidence of cancer in patients with the acquired immunodeficiency disorders (e.g., AIDS) and other primary and secondary immunodeficiency disorders. Also, spontaneous regression of some malignancies have been reported occasionally,[261] and in some instances, these have occurred during periods of immune activation (such as an acute bacterial infection).[262,263] The incidence of many cancers also is higher in neonates and in the elderly, groups whose immune systems may not be functioning optimally.

Sophisticated immunologic techniques and recombinant DNA and hybridoma technologies have further elucidated the role of the immune system in tumor surveillance. Subsets of T lymphocytes can recognize and lyse autologous tumor cells while not affecting autologous normal cells.[260] Specific cytokines produced by cells of the immune system (either lymphokines produced by lymphocytes or monokines produced by monocytes) regulate their activity. (See Table 90.16.) Thus, the ability to produce large quantities of these cytokines through recombinant DNA technology has opened a new era in the immunologic treatment of cancer.

Immunotherapy Strategies

Immunotherapy strategies used to treat cancer generally are divided into active and passive approaches.[260] Active immunotherapy attempts to induce immune responsiveness by the host against the tumor through specific and nonspecific strategies. Nonspecific strategies include the use of general immunostimulants which produce a response against a variety of antigens, while specific strategies attempt to induce a response to a specific tumor antigen. In passive immunotherapy, immunologically active cells or antibodies which have the ability to mediate an antitumor response are given to the tumor-bearing host.[260,264] The term adoptive immunotherapy often is used to describe the use of cells in passive immunotherapy. Examples of active and passive immunotherapeutic strategies which are in clinical use or evaluation are listed in Table 90.17.

Interferon Alfa

The first recombinant cytokine to become available for the treatment of cancer was interferon alfa. Interferon alfa affects tumor cells by several different mechanisms including: 1) a direct antiproliferative effect; 2) immunomodulatory effects on natural killer cells, T-cells, B-cells, and macrophages; 3) induction of tumor cell antigens, and 4) differentiating effects on tumor cells. Alfa interferon has demonstrated antitumor effects in several human malignancies. Currently, evaluations of interferon alfa in combination with radiation therapy, other biologic therapies, and cytotoxic chemotherapy are underway. Most patients experience a flu-like illness (i.e., fever, chills, myalgias) following the initial doses of interferon; however, tolerance to these effects develops within one to two weeks. The symptoms of dose-limiting toxicity include profound fatigue, weakness, anorexia, weight loss, lethargy, and disordered mentation. Other organ system toxicities occur less commonly.[265–267]

Interleukin-2 (IL-2)

Interleukin-2 is a lymphokine which has numerous immunoregulatory functions and is produced by activated T-cells. Its primary effect is stimulation of activated T-cell proliferation.[268] Lymphoid cells incubated with IL-2 develop the capacity to lyse tumor cells [lymphokine-activated killer cells (LAK cells)].[269,270] This observation served as the basis for the development of adoptive immunotherapies.[260]

Initial studies used priming doses of IL-2 followed by leukapheresis and incubation of lymphocytes in additional IL-2 to generate LAK cells. These cells then were reinfused in conjunction with IL-2 administration.[271,272] Evidence of tumor regression was observed in patients with advanced tumors such as renal cell carcinoma and malignant melanoma which are generally refractory to other forms of treatment. Subsequent studies using high doses of IL-2 alone (without LAK cells) also have reported responses in similar patients with advanced disease.[273] In all studies, however, toxicity has been severe and dose related. Most serious toxicities (hypotension, pulmonary edema, oliguria, increased bilirubin) appear to be related to a diffuse capillary leak which develops during IL-2 therapy; these resolve promptly after therapy is discontinued. Recently, lower doses of IL-2 that produce less toxicity have demonstrated antitumor responses in renal cell carcinoma.[274–276]

Handling of Cytotoxic Drugs
Impact Upon the Pharmacy

9. **The administrator of a health plan recently has announced that 2 medical oncologists will be joining the profes-**

Table 90.16	Clinically Useful Tumor Markers
Tumor Marker	**Cancers Associated with ↑ Levels**
Alpha fetoprotein	Liver, testis
CA-125	Ovary
Carcinoembryonic antigen	Colon, lung, breast
Human chorionic gonadotropin	Trophoblastic tumors, germ cells tumors of testis
Immunoglobulins	Multiple myeloma
Prostatic acid phosphatase	Prostate
Prostate-specific antigen	Prostate

Table 90.17	Immune Response to Neoplastic Growth
Cell-Mediated Response	
T-cells	Recognize tumor antigen. Lyse tumor cells (following activation). Secrete cytokines
Natural killer cells	Lyse tumor cells
Macrophages	Destroy tumor cells by both lysis and phagocytosis
Cytokines (secreted by T-cells)[a]	*Interleukin 2:* ↑ the number and lytic activity of NK cells
	Interferons: simulate NK cell and macrophage activity
Humoral Response	
Immunoglobulins[a]	In the presence of complement, both IgM and some types of IgG can directly lyse tumor cells
Antibodies	Antibodies are produced against antigen expressed on tumor cells

[a] IgG = Immunoglobulin G; IgM = Immunoglobulin M; NK = Natural killer.

sional staff. In the past, patients were referred to outside oncologists and no cytotoxic drugs were prepared or administered at the clinics. What implications will the addition of these physicians have on the pharmacy department?

The impact of the new oncologists can be divided into three areas: 1) budgetary impact; 2) the development of policies and procedures for handling cytotoxic drugs; and 3) a staff development program to educate the pharmacy staff about the safe handling procedures for chemotherapeutic agents and their clinical use. The budgetary impact includes the effects of the additional workload on personnel time, the impact on the drug budget, and the purchase of equipment and supplies which will be necessary to implement the new cytotoxic handling procedures. To accurately predict the first two budgetary items, a pharmacist should meet with the oncologists to discuss the anticipated volume of chemotherapy orders and the drugs which must be added to the formulary (e.g., cytotoxics, hormones, antiemetics, analgesics). Other aspects of the oncologists' practice which could affect the pharmacy department include the use of investigational drugs, the development of an ambulatory infusion program, and clinical pharmacy services.

Risks

8. **What are the potential risks of handling cytotoxic drugs and what resources are available to assist the director and the pharmacy staff in the development of policies and procedures?**

For over a decade, the potential hazards of cytotoxic drugs have received considerable attention. Many of these drugs are carcinogenic, teratogenic, or mutagenic in animal models or when used therapeutically.[277–282] The danger to health care personnel handling such agents results from both the inherent toxicities of the drugs and the extent to which the workers are exposed during drug handling.[283] Various studies have attempted to assess the impact of occupational exposure of hazardous drugs on health care workers. These have included measurements of urine mutagenicity, chromosomal damage, and drug absorption.[283–289] Although somewhat controversial, the documentation of urine mutagenicity or chromosomal damage was thought to be a direct result of cytotoxic exposure. Other reports correlate reproductive and birth defect risks in pregnant workers handling cytotoxic drugs.[290,291] Results of these reports together with the toxicities observed in patients receiving therapeutic doses led the American Society of Hospital Pharmacists to conclude that ''health care workers exposed to hazardous drugs during their work may be absorbing these drugs and may be at risk for adverse outcomes.''[283]

In response to the concerns regarding occupational exposure to hazardous drugs, several groups have published guidelines for the handling of these agents in the workplace (i.e., storage, preparation, administration, disposal).[283,292–295] These documents will be very helpful to the pharmacy department when developing policies and procedures.

Policies and Procedures

9. What specific policies and procedures are necessary and what other departments should be consulted during the development and implementation of the handling guidelines?

Policies must be developed regarding the entire scope of potential occupational exposures within the workplace. These include: 1) workers' right to know of potential hazards; 2) education and training of workers involved with hazardous drug handling; 3) quality assurance and monitoring of adherence to handling procedures; and 4) guidelines for pregnant and nursing women or those attempting to become pregnant or father a child.

Specific procedures should be developed which detail the appropriate handling of hazardous drugs during all aspects of institutional storage, use, and disposal. These include: 1) procedures for appropriate storage in the receiving and storeroom areas; 2) preparation of parenteral formulations; 3) manipulation and dispensing of oral and topical formulations; 4) administration of parenteral drugs; 5) clean up of spills; 6) management of acute exposures; and 7) disposal of hazardous drugs and supplies used in their preparation and disposal. In addition, if the oncology program includes ambulatory infusion or homecare components, procedures must be developed regarding the appropriate handling and disposal of these products in the home.

Other departments which may be impacted by these guidelines include the medical staff, nursing, housekeeping (in the clean-up of spills and equipment), maintenance (upkeep of equipment), and the receiving area (where cytotoxic drugs may be received from suppliers). In addition, the institutional safety office and legal staff also should be consulted.

Necessary Equipment and Supplies

10. What equipment and supplies are necessary for the handling of hazardous drugs?

Various equipment and supplies can minimize occupational exposure in the healthcare workplace thus, protecting both the worker and the environment. Since most patients who will be receiving these drugs are immunosuppressed, it is also of great importance to maintain the sterile integrity of all parenteral products. All handling guidelines recommend that manipulations (e.g., reconstitution, admixing) of hazardous drugs should be done in a Class II biological safety cabinet to provide maximum protection for the worker and the work environment. Workers also should wear gloves (one or two pairs) and a disposable, closed-front gown of lint-free low permeability fabric with a solid front, long sleeves, and knit cuffs. In addition, only syringes and IV sets with luer-lock fittings should be used. Final products (i.e., syringes, IV bags or bottles) should be placed in sealable containers such as zipper closure plastic bags and clearly labeled as a hazardous drug. Other supplies which may be necessary for the sterile product preparation area include plastic-back paper liners for the bottom surface of the biological safety cabinet and 0.2 μm hydrophobic filters.

The disposal of hazardous waste also requires specific receptacles which are placed in all areas where these drugs are used. These must be disposed of according to institutional and/or state and local regulations. Materials for the clean up of spills (e.g., absorbent material, plastic bags or containers, protective garments) also must be kept in all areas where hazardous drugs are stored, prepared, or administered.

References

1 **Miller BA et al.** SEER cancer statistics review: 1973–1991. Bethesda, MD: National Cancer Institute, 1994; NIH Publication no. 94-2789.

2 **Wingo PA et al.** Cancer statistics, 1995. CA Cancer J Clin. 1995;45:8.

3 **Squire J, Phillips RA.** Genetic basis of cancer. In: Tannock IF, Hill RP, eds. The Basic Science of Oncology. 2nd ed. New York: Pergamon Press; 1992: 41–60.

4 **Shields PG, Harris CC.** Principles of carcinogenesis: chemical. In: DeVita VT et al., eds. Cancer. Principles and Practice of Oncology. 4th ed. Philadelphia: Lippincott; 1993:200–12.

5 **Herity B et al.** The role of tobacco and alcohol in the aetiology of lung and larynx cancer. Br J Cancer. 1982;46:961.

6 **Willett WC et al.** Moderate alcohol consumption and the risk of breast cancer. N Engl J Med. 1987;316:1174.

7 **Doll R, Peto R.** The Causes of Cancer. New York: Oxford University Press; 1981.

8 **Herbst AL.** Clear cell adenocarcinoma and the current status of DES-exposed females. Cancer. 1981;48:484.

9 **Huggins GR, Zucker PK.** Oral contraceptives and neoplasia. 1987 update. Fertil Steril. 1987;47:733.

10 **Hoover R, Fraumeni JF.** Drug-induced cancer. Cancer. 1981;47:1071.

11 **Hall EJ.** Principles of carcinogenesis: physical. In: DeVita VT et al., eds. Cancer. Principles and Practice of Oncology. 4th ed. Philadelphia: Lippincott; 1993:213–37.

12 **Minden MD, Pawson AJ.** Oncogenes. In: Tannock IF, Will RP, eds. The Basic Science of Oncology. 2nd ed. New York: Pergamon Press; 1992:61–87.

13 **Weinberg RA.** Oncogenes of spontaneous and chemically induced tumors. Adv Cancer Res. 1982;36:149.

14 **Sukumar S et al.** A transforming ras gene in tumorigenic guinea pig cell lines initiated by diverse chemical carcinogens. Science. 1984;223:1197.

15 **Wattenberg LW.** Chemoprevention of cancer. Cancer Res. 1985;45:1.

16 **Kelloff GJ et al.** Progressive cancer chemoprevention: perspectives on agent selection and short term clinical intervention trials. Cancer Res. 1994; 54(Suppl.):2015s.

17 **Malone WF et al.** Chemoprevention and modern cancer prevention. Preventive Medicine. 1989;18:553.

18 **Hannes BS et al.** Plasma antioxidant vitamins and subsequent cancer mortality in the 12-year follow-up of the prospective Basel study. Am J Epidemiol. 1991;133:766.

19 **Paul K et al.** Dietary antioxidants and the risk of lung cancer. Am J Epidemiol. 1991;134:471.

20 **Hong WK et al.** 13-cis-retinoic acid in the treatment of oral leukoplakia. N Engl J Med. 1986;315:1501.

21 **The α-Tocopherol, β Carotene Cancer Prevention Study Group.** The effect of vitamin E and β carotene on the incidence of lung cancer and other cancer in male smokers. N Engl J Med. 1994;330:1029.

22 **Ziegler RG.** Vegetables, fruits, and carotenoids, and the risk of cancer. Am J Clin Nutri. 1991;53:251.

23 **Thun MJ.** Aspirin use and reduced risk of fatal colon cancer. N Engl J Med. 1991;325:1593.

24 **Burkitt DP.** Epidemiology of cancer of the colon and rectum. Cancer. 1971: 28:3.

25 **Buell P.** Changing incidence of breast cancer in Japanese American women. J Natl Cancer Inst. 1973;51:1479.

26 **Mackie RM et al.** Personal risk factor chart for cutaneous melanoma. Lancet. 1989;2(8661):487.

27 **Lynch HT, Fusarp RM.** The surgeon, genetics and malignant melanoma. Arch Surg. 1992;127:317.

28 **Zanowiak P.** Protecting the skin from solar radiation. U.S. Pharmacist. 1993: 14.

29 **Nowell PC.** The clonal evolution of tumor cell populations. Science. 1976; 194:23.

30 **Heppner GH.** Tumor heterogeneity. Cancer Res. 1984;44:2259.

31 **Buick RN, Tannock IF.** Properties of malignant cells. In: Tannock IF, Hill RP, eds. The Basic Science of Oncology. 2nd ed. New York: Pergamon Press; 1992:139–53.

32 **Shapiro JR, Shapiro WR.** Clonal tumor cell heterogeneity. Prog Exp Tumor Res. 1984;27:49.

33 **Tannock IF.** Cell proliferation. In: Tannock IF, Hill RP, eds. The Basic Science of Oncology. 2nd ed. New York: Pergamon Press; 1992:154–77.

34 **Barlogie B et al.** Flow cytometry in clinical cancer research. Cancer Res. 1983;43:3982.

35 **Chabner BA.** Clinical strategies for cancer treatment: the role of drugs. In: Chabner BA, Collins JM, eds. Cancer Chemotherapy. Principles and Practice. Philadelphia: Lippincott; 1990:1–15.

36 **Hill RP.** Metastasis. In: Tannock IF, Hill RP, eds. The Basic Science of Oncology. 2nd ed. New York: Pergamon Press; 1992:178–94.

37 **Sugarbaker EV.** Patterns of metastasis in human malignancies. Cancer Biol Rev. 1981;2:235.

38 **Mettlin C, Dodd CD.** The American Cancer Society guidelines for the cancer-related check: an update. CA Cancer J Clin. 1991;41:279–82.

39 **Bloom JR.** Early detection of cancer. Cancer. 1994;74:1464.

40 **American Joint Committee on Cancer.** Manual for cancer staging. Philadelphia: Lippincott; 1993.

41 **Beahrs OH et al.,** eds. American Joint Committee on Cancer. Manual for staging of cancer, fourth edition. Philadelphia: Lippincott; 1993:161.

42 **Longo DL et al.** Twenty years of MOPP chemotherapy for Hodgkin's disease. J Clin Oncol. 1986;4:1295.

43 **Rosenberg SA.** Principles of surgical oncology. In: DeVita VT et al., eds. Cancer. Principles and Practice of Oncology, 4th ed. Philadelphia: Lippincott; 1993:238–47.

44 **Silberman AW.** Surgical debulking of tumors. Surg Gynecol Obstet. 1982; 155:577.

45 **Rubin P, Siemann D.** Principles of radiation oncology and cancer radiotherapy. In: Rubin P, ed. Clinical Oncology for Medical Students and Physicians. 6th ed. New York: American Cancer Society; 1983:58–71.

46 **Perez CA, Brady LW.** Introduction. In: Perez CA, Brady LW, eds. Principles and Practice of Radiation Oncology. Philadelphia: Lippincott; 1987:1–19.

47 **Magrath IT.** New directions in cancer treatment: an overview. In: Magrath I, ed. New Directions in Cancer Treatment. New York: Springer-Verlag; 1989:1–27.

48 **Hersh SM.** Chemical and biological warfare: America's hidden arsenal. New York: Bobbs Merril; 1968.

49 **Marshall EK Jr.** Historical perspectives in chemotherapy. In: Goldin A, Hawking IF, eds. Advances in Chemotherapy, Vol. 1. New York: Academic Press; 1964:1–8.

50 **Newell D et al.** N-methylantitumor agents: a distinct class of anticancer drugs? Cancer Chemother Pharmacol. 1987;19:91.

51 **Foster BJ et al.** Hexamethylmelamine: a critical review of an active drug. Cancer Treat Rev. 1986;13:197.

52 **D'Incalci et al.** Variable oral absorption of hexamethylmelamine in man. Cancer Treat Rep. 1983;62:2117.

53 **Wilson WL et al.** Phase II study of hexamethylmelamine (NSC-13875). Cancer. 1969;23:132.

54 **Chabner BA.** Enzyme therapy: L-asparaginase. In: Chabner BA, Collins JM, eds. Cancer Chemotherapy. Principles and Practice. Philadelphia: Lippincott; 1990:397–407.

55 **Peterson RC et al.** Immunological responses to L-asparaginase. J Clin Invest. 1971;1080.

56 **Capizzi RL et al.** L-asparaginase: clinical, biochemical, pharmacological and immunological studies. Ann Intern Med. 1971;74:893.

57 **Chabner BA.** Bleomycin. In: Chabner BA, Collins JM, eds. Cancer Chemotherapy. Principles and Practice. Philadelphia: Lippincott; 1990:341–55.

58 **Crooke ST et al.** Bleomycin serum pharmacokinetics as determined by a radioimmunoassay and a microbiologic assay in a patient with compromised renal function. Cancer. 1977;39:1430.

59 **Bennett WM et al.** Fatal pulmonary bleomycin toxicity in cisplatin-induced acute renal failure. Cancer Treat Rep. 1980;64:921.

60 **Crooke ST et al.** Effects of variations in renal function on the clinical pharmacology of bleomycin administered as an IV bolus. Cancer Treat Rep. 1977;61:1631.

61 **Blum RH et al.** A clinical review of bleomycin—a new antineoplastic agent. Cancer. 1973;31:903.

62 **Burrough's Wellcome Co.** Myleran package insert. 1989.

63 **Knoben JE, Anderson PO, eds.** Clinical Drug Data. 6th ed. Hamilton: Drug Intelligence Publications; 1988.

64 **Heard BE, Cooke RA.** Busulfan lung. Thorax. 1968;23:187.

65 **Wilson JKV.** Pulmonary toxicity of antineoplastic drugs. Cancer Treat Rep. 1978;62:2003.

66 **Reed E, Kohn KW.** Platinum analogues. In: Chabner BA, Collins JM, eds. Cancer Chemotherapy. Principles and Practice. Philadelphia: Lippincott; 1990:465–90.

67 **Oguri S et al.** Clinical pharmacokinetics of carboplatin. J Clin Pharmacol. 1988;28:1223.

68 **Paraplatin manufacturer's package insert.** Bristol-Myers Oncology Division. 1989.

69 **Egorin MJ et al.** Pharmacokinetics and dosage reduction of cis-diammine (1,1-cyclobutanedicarboxylato) platinum in patients with impaired renal function. Cancer Res. 1984;44:5432.

70 **Calvert AH et al.** Carboplatin dosage: prospective evaluation of a simple formula based on renal function. J Clin Oncol. 1989;7:1748.

71 **DeVita VT et al.** The physiological disposition of the carcinostatic 1,3-bis(2-chloroethyl)-1-nitrosourea (BCNU) in man and animals. Clin Pharmacol Ther. 1965;8:566.

72 **Young RC et al.** Treatment of advanced Hodgkin's disease with [1,3 bis (2-chloroethyl)-1-nitrosourea] BCNU. N Engl J Med. 1971;285:475.

73 **Durant JR et al.** Pulmonary toxicity associated with bischloroethylnitrosourea (BCNU). Ann Intern Med. 1979; 90:191.

74 **Colvin M, Chabner BA.** Alkylating agents. In: Chabner BA, Collins JM, eds. Cancer Chemotherapy. Principles and Practice. Philadelphia: Lippincott; 1990:276–313.

75 **McLean A et al.** Pharmacokinetics and metabolism of chlorambucil in patients with malignant disease. Cancer Treat Rev. 1979;6(Suppl.):33.

76 **Adair CG et al.** Can food affect the bioavailability of chlorambucil in patients with haematological malignancies? Cancer Chemother Pharmacol. 1986;17:99.

77 **Lane SD et al.** Fatal interstitial pneumonitis following high-dose chlorambucil therapy for chronic lymphocytic leukemia. Cancer. 1981;47:32.

78 **Saven A, Piro LD.** 2-chlorodeoxyadenosine: a newer purine analog active in the treatment of indolent lymphoid malignancies. Ann Intern Med. 1994;120:784.

79 **Baltz JK, Montello MJ.** Cladribine for the treatment of hematologic malignancies. Clin Pharm. 1993;12:805.

80 **Beutler E.** Cladribine (2-chlorodeoxyadenoside). Lancet. 1992;340:952.

81 **Gormley PE et al.** Kinetics of cis-dichlorodiammineplatinum. Clin Pharmacol Ther. 1979;25:351.

82 **Weiner MW, Jacobs C.** Mechanism of cisplatin nephrotoxicity. Fed Proc. 1983;42:2794.

83 **Finley RS et al.** Cisplatin nephrotoxicity: a summary of preventive interventions. Drug Intell Clin Pharm. 1985; 19:362.

84 **Bohein K, Bichler E.** Cisplatin-induced ototoxicty: audiometric findings and experimental chochlear pathology. Arch Otorhinolaryngol. 1985;242:1.

85 **Legha SS, Dimery IW.** High-dose cisplatin administration without hypertonic saline: observation of disabling neurotoxicity. J Clin Oncol. 1985;3:1373.

86 **Brock N et al.** Activation of cyclophosphamide in man and animals. Cancer. 1971;6:1512.

87 **Bagley CM et al.** Clinical pharmacology of cyclophosphamide. Cancer Res. 1973;33:226.

88 **Mouridsen HT, Jacobsen E.** Pharmacokinetics of cyclophosphamide in renal failure. Acta Pharmacol Toxicol. 1975;36:409.

89 **Juma FD et al.** Pharmacokinetics of cyclophosphamide and alkylating activity in man after intravenous and oral administration. Br J Clin Pharmacol. 1979;8:209.

90 **Grochow LB, Colvin M.** Clinical pharmacokinetics of cyclophosphamide. Clin Pharmacokinet. 1979;4:380.

91 **Chabner BA.** Cytidine analogs. In: Chabner BA, Collins JM, eds. Cancer Chemotherapy. Principles and Practice. Philadelphia: Lippincott; 1990:154–79.

92 **Ho DHW, Frei E.** Clinical pharmacology of 1-B-D-arabinofuranosylcytosine. Clin Pharmacol Ther. 1971;12:944.

93 **Van Prooijen R et al.** Pharmacokinetics of cytosine arabinoside in acute myeloid leukemia. Clin Pharmacol Ther. 1977;21:744.

94 **Slavin RE et al.** Cytosine arabinoside-induced gastrointestinal toxic alterations in sequential chemotherapeutic protocols. Cancer. 1978;42:1747.

95 **Averbach SD.** Nonclassic alkylating agents. In: Chabner BA, Collins JM, eds. Cancer Chemotherapy. Principles and Practice. Philadelphia: Lippincott; 1990:314–40.

96 **Breithaupt H et al.** Pharmacokinetics of dacarbazine (DTIC) and its metabolite 5-aminoimidazole-4-carboxamide (AIC) following different dose schedules. Cancer Chemother Pharmacol. 1982;9:103.

97 **Loo TL et al.** Mechanism of action and pharmacology studies with DTIC (NSC-45388). Cancer Treat Rep. 1976; 60:149.

98 **Buesa JM et al.** Phase I trial of intermittent high-dose dacarbazine. Cancer Treat Rep. 1984;68:499.

99 **Feaux de L et al.** Acute liver dystrophy with thrombosis of hepatic veins: a fatal complication of dacarbazine therapy. Cancer Treat Rep. 1983;67:784.

100 **Cici G et al.** Fatal hepatic vascular toxicity of DTIC: is it really a rare event? Cancer. 1988;61:1988.

101 **Kamawata J, Imoniski M.** Interaction of actinomycin with DNA. Nature. 1960;187:1112.

102 **Tattersall MHM et al.** Pharmacokinetics of actinomycin D in patients with malignant melanoma. Clin Pharmacol Ther. 1975;17:701.

103 **Frei E.** The clinical use of actinomycin. Cancer Chemother Rep. 1974;58:49.

104 **Myers CE, Chabner BA.** Anthracyclines. In: Chabner BA, Collins JM, eds. Cancer Chemotherapy. Principles and Practice. Philadelphia: Lippincott; 1990:356–81.

105 **Tewey KM et al.** Intercalative antitumor drugs interfere with the breakage-reunion reaction of mammalian DNA topoisomerase. J Biol Chem. 1984;259:9182.

106 **Bachur NR et al.** A general mechanism for microsomal activation of quinone anticancer agents to free radicals. Cancer Res. 1977;38:1745.

107 **Von Hoff DD et al.** Daunomycin-induced cardiotoxicity in children and adults. Am J Med. 1977;62:100.

108 **Huffman DH et al.** Daunorubicin metabolism in acute nonlymphocytic leukemia. Clin Pharmacol Ther. 1972;13:895.

109 **Gianni L.** The biochemical basis of anthracycline toxicity and antitumor action. Rev Biochem Toxicol. 1983;5:1.

110 **Legha SS et al.** Reduction of doxorubicin cardiotoxicity by prolonged continuous intravenous infusion. Ann Intern Med. 1982;96:133.

111 **Von Hoff DD et al.** Risk factors for doxorubicin-induced congestive heart failure. Ann Intern Med. 1979;91:710.

112 **Benjamin RS et al.** Adriamycin chemotherapy—efficacy, safety, and pharmacological basis of an intermittent single high-dosage schedule. Cancer. 1974;33:19.

113 **Hauser AR, Merryman R.** Estramustine phosphate sodium. Drug Intell Clin Pharm. 1984;18:368.

114 **Forshell GP et al.** The absorption, metabolism, and excretion of Estracyt (NSC 89199) in patients with prostatic cancer. Invest Urol. 1976;14:128.

115 **Arbuck SG et al.** Etoposide pharmacokinetics in patients with normal and abnormal organ function. J Clin Oncol. 1986;4:1690.

116 **Smyth RD et al.** Bioavailability and pharmacokinetics of etoposide (VP-16). Semin Oncol. 1985;12(Suppl. 2):48.

117 **Stewart DJ et al.** Bioavailability, pharmacokinetics, and clinical effects of an oral preparation of etoposide. Cancer Treat Rep. 1985;69:269.

118 **Harvey VJ et al.** The pharmacokinetics of VP-16 (etoposide) and bioavailability following different methods of administration. Br J Pharmacol. 1984;17:204P.

119 **Bender RA et al.** Plant alkaloids. In: Chabner BA, Collins JM, eds. Cancer Chemotherapy. Principles and Practice. Philadelphia: Lippincott; 1990:253–75.

120 **D'Incalci M et al.** Pharmacokinetics of etoposide in patients with abnormal renal and hepatic function. Cancer Res. 1986;46:2566.

121 **O'Dwyer PJ et al.** Etoposide (VP-16-213): current status of an active anticancer drug. N Engl J Med. 1985;312:692.

122 **Grem JL.** Fluorinated pyrimidines. In: Chabner BA, Collins JM, eds. Cancer Chemotherapy. Principles and Practice. Philadelphia: Lippincott; 1990:180–224.

123 **Santi DV et al.** Mechanisms of interactions of thymidylate synthetase with 5-fluorodeoxyuridylate. Biochem. 1974; 13:471.

124 **Wilkinson DS et al.** The inhibition of ribosomal RNA synthesis and maturation in Novikiff hepatoma cells by 5-fluorouridine. Cancer Res. 1975;35:3014.

125 **Hood MA, Finley RS.** Fludarabine: a review. DICP. 1991;25:518.

126 **Plunkett W et al.** Metabolism and action of fludarabine phosphate. Semin Oncol. 1990;17(Suppl. 8):3.

127 **Malspeis L et al.** Pharmacokinetics of 2-F-araA (9-B-arabinofuranosyl-2-fluoradenine) in cancer patients during the phase I clinical investigation of fludarabine phosphate. Semin Oncol. 1990;17(Suppl. 8):18.

128 **Chun HG et al.** Central nervous system toxicity of fludarabine phosphate. Cancer Treat Rep. 1986;70:1225.

129 **Weiss HD et al.** Neurotoxicity of commonly used antineoplastic agents. N Engl J Med. 1974;291:75, 127.

130 **Donagin WG.** Clinical toxicity of chemotherapeutic agents: dermatologic toxicity. Semin Oncol. 1982;9:14.

131 **Spaeth PAJ et al.** Idarubicin versus daunorubicin: preclinical and clinical pharmacokinetic studies. Semin Oncol. 1989;16(Suppl. 2):2.

132 **Neidle S.** A hypothesis concerning possible new derivative of daunorubicin and Adriamycin with enhanced DNA-binding properties. Cancer Treat Rep. 1977;61:928.

133 **Berman E et al.** Phase I and clinical pharmacology studies of intravenous and oral administration of 4-demethoxydaunorubicin in patients with advanced cancer. Cancer Res. 1983;43:6096.

134 **Wiernik PH et al.** A multicenter trial of cytarabine plus idarubicin or daunorubicin as induction therapy for adult nonlymphocytic leukemia. Semin Oncol. 1989;16(Suppl. 2):25.

135 **Vogler WR et al.** A phase-three trial comparing daunorubicin or idarubicin combined with cytosine arabinoside in acute myelogenous leukemia. Semin Oncol. 1989;16:21.

136 **Bristol-Myers Oncology Division.** Ifex package insert. Dec 1992.

137 **Allen LM et al.** Studies on the human pharmacokinetics of ifosfamide (NSC-109724). Cancer Treat Rep. 1976;60:451.

138 **Zalupski M et al.** Ifosfamide. J Natl Cancer Instit. 1988;80:556.

139 **Pratt CB et al.** Central nervous system toxicity following the treatment of pediatric patients with ifosfamide/mesna. J Clin Oncol. 1986;4:1253.

140 **Calabresi P, Parks RE.** Antiproliferative agents and drugs used for immunosuppression. In: Gilman AG et al., eds. The Pharmacological Basis of Therapeutics. 6th ed. New York: MacMillan; 1985:1247–1308.

141 **Bristol Myers Oncology Division.** CeeNu package insert. Dec 1990.

142 **Wheeler GP et al.** Comparison of the properties of metabolites of CCNU. Biochem Pharmacol. 1977;26:2331.

143 **Merck, Sharp and Dohme.** Mustargen package insert. July 1987.

144 **Spitz S.** The histological effects of nitrogen mustards on human tumors and tissues. Cancer. 1948;1:383.

145 **Horning SJ et al.** Female reproductive potential after treatment for Hodgkin's disease. N Engl J Med. 1981;304:1377.

146 **Alberts DS et al.** Oral melphalan kinetics. Clin Pharmacol Ther. 1979;26:737.

147 **Taetle R et al.** Pulmonary histopathologic changes associated with melphalan therapy. Cancer. 1978;42:1239.

148 **Adair CG et al.** Renal function in the elimination of oral melphalan in patients with multiple myeloma. Cancer Chemother Pharmacol. 1986;17:185.

149 **McCormack JJ, Johns DG.** Purine and purine nucleoside antimetabolites. In: Chabner BA, Collins JM, eds. Cancer Chemotherapy. Principles and Practice. Philadelphia: Lippincott; 1990:234–52.

150 **Zimm S et al.** Variable bioavailability of oral 6-mercaptopurine: is maintenance chemotherapy in acute lymphoblastic leukemia being optimally delivered? N Engl J Med. 1983;308:1005.

151 **Allegra CJ et al.** The effect of methotrexate on intracellular folate pools in human MCF-7 breast cancer cells: evidence for direct inhibition of purine synthesis. J Biol Chem. 1986;261:6478.

152 **Matherly LH et al.** The effects of 4-aminoantifolates on 5-formyltetrahydrofolate metabolism in L1210 cells. J Biol Chem. 1987;262:710.

153 **Kearny PJ et al.** Unpredictable serum levels after oral methotrexate in children with acute lymphoblastic leukemia. Cancer Chemother Pharmacol. 1979;3:117.

154 **Wan SH et al.** Effect of route of administration and effusion on methotrexate pharmacokinetics. Cancer Res. 1974;34:3487.

155 **Chabner BA et al.** Methotrexate disposition in humans: case studies in ovarian cancer and following high dose infusion. Drug Metab Rev. 1978;8:107.

156 **Crom WR, Evans WE.** Methotrexate. In: Evans WE et al., eds. Applied Pharmacokinetics: Principles of Therapeutic Drug Monitoring. 3rd ed. Vancouver: Applied Therapeutics; 1992:29-1.

157 **Bristol-Myers Oncology Division.** Lysodren package insert. May 1987.

158 **Gutierres ML et al.** Mitotane. Cancer Treatment Rev. 1980;7:49.

159 **Calabresi P, Chabner BA.** Chemotherapy of neoplastic diseases. In: Gilman AG et al., eds. Goodman and Gilmans: The Pharmacological Basis of Therapeutics. 8th ed. New York: Pergamon Press; 1990:1202–263.

160 **Foye WD et al.** DNA binding specificity and RNA polymerase inhibitory activity of bis(aminoalkyl)anthraquinones and bis(methythio) vinyl quinolinium iodides. J Pharm Sci. 1982;71:253.

161 **Lederle laboratories.** Novantrone package insert. May 1994.

162 **Batra VJ et al.** Pharmacokinetics of mitoxantrone in man and laboratory animals. Drug Metabol Rev. 1986;17:311.

163 **Shenkenberg RD, VonHoff DD.** Mitoxantrone: a new anticancer drug with significant clinical activity. Ann Intern Med. 1986;105:67.

164 **Benjamin RS et al.** Evaluation of mitoxantrone cardiac toxicity by nuclear angiography and endomyocardial biopsy: an update. New Drugs. 1985;3:117.

165 **Underferth DV et al.** Cardiac evaluation of mitoxantrone. Cancer Treat Rep. 1983;67:343.

166 **Smyth JF et al.** The clinical pharmacology of mitoxantrone. Cancer Chemother Pharmacol. 1986;17:149.

167 **Rowinsky EK et al.** Taxol: the first of the taxanes, an important new class of antitumor agents. Semin Oncol. 1992; 19:646.

168 **Gregory RE, DeLisa AF.** Paclitaxel: a new antineoplastic agent for refractory ovarian cancer. Clin Pharm. 1993; 12:401.

169 **Weiss RB et al.** Hypersensitivity reactions from taxol. J Clin Oncol. 1990; 8:1263.

170 **Rowinsky EK et al.** Cardiac disturbances during the administration of taxol. J Clin Oncol. 1991;9:1704.

171 **Lipton RB et al.** Taxol produces a predominantly sensory neuropathy. Neurol. 1989;39:368.

172 **O'Dwyer PJ et al.** 2′-deoxycoformycin (pentostatin) for lymphoid malignancies. Ann Inter Med. 1988;108:733.

173 **Cassileth PA et al.** Pentostatin induces durable remissions in hairy cell leukemia. J Clin Oncol. 1991;9:243.

174 **Kraut EH et al.** Immunosuppressive effects of pentostatin. J Clin Oncol. 1990;8:848.

175 **Hande KR et al.** Cimetidine prolongs half life of procarbazine and hexamethylmelamine. Proc Am Soc Clin Oncol. 1983;24:287. Abstract.

176 **DeVita VT et al.** Monoamine oxidase inhibition by a new carcinostatic agent procarbazine. Proc Soc Biol Med. 1965; 120:561.

177 **Spivack SD.** Procarbazine. Ann Intern Med. 1974;81:795.

178 **Adolphe AB et al.** Fate of streptozotocin (NSC 85998) in patients with advanced cancer. Cancer Chemother Rep. 1975;59:547.

179 **Bhuyan BK et al.** Tissue distribution of streptozotocin (NSC-85998). Cancer Chemother Rep. 1974;58:157.

180 **Karunanayake EH et al.** The metabolic fate and elimination of streptozotocin. Biochem Soc Trans. 1975;3:410.

181 **Clark PI, Slevein ML.** The clinical pharmacology of etoposide and teniposide. Clin Pharmacokinet. 1987;12:223.

182 **O'Dwyer PJ et al.** Hypersensitivity reactions to teniposide (VM-26): an analysis. J Clin Oncol. 1986;4:1262.

183 **Pui CH et al.** Acute myeloid leukemia in children treated with epipodophyllotoxins for acute lymphoblastic leukemia. N Engl J Med. 1991;325:1682.

184 **Brox LW et al.** Clinical pharmacology of oral thioguanine in acute myelogenous leukemia. Cancer Chemother Pharmacol. 1981;6:35.

185 **Cohen BE et al.** Human plasma pharmacokinetics and urinary excretion of thiotepa and its metabolites. Cancer Treat Rep. 1986;70:859.

186 **Owellen RJ et al.** Inhibition of tubulin-microtubulin polymerization by drugs of the vinca alkaloid class. Cancer Res. 1976;36:1499.

187 **Carter SK et al.,** eds. Chemotherapy of Cancer, 3rd ed. New York: John Wiley & Sons; 1987:82–3.

188 **Weiss HD et al.** Neurotoxicity of some commonly used antineoplastic agents. N Engl J Med. 1974;291:127.

189 **Nelson RL.** The comparative clinical pharmacology and pharmacokinetics of vindesine, vincristine, and vinblastine in human patients with cancer. Med Pediatr Oncol. 1982;10:115.

190 **Bender RA.** The pharmacokinetics of H-vincristine in man. Clin Pharmacol Ther. 1977;22:430.

191 **Jackson DV.** Pharmacokinetics of vincristine in the cerebrospinal fluid. Cancer Res. 1981;41:1466.

192 **Chevalier TL et al.** Randomized study of vinorelbine and cisplatin versus vindesine and cisplatin versus vinorelbine alone in advanced non-small-cell lung cancer: results of a European multicenter trial including 612 patients. J Clin Oncol. 1994;12:360.

193 **O'Rourke M et al.** Survival advantage for patients with stage IV NSCLC treated with single agent navelbine in a randomized controlled trial. Proc Am Soc Clin Oncol. 1993;12:343. Abstract.

194 **Krikorian A et al.** Pharmacokinetics and metabolism of navelbine. Semin Oncol. 1989;16:21.

195 **Marty M et al.** Advances in vinca-alkaloids: navelbine. Nouv Rev Fr Haematol. 1989;31:77.

196 **Skipper HE et al.** Experimental evaluation of potential anticancer agents: XII. On the criteria and kinetics associated with "curability" of experiment leukemia. Cancer Chemother Rep. 1964;35:1–111.

197 **Skipper HE.** Reasons for success and failure in treatment of murine leukemias with the drugs now employed in treating human leukemias. Cancer Chemotherapy, Vol 1. Ann Arbor: University Microfilms International; 1978:1–166.

198 **DeVita VT.** Principles of chemotherapy. In: DeVita VT et al., eds. Cancer. Principles and Practice of Oncology. 3rd ed. Philadelphia: Lippincott; 1989:276–300.

199 **Hryniuk W.** The importance of dose intensity in the outcome of chemotherapy. In: DeVita VT et al., eds. Important Advances in Oncology 1988. Philadelphia: Lippincott; 1988:121–42.

200 **Skipper H.** Data and analysis having to do with the influence of dose intensity and duration of treatment (single drugs and combinations) on lethal toxicity and the therapeutic response of experimental neoplasms. Southern Research Institute. Booklets 1, 1986, and 2–13, 1987.

201 **DeVita VT et al.** The chemotherapy of lymphomas: looking back, moving forward. The Richard and Hinda Rosenthal Foundation Award Lecture. Cancer Res. 1987;47:5810.

202 **Levin L, Hryniuk W.** Dose intensity analysis of chemotherapy regimens in ovarian carcinoma. J Clin Oncol. 1987; 5:756.

203 **Cheson BD et al.** Autologous bone marrow transplantation. Ann Intern Med. 1989;110:51.

204 **Laver J, Moore MAS.** Clinical use of recombinant human hematopoietic

growth factors. J Natl Cancer Instit. 1989;81:1370.

205 **Morstyn G et al.** Clinical experience with recombinant human granulocyte colony-stimulating factor and granulocyte macrophage colony-stimulating factor. Semin Hematol. 1989;26(Suppl. 2):9.

206 **Antman KS et al.** Effect of recombinant human granulocyte-macrophage colony-stimulating factor on chemotherapy-induced myelosuppression. N Engl J Med. 1988;319:593.

207 **Goldie JH, Coldman AJ.** A mathematic model for relating the drug sensitivity of tumors to the spontaneous mutation rate. Cancer Treat Rep. 1979; 63:1727.

208 **Fox BW, Fox M, eds.** Antitumor drug resistance. Berlin: Springer Verlag; 1984.

209 **Tannock IF.** Experimental chemotherapy. In: Tannock IF, Hill RP, eds. The Basic Science of Oncology. New York: Pergamon; 1987:308–25.

210 **Biedler JL, Riehm J.** Cellular resistance to actinomycin D in Chinese hamster cells in vitro: cross-resistance, radioautographic and cytogenic studies. Cancer Res. 1970;30:1174.

211 **Juliano RL, Ling V.** A surface glycoprotein modulating drug permeability in Chinese hamster ovary cell mutants. Biochem Biophys Acta. 1976; 455:152.

212 **Bech-Hanson NT et al.** Pleiotropic phenotype of colchicine-resistant CHO cells: cross-resistance and collateral sensitivity. J Cell Physiol. 1976;88:23.

213 **Pommier Y et al.** Altered DNA topoisomerase II activity in Chinese hamster cells resistant to topoisomerase II inhibitors. Cancer Res. 1986;46:3075.

214 **Deffie AM et al.** Direct correlation between topoisomerase II activity and cytotoxicity in adriamycin-sensitive and -resistant P388 leukemia cell lines. Cancer Res. 1989;49:58.

215 **Hamburger AW, Salmon SE.** Primary bioassay of human tumor stem cells. Science. 1977;197:461.

216 **Salmon SE et al.** Clinical correlations of drug sensitivity in the human tumor stem cell assay. Recent Results Cancer Res. 1980;74:300.

217 **Tancini G et al.** Adjuvant CMF in breast cancer: comparative 5-year results of 12 versus 6 cycles. J Clin Oncol. 1983;1:2.

218 **Bull JM et al.** A randomized comparative trial of Adriamycin versus methotrexate in combination drug therapy. Cancer. 1978;41:1649.

219 **Tranum B et al.** Adriamycin in combination for the treatment of breast cancer. Cancer. 1978;41:2078.

220 **Smalley R et al.** A comparison of cyclophosphamide, Adriamycin, 5-fluorouracil (CAF) and cyclophosphamide, methotrexate, 5-fluorouracil, vincristine, prednisone (CMFVP) in patients with metastatic breast cancer. Cancer. 1977;40:625.

221 **Poon MA et al.** Biochemical modulation of fluorouracil: evidence of significant improvement of survival and quality of life in patients with advanced colorectal carcinoma. J Clin Oncol. 1989;7:1407.

222 **Petrelli N et al.** The modulation of fluorouracil with leucovorin in metastatic colorectal carcinoma: a prospective randomized phase III trial. J Clin Oncol. 1989;7:1419.

223 **Poon Ma et al.** Biochemical modulation of fluorouracil with leucovorin: confirmatory evidence of improved therapeutic efficacy in advanced colorectal cancer. J Clin Oncol. 1991;9:1967.

224 **Moertel CG et al.** Levamisole and fluorouracil for surgical adjuvant therapy of colon carcinoma. N Engl J Med. 1990;322:352.

225 **MacDonald JS et al.** 5-fluorouracil, doxorubicin, and mitomycin (FAM) combination chemotherapy for advanced gastric cancer. Ann Intern Med. 1980;93:533.

226 **Preusser P et al.** Phase II study with the combination etoposide, doxorubicin, and cisplatin in advanced measurable gastric cancer. J Clin Oncol. 1989; 7:1310.

227 **Leichman L et al.** Nonoperative therapy for squamous-cell cancer of the esophagus. J Clin Oncol. 1987;5:365.

228 **Rothman H et al.** Continuous infusion 5-fluorouracil plus weekly cisplatin for pancreatic carcinoma. A Mid-Atlantic Oncology Program study. Cancer. 1991; 68:264.

229 **Decker DG et al.** Cyclophosphamide plus cisplatinum in combination: treatment program for stage III or IV ovarian carcinoma. Obstet Gynecol. 1982; 60:481.

230 **Young RC et al.** Advanced ovarian adenocarcinoma: a prospective clinical trial of melphalan (L-PAM) versus combination chemotherapy. N Engl J Med. 1978;299:1261.

231 **Greco FA et al.** Advanced ovarian cancer: Brief intensive combination chemotherapy and second look operation. Obstet Gynecol. 1981;58:199.

232 **McGuire WP et al.** A phase III trial comparing cisplatin/cytoxan (PC) and cisplatin/taxol in advanced ovarian cancer (AOC) Proc Am Soc Clin Oncol. 1993;12:255. Abstract.

233 **Williams SD et al.** Treatment of disseminated germ-cell tumors with cisplatin, bleomycin, and either vinblastine or etoposide. N Engl J Med. 1987; 316;1435.

234 **Loehrer PJ et al.** Salvage therapy in recurrent germ cell cancer: ifosfamide and cisplatin plus either vinblastine or etoposide. Ann Intern Med. 1988;109: 540.

235 **Sternberg CN et al.** Preliminary results of M-VAC (methotrexate, vinblastine, doxorubicin and cisplatin) for transitional cell carcinoma of the urothelium. J Urol. 1985;133:403.

236 **Evans WK et al.** VP-16 and cisplatin as first line therapy for small cell lung cancer. J Clin Oncol. 1985;3:1471.

237 **Aisner J et al.** Doxorubicin, cyclophosphamide, etoposide and platinum, doxorubicin, cyclophosphamide, and etoposide for small cell carcinoma of the lung. Semin Oncol. 1986;3(Suppl. 3):54.

238 **Goldhirsch A et al.** Cis-dichlorodiammineplatinum (II) and VP 16-213 combination chemotherapy for non-small cell lung cancer. Med Pediatr Oncol. 1981;9:205.

239 **Dhingra HM et al.** Chemotherapy for advanced adenocarcinoma and squamous cell carcinoma of the lung with etoposide and cisplatin. Cancer Treat Rep. 1984;68:671.

240 **Ruckdeschel JC et al.** Chemotherapy for metastatic non-small cell bronchogenic carcinoma: EST 2575, Generation V—a randomized comparison of four cisplatin-containing regimens. J Clin Oncol. 1985;3:72.

241 **Kish JA et al.** A randomized trial of cisplatin (CACP) + 5-fluorouracil (5-FU) infusion and CACP + 5-FU bolus for recurrent and advanced squamous cell carcinoma of the head and neck. Cancer. 1985;56:2740.

242 **Armitage JO et al.** Predicting therapeutic outcome in patients with diffuse histiocytic lymphoma treated with cyclophosphamide, adriamycin, vincristine, and prednisone (CHOP). Cancer. 1982;50:1695.

243 **Skarin A et al.** Moderate dose methotrexate (m) combined with bleomycin (B), adriamycin (A), cyclophosphamide (C), oncovin (O) and dexamethasone (D), m-BACOD in advanced diffuse histiocytic lymphoma (DHL). Proc Amer Soc Clin Oncol. 1983;2: 220.

244 **Klimo P, Connors JM.** MACOP-B chemotherapy for the treatment of diffuse large cell lymphoma. Ann Intern Med. 1985;102:596.

245 **Canellos GP et al.** EVA: etoposide, vinblastine, doxorubicin (adriamycin)—an effective regimen for the treatment of Hodgkin's disease in relapse following MOPP. A Study of the Cancer and Leukemia Group B. Proc Am Soc Clin Oncol. 1991;10:273.

246 **DeVita VT et al.** Combination chemotherapy in the treatment of advanced Hodgkin's disease. Ann Intern Med. 1970;73:881.

247 **Santoro A et al.** Alternating drug combinations in the treatment of advanced Hodgkin's disease. N Engl J Med. 1982;306:770.

248 **Barlogie B et al.** Effective treatment of advanced multiple myeloma refractory to alkylating agents. N Engl J Med. 1984;310:1353.

249 **Alexanian R et al.** Combination chemotherapy for multiple myeloma. Cancer. 1972;30:382.

250 **Mandelli F et al.** Maintenance treatment with recombinant interferon alfa-2b in patients with multiple myeloma responding to conventional induction chemotherapy. N Engl J Med. 1990; 322:1430.

251 **Link MP et al.** The effect of adjuvant chemotherapy on relapse-free survival in patients with osteosarcomas of the extremity. N Engl J Med. 1986;314: 1600.

252 **Eilber F et al.** Adjuvant therapy for osteosarcoma: a randomized prospective trial. J Clin Oncol. 1987;5:21.

253 **Wilson SE et al.** Current status of vascular access techniques. Surg Clin N Am. 1982;62:531.

254 **World Health Organization.** Recommendations for grading of acute and subacute toxic effects. In: WHO Handbook for Reporting Results of Cancer Treatment. Geneva: World Health Organization; 1979:16–21.

255 **Anon.** Common toxicity criteria for cancer clinical trials. In: Wittes RE, ed. Manual of Oncologic Therapeutics 1989/1990. Philadelphia: Lippincott; 1989:628–32.

256 **Schipper H, Leavitt M.** Measuring quality of life: risks and benefits. Cancer Treat Rep. 1985;69:1115.

257 **Moinpour CM et al.** Quality of life end points in cancer clinical trials: review and recommendations. JNCI. 1989;81:485.

258 **Virji MA et al.** Tumor markers in cancer diagnosis and prognosis. CA Cancer J Clin. 1988;38:104.

259 **Sutherland DJ.** Hormones and cancer. In: Tannock IF, Hill RP, eds. The Basic Science of Oncology. New York: Pergamon Press; 1987:204–22.

260 **Rosenberg SA et al.** Principles and applications of biologic therapy. In: DeVita VT et al., eds. Cancer. Principles and Practice of Oncology. 3rd ed. Philadelphia: Lippincott; 1989:301–47.

261 **Everson TC, Cole WH.** Spontaneous regression of cancer. Philadelphia: WB Saunders; 1966.

262 **Coley WB.** The treatment of malignant tumors by repeated inoculations of erysipelas: with a report of ten original cases. Am J Med Sci. 1893;105:487.

263 **Gressler I.** A Chekhov and Coley's toxins. N Engl J Med. 1987;317:457. Letter.

264 **Lotze MT, Rosenberg SA.** The immunologic treatment of cancer. CA Cancer J Clin. 1988;38:68.

265 **Balmer CM.** The new α interferons. Drug Intell Clin Pharm. 1985;19:887.

266 **Goldstein D, Laszlo J.** The role of interferon in cancer therapy: a current perspective. CA Cancer J Clin. 1988; 38:258.

267 **Quesada JR et al.** Clinical toxicity of interferons in cancer patients: a review. J Clin Oncol. 1986;4:234.

268 **Morgan DA et al.** Selective in vitro growth of T lymphocytes from normal human bone marrow. Science. 1986; 193:1007.

269 **Lotze MT et al.** In vitro growth of cytotoxic human lymphocytes IV: lysis of fresh and cultured autologous tumor by lymphocytes cultured in T cell growth factor (TCGF). Cancer Res. 1981;41:4420.

270 **Rayner AA et al.** Lymphokine-activated killer (LAK) cell phenomenon: analysis of factors relevant to the immunotherapy of human cancer. Cancer. 1985;55:1327.

271 **West WH et al.** Constant-infusion recombinant interleukin-2 in adoptive immunotherapy of advanced cancer. N Engl J Med. 1987;316:898.

272 **Rosenberg SA et al.** Observations on the systemic administration of autologous lymphokine-activated killer cells and recombinant interleukin-2 to patients with metastatic cancer. N Engl J Med. 1985;313:1485.

273 **Rosenberg SA et al.** A progress report on the treatment of 157 patients with advanced cancer using lymphokine-activated killer cells and interleukin-2 or high-dose interleukin-2 alone. N Engl J Med. 1987;316:889.

274 **Sleijfer DT et al.** Phase II study of subcutaneous interleukin-2 in unselected patients with advanced renal cell cancer on an outpatient basis. J Clin Oncol. 1992;10:1119.

275 **Caligiuri MA et al.** Extended contin-

uous infusion low-dose recombinant interleukin-2 in advanced cancer: prolonged immunomodulation without significant toxicity. J Clin Oncol. 1991; 9:2110.

276 Vogelzang NJ et al. Subcutaneous interleukin-2 plus interferon alfa-2a in metastatic renal cancer: an outpatient multicenter trial. J Clin Oncol. 1993; 11:1809.

277 Berk PD et al. Increased incidence of leukemia in polycythemia vera associated with chlorambucil therapy. N Engl J Med. 1981;304:441.

278 Schafer AI. Teratogenic effects of antileukemic therapy. Arch Intern Med. 1981;141:514.

279 Stephens JD et al. Multiple congenital abnormalities in a fetus exposed to 5-fluorouracil during the first trimester. Am J Obstet Gynecol. 1980;137:747.

280 Benedict WF et al. Mutagenicity of

cancer chemotherapeutic agents in the Salmonella/microsome test. Cancer Res. 1977;37:2209.

281 Rieche K. Carcinogenicity of antineoplastic agents in man. Cancer Treat Rev. 1984;11:39.

282 Palmer RG et al. Chlorambucil-induced chromosome damage to human lymphocytes is dose-dependent and cumulative. Lancet. 1984;1:246.

283 ASHP technical assistance bulletin on handling cytotoxic and hazardous drugs. Am J Hosp Pharm. 1990;47: 1033.

284 Anderson RW et al. Risk of handling injectable antineoplastic agents. Am J Hosp Pharm. 1982;39:1881.

285 Falck K et al. Mutagenicity in urine of nurses handling cytostatic drugs. Lancet. 1979;1:1250.

286 Waksvik H et al. Chromosome analyses of nurses handling cytostatic

agents. Cancer Treat Rep. 1981;65: 607.

287 Chrysotomou A et al. Mutation frequency in nurses and pharmacists working with cytotoxic drugs. Aust N Z Med. 1984;14:831.

288 Hirst M et al. Occupational exposure to cyclophosphamide. Lancet. 1984;1: 186.

289 Venitt S et al. Monitoring exposure of nursing and pharmacy personnel to cytotoxic drugs: urinary mutation assays and urinary platinum as markers of absorption. Lancet. 1984;1:74.

290 Selevan SH et al. A study of occupational exposure to antineoplastic drugs and fetal loss in nurses. N Engl J Med. 1985;333:1173.

291 Hemminki K et al. Spontaneous abortions and malformations in the offspring of nurses exposed to anesthetic gases, cytostatic drugs and other poten-

tial hazards in hospitals, based on registered information outcome. J Epidemiol Community Health. 1985;39:141.

292 Yodaiken R. Safe handling of cytotoxic drugs by health care personnel. Washington, DC: Occupational Safety and Health Administration; 1986. (Instructional publication 8-1.1)

293 U.S. Public Health Service, National Institutes of Health. Recommendations for the safe handling of parenteral antineoplastic drugs. Washington, DC: U.S. Department of Health and Human Services, 1983; NIH publication no. 83-2621.

294 National Study Commission on Cytotoxic Exposure. Recommendations for handling cytotoxic agents. 1987.

295 AMA Council on Scientific Affairs. Guidelines for handling parenteral antineoplastics. JAMA. 1985;253:1590.

Adverse Effects of Chemotherapy

Celeste Lindley
Rebecca S Finley
Cynthia L LaCivita

Common and Acute Toxicities 91-2
  Hematologic Toxicities 91-2
    Effects of chemotherapy on bone marrow 91-2
      Myelosuppression 91-2
        Prevention 91-3
        Treatment 91-4
    Anemia and erythropoietin 91-4
    Chemotherapy and coagulation 91-4
      Thrombotic events 91-4
  Gastrointestinal (GI) Toxicities 91-5
    Complications of the oral cavity 91-5
    Esophagitis 91-5
    Nausea and vomiting 91-5
    Lower gastrointestinal tract complications 91-5
      Xerostomia 91-6
      Mucositis/stomatitis 91-7
        Treatment 91-7
        Prevention 91-7
  Dermatologic Toxicities 91-8
    Alopecia 91-8
      Pathogenesis 91-8
      Prevention 91-8
    Skin and nail changes 91-9
      Nail changes 91-9
      Dermatological pigment changes 91-9
      Hand-foot syndrome 91-10
      Dry skin 91-10
    Interactions with radiation 91-10
    Irritant and vesicant reactions 91-11
  Hypersensitivity Reactions 91-13
Specific Organ Toxicities 91-14
  Neurotoxicity 91-14
    Cytarabine and L-asparaginase 91-14
    Other agents 91-15
      Methotrexate 91-15
      Fluorouracil (FU) 91-15

      Fludarabine 91-15
      Carmustine and other nitrosureas 91-15
    Peripheral nerve toxicity 91-15
    Cranial nerve toxicity 91-17
    Autonomic neuropathy 91-17
  Cardiac Toxicities 91-17
    Doxorubicin 91-17
    Other agents 91-18
      Daunorubicin 91-18
      Idarubicin 91-18
      Mitoxantrone 91-18
    Prevention 91-18
    Management 91-19
    Other cardiac toxicities 91-19
      Fluorouracil 91-19
  Nephrotoxicity 91-19
    Cisplatin-induced 91-19
      Prevention 91-20
    Other nephrotoxic agents 91-21
      Methotrexate 91-21
      Ifosfamide 91-21
        Pathogenesis 91-21
        Clinical presentation 91-22
        Prevention 91-22
  Pulmonary Toxicities 91-22
    Management 91-23
  Hepatotoxicity 91-23
Long-Term Complications of Chemotherapy 91-25
  Second Malignancies after Chemotherapy 91-25
    Acute nonlymphocytic leukemia (ANLL) 91-25
      Therapy and prognosis 91-26
  Fertility and Teratogenicity 91-26
    Effects on oogenesis 91-26
    Effects on spermatogenesis 91-27
    Teratogenicity 91-28

Antineoplastic agents are toxic not only to cancer cells, but have effects on a variety of host tissues and organs as well. The toxicities of chemotherapy can be classified as common and acute toxicities, specific organ toxicities, and long-term complications. *Common and acute toxicities* generally include those adverse effects which occur as a result of inhibition of host cell division. One of the first observations made in animals and humans treated with early nitrogen mustard analogues was that the host tissues susceptible to these agents were those with renewal cell populations, primarily the lymphoid tissues, the bone marrow, the epithelium of the gastrointestinal (GI) tract and skin. A number of additional toxicities that will be discussed under the category of common and acute toxicities do not occur as the result of inhibition of host cell division, but are observed frequently in patients receiving combination chemotherapy regimens and usually occur shortly after the administration of antineoplastic agents (e.g., nausea and vomiting and hypersensitivity reactions). *Specific organ toxicities* often are at-

tributed to a unique uptake of the drug by the organ or a selective toxicity of the drug to the organ. *Long-term complications* are problems attributed to chemotherapy that occur months to years after the administration of chemotherapy. It is important to emphasize that these categories of toxicities overlap. For example, many of the specific organ toxicities will be evident within days following drug administration, whereas others present months after initiation of therapy. This classification system is helpful only in providing some framework to the very complex topic of adverse effects of chemotherapy.

The toxicity of cancer chemotherapy is the most important factor limiting the use of drugs that might be curative more often if higher doses could be used. Therefore, all discussions regarding the benefits of antineoplastic agents must include a discussion of the risks and toxicities associated with their use. Concerns regarding the toxicity of chemotherapy include the incidence or rate at which these adverse reactions occur, the predictability of their occurrence, and the severity and reversibility of the adverse effect. Although the incidence and predictability may be defined in specific patient populations, there appears to be significant individual susceptibility. In addition, adverse effects of chemotherapy are influenced by the specific agent or agents administered, as well as the dose and duration of their use. Therefore, it often is difficult to predict the specific adverse effects that an individual patient will experience. However, a number of toxicities of chemotherapy do have well-defined characteristics and occur with a frequency that merits baseline knowledge on the part of the clinician providing services to this ever-growing patient population.

Many patients receiving chemotherapy also have significant disease involvement and impairment of organ function due to the presence of malignant cells. In addition, patients with cancer commonly receive many other agents (e.g., antibiotics, analgesics). Thus, when a new symptom becomes evident, it may be difficult to determine whether it is occurring secondary to chemotherapy, concurrently administered medications, or disease progression. Therefore, it is important to be aware of the presentation, management, and methods of preventing most common toxicities that would be expected to occur in patients receiving chemotherapy agents.

Common and Acute Toxicities

Hematologic Toxicities

Effects of Chemotherapy on Bone Marrow

The bone marrow contains a population of pluripotent stem cells capable of differentiation into any mature blood cell. The pluripotent stem cells have self-renewal capacity. However, at some point, their progeny will commit to either the myeloid or lymphoid line. The myeloid stem cell will further commit to development along the erythrocyte, megakaryocyte, granulocyte, or the monocyte line. Once committed to a particular cell line, these bone marrow precursor cells undergo a series of divisions (mitosis) whereby their numbers increase. This is followed by a series of stages of development during which the cells become more mature and differentiate into the final forms in which they leave the bone marrow (postmitotic). The total time required for a cell to pass through the mitotic and postmitotic pool under normal resting conditions is approximately 10 to 14 days. This process is regulated by a number of cytokines, many of which have been identified and several of which are now produced through recombinant DNA technology. These growth factors cause expansion of the mitotic pool and accelerate the process of maturation and differentiation, decreasing the total time spent in these stages to approximately five to seven days.

The pharmacokinetics of hematopoietic cell lines affected by chemotherapy determine the severity of the depression of that cell line and the time course in which obvious depression occurs. Red blood cells (RBCs) survive approximately 120 days in the peripheral blood. Thus, if red blood cell production is impaired for a short period of time, clinically significant anemia is not likely to result. Instead, anemia develops slowly, usually after several courses of chemotherapy. On the other hand, the survival time of platelets is approximately ten days and that of granulocytes is approximately six to eight hours. Thus, neutropenia generally is more severe and occurs before thrombocytopenia. Neutropenia and thrombocytopenia may be observed following the first or any subsequent course of chemotherapy. The bone marrow is the organ affected most consistently and frequently by cancer chemotherapy. The depression of peripheral blood cells following chemotherapy is used in determining the dose, drug combinations, and mode and frequency of administration for subsequent chemotherapy. Life-

threatening neutropenia or thrombocytopenia necessitates some action to eliminate risk to the patient with subsequent chemotherapy cycles. In the past, this action has consisted of reducing the dose of the myelosuppressive agents. However, the availability of colony-stimulating factors (CSFs) provides an alternative approach to reducing the frequency and the duration of chemotherapy-induced neutropenia. To date, a specific stimulating factor that supports or enhances platelet production is not available commercially. Thus, the mainstay of managing severe thrombocytopenia is the use of platelet transfusions.

1. **Myelosuppression. J.T., a 45-year-old, 70 kg male with no significant past medical history, presents to the University Hospital with complaints of cough and shortness of breath (SOB). Chest x-ray reveals a lesion in the right upper lobe; bronchoscopy washings and cytology are positive for small cell lung cancer. A metastatic work-up is negative. J.T. is diagnosed with small cell lung cancer limited to one lobe and plans are to initiate radiation therapy to the right upper lobe with concurrent cyclophosphamide 800 mg/m^2 on Day 1, doxorubicin 45 mg/m^2 on Day 1, and etoposide 100 mg/m^2 on Days 1–3 Q 21 days. You will discuss with J.T. the toxicities that might be expected to occur with this regimen. What effects on the bone marrow can be anticipated and how will they present clinically in J.T.? What factors can influence the likelihood that these effects will occur and their severity? When can J.T. expect these effects to occur?**

A number of toxicities commonly are associated with cyclophosphamide, doxorubicin, and etoposide and each should be identified and discussed with J.T. However, one of the most predictable and dangerous toxicities associated with this regimen is myelosuppression. Myeloid elements include red blood cells, granulocytes (i.e., neutrophils, eosinophils, and basophils), monocytes, and platelets. The bone marrow suppressive effect of chemotherapy is reflected by peripheral cytopenias. Depression of red blood cell precursors gives rise to anemia with symptoms of fatigue and decreased exercise tolerance. Growth inhibition of granulocyte precursors results in a reduction in circulating neutrophils which significantly increases the risk of a patient developing bacterial infections. Reduction in platelet precursors results in a decreased number of platelets in the peripheral blood which can lead to bleeding, usually from the gastrointestinal and genitourinary tract. Reductions in non-neutrophil granulocytes and monocytes are not associated with clinically important consequences.

The degree of cytopenia induced by a particular agent is influenced by the agent administered, the dose, and the schedule of administration. In addition, since these agents almost always are given in combination, it must be kept in mind that their individual myelosuppressive effects may be intensified by the effects of other drugs. The degree of cytopenia induced by a particular agent also will be influenced by a number of factors involving the host which specifically affect the cellularity of the bone marrow compartment. These factors include: patient age (younger patients have a much more cellular marrow with a decreased percentage of fat and, therefore, are more tolerant of a given dose of drug than are elderly patients); the degree of bone marrow reserve in relation to the amount of involvement by a particular neoplastic process (fibrosis and tumor cells including leukemic cells in the marrow); the degree of compromise by previous chemotherapy, radiotherapy, or both (prior chemotherapy and radiotherapy to fields involving marrow-producing bone reduce bone marrow reserves); the nutritional status of the patient (the greater the negative nitrogen balance with its associated loss of weight, the less the tolerance); and the ability of the liver or kidneys to metabolize and/or excrete the compounds administered.[1]

With most agents, the patient's white blood cell (WBC) and platelet counts will begin to fall within five to seven days, nadir at seven to ten days, and recover in about 14 to 26 days. Those antineoplastic agents that are active in a specific phase of the cell cycle (i.e., cell-cycle phase specific) such as the antimitotics and antimetabolites produce a fairly rapid cytopenia with faster recovery than agents that are cell-cycle phase nonspecific such as alkylating agents and most of the antitumor antibiotics. For poorly understood reasons, nitrosureas typically produce late and often severe neutropenia and thrombocytopenia that occur four to six weeks after the administration of the agent. Other agents that exhibit this pattern include mitomycin and mechlorethamine. The most common explanation offered for these late effects is that these drugs exert inhibitory effects on cells in the resting phase and when resting but damaged cells enter a growth phase, the delayed cytopenias become evident. With this last group of agents, there are often two nadirs in neutrophils and platelets associated with their administration, one at the conventional time expected of cell cycle non-phase specific agents and then the later effect at approximately four to six weeks post dose administration. Many combination regimens that employ these agents call for six-week cycles to avoid administration before the second nadir.

All of the agents included in J.T.'s regimen have marked myelosuppressive activity. Thus, J.T. should be carefully counseled to contact his physician or report to the emergency room (ER) should he experience signs or symptoms of infection or bleeding. Both of these conditions most commonly would be observed 10 to 14 days after Day 1 of his chemotherapy regimen.

2. Prevention. About 9 days after the first course of chemotherapy, J.T. developed a severe sore throat and fever that were managed with hospitalization and administration of intravenous (IV) antibiotics. At the time, his WBC count was 300/mm^3. His febrile illness resolved 3 days after admission and all cultures were negative; it is now 3 weeks after his chemotherapy and he is scheduled for his second course. Should he receive the same doses he was given initially?

In the past, the doses of antineoplastic agents would have been reduced (usually by 25%) in all subsequent cycles for a patient like J.T. Although dose reduction clearly results in reduced neutropenia, the response and survival of patients with chemotherapy-sensitive tumors also is compromised. J.T. has limited stage small cell lung cancer which is both chemosensitive and potentially curable. Therefore, dose reduction is undesirable in this case.

Two major approaches to overcoming myelosuppression from chemotherapy developed in the early 1990s. First, alterations in the rate of dose administration may change the hematotoxicity of certain chemotherapeutic agents.[2] For agents that are cell-cycle phase-specific, administering the same dose over a short period of time (i.e., 1 to 3 hours) has been found to result in less myelosuppression than more prolonged administration of the same dose (i.e., over 24 hours). The greater myelosuppression seen with prolonged infusions likely is due to increased exposure of dividing cells at their susceptible times for inhibition by cell-cycle phase specific agents. Most cell-cycle phase nonspecific agents do not demonstrate major differences in hematotoxicity based upon rate or duration of dose administration.

The other method available to protect against the myelosuppressive effects of chemotherapy is the prophylactic administration of growth factors. At least six colony stimulating factors are under development in the U.S., but only two, granulocyte colony stimulating factor [G-CSF (Filgrastim)] and granulocyte monocyte colony stimulating factor [GM-CSF (Sargramostim)] are available commercially. These products were approved by the Food and Drug Administration (FDA) in 1991 to enhance neutrophil recovery following chemotherapy administration. The primary licensing trial demonstrating the safety and efficacy of G-CSF was conducted in patients like J.T. who had small cell lung cancer and were receiving cyclophosphamide, adriamycin, and etoposide.[3] Thus, use of CSFs in J.T. may be recommended.

3. How are CSFs dosed to prevent chemotherapy-induced neutropenia?

Although the two commercially available colony-stimulating factors often are used interchangeably in clinical trials, their approved indications and dosage guidelines are different. Filgrastim is indicated for prevention of neutropenic fever in patients with non-myeloid malignancies receiving antineoplastic therapy. An initial dose of 5 µg/kg/day as a single daily injection by subcutaneous (SQ) bolus, short intravenous infusion (15 to 30 minutes), or by continuous SQ or IV infusion is recommended. A subcutaneous bolus is the commonly preferred route and method of administration. The manufacturer recommends that therapy with Filgrastim be continued until the patient's neutrophil count exceeds 10,000 cells/mm^3 after the expected chemotherapy-induced neutrophil nadir.

Sargramostim, the only commercially available GM-CSF product, has a narrower FDA approved indication than Filgrastim; it has been approved to accelerate recovery of neutrophils following high dose chemotherapy and autologous bone marrow transplant in patients with lymphoid malignancies. The recommended initial dose of Sargramostim is 250 µg/m^2/day for 21 days as a two-hour IV infusion beginning two to four hours after the autologous bone marrow infusion, not less than 24 hours after the last dose of chemotherapy, and 12 hours after the last dose of radiotherapy.

The recommended dose of G-CSF is expressed in µg/kg and GM-CSF in µg/m^2. It is helpful to keep in mind that a dose in µg/m^2 can be divided by 40 to obtain a rough estimate of equivalent dose in µg/kg. Thus, the recommended initial dose of GM-CSF (6 µg/kg) is roughly equivalent to that of G-CSF (5 µg/kg). Clinical trials are further addressing questions related to optimal dose and scheduling of CSFs to prevent febrile neutropenia following myelotoxic chemotherapy.

Phase I to II dose escalation trials with G-CSF and GM-CSF in patients receiving standard dose chemotherapy regimens have shown a steep dose response for neutrophils with G-CSF doses ranging from 1 to 40 µg/kg/day and GM-CSF doses ranging from 0.3 to 32 µg/kg/day. [5,6] These early studies, as well as later dose-ranging trials, appear to indicate that doses higher than 5 to 10 µg/kg/day of GM-CSF and G-CSF are not superior in preventing neutropenia in patients receiving standard dose chemotherapy and may in fact be less effective and more toxic than 5 to 10 µg/kg/day.[7,8] Data are limited at this time regarding optimal dose and schedule of CSFs in "high-dose" or "dose-intense" regimens.

The optimum dose for a particular patient receiving standard combination chemotherapy is unknown. For this reason, many authorities recommend standardizing the dose based upon the patient's weight and commercially available product vial size is recommended. For example, the University of California at San Francisco has established the following CSF dosage standardization policy for adult patients: Patients <75 kg receive 300 µg G-CSF daily and patients >75 kg receive 480 µg G-CSF daily.[9] Commercially available vials contain 300 and 480 µg. Due to differences in commercially available vial sizes, the weight breakpoint for GM-CSF is slightly different; patients who weigh ≥60 kg receive 500 µg/day and patients weighing <60 kg receive 250 µg/day. The Cancer and Leukemia Group B released a Filgrastim dosing policy that recommends rounding the dose to the nearest 0.1 mL (30 µg). If the calculated dose is 330 µg or less, the entire

300 µg (1 mL) vial should be administered. If the dose is 330 µg or greater, the entire 480 µg (1.6 mL) vial should be administered.

Another modification of manufacturer's recommended use of these agents relates to duration of administration. Currently, discontinuation of G-CSF is recommended when the neutrophil count reaches or exceeds 10,000/mm^3 after the expected chemotherapy nadir. This is based upon the observation that the neutrophil count falls following CSF discontinuation by roughly 50%. However, the risk of bacterial infection is highest in patients with neutrophil counts of less than 500 to 1000/mm^3; patients with neutrophil counts above 500 to 1000/mm^3 are not thought to be at high risk for developing bacteria infection. Thus, many clinicians elect to discontinue CSFs when the neutrophil count reaches 2,000 to 4,000/mm^3 following the chemotherapy nadir. This reduces the number of CSF treatment days and the cost associated with therapy without placing the patient at excessive risk for bacterial infection following CSF discontinuation.

In summary, J.T. should be given G-CSF 300 µg/day subcutaneously beginning the day following his last dose of chemotherapy and continuing until his absolute neutrophil count reaches 2,000 to 4,000/mm^3. This is consistent with guidelines recommended by the American Society of Clinical Oncology (ASCO). Aside from high cost and inconvenience, the only negative effect of G-CSF therapy is mild transient bone pain.

4. Treatment. **If J.T. was not given G-CSF and then presented with febrile neutropenia, would G-CSF therapy be helpful?**

CSFs accelerate hematopoiesis by expanding the mitotic pool of committed progenitor cells and shortening the period of time spent in the postmitotic pool from five to six days to one day. The major benefit of CSFs is their ability to reduce the duration of neutropenia, since the latter is the most significant prognostic factor in patients with established febrile neutropenia. If CSFs reduced the duration of neutropenia in patients who present with febrile neutropenia, there should be a significant reduction in morbidity, mortality, and cost. The ability of CSFs to reduce the duration of neutropenia in patients with febrile neutropenia has been addressed in at least three randomized double-blind, placebo-controlled trials, all of which have been reported only in abstract form.[10–12]

These abstracts suggest that either G-CSF or GM-CSF administered in doses of 5 µg/kg/day reduces days with neutropenia, length of hospitalization, and duration of antibiotic therapy. However, the combined data for G-CSF and GM-CSF reveal minimal to moderate benefit in reducing hospital stays. Furthermore, several groups have questioned whether all patients with febrile neutropenia require hospitalization.[13–15] Therefore, although colony-stimulating factors do appear to hasten neutrophil recovery, the true cost-benefit associated with the use of these products in established febrile neutropenia remains to be determined. The ASCO Clinical Practice Guidelines do not support routine use of CSFs in febrile neutropenic patients, but do recognize that certain febrile neutropenic patients with prognostic factors predictive of clinical deterioration (e.g., pneumonia, fungal infection, sepsis syndrome) may benefit from use of CSFs.

Anemia and Erythropoietin

5. Is erythropoietin useful in cancer patients with anemia?

Anemia usually is not a dose-limiting toxicity of chemotherapy because of the long survival time of the red blood cell (120 days). The predominant effects of chemotherapy on red blood cells are anisocytosis and macrocytosis. These effects are related to inhibition of DNA synthesis and are associated predominantly with the folic acid antagonists, hydroxyurea, purine, and pyrimidine antagonists. Anemia commonly does not accompany this red blood cell size change, and chemotherapy-induced effects on red blood cells infrequently are the sole factor producing a hemoglobin (Hgb) level that necessitates RBC transfusion.

Nevertheless, anemia is not uncommon in cancer patients and most often is the result of the primary disease. The exact mechanism by which this anemia occurs is not well understood. Impaired erythrocyte response to erythropoietin [possibly mediated by IL-1 and tumor necrosis factor (TNF) elaborated in association with malignant disease], reduced hematopoietic precursors due to chemotherapy and/or irradiation, and disruption of the marrow architecture by invasion of malignant cells all seem to play a role in the anemia of cancer. Erythropoietin treatment has been shown to ameliorate anemia associated with cancer and chemotherapy, reduce the need for transfusions, and enhance the patient's quality of life.[16–20] Due to its high cost, erythropoietin generally is reserved for patients who either require red blood cell transfusions to alleviate symptoms of anemia or whose downward trend in hemoglobin/hematocrit counts suggests that intervention will be required to avoid transfusion. The recommended starting dose for erythropoietin is 150 U/kg three times a week, which is significantly higher than that recommended for the anemia of renal failure. Dose escalation often is required. Up to eight weeks of treatment may be required to achieve a significant decrease in transfusion requirements. Adverse effects of hypertension, seizures, and angina which occurred in renal failure patients with rapid erythropoietin dose escalation or normalization of hematocrit (Hct) have not been observed in cancer patients. Pretreatment erythropoietin levels correlate with the rate and likelihood of response in patients who are not receiving chemotherapy with nonresponders having higher endogenous erythropoietin levels. Treatment with erythropoietin is not recommended for patients who have baseline serum erythropoietin levels >200 mU/mL. The reduced need for transfusion therapy must be weighed against the cost and inconvenience of erythropoietin therapy for anemia associated with cancer and chemotherapy.

Chemotherapy and Coagulation

6. What effect does chemotherapy have on blood coagulation?

The most common coagulation effect observed in patients receiving chemotherapy is bleeding secondary to thrombocytopenia caused by direct suppression of platelet production by the bone marrow. However, chemotherapy can affect coagulation factors which may result in coagulation disorders.

L-asparaginase can decrease the synthesis of fibrinogen and other specific coagulation factors produced by the liver under the influence of Vitamin K.[21,22] This is because L-asparaginase has a widespread effect on protein synthesis, and many plasma protein factors are depressed shortly after the administration of this drug. When tests of coagulation are obtained, prolongation of the prothrombin time (PT), partial thromboplastin time (PTT), and thrombin time are observed. However, bleeding or thrombosis occurring as a direct result of alterations in coagulation proteins has been reported rarely and not documented conclusively. Coagulation factors may return to normal levels with continued administration of the drug which suggests that the impairment of protein synthesis created by L-asparaginase is partially overcome by the liver. Specific treatment of prolonged PT, PTT, and thrombin clotting time with coagulation factors, fibrinogen or Vitamin K is not indicated.

Thrombotic events have been associated with the administration of chemotherapy.[23] Evidence of intravascular coagulation from the presence of plasma fibrinopeptide A, a specific activation peptide of fibrinogen, has been reported after the initiation of chemotherapy.[24] Conversely, a decrease in fibrinolytic activity reflected by a decrease in functional plasminogen activator also has been reported.[24] Other protein abnormalities associated with thrombosis, including a decrease in Protein C antigen and activity and a decrease in total and free Protein S levels,[25,26] have occurred following chemotherapy administration. Protein C and Protein S are naturally occurring anticoagulants; deficiencies of these proteins have been reported to result in spontaneous thrombosis.

Assessing the risk of thrombosis from administration of chemotherapy is complicated by the fact that many cancers are associated with an increased incidence of thrombosis. This is particularly true in tumors of the GI tract and acute promyelocytic leukemia. Trousseau[27] was the first to report an increased incidence of venous thrombosis in patients with cancer; however, many investigators have since confirmed the relationship of multiple or migratory venous thrombosis in up to 15% of cancer patients.[28] Up to one-third of apparently healthy adults who develop otherwise unexplained deep vein thrombosis eventually prove to have malignancy.[29,30] Removal of the tumor often is associated with disappearance of thrombotic episodes. Warfarin or heparin therapy may be beneficial; however, thrombosis in cancer patients often is resistant to anticoagulant therapy.

Initiating treatment for acute promyelocytic leukemia commonly is associated (i.e., up to 85%) with disseminated intravascular coagulation.[31] This is thought to occur secondary to release of a procoagulant from lysed tumor cells. Heparin generally has been accepted as beneficial in induction treatment of acute promyelocytic leukemia; however, other investigators have reported excellent results in patients treated almost entirely with blood product support (fibrinogen and/or antithrombin III) without heparin.[31] With the exception of acute promyelocytic leukemia, no general guidelines are recommended to prevent thrombosis associated with cancer or chemotherapy.

It is important to remember that patients receiving cancer chemotherapy often have multiple other illnesses that may predispose them to the development of thrombosis. In addition, surgical procedures and bed rest are known to increase the risk of thrombosis. Thus, one should maintain a high index of suspicion when a patient with cancer presents with signs or symptoms of thrombotic disease.

Gastrointestinal (GI) Toxicities

The gastrointestinal tract may be second only to the bone marrow in its susceptibility to toxic effects produced by chemotherapy. GI toxicities include oral complications, esophagitis, nausea and vomiting, and lower bowel disturbances.

Complications of the Oral Cavity

Complications of the oral cavity include mucositis, xerostomia (dry mouth), infection, and bleeding. Approximately 40% of patients treated with chemotherapy develop oral complications and virtually all patients who receive radiation to the head and neck develop oral complications.[32] These toxicities are the consequence of the nonspecific effect of cancer chemotherapy on cells undergoing cell division. Cells of the mouth undergo rapid renewal with a turnover time of 7 to 14 days. Chemotherapy causes a reduction in the renewal rate of the basal epithelium, which results in mucosal atrophy, as well as glandular and collagen degeneration.[33] Radiation therapy to the head and neck also results in mucosal atrophy due to decreased cell renewal; fibrosis of the salivary glands, muscles, ligaments, and blood vessels; and damage to the taste buds.[34] The combined effects of chemotherapy and radiation therapy on the oral mucosa are profound. Infection and bleeding in the oral cavity also are common in patients receiving chemotherapy and/or radiation therapy to the head and neck. These actually result from the effects of chemotherapy on the bone marrow which result in thrombocytopenia and neutropenia. The oral mu-

cosa is highly vascular and frequently traumatized; thus, bleeding occurs commonly when platelets are reduced in number or function. The oral cavity harbors an extensive microbial flora and this flora is altered by both chemotherapy and the absence of neutrophils. Oral bleeding and infection of the oral mucosa most commonly are noted in the presence of neutropenia and thrombocytopenia, and most often occur approximately two weeks after the administration of chemotherapy. Often, oral complications compound one another. For example, xerostomia has been shown to accelerate the development of mucositis, as well as the formation of dental caries and local infection. Mucositis clearly predisposes the oral cavity to local bleeding and infection, as well as sepsis. In addition, all of these oral complications are associated with varying degrees of discomfort and adversely affect the patient's ability to eat. This, in turn, may compromise the patient's nutritional status. Topical treatments of oral complications are summarized in Table 91.1.

Esophagitis

Chemotherapy and radiation therapy also may damage the mucosa lining the esophagus; this is manifested most commonly by dysphagia. Symptomatic management of esophagitis is similar to that of mucositis. Careful monitoring of patients with severe esophagitis is required to assure adequate oral hydration and nutritional intake. Acidic or irritating foods should be avoided. Oftentimes, bacterial, viral, and fungal cultures are necessary to rule out an infectious etiology.

Nausea and Vomiting

Nausea and vomiting are common and serious complications associated with most antineoplastic agents. Chemotherapeutic agents, their metabolites, or neurotransmitters may stimulate receptors such as dopamine or serotonin in the GI tract, the chemoreceptor trigger zone, or the central nervous system (CNS) that ultimately act on the vomiting center to cause nausea and vomiting. Emesis is most common on the first day of chemotherapy administration and often persists for several days thereafter.[35] Most patients who receive cancer chemotherapy require antiemetic premedication and continued therapy for a period of time sufficient to control these symptoms in the postchemotherapy days. Selection of the most appropriate antiemetic regimen for a given patient and monitoring parameters are important areas for pharmacist involvement.

Lower Gastrointestinal Tract Complications

Lower GI tract complications of chemotherapy include malabsorption, diarrhea, and constipation. Several investigators have noted villus atrophy and cessation of mitosis within crypts in patients and animals treated with combination chemotherapy.[36-38] Other changes consisting of swelling and dilation of mitochondria and endoplasmic reticulum and shortening of the microvilli have been noted. It is likely that these or other changes to small and large bowel integrity may result in decreased absorption of drugs whose major site of absorption is the upper part of the small intestine. Decreased absorption of phenytoin, verapamil, and digoxin following administration of antineoplastic agents has been reported.[39-41]

Drug-induced intestinal changes also may be responsible for *diarrhea* which is noted frequently with such regimens as high-dose cytarabine (ARA-C) and fluorouracil [5-Fluorouracil (5-FU)]. With the exception of the vinca alkaloids, which produce colicky abdominal pain, constipation, and adynamic ileus due to autonomic nerve dysfunction (see Neurotoxicity), constipation has not been recognized as a common complication of antineoplastic agents. The true incidence of diarrhea and constipation associated with

Table 91.1	Topical Medications for Oral Complications of Chemotherapy and/or Radiation Therapy	
Problem	Products	Use
Xerostomia	Pilocarpine 5 mg tablet	1–2 tablets TID–QID
	Saliva substitutes *and/or*	Rinse or spray PRN
	Sugar-free hard candy; sugar-free gum; ice chips	PRN
Mucositis		
Generalized	Dyclonine HCl 0.5% or 1% solution *or*	Swish and expectorate 5–15 mL Q 2–3 hr PRN
	Viscous lidocaine 2% solution *or*	Swish and expectorate 5–15 mL Q 2–3 hr PRN
	Diphenhydramine capsules (125 mg) Dyclonine 1% 30 cc Nystatin 1 cc and ≤120 cc Maalox *or*	Swish and expectorate 5–15 mL Q 2–3 hr PRN
	Diphenhydramine + nystatin + hydrocortisone (various formulations) *or*	Swish and expectorate 5–15 mL Q 2–3 hr PRN
	Sucralfate suspension (8 tablets in 40 mL sterile water plus 40 mL 70% sorbitol. Shake well and add water to 120 mL	Swish and expectorate 5–15 mL Q 2–3 hr PRN
Localized	Benzocaine in orabase	Apply to affected dried area Q 2–3 hr. Not to be used in the presence of an infection
Local bleeding (gingival)	Topical thrombin solution	Apply to affected area with gauze sponge and hold in place with pressure for 30 min. Do not remove formed clots
Mucosal surface bleeding	Microfibrillar collagen	Apply to dried site with dry sponge for 1–5 min. Do not use in closure of mucosal incisions
General infection control	Chlorhexidine gluconate 0.12% oral rinse	Rinse BID after breakfast and at HS for 30 sec. Do not swallow
Prevention and treatment of oral candidiasis	Nystatin oral suspension	Rinse and swallow (if tolerated) 500,000–1,000,000 units TID–QID
	or Clotrimazole troche 10 mg	Dissolve 1 tablet 5 times/day
Prevention of caries	Acidulated fluoride rinse	Rinse daily for 1 min with 5–10 mL. Do not swallow. Switch to neutral fluoride if mucositis is present
	or Neutral fluoride rinse	Rinse daily for 1 min with 5 mL. Do not swallow. Switch back to acidulated fluoride rinse when mucositis resolves
	or Stannous fluoride gel 0.4%	Brush daily at HS. Swish for 30 sec. Spit out and rinse
	or Sodium fluoride gel 1.1%	Brush daily at HS. Swish for 30 sec. Spit out and rinse

antineoplastic drugs is unknown and would be difficult to identify in a setting where many agents with known tendencies to produce these symptoms (e.g., opioid analgesics, antiemetics, antacids) are administered concurrently with chemotherapy.

7. Xerostomia. J.B. is a 55-year-old male with newly-diagnosed, locally advanced head and neck cancer. Neoadjuvant chemotherapy consisting of cisplatin, methotrexate (MTX), and fluorouracil (5-FU), followed by a 2-week course of radiotherapy at 200 rads/day for 3 cycles, followed by surgical resection of persistent residual disease is planned. A review of systems suggests that J.B. has poor oral hygiene and a decision is made to consult the dental department of the University Hospital before initiating radiation and chemotherapy. Is J.B. at risk for developing oral complications of chemotherapy? Is there anything that should be done at this point to decrease his risk?

J.B. is at high risk for several of the oral complications as described earlier. Xerostomia is one of the most frequent side effects of irradiation to the head and neck and is due to changes in the salivary glands. There is a direct relationship between the dose of irradiation to the salivary glands and the extent of glandular changes.[34] In most patients treated with under 6000 rads, changes in the salivary glands induced by irradiation are reversible 6 to 12 months following completion of therapy. However, J.B. also will be receiving chemotherapy drugs (i.e., MTX, 5-FU) which have been associated with xerostomia and this may compound toxicity to the salivary glands. Clinically, xerostomia has been reported with as little as two to three radiation doses of 200 rads.[34]

Damage to the salivary glands results in loss of salivary buffering capacity, lowered salivary pH, elimination of mechanical flushing, and decreased salivary IgA. In addition, the patient's sense of taste is altered; most often, patients lose their ability to differentiate between sweet and salty foods and avoid foods with these tastes. A bitter taste also is common. The most consistent consequence of xerostomia is the development of caries. Caries and decalcification may become so severe that the integrity of the tooth is compromised and fracture occurs. Xerostomia also predisposes patients to increases in oral bacteria because saliva is no longer available to help clear bacteria from the mouth.

The two primary treatment modalities for xerostomia are stimulation of existing salivary flow and replacement of lost secretions. Relatively low doses of systemically administered *pilocarpine* (5 to 10 mg TID) may stimulate salivary flow and produce clinically significant benefits in patients with postirradiation xerostomia.[42,43] Dose-related adverse effects include sweating, rhinitis, headache, nausea, and abdominal cramps. Stimulation of salivation also can be accomplished with sucrose-free hard candy and sugar-free chewing gum, although these are considered by some authorities to be oral comfort agents not unlike saliva substitutes.

A variety of commercially available *saliva substitutes* generally are recommended for use before meals and at bedtime. They are available in a number of dosage formulations including sprays, rinses, and chewing gums. Patients who find one product or formulation unacceptable or unsuccessful may benefit from experimenting with other formulations or product lines. Studies have shown that salivary substitutes containing carboxymethylcellulose or hydroxyethylcellulose are more effective in relieving dryness than water- or glycerin-based solutions.[44,45]

Prevention of radiation-induced caries is accomplished best by the aggressive use of fluorides.[46] Generally, acidulated fluorides are the most effective, although neutral fluorides may become necessary in patients with mucositis. Patients are instructed to rinse daily for one minute with 5 to 10 mL of these fluoride rinses. In addition, the use of stannous fluoride gels 0.4% or sodium fluoride gel 1.1% as toothbrushing agents may be recommended. Meticulous attention to oral hygiene with regular dental checkups and avoidance of sucrose is essential to minimize the development of caries.

In general, patients who are to receive radiation to the head and neck or chemotherapeutic drugs with a high risk of oral complications are seen by a dentist before therapy is initiated. This includes patients with hematological malignancies, particularly those in whom profound myelosuppression for prolonged periods of time is expected. Oral evaluation before therapy, intervention to eliminate potential sources of infection or irritation, and preventive measures taken during therapy can decrease the frequency of oral complications dramatically.[47] Given J.B.'s risk factors, a dental examination is indicated before initiating therapy.

8. Mucositis/Stomatitis. J.B. successfully completes his first 2-week course of combined chemo- and radiation-therapy; however, 3 days into his second 2-week cycle, he complains of generalized burning, discomfort, and pain of the ventral surface of his tongue. On clinical observation, both the ventral surface of his tongue and the floor of his mouth appear erythematous and several discrete lesions are appreciated involving both of those areas. What is the most likely explanation for J.B.'s new onset of symptoms? What treatment is indicated at this time?

J.B.'s symptoms are consistent with therapy-related stomatitis/mucositis. As discussed earlier, this complication is a consequence of the nonspecific effect of antineoplastic agents and radiation therapy on the basal epithelium which results in mucosal atrophy. Nonkeratinized mucosa is affected most often. The buccal, labial, and soft palate mucosa, along with the ventral surface of the tongue and the floor of the mouth are the most common sites. Lesions are discrete initially, but often progress to produce large areas of ulceration; although they do not progress outside the mouth they may extend to the esophagus and involve the entire GI tract.

Pain is the most common presenting symptom of mucositis. Signs and symptoms of mucositis generally occur approximately five to seven days after the administration of chemotherapy or at almost any point in a course of radiation. Many antineoplastic agents are capable of producing direct stomatotoxicity including antimetabolites (in particular, methotrexate, fluorouracil, and cytarabine) as well as many "antitumor antibiotics." Lesions generally regress and resolve completely in approximately one to three weeks depending upon the severity of the lesions.

The major clinical problem associated with direct stomatotoxicity is pain, often severe enough to require parenteral narcotic analgesics. Even less severe cases interfere with the patient's ability to eat and speak. Bacterial, fungal, and herpetic infection from mucosal lesions also can occur. Oral lesions vary in size and the appearance of the lesion does not always relate directly to the causative microbial agent. This is particularly true in neutropenic patients who are unable to mount a full inflammatory response; here the clinical appearance of an infected lesion may be muted relative to the presence or number of pathogens. The most life-threatening complication of stomatotoxicity is the development of sepsis related to a mucosal infection. Under normal conditions, the mucosa provides a natural barrier to the entry of normal oral flora into the bloodstream. When the integrity of the mucosa is disrupted, these organisms may invade the bloodstream more easily.

Treatment of mucositis is palliative. Topical anesthetics, including viscous lidocaine or dyclonine hydrochloride 0.5% or 1%, often are recommended due to their local anesthetic properties. Equal portions of Kaopectate, diphenhydramine elixir, and magnesium- and aluminum-containing antacids also may be beneficial due to their astringent and anesthetic properties. Many institutions may compound mouthwash products containing such ingredients as di-

phenhydramine, antibiotics, nystatin, and a corticosteroid. In these cases, the corticosteroid and the diphenhydramine are used for their anti-inflammatory and anesthetic properties, and the antibiotic and antifungal ingredients are intended to reduce the bacterial or fungal content of the oral mucosa. Sucralfate suspension also has been used to treat mucositis. All of these topically applied products are used for symptom control only and data supporting superior efficacy of one product over another in relieving pain are lacking.

All of the topical anesthetic-type preparations are recommended for use as "swish-and-spit" preparations. Generally, 5 to 10 mL are applied three to six times a day. The longer the patient can hold the solution in the mouth, the longer the contact, and, theoretically, the better the results. Therefore, patients should be advised to hold and swish the solution around the mouth for as long as possible before spitting it out. For small localized lesions, ointments such as benzocaine in Orabase may be applied to the affected area after it is dried with a sponge. Patients often find cold ice chips soothing; however, in most cases, systemic analgesics will be required as well.

J.B. appears to have a mild case of stomatitis and mucositis at this time; however, the lesions may progress over the next several days. Appropriate treatment may include the use of any of the topical products listed in Table 91.1. Table 91.2 lists additional guidelines for management of stomatitis.

9. Prevention. Could J.B.'s mucositis have been prevented?

Historically, treatment of chemotherapy- and radiation-induced mucositis has been aimed at reducing symptoms once they occur and avoiding further trauma to the oral mucosa. Specific measures to reduce the incidence or severity of chemotherapy-induced mucositis have received some attention in the past few years. *Cryotherapy* has been reported to be marginally effective in reducing the severity of chemotherapy-induced mucositis.[48] Cryotherapy consists of placing ice chips in the mouth five minutes before chemotherapy begins and continuing for 30 minutes. The rationale for this procedure is to reduce blood flow to the mouth and thus, protect the dividing cell population from toxins. The use of *allopurinol* to prevent mucositis induced by fluorouracil has been reported to have some efficacy in two studies; however, a larger, well-controlled investigation failed to substantiate this claim.[49-51] *Chlorhexidine* gluconate 0.12% also may reduce the frequency and severity of mucositis infection associated with chemotherapy and radiation therapy;[52,53] however, not all studies have shown benefit. This solution is used twice daily as a rinse. Side effects are minimal

Table 91.2	Guidelines for the Management of Stomatitis

Remove dentures to prevent further irritation and tissue damage

Maintain gentle brushing of teeth with a soft toothbrush

Avoid mouthwashes or rinses that contain alcohol because they may be painful and cause drying of the mucosa

Lubricants, such as artificial saliva, may loosen mucus and prevent membranes from sticking together. Avoid mineral oil and petroleum jelly because they can be aspirated

Apply local anesthetics for localized pain control, especially before meals. Systemic analgesics may be required to control pain associated with severe mucositis

Ensure that adequate hydration and nutrition are maintained
- Eat a bland diet, avoiding spiced, acidic, and salted foods
- Avoid rough food; process in a blender if necessary
- Use sugar-free gum or sugar-free hard candy to stimulate salivation and facilitate mastication
- If necessary, provide IV support

and include occasional burning (which is thought to be due to the product's alcohol content and can be reduced by diluting it with water) and brown superficial tooth staining which can be polished off easily. The mechanism by which chlorhexidine reduces the frequency and severity of mucositis is by elimination of microorganisms in the oral cavity. Preliminary and anecdotal data suggest that some *growth factors* may positively modify mucositis in myelosuppressed cancer patients.[54] This also may be related to reduction of the bacterial population in the oral cavity.

Unfortunately, there are no proven methods to prevent chemotherapy- or radiation-induced mucositis. The only sure way to decrease the incidence and severity of the symptoms is to reduce the dose of chemotherapy or the amount of radiation therapy that the patient is receiving. Although this usually is not desirable, stomatitis is a dose-limiting toxicity associated with many chemotherapy regimens.

Dermatologic Toxicities

Dermatologic toxicities, such as alopecia, nail changes, dry skin, and blistering, appear to result from the ability of antineoplastic agents to reduce or inhibit mitotic activity in the epidermis and nail matrix. Cancer chemotherapy also causes a number of skin reactions when it interacts with ultraviolet (UV) light, radiation, or vesicant antineoplastic agents which have extravasated from the veins into surrounding soft tissue. In addition, a number of antineoplastic agents produce specific skin eruptions, nonspecific eruptions, or ''rashes'' by unknown mechanisms. A number of reviews serve as excellent references.[55-57]

Alopecia

10. Pathogenesis. C.W., a 45-year-old female with recently diagnosed breast cancer, had a lumpectomy to be followed by 20 courses of radiation to the affected breast. She is in the clinic today to receive the first of 6 cycles of cyclophosphamide, doxorubicin, and fluorouracil. C.W. had minimal problems with surgery; however, she is particularly fearful of receiving combination chemotherapy. You are counseling C.W. regarding the most common toxicities and begin by reviewing with her the likelihood of myelosuppression, nausea, and vomiting and the management of these conditions. C.W. is appropriately attentive as you discuss these with her; however, her overriding concern is whether or not she will lose her hair. Is C.W.'s concern typical of most cancer patients? How would you respond?

C.W.'s concern regarding hair loss is typical of cancer patients embarking on a course of chemotherapy. In fact, a number of investigators have reported that hair loss ranks second only to nausea and vomiting as a cancer patient's greatest fear. Because hair bulb cells replicate every 12 to 24 hours, they are quite susceptible to a variety of cytotoxic agents. Normally, hair follicles independently move through phases of growth (anagen), involution or transition (catagen), and rest (telogen) in a cyclic fashion. About 100 scalp hairs are lost daily, but of the approximately 100,000 follicles in a typical scalp, approximately 85% to 90% are in anagen or the growth phase of the hair cycle. Cytotoxic drugs may inhibit mitosis partially or completely or impair metabolic processes in the hair matrix. This results in either a thinned, weakened hair shaft or a complete failure to form hair. Even mild trauma, such as normal hair grooming or rubbing the head on a pillow, can fracture the thinned shaft leading to hair loss. Hair loss usually begins seven to ten days after a single treatment with chemotherapy and generally is quite prominent within one or two months. Other terminal hairs, such as beards, eyebrows, eyelashes, axillary, and pubic hair are affected; however, these effects are somewhat variable depending upon the rate of mitosis and the percentage of hairs in anagen.[55-57]

It should be emphasized to C.W. that alopecia from chemotherapy is reversible and that hair regeneration will begin one to two months after therapy is discontinued. The color and texture of her hair may be altered, however. C.W.'s new hair may be lighter or darker in color and may be curlier as it regrows. Drugs most commonly associated with severe alopecia are listed in Table 91.3.

Prevention. A number of interventions have been proposed to prevent scalp hair loss during chemotherapy. These procedures attempt to prevent drug circulation to the hair follicles by causing temporary vasoconstriction with either an occlusive scalp tourniquet or an ice cap producing localized hypothermia. Generally, the correct use of these caps or scalp tourniquets includes occlusion of the superficial scalp vein by the cap/tourniquet before the antineoplastic agent is given and for several hours following the time of peak drug concentration. Recognizing that such devices create a refuge for tumor cells, these procedures are contraindicated in patients with hematologic malignancies and in other individuals at risk for scalp metastases. Although these scalp icing devices had been manufactured by several U.S. companies and had been marketed for a number of years, the FDA reviewed these devices early in 1990 and became concerned that their safety and efficacy had not been substantiated by adequate clinical data.[59-63] The FDA halted the commercial distribution of these devices at that time and requested evidence or data to address the following concerns:

- The potential for scalp metastases posed by the use of these devices;

- The potential for reducing drug circulation to other anatomic sites beyond the scalp, such as the skull and possibly the brain; and

- The effectiveness of these devices in preventing hair loss and how specific cytotoxic doses and other variables affected the results achieved.

No company has come forward to date with clinical evidence supporting the reasonable safety and effectiveness of these devises. Although these devices are not available commercially, there are other ways to induce scalp hypothermia or create a scalp tourni-

Table 91.3	Single Agents Associated with Alopecia, Pigmentation Changes, and Nail Disorders	
	Frequent	Occasional
Alopecia[a]	Cyclophosphamide	Mechlorethamine
	Ifosfamide	Thiotepa
	Fluorouracil	Methotrexate
	Dactinomycin	Vinblastine
	Daunorubicin	Vincristine
	Doxorubicin	Etoposide
	Bleomycin	BCNU
	Vindesine	Hydroxyurea
	Paclitaxel	
Pigmentation	Busulfan	Cyclophosphamide
	Fluorouracil	Methotrexate
	Doxorubicin	Dactinomycin
	Bleomycin	Daunorubicin
		Hydroxyurea
Nail	—	Cyclophosphamide
		Fluorouracil
		Daunorubicin
		Doxorubicin
		Bleomycin
		Hydroxyurea

[a] Degree and onset of alopecia are dependent upon dose, schedule of administration, rate and route of delivery, and various combinations of agents.

quet. The questions of safety and efficacy raised by the FDA should be discussed with patients seeking information about these devices and hair preservation techniques.[59-63]

C.W.'s concern is a legitimate one expressed by many cancer patients, not just those with breast cancer. Unfortunately, she is likely to experience near or complete hair loss depending upon the thickness of her hair and its growth rate. Thus, she should be told how to minimize the impact of alopecia on her appearance through the use of hair pieces or stylish head scarves, turbans, or hats. She also should be referred to volunteer groups and organizations that can help her through this difficult time. For example, several small private businesses have been started by former patients who distribute or sell hair coverings of various designs. Hair pieces are tax deductible as a medical expense and are covered by some health insurance policies. If C.W. thinks she will use a hair piece, she should be advised to select a wig soon, before hair loss begins, so that she will have a piece that matches the color and style of her hair when alopecia or significant hair loss occurs. Other resources include the American Cancer Society's rehabilitation program called "Look Good Feel Better" which was developed to assist women compensating for hair loss and skin changes during cancer treatment. Also, the American Cancer Society Hot-Line (1–800–395–LOOK) can help C.W. find volunteer beauticians and cosmetologists who help women look and feel more comfortable with changes in their appearance caused by chemotherapy including dry, discolored, or blotching skin; discolored nails; and alopecia. (See Table 91.4 for other resources for breast cancer patients.)

Skin and Nail Changes

11. Besides alopecia, what other skin or nail changes should C.W. anticipate?

Several skin and nail changes have been associated with chemotherapy which C.W. may find disturbing. Fortunately, the major consequences of these toxicities are cosmetic and resolution can be expected 6 to 12 months after chemotherapy has been completed.

Nail Changes. The growth of fingernails and toenails is arrested in a manner similar to hair growth. A reduction or a cessation of mitotic activity in the nail matrix results in a horizontal depression of the nail plate. Within weeks, these pale horizontal lines ("Beau's lines") begin to appear in the nail beds and are most commonly observed in patients who have received chemotherapy for six months or more. These *growth arrest* lines move distally as the nail grows and normally disappear from the fingernails in approximately six months.[64] Less well understood are the changes in nail pigmentation associated with cyclophosphamide, fluorouracil, daunorubicin, doxorubicin, and bleomycin.[65-72] Brown or blue lines are deposited as horizontal or vertical bands in the nails and are seen more commonly in dark skinned individuals.[71] Like Beau's lines, these pigmentation lines generally grow out with the nail.

Dermatological pigment changes are among the most common and least well understood side effects of cancer chemotherapy. Hyperpigmentation is by far the most frequently seen pigmentation abnormality, but hypopigmentation has been reported occasionally. In the majority of patients who demonstrate hyperpigmentation, there is no identifiable cause and no systemic toxicity associated with it. Hyperpigmentation following antitumor medications commonly is diffuse and generalized; however, it may be quite localized, involving only the mucus membrane, hair, or nails.

Wide-spread cutaneous hyperpigmentation has been reported following busulfan, cyclophosphamide, fluorouracil, dactinomycin, and hydroxyurea.[66,73-78] An Addisonian-like syndrome consisting of diffuse cutaneus hyperpigmentation, weakness, weight

Table 91.4	Information and Toll-Free Hotlines for Cancer Support

Toll-Free Hotlines

- The American Cancer Society's (ACS) National Toll-Free Hotline: 800 ACS-2345
- The American College of Radiology (ACR): 800 648-8900
- The American Society of Plastic and Reconstructive Surgeons: 800 635-0635
- Breast Settlement Information Line: 800 887-6828
- The FDA Breast Implant Hotline: 800 532-4440
- National Bone Marrow Transplant Link: 800 546-5268
- The National Cancer Institute (NCI): 800 4-CANCER
- The National Cancer Information Service (NCI): 800 4-CANCER
- The National Consumer Insurance Helpline (HIAA): 800 942-4242
- The National Council Against Health Fraud: 800 821-6671
- The National Lymphedema Network: 800 541-3259
- PDQ (Physicians Data Query): 800 4-CANCER
- The Susan Komen Alliance Treatment and Information Line: 800 462-9273 [800-I'M AWARE]
- The Susan G. Komen Breast Cancer Foundation: 800 462-9273 [800-I'M AWARE]
- The Y-ME National Organization for Breast Cancer Information and Support's National Toll-free Hotline: 800 221-2141[a]

Organizations for Information and Support

- Cancer Care, Inc., and the National Cancer Care Foundation: (212) 221-3300
- Cancer Research Council: (301) 654-7933
- The Chemotherapy Foundation: (212) 213-9292
- The Health Insurance Association of America (HIAA): (202) 866-6244
- The National Alliance of Breast Cancer Organizations (NABCO): (212) 719-0154
- The National Breast Cancer Coalition: (202) 296-7477
- The National Coalition for Cancer Survivorship: (505) 764-9956

[a] A support line for husbands.

loss, and diarrhea has been reported in patients receiving busulfan. Pulmonary fibrosis is more common in patients with this form of hyperpigmentation,[57] and the pigmentation change usually resolves when busulfan is discontinued. Despite extensive evaluation, endocrine abnormalities consistent with Addison's disease have not been documented.

A peculiar serpiginous hyperpigmentation has been observed over veins used to administer fluorouracil and bleomycin.[71-80] Some investigators have attributed this phenomenon to a subclinical phlebitis. Hyperpigmentation over pressure points has been noted following the use of bleomycin, and hyperpigmentation caused by hydroxyurea has been described as more prominent in traumatized areas. Peculiar linear or flagellate streaks of hyperpigmentation have been described in association with bleomycin administration. Because of their characteristic location and appearance, it has been assumed that these streaks result from scratching during therapy; however, attempts to reproduce these lesions iatrogenically thus far have been unsuccessful. Thiotepa has been reported to cause hyperpigmentation in areas of skin occluded by bandages, presumably by toxicity to the skin from thiotepa secretion in sweat.[81] Interestingly, skin contact with thiotepa has been reported to cause hypopigmentation.[82] Topical contact with mechlorethamine and carmustine has been reported to cause hyperpigmentation.[83,84]

Table 91.5	Chemotherapy and Radiation Reactions	
Radiation Enhancement Reactions		
Bleomycin	Doxorubicin	Hydroxyurea
Dactinomycin	Fluorouracil	Methotrexate
Radiation Recall Reactions		
All of the above *plus:*		
Etoposide	Vinblastine	Paclitaxel
Reactions with Ultraviolet Light		
Phototoxic reactions		
Dacarbazine	Thioguanine	
Fluorouracil	Vinblastine	
Reactivation of sunburn		
Methotrexate		

Although hyperpigmentation of the nails and skin is quite common, methotrexate is the only antineoplastic agent to date that has been reported to cause hyperpigmented banding of light colored hair. This has been described in a patient receiving intermittent high-dose methotrexate and has been referred to by some investigators as the "flag sign" of chemotherapy.[85]

As previously stated, pigmentary changes which occur in individuals receiving chemotherapy are basically a cosmetic concern. It is important to anticipate these distressing side effects and educate patients in appropriate cases. At this time, it may be appropriate to explain to C.W. that these side effects may occur since she will be receiving a number of the agents that have been implicated in producing both diffuse, as well as localized, cutaneous nail hyperpigmentation. She should be reassured that should hyperpigmentation occur, it usually resolves with time.

Hand-Foot Syndrome. There are numerous reports of patients receiving chemotherapy who develop tender, erythematous skin on their palms and, sometimes, on the soles of their feet. Complaints of tingling or burning also may be present. These changes may resolve after several days or progress to bullous lesions which desquamate. This reaction is referred to as "chemotherapy-associated acral erythema" or "the palmar-plantar erythrodysesthesia syndrome." Drugs reported to cause this reaction include cytarabine, fluorouracil, doxorubicin, methotrexate, and hydroxyurea.[56,57] Most of the reported cases involve leukemia patients who have received bone marrow transplants or blood products or patients receiving continuous infusions or large doses of the agents listed above.

Dry Skin. Many chemotherapeutic agents (especially bleomycin, hydroxyurea, and fluorouracil) can cause dry skin with fine scaling on the surface. This effect has been attributed to the cytostatic effect of antineoplastics on biologically active sebaceous and sweat glands. Normally, sebaceous and sweat glands provide lipids, lactates, and other products which contribute to the pliability and moisture retention of the stratum corneum. Topical application of emollient creams may provide some symptomatic relief of this dryness.

Interactions with Radiation

12. C.W. recently completed her course of total breast irradiation. She also plans to leave for a 1-week vacation in Florida 3 days after this clinic visit. Are there any interactions between radiation therapy and sunlight exposure with chemotherapeutic agents? Are there any specific precautions that C.W. should take, or signs and symptoms of toxicity that she should be made aware of?

The interactions between chemotherapy and radiation, or UV light (from both external beam and natural sources) can be divided into radiation enhancement, radiation recall, photosensitivity reactions, and sunburn reactivation (see Table 91.5). A number of

excellent reviews are available which describe each of these interactions in great detail. The important principles of the interaction between radiation and chemotherapy are described below.[55–57]

There is a synergistic interaction between a small number of antineoplastic agents and irradiation that results in enhanced radiation effect. The leading explanation for this enhancement of radiation effect is that these agents interfere with the cellular process of radiation repair. Radiation causes alterations in the molecular structure of DNA. A mechanism of excision repair can remove small damaged portions of one strand of DNA and insert new bases using the other strand as a template. Excision repair requires several enzymes including DNA polymerase. Chemotherapy drugs may interfere with some of the enzymes and synthetic mechanisms needed to rejuvenate sublethally damaged cells. Obviously, the synergistic effect of radiation and chemotherapy can be exploited therapeutically and often is in the treatment of solid tumors. Unfortunately, this same reaction inadvertently may cause undesirable reactions in non-neoplastic tissues, especially the skin, esophagus, lung, and GI tract. The skin is the most common target of radiation enhancement reactions. However, radiation enhancement in the skin, as well as other organs, may produce tissue necrosis severe enough to delay or discontinue further therapy and/or significantly compromise the functions of vital organs.

The primary distinction between radiation enhancement reactions and radiation recall reactions lies in the temporal relationship between radiation and chemotherapy. Generally, enhancement reactions occur when chemotherapy is given concurrently or within one week of irradiation. Radiation recall reactions occur when treatment with a chemotherapeutic drug causes an inflammatory reaction in a tissue that was previously treated with irradiation (e.g., when chemotherapy is administered several weeks to years after radiation therapy). Radiation recall is independent of previous, clinically-apparent radiation damage. Not surprisingly, the chemotherapeutic agents that have been associated with radiation enhancement reactions and radiation recall reactions are the same. Drugs most commonly associated with these reactions include the antitumor antibiotics dactinomycin and doxorubicin; however, bleomycin, fluorouracil, hydroxyurea, methotrexate, etoposide, vinblastine, and paclitaxel also have been implicated.

Ultraviolet light has sufficient energy to cause photochemical alterations in biologic molecules. Chemotherapy drugs may interact with UV light, but the reactions usually are less severe than x-ray-enhancing reactions and may well be due to a different mechanism. Photosensitivity reactions, defined as enhanced erythema responses to UV light, have been reported with dacarbazine, fluorouracil, methotrexate, and vinblastine. Reactivation of sunburn has been reported after methotrexate therapy. This is similar to,

Table 91.6	Chemotherapeutic Drugs Reported to Produce Local Toxicities	
Potential Vesicants		
Dactinomycin	Mitomycin	
Daunorubicin	Plicamycin	
Doxorubicin	Streptozocin	
Idarubicin	Vinblastine	
Mechlorethamine	Vincristine	
Potential Irritants		
Carmustine	Etoposide	
Cisplatin	Mitoxantrone	
Dacarbazine		
Drugs That Produce Local Hypersensitivity Reactions		
Daunorubicin	Idarubicin	
Doxorubicin	Mechlorethamine	

although generally far less severe than, the radiation recall reactions described previously. The reaction may be more severe than the initial sunburn, resulting in severe blisters, and occurs only in patients who receive large doses of methotrexate. The precise incidences of photosensitivity reactions caused by chemotherapeutic drugs are unknown, but they may be more common than generally believed. For example, photosensitivity may account for many of the erythematous periodic rashes attributed to allergy.

C.W. received doxorubicin and fluorouracil, both of which can interact with radiation. Although not commonly reported, doxorubicin also may cause some increased erythema in the specific area of skin at which irradiation was directed. Since C.W. may be at some increased risk for a photosensitivity reaction, she should be advised to avoid direct exposure to the sunlight for several days to a week following chemotherapy administration. Although no data exist regarding the efficacy of sunscreens in this patient population, C.W. should be advised to use a protective sunscreen with a high sun protective factor when she cannot avoid sun exposure. Furthermore, she should periodically assess her skin's reaction to the sun with intermittent periods of rest and observation throughout the day.

13. How will C.W. know if she has a radiation reaction? How should she be managed if a such a reaction occurs?

If C.W. has a radiation reaction, she will experience "easy burning" and erythema or redness, followed by dry desquamation. However, if her reaction is more severe, small blisters (vesicles) and oozing can develop. Necrosis with persistent painful ulceration occurs in the most severe cases. Post-inflammatory hyperpigmentation or depigmentation may follow.

Milder cases can be treated with topical steroids in an emollient cream base and cool wet compresses. Necrosis and ulcers are notoriously difficult to treat because irradiated skin does not heal well. When ulcers occur, treatment is aimed at keeping the ulcer clean with surgical debridement. Even when the ulcers are clean, there may be persistent exudation and bacterial contamination. Radiation reactions which occur in tissues other than the skin (e.g., the lungs, esophagus, GI tract) often are managed with oral corticosteroids, although data regarding the efficacy of these agents in ameliorating the symptoms or reducing the extent of damage are lacking.

Irritant and Vesicant Reactions

14. C.W. complained of pain and burning at the injection site immediately following the administration of her third course of IV chemotherapy with cyclophosphamide, doxorubicin, and fluorouracil. She described the sensation as being distinctly different from the mild discomfort she had experienced with previous chemotherapy administration. Physical examination of the injection site revealed mild erythema and slight induration. What types of local reactions can occur following the administration of chemotherapy?

Several distinct types of local reactions (ranging from transient local irritation to severe tissue necrosis of the skin, surrounding vasculature, and supporting structures) have been reported following the administration of chemotherapy.[86,87] (See Table 91.6.) Some of these reactions (particularly those associated with anthracycline antitumor antibiotics) may be the result of local hypersensitivity reactions. These reactions usually are characterized by immediate local burning, itching, and erythema and some patients may experience a "flare" reaction along the length of the vein used for drug injection.[88,89] Hypersensitivity reactions usually are self-limited and subside within a few hours. Administration of the antihistamine, diphenhydramine, before the next course of chemotherapy may reduce the severity or duration of hypersensitivity

reactions.[88,89] In some cases, irritation of the vein (or phlebitis) due to the irritant properties of a drug (e.g., mechlorethamine) or a diluent (e.g., carmustine) occurs.

Local reactions resulting from the extravasation of vesicant or irritant drugs may be much more severe. All vesicant drugs potentially can produce these devastating reactions; however, drugs known to bind to DNA (i.e., the anthracyclines) have the propensity to produce the most severe damage. Administration of an antineoplastic agent may produce phlebitis and pain, and extravasations may cause local irritation or soft tissue ulcers depending upon the amount, drug, and concentration of the extravasate. In addition, there is no clear agreement regarding the vesicant potential of many antineoplastic agents and various references may categorize vesicant versus irritant agents differently. Initially, it may be impossible to distinguish a local irritant reaction from a vesicant extravasation; therefore, if a vesicant or irritant drug has been administered, the reaction should be treated as though it is a potential extravasation.

Infiltration of a vesicant into tissue often produces a severe burning sensation which may persist for hours. However, in some cases no immediate symptoms or signs are evident. In the days to weeks that follow, the skin overlying the extravasation site may become reddened and firm. Redness may gradually diminish, or progress to ulceration and necrosis. Histologically, inflammatory cells rarely are observed in either human tissue samples or experimental animal models.[90,91]

Table 91.7	Guidelines for Administration of Cytotoxic Agents[92,93,102]

- Administration of chemotherapy should be performed only by individuals familiar with its toxic effects
- The site of infusion is selected with consideration of visualization of the vessel, its size, and potential damage if extravasation occurs in the following order of preference: forearm > dorsum of the hand > wrist > antecubital fossa
  - Limbs with compromised circulation (e.g., invading neoplasm, axillary dissection, severe bruising) should not be used
  - The lower extremities should not be used
  - Pre-existing IV lines should not be used because the site may already have occult vein or tissue irritation or phlebitis
- A 23 or 25 gauge scalp vein ("butterfly") needle is inserted into the vein. Only 1 venipuncture should be performed on a vein to avoid leakage
- The wings of the needle should be lightly taped in place with care not to obscure the injection site so that it may be visualized during injection
- Test the integrity of the IV line by injecting a small volume of saline solution and withdrawing a small amount of blood. If extravasation of the saline is obvious, select another vein or a site proximal on the same vein to avoid upstream leakage
- Administer the drug at the recommended rate (preferably through the tubing of an IV running by gravity to assess for back pressure)
- During the administration, question the patient about discomfort, check for blood return by aspirating the syringe gently, observe the continuous flow of the running IV and visualize the IV site frequently. If the patency of the line is in doubt at any time, the injection should be stopped and an alternate site selected
- After administration, the IV line should be flushed with at least 10 mL of saline or other IV fluid to flush the needle and tubing of all drug
- If multiple drugs are to be given, the IV should be flushed between each drug
- Apply pressure with sterile gauze for 3–4 minutes after the needle is removed. Inspect the site before applying bandage

Table 91.8	Suggested Procedures for Management of Suspected Extravasation of Vesicant Drugs[92,93,102]

Stop the injection immediately, but do not remove the needle. Any drug remaining in the tubing or needle, as well as the infiltrated area should be aspirated

Contact a physician as soon as possible

If deemed appropriate, instill an antidote in the infiltrated areas (via the extravasated IV needle if possible)

Remove the needle

Apply ice to the site and elevate the extremity for the first 24 to 48 hr. (If vinca or podophyllotoxin, use warm compresses)

Document the drug, suspected volume extravasated, and the treatment in the patient's medical record

Check the site frequently for 5–7 days

Consult a surgeon familiar with extravasations early so that they can periodically review the site and if ulceration begins they can rapidly assess if surgical debridement or excision is necessary

15. What factors increase the risk of extravasation and what administration techniques and precautions can minimize these risks?

Several factors have been associated with an increased risk of extravasation and subsequent tissue damage following administration of chemotherapy. These include: 1) generalized vascular disease such as that found in elderly and debilitated patients or in patients who have undergone frequent venipuncture and administration of irritating chemotherapy (the latter causes venous fragility, instability, or decreased local blood flow); 2) elevated venous pressure such as that which occurs in patients with tumor obstruction of the superior vena cava or obstructed venous drainage following axillary dissection; 3) prior radiation therapy to the site of injection; 4) recent venipuncture in the same vein which may result in drug leakage; and 5) use of injection sites over joints where there may be an increased risk of needle dislodgement.[92,93] In addition, tissue damage may be more severe if extravasation occurs in areas where there is only a small amount of subcutaneous tissue (e.g., the back of the hand or wrist) because wound healing is difficult and there is increased exposure of deeper structures such as the tendons.[89] Also, in an experimental model, the size and healing times for skin ulcers increased with the volume and con-

centration of doxorubicin administered.[94] These risks have led to the increased use of indwelling central catheters in patients receiving vesicant chemotherapy.

Extravasations of vesicant drugs can produce such devastating tissue damage that loss of an extremity or death can result; therefore, major emphasis must be placed on prevention. All individuals who administer vesicant or irritant chemotherapy should be skilled in IV drug administration and must receive special instruction before administering these drugs. The patient also must be told how drug administration should feel and to report any change in sensation including pain, burning, or itching immediately. Recommendations to reduce the risk of local complications during cytotoxic drug administration are outlined in Table 91.7 on page 91–11.

16. The oncology nurse believes that the doxorubicin may have extravasated during C.W.'s chemotherapy administration. How should this be managed? Do management guidelines differ for other vesicant drugs?

Immediate management of a potential vesicant extravasation should include stopping the injection if all the drug has not been administered. Various other measures have been recommended which may minimize vesicant exposure and subsequent tissue damage (see Table 91.8). These include application of cold compresses to the extravasation site and elevation of the extremity. Warm compresses are recommended for vinca alkaloids and podophyllotoxins.[86,87] Specific antidotes thought to inactivate the extravasated drug have been suggested; however, many of these antidotes are based upon observations in a very few patients or animal models and their effectiveness, in many cases, is unsubstantiated. Some have suggested that antidotes recommended in some guidelines may actually worsen tissue damage (e.g., sodium bicarbonate for doxorubicin). Recommended treatments for suspected extravasation of vesicant drugs are outlined in Table 91.9.[86,87]

Since doxorubicin skin damage may be related to the formation of toxic free radicals of oxygen, a free radical scavenger may prevent ulceration. Dimethyl sulfoxide (DMSO) is a potent free radical scavenger that penetrates all tissue planes. In pig and rat models, topical DMSO has decreased doxorubicin-induced skin ulcers.[95] Several series of case reports and a single-arm clinical study have reported that topical application of DMSO is safe and beneficial for anthracycline extravasation.[96–99] DMSO also has been reported to be beneficial in patients with mitomycin extravasations.[100]

Table 91.9	Recommended Extravasation Antidotes[a]	
Class/Specific Agents	Local Antidote Recommended	Specific Procedure
Alkylating agents Cisplatin[b] Mechlorethamine	1/6 or 1/3 M solution sodium thiosulfate	Mix 4–8 mL 10% sodium thiosulfate USP with 6 mL of sterile water for injection, USP for a 1/6 or 1/3 M solution. Into site inject 2 mL for each mg of mechlorethamine or 100 mg of cisplatin extravasated
Mitomycin-C	Dimethylsulfoxide 50%–99% (w/v)	Apply 1–2 mL to the site Q 6 hr for 14 days. Allow to air-dry; do not cover
DNA intercalators Doxorubicin Daunorubicin	Cold compresses Dimethylsulfoxide 50%–99% (w/v)	Apply immediately for 30–60 min for 1 day Apply 1–2 mL to the site Q 6 hr for 14 days. Allow to air-dry; do not cover
Vinca alkaloids Vinblastine Vincristine	Warm compresses Hyaluronidase	Apply immediately for 30–60 min, then alternate off/on every 15 min for 1 day Inject 150 U hyaluronidase (Wydase) into site
Epipodophyllotoxins[b] Etoposide Teniposide	Warm compresses Hyaluronidase	Apply immediately for 30–60 min, then alternate off/on every 15 min for 1 day. Inject 150 U hyaluronidase (Wydase) into site

[a] Reprinted with permission from Reference 86.
[b] Treatment indicated only for large extravasations (e.g., doses one half or more of the planned total dose for that course of therapy).

Table 91.10		National Cancer Institute Common Toxicity Criteria			
Toxicity[a]	Grade 0[a]	Grade 1	Grade 2[a]	Grade 3	Grade 4
Hematologic					
WBC	≥4.0	3.0–3.9	2.0–2.9	1.0–1.9	<1.0
Platelets	WNL	75.0–Normal	50.0–74.9	25.0–49.9	<25.0
Hgb gm/100 mL	WNL	10.0–Normal	8.0–10.0	6.5–7.9	<6.5
gm/L	WNL	100–Normal	80–100	65–79	<65
mmol/L	WNL	6.2–Normal	4.95–6.2	4.0–4.9	<4.0
Granulocytes/bands	≥2.0	1.5–1.9	1.0–1.4	0.5–0.9	<0.5
Lymphocytes	≥2.0	1.5–1.9	1.0–1.4	0.5–0.9	<0.5
Hematologic (other)	None	Mild	Moderate	Severe	Life-threatening
Hemorrhage (Clinical)	None	Mild, no transfusion	Gross, 1–2 units transfusion per episode	Gross, 3–4 units transfusion per episode	Massive, >4 units transfusion per episode
Infection	None	Mild, no active treatment	Moderate, PO antibiotic	Severe, IV antibiotic, antifungal, or hospitalization	Life-threatening
Gastrointestinal					
Nausea	None	Able to eat reasonable intake	Intake significantly ↓ but can eat	No significant intake	—
Vomiting	None	1 episode in 24 hr	2–5 episodes in 24 hr	6–10 episodes in 24 hr	>10 episodes in 24 hr or requiring parenteral support
Diarrhea	None	↑ of 2–3 stools/day over pretreatment	↑ of 4–6 stools/day or nocturnal stools, or moderate cramping	↑ of 7–9 stools/day or incontinence, or severe cramping	↑ of ≥10 stools/day or grossly bloody diarrhea, or need for parenteral support

[a] PO = Orally; WBC = White blood cell; WNL = Within normal limits.

Hypersensitivity Reactions

All cancer chemotherapeutic agents except altretamine, the nitrosureas, and dactinomycin, have produced at least an isolated instance of a hypersensitivity reaction.[102,103] All types of hypersensitivity reactions are represented in the reactions produced by antitumor drugs, although Type 1 is the most common. Type 1 hypersensitivity reactions occur when an antigen interacts with IgE bound to a mast cell membrane, causing degranulation of mast cells. Major signs and symptoms of Type 1 reactions include urticaria, angioedema, rash, bronchospasm, abdominal cramping, and hypotension. Although many reactions from cytotoxic agents probably are immunologically mediated, there are other possible mechanisms for Type 1 or immediate reactions. These include the degranulation of mast cells and basophils through a direct effect on the cell surface, thus releasing histamine and other vasoactive substances. Activation of the alternative complement pathway also can result in the release of vasoactive substances from mast cells. When non-IgE mediated mechanisms account for the symptoms of a Type 1 reaction, it is called an ''anaphylactoid reaction.''

Many of the Type 1 hypersensitivity reactions produced by chemotherapeutic agents appear to be mediated by non-IgE mechanisms. Although little research has been done to elucidate the mechanism for most hypersensitivity reactions produced by antineoplastic agents, two features of these reactions suggest that they are not IgE mediated. The first is that many of these reactions occur following the first dose of an agent. This is in contrast to immunological reactions that require prior exposure (i.e., one must be sensitized before becoming hypersensitized). In addition, certain symptoms or complexes are more diagnostic of immunologically-mediated disorders. These include urticaria, angioedema, bronchospasm, laryngeal spasm, cytopenias, arthritis, mucositis, vasculitic syndromes, and vesicular dermatitis. The absence of any of these symptoms or an adverse reaction soon after the first dose makes it less likely that the patient has had an immunologically-mediated hypersensitivity reaction. Although the spectrum of symptoms and their severity varies widely in the cases reported, most hypersensitivity reactions that occur with antineoplastic agents are classified as Grade 1 (transient rash, mild) or Grade 2 (mild bronchospasm, moderate) by the National Cancer Institute (NCI) Common Toxicity Criteria and do not include all of these symptoms. Furthermore, a patient who has had a reaction to an agent safely can be given subsequent courses if appropriate premedication is given in many instances. For example, preventive medication allows many (>60%) patients who have previously experienced a hypersensitivity reaction secondary to paclitaxel to continue therapy and also reduces the incidence of hypersensitivity reactions associated with short duration of infusion (i.e., 3 hours).[104] (See Table 91.10 for NCI Common Toxicity Criteria.)

Antineoplastic agents most frequently reported to produce hypersensitivity reactions and their characteristic reactions are listed in Table 91.11. Available information is largely from patient series and case reports and often is conflicting and contradictory, particularly with respect to incidence, severity, characteristic symptoms, time course, and the success of rechallenge. If a patient experiences a hypersensitivity reaction or a suspected hypersensitivity reaction and continued therapy is desired, a full review of all of the relevant literature as well as manufacturer's data is advised. A number of excellent reviews are available to assist in this effort.[102,103]

If a patient develops a severe Type 1 hypersensitivity reaction to any antitumor drug, treatment usually is stopped. If available, an analog or another drug in the same chemical class could be substituted in hopes that cross-reactivity will not occur. Recommended treatment of hypersensitivity reactions is reviewed in Table 91.12. If the reaction is mild or moderate, another course of the drug may be possible if it is preceded by methods to prevent or minimize hypersensitivity reactions. Although true Type 1 anaphylactic reactions seldom are circumvented by preventive measures, use of pretreatment antihistamines and corticosteroids will reduce the incidence and severity of Type 1 anaphylactoid reactions caused by roentgenographic contrast agents.[105,106] General recommendations for preventing anaphylactoid reactions are found in Table 91.11. Although pretreatment with prednisone and diphenhydramine results in a marked decrease in the frequency and severity of anaphylactoid reactions, the value of H_2-receptor antagonists and ephedrine is more controversial. Since the success of these preventive measures will depend upon the likelihood that the reaction truly was immunologically mediated or anaphylactoid in nature, the aforementioned characteristics of Type 1 reactions should be used to assess the underlying pathogenesis. Another important consideration is that other chemicals present in the drug product or other drugs administered concomitantly may be the cause of the hypersensitivity reaction. Potential allergens included in the diluent or formulation of antitumor agents include Cremophor EL (present in Paclitaxel and Teniposide) and benzyl alcohol (present in the parenteral form of methotrexate and cytarabine).

Specific Organ Toxicities

Neurotoxicity

Cytarabine and L-Asparaginase

17. A.L., a 39-year-old female with acute lymphoblastic leukemia, has been admitted to the hospital for induction chemotherapy. Cytarabine 5 gm Q 12 hr for 8 doses, vincristine 2 mg IV push weekly, prednisone 100 mg/day, L-asparaginase 15,000 U/day for 14 days, and allopurinol 300 mg/day are ordered. Laboratory data obtained on admission include a WBC of 120,000/mm³ (Normal: 3.2–9.8) with 9% neutrophils (Normal: 54–62), 11% lymphocytes (Normal: 25–33), and 80% blasts and a uric acid of 7.5 mg/dL (Normal: 2–7). On Day 3, A.L. is confused and has difficulty performing a finger-to-nose neurologic examination. After 3 weeks, she complains of numbness in her fingers and on the soles of her feet; eyelid lag also is noted. A.L. is ataxic and has severe constipation. What is the possible cause A.L.'s mental status? Should chemotherapy be continued? [SI units: uric acid 446 µmol/L]

High doses of cytarabine (>1 gm/m² in multiple doses) are associated with central nervous system toxicity in 15% to 37% of patients.[140,141] These neurotoxicities are dose and schedule related. Increasing doses, greater than 18 gm/m² per course, results in an increasing frequency of neurotoxicity. Older patients are more susceptible than younger patients, and the prevalence seems higher in subsequent versus initial courses of therapy. As illustrated by A.L., neurotoxicity may become evident within a few days of cytarabine administration and is manifested most commonly by generalized encephalopathy with symptoms such as confusion, obtundation, seizures, and coma. Cerebral dysfunction, presenting as ataxia, gait and coordination difficulties, dysmetria (inability to arrest muscular movement when desired and lack of harmonious action between muscles when executing voluntary movement), is observed frequently in patients receiving high-dose cytarabine therapy. Once the drug is stopped, neurological symptoms appear to resolve over days to weeks, at least partially, in most patients. Progressive leukoencephalopathy also has been reported and is characterized clinically by progressive personality and intellectual decline, dementia,

Table 91.11			Cancer Chemotherapeutic Agents Commonly Causing Hypersensitivity		
Drug	Frequency	Risk Factors	Manifestations	Mechanism[a]	Comments
L-Asparaginase[107–110]	10%–20%	Increasing doses; Interval (weeks-months) between doses; IV administration; History of atopy/allergy; Use without prednisone 6 MP and/or vincristine	Pruritus, dyspnea agitation, urticaria angioedema, laryngeal spasm	Type I	Substitute PEG-L-asparaginase,[b] but up to 32% may demonstrate mild hypersensitivity
Paclitaxel[111]	Up to 10% 1st or 2nd dose	None known	Rashes, dyspnea, bronchospasm, hypotension	Nonspecific release of mediators; ? Cremophor	Premedicate with diphenhydramine, corticosteroids
Teniposide[112–117]	6%–40%; can occur with 1st dose	Increasing doses or number of doses. Young age/leukemia	Dyspnea, wheezing, hypotension, rash, facial flushing	Type I versus nonspecific; ? Cremophor	Etoposide may be substituted in some cases; ↓ rate of infusion
Cisplatin[118–123]	Up to 20% intravesicular; 5%–10% systemic. Case reports of hemolytic anemia	Increasing number of doses. *Anemia:* None known	Rash, urticaria, bronchospasm *Anemia:* Hemolytic anemia	Type I *Anemia:* Type III	Carboplatin may be substituted in some cases but cross reactivity has been reported
Procarbazine[124–129]	Up to 15% Case reports	None known	Urticaria Pneumonitis	Type I Type III	All patients rechallenged had prompt return of symptoms
Anthracyclines[130–136]	1%–15% depending upon anthracycline	None known	Dyspnea, bronchospasm angioedema	Unknown; ? nonspecific release	Cross reactivity documented but incidence and likelihood unknown
Bleomycin[137–139]	Common	Lymphoma	Fever (up to 42 °C) tachypnea	Endogenous pyrogen release	Not technically classified as HSR[b]. Premedicate with acetaminophen and diphenhydramine

[a] Type I: Antigen interaction with IgE bound to mast cell membrane causes degranulation. Drug binding to mast cell surface causes degranulation. Activation of classic or alternative complement pathways produces anaphylatoxins. Neurogenic release of vasoactive substances. Type III: Antigen-antibody complexes form intravascularly and deposit in or on tissues.

[b] PEG-L-asparaginase = Pegaspargase; HSR = Hypersensitivity reaction.

hemiparesis, and, sometimes, seizures. Intrathecal administration of cytarabine can cause chemical meningitis (see Chapter 92: Hematological Malignancies).

L-asparaginase frequently causes encephalopathy which presents most commonly as lethargy and confusion.[142] Severe cerebral dysfunction occurs occasionally and is manifested by stupor, coma, excessive somnolence, disorientation, hallucination, or severe depression. Symptoms can occur early (within days of administration of L-asparaginase) or have a more delayed onset.[143,144] The acute syndrome usually clears rapidly, but the delayed form may last several weeks.

A.L.'s symptoms most likely are due to CNS toxicity caused by both cytarabine and L-asparaginase. A decision regarding further treatment with these agents is complicated, since decreasing the dose of cytarabine and/or L-asparaginase would compromise the likelihood of obtaining a complete remission in A.L. Because these CNS neurotoxicities are reversible in most cases, continuing the full dose regimen to completion is not unreasonable. Alternatively, therapy can be discontinued until the CNS toxicity resolves.

Other Agents

18. What other chemotherapy agents produce CNS toxicity?

Other agents that produce CNS toxicities include methotrexate, fluorouracil, fludarabine, BCNU, hexamethylmelamine, procarbazine, and ifosfamide. (See Table 91.13.)

Methotrexate has little or no neurotoxicity when used orally or intravenously in usual doses; however, high-dose intravenous use (usually >1 gm/m^2) occasionally is followed by acute encephalopathy which usually is transient and reversible. A progressive leukoencephalopathy similar to that described for cytarabine may follow high-dose intravenous methotrexate as well. The risk of leukoencephalopathy appears to be increased with increasing cumulative doses of methotrexate and by concurrent cranial radiotherapy.[145–147] Intrathecal methotrexate has been associated with chemical meningitis and, less commonly, with myelopathy and paraplegia (see Chapter 92: Hematological Malignancies).

Fluorouracil (FU) can cause acute cerebellar dysfunction characterized by the rapid onset of gait ataxia, limb incoordination, dysarthria, and nystagmus.[148–150] The prevalence of this effect is 5% to 10% and occurs with all schedules of administration in common use. A more diffuse encephalopathy presenting as headache, confusion, disorientation, lethargy, and seizures sometimes is seen and is reversible if the drug is discontinued or the dose is reduced. Rare reports of optic neuropathy and decreased vision have been recorded.

Fludarabine was associated with severe neurotoxicity when used in doses higher than 90 mg/m^2 for five to seven days to treat acute leukemia.[150,151] Symptoms of altered mental status, photophobia, amaurosis (blindness that usually is temporary without change in the eye itself), generalized seizures, spastic or flaccid paralysis, quadriparesis, and coma were observed and, in some instances, progressed to death despite discontinuation of therapy. The CNS toxicity of fludarabine clearly is dose related and, with the current recommended dose of fludarabine 25 mg/m^2/day for five days, few and mild neurologic symptoms are reported.[152] However, even these substantially lower doses have caused severe CNS toxicity[151,153] and optic demyelination.

Carmustine and other nitrosureas have little or no neurotoxicity at the usual intravenous dose. Doses higher than 600 to 800 mg/m^2 have produced an encephalopathy with confusion and seizures.[154] Concurrent cranial radiotherapy and intracarotid carmustine chemotherapy may increase the risk of neurotoxicity.[155,156] Other alkylating agents reported to produce CNS toxicity include ifosfamide,[157,158] procarbazine,[159] altretamine,[160] and cisplatin.[161–169]

Table 91.12	Prophylaxis and Treatment of Hypersensitivity Reactions from Antitumor Drugs[a]

Prophylaxis

IV access must be established

BP monitoring must be available

Premedication
- Dexamethasone 20 mg PO and diphenhydramine 50 mg PO 12 and 6 hr before treatment then the same doses IV immediately before treatment
- Consider addition of H$_2$-antagonist with similar schedule

Have epinephrine and diphenhydramine readily available for use in case of a reaction

Observe the patient up to 2 hr after antitumor drug administration is completed

Treatment

Discontinue the drug (immediately if being administered IV)

Administer epinephrine 0.35–0.5 mL IV Q 15–20 min until reaction subsides or a total of 6 doses administered

Administer diphenhydramine 50 mg IV

If hypotension is present that does not respond to epinephrine, administer IV fluids

If wheezing is present that does not respond to epinephrine, administer nebulized albuterol solution 0.35 mL

Although corticosteroids have no effect on the initial reaction, they can block late allergic symptoms. Thus, administer methylprednisolone 125 mg (or its equivalent) IV to prevent recurrent allergic manifestations

[a] BP = Blood pressure; IV = Intravenous.

Each of these agents has been associated with encephalopathy manifested by confusion, lethargy, and, in some instances, psychosis and depression. These appear to be dose-related toxicities in that they are reported more frequently in patients receiving high doses of these agents.

Peripheral Nerve Toxicity

19. What is the cause of A.L.'s numbness?

Paresthesias (numbness and tingling) involving the feet and hands (or both) is an early subjective manifestation of vincristine neurotoxicity, often appearing within the first few weeks of therapy. This peripheral nerve toxicity commonly is bilateral and symmetrical and often referred to as a "stocking-glove" neuropathy. Symptoms initially consist of paresthesias, loss of ankle jerks, and depression of deep tendon reflexes. Areflexia (absent reflexes) is very common, occurring in about 50% to 70% of patients treated with a cumulative dose of 6 to 8 mg of vincristine. Paresthesias are almost as common as the loss of deep tendon reflexes. Although older patients appear to be more susceptible to this neurologic toxicity than younger patients, the almost universal finding of paresthesias in patients receiving combination chemotherapy regimens which incorporate vincristine or vinblastine questions the significance of this distinction. Pin and temperature sensory loss is more pronounced than vibration and proprioception sensory loss. Motor weakness with foot drop and muscle atrophy is one of the most disabling manifestations of vincristine neurotoxicity, and occasionally is accompanied by muscle wasting. True motor weakness is infrequent; the majority of patients' complaints regarding stumbling and falling appear to occur when darkness sets in and proprioception is lost due to lack of visual orientation. These complications are reversible either partially or completely, but recovery may take several months.[165,166]

20. What other drugs may cause similar complaints of numbness?

Table 91.13

Neurotoxicity of Selected Chemotherapeutic Agents[a]

	Alkylating Agents							Antimetabolites				Plant Alkaloids				Misc.
	CTX	IFX	TT	CIS	CARB	ALTRET	PCZ	FU	FLUD	CTB	MTX	VCR	VLB	ETOP	TAX	ASP
Encephalopathy																
Acute		+		+		+	++		+	+	+			+		++
Chronic			+							+	+				+	+
Cerebellar syndrome		+				+	+	++	+							
Peripheral neuropathy		+		++	+	++	+	+				++	++	+	+	
Cranial neuropathy		+		++	+			+				++	++			
Autonomic neuropathy												++	++			
Arachnoiditis (IT Dose)			+							+	+					
Stroke-like syndrome											+					
SIADH	+											+				

[a] + = Reported but appears rare; ++ = Common in some cases and may present a clinical problem; +++ = Common and/or dose-limiting; ALTRET = Altretamine; ASP = Asparaginase; CARB = Carboplatin; CIS = Cisplatin; CTB = Cytarabine; CTX = Cyclophosphamide; ETOP = Etoposide; FLUD = Fludarabine; FU = Fluorouracil; IFX = Ifosfamide; IT = Intrathecal; MTX = Methotrexate; PCZ = Procarbazine; SIADH = Syndrome of inappropriate antidiuretic hormone; TAX = Taxol; TT = Thiotepa; VCR = Vincristine; VLB = Vinblastine.

Other agents classified as mitotic inhibitors frequently share the peripheral nerve toxicity of vincristine. These include vinblastine, cisplatin, carboplatin, etoposide, and paclitaxel. Many of the agents associated with CNS toxicity have been reported to result in toxicity to the peripheral nervous system as well. It is important to point out that none of these agents are as likely to result in the loss of reflexes, paresthesias, or weakness as the vinca alkaloids. Like those experienced with the vinca alkaloids, these side effects generally are not dose limiting and are reversible upon discontinuation of the agents. Several reviews provide detailed references for this information.[167,168]

Cranial Nerve Toxicity

21. What is the significance of A.L.'s lid lag?

Cranial nerve toxicity occurs in 1% to 10% of patients receiving vinca alkaloids and generally consists of ptosis or ophthalmoplegia.[169,170] This toxicity probably is the result of damage to the third cranial nerve. Toxicity to other cranial nerves may result in trigeminal neuralgia, facial palsy, depressed corneal reflexes, and vocal cord paralysis.[171] An unusual nerve toxicity, jaw pain, can occur after the first or second injection;[171] the pain usually resolves spontaneously and does not recur with subsequent doses. Several of the cranial nerve toxicities associated particularly with vincristine do appear to be dose related in that there is an increasing prevalence associated with increasing doses. A.L.'s eyelid lag probably is due to vincristine.

22. Do other antineoplastic agents produce cranial nerve toxicity?

Cranial neuropathies have been reported with ifosfamide, vinblastine, cisplatin, and several experimental antineoplastic agents which are not yet commercially available. Intra-arterial administration of antineoplastics may increase the risk of encephalopathy and cranial neuropathies.[167,168]

Ototoxicity, characterized by a progressive, high-frequency, sensorineural hearing loss commonly is associated with cisplatin.[172,173] The most likely mechanism is direct toxicity of cisplatin on the cochlea. This reaction is dose related, exacerbated by concurrent cranial radiotherapy, and more pronounced in children. The reversibility of cisplatin ototoxicity is questionable. At some centers, routine audiometric tests are performed in patients receiving cisplatin. This results in a greater percentage of patients documented or found to have experienced a decrease in audio acuity than is observed clinically. Early cessation of cisplatin therapy may result in greater improvement in hearing. Ototoxicity does not appear to be a major toxicity of carboplatin in that only 8 of 710 (1.1%) patients in a study experienced clinical hearing deficits (mainly tinnitus).[174]

Autonomic Neuropathy

23. What is the cause of A.L.'s constipation and how might this problem have been prevented?

Vincristine, as well as vinblastine, commonly cause an autonomic neuropathy. The earliest symptoms (i.e., colicky abdominal pain with or without constipation) are reported by one-third to one-half of patients receiving these drugs.[169,171] The constipation is troublesome sometimes in that it might be quite severe and progress to or include adynamic ileus. Prophylactic laxatives are recommended on a regular basis for patients receiving vincristine and vinblastine, and stimulant laxatives such as the senna derivatives or bisacodyl are felt to be the most effective agents for treating vincristine-induced constipation. Stool-softeners also may be used concurrently. Unfortunately, there is no compelling evidence that use of laxatives prevents constipation. Other less frequent manifestations of autonomic dysfunction associated with vinca alka-

loids include bladder atony with urinary retention, impotence, and orthostatic hypotension.[175,176]

Cardiac Toxicities

Doxorubicin

24. D.A., a 35-year-old male with Stage IV Hodgkin's disease, is receiving CHOP (cyclophosphamide 750 mg/m² Day 1, doxorubicin 50 mg/mm³ IV Day 1, vincristine 2 mg IV Day 1, and prednisone 100 mg PO Days 1–5) and concurrent radiotherapy to a large mediastinal mass. He is in clinic today to receive his fifth cycle of CHOP and complains of tachycardia, SOB, and a nonproductive cough. Physical examination reveals neck vein distention, pulmonary rales, and ankle edema. What is the most likely cause of D.A.'s current symptoms?

D.A. is experiencing symptoms of congestive heart failure (CHF) most likely induced by doxorubicin therapy. Doxorubicin is an anthracycline antibiotic whose dose-limiting toxicity is the development of dose-dependent cardiomyopathy that generally occurs with repeated administration. It appears that doxorubicin causes myocyte damage by a mechanism different from its cytotoxic effects on tumor cells. This is because myocytes stop dividing in infancy and presumably would not be affected by an agent whose cytotoxicity is reliant on actively cycling cells. Many mechanisms have been proposed to explain the cardiac toxicity associated with doxorubicin.[177,178]

D.A.'s presentation is fairly typical of doxorubicin cardiomyopathy; however, his case is unusual in that he has very few of the risk factors usually associated with development of CHF. The total cumulative dose of doxorubicin is the most clearly established risk factor for the development of congestive heart failure.[179–181] For patients like D.A. receiving full doses of doxorubicin at the standard three-week interval, the risk of CHF remains very low until a total dose of 450 to 550 mg/m² has been reached. After 550 mg/m², the risk of CHF rises rapidly; the risk of CHF in unselected patients receiving less than 550 mg/m² of doxorubicin is 0.1% to 1.2%, whereas for patients receiving more than 550 mg/m², the risk rises more or less linearly such that patients receiving a total of 1000/m² may have nearly a 50% probability of developing CHF.[181] Factors that would increase D.A.'s risk of developing doxorubicin cardiomyopathy include mediastinal irradiation, pre-existing cardiac disease, hypertension, and age. Young children, as well as the elderly are likely to experience congestive heart failure at a lower cumulative dose. Concomitant administration of other chemotherapy drugs also has been implicated as a potentiator of doxorubicin cardiac toxicity. Drugs include cyclophosphamide, etoposide, actinomycin-D, mitomycin, melphalan, vincristine, and bleomycin.[182] The relationship between risk factors and the total cumulative dose of doxorubicin is strong enough to warrant guidelines restricting the total cumulative dose of doxorubicin to 450 mg/m² in patients with one or more identified risk factors (high risk patients) and 550 mg/m² in patients without risk factors (low risk patients).

It is unusual that D.A., a 35-year-old male who has received only 200 mg/m² of doxorubicin, would be presenting with symptoms of CHF. However, perhaps mediastinal irradiation, cyclophosphamide, or underlying cardiac disease not previously appreciated may have contributed to this unfortunate event. In addition, Hodgkin's disease involving the myocardium may be responsible for this presentation.

25. Is routine cardiac monitoring recommended in patients receiving doxorubicin?

Prevention of cardiomyopathy is achieved primarily by limiting the total cumulative dose. This is not entirely adequate for two reasons. First, there is a range of individual tolerance to doxorubicin which varies such that cardiotoxicity may occur before the arbitrary dose limit; secondly, there are clinical situations in which exceeding the dose limit may have positive effects on patient outcomes. Early efforts focused on monitoring systolic time intervals, QRS voltage loss, or ST-T segment changes on electrocardiogram (ECG). However, these changes were too nonspecific or occurred too late in the evolution of cardiac damage to be useful for prevention. Serial echocardiography has some usefulness in children;[183,184] however, current state-of-the-art monitoring for anthracycline cardiomyopathy includes radionuclide ventriculography (RNV) and endomyocardial biopsy. The use of radionuclide ventriculography [also referred to as radionuclide cardiac angiography; gated blood pool imaging; multiple gated acquisition (MUGA)] for early detection of doxorubicin-induced cardiac dysfunction has been investigated extensively.[185] RNV is very accurate in detecting functional cardiac status, but is not particularly sensitive in detecting patients who have early myocyte damage. Augmenting the RNV with exercise appears to give a more accurate picture of functional cardiac reserve. Because myocyte damage usually occurs days to weeks after doxorubicin is administered, the RNV should be obtained just before a course of the drug, rather than just afterwards. Although guidelines vary, most institutions recommend obtaining an RNV before the administration of any doxorubicin and obtaining additional RNVs if signs or symptoms of CHF become evident, or at a cumulative dose of 450 mg/m^2 in low risk patients or 350 mg/m^2 in high risk patients if continued therapy with doxorubicin is desired. Most guidelines call for cessation of doxorubicin or an endomyocardial biopsy when an absolute decrease in the RNV exceeds 10%, the decline reaches a level of less than 50%, and/or the RNV fails to increase by more than 5% with exercise.[182]

Endomyocardial biopsies along with a quantitative assessment of morphologic changes provide the most specific evaluation of myocardial damage induced by anthracyclines. Progressive myocardial pathology is graded on a scale (the "Billingham Score") of 0 (no change from normal) to 3 (diffuse cell damage in >35% of total number of cells with marked change in cardiac ultrastructure).[186] The prevalence of abnormal RNVs and the appearance of signs and symptoms of CHF correlate with biopsy scores. Usually, a significant change in cardiac function is not seen with scores less than 2 to 2.5. The predictive value of this technique has been evaluated by several investigators. With a score of ≤2, a patient has less than a 10% chance of developing heart failure if 100 mg more of doxorubicin is given.[187–189] There are occasional false negative biopsies and fatal CHF has been encountered in at least one patient with a relatively normal (1.0) biopsy score.[190] The most important morbidity associated with endomyocardial biopsy is perforation of the right ventricle with associated tamponade; this occurs rarely and is dependent largely upon the experience of the operator.

In summary, the RNV and endomyocardial biopsy are complementary procedures which when used together can provide a degree of confidence in predicting tolerance of additional doxorubicin dosing. The value of the endomyocardial biopsy is that, unlike the RNV, early myocyte damage can be appreciated.

Other Agents

26. How do the other members of the anthracycline class compare to doxorubicin in terms of cardiotoxicity and clinical usefulness?

Daunorubicin differs from doxorubicin only by hydroxylation of the fourteenth carbon and is used to treat acute nonlymphocytic leukemia. The reason that doxorubicin is employed most commonly in solid tumors relates to the poor understanding of dose-schedule toxicity relationships for daunorubicin during its initial clinical evaluations 25 years ago. Excessive mucositis and myelosuppression were encountered routinely as antileukemic dosages of daunorubicin were applied in therapy of solid tumors, and it became known on some hospital wards as "the red death." In more modern clinical trials, with better appreciation of its side effects and better supportive care procedures available, daunorubicin has been found to produce clinical responses in Hodgkin's disease, nonHodgkin's lymphomas, malignant melanoma, sarcomas, and carcinomas of the lung, breast, and gastrointestinal tract.[191] Randomized trials comparing daunorubicin with doxorubicin actually have shown a lesser incidence of mucositis, with a lower incidence of colonic damage and perforation with daunorubicin.[192] Similar pathological and cardiac toxicities are seen with daunorubicin, although somewhat higher cumulative doses of daunorubicin may be tolerated.[193] Risk factors appear to be equivalent and assessment of cardiotoxicity is the same.

Idarubicin is a relatively new anthracycline that has been approved in the U.S. for the treatment of acute leukemias. It is unclear how idarubicin's cardiotoxicity compares to that of doxorubicin and daunorubicin. It is less cardiotoxic than doxorubicin in animal models[194] and appears to be less cardiotoxic than daunorubicin in some early clinical trials;[195–197] however, other studies have shown that when equivalent myelosuppressive doses are employed, the cardiotoxicity of idarubicin may be comparable to that of other anthracyclines (i.e., doxorubicin and daunorubicin).[198,199]

Mitoxantrone is an anthracenedione structurally similar to the anthracyclines. Typically it is dosed as one-fifth the dose of doxorubicin or 12 to 14 mg/m^2 every three weeks. As with doxorubicin, the important risk factors for mitoxantrone cardiotoxicity are a history of mediastinal irradiation, cardiovascular disease, and anthracycline exposure. Predicting mitoxantrone cardiotoxicity is similar to that of doxorubicin and daunorubicin. In patients without risk factors, the risk for cardiotoxicity does not begin to rise significantly until a dose of about 160 mg/m^2 has been reached. This is equivalent to about 800 mg/m^2 of doxorubicin. For patients who have received doxorubicin (mean cumulative dose: 239 mg/m^2), the risk starts to rise when the cumulative mitoxantrone dose reaches about 100 mg/m^2.[200–202]

Prevention

27. Can CHF be prevented by the use of a different dose or dosing schedule or by agents that protect the myocardium?

Altering the dose schedule of doxorubicin to more frequent, lower doses, while maintaining dose intensity, consistently has resulted in reduction of cardiotoxicity without obvious compromise of antitumor effects.[203–208] Several reports suggest that peak plasma levels as well as cumulative dose have an important relationship to doxorubicin cardiotoxicity. Low doses of doxorubicin administered weekly or prolonged continuous IV infusions (48 to 96 hours) can be relatively cardiac sparing, allowing higher cumulative doses to be administered. In a retrospective, uncontrolled study of 1000 patients receiving weekly doxorubicin, a total dose of 900 to 1200 mg/m^2 of doxorubicin given in weekly fractions had the equivalent cardiotoxicity of 550 mg/m^2 given in every three week fractions.[204] Although it could be argued that well-designed studies comparing cardiac toxicity of bolus doses of doxorubicin to fractionated or continuous infusion schedules are lacking, it would appear prudent to adopt the use of one of these altered dosing schedules in patients with pre-existing risk factors or in patients for whom doxorubicin doses exceeding 450 to 550 mg/m^2 may be desirable.

Protecting the myocardium with the use of free radical scavengers has received the most preclinical and clinical attention.

Agents such as alpha-tocopherol and n-acetyl-cysteine have been shown to have a cardioprotective effect in some animal models; however, human studies have been disappointing.[209,210] ICRF-187, an investigational drug, was found to offer significant cardioprotection without affecting the antitumor action of doxorubicin in a prospective randomized trial.[211] The mechanism of action of this cardioprotectant is thought to be related to its ability to chelate iron, which would impair the subsequent generation of a singlet oxygen by doxorubicin. This agent has been reviewed by the FDA which found the data insufficient to support a cardioprotective effect of ICRF-187.

Animal model research to reduce anthracycline cardiotoxicity has included administration of agents that block vasoactive amines (H_1- and H_2-receptor antagonists, α- and β-adrenergic blockers) and calcium antagonists. Results have been positive,[212–214] but comparable studies are lacking in humans. An unusual approach to protecting against doxorubicin cardiotoxicity has been to deliver the drug encapsulated in liposomes.[215,216]

Management

28. How should doxorubicin- or other anthracycline-induced CHF be managed clinically?

Anthracycline-induced CHF presents no differently from other forms of biventricular congestive heart failure. Heart failure may occur between 0 to 231 days after the last dose of doxorubicin (mean: 33 days). Like other forms of CHF, it is treated with diuretics, activity restriction, inotropes, and vasodilators; however, these measures often are ineffective. The clinical course varies in that it may stabilize, and occasionally improve. Before cardiotoxicity was widely recognized, the course of anthracycline-induced CHF was characterized by rapid progression generally leading to death in a few weeks. However, now that anthracycline therapy is discontinued at the first appearance of signs and symptoms, if not sooner, the high fatality rates and failure of CHF to respond to conventional therapy reported in the older literature may not hold true today.

Other Cardiac Toxicities

29. What other cardiac toxicities have been associated with antineoplastic drugs?

Electrocardiographic changes have been observed during or following the administration of *doxorubicin* as well as other anthracyclines, cisplatin, etoposide, paclitaxel, cyclophosphamide, and mechlorethamine. ECG changes which occur most commonly involve ST-T segment changes, decreases in voltage, T-wave flattening, and atrial and ventricular ectopy. Other ECG abnormalities may be seen as well. Most studies suggest that dysrhythmias occur in 6% to 40% of patients receiving bolus doxorubicin.[217] Paclitaxel has been associated with significant rhythm and conduction defects in Phase I and II trials;[218] sinus bradycardia is the most common effect reported. For most of the other antineoplastic agents mentioned, there have been scattered reports of arrhythmias. Transient ECG changes are not thought to have clinical significance. Except for the documentation of serious cardiac dysrhythmias, transient ECG changes are not considered clinically important and are not an indication to discontinue doxorubicin therapy.

Fluorouracil (FU) has been associated with angina pectoris and myocardial infarction. The prevalence of angina in the series reported ranges from 1.6% to 18%[219–221] and appears to be higher in patients with a history of ischemic cardiomyopathy and in those receiving five-day infusions of FU. Angina has been associated with both initial and subsequent courses and although it occurs most frequently during continuous infusion, it occasionally is delayed 3 to 18 hours after fluorouracil administration and has been reported after an oral dose. The cause of fluorouracil cardiotoxicity is uncertain. Direct myocyte damage is suggested from animal studies; however, human studies suggest that coronary artery spasm is the most likely cause of angina. Since the chest pain associated with FU responds to nitrates,[219] theoretically, it could be addressed prophylactically or therapeutically with long-acting nitrates or calcium channel blockers. Other agents for which case reports of chest pain or infarction have appeared in the literature include vincristine, vinblastine, etoposide, paclitaxel and bleomycin.[182]

Myocardial necrosis rarely has been reported with the alkylating agents, cyclophosphamide, ifosfamide, busulfan, and mechlorethamine. This is particularly true when the drugs are given at very high doses, such as those used in bone marrow ablation. Pericarditis and hemorrhagic myocardial necrosis also have been reported in these cases. Risk factors are similar to those associated with doxorubicin and daunorubicin; however, a clear relationship between dose and cardiac dysfunction has not been demonstrated consistently in all case reports.[182]

Nephrotoxicity

Cisplatin-Induced

30. T.J., a 58-year-old male with nonresectable head and neck cancer, is being treated with cisplatin 100 mg/m² on Day 1 and fluorouracil 1 gm/m²/day for 5 days. He presents today for the third cycle of this regimen. A 24-hour urine for creatinine collected by T.J. at home revealed a creatinine clearance (Cl_{Cr}) of 75 mL/min, down from 110 mL/min at baseline. Other abnormalities include a serum magnesium (Mg) of 1.2 mEq/L; all other electrolyte values are within normal range. Is cisplatin responsible for T.J.'s decreased glomerular filtration rate (GFR) and serum magnesium levels?[SI units: Cl_{Cr} 1.25 mL/s; Mg 0.6 mmol/L]

Cisplatin is a heavy-metal complex which has high activity in a variety of solid tumors and is widely used clinically. The major dose-limiting toxicity of cisplatin is nephrotoxicity. A variety of renal and electrolyte disorders, both acute and chronic, have been associated with cisplatin. In the early 1970s, before the need for vigorous hydration was recognized, cisplatin-induced acute renal failure occurred frequently. Acute renal failure is uncommon today if vigorous hydration is employed; however, tubular dysfunction and a decrease in glomerular filtration rate are still problematic.

Morphological damage is greatest in the straight segment of the proximal tubules where the highest concentration of platinum occurs. Acute and cumulative renal tubular damage due to cisplatin has been demonstrated by increased urinary excretion of proximal tubular enzymes such as β_2 microglobulin, alanine aminopeptidase, and n-acetyl glucosamine. Proximal tubular enzyme elevations correlate well with urinary excretion of protein, magnesium, and a decrease in proximal tubular salt and water reabsorption. T.J. has hypomagnesemia which is the most prominent and well-described electrolyte abnormality induced by cisplatin. This disorder appears to be dose related but can occur after a single treatment. Magnesium deficit requires replacement with oral magnesium and patients may have persistent renal losses of magnesium and decreased serum magnesium levels for months or even years after they complete cisplatin therapy. Cisplatin is associated less frequently with hypocalcemia and hyponatremia. The etiology of these electrolyte abnormalities is thought to be similar to that of hypomagnesemia in that a proximal tubular defect occurs which interferes with reabsorption of these electrolytes.[222,223]

Chronic renal toxicity associated with cisplatin presents as a decrease in the glomerular filtration rate. Published reports suggest that the GFR decreases by 12% to 25% in the majority of patients receiving multiple courses.[222-225] This decrease in GFR appears to be persistent and only partially reversible. These abnormalities are not necessarily characterized by a remarkable increase in serum creatinine or a decrease in creatinine clearance and are better identified by sensitive measures of renal function such as radioisotope clearance. Unfortunately, these methods are not widely available at most institutions. Patients who are to receive cisplatin therapy must have their renal function evaluated, since dosage reductions may be necessary if the creatinine clearance decreases. Methods to estimate creatinine clearance based upon serum creatinine should be avoided, especially in patients with borderline renal function, because poor correlation has been demonstrated in some cancer patient populations. In addition, changes in creatinine clearance are not always reflected by changes in serum creatinine in these patients. Until a more sensitive and specific determinant of GFR becomes widely available, creatinine clearance should be determined using a 12 to 24 hour urine collection for creatinine.

T.J.'s decreased GFR and serum magnesium likely are due to cisplatin therapy. Although a dose reduction of cisplatin generally is not recommended for clearances in this range, attention should be paid to adequate and aggressive hydration to prevent cisplatin nephrotoxicity. In addition, an oral magnesium supplement should be instituted. Magnesium replacement usually requires intravenous administration of large doses of magnesium sulfate. Typically, therapy would begin with 5 gm of $MgSO_4$ (40 mEq) in 500 mL of fluid infused over five hours followed by measurement of serum magnesium levels and repeated courses as necessary. Oral supplementation is possible in some cases; however, diarrhea usually limits the use of the oral route when large doses are necessary.

31. Prevention. What measures should be taken to prevent cisplatin nephrotoxicity in T.J.?

Several measures have been used to minimize or prevent cisplatin-induced nephrotoxicity; but of them all, hydration with saline, mannitol, and prophylactic magnesium are the least controversial. The patient should be vigorously hydrated with 2 to 3 L of normal saline over 8 to 12 hours to maintain a urine output of 100 to 200 mL/hour just before and at least six hours after cisplatin administration.[226-228] A loop diuretic such as furosemide may be required to eliminate excess sodium in elderly patients or those with compromised cardiac reserve, but its use is not routine. Mannitol (25 to 50 gm) also can be administered just before chemotherapy to prevent cisplatin-induced renal artery vasoconstriction which increases the concentration of platinum in the renal tubules.[228,229] Patients who received prophylactic magnesium 16 mEq IV daily during a five-day course of cisplatin followed by 60 mEq orally (20 mEq TID) between courses experienced less nephrotoxicity compared to those who received no supplements in a prospective trial of 16 patients with testicular carcinoma.[230]

Other more controversial interventions include admixing cisplatin in 3% sodium, decreasing the dose of cisplatin, administering the drug by continuous infusion, administering sodium thiosulfate concurrently to complex cisplatin in the renal tubule, and avoiding the concurrent administration of aminoglycosides. Animal studies support the notion that 3% sodium chloride decreases the formation of the aquated moiety of cisplatin [replacement of chloride ions with "water of hydration" (i.e., OH⁻)] which is thought to be nephrotoxic,[231,232] but the admixture also may have diminished antitumor activity.[233,234] Although cisplatin must be mixed in a

Table 91.14	Chemotherapeutics Requiring Dose Modification in Renal Failure[370]			
Drug	>60 mL/min	30–60 mL/min	10–30 mL/min	<10 mL/min
Bleomycin	NC[a]	75	75	50
Carboplatin (see below)	—	—	—	—
Cisplatin	NC	50	Omit	Omit
Cyclophosphamide	NC	NC	NC	50
Methotrexate	NC	50	Omit	Omit
Mitomycin	NC	75	75	50
Nitrosureas	NC	Omit	Omit	Omit

Carboplatin Dosing Recommendation

Calvert Equation[366]

$$\frac{\text{Dose}}{(\text{mg})} = \text{Target AUC}(\text{mg/mL} \times \text{min}) \times \left[\text{GFR}(\text{mL/min}) + 25\right]$$

Suggested Target AUC for adults

Single agent, untreated	7 mg/mL/min
Single agent, previously treated	5 mg/mL/min
Combination chemotherapy	4.5 mg/mL/min

Egorin Formula[367]

For patients heavily pretreated with myelosuppressive agents

$$\frac{\text{Dose}}{(\text{mg/m}^2)} = (0.091)\left(\frac{\text{Cl}_{\text{Cr}}}{\text{BSA}}\right)\left[\left(\frac{\text{Pretreatment Platelet Count} - \text{Platelet Nadir Desired}}{\text{Pretreated Platelet Count}} \times 100\right) - 17\right] + 86$$

For previously untreated patients

$$\frac{\text{Dose}}{(\text{mg/m}^2)} = (0.091)\left(\frac{\text{Cl}_{\text{Cr}}}{\text{BSA}}\right)\left(\frac{\text{Pretreatment Platelet Count} - \text{Platelet Nadir Desired}}{\text{Pretreated Platelet Count}} \times 100\right) + 86$$

[a] AUC = Area under the concentration-time curve; BSA = Body surface area; Cl$_{Cr}$ = Creatinine clearance; GFR = Glomerular filtration rate; NC = No change.

chloride-containing vehicle, the additional protective effects of 3% versus normal (0.9%) saline are unclear. Since acute nephrotoxicity correlates with high levels of unbound platinum five minutes after administration, maneuvers to decrease peak concentrations theoretically could decrease nephrotoxicity. Cisplatin has been given by infusion and the total dose has been divided over three to five days,[235,236] and these measures seem to decrease acute and chronic toxicity. However, since platinum is rapidly bound to protein, some have questioned the benefits of these maneuvers. Administration of cisplatin in the evening and night (circadian timing) also reduces renal injury.[234]

Sodium thiosulfate is concentrated in the renal tubules where it could complex and neutralize cisplatin. However, because of concern that complexation could occur in the serum, IV sodium thiosulfate is given only when high-dose cisplatin is administered intraperitoneally or intrapleurally.[222] The concurrent administration of aminoglycosides with cisplatin may augment the nephrotoxicity of both agents in animal models.[239-241] Although it would be ideal to avoid aminoglycosides, this often is not possible clinically. When both must be given, aminoglycoside levels and renal function should be monitored meticulously and the patient hydrated before and after cisplatin administration.

32. At what point would cisplatin therapy be discontinued in a patient with a diminished GFR?

Guidelines to modify the dose of cisplatin in patients with decreased renal function are available. Most suggest a 50% dose reduction when the glomerular filtration rate decreases to 30 to 60 mL/minute[222] and discontinuation when the GFR falls to less than 30 mL/minute (see Table 91.14). Percentage dose reduction generally refers to the recommended dose for a specific cancer in a given combination chemotherapy regimen. Since the cisplatin dose ranges from 50 to 150 mg/m^2, the precise dose for a patient with a GFR of less than 60 mL/minute must be individualized to the situation. In tumors that are known to be responsive, carboplatin may be substituted for cisplatin in patients with diminished renal function. Carboplatin is not nephrotoxic; however, since it is eliminated almost entirely by renal mechanisms, its dose also must be modified in patients with decreased glomerular filtration rates. Recommendations are included in the manufacturer's product information.

Other Nephrotoxic Agents

33. What other antineoplastic agents are known nephrotoxins? What are the clinical consequences of nephrotoxicity produced by these agents?

Other agents reported to cause renal tubular defects include streptozotocin, lomustine (CCNU), carmustine (BCNU), plicamycin, and ifosfamide.[222,223] Nephrotoxicity appears to be dose related for total cumulative dose for streptozocin, BCNU, CCNU, and plicamycin. A clear relationship between dose and schedule and renal tubular toxicity with ifosfamide has not been established; however, originally it was the renal abnormality associated with high doses of bolus ifosfamide which led to the use of fractionated dose administration. Plicamycin is associated infrequently with signs of nephrotoxicity in the doses used for the management of hypercalcemia of malignancy.[222,223]

The primary renal lesion associated with each of these agents occurs in the proximal renal tubule and is manifested by loss of protein, glucose, bicarbonate, and potassium. Serum creatinine, bicarbonate, potassium, urinary pH, protein, and glucose should be monitored closely in patients receiving these agents. If the serum creatinine rises or there is an alteration in electrolyte status, these agents should be discontinued since reversibility of the lesions varies among clinical reports and a significant number of patients who develop renal toxicity with these agents require dialysis.[222,223]

The antitumor antibiotic mitomycin has been associated with a hemolytic uremic syndrome.[222,234,242] This syndrome, which often is fatal, most commonly occurs after several courses of therapy, but may occur earlier. It is characterized by the abrupt onset of microangiopathic hemolytic anemia, increasing serum creatinine, increased fibrin degradation products, thrombocytopenia, and hypertension. The syndrome also has been associated with combination chemotherapy (bleomycin, cisplatin, and vincristine or;[243] bleomycin, cisplatin, and methotrexate[244]) and with carboplatin alone.[245] Early recognition and prompt treatment with plasmapheresis and hemodialysis may be beneficial.[242]

34. Methotrexate. J.R., a 15-year-old male with osteogenic sarcoma of the right knee, was treated with amputation of his right leg. His leg is now healed and chemotherapy consisting of high-dose methotrexate, leucovorin rescue, doxorubicin, dactinomycin, bleomycin, cisplatin, and ifosfamide is planned. The dose of methotrexate is 15 gm/m^2 administered over 3 hours. What precautions are necessary to prevent the renal and other toxicities associated with high-dose methotrexate therapy in J.R.?

Methotrexate normally is not nephrotoxic, although 90% of the drug is excreted unchanged in the urine; however, acute tubular obstruction may occur with high-dose methotrexate if appropriate precautions are not taken. This phenomenon is caused by secondary tubular precipitation of methotrexate which is poorly soluble at a pH less than 7.0. To prevent this occurrence, preventive measures should be planned for J.R. These include brisk diuresis to produce urine outputs in the range of 100 to 200 mL/hour for at least 24 hours following the administration of high-dose methotrexate and urinary alkalinization. A urine pH above 7.0 usually can be assured by administration of 25 to 50 mEq/L sodium bicarbonate/L of hydration fluid. Acetazolamide, a carbonic anhydrase inhibitor, promotes urinary bicarbonate excretion and is used by some clinicians to assist in maintaining urinary pH above 7.0. J.R.'s urine output and pH must be monitored closely to prevent acute tubular obstruction associated with high-dose methotrexate therapy.[222,223]

If J.R. has any existing renal insufficiency, methotrexate excretion will be decreased significantly and he may suffer greater bone marrow suppression and gastrointestinal side effects due to prolonged exposure to high serum methotrexate levels. Therefore, it is very important to assure that appropriate leucovorin rescue is initiated within 48 hours after high-dose methotrexate infusion. There is considerable intra- and interpatient variability in methotrexate clearance, particularly when high doses of methotrexate therapy are employed. Renal excretion of methotrexate is a complex process involving glomerular filtration, tubular reabsorption, and secretion. Concentrations of methotrexate obtained within 24 hours after the infusion often are not predictive of concentrations at 48 hours. Therefore, methotrexate concentrations between 24 and 48 hours must be monitored in J.R. and in all patients receiving high-dose therapy. Methotrexate levels are necessary to optimize leucovorin rescue (see Chapter 93: Solid Tumors). However, leucovorin rescue does not affect the renal toxicity of methotrexate. Acute tubular obstruction associated with high-dose methotrexate therapy can be prevented only by appropriate attention to optimal urinary output before and for at least 24 hours after high dose methotrexate administration and urinary alkalization.

35. Ifosfamide. J.R. also is receiving ifosfamide. What unique bladder toxicity occurs with ifosfamide that requires attention before its administration?

Pathogenesis. Ifosfamide, a structural analog of cyclophosphamide, belongs to the oxazaphosphorine class of antitumor alkylating agents which must be activated by the mixed function oxidase system of the liver. The 4-hydroxy oxazaphosphorines are a reactive species capable of interacting with nucleic acids and cellular materials to cause cell damage and death. The 4-hydroxy metabolite spontaneously liberates acrolein in many sites throughout the body and it is this substance that is responsible for oxazaphosphorine urotoxicity. Both ifosfamide and cyclophosphamide produce cystitis characterized by tissue edema and ulceration followed by sloughing of mucosal epithelial cells, necrosis of smooth muscle fibers and arteries, and culminating in focal hemorrhage. The selective urotoxicity of oxazaphosphorine occurs because the bladder contains a very low concentration of thiol compounds (glutathione, cysteine) which, by virtue of their nucleophilic sulfhydryl groups, are able to react and neutralize many reactive chemicals. Because the metabolic activation of ifosfamide proceeds more slowly than that of cyclophosphamide, doses of ifosfamide are three to four times higher than those of cyclophosphamide. This explains the higher incidence of urotoxicity associated with ifosfamide.

Clinical Presentation. Patients with oxazaphosphorine-induced hemorrhagic cystitis initially go through an asymptomatic stage characterized by complaints of brief episodes of painful urination, frequency, and hematuria. The symptoms may subside over a period of several days or weeks after the drug has been discontinued. The course of oxazaphosphorine-induced hemorrhagic cystitis usually is relatively benign although death from massive refractory hemorrhage has occurred. Factors which may predispose J.R. to hemorrhagic cystitis include IV administration, large doses, and his young age.

Prevention. Forced hydration is the primary method used to prevent hemorrhagic cystitis in patients treated with cyclophosphamide therapy.[251] Theoretically, hydration flushes the toxic metabolites out of the bladder so there is insufficient time to set up the tissue reaction. The more urotoxic agent ifosfamide was introduced to the market with the uroprotective agent, Mesna. Mesna liberates free thiol groups in the bladder which then can react with and neutralize the oxazaphosphorine metabolite. When administered in an appropriate dosing schedule, Mesna can prevent the bladder toxicity completely.

The manufacturer recommends a parenteral Mesna dose of 20% weight/weight of the ifosfamide dose given intravenously at zero, four, and eight hours after the ifosfamide dose (total of 60% weight/weight).[252] The goal is to maintain Mesna levels within the urinary tract beyond the time of administration of ifosfamide to provide adequate uroprotection. Repeated administration is required because Mesna has a short elimination half-life (<1 hour).

A variety of other Mesna dosing guidelines are used clinically, but actual trials comparing Mesna doses and schedules when used with ifosfamide are lacking. One author suggests that a total Mesna dose equivalent to 17% weight/weight of the ifosfamide dose was just as effective in preventing urotoxicity as the 60% weight/weight dose.[253] Many investigators employ a 1:1 weight/weight dose of Mesna to ifosfamide when administered by continuous infusion.

The lack of data as well as the unique pharmacokinetic properties of ifosfamide have caused some concerns about the current dosing guidelines. The pharmacokinetics of ifosfamide are dose dependent.[254] The elimination half-life associated with doses of 2.5 gm/m^2 is six to eight hours, whereas the elimination half-life associated with doses of 3.5 to 5 gm/m^2 is 14 to 16 hours. The current recommendations for Mesna administration provide protection for approximately 12 hours after an ifosfamide bolus infusion. With higher doses of ifosfamide, Mesna should be infused beyond the recommended eight hours post-ifosfamide to keep the bladder protected. Based upon pharmacokinetic data of ifosfamide

and Mesna following continuous infusion and clinical evidence of hematuria developing one to two days after the end of a combined ifosfamide and Mesna infusion, Klein et al. recommended that Mesna infusion be continued for some period of time following discontinuation of ifosfamide.[259] Also, there is concern that the four-hour dosing interval may be inadequate to maintain sufficient Mesna levels within the bladder. Although the majority of the Mesna dose after intravenous administration is eliminated within four to six hours, the data demonstrate that elimination rates (mg/kg/hour) are highest in the first two hours after intravenous administration.[255,256] Thus, some have suggested that Mesna be given more frequently than every four hours. Indeed, a number of clinicians opt to administer Mesna by continuous infusion to avoid the need for frequent bolus dosing. Since ifosfamide and Mesna are compatible in solution, combined continuous infusion is convenient.

A third question concerning the influence of micturition on the efficacy of Mesna uroprotection also has been raised. Several authors have suggested that the frequency of Mesna doses be adjusted based upon frequency and amount of micturition.[258,259] Although forced hydration has been the mainstay for prevention of cyclophosphamide-induced hemorrhagic cystitis, it is unnecessary and potentially disadvantageous when Mesna is administered with ifosfamide or cyclophosphamide. This is because increased micturition increases the evacuation of Mesna from the bladder.

The bioavailability of oral Mesna is approximately one-half that of IV Mesna. This has led to the recommendation that the oral dose of Mesna should be double that of the IV dose. The manufacturer recommends an oral regimen of 40% weight/weight of the ifosfamide bolus dose two hours before and four and eight hours after the ifosfamide administration. Others have recommended that a dose also be given with the ifosfamide dose. A number of centers administer the first dose of Mesna intravenously followed by oral doses at four and eight hours, particularly in the outpatient clinic setting.

For patients receiving cyclophosphamide in low oral doses for prolonged periods or high intravenous doses, hydration is necessary. When cyclophosphamide is used in bone marrow transplant regimens at doses which would be expected to produce significantly more of the urotoxic metabolites than with conventional dosing, other measures are used to prevent hemorrhagic cystitis. (See Chapter 94: Bone Marrow Transplantation.)

36. If J.R. develops hemorrhagic cystitis, how should it be treated?

Once hemorrhagic cystitis develops, the chemotherapeutic drug causing the disorder must be discontinued and vigorous hydration initiated. If gross hematuria is present, a large bore catheter should be inserted since clot formation and obstruction of the urethra can occur. Some clinicians also use continuous silver nitrate irrigation, local instillation of formalin, or electrocauterization of bladder blood vessels. If these measures fail, surgical intervention to divert urine flow away from the bladder is indicated.[260,261]

Pulmonary Toxicities

37. J.A., a 67-year-old male with an 8-year history of chronic lymphocytic leukemia (CLL), was treated intermittently for 7 years with chlorambucil and prednisone. About 1 year ago, increasing lymphadenopathy was noted and a biopsy revealed that his CLL had transformed to large-cell lymphoreticular lymphoma. (This transformation is called Richter's syndrome.)[262,263] At that time he was started on a chemotherapeutic regimen of cyclophosphamide, doxorubicin, vincristine, prednisone, and bleomycin (CHOP-Bleo) and his disease stabilized. Three weeks after his ninth course, he developed dys-

pnea, a nonproductive cough, and fever. Chest x-ray showed diffuse bilateral infiltrates, his respiratory rate (RR) was 36/min, and the arterial blood gases (ABGs) were: pH 7.50, PO_2 62, PCO_2 28, and O_2 saturation of 92%. What are the possible etiologies of his new pulmonary findings?

J.A. is at risk for several processes which could produce diffuse pulmonary infiltrates and dyspnea. He undoubtedly is immunosuppressed secondary to both his lymphoma and the chemotherapy and is, therefore, at risk for infection [e.g., *Pneumocystis carinii* or cytomegalovirus (CMV)]. In addition, his lymphoma now may be resistant to the therapy and the infiltrates may represent progression of the disease. Pulmonary infiltrates also may represent toxicity resulting from one or more of the chemotherapeutic agents which he has received. Further diagnostic work-up is necessary to establish the etiology.

38. A bronchoscopy with bronchoalveolar lavage and a biopsy with pathologic and microbiologic evaluations were performed. Bacterial, fungal, and viral cultures were negative, and the biopsy revealed inflammation and fibrosis with no evidence of lymphoma. These results are highly suggestive of drug-induced pulmonary damage. (*Note:* If the results of the bronchoscopy had not been helpful in establishing a diagnosis, an open lung biopsy would have been recommended.) Which of the drugs that J.A. received are associated with pulmonary toxicity and what other factors may have increased his risk of pulmonary toxicity?

Many chemotherapeutic drugs have been associated with pulmonary toxicity (see Table 91.15). Of these, J.A. has received chlorambucil, cyclophosphamide, and bleomycin. Factors that may increase the risk of drug-induced pulmonary toxicity are listed in Table 91.16. Because J.A. has received three potentially pulmonary toxic agents, his risk may be increased; his age also may play a role in the development of this toxicity.

Among the chemotherapeutic agents, *bleomycin* most commonly causes pulmonary toxicity. Although several forms have been reported, the most frequent is interstitial pneumonitis followed by pulmonary fibrosis.[264-268] Patients generally present with a nonproductive cough and dyspnea; fine crackling bibasilar rales that progress to coarse rales are the earliest physical finding. Chest x-ray may be normal in the early stages; however, as illustrated by J.A., bilateral alveolar and interstitial infiltrates will develop. Arterial blood gases show hypoxia and pulmonary function tests generally show a progressive fall in the diffusing capacity without a significant decrease in the forced vital capacity.[264] The cumulative dose of bleomycin is the most significant factor associated with the development of pulmonary toxicity. At total doses below 400 mg, there is a constant low incidence of 10% or less. When the cumulative dose reaches 450 to 500 mg, the dose-related effect becomes more prominent. The incidence may be lower when the bleomycin is administered as a continuous infusion.[269] A rarer, hypersensitivity type of pulmonary toxicity which produces fever, eosinophilia, and diffuse infiltrates and is not dose related also has been reported. The mortality associated with bleomycin pulmonary toxicity is about 50%.[264,266] If bleomycin is discontinued while symptoms are minimal and before pulmonary function has decompensated significantly, the damage may not progress. In contrast, patients with prominent physical and radiographic findings generally die due to pulmonary complications.

Less commonly, *chlorambucil* and *cyclophosphamide* induce pulmonary toxicities similar to bleomycin. Chlorambucil-induced lung damage appears to be dose related in that most cases have occurred in patients who had received a total dose exceeding 2 gm over more than six months.[264] In most instances, patients died of severe interstitial pulmonary fibrosis. Cyclophosphamide pulmo-

nary toxicity does not appear to be related to dose or schedule of administration and about 50% to 65% of patients improve clinically after withdrawal of therapy.

39. Are routine pulmonary evaluations indicated in patients like J.A. who receive bleomycin or other pulmonary toxic drugs?

Because a dose-related decrease in diffusing capacity has been observed in patients receiving bleomycin before the onset of clinical symptoms, routine baseline and serial pulmonary function studies are recommended.[270] Bleomycin therapy should be withheld if the diffusing capacity falls below 40% of the baseline value, if the forced vital capacity falls below 75% of the baseline value, or if patients develop any signs or symptoms of pulmonary damage.[264] Some practitioners also recommend limiting the total cumulative dose to 450 mg or less. Specific screening is not routinely recommended for patients receiving other pulmonary toxic agents; however, if patients develop any symptoms or clinical findings, therapy should be withheld until the etiology can be determined.

Management

40. How should J.A.'s drug-induced pulmonary toxicity be managed?

The most effective way to manage pulmonary toxicity is to prevent it. However, if it does occur, as in the case of J.A., all drugs felt to be responsible (bleomycin, chlorambucil, and cyclophosphamide) should be discontinued and the patient given symptomatic support as indicated by his physical condition (e.g., oxygen). As illustrated by J.A., other treatable causes of pulmonary infiltrates (e.g., infection) also should be ruled out. Unfortunately, in many cases, pulmonary toxicity is irreversible and progressive, and effective treatments are unavailable. Corticosteroids often are administered but probably are effective only in cases of pulmonary damage due to hypersensitivity. Nevertheless, since other effective treatments are lacking, a trial of steroids generally is indicated for all patients; if steroids are discontinued, they must be tapered carefully to avoid clinical deterioration.

Hepatotoxicity

41. J.D. has received 2 courses of chemotherapy with cytarabine and daunorubicin. Before chemotherapy was started, his liver function tests (LFTs) and coagulation studies were within normal limits. His current laboratory values are aspartate aminotransferase (AST) 204 U/L (Normal: 8–46), alanine aminotransferase (ALT) 197 U/L (Normal: 7–46), lactate dehydrogenase (LDH) 795 U/L (Normal: 100–190), alkaline phosphatase 285 U/L (Normal: 25–100), bilirubin 1.2 mg/dL (Normal: <1.5), and PT 13.1 seconds (Normal: 11–16). Could J.D.'s chemotherapy be responsible for these laboratory abnormalities? [SI units: AST 3.4 μkat/L; ALT 22.98 μkat/L; LDH 13.25 μkat/L; alkaline phosphatase 4.75 μkat/L; bilirubin 20.52 μmol/L]

Elevated LFTs occur frequently in cancer patients and their causes are listed in Table 91.17. In addition, patients also may present with jaundice, nausea, vomiting, abdominal pain, and, rarely, encephalopathy. Initially, it is important to rule out causes which may require immediate attention such as tumor involvement of the liver or infection. In addition, other nonessential medications which may contribute to hepatotoxicity should be discontinued.

Several cytotoxic drugs, including cytarabine given to J.D., have been associated with hepatocellular damage (see Table 91.18). Those most commonly associated with hepatotoxicity include asparaginase, carmustine, cytarabine, mercaptopurine, and streptozocin. Both methotrexate and mithramycin have caused hepatotoxicity when given on a daily schedule; however, if they are given on an intermittent basis, the incidence of toxicity decreases significantly.[299-302]

Table 91.15	Chemotherapy-Induced Pulmonary Toxicity		
Drug	Histopathology	Clinical Features	Treatment/Outcome
Bleomycin[2,85,270]	Interstitial edema and hyaline membrane formation; mononuclear cell infiltration; pneumonitis with progression to fibrosis. Eosinophilic infiltrations seen in patients with suspected hypersensivity-type reactions	Cumulative dose-related toxicity with risk increasing substantially with total dose >450 mg or 200 mg/m². may occur during or following treatment. Clinical presentation: cough, fever, dyspnea, tachypnea, rales, hypoxemia, bilateral infiltrates, dose-related ↓ in diffusing capacity	Recovery if bleomycin is discontinued while symptoms and radiologic changes still minimal; progressive and usually fatal if symptoms severe. Avoid cumulative doses >200 mg/m²; monitor serial pulmonary function tests. Discontinue therapy if diffusing capacity ≤40% of baseline, FVC[a] <25% of baseline, or if any signs or symptoms suggestive of pulmonary toxicity occur. Steroids may be helpful if toxicity is result of hypersensitivity
Busulfan[264,285]	Pneumocyte dysplasia; mononuclear cell infiltrations; fibrosis	Does not appear to be dose-related, but no cases reported with total doses <500 mg. Clinical presentation: insidious onset of dyspnea, dry cough, fever, tachypnea, rales, hypoxemia, diffuse linear infiltrate, ↓ in diffusing capacity	Fatal in most patients. Progressive despite discontinuation of busulfan. High-dose steroids (50–100 mg prednisone daily) have been helpful in a few cases
Carmustine[264, 284, 296, 287]		Dose-related. Usually occurs with doses >1400 mg/m². Clinical presentation: dyspnea, tachypnea, dry hacking cough, bibasilar rales, hypoxemia, interstitial infiltrates. Spontaneous pneumothorax has been reported	May continue to progress after carmustine discontinued. No evidence that steroids improve or alter incidence. High mortality rate if symptoms severe. Serial pulmonary function studies recommended. Total cumulative dose should not exceed 1400 mg/m²
Chlorambucil[264]	Pneumocyte dysplasia; fibrosis	Usually occurs after at least 6 months of treatment with total cumulative doses of >2 gm. Clinical presentation: dyspnea, dry cough, anorexia, fatigue, fever, hypoxemia, bibasilar rales, localized infiltrates progressing to diffusing involvement of both lung fields	Fatal in most cases despite discontinuation of chlorambucil and treatment with high-dose steroids
Cyclophosphamide[264, 288]	Endothelial swelling, pneumocyte dysplasia, lymphocyte infiltration; fibrosis	Does not appear to be schedule- or dose-related and may occur after discontinuation. Clinical presentation: progressive dyspnea, fever, dry cough, tachypnea, fine rales, ↓ diffusing capacity and restrictive ventilatory defect, bilateral interstitial infiltrates	Clinical recovery reported in about 50% of patients within 1–8 weeks if therapy stopped. Some of these patients received steroid therapy; however, others have died despite steroid therapy. Occasionally, therapy has been restarted without recurrence
Cytarabine[289]	Pulmonary edema	Clinical presentation: tachypnea, hypoxemia, interstitial/alveolar infiltrates	Not always fatal
Fludarabine[2, 90]	Interstitial infiltrates, alveolitis, centrilobular emphysema	Clinical presentation: fever, dyspnea, cough, hypoxia; onset 3–28 days after 3rd or 4th course; bilateral infiltrates and effusions	Resolves spontaneously over several weeks with or without corticosteroids
Melphalan[264]	Pneumocyte dysplasia	Not dose-related. Clinical presentation: dyspnea, dry cough, fever, tachypnea, rales, pleuritic chest pain, hypoxemia. Usually progresses rapidly	Most patients die due to progressive pulmonary disease. Most reported cases occurred while patients were receiving concomitant prednisone therapy
Methotrexate[264, 291–294] Delayed	Nonspecific changes; occasional fibrosis	No evidence that dose related. Daily or weekly schedules more likely to cause toxicity than monthly dosing. Clinical presentation: headache, malaise prodrome, dyspnea, dry cough, fever, hypoxemia, tachypnea, rales, eosinophilia, cyanosis in up to 50% of patients, interstitial infiltrates, ↓ diffusing capacity, restrictive ventilatory defect	Most patients recover within 1–6 weeks (some may have persistent infiltrates or ↓ pulmonary function parameters). Steroids may produce more rapid resolution. May resolve despite continuation of methotrexate, but discontinuation may speed resolution. Rarely fatal
Noncardiac pulmonary edema	Acute pulmonary edema	Occurs very rarely 6–12 hr after PO or IT[a] methotrexate	Fatal in 2 of 3 reported cases. Resolved within 3 days in 1 case

Continued

Table 91.15		Chemotherapy-Induced Pulmonary Toxicity (Continued)	
Drug	Histopathology	Clinical Features	Treatment/Outcome
Pleuritic chest pain		Not related to other methotrexate toxicities or serum levels. May not occur with each course of therapy. *Clinical presentation:* right-sided chest pain, occasional pleural effusion or collapse of lung, thickened pleural densities	Usually resolves within 3–5 days
Mitomycin[2,65,264]	Similar to bleomycin	*Clinical presentation:* dyspnea, dry cough, basilar rales, hypoxemia, bilateral interstitial or finely nodular infiltrates, ↓ diffusing capacity	Fatal in ≈50% of cases. Complete resolution reported in some patients, including some who received steroid therapy
Procarbazine[295, 296]	Hypersensitivity pneumonitis with eosinophilia and interstitial fibrosis	*Clinical presentation:* nausea, fever, dry cough, dyspnea within a few hours of ingestion, bilateral interstitial infiltrates, and pleural effusion	Rapid resolution after discontinuation of procarbazine
Vinblastine[297]	Hyperplasia, dysplasia, interstitial edema and fibrosis	Associated with concomitant treatment with mitomycin. *Clinical presentation:* acute respiratory distress, bilateral infiltrates	Initial improvement with subsequent progression

ᵃ FVC = Forced vital capacity. IT = Intrathecal.

The liver is unique in that it receives a dual blood supply from the portal and superior mesenteric veins. Its major function is to detoxify or inactivate noxious substances which are ingested or absorbed by the body, and thus most antineoplastics are oxidized, reduced, hydrolyzed, and/or conjugated by the liver.

The exact mechanisms by which cytotoxic agents damage the liver are unknown but it is believed that most of these drugs probably produce hepatic damage by: 1) interfering with the mitochondrial function of the hepatocyte; 2) depleting hepatic glutathione stores; 3) eliciting hypersensitivity reactions; 4) decreasing bile flow; or 5) causing phlebitis of the central hepatic vein to produce veno-occlusive disease.[298]

Serum transaminases, alkaline phosphatase, and bilirubin levels should be monitored routinely in patients receiving hepatotoxic chemotherapy. Although these laboratory indices are sensitive indicators of liver injury, they are nonspecific for the type of liver disease and do not necessarily correlate with hepatic function. Serum levels of proteins produced by the liver such as ferritin, albumin, prealbumin, or retinol binding protein also may be helpful in assessing liver function.

The decision of whether to continue chemotherapy in patients with apparent hepatic dysfunction is difficult. If the chemotherapy is the suspected cause, therapy should be withheld until liver function tests are within normal ranges. It also may be appropriate to consider alternative (nonhepatotoxic) chemotherapy for future treatment. In addition, drugs which are cleared predominantly via the liver may require dosage adjustments and should be administered cautiously (see Table 91.19).

It is likely that J.A.'s therapy is responsible for his elevated liver enzymes. Therefore, costly work-up should be deferred to allow recovery of liver function. This likely is to occur within two weeks of chemotherapy administration. If full recovery does not occur, further therapy (agents and/or doses) may require modification.

Long-Term Complications of Chemotherapy
Second Malignancies after Chemotherapy
Acute Nonlymphocytic Leukemia (ANLL)

42. T.D., a 60-year-old woman, was diagnosed with epithelial carcinoma of the ovary Stage 1, 40 months before this admission. She underwent a total abdominal hysterectomy, bilateral salpingo-oophorectomy, and omentectomy. Pathological features suggested that she may be at a high risk for recurrent disease and that adjuvant therapy could be beneficial. Consequently, T.D. received a course of melphalan 0.2 mg/kg/day PO for 5 days Q 4 weeks for 10 courses. On this admission, she has no evidence of ovarian cancer; however, she has complaints of increasing fatigue, fever, and chills. A peripheral blood smear shows a WBC of 120,000/mm³ with a differential of >90% leukemic blasts, a bone marrow examination confirms ANLL. Subsequent cytogenetic analysis revealed abnormalities of chromosomes 5 and 7. What factors support the diagnosis of chemotherapy-associated acute leukemia in T.D.?

Acute leukemia has been associated with chemotherapy administered to treat hematological malignancies, solid tumors, and nonmalignant diseases.[320] Myelodysplastic syndrome (preleukemia changes) commonly is observed in 50% of patients before overt acute leukemia appears.[321,322] The median duration from the initiation of chemotherapy to the development of overt leukemia is three to four years.[323] Although all alkylating agents have been implicated, melphalan appears to be the most potent leukemogenic agent in this class; other classes of antineoplastic agents do not appear to carry as significant a risk. Large doses, continuous daily dosing, and prolonged treatment periods may increase the risk of developing acute leukemia. In addition to dose intensity, age greater than 40 years, concomitant radiation therapy, and a number of additional factors also may increase the risk.[324–327]

ANLL also has been reported following combination chemotherapy that includes teniposide or etoposide.[328] These leukemias differ from those that follow alkylating agents in that they occur sooner, are not preceded by myelodysplasia, frequently are associated with FAB M4 or M5, and the most frequent chromosomal abnormalities involve chromosome 11q23. Cumulative risks of 4% to 12% have been reported with the higher prevalence observed in children treated with relatively high doses of teniposide and other drugs with or without radiation for acute lymphocytic leukemia. It is unclear what role other antineoplastic agents and radiation played in these reports. Nonetheless, it does appear that combination chemotherapy with podophyllotoxins confers some risk of leukemia. This is an important area for research given the widespread and increasing use of these agents in curable disease.

Table 91.16	Factors Associated with Increased Risk of Chemotherapy-Induced Pulmonary Toxicity[a]
Risk Factor	**Drug(s)**
Total cumulative dose	Bleomycin,[264,268] carmustine[264]
Age	Bleomycin[268]
Oxygen therapy	Bleomycin,[271–273] cyclophosphamide,[272] mitomycin[273]
Irradiation to lungs	Bleomycin,[284,285] busulfan,[286] carmustine,[277] mitomycin[274]
Concurrent therapy with other drugs	Bleomycin,[279, 280] carmustine,[277, 278] cyclophosphamide,[279, 281] methotrexate,[281] mitomycin,[283,282] vinblastine[283]
Pre-existing pulmonary disease	Carmustine[284]
Tobacco use	Carmustine[284]

[a] Adapted from Reference 266.

There also is strong evidence that chemotherapy can cause secondary lymphoid malignancies, particularly nonHodgkin's lymphoma. The primary cause in this case may be immunosuppression from the disease and its treatment rather than the particular antineoplastic agent. Solid tumors have been associated with superficial bladder cancer in patients treated with daily oral cyclophosphamide and bone sarcoma following treatment with alkylating agents.[329] The development of a secondary solid tumor in patients treated with other antineoplastic agents currently is considered coincidental.[330,331]

It is likely that T.D.'s acute nonlymphocytic leukemia is the result of her previous melphalan therapy. The agent used, as well as the time course for the development of her acute leukemia, is consistent with alkylating agent-induced malignancies. In addition, cytogenetic abnormalities occur in more than 90% of those patients who have received chemotherapy or radiotherapy and subsequently developed therapy-related myelodysplastic syndrome or acute nonlymphocytic leukemia.[322] Chromosomes 5 and 7 are involved in almost 90% of those with cytogenetic abnormalities.[333] Deletions of all or part of chromosomes 5 and 7 in T.D. strongly support the diagnosis of chemotherapy-associated acute leukemia rather than de novo (naturally occurring or no known cause or "from the beginning") leukemia.

43. Therapy and Prognosis. Are the therapy and prognosis of T.D. with treatment-associated ANLL similar to that of patients with de novo ANLL?

Therapy of patients with treatment-associated acute nonlymphocytic leukemia compares poorly to that of patients with de novo leukemia. Complete remissions with standard cytarabine and daunorubicin regimens are obtained in less than one-half of patients with treatment-associated ANLL compared to a complete remission rate of 70% to 80% in patients with de novo leukemia.[334,335] (See Chapter 92: Hematological Malignancies.) High-dose cytarabine produced remissions in 10 of 11 patients with acute nonlymphocytic leukemia secondary to chemotherapy in one series.[336] However, most series reported a lower response rate, with responses of very short duration and a median survival of only three to four months. Isolated case reports suggest that bone marrow transplantation may benefit younger patients and those with human leukocyte antigen (HLA) identical donors.[338–340]

The best "treatment" of therapy-associated ANLL is prevention. In patients like T.D. with curable malignancies, avoiding the use of alkylating agents is strongly encouraged. Efforts to eliminate alkylating agents from regimens used to treat patients with curable disease are ongoing. Although the choice of melphalan therapy for adjuvant treatment of T.D.'s ovarian cancer was not inappropriate at the time (over three years ago) it was initiated, it is far less likely that it would be employed today.

Fertility and Teratogenicity

Effects on Oogenesis

44. C.L., a 32-year-old female with recently diagnosed Stage II breast cancer, underwent a lumpectomy and external beam radiation therapy and is scheduled to begin adjuvant chemotherapy with cyclophosphamide, doxorubicin, and fluorouracil (CAF). C.L. was married 12 months before her diagnosis and wishes to have children. What are C.L.'s prospects for fertility following adjuvant chemotherapy?

Chemotherapy is potentially gonadotoxic in humans. Ovarian biopsies taken from women treated for cancer demonstrate loss of ova and follicular elements.[341,342] This injury is evident even in prepubertal females treated for cancer.[343,344] Ova die or become nonfunctional by direct injury to the ova or indirect injury resulting from loss of supporting follicular cells. If the damage to the follicular elements is extensive and irreversible, fertility is impaired even if the ova are spared.

Drug-induced injury to ova and follicular elements reduces ovarian estrogen and progesterone secretion in menstruating women. This causes the hypothalamus and pituitary to secrete more follicle-stimulating hormone (FSH) and luteinizing hormone (LH) which, in turn, increase follicular recruitment and the number of follicles vulnerable to cytotoxic agents. If the gonadal toxicity is profound and/or prolonged, enough depletion of ova and follicles occurs to produce permanent ovarian failure; however, recovery of some of the affected follicles often occurs and this may be manifested by irregular menses or delayed recovery of menses. If ova are spared and follicular cells recover sufficiently, ovulation and pregnancy may occur, but premature ovarian failure is inevitable in most women treated with large doses of gonadotoxic agents given over long periods. Prepubertal girls have a greater reserve of primary follicles and since their ovaries are not producing estrogen and progesterone, increases in FSH and LH with resultant recruitment of follicular elements does not occur. For this reason, prepubertal girls can sustain substantial doses without apparent effects even if the pathology described above occurs. The gonadal effects of chemotherapy in women and girls are described in a number of reviews.[343,344]

C.L. is going to receive one of the alkylating drugs which are the most potent gonadotoxic agents. Cyclophosphamide is well known for producing infertility in men and women and gonadal failure even in children. The effect is influenced strongly by the total dose of cyclophosphamide and the patient's age at the onset of chemotherapy. Nearly 100% of women over 29 years of age develop amenorrhea when the mean total dose is 20.8 gm/m². The

Table 91.17	Common Causes of Elevated LFTs in Patients with Cancer[a]

Primary or metastatic tumor involvement of the liver

Hepatotoxic drugs [e.g., cytotoxics, hormones (estrogens, androgens), antiemetics (phenothiazines), antimicrobials (rifampin, isoniazid)]

Infections (e.g., hepatic candidiasis, viral hepatitis)

Parenteral nutrition

Allopurinol

[a] LFTs = Liver function tests.

Table 91.18	Hepatotoxicity from Antineoplastic Drugs	
Drug/Schedule	**Prevalence**	**Type**
Asparaginase[304–306]		
Daily	Frequent	Hepatocellular fatty meta-morphosis
Carmustine[307,308]		
Weekly bolus	Common	Hepatocellular
Daily x 3	Common	
Bolus	Infrequent	
Cytarabine[309]		
Daily	Common	Cholestatic
Dacarbazine[310,311]		
Daily x 5	Infrequent	Hepatocellular
Bolus		
Etoposide[312]		
High dose	Common with high dose	Hepatocellular
Lomustine[313,314]	Infrequent	
Mercaptopurine[315,316]		
Daily	Common	Cholestatic
High dose		Hepatocellular
Methotrexate[299,300]		
Daily	Common	Hepatocellular
Weekly bolus	Rare	Hepatocellular
High dose	Uncommon	Hepatocellular
Mitomycin[317]		
High dose	Infrequent	Veno-occlusive disease
Plicamycin[301,302]		
Daily x 5	Common	Hepatocellular
Streptozocin[318]		
Bolus	Common	Hepatocellular
Thioguanine[319]		
Daily	Rare	Veno-occlusive disease

same consequence can be expected in those 30 to 39 years of age who receive 7.55 gm/m^2 and in those 40 years of age and older who receive 3.25 gm/m^2. Depending upon the exact dose of cyclophosphamide in the CAF regimen planned, C.L. may or may not fall into a dose range which would be expected to produce permanent amenorrhea.

One also must consider that a synergistic gonadotoxic effect has been reported when doxorubicin is combined with cyclophosphamide. The onset of amenorrhea may occur at one-half the total dose of cyclophosphamide after therapy with doxorubicin and cyclophosphamide than after treatment with cyclophosphamide, methotrexate, and fluorouracil. Fluorouracil is unlikely to play any role in producing ovarian failure. Aside from the alkylating agents, the only antineoplastic agents with strong evidence of gonadal toxicity include vinblastine, etoposide, and cisplatin. A number of excellent reviews discuss the doses of antineoplastic agents, used both alone and in combination, and specific incidences of associated gonadotoxicity, as well as the prevalence of temporary and permanent amenorrhea.[345,346]

It is highly likely that C.L. will experience amenorrhea along with the signs and symptoms of menopause as estrogen and progesterone production diminish during chemotherapy. As previously discussed, C.L. may recover from chemotherapy-induced amenorrhea months to years following completion of her therapy. Recovery may be manifested partially by amenorrhea interspersed with normal menstrual periods. Pregnancy is possible during periods of normal menstruation since ovulation does occur in most instances. However, premature menopause is inevitable. Because the greatest risk of pregnancy exists early in the course of chemotherapy C.L. should be counseled to practice birth control while receiving chemotherapy. Oral contraceptives generally are considered contraindicated in breast cancer patients. Barrier methods (i.e., diaphragm, condoms, spermicide) may be well advised.

Effects on Spermatogenesis

45. J.K., a 25-year-old male with recently diagnosed Stage IV Hodgkin's lymphoma, will receive systemic chemotherapy. What effects does systemic chemotherapy have on male gonadal function?

The primary gonadal toxic effect of chemotherapeutic agents in males is one of progressive dose-related depletion of the germinal epithelium lining the seminiferous tubule.[347–349] The clinical manifestations of germinal depletion include a marked reduction in testicular volume and azoospermia. The Leydig cells responsible for testosterone production remain morphologically intact, although mild functional impairment occurs rarely. Thus, the major toxicity of chemotherapy in males is loss of reproductive capacity. During treatment, libido and sexual activity may decline, but the majority of men report a return to pretreatment sexual function following chemotherapy.[347–349]

Of the chemotherapeutic drugs, alkylating agents most commonly are associated with azoospermia. Progressive dose-related oligospermia occurs in men receiving chlorambucil,[350,351] cyclophosphamide,[352,353] nitrogen mustard, busulfan, procarbazine, and nitrosureas; procarbazine appears to be the most gonadotoxic alkylating agent in men. Doxorubicin, vinblastine, cytarabine, and cisplatin also have been associated with azoospermia,[354] and doxorubicin appears to have a synergistic toxic effect in men when given with cyclophosphamide similar to that described above in women. The antimetabolite and antimitotic agents which generally are cell cycle-specific seem unlikely to produce azoospermia when used alone but may play a minor role in combination chemotherapy regimens.

In contrast to oogenesis, in which women are born with a full complement of ova, spermatogenesis occurs in a continuous cycle of regeneration, differentiation, and maturation beginning in the second month of embryogenesis and continuing through old age. Although different chemotherapeutic drugs appear to exert more damage to germ cells in specific phases of spermatogenesis in animal models, in humans, gonadotoxic drugs generally are used in large enough doses to affect varying proportions of maturing sperm cells in any stage of development. This has two very realistic implications. The first is that since spermatogenesis must start at the beginning after drug-induced azoospermia occurs, the length of recovery is prolonged, usually lasting at least two to three years. The second is that the relationship of age to the development of azoospermia is far less clear than the relationship of age to ovarian suppression. Although conventional wisdom holds that prepubertal males are less likely to be affected by chemotherapeutic agents than adult males, the reserve of primitive sperm cells in male children is far less than it is in adults. Thus, spermatogenesis potential in prepubertal testes may be more vulnerable to cytotoxic damage than that of adults. A review of the literature regarding the effects of chemotherapy administered to male children concluded that drugs and drug regimens known to be toxic in men should be considered toxic in young boys.[345] Short of a testicular biopsy, the damage cannot be detected until puberty.

Table 91.19		Chemotherapeutics Requiring Dose Modification in Hepatic Dysfunction[368]				
Bilirubin	AST[a]	Adriamycin	Daunorubicin	Vinblastine Vincristine Etoposide	Cyclophosphamide Methotrexate	5-Fluorouracil
<1.5	<60	100%	100%	100%	100%	100%
1.5–3.0	60–180	50%	75%	50%	100%	100%
3.1–5.0	>180	25%	50%	Omit	75%	100%
5.0		Omit	Omit	Omit	Omit	Omit

Paclitaxel-CALGB[a] Recommendations
For Dosing in Patients with Liver Dysfunction[369]

AST > 2 x N Bilirubin ≤1.5	<135 mg/m^2
Bilirubin = 1.6–3.0	≤75 mg/m^2
Bilirubin ≥3.1	50 mg/m^2

[a] AST = Aspartate aminotransferase; CALGB = Cancer and leukemia group B.

The two diseases most likely to affect young men concerned with fertility are Hodgkin's disease and testicular cancer. The two treatment regimens for advanced Hodgkin's disease are mechlorethamine, vincristine, prednisone, and procarbazine (MOPP) and doxorubicin, bleomycin, vinblastine, and dacarbazine (ABVD) (see Table 90.10 in Chapter 90: Neoplastic Disorders and Their Treatment: General Principles). Of the two, ABVD is considered equally efficacious and less toxic. In a comparison of these treatment regimens, azoospermia occurred in 100% of MOPP-treated patients versus 35% of those receiving ABVD. Furthermore, spermatogenesis nearly always recovered in the ABVD-treated patients.[354] This is consistent with information regarding the potential of mechlorethamine and procarbazine to produce testicular germ cell depletion when compared to the agents included in the ABVD regimen. This information may be important in planning treatment for young men with Hodgkin's disease who are concerned about preservation of fertility following treatment of their curable malignancy.

A similar scenario exists in patients about to embark on chemotherapy for testicular cancer. Evidence to date suggests that chemotherapy-induced azoospermia that follows treatment with vinblastine, bleomycin, and cisplatin for nonseminomatous testicular carcinoma is reversible within two to three years in approximately 50% of patients treated and that those individuals who recover spermatogenesis are capable of impregnating their partners.[355] In this particular patient population, it is important to recognize that retroperitoneal lymph node dissection which results in retrograde ejaculation, as well as cryptorchism which predisposes to infertility, may contribute to the lack of full recovery of fertility potential.

46. Aside from the use of chemotherapeutic agents with less gonadal toxicity, are there means of circumventing infertility in young patients receiving chemotherapy?

Sperm/gamete cryopreservation should be considered in males. A major limitation of this approach has been the finding of diminished sperm counts, sperm volume, and sperm motility in young males affected with Hodgkin's disease and testicular cancer before combination chemotherapy is initiated.[357,358] Although the published studies suggest that the quantity and motility of sperm are important determinants of successful artificial insemination, pregnancies have been reported.[359,360] Thus, sperm banking should be considered even in oligospermic males.

Oocyte and embryo cryopreservation now are feasible options for young women about to undergo cytotoxic chemotherapy. Even in the face of chemotherapy-induced ovarian failure, in vitro fertilization of an ova, and implantation into the endometrium with proper hormonal support can successfully accommodate a term pregnancy.[361,362] This may be an option for C.L. described in the Question 44.

In both genders, it has been hypothesized that gonadal toxicity from chemotherapy could be decreased by inhibiting spermatogenesis or follicular development during chemotherapy. Methods used to suppress gonadal function have included administration of testosterone in men,[363] oral contraceptives in women,[364] and gonadotropin releasing hormone analogues (LHRH analogs) in both men and women.[345,364,365] Unfortunately, none of these approaches has proven effective despite encouraging preliminary results in experimental animal and human studies.

Teratogenicity

47. If C.L. or J.K. regain fertility following their planned combination chemotherapy regimens, are they at risk of producing offspring with congenital abnormalities or an excess risk of cancer?

Most of the agents used to treat cancer are designed specifically to interfere with DNA synthesis, cellular metabolism, and cell division. Thus, there is reason to suspect that they may cause mutation of ova or spermatocytes exposed to these effects. The actual outcomes of pregnancies in survivors of cancer are published as case reports, small series, and retrospective case series. Nearly 1600 children have been born to 1078 patients previously treated for malignancy in childhood or as adults. A review of the published information suggests there is no evidence that spontaneous abortion, genetic disease, or congenital anomalies occur more frequently in the progeny of cancer survivors. Similarly, there does not appear to be an increased risk of malignancy in the offspring of patients treated for cancer.[345] The likely explanation for this is that ova and sperm cells affected by chemotherapy usually are killed. The risk of producing an abnormal offspring thus would be highest at the time of ongoing germ cell exposure. Men and women should be explicitly discouraged from conception during chemotherapy. In general, adults surviving cancer should be advised to wait two years or more after completion of therapy before attempting to parent a child; this allows time for elimination of damaged germ cells. This also provides time to assess the likelihood of the necessity for further treatment which would have grave consequences, particularly in the case of female patients.

References

1   **Gastineau DA, Hoagland HA.** Hematologic effects of chemotherapy. Semin Oncol. 1992;19(5):543–50.

2   **Carson RW, Sikic BI.** Continuous infusion or bolus injection in cancer chemotherapy. Ann Intern Med. 1983;99:823–33.

3   **Crawford J et al.** Reduction by granulocyte colony-stimulating factor of fever and neutropenia induced by chemotherapy in patients with small cell lung cancer. N Engl J Med. 1991;325:164–70.

4   **American Society of Clinical Oncology.** Recommendations for Use of Hematopoietin Colony-Stimulating Factors: Evidence-Based Clinical Practice. Guidelines. J Clin Onc. 1994;12:2471–508.

5   **Bronchud MH et al.** Phase I/II study of recombinant human granulocyte colony-stimulating factor in patients receiving intensive chemotherapy for small cell lung cancer. Br J Cancer. 1987;56:809–13.

6   **Gabrilove JL et al.** Effect of granulocyte colony-stimulating factor on neutropenia and associated morbidity due to chemotherapy for transitional-cell carcinoma of the urothelium. N Engl J Med. 1988;318:1414–422.

7   **Hamm JT et al.** Dose ranging study of recombinant human granulocyte-macrophage colony-stimulating factor in small cell lung cancer. Proc Am Soc Clin Oncol. 1993;12:335.

8   **Maugard-Louboutin C et al.** Dose effect relationship of granulocyte colony-stimulating factor (G-CSF): PE 2601 in patients with advanced breast carcinoma (ABC) treated by intensive chemotherapy. Proc Am Soc Clin Oncol. 1993;12:P90. Abstract.

9   **Corelli RL.** Management of the colony-stimulating factors. Pharmacy Practice News. 1993;20(9):3–4,26.

10 **Maher D et al.** Randomized, placebo-controlled trial of filgrastim (r-met-HuG-CSF) in patients with febrile neutropenia (FN) following chemotherapy (CT). Proc Am Soc Clin Oncol. 1993;12:P884. Abstract.

11 **Mayordomo JI et al.** Decreasing morbidity and cost of treating febrile neutropenia by adding G-CSF and GM-CSF to standard antibiotic therapy: Results of a randomized trial. Proc Am Soc Clin Oncol. 1993;12:437.

12 **Pekka Riikonen et al.** rh GM-CSF in the treatment of fever and neutropenia: a double-blind, placebo-controlled study in children with malignancy. Proc Am Soc Clin Oncol. 1993;12:443.

13 **Tomaik A et al.** Duration of intravenous (IV) antibiotic and hospital stay for patients with febrile neutropenia after chemotherapy; experience of Ottawa Regional Cancer Centre. Proc Am Soc Clin Oncol. 1993;12:435.

14 **Rolston K et al.** Outpatient treatment of febrile episodes in low-risk neutropenia cancer patients. Proc Am Soc Clin Oncol. 1993;12:436. Abstract.

15 **El-Dairy W, Morris L.** High cost of hospital admissions for cancer patients at low risk to develop complications

16 **Doweiko JP, Goldberg MA.** Erythropoietin therapy in cancer patients. Oncology. 1991;5:31–7.

17 **Abels RI, Rudnick SA.** Erythropoietin: evolving clinical applications. Exp Hematol. 1991;19:842–50.

18 **Ludwig H et al.** Erythropoietin treatment of anemia associated with multiple myeloma. N Engl J Med. 1990;322:1693–699.

19 **Oster W et al.** Erythropoietin for the treatment of anemia of malignancy associated with neoplastic bone marrow infiltration. J Clin Oncol. 1990;8:956–62.

20 **Platanias LC et al.** Treatment of chemotherapy-induced anemia with recombinant human erythropoietin in cancer patients. J Clin Oncol. 1991;9:2021–026.

21 **Whitecare JP Jr et al.** L-Asparaginase. N Engl J Med. 1970;282:732–34.

22 **Ramsay NKC et al.** The effect of L-Asparaginase on plasma coagulation factors in acute lymphoblastic leukemia. Cancer. 1977;40:1398–401.

23 **Levine MN et al.** The thrombogenic effect of anticancer drug therapy in women with stage II breast cancer. N Engl J Med. 1988;318:404–07.

24 **Ruiz MA et al.** The influence of chemotherapy on plasma coagulation and fibrinolytic systems in lung cancer patients. Cancer. 1989;63:643–48.

25 **Rogers JS II et al.** Chemotherapy for breast cancer decreases plasma protein C and protein S. J Clin Oncol. 1988;6:276–81.

26 **Kaufman PA et al.** Autologous bone marrow transplantation and factor XII, factor VII, and protein C deficiencies: report of a new association and its possible relationship to endothelial cell injury. Cancer. 1990;66:515–21.

27 **Trousseau A.** Phlegmasia alba dolens. Clinique medicale de L'Hotel-Dieu de Paris. London, The New Sydenham Society. 1865;3:94.

28 **Sack GH Jr et al.** Trousseau's syndrome and other manifestations of chronic disseminated coagulopathy in patients with neoplasms: clinical, pathophysiologic, and therapeutic features. Medicine. 1977;56:1–37.

29 **Aderka D et al.** Idiopathic deep vein thrombosis in an apparently healthy patient as a premonitory sign of occult cancer. Cancer. 1986;57:1846–849.

30 **Goldberg RJ et al.** Occult malignant neoplasm in patients with deep venous thrombosis. Arch Intern Med. 1987;147:251–53.

31 **Goldberg MA et al.** Is heparin administration necessary during induction chemotherapy for patients with acute promyelocytic leukemia? Blood. 1987;69:187–91.

32 **Sonis ST et al.** Oral complications in patients receiving treatment for malignancies other than of the head and neck. J Am Dent Assoc. 1978;97:468–72.

33 **Lockhart PB, Sonis ST.** Alterations in the oral mucosa caused by chemother-

apeutic agents. J Dermatol Surg Oncol. 1981;7:1019–025.

34 **Eneroth CM et al.** Effects of fractionated radiotherapy on salivary gland function. Cancer. 1972;30:1147–153.

35 **Lindley CM.** Incidence and duration of chemotherapy-induced nausea and vomiting in an outpatient cancer population. J Clin Oncol. 1989;7:1142–149.

36 **Shaw MT et al.** Effects of cancer, radiotherapy and cytotoxic drugs on intestinal structure and function. Cancer Treat Rev. 1979;6:141–51.

37 **Wurth MA, Musacchila XJ.** Mechlorethamine effects on intestinal absorption in vitro and on cell proliferation. Am J Physiol. 1973;225:73–80.

38 **Roche AC et al.** Correlation between the histologic changes and glucose intestine absorption following a single dose of 5-fluorouracil. Digestion. 1970;3:195–212.

39 **Kuhlmann J et al.** Effects of cytostatic drugs on plasma levels and renal excretion of B-acetyldigoxin. Clin Pharmacol Ther. 1981;30:519–27.

40 **Finchman R, Stoccelius D.** Decreased phenytoin levels in antineoplastic therapy. Ther Drug Monit. 1984;6:302–05.

41 **Kuhlmann J et al.** Verapamil plasma concentrations during treatment with cytostatic drugs. J Cardiovasc Pharmacol. 1985;7:1003–005.

42 **LeVeque FG et al.** A multicenter, randomized, double-blind, placebo-controlled, dose-titration study of oral pilocarpine for treatment of radiation-induced xerostomia in head and neck cancer patients. J Clin Oncol. 1993;11:1123–131.

43 **Johnson JT et al.** Oral pilocarpine for post-irradiation xerostomia in patients with head and neck cancer. N Engl J Med. 1993;329:390–95.

44 **Donatsky O et al.** Effect of Saliment on parotid salivary gland secretion and on xerostomia caused by Sjögren's syndrome. Scand J Dent Res. 1982;90:157.

45 **Klestov AC et al.** Treatment of xerostomia: A double-blind trial of 108 patients with Sjörgren's syndrome. Oral Surg Oral Med Oral Pathol. 1981;51:594.

46 **Keys HM, McCasland JP.** Techniques and results of a comprehensive dental care program in head and neck cancer patients. Int J Radiat Oncol Biol Phys. 1976;1:859–65.

47 **Sonis ST et al.** Pretreatment oral assessment. J Natl Cancer Inst. 1990;9:29–32.

48 **Mahood D et al.** Inhibition of fluorouracil-induced stomatitis by oral cryotherapy. J Clin Oncol. 1991;9:449–52.

49 **Clark PI, Sleven ML.** Allopurinol mouthwash and 5-fluorouracil induced oral toxicity. Eur J Surg Oncol. 1985;11:267–68.

50 **Tsavaris N et al.** Reduction of oral toxicity of 5-fluorouracil by allopurinol mouthwashes. Eur J Surg Oncol. 1988;14:405–06.

51 **Loprinzi CL et al.** A controlled evaluation of an allopurinol mouthwash as prophylaxis against 5-fluorouracil-

induced stomatitis. Cancer. 1990;65:1879–882.

52 **Ferretti GA et al.** Chlorhexidine in prophylaxis against oral infections and associated complications in patients receiving bone marrow transplantation. J Am Dent Assoc. 1987;114:292–94.

53 **Ferretti GA et al.** Chlorhexidine prophylaxis for chemotherapy and radiotherapy-induced stomatitis: a randomized, double-blind trial. Oral Surg Med Oral Pathol. 1990;69:331–38.

54 **Gabrilove JL et al.** Effect of granulocyte colony-stimulating factor on neutropenia and associated morbidity due to chemotherapy for transitional-cell carcinoma of the urothelium. N Engl J Med. 1988;318:1414–422.

55 **Hood AF.** Cutaneous side effects of cancer chemotherapy. Med Clin North Am. 1986;70:187–209.

56 **DeSpain JD.** Dermatologic toxicity of chemotherapy. Semin Oncol. 1992;19:501–07.

57 **Dunagin WG.** Dermatologic toxicity. In: Perry MC, Yarbro JW, eds. Toxicity of Chemotherapy. Orlando: Grune & Stratton; 1984:125–54.

58 **Claudia Seipp.** Alopecia. In: De Vita VT et al, eds. Cancer: Principles and Practice of Oncology. 4th ed. Philadelphia: JB Lippincott; 1993:2394–393.

59 **Middleton J et al.** Failure of scalp hypothermia to prevent hair loss when cyclophosphamide is added to doxorubicin and vincristine. Cancer Treat Rep. 1985;69:373–75.

60 **Wheelock JB et al.** Ineffectiveness of scalp hypothermia in the prevention of alopecia in patients treated with doxorubicin and cis-platin combinations. Cancer Treat Rep. 1984;68:1387–388.

61 **Seipp CA.** Scalp hypothermia: indicators for precaution. Oncol Nurs Forum. 1983;10:12. Letter.

62 **Whitman G et al.** Misuse of scalp hypothermia. Cancer Treat Rep. 1981;65:507–08.

63 **Camp Sorrell D.** Scalp hypothermia devices: current status. ONS News. 1991;7:1.

64 **Singh M, Kaur S.** Chemotherapy-induced multiple Beau's lines. Int J Dermatol. 1986;25:590–91.

65 **Jessen RT et al.** Cutaneous and other complications of cyclophosphamide: a brief review. Rocky Mt Med J. 1978;75:204–06.

66 **Faulkson G, Schulz EJ.** Skin changes in patients treated with 5-fluorouracil. Br J Dermatol. 1962;74:229–36.

67 **Harrison BM, Wood CBS.** Cyclophosphamide and pigmentation. Br Med J. 1972;2:352.

68 **deMarinis M et al.** Nail pigmentation with daunorubicin therapy. Ann Intern Med. 1978;89:516–17.

69 **Priestman TJ, James KW.** Adriamycin and longitudinal pigmented banding of fingernails. Lancet. 1975;1:1337–338.

70 **Rothberg H et al.** Adriamycin (NSC-123127) toxicity: unusual melanotic reaction. Cancer Chemother Rep. 1974;58:749–51.

71 **Pratt CB, Shanks EC.** Hyperpigmentation of nails from doxorubicin. JAMA. 1974:228:460.

72 **Shetty MR.** Case of pigmented banding of the nail caused by bleomycin. Cancer Treat Rep. 1977;61:501–02.

73 **Adrian RM et al.** Mucocutaneous reactions to neoplastic agents. CA Cancer J Clin. 1980;30:143–57.

74 **Ma HK et al.** Actinomycin D in the treatment of methotrexate-resistant trophoblastic tumours. J Obstet Gynaecol Br Commonw. 1971;78:166–71.

75 **Kennedy BJ et al.** Skin changes secondary to hydroxyurea therapy. Arch Dermatol. 1975;111:183–87.

76 **Harrold BP.** Syndrome resembling Addison's disease following prolonged treatment with busulfan. Br Med J. 1966;1:463–64.

77 **Kyle RA et al.** A syndrome resembling adrenal cortical insufficiency associated with long-term busulfan (Myleran) therapy. Blood. 1961;18:497–510.

78 **Delmonte L, Jukes TH.** Folic acid antagonists in cancer chemotherapy. Pharmacol Rev. 1962;14:91–135.

79 **Hrushesky WJ.** Serpentine supravenous fluorouracil hyperpigmentation. JAMA. 1976;236:138.

80 **Fernandez-Obregon AC et al.** Flagellate pigmentation from intrapleural bleomycin. A light microscopy and electron microscopy study. J Am Acad Dermatol. 1985;13:464–68.

81 **Horn TD et al.** Observations and proposed mechanisms of N,N',N''-triethylenethio-phosphoramide (Thio-TEPA)-induced hyperpigmentation. Arch Dermatol. 1989;125:524–27.

82 **Harben DJ et al.** Thiotepa-induced leukoderma. Arch Dermatol. 1979;115:973–74.

83 **Vonderheid EC.** Topical mechlorethamine chemotherapy. Int J Dermatol. 1984;23:180–86.

84 **DeVita VT et al.** Clinical trials with 1,3Bis(2-chloroethyl)-1-nitrosourea, NSC-409962. Cancer Res. 1965;25:1876–881.

85 **Wheeland RG et al.** The flag sign of chemotherapy. Cancer. 1983;51:1356–358.

86 **Dorr RT.** Pharmacologic management of vesicant chemotherapy reactions. In: Dorr RT, Von Hoff DD, eds. Cancer Chemotherapy Handbook. 2nd ed. East Norwalk: Appelton and Lange; 1993:109–18.

87 **Gallina C, Ellen J.** Practical guide to chemotherapy administration for physicians and oncology nurses. In: De Vita VT et al., eds. Cancer: Principles and Practice of Oncology. 4th ed. Philadelphia: JB Lippincott; 1993:2570–580.

88 **Vogelzang NJ.** "Adriamycin flare": a skin reaction resembling extravasation. Cancer Treat Rep. 1979;63:2067.

89 **Souhami L, Feld R.** Urticaria following intravenous doxorubicin administration. JAMA. 1978;240:1624.

90 **Luedke DW et al.** Histopathogenesis of skin and subcutaneous injury induced by adriamycin. Plast Reconstr Surg. 1979;63:463.

91 **Rudolph R et al.** Skin ulcers due to adriamycin. Cancer. 1976;38:1087.

92 **Ignoffo RJ, Friedman MA.** Therapy of local toxicities caused by extravasation of cancer chemotherapeutic drugs. Cancer Treat Rev. 1980;7:17.

93 **Rudolph R, Larson DL.** Etiology and treatment of chemotherapeutic agent extravasation injuries: a review. J Clin Oncol. 1987;5:1116.

94 **Rudolph R et al.** Experimental skin necrosis produced by adriamycin. Cancer Treat Rep. 1979;63:529.

95 **Desao MH, Teres D.** Prevention of doxorubicin-induced skin ulcers in the rat and pig with dimethyl sulfoxide (DMSO). Cancer Treat Rep. 1982;66:1371.

96 **Bertelli G et al.** Dimethyl sulfoxide and cooling after extravasation of antitumor agents. Lancet. 1993;341:1098.

97 **Lawrence HJ, Goodnight SH.** Dimethyl sulfoxide and extravasation of anthracycline agents. Ann Intern Med. 1983;98:1026. Letter.

98 **Olver IN et al.** A prospective study of topical dimethyl sulfoxide for treating anthracycline extravasation. J Clin Oncol. 1988;6:1732.

99 **Ludwig CU et al.** Prevention of cytotoxic drug-induced skin ulcers with dimethyl sulfoxide (DMSO) and alpha-tocopheral. Eur J Cancer Clin Oncol. 1987;23:327.

100 **Alberts DS, Dorr RT.** Case Report: Topical DMSO for mitomycin C-induced skin ulceration. Oncol Nurs Forum. 1991;19:693–95.

101 **Van Slotten-Harwood K, Aisner J.** Treatment of chemotherapy extravasation: current status. Cancer Treat Rep. 1984;7–8:939.

102 **Weiss RB.** Hypersensitivity reactions. Semin Oncol. 1992;19:458–77.

103 **Weiss RB.** Hypersensitivity reactions. In: Perry MC, ed. The Chemotherapy Source Book. Baltimore: Williams & Wilkins; 1992:555–70.

104 **Swenerton K et al.** Taxol in relapsed ovarian cancer: high vs. low and short vs. long infusion: a European-Canadian study coordinated by the NCI Canada Clinical Trials Group. Proc Am Soc Oncol. 1993;12:256. Abstract.

105 **Greenberger PA et al.** Pretreatment of high-risk patients requiring radiographic contrast media studies. J Allergy Clin Immunol. 1981;67:185–87.

106 **Greenberger PA et al.** Emergency administrations of radio contrast media in high-risk patients. J Allergy Clin Immunol. 1986;77:630–34.

107 **Evans WE et al.** Anaphylactoid reactions to *Escherichia coli* and *Erwinia* asparaginase in children with leukemia and lymphoma. Cancer. 1982;49:1378–383.

108 **Clavell LA et al.** Four-agent induction and intensive asparaginase therapy for treatment of childhood acute lymphocytic leukemia. N Engl J Med. 1986;315:657–63.

109 **Rausen AR et al.** Superiority of L-asparaginase combination chemotherapy in advanced acute lymphocytic leukemia of childhood. Randomized comparative trial of combination versus solo therapy. Cancer Clin Trials. 1979;1:137–44.

110 **Land VJ et al.** Unexpectedly high incidence of allergic reactions with high dose (HD) weekly asparaginase (ASP) consolidation (cons) therapy (Rx) in children with newly diagnosed non-T, non-B acute lymphoblastic leukemia (ALL): a Pediatric Oncology Group (POG) study. Proc Am Soc Clin Oncol. 1989;8:215. Abstract.

111 **Weiss RB et al.** Hypersensitivity reactions from taxol. J Clin Oncol. 1990;8:1263–268.

112 **O'Dwyer PJ et al.** Hypersensitivity reactions to teniposide (VM-26): an analysis. J Clin Oncol. 1986;4:1262–269.

113 **Hayes FA et al.** Allergic reactions to teniposide in patients with neuroblastoma and lymphoid malignancies. Cancer Treat Rep. 1985;69:439–41.

114 **Carstensen H et al.** Hypersensitivity reactions to teniposide in children. J Clin Oncol. 1987;5:1491–492.

115 **Canal P et al.** Phase I/pharmacokinetic study of intraperitoneal teniposide (VM 26). Eur J Cancer Clin Oncol. 1989;25:815–20.

116 **O'Dwyer PJ, Weiss RB.** Hypersensitivity reactions induced by etoposide. Cancer Treat Rep. 1984;68:959–61.

117 **Tucci E, Pirtoli L.** Etoposide-induced hypersensitivity reactions. Report of two cases. Chemioterapia. 1985;4:460–62.

118 **Anderson T et al.** Chemotherapy for testicular cancer: current status of the National Cancer Institute combined modality trial. Cancer Treat Rep. 1979;63:1687–692.

119 **Denis L.** Anaphylactic reactions to repeated intravesical instillation with cisplatin. Lancet. 1983;1:1378–379.

120 **Getaz EP et al.** Cisplatin-induced hemolysis. N Engl J Med. 1980;302:334–35.

121 **Levi JA et al.** Haemolytic anemia after cisplatin treatment. Br Med J. 1981;282:2003–004.

122 **Bacha DM et al.** Phase I study of carboplatin (CBDCA) in children with cancer. Cancer Treat Rep. 1986;70:865–69.

123 **Allen JC et al.** Carboplatin and recurrent childhood brain tumors. J Clin Oncol. 1987;5:459–61.

124 **Glovsky MM et al.** Hypersensitivity to procarbazine associated with angioedema, urticaria, and low serum complement activity. J Allergy Clin Immunol. 1976;57:134–40.

125 **Eyre HJ et al.** Malignant glioma: a randomized trial of radiotherapy plus BCNU, procarbazine, or DTIC; a SWOG study. Proc Am Soc Clin Oncol. 1982;1:180. Abstract.

126 **Brunner KW, Young CW.** A methylhydrazine derivative in Hodgkin's disease and other malignant neoplasms. Ann Intern Med. 1965;63:69–86.

127 **Lokich JJ, Moloney WC.** Allergic reaction to procarbazine. Clin Pharmacol Ther. 1972;13:573–74.

128 **Jones SE et al.** Hypersensitivity to procarbazine (Matulane) manifested by fever and pleuropulmonary reaction. Cancer. 1972;29:498–500.

129 **Ecker MD et al.** Procarbazine lung. Am J Roentgenol. 1987;131:527–28.

130 **Arnold DJ, Stafford CT.** Systemic allergic reaction to adriamycin. Cancer Treat Rep. 1979;63:150–51.

131 **Solimando DA, Wilson JP.** Doxorubicin-induced hypersensitivity reactions. Drug Intell Clin Pharm. 1984;18:808–11.

132 **Collins JA.** Hypersensitivity reaction to doxorubicin. Drug Intell Clin Pharm. 1984;18:402–03.

133 **Etcubanas E, Wilbur JR.** Uncommon side effects of adriamycin (NSC-123127). Cancer Chemother Rep (Part 1). 1974;58:757–58.

134 **Crowther D et al.** Management of adult acute myelogenous leukaemia. Br Med J. 1973;1:131–37.

135 **Mathé G et al.** Phase II trial of THP-Adriamycin (pirarubicin), the most efficient and least toxic anthracycline in breast cancer. In: Kuemmerle H-P, ed. Advances in Experimental and Clinical Chemotherapy. Landsberg, Germany: Ecomed; 1988:51–5.

136 **Tan CTC et al.** Phase I trial of rubidzone (NSC 164011) in children with cancer. Med Pediatr Oncol. 1981;9:347–53.

137 **Rosenfelt F et al.** A fatal hyperpyrexial response to bleomycin following prior therapy: a case report and literature review. Yale J Biol Med. 1982;55:529–31.

138 **Leung W-H et al.** Fulminant hyperpyrexia induced by bleomycin. Postgrad Med J. 1989;65:417–19.

139 **Bochner BS, Lichtenstein LM.** Anaphylaxis. N Engl J Med. 1991;324:1785–790.

140 **Baker WJ et al.** Cytarabine and neurologic toxicity. J Clin Oncol. 1991;9:679–93.

141 **Graves T, Hooks MA.** Drug-induced toxicities associated with high-dose cytosine arabinoside infusions. Pharmacotherapy. 1989;9:23–8.

142 **Pratt CB et al.** Low dose asparaginase treatment of childhood acute lymphocytic leukemia. Am J Dis Child. 1971;121:406.

143 **Weiss HD et al.** Neurotoxicity of commonly used antineoplastic agents. N Engl J Med. 1974;297:127.

144 **Ohnuma T et al.** Biochemical and pharmacological studies with asparaginase in man. Cancer Res. 1970;30:2297.

145 **Allen JC, Rosen G.** Transient cerebral dysfunction following chemotherapy for osteogenic sarcoma. Ann Neurol. 1978;3:441–44.

146 **Bleyer WA, Griffin TW.** White matter necrosis mineralizing microangiopathy, and intellectual abilities in survivors of childhood leukemia: associations with central nervous system irradiation and methotrexate therapy. In: Gilbert HA, Kagan AR, eds. Radiation Damage to the Nervous System. New York: Raven Press; 1980:155–74.

147 **Allen JC et al.** Leukoencephalopathy following high-dose IV methotrexate chemotherapy with leucovorin rescue. Cancer Treat Rep. 1980;64:1261–273.

148 **Moertel CG et al.** Cerebellar ataxis associated with fluorinated pyrimidine therapy. Cancer Chemother Rep. 1964;41:15–8.

149 **Lynch HT et al.** "Organic brain syndrome" secondary to 5-fluorouracil toxicity. Dis Colon Rectum. 1981;24:130–31.

150 **Warrell RP, Berman E.** Phase I and II study of fludarabine phosphate in leukemia: therapeutic efficacy with delayed central nervous system toxicity. J Clin Oncol. 1986;4:74–9.

151 **Chun HG et al.** Central nervous system toxicity of fludarabine phosphate. Cancer Treat Rep. 1986;70:1225–228.

152 **Puccio CA et al.** A loading/continuous infusion schedule of fludarabine phos-

phate in chronic lymphatic leukemia. J Clin Oncol. 1991;9:1562–569.

153 **Merkel DE et al.** Central nervous system toxicity with fludarabine. Cancer Treat Rep. 1986;70:1449–450.

154 **Phillips GL et al.** Intensive 1, 3-bis (2-chloroethyl)-1-nitrosourea (BCNU) monochemotherapy and autologous marrow transplantation for malignant glioma. J Clin Oncol. 1986;4:639–45.

155 **Shapiro WR, Green SB.** Re-evaluating the efficacy of intra-arterial BCNU. J Neurosurg. 1987;66:313–15.

156 **Mahaley MS Jr et al.** Central neurotoxicity following intracarotid BCNU chemotherapy for malignant gliomas. J Neurooncol. 1986;3:297–314.

157 **Watkin SW et al.** Ifosamide encephalopathy: a reappraisal. Eur J Cancer Clin Oncol. 1989;25:1303–310.

158 **Merimsky O et al.** Ifosfamide-related acute encephalopathy: clinical and radiological aspects. Eur J Cancer. 1991; 27:1188–189.

159 **Brunner KW, Young CW.** A methylhydrazine-derivative in Hodgkin's disease and other malignant neoplasms: therapeutic and toxic effects studied in 51 patients. Ann Intern Med. 1965;63:69–86.

160 **Weiss RB.** The role of hexamethylmelamine in advanced ovarian carcinoma treatment. Gynecol Oncol. 1981; 12:141–49.

161 **Gerritsen van der Hoop R et al.** Incidence of neuropathy in 395 patients with ovarian cancer treated with or without cisplatin. Cancer. 1990;66: 1967–702.

162 **Legha SS, Dimery IW.** High dose cisplatin administration without hypertonic saline: observation of disabling neurotoxicity. J Clin Oncol. 1985;3: 1373–378.

163 **Cersosimo RJ.** Cisplatin neurotoxicity. Cancer Treat Rev. 1989;16:195–211.

164 **Thompson SW et al.** Cisplatin neuropathy: clinical, electrophysiologic, morphologic, and toxicologic studies. Cancer. 1984;54:1269–275.

165 **Sandler SG et al.** Vincristine-induced neuropathy: a clinical study of fifty leukemic patients. Neurology. 1969;19: 367–74.

166 **Casey EG et al.** Vincristine neuropathy: clinical and electrophysiological observations. Brain. 1973;96:69–86.

167 **Weiss RB, Vogelzang NJ.** Miscellaneous toxicities. In: De Vita VT, Cancer: Principles and Practice of Oncology. 4th ed. Philadelphia: Lippincott; 1993.

168 **MacDonald, DR.** Neurotoxicity of chemotherapeutic agents. In: Perry MC, ed. The Chemotherapy Source Book. Baltimore: Williams & Wilkins; 1992: 666–80.

169 **Sandler SG et al.** Vincristine-induced neuropathy: a clinical study of fifty leukemic patients. Neurology (Minn). 1969;19:367–74.

170 **Albert DM et al.** Ocular complications of vincristine therapy. Arch Ophthalmol. 1967;78:709–13.

171 **Holland JF et al.** Vincristine treatment of advanced cancer: a cooperative study of 392 cases. Cancer Res. 1973; 33:1258–264.

172 **Granowetter L et al.** Enhanced cisplatinum neurotoxicity in pediatric patients with brain tumors. J Neurooncol. 1983;1:293–97.

173 **Schaefer SD et al.** Ototoxicity of low- and moderate-dose cisplatin. Cancer. 1985;56:1934–939.

174 **Canetta R et al.** Carboplatin, the clinical spectrum to date. Cancer Treatment Rev. 1985;12(A):125–36.

175 **Carmichael SM et al.** Orthostatic hypotension during vincristine therapy. Arch Intern Med. 1973;126:290.

176 **Gottlieb RJ et al.** Vincristine-induced bladder atony. Cancer. 1971;28:674.

177 **Allen A.** The cardiotoxicity of chemotherapeutic drugs. In: Perry MC, ed. The Chemotherapy Source Book. Baltimore: Williams & Wilkins; 1992: 582–98.

178 **Alexander J et al.** Serial assessment of doxorubicin cardiotoxicity with quantitative radionuclide angiography. N Engl J Med. 1979;300:278–83.

179 **Tan C et al.** Adriamycin—an antitumor antibiotic in the treatment of neoplastic diseases. Cancer. 1973;32:9–17.

180 **Lefrak EA et al.** A clinicopathologic analysis of adriamycin cardiotoxicity. Cancer. 1973;32:302–14.

181 **Von Hoff DD et al.** Risk factors for doxorubicin induced congestive heart failure. Ann Intern Med. 1977;62: 200–08.

182 **Allen A.** The cardiotoxicity of chemotherapeutic drugs. Semin Oncol. 1992;19:529–42.

183 **Bloom K et al.** Echocardiography in adriamycin cardiotoxicity. Cancer. 1978;41:1265–269.

184 **Biancaniello T et al.** Doxorubicin cardiotoxicity in children. J Pediatr. 1980; 97:45–50.

185 **Steinberg JS, Wasserman AG.** Radionuclide ventriculography for evaluation and prevention of doxorubicin cardiotoxicity. Clin Ther. 1985;7:660–67.

186 **Isner JM et al.** Clinical and morphologic cardiac findings after anthracycline chemotherapy. Analysis of 64 patients studied at necropsy. Am J Cardiol. 1983;51:1167–174.

187 **Bristow MR.** Toxic cardiomyopathy due to doxorubicin. Hosp Pract. 1982; 17:101–11.

188 **Bristow MR et al.** Dose-effect and structure-function relationships in doxorubicin cardiomyopathy. Am Heart J. 1981;102:709–18.

189 **Bristow MR et al.** Efficacy and cost of cardiac monitoring in patients receiving doxorubicin. Cancer. 1982;50:32–41.

190 **Bristow MR et al.** Doxorubicin cardiomyopathy: evaluation by phonocardiography, endomyocardial biopsy, and cardiac catheterization. Ann Intern Med. 1978;88:168–75.

191 **Von Hoff DD.** Use of daunorubicin in patients with solid tumors. Semin Oncol. 1984;11(Suppl. 3):23–7.

192 **Yates J et al.** Cytosine arabinoside with daunorubicin or adriamycin for therapy of acute myelocytic leukemia. A GALGB study. Blood. 1982;60: 454–62.

193 **Von Hoff DD et al.** Daunomycin-induced cardiotoxicity in children and adults. Am J Med. 1977;62:200–08.

194 **Cassaza AM.** Effects of modifications in position 4 of the chromophore or in position 4′ of the amino sugar on the antitumor activity and toxicity of daunorubicin and doxorubicin. In: Crooke ST, Reich SD, eds. Anthracyclines: Current Status and New Developments. New York: Academic Press; 1980:403–30.

195 **Hurteloup P, Ganzina F.** Clinical studies with new anthracyclines: epirubicin, idarubicin, esorubicin. Drugs Exp Clin Res. 1986;12:233–46.

196 **Hurteloup P et al.** Phase II trial of idarubicin (4-demethoxydaunorubicin) in advanced breast cancer. Eur J Cancer Clin Oncol. 1989;25:423–28.

197 **Villani F et al.** Evaluation of cardiac toxicity of idarubicin (4-demethoxy-daunorubicin). Eur J Clin Oncol. 1989; 25:13–8.

198 **Tan CT et al.** Phase I and clinical pharmacological studies with 4-demethoxydaunorubicin (Idarubicin) in children with advanced cancer. Cancer. 1987;47:2990–995.

199 **Feig SA et al.** Determination of the maximum tolerated dose of idarubicin when used in a combination chemotherapy program of reinduction childhood ALL at first marrow relapse and a preliminary assessment of toxicity compared to that of daunorubicin: a report from the Children's Cancer Study Group. Med Pediatr Oncol. 1992;20: 124–29.

200 **Crossley RJ.** Clinical safety and tolerance of mitoxantrone. Semin Oncol. 1984;11(Suppl. 1):54–8.

201 **Posner LE et al.** Mitoxantrone: an overview of safety and toxicity. Invest New Drugs. 1985;3:123–32.

202 **Henderson IC et al.** Randomized clinical trial comparing mitoxantrone with doxorubicin in previously treated patients with breast cancer. J Clin Oncol. 1989;7:560–71.

203 **Weiss AJ et al.** Studies on adriamycin using a weekly regimen demonstrating its clinical effectiveness and lack of cardiac toxicity. Cancer Treat Rep. 1976;60:813–22.

204 **Weiss AJ.** Studies on cardiotoxicity and antitumor effect of doxorubicin administered weekly. Cancer Treat Symp. 1984;3:91–4.

205 **Jain KK et al.** A randomized comparison of weekly (Arm I) vs monthly (Arm II) doxorubicin in combination with mitomycin C in advanced breast cancer. Proc Am Soc Clin Oncol. 1983; 2:206. Abstract.

206 **Torti FM et al.** Reduced cardiotoxicity of doxorubicin delivered on a weekly schedule. Assessment by endomyocardial biopsy. Ann Intern Med. 1983;99: 745–49.

207 **Valdivieso M et al.** Increased therapeutic index of weekly doxorubicin in the treatment of non-small cell lung cancer: a prospective, randomized study. J Clin Oncol. 1984;2:207–14.

208 **Lum BL et al.** Doxorubicin: alteration of dose scheduling as a means of reducing cardiotoxicity. Drug Intell Clin Pharm. 1985;19:259–64.

209 **Legha SS et al.** Evaluation of alphatocopherol against adriamycin cardiotoxicity in humans. Proc of AACR. 1981:176. Abstract.

210 **Myers CE et al.** A randomized controlled trial assessing the prevention of doxorubicin cardiomyopathy by N-acetylcysteine. Semin Oncol. 1983;10: 53–5.

211 **Speyer JL et al.** Protective effect of the bispiperazinedione ICRF-187 against doxorubicin-induced toxicity in women with advanced breast cancer. N Engl J Med. 1988;319:745–52.

212 **Bristow MR et al.** Acute and chronic cardiovascular effects of doxorubicin in the dog: the cardiovascular pharmacology of drug-induced histamine release. J Cardiovasc Pharmacol. 1980; 2:487–515.

213 **Bristow MR et al.** Anthracycline-associated cardiac and renal damage in rabbits. Evidence for mediation by vasoactive substances. Lab Invest. 1981; 45:157–68.

214 **Nooter K et al.** Effects of verapamil on the pharmacokinetics of daunomycin in the rat. Cancer Chemother Pharmacol. 1987;20:176–78.

215 **Rahman A et al.** Doxorubicin-induced chronic cardiotoxicity and its protection by liposomal administration. Cancer Res. 1982;42:1817–825.

216 **Herman EH et al.** Prevention of chronic doxorubicin cardiotoxicity in beagles by liposomal encapsulation. Cancer Res. 1983;43:5427–432.

217 **Wortman JE et al.** Sudden death during doxorubicin administration. Cancer. 1979;44:1588–591.

218 **Rowinsky EK et al.** Cardiac disturbances during the administration of Taxol. J Clin Oncol. 1991;9:1704–712.

219 **Labianca R et al.** Cardiac toxicity of 5-fluorouracil: A study on 1083 patients. Tumori. 1982;68:505–10.

220 **Eskilsson J et al.** Adverse cardiac effects during induction chemotherapy treatment with cisplatin and 5-fluorouracil. Radiother Oncol. 1988;13:41–6.

221 **Pottage A et al.** Fluorouracil cardiotoxicity. Br Med J. 1978;6112:547.

222 **Patterson WP, Reams GP.** Renal and electrolyte abnormalities due to chemotherapy. In: Perry MC, ed. The Chemotherapy Source Book. Baltimore: Williams & Wilkins; 1992:648–65.

223 **Patterson WP, Reams GP.** Renal toxicities of chemotherapy. Semin Oncol. 1992;19:521–28.

224 **Fjeldborg P et al.** The long-term effect of cisplatin on renal function. Cancer. 1986;58:2214–217.

225 **Macleod PM et al.** The effect of cisplatin on renal function in patients with testicular tumors. Clin Radiol. 1988; 39:190–92.

226 **Ries F, Klastersky J.** Nephrotoxicity induced by cancer chemotherapy with special emphasis on cisplatin toxicity. Am J Kidney Dis. 1986;8:368–79.

227 **Finley RS et al.** Cisplatin nephrotoxicity: a summary of preventative interventions. Drug Intell Clin Pharm. 1985;19:362–67.

228 **Pera MF et al.** Effects of mannitol or furosemide diuresis on the nephrotoxicity and physiological disposition of cis-dichlorodiammineplatinum-(II). Cancer Research. 1979;39:1269–278.

229 **Ries F, Klastersky J.** Nephrotoxicity induced by cancer chemotherapy with special emphasis on cisplatin toxicity. Am J Kidney Dis. 1986;8:368–79.

230 **Willox JC et al.** Effects of magnesium supplementation on testicular cancer patients receiving cis-platin: a randomized trial. Br J Cancer. 1986;54:12–23.

231 **Fuks JZ et al.** Phase I and II agents in cancer therapy: two cisplatin analogues and high-dose cisplatin in hypertonic saline or with thiosulfate protection. J Clin Pharmacol. 1987;27:357–65.

232 **Ozols RF et al.** High-dose cisplatin in hypertonic saline. Ann Intern Med. 1984;100:19–24.

233 **Aamdal S et al.** Reduced antineoplastic activity in mice of cisplatin administered with high salt concentration in the vehicle. J Natl Cancer Inst. 1984; 73:743–51.

234 **Hrushesky AD.** Chemotherapy: circadian timing and toxicity. In: Perry MC, ed. The Chemotherapy Source Book. Baltimore: Williams & Wilkins; 1992: 165–212.

235 **Salem P et al.** Cis-diamminedichloroplatinum (II) by 5-day continuous infusion. Cancer. 1984;53:837–40.

236 **Posner MR et al.** A phase I trial of continuous infusion cisplatin. Cancer. 1987;59:15–8.

237 **Belliveau JF et al.** Cis-platin administered as a continuous 5-day infusion: plasma platinum levels and urine platinum excretion. Cancer Treat Rep. 1986;70:1215–217.

238 **Forastiere AA et al.** Pharmacokinetic and toxicity evaluation of five-day continuous infusion versus intermittent bolus cis-diamminedichloroplatinum (II) in head and neck cancer patients. Cancer Res. 1988;48:3869–874.

239 **Kawamura J et al.** Nephrotoxicity of cis-diamminedichloroplatinum (II) (cisplatinum) and the additive effects of antibiotics: morphological and functional observation in rats. Toxicol Appl Pharmacol. 1981;38:535–41.

240 **Bregman CL, Williams PD.** Comparative nephrotoxicity of carboplatin and cisplatin in combination with tobramycin. Cancer Chemother Pharmacol. 1986;18:117–23.

241 **Jongejan HTM et al.** Potentiation of cis-dimminedichloroplatinum nephrotoxicity by amikacin in rats. Cancer Chemother Pharmacol. 1988;22:178–80.

242 **Fields S, Lindley CM.** Thrombotic microangiopathy associated with chemotherapy: case report and review of the literature. DICP, Ann Pharmacother. 1989;23:582–88.

243 **Angiola G et al.** Hemolytic-uremic syndrome associated with neoadjuvant chemotherapy in the treatment of advanced cervical cancer. Gynecol Oncol. 1990;39:214–17.

244 **Gradishar WJ et al.** Chemotherapy-related hemolytic-uremic syndrome after the treatment of head and neck cancer: a case report. Cancer. 1990;66: 1914–918.

245 **Walker RW et al.** Carboplatin-associated thrombotic microangiopathic hemolytic anemia. Cancer. 1989;64:1017–020.

246 **Richtsmeier AJ.** Urinary bladder tumors after cyclophosphamide. N Engl J Med. 1975;293:1045.

247 **Worth PHL.** Cyclophosphamide and the bladder. Br Med J. 1971;3:182.

248 **Wali RL et al.** Carcinoma of the urinary bladder in patients receiving cyclophosphamide. N Engl J Med. 1975; 293:271.

249 **Johnson W et al.** Urinary bladder fibrosis and telangiectasia associated with long-term cyclophosphamide therapy. N Engl J Med. 1971;284:290.

250 **Aptekar RG et al.** Cyclophosphamide-induced, non-hemorrhagic cystitis with abnormal bladder cells. Arthritis Rheum. 1972;15:530.

251 **Droller MJ et al.** Prevention of cyclophosphamide-induced hemorrhagic cystitis. Urology. 1982;20:256.

252 **Schoenike SE, Dana WJ.** Ifosfamide and mesna. Clin Pharm. 1990;9:179–91.

253 **Scheef W et al.** Controlled clinical studies with an antidote against the urotoxicity of oxazaphosphorines: preliminary results. Cancer Treat Rep. 1982; 18:1377–387.

254 **Allen LM et al.** Studies of the human pharmacokinetics of ifosfamide (NSC-109724). Cancer Treat Rep. 1976;60: 451–58.

255 **Ormstad K.** Pharmacokinetics and metabolism of sodium 2-mercaptoethanesulfonate in the rat. Cancer Res. 1983;43:333–38.

256 **Brock N et al.** Studies of the urotoxicity of oxazaphosphorine cytostatics and its prevention. 2. Comparative study of the uroprotective efficacy of thiols and other sulfur compounds. Eur J Cancer Clin Oncol. 1981;17:1155–163.

257 **Klein HO et al.** High-dose ifosfamide and mesna as continuous infusion over five days—a phase I/II trial. Cancer Treat Rev. 1983;10(Suppl. A):167–73.

258 **Shaw IC, Graham MI.** Mesna—a short review. Cancer Treat Rev. 1987; 14:67–86.

259 **Finn GP et al.** Protecting the bladder from cyclophosphamide with mesna. N Engl J Med. 1986;314:61. Letter.

260 **Klein FA, Smith MJV.** Urinary complications of cyclophosphamide therapy: etiology, prevention, and management. South Med J. 1983;76:1413–416.

261 **Jerkins GR et al.** Treatment of complication of cyclophosphamide cystitis. J Urol. 1988;139:923–25.

262 **Trump DL et al.** Richter's syndrome: diffuse histiocytic in patients with chronic lymphocytic leukemia: a report of 5 cases and review of the literature. Am J Med. 1980;68:539.

263 **Harousseau JL et al.** Malignant lymphoma supervening in chronic lymphocytic leukemia and related disorders. Richter's syndrome: a study of 25 cases. Cancer. 1981;48:1302.

264 **Ginsberg SJ, Comis RL.** The pulmonary toxicity of antineoplastic agents. In: Perry MC, Yarbro JW, eds. Toxicity of Chemotherapy. Orlando: Grune and Stratton; 1984;224–46.

265 **Muggia FM.** Pulmonary toxicity of antitumor agents. Cancer Treat Rev. 1983;10:221.

266 **Stover RR.** Pulmonary toxicity. In: De Vita VT et al., eds. Cancer: Principles and Practice of Oncology. 3rd ed. Philadelphia: Lippincott; 1989;2162–170.

267 **Weiss RB, Muggia FM.** Cytotoxic drug-induced pulmonary disease: update 1980. Am J Med. 1980;68:259.

268 **Blum RH et al.** A clinical review of bleomycin—a new antineoplastic agent. Cancer. 1973;31:903.

269 **Sikic BI et al.** Improved therapeutic index of bleomycin when administered by continuous infusion in mice. Cancer Treat Rep. 1978;62:2011.

270 **Comis RL et al.** Role of single breath carbon monoxide diffusing capacity in monitoring the pulmonary effects of bleomycin in germ cell tumor patients. Cancer Res. 1979;39:5076.

271 **Goldiner PL et al.** Factors influencing postoperative morbidity and mortality in patients treated with bleomycin. Br Med J. 1978;1:1664.

272 **Hakkinen PJ et al.** Nyperoxia, but not thoracic x-irradiation potentiates bleomycin and cyclophosphamide-induced lung damage in mice. Am Rev Respir Dis. 1982;126:281.

273 **Tryka AF et al.** Differences in effects of immediate and delayed hyperoxia exposure on bleomycin-induced pulmonary injury. Cancer Treat Rep. 1984;68:759.

274 **Einhorn L et al.** Enhanced pulmonary toxicity with bleomycin and radiotherapy in oat cell cancer. Cancer. 1976;37: 2414.

275 **Samuels ML et al.** Large-dose bleomycin therapy and pulmonary toxicity; a possible role of prior radiotherapy. JAMA. 1976;235:1117.

276 **Soble AR, Perry H.** Fatal radiation pneumonia following subclinical busulfan injury. AJR. 1977;128:15.

277 **Durant JR et al.** Pulmonary toxicity associated with bischloroethylnitrosurea (BCNU). Ann Intern Med. 1979; 90:191.

278 **Schreml W et al.** Progressive pulmonary fibrosis during combination chemotherapy with BCNU. Blut. 1978;36: 353.

279 **Skarin AT et al.** The treatment of advanced non-Hodgkin's lymphoma (NHL) with bleomycin, adriamycin, cyclophosphamide, vincristine and prednisone. Blood. 1977;49:759.

280 **Bauer KA et al.** Pulmonary complications associated with combination chemotherapy programs containing bleomycin. Am J Med. 1983;74:557.

281 **White DA et al.** Chemotherapy-associated pulmonary toxic reactions during treatment for breast cancer. Arch Intern Med. 1984;144:953.

282 **Luedke D et al.** Mitomycin C and vindesine-associated pulmonary toxicity with variable clinical expression. Cancer. 1985;55:542.

283 **Konits PH et al.** Possible pulmonary toxicity secondary to vinblastine. Cancer. 1982;50:2771.

284 **Aronin PA et al.** Prediction of BCNU pulmonary toxicity in patients with malignant gliomas: an assessment of risk factors. N Engl J Med. 1980;303:183.

285 **Oliner H et al.** Interstitial pulmonary fibrosis following busulfan therapy. Am J Med. 1961;31:134.

286 **Holoye PY et al.** Pulmonary toxicity in long-term administration of BCNU. Cancer Treat Rep. 1976;60:1691.

287 **Wilson KS et al.** Fatal pneumothorax in "BCNU lung." Med Rad Oncol. 1982;10:195.

288 **Stutz FH et al.** Non-bacterial pneumonitis with multidrug antineoplastic therapy in breast carcinoma. Can Med Assoc J. 1973;108:710.

289 **Haupt HM et al.** Ara-C lung: noncardiogenic pulmonary edema complicating cytosine arabinoside therapy of leukemia. Am J Med. 1981;70:256.

290 **Hurst PG et al.** Pulmonary toxicity associated with fludarabine monophosphate. Invest New Drugs. 1987;5:207–10.

291 **Wall MA et al.** Lung function in adolescents receiving high-dose methotrexate. Pediatrics. 1979;63:741.

292 **Zusman J et al.** Rapid resolution of "methotrexate lung" with preoperative steroids. Proc Am Assoc Cancer Res. 1979;20:412. Abstract.

293 **Lascari AD et al.** Methotrexate-induced sudden fatal pulmonary reaction. Cancer. 1977;40:1393.

294 **Walden PAM et al.** Pleurisy and methotrexate treatment. Br Med J. 1977;2:867.

295 **Jones SE et al.** Hypersensitivity to procarbazine (Mutalane) manifested by fever and pleuropulmonary reaction. Cancer. 1972;29:498.

296 **Lokich JJ.** Allergic reaction to procarbazine. Clin Pharmacol Ther. 1972;13: 573.

297 **Konits PH et al.** Possible pulmonary toxicity secondary to vinblastine. Cancer. 1982;50:2771.

298 **Woodley PV.** Hepatic and pancreatic damage produced by cytotoxic drugs. Cancer Treat Rev. 1983;10:17.

299 **Dahl MGC et al.** Methotrexate hepatotoxicity in psoriasis—comparison of different dosage regimens. Br Med J. 1972;1:654.

300 **Podugiel BJ et al.** Liver injury associated with methotrexate therapy for psoriasis. Mayo Clin Proc. 1973;48:787.

301 **Kennedy BJ.** Metabolic and toxic effects of mithramycin tumor therapy. Am J Med. 1970;49:494.

302 **Perlia CP.** Mithramycin treatment of hypercalcemia. Cancer. 1970;25:389.

303 **Lawrence MJ et al.** AMSA—a promising new agent in refractory acute leukemia. Cancer Treat Rep. 1982;66: 1475.

304 **Pratt CB et al.** Duration and severity of fatty metamorphosis of liver following L-asparaginase therapy. Cancer. 1971;28:361.

305 **Ohnuma T et al.** Biochemical and pharmacological studies with L-asparaginase in man. Cancer Res. 1970;30: 2297.

306 **Oettgen HF et al.** Toxicity of E. coli L-asparaginase in man. Cancer. 1969; 25:253.

307 **DeVita VT et al.** Clinical trials with 1,3-Bis(2-chloroethyl)-1-nitrosurea, NSC-79037. Cancer. 1965;25:1876.

308 **Takvorian T et al.** Single high-dose of BCNU with autologous bone marrow (ABM). Proc Am Soc Clin Oncol. 1980;21:341.

309 **Slavin RE et al.** Cytosine arabinoside-induced gastrointestinal toxic alterations in sequential chemotherapeutic protocols. Cancer. 1978;42:1747.

310 **Fosch PJ et al.** Hepatic failure in a patient treated with DTIC for malignant melanoma. J Cancer Res Clin Oncol. 1979;95:281.

311 **Ceci G et al.** Fatal hepatic vascular toxicity of DTIC: is it really a rare event? Cancer. 1988;61:1691.

312 **Johnson D et al.** Etoposide-induced hepatic injury: a potential complication of high-dose therapy. Cancer Treat Rep. 1983;67:1023.

313 **Hoogstraten B et al.** CCNU and bleomycin in the treatment of cancer: a Southwest Oncology Group Study. Med Pediatr Oncol. 1975;1:95.

314 Hoogstraten B et al. CCNU (1,(2-chloroethyl)-3-cyclohexyl-1-nitrosurea, NSC-79037) in the treatment of cancer. Cancer. 1973;32:38.

315 Einhorn M et al. Hepatotoxicity of 6-mercaptopurine. JAMA. 1964;188: 802.

316 Clark PA et al. Toxic complications of treatment with 6-mercaptopurine: two cases with hepatic necrosis and intestinal ulceration. Br Med J. 1960;1: 393.

317 Lazarus HM et al. Veno-occlusive disease of the liver after high-dose mitomycin C therapy and autologous bone marrow transplantation. Cancer. 1982;49:1789.

318 Schein PS et al. Clinical antitumor activity and toxicity of streptozotocin (NSC-85998). Cancer. 1974;34:993.

319 Gill RA et al. Hepatic veno-occlusive disease caused by 6-thioguanine. Ann Intern Med. 1982;96:58.

320 Dorr FA, Coltman CA Jr. Second cancers following antineoplastic therapy. Curr Probl Cancer. 1985;9:1–43.

321 De Gamont A et al. Preleukemic changes in cases of non-lymphocytic leukemia secondary to cytotoxic therapy: analysis of 105 cases. Cancer. 1986;58:630–34.

322 Kantarjian HM et al. Therapy-related leukemia and myelodysplastic syndrome: clinical, cytogenic, and prognostic features. J Clin Oncol. 1986;4: 1748–757.

323 Casciato DA, Scott JL. Acute leukemia following prolonged cytotoxic agent therapy. Medicine (Baltimore). 1979;58:32–47.

324 Tucker MA et al. Leukemia after therapy with alkylating agents for childhood cancer. J Natl Cancer Inst. 1987; 78:459–64.

325 Kaldor JM et al. Leukemia following chemotherapy for ovarian cancer. N Engl J Med. 1990;332:1–6.

326 Kaldor JM et al. Leukemia following Hodgkin's disease. N Engl J Med. 1990;322:7–13.

327 Kyle RA, Gertz MA. Second malignancies after chemotherapy. In: Perry MC, ed. The Chemotherapy Source Book. Baltimore: Williams & Wilkins; 1992:689–702.

328 Pedersen-Bjergaard J et al. Increased risk of myelodysplasia and leukaemia after etoposide, cisplatin, and bleomycin for germ-cell tumors. Lancet. 1991; 338:359–63.

329 Tucker MA et al. Bone sarcomas linked to radiotherapy and chemotherapy in children. N Engl J Med. 1987; 317:588–93.

330 Stegman R, Alexanian R. Solid tumors in multiple myeloma. Ann Intern Med. 1979;90:780–82.

331 Zarrabi MH. Association of non-Hodgkin's lymphoma (NHL) and second neoplasms. Semin Oncol. 1980;7: 340–51.

332 Michels SD et al. Therapy-related acute myeloid leukemia and myelodysplastic syndrome: a clinical and morphologic study of 65 cases. Blood. 1985;65:1364–372.

333 Le Beau MM et al. Clinical and cytogenetic correlations in 63 patients with therapy-related myelodysplastic syndromes and acute non-lymphocytic leukemia: further evidence for characteristic abnormalities of chromosomes no. 5 and 7. J Clin Oncol. 1986;4: 325–45.

334 Pedersen-Bjergaard J et al. Acute non-lymphocytic leukemia, preleukemia, and acute myeloproliferative syndrome secondary to treatment of other malignant diseases. Clinical and cytogenetic characteristics and results of in vitro culture of bone marrow and HLA typing. Blood. 1981;57:712–23.

335 Bloomfield CD et al. Treatment-induced acute non-lymphocytic leukemia (t-ANLL): response to cytarabine-anthracycline therapy. Blood. 1982;60 (Suppl. 1):152. Abstract.

336 Preisler HD et al. Therapy of secondary acute non-lymphocytic leukemia with cytarabine. N Engl J Med. 1983; 308:21–3.

337 Pui CH et al. Acute myeloid leukemia in children treated with epipodophyllotoxins for acute lymphoblastic leukemia. N Engl J Med. 1991;325:1682–687.

338 Marmont AM et al. Bone marrow transplantation for secondary (therapy-related) acute non-lymphoblastic leukaemia: report of a case associated with adoptive beta-thalassemia. Bone Marrow Transplant. 1987;2:91–7.

339 Geller RB et al. Successful marrow transplantation for acute myelocytic leukemia following therapy for Hodgkin's disease. J Clin Oncol. 1988;6: 1558–561.

340 Brusamolino E et al. Treatment-related leukemia in Hodgkin's disease: a multi-institution study of 75 cases. Hematol Oncol. 1987;5:83–98.

341 Belohorsky B et al. Comments on the development of amenorrhea caused by myleran in cases of chronic myelosis. Neoplasma. 1960;7:397–403.

342 Sobrinho LG et al. Amenorrhea in patients with Hodgkin's disease treated with antineoplastic agents. Am J Obstet Gynecol. 1971;109:135–39.

343 Himelstein-Braw R et al. Influence of irradiation and chemotherapy on the ovaries of children and abdominal tumors. Br J Cancer. 1977;36:269–75.

344 Nicosia SV et al. Gonadal effects of cancer therapy in girls. Cancer. 1985; 55:2364–372.

345 Chapman RM. Gonadal toxicity and teratogenicity. In: Perry MC, ed. The Chemotherapy Source Book. Baltimore: Williams & Wilkins; 1992:710–55.

346 Myers SE, Schilsky RL. Prospects for fertility after cancer. Semin Oncol. 1992;19:597–604.

347 Griffin JE, Wilson JD. Disorders of the testes and male reproductive tract. In: Wilson JD, Foster DW, eds. Williams Textbook of Endocrinology. Philadelphia: WB Saunders; 1985:259–311.

348 Monesi V. Spermatogenesis. In: Austin CR, Short RV, eds. Reproduction in Mammals. Book 1: Germ Cells and Fertilization. Oxford: Cambridge University Press; 1972:1–55.

349 Meistrich ML. Critical components of testicular function and sensitivity to disruption. Biol Reprod. 1986;34:17–28.

350 Miller DG. Alkylating agents and human spermatogenesis. JAMA. 1971; 217:1662–665.

351 Cheviakoff S et al. Recovery of spermatogenesis in patients with lymphoma after treatment with chlorambucil. J Reprod Fertil. 1973;33:155–57.

352 Fairley KF et al. Sterility and testicular atrophy related to cyclophosphamide therapy. Lancet. 1972;1:568–69.

353 Buchanan JD et al. Return of spermatogenesis after stopping cyclophosphamide therapy. Lancet. 1975;2:156–57.

354 Vivani S et al. Gonadal toxicity after combination chemotherapy for Hodgkin's disease: comparative results of MOPP vs ABVD. Eur J Cancer Clin Oncol. 1985;21:601–05.

355 Drasga RE et al. Fertility after chemotherapy for testicular cancer. J Clin Oncol. 1983;1:179–83.

356 Nijman JM et al. Gonadal function after surgery and chemotherapy in men with stage II and III nonseminomatous testicular tumors. J Clin Oncol. 1987; 5:651–56.

357 Fossa SD et al. Recovery of impaired pretreatment spermatogenesis in testicular cancer. Fertil Steril. 1990;54:493–96.

358 Einhorn LH, Donahur J. Cis-diammine-dichloroplatinum, vinblastine and bleomycin combination chemotherapy in disseminated testicular cancer. Ann Intern Med. 1977;87:293–98.

359 Lange PH et al. Fertility issues in the therapy of nonseminomatous testicular tumors. Urol Clin North Am. 1987;14: 731–47.

360 Berthelsen JG, Skakkebaek NE. Sperm counts and serum follicle-stimulating hormone levels before and after radiotherapy and chemotherapy in men with testicular germ cell cancer. Fertil Steril. 1984;41:281–86.

361 Tournage H et al. In vitro fertilization techniques with frozen-thawed sperm: a method for preserving the progenitive potential of Hodgkin's patients. Fertil Steril. 1991;55:443–45.

362 Davis OK et al. Pregnancy achieved through in vitro fertilization with cryopreserved semen from a man with Hodgkin's lymphoma. Fertil Steril. 1990;53:377–78.

363 Redman J et al. Prospective, randomized trial of testosterone cypionate to prevent sterility in men treated with chemotherapy for Hodgkin's disease: preliminary results. In: Proceedings of the 14th International Cancer Congress, Budapest. Basel: S. Karger; 1986:440.

364 Chapman RM, Sutcliffe SB. Protection of ovarian function by oral contraceptives in women receiving chemotherapy for Hodgkin's disease. Blood. 1981;58:849–51.

365 Johnson DH et al. Effect of luteinizing hormone-releasing hormone agonist given during combination chemotherapy on post-therapy fertility in male patients with lymphoma: preliminary observations. Blood. 1985;65:832–36.

366 Calvert AH et al. Carboplatin dosage: prospective evaluation of a simple formula based on renal function. J Clin Oncol. 1989;7:1748–756.

367 Egorin MJ et al. Prospective validation of a pharmacologically base dosing schem for the cis-diamminedichloroplatinum (II) analogue diamminecyclobutanedicarboxylatoplatinum. Cancer Res. 1985;45:6502–506.

368 Perry MC. Hepatotoxicity of chemotherapeutic Agents. In: Perry MC, ed. The Chemotherapy Sourcebook. Baltimore: Williams & Wilkins. 1992: 635–647.

369 Venook AP, et. al. Paclitaxel (Taxol) in Patients with Liver Dysfunction. Proc Am Soc Clin Oncol. 1994;13:139.

370 Patterson WP, Reams GP. Renal abnormalities. In: Perry MC, eds. The Chemotherapy Sourcebook, chapter 38. Williams & Wilkins. 1992:635.

Chapter 92

Hematologic Malignancies

Adult: Rebecca S Finley
Cynthia L LaCivita
Celeste Lindley
Pediatric: Mark T Holdsworth

Definitions and Classification 92-2
 Leukemias (See Table 92.1) 92-2
 Lymphomas (See Table 92.2) 92-2
 Plasma cell disorders (PCDs) 92-2
Acute Nonlymphocytic Leukemia (ANLL) 92-3
 Signs and Symptoms 92-3
 Classification and Diagnosis (See Table 92.3) 92-3
 Treatment 92-4
  Goal of therapy 92-4
  Induction therapy 92-4
   Choice of anthracycline 92-4
   Acute promyelocytic leukemia (APL)
    and tretinoin 92-4
   Complications of induction therapy 92-5
    Tumor lysis syndrome (TLS)
     (See Table 92.4) 92-5
    Myelosuppression 92-5
 Postremission Therapy 92-6
  Rationale 92-6
  High dose cytarabine 92-6
   Ocular toxicity 92-6
   Dermatologic toxicity 92-6
 Acute Leukemia in the Elderly 92-6
Chronic Myelogenous Leukemia (CML) 92-6
 Signs and Symptoms 92-6
 Staging and Prognosis 92-7
 Treatment 92-7
  Busulfan 92-7
  Hydroxyurea 92-7
  Interferon alfa 92-7
  Bone marrow transplantation 92-7
Chronic Lymphocytic Leukemia (CLL) 92-7
 Signs and Symptoms 92-7
 Staging and Prognosis 92-8
 Treatment 92-8
  Chlorambucil 92-8
  Corticosteroids 92-8
  Immune-mediated thrombocytopenia 92-8
  Fludarabine 92-8
 Infectious Complications 92-9
NonHodgkin's Lymphoma (Also see
 Pediatric NonHodgkin's Lymphoma) 92-9
 Clinical Presentation and Prognosis 92-9
  Human immunodeficiency virus (HIV)-positive
   patients versus other patients 92-9
 Treatment 92-9
  Combination chemotherapy 92-9
  Corticosteroids 92-10
 Malignant Pleural Effusion 92-10
  Sclerosing agents and thoracostomy 92-10
**Acute Lymphoblastic Leukemia (ALL)
 of Childhood** 92-10
 Etiology 92-11

Pathophysiology 92-11
Clinical Presentation 92-11
Prognostic Variables 92-11
 Clinical variables (See Table 92.5) 92-11
  White blood cell (WBC) count
   (See Figure 92.1) 92-11
  Age (See Figure 92.2) 92-11
  Sex 92-11
  Race 92-12
  Morphology 92-12
 Immunologic variables (See Table 92.6) 92-12
 Cytogenetic variables (See Figure 92.3) 92-13
 Additional variables 92-13
  Lactate dehydrogenase (LD) 92-13
  Receptors for corticosteroids on leukemic cells ... 92-13
Treatment 92-14
 Remission induction therapy 92-14
  Allopurinol interaction 92-14
  Goal of induction 92-14
  Induction combination chemotherapy 92-14
 Vincristine toxicity 92-15
 CNS preventative therapy 92-15
  Purpose 92-15
  Craniospinal radiation 92-15
  Intrathecal chemotherapy 92-16
   Chronic adverse effects 92-16
   Dosage (See Table 92.8) 92-16
   Acute adverse effects 92-16
 Maintenance therapy 92-16
  Purpose 92-16
  Chemotherapy regimens 92-17
   Potential problems 92-17
   Duration of therapy 92-17
 High-risk ALL 92-17
  Asparaginase 92-17
   Adverse effects 92-17
    Pancreatitis 92-17
    Hypersensitivity reactions 92-18
   Preparations 92-18
  Etoposide 92-18
   Hypersensitivity reactions 92-18
   Secondary AML 92-19
  Methotrexate concentration monitoring 92-19
 Relapsed ALL 92-19
Pediatric NonHodgkin's Lymphoma
(Also see NonHodgkin's Lymphoma) 92-19
 Classification 92-20
 Clinical Presentation 92-20
 Staging 92-20
 Treatment 92-20
  Lymphoblastic (T-cell)
   (See Tables 92.10 and 92.11) 92-20
  Small noncleaved (B-cell) 92-21

(Continued)

Large cell 92-21
Lymphoblastic Lymphoma 92-21
    Treatment 92-21
        Acute treatment 92-21
        Adverse effects 92-21
Antiemetic regimen 92-22
CNS prophylaxis 92-22
    Precautions 92-22
Myelosuppression and Hematopoietic Recovery 92-22
    Modification for delayed recovery 92-22

Definitions and Classification

Cancers that arise from the bone marrow and lymphoreticular system are referred to as *hematologic malignancies*. Major categories of hematologic malignancies include the leukemias, lymphomas, and plasma cell disorders (PCDs). Although these malignancies collectively will account for less than 10% of all new cancers diagnosed in the U.S. in 1995; they are particularly important to the pharmacist because they are diseases that are very commonly managed with systemic chemotherapy. Since these disorders usually are disseminated at the time of diagnosis, localized treatment methods of surgery and irradiation are not as commonly employed as in solid tumors. Although there are exceptions, the growth rate of most hematologic malignancies is rapid, and aggressive combination chemotherapy regimens result in high response rates, and in some cases, cure of disease. In addition, the hematologic malignancies have served as the most common experimental laboratory models of cancer growth, biology, and the effects of treatment.

Leukemias

Leukemia is defined as progressive proliferation of leukocytes. Leukemias are classified as *lymphocytic* (of lymphocyte origin) or *nonlymphocytic*. Nonlymphocytic leukemias also are referred to as myeloid leukemias. Although the true definition of "myeloid" (pertaining to the bone marrow) is broad, nonlymphocytic or myeloid leukemia commonly refers to a disorder of hematopoietic cells that are not of lymphoid origin which include granulocytes, monocytes, red cells, or platelets.

Leukemias are further classified as "acute" or "chronic." Acute leukemia is the result of proliferation and impaired differentiation of immature hematopoietic cells. This proliferation results in the appearance of large numbers of immature cells (blasts) in the bone marrow and peripheral blood and in rapid bone marrow failure. These immature blast cells generally retain some features indicative of their origin in the hematopoietic lineage. If the blasts have lymphoid features, the leukemia is acute lymphocytic leukemia (ALL). If myeloid features predominate, the disease is acute nonlymphocytic leukemia (ANLL) or acute myelogenous leukemia (AML). Clinical and laboratory distinction of ANLL from ALL is illustrated in Table 92.1. The laboratory distinction of ANLL from ALL is based upon morphological examination of the bone marrow and blood with the addition of cytochemical stains, surface membrane phenotyping, and chromosomal analysis. Acute leukemias appear suddenly and progress very rapidly. Death occurs within weeks to months if the patient is not effectively treated.

Chronic leukemias differ from acute leukemias in that they follow a more insidious onset and course. Chronic leukemias, unlike acute leukemias, are associated with proliferation of a mature cell. Chronic lymphocytic leukemia (CLL) is characterized by overproduction of mature lymphocytes. Chronic granulocytic or myelocytic leukemia (CGL or CML) is associated with overproduction of mature neutrophil granulocytes. Accumulation of these cells in various organs of the body, as well as high levels in the circulatory system, have profound and unique consequences that will be discussed in subsequent cases. In addition, as the energy of the bone marrow is channeled towards production of these specific cell lines, decreased production of red blood cells (RBCs) and platelets

occurs. Although patients with chronic leukemias may survive for years with suppressive therapies, these disorders are not curable with conventional treatment approaches. Other less common chronic leukemias include hairy cell leukemia and chronic myelomonocytic leukemia.

Lymphomas

The lymphomas are a heterogeneous group of neoplasms that originate from lymphoid cells. A lymphoma may arise within the lymph node itself or in extranodal sites involving the lymphoid tissue of such diverse organs as the gastrointestinal (GI) tract, central nervous system (CNS), and bone. There are two major types of lymphoma, Hodgkin's disease (HD) and nonHodgkin's lymphoma (NHL), which together account for more than 30,000 new cases annually. NHL is three times as common as HD and represents a spectrum of diseases marked by different pathological features, natural history, and prognosis. As addressed in the case, NHLs are divided into three broad groups (low, intermediate, and high grade) based upon their histology. Table 92.2 compares the disease characteristics of Hodgkin's disease, low grade NHL, and intermediate to high-grade NHL.

Plasma Cell Disorders (PCDs)

Plasma cell disorders include a group of neoplasms that arise from immunoglobulin secreting cells that produce excessive amounts of an immunoglobulin or part of an immunoglobulin. If

Table 92.1	Distinction of Acute Myelogenous from Acute Lymphocytic Leukemia[a]	
	AML	**ALL**
Clinical Features		
Age	Commonly adults	Commonly children
Lymphadenopathy	Rare	Common
CNS involvement	Unusual	5%
Cytochemical Stains		
Myeloperoxidase	Positive	Negative
Periodic acid (Schiff)	Negative (except M_6)	Positive
Other Studies		
Surface markers	Myeloid	Lymphoid
CALLA	No	In early pre-B lineage ALL
Tdt	Absent	Present
Gene Arrangement Studies		
T-cell receptor	Absent	Present in T-cell ALL
Immunoglobulin	Absent	Present in B-cell ALL
Common Cytogenic Abnormalities	t(9,22)	t(9,22)
	t(8,21)	t(4,11) null cell ALL
	t(15,17) in AML-M_3	t(8,14) B-cell Burkitt's type
	5q-, 7q-	t(11,14) B-cell
	Inv 16 in AML-M_4Eo	t(1,19) B-cell

[a] ALL = Acute Lymphocytic Leukemia; AML = Acute Myelogenous Leukemia; CALLA = Common ALL antigen; CNS = Central nervous system.

Table 92.2	Comparison of Hodgkin's Disease and NonHodgkin's Lymphomas		
		NonHodgkin's Lymphomas	
Characteristic	Hodgkin's Disease	Low Grade	Intermediate– High Grade
Site(s) of origin	Nodal	Extranodal (≈10%)	Extranodal (≈35%)
Nodal distribution	Axial (centripetal)	Centrifugal	Centrifugal
Nodal spread	Contiguous	Noncontiguous	Noncontiguous
CNS involvement	Rare (<1%)	Rare (<1%)	Uncommon (<10%)
Hepatic involvement	Uncommon	Common (>50%)	Uncommon
Bone marrow involvement	Uncommon (<10%)	Common (>50%)	Uncommon (<20%)
Marrow involvement adversely affects prognosis	Yes	No	Yes
Curable by chemotherapy	Yes	No	Yes

the immunoglobulin (Ig) is of the IgM class, the disease is Waldenström's macroglobulinemia and the malignant cells are plasmacytoid lymphocytes. If the immunoglobulin is of the IgG, IgA, IgD, or IgE class, the disease is multiple myeloma and the malignant cells are plasma cells. High immunoglobulin levels can be found in conditions other than multiple myeloma or Waldenström's macroglobulinemia. However, the amount of the specific immunoglobulin produced by malignant cells is far greater than in these other conditions. Overproduction of proteins in plasma cell disorders is associated with a number of clinical manifestations including osteoporosis, hypercalcemia, renal disease, and decreased production of red blood cells and platelets. PCDs are less common than leukemias and lymphomas, and the reader is referred to hematology or oncology texts for a more in-depth discussion of these disorders.

Acute Nonlymphocytic Leukemia (ANLL)

Signs and Symptoms

1. G.M., a 35-year-old female, presented to University Hospital with increasing fatigue, fever, and night sweats. Over the past week a peripheral blood smear (CBC) revealed a white blood cell (WBC) count of 120,000/mm³ (Normal: 400–11,000) with a differential of >90% leukemic blasts (Normal: 0%), a hematocrit (Hct) of 31% (Normal: 40–44), and a platelet count of 46,000/mm³ (Normal: >150,000). A bone marrow aspirate confirmed the diagnosis of ANLL. [FAB-M2 myeloid with maturation; 60% blasts myeloperoxidase positive; CD 13 CD 33 positive] All serum chemistry values were within normal limits with the exception of potassium (K) 3.2 mEq/L (Normal: 3.5–5.5), phosphorus 5.5 mg/dL (Normal: 2.5–4.5), and LD 3000 mU/mL (Normal: 30–120). Physical examination was unremarkable except for a perirectal cellulitis. Which signs and symptoms exhibited by G.M. are consistent with ANLL? [SI units: WBC count 120 × 10⁹/L (Normal: 4–11) with differential >0.09 leukemic blasts (Normal: 0); Hct 0.31 (Normal: 0.40–0.44); platelets 46 × 10⁹/L (Normal: >150); K 3.2 mmol/L (Normal: 3.5–5.5); phosphorus 1.78 mmol/L (Normal: 0.08–1.78); LD 30 (Normal: 30–120)]

G.M.'s symptoms of increasing fatigue, fever, and night sweats of one week duration are consistent with a rapid reduction in red

blood cells leading to anemia (Hct 31%) and low neutrophil counts leading to infection (perirectal cellulitis). Although her WBC is high, the differential reveals that over 90% are "blasts" which are immature, nonfunctional cells of myeloid or lymphoid bone marrow origin. Circulating blast cells are not typically present in chronic leukemias or infection; however, a small number may be observed on the peripheral smear in patients with anemia associated with primary bone marrow dysfunction (myelodysplastic syndromes). They also are present in patients with severe infection, stress or trauma, and those with chronic granulocytic leukemia in "transformation" to acute leukemia. G.M.'s platelet count is also low and although she has not experienced bleeding or bruising, these are frequently presenting symptoms of acute leukemia.

G.M.'s symptoms are consistent with acute leukemia of either myeloid or lymphoid origin. The major difference in presentation of these two types of leukemia is that lymphadenopathy and hepatosplenomegaly commonly accompany acute leukemia of lymphoid origin. It is very important to distinguish between these two disorders since treatment regimens differ significantly. ANLL is far more common in adults than pediatric patients. [For a complete discussion of ALL see Acute Lymphoblastic Leukemia (ALL) of Childhood.]

Classification and Diagnosis

A diagnosis of ANLL is established when ≥30% of all nucleated bone marrow cells are immature (blast) cells of myeloid origin. This subset of acute leukemia was historically referred to as acute myelogenous leukemia (AML). However, since leukemic transformation of erythroid and megakaryocytic progenitor cells also occurs, the nomenclature acute nonlymphocytic leukemia (ANLL) is considered technically more accurate. Seven major variants of ANLL are defined by the French-American-British (FAB) classification system based upon morphologic and cytochemical characteristics. (See Table 92.3.) Cells of myeloid origin commonly contain myeloperoxidase enzymes and express surface markers CD13, CD33, CD14, and CD15. Specific clonal chromosomal abnormalities are associated with several ANLL subtypes. These aberrations include gains or losses of whole chromosomes or the long (q) or short (p) arms of chromosomes as well as a variety of structural rearrangements (e.g., translocations, inversions, or insertions).[1] A number of cytogenetic abnormalities in ANLL have suggested molecular-clinical syndromes which are now being analyzed at the gene level. The most dramatic of these to date is the translocation t(15, 17) (q22, q12), the cytogenetic hallmark of acute promyelocytic leukemia (ANLL-M3). On a molecular level, this translocation splits the retinoic acid receptor gene on chromosome 17 and blocks expression of retinoic acid-controlled genes required for cell differentiation. Treatment of patients with acute promyelocytic leukemia with all-trans retinoic acid (Vesanoid) has been effective, and complete morphologic responses have been obtained. Although this field of research is in its infancy, defining cytogenetic events of chromosomal abnormalities in acute leukemia is critical to understanding its pathophysiology and identifying optimal treatment of acute leukemias.

G.M. has M2 (myelomonocytic) ANLL. Ten to twenty percent of patients with M2 leukemias manifest a translocation of t(8,21) (q22 q22). This translocation usually is seen in young patients like G.M. and is associated with a favorable response to therapy although their overall survival is not clearly better than average. G.M.'s bone marrow has been sent for cytogenetic analysis; however, results will not be available for several weeks. It is in many institutions and in most research protocols routine procedure to obtain cytogenetic analysis in patients with acute leukemia. Al-

Table 92.3		Classification of Acute Nonlymphocytic Leukemia (ANLL) and Acute Myeloid Leukemia(AML)[a]				
	ANLL					AML
Designation	Name	Predominant Cell Type	Cytogenetics	Frequency (%)		Morphology
M_0	Undifferentiated myeloblastic					No maturation of myeloblasts
M_1	Undifferentiated myelocytic	Myeloblasts	t(9;22) + 8 del(5), del(7)	2–3		Minimal maturation of myeloblasts
M_2	Myelocytic	Myeloblasts, promyelocytes, myelocytes	t(8;21) + 8 del(5), del(7)	20		Prominent maturation of myeloblasts
M_3	Promyelocytic	Hypergranular promyelocytes	t(15;17)	25–30		Promyelocytic
M_3 variant						Promyelocytic in marrow; atypical monocytes in blood
M_4	Myelomonocytic	Promyelocytes, myelocytes, promonocytes, monocytes	t(4;11), t(9;11) + 8 del(5), del(7)	8–15		Myelomonocytic
M_4Eo			inv(16)			With atypical eosinophils
M_{5a}	Monoblastic	Monoblasts	t(9;11) + 8 del(5), del(7)			Monoblastic
M_{5b}	Differentiated monocytic	Monoblasts, promonocytes, monocytes		20–25		Promonocytic
M_6	Erythroleukemia	Erythroblasts	+ 8 del(5), del(7)	5		Erythroblastic
M_7	Megakaryocytic	Megakaryocytes		1–2		Megakaryoblastic

[a] French-American-British (FAB) classification system.

though results will not alter treatment recommendations for G.M. at this time, it is probable that cytogenetic abnormalities will influence management and prognosis of ANLL in the future as more information accrues.

Treatment

Goal of Therapy

2. What is the goal of treatment and what type of therapy is indicated for G.M. at this time?

The leukemic cells populating G.M.'s blood are abnormal and incapable of fighting infection. Their rapid proliferation also is suppressing red blood cell and megakaryocyte production in the bone marrow; therefore, G.M. is experiencing symptoms of anemia and her platelet count is low. She is at substantial risk for both life-threatening infections and bleeding complications. The goal of the initial chemotherapy is to clear the bone marrow and peripheral blood of all leukemic blast cells so that normal blood cell components can regenerate.

Induction Therapy

Standard induction chemotherapy for ANLL includes anthracycline (daunorubicin, doxorubicin, or idarubicin) and cytarabine, an antimetabolite. One commonly used regimen includes daunorubicin 45 mg/m^2/day on days one, two, and three as an intravenous (IV) bolus injection plus cytarabine 200 mg/m^2/day as a continuous intravenous infusion on days one through seven. This combination is one of the most successful chemotherapy regimens used in the treatment of ANLL. As single agent therapy, daunorubicin and cytarabine produce complete response rates of 50% and 25%, respectively. When used in combination, complete response rates of 60% to 80% have been reported.[3,4] The schedule of drug delivery also appears to affect tumor response. Continuous infusions of cytarabine produce higher response rates than bolus injections.[5,6] Other agents to which ANLL responds include mitoxantrone (which may be substituted for daunorubicin in the above regimen), thioguanine, and amsacrine (investigational).

3. Choice of Anthracycline. Is there any advantage to using doxorubicin or idarubicin instead of daunorubicin in the induction regimen?

Daunorubicin was the anthracycline used in initial successful treatment for regimens and for many years it has been the preferred anthracycline for ANLL induction. Because the major metabolite of idarubicin, idarubicinol has a long half-life and is active against leukemia cells, it has been suggested as an alternative to daunorubicin. Randomized trials comparing daunorubicin to idarubicin in standard induction regimens have demonstrated higher remission rates and longer survival times for the idarubicin arms.[7,8] However, these studies have been questioned because the remission rates and duration reported for receiving daunorubicin were inferior to those reported previously.

4. Acute Promyelocytic Leukemia (APL) and Tretinoin. Would induction treatment for other FAB subtypes of ANLL differ from that described above?

Induction therapy is standard for all with one exception: FAB type M3 or acute promyelocytic leukemia (APL). APL is characterized by disseminated intravascular coagulation and associated bleeding complications. These complications are caused by myeloperoxidase and procoagulant substances released from granules contained within the leukemia cells. Heparin frequently is used to correct coagulation abnormalities from the time of initial diagnosis (or relapse) until leukemia cells have been eradicated.[9] As discussed previously the apparent mechanism of tretinoin or all-trans-retinoic acid (ATRA) is induction of promyelocyte differentiation and maturation.[10] In clinical trials, ATRA has induced complete remissions in a high proportion of patients with APL. Serial bone marrow aspirations following initiation of ATRA therapy demonstrate progressive differentiation without hypoplasia.[11–13] After remission with ATRA is achieved, patients typically receive standard induction therapy to maintain the remission. ATRA therapy, while avoiding life-threatening myelosuppression, can produce significant toxicities including hyperleukocytosis and the "retinoic acid syndrome" (fever, pulmonary infiltrates, pulmonary capillary leak and acute renal failure).[14] If the "retinoic acid syndrome" develops, the all-trans retinoic acid should be stopped and corticosteroid therapy initiated. Therapy with all-trans retinoic acid may be reinstituted at a lower dose once the syndrome resolves. All-trans retinoic acid also causes dryness of the lining of the mouth, rectum, and skin; hair loss; skin rash; blepharoconjunctivitis; corneal erosions; muscle weakness; nail changes; depression; elevated liver enzymes; and high cholesterol.

5. Complications of Induction Therapy. Twenty-four hours after G.M.'s induction chemotherapy was initiated the following laboratory values were obtained: WBC count 58,000/mm³, K 5.3 mEq/L, phosphorus 6.0 mg/dL, uric acid 9.8 mg/dL (Normal 2.5–8), calcium 6.0 mg/dL (Normal 9.0–11.5), and creatinine 1.6 mg/dL (Normal: 1–2). Why have these laboratory values changed so suddenly? Could they have been minimized or prevented? How should these metabolic disturbances be managed? [SI units: WBC count 58 × 10⁹/L; K 5.3 mmol/L; phosphorus 1.94 mmol/L; uric acid 582.9 μmol/L (Normal: 148.7–475.84); calcium 1.5 mmol/L (Normal: 2.25–2.875); creatinine 141.44 μmol/L (Normal: 88.4–176.8)]

Tumor Lysis Syndrome (TLS). G.M. presented with a very high circulating leukemic cell count. Consequently, chemotherapy resulted in rapid lysis of the leukemic cells or tumor lysis syndrome. TLS can occur 12 to 24 hours after chemotherapy is initiated and is caused by the release of the cellular contents into the blood. This can produce a tremendous metabolic burden for the kidneys and, ultimately, several metabolic abnormalities may occur which can lead to renal failure and electrocardiographic (ECG) abnormalities. (See Table 92.4.) TLS may occur following therapy for other malignancies, particularly those with a high tumor burden such as high grade lymphomas and acute lymphocytic leukemia. TLS rarely occurs following therapy for solid tumors.

Before initiating chemotherapy, leukophoresis to reduce G.M.'s peripheral WBC may have helped to minimize TLS. Alternatively, hydroxyurea, 2 to 4 gm orally, could have been administered to lower the tumor burden. However, neither of these approaches are definitive therapies for the leukemia. Thus, induction therapy should be initiated as soon as possible to treat the underlying leukemia. Because of the immediacy of the need for definitive anti-leukemic therapy leukophoresis and/or hydroxyurea are not routinely administered unless the patient is experiencing symptoms of hyperviscosity (ringing ears, stroke, blindness, headache) due to impaired oxygen delivery to the nervous system.

As the tumor cells lyse, the serum uric acid often rises due to the breakdown of nucleoproteins which are replaced.

Patients should receive intravenous hydration (2 to 3 L/day) beginning 24 to 48 hours before chemotherapy to 1) maintain renal perfusion; 2) and optimize the solubility of tumor lysis products; and 3) compensate for fluid losses due to fever or vomiting. Alkalinization of the urine also may reduce or prevent uric acid precipitation in the renal tubules and collection ducts by maintaining the urate in its ionized state. However, increased serum pH may increase the risk of precipitation of calcium phosphate in the kidney tubules.

Table 92.4	Complications Associated with Acute Tumor Lysis Syndrome

Hypocalcemia
Hyperkalemia
Hyperphosphatemia
Hyperuricemia
Renal failure
Electrocardiogram changes
Metabolic acidosis

Allopurinol which inhibits xanthine oxidase and thereby the conversion of hypoxanthine and xanthine to uric acid, should be started before chemotherapy. Recommended dosages range from 200 to 400 mg/m²/day. G.M.'s serum uric acid as well as electrolytes should be monitored daily for several days after initiating chemotherapy and if severe abnormalities occur, more aggressive measures (described below) should be initiated. When G.M.'s chemotherapy is completed and her WBC count is low (e.g., ≤500 WBC/mm³), the threat of further tumor lysis is minimal and the allopurinol may be discontinued if the serum uric acid is within normal limits.

While G.M. is receiving allopurinol, the clinician should be alert for potential adverse effects. A high incidence of skin rash also has been associated with allopurinol use in patients with acute leukemia. However, these often are difficult to differentiate from those caused by other drug therapy (e.g., antibiotics, cytarabine) or leukemic infiltrations of the skin. G.M.'s renal function appears to be within normal limits, but if it deteriorates, the dose of allopurinol should be reduced according to recommended guidelines[16] since hepatotoxicity[15] and life-threatening syndrome of erythematous desquamative skin rash, fever, hepatitis, eosinophilia, and worsening renal function have been described in patients with renal insufficiency.[16] (Also see Chapter 40: Gout and Hyperuricemia.)

Although G.M.'s serum potassium was low on admission it has increased significantly as a result of tumor cell lysis. For this reason, replacement potassium therapy is not recommended before chemotherapy to allow for acute electrolyte changes that my result from acute TLS. In extreme circumstances, dialysis may be required to correct severe metabolic and electrolyte disturbances.

6. *Myelosuppression.* G.M. received allopurinol therapy and aggressive hydration throughout her induction chemotherapy. As her WBC count declined and tumor lysis diminished, the metabolic abnormalities gradually resolved. What other complications may occur during induction therapy. Can they be treated?

Myelosuppression is a common and dose-limiting effect of cytotoxic chemotherapy and is further described in Chapter 91: Adverse Effects of Chemotherapy. The unavoidable eradication of WBC and platelet precursors caused by chemotherapy and the disease itself results in infection and bleeding.

It may seem rational to treat granulocytopenia with colony stimulating factors (CSFs). However, since filgrastim (G-CSF) and sargramostim (GM-CSF) stimulate leukemic cells as well as normal granulocyte precursors *in vitro*, their use has been cautioned.[17,18] A Japanese study has demonstrated that if G-CSF is initiated after leukemic blasts cells are eradicated from peripheral blood and bone marrow, it significantly accelerates myeloid recovery without compromising remission rate or duration.[19] Currently, G-CSF is reserved for patients with life-threatening infections and minimal numbers of residual leukemia cells.

Patients receiving cytarabine and daunorubicin induction therapy become profoundly granulocytopenic (e.g., <100 WBC/mm³) and thrombocytopenic (<20,000 platelets/mm³) shortly after therapy is initiated and this persists for 21 to 28 days. All infectious complications must be considered life-threatening in severely immunocompromised patients like G.M. (see Chapter 67: Infections in Immunocompromised Hosts).

Severe thrombocytopenia may result in bleeding episodes that range in severity from oozing gums to massive gastrointestinal hemorrhage. Serious bleeding complications usually can be avoided if patients receive platelet transfusions when their platelet counts drop below 20,000/mm³ or if bleeding occurs. Because G.M. is premenopausal, she has a significant risk of excessive vaginal bleeding if she begins a menstrual period while she is thrombocytopenic. To minimize this risk menstrual periods may be suppressed with daily uninterrupted oral contraceptives or progesterone (e.g., medroxyprogesterone 10 to 20 mg QD). If spotting occurs, dosages should be increased until bleeding stops. After G.M.'s platelet count returns to normal suppressive therapy can be discontinued.

Other common drug-induced complications which may occur during induction therapy include nausea and vomiting, fever, and skin rash. (See Chapter 105: Nausea and Vomiting.)

Postremission Therapy

Rationale

7. Following completion of her induction chemotherapy, G.M.'s WBC count fell to <100/mm³ and her platelet count to 10,000/m³. She received platelet transfusions approximately every 3–5 days to avoid bleeding complications. On day 9 she became profoundly granulocytopenic. She was started immediately on empiric, broad-spectrum antibiotic therapy. Her fever resolved and on day 29 her WBC count was 5,600/mm³ with a normal differential and a platelet count of 168,000/mm³. She received transfusions of packed RBCs on 2 separate occasions when her Hct fell below 30%. A repeat bone marrow aspirate showed no evidence of persistent leukemia and G.M. was told that her leukemia was in remission. Nevertheless, her oncologist recommended additional chemotherapy and G.M. questions why this is necessary? Is postremission therapy necessary and if so, what therapeutic options are available to G.M.?

Although more than 60% of patients treated for ANLL achieve complete remission, the median duration of the remission is only about 12 to 18 months and only 20% to 30% of patients have a disease-free survival exceeding five years.[20-23] Shortened relapse has been attributed to proliferation of clinically undetectable leukemic cells. Thus, the rationale for administering chemotherapy after remission is to eradicate these residual cells.

Strategies used to lengthen remissions have ranged from low-dose chronic maintenance therapy lasting several years to several monthly courses of high-dose chemotherapy. The latter approach is called intensification therapy. Recent literature suggests those receiving aggressive postremission therapy have a higher percentage of disease-free survivors at two to five years than those who have received no or low-dose postremission chemotherapy.[21-25] Postremission therapy regimens usually include high-dose cytarabine alone or in combination with one or more agents such as mitoxantrone, daunorubicin, or etoposide. Elderly patients or those with other underlying medical conditions may not be able to tolerate intensive postremission therapy. In these circumstances, the risk of life-threatening toxicity may outweigh the potential benefits of postremission chemotherapy.

Allogeneic bone marrow transplantation also has been studied in the postremission treatment of ANLL and is addressed in Chapter 94: Bone Marrow Transplantation.

High-Dose Cytarabine

8. G.M. does not have an identical HLA donor who could be harvested for a bone marrow transplant. Consequently, her oncologist recommends 4 courses of high-dose cytarabine as postremission therapy. One week after she was declared to be in remission, G.M. is re-admitted to the hospital to receive cytarabine 2 gm/m² Q 12 hr on days 1, 3, and 5. Each dose is to be infused over 6 hours. What are the potential acute and delayed toxicities associated with high-dose cytarabine and how can these effects be prevented?

At conventional doses of 100 to 200 mg/m²/day, cytarabine adverse effects include myelosuppression, moderate nausea and vomiting, fever, and skin rashes. Occasionally, liver enzymes rise transiently. In addition to these adverse effects high doses of cytarabine also produce major central nervous system, skin, and ocular toxicities.[26-28] (Also see Chapter 91: Adverse Effects of Chemotherapy.)

Ocular toxicity results from damage to corneal epithelium when cytarabine penetrates the epithelium through the anterior chamber of the eye or in the tears. Symptoms include conjunctivitis, excessive lacrimation, ''burning'' ocular pain, photophobia, and blurred vision.[28] Either artificial tear products or corticosteroid eye drops (e.g., dexamethasone 0.1% in each eye Q 6 hr) initiated before high-dose cytarabine generally prevents these symptoms.[29]

Dermatologic toxicity may be manifested as a rash covering most of the body (similar to that seen with conventional doses) or plantar-palmer erythema which may progress to desquamation of the palms and soles.[26] This may be extremely painful, requiring analgesic therapy; desquamation also creates a portal of entry for pathogenic organisms.

Acute Leukemia in the Elderly

9. Would recommendations for induction and postremission therapy differ if G.M. were elderly?

The incidence of ANLL gradually increases with age; and about 30% of patients with ANLL are more than 60 years old.[26] The proportion of patients achieving a complete remission, however, declines with advancing age.[30] This is partially due to a higher death rate during induction therapy. The elderly may have a decreased tolerance to chemotherapy due to concomitant illness and compromised organ function. They also appear to have an increased risk for complications including serious infections.[30] Whether the elderly should receive aggressive chemotherapy is often debated.[30-32] Poor prognostic factors include documentation of a preleukemic syndrome, hypocellular bone marrow at initial presentation, or a history of prior radiation therapy or chemotherapy.[30,31] Nevertheless, many oncologists believe aggressive therapy is warranted in most cases. Two studies indicate that moderate dose reductions of the anthracyclines are more effective than standard dose in the elderly patients.[32,34]

Postremission therapy is difficult in elderly patients because they have a higher risk of morbidity and mortality. The intensity of the regimens often must be attenuated because the risk of serious toxicities (e.g., neurotoxicity associated with high-dose cytarabine) increases with age.[35]

Chronic Myelogenous Leukemia (CML)
Signs and Symptoms

10. P.D., a 32-year-old female, recently sought medical attention for increasing fatigue and decreased exercise tolerance. A CBC showed a WBC count of 60,000/mm³ with 90% neutrophils, an Hct of 30%, and a platelet count 1,300,000/mm³. The only physical finding was splenomegaly. A bone marrow aspirate revealed a hypercellular marrow and biopsy confirmed a diagnosis of Philadelphia chromosome-positive CML. Explain P.D.'s high WBC counts. What are the possible clinical consequences of these abnormal values? [SI units: WBC count 60 × 10⁹/L with 0.9 neutrophils; Hct 0.3, platelets 1.300 × 10⁹/L]

Chronic myelogenous leukemia is a myeloproliferative disorder characterized by unregulated granulocyte proliferation in the bone marrow and an increase in mature granulocytes in the peripheral blood. Progressive leukocytosis may be associated with increased blood viscosity causing headaches, other CNS symptoms (including stroke), and pulmonary leukostasis. Plasma and leukocyte levels of histamine and histamine metabolites may cause pruritus. The accelerated rate of cell production and turnover may lead to increased uric acid and acute gouty arthritis and nephrolithiasis.

Splenomegaly results from increased activity of the reticuloendothelial system for removal of excessive white blood cells. Low grade fever also may result from release of granulocyte lysozymes.[36,37]

11. Why is P.D.'s hematocrit low and platelet count high?

Many patients with CML present with a normochromic, normocytic anemia resulting from suppression of erythroid precursors in the bone marrow and shortened RBC life span in the peripheral blood. Increased megakaryocytes often are observed in the marrow with accompanying thrombocytosis in peripheral blood. Thrombotic episodes and hemorrhagic complications may result from the thrombocytosis and impaired platelet function. While many patients present with thrombocytosis, others may present with normal platelet counts or even thrombocytopenia.

Staging and Prognosis

12. What is the expected disease progression for P.D. and others with newly-diagnosed CML?

The natural history of CML can be divided into three distinct phases. Early in the disease, a chronic phase is seen in which patients exhibit leukocytosis and associated symptoms as described above. The duration of the chronic phase may range from a few weeks to many years, with the median being about three years.[37] Since symptoms may be nonspecific and relatively minor, CML may remain undiagnosed until it progresses in some patients.

During the second phase of the disease, the accelerated phase, leukocytosis progresses (despite therapy) and an increased number of immature leukocytes (blasts) appear in the peripheral blood; symptoms become more problematic. The accelerated phase generally lasts less than six weeks. The final phase of the disease is characterized by a predominance of immature cells and is called blast crisis. This is characterized by exacerbating symptoms including bone pain, fatigue and worsening anemia, infections, and bleeding complications. The blast phase is usually refractory to treatment and median survival is less than three months. Since there are no blast cells present and P.D.'s symptoms are mild, she is in the chronic phase of the disease.

Treatment

13. What therapy is appropriate for P.D.?

Busulfan

The goal of therapy during the chronic phase of CML is to reduce leukocytosis and its related symptoms. Hydroxyurea, busulfan, and interferon alfa have been most widely used to reduce leukocyte counts.[38,39] Busulfan is an alkylating agent which appears to be selectively toxic to hematopoietic stem cells. Busulfan is given orally in dosages of 4 to 6 mg/day. P.D.'s complete blood count should be monitored weekly and the dose reduced as the WBC count decreases until it reaches 25,000/mm³. At that time, therapy should be discontinued because the WBC and platelet count will continue to decline. Thereafter, maintenance doses of 2 mg every other day to 4 mg/day can be given to maintain the leukocyte count at this level. Intermittent pulse dosing (50 to 150 mg every 2 to 4 weeks) also has been used. In either case, doses require careful titration. Toxicities associated with chronic busulfan ingestion include sterility, hyperpigmentation, adrenal insufficiency, and pulmonary fibrosis.

Hydroxyurea

In recent years, hydroxyurea has been more widely used than busulfan. It has a more rapid onset of effect and a shorter duration of action which avoids the prolonged, profound marrow aplasia that sometimes occurs with busulfan therapy. Treatment is initiated with 2 gm/day orally and the dose is titrated to the desired neutrophil count. A small decrease in dose often will permit a considerable rise in leukocyte count in one or two days. Hydroxyurea is remarkably free of side effects.

Interferon Alfa

Interferon alfa has a direct antiproliferative effect on the leukemic cells and platelets and is given in doses of 5 million units/m²/day subcutaneously (SQ). Fifty to sixty percent of patients respond completely or partially, although the maximal effect may take weeks to months.[40,41] In about 50% of patients partial suppression of the Philadelphia chromosome is observed although it is unclear whether this effect influences survival or the natural history of CML.[42,43] However, several groups of investigators have reported that patients randomized to receive interferon therapy either have a longer duration in chronic phase or survive longer than patients receiving busulfan or hydroxyurea. Toxicities of interferon can be more severe than busulfan and hydroxyurea. Initially, all patients experience fever, chills, myalgias, malaise, and headache. Although tolerance develops to these effects, many develop chronic fatigue and neurological symptoms such as impaired cognition and depression.

While all three of these agents are effective in reducing leukocytosis, it is controversial if interferon is clearly superior to the others. Furthermore, whether control of leukocytosis prolongs overall survival and alters the natural history of this disease is unknown. Treatment choice is, therefore, based upon prescriber preference, risk of treatment-associated toxicities, and cost.

Bone Marrow Transplantation

14. What is the role of bone marrow transplantation in the treatment of CML?

Over 2000 patients with CML have received bone marrow transplants from HLA identical donors. When patients are not transplanted until the blast phase only 10% to 20% survive five years or more. If patients are transplanted in the chronic phase, 50% to 60% are alive and disease-free at five years and less than 20% have relapsed.[44,45] The highest rate of prolonged disease-free survival occurs in younger patients transplanted within one year of initial diagnosis during the chronic phase.

Chronic Lymphocytic Leukemia (CLL)
Signs and Symptoms

15. G.L., a 63-year-old female, recently presented to her family physician with a persistent cough. A routine CBC revealed a Hct of 39% with normal indices, a WBC count of 25,000/mm³ with 80% lymphocytes, and a platelet count of 175,000/mm³. Physical examination and chest x-ray were unremarkable and she was afebrile. Blood pressure was 120/70 mm Hg, heart rate 70 beats/min, and respiratory rate 20 breaths/min. She was prescribed azithromycin for presumptive mycoplasma pneumonia and scheduled for a return visit in 2 weeks. At that time, her CBC was as follows: Hct 39% with normal indices, WBC count 28,000/mm³ with 82% lymphocytes, and platelets 168,000/mm³. Physical examination was unchanged and her cough had resolved. G.L. was referred to a hematologist for evaluation of her persistent lymphocytosis. What is the most likely cause of persistent lymphocytosis in G.L.? [SI units: Hct 0.39; WBC count 25 × 10⁹/L with 0.8 lymphocytes and 28 × 10⁹/L with 0.82 lymphocytes, respectively; platelets 175 × 10⁹/L and 168 × 10⁹/L]

Causes of lymphocytosis (>5000 lymphocytes/mm³ in peripheral blood) include infectious mononucleosis, pertussis, acute infectious lymphocytosis (viral and other infections), chronic lymphocytic leukemia, and acute lymphocytic leukemia (ALL). Examination of the peripheral blood lymphocyte morphology by an experienced hematologist or pathologist may be helpful in distinguishing these disorders. Patients with ALL commonly have lymphoblasts in the peripheral blood and other disorders, including mononucleosis, are characterized by a high percentage of atypical lymphocytes. Because G.L. has no fever or systemic symptoms of infection and her lymphocytes in the peripheral blood are mature, the most likely diagnosis is CLL. Bone marrow aspiration, biopsy, and cell surface markers are required to determine the definitive diagnosis.

Staging and Prognosis

16. Bone marrow examination revealed normal cellularity and >30% of nucleated cells were lymphocytes. The phenotype indicated peripheral blood lymphocytes were predominately of B-cell lineage. A diagnosis of CLL is confirmed. What is the usual presentation and prognosis of CLL? What treatment is indicated at this time?

CLL is a monoclonal neoplasm of slowly proliferating, long-lived lymphocytes which are immunologically incompetent. CLL is the most common type of leukemia and it occurs twice as commonly in men as women. It is predominant in individuals over the age of 55.[46] The etiology is unknown, although there does appear to be some genetic predisposition.[47] Like G.L., about 25% of patients are asymptomatic at initial presentation. Survival is quite variable and dependent upon the stage of disease at diagnosis. CLL is staged based upon the lymphocyte count in the periphery; enlargement of the lymph nodes, liver, and spleen; and presence of anemia and thrombocytopenia. G.L. has very early stage disease since her only finding is absolute lymphocytosis. The prognosis for patients with early disease is good, with a median survival of over ten years.[48]

Studies have demonstrated that there is no clear advantage in treating asymptomatic patients with early stage disease; therefore, it is reasonable to observe G.L. at this time.[49,50] If the CLL progresses she may become less able to produce antibodies (immunologically incompetent). At this stage vaccination against pneumococcal, haemophilus, and meningococcal disease may be advisable.

Treatment

17. G.L. returns to the hematologist every 3 months and does well for about 2 years. Physical examination at this visit reveals enlargement of cervical, inguinal, and axillary lymph nodes. Her liver is palpable to 7 cm below the costal margin and she has splenomegaly. Her lymphocyte count has increased from 35,000/mm³ six months ago to 63,000/mm³ today; the Hct is 35% and platelet count is 140,000/mm³. Is treatment now indicated? [SI units: lymphocyte count 35 × 10⁹/L and 63 × 10⁹/L, respectively; Hct 0.35; platelets 140 × 10⁹/L]

G.L.'s CLL has obviously progressed as indicated by the enlarged lymph nodes, hepatomegaly, splenomegaly, and progressive lymphocytosis (doubling of count in <6 months). Other indications for initiating treatment in a patient with CLL might include the development of anemia or thrombocytopenia which are not immune-mediated or due to recurrent infections.[46,47] Treatment should be initiated at this time to prevent further deterioration of G.L.'s hematologic and immune functions.

Chlorambucil

Initial treatment of CLL usually consists of chlorambucil with or without prednisone. Approximately 70% of previously untreated patients will respond satisfactorily to chlorambucil, administered daily or intermittently.[51,52] Daily therapy usually consists of 6 to 14 mg which is given until signs and symptoms diminish. At that time, lower doses may be given for an additional six months. Intermittent therapy usually consists of 0.7 mg/kg given over two to four days and repeated every three weeks until the disease stabilizes. Many variations of these regimens produce similar response rates.

Corticosteroids

Controversy exists regarding whether all patients should receive a corticosteroid. Although response rates may be modestly better for the combination, considerable risks may be associated with high-dose steroid therapy in this elderly population.[53] Currently, experts recommend that steroids be included only for the 15% of patients who also have immune complications such as autoimmune hemolytic anemia or thrombocytopenia.[48] When corticosteroids are indicated, oral prednisone is given 30 to 60 mg/m²/day for five to seven days each month.

Once therapy is initiated, patients require frequent monitoring of blood counts and physical findings. Doses of all drugs must be adjusted to maximize their benefits while avoiding serious toxicities.

Immune-Mediated Thrombocytopenia

18. G.L. receives chlorambucil on the intermittent schedule and this produces regression of her lymph adenopathy and hepatosplenomegaly. Her lymphocyte count decreases to 30,000/mm³. Six months later, just before her 8th course of chlorambucil, a CBC is obtained which reveals: Hct 33%, platelets 10,000/mm³, and WBC 36,000/mm³ with 80% lymphocytes. Why is G.L. profoundly thrombocytopenic? [SI units: Hct 0.33, platelets 10 × 10⁹/L; WBC count 36 × 10⁹/L]

The most likely explanation is immune-mediated thrombocytopenia. Chemotherapy-associated myelosuppression is an unlikely cause because she has adequate granulocytes and only mildly suppressed RBCs. If thrombocytopenia is due to autoimmune destruction in the periphery, normal or increased numbers of megakaryocytes should be seen in the bone marrow, despite low levels in peripheral blood.

High-dose corticosteroids (60 to 100 mg of prednisone daily for 5 days) should be added to G.L.'s therapy.[46] If the platelet count does not begin to increase in three to five days or if bleeding occurs, intravenous immune globulin in doses of 1 gm/kg every 12 hours for two doses may be administered.[55,56]

Fludarabine

19. Five days after initiation of prednisone, G.L.'s platelet count has increased to 89,000/mm². Prednisone therapy is continued and the dosage is gradually tapered. Prednisone will now be added to her monthly cycles of chlorambucil. While on chlorambucil and prednisone, G.L. experienced 2 infections (sinusitis and pneumonia) requiring hospitalization and IV antibiotics. Her neutrophil count was within normal limits and quantification of serum immunoglobulins reveals hypogammaglobulinemia. G.L.'s Hct is 29% and her lymphocyte count has increased to 60,000/mm³. Lymphadenopathy also has returned. Are changes in G.L.'s therapy indicted? [SI unit: Hct 0.29]

G.L. now has evidence of disease progression (anemia, lymphocytosis, lymphadenopathy) and has experienced recurrent infections related to her hypogammaglobulinemia, a complication of advanced CLL. A change in therapy is indicated. Fludarabine, a pyrimidine analog, is approved for the treatment of CLL refractory to an alkylating agent. Studies conducted at the MD Anderson Cancer Center and the Southwest Oncology Group demonstrated that fludarabine 20 to 25 mg/m² IV daily for five days, produced responses in approximately 50% of patients who had progressed while receiving alkylating agents, including chlorambucil.[57,58] Other studies have confirmed these results. Courses of fludarabine are repeated every four weeks and toxicities are generally mild.

Concurrent corticosteroids do not appear to improve the response to fludarabine; however, in G.L.'s case they may be necessary to control her autoimmune thrombocytopenia. If her response to fludarabine is favorable, prednisone can be discontinued.

The high rate of complete responses to fludarabine in patients unresponsive to alkylating agents coupled with its low toxicity has stimulated interest in the use of this agent as first line therapy for CLL.

Combination therapy with agents such as cyclophosphamide, doxorubicin, vincristine, prednisone, and cytarabine also has been studied in patients with advanced and refractory CLL. Currently, there are no obvious benefits over chlorambucil and fludarabine.

Infectious Complications

20. Are prophylactic antibiotics indicated to prevent infection in G.L.? What other options are available?

Infections in patients with advanced CLL like G.L. usually are related to hypogammaglobulinemia. Currently, there is not good evidence to support the use of prophylactic antibiotics. However, quinolones or cotrimoxazole are sometimes prescribed for patients with past infections who are receiving chemotherapy. In two studies, administration of IVIG, 400 mg/kg every three weeks, reduced the incidence of major bacterial infections in patients with hypogammaglobulinemia associated with CLL.[59,60] Its use appears to be justified in patients who have experienced recurrent severe infections.

NonHodgkin's Lymphoma
Clinical Presentation and Prognosis

21. K.G., a 39-year-old male, recently presented with bilateral lower extremity weakness and occasional dyspnea. K.G. reported that he had been diagnosed as human immunodeficiency virus (HIV) positive for about 7 months and that over the past 2 months he had noticed increased swelling in his lymph nodes, occasional fevers, and night sweats. He also reported a 35-pound weight loss. Physical examination revealed marked supraclavicular and inguinal adenopathy, decreased strength in both lower extremities, a large abdominal mass, and decreased breath sounds over the base of the right lung. CT scans showed a vertebral erosion with a compression fracture at L_2, a large abdominal mass involving the large bowel, and a pleural effusion at the right lung base. A myelogram confirmed that the L_2 fracture was causing epidural spinal cord compression. He underwent emergency laminectomy to repair the vertebral fracture. Biopsy done at the time of surgery revealed evidence of malignant cells. Laparotomy and biopsy confirmed the diagnosis of small, noncleaved lymphoma, Burkitt's type. What is this lymphoma? Is this a typical presentation? Is its diagnosis related to K.G.'s HIV infection?

Burkitt's lymphoma is a high-grade lymphoma and among the most common nonHodgkin's lymphomas (NHLs) seen in HIV-positive patients. All NHLs are divided into three broad groups based upon their histology. Low-grade lymphomas tend to be more indolent in their natural history, and although they are not curable, these patients survive for prolonged periods with minimal symptoms. In contrast, high-grade lymphomas spread rapidly to other organs and will result in death within weeks to months if untreated. However, these lymphomas are often very responsive to chemotherapy and up to 60% to 70% of patients (non-HIV positive) may be cured with combination chemotherapy. Intermediate-grade lymphomas have an intermediate natural history and prognosis. The most common clinical presentation of lymphoma is painless enlargement of one or more lymph nodes. Fever and night sweats are constitutional symptoms that frequently constitute initial symptoms of lymphoma as well. In addition, weight loss and alcohol induced pain are also common. K.G. did report increased swelling in his lymph nodes, occasional fever and night sweats, and a 35-pound weight loss over the past two months. Physical examination revealed significant lymph node enlargement in the supraclavicular and inguinal areas as well. A large abdominal mass resulted in a malignant pleural effusion, and spinal cord compression. K.G.'s tumor burden is obviously very large which is not uncommon in patients with high grade lymphoma.

The risk of NHL is increased in HIV-positive patients by 60- to 100-fold over the general population.[60,61] The case definition of acquired immunodeficiency syndrome (AIDS) includes either intermediate- or high-grade lymphomas of B-cell origin in the presence of seropositivity against HIV.[62]

Human Immunodeficiency Virus (HIV)-Positive Patients versus Other Patients

22. Do the clinical features and prognosis of this high-grade lymphoma differ in patients who are HIV positive compared to those who are not?

Patients who are HIV positive may present with lymphomas as their initial clinical presentation or during the course of their disease.[63] HIV-positive patients are more likely to develop widely disseminated lymphoma (GI tract, CNS, bone marrow, liver) than those who are not HIV positive. Unusual sites of lymphoma involvement such as the rectum, myocardium, adrenals, popliteal fossa, gallbladder, and orbit also have been described in patients with AIDS.[60,64] In addition, HIV-positive patients are more likely to complain of fever, night sweats, and weight loss.

The prognosis for patients who are HIV positive with lymphoma is significantly poorer than those who are HIV negative. Their median survival is generally only five to six months and is related to their profound immunosuppression and unresponsiveness to chemotherapy.[64,65] However, occasional patients responded well to chemotherapy and survive more than one to two years.[66]

Treatment
Combination Chemotherapy

23. K.G. received combination chemotherapy consisting of cyclophosphamide, doxorubicin, vincristine, and prednisone (CHOP). Is this considered standard therapy?

Optimal therapy for HIV-associated NHL is difficult to define due to widespread differences in underlying immunosuppression and related complications in this population. Although the effects of numerous combination chemotherapy regimens have been described in this high risk group, there have been few controlled clinical trials. Furthermore, the heterogeneity of this patient population makes this information difficult to interpret. Although high response rates have been associated with aggressive, multidrug chemotherapy such as the methotrexate, doxorubicin, cyclophosphamide, prednisone, and bleomycin (MACOP-B) regimen, many HIV-positive patients cannot tolerate the associated toxicities. Patients who are most likely to respond include those who have: 1) less extensive disease involvement, 2) no prior history of AIDS or AIDS-related complex (ARC) symptoms including opportunistic infections and Kaposi's sarcoma, 3) no bone marrow or central nervous system involvement, and 4) a good performance status at the time of diagnosis.[63,66-68] Although patients with few complications of the underlying disorder may do well with dose-intensive combination chemotherapy regimens, overall response rates have been lower than those reported for non-HIV patient populations. HIV-positive patients also have a high mortality rate due to opportunistic infectious complications and tend to relapse (often in the CNS) early even if remission is achieved.[60,69-71] Current strategies emphasize less myelosuppressive therapy combined with prophylaxis for central nervous disease [e.g., intrathecal (IT) cytarabine] and pneumocystis infection.[72] CHOP chemotherapy is an appropriate choice for K.G. due to his tumor volume, otherwise good functional status, and recent AIDS diagnosis. Antiretroviral therapy and marrow protective therapy with G-CSF or GM-CSF may be used in conjunction with his chemotherapy.

Corticosteroids

24. What are the toxic effects of chemotherapy in this patient group? Is the use of corticosteroids as part of the chemotherapy regimen contraindicated in these patients who already have considerable immunosuppression?

The toxicity associated with intensive chemotherapy regimens has been substantial in some series. Severe mucositis, leukopenia, and associated sepsis have been common in patients who have previously had opportunistic infections or other AIDS-related symptoms.[66] One group of researchers reported that such regimens were associated with a significant risk of early death due to opportunistic infections and advocated the use of less intensive regimens.[73]

There is considerable controversy regarding the use of corticosteroids in the HIV-positive population because it might contribute to additional immunosuppression.[74] However, most of the recommended chemotherapy regimens include corticosteroids. In one study, HIV-positive patients who had not experienced opportunistic infections before the diagnosis of NHL, did not experience a significant increase in these complications.[66] The total duration of chemotherapy may have a greater impact on the overall immune status of the patient and should be considered when selecting therapy. Regimens such as the MACOP-B may be completed in two to three months, whereas others may require five to six months thereby prolonging the period of enhanced immunosuppression.[66,73]

Malignant Pleural Effusion

25. Before chemotherapy was started, thoracentesis was performed to remove the pleural effusion and to relieve K.G.'s shortness of breath. One liter of blood-tinged serous fluid was removed and K.G. improved symptomatically. The fluid was exudative and cytology was positive for malignant cells consistent with Burkitt's lymphoma. Are pleural effusions common complications of malignancy? Will treatment of the systemic disease be adequate therapy to prevent the reaccumulation of pleural effusion?

Pleural effusions frequently are associated with advanced malignancies such as lymphomas and lung, breast, gastric, esophageal, and prostate cancers. They are accumulations of fluid in the pleural space (i.e., the space between the visceral pleura and the chest wall parietal pleura). They are believed to be the result of increased capillary permeability due to inflammation, disruption of the capillary endothelium by tumor, or impaired lymphatic drainage secondary to obstruction.[75] Typically, malignant pleural effusions are exudative with a protein content of greater than 3 gm/dL, specific gravity greater than 1.015, a pleural protein/serum protein ratio of greater than 0.5, and a pleural lactic dehydrogenase (LD)/serum LD ratio greater than 0.6.[76] Dyspnea, cough, and chest pain are common presenting symptoms and physical findings include tachypnea, labored breathing, and restricted chest wall expansion. Thoracentesis provides symptomatic improvement; however, without more definitive therapy the effusion usually will reaccumulate. If the underlying malignancy is treated, the pleural effusion may be controlled by performing periodic thoracentesis until the underlying pathology is corrected. Unfortunately, systemic treatment is not effective in many patients with advanced disease and additional local measures must be initiated to control reaccumulation of pleural fluid and diminish or eliminate the need for repeated thoracenteses.[76] In K.G.'s case it is probably reasonable to delay local therapy of the pleural effusion because lymphomas often respond to chemotherapy very rapidly.

Sclerosing Agents and Thoracostomy

26. Two days after the thoracentesis K.G. was once again short of breath and a chest-x-ray confirmed that the pleural effusion had reaccumulated. A chest tube was placed in the pleural space and drainage over the first 24 hours was about 200 mL. What is the function of the chest tube? Should local therapy be initiated?

The thoracostomy or chest tube is placed into the area of the effusion and is connected to a continuous, underwater-seal suction to provide drainage and subsequent obliteration of the space occupied by the effusion. Unfortunately, the effectiveness of a chest tube alone is only about 20%.[75] Instillation of a sclerosing drug through the chest tube can produce pleurodesis (i.e., fusion of the pleural membranes). However, this approach is usually only successful if the chest tube drainage is minimal (i.e., <100 mL/24 hours). Otherwise, the sclerosing agent will be diluted in the effusion to an ineffective concentration.

Historically, many agents have been used as sclerosing agents. Most of these have been abandoned because their local or systemic toxicities have been excessive or they have not been efficacious. Tetracycline (0.5 to 1.0 gm) and bleomycin (60 mg) and talc have been the most widely used in the past.[2,76–86] These agents control malignant pleural effusions in ≥70% patients probably by inducing inflammation which causes secondary sclerosis.[81] A single randomized trial comparing tetracycline and bleomycin reported equal response rates.[81] However, bleomycin does appear to cause less pain during and following the instillation procedure. Unfortunately, parenteral tetracycline is no longer commercially available in the U.S., but doxycycline and minocycline also appear to be effective. A comparative trial of talc with both bleomycin[86] and tetracycline[2] supports a greater success rate with talc than with either of these other agents. However, these results are inconclusive because of the difficulties with study design and inconsistencies in evaluating patients. Sterile talc is not commercially available and, therefore, it must be sterilized before its use. The administration of talc, both as powder and as suspension, is considered to be rather complicated and associated with severe pain and some risk. Moreover, talc insufflation into the pleural space requires general anesthesia, which increases the risk of morbidity and mortality of the procedure. Because of the complications associated with the use of this agent, its use is generally recommended only for symptomatic patients with a significant life expectancy whose therapy with other sclerosing agents has failed.

All patients should receive systemic analgesics about 30 minutes before instillation of the sclerosing agent, and lidocaine 150 mg also has been added to tetracycline solutions to decrease pain. The sclerosing agent is diluted in 50 to 100 mL of saline and instilled directly through the chest tube with an irrigating syringe. The chest tube is then clamped and the patient is instructed to change positions every 15 minutes for four hours to ensure adequate distribution throughout the pleural cavity. At the end of four hours the tube is unclamped and the fluid is drained with suction for about 24 hours.[76]

Acute Lymphoblastic Leukemia (ALL) of Childhood

Acute lymphoblastic leukemia is the most common childhood cancer, accounting for approximately 30% of all malignancies in children.[87] Approximately 2000 new cases of childhood ALL occur each year in the U.S., with an estimated incidence of 4 cases per 100,000 in children less than 15 years.[88] Before the early 1970s, ALL was a fatal illness and most children did not survive more than two to three months following diagnosis. Today, over 70% of children will achieve prolonged survival with antileukemic therapy and the majority of these will be cured.[89–91]

Etiology

The etiology of ALL is unknown; however, several interesting associations have been discovered. A high incidence of leukemia was found among survivors of the atom bomb explosion in Japan during World War II, and those closest to the epicenter of the blast were at greatest risk.[92,93] Leukemia also occurs in children exposed to radiation *in utero*.[94] Other factors which have been suggested to cause ALL include exposure to electromagnetic fields, pesticides, maternal use of alcohol, contraceptives, and cigarettes.[95–98] Viruses have not been proven to cause childhood ALL.[99]

Evidence supporting an association between ALL and electromagnetic field exposure is currently inadequate.[100] In particular, the incidence of childhood ALL has not increased markedly over the past 40 years during a time when electricity use has seen a large increase.[101] Nevertheless, the lay press has succeeded in generating considerable public anxiety regarding this potential risk factor, based upon a cluster of ALL cases.[102] Clusters of leukemia cases which occur over certain time frames and places may merely represent instances of statistical coincidence.[103]

Pathophysiology

The pathophysiology of ALL involves the replacement of normal bone marrow elements with an accumulation of immature lymphoid cells. The essential lesion in ALL is a stabilization of a transit cell in the lymphocyte differentiation process. Many factors are involved in the control of normal cellular proliferation. Leukemia may represent a disruption in one or more of the normal relationships within the cell proliferation pathway, such as an abnormal response to lymphoid cell growth factors.[104]

With the availability of classification systems of lymphoblasts based upon morphology, immunology, and cytogenetics, it has become clear that ALL is a heterogenous disease. The heterogeneity results from leukemic transformation at any stage of lymphocyte differentiation. As discussed later, each of these classifications has important prognostic significance.

Clinical Presentation

The signs and symptoms of ALL are nonspecific, and many are shared with other childhood diseases such as juvenile rheumatoid arthritis. These signs and symptoms reflect the uncontrolled growth and differentiation of the immature lymphoid clone and the resulting deficiency in normal bone marrow elements: namely neutrophils, red blood cells, and platelets. Frequent clinical findings include fever (61%), bleeding (48%), and bone pain (23%).[105] Bone pain is believed to be the result of a hypercellular bone marrow and infiltration of leukemic lymphoblasts into pain sensitive structures such as the periosteum. Although bone pain may be severe, it quickly resolves once chemotherapy is initiated. On physical examination many patients have lymphadenopathy (50%), splenomegaly (63%), and/or hepatosplenomegaly (68%).[105]

A complete blood count will demonstrate that at least 59% of patients have a normal or low WBC count, the remainder have elevated counts.[105] The WBC differential reveals a low percentage of neutrophils and bands and a marked lymphocytosis. Lymphoblasts may be present in the peripheral blood even with a low WBC

count (e.g., 2000 to 4000/mm³), but they are more likely to be present when the WBC count is high.[105] A normochromic, normocytic anemia along with thrombocytopenia will be present in the majority of patients.[105]

A bone marrow biopsy is necessary to confirm the diagnosis of ALL. The diagnosis of ALL is made when at least 25% of lymphoid cells in the bone marrow are blasts.[88] Most ALL patients have greater than 25% blasts and many have complete replacement of bone marrow with lymphoblasts. Once a child is diagnosed with ALL, it is important to determine morphologic, immunologic, and cytogenetic characteristics which influence treatment decisions and the prognosis.

Prognostic Variables

Clinical Variables

Clinical and laboratory findings which are present at diagnosis and are important in predicting a child's prognosis are provided in Table 92.5.

White Blood Cell (WBC) Count. The initial WBC count is considered to be among the most important predictors of outcome in childhood ALL. Its importance as a prognostic feature is often retained following the adjustment for other important prognostic criteria.[88] Children with the highest WBC counts at presentation have the shortest duration of complete remissions.[106–112] There appears to be a linear relationship between the duration of remission and the white blood cell count at presentation (see Figure 92.1). Although it is unknown exactly where the demarcation line is for predicting a good or a poor prognosis, an initial white blood cell count greater than 50,000/mm³ generally is associated with a poor prognosis.[87] The degree of hepatosplenomegaly and lymphadenopathy are thought to be indicative of the extent of extramedullary leukemic infiltration and to have important prognostic significance as well.[107]

Age. Patients younger than two years or greater than ten years of age at diagnosis tend to have a worse prognosis (see Figure 92.2). Age is the most ominous predictor of prognosis with regard to infants, a group in which survival is exceedingly poor compared with other age groups.[113–117]

Sex also has been shown to be an important prognostic factor in several studies.[112,118,119] Although testicular relapse in males is responsible for a somewhat worse prognosis in males, it does not completely account for the better prognosis of females. Other factors which may be of importance are the higher incidence of a worse type of leukemia in males[87] and the inherent ability of males

Table 92.5	Clinical Predictors of Prognosis in Childhood Acute Lymphocytic Leukemia[a,107–119,122–135]	
Predictor	**Better Prognosis**	**Worse Prognosis**
Age	>2 yr, <10 yr	<2 yr, >10 yr
Race	Caucasian	Black, Native American
Initial leukocyte count	<20,000/mm³	>20–50,000/mm³
Cellular morphology FAB class[b]	L1	L2, L3
Sex	Female	Male
Mediastinal mass	Absent	Present
Central Nervous System disease	Absent	Present

[a] The value of predicting prognosis varies and not all studies confirm the same factors as being important.
[b] French-American-British classification system.

Fig 92.1 Percent of Children with ALL in Continuous Complete Remission Stratified According to Their WBC Count at the Time of Diagnosis
Reprinted with permission. Wiley-Liss, reference 118.

to tolerate higher doses of chemotherapy.[120] This greater tolerance in males suggests the need to use higher doses to produce the same therapeutic effect achieved in females at lower doses. This finding may be due to a sex difference in the metabolism of certain chemotherapy agents.[121]

Race. Several studies have shown that black children appear to have a higher relapse rate than Caucasian children.[122–124] Native American males also appear to fair worse than Caucasian children.[125] The differences in outcome for blacks and Native Americans do not appear to be the result of an alteration in therapy, but to a more severe form of ALL in these patient populations.[124,125] The prognosis of Hispanic children does not appear to differ from that of Caucasian children.[125]

Morphology. Cells with the L1 morphology are the most common in childhood ALL and are associated with the best prognosis. Cells with an L3 morphology, associated with B-cell leukemia and Burkitt's lymphoma, historically have been associated with a poor prognosis. The L2 morphology has been associated with a poor prognosis in several studies.[126–128] Patients tend to have a worse outcome when more than 10% of their leukemic lymphoblasts have the L2 subtype.[107,126] Other studies, however, have not found the L2 morphology to be an important independent predictor of prognosis.[106,129]

Immunologic Variables

ALL is classified into different immunologic subsets based upon cell surface markers and/or antigens present on the leukemic lymphoblasts at diagnosis (see Table 92.6). These can be divided into cells of B-cell and T-cell origin. The B-cell lineage is further classified into various subtypes through the use of monoclonal antibodies. These subtypes reflect the various stages of differentiation at which leukemia may develop. Approximately 20% of children with ALL have leukemia with a T-cell lineage[130,131] and 1% to 2% of patients have leukemia with a mature B-cell origin.[131,132] Using more sophisticated diagnostic techniques available in recent

years, the majority of patients who were previously classified as non-T, non-B cell ALL are now known to have leukemia of a more immature B-cell lineage.[133–135] Most patients with B-cell lineage ALL (80%) have cells positive for the common ALL antigen (CALLA) on their surface.[136,137] This is referred to as "common" ALL. The cell surface marker cytoplasmic immunoglobulin has been used to further determine the level of differentiation of leukemic cells of the B-cell lineage. Intermediate cells of the B-cell lineage (pre-B cells) possess this marker, but more immature cells (early pre-B cells) do not.[135,138] Over 60% of children with ALL have a leukemia of the early pre-B subtype and approximately 20% have a leukemia of pre-B cells.

Mature B-cell ALL traditionally has been associated with a poor prognosis,[135,139,140] although more aggressive treatment than that used in standard ALL treatment has resulted in a marked improvement in overall survival in recent years.[141,142] Patients with pre-B ALL also do less well than patients with the early pre-B subtype.[135,143] Patients with lymphoblasts positive for CALLA and of an early pre-B subtype tend to have the best prognosis.[135,143–145] However, when other prognostic factors are considered and when effective therapy is employed, these differences in prognosis may not be evident.[118,146,147]

Patients with T-cell ALL have several distinguishing features. These include a greater likelihood of being older males with high initial white blood cell counts and the presence of a mediastinal mass and/or initial leukemic involvement of the central nervous system.[148,149] Patients with T-cell ALL characteristically have a decreased survival, although more intensive treatment is improving their outcome.[106,107,150] There are subgroups of T-cell ALL based upon such factors as initial white blood cell count and splenomegaly.[151] Since T-cell ALL occurs in older patients with high initial white blood cell counts, it is unclear if T-cell ALL is an independent predictor of prognosis.[105,106,144]

Patients with ALL often present with a mixed cell lineage with leukemic blasts that express both lymphoid and myeloid antigens.

Percent

p (trend) = <0.0001

1-9 yr   n / 3827

>10 yr   959

<1 yr   112 / 4898

Years

Fig 92.2   Percent of Children with ALL in Continuous Complete Remission Stratified Into Three Age Groups   Reprinted with permission. Wiley-Liss, reference 32.

Expression of myeloid antigens may be an important prognostic factor in predicting the risk of relapse,[152] although this has been questioned by others.[153]

Cytogenetic Variables

Recent advances in chromosomal analysis and cell culture techniques (cytogenetics) have improved our understanding of ALL biology. Abnormalities in both chromosome number (ploidy) and structure of the leukemic clone have been found in more than 90% of ALL cases; these appear to have prognostic importance.[154-158] Ploidy is represented by the DNA index. A value of one indicates a normal number of chromosomes and a value greater than one indicates a greater than normal number of chromosomes by a multiplication factor of the normal chromosome number. Children with greater than 50 chromosomes (DNA index >1.16, hyperdiploid), appear to have an improved response and an increased probability of continuous complete remission versus patients with a diploid chromosome complement or with a DNA index less than 1.16 (see Figure 92.3).[156] Approximately 30% of ALL cases have a DNA index greater than 1.16.[159] Patients whose ALL cells are hyperdiploid also tend to have other favorable prognostic features.[156]

Translocations are the most common structural abnormalities occurring in leukemic cells[160,161] and occur in approximately 30% of childhood ALL cases.[162] Translocation is a poor prognostic sign associated with treatment failure and relapse.[155,157,163] The translocations most commonly associated with treatment failure are t(8;14), t(9;22), and t(4;11).[155,162] Approximately 50% of the translocations found in childhood ALL are unique to specific ALL cases and are uncommon (random translocations).[157] There may be an association between translocation and both immunologic classifi-

cation and age.[157,163,164] Once a patient achieves complete remission, abnormalities of both ploidy and structure are not evident. If relapse does occur, the leukemic cell cytogenetic characteristics are usually identical to those observed at diagnosis.[161]

Additional Variables

Other features also may be important in predicting the outcome of childhood ALL.

Lactate Dehydrogenase (LD). A longer duration of remission is more likely in patients with a lower serum LD.[165]

Receptors for Corticosteroids on Leukemic Cells. The greatest number of these receptors appears to be found on early pre-B cells, followed by pre-B cells, T-cells, and finally B-cells.[166] Low numbers of these receptors are associated with decreased responses to therapy and shorter remissions.[167-169]

All of these prognostic variables can be used to assign patients to various categories, based upon their risk of relapse. These categories are important in determining the therapy which patients

Table 92.6	Immunologic Classifications of Childhood Acute Lymphocytic Leukemia (ALL)	
Cell type	% of ALL Cases	Prognosis
B-Cell Subtypes		
Mature B-cell	1–2	Poor[a]
Pre-B	20	Intermediate
Early pre-B	60	Good
T-Cell	20	Intermediate

[a] New treatment approaches have resulted in a considerable improvement in prognosis.

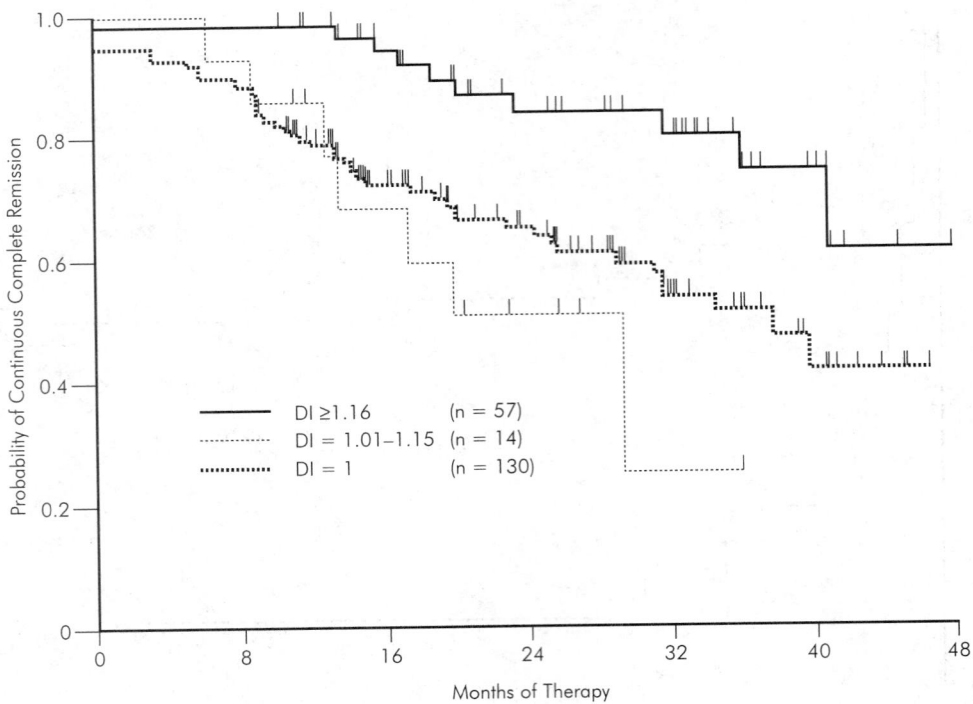

Fig 92.3   Time-to-Fail Curves for 201 Patients with DNA Index equal to 1.0 (Diploid); Ranging from 1.01 to 1.15; or ≥1.16   Reprinted with permission. WB Saunders Co., reference 156.

will receive. While there is considerable agreement as to the importance of certain variables in assigning patients to a defined risk group (e.g., age, initial WBC, DNA index, translocations), institutions which treat ALL differ in their definitions of high-risk and standard-risk patients. This makes it difficult to compare treatment results from different institutions or treatment groups.

Treatment

Remission Induction Therapy

27. Allopurinol Interaction. J.B. is a 4-year-old Hispanic male presenting with a 2-week history of an upper respiratory tract infection and a 1-week history of otitis media. His symptoms have worsened and he now presents with nosebleed and fatigue as well. Physical examination reveals appreciable pallor and hepatosplenomegaly. A CBC with differential reveals a normochromic, normocytic anemia with a Hct of 15.7% (Normal: 39–49), Hgb of 5.7 gm/dL (Normal: 14–18), WBC count of 4300/mm³ (Normal: 3200–9800), and platelet count of 13,000/mm³ (Normal: 150,000–400,000). A differential on the WBC count reveals 82% lymphocytes (Normal: 30–40), 7% neutrophils (Normal: 50–60), and 11% lymphoblasts (Normal: 0). Based upon these findings, a bone marrow biopsy is performed which reveals 95% lymphoblasts. A diagnosis of ALL is made. The ALL is morphologically an L1 type, and the immunologic class is early pre-B cell. Analysis of the chromosomes reveals no translocations and a DNA index = 1.24. The chest x-ray does not reveal a mediastinal mass and a lumbar puncture shows that there are no leukemic lymphoblasts in the cerebrospinal fluid (CSF). J.B. is hydrated and treated with allopurinol 200 mg/m²/day PO, with a plan to institute induction therapy the next day. (For a discussion of the use of allopurinol in induction chemotherapy for the prevention of tumor lysis syndrome, see Adult Nonlymphocytic Leukemia: Complications of Induction Therapy.) Within a few days, J.B. will be treated with several drugs for his leukemia. Do any of the agents which are likely to be utilized in J.B. exhibit significant drug interactions with allopurinol? [SI units: Hct 0.157 (Normal:

0.39–0.49); Hgb 57 gm/L (Normal 140–180); WBC count 4.3 × 10⁹/L (Normal: 3.2–9.8) with 0.82 lymphocytes (Normal: 0.3–0.4), 0.07 neutrophils (Normal: 0.5–0.6), 0.11 lymphoblasts (Normal: 0); platelets 13 × 10⁹/L (Normal 150–400)]

Xanthine oxidase, the enzyme inhibited by allopurinol, also converts mercaptopurine to 6-thiouric acid.[170] Thus, allopurinol may markedly increase the plasma concentrations of oral mercaptopurine by inhibiting first-pass metabolism and this may lead to toxicity.[171] Although this is a potentially serious drug interaction, it is usually irrelevant for most patients with ALL since these agents are rarely used together. Allopurinol usually is employed early in the first week of induction therapy, and patients do not receive mercaptopurine until they finish induction therapy and enter the continuation or maintenance phase of leukemia treatment approximately four to eight weeks later.

28. What is the goal of the induction therapy which J.B. will receive and which agents should be utilized to achieve this goal?

Goal of Induction. The goal of remission induction therapy is complete remission (i.e., the inability to detect leukemic cells in the peripheral blood or the bone marrow). J.B.'s peripheral blood values must be within the normal range and the bone marrow must reveal less than 5% lymphoblasts.[87,172] This definition also assumes the absence of lymphoblasts in the cerebrospinal fluid. While these findings indicate an adequate response to chemotherapy, they do not indicate a cure. Most patients have a total of 10¹² cells at diagnosis, and successful induction regimens reduce this cell load by 99% to 10⁹.[173,174] Therefore, continuation of therapy will be required for J.B. to further reduce the leukemic cell population and to increase his chances of long-term survival. Without continuation of therapy, the vast majority of patients will relapse within one to two months.[175,176]

Induction Combination Chemotherapy. The agents most commonly used in remission induction therapy are vincristine (Oncovin) and prednisone (Deltasone). The prednisone dose is not routinely tapered at the end of induction treatment.[89,90] This two-drug combination (see Table 92.7) is effective in inducing remissions in approximately 85% of children with ALL.[177–179] While no chemotherapy drug meets the criteria of an ideal agent (i.e., toxic only to leukemic cells and active in all phases of the cell cycle), prednisone and vincristine come closest to this ideal. To improve the success in attaining complete remission, additional agents have been added to vincristine and prednisone (see Table 92.7). The two most frequently employed agents are L-asparaginase (Elspar) and an anthracycline, such as daunorubicin (Cerubidine) or doxorubicin (Adriamycin). The addition of a third drug improves the remission induction rate and prolongs remission duration.[190–194] It is still controversial whether a fourth drug adds additional benefit to induction therapy. However, a four-drug regimen plus a more intense continuation therapy has improved remission duration.[90,91,150] The fourth drug varies from institution to institution. Some use a single high dose of methotrexate in place of L-asparaginase for remission induction.[90,195,196]

If complete remission is not achieved with three agents by the end of induction, patients are treated with additional agents (e.g., an additional 2 to 4 weeks of daunorubicin and prednisone, initiation of cytarabine with additional asparaginase, vincristine and prednisone × 1 to 2 weeks).[191,197] There is no consensus about the most effective agents or schedules when a complete remission has not been attained by the end of the induction period. Most such patients have a decreased survival and a higher relapse rate.[198]

Early intensive treatment with a three or four drug induction regimen has benefits for the majority of children with ALL. This treatment strategy supports the hypothesis of Goldie and Coldman, that intensification of early treatment may decrease the chance that drug resistance will develop, therefore, potentially increasing the proportion of long-term relapse-free survivors.[199] Although J.B. is a patient with a low risk of relapse, a three-drug induction regimen consisting of vincristine, prednisone, and L-asparaginase may further improve his chances for long-term, disease-free survival. However, use of a two-drug regimen in children such as J.B. with no high risk features is not unreasonable and is usually quite successful. Since most of the studies which determined the value of three- or four-drug induction were performed before risk criteria were refined, the number of low- versus high-risk patients included in these studies is unclear as is the number of low risk patients who were candidates for two-drug induction therapy.

Vincristine Toxicity

29. J.B. is discharged from the hospital during the second week of induction chemotherapy. Results of his CBC and differential indicate that he is responding well to his chemotherapy (i.e., WBC count 2600/mm³, neutrophils 69%, lymphocytes 22%, platelets 229,000/m³, Hct 28.6%, and blasts 0). However, during the third week of induction chemotherapy, J.B. develops severe abdominal pain. It is discovered that he has not had a bowel movement in 6 days. J.B. also has been exhibiting "acting out" behaviors in recent days. How might these symptoms be explained? [SI units: WBC count 2.6 × 10⁹/L; neutrophils 0.69; lymphocytes 0.22; platelets 229 × 10⁹/L; Hct 0.286; blasts 0]

The use of vincristine is associated with an autonomic neuropathy, which may substantially reduce gastrointestinal motility;[200] in severe cases, paralytic ileus may result. Constipation often is accompanied by colicky abdominal pain which may be quite distressing.[201] These symptoms usually become apparent three to ten days following drug administration and usually resolve over several days. Prophylactic use of a stool softener [docusate (Colace)] or laxative [senna (Senokot)] may lessen the severity of J.B.'s constipation and facilitate defecation.

J.B.'s emotional changes are likely the result of the prednisone he is receiving. Emotional lability, sleep disturbances, depressed mood, and listlessness have occurred during corticosteroid therapy in children with ALL.[202] These behavioral changes can be quite disruptive and parents should be prepared for them in advance. Behavioral disturbances resolve within two weeks following prednisone discontinuation.[202]

CNS Preventative Therapy

30. In addition to the above mentioned drugs, J.B. also receives intrathecal (IT) chemotherapy for CNS prophylaxis with methotrexate, cytarabine (Cytosar-U), and hydrocortisone (Solu-Cortef) at the beginning (week 1) and end (week 4) of induction therapy. What is the purpose of intrathecal chemotherapy? What are the various treatments available for intrathecal chemotherapy and what determines which one was chosen for J.B.?

Purpose. The purpose of intrathecal or central nervous system preventative therapy is to decrease the chance of relapse within the central nervous system and increase J.B.'s chance of long-term survival. Before CNS preventative therapy was routine, the CNS was the most common site of leukemic relapse and predicted bone marrow relapse.[203,204] Patients at greatest risk for CNS relapse include those with very high initial white blood cell counts, T-cell ALL, and infants.[113,205,206] Since many antileukemic agents do not distribute into the cerebrospinal fluid, it may function as a sanctuary site for leukemic lymphoblasts. The aim is to eradicate any CNS leukemic lymphoblasts present at diagnosis and to prevent the emergence of a relapse within the CNS.

Craniospinal Radiation. All centers treating childhood ALL employ some form of CNS preventative therapy, although different regimens are used. The first successful CNS prophylaxis treatments were 2400 cGy of craniospinal radiation with or without IT methotrexate, which markedly reduced the CNS relapse rate.[207,208] To avoid the myelosuppression and reductions in spinal growth due to craniospinal irradiation, the standard CNS preventative therapy was modified to 2400 cGy of cranial irradiation along with IT methotrexate. This standard therapy was questioned with the emergence of adverse effects such as decreased intellectual function and dysfunctions of the neuroendocrine system.[209–212] As a result, clinicians began to seek alternative, potentially safer forms of CNS preventative therapy. For example lower doses (1800 cGy) of cranial irradiation were combined with IT methotrexate to reduce the CNS effects.[205,213] The 1800 cGy dose has proven to be equivalent to 2400 cGy in preventing CNS relapse,[213] and the results of a long-term follow-up study indicate mild, but diffuse deficits in information processing in patients receiving 2400 cGy of cranial irradiation but not in patients treated with 1800 cGy. This suggests that the lower radiation dose reduces neuropsychological morbidity.[214] Other approaches include the use triple intrathecal chemotherapy (methotrexate, cytarabine, and hydrocortisone), intermediate dose methotrexate either alone or with IT methotrexate, and high-dose methotrexate.[215–219] Patients receiving triple IT chemotherapy may be administered all three of these agents as a

Table 92.7	Induction Regimens for Childhood Acute Lymphocytic Leukemia[89,90,177,179–194]	
Agent	Route	Dose/Schedule
Prednisone	PO	40 mg/m²/day × 28 days
Vincristine with:	IV	1.5 mg/m²/week (*max*: 2 mg) × 4
Asparaginase *and/or*	IM	10,000 units/m² 3 × week × 9 doses
Daunorubicin *and/or*	IV	25 mg/m² on days 2, 8, ±15
Methotrexate	IV	4 gm/m² on day 1

single injection since they are all compatible when admixed together in 0.9% sodium chloride.[220]

Intrathecal Chemotherapy: Chronic Adverse Effects. The chronic toxicities of IT chemotherapy are now being determined. When examined for effects on growth, triple IT chemotherapy demonstrated no effect on the final height achieved by children in contrast to a reduced final height in patients receiving cranial irradiation.[221] It is still unclear whether IT chemotherapy results in neuropsychological deficits. At least one study of patients receiving IT chemotherapy without cranial irradiation has demonstrated deficits in higher order cognitive function tasks and learning disabilities in mathematics.[222] However, these learning deficits may be due to IT chemotherapy, systemic chemotherapy, missed school days, or a combination of factors.

Since patients differ in their risk of developing CNS leukemia, CNS preventative therapy should be tailored accordingly. For patients with standard-risk ALL, cranial irradiation is unnecessary.[205] Patients at low risk of relapse may be treated with either triple IT chemotherapy or IT methotrexate, depending upon the institutional protocol.[216,223] For patients with a greater risk of CNS relapse, several regimens offer equivalent protection: triple IT chemotherapy, IT chemotherapy combined with intermediate dose methotrexate, high dose methotrexate, or cranial irradiation (1800 cGy) combined with IT methotrexate.[216,217,224] Most centers give cranial irradiation along with IT methotrexate in patients at high risk of CNS relapse, such as those with T-cell ALL. However, recent evidence suggests that the use of high-dose methotrexate may be equivalent.

31. Dosage. J.B. is at a low risk for CNS relapse and the decision is made to treat him with the triple IT combination. How should J.B.'s IT chemotherapy be dosed?

High chemotherapy concentrations can be attained within the CSF with relatively low doses because the cerebral spinal fluid volume of distribution is small relative to the peripheral plasma volume (140 versus 3500 mL).[225,226] Drug exposure also is maximized by the longer half-life of most drugs in the CSF.[227] The approach used for IT dosing differs from systemic administration which is based upon body weight or body surface area. CSF methotrexate concentrations appear to correlate better with patient age than size.[228] As seen in Figure 92.4, the CSF volume in children approaches that of an adult by the age of three years. Since CSF volume does not correlate with body surface area, IT doses based upon body size will result in subtherapeutic concentrations in children and potentially toxic concentrations in adults. The age-based dosing regimens shown in Table 92.8 are less neurotoxic and as-

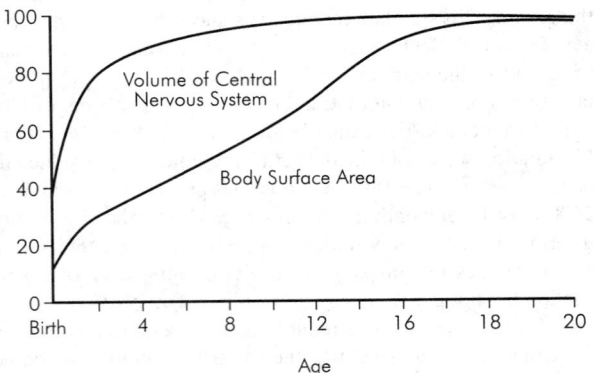

Fig 92.4 Relationship Between Body Surface Area and CNS Volume as a Function of Age CNS volume increases at a more rapid rate than body surface area, reaching adult volume by three years of age. Reprinted with permission from PRR Inc. Oncology 1991;5:107.

Table 92.8	Dosage Regimen for IT Methotrexate Based Upon Patient Age[a]		
Patient Age	Methotrexate	Hydrocortisone	Cytarabine
<1 yr	6 mg	6 mg	12 mg
1 yr	8 mg	8 mg	16 mg
2 yr	10 mg	10 mg	20 mg
≥3 yr	12 mg	12 mg	24 mg
≥9 yr	15 mg	15 mg	30 mg
[a] Adapted from reference 228.			

sociated with a lower rate of CNS relapse than doses based upon size.[229] Using this dosing regimen, J.B.'s dose of IT methotrexate should be 12 mg. The doses of intrathecal cytarabine and hydrocortisone will by 24 mg and 12 mg, respectively. These doses also are based upon age, but no literature exists to support how they were derived. Nevertheless, empirical evidence supports their efficacy.[216]

32. Acute Adverse Effects. J.B. develops severe nausea and vomiting following his triple IT chemotherapy treatment. Is this common following IT chemotherapy? What can be done to decrease this toxicity for future IT chemotherapy treatments?

Several acute toxicities have been reported following IT chemotherapy. Acute arachnoiditis may occur 12 to 24 hours after injection, resulting in headaches, nausea, vomiting, and various other signs of increased intracranial pressure.[230] Severe symptoms occurred in 4 of 91 children receiving combination intrathecal chemotherapy.[231] Intrathecal methotrexate alone produces these side effects in 38% of cases.[232] Fortunately, these reactions are usually self limiting and can be reduced by use of doses based upon patient age.[229]

Nausea and vomiting due to IT chemotherapy can be quite severe[233] and probably are caused by direct contact between the chemotherapy and the chemoreceptor trigger zone. Intravenous ondansetron (a 5-HT$_3$ antagonist) at a dose of 0.15 mg/kg before and three to four hours following IT chemotherapy can markedly reduce the incidence and severity of nausea and vomiting secondary to triple IT chemotherapy.[233] The efficacy of ondansetron is consistent with animal data demonstrating that 5-HT$_3$ antagonists administered directly into the brain stem can block the emetic response of systemically administered chemotherapy.[234] (Also see Chapter 105: Nausea and Vomiting.)

Rarely, a form of methotrexate neurotoxicity resulting in either paraplegia or necrotizing leukoencephalopathy may occur.[235–237] Leukoencephalopathy is associated with cranial irradiation given before or during intrathecal therapy.[237] The preservatives in the chemotherapy diluents (methylhydroxylbenzoate and benzyl alcohol) rather than the chemotherapy agents are thought to be responsible for the paraplegia. This emphasizes the importance of diluting intrathecal chemotherapy with a preservative-free diluent.[235]

Maintenance Therapy

33. Following completion of his induction treatment, J.B. is scheduled to receive maintenance treatment. His parents are shocked treatment will be of such a long duration and question whether this is necessary since J.B. is already in remission. What is the purpose of J.B.'s maintenance or continuation treatment for his ALL? Which agents should be used in J.B. for this phase of therapy?

Purpose. The purpose of maintenance or continuation treatment is to sustain the complete remission achieved from induction chemotherapy. Early trials have shown that without maintenance treatment, the majority of ALL patients will relapse within one to two months.[175,176] It must be stressed that patients who have successfully responded to induction therapy will still have a high leukemic cell burden (although undetectable) which must be eradicated by additional treatment. This is supported by the results of bone marrow biopsies from patients who have relapsed after several months to years of treatment. The cytogenetic characteristics of the leukemic cells in relapsed patients are identical to those at the time of diagnosis.[238,239]

Chemotherapy Regimens. Drugs that are effective during induction therapy cannot, by themselves, prolong remission during maintenance therapy.[88] However, other agents are quite effective in sustaining a complete remission. Two of the most effective drugs are mercaptopurine (Purinethol) and methotrexate.[191,240,242] Methotrexate is most effective and least toxic when administered intermittently, usually on a weekly basis in oral doses of 20 mg/m^2/week. Mercaptopurine, however, is effective and well tolerated orally when dosed on a daily bases, usually at a dose of 50 mg/m^2/day.

Other agents have been added to or used in place of standard maintenance therapy with mercaptopurine and methotrexate to improve remission duration and to increase a patient's chances for long-term survival. These newer, more aggressive maintenance regimens include intermittent pulses of vincristine and prednisone, intensification phases with etoposide (Vepesid) and cytarabine, intermediate-dose methotrexate, and rotational combinations of various agents.[89–91,106,150,243–245] The value of these additional agents and more aggressive dosing schemes is still controversial.[245] Impressive improvements in disease-free survival are achieved with several of these regimens, especially in patient populations with a high risk of relapse.[89–91] There is also emerging evidence that monthly pulses of vincristine and prednisone offer advantages (lower bone marrow and testicular relapse rates) in standard-risk patients as well.[246] It is also unclear which regimen is most optimal for specific patients because risk criteria used to assign patients to intensive maintenance protocols have varied among investigators and those who have received more intensive maintenance treatment oftentimes have received more intensive induction treatment as well.

The available evidence suggests that a patient like J.B. with standard-risk ALL will benefit from use of daily mercaptopurine 50 mg/m^2 orally and weekly methotrexate 20 mg/m^2 orally along with periodic pulse therapy with vincristine 1.5 mg/m^2 for one day and prednisone 40 mg/m^2 orally for seven days every four weeks. In addition, IT chemotherapy should be repeated every 8 to 12 weeks.

34. *Potential Problems.* **What potential problems with mercaptopurine and methotrexate might J.B. experience that could increase his risk of treatment failure?**

Diurnal variation of methotrexate concentration and marked interpatient variability in absorption and metabolism of mercaptopurine have been described.[247–249] Patients receiving half-doses of these agents have shorter remission durations,[250] but those who tolerate maximal protocol dosages also may be at greater risk of relapse.[120] Patients who are able to tolerate maximal doses without significant myelosuppression may require even higher doses than are recommended in some protocols. Since bioavailability is a concern for both agents and since some patients, particularly males, may be able to tolerate high dosages without toxicity, some have suggested that the dose be adjusted upward based upon the degree of leukopenia (i.e., WBC <3500/mm^3).[251] Although no definitive guidelines have been developed, dose increases of 10% to 25% of both methotrexate and mercaptopurine every three to four weeks may allow the target WBC (1500–3500/mm^3) to be achieved.

For J.B., this means an increase in mercaptopurine to an alternating daily schedule of 50 mg with 75 mg and a methotrexate dose of 22.5 mg/week. Although parenteral administration of methotrexate is logical, it does not consistently improve the results of therapy.[252,253] To assess whether J.B. is receiving an adequate dose, weekly WBC counts are essential. This will allow one to accurately appraise the adequacy of his dose and follow his disease status to assure that remission is continuing. If an inadequate degree of myelosuppression is demonstrated, J.B.'s compliance should be investigated since decreased compliance is a frequent problem in the therapy of childhood ALL.[125,254,255]

35. *Duration of Therapy.* **How long should J.B.'s maintenance therapy be continued?**

Most centers treat children with ALL for two and one-half to three years, which includes the length of induction therapy.[256–258] Extending maintenance treatment to five or six years adds no benefit.[256,257] Other data suggest that a shorter duration of 18 months may be adequate for girls, but not for boys.[259] The majority of patients who relapse do so during therapy or within the first year of completing therapy. Following the second year of therapy and for every year thereafter, relapses become much less common but are occasionally observed. Some centers are exploring whether more intensive treatment protocols could decrease the duration of maintenance treatment, since the optimal duration is based upon less aggressive protocols. Until there is more conclusive evidence regarding the duration of ALL maintenance therapy, patients with J.B.'s characteristics should receive chemotherapy for two and one-half to three years.

High-Risk ALL

36. *Asparaginase: Adverse Effects.* **N.B. is a 12-year-old Native American male with a 3-week history of increasing fatigue, recurrent sore throat and fever, and diffuse bone pain. Upon physical examination, he is found to have considerable pallor and hepatosplenomegaly. The CBC reveals a WBC count of 30,000/mm^2 (95% lymphocytes and 5% neutrophils), hematocrit of 18.2%, and a platelet count of 19,000/mm^3. A bone marrow biopsy confirms the diagnosis of ALL and shows that 95% of the bone marrow is replaced by leukemic lymphoblasts. The leukemic cells are pre-B and their DNA index is 1.0. A lumbar puncture reveals no blasts within the CSF.**

N.B. is started on allopurinol 200 mg/day PO along with hydration and blood and platelet transfusions. Based upon his age and DNA index, N.B. is judged to have high-risk ALL and is begun on an intensive protocol. The induction regimen consists of 4 drugs including prednisone 40 mg/m^2/day PO on days 1–29, vincristine 1.5 mg/m^2 IV weekly × 4 weeks, asparaginase 10,000 units/m^2 IM on days 2, 5, 8, 12, 15, and 19, and daunorubicin 25 mg/m^2 IV on days 2, 8, and 15. Triple IT therapy consists of methotrexate 15 mg, cytarabine 30 mg, and hydrocortisone 15 mg on days 2 and 22.

N.B. achieves a complete remission based upon the results of a bone marrow specimen on day 14, but he develops severe abdominal pain and hyperglycemia on day 20 of induction. N.B. has been having normal bowel movements and does not have abdominal distention. The serum amylase is markedly elevated to 450 IU/L (Normal: 111–296). Which agent is likely responsible for N.B.'s abdominal pain? What other complications are associated with this chemotherapy agent? [SI units: WBC count 30 × 10^9/L with 0.95 lymphocytes and 0.05 neutrophils; Hct 0.182; platelets 19 × 10^9/L; amylase 450 U/L (Normal: 111–296)]

Pancreatitis has been noted in children following the administration of asparaginase.[260] As illustrated by N.B., this often presents as abdominal pain accompanied by an elevated serum amylase and hyperglycemia. Insulin may be required to control the hyperosmotic, nonketotic hyperglycemia which may result.[261,262] The pancreatitis is occasionally severe and fatalities have been reported.[263]

Unfortunately, the serum amylase may not predict whether patients will develop acute fatal pancreatitis.[263] N.B.'s pancreatitis secondary to asparaginase makes further treatment with this agent inadvisable. Since this reaction is not a hypersensitivity reaction, further therapy with the Erwinia form of asparaginase is also not recommended. N.B. may be treated with supportive care and insulin therapy. He should recover fully and be able to receive further chemotherapy.

Hypersensitivity reactions are frequent, occurring in 20% to 35% of patients and they are usually mild. The mild reactions generally present as urticarial eruptions which can sometimes be controlled with antihistamines.[261] Severe anaphylactoid reactions may occur and can be fatal.[264] Clinical reactions correlate better with asparaginase-specific IgG rather than IgE antibodies, and severe hypersensitivity reactions can be explained in most instances by complement activation.[267,268]

Anaphylactoid reactions appear to be less common when asparaginase is administered intramuscularly (IM).[265,266] This is because the slow absorption of asparaginase following IM administration results in delayed, less severe acute reactions. Because these reactions can be delayed, prolonged monitoring is recommended after IM asparaginase.[269] The majority of serious hypersensitivity reactions tend to occur after the patient has received several doses.

Preparations. Asparaginase is available from two natural sources, *Escherichia coli* (commercially available) and Erwinia (investigational, available from the National Cancer Institute). Since these two preparations may not be cross-reactive, the Erwinia product may be substituted for the *E. coli* product when hypersensitivity reactions occur and further dosing is planned.[270] However, while most patients do not appear to be cross-reactive to the Erwinia product, cross reactions occur in 17% to 26% of patients.[90,197,271] The incidences of hypersensitivity reactions are equivalent for these two preparations.[270]

Asparaginase also is available as an altered form known as PEG-asparaginase (Oncaspar). This agent is formed by covalently linking monomethoxypolyethylene glycol (PEG) to *E. coli* asparaginase. PEG-asparaginase has a prolonged half-life of 5.8 days versus 1.2 days for *E. coli* asparaginase and appears to be safe and effective even in patients with prior reactions to *E. coli* and Erwinia asparaginase.[272] The prolonged half-life allows for less frequent (i.e., every 2 week) dosing of PEG-asparaginase than for the natural source asparaginase products (i.e., 3 times a week).[273] For all three preparations of asparaginase, some patients without acute allergic reactions may develop anti-asparaginase antibodies that are associated with rapid clearance of asparaginase from the circulation and possible development of drug resistance.[272–275] Therefore, an unknown number of patients treated with asparaginase may not benefit due to rapid clearance. While plasma concentration monitoring would be helpful, convenient assay methods are not available for routine use.

37. Etoposide. N.B. is continued on treatment with an intensification or consolidation phase for 3 weeks (see Table 92.9). This consists of 3 treatments of IV teniposide (Vumon) 200 mg/m² and cytarabine 300 mg/m², two IV (high-dose) methotrexate 2 gm/m² treatments, and a third IT treatment. Following completion of the intensification therapy, N.B. is started on a rotating continuation regimen (see Table 92.9). This consists of 4 pairs of drugs rotating weekly over 120 weeks as follows: IV etoposide 300 mg/m² and cyclophosphamide (Cytoxan) 300 mg/m², PO mercaptopurine 75 mg/m² and IM methotrexate 40 mg/m², IV teniposide 150 mg/m² and cytarabine 300 mg/m², and IV vincristine 1.5 mg/m² and PO prednisone 40 mg/m². He also receives triple IT therapy every 8 weeks. These agents are delayed by 1 week if the absolute neutrophil count (ANC) is <1000/mm³ or platelets are <100,000/mm³. During the tenth

Table 92.9	Intensification and Continuation Protocol for High-Risk Acute Lymphocytic Leukemia[a]		
Agent	Dose/m²	Route[d]	Schedule
Intensification			
Teniposide	200 mg	IV	Days 29, 32, 36
Cytarabine	300 mg	IV	Days 29, 32, 36
Methotrexate	15 mg	IT[b]	Day 36
Hydrocortisone	15 mg	IT	Day 36
Cytarabine	30 mg	IT	Day 36
Methotrexate	2000 mg	IV	Days 44, 51
Continuation[c]			
Etoposide	300 mg	IV × 1	Week 1
Cyclophosphamide	300 mg	IV × 1	Week 1
Mercaptopurine	75 mg	PO daily	Week 2–4
Methotrexate	40 mg	IM weekly	Week 2–4
Teniposide	150 mg	IV × 1	Week 6
Cytarabine	300 mg	IV × 1	Week 6
Prednisone	40 mg	PO daily	Week 7
Vincristine	1.5 mg	IV × 1	Week 7
Methotrexate	15 mg	IT	Week 7
Hydrocortisone	15 mg	IT	Week 7
Cytarabine	30 mg	IT	Week 7

[a] Adapted from references 89 and 90.
[b] IT dosing is based upon patient age, with a maximum dose of 15 mg.
[c] Continuation is repeated approximately every 8 weeks.
[d] IM = Intramuscular; IT = Intrathecal; IV = Intravenous; PO = Oral.

dose of etoposide, N.B. develops flushing, chills, urticaria, and hypotension. This reaction responds to discontinuation of the etoposide infusion and administration of IV diphenhydramine. Is this reaction common with epipodophyllotoxins such as etoposide? Is it possible for N.B. to receive additional etoposide and teniposide?

Hypersensitivity reactions, usually characterized by flushing, chills, and occasionally by bronchospasm and hypotension, are common following both teniposide and etoposide. In a recent trial, approximately one-half of children, receiving these agents repeatedly, experienced a hypersensitivity reaction.[276] Previous studies document hypersensitivity reactions in 2% to 11% of patients receiving teniposide.[277,278] These reactions appear to be more common in children with neuroblastoma and brain tumors (account for 45% to 82% of reactions) than in patients with other malignancies.[278,279] The higher incidence of hypersensitivity in the recent study is attributed to repeated epipodophyllotoxin exposure during prolonged therapy.[276] Fortunately, less than 2% of scheduled doses were discontinued due to severe reactions.[276] This trial also demonstrated that the risk of hypersensitivity reactions increased with the total cumulative dose up to an eventual plateau for both of these agents. These reactions may not become manifest until the infusion is complete. It does not appear that the excipients used in the formulation of teniposide and etoposide account for these reactions.[280] Rather, it appears that these reactions are concentration dependent, are not mediated by IgE, and are not related to Cremophor in the formulation.[280] Patients reacting to one of these agents are quite likely to experience a cross-reaction to the other.[276] The reactions often can be managed successfully with an antihistamine with or without a corticosteroid, and do not preclude additional courses.[276] When patients develop subsequent reactions, they are generally similar in severity to the initial reaction, with no worsening trend.[276] Thus, N.B. may continue to receive additional doses of teniposide and etoposide, but he should be premedicated with antihistamines with or without corticosteroids and he should be monitored closely for signs of hypersensitivity.

38. Secondary Acute Myelogenous Leukemia (AML). **Are there any long-term complications peculiar to the use of epipodophyllotoxins?**

Patients with childhood ALL who are receiving epipodophyllotoxins appear to be at increased risk for developing secondary acute myelogenous leukemia,[281] which is unresponsive to standard AML therapy.[281] No definitive data exist to predict an individual patient's risk for developing secondary AML, but rate estimates published by several investigators report 3.2% at six years; a cumulative risk at six years of 3.8% to 12.4%; and a relative risk of 3.4 to 39.4.[281–283] The higher risk values are associated with higher doses and more frequent administration of epipodophyllotoxins.[281,283] A significant risk of developing this complication exists, and should be weighed against the benefits of including epipodophyllotoxins in regimens of childhood ALL.

39. Methotrexate Concentration Monitoring. **N.B.'s methotrexate serum concentrations are monitored after the administration of high-dose methotrexate during the intensification phase, but not during the low-dose methotrexate used in the continuation phase. Why is concentration monitoring important when giving higher doses of methotrexate? Are methotrexate concentrations important in predicting the outcome of ALL therapy?**

Following high-dose methotrexate administration, concentration monitoring is crucial to establish the dose of leucovorin needed to prevent systemic methotrexate toxicity.[284] Before serum methotrexate concentrations were routinely monitored after high-dose methotrexate, severe gastrointestinal desquamation and myelosuppression led to fatalities in as many as 6% of patients.[285] Methotrexate concentrations are measured approximately 12 hours following completion of the methotrexate infusion and repeated daily until the concentration falls below the toxic threshold of 0.05 µmol/L. Patients who have unexpectedly high concentrations following high-dose methotrexate may require higher doses of leucovorin to circumvent methotrexate toxicity.[284] (See Chapter 93: Solid Tumors: Pediatric Osteosarcoma for details on monitoring methotrexate concentrations and dosing leucovorin.)

Recent reports have described the influence of serum concentrations of methotrexate on the outcome of ALL patients.[285,286] These studies have determined that children with higher methotrexate clearance values appear to be at higher risk of relapse, and suggest that concentration monitoring also may play a role in enhancing the long-term survival of these patients.[286] However, when follow-up was extended, the survival advantage reported in one of these studies was lost.[286,287] Data examining the predictive value of serum methotrexate concentrations in patients receiving lower doses of methotrexate did not demonstrate improved survival with either higher peak concentrations or drug exposure [i.e., area under the curve (AUC)].[252]

Thus, dose adjustment of methotrexate based upon serum concentrations is not warranted in N.B. and is not likely to influence his long-term survival. Dosage adjustment of high-dose methotrexate concentrations is only necessary for patients experiencing excess toxicity. N.B.'s low dose IM methotrexate therapy may be monitored using serial CBC determinations with dose adjustment based upon the degree of myelosuppression. It has been suggested that patients receiving low-dose methotrexate and mercaptopurine may benefit from administering both agents at maximally tolerated dose to achieve an ANC of 1000 to 2000/mm³ since the latter may be a more important indicator of long-term survival than serum methotrexate concentrations.[251,252]

Relapsed ALL

40. After 1 year of continuation therapy, N.B. develops leg pain. A CBC reveals an Hct of 29.5%, a platelet count of 39,000/mm³, and a WBC count of 12,300/mm³ with 80% lymphocytes, 18% blasts, and 2% neutrophils. A bone marrow biopsy confirms relapsed ALL, but the CSF is free of leukemic lymphoblasts. Would routine bone marrow biopsies of N.B. have allowed for early detection of N.B.'s relapse and an increased chance for long-term survival? What are N.B.'s chances of achieving a second remission and long term survival? Which treatments could be used in N.B. in an attempt to attain a complete remission and improve his chances of long-term survival? [SI units: Hct 0.295; platelets 39 × 10⁹/L; WBC count 12.3 × 10⁹/L with 0.8 lymphocytes, 0.18 blasts, and 0.02 neutrophils]

Unlike N.B., the majority of patients experiencing a relapse of ALL are asymptomatic and are diagnosed by routine bone marrow biopsies.[288] Although routine bone marrow biopsies will identify some bone marrow relapses before they become evident on a complete blood count, it has not been demonstrated that earlier identification of relapse (usually by a matter of a few weeks) impacts long-term survival.

N.B.'s chances of achieving a second remission are good. Approximately 80% to 85% of relapsed patients will attain a second complete remission with further chemotherapy.[288–291] Unfortunately, however, bone marrow relapse in childhood ALL is associated with poor long-term survival.[288–294] Only 6% to 29% of patients with bone marrow relapse may be rendered disease free for two years following relapse.[292–294] Allogeneic bone marrow transplantation for ALL in relapse results in a 10% to 20% long term leukemia-free survival.[295] However, better results with bone marrow transplantation are possible after a second remission has been achieved. Studies of children with ALL receiving bone marrow transplantation in second remission report five-year, disease-free survival rates of 40% and 64%.[296,297] These results are superior to those of chemotherapy in patients like N.B. who relapse within 18 months of achieving a complete remission.[298,299] Children who relapse beyond 18 months do not appear to gain additional benefit from bone marrow transplantation. N.B.'s family should be offered the option of a bone marrow transplant if testing determines that he has an acceptable bone marrow donor match in his family.

Agents used in salvage regiments are similar to those used in high-risk ALL regiments. In general, treatment usually consists of an intensive three- or four-agent induction regiment of vincristine, prednisone, and daunorubicin with or without asparaginase. This is accompanied by radiotherapy to sites of local relapse (e.g., testis, CNS) or IT chemotherapy in patients without concomitant CNS relapse.[290,293,294] After this regimen has been completed, the patient may continue with courses of intensification therapy, continuation therapy with triple IT therapy, and rotating cycles of chemotherapy similar to that described previously.[293,294] N.B. has already been treated with many of the chemotherapeutic agents: therefore, the regimen selected should include agents to which N.B. has had little or no exposure. This will theoretically increase his chances of maintaining a second remission. For example, a regimen that includes doxorubicin, asparaginase, and cyclophosphamide appears most appropriate for N.B.

Pediatric NonHodgkin's Lymphoma (NHL)

Lymphomas account for approximately 10% of all childhood malignancies,[300] although they are less common in children than in adults. Children under 16 years account for only 3% of all lymphoma cases.[301] The malignancy can occur in any lymphoid cell at any level of differentiation and appears to be a consequence of a genetic alteration.

Classification

Numerous classification systems for nonHodgkin's lymphoma (NHL) exist, and there is considerable variation in terminology between these systems.[302–306] Pediatric NHLs are best classified using histopathology which divides them into three different categories: lymphoblastic, small noncleaved, and large cell lymphomas.[307,308] This is a narrower range of histologic types than in adults.

Lymphoblastic lymphomas account for approximately 30% of childhood NHL, small noncleaved for about 50%, and large cell for the remainder.[309] The lymphoblastic lymphomas are usually immature T-cells that are histologically identical to the cells of acute lymphoblastic leukemia. The distinction between lymphoblastic lymphoma and ALL is made on the basis of bone marrow involvement, with ALL being diagnosed if there is greater than 25% bone marrow infiltration. This distinction is made by the amount of bone marrow infiltration that is present at the time of diagnosis. Small noncleaved lymphomas are B-cells and these may be further divided into Burkitt's and nonBurkitt's lymphomas. Large cell lymphomas may be T-cell or, more commonly B-cell in origin. They differ from small noncleaved lymphomas primarily in their larger cell size. Other lymphomas frequently included in this category but which do not possess all of the features of large cell lymphomas are immunoblastic lymphomas and Ki-1 anaplastic lymphomas.

Clinical Presentation

Pediatric patients with NHL may present with a number of different symptoms, many of which are related to the cell type of NHL. In general, these symptoms differ from those in adults due to the propensity of pediatric NHL to be extranodal in origin in contrast to the common nodal presentation of adult NHL.[309] Patients with lymphoblastic lymphoma commonly present with a mediastinal mass and/or pleural effusions.[309] They also may have pain, dyspnea, or swelling of the face and upper arms if superior vena caval obstruction is present. Lymphoblastic lymphoma also has a predilection for the bone marrow and the central nervous system.[310,311] Lymphadenopathy in patients with lymphoblastic lymphoma tends to be supradiaphragmatic. Patients with small noncleaved NHL typically present with an abdominal tumor along with abdominal pain and an alteration in bowel function, and possibly nausea and vomiting.[312] In addition, many cases of small noncleaved NHL present with bone marrow involvement.[313] Lymphadenopathy in these patients occurs typically below the diaphragm in the inguinal or iliac area. Large cell lymphomas may involve the gut or unusual sites such as the lung, face, or central nervous system.[309]

Staging

Several staging systems for pediatric NHL are used.[312] Most include four or more stages with stage I being defined as a single tumor and higher stages including cases with more than one anatomic site involved. The highest stage usually refers to patients with bone marrow and/or CNS involvement. The main predictor of outcome in pediatric NHL is tumor burden at presentation.[314,315] Serum concentrations of several different molecules, particularly interleukin IIR, help clinicians estimate tumor burden.[314–316]

Treatment

Lymphoblastic (T-Cell)

The primary treatment for all stages and histologic types of pediatric NHL is combination chemotherapy, because it is a generalized disease at the time of diagnosis.[309] Two of the most effective

protocols studied in lymphoblastic lymphoma are the German BFM and the Memorial Sloan-Kettering LSA_2L_2 protocols (see Table 92.10).[317–319] Both protocols employ an intensive scheme of eight to ten chemotherapy agents administered in two- or four-drug rotational combination cycles for a treatment duration of approximately two years. Agents which demonstrate efficacy in pediatric NHL include methotrexate, cyclophosphamide (Cytoxan), vincristine (Oncovin), daunorubicin (Cerubidine), cytarabine (Cytosar-U), asparaginase (Elspar), carmustine (BiCNU), mercaptopurine (Purinethol), hydroxyurea (Hydrea), thioguanine, prednisone (Deltasone), and teniposide (Vumon). Long-term disease free survival with the LSA_2L_2 protocol is approximately 60% to 80% for patients with advanced-stage disease and even higher for patients with early-stage disease.[320,321] Patients with localized small noncleaved lymphomas respond as adequately to a four-drug regimen (COMP, see Table 92.11) as they do to a ten-drug regimen.[319] Recent evidence suggests that a six-month course is as efficacious as the previously employed 18-month course for patients with localized small noncleaved lymphomas.[322] It is interesting that for patients with advanced stage small noncleaved lymphomas the treatment strategies useful in advanced stage lymphoblastic lymphoma have resulted in lower failure-free survival rates.[319–321] These patients with advanced stage small noncleaved lymphomas have responded adequately to protocols employing cyclophosphamide containing combinations with intermediate or high-dose

Table 92.10	LSA_2L_2 Regimen for Lymphoblastic Lymphomas[a]
Induction	
Cyclophosphamide	1 gm/m^2 IV on day 1
Vincristine	1.5 mg/m^2 IV (*max*: 2 mg) IV on days 1 and 4
Methotrexate	12 mg[b] IT on days 5, 31 and 34
Daunorubicin	60 mg/m^2 IV on days 12 and 13
Prednisone	60 mg/m^2 (*max*: 60 mg) PO daily in 3 divided doses on days 3–30, with doses decreasing to 0 on days 31–37
Consolidation	
Cytarabine	100 mg/m^2 daily × 5 days × 4 weeks
Thioguanine	50 mg/m^2 PO 8–12 hr after each cytarabine dose
Asparaginase	6000 units/m^2 IM daily × 14 days following completion of cytarabine
Methotrexate	12 mg IT twice (3 days apart) beginning 3 days after last asparaginase dose
Carmustine	60 mg/m^2 IV × 1, given 2–3 days after completion of methotrexate
Maintenance (Cycles Separated by 1–2 Weeks and Repeated For ≈15 Months)	
1) Thioguanine	300 mg/m^2 PO on days 1–4
Cyclophosphamide	600 mg/m^2 IV on day 5
2) Hydroxyurea	2.4 gm/m^2 PO on days 1–4
Daunorubicin	45 mg/m^2 IV on day 5
3) Methotrexate	10 mg/m^2 PO on days 1–4
Carmustine	60 mg/m^2 IV on day 5
4) Cytarabine	150 mg/m^2 IV on days 1–4
Vincristine	2 mg/m^2 (*max*: 2 mg) IV on day 5
5) Methotrexate	12 mg IT × 2 (3 days apart)

[a] Adapted from reference 319.
[b] Dosage based upon patient age.
[c] IM = Intramuscular; IT = Intrathecal; IV = Intravenous; PO = Oral.

methotrexate (e.g., COMP) and achieve overall survival rates of 50% to 75% as long as they do not have central nervous system or bone marrow involvement.[315,317,319,323] It has been demonstrated that treatment of patients with small noncleaved lymphomas without central nervous system involvement may require no more than three to four months of chemotherapy, with results equal or superior to earlier protocols of one to two years duration.[324–326] These results provide good evidence for limiting the treatment of patients with small noncleaved lymphoma to a few months.

Small Noncleaved (B-Cell)

The main differences between the treatment of lymphoblastic and small noncleaved lymphoma are the use of more agents including more frequent use of anthracyclines in the former and a shorter treatment duration and more frequent use of methotrexate in the latter. It appears that lymphoblastic lymphomas should be treated more like leukemias, with both a longer treatment duration and a greater number of agents. Patients with small noncleaved lymphoma with bone marrow or central nervous system involvement have recently been treated with both high-dose cytarabine and high-dose methotrexate with an impressive failure-free survival of 72%.[327]

Large Cell

Large cell lymphomas have responded well to both types of regimens.[319,328,329] Thus, the use of the shorter, less complicated small noncleaved cell protocols is appropriate. Patients who fail to respond may be treated with additional courses of their prescribed protocol in hopes of eventually inducing a response. They also may be candidates for autologous bone marrow transplantation.[330] Patients who relapse may be reinduced with intensive chemotherapy, but their prognosis for long-term survival is unfavorable.

Lymphoblastic Lymphoma

Treatment

41. Acute Treatment. D.B., a 16-year-old female, presents with a history of shortness of breath and chest pain for 3 weeks before admission. A mediastinal mass is found and a biopsy confirms a lymphoblastic (T-cell) lymphoma. A chest x-ray reveals a right pleural effusion. Laboratory values show: erythrocyte sedimentation rate (ESR) 35 (Normal: 0–20), WBC count 22,000/mm³ (Normal: 4500–11,000), and LD 1259 U/L (Normal: 280–540). The bone marrow, central nervous system, and abdomen are negative for lymphoma. How should D.B. be managed acutely? Besides chemotherapy, what types of adjunctive therapies should be initiated to minimize the acute effects of treatment?

Given D.B.'s shortness of breath and chest pain, it is likely that her mediastinal mass may be obstructing the superior vena cava. To alleviate this obstruction, the most appropriate course of action is to decrease the tumor mass by initiating chemotherapy as soon as possible. Radiation therapy offers no additional benefit in patients such as D.B., with a tumor such as NHL which is highly responsive to chemotherapy.[331] Due to the high cell kill which will result from the initial chemotherapy treatment, uric acid nephropathy is also possible. However, the risk of this complication is probably greater in patients with small noncleaved NHL where the fraction of cells in S-phase is higher.[332,333]

Alkaline diuresis and allopurinol should be instituted before chemotherapy to prevent this complication (see Acute Lymphoblastic Leukemia of Childhood). Since D.B. has a pleural effusion, fluids may collect in this third space resulting in weight gain and decreased urine output. Thus, in addition to placement of a chest tube with suction, D.B. should be given diuretics to maintain an adequate urine output. To minimize intravascular volume depletion

Table 92.11	COMP Protocol for Localized Small Noncleaved Lymphoma[a]
Induction	
Cyclophosphamide	1.2 gm/m² IV on day 1
Vincristine	2 mg/m² (*max*: 2 mg) IV on days 3, 10, 17, and 24
Methotrexate	12 mg[b] IT on days 5, 31, and 34
Methotrexate	300 mg/m² IV on day 12
Prednisone	60 mg/m² (*max*: 60 mg) PO daily in 3 divided doses on days 3–30, with doses decreasing to 0 on days 31–37
Maintenance (Repeated Q 28 days × 5)	
Cyclophosphamide	1 gm/m² IV on day 1
Vincristine	1.5 mg/m² (*max*: 2 mg) IV on days 1 and 15
Methotrexate	12 mg IT on day 1
Methotrexate	300 mg/m² IV on day 15
Prednisone	60 mg/m² (*max*: 60 mg) on days 1–5 (excluded from 1st maintenance cycle)

[a] Adapted from references 319 and 322.
[b] Dosage based upon patient age.

and maintain electrolyte balances, fluid inputs and outputs, body weight, and electrolyte panels should be monitored daily. These values should be used to make appropriate adjustments in her electrolyte and fluid balance.

42. Adverse Effects. D.B. is treated with a combination chemotherapy regimen designed from experience with the two most effective regiments used to date, the BFM and LSA₂L₂ treatment programs. She is to receive induction therapy for one month (1 cycle): cyclophosphamide 1000 mg/m² on day 1, weekly vincristine 1.5 mg/m² (maximum: 2.0 mg) on days 1, 8, 15, and 22, doxorubicin 50 mg/m² IV on days 12 and 13, and prednisone 40 mg/m²/day (divided into TID dosing) on days 1–28 with doses decreasing to 0 on days 29–35. Which acute adverse effects is D.B. likely to experience with these agents? How can they be monitored, minimized, and treated?

Several toxicities are expected with the four chemotherapy agents employed. For vincristine, both *constipation* and *neuropathy* are likely to appear during or following the four weeks of therapy.[334] Constipation can be prevented or minimized by use of stool softeners with or without a laxative.[335] Neuropathy may be painful (especially when jaw pain occurs), but can be managed with mild analgesic regimens consisting of NSAIDs and/or acetaminophen with codeine. Both toxicities are self-limiting and are not reasons to discontinue or decrease the dose of vincristine unless neuromuscular toxicity which presents as motor weakness develops.

Prednisone is likely to increase D.B.'s appetite and may cause gastritis, although divided doses will help to decrease stomach upset. In addition, prednisone-induced behavioral disturbances are not uncommon.[336]

Unlike prednisone and vincristine, both daunorubicin and cyclophosphamide produce significant *myelosuppression*. Leukopenia is the primary sign with the nadir occurring in approximately 8 to 14 days and recovery occurring by approximately day 21 following administration.[335] To allow for bone marrow recovery, additional treatment with myelosuppressive chemotherapy will not be given for about two to three weeks following administration.

Hemorrhagic cystitis may occur with cyclophosphamide, but it usually is associated with high-dose therapy or with prolonged administration,[335] which D.B. is not receiving. Vigorous intravenous hydration to maintain urine output of approximately 50 cc/hour/m^2 should reduce the risk of this toxicity at this dose. Since most of the induction regimen will be administered on an outpatient basis, patients and/or parents should be instructed to report signs or symptoms of infection (e.g., febrile episodes) immediately so that proper treatment may be instituted as soon as possible. To decrease the risk of hemorrhagic cystitis, parents should be instructed to report if patients are not urinating regularly following cyclophosphamide.

Nausea and vomiting are likely to be induced by both doxorubicin and cyclophosphamide.[337] D.B.'s chemotherapy regimen includes a corticosteroid (prednisone) which may provide some antiemetic activity.[338] However, to maximize tolerance to her chemotherapy, D.B. should receive a potent antiemetic. Ondansetron may be employed in this setting and is more effective than metoclopramide when either is combined with a corticosteroid.[180] Ondansetron also has a safety profile that is superior to that of metoclopramide in children.[181–183] Although ondansetron is synergistic with corticosteroids, D.B. may not require additional amounts since prednisone already is included in her chemotherapy regimen. Furthermore, ondansetron alone (0.15 mg/kg IV every 4 hours × 3) has been shown to be efficacious against cyclophosphamide-induced emesis.[184] If necessary, an additional dose of a corticosteroid (e.g., dexamethasone 0.25 to 0.5 mg/kg once) may be added to the antiemetic regimen without changing the prednisone dose.

CNS Prophylaxis

43. What is the importance of CNS prophylaxis for D.B. and what type of treatment regimen is typically employed?

All pediatric patients with NHL should receive some form of CNS prophylaxis. Although lymphoblastic lymphoma rarely presents with CNS involvement as illustrated by D.B., it was a common site of relapse before CNS prophylaxis was included as a routine part of the chemotherapy regimen.[310,311] Recurrence of NHL within the CNS is rare when intrathecal methotrexate and/or cytarabine are employed.[315,319] D.B. will be treated with triple intrathecal therapy consisting of methotrexate, hydrocortisone, and cytarabine every other week for eight doses for her initial phase of treatment.

44. Precautions. D.B.'s triple IT chemotherapy is to be administered on the same day as her vincristine dose. Are there any special precautions which should be taken when these medications are administered in close proximity?

Inadvertent intrathecal administration of vincristine is almost uniformly fatal,[185–187] although there is one report of a patient in whom death was prevented.[188] The clinical course in patients mistakenly given intrathecal vincristine typically has progressed from backache and headache on day one, muscle weakness (generalized) on day two, apnea on day five, loss of evidence of electroencephalographic activity by days seven to nine, and death on day 12.[185] To avoid the tragedy of intrathecal vincristine administration, vincristine should be admixed separately from intrathecal medications, specially labeled, and preferably delivered to the patient area for intravenous infusion following the administration of intrathecal medications.

Myelosuppression and Hematopoietic Recovery

45. Following completion of initial therapy, the chemotherapy plan for D.B. consists of a continuation regimen of 10 nine-week treatment cycles. Each cycle includes the following sequence of agents: 1) cytarabine 150 mg/m^2/day by continuous IV infusion × 72 hours and cyclophosphamide 75 mg/m^2 by slow IV push Q 12 hr × 6 doses (during cytarabine infusion); 2) vincristine 2.0 mg/m^2 (maximum: 2 mg) IV push, doxorubicin 30 mg/m^2 IV over 15 minutes, and both prednisone 120 mg/m^2/day PO and mercaptopurine 300 mg/m^2/day PO divided TID × 5 days; 3) teniposide 150 mg/m^2 by IV infusion over 45 minutes and cytarabine 300 mg/m^2 IV push following teniposide, repeated 3 days later. A repeat triple IT treatment also will be given during the teniposide/cytarabine sequence. Each cycle will be separated by ≈3 weeks to allow for hematopoietic recovery. How should D.B.'s hematopoietic recovery be monitored and what guidelines may be used to determine when it is appropriate for her to receive the next sequence of a treatment cycle?

D.B.'s hematopoietic recovery should be monitored weekly throughout the continuation phase with white blood cell and differential, platelet, and red blood cell counts. Hematopoietic recovery may be considered adequate for the next treatment if the absolute neutrophil count is ≥500/mm^3 and platelets have recovered to 100,000/mm^3. An ANC of less than 1000/mm^3 may sometimes lead to delayed myelosuppression with subsequent treatments, leading some clinicians to use an ANC of ≥1000/mm^3 as the threshold for initiating the next chemotherapy treatment.

Modification for Delayed Recovery

46. D.B. has received 6 of the 10 nine-week treatment cycles and has done well with no severe drug toxicities or signs of recurring NHL. After her last treatment with vincristine/doxorubicin/prednisone/mercaptopurine, her WBC count was slow to recover. Her ANC was 200/mm^3 2 weeks later and this caused a 1 week delay in the next treatment (teniposide/cytarabine). What modifications should be made with her next 4-day treatment sequence?

Delayed recovery after repeated courses of myelosuppressive chemotherapy is common. The myelosuppressive agents in this four-drug regimen which have likely resulted in delayed recovery are doxorubicin and mercaptopurine. Thus, doses of these agents should be reduced by 25% in subsequent treatments. These reductions usually will not compromise antitumor efficacy and will allow subsequent chemotherapy treatments to be given on schedule. Recent work with the colony stimulating factor, sargramostim (GM-CSF), indicates that it may decrease the risk for septicemia and enhance on-schedule administration of aggressive chemotherapy in pediatric patients with NHL.[189]

References

1   **Devine SM, Larson RA.** Acute leukemia in adults: recent developments in diagnosis and treatment. CA Cancer J Clin. 1994;44:326.

2   **Fentiman IS et al.** A comparison of intracavitary talc and tetracycline for the control of pleural effusions secondary to breast cancer. Eur J Cancer Clin Oncol. 1986;22:1079–81.

3   **Crowther D et al.** Management of adult acute myelogenous leukemia. Br Med J. 1973;1:131.

4   **Wiernik PH.** Acute leukemias. In: DeVita VT et al., eds. Cancer. Principles and Practice of Oncology. 3rd ed. Philadelphia: Lippincott; 1989:1809–835.

5   **Frei E et al.** Dose schedule and antitumor studies of arabinosylcytosine. Cancer Res. 1967;29:1325.

6   **Rai KR et al.** Treatment of acute myelocytic leukemia: a study by Cancer and Leukemia Group B. Blood. 1981; 58:1203.

7   **Wiernik PJ et al.** Cytarabine plus idarubicin or daunorubicin as induction and consolidation therapy for previously untreated adults with newly diagnosed acute myelogenous leukemia. Blood. 1992:313.

8   **Berman E et al.** Results of a randomized trial comparing idarubicin and cytosine arabinoside with daunorubicin and cytosine arabinoside in adult patients with newly diagnosed acute myelogenous leukemia. Blood. 1991;77: 1666.

9   **Stone RM, Mayer RJ.** The unique aspections of acute promyelocytic leukemia. J Clin Oncol. 1990;8:1913.

10 **Brietman TR et al.** Terminal differentiation of human promyelocytic leukemic cells in primary culture in response to retinoic acid. Blood. 1981; 57:1000.

11 **Warrell RP et al.** Differentiation therapy of acute promyelocytic leukemia with tretinoin (all-trans-retinoic acid). N Engl J Med. 1991;324:1385–393.

12 **Fenaux P et al.** Effect of all transretinoic acid in newly diagnosed acute promyelocytic leukemia: results of a multi center randomized trial. Blood. 1993;82:3241.

13 **Castaigne S et al.** All-trans retinoic acid as a differentiation therapy for acute promyelocytic leukemia: I. Clinical results. Blood. 1990;76:1704.

14 **Frankel SR et al.** The "retinoic acid syndrome" in acute promyelocytic leukemia. Ann Intern Med. 1992;117:292.

15 **Al-Kawas FH et al.** Allopurinol hepatotoxicity. Ann Intern Med. 1981;95: 588.

16 **Hande KR et al.** Severe allopurinol toxicity. Am J Med. 1984;76:47.

17 **Souza LM et al.** Recombinant human granulocyte-colony stimulating factor: effects on normal and leukemic myeloid cells. Science. 1986;232:61.

18 **American Society of Clinical Oncology (ASCO).** ASCO recommendations for the use of hematopoietic colony-stimulating factors: evidence-based, clinical practice guidelines. J Clin Oncol. 1994;12:2471–508.

19 **Ohno R et al.** Effect of granulocyte colony stimulating factor after intensive induction therapy in relapsed or refractory acute leukemia: a randomized controlled study. N Engl J Med. 1990; 323:871.

20 **Van Sloten K et al.** Evaluation of levamisole as an adjuvant to chemotherapy for treatment of ANLL. Cancer. 1983;51:1576.

21 **Cassileth PA et al.** Prolonged unmaintained remission after intensive consolidation therapy in adult acute nonlymphocytic leukemia. Cancer Treat Rep. 1987;71:137.

22 **Tallman MS et al.** Evaluation of intensive postremission chemotherapy for adults with acute nonlymphocytic leukemia using high-dose cytosine arabinoside with L-asparaginase and amsacrine with etoposide. J Clin Oncol. 1987;5:918.

23 **Wolff SN et al.** High-dose cytosine arabinoside and daunorubicin as consolidation therapy for acute nonlymphocytic leukemia in first remission: an update. Semin Oncol. 1987;14(Suppl. 1): 12.

24 **Buchner T et al.** Intensified induction and consolidation with or without maintenance chemotherapy for acute myeloid leukemia (AML): two multicenter studies of the German AML cooperative group. J Clin Oncol. 1985;3: 1583.

25 **Rohatiner AZ, Lister TA.** The treatment of acute myelogenous leukemia. In: Henderson E, Lister TA, eds. Leukemia. 5th ed. WB Saunders: Philadelphia; 1990:485–514.

26 **Graves T, Hooks MA.** Drug-induced toxicities associated with high-dose cytosine arabinoside infusions. Pharmacotherapy. 1989;9:23.

27 **Herzig RH et al.** Central nervous system toxicity with high-dose cytosine arabinoside. Semin Oncol. 1985;12 (Suppl. 3):233.

28 **Ritch PS et al.** Ocular toxicity from high-dose cytosine arabinoside. Cancer. 1983;51:430.

29 **Barnett M et al.** Central nervous system toxicity of high-dose cytosine arabinoside. Semin Oncol. 1985;12 (Suppl. 3):227.

30 **Champlin RE et al.** Treatment of acute myelogenous leukemia in the elderly. Semin Oncol. 1989;16:51.

31 **Foon KA et al.** Intensive chemotherapy is the treatment of choice for elderly patients with acute myelogenous leukemia. Blood. 1981;58:467.

32 **Beguin Y et al.** Treatment of acute nonlymphocytic leukemia in young and elderly patients. Cancer. 1985;56: 41.

33 **Yates J et al.** Cytosine arabinoside with daunorubicin or Adriamycin for therapy of acute myelocytic leukemia. A CALGB study. Blood. 1982;60:454.

34 **Kahn SB et al.** Full-dose versus attenuated dose daunorubicin, cytosine arabinoside and 6-thioguanine in the treatment of acute nonlymphocytic leukemia in the elderly. J Clin Oncol. 1984; 2:865.

35 **Herzig RH et al.** Cerebellar toxicity with high dose cytosine arabinoside. J Clin Oncol. 1987;5:927.

36 **Silver RT.** Chronic myeloid leukemia. Hematol Oncol Clin North Am. 1990; 4:319.

37 **Morrison VA.** Chronic leukemias. CA Cancer J Clin. 1994;44:353.

38 **Sokal JE.** Evaluation of survival data from chronic myelocytic leukemia. Am J Hematol. 1979;1:493–500.

39 **Hehlmann R et al.** Randomized comparison of interferon-alpha with busulfan and hydroxyurea in chronic myelogenous leukemia. The German CML Study Group. Blood. 1994;84(12): 4064–77.

40 **Ozer H.** Biotherapy of chronic myelogenous leukemia with interferon. Semin Hematol. 1988;15(Suppl. 5):14.

41 **Alimena G et al.** Interferon alpha-2b as therapy for Ph1-positive chronic myelogenous leukemia. A study of 82 patients treated with intermittent or daily administration. Blood. 1988;72: 642.

42 **Talpaz M.** Use of interferon in the treatment of chronic myelogenous leukemia. Semin Oncol. 1994;21(6 Suppl. 14):3–7.

43 **Italian Cooperative Study Group on Chronic Myeloid Leukemia.** Interferon alfa-2a as compared with conventional chemotherapy for the treatment of chronic myeloid leukemia. N Engl J Med. 1994;330:820.

44 **Talpaz M et al.** Interferon-alpha produces sustained cytogenetic responses in chronic myelogenous leukemia. Philadelphia chromosome-positive-patients. Ann Intern Med. 1991;114:532.

45 **McGlave PB et al.** Allogeneic bone marrow transplantation as treatment for accelerating chronic myelogenous leukemia. Blood. 1984;63:219.

46 **Deisseroth AB et al.** In: DeVita VT et al., eds. Cancer. Principles and Practice of Oncology. 4th ed. Philadelphia: Lippincott; 1993:1965.

47 **Conley CL et al.** Genetic factors predisposing to chronic lymphocytic leukemia and to autoimmune disease. Medicine (Baltimore). 1980;5:323.

48 **Foon KA et al.** Chronic lymphocytic leukemia: new insights into biology and therapy. Ann Intern Med. 1990; 113:525.

49 **Han T et al.** Benign monoclonal B cell lymphocytosis—a benign variant of CLL: clinical, immunologic, phenotypic, and cytogenic studies in 20 patients. Blood. 1984;64:244.

50 **The French Cooperative Group on Chronic Lymphocytic Leukemia.** Effect of chlorambucil and therapeutic decision in initial forms of chronic lymphocytic leukemia (stage A): results of a randomized clinical trial on 612 patients. Blood. 1990;75:1414.

51 **Knospe WH et al.** Bi-weekly chlorambucil treatment of chronic lymphocytic leukemia. Cancer. 1974;33:555.

52 **Sawitsky A et al.** Comparison of daily versus intermittent chlorambucil and prednisone therapy in the treatment of patients with chronic lymphocytic leukemia. Blood. 1977;50:1049.

53 **Han T et al.** Chlorambucil vs. combined chlorambucil-corticosteroid therapy in chronic lymphocytic leukemia. Cancer. 1973;31:502.

54 **Han T, Rai KR.** Management of chronic lymphocytic leukemia. Hematol Oncol Clin North Am. 1990;4:431.

55 **Besa EC.** Use of intravenous immunoglobulin in chronic lymphocytic leukemia. Am J Med. 1984;76:209.

56 **Bussel JB et al.** Maintenance treatment of adults with chronic refractory immune thrombocytopenia purpura using repeated intravenous infusions of gammaglobulin. Blood. 1988;72:121.

57 **Grever MR et al.** Fludarabine monophosphate: a potentially useful agent in chronic lymphocytic leukemia. Nouv Rev Fr Hematol. 1988;30:457.

58 **Keating MJ et al.** Fludarabine: a new agent with marked cytoreductive activity against chronic lymphocytic leukemia. Blood. 1989;74:19.

59 **Cooperative Group for the Study of Immunoglobulin in Chronic Lymphocytic Leukemia.** Intravenous immunoglobulin for the prevention of infection in chronic lymphocytic leukemia: a randomized, controlled clinical trial. N Engl J Med. 1988;319:902.

60 **Levine AM.** AIDS-related malignancies: the emerging epidemic. J Nat Cancer Instit. 1993;85:1382.

61 **Biggar RJ.** Cancer in acquired immunodeficiency syndrome: an epidemiological assessment. Semin Oncol. 1990; 17:251.

62 **Centers for Disease Control.** Revision of the CDC surveillance definition for acquired immunodeficiency syndrome. MMWR. 1987;36(Suppl.):1S.

63 **Ziegler JL et al.** Non-Hodgkin's lymphoma in 90 homosexual men. N Engl J Med. 1984;311:565.

64 **Levine AM.** Lymphoma in acquired immunodeficiency syndrome. Semin Oncol. 1990;17:104.

65 **Karp JE et al.** Cancer in AIDS. In: Devita VT et al., eds. Cancer. Principles and Practice of Oncology. 4th ed. Philadelphia: Lippincott; 1993:2100.

66 **Bermudez MA et al.** Non-Hodgkin's lymphoma in a population with at risk for acquired immunodeficiency syndrome: indications for intensive chemotherapy. Am J Med. 1989;86:71.

67 **Raphael BG, Knowles DM.** Acquired immunodeficiency syndrome-associated non-Hodgkin's lymphoma. Semin Oncol. 1990;17:361.

68 **Levine AM et al.** HIV-positive high or intermediate grade lymphoma: prognostic factors related to survival. Blood. 1988;72:247. Abstract.

69 **Karp JE et al.** Cancer in AIDS. In: Devita VT et al., eds. Cancer. Principles and Practice of Oncology. 4th ed. Philadelphia: JB Lippincott; 1993: 2093–110.

70 **Gill P et al.** AIDS-related malignant lymphoma. Results of prospective treatment trials. J Clin Oncol. 1987;5: 1322.

71 **Kaplan LD et al.** AIDS-associated non-Hodgkin's lymphoma in San Francisco. JAMA. 1989;261:719.

72 **Levine AM et al.** Low-dose chemotherapy with central nervous system prophylaxis and azidothymidine maintenance in AIDS-related lymphoma: a prospective multi-institutional trial. JAMA. 1991;266:84.

73 **Gill PS et al.** AIDS-related malignant lymphoma: results of prospective treatment trials. J Clin Oncol. 1987;5:1322.

74 **Krown SE.** Neoplasia in AIDS. Bull N Y Acad Med. 1987;63:679.

75 **Hausheer FH, Yarbro JW.** Diagnosis and treatment of malignant pleural effusion. Semin Oncol. 1985;12:54.

76 **Pass HI.** Treatment of malignant pleural and pericardial effusions. In: DeVita VT et al., eds. Cancer. Principles and Practice of Oncology. 3rd ed. Philadelphia: Lippincott; 1989:2317–327.

77 **Ostrowski MJ.** An assessment of the long-term results of controlling the reaccumulation of malignant effusions using intracavitary bleomycin. Cancer. 1986;57:721.

78 **Paladine W et al.** Intracavitary bleomycin in the management of malignant effusions. Cancer. 1976;38:1903.

79 **Wallach HW.** Intrapleural tetracycline for malignant pleural effusions. Chest. 1975;68:510.

80 **Fox GN.** Intrapleural tetracycline therapy. JAMA. 1979;242:1362. Letter.

81 **Gupta N et al.** Intrapleural bleomycin vs tetracycline for control of malignant pleural effusions. A randomized trial. Proc Am Soc Clin Oncol. 1980:366. Abstract.

82 **Mansson T.** Treatment of malignant pleural effusion with doxycycline. Scand J Infect Dis. 1988;53:29.

83 **Kitamura S et al.** Intrapleural doxycycline for control of malignant pleural effusion. Curr Ther Res. 1981;30:515.

84 **Ruckdeschel JC.** Management of malignant pleural effusion: an overview. Semin Oncol. 1988;15(Suppl. 3):24.

85 **Andrews CO, Gora ML.** Pleural effusions: pathophysiology and management. Ann Pharmacother. 1994;28: 894–902.

86 **Hamed H et al.** Comparison of intracavitary bleomycin and talc for control of pleural effusions secondary to carcinoma of the breast. Br J Surg. 1989; 76:1266–267.

87 **Pierce MI et al.** Epidemiological factors and survival experience in 1770 children with acute leukemia treated by members of Children's Study Group A

between 1957 and 1964. Cancer. 1969; 23:1296.

88 **Poplack DG.** Acute lymphoblastic leukemia. In: Pizzo PA, Poplack DG, eds. Management of Common Cancers of Childhood. Philadelphia: JB Lippincott; 1989:323.

89 **Rivera GK et al.** Improved outcome in childhood acute lymphoblastic leukaemia with reinforced early treatment and rotational combination chemotherapy. Lancet. 1991;337:61.

90 **Clavell LA et al.** Four-agent induction and intensive asparaginase therapy for treatment of childhood acute lymphoblastic leukemia. N Engl J Med. 1986; 315:657.

91 **Riehm H et al.** Acute lymphoblastic leukemia: treatment results in three BFM studies (1970–1981). In: Murphy SB, Gilbert JR, eds. Leukemia Research: Advances in Cell Biology and Treatment. New York: Elsevier; 1983: 251.

92 **Bizzozzero OJ Jr et al.** Radiation-related leukemia in Hiroshima and Nagasaki, 1946–64: I. Distribution, incidence and appearance in time. N Engl J Med. 1966;274:1095.

93 **Folley JH et al.** Incidence of leukemia in survivors of the atomic bomb in Hiroshima and Nagasaki, Japan. Am J Med. 1952;13:311.

94 **Morgan KZ.** Radiation-induced health effects. Science. 1977;195:344.

95 **Van Steensel-Moll HA et al.** Are maternal fertility problems related to childhood leukemia? Int J Epidemiol. 1985;14:555.

96 **Stjernfeldt M et al.** Maternal smoking during pregnancy and risk of childhood cancer. Lancet 1986;1:1350.

97 **London SL et al.** Exposure to residential electric and magnetic fields and risk of childhood leukemia. Am J Epidemiol. 1991;134:923.

98 **Greenberg RS, Shuster JL.** Epidemiology of cancer in children. Epidemiol Rev. 1985;7:22.

99 **Wyke J.** Principles of viral leukemogenesis. Semin Hematol. 1986;23:189.

100 **Michaelson SM.** Household magnetic fields and childhood leukemia: a critical analysis. Pediatrics. 1991;88:630.

101 **Pool R.** Is there an EMF-cancer connection? Science. 1990;249:1096.

102 New study adds evidence electric wires may boost risk of childhood leukemia. Wall St J. 1991 Feb 8.

103 **Lewis MS.** Spatial clustering in childhood leukemia. J Chronic Dis. 1980; 33:703.

104 **Miller DR.** Childhood acute lymphoblastic leukemia: 1. Biological features and their use in predicting outcome of treatment. Am J Pediatr Hematol Oncol. 1988;10:163.

105 **Miller DR.** Acute lymphoblastic leukemia. Pediatr Clin North Am. 1980; 27:269.

106 **Kalwinsky DK et al.** Clinical relevance of lymphoblast biological features in children with acute lymphoblastic leukemia. J Clin Oncol. 1985;3: 477.

107 **Hammond GD et al.** Stratification by prognostic factors in the design and analysis of clinical trials for acute lymphoblastic leukaemia. Haematology and blood transfusion. In: Buchner T et

al., eds. Acute Leukemias. Berlin: Springer-Verlag; 1987:161.

108 **Simone JV et al.** Initial features and prognosis in 363 children with acute lymphocytic leukemia. Cancer. 1975; 36:2009.

109 **Sather HN.** Statistical evaluation of prognostic factors in ALL and treatment results. Med Pediatr Oncol. 1986; 14:158.

110 **Bleyer WA et al.** The staging of childhood acute lymphoblastic leukemia: strategies of the Children's Cancer Study Group and a three-dimensional technique of multivariate analysis. Med Pediatr Oncol. 1986;14:271.

111 **Mastrangelo R et al.** Report and recommendations of the Rome Workshop concerning poor-prognosis acute lymphoblastic leukemia in children: biologic bases for staging, stratification, and treatment. Med Pediatr Oncol. 1986;14:191.

112 **Robison L et al.** Assessment of the interrelationship of prognostic factors in childhood acute lymphoblastic leukemia. Am J Pediatr Hematol Oncol. 1980;2:3.

113 **Reaman G et al.** Acute lymphoblastic leukemia in infants less than one year of age: a cumulative experience of the Children's Cancer Study Group. J Clin Oncol. 1985;3:1513.

114 **Leiper AD, Chessells J.** Acute lymphoblastic leukaemia under 2 years. Arch Dis Child. 1986;61:1007.

115 **Leverger G et al.** Acute lymphoblastic leukemia in very young children. Am J Pediatr Hematol Oncol. 1986;8:213.

116 **Crist W et al.** Clinical and biologic features predict a poor prognosis in acute lymphoid leukemias in infants: a Pediatric Oncology Group Study. Blood. 1986;67:135.

117 **Sather HN.** Age at diagnosis of childhood acute lymphoblastic leukemia. Med Pediatr Oncol. 1986;14:166.

118 **Hammond D et al.** Analysis of prognostic factors in acute lymphoblastic leukemia. Med Pediatr Oncol. 1986;14: 124.

119 **Lanning M et al.** Superior treatment results in females with high-risk acute lymphoblastic leukemia in childhood. Acta Paediatr. 1992;81:66.

120 **Hale JP, Lilleyman JS.** Importance of 6-mercaptopurine dose in lymphoblastic leukaemia. Arch Dis Child. 1991; 66:462.

121 **Lilleyman JS et al.** Childhood lymphoblastic leukemia: sex difference in 6-mercaptopurine utilization. Br J Cancer. 1984;49:703.

122 **Kalwinsky DK et al.** Variation by race in presenting clinical and biologic features of childhood acute lymphoblastic leukaemia: implications for treatment outcome. Leuk Res. 1985;9:817.

123 **Sklo M et al.** The changing survivorship of white and black children with leukemia. Cancer. 1978;42:59.

124 **Walters TR et al.** Poor prognosis in Negro children with acute lymphoblastic leukemia. Cancer. 1972;29:210.

125 **Foucar K et al.** Survival of children and adolescents with acute lymphoid leukemia: a study of American Indians and Hispanic and non-Hispanic Whites treated in New Mexico. (1969 to 1986). Cancer. 1991;67:2125.

126 **Miller DR et al.** Prognostic implica-

tions of blast cell morphology in childhood acute lymphoblastic leukemia: a report from the Children's Cancer Study Group. Cancer Treat Rep. 1985; 69:1211.

127 **Lilleyman JS et al.** The clinical significance of blast cell morphology in childhood lymphoblastic leukemia. Med Pediatr Oncol. 1986;14:144.

128 **Miller DR et al.** Prognostic importance of morphology (FAB classification) in childhood acute lymphoblastic leukemia. Br J Haematol. 1981;48:199.

129 **van Eyes J et al.** The French-American-British (FAB) classification of leukemia. The Pediatric Oncology Group experience with Lymphocytic leukemia. Cancer. 1986;57:1046.

130 **Gupta S, Good RA.** Markers of human lymphocyte subpopulations in primary immunodeficiency and lymphoproliferative disorders. Semin Hematol. 1980;17:1.

131 **Brouet JC et al.** The use of B and T membrane markers in the classification of human leukemias, with special reference to acute lymphoblastic leukemia. Blood Cells. 1975;1:81.

132 **Brouet JC, Seligmann M.** The immunological classification of acute lymphoblastic leukemias. Cancer. 1978; 42:817.

133 **Cossman J et al.** Induction of differentiation in the primitive B-cells of common, acute lymphoblastic leukemia. N Engl J Med. 1982;307:1251.

134 **Nadler LM et al.** Induction of human B-cell antigens in non-T-cell acute lymphoblastic leukemia. J Clin Invest. 1982;70:433.

135 **Crist WM et al.** Immunologic markers in childhood acute lymphocytic leukemia. Semin Oncol. 1985;12:105.

136 **Pesando JM et al.** Leukemia-associated antigens in ALL. Blood. 1979;54: 1240.

137 **Ritz J et al.** A monoclonal antibody to human acute lymphoblastic leukemia antigen. Nature. 1980;283:583.

138 **Pullen DJ et al.** Southwest Oncology Group experience with immunological phenotyping in acute lymphocytic leukemia of childhood. Cancer Res. 1981; 41:4802.

139 **Magrath IT et al.** Bone marrow involvement in Burkitt's lymphoma and its relationship to acute B cell leukemia. Leuk Res. 1979;4:33.

140 **Flandrin G et al.** Acute leukemia with Burkitt's tumor cells: a study of six cases with special reference to lymphocyte surface markers. Blood. 1975;45: 183.

141 **Reiter A et al.** Favorable outcome of B-cell acute lymphoblastic leukemia in childhood: a report of three consecutive studies of the BFM group. Blood. 1992;80:2471.

142 **Murphy SB et al.** Results of treatment of advanced-stage Burkitt's lymphoma and B cell (SIg +) acute lymphoblastic leukemia with high-dose fractionated cyclophosphamide and coordinated high-dose methotrexate and cytarabine. J Clin Oncol. 1986;4:1732.

143 **Crist WM et al.** Pre B-cell leukemia responds poorly to treatment: a Pediatric Oncology Group Study. Blood. 1984;63:407.

144 **Greaves MF et al.** Immunologically defined subclasses of acute lymphob-

lastic leukemia in children: their relationship to presentation features and prognosis. Br J Haematol. 1981;48: 179.

145 **Pullen J et al.** How important is common acute lymphocytic leukemia antigen (CALLA) negativity as a prognostic factor in children excluding infants with B-precursor acute lymphocytic leukemia (ALL): a Pediatric Oncology Group (POG) study. Proc Am Soc Clin Oncol. 1987;6:151. (Abstract.)

146 **Look AT.** The emerging genetics of acute lymphoblastic leukemia: clinical and biological implications. Semin Oncol. 1985;12:92.

147 **Lampert F et al.** Acute lymphoblastic leukemia: current status of therapy in children. Recent Results Cancer Res. 1984;93:159.

148 **Bowman WP et al.** Cell markers in lymphomas and leukemias. In: Stollerman GH, ed. Advances in Internal Medicine. Chicago: Year Book Medical Publishers; 1980;25:391.

149 **Sallan SE et al.** Cell surface antigens: prognostic implications in childhood acute lymphoblastic leukemia. Blood. 1980;55:395.

150 **Steinherz PG et al.** Improved disease-free survival of children with acute lymphoblastic leukemia at high risk for early relapse with the New York regimen—a new intensive therapy protocol: a report from the Children's Cancer Study Group. J Clin Oncol. 1986; 4:744.

151 **Shuster JJ et al.** Prognostic factors in childhood T-cell acute lymphoblastic leukemia: a Pediatric Oncology Group study. Blood. 1990;75:166.

152 **Wiersma SR et al.** Clinical importance of myeloid-antigen expression in acute lymphoblastic leukemia in childhood. N Engl J Med. 1991;324:800.

153 **Pui C-H et al.** Myeloid-antigen expression in childhood acute lymphoblastic leukemia. N Engl J Med. 1991; 325:1378.

154 **Yunis JJ et al.** Prognostic significance of chromosomal abnormalities in acute leukaemias and myelodysplastic syndromes. Clin Haematol. 1986;15:597.

155 **Bloomfield CD et al.** Chromosomal abnormalities identify high-risk and low-risk patients with acute lymphoblastic leukemia. Blood. 1986;67:415.

156 **Look AT et al.** Prognostic importance of blast cell DNA content in childhood acute lymphoblastic leukemia. Blood. 1985;65:1079.

157 **Williams DL et al.** Chromosomal translocations play a unique role in influencing prognosis in childhood acute lymphoblastic leukemia. Blood. 1986; 68:205.

158 **Pui C-H et al.** Hypodiploidy is associated with a poor prognosis in childhood acute lymphoblastic leukemia. Blood. 1987;70:247.

159 **Secker-Walker LM et al.** Cytogenetics of acute lymphoblastic leukaemias in children as a factor in the prediction of long-term survival. Br J Haematol. 1982;52:389.

160 **Rowley JD.** The cytogenetics of acute leukaemia. Clin Haematol. 1978;7:385.

161 **Look AT.** The cytogenetics of childhood leukemia: clinical and biological implications. Pediatr Clin North Am. 1988;35:723.

162 **Loot AT.** The emerging genetics of acute lymphoblastic leukemia: clinical and biologic implications. Semin Oncol. 1985;12:92.

163 **Third International Workshop on Chromosomes in Leukemia.** Chromosomal abnormality and their clinical significance in acute lymphoblastic leukemia. Cancer Res. 1983;43:868.

164 **Kocova M et al.** Translocation 4;11 acute leukemia: three case reports and review of the literature. Cancer Genet Cytogenet. 1985;16:21.

165 **Kornberg A, Polliack A.** Serum lactic dehydrogenase (LDH) levels in acute leukemia: marked elevations in lymphoblastic leukemia. Blood. 1980;56:351.

166 **Quddus FF et al.** Glucocorticoid receptors in immunological subtypes of childhood acute lymphocytic leukemia cells: a Pediatric Oncology Group study. Cancer Res. 1985;45:6482.

167 **Lippman ME et al.** Clinical implications of glucocorticoid receptors in human leukemia. Cancer Res. 1976;38:4251.

168 **Mastrangelo R et al.** Clinical implications of glucocorticoid receptors studied in childhood acute lymphoblastic leukemia. Blood. 1980;56:1036.

169 **Pui C-H et al.** Impact of treatment efficacy on the prognostic value of glucocorticoid receptor levels in childhood acute lymphoblastic leukemia. Leuk Res. 1984;8:345.

170 **Elion GB et al.** Relationship between metabolic rates and antitumor activities of thiopurines. Cancer Res. 1963;23:1207.

171 **Zimm S et al.** Inhibition of first pass metabolism in cancer chemotherapy: interaction of 6-mercaptopurine and allopurinol. Clin Pharmacol Ther. 1983;34:810.

172 **Bisel HF.** Criteria for the evaluation of response to treatment in acute leukemia. Blood. 1956;11:676.

173 **Skipper HE, Perry SE.** Kinetics of normal and leukemic leukocyte populations— relevance to chemotherapy. Cancer Res. 1970;30:1883.

174 **Hart JS et al.** The mechanism of induction of complete remission in acute myeloblastic leukemia in man. Cancer Res. 1969;29:2300.

175 **Frei E III.** Progress in treatment for the leukemias and lymphomas. Cancer. 1965;18:1580.

176 **Lonsdale D et al.** Interrupted vs continued maintenance therapy in childhood leukemia. Cancer. 1975;336:342.

177 **Aur RJA et al.** Central nervous system therapy and combination chemotherapy of childhood lymphocytic leukemia. Blood. 1971;37:272.

178 **George P et al.** A study of ''total therapy'' of acute lymphocytic leukemia in children. J Pediatr. 1968;72:399.

179 **Haghbin M.** Chemotherapy of acute lymphoblastic leukemia in children. Am J Hematol. 1976;1:201.

180 **Roila F.** Ondansetron plus dexamethasone compared to the 'standard' metoclopramide combination. Oncology. 1993;50:163.

181 **Bryson JC.** Clinical safety of ondansetron. Semin Oncol. 1992;19(Suppl. 15):26.

182 **Terrin BN et al.** Side effects of metoclopramide as an antiemetic in childhood cancer chemotherapy. J Pediatr. 1984;104:138.

183 **Howrie DL et al.** Metoclopramide as an antiemetic agent in pediatric oncology patients. Drug Intell Clin Pharm. 1986;20:122.

184 **Cubeddu LX et al.** Antagonism of serotonin S3 receptors with ondansetron prevents nausea and emesis induced by cyclophosphamide-containing chemotherapy regimens. J Clin Oncol. 1990;8:1721.

185 **Shepherd DA et al.** Accidental intrathecal administration of vincristine. Med Pediatr Oncol. 1978;5:85.

186 **Bain PG et al.** Intrathecal vincristine: a fatal chemotherapeutic error with devastating central nervous system effects. J Neurol. 1991;238:230.

187 **Solimando DA, Wilson JP.** Prevention of accidental intrathecal administration of vincristine sulfate. Hosp Pharm. 1982;17:540.

188 **Dyke RW.** Treatment of inadvertent intrathecal injection of vincristine. N Engl J Med. 1989;321:1270.

189 **Magrath I et al.** Preliminary results of an intensive protocol, including GM-CSF, for patients with small, noncleaved cell and immunoblastic lymphomas. Blood. 1991;78:114. Abstract.

190 **Vietti TJ et al.** Vincristine, prednisone and daunomycin in acute leukemia of childhood. Cancer. 1971;27:602.

191 **Aur RJA et al.** Childhood acute lymphocytic leukemia: study VIII. Cancer. 1978;42:2123.

192 **Pinkel D.** Treatment of acute leukemia. Pediatr Clin North Am. 1976;23:117.

193 **Ortega JA et al.** L-asparaginase, vincristine, and prednisone for induction of first remission in acute lymphocytic leukemia. Cancer Res. 1977;37:535.

194 **Simone JV.** Factors that influence haematological remission duration in acute lymphocytic leukemia. Br J Haematol. 1976;32:465.

195 **Niemeyer CM et al.** Low-dose versus high-dose methotrexate during remission induction in childhood acute lymphoblastic leukemia (protocol 81-01 update). Blood. 1991;78:2514.

196 **Barr RD et al.** Management of children with acute lymphoblastic leukemia by the Dana-Farber Cancer Institute protocols: an update of the Ontario experience. Am J Pediatr Hematol Oncol. 1992;14:136.

197 **Evans WE et al.** Anaphylactoid reactions to escherichia coli and erwinia asparaginase in children with leukemia and lymphoma. Cancer. 1982;49:1378.

198 **Miller DR.** Prognostic factors in childhood lymphoblastic leukemia. J Pediatr. 1974;87:672.

199 **Goldie JH et al.** Rationale for the use of alternating non-cross-resistant chemotherapy. Cancer Treat Rep. 1982;66:439.

200 **Kaplan RS, Wiernik PH.** Neurotoxicity of antineoplastic drugs. Semin Oncol. 1982;9:103.

201 **Legha SS.** Vincristine neurotoxicity: pathophysiology and management. Med Toxicol. 1986;1:421.

202 **Drigan R et al.** Behavioral effects of corticosteroids in children with acute lymphoblastic leukemia. Med Ped Oncol. 1992;20:13.

203 **Price RA, Johnson WW.** The central nervous system in childhood leukemia: I. The arachnoid. Cancer. 1973;31:520.

204 **Evans AE et al.** The increasing incidence of central nervous system leukemia in children. Cancer. 1970;26:404.

205 **Bleyer WA, Poplack DG.** Prophylaxis and treatment of leukemia in the central nervous system and other sanctuaries. Semin Oncol. 1985;12:131.

206 **Reaman GH et al.** Prognostic factors for central nervous system (CNS) relapse in acute lymphoblastic leukemia (ALL) of childhood. Proc Am Soc Clin Oncol. 1984;3:202. Abstract.

207 **Aur RJA et al.** A comparative study of central nervous system irradiation and intensive chemotherapy early in remission of childhood acute lymphocytic leukemia. Cancer. 1972;29:381.

208 **Aur RJA et al.** Central nervous system therapy and combination chemotherapy of childhood lymphocytic leukemia. Blood. 1971;37:272.

209 **Brouwers P et al.** Long-term neuropsychological sequelae of childhood leukemia: correlation with CT brain scan abnormalities. J Pediatr. 1985;106:723.

210 **Meadows A et al.** Declines in IQ scores and cognitive dysfunction in children with acute lymphocytic leukemia treated with cranial irradiation. Lancet. 1981;1:1015.

211 **Oliff A et al.** Hypothalamic-pituitary dysfunction following CNS prophylaxis in acute lymphocytic leukemia: correlation with CT scan abnormalities. Med Pediatr Oncol. 1979;7:141.

212 **Pizzo P et al.** Neurotoxicities of current leukemia therapy. Am J Pediatr Hematol Oncol. 1979;1:127.

213 **Nesbit ME Jr et al.** Presymptomatic central nervous system therapy in previously untreated childhood acute lymphoblastic leukemia: comparison of 1800 rad and 2400 rad. A report for Children's Cancer Study Group. Lancet. 1981;1:461.

214 **Halberg FE et al.** Prophylactic cranial irradiation dose effects on late cognitive function in children treated for acute lymphoblastic leukemia. Int J Radiat Oncol Biol Phys. 1991;22:13.

215 **Haghbin M et al.** Treatment of acute lymphoblastic leukemia in children with ''prophylactic'' intrathecal methotrexate and intensive systemic therapy. Cancer Res. 1975;35:807.

216 **Sullivan MP et al.** Equivalence of intrathecal chemotherapy and radiotherapy as central nervous system prophylaxis in children with acute lymphatic leukemia: a Pediatric Oncology Group Study. Blood. 1982;60:948.

217 **Freeman AT et al.** Comparison of intermediate-dose methotrexate with cranial irradiation for postinduction treatment of acute lymphocytic leukemia in children. N Engl J Med. 1983;308:477.

218 **Komp DM et al.** CNS prophylaxis in acute lymphoblastic leukemia. Cancer. 1982;50:1031.

219 **Moe PJ et al.** Methotrexate infusions in poor prognosis acute lymphoblastic leukemia: II. High-dose methotrexate (HDM) in acute lymphoblastic leukemia in childhood: a pilot study from April 1981. Med Pediatr Oncol. 1986;14:189.

220 **Perry MC, ed.** The Chemotherapy Source Book. Baltimore: Williams & Wilkins; 1992:843.

221 **Katz JA et al .** Final attained height in patients successfully treated for childhood acute lymphoblastic leukemia. J Pediatr. 1993;123:546.

222 **Brown RT et al.** Chemotherapy for acute lymphocytic leukemia: cognitive and academic sequelae. J Pediatr. 1992;121:885.

223 **Littman P et al.** Central nervous system (CNS) prophylaxis in children with low risk acute lymphoblastic leukemia (ALL). Int J Radiat Oncol Biol Phys. 1987;13:1443.

224 **Poplack DG et al.** Central nervous system preventive therapy with high-dose methotrexate in acute lymphoblastic leukemia: a preliminary report. Proc Am Soc Clin Oncol. 1984;3:204. Abstract.

225 **Collins JM.** Regional therapy: an overview. In: Poplack DG et al., eds. The Role of Pharmacology in Pediatric Oncology. Boston: Martinus Nijhoff; 1987:125.

226 **Poplack DG et al.** Pharmacologic approaches to the treatment of central nervous system malignancy. In : Poplack DG et al., eds. The Role of Pharmacology in Pediatric Oncology. Boston: Martinus Nijhoff; 1987:125.

227 **Poplack DG et al.** Pharmacology of antineoplastic agents in cerebrospinal fluid. In: Wood JH, ed. Neurobiology of Cerebrospinal Fluid. New York: Plenus Press; 1980;2:561.

228 **Bleyer WA.** Clinical pharmacology of intrathecal methotrexate. II. An improved dosage regimen derived from age-related pharmacokinetics. Cancer Treat Rep. 1977;61:1419.

229 **Bleyer WA et al.** Reduction in central nervous system leukemia with a pharmacokinetically derived intrathecal methotrexate dosage regimen. J Clin Oncol. 1983;1:317.

230 **Geiser CF et al.** Adverse effects of intrathecal methotrexate in children with acute leukemia in remission. Blood. 1975;45:189.

231 **Sullivan MP et al.** Combination intrathecal therapy for meningeal leukemia: two versus three drugs. Blood. 1977;50:471.

232 **Sullivan MP et al.** Remission maintenance for meningeal leukemia: intrathecal methotrexate vs. intravenous bis-nitrosourea. Blood. 1971;38:680.

233 **Holdsworth MT et al.** Assessment of emetogenic potential of intrathecal chemotherapy in pediatric patients and evaluation of the antiemetic efficacy of ondansetron vs. chlorpromazine. Pharmacotherapy. 1993;13:277. Abstract.

234 **Higgins GA et al.** 5-HT₃ receptor antagonists injected in the area postrema inhibit cisplatin— induced emesis in the ferret. Br J Pharmacol. 1989;97:247.

235 **Saiki JG et al.** Paraplegia following intrathecal chemotherapy. Cancer. 1972;29:370.

236 **Gagliano R, Costani J.** Paraplegia following intrathecal methotrexate; report of a case and review of the literature. Cancer. 1976;37:1663.

237 **Rubinstein LJ et al.** Disseminated necrotizing leukoencephalopathy: a complication of treating central nervous system leukemia and lymphoma. Cancer. 1975;35:291.

238 **Wright JJ et al.** Gene rearrangements

as markers of clonal variation and minimal residual disease in acute lymphoblastic leukemia. J Clin Oncol. 1987;5: 735.

239 **Secker-Walker LM et al.** Bone marrow chromosomes in acute lymphoblastic leukemia: a long-term study. Med Pediatr Oncol 1979;7:371.

240 **Freireich EJ et al.** The effect of 6-mercaptopurine on the duration of steroid induced remission in acute leukemia: a model for evaluation of other potentially useful therapy. Blood. 1963;21:699.

241 **Mauer AM, Simone JV.** The current status of the treatment of childhood acute lymphoblastic leukemia. Cancer Treat Rev. 1976;3:17.

242 **Holland JV, Glidewell OA.** Chemotherapy of acute lymphocytic leukemia of childhood. Cancer. 1972;30:1480.

243 **Leikin S et al.** Reinduction and pulse therapy in acute lymphocytic leukemia. Proc Am Soc Clin Oncol. 1981;1:486.

244 **Niemeyer CM et al.** Comparative analysis of treatment programs for childhood acute lymphoblastic leukemia. Semin Oncol. 1985;12:122.

245 **Rivera GK, Mauer AM.** Controversies in the management of childhood acute lymphoblastic leukemia: treatment intensification, CNS leukemia, and prognostic factors. Semin Hematol. 1987;24:12.

246 **Bleyer WA et al.** Monthly pulses of vincristine and prednisone prevent bone marrow and testicular relapse in low-risk childhood acute lymphoblastic leukemia: a report of the CCG-161 study by the Children's Cancer Study Group. J Clin Oncol. 1991;9:1012.

247 **Ferrazzini G et al.** Diurnal variation of methotrexate disposition in children with acute leukaemia. Eur J Clin Pharmacol. 1991;41:425.

248 **Kato Y et al.** Dose-dependent kinetics of orally administered 6-mercaptopurine in children with leukemia. J Pediatr. 1991;119:311.

249 **Lennard L, Lilleyman JS.** Variable mercaptopurine metabolism and treatment outcome in childhood lymphoblastic leukemia. J Clin Oncol. 1989;7: 1816.

250 **Pinkel D et al.** Drug dosage and remission duration in childhood lymphocytic leukemia. Cancer. 1971;27:247.

251 **Schmiegelow K, Pulczynska MK.** Maintenance chemotherapy for childhood acute lymphoblastic leukemia: should dosage be guided by white blood cell counts? Am J Pediatr Hematol Oncol. 1990;12:462.

252 **Pearson ADJ et al.** The influence of serum methotrexate concentrations and drug dosage on outcome in childhood acute lymphoblastic leukemia. Br J Cancer. 1991;64:169.

253 **Chessels JM et al.** Oral methotrexate is as effective as intramuscular in maintenance therapy of acute lymphoblastic leukemia. Arch Dis Child. 1987;62:172.

254 **Festa RS et al.** Therapeutic adherence to oral medication regimens by adolescents with cancer. I. Laboratory assessment. J Pediatr. 1992;120:807.

255 **Kamen BA et al.** Methotrexate and folate content of erythrocytes in patients receiving oral vs intramuscular therapy with methotrexate. J Pediatr. 1984;104: 131.

256 **Land VJ et al.** Long term survival in childhood acute leukemia: "late" relapses. Med Pediatr Oncol. 1979;7:19.

257 **Nesbit ME et al.** Randomized study of 3-years versus 5-years of chemotherapy in childhood acute lymphoblastic leukemia. J Clin Oncol. 1983;1:308.

258 **Working Party on Leukaemia in Childhood.** Treatment of acute lymphoblastic leukaemia: effect of variation in length of treatment on duration of remission. Br Med J. 1977;2:495.

259 **Medical Research Council Working Party on Leukaemia in Childhood.** Duration of chemotherapy in childhood acute lymphoblastic leukemia. Med Pediatr Oncol. 1982;10:511.

260 **Haskell CM et al.** L-asparaginase: therapeutic and toxic effects in patients with neoplastic disease. N Engl J Med. 1969;281:1028.

261 **Capizzi RL et al.** L-asparaginase. Abstract Annu Rev Med. 1970;21:2433.

262 **Faletta JM et al.** Nonketotic hyperglycemia due to prednisone (NSC-10023) following ketotic hyperglycemia due to L-asparaginase (NSC-109229) plus prednisone. Cancer Chemother Rep. 1972;56:781.

263 **Land VJ et al.** Toxicity of L-asparaginase in children with advanced leukemia. Cancer. 1972;30:339.

264 **Zubrod CG.** The clinical toxicities of L-asparaginase in treatment of leukemia and lymphoma. Pediatrics. 1970; 45:555.

265 **Nesbit M et al.** Evaluation of intramuscular versus intravenous administration of L-asparaginase in childhood leukemia. Am J Pediatr Hematol Oncol. 1979;1:9.

266 **Lobel JS et al.** Methotrexate and asparaginase combination chemotherapy in refractory acute lymphoblastic leukemia of childhood. Cancer. 1979;43: 1089.

267 **Fabry U et al.** Anaphylaxis to L-asparaginase during treatment for acute lymphoblastic leukemia in children—evidence of a complement-mediated mechanism. Pediatr Res. 1985;19:400.

268 **Cheung N-KV et al.** Antibody response to escherichia coli L-asparaginase: prognostic significance and clinical utility of antibody measurement. Am J Pediatr Hematol Oncol. 1986;8: 99.

269 **Spiegel RJ et al.** Delayed allergic reactions following intramuscular L-asparaginase. Med Pediatr Oncol. 1980; 8:123.

270 **Dellinger CT, Miale TD.** Comparison of anaphylactic reactions to asparaginase derived from Escherichia coli and from Erwinia cultures. Cancer. 1976; 38:1843.

271 **Land VJ et al.** Unexpectedly high incidence of allergic reactions with high dose weekly asparaginase consolidation therapy in children with newly diagnosed non-T, non-B acute lymphoblastic leukemia: a Pediatric Oncology Group study. Proc Am Soc Clin Oncol. 1989;8:215. Abstract.

272 **Kurtzberg J et al.** The use of polyethylene glycol-conjugated L-asparaginase in pediatric patients with prior hypersensitivity to native L-asparaginase. Proc Am Soc Clin Oncol. 1990;9:219. Abstract.

273 **Capizzi RL, Holcenberg JS.** Asparaginase. In: Holland JF, ed. Cancer Medicine. 3rd ed. Philadelphia: Lea & Febiger; 1993:796.

274 **Capizzi RL et al.** L-asparaginase: clinical, biochemical, pharmacological and immunological studies. Ann Intern Med. 1971;74:893.

275 **Ohnuma T et al.** Biochemical and pharmacological studies with asparaginase in man. Cancer Res. 1970;30: 2297.

276 **Kellie SJ et al.** Hypersensitivity reactions to epipodophyllotoxins in children with acute lymphoblastic leukemia. Cancer. 1991;67:1070.

277 **Weiss RB, Bruno S.** Hypersensitivity reactions to cancer chemotherapeutic agents. Ann Intern Med. 1981;94:66.

278 **O'Dwyer PJ et al.** Hypersensitivity reactions to teniposide (VM-26): an analysis. J Clin Oncol. 1986;4:1262.

279 **Hayes FA et al.** Allergic reactions to teniposide in patients with neuroblastoma and lymphoid malignancies. Cancer Treat Rep. 1985;69:439.

280 **Nolte H et al.** VM-26 (teniposide)-induced hypersensitivity and degranulation of basophils in children. Am J Pediatr Hematol Oncol. 1988;10:308.

281 **Pui C-H et al.** Secondary acute myeloid leukemia in children treated for acute lymphoid leukemia. N Engl J Med. 1991;325:1682.

282 **Smith MA et al.** Report of the Cancer Therapy Evaluation Program Monitoring Plan for secondary acute myeloid leukemia following treatment with epipodophyllotoxins. J Natl Cancer Inst. 1993;85:554.

283 **Hawkins MM et al.** Epipodophyllotoxins, alkylating agents, and radiation and risk of secondary leukaemia after childhood cancer. Br Med J. 1992;304: 951.

284 **Crom WR, Evans WE.** Methotrexate. In: Evans WE et al., eds. Applied Pharmacokinetics: Principles of Therapeutic Drug Monitoring. Vancouver: Applied Therapeutics; 1992:29-1.

285 **Borsi JD, Moe PJ.** Systemic clearance of methotrexate in the prognosis of acute lymphoblastic leukemia in children. Cancer. 1987;60:3020.

286 **Evans WE et al.** Clinical pharmacodynamics of high-dose methotrexate in acute lymphocytic leukemia: identification of a relation between concentration and effect. N Engl J Med. 1986; 314:471.

287 **Evans WE et al.** Reappraisal of methotrexate clearance as a prognostic factor in childhood acute lymphocytic leukemia. Proc Amer Assoc Canc Res. 1989;30:241. Abstract.

288 **Rivera G et al.** Recurrent childhood lymphocytic leukemia: clinical and cytokinetic studies of cytosine arabinoside and methotrexate for maintenance of second hematologic remission. Cancer. 1978;42:2521.

289 **Ekert H et al.** Poor outlook for childhood acute lymphoblastic leukemia with relapse. Med J Aust. 1979;2:224.

290 **Amadori S et al.** Combination chemotherapy for marrow relapse in children and adolescents with acute lymphocytic leukemia. Scand J Haematol. 1981;26:292.

291 **Amato KR et al.** Combination chemotherapy in relapsed childhood acute lymphoblastic leukemia. Cancer Treat Rep. 1984;68:411.

292 **Baum E et al.** Prolonged second remission in childhood acute lymphocytic leukemia: a report from the Children's Cancer Study Group. Med Pediatr Oncol. 1983;11:1.

293 **Rivera GK et al.** Intensive treatment of childhood acute lymphoblastic leukemia in first bone marrow relapse. N Engl J Med. 1986;315:273.

294 **Culbert SJ et al.** Remission induction and continuation therapy in children with their first relapse of acute lymphoid leukemia: a Pediatric Oncology Group Study. Cancer. 1991;67:37.

295 **Champlin R, Gale RP.** Acute lymphoblastic leukemia: recent advances in biology and therapy. Blood. 1989; 73:2051.

296 **Sanders JE et al.** Marrow transplantation for children with acute lymphoblastic leukemia in second remission. Blood. 1987;70:324.

297 **Brochstein JA et al.** Allogeneic marrow transplantation after hyperfractionated total body irradiation and cyclophosphamide in children with acute leukemia. N Engl J Med. 1987;317: 1618.

298 **Barret AJ et al.** Prediction and prevention of relapse of acute lymphoblastic leukemia after bone marrow transplantation. Br J Haematol. 1986; 64:179.

299 **Butturini A et al.** Which treatment for childhood acute lymphoblastic leukemia in second remission? Lancet. 1987; 1:429.

300 **Young JL et al.** Cancer incidence, survival and mortality for children younger than age 15 years. Cancer. 1986;58:598.

301 **West R.** Childhood cancer mortality: International comparisons 1955-1974. World Health Stat. 1984;37:98.

302 **Nathwani BW et al.** Malignant lymphoma, lymphoblastic. Cancer. 1976; 38:964.

303 **Bennett HM et al.** Classification of non-Hodgkin's lymphomas. Lancet. 1974;1:1295.

304 **Lennert K et al.** The histopathology of malignant lymphoma. Br J Haematol. 1975;31(Suppl.):193.

305 **Lukes RJ et al.** New approaches to the classification of the lymphomata. Br J Cancer. 1975;31(Suppl. 2):1.

306 **National Cancer Institute sponsored study of classifications of non-Hodgkin's lymphomas.** Summary and description of a working formulation for clinical usage. Cancer. 1982;49:2112.

307 **Magrath IT.** Lymphocyte differentiation pathways-An essential basis for the comprehension of lymphoid neoplasia. J Natl Cancer Inst. 1981;67:501.

308 **Magrath IT.** Malignant lymphomas. In: Levine AS, ed. Cancer in the Young. New York: Masson; 1982:473.

309 **Magrath IT.** Malignant non-Hodgkin's lymphomas. In: Pizzo PA, Poplack DG, eds. Management of Common Cancers in Childhood. Philadelphia: JB Lippincott; 1989:415.

310 **Wanatabe A et al.** Undifferentiated lymphoma, non-Burkitt's type: Meningeal and bone marrow involvement in children. Am J Dis Child. 1973;125:57.

311 **Hutter JJ et al.** Non-Hodgkin's lymphoma in children. Correlation of CNS

disease with initial presentation. Cancer. 1975;36:2132.

312 **Magrath IT.** Burkitt's lymphoma. In: Mollander D, ed. Diseases of the Lymphatic System: Diagnosis and Therapy. Heidelberg: Springer-Verlag; 1983:103.

313 **Magrath IT et al.** Bone marrow involvement in Burkitt's lymphoma and its relationship to acute B-cell leukemia. Leuk Res. 1980;4:33.

314 **Magrath IT et al.** Prognostic factors in Burkitt's lymphoma: Importance of total tumor burden. Cancer. 1980;45:1507.

315 **Magrath IT et al.** An effective therapy for both undifferentiated (including Burkitt's) lymphomas and lymphoblastic lymphomas in children and young adults. Blood. 1984;63:1102.

316 **Wagner DK et al.** Soluble interleukin II receptor levels in patients with undifferentiated and lymphoblastic lymphomas. J Clin Oncol. 1987;5:1262.

317 **Muller-Weihrich S et al.** BFM trials for childhood non-Hodgkin's lymphomas. In: Cavalli F et al., eds. Malignant Lymphomas and Hodgkin's Disease: Experimental and Therapeutic Advances. Boston: Martinus Nijhoff; 1985:633.

318 **Wollner N et al.** Non-Hodgkin's lymphoma in children: a comparative study of two modalities of therapy. Cancer. 1976;37:123.

319 **Anderson Jr et al.** The results of a randomized therapeutic trial comparing a 4-drug regimen (COMP) with a 10-drug regimen (LSA^2-L^2). N Engl J Med. 1983;308:559.

320 **Pichler E et al.** Results of LSA^2-L^2 therapy in 26 children with non-Hodgkin's lymphoma. Cancer. 1982;50:2740.

321 **Bogusawska-Jaworska J et al.** Evaluation of the LSA^2-L^2 protocol for treatment of childhood non-Hodgkin's lymphoma. A report from the Polish Children's Leukemia/Lymphoma Study Group. Am J Pediatr Hematol Oncol. 1984;6:363.

322 **Meadows AT et al.** Similar efficacy of 6 and 18 months of therapy with four drugs (COMP) for localized non-Hodgkin's lymphoma of children: A report from the Children's Cancer Study Group. J Clin Oncol. 1989;7:92.

223 **Patte C et al.** Improved survival rate in children with stage III and IV B cell non-Hodgkin's lymphoma and leukemia using multi-agent chemotherapy: results of a study of 114 children from the French Pediatric Oncology Society. J Clin Oncol. 1986;4:1219.

324 **Patte C et al.** High survival rate in advanced-stage B-cell lymphomas and leukemias without CNS involvement with a short intensive polychemotherapy: results from the French Pediatric Oncology Society of a randomized trial of 216 children. J Clin Oncol. 1991;9:123.

325 **Murphy SB, Magrath I.** Pediatric lymphomas: current results and prospectus. Ann Oncol. 1991;2(Suppl. 2):219.

326 **Gadner H et al.** Treatment strategies in malignant non-Hodgkin lymphomas in childhood. Onkologie. 1986;9:126.

327 **Schwenn MR et al.** HiC-COM: a 2-month intensive chemotherapy regimen for children with stage III and IV Burkitt's lymphoma and B-cell acute lymphoblastic leukemia. J Clin Oncol. 1991;9:133.

328 **Weinstein HJ et al.** APO Therapy for malignant lymphoma of large cell "histiocytic" type of childhood: analysis of treatment results for 29 patients. Blood. 1984;64:422.

329 **Murphy SB et al.** Non-Hodgkin's lymphomas of childhood: An analysis of the histology, staging, and response to treatment of 338 cases at a single institution. J Clin Oncol. 1989;7:186.

330 **Phillip T et al.** High-dose therapy and autologous BMT in partial remission after induction. J Clin Oncol. 1988;6:1118.

331 **Mott MG et al.** Adjuvant low dose radiation in childhood T cell leukaemia/lymphoma (report from the United Kingdom childrens cancer study group—UKCCSG). Br J Cancer. 1984;50:457.

332 **Murphy SB et al.** Correlation of tumor cell kinetic studies with surface marker results in childhood non-Hodgkin's lymphoma. Cancer Res. 1979;39:1534.

333 **Hirt A et al.** Differentiation and cytokinetic analysis of normal and neoplastic lymphoid cells in B and T cell malignancies of childhood. Br J Haematol. 1984;58:241.

334 **Kaplan RS, Wiernik PH.** Neurotoxicity of antineoplastic drugs. Semin Oncol. 1982;9:103.

335 **Vincristine Sulfate.** In: Dorr RT, Von Hoff DD, eds. Cancer Chemotherapy Handbook (2nd ed.). Norwalk: Appleton and Lange; 1994:951.

336 **Drigan R et al.** Behavioral effects of corticosteroids in children with acute lymphoblastic leukemia. Med Pediatr Oncol. 1992;20:13.

337 **Tortorice PV, O'Connell MB.** Management of chemotherapy-induced nausea and vomiting. Pharmacotherapy. 1990;12:129.

338 **Mehta P et al.** Methylprednisolone for chemotherapy-induced emesis: A double-blind randomized trial in children. J Pediatr. 1986;108:774.

Solid Tumors

Adult: Rebecca S Finley
Celeste M Lindley
Cynthia L LaCivita
Pediatric: David W Henry

Breast Cancer 93-2
Premenopausal Women 93-2
Risk factors 93-2
Screening 93-2
Surgery 93-3
Adjuvant therapy (See Table 93.2) 93-3
Recommended regimens 93-4
Dose intensity 93-4
Tamoxifen 93-5
Metastatic Disease 93-5
Prognosis 93-5
Treatment 93-5
Combination and single agent chemotherapy 93-5
High-dose chemotherapy with autologous
bone marrow transplant (HDC-ABMT) 93-6
Spinal cord compression 93-6
Postmenopausal Women 93-6
Hormonal therapy 93-6
Estrogen and progesterone receptors 93-6
Tamoxifen 93-6
Flare reactions 93-6
Disease progression 93-6

Colon Cancer 93-7
Screening 93-7
Digital rectal examination (DRE) 93-7
Fecal occult blood testing 93-7
Prognosis 93-7
Treatment 93-8
Adjuvant therapy 93-8
Fluorouracil (FU) and levamisole 93-8
Follow-up care 93-8
Recurrent Disease 93-8
Rising carcinoembryonic (CEA) level 93-8
Chemotherapy 93-8
Fluorouracil (FU) and floxuridine (FUDR)
combinations 93-9
Hepatic Metastases 93-9
Hepatic intra-arterial (IA) chemotherapy 93-9
Floxuridine (FUDR) toxicity 93-9
Embolization 93-9

Small Cell Lung Cancer (SCLC) 93-9
Clinical Presentation 93-9
Prevalence and Risk Factors 93-10
Screening 93-10
Small Cell Lung Cancer (SCLC) versus Nonsmall
Cell Lung Cancer (NSCLC) 93-10
Staging 93-11
Cancer Cachexia 93-11
Causes 93-11
Management 93-11
Chemotherapy 93-11
Combination chemotherapy 93-11
Etoposide capsules 93-11
Follow-up care 93-12

Duration of therapy and prophylactic
irradiation 93-12
Ovarian Cancer 93-12
Clinical Presentation and Risk Factors 93-12
Detection and the Papanicolaou (Pap) Test 93-12
Chemotherapy 93-13
Cisplatin dosing 93-13
Intraperitoneal (IP) chemotherapy 93-13
Recurrent disease 93-13
Bladder Cancer 93-13
Clinical Presentation and Risk Factors 93-13
Treatment 93-14
Intravesicular chemotherapy 93-14
Neoadjuvant therapy 93-14
Metastatic Disease 93-14
Melanoma 93-14
Danger Signs (See Table 93.4) 93-15
Treatment 93-14
Interferon alpha 93-15
Interleukin-2 (IL-2) 93-15
Interleukin-2 (IL-2) plus chemotherapy 93-16
Tamoxifen 93-16
Risk Factors 93-16
Prostate Cancer 93-16
Etiology and Risk Factors 93-16
Staging 93-16
Treatment (See Figure 93.1) 93-16
Choice of therapy 93-17
Bilateral orchiectomy 93-17
Diethylstilbestrol (DES) 93-17
Leuprolide and goserelin (LHRH analogs) 93-17
Antiandrogens 93-17
Monitoring therapy 93-18
Second-line therapies 93-18
Aminoglutethimide 93-18
Ketoconazole 93-18
Spinal cord compression 93-18
Cytotoxic chemotherapy 93-18
Testicular Cancer 93-18
Clinical Presentation 93-18
Histologic Classification (See Table 93.5) 93-19
Staging 93-19
Treatment 93-19
Adjuvant chemotherapy 93-19
Metastatic disease: chemotherapy 93-19
Monitoring therapy 93-19
Pediatric Solid Tumors 93-20
Statistics (See Figure 93.2) 93-20
Small Round Cell Tumors 93-20
Genetics 93-20
Carcinogens 93-20
Patient Age 93-20

(Continued)

Multi-Institutional Research Groups 93-21
Neuroblastoma 93-21
    Staging (See Table 93.6 and Question 67) 93-21
    Prognostic factors (See Table 93.7) 93-22
    Clinical presentation 93-21
    Treatment (See Table 93.8) 93-21
        Monitoring vital signs for etoposide 93-22
        Monitoring hydration for cisplatin 93-22
        Adjustment of creatinine clearance (Cl$_{Cr}$)
            to adult size 93-22
        Recurrent disease 93-22
            Bone marrow transplant 93-22
            Investigational treatments based upon
                disease biology 93-22
Wilms' Tumor 93-22
    Clinical presentation and treatment
        (See Table 93.9) 93-23

Dosing chemotherapy in infants 93-23
    Interaction of chemotherapy with radiation 93-23
    Doxorubicin cardiotoxicity in pediatrics 93-23
    Dactinomycin hepatotoxicity 93-24
Osteosarcoma 93-24
    Clinical presentation and prognostic factors
        (Also see Question 77) 93-24
    Treatment 93-24
        Delayed clearance after high-dose methotrexate ..93-24
        Leucovorin rescue 93-24
Rhabdomyosarcoma 93-25
    Clinical presentation and prognostic factors 93-25
    Treatment 93-25
        Trimethoprim-sulfamethoxazole (TMP-SMX)
            prophylaxis and filgrastim for
            myelosuppression 93-25
        Renal Fanconi's syndrome with ifosfamide 93-26

Solid tumors include the malignancies that initially present as discrete masses. They arise from malignant transformations of cells within virtually any organ system except the hematopoietic system. Solid tumors are far more common than hematologic malignancies and represent the major causes of cancer-related morbidity and mortality. Depending upon the specific type of cancer and its stage, surgery, radiation, chemotherapy, immunotherapy, and hormonal manipulation all play important roles in patient management. The types of solid tumors which occur in adults versus pediatric populations are distinctively different. Specific tumors which are commonly treated with drug therapy are included in this chapter.

Breast Cancer

Premenopausal Women

Risk Factors

1. B.W., a 37-year-old female, was found to have a 2.2 cm mass in the upper, outer quadrant of her left breast during routine screening mammography. Biopsy of the mass revealed infiltrating ductal carcinoma. Physical examination at that time was unremarkable and she had no complaints. All laboratory values including the complete blood count (CBC) and liver function tests were within normal limits and a chest x-ray was negative. Her family history was significant in that her mother died at age 42 of breast cancer and her 44-year-old sister had a breast tumor removed about 5 years ago. B.W. reported that she had her first menstrual cycle at age 10 and has had regular periods since that time. She is married but has never been pregnant. What is the incidence of breast cancer in premenopausal women? Did any factors place B.W. at an increased risk of developing breast cancer?

Overall, breast cancer is the most common cancer in women in the U.S. and accounts for 27% of their cancers.[1] About one in eight women will develop breast cancer with the greatest risk occurring after age 65.[2] For women age 35 or less, the chance of developing breast cancer is less than 1%; however, a strong family history of breast cancer increases the relative risk.[3,4]

Although any family history of breast cancer increases an individual's risk of the disease, it is highest among women with first degree relatives (i.e., mother, sister, daughter) who have had breast cancer.[4,5] In B.W.'s case, her mother and sister both had breast cancer. Some studies have indicated an even greater risk when more than one relative is affected, but other studies have not substantiated this observation. Several additional factors have been associated with an increased risk of developing breast cancer. (See

Table 93.1.) Nulliparous women like B.W. also have a higher incidence of breast cancer than women who have had one or more pregnancies, but age at first pregnancy appears to be an even more important determinant. One study indicated that there was a substantially higher risk of developing breast cancer in women whose first pregnancy was after age 30, than compared with those whose first pregnancy was before age 18. Early menarche also has been associated with an increased risk of breast cancer.[3,5]

Screening

2. Is routine screening mammography recommended for B.W. because of her increased risk of breast cancer? Is it recommended for all women?

Women with a positive family history often are instructed to begin screening at an earlier age.[1] Several different guidelines for breast cancer screening are available.[6] (See Chapter 90: Neoplastic Disorders and Their Treatment: General Principles, Table 90.5.) It generally is agreed that beginning at age 20, women should perform monthly breast self-examinations. They should undergo a clinical breast examination every three years until age 40 when it should be done annually.

Nearly 75% of breast cancers occur in women over 50 years of age. The American Cancer Society (ACS) recommends that women in this age group have annual mammography. Data strongly support mammography in this age group since it can reduce mortality by 20% to 39%.[7] The value of routine mammography for women in B.W.'s age group (<50 years) is less clear. Interpretation of abnormal findings is more difficult and varies considerably for this age group.

Based upon the data from eight major randomized controlled trials of breast cancer screening performed over the last 30 years, it was concluded that for women who had been screened between the ages 40 to 49 there was no apparent benefit at five to seven years after enrollment into any of the studies. After 10 to 12 years, the Swedish studies did show a 13% reduction in mortality; however, this reduction did not reach statistical significance. Follow-up of one trial at 10 to 18 years did show a 25% decrease in mortality which reached questionable statistical significance.[8]

Failure to document the same decrease in mortality for women ages 40 to 49 was likely because this subgroup was not large enough to detect a difference. For this age group, experts project that over 500,000 women would be needed for a trial to have statistical power to detect a 25% reduction in mortality.[9] Other variables which may have affected the results include differences in mammography techniques, increased breast density, and less than optimal intervals between screenings. If it is true that mammography has the advantage of detecting breast cancer two years before physical examinations, the two-year interval recommended for the 40- to 49-year-old group maybe be too long to reduce mortality.[9] For all these reasons, women younger than 50 years of age should not be denied mammography.[11]

It is not clear how long screening should be continued. Women older than 70 years of age are at increased risk for developing breast cancer; however, there are no randomized trials evaluating the merits of annual mammography in this group.[7] For women 70 years and older, the decision to continue screening must be made taking into consideration the patient's overall health.

Surgery

3. Following the results of the biopsy, B.W. underwent a partial mastectomy, full axillary lymph node dissection, and local radiation therapy. Tissue sample of the tumor was estrogen- and progesterone-receptor negative and 4 of 20 lymph nodes were positive for tumor involvement. Is the partial mastectomy as effective as more extensive surgical procedures such as the modified radical mastectomy? Was radiation indicated following surgery?

Historically, radical mastectomy (removal of the breast, axillary lymph nodes, and pectoralis muscles) and modified radical mastectomy (radical mastectomy with preservation of the pectoralis muscles) have been the standard surgical procedures used for primary breast cancer. However, the psychological and cosmetic effects of breast loss can be substantial. This has led to increased interest in more conservative surgical procedures such as lumpectomy and partial mastectomy. Lumpectomy consists of gross removal of the tumor without attention to margins; a partial mastectomy includes excision of the tumor with clean surgical margins. Early trials evaluating conservative procedures without treatment of the remaining breast tissue or axillary lymph nodes reported high failure rates. Failures were primarily recurrences in the remaining breast tissue or axilla.[12–14] Postoperative radiation therapy reduces the risk of local recurrence. Several randomized trials have indicated no difference in survival between patients undergoing conservative surgery (e.g., partial mastectomy) followed by local radiation therapy and those treated with radical surgery.[12–14]

Adjuvant Therapy

4. B.W. recalled that her sister also received chemotherapy after her surgery for breast cancer. She now questions whether she should receive any additional therapy and what the chances are that she has been cured. What factors determine the need for adjuvant systemic therapy following surgery and what are the indications for administering adjuvant chemotherapy or hormonal therapy?

The benefit of systemic adjuvant therapy is directly related to the likelihood of disease recurrence. Size of the primary tumor, presence and number of involved axillary lymph nodes, nuclear or histologic grade, and the presence of hormone receptors (estrogen and/or progesterone) appear to be the most important factors that predict prognosis.[3,15] Additional potential prognostic factors include tumor growth fraction (S-Phase), oncogene amplification, ploidy (DNA content), and cathepsin D expression.[16] Intense research in this area is ongoing.

The single most important factor that predicts recurrence of breast cancer in patients like B.W. whose tumor is initially small and localized is the presence and extent of lymph nodes positive for cancer. Women with positive lymph nodes (Stage II disease) have a 40% to 60% chance of being cured with surgery alone. Women with negative lymph nodes (Stage I disease) have a 70% to 90% chance of cure with surgery alone. Therefore, B.W. who has four positive nodes and negative hormone receptors would be considered at high risk of recurrence.[3]

Trials of systemic adjuvant therapy in women with breast cancer began in the 1960s. These trials originally focused on patients with Stage II disease; however, recognizing the significant rate of disease recurrence in patients with Stage I disease, later trials included Stage I patients as well. Many trials have been conducted over the past 40 years evaluating the effects of systemic adjuvant chemotherapy, endocrine therapy, and combined chemoendocrine therapy. Since many of the individual trials have included relatively small numbers of patients, multiple patient subsets, or different therapeutic strategies, a series of meta-analyses has been performed by the Early Breast Cancer Trialists' Collaborative Group.[17,18] The most recent meta-analysis reviewed data from 133 randomized clinical trials conducted worldwide which included 75,000 women with Stage I and II breast cancer. The overview concluded that systemic adjuvant therapy reduces the relative risk of death by 30% to 40% compared to untreated controls. The proportional reduction in risk of death in Stage I and II is approximately equivalent; however, the absolute survival difference is greater in Stage II patients who would have a higher risk of recurrence. In B.W.'s case, her risk of recurrence is approximately 50% and systemic adjuvant therapy would be expected to improve her chances of cure by approximately 10%.

Treatment recommendations for patients with Stage I and II breast cancer continue to evolve.[19–21] The earliest guidelines were based upon menopausal status (if unknown, based upon age over or under 50) and the presence of involved axillary lymph nodes at the time of the initial surgery. The results of these early studies demonstrated conclusively that premenopausal women, particularly those with ≥4 positive lymph nodes, who received chemotherapy had significant prolongation in disease-free and overall survival compared to untreated controls. These trials also demonstrated that postmenopausal women treated with adjuvant tamoxifen had significant improvement in disease-free and overall survival compared to untreated controls. Thus, chemotherapy was recommended for premenopausal women and tamoxifen for postmenopausal women.

The significance of menopausal status for adjuvant therapy is related to the presence of hormone receptors in the primary tumor. The majority of premenopausal women are hormone receptor negative, while the majority of postmenopausal women are hormone receptor positive. Tamoxifen is most likely to benefit women with positive hormone receptors. In early studies, hormone receptor as-

Table 93.1	Risk Factors Associated with Development of Breast Cancer

Strong Risk Factors
- History of breast cancer in the contralateral breast
- Family history of breast cancer, especially in 1st degree relatives
- Benign breast "cancer" (i.e., atypical hyperplasia)
- Early menarche, late menopause
- Late 1st pregnancy greater than no pregnancy
- Advancing age

Possible Risk Factors
- Obesity
- High fat diet
- Long-term use of exogenous estrogens
- Alcohol

says were not available and menopausal status served as a surrogate marker of hormone receptor positivity. Although current adjuvant treatment guidelines retain the categories of pre- and postmenopause, they also incorporate hormone receptor status.

The most recent adjuvant therapy guidelines hail from the Fourth International Conference on Adjuvant Therapy of Primary Breast Cancer held in St. Gallen, Switzerland in February 1992.[21] This conference brought together experts from around the world to review the updated results (10 year overview) of the Early Breast Cancer Trialists Collaborative Group as well as new scientific findings regarding prognostic factors in early breast cancer. The St. Gallen treatment recommendations are based upon the presence of tumor in axillary lymph nodes, menopausal, and hormone receptor status. (See Table 93.2.)

Treatment recommendations for node negative patients are based upon prognostic factors that define risk of disease recurrence. *Minimal/low risk* includes patients with noninvasive tumors (ductal carcinoma *in situ*), tumors ≤1 cm in diameter, or tumors classified histologically as tubular, colloid (mucinous), or papillary. These patients are considered to have an excellent prognosis with less than 10% recurrence at ten years. The *good risk* category includes patients with estrogen receptor positive tumors greater than 1 cm but ≤2 cm. The *high risk* node negative group includes estrogen receptor negative tumors ≥1 cm, estrogen receptor positive tumors larger than 2 cm, and nuclear grade III (i.e., poor) tumors. The consensus conference acknowledged that additional prognostic factors, such as growth fraction, can be added to the prognostic profile to guide the clinician and individual patient. The patient's general medical condition and psychological status and social support also must be considered in making adjuvant therapy selection.

5. Recommended Regimens. **Based upon these guidelines and the estrogen receptor negativity of her tumor, B.W.'s physician recommended that she receive adjuvant cytotoxic chemotherapy. What regimens are currently recommended?**

No clear consensus exists regarding the optimal adjuvant chemotherapy regimen for estrogen-receptor negative breast cancer in premenopausal women. Regimens such as cyclophosphamide, methotrexate, fluorouracil (CMF); and cyclophosphamide, doxorubicin, fluorouracil (CAF) have been widely studied. Doxorubicin generally is regarded as the most active agent for the treatment of metastatic (advanced) breast cancer and it often is included in adjuvant regimens for node positive, hormone receptor negative women who are at high risk of relapse.[22-24]

6. Dose Intensity. **Twenty-one days after surgery, B.W. started chemotherapy with cyclophosphamide 600 mg/m^2, doxorubicin 60 mg/m^2, and fluorouracil 600 mg/m^2. She is to receive a course of therapy Q 21 days for the next 4 months. At the time of chemotherapy administration she received antiemetic therapy. (See Chapter 105: Nausea and Vomiting.) Two weeks after completing her second course of chemotherapy, B.W. became febrile while granulocytopenic and was admitted to the hospital for empiric antibiotic treatment. B.W. asked her physician if the doses of chemotherapy could be reduced to avoid infection after her next courses of chemotherapy. Her physician advised her against reducing the doses of chemotherapy; however, he did initiate filgrastim following the next course of chemotherapy. Why is it inadvisable to decrease the dose of chemotherapy in this case?**

Variables which may influence the effectiveness of adjuvant therapy besides the choice of drugs include the dose, duration of therapy, and time interval between surgery and the initiation of chemotherapy. Two retrospective analyses of adjuvant chemotherapy trials found that survival correlated positively with dose intensity (i.e., the amount of drug administered per unit of time).[25,26] B.W.'s physician was correct in recommending that she receive full dose therapy because evidence suggests that the dose-related response of chemotherapy in this disease is important. Either a decrease in the amount of each drug administered per course or a lengthening of the interval between courses would result in a net decrease in dose intensity.

A major area of investigation is the use of more intensive chemotherapy regimens as adjuvant therapy. Since bone marrow suppression is the major dose-limiting toxicity of many chemotherapeutic agents, regimens that incorporate high doses of myelosuppressive agents followed by administration of growth factors, peripheral blood progenitor cells, autologous bone marrow stem cells, or some combination of these have been tried. Trials to define the usefulness of dose-intense regimens in the adjuvant setting are justified based upon the encouraging response rates seen in patients with advanced stages (i.e., III and IV).[27-29] Single institution studies using high-dose chemotherapy with autologous bone marrow transplant (HDC-ABMT) for high risk Stage II and III breast cancer have preliminarily reported prolonged disease-free survival.[30] Cooperative groups have initiated prospective randomized trials in this population to further delineate the risks and benefits of dose intensity in adjuvant therapy for breast cancer.

B.W. is scheduled to receive four courses of cyclophosphamide, doxorubicin, and fluorouracil. Several adjuvant trials also have evaluated the effect of duration of therapy. To date, no trials have

Table 93.2	Adjuvant Therapy for Breast Cancer[a]		
	Treatment Recommendations		
	Node-Negative (Minimal to Good Risk)	Node-Negative (High Risk)	Node-Positive
Premenopausal			
Receptor positive	No treatment or tamoxifen	Chemotherapy ± tamoxifen	Chemotherapy ± tamoxifen
Receptor negative	No treatment or tamoxifen	Chemotherapy	Chemotherapy
Postmenopausal			
Receptor positive	No treatment or tamoxifen	Tamoxifen ± chemotherapy	Tamoxifen ± chemotherapy
Receptor negative	No treatment or tamoxifen	Chemotherapy ± tamoxifen	Chemotherapy ± tamoxifen
Elderly (>70 yr)			
Receptor positive	No treatment or tamoxifen	Tamoxifen (chemotherapy, if tolerated)	Tamoxifen
Receptor negative	No treatment or tamoxifen	Tamoxifen (chemotherapy, if tolerated)	Chemotherapy[b]

[a] Recommendations of the 1992 St. Gallen Conference. See reference 21.
[b] In selected circumstances, given the patient's medical condition and own treatment preference, chemotherapy could be administered.

demonstrated a significant survival benefit for patients given treatment for longer than six months.[31] Guidelines generally recommend that adjuvant therapy begin within two or three weeks following surgery. Some advocate therapy immediately after surgery or even perioperatively.[32]

7. Tamoxifen. Should B.W. receive adjuvant tamoxifen therapy in addition to chemotherapy?

Chemotherapy is clearly indicated in B.W. because she is premenopausal and has positive lymph nodes. Since her tumor was negative for hormone receptors, tamoxifen therapy is not indicated. However, in premenopausal women with positive hormone receptors combined chemoendocrine therapy may be beneficial. Results of the meta-analysis found that ovarian ablation in patients under age 50 was as effective as chemotherapy in reducing recurrence and mortality.[18] This is, however, an indirect comparison of results of trials employing ovarian ablation to those using combination chemotherapy. Furthermore, hormone receptor status was not assessed in a number of the trials included in the analysis. Nonetheless, this report has stimulated renewed interest in the value of endocrine therapy (ovarian ablation, tamoxifen, or LHRH analogs) in premenopausal women. Combination chemotherapy often produces permanent ovarian failure in premenopausal women and evidence exists that this is associated with a favorable prognosis.

If B.W.'s tumor had been hormone receptor positive, chemoendocrine therapy would have been indicated. In the meta-analysis, chemoendocrine therapy was associated with the greatest reduction in risk of death in women ages 50 to 69 years.[18] Consequently, chemoendocrine therapy is now recommended for a number of patient subgroups, representing a significant shift in adjuvant treatment of breast cancer over the past decade.

Adjuvant tamoxifen therapy consists of 20 mg administered as two 10 mg doses or one 20 mg dose daily. The optimal duration of therapy is unknown; however, five years is currently recommended. Laboratory and some clinical evidence suggest that the cytostatic effect of tamoxifen interferes with the cytocidal effect of chemotherapy.[33,34] Therefore, sequential use of chemotherapy and tamoxifen, or withholding initiation of tamoxifen until chemotherapy administration is complete is advised.

Metastatic Disease

Prognosis

8. About 7 months after completing adjuvant chemotherapy, B.W. began experiencing back pain which was partially relieved by ibuprofen 400 mg PRN. Since the pain was temporally related to moving some furniture in her living room, she did not seek medical attention. Five days after the onset of the back pain her husband noted that she was "sleepy" and mildly confused. He contacted her physician who suggested she come to the clinic immediately. Physical examination was negative for lymphadenopathy or breast masses and chest and abdominal examinations were unremarkable. Pertinent laboratory values were as follows: calcium (Ca) 15 mg/dL (Normal: 9.0–11.5), phosphorus 4.2 mg/dL (Normal: 2.5–4.5), sodium (Na) 138 mEq/L (Normal: 136–145), potassium (K) 4.3 mEq/L (Normal: 3.5–5.5), albumin 3.0 gm/dL (Normal: 3.5–5.5), alkaline phosphatase 580 mU/mL (Normal: 15–70), aspartate aminotransferase (AST) 258 mU/mL (Normal: 5–20), and alanine aminotransferase (ALT) 96 mU/mL (Normal: 5–24). The CBC was within normal limits. Spinal cord x-rays revealed several lytic vertebral lesions consistent with metastatic carcinoma, but a myelogram did not show any evidence of spinal cord compression.

B.W. was admitted to the hospital for acute management of hypercalcemia (see Chapter 28: Fluid and Electrolyte Disorders) and re-staging of her breast cancer to determine the ex-

tent of tumor spread. A bone scan showed positive uptake in the spine and right scapula and a liver scan revealed 2 small nodules consistent with metastatic disease. A CT scan of the brain was negative. Is any further assessment of the disease stage necessary at this time? What is the prognosis now that B.W.'s disease has metastasized? [SI units: Ca 3.75 mmol/L (Normal: 2.25–2.88); phosphorus 1.36 mmol/L (Normal: 0.81–1.45); Na 138 mmol/L (Normal: 136–145); K 4.3 mmol/L (Normal: 3.5–5.5); albumin 30 gm/L (Normal: 35–55); alkaline phosphatase 580 U/L (Normal: 15–70); AST 258 U/L (Normal: 5–20); ALT 96 U/L (Normal: 5–24)]**

The most common sites of metastatic spread of breast cancer are listed in Table 90.4 in Chapter 90: Neoplastic Disorders and Their Treatment: General Principles. The purpose of documenting all sites of disease involvement is to enable the evaluation of the effect of treatment and to identify any disease sites which may require immediate therapy to avoid life-threatening complications (e.g., brain metastases). B.W. has documented disease in the liver and bones. Other common sites of disease are the remaining breast tissue, bone marrow, and the lungs. Because her CBC is normal, further examination of the bone marrow is not necessary at this time; however, a chest x-ray should be ordered to rule out involvement of the lungs.

Metastatic breast cancer is rarely curable. After metastatic disease is documented, survival may range from a few months to several years depending upon the site(s) and number of metastases, and the rate of growth of the tumor (which may be assessed by the disease-free interval). The median duration of survival after recurrence is about two years.[35] Multiple sites of metastatic disease, a relatively short disease-free interval (<1 year), liver involvement, negative estrogen and progesterone receptors at the time of diagnosis, and premenopausal status all confer a poor prognosis for B.W.[3]

Treatment

9. Combination and Single Agent Chemotherapy. What treatment options are available for B.W. at this time?

B.W. has tumor in both the liver and bones, and systemic therapy is necessary to simultaneously treat both disease sites. She is unlikely to respond to endocrine manipulations such as hormonal therapy or oophorectomy because her tumor is hormone receptor negative and she is premenopausal.[3] Liver metastases also do not respond well to hormonal therapy. Patients like B.W. who are symptomatic and unlikely to benefit from hormonal therapy should receive combination chemotherapy.

Many cytotoxic agents have demonstrated activity in breast cancer including doxorubicin, cyclophosphamide, mitoxantrone, fluorouracil, methotrexate, mitomycin, vinblastine, paclitaxel, vinorelbine, and thiotepa.[3,36–38] Several combination regimens which have been widely used in advanced breast cancer are listed in Table 90.12 in Chapter 90: Neoplastic Disorders and Their Treatment: General Principles.

Response rates to combination chemotherapy regimens in metastatic disease in patients who have not received prior chemotherapy are high (approximately 50% to 80%). Unfortunately, the response rates to chemotherapy in patients who have had prior exposure to chemotherapy are low. Although doxorubicin is considered to be one of the most active agents against breast cancer, the overall response rate to chemotherapy in patients who have had prior doxorubicin is only about 20%.[36,39] The median survival of these patients is four to six months.[36] Paclitaxel (Taxol) was recently approved for treatment of breast cancer after failure of combination chemotherapy for metastatic disease or relapse within six months of adjuvant chemotherapy. Prior therapy should have included an anthracycline unless clinically contraindicated. Response rates to single agent paclitaxel (250 mg/m²) of 63% have been reported in patients who developed metastatic disease 12 or more months following adjuvant chemotherapy with CMF or CAF; however, the response rate was only 22% in patients receiving 200 mg/m^2 who had received three to six prior chemotherapy regimens.[40]

B.W. received cyclophosphamide, doxorubicin, and fluorouracil as adjuvant therapy only a few months before the relapse of her breast cancer. This suggests that her disease is resistant to these drugs. Consequently, further therapy with these drugs is unlikely to produce a significant response. Single agent paclitaxel may be the most appropriate therapy for B.W. at this time. Regimens consisting of other active agents (e.g., mitomycin plus vinblastine or vincristine, methotrexate plus thiotepa) are potential alternatives to paclitaxel for B.W.[41,42] Single agent mitomycin also has been suggested as a reasonable alternative in patients who have failed doxorubicin.[3]

10. High-Dose Chemotherapy with Autologous Bone Marrow Transplant (HDC-ABMT). Is B.W. a candidate for high-dose chemotherapy with autologous bone marrow transplant?

Early studies of HDC-ABMT in patients with advanced metastatic breast cancer demonstrated high response rates of relatively short duration.[26] These led to trials that investigated HDC-ABMT as intensification therapy for patients with metastatic breast cancer who had complete or near complete responses to induction therapy with standard chemotherapy regimens for advanced disease. Results of the second generation trials using HDC-ABMT as intensification therapy indicate that 15% to 30% of women have remained disease-free for median follow-up period approaching 36 months in the larger series.[28,43,44] This has led some experts to conclude that this approach may provide curative therapy for the subset of women who achieve a complete or near complete response to standard combination chemotherapy for metastatic breast cancer. Although longer follow-up is required to demonstrate cure of these patients, the long period of disease-free survival demonstrated in these trials is impressive. If B.W. achieves a complete or near complete response to paclitaxel or an alternative regimen, she would be a candidate for HDC-ABMT.

11. Spinal Cord Compression. If B.W.'s myelogram had indicated impending spinal cord compression what therapy would have been appropriate?

Bone pain in patients with breast cancer without evidence of epidural spinal cord compression should be treated first with systemic chemotherapy, as suggested for B.W. Radiation therapy may be added later if systemic treatment is not effective in relieving symptoms. Compression of the spinal cord by expansion of the tumor or fracture of the vertebrae can result in paralysis and anal sphincter dysfunction. If there is a potential impending compression, high-dose steroids (e.g., dexamethasone 10 to 25 mg Q 6 hr then titrated for maximum response) should be initiated immediately followed by radiation therapy. Steroids decrease edema and inflammation around the tumor mass and contribute to pain relief. In some instances, steroid therapy also may produce some cytotoxic effect.[45,46]

Postmenopausal Women

Hormonal Therapy

12. Estrogen and Progesterone Receptors. M.L., a 68-year-old female with breast cancer, underwent a modified radical mastectomy followed by radiation therapy 7 years ago. At that time she had been postmenopausal for about 10 years and her tumor was documented to have high concentrations of both estrogen and progesterone receptors. She remained disease-free until recently when she was found to have bone metastases in her left scapula and several ribs. No other sites of disease involvement were identified. Her only symptom is shoulder pain. Would it be appropriate to treat M.L. with hormonal therapy at this time?

Breast cancer is one of the few human tumors which may be very sensitive to hormonal manipulations; however, it is also well recognized that only a subset of patients with breast cancer respond to the various endocrine therapies. Patients with tumors that are potentially endocrine-sensitive tumors can be identified by the measuring estrogen and progesterone receptors in the tumor tissue. Patients whose tumors are positive for both estrogen receptors (ER+) and progesterone receptors (PR+) have a much higher response rate to endocrine therapy than patients without either receptor (about 70% versus 10%). Patients with ER+, PR− tumors have an intermediate response rate (30%).[47] Patients with higher concentrations of ER are also more likely to have PR+ tumors and are more likely to respond. Patients with endocrine-responsive tumors also are reported to have longer disease-free intervals after initial surgery, such as M.L. experienced.[47,48] In addition, they may have a longer survival after the documentation of metastatic disease. M.L.'s tumor was strongly ER+ and PR+ and she had a long disease-free interval (7 years); therefore, she is likely to respond to endocrine therapy.

13. Tamoxifen. M.L. was started on tamoxifen 10 mg BID. Is this a reasonable approach? How soon after the start of treatment will antitumor effects be seen?

Hormonal agents including tamoxifen, progesterone (e.g., megestrol acetate), aminoglutethimide, and estrogens are probably equally effective for the initial treatment of endocrine-responsive breast cancer. However, tamoxifen generally is considered the first-line endocrine therapy because it has a low toxicity profile and there is widespread experience with its use. Before tamoxifen was available, diethylstilbestrol (DES) was widely used, but side effects (e.g., vomiting, fluid retention) were more common with DES and its use in breast cancer is now considered third- or fourth-line therapy.

Following the initiation of endocrine therapy, it usually takes four to six weeks before the therapeutic response can be assessed. In patients like M.L. with only bone metastases, assessment may be difficult because it may take four to six months to reossify the involved bones. In such cases, the decision to continue therapy may be based upon the lessening of bone pain and the appearance of no new sites of metastases (i.e., disease stabilization). Steady-state tamoxifen levels will not be achieved for about 16 weeks; however, loading doses or higher doses have not improved response rates.[49,50]

14. Flare Reactions. Two days after starting tamoxifen, M.L. began experiencing increased pain in her shoulder and became concerned that the cancer was worsening. Repeat laboratory values including serum calcium were unchanged, and M.L. was instructed to continue taking the tamoxifen. Is her increased pain related to the tamoxifen therapy?

Many patients who receive endocrine therapy may experience a transient worsening of symptoms within hours or days after therapy is started. This is referred to as a flare reaction.[5] Patients with bone metastases often report a significant increase in pain severity and patients with skin or soft tissue disease may notice erythema and swelling of nodules. Some patients, especially those with bone metastases, also may develop hypercalcemia. In most cases, therapy should be continued since symptoms generally subside within a month. If hypercalcemia is severe, therapy may have to be interrupted until the serum calcium level declines. Endocrine therapy may then be restarted cautiously at a lower dosage with gradual escalation. In either case, patients should be reassured that the flare reaction does not represent disease progression and that patients with flare reactions are as likely to respond to therapy as are those who have no initial worsening of symptoms.

15. Disease Progression. Over the next 18 months, M.L. continued tamoxifen therapy and had a complete resolution of her

shoulder pain with considerable improvement of the x-rays and no appearance of new lesions. At that time, she began experiencing left hip pain and a bone scan documented new metastatic disease. What therapy should be considered at this time?

Because M.L. had a good initial response to tamoxifen, she is very likely to respond again to another type of endocrine therapy. Therefore, a progesterone such as megestrol acetate should be considered. Megestrol acetate, in doses of 160 to 320 mg/day, is well tolerated and associated with response rates of 14% to 56% in patients who had initially responded to tamoxifen. When used as first-line endocrine therapy, megestrol produces response rates equivalent to those of tamoxifen.[51] However, response rates diminish if megestrol is used after two or three prior hormone treatments.[51] Aminoglutethimide, fluoxymesterone, and LHRH analogs (i.e., leuprolide, goserelin) are alternative second- or third-line hormonal therapies. Radiation therapy also may provide M.L. with palliative relief of pain. If M.L. had rapidly worsening disease involving a visceral organ such as the liver or if she had not responded well to prior endocrine therapy, cytotoxic chemotherapy may have been more appropriate.

Colon Cancer

Screening

Digital Rectal Examination (DRE)

16. E.R., a 57-year-old black male, is undergoing his first physical examination in over 10 years. His physician recommends that a digital rectal exam (DRE) be performed during this visit as a screening tool for colorectal disease. E.R. questions if this is really necessary. Are there any other tests or procedures which should be done?

To screen for colorectal disease in asymptomatic patients, the ACS recommends a digital rectal exam, fecal occult blood tests, and proctosigmoidoscopy. The DRE should be performed annually after age 40 as part of the regular physical examination. DRE is a simple and inexpensive screening tool for colorectal cancers located in the first 10 to 12 cm of the rectum. Operator skill and experience are crucial to detection of abnormal findings. Beginning at age 50, the stool should be tested for occult blood annually and sigmoidoscopy (preferably flexible) should be performed every three to five years. Detection of adenomatous colon polyps and precancerous lesions depends upon the type of proctosigmoidoscopy and the ability to visualize all or a portion of the colon; the rigid sigmoidoscope has limited visualization of the colon. Flexible 60 and 35 cm sigmoidoscopes can reach 55% and 40% of neoplastic lesions, respectively; the colonoscope can reach the cecum enabling detection of nearly all neoplastic lesions. Biopsies can be taken through the scope, thus eliminating inaccurate reporting based upon visual observations. Lack of patient acceptance, discomfort, and cost are the major drawbacks to this screening procedure.

Fecal Occult Blood Testing

17. What methods to detect fecal occult blood are available and are there any advantages of one method over another?

Annual fecal occult-blood testing decreases the cumulative mortality of colorectal cancer by 33% over 13 years.[52] This test can detect 20% to 70% of all colorectal cancers and may increase the proportion of tumors detected at an early (curable) stage.[53,54] Of the three methods used, the guaiac test is common, although newer methods may be more sensitive and specific. It is a colorimetric test in which guaiac dye is oxidized to a bluish quinone compound in the presence of a peroxidase (e.g., hemoglobin). Foods, other substances, and medical conditions which contain or produce peroxidase activity may yield false readings (see Table 93.3). Conversely, large amounts of ascorbic acid may produce false negative guaiac tests.

Table 93.3	Causes of Positive Fecal Guaiac Test	
Foods with Peroxidase Activity	Medications Which Interfere with Fecal Blood Testing	Common Causes of Blood in the Stool
Broccoli	Steroids	Colorectal cancer
Cauliflower	NSAIDs	Colorectal polyps
Turnips	Reserpine	Diverticulitis
Horseradish		Hemorrhoids
Cabbage		Fissures
Potatoes		Proctitis
Cucumbers		Inflammatory bowel disease
Mushrooms		
Artichokes		

A second method, the Hemo-Quant test (Smith Kline Diagnostics), is a quantitative test based upon fluorometry of heme-derived porphyrin. During intestinal transit hemoglobin is broken down to porphyrin. The third method is an immunochemical test (e.g., HemeSelect) which uses antiserum to human hemoglobin to detect blood in the feces. This test is very sensitive and specific; however, it does lose sensitivity if the bleeding is from the proximal colon because bacteria alter the globin.[55] The immunochemical test eliminates the need for dietary restrictions; however, there is a 24-hour delay in reading the results because an extract needs to be prepared from the stool sample. Red meat should be eliminated from the diet for three days before occult blood is tested using the guaiac methods and for four days before testing using methods based upon heme-derived porphyrins.[56]

Prognosis

18. E.R.'s digital rectal examination was normal; however, fecal occult blood tests were positive on specimens obtained on 2 consecutive days before the examination. Sigmoidoscopy revealed a 2.5 cm mass. Biopsy of the lesion was interpreted as adenocarcinoma of the colon and a surgical resection of the mass and regional lymph nodes was performed. The tumor was confined to the bowel wall, although 4 regional lymph nodes showed evidence of tumor involvement. There was no evidence of distant metastases of the tumor at that time and his colon cancer was staged as Dukes C. E.R.'s physical examination was otherwise unremarkable and all laboratory values were within normal limits except for an elevated lactate dehydrogenase (LD) and a carcinoembryonic antigen (CEA) level of 647 ng/mL (Normal: <5 ng/mL) before the surgical procedure. What is the prognosis for stage C colon cancer? Could earlier detection have improved the prognosis?

Colorectal cancer is the second leading cause of cancer deaths in the U.S. adult population.[1] However, when it is diagnosed in the early stages it is curable with surgical intervention and over 90% of patients survive five years. The five-year survival rate declines to 40% to 50% in patients like E.R. with stage C disease.[57–59] The Dukes staging system is most commonly used for colon cancer. Stage A indicates penetration into but not through the bowel wall, Stage B indicates penetration through the bowel wall, and Stage C indicates lymph node involvement. Patients with early stage colorectal cancer often are asymptomatic; therefore, intensive screening programs as described above have been advocated to reduce the mortality of this disease. Sixty to ninety percent of patients with metastatic and recurrent colorectal cancer have elevated CEA levels. Levels are elevated in relation to the stage and extent of disease, the degree of tumor differentiation, and the site of metastases. If the CEA level is elevated at the time of initial diagnosis, like E.R., it may be monitored after surgical resection of the tumor for evidence of recurrent disease.

Treatment

Adjuvant Therapy

19. All evidence of tumor was removed and E.R.'s CEA level declined. Therefore, the surgery may be considered potentially curable. Should E.R. receive any additional therapy at this time?

Tumor recurrence is a significant problem in stage C colon and rectal cancers with up to 60% of all surgically treated patients eventually having local recurrences.[57-60] Causes of these relapses may include peritoneal seeding due to exfoliation of tumor cells in the colonic lumen and spillage during surgery. Most tumor recurrences are secondary to either disease spread to the regional lymph nodes or extension of the tumor into the bowel wall, with subsequent hematogenous dissemination. The risk of lymphatic and hematogenous spread increases when the bowel wall has been penetrated.[61] Metastasis to the liver via hematogenous spread (through the portal circulation) is the most common site of disease spread beyond the regional lymph nodes and occurs in 50% of patients with invasive disease.[62] Lung metastases (in the absence of liver metastases) occur rarely and generally are associated with lesions in the lower rectum.

Because of the significant relapse rate in patients with stage C colon cancer, adjuvant chemotherapy has been extensively studied and shown to improve disease-free survival in those patients who have had "potentially curative surgery" such as E.R. Treatment options have been somewhat limited due the paucity of chemotherapeutic agents with significant activity. The most widely studied have been the fluorinated pyrimidines, fluorouracil (FU) and floxuridine (FUDR), mitomycin, and thiotepa. Because single agent therapy has been less than optimal, combination therapy as well as biochemical and immunological modulation of FU have been studied in an effort to improve long-term survival. In 1989, two studies using FU in combination with levamisole reported very promising results which led to the commercial availability of levamisole in 1990.

20. Fluorouracil (FU) and Levamisole. E.R. began adjuvant therapy with FU and levamisole 3 weeks following surgery. The regimen consists of: FU 450 mg/m²/day for 5 consecutive days as a rapid intravenous (IV) bolus, followed by weekly FU doses of 450 mg/m² beginning on day 28. Levamisole 50 mg PO was given Q 8 hr for 3 days every 2 weeks. All therapy is to continue for 1 year.[63,64] What is levamisole and what is the rationale for including it with FU?

Levamisole, an imidazothiazole derivative, has been used as an antihelmintic in humans and in veterinary medicine. It has immunomodulating activity and in tumor-bearing animal models has demonstrated antineoplastic activity, although it does not appear to be directly cytolytic.[65] Levamisole's antitumor activity may be indirect via augmentation of immune functions, particularly in patients who are immunosuppressed.[66] Alternatively, it may augment the cytotoxicity of fluorouracil.[67] Side effects associated with levamisole are dose related and reversible when therapy is stopped. Common adverse effects include granulocytopenia, nausea and vomiting, abdominal pain, diarrhea, altered or metallic taste, flu-like symptoms, mood elevation, insomnia, hyperalertness, dizziness, and headache.[68]

In two trials, patients whose colorectal cancer had been completely resected and staged as either stage B or C were randomized to receive no further treatment, levamisole alone, or levamisole plus fluorouracil. The combination of FU and levamisole was shown to reduce liver recurrences and improve survival. Patients with stage C disease derived the most benefit from this therapy.[63,64] In addition to the usual adverse effects of the fluorouracil and levamisole, liver function abnormalities (usually manifested by an increase in serum alkaline phosphatase or aminotransferase) have been reported in 39% of patients receiving the combination. Neurotoxicity manifested by cerebellar signs and symptoms or impaired thinking also have been reported in a few patients.[69]

The National Institutes of Health Consensus Development Conference on Adjuvant Therapy for Patients with Colon and Rectum Cancer held in 1990 considered the FU and levamisole regimen to be an appropriate control regimen for ongoing clinical trials and advocated this regimen for patients who are unable to participate in a clinical trial.[70] Current adjuvant trials in colon cancer are evaluating the three-drug combination of fluorouracil, levamisole, and leucovorin.

Follow-Up Care

21. Within six months after surgery, E.R.'s CEA level had fallen to <2.5 ng/mL and he completed the adjuvant therapy without serious sequelae. What follow-up care is recommended at this time?

E.R. continues to be at significant risk of developing recurrent disease. If recurrences are detected early, it is possible to cure them with additional surgery. In most cases, patients with early recurrences are asymptomatic; therefore, an active follow-up program is necessary to detect them. Physical examinations, fecal occult blood testing, sigmoidoscopy, and serum CEA level monitoring are recommended every three to four months for three years, then every six months for two years. Colonoscopy is recommended every six months and a chest x-ray should be done yearly. Additional tests, such as abdominal and pelvic computed tomography (CT) scans and liver function chemistries should be done if routine tests are abnormal or if symptoms are suggestive of recurrent disease.[71]

Recurrent Disease

Rising Carcinoembryonic (CEA) Level

22. Eighteen months after completing adjuvant chemotherapy, E.R.'s serum LD and CEA levels began to rise. What is the significance of a rising CEA level?

Although widespread serum CEA level monitoring is not an efficient way to screen for colorectal cancer in the general population, a rising CEA level in a patient with a history of colorectal cancer may be the first indication of recurrent disease if the patient had an elevated CEA level at the time of original diagnosis. Generally, the CEA level is measured every two to four months for three years and then every six months for two years. Over 50% of patients who have recurrent disease have been reported to have elevated CEA levels.

Chemotherapy

23. A CT scan of E.R.'s liver showed 2 discrete nodules which were consistent with metastatic disease, but E.R. was feeling well and had no symptoms suggestive of metastases. What is the role of further chemotherapy now that E.R. has recurrent disease?

A variety of approaches using chemotherapy have been employed to manage patients with advanced colorectal cancer. These include single agent intravenous therapy (primarily with FU or FUDR), combination chemotherapy, biological response modifiers, and hepatic intra-arterial administration of chemotherapy agents to treat localized liver metastases. Reported response rates for single agent intravenous FU have ranged from 8% to 85%, but most feel that the overall response rate is about 20%.[71] Factors which appear to influence response include the sites and extent of metastases, the patient's underlying condition, and the FU dosage.

Fluorouracil (FU) and Floxuridine (FUDR) Combinations. Combinations of FU or FUDR with other cytotoxic drugs or modulating agents also have been widely studied in advanced colorectal cancer. The most promising systemic regimen thus far is the biochemical modulation of fluorouracil with a reduced folate (i.e., leucovorin).[72–74] FU exerts its cytotoxic activity by inhibiting thymidylate synthase which ultimately results in the inhibition of DNA synthesis. *In vitro* tests have shown that by increasing the intracellular concentration of a reduced folate, the formation of a stable complex of the FU metabolite (FUMP), the reduced folate, and the thymidylate synthase will be favored, thus augmenting the cytotoxicity of FU by blocking further steps toward DNA synthesis.[72–74] Numerous FU and leucovorin regimens (changes in schedule, dose, and route of administration) have been studied in metastatic colorectal cancer and some have been associated with improved survival when compared with untreated controls.[67] A review of the randomized clinical trials to date suggests that regimens using weekly high-dose intravenous leucovorin (e.g., 500 mg/m^2) with FU (600 mg/m^2) and those using a schedule of five day low-dose intravenous leucovorin (20 mg/m^2/day) with FU (370 to 425 mg/m^2) have shown improved survival over fluorouracil alone.[67,75] One trial comparing the high-dose weekly regimen to the five-day schedule reported a slightly higher response rate for the five-day regimen, but no difference in survival.[76] The five-day regimen, however, appears to be associated with substantially less toxicity and is less costly.

In vitro studies have indicated that interferon alfa enhances the activity of FU in colon cell cultures, and a preliminary clinical trial reported a response rate of 63% in previously untreated patients.[77] Interferon is believed to modulate the cytotoxicity of FU as well as reduce FU clearance, thus increasing FU exposure.[78,79] Additional clinical trials will be necessary to substantiate these data.

Hepatic Metastases

Because the liver is the most common site of metastatic colorectal cancer, many patients could potentially benefit from effective therapy for hepatic metastases. These tumors derive most of their blood supply from the hepatic artery, and direct administration of effective anticancer drugs into the hepatic artery provides high drug concentrations to the area of tumor involvement.[80] Hepatic intra-arterial administration of fluorouracil, floxuridine, or other chemotherapeutic agents also has been extensively studied in patients with metastases confined to the liver.[81–86]

Hepatic Intra-Arterial (IA) Chemotherapy

24. E.R. underwent a laparotomy during which the hepatic artery was canalized and an Infusaid pump implanted. (No additional sites of metastases were observed.) He subsequently received a continuous hepatic arterial infusion of FUDR 0.2 mg/kg/day for 14 days every 28 days. Does this method of drug delivery produce increased antitumor effects over conventional IV infusions?

Optimal characteristics for a drug to be administered by this method should include: 1) efficacy against colorectal carcinoma; 2) high extraction by the liver; and 3) rapid clearance of the drug once it reaches systemic circulation. Therefore, FUDR is a logical agent because 95% of the dose is extracted by the liver and it has a half-life of only about 20 minutes when it does reach the systemic circulation.[87]

Initial uncontrolled trials using intrahepatic FUDR reported response rates of 29% to 88% and suggested that this mode of therapy may be superior to conventional systemic therapy.[85,86] Several randomized trials of intravenous versus hepatic intra-arterial FUDR administration have been reported.[82–84,88,89] Intra-arterial

floxuridine consistently produced significantly higher response rates (complete plus partial responses) than intravenous administration (40% to 60% versus 10% to 20%); however, survival was not improved in four of these five major trials.

25. Floxuridine (FUDR) Toxicity. Are the toxicities produced by IA FUDR similar to those common with IV FUDR? What follow-up monitoring is recommended?

Toxicities associated with FUDR (and FU) therapy depend upon the dose, route, and schedule of administration. When administered by IV bolus injections each week, the dose-limiting toxicity is usually myelosuppression. However, when the dose is given as a continuous intravenous infusion over several days, the dose-limiting toxicities are mucositis and diarrhea.[82,84] If these toxicities begin during therapy, the decision may be made to discontinue the infusion before completion in order to avoid life-threatening toxicity. Nausea and vomiting associated with FU or FUDR therapy are dose related and generally only mild to moderate in severity. Dermatologic changes are more commonly associated with continuous infusion therapy and include alopecia, onycholysis, acral erythema, and dermatitis.[90]

The dose-limiting toxicities associated with IA infusions are generally hepatic or gastrointestinal in nature. Cumulative FUDR-associated hepatobiliary toxicity which can progress to biliary sclerosis and liver failure has been related both to the total dose administered and the duration of therapy.[82] The initial sign of hepatic toxicity is usually an elevation of alkaline phosphatase and when this occurs, the dosage should be reduced or treatment interrupted until normalization occurs. Failure to do so may result in severe jaundice and chemical cholecystitis and eventual biliary sclerosis.[91,92] Patients also may experience transient increases in AST and LD. Gastritis and gastric ulcers also have been associated with intra-arterial FUDR therapy. This probably is related to inadvertent perfusion of the gastric artery.

Before initiating therapy, E.R. should have a baseline CT scan of the liver and liver function tests. Physical examination and liver function tests should be repeated before and after each course of therapy. Although myelosuppression is unusual following IA floxuridine, E.R. also should have a complete blood count done periodically. Serum chemistries also should be evaluated before each course.

Embolization

26. Is chemo-embolization the same technique as intra-arterial chemotherapy? Would E.R. benefit from this therapy? Is E.R. a candidate for chemo-embolization?

Embolization is a technique which involves deliberate obstruction of the artery which supplies blood to the tumor site resulting in necrosis. This procedure also results in necrosis of the organ where the tumor is located. Because the liver has a dual blood supply, a tumor can be embolized through the hepatic artery while the parenchyma is sustained by portal venous inflow.[93] Chemoembolization combines intra-arterial chemotherapy with obstruction of the vasculature thus prolonging the exposure of the tumor to the drug. This may be associated with substantial complications including infection, severe adhesions, infarction, and abscesses. Although this type of therapy is promising it is not clear which patients are most likely to benefit or if survival is significantly impacted.[94]

Small Cell Lung Cancer (SCLC)

Clinical Presentation

27. H.H., a 57-year-old, white female with a 6-month history of weight loss and increasing fatigue, recently noted shortness of breath (SOB) and fever. She also complains of joint pain in

her knees and elbows and has noticed a change in her fingers and nails over the last several months. Physical examination was significant for swelling and tenderness over her knees and elbows as well as hypertrophy and clubbing of the distal joints of both hands. A chest x-ray and CT scan revealed a central mass causing obstruction of the middle right lobe as well as mediastinal lymphadenopathy. Bronchoscopy washings and cytology were positive for small cell lung carcinoma. H.H. denied exposure to any environmental or occupational carcinogens but did admit to a 40-pack-year history of cigarette smoking. Are H.H.'s symptoms typical of those associated with lung cancer?

Signs and symptoms associated with lung cancer are dependent upon the size and location of the tumor and degree of spread outside of the lungs. The most common symptoms at presentation are those associated with the primary tumor and include cough, wheezing, chest pain, hemoptysis, and dyspnea.[45] However, because many patients have other medical problems such as chronic obstructive airways disease related to cigarette smoking, the worsening of these symptoms may go unnoticed for a period of time or may be attributed to other smoking-related illnesses. A large tumor may result in obstruction leading to fever and other evidence of pneumonia.

Regional spread to lymph nodes and other structures within the thorax may result in dysphagia, superior vena cava obstruction, pleural effusion, and hoarseness. Patients with distant metastatic spread may have findings associated with the site of disease involvement. For example, if the tumor has spread to the liver they are likely to have elevated liver functions tests or if they have brain metastases they may have severe headache, neurological impairment, or seizures.

Lung cancers also often are associated with distant or paraneoplastic syndromes. Almost one-third of patients with lung cancer present with anorexia and weight loss.[96] (See Question 32.) Hypertrophic pulmonary osteoarthropathy with inflammation of the outer covering of bones and clubbing can cause pain, tenderness, and swelling over the affected bones such as that experienced by H.H. This often mimics bone metastases (bone scans also may be positive); however, further studies will reveal no evidence of direct tumor involvement of the bones. Other paraneoplastic syndromes commonly seen in patients with small cell lung cancer include ectopic Cushing's syndrome and the syndrome of inappropriate antidiuretic hormone secretion (SIADH). Characteristically, paraneoplastic syndromes improve after successful treatment of the tumor.

Prevalence and Risk Factors

28. How common is small cell lung cancer and what factors place H.H. at risk for SCLC?

The American Cancer Society estimates that 172,000 new cases of lung cancer will be diagnosed in 1994. Although the World Health Organization recognizes that there are more than ten types of primary pleuropulmonary malignancies, four major types of carcinomas account for up to 95% of all lung cancers.[97,98]

The relative prevalence of the four major types are as follows: epidermoid carcinoma (also called squamous cell carcinoma) 30% to 35%; adenocarcinomas 25% to 29%; large cell carcinomas 14% to 19%; and small cell carcinomas 25%.[99] Commonly, the first three are grouped together and referred to as nonsmall cell lung cancers because they are similar in prognosis and response to therapy.

Cigarette smoking is the predominant cause of lung cancer worldwide and the risk appears to increase with the number of cigarettes smoked each day.[95,100] About 75% to 80% of lung cancer cases are attributable to smoking.[100] Although the risk of de-

veloping any type of lung cancer increases with cigarette smoking, the relative risk of small cell lung cancer is among the highest.[96] Therefore, individuals such as H.H. who have a long history of cigarette smoking have the highest risk of developing lung cancer relative to any other population. Other risk factors for lung cancer include exposure to passive smoke (i.e., nonsmokers who live with smokers); pipe and cigar smoking; and exposure to asbestos, radon, or other occupational carcinogens such as heavy metals, chloromethyl ether, and arsenic.[96,101,102]

Screening

29. What are the current recommendations for screening or early detection of lung cancer in patients like H.H.?

Unfortunately, no specific recommendations for lung cancer screening have affected overall mortality. In the early 1970s, the National Cancer Institute (NCI) launched three studies evaluating sputum cytology and chest radiography as lung cancer screening tests. Individuals at the Johns Hopkins Hospital in Baltimore and Memorial Sloan-Kettering Cancer Center in New York received annual chest radiography and every four months their sputum cytology was evaluated. At the Mayo Clinic, the control group received only standard medical advice and the treatment group was screened as described above. The overall mortality rates in the two groups did not differ significantly.[103]

Small Cell Lung Cancer (SCLC) versus Nonsmall Cell Lung Cancer (NSCLC)

30. How do treatment and prognosis differ for SCLC and nonsmall cell lung cancer?

The natural history and response to treatments between SCLC and the nonsmall cell lung cancers differ significantly. Therefore, it is extremely important to establish a histologic diagnosis before contemplating treatment. In general, the NSCLCs are less likely to metastasize early in the course of the disease and are less sensitive to chemotherapy than SCLCs. In contrast, SCLC progresses very rapidly and is sensitive to many chemotherapeutic agents.

Surgery is curative only in early stages of NSCLC.[104] Radiation therapy may be considered an alternative for patients who are poor surgical risks. Radiotherapy also is used to treat NSCLC characterized by large tumors or extensive lymph node involvement. In advanced stages of NSCLC, overall response rates to combination chemotherapy are 20% to 40%, with fewer than 5% of patients achieving a complete response.[105] The highest response rates for chemotherapy in NSCLC have been achieved with regimens utilizing high-dose cisplatin (≥ 100 mg/m^2) combined with etoposide, mitomycin, or vinblastine.

Because small cell lung cancer disseminates early in the disease, surgery is almost never indicated. The only exception is the rare patient who presents with very early stage disease. Such patients may benefit by resection of the tumor followed by combination chemotherapy. Overall, the use of combination chemotherapy regimens for SCLC has increased median survival by four- to five-fold.[106] In disease which is limited to the thoracic cavity, optimal chemotherapy regimens produce response rates of 85% to 95%, with 50% to 60% of patients achieving a complete response. Although many patients initially respond to therapy, most eventually relapse and die from their small cell lung cancer. The median duration of survival is 12 to 16 months and the two-year disease-free survival rate is usually 15% to 20% for patients with limited disease. Response rates are somewhat lower for patients with disease outside the thoracic cavity and the median survival is only 7 to 11 months. The two-year disease-free survival for these patients is less than 2%.[96]

Staging

31. What information, in addition to the histologic type, is necessary before H.H.'s treatment can be initiated?

Before initiating therapy, the stage of H.H.'s disease should be evaluated. This will help to establish a prognosis and identify tumor lesions that can be monitored to evaluate the response to therapy. Staging also will assist in determining if H.H. will benefit from radiation therapy in addition to chemotherapy. Because the TNM staging factors do not appear to correlate with survival, a simple two-stage system is used for SCLC. Limited disease is defined as that confined to one hemithorax and the regional lymph nodes, whereas extensive disease is that which extends beyond the thorax. Staging procedures should include a thorough work-up of any areas that are suspicious for tumor involvement as well as the chest x-ray and CT scans, liver function tests and physical examination of the liver, CBC, and neurologic exam. In addition, an assessment of H.H.'s physiologic and performance status should be made to determine her ability to tolerate the aggressive chemotherapy and possible radiation therapy. This includes evaluation of her nutritional, cardiac, and pulmonary status. Renal and hepatic function also should be evaluated to determine if chemotherapy elimination will be normal.

Cancer Cachexia

32. Results of H.H.'s staging procedures determined that she had limited stage SCLC. However, her body weight is 25% below her ideal weight and her serum albumin is 3.0 gm/dL (Normal: 3.5–4.5). H.H. states that she has very little appetite and has not been eating much for several months. Her oncologist is concerned because chemotherapy is likely to worsen H.H.'s anorexia. Are H.H.'s anorexia and weight loss related to her cancer? Should chemotherapy be withheld until the anorexia is corrected? Can anything be done to stimulate her appetite? [SI units: albumin 30 gm/L (Normal: 35–45)]

Malnutrition is a common complication of cancer. Weight loss and poor nutritional status do not necessarily correlate with tumor histology, disease stage, or absolute caloric intake. The syndrome of cancer cachexia is complex and multifactorial and ultimately, effective therapy for the tumor results in successful treatment of the cachexia. Therefore, H.H. should receive chemotherapy.

Causes

Cancer cachexia has many causes. The most obvious are *mechanical alterations* caused by the tumor mass or complications from treatment that result in the loss or failure of organ function (e.g., liver, gastrointestinal tract), infections, or tissue damage (e.g., stomatitis, esophagitis). Frequently, patients with cancer have *taste alterations* such as a decreased tolerance to sweetness, an aversion to meat, and an increase in the tolerability of salty and sour foods.[107–110] These taste abnormalities usually resolve following effective treatment of the tumor. *Psychological factors* also can cause or contribute to anorexia in the cancer patient. Emotional stress can stimulate the release of catecholamines which have a negative effect on appetite.[18] Depression as well as food aversions which were learned during emetogenic chemotherapy also influence appetite.

Cancer cachexia cannot always be readily attributed to reduced caloric intake secondary to these factors. Even in advanced disease, the tumor mass is only a small percentage of the patient's total body weight, and it is unlikely that it competes with the host for sources of energy to the point of starvation. Changes in plasma protein concentrations and alterations in metabolic rates also occur in cancer patients.[112] The most common theory of cancer cachexia is that neoplastic cells produce or stimulate the secretion of circulating substances which alter energy utilization or conservation (i.e., a paraneoplastic effect).[113] *Cachectin* [also called tumor necrosis factor (TNF)] is produced by macrophages in response to endotoxin stimulation; the latter may not be specific for malignancy but a physiological response to tissue injury.[112,114] Cachectin is reported to cause anorexia and to alter the activity of adipocyte lipogenic enzymes.[114–116]

Management

Calorie supplements and alternate feeding methods may play a supportive role when anorexia, nausea, and vomiting limit administration of appropriate treatment for the underlying malignancy. High-dose megestrol acetate has been shown to increase appetite and cause weight gain in cancer patients and Tchekmedyian et al. reported significant weight gain in patients with advanced breast cancer receiving 480 to 1600 mg/day orally. Weight gain occurred regardless of pretreatment weight, response of the breast cancer, or the extent of disease spread.[117] Megestrol acetate or one of its metabolites may exert an effect at the cellular level to enhance appetite and metabolic activity.[118] Dronabinol or delta-9-tetrahydrocannabinol (Marinol) can stimulate appetite and weight gain in patients with the acquired immunodeficiency syndrome (AIDS).[119] The doses of dronabinol used in these trials (5 to 10 mg BID) are lower than those used for chemotherapy-induced emesis and side effects were rare.[119] Hydrazine sulfate is thought to augment appetite and retard weight loss through the inhibition of phosphoenol pyruvate kinase. However, controlled trials have failed to demonstrate any benefit.[120,121]

Chemotherapy

Combination Chemotherapy

33. H.H. is to be started on a chemotherapeutic regimen of cisplatin 100 mg/m^2 IV on day 1, etoposide 50 mg/m^2 IV on days 1–5, and vincristine 2 mg IV on day 1. The chemotherapy is to be repeated every 28 days. She also will receive radiation therapy to the area of tumor involvement. Is H.H. likely to benefit from the addition of other cytotoxic agents to her regimen?

Although combination chemotherapy is clearly superior to single-agent therapy in the treatment of SCLC, there are no major differences between a number of combination chemotherapy regimens which have been widely studied in terms of response rate or survival.[122] Cyclophosphamide, doxorubicin, etoposide, carboplatin, vincristine, and methotrexate are among many agents with significant activity against this disease and these drugs have been studied in many three- and four-drug regimens. Most of these agents cause dose-related bone marrow suppression, necessitating individual dosage reductions that could adversely effect antitumor activity. Currently, there is little evidence to support the use of more than three or four drugs simultaneously.[122] Because of the myelosuppressive effects of these regimens, filgrastim often is initiated following courses of chemotherapy to ameliorate granulocytopenia.[123]

Cisplatin has only modest activity as a single agent in SCLC patients who have failed prior therapy. However, its synergistic activity with etoposide in experimental systems has led to the evaluation of this combination in many human tumors including small cell lung cancer.[124] Early trials of the cisplatin and etoposide regimen in patients with refractory SCLC produced encouraging reports and led to its evaluation as first-line therapy.[125]

Etoposide Capsules

34. Can oral etoposide be substituted for the IV administration, and if so, are equivalent dosages used?

Etoposide capsules are available for use in combination with other agents in the treatment of SCLC and clinical trials in patients with small cell lung cancer, have demonstrated that regimens containing oral etoposide produce results comparable to those achieved with the intravenous formulation.[126] Since pharmacokinetic studies have indicated that the bioavailability of etoposide capsules is about 50%, the recommended oral dose is double the intravenous dose rounded to the nearest 50 mg.

However, because of the severe nausea and vomiting which may be caused by the cisplatin given on day 1, H.H. should receive the etoposide intravenously to avoid vomiting the capsules. If her vomiting is controlled by day 2 she can take the remaining doses orally. H.H. should contact her physician immediately if she experiences any vomiting.

More protracted schedules (2 to 3 weeks) of daily oral etoposide have shown activity in previously-treated and newly-diagnosed patients with SCLC; however, it is not known whether this schedule is superior to the schedule that H.H. will receive.[127,128]

Follow-Up Care

35. How should H.H. be monitored during therapy?

Follow-up care of a patient receiving chemotherapy should include: 1) assessment of chemotherapy-associated toxicities (e.g., mucositis, CBC, renal function, electrolytes) so that appropriate interventions may be initiated; 2) regular re-evaluation of renal, hepatic, and bone marrow function to assess the patient's ability to tolerate further treatment; and 3) assessment of the antitumor effects of the treatment.

Myelosuppression (i.e., granulocytopenia, thrombocytopenia) is generally only moderate with cisplatin-etoposide regimens; however, the addition of radiation therapy is likely to increase its severity. Therefore, H.H. should have her complete blood count monitored weekly once therapy begins. Because nephrotoxicity is the usual dose-limiting toxicity of cisplatin, renal function must be evaluated frequently.

Chest x-rays and CT scans should be repeated after every two courses of therapy to assess antitumor effects. Therapy should be continued if the tumor is responding to treatment and discontinued or changed if there is evidence of tumor progression.

Duration of Therapy and Prophylactic Irradiation

36. After 6 courses of this regimen, repeat chest x-rays and CT scans reveal no evidence of residual tumor in H.H. A repeat bronchoscopy is also negative. Is additional treatment indicated?

Despite the high recurrence rate for patients with SCLC who achieve a complete response, there is currently no evidence to support prolonged administration of chemotherapy after complete response is achieved. Long-term survival rates appear to be similar for patients who receive four to six months of treatment and those who receive 12 to 24 months.[96] In addition, patients who receive a shorter duration of chemotherapy exposure are less likely to suffer major toxicities.

Unfortunately, at least 20% to 25% of patients with SCLC eventually develop brain metastases which produce significant morbidity. Clinical trials have demonstrated that prophylactic cranial irradiation significantly reduces the incidence of subsequent brain metastases in patients achieving a complete remission following chemotherapy.[129–131] Therefore, prophylactic cranial irradiation is recommended for H.H. at this time. She also may require antiemetics to alleviate nausea.

Ovarian Cancer

Clinical Presentation and Risk Factors

37. C.R., a 50-year-old white female, presented to her family physician complaining of vague abdominal pain over the last

several weeks. A detailed history revealed that she had experienced increasing abdominal girth without significant weight gain and a change in her usual bowel habits. An abdominal and pelvic ultrasound showed a 6×10 cm mass, and her serum CA-125 antigen was markedly elevated. C.R. was then referred to a surgical gynecologist who performed a total abdominal hysterectomy and bilateral salpingo-oophorectomy. Pathological examination of the mass determined it to be epithelial carcinoma of the ovary. The large intra-abdominal mass and numerous peritoneal tumor implants were resected during surgery; however, several small (<0.5 cm) tumor implants were not resectable. What factors are associated with an increased risk of ovarian cancer? Are C.R.'s symptoms consistent with ovarian cancer?

Ovarian cancer is one of the leading causes of cancer deaths in women.[1] Industrialized countries have the highest incidence of ovarian cancer with the exception of Japan. Postmenopausal women (40 to 70+ years) are most likely to develop carcinoma of the ovary, while germ cell neoplasms are more common in younger women. Other factors which appear to increase the risk of ovarian cancer include endocrine disorders; nulliparity or a low number of pregnancies; positive family history; and a history of previous malignancies, particularly breast cancer.[132]

As in C.R.'s case, patients with early stages of ovarian cancer may be relatively asymptomatic. The patient's only complaint may be vague abdominal symptoms and she may not seek medical attention until symptoms become significantly worse. Unfortunately, ovarian carcinoma usually has extended beyond the pelvis at the time of diagnosis. Pain, abdominal distention, and vaginal bleeding are the most common symptoms in patients with advanced disease.[133,134] Other symptoms may include weight loss, nausea, or a change in bowel or bladder habits if the tumor mass is compressing adjacent structures.

Detection and the Papanicolaou (Pap) Test

38. C.R. was surprised by the diagnosis and questions why the cancer was not diagnosed earlier. She has always had routine annual physical and gynecologic examinations which included the Papanicolaou test.

Although the Papanicolaou (Pap) test is the single most successful screening test used in gynecology, it is not useful for detecting ovarian cancer.[135,136] The dramatic decrease in invasive cancers along with a 70% reduction in mortality confirms the efficacy of the Pap test as a screening tool for uterine cervical cancer.[137] (See Chapter 90: Neoplastic Disorders and Their Treatment: General Principles, Table 90.5.)

Although, the pelvic examination is the most common method of screening for ovarian cancer, it has a very low sensitivity; for every 10,000 examinations, approximately one tumor is detected.[138] Laparoscopy should not be used as a diagnostic tool for ovarian carcinoma because of the potential for spilling malignant cells into the peritoneal cavity and spreading the disease.[139]

Ovarian cancer has a low prevalence (13.8/100,000); however, women with a family history have increased risk for developing the disease. Ovarian masses may become large before they are detected since the ovaries are suspended by ligaments in a large spacious pelvic cavity. At the time of diagnosis, 75% of women with ovarian cancer have evidence of spread beyond the ovaries and in 60%, the cancer has spread beyond the pelvis.[139] The high incidence of ovarian cancer in women with a family history emphasizes the need for an effective screening program.

Abdominal ultrasounds produce a high number of false positives, even in high-risk populations. Andolf et al. used ultrasound as an adjunct to pelvic examination in 801 women ages 40 to 71 years who presented with gynecological complaints. There were

163 patients with abnormal ultrasounds and further work-up revealed only two endometrial cancers and one borderline ovarian cancer. They concluded that ultrasound does not have a role in screening for ovarian cancer.[140] Transvaginal sonography produces clearer images than abdominal scanning and more accurately identifies intrapelvic disease. Currently, neither test is recommended for screening women in the general populations.[141,142]

CA-125 is a monoclonal antibody which reacts to a tumor specific antigen. It is the most promising of the monoclonal antibodies, but unfortunately lacks sensitivity in detecting early ovarian cancer in that it is elevated in various nonmalignant states. Elevated CA-125 levels become more sensitive as the clinical stage of ovarian cancer advances: 50% for stages 1 and 2 and 90% for stage 3 and 4.[143,144]

Chemotherapy

39. Following surgery, C.R. was advised that she should receive chemotherapy to eradicate the small amounts of tumor cells that remain. Which antineoplastic drugs are effective in advanced ovarian carcinoma?

Single agents that have exhibited activity in the treatment of advanced ovarian cancer include cisplatin, doxorubicin, altretamine, fluorouracil, methotrexate, and the alkylating agents.[145] Most first-line regimens currently include cisplatin and cyclophosphamide, and it is questionable whether the addition of any other agents improves response rates or survival. Their addition will, however, increase toxicity.[146,147] When comparing combination chemotherapy regimens, those containing cisplatin appeared to have superior results which, in some trials, translated into improved survival durations.[148–150] When cisplatin was omitted from the cyclophosphamide, doxorubicin (Adriamycin), cisplatin (Platinol) (CAP) regimen, the complete response rate was 26% for the two-drug combination versus 51% for the three-drug regimen. The median survival was also significantly longer for the cisplatin-containing regimen (19.7 versus 15.7 months).[150]

Clearly, cisplatin plays a major role in the management of advanced ovarian cancer and is probably one of the most active agents against it. Whether doxorubicin adds therapeutic value to the CAP regimen is controversial. Several studies have compared the CAP regimen to cisplatin and have not demonstrated improved survival in patients receiving the three-drug regimen.[151–154] Carboplatin also has significant activity in ovarian cancer.[155–157]

Paclitaxel (Taxol) also has been evaluated in combination with cisplatin for newly-diagnosed disease. An initial trial reported modest increases in both response rate (79% versus 63%) and median survival (17.9 versus 23.8 months) for patients receiving the cisplatin and paclitaxel combination as compared to a standard cisplatin and cyclophosphamide regimen.[158]

Cisplatin Dosing

40. C.R. is to receive 6 courses of cisplatin 50 mg/m^2 plus cyclophosphamide 600 mg/m^2. Both drugs are to be given intravenously every 28 days. Would there be any potential increased benefit if the dose of either was escalated?

Dose intensity may influence survival in advanced ovarian cancer. When several different studies using the combination of cisplatin and cyclophosphamide are compared, the median survival durations increase with the dose intensity of cisplatin. Although this trend is encouraging, it is important to note that this observation does not represent a randomized trial and that many other factors such as study design, stage of disease, tumor burden, and cyclophosphamide dose differed among these studies.[147,148,151,159,160] Therefore, it would be reasonable to consider higher doses of cisplatin for C.R. if she can tolerate the renal and emetogenic effects.

Intraperitoneal (IP) Chemotherapy

41. What is the role of IP chemotherapy in ovarian cancer?

Advanced ovarian carcinoma usually is limited to the peritoneal cavity. Commonly, tumor plaques are attached to the underside of the diaphragm as well as the exterior of other organs within the abdominal cavity. Even following meticulous surgical removal of the tumor, there is nearly always some residual disease. Thus, intraperitoneal instillation of chemotherapeutic agents allows drug delivery directly to the site of the tumor and produces higher concentrations of drug at the tumor than could be attained by systemic administration. Although drug delivery to the tumor is primarily by surface diffusion, agents which are then absorbed systemically from the peritoneum also reach the tumor via capillary flow.[160] IP cisplatin has been the most widely studied and some patients (i.e., those with minimal disease, no large tumor masses, no adhesions) have responded.[161–163] Toxicities of intraperitoneal therapy include chemical peritonitis, fibrosis, and pain. Despite the theoretical advantages of IP chemotherapy, clinical trials have not substantiated that it improves survival for patients with advanced ovarian cancer.[164] In addition to therapeutic anticancer IP chemotherapy, drugs or radioisotopes occasionally are injected into the peritoneal cavity to control malignant ascites. Such instillation provides symptomatic relief with minimal treatment-related toxicity.[165]

Recurrent Disease

42. After 6 courses of cisplatin and cyclophosphamide, C.R. had no remaining evidence of ovarian cancer. Planned follow-up for C.R. included repeat serum CA-125 levels and CT scans at 3-month intervals. Six months after completing chemotherapy the CA-125 level was increased and a CT scan of the abdomen revealed several new masses. Should C.R. receive more cisplatin and cyclophosphamide therapy at this time?

Patients with disease that recurs within six months after treatment are unlikely to benefit from additional cisplatin therapy.[166,167] Therefore, it is most appropriate to treat C.R.'s cancer with a drug that has a different mechanism of action and, hopefully, a different pattern of resistance. Paclitaxel exerts its cytotoxic effect through a unique mechanism involving microtubule polymerization. This renders the mitotic spindle dysfunctional and arrests cell division in the late G_2 or early M phase of the cell cycle. Early clinical trials with paclitaxel as a single agent indicated that 25% to 35% of women with ovarian cancer who initially had been refractory to cisplatin or had relapsed following cisplatin therapy responded to 110 to 250 mg/m^2.[168–170] Although a few complete responses were documented in these trials, most patients had partial responses lasting about six months. Because toxicity (e.g., myelosuppression, neurotoxicity) was unacceptable at the higher dosages (especially in women who had received prior chemotherapy), the recommended dose of paclitaxel in ovarian cancer is 135 mg/m^2 repeated every three weeks.

Bladder Cancer
Clinical Presentation and Risk Factors

43. B.B., a 65-year-old male, presented with complaints consistent with cystitis including burning and pain on urination. Urinalysis (UA) reveals no WBC or bacteria and 10 red blood cells (RBCs)/high powered field (HPF). B.B. is a textile worker who smokes cigarettes but does not drink alcohol. He is referred to a urologist for cystoscopy, and the biopsy is consistent with multifocal, transitional cell carcinoma of the bladder, grade 3. What factors placed B.B. at risk for bladder cancer?

Risk factors for bladder cancer include age greater than 60 years, male gender, occupational exposure to chemical carcinogens (aryl amines including organic chemical, aniline dye, rubber and paint industries), cigarette smoking, drugs (cyclophosphamide and phenacetin), and chronic urinary tract infections.[171,172] Since the whole uroepithelium is chronically exposed to carcinogens excreted in the urine, these cancers tend to recur in multiple sites even after surgical resection. B.B.'s male gender, long career as a textile worker coupled with his significant history of cigarette smoking placed him at increased risk of bladder cancer.

The only symptom many patients experience before diagnosis is bladder irritation; in women, this may be mistaken for interstitial cystitis. Microscopic or gross hematuria is often the finding which prompts the patient to seek medical intervention. Patients with more extensive tumors may experience flank pain, constipation, or lower extremity edema.

Treatment

44. Further workup establishes that B.B.'s tumor is superficial (stage A). B.B. undergoes endoscopic resection and fulguration (tumor is charred and then scraped with a curet). Is further therapy indicated at this time?

Although resection is highly effective in eradicating existing lesions, 30% to 85% of patients eventually will develop new lesions.[173] B.B.'s tumor is also grade 3 (poorly differentiated) and multifocal which further increases his risk for recurrence.[174] Cystoscopy should be repeated at least every three months to detect new tumor loci. Until there is evidence of recurrence, no therapy is indicated.

Intravesical Chemotherapy

45. B.B.'s first follow-up cystoscopy reveals multifocal, superficial recurrent foci. How should this recurrent bladder cancer be managed?

Transurethral resection (TUR) of the cancer should be repeated and prophylactic (adjuvant) intravesical (instillation into the urinary bladder) therapy should be initiated. This route places high concentrations of the drug into direct contact with the bladder mucosa and can delay or prevent progression of disease (which could require cystectomy) or systemic chemotherapy.[175] The limited systemic absorption of intravesicular therapy also minimizes the risk of serious systemic toxicities.

Drugs which have been used intravesicularly include thiotepa, doxorubicin, mitomycin, and Bacillus-Calmette-Guerin (BCG). The few randomized studies that have been conducted suggest that BCG is superior to thiotepa and doxorubicin.[176,177] Definitive studies have not established superiority of BCG over mitomycin, but the trend clearly favors BCG.[175] Some patients experience a dose-limiting local irritation following BCG therapy which presents as dysuria, hematuria, and increased urinary frequency. Approximately 6% of patients experience severe systemic effects including fever, chills, and joint pain. There also have been cases of patients converting from negative to positive PPD skin test, as well as rare cases of active tuberculosis.[178] Other systemic effects following intravesical therapy are rare; however, myelosuppression is seen in approximately 20% of patients receiving thiotepa. Chemical cystitis is also a frequent toxicity following both mitomycin and doxorubicin therapy, with some patients experiencing contact dermatitis in the urogenital area.

The agents usually are given diluted in sterile saline or water and administered via catheter into an empty bladder. Patients are asked to retain the dose for two hours. Doses used are 30 to 60 mg of thiotepa, 20 to 80 mg of doxorubicin, or 20 to 60 mg of mitomycin C, each diluted in 60 mL. BCG is given in a dose of 120 mg in sterile saline. Of the seven substrains of BCG, the TICE, RIMV (Rotterdam Institute of Veterinary Medicine), Pasteur, Jap-

anese, Connaught, and Armand Frappeir strains appear to be effective, while the Glaxo strain appears to be relatively ineffective.[179] Although schedules vary, they generally consist of an initial weekly induction phase that lasts six weeks followed by monthly maintenance instillations for up to 12 months.

Neoadjuvant Therapy

46. After 4 months of BCG therapy, B.B. developed a local disease recurrence which had invaded through the bladder wall. Can cystectomy be avoided at this time?

Cystectomy or removal of the urinary bladder is a major surgical procedure which often is complicated by significant blood loss, infection, male impotence, and neurological impairment. Neoadjuvant chemotherapy with regimens such as methotrexate, vinblastine, doxorubicin, and cisplatin (i.e., M-VAC) with or without radiation therapy have produced pathological complete responses in approximately 30% of patients and delayed the need for radical surgery.[180–182] Response rates are inversely correlated with the depth of tumor invasion. Bladder preservation is possible in many cases; however, for patients with very advanced local disease avoidance of cystectomy is not realistic. For these patients, cystectomy followed by postoperative adjuvant therapy with a similar regimen (i.e., M-VAC) may represent a better strategy. Although the results of neoadjuvant and adjuvant therapy are encouraging it should be emphasized that neither approach has been shown to improve survival definitively.

Metastatic Disease

47. Following 2 courses of neoadjuvant M-VAC therapy and radiation, B.B. is able to undergo another endoscopic resection that renders him free of disease. What would be the usual pattern of disease recurrence and how should B.B. be monitored?

Approximately 40% of patients with bladder cancer develop metastatic disease during their clinical course. The most common sites of disease spread the are lymph nodes, liver, lung, and bone. Follow-up histories, physical examinations, and assessments should focus on these areas. Once the disease disseminates to a distant site, the prognosis is poor. Further chemotherapy with regimens such as M-VAC; cisplatin, cyclophosphamide and doxorubicin (CISCA); or investigational therapies may be considered if the patient is able to tolerate aggressive therapy. The likelihood of meaningful response is low in patients who have had prior exposure to these chemotherapeutic agents in the past, however.

Melanoma

Treatment

48. B.C., a 35-year-old white male, has worked for the last 12 years as a landscaper in south Florida. Two years before this admission he had undergone surgical resection of a stage II malignant melanoma. He underwent a wide excision of the area, but since he did not have lymphadenopathy, the regional lymph nodes were not dissected. B.C. now presents with complaints of enlarging, painful lymph nodes in his groin, and physical examination reveals several enlarged inguinal nodes and hepatomegaly. A lymph node biopsy confirms recurrence of malignant melanoma and liver function tests were as follows: AST 190 IU/L, ALT 165 IU/L, and bilirubin 2.2 mg/dL. Is chemotherapy indicated for B.C. who has metastatic malignant melanoma? [SI units: AST 190 U/L, ALT 165 U/L, bilirubin 37.62 μmol/L]

Today, melanoma accounts for only 3% of all cancer diagnoses in the U.S.; however, it is estimated that by the year 2000 that one in every 90 to 150 individuals in the U.S. will develop a melanoma. This represents the most dramatic increase in incidence of any of the neoplastic diseases. Melanoma can occur in adults of all age groups and affects Caucasians predominantly. The precise cause of melanoma is unknown; however, epidemiologic studies suggest that sunlight is the most important factor in its pathogenesis.[183] (Also see Question 49.) Melanocytes, the normal precursor cells, are found in the skin and other peripheral sites and synthesize melanin, which protects against ultraviolet damage. Various growth factor receptors, binding proteins, and other surface antigens have been identified on the surface of melanocytes at different stages during their transformation to malignant melanoma cells. Research is now focused on elucidation of the role of these antigens in the malignant transformation and their potential as targets for therapeutic interventions.

Cutaneous melanoma can arise on any surface of the skin and is perhaps the most visible of malignancies; therefore, it can be detected in asymptomatic individuals. Physical characteristics of melanoma are described in Table 93.4. Early detection and recognition of melanoma are essential for possible cure. Occasionally melanomas develop in noncutaneous tissues (e.g., the retina). The most critical factor in determining the prognosis following surgical removal of a melanoma is the vertical extension of the lesion into the skin and subcutaneous tissue; those that extend into the subcutaneous fat have a high rate of tumor recurrence and a grave prognosis. Once the melanoma has metastasized, surgery is no longer a therapeutic option.

To date, the results of chemotherapy in the treatment of melanoma have been disappointing. Single agents which have demonstrated modest activity include alkylating agents such as dacarbazine, carboplatin, carmustine, and cisplatin. However, most responses are only partial and the duration of response is generally only three to six months. Combination therapy using these agents as well as vincristine or vinblastine has produced only slightly improved response rates (overall response rate of about 30%).[183,184]

For several reasons, melanoma has been one of the most widely studied tumors in the area of immunotherapy. Commonly, melanoma cells express surface antigens which can be targeted by specific immunotherapy (e.g., monoclonal antibodies) and these surface antigens enhance recognition by the host's own immune system.[185,186] The latter is supported by the lymphocytic infiltrates frequently observed in tumor biopsies.[187] In addition, melanoma and its normal precursor cells, melanocytes, require growth factors for proliferation. Although melanocytes require exogenous growth factors, melanoma cells (at least sometimes) produce their own. This may explain, in part, the progressive nature of malignant melanomas.[188,189] The interferons and interleukin-2 are immunotherapies which have been most widely studied in the treatment of melanoma. Other immunotherapies which are under intense investigation include monoclonal antibodies, active immunotherapy by vaccination, and adoptive immunotherapy using tumor-infiltrating lymphocytes or lymphokine-activated killer cells.

Interferon Alpha

Early studies using interferon alfa demonstrated overall response rates of 15% to 20% with survival durations and time to progression of disease approximating that demonstrated by cytotoxic chemotherapy regimens.[186] In many cases, it may take three to six months for patients to achieve the maximum response to interferon. Patients most likely to respond include those with only cutaneous or pulmonary disease who have small tumor burdens. The optimal dose of interferon in melanoma has not been clearly defined; similar responses have been reported for doses ranging from 10 million units/m^2/day to 50 million units/m^2 every other day.

Interleukin-2 (IL-2)

Initial studies using high-dose interleukin-2 (IL-2) either alone or in combination with lymphokine-activated killer (LAK) cells produced overall response rates of only 10% to 20%. Importantly, about 5% of patients responded completely, most of whom have been maintained for many years.[190,191] Partial responses are typically of brief duration.

Several different preparations of IL-2 have been used in clinical trials, and some confusion regarding various clinical trials has resulted because of variations in administration (on a per m^2 or per kg of body weight basis) as well as the use of different unit standards. The World Health Organization has now defined international units.[192,193] In the case of the commercially available aldesleukin (Proleukin Chiron Therapeutics, Inc), a milligram which had previously been defined as equivalent to 3 million Cetus units, is now defined as equivalent to 18 million international units. Attention to the formulation and units is crucial for ensuring appropriate dosage.

Regimens using high doses of interleukin-2 (e.g., 600,000 international units/kg Q 8 hr for 15 days) have been associated with considerable dose-related toxicities.[188,190–194] Most of these can be included in a "diffuse capillary leak syndrome" characterized by intravascular volume depletion, oliguria, and edema of all major organs resulting in multiorgan dysfunction. Once therapy is discontinued, the capillary leak and related toxicities resolve quickly. During therapy, fluid balance must be carefully and frequently evaluated and intravenous hydration administered cautiously. Early administration of vasopressors is usually necessary when patients receive high-dose therapy to maintain systemic perfusion and enhance urinary output. Patients also require H$_2$-receptor antagonists to prevent gastritis and premedication with acetaminophen and a nonsteroidal anti-inflammatory drug (such as indomethacin) to prevent fever and chills associated with IL-2 administration. Meperidine is usually effective in attenuating chills when they occur. Concurrent with resolution of widespread edema, desquamation and intense pruritus often is observed which can be managed with emollients. Corticosteroids should not be given because they may attenuate the immunomodulatory effects of IL-2. Even though patients receiving single agent IL-2 do not become neutropenic, a high incidence of staphylococcal bacteremia also has been observed and prophylactic treatment with systemic vancomycin has been recommended.

Table 93.4	Danger Signs of Malignant Melanoma[199]

Examine Skin Lesions for:

Change in Color
Especially multiple shades of dark brown or black; red, white, and blue; spread of color from the edge of the lesion into surrounding skin

Change in Size
Especially sudden or continuous enlargement

Change in Shape
Especially development of irregular margins

Change in Elevation
Especially sudden elevation of a previously macular pigmented lesion

Change in Surface
Especially scaliness, erosion, oozing, crusting, ulceration, bleeding

Change in Surrounding Skin
Especially redness, swelling, satellite pigmentations

Change in Sensation
Especially itching, tenderness, pain

Change in Consistency
Especially softening or friability

Costs associated with high-dose IL-2 therapy are high. The average cost of the drug itself for a single course of therapy is approximately $15,000 to $20,000. Hospitalization and ancillary therapies add another several thousand dollars to overall treatment costs.

Interleukin-2 (IL-2) Plus Chemotherapy

More recently, interleukin-2 has been given in lower dosages and in combination with cytotoxic agents (e.g., dacarbazine, cisplatin, cyclophosphamide, carmustine) or interferon alfa in the treatment of malignant melanoma.[195-197] Response rates reported with some of these early trials have been encouraging. Using a regimen including IL-2, interferon alfa, carmustine, dacarbazine, cisplatin, and tamoxifen, Richard et al. reported an overall response rate of 55% with 24% achieving a complete response.[195]

Tamoxifen was initially added to many combination chemotherapy regimens for melanoma because of the presence of estrogen receptors on some melanoma cells.[198] A randomized trial comparing dacarbazine alone to dacarbazine plus tamoxifen reported a higher response rate (28% versus 12%) and a longer survival (48 versus 29 weeks) for patients receiving tamoxifen.[198] In other nonrandomized trials, the impact of tamoxifen has been controversial.[220]

Toxicities of these combination regimens are acceptable. Because lower overall dosages of IL-2 generally are used, few patients develop the acute capillary leak syndrome; however, patients do experience severe fever and chills and chronic malaise which may be attributed to the IL-2 or interferon. In addition, the cytotoxic agents cause many patients to experience periods of profound neutropenia and many require platelet transfusions for thrombocytopenia. Patients receiving combinations that include emetogenic chemotherapy also require aggressive prophylactic antiemetic therapy. Even though advances in the treatment of metastatic melanoma have been made, response rates are low and duration of survival is usually brief. Therefore, when possible, patients should be included in clinical research protocols. When this is not possible, cisplatin-based combination chemotherapy with or without IL-2 should be considered; however, the risks of serious toxicities and the impact of this therapy on quality of life must be carefully weighed against its poor potential benefits.

Risk Factors

49. Are B.C.'s children at risk for developing skin cancer? Should they receive any counseling on early detection of skin cancers or self-examination of the skin?

B.C.'s children may be at increased risk for developing malignant melanoma, particularly if they are fair skinned, tan poorly (e.g., a history of freckling or severe sunburns) and have red hair or lightly pigmented eyes. Those with a hereditary dysplastic nevus syndrome also have a high risk of subsequent malignant melanoma. Offspring should be evaluated for such risk factors, since early diagnosis can be lifesaving.

Risk should be assessed during routine physical examinations. Charting or mapping unusually pigmented lesions, surveillance photography, and monthly self-examination may be particularly helpful in high-risk individuals. Adults should examine the skin for any noticeable changes in existing lesions or for new ones and report them. (See Table 93.4.)

Prostate Cancer

Etiology and Risk Factors

50. J.D., a 65-year-old black male, was diagnosed with prostate carcinoma 18 months ago. At that time, he underwent a radical prostatectomy and was found to have stage B disease (confined to the prostate). Before surgery, his prostate specific antigen (PSA) was 25 ng/mL (Normal: <3.0). At a regular follow-up examination J.D.'s only complaint was mild backache which he attributed to strain. His PSA was found to be 100 ng/mL and a CT scan of the pelvis showed a number of enlarged lymph nodes consistent with metastatic prostate cancer. Bone scan revealed blastic lesions in the lumbar region of the spine. J.D. was otherwise asymptomatic and his only other medical problems are 20-year history of essential hypertension and evidence of early congestive heart failure. What are J.D.'s risk factors for prostate cancer?

Although adenocarcinoma of the prostate is the most common malignancy in adult males in the U.S., specific risk factors (other than male gender and increasing age) have not been identified. Unfortunately, the highest incidence worldwide is in black males. In this group, the incidence is 1.7 times that of Caucasian males in the U.S.[200,201]

The etiology of prostate cancer is unknown. Regional variation in incidence worldwide suggests that environmental factors may have a role. Nationalized males have incidence rates that are intermediate between those born in the U.S. and those who have remained in their native country which suggests that environmental factors also contribute. Increased risk also has been linked to high meat and saturated fat diets and exposure to cadmium. High levels of testosterone also have been implicated in prostate cancer development. Support for a hormonal etiology includes the hormone dependence of prostate cancer, the absence of prostate cancer in eunuchs, and the increased incidence in male populations with higher testosterone levels. An increased risk of prostate cancer in patients with benign prostatic hyperplasia has been suggested, although others have not observed this association. Case reports have suggested those with a family history of the disease or prior venereal disease may be at increased risk.

The value of widespread screening and early detection of prostate cancer is questionable at present, because the optimum management of early stage prostate cancer is not well-defined and there is not clear-cut evidence that early intervention will affect overall survival.[200]

Staging

51. Is J.D.'s disease still considered stage B?

No. Stage B disease is confined to the prostate, and J.D. now has obvious spread to the pelvic lymph nodes and bone (stage D). The stage of the disease determines the most appropriate therapy. Whereas stage B usually is treated with surgery (radical prostatectomy) or radiation therapy, the mainstay of treatment for symptomatic stage D prostate cancer is hormonal manipulation.

Treatment

52. Does J.D.'s disease require therapy at this time?

Yes. J.D. has advanced disease and is experiencing symptoms which could progress and cause him considerable pain and loss of neurologic function if left untreated. If he had been asymptomatic with progressing disease (i.e., an increasing PSA level with no identifiable site of disease), it is unlikely that therapy would be beneficial because available therapies (e.g., hormonal manipulations) provide only suppressive effects and are not curative.

Hormonal manipulation that reduces testosterone to levels consistent with castration is the mainstay of pharmacotherapy for advanced symptomatic prostate cancer. Testosterone deprivation is effective against prostate tumor cells because the growth of both normal and malignant prostate tissue depends upon testosterone.

There are multiple hormonal manipulations which may be employed. These include: 1) ablation of androgen sources, 2) inhibition of testosterone production, and 3) interference of testosterone binding at its receptor site. (See Figure 93.1.)

Testosterone is produced by the testicles in response to pituitary FSH and LH and also by metabolic conversion of androgens produced by the adrenal glands. Testosterone is converted by alpha reductase enzymes to dihydrotestosterone, the major intracellular androgen, which then binds to a specific cytoplasmic receptor protein. The receptor-dihydrotestosterone complex is then translocated into the prostatic nucleus where it binds to and activates DNA, to induce the production of messenger RNA. Messenger RNA then codes for proteins that are essential for the metabolic functions of the prostate cells, including prostate cancer cells.

Therapeutic options for J.D. at this time include: 1) orchiectomy; 2) DES or LHRH analogs (leuprolide or goserelin) which decrease FSH and LH synthesis and production which in turn decreases testosterone production; or 3) flutamide which inhibits dihydrotestosterone binding to its receptor.

Choice of Therapy

53. Which therapy would be the most appropriate choice for J.D. at this time?

Bilateral orchiectomy is considered by many to be the therapy of choice because it permanently removes the primary source of testosterone production (95%) with few surgical complications. Orchiectomy does cause impotence (as do all forms of testosterone ablation)[202] but avoids the need for regular long-term administration of drugs with potential side effects. Nevertheless, some patients find this procedure unacceptable.

Diethylstilbestrol (DES) (1 mg TID) decreases serum testosterone to castration levels. Although the efficacy was similar, lower dosages of DES (i.e., 1 mg/day) have produced inconsistent suppression, whereas higher dosages (i.e., 5 mg/day) have been associated with increased thromboembolic complications and cardiovascular deaths. The relative risk of cardiovascular complications (stroke, deep venous thrombosis, myocardial infarction) has not been firmly established for the 3 mg/day dose; however, it is less than the 5 mg/day dose. These side effects are relevant in J.D. who has hypertension and early signs of congestive heart failure. Other complications of DES therapy include fluid retention, nausea, vomiting, and gynecomastia. The latter can be attenuated by radiating the breasts before estrogen therapy.[202]

Leuprolide and Goserelin (LHRH Analogs). Leuprolide (Leupron) and goserelin (Zoladex) are LHRH analogs. Like LHRH itself, they stimulate the release of FSH and LH by the pituitary which leads to an increase in production of testosterone. When therapy is initiated, there is an initial testosterone surge which produces transient worsening of symptoms such as pain (i.e., flare reactions). In severe cases, local tumor growth can result in urinary obstruction or spinal cord compression. However, over several weeks, the LHRH receptors in the pituitary are down-regulated by the continuous onslaught of synthetic LHRH, and there is a decline in the release of LH. Ultimately, the level of FSH, LH, and testosterone become profoundly suppressed.

In a large comparison of leuprolide with DES, response rates were equivalent and toxicity was less in the leuprolide group.[203] Leuprolide and goserelin are long-acting formulations which require monthly injections. The efficacy of leuprolide (7.5 mg IM monthly) and goserelin [3.6 mg subcutaneously (SQ) monthly] appear to be similar, although large scale comparative trials have not been completed. Goserelin often is less expensive; however, some patients find injection of the goserelin dosage form (pellet) to be painful. Therapy with either drug is continued until the disease progresses (i.e., new metastatic sites).

Antiandrogens. Monotherapy with antiandrogens such as flutamide, megestrol, and cyproterone has been evaluated in a small number of trials. Flutamide blocks androgen uptake and receptor binding. In 72 previously untreated patients with advanced prostate cancer flutamide, 250 mg three times daily, produced responses in 88% of patients;[204] however, monotherapy with flutamide can induce a compensatory increase in LH release resulting in a gradual increase in testosterone levels. This ultimately reverses androgen blockade.[200] Flutamide can cause gynecomastia, gastrointestinal disturbances, and chemical hepatitis. However, because it does not directly reduce testosterone levels, patients often can maintain sexual potency.

A clinical trial which compared leuprolide alone to leuprolide plus flutamide demonstrated longer median survival (28.3 versus 35.6 months) and fewer acute flare reactions in the combination arm.[205] This approach suppresses testosterone production by the testes and receptor blockade of adrenally-produced testosterone, and frequently is referred to as "total androgen blockade." Collectively, large studies addressing combined androgen blockade

Complete Androgen Withdrawal
LHRH-A + Anti-Androgen

a) LHRH-A blocks the formation of male hormones (androgens) by the testis
b) Anti-androgen prevents the action of androgens of adrenal and testicular origin
c) Combination of both drugs should exert maximal inhibitory effects on cancer growth by eliminating all androgenic stimulation

Advantages

— Eliminates the action of all androgens
— No secondary effects
— Can be administered early in order to prevent dissemination of cancer to other tissues and development of androgen-insensitive cell clones

Fig 93.1 Complete Androgen Withdrawal in Prostate Cancer LHRH = Luteinizing hormone-releasing hormone; LHRH-A = LHRH analog; LH = Luteinizing hormone; ACTH = Adrenocorticotropic hormone; CRF = Corticotropin-releasing factor. Reprinted with permission from reference 202.

have shown that for patients with widespread disease and poor performance status, combined therapy offers no advantage over LHRH agonists alone or orchiectomy.[206-208] For patients, like J.D., with minimal metastatic disease there appears to be a survival advantage with combined therapy of six months to two years.

Because of his pre-existing cardiovascular disease, DES would not be an appropriate choice for J.D. Combined androgen therapy (leuprolide plus flutamide) or orchiectomy plus flutamide would be appropriate choices given his minimal disease and good performance status.

Monitoring Therapy

54. J.D. was started on leuprolide 7.5 mg IM monthly and flutamide 250 mg TID. How should his response therapy be monitored?

Blastic bone lesions heal slowly and have been shown to persist even when biopsy documents absence of disease. A repeat bone scan, therefore, would not be a useful indicator of response; however, it may be used to rule out new lesions or progressive disease. If bony lesions improve, it may take up to six months for resolution on the bone scan due to slow bone remodeling in elderly men.

Measurement of PSA is the most useful tool to follow response to therapy. Because the serum half-life of PSA is only two to four days, serial measurements provide a rapid indication of tumor status. It also is less expensive and more sensitive than imaging techniques (e.g., CT scans, bone scans). Control of symptoms such as pain and maintenance of quality of life are important outcome indicators in this disease and should be monitored frequently.

Second-Line Therapies

55. Following initiation of treatment, J.D.'s PSA level fell to 20 ng/mL and remained stable for the next 18 months. During this time, he had no clinical evidence of disease progression. However, his most recent clinic visit revealed an increase in his PSA level to 75 ng/mL and a repeat bone scan and pelvic CT showed some progression. Is a change in therapy warranted at this time?

Various second-line hormonal therapies have been studied. In most cases, the response rate was about 20% in patients who had previously responded to hormonal manipulation and the duration of responses was less than six months. In patients who have received monotherapy with a DES or an LHRH agonist, androgen receptor blockade with flutamide or inhibition of adrenal androgen synthesis with aminoglutethimide or ketoconazole are the most widely used approaches. Because J.D. has already been receiving flutamide, addition of aminoglutethimide or ketoconazole to the existing regimen may be beneficial. Leuprolide and flutamide should not be discontinued because they will continue to suppress testosterone production and block receptor binding, respectively. Withdrawal of either agent could lead to accelerated disease progression.

Aminoglutethimide inhibits the desmolase enzyme complex in the adrenal gland thereby preventing synthesis of all adrenally-derived steroids. Therefore, concurrent physiological replacement of glucocorticoids is essential, and mineralocorticoid replacement may be necessary in selected patients. Therapy usually is initiated with 250 mg twice a day and gradually increased to 250 mg four times a day as the patient tolerates therapy. Responses to aminoglutethimide may take up to four to six weeks. Approximately 50% of patients experience adverse effects which may include central nervous system effects (lethargy, ataxia, dizziness) and a morbilliform, pruritic rash which is self-limiting and usually resolves within five to eight days with continued therapy.

Ketoconazole, an imidazole antifungal agent, interferes with both adrenal and testicular steroidogenesis. In doses of 400 mg

every eight hours response is rapid and adverse effects include gastrointestinal intolerance, transient increases in liver and renal function tests, weakness, lethargy, and skin pigmentation. Concurrent physiological replacement of glucocorticoids also is recommended.

J.D. is not experiencing progressive symptoms at this time and therefore the benefits of addition therapy with either aminoglutethimide or ketoconazole probably do not outweigh the potential risks and complications of treatment and its associated costs.

Spinal Cord Compression

56. Three weeks after his last clinic visit, J.D. phoned his physician with complaints of worsening back pain and new onset tingling in his lower extremities. Upon questioning, he denied being incontinent of either urine or stool. He was instructed to return to the hospital immediately and an emergency MRI of the spine showed epidural compression at the level of L3 and L4. How should J.D.'s spinal cord compression be treated?

Spinal cord compression by tumor is considered an oncologic emergency which requires immediate intervention to avoid irreversible paralysis and loss of bladder and bowel function. High dose corticosteroids (e.g., minimum dose of dexamethasone 10 mg Q 6 hr) should be initiated immediately to improve neurologic function and alleviate pain. If improvement is not demonstrated, higher dosages of dexamethasone (up to 100 mg/day) have been reported to produce dose-related improvement. Definitive therapy with radiotherapy or surgery followed by radiotherapy should then be employed.

Cytotoxic Chemotherapy

57. Despite effective treatment of his spinal cord compression, J.D.'s remaining metastatic disease continued to progress. Would cytotoxic chemotherapy be beneficial at this time?

A large number of clinical trials have evaluated the use of chemotherapeutic agents in patients with progressive prostate cancer after hormonal therapy. Several chemotherapeutic agents including doxorubicin, cisplatin, and cyclophosphamide have demonstrated modest activity against prostate cancer. Such agents appear to produce objective response rates in 10% to 30% of patients with an additional 20% to 30% of patients experiencing transient stabilization of their disease progression. The efficacy of combination chemotherapy is not consistently superior to single agents and is frequently associated with more unacceptable toxicities in this elderly patient group. Consequently, a single agent such as doxorubicin 45 mg/m^2 every three weeks is used most frequently. *Suramin*, an investigational antineoplastic agent, blocks the action of a wide range of cytokines, including growth factors that are involved in the regulation of prostatic epithelium. Phase II trials have reported response rates of greater than 40%; however, serious side effects have been associated with treatment.[209,210]

Testicular Cancer

Clinical Presentation

58. M.W., a 26-year-old male, noticed painless swelling of his left testicle about 2 or 3 weeks before seeing his family physician. Physical examination revealed an indurated mass located in the lower pole of the left testicle. Epididymitis was ruled out due to the location. Alpha fetoprotein (AFP) was 300 ng/mL (Normal: <40), beta human chorionic gonadotropin (BHCG) (<5 IU/L) was negative, and LD was 43 U/L. He was referred to a urologist who performed an orchiectomy. The pathology report revealed embryonal carcinoma. Following orchiectomy the AFP was 270 ng/mL, but a metastatic work up including chest x-ray and CT scan of the abdomen and pelvis

revealed no evidence of disease. Is this a typical presentation of testicle cancer? [SI units: AFP 300 and 270 µg/L, respectively (Normal: <40); LD 43 U/L]

Testes cancer is the most common malignancy in men between ages 15 and 35 years. M.W.'s presentation is typical in that the cancer presents as a painless swelling in one gonad. The cause of testicular cancer is unknown, but about 10% of patients have a history of cryptorchidism.[211] Other possible risk factors include race (the incidence is much lower among black males) and family history.[212]

Histologic Classification

59. Does histologic classification provide a clinical basis for therapeutic decisions?

Germinal neoplasms are divided into seminomas and a variety of other types known collectively as nonseminomatous germ cell tumors. (See Table 93.5.) Seminomas arise from malignant transformations of spermatocytes whereas nonseminomas arise from transformation of germ cells of placental origin. Although treatment of advanced disease is similar, seminoma is exquisitely sensitive to radiation and therefore early stages of the disease are more frequently treated with radiotherapy.[213] The determination of the most appropriate therapy is dependent upon both the histology and the stage of the disease. Since M.W. has a nonseminoma (i.e., embryonal carcinoma), initial radiation is not indicated.

Staging

60. What is the stage of M.W.'s disease?

Stage I disease is limited to the testes; stage II disease involves the testes and lymph nodes; and stage III disease includes all metastatic tumors. Because M.W. had two positive lymph nodes, his disease is classified as stage II.

Treatment

61. Was the initial management of M.W.'s disease appropriate?

Radical inguinal orchiectomy is required to make the diagnosis of testicular cancer. Following orchiectomy, a metastatic work-up was completed to rule out spread of the disease. This work-up should include chest x-ray, evaluation of retroperitoneal lymph nodes, and assessment of decline in the tumor markers following orchiectomy. The persistent elevation of M.W.'s AFP following orchiectomy was indicative of residual tumor which led to dissection of the retroperitoneal lymph nodes, the most likely site of residual disease.

Adjuvant Chemotherapy

62. Retroperitoneal lymph node dissection was performed and 2 of 8 nodes were found to be positive for tumor. Following the node dissection the AFP and BHCG declined exponentially. Is adjuvant chemotherapy indicated at this time?

Table 93.5	Histologic Classification of Primary Tumors of the Testes

Germinal Neoplasms
    Seminoma
    Embryonal carcinoma
    Teratoma
    Choriocarcinoma
    Yolk sac tumor

Nongerminal Neoplasms
    Specialized gonadal stromal neoplasms (e.g., Leydig cell tumor)
    Gonadoblastoma
    Miscellaneous (e.g., adenocarcinoma, carcinoid, mesenchymal)

About 50% of patients like M.W. whose disease is apparently completely resected (AFP declined following lymph node dissection) ultimately relapse,[213] and adjuvant chemotherapy dramatically reduces this risk. However, if patients do not receive adjuvant chemotherapy and are monitored closely for early detection of relapse, the chance of cure following aggressive induction chemotherapy is still very high (>80%).[214]

Metastatic Disease: Chemotherapy

63. It is decided that M.W. will not receive adjuvant therapy at this time but will be followed by a monthly history, physical examination, and AFP for the first year, every 2 months during the second year, and every 6 months thereafter. After 4 months M.W. is lost to follow-up. He returned to his urologist 1 year later with complaints of abdominal discomfort and SOB. Chest x-ray revealed multiple nodules in the lung and an abdominal CT revealed a 6 × 10 cm mass. His AFP was 360 ng/mL and the BHCG was 290 ng/mL. Is chemotherapy indicated at this time? [SI unit: AFP 360 µg/L]

M.W. now has metastatic testicular cancer and should receive systemic chemotherapy. For many years the combinations of either cisplatin, vinblastine, and bleomycin or cisplatin or etoposide plus bleomycin have produced responses in almost all men and complete responses in 60% to 80%.[215–217] A randomized trial demonstrated a higher long-term survival rate for patients who had received etoposide and this combination is most widely used today.[217]

Before chemotherapy, pulmonary function tests, an audiogram, and a 24-hour urinary creatinine clearance were obtained. M.W. was hydrated with intravenous D5/0.45 NaCl and chemotherapy was initiated with cisplatin 20 mg/m²/day for five days, etoposide 100 mg/m² on days one to five, and bleomycin 30 mg on days 2, 9, and 16. Courses were repeated every 21 days.

64. Monitoring Therapy. How should M.W. be monitored for therapeutic and toxic responses to chemotherapy?

Response to chemotherapy would be demonstrated by a reduction in the size of the abdominal mass, a reduction in the size and number of pulmonary nodules, and a steady decrease in the AFP and BHCG without any other evidence of disease progression. CT scans, chest x-ray, and tumor markers are typically re-evaluated after every second course of therapy.

The most significant toxicities associated with this regimen include myelosuppression and the nephrotoxicity and neurotoxicity associated with cisplatin. A CBC with differential and platelet count should be done once or twice weekly until the myelosuppression has resolved and just before the next course. Serum creatinine, BUN, and electrolytes (including magnesium) should be done daily during chemotherapy and weekly thereafter. If evidence of toxicity appears, more intense monitoring may be recommended. Weekly symptom analysis and physical examination should include assessment for cisplatin neurotoxicity and other chemotherapy-associated toxicities. In order to assess bleomycin lung toxicity baseline pulmonary function tests should be done before the first course and after every second or third course.

65. M.W.'s AFP and BHCG dropped dramatically following his first course of chemotherapy and less so after his second course; however, they appeared to plateau at an AFP of 170 ng/mL and BHCG of 200 ng/mL following the third course. There is no evidence of tumor on the abdominal CT scan or chest x-ray. Should the fourth and fifth cycles of chemotherapy be administered? [SI unit: AFP 170 µg/L]

The plateau of the tumor markers confirms that M.W.'s disease is not continuing to regress after chemotherapy. First line cisplatin-based combination chemotherapy cures 70% of patients with disseminated germ cell tumors.[215–217] The remaining 30% of patients are candidates for salvage chemotherapy at the time of relapse or disease progression. Additional cycles of chemotherapy with the same regimen are unlikely to produce further tumor regression and normalization of the tumor markers. Because he had an initial good response to cisplatin therapy it is reasonable to continue cisplatin in this circumstance.[211] M.W. should receive salvage chemotherapy with cisplatin 20 mg/m^2/day for five days, vinblastine 0.11 mg/kg on days 1 and 2, and ifosfamide 1.2 gm/m^2/day for five days. (See Chapters 90: Neoplastic Disorders and Their Treatment: General Principles and 91: Adverse Effects of Chemotherapy.) As a single agent, ifosfamide produces responses in about 22% of patients with refractory germ cell tumors.[218] In patients like M.W., the combination of ifosfamide with cisplatin and vinblastine has produced a 36% complete response rate with a median duration of remission of 34 months.[219] Mesna should be administered concurrently with ifosfamide to prevent hemorrhagic cystitis. (See Chapter 91: Adverse Effects of Chemotherapy.)

The response and long-term survival rates reported with both first-line and salvage chemotherapy for testicular cancer are considerably higher than for most solid tumors. Because of the likelihood of long-term survival, efforts are now focused on minimizing the long-term sequelae of chemotherapy (e.g., secondary malignancies, sterility).

Pediatric Solid Tumors

Statistics

In the U.S., more children between 1 and 14 years of age die of cancer than any other disease.[222] Yet, many common pediatric cancers which had very low cure rates before the advent of chemotherapy now have five-year survivals above 65%. Acute leukemias are the most common malignancies of childhood (see Figure 93.2), with the solid tumors in this chapter each representing 3% to 8% of all childhood malignancies.[223] Many common pediatric solid tumors are uncommon in adults. Likewise, many tumors common in adults occur infrequently in children. In general, sarcomas are common in children, while carcinomas predominate in adults.

Small Round Cell Tumors

Several pediatric malignancies present as small round cell tumors, making morphological diagnosis by traditional light microscopy more difficult.[224,225] The biggest diagnostic problems are the less typical forms of these diseases. The list commonly includes peripheral primitive neuroectodermal tumors, extraosseous Ewing's sarcoma, extranodal lymphoma, rhabdomyosarcoma, metastatic neuroblastoma, and some bone sarcomas. Problems involved with diagnosing these tumors have stimulated the development of newer techniques aimed at detecting tumor-specific antigens or chromosomal aberrations. This information may prove useful in identifying prognostic subgroups as well as tumor types in children and adults with cancer.

Genetics

Similar to adult cancers, the association between many pediatric cancers and chromosomal aberrations or genetic defects is well confirmed. Examples include the association of Wilms' tumor with congenital malformations,[224] acute lymphoblastic leukemia with Down's syndrome,[226] and the association of some pediatric cancers with loss of the p53 or retinoblastoma genes.[225] The latter are tumor suppressor genes.

Carcinogens

The role of carcinogens in pediatric cancer is probably less than in adults due to the long latency periods required. However, carcinogens are implicated in the etiology of some childhood cancers.[227] Postnatal exposure to ionizing radiation is associated with acute leukemias, chronic myelogenous leukemia, and solid tumors such as those affecting the brain, thyroid, salivary gland, bone, and other sarcomas.[227] Treatment of pediatric malignancies with alkylators is associated with an increased risk of leukemias.[228] Etoposide and teniposide are associated with an increased risk of secondary acute myelogenous leukemia.[229] Treatment of childhood acute lymphoblastic leukemia, especially in those less than five years of age who received irradiation, results in an increased risk of central nervous system neoplasms, leukemia, lymphoma, and other neoplasms later in life.[230] The only well documented prenatal carcinogen is diethylstilbestrol (DES), which is associated with an increased risk of vaginal or cervical cancer in offspring.[231]

Patient Age

Patient age can be a factor in pediatric cancers and their treatment. Neuroblastoma is the most common malignancy in infants;

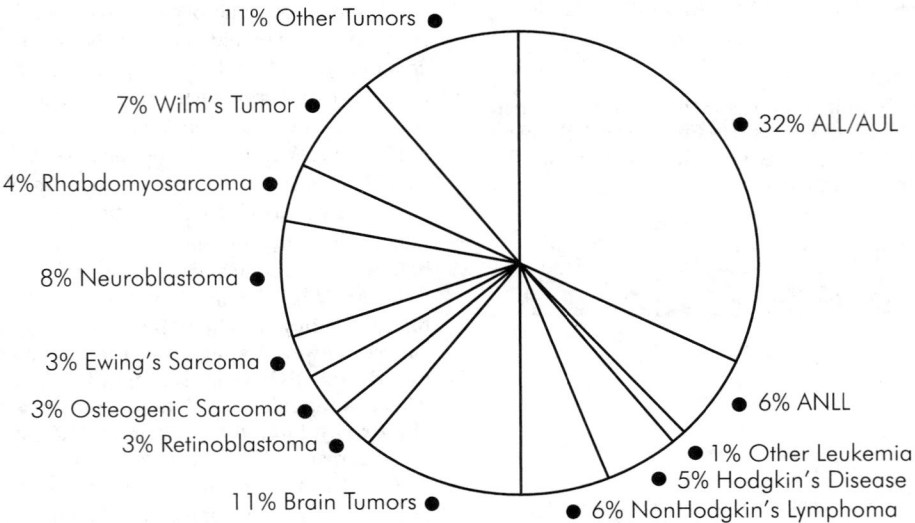

Fig 93.2   Approximate Percent Distribution of Common Pediatric Cancers, Using Data from the Children's Study Group   Reprinted with permission.
Nursing Clinics of North America, reference 4.

however, an infant's prognosis is typically better than a child's. This is apparently due to the biology of the disease in this age group.[232] Infants with acute lymphoblastic leukemia tend to have a worse prognosis than older children.[233] The biology and location of rhabdomyosarcoma are often different in younger versus older children, with younger children having the better overall survival.[234]

Similarly, age may be a consideration regarding toxicity of treatments. Children may have increased susceptibility to toxicity from irradiation. Normal organ development may be disrupted, especially that of the skeletal system,[232] and in children under four years old, the brain.[235] Prepubertal children may have a decreased risk of fertility problems from chemotherapy relative to older children and adults,[235] and conversely, children appear to have a greater risk than adults for cardiovascular toxicity from anthracyclines.[236]

Multi-Institutional Research Groups

With the exception of a few pediatric oncology centers, most treatment centers do not have enough patients with specific diagnoses to scientifically establish the efficacy of therapeutic regimens within a reasonable timeframe. Thus, most centers join multi-institutional research groups such as the Pediatric Oncology Group (POG) or the Children's Cancer Group (CCG) to pool their patients. Through this mechanism, clinical trials often can be finished over three to four years, allowing for more rapid progress in the treatment of pediatric cancers.

With the number of childhood cancer survivors increasing, research is focusing on reducing the long-term risks and complications of treatment modalities. It is important to determine which patients are at the greatest risk from their cancer and to stratify treatments such that the minimum treatment to cure is given where prognoses are good, and maximal treatment is given where the potential benefit outweighs the risks. Progress is already being made in this direction, and the future holds promise, especially with rapid gains in our understanding of the biology of cancers.

Neuroblastoma

Neuroblastoma develops in immature cells of sympathetic nervous system origin.[237] It is the most common extracranial tumor of childhood, representing approximately 8% of all childhood cancers.[223] The median age at diagnosis is 22 months; 36% occur below 1 year, and 79% before 4 years of age.[237] Sixty five percent of neuroblastomas are abdominal (half of these adrenal) and 20% thoracic.[237] Neuroblastoma often presents as a fixed, hard, abdominal mass noted by the family or physician without any other signs or symptoms, although other findings may be present depending upon the location of the primary tumor and metastases. For example, gastrointestinal fullness, discomfort, or dysfunction can occur. Other less common but characteristic signs include proptosis with peri-orbital ecchymoses, increased-renin hypertension, secretory diarrhea with increased vasoactive intestinal peptide, opsomyoclonus, and unilateral ptosis.[237] The catecholamine metabolites vanillylmandelic acid (VMA) and homovanillic acid (HVA) are elevated in the urine of 90% of neuroblastoma patients.[238,239] The most common sites of metastases are bone marrow, bone, liver, and skin.[237]

The older staging systems have been combined into an international staging system (see Table 93.6).[240] Forty-three percent of infants (<1 year) and 78% of children have stage 3 or 4 disease at the time of diagnosis.[237] Two-year disease-free survival for patients with stages 3 or 4 is 10% to 30% and for patients with 1, 2, or 4S is 75% to 90%.[237] Other prognostic factors are listed in Table

Table 93.6	International Neuroblastoma Staging System (Abbreviated)[240]
Stage 1	Local tumor with complete gross excision
Stage 2A	Unilateral tumor with incomplete gross excision
Stage 2B	Unilateral tumor, complete or incomplete excision, with ipsilateral lymph node spread
Stage 3	Involves both sides of the midline
Stage 4	Distant lymph node or organ involvement
Stage 4S	Localized primary tumor (Stage 1 or 2) with dissemination limited to liver, skin and/or bone marrow

93.7. Histopathologic grading systems such as those by Shimada or Joshi and genetic subtyping may become important in classifying risk categories in the future.[241,251-253]

Surgical excision may be used initially to treat localized tumors or in patients with metastatic disease after they have partially responded to initial chemotherapy. Chemotherapy is used in all but Stage 1 or sometimes Stage 4S disease; irradiation is important in a few circumstances.[237] Drugs commonly used in neuroblastoma include cisplatin (Platinol), etoposide (VePesid) or teniposide (Vumon), cyclophosphamide (Cytoxan), doxorubicin (Adriamycin), vincristine (Oncovin), carboplatin (Paraplatin), ifosfamide (Ifex), and melphalan (Alkeran).[254-261] Examples of chemotherapy regimens for neuroblastoma by stage and age are given in Table 93.8. Note that infants have better outcomes for the same stage of disease and Stage 4S has a significant incidence of spontaneous regression or regression with minimal treatment.[237,262-264]

Clinical Presentation

66. A.N. is a 4-year-old white female with an abdominal mass, 6 pound weight loss, decreased appetite, 2 cm supraclavicular nodule, and intermittent fever, chills, and abdominal pain for 2 months. Her Hgb is 9.0 gm/dL (Normal: 10–14); WBCs, differential, and platelets are within normal limits. Serum sodium, potassium, chloride, creatinine, and glucose are within normal limits. LD is 1341 U/L (Normal: 322–644), erythrocyte sedimentation rate (ESR) 98 mm/hr (Normal: <10), and ferritin 227 ng/mL (Normal: 15–220). Urine HVA is 245 μg/mg, Cr (Normal: <17 μg/mg) and VMA 124 μg/mg Cr (Normal: <8). Biopsies of the abdominal mass and supraclavicular lymph node are positive for neuroblastoma. Bone marrow aspirate and further scans are negative for other sites of disease. Are these signs, symptoms, and laboratory results consistent with a diagnosis of neuroblastoma? [SI units: Hgb 90 gm/L (Normal: 100–140); LD 1341 U/L (Normal: 322–644); ferritin 227 μg/L (Normal: 15–220)]

Virtually all of A.N.'s findings are consistent with neuroblastoma. However, the low hemoglobin and high lactate dehydrogenase and ESR are not specific for this cancer. In addition to the biopsy, the elevated urine VMA and HVA (catecholamine metabolites) are most helpful in confirming the diagnosis. Neuroblastomas can contain malignant (neuroblastoma) and benign (ganglioneuroma) cells within the same tumor, which is referred to as ganglioneuroblastoma.[237] In A.N., biopsies of the lymph nodes and primary tumor are necessary to demonstrate neuroblastoma at both sites for staging purposes. Although there is no special risk of infection in A.N., the fever and chills require cultures to rule out an infection.

Treatment

67. What stage of disease does A.N. have? What treatment will she receive?

A.N.'s abdominal disease with distant lymph node involvement indicates stage 4 disease. Considering her age and disease stage, A.N. has a high risk of dying from her disease. Therefore, she is started on chemotherapy consisting of cycles of cisplatin (40 mg/m^2/day on days 1 to 5) and etoposide (200 mg/m^2/day on days 2 to 4) alternating with cyclophosphamide (600 mg/m^2/day on days 1 to 2 with Mesna to reduce the risk of hemorrhagic cystitis), doxorubicin (35 mg/m^2/day on day 1), and vincristine (1.5 mg/m^2/day on days 1, 8, and 15).

68. A.N. is 105 cm, 17.5 kg, and 0.74 m^2. She is started on cisplatin and etoposide with hydration fluids of 5% dextrose with 0.45% sodium chloride at 93 mL/hr. Urine output is 3 mL/kg/hr. How does the monitoring of A.N.'s chemotherapy differ from that of an adult?

Monitoring Vital Signs for Etoposide. Although prevention and monitoring of toxicities to chemotherapy agents in children follow the same basic rules as in adults, there are some differences. When monitoring vital signs for hypotensive reactions to etoposide, normal blood pressure will be lower (90th percentile 108/69 for a 4-year-old girl) and the pulse higher (mean: 108 beats/minute for a 4-year-old) than that of adults.[265] It is important to have baseline vital signs so that hypotension or tachycardia will be recognized.

Monitoring Hydration for Cisplatin. In adults receiving cisplatin, hydration often is standardized with 1 to 2 L of IV fluids given before the drug, 1 to 2 L with the drug, and continuous hydration for at least 24 hours after the dose.[266] In children, hydration volumes should be calculated based upon size. For cisplatin, most protocols recommend IV fluids at twice maintenance rates to maintain urine outputs of at least 2 mL/kg/hour which should help prevent nephrotoxicity. The Pediatric Oncology Group calculates maintenance fluids as 1500 mL/m^2/24 hours, so A.N. should receive 3000 mL × 0.74 m^2 = 2220 mL over 24 hours (92.5 mL/hour). A.N.'s measured urine output is 3 mL/kg/hour which should be adequate to prevent nephrotoxicity. Weight also should be monitored throughout cisplatin administration to ensure fluid balance. Acute weight gain may require diuretics to prevent overhydration, and weight loss may indicate dehydration with impending reduced urine output which could lead to acute nephrotoxicity. Increased IV fluids would help prevent the latter.

69. Adjustment of Creatinine Clearance (Cl$_{Cr}$) to Adult Size. **A.N.'s measured creatinine clearance (Cl$_{Cr}$) is 45 mL/min. Should her cisplatin be withheld or the dose adjusted due to low Cl$_{Cr}$?** [SI unit: Cl$_{Cr}$ 0.75 mL/s]

Often cisplatin is not administered when the creatinine clearance is below 50 mL/minute/1.73 m^2.[267] A.N.'s creatinine clearance of 45 mL/minute appears to be low, but it is reported for the patient's size (i.e., 45 mL/minute/0.74 m^2). Guidelines for dosing drugs cleared by glomerular filtration are based upon creatinine clearance for normal adult body size, 1.73 m^2. Therefore, it is important to correct A.N.'s creatinine clearance to adult body size.[268] Multiplying by 1.73/0.74, her creatinine clearance is 105 mL/minute/1.73

Table 93.7	Factors Associated with a Poor Prognosis in Neuroblastoma[241–250]

- Stage 3 or 4 disease
- Age >1 yr
- Ferritin >142 ng/mL
- Neuron-specific enolase >100 ng/mL
- Lactate dehydrogenase >1500 units/mL in infants
- DNA index = 1 (diploid)
- N-myc oncogene amplification
- Deletions of the short arm of chromosome 1

Table 93.8		Typical Neuroblastoma Chemotherapy by Age and Stage[237,262–264]
Age	**Stage**	**Treatment**
All	1	Often surgery alone, with chemotherapy reserved for recurrence
All	4S	Varies from observation to surgery, low dose irradiation, or chemotherapy like stage 2A
All	2A	5 courses of cyclophosphamide and doxorubicin with failures receiving cisplatin
Infants	2B, 3	Same as 2A
Infants	4	Same as 2A, or like children with 2B or 3. More intensive treatment used only with high risk factors or in treatment failures
Children	2B, 3	Cyclophosphamide and doxorubicin for remission, then cisplatin and teniposide or etoposide for maintenance. Irradiation improves survival in these intermediate stage patients
Children	4	Cyclophosphamide, doxorubicin, cisplatin, and etoposide or teniposide and/or intensive chemotherapy regimens with autologous bone marrow rescue

m^2, so this is not a reason to withhold cisplatin. One precaution is that the accuracy of serum creatinine and creatinine clearance in assessing renal function during cisplatin therapy in children has been questioned.[269]

70. Recurrent Disease. **A.N. obtains a partial response to the above regimen with reduction of urine VMA and HVA concentrations and disappearance of disease at the supraclavicular nodes, but minimal decrease in size of the residual primary tumor in the abdomen. Repeat biopsy determines that the residual tumor contains mature (benign) ganglioneuroma cells, but neuroblastoma cells are still present. What alternative therapies are available for A.N.?**

Bone Marrow Transplant. The best chance for prolonged disease-free survival for A.N. is dose-intensive chemotherapy combined with autologous bone marrow rescue. Although long-term disease-free survival has not been improved in all trials, two- to three-year disease-free survival is significantly better in those receiving intensive chemotherapy and autologous bone marrow rescue.[270–273] The plan for A.N. is to proceed to high-dose chemotherapy with an autologous bone marrow rescue.

Investigational Treatments Based Upon Disease Biology. With rapid advances in neuroblastoma biology being made, future alternatives may include biological treatments. Two treatments that are in the early stages of clinical trials are anti-GD2 ganglioside monoclonal antibodies and deferoxamine (Desferal).[274–277] Deferoxamine binds intracellular iron and increases its excretion, resulting in growth inhibition of neuroblastoma cells.[278] Deferoxamine has shown activity for purging autologous bone marrow grafts,[275] and has shown activity alone[276] or with chemotherapy[277] in neuroblastoma patients. The utility of these treatments is not yet established.

Wilms' Tumor

Wilm's tumor, also known as nephroblastoma, is a kidney tumor composed of various types of renal cells at different stages of maturation.[279] It represents 5% to 6% of all childhood cancers and is the most common intra-abdominal tumor of childhood.[223] The peak incidence occurs at two to three years of age.[280] Wilm's tumor frequently presents as an asymptomatic abdominal mass, although malaise and/or pain may be reported.[279] Hematuria and high renin hypertension each occur in approximately 25% of patients. Metastases, when present at diagnosis, involve the lung (80%) or the liver (15%) most commonly.

Overall, Wilm's tumor has an excellent prognosis. Treatment is based upon disease stage following any surgical resection that can be performed and favorable versus unfavorable (anaplastic) histology. A simplified description of the staging is as follows: stage I is limited to the kidney and completely removed surgically, stage II is extended beyond the kidney but completely excised, stage III is residual tumor confined to the abdomen, stage IV is distant metastases, and stage V is bilateral disease.[281] Metastases are present in only 15% of patients at diagnosis, and even these patients have relatively good prognoses. Four-year relapse-free survival rates from the third National Wilms' Tumor Study (NWTS-3) range from 55% for stage IV with unfavorable histology to 75% for stage IV with favorable histology.[281] It is approximately 90% for stage I patients regardless of histology.

Clinical Presentation and Treatment

71. D.S., a 6-month-old male, developed fever 2 days before admission. His physician discovered a mass on the right side of the abdomen. Scans showed a right renal mass with 2 pulmonary nodules and no disease in the liver and bones. His primary tumor was surgically removed and his diagnosis was Stage IV, favorable histology Wilms' Tumor. D.S. is entered in the National Wilms' Tumor Studies (NWTS) and will be randomized to receive chemotherapy as "standard" therapy or "pulse-intensive" therapy, and he will receive radiation therapy to the lungs if his metastases do not completely respond after the first 4 weeks of chemotherapy with dactinomycin (Cosmegen) and vincristine. Doxorubicin begins at week 6. Chemotherapy will continue for 26 weeks, and then D.S. will be randomized again to stop treatment or continue to 65 weeks. What is the rationale for randomizing patients in the different treatment groups?

The series of four National Wilms' Tumor Studies have sought to progressively minimize toxicities from radiation and chemotherapy while maintaining the excellent cure rate. The NWTS-4 randomizes stage I anaplastic and all favorable histology patients to drug regimens that are either standard or pulse-intensive (higher doses over a shorter time). The latter regimen should result in fewer physician visits. The second randomization, for patients with favorable histology stage II and above, divides each group into those completing therapy at five to six months and those continuing for approximately 12 to 15 months, to determine if shorter duration therapy can maintain the cure rates. Stage I and II therapy includes vincristine and dactinomycin. Stages III and IV add doxorubicin (see Table 93.9).

72. Dosing Chemotherapy in Infants. Are there any special precautions for dosing chemotherapy in D.S.?

Doses of chemotherapy agents for infants under 1 year on the NWTS-4 are 50% less than other children to reduce the incidence of toxicities in this age group. When excessive toxic deaths were noticed in NWTS-2 in good-prognosis infants, a change in the dosing was made.[282] After chemotherapy doses were reduced by 50%, severe hematologic toxicity, toxic deaths, and pulmonary and hepatic complications were reduced,[283] without a decrease in therapeutic effect. Reduction of chemotherapy doses in infants may be considered for other pediatric cancers also.[284-286] Reasons for increased toxicity may include altered pharmacokinetics or organ sensitivity, but it is probably important to note that infants have a larger body surface area/kg relative to children and adults.[284] Another mechanism used in protocols for reducing doses is to convert the normal dose/m^2 into a dose/kg. By assuming the average 1 m^2 child weighs 30 kg, one can divide the dose/m^2 by 30 and arrive at a dose/kg to be used in dosing calculations.

73. Interaction of Chemotherapy with Radiation. Are there any dosing precautions required due to potential interactions between D.S.'s treatments?

Another drug-related problem which may arise in D.S. is the interaction between dactinomycin or doxorubicin with radiation therapy.[287-291] Two effects have been reported. One is acute enhancement of radiation effects, and the other is recurrence (recall) of radiation effects up to several weeks later, especially in the skin and mucous membranes. If D.S. requires pulmonary radiation to treat metastases, his doses of dactinomycin and doxorubicin should be reduced an additional 50% during and for four to six weeks after the radiation treatment.

74. Doxorubicin Cardiotoxicity in Pediatrics. If D.S. receives lung irradiation for his metastases, how will it affect the doxorubicin he is scheduled to receive?

Although it is well known that mediastinal irradiation can increase the risk of anthracycline-induced cardiac toxicity,[292] the only adjustment for D.S. would be temporary reduction of doxorubicin doses as described in Question 73. The total doxorubicin dose for his protocol is already limited to no more than 270 mg/m^2. Recent reports have demonstrated that cardiovascular toxicity may occur as long as 20 years after the end of therapy in children, with an apparent decrease in left ventricular free wall thickness and increased ventricular afterload, probably related to inadequate numbers of myocytes.[293-295] These reports emphasize the need to minimize chemotherapy in good-prognosis patients as the NWTS is doing. New recommendations include better standardization of cardiac monitoring and continuation of monitoring for life in survivors of childhood cancer who receive cardiotoxic agents.[296,297]

Table 93.9		NWTS-4 Drug Treatment of Stage III-IV Favorable Histology Wilms' Tumor[a]	
Drug	**Dose**	**Short Protocol**	**Long Protocol**
Standard Regimen			
Dactinomycin	15 µg/kg/day × 5 days Q 13 weeks	Week 0–26	Through week 65
Vincristine	1.5 mg/m^2 weekly	Week 1–10	No difference
Vincristine	1.5 mg/m^2 days 1 and 5 Q 13 weeks	Week 13 and 26	Through week 65
Doxorubicin	20 mg/m^2/day × 3 days Q 13 weeks	Week 6 and 19	Through week 58
Pulse-Intensive Regimen			
Dactinomycin	0.45 mg/kg Q 6 weeks	Week 6–24	Through week 54
Doxorubicin	45 mg/m^2 Q 6 weeks	Week 3 and 9	No difference
Doxorubicin	30 mg/m^2 Q 6 weeks	Week 15 and 21	Through week 51
Vincristine	1.5 mg/m^2 weekly	Week 1–10	No difference
Vincristine	2 mg/m^2 Q 3 weeks	Week 12–24	Through week 54

[a] Doses subject to many modifications. Please see full protocol.

75. Dactinomycin Hepatotoxicity. D.S. is randomized to receive the standard-dose chemotherapy regimen. During the third week of treatment, his ALT is elevated to 97 U/dL (Normal: 7–55). Is this related to his drug therapy?

Early in the NWTS-4, an increased incidence (14.3%) of severe hepatotoxicity (elevation of AST and/or ALT 10 times normal with or without ascites) was reported with the pulse-intensive dactinomycin doses (60 µg/kg/single dose) in patients receiving no abdominal radiation.[298] Dactinomycin doses were reduced. Follow-up has determined that the incidence of hepatotoxicity in patients receiving the new 45 mg/kg pulse doses (3.7%), as well as in those receiving the standard 15 mg/kg/day for five days (2.8%), is still elevated compared to NWTS-3 results (0.4%) which used 15 mg/kg/day for five days.[299] The reasons for the increased hepatotoxicity are unknown. Liver function usually returns to baseline within one to two weeks after chemotherapy is discontinued. Chemotherapy was restarted in some patients, although frequently at lower doses or without dactinomycin. D.S. should be monitored closely in case his liver enzymes continue to rise. If his ALT rises to two to five times normal, or his total bilirubin is 3 to 5 mg/dL, the doses of all of his drugs should be reduced by 50%. If his ALT or bilirubin continue to rise, then the drugs should be withheld until laboratory values return to the above range.

Osteosarcoma

Osteosarcoma is a malignant bone tumor which occurs most commonly in children in the second decade of life.[300] It occurs most frequently in the metaphyseal ends of the distal femur, proximal tibia, or proximal humerus, but can occur in the flat bones as well.[301] The age range and bones involved suggest a malignant response associated with normal childhood growth spurts.[300]

The most common manifestation at diagnosis is pain at the site, which can sometimes be present for several weeks to months.[300] Clinically detectable metastases are present in 10% to 12% of patients, usually in the lungs but occasionally in other bones.

If surgery alone is used for treatment, 80% of patients will die within five years of recurrent metastatic disease, indicating the presence of subclinical micrometastases at the time of diagnosis.[301,302] Although surgery is the main treatment of the primary tumor, chemotherapy is used to prevent metastases. Drugs frequently used for osteosarcoma include high-dose methotrexate,[303] cisplatin,[304,305] doxorubicin,[306] ifosfamide,[307] bleomycin (Blenoxane), cyclophosphamide, and dactinomycin.[308,309] The tumor is relatively resistant to radiation therapy, which usually is reserved for cases in which control cannot be achieved surgically.[300,310] When chemotherapy is used with surgery, long-term (2 to 5 year) disease-free survival estimates are typically 50% to 75%.[301,302,309]

Clinical Presentation and Treatment

76. K.F., an 11-year-old female, experienced pain with no apparent trauma in her right thigh 2 months before admission. The pain continued until she was placed on ibuprofen which provided good relief. When the ibuprofen was discontinued, the pain recurred and x-rays revealed a tumor. A bone biopsy later confirmed osteosarcoma, but CT and bone scans revealed no metastases. K.F. is begun on neo-adjuvant (presurgical) chemotherapy consisting of high-dose methotrexate alternating with cisplatin and doxorubicin. Two cycles of this chemotherapy will be given before her surgery, and then it is to be continued after surgery for approximately 1 year. What is the goal of chemotherapy? What is the role of presurgical chemotherapy in K.F.?

Since K.F.'s osteosarcoma is in her distal femur, the surgeon should have no trouble removing the primary tumor using one of the variety of operations which have been described elsewhere.[300]

Osteosarcoma patients usually die from metastases, and the goal of the chemotherapy is to eradicate micrometastases. Neo-adjuvant chemotherapy of osteosarcoma was developed to treat micrometastases while waiting for limb salvage surgeries to be arranged, performed, and healed. Neo-adjuvant therapy also may facilitate limb sparing surgery by shrinking the tumor, and it allows for histologic grading of the response to initial chemotherapy at surgery, a prognostic factor for risk of relapse. Although comparisons of neo-adjuvant to adjuvant chemotherapy in osteosarcoma continue, there is no convincing evidence to date that disease-free survival is better for neo-adjuvant than adjuvant chemotherapy.[309,311]

Prognostic Factors

77. At surgery, K.F.'s tumor shows excellent histologic response, with almost 100% necrosis. At diagnosis, her LD was 602 IU/L (Normal: 297–537). Both of these factors indicate that K.F. is a good risk patient. What role do prognostic factors play in the therapy of osteosarcoma? [SI units: LD 602 U/L (Normal: 297–537)]

Clinically apparent metastases or a location which does not allow complete surgical removal of the primary tumor are associated with a poor prognosis.[309] Although newer surgical techniques and treatments have improved the outlook,[312] patients with these poor prognostic factors are less likely to benefit from conventional surgery and chemotherapy. Therefore, newer investigational treatments are considered for poor-risk patients. Other potential prognostic factors have been identified; however, few of these factors have been used to stratify patients to different treatment regimens.[309,311] One exception is the histologic grade of the tumor at surgery. If a poor response to initial treatment is seen, chemotherapy often is intensified after surgery, although there is little evidence for improved outcomes when this is done.

78. Delayed Clearance After High-Dose Methotrexate. K.F. restarts high-dose methotrexate 3 weeks after her surgery. Recorded urine specific gravities are <1.015, urine pHs are >6.5, creatinine has remained at baseline, and urine output is >2 mL/kg/hr. However, her 72-hour methotrexate concentration has stabilized at 0.2 µm/L instead of continuing to decline, and leucovorin rescue (15 mg IV Q 6 hr) is continued. What potential problems could be causing her retention of methotrexate?

Accumulations of protein-containing "third-space" fluids such as pleural effusions and ascites or gastrointestinal obstruction, may retain methotrexate and cause slow terminal excretion.[313–315] Many drugs interact with methotrexate. Cisplatin reportedly reduces the excretion of methotrexate; however, this is more likely at cumulative doses above 300 mg/m² which K.F. has not yet received.[316] Also, she has not received concomitant nephrotoxins such as aminoglycosides or amphotericin B. Weak organic acids such as salicylates, ketoprofen, or trimethoprim-sulfamethoxazole can compete with methotrexate for renal tubular secretion.[317,318] If trimethoprim had been given to K.F., another consideration would have been a false elevation of methotrexate concentration caused by trimethoprim competing for bacterial dihydrofolate reductase used in the radioenzymatic assay.[314,319] Other methods of measuring concentrations would avoid this problem.

Although her renal function appears to be adequate, serum creatinine is not always a precise indicator, so it is possible that K.F. has suffered some renal damage that is not apparent from her serum creatinine concentrations.[269] A measured creatinine clearance may or may not help, since it also has been reported to be inaccurate when compared to ^{51}Cr-EDTA measurement of glomerular filtration rate. It is not apparent why K.F. is retaining methotrexate; future courses of methotrexate will require close monitoring.

79. Leucovorin Rescue. How long should leucovorin be administered to K.F.?

Cytotoxic effects of methotrexate depend upon concentration and duration of exposure.[320] Many high-dose methotrexate protocols continue leucovorin rescue until serum methotrexate concentrations are 0.1 μm/L. Since K.F. has delayed clearance with persistence of low methotrexate levels, prevention of gastrointestinal and bone marrow cytotoxicity may require continuation of leucovorin rescue until methotrexate concentrations are below 0.01 to 0.05 μm/L.[314] Other considerations may be important in other patients receiving leucovorin rescue. Due to the competitive nature of leucovorin rescue, higher leucovorin doses may be needed in patients with methotrexate concentrations above the usual range at a specified time after the dose. Crom and Evans have published a figure (see Figure 93.3) which helps identify patients who are at high risk for methotrexate toxicity if given the usual low doses of leucovorin rescue.[314] Using their guidelines, if K.F.'s methotrexate concentrations had remained between 1 and 5 μm/L 42 hours after the beginning of the infusion, recommendations would include increasing the dose of the leucovorin to 30 mg/m^2 every six hours until methotrexate concentrations fall below 1 μm/L. Oral leucovorin administration should not be used when the patient has emesis or when receiving larger doses (>50 mg) which are often poorly absorbed.[314]

Rhabdomyosarcoma

Rhabdomyosarcoma is the most common soft tissue sarcoma of childhood, occurring in 5% to 8% of all children with cancer.[223,234] The two most common histologic types are embryonal and alveolar.[234] Embryonal rhabdomyosarcoma cells resemble striated muscle and occur most frequently in young children with involvement in the head and neck or genitourinary tract. Alveolar rhabdomyosarcoma cells resemble lung parenchymal cells and occur more frequently in older children or adolescents with involvement of the trunk or extremities. The clinical presentation of rhabdomyosarcoma varies with the location.

Treatment combines surgery, irradiation, and chemotherapy. Complete surgical removal is often difficult given the locations of this tumor and that it generally infiltrates neighboring tissues.[234] Irradiation is used to gain further local control. Combination chemotherapy is necessary because the five-year survival with local control alone is 10% to 30%. Vincristine, dactinomycin, and cyclophosphamide (VAC regimen) have been used extensively to treat rhabdomyosarcoma.[321] Other agents producing responses include doxorubicin,[322] ifosfamide,[323] etoposide,[324] cisplatin,[325] dacarbazine,[326] and methotrexate.[327] Melphalan (Alkeran) has little activity in heavily pretreated patients (8% partial responses), but previously untreated patients respond well (77% partial responses).[328] The Intergroup Rhabdomyosarcoma Study III had a three-year progression-free survival of 67% using chemotherapy with local treatment.[329]

Clinical Presentation and Prognostic Factors

80. K.W. is a 22-month-old female with a 3-week history of a bulging right eye (exophthalmos) and infraorbital ecchymosis. Her ophthalmologist discovered a tumor with nearby skull erosion on a CT scan, and a biopsy was performed. K.W. has no complaints. Further work-up includes an MRI which shows possible extension to the right lateral cortex, but the bone marrow and cerebrospinal fluid are negative for disease. The diagnosis is embryonal rhabdomyosarcoma.

K.W. is begun on radiation therapy and combination chemotherapy: vincristine 1.5 mg/m^2 weekly with ifosfamide 1.8 g/m^2/day × 5 days (every 3 weeks) with 4 doses of Mesna 360 mg/m^2 every 3 hours each day of ifosfamide. Etoposide 100 mg/m^2/day will be added on the same days as ifosfamide after radiation therapy is finished. Trimethoprim-sulfamethoxazole

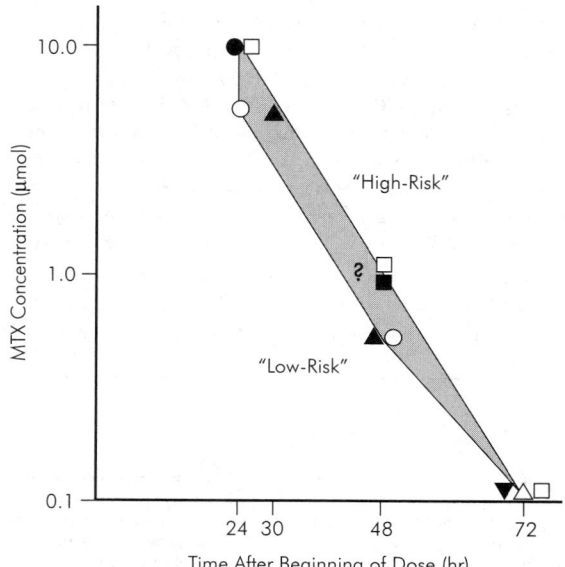

Fig 93.3 Composite Semi-Logarithmic Plot of Serum Methotrexate (MTX) Concentrations Which Have Been Proposed to Identify Patients at "High Risk" to Develop Toxicity From High Dose Methotrexate (HDMTX) if Conventional Low-Dose Leucovorin Is Administered Data obtained from reports of (▲) Evans,[336] (△) Tattersal,[337] (●) Isacoff,[338] (○) Isacoff,[339] (□) Nirenberg,[340] (■) Stoller,[341] (▼) Rechnitzer.[342] Reprinted from Evans et al. Applied Pharmacokinetics: Principles of Therapeutic Drug Monitoring. Applied Therapeutics: 1992.

(TMP-SMX) is begun at 150 mg/m^2/day (TMP) divided BID for 3 consecutive days per week. After each course of chemotherapy K.W. is to receive filgrastim (Neupogen) 5 μg/kg/day SQ for 14 days or until the ANC is >1000. What factors in K.W. are associated with a good prognosis?

The embryonal histopathological classification has a better prognosis than the alveolar one, although there is evidence that the primary tumor site is more important than histology.[234,330,331] The primary site affects resectability, route of spread, and how early the diagnosis is made. The Intergroup Rhabdomyosarcoma Studies (IRS) have used a clinical grouping system (groups I to IV) which is based upon spread of the disease and extent of resection. This system has been useful due to its correlation with prognosis; complete surgical removal and lack of metastases both correlate with good prognosis.[234] The fourth IRS study is comparing the clinical grouping system to a TNM staging system similar to that used in adult cancers. In rhabdomyosarcoma, the tumor site is one important part of the T rating in the staging system. K.W. has cranial parameningeal disease due to her orbital tumor with erosion into the skull, and surgical resection cannot be done due to the orbital location. Therefore, her disease is both stage and clinical group III, giving her approximately a 70% to 80% chance of three-year survival based upon IRS-II and IRS-III results.[234,329]

Treatment

81. Trimethoprim-Sulfamethoxazole (TMP-SMX) Prophylaxis and Filgrastim for Myelosuppression. What are the reasons for adding TMP-SMX and filgrastim to K.W.'s regimen?

K.W.'s vincristine, ifosfamide, etoposide (VIE) as well as regimens it is being compared to in the fourth IRS study, VAC (vincristine, dactinomycin, and cyclophosphamide) and VAI (vincristine, dactinomycin, and ifosfamide) were shown to be highly myelosuppressive in pilot studies.[332] Due to the frequency of severe myelosuppression, TMP-SMX is used until six months after chemotherapy for prophylaxis against *Pneumocystis carinii*. Filgrastim is used to minimize neutropenia while maintaining dose-intensity. The benefit of using a post-nadir ANC of 1000 as an endpoint for filgrastim therapy is unknown. The median time to neutrophil nadir was 11 days in the VAI pilot study.[332]

82. Renal Fanconi's Syndrome With Ifosfamide. During her seventh course of chemotherapy, K.W.'s UA is negative for hematuria, but she has 2+ ketonuria and 1+ glycosuria in spite of a serum glucose of 125 mg/dL (Normal: 70–115). Does this relate to her treatment? [SI units: 6.94 mmol/L (Normal: 3.89–6.38)]

Ifosfamide has been associated with renal Fanconi's syndrome, a proximal tubular defect which is characterized by wasting of electrolytes, glucose, and amino acids, as well as renal tubular acidosis and increased serum creatinine. Data suggest that the following increase the risk of Fanconi's syndrome: greater than three years old, total doses above 72 gm/m^2, hydronephrosis, a single kidney, elevated serum creatinine, or previous platinum therapy.[333–335] Protocol guidelines for this study switch all patients from ifosfamide to cyclophosphamide after a total dose of 72 gm/m^2 has been given. K.W. is one course short of 72 gm/m^2, but due to her mild glycosuria she will receive no ifosfamide in her next course of chemotherapy. Subsequently, it may be reinstituted at 50% of the dose. If K.W. had the full manifestations of Fanconi's syndrome she would be immediately switched to cyclophosphamide. K.W.'s ketonuria is most likely due to her Mesna therapy, which has been reported to routinely cause false-positive ketone tests.[343]

References

1   **American Cancer Society.** Cancer Facts and Figures— 1995.

2   **Feuer EJ et al.** The lifetime risk of developing breast cancer. J Natl Cancer Inst. 1993;85:892–897.

3   **Henderson IC et al.** Cancer of the breast. In: DeVita VT et al., eds. Cancer. Principles and Practice of Oncology. 3rd ed. Philadelphia: Lippincott; 1989:1197–268.

4   **Sattin RW et al.** Family history and the risk of breast cancer. JAMA. 1985; 253:1908.

5   **Harris JR et al.** Breast cancer (second of 3 parts). N Engl J Med. 1992;327: 390–398.

6   **Bloom JR.** Early detection of cancer. Cancer. 1994;74:1464.

7   **Harris JR et al.** Breast cancer (first of 3 parts). N Engl J Med. 1992;327:319.

8   **Brinton LA et al.** Reproductive factors in the aetiology of breast cancer. Br J Cancer. 1983;47:757.

9   **Pike MC et al.** Oral contraceptive use and early abortion as risk factors for breast cancer in young women. Br J Cancer. 1981;43:72.

10 **Haagensen CD.** Treatment of curable carcinoma of the breast. Int J Radiat Oncol Biol Phys. 1977;2:975.

11 **Shapiro S et al.** Ten- to fourteen-year effect of screening on breast cancer mortality. J Natl Cancer Instit. 1982; 69:349.

12 **Hermann RE et al.** Results of conservative operations for breast cancer. Arch Surg. 1985;120:746.

13 **Veronesi U et al.** Comparing radical mastectomy with quadrantectomy, axillary dissection and radiotherapy in patients with small cancers of the breast. N Engl J Med. 1981;305:6.

14 **Fisher B et al.** Five-year results of a randomized clinical trial comparing total mastectomy and segmental mastectomy with or without radiation in the treatment of breast cancer. N Engl J Med. 1985;312:666.

15 **McGuire WL et al.** Prognostic factors and treatment decisions in axillary node negative breast cancer. N Engl J Med. 1992;326:1765.

16 **Hams JR et al.** Breast cancer (3rd of three parts). N Engl J Med. 1992;327: 473.

17 **Early Breast Cancer Trialists' Collaborative Group.** Effects of adjuvant tamoxifen and of cytotoxic chemotherapy on mortality in early breast cancer. N Engl J Med. 1988;319:1681.

18 **Early Breast Cancer Trialists' Collaborative Group.** Systemic treatment of early breast cancer by hormonal cytotoxic or immune therapy. Lancet. 1992;339:1–15, 81–5.

19 **Consensus Conference.** Adjuvant chemotherapy for breast cancer. JAMA. 1991;265:391.

20 **NIH Consensus Conference.** Treatment of early stage breast cancer. JAMA. 1991;265:391.

21 **Glick JH et al.** Meeting highlights: adjuvant therapy for primary breast cancer. J Natl Cancer Inst. 1992;84:1479.

22 **Brooks RJ et al.** Improved outcome with early treatment in a adjuvant breast cancer program. Proc Am Soc Clin Oncol. 1983;2:110. Abstract.

23 **Mathe G et al.** Consistencies and variations of observations during serial analysis of a trial of adjuvant chemotherapy in breast cancer. In: Salmon SE, ed. Adjuvant Chemotherapy for Cancer. Orlando: Grune and Stratton; 1987:271–80.

24 **Fisher B.** Doxorubicin-containing regimens for the treatment of stage II breast cancer: the National Surgical Adjuvant Breast and Bowel Project experience. J Clin Oncol. 1989;7:572.

25 **Hryniuk W, Levine MN.** Analysis of dose intensity for adjuvant chemotherapy trials in stage II breast cancer. J Clin Oncol. 1986;4:1162.

26 **Bonadonna G, Valagussa P.** Dose-response effect of adjuvant chemotherapy in breast cancer. N Engl J Med. 1981;304:10.

27 **Peters WP et al.** High-dose combination alkylating agents with bone marrow support as initial treatment for metastatic breast cancer. J Clin Oncol. 1988;6:1368.

28 **Williams SF et al.** High-dose consolidation therapy with autologous stem-cell rescue in stage IV breast cancer: follow-up report. J Clin Oncol. 1992; 10:1743.

29 **Eder JP et al.** High-dose combination alkylating agent chemotherapy with autologous bone marrow support for metastatic breast cancer. J Clin Oncol. 1986;4:1592.

30 **Peters WP et al.** High-dose chemotherapy and autologous bone marrow support as consolidation after standard-dose adjuvant therapy for high-risk primary breast cancer. J Clin Oncol. 1993; 11:1132.

31 **Henderson IC et al.** Duration of therapy in adjuvant chemotherapy trials. NCI monograph. 1986;1:95.

32 **Nissen-Meyer R et al.** Adjuvant chemotherapy in breast cancer. Rec Res Cancer Res. 1982;80:142.

33 **Osborne CK et al.** Antagonisms of chemotherapy-induced cytotoxicity for human breast cancer cells by antiestrogens. J Clin Oncol. 1989;7:710.

34 **Clarke R.** Effect of cytotoxic drugs on estrogen receptor expression and response to tamoxifen on MCF-7 cells. Cancer Res. 1986;46:6116.

35 **Fey MF et al.** Prognostic factors in metastatic breast cancer. Cancer Clin Trials. 1981;4:237.

36 **Henderson IC.** Chemotherapy for advanced disease. In: Harris JR et al., eds. Breast Diseases. Philadelphia: Lippincott; 1987:428–79.

37 **Holmes FA et al.** Phase II trial of taxol, an active drug in metastatic breast cancer. J Natl Cancer Inst. 1991;83:1797.

38 **Canobbio L et al.** Phase II study of navelbine in advanced breast cancer. Sem Oncol. 1989;16:33.

39 **Brambilla C.** Response and survival in advanced breast cancer after two non-cross-resistant combinations. Br Med J. 1976;1:801.

40 **Nabholtz JM et al.** (1993) Randomized trial of two doses of taxol in metastatic breast cancer: an interim analysis. Proc Am Soc Clin Oncol. 12:60. Abstr.

41 **Konits P et al.** Mitomycin C and vinblastine chemotherapy for advanced breast cancer. Cancer. 1981;48:1295.

42 **Garewal HS et al.** Treatment of advanced breast cancer with mitomycin C combined with vinblastine or vindesine. J Natl Cancer Inst. 1983;1:772.

43 **Antman K et al.** A phase II study of high dose cyclophosphamide, thiotepa, and carboplatin with autologous marrow support in women with measurable advanced breast cancer responding to standard dose therapy. J Clin Oncol. 1992;10:102.

44 **Elias AD et al.** Mobilization of peripheral blood progenitor cells by chemotherapy and GM-CSF for hematologic support after high-dose intensification for breast cancer. Blood. 1992;79: 3036.

45 **Rodriques M, Dinapoli RP.** Spinal cord compression with special reference to metastatic epidural tumors. Mayo Clin Proc. 1980;55:442.

46 **Gilbert RW et al.** Epidural spinal cord compression from metastatic tumor: diagnosis and treatment. Ann Neurol. 1978;3:40.

47 **McGuire WL.** Hormone receptors: their role in predicting prognosis and response to endocrine therapy. Semin Oncol. 1978;5:428.

48 **Singhakowinta A et al.** Estrogen receptor and natural course of breast cancer. Ann Surg. 1976;183:84.

49 **Bratherton DG et al.** A comparison of two doses of tamoxifen (Nolvadex) in postmenopausal women with advanced breast cancer: 10 mg versus 20 mg BD. Br J Cancer. 1984;50:199.

50 **Fabian C et al.** Clinical pharmacology of tamoxifen in patients with breast cancer: comparison of traditional and loading dose schedules. Cancer Treat Rep. 1980;64:765.

51 **Hams JR et al.** Cancer of the breast. In: DeVita VT et al., eds. Cancer. Principles and Practice of Oncology. 4th ed. Philadelphia: Lippincott; 1993: 1352.

52 **Mandel JS et al.** Reducing mortality from colorectal cancer by screening for fecal occult blood. N Engl J Med. 1993;319:1365.

53 **Winawer SJ et al.** Screening for colorectal cancer with fecal occult blood testing and sigmoidoscopy. J Natl Cancer Inst. 1993;85:1311.

54 **Division of Cancer Prevention and Control, National Cancer Institute.** Working Guidelines for Early Detection; Rationale and Supporting Evidence to Decrease Mortality. Bethesda, MD: National Institutes of Health; 1987:1.

55 **Adams EC, Layman KM.** Immunochemical confirmation of gastrointestinal bleeding. Ann Clin Lab Sci. 1974; 4:343.

56 **Feinberg EJ et al.** How long to abstain from eating red meat before fecal occult blood tests. Ann Intern Med. 1990; 113:403.

57 **Willett CG et al.** Failure patterns following curative resection of colonic carcinoma. Ann Surg. 1984;200:685.

58 **Eisenberg BL.** Carcinoma of the colon and rectum: the natural history review in 1704 patients. Cancer. 1982; 49:1131.

59 **Panettiere FJ, Chenn TT.** The SWOG large bowel study benefits from therapy. Proc Am Soc Clin Oncol. 1985;4: 76. Abstract.

60 **Cass AW et al.** Patterns of reoccurr-

ence following surgery alone for adenocarcinoma of the colon and rectum. Cancer. 1976;37:2861.

61 Grinnell RS. The chance of cancer and lymphatic metastasis in small colon tumors discovered on x-ray examination. Ann Surg. 1964;159:132.

62 Weiss L et al. Hematogenous metastatic patterns in colonic carcinoma: an analysis of 1541 necropsies. J Pathol. 1986;150:195.

63 Moertel CG et al. Levamisole and fluorouracil for surgical adjuvant therapy of colon carcinoma. N Engl J Med. 1990;322:352.

64 Laurie JA et al. Surgical adjuvant therapy of large-bowel carcinoma: an evaluation of levamisole and the combination of levamisole and fluorouracil. J Clin Oncol. 1989;7:1447.

65 Goldin A et al. Biologic response modifiers and adjuvant chemotherapy. Recent Results Cancer Res. 1982;80: 351.

66 Spreafico F. Use of levamisole in cancer patients. Drugs. 1981;19:105.

67 Moertel CG. Chemotherapy for colorectal cancer. N Engl J Med. 1994;330: 1136.

68 Mutch RS, Hutson PR. Levamisole in the treatment of colon cancer. Clin Pharm. 1991;10:95.

69 Hook CC et al. Multifocal inflammatory leukoencephalopathy with 5-fluorouracil and levamisole. Ann Neurol. 1992;31:262.

70 NIH Consensus Development Conference. Adjuvant therapy for patients with colon and rectum cancer. Bethesda, MD: 1990 April 16–18.

71 Cohen AM et al. Colorectal cancer. In: DeVita VT et al., eds. Cancer. Principles and Practice of Oncology. 4th ed. Philadelphia: Lippincott; 1993:929–77.

72 Poon MA et al. Biochemical modulation of fluorouracil: evidence of significant improvement of survival and quality of life in patients with advanced colorectal carcinoma. J Clin Oncol. 1989;7:1407.

73 Petrelli N et al. The modulation of fluorouracil with leucovorin in metastatic colorectal carcinoma: a prospective randomized phase III trial. J Clin Oncol. 1989;7:1419.

74 Valone FH et al. Treatment of patients with advanced colorectal carcinoma with fluorouracil alone, high dose leucovorin plus fluorouracil, or sequential methotrexate, fluorouracil and leucovorin: a randomized trial of the Northern California Oncology Group. J Clin Oncol. 1989;7:1427.

75 Poon MA et al. Biochemical modulation of fluorouracil with leucovorin; confirmatory evidence of improved therapeutic efficacy in advanced colorectal cancer. J Clin Oncol. 1991;9: 1967.

76 Gerstner J et al. A prospective randomized clinical trial comparing 5-FU combined with either high or low dose leucovorin for the treatment of colorectal carcinoma. Proc Am Soc Clin Oncol. 1991;10:134. Abstract.

77 Wadler S, Wiernik P. Clinical update on the role of fluorouracil and recombinant interferon alfa-2a in the treatment of colorectal carcinoma. Semin Oncol. 1990;17(Suppl.):16.

78 Wadler S et al. Interaction of fluorouracil and interferon in human colon cancer cell lines: cytotoxic and cytokinetic effects. Cancer Res. 1990;50: 5735.

79 Grem JL et al. A pilot study of interferon alfa-2a in combination with fluorouracil plus high dose leucovorin in metastatic gastrointestinal carcinoma. J Clin Oncol. 1991;9:1811.

80 Breedis C, Young C. The blood supply of neoplasms in the liver. Am J Path. 1954;30:969.

81 Stagg RJ et al. Hepatic arterial chemotherapy for colorectal cancer metastatic to the liver. Ann Intern Med. 1984;100:736.

82 Hohn DC et al. A randomized trial of continuous intravenous versus hepatic intraarterial floxuridine in patients with colorectal cancer metastatic to the liver: the Northern California Oncology Group trial. J Clin Oncol. 1989;7: 1646.

83 Chang AE et al. A prospective randomized trial of regional versus systemic continuous 5-fluorodeoxyuridine chemotherapy in the treatment of colorectal metastases. Ann Surg. 1987; 206:685.

84 Kemeny N et al. Intrahepatic or systemic infusion of fluorodeoxyuridine in patients with liver metastases from colorectal carcinoma. Ann Intern Med. 1987;107:459.

85 Weiss GR et al. Long-term hepatic arterial infusion of 5-fluorodeoxyuridine for liver metastases using an implantable infusion pump. J Clin Oncol. 1983;1:337.

86 Balch CM et al. A prospective phase II clinical trial of continuous FUDR regional chemotherapy for colorectal metastases to the liver using a totally implantable drug infusion pump. Ann Surg. 1983;198:567.

87 Ensminger W. A clinical-pharmacological evaluation of hepatic arterial infusions of 5-fluoro-2'-deoxyuridine and 5-fluorouracil. Cancer Res. 1978; 38:3784.

88 Rougier P et al. Hepatic arterial infusion of floxuridine in patients with liver metastases from colorectal carcinoma: long-term results of a prospective randomized trial. J Clin Oncol. 1992;10: 1112.8

89 Martin JK et al. Intra-arterial floxuridine vs systemic fluorouracil for hepatic metastases from colorectal cancer: a randomized trial. Arch Surg. 1990;125:1022.

90 Donagen WG. Clinical toxicity of chemotherapeutic agents: dermatologic toxicity. Semin Oncol. 1982;9:14.

91 Hohn DC et al. Biliary sclerosis in patients receiving hepatic arterial infusion of floxuridine. J Clin Oncol. 1985;3:98.

92 Kemeny N et al. Sclerosing cholangitis after continuous hepatic artery infusion of FUDR. Ann Surg. 1985;202: 176.

93 Allison DJ, Booth A. Arterial embolization in the management of liver metastases. Cardiovasc Intervent Radiol. 1990;13:161.

94 Miller DL, Doppman JL. Interventional radiology in oncology. In: DeVita VT et al., eds. Cancer. Principles and Practice of Oncology. 4th ed. Philadelphia: Lippincott; 1993:542–55.

95 Cohen MH. Signs and symptoms of bronchogenic carcinoma. In: Straus MJ, ed. Lung Cancer: Clinical Diagnosis and Treatment. New York: Grune and Stratton; 1977:85–94.

96 Minna JD et al. Cancer of the lung. In: DeVita VT et al., eds. Cancer. Principles and Practice of Oncology. 3rd ed. Philadelphia: Lippincott; 1989: 591–705.

97 Kreyberg L. Histologic typing of lung tumors. In: Kreyberg L, ed. International Histological Classification of Tumors. No. 1. Geneva: World Health Organization; 1967:19–26.

98 Yesner R et al. Application of the World Health Organization classification of lung carcinoma to biopsy material. Ann Thorac Surg. 1965;1:33.

99 Matthews MJ, Gordon PR. Morphology of pulmonary and pleural malignancies. In: Strauss MJ, ed. Lung Cancer: Clinical Diagnosis and Treatment. New York: Grune and Stratton; 1977: 49–69.

100 National Academy of Sciences. Environmental Tobacco Smoke: Measuring Exposures and Assessing Health Effects. Appendix D. Washington, DC: National Academy Press; 1986.

101 Speizer FE. Overview of the risk of respiratory cancer from airborne contaminants. Environ Health Perspect. 1986;70:9.

102 Omenn GS et al. Contribution of environmental fibers to respiratory cancer. Environ Health Perspect. 1986;70: 51.

103 Berlin NI et al. The National Cancer Institute Cooperative Early Lung Cancer Detection Program: results of the initial screen (prevalence). Early lung cancer detection: introduction. Am Rev Respir Dis. 1984;13:545.

104 Martini N. Preoperative staging and surgery for non-small cell lung cancer. In: Aisner JA, ed. Lung Cancer. New York: Churchill Livingstone; 1985: 101–30.

105 Mulshine J, Ruckdeschel JC. The role of chemotherapy in the management of disseminated non-small cell lung cancer. Roth JA et al., ed. Thoracic Oncology. Philadelphia: WB Saunders; 1989:220–28.

106 Hansen HH et al. Management of small-cell carcinoma of the lung. In: Aisner JA, ed. Lung Cancer. New York: Churchill Livingstone; 1985: 269–85.

107 Carson JAS et al. Taste acuity and food attitudes of selected patients with cancer. J Am Diet Assoc. 1977;70:361.

108 DeWys WD. Changes in taste sensation and feeding behavior in cancer patients: a review. J Hum Nutr. 1978;32: 447.

109 Gorshein D. Posthypophysectomy taste normalities: their relationship to remote effects of cancer. Cancer. 1977;39: 1700.

110 Williams LR et al. Altered taste thresholds in lung cancer. Am J Clin Nutr. 1978;31:122.

111 DeWys WD. Anorexia as a general effect of cancer. Cancer. 1979;43:2013.

112 Terrell M et al. Plasma protein synthesis in experimental cancer compared to paraneoplastic conditions, including monokine administration. Cancer Res. 1987;47:5825.

113 Theologides A. Anorexins, asthenins, and cachectins in cancer. Am J Med. 1986;81:696.

114 Torti FM et al. A macrophage factor inhibits adipocyte gene expression: an in vitro model of cachexia. Science. 1985;229:867.

115 Beck SA, Tisdale MJ. Production of lipolytic and proteolytic factors by a murine tumor producing cachexia in the host. Cancer Res. 1987;47:5919.

116 Beutler B et al. Identity of tumor necrosis factor and the macrophage-secreted factor cachectin. Nature. 1985; 316:552.

117 Tchekmedyian NS et al. High-dose megestrol acetate. JAMA. 1987;257: 1195.

118 Aisner J et al. Studies of high-dose megestrol acetate: potential applications in cachexia. Semin Oncol. 1988; 15:88.

119 Struwe M et al. Effect of dronabinol on nutritional status in HIV infection. Ann Pharmacother. 1993;27:827.

120 Loprinzi CL et al. Randomized placebo-controlled evaluation of hydrazine sulfate in patients with advanced colorectal cancer. J Clin Oncol. 1994; 12:1121–125.

121 Loprinzi CL et al. Placebo controlled trial of hydrazine sulfate in patients with newly diagnosed non-small-cell lung cancer. J Clin Oncol. 1994;12: 1126–129.

122 Markham M. Chemotherapy with curative potential in small cell carcinoma of the lung. Hematol Oncol Clin North Am. 1988;2:375.

123 Crawford J et al. Reduction by granulocyte colony-stimulating factor of fever and neutropenia induced by chemotherapy in patients with small-cell lung cancer. N Engl J Med. 1991;325: 164.

124 Schabel FM et al. Cisdichlorodiaminneplatinum(II): combination chemotherapy and cross-resistance studies with tumors of mice. Cancer Treat Rep. 1979;63:1459.

125 Evans WK et al. Etoposide (VP-16) and cisplatin: an effective treatment for relapse of small cell lung cancer. J Clin Oncol. 1985;3:65.

126 Comis R. Oral etoposide in small cell lung cancer. Semin Oncol. 1986;13 (Suppl. 3):40.

127 Johnson DH et al. Prolonged administration of oral etoposide in patients with relapsed or refractory small-cell lung cancer: a phase II trial. J Clin Oncol. 1990;8:1613.

128 Clark PI et al. Prolonged administration of single agent etoposide in patients with untreated small cell lung cancer. Proc Am Soc Clin Oncol. 1990; 9:226. Abstract.

129 Bleehen NM et al. Role of radiation therapy in small cell anaplastic carcinoma of the lung. Cancer Treat Rep. 1983;67:11.

130 Rosen RT et al. Role of prophylactic cranial irradiation in prevention of central nervous system metastases in small cell lung cancer: potential benefit restricted to patients with complete response. Am J Med. 1983;74:615.

131 Aroney RS et al. Value of prophylactic cranial irradiation given at complete remission in small cell lung carcinoma. Cancer Treat Rep. 1983;67:675.

132 **Young RC et al.** Cancer of the ovary. In: DeVita VT et al., eds. Cancer. Principles and Practice of Oncology. 3rd ed. Philadelphia: Lippincott. 1989; 1162–196.

133 **Kent SW, McKay DG et al.** Primary cancer of the ovary. Am J Obstet Gynecol. 1960;80:430.

134 **Pearse WH, Behrman SJ.** Carcinoma of the ovary. Obstet Gynecol. 1954;3: 32.

135 **Averette HE et al.** Screening in gynecologic cancers. Cancer. 1993;72: 1043–49.

136 **Comprehensive Text Book of Oncology.** Vol. 2. Cap 98.

137 **Koss LG.** Cervical (PAP) Smear. Cancer. 1993;71:1406–412.

138 **Creasman WT, DiSaia PJ.** Screening in ovarian cancer. Am J Obstet Gynecol. 1991;165:7–10.

139 **Young RC et al.** Cancer of the ovary. In: DeVita VT et al., eds. Cancer. Principles and Practice of Oncology. 4th ed. Philadelphia: JB Lippincott; 1993: 1226.

140 **Andolf E et al.** Ultrasound examination for detection of ovarian carcinoma in risk groups. Obstet Gynecol. 1990; 75:106–9.

141 **Bourne TH et al.** Screening for early ovarian cancer. Br J Hosp Med. 1992; 48(8):454–59.

142 **Andolf E.** Ultrasound screening in women at risk for ovarian cancer. Clin Obstet and Gynecol. 1993;36(2):422–32.

143 **Zurawski VR Jr et al.** An initial analysis of preoperative serum CA-125 levels in patient with early stage ovarian carcinoma. Gynecol Oncol. 1988;30: 7–14.

144 **Jacobs I, Bast RC Jr.** The CA-125 tumor associated antigen; a review of literature. Hum Reprod. 1989;4:1–12.

145 **Thigpin JT.** Single agent chemotherapy in the management of ovarian carcinoma. In: Alberts DS, Surwit EA, eds. Ovarian Cancer. Boston: Martinus Nijhoff; 1985:115–46.

146 **Ozols R.** Chemotherapy of ovarian cancer. In: Updates. Cancer Principles and Practice of Oncology. 2nd ed. Philadelphia: Lippincott; 1988.

147 **Neijt JP et al.** Randomized trial comparing two combination chemotherapy regimens (CHAP-5 v CP) in advanced ovarian carcinoma. J Clin Oncol. 1987; 5:1157.

148 **Decker DG et al.** Cyclophosphamide plus cisplatinum in combination: treatment program for stage III or IV ovarian carcinoma. Obstet Gynecol. 1982; 60:481.

149 **Neijt JP.** Randomized trial comparing two combination chemotherapy regimens (Hexa-CAF vs CHAP-5) in advanced ovarian carcinoma. Lancet. 1984;2:294.

150 **Omura G et al.** A randomized trial of cyclophosphamide and doxorubicin with or without cisplatin in advanced ovarian carcinoma. Cancer. 1986;56: 1725.

151 **Conte PF et al.** A randomized trial comparing cisplatin plus cyclophosphamide versus cisplatin, doxorubicin and cyclophosphamide in advanced ovarian cancer. J Clin Oncol. 1986;4: 965.

152 **Gruppe Interginale Cooperativo Ginecolgia.** Randomized comparison of cisplatin with cyclophosphamide/cisplatin and with cyclophosphamide/doxorubicin/cisplatin in advanced ovarian cancer. Lancet. 1987;11:353.

153 **Bertelsen K et al.** A randomized study of CP versus CAP in advanced ovarian cancer: proceedings of the European Society of Medical Oncol. Cancer Chemother Pharmacol. 1986;18:7. Abstract.

154 **Omura GA et al.** A randomized trial of cyclophosphamide plus cisplatin with or without adriamycin in ovarian carcinoma. Proc Am Soc Clin Oncol. 1987;6:112. Abstract.

155 **Alberts DS et al.** Improved efficacy of carboplatin (CarboP)/cyclophosphamide (CPA) vs cisplatin (CisP)/CPA: preliminary report of a phase III randomized trial in stages II-IV suboptimal ovarian cancer (OV CA). Proc Am Soc Clin Oncol. 1989;8:151. Abstract.

156 **McVie JG et al.** Carboplatin and cyclophosphamide in relapsing ovarian cancer patients. Proc Am Soc Clin Oncol. 1989;8:161. Abstract.

157 **Eisenhauer EA et al.** Phase II study of carboplatin in patients with ovarian carcinoma: a National Cancer Institute of Canada clinical trials group study. Cancer Treat Rep. 1986;70:1195.

158 **McGuire WP et al.** A phase III trial comparing cisplatin/cytoxan (PC) and cisplatin/taxol (PT) in advanced ovarian cancer (AOC). Proc Am Soc Clin Oncol. 1993;12:255. Abstract.

159 **Ozols RF et al.** Ovarian cancer. Curr Probl Cancer. 1987;11:59.

160 **Piccart MJ et al.** Advanced ovarian cancer: three year results of a 6–8 month, 2 drug cisplatin-containing regimen. Eur J Clin Oncol. 1987;23:631.

161 **Markman M.** Intraperitoneal antineoplastic agents for tumors principally confined to the peritoneal cavity. Cancer Treat Rev. 1986;13:219.

162 **Brenner DE.** Intraperitoneal chemotherapy: a review. J Clin Oncol. 1986; 4:1135.

163 **Dunnick NR et al.** Intraperitoneal contrast infusion for assessment of intraperitoneal fluid dynamics. AJR. 1979; 133:221.

164 **Ozols RF.** Intraperitoneal therapy in ovarian cancer: times up! J Clin Oncol. 1991;12:197.

165 **Baker AR, Weber JS.** Treatment of malignant ascites. DeVita VT et al., eds. Cancer. Principles and Practice of Oncology. 4th ed. Philadelphia: JB Lippincott; 1993:2255–261.

166 **Markman M et al.** Second-line platinum therapy in patients with ovarian cancer previously treated with cisplatin. J Clin Oncol. 1991;9:389.

167 **Cannistra SA.** Cancer of the ovary. N Engl J Med. 1993;329:1550.

168 **McGuire WP et al.** Taxol: a unique antineoplastic agent with significant activity in advanced ovarian epithelial neoplasms. Ann Intern Med. 1989;111: 273.

169 **Thigpen T et al.** Phase II trial of taxol as second-line therapy for ovarian carcinoma: a gynecologic oncology group study. Proc Am Soc Clin Oncol. 1990; 9:604. Abstract.

170 **Einzig AI et al.** Phase II study and long-term follow-up of patients treated with taxol for advanced ovarian cancer. J Clin Oncol. 1992;10:1748.

171 **Fair WR et al.** Cancer of the bladder. In: DeVita VT et al., eds. Cancer. Principles and Practice of Oncology. 4th ed. Philadelphia: Lippincott; 1993: 1052.

172 **Batts CN.** Adjuvant intravesical therapy for superficial bladder cancer. Ann Pharmacother. 1992;26:1270.

173 **Heney NM et al.** TA and T1 bladder cancer: occasion, recurrence and progression. Br J Urol. 1982;54:152.

174 **Jaske G et al.** Stage T_1, grade 3 transitional cell carcinoma of the bladder: an unfavorable tumor? J Urol. 1987; 137:39.

175 **Herr HW.** Intravesical therapy. Hematol Oncol Clin North Am. 1992;6:1.

176 **Lamm DS et al.** BCG vs adriamycin intravesical therapy for in situ and papillary transitional cell carcinoma of the urinbladder: a Southwest Oncology Group study. Proc Am Soc Clin Oncol. 1989;8:504. Abstract.

177 **Lamm DL et al.** A randomized trial of intravesical doxorubicin and immunotherapy with Bacille Calmette-Guerin for transitional-cell bladder carcinoma of the bladder. N Engl J Med. 1991; 325:1205.

178 **Brosman SA, Lamm DL.** The preparation, handling and use of intravesical bacillus Calmette-Guerin for the management of stage T_a, T_1, carcinoma-in-situ and transitional cell cancer. J Urol. 1990;144:313.

179 **Vogelzang NJ.** Chemotherapy of genitourinary cancer. In: Perry MC, ed. The Chemotherapy Sourcebook. Baltimore: Williams & Wilkens; 1992: 1008.

180 **Sher H.** Chemotherapy for invasive bladder cancer: neoadjuvant versus adjuvant. Semin Oncol. 1990;17:555.

181 **Sher H et al.** Neoadjuvant M-VAC (methotrexate, vinblastine, adriamycin and cisplatin): the effect on primary bladder tumors. J Urol. 1988;139:470.

182 **Kaufman DS et al.** Selective bladder preservation by combination treatment of invasive bladder cancer. N Engl J Med. 1993;329:1377.

183 **Koh HK.** Cutaneous melanoma. N Engl J Med. 1991;325:171.

184 **Creagan ET.** Regional and systemic strategies for metastatic malignant melanoma. Mayo Clin Proc. 1989;64:852.

185 **Thomson TM et al.** Differentiation antigens of melanocytes and melanoma: analysis of melanosome and cell surface markers of human pigmented cells with monoclonal antibodies. J Invest Dermatol. 1988;90:459.

186 **Kirkwood JM, Ernstoff MS.** Cutaneous melanoma. In: DeVita VT et al., eds. Biologic Therapy of Cancer. Philadelphia: Lippincott; 1991:311–33.

187 **Kirkwood JM, Ernstoff MS.** Potential applications of interferons in oncology: lessons drawn from studies of human melanoma. Semin Oncol. 1986; 13(Suppl. 2):48.

188 **Balch CM et al.** Cutaneous melanoma. In: DeVita VT et al., eds. Cancer. Principles and Practice of Oncology. 4th ed. Philadelphia: Lippincott; 1993: 1612–661.

189 **Herlyn M et al.** Biology of melanocytes and melanoma. In: Balch CM et al., eds. Cutaneous Melanoma. 2nd ed. Philadelphia: Lippincott; 1992:234–43.

190 **Rosenberg SA et al.** A progress report on the treatment of 157 patients with advanced cancer using lymphokine-activated killer cells and interleukin-2 or high-dose interleukin-2 alone. N Engl J Med. 1987;316:889.

191 **Parkinson DR et al.** Interleukin-2 therapy in patients with metastatic malignant melanoma. J Clin Oncol. 1990; 8:1650.

192 **Lotze MT, Rosenberg SA.** Interleukin-2: clinical applications. In: DeVita VT et al., eds. Biologic Therapy of Cancer. Philadelphia: Lippincott; 1991: 159–77.

193 **Gearing AJH, Thorpe R.** The international standard for human interleukin-2: calibration by international collaborative study. J Immunol Meth. 1988;114:3.

194 **Siegal JP, Puri RK.** Interleukin-2 toxicity. J Clin Oncol. 1991;9:694.

195 **Richards J et al.** Sequential chemoimmunotherapy in the treatment of metastatic melanoma. J Clin Oncol. 1992; 10:1338.

196 **Flaherty LE et al.** A phase I-II study of dacarbazine in combination with outpatient interleukin-2 in metastatic malignant melanoma. Cancer. 1990; 65:2471.

197 **Stoter G et al.** Sequential administration of recombinant human interleukin-2 and dacarbazine in metastatic melanoma: a multicenter phase II trial. J Clin Oncol. 1991;9:1687.

198 **Cocconi G et al.** Treatment of metastatic malignant melanoma with dacarbazine plus tamoxifen. N Engl J Med. 1992;327:516.

199 **Friedman RJ et al.** Malignant melanoma in the 1990s: the continual importance of early examination and the role of physician examination and self examination of the skin. CA A Cancer Journal for Clinicians. 1991;41:201.

200 **Hanks GE, Myers CE, Scardino PT.** Cancer of the prostate. In: DeVita VT et al., eds. Cancer. Principles and Practice of Oncology. 4th ed. Philadelphia: Lippincott; 1993:1073–113.

201 **Pienta KJ, Esper PS.** Risk factors for prostate cancer. Ann Intern Med. 1993; 118:793.

202 **Perez CA et al.** Carcinoma of the prostate. In: DeVita VT et al., eds. Cancer. Principles and Practice of Oncology. 3rd ed. Philadelphia: Lippincott; 1989; 1023–58.

203 **Leuprolide Study Group.** Leuprolide versus diethylstilbestrol for metastatic prostate cancer. N Engl J Med. 1984; 311:1281.

204 **Baccon-Gibod L.** Nonsteroidal antiandrogen monotherapy of metastatic cancer of the prostate. Eur Urol. 1993;24 (Suppl. 2):77–80.

205 **Crawford ED et al.** A controlled trial of leuprolide with and without flutamide in prostatic carcinoma. N Engl J Med. 1989;321:419.

206 **Newling DWW et al.** Orchiectomy versus goserelin and flutamide in the treatment of newly diagnosed metastatic prostate cancer: analysis of the criteria of evaluation used in the European Organization for Research and Treatment of Cancer—Genitourinary Group Study 30853. Cancer. 1993;72 (Suppl.).:3793.

207 **Iversen P et al.** Long-term results of

Danish Prostatic Group Trial 86: goserelin acetate plus flutamide versus orchiectomy in advanced prostate cancer. Cancer. 1993;72(Suppl.):3851.

208 **Robinson MRG.** A further analysis of European Organization for Research and Treatment of Cancer Protocol 30805: orchidectomy versus orchidectomy plus cyproterone acetate versus low-dose diethylstilbestrol. Cancer. 1993;72(Suppl.):3855.

209 **Myers C et al.** Suramin: a novel growth factor antagonist with activity in hormone-refractory metastasis prostate cancer. J Clin Oncol. 1992;10:881.

210 **Jodrell DI et al.** Suramin: development of a population pharmacokinetic model and its use with intermittent short infusions to control plasma drug concentration in patients with prostate cancer. J Clin Oncol. 1994;12:166–75.

211 **Richie JP.** Detection and treatment of testicular cancer. CA— A Cancer J for Clinicians. 1993;43:151.

212 **Brodsky GL.** Pathology of testicular germ cell tumors. Hematol Oncol Clin North Am. 1991;5:1095.

213 **Bosl G.** Germ cell tumors. In: Wittes R, ed. Manual of Oncologic Therapeutics 1991–1992. Philadelphia: Lippincott; 1991:189–94.

214 **Williams SD et al.** Pathologic stage II testis cancer: immediate adjuvant chemotherapy versus observation with treatment relapse— a report from the Testicular Cancer Intergroup Study. N Engl J Med. 1987;317:1433.

215 **Einhorn LH, Donohue J.** Cis-diamminechloroplatinum, vinblastine, and bleomycin combination chemotherapy in disseminated testicular cancer. Ann Intern Med. 1977;87;1339.

216 **Einhorn LH et al.** The role of maintenance therapy in disseminated testicular cancer. N Engl J Med. 1981;305:727.

217 **Williams SD et al.** Treatment of disseminated germ cell tumors with cisplatinum, bleomycin and either vinblastine or etoposide. N Engl J Med. 1987;316:1435.

218 **Wheeler BM et al.** Ifosfamide in refractory germ cell tumors. J Clin Oncol. 1986;4:28.

219 **Loehrer PJ et al.** Salvage therapy in recurrent germ cell cancer: ifosfamide and cisplatin plus either vinblastine or etoposide. Ann Intern Med. 1988;109:540.

220 **Buzaid AC.** High-dose cisplatin with dacarbazine and tamoxifen in the treatment of metastatic melanoma. Cancer. 1991;68:1230.

221 **Sieman AD et al.** Preliminary experience with paclitaxel (Taxol) plus recombinant human granulocyte colony-stimulating factor in the treatment of breast cancer. Sem Oncol. 1993;20:40.

222 **Miller BA et al.,** eds. Cancer statistics review: 1973–1989. Bethesda, MD: National Cancer Institute, 1992; NIH publication no. 92-2789.

223 **Wasterwitz MJ, Ruccione K.** An overview of cancer in children in the 1980's. Nurs Clin North Am. 1985;20:5.

224 **Pui CH, Crist WM.** Pediatric solid tumors. In: Holleb AI et al., eds. Textbook of Clinical Oncology. 1st ed. Atlanta: American Cancer Society; 1991:453.

225 **Triche TJ.** Pathology of pediatric malignancies. In: Pizzo PA, Poplack PG, eds. Principles and Practice of Pediatric Oncology. 2nd ed. Philadelphia: JB Lippincott; 1993:11.

226 **Pui CH, Crist WM.** Childhood leukemias. In: Holleb AI et al., eds. Textbook of Clinical Oncology. 1st ed. Atlanta: American Cancer Society; 1991:435.

227 **Mulvihill JJ.** Childhood cancer, the environment and heredity. In: Pizzo PA, Poplack PG, eds. Principles and Practice of Pediatric Oncology. 2nd ed. Philadelphia: JB Lippincott; 1993:11.

228 **Tucker MA et al.** Leukemia after therapy with alkylating agents for childhood cancer. J Natl Cancer Inst. 1987;78:459.

229 **Pui CH et al.** Acute myeloid leukemia in children treated with epipodophyllotoxins for acute lymphoblastic leukemia. N Engl J Med. 1991;325:1682.

230 **Neglia JP et al.** Second neoplasms after acute lymphoblastic leukemia in childhood. N Engl J Med. 1991;324:1330.

231 **Melnick S et al.** Rates and risks of diethylstilbestrol-related clear-cell adenocarcinoma of the vagina and cervix: an update. N Engl J Med. 1987;316:514.

232 **Reamon GH.** Special considerations for the infant with cancer. In: Pizzo PA, Poplack DG, eds. Principles and Practice of Pediatric Oncology. 2nd ed. Philadelphia: JB Lippincott; 1993:303.

233 **Crist W et al.** Clinical and biologic features predict a poor prognosis in acute lymphoid leukemias in infants: Pediatric Oncology Group study. Blood. 1986;67:135.

234 **Raney RB Jr et al.** Rhabdomyosarcoma and the undifferentiated sarcomas. In: Pizzo PA, Poplack DG, eds. Principles and Practice of Pediatric Oncology. 2nd ed. Philadelphia: JB Lippincott; 1993:769.

235 **Blatt J et al.** Late effects of childhood cancer and its treatment. In: Pizzo PA, Poplack DG, eds. Principles and Practice of Pediatric Oncology. 2nd ed. Philadelphia: JB Lippincott; 1993:1091.

236 **Von Hoff DD et al.** Daunomycin induced cardiotoxicity in children and adults. Am J Med. 1977;62:200.

237 **Brodeur GM, Castleberry RP.** Neuroblastoma. In: Pizzo PA, Poplack DG, eds. Principles and Practice of Pediatric Oncology. 2nd ed. Philadelphia: JB Lippincott; 1993:739–747.

238 **Laug WE et al.** Initial urinary catecholamine metabolite concentrations and prognosis in neuroblastoma. Pediatrics. 1978;62:77.

239 **LaBrosse EH et al.** Urinary excretion of 3-methoxy-4-hydroxymandelic acid and 3-methoxy-4-hydroxy-phenylacetic acid by 288 patients with neuroblastoma and related neural crest tumors. Cancer Res. 1980;40:1995.

240 **Brodeur GM et al.** International criteria for diagnosis, staging and response to treatment in patients with neuroblastoma. J Clin Oncol. 1988;6:1874.

241 **Evans AE et al.** Prognostic factors in neuroblastoma. Cancer. 1987;59:1853.

242 **Coldman AJ et al.** Neuroblastoma: influence of age at diagnosis, stage, tumor site, and sex on prognosis. Cancer. 1980;46:1896.

243 **Carlsen NLT et al.** Prognostic factors in neuroblastomas treated in Denmark from 1943 to 1980. A statistical estimate of prognosis based on 253 cases. Cancer. 1986;58:2726.

244 **Breslow N et al.** Statistical estimation of prognosis for children with neuroblastoma. Cancer Res. 1971;31:2098.

245 **Hann HWL et al.** Serum ferritin as a guide to therapy in neuroblastoma. Cancer Res. 1980;40:1411.

246 **Hann HWL et al.** Basic and acidic isoferritins in the sera of patients with neuroblastoma. Cancer. 1988;62:1179.

247 **Zeltzer PM et al.** Serum neuron-specific enolase in children with neuroblastoma. Relationship to stage and disease course. Cancer. 1986;57:1230.

248 **Quinn JJ et al.** Serum lactic dehydrogenase, an indicator of tumor activity in neuroblastoma. J Pediatr. 1980;97:89.

249 **Look AT et al.** Clinical relevance of tumor cell ploidy and N-myc gene amplification in childhood neuroblastoma. A Pediatric Oncology Group study. J Clin Oncol. 1991;9:581.

250 **Brodeur GM, Fong CT.** Molecular biology and genetics of human neuroblastoma. Cancer Genet Cytogenet. 1989;41:153.

251 **Shimada H et al.** Histopathologic prognostic factors in neuroblastic tumors: definition of subtypes of ganglioneuroblastoma and an age-linked classification of neuroblastomas. J Natl Cancer Inst. 1984;73:405.

252 **Joshi VV et al.** Age-linked prognostic categorization based on a new histologic grading system of neuroblastomas: a clinicopathologic study of 211 cases from the Pediatric Oncology Group. Cancer. 1992;69:2197.

253 **Joshi VV et al.** Correlation between morphologic and other prognostic markers of neuroblastoma. Cancer. 1993;71:3173.

254 **Hartman O et al.** Very high-dose cisplatin and etoposide in children with untreated advanced neuroblastoma. J Clin Oncol. 1988;6:44.

255 **Green AA et al.** Sequential cyclophosphamide and adriamycin for induction of complete remissions in children with disseminated neuroblastoma. Cancer. 1982;48:2310.

256 **Fairclough DL et al.** Received dose intensity and outcome in disseminated neuroblastoma over 1 year of age. Proc ASCO. 1992;11:368. Abstract 1271.

257 **Shafford EA et al.** Advanced neuroblastoma: improved response rate using a multiagent regimen (OPEC) including sequential cisplatin and VM-26. J Clin Oncol. 1984;2:742.

258 **Sullivan MP et al.** Evaluation of vincristine sulfate and cyclophosphamide chemotherapy for metastatic neuroblastoma. Pediatrics. 1969;44:685.

259 **Michon J et al.** The use of VP16 and carboplatin in localized neuroblastoma. Results of a SFOP Pilot study. Proc ASCO. 1993;12:418. Abstract 1437.

260 **Marina N et al.** Ifosfamide, carboplatin and etoposide (ICE) combined with human granulocyte-macrophage colony-stimulating factor (GM-CSF) in children with recurrent solid tumors.

Proc ASCO. 1993;12:422. Abstract 1453.

261 **Morris J et al.** Bone marrow transplantation for advanced stage neuroblastoma. Proc ASCO. 1992;11:364. Abstract 1252.

262 **Evans A et al.** Do infants with stage IV-S neuroblastoma need treatment? Arch Dis Child. 1981;56:271.

263 **McWilliams NB.** IV-S neuroblastoma: treatment controversy revisited. Med Pediatr Oncol. 1986;14:41.

264 **Stokes SH et al.** Stage IV-S neuroblastoma—results with definitive therapy. Cancer. 1984;53:2083.

265 **Phoon C.** Cardiology. In: Johnson KB, ed. The Harriot Lane Handbook. 13th ed. St. Louis: Mosby; 1993:101.

266 **Bristol Laboratories Oncology Products.** Platinol-AQ package insert. Evansville, IN: 1991 Jan.

267 **McEvoy GK et al.,** eds. AHFS Drug Information 93. Bethesda, MD: American Society of Hospital Pharmacists; 1993:543.

268 **D'Angio R et al.** Creatinine clearance: corrected versus uncorrected. Drug Intel Clin Pharm. 1988;22:32. Letter.

269 **Womer RB et al.** Renal toxicity of cisplatin in children. J Pediatr. 1985;106:659.

270 **Dini G et al.** Bone marrow transplantation for neuroblastoma: a review of 509 cases. Bone Marrow Transplant. 1989;4(Suppl. 4):42.

271 **Hartman O et al.** Repeated high-dose chemotherapy followed by purged autologous bone marrow transplantation as consolidation therapy in metastatic neuroblastoma. J Clin Oncol. 1987;5:1205.

272 **Graham-Pole J.** High-dose chemoradiotherapy supported by marrow infusions for advanced neuroblastoma: a Pediatric Oncology Groups study. J Clin Oncol. 1991;9:152.

273 **Ladenstein R.** Analysis of risk-factors in 550 stage 4 neuroblastoma patients older than 12 months at diagnosis consolidated by megatherapy and bone marrow transplantation. A survey on the European experience. Proc ASCO. 1993;12:419. Abstract 1440.

274 **Yu A et al.** Phase I clinical trial of CH14.18 in patients with refractory neuroblastoma. Proc ASCO. 1991;10:318. Abstract 1118.

275 **Skala JP et al.** Deferoxamine as a purging agent for autologous bone marrow graft in neuroblastoma. Prog Clin Biol Res. 1992;377:71.

276 **Donfrancesco A et al.** Effects of a single course of deferoxamine in neuroblastoma patients. Cancer Res. 1990;50:4929.

277 **Donfrancesco A et al.** D-CECaT: a breakthrough for patients with neuroblastoma. Anticancer Drugs. 1993;4:317.

278 **Becton DL, Bryles P.** Deferoxamine inhibition of human neuroblastoma viability and proliferation. Cancer Res. 1988;48:7189.

279 **Green DM et al.** Wilms' tumor (nephroblastoma, renal embryoma). In: Pizzo PA, Poplack DG, eds. Principles and Practice of Pediatric Oncology. 2nd ed. Philadelphia: JB Lippincott; 1993:713.

280 **Breslow NE et al.** Age distribution of Wilms' tumor: report from the Nation-

al Wilms' Tumor Study. Cancer Res. 1988;48:1653.

281 D'Angio GJ et al. Treatment of Wilms' tumor; results of the third National Wilms' Tumor Study. Cancer. 1989;64:349.

282 Jones B et al. Toxic deaths in the second National Wilms' Tumor Study. J Clin Oncol. 1984;2:1028.

283 Morgan E et al. Chemotherapy-related toxicity in infants treated according to the second National Wilms' Tumor Study. J Clin Oncol. 1988;6:51.

284 Woods WG et al. Life-threatening neuropathy and hepatotoxicity in infants during induction therapy for acute lymphoblastic leukemia. J Pediatr. 1981;98:642.

285 Allen JC. The effects of cancer therapy on the nervous system. J Pediatr. 1978; 93:903.

286 Reaman G et al. Acute lymphoblastic leukemia in infants less than one year of age: a cumulative experience of the Children's Cancer Study Group. J Clin Oncol. 1985;3:1513.

287 D'Angio GJ et al. Potentiation of x-ray effects by actinomycin D. Radiology. 1959;73:175.

288 Tan CTC et al. The effect of actinomycin D on cancer in childhood. Pediatrics. 1959;24:544.

289 Donaldson SS et al. Adriamycin activating a recall phenomenon after radiation therapy. Ann Intern Med. 1974; 81:407.

290 Greco FA et al. Adriamycin and enhanced radiation reaction in normal esophagus and skin. Ann Intern Med. 1976;85:294.

291 Phillips TL, Fu KK. Acute and late effects of multimodal therapy on normal tissues. Cancer. 1977;40:489.

292 Merrill J et al. Adriamycin and radiation-synergistic cardiotoxicity. Ann Intern Med. 1975;82:122.

293 Goorin AM et al. Initial congestive heart failure, six to ten years after doxorubicin chemotherapy for childhood cancer. J Pediatr. 1990;116:144.

294 Lipshultz SE et al. Late cardiac effects of doxorubicin therapy for acute lymphoblastic leukemia in childhood. N Engl J Med. 1991;324:808.

295 Steinherz LJ et al. Cardiac toxicity 4 to 20 years after completing anthracycline therapy. J Am Med Assoc. 1991; 266:1672.

296 Steinherz LJ et al. Guidelines for cardiac monitoring of children during and after anthracycline therapy: report of the Cardiology Committee of the Children's Cancer Study Group. Pediatrics. 1992;89:942.

297 Jakacki RI et al. Comparison of cardiac function tests after anthracycline therapy in childhood. Cancer. 1993;72:2739.

298 Green DM et al. Severe hepatic toxicity after treatment with single-dose dactinomycin and vincristine. Cancer. 1988;62:270.

299 Green DM et al. Severe hepatic toxicity after treatment with vincristine and dactinomycin using single-dose or divided-dose schedules: a report from the National Wilms' Tumor Study. J Clin Oncol. 1990;8:1525.

300 Link MP, Eilber F. Osteosarcoma. In: Pizzo PA, Poplack DG, eds. Principles and Practice of Pediatric Oncology. 2nd ed. Philadelphia: JB Lippincott; 1993;841.

301 Goorin AM et al. Osteosarcoma: fifteen years later. N Engl J Med. 1985; 313:1637.

302 Link MP et al. The effect of adjuvant chemotherapy on relapse-free survival in patients with osteosarcoma of the extremity. N Engl J Med. 1986;314:1600.

303 Pratt C et al. High dose methotrexate used alone and in combination for measurable primary and metastatic osteosarcoma. Cancer Treat Rep. 1980; 64:11–20.

304 Ochs JJ et al. Cis-dichlorodiammineplatinum (II) in advanced osteogenic sarcoma. Cancer Treat Rep. 1978;62:239.

305 Baum ES et al. Phase II study of cis-dichlorodiammineplatinum (II) in childhood osteosarcoma: Children's Cancer Study Group report. Cancer Treat Rep. 1979;63:1621.

306 Cortes EP et al. Doxorubicin in disseminated osteosarcoma. J Am Med Assoc. 1972;221:1132.

307 Marti C et al. High-dose ifosfamide in advanced osteosarcoma. Cancer Treat Rep. 1985;69:115.

308 Mosende C et al. Combination chemotherapy with bleomycin, cyclophosphamide and dactinomycin for the treatment of osteogenic sarcoma. Cancer. 1977;40:2779.

309 Meyers PA et al. Chemotherapy for nonmetastatic osteogenic sarcoma: the Memorial Sloan-Kettering experience. J Clin Oncol. 1992;10:5.

310 Jenkin R et al. Osteosarcoma: an assessment of management with particular reference to primary irradiation and selective delayed amputation. Cancer. 1972;30:393.

311 Simone JV, Link MP. Osteosarcoma: good news despite crude tools. J Clin Oncol. 1992;10:1. Editorial.

312 Pastorino U et al. The contribution of salvage surgery to the management of childhood osteosarcoma. J Clin Oncol. 1991;9:1357.

313 Evans WE, Pratt CB. Effect of pleural effusion on high-dose methotrexate kinetics. Clin Pharmacol Ther. 1978;23:68.

314 Crom WR, Evans WE. Methotrexate. In: Evans WE et al., eds. Applied Pharmacokinetics. 3rd ed. Vancouver: Applied Therapeutics; 1992;29–12.

315 Evans WE et al. Pharmacokinetics of sustained serum methotrexate concentrations secondary to gastrointestinal obstruction. J Pharm Sci. 1981;70:1194.

316 Crom WR et al. The effect of prior cisplatin therapy on the pharmacokinetics of high-dose methotrexate. J Clin Oncol. 1984;2:655.

317 Hansten PD, Horn JR, eds. Drug Interactions & Updates Quarterly. Vancouver: Applied Therapeutics; 1994:414.

318 Gerrazzini G et al. Interaction between trimethoprim-sulfamethoxazole and methotrexate in children with leukemia. J Pediatr. 1990;117:823.

319 Hande K et al. Trimethoprim interferes with serum methotrexate assay by the competitive protein binding technique. Clin Chem. 1980;26:1617.

320 Pinedo HM, Chabner BA. Role of drug concentration, duration of exposure and endogenous metabolites in determining methotrexate cytotoxicity. Cancer Treat Rep. 1977;61:709.

321 Wilbur JR. Combination chemotherapy for embryonal rhabdomyosarcoma. Cancer Chemother Rep. 1974;58:281.

322 Tan C et al. Adriamycin—an antitumor antibiotic in the treatment of neoplastic diseases. Cancer. 1973;32:9.

323 Miser JS et al. Ifosfamide with mesna uroprotection and etoposide: an effective regimen in the treatment of recurrent sarcomas and other tumors of children and young adults. J Clin Oncol. 1987;5:1191.

324 Chard RL Jr et al. Phase II study of VP-16-213 in childhood malignant disease: a Children's Cancer Study Group report. Cancer Treat Rep. 1979;63:1755.

325 Crist W et al. Intensive chemotherapy including cisplatin with or without etoposide for children with soft-tissue sarcomas. Med Pediatr Oncol. 1987;15:51.

326 Finkelstein JZ et al. 5-(3,3-dimethyltriazeno) imidazole-4-carboxamide (NSC-45388) in the treatment of solid tumors in children. Cancer Chemother Rep. 1975;59:351.

327 Bode U. Methotrexate as relapse therapy for rhabdomyosarcoma. Am J Pediatr Hematol Oncol. 1986;8:70.

328 Horowitz ME et al. Phase II testing of melphalan in children with newly diagnosed rhabdomyosarcoma: a model for anticancer drug development. J Clin Oncol. 1988;6:308.

329 Ragab A et al. Intergroup Rhabdomyosarcoma Study (IRS) III: preliminary report of the major results. Proc ASCO. 1992;11:363.

330 Crist WM et al. Prognosis in children with rhabdomyosarcoma: a report of the Intergroup Rhabdomyosarcoma Studies I and II. J Clin Oncol. 1990;8:443.

331 Rodary C et al. Prognostic factors in 281 children with non-metastatic rhabdomyosarcoma (RMS) at diagnosis. Med Pediatr Oncol. 1988;16:71.

332 Ortega J et al. Ifosfamide, actinomycin-D, and vincristine for the treatment of childhood rhabdomyosarcoma: a feasibility and toxicity study. A report for the Intergroup Rhabdomyosarcoma Study IV. Proc ASCO. 1991;10:314. Abstract 1102.

333 Raney B et al. Renal toxicity in patients receiving ifosfamide/mesna on intergroup rhabdomyosarcoma study (IRS)-IV Pilot regimens for gross residual sarcoma. Proc ASCO. 1993;12:418. Abstract 1435.

334 Rossi R et al. Unilateral nephrectomy and cisplatin as risk factors of ifosfamide-induced nephrotoxicity: analysis of 120 patients. J Clin Oncol. 1994;12:159.

335 Suarez A et al. Long-term follow-up of ifosfamide renal toxicity in children treated for malignant mesenchymal tumors: an International Society of Pediatric Oncology report. J Clin Oncol. 1991;9:2177.

336 Evans WE et al. Pharmacokinetic monitoring of high-dose methotrexate: early recognition of high-risk patients. Cancer Chemother Pharmacol. 1979;3:161.

337 Tattersall MHN et al. Clinical pharmacology of high-dose methotrexate (NSC-740). Cancer Chemother Rep. 1975;6(pt. 3):25.

338 Isacoff WH et al. High-dose methotrexate therapy of solid tumors: observations relating to clinical toxicity. Med Pediatr Oncol. 1976;2:319.

339 Isacoff WH et al. Pharmacokinetics of high-dose methotrexate with citrovorum factor rescue. Cancer Treat Rep. 1977;61:1665.

340 Nirenberg A et al. High dose methotrexate with CF rescue: predictive value of serum methotrexate concentrations and corrective measures to avert toxicity. Cancer Treat Rep. 1977;61:779.

341 Stoller RC et al. Use of plasma pharmacokinetics to predict and prevent methotrexate toxicity. N Engl J Med. 1977;297:630.

342 Rechnitzer C et al. Methotrexate in the plasma and cerebrospinal fluid of children treated with intermediate dose methotrexate. Acta Paediatr Scand. 1981;70:615.

343 Yehuda AB et al. False positive reaction for urinary ketones with mesna. Drug Intell Clin Pharm. 1987;21:547. Letter.

Bone Marrow Transplantation

Dayna L McCauley
Pamala Jacobson

Overview (See Figures 94.1 and 94.2) 94-1
   Allogeneic Bone Marrow Transplantation (BMT)
   (See Table 94.1) 94-1
      Histocompatibility considerations (Figure 94.3) 94-2
      Preparative regimens (See Table 94.2) 94-2
      Immunosuppressive therapy 94-3
      Technique for obtaining bone marrow 94-3
      Indications for allogeneic bone marrow
      transplantation (See Table 94.1) 94-4
      Supportive care 94-5
   Autologous Bone Marrow Transplantation and
   Peripheral Blood Stem Cell (PBSC) Rescue 94-5
      High-dose chemotherapy (See Table 94.2) 94-6
      Technique for harvesting stem cells 94-6
      Autologous bone marrow 94-6
      Peripheral blood stem cells 94-6
      Indications for high-dose chemotherapy and
      stem cell support (Table 94.1) 94-6
      Supportive care 94-7
      Hematopoietic growth factors 94-7
      Comparison to allogeneic bone marrow
      transplantation 94-7
   Bone Marrow Transplantation in AML 94-22
Complications Associated with Bone
Marrow Transplantation (See Figure 94.4,
Tables 94.3 and 94.4) 94-7
   Regimen-Related Toxicities 94-8
      Dose calculations in obesity 94-8
      Busulfan-induced neurotoxicity 94-9
      Hemorrhagic cystitis 94-9
      Veno-occlusive disease (VOD) of the liver 94-10
      Signs and symptoms (See Table 94.5) 94-10

      Mortality and treatment 94-10
Graft Failure 94-11
Graft-versus-Host Disease (GVHD) 94-11
   Acute GVHD (See Table 94.6 and Table 94.7) 94-12
      Clinical presentation 94-12
      Risk factors (See Figure 94.5) 94-13
      Immunosuppressive prophylaxis (See Table 94.8
      and Table 94.9) 94-13
      Guidelines for use of immunosuppressants 94-14
      Role of cyclosporine pharmacokinetic
      monitoring 94-15
      Investigational therapies for prophylaxis 94-15
      Treatment of established acute GVHD 94-15
   Chronic GVHD 94-16
      Clinical presentation (See Table 94.10) 94-16
      Pharmacologic management 94-17
      Adjuvant therapies 94-17
Infectious Complications (See Figure 94.4) 94-17
   Prevention of herpes simplex virus (HSV) 94-17
      Acyclovir dosing 94-18
   Prevention of cytomegalovirus (CMV) disease 94-18
      Antivirals (See Table 94.11) 94-18
      Immune globulins (See Table 94.12 and
      Table 94.13) 94-19
   Diagnosis and treatment of CMV interstitial
      pneumonitis (IP) 94-19
      Diagnosis and manifestations 94-20
      Treatment of CMV interstitial pneumonitis
      (See Table 94.14) 94-20
      Treatment of CMV gastrointestinal (GI) disease .. 94-21
   Antiviral toxicity 94-21
   Prevention of Pneumocystis carinii pneumonia
   (PCP) (See Table 94.15) 94-21

Bone marrow transplantation (BMT) is defined broadly as the infusion of hematopoietic progenitor cells (stem cells) into a patient to treat disease.[1] Historically, bone marrow transplantation involved true ''transplantation'' of bone marrow from one individual to another. This technique is referred to as *allogeneic bone marrow transplantation* and commonly is used as potentially curative therapy in the treatment of diseases involving the bone marrow or immune system.[2] Recently, application of the concept of dose-intensity to the treatment of malignancy (see related information in Chapter 90: Neoplastic Disorders and Their Treatment: General Principles) has expanded this traditional concept of bone marrow transplantation. Infusion of a patient's own bone marrow (referred to as *autologous bone marrow*) has been proposed as a way to administer escalated doses of chemotherapy, radiation, or both. The bone marrow ''rescues'' the patient from otherwise dose-limiting hematopoietic toxicity. In this setting, bone marrow transplantation is defined more aptly as bone marrow rescue. In addition, peripheral-blood stem cells (PBSCs) increasingly are being used in place of, or in combination with, autologous bone marrow as a source of hematopoietic rescue. Thus, the current definition of bone marrow transplantation encompasses several techniques, including allogeneic bone marrow transplantation and stem cell rescue following high-dose chemotherapy.

The basic schema for bone marrow transplantation is depicted in Figure 94.1. Administration of near-lethal doses of chemotherapy and/or radiation is followed by a one- to two-day rest and then infusion of stem cells.[1,2] The rest period is necessary to allow for elimination of toxic metabolites from the chemotherapy that could damage infused stem cells. Following chemotherapy and radiation is a period of pancytopenia that lasts until the infused cells home to the bone marrow cavity, lodge, and re-establish functional hematopoiesis. This process is called *engraftment* and commonly is defined as the time to an absolute neutrophil count (ANC) of 500 cells/mm^3 in the peripheral blood for two to three consecutive days. The median time to engraftment is a function of several factors (see Figure 94.2).

Modifications to the basic schema for bone marrow transplantation are necessary based upon the source of stem cells infused (i.e., allogeneic, autologous, or PBSCs).

Allogeneic Bone Marrow Transplantation (BMT)

The defining characteristic of an allogeneic BMT schema is the incorporation of intensive pre- and posttransplant immunosuppres-

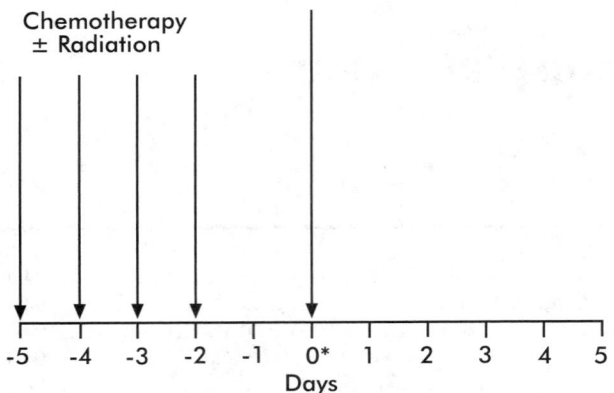

Fig 94.1   Basic Schema for Bone Marrow Transplantation   *Day 0 =
Bone marrow or stem cell infusion.

sion. Immunosuppression is needed because of histocompatibility differences between the donor and the patient. Thus, in order to understand the application of and complications following allogeneic bone marrow transplantation, a working knowledge of immunology and the major histocompatibility complex (MHC) [referred to as human leukocyte antigen (HLA) in humans] is in order. For a detailed review of this topic the reader is referred elsewhere.[3] (Also see related information in Chapter 33: Solid Organ Transplantation.) The primary indications for the use of allogeneic BMT include treatment of otherwise fatal diseases of the bone marrow or immune system (see Table 94.1).

Histocompatibility Considerations

Allogeneic bone marrow transplantation involves the transplantation of tissue (bone marrow) from a donor to a patient. Unless the donor and the patient are identical twins (referred to as a *syngeneic* BMT), the donor and the recipient are dissimilar genetically. Thus, histocompatibility considerations are of major concern. Because the tissue being transplanted in allogeneic BMT is immunologically active, there is potential for bidirectional graft rejection.[2,6] In the first scenario, recipient or host (patient) cytotoxic T-cells and natural killer (NK) cells recognize MHC antigens of the graft (donor bone marrow) and elicit a rejection response. In the second scenario, immunologically active cells in the graft can recognize host MHC antigens and elicit a rejection response. The former is referred to as host-versus-graft disease and the latter as graft-versus-host disease (GVHD). Host-versus-graft effects are more common in solid organ transplantation. When host-versus-graft effects occur in allogeneic BMT, they are referred to as graftfailure (i.e., graft-rejection). Graft-versus-host disease is more common in allogeneic BMT because immunologically active host tissue has been ablated with chemotherapy or radiation and the patient is heavily immunosuppressed.

Determination of histocompatibility between potential donors and the patient is completed before allogeneic bone marrow transplantation.[7] Human leukocyte antigen typing is performed using blood samples and compatibility for Class I MHC antigens (HLA-A, HLA-B, and HLA-C) is determined. *In vitro* reactivity between donor and recipient in mixed-lymphocyte culture (MLC) may be assessed. This test, which measures the degree of lymphocyte proliferation when lymphocytes from the donor and the recipient are mixed together, is a measure of compatibility of the MHC Class II antigens (HLA-DR, HLA-DP, HLA-DQ). A high proliferative index indicates incompatibility at the HLA-D loci. Other than syngeneic bone marrow, the source of marrow that is least likely to result in rejection reactions is allogeneic marrow that is fully matched at HLA-A, HLA-B, and HLA-DR and is nonreactive in

mixed lymphocyte culture.[7] Because the likelihood of complete histocompatibility between unrelated individuals is remote, HLA typing usually is conducted on family members. Siblings are the most likely individuals to be histocompatible within a family. However, since each offspring inherits only one parental haplotype, the chance for complete histocompatibility occurring in an individual with only one sibling is 25%.[2,6] Approximately 40% of patients with more than one sibling will have an HLA-identical match.[2] The frequency of identical (monozygotic) twins occurring spontaneously in nature is approximately 1 in 100 births. Thus, it is even less likely that a patient would have a syngeneic donor.

Lack of an HLA-matched sibling donor can be a barrier to allogeneic BMT. The use of alternative sources of allogeneic marrow, such as related donors mismatched at one or more HLA-loci, or phenotypically matched unrelated donors has been attempted. Establishment of the National Marrow Donor Program has helped increase the pool of potential donors for allogeneic bone marrow transplantation.[8] Through this program, an HLA-matched unrelated volunteer donor may be identified. Figure 94.3 depicts the chance of finding a histocompatible allogeneic donor for a given patient.

Preparative Regimens

The combination of high-dose chemotherapy or radiation used in allogeneic bone marrow transplantation is referred to as the preparative or conditioning regimen. Depending upon the disease being treated, the preparative regimen is designed to immunosuppress the patient, eradicate residual malignancy, or both.[1,2]

An immunosuppressive conditioning regimen is required when an allogeneic BMT is performed in adults or children who have functioning immune systems before bone marrow transplantation (e.g., aplastic anemia or acute myelogenous leukemia). In these examples, the preparative regimen is designed to eradicate immunologically active host tissues (lymphoid tissue and macrophages), and thus prevent or minimize the development of host-versus-graft reactions. Cyclophosphamide and radiation, both potent immunosuppressants, are the two agents commonly employed in regimens designed to immunosuppress the patient before allogeneic bone marrow transplantation. In contrast, if a histocompatible allogeneic BMT is being performed on a patient with a poorly functioning immune system [e.g., severe combined immunodeficiency disease (SCID)], an immunosuppressive pretrans-

Fig 94.2   Time to Engraftment   A = Bone marrow infusion without complications or hematopoietic growth factors. B = Accelerated engraftment with hematopoietic growth factors, PBSCs, and/or combination of bone marrow, PBSCs, and hematopoietic growth factors. C = Delayed engraftment caused by infection, purged bone marrow, and/or inadequate inoculum.

Table 94.1	Indications for BMT[a,b,1,4,5]	
	Established Role	**Promising/ Experimental**
Allogeneic		
Nonmalignant	Aplastic anemia	Sickle cell anemia
	Homozygous β-thalassemia	Severe leukocyte adhesion deficiency
	Severe combined immunodeficiency disease	X-linked agammaglobinemia
	Wiskott-Aldrich syndrome	Common variable immunodeficiency
	Fanconi's anemia	
	Infantile osteopetrosis	
	Chediak-Higashi syndrome	
Malignant	AML	CLL (young patients only)
	ALL	Multiple myeloma
	CML	Myelodysplastic
	(Intermediate and high-grade NHL)	syndrome
Autologous		
Nonmalignant	—	Genetic disorders with gene therapy
Malignant	Intermediate and high-grade NHL	Breast cancer (high risk adjuvant or metastatic)
	AML (patients who lack suitable allogeneic donors)	Multiple myeloma
		Neuroblastoma
	Relapsed or refractory HD	Small-cell lung cancer
	Testicular cancer	Ovarian cancer
		Low-grade lymphomas
		Rhabdomyosarcoma

[a] AML = Acute myelogenous leukemia; BMT = Bone marrow transplantation; CLL = Chronic lymphocytic leukemia; CML = Chronic myelogenous leukemia; HD = Hodgkin's disease; NHL = NonHodgkin's lymphoma.
[b] Timing relative to diagnosis and other therapies may vary.

plant preparative regimen is unnecessary.[4] In the absence of a functioning immune system, the likelihood of a host-versus-graft reaction to histocompatible bone marrow is small. In fact, hematopoietic progenitor cells can be infused into patients with SCID without a preparative regimen at all.[4] Similarly, patients undergoing syngeneic bone marrow transplantation do not require immunosuppressive preparative regimens before BMT because the donor and the patient are genetically identical.[2]

If allogeneic bone marrow transplantation is used to treat a hematologic malignancy (e.g., leukemia), another goal of the preparative regimen is to eradicate residual disease.[1] If patients undergo allogeneic bone marrow transplantation during periods of clinical remission, occult malignant cells still may be present. Thus, in the treatment of malignancy, chemotherapy or radiation administered as part of a preparative regimen is intended to destroy remaining malignant cells and contribute to a long-term cure.[1,2] Alkylating agents, alone or in combination with radiation, are the class of antineoplastics used most commonly. They are preferred because they exhibit a steep dose-response curve and are characterized by myelosuppression as their dose-limiting toxicity.[10] Ideally, if combinations of antineoplastics are used, they should have nonhematologic toxicities that do not overlap and are nonlife-threatening.

Examples of common preparative regimens for allogeneic bone marrow transplantation are depicted in Table 94.2. Most allogeneic preparative regimens for the treatment of hematologic malignan-

cies contain either cyclophosphamide, irradiation, or ⸺ combination of cyclophosphamide and total body irradiatio⸺ was the first preparative regimen to be used and still is used wi⸺ today.[2] This regimen is immunosuppressive and has inherent activity against hematologic malignancies (e.g., leukemias, lymphomas). Total body irradiation has the added advantages of being devoid of active metabolites that might interfere with activity of the donor marrow, as well as the ability to eradicate residual malignant cells at sanctuary sites such as the central nervous system (CNS). Modifications of the cyclophosphamide-TBI preparative regimen include replacing total body irradiation with other agents (busulfan), or adding other agents to the existing regimen (e.g., etoposide, cytarabine).[22,23] These measures are designed to minimize the long-term toxicities associated with TBI (e.g., growth retardation in children, cataracts) or provide additional antitumor activity, respectively.[22,23]

Immunosuppressive Therapy

In order to prevent or minimize the development of graft-versus-host disease, immunosuppressive therapy is administered to the patient following infusion of allogeneic bone marrow. Patients receiving syngeneic BMTs for any disease or a T-cell depleted histocompatible allogeneic bone marrow transplantation for the treatment of SCID do not receive posttransplant immunosuppressive therapy. In the former, the donor and the patient are genetically identical, and, thus, should not elicit GVHD. In the latter, the volume of donor T-cells infused into the patient usually is insufficient to elicit a significant graft-versus-host reaction.[4]

In contrast to solid organ transplantation where immunosuppressive therapy is administered for the duration of the recipient's life, immunosuppressive therapy following allogeneic bone marrow transplantation is tapered slowly and discontinued over six months to one year. This difference is accounted for by the development of a poorly understood phenomenon known as immunological tolerance.[2] Over time, the immunologically active tissue between host and recipient become tolerant of one another and cease recognizing the other as foreign.

Technique for Obtaining Bone Marrow

Allogeneic bone marrow is obtained from the donor under spinal or general anesthesia in the operating room under sterile conditions on day 0 of bone marrow transplantation.[2,24] Multiple aspirations of marrow are obtained from the anterior and posterior iliac crests until a volume with a sufficient number of stem cells is collected

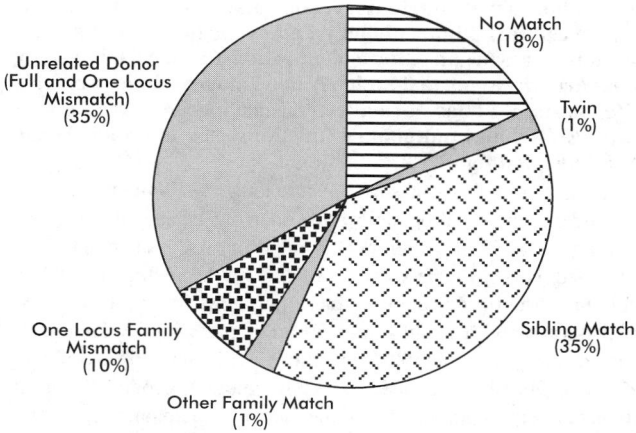

Fig 94.3 Chance of Finding a Donor for a Patient with Two Live Parents and an Average of 1.7 Siblings Also shown is the chance of finding a donor if a family donor is not available. Reproduced with permission from reference 9.

Table 94.2   Representative Preparative Regimens Used in BMT[a]

Type of BMT	Disease State	Regimen[b]	Dose/Schedule
Allogeneic[2,11]	Hematologic malignancies[b]	Cy + TBI	Cy 60 mg/kg IV on 2 consecutive days before TBI + 1000–1575 rads TBI fractionated over 1–7 days
Allogeneic[12]	Aplastic anemia	Cy	Cy 60 mg/kg IV on 4 consecutive days (−5, −4, −3, −2)
Allogeneic, Autologous[13–15]	Acute and chronic leukemias	Bu + Cy	Bu *(adult):* 16 mg/kg PO over 4 days (1 mg/kg/dose PO Q 6° × 16 doses) *Age <7 yr:* 600 mg/m² PO over 4 days (37.5 mg/m² PO Q 6° × 16 doses) + Cy 50 mg/kg IV QD × 4 days following Bu or 60 mg/kg IV QD × 2 days following Bu
Allogeneic[16]	Hematologic malignancies	TBI + VP-16	1320 rads TBI over 4 consecutive days (−7, −6, −5, −4) + VP-16 60 mg/kg IV on day −3
Allogeneic Autologous, PBSC[17,18]	Hematologic malignancies	Cy + BCNU + VP-16	Cy 1.5 gm/m² IV on 4 consecutive days (−6, −5, −4, −3) + BCNU 300 mg/m² IV × 1, day −6 + VP-16 100 mg/m² IV Q 12 hr for 6 doses (−6, −5, −4)
Autologous, PBSC[19]	HD, NHL	BCNU + VP-16 + Ara-C + Melphalan	BCNU 300 mg/m² IV × 1, day −6 + VP-16 100–200 mg/m² IV QD × 4 (days −5, −4, −3, −2) + Ara-C 200–400 mg/m² IV QD × 4 (days −5, −4, −3, −2) + Melphalan 140 mg/m² IV, day −1
Autologous, PBSC[20]	Breast	Cy + Cisplatin + BCNU	Cy 1875 mg/m² IV QD × 3 (−6, −5, −4) + CDDP 55 mg/m²/day as a 72 hr IV continuous infusion (−6, −5, −4) + BCNU 600 mg/m² IV × 1, day −6
Autologous, PBSC[21]	Testicular	Carbo + VP-16	Carbo 500 mg/m² IV QD × 3 (days −7, −5, −3) + VP-16 400 mg/m² IV QD × 3 (days −7, −5, −3)

[a] Ara-C = Cytarabine; BCNU = Carmustine; BMT = Bone marrow transplantation; Carbo = Carboplatin; CDDP = Cisplatin; Cy = Cyclophosphamide; HD = Hodgkin's disease; NHL = NonHodgkin's lymphoma; TBI = Total body irradiation; VP-16 = Etoposide.
[b] Includes acute myelogenous leukemia, acute lymphocytic leukemia, chronic myelogenous leukemia, NonHodgkin's lymphoma, and Hodgkin's disease.

(e.g., 600 to 1200 mL of bone marrow). The bone marrow then is processed to remove fat or marrow emboli and then is immediately infused intravenously into the patient like a blood transfusion. If the donor and the recipient are ABO incompatible, red blood cells (RBCs) must be removed from the marrow inoculum before infusion into the patient to prevent acute transfusion reactions.[24] In addition, as a means of reducing or preventing the development of GVHD, T-lymphocytes may be depleted from the donor marrow before infusion into the patient.[24]

Indications for Allogeneic
Bone Marrow Transplantation

1. B.S., a 22-year-old male, has acute myelogenous leukemia (AML) in complete remission following his first induction of chemotherapy with standard doses of cytarabine and daunorubicin. HLA typing performed on family members has identified a fully HLA-matched sibling donor. B.S. returns to clinic today for a pretransplant work-up. At this time, his physical examination is noncontributory, bone marrow aspirate and biopsy reveal normal morphology and cytogenetics, and a lumbar puncture is negative for leukemic infiltrates. All laboratory values are within normal limits. A bone marrow biopsy reveals <5% blasts. B.S. has normal electrocardiogram, cardiac wall motion study, and pulmonary function tests. Is an allogeneic BMT indicated for B.S.?

B.S. has a diagnosis of AML. Acute leukemia is the most common indication for allogeneic bone marrow transplantation, accounting for 47% of all allogeneic bone marrow transplantations performed worldwide between 1988 and 1990.[25] Allogeneic BMT offers the potential for curative therapy in AML by replacing diseased marrow with healthy marrow of donor origin.[2] Treatment with conventional chemotherapy alone will cure approximately 20% of patients of their disease.[11,26] In contrast, about 50% of all patients undergoing allogeneic bone marrow transplantation in first complete remission can expect to be cured.[2,11,25,26]

Eligibility criteria for allogeneic BMT vary between institutions. A matched sibling donor no longer is a requirement for allogeneic

bone marrow transplantation because improved immunosuppressive regimens and the National Marrow Donor Program have increased the use of unrelated or related mismatched bone marrow transplantations.[27] Normal renal, hepatic, pulmonary, and cardiac function are necessary for eligibility at most centers. In addition, most centers exclude patients older than 55 years from their allogeneic BMT protocols, since they are more likely to succumb to transplant-related complications.[2,11,26]

The optimal role and timing of allogeneic bone marrow transplantation relative to other therapies remains to be defined. An advantage of allogeneic BMT relative to chemotherapy includes a decreased incidence of leukemia relapse.[2,11,26] This beneficial effect of transplantation may be due to an immunologically mediated reaction known as the graft-versus-leukemia effect, which is proposed to be exerted by cytotoxic T-lymphocytes in the donor marrow.[28] The major disadvantage of allogeneic bone marrow transplantation relative to chemotherapy is a high incidence of early mortality.[11,26] This increased early mortality is caused by regimen-related toxicities, GVHD, and infectious complications that result from profound immunosuppression (see Question 2). Nonetheless, allogeneic BMT has been advocated in early first remission for eligible young patients with AML and histocompatible donors. This recommendation is based upon results demonstrating a clear relationship between long-term, disease-free survival and extent of disease at time of transplant (e.g., 51%, 31%, and 21% for patients worldwide undergoing allogeneic BMT for AML in first complete remission, second or subsequent remission, and overt relapse, respectively).[27] However, other authors have suggested that intensified consolidation therapy (e.g., with high-dose cytarabine or autologous BMT) in first complete remission produces long-term survival comparable to that obtained with allogeneic bone marrow transplantation.[29–31] A randomized, intergroup, multicenter study is currently underway comparing the relative merits of allogeneic BMT, autologous BMT, and high-dose cytarabine as consolidation therapy for AML in early first remission. Unlike other comparative trials, remission induction, consolidation and preparative regimens, and time to bone marrow transplantation are standardized between arms. Results of this trial will determine whether early first remission is the optimum timing for allogeneic bone marrow transplantation in patients with AML.

B.S. is eligible for allogeneic BMT by virtue of his diagnosis and the availability of a histocompatible donor. In addition, he meets age and organ function eligibility requirements and is in complete remission with minimal residual disease. The decision regarding timing of bone marrow transplantation relative to other therapies must be made weighing the above risks and benefits. B.S. either can undergo allogeneic BMT now or receive consolidation chemotherapy and delay BMT until early first relapse.

Supportive Care

2. B.S. is admitted for allogeneic BMT. Upon admission to the hospital the following orders are written: Admit to a positive-pressure high efficiency particulate air (HEPA)-filtered room. Triple-lumen Hickman catheter to be placed immediately. Begin strict low bacterial diet immediately and continue until neutrophils are >500/mm^3. Begin ceftazidime 2 gm intravenously (IV) Q 8 hr when ANC <500/mm^3. Transfuse 2 U of packed RBCs for hematocrit (Hct) <25% and 6 U of platelets when <20,000/mm^3 or signs of active bleeding. What is the rationale for these supportive measures?

As a result of disease-related immunosuppression, intensive preparative regimens and/or posttransplant immunosuppressive therapy, patients undergoing allogeneic bone marrow transplantation require intensive supportive care directed toward blood product support, prevention or treatment of infection, maintenance of adequate nutrition, and careful vigilance for regimen-related toxicities.

Placement of a semipermanent double- or triple-lumen central venous catheter (e.g., Hickman, Groshong, Broviac) is mandatory in all patients. The need for prolonged administration of chemotherapy, blood products, antibiotics, parenteral nutrition, and adjunctive medications such as immunoglobulin therapies preclude the use of peripheral access sites that require frequent rotation. In addition, the use of central venous catheters allows delivery of maximum concentration of all medications into an area of high blood flow, a measure that can reduce administration time and minimize daily fluid requirements.

Following administration of the preparative regimen and preceding successful engraftment, the patient undergoes a period of pancytopenia that can last from two to six weeks. During this time, patients require multiple transfusions with red blood cells and platelets. Packed red blood cells and platelets usually are given for a hematocrit less than 25% and platelets less than 20,000/mm^3, respectively.[2] The number of transfusions required to maintain hemostasis is influenced by the conditioning regimen, the underlying disease, time to successful engraftment, and the presence of posttransplant complications such as GVHD or infection. Transfusions with multiple blood products put patients at risk for blood product-derived infection [e.g., cytomegalovirus (CMV), hepatitis]. In addition, sensitization to foreign leukocyte HLA-antigens (i.e., allo-immunization) can cause immune-mediated thrombocytopenia. Thus, blood product support in the allogeneic bone marrow transplantation patient must incorporate strategies that reduce the risk of viral infection and allo-immunization. Methods used include minimizing the number of pretransplant infusions, use of single donor (rather than pooled donor) blood products, irradiating blood products, or filtering blood products with leukopoor filters.

Infection is a leading cause of morbidity and mortality in allogeneic bone marrow transplantation patients because they are neutropenic and severely immunosuppressed as a result of their pre-

parative regimens and immunosuppressive therapy. Consequently, several measures are recommended to minimize the risk of infection. The use of strict isolation rooms equipped with laminar air flow (LAF) reduces the incidence of bacterial infection and GVHD in patients undergoing allogeneic bone marrow transplantation.[32] When LAF rooms are used, all health care personnel and family members must adhere to strict aseptic technique when coming in contact with the patient. Alternatively, patients may be treated in private reverse isolation rooms equipped with positive-pressure HEPA filters. When HEPA-filtered rooms are used, health care workers and family members must adhere only to strict hand-washing technique when coming in contact with patients.

Other measures designed to reduce the risk of infection include aggressive use of antibacterial and antifungal therapy, low-bacterial diets, oral nonabsorbable antibiotics, and proper mouth hygiene. Antibiotics with a broad gram-negative spectrum may be instituted prophylactically once the patient becomes neutropenic or empirically after the patient is neutropenic and experiences a first fever. Similarly, antifungal therapy with amphotericin or fluconazole may be instituted prophylactically or following several days of persistent fever on broad-spectrum antibiotics. Low-bacterial diets are instituted upon admission and maintained throughout the period of profound neutropenia. In addition, visitors are prohibited from bringing plants, flowers, or other sources of exogenous bacteria into the patient's room. The use of oral nonabsorbable antibiotics such as polymyxin, vancomycin, or neomycin for selective decontamination of the gut is controversial. Although these oral antibiotics are used to selectively sterilize the gut and remove endogenous flora, many BMT centers have abandoned this practice due to a high rate of patient noncompliance (especially pediatric patients) and high cost. Maintaining good oral hygiene is essential during bone marrow transplantation as the mouth can be a focus of bacterial or fungal infections. Tooth-brushing or flossing is avoided during periods of thrombocytopenia and neutropenia. The mouth should be kept clean by utilizing frequent (4 to 5 times daily) mouth rinses with salt-and-soda mixtures (1 teaspoon of salt and 1 teaspoon of baking soda in 1 quart of warm water) or chlorhexidine 0.12% (Peridex).[33] Dilute solutions of hydrogen peroxide in sodium chloride also can be used to loosen scabs and debris caused by severe bleeding and mucositis. (See Chapter 67: Infections in Immunocompromised Hosts for a complete discussion of the use of antimicrobial and antifungal therapy in the immunocompromised host.)

Lastly, preparative regimens result in severe acute nausea, vomiting, and mucositis. Thus, patients such as B.S. who are undergoing BMT should be treated with antiemetics appropriate for use with highly emetogenic chemotherapy (e.g., serotonin antagonists or high-dose metoclopramide). In addition, severe mucositis may require parenteral narcotic analgesics for pain relief and total parenteral nutrition to prevent the development of nutritional deficits. (See Chapters 7: Pain and 35: Adult Parenteral Nutrition.)

Autologous Bone Marrow Transplantation and Peripheral Blood Stem Cell (PBSC) Rescue

The defining characteristic of autologous marrow or PBSC rescue (stem cell support) is that the donor and the patient are the same individual. Consequently, pre- and posttransplant immunosuppression are unnecessary. Another difference is the need to obtain autologous marrow or PBSC before chemotherapy is administered. Thus, unlike allogeneic bone marrow which is harvested the day of infusion, autologous marrow or PBSCs are harvested and stored for future use. Stem cell support with autologous marrow or PBSCs is used to treat a variety of malignancies (see Table

94.1). In the treatment of chemotherapy-responsive solid tumors or hematologic malignancies, stem cell support circumvents the myelosuppression following high-dose chemotherapy. In addition, autologous bone marrow obtained during complete remission is an alternative to allogeneic marrow for the treatment of acute leukemias in patients who do not meet allogeneic eligibility criteria by virtue of age or donor limitations.

High-Dose Chemotherapy

Occasionally, the high-dose chemotherapy or radiation programs used with autologous stem cell support are referred to as preparative regimens. Increasingly, however, they simply are referred to as high-dose or intensified chemotherapy. The sole goal of this high-dose therapy is to eradicate residual malignancy. Since the donor and the recipient are genetically identical, there is no need to provide immunosuppression.[1] Consequently, if radiation is used in conjunction with high-dose chemotherapy and stem cell support, it is because radiation has inherent activity against the tumor being treated (e.g., malignant lymphomas).

Combination chemotherapy with multiple alkylating agents comprise the most common high-dose regimens before stem cell rescue. Alkylating agents are employed because they exhibit a steep dose-response curve for various malignancies and are characterized by dose-limiting bone marrow suppression.[10] Examples of common high-dose chemotherapy regimens used with stem cell support are depicted in Table 94.2.

Technique for Harvesting Stem Cells

Autologous bone marrow is obtained from the iliac crests using the same technique described for allogeneic BMT. Because the harvest occurs before high-dose chemotherapy, the bone marrow must be cryopreserved and stored for future use.[24] Before storage, autologous marrow may be manipulated *ex vivo* to remove occult malignant cells (referred to as "purging"). Although several chemical and physical purging methods are available, the most widely used method employs a metabolite of cyclophosphamide, 4-hydroperoxy-cyclophosphamide (4-HC) to purge autologous bone marrow in patients with AML.[24,34] At the time of stem cell rescue, the autologous bone marrow is thawed and then infused into the patient like a blood transfusion.

Peripheral blood stem cells are obtained in apheresis, an outpatient procedure similar to dialysis.[35] Daily aphereses are performed until an adequate number of hematopoietic progenitor cells have been obtained.[35]

Chemotherapy and hematopoietic growth factors often are used as priming agents to increase the yield of progenitor cells in the peripheral blood. When chemotherapy is used as a priming agent, apheresis begins when the peripheral white blood cell count (WBC) begins to recover. An example includes single-agent cyclophosphamide 4 gm/m^2, administered as an intravenous infusion.[36] Peripheral blood stem cells also may be collected at the point of hematologic recovery following combination chemotherapy used to treat the underlying malignancy.[37] When hematopoietic growth factors are used as priming agents, they are administered alone or in conjunction with chemotherapy. Hematopoietic growth factors are administered daily and apheresis begins when the WBC increases or progenitor cells are detected in the peripheral blood.[35,38,39] The patient continues to receive daily injections of hematopoietic growth factor and is apheresed simultaneously until an adequate number of progenitor cells have been harvested. Both granulocyte-macrophage colony stimulating factor (sargramostim, Leukine, Prokine) and granulocyte-colony stimulating factor (filgrastim, Neupogen) are used as priming agents for PBSC collec-

tion.[35,37] A typical dose of sargramostim is 250 to 500 µg/m^2/day administered subcutaneously (SQ) or intraveneously.[35,37] Doses of filgrastim range from 5 to 15 µg/kg/day.[35,37] Following aphereses, PBSCs are cryopreserved, stored, thawed, and infused into the patient as described for autologous bone marrow.[35]

3. Indications for High-Dose Chemotherapy and Stem Cell Support. P.J., a 46-year-old male, has standard risk, high-grade nonHodgkin's lymphoma (NHL) in first relapse after a complete remission of 1 year's duration. A 50% reduction in measurable disease is noted after 1 cycle of dexamethasone, high-dose cytarabine, *cis*-platinum (DHAP) salvage chemotherapy. P.J.'s bone marrow biopsy and lumbar puncture are negative. Autologous bone marrow is harvested, cryopreserved, and stored. P.J. is scheduled for admission to the University Hospital in 4 weeks following recovery of his peripheral blood counts. Is autologous BMT indicated in P.J.?

Relapsed intermediate and high-grade NHLs are common indications for high-dose chemotherapy and stem cell rescue with autologous marrow or peripheral blood stem cells.[40] Non-Hodgkin's lymphoma is considered a chemotherapy-sensitive malignancy where the principles of dose intensity can be applied. In the treatment of NHL, allogeneic, autologous, and PBSCs all have been used as stem cell rescue.[41,42] Although NHL is classified as a hematologic malignancy and can metastasize to bone marrow, it is not a disease of the bone marrow *per se*. Consequently, allogeneic bone marrow is not necessary for curative therapy. Indeed, there appears to be no difference in long-term disease-free survival following either allogeneic or autologous bone marrow transplantation in the treatment of NHL.[41,43] Autologous bone marrow transplantation and PBSC support are preferable because they circumvent the need for histocompatible donors, are associated with lower procedure-related mortality, and are not restricted by age to patients under 55 years.

The primary eligibility criteria for autologous marrow or PBSC support is demonstrated chemotherapy-sensitive disease since patients who do not respond to chemotherapy are unlikely to respond to autologous BMT.[19,42] For example, in a study of 100 patients undergoing autologous bone marrow transplantation for intermediate- or high-grade NHL, three-year disease-free survivals of 36%, 14%, and 0% were reported for patients with chemotherapy-sensitive relapse, resistant disease, or no complete remission, respectively.[42]

The most appropriate patient population and timing for autologous bone marrow transplantation in the treatment of NHL is being defined. A significant percentage of patients with standard-risk nonHodgkin's lymphoma are cured with conventional chemotherapy alone. Thus, advocating high-dose therapy and stem cell rescue as consolidation therapy for all patients in first complete remission would needlessly expose some patients that are already cured to the toxic effects of high-dose therapy. Consequently, initial trials have focused on patients with relapsed or refractory NHL.[40–42] Uses under investigation include consolidation therapy in first remission for patients at high risk of relapse, initial therapy for aggressive NHL, and low-grade lymphomas.[40,44]

Peripheral blood stem cells can be used as a substitute for autologous bone marrow as a source of stem cell rescue.[35,38,45] PBSCs were advocated first as a means of obtaining hematopoietic stem cells in patients when autologous marrow was difficult to harvest (e.g., patients with bone marrow involvement or who had received prior pelvic irradiation). However, PBSCs have become the preferred source of hematopoietic rescue in an increasing number of centers because of rapid hematopoietic engraftment.[35,37] Autologous bone marrow was obtained in P.J. because he does not have bone marrow involvement. If his bone marrow biopsy had been positive, PBSCs would have been obtained instead.

P.J. has minimal residual disease and has demonstrated chemotherapy-sensitive disease. Without further therapy, his long-term prognosis is poor. Thus, autologous BMT is indicated.

Supportive Care

4. Hematopoietic Growth Factors. P.J. receives high-dose chemotherapy with cyclophosphamide, carmustine, and etoposide (CBV). An order is written to begin sargramostim 250 mg/m² IV over 2 hours beginning day 0 and continuing until day +21. What is the rationale for sargramostim in P.J.?

Following high-dose therapy and autologous bone marrow transplantation, peripheral blood counts drop rapidly, resulting in a period of profound aplasia of approximately 20 to 30 days' duration (see Figure 94.2). During this period of aplasia, patients are at high risk for complications such as bleeding and infection. Sargramostim is a multilineage hematopoietic growth factor used as an adjunct to autologous BMT to accelerate hematopoietic engraftment. Sargramostim exerts its effects by stimulating the proliferation of committed progenitor cells; hence, once engraftment occurs, hematopoietic recovery is accelerated under the influence of sargramostim. The benefits of sargramostim noted in small uncontrolled trials[46,47] have been confirmed in a large multicenter, randomized, double-blinded, placebo-controlled trial.[48] Neumunaitis et al. randomized 128 patients undergoing autologous BMT for the treatment of lymphoid malignancies to receive sargramostim 250 µg/m² or placebo (both administered IV over 2 hours) daily for 21 days beginning the day of marrow infusion (day 0).[48] Time to engraftment, defined as time to an ANC greater than 500 cells/mm³ for two consecutive days, was significantly shorter in sargramostim-treated patients when compared to patients receiving placebo (19 versus 26 days). In addition, accelerated engraftment in sargramostim-treated patients resulted in fewer days of antibiotics (24 versus 27 days), fewer documented bacterial infections (17% versus 30%), and a shorter initial hospital stay (27 versus 33 days).

Sargramostim and filgrastim are approved by the Food and Drug Administration (FDA) for accelerating engraftment; however, filgrastim often is used preferentially for this indication in clinical practice.[20,37,49,50] The most common reason cited for using filgrastim is the desire to avoid febrile reactions associated with sargramostim which complicate interpretation of febrile neutropenia. This fear probably is unfounded, however, as no statistically significant difference in toxicity (including fever) was noted between sargramostim and placebo in the randomized trial cited above.[48] Both sargramostim and filgrastim can be administered intravenously or subcutaneously.

Several factors need to be considered when discussing the role of hematopoietic growth factors in accelerating engraftment following bone marrow transplantation. First, although both filgrastim and sargramostim successfully hasten neutrophil recovery, neither agent stimulates platelet production or augments platelet recovery.[46-50] This is an important consideration since thrombocytopenia often is a cause of prolonged hospitalization in the BMT patient even when neutrophils have recovered. Successful engraftment of all hematopoietic cell lines likely will require combinations of growth factors that work in concert to augment hematopoiesis. Second, the role of hematopoietic growth factors in accelerating engraftment following allogeneic bone marrow transplantation is controversial. Fear of exacerbating graft-versus-host disease by stimulating macrophage production [and, hence, tumor necrosis factor (TNF), a cytokine implicated in the pathogenesis of GVHD] particularly has limited the use of sargramostim. Enhanced GVHD has been reported with sargramostim following allogeneic bone marrow transplantation in a small number of patients.[51] In contrast, other trials,[52,53] including a randomized, placebo-controlled trial,[54] have failed to substantiate this concern. Because filgrastim exerts its effects on granulocytes and does not stimulate monocytes or macrophages, it is the preferred agent in allogeneic bone marrow transplantation. However, only a few patients have been treated with filgrastim for this indication.[55] Third, despite concern regarding the theoretical potential for sargramostim or filgrastim to stimulate proliferation of leukemia myeloblasts, there is no evidence to date that suggests that the incidence of leukemia relapse is higher in patients who receive these hematopoietic growth factors following autologous or allogeneic BMT.[52-54] This may be due to the fact that patients with leukemia usually are in remission at the time of transplant. Thus, the population of residual leukemia cells probably is minimal.

In summary, P.J. is undergoing autologous bone marrow transplantation for the treatment of a lymphoid malignancy. Thus, either sargramostim or filgrastim is an acceptable option for accelerating engraftment. A complete blood count (CBC) with differential should be obtained daily. Sargramostim should be continued until day +21 or evidence of engraftment has occurred.

5. Comparison to Allogeneic Bone Marrow Transplantation. How do supportive care strategies used for high-dose chemotherapy with autologous BMT or PBSCs (stem cell rescue) differ from those described for high-dose chemotherapy followed by allogenic BMT described in Question 2?

Similar supportive care strategies used for both stem cell rescue and allogeneic bone marrow transplantation include use of indwelling central venous catheters, blood product support, and pharmacologic management of nausea, vomiting, mucositis, and pain. These similarities are a function of the toxic effects from high-dose chemotherapy which is a component of both procedures.

Disparity in the degree of immunosuppression accounts for the differences in supportive care strategies used for stem cell rescue and allogeneic bone marrow transplantation. Because the combination of high-dose chemotherapy and stem cell rescue is not complicated by profound immunosuppression and graft-versus-host disease, supportive care for patients undergoing stem cell rescue does not differ significantly from patients undergoing chemotherapy without stem cell support. Isolation and use of LAF rooms are unnecessary, although most centers continue to provide care for patients undergoing autologous bone marrow transplantation in HEPA-filtered rooms. In addition, gut decontamination with oral nonabsorbable antibiotics is unnecessary.

Bacterial infections remain a common complication in patients undergoing autologous BMT or PBSC support. With the use of hematopoietic growth factors, the duration of neutropenia and infectious risk appears to decrease.[37,48] Indeed, novel combinations of oral prophylactic antibiotics and once-daily dosing of IV antibiotics are being used at one center to facilitate the outpatient treatment of patients undergoing stem cell rescue.[56] It is likely that new combinations of hematopoietic growth factors or *ex vivo* expansion of stem cells will further reduce the duration of neutropenia. Advances such as these could move autologous bone marrow transplantation or PBSC support exclusively to the outpatient setting.[56,57]

Complications Associated with Bone Marrow Transplantation

When used in conventional doses, myelosuppression is the dose-limiting toxicity for antineoplastics employed in bone marrow transplantation. Because myelosuppression is circumvented with hematopoietic rescue, nonhematologic (i.e., extramedullary) toxicities have emerged as the dose-limiting factors. Table 94.3 lists the dose-limiting extramedullary toxicities for single-agent therapies commonly employed in bone marrow transplantation.

Table 94.3	Single-Agent Dose Escalation[58,59]		
Agent	Usual Dose (mg/m^2)	Max Dose with Stem Cell Rescue (mg/m^2)	Extra-Medullary Toxicity
Total body irradiation	—	1300–1500 rads[a]	Hepatic, pulmonary
Cyclophosphamide	500–1000	7500 (200 mg/kg)	Cardiac, bladder
Busulfan	2–8 mg/day	16 mg/kg	Hepatic (VOD)
Carmustine	200	1200	Pulmonary, hepatic
Melphalan	40	200	Mucositis[b]
Thiotepa	50	1135	Mucositis,[b] CNS
Etoposide	200	2400 (60 mg/kg)	Mucositis[b]
Carboplatin	400	2000	Renal, hepatic
Cisplatin	100	200	Renal

[a] Administered in fractionated doses.
[b] Mucositis requiring airway protection, parenteral nutrition, and IV narcotic analgesics.

All patients undergoing bone marrow transplantation experience toxicities commonly associated with chemotherapy (i.e., alopecia, mucositis, nausea and vomiting, sterility). (Also see related information in Chapter 91: Adverse Effects of Chemotherapy.) However, in the BMT population, these toxicities are magnified. For example, mucositis often is severe enough to warrant airway protection, preclude oral intake, and require intravenous narcotics for pain control. Table 94.4 depicts a range of toxicities that can occur following bone marrow transplantation, and Figure 94.4 depicts the time course for complications following BMT. Specific toxicities are discussed in detail below.

Regimen-Related Toxicities

Dose Calculations in Obesity

6. K.M. is a 36-year-old female with AML. Following her initial diagnosis, an unsuccessful search for an allogeneic donor was conducted. Autologous marrow was harvested during her first complete remission and purged *ex vivo* with 4-hydroperoxy-cyclophosphamide (perfosfamide). K.M. now is in her second complete remission and is being admitted for autologous BMT. Orders for K.M.'s preparative regimen are written as follows: Actual body weight (ABW) = 85 kg; ideal body weight (IBW) = 62 kg; body surface area (BSA) = 1.7 m^2. Busulfan 16 mg/kg total dose to be administered over 4 days (1 mg/kg/dose PO Q 6 hr for 16 doses, days −9, −8, −7, and −6). If K.M. vomits within 1 hour of a dose, repeat a dose of 0.5 mg/kg PO. Cyclophosphamide 50 mg/kg IV days −5, −4, −3, and −2. Day −1 is a "rest" day followed by infusion of bone marrow on day 0. Hydration: 3000 mL/m^2/day with D$_5$W/0.9% NaCl at 250 mL/hr beginning 24 hours before cyclophosphamide and continuing for 24 hours postcyclophosphamide, then change to D$_5$W/0.45% NaCl + 20 mEq KCl/L to run at 150 mL/hr. Mesna to be given concurrently with cyclophosphamide as 30% of the cyclophosphamide dose administered IV at hours 0, 3, 6, and 9 after cyclophosphamide (total mesna dose = 120% of cyclophosphamide dose). Beginning on day −5 weigh patient BID, check inputs and outputs BID, and urine specific gravity and urine heme testing Q 1 hr. If urine output drops below 300 mL/2 hr, administer an IV bolus of 250 mL normal saline (NS) and give Lasix 10 mg/m^2, not to exceed 20 mg IV. On the day of admission (day −10) administer a phenytoin loading dose (15 mg/kg, not to exceed 1 gm) orally in divided doses (300, 300, and 400 mg Q 2 hr). Continue 300 mg PO QD from days −9 to −6. Which weight should be used to calculate doses of K.M.'s preparative regimen?

K.M.'s ideal body weight is 62 kg and her actual body weight is 85 kg. Thus, she is 37% over her IBW. There are few dosing guidelines for chemotherapy drugs in clinically obese patients (defined as a ABW 20% greater than IBW)[60–62] and even fewer guidelines for patients undergoing bone marrow transplantation.[63] Because the doses of chemotherapy used in BMT preparative regimens approach the lethal limit for nonhematologic toxicities,[10] the weight used is critical. Unfortunately, the weight that is most accurate for clinically obese patients is difficult to determine. Using a weight that is too high can cause lethal toxicity, while using one that is too low could result in inadequate marrow ablation or disease eradication. To date, only one report addresses body weight and conditioning regimens for bone marrow transplantation.[63] In this report, data from 16 patients of varying body weights receiving busulfan and cyclophosphamide were assessed for toxicity. Veno-occlusive disease (VOD) of the liver, a common toxicity of busulfan-containing regimens, occurred in four patients, all of whom had a ratio of actual body weight:ideal body weight of 1.22. None of the patients with an ABW:IBW ratio of approximately 1.0 developed VOD. These authors concluded that busulfan-cyclophosphamide containing regimens should be based upon ideal body weight estimates for obese patients (>20% above IBW) and upon actual body weight for patients whose weight is equal to or less than ideal body weight.[63]

At least two other methods have been described for dosing chemotherapy in preparative regimens. For patients whose weight exceeds 20% of the ideal body weight, Peters et al. recommend dosing cyclophosphamide, cisplatin, and carmustine on the basis of an average body surface area calculated from actual and ideal body weights.[20] The national intergroup study evaluating the role of allogeneic, autologous, and high-dose cytarabine as consolidation therapy in first complete remission for AML recommends using an adjusted body weight for calculating busulfan and cyclophosphamide in clinically obese patients. The adjusted weight is ideal body weight plus 25% of the obese weight (i.e., adjusted weight = IBW + 0.25(ABW − IBW).

K.M.'s busulfan dose should not be based upon her actual body weight, as this may predispose her to veno-occlusive disease of the liver. Her chemotherapy doses should be based upon her ideal body weight or an adjusted ideal body weight as described above.

Table 94.4	Common Toxicities Associated with BMT[a]
Early	Late
Nausea, vomiting, diarrhea	Cardiotoxicity
Mucositis	Cataracts
Infectious complications	Sterility
Hemorrhagic cystitis	Delayed puberty
Renal dysfunction	Growth retardation
VOD	Second malignancies
Acute GVHD	Chronic GVHD
Cardiotoxicity	
Idiopathic pneumonitis	
Viral pneumonitis	
Graft failure, graft rejection	

[a] BMT = Bone marrow transplantation; GVHD = Graft-versus-host disease; VOD = Veno-occlusive disease.

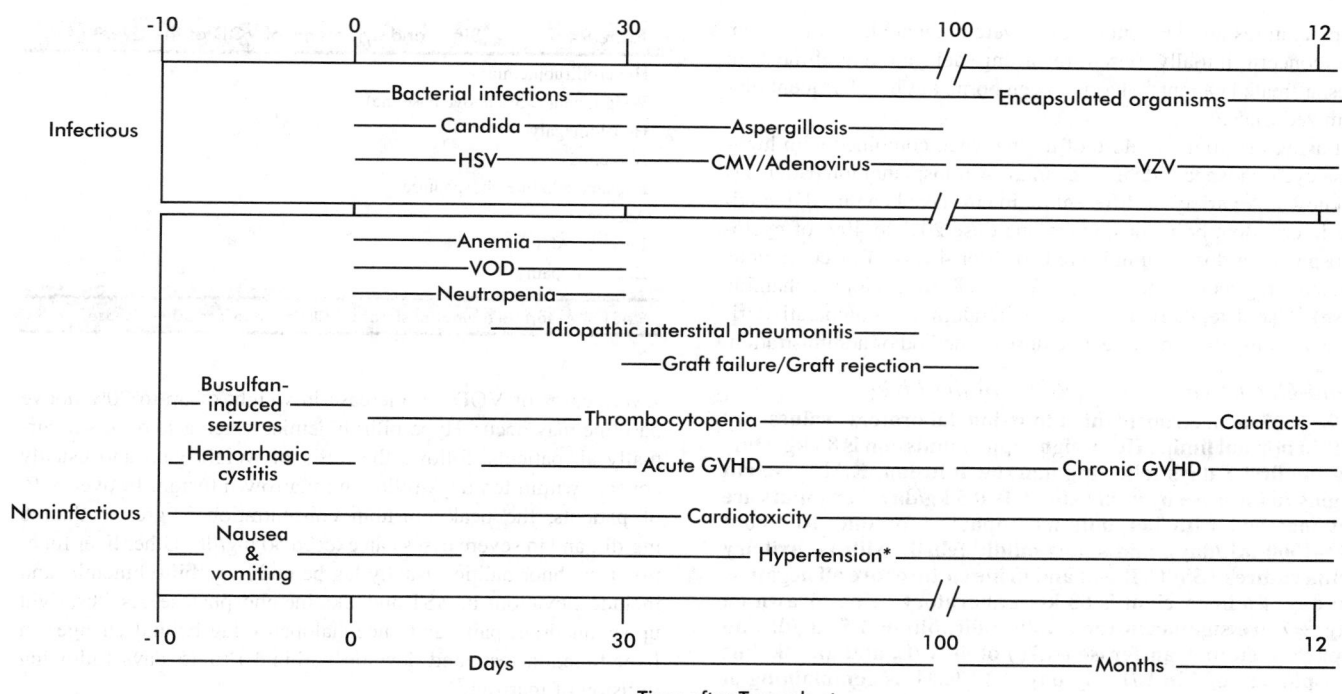

Fig 94.4 Complications Following Bone Marrow Transplantation by Time   *Patients undergoing allogeneic bone marrow transplantation only. HSV = Herpes simplex virus; CMV = Cytomegalovirus; VZV = Varicella zoster virus; VOD = Veno-occlusive disease; GVHD = Graft-versus-host disease.

Busulfan-Induced Neurotoxicity

7. On day −5, 14 hours after the last dose of busulfan, the nurse noticed that K.M.'s hands and legs jerked rapidly. This was followed by a loss of consciousness, urinary incontinence, and a generalized tonic seizure of approximately 30-second duration. Since then, no other convulsions have occurred. All laboratory values were within normal limits and a computed tomography (CT) scan of the brain is normal. Since this episode, K.M. has had no neurologic deficits. What was the cause of K.M.'s seizure?

Seizures have been reported in patients receiving busulfan for bone marrow transplantation preparative regimens.[64–67] Busulfan is highly lipophilic and is known to cross the blood brain barrier with a CSF:plasma ratio of approximately 1.0.[68] Although the exact incidence of busulfan-induced neurotoxicity is unknown, 7.5% of 123 children experienced seizures from busulfan in one series.[64] Busulfan-induced neurotoxicity usually is characterized by a single seizure episode that occurs after at least 6 or 7 of the 16 total doses have been administered. Seizures have occurred in both children and adults, can occur despite the use of prophylactic anticonvulsants, and usually do not result in permanent neurologic deficits. Recent evidence suggests that the neurotoxicity may be dose related, as the incidence of seizures is significantly higher in children whose mean CSF:plasma ratio is 1.4 compared to 0.92.[64]

To assure adequate antiseizure prophylaxis, it would have been prudent to administer K.M.'s phenytoin as an intravenous infusion before oral busulfan was initiated. In addition, daily IV doses could have been administered during the four days of busulfan therapy and for 48 hours after the last dose.

Hemorrhagic Cystitis

8. What is the most effective method to prevent hemorrhagic cystitis in the BMT patient? What dose and schedule of mesna is most appropriate?

Cyclophosphamide-induced hemorrhagic cystitis reportedly occurs in 12% to 73% of bone marrow transplantation patients.[69–72]

Consequently, all transplant centers incorporate some method of prophylaxis against hemorrhagic cystitis into their protocols. The methods employed include forced hydration with NS or D_5NS 3000 mL/m^2/day, continuous bladder irrigation with NS 200 to 1000 mL/hour via a three-way Foley catheter, and/or concomitant use of the uroprotectant, mesna. There is no consensus with regard to the most effective method of prophylaxis. In a survey of BMT units, 55% incorporated mesna, with or without forced hydration or bladder irrigation.[73] The relative merits of mesna versus forced hydration with or without the addition of continuous bladder irrigation for prevention of cyclophosphamide-induced hemorrhagic cystitis in bone marrow transplantation patients have been evaluated in three randomized trials.[69,70,72] The definition of microscopic, macroscopic, and severe hematuria varies between these studies, which complicates interpretation of the results. Nonetheless, results are equivocal. All three studies report decreased hematuria (of any grade or severity) in mesna-treated patients when compared to patients receiving forced hydration or bladder irrigation.[69,70,72] However, this difference was statistically significant in only two of these studies.[69,70] In contrast, when only those patients developing severe hematuria are compared, there is no significant difference between mesna-treated patients and those who did not receive mesna.[70,72] Importantly, hematuria or hemorrhagic cystitis can occur despite the use of any of these methods.[69–72] Thus, the decision to use one method over another will depend upon the relative merits of the various methods, and the preference of the BMT center personnel. Disadvantages of Foley catheter irrigation include intensive nursing time, patient dissatisfaction, and a higher incidence of microbiologically detected urinary tract infections.[70] Furthermore, Foley trauma itself can cause hematuria, which can confuse the diagnosis of cyclophosphamide-induced hemorrhagic cystitis. Potential disadvantages of mesna include delayed engraftment and cost.[69] However, in a cost analysis comparing Foley bladder irrigation with mesna, there was very little difference between the two methods when total costs, including urine cultures and laboratory tests, were compared.[70] In addition, the concern initially posed regarding delayed engraftment in mesna-treated patients[69] has not been borne out in subsequent randomized trials.[70,72]

Lastly, the optimum dose of mesna when combined with high-dose cyclophosphamide in bone marrow transplantation patients is unknown. A variety of different regimens have been used, including intermittent bolus dosing (mesna dose 20% to 40% of cyclophosphamide dose, administered for 3 or 4 doses) or continuous infusion regimens (mesna 80% to 160% of cyclophosphamide dose).[73] To date, there have been no randomized, comparative trials evaluating the most effective dose or method of administration.

Veno-Occlusive Disease (VOD) of the Liver

9. K.M.'s pretransplant admission laboratory values are within normal limits. Her weight upon admission is 85 kg. During the first 5 days following marrow infusion, K.M.'s weight begins to increase by approximately 0.5 kg/day, her inputs are not matched with her outputs (inputs > outputs by about 500–1000 mL/day), and she is mildly febrile with an axillary temperature of 38 °C. Blood and urine cultures are all negative. On day +6 her weight is 88 kg. Laboratory values drawn on day +7 are significant for a total bilirubin of 1.5 mg/dL, an aspartate aminotransferase (AST) of 40 U/L, and an alkaline phosphatase of 120 U/L. By day +10 K.M. is complaining of midepigastric and right upper quadrant (RUQ) pain and a liver that is tender to palpation. Over the next few days K.M. begins to look icteric. Her liver function tests (LFTs) continue to rise slowly, until day +18 when they reach the following peak values: total bilirubin 5.0 mg/dL, AST 150 U/L, alkaline phosphatase 180 U/L. On day +18 K.M.'s weight is 95 kg. "Rule out VOD of the liver" is listed on her problem list in the medical record. What is VOD? [SI units: total bilirubin 25.65 and 85.5 μmol/L, respectively; AST 0.67 and 2.5 μkat/L, respectively; alkaline phosphatase 2.0 and 3.0 μkat/L, respectively]

Veno-occlusive disease of the liver is a life-threatening complication that may occur secondary to high-dose chemotherapy or radiation used in bone marrow transplantation. VOD is defined histologically as a fibrous narrowing or obliteration of the small hepatic venules,[74] and clinically as a constellation of signs and symptoms associated with hepatic failure.[75] Although the pathogenesis is not understood completely, several mechanisms have been proposed. Chemotherapy and radiation are thought to directly damage the endothelium of the hepatic venules, activating the coagulation cascade and occluding small vessels. In addition, elevated levels of cytokines such as tumor necrosis factor-alpha (TNF-alpha) and interleukin-1 have been implicated in contributing to the development of this syndrome. In one study of patients undergoing allogeneic bone marrow transplantation, increased levels of TNF-alpha preceded major transplant-related complications (including VOD) in the first 100 days following bone marrow transplantation.[76] TNF-alpha, which is proposed to be released from residual host tissue macrophages damaged by the pretransplant conditioning regimen, elicit a variety of effects on endothelial cells that may exacerbate tissue injury.[76]

10. Signs and Symptoms. What signs and symptoms in K.M. are consistent with a diagnosis of VOD?

The signs and symptoms associated with VOD are depicted in Table 94.5. Insidious weight gain exceeding 5% of baseline usually is the first manifestation of impending VOD, occurring in over 90% of patients within three to six days following marrow infusion.[75] Weight gain is caused by sodium and water retention, as evidenced by decreased renal sodium excretion, and usually is distinguished from cyclophosphamide-induced syndrome of inappropriate secretion of antidiuretic hormone (SIADH) by the time course relative to administration of the preparative regimen. In

Table 94.5	Signs and Symptoms of VOD of the Liver[a,77]
Hyperbilirubinemia	
Weight gain (>5% above baseline)	
Hepatomegaly	
Azotemia	
Elevated alkaline phosphatase	
Ascites	
Elevated AST	
Encephalopathy	

[a] AST = Aspartate aminotransferase; VOD = Veno-occlusive disease.

severe cases of VOD, an increase in weight of up to 20% above baseline may occur. Hyperbilirubinemia, which also occurs in virtually all patients, follows the onset of weight gain and usually appears within ten days following marrow infusion. In over 50% of patients, the peak bilirubin concentration is greater than 6 mg/dL, and in severe cases can exceed 50 mg/dL. Other liver function test abnormalities usually lag behind hyperbilirubinemia, and include elevations in AST and alkaline phosphatase. Ascites, right upper quadrant pain, and encephalopathy lag behind changes in liver function tests and develop within 10 to 15 days following infusion of marrow.[75]

A clinical diagnosis of VOD is made when two of the following features occur within the first 30 days following bone marrow transplantation: 1) hyperbilirubinemia and jaundice; 2) hepatomegaly and RUQ pain; or 3) ascites and/or unexplained weight gain of more than 5% from baseline.[75,77–79] In order to make a clinical diagnosis of VOD, the features listed above must occur in the absence of other causes of posttransplant liver failure, including graft-versus-host disease, viral hepatitis, fungal abscesses, or drug reactions. A clinical diagnosis can be confirmed histologically via liver biopsy. Histologic changes consistent with VOD include concentric subintimal thickening or luminal narrowing of the terminal hepatic venules or sublobular veins caused by either edematous reticulum fibers or collagen.[74,80] Using these criteria, the prevalence of VOD is reported to range from 4% to 54%.[77–80]

In summary, the signs and symptoms consistent with VOD in K.M. include insidious weight gain, fever, hyperbilirubinemia, elevated transaminases, and RUQ pain. The onset and timing of these signs and symptoms are consistent with a diagnosis of VOD and occurred in the absence of other causes for hepatic toxicity.

11. Mortality and Treatment. What is the likelihood that K.M. will recover from her VOD? How should K.M. be treated?

The overall mortality for all patients who develop VOD is approximately 50% and is correlated with the onset and severity of disease.[75,77,79] For example, patients with early weight gain, severely elevated bilirubin, AST, or presence of encephalopathy are more likely to die of VOD when compared to patients with mild elevations of liver function tests and no encephalopathy.[77] Mortality for patients with severe VOD exceeds 90% and usually is accompanied by multiorgan system failure.[79]

The mainstay of treatment for established VOD is supportive care aimed at increasing intravascular volume, decreasing extracellular fluid accumulation, and minimizing factors that contribute to or exacerbate encephalopathy. Thus, volume expanders such as albumin and colloids can be used to maintain intravascular volume, spironolactone can be used to minimize extravascular fluid accumulation, and protein restriction and lactulose can be used if encephalopathy develops. In addition, avoidance of CNS-active drugs, if possible, helps to provide an accurate assessment and interpretation of the patient's mental status.

Because mortality following development of severe VOD is high and treatment options are limited, investigational alternatives are being sought. Bearman et al. reported a pilot study using recombinant human tissue plasminogen activator (rh-TPA) for the treatment of established severe VOD.[81] Patients with a serum bilirubin greater than 15 mg/dL by day +20, weight gain greater than 5% from baseline, or presence of encephalopathy were treated with 10 mg of rh-TPA daily for two to four days via IV infusion over four to six hours. In addition, patients were started simultaneously on heparin 150 U/kg/day via IV continuous infusion. A total of seven out of ten patients responded, with decreases in bilirubin, diuresis, and weight loss. Five out of ten patients (50%) survived. Four patients had bleeding episodes, none of which were classified as life-threatening and were manageable by adjusting or discontinuing the heparin infusion. Thus, this initial study provides some evidence that rh-TPA may be of benefit in the treatment of severe VOD. Given the inherent risks of bleeding and expense of this therapy, investigators currently are evaluating models that could help predict which patients might benefit.[82]

Other therapies directed at either modulating the coagulation cascade or concentration of inflammatory mediators have been employed in an attempt to prevent the development of VOD. Continuous-infusion heparin has been used unsuccessfully to prevent VOD in a limited number of patients.[83] In addition to its lack of efficacy, this modality was complicated by a high incidence of bleeding. Prostaglandin-E_1 (PGE_1) 500 μg/day administered as a continuous intravenous infusion from days −8 to +30 has been used successfully to reduce the incidence of VOD in one study.[84] Adverse effect data (e.g., nausea, flushing, hypotension) were not reported. Pentoxifylline, a synthetic xanthine derivative, has been explored for prophylaxis of VOD. It is thought to inhibit production of TNF-alpha from monocyte-macrophages, thereby ameliorating regimen-related toxicities, including VOD. Although preliminary evidence suggested beneficial effects of pentoxifylline,[85] a prospective randomized, placebo-controlled trial has failed to document these findings.[86] In the trial by Clift et al., 88 patients matched for age, disease, and preparative regimen undergoing allogeneic bone marrow transplantation were randomized to receive 600 mg of pentoxifylline orally four times daily or placebo beginning at the time of conditioning and continuing for 70 days post-transplant.[86] Pentoxifylline did not significantly decrease the incidence of VOD or other transplant-related toxicities when compared to placebo. In addition, patients in the pentoxifylline arm experienced significantly more nausea and emesis when compared to patients receiving placebo. Lastly, pentoxifylline is commercially available only as tablets. Thus, it frequently must be crushed for administration to patients with severe mucositis, which limits the practical utility of this agent in the bone marrow transplantation patient population.

K.M. does not meet the criteria for severe VOD. Therefore, rh-TPA is not indicated. She should be managed conservatively with fluid restriction and spironolactone. Her signs and symptoms should resolve over the next two weeks. Because she has mild VOD, she has a 50% chance of recovering completely without sequelae.

Graft Failure

12. It now is day +40 and K.M.'s CBC reveals the following: WBC <0.1 cells/mm³; no granulocytes or monocytes are detected on differential; platelets 18,000/mm³, and Hct 22%. A bone marrow biopsy reveals a hypocellular bone marrow with no evidence of leukemic infiltrates. What is K.M. experiencing and how should she be treated?

Engraftment usually is evident by day +25 in patients undergoing autologous bone marrow transplantation without hematopoietic growth factor support. Because K.M. has no evidence of engraftment at day +40, she most likely is experiencing primary graft failure.

Graft failure is defined as the lack of functional hematopoiesis following bone marrow transplantation[28,87] and is classified as primary graft failure (failure to engraft) or graft rejection. Primary graft failure is more likely to occur following autologous BMT. Prior treatment with intensive chemotherapy is likely to reduce the inoculum or viability of hematopoietic progenitor cells. In addition, residual malignancy in patients with leukemias or lymphomas, or use of *ex vivo* purging methods that indiscriminately remove stem cells is likely to contribute to graft failure.[87] In allogeneic bone marrow transplantation, primary graft failure is uncommon because the donor marrow is unmanipulated and is free from the toxic effects of prior chemotherapy.[28,87] Instead, graft rejection caused by residual host-versus-graft effects is more likely to occur. The incidence of graft rejection is higher in patients with aplastic anemia, or patients undergoing BMT with histoincompatible marrow or T-cell-depleted marrow.[28,88] Graft rejection is uncommon in patients undergoing allogeneic bone marrow transplantation with histocompatible donors for the treatment of leukemia. The pathogenesis of graft rejection is complex and most likely involves a delicate balance between host and donor effector cells.[87]

Therapeutic options for the treatment of graft rejection or graft failure are limited. A second bone marrow transplantation is the most definitive therapy although the toxicities are formidable.[89] Graft rejection is best managed with immunosuppressants such as antithymocyte globulin. Primary graft failure occasionally can be treated successfully using hematopoietic growth factors.[90,91] Patients least likely to respond to hematopoietic growth factors are those who have received purged autografts.[90,92] The reason for this is unknown, but it is likely due to an insufficient inoculum of hematopoietic progenitor cells.

K.M. has primary graft failure. Although she has no evidence of residual leukemia, she has a history of extensive prior chemotherapy and has received a purged autograft. Because she has evidence of other organ dysfunction (i.e., VOD), a second bone marrow transplantation would incur excessive toxicity. Thus, a trial of sargramostim is indicated. K.M. should receive sargramostim 250 μg/m²/day IV; the intravenous route is indicated because of her severe thrombocytopenia. K.M.'s hematopoietic function should be monitored with daily CBCs and a bone marrow biopsy every two weeks. If there is no evidence of engraftment after two weeks of therapy, her dose can be doubled to 500 μg/m²/day. Two to three weeks of therapy often is necessary before engraftment is noted.

Note: K.M. underwent therapy with sargramostim, but failed to respond to either dose. She expired on day +70 from an overwhelming fungal sepsis.

Graft-versus-Host-Disease (GVHD)

Graft-versus-host disease is one of the most serious complications following transplantation of allogeneic bone marrow. The pathophysiology of GVHD is extremely complex and involves a myriad of immune system effector cells (e.g., monocytes, macrophages, a variety of T-cell subsets) and amplified secretion of several soluble mediators (e.g., interleukin-1, interleukin-2, TNF-alpha). For a detailed review of the pathogenesis of GVHD the reader is referred elsewhere.[6] Simplistically, GVHD is caused by immunocompetent T-cells in the donor bone marrow that recognize host histocompatibility antigens as foreign, ultimately triggering a series of events that culminate in a rejection response. Although the incidence of GVHD varies widely from center to center, the International Bone Marrow Transplant Registry (IBMTR) reported an overall prevalence of GVHD of 45% when data from over 2000 allogeneic bone marrow transplantations worldwide were analyzed.[93,94] Mortality following the onset of GVHD is high and correlates with the severity of the disease. Data from the IBMTR indicate an overall mortality of 48% for patients who developed moderate to severe GVHD (grade II to IV).[93,94] However, mortality increases to over 90% for patients with severe (grade IV) GVHD.[6] Thus, graft-versus-host disease is a serious complication associated with a high mortality.

Graft-versus-host disease is classified as acute or chronic based upon clinical manifestations and an arbitrarily designated time relative to day 0 of bone marrow transplantation. Acute GVHD is a clinical syndrome affecting primarily the skin, liver, and gastrointestinal (GI) tract and usually occurs in the first 100 days following bone marrow transplantation. In contrast, chronic GVHD can affect almost any organ system, closely resembles several autoimmune diseases, and usually occurs after day 100 following bone marrow transplantation. Immune-mediated destruction of tissues, a hallmark of GVHD, disrupts the integrity of protective mucosal barriers and thus provides an environment that favors the establishment of opportunistic infections. The combination of GVHD and infectious complications is a leading cause of mortality for BMT patients.

Acute GVHD

13. Clinical Presentation. M.P., a 22-year-old, 70 kg male, undergoes a 1 antigen mismatched allogeneic BMT from his sister for the diagnosis of chronic myelogenous leukemia (CML) in chronic phase. Following a preparative regimen of cyclophosphamide and TBI, the following immunosuppressive regimen is ordered: Cyclosporine 1.5 mg/kg IV Q 12 hr from days −1 to +7, then switch to CSA 6.25 mg/kg PO Q 12 hr until day +50. Methotrexate 15 mg/m² IV on day +1, then 10 mg/m² day +3, +6, and +11. On day +14, the time at which engraftment occurred, M.P. is noted to have a diffuse macular papular rash on his arms, hands, and trunk. He does not have diarrhea and his LFTs are within normal limits. At the onset of his rash, M.P.'s empiric antibiotics are changed from vancomycin, piperacillin, and gentamicin to ceftazidime, gentamicin, and vancomycin. Despite the change in antibiotics, M.P.'s rash persists. How is M.P.'s presentation consistent with acute GVHD?

Table 94.6	Proposed Clinical Stage of GVHD According to Organ System[a,b]		
Stage	Skin	Liver	GI Tract
+	Maculopapular rash 25% of BSA	Bilirubin 2–3 mg/dL	>500 mL/day diarrhea
++	Maculopapular rash 25%–50% of BSA	Bilirubin 3–6 mg/dL	>1000 mL/day diarrhea
+++	Generalized erythroderma	Bilirubin 6–15 mg/dL	>1500 mL/day diarrhea
++++	Generalized erythroderma with bullous formation and desquamation	Bilirubin >15 mg/dL	Severe abdominal pain with or without ileus

[a] BSA = Body surface area; GI = Gastrointestinal; GVHD = Graft-versus-host disease.
[b] Reproduced with permission from reference 28.

Table 94.7	Overall Clinical Grading of Severity of GVHD[a,b]
Grade	Degree of Organ Involvement
I	+ to ++ skin rash; no gut involvement; no liver involvement; no ↓ in clinical performance
II	+ to +++ skin rash; + gut involvement or + liver involvement (or both); mild ↓ in performance status
III	++ to +++ skin rash; ++ to +++ gut involvement or ++ to ++++ liver involvement (or both); marked ↓ in performance status
IV	Similar to grade III with ++ to ++++ organ involvement and extreme ↓ in clinical performance

[a] GVHD = Graft-versus-host disease.
[b] Reproduced with permission from reference 28.

The primary targets of immune-mediated destruction of host tissue by donor lymphocytes in acute graft-versus-host disease are the skin, liver, and GI tract.[6,28] Why these three organ systems are involved and others are spared remains unknown. Acute GVHD of the skin usually manifests as a diffuse maculopapular rash that starts on the palms of the hands or soles of the feet or behind the ears. In more severe cases, skin GVHD can progress to a generalized total body erythroderma, bullous formation, and skin desquamation.[28] The primary manifestation of acute GVHD in the gastrointestinal tract is the development of watery or bloody diarrhea. In severe cases, electrolyte abnormalities, dehydration, and abdominal pain or ileus can occur. Clinical manifestations of liver GVHD include elevated bilirubin, alkaline phosphatase, and hepatic transaminases, which often progress to fulminant hepatic failure. Acute GVHD usually is not evident until the time of engraftment, when donor lymphoid elements begin to proliferate. The skin usually is the first organ to be involved. The onset of liver or gastrointestinal GVHD usually lags behind the onset of skin GVHD by approximately one week, and rarely occurs in the absence of skin GVHD.[28]

Acute GVHD must be distinguished accurately from other causes of skin, liver, or GI toxicity in the bone marrow transplantation patient. For example, a macular papular rash which may occur as a manifestation of an allergic reaction to antibiotics, usually begins on the trunk or upper extremities and rarely presents on the palms of the hands or soles of the feet. Diarrhea can be caused by chemotherapy, radiation, infection, or antibiotic therapy. However, diarrhea caused by the conditioning regimen is rarely bloody and usually resolves within three to seven days following discontinuation of drugs and radiation. Diarrhea caused by infectious agents such as *Clostridium difficile* or cytomegalovirus can be distinguished from GVHD by stool culture. Liver GVHD must be distinguished primarily from VOD, and to a lesser extent, hepatitis induced by drugs, blood products, or parenteral nutrition. Although liver function test abnormalities between these syndromes are similar, liver GVHD rarely is associated with insidious weight gain or right upper quadrant pain. A tissue biopsy of the affected organ in conjunction with clinical evidence is the only way to definitively diagnose acute GVHD. Acute GVHD is associated with characteristic histologic changes to affected organs.[6,28] A staging system based upon clinical criteria is used to grade acute GVHD. The severity of organ involvement is determined first (see Table 94.6), and then an overall grade is established based upon number and extent of involved organs (see Table 94.7).[28]

M.P. developed a rash at the time of engraftment that could have been consistent with either an antibiotic-induced rash or acute GVHD. Although it was appropriate to change antibiotics, the fact that M.P.'s rash did not improve is suggestive of acute GVHD.

Since there are no signs of gastrointestinal or liver involvement at this time, M.P. is likely to have Grade I acute GVHD.

14. Risk Factors. What factors are associated with an increased risk of acute GVHD?

The single most important factor associated with the development of GVHD is the degree of histocompatibility between donor and recipient. As mentioned previously, for patients receiving allogeneic marrow from genotypically identical sibling donors, the overall incidence of acute GVHD (grade II to IV) worldwide is approximately 45%. Why such a high incidence of GVHD occurs despite the use of genotypically HLA-matched, MLC nonreactive marrow is unclear. Other histocompatibility antigens that are not yet identified may play a role in the development of this syndrome. Alternatively, the influence of existing HLA loci (HLA-C, HLA-E, DP) in determining alloreactivity may be understood poorly.[28,95,96] Nonetheless, when patients receive allogeneic marrow from donors that are mismatched at more than one known HLA loci, the prevalence of GVHD increases significantly, occurring in more than 70% of patients.[88,96,97] In addition, the onset of acute GVHD is earlier and severity is increased in mismatched donor-recipient pairs when compared to matched donor-recipient pairs.[88] The prevalence of severe acute GVHD (grade III to IV) by degree of histocompatibility between donor and recipient is depicted in Figure 94.5. Other factors that consistently increase the risk of developing GVHD include patient age (>20 years) and donor-recipient gender mismatch.[28,93,94,98,99,101-103]

M.P. is receiving allogeneic marrow from a female sibling donor that is mismatched at one HLA antigen. These two factors increase his risk of developing acute GVHD.

15. Immunosuppressive Prophylaxis. Why did M.P. receive prophylactic immunosuppressive therapy with cyclosporine and methotrexate?

Because GVHD is a leading cause of morbidity and mortality following allogeneic bone marrow transplantation, efforts to improve survival have focused on identifying therapies that can prevent or minimize its development. Two approaches have been taken. The first and most common method is to administer post-transplant immunosuppressive therapy. The second approach involves *ex vivo* removal of immunocompetent T-cells in donor bone marrow before bone marrow transplantation (referred to as T-cell-depleted bone marrow).

Historically, single-drug therapy was employed for the prevention of acute GVHD. Antithymocyte globulin (ATG), cyclophosphamide, methotrexate, and cyclosporine all have been used as single-agent therapy (see Table 94.8). ATG, which modulates GVHD by removing cytotoxic T-lymphocytes, no longer is used routinely as single-agent therapy. Its nonspecific binding to mononuclear cells depletes hematopoietic progenitor cells in addition to lymphocytes. Consequently, ATG has fallen out of favor for fear of a high incidence of graft failure.[105] Similarly, single-agent therapy with cyclophosphamide, methotrexate, or cyclosporine is used rarely as prophylaxis against acute GVHD. Although these agents effectively reduce the incidence of acute GVHD, randomized comparative trials have documented the superiority of combination immunosuppressive therapy in most patient populations (e.g., CML, aplastic anemia).[102,103,108,109,112] The exception to this rule includes patients with acute leukemia who are at high risk of relapse. In this patient population, the early decrease in mortality from acute GVHD provided by combination immunosuppressive therapy is offset by an increase in late mortality caused by an increased incidence of leukemic relapse.[109] Acute GVHD appears to mediate a beneficial graft-versus-leukemia (GVL) effect.[2,113] Indeed, an inverse relationship between acute GVHD and leukemic relapse has been observed.[2,113] Consequently, patients with acute leuke-

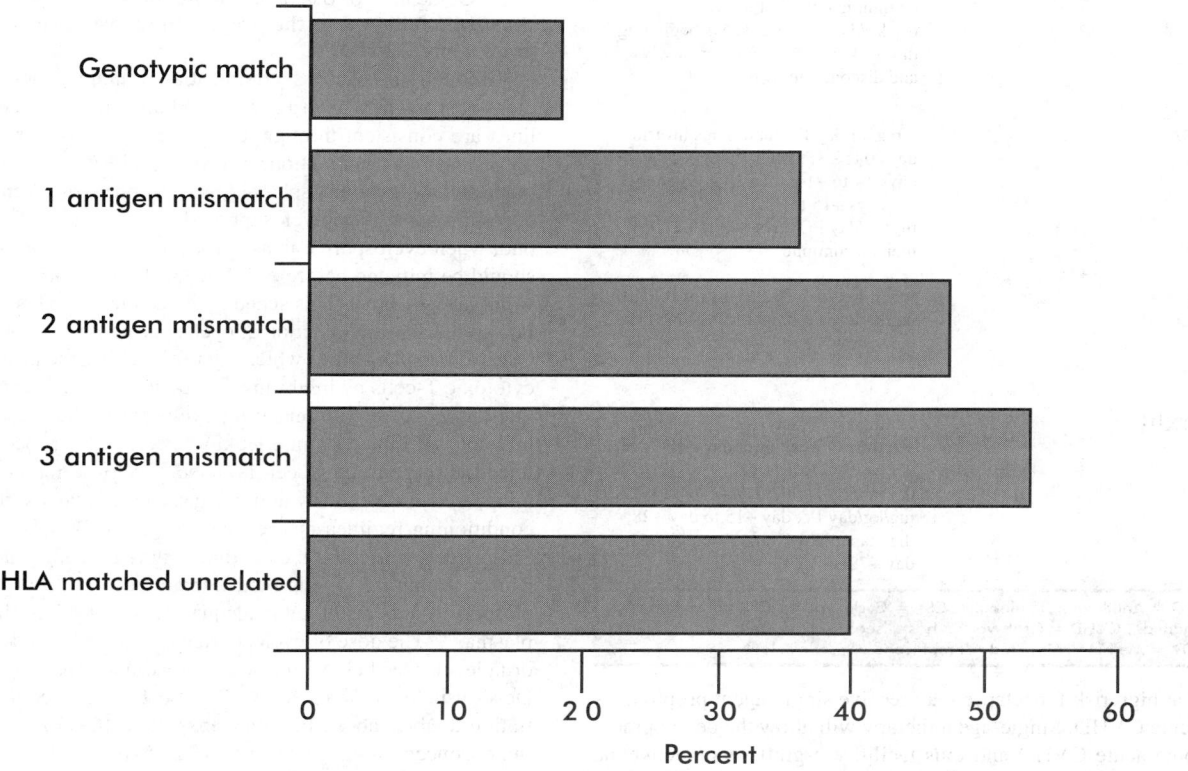

Fig 94.5 Probability of Developing Severe Acute (Grade III–IV) Graft-versus-Host Disease by Degree of Histocompatibility This graph assumes all patients received combination therapy with methotrexate and cyclosporine for prevention of acute GVHD. Reproduced with permission from reference 9.

Table 94.8	Regimens of Prophylaxis of Acute GVHD[a]
Drug	**Regimen**
Single Agent	
MTX "long course"[2]	15 mg/m^2 IV, day +1 10 mg/m^2 IV, day +3, +6, +11; then Q week until day 100
MTX "short course"	Same dose but no doses after day +11
CTX[104]	7.5 mg/kg IV, day +1, +3, +5, +7, +9; then Q week until day +10
ATG[105]	7 mg/kg IV over 6 hr QOD x 6 doses, days +8 to +29
CSA[101,106,107]	1.5 mg/kg IV or 6.25 mg/kg PO Q 12 hr, days −1 to +50. Then taper 5% per week and discontinue by day +180
Combination Therapy	
MTX "short course"[103,108,109] +	15 mg/m^2 IV, day +1; 10 mg/m^2, days +3, +6, +11
CSA	1.5 mg/kg IV Q 12 hr (or 6.25 mg/kg PO Q 12 hr), days −1 to +50; then taper by 5% per week and discontinue by day +180
MTX[110] +	15 mg/m^2 IV, days +1, +3, +6
CSA	5 mg/kg/day IV continuous infusion, day −2 to +3, then 3–3.75 mg/kg IV until day +35; then switch to 10 mg/kg/day PO and taper by 20% Q 2 weeks; then discontinue by day +180 (dose adjusted to maintain serum concentration between 200–600 ng/mL)
+ Pred	0.5 mg/kg/day IV for 1 week beginning day +7; then 1.0 mg/kg/day IV for 2 weeks beginning day +14 or +15; then taper slowly and discontinue by day +180
CSA[111]	5 mg/kg/day IV continuous infusion days 0 to +3; then 3.75 mg/kg/day IV days +4 to +14; then 10 mg/kg/day PO days +15 to +42; then 7.5 mg/kg/day PO days +43 to +180; then discontinue
+ MP	0.5 mg/kg/day IV day +8 to +14; 1.0 mg/kg/day IV days +15 to +28; then taper slowly and discontinue by day +72
CTX[111] +	7.5 mg/kg IV, days +1, +3, +5, +7, +9; then Q week until day +100
MP	0.5 mg/kg/day IV day +8 to +14; 1.0 mg/kg/day IV, day +15 to day +28; then taper slowly and discontinue by day +72

[a] ATG = Antithymocyte globulin; CSA = Cyclosporine; CTX = Cyclophosphamide; GVHD = Graft-versus-host disease; MP = Methylprednisolone; MTX = Methotrexate; Pred = Prednisone or prednisolone.

mias at high risk for relapse may receive single-agent prophylaxis for acute GVHD. Single-agent therapy will allow the development of some acute GVHD and thus facilitate a graft-versus-leukemia effect. Methotrexate is the agent of choice in this setting because it also provides inherent antileukemic activity.

A variety of two- and three-drug combination immunosuppressive regimens have been used for prophylaxis against GVHD (see Table 94.8). Methotrexate, cyclosporine, and corticosteroids are the three agents most commonly incorporated into combination immunosuppressive regimens. Characteristics of regimens containing these agents are depicted in Table 94.9. Although the most widely published regimen is "short course" methotrexate plus cyclosporine (Seattle regimen),[103,108] there is no national consensus with regard to the most effective regimen. In addition, there is insufficient evidence to date to determine whether three-drug combinations are superior to two-drug combinations for histocompatible allogeneic bone marrow transplantation. Most centers utilize three-drug combination immunosuppressive therapy only in mismatched or unrelated allogeneic BMT where the risk of acute GVHD is increased.

The use of T-cell depleted bone marrow is another method used to prevent acute GVHD. Depletion of T-lymphocytes in donor marrow is completed *ex vivo* using a variety of techniques.[114] Following infusion of T-cell depleted bone marrow, no further immunosuppressive therapy is administered. Regardless of the purging method employed, use of T-cell depleted marrow grafts reduces the incidence of GVHD.[114–116] Complications associated with T-cell depleted grafts include a high incidence of graft failure and an increased incidence of relapse in patients with leukemia. The reasons behind these complications are not understood fully, but may involve nonspecific depletion of other T-cell subsets that are responsible for promoting engraftment or modulating the graft-versus-leukemia effect.[114]

M.P. received prophylactic immunosuppressive therapy with a two-drug regimen of short-course methotrexate and cyclosporine for prophylaxis of acute GVHD. This regimen has been shown to be effective for the prophylaxis of acute GVHD in patients with chronic myelogenous leukemia undergoing allogeneic bone marrow transplantation.[106]

16. Guidelines for Use of Immunosuppressants. **What guidelines should be followed in the use of immunosuppressants to suppress acute GVHD?**

Although the various combination immunosuppressive regimens vary slightly by drug, dose, and combination, several guidelines are consistent throughout all the regimens. First, cytotoxic agents used in combination for prophylaxis of acute GVHD (e.g., methotrexate, cyclophosphamide) are withheld or given in reduced doses if mucositis or myelosuppression is severe.[103,108,110,111] Second, when cyclosporine is used for prophylaxis against GVHD, it should be initiated before or immediately following marrow infusion (day −1 or 0). This schedule is recommended because of the known mechanism of action of cyclosporine (see Chapter 33: Solid Organ Transplantation) which entails blocking the proliferation of cytotoxic T-cells by inhibiting production of T-helper cell-derived interleukin-2. By administering cyclosporine before the marrow infusion, inhibition of interleukin-2 secretion can occur before a rejection response has been initiated. Cyclosporine usually is administered intravenously until the gastrointestinal toxicity from the conditioning regimen has resolved (e.g., for 7 to 14 days).[103,108] Side effects caused by the conditioning regimen, including severe nausea, vomiting, or diarrhea impair the oral absorption of cyclosporine and result in inadequate concentrations in blood or plasma.[117] The dose of cyclosporine is adjusted based upon serum drug levels (see below) and serum creatinine (SrCr) concentration. Doses usually are reduced by 50% if the serum creatinine concentration doubles above baseline, and are withheld for serum creatinine concentrations greater than 2 mg/dL.[101,103,106–108] When corticosteroids are added to combination immunosuppressive regimens, they usually are withheld until engraftment is expected (7

Table 94.9	Characteristics of Combination Regimens for Prophylaxis of Acute GVHD[a]
Regimens Containing	Characteristic
MTX	Delayed engraftment ↑ time to platelet independence ↑ incidence and severity of mucositis Elevations in LFTs
CSA	Marrow sparing ↑ incidence of nephrotoxicity ↑ incidence of neurotoxicity ↑ incidence of hypertension ↓ clearance of MTX if nephrotoxicity develops
Corticosteroids	↑ infectious complications ↑ incidence of hypertension in combination with CSA Hyperglycemia

[a] CSA = Cyclosporine; GVHD = Graft-versus-host disease; LFTs = Liver function tests; MTX = Methotrexate.

to 14 days after marrow infusion). Administering corticosteroids earlier in the post-transplant period (e.g., day 0) paradoxically increases the incidence of GVHD when used in combination with methotrexate and cyclosporine.[118] The reason for this is unknown.

Tapering schedules for cyclosporine and corticosteroids vary widely between institutions. The general goal is to keep doses of both agents stable up to day +50, and then taper slowly with the intent to discontinue all immunosuppressives by six months following the transplant. By this time, immunological tolerance has developed and patients no longer require immunosuppressive therapy. The rate at which tapering occurs depends upon the patient. Patients who develop acute GVHD or who experience flares of existing GVHD during a tapering trial will have to have their doses increased or tapered more slowly as tolerated.

17. Role of Cyclosporine Pharmacokinetic Monitoring. On day +18, a cyclosporine level is drawn right before the morning dose and is reported to be 150 ng/mL [by radioimmunoassay (RIA)]. Why are cyclosporine levels being obtained?

The role of pharmacokinetic monitoring of cyclosporine in BMT patients is not well defined. Early studies could not identify a relationship between cyclosporine concentration and incidence of acute GVHD.[119-121] In contrast, more recent studies suggest that the incidence of acute GVHD is significantly higher in patients whose trough cyclosporine concentrations are less than 200 ng/mL.[111,122-124] Pharmacokinetic monitoring may play a more important role in preventing or minimizing cyclosporine-induced nephrotoxicity. Although the distinction between safe and unsafe cyclosporine concentrations is unknown, trough concentrations greater than 400 ng/mL (via RIA and high-pressure liquid chromatography assay) are associated with a higher incidence of nephrotoxicity in some series.[119,125,126] It is important to note, however, that cyclosporine-induced nephrotoxicity can occur despite low or normal concentrations of cyclosporine and may be a consequence of other drug or disease-related factors known to influence the development of nephrotoxicity (e.g., concurrent use of other nephrotoxic agents, sepsis).

Based upon the above information, it is reasonable to attempt to maintain cyclosporine concentrations between 200 and 400 ng/mL in patients undergoing allogeneic bone marrow transplantation. Recommendations for dose adjustments should be made considering cyclosporine levels and serum creatinine concentration. Dose adjustments should be made for serum creatinine, regardless of cyclosporine concentration, as recommended above. For patients with serum creatinine concentrations less than 2.0

mg/dL and cyclosporine concentrations less than 200 ng/mL, the dose can be increased by 25%. Conversely, the dose of cyclosporine should be decreased by 25% if cyclosporine concentrations are greater than 400 ng/mL. M.P. has a normal serum creatinine and his cyclosporine level is less than 200 ng/mL. Therefore, his cyclosporine dose should be increased by 25%.

18. Investigational Therapies for Prophylaxis. What other therapies have been proposed for the prophylaxis of acute GVHD?

Pentoxifylline has been evaluated as an adjunctive medication for decreasing regimen-related toxicities, including acute graft-versus-host disease.[86,127] Support for the use of this agent is based upon findings that patients who develop acute GVHD (grade II to IV) have elevated levels of circulating TNF-alpha when compared to patients who have no evidence of GVHD or develop a mild acute GVHD (grade 0 to I).[76] However, two prospective, randomized, placebo-controlled trials evaluating pentoxifylline 400 to 600 mg four times daily have failed to establish a role for this agent in modulating acute GVHD.[86,127]

A role for the use of *intravenous immunoglobulin (IVIG)* in GVHD has been defined. Intravenous immunoglobulin therapy is administered routinely to patients undergoing allogeneic bone marrow transplantation to prevent or treat viral infections. Two large studies have noted a relationship between administration of immunoglobulins and a decreased prevalence of acute GVHD.[128,129] Although the exact mechanism is unknown, immunoglobulins may manifest their beneficial effects by blocking immunologic reactions between donor effector cells and host histocompatibility antigens. Doses ranging from 100 to 500 mg/kg/dose, with the first dose administered pretransplantation and subsequent doses administered weekly for three months have been used for the prophylaxis of acute GVHD.[128,129] Currently, Gamimune-N is the only immunoglobulin product which has been approved by the FDA to prevent GVHD in patients undergoing allogeneic bone marrow transplantation.[130] To date, there have been no published studies comparing the efficacy of different immunoglobulin preparations for this indication. Nonetheless, given the multitude of other factors that influence the development of acute GVHD (e.g., histocompatibility between donor and recipient, donor-recipient gender disparity, underlying disease, prophylactic immunosuppressive therapy) it is unlikely that minimal differences between products would result in major differences in the incidence of acute GVHD.

Investigational agents being considered for a role in preventing acute GVHD include anti-interleukin-2 receptor murine monoclonal antibody,[131-133] antiCD5 ricin immunotoxin (XomaZyme-H65),[134-137] tacrolimus (FK-506),[138] and antiTNF-alpha monoclonal antibody.[139] The role of these agents is yet to be defined.

19. Treatment of Established Acute Graft-versus-Host Disease. On day +23 the suspicion of acute Grade I skin GVHD is confirmed by biopsy. The physician orders the application of topical triamcinolone 0.1% to affected areas on M.P.'s trunk and hands and hydrocortisone 0.5% to be applied sparingly to his face. Topical steroids stabilize M.P.'s skin GVHD temporarily; however, 3 days later his rash begins to progress, he develops diarrhea, and is noted to have increased LFTs. M.P. is started on prednisolone 35 mg IV Q 6 hr. What is the rationale for triamcinolone and prednisolone therapy in M.P.?

As mentioned previously, the most effective way to treat graft-versus-host disease is to prevent its development. However, once GVHD has manifested itself, the best treatment is early intervention, since only 40% of patients respond to first-line therapy for treatment of established disease.[99,114,140] In addition, patients with mild to moderate (Grade I to III) acute GVHD who respond to initial therapy have a significantly better survival advantage when compared to patients with severe acute GVHD or disease that does not respond to initial therapy. Patients who do not respond to therapy or have ongoing severe GVHD usually die from a combination of GVHD and infectious complications.[99,140–144] M.P. has objective evidence of established acute GVHD. Initially, his disease was localized (Grade I skin GVHD only), and topical corticosteroids are the therapy of choice for limited skin GVHD.[114,145] Furthermore, topical therapy can stop progression or reverse existing limited disease while avoiding the systemic toxicities associated with intravenous or oral corticosteroids.

M.P. also was given systemic steroids at the first sign of progressive disease. This was appropriate, since single-agent corticosteroids are considered by many to be the therapy of choice for established acute GVHD.[140,146] Corticosteroids indirectly halt the progression of immune-mediated destruction of host tissues by blocking macrophage-derived interleukin-1 secretion. Interleukin-1 is a primary stimulus for T-helper cell-induced secretion of interleukin-2 which in turn is responsible for stimulating proliferation of cytotoxic T-lymphocytes (see Chapter 33: Solid Organ Transplantation). The recommended dose of prednisolone for the treatment of established acute GVHD is 2 mg/kg/day, given intravenously or orally in four divided doses for a minimum of 14 days, followed by a tapering schedule that is dependent on patient response.[140–142,146,147] The dose of prednisolone in M.P. (35 mg IV Q 6 hr) is approximately 2 mg/kg/day and thus is consistent with these recommendations. In the only comparative trial evaluating corticosteroid dose in acute GVHD, low-dose prednisolone 2.5 mg/kg/day was found to be just as effective as higher-dose therapy.[147] Nonetheless, high-dose pulse therapy with intravenous methylprednisolone 20 to 60 mg/kg/day or 500 mg/m^2 every six hours followed by a rapid taper has been advocated by some investigators.[143–145]

Other therapies that have been used to treat established acute GVHD include antithymocyte globulin 15 mg/kg/dose intravenously every other day for three to ten doses,[142,146] cyclosporine 3 mg/kg/day intravenously or 12.5 mg/kg/day orally,[141,142] and murine monoclonal antibody (OKT$_3$) 5 mg/day intravenously for 14 days.[148] Single-agent and combination therapy also have been used, although a high incidence of death due to infection is seen when more than two agents are used;[145] the latter is most likely caused by enhanced immunosuppression. Cyclosporine is used only to treat established GVHD in patients who did not receive cyclosporine as part of their prophylactic regimen. In addition, cyclosporine levels do not correlate with response in the setting of acute GVHD.[141,145] If a patient fails to respond to one drug, switching to another agent for rescue therapy occasionally is successful; however, response rates to salvage therapy for acute GVHD are low.[140,149]

Two new agents directed against blocking the accelerated cytokine cascade are under investigation for the treatment of established acute GVHD. These include anti-interleukin-2 receptor monoclonal antibody and monoclonal antiTNF-alpha antibody.[150–153] The most effective dose, timing, or combination of these new therapies still is unknown.

M.P. should be evaluated for response to prednisolone after seven days. If his acute GVHD has improved or stabilized, he should continue on therapy at this dose for a total of 14 days. If M.P. responds to therapy, his steroid dose should be tapered slowly over a minimum of one month, and he should be monitored for any evidence of recurrent graft-versus-host disease. If GVHD flares during his steroid taper (as evidenced by worsening skin reactions or increased diarrhea volume) the dose should be increased again until his disease is stable, with the subsequent taper initiated at a slower rate. If he fails to respond to first-line therapy with prednisolone, he should receive salvage therapy with either ATG, OKT$_3$, or an investigational drug on protocol.

Chronic GVHD

20. Clinical Presentation. M.P. was successfully treated for his acute GVHD, is now off prednisolone, and currently is tapering his cyclosporine. On day + 120 M.P. comes to clinic for follow-up after a 2-week vacation in Florida. Upon examination, M.P. has a mild skin rash on his arms and legs, hyperpigmentation of the tissue surrounding the eyes, and white plaque-like lesions in his mouth. He also is complaining of dry eyes. Laboratory tests reveal an increased alkaline phosphatase and total bilirubin concentration. What is the most likely cause of M.P.'s findings?

Chronic graft-versus-host disease occurs in approximately 45% of patients undergoing allogeneic bone marrow transplantation and is unrelated to the regimen used for prophylaxis of acute GVHD.[101,102,105,107,109,110,146] Increased patient age and history of acute GVHD are the two single most important factors predicting the development of chronic GVHD.[6,154] In addition, the grade of acute GVHD experienced by the patient influences the incidence of chronic GVHD. For example, in one study, the incidence of chronic GVHD was 57%, 80%, and 100% in patients with preexisting grade I, II to III, and IV acute GVHD, respectively.[155] Death from complications relating to chronic GVHD and concomitant infection occurs in approximately 40% of patients.[154]

The time course for the onset of chronic GVHD follows three typical patterns: *progressive*, *quiescent*, or *de novo*.[156,157] Progressive chronic GVHD evolves directly from acute GVHD, with no resolution of acute disease in between. This form of chronic GVHD carries the worst prognosis.[154] Quiescent chronic GVHD appears slowly following a period of complete resolution of acute GVHD, and *de novo* late onset chronic GVHD occurs spontaneously in the absence of a history of acute GVHD.

The clinical course of chronic GVHD is multifaceted, involving almost any organ in the body. Because of its diffuse nature, chronic GVHD is not graded by organ system, and instead is described as *limited* or *extensive*, based upon the extent of involvement. Limited chronic GHVD is characterized by localized skin or liver involvement. Extensive chronic GVHD is characterized by extensive skin or hepatic involvement, mucosal changes, and/or involvement of

Table 94.10	Signs and Symptoms of Chronic GVHD[a,156,157]
Affected Organ	**Clinical Manifestations**
Skin	Rash, hypo- or hyperpigmentation, erythema, alopecia, sclerosis, or scleroderma with joint contractures if severe, lichen planus lesions
Eyes	↓ tear formation, dry eyes, burning, photophobia
GI tract	↓ saliva production, dry mouth leading to cracking or fissure formation, change in taste sensation, diarrhea and abdominal pain, fat malabsorption, chronic malnutrition, web formation
Liver	Increased LFTs, histologic changes consistent with combined hepatocellar injury and cholestasis
Lungs	Nonproductive cough, wheezing, bronchospasm, diffuse interstitial pneumonitis, restrictive or obstructive abnormalities on PFTs
Bone marrow	Eosinophilia, thrombocytopenia, ↓ antibody formation and subclass distribution
Musculoskeletal	Myalgias, arthralgias, clinical picture resembling systemic lupus erythematosus or rheumatoid arthritis
Miscellaneous	Circulating autoantibodies (antinuclear antibody, rheumatoid factor, positive direct Coombs' test)

^{a} GI = Gastrointestinal; GVHD = Graft-versus-host disease; LFTs = Liver function tests; PFTs = Pulmonary function tests.

any other organ system. Signs and symptoms of chronic GVHD in various organ systems are listed in Table 94.10.

The signs and symptoms of chronic GVHD in M.P. include a rash in sun-exposed areas of the skin, hyperpigmentation of tissues surrounding his eyes, white plaque-like lesions in the mouth, dry mucous membranes, and increased alkaline phosphatase and total bilirubin. These symptoms appeared following a period of complete resolution of his acute GVHD. Thus, M.P. has limited-involvement, quiescent chronic GVHD.

21. Pharmacologic Management. M.P. is started on oral azathioprine 125 mg PO QD for the treatment of his chronic GVHD. Is this therapy rational? What other agents are available to treat chronic GVHD?

The mainstay of therapy for the treatment of chronic graft-versus-host disease is long-term immunosuppressive therapy. Although oral prednisone, azathioprine, procarbazine, and cyclophosphamide all have been used, prednisone, azathioprine, and cyclosporine have emerged as the most commonly used agents with the best efficacy and toxicity profiles.[157,158] M.P. was started on single agent azathioprine, for the treatment of his chronic GVHD. This is a reasonable decision since single-agent immunosuppressive therapy is the treatment of choice for standard-risk (i.e., limited involvement quiescent or *de novo* chronic GVHD) patients. The use of combination immunosuppressive therapy in this setting results in an unacceptably high incidence of infectious complications when compared to single agent therapy.[158] However, if M.P. fails to respond to azathioprine or if he had presented initially with progressive or extensive chronic GVHD, combination therapy with prednisone and azathioprine would be a reasonable alternative.[157]

When used as a single agent, or in combination, the dose of azathioprine is 1.5 mg/kg/day. M.P. is 60 kg, so his calculated dose is 90 mg/day. Since azathioprine is available only as scored 50 mg tablets, the dose must be rounded up or down in 25 mg increments. When used alone or in combination, the dose of prednisone for the treatment of chronic GVHD is 1.0 mg/kg/day, administered orally in divided doses for 30 days. After 30 days, the dose is converted slowly to alternate day therapy by increasing the "on-day" and decreasing the "off-day" dose until a total of 2 mg/kg/day on alternate days is administered.[157–159] Once the alternate day conversion has occurred, the patient is tapered slowly to the final dose of 1 mg/kg every other day. Alternate day therapy is preferred to minimize adrenocortical suppression.[157–159]

Other therapies may be required for patients considered to be at high-risk for developing chronic GVHD (defined as patients with GVHD that progresses from acute GVHD or the presence of thrombocytopenia). Cyclosporine is used in combination with prednisone in an alternating sequence for this patient population.[158] The dose of cyclosporine is 6 mg/kg orally every 12 hours every other day, alternating with prednisone 1 mg/kg orally every other day.[158] Thalidomide, a sedative hypnotic with immunosuppressive properties, also has been evaluated on an investigational basis for the treatment of chronic GVHD in high-risk patients.[160] The dose of thalidomide used for this indication is 200 mg orally four times daily in adults and 3 mg/kg orally four times daily in children. Toxicity associated with thalidomide includes sedation, neurotoxicity, and teratogenicity.[160]

Once immunosuppressive therapy is initiated, one to two months may pass before an improvement in clinical symptoms is noted; therapy usually is continued for 9 to 12 months. If after this time there has been resolution of signs and symptoms of chronic GVHD, immunosuppressive therapy can be tapered slowly. If a flare of chronic GVHD occurs during the tapering schedule or after therapy is discontinued, immunosuppressive therapy is reinstituted.

When immunosuppressive therapy is administered for long periods, the patient must be monitored closely for chronic toxicity. Blood counts should be monitored routinely in patients on azathioprine, since hematologic toxicity resulting in infection and bleeding may occur. Cushingoid effects, aseptic necrosis of the joints, and diabetes can develop with long-term corticosteroid use. Other severe complications include a high incidence of infection with atypical pathogens such as *Pneumocystis carinii* pneumoniae, cytomegalovirus, and herpes zoster. Cyclosporine therapy is associated with nephrotoxicity, neurotoxicity, and hypertension, although these effects are minimized with an alternate day schedule.

22. Adjuvant Therapies. Suggest some adjuvant therapies that should be instituted in a patient like M.P. with chronic GVHD.

Patients being treated for chronic GVHD should receive trimethoprim-sulfamethoxazole for prophylaxis of *P. carinii*. In addition, the use of artificial tears and saliva may improve lubrication and decrease the occurrence of cracking and fissures in mucous membranes. If nutritional intake is poor, consultation with a clinical nutritionist and use of oral nutritional supplementation may be advisable. In addition, patients should be instructed to use sunscreens to exposed areas whenever prolonged sun exposure is anticipated. Lastly, patient education regarding the delay in improvement of symptoms, anticipated duration of therapy, and importance of compliance with oral immunosuppressive therapy is essential.

Infectious Complications

Infections are a major source of morbidity and mortality following marrow transplantation. Three major periods of infectious risks have been described (see Figure 94.4). During the early period when neutropenia and severe mucosal damage are present, the primary pathogens are aerobic bacteria and herpes simplex virus (HSV). Because all patients undergoing marrow transplantation have indwelling intravenous central catheters, *Staphylococcus* is a predominant organism. *Streptococcus viridans* is common and enters the systemic circulation from the GI tract and oral mucosa. Aerobic gram-negative organisms primarily originate from the gastrointestinal tract. Chemotherapy-induced mucosal damage serves as a portal of entry for most of the bacteria into the blood stream. Herpes simplex, also a major organism during this period, rarely occurs now with the routine use of antiviral prophylaxis. Systemic and oral candidiasis may occur during this period.

The second or middle period of infectious risk occurs following marrow engraftment to posttransplant day +100. Pathogens such as cytomegalovirus, adenovirus, and aspergillosis are common during this period. Interstitial pneumonitis (IP) is a frequent manifestation of infection and can be caused by several infectious agents including cytomegalovirus, adenovirus, and *Pneumocystis carinii*.

During the late period (after day +100), the predominant organisms are the encapsulated bacteria (e.g., *Streptococcus pneumoniae*, *Haemophilus influenzae*, *Neisseria meningitidis*) and *Varicella zoster* virus (VZV). The encapsulated organisms commonly cause sinopulmonary infections.

Prevention of Herpes Simplex Virus (HSV)

23. D.W., a 35-year-old male with nodular sclerosing Hodgkin's disease, stage IIIB, has been treated with 8 cycles of cyclophosphamide, doxorubicin (Hydroxyldaunorubicin), vincristine (Oncovin), Prednisone (CHOP) and 5 cycles of bleomycin, lomustine (CCNU), doxorubicin (Adriomycin), vinblastine (B-CAVe) after which he achieved a complete remission. His disease recurred 5 years later and was treated with radiation therapy. One year later he presented with an Hgb of 9.0 gm/dL, an Hct of 27.2%, and normal RBCs. A bone marrow biopsy was performed and showed dysplasia of all 3 cell

lines. The diagnosis of myelodysplastic syndrome secondary to previous chemotherapy and radiotherapy was made. He was referred for an allogeneic BMT from a HLA-identical matched sister. His preparative regimen included 2 days of IV cyclophosphamide (60 mg/kg/day) and 4 days of TBI. Pretransplant viral titers were positive for CMV, HSV, and VZV. The hepatitis screen was negative. Creatinine clearance (Cl_{Cr}) upon admission was 111 mL/min. Pertinent laboratory values are: WBC 1700/mm^3, platelets 44,000/mm^3, ANC 561 cells/µL, Hgb 7.4 gm/dL, Hct 21.8%. What is the significance of D.W.'s positive HSV antibody titer before transplant? What prophylaxis will he receive because of it? [SI unit: Cl_{Cr} 1.85 mL/s; WBC 1700 × 10^6 cells/L; platelets 44 × 10^9/L; ANC 561 × 10^6 cells/L; Hct 0.27 and 0.21, respectively; Hgb 90 and 74 mmol/L, respectively]

Patients who are herpes simplex virus antibody seropositive before transplant are at high risk for reactivation of their HSV infection. Reactivation occurs in 43% to 70% of HSV-seropositive patients undergoing allogeneic transplant.[161,162] Thus, prophylactic acyclovir is used routinely in most allogeneic and autologous transplant centers in HSV-seropositive patients. Acyclovir is highly effective in preventing HSV reactivation, reducing its occurrence to 0% to 45% of patients.[161–168] Patients who are HSV seronegative rarely develop HSV infection and prophylactic acyclovir is not warranted. If HSV does occur, lesions usually appear on the oral mucosa, nasolabial mucous membranes, or genital mucocutaneous area. Oral lesions can be nondescript and confused with chemotherapy-induced stomatitis. Diagnosis can be confirmed with culture of the lesion. Since D.W. is HSV seropositive, he is at risk of reactivating his HSV and will be given prophylactic acyclovir.

24. Acyclovir Dosing. What would be an appropriate dose of acyclovir for HSV prophylaxis?

Doses, routes of administration, and duration of prophylaxis have varied widely in published trials. Intravenous acyclovir is generally given from the day of admission until the patient is able to tolerate and reliably absorb oral medications. Intravenous acyclovir appears to be slightly more effective than oral therapy in preventing reactivation early posttransplant. This may be due to poor compliance or absorption of the drug due to chemotherapy-induced nausea, vomiting, and mucositis. When oral acyclovir is given, the total dose administered varies from 800 to 3200 mg/day divided in two to four doses a day and continued until day +30 to +180.[162–167] One commonly used regimen is to administer acyclovir 250 mg/m^2 (5 mg/kg) IV every 12 hours[161,163,167] and convert to oral acyclovir (400 mg TID >7 years old and 200 mg TID if <7 years old) when the patient is able to tolerate oral medications. Patients on ganciclovir prophylaxis for cytomegalovirus infection do not require acyclovir prophylaxis against HSV.

Prevention of Cytomegalovirus (CMV) Disease

25. D.W. also is CMV seropositive. What is the significance of this finding and what measures can be taken to prevent reactivation of CMV?

Primary cytomegalovirus can be prevented in the CMV seronegative recipient by avoiding exposure to the virus. This can be accomplished by transplantation of marrow from a CMV seronegative donor and transfusion of blood products from CMV seronegative donors. However, transplantation of marrow from a CMV seronegative donor into a CMV seronegative recipient is not always possible. The exclusive use of blood products from CMV seronegative donors is difficult for a blood bank to support due to the difficulty in obtaining CMV-negative products. Thus, other strategies, such as the use of filtered blood products (leukopoor), immune globulin, prophylactic antiviral therapy, or a combination of these may be employed. To prevent secondary CMV or its reactivation in the seropositive recipient, high-dose acyclovir, gan-

ciclovir, and immune globulin are used. CMV occurs rarely in the autologous transplant recipient; therefore, CMV prophylactic measures probably are not necessary and in most centers restricted to the allogeneic transplant recipient. CMV is common following allogeneic transplantation and the morbidity and mortality associated with this infection are high; however, appropriate CMV prophylaxis has resulted in dramatic reductions in mortality.

Antivirals. High-dose IV acyclovir (500 mg/m^2 Q 8 hr from day −5 to +30) may prevent CMV reactivation following allogeneic transplantation.[169] Acyclovir has no benefit in the treatment of CMV but reduces the incidence of CMV infection and disease when given prophylactically in high doses. The probability of developing CMV in the first 30 days posttransplant is very low. Thus, although it has been a standard of practice to administer high-dose acyclovir during neutropenia, this practice now is being reconsidered in many institutions due to the significant cost and relatively low risk of CMV during this period. Because acyclovir does not have hematological side effects, its use during engraftment is relatively safe.

The use of ganciclovir for CMV prophylaxis postengraftment is more practical and it is used widely following allogeneic marrow transplantation. Ganciclovir decreases the incidence of CMV infection and disease in seropositive allogeneic marrow recipients; however, their overall long-term survival is not changed.[170,171] Table 94.11 outlines the commonly used ganciclovir and foscarnet prophylaxis regimens. Typically, ganciclovir prophylaxis is begun when the absolute neutrophil count is greater than 750 or 1000 cells/µL for at least two consecutive days. It is not given during neutropenia because it could impair hematological recovery. Neutropenia occurs in a significant number of prophylactic ganciclovir recipients; and as a consequence, patients may be more likely to develop bacterial and fungal infections, although this has not been demonstrated in all trials. Less commonly, ganciclovir may cause thrombocytopenia or delayed platelet engraftment.[171] Careful follow-up with regular complete blood counts with platelets and differential is necessary if ganciclovir prophylaxis is used. The cessation of ganciclovir due to neutropenia during prophylaxis is common, occurring in 30% to 58% of patients within a median of 36 days after initiation of prophylaxis.[170,171] Cell counts usually recover to an absolute neutrophil count greater than 1000 cells/µL within two weeks and ganciclovir can be reinstituted safely, but usually on an every-other-day or Monday, Wednesday, Friday schedule.

Foscarnet may be used in patients unable to tolerate ganciclovir prophylaxis. Conclusive efficacy data for foscarnet are lacking; however, it probably is similar to that of ganciclovir.[172] No conclusive data are available evaluating the efficacy of foscarnet and ganciclovir following autologous transplantation. Since the incidence of CMV disease is significantly less in the autologous pop-

Table 94.11	Prophylactic IV Ganciclovir and Foscarnet in CMV Seropositive Patients[a]
Drug	**Regimen**
Ganciclovir	5 mg/kg Q 12 hr x 5 days then 5 mg/kg/day until day +100 (beginning after engraftment)[170]
	Or
	2.5 mg/kg Q 8 hr (admission to day −1); then 6 mg/kg/day Mon–Fri only until day +120 (beginning after engraftment)[171]
Foscarnet	40 mg/kg Q 8 hr (day −7 to +30) then 60 mg/kg QD until day +75[172]

a CMV = Cytomegalovirus.

Table 94.12	Immune Globulin Products
Product	**Manufacturer**
Unselected IVIG	
Polygam	American Red Cross
Gamimune-N	Cutter Biological
Gammagard S/D	Hyland
Iveegam	Immuno US
Sandoglobulin	Sandoz
Venoglobulin-S	Alpha Therapeutic
Gammar-IV	Armour
CMV Hyperimmune Globulin	
CytoGam	Connaught

ulation, it is the author's opinion that the benefits of CMV prophylaxis do not justify the potential risk or expense.

D.W.'s absolute neutrophil count recovers to over 1000 cells/μL on day +20 and prophylactic ganciclovir IV 5 mg/kg/day is begun. Ganciclovir will be continued until day +100. Prophylactic acyclovir is discontinued. If D.W. were receiving an autologous transplant he would not require ganciclovir prophylaxis because the risk of CMV would be low.

Immune Globulins. Immune globulin products consist primarily of IgG antibody, although small amounts of IgA and IgM may be present. Unselected intravenous immune globulin (IVIG) has IgG antibody to a broad spectrum of bacteria and virus including CMV. Cytomegalovirus hyperimmune globulin (CMV-IVIG) is obtained from donors with known high antibody titers to CMV; therefore, the product contains higher amounts of IgG antibody to CMV than the unselected IVIG products. See Table 94.12 for a list of currently available immune globulin products.

Humoral immunity is depressed following autologous and allogeneic bone marrow transplantations, although immunity recovers more rapidly in the patient who has received an autologous transplant. Serum immune globulins such as IgG and IgM may be reduced for three to four months following transplantation; IgA may be reduced for years.[173] In addition, once immune globulin levels are normal, antibody function may still be impaired. Serum IgG$_2$ and IgG$_4$ subclass deficiencies may occur; however, the significance is unknown. Patients developing chronic graft-versus-host disease may have extensive hypogammaglobulinemia and require frequent immune globulin infusions.

The administration of immune globulin following allogeneic marrow transplantation has several possible advantages. It provides passive immunity (especially to CMV and bacteria), potentiates complement activation, and augments opsonic and neutrophil function. It probably also has an immunomodulatory effect that modifies graft-versus-host disease.[129]

Numerous studies have evaluated the use of immune globulin prophylaxis in marrow transplant recipients,[128,174–188] and most have demonstrated a reduction in CMV infection and interstitial pneumonitis. Comparing studies is difficult because they differ with regard to GVHD prophylactic regimen, use of other antiviral prophylactic agents, granulocyte transfusions, type of blood products, immune globulin product viral titers, doses, schedules, and duration of therapy.

Recent immune globulin studies using unselected IVIG have demonstrated a reduction in septicemia and GVHD;[129,189] however, overall improvement in survival has not been demonstrated in all trials. Minimal data in autologous transplantation are available, but to date immune globulin has not been demonstrated to be beneficial.[190,191] Most transplant centers use unselected IVIG for

prophylaxis. The optimal immune globulin dose and schedule regimen is unknown. (Table 94.13 outlines some of the commonly used unselected IVIG prophylactic regimens.) Alternatively, some centers follow serum IgG levels and administer immune globulin when the level is less than 650 mg/dL. Patients with GVHD often require more frequent infusions and IgG levels are helpful in determining the optimal dose requirements.

Minimal data are available regarding the comparative efficacy of the various unselected IVIG products,[193] and it is unlikely that a large comparative trial will ever be performed. Although Gamimune-N is the only product approved by the FDA for bone marrow transplant, all products appear similar with regard to their side effects, pharmacokinetics, ability to modify infection, and possibly graft-versus-host disease. Therefore, the ideal unselected IVIG should contain a broad spectrum of antibodies (IgG subclasses), be easy to prepare, be available in varied concentrations (since fluid restriction is common), and have a low price.

D.W. is given Sandoglobulin IV 500 mg/kg weekly during hospitalization and then monthly until posttransplant day +90 to prevent viral and bacterial infections and, perhaps, graft-versus-host disease.

Diagnosis and Treatment of CMV Interstitial Pneumonitis (IP)

26. P.N., a 30 kg, 85 cm, 12-year-old male, is on day +245 following a third allogeneic, mismatched, T lymphocyte-depleted bone marrow transplant for Philadelphia chromosome-positive CML. He presents to the clinic with increased difficulty breathing, a nonproductive cough, and a fever of 101.1 °F. Significant past medical history includes chronic pulmonary and skin GVHD which is stable on prednisone and chronic pulmonary insufficiency secondary to fibrosis. He requires 1 to 2 L/minute of oxygen to maintain O$_2$ saturations >90%. P.N. has chronic renal insufficiency, a history of pansinusitis and bilateral otitis media, each treated with several courses of antibiotics over the past few months. He has been unable to maintain his weight due to nausea, vomiting, and anorexia and is on home total parenteral nutrition. Pertinent laboratory values are: glucose 97 mg/dL, Na 138 mEq/L, K 3.6 mEq/L, Cl 102 mEq/L, CO$_2$ 21 mEq/L, blood urea nitrogen (BUN) 31 mg/dL, SrCr 1.1 mg/dL, lactate dehydrogenase (LDH) 367 U/L, AST 39 U/L, alanine aminotransferase (ALT) 28 U/L, total bilirubin 0.6 mg/dL, Mg 1.6 mg/dL, WBC 6,100/mm^3, platelets 164,000/mm^3, ANC 4819 cells/×L, and Hgb 10.8 g/dL. He was CMV and HSV antibody seropositive before transplant. Oral medications include: Prednisone 15 mg alternating with 7.5 mg BID, furosemide 30 mg QD, K-Dur 40 mEq BID, ranitidine 75 mg HS, Septra 80/400 BID on Monday, Wednesday, Friday Magnesium oxide 400 mg BID, sucralfate 500 mg QID, and a Flintstone vitamin QD. He receives Sandoglobulin IV 15 gm (500 mg/kg) every month.

Table 94.13	Common Unselected IVIG Prophylactic Regimens[a]
Dose and Schedule	
500 mg/kg Q week to day +90; then Q month to day +360[129]	
500 mg/kg Q week for 12–16 weeks[189]	
300 mg/kg Q 2–3 weeks for 12–16 weeks[189]	
1 gm/kg Q week until day +120[128]	
500 mg/kg Q 2 weeks until day +120 then Q month until day +360[175]	
500 mg/kg Q 2 weeks until day +90[192]	

[a] IVIG = Intravenous immune globulin.

Upon physical examination P.N. is a slightly malnourished child with moon facies, dry skin with thickened areas, and thinning hair. Rales are heard throughout the lung fields and a chest x-ray shows bilateral diffuse interstitial infiltrates. P.N. is admitted and an open lung biopsy is performed. Blood cultures are sent for CMV shell vial and buffy coat. Twenty-four hours later shell vial cultures from the lung biopsy and blood were positive for CMV antigen. The diagnosis of CMV interstitial pneumonitis (CMV-IP) is made. What signs and symptoms of CMV-IP does P.N. display? [SI units: glucose 5.38 mmol/L; Na 138 mmol/; K 3.6 mmol/L; Cl 102 mmol/L; CO_2 21 mmol/L; BUN 11.1 mmol/L; SrCr 83.9 μmol/L; LDH 6.12 μkat/L; AST 0.65 μkat/L; ALT 0.47 μkat/L; total bilirubin 10.26 μmol/L; Mg 0.65 mmol/L; WBC 6100 × 10^6 cells/L; platelets 164 × 10^9/L; ANC 4819 × 10^6 cells/L; Hgb 108 gm/L]

Cytomegalovirus is one of the most serious infectious complications that can occur following marrow transplantation. It can occur at anytime but generally has an onset between days + 30 and + 90. It is associated most commonly with allogeneic transplantation and rarely occurs following autologous or syngeneic transplantation.[194,195] CMV most often is the result of a reactivation of a latent virus; less frequently, it is acquired through primary transmission from the bone marrow of a CMV seropositive donor or unscreened blood products. Primary disease occurs in recipients who were CMV seronegative before transplant, indicating no prior CMV infection.

Diagnosis and Manifestations. Cytomegalovirus usually manifests itself as interstitial pneumonitis or gastrointestinal disease in the bone marrow transplantation patient and less often as hepatitis. In rare cases, it may infect the bone marrow resulting in delayed engraftment and/or neutropenia and thrombocytopenia. Unexplainably, CMV retinitis is uncommon in the bone marrow transplantation population.

Diagnosis of CMV is difficult and is based upon clinical and laboratory findings. The documented presence of CMV without associated signs and symptoms of organ damage is referred to as CMV infection and treatment is controversial. CMV disease is the documented or strongly suspected presence of CMV accompanied by signs and symptoms and organ damage; it is treated aggressively. CMV infection occurs more often than CMV disease.

As illustrated by P.N., CMV-IP commonly presents as fever, nonproductive cough, dyspnea, and hypoxia with a diffuse pulmonary infiltrate on chest x-ray. Other opportunistic pathogens such as P. carinii pneumonia and pulmonary damage secondary to chemotherapy may present as interstitial pneumonitis; thus, detection of CMV in the lungs by bronchoalveolar lavage (BAL) or biopsy is important in confirming the diagnosis.

Gastrointestinal CMV is an erosive or ulcerative process that can occur at any location in the gut. It usually presents as epigastric pain, nausea, vomiting, diarrhea, anorexia, weight loss, or GI hemorrhage.[196] Stool cultures and endoscopic evaluation with gastrointestinal tissue biopsy and culture may aid in the diagnosis of CMV.

Laboratory diagnosis of CMV may be based upon several laboratory findings. Viral cultures of the blood buffy coat, body fluids, or tissue isolates are the diagnostic gold standard; however, detection of the virus by this method may take two to three weeks. The shell vial culture technique is a monoclonal antibody test that detects the presence of early CMV antigen by immunofluorescence on cultured cells which produce a reliable and rapid result. Thus, earlier treatment of CMV is possible. Fluid from BAL or biopsy tissue also may be examined; cells infected with CMV appear to have large intranuclear inclusion bodies. Detection of CMV IgG or IgM antibody may aid in the diagnosis but should not be used as sole method for diagnosis. CMV antibodies contained in immune globulin preparations may result in a transient presence of

CMV IgG antibodies and cannot be relied upon to confirm CMV infection or disease. Isolation of CMV from the blood, urine, or BAL fluid in an asymptomatic patient is not an indication of disease but is a significant risk factor in the marrow transplant patient for the development of disease.[197,198] Therefore, routine viral surveillance cultures may be useful in identifying patients at risk for developing CMV disease.

P.N.'s diagnosis is based upon his clinical and laboratory signs. Clinical findings suggestive of CMV disease include fever, nonproductive cough, and hypoxia. P.N.'s chest x-ray is consistent with CMV pneumonitis which is confirmed by positive shell vial cultures from the lung biopsy and blood culture. A buffy coat blood culture for CMV is pending and results will not be known for two to three weeks. Since other organisms may cause the same changes on chest x-ray, cultures are important in confirming the diagnosis. In addition, P.N. has chronic graft-versus-host disease and is CMV antibody seropositive, both of which are known to be risk factors for CMV. Although P.N. did not undergo endoscopy or GI biopsy, his persistent inability to eat and maintain weight is suggestive of CMV gastroenteritis.

27. P.N. is given ganciclovir and unselected IVIG to treat the CMV-IP. Is combination therapy necessary and, if so, why?

Treatment of CMV Interstitial Pneumonitis. Cytomegalovirus IP is the most serious manifestation of CMV. Morbidity and mortality due to CMV-IP are high and, if left untreated, mortality occurs in 80% to 90% of patients. The availability of ganciclovir and foscarnet has led to dramatic changes in the mortality due to CMV-IP. When single agent ganciclovir or CMV hyperimmune globulin is used as monotherapy for treatment of CMV-IP, improvement or increased survival rates occur in 10% to 48% of the patients.[199-204] However, when ganciclovir is combined with unselected IVIG, survival rates increase to 85% to 100%.[205,206] When combined with CMV hyperimmune globulin, reported response rates are lower.[207-209] (See Table 94.14.)

Unlike cytomegalovirus disease in patients who have received a solid organ transplant or in patients with AIDS, which responds to ganciclovir or foscarnet alone, CMV in the marrow transplant patient rarely does. Thus, treatment regimens for marrow transplant patients uniquely combine immune globulin with induction and maintenance courses of an antiviral agent. The reason for the increased efficacy of combination therapy in marrow transplant patients is unknown, but it may be due to blockade of CMV-specific cytotoxic T-lymphocyte effector cells in the lungs by the CMV antibodies contained in the immune globulin. This blockage may modify the immunologic response that results in pulmonary damage. Ganciclovir and foscarnet have a direct effect by inhibiting viral replication.

Although data are limited with foscarnet, it also is not very effective when used as monotherapy for CMV-IP.[210,211] No published trials have evaluated its use in combination with intravenous immunoglobulin. Trials have not been performed comparing ganciclovir to foscarnet for the treatment of CMV-IP.

In summary, induction therapy for the treatment of CMV-IP should consist of ganciclovir or foscarnet combined with CMV hyperimmune globulin or unselected intravenous immune globulin. Unselected IVIG is the author's preference because it is more widely available and data supporting increased efficacy of CMV-IVIG are inconclusive. None of the unselected IVIG products are FDA-approved for the treatment of CMV-IP; however, all are effective. Induction therapy should be administered for three weeks. Maintenance therapy is necessary, and although the optimal maintenance regimen is unknown, combination maintenance therapy should be administered for an additional two to three weeks or longer if pulmonary symptoms persist.

Table 94.14	Treatment of CMV-IP[a]	
Induction	Maintenance	Outcome
Ganciclovir 5 mg/kg Q 12 hr IV (range: 10–59 days); + IVIG (Gammagard) 500 mg/kg QOD (range: 10–59 days)	Ganciclovir 5 mg/kg/dose 5 days/week + IVIG 500 mg/kg Q week	11/13 (85%) responded 9/13 (69%) alive at median of 211 days[205]
Ganciclovir 2.5 mg/kg Q 8 hr IV × 20 days; + IVIG (Gammagard) 500 mg/kg QOD × 10 doses	Ganciclovir 5 mg/kg/dose 3–5 days/week × 20 doses + IVIG (Gammagard) 500 mg/kg 2×/week × 8 doses	10/10 (100%) responded 7/10 (70%) alive at median of 10 months[206]
Ganciclovir 2.5 mg/kg Q 8 hr IV × 14 days; + CMV-IVIG 400 mg/kg on days 1, 2, 7; 200 mg/kg on day 14	Ganciclovir 5 mg/kg/day × 14 days; + CMV-IVIG 200 mg/kg on day 21 (only received maintenance if symptomatic after completion of induction)	13/25 (52%) survived initial episode 8/25 (32%) long-term survival[207]
Ganciclovir 2.5 mg/kg Q 8 hr IV; + CMV-IVIG 20 gm QOD until signs and symptoms resolved	None	4/6 died[208]

[a] CMV-IP = Cytomegalovirus interstitial pneumonitis; IVIG = Intravenous immune globulin; CMV-IVIG= Cytomegalovirus hyperimmune globulin.

Treatment of CMV Gastrointestinal (GI) Disease. In the normal host, gastrointestinal CMV frequently is self-limited but in the marrow transplant patient it can be progressive and requires aggressive therapy. Ganciclovir has not yet demonstrated a definitive benefit in the treatment of gastrointestinal CMV.[212] However, due to the progressive nature and debilitating symptoms of gastroenteritis, it usually is treated with IV ganciclovir 2.5 mg/kg every eight hours or 5 mg/kg every 12 hours for two to three weeks. Maintenance therapy similar to that given for CMV-IP may be used to prevent or delay recurrences. The appropriate length of maintenance therapy is unknown. No data are available describing the use of foscarnet for the treatment of CMV gastroenteritis in marrow transplant patients. Patients who are not candidates for or are unable to tolerate ganciclovir can be treated with foscarnet 60 mg/kg IV every eight hours for two to three weeks followed by a maintenance dose of 60 mg/kg/day IV. Immune globulin in combination with ganciclovir or foscarnet may be of benefit; justification for combination therapy in gastroenteritis is based upon the CMV-IP data.

P.N.'s CMV-IP was treated with IV ganciclovir 75 mg/day and unselected IVIG 15 gm (500 mg/kg) every other day. The dose of ganciclovir had to be reduced from the standard dose of 5 mg/kg every 12 hours because of his renal insufficiency. Monthly prophylactic immune globulin was discontinued during his CMV therapy. The plan is to administer induction therapy for three weeks followed by an indefinite course of maintenance therapy. Discontinuation of maintenance therapy will depend upon P.N.'s clinical course. His white blood cell and platelet counts will be checked three times a week; electrolytes and liver function tests will be checked once a week.

Antiviral Toxicity

28. By day 15 of ganciclovir induction P.N.'s WBC count had gradually fallen to 1900 cells/mm³, ANC 930 cells/μL, and platelets 151,000/mm³. What is the most likely cause of the falling WBC count and what change in therapy should be made? [SI units: WBC 1900 × 10⁶ cells/L; ANC 930 × 10⁶ cells/L; platelets 151 × 10⁹/L]

Development of neutropenia and thrombocytopenia while on ganciclovir induction or maintenance therapy is a significant problem, particularly in bone marrow transplantation. If leukopenia develops, ganciclovir should be discontinued until the counts recover. Sargramostim (250 μg/m²/day) or filgrastim (5 μg/kg/day) IV or SQ may be used to speed recovery and titrated to maintain the absolute neutrophil count over 1000 cells/μL. However, the type of underlying malignancy should be considered before instituting a cytokine due to the potential for stimulation of residual leukemic cells. Alternatively, foscarnet may be substituted for ganciclovir. Foscarnet lacks hematologic toxicity, but it has significant renal toxicity; thus, its use should be considered carefully if other nephrotoxins such as cyclosporine and amphotericin B are used concurrently. Adequate hydration is important in minimizing renal toxicity.[213]

P.N.'s ganciclovir should be held until his absolute neutrophil count (ANC) recovers to above 1000 cells/μL. Optimally, it should be reinstituted at the same dose; however, if he is unable to maintain his ANC over 1000 cells/μL, it may require administration on an every-other-day regimen. If he has not improved clinically then an every-other-day regimen would not be acceptable because the serum concentrations may not be adequate to treat active CMV disease. Therefore, IV foscarnet induction (60 mg/kg Q 8 hr) should be instituted. However, P.N. has chronic renal insufficiency and may not tolerate the renal toxic effects of foscarnet. If P.N. receives foscarnet, he should be hydrated adequately with fluids during treatment and the dose appropriately reduced for renal insufficiency. If P.N. is unable to tolerate foscarnet, then ganciclovir should be used in combination with filgrastim 5 μg/kg/day SQ and titrated to maintain his absolute neutrophil count above 1000 cells/μL.

Prevention of Pneumocystis Carinii Pneumonia (PCP)

29. P.N. is receiving Septra, 1 single strength tablet PO BID on Mondays, Wednesdays, and Fridays. What is the rationale for its use in P.N.?

Pneumocystis is a common cause of infection in postallogeneic bone marrow transplant patients and has a high mortality rate if left untreated. (See Chapter 68: Human Immunodeficiency Virus (HIV) Infection for description, diagnosis, and treatment.) PCP prophylaxis is routine following allogeneic BMT. Data are lacking as to the best regimen in bone marrow transplantation and current practices primarily are based upon the pediatric cancer literature.[214,216] Most centers administer co-trimoxazole for PCP prophylaxis or pentamidine in patients who are allergic to sulfa drugs or who do not tolerate co-trimoxazole. See Table 94.15 for common prophylactic regimens.

PCP most commonly occurs after engraftment; therefore, co-trimoxazole usually is begun after the counts have recovered to an ANC greater than 1000 cells/μL. However, some centers admin-

Table 94.15	Common PCP Prophylactic Regimens[a]
Co-trimoxazole	5 mg/kg QD divided in 2 doses on 2 or 3 consecutive days of the week or Mon–Wed–Fri
Pentamidine aerosolized	4 mg/kg or 300 mg Q month
Pentamidine IV	4 mg/kg or 300 mg Q 2–4 weeks

[a] PCP = *Pneumocystis carinii* pneumonia.

ister co-trimoxazole throughout the neutropenic period. Because of the myelosuppressive effects of co-trimoxazole, this practice is approached with some caution and, although not proven, may delay or prevent engraftment. It is common for co-trimoxazole prophylaxis to be held postengraftment if white blood cell or platelet counts fall unexplainably. This occurs more often in patients receiving ganciclovir for CMV prophylaxis or methotrexate for graft-versus-host disease prophylaxis. Rash may occur secondary to the sulfa component in co-trimoxazole and require discontinuation. Co-trimoxazole usually is avoided on days of methotrexate administration due to the ability of sulfonamides to displace methotrexate from plasma binding sites and decrease renal MTX clearance resulting in higher methotrexate concentrations. Prophylaxis usually is continued for six months to one year posttransplant.

The routine use of PCP prophylaxis following autologous marrow transplantation is controversial and practices vary widely among centers. Autologous bone marrow recipients do not receive posttransplant immunosuppression; thus, their risk of developing PCP is lower. PCP prophylaxis probably is not necessary due to its low occurrence rate following autologous transplantation.

Update

The material presented in this section updates the information presented in Question 1 page 94-4 regarding the role of allogeneic bone marrow transplantation in the treatment of AML in first remission.

Bone Marrow Transplantation in Acute Myelogenous Leukemia (AML)

A large European multicenter, intergroup study evaluated three post-remission therapies for the treatment of AML in first remission.[217] Patients 10 to 59 years of age with previously untreated AML were eligible for the study. All patients received standardized induction and consolidation chemotherapy. Patients who achieved complete remission and had an identified HLA-matched sibling donor were scheduled for allogeneic BMT. All remaining patients who achieved complete remission were randomly assigned to undergo either an autologous BMT or a second course of consolidation chemotherapy. The conditioning regimen did not vary between the allogeneic or autologous arms and included either cyclophosphamide and total body irradiation or cyclophosphamide and busulfan. Nine hundred forty-one patients were enrolled in the trial: 144, 95, and 104 patients underwent allogeneic, autologous, and intensive chemotherapy, respectively. At a median follow-up of 3.3 years, the projected disease-free survival was higher in both bone marrow transplantation arms when compared to intensive consolidation chemotherapy (55%, 48%, and 30% for the allogeneic BMT, autologous BMT, and intensive chemotherapy arms, respectively). However, overall survival after achieving complete remission was not significantly different between the three groups (59%, 56%, and 46% for the allogeneic BMT, autologous BMT, and intensive chemotherapy arms, respectively).

Results of this well designed trial confirm results previously noted in smaller single institution studies. Compared with intensive chemotherapy, BMT improves disease-free survival for patients with AML in first remission.[217] However, higher early mortality in the BMT arms, a higher incidence of relapse in chemotherapy-treated patients and subsequent successful salvage with autologous BMT for patients previously treated with only intensified chemotherapy all combine to equalize overall survival. Whether allogeneic bone marrow transplantation is superior to autologous BMT is open to debate. Although disease-free survival favored allogeneic BMT, the difference was not statistically significant. For older patients or patients who do not have an appropriate allogeneic donor, the decision to proceed with autologous BMT in first remission appears clear. For a patient like B.S., who is young and has an identified allogeneic donor, the decision between allogeneic or autologous bone marrow transplantation is a difficult one. Either allogeneic or autologous BMT is an appropriate option. Patient specific factors and preferences of various BMT centers will determine whether a patient is treated with allogeneic or autologous bone marrow transplantation.

References

1   **Armitage JO.** Bone marrow transplantation. N Engl J Med. 1994;330:827.

2   **Thomas ED et al.** Bone-marrow transplantation. N Engl J Med. 1975;292:832.

3   **Bach FH, Sachs DH.** Current concepts: immunology. Transplantation immunology. N Engl J Med. 1987;317:489.

4   **Pinkel D.** Bone marrow transplantation in children. J Pediatr. 1993;122:331.

5   **Lenarsky C, Parkman R.** Bone marrow transplantation for the treatment of immune deficiency states. Bone Marrow Transplant. 1990;6:361.

6   **Ferrara JLM, Deeg HJ.** Graft-versus-host disease. N Engl J Med. 1991;324:667.

7   **Hansen JA et al.** The HLA system in clinical marrow transplantation. Hematol Oncol Clin North Am. 1990;4:507.

8   **McCullough J et al.** Development and operation of a program to obtain volunteer bone marrow donors unrelated to the patient. Transfusion. 1986;26:315.

9   **Beatty PG, Anasetti C.** Marrow transplantation from donors other than HLA identical siblings. Hematol Oncol Clin North Am. 1990;4:677.

10 **Keating A.** Autologous bone marrow transplantation. In: Armitage JO, Antman KH, eds. High-Dose Cancer Therapy. Pharmacology, Hematopoietins, Stem Cells. Baltimore: Williams & Wilkins; 1992:162.

11 **Applebaum FR et al.** Bone marrow transplantation or chemotherapy after remission induction in adults with acute nonlymphoblastic leukemia. Ann Intern Med. 1984;101:581.

12 **Storb R et al.** Allogeneic marrow grafting for treatment of aplastic anemia. Blood. 1974;43:157.

13 **Santos GW et al.** Marrow transplantation for acute nonlymphocytic leukemia after treatment with busulfan and cyclophosphamide. N Engl J Med. 1983;309:1347.

14 **Tutschka PJ et al.** Bone marrow transplantation for leukemia following a new busulfan and cyclophosphamide regimen. Blood. 1987;70:1382.

15 **Vassal G et al.** Is 600 mg/m^2 the appropriate dosage of busulfan in children undergoing bone marrow transplantation? Blood. 1992;79:2475.

16 **Blume KG et al.** Total body irradiation and high-dose etoposide: a new preparatory regimen for bone marrow transplantation in patients with advanced hematologic malignancies. Blood. 1987;69:1015.

17 **Zander AR et al.** High dose cyclophosphamide, BCNU, and VP-16 (CBV) as a conditioning regimen for allogeneic bone marrow transplantation for patients with acute leukemia. Cancer. 1987;59:1083.

18 **Jagannath S et al.** High-dose cyclophosphamide, carmustine, and etoposide and autologous bone marrow transplantation for relapsed Hodgkin's Disease. Ann Intern Med. 1986;104:163.

19 **Gribben JG et al.** Effectiveness of high-dose combination chemotherapy and autologous bone marrow transplantation for patients with non-Hodgkin's lymphomas who are still responsive to conventional-dose therapy. J Clin Oncol. 1989;7:1621.

20 **Peters WP et al.** High-dose chemotherapy and autologous bone marrow support as consolidation after standard-dose adjuvant therapy for high-risk primary breast cancer. J Clin Oncol. 1993;11:1132.

21 **Nichols CR et al.** High-dose carboplatin and etoposide with autologous bone marrow transplantation in refractory germ cell cancer: an eastern cooperative oncology group protocol. J Clin Oncol. 1992;10:558.

22 **Aurer I, Gale RP.** Are new conditioning regimens for transplants in acute myelogenous leukemia better? Bone Marrow Transplant. 1991;7:255.

23 **Copelan EA, Deeg HJ.** Conditioning for allogeneic marrow transplantation in patients with lymphohematopoietic malignancies without the use of total body irradiation. Blood. 1992;80:1648.

24 **Jones R, Burnett AK.** How to harvest bone marrow for transplantation. J Clin Pathol. 1992;45:1053.

25 **Bortin MM et al.** Increasing utilization of allogeneic bone marrow transplantation. Results of the 1988–1990 survey. Ann Intern Med. 1992;116:505.

26 **Champlain RE et al.** Treatment of acute myelogenous leukemia. A prospective controlled trial of bone marrow transplantation versus consolida-

tion chemotherapy. Ann Intern Med. 1985;102:285.

27 **Bortin MM et al.** Progress report from the international bone marrow transplant registry. Bone Marrow Transplant. 1992;10:113.

28 **Thomas ED et al.** Bone-marrow transplantation. N Engl J Med. 1975;292: 895.

29 **Cassileth PA et al.** Varying intensity of postremission therapy in acute myeloid leukemia. Blood. 1992;79:1924.

30 **Champlain R et al.** Postremission chemotherapy for adults with acute myelogenous leukemia: improved survival with high-dose cytarabine and daunorubicin consolidation treatment. J Clin Oncol. 1990;8:1199.

31 **Wolff SN et al.** High-dose cytarabine and daunorubicin as consolidation therapy for acute myeloid leukemia in first remission: long-term follow-up and results. J Clin Oncol. 1989;7:1260.

32 **Storb R et al.** Graft-versus-host disease and survival in patients with aplastic anemia treated by marrow grafts from HLA-identical siblings. Beneficial effect of a protective environment. N Engl J Med. 1983;308:302.

33 **Epstein JB et al.** Efficacy of chlorhexidine and nystatin rinses in prevention of oral complications in leukemia and bone marrow transplantation. Oral Surg Oral Med Oral Path. 1992;73:682.

34 **Yeager AM et al.** Autologous bone marrow transplantation in patients with acute nonlymphocytic leukemia, using ex vivo marrow treatment with 4-hydroperoxycyclophosphamide. N Engl J Med. 1986;315:141.

35 **Kessinger A.** Utilization of peripheral blood stem cells in autotransplantation. Hematol Oncol Clin North Am. 1993; 7:535.

36 **To LB et al.** Single high doses of cyclophosphamide enable the collection of high numbers of hemopoietic stem cells from the peripheral blood. Exp Hematol. 1990;18:442.

37 **Peters WP.** Comparative effects of granulocyte-macrophage colony-stimulating factor (GM-CSF) and granulocyte colony-stimulating factor (G-CSF) on priming peripheral blood progenitor cells for use with autologous bone marrow after high-dose chemotherapy. Blood. 1993;81:1709.

38 **Haas R et al.** Successful autologous transplantation of blood stem cells mobilized with recombinant human granulocyte-macrophage colony-stimulating factor. Exp Hematol. 1990;18:94.

39 **Siena S et al.** Flow cytometry for clinical estimation of circulating hematopoietic progenitors for autologous transplantation in cancer patients. Blood. 1991;77:400.

40 **Vose JM, Armitage JO.** Role of autologous bone marrow transplantation in non-Hodgkin's lymphoma. Hematol Oncol Clin North Am. 1993;7:577.

41 **Appelbaum FR et al.** Treatment of malignant lymphoma in 100 patients with chemotherapy, total body irradiation, and marrow transplantation. J Clin Oncol. 1987;5:1340.

42 **Philip T et al.** High-dose therapy and autologous bone marrow transplantation after failure of conventional chemotherapy in adults with intermediate-grade or high-grade non-Hodgkin's

lymphoma. N Engl J Med. 1987;316: 1493.

43 **Chopra R et al.** Autologous versus allogeneic bone marrow transplantation for non-Hodgkin's lymphoma: a case-controlled analysis of the European bone marrow transplant group registry data. J Clin Oncol. 1992;10:1690.

44 **Nademanee A et al.** High-dose chemoradiotherapy followed by autologous bone marrow transplantation as consolidation therapy during first complete remission in adult patients with poor-risk aggressive lymphoma: a pilot study. Blood. 1992;80:1130.

45 **Kessinger A et al.** Autologous peripheral hematopoietic stem cell transplantation restores hematopoietic function following marrow ablative therapy. Blood. 1988;71:723.

46 **Brandt ST et al.** Effect of recombinant human granulocyte-macrophage colony-stimulating factor on hematopoietic reconstitution after high-dose chemotherapy and autologous bone marrow transplantation. N Engl J Med. 1988; 318:869.

47 **Devereaux S et al.** GM-CSF accelerates neutrophil recovery after autologous bone marrow transplantation for Hodgkin's disease. Bone Marrow Transplant. 1989;4:49.

48 **Nemunaitis J et al.** Recombinant granulocyte-macrophage colony-stimulating factor after autologous bone marrow transplantation for lymphoid cancer. N Engl J Med. 1991;324:1773.

49 **Taylor KM et al.** Recombinant human granulocyte colony-stimulating factor hastens granulocyte recovery after high-dose chemotherapy and autologous bone marrow transplantation in Hodgkin's disease. J Clin Oncol. 1989; 7:1791.

50 **Sheridan WP et al.** Granulocyte colony-stimulating factor and neutrophil recovery after high-dose chemotherapy and autologous bone marrow transplantation. Lancet. 1989;2:891.

51 **Atkinson K et al.** GM-CSF after allogeneic bone marrow transplantation: accelerated recovery of neutrophils, monocytes and lymphocytes. Aust N Z J Med. 1991;21:868.

52 **De Witte T et al.** Recombinant human granulocyte-macrophage colony-stimulating factor accelerates neutrophil and monocyte recovery after allogeneic T-cell-depleted bone marrow transplantation. Blood. 1992;79:1359.

53 **Nemunaitits J et al.** Phase II trial of recombinant human granulocyte-macrophage colony-stimulating factor in patients undergoing allogeneic bone marrow transplantation from unrelated donors. Blood. 1992;79:2572.

54 **Powles R et al.** Human recombinant GM-CSF in allogeneic bone-marrow transplantation for leukaemia: double-blind, placebo-controlled trial. Lancet. 1990;336:1417.

55 **Masaoka T et al.** Recombinant human granulocyte colony-stimulating factor in allogeneic bone marrow transplantation. Exp Hematol. 1989;17:1047.

56 **Gilbert C et al.** Sequential prophylactic oral and empiric once-daily parenteral antibiotics for neutropenia and fever after high-dose chemotherapy and autologous bone marrow support. J Clin Oncol. 1994;12:1005.

57 **Peters WP et al.** Role of cytokines in autologous bone marrow transplantation. Hematol Oncol Clin North Am. 1993;7:737.

58 **Chao NJ, Blume KG.** Bone marrow transplantation. Part II-Autologous. West J Med. 1990;152:46.

59 **Gulati S.** Autologous bone marrow transplantation. Curr Probl Cancer. 1991;15:5.

60 **Anon.** Health Implications of Obesity. National Institutes of Health Consensus Development Conference Statement. Ann Intern Med. 1985;103:1073.

61 **Grochow LB et al.** Is dose normalization to weight or body surface area useful in adults? J Natl Cancer Inst. 1990;82:323. Letter.

62 **Smith TJ, Resch CE.** Neutropenia-wise and pound-foolish: safe and effective chemotherapy in massively obese patients. Southern Med J. 1991;84:883.

63 **Kasai M et al.** Toxicity of high-dose busulfan and cyclophosphamide as a preparative regimen for bone marrow transplantation. Transplant Proc. 1992; 24:1529.

64 **Vassal G et al.** Dose-dependent neurotoxicity of high-dose busulfan in children: a clinical and pharmacokinetic study. Cancer Res. 1990;50:6203.

65 **De La Camara R et al.** High dose busulfan and seizures. Bone Marrow Transplant. 1991;7:363.

66 **Sureda A et al.** High dose busulfan and seizures. Ann Intern Med. 1989; 111:543.

67 **Grigg A et al.** Busulfan and phenytoin. Ann Intern Med. 1989;111:1049.

68 **Vassal G et al.** Pharmacokinetics of high-dose busulfan in children. Cancer Chemother Pharmacol. 1989;24:386.

69 **Hows JM et al.** Comparison of mesna with forced diuresis to prevent cyclophosphamide induced haemorrhagic cystitis in marrow transplantation: a prospective randomized study. Br J Cancer. 1984;50:753.

70 **Vose JM et al.** Mesna compared with continuous bladder irrigation as uroprotection during high-dose chemotherapy and transplantation: a randomized trial. J Clin Oncol. 1993;11:1306.

71 **Atkinson K et al.** Bladder irrigation does not prevent haemorrhagic cystitis in bone marrow transplant recipients. Bone Marrow Transplant. 1991;7:351.

72 **Shepherd JD et al.** Mesna versus hyperhydration for the prevention of cyclophosphamide-induced hemorrhagic cystitis in bone marrow transplantation. J Clin Oncol. 1991;9:2016.

73 **Nicolau DP, Hogan KR.** National survey of use of mesna for the prevention of cylcophosphamide-induced hemorrhagic cystitis in recipients of bone marrow transplants. Mayo Clin Proc. 1992;67:611. Letter.

74 **Shulman HM et al.** An analysis of hepatic veno-occlusive disease and centrilobular hepatic degeneration following bone marrow transplantation. Gastroenterology. 1980;79:1178.

75 **McDonald GB et al.** The clinical course of 53 patients with veno-occlusive disease of the liver after marrow transplantation. Transplantation. 1985; 39:603.

76 **Holler E et al.** Increased serum levels of tumor necrosis factor α precede major complications of bone marrow

transplantation. Blood. 1990;75:1011.

77 **Jones RJ et al.** Veno-occlusive disease of the liver following bone marrow transplantation. Transplantation. 1987; 14:778.

78 **Ayash LJ et al.** Hepatic veno-occlusive disease in autologous bone marrow transplantation of solid tumors and lymphomas. J Clin Oncol. 1990;8:1699.

79 **McDonald GB et al.** Veno-occlusive disease of the liver and multiorgan failure after bone marrow transplantation: a cohort study of 355 patients. Ann Intern Med. 1993;118:255.

80 **McDonald GB et al.** Veno-occlusive disease of the liver after bone marrow transplantation: diagnosis, incidence, and predisposing factors. Hepatology. 1984;4:116.

81 **Bearman SI et al.** Recombinant human tissue plasminogen activator for the treatment of established severe veno-occlusive disease of the liver after bone marrow transplantation. Blood. 1992;80:2458.

82 **Bearman SI et al.** Veno-occlusive disease of the liver: development of a model for predicting fatal outcome after marrow transplantation. J Clin Oncol. 1993;11:1729.

83 **Bearman SI et al.** A pilot study of continuous infusion heparin for the prevention of hepatic veno-occlusive disease after bone marrow transplantation. Bone Marrow Transplant. 1990;5:407.

84 **Gluckman E et al.** Use of prostaglandin E1 for prevention of liver veno-occlusive disease in leukaemic patients treated by allogeneic bone marrow transplantation. Br J Haematol. 1990; 74:277.

85 **Bianco JA et al.** Phase I-II trial of pentoxifylline for the prevention of transplant-related toxicities following bone marrow transplantation. Blood. 1991; 78:1205.

86 **Clift RA et al.** A randomized controlled trial of pentoxifylline for the prevention of regimen-related toxicities in patients undergoing allogeneic marrow transplantation. Blood. 1993; 82:2025.

87 **Quinones RR.** Hematopoietic engraftment and graft failure after bone marrow transplantation. Am J Pediatr Hematol Oncol. 1993;15:3.

88 **Beatty PG et al.** Marrow transplantation from related donors other than HLA-identical siblings. N Engl J Med. 1985;313:765.

89 **Kernan NA et al.** Graft failure after T-cell-depleted human leukocyte antigen identical marrow transplants for leukemia: I. Analysis of risk factors and results of secondary transplants. Blood. 1989;74:2227.

90 **Nemunaitis J et al.** Use of recombinant human granulocyte-macrophage colony-stimulating factor in graft failure after bone marrow transplantation. Blood. 1990;76:245.

91 **Vose JM et al.** The use of recombinant human granulocyte-macrophage colony stimulating factor for the treatment of delayed engraftment following high dose therapy and autologous hematopoietic stem cell transplantation for lymphoid malignancies. Bone Marrow Transplant. 1991;7:139.

92 **Blazer BR et al.** In vivo administration of recombinant human granulocyte/macrophage colony-stimulating factor in acute lymphoblastic leukemia patients receiving purged autografts. Blood. 1989;73:849.

93 **Bortin MM.** Acute graft-versus-host disease following bone marrow transplantation in humans: prognostic factors. Transplant Proc. 1987;19:2655.

94 **Gale RP et al.** Risk factors for acute graft-versus-host disease. Br J Haematol. 1987;67:397.

95 **Beatty PG.** Results of allogeneic bone marrow transplantation with unrelated or mismatched donors. Semin Oncol. 1992;19(Suppl. 7):13.

96 **Anasetti C et al.** Effect of HLA compatibility on engraftment of bone marrow transplants in patients with leukemia or lymphoma. N Engl J Med. 1989; 320:197.

97 **Anasetti C et al.** Effect of HLA incompatibility on graft-versus-host disease, relapse, and survival after marrow transplantation for patients with leukemia or lymphoma. Hum Immunol. 1990;29:79.

98 **Bross DS et al.** Predictive factors for acute graft-versus-host disease in patients transplanted with HLA-identical bone marrow. Blood. 1984;63:1265.

99 **Weisdorf D et al.** Risk factors for acute graft-versus-host disease in histocompatible donor bone marrow transplantation. Transplantation. 1991; 51:1197.

100 **Nash RA et al.** Acute graft-versus-host disease: analysis of risk factors after allogeneic marrow transplantation and prophylaxis with cyclosporine and methotrexate. Blood. 1992;80:1838.

101 **Deeg HJ et al.** Cyclosporine as prophylaxis for graft-versus-host disease: a randomized study in patients undergoing marrow transplantation for acute nonlymphoblastic leukemia. Blood. 1985;65:1325.

102 **Ramsay NK et al.** A randomized study of the prevention of acute graft-versus-host disease. N Engl J Med. 1982;306: 392.

103 **Storb R et al.** Marrow transplantation for severe aplastic anemia: methotrexate alone compared with a combination of methotrexate and cyclosporine for prevention of acute graft-versus-host disease. Blood. 1986;68:119.

104 **Santos GW et al.** Marrow transplantation for acute non-lymphocytic leukemia after treatment with busulfan and cyclophosphamide. N Engl J Med. 1983;309:1347.

105 **Weiden PL et al.** Anti-human thymocyte globulin (ATG) for prophylaxis and treatment of graft-versus-host disease in recipients of allogeneic marrow grafts. Transplant Proc. 1978;10:213.

106 **Storb R et al.** Marrow transplantation for chronic myelocytic leukemia: a controlled trial of cyclosporine versus methotrexate for prophylaxis of graft-versus-host disease. Blood. 1985;66:698.

107 **Irle C et al.** Marrow transplantation for leukemia following fractionated total body irradiation. A comparative trial of methotrexate and cyclosporine. Leukemia Res. 1985;9:1255.

108 **Storb R et al.** Methotrexate and cyclosporine compared with cyclosporine alone for prophylaxis of acute graft versus host disease after marrow transplantation for leukemia. N Engl J Med. 1986;314:729.

109 **Storb R et al.** Methotrexate and cyclosporine versus cyclosporine alone for prophylaxis of graft-versus-host disease in patients given HLA-identical marrow grafts for leukemia: long-term follow-up of a controlled trial. Blood. 1989;73:1729.

110 **Chao NJ et al.** Cyclosporine, methotrexate, and prednisone compared with cyclosporine and prednisone for prophylaxis of acute graft-versus-host disease. N Engl J Med. 1993;329:1225.

111 **Santos GW et al.** Cyclosporine plus methylprednisolone versus cyclophosphamide plus methylprednisolone as prophylaxis for graft-versus-host disease: a randomized double-blind study in patients undergoing allogeneic marrow transplantation. Clin Transplant. 1987;1:21–28.

112 **Storb R et al.** Marrow transplantation for leukemia and aplastic anemia: two controlled trials of a combination of methotrexate and cyclosporine v cyclosporine alone or methotrexate alone for prophylaxis of acute graft-v-host disease. Transplant Proc. 1987;19:2608.

113 **Butturini A et al.** Graft-versus-leukemia following bone marrow transplantation. Bone Marrow Transplant. 1987; 2:233.

114 **Pietryga D.** Prevention and treatment of acute graft-vs.-host disease. Am J Pediatr Hematol Oncol. 1993;15:28.

115 **Martin PJ et al.** Effects of in vitro depletion of T cells in HLA-identical allogeneic marrow grafts. Blood. 1985; 66:664.

116 **Prentice HG et al.** Depletion of T lymphocytes in donor marrow prevents significant graft-versus-host disease in matched allogeneic leukemic marrow transplant recipients. Lancet. 1984;1: 472.

117 **Atkinson K et al.** Detrimental effect of intestinal disease on absorption of orally administered cyclosporine. Transplant Proc. 1983;15(Suppl. 1):2446.

118 **Storb R et al.** What role for prednisone in prevention of acute graft-versus-host disease in patients undergoing marrow transplants? Blood. 1990;76:1037.

119 **Gluckman E et al.** Use of cyclosporine as prophylaxis of graft-vs.-host disease after human allogeneic bone marrow transplantation: report of 38 patients. Transplant Proc. 1983;15(No. 4, Suppl. 1):2628.

120 **Barrett AJ et al.** Cyclosporine A as prophylaxis against graft-versus-host disease in 36 patients. Br Med J. 1982; 285:162.

121 **Gratwohl A et al.** Cyclosporine in human bone marrow transplantation. Serum concentration, graft-versus-host disease, and nephrotoxicity. Transplantation. 1983;36:40.

122 **Yee GC et al.** Serum cyclosporine concentration and risk of acute graft-versus-host disease after allogeneic marrow transplantation. N Engl J Med. 1988;319:65.

123 **Przepiorka D et al.** Cyclosporine and methylprednisolone after allogeneic marrow transplantation: association between low cyclosporine concentration and risk of acute graft-versus-host disease. Bone Marrow Transplant. 1991; 7:461.

124 **Schmidt H et al.** Correlation between low CSA plasma concentration and severity of acute GvHD in bone marrow transplantation. Blut. 1988;57:139.

125 **Kennedy MS et al.** Cyclosporine in marrow transplantation: concentration-dependent toxicity and immunosuppression in vivo. Transplant Proc. 1983;15:471.

126 **Hows JM et al.** Use of cyclosporine A in allogeneic bone marrow transplantation for severe aplastic anemia. Transplantation. 1982;33:382.

127 **Attal M et al.** Prevention of regimen-related toxicities after bone marrow transplantation by pentoxifylline: a prospective, randomized trial. Blood. 1993;82:732.

128 **Winston DJ et al.** Intravenous immune globulin for prevention of cytomegalovirus infection and interstitial pneumonia after bone marrow transplantation. Ann Intern Med. 1987;106:12.

129 **Sullivan et al.** Immunomodulatory and antimicrobial efficacy of intravenous immunoglobulin in bone marrow transplantation. N Engl J Med. 1990;323: 705.

130 **Anon.** Miles's Gamimune N recommended for approval in bone marrow transplants. FDC Rep. 1993;51(Apr 12):T&G7.

131 **Belanger C et al.** Use of an anti-interleukin-2 receptor monoclonal antibody for GVHD prophylaxis in unrelated donor BMT. Bone Marrow Transplant. 1993;11:293.

132 **Blaise D et al.** Prevention of acute GVHD by in vivo use of anti-interleukin-2 receptor monoclonal antibody (33B3.1): a feasibility trial in 15 patients. Bone Marrow Transplant. 1991; 8:105.

133 **Anasetti C et al.** Prophylaxis of graft-versus-host disease by administration of the murine anti-IL-2 receptor antibody 2A3. Bone Marrow Transplant. 1991;7:375.

134 **Gajewski J et al.** Anti-CD5-Ricin A chain immunotoxin for prevention of acute graft-versus-host disease in closely HLA matched unrelated donor bone marrow transplants. Exp Hematol. 1990;18:712. Abstract.

135 **Nevill TJ et al.** Efficacy of combined cyclosporine (CSP), methotrexate (MTX) and xomazyme-H65 prophylaxis for patients (PTS) at high risk of acute graft-versus-host disease (GVHD) after allogeneic bone marrow transplantation (BMT). Blood. 1991; 78(Suppl. 1):233a. Abstract.

136 **Przepiorka D et al.** Cyclosporine (CsA) enhances the toxicity of anti-CD5 ricin A chain immunotoxin when used to prevent acute graft-vs-host disease (AGVHD) after allogeneic marrow transplantation (BMT). Blood. 1991;78(Suppl. 1):230a. Abstract.

137 **Krance R et al.** Anti-pan T lymphocyte ricin A chain immunotoxin (H65-RTA) and methylprednisolone for acute GVHD prophylaxis following allogeneic BMT form HLA-identical sibling donors. Bone Marrow Transplant. 1993;11:33.

138 **Fay JW et al.** FK506 monotherapy for prevention of graft versus host disease after histocompatible sibling marrow transplantation. Blood. 1992;80(Suppl. 1):135a. Abstract.

139 **Holler E et al.** Role of tumor necrosis factor α in acute graft-versus-host disease and complications following allogeneic bone marrow transplantation. Transplant Proc. 1993;25:1234.

140 **Martin PJ et al.** A retrospective analysis of therapy for acute graft-versus-host disease: initial treatment. Blood. 1990;76:1464.

141 **Kennedy MS et al.** Treatment of acute graft-versus-host disease after allogeneic marrow transplantation. Randomized study comparing corticosteroids and cyclosporine. Am J Med. 1985;78: 978.

142 **Deeg HJ et al.** Treatment of human acute graft-versus-host disease with antithymocyte globulin and cyclosporine with or without methylprednisolone. Transplantation. 1985;40:162.

143 **Kanojia MD et al.** High-dose methylprednisolone treatment for acute graft-versus-host disease after bone marrow transplantation in adults. Transplantation. 1984;37:246.

144 **Bacigalupo A et al.** High dose bolus methylprednisolone for the treatment of acute graft versus host disease. Blut. 1983;46:125.

145 **Neudorf S et al.** Prevention and treatment of acute graft-versus-host disease. Semin Hematol. 1984;21:91.

146 **Doney KC et al.** Treatment of graft-versus-host disease in human allogeneic marrow graft recipients: a randomized trial comparing antithymocyte globulin and corticosteroids. Am J Hematol. 1981;11:1.

147 **Vogelsang GB et al.** Acute graft-versus-host disease: clinical characteristics in the cyclosporine era. Medicine. 1988;67:163.

148 **Gratama JW et al.** Treatment of acute graft-versus-host disease with monoclonal antibody OKT3. Clinical benefits and effect on circulating T lymphocytes. Transplantation. 1984;38:469.

149 **Weisdorf D et al.** Treatment of moderate/severe acute graft-versus-host disease after allogeneic bone marrow transplantation: an analysis of clinical risk features and outcome. Blood. 1990;75:1024.

150 **Tiley C et al.** Treatment of acute graft versus host disease with a murine monoclonal antibody to the IL-2 receptor. Bone Marrow Transplant. 1991; 7(Suppl. 2):151.

151 **Cuthbert RJG et al.** Anti-interleukin-2 receptor monoclonal antibody (BT 563) in the treatment of severe acute GVHD refractory to systemic corticosteroid therapy. Bone Marrow Transplant. 1992;10:451.

152 **Herve P et al.** Use of monoclonal antibodies in vivo as a therapeutic strategy for acute GvHD in matched and mismatched bone marrow transplantation. Transplant Proc. 1991;23:1692.

153 **Herve P et al.** Monoclonal anti TNF α antibody in the treatment of acute GvHD refractory both to corticosteroids and anti IL-2 R antibody. Bone Marrow Transplant. 1991;7(Suppl. 2): 149.

154 **Wingard JR et al.** Predictors of death from chronic graft-versus-host disease after bone marrow transplantation. Blood. 1989;74:1428.

155 **Storb R et al.** Predictive factors in chronic graft-versus-host disease in patients with aplastic anemia treated by marrow transplantation from HLA-identical siblings. Ann Intern Med. 1983;98:461.

156 **Shulman HM et al.** Chronic graft-versus-host syndrome in man. A long-term clinicopathologic study of 20 Seattle patients. Am J Med. 1980;69:204.

157 **Sullivan KM et al.** Chronic graft-versus-host disease in 52 patients: adverse natural course and successful treatment with combination immunosuppression. Blood. 1981;57:267.

158 **Sullivan KM et al.** Alternating-day cyclosporine and prednisone for treatment of high-risk chronic graft-v-host disease. Blood. 1988;72:555.

159 **Sullivan KM et al.** Prednisone and azathioprine compared with prednisone and placebo for treatment of chronic graft-v-host disease: prognostic influence of prolonged thrombocytopenia after allogeneic marrow transplantation. Blood. 1988;72:546.

160 **Vogelsang GB et al.** Thalidomide for the treatment of chronic graft-versus-host disease. N Engl J Med. 1992;326:1005.

161 **Saral R et al.** Acyclovir prophylaxis of HSV infections: a randomized double blind, controlled trial in bone marrow transplant recipients. N Engl J Med. 1981;305:63.

162 **Selby PJ et al.** The prophylactic role of intravenous and long term oral acyclovir after allogeneic bone marrow transplantation. Br J Cancer. 1989;59:434.

163 **Lundgren G et al.** Acyclovir prophylaxis in bone marrow transplant recipients. Scand J Infect Dis. 1985;(Suppl. 47):137.

164 **Hann IM et al.** Acyclovir prophylaxis against Herpes virus infections in severely immunocompromised patients: randomized double blind trial. Br Med J. 1983;287:384.

165 **Wade JC et al.** Oral acyclovir for the prevention of HSV reactivation after marrow transplantation. Ann Intern Med. 1984;100:823.

166 **Gluckman E et al.** Oral acyclovir prophylactic treatment of Herpes simplex infection after bone marrow transplantation. J Antimicrob Chemother. 1983;12(Suppl. B):161.

167 **Shepp DH et al.** Sequential intravenous and twice-daily oral acyclovir for extended prophylaxis of HSV infection in marrow transplant patients. Transplantation. 1987;43:654.

168 **Engelhard D et al.** Prevention of herpes simplex virus (HSV) infection in recipients of HLA-matched T-lymphocyte depleted bone marrow allografts. Isr J Med Sci. 1988;24:145.

169 **Meyers JD et al.** Acyclovir for prevention of cytomegalovirus infection and disease after allogeneic marrow transplantation. N Engl J Med. 1988;318:70.

170 **Goodrich JM et al.** Ganciclovir prophylaxis to prevent cytomegalovirus disease after allogeneic bone marrow transplant. Ann Intern Med. 1993;118:173.

171 **Winston DJ et al.** Ganciclovir prophylaxis of cytomegalovirus infection and disease in allogeneic bone marrow transplant recipients. Ann Intern Med. 1993;118:179.

172 **Reusser P et al.** Phase I-II trial of foscarnet for prevention of cytomegalovirus infection in autologous and allogeneic marrow transplant recipients. J Infect Dis. 1992;166:473.

173 **Lenarsky C.** Mechanisms in immune recovery after bone marrow transplantation. J Ped Hem Onc. 1993;15:49.

174 **Fehir KM et al.** Immune globulin (Gammagard) prophylaxis of CMV infections in patients undergoing organ transplantation and allogeneic bone marrow transplantation. Transplant Proc. 1989;21:3107.

175 **Kapoor N et al.** Cytomegalovirus infection in bone marrow transplant recipients: use of intravenous gamma globulin as a prophylactic and therapeutic agent. Transplant Proc. 1989;21:3095.

176 **Winston DJ et al.** Intravenous immunoglobulin for modification of cytomegalovirus infections associated with bone marrow transplantation. Preliminary results of a controlled trial. Am J Med. 1984;76(3A):128.

177 **Elfenbein G et al.** Preliminary results of a multicenter trial to prevent death from cytomegalovirus pneumonia with intravenous immunoglobulin after allogeneic bone marrow transplantation. Transplant Proc. 1987;19:138.

178 **Einsele H et al.** Significant reduction of cytomegalovirus (CMV) disease by prophylaxis with CMV hyperimmune globulin plus oral acyclovir. Bone Marrow Transplant. 1988;3:607.

179 **Winston DJ et al.** Cytomegalovirus immune plasma in bone marrow transplant recipients. Ann Intern Med. 1982;97:11.

180 **Kubanek B et al.** Preliminary data of a controlled trial of intravenous hyperimmune globulin in the prevention of cytomegalovirus infection in bone marrow transplant recipients. Transplant Proc. 1985;17:468.

181 **Jacobsen N et al.** Intravenous hyperimmune immune globulin prophylaxis against cytomegalovirus interstitial pneumonitis after allogeneic bone marrow transplantation. Tokai J Exp Clin Med. 1985;10:193.

182 **Einsele H et al.** Prevention of CMV infection after BMT in high-risk patients using CMV hyperimmune globulin. Can Detect Prevent. 1988;12:637.

183 **Petersen RB et al.** The effect of prophylactic intravenous immune globulin on the incidence of septicemia in marrow transplant recipients. Bone Marrow Transplant. 1987;2:141.

184 **O'Reilly RJ et al.** A randomized trial of intravenous hyperimmune globulin for the prevention of cytomegalovirus (CMV) infections following marrow transplantation: preliminary results. Transplant Proc. 1983;15:1405.

185 **Vu Van H et al.** A pilot study with high titered anti-cytomegalovirus globulin in patients with bone marrow transplantation. Exp Hematol. 1984;12(Suppl. 15):109.

186 **Bordigoni P et al.** Evaluation clinique et biologique du role prophylactique des immunoglobulines specifiques anti-cytomegalovirus dans les graffes medullaires. Rev Fr Hematol. 1987;29:289.

187 **Ringden O et al.** Failure to prevent cytomegalovirus infection by cytomegalovirus hyperimmune plasma: a randomized trial by the Nordic Bone Marrow Transplantation Group. Bone Marrow Transplant. 1987;2:299.

188 **Meyers JD et al.** Prevention of cytomegalovirus infection by cytomegalovirus immune globulin after marrow transplantation. Ann Intern Med. 1983;98:442.

189 **Graham-Pole J et al.** Intravenous immunoglobulin may lessen all forms of infection in patients receiving allogeneic bone marrow transplantation for acute lymphoblastic leukemia: a pediatric oncology group study. Bone Marrow Transplant. 1988;3:559.

190 **Wolff SN et al.** High-dose weekly intravenous immunoglobulin to prevent infections in patients undergoing autologous bone marrow transplantation or severe myelosuppressive therapy. Ann Intern Med. 1993;118:937.

191 **Horowitz LJ et al.** Intravenous and/or oral immunoglobulin for autologous marrow transplantation: an interim report. Autologous Bone Marrow Transplantation Proceeding of the Fourth International Symposium. University of Texas MD Anderson Cancer Center. 1989.

192 **Rowe JM et al.** Recommended guidelines for the management of autologous and allogeneic bone marrow transplant: a report from the Eastern Cooperative Oncology Group (ECOG). Ann Intern Med. 1994;120:143.

193 **Peltier N et al.** Randomized double-blinded comparison or three intravenous immune globulins products in bone marrow transplantation. Sem Hematol 1992;29(Suppl. 2):112.

194 **Reusser R et al.** CMV infection after autologous bone marrow transplantation: occurrence of CMV disease and effect on engraftment. Blood. 1990;75:1888.

195 **Wingard JR et al.** CMV infection after autologous bone marrow transplantation with comparison to infection after allogeneic bone marrow transplantation. Blood. 1988;71:1432.

196 **Goodgame RW.** Gastrointestinal cytomegalovirus disease. Ann Intern Med. 1993;119:924.

197 **Goodrich JM et al.** Early treatment with ganciclovir to prevent cytomegalovirus disease after allogeneic bone marrow transplantation. N Engl J Med. 1991;325:1601.

198 **Schmidt GM et al.** A randomized trial of prophylactic ganciclovir for cytomegalovirus pulmonary infection in recipients of allogeneic bone marrow transplants. N Engl J Med. 1991;324:1005.

199 **Reed EC et al.** Efficacy of cytomegalovirus immunoglobulin in marrow transplant recipients with cytomegalovirus pneumonia. J Infect Dis. 1987;156:641.

200 **Ettinger NA et al.** Cytomegalovirus pneumonia: the use of ganciclovir in marrow transplant recipients. J Antimicrob Chemother. 1989;24:53.

201 **Crumpacker C et al.** Treatment of cytomegalovirus pneumonia. R Infect Dis. 1988;10:S3:S538.

202 **Thomson MH, Jeffries DJ.** Ganciclovir therapy in iatrogenically immunosuppressed patients with cytomegalovirus disease. J Antimicrob Chemother. 1989;23:SE:61.

203 **Winston DJ et al.** Ganciclovir therapy for cytomegalovirus infections in recipients of bone marrow transplants and other immunosuppressed patients. R Inf Dis. 1988;10:S3:S547.

204 **Shepp DH et al.** Activity of 9- [2-hydroxy-1-(hydroxymethyl)ethoxymethyl] guanine in the treatment of cytomegalovirus pneumonia. Ann Intern Med. 1985;103:368.

205 **Schmidt GM et al.** Ganciclovir/Immunoglobulin combination therapy for the treatment of human cytomegalovirus associated interstitial pneumonia in the bone marrow allograft recipients. Transplantation. 1988;46:905.

206 **Emanuel D et al.** Cytomegalovirus pneumonia after bone marrow transplantation successfully treated with the combination of ganciclovir and high-dose intravenous immune globulin. Ann Intern Med. 1988;109:777.

207 **Reed EC et al.** Treatment of cytomegalovirus pneumonia with ganciclovir and intravenous cytomegalovirus immunoglobulin in patients with bone marrow transplants. Ann Intern Med. 1988;109:783.

208 **Aulitzky WE et al.** Ganciclovir and hyperimmunoglobulin for treating cytomegalovirus infection in bone marrow transplant recipients. J Infect Dis. 1988;158:488.

209 **Verdonck LF et al.** Treatment of cytomegalovirus pneumonia after bone marrow transplantation with cytomegalovirus immunoglobulin combined with ganciclovir. Bone Marrow Transplant. 1989;4:187.

210 **Klintman G et al.** Intravenous foscarnet for the treatment of severe cytomegalovirus infection in allograft recipients. Scand J Infect Dis. 1985;17:157.

211 **Ringden O et al.** Pharmacokinetics, safety and preliminary clinical experiences using foscarnet in the treatment of cytomegalovirus infections in bone marrow and renal transplant recipients. J Antimicrob Chemother. 1986;17:373.

212 **Reed EC et al.** Ganciclovir for the treatment of cytomegalovirus gastroenteritis in bone marrow transplant patients; a randomized, placebo controlled trial. Ann Intern Med. 1990;112:505.

213 **Deray G et al.** Foscarnet nephrotoxicity: mechanism, incidence and prevention. Am J Nephrol. 1989;9:316.

214 **Hughes WT et al.** Successful chemoprophylaxis for *Pneumocystis carinii* pneumonitis. N Engl J Med. 1977;297:1419.

215 **Hughes WT et al.** Successful intermittent chemoprophylaxis for *Pneumocystis carinii* pneumonitis. N Engl J Med. 1987;316:1627.

216 **Harris RE et al.** Prevention of Pneumocystis pneumonia: use of continuous sulfamethoxazole-trimethoprim therapy. Am J Dis Child. 1980;134:35.

217 **Zittoun RA et al.** Autologous or allogeneic bone marrow transplantation compared with intensive chemotherapy in acute myelogenous leukemia. N Engl J Med. 1995;332:217–23.

Pediatric Considerations

Ann M Bolinger
CY Jennifer Chan

Teething	95-2
Natal Teeth	95-2
Normal Eruption of Primary Teeth	95-2
Signs and symptoms	95-2
Treatment	95-2
General management	95-2
Aspirin and acetaminophen	95-2
Diaper Rash	95-2
Etiology	95-2
Clinical presentation	95-3
Treatment	95-3
Fever	95-3
Clinical Presentation and Treatment	95-3
Risk of febrile seizures	95-3
Antipyretic therapy	95-3
Vomiting and Diarrhea	95-4
Pathogenesis (See Table 95.1)	95-4
Treatment	95-4
Viral gastroenteritis (See Table 95.2)	95-4
Assessment of dehydration	95-5
Oral replacement therapy (See Table 95.3)	95-5
Reinstitution of oral feedings	95-6
Drug therapy	95-6
Gastroesophageal Reflux (GER)	95-6
Treatment	95-6
Positional and dietary measures	95-6
Drug therapy (See Table 95.4)	95-7
Bethanechol	95-7
Prokinetic agents	95-7
Immunizations (See Table 95.5)	95-7
Guidelines and Routine Schedule (See Table 95.6)	95-7
Contraindications	95-9
Adverse Effects (See Table 95.7)	95-9
Pertussis	95-9
Adverse effects	95-9
Acellular vaccine	95-11
Tetanus (See Table 95.8)	95-11
Polio	95-11
Measles/Mumps/Rubella (MMR)	95-12
Measles	95-12
Mumps	95-12
Rubella	95-12
Haemophilus influenzae Type b (Hib) Vaccine	95-12
Varicella Vaccine	95-13; 95-25
Recommendations for Immunocompromised Patients	95-13
Hemolytic Uremic Syndrome (HUS)	95-14
Clinical Presentation	95-14
Treatment	95-14
Correction of hemostatic and electrolyte imbalances	95-14
Antiplatelet agents	95-14
Plasmapheresis	95-15
Heparin	95-15
Vitamin E	95-15
Thrombolytic drugs	95-15
Exchange transfusion and fresh frozen plasma	95-15
Prognosis	95-15
Short Stature	95-15
Growth Hormone Deficiency (GHD)	95-15
Growth hormone replacement	95-15
Adverse effects	95-16
Growth hormone-releasing factor (GHRF)	95-16
Dopamine agonists and clonidine	95-16
Other Diagnoses	95-16
Idiopathic Thrombocytopenic Purpura (ITP)	95-17
Clinical Presentation	95-17
Treatment	95-17
Splenectomy	95-17
Steroids	95-17
Intravenous gamma globulin (IVIG)	95-18
Dosing (See Table 95.9)	95-18
Goals of therapy	95-18
Prognosis	95-18
Chronic idiopathic thrombocytopenic purpura	95-18
Enuresis	95-19
Evaluation	95-19
Treatment	95-19
Conditioning therapy	95-19
Bladder training	95-20
Motivational counseling	95-20
Drug therapy	95-20
Imipramine	95-20
Oxybutynin	95-20
Desmopressin (DDVAP)	95-20
Sedation and Analgesia	95-20
Sedation	95-20
Conscious sedation	95-20
Intensive care unit (ICU) sedation	95-22
Analgesia	95-22
Administration schedules	95-22
Routes of administration	95-23
Narcotic agents (See Table 95.11)	95-23
Nonnarcotic analgesics	95-23
Adverse effects	95-23
Tolerance and drug withdrawal	95-23
Topical Anesthetics (See Table 95.12)	95-24
Drug Administration	95-25
Oral Medications	95-25
Ear Drops	95-25
Nose Drops	95-25
Eye Drops	95-25

Drug therapy in pediatric patients presents a unique dilemma in the management and monitoring of disease. Establishing safe and effective therapeutic regimens for children is challenging. From birth through adolescence, the pediatric patient is continually changing with respect to growth, psychosocial development, and pharmacodynamic response. In addition, information on drug therapy in pediatric patients is limited. Approximately 75% of all drugs do not have approval by the Food and Drug Administration (FDA) for use in children. This is due to many factors including a lack of interest by clinicians and manufacturers to seek FDA approval, difficulty with parental consent, and significant pharmacokinetic interpatient variability. As a result, many indications and drug dosages are based upon clinical experience instead of large clinical trials.

Child health maintenance, prevention of common childhood diseases, and supportive care are important aspects of pediatric practice. This chapter addresses issues of disease prevention, supportive care, and the management of selected problems in the pediatric population.

Teething

The growth and development of teeth begin as early as the sixth week of embryonic life. By the sixth month of gestation, all 20 teeth are formed and calcification of the enamel and dentin has begun. At birth, the deciduous cuspids are partially calcified and the development of permanent teeth is underway.[1]

Normal eruption of primary or deciduous teeth rarely begins before four to five months of age and usually is completed by 30 months of age. Premature infants usually exhibit delayed eruption of their deciduous teeth based upon chronological age. Based upon conceptual age, however, premature infants will get their first tooth at the same time as full-term infants.[1] Teething usually is uneventful and often asymptomatic.

A significant number of full-term infants erupt no teeth until the end of the first year. Delayed eruption of all teeth, however, may indicate systemic or nutritional disturbances such as hypothyroidism, hypopituitarism, rickets, or a prenatal event.[2] Early eruption is less common but has been associated with hyperthyroidism, precocious puberty, and long-term steroid therapy.

Natal Teeth

1. C.J., a baby girl, was born with a tooth that was removed postpartum. While obtaining discharge medications, her mother expresses concern regarding the baby's dental care. C.J.'s mother is worried that C.J. will not develop baby teeth normally. What information should the mother receive?

Occasionally, infants may be born with teeth, called natal teeth. Usually there are two in the position of the mandibular central incisors. The incidence of natal teeth is approximately 1 in 2000 to 3500 live births. Treatment of this problem depends upon the maturity of the crown and root and the danger of dislodgment. Often these teeth are poorly formed with minimal root structure and thus are very loose. These rudiments, therefore, should be extracted to prevent their aspiration by the infant. If the teeth are well developed, calcified, and firm, they do not have to be removed. The mother should be told that the presence and removal of natal teeth will not interfere with the normal eruption of primary teeth.

Occasionally, the mother may experience some breast irritation from the natal teeth. Application of collodion to the areola of the breast may protect it from abrasion.

Normal Eruption of Primary Teeth

Signs and Symptoms

2. Six months later, C.J. has become increasingly irritable and has been waking up 4 to 5 times a night. She also seems to be drooling excessively and biting on hard objects constantly. A brief examination of C.J.'s mouth shows red and tender gums. No teeth are present, and C.J. is afebrile. The mother is concerned that her baby's teething has caused a secondary illness. Are these symptoms unusual?

C.J.'s regular sleeping pattern has been disturbed by symptomatic teething. As the teeth penetrate the gums, the site may become tender; this process also may be associated with increased salivation. Bacterial invasion through a break in the tissue or under a gingival flap covering the teeth may cause inflammation and edema, but "teething" does not cause systemic disturbances.[3] In general, tooth eruption bears no relationship to the incidence of pediatric infections, diarrhea, fever, rashes, or convulsions. Teething, however, has been associated with restlessness, increased salivation, thumb-sucking, gum-rubbing, and sometimes, a decreased appetite. Some investigators believe that the signs and symptoms which appear during the teething period are coincidental and related to normal physiologic growth and development.[4]

Treatment

3. What course of treatment can be suggested for C.J.?
General Management. Gentle irrigation with water often relieves the inflammation around a gum flap. A topical anesthetic applied with a cotton-tipped applicator may be rubbed gently on the mucous membranes overlying the erupting tooth. Although the American Dental Association has not endorsed any product for teething, a number of nonprescription products are available.[5] Long-term use of local anesthetics is not recommended. Topical anesthetics containing lidocaine are not recommended for the symptomatic relief of deciduous teeth because infants may absorb significant amounts of lidocaine, which can lead to systemic toxicity.

Other palliative measures include having the child chew on a blunt, firm object or cracked ice wrapped in a soft cloth to hasten tooth eruption and relieve pain. Rubber teething rings of various shapes may be beneficial; however, trauma from the teething ring can lead to angular cheilitis.[6] In addition, water-containing rings should be avoided since these can become infected with bacteria. Gingival incision for teething is rarely indicated. Proprietary teething aids which contain mercurial compounds should not be used because of possible systemic toxicity.

Aspirin and Acetaminophen. Both analgesics are commonly prescribed for younger children to relieve pain associated with the eruption of primary dentition. Since both drugs can produce serious side effects, dosage recommendations should be strictly followed. Topical aspirin should never be used because it can cause oral chemical burns.

Diaper Rash
Etiology

Dermatitis limited to the diaper area is a frequent problem in pediatric practice. Most authorities believe these rashes represent contact dermatitis caused by prolonged contact with urine or stool. While the pathogenesis of diaper dermatitis is not well defined, a combination of factors is associated with skin inflammation in the diaper area. These include irritants, occlusion, friction, and fungal or bacterial overgrowth.[7,8]

Various components of urine or stool have been implicated, including ammonia, bacteria, bacterial by-products, urine and fecal pH, *Candida albicans*, and water alone; however, no single cause can be isolated. The theory of ammonia-induced rashes has been challenged by studies which have demonstrated similar urine ammonia concentrations in infants with and without diaper rash. Once the skin integrity has been compromised by prolonged exposure to moisture and friction, however, ammonia does produce a more severe inflammatory state than saline alone.[9]

Direct irritation by an alkaline urine (pH 8 to 9) or stool may be responsible.[8] A persistent rash may represent infection with *C.

albicans. Other potential irritants which should be suspected include residual chemicals or laundry detergents in the diaper (cloth or disposable), or a soap, medication, or lotion that has been applied directly to the infant's skin.

Plastic pants or waterproof disposable diapers are associated with a higher prevalence of diaper rash.[10] A moisture-proof barrier, however, will not result in more favorable growth conditions for skin bacteria if the wet diaper is changed promptly.

Clinical Presentation

There are four clinical presentations of dermatitis associated with diaper wear: 1) a mild, scaling rash in the perianal area; 2) a sharply demarcated confluent erythema; 3) ulceration distributed through the diaper area; and 4) a beefy red confluent erythema with satellite lesions, vesiculopustular lesions, and diffuse involvement of the genitalia.

Treatment

4. K.G., a 3-month-old infant, has had a severe "diaper rash" for the past 4 days. It is confined to the diaper area, is very inflamed and tender, and there are vesicular satellite lesions on the periphery of the main erythematous area. K.G.'s mother uses only cloth diapers and has not changed soap or her normal pattern of diaper care since K.G. was born. Based upon the clinical appearance of the rash and its long duration, the clinician prescribed nystatin (Mycolog II) ointment and gave the mother instructions for treatment. Why was nystatin prescribed? How should diaper rash be treated and prevented?

K.G.'s rash is consistent with a candidal infection which typically is beefy red and associated with vesicular satellite lesions. Presence of a rash for more than three days and diffuse involvement of the genitalia and inguinal folds also are characteristic of this form of diaper rash. K.G.'s rash can be treated with nystatin powder or ointment applied to the rash four times daily until it has resolved. Alternatively, clotrimazole cream (Lotrimin) can be used.

General treatment measures include removal of the primary irritant by gentle rinsing with plain water, followed by application of a drying agent, such as cornstarch, to minimize friction. Talcum powder should be avoided or used cautiously since the infant may aspirate the talc particles, which potentially is fatal.[11] Baking soda should be avoided as well since transcutaneous absorption of sodium bicarbonate can cause metabolic alkalosis.[12] Although many believe that cornstarch is a culture media for *C. albicans*, this has not been substantiated.[13] Its use, therefore, appears to be both safe and effective.

Other prevention and treatment measures should include the following: 1) Change the diaper as soon as it is wet or at least every two to four hours, including a change at night. 2) Avoid the overnight use of plastic pants or disposable diapers; instead, "triple diaper" the infant with cotton diapers and use a rubber pad. 3) Expose the diaper area to air as frequently as possible. 4) If cotton diapers are used, rinse with diluted vinegar (i.e., 1 cup of white vinegar in ½ of a washing machine full of water for ½ hour) to reduce the alkalinity of the diaper. 5) Apply 0.5% to 1% hydrocortisone ointment twice daily for up to one week when severe inflammation is present.[8]

Fever

Fever is a symptom that frequently causes parents to seek medical care for their children. Fever is defined as an oral temperature greater than 37.3 °C or in children less than five years of age, a rectal temperature greater than 37.9 °C. Children with fevers may or may not have other signs or symptoms suggesting a focus or cause of illness. In general, four groups of children having fever require special attention: infants less than two months of age with any fever; children between 6 and 24 months of age with temperature measurements greater than 38.9 °C accompanied by abnormal white blood cell (WBC) counts; all children with temperature measurements greater than 41.0 °C; and children with fever who have been diagnosed with asplenia.[14]

Fever in children less than two months of age is not predictive of the degree of illness. Clinical manifestations of a serious infection often are subtle and nonspecific. Therefore, any child less than two months of age who develops a fever requires a complete evaluation that includes blood culture, urinalysis, and lumbar puncture. In addition, antibiotic therapy should be initiated while awaiting the results of the studies.

Children between 6 and 24 months of age with fever greater than 38.9 °C and WBC counts less than 5000/mm³ or greater than 15,000/mm³ are at an increased risk for bacteremia. Blood cultures, lumbar puncture, urinalysis, and chest x-ray should be considered on an individual basis to help determine the cause of infection.

Children with functional or anatomic asplenia are at an increased risk of fulminant infection caused by *S. pneumonia*, *Salmonella sp.*, *E. coli*, and other gram-negative organisms. Febrile children with asplenia should receive prompt antibiotic therapy.

Temperature elevations greater than 41 °C frequently are associated with bacterial disease. Children of any age who develop a fever greater than 41 °C should be evaluated for bacteremia and meningitis.

Clinical Presentation and Treatment

5. R.B. is a 12-month-old, 10 kg baby boy. His mother calls to request advice about the treatment of a fever in R.B. She states that R.B. was well until yesterday afternoon when he felt warm to her touch. For the past 24 hours, he has remained warm and is fussy and less active. A rectal temperature taken 15 minutes ago was 39 °C. Although the pediatrician said that R.B. only has a viral infection, she is worried that R.B.'s temperature will continue to rise and that he might have a seizure. She asks what can be done to safely lower R.B.'s temperature. Are R.B.'s mother's concerns valid? How should R.B.'s febrile illness be treated?

Risk of Febrile Seizures

Febrile seizures occur in approximately 4% of children between the ages of six months and six years who have temperature elevations greater than 38 °C.[15,16] The etiology and pathogenesis are not known but the absolute temperature recording and the rate of temperature increase appear to be important factors.[17] In addition, there appears to be a genetic influence as febrile seizures occur with greater frequency among family members.[18] There are two types of febrile seizures: simple and complex. Simple febrile seizures last less than 15 minutes and do not have significant focal features. Complex febrile seizures have a longer duration, occur in series, and are associated with focal changes. Typically, febrile seizures occur within the first 24 hours of a febrile episode.[15] Although R.B. is in the age group at greatest risk for having a febrile seizure, he has been febrile for more than 24 hours and it is unlikely that a seizure will occur during this illness.

Antipyretic Therapy

Acetaminophen is the most common antipyretic agent used in children. The usual oral or rectal dose is 10 to 15 mg/kg/dose administered every four to six hours as needed to a maximum of 65 mg/kg/day. Other alternatives include aspirin or ibuprofen. Aspirin also is recommended to be administered orally (PO) or rectally (PR) as 10 to 15 mg/kg/dose, although caution should be used as salicylic acid may accumulate with repeated dosing when using the upper range of this guideline.[19] Aspirin therapy is not recommended for treatment of fever in children or adolescents with chickenpox or respiratory viral infections because of its association with Reye's syndrome.[20-22] Reye's syndrome is a rare illness affecting otherwise healthy children that consists of an acute non-inflammatory encephalopathy, hepatic dysfunction, and various metabolic derangements.[20] Reye's syndrome is associated with a 10% to 40% mortality, although these numbers have decreased in recent years due to early diagnosis and aggressive therapy.[21,23]

Ibuprofen was approved for use as an antipyretic in children in 1989. It is administered as 5 to 10 mg/kg/dose orally every six to eight hours as needed to a maximum of 40 mg/kg/day. Controlled studies have demonstrated that as an antipyretic, ibuprofen is as effective as acetaminophen.[24-26] These studies also reported a low incidence of adverse effects when ibuprofen was used to treat fever.

Acetaminophen, aspirin, and ibuprofen all would be effective in lowering R.B.'s fever. However, it also is important to consider potential adverse effects when selecting therapy. Acetaminophen clearly is the safest agent and typically is considered to be a first-line drug in children. Aspirin, because of its association with Reye's syndrome, is avoided in pediatric patients with viral infections. Ibuprofen is an alternative in R.B. since studies have documented only limited adverse effects when it is used for antipyresis. However, since experience with this agent still is relatively limited, it should be considered second-line therapy at this time.

Vomiting and Diarrhea

Vomiting and diarrhea are two commonly encountered complaints in pediatric practice. Most cases are self-limited but severe cases can result in serious complications, such as dehydration, metabolic disturbances, and even death. Infants and young children are particularly prone to more severe complications.

Pathogenesis

Vomiting or emesis is defined as forceful expulsion of gastrointestinal (GI) contents through the mouth or nose. In newborns, regurgitation of small amounts of formula after feeding, especially when burping, is common. In most cases, regurgitation usually resolves by one year of age and rarely causes a problem.[27] Therefore, extensive evaluation is not needed in a child who is growing well. Other causes of vomiting during the newborn period include pyloric stenosis, gastroesophageal reflux, overfeeding, food intolerance, and GI obstruction. Beyond the neonatal period, the most common cause of vomiting is infection.

Conditions causing emesis in older infants and children range from viral gastroenteritis to more severe illnesses that require immediate medical attention such as bowel obstruction or head injury (see Table 95.1).[27,28] Acute vomiting also may result from medication or toxic ingestions. Other pathologic vomiting in infants and children may be caused by central nervous system (CNS) disease (e.g., intracranial tumors), metabolic disease (e.g., urea cycle disorder), inflammatory bowel disease, and ulcers. In teenagers, psychological or emotional disorders such as bulimia also should be considered.

Diarrhea refers to an increase in frequency, volume, or liquidity of stool when compared to the child's normal bowel movements. In developing countries, diarrhea is a common cause of death. In the U.S., it is estimated that 16.5 million children less than five years of age have between 21 and 37 million cases of diarrheal disease each year. Of these cases, 10% lead to a physician visit and a total of 220,000 children are hospitalized.[29]

Acute diarrhea is abrupt in onset and usually lasts a few days with most cases having a viral etiology. Infectious diarrhea will be

Table 95.1	Causes of Vomiting in Infants and Children[a,27,28]
Causes	**Other Signs and Symptoms**
Drug-induced	Nausea
Cancer chemotherapy	
Narcotics	
Theophylline/aminophylline	
Antibiotics	
Alcohol	
Anesthetics	
Metabolic or endocrine disorders	Alteration in behavior
Infectious diseases	Fever
Otitis media	Symptoms of otitis media
Meningitis	Stiff neck, toxic appearance
Appendicitis	Abdominal pain
Urinary tract infection/pyelonephritis	Dysuria, frequency and urgency in older children
Viral or bacterial gastroenteritis	Diarrhea
Mechanical obstruction	
Bowel obstruction	Abdominal distention, green emesis
Pyloric stenosis	Projectile nonbilious vomiting
Inflammatory	Abdominal pain
Pancreatitis	
Inflammatory bowel	Diarrhea
PUD	Black or red vomitus
Psychological	
Chemotherapy	
Bulimia	
Miscellaneous	
Gastroesophageal reflux	Usually self-limited. Indications for evaluation include recurrent pneumonia, poor growth, GI blood loss, dysphagia or heartburn
↑ intracranial pressure	Mental status alternation
Head injury/trauma	History of trauma, mental status changes
Food or milk intolerance or allergy	Irritability, loose stool, blood in stool

a GI = Gastrointestinal; PUD = Peptic ulcer disease.

discussed in Chapter 60: Gastrointestinal Infections. Chronic diarrhea is caused by a variety of problems including malabsorption, inflammatory disease, alteration of intestinal flora, milk or protein intolerance, and drugs.[27]

Infants and children are at high risk for morbidity and mortality secondary to diarrhea for several reasons. Once a child no longer benefits from the passive immunity provided by breast milk, he becomes susceptible to potential pathogens until he develops his own immunity. Also, acute net intestinal fluid losses are relatively much greater in young children than in adults, possibly due to inefficient transport systems in the developing intestine. In addition, the percent of total body water in children is higher than adults; thus, they are more susceptible to body fluid shifts. Total body water changes from 87% of total body weight in premature infants to 77% in full-term infants, and 56% in adults.[30] Lastly, the renal capacity to compensate for fluid and electrolyte imbalances in the infant is limited compared to an adult's.[31]

Treatment

Viral Gastroenteritis

6. J.R., a 15-month-old male infant, began vomiting this morning but has not had a fever or diarrhea. Upon questioning, you discover that many children attending day care with J.R. are experiencing vomiting, diarrhea, and low-grade temperatures. How should J.R.'s vomiting be treated?

Routine use of antiemetics for acute vomiting in children is not recommended because the effectiveness of antiemetics in viral gastroenteritis has not been demonstrated and side effects commonly are reported. In addition, it may delay the diagnosis of a treatable illness.[32-34]

Parents should be educated on the signs and symptoms of serious illness that warrant medical attention. A pediatrician should be contacted if a child is toxic-appearing or has unusual behavior, abdominal pain or distention, red or black vomitus, or signs of an ear infection. In addition, a pediatrician should be called if there is a history or suspicion of toxic ingestion or head trauma. Fever may accompany vomiting in viral gastroenteritis. A physician should be notified of any fever occurring in a neonate; in older infants and children, a change in fever pattern or prolonged fever also warrant seeking medical attention.

When communicating information regarding a vomiting child, it is helpful if the parents have knowledge of the child's fluid intake along with the frequency of vomiting and urination. It is easy to overestimate the amount of vomitus. To estimate volume, one tablespoon makes a spot four inches in diameter and a quarter-cup makes a spot approximately eight inches in diameter.[28]

Vomiting associated with gastroenteritis usually resolves in 24 to 48 hours. The most important treatment during this period is fluid and electrolyte replacement (see Question 8). Infants are particularly susceptible to the development of fluid and electrolyte abnormalities.

J.R.'s vomiting should be managed by withholding food or drink for two hours. Then, 5 to 10 mL of an oral rehydration solution should be administered every 10 to 15 minutes, increasing the volume gradually as tolerated. If vomiting recurs, wait 30 to 60 minutes and repeat the hydration fluid.[35-37] The minimum amount of fluid required to maintain fluid balance is listed in Table 95.2. More than 90% of infants will tolerate hydration fluid when frequent small amounts are given. Using a spoon to administer the fluid may be more effective than using a nipple or cup.[28,38] After 24 hours, J.R. may be given carbohydrate-containing solids such as crackers or jello. A normal diet may be resumed in 48 to 72 hours.

Assessment of Dehydration

7. On the 2nd day of illness, J.R. develops a mild fever and diarrhea that has increased in frequency and water content. How can the severity of J.R.'s diarrhea be assessed? Should he be hospitalized for intravenous (IV) fluid replacement, or can he be treated on an outpatient basis?

To determine whether intravenous fluid replacement is needed, consider the following questions: Does the child have any of the following signs and symptoms of dehydration? A depressed fontanel (useful up to 6 months of age), sunken eyes, dry mucus membranes, crying without tears, a diminished urine output, a fever without perspiration, or thirst.

Are a large number of copious stools still being produced? Is there a risk of dehydration from inadequate monitoring, or is the parent unable to care for the child? Specific inquiries should be made about the number and consistency of stools in children with

diarrhea. Are other signs and symptoms present, such as lethargy, severe emesis, or a history of convulsions, that preclude management at home? Estimating the degree of dehydration is particularly valuable in assessing the patient with diarrhea; weight loss is a good criterion. A 5% weight loss is considered mild dehydration; up to 10% is considered moderate, and greater than 10% is severe or life-threatening dehydration. See Chapter 99: Pediatric Nutrition for a discussion on IV replacement therapy in children with ≥10% dehydration.

Oral Replacement Therapy

8. Upon questioning, it is determined that J.R. is not dehydrated. What recommendations can be made regarding the management of J.R. on an outpatient basis?

The object of therapy is to avoid significant dehydration and restore or maintain adequate hydration and electrolyte balance. Mild to moderate diarrhea *without dehydration* generally is managed at home by discontinuing intake of solids and giving the child oral hypotonic electrolyte solutions containing glucose.[39,40] Glucose provides a caloric source and enhances the absorption of salt and water in the small intestine by mechanisms that usually are unimpaired in many toxin-induced diarrheas. Previously, parents were instructed to prepare salt and sugar solutions at home; however, frequent errors in preparing the solutions led to problems in fluid and electrolyte balance. Commercially available oral electrolyte solutions containing glucose should be used in infants and young children because of their susceptibility to imbalance. Gatorade is an alternative for older children. Other liquids which can be used at home include "decarbonated" beverages, flavored gelatin products mixed at half the strength recommended on the package, or fruit juices. Homemade remedies do not contain appropriate compositions of electrolytes and should not be used exclusively.[41]

The World Health Organization (WHO) has promoted the use of an oral replacement solution (WHO formula) containing sodium (90 mEq/L), potassium (20 mEq/L), bicarbonate (30 mEq/L), chloride (80 mEq/L), and 2.5% glucose for the widespread management of acute diarrhea. This has resulted in a new generation of oral electrolyte solutions which differ in two significant ways: glucose concentrations have been decreased and sodium concentrations have been increased. The quantity of sodium loss in secretory diarrhea ranges from 60 mEq/L to as high as 120 mEq/L. Malabsorptive diarrheas, such as those secondary to rotavirus infections, have much lower sodium concentrations, usually less than 40 mEq/L. Unlike sodium, potassium concentrations in the stool do not vary according to the infecting organism. These concentrations range from 20 to 35 mEq/L of stool water.[42] Glucose is added to oral electrolyte solutions to enhance glucose-coupled sodium transport; however, concentrations greater than 3% may actually impair sodium absorption. At this level the glucose-coupled sodium transport system is saturated and any additional glucose acts as an osmotically active solute in the bowel lumen. The electrolyte content of commonly used oral solutions is provided in Table 95.3.

9. How should J.R. be managed if his diarrhea causes mild dehydration? Can oral hydration be employed in J.R.? When should oral feeding be reinstituted?

Oral electrolyte solutions can be used to treat mild dehydration and maintain fluid balance.

Oral replacement is contraindicated in the presence of: 1) shock with inability to drink, 2) persistent vomiting, and 3) stool losses exceeding 100 mL/kg/hour which makes oral replacement impractical.

The American Academy of Pediatrics recommends that oral electrolyte solutions containing 75 to 90 mEq/L of sodium be used for rehydration in situations of mild dehydration caused by diar-

Table 95.2	Oral Fluid Requirements[28]
Weight	Minimum Amount of Fluid/Day
10 lb (4.5 kg)	450 mL (15 oz)
20 lb (9.1 kg)	690 mL (23 oz)
30 lb (13.6 kg)	1050 mL (35 oz)
40 lb (18.1 kg)	1200 mL (40 oz)

Table 95.3   Oral Electrolyte Solutions[28,35,36,41]

Solution	Sodium (mEq/L)	Potassium (mEq/L)	Carbo-hydrate (gm/L)	Osmolality
Rehydration				
Rehydralyte	75	20	25	305
WHO formula	90	20	25	310
Maintenance				
Infalyte	50	25	20	290
Pedialyte	45	20	25	250
Resol	50	20	20	270
Ricelyte	50	25	30	200
Home remedies				
Jell-O	15–27	0.1–20	100–150	570–640
Apple juice	0.1–3.5	24–32	120	650–734
Gatorade	20	3	46	330
Gingerale	0.8–5.5	0.1–1.5	53	520–560
Chicken broth	140–251	1.5–8.2	—	380–500

rhea. Volume equal to estimated fluid deficit (usually 40 to 50 mL/kg) should be given over about four hours. The patient should be reassessed after completion of rehydration. For maintenance therapy, solutions containing 40 to 60 mEq/L of sodium should be used. Maintenance hydration also should include replacement of ongoing losses. For each diarrheal stool, approximately 10 mL/kg of oral electrolyte solution should be given. It is recommended that the volume of solutions containing 40 to 60 mEq/L of sodium should not exceed 150 mL/kg/day. If additional fluid is needed, water or breast milk should be used.[37,38]

Reinstitution of Oral Feedings. Refeeding children after a bout of diarrhea may present some problems. In the past, delayed feeding has been recommended to avoid the consequences of malabsorption. Malabsorption of carbohydrate, especially lactose, is common during and after diarrhea but typically is self-limited; malabsorption of fat and protein also may be present. Currently, mothers are encouraged to continue breast-feeding their children during the episode or to reinstitute breast-feeding six to eight hours after oral replacement of fluid losses.[43] Theoretical advantages of continued feeding during diarrhea include: prevention of protein and energy deficits, maintenance or repair of intestinal mucosa and enzyme concentration, and sustained breast-feeding.[44]

If the child has been receiving solids before the bout of diarrhea, a gradual return of these foods is suggested. High-carbohydrate foods present a significant osmotic load to the damaged intestinal lumen and should be avoided. The milk or formula the child has been receiving should be restarted at half-strength for a day or two, then full-strength can be given.[31,45] If the child is lactose intolerant, a lactose-free formula may be substituted for two to six weeks until normal function of gastrointestinal lactase returns.

Drug Therapy

10. What medications can be recommended for the treatment of diarrhea in children?

Medications play a minor role in the treatment of acute infantile diarrhea. Antibiotics should only be used when systemic bacteremia is suspected, in infants with compromised defenses, or in any child with a persistent enteric infection that is sensitive to antibiotics.[31] Antidiarrheal preparations which contain anticholinergic agents should not be used in children less than two years old.[46] Deaths have been reported in infants who received anticholinergic agents and continued to accumulate fluid in the GI tract. Drugs which alter gastrointestinal motility should be avoided, especially in those children with high fever, toxemia, or bloody, mucoid stools, since they may worsen the clinical course of the bacterial infection. Other supportive therapies with agents such as lactobacillus preparations, which are given to recolonize the intestine with saccharolytic flora and to alter the intestinal pH, are ineffective.[47] Adsorbents, such as Kaopectate, adsorb bacterial toxins and water and improve the symptoms of diarrhea by producing more formed stools; however, they do not decrease the duration of diarrhea, or fluid and electrolyte losses. Their disadvantages include adsorption of nutrients, enzymes, and antibiotics, especially with prolonged use.[48]

Gastroesophageal Reflux (GER)

Gastroesophageal reflux is a common disorder in infants. GER also occurs in older children, but it runs a different course which is similar to GER in adults. There are a number of factors involved in the pathogenesis of infant GER. Occasionally, a hiatal hernia is involved. Other factors include decreased lower esophageal sphincter (LES) pressure, decreased muscle mass, motor dysfunction of the esophagus, and decreased gastric emptying.[49,50] Possible complications of untreated GER include strictures secondary to esophagitis, gastrointestinal hemorrhage, aspiration leading to chronic respiratory disease, and apnea. Deaths have occurred secondary to aspiration, malnutrition, or prolonged apnea.

The most common symptom of GER in infants is vomiting or regurgitation. Other signs and symptoms include failure to thrive, recurrent pneumonia, apnea, dysphagia, hematemesis, and anemia.[51] The diagnosis is based upon the clinical presentation and tests that measure upper GI motility and acid reflux. Endoscopy is indicated in infants with symptoms of esophagitis.

Since GER often resolves spontaneously by 18 months to two years of age, therapy is aimed at preventing complications so that surgery can be avoided.[52] Resolution of GER after two years of age is associated with the introduction of solid foods and maintenance of an upright position for longer periods during the day.[33] The first line of therapy is a combination of general and dietary measures. The second step includes addition of drugs that will either restore normal gastrointestinal motility or neutralize or decrease acid secretion. Surgery is the last resort except in infants with strictures or those presenting with recurrent apnea and aspiration.[49]

Treatment

Positional and Dietary Measures

11. S.B., a 3-month-old, 6 kg, 60 cm male infant, has a 2-week history of regurgitation after each feeding. The pediatrician noted that S.B. had not gained weight since his last visit 1 month earlier. A presumptive diagnosis of failure to thrive (FTT) secondary to GER was made, and S.B. was referred to a pediatric gastroenterologist. The gastroenterologist admitted S.B. to the hospital and confirmed the diagnosis using 24-hour pH monitoring. How should S.B. be managed initially?

Since S.B. does not have life-threatening complications, he should be treated conservatively. Dietary and positional measures should be tried first. Dietary measures include thickening his foods with rice cereal and feeding the infant smaller volumes more frequently. Positional therapy consists of maintaining the infant in a semiupright position 24 hours a day to promote clearance of acid from the esophagus and to minimize reflux after meals. S.B. should be kept at a 60-degree angle while sitting and a 30-degree position at night. Infants with milder cases of GER can be managed successfully by dietary measures alone and by propping them upright during and one hour after feedings.[52,53]

Drug Therapy

12. Four weeks after instituting positional and dietary measures, S.B. continued to vomit; he again failed to gain weight. Upon physical examination, the gastroenterologist notes bilateral wheezes, and endoscopy rules out esophagitis. What would be the next line of therapy?

A course of drug therapy should be tried before resorting to surgery. A variety of drugs have been used to treat infant GER (see Table 95.4). Since S.B. does not have esophagitis, antacids, H_2-antagonists, and omeprazole are not indicated. Bethanechol or a prokinetic agent can be used to enhance gastric emptying.

Bethanechol. There are a number of reasons why bethanechol (Urecholine) is not the drug of choice in S.B. It is a cholinergic agent and may exacerbate S.B.'s wheezing by inducing bronchospasm; it can stimulate gastric acid secretion; and a pediatric dosage form is unavailable.[55] If used, the injectable form must be administered orally or a suspension must be specially prepared from the tablets.

Prokinetic Agents. Metoclopramide (Reglan), domperidone, and cisapride (Propulsid) are prokinetic agents. They improve gastric emptying, increase LES pressure, and enhance esophageal clearance. Domperidone has been studied more extensively than metoclopramide in infant GER, but it currently is unavailable in the U.S.[64] Cisapride may be more effective than metoclopramide in relieving the symptoms of GER.[61]

Both metoclopramide and domperidone are dopamine antagonists and stimulate prolactin release. Although rare, gynecomastia and galactorrhea have been reported.[65] Metoclopramide has been associated with CNS effects including restlessness, drowsiness, and extrapyramidal reactions. However, such adverse reactions are uncommon at doses used for GER. Domperidone does not cross the blood brain barrier and is less likely to cause CNS side effects.[50,64] Cisapride has no antidopaminergic activity and, therefore, is not associated with extrapyramidal reactions, prolactin release, or CNS depression.[61]

Metoclopramide and cisapride are the agents of choice for S.B. Metoclopramide is available as an oral solution. A dose of 0.6 mg should be administered four times daily, 30 minutes before meals and at bedtime. This dose may be doubled based upon his response. Cisapride is not commercially available in a liquid formulation. However, a 1 mg/1 mL suspension stable for 21 days at room temperature can be compounded using the tablets.[62]

Treatment should be continued for at least three to four months although the optimal duration of therapy is unknown. If S.B. requires drug therapy to control symptoms of GER beyond two years of age, surgery should be considered since GER is unlikely to resolve spontaneously after this age.[51] Surgery should be considered earlier if he develops an esophageal stricture, apnea, or recurrent respiratory disease.[49]

Immunizations

Many viral and bacterial diseases can be prevented by immunization at an early age. Information about some of the more common childhood infections is summarized in Table 95.5. Vaccines are available for all of these except chickenpox (varicella zoster); however, a vaccine for this condition currently is under investigation.

Guidelines and Routine Schedule

13. M.K., a 2-month-old female infant, is brought to the clinic for her first scheduled well-baby visit. M.K.'s mother inquires about immunization for M.K. What are the present recommendations for immunizing pediatric patients? When should these immunizations be given?

The goal of pediatric immunization is to prevent specific infectious diseases and their sequelae. For maximum effectiveness, vaccines must be administered to appropriate populations before they have been exposed to the pathogen. However, the earliest recommended age for initiation of most immunizations is two months. Before this age, the infant's immune mechanisms are considered too immature to respond with sufficient antibody production. In addition, for the first few months of life, resistance to certain infectious diseases is provided by antibodies which were transferred from the mother through the placenta.

The schedule for routine active immunization of normal infants and children listed in Table 95.6 can be adjusted to meet individual needs. Immunizations may begin at any time of the year. An interruption in the recommended schedule does not interfere with the final immunity gained.

14. M.K.'s mother states that even though she was found to be hepatitis B surface antigen (HBsAg)-negative before delivery, M.K. received Engerix-B shortly after birth. Does M.K. need further protection against hepatitis B? If so, when should this vaccine be administered?

Although the hepatitis B vaccine has been available since 1982, there have been many reported cases of hepatitis infection. Acute disease can progress to a chronic carrier state which can lead to chronic liver disease and primary hepatocellular carcinoma. Previous vaccination guidelines recommended administration only to

Table 95.4	Oral Drugs Used to Treat GER in Infants[a,49,51,52,54–63]	
Agent	Mode of Action	Oral Dose
Antacids (aluminum/magnesium hydroxide)	Neutralizes acid; ↑ LES pressure	0.5–1.0 mL/kg/dose before and after feeding (*max*: 15 mL/dose)
Bethanechol	↑ LES pressure; augments esophageal clearance; corrects delayed gastric emptying	0.1–0.2 mg/kg/dose QID given 30–60 min before feeding and HS
Cimetidine	Blocks H_2-receptors; ↓ acid secretion	5–10 mg/kg/dose QID
Cisapride	Prokinetic agent; corrects delayed gastric emptying; ↑ LES pressure; augments esophageal clearance	0.2 mg/kg/dose TID–QID given 30 min before meals and HS
Metoclopramide	Prokinetic agent; corrects delayed gastric emptying; ↑ LES pressure; augments esophageal clearance	0.1–0.2 mg/kg/dose QID given 30 min before feeding and HS
Omeprazole	Inhibits gastric secretion via inhibition of gastric hydrogen-potassium adenosine triphosphatase	0.7–1.9 mg/kg/day Q AM. Used for resistant GER
Ranitidine	Blocks H_2-receptors; ↓ acid secretion	1.25–2.5 mg/kg/dose BID

[a] GER = Gastroesophageal reflux; LES = Lower esophageal sphincter.

Table 95.5			Common Childhood Communicable Diseases[a,66,71–73]		
Disease	**Organism**	**Incubation Period**	**Communicability**	**Treatment**	**Immunization**
Chickenpox	Varicella zoster virus	10–21 days	1–2 days before and 5–6 days after rash	*Patient*: Acyclovir *Contact*: VZIG	*Active*: Vaccine *Passive*: VZIG
Diphtheria	*C. diphtheria*	2–6 days	2–4 weeks untreated; 1–2 days after antibiotics initiated	*Patient*: Diphtheria antitoxin combined with penicillin or erythromycin *Contact*: 1) Oral erythromycin or IM benzathine penicillin; 2) diphtheria toxoid immunization	*Active*: Diphtheria toxoids *Passive*: Diphtheria/toxoid antitoxin
Hepatitis	Hepatitis B	120 days	Transmission via contaminated blood, sexual intimacy and perinatal transmission from a HBsAg-positive mother to her child	*Patient*: HBIG *Contact*: HBIG and Hepatitis B vaccine series	*Active*: Hepatitis B vaccine series *Passive*: HBIG
Invasive bacteremic disease	*H. influenzae*, type b (Hib)			*Patient*: Ampicillin combined with chloramphenicol or 3rd-generation cephalosporin *Contact*: Rifampin 20 mg/kg/day QD × 4 days	*Active*: HbCV vaccine
Measles (Rubeola)	Measles virus	10–12 days	Beginning 5th day of incubation through 1st few days of rash	*Patient*: None *Contact*: As under immunizations	*Active*: Measles virus vaccine *Passive*: Unvaccinated normal children with severe systemic infection: IVIG 500 mg/kg. Unvaccinated immuno-suppressed children: IVIG 500 mg/kg
Mumps	Mump virus	14–21 days	7 days before and 9 days after parotid swelling	*Patient*: None *Contact*: Mumps immune serum globulin	*Active*: Mumps virus vaccine *Passive*: Mumps immune globulin
Pertussis	*B. pertussis*	5–21 days	Greatest during disease; ranges include 4 weeks; lessened with antibiotics	*Patient*: Erythromycin *Contact*: Erythromycin or ampicillin for 10 days after contact or for duration of cough in contacted patient	*Active*: Pertussis vaccine *Passive*: None
Polio	Polio viruses Type 1, 2, 3	7–14 days	Virus persists in throat 1 week after onset of symptoms, also may be excreted in feces 4–6 weeks	*Patient*: none Contact: TOPV	*Active*: TOPV or IPV *Passive*: None
Rubella (German measles)	Rubella virus	14–21 days	7 days before and 5 days after appearance of rash	*Patient*: None *Contact*: See text	*Active*: Rubella virus vaccine *Passive*: ISG
Tetanus (Lock jaw)	*C. tetani*	3 days–3 weeks	None	*Patient*: Tetanus immune globulin (human), penicillin G, or tetracycline *Contact*: None required	*Active*: Tetanus toxoid *Passive*: Tetanus immune globulin (human)

[a] HbCV = *H. influenzae* type b conjugate vaccine; HBIG = Hepatitis B immune globulin; IPV = Inactive polio vaccine; ISG = Immune serum globulin; IVIG = Intravenous immune globulin; TOPV = Trivalent oral polio vaccine; VZIG = Varicella zoster immune globulin.

infants born to mothers who were HBsAg-positive, children who were household contacts of chronic hepatitis B virus carriers, and others at high risk including health care workers and IV drug abusers.[67,68] In 1991, in an effort to eliminate hepatitis B transmission, the guidelines were expanded to include all newborn infants and adolescents in high-risk groups.[69]

There are two hepatitis B vaccines (HepB) currently available for use in the U.S. Recombivax-HB and Engerix-B are yeast-derived recombinant vaccines administered as a three-dose series usually at birth, one to two months, and six months. A schedule of doses administered at one to two months, four months, and six months also has induced adequate levels of antiHBs.[70] Adolescents and adults also should follow a three-dose schedule. Dialysis patients and other immunocompromised patients should receive a four-dose series at zero, one, two, and six months apart.[70] Dosage recommendations depend upon if the patient is in a high-risk group, what vaccine is used, and the patient's age.[69] For more information on the use of HepB, see Chapter 62: Acute and Chronic Hepatitis.

M.K. appropriately received immunization against hepatitis B at birth. She should receive her second dose at this visit. Either formulation may be used as the immune response from a course using different vaccines has been found to be comparable to that of a full series using a single vaccine.[66]

Contraindications

15. What are contraindications for vaccination? Should M.K. receive additional immunizations on this visit? If so, which should she receive?

There are many misconceptions regarding true contraindications and precautions for immunization which lead to missed opportunities to provide needed immunizations. True contraindications to both live and killed vaccines include: 1) a history of anaphylaxis to the vaccine or vaccine components; and 2) moderate to severe illness with or without a fever. Immunization of a child with a history of anaphylaxis should be withheld unless the child has undergone desensitization. Immunization of a child with a minor illness (upper respiratory tract infection or diarrhea) with or without fever should not be delayed.[66]

Contraindications to live, attenuated virus vaccines and live bacterial vaccines also include: 1) immunosuppressive therapy; 2) congenital or acquired immunodeficiency disorders; 3) leukemia, lymphoma or generalized malignancies; and 4) pregnancy (although the risk in pregnancy is largely theoretical). Administration of immune globulin can impair the immune response to measles, mumps, rubella (MMR) for 8 to 12 months following IV doses used in the treatment of idiopathic thrombocytic purpura (ITP), Kawasaki's disease, or replacement of humoral immune deficiencies [e.g., children with human immunodeficiency virus (HIV) infection]. Response to MMR also can be diminished for three to seven months following administration of whole blood, plasma, or platelet transfusions and for three to five months following passive immune globulin prophylaxis, blood, plasma or platelet transfusions.[66]

Since M.K. does not have any contraindications, she can continue her active immunization series. In addition to HepB, M.K. should receive her first doses of diphtheria/tetanus/pertussis (DTP) vaccine, oral polio vaccine (OPV) and *Haemophilus influenzae*, type b conjugate vaccine (HbCV) at this visit.

Adverse Effects

16. Should M.K.'s mother be warned of any potential adverse effects of the vaccines?

Hypersensitivity reactions to vaccines are rare. An allergic reaction may occur as a result of a specific allergy to the vaccine itself or to trace components in the vaccine (e.g., egg protein, preservatives, antibiotics). Children with allergies to eggs can receive vaccines grown in chick or duck fibroblast tissue culture (e.g., measles, rubella, mumps). Egg albumin and yolk components essentially are absent from the fibroblast cultures. Refer to Table 95.7 for specific risks and benefits of the routine immunizations.

Pertussis

Adverse Effects

17. At 4 months of age, M.K. received her 2nd DTP immunization. That evening she became quite "fussy" and febrile (103 °F). M.K.'s leg was swollen at the site of the injection and warm to touch; she cried when it was moved to change her clothes. Assess the cause of M.K.'s reaction. Should her DTP series be continued?

No other vaccine has generated as much controversy as pertussis. The DTP vaccine has been associated with various adverse reactions, the most significant being permanent neurologic sequelae. The pertussis component, a whole-cell vaccine, contributes most significantly to the febrile, behavioral, and local reactions in addition to the more severe CNS toxicity.[74]

When DTP and diphtheria tetanus (DT) were compared, it was found that redness, swelling, and pain at the injection site occurred

Table 95.6	Recommended Schedule of Active Immunizations[a]
Age	Immunization[b]
Normal infants and children	
Birth	HepB[c]
2 months	HepB, DTP, OPV, HbCV[d]
4 months	DTP, OPV, HbCV[d]
6 months	HepB, DTP, OPV, HbCV[d]
12 months	MMR
15 months	DTaP, HbCV[d]
4–6 years	DTaP, OPV, MMR
14–16 years	Td
Q 10 yr	Td
Children <7 years old, not immunized in infancy	
1st visit	DTP, OPV, HbCV,[e] HepB, MMR[f]
1 month after 1st visit	DTP, HbCV, HepB
2 months after 1st visit	DTP, OPV, HbCV
4 months after 1st visit	OPV
8–12 months after 1st visit	DTaP, HbCV, HepB
4–6 years	DTaP,[g] OPV,[g] MMR
14–16 years	Td
Q 10 yr	Td
Children >7 years old, not immunized in infancy	
1st visit	Td, OPV, MMR, HepB
2 months after 1st visit	Td, OPV, MMR, HepB
8 months after 1st visit	Td, OPV, HepB
Q 10 yr	Td
Unimmunized adults	
1st visit	Td, IPV
Q 10 yr	Td, IPV

[a] Adapted from reference 66.

[b] DTaP = Diphtheria-tetanus-acellular pertussis; DTP = Pediatric diphtheria-tetanus-pertussis; HbCV = *Haemophilus influenzae* type b conjugate vaccine; HepB = Hepatitis B; IPV = Inactivated polio vaccine; MMR = Measles/mumps/rubella; OPV = Oral polio vaccine; Td = Adult tetanus-diphtheria.

[c] For infants born to HBsAg-negative mothers. First dose given during newborn period, preferably before hospital discharge but no later than 2 months. All infants born to HBsAg-positive mothers should receive immunoprophylaxis for hepatitis B as soon as possible after birth.

[d] HbCV schedules in infants vary depending upon product used; HbOC/PRP-T: primary series given at 2, 4, and 6 months with a booster at 15 months; PRP-OMP: primary series given at 2 and 4 months with a booster at 12 months. After the primary HbCV series, any of the licensed HbCV may be used as a booster dose.

[e] The recommended schedule varies depending upon the product used and the age when the series is initiated. See text.

[f] If the child is 12 months old.

[g] Preschool doses (age: 4–6 years) are not necessary if the 4th dose of DTP and 3rd dose of OPV are given after 4 years of age.

in 50% of DTP recipients as compared to 18% of DT recipients. Fever was seen in 48% of those given DTP and 10% of those given DT. "Drowsiness" and "fretfulness" occurred twice as frequently in DTP recipients. Historically, four neurologic reactions to pertussis vaccination have been identified: 1) prolonged uncontrollable crying beginning a few hours after the injection and lasting at least one hour; 2) excessive somnolence which begins several hours after the injection; 3) febrile seizures; and 4) gross encephalopathy.[75] More recently, a population-based, case-controlled study evaluated the association between serious acute neurological illness and the receipt of DTP vaccine. The study monitored 218,000 children and did not find any statistically significant increased risk in the onset of serious acute neurologic illness within seven days of receiving DTP vaccine.[76] The results of this study are consistent with other controlled studies that have not found a significant increase in the rate of acute neurological illness with DTP.[77,78] Although a relationship between DTP vaccine and acute

Table 95.7	Benefits and Reactions from Immunizations[76]
Disease	**Vaccine**
Diphtheria Occurs primarily in children. Attacks throat and nasal passages. Toxin damages heart, kidney, and nerves. 10% case fatality	**Tetanus diphtheria toxoid (Td)** Almost 100% protection from primary series plus booster. Sore arm or bump at injection site and possible fever for 12–24 hours after injection. Severe reactions very rare
Tetanus (lock jaw) Caused by contaminated dirt entering wound. Causes painful muscular contractions. 50% case fatality	**Diphtheria/tetanus/pertussis (DTP)** Administered to children <6 years of age. Most children protected after completing primary series and booster. Sore arm or bump at injection site and fever 12–24 hours after injection. Very rarely causes seizure, hypotonic-hyperresponse episode, or permanent neurologic injury
Pertussis (whooping cough) Most severe in young infants. Can cause ear infections, pneumonia, and convulsions; rarely causes permanent neurologic injury	**Diphtheria/tetanus/acellular pertussis (DTaP)** Recommended for use as the 4th and/or 5th doses of the DTP series in children 15 months to 6 years of age. Side effects reported to occur less frequently than those seen with whole cell DTP
Polio Attacks the nervous system. Causes muscular and/or respiratory paralysis. 10% case fatality	**Oral polio vaccine (OPV, Live, Sabin)** 90% receiving primary series plus booster protected. Given by oral drops. No common reactions. Paralytic reaction to the vaccine occurs in person vaccinated or a close contact 1 in 3 million doses **Inactivated polio vaccine (IPV, Killed, Salk)** 90% protection after receiving primary series plus booster. Administered by injection. No common reactions
Measles Most common childhood disease. Causes high fever (103–105 °F) and rash. May cause pneumonia or encephalopathy. Causes deafness, blindness, convulsions, brain disorders in 1 of every 1000 children contracting the disease. Children who develop a brain disorder from measles have a 10% fatality rate	**Measles vaccine** 95% protection after 1 dose. 10%–20% of immunized children may have a mild fever and rash within 10 days. Very rarely causes neurologic problems
Rubella Usually mild disease with mild fever, rash, and swollen glands. When contracted by pregnant women, can cause miscarriage, stillbirth, or multiple birth defects including blindness, deafness, and heart disease	**Rubella vaccine** 90% of persons receiving 1 dose will be protected. Approximately 1% of young children and 5%–10% of teenagers may develop temporary arm, leg, or joint pains. Very rarely may cause rash. Children of pregnant women can be vaccinated
Mumps Usually causes fever and swelling of salivary glands. May cause inflammation of testicles in adolescent and adult males, pancreatitis, temporary brain disorder, and permanent deafness	**Mumps vaccine** 90% of persons immunized will be protected. Very rarely, fever, and swelling of salivary glands occur after vaccination
Invasive *H. influenzae*, type b (Hib) Most common cause of bacterial meningitis. 5% mortality rate. Neurologic sequelae observed in 25%–35%. May cause other invasive diseases	**HbCV vaccines** Mild local and febrile reactions commonly resolve in 24 hours. Rare anaphylactic reactions may occur. 95% protection after completing primary series and booster
Hepatitis B Chronic infection can lead to long-term problems with chronic liver disease	**Hep B vaccines** Administered to newborn infants and adults and adolescents felt to be at high risk of contracting disease. 95% seroconversion with adequate antiHBs when administered as a 3-dose series. Side effects include pain at the injection site and fever

neurologic illness cannot be ruled out completely by these studies, the risk appears to be very low. This helps to further reinforce the consensus that the benefits of preventing the morbidity and mortality associated with pertussis infection outweigh the potential risks of adverse effects associated with the vaccine.

Pertussis is a highly communicable infection caused by *Bordetella pertussis*. Attack rates of over 90% have been reported in nonimmunized household contacts.[79] The syndrome is characterized by a triphasic course: a paroxysmal cough with a whoop-like, high-pitched inspiratory noise, vomiting, and lymphocytosis. Morbidity and mortality rates following infection are high, with a 0.3% to 14% incidence of encephalopathy, 0.1% to 4% incidence of death, and a 0.6% to 2% incidence of permanent neurologic damage.[80] The efficacy of the DTP vaccine against pertussis following primary immunization is greater than 80%.[81]

M.K. developed a fever of 103 °F, had pain at the site of injection, and became fussy. Weighing the risks associated with pertussis disease with the risks associated with the vaccine, M.K. should continue with her DTP series.

Infants experiencing a temperature ≥105 °F after the administration of pertussis-containing vaccines should not receive additional doses. Other contraindications include severe changes in consciousness, focal neurological signs, and hypersensitivity to the vaccine. If an evolving neurologic disorder is present, pertussis immunization should be deferred. Pre-existing static neurological conditions, such as well-controlled seizures, do not constitute a contraindication because the benefits of pertussis immunization outweigh the risks.[82] A minimum of three doses of DTP given at intervals of at least four weeks is required for adequate protection. A fourth dose also is recommended 6 to 12 months later.

Because M.K. developed a fever, she should receive antipyretic therapy with each immunization. Acetaminophen also may help to minimize pain associated with the local reaction. The Advisory Committee on Immunization Practice (ACIP) strongly discourages any variation from the recommended volume or the recommended number of doses of a vaccine. Partial doses should not be administered, and all children require the full series of immunizations to be adequately protected.

Acellular Vaccine

18. In view of the controversy associated with its use, should pertussis be eliminated from the vaccination program? Are less toxic forms of vaccination available?

Pertussis still is an integral part of a pediatric immunization program. Epidemic outbreaks of whooping cough occurred in England, Japan, and Sweden following discontinuation of the pertussis vaccine. Therefore, elimination of the pertussis vaccine is not recommended.[80] Much research has gone into the development of an acellular vaccine that is protective but less likely to induce reactions.[83,84] Testing in Japan and the U.S. has indicated that the prevalence of febrile responses associated with the acellular vaccine is significantly lower than that associated with the whole-cell vaccine; however, the prevalence of local reactions is similar.[85–87] In Japan, acellular DTP (DTaP) vaccines have been used in children older than two years of age since 1981 and in children three months of age since 1989.[88–90] DTaP vaccine contains two proteins felt to be important for immunity: lymphocytosis promoting factor and filamentous hemagglutinin. Unlike the whole-cell vaccine, it has a reduced amount of lipopolysaccharide, which may be the cause of fever and toxic reactions to the whole-cell vaccine. The acellular vaccine is detoxified further by formalin treatment. In 1991 the FDA approved a DTaP vaccine (ACEL-IMUNE) for use as the fourth and fifth doses of the DTP series.[91] Although either whole cell DTP or DTaP may be used for the fourth and fifth doses, the ACIP recommends the use of DTaP due to the decreased incidence of adverse reactions.[92,93] DTaP currently is under evaluation for use in younger children and it is likely that it will be approved soon for routine use in infants two, four, and six months of age.

Tetanus

19. J.W., a 9-year-old male, stepped on a rusty nail at school. The wound was cleaned and treated with an antiseptic by the school nurse who also notes that the child received his last tetanus "shot" 7 years ago. Should J.W. receive tetanus immunoglobulin (TIG) or tetanus toxoid (Td)?

Tetanus is a noncommunicable childhood disease. It results from puncture wounds caused by contaminated articles, and it is associated with a very high mortality rate. The etiologic agent, *Clostridium tetani*, an anaerobic, spore-forming, gram-positive rod, exists in nature as an extremely resistant spore. All the clinical features of tetanus, specifically the painful muscular contractions, are produced by an exotoxin; the organism itself causes no disease.[94]

There is no natural immunity to tetanus. Prophylaxis can be achieved through active stimulation of antibody formation against the toxin through immunization with tetanus toxoid. Passive immunity can be achieved through administration of tetanus immunoglobulin. Immunization affords extremely high protection with minimal risk. It is controversial whether the vaccine should be administered to patients who cannot recall their last immunization or who have not received an immunization in quite some time, as in R.D. Nevertheless, based upon current recommendations (see Table 95.8), R.D. should receive tetanus toxoid, since his immunizations were complete up to his fourth dose at 18 months of age, and it has been more than five years since his last dose. If tetanus toxoid is administered too frequently, a serum reaction and a qualitative change in the spectrum of antibodies produced may result.[94,95]

Polio

20. The mother of T.C., a 6-month-old, breast-fed female infant, brings the child to the community clinic for polio vac-

Table 95.8	Tetanus Prophylaxis in Routine Wound Management[a,b]			
	Clean, Minor Wounds		All Other Wounds[c]	
Tetanus Toxoid Adsorbed History	Td	TIG	Td	TIG
Not known or <3 doses	Yes	No	Yes	Yes
≥3 doses[d]	No[e]	No	No[f]	No

[a] Adapted from reference 73.
[b] Td = Adult tetanus and diphtheria toxoids, adsorbed; for children <7 years old, use DTP or DT; TIG = Tetanus immune globulin.
[c] Including, but not limited to, wounds contaminated with saliva, soil, feces, dirt; puncture wounds; avulsions; and wounds from crushing, burns, or frostbite.
[d] If only 3 doses of tetanus toxoid have been received, a 4th dose (using tetanus toxoid adsorbed) should be given.
[e] Yes, if >10 years since last dose.
[f] Yes, if >5 years since last dose.

cination. The mother has never been immunized nor have her 18-year-old son, husband, and pregnant sister. All have moved recently to this country. How should this situation be handled?

Since the advent of the trivalent oral polio vaccine (TOPV) and inactivated polio vaccine (IVP), the number of reports of paralytic polio has been reduced to fewer than a dozen cases annually. Debate continues over which immunization, TOPV or IVP, should be recommended and used in pediatric immunization programs.

The oral polio virus vaccine (TOPV) or Sabin Vaccine has been the vaccine of choice since 1962 in the U.S. Its advantages include low cost and ease of administration. TOPV induces lifelong immunity similar to that observed after natural infection. In addition, TOPV provides gut immunity, thus preventing the carrier state. Lastly, the fecal shedding of vaccine virus after Sabin vaccine administration is an effective way to immunize or boost the pre-existing immunity in close contacts.[96] Despite these benefits, TOPV carries the risk of paralytic disease, especially after the first dose. The current rate of paralytic disease following the first dose is approximately one case per 0.5 to 1.5 million vaccinations.

In contrast to TOPV, the Salk vaccine (IPV) has been associated with no severe reactions. More potent forms of IPV have been used successfully in many European countries. Unfortunately, it must be administered by injection; the induced immunity is not lifelong, so booster doses are required; and gut immunity is not produced.

In this case, T.C. must begin her routine immunizations. TOPV appears to be suitable for breast-fed children. The passive transfer of antibodies from the mother through the breast milk does not seem to interfere with the vaccine-induced antigen-antibody response. Studies have shown similar antibody titers in both bottle-fed and breast-fed infants.

Since T.C. will shed the vaccine virus in her stool, all nonimmunized household contacts also must be immunized against polio. Persons over 18 years of age are more susceptible to TOPV-associated polio. To prevent iatrogenic paralytic disease, some have suggested the use of IPV in adult household contacts and other high-risk (immunocompromised) susceptible contacts of children receiving their first TOPV dose. T.C.'s parents and 18-year-old brother should be immunized with IPV monthly for three doses before T.C. receives her first TOPV dose.[96] Alternatively, T.C. could receive a single IPV dose in the initial routine immunization schedule with DTP to avoid a three-month delay in starting her polio (TOPV) immunizations. The pregnant sister should receive IPV injections along with the other adult household contacts.

21. What are the recommendations for nonimmunized individuals traveling to polio-endemic areas and during a domestic outbreak?

Persons traveling to an area endemic for polio should be given IPV, assuming sufficient time is available. If travel must be taken on short notice, the patient and physician must weigh the risk of TOPV use against the risk of infection abroad. In domestic outbreaks of polio, TOPV is routinely given to adult contacts since the risk of natural disease is much greater than the risk of paralysis from TOPV. Pregnancy is not a contraindication to TOPV immunization when protection is needed as during an epidemic.

Measles/Mumps/Rubella (MMR)

22. At 12 months, M.K. (see Question 13) is scheduled to receive her MMR vaccination. What is MMR? Why is each component administered? M.K.'s mother, who has never been immunized, now is pregnant with a 2nd child. Should M.K.'s immunization be delayed?

MMR is a combination vaccine containing live-attenuated measles, mumps, and rubella viruses.

Measles is a highly contagious and previously common disease of childhood. Symptoms include high fever, rash, cough, rhinitis, and conjunctivitis. Complications, although uncommon, may include pneumonia and encephalitis. Live-attenuated measles virus vaccine produces a benign infection which is thought to produce lifelong immunity. When the measles vaccine was first licensed in 1963, a single dose was administered at age nine months. In 1965 the age of immunization was increased to 12 months due to primary vaccine failure in younger children. In 1976 the age of immunization was raised to 15 months because of greater vaccine efficacy in children older than 15 months of age.[97]

Because of endemic outbreaks, a two-dose schedule now has been recommended. The first dose should be given as MMR at age 12 months followed by a second dose of MMR at entrance to grade school (age 5 to 6 years).[66] During an epidemic outbreak, infants can be immunized at age six to nine months with single-antigen measles, followed by a dose of MMR at age 12 months and a dose of MMR at age five to six years.[98,99] Two doses of measles vaccine also should be administered to persons born in or after 1957 and before 1968 who have no record of vaccination or proof of immunity. Persons born after 1968 should receive one dose of a measles-containing vaccine.[98]

Mumps immunization remains controversial in childhood since mumps illness in children rarely produces complications. Meningo-encephalitis generally is a benign meningitis, and postinfectious encephalitis, a serious disease, is extremely rare (1/6000). Deafness, frequently considered a risk of mumps, occurs rarely (1/15,000) and usually is unilateral. Orchitis primarily is a complication in infected adult males. Controversy exists because vaccination at 12 months of age may not protect male children into their adult years while administration of a second dose of MMR at age four to six years may provide longer protection; current immunization practices are aimed at eliminating the mumps virus from the pool of young children, thereby minimizing the exposure of nonimmunized adults.[95] The mumps virus vaccine temporarily suppresses the reaction to tuberculin skin tests; therefore, tuberculin skin testing should be performed before, simultaneously with, or six weeks after administration of the vaccine.

Rubella is a common childhood infection which often is misdiagnosed because its signs and symptoms vary widely. The most common symptoms include postauricular and suboccipital lymphadenopathy, arthralgia, transient erythematous rash, and low fever. The most important consequences of rubella occur in pregnant women and include abortions, miscarriages, still births, and fetal anomalies. This is especially true if the infection occurs during the first trimester. Preventing congenital rubella through elimination of the viral pool is the primary objective of rubella immunization programs since approximately 10% to 20% of women of child-bearing age have not acquired natural immunity.

Live rubella virus vaccination is recommended for all children at 12 months of age. Immunization and/or rubella antibody titer screening of women at premarital examinations and postpartum also is recommended. Women of child-bearing age receiving the rubella vaccine should use contraception for at least two months after immunization. Antibody titers should be measured six to eight weeks after immunization to evaluate antibody response in women who have received blood products or immunoglobulin within eight weeks of immunization. The latter may inhibit antibody stimulation.[100,101]

Previously, when rubella immunization was administered to women who were unknowingly pregnant, approximately 10% of fetuses acquired congenital rubella infection. The new RA27/3 vaccine, reformulated in 1979, dramatically reduces this risk of fetal infection;[102,103] however, more studies are required before the vaccine can be recommended for pregnant women.[104]

M.K.'s mother should have rubella antibody titers measured. If she does not have natural immunity to rubella, she should receive MMR postpartum. M.K.'s MMR vaccination is not contraindicated at this time and should not be deferred until her mother has delivered the child.

Haemophilus Influenzae Type b (Hib) Vaccine

23. M.K. will be attending day care. Are there any vaccinations available which will minimize infections she is likely to encounter in this environment?

In 1985 a new polysaccharide vaccine against invasive bacteremic disease caused by *H. influenzae* type b was added to the routine schedule of pediatric immunizations. Hib is the most common cause of bacterial meningitis and a leading cause of serious, systemic bacterial diseases in children less than five years of age.[105–107] The mortality rate associated with Hib meningitis is approximately 5%, and neurological sequelae are observed in 25% to 35% of survivors.[108,109] Other invasive Hib infections include epiglottitis, sepsis, cellulitis, septic arthritis, osteomyelitis, pericarditis, and pneumonia. Hib strains account for only 5% to 10% of *H. influenzae*-causing otitis media and other upper respiratory tract infections.[110]

The emergence of antibiotic resistance, especially to ampicillin, has created problems in the treatment of Hib meningitis. In addition, cross-transmission in families and in day care centers places children of susceptible age at risk for secondary infections. Immunization and chemoprophylaxis with antibiotics such as rifampin have been studied as ways of preventing these infections; only immunization would have general applicability.

The first Hib polysaccharide vaccine stimulated an adequate immune response in children older than two years of age. Children 18 to 23 months of age responded partially but required a booster dose at 24 months of age.[111–112] To improve the response in younger children, the polysaccharide vaccine was conjugated to carrier proteins. Currently, four such Hib polysaccharide conjugate vaccines (HbCV) are available: Hib diphtheria toxoid conjugate vaccine or PRP-D (ProHibit); Hib meningococcal protein conjugate vaccine or PRP-OMP (PedvaxHIB); Hib tetanus toxoid conjugate vaccine or PRP-T (ActHIB, OmniHIB); and Hib diphtheria CRM197 protein conjugate vaccine or HbOC (HibTITER). Like the original polysaccharide vaccine, immunogenicity of the conjugate vaccine is age-dependent, with an improved immune response seen in older children.[113,114]

In October 1990, the FDA approved the use of HbOC (Hib-TITER) in infants, the group at highest risk for *H. influenzae* infection.[115] A three-dose schedule administered at ages two, four, and six months is recommended with a booster at age 15 months. Approval was based upon an efficacy trial in a study population of 48,000 infants. *H. influenzae* type b invasive disease occurred in 12 unvaccinated children while no cases were reported in children who were fully vaccinated. The results of this study are similar to the Finland trial that demonstrated 90% efficacy when HbCV was administered in three doses early in infancy.[116] Shortly thereafter, PRP-OMP (PedvaxHIB) and PRP-T (ActHIB, OmniHIB) also were approved for use in infants. PRP-T employs the same schedule as HibTITER while PRP-OMP uses a different schedule, administering the primary series at two and four months of age. A booster dose should be administered at age 12 months.

Ideally, the primary series should be completed with the same HbCV. Any of the licensed conjugate vaccines can be used for the recommended booster dose at age 12 to 18 months.[66] Children who begin HbCV at 7 to 11 months of age should receive a primary series of two doses of a HbOC, PRP-T, or PRP-OMP containing vaccine followed by a booster dose at 12 to 18 months of age administered at least two months after the previous dose. Children ages 12 to 15 months should receive a primary series of one dose followed by a booster dose two months later. If a child reaches 15 months of age without receiving HbCV, only one dose is necessary. HbCV should not be administered to children age ≥ 5 years unless there are special circumstances such as anatomic or functional asplenia, sickle cell anemia, or immunosuppression due to malignancy that might place a child at an increased risk of infection.[66]

Availability of HbCV for infants and children has reduced the incidence of invasive Hib infections dramatically. M.K. started her primary series with a HbCV approved for infants at age two months (see Question 14). To ensure protection she should receive a booster dose now or at 15 months of age.

24. M.K.'s mother is concerned about the number of injections M.K. is to receive at each office visit. Can any of the immunizations be given together in the same syringe to minimize the number of "sticks"?

Ideally, pediatricians and parents would like to be able to deliver all of the needed vaccines with the fewest injections over the shortest time period. TETRAMUNE, containing DTP and HbOC, currently is the only commercially available combination vaccine. However, the PRP-T preparations (ActHIB, OmniHIB) can be reconstituted with the DTP vaccine manufactured by Connaught to result in a combination product. Both combination preparations are felt to have equivalent immunogenicity compared to administering DTP and HbOC or PRP-T separately.[117–119] Combination products that contain HbCV, DTP, and IPV also are being evaluated.[120] If the combination preparations are not used, administering the vaccines at different anatomic sites is recommended particularly if one of the vaccines used is DTP. If more than one injection must be administered in the same limb, the thigh is the preferred location due to the greater muscle mass.

To minimize the number of "sticks" M.K. must receive, one of the combination preparations can be used to administer DTP and HbCV.

Varicella Vaccine

25. A working mother of 3 preschool-aged children has received a notice that there has been a case of chickenpox in their school. Can her children be immunized against this infection?

A live attenuated vaccine against varicella zoster (chickenpox) developed in Japan in the early 1970s has been under investigation in the U.S. for more than a decade.[121,122] It is the first herpes virus vaccine to be widely tested in healthy and high-risk children and adults. Chickenpox is a highly contagious, mild childhood disease in normal children, but it can be severe and even fatal in the immunocompromised patient. Unusual complications, such as severe bacterial superinfections, Reye's syndrome, and other encephalopathies, are worth preventing with an immunization program.

While most children recover from chickenpox, there are many direct and indirect costs associated with chickenpox. Direct costs include nonprescription and prescription (i.e., acyclovir) medications used in the treatment of the illness while indirect costs are those associated with missed work to be home to care for an ill child.[123] It is likely that universal immunization to prevent chickenpox would be less costly than universal treatment with oral acyclovir, even if a two-dose schedule is used for maximal protection.

In healthy children, the vaccine has been efficacious in preventing varicella.[124] In the immunocompromised patient, a low clinical attack rate has been observed. While the vaccine may not entirely prevent chickenpox from occurring, one of its effects may be to modify the disease. In the Collaborative Varicella Vaccine Study sponsored by the National Institutes of Health, a seroconversion rate of only 85% after a single dose was observed in adults, compared to 95% in healthy children and 90% in children with leukemia.[125] Therefore, two doses generally are given to adults. In addition, the vaccine also may be given to healthy varicella-susceptible children, such as those described in this case who already have been exposed. Chickenpox usually can be prevented if no more than three days has passed since exposure.[126]

Concern regarding the varicella vaccine focuses on the potential of breakthrough varicella (BV) occurring in children previously vaccinated with live varicella vaccine and that BV would become more severe as the time from immunization increased. Breakthrough cases occurring up to eight years after vaccination were reported to be clinically mild with one-sixth fewer total and vesicular lesions and a shorter duration of illness when compared to natural varicella infection.[128]

The use of the varicella virus vaccine, formerly restricted to immunocompromised patients or children and adults under specific investigative protocols, is now available (see Update page 95.25).

Recommendations for Immunocompromised Patients

26. B.R., a 15-month-old boy diagnosed with HIV infection, lives with foster parents taking care of 2 other chronically ill children. He is taking zidovudine 180 mg/m^2 PO QID, pentamidine 4 mg/kg IV once monthly, and intravenous gamma globulin (IVIG) 400 mg/kg once monthly. B.R. currently is asymptomatic. What immunizations are recommended for immunocompromised children and their close contacts?

Administration of live virus vaccines in immunocompromised patients is controversial due to the possibility of excessive virus replication and serious complications. Immunocompromised patients include those with acquired or congenital immunodeficiencies, leukemia, lymphoma, or generalized malignancies. Patients receiving cancer chemotherapy or other immunosuppressive agents also are considered immunocompromised.

Scheduled inactivated vaccines should be administered to all HIV-infected children, although an adequate immune response cannot be guaranteed. IPV is the polio immunization of choice for children known to be HIV-positive. TOPV has been administered to asymptomatic HIV-infected children without problems; however, use of IPV eliminates the potential risk to the patient as well as spread of vaccine virus to other close contacts who may be immunocompromised. IPV should be used when polio immunization is indicated for household members or other close contacts of immunocompromised children.[66,127]

Because of the risk of serious measles infection, MMR should be administered to all asymptomatic HIV-infected patients and considered in children with symptomatic HIV infection. Although studies are limited, adverse effects following administration of MMR to both asymptomatic and symptomatic children have not been reported.[127]

Many children known to be infected with HIV receive IVIG for prophylaxis of bacterial and viral infections. Vaccine-induced immunity to MMR may be compromised in patients who receive IVIG. Because of the potential benefit, MMR should be given two weeks before the next dose of IVIG even though an adequate immune response is unlikely.[66]

In summary, although B.R.'s ability to mount an antibody response cannot be determined, he should continue to receive all inactivated vaccines as scheduled. To minimize potential risks, B.R. and his close contacts should receive IPV instead of TOPV. Since B.R. is asymptomatic from his HIV infection, MMR should be administered to protect him from a serious measles infection. MMR is not contraindicated in close contacts of immunosuppressed patients.

Hemolytic Uremic Syndrome (HUS)

Hemolytic uremic syndrome is a common cause of renal failure in children. It is characterized by microangiopathic hemolytic anemia, thrombocytopenia, and acute renal failure. HUS typically occurs several days to two weeks after an episode of gastroenteritis, upper respiratory tract infection, or an acute, flu-like illness. Pathologically, white blood cell activation and endothelial cell injury in the kidney lead to fibrin deposition and platelet adherence to vessel walls. Glomerular lumens are swollen and occluded resulting in renal insufficiency. Red blood cells (RBCs) and platelets are damaged by the fibrin strands as they pass through the narrowed vessels. Abnormalities in coagulation involving prostacyclin-thromboxane axis and von Willebrand factor have been implicated in the pathogenesis of thrombocytopenia.[129–132]

Hemolytic uremic syndrome is classified into diarrhea-associated and nondiarrhea-associated (atypical) illness. Diarrhea-associated HUS is more frequent, has seasonal variation, and occurs primarily between six months and four years of age. It most often is associated with cytotoxin-producing bacteria, such as *Escherichia coli* (usually subtype 0157:H7) and *Shigella dysenteriae* type 1. These organisms are spread by contaminated and/or undercooked food and person to person contact. Other bacteria and viruses associated with HUS include *Salmonella*, *Campylobacter*, *Yersinia*, *Pseudomonas*, *Bacteroides*, *Aeromonas*, *Coxsackie*, *Influenza*, and *Epstein Barr*.[129,132–136] Atypical HUS may be inherited or caused by oral contraceptives, cyclosporin, or cancer chemotherapeutic agents. It also has been seen following pregnancy, Kawasaki's disease, or bone marrow transplant.[129,137] The estimated prevalence of HUS in the U.S. ranges from 0.3 to 10 per 10,000 children; children with nondiarrhea-associated HUS appear to have a worse prognosis.[133–135,137,138]

Clinical Presentation

27. B.J., a 3-year-old, 15 kg male, has been increasingly lethargic over the past 3 days. The sudden appearance of dark urine 24 hours ago and no urine output over the last 12 hours caused his mother to bring him in for evaluation. His recent medical history was significant for a 4-day bout of gastroenteritis which resolved 2 days before the onset of his present illness. His past medical history was normal and his family medical history is negative for HUS.

Upon physical examination, B.J. was pale, somnolent, and had several large purple bruises over his arms and legs. Significant laboratory results were as follows: partial thromboplastin time (PTT) 26 seconds (Normal: 25–35); hemoglobin (Hgb) 5 gm/dL (Normal: 12.8); hematocrit (Hct) 16% (Normal: 37%); platelet count 50,000 cells/mm^3 (Normal: 250,000–350,000); reticulocytes 14% (Normal: 0.6%–1.7%); blood urea nitrogen (BUN) 245 mg/dL (Normal: 6–23); serum creatinine (SrCr) 7 mg/dL (Normal: 0.3–0.8); potassium (K) 6.5 mEq/L (Normal: 3.5–5.5); urinalysis 3 + protein and hematuria; blood smear, schistocytes (fragmented RBCs); factor V and VIII within normal limits; fibrinogen within normal limits; and fibrin split within normal limits. B.J. was admitted to the hospital with a diagnosis of HUS. Which signs, symptoms, and laboratory tests are consistent with HUS in B.J.? [SI units: Hgb 50 gm/L (Normal: 128); Hct 0.16 (Normal: 0.37); platelet count 50 × 10^9/L (Normal: 250–350); reticulocytes 0.14 (Normal: 0.006–0.017); BUN 87.8 mmol/L (Normal: 2.1–8.2); SrCr 618.8 μmol/L (Normal: 26.5–70.7); K 6.5 mmol/L (Normal: 3.5–5.5)]

B.J. exhibits many signs and symptoms associated with HUS. His lethargy, change in mental status, and pale color are symptoms of anemia. The dark color of his urine is indicative of hemolysis and renal damage; other signs of renal damage include anuria and hypertension. The purpura (i.e., bruises) on his arms and legs is evidence for thrombocytopenia.

B.J.'s laboratory abnormalities also help confirm a diagnosis of HUS. The low hemoglobin and hematocrit are consistent with anemia, while the high reticulocyte count and presence of schistocytes indicate hemolysis. Nephropathy in B.J. is manifested by proteinuria and elevations in BUN and creatinine. The hyperkalemia is a sign of both nephropathy and hemolysis. Finally, normal coagulation studies, absence of fibrin split products, and normal levels of clotting factors and fibrinogen indicate that B.J., like many children with HUS, does not have active disseminated intravascular coagulation (DIC) at initial presentation.

Treatment

28. How should B.J. be managed initially?

Therapeutic approaches to B.J. include supporting him until his renal function normalizes, limiting the hemostatic response, and limiting or preventing endothelial cell breakdown. Currently, supportive care (which includes dialysis) is the only widely accepted form of therapy. Other treatment regimens are either controversial or not well studied.[139–142]

Correction of Hemostatic and Electrolyte Imbalances. B.J.'s hemostatic and electrolyte imbalances need to be corrected first. Packed red blood cells should be given to increase his hemoglobin and hematocrit. If his platelet count declines to less than 20,000 cells/mm^3, platelets should be administered as well. Dialysis is needed to control uremia and hyperkalemia; a dose of Kayexalate can be given before dialysis is initiated to lower his serum potassium (see Chapter 28: Fluid and Electrolyte Disorders). His blood pressure should be controlled with an antihypertensive agent such as hydralazine.[131] B.J. will have to be monitored closely for seizures, a complication of HUS.[142]

29. Upon admission, B.J. received 15 gm of Kayexalate (1 gm/kg), packed RBCs, and 1.5 mg of hydralazine (0.1 mg/kg) IV. Peritoneal dialysis was instituted within 24 hours along with 81 mg aspirin PO QD and 25 mg dipyridamole PO BID. On day 3, plasmapheresis was performed; 12 hours later, B.J. began producing urine. What is the rationale for using antiplatelet drugs and plasmapheresis?

Antiplatelet agents are thought to decrease the formation of platelet thrombi on damaged endothelium and to secondarily limit renal damage.[143] Aspirin in doses ranging from 1 to 60 mg/kg/day and dipyridamole in doses of 3 to 10 mg/kg/day in two doses have been used singly or in combination, but studies have not documented clinical efficacy.[139,144,145]

Plasmapheresis is not a well-established treatment for HUS. It theoretically increases prostacyclin production by replacing a plasma factor which stimulates release of vascular prostacyclin or by removing an inhibitor of prostacyclin synthesis. Increased prostacyclin levels may decrease platelet aggregation in renal capillaries, thereby improving renal function indirectly. Some physicians believe that the beneficial effects of antiplatelet agents are enhanced by plasmapheresis.[146]

30. Heparin. B.J.'s nephrologist also considered treating him with heparin. What are the risks and benefits of heparin therapy?

Theoretically, anticoagulants prevent further fibrin deposition in the kidneys, thereby limiting progression of nephropathy. Unfortunately, anticoagulants do not affect the outcome of children with HUS.[141,142,144] Anticoagulants probably are not beneficial for most children with HUS because significant fibrin deposition usually has occurred by the time a child is first seen by a physician. Also, most children with HUS do not have active disseminated intravascular coagulation at initial presentation.[140,144] Since B.J. is predisposed to bleeding and does not have DIC, the risks of heparin therapy outweigh the potential benefits in this case. Anticoagulants may be beneficial in the small subgroup of children with HUS who have active DIC.[144,147]

31. What other modes of therapy have been used to treat HUS in children?

Vitamin E is used for its antioxidant effects. It is thought to stabilize red blood cell lipid peroxides which, if released, can inhibit prostacyclin synthetase. The risks of vitamin E therapy are negligible.[146,148]

Thrombolytic Drugs. Streptokinase and urokinase might limit renal damage by lysing fibrin in renal blood vessels. Although these drugs should hasten resolution of nephropathy in HUS, they do not improve prognosis.[140,144] Since B.J. is at high risk for bleeding and the benefits from therapy are low, thrombolytic agents should not be used in his case.

Exchange transfusion and fresh frozen plasma are thought to benefit children with HUS by normalizing prostacyclin synthesis. The risks of these treatments are those associated with blood transfusion (i.e., hepatitis, transfusion reactions).[146,149] They cannot be recommended for B.J. since the benefits are not well established.

Prognosis

32. What is B.J.'s prognosis?

B.J.'s prognosis is good since he has a common or typical form of HUS (i.e., age <4 years, negative family history). In 80% to 90% of children with the common form of HUS, renal function normalizes within one to two months with supportive care only.[130,150] The remaining children either die during the acute phase; progress to end-stage renal disease; or develop persistent hypertension, proteinuria, or mild azotemia.[142] The outlook is worse for children with recurrent HUS, those who are older than four years of age, and for children of families with ≥two affected children.[149] More aggressive treatments may benefit these children.

Short Stature

Short stature, defined as a height ≥3 standard deviations below the mean for age and sex, is the most common complaint of children and adolescents referred to pediatric endocrine clinics.[151] Three out of every 100 children are short. Evaluation of a child with short stature is complex.[152] Short children should be monitored over a 6- to 12-month period to calculate growth velocity

and construct a growth curve. Bone age determination is helpful in determining prognosis since patients with a delayed bone age are most likely to respond to therapy.[153] Body proportions also should be evaluated to help make a differential diagnosis since short children with abnormal proportions are likely to have skeletal or endocrine disorders.

The three main types of short stature are intrinsic shortness, delayed growth, and attenuated growth. Children with intrinsic shortness have inherent limitations to bone growth and are destined to be short adults. They have growth velocities within normal limits and growth curves parallel to those of normal children. Children with delayed growth have delayed puberty but ultimately reach normal adult height. Children with attenuated growth have a subnormal growth rate but their adult height potential is normal. Their growth curves clearly are abnormal.[154]

The majority of short children are normal; that is, they are intrinsically short or their growth is delayed.[151] Growth hormone deficiency (GHD) is a relatively rare cause of short stature, and idiopathic GHD is the most common type of GHD.[154]

Treatment varies with the type and etiology of short stature. The treatment of classic GHD with growth hormone (GH) is well established but treatment of other types of short stature is not. Controversy exists over whether short children with diagnoses other than GHD should receive GH.[155] Concern also exists over the possible abuse of GH since supplies of synthetic GH are unlimited.[156] Alternative drugs for treating short stature are androgens and anabolic steroids; other agents are available, but they are experimental or are not approved for the treatment of GHD. Short children with underlying disease may respond to specific treatment of that disease.

Growth Hormone Deficiency (GHD)

33. C.T., a 6-year-old, healthy, 20 kg girl, was referred to a pediatric endocrinologist for short stature. Her height of 100 cm fell below the 5th percentile. Also, she grew only 1 cm over the past 6 months. This growth rate fell below the 3rd percentile for her age and sex. A growth hormone level obtained after 30 minutes of exercise was low and a preliminary diagnosis of GHD was made. She was hospitalized for further testing. Upon admission, C.T. was given 10 gm of arginine 10% IV (0.5 gm/kg) over 30 minutes and later 2 units of regular human insulin IV (0.1 unit/kg) to stimulate GH secretion. GH levels drawn after administration of both of these agents rose to 3 ng/mL (Normal: 7–10). A definitive diagnosis of GHD was made. What is the appropriate treatment for C.T.? [SI unit: GH 3 μg/L (Normal: 7–10)]

Growth Hormone Replacement

Growth hormone replacement is the treatment of choice for children with GHD who have open epiphyses (i.e., children with a bone age <12 or 13 years). Since GH is species-specific, only human GH is effective in children.[154]

There are two types of human GH: synthetic and pituitary-derived. Synthetic GH is obtained using DNA recombinant technology and is available in two forms: Somatrem (Protropin) and Somatropin (Humatrope).[157,158] Both are as potent as natural GH in promoting growth. Somatrem differs from natural GH by one additional methionine at the amino terminal, while synthetic Somatropin has the same amino acid sequence as natural GH. Pituitary GH, also known as Somatropin, is extracted from human cadaver pituitary glands. All sources of pituitary GH were withdrawn from the market in 1985 after four young adults who had received GH as children died of Creutzfeldt-Jacob disease (CJD), a rapidly fatal degenerative neurologic disorder that may be caused by the scrapie virus.[159] Pituitary GH will remain off the market until animal studies show that lots produced by refined purification methods are not contaminated with the virus.[160]

The optimal GH dosing regimen is unknown. Also, there is some evidence that doses higher than those currently recommended are more effective.[158] The initial dose of Somatrem ranges from 0.05 mg/kg/dose (0.13 unit/kg/dose) to a maximum of 0.1 mg/kg/dose (0.26 units/kg/dose).[161,162] The recommended dose of synthetic Somatropin is 0.06 mg/kg/dose. It is unknown why the recommended doses of these GH products differ when they are equipotent.[158] All products are given intramuscularly (IM) three times a week.[153,154] GH should be given during the evening hours to mimic endogenous GH secretion which predominantly takes place during the first hours of sleep.

Currently used GH regimens may not be ideal because they produce abnormal GH profiles. Daily GH dosing may be more effective, for example, since GH normally is secreted in daily episodic bursts.[163] Daily injections can be more effective than three times weekly IM dosing and can result in an improved growth rate.[164] Other clinicians believe that twice-weekly dosing should be used in the second year of therapy to improve patient convenience since one study showed that twice-weekly dosing was as effective as three times weekly dosing in the second year.[162]

Also, subcutaneous injection may be a better route since it is less painful and just as effective as the intramuscular injections.[163,165] Some clinicians discourage subcutaneous administration because the incidence of lipoatrophy or antibody formation may be increased. However, several studies using purer forms of GH have not substantiated these concerns.[165,166]

C.T. is an ideal candidate for GH therapy because she has documented GHD and probably has open epiphyses. A synthetic form of GH must be used since the pituitary form is off the market. Somatrem 2 mg (0.1 mg/kg) or synthetic Somatropin 1.6 mg IM every Monday, Wednesday, and Friday evening are adequate initial regimens. Although synthetic Somatropin is not more effective than Somatrem, it may be the preferred product because it is less antigenic.[158] Treatment is continued until a satisfactory adult height is attained, the epiphyses close, or the patient ceases to respond.

The benefits of exogenous GH may be substantial in C.T. A satisfactory response is an increase in growth velocity to over 5 cm a year or a doubling of the previous growth rate. The greatest response is seen during the first year of therapy.[154]

Methods of enhancing the response to GH include withdrawal of therapy for several months or coadministration of anabolic steroids. Anabolic steroids must be used cautiously, however, since they accelerate epiphyseal closure, which would preclude any further response to GH. Liver function tests should be monitored since anabolic steroids occasionally are hepatotoxic and in rare cases have been associated with hepatic tumors. Also, anabolic steroids may cause unacceptable virilizing side effects in females.[153]

Inexplicably, only one-half of patients treated with pituitary GH attain normal adult height. Long-term responses to both forms of synthetic GH should be similar since initial responses are similar to those seen with the pituitary form.[155,158] Ten percent of children with GHD do not respond to GH, and this may be related to a GH-receptor defect.

Adverse Effects. Growth hormone therapy is relatively safe and serious side effects are rare. All forms of GH stimulate antibody formation, but Somatrem does so to the greatest extent.[158,167] Fortunately, less than 5% of patients receiving Somatrem develop titers of potent neutralizing antibodies capable of interfering with the GH response.[154,155] The increased antigenicity of Somatrem appears to be due to imperceptible quantities of protein from the

E. coli used to synthesize this form of GH rather than to the extra methionine residue.[155] Local tenderness at the injection site is an occasional side effect, and hypothyroidism and hypertension are uncommon side effects. Glucose intolerance and acromegaly accompany the use of suprapharmacologic doses.[167] An increased rate of tumor recurrence in children with GHD secondary to an intracranial malignancy is a potential side effect. Although this has not been confirmed, caution should be exercised when GH is given to such children.[168] Before GH therapy is initiated, intracranial lesions must have been inactive for one year and antitumor therapy must have been completed.

34. If C.T. has an unsatisfactory response to GH, with and without anabolic steroids, what other treatments could be used?

Growth Hormone-Releasing Factor (GHRF)

Growth hormone-releasing factor, dopaminergic drugs, and clonidine are alternative agents for treatment of GHD. GHRF is secreted by the hypothalamus and controls pituitary growth hormone secretion. Initial studies have shown that synthetic GHRF can promote growth hormone secretion and stimulate growth in children with GHD.[169–171] It has been administered subcutaneously in multiple pulses throughout the day to approximate a normal physiological state. Growth hormone-releasing factor may be the treatment of choice for children with idiopathic GHD since 60% of these children have hypothalamic rather than pituitary deficiencies.[169]

Dopamine Agonists and Clonidine

Dopamine agonists stimulate GH secretion directly or by a noradrenergic mechanism. These drugs have been used alone or in combination with exogenous GH with positive results. Levodopa and bromocriptine have been administered orally in doses of 15 mg/kg every six hours or 1.25 mg every 12 hours, respectively.[172] Clonidine (Catapres), an α-adrenergic agonist, promotes growth through stimulation of GH secretion. This effect may be secondary to enhancement of GHRF secretion from the hypothalamus. Clonidine (0.05 to 0.15 mg/m²) given orally twice a day for 60 days stimulated linear growth in two out of four children with GHD in one study.[173] Dopamine agonists and clonidine may be effective in children with idiopathic GHD because many of these cases are likely to be secondary to decreased dopaminergic or noradrenergic tone in the central nervous system. More studies are needed to determine optimal dosing regimens for all of these agents.

Other Diagnoses

35. If C.T. had short stature secondary to a diagnosis other than GHD, how would her management have differed?

Treatment of short children with diagnoses other than GHD is not well established. Use of GH is controversial since this agent is approved for use only in children who meet the standard criteria of GHD. Restricting GH use to these children, however, may be inappropriate since other short children may respond to GH.[156,174]

Treatment of boys with constitutional growth delay is controversial since these children eventually attain a normal adult height.[153] Therefore, treatment is reserved for patients who meet the following criteria: 1) height below the third percentile; 2) prepubertal; 3) bone age at least two years behind chronologic age; and 4) psychological problems secondary to short stature. Testosterone enanthate (Testaval) 100 to 200 mg is given intramuscularly once a month for three to four months or every three weeks for four doses.[175] A short course is given to prevent untoward acceleration of epiphyseal closure which would compromise final height. Insufficient data are available to evaluate the benefits of GH for this form of short stature.

Treatment of children with attenuated growth secondary to an endocrinopathy other than GHD, severe malnutrition, or chronic disease also is not well established. Short children with hypothyroidism will respond to thyroid replacement.[153] Short boys with chronic diseases such as cystic fibrosis may respond to testosterone.[176] GH treatment of these children is not well documented.

Most debates over therapy of short stature surround the treatment of children who are intrinsically short. Some clinicians feel that most of these children are normal and will not benefit from therapy. Others believe a subgroup of these children have a subtle or partial form of GHD and may respond to GH.[161,177] Children who are considered variants of normal or those with familial short stature have been treated with GH with positive short-term results.[177–181] Whether GH can increase the final adult height of these children is unknown.[182] Supraphysiologic doses of GH may be more effective, but they also are more toxic.

Girls with Turner's Syndrome, an x-chromosome anomaly, are thought to have intrinsic shortness but actually may have a relative deficiency of GH.[179] Anabolic steroid and sex hormone replacement are standard therapy. Estrogens with progesterone are started between 12 and 14 years of age. GH has been used to treat Turner's Syndrome alone or in combination with oxandrolone with good results in a few studies.[183,184] However, oxandrolone production was discontinued by the manufacturer in May of 1989. More studies are needed before GH can be recommended as part of the standard treatment regimen for short stature associated with Turner's Syndrome.

In conclusion, long-term studies are needed before GH can be recommended routinely for short children without classic GHD.[154] A potential problem with the use of GH in these children and other apparently normal children is induction of antibodies which could interfere with the function of endogenous GH.[154,156]

In this case, C.T.'s management would depend upon the etiology of her short stature. A 6- to 12-month trial of GH could be administered since some children without classic GHD respond to GH. C.T.'s parents would need to be informed of the risks of such therapy and the poorly documented, long-term benefits of using GH in short children without GHD. C.T. should be monitored closely for antibody production and growth response.

Idiopathic Thrombocytopenic Purpura (ITP)

Idiopathic thrombocytopenic purpura in children generally is an acute, self-limited, benign disease with spontaneous remission occurring in 80% to 90% of cases within six months of diagnosis.[185] Chronic ITP evolves from the acute form in less than 20% of cases.[186] Mortality rates are low, ranging from 0.21% to 2.1%, and most deaths can be attributed to intracranial hemorrhage, which usually occurs within the first few weeks of diagnosis.[187,188] The social and psychological effects that occur secondarily to restriction of normal childhood physical activity constitute the primary forms of morbidity.

The etiology of ITP in children is unknown. Also, the pathogenesis of the acute form probably is not the same as chronic ITP since children with these two types of ITP exhibit different characteristics. Acute ITP is thought to be triggered by a viral infection which induces formation of antigen-antibody complexes. These complexes adhere to platelets, resulting in increased platelet consumption by the reticuloendothelial system (RES). The chronic form, which is similar to adult ITP, may be due to production of auto-antibodies to platelet antigens.[185,187,188]

Clinical Presentation

36. J.T., a 3-year-old, 15 kg, previously healthy girl, presented with a 3-week history of increased bruising and repeated nose- **bleeds after an episode of gastroenteritis. Physical examination was remarkable for generalized petechiae and scattered bruising. Her Hgb, Hct, WBC count and differential were within normal limits, but the platelet count was 10,000/mm^3 (Normal: 250,000–350,000). A bone marrow aspiration was normal except for increased numbers of platelet precursors. She was admitted to the hospital with a diagnosis of acute ITP. Which signs, symptoms, and laboratory tests in J.T. are consistent with ITP?**
[SI unit: platelet count 10×10^9/L (Normal: 250–350]

Diagnosis of idiopathic thrombocytopenic purpura is based upon clinical presentation, complete blood count (CBC), and bone marrow aspiration.[189] As illustrated by J.T., children with acute ITP classically present with a sudden appearance of purpura or petechiae within a month of the onset of a viral infection.[190] Approximately 25% of children with acute ITP have epistaxis (nosebleeds), 5% have hematuria, and less than 4% have massive purpura or retinal hemorrhages. The marked decrease in J.T.'s platelet count to below 50,000 cells/mm^3 with a normal CBC is indicative of idiopathic thrombocytopenic purpura. Eosinophilia is seen in 15% to 20% of cases; a relative lymphocytosis also is common. J.T.'s bone marrow examination is typical in that it reveals a normocellular marrow with the exception of an increased number of megakaryocytes (i.e., platelet precursors).[185] A bone marrow examination also is useful for ruling out diseases that can mimic ITP, such as acute leukemia and aplastic anemia, but some clinicians believe it is not routinely indicated.[189]

Treatment

37. How should J.T. be managed initially?

J.T. can be managed conservatively since she is not massively hemorrhaging. Medical treatment, however, may be indicated because most cases of intracranial hemorrhage have occurred in children with platelet counts below 20,000 cells/mm^3.[187] If J.T.'s platelet count were higher, some clinicians would delay treatment since the risk of spontaneous, severe bleeding is low if platelet counts remain above 30,000/mm^3. Also, other clinicians would not treat children, like J.T., who are not massively hemorrhaging or bleeding internally, regardless of the platelet count, because they believe the incidence of catastrophic hemorrhage is very low.[191]

Splenectomy

The treatment of choice is controversial since the mortality rate is low, the rate of spontaneous remission is high, and data for different therapies are inconsistent.[189] The only therapeutic modality with undisputed efficacy is splenectomy. However, since splenectomy is a major surgical procedure leaving a child at risk for serious infection, and intravenous gamma globulin (IVIG) therapy is associated with good results, many clinicians reserve splenectomy for children with resistant cases of ITP.[192–195]

38. What treatments are available for acute ITP?

Splenectomy, plasmapheresis, steroids, and IVIG have been used to treat acute idiopathic thrombocytopenic purpura. Platelet transfusions are ineffective since infused platelets are removed rapidly by the reticuloendothelial system. Splenectomy is the only treatment that can be considered curative because the major site of platelet phagocytosis and antibody formation is removed. Splenectomy is performed in children with acute ITP only if they have a catastrophic hemorrhage (e.g., intracranial bleeding). Plasmapheresis is an investigational treatment for acute ITP and its place in the treatment scheme has not been determined; its efficacy may be due to the removal of antigen-antibody complexes.[186]

Steroids

Steroids have been used as treatment for acute ITP for many years, but their benefits and indications are controversial.[188,189,193]

Steroids may decrease the duration of thrombocytopenia by inhibiting platelet phagocytosis. They also may lower the risk of hemorrhage by increasing capillary integrity.

The efficacy of steroids has been disputed. First, not all studies have shown that steroids induce a more rapid rise in platelet levels than would occur spontaneously. Second, there is not enough evidence to support the claim that steroids increase capillary integrity. Also, indications for using steroids vary among clinicians. Most agree that steroids should be given if the patient's platelet count is below 10,000/mm³ or if there is severe bleeding. Disagreement over steroid use arises when platelet counts are over 10,000 to 20,000/mm³ and the child is minimally symptomatic.[185,188,189]

The optimum steroid regimen for acute ITP has not been determined. Prednisone doses have ranged from 1.5 to 3 mg/kg/day for two to three weeks to 60 mg/m²/day for three weeks.[185,188,189,193] Intravenous steroids and/or higher doses have been used for intracranial bleeding.[196] The risks of using steroids are low since they are used for a short time period. One reported side effect is transient rebound thrombocytopenia following their discontinuation.[185] In addition, since steroids can mask leukemia, a bone marrow aspiration must be performed to rule out malignancy before they are prescribed.

Intravenous Gamma Globulin (IVIG)

Intravenous gamma globulin is a commonly used therapy for acute idiopathic thrombocytopenic purpura. IVIG induces a rapid rise in platelet counts, and this action may prevent hemorrhage. An advantage of IVIG is that it may induce a more rapid increase in platelet levels than steroids.[188,193,197] Platelet counts may take two to three weeks to return to normal if steroids are used.[188,190,198] In contrast, platelet counts begin to increase within 24 hours and usually peak in the normal range within five to ten days after completion of an IVIG course.[188,198] Although the platelet increase may be transient, platelet counts still may remain high enough to maintain hemostasis.[191,199]

The exact mechanism of action of IVIG is not clear. IVIG may work by blocking phagocytosis of antibody-coated platelets by the reticuloendothelial system or by eliminating circulating immune complexes and microbial antigens.[197,198,200] Adverse reactions to IVIG usually are mild (see Question 42) and related to the rate of administration. Reactions may include flushing, chills, fever, headache, dizziness, diaphoresis, and nausea and can be minimized by stopping the infusion or decreasing the infusion rate. Hypotension, dyspnea, myalgias, joint pain, and abdominal pain also have been reported. Anaphylactic reactions have been reported in patients with IgA deficiency. Another consideration is the relatively high cost of IVIG therapy.

Steroids or IVIG are reasonable treatments for J.T. because she is at high risk for bleeding. On the other hand, other clinicians might elect to monitor J.T. closely but avoid treatment.

39. Dosing. The hematologist decided to treat J.T. with IVIG and ordered Gammagard 15 gm IV QD for 3 days. Is this regimen optimal?

The optimal IVIG regimen is unknown. Early studies used 400 mg/kg/day for five days.[191,192,197] Doses up to 1 gm/kg/day for one to three days also have been effective.[194,198] Kurlander et al. compared the efficacy of 400 mg/kg/day for five days to 1 gm/kg/day for two days in 27 adult patients with ITP. Although a higher response rate was seen in the group receiving 1 gm/kg, the patients in the 400 mg/kg group had a better quality of response.[194]

Proper IVIG administration can reduce the incidence of side effects. Headaches, nausea, chills, fever, and hypotension may be avoided by infusing IVIG slowly.[192] Premedication with an anti-

pyretic or an antihistamine also may help minimize these adverse reactions.[197,198] Other side effects include cutaneous rashes and local reactions at the injection site. Recommended infusion rates differ for each of the preparations (see Table 95.9). To avoid an inflammatory response, infusions of IVIG should begin at a low rate and be increased as tolerated.

J.T.'s dose of IVIG is 1 gm/kg/day for three days. The optimal dose of IVIG to treat ITP is unknown. The 15 gm dose should be infused over several hours. The infusion should be initiated at a rate of 7.5 mL/hour (0.5 mL/kg/hour) and doubled every 30 minutes as tolerated to a maximum of 60 mL/hour (4 mL/kg/hour). To minimize adverse effects, 200 mg acetaminophen (12 mg/kg/dose) and 15 mg diphenhydramine (1 mg/kg/dose) can be administered 30 to 60 minutes before starting the IVIG infusion. Epinephrine and hydrocortisone should be readily available in the event of an anaphylactic reaction.

Goals of Therapy

40. What are the goals of therapy?

The ultimate goal of therapy is induction of remission. If remission does not occur, therapy is aimed at maintenance of hemostatic platelet levels (i.e., platelet counts >50,000/mm³) and prevention of catastrophic hemorrhage.[199] Unfortunately, severe internal bleeding has occurred in patients despite treatment with steroids or IVIG. Another goal of therapy is to avoid performing a splenectomy, which would put the child at an increased risk for infection.[186]

Prognosis

41. What is J.T.'s prognosis?

J.T.'s prognosis is good, much better than the prognosis of adults with ITP.[187] Over 50% of untreated children with acute ITP will achieve a spontaneous remission within three weeks of diagnosis, and another 30% to 40% will enter remission six months after diagnosis.[197] Children with chronic ITP will enter remission slowly over a period of years or after a splenectomy.[199] Although early institution of nonsurgical treatments for acute ITP can decrease morbidity and mortality, they probably cannot prevent the development of chronic ITP.[190,192]

Chronic Idiopathic Thrombocytopenic Purpura

42. J.T.'s platelet count rose to 260,000/mm³ after she received the IVIG, and her counts have remained within normal limits for the past year. J.T. appears to be in remission. If she had developed chronic ITP, how would she have been managed? [SI unit: platelet count 260 × 10⁹/L]

Chronic idiopathic thrombocytopenic purpura is defined as thrombocytopenia lasting for more than six months. There are different approaches to the treatment of chronic ITP, but all agree that splenectomy should be delayed to allow for spontaneous remission as long as hemostatic platelet counts are maintained and the child remains asymptomatic.

Steroids or IVIG can be used to maintain adequate platelet counts or control symptoms before a splenectomy.[185] IVIG sometimes is cited as the treatment of choice for chronic ITP because it has relatively few side effects.[197,199] IVIG may induce a remission or a transient rise in platelet counts even in steroid-resistant patients.[198] Booster doses may be required to maintain hemostatic platelet counts and have been given in doses ranging from 400 mg/kg to 1 gm/kg as frequently as once a week.[197–202] Long-term steroid use is discouraged because it may exacerbate thrombocytopenia, delay bone growth, and cause a Cushingoid state.

Children with steroid and IVIG-resistant chronic ITP may respond to plasmapheresis or immunosuppressive therapy. Plasmapheresis has been effective in a small number of children and, in

Table 95.9	Preparation and Administration of Intravenous Products[a,b]				
Item	Sandoglubulin	Venoglobulin-L	Gamimune N	Gammagard	Iveegam
Diluent(s)	SWI, NS, D5W[c]	SWI	None	SWI	SWI
Filter	No	No	No	Yes[d]	Yes[d]
Initial concentration to be infused (%)	3	5	5	5	5
Initial infusion rate	0.5–1.0 mL/min	0.01–0.02 mL/kg/min	0.01–0.2 mL/kg/min	0.5 mL/kg/hr	1.0 mL/min
Rate to which infusion may be ↑	2.0–2.5 mL/min	0.04 mL/kg/min	0.08 mL/kg/hr	4.0 mL/kg/hr	2.0 mL/min
Subsequent maximum concentration (%)	6 and 12	5	5	—[c]	—[e]
IV solutions with which compatible	NS, D5W,[c] SWI, 0.45 NaCl, 0.22% NaCl	NS[c]	—[f,g]	—[c]	—[e]

[a] Reprinted with permission from reference 201.
[b] D5W = 5% dextrose injection; NaCl = Sodium chloride injection; NS = 0.9% sodium chloride injection; SWI = Sterile water for injection.
[c] Not mentioned in package insert.
[d] Provided by manufacturer.
[e] Information not available at this writing.
[f] Manufacturer recommends infusing in a separate IV line.
[g] Manufacturer recommends infusing in a separate IV line; however, the diluent used for this product is 5% dextrose injection.

some cases, has restored responsiveness to IVIG.[199] Immunosuppressive drugs have been used before and after surgery but generally are reserved for children with ITP resistant to splenectomy. Azathioprine (Imuran), cyclophosphamide (Cytoxan), vincristine (Oncovin), vinblastine (Velban), and 6-mercaptopurine have been used with variable success.[189,191]

Splenectomy is effective in 70% of children with chronic ITP and is indicated in symptomatic children with platelet counts that have remained below 50,000/mm^3 for 12 months.[187,191] It also is used in asymptomatic children who are physically active and is definitely indicated for children who develop severe bleeding. Steroids or IVIG can be given before splenectomy to obtain platelet counts that will maintain hemostasis during surgery.[186] Therefore, if J.T. develops chronic ITP, she could receive a repeat course of IVIG with booster doses to maintain hemostasis; a second line of therapy would be steroids or plasmapheresis. Splenectomy and immunosuppressive drugs would be considered last resorts.

Finally, patients with ITP should avoid medications with antiplatelet effects [e.g., aspirin, dipyridamole, nonsteroidal anti-inflammatory drugs (NSAID)]. The child and/or the child's parents should be informed of common aspirin-containing medications. Parents also should be instructed to monitor their child's physical activity to avoid any trauma that could precipitate life-threatening hemorrhage.

Enuresis

Enuresis is involuntary voiding of urine in the absence of any organic lesion after the age of five to six.[203] This problem occurs in 20% of children at age five, 10% at age six, 3% at age 12, and 1% at age 18.[204] Most children become dry at night between the ages of 18 months and four years, usually after daytime control is achieved.[205] Enuresis is a benign condition which is encountered more often in males than in females.

The pathology of nocturnal enuresis is not well understood. Somatic and psychogenic causes have been proposed, but an inherited predisposition also must be considered. Additionally, some children are thought to have a small bladder capacity. An organic etiology is present in 2% of cases. Norgaard et al. reported that unlike normal children, enuretic patients do not have a normal nighttime peak in antidiuretic hormone levels.[206] In this study, enuretic patients were found to have normal bladder capacity with a high urine output at night.

Evaluation

43. S.N., a 6-year-old male, is brought to his pediatrician because he still wets the bed; punishing him only seems to worsen the situation. Within the past year, S.N. achieved daytime bladder control, but now he wets his bed once or twice a week. How should S.N.'s problem be evaluated and classified?

A thorough medical history is required including a detailed family history, a review of psychosocial aspects of the child's family life, and information concerning day and night wetting patterns and fluid intake. If both parents are enuretic, 77% of their children will have nocturnal enuresis.[207] With only one enuretic parent, 44% tend to be enuretic, and when the family history is negative, a 15% prevalence of enuresis can be expected.[207]

The child's evaluation also should include a general physical examination to rule out any urologic abnormality or spinal cord lesion. A neurological examination should include an assessment of muscle tone, reflexes, and sensory response.[203]

A urinalysis should be performed to rule out organic causes such as diabetes insipidus, diabetes mellitus, or urinary tract infections. Radiographic studies are not indicated unless the child has a urinary tract infection (≥2 cases of infection in girls) or an abnormal urine stream.[208,209]

Treatment

44. How might S.N.'s enuresis be treated?

Enuretic children exhibit a 15% spontaneous cure rate per year after age six, and this must be considered when evaluating various treatment modes. Spontaneous cures after age 14 are rare. In all situations, counseling for emotional problems should be offered to the patient and parents if warranted.

Conditioning therapy involves a signal alarm that arouses the child as soon as urine moistens a special, electrically wired mattress pad that is connected to a buzzer. These older devices were referred to as "the bell and pad" model alarms. Two enuresis alarms now are available which have revolutionized the treatment of enuresis. These awakening devices run on a hearing aid battery, are easy to set up, are sensitive to a few drops of urine, and are relatively inexpensive. An alarm sounds when urine completes the transistorized circuit between two electrodes attached to the front of the child's underwear. The bell and pad alarms are effective in 30% to 50% of enuretic patients and should be continued for several weeks (usually 3) after the child has stopped wetting. Success rates as high as 75% have been reported with the newer devices.[210]

Approximately 10% to 15% of the patients using a newer device may relapse after therapy is discontinued; however, they frequently will respond to retreatment.[211] The use of these devices is relatively safe, but rashes from urinary sodium chloride electrolysis and electrical burns from faulty apparatus have been reported.[212]

Bladder training consists of stretching exercises to increase the functional bladder capacity and stream interruption exercises to increase the ability of the sphincter to withstand bladder spasms. Some enuretic children appear to have small functional bladder capacities for their age and, therefore, tend to void more frequently during the day.[207] Normal bladder capacity can be estimated using the following equations: Ounces = Age (years) + 2.[207] An adult has a bladder capacity of 350 to 500 mL.[211] Increased daytime fluid intake also may be an important component of bladder stretching exercises. The child is encouraged to hold the urine as long as possible during the daytime. During urination, the child is instructed to practice stopping the flow midstream to increase his sphincter tone. In an uncontrolled study, these exercises resulted in improvement in bladder capacity in 66% of cases, with cure reported in 30%.[213]

Motivational counseling is an important adjunct in the treatment of an enuretic child. Counseling is geared toward increasing the patient's commitment to a treatment goal. The child is encouraged to play an active role; the physician can provide reassurance about the etiology and prognosis of enuresis; and parents can provide positive reinforcement for "dry nights." Punishment for bedwetting must be discontinued.

Drug therapy is used frequently to manage enuresis. Because of its rapid onset of action, drug therapy can help an enuretic child with special situations, such as family vacations, camp, or slumber parties. In general, drugs should be prescribed only in conjunction with motivational techniques and bladder exercises.

Imipramine, a tricyclic antidepressant (TCA), is used frequently and is the drug of choice for enuresis. The basis for the antienuretic action of TCAs is unknown but may be the result, in part, of its anticholinergic effect. Kales et al. have suggested that early in the night, when sleep is deepest, imipramine decreases bladder excitability and/or increases its capacity. The child thus is permitted to sleep without wetting until later in the night when sleep is lighter and the child is more responsive to bladder stimuli.[213] In contrast to the drug's delayed antidepressant effect, the onset of the antienuretic effect is immediate.[207,213] Some investigators have suggested that the plasma imipramine concentration plus that of its active metabolite, desipramine, should be above 60 ng/mL; others believe a level of ≥150 ng/mL is needed. Studies have not substantiated a correlation between plasma drug concentration and clinical response in enuretic patients; however, there does seem to be a high correlation between drug concentration and toxicity.[214,215]

The initial dose ranges from 1 to 1.5 mg/kg/day (25 to 50 mg) and may be titrated to a maximum of 2.5 mg/kg/day (75 to 100 mg). Imipramine is recommended for use only in children older than six years and should be administered one to two hours before bedtime.[207]

45. S.N. was given bladder training exercises and started on imipramine therapy. What information about imipramine's efficacy and side effects should S.N.'s parents receive?

Although the drug usually is effective, some patients do not respond or develop an apparent tolerance to the antienuretic effect of imipramine.[213] Success occurs in 40% of patients, although relapse following discontinuation of the drug is high, especially if it is stopped abruptly.[207] Side effects generally are mild and dose-related; however, these drugs are potentially lethal in overdose

situations and should be kept out of the reach of small children. When dispensing imipramine, the total amount should be limited, and syrup of ipecac should be dispensed as well. If an overdose occurs, S.N.'s parents should be instructed to contact his physician or poison control center immediately.

46. Are there other agents used to treat enuresis which might offer S.N. a safe and effective alternative to imipramine?

Oxybutynin (Ditropan) is an antispasmodic agent that reduces uninhibited detrusor muscle contractions. Unlike imipramine, oxybutynin has a direct spasmolytic effect on the bladder and thereby minimizes spasms. Efficacy of oxybutynin for nocturnal enuresis is questionable. In a prospective, double-blind, crossover study, no difference was found in response to oxybutynin compared to placebo.[216] The recommended dose is 0.4 to 0.6 mg/kg/day in two or three divided doses (maximum: 10 to 15 mg/day).

Desmopressin (DDVAP). Another alternative to imipramine is desmopressin, a synthetic, long-acting analog of vasopressin. Some studies have indicated that nocturnal bedwetting can be reduced by decreasing urine output with DDAVP. In one study, doses of 40 µg at bedtime allowed 51% of patients to achieve total dryness.[217] Gradual tapering of the dose led to a small relapse rate. In another study, doses of 40 µg were found to be more effective than 20 µg, although both had a significant response when compared to placebo.[218] Although desmopressin therapy is expensive, adverse effects are minimal. Further studies are needed to determine the appropriate dose and duration of therapy.

Sedation and Analgesia
Sedation

Sedation frequently is required for pediatric patients undergoing diagnostic or therapeutic procedures or for children in an intensive care setting. Various medications and routes of administration have been used to produce sedative effects (see Table 95.10). In general, drugs administered intravenously produce a rapid rise of serum concentrations; thus, a more rapid onset of action. Therefore, caution should be exercised when using the IV route to administer sedatives. Absorption of drugs administered intramuscularly, rectally, or orally may be variable, especially in infants and young children.[219,220]

Conscious Sedation

47. A.J., a 3-year-old, 15-kg female, is admitted for evaluation of abdominal mass. A computed tomography scan is ordered. What regimen should be used to sedate A.J.?

Ideally, sedative agents should be easy to administer, have a rapid and predictable onset, have minimal adverse effects and a duration that is just long enough to complete the procedure. Unfortunately, a sedative regimen that meets all of these requirements is not available. However, many agents, when properly used, can achieve some of these goals. Historically, these agents include chloral hydrate, barbiturates, narcotic analgesics, and benzodiazepines.

Chloral hydrate is one of the oldest available sedative hypnotics. Although it often is thought to be an ideal hypnotic agent, it was in widespread use before the FDA began regulating drugs in 1938 and has never been tested comprehensively for toxicity or efficacy.[221] Recently, chloral hydrate has been alleged to have potential carcinogenicity and genotoxicity.[222] These concerns surfaced because chloral hydrate is a metabolite of trichloroethylene, an industrial solvent and cleaning fluid found to induce cancer following daily administration in rodents. While it is difficult to extrapolate animal data to humans and much of the evidence for carcinogenesis is largely theoretical, this controversy was alarming

Table 95.10	Drugs Commonly Used for Conscious Sedation[224]			
Drug	Dosage[a]	Onset of Action	Duration	Comments
Chloral hydrate	*Adults*: 500–1000 mg *Children*: 25–100 mg/kg (*max*: 1 gm/dose to a total of 2 gm) *Route*: PO, PR	20–30 min	Unpredictable	Rapidly metabolized to active metabolite trichloroethanol. Paradoxical excitation may occur. Hyperbilirubinemia has been associated with chloral hydrate (repeated doses) in premature infants and neonates
Diazepam (Valium)	*Adults*: PO: 5–20 mg IV: 5–7.5 mg *Children*: IV: 0.05–0.2 mg/kg (*max*: 10 mg) PO: 0.1–0.5 mg/kg (*max*: 10 mg)	IV: 2–3 min PO: 30–45 min	2–6 hours	May burn when given IV (lipid soluble). Do not use small veins. Infuse IV over 3 min and at most 5 mg/min. Potentiates the effect of narcotics and barbiturates
Fentanyl (Sublimaze)	*Adults*: IV: 0.5–1.0 µg/kg *Children*: IV: 1–2 µg/kg (up to 100 µg/dose) PO: 5–15 µg/kg (*max*: 400 µg)	IV: 1–1.5 min IM: 7–8 min PO: 5–15 min	IV: 30–60 min IM: 1–2 hours PO: 1–2 hours	Infuse IV over 3–5 min. Effects potentiated by benzodiazepines. Oralet available in 200, 300, and 400 µg doses
Lorazepam (Ativan)	*Adults*: IV: 2 mg/dose PO: 2–4 mg/dose *Children*: IV: 0.05 mg/kg PO: 0.05–0.1 mg/kg	IV: 2–5 min IM: 15–30 min PO: 30–60 min	6–24 hours	Infuse IV over 2–3 min, not to exceed 2 mg/min. Potentiates the effect of narcotics and barbiturates
Meperidine (Demerol)	*Adults*: IV/IM: 50–100 mg *Children*: IV: 0.5–1.0 mg/kg SQ/IM: 1–2 mg/kg (*max*: 100 mg/dose) See Combination Drugs below for Demerol/Phenergan/Thorazine dosage	IV: 1–5 min SQ/IM: 10 min	IV: 1–2 hours SQ/IM: 2–4 hours	Metabolite (normeperidine) has neurotoxic effect. Accumulation of normeperidine may result in CNS manifestation. Caution in patients with renal impairment after high or repeated doses. Infuse IV dose over 3–5 min
Midazolam (Versed)	*Adults*: IV: 0.5–2.0 mg/dose; may repeat to total dose of 2.5–5 mg *Children*: IV: 0.05–0.1 mg/kg Intranasal: 0.2–0.3 mg/kg PO: 0.2–0.4 mg/kg (*max*: 15 mg)	IV: 1–3 min IM: 10–15 min Intranasal: 5 min PO: 5–10 min	IV: 30–60 min IM: 2–6 hours Intranasal: 40–75 min PO: 30–90 min	3–4 times potency of diazepam. Potentiates the effect of narcotics. Infuse IV dose over 1–2 min
Morphine	*Adults*: IV: 2–15 mg/dose *Children*: IV: 0.05–0.1 mg/kg	IV: 1.0–2.5 min	1–2 hours	Maximal respiratory depression occurs within 7 min. Effect potentiated by benzodiazepines. Infuse IV dose over 3–5 min
Pentobarbital (Nembutal)	*Adults*: PO/IV: 100 mg *Children*: PO/PR/IM: 2–6 mg/kg (*max*: 100 mg/dose) IV: 1–3 mg/kg in increments of 1 mg/kg (*max*: 100 mg/dose)	PO/PR: 15–60 min IM: 10–25 min IV: 1–2 min	PO/PR: 1–4 hours IM: 30–60 min IV: 15–20 min	IV administration over at least 1 min or not to exceed 50 mg/min
Combination drugs Demerol/ Phenergan/ Thorazine	IM: *Demerol*: 2 mg/kg (up to 50 mg) *Phenergan*: 1 mg/kg (up to 12.5 mg) *Thorazine*: 1 mg/kg (up to 12.5 mg) IV: ½ of IM dose	IM: 10–15 min IV: 5–10 min	2–5 hours	Infuse IV dose over 5 min. Hypotension can occur with rapid IV infusion. May be mixed in the same syringe

[a] Use low end of the dose if combined with another agent(s).

to clinicians who have used the drug for many years without evidence of problems.[221] The American Academy of Pediatrics feels that many practitioners are familiar with the use of chloral hydrate and that it is an effective agent with a low incidence of toxicity. They are concerned that a sudden switch by practitioners to an agent that they are less familiar with might pose a greater risk than a theoretical risk of carcinogenesis.[223] While it is unreasonable to ban a drug like chloral hydrate based upon limited animal data, it may be reasonable for practitioners to become familiar with ad-

ditional agents, especially in situations where chloral hydrate fails to produce the desired sedative effect. Additional studies directed at pediatric risks of chloral hydrate also would be beneficial.

The reported dosage range of chloral hydrate is 25 to 100 mg/kg/dose to a maximum total dose of 2 gm.[224] Most children require 50 to 75 mg/kg to achieve the desired effect although a lower dose may be sufficient in infants.[220,223,225–229] Repetitive dosing of chloral hydrate to maintain prolonged sedation in infants and children during mechanical ventilation currently is not recommended due to accumulation of metabolites which can produce excessive central nervous system depression and other complications.[221,223] Chloral hydrate may be particularly useful for sedating infants and children in situations where there are limited alternatives such as electroencephalogram and pulmonary function tests.

Pentobarbital is another effective agent commonly used for sedation in children. It has a more rapid onset of action and shorter duration of action than chloral hydrate. Caution should be used in that the mg/kg dose required by older patients is much less than that needed in younger infants and children. Doses greater than 100 mg are rarely needed.[230] When given by the IV route, doses should be given in increments of 1 mg/kg to minimize risk of respiratory depression.[220,229-231] Barbiturates sometimes are associated with paradoxical reactions that include excitation and hyperactivity. If this reaction occurs, additional doses will only make the situation worse. Instead, administration of a narcotic such as morphine to the excited child will increase the chance of a peaceful sedation.

Narcotics such as morphine, fentanyl, and meperidine are used sometimes for sedation. These agents have the advantage of providing both sedation and analgesia and are useful in patients undergoing painful procedures, such as bone marrow biopsy. However, since analgesic effects occur at lower doses than those required for sedation, narcotics rarely are used alone for sedation. An oral preparation of fentanyl is available for use in preprocedure sedation. The oral fentanyl (Oralat) is available in doses of 200, 300, and 400 µg. The child is allowed to suck on the flavored product until she falls asleep.[232] Although the studies have reported successful sedation, some clinicians are concerned about associating drug therapy with candy-like preparations. Narcotic analgesics can induce respiratory depression which is reversed easily by administering naloxone. The risk of respiratory depression increases when narcotics are used in combination with benzodiazepines.[220,225,235-241]

Benzodiazepines (lorazepam, diazepam, and midazolam) produce sedation, hypnosis, muscle relaxation, and amnesia. In addition, they decrease anxiety in patients undergoing procedures.[233-236] These agents usually are administered intravenously before the procedure, although midazolam also has produced successful sedation when administered intranasally.[237,238] Flumazenil, a specific benzodiazepine antagonist, can be used for complete or partial reversal of the sedative effects of benzodiazepines.[239,240]

Combination agents also have been used to accomplish sedation. Meperidine (Demerol), promethazine (Phenergan), and chlorpromazine (Thorazine), also known as "DPT" or "pedi cocktail", is a popular sedative combination administered as a single injection. Although this regimen produces sedation in a majority of patients, it has been associated with a prolonged duration of action. In one study, approximately 70% of patients were sedated for ≥7 hours.[241] Therefore, patients receiving this "DPT" should be monitored closely for several hours.[241-243] Other combination regimens include fentanyl and midazolam; meperidine and pentobarbital; and morphine and various benzodiazepines. These combinations also have been associated with adverse effects and a prolonged duration of action.[225,235]

Available data do not indicate that one particular sedative regimen is superior to another. The choice and dosage of medication(s) usually depend upon the type of procedure and the degree of sedation required. Other important considerations include the age of the patient and their clinical condition. For A.J., use of intravenous or oral pentobarbital might be considered. It has a rapid onset and a shorter duration of action than chloral hydrate. Any previous history of successful sedation also can be helpful. Re-

gardless of the choice, appropriate monitoring should be performed during and after the procedure. In addition, adequate personnel and resuscitation equipment should be readily available.[244]

Intensive Care Unit (ICU) Sedation

48. M.P., a 5-year-old boy, is admitted to the pediatric ICU for sepsis. He currently is intubated and paralyzed. What are the considerations when sedating critically ill patients such as M.P.?

Children who require mechanical ventilation frequently receive medication to induce sedation to promote optimal ventilator manipulation without resistance from the patient. In children receiving paralytic agents, adequate sedation is particularly important to avoid the fear associated with being aware but unable to move.

Critically ill patients often require constant sedation. Therefore, scheduled administration (not PRN) or continuous infusions are recommended. Intermittent administration of medication results in peak and trough effects. Continuous infusions provide a more constant serum concentration and, therefore, more constant sedation; however, compatibility with other medications often is a problem. Intramuscular administration should be avoided. It causes pain with each injection and absorption of the drug is erratic and unpredictable in critically ill patients, partly due to decreased musculoskeletal activity. Oral administration can be used if the patient has demonstrated an ability to absorb oral medication but it often is impractical to manage sedation with oral medication in an intensive care setting.

Narcotic analgesics and benzodiazepines are the most commonly used agents for sedation in the ICU. Chloral hydrate, although not currently recommended for chronic sedation, also has been used.[245] With repetitive administration, it is important to consider the potential for accumulation of both the drugs and their metabolites, especially in patients with impaired hepatic and/or renal function. Repeated doses of chloral hydrate lead to accumulation of active metabolites, resulting in hyperbilirubinemia in newborns and respiratory depression and hypotonia in infants. Normeperidine, an active metabolite of meperidine, can cause seizures in patients with renal impairment after high or repeated doses.

Other problems with sedation include the development of tolerance. Children who receive repeated doses of agents for sedation may begin to require larger doses to achieve the desired effect. In addition, pediatric patients who receive narcotics or benzodiazepines for several days to weeks are at risk for developing symptoms of drug withdrawal.[246-248] Therefore, agents used for sedation should never be discontinued abruptly; instead, they should be tapered over several days. If this is impractical, an alternative is to switch the child to a long-acting agent, like phenobarbital, to minimize problems associated with acute withdrawal.

Analgesia

Inadequate pain control in children usually is a result of difficulty in pain assessment or misconceptions about pain.[249] During the last 20 years, much attention has been placed on the undertreatment of pain experienced by infants and children. In addition, clinical studies have documented that pain experienced by children is treated less aggressively than adult pain.[249,250] As the effects of pain on psychologic, physiologic, and endocrine systems have been better understood, there has been an increased emphasis to ensure adequate pain control in pediatric patients.[251-254]

Administration Schedules

The choice of drug, dose, frequency and route of administration must be individualized. As-needed dosing schedules require patients to endure and/or complain about pain before receiving analgesia. It takes less medication to prevent the return of pain than to control it; therefore, scheduled (around the clock) administration may require less overall medication to provide pain control. Continuous infusion of pain medication maintains more constant blood levels and avoids peak (sedation) and trough (return of pain) effects.

Patient-controlled analgesia (PCA) is an alternative which allows the patient to administer small boluses of analgesia. This method eliminates time between pain perception and relief, and gives the patient control over pain therapy. Several studies have demonstrated safety and effectiveness of PCA in children and adolescents.[255-259] Children as young as six years of age can be taught to use PCA devices, although some institutions restrict use to children who are ≥10 years of age.[259-261] A low-dose continuous infusion combined with PCA has the added benefit of providing baseline pain relief, especially while the patient is sleeping.

Routes of Administration. Typically, pain medication is administered intravenously, intramuscularly, or orally. The IV route provides the most rapid onset of action. When medication is administered intramuscularly, children may deny pain to avoid injections. When changing from parenteral to oral route, bioavailability and absorption need to be considered. Sustained-release products may be useful in children with chronic pain, but use of such products often is limited by the ability of the patient to swallow whole tablets.

Epidural analgesia is another effective approach to drug administration that can provide significant analgesia for long time periods with minimal sedation. Anesthesia can be obtained through the administration of local anesthetics (e.g., bupivacaine, lidocaine) or narcotics (e.g., morphine, fentanyl). The epidural route is being used with increasing frequency and has contributed significantly to the pain management of children.[254,262,263] The transdermal fentanyl patch also offers a unique approach to pain control, but due to limited data, the patches are not used frequently in the pediatric population.[264]

49. S.C., a 7-year-old boy, is admitted to the hospital after being hit by a car while riding his bicycle. He sustained multiple fractures and has just returned from surgery after an open reduction and internal fixation of his left femur and left humerus. He is tearful and states that he is in a lot of pain. What classes of pain medication are available for use in children? What problems can be anticipated following the use of analgesics in children?

Narcotic Agents

Narcotic analgesics are one of the most important classes used in the management of postoperative pediatric pain (see Table 95.11).[260] The use of morphine, meperidine, and fentanyl to treat moderate to severe pain in pediatric patients is well documented in the literature. Morphine is one of the most frequently used agents. The elimination and clearance of morphine in children older than five months of age is similar to that seen in adults. Neonates demonstrate decreased clearance and a longer elimination half-life when compared to older infants and children.[265] In neonates, the prolonged half-life may allow for adequate pain control when using intermittent bolus doses. However, older infants and children will require redosing every two to three hours with intermittent administration. This frequent dosing schedule has led to an increased use of continuous infusion regimens and PCA. Morphine also may be administered by epidural infusion.

Meperidine also is used frequently for the management of postoperative pain in pediatric patients even though the pharmacokinetic data in children are somewhat limited. At equipotent doses,

meperidine will exhibit the same degree of pain relief when compared to morphine. One advantage of meperidine is its 50% to 75% bioavailability when administered orally.[266]

Fentanyl is a popular analgesic because of its rapid onset and short duration of action. Fentanyl is approximately 100 times more potent than morphine. It most often is administered as a continuous or epidural infusion for the management of postoperative pain. It also is administered as an intermittent bolus for short procedures. Fentanyl is highly lipophilic and rapidly penetrates the blood brain barrier. Because of a larger volume of distribution, neonates, infants, and toddlers may require higher doses to achieve a desired effect.[265] Neonates also exhibit a prolonged elimination half-life of fentanyl which can lead to accumulation of drug with repeated doses or continuous infusions.[265]

Codeine frequently is administered in combination with acetaminophen for the treatment of mild to moderate pain. Although it can be administered intramuscularly, it offers no advantage over IM administration of morphine or meperidine.[265]

Nonnarcotic Analgesics. Acetaminophen, salicylates or NSAIDs commonly are used for mild to moderate pain. (See Table 95.11.) Salicylates and NSAIDs are useful in pain associated with inflammatory processes or bone metastases. Because of its association with Reye's syndrome, aspirin is not used routinely. Ketorolac (Toradol) is the only NSAID available parenterally. It is approved for IM administration but IV use has been reported for both adult and pediatric patients.[253,267-269]

Adverse Effects. At equipotent doses, all narcotic analgesic agents will cause a similar degree of respiratory depression and constipation. Nausea and vomiting occur secondary to stimulation of the chemoreceptor trigger zone in the brain. Fentanyl produces less sedation than meperidine and morphine. Morphine can produce peripheral vasodilation and significant hypotension can occur in hypovolemic patients. Meperidine should be avoided in patients with renal failure as accumulation of its metabolite, nor-meperidine, has been associated with seizures. The most serious side effect following administration of opioid analgesics is respiratory depression. Infants less than three months of age are particularly susceptible because of their immature blood brain barrier and decreased clearance of narcotics.[265] Patients receiving concomitant therapy with benzodiazepines or barbiturates may have an increased risk of cardiorespiratory side effects.

Adverse effects associated with epidural administration of morphine include nausea, pruritus, urinary retention, and late respiratory depression. Although late respiratory depression appears to be less common in children than adults, the possibility requires close monitoring of respiratory status for up to 12 hours after administration.[265]

Side effects associated with salicylates and NSAIDs are minimal although gastritis may occur, especially following prolonged use. NSAIDs also have been associated with renal toxicity.

Tolerance and Drug Withdrawal. Tolerance may occur in some children receiving several days of narcotic therapy resulting in the need of an increased dose to produce the same pain relief. If the patient continues to have a reason for pain, doses should be adjusted accordingly. If narcotics are being used for sedation, an alternative agent should be considered.

Withdrawal can occur when opioids are discontinued abruptly after continued use for more than seven to ten days. Withdrawal can be managed by slowly tapering the drug over several days. Another alternative is to switch to a longer-acting agent like methadone, which can be given at less frequent dosing intervals. Phenobarbital also can be used to minimize the agitation associated with withdrawal.

Topical Anesthetics

50. M.M., a 3-year-old boy, is brought to the emergency room (ER) by his parents for repair of a facial laceration. The physician in the ER orders TAC solution for repair of M.M.'s wound. What is TAC solution?

TAC solution is a topical anesthetic that contains tetracaine, adrenaline (epinephrine), and cocaine that is used for minor procedures such as laryngoscopy, bronchoscopy, and suturing of minor lacerations.[270] Tetracaine and cocaine are potent local anesthetics. Adrenaline and cocaine have vasoconstrictive effects, helping to decrease bleeding and systemic absorption of the solution. TAC typically is supplied as tetracaine 0.5%, epinephrine 1:2000, and cocaine 10% to 11.8%, although it has been suggested that half-strength solution is equally effective.[270,271]

TAC offers an advantage over local infiltration of anesthetics (e.g., lidocaine) for wound repair. Lidocaine infiltration is painful and has the potential to distort wound edges. In comparison studies, topical anesthetics result in better patient acceptability and more cooperative patients.[272,273]

TAC is not effective when applied to intact skin. However, rapid absorption can occur from mucosal surfaces resulting in toxic reactions. Death, seizures, and other CNS effects have been associated with accidental or deliberate applications of the solution to mucosal membranes or burn wounds. Therefore, TAC should not be used on mucosal surfaces, burns, or large wounds (>10 cm) because of the increased potential for absorption. TAC also should not be administered to areas where vasoconstriction may compromise vascularity (e.g., ear lobes, tip of nose, digits, penis).[265,270,272] Lastly, to avoid complications, TAC should not be used in patients with a history of seizures or cardiac dysrhythmias.

The following guidelines should be used to ensure the safety and efficacy of TAC:[265,270,274]

- Determine allergy history;
- Thoroughly clean wound and surrounding tissue;
- Saturate a sterile gauze pad or cotton ball with TAC solution (children: 0.05 mL/kg; maximum: 3 mL) and cover wound surface;
- Let stand for 10 to 20 minutes;
- Check for loss of pain sensation before wound repair.

Other important considerations include parental acceptance of the solution (due to concern about the cocaine component) and the time period between TAC application and the repair procedure. If adequate analgesia is not achieved after proper application of TAC or wound repair is delayed, TAC solution may be reapplied to a maximum total dose of 3 mL.[265,271] However, to avoid exposure to excessive amounts of cocaine, supplemental lidocaine infiltration may be a better alternative than reapplication of TAC.

51. K.M., a 6-year-old girl, comes to the cancer clinic for a lumbar puncture and intrathecal chemotherapy. EMLA is ordered for the procedure. What is EMLA? How is it administered?

Eutectic mixture of local anesthetics (EMLA), which has been widely used in Canada, Europe, and Australia as a transdermal local anesthetic for several years, is available now in the U.S. EMLA contains 2.5% lidocaine and 2.5% prilocaine. It reduces pain associated with venipuncture, intravenous cannulation, and lumbar puncture. EMLA is applied to intact skin at least one hour before the procedure. Systemic absorption is related to the duration of application and the application size (see Table 95.12).[275] Side effects include local reactions which usually resolve spontaneously within one to two hours, and allergic reactions to lidocaine or prilocaine. Systemic reaction is rare but one case of methemoglobinemia has been reported in a three-month-old infant.[276–279]

EMLA has been evaluated for reduction of pain from venipuncture in several trials.[276,280,281] Overall, these studies have concluded that EMLA is safe and effective in relieving pain associated with venipuncture. EMLA was felt to produce analgesia comparable to that of lidocaine infiltration without requiring an injection. EMLA also has been evaluated for use in procedure related pain. Children receiving EMLA as premedication to lumbar puncture reported significantly less pain than those receiving placebo.[278,282] Pain of vaccine injection decreased following administration of EMLA.[279] EMLA-treated infants appeared to have less pain, cry-

Table 95.11	Analgesic Agents Used in Children[a,224]	
Product	**Initial Dose**	**Comments**
Nonopioid		
Acetaminophen	10–15 mg/kg/dose Q 4–6 hr	No anti-inflammatory effect
Salicylates	10–15 mg/kg/dose Q 4–6 hr	Associated with Reye's syndrome; has anti-inflammatory effect
NSAIDs		
Ibuprofen	5–10 mg/kg/dose Q 6–8 hr	Gastritis with prolonged use
Naprosyn	5–7 mg/kg/dose Q 8–12 hr	
Ketorolac	*Adults:* 30–60 mg loading dose then 15–30 mg IM Q 6 hr *Children:* Not well established; 0.5–1.0 mg/kg loading dose then 0.25–0.5 mg/kg has been used	IV administration has been used
Opioids		
Codeine	0.5–1.0 mg/kg/dose Q 4–6 hr (*Adults:* 30–60 mg/dose)	Frequently combined with acetaminophen
Fentanyl	1–2 µg/kg/dose IV/IM (*Adults:* 50–100 µg/dose) *Infusion:* 3–10 µg/kg/hr	Chest wall rigidity, especially after rapid IV administration
Meperidine	*IV/IM:* 1.0–1.5 mg/kg Q 2–4 hr *PO:* 1–2 mg/kg Q 3–4 hr (*Adults:* 50–100 mg/dose)	Active metabolite has neurotoxic effect; avoid in renal failure
Morphine	*IV:* 0.1 mg/kg/dose Q 2–4 hr *IM:* 0.1–0.2 mg/kg Q 3–4 hr *PO:* 0.3–0.6 mg/kg Q 3–4 hr *IV infusion:* 0.05–0.1 mg/kg/hr	When changing to sustained release formulation, give daily dose as 2–3 divided doses

[a] IM = Intramuscular; IV = Intravenous; NSAID = Nonsteroidal anti-inflammatory drug; PO = Oral.

ing, and tenderness around the vaccination site. However, there was no difference in regard to fear exhibited by the children.[279,283]

Drug Administration

The administration of drugs to children requires special knowledge and expertise primarily because doses prescribed for children often are in amounts which are not commercially available. Guidelines or recipes are available for the extemporaneous preparation of medications that are available only in adult strengths or dosage forms. Caution must be used, however, since stability and bioavailability data often are unavailable for these extemporaneous preparations.

Oral Medications

The administration of oral medicines to an infant is not difficult as long as caution is exercised not to choke the patient. Liquid medications should be placed on the middle of the tongue or in the buccal cavity, preferably through a dropper. Oral syringes also are available for drug administration. These syringes are designed to prevent the attachment of intravenous needles and the inadvertent parenteral administration of an oral medication. They must be used with care since rapid administration or squirting can result in aspiration of the liquid.

It is common practice in pediatrics to disguise the taste of some medications in juice, Karo syrup, applesauce, ice cream, or another palatable vehicle to increase compliance. Children always should be encouraged and praised for their cooperation in taking their medicine.

Ear Drops

The methods used to administer otic medications in the outer ear of a child and to irrigate the ear are the same as for adults with one exception: the auricle of the ear in older patients is held up and back to straighten the canal. For children up to two or three years of age, however, the auricle is held down and out. This facilitates delivery of the medication to the middle ear.

Nose Drops

Administration of nose drops in children varies from nasal instillation in adults. The child is placed on his back, across the bed, with his shoulders projecting over the edge so that his head is lower than his body. The prescribed number of drops are instilled, and the patient is kept in this position for two to five minutes. Afterwards, the patient is placed on his abdomen facing directly down toward the mattress.

Eye Drops

Eye drops must be administered with extreme caution. Positioning and proper restraint of the child are necessary to prevent injury to the eye. The child's neck should be hyperextended with support provided under the shoulders. By having the head lower than the rest of the body, gravity will help to dispense the medication over the cornea. First, the lower lid must be retracted gently by using

Table 95.12	Maximum Application Area for EMLA[a],[272]
Body Weight	Maximum Application Area (cm^2)
≤10 kg	100
10–20 kg	600
>20 kg	2000

[a] EMLA = Eutectic mixture of local anesthetics.

the thumb to pull down on the skin beneath the lower eyelid. The prescribed number of drops then is instilled into the eye. The hand holding the dropper should be balanced on the head of the patient, so that the hand moves with the head if there is any inadvertent turning or jumping. This prevents any injuries to the eye secondary to collision with the dropper. The same technique can be used to apply ophthalmic ointments. After a thin line of ointment is placed in the cul-de-sac of the lower lid, the lid margin is closed. The child should remain still with his eyes closed for several minutes.

Note to the reader. The treatment of pediatric patients is considered throughout this text. (Also see the index or specific disease state chapters for a full discussion of other pediatric disorders.)

Update

Varicella Vaccine

The material in this section updates recommendations for varicella vaccine in Question 25.

The varicella vaccine, Varivax, was approved for use in healthy children on March 17, 1995. The American Academy of Pediatrics Committee of Infectious Diseases recommends administering a single dose of the vaccine to children age 12 months to 12 years who lack a reliable history of varicella infection and two injections four to eight weeks apart to children age 13 years or older.[284] Varicella vaccine is a live-attenuated vaccine and should not be routinely administered to children who are immunocompromised, including those with symptomatic or asymptomatic HIV infection and children on high systemic doses of corticosteroids. Although the vaccine is not licensed for routine use in children with acute lymphocytic leukemia, immunization is available for patients enrolled in specific research protocols. It also is recommended that salicylates not be given for six weeks following administration of the varicella vaccine because of the association between chickenpox and Reye's Syndrome. The Washington State Department of Health also has issued an advisory on the use of ibuprofen for children with chickenpox. Nine of twelve children with varicella who developed necrotizing fasciitis had received ibuprofen. A causal relationship, however, has not been established.

The FDA has requested that additional studies be carried out to determine the need for booster doses. Studies also are underway to evaluate the safety and efficacy of a quatravalent vaccine that includes the varicella vaccine and MMR (measles, mumps, rubella). At this time, Varivax may be administered at the same time as MMR but at separate sites. If not given simultaneously, varicella vaccine and MMR should be give at least one month apart.

References

1 **Golden NL et al.** Teething age in prematurely born infants. Am J Dis Child. 1981;135:903.

2 **Anomalies associated with tooth development.** In: Vaughan VC, Behrman RE, eds. Nelson's Textbook of Pediatrics. 13th ed. Philadelphia: WB Saunders; 1987:756.

3 **Developmental disorders of the teeth and supporting structures.** In: Rudolph AM, ed. Pediatrics. Norwalk: Appleton and Lange; 1991:976.

4 **Bradshaw TW.** Teething. Pediatr Nurs. 1981;7:41.

5 **Walker JA, Helling DK.** Oral health products. In: Handbook of Nonprescription Drugs. 8th ed. Washington, DC: American Pharmaceutical Association; 1986:492,504.

6 **Skoglund RR.** Teething ring cheilitis. Cutis. 1984;34:362.

7 **Honig PJ.** Diaper dermatitis—factors to consider in diagnosis and treatment. Postgrad Med. 1983;74:79.

8 **Weston WL et al.** Diaper dermatitis: current concepts. Pediatrics. 1980;66:532.

9 **Leyden JJ et al.** Urinary ammonia and ammonia-producing microorganisms in infants with and without diaper dermatitis. Arch Dermatol. 1977;113:1673.

10 **Jordon WE.** Relationship of diapers to diaper rashes. J Pediatr. 1980;96:957.

11 **Mofenson HC et al.** Baby powder—a hazard. Pediatrics. 1981;68:265.

12 **Gonzalez J, Hogg RJ.** Metabolic alkalosis secondary to baking soda. Treatment of a diaper rash. Pediatrics. 1981;67:820.

13 **Leyden JJ.** Corn starch, *Candida albicans* and diaper rash. Pediatr Dermatol. 1984;1:322.

14 **Black SB, Grossman M.** Fever in infants and young children. In: Rudolph AM, ed. Pediatrics. 19th ed. Norwalk: Appleton-Lange; 1991:545.

15 **Consensus Development Panel.** Febrile seizures: long term management of children with fever-associated seizures. Pediatrics. 1980;66:1009.

16 **Hirtz DG.** Generalized tonic clonic and febrile seizures. Pediatr Clin North Am. 1989;36:365.

17 **Applegate MS, Lo W.** Febrile seizures: current concepts concerning prognosis and clinical management. J Fam Pract. 1989;29:422–28.

18 **Fishman MA.** Febrile Seizures. In: Rudolph AM, ed. Pediatrics. 19th ed. Norwalk: Appleton and Lange; 1991: 1793.

19 **Wilson JT et al.** Efficacy, disposition and pharmacodynamics of aspirin, acetaminophen and choline salicylate in young febrile children. Ther Drug Monit. 1982;4:147.

20 **Sarnaik AP.** Diagnosis and management of Reye's syndrome. Compr Ther. 1982;8:47.

21 **Rockoff MA, Pascucci RC.** Reye's syndrome. Emerg Med Clin North Am. 1983;1:87.

22 **Rowe PC et al.** Inborn errors of metabolism in children referred with Reye's syndrome. JAMA. 1988;260 (21):3167.

23 **Rogers MF et al.** National Reye's syndrome surveillance, 1982. Pediatrics. 1985;75:260.

24 **Walson PD et al.** Ibuprofen, acetaminophen, and placebo treatment of febrile children. Clin Pharmacol Ther. 1989; 46:9.

25 **Wilson JT et al.** Single dose, placebo-controlled comparative study of ibuprofen and acetaminophen antipyresis in children. J Pediatr. 1991;119:803.

26 **Sidler J et al.** A double-blind comparison of ibuprofen and paracetamol in juvenile pyrexia. Br J Clin Pract. 1990; 44(Suppl. 7):22.

27 **Vanderhoof JA.** The gastrointestinal tract. In: Rudolph AM, ed. Pediatrics. 19th ed. Norwalk: Appleton and Lange; 1991:987.

28 **Book LS.** Vomiting and diarrhea. Pediatrics. 1984;74(Suppl.):950.

29 **Glass RI et al.** Estimates of morbidity and mortality rates for diarrheal diseases in American children. J Pediatr. 1991;118:S27.

30 **Stewart CF, Hampton EM.** Effect of maturation on drug disposition in pediatric patients. Clin Pharm. 1987;6: 548.

31 **Hamilton JR.** Treatment of acute diarrhea. Pediatr Clin North Am. 1985; 32:419.

32 **Anquist KW et al.** Diagnostic delay after dimenhydrinate use in vomiting children. Can Med Assoc J. 1991;145: 965.

33 **Anderson OW.** Antinausea drugs in treatment of epidemic or virus gastritis? Pediatrics. 1980;46:319. Letter.

34 **Offit PA.** Viral Gastroenteritis. In: Rudolph AM, ed. Pediatrics. 19th ed. Norwalk: Appleton and Lange; 1991:670.

35 **Avery ME et al.** Oral therapy for acute diarrhea. N Engl J Med. 1990;323:891.

36 **DeWitt TG.** Acute diarrhea in children. Pediatr Rev. 1989;11:6.

37 **Santosham M et al.** Oral rehydration therapy: a global perspective. J Pediatr. 1991;118:S44.

38 **American Academy of Pediatrics Committee on Nutrition.** Use of oral fluid therapy and posttreatment feeding following enteritis in children in a developed country. Pediatrics. 1985;75: 358.

39 **Finberg L.** The role of oral electrolyte-glucose solutions in hydration for children—international and domestic aspects. J Pediatr. 1980;96:51.

40 **Nalin DR et al.** Comparison of low and high sodium and potassium content in oral rehydration solutions. J Pediatr. 1980;97:848.

41 **Snyder JD et al.** Home-based therapy for diarrhea. J Pediatr Gastroenterol Nutr. 1990;11:438.

42 **Klish WJ.** Use of oral fluids in treatment of diarrhea. Pediatr Rev. 1985;7: 27.

43 **Tolia VK, Dubois RS.** Update on oral rehydration: its place in treatment of acute gastroenteritis. Pediatr Ann. 1985; 14:295.

44 **Brown KH.** Dietary management of acute childhood diarrhea: optimal timing of feeding and appropriate use of milks and mixed diets. J Pediatr. 1991; 118:S92.

45 **Lifshitz F.** Refeeding of infants with acute diarrheal disease. J Pediatr. 1991; 118:S99.

46 **Randall DL.** Therapy of acute diarrhea diseases in children. Drug Ther. 1973; 5:77.

47 **Pearce JL et al.** Controlled trial of orally-administered lactobacilli in acute infantile diarrhea. J Pediatr. 1974;84: 261.

48 **Pickering LK.** Antimicrobial therapy of gastrointestinal infections. Pediatr Clin North Am. 1983;30:373.

49 **Levin G, Fisher RS.** Gastroesophageal reflux disease. Clin Ther. 1983;6:4.

50 **Cucchiara S et al.** Esophageal motor abnormalities in children with gastroesophageal reflux and peptic esophagitis. J Pediatr. 1986;108:907.

51 **Cucchiara S et al.** Antacids and cimetidine treatment for gastroesophageal reflux and peptic oesophagitis. Arch Dis Child. 1984;59:842.

52 **Carre IJ.** Management of gastroesophageal reflux. Arch Dis Child. 1985;60:71.

53 **Nelson HS.** Gastroesophageal reflux and pulmonary disease. J Allergy Clin Immunol. 1984;73:547.

54 **Euler AR.** Use of bethanechol for the treatment of gastroesophageal reflux. J Pediatr. 1980;96:321.

55 **Tolia V, Dubois RS.** Gastroesophageal reflux in children. Lancet. 1982:738.

56 **Sondheimer JM et al.** Bethanechol treatment of gastroesophageal reflux in infants: effect on continuous esophageal pH records. J Pediatr. 1984;104: 128.

57 **Angelides A, Fitzgerald JF.** Pharmacologic advances in the treatment of gastrointestinal diseases. Pediatr Clin North Am. 1981;28:95.

58 **Sutphen JL et al.** Antacid and formula effects on gastric acidity in infants with gastroesophageal reflux. Pediatrics. 1986;78:55.

59 **Sondheimer JM et al.** Effects of bethanechol (B) on esophageal infants with gastroesophageal reflux (GER). Pediatr Res. 1983;17:201A.

60 **Hitch DG et al.** Enhanced gastroduodenal motility in children. Am J Dis Child. 1982;136:299.

61 **Baron JA.** Cisapride: a gastrointestinal prokinetic agent. Ann Pharm. 1994; 28(4):488–99.

62 **Horn JR, Anderson GD.** Stability of an extemporaneously compounded cisapride suspension. Clin Ther. 1994;16: 169.

63 **Gunasekaran TS, Hassall EG.** Efficacy and safety of omeprazole for severe gastroesophageal reflux in children. J Pediatr. 1993;123:148.

64 **Grill BB et al.** Effects of domperidone therapy on symptoms and upper gastrointestinal motility in infants with gastroesophageal reflux. J Pediatr. 1985; 106:311.

65 **Vandersteen M et al.** Gynaecomastia in a male infant given domperidone. Lancet. 1982;8303:884.

66 **Advisory Committee on Immunization Practices.** General recommendations on immunization. MMWR. 1994; 43(RR-1):1.

67 **Kane MA et al.** Hepatitis b infection in the United States. Am J Med. 1989; 87(S-3A):11S.

68 **Tong MJ.** Hepatitis b vaccination of neonates and children. Am J Med. 1989;87(S-3A):33S.

69 **Immunization Practices Advisory Committee (ACIP).** Hepatitis b virus: a comprehensive strategy for eliminating transmission in the United States through universal childhood vaccination. MMWR. 1991;40:1.

70 **Hollinger FB.** Factors influencing the immune response to hepatitis b vaccine, booster guidelines and vaccine protocol recommendations. Am J Med. 1989;87(S-3A):36S–40S.

71 **Harrison HR, Fulginiti VA.** Bacterial immunizations. Am J Dis Child. 1980; 134:184.

72 **Centers for Disease Control.** Polysaccharide vaccine for prevention of haemophilus influenza type b disease. MMWR. 1985;34:201.

73 **Tetanus: United States 1987 and 1988.** MMWR. 1990;39(3):37.

74 **Barkin RM et al.** Pediatric diphtheria and tetanus toxoids vaccine: clinical and immunologic response when administered as the primary series. J Pediatr. 1985;106:779.

75 **Mortimer EA.** Pertussis immunization: problems, perspectives, prospects. Hosp Pract. 1980;15:130.

76 **Gale JL et al.** Risk of serious acute neurological illness after immunization with diphtheria-tetanus-pertussis vaccine. JAMA. 1994;271(1):37.

77 **Walker AM et al.** Neurologic events following diphtheria-tetanus-pertussis immunization. Pediatrics. 1988;81:345.

78 **Griffen MR et al.** Risk of seizures and encephalopathy after immunization with diphtheria-tetanus-pertussis vaccine. JAMA. 1990;263:1641.

79 **Centers for Disease Control.** Diphtheria, tetanus and pertussis: guidelines for vaccine prophylaxis and other preventive measures. MMWR. 1981;30: 392.

80 **Katz SL.** Controversies in immunization. Pediatr Infect Dis J. 1987;6:607.

81 **Hinman AR, Koplan JP.** Pertussis and pertussis vaccine: reanalysis of benefit and costs. JAMA. 1984;251: 3109.

82 **Centers for Disease Control.** Supplementary statement of contraindications to receipt of pertussis vaccine. MMWR. 1984;33:170.

83 **Edwards KM, Karzon DT.** The search for an improved pertussis vaccine. Pediatr Ann. 1990;19:695.

84 **Robinson A, Funnell SGP.** Potency testing of acellular pertussis vaccines. Vaccine. 1992;10(3):139.

85 **Blenow M et al.** Primary immunization of infants with an acellular pertussis vaccine in a double-blind randomized clinical trial. Pediatrics. 1988; 82(3):293.

86 **Isomura S.** Efficacy and safety of acellular pertussis vaccine in Aichai Perfecture, Japan. Pediatr Infect Dis J. 1988;7:258.

87 **Aoyama T et al.** Adverse reactions and antibody responses to acellular pertussis vaccine. J Pediatr. 1986;109:925.

88 **Mortimer EA et al.** Protective efficacy of the takeda acellular pertussis vaccine combined with diphtheria and tetanus toxoids following household exposure of Japanese children. Am J Dis Child. 1990;144:899.

89 **Noble GR et al.** Acellular and whole cell pertussis vaccines in Japan: report of a visit by US scientists. JAMA. 1987;257:1351.

90 **Aoyama T et al.** Efficacy of an acellular pertussis vaccine in Japan. J Pediatr. 1985;107:180.

91 **Auerbach BS et al.** Dose response to acellular pertussis vaccine and comparison with whole cell pertussis vaccine at 15–24 months and 4–6 years of age. Vaccine. 1992;10(1):14.

92 **Pertussis vaccination: acellular pertussis vaccine for reinforcing and booster use.** Supplementary ACIP statement. MMWR. 1992;41(1):1.

93 **New recommendations for immunization against pertussis and hepatitis b.** Med Lett Drugs Ther. 1993;34(875): 69.

94 **Tetanus.** In: Report of the Committee on Infectious Diseases (Redbook). 21st ed. Peter G et al., eds. Elk Grove: American Academy of Pediatrics; 1988:409.

95 **Shaw ER.** Commentary on immunization. Am J Dis Child. 1980;134:130.

96 **Ogra PL, Faden HS.** Poliovirus vaccine: live or dead. J Pediatr. 1986;108: 1031.

97 **Markowitz LE et al.** Duration of live measles vaccine-induced immunity. Pediatr Infect Dis. 1990;9:101.

98 **American Academy of Pediatrics Committee on Infectious Disease.** Measles: reassessment of the current immunization policy. Pediatrics. 1989; 84(6):1110.

100 **Landes RD et al.** Neonatal rubella following postpartum maternal immunization. J Pediatr. 1980;97:465.

101 **Centers for Disease Control.** Rubella prevention—recommendation of the immunization practices advisory committee. Ann Intern Med. 1984;101:505.

102 **Balfour HH et al.** RA 27/3 rubella vaccine: a four-year follow up. Am J Dis Child. 1980;134:350.

103 **Bernstein DI et al.** Feto maternal aspects of immunization with RA 27/3 live attenuated rubella virus vaccine during pregnancy. J Pediatr. 1980;97:467.

104 **Centers for Disease Control.** Rubella vaccination during pregnancy— United States 1971–1982. MMWR. 1983;32:429.

105 **Fraser DW.** Haemophilus influenza in the community and the home. In: Sell SH, Wright PF, eds. Haemophilus influenza: Epidemiology, Immunology, and Prevention of Disease. New York: Elsevier Science; 1982:11.

106 **Schlech W et al.** Bacterial meningitis in the United States, 1978 through 1981. JAMA. 1985;253:1749.

107 **Dajani AS et al.** Systemic *haemophilus influenza* disease: an overview. J Pediatr. 1979;98:355.

108 **Taylor HG et al.** Intellectual, neuropsychological, and achievement outcomes in children six to eight years after recovery from *Haemophilus influenza* meningitis. Pediatrics. 1984;74:198.

109 **Peltoa H et al.** Prevention of *Haemophilus influenza* type b bacteremic infections with the capsular polysaccharide vaccine. N Engl J Med. 1984;310:1566.

110 **Anon.** Polysaccharide vaccine for prevention of *Haemophilus influenza* type b disease. JAMA. 1985;253:2630.

111 **Black SB et al.** Efficacy of *Haemophilus influenzae* type b capsular polysaccharide vaccine. Pediatr Infect Dis. 1988;7:149.

112 **Harrison LH et al.** *Haemophilus influenzae* type b polysaccharide vaccine: an efficacy study. Pediatrics. 1989;84(2):255.

113 **Lepow ML et al.** Safety and immunogenicity of *Haemophilus influenzae* type b diphtheria toxoid conjugate vaccine (PRP-D) in infants. J Infect Dis. 1987;156:591.

114 **American Academy of Pediatrics Committee on Infectious Diseases.** Haemophilus influenzae type b conjugate vaccines: update. Pediatrics. 1989;84(2):386.

115 **Food and Drug Administration** approval of use of Haemophilus b conjugate vaccine for infants. MMWR. 1990;39(39):698.

116 **Eskola J et al.** Efficacy of *Haemophilus influenzae* type b polysaccharide-diphtheria toxoid conjugate vaccine in infancy. N Engl J Med. 1987;317:717.

117 **Paradiso P et al.** Safety and immunogenicity of a combined diphtheria, tetanus, pertussis and *Haemophilus influenzae* type b vaccine in young infants. Pediatrics. 1993;92(6):827.

118 **Watemburg N et al.** Safety and immunogenicity of *Haemophilus influenzae* type b tetanus protein conjugate vaccine, mixed in the same syringe with diphtheria-tetanus-toxoid-pertussis vaccine in young infants. Pediatr Infect Dis J. 1991;10:758.

119 **Avendano A et al.** *Haemophilus influenzae* type b polysaccharide-tetanus toxoid protein conjugate vaccine does not depress serologic responses to diphtheria, tetanus or pertussis antigens when coadministered in the same syringe with diphtheria-tetanus toxoid-pertussis vaccine at two, four and six months of age. Pediatr Infect Dis J. 1993;12:638.

120 **Gold R et al.** Safety and immunogenicity of *Haemophilus influenzae* vaccine (tetanus toxoid conjugate) administered concurrently or combined with diphtheria and tetanus toxoids-pertussis vaccine and inactivated poliomyelitis vaccine to healthy infants at two, four and six months of age. Pediatr Infect Dis J. 1994;13:348.

121 **Gershon AA.** Live attenuated varicella vaccine. Pediatr Ann. 1984;13:653.

122 **Arbeter AM et al.** Immunization of children with acute lymphoblastic leukemia with live attenuate varicella vaccine without complete suspension of chemotherapy. Pediatrics. 1990;85(3):338.

123 **Lieu AT et al.** The cost of childhood chickenpox: parents' perspective. Pediatr Infect Dis J. 1994;13:173–77.

124 **Weibel RE et al.** Live attenuated varicella virus vaccine—efficacy trial in healthy children. N Engl J Med. 1984;310:1409.

125 **Gershon A et al.** NIAID varicella vaccine collaborative study group. Live attenuated varicella vaccine in immunocompromised children and healthy adults. Pediatrics. 1986;78:757.

126 **Arbeter AM et al.** Varicella vaccine studies in healthy children and adults. Pediatrics. 1986;78:748.

127 **McLaughlin M et al.** Live virus vaccines in human immunodeficiency virus-infected children: a retrospective survey. Pediatrics. 1988;82(2):229.

128 **Bernstein HH et al.** Clinical survey of natural varicella compared with breakthrough varicella after immunization with live attenuated oka/Merke varicella vaccine. Pediatrics. 1993;92(6):833.

129 **Pickering LK, Obrig TG and Stapleton FB.** Hemolytic-uremic syndrome and enterohemorrhagic Escherichia coli. Pediatr Infect Dis J. 1994;13:459.

130 **Robson WLM et al.** Hemolytic-uremic syndrome. Curr Probl Pediatr. 1993;23:16.

131 **Stewart CL et al.** Hemolytic uremic syndrome. Pediatr Rev. 1993;14:218.

132 **Byrnes JJ et al.** Thrombotic thrombocytopenic purpura and the haemolytic-uraemic syndrome: evolving concepts of pathogenesis and therapy. Clin Haematol. 1986;15:413.

133 **Griffin PM et al.** The epidemiology of infections caused by *Escherichia coli* 0157:H7, other enterohemorrhagic *E. Coli* and the associated hemolytic uremic syndrome. Epidemiol Rev. 1991;13:60.

134 **Cleary TG et al.** Cytotoxin-producing *Escherichia coli* and the hemolytic uremic syndrome. Ped Clin North Am. 1988;35:485.

135 **Parsonnet J et al.** Hemolytic uremic syndrome: clinical picture and bacterial connection. Curr Clin Top Infect Dis. 1993;13:172.

136 **Robson WLM et al.** Hemolytic-uremic syndrome in children: a serious hazard of undercooked beef. Postgrad Med. 1990;88:135.

137 **Loomis LJ et al.** Hemolytic uremic syndrome following bone marrow transplantation: a case report and review of the literature. Am J Kidney Dis. 1989;14:324.

138 **Lesesne JB et al.** Cancer-associated hemolytic-uremic syndrome: analysis of 85 cases from a national registry. J Clin Oncol. 1989;7:781.

139 **O'Reyan S et al.** Aspirin and dipyridamole therapy in the hemolytic-uremic syndrome. J Pediatr. 1980;97:473.

140 **Jones RWA et al.** Endarterial urokinase in childhood hemolytic-uremic syndrome. Kidney Int. 1981;20:723.

141 **Coalthard MG.** An evaluation of treatment with heparin in the haemolytic-uraemic syndrome successfully treated by peritoneal dialysis. Arch Dis Child. 1980;55:393.

142 **Binda KI et al.** The haemolytic uraemic syndrome in childhood: a study of the long-term prognosis. Eur J Pediatr. 1981;136:237.

143 **Arenson EB et al.** Preliminary report: treatment of the hemolytic uremic syndrome with aspirin and dipyridamole. J Pediatr. 1975;86:957.

144 **Bergstein JM.** Anticoagulant therapy in human renal disease. Int J Pediatr Nephrol. 1981;2:1.

145 **Hathaway WE.** Use of antiplatelet agents in pediatric hypercoagulable states. Am J Dis Child. 1984;138:301.

146 **Scully RE et al.** Case 15–1986. N Engl J Med. 1986;314:1032.

147 **Monnens L et al.** "Active" intravascular coagulation in the epidemic form of hemolytic-uremic syndrome. Clin Nephrol. 1982;17:284.

148 **Powell HR et al.** Vitamin E treatment of haemolytic uraemic syndrome. Arch Dis Child. 1984;59:401.

149 **Gillor A.** Plasmapheresis as a therapeutic measure in hemolytic-uremic syndrome in children. Klin Wochenschr. 1983;61:363.

150 **Robson WLM et al.** Prognostic factors in typical postdiarrhea hemolytic-uremic syndrome. Child Nephrol Urol. 1987;9:203.

151 **Wright JC.** Evaluation of short stature in children and adolescents. Indiana Med. 1984:515.

152 **Lindsay R et al.** Utah growth study: growth standard and the prevalence of growth hormone deficiencies. J Pediatr. 1994;125(1):29.

153 **Frasier SD.** Short stature in children. Pediatr Rev. 1981;3:171.

154 **Schaff-Blass E et al.** Advances in diagnosis and treatment of short stature, with special reference to the role of growth hormone. J Pediatr. 1984;104:801.

155 **Underwood LE.** Report of the conference on uses and possible abuses of biosynthetic human growth hormone. N Engl J Med. 1984;311:606.

156 **Milner RDG.** Which children should have growth hormone therapy? Lancet. 1986;8479:483.

157 **Kaplan SL et al.** Clinical studies with recombinant-DNA derived methionyl human growth hormone in growth hormone-deficient children. Lancet. 1986;8483:697.

158 **Anon.** A new biosynthetic human growth hormone. Med Lett Drugs Ther. 1987;29:73.

159 **Gajduske DC et al.** Potential epidemic of Creutzfeldt-Jakob disease from human growth hormone therapy. N Engl J Med. 1985:312.

160 **Underwood LE et al.** Degenerative neurologic disease in patients formerly treated with human growth hormone. J Pediatr. 1985;107:10.

161 **Bercu BB.** Growth hormone treatment and the short child; to treat or not to treat? J Pediatr. 1987;110:991.

162 **Moore WV et al.** Comparison of dose frequency of human growth hormone in treatment of organic and idiopathic hypopituitarism. J Pediatr. 1987;110:144.

163 **Christensen JS et al.** Higher plasma somatomedin A (biological) and C (immunological) levels with SC than with IM growth hormone replacement therapy. Acta Endocrinol (Copenh). 1985;109:169.

164 **Hermansussen M et al.** Catch-up growth following transfer from three times weekly IM to daily SC administration of hgH in GH-deficient patients, monitored by kinemometry. Acta Endocrinol (Copenh). 1985;109:163.

165 **Wilson DM et al.** Subcutaneous versus intramuscular growth hormone therapy: growth and acute somatomedin response. Pediatrics. 1985;76:361.

166 **Albertsson-Wikland K et al.** Daily subcutaneous administration of human growth hormone in growth hormone-deficient children. Acta Paediatr Scand. 1986;75:98.

167 **Glasbrenner K.** Technology spurt resolves growth hormone problem, ends shortage. JAMA. 1986;255:581.

168 **Arslanian SA et al.** Growth hormone therapy and tumor recurrence. Am J Dis Child. 1985;139:347.

169 **Thorner MO et al.** Acceleration of growth in two children treated with human growth hormone-releasing factor. N Engl J Med. 1985;312:4.

170 **Grossman A et al.** The use of growth hormone-releasing hormone in the diagnosis and treatment of short stature. Horm Res. 1985;22:52.

171 **Gelato MC et al.** Effects of pulsatile administration of growth hormone (GH)—releasing hormone on short-term linear growth in children with GH deficiency. J Clin Endocrinol Metab. 1985;61:444.

172 **Huseman CA, Hassing JM.** Evidence for dopaminergic stimulation of growth velocity in some hypopituitary children. J Clin Endocrinol Metab. 1984;58:419.

173 **Pintor C et al.** Clonidine accelerates growth in children with impaired growth hormone secretion. Lancet. 1985;8444:1482.

174 **Moore KC et al.** Clinical diagnosis of children with extremely short stature and their response to growth hormone. J Pediatr. 1993;122(5):687.

175 **Rosenfeld RG.** Evaluation of growth and maturation in adolescence. Pediatr Rev. 1982;4:175.

176 **Landon C, Rosenfeld RG.** Short stature and pubertal delay in male adolescents with cystic fibrosis. Am J Dis Child. 1984;138:388.

177 **Spiliotis BE et al.** Growth hormone

neurosecretory dysfunction. JAMA. 1984;251:2223.

178 **Van Vliet G et al.** Growth hormone treatment for short stature. N Engl J Med. 1983;309:1016.

179 **Gertner JM et al.** Prospective clinical trial of human growth hormone in short children without growth hormone deficiency. J Pediatr. 1984;104:172.

180 **Rudman D et al.** The short child with subnormal plasma somatomedin C levels. Pediatr Res. 1985;19:975.

181 **Grunt JA et al.** Comparison of growth and somatomedin C responses following growth hormone treatment in children with small-for-date short stature, significant idiopathic short stature, and hypopituitarism. Acta Endocrinol (Copenh). 1984;106:168.

182 **Loche S et al.** Final height after growth hormone therapy in non growth hormone deficient children with short stature. J Pediatr. 1994;125:196.

183 **Ross JL et al.** Growth hormone secretory dynamics in Turner Syndrome. J Pediatr. 1985;106:202.

184 **Rosenfeld RG et al.** Methionyl human growth hormone and oxandrolone in Turner's Syndrome: preliminary results of a prospective randomized trial. J Pediatr. 1986;109:936.

185 **Lusher JM et al.** Idiopathic thrombocytopenic purpura in children. Am J Pediatr Hematol Oncol. 1984;6:149.

186 **Russell EC, Maurer HM.** Alternatives to splenectomy in the management of chronic idiopathic thrombocytopenic purpura in children. Am J Pediatr Hematol Oncol. 1984;6:175.

187 **Schulman I.** Idiopathic (immune) thrombocytopenic purpura in children: pathogenesis and treatment. Pediatr Rev. 1983;5:173.

188 **Dunn NL, Maurer HM.** Prednisone treatment of acute idiopathic thrombocytopenic purpura of childhood. Am J Pediatr Hematol Oncol. 1984;6:159.

189 **Dubansky AS, Osk FA.** Controversies in the management of acute idiopathic thrombocytopenic purpura: a survey of specialists. Pediatrics. 1986;77:49.

190 **Sartorious JA.** Steroid treatment of idiopathic thrombocytopenic purpura in children. Am J Pediatr Hematol Oncol. 1984;6:165.

191 **Wordell CJ et al.** Immune globulin in the treatment of auto immune thrombocytopenic purpura. Clin Pharm. 1985;4:206.

192 **Bussel JB, Cunningham-Rhodes C.** Intravenous usage of gamma globulin: humoral immunodeficiency, immune thrombocytopenic purpura, and newer indications. Cancer Invest. 1985;3:361.

193 **Lusher JM, Warrier I.** Use of intravenous gamma globulin in children and adolescents with idiopathic thrombocytopenic purpura and other immune thrombocytopenias. Am J Med. 1987; 83(4A):10.

194 **Kurlander R et al.** Comparison of the efficacy of a two-day and a five-day schedule for infusing intravenous gamma globulin in the treatment of immune thrombocytopenic purpura in adults. Am J Med. 1987;83(4A):17.

195 **Newland AC.** Idiopathic thrombocytopenia purpura and IgG: a review. J Infect. 1987;15(Suppl. I):41.

196 **Lotan CS et al.** Intracranial hemorrhage simulating brain tumor in immune thrombocytopenic purpura. Eur J Pediatr. 1983;141:127.

197 **Bussel JB et al.** Intravenous gamma globulin treatment of chronic idiopathic thrombocytopenic purpura. Blood. 1983;62:480.

198 **Bussel JB et al.** Intravenous gamma globulin treatment of chronic idiopathic thrombocytopenic purpura. Blood. 1983; 62.480.

199 **Bussel JB et al.** Treatment of acute idiopathic thrombocytopenia of childhood with intravenous infusions of gamma globulin. J Pediatr. 1985;106: 886.

200 **Uchino H et al.** A cooperative clinical trial of high-dose immunoglobulin therapy in 177 cases of idiopathic thrombocytopenic purpura. Thromb Haemost. 1984;51:182.

201 **Knapp MJ, Colburn PA.** Clinical uses of intravenous immune globulin. Clin Pharm. 1990;9(7):509.

202 **Blachette VS.** Intravenous gamma globulin (Sandoglobulin) therapy in the management of four patients with immune thrombocytopenic purpura. Vox Sang. 1985;49(Suppl. 1):32.

203 **McClain LG.** Childhood enuresis. Curr Probl Pediatr. 179;9:1.

204 **DeJonge GA.** Epidemiology of enuresis: a survey of the literature. In: Kelvin I et al., eds. Bladder Control and Enuresis. Clin Dev Med. London: WM Heinemann Med; 1973:39.

205 **Dische S.** Childhood enuresis—a family problem. Practitioner. 1978;221: 323.

206 **Norgaard JP et al.** Nocturnal enuresis: an approach to treatment based on pathogenesis. J Pediatr. 1989;114(4): 705.

207 **Rushton HG.** Nocturnal enuresis. Epidemiology evaluation and currently available treatment options. J Pediatr. 1989;114(4):691.

208 **American Academy of Pediatrics: Committee on Radiology.** Excretory urography for evaluation of enuresis. Pediatrics. 1980;65:644.

209 **Redman JF, Seibert JJ.** The uroradiographic evaluation of the enuretic child. J Urol. 1979;122:799.

210 **Schmitt BD.** Nocturnal enuresis: an update on treatment. Pediatr Clin North Am. 1982;29:21.

211 **Forsythe WI, Butler RJ.** Fifty years of enuretic alarms. Arch Dis Child. 1989;64:879.

212 **Starfield B.** Increase in functional bladder capacity and improvements in enuresis. J Pediatr. 1968;72:483.

213 **Kales A et al.** Effects of imipramine on enuretic frequency and sleep stages. Pediatrics. 1971;60:431.

214 **DeVane CL et al.** Concentrations of imipramine and its metabolites during enuresis therapy. Pediatr Pharmacol. 1984;4:245.

215 **Rapoport JL et al.** Childhood enuresis II. Psychopathology, tricyclic concentration in plasma, and antineuritic effect. Arch Gen Psychiatry. 1980;37: 1146.

216 **Lovering JS et al.** Oxybutynin efficacy in treatment of primary enuresis. Pediatrics. 1988;82:104.

217 **Miller K et al.** Nocturnal enuresis. Experience with long-term use of intranasally-administered desmopressin. J Pediatr. 1989;114(4):723.

218 **Klauber GT.** Clinical efficacy and safety of desmopressin in the treatment of nocturnal enuresis. J Pediatr. 1989; 114(4):719.

219 **Kearns GL et al.** Clinical pharmacokinetics in infants and children. A reappraisal. Clin Pharmacokinet. 1989; 17(Suppl. 1):29.

220 **Keeter S et al.** Sedation in pediatric CT: national survey of current practice. Radiology. 1990;175:745.

221 **Steinburg AD.** Should chloral hydrate be banned? Pediatrics. 1993;92(3):442.

222 **Smith MT.** Chloral hydrate warning. Science. 1990;250:359.

223 **Committee on Drugs and Committee on Environmental Health, AAP.** Use of chloral hydrate for sedation in children. Pediatrics. 1993;92:471.

224 **Taketomo KC et al.,** eds. Pediatric Dosage Handbook. 2nd ed. Hudson: LexiComp Inc.; 1993.

225 **Mitchell AA et al.** Risk to children from computed tomographic scan premedication. JAMA. 1982;247:2385.

226 **Weir MR et al.** Sedation for pediatric procedures. Milit Med. 1986;151.

227 **Sander JE et al.** Computed tomographic premedication in children. JAMA. 1983;249:2639. Letter.

228 **Thompson JR et al.** The choice of sedation for computed tomography in children: a prospective study. Radiology. 1982;143:475.

229 **Jaffe RB et al.** Introduction: sedation and imaging protocol. Semin Ultrasound CT MR. 1990;11:181.

230 **Strain JD et al.** Intravenously administered pentobarbital sodium in sedation in pediatric CT. Radiology. 1986; 161:105.

231 **Strain JD et al.** IV nembutal: safe sedation for children undergoing CT. AJR. 1988;151:975.

232 **Streisand JB et al.** Absorption and bioavailability of oral transmucosal fentanyl citrate. Anesthesiology. 1991; 75:223.

233 **Streisand JB et al.** Oral transmucosal fentanyl premedication in children. Anesth Analg. 1989;69:28.

234 **Henry D et al.** Determination of sedative and amnestic doses of lorazepam in children. Clin Pharm. 1991;10:625.

235 **Yaster M et al.** Midazolam-fentanyl intravenous sedation in children: case report of respiratory arrest. Pediatrics. 1990;86:463.

236 **Milligan DW et al.** Premedication with lorazepam before bone marrow biopsy. J Clin Pathol. 1987;40:696.

237 **Latson LA et al.** Midazolam nose drops for outpatient echocardiography sedation in infants. Am Heart J. 1991; 121(1):209.

238 **Walbergh EJ et al.** Plasma concentrations of midazolam in children following intranasal administration. Anesthesiology. 1991;75:233.

239 **Anderson JA.** Reversal agents in sedation and anesthesia: a review. Anesth Prog. 1988;35:43.

240 **Rodrigo MR et al.** Flumazenil reversal of conscious sedation for minor oral surgery. Anaesth Intensive Care. 1992; 20:174.

241 **Nahata MC et al.** Adverse effects of meperidine, promethazine and chlorpromazine for sedation in pediatric patients. Clin Pediatr. 1985;24:558.

242 **Snodgrass WR et al.** Lytic "DPT" cocktail: time for rational and safe alternative. Pediatr Clin North Am. 1989; 36:1285.

243 **Terndruys TE et al.** Intramuscular meperidine, promethazine and chlorpromazine: analysis of use and complications in 487 pediatric emergency department patients. Ann Emerg Med. 1989;18:528.

244 **Committee on Drugs, AAP.** Guidelines for monitoring and management of pediatric patient during and after sedation for diagnostic and therapeutic procedures. Pediatrics. 1992;89:1110.

245 **Reimche LD et al.** Chloral hydrate sedation in neonates and infants—clinical and pharmacologic considerations. Dev Pharmacol Ther. 1989;12:57.

246 **Sury MRJ et al.** Acute benzodiazepine withdrawal syndrome after midazolam infusions in children. Crit Care Med. 1989;17:301.

247 **Arnold JH et al.** Tolerance and dependence in neonates sedated with fentanyl during extracorporeal membrane oxygenation. Anesthesiology. 1990;73: 1136.

248 **Yaster M et al.** Management of pediatric pain with opioid analgesics. J Pediatr. 1988;113:421.

249 **Beyer JE, Wells N.** The assessment of pain in children. Pediatr Clin North Am. 1989;36:837.

250 **Schechter NL.** The undertreatment of pain in children: an overview. Pediatr Clin North Am. 1989;36:781–94.

251 **Anand KJS et al.** Pain and its effects in the human neonate and fetus. N Engl J Med. 1987;317:1321.

252 **Anand KJS et al.** Halothane-morphine compared with high-dose sufentanil for anesthesia and postoperative analgesia in neonatal cardiac surgery. N Engl J Med. 1992;326:1.

253 **Brill JE.** Control of pain. Crit Care Clin. 1992;8:203.

254 **Yaster M et al.** Management of pediatric pain with opioid analgesics. J Pediatr. 1988;113:421.

255 **Rodgers BM et al.** Patient-controlled analgesia in pediatric surgery. J Pediatr Surg. 1988;23:259.

256 **Gaukroger PB et al.** Patient-controlled analgesia in children. Anaesth Intensive Care. 1989;17:264.

257 **Berde CB et al.** Patient-controlled analgesia in children and adolescents: A randomized prospective comparison with intramuscular administration of morphine for postoperative analgesia. J Pediatr. 1991;118:460.

258 **Broadman LM et al.** Patient controlled analgesia in children and adolescents: A report of postoperative pain management in 150 patients. Anesthesiology. 1989;71:A1170.

259 **Rodgers BM et al.** Patient controlled analgesia in paediatric surgery. J Paediatric Surg. 1988;23:259.

260 **Berde CB.** Pediatric postoperative pain management. Pediatr Clin North Am. 1989;36:921.

261 **Brown RE, Broadman LM.** Patient controlled analgesia (PCA) for postoperative pain control in adolescents. Anesth Analg. 1987;66:S22.

262 **Shapiro LA et al.** Epidural morphine analgesia in children. Anesthesiology. 1984;61:210.

263 **Attia J et al.** Epidural morphine in children: Pharmacokinetics and CO_2

sensitivity. Anesthesiology. 1986;65:590.

264 **Levron JC et al.** Pharmacokinetics and tolerance of transdermal fentanyl in young children. Anesthesiology. 1992;77:A1204 (abstract).

265 **Bhatt-Mehta V, Rosen DA.** Management of acute pain in children. Clin Pharm. 1991;10:667.

266 **Yaster M, Deshpande JK.** Management of pediatric pain with opioid analgesics. J Pediatr. 1988;113(3):421.

267 **Olkkola KT et al.** The pharmacokinetics of postoperative intravenous ketorolac tromethamine in children. Br J Clin Pharmacol. 1991;31:182.

268 **Maunuksela EL et al.** Comparison of intravenous ketorolac with morphine for postoperative pain in children. Clin Pharmacol Ther. 1992;52:436.

269 **Watcha MF et al.** Comparison of ke-torolac and morphine as adjuvants during pediatric surgery. Anesthesiology. 1992;76:368.

270 **Berde CB.** Toxicity of local anesthetics in infants and children. J Pediatrics. 1993;122:S14.

271 **Bonadio WA et al.** Half-strength TAC topical anesthetic. Clin Pediatr. 1988;10:495.

272 **Cannon CR et al.** Topically applied tetracaine, adrenaline and cocaine in the repair of traumatic wounds of the head and neck. Otolaryngol Head Neck Surg. 1989;100:78.

273 **Pryor GJ et al.** Local anesthesia in minor lacerations: topical TAC versus lidocaine infiltration. Ann Emerg Med. 1980;9:568.

274 **Yaster M et al.** Local anesthetics in the management of acute pain in children. J Pediatr. 1994;124(2):165.

275 **ASTRA USA, Inc.** EMLA package insert. Westborough, MA: 1993 April.

276 **Halperin DL et al.** Topical skin anesthesia for venous, subcutaneous drug reservoir and lumbar punctures in children. Pediatrics. 1989;84:281.

277 **Cooper CM et al.** EMLA cream reduces the pain of venipuncture in the children. Eur J Anaesthesiol. 1987;4:441.

278 **Kapelushrik J et al.** Evaluating the efficacy of EMLA in alleviating pain associated with lumbar puncture; comparison of open and double-blinded protocols in children. Pain. 1990;42:31.

279 **Uhare M.** A eutectic mixture of lidocaine and prilocaine for alleviating vaccination pain in infants. Pediatrics. 1993;92:719.

280 **Joyce TH et al.** Dermal anesthesia us-ing a eutectic mixture of lidocaine and prilocaine (EMLA) for venipuncture in children. Pain Digest. 1992;2:137.

281 **Maunuksela E-L, Korpela R.** Double blind evaluation of a lignocaine-prilocaine cream (EMLA) in children: effect on the pain associated with venous cannulation. Br J Anaesth. 1986;58:1242.

282 **Koren G.** Use of the eutectic mixture of local anesthetics in young children for procedure related pain. J Pediatr. 1993;122:S30.

283 **Taddio H et al.** Effect of lidocaine-prilocaine cream on pain from subcutaneous injection. Clin Pharm. 1992;11:347.

284 **American Academy of Pediatrics Committee on Infectious Diseases.** Recommendations for the use of Live Attenuated Varicella Vaccine. Pediatrics 1995;95:791.

Neonatal Therapy

Donna M Kraus
Fotini K Hatzopoulos

Overview 96-2
   Terminology 96-2
   Neonatal Monitoring Parameters 96-2
Neonatal Pharmacokinetics 96-2
   Drug Absorption 96-2
      Gastrointestinal (GI) absorption 96-2
      Rectal absorption 96-3
      Intramuscular (IM) absorption 96-3
      Percutaneous absorption 96-3
   Drug Distribution 96-4
      Water compartments 96-4
      Adipose tissue 96-4
      Protein binding 96-4
      Other factors 96-5
   Metabolism 96-5
      Phase I biotransformation reactions ... 96-5
      Oxidation 96-5
      Hydrolysis 96-5
      Demethylation 96-5
      Phase II reactions 96-6
      Glucuronide conjugation 96-6
      Glycine conjugation 96-6
      Induction of enzymes 96-6
      Other effects 96-6
   Renal Elimination 96-6
      Glomerular filtration 96-6
      Tubular secretion 96-7
      Tubular reabsorption 96-7
      Clinical relevance to dosing 96-7
Respiratory Distress Syndrome (RDS) ... 96-7
   Clinical Presentation 96-8
   Prevention 96-8
   Treatment 96-8
      Surfactant therapy 96-8
      Pharmacologic and long-term effects ... 96-9
      Number of doses 96-9
      Prophylactic administration 96-9
      Complications 96-9
      Product selection 96-9
     Diuretics 96-10
      Routine use 96-10
      Selective use 96-10
Patent Ductus Arteriosus (PDA) 96-11
   Pathogenesis 96-11
      Fetal circulatory anatomy 96-11
      Fetal circulation 96-11
      Changes at birth 96-12
      Closure of the foramen ovale 96-12
      Closure of the ductus arteriosus 96-12
   Clinical Presentation 96-12
   Treatment 96-13
      Indomethacin 96-13
      Monitoring therapy 96-13
      Recurrence 96-14
      Prophylactic administration 96-14
Necrotizing Enterocolitis (NEC) 96-14

   Pathogenesis 96-14
   Classification 96-15
   Treatment 96-15
      General management 96-15
      Antibiotics 96-16
        Enteral antibiotics 96-16
        Additional antibiotics 96-16
   Prognosis 96-16
Neonatal Sepsis and Meningitis 96-16
   Pathogenesis and Clinical Presentation ... 96-16
      Common pathogens 96-17
   Treatment of Sepsis 96-17
      Antibiotic selection 96-17
      Dosage and route of administration ... 96-18
      Duration of therapy 96-18
   Treatment of Meningitis 96-18
      Antibiotic selection 96-18
      Duration of therapy 96-19
   Intravenous Immune Globulin (IVIG) 96-19
      Rationale 96-19
      Efficacy 96-19
      Initiation of therapy 96-19
      Dosing, administration, and adverse effects ... 96-19
Congenital Infections 96-20
   TORCH Titers 96-20
   Congenital Herpes 96-20
      Treatment 96-20
Apnea 96-21
   Pathogenesis 96-21
   Treatment 96-21
      Methylxanthines 96-21
        Rationale 96-21
        Dosing considerations 96-22
        Dosing and administration 96-22
      Pharmacokinetics 96-23
      Efficacy, toxicity, and dosing 96-23
      Other agents 96-23
**Periventricular-Intraventricular Hemorrhage
(PV-IVH)** 96-24
   Pathogenesis 96-24
   Treatment 96-24
Neonatal Seizures 96-24
   Pathogenesis and Diagnosis 96-24
   Treatment of Hypocalcemia and Hypomagnesemia 96-25
   Treatment with Antiepileptic Drugs (AEDs) 96-25
      AED Maintenance Doses 96-26
Neonatal Abstinence Syndrome 96-26
   Clinical Presentation 96-26
   Treatment 96-27
      Supportive care 96-27
      Monitoring and indications for pharmacological
        treatment 96-27
      Phenobarbital 96-28
      Narcotic agents 96-28
      Diazepam and chlorpromazine 96-28

(Continued)

Sedation and Paralysis during Ventilation 96-28
   Pharmacology and Monitoring Parameters 96-28
   Drug/Disease Interactions 96-29
   Toxicity 96-29
Use and Administration of Medications 96-30

Drug Formulation Problems 96-30
   Lack of nonsolid enteral dosage formulations 96-30
   Inappropriate concentrations 96-30
   Hypertonicity 96-30
   Pharmaceutical adjuvants 96-31
Drug Administration 96-31

The rational use of medications in neonates is dependent upon an appreciation of both the physiologic immaturity and developmental maturation that influence neonatal drug disposition and pharmacologic effects. Much progress has been made to decrease neonatal mortality and to increase survival of more premature and lower birth weight newborns. Neonates, particularly those of extremely low birth weights, pose a pharmacotherapeutic challenge to the clinician. The alterations of body composition, weight, size, and physiologic and pharmacokinetic parameters that occur with normal growth and maturation during the first few months of life are greater than at any other time. Although the amount of neonatal drug information is increasing, the overall lack of well designed pharmacokinetic and pharmacodynamic studies still hinders the clinical use of many drugs in this population. This is especially true for newborns of the lowest birth weights (<750 gm).

The term "therapeutic orphans,"[1] which was coined over 25 years ago to describe the lack of medications labeled for use in children, unfortunately still is applicable today. Only 38% of medications listed in the 1991 *Physician's Desk Reference* have Food and Drug Administration (FDA)-approved labeling for use in pediatrics and even less (19%) have approved labeling for use in neonates.[2] Practical issues such as technical problems of drug delivery and a lack of suitable dosage formulations further complicate neonatal pharmacotherapeutics.

Terminology. An understanding of common neonatal terminology is important as every newborn is evaluated and classified at birth according to birth weight, gestational age, and intrauterine growth status. These factors influence patient outcome and long-term prognosis.[3] Common neonatal terminology is listed in Table 96.1. Pharmacokinetic parameters, pharmacodynamics, and dosing recommendations often are specified according to these terms.

Neonatal Monitoring Parameters. Many pharmacotherapeutic monitoring parameters used in adults also are used in neonates. However, normal values for neonates may differ. In order to adequately monitor pharmacotherapy in neonates, one must be aware of the differences in normal vital signs and laboratory parameters. For example, neonates have a greater heart rate (HR) and respiratory rate (RR) and lower blood pressures (BP) compared to adults. Appropriate texts should be consulted for neonatal normal values when providing comprehensive pharmacy care.[4,5]

The physiologic transitions from intrauterine to extrauterine life may influence disease states and drug disposition. For example, the change from fetal to adult circulation results in an increase in perfusion of organs that are responsible for the elimination of drugs. The developmental changes in absorption, distribution, metabolism, and excretion affect drug disposition and ultimately neonatal drug dosing. This chapter will focus on the applied therapeutics for common neonatal disease states and the safe and effective use of drugs in the neonate.

Neonatal Pharmacokinetics

Drug Absorption

Gastrointestinal (GI) Absorption

Numerous developmental factors, including gastric acidity, gastric emptying time, intestinal integrity and motility, and bacterial colonization may influence the absorption of enterally adminis-

tered drugs during the neonatal period. Neonates, especially preterm newborns, have a decreased capacity to secrete gastric acid compared to adults.[6] This relative lack of gastric acid output may be referred to as "relative achlorhydria" or "hypochlorhydria." Although the exact maturational pattern of gastric acid secretion needs more clarity, a biphasic pattern in term infants usually is described. At birth, the pH of gastric contents is neutral due to the presence of residual amniotic fluid. (Amniotic fluid is swallowed regularly during intrauterine life.) In term infants, acid output begins within minutes after birth and gastric pH decreases to 1.5 to 3 within a few hours. Gastric acidity then decreases (pH increases) over the next ten days: subsequently, basal acid output gradually rises. This maturational pattern of acid secretion in term infants is different in preterm neonates. Gastric acid rarely is present in the fetal stomach before 32 weeks of gestation and the early decrease in gastric pH usually is not seen or may be delayed in preterm neonates. Hypochlorhydria with a basal pH greater than 4.0 is present in about 20% of preterm neonates one to two weeks of age. After six weeks of life, gastric pH falls to less than 4.[7] Although gastric acid production correlates with postnatal age, extrauterine factors (e.g., initiation of enteral feedings) appear to be responsible for the stimulation of gastric acid output.[7] In general, gastric acidity is lower during the neonatal period and adult values for maximal acid output are not reached until two years of age.[6,8]

Both gastric and duodenal pH affect drug ionization and absorption.[8,9] Generally, an acidic environment favors absorption of

Table 96.1	Common Neonatal Terminology[3]
Term	**Definition**
Gestational age	*By Dates*: The number of weeks from the onset of the mother's last menstrual period until birth
	By Exam: Assessment of gestational maturity by physical and neuromuscular examination. Gestational age estimates the time from conception until birth
Postnatal age	Chronological age after birth
Postconceptional age	Gestational age plus postnatal age
Corrected age	Postconceptional age in weeks minus 40. Represents postnatal age if neonate had been born at term (40 weeks gestational age)
Preterm	<38 weeks gestational age at birth
Term	38–42 weeks gestational age at birth
Postterm	≥43 weeks gestational age at birth
Extremely low birth weight	Birth weight <1 kg
Very low birth weight	Birth weight <1.5 kg
Low birth weight	Birth weight <2.5 kg
Small for gestational age	Birth weight below 10th percentile for gestational age
Appropriate for gestational age	Birth weight between 10th and 90th percentiles for gestational age
Large for gestational age	Birth weight above 90th percentile for gestational age

acidic drugs, as these drugs will be unionized and, therefore, more lipid soluble. Basic drugs, however, will be mostly ionized in an acid environment. As a result, basic drugs in an acidic environment are hydrophilic and less well absorbed. Likewise, an acidic drug in an alkaline environment also will be primarily in the ionized form and less well absorbed. Therefore, the hypochlorhydria (i.e., relatively alkaline gastric pH) in neonates can result in decreased bioavailability of acidic drugs (e.g., phenobarbital, phenytoin), as well as increased bioavailability of weakly basic drugs or acid-labile drugs (e.g., penicillin, ampicillin, erythromycin) compared to adults.[8,10]

Since most drugs are absorbed in the small intestine, gastric emptying time plays an important role in both the rate and degree of drug absorption. During the neonatal period, gastric emptying time can be prolonged up to six to eight hours and may not attain adult values until six to eight months of age.[8] The rate of gastric emptying is affected by gestational age, disease states, and dietary intake. Prematurity, respiratory distress syndrome, congenital heart disease, and ingestion of long-chain fatty acids will prolong gastric emptying time. The rate of gastric emptying is increased with consumption of human milk and hypocaloric feedings but is unaffected by osmolality and posture. A prolonged gastric emptying time may delay drug absorption resulting in a longer time to reach maximal serum drug concentrations and a decrease in the peak concentration.

Motility of the small intestine is irregular in both neonates and young infants.[10] This may make it difficult to predict the time for peak absorption or the extent of absorption of enterally administered drugs. In addition, the immature or altered permeability of the intestinal mucosa, which may result in increased drug absorption, actually may be more important than both gastric emptying time and intestinal motility.[11] Osmolality also may influence gastrointestinal tract integrity and absorption, particularly in preterm infants.[10] Enteral administration of drugs or solutions with high osmolalities may destroy GI tract integrity and increase the risk of necrotizing enterocolitis in neonates.

Drug absorption in the neonate also can be affected by other factors. For example, the reduced rate of bile acid synthesis and pancreatic secretions in preterm neonates may decrease the absorption of fat-soluble vitamins D and E.[9,10,12] Absorption of these vitamins may be reduced further by cholestasis, and water-soluble forms of these vitamins may be indicated. Short-bowel syndrome (which may occur as a result of necrotizing enterocolitis) may decrease the intestinal surface area available for drug absorption and result in decreased drug bioavailability. Changes in bacterial colonization of the GI tract during the neonatal period can influence the fate of conjugated forms of drugs excreted in bile. The high activity of beta-glucuronidase in the neonatal intestinal lumen results in hydrolysis of drug glucuronide conjugates and potentially alters the disposition of the parent drug or metabolite.[8,10]

During the neonatal period, drugs such as phenobarbital, digoxin, and sulfonamides are absorbed at a slower rate but the total amount absorbed is similar to that of older children.[11] In contrast, the total absorption of drugs such as phenytoin, acetaminophen, carbamazepine, and rifampin is decreased in neonates.[8,10,12]

Rectal Absorption

The routine utilization of the rectum for administration of drugs such as aminophylline has been discouraged because of erratic drug absorption and toxicities.[10] With the proper drug and dosage formulation, however, the rectum can be an important alternate route for drug administration with rapid and efficient absorption.[8,10] For example, rectal administration of diazepam solution for injection produces serum concentrations similar to those from intravenous (IV) administration.[13] This route is therapeutically important in the neonate with seizure activity in whom rapid intravenous access is not available.

Intramuscular (IM) Absorption

Many physiologic factors, as well as physicochemical characteristics of drugs, influence intramuscular absorption.[8-10] During the first few days of life, both the rate and the amount of intramuscular absorption may be reduced due to the relatively decreased muscle blood flow, higher percentage of water in muscle mass, and diminished strength of muscular contractions.[8] Both the amount of muscle and subcutaneous tissue in the newborn are directly proportional to gestational age. The low muscle mass to total body mass ratio in neonates can result in decreased absorption of an intramuscularly administered drug because absorption is influenced by the surface area of the muscle that comes into contact with the injected medication. In addition, the degree of muscle activity, which directly affects the rate of drug absorption from both intramuscular and subcutaneous injections, can be greatly decreased in the severely ill, immobile, or paralyzed neonate.[8-10] Adequate perfusion of the injection site also is required for systemic absorption to occur. Blood supply to muscles may be compromised in the critically ill neonate with low cardiac output or hypotensive states such as patent ductus arteriosus, sepsis, or respiratory distress syndrome.[9,14] Drugs that more commonly may be administered intramuscularly to neonates are vitamin K, aminoglycosides, phenobarbital, and penicillins.[5,9]

Percutaneous Absorption

Percutaneous absorption is increased in neonates (and especially in preterm newborns) because of decreased thickness of the stratum corneum, increased skin hydration, and increased ratio of surface area per kilogram body weight.[8-10] Since the epidermis is barely present before 34 weeks gestation age, preterm newborns (especially those <2 weeks postnatal age) are at greatest risk for percutaneous drug absorption. After two to three weeks postnatal age, the epidermis of the preterm newborn histologically matures to that seen at term. Although the epidermis of a term neonate is functionally intact, the epidermis continues to develop through four months of age. The newborn's ratio of skin surface area to body weight is approximately three times that of an adult. Therefore, for the same percutaneous dose, the neonate would absorb three times more drug per kilogram compared to an adult. In addition, occlusive dressings or an interruption in the integrity of the skin (e.g., abrasion) will increase the amount of drug absorbed percutaneously. Various toxicities have been described in neonates after topical administration of iodine, hexachlorophene, boric acid, salicylic acid, alcohol, epinephrine, corticosteroids, and triple antibiotic (bacitracin, neomycin, polymyxin B) spray.[15]

The increased percutaneous absorption of drugs in preterm newborns has potential therapeutic implications. For example, transdermal theophylline, administered as a gel with an occlusive dressing, produced therapeutic serum concentrations in preterm newborns ≤30 weeks gestational age and ≤20 days postnatal age.[16] The technological feasibility of a neonatal transdermal theophylline patch also has been demonstrated.[17] Clinical application of transdermal drug delivery in preterm newborns appears promising and may avoid problems associated with other routes of administration. However, transdermal drug delivery appears to be limited by the normal maturation of the epidermis because drug absorption decreases with increasing postnatal age and in newborns greater than 32 weeks gestational age.[16,17]

Drug Distribution

Drug distribution, the process of drug partition among various body organs, fluids, and tissues, is dependent upon pH, composition and size of body compartments (e.g., total body water, intracellular and extracellular water, and adipose tissue mass), protein binding, membrane permeability, and hemodynamic factors such as cardiac output and regional blood flow.[18]

Water Compartments

Total body water, as a percentage of body weight, is increased in the newborn (especially the preterm neonate) and decreases with increasing age. The total body water of a preterm 1 kg newborn is 80% and that of a term newborn is 75%. These values are much higher than those of a three-month-old (60%) or an adult (55%).[19] Newborns also have an increase in extracellular water as a percentage of body weight, and an increase in the extracellular water to intracellular water ratio. Extracellular water decreases from approximately 40% at term to about 20% at three months of age.[19] The higher total body water and extracellular water in newborns typically result in larger volumes of distribution (Vd) for water soluble drugs.[5,9,20,21] (See Table 96.2.) In addition, the volume of distribution for water-soluble drugs that distribute to the extracellular water compartment (e.g., gentamicin) roughly parallels extracellular water as a percentage of body weight. Since the Vd in newborns usually is larger for water-soluble drugs, larger mg/kg loading doses of these agents are needed in neonates, particularly preterm newborns, to achieve similar initial concentrations to that of an adult. As the neonate grows and matures, total body water and extracellular water decrease, causing the volume of distribution for water-soluble drugs and, therefore, mg/kg loading doses to decrease with increasing age.

Adipose Tissue

In contrast to total body water, the neonate has much less adipose tissue compared to adults. A preterm newborn is comprised of only 1% to 2% fat, while a term neonate is about 15% fat.[19] Neonatal adipose tissue also contains more water. The decreased amount of adipose tissue and the higher water content in the newborn may decrease the Vd for fat-soluble drugs (e.g., diazepam). Due to the smaller volume of distribution for fat-soluble or lipophilic drugs, smaller mg/kg loading doses should be administered in neonates.

Protein Binding

In general, neonatal protein binding of drugs is decreased compared to adults (see Table 96.2). The decrease in plasma-protein binding is a result of several factors including: a lower concentration of binding proteins (e.g., albumin, lipoproteins, α_1-acid glycoprotein, and beta globulins); the presence of fetal albumin which has decreased affinity for drugs; a lower plasma pH which can decrease protein binding of acidic drugs; and the presence of endogenous substances (e.g., bilirubin and free fatty acids) or transplacentally acquired interfering substances (e.g., hormones and pharmacologic agents) that may compete for protein-binding sites.[8,22] Decreased protein binding (increased free fraction) has been described in neonates for many drugs including ampicillin, carbamazepine, diazepam, lidocaine, penicillin, phenobarbital, phenytoin, propranolol, salicylic acid, sulfonamides, and theophylline.[8,9,22] Total plasma-protein concentration, as well as the affinity of albumin for acidic drugs, increases with age and may approach adult values at 10 to 12 months.[9] Therefore, as the newborn grows and matures, protein binding also will increase.

A decrease in protein binding may result in an increased volume of distribution, increased free (unbound) fraction, or increased free concentration of a drug. Drugs that have an increased Vd may require larger mg/kg loading doses in neonates to attain the same total serum concentration as that of an adult. However, for a given total serum concentration, the increased free fraction will result in a higher free concentration. The increased free concentration may result in increased therapeutic or toxic effects. For example, protein binding of theophylline in full-term newborns (36%) is decreased compared to adults (56%).[23] The commonly accepted total theophylline serum concentration of 10 to 20 µg/mL in adults produces free theophylline serum concentrations of 4.4 to 8.8 µg/mL in adults but 6.4 to 12.8 µg/mL in newborns (i.e., $\approx$1.5 times the adult free concentrations). Since the pharmacologic and toxic effects of drugs are related to the free concentration (i.e., the amount of drug that can pass through membranes and reach the receptor), the total theophylline serum concentration range used in adults (10 to 20 µg/mL) could result in toxicities if applied to the neonatal population. In neonates, a total theophylline serum concentration of approximately 7 to 14 µg/mL would produce free concentrations comparable to those seen with total concentrations of 10 to 20 µg/mL in adults.[23] Likewise, the decreased protein binding of phenytoin in neonates and resultant increased free fraction suggests

Table 96.2	Pharmacokinetics of Selected Drugs in Neonates and Adults[a,5,9,20,21]					
	Plasma t½ (hr)		Vd (L/kg)		% Protein Bound	
Drug	Neonates	Adults	Neonates	Adults	Neonates	Adults
Caffeine	40–230	3–7	1.0	0.5–0.6	NA	30–40
Diazepam	25–100	20–30	1.8–2.1	1.6–3.2	84–86	94–98
Digoxin	20–80	25–50	4–10	7	14–26	23–40
Gentamicin	3–12	1.5–3	0.4–0.7	0.2–0.3	<10	<10
Indomethacin	15–30	4–10	0.35–0.53	0.15–0.26	95–98	90–95
Morphine	5–14	2–4	1.7–4.5	2.4–4.2	18–22	33–37
Phenobarbital	40–400	50–180	1.0	0.6–0.7	28–43	45–50
Phenytoin	15–105	15–30	1.0	0.6–0.7	70–90	89–93
Theophylline	20–60	6–12	1.0	0.45	36–50	50–65
Vancomycin	6–12	5–8	0.48–0.97	0.3–0.7	NA	30–55

a NA = Not available; t½ = Half-life; Vd = Volume of distribution.

that total phenytoin therapeutic serum concentrations in newborns should be 8 to 15 μg/mL instead of the 10 to 20 μg/mL as accepted in adults.

Decreased protein binding also may be a result of endogenous or exogenous substances displacing highly protein-bound drugs from protein binding sites. Higher concentrations of free fatty acids in neonates may be responsible for the decreased protein binding of diazepam, propranolol, salicylates, and valproic acid.[22] In addition, bilirubin may displace acidic drugs, such as phenytoin, from albumin binding sites. A positive correlation between total bilirubin concentrations and free fraction of phenytoin has been described. Unbound phenytoin was reported as 11% in normal newborns, but approximately 20% in neonates when bilirubin concentrations were 20 mg/dL.[24]

Some drugs (e.g., sulfonamides) or free fatty acids can displace bilirubin from albumin binding sites, facilitating the deposition of unconjugated bilirubin in the brain which may produce neurological injury and cell death, usually in the basal ganglia and brain stem. This condition, known as kernicterus or bilirubin encephalopathy, is frequently fatal but survivors experience central hearing loss, ataxia, and choreoathetosis.[25] The displacement of bilirubin from albumin binding sites is dependent upon several factors including: pH; the affinity of albumin for the drug and bilirubin; and the individual molar concentrations of the drug, bilirubin, and albumin. Preterm newborns may be at an increased risk for bilirubin displacement due to: lower albumin concentrations, decreased albumin affinity for bilirubin, lower pH, and higher bilirubin concentrations (secondary to overproduction or decreased hepatic glucuronide conjugation). In order to displace bilirubin, a specific molar concentration of a drug is necessary to occupy a critical portion of the reserve albumin. Generally, if the molar concentration of a drug is much lower than the molar concentration of albumin, then displacement of bilirubin from albumin binding sites is unlikely.[9,26] For example, highly protein-bound drugs such as furosemide, indomethacin, and cardiac glycosides can be administered to neonates without fear of displacing bilirubin from albumin (even though some of them are potent displacers of bilirubin) because they achieve low plasma concentrations.[9] In contrast, ceftriaxone and moxalactam significantly displace bilirubin off albumin binding sites and, therefore, should be avoided in the presence of hyperbilirubinemia.[27,28] Sulfonamides are associated with the development of kernicterus and, therefore, generally are avoided in neonates and infants less than two months of age. However, not all sulfonamides have the same ability to displace bilirubin. Therapeutic concentrations of trimethoprim-sulfamethoxazole do not alter albumin's capacity to bind bilirubin and this drug occasionally is used in neonates if no reasonable alternative antibiotic exists.[29]

Other Factors

Decreased skeletal muscle mass and alterations in tissue affinity, membrane permeability, and hemodynamics also may influence drug distribution in neonates. The increased permeability of the central nervous system (CNS) to certain lipophilic drugs, such as phenytoin, may be due to the composition of the immature brain (lower myelin content) and the higher cerebral blood flow as compared to adults.[8] The increased permeability of drugs into neonatal tissues, such as the CNS or red blood cells (e.g., digoxin, theophylline), also may contribute to the increased Vd observed in newborns.[18]

Metabolism

Most drugs are lipophilic and require biotransformation into more water-soluble substances before they can become inactivated and eliminated from the body. Although biotransformation may take place at various sites (e.g., plasma, skin, lungs, and kidney),

the majority occurs in the liver with subsequent elimination of metabolites via the kidneys, lungs, or biliary tract. Hepatic biotransformation may include Phase I (oxidation, reduction, hydrolysis, and demethylation) and Phase II reactions (conjugation with sulfate, glucuronide, glycine, glutathione, and hippurate; acetylation; and methylation).[30] In general, hepatic metabolism is reduced in the neonate due to decreases in hepatic blood flow, cellular uptake of drugs, hepatic enzyme capacity, and biliary excretion. Hepatocellular uptake and intrahepatic transport of drugs may be decreased at birth due to reduced concentrations of hepatocyte acceptor proteins, Y and Z. This may result in decreased hepatic clearance for capacity-limited drugs (i.e., drugs with low extraction ratios and low intrinsic clearance).[8,9] Concentrations of acceptor proteins significantly increase during the first ten days of life.[9,30]

Phase I Biotransformation Reactions

Phase I biotransformation reactions are significantly reduced in the newborn but increase with both gestational age and postnatal age.[8] Maturation of enzyme activity (Phase I and Phase II) occurs at different ages for different metabolic pathways, may be regulated by endogenous hormones (e.g., growth hormone or corticosteroids), and may be substrate-specific. The development of isoenzymes, presence of endogenous competitive substrates, and in utero or postnatal induction of hepatic enzymes may alter the maturation of drug metabolism.

Oxidation

In full-term newborns, activity of cytochrome P450 enzymes and NADPH-cytochrome-C-reductase is approximately 50% of the adult value.[31] This decreased oxidative capacity results in a reduced clearance of some drugs (e.g., diazepam, phenobarbital, phenytoin, valproic acid, theophylline, indomethacin, and metronidazole), particularly in the first few weeks of life.[8,30] Compared to other enzyme systems, maturation of oxidative reactions occurs rapidly after birth. For example, in full-term newborns hydroxylation of phenytoin and phenobarbital matures as early as two to four weeks postnatal age.[30] In preterm infants, however, the rapid postnatal maturation of hydroxylation is delayed. Hydroxylation of theophylline is related primarily to postconceptional age and approaches adult values by 40 weeks postconceptional age.[32] In general, oxidative biotransformation pathways have one-third to one-half the adult activity at birth but increase to two to five times that of an adult by one year postnatal age.

Hydrolysis

Hepatic and plasma esterase activity is reduced in neonates, especially preterm newborns, and reaches adult values within 10 to 12 months.[8] The decreased esterase activity results in reduced elimination of ester anesthetics such as procaine, tetracaine, and cocaine. This may explain the increased effects and cardiorespiratory depression seen in newborns exposed to local anesthetics.

Demethylation

The dealkylation pathway for some drugs (e.g., diazepam and lidocaine) may be less impaired than the hydroxylation pathway at birth.[8] In contrast, the N-demethylation pathways of theophylline are greatly reduced in comparison to hydroxylation.[32] Maturation of theophylline N-demethylation occurs at 55 weeks postconceptional age and lags behind the maturation of the oxidation pathways seen at 40 weeks postconceptional age. Despite the earlier maturation of theophylline hydroxylation, theophylline clearance is not increased significantly until the N-demethylation pathway matures.[32] Clearances of other drugs such as diazepam, morphine, and meperidine also are affected by low N-demethylation activity.

Phase II Reactions

Most Phase II reactions are decreased in the newborn. Sulfation, however, is more developed than other conjugation reactions as sulfotransferase activity may approximate adult values at birth (e.g., estrogen sulfotransferase).[30] Methylation also is functional at birth as demonstrated by the ability of both full-term and preterm newborns to methylate theophylline to caffeine. Methyltransferase activity is known to be present even in the fetus because methylation is required for synthesis of pulmonary surfactant. In contrast, acetylation of sulfonamides is decreased in neonates, especially preterm newborns.[30] Other drugs such as hydralazine that are eliminated via acetylation may have decreased hepatic clearance in the neonate.

Glucuronide Conjugation

Uridine diphosphate (UDP)-glucuronyl transferase activity is significantly reduced at birth and reaches adult levels within three years postnatal age.[9] As a result, metabolism is significantly decreased in the neonate for compounds that undergo glucuronidation [e.g., chloramphenicol, morphine, corticosteroids, bilirubin, and trichloroethanol (the active metabolite of chloral hydrate)]. Toxic effects of these agents may be seen unless doses are decreased appropriately. Reduced glucuronidation with resultant accumulation of chloramphenicol was responsible for the toxic symptoms of the "gray baby syndrome" (i.e., cardiovascular collapse and shock).

The effects of decreased glucuronidation may not be as dramatic for drugs that have alternate metabolic pathways since a shift to a more mature pathway may occur. For example, in neonates, the decreased glucuronidation of acetaminophen is partially offset by an increase in acetaminophen sulfate conjugation. This change to sulfation only partially compensates for decreased glucuronidation as acetaminophen half-life is still prolonged in the newborn.[9]

Glycine Conjugation

Glycine conjugation is decreased in newborns but increases to adult levels by approximately eight weeks of age. In adults, benzyl alcohol (a preservative) is converted to benzoic acid (benzoate) which then is detoxified in the liver through conjugation with glycine to form hippuric acid. Since neonates have a decreased capacity to conjugate p-amino benzoate and benzoate with glycine, benzoic acid can accumulate in newborns given excess benzyl alcohol or benzoic acid.[33] Accumulation of benzoic acid results in the "gasping syndrome" which consists of multiple organ system failure, severe metabolic acidosis, and gasping respirations. This potentially fatal syndrome is associated with cumulative benzyl alcohol doses greater than 99 mg/kg in preterm neonates.[34] As recommended by the FDA, drugs containing the preservatives benzyl alcohol or benzoic acid should not be used in neonates.[35] The use of preservative-free IV solutions, diluents, and medications is advised.

Induction of Enzymes

Maturation of hepatic enzymes can be influenced by *in utero* or postnatal exposure to enzyme-inducing agents.[30] Neonatal enzymes may have a faster and greater response to inducing agents compared to adults. Hydroxylation and glucuronidation pathways are especially affected.[8] For example, the plasma half-life of diazepam is 40 to 100 hours in preterm neonates and 20 to 45 hours in full-term neonates, but only 11 to 18 hours in neonates briefly exposed to the enzyme-inducing drug, phenobarbital.[36,37] This shortened diazepam half-life is a result of an increase in the hydroxylation and conjugation pathways. Since phenobarbital can induce UDP-glucuronyl transferase (and therefore, glucuronide conjugation), it sometimes is used to treat neonatal unconjugated hyperbilirubinemia. Antenatal corticosteroid administration which commonly is used to promote fetal lung maturation, also can induce postnatal metabolism of both theophylline and metronidazole.[8]

Other Effects

Decreased cardiac output, respiratory distress, decreased liver perfusion, or hypoxia may further decrease neonatal hepatic enzymatic activity.[8] Decreased phenobarbital clearance has been demonstrated in asphyxiated neonates.[38]

Renal Elimination

Glomerular filtration, tubular secretion, and tubular reabsorption are decreased in preterm and full-term newborns compared to adults. Since most drugs and metabolites are eliminated renally, clearance generally is decreased in neonates. As a result, maintenance doses of drugs that are eliminated renally must be decreased. Although overall renal function increases with age, the maturational rates of individual physiologic functions vary. For example, glomerular filtration matures several months before tubular secretion and factors increasing tubular reabsorption mature after tubular secretion. Since renal elimination is dependent upon the balance of filtration, secretion, and reabsorption, predictions of renal clearance of drugs eliminated by more than one of these mechanisms may be difficult in the maturing neonate.

Glomerular Filtration

At birth, glomerular filtration rate is significantly decreased. The glomerular filtration rate (GFR) for full-term newborns is 2 to 4 mL/minute or approximately 10 to 20 mL/minute/1.73 m^2. For preterm newborns, glomerular filtration rate is only 0.7 to 0.8 mL/minute or about 0.5 % of an adult.[39] In full-term newborns glomerular filtration rate increases markedly after birth, doubling by one to two weeks postnatal age. Despite the continued increase postnatally, glomerular filtration rate is only 50 mL/minute/1.73 m^2 at 2.5 weeks postnatal age[40] and does not reach adult values until three to five months postnatal age.

In preterm neonates, postnatal development of glomerular filtration rate is delayed and a lower glomerular filtration rate persists beyond the first few months of life, especially in very low birthweight newborns ≤30 weeks gestational age. Even at a corrected postnatal age of nine months (i.e., 18 months postconceptional age), glomerular filtration rate is significantly decreased in very low birthweight infants compared to term infants of the same postconceptional age.[40] Although the exact age at which glomerular filtration rate matures in very low birthweight infants is not known, a normal glomerular filtration rate should not be assumed in older preterm infants even up to one to two years postnatal age.

Serum creatinine (SrCr) concentrations in all neonates are elevated at birth reflecting maternal concentrations. In healthy newborns greater than 30 weeks gestational age, serum creatinine steadily decreases throughout the first week of life to approximately 0.4 mg/dL. Serum creatinine concentrations in very low birthweight infants born ≤30 weeks gestational age are significantly higher than their term counterparts, even at a corrected postnatal age of nine months.[40]

Clearance of drugs primarily eliminated by glomerular filtration (e.g., digoxin, vancomycin, and the aminoglycosides) is well correlated with glomerular filtration rate. Therefore, maturation of glomerular filtration rate must be considered when developing dosing guidelines for these medications. For example, gentamicin clearance has been found to correlate with postnatal age, weight, and creatinine clearance (Cl$_{Cr}$), as well as postconceptional age.[41–43] Guidelines that incorporate these patient factors, therefore, are more likely to result in therapeutic serum concentrations in the developing neonate. An example of neonatal gentamicin dosing guidelines[44,45] that are used commonly is given in Table 96.3.

Other conditions such as asphyxia, decreased cardiac output, renal disease, or indomethacin therapy may further decrease glomerular filtration rate and drug clearance during the perinatal period.[46-48] The hypoxia, hypercarbia, hypotension, and decreased cardiac output that occur during asphyxia will cause significant decreases in glomerular filtration rate. In addition, compensatory mechanisms such as an increased formation of renovascular constricting prostaglandins may aggravate this condition further.[39] Therefore, dosage regimens of renally eliminated drugs should be empirically decreased in severely asphyxiated neonates. Dosage reduction before indomethacin therapy also is necessary as significant elevations of aminoglycoside and digoxin serum concentrations have resulted with concomitant indomethacin therapy.[47,48] For example, a 50% dosage reduction of digoxin is recommended in preterm infants receiving indomethacin.[48]

In contrast, an increase in dosage may be required for drugs (e.g., thiazide and loop diuretics) that depend upon glomerular filtration rate for sufficient intraluminal concentrations and pharmacologic effect. A diminished diuretic response may be seen in preterm neonates particularly during the first month of life. Since furosemide is less dependent upon glomerular filtration rate, it is the preferred diuretic in neonates.

Tubular Secretion

Tubular secretion is approximately 20% to 30% of adult values at birth and matures more slowly than glomerular filtration rate. Despite a doubling over the first seven days of life, tubular secretion does not reach adult values until 30 to 40 weeks postnatal age. By one year of age, tubular secretion is ten times higher than at birth.[8,9]

In neonates, therefore, a decreased clearance is seen for drugs that are eliminated by proximal tubular secretion (e.g., furosemide, penicillins, thiazides, tolazoline, atropine, and morphine). Tubular secretion, however, can be enhanced in the immature kidney after continued exposure to certain drugs. Substrate stimulation of tubular secretory pathways and subsequent increases in elimination (and therefore, dosing requirements) have been reported for penicillin, ampicillin, and dicloxacillin.[9,49]

Tubular Reabsorption

Tubular reabsorption, a passive process that is concentration dependent, is decreased in the neonate due to the decreased glomerular filtration rate and reduced filtrate load.[8] The low urinary pH seen in neonates results in an increase in reabsorption of weak acids (decreased clearance) and a decrease in reabsorption of weak ba-

ses. In addition, the normal diurnal variation in urine pH is not present until two years postnatal age.[8]

Clinical Relevance to Dosing

The decreased enzyme activity and renal function seen in neonates result in a decreased clearance and prolonged half-life for many drugs. (See Table 96.2.) Since drug clearance determines the maintenance dose, mg/kg/day dosages must be reduced in neonates, particularly preterm neonates, to avoid toxicities. As biotransformation reactions and renal function mature, daily dosages subsequently must be increased with age to prevent subtherapeutic concentrations. Because of these dynamic changes, periodic clinical assessment and therapeutic drug monitoring are extremely important in neonates.

Respiratory Distress Syndrome (RDS)

Respiratory distress syndrome is the major cause of morbidity and mortality in preterm neonates. This clinical syndrome is characterized by respiratory failure with atelectasis, hypoxemia, decreased lung compliance, small airway epithelial damage, and pulmonary edema. The principle cause of respiratory distress syndrome is surfactant deficiency. Pulmonary surfactant decreases the surface tension at the air:fluid interface in the alveoli and prevents alveolar collapse. Surfactant also facilitates the clearance of pulmonary fluid, prevents pulmonary edema, and stabilizes alveoli during aeration. At birth, the clearance of residual fetal lung fluid is accompanied by an increase in pulmonary blood flow which facilitates the transition from fetal to adult circulation.[50]

In the fetus, endogenous cortisol stimulates the synthesis and secretion of pulmonary surfactant at 30 to 32 weeks gestational age. However, sufficient amounts of pulmonary surfactant for normal lung function are not present before 34 to 36 weeks gestation. Therefore, the incidence and severity of respiratory distress syndrome increase as gestational age decreases. Respiratory distress syndrome occurs in 20% of neonates born at 30 to 32 weeks gestational age but in 60% to 80% of neonates born at 26 to 28 weeks gestational age.[51]

Without adequate amounts of surfactant, the surface tension within the alveoli is so great that the alveoli collapse (atelectasis), resulting in poor gas exchange (e.g., hypoxemia, hypercapnia). Low lung compliance also results and large inspiratory pressures are needed to aerate the lungs. Unfortunately, the extremely compliant neonatal chest wall makes it difficult to create the large negative inspiratory pressures necessary to open the alveoli. This results in an increased work of breathing and uneven ventilation.

Aeration of the surfactant-deficient lung also results in the cyclic collapse and distention of bronchioles with resultant bronchiolar epithelial injury and necrosis. This epithelial damage causes pulmonary edema by allowing fluid and proteins to leak from the intravascular space into the air spaces and interstitium of the lung. The necrotic epithelial debris and proteins then form fibrous hyaline membranes. Hyaline membranes and pulmonary edema further impair gas exchange. The term hyaline membrane disease has been used to describe the presence of these fibrous membranes. However, since hyaline membrane disease is not specific to surfactant deficiency, the term respiratory distress syndrome is preferred.

The inadequate oxygenation and ventilation and increased work of breathing caused by respiratory distress syndrome may result in the need for assisted positive-pressure ventilation. Complications of respiratory distress syndrome may be related to mechanical ventilation and include: pulmonary barotrauma (e.g., pneumothorax and pulmonary interstitial emphysema), intraventricular hemorrhage, patent ductus arteriosus, retinopathy of prematurity, and

Table 96.3	Gentamicin Dosing Guidelines for Neonates and Infants[a]		
Postconceptional Age (weeks)	Postnatal Age (days)	Dose (mg/kg/dose)	Interval (hr)
≤ 29 or significant asphyxia	0–28	2.5	24
	>28	3.0	24
30–36	0–14	3.0	24
	>14	2.5	12[b]
≥ 37	0–7	2.5	12
	>7	2.5	8

[a] Adapted with permission from reference 44.
[b] Use 18–24 hours if birthweight ≤1200 gm and postnatal age <28 days.[45]

chronic lung disease or bronchopulmonary dysplasia.[51-53] (Also see Chapter 98: Bronchopulmonary Dysplasia.)

Clinical Presentation

1. L.D., an 800 gm male, was precipitously born at 27 weeks gestational age to a 38-year-old gravida6para5 female. Apgar scores were 5 at 1 minute and 7 at 5 minutes. One hour after birth, L.D. appears cyanotic and has retracting respirations with grunting and nasal flaring. HR is 160 beats/min and RR is 65 breaths/min. An arterial blood gas (ABG) on 100% oxygen by nasal cannula is: pH 7.26, pCO$_2$ 50 mm Hg, pO$_2$ 53 mm Hg, and base deficit 7. Arterial to alveolar oxygen tension ratio (a/A) is <0.2. L.D. is intubated immediately and placed on positive pressure assisted ventilation. A catheter is inserted in his umbilical artery for frequent ABG monitoring and an umbilical vein catheter is inserted for central venous access. L.D.'s chest x-ray shows moderate hyaline membrane disease. Ampicillin 50 mg/kg Q 12 hr and gentamicin 2.5 mg/kg Q 24 hr are ordered IV to rule out sepsis. What risk factors does L.D. have for RDS? What signs and laboratory data are consistent with RDS? [SI units: pCO$_2$ 6.67 kPa; pO$_2$ 7.1 kPa]

L.D.'s risk factors for respiratory distress syndrome are prematurity and male gender. Other risk factors include gestational diabetes, asphyxia, Cesarean section with no labor, and second-born twins.[53,54] Clinical signs and laboratory data consistent with respiratory distress syndrome in L.D. include tachypnea (respiratory rate 65 breaths/minute), cyanosis, retracting respirations, grunting, nasal flaring, hypoxemia (pO$_2$ 53 mm Hg), hypercapnia (pCO$_2$ 50 mm Hg), and a mixed respiratory and metabolic acidosis.

Tachypnea, the first sign of respiratory distress, is an attempt to compensate for the inadequate ventilation, hypercapnia, and acidosis. L.D.'s retracting respirations (the use of intercostal, subcostal, suprasternal, or sternal accessory muscles) reflect the increased work of breathing necessary to maintain ventilation. His nasal flaring decreases resistance during inspiration and increases oxygenation. Grunting is the result of forceful exhalation against a partially closed glottis in an effort to prolong expiration and maximize oxygenation. Grunting also increases intrathoracic pressure during expiration in an attempt to stabilize the alveoli and prevent atelectasis. L.D.'s cyanosis, hypoxemia, hypercapnia, and mixed respiratory and metabolic acidosis are consequences of inadequate oxygenation and poor ventilation and are consistent with respiratory distress syndrome.[52,53]

Prevention

2. What maternal treatment might have prevented RDS in L.D.?

Respiratory distress syndrome may be prevented if pregnancy can be prolonged long enough for fetal lungs to mature or if production of pulmonary surfactant can be accelerated *in utero*. Premature labor can be suppressed pharmacologically with drugs that inhibit uterine contractions (tocolytic agents). Tocolytic agents such as the β-adrenergic agonists (e.g., ritodrine, terbutaline) and magnesium sulfate may be administered parenterally to stop uterine activity. Therapy then may be continued with oral beta agonists.[55] (See Chapter 44: Obstetrics.)

Maternal administration of glucocorticoids can accelerate fetal lung maturation and decrease the incidence and severity of respiratory distress syndrome. If pregnancy could have been prolonged for at least 24 and preferably 48 hours, L.D.'s mother could have received either dexamethasone or betamethasone.[56] This may have decreased L.D.'s risk and severity of respiratory distress syndrome. Although older literature supports the greatest benefit in fetuses between 30 and 32 weeks gestational age, antenatal corticosteroids commonly are administered when preterm labor occurs at 24 to 34

weeks gestation.[57,58] A recent meta-analysis of 12 antenatal corticosteroid trials with over 3000 participants demonstrated a significant reduction in respiratory distress syndrome along with significant decreases in necrotizing enterocolitis, intraventricular hemorrhage, and neonatal death. The decrease in respiratory distress syndrome, however, was not significant for newborns greater than 34 weeks gestational age.[59]

The most commonly used regimens are betamethasone injection 12 mg IM every 12 to 24 hours for two doses, dexamethasone injection 5 mg IM or IV every 12 hours for four doses, or dexamethasone injection 4 mg IM or IV every eight hours for six doses. The risk of respiratory distress syndrome is significantly decreased if the mother receives the last dose of corticosteroid at least 24 hours but no more than seven days before delivery. Therefore, treatment is repeated every seven to ten days until 34 weeks gestation or until amniotic fluid testing reveals mature fetal lungs. Fetal lung maturity can be assessed by measuring certain components (e.g., lecithin and sphingomyelin) of lung surfactant found in amniotic fluid. A ratio of lecithin:sphingomyelin greater than two indicates functionally mature fetal lungs and a decreased risk for respiratory distress syndrome.[56]

Maternal administration of glucocorticoids increases the production of fibroblast pneumocyte factor which stimulates the biosynthesis of surfactant in type II pneumocytes. This mimics the physiologic response of fetal lungs to the increased cortisol production that normally begins at 30 to 32 weeks gestation.[54] Certain obstetrical conditions may stress the fetus and stimulate adrenal activity and corticosteroid release *in utero*, thereby enhancing fetal lung maturity. For example, an unusually low incidence of respiratory distress syndrome occurs in neonates born prematurely to mothers with hypertension, infection, sickle cell disease, heroin addiction, premature rupture of membranes greater than 48 hours, and decreased placental function.[53,57] Antenatal steroids also improve postnatal responsiveness to exogenous surfactant administration.[60-62]

Treatment

Surfactant Therapy

3. What treatments should be initiated for L.D.?

Before treating L.D. for respiratory distress syndrome, other causes of respiratory distress must be ruled out. Infections, for example, (particularly group B *streptococcal* sepsis or pneumonia) often may present with respiratory distress. L.D. was started empirically on antibiotics and a complete evaluation of possible sepsis should be performed.

Exogenous surfactant should be administered intratracheally to L.D. as soon as possible. Surfactant is the most comprehensively studied new therapy in neonatal medicine.[60-63] Until the late 1980s, oxygen supplementation, mechanical ventilation, fluid restriction, and supportive care were the general treatment measures for respiratory distress syndrome. Since respiratory distress syndrome primarily is a consequence of surfactant deficiency, the administration of exogenous surfactant should decrease the severity of respiratory distress syndrome and the risk of death.[62,63]

Three types of exogenous surfactants have been evaluated clinically: natural, modified natural, and synthetic. Natural surfactants are derived from bovine or porcine lung lipid or lavage extracts, or from human amniotic fluid. Modified natural surfactants are lung lipid extracts supplemented with phospholipids or other components.[60] Two surfactant products currently are licensed in the U.S.: Exosurf (colfosceril palmitate) is synthetic and Survanta (beractant) is a modified natural surfactant. Both are indicated for the prevention and treatment (i.e., rescue therapy) of respiratory distress syndrome.

Human surfactant contains phospholipids, neutral lipids, and proteins. The major surface-active component is dipalmitoylphosphatidylcholine (DPPC), also known as colfosceril or lecithin. However, this phospholipid slowly adsorbs to the air:fluid interface in the alveoli. Other phospholipids, such as phostidylcholine and phosphatidylglycerol, and three surfactant proteins (SP-A, SP-B, and SP-C) enhance spreadability and surface adsorption.[60,61] Adsorption and surface spreading of the surfactant in the alveoli are important determinants of surface tension activity.

Exosurf is protein-free and contains DPPC, cetyl alcohol to enhance surface activity, and tyloxapol to facilitate spreading and adsorption.[60-62,64] Survanta is a modified bovine extract with added DPPC and lipids to improve surface activity. It has similar phospholipid composition to human surfactant and contains SP-B and SP-C, but not SP-A.[60,61,65,66] Other comparisons between these two products are listed in Table 96.4.

4. Pharmacologic and Long-Term Effects. What are the effects of exogenously administered surfactant in respiratory distress syndrome?

Oxygenation and lung compliance rapidly and markedly improve after the administration of surfactant. Supplemental oxygen and mechanical ventilation can be reduced significantly. The increased lung compliance and decreased need for high inspiratory pressures result in a dramatic decrease in the incidence of pneumothorax and pulmonary interstitial emphysema. Neonatal mortality is decreased by approximately 33% and survival increases by 17% in patients without bronchopulmonary dysplasia or chronic lung disease.[60] Other complications of respiratory distress syndrome such as intraventricular hemorrhage and patent ductus arteriosus have not been decreased consistently with surfactant therapy.[61]

5. Number of Doses. At 3 hours of age, 5 mL/kg of Exosurf was administered to L.D. intratracheally. Within 2 hours, oxygenation improved and the FiO2 was weaned from 100% to 80%. Ten hours later, the ABGs were pH 7.36, pCO2 45 mm Hg, pO2 80 mm Hg, base deficit 2, and O2 saturation of 94% on the following ventilator settings: FiO2 0.73, IMV 40, PiP 18, and PEEP +3. The a/A ratio is <0.2. Should another dose of Exosurf be administered? [SI units: pCO2 6.0 kPa; pO2 10.7 kPa]

Because the response to a single dose usually is transient, more than one dose of surfactant is needed. Response to surfactant therapy can be variable, especially in preterm newborns less than 750 gm.[60] Reasons for nonresponse include: surfactant inhibition by proteins that have leaked into the alveolar spaces, inactivation of surfactant by inflammatory mediators (i.e., free oxygen radicals, proteases), presence of conditions such as pulmonary edema that can decrease surfactant effectiveness, or poor delivery of surfactant to the alveoli. The degree of responsiveness to surfactant also decreases with increasing postnatal age.[60]

Although the indications for subsequent doses of surfactant have varied in investigational studies, persistence of respiratory failure is the major clinical indicator for retreatment. A second dose of Exosurf should be given to L.D. since he still requires mechanical ventilation with relatively high inspiratory pressures and supplemental oxygen (FiO2 ≥0.3) to maintain an arterial pO2 ≥50 mm Hg and oxygen saturation of 90%. Also, most clinicians would agree that an a/A ratio of less than 0.2 is an indication for repeat dosing.[64] Administration of a third and fourth dose of Exosurf, however, does not significantly increase therapeutic benefits.[67]

6. Prophylactic Administration. Could prophylactic administration of surfactant have prevented RDS in L.D.?

Prophylactic administration of surfactant may reduce the incidence and severity of respiratory distress syndrome, but does not always prevent the disease.[52] Theoretically, the first dose of surfactant could be given before the newborn's first breath or before positive pressure ventilation.[61] This would avoid the early lung injury seen in respiratory distress syndrome that may interfere with surfactant distribution, bioavailability, and effectiveness.[60,68] However, this strategy would increase the cost of care because newborns who may never go on to develop respiratory distress syndrome would be intubated and treated unnecessarily.[60,62] In addition, delivery-room treatment may interfere with resuscitation and stabilization of the neonate.[61,68]

More importantly, prophylactic administration of surfactant within four hours of birth is not any better than rescue treatment after the onset of respiratory distress syndrome.[68] Therefore, current recommendations include surfactant treatment as soon as clinical signs of respiratory distress syndrome appear.[61,68] Early rescue therapy avoids progression of the disease and the potential for decreased surfactant effectiveness. Thus, prophylactic administration in the delivery room should be reserved for extremely premature neonates who are at the highest risk for respiratory distress syndrome.[61]

Unfortunately, the incidence of bronchopulmonary dysplasia after prophylactic surfactant administration is not reduced[62] and may even be increased in extremely low birthweight infants.[68] Extremely low birthweight infants who receive prophylactic surfactant also have a poorer neurodevelopmental outcome at one year postnatal age.[68] It is thought that prophylactic surfactant administration may increase the survival of the most critically ill neonates who then are at the highest risk for developing bronchopulmonary dysplasia.[62]

7. Complications. What complications of surfactant treatment is L.D. at risk of developing?

The most common adverse effects of surfactant therapy are related to its administration method.[64,65] During administration, bradycardia and oxygen desaturation may occur secondary to vagal stimulation and airway obstruction.[61] These adverse events may require surfactant administration to be discontinued temporarily and ventilator support to be increased temporarily. Rarely, mucous plugging with obstruction also may occur.[64,65] Airway obstruction may be decreased by delivering surfactant as a continuous intratracheal infusion over 10 to 20 minutes via an infusion pump.[69]

Surfactant therapy may increase the risk of pulmonary hemorrhage. Although the exact mechanism is unknown, surfactant may increase pulmonary blood flow through the ductus arteriosus, increase pulmonary microvascular pressures, and cause hemorrhagic pulmonary edema.[62,63,70] The benefits of surfactant therapy, however, far outweigh the increased risk of pulmonary hemorrhage.[70] The incidence of pulmonary hemorrhage is similar for both Exosurf and Survanta.[71]

Neonates given surfactant may be at a greater risk for apnea requiring methylxanthine treatment. Since surfactant-treated neonates can be weaned from ventilator support sooner, they may display apnea more easily.[62] Individual trials with natural surfactants have suggested an increased incidence of sepsis, but the majority of studies have not validated this finding.[63] No difference in the incidence of sepsis or apnea treated with methylxanthines was noted between Exosurf or Survanta.[71]

8. Product Selection. Are there any advantages of one surfactant product over the other?

Not enough data exist to label one commercially available product superior to the other. In a randomized comparative trial, Survanta-treated neonates responded more rapidly (i.e., oxygen and ventilator pressures were able to be decreased sooner) than those who received Exosurf. Despite Survanta's faster onset of action, the incidence of death and bronchopulmonary dysplasia were similar in the two groups.[71]

Table 96.4	Comparison of Currently Marketed Surfactant Products[a,64–66]	
Variable	Colfosceril (Exosurf)	Beractant (Survanta)
Type and source	Synthetic	Modified natural surfactant, calf lung extract
Phospholipids	Synthetic DPPC (hexadecanol and DPPC)	Natural and supplemented DPPC and mixed phospholipids
Proteins	None	Bovine proteins SP-B and SP-C
Dispersing and adsorption agents	Cetyl alcohol, tyloxapol	Proteins SP-B and SP-C
Recommended dose	5 mL/kg (DPPC 67.5 mg/kg)	4 mL/kg (phospholipids 100 mg/kg)
Indications	Prophylaxis or rescue therapy	Prophylaxis or rescue therapy
Criteria for prophylaxis	Birth weight <1350 gm with risk for respiratory distress syndrome. Birth weight >1350 gm with evidence of lung immaturity	Birth weight <1250 gm or evidence of surfactant deficiency
Recommended regimen for prophylaxis	Give 1st dose ASAP after birth; give 2nd and 3rd doses 12 and 24 hours later to all who remain on ventilator	Give 1st dose ASAP after birth, preferably within 15 min; give 2nd–4th doses if respiratory distress syndrome develops and mechanical ventilation required with $FiO_2 \geq 0.30$
Criterion for rescue therapy	FiO_2 >0.3 at arterial pO_2 <80 mm Hg (a/A <0.22)	FiO_2 >0.3 at arterial pO_2 <80 mm Hg (a/A <0.22)
Recommended regimen for rescue therapy	Give 1st dose ASAP after respiratory distress syndrome diagnosed; give 2nd dose 12 hr later to all who remain on ventilator	Give 1st dose ASAP after respiratory distress syndrome diagnosed, preferably by 8 hr postnatal age. Re-evaluate to determine need for doses 2–4. Do not give more frequently than Q 6 hr; no more than 4 doses within 48 hours
Recommended administration technique	Administer through ETT adapter via ventilator, divide dose into 2 aliquots with position change	Administer through disconnected ETT via 5 French catheter, divide dose into 4 aliquots with position change
Formulation	Lyophilized powder	Suspension
Storage	Room temperature	Refrigerate 2–8 °C
Volume/vial	8 mL (after reconstitution)	8 mL
Special instructions	Reconstitute with 8 mL of preservative-free sterile water for injection, follow mixing procedures carefully, do not shake	Warm to room temperature before use, do not shake
Stability	Stable up to 12 hr after reconstitution	If warmed to room temperature for <8 hr, unopened, unused vials may be returned only once to refrigerator
Cost per vial[b]	$659	$689

a a/A = Arterial to alveolar oxygen tension ratio; ASAP = As soon as possible; DPPC = Dipalmitoylphosphatidylcholine; ETT = Endotracheal tube; FiO_2 = Fractional inspired oxygen; pO_2 = Oxygen pressure.
b Average wholesale price 1994 Red Book.

Since Exosurf comes with various sized endotracheal tube adapters, neonates do not need to be disconnected from the ventilator during administration. According to the package insert for Survanta, neonates must be disconnected from the ventilator before surfactant administration. As a result, clinicians will transiently increase both FiO_2 and peak inspiratory pressures before disconnecting the ventilator. These higher settings and interruption from the ventilator may be avoided, however, if Survanta is given through a neonatal suction valve. This method has been shown to be equally effective, simpler, and possibly safer than methods with ventilator disconnection.[72]

Since Survanta is a modified natural surfactant, it contains proteins that are potentially antigenic. Thus, theoretically, it may cause an immunologic response. However, there are no reports of Survanta-induced hypersensitivity reactions.[63]

Diuretics

9. What is the role of diuretics in the management of respiratory distress syndrome?

The therapeutic role of diuretics in respiratory distress syndrome is controversial. In the natural course of respiratory distress syndrome, an abrupt diuresis (urine output >80% of fluid intake) occurs within the first 48 to 72 hours of life. This diuresis is followed by an improvement in pulmonary function which is thought to be due to a decrease of alveolar or interstitial pulmonary fluid. Before surfactant was commercially available, neonates who did not have this diuresis (or had it after 72 hours) were more likely to develop bronchopulmonary dysplasia.

Routine Use. Routine early administration of furosemide to pharmacologically mimic the natural course of respiratory distress syndrome may facilitate diuresis and weaning from mechanical ventilation. However, diuretics do not decrease the incidence of bronchopulmonary dysplasia.[73,74] In addition, treatment with furosemide may promote patency of the ductus arteriosus which may further worsen pulmonary edema.[73,75] Therefore, routine administration of diuretics in respiratory distress syndrome is not indicated.[74]

Selective Use. Since pulmonary edema is present in respiratory distress syndrome, furosemide occasionally is administered to enhance lung fluid elimination and decrease pulmonary edema. If L.D. had signs of pulmonary edema with compromised pulmonary function (e.g., hypoxemia and hypercapnia), furosemide 1 mg/kg IV push could be given.

Patent Ductus Arteriosus (PDA)

Pathogenesis

Several major differences between adult and fetal circulation exist. In order to understand the pathophysiology and clinical manifestations of patent ductus arteriosus, fetal circulation and the cardiovascular changes that occur at birth will be reviewed.

Fetal Circulatory Anatomy

The fetus has three unique circulatory structures that differ from the adult: 1) the ductus venosus, which permits blood to bypass the liver; 2) the foramen ovale, which allows blood to pass from the right atrium into the left atrium; and 3) the ductus arteriosus, the structure that connects the pulmonary artery to the descending aorta and allows blood to bypass the lungs. (See Figure 96.1.)

In addition to these structural differences, vascular resistance and pressure play important roles in determining the pathway of fetal circulation. For example, the relative hypoxia that occurs *in utero* causes pulmonary vasoconstriction. Pulmonary vasoconstriction, along with compression of pulmonary blood vessels by unexpanded fetal lung mass, results in a high pulmonary vascular resistance and decreased pulmonary blood flow. This decreased pulmonary blood flow is acceptable *in utero*, since the lungs essentially are nonfunctional. Large amounts of blood, however, must be pumped through the placenta where gas exchange occurs.

Fetal Circulation

Maximally oxygenated blood (PO_2 30 to 35 mm Hg) flows from the placenta to the fetus through the umbilical vein. (See Figure 96.1.) About 50% of the umbilical venous blood is shunted away from the liver through the ductus venosus and directed into the inferior vena cava. Blood from the inferior vena cava and superior vena cava then enters the right atrium. Most of the blood from the inferior vena cava, which is well oxygenated, is directed in a straight pathway across the right atrium through the foramen ovale directly into the left atrium. It then enters the left ventricle through

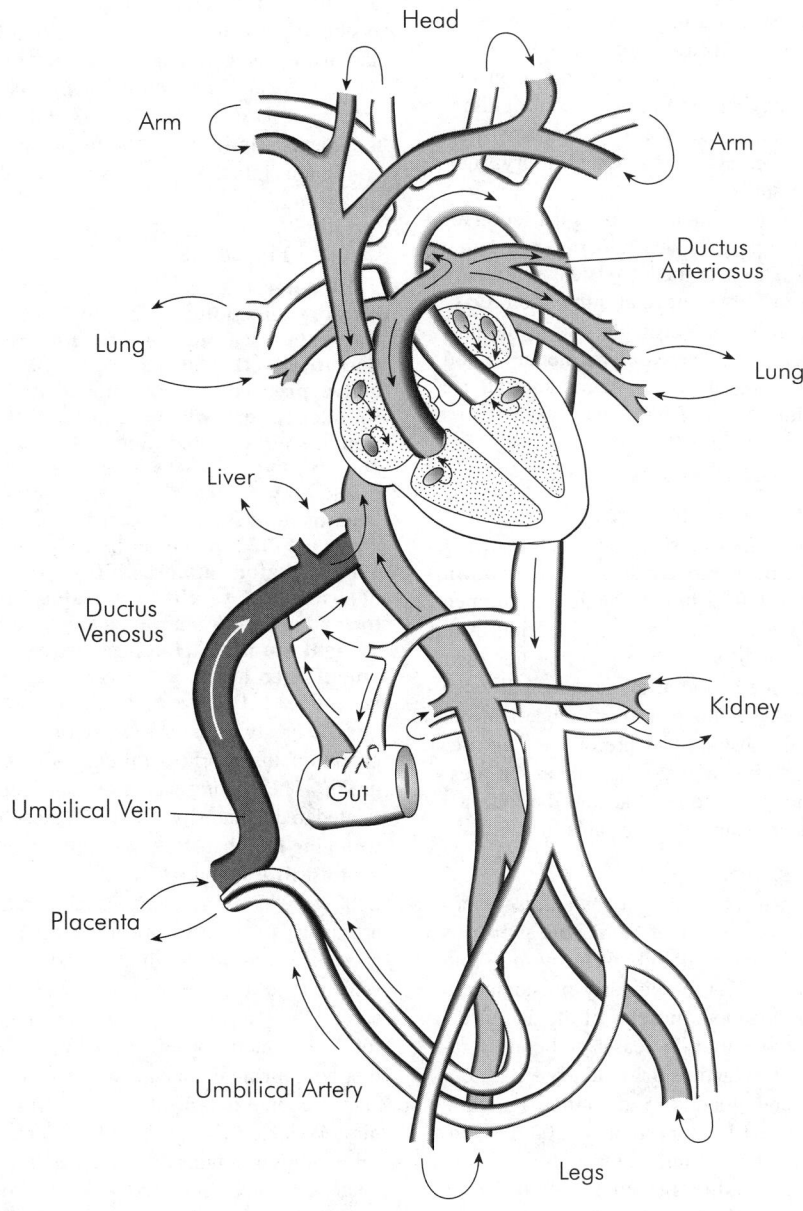

Fig 96.1 Fetal Circulation   Reprinted with permission from Friedman WF. Congenital heart disease in infancy and childhood. In: Braunwald E, ed. Heart Disease: A Textbook of Cardiovascular Medicine. 4th ed. Philadelphia: WB Saunders; 1992:893.

the mitral valve and is pumped into the vessels of the head and forelimbs. Thus, the fetal brain is preferentially perfused with blood containing a higher amount of oxygen. Deoxygenated blood returning from the head region via the superior vena cava enters the right atrium and is directed through the tricuspid valve into the right ventricle where it then is pumped into the pulmonary artery. Most of this blood is diverted through the ductus arteriosus into the descending aorta and then through the two umbilical arteries to the placenta. A small percentage of the blood flows to the lower extremities and then is returned to the heart via the inferior vena cava.[76]

Changes at Birth

At birth, major circulatory changes result from umbilical cord clamping, aeration and expansion of the lungs, and an increase in arterial pO_2. These changes are important in the transition from fetal to adult circulation. When the umbilical cord is clamped, blood flow decreases through the ductus venosus which then closes within three to seven days. Clamping of the umbilical cord also results in a twofold increase in systemic vascular resistance. This increase in systemic vascular resistance increases aortic, left ventricular, and atrial pressures and cardiac output. Changes in pulmonary pressures and blood flow also occur. After the neonate's first breath, the lungs expand, oxygenation improves, and pulmonary vascular resistance immediately drops. This increases pulmonary blood flow causing a decrease in pulmonary artery, right ventricle, and right atrium pressures.

If hypoxia occurs after delivery, pulmonary vasoconstriction results and the neonate may develop pulmonary hypertension with a persistence of fetal circulation. This is termed persistent pulmonary hypertension of the newborn or persistent fetal circulation. Oxygenation of these neonates is extremely difficult, due to the pulmonary vasoconstriction and resultant decreased pulmonary blood flow. Systemic alkalization (through hyperventilation and the use of sodium bicarbonate), administration of pulmonary vasodilators (e.g., tolazoline), and inotropic support often are necessary.[77] Severe cases may require extra corporeal membrane oxygenation.[78]

Closure of the Foramen Ovale

Due to the decreased right atrium pressure and increased left atrium pressure that occur after birth, blood attempts to flow down the pressure gradient from the left atrium through the foramen ovale into the right atrium. This is in the opposite direction from what occurs in fetal life. The small valve-like flap that lies over the foramen ovale on the left side of the atrial septum will close over the foramen ovale opening when the pressure in the left atrium exceeds the pressure in the right atrium. Closure of this flap prevents further flow through the foramen ovale. As long as the pressure in the left atrium is higher than the right atrium the foramen ovale remains functionally closed, until it closes anatomically.

Closure of the Ductus Arteriosus

Closure of the ductus arteriosus is more complex and is dependent upon many factors. *In utero*, patency of the ductus arteriosus is maintained through the vasodilatory effects of a low pO_2 and high concentrations of prostaglandins, particularly prostaglandin E_2 (PGE_2).[78-81] After birth, the smooth muscles of the ductus arteriosus constrict as arterial oxygenation increases and concentrations of placentally derived prostaglandins, particularly PGE_2, decrease. *In utero*, pO_2 of the ductal blood is 15 to 20 mm Hg, while after birth in a full-term neonate, it is approximately 100 mm Hg. Normally, the ductus arteriosus of a full-term neonate functionally closes within the first few days of life and anatomically closes within two weeks postnatal age.[81] When the ductus arteriosus fails to close, it is called patent ductus arteriosus. In a full-term neonate,

a patent ductus arteriosus beyond the first few days of life generally is permanent. It usually is secondary to an anatomic defect in the wall of the ductus arteriosus and requires surgical ligation. In contrast, a patent ductus arteriosus in a preterm neonate may persist for weeks and still undergo spontaneous closure.

When the ductus arteriosus fails to close, blood can flow from the aorta into the pulmonary circulation. Since systemic vascular resistance and aortic pressure are increased and pulmonary vascular resistance and pulmonary artery pressure are decreased after birth, blood pumped from the left ventricle into the aorta flows from the aorta (a high pressure area) through the patent ductus arteriosus and into the pulmonary artery (a lower pressure area). This flow is called left-to-right shunting and is in contrast to the right-to-left shunting that occurs through the patent ductus arteriosus during fetal life.

Although the persistence of a patent ductus arteriosus is pathologic, it is necessary for the survival of patients with cyanotic congenital heart disease while awaiting corrective or palliative cardiac surgery. These patients have congenital cardiac defects that depend upon the ductus arteriosus to maintain cardiac output and systemic perfusion (e.g., coarctation of the aorta, aortic stenosis, and hypoplastic left heart syndrome) or to provide pulmonary blood flow and maintain systemic oxygenation (e.g., pulmonary artery atresia or severe stenosis and tricuspid atresia). Patency of the ductus arteriosus can be maintained pharmacologically with a continuous infusion of alprostadil [(PGE_1) initial starting dose: 0.1 µg/kg/minute].[78,81]

Clinical Presentation

10. After L.D. received a second dose of Survanta, his respiratory function greatly improved and no further doses of Survanta were required. On the 3rd day of life, his nurse noticed that L.D. had tachycardia, a systolic murmur, a hyperactive precordium, and a widened pulse pressure. He also sounded "wet" when the nurse listened to his lungs. In addition, his nurse noted that L.D.'s combined IV fluid rates total 160 mL/kg/day instead of the desired fluid intake of 120 mL/kg/day. Current vital signs are: HR 190 beats/min; RR 65 breaths/min; BP 55/23 mm Hg; O_2 saturation 89%; ABGs include pH 7.22, pCO_2 55 mm Hg, pO_2 77 mm Hg, base deficit 10. Ventilator support is increased to compensate for L.D.'s deteriorating respiratory status. Echocardiography is performed and shows a moderate-sized PDA with significant left-to-right shunting. The chest x-ray shows pulmonary edema and an enlarged heart. What risk factors for patent ductus arteriosus does L.D. have? [SI units: pCO_2 7.33 kPa; pO_2 10.3 kPa]

L.D. has two major risk factors for developing a symptomatic patent ductus arteriosus: prematurity and respiratory distress syndrome. The occurrence of a patent ductus arteriosus is inversely related to the maturity of the neonate. Greater than 80% of neonates weighing less than 1000 gm develop a patent ductus arteriosus, in contrast to less than 10% to 15% of neonates weighing 1500 to 2000 gm.[80] Preterm neonates are at a higher risk for patent ductus arteriosus than term newborns because the immature ductus is more sensitive to the dilatory effects of prostaglandins and less sensitive to the constrictive effects of increased oxygen tension.[78,79,81] Respiratory distress syndrome also increases the risk for patent ductus arteriosus, and patent ductus arteriosus can further complicate the course of respiratory distress syndrome.[78,79,82] L.D.'s course is typical of a preterm neonate with resolving respiratory distress syndrome. L.D.'s pulmonary function improved following surfactant administration. Consequently, pulmonary vascular resistance decreased and the degree of left-to-right shunting across the ductus arteriosus increased, causing a deterioration in respiratory status. In addition, the excess fluid that L.D. received is an iatrogenic factor that may have increased the shunting across the patent ductus arteriosus, aggravating the degree of pulmonary congestion.[79]

11. How is L.D.'s presentation consistent with that of PDA?

L.D.'s clinical presentation is due to the increased pulmonary blood flow, decreased systemic perfusion, and left-ventricular volume overload which resulted from the shunting of left ventricular cardiac output through the patent ductus arteriosus into the lungs. In order to compensate for the inadequate peripheral perfusion, heart rate increases. This results in an increase in cardiac output and a greater left-to-right shunt through the patent ductus arteriosus, creating a vicious cycle. The widened pulse pressure (32 mm Hg) is a result of diversion of aortic blood flow through the patent ductus arteriosus which is causing the bounding pulses. Tachycardia, hyperactive precordium, and a continuous murmur, although not always present, are results of the left-to-right shunting through the ductus arteriosus during systole.[79,81,83]

12. What are the potential complications of this hemodynamically significant PDA in L.D.?

The increased pulmonary blood flow and resultant pulmonary edema will worsen L.D.'s respiratory disease and increase the need for ventilatory support. The higher ventilatory settings will place L.D. at risk for developing bronchopulmonary dysplasia. If the patent ductus arteriosus is left untreated, L.D. may develop congestive heart failure (CHF) secondary to an increased left ventricular end-diastolic volume. A hemodynamically significant patent ductus arteriosus also places L.D. at risk for intraventricular hemorrhage and necrotizing enterocolitis.[78,79]

Treatment

13. How should PDA be managed in L.D.?

There are three treatment options for L.D.'s symptomatic patent ductus arteriosus: 1) fluid management, consisting of diuretic therapy and fluid restriction; 2) pharmacologic therapy with indomethacin; and 3) surgical ligation. L.D. should first be given furosemide 1 mg/kg IV push immediately to treat his pulmonary edema. (See Question 9.) In addition, L.D.'s fluid intake should be restricted to 100 to 120 mL/kg/day to avoid worsening of his pulmonary edema and to prevent CHF.[79,80] Because of L.D.'s gestational age, birthweight, and size of patent ductus arteriosus, it is unlikely that he will respond to these general measures alone. Therefore, L.D. will require treatment with indomethacin. Indomethacin nonspecifically inhibits prostaglandin synthesis, thereby eliminating the vasodilator effects of the PGE series on the ductus arteriosus. The third option for L.D. is surgical ligation of the patent ductus arteriosus. Ligation generally is reserved for neonates who do not respond to indomethacin therapy or those in whom indomethacin therapy is contraindicated. (See Question 15.)[79,82]

Indomethacin

14. What is the dose of indomethacin and what route should be used for its administration?

The treatment of choice for L.D. is pharmacologic therapy with IV indomethacin. Enteral indomethacin is less effective than IV indomethacin.[79,80] This reduced effectiveness may be due to the formulation of the suspension and decreased, erratic, enteral absorption.[79]

A large interpatient variability of indomethacin pharmacokinetics occurs in preterm neonates.[79,80] Serum concentrations do not correlate consistently with therapeutic or adverse effects.[79-81,84] Furthermore, the optimal therapeutic serum concentration is not yet defined. Although many dosage regimens have been reported, dosing guidelines from the National Collaborative Study are used most commonly.[82] Three indomethacin doses are given in 12- to 24-hour intervals, with the first dose equal to 0.2 mg/kg IV in all neonates. Since indomethacin clearance is directly proportional to postnatal age, the second and third doses are determined by postnatal age at initiation of indomethacin therapy.[85] If onset of treatment was at less than two days postnatal age, neonates receive 0.1 mg/kg/dose; if initiation of therapy occurred at two to seven days postnatal age, neonates receive 0.2 mg/kg/dose; and if therapy began greater than seven days postnatal age, neonates receive 0.25 mg/kg/dose. Second and third doses are administered at 12- to 24-hour intervals. No specific guidelines exist as to which patients receive every 12 hour versus every 24 hour dosing; however, the individual dosing interval generally is determined by the neonate's urine output.[79] If urine output remains greater than 1 mL/kg/hour after an indomethacin dose, then the next dose may be given in 12 hours. If urine output is less than 1 mL/kg/hour but greater than 0.6 mL/kg/hour, then the dosing interval may be extended to 24 hours. Response to indomethacin therapy can be determined by assessing the clinical signs of patent ductus arteriosus such as tachycardia, widened pulse pressure, bounding pulses, and heart murmur, and the ability to wean ventilator support. In certain cases, echocardiography may be performed to confirm closure of a patent ductus arteriosus.

15. Monitoring Therapy. What clinical and laboratory data should be monitored during L.D.'s indomethacin therapy?

Before initiating indomethacin therapy, L.D. should receive an echocardiogram to rule out ductal dependent congenital heart disease and to confirm the presence of a patent ductus arteriosus. In addition, a serum creatinine and blood urea nitrogen (BUN) should be obtained from L.D. before indomethacin therapy because nephrotoxicity is the most common adverse effect. Approximately 40% of neonates receiving indomethacin develop transient oliguria with increased serum creatinine. This occurs as a result of indomethacin-induced decreases in renal blood flow and glomerular filtration rate.[82] Dilutional hyponatremia may occur secondary to either decreased urine output or decreased free water diuresis due to increased antidiuretic hormone activity.[80,81] Treatment of hyponatremia should be aimed at decreasing free water intake through fluid restriction rather than by sodium supplementation. In general, indomethacin therapy is contraindicated in neonates with renal failure, urine output less than 0.6 mL/kg/hour, or serum creatinine $\geq$1.8 mg/dL.[82] Indomethacin-induced nephrotoxicity may be reduced in neonates concurrently receiving furosemide without affecting patent ductus arteriosus closure.[86] In addition, serum concentrations of aminoglycosides, digoxin, and other renally eliminated drugs should be monitored carefully. Indomethacin therapy may decrease renal drug clearance and cause accumulation of these agents.[87]

A platelet count should also be obtained from L.D. before therapy, since indomethacin may decrease platelet aggregation. Thrombocytopenia (platelet count <50,000 to 60,000/mm^3) is a contraindication to indomethacin therapy.[79,81,82] In cases of thrombocytopenia, indomethacin may be withheld temporarily until a platelet transfusion can be given. Other potential contraindications to indomethacin therapy include active bleeding and clinical evidence of necrotizing enterocolitis, since gastrointestinal bleeding, perforation, and necrotizing enterocolitis have been reported with indomethacin use.[79,82] These GI effects may be related to decreases in intestinal blood flow. Significant decreases in intestinal blood flow occur with rapid IV push and can be avoided by infusing indomethacin over 30 minutes.[88] Grade II to IV intraventricular hemorrhage also is frequently quoted as a contraindication to indomethacin therapy; however, indomethacin treatment probably is not associated with progression of intraventricular hemorrhage.[89]

16. Recurrence. **L.D. completes a course of indomethacin 0.16 mg IV push Q 12 hr × 3 doses. The physicians were able to decrease L.D.'s ventilator support within the first 12 to 24 hours after starting indomethacin treatment. After 3 to 4 days of gradual and consistent ventilator weaning, ventilator settings could not be decreased further. Over the following 2 to 3 days, L.D.'s respiratory status deteriorated and he required increased ventilator support. L.D. now has tachycardia, a widened pulse pressure, bounding pulses, and a hyperactive precordium. Repeat echocardiogram shows a small- to moderate-sized PDA. Current data includes: BUN 10 mg/dL, SrCr 1.1 mg/dL, sodium (Na) 134 mEq/L, potassium (K) 4.9 mEq/L, chloride (Cl) 97 mEq/L, urine output 2.3 mL/kg/hr, fluid intake 130 mL/kg/day, and platelets 180,000/mm³. Why did PDA recur in L.D.?** [SI units: BUN 3.6 mmol/L of urea; SrCr 97.2 µmol/L; Na 134 mmol/L; K 4.9 mmol/L; Cl 97 mmol/L; platelets 180 × 10⁹/L]

Unsuccessful closure of the patent ductus arteriosus occurs with indomethacin therapy in 10% to 40% of cases. Even neonates that initially respond to indomethacin will reopen their ductus arteriosus 20% to 35% of the time. Recurrence of patent ductus arteriosus occurs especially in infants less than 1000 gm.[90] Several reasons have been proposed to explain L.D.'s transient response to indomethacin. Recurrence of patent ductus arteriosus is inversely proportional to birthweight with the highest recurrence in neonates weighing less than 700 gm at birth.[91] The higher recurrence in younger gestational age neonates may be due to resumption of PGE_2 production after indomethacin serum concentrations decline and heightened sensitivity of the immature ductus arteriosus to the dilating effects of PGE.[91,92] This is particularly important in ventilator-dependent patients such as L.D., since mechanical ventilation increases circulating vasodilating prostaglandins.[92] Because anatomic closure of a patent ductus arteriosus may be delayed for a couple of weeks, it is not surprising that the ductus arteriosus reopened in L.D. after his initial response to indomethacin.[91,92]

Prolonged indomethacin therapy may prevent recurrences and allow for permanent closure of the ductus arteriosus. Several prolonged treatment regimens have been successful in preventing ductal reopening.[90,93] One such regimen (indomethacin 0.2 mg/kg/dose IV Q 12 hr × 3 doses followed by 0.2 mg/kg/dose Q 24 hr × 5 doses) was able to significantly decrease the recurrence of patent ductus arteriosus in neonates less than 1500 gm from 47% to 10% without increasing toxicity. The need for surgical ligation also was decreased significantly.[90]

17. Should indomethacin be given to L.D. again? Can future recurrences be prevented?

L.D. remains ventilator dependent and is at increased risk for developing bronchopulmonary dysplasia. Since he has no contraindications to indomethacin therapy, a second course should be given. To prevent further recurrences, an additional five doses of indomethacin (0.16 mg IV Q 24 hr) may be given to L.D. after he completes the standard three-dose regimen. If the patent ductus arteriosus fails to respond to this prolonged regimen or if it recurs again after an initial response and L.D. remains ventilator dependent, surgical ligation most likely will be required to permanently close the patent ductus arteriosus.

18. Prophylactic Administration. **Could prophylactic indomethacin have prevented the development of a symptomatic PDA?**

In neonates who have echocardiographic evidence but no clinical signs of patent ductus arteriosus, prophylactic indomethacin decreases the incidence of hemodynamically significant (i.e., symptomatic) patent ductus arteriosus.[94] Even one dose of indomethacin (0.2 mg/kg) given intravenously within the first 24 hours after birth to neonates with respiratory distress syndrome decreases the incidence of a symptomatic patent ductus arteriosus.[95] Unfortunately, most studies have not been able to show that prophylactic

ductal closure with indomethacin decreases the incidence of death or bronchopulmonary dysplasia.[78,94,95] Therefore, routine prophylactic administration is not warranted. Preterm neonates, particularly those at high risk for developing a large patent ductus arteriosus (e.g., extremely low birthweight neonates), should be treated as soon as clinical signs appear.[78]

Necrotizing Enterocolitis (NEC)

Pathogenesis

19. C.D., an 11-day-old female neonate, was born at 28 weeks gestational age with a birthweight of 908 gm. Her postnatal course has been complicated by RDS, sepsis, and PDA for which she required intubation and mechanical ventilation, 2 doses of Survanta, a 7-day course of ampicillin and gentamicin, and indomethacin. Enteral feedings with a standard preterm 24 cal/oz formula were started on day 7 of life at 5 mL Q 3 hr. Feedings were increased by 5 mL/feed on days 8–10 to 20 mL/feed Q 3 hr on day 10 of life. This morning C.D. developed a distended abdomen, bloody stools, multiple episodes of apnea that required reintubation and assisted ventilation, and metabolic acidosis. ABG results were: pH 7.20, pCO₂ 47 mm Hg, and pO₂ 55 mm Hg. An abdominal x-ray revealed pneumatosis intestinalis (the presence of gas in the intestinal submucosa). C.D. is to take nothing by mouth (NPO) and gentamicin 2.5 mg/kg IV infusion Q 24 hr and ampicillin 50 mg/kg IV push Q 12 hr are restarted. What clinical signs of NEC does C.D. have? What is the pathogenesis of necrotizing enterocolitis and what risk factors for necrotizing enterocolitis does C.D. have?

Necrotizing enterocolitis, a type of acute intestinal necrosis, is the most common life-threatening nonrespiratory condition affecting newborns.[96] It primarily occurs in preterm neonates, but up to 20% of cases occur in full term infants. Necrotizing enterocolitis occurs in 3% to 15% of neonatal intensive care unit (ICU) admissions and accounts for at least 10% of all deaths in extremely low birthweight infants.[97,98] C.D. has several clinical signs of necrotizing enterocolitis including abdominal distention, bloody stools, apnea, metabolic acidosis, and pneumatosis intestinalis on abdominal x-ray. Gastric retention of feedings, occult blood in stools, lethargy, temperature instability, thrombocytopenia, and neutropenia also may occur. Necrotizing enterocolitis may progress to bowel perforation, peritonitis, sepsis, and shock. On abdominal x-ray, the presence of gas in the intestinal mucosa or in the portal venous system is diagnostic for necrotizing enterocolitis and free air in the abdomen is observed with bowel perforation. Although these x-ray findings confirm the diagnosis of necrotizing enterocolitis, a lag time may occur between the initial clinical signs of necrotizing enterocolitis and radiologic confirmation.[96,97]

The exact pathogenesis of necrotizing enterocolitis is unknown but appears to be multifactorial. Most likely, necrotizing enterocolitis results from the effects of intestinal bacteria and other factors, on injured intestinal mucosa (see Figure 96.2). The neonatal intestinal mucosa is prone to injury due to its: 1) increased permeability to potentially harmful substances, such as bacteria and proteins; 2) decreased immunologic host defenses, including low concentrations of IgA in intestinal mucosa; and 3) decreased nonimmunologic defenses, such as decreased concentrations of proteases and gastric acid. In addition, numerous factors can injure the neonatal intestinal mucosa including ischemia, malnutrition, infection, hemodynamically significant patent ductus arteriosus, congenital GI anomalies, cyanotic heart disease, toxins, hyperosmolar substances (e.g., feedings, medications), and exchange transfusions. The two most significant clinical risk factors for necrotizing enterocolitis are prematurity and polycythemia.[99]

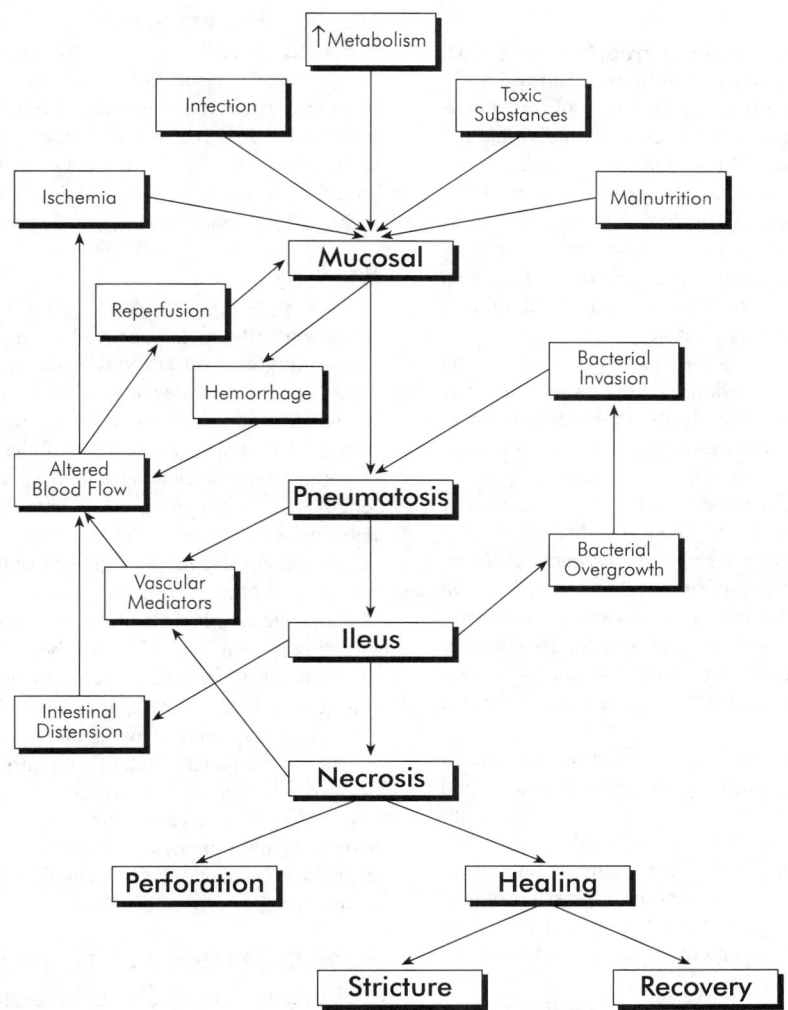

Fig 96.2 Necrotizing Enterocolitis (NEC) This schematic is a composite of the theories about factors believed to be involved in the pathogenesis of NEC. The progression of this disease is denoted in large type. The factors believed to initiate or propagate the disease process are in smaller type. Reprinted with permission from Crouse DT. Necrotizing enterocolitis. In: Pomerance JJ, Richardson CJ, eds. Neonatology for the Clinician. Norwalk: Appleton & Lange; 1993:364.

Approximately 90% to 95% of infants with necrotizing enterocolitis have received enteral feedings.[100] Early feeding and rapid advancements in the volume of feeds increases the risk of necrotizing enterocolitis. It is recommended that feedings be increased by no more than 10 to 20 mL/kg/day; increases greater than 35 mL/kg/day can place the infant at risk for necrotizing enterocolitis.[101] C.D. was started at 44 mL/kg/day and increased by 44 mL/kg/day. If C.D. was appropriately fed, she would have reached full feedings at 7 to 14 days of life instead of day four. C.D. also had a patent ductus arteriosus which may have contributed to the development of her necrotizing enterocolitis. Her patent ductus arteriosus may have caused a decrease in mesenteric blood flow with resultant ischemia and intestinal mucosal injury.

Classification

Necrotizing enterocolitis can evolve slowly over a period of 24 to 48 hours, from a clinically benign course to an advanced stage of shock, peritonitis, and widespread intestinal necrosis. A staging system has been developed to permit a more consistent evaluation and treatment of patients. Stage I necrotizing enterocolitis includes neonates and infants with suspected disease or "rule out" necrotizing enterocolitis. These patients may have mild GI problems such as emesis or an ileus. C.D.'s presentation is most consistent with Stage II necrotizing enterocolitis: signs of necrotizing enterocolitis (abdominal distension, bloody stools) confirmed by the presence of pneumatosis intestinalis on x-ray. Stage II disease usually requires 7 to 14 days of bowel rest (NPO) and parenteral antibiotics, with length of therapy determined by the severity of systemic illness (e.g., metabolic acidosis, thrombocytopenia). Stage III is advanced disease with peritonitis, shock, and possible intestinal perforation. Stage III requires fluid resuscitation, administration of inotropic agents such as dopamine and dobutamine, and surgical intervention.[99]

Treatment

General Management

20. How should C.D. be managed?

Significant abdominal distention may compromise respiratory function and blood flow to the intestines. Therefore, feedings should be stopped immediately and orogastric suction initiated to decompress the abdomen. Blood, urine, and stool cultures should be obtained and parenteral antibiotics started as soon as possible. C.D. also will require total parenteral nutrition until 10 to 14 days after the resolution of the acute period. At that time, enteral nutrition may be introduced gradually.

Antibiotics

21. Are ampicillin and gentamicin appropriate since C.D. just completed a 7-day course of ampicillin and gentamicin?

The selection of antibiotics for necrotizing enterocolitis depends upon the common micro-organisms observed in an individual neonatal unit and their sensitivities. Many organisms have been implicated in necrotizing enterocolitis including *Enterobacteriaceae*, *Pseudomonas*, methicillin-resistant *Staphylococcus aureus*, *Staphylococcus epidermidis*, *Clostridia*, *enteroviruses*, and *rotaviruses*.[97,99,100] For most cases of necrotizing enterocolitis, treatment with a broad-spectrum penicillin, such as ampicillin, and an aminoglycoside (e.g., gentamicin) is appropriate.

However, in some nurseries, *S. epidermidis* is the most common cause of neonatal nosocomial infections. Increases in *S. epidermidis*-associated necrotizing enterocolitis also have been reported. Therefore, vancomycin and an aminoglycoside are used as routine treatment in some nurseries or in specific patients at risk for *Staphylococcus* infections (e.g., neonates with central catheters or prolonged ICU stays). Vancomycin may be more appropriate than ampicillin since vancomycin has coverage against methicillin-resistant *S. epidermidis*, as well as *enterococcal* and *streptococcal* species. Since C.D. has been hospitalized for over a week, vancomycin and gentamicin may be more appropriate, especially if her neonatal ICU has a high incidence of *staphylococcal* nosocomial infections. C.D. should be treated with parenteral antibiotics for 10 to 14 days.

Other antibiotic combinations used to treat necrotizing enterocolitis include cefotaxime and vancomycin, and cefotaxime and ampicillin. The combination of cefotaxime and vancomycin has been shown to prevent severe peritonitis and death in less than 2200 gm birthweight neonates with necrotizing enterocolitis, whereas gentamicin and ampicillin have not. Suppression of aerobic fecal floral by the combination of cefotaxime and vancomycin, but not by ampicillin and gentamicin, may explain these findings.[102]

22. Enteral Antibiotics. The neonatologist would like to give gentamicin 2.5 mg/kg via the orogastric tube Q 12 hr in addition to parenteral antibiotics. Is there any added benefit to adding enteral gentamicin to the current parenteral antibiotic regimen?

Enteral administration of aminoglycosides does not prevent GI perforation or change the course of necrotizing enterocolitis. In addition, enteral aminoglycosides can be absorbed systemically in neonates with necrotizing enterocolitis, via the inflamed intestinal mucosa.[103] Systemic absorption may significantly increase the serum concentrations of concomitantly administered parenteral aminoglycosides. Therefore, routine enteral administration of gentamicin is not warranted for C.D. In select patients and during necrotizing enterocolitis epidemics, however, prophylactic administration of enteral aminoglycoside antibiotics or vancomycin decreases the incidence of necrotizing enterocolitis.[104] Systemic absorption of enterally administered vancomycin also can occur through inflamed intestinal mucosa.

23. Additional Antibiotics. Two days later, C.D. develops peritonitis with ascites, hypotension, metabolic acidosis, neutropenia, and disseminated intravascular coagulation. She is administered IV fluids and dopamine 10 μg/kg/min for the hypotension, fresh frozen plasma and whole blood for her coagulopathy, and morphine injection 0.05 mg/kg IV push Q 4 hr PRN for pain control. Free air in the abdomen is observed on abdominal x-ray. Blood and urine cultures have had no growth for 48 hours. What additional antimicrobial coverage should be provided?

Peritonitis secondary to intestinal perforation may be polymicrobial involving both aerobes and anaerobes. Therefore, an antimicrobial agent with anaerobic activity should be added to C.D.'s current regimen.[105] The two most commonly used agents are clindamycin and metronidazole. Empiric anaerobic coverage in the treatment of necrotizing enterocolitis without perforation is controversial.[97] Routine use of clindamycin in the treatment of necrotizing enterocolitis has not decreased the incidence of intestinal gangrene or perforation. In addition, it has been associated with an increased incidence of abdominal strictures.[106]

Prognosis

24. C.D. is taken urgently to the operating room and 10 cm of necrotic ileum is removed along with the ileocecal valve. What long term nutritional problems is C.D. likely to develop?

C.D. is at risk of developing short-bowel syndrome, a condition of malabsorption and malnutrition that results from surgical removal of a significant portion of the small intestine. The most important factors that determine short-bowel syndrome are the length of the remaining small intestine and the presence of the ileocecal valve. Since C.D. has had a majority of her ileum and her ileocecal valve removed, she most likely will suffer from short-bowel syndrome.

Since the terminal ileum is an important site for absorption of vitamins and nutrients, C.D. will be at risk for decreased absorption of these substances. C.D. also will have a faster gastrointestinal transit time and diarrhea, since her ileocecal valve was removed. (The ileocecal valve plays a major role in controlling intestinal transit time.) Absorption of enterally administered medications also may be decreased in patients with short-bowel syndrome. As C.D. starts to receive the majority of her nutrition enterally, she should be monitored for fat malabsorption and other nutritional deficiencies (e.g., deficiencies in vitamin A, B_{12}, D, E, and K), and supplemented accordingly.[107]

Neonatal Sepsis and Meningitis
Pathogenesis and Clinical Presentation

25. J.E., a 28-week gestation, 850 gm male, was born to a mother with prolonged rupture of membranes >72 hours. The newborn's mother is febrile with a white blood cell count (WBC) of 20 × 10³/mm³ and differential of 70% segmented neutrophils, 20% bands, 7% lymphocytes, and 3% monocytes. J.E. had Apgar scores of 4 at 1 min and 3 at 5 min after birth. Mechanical ventilation was instituted and J.E. was admitted to the neonatal ICU. Vital signs upon admission were: HR 190 beats/min, temperature 35.8 °C, and BP 56/33 mm Hg. Blood and urine cultures are pending. Significant laboratory data include: WBC 3000 cells/mm³ with a differential of 50% segmented neutrophils, 30% bands, 15% lymphocytes, and 5% monocytes; platelets 75,000/mm³. What is the etiology and pathogenesis of neonatal sepsis? What risk factors for sepsis does J.E. have? What clinical signs and laboratory evidence of sepsis are apparent in J.E.? [SI units: WBC 3000 × 10⁶ cells/L with 0.5 neutrophils, 0.3 bands, 0.15 lymphocytes, and 0.05 monocytes; platelets 75 × 10⁹/L]

Bacterial sepsis significantly contributes to neonatal morbidity and mortality. Neonates, especially preterm newborns, are at increased risk for infections and should be considered as immunocompromised. The neonate's decreased immune function (e.g., immature function of neutrophils, lower amounts of immunoglobulin), also results in a reduced ability to localize infections. Once a tissue site becomes infected, bacteria can spread easily, resulting in disseminated disease.

The incidence of neonatal sepsis varies from one to ten cases per 1000 live births.[108] Risk factors (as demonstrated in J.E.) include prematurity, low birthweight, and predisposing maternal conditions (e.g., prolonged rupture of membranes, maternal fever, and elevated maternal WBC or left shift).[109] Despite treatment, mortality from neonatal sepsis ranges from 20% to 75% with the highest mortality observed in newborns less than 1000 gm.[108,110] Meningitis occurs as a complication of bacterial sepsis in 25% to 30% of septic neonates.[108,111]

Common Pathogens

Early-onset neonatal sepsis (i.e., sepsis that presents during the first 5 to 7 days of life) usually is caused by organisms acquired from the maternal genital tract. The primary pathogens found in neonatal sepsis are group B *Streptococcus*, *Escherichia coli*, and other gram-negative bacilli (e.g., *Klebsiella pneumoniae*, *Proteus sp.*), *Listeria monocytogenes*, and *Enterococcus*. Late-onset sepsis (sepsis presenting after 5 to 7 days postnatal age) usually is caused by these primary organisms or by nosocomial pathogens, such as coagulase-negative *Staphylococcus* (particularly *S. epidermidis*), *S. aureus*, *Pseudomonas* species, anaerobes, and *Candida* species.[109,112] Risk factors for nosocomial infections include prolonged hospital stay, prior antibiotic use, presence of indwelling devices (e.g., endotracheal tubes, central venous catheters, ventriculoperitoneal shunts), invasive procedures, and low birthweight.

Coagulase-negative *Staphylococcus* has emerged as a major cause of neonatal nosocomial infections and the primary pathogen of bacteremia in low birthweight newborns.[113,114] Only 50% of coagulase-negative *staphylococcal* bacteremias in neonates are associated with the presence of a central venous catheter.[114] More disturbing, however, is the reported persistence of coagulase-negative *staphylococcal* bacteremia, despite appropriate treatment in low birthweight neonates *without* central venous catheters.[115]

Neonatal sepsis may present with nonspecific or subtle signs such as poor feeding, temperature instability, lethargy, or apnea. Clinical signs and laboratory evidence of neonatal sepsis observed in J.E. include tachycardia (heart rate 190 beats/minute), hypothermia (temperature 35.8 °C), neutropenia (WBC $3 \times 10^3/\text{mm}^3$), a left shift in the differential, and thrombocytopenia (platelets 75,000/mm³). Hypothermia is more common than fever in neonatal sepsis, especially in preterm newborns. However, if fever is present, it is strongly associated with bacterial infection. Neutropenia, especially with a left shift (as seen in J.E.) can be a sign of WBC depletion from bone marrow due to overwhelming sepsis. An elevated WBC also can indicate a neonatal infection, but may be less specific.[109] Other signs of neonatal sepsis include tachypnea, vomiting, and diarrhea. Late signs of neonatal infection include jaundice, hepatosplenomegaly, and petechiae. A bulging fontanelle, posturing, or seizures would indicate meningitis, although these CNS signs are not always present when meningitis exists. Neonatal cerebrospinal fluid (CSF) Gram's stain, culture, and cell counts are useful for the diagnosis of meningitis. However, neonatal CSF cell counts are difficult to interpret because values may overlap with normal neonatal values. The diagnosis of neonatal sepsis is confirmed by isolation of the pathogen from blood, urine, CSF, or other body sites. Latex agglutination tests which detect antigens (e.g., bacterial cell wall fragments) of group B *streptococci*, *E. coli*, *S. pneumonia*, *N. meningitidis*, and *H. influenzae* type B in body fluids can facilitate a prompt diagnosis, especially in patients who previously were treated with antibiotics.[108]

Treatment of Sepsis

Antibiotic Selection

26. What antibiotic regimen should be prescribed for J.E.?

Empiric treatment with appropriate IV antibiotics must be initiated immediately in J.E. Significant morbidity or fatality would occur if antibiotics were withheld until a diagnosis was confirmed by culture results (i.e., in 24 to 72 hours). This is especially true

in cases where meningitis is suspected. The initial empiric antibiotic treatment of choice for early onset neonatal sepsis and meningitis is ampicillin plus an aminoglycoside. These antibiotics are used because they: 1) are bactericidal against the common neonatal pathogens; 2) penetrate into the central nervous system; 3) are relatively safe; and 4) have proven clinical efficacy.

Therefore, ampicillin 45 mg every 12 hours intravenously plus an aminoglycoside (e.g., gentamicin 2.1 mg Q 24 hr IV) should be started in J.E. for suspected neonatal sepsis and possible meningitis. Meningitic doses of ampicillin should be used in J.E. until meningitis can be ruled out. Ampicillin is active against group B *streptococci*, group D *streptococci*, *Listeria*, and most strains of *E. coli*. Aminoglycoside antibiotics (e.g., gentamicin or tobramycin) usually are active against gram-negative bacilli. In addition, aminoglycosides may provide synergy with ampicillin against *Listeria* and group B *Streptococcus*.[109] Selection of the specific aminoglycoside should be determined by antibiotic resistance patterns within the neonatal ICU. Amikacin should be reserved for gram-negative organisms resistant to gentamicin and tobramycin. Aminoglycoside regimens need to be designed to achieve safe and therapeutic serum concentrations (gentamicin and tobramycin peak 6 to 8 µg/mL, trough <2 µg/mL; amikacin peak 20 to 30 µg/mL, trough <10 µg/mL).[5,42]

In some nurseries, a third-generation cephalosporin [e.g., cefotaxime (Claforan) or ceftriaxone (Rocephin)], instead of an aminoglycoside, is added to ampicillin for initial empiric treatment of early-onset neonatal sepsis and meningitis.[109,112,116] The spectrum of activity of these third-generation cephalosporins includes many gram-negative organisms and group B *streptococci*. However, third-generation cephalosporins do not have sufficient activity against *Listeria* or group D *streptococci*. Therefore, these agents must be used in combination with ampicillin for empiric neonatal therapy.

The third-generation cephalosporins have advantages over the aminoglycosides including better CNS penetration and the elimination of serum concentration measurements. However, these cephalosporins do not significantly improve clinical or microbiological endpoints compared to the standard ampicillin and gentamicin regimen. Furthermore, extensive use of the third-generation cephalosporins in neonatal ICUs may lead to rapid emergence of resistant gram-negative bacilli.[109] Thus, combinations such as ampicillin and cefotaxime should be reserved for the following situations: 1) neonatal ICUs where aminoglycoside resistance to gram-negative enteric bacilli is of concern; 2) neonatal ICUs where serum concentrations of aminoglycosides cannot be measured; and 3) specific neonates in whom aminoglycoside therapy could be of concern (e.g., neonates with known renal failure).[116]

Therapy for late-onset sepsis or meningitis is directed towards nosocomial pathogens plus the primary pathogens of early-onset infection (see Question 25). Selection of initial antibiotic therapy should consider the specific neonatal ICU's nosocomial pathogen and antibiotic resistance patterns, as well as the neonate's risk factors, clinical condition, and previous antibiotic therapy.[117] For example, if J.E. had a central venous catheter and presented with a late-onset sepsis, the initial antibiotics should include an aminoglycoside (for gram-negative coverage) plus nafcillin or methicillin for activity against *S. aureus* and *S. epidermidis*.[112] However, in neonatal ICUs with methicillin-resistant *S. aureus* or a high percent of nosocomial infections due to coagulase-negative *staphylococci*, vancomycin should be used in place of the antistaphylococcal penicillin.[117] In general, methicillin resistance occurs in 10% to 40% of cases of coagulase-negative *Staphylococcus*.[114] However, some neonatal ICUs have reported methicillin resistance in as high as 80% of coagulase-negative *staphylococcal* isolates.[117]

If *Pseudomonas* infection is suspected, ticarcillin or mezlocillin combined with an aminoglycoside should be used for their synergistic bacterial activity. For systemic fungal infections, amphotericin B (with or without flucytosine) is considered to be the initial treatment of choice.[118] Since uncommon organisms are not suspected in J.E., the regimen of ampicillin 45 mg IV every 12 hours plus gentamicin 2.1 mg IV every 24 hours is appropriate.

Dosage and Route of Administration

Dosage regimens for the antimicrobial agents commonly used in neonates[44,45,119] are listed in Tables 96.3 and 96.5. Dosing guidelines for tobramycin and netilmicin are the same as gentamicin (see Table 96.3). The intravenous route is preferred for treatment of all septic neonates. If the IV route is not available, the intramuscular route can be used in neonates with sufficient muscle mass, adequate peripheral perfusion, and a normal stable coagulation status. Oral administration almost never is used in serious neonatal infections because gastrointestinal drug absorption is extremely variable during this age. Meningitic doses of antibiotics should be used for the treatment of any seriously ill neonate until meningitis is excluded by negative CSF cultures.

Once a pathogen is isolated, the antimicrobial susceptibilities should be evaluated and the drug therapy modified appropriately. Blood, CSF, or urine cultures should be repeated to document bacterial sterilization after 24 to 48 hours of appropriate therapy. J.E. should be evaluated carefully for the development of serious bacterial complications such as meningitis, osteomyelitis, abscess formation, or endocarditis.[109,112]

Duration of Therapy

As long as there is no evidence of meningitis or other focal infection (e.g., abscess formation), the duration of therapy for most systemic bacterial infections is seven to ten days (or ≈5 to 7 days after significant clinical improvement). Antibiotic therapy may need to be continued for 14 to 21 days if the neonate's clinical response is slow or if multiple organ systems are involved.[112] If cultures are negative at 72 hours, and the infant does not have any clinical or laboratory signs of sepsis, antibiotics can be discontinued. In neonates presenting with signs of severe infection followed by improvement after initiation of antibiotics, therapy may be continued despite negative cultures.

Treatment of Meningitis

27. How should J.E. be treated if meningitis is suspected?

Antibiotic Selection

The major pathogens causing neonatal sepsis also are the primary pathogens that cause neonatal meningitis. Seventy-five percent of neonatal meningitis is caused by group B *streptococci* and *E. coli*, and *L. monocytogenes* is the third most common organism.[112,116] Initial empiric antibiotic therapy of choice consists of ampicillin plus an aminoglycoside.[116] Ampicillin plus a third-generation cephalosporin (cefotaxime or ceftriaxone) may be used em-

Table 96.5	Antibiotic Dosage Regimens for Neonates: Dosages and Intervals of Administration[a]				
	Weight <1200 gm[45]	Weight 1200–2000 gm		Weight >2000 gm	
Drug	0–4 Weeks[b] (mg/kg)	0–7 Days[b] (mg/kg)	>7 Days[b] (mg/kg)	0–7 Days[b] (mg/kg)	>7 Days[b] (mg/kg)
Ampicillin					
meningitis	50 Q 12 hr	50 Q 12 hr	50 Q 8 hr	50 Q 8 hr	50 Q 6 hr
other diseases	25 Q 12 hr	25 Q 12 hr	25 Q 8 hr	25 Q 8 hr	25 Q 6 hr
Cefazolin	20 Q 12 hr	20 Q 12 hr	20 Q 12 hr	20 Q 12 hr	20 Q 8 hr
Cefotaxime	50 Q 12 hr	50 Q 12 hr	50 Q 8 hr	50 Q 12 hr	50 Q 8 hr
Ceftazidime	50 Q 12 hr	50 Q 12 hr	50 Q 8 hr	50 Q 8 hr	50 Q 8 hr
Ceftriaxone	50 Q 24 hr	50 Q 24 hr	50 Q 24 hr	50 Q 24 hr	75 Q 24 hr
Chloramphenicol	22 Q 24 hr	25 Q 24 hr	25 Q 24 hr	25 Q 24 hr	25 Q 12 hr
Clindamycin	5 Q 12 hr	5 Q 12 hr	5 Q 8 hr	5 Q 8 hr	5 Q 6 hr
Erythromycin	10 Q 12 hr	10 Q 12 hr	10 Q 8 hr	10 Q 12 hr	10 Q 8 hr
Methicillin					
meningitis	50 Q 12 hr	50 Q 12 hr	50 Q 8 hr	50 Q 8 hr	50 Q 6 hr
other diseases	25 Q 12 hr	25 Q 12 hr	25 Q 8 hr	25 Q 8 hr	25 Q 6 hr
Metronidazole	7.5 Q 48 hr	7.5 Q 24 hr	7.5 Q 12 hr	7.5 Q 12 hr	15 Q 12 hr
Mezlocillin	75 Q 12 hr	75 Q 12 hr	75 Q 8 hr	75 Q 12 hr	75 Q 8 hr
Oxacillin	25 Q 12 hr	25 Q 12 hr	25 Q 8 hr	25 Q 8 hr	25 Q 6 hr
Nafcillin	25 Q 12 hr	25 Q 12 hr	25 Q 8 hr	25 Q 8 hr	25 Q 6 hr
Penicillin G					
meningitis	50,000 units Q 12 hr	50,000 units Q 12 hr	75,000 units Q 8 hr	50,000 units Q 8 hr	50,000 units Q 6 hr
other diseases	25,000 units Q 12 hr	25,000 units Q 12 hr	25,000 units Q 8 hr	25,000 units Q 8 hr	25,000 units Q 6 hr
Piperacillin	75 Q 12 hr	75 Q 12 hr	75 Q 8 hr	75 Q 8 hr	75 Q 6 hr
Ticarcillin	75 Q 12 hr	75 Q 12 hr	75 Q 8 hr	75 Q 8 hr	75 Q 6 hr
Vancomycin	15 Q 24 hr[c]	20 Q 24 hr	15 Q 12 hr	15 Q 12 hr	15 Q 8 hr

[a] Adapted with permission from Nelson JD. Pocketbook of Pediatric Antimicrobial Therapy. 11th ed. Baltimore: Williams & Wilkins: 1995:16.
[b] Postnatal age.
[c] If weight <750 gm and postnatal age <14 days, use 10.0–12.5 mg/kg Q 24 hr.

pirically for early onset neonatal meningitis in situations as outlined above for early-onset neonatal sepsis (see Question 26). In addition, due to their greater CSF penetration compared to the aminoglycosides, the combination of a third-generation cephalosporin with ampicillin may be preferred when the CSF Gram's stain indicates a gram-negative infection. Initial empiric antibiotic treatment of late-onset meningitis should follow similar guidelines as late onset sepsis with consideration of nosocomial as well as primary pathogens (see Question 26). As with neonatal sepsis, once an organism is recovered from the CSF, the most appropriate antibiotic is selected based upon susceptibility.

Duration of Therapy

If CSF cultures are positive, repeat CSF cultures should be obtained daily or every other day in J.E. to document when the CSF becomes sterilized. Appropriate antibiotics should be continued for a minimum of 14 days after the CSF is sterilized. This is equivalent to a duration of antibiotic therapy for a minimum of 21 days for gram-negative organisms and at least 14 days for gram-positive pathogens. As a general rule, it takes longer to sterilize the CSF of neonates infected by gram-negative enteric bacilli than those infected by gram-positive bacteria. (See Chapter 56: Central Nervous System Infections.)

Intravenous Immune Globulin (IVIG)

28. On day 2 of life, J.E.'s blood culture is reported as positive for group B *Streptococcus*. His current vital signs are: HR 135 beats/min, temperature 37 °C, and BP 59/40 mm Hg. Laboratory data include: WBC 7000 cells/mm³ with a differential of 53% segmented neutrophils, 15% bands, 25% lymphocytes, and 7% monocytes; platelets 150,000/mm³. J.E.'s ventilatory settings are slightly improved. Why should IVIG be considered for treatment of J.E.? [SI units: WBC 7000 × 10⁶ cells/L with 0.53 neutrophils, 0.15 bands, 0.25 lymphocytes, and 0.07 monocytes; platelets 150 × 10⁹/L]

Rationale

Neonatal IgG is obtained by transplacental transport of maternal IgG to the fetus, the majority of which takes place after 34 weeks gestation.[120] Neonates born before this time, therefore, will have very low IgG concentrations. In addition, due to the neonate's poor antibody response to antigenic stimuli, these low concentrations of IgG can decrease further during the first three months of life. Low IgG concentrations, as well as a lack of micro-organism-specific antibodies, significantly contribute to the neonate's increased susceptibility to infections. Therefore, administration of IVIG to correct low IgG serum concentrations has been proposed for the prevention and treatment of neonatal infections.

Efficacy

The efficacy of IVIG as an adjunct to antimicrobial therapy has been assessed in four neonatal studies and is reviewed elsewhere.[121,122] Three of the studies did not find a statistically significant difference in mortality between IVIG-treated and control neonates. Unlike the other studies, the fourth and largest study[123] used IVIG lots preselected for their specific opsonic activity against group B *streptococci* and IVIG was administered as a single dose of 500 mg/kg within 12 hours postnatal age. This study found a significant increase in survival at seven days postinfusion in the IVIG-treated neonates (100%) versus albumin-treated controls (70%). The overall survival, at 56 days postnatal age, however, was not significantly different.[123] This latter study demonstrates the potential use of preselected lots of IVIG that possess antibodies against specific neonatal pathogens. However, further studies are required to determine the optimal dosage regimen, including dose/kg, number of doses, and timing of treatment. Unla-

beled or low concentrations of antibodies against the primary pathogens of neonatal sepsis may limit the use of commercial IVIG preparations. Other immunologic agents, such as monoclonal antibodies and hyperimmune immunoglobulin preparations, may be more effective and currently are being investigated.

Results from studies evaluating the use of IVIG to prevent neonatal sepsis are conflicting.[122] Findings may differ due to variations in study design, sample size, IVIG product, specific product lot, or dosage regimen used. Although repeated prophylactic infusions of IVIG decrease neonatal nosocomial infections, no difference in mortality has been observed.[124] Furthermore, the largest study to date did not find any difference in nosocomial infection rates, duration of hospitalization, morbidity, or mortality between neonates given repeated doses of IVIG and untreated neonates.[125]

Initiation of Therapy

At this time, routine use of IVIG for all newborns to prevent or treat neonatal sepsis is not indicated.[122] However, the prophylactic use of IVIG should be strongly considered in preterm neonates with recurrent infections or in neonatal ICUs with extremely high infection rates. Septic neonates who are not responding to standard antibiotic treatment and supportive care, or preterm neonates with documented low serum IgG concentrations, also may benefit.[122] Since J.E. has responded to antibiotic therapy, as evidenced by his improvement in vital signs, WBC, differential, platelet count, and ventilatory settings, IVIG would not be indicated.

Dosing, Administration, and Adverse Effects

29. IVIG 500 mg/kg IV push weekly × 4 doses has been ordered for J.E. because of prescriber preference. How should IVIG be administered and what should be monitored for adverse effects?

The optimal dose of IVIG has not been established. The National Institute of Child Health and Human Development (NICHD) study used prophylactic doses of 900 mg/kg for neonates 501 to 1000 gm and 700 mg/kg for neonates 1001 to 1500 gm to attain IgG serum concentrations of 700 mg/dL.[125] Doses were repeated every two weeks. Trough concentrations after the first dose were ≥700 mg/dL in approximately 50% of the neonates. Only 13% of neonates had all trough concentrations at or above the target concentration during the study period.[125] These findings suggest that the clinical use of these doses or even slightly higher doses would be adequate. However, the optimal total IgG serum concentration for treatment or prophylaxis of neonatal sepsis has not been established. In addition, the amount of specific immunoglobulins directed against the primary neonatal pathogens may be more important. Although many dosing regimens have been studied,[122-125] doses of 500 to 750 mg/kg given every one to two weeks commonly are used. Some institutions use 1000 mg/kg in extremely low birthweight neonates. Doses ≥1000 mg/kg may not be more effective and may have toxic effects. Suppression of opsonophagocytosis and decreased bacterial clearance have been reported with high-dose IVIG in neonatal animal models.[126]

Although the dose of IVIG prescribed for J.E. is reasonable, IVIG should *never* be administered via IV push. Rapid IV administration may result in significant adverse effects. Administration rates for IVIG are product-specific and most neonatal doses should be infused intravenously over two to six hours. Since anaphylaxis can occur, slower initial infusion rates are recommended. In this case, the specific IVIG product used in J.E.'s neonatal ICU should be identified and an appropriate text[5] or the package insert should be consulted for proper administration rates. Neonates receiving IVIG should be monitored routinely for adverse effects such as tachycardia, dyspnea, hypotension, hypertension, fever, flushing, irritability, tremors, restlessness, and emesis.[124,125,127] These reactions may be related to the rate of infusion and generally resolve when the infusion rate is decreased or when the infusion is discontinued temporarily. An association between IVIG and necrotizing enterocolitis currently is being investigated.[125] In the NICHD study, the overall rate of necrotizing enterocolitis in the IVIG group (12%) was not statistically higher than the control group (9.5%). However, a significantly greater number of necrotizing enterocolitis cases occurred during phase 2 of the study in the IVIG group (12%) as compared to placebo (8.3%).[125] Therefore, due to the potential association with necrotizing enterocolitis, indiscriminate use of IVIG is not warranted. Other adverse effects may be identified as neonatal investigations continue with IVIG use.

Congenital Infections
TORCH Titers

30. S.Y., a 2000 gm female, was born at 34 weeks gestational age by vaginal delivery. She was born at another institution and transferred to your hospital on day 3 of life. S.Y.'s birth was complicated by prolonged rupture of membranes >72 hours, a difficult labor and delivery, and fetal distress requiring a fetal scalp monitor. Upon physical examination, S.Y. is an extremely irritable newborn with a RR of 60 breaths/min. Several vesicular skin lesions located on the scalp and around the eyes are noted. Conjunctivitis also is present. S.Y. is placed on supplemental oxygen and ABGs are obtained. Blood, CSF, and urine were cultured for bacteria and fungus and S.Y. was started on ampicillin 75 mg IV Q 12 hr and gentamicin 4.5 mg IV Q 24 hr for rule out sepsis. Antimicrobial therapy will not be altered until culture results are available. What other tests and/or information is needed for S.Y. at this time?

Certain bacteria, viruses, and protozoa can cause fetal infections that may result in fetal death, congenital anomalies, serious CNS sequelae, intrauterine growth retardation, or preterm birth.[128,129] The primary organisms that cause these infections can be remembered by the acronym, TORCH: T = Toxoplasmosis; O = Other (i.e., syphilis, gonorrhea, hepatitis B, listeria); R = Rubella; C = Cytomegalovirus; H = Herpes simplex. Due to the potential severity of these diseases, newborns who display any signs of infection (e.g., irritability, fever, thrombocytopenia, hepatosplenomegaly) need to be evaluated for these intrauterine and perinatally acquired infections. A complete infectious disease work-up should include specific antibody titer measurements to the above organisms.

Primary clinical manifestations and treatment[130,131] for selected congenital infections are listed in Table 96.6. The clinical signs of these infections may overlap and concurrent infection with two or more micro-organisms is possible. The detection of congenital infections oftentimes is difficult as many neonates are asymptomatic at birth. Prenatal maternal screening and accurate evaluation of maternal history for risk factors, therefore, are very important. Other organisms that can cause congenitally acquired infections include human immunodeficiency virus, human parvovirus, varicella-zoster virus, and measles virus.[128]

Because S.Y. has signs of a congenital infection (i.e., respiratory distress, skin rash, and conjunctivitis), TORCH titers should be measured.[132] A complete maternal history along with the results of recent maternal vaginal cultures also should be obtained. Due to the nature of the skin rash (i.e., vesicular), infection with the herpes simplex virus (HSV) should be highly suspected. Skin vesicles, conjunctiva, oropharynx, rectum, urine, and CSF should be cultured for HSV and other organisms known to cause congenital infections. Other appropriate tests for the diagnosis and work-up of congenital infections also should be performed [e.g., liver enzymes, prothrombin time, partial thromboplastin time, electroencephalogram (EEG), computed tomography (CT) scan or magnetic resonance imaging (MRI)].[128,129,132,133]

Congenital Herpes

31. Upon investigation it is discovered that S.Y.'s mother has genital herpes. This infection is her first known genital HSV episode and was accompanied by fever and headache. S.Y.'s mother had herpes genital lesions present during the vaginal delivery of S.Y. What are risk factors for HSV infection in S.Y.? What interventions could have lowered S.Y.'s risk for HSV?

Neonatal herpes simplex virus may be acquired *in utero* by either transplacental or ascending vaginal and cervical infections, perinatally via passage through a birth canal with active herpes lesions, or postnatally.[133] Ascending infections are more likely to occur with prolonged rupture of membranes. Factors that increased the risk of HSV in S.Y. include primary maternal infection during delivery, prolonged rupture of membranes, presence of active lesions at vaginal birth, and use of a fetal scalp monitor during active herpes infection.[133] The most important of these risk factors is primary maternal genital HSV infection at the time of delivery. Neonates born vaginally to these women are ten times more likely to develop HSV infections than neonates born vaginally to women with recurrent HSV infection (33% risk of HSV versus 3%).[134] Identification of newborns at high risk for HSV is difficult, however, because the majority of women who give birth to HSV infected neonates have asymptomatic or unrecognized HSV infection at the time of delivery. These women also have negative histories for HSV genital infections.[132,133]

In women with active genital herpes lesions, delivery by cesarean section can reduce the newborn's exposure to HSV lesions and, therefore, decrease the risk of perinatal transmission. Prolonged rupture of membranes, however, can lessen the protective effect of cesarean delivery by increasing the risk of an ascending HSV infection. In S.Y.'s case, delivery by cesarean section may have decreased S.Y.'s risk for HSV infection, especially if performed before or shortly (within 4 to 6 hours) after the rupture of membranes.[128]

Treatment

32. Cultures for HSV and other organisms have been obtained from S.Y. as described in Question 30. Why should therapy be initiated before culture results are available?

Neonatal HSV infections can result in significant morbidity and mortality. Given S.Y.'s signs of infection and risk factors, she should be treated as a case of probable HSV infection until culture results confirm the diagnosis. Three patterns of neonatal HSV infection can occur: 1) disseminated infection (multiple organ involvement) with or without encephalitis; 2) localized CNS infection; and 3) localized infection of the skin, eyes, or mouth (SEM). S.Y. has several signs of disseminated infection including irritability, respiratory distress, and skin vesicles. Other signs of disseminated disease include seizures, coagulopathy, jaundice, and shock. Untreated disseminated infections have the worst prognosis with mortality rates of 90%.[133] Morbidity and mortality for neonatal HSV infections can be decreased with appropriate treatment. Early treatment also is important as it can halt the progression of less severe SEM infections to more severe forms (i.e., encephalitis and disseminated disease).[135]

Although acyclovir and vidarabine are equally effective in neonatal HSV infections, acyclovir is preferred due to its ease of administration.[135] Vidarabine must be administered in a large amount of fluid which is not practical in the neonate. S.Y. should receive acyclovir 20 mg intravenously every eight hours for 14

Table 96.6	Selected Congenital and Perinatal Infections in the Neonate[a,128–131]	
Organism	Primary Clinical Manifestations	Treatment of Proven or Highly Probable Disease
Treponema pallidum[b]	Skin rash (maculopapular or vesiculo-bullous), rhinitis, periostitis, osteochondritis, hepatosplenomegaly, lymphadenopathy, meningitis, prematurity	Aqueous crystalline penicillin G × 10–14 days IV: ≤7 days postnatal age: 50,000 units/kg Q 12 hr >7 days postnatal age: 50,000 units/kg Q 8 hr **OR** Procaine penicillin G 50,000 units/kg/day IM Q 24 hr × 10–14 days
Neisseria gonorrhea[b]	Ophthalmia neonatorum, scalp abscess, sepsis, arthritis, meningitis, endocarditis	*Nondisseminated (including opthalmia neonatorum):* Ceftriaxone 25–50 mg/kg IV or IM × 1 (max dose: 125 mg); if hyperbilirubinemic, use cefotaxime 25–50 mg/kg IM or IV Q 12 hr × 7 days. Use saline eye irrigations for opthalmia neonatorum *Disseminated:* Ceftriaxone 25–50 mg/kg IV or IM Q 24 hr × 10–14 days or cefotaxime 25–50 mg/kg IV or IM Q 12 hr × 10–14 days
Hepatitis B[c]	Prematurity; usually asymptomatic; long-term effects include chronic hepatitis, liver failure, hepatocellular carcinoma	*Perinatal Exposure (maternal HBsAg-positive):* HBIG 0.5 mL IM and hepatitis B vaccine IM (different IM sites) within 12 hr after birth. Repeat hepatitis B vaccine at 1 and 6 months
Rubella	Hepatosplenomegaly, hepatitis, jaundice, purpura, bone lesions, microcephaly, deafness, heart defects, eye lesions, IUGR; rarely acquired perinatally	Supportive care
Herpes Simplex[b,d]	Cutaneous vesicles, keratoconjunctivitis, microcephaly, CNS infection, hepatitis, pneumonitis, prematurity. (See text)	*Acyclovir:* Term neonate: 10 mg/kg Q 8 hr IV × 14–21 days; preterm <33 weeks gestational age: 10 mg/kg Q 12 hr IV × 14–21 days *Ocular Involvement:* Acyclovir IV plus topical therapy: 1%–2% trifluridine, 1% iododeoxyuridine, or 3% vidarabine

[a] CNS = Central nervous system; HBIG = Hepatitis B immune globulin; HBsAg = Hepatitis B surface antigen; IM = Intramuscular; IUGR = Intrauterine growth retardation; IV = Intravenous.
[b] See Chapter 64: Sexually Transmitted Diseases.
[c] See Chapter 62: Acute and Chronic Hepatitis.
[d] See Chapter 70: Viral Infections.

days plus topical antiviral ophthalmic therapy (see Table 96.6). Liver enzymes, serum creatinine, BUN, and complete blood count (CBC) should be monitored for adverse effects of acyclovir. Phlebitis at the injection site also may occur.[5] Studies are underway to determine if higher acyclovir doses (e.g., 45 to 60 mg/kg/day) and routine use of a longer duration of therapy (e.g., 21 days) improve outcome and decrease HSV recurrences.[130,135]

Apnea

Pathogenesis

Apnea in neonates is a life-threatening condition that occurs more frequently in premature newborns and newborns of lower birthweights. Only 7% of infants 34 to 35 weeks gestational age have apnea.[136] In contrast, the incidence of apnea has been reported to be 78% in infants 26 to 27 weeks gestational age[136] and 84% in infants with birthweights less than 1000 gm.[137] Although several definitions exist,[138,139] clinically significant apnea may be defined as cessation of breathing for ≥15 seconds or less if accompanied by bradycardia (heart rate <100 beats/minute), significant hypoxemia, or cyanosis.[140–142] Pallor or hypotonia also may occur.

In neonates, apnea may be caused by a severe underlying illness or by prematurity itself (see Figure 96.3). Appropriate patient history, physical examination, and laboratory tests must be evaluated to rule out other causes of apnea before the diagnosis of apnea of prematurity can be made.[140,141] It is especially important to rule out sepsis before apnea of prematurity is presumed. If an etiology other than prematurity is identified, therapy would be directed towards that specific cause. For example, antibiotics would be used to treat neonatal sepsis with secondary apnea.

In apnea of prematurity, approximately 40% of apneic episodes are of central origin (i.e., no respiratory effort), 10% are due to obstruction and 50% are due to both (i.e., mixed events).[143] Treatment of apnea of prematurity includes the use of supplemental oxygen, gentle tactile stimulation, environmental temperature control, oscillation water beds, methylxanthines, nasal continuous positive airway pressure, and positive pressure ventilation.[140,141]

Treatment

Methylxanthines

33. S.M., a premature male newborn of 29 weeks gestational age, has a birthweight of 995 gm. On day 2 of life, he develops 7 episodes of apnea followed by bradycardia with heart rates as low as 85 beats/min. These episodes last 20 to 30 seconds in duration and require administration of oxygen and tactile stimulation. Three prolonged episodes required bag and mask ventilation. Between apneic spells the newborn appears well; physical examination and laboratory tests are normal for gestational age. Appropriate cultures are drawn for a septic work-up and ampicillin and gentamicin are initiated. The decision is made to begin aminophylline. What is the rationale for the use of methylxanthines in apnea of prematurity and what dosing considerations must be addressed?

Rationale. Methylxanthine therapy generally is initiated for apnea of prematurity when apneic episodes are frequent (e.g., >3 episodes), prolonged (e.g., duration >20 to 30 seconds), or severe in nature (e.g., accompanied by significant bradycardia or cyanosis) or are not controlled by nonpharmacologic means (e.g., gentle tactile stimulation, environmental temperature control, or oscillation water beds). This infant's apneic episodes are frequent, prolonged, and severe and, therefore, will require pharmacologic intervention.

Methylxanthines, specifically theophylline and caffeine, are widely accepted as the initial pharmacologic approach for the treatment of idiopathic apnea of prematurity.[141,144] These agents decrease apneic episodes via both central and peripheral effects. Methylxanthines stimulate the medullary respiratory center and increase receptor responsiveness to carbon dioxide. This results in an increase in respiratory drive and minute ventilation.[140,144] Central stimulatory effects may be mediated by adenosine receptor blockade. Adenosine is a known inhibitor of respiration and

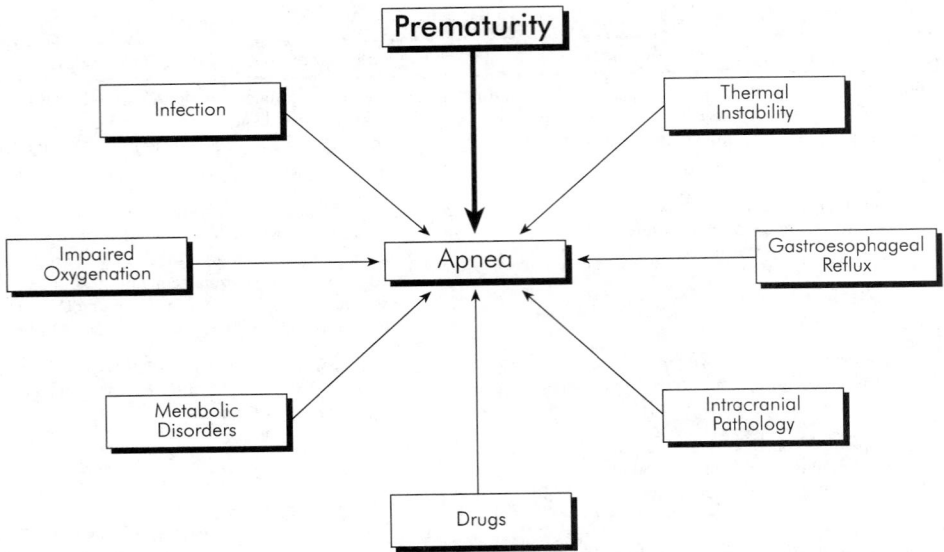

Fig 96.3 Causes of Apnea in the Neonate   Reproduced with permission from Martin RJ et al. Pathogenesis of apnea in preterm infants. J Pediatr. 1986;109:738.

both theophylline and caffeine competitively inhibit adenosine at the receptor level.[145] Other central effects, such as alteration of sleep-awake patterns, also may be important.[146] Peripherally, methylxanthines increase diaphragmatic contractility, decrease diaphragmatic fatigue, and improve respiratory muscle contraction.[144,147,148] In addition, methylxanthines increase catecholamine release and metabolic rate. This may improve cardiac output and oxygenation, lessen hypoxic episodes, and decrease apneic spells.

Dosing Considerations. Several developmental pharmacokinetic and pharmacodynamic factors need to be considered when dosing theophylline in neonates. Protein binding of theophylline is decreased in full-term newborns (36%) compared to adults (65%).[23] The decreased protein binding along with an increased tissue distribution results in a larger volume of distribution (Vd) of theophylline in neonates (see Table 96.2). This larger volume of distribution results in larger loading dose requirements to attain similar serum concentrations.

Theophylline clearance in preterm newborns (17.6 mL/hour/kg) is much slower than that observed in young children 1 to 4 years of age (100 mL/hour/kg).[23] As a result, smaller theophylline maintenance doses are required in neonates. Theophylline clearance increases dramatically during the first year of life approaching adult values at 55 weeks postconceptional age.[32] Theophylline clearance and, therefore, maintenance doses increase with increasing postconceptional age. Adjustment of maintenance doses is especially important in infants 40 to 50 weeks postconceptional age when the greatest maturational changes in theophylline clearance occur.[32]

In adults, theophylline is eliminated primarily via hepatic metabolism by C-8 oxidation to 1,3-methyluric acid (39% of a dose) and by N-demethylation to 3-methylxanthine (16%) and 1-methyluric acid (20%).[149] Small amounts of theophylline are eliminated unchanged in the urine (13%) and 6% of the dose is N-methylated to caffeine.[149,150] In contrast, the primary route of theophylline elimination in neonates is renal excretion of unchanged drug (55%).[32] Hepatic metabolism of theophylline (especially N-demethylation) is decreased in the neonate. Lower amounts of theophylline are eliminated by C-8 oxidation to 1,3-methyluric acid (24%) and by N-demethylation to 3-methylxanthine (1.4%) and 1-methyluric acid (8.2%).[32] As in adults, theophylline is methylated to caffeine in the neonate. The neonate's decreased demethylation

pathway, however, results in a decrease in caffeine elimination and significant serum caffeine accumulation. On average, serum caffeine concentrations can be 40% of the serum theophylline concentration.[32] The theophylline-derived caffeine may contribute to the pharmacologic and toxic effects seen in neonates receiving theophylline. After 50 weeks postconceptional age, the theophylline-derived serum caffeine concentrations become insignificant.

The generally accepted therapeutic range of theophylline for apnea of prematurity is 6 to 12 μg/mL. This range is lower than that which is normally accepted for the treatment of asthma (10 to 20 μg/mL) due to several reasons: 1) the higher free fraction of theophylline found in neonates results in a higher free concentration at any given total concentration; 2) there is a significant accumulation of the unmeasured active metabolite, caffeine; and 3) a different mechanism of action for theophylline is being exploited for apnea (i.e., central stimulation versus bronchodilation for asthma). Although some neonates may respond to theophylline serum concentrations as low as 2.8 μg/mL,[146] the majority require concentrations in the generally accepted therapeutic range.[151]

Dosing and Administration. Although oral aminophylline and theophylline are considered to be well absorbed in the neonate, many neonates initially have feeding problems when apnea and bradycardia are present. Therefore, S.M. should initially receive IV therapy and an oral nonalcoholic solution can be used when S.M. is stable and tolerating oral feedings. It should be remembered that depending upon the specific product used, aminophylline is 80% to 85% theophylline.

An aminophylline IV loading dose of 6 to 7 mg/kg (4.8 to 5.6 mg/kg of theophylline) will produce theophylline levels of approximately 6.4 to 7.5 μg/mL. Most centers use initial maintenance doses of aminophylline in the range of 1 to 2 mg/kg/dose given every 8 to 12 hours, with the lower doses in this range used in younger, more premature infants. An aminophylline maintenance dose for S.M. of 1 mg/kg/dose every eight hours should produce steady-state theophylline serum concentrations in the midtherapeutic range. Lower doses, for S.M. as recommended by the FDA guidelines (theophylline 1 mg/kg given Q 12 hr),[152] will result in serum concentrations below 5 μg/mL in the majority of infants less than 40 weeks postconceptional age.[153] Concomitant drug therapy and disease states (e.g., hepatic or renal dysfunction) also should be taken into consideration when selecting initial theophylline doses.

34. S.M. was given aminophylline 6 mg (6 mg/kg of aminophylline, 4.8 mg/kg theophylline) as an IV loading dose over 20 min. Maintenance doses of 1 mg Q 8 hr have been ordered. Describe your pharmacotherapeutic monitoring plan for S.M. Include monitoring parameters for efficacy and toxicity and duration of therapy.

The goal of methylxanthine therapy in the treatment of apnea of prematurity is to decrease the number of episodes of apnea and bradycardia. Continuous monitoring of heart rate and respiratory rate is required for proper evaluation. The time, duration, and severity of episodes; activity of the infant; and any necessary intervention performed should be documented. Relationships between the apneic episodes and the feeding schedule and volume of feeds, as well as the dosing schedule of theophylline (e.g., trough), should be examined.

Apnea of prematurity usually resolves after 36 weeks postconceptional age; however, it may persist in some infants up to or beyond 40 weeks postconceptional age.[136] Therefore, methylxanthine therapy usually is discontinued at 35 to 37 weeks postconceptional age provided that the infant has not been having apneic spells.[141] Infants that require therapy for longer periods of time may be discharged home on methylxanthines with apnea monitors.

Toxicities noted in neonates include tachycardia, agitation, irritability, hyperglycemia, feeding intolerance, gastroesophageal reflux, and emesis or occasional spitting up of food. Tachycardia is the most common toxicity and usually responds to a downward adjustment of the theophylline dose. Tachycardia may persist for one to three days after dosage reductions due to the decreased elimination of theophylline-derived caffeine. Seizures also have been reported with accidental overdoses. Methylxanthine toxicity can be minimized with careful dosing and appropriate monitoring of serum concentrations. Serum theophylline concentrations should be monitored 72 hours after initiation of therapy or after a change in dosage. Serum concentrations of theophylline also should be measured if the infant experiences an increase in the number of apneic episodes, signs or symptoms of toxicity, or a significant increase in weight. In asymptomatic neonates, once steady-state levels are obtained, theophylline concentrations may be monitored every two weeks.

35. S.M. now is 3 weeks old (32 weeks postconceptional age) and weighs 1100 gm. His septic work-up was negative. Currently S.M. has several apneic spells per day which respond to tactile stimulation; his apneic episodes have not required ventilatory assistance. S.M. receives 1 mg aminophylline IV Q 8 hr and his trough theophylline level this morning was 5.7 μg/mL. The medical team is considering switching S.M.'s theophylline therapy to caffeine because of possible improved benefits. How does caffeine compare to theophylline with regard to its pharmacokinetics, efficacy, and toxicity? What treatment should be selected?

Pharmacokinetics. The plasma clearance of caffeine is considerably lower and the half-life is extremely prolonged in the premature newborn (see Table 96.2). The low clearance is a reflection of the decreased neonatal hepatic metabolism and a resultant dependence of elimination on the slow urinary excretion. In the preterm neonate, the amount of caffeine excreted unchanged in the urine is 85%, compared to less than 2% in adults. Adult urinary metabolite patterns are seen by seven to nine months of age.[154] The half-life of caffeine decreases with increasing postconceptional age[155] and plasma clearance reaches adult levels after 3 to 4.5 months of life.[156] As a result of the maturational changes, doses usually need to be adjusted after 38 weeks postconceptional age and dosing intervals need to be shortened to eight hours after 50 weeks postconceptional age.[155]

Efficacy, Toxicity, and Dosing. Comparative studies have found similar efficacy for theophylline and caffeine in the control of apnea of prematurity.[157,158] Caffeine, however, may have some advantages over theophylline including a wider therapeutic index. Adverse effects such as tachycardia, CNS excitation, and feeding intolerance are reported more frequently with theophylline than with caffeine. The prolonged half-life of caffeine in premature neonates results in less fluctuation in plasma concentrations and permits the use of a 24-hour dosing interval. Since the half-life is prolonged and dosing requirements do not change quickly over time, caffeine serum concentrations can be monitored less frequently. Oral or IV loading doses of 10 mg/kg of caffeine base (20 mg/kg of caffeine citrate), followed by maintenance doses of 2.5 mg/kg (5 mg/kg caffeine citrate) given daily will maintain plasma caffeine concentrations in the therapeutic range (5 to 20 μg/mL).[144]

Although infants who are unresponsive to theophylline may respond to caffeine,[159] S.M.'s theophylline therapy presently is not optimized; his serum concentration is less than 6 μg/mL. S.M. appears to have partially responded to theophylline and may benefit from an increase in the dose with resultant therapeutic serum concentrations. S.M.'s aminophylline dose should be increased to 1.5 mg every eight hours to achieve serum concentrations of around 8 μg/mL. Although caffeine may have several advantages over theophylline, the IV product marketed in the U.S. is only available as the sodium benzoate salt. Benzoic acid has been associated with the gasping syndrome and also may displace bilirubin from albumin binding sites.[34,35] Because of these toxicities, caffeine sodium benzoate should not be used in neonates. It is possible, however, to compound an acceptable IV and oral caffeine preparation.[160] As for any compounded injectable preparation, quality control must be done to assure sterility, stability, and lack of pyrogen contamination. If the hospital currently is not compounding an IV caffeine product, it could take months to institute quality control measures.

Other Agents

36. S.M.'s dose of theophylline has been optimized and theophylline serum concentrations now are 12.4 μg/mL. S.M. continues to have apneic episodes. What other pharmacologic agents can be used?

Doxapram, an analeptic agent, has been shown to be as effective as theophylline for the treatment of apnea of prematurity.[161,162] Due to the limited number of investigations and uncertain side effects, however, the use of doxapram should be restricted to patients who are refractory to methylxanthine therapy.[144] In addition, the IV preparation commercially available in the U.S. contains 0.9% benzyl alcohol and should be used with caution. Although doses are not well defined, a loading dose of 2.5 to 3 mg/kg given IV over 15 to 30 minutes followed by a 1 mg/kg/hour continuous infusion has been recommended.[144,163] Doses may be increased by 0.5 mg/kg/hour increments to a maximum dose of 2.5 mg/kg/hour.[144] Lower doses have been used in infants receiving concomitant methylxanthine therapy with approximately 50% responding to IV doxapram doses of 0.5 mg/kg/hour.[164] A few studies have administered doxapram enterally; however, bioavailability in preterm newborns is not yet well defined.[144,165] Side effects associated with doxapram include: increased blood pressure (usually with doses >1.5 mg/kg/hour);[164] GI disturbances such as abdominal distension, regurgitation, increased gastric residuals, and vomiting; and CNS adverse effects such as increased agitation, excessive crying, jitteriness, irritability, disturbed sleep, and seizures. Further studies of doxapram are needed in order to better delineate its adverse effects and to help define its safety and efficacy for the treatment of apnea of prematurity.

Periventricular-Intraventricular Hemorrhage (PV-IVH)

Pathogenesis

37. M.C., a 3-day-old male infant, was born at 28 weeks gestation with a birth weight of 980 gm. He was intubated shortly after birth for respiratory distress and last night developed a pneumothorax. This morning, M.C. required a blood transfusion due to a significant drop in hematocrit (Hct). Hypotension, hypotonia, and decreased responsiveness now are noted upon physical examination. An ultrasound of the head was ordered to confirm the suspicion of an intraventricular bleed. What factors are associated with an increased risk for the development of PV-IVH?

Periventricular-intraventricular hemorrhage is the second highest cause of death in premature newborns and is the most common serious neurologic injury that occurs during the neonatal period. It occurs in 40% to 50% of premature newborns less than 1500 gm birthweight or less than 35 weeks gestation.[166]

The most common site for the origin of the hemorrhage is the periventricular germinal matrix, a highly vascularized cellular region that contains neuronal precursor cells. This vascular network, which is prominent at 26 to 34 weeks gestational age, contains poorly supported blood vessels that are fragile and vulnerable to injury.[166] Most factors associated with an increased risk of PV-IVH alter cerebral blood flow or arterial blood pressure which results in damage to these vessels. Associated risk factors include prematurity, very low birthweight, respiratory failure requiring mechanical ventilation, pneumothorax, hypotension, hypertension, hypoxia, hypercapnia, asphyxia, acidosis, rapid volume expansion, coagulation defects, infusion of hyperosmolar substances (e.g., sodium bicarbonate), hypernatremia, hyperglycemia, seizures, tracheal suctioning, and inadvertent noxious stimulation.[166–168]

Common signs and symptoms of PV-IVH include hypotension, hypotonia, a drop in hematocrit, and a decrease in responsiveness as illustrated by M.C. Apnea, areflexia, tonic posturing, seizures, and death also may occur.[169] Prognosis for normal neurological development in survivors depends upon location and severity of the bleed. Mild hemorrhages (Grade I: isolated germinal matrix hemorrhage and Grade II: hemorrhage extending into normal sized ventricles) have a better prognosis, but may result in cognitive deficits such as reading disabilities. Infants with moderate (Grade III: hemorrhage extending into enlarged ventricles) or severe hemorrhages (Grade IV: intraparenchymal hemorrhage) do worse with an increase in major motor (e.g., spastic hemiparesis) and intellectual deficits. Infants with moderate and severe bleeds also are more likely to develop posthemorrhagic hydrocephalus and seizure activity.

Treatment

38. How is PV-IVH managed and what therapies have been investigated to prevent PV-IVH?

Management and prevention of PV-IVH include the reduction or elimination of known risk factors. Wide variations in blood pressures and cerebral blood flow, abnormalities in serum osmolality and blood gases, and noxious stimulations should be avoided.[170]

Several drugs including phenobarbital, indomethacin, ethamsylate, vitamin E, and pancuronium have been investigated for the prevention of PV-IVH.[167] At the present time, none of these are widely accepted for routine use in newborn infants. Of the agents studied, low-dose indomethacin offers the best potential for PV-IVH prophylaxis.[171,172] A multicenter, randomized, placebo controlled trial using indomethacin (0.1 mg/kg/dose IV at 6 to 12 hours after birth and Q 24 hr for 2 additional doses) significantly lowered the incidence and severity of intraventricular hemorrhage in neonates of 600 to 1250 gm birthweight.[172] Indomethacin, a cyclooxygenase inhibitor, may prevent intraventricular hemorrhage by reducing the synthesis of vasodilating prostanoids and prostaglandins. This results in a decrease in baseline cerebral blood flow and changes in cerebral blood flow modulation. Inhibition of cyclooxygenase also may decrease formation of harmful free radicals. Although it appears promising, long-term follow-up investigations are needed before the use of low-dose indomethacin in premature infants can be recommended universally.[170,173]

Neonatal Seizures

Pathogenesis and Diagnosis

39. F.H., a full-term female newborn (weight 3.5 kg), has a history of perinatal asphyxia. Apgar scores were 2 and 4 at 1 and 5 min, respectively. Forty-eight hours after birth, F.H. begins to have rhythmic clonic twitching of the right hand, repetitive chewing movements, fluttering of the eyelids, and occasional pendular movements of the extremities that resemble swimming motions. What interventions should be initiated immediately for F.H.?

Seizure activity may be difficult to recognize in the full-term or premature neonate. Due to the immaturity of the cortex, neonatal seizures rarely are generalized tonic-clonic events, but can be clonic (focal or multifocal), tonic (focal or generalized), myoclonic (focal, multifocal, or generalized), or subtle in nature.[174] Subtle seizures include activities such as abnormal oral-buccal-lingual movements; ocular movements; swimming, pedaling, or stepping movements; and occasionally apnea. In addition, autonomic nervous system signs such as changes in heart rate, blood pressure, respirations, salivation, or pupil size may occur. Clinical neonatal seizures may or may not be associated with EEG changes.[175]

Neonatal seizure activity is a common manifestation of a life-threatening underlying neurological process (see Table 96.7) and, therefore, initial efforts may not include antiepileptic drug therapy. Definitive treatment is directed toward specific identified etiologies. The acute evaluation of neonatal seizures includes assessment of the infant's airway, breathing, and circulation and a review of the infant's history, physical examination, and laboratory studies. Every neonate with seizure activity should have a bedside determination of glucose; laboratory determinations of serum electrolytes including sodium, BUN, glucose, calcium (Ca), and magnesium (Mg); blood gases; bilirubin; and an infectious disease work-up including CBC with platelets, blood culture, urine culture, lumbar puncture with CSF analysis (cell count, protein, glucose), and CSF culture.[174,176] Treatment with antiepileptic drugs is indicated after correction of known electrolyte abnormalities. Antiepileptic drug therapy can be initiated (after correction of hypoglycemia) while laboratory test results are pending.

If the above tests do not reveal any abnormalities, an EEG and a metabolic disease work-up (serum ammonia, urine amino acids, and organic acids) can be performed. Intrauterine infections that are associated with congenital neurological abnormalities and seizures can be identified by obtainment of TORCH titers. (See Question 30.) CT scans and MRIs may be obtained to identify infarcts, hemorrhages, calcifications, or cerebral malformations which may cause seizure activity.[174,177]

40. The physician assesses F.H. as having adequate ventilation and circulation. She establishes an IV line and sends blood samples for electrolytes, Ca and Mg. A Chemstrip reveals a blood glucose of 20 mg/dL. What is your assessment and recommendation at this time?

It would appear that hypoglycemia is the cause of F.H.'s seizure activity. Hypoxic ischemic encephalopathy (secondary to asphy-

Table 96.7	Causes of Neonatal Seizures[a]
Asphyxia	
Hypoxic ischemic encephalopathy	Subependymal hemorrhage
Trauma	
Subdural hematoma	Cortical vein thrombosis
Intracortical hemorrhage	
Congenital Abnormalities (Cerebral Dysgenesis)	
Hypertension	
Metabolic	
Hypocalcemia	
Hypomagnesemia	Hypoparathyroidism
High phosphate load	Maternal hyperparathyroidism
Infant of diabetic mother	Idiopathic
Hypoglycemia	
Galactosemia	Glycogen storage disease
Intrauterine growth retardation	Idiopathic
Infant of diabetic mother	
Electrolyte imbalance	
Hypernatremia	Hyponatremia
Infections	
Bacterial meningitis	Cytomegalovirus
Cerebral abscess	Toxoplasmosis
Herpes encephalitis	Syphilis
Coxsackie meningoencephalitis	
Drug Withdrawal	
Methadone	Barbiturate
Heroin	Propoxyphene
Pyridoxine Dependency	
Amino Acid Disturbances	
Maple syrup urine disease	Nonketotic hyperglycinemia
Urea cycle abnormalities	Ketotic hyperglycinemia
Toxins	
Local anesthetics	Bilirubin
Isoniazid	Maternal cocaine
Familial Seizures	
Neurocutaneous Syndromes	
Tuberous sclerosis	Incontinentia pigmenti
Genetic Syndromes	
Zellweger	Neonatal adrenoleukodystrophy
Smith-Lemli-Opitz	
Benign Familial Epilepsy	

[a] Adapted with permission from reference 235.

xia), however, is the most common cause of neonatal seizures and can be associated with metabolic abnormalities such as hypoglycemia, hypocalcemia, and hypomagnesemia.[174] Hypoglycemia is defined as a whole blood glucose less than 20 mg/dL for premature infants and less than 30 mg/dL for full-term infants during the first 72 hours of life and less than 40 mg/dL for any neonate after 72 hours of age. In clinical practice, however, a glucose less than 40 mg/dL in a symptomatic neonate of any age would be treated.[178]

F.H. should receive an IV bolus dose of 7 to 14 mL (2 to 4 mL/kg) of dextrose 10% (200 to 400 mg/kg) given over two to three minutes, followed by a continuous infusion of dextrose 10% at an initial dose of 12.6 to 16.8 mL/hour (6 to 8 mg/kg/minute or 3.6 to 4.8 mL/kg/hour).[177] Serum glucose should be monitored and the dextrose infusion should be titrated as needed. If hypoglycemia persists, possible etiologies such as islet tumor of the pancreas, adrenal insufficiency, and inborn errors of metabolism should be investigated. Corticosteroids, glucagon, and diazoxide have been used to treat persistent hypoglycemia.[178]

Treatment of Hypocalcemia and Hypomagnesemia

41. The physician administers 10 mL (1 gm) of 10% dextrose solution IV and starts an IV infusion of glucose at 8 mg/kg/min. A repeat Chemstrip reveals a blood glucose of 80 mg/dL, but F.H. continues to have seizure activity. F.H.'s laboratory results come back as: Na 137 mEq/L, K 4.3 mEq/L, CO_2 22 mEq/L, Cl 104 mEq/L, BUN 7 mg/dL, SrCr 0.7 mg/dL, glucose 25 mg/dL, Mg 1.0 mEq/L, and Ca 5 mg/dL. What should be done next to control F.H.'s seizures? [SI units: Na 137 mmol/L; K 4.3 mmol/L; CO_2 22 mmol/L; Cl 104 mmol/L; BUN 2.5 mmol/L of urea; SrCr 61.9 μmol/L; glucose 1.4 mmol/L; Mg 0.5 mmol/L; Ca 1.25 mmol/L]

F.H. also has hypocalcemia and hypomagnesemia, both of which may cause seizure activity. Neonatal hypocalcemia is defined as a serum calcium less than 7 mg/dL[174] or an ionized serum calcium less than 3 mg/dL.[177] Hypomagnesemia (defined as a serum magnesium <1.5 mEq/L) is rare but may coexist with hypocalcemia. Hypomagnesemia should be suspected when hypocalcemia cannot be corrected despite large doses of calcium.[179]

F.H. should receive calcium gluconate 700 mg (200 mg/kg) given slowly intravenously as a 10% solution[176] and magnesium sulfate 25 to 50 mg/kg/dose (0.2 to 0.4 mEq/kg/dose) intramuscularly as a 50% solution or intravenously as a dilute solution (maximum concentration: 100 mg/mL) administered over two to four hours.[5] Doses of calcium gluconate and magnesium sulfate may be repeated based upon serum determinations. If IV calcium is administered too quickly, vasodilation, hypotension, bradycardia, and cardiac arrhythmias may occur. Calcium gluconate may be administered intravenously at a maximum rate of 50 mg/minute while monitoring heart rate, blood pressure, and electrocardiogram (ECG).[5] To avoid IV extravasation with resultant severe dermal necrosis, calcium salts should be administered through a properly working IV line and the IV site should be monitored for signs of infiltration.

Treatment with Antiepileptic Drugs (AEDs)

42. Despite the normalization of his laboratory tests, F.H. continued to have seizure activity. Phenobarbital 35 mg IV push over 1 min was administered. Ten minutes later, F.H. continued to have intermittent seizure activity. Describe a pharmacotherapeutic plan to control F.H.'s seizure activity.

Phenobarbital is the initial antiepileptic drug of choice for neonatal seizures: phenytoin and lorazepam usually are considered the second and third drugs of choice.[180] Due to the large volume of distribution of phenobarbital in neonates ($\approx$1 L/kg),[174,181] large initial loading doses of 20 mg/kg are required to produce therapeutic serum concentrations. (See Table 96.8.) Since F.H. only received a 10 mg/kg dose (35 mg) of phenobarbital, an additional 10 mg/kg should be given now. Phenobarbital should be administered intravenously at a rate of $\leq$1 mg/kg/minute,[5] so this 35 mg dose should be given over at least ten minutes, not over one minute. Rapid administration of phenobarbital may cause respiratory depression, apnea, or hypotension. If F.H. continues to have seizure activity after a total phenobarbital loading dose of 20 mg/kg, additional 5 to 10 mg/kg loading doses may be given every 15 to 20 minutes as needed up to a total loading dose of 30 mg/kg before the administration of phenytoin. Ventilatory support may be required when using these higher doses and serum phenobarbital concentrations should be monitored. Phenobarbital's therapeutic effect of controlling neonatal seizures plateaus at serum concentrations of 40 μg/mL, with an increase in adverse effects at higher serum concentrations.[182]

If seizure activity is not controlled in F.H. (despite optimal phenobarbital loading doses), a phenytoin loading dose of 70 mg (20 mg/kg) should be administered IV at a rate $\leq$1 mg/kg/minute.[176] Rapid IV administration of phenytoin may cause cardiac arrhyth-

Table 96.8   Pharmacotherapy of Neonatal Seizures[a,b]

Drug	Loading Dose	Maintenance Dose	Therapeutic Concentration
Phenobarbital	*IV:* Initial: 20 mg/kg then 5–10 mg/kg Q 15–20 min if needed until total load of 30–40 mg/kg	*IV PO:* Initial: Premature: 3 mg/kg/day Full-term: 4 mg/kg/day May need to ↑ to 4–5 mg/kg/day by 2–4 weeks of therapy	20–40 μg/mL
Phenytoin	*IV:* 20 mg/kg	*IV:* Initial: 3–4 mg/kg/day May need to ↑ to ≥10 mg/kg/day by 2–4 weeks of therapy	8–15 μg/mL
Lorazepam	*IV:* 0.05–0.1 mg/kg	May repeat doses if needed Q 10–15 min	—
Diazepam	*IV:* 0.1–0.3 mg/kg	May repeat doses if needed Q 10–15 min	—
Pyridoxine	*IV:* 50–100 mg	*IV PO:* 20–50 mg/day; ↑ dose PRN with age	—
Paraldehyde	*Rectal:* 0.3 mL/kg; dilute 2:1 with mineral oil	May repeat dose if needed	—
Valproic acid	*PO:* 20 mg/kg	*PO:* 10 mg/kg/dose Q 12 hr	40–50 μg/mL

[a] See text for comments on appropriate IV administration and monitoring.
[b] IV = Intravenous; PO = Oral.

mias, bradycardia, or hypotension. Phenytoin also may cause severe damage to tissues if extravasation occurs. Therefore, blood pressure, heart rate, ECG, and the IV site of infusion should be monitored.

Lorazepam or diazepam may be used to treat F.H.'s seizures if they are unresponsive to phenobarbital and phenytoin.[183,184] Although lorazepam offers the advantage of a longer duration of effect than diazepam, the use of either agent (especially in combination with phenobarbital) may cause respiratory and CNS depression. Respiratory rate, blood pressure, and heart rate should be monitored. Both IV preparations contain propylene glycol and benzyl alcohol. Although these substances have been reported to cause toxicities in newborns, the actual amount administered when using appropriate benzodiazepine doses is minimal and should not pose a significant risk.[183] Doses of lorazepam should be diluted with an equal volume of D_5W, normal saline, or sterile water for injection before IV use and administered slowly over two to five minutes. The relatively high concentration of diazepam injection (which results in <0.1 mL doses) and its physical incompatibility with most diluents, make it impractical to use in small neonates. As a result, lorazepam has become the preferred benzodiazepine in many neonatal ICUs.

If F.H. continues to have seizure activity, IV pyridoxine, rectal paraldehyde, or oral valproic acid should be considered.[174,176,185] Pyridoxine is a cofactor required for the synthesis of the inhibitory neurotransmitter gamma-amino-butyric acid (GABA). Patients with pyridoxine dependency require higher amounts of pyridoxine for proper GABA synthesis. Pyridoxine dependency is a rare disorder but should be considered in neonates with seizure activity unresponsive to antiepileptic drug therapy. Supplementation of pyridoxine is required for life in these patients.

AED Maintenance Doses

43. F.H.'s seizure activity stopped after receiving a total loading dose of 105 mg of phenobarbital and 70 mg of phenytoin. A serum phenobarbital concentration of 35 μg/mL and a phenytoin concentration of 17 μg/mL were measured 1 hour after the phenytoin loading dose (2 hours after the last phenobarbital loading dose). How should maintenance doses of AEDs be instituted in F.H.?

F.H. should be placed on maintenance doses of both phenobarbital and phenytoin, since both drugs were needed to control her seizure activity. Since the half-life of phenobarbital is prolonged in neonates (≈100 to 150 hours), maintenance doses can be instituted 24 hours after the loading dose at 3 to 4 mg/kg/day[181,186,187]

as a single daily dose (see Table 96.8). Although this newborn is full-term, she should receive a lower dose of phenobarbital (2.5 to 3 mg/kg/day) due to her history of asphyxia. Asphyxiated neonates have a decrease in phenobarbital clearance and, therefore, require lower maintenance doses than nonasphyxiated neonates to achieve similar phenobarbital serum concentrations.[38] Maintenance doses of phenytoin (3 to 4 mg/kg/day given in divided doses Q 12 hr) may be initiated 12 to 24 hours after the loading dose. Serum concentrations of these agents should be monitored periodically, as maintenance dose requirements will increase with time (usually by the second to fourth week of therapy).[181,187] This may be due to a normal maturation of hepatic enzyme systems with age or induction of P450 enzymes. In neonates, oral phenytoin is poorly absorbed and should be avoided in the acute setting. A routine 25% increase in the dose is needed when converting intravenous phenytoin to oral to attain similar serum concentrations. In addition, after two to four weeks of age, dosing intervals of every eight hours may be needed.

Neonatal Abstinence Syndrome

A disturbing incidence of maternal substance abuse and associated obstetric and neonatal complications exists.[188,189] Drugs such as alcohol, opiates, barbiturates, and benzodiazepines, readily cross the placenta and may induce fetal dependency. In addition to neonatal abstinence syndrome, other problems seen in infants of addicted mothers must be recognized in order to optimize patient care. *In utero* exposure to drugs of abuse may have serious short- and long-term consequences on fetal growth, physiologic functions, and neurologic development. The use of cocaine during pregnancy may cause complications such as fetal distress, preterm labor, spontaneous abortion, or congenital malformations.[188] Intrauterine growth retardation and sudden infant death syndrome have been associated with heroin, methadone, and cocaine abuse during pregnancy. Neonatal systolic hypertension, abnormal thyroid function, hyperbilirubinemia, and thrombocytosis have been reported with maternal methadone use.[188] The increase of polydrug abuse during pregnancy also may complicate treatment. Investigations assessing long-term neurologic outcome and behavioral development of drug-exposed infants are needed to evaluate current recommended therapies.[190]

Clinical Presentation

44. A.K., a 38-week gestation, 2000 gm, small for gestational age female, was born to a gravida₃ para₂ mother with a history

of frequent heroin use during pregnancy. A.K.'s mother was enrolled in a methadone maintenance program 1 month ago and her last dose of methadone was 12 hours before delivery. Upon further questioning, A.K.'s mother admits to the continued use of heroin and occasional use of "crack" cocaine. Her last "fix" was 3 hours before delivery. On the 1st day of life, A.K. became restless, irritable, and tachypneic and displayed spontaneous tremors and a high-pitch cry. A.K. developed vomiting and diarrhea on day 2 of life after starting feedings with a standard formula. Although A.K. frequently would suckle on her fist, she was not able to suckle properly while feeding. A.K.'s drug screen was positive for cocaine, opiates, and methadone. What clinical symptoms of neonatal drug abstinence does A.K. demonstrate? How do the onset, severity, and duration of neonatal abstinence syndrome vary with various commonly abused substances?

Symptoms of drug withdrawal occur in 55% to 95% of infants born to narcotic-dependent mothers.[190] Neonatal abstinence syndrome is a generalized disorder characterized by central nervous system hyperirritability (e.g., hyperactivity, irritability, high-pitched or prolonged cry, hyperreflexia, fist sucking, abnormal sleep pattern, tremor, and rarely, seizures); respiratory difficulties (e.g., stuffy nose, rhinorrhea, respiratory distress, tachypnea, respiratory alkalosis, and apnea); gastrointestinal dysfunction (e.g., regurgitation, vomiting, diarrhea, uncoordinated suck and swallow reflex, and poor feeding); and vague autonomic symptoms (e.g., sneezing, yawning, sweating, lacrimation, hyper- or hypothermia, and skin mottling).[188–190]

The onset, severity, and duration of neonatal abstinence syndrome may be influenced by many factors including the specific drug(s) abused, time and amount of the mother's last dose before delivery, elimination of the drug by the infant, and the gestational age of the infant at birth.[189–191] Preterm infants display a less severe abstinence syndrome compared to term infants, possibly due to their CNS immaturity or a decreased total in utero drug exposure.[191] Neonatal methadone withdrawal may be more severe than heroin withdrawal,[192] while withdrawal from nonnarcotic drugs usually is less severe.[190] Typically, the cocaine-exposed newborn is hypertonic when alert, irritable, and tremulous. Infants may display decreased interactive behavior, disorganized sleeping and feeding patterns, and may be intermittently lethargic. The CNS irritability and tremulousness may be signs of cocaine toxicity rather than withdrawal per se.[189,193,194]

The onset of narcotic drug withdrawal ranges from minutes after delivery to two weeks of age, with the majority of symptoms appearing within 72 hours. Withdrawal from methadone, however, may be delayed with symptoms presenting as late as two to four weeks of age.[195] Similarly, symptoms of barbiturate withdrawal usually appear at 10 to 14 days. The long elimination half-life of these abused substances contributes to the delayed onset of drug withdrawal (and possibly a greater duration of symptoms). Major symptoms of opiate withdrawal usually continue for two to three weeks, but some may persist for two to six months.[189,190] In mild cases, significant symptoms may subside within a week. Maternal polydrug abuse, as seen in A.K., may result in biphasic patterns or recurrence of abstinence syndrome.[190]

A.K.'s presentation is consistent with neonatal narcotic abstinence syndrome. However, clinical manifestations of neonatal abstinence syndrome are similar to other serious neonatal diseases. Disorders such as infection (sepsis, meningitis), metabolic abnormalities (hypoglycemia, hypocalcemia), endocrine dysfunction (adrenal insufficiency, hyperthyroidism), and CNS abnormalities (hemorrhage and anoxia) must be ruled out before specific neonatal abstinence therapy is begun. Failure to recognize and treat the above diseases would have dire consequences for A.K. A.K. also

may be at risk for hepatitis and sexually transmitted diseases. Therefore, an accurate maternal history or testing also should be performed.

Treatment

45. What initial therapy is recommended for A.K.'s narcotic withdrawal symptoms?

Supportive Care

Since pharmacologic therapy may prolong A.K.'s hospital stay or expose her to unnecessary adverse effects, initial treatment should include nonpharmacologic measures directed at decreasing sensory stimulation. Provision of a quiet, dark, warm environment, gentle handling, and swaddling can be beneficial. Use of a pacifier for nonnutritive, excessive sucking also may help. Hypercaloric formulas (24 cal/oz) should be given as frequent small feedings to supply the additional calories that these infants require (150 to 250 cal/kg/day). Changes in severity of symptoms, vital signs, sleeping and feeding patterns, and weight loss or gain should be monitored. Successful management of 40% to 50% of symptomatic infants can be accomplished with supportive care alone.[189] In addition, the majority of infants who are exposed to cocaine as the primary drug of abuse, can be managed successfully without pharmacologic intervention.[189]

Monitoring and Indications for Pharmacological Treatment

An abstinence scoring system should be used to more objectively assess symptoms of withdrawal and the need for pharmacologic treatment or dosage adjustment. The abstinence scoring sheet lists common signs and symptoms of neonatal opiate withdrawal. The infant is monitored and a number score that indicates severity is assigned to each observed symptom. A "total score" is calculated for each four- or eight-hour observation period and is used to initiate, increase, decrease, or discontinue pharmacologic therapy.[189] Standardized scoring systems currently are used for all neonates regardless of gestational age; however, one study suggests the need for development of specific scoring systems for preterm newborns.[191] In general, indications for pharmacologic treatment include seizures, excessive weight loss or dehydration due to diarrhea or vomiting, severe hyperactivity or tachypnea that interferes with feeding, inability to sleep, and significant hypo- or hyperthermia.[188–190]

A.K. should be monitored closely and if her symptoms are not controlled with supportive care, pharmacologic therapy would be indicated. The most common agents used to treat neonatal narcotic or CNS depressant withdrawal are phenobarbital, paregoric (camphorated tincture of opium), diluted tincture of opium, and diazepam. The choice of agent depends upon the specific nursery, the predominant symptoms displayed, and the substance of abuse. For example, diazepam would be the preferred agent in neonatal withdrawal from maternal benzodiazepine abuse. Doses of these agents should be initiated at lower amounts and titrated upward to a dose that controls withdrawal symptoms but does not produce toxicity. Once A.K. is symptom-free for three to five days, the dose should be decreased gradually by 10% to 20% per day with close patient monitoring. The goals of pharmacologic therapy are to control the symptoms of withdrawal and wean the patient completely off therapy.

46. A.K.'s laboratory tests were within normal limits and other diseases have been ruled out. Her symptoms have worsened despite supportive care and pharmacologic therapy for neonatal abstinence syndrome is initiated. Phenobarbital was started on day 3 of life with an IV dose of 10 mg given Q 12 hr for 4 doses, followed with 3 mg Q 8 hr. This morning's phenobarbital serum concentration was 27 µg/mL. A.K. is less

irritable today (day 6 of life) and no longer is tachypneic. Her tremors have decreased significantly and she no longer has a high-pitched cry. She continues to have significant diarrhea and is feeding poorly. A.K. has not gained weight in the past 4 days. Evaluate A.K.'s therapy. What are your recommendations?

Phenobarbital

Phenobarbital is the drug of choice for neonatal abstinence syndrome due to barbiturate, alcohol, and polydrug abuse[189,190] and is the second-line agent for treatment of seizures due to withdrawal. Phenobarbital is effective in approximately 50% of infants and is especially useful (as demonstrated in A.K.) for controlling symptoms of CNS hyperirritability.[189] GI symptoms of withdrawal, however, do not respond well to phenobarbital. A.K. received the proper phenobarbital total loading dose (20 mg/kg) and maintenance therapy (4.5 mg/kg/day). Recommended loading doses range from 15 to 20 mg/kg and usually are divided over 24 to 48 hours. A single intravenous or oral loading dose may be given when rapid control of symptoms is desired. However, single loading doses may be associated with CNS and respiratory depression (e.g., sedation, apnea, or an increase in periodic breathing). Maintenance doses range from 2 to 6 mg/kg/day.[189] Doses should be adjusted according to symptoms and serum concentrations should be monitored to avoid toxicity. High doses of phenobarbital may result in oversedation and impairment of the suck reflex. The therapeutic serum concentration for control of withdrawal symptoms has not been clearly identified; however, 20 to 30 μg/mL has been suggested.[196] Although A.K.'s serum phenobarbital concentration is within the normal range, she continues to have diarrhea and has not gained weight. Since gastrointestinal symptoms do not respond well to phenobarbital, an alternative agent (preferably a narcotic) should be selected.

Narcotic Agents

Because paregoric (0.4 mg/mL anhydrous morphine), tincture of opium (10 mg/mL morphine), morphine, and methadone are narcotics, they may have a physiologic advantage over nonnarcotics in the treatment of neonatal opiate withdrawal syndrome.[190] In addition, the constipating side effects of narcotics may be advantageous when diarrhea is part of withdrawal symptoms. Although any narcotic theoretically could be used, most studies assessing opioid treatment have used paregoric. Paregoric is easy to administer and controls withdrawal symptoms in 90% of infants. In comparative studies, paregoric improved sucking coordination, nutrient ingestion, and weight gain better than diazepam or phenobarbital. Infants treated with paregoric also may have a lower incidence of seizure episodes than those treated with phenobarbital or diazepam. Unfortunately, large doses of paregoric often are needed and the duration of treatment usually is longer than with other agents.[189] In addition to opium alkaloids, paregoric contains unwarranted compounds such as camphor (a CNS stimulant that is eliminated slowly), high concentrations of alcohol (44% to 46%), anise oil, benzyl alcohol, and glycerine. Since some of these substances may have adverse effects on the newborn, a 25-fold dilution of tincture of opium with water (final concentration 0.4 mg/mL morphine) now is preferred. The dilution of tincture of opium is free of unnecessary ingredients and has a lower alcohol concentration.[197] For full-term infants, the dose of paregoric (or a 25-fold dilution of tincture of opium) is 0.2 mL to 0.5 mL/dose (0.08 to 0.2 mg morphine) given orally every three to four hours until control of withdrawal symptoms.[197] A.K.'s dose may be initiated at 0.2 mL/dose and titrated upwards as needed by 0.05 to 0.1 mL/dose every three hours.[5,190] A.K. also should be monitored for signs of overtreatment such as hypotonia, lethargy, irregular respirations, and bradycardia.[189]

The use of oral morphine to control neonatal withdrawal symptoms has not been well studied; however, oral preparations of 2 and 4 mg/mL may be used.[197] Parenteral morphine has been used in infants to treat narcotic withdrawal seizures unresponsive to antiepileptic agents[198] and vasomotor collapse secondary to heroin withdrawal.[199] Parenteral morphine may be used if A.K. is unable to take oral medications and a narcotic agent is desired. Methadone (in doses of 0.5 mg/kg/day given Q 8 hr) also may be used, but the prolonged elimination half-life (26 hours) makes tapering the dosage difficult.

Diazepam and Chlorpromazine

Diazepam (0.3 to 0.5 mg/kg given Q 8 hr) can be used to control the CNS hyperactivity associated with neonatal narcotic withdrawal symptoms.[188] Adverse effects, however, which may be related to prolonged elimination and accumulation of diazepam and metabolites, can limit the drug's usefulness (e.g., depression of the suck reflex, late onset seizures, and bradycardia).[190] In addition, the parenteral formulation contains substances known to cause problems in the newborn.[190,197] (See Question 42.) Chlorpromazine (0.5 to 0.7 mg/kg given Q 6 hr) controls the CNS and GI symptoms of neonatal withdrawal. Disadvantages of chlorpromazine include a wide spectrum of pharmacologic effects, possible prolonged elimination in the neonate, rare reports of hypothermia and eosinophilia, and lack of long-term studies on behavioral outcomes.[190] As a result, chlorpromazine rarely is used to treat neonatal abstinence syndrome.

A.K. should receive long-term follow-up to monitor for potential developmental problems. Since A.K. is at risk for recurrence of drug withdrawal, her parents should receive information on recognition of symptoms. Her parents will need instructions of how to care for this drug-exposed infant as well as counseling for drug addiction.

Sedation and Paralysis During Ventilation
Pharmacology and Monitoring Parameters

47. M.M., a 42 week-gestation (postterm), 3500 gm male, presents with meconium-stained amniotic fluid. At birth, meconium was removed by suction from M.M.'s nose and mouth. M.M. was tachypneic (RR 80 breaths/min), cyanotic, and had decreased peripheral perfusion. His Apgar score at 1 min was 5. M.M. was intubated shortly after delivery and his trachea suctioned to remove meconium. Immediate ABGs, obtained while M.M. was intubated and ventilated with an Ambu bag at 60 breaths/min and 100% oxygen, revealed: pH 7.18, pCO$_2$ 55 mm Hg, and pO$_2$ 50 mm Hg. M.M.'s clinical condition and ABG results (acidosis, increased pCO$_2$, and hypoxia) were consistent with persistent pulmonary hypertension of the newborn and appropriate tests confirmed the diagnosis. He currently is receiving mechanical ventilation using hyperoxia and hyperventilation to achieve a target pCO$_2$ of 30 mm Hg and pH of 7.5. M.M. had been "fighting the ventilator" and pancuronium bromide 0.35 mg given IV Q 2–4 hr as needed for spontaneous movement was initiated. M.M.'s other medications are: ampicillin and gentamicin to rule out sepsis, and tolazoline, dopamine, and sodium bicarbonate for his persistent pulmonary hypertension of the newborn. After evaluating M.M's paralysis therapy what medications should be started immediately for him? [SI units: pCO$_2$ 7.33 kPa, 4.0 kPa; pO$_2$ 6.7 kPa]

Neonates with severe lung disease (e.g., RDS, persistent pulmonary hypertension of the newborn, pneumonia) may require mechanical ventilation with high ventilatory settings (high rates or pressures). Ineffective mechanical ventilation results when neonates "fight the ventilator" (i.e., spontaneously breathe asynchronously or out of phase with mechanical ventilation). Sedation generally is indicated when high ventilator settings are used or when patients "fight the ventilator." Paralysis usually is reserved for cases when sedation alone does not improve the effectiveness of mechanical ventilation. Typically, paralysis is required in severely ill, hypoxic neonates such as M.M. Paralysis increases chest wall compliance and allows for adequate oxygenation and ventilation.[200,201] It also decreases oxygen consumption, improves blood gases, and may decrease the risk for pneumothorax.[200,202] In addition, paralysis of neonates with persistent pulmonary hypertension of the newborn (like M.M.) indirectly decreases right-to-left shunting through the ductus arteriosus and foramen ovale and results in increased oxygenation.[203]

Pancuronium bromide causes skeletal muscle paralysis by competitively blocking acetylcholine at postsynaptic nicotinic cholinergic receptors located on the muscle fiber (motor endplate) of the neuromuscular junction.[202,204] At normal clinical doses, pancuronium has minimal ganglionic blocking effects and possesses little histamine releasing activity.[202,204] Onset of effect occurs within minutes and duration, which typically lasts 30 to 60 minutes following a single dose, increases with incremental dosing. M.M.'s dose of pancuronium is appropriate. Although lower neonatal doses (0.03 to 0.09 mg/kg) have been recommended,[205] doses of 0.1 mg/kg every two to four hours given intravenously as needed for spontaneous movement generally are required.

The greatest danger of using any neuromuscular blocking agent is inadvertent disconnection from the ventilator with resultant apnea. When paralytic agents are initiated, adjustments in ventilator settings usually are required to avoid hypoventilation. Clinically important adverse effects include tachycardia and fluid retention with significant edema.[202,206] Although pancuronium usually does not have a significant effect on blood pressure,[206] hypertension[207] and occasional reports of hypotension[208] (usually in marginally hypovolemic neonates) have been reported. Ventilatory settings, blood gases, spontaneous movements, daily weights, fluid intake and output, heart rate, and blood pressure should be monitored. If tachycardia becomes serious, another nondepolarizing neuromuscular blocking agent with fewer cardiovascular effects, such as vecuronium, can be used.

Paralysis, as well as intubation and mechanical ventilation, may be extremely stressful to the neonate. Neuromuscular blocking agents, however, do *not* possess any analgesic, sedative, or amnestic effects.[202,204] Therefore, sedation therapy should be instituted as soon as possible in M.M. Neonates and even premature newborns have the anatomical structures and physiological capacity to sense pain.[209–211] Since clinical symptoms of pain may go undetected in paralyzed neonates, a sedative/analgesic such as morphine may be preferred for sedation. In addition, administration of analgesics for painful procedures may be easily forgotten when neonates are sedated with nonanalgesics such as phenobarbital, benzodiazepines, or chloral hydrate. Since paralysis will mask the clinical symptoms of seizures,[202] M.M. should be monitored carefully for rhythmic fluctuations in heart rate, blood pressure, ECG, and oxygenation. These rhythmic changes may indicate seizure activity in a paralyzed neonate and if observed, electroencephalogram testing is indicated.[212] The EEG also may be monitored in paralyzed newborns who are at high risk for seizure activity (e.g., asphyxiated neonates). Alternatively, some clinicians advocate routine sedation with phenobarbital (rather than morphine) which also would treat any clinically unapparent seizure activity.

Morphine usually is administered by slow IV push over one to two minutes at initial doses of 0.05 to 0.1 mg/kg every two to four hours.[213] Adverse effects include hypotension, decreased GI mo-

tility, respiratory depression, tolerance, and physiologic dependence with prolonged use. The use of morphine in neonates may be limited by histamine release and the development of hypotension. Fentanyl, a synthetic opiate with less histamine-releasing activity and fewer cardiovascular effects, may be used as an alternative agent. Fentanyl has a shorter duration of action and, therefore, usually is administered by continuous IV infusion (0.5 to 2 μg/kg/hour).[214] Continuous infusion of fentanyl, however, may be associated with a greater development of tolerance and physical dependence compared with intermittent morphine administration.[215,216] Continuous fentanyl infusions of five and nine or more days have been associated with a greater than 50% and a 100% chance, respectively, of developing withdrawal symptoms,[217] and withdrawal has been reported after as few as three days.[218]

At this time, recommendations for M.M. should include the addition of morphine as a sedative agent (0.2 mg IV Q 4 hr) and an ocular lubricant to prevent corneal abrasions. Neuromuscular blocking agents prevent blinking and corneal abrasions may occur. Since tolerance to opiates develops, the morphine dose will need to be increased with continued use. Determination of adequate sedation is difficult in paralyzed infants but increases in heart rate and blood pressure or decreases in oxygenation may indicate inadequate sedation.

Drug/Disease Interactions

48. Morphine (0.2 mg IV Q 4 hr) and an ocular lubricant (as an ophthalmic ointment applied to both eyes Q 6 hr PRN) were added to M.M.'s therapy. On day 2 of life, M.M. continues on mechanical ventilation with hyperoxia and hyperventilation. His ABG is pH 7.5, pCO_2 30 mm Hg, and pO_2 55 mm Hg. Mylanta 3.5 mL given NG Q 3 hr was added for gastric ulcer prophylaxis due to tolazoline therapy. M.M. continues to receive IV ampicillin, gentamicin, tolazoline, dopamine, sodium bicarbonate, and pancuronium. What factors may influence the neuromuscular blocking effect of pancuronium in M.M.? What adjustments to his dosing schedule should be made? [SI units: pCO_2 4.0 kPa; pO_2 7.33 kPa]

Both alkalosis and gentamicin may potentiate the neuromuscular blocking effects of pancuronium in M.M.[202] Although alkalosis may potentiate and acidosis may antagonize the effects of pancuronium, the opposite effects have been reported with vecuronium.[202] Pancuronium already is being dosed in M.M. on an "as needed" basis. Monitoring for spontaneous movement should continue and a longer required dosing interval may be noted. If gentamicin then is discontinued or pH is normalized, the duration of effect may shorten. Other factors such as electrolyte status, disease states, and other medications may influence the pharmacodynamics of neuromuscular blocking agents.[202] For instance, renal or hepatic impairment (such as cholestasis) may result in accumulation of drug or active metabolite (3-hydroxypancuronium) and a prolonged effect.

Toxicity

49. Sodium bicarbonate, tolazoline, and dopamine were discontinued on day 3 of life. On day 4 of life, Mylanta was stopped and M.M.'s antibiotics were discontinued after culture results ruled out infection. On Friday (day 5 of life), pancuronium was discontinued and M.M. remained intubated. Concerns about morphine "addiction" resulted in the discontinuation of morphine and the initiation of chloral hydrate 250 mg NG Q 4 hr for sedation. On Monday morning, M.M. was noted to have severe lethargy, decreased deep tendon reflexes, and respiratory depression requiring an increase in ventilator settings. Bowel sounds were absent and M.M. had marked ab-

dominal distension. **Is M.M. experiencing prolonged paralysis from pancuronium? What is your assessment of this situation?**

Administration of opiates for sedation or analgesia does not cause "addiction."[219] The term "addiction" should only be used to describe complex behavioral patterns characterized by a preoccupation with obtainment of a drug (drug-seeking behavior) and compulsive drug use. Prolonged administration of opiates may cause tolerance (i.e., a decreased effect after repeated administration of the original dosage or an increasing dosage requirement to attain the original effect) or physical dependence. Physical dependence requires the continued administration of a medication in order to prevent symptoms of withdrawal. Although symptoms of withdrawal may occur when opiates are discontinued, careful weaning of the opiate and appropriate monitoring of symptoms using an abstinence scoring method will lessen withdrawal severity. Opioids may be weaned in less than 72 hours when low to moderate doses have been used for less than one week. Typically, the dose is decreased by 25% to 50% initially (and by 20% subsequently) every six to eight hours. If opioids are used for greater than one week, smaller decreases in doses, a longer total weaning time, and conversion to an oral agent usually are required.[219] In M.M.'s case, IV morphine could have been continued for sedation or an appropriate oral agent could have been used if normal bowel function was apparent.

Disuse atrophy, muscle weakness, joint contractures, and prolonged paralysis have been reported after discontinuing neuromuscular blocking agents.[202] Prolonged neuromuscular blockade may be more common in patients with renal or hepatic dysfunction or with the use of continuous infusion, prolonged therapy, or certain concomitant medications. In particular, prolonged paralysis may be seen after discontinuation of steroidally-based neuromuscular blocking agents (e.g., pancuronium, vecuronium) when these agents have been administered with corticosteroids.[220] In this case, M.M. did not have any apparent renal or hepatic disease, was treated with intermittent "as needed" doses, received short-term paralysis, and did not receive corticosteroids. Therefore, M.M. would be at a low risk for developing prolonged paralysis after discontinuation of pancuronium.

The most likely cause of M.M.'s current symptoms is chloral hydrate intoxication. The recommended initial dose of chloral hydrate for prolonged sedation in neonates is 10 to 30 mg/kg/dose given every six to eight hours on an "as needed" basis.[221] Although some clinicians recommend 20 to 40 mg/kg/dose every four to six hours as needed (80 to 240 mg/kg/day),[213] toxicity has been reported in a term infant with persistent pulmonary hypertension of the newborn receiving doses of 44 to 50 mg/kg every six hours (176 to 200 mg/kg/day).[221] M.M. received approximately 70 mg/kg/dose every four hours around the clock for three days.

Chloral hydrate is metabolized quickly in erythrocytes and the liver by alcohol dehydrogenase to trichloroethanol, an active metabolite. Trichloroethanol is metabolized to trichloroacetate and to trichloroethanol glucuronide in the liver and renally eliminated. The conversion of chloral hydrate to trichloroethanol may not be as rapid in neonates[222] and both chloral hydrate and trichloroethanol may be responsible for the sedative effects seen in neonates.[223] The parent drug (chloral hydrate) may be responsible for the immediate short-term sedative effects while trichloroethanol may be responsible for long-term effects. The short duration of sedation (2 hours) necessitates frequent repeated dosing that unfortunately results in accumulation of the active metabolite, trichloroethanol, and toxic effects. The half-life of trichloroethanol is prolonged in preterm (40 hours) and term neonates (28 hours).[222] Because trichloroethanol may accumulate, chloral hydrate should

only be used on an as needed basis for long-term sedation in neonates. The lower end of the recommended dosage range should be used for preterm newborns and all neonates, especially those who require frequent repeated doses, should be monitored for toxic effects.

Toxicities of chloral hydrate include central nervous system, respiratory and myocardial depression, gastric irritation, adynamic ileus, cardiac arrhythmias, hypotension, renal impairment, bladder atony, and direct hyperbilirubinemia.[221] Although M.M. is showing signs of CNS depression (lethargy, decreased deep tendon reflexes), respiratory depression (increased ventilator settings), and GI effects (absent bowel sounds, abdominal distension), a physical examination and appropriate laboratory tests should be performed to identify other known toxicities (e.g., serum BUN and SrCr to detect renal impairment). In addition, other etiologies for M.M.'s current condition also should be ruled out (e.g., sepsis, meningitis, intracranial hemorrhage, metabolic disorder). Chloral hydrate should be discontinued and trichloroethanol serum concentrations determined if available. Supportive care should be given and severe toxicities may require exchange transfusions.[221]

Use and Administration of Medications

Drug Formulation Problems

50. What problems are encountered with the use of commercially available medications in the neonate?

The lack of appropriate enteral and parenteral formulations results in many unique problems of drug use and administration in the neonatal population.

Lack of Nonsolid Enteral Dosage Formulations

Many drugs used in neonates and infants are not commercially available in an enteral liquid dosage form including acetazolamide, caffeine, captopril, clonazepam, isoniazid, rifampin, and spironolactone. For some medications, the liquid injectable form can be given enterally. Otherwise, extemporaneous powder formulations or liquid preparations must be made from the solid dosage forms.[5,224]

Little information exists regarding the preparation and stability of extemporaneous formulations.[224] Formulations intended for neonates should limit the use of pharmaceutical adjuvants, unnecessary ingredients (e.g., flavoring agents for drugs administered via nasogastric tubes), and other substances that would increase osmolality.

Inappropriate Concentrations

Most drugs are formulated for use in the adult population. As a result, the available concentrations of liquid formulations will result in appropriate volumes for adult doses, but extremely small volumes for the doses required by neonates. Frequently, these volumes are too small to accurately measure (i.e., <0.1 mL). Therefore, dilutions of commercially available injections (e.g., aminophylline, digoxin, morphine, phenobarbital) are necessary to accurately measure the small doses required by neonates. Proper diluents and dilutional techniques must be assured, as inappropriate dilutions are a common source of potentially fatal medication errors.[213,225] (See Table 96.9.)

Hypertonicity

In the neonate, parenteral and enteral administration of hypertonic medications may result in severe adverse effects.[226,227] Necrotizing enterocolitis and intraventricular hemorrhage have been associated with IV administration of hyperosmolar drugs, such as radiographic contrast media or sodium bicarbonate. Infusions of

Table 96.9	Potential Errors in Drug Administration Techniques[a,b]

Factors Involving Drug (Dose) Preparation

Inappropriate dilutions

Similarity in appearance of dose units

Loss of potentially large amounts of drug dose in the dead space of a syringe or infusion Y site

Unsuitable drug formulations for administration

Unlabeled or undesirable ingredients in dosage forms

Undesirable drug concentrations and/or osmolalities

Errors in interpreting drug orders and/or dose calculations

Factors Involving IV Drug Administration

Loss of drug consequent to routine changing of IV sets

Reduction in serum concentrations for drugs with rapid plasma clearance that are infused slowly

Extreme ↑ in plasma concentrations consequent to rapid infusion of drugs with small central compartment Vd

Delayed infusion of total dose when IV line is not flushed

Inadvertent admixture of drugs by the manual IV retrograde method

Large distance between the site of drug infusion into an IV line and the insertion of the line into the patient

Potential loss of large volume doses in the overflow syringe with the IV retrograde technique

Possible loss of drug because of binding to IV tubing

Use of large intraluminal diameter tubing for small patients

Infiltrations not detected by pump alarms

Infusion of multiple medications/fluids at different rates by means of a common "hub"

Oscillations in fluid/dose rate of potent medications infused with piston-type pumps

Factors Involving Other Routes of Drug Administration

Loss of delivery (NG tube dead space) or from oral cavity

Leakage of drug from IM or SQ injection site

Expulsion of drug from the rectum

Misapplication to external sites (i.e., ophthalmic ointment in young infants)

---

[a] Reproduced with permission from Blumer JL, Reed MD. Principles of neonatal pharmacology. In: Yaffe SJ, Aranda JV, eds. Pediatric Pharmacology: Therapeutic Principles in Practice. 2nd ed. Philadelphia: WB Saunders; 1992;168.

[b] IM = Intramuscular; IV = Intravenous; NG = Nasogastric; SQ = Subcutaneous; Vd = Volume of distribution.

---

hypertonic medications directly into the umbilical or portal vein have resulted in severe hepatic injury. In addition, enteral administration of hyperosmolar medications and feedings have been associated with necrotizing enterocolitis.[226,227] Therefore, appropriate dilutions of hypertonic medications should be made before administration to neonates.

Pharmaceutical Adjuvants

Ingredients used for the enhancement of bioavailability, stability, taste, or appearance of medications can cause adverse effects in neonates.[228] Preservatives such as benzyl alcohol or methylparaben may displace bilirubin from albumin binding sites.[22] Benzyl alcohol also may cause the potentially fatal "gasping syndrome." (Also see Neonatal Pharmacokinetics: Metabolism.) Propylene glycol, a solubilizing agent, may cause several toxicities in neonates including hyperosmolality, lactic acidosis, hypotension, and dysrhythmias.[228,229] Emulsifiers, such as Polysorbate 20 and Polysorbate 80, have been associated with hypotension, renal dysfunction, and hepatotoxicity.[230] Unfortunately, these undesired substances may not even be listed in the package insert of oral medications.[231] The safety of pharmaceutical adjuvants should be

examined thoroughly before these substances are used in the neonatal population. In addition, further studies are required to identify other pharmaceutical ingredients that may be potentially toxic to the neonate.

Drug Administration

51. D.S., a 4-day-old female neonate born at 30 weeks gestational age with a current weight of 1200 gm, has a birth history of prolonged rupture of membranes and a difficult delivery. Her current problems include rule out sepsis and apnea of prematurity. D.S. receives the following: ampicillin 60 mg IV Buretrol Q 12 hr at 2 a.m. and 2 p.m. (100 mg/kg/day); gentamicin 3.6 mg IV Buretrol Q 24 hr at 7 a.m. (3 mg/kg/day); aminophylline 1.2 mg IV Buretrol Q 12 hr at 10 a.m. and 10 p.m. (2 mg/kg/day); and dextrose 5%/NaCl 0.2% with KCl 1.8 mEq/day and calcium gluconate 250 mg/day at 6 mL/hr. Gentamicin serum concentrations were obtained today (day 4 of antibiotic therapy) and reported as a trough of 1.2 µg/mL at 6:50 a.m. and a peak of 2.8 µg/mL at 8 a.m. Using standard pharmacokinetic equations you calculate a Kd of 0.037 hr^{-1}, half-life of 18.7 hours, and Vd of 1.8 L/kg. What should be done next for D.S.?

Serum concentrations of aminoglycosides and other drugs can be affected significantly by the IV drug delivery system.[232,233] The low IV infusion rates required by neonates will significantly delay drug delivery, especially if medications are administered via volumetric chamber devices (e.g., Buretrol or Metriset) or via the Y-site injection port distal to the patient. Even when factors such as injection site, infusion rate, drug volume, and tubing diameter are considered, actual drug delivery may be delayed up to two hours using volumetric chamber devices.[232] If aminoglycosides are administered by Y-site injection, peak concentrations can be decreased by a mean of 2.5 µg/mL and delayed by one and one-half hours compared to IV syringe pump administration.[234] Trough concentrations, however, are not significantly affected. As a result of inappropriate administration methods, a larger volume of distribution and prolonged half-life would be calculated, as demonstrated in D.S.

D.S.'s unbelievably large volume of distribution should lead to suspicion of the method of drug administration. At this time, no dosage change can be recommended for D.S. Serum aminoglycoside concentrations should be repeated after an appropriate IV administration method is instituted. This method should include the use of a neonatal syringe pump, low volume IV tubing, and drug injection into the port most proximal to the neonate.[232,233]

Other potential neonatal IV drug administration errors are listed in Table 96.9. Additional problems include significant overdoses resulting from the unintended delivery of residual drug from the hub or needle of syringes (i.e., dead spaces), and underdoses due to trapping of medications in IV filters.[213,225] In addition, the neonate's limited ability to tolerate excess fluid prohibits drug delivery via IV riders or "piggybacks" which would significantly increase fluid administration. Neonates also require special IV rates of drug infusion (i.e., mg/kg/minute) to avoid significant adverse effects. Appropriate references should be consulted for drug-specific methods and rates of infusion, appropriate final concentrations, and other special neonatal considerations.[5,44]

Dedication

Dr. Fotini Hatzopoulos would like to dedicate her work to the loving memory of her father and friend Konstantin N Hatzopoulos who passed away during the preparation of this chapter.

References

1　**Shirkey H.** Therapeutic orphans. J Pediatr. 1968;72:119. Editorial.

2　**Gilman JT, Gal P.** Pharmacokinetic and pharmacodynamic data collection in children and neonates: a quiet frontier. Clin Pharmacokinet. 1992;23:1.

3　**Fletcher MA.** Physical assessment and classification. In: Avery GB et al., eds. Neonatology: Pathophysiology and Management of the Newborn. 4th ed. Philadelphia: JB Lippincott; 1994:269.

4　**Avery GB et al.,** eds. Neonatology: Pathophysiology and Management of the Newborn. 4th ed. Philadelphia, PA: JB Lippincott; 1994:1389.

5　**Taketomo CK et al.** Pediatric Dosage Handbook. 2nd ed. Hudson, OH: Lexi-Comp; 1993.

6　**Yahav J.** Development of parietal cells, acid secretion, and response to secretagogues. In: Lebenthal E, ed. Human Gastrointestinal Development. New York: Raven Press; 1989:341.

7　**Hyman PE et al.** Gastric acid secretory function in preterm infants. J Pediatr. 1985;106:467.

8　**Morselli PL.** Clinical pharmacology of the perinatal period and early infancy. Clin Pharmacokinet. 1989;17(Suppl. 1):13.

9　**Besunder JB et al.** Principles of drug disposition in the neonate. A critical evaluation of the pharmacokinetic-pharmacodynamic interface. Part I. Clin Pharmacokinet. 1988;14:189.

10　**Radde IC.** Mechanisms of drug absorption and their development. In: Radde IC, MacLeod SM, eds. Pediatric Pharmacology and Therapeutics. St. Louis: Mosby Year Book; 1993:16.

11　**Heimann G.** Enteral absorption and bioavailability in children in relation to age. Eur J Clin Pharmacol. 1980;18:43–50.

12　**Stewart CF, Hampton EW.** Effect of maturation on drug disposition in pediatric patients. Clin Pharm. 1987;6:548.

13　**Seigler RS.** The administration of rectal diazepam for acute management of seizures. J Emerg Med. 1990;8:155.

14　**Wu PYK et al.** Peripheral blood flow in the neonate. 1. Changes in total, skin, and muscle blood flow with gestational and postnatal age. Pediatr Res. 1980;14:1374.

15　**Rutter N.** Percutaneous drug absorption in the newborn: hazards and uses. Perinat Pharmacol. 1987;14:911.

16　**Evans NJ et al.** Percutaneous administration of theophylline in the preterm infant. J Pediatr. 1985;107:307.

17　**Micali GM et al.** Evaluation of transdermal theophylline pharmacokinetics in neonates. Pharmacotherapy. 1993;13:386.

18　**Radde IC.** Growth and drug distribution. In: Radde IC, Macleod SM, eds. Pediatric Pharmacology and Therapeutics. St. Louis: Mosby Year Book; 1993:43.

19　**Friis-Hansen B.** Water distribution in the foetus and newborn infant. Acta Paediatr Scand. 1983;305(Suppl.):7.

20　**Morselli PL et al.** Clinical pharmacokinetics in newborns and infants. Clin Pharmacokinet. 1980;5:485.

21　**Besunder JB et al.** Principles of drug disposition in the neonate. A critical evaluation of the pharmacokinetic-pharmacodynamic interface. Part II. Clin Pharmacokinet. 1988;14:261.

22　**Radde IC.** Drugs and protein binding. In: Radde IC, Macleod SM, eds. Pediatric Pharmacology and Therapeutics. St. Louis: Mosby Year Book; 1993:31.

23　**Aranda JV et al.** Pharmacokinetic aspects of theophylline in premature newborns. N Engl J Med. 1976;295:413.

24　**Rane A et al.** Plasma protein binding of diphenylhydantoin in normal and hyperbilirubinemic infants. J Pediatr. 1971;78:877.

25　**Cashore WJ.** Hyperbilirubinemia. In: Pomerance JJ, Richardson CJ, eds. Neonatology for the Clinician. Norwalk: Appleton & Lange; 1993:231.

26　**Robertson A, Brodersen R.** Effect of drug combinations on bilirubin-albumin binding. Dev Pharmacol Ther. 1991;17:95.

27　**Martin E et al.** Ceftriaxone-bilirubin-albumin interactions in the neonate: an in vivo study. Eur J Pediatr. 1993;152:530.

28　**Stutman HR et al.** Potential of moxalactam and other new antimicrobial agents for bilirubin-albumin displacement in neonates. Pediatrics. 1985;75:294.

29　**Springer C, Eyal F.** Pharmacology of trimethoprim-sulfamethoxazole in newborn infants. J Pediatr. 1982;100:647.

30　**Radde IC, Kalow W.** Drug biotransformation and its development. In: Radde IC, Macleod SM, eds. Pediatric Pharmacology and Therapeutics. St. Louis: Mosby Year Book; 1993:57.

31　**Aranda JV et al.** Hepatic microsomal drug oxidation and electron transport in newborn infants. J Pediatr. 1974;85:534.

32　**Kraus DK et al.** Alterations in theophylline metabolism during the first year of life. Clin Pharmacol Ther. 1993;54:351.

33　**LeBel M.** Benzyl alcohol metabolism and elimination in neonates. Dev Pharmacol Ther. 1988;11:347.

34　**Gershanik J et al.** The gasping syndrome and benzyl alcohol poisoning. N Engl J Med. 1982;307:1384.

35　**Food and Drug Administration.** Benzyl alcohol may be toxic to newborns. FDA Drug Bulletin. 1982;12:10.

36　**Morselli PL et al.** Diazepam elimination in premature and full-term infants and children. J Perinat Med. 1973;1:133.

37　**Sereni F et al.** Induction of drug metabolizing enzyme activities in the human fetus and in the newborn infant. Enzyme. 1973;15:318.

38　**Gal P et al.** The influence of asphyxia on phenobarbital dosing requirements in neonates. Dev Pharmacol Ther. 1984;7:145.

39　**Radde IC.** Renal function and elimination of drugs during development. In: Radde IC, Macleod SM, eds. Pediatric Pharmacology and Therapeutics. St. Louis: Mosby Year Book; 1993:87.

40　**Vanpee M et al.** Renal function in very low birth weight infants: normal maturity reached during early childhood. J Pediatr. 1992;121:784.

41　**Rodvold et al.** Prediction of gentamicin concentrations in neonates and infants using a bayesian pharmacokinetic model. Dev Pharmacol Ther. 1993;20:211–19.

42　**Kildoo C et al.** Developmental pattern of gentamicin kinetics in very low weight (VLBW) sick infants. Dev Pharmacol Ther. 1984;7:345.

43　**Kasik JW et al.** Postconceptional age and gentamicin elimination half-life. J Pediatr. 1985;106:502.

44　**Young TE, Mangum OB.** Neofax '94: A Manual of Drugs Used in Neonatal Care. 7th ed. Columbus, OH: Ross Products Division, Abbott Laboratories; 1994:26.

45　**Prober CG et al.** The use of antibiotics in neonates weighing less than 1200 grams. Pediatr Infect Dis J. 1990;9:111.

46　**Friedman CA et al.** Gentamicin disposition in asphyxiated newborns: relationship to mean arterial pressure and urine output. Pediatr Pharmacol. 1982;2:189.

47　**Zarfin Y et al.** Possible indomethacin-aminoglycoside interaction in preterm infants. J Pediatr. 1985;106:511.

48　**Koren G et al.** Effects of indomethacin on digoxin pharmacokinetics in preterm infants. Pediatr Pharmacol. 1984;4:25.

49　**Hook JB, Hewitt WR.** Development of mechanisms for drug excretion. Am J Med. 1977;62:497.

50　**Jobe AH.** Pathophysiology of respiratory distress syndrome. In: Fanaroff AA, Martin RJ, eds. Neonatal-Perinatal Medicine: Diseases of the Fetus and Infant. 5th ed. St. Louis: Mosby Year Book; 1992:995.

51　**Jobe A, Ikegami M.** Surfactant for the treatment of respiratory distress syndrome. Am Rev Respir Dis. 1987;136:1256.

52　**Jobe AH.** Surfactant therapy for respiratory distress syndrome. In: Pomerance JJ, Richardson CJ, eds. Neonatology for the Clinician. Norwalk: Appleton & Lange; 1993:257.

53　**Hagedorn MI et al.** Respiratory diseases. In: Merenstein GB, Gardner SL, eds. Handbook of Neonatal Intensive Care. 3rd ed. St. Louis: Mosby Year Book; 1993:311.

54　**Stark AR, Frantz ID.** Respiratory distress syndrome. Pediatr Clin North Am. 1986;33:533.

55　**Papke KR.** Management of preterm labor and prevention of premature delivery. Nurs Clin North Am. 1993;28:279.

56　**Allbert J, Morrison JC.** Glucocorticoids and fetal pulmonary maturity. In: Rayburn WF, Zuspan FP, eds. Drug Therapy in Obstetrics and Gynecology. St. Louis: Mosby Year Book; 1992:90.

57　**Bishop EH.** Acceleration of fetal pulmonary maturity. Obstet Gynecol. 1981;58:48S.

58　**Kwong MS, Egan EA.** Reduced incidence of hyaline membrane disease in extremely premature infants following delay of delivery in mother with preterm labor: use of ritodrine and betamethasone. Pediatrics. 1986;78:767.

59　**Crowley P et al.** The effects of corticosteroid administration before preterm delivery: an overview of the evidence from controlled trials. Br J Obstet Gynaecol. 1990;97:11.

60　**Hallman M et al.** The fate of exogenous surfactant in neonates with respiratory distress syndrome. Clin Pharmacokinet. 1994;26:215.

61　**Jobe AH.** Pulmonary surfactant therapy. N Engl J Med. 1993;328:861.

62　**Corbet A.** Clinical trials of synthetic surfactant in the respiratory distress syndrome of premature infants. Clin Perinatol. 1993;20:737.

63　**Mercier CE, Soll RF.** Clinical trials of natural surfactant in respiratory distress syndrome. Clin Perinatol. 1993;20:711.

64　**Burroughs Wellcome Co.** Exosurf neonatal for intratracheal suspension. Research Triangle Park, NC: 1990 Aug.

65　**Ross Laboratories.** Survanta intratracheal suspension package insert. Columbus, OH: 1991 June.

66　**Prevost RR.** Comparing surfactant products. Clin Pharm. 1991;10:909.

67　**OSIRIS Collaborative Group.** Early versus delayed neonatal administration of a synthetic surfactant— the judgement of OSIRIS. Lancet. 1992;340:1363.

68　**Vaucher YE.** Outcome at twelve months of adjusted age in very low birth weight infants with lung immaturity: a randomized, placebo-controlled trial of human surfactant. J Pediatr. 1993;122:126.

69　**Sitler CG et al.** Pump administration of exogenous surfactant: effects on oxygenation, heart rate, and chest wall movement of premature infants. J Perinatol. 1993;13:197.

70　**Raju TNK, Langenberg P.** Pulmonary hemorrhage and exogenous surfactant therapy: a metaanalysis. J Pediatr. 1993;123:603.

71　**Horbar JD et al.** A multicenter randomized trial comparing two surfactants for the treatment of neonatal respiratory distress syndrome. J Pediatr. 1993;123:757.

72　**Zola EM et al.** Comparison of three dosing procedures for administration of bovine surfactant to neonates with respiratory distress syndrome. J Pediatr. 1993;122:453.

73　**Green TP et al.** Diuresis and pulmonary function in premature infants with respiratory distress syndrome. J Pediatr. 1983;103:618.

74　**Yeh TF et al.** Early furosemide therapy in premature infants (≤2000 gm) with respiratory distress syndrome: a randomized controlled trial. J Pediatr. 1984;105:603.

75　**Green TP et al.** Furosemide promotes patent ductus arteriosus in premature infants with the respiratory distress syndrome. N Engl J Med. 1983;308:743.

76　**Guyton AC.** Textbook of Medical Physiology. Philadelphia, PA: WB Saunders; 1991:929.

77 **Hammerman C et al.** Persistent pulmonary hypertension of the newborn. Managing the unmanageable? Clin Perinatol. 1989;16:137.

78 **Barst RJ, Gersony WM.** The pharmacologic treatment of patent ductus arteriosus. A review of the evidence. Drugs. 1989;38:249.

79 **Bhatt V, Nahata MC.** Pharmacologic management of patent ductus arteriosus. Clin Pharm. 1989;8:17.

80 **Douidar SM et al.** Role of indomethacin in ductus closure: an update evaluation. Dev Pharmacol Ther. 1988;11:196.

81 **Chessman KH, Alpert BS.** Pharmacologic manipulation of the ductus arteriosus in neonates. Hosp Pharm. 1988;23:825.

82 **Gersony WM et al.** Effects of indomethacin in premature infants with patent ductus arteriosus: results of a national collaborative study. J Pediatr. 1983;102:895.

83 **Daberkow E, Washington RL.** Cardiovascular and surgical interventions. In: Merenstein GB, Gardner SL, eds. Handbook of Neonatal Intensive Care. St. Louis: Mosby Year Book; 1993:365.

84 **Weist DB.** Population pharmacokinetics of intravenous indomethacin in neonates with symptomatic patent ductus arteriosus. Clin Pharmacol Ther. 1991;49:550.

85 **Yaffe SJ et al.** The disposition of indomethacin in preterm babies. J Pediatr. 1980;97:1001.

86 **Yeh TF et al.** Furosemide prevents the renal side effects of indomethacin therapy in premature infants with patent ductus arteriosus. J Pediatr. 1982;101:433.

87 **Gal P, Gillman JT.** Drug disposition in neonates with patent ductus arteriosus. Ann Pharmacother. 1993;27:1383.

88 **Coombs RC et al.** Gut flow velocities in the newborn: effects of patent ductus arteriosus and parenteral indomethacin. Arch Dis Child. 1990;65:1067.

89 **Ment LR et al.** Low-dose indomethacin therapy and extension of intraventricular hemorrhage: a multicenter randomized trial. J Pediatr. 1994;124:951.

90 **Hammerman C, Aramburo MJ.** Prolonged indomethacin therapy for the prevention of recurrences of patent ductus arteriosus. J Pediatr. 1990;117:771.

91 **Mellander M et al.** Recurrence of symptomatic patent ductus arteriosus in extremely premature infants, treated with indomethacin. J Pediatr. 1984;105:138.

92 **Seyberth HW et al.** Recovery of prostaglandin production associated with reopening of the ductus arteriosus after indomethacin treatment in preterm infants with respiratory distress syndrome. Pediatr Pharmacol. 1982;2:127.

93 **Rennie JM, Cooke RWI.** Prolonged low dose indomethacin for persistent ductus arteriosus of prematurity. Arch Dis Child. 1991;66:55.

94 **Hammerman C et al.** The silent ductus: its precursors and its aftermath. Pediatr Cardiol. 1986;7:121.

95 **Krueger E et al.** Prevention of symptomatic patent ductus arteriosus with a single dose of indomethacin. J Pediatr. 1987;111:749.

96 **Egan EA, Agarwal S.** Neonatal necrotizing enterocolitis. In: Lebenthal E, ed. Textbook of Gastroenterology and Nutrition in Infancy. 2nd ed. New York: Raven Press; 1989:1071.

97 **Crouse DT.** Necrotizing enterocolitis. In: Pomerance JJ, Richardson CJ, eds. Neonatology for the Clinician. Norwalk: Appleton & Lange; 1993:363–64.

98 **MacKendrick W, Caplan M.** Necrotizing enterocolitis. New thoughts about pathogenesis and potential treatments. Pediatr Clin North Am. 1993;40:1047.

99 **Walsh MC, Kliegman RM.** Necrotizing enterocolitis: treatment based on staging criteria. Pediatr Clin North Am. 1986;33:179.

100 **Kliegman RM, Fanaroff AA.** Necrotizing enterocolitis. N Engl J Med. 1984;310:1093.

101 **McKeown RE et al.** Role of delayed feeding and of feeding increments in necrotizing enterocolitis. J Pediatr. 1992;121:764.

102 **Scheifele DW et al.** Comparison of two antibiotic regimens for neonatal necrotizing enterocolitis. J Antimicrob Chemother. 1987;20:421.

103 **Grylack L et al.** Serum concentrations of gentamicin following oral administration to preterm infants. Dev Pharmacol Ther. 1982;5:47.

104 **Han VKM et al.** An outbreak of clostridium difficile necrotizing enterocolitis: a case for oral vancomycin therapy. Pediatrics. 1983;71:935.

105 **George WL.** Peritonitis and intra-abdominal abscess. In: Feigin RD, Cherry JD, eds. Textbook of Pediatric Infectious Diseases. 3rd ed. Philadelphia: WB Saunders; 1992:722.

106 **Faix RG et al.** A randomized controlled trial of parenteral clindamycin in neonatal necrotizing enterocolitis. J Pediatr. 1988;112:271.

107 **Schwartz MZ, Maeda K.** Short bowel syndrome in infants and children. Pediatr Clin North Am. 1985;32:1265.

108 **Seigel JD, McCracken GH.** Sepsis neonatorum. N Engl J Med. 1981;304:642.

109 **Smith JB.** Bacterial and fungal infections of the neonate. In: Pomerance JJ, Richardson CJ, eds. Neonatology for the Clinician. Norwalk: Appleton & Lange; 1993:185.

110 **Weisman LE et al.** Early-onset group B streptococcal sepsis: a current assessment. J Pediatr. 1992;121:428.

111 **Klein JO et al.** Report of the task force on diagnosis and management of meningitis. Pediatrics. 1986;78:959.

112 **Freij BJ, McCracken GH.** Acute infections. In: Avery GB et al., eds. Neonatology: Pathophysiology and Management of the Newborn. 4th ed. Philadelphia: JB Lippincott; 1994:1082.

113 **Hall SL.** Coagulase-negative staphylococcal infections in neonates. Pediatr Infect Dis J. 1991;10:57.

114 **Patrick CC.** Coagulase-negative staphylococci: pathogens with increasing clinical significance. J Pediatr. 1990;116:497.

115 **Patrick CC et al.** Persistent bacteremia due to coagulase-negative staphylococci in low birth weight neonates. Pediatrics. 1989;84:977.

116 **McCracken GH.** Current management of bacterial meningitis in infants and children. Pediatr Infect Dis J. 1992;11:169.

117 **Payne NR et al.** Selecting antibiotics for nosocomial bacterial infections in patients requiring neonatal intensive care. Neonatal Netw. 1994;13:41.

118 **Baley JE.** Neonatal candidiasis: the current challenge. Clin Perinatol. 1991;18:263.

119 **Nelson JD.** Pocketbook of Pediatric Antimicrobial Therapy. 11th ed. Baltimore, MD: Williams & Wilkins; 1995:16.

120 **Ballow M et al.** Development of the immune system in very low birth weight (less than 1500 g) premature infants: concentrations of plasma immunoglobulins and patterns of infections. Pediatr Res. 1986;20:899.

121 **Weisman LE.** Advances in the treatment of neonatal sepsis and meningitis. Isr J Med Sci. 1994;30:455.

122 **Fischer GW.** Use of intravenous immune globulin in newborn infants. Clin Exp Immunol. 1994;97(Suppl. 1):73.

123 **Weisman LE et al.** Intravenous immune globulin therapy for early-onset sepsis in premature neonates. J Pediatr. 1992;121:434.

124 **Baker CJ et al.** Intravenous immune globulin for the prevention of nosocomial infection in low-birth-weight neonates. N Engl J Med. 1992;327:213.

125 **Fanaroff AA et al.** A controlled trial of intravenous immune globulin to reduce nosocomial infections in very-low-birth-weight infants. N Engl J Med. 1994;330:1107.

126 **Weisman LE, Lorenzetti PM.** High intravenous doses of human immune globulin suppress neonatal group B streptococcal immunity in rats. J Pediatr. 1989;115:445.

127 **Bell SG.** Intravenous immunoglobulin therapy in neonatal sepsis. Neonatal Netw. 1991;9:9.

128 **Smith JB.** Congenital viral and protozoan infections. In: Pomerance JJ, Richardson CJ, eds. Neonatology for the Clinician. Norwalk: Appleton & Lange; 1993:173.

129 **Bale JF, Murph JR.** Congenital infections and the nervous system. Pediatr Clin North Am. 1992;39:669.

130 **American Academy of Pediatrics.** Peter G, ed. 1994 Red Book; Report of the Committee on Infectious Diseases. 23rd ed. Elk Grove Village, IL: American Academy of Pediatrics; 1994.

131 **Englund JA et al.** Acyclovir therapy in neonates. J Pediatr. 1991;119:129.

132 **Overall JC.** Herpes simplex virus infection of the fetus and newborn. Pediatr Ann. 1994;23:131.

133 **Whitley RJ.** Neonatal herpes simplex virus infections. J Med Virol. 1993;41(Suppl. 1):13.

134 **Brown ZA et al.** Neonatal herpes simplex virus infection in relation to asymptomatic maternal infection at the time of labor. N Engl J Med. 1991;324:1247.

135 **Whitley R.** A controlled trial comparing vidarabine with acyclovir in neonatal herpes simplex virus infection. N Engl J Med. 1991;324:444.

136 **Henderson-Smart DJ.** The effect of gestational age on the incidence and duration of recurrent apnoea in newborn babies. Aust Paediatr J. 1981;17:273.

137 **Alden ER et al.** Morbidity and mortality of infants weighing less than 1000 grams in an intensive care nursery. Pediatrics. 1972;50:40.

138 **Barrington K, Finer N.** The natural history of the appearance of apnea of prematurity. Pediatr Res. 1991;29:372.

139 **Consensus Statement.** National Institutes of Health consensus development conference on infantile apnea and home monitoring, Sept 29 to Oct 1, 1986. Pediatrics. 1987;79:292.

140 **Martin GI.** Infant apnea. In: Pomerance JJ, Richardson CJ, eds. Neonatology for the Clinician. Norwalk: Appleton & Lange; 1993:267.

141 **Miller MJ, Martin RJ.** Apnea of prematurity. Clin Perinatol. 1992;19:789.

142 **Martin RJ et al.** Pathogenesis of apnea in preterm infants. J Pediatr. 1986;109:733, 738.

143 **Finer NN et al.** Obstructive, mixed, and central apnea in the neonate: physiologic correlates. J Pediatr. 1992;121:943.

144 **Aranda JV et al.** Drug treatment of neonatal apnea. In: Yaffe SJ, Aranda JV, eds. Pediatric Pharmacology: Therapeutic Principles in Practice. Philadelphia: WB Saunders; 1992:193.

145 **Darnall RA.** Aminophylline reduces hypoxic ventilatory depression: possible role of adenosine. Pediatr Res. 1985;19:706.

146 **Myers TF et al.** Low-dose theophylline therapy in idiopathic apnea of prematurity. J Pediatr. 1980;96:99.

147 **Kritter KE, Blanchard J.** Management of apnea in infants. Clin Pharm. 1989;8:577.

148 **Lopes JM et al.** The effects of theophylline on diaphragmatic fatigue in the newborn. Pediatr Res. 1982;16:355A.

149 **Tang-Lui DDS et al.** Nonlinear theophylline elimination. Clin Pharmacol Ther. 1982;31:358.

150 **Tang-Lui DD, Reigelman S.** Metabolism of theophylline to caffeine in adults. Res Commun Chem Pathol Pharmacol. 1981;34:371.

151 **Muttitt SC et al.** The dose response of theophylline in the treatment of apnea of prematurity. J Pediatr. 1988;112:115.

152 **Willis J, ed.** Use of theophylline in infants. FDA Drug Bull. 1985;15:16.

153 **Kraus DM et al.** Pharmacokinetic evaluation of two theophylline dosing methods for infants. Ther Drug Monit. 1994;16:270.

154 **Aldridge A et al.** Caffeine metabolism in the newborn. Clin Pharmacol Ther. 1979;25:447.

155 **LeGuennec JC et al.** Maturational changes of caffeine concentration and disposition in infancy during maintenance therapy for apnea of prematurity: influence of gestational age, hepatic disease, and breast-feeding. Pediatrics. 1985;76:834.

156 **Aranda JV et al.** Maturation of caffeine elimination in infancy. Arch Dis Child. 1979;54:946.

157 **Brouard C et al.** Comparative efficacy of theophylline and caffeine in the treatment of idiopathic apnea in premature infants. Am J Dis Child. 1985;139:698.

158 **Bairam A et al.** Theophylline versus caffeine: comparative effects in treatment of idiopathic apnea in the preterm infant. J Pediatr. 1987;110:636.

159 **Davis JM et al.** Use of caffeine in infants unresponsive to theophylline in apnea of prematurity. Pediatr Pulmonol. 1987;3:90.

160 **Eisenberg MG, Kang N.** Stability of citrated caffeine solutions for injectable and enteral use. Am J Hosp Pharm. 1984;41:2405.

161 **Eyal F et al.** Aminophylline versus doxapram in idiopathic apnea of prematurity: a double-blind controlled study. Pediatrics. 1985;75:709.

162 **Peliowski A, Finer NN.** A blinded, randomized, placebo-controlled trial to compare theophylline and doxapram for the treatment of apnea of prematurity. J Pediatr. 1990;116:648.

163 **Bairam A et al.** Doxapram for the initial treatment of idiopathic apnea of prematurity. Biol Neonat. 1992;61:209.

164 **Barrington KJ et al.** Dose-response relationship of doxapram in the therapy for refractory idiopathic apnea of prematurity. Pediatrics. 1987;80:22.

165 **Tay-Uyboco J et al.** Clinical and physiological responses to prolonged nasogastric administration of doxapram for apnea of prematurity. Biol Neonate. 1991;59:190.

166 **Papile LA.** Central nervous system disturbances, part four: periventricular-intraventricular hemorrhage. In: Fanaroff AA, Martin RJ, eds. Neonatal-Perinatal Medicine: Diseases of the Fetus and Infant. 5th ed. St. Louis: Mosby Year Book; 1992:719.

167 **Papile LA, Brann BS IV.** Intracranial hemorrhage: periventricular, intraventricular hemorrhage. In: Pomerance JJ, Richardson CJ, eds. Neonatology for the Clinician. Norwalk: Appleton & Lange; 1993:425.

168 **Volpe JJ.** Intraventricular hemorrhage and brain injury in the premature infant: neuropathology and pathogenesis. Clin Perinatol. 1989;16:361.

169 **Minarcik CJ Jr, Beachy P.** Neurologic disorders. In: Merenstein GB, Gardner SL, eds. Handbook of Neonatal Intensive Care. 3rd ed. St. Louis: Mosby Year Book; 1993:430.

170 **Volpe JJ.** Intraventricular hemorrhage and brain injury in the premature infant: diagnosis, prognosis, and prevention. Clin Perinatol. 1989;16:387.

171 **Lamp KC, Reynolds MS.** Indomethacin for prevention of neonatal intraventricular hemorrhage. DICP, Ann Pharmacother. 1991;25:1344.

172 **Ment LR et al.** Low-dose indomethacin and prevention of intraventricular hemorrhage: a multicenter randomized trial. Pediatrics. 1994;93:543.

173 **Volpe JJ.** Brain injury caused by intraventricular hemorrhage: is indomethacin the silver bullet for prevention? Pediatrics. 1994;93:673.

174 **Rust RS, Volpe JJ.** Neonatal seizures. In: Dodson WE, Pellock JM, eds. Pediatric Epilepsy: Diagnosis and Therapy. New York: Demos; 1993:107.

175 **Mizrahi EM.** Consensus and controversy in the clinical management of neonatal seizures. Clin Perinatol. 1989; 16:485.

176 **Painter MJ.** Therapy of neonatal seizures. Cleve Clin J Med. 1988;56 (Suppl.):S124.

177 **Morrison A.** Neonatal seizures. In: Pomerance JJ, Richardson CJ, eds. Neonatology for the Clinician. Norwalk: Appleton & Lange; 1993:411.

178 **Haymond MW.** Hypoglycemia in infants and children. Endocrinol Metab Clin North Am. 1989;18:221.

179 **Tsang RC.** Neonatal magnesium disturbances. Am J Dis Child. 1972;124:282.

180 **Massingale TW, Buttross S.** Survey of treatment practices for neonatal seizures. J Perinatol. 1993;13:107.

181 **Painter MJ et al.** Phenobarbital and diphenylhydantoin levels in neonates with seizures. J Pediatr. 1978;92:315.

182 **Gilman JT et al.** Rapid sequential phenobarbital treatment of neonatal seizures. Pediatrics. 1989;83:674.

183 **Deshmukh A et al.** Lorazepam in the treatment of refractory neonatal seizures: a pilot study. Am J Dis Child. 1986;140:1042.

184 **McDermott CA et al.** Pharmacokinetics of lorazepam in critically ill neonates with seizures. J Pediatr. 1992; 120:479.

185 **Gal P et al.** Valproic acid efficacy, toxicity, and pharmacokinetics in neonates with intractable seizures. Neurology. 1988;38:467.

186 **Fischer JH et al.** Phenobarbital maintenance dose requirements in treating neonatal seizures. Neurology. 1981;31:1042.

187 **Painter MJ et al.** Phenobarbital and phenytoin in neonatal seizures: metabolism and tissue distribution. Neurology. 1981;31:1107.

188 **Rosen TS.** Infants of addicted mothers. In: Fanaroff AA, Martin RJ, eds. Neonatal-Perinatal Medicine: Diseases of the Fetus and Infant. 5th ed. St. Louis: Mosby Year Book; 1992:574.

189 **Finnegan LP, Weiner SM.** Drug withdrawal in the neonate. In: Merenstein GB, Gardner SL, eds. Handbook of Neonatal Intensive Care. 3rd ed. St. Louis: Mosby Year Book; 1993:40.

190 **Levy M, Spino M.** Neonatal withdrawal syndrome: associated drugs and pharmacological management. Pharmacotherapy. 1993;13:202.

191 **Doberczak TM et al.** Neonatal opiate abstinence syndrome in term and preterm infants. J Pediatr. 1991;118:933.

192 **Zelson C et al.** Neonatal narcotic addiction: comparative effects of maternal intake of heroin and methadone. N Engl J Med. 1973;289:1216.

193 **Greenglass EJ.** The adverse effects of cocaine on the developing human. In: Yaffe SJ, Aranda JV, eds. Pediatric Pharmacology: Therapeutic Principles in Practice. Philadelphia: WB Saunders; 1992:598.

194 **Neuspeil DR, Hamel BC.** Cocaine and infant behavior. J Dev Behav Pediatr. 1991;12:55.

195 **Kandall SR, Gartner LM.** Late presentation of drug withdrawal symptoms in newborns. Am J Dis Child. 1974;127:58.

196 **Finnegan LP et al.** Management of neonatal narcotic abstinence utilizing a phenobarbital loading dose method. Natl Inst Drug Abuse Res Monogr Ser. 1979;27:247.

197 **American Academy of Pediatrics, Committee on Drugs.** Neonatal drug withdrawal. Pediatrics. 1983;72:895.

198 **Wijburg FA et al.** Morphine as an anti-epileptic drug in neonatal abstinence syndrome. Acta Paediatr Scand. 1991;80:875.

199 **Hill RM, Desmond MM.** Management of the narcotic withdrawal syndrome in the neonate. Pediatr Clin North Am. 1963;10:67.

200 **Stark AR et al.** Muscle relaxation in mechanically ventilated infants. J Pediatr. 1979;94:439.

201 **Crone RK, Favorito J.** The effects of pancuronium bromide on infants with hyaline membrane disease. J Pediatr. 1980;97:991.

202 **Buck ML, Reed MD.** Use of nondepolarizing neuromuscular blocking agents in mechanically ventilated patients. Clin Pharm. 1991;10:32.

203 **Carlo WA et al.** Assisted ventilation and the complications of respiratory distress. In: Fanaroff AA, Martin RJ, eds. Neonatal-Perinatal Medicine: Diseases of the Fetus and Infant. 5th ed. St. Louis: Mosby Year Book; 1992:827.

204 **Taylor P.** Agents acting at the neuromuscular junction and autonomic ganglia. In: Gilman AG et al., eds. Goodman and Gilman's The Pharmacological Basis of Therapeutics. 8th ed. New York: Pergamon Press; 1990:166.

205 **Bennett EJ et al.** Pancuronium and the neonate. Br J Anaesth. 1975;47:75.

206 **Greenough A et al.** Investigation of the effects of paralysis by pancuronium on heart rate variability, blood pressure and fluid balance. Acta Paediatr Scand. 1989;78:829.

207 **Cabal LA et al.** Cardiovascular and catecholamine changes after administration of pancuronium in distressed neonates. Pediatrics. 1985;75:284.

208 **Piotrowski A.** Comparison of atracurium and pancuronium in mechanically ventilated neonates. Intensive Care Med. 1993;19:401.

209 **American Academy of Pediatrics.** Committee on fetus and newborn, committee on drugs, section on anesthesiology, section on surgery. Neonatal anesthesia. Pediatrics. 1987;80:446.

210 **Anand KJS, Hickey PR.** Pain and its effects in the human neonate and fetus. N Engl J Med. 1987;317:1321.

211 **Shapiro C.** Pain in the neonate: assessment and intervention. Neonatal Netw. 1989;8:7.

212 **Goldberg RN et al.** Detection of seizure activity in the paralyzed neonate using continuous monitoring. Pediatrics. 1982;69:583.

213 **Zenk KE.** Practical pharmacology for the clinician caring for the newborn. In: Pomerance JJ, Richardson CJ, eds. Neonatology for the Clinician. Norwalk: Appleton & Lange; 1993:59.

214 **Roth B et al.** Analgesia and sedation in neonatal intensive care using fentanyl by continuous infusion. Dev Pharmacol Ther. 1991;17:121.

215 **Norton SJ.** After effects of morphine and fentanyl analgesia: a retrospective study. Neonatal Netw. 1988;7:25.

216 **Arnold JH et al.** Changes in the pharmacodynamic response to fentanyl in neonates during continuous infusion. J Pediatr. 1991;119:639.

217 **Katz R et al.** Prospective study on the occurrence of withdrawal in critically ill children who receive fentanyl by continuous infusion. Crit Care Med. 1994;22:763.

218 **Lane JC et al.** Movement disorder after withdrawal of fentanyl infusion. J Pediatr. 1991;119:649.

219 **Anand KJS, Arnold JH.** Opioid tolerance and dependence in infants and children. Crit Care Med. 1994;22:334.

220 **Watling SM, Dasta JF.** Prolonged paralysis in intensive care unit patients after the use of neuromuscular blocking agents: a review of the literature. Crit Care Med. 1994;22:884.

221 **Anyebuno MA, Rosenfeld CR.** Chloral hydrate toxicity in a term infant. Dev Pharmacol Ther. 1991;17:116.

222 **Mayers DJ et al.** Chloral hydrate disposition following single-dose administration to critically ill neonates and children. Dev Pharmacol Ther. 1991; 16:71.

223 **Mayers DJ et al.** Sedative/hypnotic effects of chloral hydrate in the neonate: trichloroethanol or parent drug? Dev Pharmacol Ther. 1992;19:141.

224 **Nahata MC, Hipple TF.** Pediatric Drug Formulations. 2nd ed. Cincinnati, OH: Harvey Whitney Books; 1992.

225 **Blumer JL, Reed MD.** Principles of neonatal pharmacology. In: Yaffe SV, Aranda JV, eds. Pediatric Pharmacology: Therapeutic Principles in Practice. 2nd ed. Philadelphia: WB Saunders; 1992:164, 168.

226 **Ernst JA et al.** Osmolality of substances used in the intensive care nursery. Pediatrics. 1983;72:347.

227 **White KC, Harkavy KL.** Hypertonic formula resulting from added oral medications. Am J Dis Child. 1982;136:931.

228 **American Academy of Pediatrics, Committee on Drugs.** "Inactive" ingredients in pharmaceutical products. Pediatrics. 1985;76:635.

229 **Glasgow AM et al.** Hyperosmolality in small infants due to propylene glycol. Pediatrics. 1983;72:353.

230 **Balistreri WF et al.** Lessons from the E-Ferol tragedy. Pediatrics. 1986;78:503.

231 **Kumar A et al.** The mystery ingredients: sweeteners, flavorings, dyes, and preservatives in analgesic/antipyretic, antihistamine/decongestant, cough and cold, antidiarrheal, and liquid theophylline preparations. Pediatrics. 1993;91:927.

232 **Nahata MC.** Intravenous infusion conditions: implications for pharmacokinetic monitoring. Clin Pharmacokinet. 1993;24:221.

233 **Roberts RJ.** Issues and problems associated with drug delivery in pediatric patients. J Clin Pharmacol. 1994;34:723.

234 **Nahata MC et al.** Effect of infusion methods on tobramycin serum concentrations in newborn infants. J Pediatr. 1984;104:136.

235 **Painter MJ et al.** Neonatal Seizures. Pediatr Clin North Am. 1986;33:95.

236 **Friedman WF.** Congenital heart disease in infancy and childhood. In: Braunwald E, ed. Heart Disease: A Textbook of Cardiovascular Medicine. 4th ed. Philadelphia: WB Saunders; 1992:893.

Pediatric Infectious Diseases

Chris Paap

Immunology (See Table 97.1) 97-2
Microbiology (See Table 97.2) 97-3
Otitis Media 97-2
Clinical Presentation and Classification 97-2
Acute 97-2
Chronic 97-3
Recurrent 97-3
Microbiology 97-3
Treatment 97-8
Antibiotic therapy (See Table 97.3) 97-8
Acute otitis media 97-8
Chronic otitis media with effusion 97-9
Adjunctive therapy 97-9
Corticosteroids 97-9
Sinusitis 97-9
Acute Sinusitis 97-9
Clinical presentation 97-9
Microbiology 97-10
Treatment 97-10
Antibiotic therapy 97-10
Adjunctive therapy 97-10
Chronic Sinusitis 97-10
Antibiotic therapy 97-10
Medication history 97-10
Pharyngitis 97-11
Clinical Presentation 97-11
Microbiology 97-11
Complications of Group A Beta Hemolytic Streptococci
(GABHS) Infection (Also see Questions 17 to 19) 97-11
Treatment 97-12
Antibiotic therapy (Also see Question 14) 97-12
Prophylaxis of household members 97-12
Rheumatic Fever/Endocarditis (Also see Question 14) ..97-13
Clinical presentation and diagnosis
(See Table 97.4) 97-13

Treatment 97-13
Prophylaxis (See Table 97.5) 97-13
Bronchiolitis 97-14
Clinical Presentation and Classification
(See Table 97.6) 97-14
Treatment 97-14
Bronchodilators 97-14
Ribavirin 97-15
Risks to health care workers 97-15
Adjunctive therapies 97-15
Croup Syndrome 97-15
Clinical Presentation and Classification
(See Table 97.7) 97-15
Treatment 97-16
Laryngotracheobronchitis 97-16
Epinephrine 97-16
Corticosteroids 97-16
Antibiotics 97-16
Supraglottitis 97-17
Pertussis 97-17
Clinical Presentation 97-17
Treatment: Erythromycin (See Table 97.8) 97-17
Prophylaxis 97-17
Measles 97-17
Kawasaki's Disease 97-18
Clinical Presentation and Diagnosis 97-18
Treatment 97-18
Aspirin therapy 97-18
Dose and monitoring 97-19
Intravenous immunoglobulin (IVIG) 97-19
Rickettsial Diseases 97-19
Rocky Mountain Spotted Fever (RMSF) 97-19
Clinical presentation 97-19
Treatment 97-19
Monitoring 97-20

Infectious diseases account for a vast majority of visits to the pediatrician. Acute febrile illnesses, either viral or bacterial, occur on average six to eight times a year in pediatric patients. For this reason, the management of pediatric infectious diseases remains a significant component of care. Many infectious diseases take place in children, however, some are specific only to this patient population.

The relatively high incidence of infectious diseases in pediatric patients is due to a combination of host and microbial factors. The ontogeny of immune function in newborns, infants, and children has been studied extensively. Deficits in both cellular and humoral immunity have been described in the immediate newborn period as well as the first several years of life. Table 97.1 summarizes the relative immunologic deficiencies in children during the first years of life.[1] Concentrations of all the immunoglobulins (IgG, IgM, IgD, IgE, and IgA) are diminished at birth, particularly in the premature neonate.[2] While there is some maternal transfer of immunoglobulin G (IgG) to the newborn, this is generally a short-lived effect that dissipates during the first year of life. There are also deficits in complement and C-reactive protein causing decreased opsonization. Also, the phagocytic and intracellular killing functions of neutrophils and macrophages are depressed which affects overall immunity in the newborn and infant. It is also equally important to consider the microbial naivety of children and the significant impact it has on their ability to fight infection. The newborn and infant have not developed a full complement of normal bacterial flora. As a result, potential pathogens can colonize and cause clinical infection much easier. Secondly, children must begin acquiring their own immunity to organisms by becoming exposed to antigens, developing an immune response, and generating lasting-memory immunity cells. These microbiologic and immunologic processes are vital to the development of an adequate immune defense against infection. Unfortunately, children are not born with these components of our physiologic defense mechanisms.

Children also are exposed increasingly to more potential pathogens. About 50% of households with children under six years of age have a single working parent or both parents are employed outside of the home.[3] As a result, children are increasingly attending daycare and school environments at an earlier age. Thus, children may be more likely to come in contact with another infected child or caregiver resulting in increased environmental exposure and risk for infection.[4]

Bacterial and viral pathogens that most commonly affect pediatric patients are summarized in Table 97.2.[5] The age of the child as well as the site of infection implicate different potential pathogens, however there is significant overlap and it is evident that the most common bacterial pathogens among pediatric infections are caused by *Streptococcus pneumoniae*, *Haemophilus influenzae*, and *Moraxella catarrhalis*. Thus, antimicrobial therapy in pediatric patients almost always includes an agent that is active against these pathogens. Viral infections are caused by many different viruses and are not commonly cultured clinically because treatments are not readily available. Respiratory syncytial virus (RSV), however, is a common viral pathogen that causes respiratory tract infection in pediatric patients and a treatment option is available for this particular pathogen.

Otitis Media

Otitis media is simply an inflammation of the middle ear. Otitis media is very common, occurring in more than 75% of all children by the age of two.[6] The middle ear is the anatomical location of the hearing apparatus. The middle ear is separated from the outer ear canal by the tympanic membrane (ear drum) and has drainage into the nasopharynx via the eustachian tubes. The tympanic membrane is commonly visualized by otoscopy for the diagnosis of otitis media. The presence of a dull, red, bulging, tympanic membrane that does not fluctuate during insufflation (application of slight changes in air pressure in the ear canal) of the ear canal, is diagnostic for acute otitis media. Otitis media has a peak incidence between six months and three years of age and is thought to be most likely due to eustachian tube obstruction and secondarily due to the decreased immunocompetence.[7] Eustachian tube dysfunction has been associated with preceding upper respiratory tract infections[8,9] and allergies.[7] Some ''otitis prone'' children may have three or four infections a year or continuous ''chronic'' otitis media for a prolonged period of time (>3 months).

Otitis media infections can be caused by viral or bacterial pathogens. A majority of otitis media is due to viral causes, unfortunately it is difficult to distinguish viral from bacterial etiology based upon clinical presentation and otoscopic examination. The only definitive method for determining bacterial disease would require invasive and painful culturing of middle ear fluid. Over 70% of bacterial disease is caused by *Streptococcus pneumoniae*, *Haemophilus influenzae*, and *Moraxella catarrhalis*.[10] Since there is such a high prevalence of these organisms, empiric antibiotic therapy targeted at these pathogens often is prescribed without obtaining cultures from the middle ear. Table 97.3 summarizes the oral antibiotics that are commonly used to treat otitis media.

Clinical Presentation and Classification

1. J.S., an 11-month-old, 10 kg female, is brought to a central Texas clinic with a history of increased irritability and fever over the last 2 days. She has been observed pulling on her right ear and is refusing to take her bottle feedings. She is currently in daycare 5 days a week and had 1 previous episode of left ear otitis media 3 months ago which was treated with amoxicillin/clavulanate (Augmentin) 40 mg/kg/day (amoxicillin) Q 8 hr for 10 days. She was evaluated after completion of the course of antibiotics and still had an accumulation of serous (clear) fluid behind the tympanic membrane but had no signs of acute infection (redness, bulging, opaque appearance, or pain). However, the mother complained that the child had loose, frequent stools during the entire course of the antibiotic which caused a severe diaper rash. Her vaccinations were up to date and include: Hepatitis B, Diphtheria, pertussis, tetanus (DTP), oral polio virus (OPV), and *Haemophilus influenzae*, type b. On physical examination the right tympanic membrane appears red, inflamed, and opaque (indicating pus in the middle ear), causing it to bulge. Upon gentle air insufflation, the tympanic membrane is immobile and is very painful. The left ear has an accumulation of serous (clear) fluid behind the tympanic membrane but is not red or bulging and is mobile and not painful upon air insufflation. A tympanogram of the left ear indicates the presence of fluid in the middle ear. How would you classify the diagnosis of otitis media in J.S. based upon the presenting symptoms, history, and physical examination?

Acute Otitis Media

The clinical presentation of otitis media varies widely and many different terms are given to its diagnostic description. For the purposes of treatment differentiation three basic diagnostic categories are: acute otitis media, recurrent otitis media, and chronic otitis media.[11] The infection present in the right ear of J.S. represents the most common and clearly defined classification, acute otitis media. Acute otitis media presents with a history of ear pain, irritability, and fever. Fever may not be present in up to 50% of cases,[11] however it is present in J.S. and is indicative of an acute infectious process. The otoscopic examination of the right ear in J.S. is also typical of acute otitis media. The tympanic membrane appears opaque and bulging due to the accumulation of pus in the middle ear behind the membrane. The tympanic membrane is red due to inflammation and is painful. The immobility of the tympanic membrane during insufflation indicates significant fluid accumulation behind the membrane in the middle ear.

Table 97.1	Immunologic Parameters in Infants, Children, and Adults[a]				
	Birth	1 Month	1 Year	5 Years	Adult
Average white blood cell count (cells/mm^3)	18,100	10,800	10,600	8500	7400
Average neutrophil count (cells/mm^3)	8500	2700	2900	3200	3700
Average lymphocyte count (cells/mm^3)	4300	6000	6400	3200	2500
Average serum immunoglobulin G concentration (mg/dL)	1100	650	800	900	1000
Average serum immunoglobulin M concentration (mg/dL)	15	80	140	150	200
Average serum immunoglobulin A concentration (mg/dL)	3	35	140	120	230
Average complement C$_3$ concentration (mg/dL)	—	110	130	140	130
Average complement C$_4$ concentration (mg/dL)	—	25	25	25	30

[a] Compiled from reference 1.

Table 97.2	Common Viral and Bacterial Pathogens Associated with Specific Pediatric Infectious Diseases[a,b]				
	Otitis Media	Sinusitis	Pharyngitis	Bronchiolitis	Croup Syndrome[c]
Viral[d]					
Parainfluenza	+	+	++	++	+++
Influenza	++	+	++		++
Adenovirus	+	+	+++	+	+
Rhinovirus		++	+		+
RSV	+++	+	+	+++	+
Coronavirus		++			+
Enterovirus	+	+	+++		+
EBV			++		
Bacterial					
S. pneumoniae	+++	+++	+		
S. pyogenes	+	+	+++		
S. aureus		+[e]	+		+[f]
H. influenzae	++	++	++		+[f]
M. catarrhalis	++	++			
C. diphtheria			+		+
Oral anaerobes		+[e]	+		
M. pneumoniae	+	+	+	+	+

[a] Adapted with permission from the University of Kentucky College of Pharmacy Office of continuing Education Independent Study Program entitled, Pediatric Pharmacotherapy.

[b] +++ = Most common pathogens; ++ = Common pathogens; + = Occasional pathogens.

[c] See Table 97.7 for specific bacterial pathogens for Croup Syndrome.

[d] RSV = Respiratory syncytial virus; EBV = Epstein-Barr virus.

[e] Mostly isolated to chronic infections.

[f] Most common bacterial pathogens, but are rare overall. S. aureus more common than H. influenzae as cause of bacterial tracheitis, but H. influenzae more common as cause for supraglottitis.

Chronic Otitis Media

J.S. has a different process occurring in the left ear which is representative of chronic otitis media with effusion. J.S. has no complaints of pain in the left ear. Fluid behind the tympanic membrane is visualized with an otoscope and air insufflation does not elicit pain. Chronic otitis media also can be present with signs and symptoms similar to acute otitis media or with subtle changes in balance, lack of speech development, and deafness.[12] A tympanogram is a diagnostic test that measures impedance of the tympanic membrane to determine whether fluid is in the middle ear. While tympanograms can be helpful in identifying middle ear effusions, the test requires special equipment and is not superior to pneumatic otoscopy.[13] J.S. has a history of otitis media in the left ear that was treated three months ago. Although fluid accumulated despite a ten-day course of amoxicillin/clavulanate, this is not uncommon and occurs in about 70% of all patients with otitis media.[14] The effusion generally is not treated following an acute otitis media because it will resolve spontaneously in a vast majority of patients within three months.[14] However, J.S. has a persistent effusion in the left ear that has been present for at least three months and should be treated.

Recurrent Otitis Media

Recurrent otitis media is the third major classification of otitis media that requires therapeutic consideration. J.S. experienced two acute otitis media infections in a three-month period, but these episodes do not meet the established definition of recurrent otitis media. Recurrent otitis media generally is defined as three episodes of otitis media in a six-month period or ≥4 episodes in a year.[12] If J.S. were to get another acute otitis in the next three months, or

two more infections in the next nine months, the diagnosis of recurrent otitis media would be appropriate for J.S. Since J.S. is in full time daycare, the risk of recurrent otitis media is increased.[15] J.S. also has had two middle ear infections in the first year of life which is another prognostic factor that suggests J.S. will develop recurrent otitis media. Antimicrobial prophylaxis can decrease the incidence of recurrent otitis media.[16–18] The most common regimens are amoxicillin 20 mg/kg,[16] sulfisoxazole 50 mg/kg,[16,17] or trimethoprim-sulfamethoxazole (TMP-SMX) 4/20 mg/kg[18] given once daily for periods up to six months.

Microbiology

2. What are the most likely organisms causing J.S.'s middle ear infection?

The most likely bacterial organisms causing otitis media in J.S. are *S. pneumoniae*, *H. influenzae*, and *M. catarrhalis*, respectively and these three organisms account for nearly 70% of all bacterial otitis media infections.[10] Other organisms such as *Staphylococcus aureus*, Group A *Streptococcus*, and gram-negative rods also can cause otitis media.[10] Gram-negative rods, such as *Escherichia coli*, occur in newborns with otitis media; however, middle ear infection in this age population is rare and generally is managed as a possible sepsis. (See Chapter 96: Neonatal Therapy.) Although other atypical organisms such as *Chlamydia trachomatis* and *Mycoplasma pneumoniae* have been isolated from middle ear fluid, these are not common causes of otitis media.[19] It is important to recognize that up to 50% of acute otitis media may be caused by viral infection which will resolve regardless of antibiotic therapy. However, it is difficult to determine whether J.S. has viral or bacterial disease

Table 97.3 Oral Antibiotics for the Treatment of Common Pediatric Infectious Diseases

Antibiotic	Dose	S. aureus	S. pneumonia	H. influenzae	M. catarrhalis	Group B β-Hemolytic Strep	β-Lactamase Stable	Compliance Factor Ratings[c]	Side Effects/Comments	Cost[b]
Penicillins										
Penicillin VK,[d] Penicillin V	250 mg = 400,000 units of Pen G. 25–50 mg/kg/day divided Q 6 hr (*max:* 3 gm/day)	+	+++	—	—	+++	—	1	Allergy, drug fever, eosinophilia, interstitial nephritis, CNS toxicity. ↓ dose in renal failure	$2.86
Penicillinase-Resistant Penicillins										
Dicloxacillin[e]	25–50 mg/kg/day divided Q 6 hr	+++	+++	—	—	+++	+++	1	Mild GI symptoms, diarrhea	$9.84 C $15.53 S
Cloxacillin[f]	50–100 mg/kg/day divided Q 6 hr	+++	+++	—	—	+++	+++	1	Mild GI symptoms, diarrhea	$15.45
Broad-Spectrum Penicillins										
Amoxicillin[g]	20–40 mg/kg/day divided Q 8 hr	+	+++	++	+	+++	—	2	↓ dose in renal failure. Good activity against *Salmonella*; poor against *Shigella*	$3.27
Amoxicillin-clavulanate[h]	20–40 mg/kg/day divided Q 8 hr	+++	+++	+++	+++	+++	+++	2	Nausea, vomiting, diarrhea, abdominal cramps. Take with food. Do not give 2 of the 250 mg amoxicillin/125 mg clavulanate at one time. May result in GI toxicity	$44.55
Ampicillin[i]	50–100 mg/kg/day divided Q 6 hr	+	+++	++	+	+++	—	1	Useful in treatment of *Shigella*. Fair to good activity against *Salmonella*	$5.37 C $8.28 S
Cephalosporins (All Adjusted in Renal Failure)										
1st Generation Cephalexin (Keflex)[j]	25–50 mg/kg/day divided Q 6 hr	+++	+++	+	+	+++	+	2	GI distress, dizziness, fatigue, headache, neutropenia, rash, ↑ AST, false-positive test for urinary reducing substances	$10.44
Cephradine (Velosef, Anspor)[k]	25–50 mg/kg/day divided Q 6 hr	+++	+++	+	+	+++	+	2	GI distress, diarrhea, pseudomembranous colitis, rash, joint pains, transient leukopenia or neutropenia, ↑ hepatic enzymes or bili	$34.02
Cefadroxil (Duricef)[l]	30 mg/kg/day divided Q 12 hr	+++	+++	+	+	+++	+	3	Allergy, GI distress, transient neutropenia, pruritus	$30.62

Drug	Dosage							Comments	Cost
2nd Generation									
Cefaclor (Ceclor)[m]	20–40 mg/kg/day divided Q 8–12 hr	+	++	++	+	+	3	GI distress, eosinophilia, pruritus, positive Coombs, false-positive test for urinary glucose	$54.96 C $47.60 S
Loracarbef (Lorabid)[n]	15 mg/kg/day divided Q 12 hr	++	+++	+++	++	++	3	GI distress, eosinophilia, pruritus, positive Coombs, false-positive test for urinary glucose	≈$37.50
Cefuroxime axetil (Ceftin)[o]	30 mg/kg/day divided Q 12 hr (40 mg/kg/day for otitis)	+++	+++	+++	+++	++	1	Minor GI complaints	$55.86 T $48.00 S
3rd Generation									
Cefixime (Suprax)[p]	8 mg/kg/day divided Q 12–24 hr	+	++	+++	+++	+++	3	GI distress	$52.94
Cefpodoxime (Vantin)[q]	10 mg/kg/day divided Q 12 hr	++	+++	+++	+++	+++	3	Not approved in <6 months of age. Suspension contains phenylalanine. Side effects include GI distress, ↑ liver enzymes, allergy, dizziness, ↓ leukocytes, eosinophilia. Suspension does not contain phenylalanine	≈$42.00
Cefprozil (Cefzil)[r]	30 mg/kg/day divided Q 12 hr	+++	++	+++	+++	+++	3	Not approved in <6 months of age. Suspension contains phenylalanine. Side effects include GI distress, ↑ liver enzymes, allergy, dizziness, ↓ leukocytes, eosinophilia	$41.28
Macrolides									
Erythromycin[s]	30–50 mg/kg/day divided Q 6 hr *<4 months of age:* 20–40 mg/kg/day divided Q 6 hr	+	+++	+	++	+++	1	In pediatrics, estolate has greater bioavailability than ethylsuccinate. Absorption not affected by food. No adjustment in renal failure. Avoid in hepatic failure. GI: epigastric distress, diarrhea. Drug interactions with theophylline, carbamazepine, digoxin, cyclosporine	Estolate $10.78 Ethylsuccinate $5.40
Clarithromycin (Biaxin)[t]	15 mg/kg/day divided BID	+	++	+++	++	+++	2	GI side effects less than erythromycin. Drug interactions include ↑ theophylline and carbamazepine concentrations, failure of oral contraceptives	$50.00 T $36.80 S

Continued

Table 97.3

Oral Antibiotics for the Treatment of Common Pediatric Infectious Diseases (Continued)

Antibiotic	Dose	Spectrum[a]						Compliance Factor Ratings[c]	Side Effects/Comments	Cost[b]
		S. aureus	S. pneumonia	H. influenzae	M. catarrhalis	Group B β-Hemolytic Strep	β-Lactamase Stable			
Others										
TMP-SMX[u]	6–12 mg TMP/30–60 mg SMX/kg/day divided Q 12 hr	+	+++	+++	+++	—	+++	3	Not in patients <2 months (kernicterus). Mild GI symptoms, skin rash, thrombocytopenia (rare); neutropenia (rare). ↑ half-life of phenytoin	$5.49
Erythromycin-sulfisoxazole[v] (Pediazole)	40 mg/kg/day of erythromycin divided Q 6–8 hr	++	+++	+++	+++	+++	+++	1	Same as erythromycin. Also, neutropenia, agranulocytosis, thrombocytopenia, aplastic anemia, allergy, GI distress, crystalluria	$27.29 brand $15.30 generic
Metronidazole[w]	15–35 mg/kg/day divided Q 6 hr	—	—	—	—	—	+++	1	Anaerobic infections, C. difficile colitis, alcohol intolerance, GI distress, metallic or unpleasant taste	$6.65
Tetracycline[x]	25–50 mg/kg/day divided Q 6 hr. **Use only in patients >9 yr**	++	++	+	+	+++	+++	1	Depress bone growth, discolor teeth, enamel hypoplasia, photosensitivity, nausea, vomiting, epigastric distress, esophageal ulceration	$1.62
Doxycycline[y]	2–4 mg/kg/day divided Q 12 hr on day 1, then ½ dose Q 24 hr. **Use only in patients >9 yr**	++	++	+	+	+++	+++	2	Depress bone growth, discolor teeth, enamel hypoplasia, photosensitivity, nausea, vomiting, epigastric distress, esophageal ulceration	$9.51
Clindamycin[z]	20–30 mg/kg/day divided Q 6–8 hr	+++	+++	—	+	+++	+++	2	C. difficile diarrhea, allergy, minor ↑ in hepatocellular enzymes, neutropenia, thrombocytopenia	$12.37 S

	Cost	FR							
Rifampin[aa] H. influenzae: 20 mg/kg/day QD × 4 days N. meningitidis: 20 mg/kg/day divided BID × 2 days	$3.93	2	+++	+++	++	+++	+++	++	+++	Resistance develops rapidly. Drug interactions with theophylline, cyclosporine, ketoconazole, beta-blockers, digoxin, verapamil, phenytoin. Adverse effects include allergy, ↑ cortisol metabolism, flu-like syndrome, hepatotoxicity, exudative conjunctivitis

a +++ = Good; ++ = Average; + = Minimal; — = None.
b Cost = Cost based upon 10-day course at average wholesale price; maximal dose for a 15–20 kg child. C = Capsule; S = Suspension; T = Tablet.
c FR = Factor Ratings; 1 = Less favorable; 2 = Average; 3 = More favorable.
d Penicillin VK available as 125, 250, 500 mg tablets; 125, 250 mg/5 mL suspension; Penicillin V available as 250, 500 mg tablets; 125, 250 mg/5 mL suspension.
e Dicloxacillin available as 250, 500 mg capsules; 62.5 mg/5 mL suspension.
f Cloxacillin available as 250, 500 mg capsules; 125 mg/5 mL suspension.
g Amoxicillin available as 250, 500 mg capsules; 125, 250 mg chewable tablets; 125, 250 mg/5 mL suspension.
h Amoxicillin-clavulanate available as 250 mg amoxicillin/125 clavulanate chewable tablets, 500 mg amoxicillin/125 mg clavulanate chewable tablets; 250 mg amoxicillin/62.5 mg clavulanate/5 mL suspension.
i Ampicillin available as 250, 500 mg capsules; 125, 250 mg/5 mL suspension.
j Cephalexin available as 250, 500 mg capsules; 125, 250 mg/5 mL suspension.
k Cephradine available as 250, 500 mg capsules; 125, 250 mg/5 mL suspension.
l Cefadroxil available as 50 mg, 1 gm capsules; 125, 250, 500 mg/5 mL suspension.
m Cefaclor available as 250, 500 mg capsules; 125, 187, 250, 375 mg/5 mL suspension.
n Loracarbef available as 200 mg pulvules; 100 mg/5 mL suspension.
o Cefuroxime axetil available as 125, 250, 500 mg tablets; 125 mg/5 mL suspension.
p Cefixime available as 200, 400 mg tablets; 100 mg/5 mL suspension.
q Cefpodoxime available as 100, 200 mg capsules; 50, 100 mg/5 mL suspension.
r Cefprozil available as 250, 500 mg tablets; 125, 250 mg/mL suspension.
s Erythromycin available as Estolate: 125, 250 mg/5 mL suspension; ethylsuccinate available as 200, 400 mg/5 mL suspension; base available as 400 mg tablets; stearate available 250, 500 mg tablets.
t Clarithromycin available as 250, 500 mg tablets; 125, 250 mg/5 mL suspension.
u TMP-SMX = Trimethoprim-sulfamethoxazole. Regular strength tablets: 80 mg TMP/400 mg SMX; Double strength tablets: 160 mg TMP/800 mg SMX; Suspension: 40 mg TMP/200 mg SMX/5 mL.
v Erythromycin-sulfisoxazole available as 200 mg erythromycin + 600 mg sulfisoxazole/5 mL.
w Metronidazole available as 250, 500 mg tablets.
x Tetracycline available as 250, 500 mg capsules.
y Doxycycline available as 50, 100 mg capsules and tablets; 25 mg/5 mL suspension; 50 mg/5 mL syrup.
z Clindamycin available as 75, 150, 300 mg capsules; 75 mg/5 mL suspension.
aa Rifampin available as 150, 300 mg capsules; suspension can be compounded.

based upon the clinical presentation. While J.S. has been immunized against *H. influenzae* type b, most otitis media caused by *H. influenzae* is nontypable (90%) and the vaccine does not confer protection against nontypable strains. Tympanocentesis, a procedure in which the tympanic membrane is punctured and an aspirate of middle ear fluid is obtained, can be performed but is not done routinely because it is quite painful. Since most bacterial disease is caused by *S. pneumoniae*, *H. influenzae*, and *M. catarrhalis*, antibiotic therapy often is prescribed empirically which will be effective against these most common pathogens (see Table 97.3).

Resistant strains of *H. influenzae* and *M. catarrhalis* have become more prevalent. These organisms produce beta-lactamase enzymes which inactivate beta-lactam antibiotics that are not beta-lactamase stable (see Table 97.3). In the geographical region that J.S. lives in, over 50% of *H. influenzae* and 95% of *M. catarrhalis* isolates are beta-lactamase producers. It is important to know the local resistance patterns of these common pathogens. Of increasing concern is the emerging resistance of *S. pneumoniae*. This organism has developed multiple mechanisms of resistance to commonly used antibiotics such as erythromycin, TMP-SMX, and beta-lactams. Erythromycin and TMP-SMX resistance has been increasing in Europe and in the U.S. and varies depending upon local susceptibility patterns. Accurate determination of the relative rate of resistance of pneumococcus against these two antibiotics is difficult since susceptibility testing is not routinely performed in the central Texas community that J.S. lives in. *Streptococcus pneumoniae* resistance to penicillin and other beta-lactam antibiotics has become increasingly evident in the U.S.[20] and central Texas. The mechanism of *S. pneumoniae* resistance is a genetic alteration in the penicillin-binding protein which decreases the affinity of beta-lactam antibiotics for its target site and is not mediated through beta-lactamase production. In the central Texas region where J.S. lives, nearly 25% of *S. pneumoniae* isolates have developed ''relative resistance'' to penicillin [minimum inhibitory concentration (MIC) 0.12 to 1.0 mg/L] with only 3% having ''high level resistance'' to penicillin (MIC >1.0 mg/L).

Treatment

Antibiotic Therapy

3. Why was amoxicillin/clavulanate a good (or poor) choice for the treatment of the otitis media 3 months ago in J.S.?

Many clinicians strongly advocate a stepped approach to the antimicrobial therapy of acute otitis media. This approach would indicate that J.S. should have been initially treated with amoxicillin or trimethoprim-sulfamethoxazole at the doses listed in Table 97.3. If the initial antibiotic regimen does not reduce symptoms within two to three days, then therapy should be switched to a broad-spectrum, beta-lactamase stable oral antibiotic. If the initial antibiotic regimen does not reduce symptoms within two to three days, then a change in therapy should be considered. If amoxicillin was used initially, potential beta-lactamase inactivation could be the cause for failure and a switch to a broad-spectrum, beta-lactamase stable antibiotic would be appropriate. If TMP-SMX was used initially, potential multidrug resistance, as well as the bacteriostatic mechanism of TMP-SMX, may be the cause for failure and a switch to a bactericidal agent such as a beta-lactam agent would be appropriate. However, J.S. lives in a community with a relatively high resistance pattern with over 50% of *H. influenzae* and 95% of *M. catarrhalis* strains producing beta-lactamase enzymes. Thus amoxicillin would be ineffective against otitis media caused by these resistant strains and the choice of amoxicillin/clavulanate as initial therapy in J.S. may be appropriate due to the relative resistance patterns in the community. Recently, even a single 50

mg/kg dose of ceftriaxone has been shown to be as effective as ten days of amoxicillin.[21] While such a treatment strategy seems appealing, it may lead to further bacterial resistance in the future. The cost of an initial treatment failure is higher than merely the cost of the initial antibiotic; the caregiver may have to miss additional days at work and also must pay for another physician visit. In communities where the *H. influenzae* beta-lactamase resistance is less than 30% to 40%, amoxicillin remains the drug of choice as initial therapy for acute otitis media.[22]

Table 97.3 summarizes the available oral agents which are commonly used to treat otitis media. Selection of the most appropriate agent should be guided by several factors: 1) clinical efficacy, 2) side effect and toxicity profile, 3) optimal compliance factors, and 4) cost, respectively. Clinical efficacy for the treatment of otitis media should be established in patient populations in which the drug is intended to be used. Nearly all antibiotics in Table 97.3 have published data documenting their efficacy in the treatment of otitis media.[22] The side effect and toxicity profile should be taken into consideration when selecting an agent since the treatment could be worse than the disease. It is difficult to prospectively predict which patient is going to develop a particular side effect to any given antibiotic, thus side effect profiles of the oral antibiotics become a secondary consideration. J.S. has a history of diarrhea from amoxicillin/clavulanate that should be noted and taken into consideration. Compliance to the medication regimen is essential for optimal results. The regimen should have a convenient dosing schedule and storage requirements, palatable taste, minimal side effects, and affordable price. J.S. is in daycare fulltime, therefore a medication that only has to be given twice a day would eliminate the need for a mid-day dose at daycare. The taste of antibiotic suspensions is somewhat subjective; however, there has been a controlled study evaluating their palatability.[23] Therapy must be individualized based upon specific patient and antibiotic characteristics.

4. What would be the recommended antibiotic treatment for the current episode of otitis media in J.S.?

J.S. requires antibiotic therapy for two separate infections. The right ear represents an acute otitis media and the left ear represents a chronic asymptomatic middle ear effusion which also should be treated. The strategies for the management of each separate process need to be reviewed to determine the best overall plan.

Acute Otitis Media. The acute otitis media present in the right ear of J.S. can be treated with many of the antibiotics listed in Table 97.3. A systematic, individualized approach allows flexibility while optimizing therapeutic outcome. The first consideration must be based upon the identification of those drugs that are effective against the major pathogens (*S. pneumoniae*, *H. influenzae*, and *M. catarrhalis*). This would eliminate the natural penicillins, penicillinase-resistant penicillins, tetracyclines, rifampin, and erythromycin. Second, identify the drugs that would be more likely to be associated with a greater probability of side effects for the specific patient to be treated. In the case of J.S., amoxicillin/clavulanate (Augmentin) caused significant diarrhea, cefixime (Suprax) and oral cefuroxime (Ceftin) also tend to cause increased diarrhea; and erythromycin/sulfisoxazole (Pediazole) can cause gastrointestinal (GI) upset. Therefore, these drugs should be avoided in J.S. Nevertheless, all drugs have side effects and the clinician and patient must agree on which would be the most tolerable. The third consideration should focus on the drugs most likely to facilitate the patient's compliance to therapy. Erythromycin/sulfisoxazole, amoxicillin, amoxicillin/clavulanate, and cefaclor (Ceclor) require every six to eight hour dosing. Generic erythromycin/sulfisoxazole suspensions taste bad while cefaclor has been favored in taste evaluations.[23] Cefixime (Suprax), loracarbef (Lorabid), and trimethoprim-sulfamethoxazole (Bactrim) do not require refrigeration. Cost of amoxicillin and trimethoprim-sulfamethoxazole is much less than the newer cephalosporins and amoxicillin/clavulanate. Efficacy should be the most important factor in selecting the agent for therapy. An agent such as loracarbef, cefpodoxime (Vantin), cefprozil (Cefzil), or Cefuroxime (Ceftin) may be the best alternatives for therapy in J.S. Pricing could become important in selection of one of these agents over another. In this particular situation, loracarbef was the least expensive of these four drugs at the pharmacy where J.S. obtains her prescriptions. Therefore, loracarbef would be the preferred agent for her acute otitis media. Treatment for acute otitis media is usually for 10 to 14 days but there are no data to support this length of treatment over shorter courses of three to five days[24,25] or a single intramuscular injection of ceftriaxone.[21]

There have been many comparative trials between the various alternative antibiotic agents for the treatment of otitis media which report conflicting results in support of superior antibiotic agent(s). Cefaclor has been implicated as an inferior alternative agent in comparative trials, however, due to differences in study design, patient enrollment demographics, and subjective outcome variable assessments it is difficult to place much emphasis on these studies for the purposes of antibiotic selection clinically.[22]

Chronic otitis media with effusion which is representative of the process occurring in J.S.'s left ear should be considered a candidate for further antibiotic therapy if it exists for greater than two to three months after the acute otitis media infection.[26] The presence of a persistent effusion suggests chronic infection in the middle ear. The typical pathogens are the same as for acute otitis media except there should be higher suspicion of resistant organisms. The same systematic approach should be taken when evaluating antibiotic therapy for chronic otitis media which is present in J.S.'s left ear. A similar thought process would identify loracarbef for 10 to 14 days as preferred agent over cefpodoxime or cefprozil based upon cost at J.S.'s pharmacy. Single dose ceftriaxone has not been evaluated for chronic otitis media and would not be a therapeutic option for J.S.'s left ear infection. Middle ear effusions that do not resolve after a second course of antibiotic therapy should be evaluated for more aggressive adjunctive therapy or surgical correction. In this particular case, the treatment strategies for the infections in each of J.S.'s ears overlap and a single drug (loracarbef) can be used to treat both ears.

The effectiveness of the prescribed therapy should be evaluated based upon the resolution of symptoms and by otoscopic examination. The patient should be monitored for adverse drug effects based upon knowledge of the potential risk of the individual agent prescribed. The common side effects of the available oral antibiotics are described in Table 97.3. The efficacy of loracarbef therapy would be monitored in J.S. by observing for the resolution of presenting symptoms such as irritability, fever, anorexia, and tugging on the ear. Periodic otoscopic examination of the ears would provide direct evidence of infection resolution, particularly in the left ear which was asymptomatic. Monitoring for side effects and toxicity of loracarbef should focus on any gastrointestinal complaints such as vomiting and diarrhea, or any dermatologic reaction such as rash. The low incidence of hepatic and bone marrow toxicity does not warrant routine monitoring of liver function tests or complete blood count during short course treatments (<3 weeks) in otherwise healthy children.

Adjunctive Therapy

5. Would any adjunctive therapies be beneficial in J.S.?

The role of adjunctive therapies (i.e., decongestants, antihistamines, and corticosteroids) in the treatment of otitis media remains controversial. Since J.S. has both an acute and chronic otitis media, the potential benefits of adjunctive therapies on both types of infections should be considered. Multiple clinical studies have failed to demonstrate any benefit of oral or topical decongestants in the treatment of acute otitis media.[22,28] Decongestants and antihistamines may be of partial benefit in the prevention of otitis media in infants and children who have a significant allergic component causing upper airway congestion.[28] J.S. does not have a history of allergies and her episodes are not associated with a particular allergy season; thus, decongestants would not be considered a potential adjunctive therapy to reduce future episodes of otitis media in J.S.

Corticosteroids. The use of oral corticosteroids in conjunction with oral antibiotic therapy has been demonstrated to resolve bilateral middle ear effusion of chronic otitis media more effectively than antibiotics alone.[29,30] Since J.S. has a persistent middle ear effusion in her left ear, the addition of prednisone 5 mg twice a day (1 mg/kg/day) for the last seven days of loracarbef therapy may improve the resolution of effusion and be more cost effective than surgical intervention.[30] The use of corticosteroids is not without risk and some clinicians may wait until a course of antibiotics alone has failed to resolve the effusion before giving a trial of corticosteroids. However, corticosteroids without concurrent antibiotic therapy did not improve the resolution of middle ear effusion.[30]

Sinusitis

Acute Sinusitis

Clinical Presentation

6. P.L., a 4-year-old, 16 kg male from Austin, Texas, complains of headache, runny nose, cough, decreased appetite, and fever. He has had a cold for more than a week but has noted an increase in dried mucous nasal secretions that has changed from clear to a greenish-yellow appearance. P.L. has a history of recurrent otitis media: his last episode 13 months ago resolved when treated with amoxicillin/clavulanate (Augmentin). He is taking no medications and has no previous history of allergies. On physical examination, P.L. has a temperature of 102.6 °F (oral), maxillary tenderness, purulent green-yellow nasal discharge, and a mildly erythematous throat without evidence of exudates. The examination of his ear is normal. Laboratory tests indicate a white blood cell (WBC) count of 17,000/mm³ with 82% neutrophils, 10% lymphocytes, 5% monocytes, and 3% eosinophils. Sinus x-rays indicate bilateral opaque maxillary sinuses suggestive of sinusitis. What are the clinical observations in P.L. that suggest he may have sinusitis?
[SI units: WBC count 17 × 10⁹/L with 0.82 neutrophils, 0.05 lymphocytes, 0.05 monocytes, and 0.03 eosinophils]

P.L. has several distinct features of acute sinusitis. The history of an upper respiratory infection with excessive nasal discharge and cough that has persisted for over a week suggests the possibility of a secondary bacterial sinus infection. The fever and decreased appetite in P.L. are suggestive of systemic illness. The history of increased nasal discharge which has changed color to a greenish-yellow is often a sign of secondary bacterial sinusitis, although the nasal discharge also may be clear and nonpurulent. P.L. has headache which is a common symptom in adults with sinusitis but is rarely present in pediatric cases of sinusitis.[31] Maxillary tenderness and the bilateral opaque maxillary sinuses on radiography suggest maxillary sinus involvement and the erythematous throat is most likely due to postnasal mucous drip from the sinuses and nasopharynx. Although WBC counts are not routinely needed or obtained for the diagnosis of sinusitis, P.L. has an elevated white blood cell count with a predominance of neutrophils which is suggestive of bacterial infection.

Microbiology

7. What are the most likely pathogens causing sinusitis in P.L.?

Sinusitis and otitis media are very similar disease processes. Both infections involve the malfunction of the physiologic drainage of an anatomical cavity in the upper respiratory tract. It is only logical that the pathogenic organisms of sinusitis are nearly identical to otitis media. *S. pneumoniae*, *H. influenzae*, and *M. catarrhalis* are the most common bacterial organisms and are probably the cause of sinusitis in P.L.[32] Like otitis media, cultures of the nasopharynx do not correlate with the causative pathogens in the sinuses or middle ear and would be of limited clinical value in identifying the causative organism in P.L.[31] Also, similar to otitis media, obtaining sinus cultures requires direct aspiration of the sinus cavity and would subject P.L. to a rather painful procedure. Therefore, antimicrobial therapy is commonly prescribed empirically directed against the most common pathogens.

Treatment

Antibiotic Therapy

8. What treatment options are available for P.L. and which would be recommended?

Since the pathophysiology and microbiology of sinusitis and otitis media are similar, the treatment options that were discussed in Questions 3 and 4 for J.S.'s otitis media also pertain to therapy for P.L. The sinusitis in P.L. could be treated with any of the oral antibiotic agents in Table 97.3 that are effective against *S. pneumoniae*, *H. influenzae*, and *M. catarrhalis*. Amoxicillin is commonly recommended as the initial empiric therapy for acute sinusitis. Unfortunately, P.L. lives in the same community as J.S. (from Questions 1 to 5) which has a high incidence of beta-lactamase producing *H. influenzae* and *M. catarrhalis*; thus amoxicillin may be ineffective as initial therapy in P.L. The selection of a particular drug must be individualized as described in the treatment of otitis media and should include assessment of efficacy, side effects and toxicity, compliance factors, and cost. P.L. has a history of recurrent otitis media and probably has been treated with several courses of oral antibiotics for those infections. A detailed drug history from P.L.'s mother may elicit information which could help guide antibiotic selection for his current sinus infection. P.L. was treated with amoxicillin/clavulanate for his last episode of otitis media which has not recurred for 13 months; therefore, it may be a reasonable choice for the treatment of his current sinusitis. Treatment may be discontinued after 10 to 14 days if a complete response has been observed; however, any residual signs or symptoms such as nasal discharge (clear or purulent), cough, fever, or headaches, mandate an additional seven to ten days of antibiotic therapy.[31,32]

Adjunctive Therapy

9. What adjunctive therapy should be prescribed for P.L.?

P.L. has no history of allergies and the current episode was associated with a preceding upper respiratory tract infection; therefore, decongestants and antihistamines would not be of benefit in the treatment of his sinusitis.[33] In patients with a significant allergic history and nasal congestion, decongestants and antihistamines can reduce congestion and the risk of secondary bacterial sinusitis.[34] Corticosteroids have not been studied in the treatment of sinusitis. Patients that use intranasal corticosteroids for allergic rhinitis are at increased risk for fungal sinusitis. Therefore, P.L. should not be prescribed medications other than his antibiotic.

Chronic Sinusitis

Antibiotic Therapy

10. Three months later P.L. returns with a similar presentation and a history of nearly 2 months of continuous nasal discharge and cough. His symptoms reappeared about 1 week after the discontinuation of his antibiotic therapy and have progressively worsened. What considerations would be appropriate in the selection of an antimicrobial for P.L. at this visit?

P.L. has chronic sinusitis with persistent symptoms of nasal discharge, cough, and headaches for more than six weeks. P.L. may have a sinus infection caused by more atypical organisms such as *Staphylococcus aureus*, *Streptococcus pyogenes*, or anaerobes;[31] or he also may have developed a chronic infection with a resistant organism. Penicillin-resistant strains of *S. pneumoniae*, *M. catarrhalis*, and *H. influenzae* were identified in over 50% of children with chronic sinusitis.[33] While *M. catarrhalis* and *H. influenzae* convey their penicillin resistance through beta-lactamase production, *S. pneumoniae* has developed penicillin resistance because of alterations in its penicillin-binding protein. Therefore, penicillin-resistant *S. pneumoniae* cannot be treated with the addition of a beta-lactamase inhibitor such as clavulanate to the penicillin.

The selection of an appropriate antimicrobial for P.L. should be determined again by a systematic approach to the important factors: efficacy, side effects and toxicity, compliance factors, and cost. The antimicrobial should be effective against both the typical and atypical organisms described above. Amoxicillin/clavulanate (Augmentin) has the most comprehensive staphylococcidal and anaerobic activity of the broad-spectrum oral antibiotics and may be preferred based upon efficacy.[32] However, the selection of the most effective antimicrobial is more difficult this time for P.L. because he was previously treated with amoxicillin/clavulanate (40 mg/kg/day amoxicillin) for 21 days and has a recurrence of the sinusitis. A careful medication history should be obtained to assess the compliance to the previous amoxicillin/clavulanate therapy.

11. Medication History. P.L.'s parents describe a period of 5 days during which P.L. was at his grandparents' house and the medicine was not refrigerated. How does this information affect the choice of an antimicrobial for P.L. at this time?

Amoxicillin/clavulanate loses significant potency if unrefrigerated for more than 24 hours[34] and may have negatively impacted on the effectiveness of the previous treatment. Based upon this information, it may be appropriate to prescribe another 21-day course of amoxicillin/clavulanate for P.L. with additional patient counseling on the proper storage and administration of this medication. Likewise, it may be prudent to switch to an agent that does not require refrigeration and has a less frequent dosing schedule to enhance compliance if P.L. is likely to be at his grandparents' home during this time. Cefixime (Suprax) does not require refrigeration, but it may be only marginally effective against *S. aureus* and *S. pneumoniae*.[35] Cefprozil (Cefzil), cefpodoxime (Vantin), and cefuroxime (Ceftin) can be given every 12 hours, but all of these require refrigeration and their efficacy in the treatment of sinusitis needs further study. Trimethoprim-sulfamethoxazole is not effective against *S. pyogenes* and is less palatable than Augmentin or Suprax. Amoxicillin without clavulanate would not be effective against beta-lactamase producing organisms and requires every eight hour dosing. Cefaclor has been associated with treatment failures with beta-lactamase producing *M. catarrhalis* and *H. influenzae*,[36] requires refrigeration, and every eight hour dosing. Loracarbef also has limited data in the treatment of sinusitis but does not require refrigeration and can be given every 12 hours. Thus it becomes difficult to make a "most appropriate" selection but, keeping in mind that efficacy is the most important factor, amoxicillin/clavulanate and loracarbef seem to be the best options for

P.L. If refrigeration was not a concern, cefpodoxime, cefuroxime, and cefprozil also would be reasonable options.

The newer macrolide antibiotics, clarithromycin and azithromycin, could also be considered for P.L. Clarithromycin is available in a suspension and has been studied in other upper respiratory tract infections (otitis media and pharyngitis).[117,118] Five day courses of azithromycin have reported effectiveness in upper respiratory tract infections including sinusitis[119,120] but would not be a reasonable choice since it is not available in a suspension form.

Pharyngitis
Clinical Presentation

12. T.R. is a 14-year-old, 52 kg, male with a severe sore throat and fever. He states that the sore throat developed yesterday afternoon and was extremely painful when he woke up this morning. He is an otherwise healthy 8th grader with no history of allergies. Several of his classmates have been absent from school with sore throats in the last several weeks. T.R. has 2 younger brothers ages 5 and 8 and the 8 year old (C.R.) had pharyngitis 2 weeks ago that was treated with TMP-SMX. On physical examination, T.R.'s throat is erythematous with exudative patches. He has a fever of 102 °F (oral) and a respiratory rate of 30 breaths/min. Laboratory results indicate a positive streptococcal rapid antigen test of the throat. What is the likelihood that T.R. has a bacterial pharyngitis rather than a viral pharyngitis?

Differentiation between viral and bacterial pharyngitis is difficult because many of the signs and symptoms overlap considerably. Several features of T.R.'s presentation are suggestive of bacterial pharyngitis. T.R. describes a history of a family member treated for bacterial pharyngitis as well as several friends at school with sore throats (which is suggestive of an epidemic). Epidemic outbreaks of bacterial or viral pharyngitis in the community should be taken into consideration when evaluating pharyngitis in T.R. The rapid onset of symptoms, an associated high fever, and the classic exudative patches in the throat all suggest bacterial infection, however, these findings also can occur with viral etiologies. Rapid streptococcal antigen tests are throat swab tests that identify the presence of streptococcal antigens. The positive rapid streptococcal antigen test in T.R. indicates with high probability a bacterial etiology although there is a low incidence of false positives with these screening tests and a negative result would not indicate a nonbacterial infection. These screening tests provide results in ten minutes to several hours, but are only positive in about 85% of cases of streptococcal pharyngitis.[37] In patients with a negative rapid streptococcal antigen test, a throat culture should be obtained to confirm the diagnosis of bacterial pharyngitis.[37] Since T.R. has a positive rapid streptococcal antigen test as well as a history and physical examination suggestive of streptococcal pharyngitis, throat culture is not necessary and antimicrobial treatment should be considered.

Microbiology

13. What common causative viral and bacterial organisms could be responsible for T.R.'s pharyngitis?

T.R. has a clinical presentation highly suggestive of a bacterial etiology but pharyngitis is caused by viruses over 50% of the time.[38] Adenovirus and enterovirus are the most common, but parainfluenza, influenza, and Epstein-Barr viruses also can cause pharyngitis (see Table 97.2). Viral cultures are rarely ordered for pharyngitis because specific drugs are not available to treat these viruses and therapy is largely symptomatic. If T.R. did have viral pharyngitis, oral analgesics such as acetaminophen and ibuprofen could be used to relieve the pain and fever; aspirin should be avoided during acute viral infections to minimize concern about potential Reye's syndrome (see Chapter 95: Pediatric Considerations). Topical anesthetic sprays also can provide symptomatic pain relief but will not reduce fever and require frequent administration.

Group A beta hemolytic streptococci (GABHS), also known as *Streptococcus pyogenes*, accounts for a vast majority of all bacterial pharyngitis and is the most likely pathogen in T.R. The rapid streptococcal antigen test specifically identifies GABHS antigen and is highly suggestive of GABHS pharyngitis when the screening test is positive, as it is in T.R. Other less frequent causes of bacterial pharyngitis are listed in Table 97.2. *Diphtheria* should only be considered in unimmunized or immigrant patients.

Complications of Group A Beta Hemolytic Streptococci (GABHS) Infection

14. Why should antimicrobial therapy be prescribed to treat T.R.'s bacterial pharyngitis?

Bacterial pharyngitis is a self-limiting infection which usually resolves in several days without treatment in nearly all patients. A few patients develop a suppurative, toxin-related, or immunologic complication from acute GABHS pharyngitis. Suppurative complications (e.g., peritonsillar abscess, cervical lymphadenitis, otitis media, mastoiditis, and sinusitis) can occur secondary to pharyngitis.[39]

Episodes of invasive GABHS bacteremia caused by virulent serotypes of GABHS have been increasing in the U.S. These data suggest that, the virulence patterns of GABHS are significant in the development of suppurative complications. GABHS is classified by M types; M-1, M-3, and M-18 isolates have been associated with increased incidence of invasive disease.[40] Unfortunately, M-type serotyping is not available in clinical laboratories and it is unknown whether T.R. is infected with one of these invasive isolates.

Scarlet fever is an example of a toxin-mediated complication of GABHS. While scarlet fever has become nearly nonexistent in the U.S., a new streptococcal toxic-shock syndrome has emerged secondary to GABHS infections.[41] Only 10% to 20% of cases of this toxin-mediated illness have occurred after pharyngitis, but severe multisystem organ failure has resulted and it is difficult to prospectively predict whether T.R. will develop this morbid complication. The immunologic complications of GABHS infections (i.e., acute rheumatic fever and rheumatic heart disease) have declined over the last several decades in the U.S. despite occasional regional outbreaks.[42] Highly rheumatogenic strains (M-1, M-3, and M-18) have been implicated in the pathogenesis of acute rheumatic fever which may explain these outbreaks.[42] Although these complications of GABHS are associated with high morbidity, they can be prevented by antibiotic treatment of the GABHS infection.[37]

Another immunologic complication of GABHS infection is the development of post-streptococcal glomerulonephritis. Antibiotic treatment of the GABHS infection does not appear to have a direct effect on the reduction of this complication, however, antibiotic treatment does decrease the spread of infection and may indirectly decrease the incidence of this complication through decreased spread of disease.[37]

Treatment of the GABHS pharyngitis in T.R. with an antimicrobial would rapidly reduce symptoms and decrease the transmission of the infection to others. Therefore, the rapid initiation of antibiotic therapy should be prescribed for T.R. If the avoidance of rheumatic fever were the only concern, protective effects of antibiotic treatment could be delayed for up to nine days without a marked effect on the decreased rate of progression to acute rheumatic fever.[43]

Treatment

Antibiotic Therapy

15. What antibiotic and duration is most appropriate for the treatment of T.R.'s pharyngitis?

Since T.R. has an apparent GABHS pharyngitis, antibiotic therapy should be instituted. GABHS is an exquisitely sensitive organism to all beta-lactam antibiotics, including penicillin. Since nearly all oral antibiotics in Table 97.3 are effective against GABHS, other factors such as side effects, compliance, and cost become the determining factors in selecting the most appropriate therapy for T.R. Penicillin has long been the treatment of choice because of its low side effect profile and cost. Twice daily penicillin regimens are as effective as four times daily regimens for the treatment of GABHS pharyngitis.[44] However, once daily penicillin therapy is not effective,[45] thus many clinicians are hesitant to prescribe twice daily penicillin since only minor noncompliance may relegate the therapy ineffective and the cost difference between twice daily versus three or four times daily regimens is minimal. Nearly all oral antibiotics in Table 97.3 have clinical data to support their use in the treatment of GABHS pharyngitis.[46] The cephalosporins have fewer treatment failures than penicillin V, however, the difference probably is clinically insignificant.[47] In patients who are allergic to penicillins and/or beta-lactams, erythromycin is considered the alternative agent of choice, largely based upon cost. Since T.R. is not allergic to penicillin, it is the most cost effective therapy for his GABHS pharyngitis.

A five-day course of the new macrolide azithromycin has equivalent clinical and bacteriologic cure rates compared to a ten-day course of penicillin for the treatment of streptococcal pharyngitis, however the effectiveness of the five-day regimen in reducing subsequent rheumatic fever could not be determined from the study results and, therefore, cannot be recommended.[121]

T.R. should take oral penicillin for a ten-day course to achieve the maximal benefit of reducing the risk of subsequent rheumatic fever. The pharyngitis symptoms should rapidly resolve after 24 to 48 hours of penicillin therapy, but the drug should be continued for the full ten-day course. Shorter courses of therapy have unacceptably high relapse rates which may be associated with increased risk of rheumatic fever.[37,47] Clinical trials to evaluate the direct effect of treatment course duration on rheumatic fever reduction need enormous numbers of patients, and not until there is vast clinical use of a particular agent will there be a definitive answer to the issue of short-course antibiotic regimens for GABHS pharyngitis. Thus, a ten-day course of penicillin is recommended for T.R.

Prophylaxis of Household Members

16. Should efforts be made to eradicate Group A *Streptococcus* from T.R.'s household? What therapeutic regimen should be used if eradication is appropriate?

There have been two documented cases of streptococcal pharyngitis in T.R.'s household in the last two weeks and there may be a rationale for prophylaxis therapy of the household to reduce the spread to other family members. A "ping pong" effect of recurrent infections could develop in the household. However, this "ping-pong" effect is not common and routine prophylaxis of households with multiple cases of GABHS pharyngitis is not necessary. Since there is no family history of rheumatic fever, there has not been a documented reinfection of a family member, and T.R.'s family has not requested it, prophylaxis therapy to eradicate GABHS from the household is not indicated. If prophylaxis was indicated, the entire family would have cultures taken and a course of penicillin would be prescribed to all culture-positive individuals.

Table 97.4	The Modified Jones Criteria for the Diagnosis of Acute Rheumatic Fever
Clinical Findings	**Description**
Major Manifestations	
Carditis	Carditis usually manifests as a valvulitis and is associated with a systolic or diastolic murmur. Myocarditis and pericarditis in the absence of a murmur are not likely
Polyarthritis	Frequently in the larger joints and migratory in nature. Classically responds to salicylates within 48 hr
Chorea	Involuntary movements of the trunk or extremities which tend to have a delayed appearance
Erythema marginatum	The rash is a rare occurrence and is transitory and migrant. The lesions are nonpruritic, round with a pale center, and occur mostly on the trunk
Subcutaneous nodules	Firm, painless nodules develop over bony surfaces such as the elbows and knees. They move freely and are not inflamed. Most often seen in patients with carditis
Minor Manifestations	
Arthralgia	Arthralgia is a joint pain without evidence of inflammation, which would be arthritis
Fever	A temperature of at least 39 °C that usually occurs early in the course of the disease
Elevated erythrocyte sedimentation rate	↑ acute-phase reactant that is relatively nonspecific
Elevated C-reactive protein	↑ acute-phase reactant that is more specific than ESR
Prolonged PR interval	Nonspecific finding suggestive of carditis. Does not predict development of chronic heart disease
Evidence of Antecedent Group A Streptococcal Infection	
(+) Throat culture	Does not differentiate between acute infection and carrier state. Only positive in about 25% of acute rheumatic fever patients
(+) Rapid streptococcal antigen screen	Does not differentiate between acute infection and carrier state. Relatively specific but lacks sensitivity. Negative results need to be confirmed with culture
Elevated or rising antibody titers	A ≥2 dilution ↑ in titers is suggestive of recent infection. Antistreptolysin O and Anti-DNase B are the most common. Antistreptolysin O titers >320 Todd units and Anti-DNase titers >240 Todd units generally are considered elevated in children

Penicillin may be given orally for ten days at doses recommended in Table 97.3 or a single intramuscular injection of benzathine penicillin (600,000 units if <30 kg or 1,200,000 units if >30 kg) may be preferred to assure compliance. If eradication has not been achieved with two successive courses of penicillin, then rifampin 20 mg/kg/day (maximum: 300 mg) once or twice a day for the last four days of the penicillin treatment eradicated GABHS from the upper respiratory tract.[48,49]

Rheumatic Fever/Endocarditis

Clinical Presentation and Diagnosis

17. Three days later, the 8-year-old younger brother of T.R., C.R. (whose episode of pharyngitis 2 weeks ago was treated with TMP-SMX) now complains of joint pain in his knees and wrists. He also has a fever of 102 °F (oral) and a rash on his thighs and stomach. On physical examination he has a heart rate of 90 beats/min, and a respiratory rate of 24 breaths/min. On cardiac examination there is a mitral valve regurgitation murmur and inflamed hot knees that are painful and non-weight bearing. The rash is a nonpruritic rash with distinct disk-like borders. Laboratory test indicate a erythrocyte sedimentation rate (ESR) of 120 mm/hr, WBC count of 28,700 cells/mm³, and an ASO titer of 845 Todd units. A chest x-ray indicated a normal heart size and no pulmonary edema. What signs and symptoms does C.R. have that would support the diagnosis of acute rheumatic fever?

C.R. presents with significant signs and symptoms of acute rheumatic fever. Acute rheumatic fever is diagnosed based upon clinical findings called the Modified Jones criteria (see Table 97.4).[50] C.R. had a presumed GABHS pharyngitis two weeks ago that was treated with trimethoprim-sulfamethoxazole. Trimethoprim-sulfamethoxazole is ineffective against GABHS (see Table 97.3) and C.R. remained at risk for acute rheumatic fever despite antimicrobial therapy for the initial GABHS pharyngitis. Documentation of a recent GABHS infection is important for the diagnosis of acute rheumatic fever but will not be elicited in approximately 50% of cases.[50] C.R. also must have at least one of the major criteria and two minor criteria from Table 97.4, or two major criteria, for the diagnosis of acute rheumatic fever. C.R. has several major criteria present which would be diagnostic of acute rheumatic fever including the presence of polyarthritis, erythema marginatum, and carditis. C.R. also has several of the minor criteria: fever, increased erythrocyte sedimentation rate, and leukocytosis. C.R. does not appear to have any associated cardiomegaly of congestive heart failure as evidenced by lack of edema, lethargy, tachypnea, or tachycardia and the normal heart size on chest x-ray. The onset of symptoms in C.R. is typical for acute rheumatic fever which tends to occur one to three weeks following the GABHS pharyngitis. C.R. is also within the common age range for acute rheumatic fever which peaks at age eight and occurs most frequently between the ages of 6 and 15 years.

Treatment

18. What pharmacologic treatment should be considered for T.R.'s acute rheumatic fever?

Antimicrobial and anti-inflammatory therapies should be instituted in C.R. as soon as possible. Parenteral penicillin 100,000 units/kg/day divided every six hours would be the antimicrobial therapy of choice unless C.R. is allergic to penicillins. Acceptable parenteral nonbeta-lactam alternatives against *S. pyogenes* would include erythromycin and vancomycin. The parenteral antimicrobials may be converted to an oral dosage form (see Table 97.3) after the fever resolves and the rash begins to dissipate. A full ten-day antibiotic course should be prescribed. If compliance to oral therapy cannot be assured, 1.2 million units IM benzathine penicillin can be given as a one-time dose.

C.R. also requires anti-inflammatory therapy. Aspirin in doses of 100 mg/kg/day divided every six hours reduces the fever and arthritis associated with acute rheumatic fever but there is no evidence that aspirin reduces the myocardial damage associated with acute rheumatic fever.[51] Trough salicylate concentrations should be maintained in the range of 15 to 30 mg/dL (150 to 300 mg/L) for the first three to four weeks or until the erythrocyte sedimen-

tation rate normalizes (<20 mm/hour).[52] Salicylate concentrations should be monitored after two to five days of therapy to ensure steady-state serum concentrations remain 15 to 30 mg/dL.[53] The use of corticosteroids in C.R. is not indicated and should be reserved for acute rheumatic fever patients that have severe pericarditis causing congestive heart failure symptoms.[51] Like salicylates, there are no data indicating that corticosteroids reduce myocardial or valvular damage due to acute rheumatic fever.[51] Digoxin and furosemide are indicated in the management of congestive heart failure symptoms secondary to acute rheumatic fever. The effects of digoxin may be enhanced in the infected myocardium.[54]

Prophylaxis

19. What is the incidence of rheumatic fever recurrence and what advice should C.R. be given regarding antibiotic prophylaxis?

C.R. has a 75% chance of having a recurrence of rheumatic fever if long-term antibiotic prophylaxis is not prescribed.[55] Therefore, long-term penicillin prophylaxis should be initiated either as regularly scheduled benzathine penicillin intramuscular injections or daily oral penicillin.[56] Prophylactic antibiotic regimens for acute rheumatic fever patients and recommendations for penicillin-allergic patients summarized in Table 97.5 and extensively presented in Chapter 57: Endocarditis. Intramuscular benzathine penicillin should be given every three weeks or every four weeks for the prophylaxis of rheumatic fever: the four-week regimens are recommended in the U.S.[56] Although increased allergic reactions with intramuscular penicillin injections have been suspected, clinical studies have not been able to document the increased risk.[57] Intramuscular benzathine penicillin given every three or four weeks can improve compliance; however, young children such as C.R. often are reluctant to receive repeated intramuscular injections and oral therapy is preferred. Long-term prophylaxis may be discontinued after ten years or when C.R. reaches adolescence if he has no other episodes of rheumatic fever during that time period.[58] Since C.R. has evidence of rheumatic heart disease as well, he should be educated about secondary antibiotic prophylaxis before minor surgical procedures or instrumentation. Since C.R. is taking long-term penicillin prophylaxis, secondary prophylaxis during increased risk procedures should be with an antimicrobial agent other than penicillin, ampicillin, or amoxicillin.

Table 97.5	Prophylactic Antibiotic Regimens for Acute Rheumatic Fever Patients

Long-Term Antibiotic Prophylaxis for the Prevention of Secondary Rheumatic Fever or Heart Disease

Benzathine penicillin G 1.2 million units IM Q 3–4 weeks

Penicillin V 125–250 mg PO Q 12 hr (125 mg <60 pounds >250 mg)

Sulfadiazine or sulfisoxazole 500–1000 mg QD (500 mg <60 pounds >1000 mg)

Erythromycin 250 mg Q 12 hr

Prophylaxis for Endocarditis in Patients with Rheumatic Fever or Heart Disease Already Receiving Long-Term Secondary Prophylaxis

Dental, Oral and Upper Respiratory Procedures

Erythromycin ethylsuccinate or stearate PO, 20 mg/kg before procedure and 10 mg/kg 6 hr later (*max dose*: 1 gm)

Clindamycin PO or IV, 10 mg/kg before procedure and 5 mg/kg 6 hr later (*max dose*: 300 mg)

Vancomycin IV, 20 mg/kg 1 hr before procedure and no additional dose needed (*max dose*: 1 gm)

Genitourinary and Gastrointestinal Procedures

Vancomycin IV, 20 mg/kg (*max dose*: 1 gm) *and* gentamicin IV 1.5 mg/kg (*max dose*: 80 mg) both given 1 hr before procedure and may be repeated 8 hr later at ½ the initial dose

Bronchiolitis

Clinical Presentation and Classification

20. S.M. is a 14-month-old, 11 kg, female with difficulty breathing, congestion, fever, and decreased appetite. She has a 3-day history of fussiness and low-grade fever. Yesterday she developed mild wheezing, cough, and a fever of 101 °F (rectal). She has a history of reactive airway disease which is treated with nebulized albuterol and cromolyn. On physical examination, S.M. is in moderate respiratory distress. She has decreased breath sounds and expiratory wheezes bilaterally, intercostal retractions, respiratory rate of 50 breaths/min, and a heart rate of 130 beats/min. Laboratory tests indicate the following: venous blood gas pH 7.35, pCO_2 56 mm Hg, pO_2 50 mm Hg, and a pulse oximetry reading of 90% oxygen saturation. WBC count 15,100/mm^3 with 22% neutrophils, 69% lymphocytes, and 9% monocytes. A nasal swab for respiratory syncytial virus (RSV) is positive. What presenting signs and symptoms does S.M. have which suggest that she has bronchiolitis and are any of these important in assessing the severity of disease? [SI units: pCO_2 7.46 kPa; pO_2 6.67 kPa; WBC count 15.1 × 10^9/L with 0.22 neutrophils, 0.69 lymphocytes, and 0.09 monocytes]

S.M. has several typical presenting signs and symptoms of bronchiolitis. Her history of a previous upper respiratory tract infection, as evidenced by the congestion and fever, is common in infants that develop bronchiolitis. The differentiation between bronchiolitis and an acute exacerbation of reactive airway disease is difficult and the two diseases can occur concurrently. Wheezing, tachypnea, hypoxia, and hypercapnia occur frequently with both diseases; however, fever and leukocytosis are not common in reactive airway disease. S.M. also has a positive RSV swabbing of the nares which is suggestive of RSV bronchiolitis infection.

Respiratory distress or difficulty often is classified based upon signs and symptoms and typically range from mild to moderate to severe. Important parameters to assess when evaluating the severity of disease include respiratory rate, oxygenation, carbon dioxide retention, lung auscultation, and the use of respiratory accessory muscles (see Table 97.6). S.M. has a respiratory rate of 50 breaths/minute which is increased and could be contributing to the poor oxygenation and CO_2 retention secondary to inadequate ventilation. S.M. has venous blood gas results which are not useful in evaluating the oxygenation, but are still helpful in determining his acid/base and CO_2 status. The pulse oximetry provides adequate evaluation of S.M.'s oxygenation status without the need for an arterial blood gas determination. S.M. has a low oxygenation of 90% by oximetry indicating moderate hypoxia while the venous

blood gas indicates an elevated CO_2 of 56 mm Hg indicating moderate CO_2 retention. Lung auscultation findings of decreased breath sounds and expiratory wheezing suggest moderate respiratory distress since they are present throughout the entire expiratory phase, but are not present during both inspiration and expiration. The presence of intercostal muscle retractions indicates that S.M. is using her diaphragmatic muscles to assist her respirations more than usual and is suggestive of moderate to severe respiratory difficulty. Based upon the data provided, S.M. appears to be in moderate respiratory distress. However, these clinical signs and symptoms should be monitored frequently because S.M. could develop severe respiratory distress quickly.

Treatment

Bronchodilators

21. Would inhaled bronchodilators be beneficial in improving S.M.'s respiratory status?

The efficacy of bronchodilators such as beta-agonists in infants with bronchiolitis and croup is controversial. The controversy is based upon the decreased pharmacologic effect of beta-agonists in infants less than 18 months old and on the underlying pathophysiology of viral upper respiratory tract infections. Earlier data suggested that beta-agonists did not produce significant bronchodilation in infants.[59,60] These studies suffered from the absence of an objective measure of bronchodilation in this patient population which cannot produce reliable incentive spirometry data. Efforts to objectively measure infant lung function with whole body plethysmography have failed to demonstrate a benefit of beta-agonists in this age group.[61] Since an objective measure of efficacy has not been documented, the routine use of beta-agonists does not seem justified. However, several studies have documented subjective improvement in clinical symptoms with the use of inhaled beta-agonists in infants with bronchiolitis and may justify a therapeutic trial.[62,63]

S.M. may be a candidate for a trial of inhaled beta-agonist bronchodilator therapy since she has a history of reactive airway disease (RAD) and currently is being treated with albuterol nebulizations. Acute viral respiratory infections can trigger reactive airway disease in predisposed patients such as S.M. and their use may be justified in patients with a history of RAD. A trial of albuterol or other similar beta-agonist should be initiated at 0.10 to 0.15 mg/kg/dose given as often as every 30 minutes if needed to improve respiratory status.[62,63] If a response in not observed within six hours, the benefits of continued beta-agonist nebulization ther-

Table 97.6	Classification of Pediatric Respiratory Distress		
	Mild	Moderate	Severe
Respiratory rate			
6 months–1 yr	35–45	45–55	>55
>1–5 yr	25–35	35–45	>45
>6 yr	20–30	30–40	>40
Color	Normal-pink	Pink-pale	Pale-gray-blue
Dyspnea	None or with exertion	With exertion	At rest
Lung auscultation	Equal inspiratory and expiratory phases, ↓ breath sounds, end expiratory phase wheezing	Inspiratory phase > expiratory phase, dull breath sounds, entire expiratory phase wheezing	Inspiratory phase < expiratory phase, few or no breath sounds, inspiratory and expiratory phase wheezing if breath sounds present
Accessory muscle use	None	Intercostal and subcostal retractions	Also subclavicular retractions
Oxygenation (pO_2)	Normal (O_2 saturation >95%)	Low normal (O_2 saturation 90%–95%)	↓ (O_2 saturation <90%)
Ventilation (pCO_2)	Normal	↑ (pCO_2 <35 mm Hg)	↓ (pCO_2 >45 mm Hg)

apy should be re-evaluated. The indiscriminate use of beta-agonists is not recommended since not all patients will benefit and there have been reports of deterioration in respiratory status and oxygenation in infants with bronchiolitis who received inhaled beta-agonists.[64,65] These reactions may be related to the osmolality and pH of the nebulization solution.[66–68] For most infants with suspected bronchiolitis and wheezing, a four to six hour trial of beta-agonist nebulization should be considered. The patients' response to the therapy after this short trial period should be re-evaluated to determine whether it is beneficial and should be continued or whether it should be discontinued.

Ribavirin

22. Should ribavirin treatment be instituted in S.M.?

Ribavirin should not be instituted in S.M. at this time. There is significant controversy about the benefits and costs of ribavirin therapy in infants with RSV bronchiolitis. The patient population that should be considered for ribavirin therapy includes infants with the highest risk of complications from RSV infection such as those with congenital heart disease, chronic pulmonary disease, and immunodeficiency of prematurity.[69] Infants with repaired patent ductus arteriosus, pre-existing reactive airway disease, or born greater than 38 weeks gestation, are not considered high risk. Since S.M. is in moderate respiratory distress based upon her clinical presentation and does not have any high risk underlying disease states, she is not a candidate for ribavirin therapy.

However, S.M. could worsen over the course of the infection to a point where ribavirin may be considered. If S.M. should progress to severe respiratory distress as indicated by a rising pCO_2 (>60 mm Hg venous), decreased pH (<7.32 venous), and decreased oxygenation to the point of requiring supplemental oxygen ($<90\%$ O_2 saturation), then ribavirin should be considered.[69] The benefit of ribavirin in patients without underlying risk factors is unclear.[61]

The effectiveness of ribavirin therapy in mechanically ventilated patients is controversial but cannot be routinely recommended.[122,123] If S.M. had an underlying heart defect causing pulmonary hypertension, bronchopulmonary dysplasia requiring continuous home oxygen, or was a premature infant, ribavirin therapy potentially would be of benefit to her.[61]

Ribavirin aerosol therapy is initiated with a standard regimen of 6 gm ribavirin diluted in 300 mL of sterile water delivered by a small-particle aerosol generator over 18 to 20 hours daily for three to five days. An alternative dosing regimen has been proposed which uses higher doses for a short duration (60 mg/L for 2 hours TID for 4 days).[70] The efficacy and safety data are limited and high dose, short duration regimens cannot be recommended until further clinical data are available.

Close observation during therapy is required to assess therapeutic benefit. Ribavirin therapy may cause clinical deterioration or no benefit and, since the cost of therapy is considerable, the decision to continue ribavirin therapy should be determined on an ongoing basis. In patients that are intubated and requiring mechanical ventilation, close observation for clogging of the ventilation apparatus is essential to prevent complications such as respiratory failure and pneumothorax.[71] It may be difficult to differentiate response to therapy from the natural resolution of the infection in most patients treated with ribavirin.

23. Risks to Health Care Workers. What is the risk to healthcare workers exposed to ribavirin?

The effects of ribavirin on health care workers who are exposed to aerosolized ribavirin for prolonged periods while providing patient care primarily involve nurses and respiratory therapists. The potential teratogenicity of ribavirin has been documented in several animal species including the mouse and rat. Oral doses ranging from 1 to 10 mg/kg cause skeletal and gastrointestinal malformations as well as reduce the survival of offspring when given to pregnant rodents. These studies administered oral doses far exceeding the amount that a health care worker may become exposed to. Also, studies in nurses exposed to ribavirin therapy had no detectable ribavirin in the plasma or urine but detectable concentrations in circulating red blood cells.[72,73] Based largely upon these findings, recommendations regarding the exposure of health care workers to ribavirin have been established.[73] Health care workers (male or female) that are planning to have a child should avoid ribavirin therapy patient care. Brief occupational exposure by pharmacists, custodians, phlebotomists, and other health care workers is too low to be of genuine risk.

The methods of ribavirin aerosolization are currently being improved to reduce the environmental exposure of ribavirin. Containment chambers are preferred over mist and oxygen tents, while direct administration via endotracheal tube mechanical ventilation virtually eliminates the environmental risk because it is a closed system.[74–76]

Adjunctive Therapies

24. What are other therapeutic alternatives for the treatment of RSV bronchiolitis in S.M.?

Several treatment alternatives other than beta-agonists and ribavirin have been proposed for bronchiolitis. Since bronchiolitis is a viral infection, antibiotics are not indicated unless signs and symptoms of a secondary bacterial infection are present. S.M.'s WBC count is increased but does not have a predominance of neutrophils suggestive of bacterial infection and his infection is most likely caused by RSV. Other bronchodilators such as ipratropium[77,78] and theophylline[79,80] have been investigated in small clinical trials and the outcomes have been discouraging; therefore, neither agent can be recommended in the management of bronchiolitis.

Corticosteroids do not have a defined role in the treatment of bronchiolitis. While several studies have indicated potential benefit from corticosteroids for bronchiolitis,[81,82] numerous studies refute their benefit.[83,84] The lack of well-controlled clinical trials in terms of patient selection, concurrent therapies, and assessment criteria have made interpretation of the studies difficult. Perhaps the most important issue when considering the use of corticosteroids in bronchiolitis is whether the patient has pre-existing reactive airway disease. The use of corticosteroids in RAD patients[85] such as S.M. who have a history and clinical presentation of RAD in conjunction with bronchiolitis, may be beneficial, particularly when used in combination with beta-agonists.[81] The use of corticosteroids alone is of marginal benefit[83,84] which suggests that the effect of corticosteroids in the treatment of bronchiolitis may be associated with their action on increased beta receptor sensitivity as well as their anti-inflammatory properties. The appropriate corticosteroid regimen has not been firmly established but relatively high doses of either methylprednisolone (2 to 4 mg/kg/day) or dexamethasone (0.4 to 0.6 mg/kg/day) for one to four days seem reasonable; however, most infants with bronchiolitis may not benefit from corticosteroid therapy because pre-existing RAD is not common in the bronchiolitis-prone population.

Croup Syndrome

Clinical Presentation and Classification

25. F.G., a 9-month-old, 8 kg, male has been brought to the emergency room (ER) because he developed difficulty breathing in his sleep and awoke crying. The parents state that F.G. was fine in the evening but had a decreased appetite before

bedtime. Around 2:00 a.m. F.G. began having breathing difficulty that was associated with a whistling noise when he inspired. F.G. was brought in when the parents noticed his lips were turning blue. On physical examination F.G. was in moderate respiratory distress with a respiratory rate of 60 breaths/min, heart rate 150 beats/min, and a temperature of 101 °F (axillary). He had moderate inspiratory stridor and very mild wheezing in the lower lung fields. Signs of cyanosis were not present when he was in the ER. What type of croup does F.G. most likely have based upon his clinical signs and symptoms?

Croup syndrome is a spectrum of upper respiratory tract infections which affect the larynx, trachea, and upper bronchial airways. There are four basic classifications of croup syndrome but they all share similar signs and symptoms: inspiratory stridor, respiratory distress, cough, and fever (see Table 97.7). Based upon frequency, age group, and clinical presentation, F.G. most likely has spasmodic croup although he could possibly have viral croup or bacterial tracheitis. The clinical presentation of the classifications overlap significantly and may represent a continuum making definitive classification difficult. F.G. does not have signs of bacterial infection as evidenced by his WBC count and lack of toxic appearance, and bacterial causes of croup are relatively rare. The implementation of early *H. influenzae* type b vaccination has significantly reduced the incidence of *H. influenzae* type b epiglottitis which is one of the most common bacterial causes of croup syndrome. Since the management of nonbacterial croup is similar, it is not critical that F.G. have a definitive diagnostic classification of spasmodic versus viral croup.

Treatment

Laryngotracheobronchitis

26. What supportive therapies may benefit F.G.?

Nonbacterial croup is a self-limiting disease that will spontaneously resolve in nearly all patients; therefore, the treatment is mainly supportive and based upon severity of symptoms. Several treatment alternatives are available to treat F.G. including nebulized epinephrine and systemic corticosteroids.

Epinephrine. Nebulized epinephrine causes local vasoconstriction of the laryngeal and tracheal tissues due to its α-adrenergic properties. Croup symptoms such as stridor, tachypnea, and cough are thought to be due to the local inflammatory swelling of the narrow airways in the larynx and trachea. Nebulized racemic epinephrine reduces symptoms in croup patients when given in doses of 2.5 to 5 mg.[86,87] The use of pure L-epinephrine is advocated. The dose of L-epinephrine is 50% less than racemic epinephrine and dosage should be corrected accordingly based upon the strength of L-epinephrine used.[87] Rebound edema and tachycardia have been associated with the use of epinephrine in croup patients. The beneficial effects of epinephrine are rapid but short-lived and symptoms can reappear one to three hours after an epinephrine treatment. Repeated epinephrine treatments can cause rebound tissue edema and the symptoms may become worse after epinephrine action has subsided. For these reasons, close monitoring of the patient is recommended and the decision to send F.G. home after receiving nebulized epinephrine treatment in the emergency room or clinic should be individualized. Patients with a telephone and who live in close proximity to a health care facility may be able to go home after responding to nebulized epinephrine treatment.[88]

Corticosteroids. Systemic corticosteroids have been used to treat croup symptoms since the primary pathophysiology of symptoms is the inflammatory swelling and narrowing of the airways. The effectiveness of corticosteroids in the treatment of croup is variable.[89] As with bronchiolitis, if a pre-existing history of atopy or reactive airway disease is present, corticosteroids may have additional benefit. If corticosteroids are considered, adequate doses (0.6 mg/kg dexamethasone as a single dose) should be used based upon data supporting increased efficacy with increased doses.[89] Since croup is generally a self-limiting disease, lasting one to three days, multiple doses of corticosteroids are not necessary or recommended. While the risks of short-term corticosteroids are few, the potential for gastrointestinal bleeding and immunosuppression need to be considered on an individual patient basis. F.G. should receive a single dose of dexamethasone 5 mg IM as soon as possible after his initial assessment if he is considered a candidate for corticosteroid therapy.

Antibiotics. Bacterial croup also incorporates the use of systemic antibiotics directed against the most common pathogens: *H. influenzae* type b, *S. aureus*, Group A *Streptococcus*, and *S. pneumoniae*. Second- and third-generation cephalosporins such as cefuroxime, cefotaxime, and ceftriaxone are active against all of these organisms. Due to the potential for rapid deterioration in patients with bacterial causes of croup, parenteral antibiotics are recommended until the patient has adequately responded to therapy. Af-

Table 97.7	Characteristics of the Different Classifications of Croup Syndrome[a,b]			
	Spasmodic Croup	Viral Croup	Bacterial Tracheitis	Supraglottitis
Synonyms	Subglottic allergic edema	Laryngotracheitis, laryngitis, LTB	Pseudomembranous croup, LTB	Epiglottitis
Frequency	Common	Most common	Less common	Rare
Age group	3 months–3 yr	3 months–3 yr	3 months–3 yr	2–8 yr
Common pathogens	None, (parainfluenza), (influenza)	Parainfluenza, adenovirus, influenza	*S. aureus, S. pyogenes, S. pneumoniae*	*H. influenzae, S. pyogenes, S. pneumoniae*
Clinical Presentation				
Onset	Rapid, nocturnal	Gradual, preceding URI	Gradual, preceding URI	Rapid
Signs and symptoms	Afebrile, cough, stridor	Fever, cough, stridor	Fever, cough, stridor, "toxic" appearance	Fever, dysphagia, drooling, stridor, "toxic" appearance
Neck radiography	Normal	Subglottic narrowing (steeple sign)	Subglottic narrowing (steeple sign)	Swollen epiglottis (thumb sign)
Laboratory	Normal	↑ WBC count, no shift	↑ WBC count, left shift, ↑ CRP	↑ WBC count, left shift, ↑ CRP

[a] Adapted with permission from the University of Kentucky College of Pharmacy Office of Continuing Education Independent Study Program entitled, Pediatric Pharmacotherapy.
[b] CRP = C-reactive protein; LTB = Laryngotracheobronchitis; URI = Upper respiratory tract infection; WBC = White blood cell.

ter the initial response and the availability of culture and sensitivity results, oral antibiotics should be considered for the remaining ten-day course of antibiotic therapy. Refer to Table 97.3 for potential alternative antibiotics based upon patient specific characteristics.

Supraglottitis

27. How does the management of F.G. differ from that of a child with epiglottitis (supraglottitis)?

F.G. has a classic presentation of nonbacterial croup syndrome. If he had a bacterial epiglottitis, his symptoms would have been markedly different and his condition would have been considered a medical emergency. Epiglottitis occurs primarily in older infants and young children and is associated with more severe symptoms including a "toxic" appearance (see Table 97.7). A "toxic" appearance is identified by the presence of signs of systemic illness such as pallor, hypotension, tachycardia, tachypnea, dehydration, and lethargy or irritability. Epiglottitis also is commonly associated with excessive drooling and a tripod positioning secondary to the inability to swallow and maintain adequate respiration, respectively. These symptoms are precursors to acute respiratory obstruction and failure, and require immediate evaluation for intubation. Empiric parenteral antibiotics as described above and in Table 97.3 should be initiated after the airway has been evaluated and maintained. The incidence of epiglottitis has decreased significantly with universal *H. influenzae* type b vaccination, however, it should be considered one of the primary bacterial pathogens causing the disease until results from epidemiological data subsequent to the availability of HIB vaccine are published.

Pertussis

Clinical Presentation

28. L.D., a 5-month-old, 5 kg, female, has been diagnosed with pertussis. What organism causes pertussis and what are the clinical stages of presentation?

Pertussis is a relatively rare respiratory infection caused by *Bordetella pertussis* that can afflict young infants or nonimmunized children and is associated with high morbidity. Vaccination with diphtheria, pertussis, tetanus toxoid (DTP) in infants has drastically reduced the incidence of pertussis, however, a vaccine shortage in the mid-1980s led to a resurgence of the disease.[90] Pertussis typically progresses through three distinct phases. The first phase is referred to as the catarrhal phase which is very difficult to differentiate from a viral upper respiratory tract infection. The typical symptoms are coryza, congestion, low grade fever, and irritability. The second phase is when the characteristic whooping cough develops and the diagnosis of pertussis generally is made. This phase can last up to two weeks and is of variable intensity from patient to patient. The final phase is referred to as the convalescent phase in which a persistent cough may last for up to three months.[90]

Treatment: Erythromycin

29. What is the drug of choice for L.D.?

The treatment for pertussis is erythromycin.[90] (See Table 97.8.) It is important to achieve maximal erythromycin concentrations for the treatment of pertussis, thus erythromycin estolate has been the preferred formulation.[91] Erythromycin estolate has been associated with increased hepatic toxicity in adults,[92] but this has not been documented to occur in children taking the estolate preparation.[93] Although serum concentrations were increased with the newer enteric-coated pellet formulations, clinical trials have not been adequate to identify their role in the treatment of pertussis. The duration of treatment should be extended to at least 14 days to assure eradication of the organism.[90] The newer macrolides, azithromycin

and clarithromycin, may have a future role in the treatment of pertussis, however there are no clinical data to support their use currently.

Prophylaxis

30. What are the benefits and risks of pertussis prophylaxis for L.D.'s siblings?

Household prophylaxis should be considered when there is a documented case of pertussis. Households with other children at risk for pertussis should have all close contacts complete a 14-day course of erythromycin to eradicate any possible carriers.[90]

Early initiation of erythromycin estolate prophylaxis and elimination of exposure to the index case can completely abort or attenuate secondary pertussis infection in exposed contacts.[124] Early erythromycin prophylaxis also reduces *Bordetella pertussis* carrier state and subsequently reduces secondary transmission which can cause epidemic outbreaks of pertussis. Although the most effective duration of prophylaxis therapy has not been established, 14 days remains the standard regimen. Even though members of L.D.'s family may have had pertussis vaccination, antibiotic prophylaxis is still recommended because the pertussis vaccine is not completely effective and the immunity from the vaccine wanes over time. Since there is little risk associated with a two-week course of erythromycin therapy, it is clearly beneficial to initiate erythromycin prophylaxis in L.D.'s family. Newer formulations of erythromycin (i.e., ERYC), as well as the newer macrolides such as clarithromycin and azithromycin, have fewer side effects (less GI upset) and may be considered for prophylaxis therapies but their effectiveness has not been documented. Until studies document their effectiveness against pertussis, they should be reserved for patients that cannot tolerate erythromycin estolate and should not be used for the treatment of active pertussis disease.

Measles

31. Measles is a relatively self-limiting disease but can be complicated by involvement of the central nervous system and the respiratory tract. What is the role for empiric prophylactic antibiotics or adjunctive therapies in the treatment of measles?

Mild cases generally are without complications, however secondary bacterial infections can occur in 5% to 15% of patients with severe cases of measles. Otitis media and bacterial pneumonia are the most common and should be monitored diligently. The occurrence of such complications does not warrant routine antimicrobial prophylaxis but very young children (<1 year), those that have a history of recurrent bacterial respiratory tract infections (otitis media, pharyngitis, bronchitis), or that require hospitalization, may warrant empiric antibiotic therapy against the common respiratory tract pathogens (see Table 97.2).

Vitamin A is an important cofactor in the immune response, particularly to acute viral infections such as measles. Measles infection also has the propensity to induce a vitamin A deficient state during the acute infection. Thus, it has been observed that children that have decreased vitamin A stores (i.e., malnourished, short bowel syndrome, cystic fibrosis) have increased morbidity and mortality from measles infection. In two studies of African children, vitamin A benefited children with severe measles.[94,95] Vitamin A 400,000 international units within five days of the onset of the rash reduced the pulmonary complications, reduced fever, decreased hospital stay, and decreased mortality as compared to a placebo group. These studies were done in Africa where vitamin A deficiency is much more prevalent than in the U.S. and it is not clear whether these results can be generalized to all children with measles. The World Health Organization does recommend vitamin

Table 97.8	Comparison of Oral Erythromycin Products[a]				
	Ethylsuccinate	Estolate	Stearate	Base Tablets	Base Pellet Capsules
Brand Names	E.E.S., EryPed, Pediamycin, Wyamycin E	Ilosone	Erypar, Erythrocin Stearate Filmtab, Wyamycin S	Erythromycin Base Filmtab, Ilotycin, Robimycin, E-mycin, Ery-Tab	ERYC, PCE Dispertab
Can be taken with food	Yes	Yes	No	No	No
Salt form dosage adjustment	Yes 400 mg = 250 mg base	No	No	No	No
Average peak serum concentrations of free base after a 250 mg base dose	0.6 mg/L (312 mg base)	0.5 mg/L	0.5 mg/L	0.5 mg/L	1.4 mg/L
Gastrointestinal upset	High	Moderate	High	High	Moderate
Hepatotoxicity	Low	Low ($\uparrow$ in adults)	Low	Low	Low
Cost per 250 mg base dose (AWP)	T = $0.16 S = $0.24	T = $0.49 S = $0.41	T = $0.09 S = N/A	T = $0.11 S = N/A	T = $0.24 S = N/A

[a] AWP = Average wholesale price; N/A = Not available; Tab = Tablet; S = Suspension.

A supplementation in cases of measles if there is a high incidence of vitamin A deficiency in the region or if the mortality rate of measles is greater than 1% (it is <1% in the U.S.). The American Academy of Pediatrics has recommended the use of vitamin A in children with measles.[96] For infants less than six months of age a single dose of 100,000 units is recommended. For infants and children more than six months of age the recommended dose is 200,000 units as a single dose. A repeat dose 24 hours and four weeks later also is recommended if the infected patient has significant vitamin A deficiency or malnutrition.

Kawasaki Disease

Clinical Presentation and Diagnosis

32. B.C., a 2-year-old, 12 kg, Asian male, has had a fever for the last 6 days. He was prescribed amoxicillin 40 mg/kg/day 4 days ago without improvement. He has become increasingly irritable, and has developed a macular papular rash over the trunk, legs, and arms. A hot, inflamed, arthritic condition in the right knee developed yesterday morning. B.C. is an otherwise healthy boy, his immunizations are current, and he has not had any contact with animals. On physical examination B.C. has a temperature of 104 °F (oral), a red, swollen tongue with a "strawberry" appearance, cracked fissures on the lips, and enlarged cervical lymph nodes. He also has bilateral injection of the conjunctiva without discharge or pain. His heart examination is normal. Laboratory tests indicate a WBC count of 22,000 cell/mm³, an ESR of 96 mm/hr, and a platelet count of 540,000 cells/mm³. What signs and symptoms would suggest the diagnosis of Kawasaki's disease in B.C.? What is the prognosis and progression of this disease? [SI units: WBC count 22 × 10⁹/L; platelets 540 × 10⁹/L]

Kawasaki's disease is a systemic vasculitis that primarily occurs in children six months to five years of age.[97] The diagnosis of Kawasaki disease in B.C. is based upon the presence of a constellation of symptoms including fever for $\geq$5 days with at least four of the following findings: 1) mucous membrane changes such as swollen "strawberry" tongue or perioral fissures; 2) cervical lymphadenopathy; 3) bilateral conjunctivitis; 4) rash; and 5) swollen hands or feet with desquamation.[97] There are several nondiagnostic characteristics such as arthritis, irritability, lack of response to antibiotic therapy, and urethritis that occur frequently and suggest the diagnosis of Kawasaki's disease. B.C. also has several typical laboratory findings suggestive of Kawasaki's disease such as an elevated ESR and platelet count. After all other possible etiologies have been ruled out such as scarlet fever, juvenile rheumatoid arthritis, and toxic shock syndrome, the diagnosis of Kawasaki's should be considered as a diagnosis of exclusion. While numerous infectious etiologies have been proposed, the cause of Kawasaki's disease remains unknown and no specific test can confirm the diagnosis in the patient. B.C. is in the *acute phase* of Kawasaki's disease which lasts one to two weeks without treatment. The acute phase is followed by a *subacute phase* in which coronary aneurysms tend to form. In the final phase, called the *convalescent phase*, the patient may be asymptomatic and the risk of aneurysm development decreases.

Kawasaki's disease is associated with high morbidity and mortality which can be significantly reduced with rapid and appropriate therapeutic management. Approximately 20% of untreated Kawasaki's disease patients will develop coronary aneurysms secondary to the disease process and about 5% will persist beyond the convalescent phase.[99] These patients are at increased risk for serious cardiac events such as myocardial infarction and/or death.[97]

Treatment

Aspirin Therapy

33. Why should B.C. be treated with aspirin?

During the initial acute phase of the disease, aspirin is prescribed as an anti-inflammatory agent to reduce coronary aneurysm development and to modify the arthritic component of the disease if it is present. There are conflicting data as to whether aspirin reduces the risk of coronary aneurysm development,[98] and the most effective dose has not been determined for this effect;[100,101] however, high doses (50 to 100 mg/kg/day) seem to provide more benefit than lower doses and are currently recommended.[100] Arthritic pain may not respond to aspirin therapy but it tends to spontaneously resolve during the convalescent phase of the disease. High-dose aspirin therapy is recommended during the acute phase of the illness and should be continued until the erythrocyte sedimentation rate is less than 20 mm/hour. During the subacute and convalescent phase, aspirin should be continued at low doses (3 to 10 mg/kg/day) for an antithrombotic effect if the patient is at increased risk for aneurysms or has documented aneurysms already present.[102] Risk factors that have been identified for the development of coronary aneurysms include: 1) Asian descent; 2) age less than 5 years; 3) fever greater than 14 days; 4) platelet count greater than 900,000/mm³; and 5) ESR greater than 100 mm/hour.[98] Dipyridamole and warfarin also have been recommended for additional antithrombotic therapy in patients that have documented persistent coronary aneurysms greater than 8 mm in size or ocular involvement.[103]

34. Dose and Monitoring. What dose of aspirin should be prescribed for B.C. and how should this therapy be monitored?

B.C. should be started on aspirin 300 mg every six hours (100 mg/kg/day). Serum salicylate concentrations should be monitored to improve efficacy and reduce potential toxicity. Target trough salicylate concentrations of 200 to 300 mg/L (20 to 30 mg/dL) have been recommended and steady state generally is achieved after 48 hours.[104] Oral absorption of aspirin can be decreased by as much as 50% in Kawasaki's disease patients and thus higher doses may be needed to achieve desired therapeutic concentrations.[104] Close monitoring of salicylate concentrations is recommended during high dose therapy since bioavailability may change during the natural course of the disease and increase the risk of salicylate toxicity. Salicylates may cause gastrointestinal bleeding and tinnitus which also should be monitored.

Intravenous Immunoglobulin (IVIG)

35. Could B.C. benefit from intravenous immunoglobulin therapy? What would be an appropriate regimen and monitoring plan for this therapy?

Intravenous immunoglobulin therapy clearly reduces the incidence of coronary aneurysms in Kawasaki's disease from approximately 20% in untreated patients to approximately 5% in patients that receive IVIG within ten days of the onset of fever.[102] Therefore, B.C. should receive IVIG therapy based upon his diagnosis of Kawasaki's disease. Several different treatment regimens have been investigated including 400 mg/kg/day for four days,[105] 1 gm/kg as a single dose,[106] and 2 gm/kg as a single dose.[107] All regimens have proven beneficial effects in Kawasaki's disease with limited data suggesting that the single dose regimens may be more effective. The 1 gm/kg dose has not been compared against the 2 gm/kg dose. The economic advantages of the single dose therapy have made this regimen favorable, although adverse effects have been reported with this aggressive regimen including isolated reports of congestive failure and hemorrhage with the high dose regimens.[106-108] IVIG generally is well tolerated by most patients and would be a reasonably cost effective regimen for B.C. As with the administration of any blood product, B.C. should be monitored closely for changes in vital signs (hypo- or hypertension, tachycardia, tachypnea) during the infusion. IVIG should be infused slowly and rates should be increased incrementally to avoid these unwanted effects. (See Chapters 95: Pediatric Considerations and 96: Neonatal Therapy for IVIG formulations.) Most patients rapidly respond to IVIG with resolution of fever, rash, and decreased ESR within 72 hours. A repeated course of IVIG may be considered if the fever has not resolved within five days after the first dose of IVIG.[109]

Rickettsial Diseases

Rickettsial diseases are infections caused by pleomorphic bacteria called Rickettsia. Rickettsia primarily infect wild and domestic animals and are transmitted to humans via ticks. The geographic and seasonal distribution of these infections mimic the presence of the tick vector. Thus, rickettsial infections are most common in the spring and summer in the midAtlantic and Rocky Mountain regions but occur in virtually every area of the country.[110] Worldwide, rickettsial diseases vary depending upon the vector and hygiene conditions present. For example, *Rickettsia japonica* is primarily isolated to Japan and *Rickettsia sibirica* is primarily found in the Siberian region of Russia. There are other rickettsial diseases such as *Rochalimaea quintana* which affect mostly Europe and Africa

and are transmitted by louse bites. *Rickettsia rickettsii* is the tick-borne pathogen responsible for Rocky Mountain Spotted Fever, the most common rickettsial disease in the Western hemisphere including the U.S. Infection by Rickettsia causes an infectious vasculitis by invading and multiplying intracellularly in endothelial cells. The tissue damage causes typical clinical manifestations of fever, rash, headache, myalgias, and respiratory symptoms. The diagnosis of Rickettsia infections is complicated by the lack of facilities in most clinical laboratories to culture the organism *in vitro* and often is based upon clinical presentation. The availability of antibody serology tests has aided the diagnosis, but these tests require acute and convalescent titers. These serological tests will not detect antibody until seven to ten days into the course of infection and are not widely available. Rickettsial infections can be treated successfully with tetracyclines or chloramphenicol if treatment is initiated early in the course of the illness. The most common rickettsial disease in humans is Rocky Mountain Spotted Fever followed by Ehrlichiosis, Q Fever, Rickettsialpox, and Typhus. Rickettsial infections are reportable to local and state health departments.

Rocky Mountain Spotted Fever (RMSF)

Clinical Presentation

36. Z.S., a 7-year-old, 26 kg, white male, has had a fever for the last several days. He complained of headache and muscle soreness 2 days ago, and began vomiting this morning. Z.S. is an active boy who loves to go camping and ride horses. On physical examination, Z.S. has a temperature of 102.3 °F and a diffuse macular papular rash with petechial lesions on the palms of his hands and soles of his feet. There was no evidence of insect or tick bites on the body. The abdomen is tense and guarded. He has a severe headache but is neurologically intact. What signs and symptoms support a diagnosis of Rocky Mountain Spotted Fever in Z.S.?

Z.S. has several characteristic signs and symptoms of Rocky Mountain Spotted Fever and his history of frequent outdoor activity, particularly around animals, provides evidence of possible exposure to a tick vector. The lack of insect or tick bites is common in patients with RMSF since the typical incubation period from the time of inoculation to presentation of symptoms is about one week.[110] Severe headache, muscle soreness, and gastrointestinal symptoms are common findings. The characteristic rash with petechial lesions on the palms and soles is highly indicative of RMSF and should prompt its consideration in the differential diagnosis. The typical fever pattern of RMSF often is erratic with high fevers (103 °F) occurring in the afternoons and evenings and relatively afebrile periods in the mornings. Signs of severe infection include hypotension due to intravascular leakage caused by the endothelial tissue damage which can cause secondary organ failure of the CNS, liver, kidneys, and lungs.[111] Fortunately Z.S. appears to have a mild infection or it is still in its early stages where treatment is most effective.

Treatment

37. What antibiotics can be used to treat RMSF in Z.S.?

Antibiotic treatment for RMSF is very limited. Only two antibiotics have demonstrated efficacy in treating RMSF, tetracyclines and chloramphenicol. Both antibiotics are only bacteriostatic against Rickettsia but are useful if given in adequate doses early in the course of the infection. The first treatment dilemma is confirming the diagnosis early since cultures are not readily available and serologic tests require acute and convalescent titers for comparison. These limitations often will not confirm the diagnosis of RMSF until seven to ten days into the illness when antibiotic therapy becomes less successful. Therefore, therapy often must be initiated based upon clinical symptoms and history. Fortunately, Z.S. has many features of RMSF which would suggest that antibiotic treatment for RMSF be initiated immediately. The second treatment decision is selection of the least toxic antibiotic, particularly for Z.S. since he is seven years old. Tetracyclines are relatively contraindicated in children less than nine years old due to teeth adsorption and discoloration.

Chloramphenicol has a narrow therapeutic index with dose limiting bone marrow toxicities which require serum chloramphenicol concentration monitoring.[112] The decision between which agent to use may depend upon the monitoring capabilities available. If chloramphenicol concentration monitoring is available, treatment can be monitored closely and Z.S. would not have to risk the potential adverse effects of tetracycline therapy. However, if chloramphenicol monitoring is not available, then the risk of potential teeth staining from a single course of a tetracycline may be preferred over the potentially serious bone marrow toxicities of chloramphenicol without proper monitoring. If tetracycline therapy were considered the best option for Z.S., doxycycline would be the preferred agent due to its preferred pharmacokinetic profile.[113] Since chloramphenicol monitoring is available for Z.S., he should receive intravenous chloramphenicol succinate 500 mg every six hours (75 mg/kg/day).

38. Monitoring. How should chloramphenicol therapy be monitored in Z.S.?

Chloramphenicol therapy requires close monitoring to minimize the risk of hematologic toxicity and improve outcome. Since Z.S. has been experiencing vomiting, parenteral chloramphenicol therapy is preferred initially. Chloramphenicol is formulated as a succinate salt in its parenteral form which is metabolized by liver esterases after injection to active chloramphenicol base. Since the esterase-mediated metabolism does not occur in muscle and connective tissue, erratic absorption and serum concentrations have been noted after intramuscular administration and it is not recommended. The plan for Z.S. should include monitoring of serum chloramphenicol concentrations.

Hematologic toxicity has been associated with chloramphenicol concentrations greater than 25 mg/L; therefore, peak levels should be kept below this limit.[114] Since parenteral chloramphenicol is administered as an inactive succinate salt, peak concentrations should not be taken until one to two hours after the end of infusion.[112] Due to the difficulty in determining when the actual peak occurs, trough concentrations of 5 to 10 mg/L have alternatively been recommended.[115]

Concentrations of chloramphenicol are best measured by high performance liquid chromatography (HPLC) since it can differentiate active chloramphenicol base from the inactive succinate, palmitate, and glucuronidated forms. Immunoassays such as EMIT detect only the active free base and are accurate and sufficient for clinical monitoring.[116] Microbiological assays suffer from interference from other antimicrobial agents in the serum and require 24 hours before results are available.

Z.S. should receive IV therapy only until oral therapy can be reliably initiated. Oral chloramphenicol is available as base in capsules and in a palmitate suspension. The palmitate requires de-esterification in the gastrointestinal tract to the active free base while the capsules are in the active form. Both the capsules and the palmitate suspension have greater bioavailability than the succinate parenteral form; therefore, conversion of intravenous to oral doses generally requires a reduction in dose of 15% to 25%.[112] Z.S. should be monitored continuously for resolution of symptoms and signs of hematologic toxicity. Complete blood count, serum iron, and platelet counts should be obtained every other day during the first week of therapy and twice weekly thereafter.

References

1 **Rowe PC.** The Harriett Lane Handbook. Chicago, IL: Year Book Medical; 1987.

2 **Ballow M et al.** Development of the immune system in very low birth weight (less than 1500 g) premature infants: concentrations of plasma immunoglobulins and patterns of infections. Pediatr Res. 1986;20:899.

3 **Bluestone CD, Klein JO.** Otitis Media in Infants and Children. Philadelphia, PA: WB Saunders; 1988:38.

4 **Wald ER et al.** Frequency and severity of infections in daycare. J Pediatr. 1988;112:540.

5 **Paap CM, Nahata MC.** Infectious diseases IV: viral and bacterial respiratory tract infections. In: Kuhn R, ed. Pediatric Pharmacotherapy. Lexington: University of Kentucky Press; 1993:8.

6 **Teele DW et al.** The greater Boston otitis media study group epidemiology of otitis media during the first seven years of life in children in greater Boston: a prospective cohort study. J Infect Dis. 1989;160:83.

7 **Bluestone CD, Klein JO.** Otitis Media in Infants and Children. Philadelphia, PA: WB Saunders; 1988:15.

8 **Arola M et al.** Clinical role of respiratory virus infection in acute otitis media. Pediatrics. 1990;86:848.

9 **Ruuskanen O et al.** Viruses in acute otitis media: increasing evidence of clinical significance. Pediatr Infect Dis J. 1991;10:425.

10 **Bluestone CD et al.** Ten-year review of otitis media pathogens. Pediatr Infect Dis J. 1992;11:S7.

11 **Ruuskanen O, Heikkinen T.** Otitis media: etiology and diagnosis. Pediatr Infect Dis J. 1994;13:S23.

12 **Fliss DM et al.** Medical sequelae and complications of acute otitis media. Pediatr Infect Dis J. 1994;13:S34.

13 **Bluestone CD, Klein JO.** Otitis Media in Infants and Children. Philadelphia, PA: WB Saunders; 1988:69.

14 **Teele DW et al.** Epidemiology of otitis media in children. Ann Otol Rhinol Laryngol. 1980;89(68):5.

15 **Stahlberg MR et al.** Risk factors for recurrent otitis media. Pediatr Infect Dis J. 1986;5:30.

16 **Bluestone CD.** Management of otitis media in infants and children: current role of old and new antimicrobial agents. Pediatr Infect Dis. 1988;7:S129.

17 **Bluestone CD, Klein JO.** Otitis Media in Infants and Children. Philadelphia, PA: WB Saunders; 1988:163.

18 **Gaskins JD et al.** Chemoprophylaxis of recurrent otitis media using trimethoprim/sulfamethoxazole. Drug Intell Clin Pharm. 1982;16:387.

19 **Bluestone CD, Klein JO.** Otitis Media in Infants and Children. Philadelphia, PA: WB Saunders; 1988:51.

20 **Baquero F, Loza E.** Antibiotic resistance of microorganisms involved in ear, nose and throat infections. Pediatr Infect Dis J. 1994;13:S9.

21 **Green SM, Rothrock SG.** Single-dose intramuscular ceftriaxone for acute otitis media in children. Pediatrics. 1993; 91:23.

22 **Pichichero ME.** Assessing the treatment alternatives for acute otitis media. Pediatr Infect Dis J. 1994;13:S27.

23 **Ruff ME et al.** Antimicrobial drug suspensions: a blind comparison of taste of fourteen common pediatric drugs. Pediatr Infect Dis J. 1991;10:30.

24 **Chaput de Saintonge D et al.** Trial of three-day and ten-day course of amoxicillin in otitis media. Br Med J. 1982; 284:1078.

25 **Hendrickse WA et al.** Five vs ten days of therapy for acute otitis media. Pediatr Infect Dis. 1988;7:14.

26 **Paparella MM et al.** Chronic otitis media: definition and classification. Ann Otol Rhinol Laryngol. 1985;94 (Suppl. 116):8.

27 **Mandel EM et al.** Efficacy of amoxicillin with and without decongestant-antihistamine for otitis media with effusion in children: results of a double-blind randomized trial. N Engl J Med. 1987;316:432.

28 **Bluestone CD, Klein JO.** Otitis Media in Infants and Children. Philadelphia, PA: WB Saunders; 1988:165.

29 **Rosenfeld RM et al.** Systemic steroids for otitis media with effusion in children. Arch Otolaryngol Head Neck Surg. 1991;117(9):984.

30 **Berman S et al.** Theoretical cost effectiveness of management options for children with persisting middle ear effusions. Pediatrics. 1994;93:353.

31 **Wald ER.** Management of sinusitis in infants and children. Pediatr Infect Dis J. 1988;7:449.

32 **Giebink GS.** Childhood sinusitis: pathophysiology, diagnosis and treatment. Pediatr Infect Dis J. 1994;13:S55.

33 **Tinkelman DG, Silk HJ.** Clinical and bacteriologic features of chronic sinusitis in children. Am J Dis Child. 1989; 143(8):938.

34 **Augmentin stability.** Beecham labs (personal communication).

35 **Johnson CE et al.** Cefixime compared with amoxicillin for the treatment of acute otitis media. J Pediatr. 1991;119: 117.

36 **McLinn SE.** Cefaclor: a decade of experience in acute otitis media. Clin Ther. 1988;11:35.

37 **Gerber MA, Markowitz M.** Management of streptococcal pharyngitis reconsidered. Pediatr Infect Dis. 1985;4: 518.

38 **Randolph MF et al.** The effort of antimicrobial therapy on the clinical course of streptococcal pharyngitis. J Pediatr. 1985;106:870.

39 **Shulman ST.** Complications of streptococcal pharyngitis. Pediatr Infect Dis J. 1994;13:S70.

40 **Johnson DR et al.** Epidemiologic analysis of Group A streptococci serotypes associated with severe systemic infections, rheumatic fever, or uncomplicated pharyngitis. J Infect Dis. 1992; 166:374.

41 **Working group on severe streptococcal infections: defining the Group A streptococcal toxic shock syndrome.** JAMA. 1993;269:390.

42 **Taubert KA et al.** Nationwide survey of Kawasaki's disease and acute rheumatic fever. J Pediatr. 1991;119:279.

43 **Catanzaro F et al.** The role of the streptococcus in the pathogenesis of rheumatic fever. Am J Med. 1954;17: 749.

44 **Gerber MA et al.** Twice daily penicillin in the treatment of streptococcal pharyngitis. Am J Dis Child. 1985;139: 1145.

45 **Gerber MA et al.** Once daily penicillin V therapy for pharyngitis. Pediatr Infect Dis J. 1993;12.

46 **Pichichero ME.** Cephalosporins are superior to penicillin for treatment of streptococcal tonsillopharyngitis: is the difference worth it? Pediatr Infect Dis J. 1993;12:268.

47 **Holm SE.** Reasons for failures in penicillin treatment of streptococcal tonsillitis and possible alternatives. Pediatr Infect Dis J. 1994;13:S66.

48 **Chaudhary S et al.** Penicillin V and rifampin for the treatment of Groups A streptococcal pharyngitis: a randomized trial of 10 days penicillin vs 10 days penicillin with rifampin during the final four days of therapy. J Pediatr. 1985;106:481.

49 **Tanz RR et al.** Penicillin plus rifampin eradicates pharyngeal carriage of Group A streptococci. J Pediatr. 1985; 106:876.

50 **Anon.** Guidelines for the diagnosis of rheumatic fever, Jones criteria 1992. JAMA. 1992;268(15):2069.

51 **Combined Rheumatic Fever Study Group.** A comparison of short-term, intensive prednisone and acetyl-salicylic acid therapy in the treatment of rheumatic fever. N Engl J Med. 1965; 272:63.

52 **Levy G, Giacomini KM.** Rational aspirin dosage regimens. Clin Pharmacol Ther. 1978;23:247.

53 **Dromgoole SH, Furst DE.** Salicylates. In: Evans WE et al., eds. Applied Pharmacokinetics: Principles of Therapeutics Drug Monitoring. Vancouver: Applied Therapeutics; 1992:32.

54 **Olley P, Rabinovitch.** Drugs affecting the cardiovascular system. In: MacCleod SM et al., eds. Textbook of Pediatric Clinical Pharmacology. Chicago: Year Book Publishers; 1993:155.

55 **Crapo JD et al.** Medicine and Pediatrics in One Book. St. Louis, MO; 1988: 88.

56 **Peters G et al.** Report of the Committee on Infectious Diseases. Elk Grove Village, IL: American Academy of Pediatrics; 1994:438.

57 **International Rheumatic Fever Study Group.** Allergic reactions to long-term benzathine prophylaxis for rheumatic fever. Lancet. 1991;337 (8753):1308.

58 **Berrios X et al.** Discontinuing rheumatic fever prophylaxis in selected adolescents and adults. Ann Intern Med. 1993;118:401.

59 **Sly PD et al.** Do wheezy infants recovering from bronchiolitis respond to inhaled salbutamol? Pediatr Pulmonol. 1991;10:36.

60 **Lenney W, Milner AD.** At what age do bronchodilator drugs work? Arch Dis Child. 1978;53:532.

61 **Lugo RA, Nahata MC.** Pathogenesis and treatment of bronchiolitis. Clin Pharm. 1993;12:95.

62 **Schuh S et al.** Nebulized albuterol in acute bronchiolitis. J Pediatr. 1990; 117:633.

63 **Klassen TP et al.** Randomized trial of salbutamol in acute bronchiolitis. J Pediatr. 1991;118:807.

64 **Ho L et al.** Effect of salbutamol on oxygen saturation in bronchiolitis. Arch Dis Child. 1991;66:1061.

65 **Prendiville A et al.** Hypoxaemia in wheezy infants after bronchodilator treatment. Arch Dis Child. 1987;62:997.

66 **Seidenberg J et al.** Hypoxemia after nebulized salbutamol in wheezy infants: importance of aerosol acidity. Arch Dis Child. 1991;66:672.

67 **O'Callaghan C, Milner AD.** Paradoxical deterioration in lung function after nebulized salbutamol in wheezy infants. Lancet. 1986;2:1424.

68 **Balmes J et al.** Acidity potentiates bronchoconstriction induced by hypoosmolar aerosols. Am Rev Respir Dis. 1988;138:35.

69 **Peters G et al.** Report of the Committee on Infectious Diseases. Elk Grove Village, IL: American Academy of Pediatrics; 1991:581.

70 **Englund JA et al.** High-dose, short-duration ribavirin aerosol therapy in children with suspected respiratory syncytial virus infection. J Pediatr. 1990;117:313.

71 **Adderley RJ.** Safety of ribavirin with mechanical ventilation. Pediatr Infect Dis J. 1990;9:S112.

72 **Rodriguez WJ et al.** Environmental exposure of primary care personnel to ribavirin aerosol when supervising treatment of infants with respiratory syncytial virus infections. Antimicrob Agents Chemother. 1987;31:1143.

73 **Harrison R et al.** Assessing exposure of health care personnel to aerosols of ribavirin—California. MMWR. 1988; 37:360.

74 **Harrison R.** Reproductive risk assessment with occupational exposure to ribavirin aerosol. Pediatr Infect Dis J. 1990;9:S102.

75 **Bradley J.** Environmental exposure to ribavirin aerosol. Pediatr Infect Dis J. 1990;9:S95.

76 **Torres A et al.** Reduced environmental exposure to aerosolized ribavirin using a simple containment system. Pediatr Infect Dis J. 1991;10:217.

77 **Seidenberg J et al.** Effect of ipratropium bromide on respiratory mechanics in infants with acute bronchiolitis. Aust Paediatr J. 1987;23:169.

78 **Henry RL et al.** Ineffectiveness of ipratropium bromide in acute bronchiolitis. Arch Dis Child. 1983;58:925.

79 **Brooks LJ, Cropp GJA.** Theophylline therapy in bronchiolitis. Am J Dis Child. 1981;135:934.

80 **Schena JA et al.** The use of aminophylline in severe bronchiolitis. Crit Care Med. 1984;12:225. Abstract.

81 **Tal A et al.** Dexamethasone and salbutamol in the treatment of acute wheezing in infants. Pediatrics. 1983; 71:13.

82 **McGeorge M.** Severe obstructive bronchiolitis in infancy: treatment with hydrocortisone. Clin Pediatr. 1964;3: 11.

83 **Leer JA et al.** Corticosteroid treatment in bronchiolitis. Am J Dis Child. 1969; 117:495.

84 **Springer C et al.** Corticosteroids do not affect the clinical or physiological status of infants with bronchiolitis. Pediatr Pulmonol. 1990;9:181.

85 **Kelly HW, Murphy S.** Corticosteroids for acute, severe asthma. Ann Pharmacother. 1991;25:72.

86 **Taussig LM et al.** Treatment of laryngotracheobronchitis (croups): use of intermittent positive-pressure breathing and racemic epinephrine. Am J Dis Child. 1975;129:792.

87 **Waisman Y et al.** Prospective randomized double-blind study comparing L-epinephrine and racemic epinephrine aerosols in the treatment of laryngotracheitis (croup). Pediatrics. 1992;89: 302.

88 **Kelley PB, Simon JE.** Racemic epinephrine in croup and disposition. Am J Emerg Med. 1992;10:181.

89 **Kairys SW et al.** Steroid treatment of laryngotracheitis: a meta-analysis of the evidence from randomized trials. Pediatrics. 1989;83:683.

90 **Cherry JD et al.** Report of the task force on pertussis and pertussis immunization—1988. Pediatrics. 1988; (Suppl.):939.

91 **Nahata MC.** Selection of an erythromycin for the treatment of pertussis. Drug Intell Clin Pharm. 1988;22:895.

92 **Braun P.** Hepatotoxicity of erythromycin. J Infect Dis. 1969;119:300.

93 **Ginsburg CM.** The multicenter pneumonia study group. A prospective study on the incidence of liver function abnormalities in children receiving erythromycin estolate, erythromycin ethylsuccinate or penicillin V for the treatment of pneumonia. Pediatr Infect Dis. 1986;5:151.

94 **Barclay AJG et al.** Vitamin A supplements and mortality related to measles: a randomized clinical trial. Br Med J. 1987;294:294.

95 **Hussey GD, Klein M.** A randomized controlled trial of vitamin A in children with severe measles. N Engl J Med. 1990;323:160.

96 **Report of the Committee of Infectious Diseases.** American Academy of Pediatrics. Vitamin A supplementation for measles. Pediatrics. 1993;92:501.

97 **Peters G et al.** Report of the Committee on Infectious Diseases. Elk Grove Village, IL: American Academy of Pediatrics; 1994:284.

98 **Nakashima L, Edwards DL.** Treatment of Kawasaki disease. Clin Pharm. 1990;9:755.

99 **Klassen TP et al.** Economic evaluation of intravenous immune globulin therapy for Kawasaki syndrome. J Pediatr. 1993;122:538.

100 **Koren G et al.** Probable efficacy of high dose salicylates in reducing coronary involvement in Kawasaki disease. JAMA. 1985;254:767.

101 **Akagi T et al.** Salicylate treatment in Kawasaki disease: high dose or low dose? Eur J Pediatr. 1991;150:642.

102 **Third International Kawasaki Disease Symposium Participants.** Management of Kawasaki syndrome: a consensus statement prepared by the North-American participants of the third international Kawasaki syndrome symposium. Pediatr Infect Dis. 1989;8: 663.

103 **Smith LBH et al.** Kawasaki syndrome and the eye. Pediatr Infect Dis J. 1989; 8:116.

104 **Koren G, MacLeod SM.** Difficulty in achieving therapeutic serum concentrations of salicylate in Kawasaki disease. J Pediatr. 1984;105:991.

105 **Newburger JW et al.** The treatment of Kawasaki syndrome with intravenous gamma globulin. N Engl J Med. 1986; 315:341.

106 **Engle MA et al.** Clinical trial of single dose intravenous gamma globulin in acute Kawasaki disease. Am J Dis Child. 1989;143:1300.

107 **Newburger JW et al.** A single intravenous infusion of gamma globulin as compared with four infusions in the treatment of acute Kawasaki syndrome. N Engl J Med. 1991;324:1633.

108 **Comenzo RL et al.** Immune hemolysis, disseminated intravascular coagulation, and serum sickness after large doses of immune globulin given intravenously for Kawasaki disease. J Pediatr. 1992;120:926.

109 **Sundel RP et al.** Gamma globulin retreatment in Kawasaki disease. J Pediatr. 1993;123:657.

110 **Peters G et al.** Report of the Committee on Infectious Diseases. Elk Grove Village, IL: American Academy of Pediatrics; 1994:399.

111 **Roberts KB.** Rocky mountain spotted fever. In: Roberts KB, ed. Manual of Clinical Problems in Pediatrics. Boston: Little, Brown & Co. 1986:378.

112 **Nahata MC.** Chloramphenicol. In: Evans WE et al., eds. Applied Pharmacokinetics: Principles of Therapeutic Drug Monitoring. Vancouver: Applied Therapeutics; 1992:16.

113 **Yagupsky P et al.** Comparison of two dosage schedules of doxycycline in children with rickettsial spotted fever. J Infect Dis. 1987;155:215.

114 **Yunis AA et al.** Chloramphenicol-induced bone marrow suppression. Semin Hematol. 1973;10:225.

115 **Lietman PS.** Oral chloramphenicol therapy. J Pediatr. 1981;99:905.

116 **EMIT chloramphenicol assay.** 1986. Syva Co. Palo Alto, CA.

117 **Pukander JS et al.** Clarithromycin vs amoxicillin suspensions in treatment of pediatric patients with otitis media. Pediatr Infect Dis J. 1993;12:S118.

118 **Still JG et al.** Comparison of clarithromycin and penicillin VK suspensions in the treatment of children with streptococcal pharyngitis and a review of currently available alternative antibiotic therapies. Pediatr Infect Dis J. 1993;12:S134.

119 **Pestalozza G et al.** Azithromycin in upper respiratory infections: a clinical trial in children with otitis media. Scand J Infect Dis Suppl. 1992;83:22.

120 **Casiano RR.** Azithromycin and amoxicillin in the treatment of acute maxillary sinusitis. Am J Med. 1991;91:27S.

121 **Hooten TM.** A comparison of azithromycin and penicillin V for the treatment of streptococcal pharyngitis. Am J Med. 1991;91:23S.

122 **Smith et al.** A controlled trial of aerosolized ribavirin in infants receiving mechanical ventilation for severe respiratory syncytial virus infection. N Engl J Med. 1991;325:24.

123 **Meert KL et al.** Aerosolized ribavirin in mechanically ventilated children with respiratory syncytial virus lower respiratory tract disease: a prospective, double-blind, randomized trial. Crit Care Med. 1994;22:566.

124 **Bass JW.** Erythromycin for treatment and prevention of pertussis. Pediatr Infect Dis. 1986;5:154–57.

Bronchopulmonary Dysplasia

Michael A Clotz

Overview 98-1
  Definition 98-1
  Incidence 98-1
  Pathophysiology 98-1
  Signs and Symptoms 98-1
  Therapy 98-1

Therapy 98-1
  Diuretics 98-1
  Bronchodilators 98-2
    Theophylline 98-3
    Inhaled β-adrenergic agonists 98-3
  Corticosteroids 98-3
Complications of Diuretic Therapy 98-4

Definition

Bronchopulmonary dysplasia (BPD), first described in 1967,[1] is the most common form of chronic lung disease in infants.[2] In 1989, the Bureau of Maternal and Child Health and Resources defined the following four diagnostic criteria for BPD:[3]

- Positive pressure ventilation during the first two weeks of life for a minimum of three days.
- Clinical signs of respiratory compromise persisting longer than 28 days of age.
- Requirement for supplemental oxygen longer than 28 days of age to maintain a PaO_2 above 50 mm Hg.
- Chest radiograph with findings consistent with BPD (described below).

These criteria reflect the risk factors for the development of bronchopulmonary dysplasia: neonatal respiratory distress or failure, prematurity, oxygen supplementation, and intermittent positive pressure ventilation. Additionally, any event that prolongs the need for mechanical ventilation and oxygen supplementation, such as pulmonary interstitial emphysema, pneumothorax, pulmonary edema, or pulmonary infection, will increase the risk for the development of bronchopulmonary dysplasia. Causes of respiratory distress in the neonate include meconium aspiration, pneumonia, congestive heart failure, and prematurity.

Incidence

Depending upon the criteria used, bronchopulmonary dysplasia affects 10% to 30% of neonates requiring mechanical ventilation at birth.[4] Improvements in the management of respiratory distress syndrome (RDS) have led to a decreasing incidence of BPD in neonates weighing greater than 1500 gm at birth. Conversely, the increased survival of extremely low birth weight neonates (<1000 gm) has led to an increase in the incidence of BPD in these infants.[5] Therefore, the overall incidence of bronchopulmonary dysplasia seems to be unchanged.[5] While exogenously administered surfactant has reduced the mortality from RDS, it has not reduced the overall incidence of BPD since respiratory distress syndrome in low-birth weight neonates is due not only to surfactant deficiency, but also extremely immature lungs and airways.[6]

Pathophysiology

The pathophysiology of BPD is multifactorial and represents a spectrum of injury to and repair of the immature developing lung. The underlying cause of the RDS, the inspired concentration of oxygen required for its management, as well as the peak inspiratory pressures and duration of these pressures during mechanical ven-

tilation, all contribute to the eventual severity of BPD.[7] Long-term exposure to high concentrations of oxygen can lead to recruitment and activation of lung neutrophils and macrophages, precipitate necrosis of bronchiolar epithelium and type I cells, cause hyperplasia of type II cells, and lead to a marked proliferation of fibroblasts and macrophages in lung interstitium.[8]

Signs and Symptoms

Bronchopulmonary dysplasia generally is described in terms of radiographic findings, although the changes are often quite subtle. The characteristic chest x-ray will show bilateral diffuse interstitial thickening with normal to increased expansion of the lungs.[9] Infants with BPD have abnormal pulmonary function, altered gas exchange, and increased caloric expenditure due to increased work of breathing. The mechanisms by which these symptoms are manifested include: pulmonary edema, airway hyperreactivity and bronchoconstriction, airway inflammation, and chronic lung injury and repair.

Therapy

Since bronchopulmonary dysplasia has multiple risk factors, diverse clinical manifestations, and a wide spectrum of severity, the treatment of BPD is multifactorial. Also, because of the wide spectrum of the disease, controlled trials evaluating the different treatments of this disorder are difficult to perform. Agents currently used in the management of BPD reduce symptoms and improve lung function, but unfortunately do not reverse the damage already done to the developing lungs. The agents most often used for the management of bronchopulmonary dysplasia include diuretics, bronchodilators, and corticosteroids. Specific drugs and dosing are listed in Table 98.1.

Since BPD is a disease of lung damage and repair,[1] the future management of this disease will be based upon an understanding of the factors responsible for the normal repair of the damaged immature lung as well as the prevention of premature births.[10]

Therapy
Diuretics

1. M.G. is an 18-month-old, 10 kg, former 28-week gestational age, premature male infant. His past medical history is significant for mechanical ventilation from birth to 6 weeks of age, and multiple episodes of pneumonia. He is admitted to the hospital for respiratory distress. His physical examination reveals an infant in moderate respiratory distress and is remarkable for a respiratory rate of 40 breaths/min (Normal: 22–30) and a heart rate of 140 beats/min (Normal Mean: 120). His blood pressure is normal and arterial hemoglobin oxygen sat-

Table 98.1	Commonly Used Drugs in Bronchopulmonary Dysplasia
Bronchodilators	
Inhaled:	
Albuterol	0.02–0.04 mL/kg/dose 0.5% solution diluted to 2 mL with saline and nebulized Q 4–6 hr
Atropine	0.025–0.05 mg/kg/dose diluted to 2 mL with saline nebulized Q 6 hr
Ipratropium	175 µg/dose diluted to 2 mL with saline nebulized Q 6 hr
Metaproterenol	0.1–0.25 mL of 5% solution diluted to 2 mL with saline nebulized Q 6 hr
Systemic	
Albuterol	0.15 mg/kg/dose PO Q 8 hr
Caffeine base	*Loading dose:* 10 mg/kg PO/IV *Maintenance dose:* 2.5 mg/kg/dose Q 24 hr
Caffeine citrate	*Loading dose:* 20 mg/kg PO/IV *Maintenance dose:* 5 mg/kg/dose Q 24 hr
Theophylline	*Loading dose:* 5 mg/kg PO/IV *Maintenance dose:* 2–3 mg/kg/dose Q 8–12 hr
Diuretics	
Chlorothiazide	5–20 mg/kg/dose IV or PO BID
Furosemide	0.5–2.0 mg/kg/dose IV or PO BID
Hydrochlorothiazide	1–2 mg/kg/dose PO BID
Metolazone	0.1–0.2 mg/kg/dose PO QD
Spironolactone	1–2 mg/kg/dose PO BID

uration is 75% (Normal: >95%). **The decision is made to admit M.G. for treatment of acute respiratory distress associated with chronic BPD. Furosemide 10 mg IV Q 12 hr is ordered. What is the rationale for diuretic therapy in M.G.?**

Diuretics are used in the management of BPD and have been shown to improve lung function in these infants,[11–17] but the exact mechanism by which they improve lung function has not been elucidated completely. Pulmonary edema is thought to play a role in the development of bronchopulmonary dysplasia[18] resulting in reduced airway compliance and increased airway resistance. Diuretics could improve lung mechanics in infants with cardiogenic pulmonary edema; however, improvement in pulmonary function after administration of diuretics does not seem to correlate with urine output.[11,12,19] Infants with BPD have abnormal regulation of fluid balance and are, therefore, predisposed to fluid overload and the development of pulmonary edema.[20] Although diuretics increase urine output, improvement in lung function has not correlated with the magnitude of diuresis.[11,12]

Furosemide is a frequently-used diuretic in infants with BPD. In addition to its diuretic effect, furosemide also lowers pulmonary vascular resistance and improves ventilation to perfusion ratios.[21] Furosemide has been shown to effectively improve clinical respiratory status, decrease ventilation requirements, and improve lung compliance in infants with BPD.[13–17] Side effects associated with furosemide therapy include electrolyte depletion, metabolic alkalosis, cholelithiasis, hypercalciuria with nephrocalcinosis, and osteopenia.[4]

2. Evaluate the appropriateness of this furosemide dose in M.G. How would response to therapy be monitored?

Furosemide is initially administered intravenously in a dose of 1 mg/kg every 12 hours. Since M.G. weighs 10 kg, his dose is appropriate. He should be monitored for the desired outcome of therapy as evidenced by reduced work of breathing and improved oxygen saturation and blood gasses. Serum electrolytes should be monitored frequently during the initiation of diuretic therapy to avoid side effects such as hypochloremic metabolic alkalosis and hypokalemia.

3. Are there any other diuretics that could be used to manage respiratory distress in M.G.?

In addition to furosemide, thiazide diuretics (hydrochlorothiazide, chlorothiazide) and potassium-sparing diuretics (spironolactone) have been used with some success in infants with BPD. Chlorothiazide has the advantage of being the only intravenous thiazide diuretic available, although experience with this dosage form in infants is limited. In an effort to reduce the incidence of hypokalemia with thiazide diuretics alone, thiazide diuretics have been combined with the aldosterone antagonist, spironolactone. The combination of chlorothiazide and spironolactone has been shown to improve pulmonary function in nonventilator-dependent infants with moderate BPD.[22] Conversely, the combination of hydrochlorothiazide and spironolactone improved urine output, but not pulmonary function, in infants with bronchopulmonary dysplasia.[11] The reason for this discrepancy is unknown.

The possible advantage of using thiazide diuretics in place of loop diuretics is that the thiazides promote less calcium excretion which not only would reduce the risk of nephrocalcinosis, but may improve bone mineralization. Thiazide diuretics should be substituted for loop diuretics if the infant develops hematuria or other signs of nephrocalcinosis.

Bronchodilators

4. Following two doses of furosemide, M.G.'s work of breathing is somewhat improved, but oxygen saturation is still only 85%. Arterial blood gasses reveal an elevated $PaCO_2$. The decision is made to start bronchodilator therapy in M.G. What is the rationale for bronchodilator therapy in M.G.?

Bronchodilator therapy generally is begun when the infant does not respond to diuretic therapy alone, or is used chronically in children who have frequent exacerbations of respiratory distress. Bronchodilators may acutely improve pulmonary function in infants with BPD; however, the magnitude of this effect may be variable. As with diuretics, the long-term benefits of these agents have yet to be examined. The use of bronchodilators is based upon the observation that the early appearance of bronchial hyperreactivity is associated with an increased risk for the development of BPD.[23] Additionally, hyperreactivity may persist in these infants even after oxygen and mechanical ventilation are no longer required.[10]

Bronchodilator therapy can be divided into three general categories: methylxanthines, β-adrenergic agonists, and anticholinergic therapy. Caffeine and theophylline are the most commonly used methylxanthine bronchodilators in infants with BPD. Because of their respiratory stimulant activity, they effectively reduce the frequency of neonatal apnea.[24] In premature neonates, caffeine may be the preferred agent due to differences in methylxanthine metabolism compared to older infants and adults. (See Chapter 96: Neonatal Therapy for a more detailed discussion of this topic.)

Both theophylline and caffeine have been shown to improve lung mechanics in infants with bronchopulmonary dysplasia.[21,25] This improvement presumably is due to direct bronchodilation; however, diuresis, central respiratory stimulation, and stimulation of respiratory muscles may play a role as well.[10] The most frequent adverse effects of the xanthines are vomiting and diarrhea.[4] Hyperreflexia, jitteriness, tachycardia, and agitation also are reported side effects of xanthine therapy.[4]

Theophylline

5. A 50 mg IV dose of theophylline is given, followed by 30 mg PO Q 8 hr. After five days of therapy a trough theophylline serum concentration of 18 µg/mL is obtained. At the same time, M.G. is vomiting three to four times a day. Is this an appropriate dose of theophylline for M.G.? Could the vomiting be related to M.G.'s theophylline therapy? [SI units: Theophylline 9.99 µmol/L]

The typical starting regimen for theophylline in infants is a loading dose of 5 mg/kg orally or intravenously or followed by a maintenance dose of 2 to 3 mg/kg/dose orally or intravenously every 8 to 12 hours. Despite receiving a dose in the recommended range, M.G. is exhibiting adverse effects of theophylline and has a trough serum level exceeding the target range of 8 to 15 µg/mL. This is not unexpected given the unpredictable pharmacokinetics of theophylline in infants with BPD, even within the same patient.[26] For this reason, serum theophylline concentrations must be monitored in infants with bronchopulmonary dysplasia. However, even with concentrations within the therapeutic range, some infants will exhibit intolerable adverse effects. If theophylline is to be continued, the dose should be reduced to 15 mg every eight hours.

Inhaled β-Adrenergic Agonists

6. What alternative bronchodilator therapy is available for M.G.?

Inhaled β-adrenergic agonists are useful alternatives to methylxanthines for the management of BPD. Compared with the methylxanthines, inhaled β-adrenergic agonists are more potent bronchodilators.[10] In order to avoid unwanted cardiovascular side effects (e.g., tachycardia), β_2-specific agents (metaproterenol, albuterol) are preferred over nonselective beta agonists (isoproterenol). Both albuterol and metaproterenol by inhalation have been shown to improve lung function in infants with BPD.[27,28] Oral albuterol also may improve airway resistance in ventilator-dependent premature infants,[29] but with a slower onset of action and more side effects than inhalation therapy.[4] For example, Stefano et al. demonstrated significant improvement in pulmonary function following 48 hours of oral albuterol therapy (0.15 mg/kg/dose every eight hours) compared to placebo.[29] However, these children exhibited statistically significantly greater heart rates, but not blood pressure, than the placebo group (Mean: 162 beats/minute versus 152 beats/minute).

For M.G., albuterol 0.3 cc of a 0.5% solution in 2 cc saline should be administered by nebulization every four hours. Nebulization by facemask is required since infants do not have the coordination necessary to receive inhaled agents via a metered-dose inhaler. If signs and symptoms such as elevated $PaCO_2$, work of breathing, and oxygen saturation do not improve, the frequency of administration can be increased to every two hours. Once M.G.'s respiratory symptoms resolve, the frequency of albuterol can be decreased to every six hours. Upon discharge, albuterol can be administered as needed for respiratory symptoms such as wheezing, increased work of breathing, or tachypnea. Side effects to monitor with aerosolized beta agonists include tachycardia, hypertension, hyperglycemia, and tremor.

If every two-hour albuterol administration does not ameliorate M.G.'s symptoms, nebulized ipratropium could be added. Since parasympathetic stimulation is reported to contribute to the airway hyperreactivity of BPD, it is not surprising that anticholinergic therapy may reverse this effect, especially in the larger, central airways. Both inhaled atropine and ipratropium have been shown to improve lung mechanics in infants with BPD,[15,27,28] and the combination of ipratropium with albuterol seems to have at least additive effects in reducing bronchial tone in these infants.[30] Being a quaternary compound, systemic absorption of ipratropium after nebulization is less than that of atropine and, therefore, is associated with fewer cardiovascular side effects, especially tachycardia.

Corticosteroids

7. Despite diuretics, nebulized albuterol, and nebulized ipratropium for 24 hours, M.G. is showing little improvement in blood gasses, oxygen saturation, and work of breathing. Systemic corticosteroid therapy is considered. What is the rationale for the use of corticosteroids in M.G.?

Corticosteroid therapy is the most controversial aspect of the management of bronchopulmonary dysplasia. Children with BPD show signs of airway hyperresponsiveness, airflow obstruction, and inflammation. Since corticosteroids are effective in relieving similar symptoms in children with asthma, it is postulated that they also should provide symptomatic relief in infants with BPD. Despite numerous clinical trials to evaluate the effectiveness of corticosteroids in the treatment of bronchopulmonary dysplasia, direct comparisons of these trials are difficult because of a lack of consistency in dosage regimens, duration of treatment, and outcome variables. While short-term dexamethasone therapy has been shown to reduce the duration of mechanical ventilation,[31,32] no study has shown improvement in long-term morbidity or length of hospital stay.[10,32] Because systemic corticosteroid therapy is associated with significant adverse effects and because data defining benefit are lacking, some investigators caution against the long-term use of corticosteroids except in children with severe BPD. Potential candidates are infants exhibiting severe growth failure indicative of chronic hypoxia, digital clubbing, and recurrent cyanotic episodes.[8]

In an attempt to retain the benefits of corticosteroids while minimizing side effects, some investigators have examined the use of inhaled corticosteroids.[33–35] Nebulized beclomethasone and flunisolide may be effective in improving lung function in infants with BPD; however, the small number of infants studied precludes any specific recommendations regarding this therapy. Additionally, there are no dosage forms manufactured for nebulization into the lungs. Flunisolide is formulated in a solution for nasal spray, but contains preservatives that could cause bronchial irritation and bronchospasm. Konig et al. coadministered albuterol with flunisolide and encountered no adverse effects.[35]

8. Dexamethasone is begun in a dose of 2.5 mg IV Q 12 hr. Is this an appropriate dose for M.G.? How long should dexamethasone be continued?

The generally accepted starting dose is 0.5 to 0.6 mg/kg/day given every 12 hours.[36] More controversial, however, is the duration of treatment and methods of tapering. Only one trial has compared differing lengths of therapy. It found that a 42-day course of dexamethasone was superior to an 18-day course or placebo.[37] Other authors propose a 21-day course of therapy using a weekly tapering schedule.[36] Since no definitive data exist, the duration of treatment will differ between centers. A reasonable compromise is a three-week course. Should the respiratory distress recur following discontinuation of dexamethasone, the subsequent course should be longer.

9. It is decided to continue dexamethasone for three weeks in M.G. following a tapering schedule. How should adverse effects of M.G.'s dexamethasone therapy be monitored?

Systemic steroid therapy is not without significant side effects. The list of possible adverse effects include increased rate of infection, hypertension, hyperglycemia, gastrointestinal (GI) ulceration, GI bleeding and intestinal perforation, impaired growth, cardiac hypertrophy, ischemic brain injury, necrotizing enterocolitis, adrenal suppression, and poor bone mineralization.[38] Hypertension can be detected by daily blood pressure recordings. Hyperglycemia can be identified by urine glucose monitoring. Gastrointestinal disturbances can be realized easily either overtly by visualization of blood in the stool or by performing occult blood testing on M.G.'s stool.

10. Is there a role for inhaled cromolyn in M.G.'s regimen?

Since BPD is characterized by continual influx of inflammatory mediators into the airways, it is hypothesized that the use of cromolyn sodium by inhalation may be effective in the management of BPD.[37] While no controlled trials have been performed, published reports suggest that cromolyn may be of benefit in the treatment of bronchopulmonary dysplasia.[39] Studies have been unable to show, however, that cromolyn can prevent the development of bronchopulmonary dysplasia in infants with RDS.[37]

Complications of Diuretic Therapy

11. M.G.'s respiratory status improves following initiation of dexamethasone. He completes a 21-day course of therapy without incident and is discharged from the hospital. Six weeks after discharge, M.G.'s mother brings him to the clinic for follow-up. He is currently receiving furosemide 10 mg PO Q 12 hr and albuterol 0.3 cc of a 0.5% solution in 2 cc saline Q 6 hr PRN. His mother states that he has required only one dose of the albuterol since his discharge. His pulmonary function tests have returned to baseline. However, the following laboratory results are obtained: sodium (Na) 132 mEq/L (Normal: 135–145), chloride (Cl) 88 mEq/L (Normal: 94–106), potassium (K) 3.0 mEq/L (Normal: 3.5–5.0), bicarbonate 35 mEq/L (Normal: 20–25). What do the laboratory results indicate? What manipulations of therapy can help manage this development? [SI units: Na 132 mmol/L (Normal: 135–145); Cl 88 mmol/L (Normal: 94–106); K 3.0 mmol/L (Normal: 3.5–5.0); bicarbonate 35 mmol/L (Normal: 20–25)]

M.G. is displaying signs of hypokalemia and hypochloremic metabolic alkalosis. Electrolyte disturbances are the most common adverse effects of the loop diuretics.[40] Chloride depletion with resultant metabolic alkalosis also is seen frequently with long-term use of furosemide.[41]

Treatment with potassium supplements is the simplest means to treat this complication of diuretic therapy. Since chloride depletion occurs as well, potassium chloride is the supplement of choice. A dose of 1 to 2 mEq/kg/day orally in divided doses is a reasonable place to start with frequent monitoring of electrolytes guiding changes in therapy. Divided doses are necessary because of the unpalatability of the oral liquid preparation. Because potassium losses are associated with aldosterone mediated exchange of potassium and sodium, the aldosterone antagonist spironolactone could be added to furosemide therapy instead of potassium chloride.[40] The recommended starting dose is 1 to 2 mg/kg/dose of an oral suspension given twice daily.

Alternatively, since M.G.'s pulmonary function tests have returned to baseline, one could consider changing to alternate day furosemide therapy. Rush et al. have demonstrated short-term improvement in pulmonary function without significant adverse effects using alternate day furosemide therapy.[12]

References

1   **Northway WH et al.** Pulmonary disease following respiratory therapy of hyaline membrane disease: bronchopulmonary dysplasia. N Engl J Med. 1967;276:357.

2   **Northway WH.** An introduction to bronchopulmonary dysplasia. Clin Perinatol. 1992;19:489.

3   **Bureau of Maternal and Child Health and Resources.** Bronchopulmonary dysplasia (BPD). In: Guidelines for the Care of Children with Chronic Lung Disease. Pediatr Pulmonol. 1989;6(Suppl. 3):3.

4   **Davis JM et al.** Drug therapy for bronchopulmonary dysplasia. Pediatr Pulmonol. 1990;8:117.

5   **Northway WH.** Bronchopulmonary dysplasia: then and now. Arch Dis Child. 1990;65:1076.

6   **Northway WH.** Bronchopulmonary dysplasia: twenty five years later. Pediatrics. 1992;89:969.

7   **Bonikos DS et al.** Bronchopulmonary dysplasia: the pulmonary pathologic sequel of necrotizing bronchiolitis and pulmonary fibrosis. Hum Pathol. 1976; 7:643.

8   **Hazinski TA.** Bronchopulmonary dysplasia. In: Chernick V, Kendig EL Jr, eds. Disorders of the Respiratory Tract in Children. Philadelphia: WB Saunders; 1990:300.

9   **Edwards DK.** Radiologic aspects of bronchopulmonary dysplasia. J Pediatr. 1979;95:823.

10 **Rush MG et al.** Current therapy of bronchopulmonary dysplasia. Clin Perinatol. 1992;19:563.

11 **Englehardt B et al.** Effect of spironolactone-hydrochlorothiazide on lung function in infants with bronchopulmonary dysplasia. J Pediatr. 1989;114:619.

12 **Rush MG et al.** Double-blind placebo controlled trial of alternate day furosemide therapy in infants with chronic bronchopulmonary dysplasia. J Pediatr. 1990;117:112.

13 **McCann EM et al.** Controlled trial of furosemide therapy in infants with chronic lung disease. J Pediatr. 1985; 106:957.

14 **Englehardt B.** Short- and long-term effects of furosemide on lung function in infants with bronchopulmonary dysplasia. J Pediatr. 1986;109:1034.

15 **Logvinoff MM et al.** Bronchodilators and diuretics in children with bronchopulmonary dysplasia. Pediatr Pulmonol. 1985;1:198.

16 **Kao LC et al.** Furosemide acutely decreases airways resistance in chronic bronchopulmonary dysplasia. J Pediatr. 1983;103:624.

17 **Najak ZD et al.** Pulmonary effects of furosemide in preterm infants with lung disease. J Pediatr. 1983;102:758.

18 **Brown ER et al.** Bronchopulmonary dysplasia: possible relationships to pulmonary edema. J Pediatr. 1978;92:989.

19 **Hazinski TA.** Diuresis does not explain why furosemide improves lung function in infants with BPD. Pediatr Res. 1988;23:509A.

20 **Hazinski TA et al.** Control of water balance in infants with bronchopulmonary dysplasia. Role of endogenous vasopressin. Pediatr Res. 1988;23:86.

21 **Kao LC et al.** Oral theophylline and diuretics improve pulmonary mechanics in infants with bronchopulmonary dysplasia. J Pediatr. 1987;111:439.

22 **Kao LC et al.** Effects of oral diuretics on pulmonary mechanics in infants with bronchopulmonary dysplasia: results of a double-blind crossover sequential trial. Pediatrics. 1984;74:37.

23 **Goldman SL et al.** Early prediction of chronic lung disease by pulmonary function testing. J Pediatr. 1983;102:613.

24 **Aranda JV et al.** Methylxanthines in apnea of prematurity. Clin Perinatol. 1979;6:87.

25 **Davis JM et al.** Changes in pulmonary mechanics after caffeine administration in infants with bronchopulmonary dysplasia. Pediatr Pulmonol. 1989;6:49.

26 **Nahata MC et al.** Theophylline pharmacokinetics in patients with bronchopulmonary dysplasia. J Clin Pharm Ther. 1989;14:225.

27 **Kao LC et al.** Effects of inhaled metaproterenol and atropine on the pulmonary mechanics of infants with bronchopulmonary dysplasia. Pediatr Pulmonol. 1989;6:74.

28 **Wilkie RA et al.** Effect of bronchodilators on airway resistance in ventilator dependent neonates with chronic lung disease. J Pediatr. 1987;110:116.

29 **Stefano JL et al.** A randomized placebo-controlled study to evaluate the effects of oral albuterol on pulmonary mechanics in ventilator-dependent infants at risk of developing BPD. Pediatr Pulmonol. 1991;10:183.

30 **Brundage KL et al.** Bronchodilator response to ipratropium bromide in infants with bronchopulmonary dysplasia. Am Rev Respir Dis. 1990;142:1137.

31 **Avery GB et al.** Controlled trial of dexamethasone in respirator-dependent infants with bronchopulmonary dysplasia. Pediatrics. 1985;75:106.

32 **Kazzi NJ et al.** Dexamethasone effects on the hospital course of infants with bronchopulmonary dysplasia who are dependent on artificial ventilation. Pediatrics. 1990;86:722.

33 **Cloutier MM.** Nebulized steroid therapy in bronchopulmonary dysplasia. Pediatr Pulmonol. 1993;15:111.

34 **LaForce WR et al.** Controlled trial of beclomethasone dipropionate by nebulization in oxygen- and ventilator-dependent infants. J Pediatr. 1993;122:285.

35 **Konig P et al.** Clinical observations of nebulized flunisolide in infants and young children with asthma and bronchopulmonary dysplasia. Pediatr Pulmonol. 1992;13:209.

36 **Ng PC.** The effectiveness and side effects of dexamethasone in preterm infants with bronchopulmonary dysplasia. Arch Dis Child. 1993;68:330.

37 **Watterberg KL et al.** Failure of cromolyn sodium to reduce the incidence of bronchopulmonary dysplasia: a pilot study. Pediatrics. 1993;91:803.

38 **Anon.** Dexamethasone for neonatal chronic lung disease. Lancet. 1991; 338:982.

39 **Yamamoto C et al.** Disodium cromoglycate in the treatment of bronchopulmonary dysplasia. Acta Paediatr Jpn. 1992;34:589.

40 **Chemtob S et al.** Pharmacology of diuretics in the newborn. Pediatr Clin North Am. 1989;36:1231.

41 **Perlman JM et al.** Is chloride depletion an important contributing cause of death in infants with bronchopulmonary dysplasia? Pediatrics. 1986;77:212.

Pediatric Nutrition

Alvin F Wong
Ann M Bolinger
Robert C Edwards

Fluid and Electrolyte Maintenance 99-2
  Requirements (See Tables 99.1 and 99.2) 99-2
    Calculation of maintenance fluid requirements 99-2
    Adjustment for phototherapy lights 99-3
  Dehydration (See Table 99.3) 99-3
    Clinical presentation: vomiting 99-3
      Acute management 99-3
      Calculation of requirements (See Equations 99.1
        to 99.4 and Table 99.4) 99-3
          Fluid 99-3
          Sodium 99-3
          Potassium 99-3
          Chloride 99-3
      Administration of fluid requirements 99-4
    Clinical presentation: diarrhea 99-4
      Acute management 99-4
      Calculation of requirements 99-4
          Fluid 99-4
          Sodium 99-4
          Potassium 99-4
          Bicarbonate 99-4
      Replacement fluid composition 99-5
      Administration of requirements
        (See Tables 99.5 and 99.6) 99-5
Infant Nutrition 99-5
  Vitamin K 99-5
  Human Milk Feeding 99-5
  Introduction of Solid Foods 99-6
  Cow's Milk and Cow's Milk-Based Formula
    (See Table 99.7) 99-6
  Therapeutic Formulas 99-6
    Phenylketonuria (PKU) 99-6
    Other metabolic errors 99-7
Pediatric Nutritional Support 99-7
  Indications (See Table 99.8) 99-7

Extremely premature infants 99-7
Respiratory distress 99-7
Gastrointestinal (GI) anomalies 99-7
Chronic renal failure and hepatic disease 99-7
Nutritional Assessment 99-7
  Anthropometric measurements 99-7
  Biochemical measurements 99-10
Nutrient Requirements (See Table 99.1) 99-10
Route of Administration 99-10
Monitoring (See Table 99.9) 99-11
Clinical Presentation: Nutritional Assessment 99-11
Nutrient Requirements (See Table 99.10) 99-11
Total Parenteral Nutrition (TPN) 99-11
Role of Enteral Nutrition in Chronic Diarrhea 99-12
  Choice of formula 99-12
  Monitoring 99-13
  Reinstitution of standard formula 99-13
Special Considerations and Complications 99-13
Parenteral Nutrition (See Figures 99.2 and 99.3) 99-13
  Goals of long-term support 99-13
  Fat emulsions: complications 99-13
  Glucose intolerance 99-14
  Effects of bronchopulmonary dysplasia (BPD)
    and mechanical ventilation 99-16
  Pediatric amino acid formulations (PAAFs)
    (See Table 99.11) 99-16
  Protein intolerance 99-16
  Septicemia 99-17
  Rickets 99-17
    Calcium and phosphorus supplementation 99-18
  Liver disease in TPN 99-18
    Risk factors 99-18
    Prognosis 99-18
    Tolerance of conversion to enteral feeding 99-19
    Enteral refeeding 99-19

Adequate nutrition is an essential component of the health maintenance of children and, in part, has been responsible for the dramatic reduction of infant mortality seen in the U.S. during the 20th century. Clinical experience has confirmed the value of optimal nutrition in resisting the effects of disease and trauma as well as in improving the response to medical and surgical therapy. The metabolic demands of rapid growth and maturation in addition to the low nutritional reserves present during infancy make the potential benefit of good nutrition to critically ill pediatric patients even greater.

Normal oral or enteral nutrition is the preferred method for meeting the nutritional requirements of a child. Enteral feedings taken orally or delivered by a tube to the stomach or small intestine can provide partial or complete nourishment for a pediatric patient who has a functioning intestinal tract but is unable or unwilling to achieve adequate oral intake. Indications for providing enteral nutrition include malnutrition, malabsorption, hypermetabolism, failure to thrive, prematurity, and disorders of absorption, digestion, excretion, or utilization of nutrients.

Despite the many formulas and feeding techniques available, several medical and gastrointestinal (GI) dilemmas arise in infants and children that impede or limit the use of the GI tract for nutritional support. Premature infants with severe respiratory disease, congenital abnormalities of the GI tract, or necrotizing enterocolitis are typical candidates for support with parenteral nutrition. Older children with short bowel syndrome, severe malnutrition, intractable diarrhea, or inflammatory bowel disease have been successfully managed with parenteral nutrition therapy. Pediatric patients receiving chemotherapy for the treatment of malignancies or bone marrow transplant, children with severe cardiac failure, and those with extensive body surface burns also have been successfully rehabilitated with parenteral nutrition.

Many disorders that adversely affect nutrient intake or absorption also have an adverse impact on a patient's fluid and electrolyte

Table 99.1	Parenteral Nutrient Requirements in Children[45,47,48,110]
Nutrient	**Requirement**
Fluid	<10 kg — 100 mL/kg 10–20 kg — 1000 mL + 50 mL/kg for each kg >10 kg >20 kg — 1500 mL + 20 mL/kg for each kg >20 kg
Calories	<10 kg — 100 kcal/kg 10–20 kg — 1000 kcal + 50 kcal/kg for each kg >10 kg >20 kg — 1500 kcal + 20 kcal/kg for each kg >20 kg
Protein[a]	*Infants: 2–3 gm/kg* *Older children: 1.5–2.0 gm/kg* *Adolescents and beyond: 1.0–1.5 gm/kg*
Fat[a, b]	4% of calories as linoleic acid
Sodium	2–4 mEq/kg (*max:* 100–120 mEq/day)
Potassium	2–3 mEq/kg (*max:* 100–120 mEq/day)
Chloride	2–4 mEq/kg (*max:* 100–120 mEq/day)
Magnesium	0.25–0.5 mEq/kg
Calcium	0.5–3.0 mEq/kg
Phosphorus	1.0–1.5 mmol/kg
Zinc	*<3 kg*: 300 µg/kg *>3 kg*: 100 µg/kg (*max:* 4 mg/day)
Copper	20 µg/kg (*max:* 1 mg/day)
Manganese	2–10 µg/kg (*max:* 400 µg/day)
Chromium	0.1–0.5 µg/kg (*max:* 10-15 µg/day)
Selenium	3 µg/kg
Vitamin A	230 units/kg (*max:* 2300 units)
Vitamin D	40 units/kg (*max:* 400 units)
Vitamin E	0.7 units/kg (*max:* 7 units)
Vitamin K	20 µg/ kg (*max:* 200 µg)
Thiamine	0.12 mg/kg (*max:* 1.2 mg)
Niacin	1.7 mg/kg (*max:* 17 mg)
Riboflavin	0.14 mg/kg (*max:* 1.4 mg)
Pyridoxine	0.1 mg/kg (*max:* 1 mg)
Vitamin B$_{12}$	0.1 µg/kg (*max:* 1 µg)
Biotin	2 µg/kg (*max:* 20 µg)
Vitamin C	8 mg/kg (*max:* 80 mg)
Folic acid	14 µg/kg (*max:* 140 µg)

[a] "Infant" amino acids contain histidine, taurine, tyrosine, and cysteine which are essential in infants, but not older patients. No clear advantage over standard amino acid solutions.

[b] Since linoleic acid represents 54% of the fatty acid in soy bean oil and 77% in safflower oil, 7%–10% of calories must be provided as fat emulsion. This can be given daily over 24 hours (preferred in patients predisposed to sepsis and preterm infants) or 2–3 times weekly.

status. Consequently, fluid, electrolyte, and nutrient management should be approached in an integrated manner. This chapter reviews selected aspects of fluid and electrolyte management and nutrition therapy for the pediatric population.

Fluid and Electrolyte Maintenance

Management of fluid and electrolyte disturbances involves the replacement of deficits, providing normal daily maintenance requirements, and replacing ongoing losses. To design rational fluid therapy for a patient, it is necessary to know the normal composition of body water and to understand the routes through which water and solutes are lost from the body. To devise fluid therapy for a sick patient, it is important to understand how these excretory routes are affected by disease.

Requirements

The general recommendations for calculating maintenance fluid, electrolyte, and nutrient requirements on the basis of weight are

provided in Table 99.1. These requirements may be altered when there are sources of increased loss or when excretion is impaired.

When abnormal fluid losses are present from any of the sources listed in Table 99.2, they must be added to the patient's daily maintenance fluid and electrolyte formula. The electrolyte content of gastrointestinal secretions varies widely. Ideally, a sample of the fluid lost from the patient should be analyzed for electrolyte content to allow for replacement of actual losses. When this is not possible, a solution of dextrose 5% 0.45% NaCl with 20 mEq of KCl/L may be used to replace GI losses. If the electrolyte imbalance continues, the formula should be adjusted to better reflect the actual losses.

Renal dysfunction may either increase or decrease maintenance fluid requirements. In patients with severe renal dysfunction, a factor of 40 mL/kg or 300 to 500 mL/m^2 may be used to estimate all other routes of fluid loss; the patient's actual urine output (mL/day) then is added to this amount to arrive at a daily maintenance.

The requirements for fluid and calories normalized to body weight are much greater in very small children than in older children and adults as can be seen in Table 99.1. Infants have a much larger body surface area relative to weight than older patients (≈ 0.25 m^2 for a 4 kg infant versus 1.73 m^2 for a 70 kg adult). Accordingly, infants lose more fluid through evaporation and dissipate much more heat per kilogram than their older counterparts which accounts for the larger requirements seen in this population.

Calculation of Maintenance Fluid Requirements

1. P.J., a 2-day-old, 3.5 kg full-term female infant, has been feeding poorly. She has developed abdominal distention, and her feedings have been stopped. Calculate a maintenance fluid and electrolyte prescription for her. Her admission serum electrolytes include the following: sodium (Na) 137 mEq/L (Normal: 135–145); potassium (K) 4.2 mEq/L (Normal: 3.5–5); chloride (Cl) 105 mEq/L (Normal: 102–109); bicarbonate (HCO$_3^-$) 23 mEq/L (Normal: 22–29). While P.J. receives nothing by mouth (NPO), her fluid and electrolyte needs must be met intravenously. Estimate her requirements. [SI units: Na 137 mmol/L (Normal: 135–145); K 4.2 mmol/L (Normal: 3.5–5.0); Cl 105 mmol/L (Normal: 102–109); HCO$_3^-$ 23 mmol/L (Normal: 22–29)]

While a commercially available intravenous (IV) solution will be used, each component of the solution should be calculated separately. Using the guidelines in Table 99.1, P.J.'s maintenance requirements can be estimated as follows:

Table 99.2	Situations That Alter Maintenance Fluid Requirements[a]	
Situation	**Mechanism**	**Extent of Change**
Extreme prematurity	↑ skin losses	Varies
Radiant warmer use	↑ insensible water loss	20%–40%
Croup tent	↓ evaporative water loss	20%–50%
Diarrhea or vomiting	↑ GI loss	Varies
Fever	↑ insensible water loss	10%–15%/°C
Renal dysfunction	↑ or ↓ renal loss	Varies
Hyperventilation	↑ pulmonary evaporative loss	Varies
Phototherapy for hyperbilirubinemia	↑ insensible water loss	10%–20%
GI tract suction or ostomy	↑ GI loss	Varies

[a] GI = Gastrointestinal.

Severity	% Dehydration	Psyche	Thirst	Mucous Membranes	Tears	Anterior Fontanel	Skin	Urine Specific Gravity
Mild	<5	Normal	Slight	Normal to dry	Present	Flat	Normal	Slight change
Moderate	6–10	Irritable	Moderate	Dry	+/–	+/–	+/–	↑
Severe	10–15	Hyperirritable to lethargic	Intense	Parched	Absent	Sunken	Tenting	Greatly ↑

Table 99.3 — Clinical Signs of Dehydration

Fluid: 100 mL/kg × 3.5 kg = 350 mL/day or ≈5 mL/hr

Sodium: 2–4 mEq/kg/day × 3.5 kg = 7–14 mEq/day

Potassium: 2–3 mEq/kg/day × 3.5 kg = 7–10.5 mEq/day

These requirements can be met by infusing a solution of 5% dextrose with 0.2% NaCl and 20 mEq/L of KCl at 15 mL/hour. This will provide 12 mEq of NaCl and 7 mEq of KCl in 360 mL of fluid per day.

Adjustment for Phototherapy Lights

2. On the 3rd day of life, P.J.'s indirect bilirubin is 15.2 mg/dL. It is decided to treat her hyperbilirubinemia with phototherapy lights. How will this modify her maintenance fluid needs?[SI unit: 259.92 µmol/L]

Table 99.2 details situations which alter maintenance fluid needs. Phototherapy lights will increase P.J.'s maintenance fluid needs by 10% to 20%. This can be met by simply increasing her prescribed IV fluid to 17 mL/hour (116 mL/kg/day). Although her increased fluid loss will be free from solutes and the solution she is receiving contains sodium and potassium, the electrolytes she receives still will be within the range of normal, and her kidneys should be able to compensate for the small increase.

Dehydration

Clinical Presentation: Vomiting

3. Acute Management. H.S., a 2-year-old lethargic female, is seen in her pediatrician's office with a 2-day history of vomiting and minimal oral intake. Yesterday she required only 3 diaper changes instead of her usual 8 and has needed only 1 change today. Her vital signs are as follows: temperature 39 °C, pulse 140 beats/min (Normal: 80–130), respiratory rate 30/min (Normal: 30–35), blood pressure (BP) 80/45 mm Hg (80–115/50–80). Upon physical examination, her eyes appear sunken, her mucous membranes are dry, and her skin is dry and cool to touch. Although she is crying, there are no tears and the skin over her thigh tents when pinched. Her weight today is 11.4 kg; 3 weeks ago, it was 12.9 kg. What do these findings represent? What immediate treatment should be provided?

H.S.'s lethargy, decreased urine output, tearless crying, dry mucous membranes, dry skin in the presence of fever, sunken eyes, mild tachycardia with low normal blood pressure, and poor skin turgor all are signs of dehydration. This is consistent with her two-day history of vomiting and poor intake. Her weight loss of 1.5 kg gives a further clue to the extent of dehydration. Dehydration or fluid loss is determined most accurately by weight loss. The percentage dehydration can be calculated using the following formula:

$$\% \text{ Dehydration} = \frac{\text{Normal Body Weight} - \text{Actual Body Weight}}{\text{Normal Body Weight}} \times 100 \qquad Eq\ 99.1$$

If recent weights are unavailable, the extent of dehydration can be approximated from physical findings. Table 99.3 organizes some of the signs and symptoms of dehydration according to severity. The presence of tachycardia and marginal blood pressure dictate immediate intravenous rehydration. This should be achieved with

the administration of 10 to 20 mL/kg of 0.9% NaCl injection infused as rapidly as possible.

4. Calculation of Requirements. Calculate H.S.'s fluid and electrolyte needs. Her serum electrolyte results were as follows: Na 128 mEq/L, K 3.1 mEq/L, Cl 88 mEq/L, HCO₃⁻ 30 mEq/L. [SI units: Na 128 mmol/L; K 3.1 mmol/L; Cl 88 mmol/L; HCO₃⁻ 30 mmol/L]

In addition to normal maintenance fluids, H.S. must be provided with fluids and electrolytes to replace her deficit secondary to dehydration and compensate for her increased insensible water loss due to fever. Each component of the fluid should be calculated separately, using equations 99.2 to 99.4.

$$\text{Fluid Deficit} = \text{Weight Loss (kg)} \times 1000\ \text{mL/kg} \qquad Eq\ 99.2$$

$$\text{Fever Adjustment} = 10\% \times \text{Maintenance for each } °C > 37\ °C \qquad Eq\ 99.3$$

$$(CD - CO) \times F_d \times \text{Weight} = \text{mEq Required} \qquad Eq\ 99.4$$

Where CD is the concentration desired (mEq/L); CO is the concentration observed (mEq/L); and F_d is the apparent distribution factor as a fraction of body weight (see Table 99.4); and weight is the baseline weight before illness (kg). Taking both maintenance needs and current deficits, fluid and electrolyte requirements for H.S. would be as follows:

Fluid

$$\text{Maintenance: } 1000\ \text{mL} + (50 \times 2.9) = 1145\ \text{mL}$$
$$\text{Fever: } 2\ °C \times 0.1(1145) = 229\ \text{mL}$$
$$\text{Deficit: } 1.5\ \text{kg} \times 1000\ \text{mL/kg} = \underline{1500\ \text{mL}}$$
$$\text{Total Fluid} = 2874\ \text{mL}$$

Sodium

$$\text{Maintenance: } 3\ \text{mEq/kg} \times 12.9\ \text{kg} = 38.7$$
$$\text{Deficit: } (135 - 128\ \text{mEq/L}) \times 0.6\ \text{L/kg} \times 12.9\ \text{kg} = \underline{54.2}$$
$$\text{Total Sodium} = \approx93\ \text{mEq}$$

Potassium. Estimation of H.S.'s potassium deficit is complicated by the fact that potassium is primarily an intracellular ion. As a result, serum concentrations are poor reflections of total body stores. In addition, H.S.'s electrolytes indicate moderate metabolic alkalosis. In this situation, potassium moves intracellularly in exchange for hydrogen ions which maintain a normal blood pH; potassium also is excreted by the kidney in exchange for hydrogen ion conservation. All of these factors combine to make the serum potassium concentration difficult to interpret. The prudent approach is to give no potassium until urine output is clearly established. Then, only maintenance doses of potassium should be administered until a normal acid base and fluid status are established and the serum potassium can be assessed more accurately. Hence, H.S. should receive approximately 39 mEq of potassium (3 mEq/kg × 12.9 kg) once urine flow is established.

Chloride. H.S. has a mild metabolic alkalosis as evidenced by her serum bicarbonate of 30 mEq/L. This is most likely due to the loss of acid and chloride in her vomitus. Thus, both the sodium and potassium replacements should be administered as chloride salts.

5. Administration of Fluid Requirements. **How should these calculated needs be given?**

Requirements for the first 24 hours of parenteral fluid therapy should provide approximately 2875 mL of fluid, 93 mEq of sodium, and 39 mEq of potassium. If the sodium and potassium are divided into three separate liters, each liter of dextrose 5% should contain 30 mEq/L NaCl and 13 mEq/L KCl, although the potassium should be withheld until urine flow is established.

The infusion rate should be calculated to provide one-third of the daily maintenance fluid (adjusted for fever) plus one-half of the deficit replacement during the first eight hours. The remainder of the maintenance fluid (adjusted for fever) and deficit replacement should be administered over the next 16 hours. (See Figure 99.1.)

Clinical Presentation: Diarrhea

6. S.B., a 4-month-old, 5.9 kg male, is seen in his pediatrician's office because of a 4-day history of diarrhea (5–8 large, liquid stools each day). On a well-child visit 4 weeks ago his weight was 6 kg. His oral intake has been changed since the onset of diarrhea to dissolved oral rehydration salts. Physical examination reveals: temperature 39.8 °C, pulse 110 beats/min (Normal: 80–160), respirations 45/min (Normal: 20–40), and BP 100/58 mm Hg (Normal: 75–105/40–65). His skin is pale, warm, and dry but does not tent on pinching. He is very irritable, and the mucous membranes are dry. S.B.'s serum electrolytes are: Na 159 mEq/L (Normal: 135–145); K 3.3 mEq/L (Normal: 3.5–5.0); Cl 114 mEq/L (Normal: 102–109); HCO_3^- 12 mEq/L (Normal: 22–29). Correlate S.B.'s history and physical findings with the reported laboratory values. [SI units: Na 159 mmol/L (Normal: 135–145); K 3.3 mmol/L (Normal: 3.5–5.0); Cl 114 mmol/L (Normal: 102–109); HCO_3^- 12 mmol/L (Normal: 22–29)]

Diarrheal fluid losses commonly contain high concentrations of bicarbonate, accounting for S.B.'s metabolic acidosis. This, in turn, has resulted in a rapid respiratory rate as the body attempts to compensate for the acidosis by eliminating carbon dioxide. The increased insensible water losses of fever and tachypnea have resulted in the loss of water in excess of sodium, producing hypernatremia. Because hypernatremia results in increased serum osmolality with consequent movement of water from within cells into the extracellular space, the blood pressure, skin turgor, and pulse remain relatively normal despite dehydration.

7. Acute Management. **How will S.B.'s management differ from that of H.S.? (See Questions 3–5.)**

Unlike H.S., S.B. has relatively normal vital signs and will not require acute administration of a fluid load to correct hypotension. The presence of hypernatremia in S.B. will alter the haste with which electrolyte and fluid deficits are corrected. In the presence of plasma hyperosmolarity, the central nervous system (CNS) produces an endogenous intracellular osmolar load to prevent intracellular dehydration of the CNS cells. Rapid correction of peripheral hyperosmolarity results in excessive displacement of water into the cells of the CNS and has been associated with seizures. To avoid this problem, S.B.'s fluid and electrolyte deficits should be corrected over two to three days at a consistent rate rather than

Table 99.4	Electrolytes and Apparent Distribution
Electrolyte	F_d (L/kg)[a]
Sodium	0.6–0.7
Bicarbonate	0.4–0.5
Chloride	0.2–0.3

[a] F_d = Apparent distribution factor as a fraction of body weight.

Fluid Rate Calculations

Maintenance:	1145 mL/day ÷ 24 hr = 47.7 mL/hr
Fever Adjustment:	229 mL/day ÷ 24 hr = 9.5 mL/hr
Deficit Replacement:	1500 mL total to be administered as
	750 mL ÷ 8 hr = 93.7 mL/hr and
	750 mL ÷ 16 hr = 46.8 mL/hr

Recommended Fluid Rate

First 8 hr:	Maintenance	47.7 mL/hr
	Fever	9.5 mL/hr
	Deficit	93.7 mL/hr
	Total	150.9 or 150 mL/hr

Next 16 hr:	Maintenance	47.7 mL/hr
	Fever	9.5 mL/hr
	Deficit	46.8 mL/hr
	Total	104 or 100 mL/hr

Fig 99.1 Fluid Rate Calculations

rapidly, over the first 24 hours as is acceptable when the serum sodium is normal or low.

8. Calculation of Requirements. **Estimate S.B.'s fluid and electrolyte requirements to correct his deficits.**

S.B.'s requirements are estimated using the same methods described in Question 4. First, the approximate extent of dehydration must be estimated. S.B.'s weight of 6 kg at the time of his well-child visit at three months of age was at the 50th percentile. If the assumption is made that his growth has continued at this rate, his current weight should be approximately 6.5 kg. Thus, his deficit is about 0.6 L, or 9%. Using this approximation, his fluid and electrolyte requirements can be estimated as follows.

Fluid:

Maintenance: 6.5 × 100 mL/kg =	650 mL/24 hr
Fever: 2.8 °C × 0.1(650 mL) =	182 mL/24 hr
Deficit: 600 mL/3 days =	200 mL/24 hr
Total Daily Needs =	1032 mL or 43 mL/hr

Sodium:

Maintenance: 3 mEq/kg × 6.56 kg = 19.5 mEq/24 hr

Deficit: This is calculated at total body deficit (Normal = Actual)

Normal: 145 mEq/L × 0.6 L/kg × 6.6 kg = 575 mEq

Actual: 159 mEq/L × 0.6 L/kg × 5.9 kg = 563 mEq

Deficit = 12 mEq or 4 mEq/day

Potassium. As noted in Question 4, the serum potassium value of 3.3 mEq/L tells little about S.B.'s total body potassium status. In S.B.'s case, however, the presence of a metabolic acidosis should have caused exchange of hydrogen ion into the cells and compensatory movement of potassium from the intracellular to the extracellular space. Thus, the serum potassium of 3.3 mEq/L likely represents a total body deficit. Until urine output is established, potassium should be withheld. Once urine output is established, a maintenance potassium dose of 20 mEq/day (≈3 mEq/kg) should be given. Serum electrolytes should be measured every 8 to 12 hours and the intake of all electrolytes should be readjusted based upon the results.

Bicarbonate. With metabolic acidosis, bicarbonate replacement should be undertaken as well. No maintenance amount is customarily given, but deficit replacement is calculated in a manner similar to that used for sodium. (See Table 99.4.) The volume of distribution of bicarbonate is 0.5 L/kg. For S.B. the bicarbonate deficit is:

$$(23 - 12) \text{ mEq/L} \times 0.5 \text{ L/kg} \times 66 \text{ kg} = 36.3 \text{ mEq}$$

Initially, about one-half of this amount should be replaced over the first 8 to 12 hours. His serum electrolytes then should be reassessed and the prescription adjusted as indicated by the results. The entire deficit is not replaced at once because other compensatory mechanisms will contribute to endogenous bicarbonate sparing.

9. Replacement Fluid Composition. Recommend an appropriate replacement fluid for S.B.'s therapy.

Given the maintenance and deficit amounts just calculated, S.B. should receive 1000 mL of D5W with 36 mEq NaHCO$_3$ over 24 hours at a rate of 42 mL/hour. After he urinates, 20 mEq/L KCl may be added. Electrolyte concentrations should be adjusted every 8 to 12 hours based upon laboratory results. The adjustment for fever should be modified based upon his subsequent body temperature.

10. Administration of Requirements. By what route should the fluid calculated above be administered?

Rehydration of the dehydrated patient may be achieved by either the oral or intravenous route. In some patients, vomiting may preclude effective oral rehydration. If the losses are diarrheal, and there is no problem with vomiting, the oral route may be a cost-effective alternative to the parenteral route. A variety of solutions have been used to rehydrate children orally. The sodium concentration of these solutions ranges from 30 to 90 mEq/L and all are safe and effective in rehydrating children whether they are hyponatremic, isonatremic, or hypernatremic.[1–3]

The composition of several products is shown in Table 99.5. A glucose concentration of 2% will optimize water and electrolyte absorption from the gut;[4] more concentrated glucose solutions may worsen rather than ameliorate diarrhea. Use of the oral route and the more concentrated sodium solutions may allow safe rehydration of hypernatremic dehydration in a shorter time frame than the two to three days noted above.[4,5]

S.B.'s output must be measured to account for ongoing fluid loss. This often is accomplished by weighing the baby's diapers when they are dry and again when they are full. Composition of additional replacement fluids can be determined by using the average composition of the patient's losses (see Table 99.6). As an alternative, the composition of the losses may be determined by actual laboratory measurement. If prolonged therapy is necessary, specific analyses are recommended because of the wide range of normal values for diarrheal stool and other gastrointestinal tract fluids. Since frequent adjustments may be necessary, replacement fluid should be administered separately if parenteral nutrition is being utilized as a maintenance solution.

Infant Nutrition

Growth assessment is an important focus of pediatric health care during the first year of life. With the exception of the intrauterine period, the first year is the time period during which the most rapid growth occurs. Typically, healthy infants will weigh approximately three times their birthweight by their first birthday.

The American Academy of Pediatrics Committee on Nutrition has suggested that infant feeding be divided into three stages.[6] In the nursing period, only liquids are provided. During the transitional period, solid foods are introduced but milk still provides the major source of the infant's caloric and nutrient supply. In the modified adult period, the majority of nutrition is derived from the solid foods consumed by the remainder of the household.

At birth, the human GI tract is adapted for the consumption of a milk-based diet. Intestinal lactase is present from 36 weeks of gestation and exhibits its maximum activity during infancy. Pancreatic amylase secretion is low, and the bile salt pool is decreased relative to older individuals, resulting in decreased fat absorption.[7] Milk, especially human milk, provides nutrients in their most usable form for the developing GI tract.

Vitamin K

11. M.E., a full-term newborn female, has just been transferred from the delivery room into the transitional nursery. What nutrient does she need to receive now and why?

The current standard of practice in the U.S. is that newborn infants receive parenteral vitamin K within a short time of birth. This practice assures that, at least for the short term, the infant will not become vitamin K-deficient.[8] When this practice is not routine, hemorrhage in the newborn period may occur.[9] The usual neonatal vitamin K dose is 1 mg, given once intramuscularly (IM), within the first several hours of life.

Human Milk Feeding

12. M.E.'s mother has decided to breast-feed her infant. What are the nutritional implications of this decision for M.E.?

The milks of various animal species have compositions unique to that species. Hence, one can assume that human milk is the ideal food for a human infant. The protein content of human milk is of such biologic quality and bioavailability that adequate growth can be attained with a lower overall intake of protein.[10–12] Likewise, the fat in human milk is present in a highly digestible and absorbable form.[10]

Human milk provides sufficient protein, minerals, and calories regardless of the mother's nutritional status.[11] Only the vitamin content of human milk depends upon the maternal nutritional status.[11] Although the iron content of human milk falls short of the quantity generally recommended for term infants, its availability for absorption from the GI tract is adequate, and supplementation generally is unnecessary in the breast-fed infant.[13] Regardless of maternal status, the vitamin D and fluoride contents of human milk are inadequate. Thus, M.E. will require 100 to 400 international units of vitamin D and 0.25 mg/day of fluoride while she is exclusively breast-fed.[11,14]

13. Aside from nutrients, what other substances are found in human milk and what are their implications?

Table 99.5	Composition of Oral Rehydration Products				
Product	Na$^+$ (mEq/L)	K$^+$ (mEq/L)	Cl (mEq/L)	Bicarbonate Source (mEq/L)	Carbohydrate (%)
Gastrolyte	90	20	80	30 Citrate	2
Rehydrate	75	20	65	30 Citrate	2.5
Lytren	50	25	45	30 Citrate	2
Pedialyte	45	20	35	30 Citrate	2.5
WHO salts	90	20	80	30 Bicarbonate	2

Table 99.6	Body Fluid Volumes and Electrolyte Content[a]				
Source	Volume (L/day)	Na$^+$ (mEq/L)	K$^+$ (mEq/L)	Cl$^-$ (mEq/L)	HCO$_3^-$ (mEq/L)
Salivary glands	1.5 (0.5–2)	10 (2–10)	26 (20–30)	10 (8–18)	30
Stomach	1.5 (0.1–4)	60 (9–116)	10 (0–32)	130 (8–154)	—
Duodenum	(0.1–2)	140	5	80	—
Ileum	3 (0.1–9)	140 (80–150)	5 (2–8)	104 (43–137)	30
Colon	—	60	30	40	—
Pancreas	(0.1–0.8)	140 (113–185)	5 (3–7)	75 (54–95)	115
Bile	(0.05–0.8)	145 (131–164)	5 (3–12)	100 (89–180)	35

[a] Adapted from reference 140.

Human milk contains immunologically active cellular components and antibodies. These include secretory IgA, both T and B lymphocytes, macrophages, and neutrophils.[10,11] The IgA antibodies may be directed toward a variety of enteric and respiratory pathogens and may be protective against illness in the infant.[15] The lipases and amylase present in human milk may facilitate digestion of fat and carbohydrates in the still developing GI tract. Proteins present in human milk serve as carriers for trace minerals and facilitate their absorption.[11] Oligosaccharides and glycopeptides may promote the colonization of the gut by *Lactobacilli* and decrease colonization by *Bacteroides*, *Clostridia*, enterococci, and gram-negative rods, all of which may be pathogenic.[10]

Introduction of Solid Foods

14. At her 2-month-old, well-child check-up, M.E.'s mother asks her pediatrician about the introduction of ''baby foods'' into M.E.'s diet. When and how should solids be introduced?

Human milk or commercially prepared infant formula, when supplemented as noted above, provides adequate nutrition for an infant for the first six months of life. Introduction of solid foods before the age of four months, while common in the past, is discouraged because the younger infant is unprepared to swallow foods other than liquids. The American Academy of Pediatrics recommends that solids (first cereals, then fruits and vegetables) be introduced when the child has good control of the head and neck movements.[6] This occurs at the age of four to six months. At that time, the Academy recommends introduction of one new food at a time, at one-week intervals, to allow assessment of food allergy.

Cow's Milk and Cow's Milk-Based Formula

15. E.R.'s mother does not want to breast-feed her infant. She received a sample package of infant formula at the time of her discharge from the hospital. How are these products prepared and how do they differ from human milk?

Infant formulas generally begin with a cow's milk base. However, because many infants have difficulty tolerating cow's milk, a number of modifications are made.[15] The predominant protein in cow's milk is casein; in human milk it is whey. Casein is difficult for human infants to digest. Consequently, infant formulas generally have had the casein content reduced, though not to the level of human milk (40% versus 20%, respectively). The casein present also may be heat denatured to improve its digestibility. The fat content of cow's milk generally is replaced by one of several vegetable oils to provide easier digestibility, while in human milk, fat is present in a digestible form. Cow's milk-based formula is lactose or sucrose supplemented since lactose content of cow's milk is only 50% to 70% as high as human milk. Examples of infant formulas and their individual components are provided in Table 99.7.

16. At her 6-month-old, well-child check-up, E.R. is found to have a hematocrit (Hct) of 33% (Normal: 35–45). Upon questioning her mother, the pediatrician learns that E.R. was taken off infant formula 3 months ago and changed to whole cow's milk to decrease food costs. How are these two findings related? What should be added to E.R.'s diet? [SI unit: 0.35]

Unlike the iron in human milk, the minimal amount present in cow's milk is absorbed very poorly from the human GI tract. Most infant formulas are iron supplemented to compensate for this. At the same time, in infants under 140 days of age, cow's milk has caused GI blood loss that can be detected in the stool.[17] When the milk is heated hotter than the usual pasteurization temperature, as it is in formula preparation, there is no blood loss. Hence, the component responsible for the blood loss appears to be a heat labile protein.

To treat E.R.'s anemia, iron should be added to her diet. This can be done by changing back to an iron-fortified infant formula, feeding her an iron-fortified cereal, or giving a therapeutic ferrous sulfate liquid medication. The appropriate dose is 6 mg/kg/day of elemental iron. In any event, cow's milk feeding should be stopped.

Therapeutic Formulas

Phenylketonuria (PKU)

17. L.B. is a 2-week-old infant whose newborn screen is positive for PKU. Discuss the concepts behind the production of therapeutic formulas and the dietary management of patients with metabolic errors. How must L.B.'s diet be modified?

Inborn errors of metabolism are disorders in which an enzyme or its cofactor exhibits low or absent activity. As a result, there will be accumulation of one or more precursor compounds which occur in the metabolic pathway before the defective step. There also will be a corresponding deficit of one or more metabolic products which normally occur after the defective step in the metabolic pathway. These deficient products may be compounds which are further utilized in normal metabolism (such as tyrosine, which is deficient in PKU) or they may be the excretory form of an otherwise toxic substance (such as urea, which is absent in patients with urea cycle defects; this results in the accumulation of ammonia).

The dietary management of metabolic errors is based upon several strategies.

- Reduce the intake of a precursor compound which cannot be metabolized.

- Supplement the deficient compounds which would have been produced if the normal metabolic pathway had not been blocked.

- Add a substrate which provides an alternate pathway for elimination of an accumulated toxin.

Therapeutic formulas are designed to reduce the intake of precursor compounds to the amount essential for growth, eliminate those precursors which may be eliminated, or provide the deficient metabolic products. In general, the therapeutic formulas are incomplete products which require supplementation to provide complete nutrition.

In PKU, hydroxylation of phenylalanine to tyrosine does not take place. Given this information, L.B.'s diet should be modified using a formula containing little or no phenylalanine, such as Lofenalac or Phenyl-Free. Natural protein such as human milk or commercial formula will be added in carefully controlled amounts to provide L.B.'s requirement for phenylalanine. The metabolic defect in PKU produces a tyrosine deficiency which is replaced with supplemental tyrosine in the PKU formulas. As L.B. progresses to solid foods and beyond, protein must be provided from predominately phenylalanine-free sources (such as these formulas); only minimal protein can be derived from table foods.[18]

Other Metabolic Errors

18. What other metabolic errors present in infancy and may be treated by diet?

Other metabolic errors which are present in infancy include galactosemia, in which galactose cannot be metabolized to glucose; homocystinuria, in which methionine is not converted to cysteine; the urea cycle disorders, in which ammonia detoxification is impaired; and maple syrup urine disease, in which there is a block in the metabolism of the branched chain amino acids leucine, isoleucine, and valine.

These metabolic errors are managed by manipulating the diet.[19] In galactosemia, the carbohydrate source contains no galactose or lactose. In homocystinuria, methionine is kept to the minimal requirement and cysteine is supplemented. In maple syrup urine disease, natural protein is fed in small quantities to provide the minimal requirement of branched chain amino acids, and a branched chain-free supplement is added to provide adequate protein intake. In the urea cycle disorders, protein often is provided as essential amino acids only, and a high-energy diet is provided to maximize the formation of nonessential amino acids from nitrogen and to minimize ammonia production.

Pediatric Nutritional Support

Indications

In general terms, nutritional support is indicated for any patient unwilling or unable to take in sufficient nourishment to maintain normal growth. Some specific disorders are listed in Table 99.8 and several deserve special comment.

Extremely Premature Infants. The extremely premature infant requires specialized nutritional support for two distinct reasons. The third trimester *in utero* is a time of rapid body growth and rapid accumulation of body stores of protein, glycogen, fat, and minerals.[20] The infant born in the very early stages of the third trimester never accumulates these stores and, therefore, must receive nutrients earlier than a more mature infant. In addition, extreme prematurity is associated with poor coordination of the suck and swallow reflex, poor gastrointestinal motility, and incomplete absorption.[21] Therefore, enteral nutrients will need to be administered via orogastric or nasogastric tube, and parenteral supplementation probably will be needed.

Respiratory distress may preclude enteral feeding because high respiratory rates prevent coordinated breathing and swallowing. Infants who are hypoxic or at high risk for hypoxia may not receive enteral feedings during the acute phase of their illness because of a concern for bowel ischemia. Often, these situations are resolved in three to five days, but this can rarely be predicted at the outset. Nutritional support in such cases is initiated by giving parenteral fluids, which provide dextrose as a caloric source. This will allow

the infant to conserve endogenous energy substrates, an important consideration for the very low birthweight infant whose entire body may represent a three to four day energy supply.[20] Full parenteral nutrition should be initiated as soon as it becomes clear the enteral feeding will be impossible for five days or more, or when several days have elapsed and no clear time frame can be determined for the initiation of enteral feeding. While a short course (<5 days) of parenteral therapy may be used, the quantity of nutrients supplied during the process of initiation and gradual increase to full requirements is so low that extremely short courses are difficult to justify.

Gastrointestinal (GI) Anomalies. Infants with GI anomalies require parenteral nourishment because they will undergo surgical repair and because the atretic blind pouch provides no outlet for fecal waste. Infants with necrotizing enterocolitis have zones of ischemic bowel and are at risk for perforation.[22] Likewise, infants with abdominal wall defects may have infected, ischemic, or necrotic tissue in the exteriorized portion.[23] Infants with these disorders will need parenteral nutrition until viability of the entire GI tract can be assured.

Chronic renal failure and hepatic disease present the need to modify a normal diet to account for impaired protein metabolism or impaired elimination of nitrogenous waste. For example, careful caloric supplementation with a reduced amount of protein may permit normal growth while minimizing excess urea production in an infant with renal failure.

Nutritional Assessment

A nutritional assessment should be performed before beginning a regimen of nutritional support and at intervals during the course of treatment. Large surveys have shown that about one-third of children admitted to hospital inpatient services are malnourished at the time of their admission.[24] Identifying malnourished individuals may allow prediction of those who eventually will be at risk for social or intellectual difficulties.[25–27]

Factors which are used to determine nutritional status in children include dietary history, weight, height, triceps skinfold thickness (TSF), midarm circumference (MAC), and visceral protein measurements such as albumin, prealbumin, retinol binding protein, and transferrin. Other measurements used in adults, such as 24-hour creatinine excretion, 24-hour nitrogen excretion, and nitrogen balance, are reserved for older children because complete collection and accurate timing of urine samples are difficult to achieve.

Anthropometric Measurements. Of the anthropometric measurements, the most universally applied are height and weight. Using these measurements, three comparisons to standards are possible: weight for age, height for age, and weight for height.[28] An individual patient's measurements are compared to tabular or graphic representations of normal values for various age groups found in most general pediatric texts. Using only these measurements, a weight which is below the fifth percentile for the patient's height is considered an indication of acute malnutrition. Similarly, a height which is below the fifth percentile for the patient's age indicates chronic malnutrition.

Other anthropometric measurements include triceps skinfold thickness, midarm circumference, and midarm muscle circumference (MAMC). These are used as indicators of body fat and skeletal or peripheral protein stores. MAMC is derived by subtracting subcutaneous fat circumference, calculated as 3.14 × TSF, from the MAC. Though this overestimates MAMC, it correlates well with measured muscle area[29] and allows comparison to normal values. The additional measures correlate well with weight and height in supporting a diagnosis of protein-calorie malnutrition.[28,30]

Table 99.7

Examples of Infant Formulas and Their Individual Components[a],[b]

Product	Calories per 100 mL	Carbo-hydrate gm/100 mL	Caloric Source	Protein gm/100 mL	Protein Source	Fat gm/100 mL	Fat Source	Osmolality mOsm/L	Sodium mEq/L	Potassium mEq/L	Chloride mEq/L	Calcium mEq(mg)/L	Phosphorous mEq/L	Iron mg/L
Human Milk/Milk-Based/Soy-Based Formulas														
Human milk	72 ± 5	7.2 ± 0.25	Lactose	1.05 ± 0.2	Whey 70% Casein 50%	3.9 ± 0.4	Human milk fat	290 ± 5	7.8 ± 1.7	13.4 ± 0.9	11.8 ± 1.7	14 ± 1.3 (280 ± 26)	9.0 ± 1.4	0.3 ± 0.1
Enfamil with iron	67	6.9	Lactose	1.5	Whey 50% Casein 50%	3.8	Soy and coconut oils	300	7.9	18.4	11.9	23	17.4	12.6
Similac with iron	68	7.23	Lactose	1.5	Casein (nonfat milk)	3.63	Soy and coconut oils	290	10	21	15	25	25.2	12
SMA	68	7.2	Lactose	1.5	Whey 60% Casein 40% L-Methionine	3.6	Oleo, safflower oleic, soy and coconut oils	300	6.4	14	10.6	21.9	20.9	12
Isomil	68	6.83	Corn syrup solids, sucrose	1.8	Soy protein isolate, L-Methionine	3.69	Soy and coconut oils	250	14	24	12	35	32.9	12
Nursoy	68	6.9	Sucrose	2.1	Soy protein isolate, L-Methionine	3.6	Oleo, safflower oleic, soy and coconut oils	296	8.7	17.9	10.6	29.9	27.1	11.5
Soyalac	69	6.8	Corn syrup, sucrose, soy	2.1	Soybean solids, L-Methionine	3.7	Soy oil	240	13	20	13	32	12	12.8
Casein Hydrolysate/Modified Fat/Premature LBW Formulas														
Nutramigen	67	9.1	Corn syrup, solids, modified corn starch	1.9	Hydrolyzed casein	2.6	Corn oil	320	14.0	18.9	16.4	31.3	24.0	12.7
Pregestimil	67	9.1	Corn syrup solids, modified corn starch	2.4	Hydrolyzed casein	2.7	MCT oil 42%, corn oil 57%, lecithin 1%	350	14.0	19.0	16.0	31.3	24.0	12.7
Portagen 20	67	7.8	Corn syrup, sucrose	2.4	Sodium caseinate	3.4	MCT oil 86%, corn oil 12%, soy lecithin 2%	220	13.9	22.0	16.4	31.3	27.0	12.7

Formula													
Enfamil Premature Formula	67	7.4	Whey 50% Casein 50%	2.0	Corn syrup solids, lactose	3.4	MCT oil 39%, soy 39%, coconut 20%, lecithin 2%	244	11.3	19.2	16.1	39.0	22.0	1.7
Enfamil Premature Formula 24	81	8.9	Whey 50% Casein 50%	2.4	Corn syrup solids, lactose	4.1	MCT oil 39%, soy 39%, coconut 20%, lecithin 2%	300	13.9	23.0	19.5	47.0	27.0	2.0
Similac Special Care	68	7.17	Whey 60% Casein 40%	1.83	Lactose, glucose polymers	3.67	MCT, soy and coconut oils	250	15	24	17	61	35.5	2.5
Similac Special Care 24	81	8.61	Whey 60% Casein 40%	2.2	Lactose, glucose polymers	4.41	MCT, soy and coconut oils	300	18	29	21	73	42.4	3.0
Similac 24 LBW	81	8.53	Nonfat milk	2.2	Lactose, glucose polymers	4.49	MCT, soy and coconut oils	290	16	31	25	36	33.1	3.0
Hypercaloric/Low Electrolyte Formulas													
Similac 27	91	9.59	Casein (nonfat milk)	2.47	Lactose	4.81	Soy and coconut oils	410	17	32	23	41	41.3	2.0
Similac PM 60:40	68	6.9	Whey 60% Casein 40%	1.58	Lactose	3.76	Soy and coconut oils	260	7	15	11	19	11	1.5
SMA 24	81	8.6	Whey 60% Casein 40%	1.8	Lactose	4.3	Oleo, safflower, oleic, soy and coconut oils	364	7.8	17	12.7	25.1	21.7	14.4
SMA 27	91.3	9.7	Whey 60% Casein 40%	2.0	Lactose	4.9	Oleo, safflower, oleic, soy and coconut oils	416	8.8	19.3	14.3	28.2	24.4	16.2

a Adapted from information provided by the American Academy of Pediatrics.
b LBW = Low body weight; MCT = Medium chain triglyceride.

Table 99.8	Indications for Nutritional Support[a]

Extreme prematurity
Respiratory distress
GI anomalies
Duodenal atresia
   Jejunal atresia
   Tracheoesophageal fistula
   Esophageal atresia
Abdominal wall defects
   Omphalocele (herniation of viscera into the umbilical cord base)
   Gastroschisis (defect of abdominal wall, any location except umbilical cord)
Necrotizing enterocolitis
Chronic diarrhea
Inflammatory bowel disease
Cystic fibrosis
Abdominal trauma involving viscera
Adverse effects of treating neoplastic disease
   Radiation enteritis
   Nausea and vomiting
   Stomatitis, glossitis, and esophagitis
Anorexia nervosa
Chronic renal failure
Hepatic renal failure
Metabolic errors

[a] GI = Gastrointestinal.

Biochemical Measurements. Numerous biochemical indices are used in the assessment of nutritional status.[28] Several, such as the quantitative excretion of compounds like 3-methyl-histidine and creatinine, are difficult to use in children because they require cumbersome 24-hour urine collections. Also, reliable standards for very young children are unavailable.

Of the biochemical markers of nutritional status, perhaps the most readily available and widely used is the serum albumin concentration. Although a low serum albumin is a very specific indicator of protein-calorie malnutrition, its long half-life (20 days)[31] makes it an insensitive indicator for developing and resolving malnutrition.

Prealbumin, fibronectin, and retinol binding protein are plasma transport proteins which also can function as biochemical markers of nutritional status.[31–34] They have the advantage of being more sensitive than albumin to acute nutritional changes because their turnover times are shorter, and they are useful when exogenous albumin infusions are given.[35] However, because they are influenced by factors other than nutrition, such as stress, they are less specific indicators of nutritional status.[36,37]

Nutrient Requirements

The basic requirements for a parenteral nutrient regimen are listed in Table 99.1. It must be remembered that these are guidelines for use in the initiation of the nutrient regimen; individual requirements may vary from patient to patient. The correct regimen for any specific individual is that supply of nutrients which promotes a normal rate of growth without toxicity. In particular, patients with ongoing, abnormal nutrient losses may require much larger doses of certain nutrients. Individualization of the nutrient prescription cannot be overemphasized.

The vitamin doses recommended in Table 99.1 deserve special comment. Although these amounts correspond to the guidelines of the American Medical Association-Nutrition Advisory Group, clinical evaluation of these doses has revealed several problems.

Very low birthweight infants given higher doses of vitamin A than those shown still develop signs and symptoms of vitamin A deficiency.[38,39] Vitamins D and E appeared to be adequately supplied by this dose (65% of the maximum shown in Table 99.1 for preterm infants, the full maximum for term infants and older children). In contrast to vitamin A, most water-soluble vitamin levels were normal with this higher dose. Niacin, pantothenate, biotin, and vitamin C levels were above normal in premature infants. Vitamin B_{12} and folate levels were elevated in premature infants as well as older infants and children.[40] Thus, a completely satisfactory parenteral vitamin product is not available yet.

Many of the requirements listed in Table 99.1 apply to nutrients administered by the enteral route as well. In some instances, the absorption of a particular nutrient from the gastrointestinal mucosa is incomplete, and enteral requirements are substantially higher. This is particularly true of the major minerals (calcium, magnesium, and iron) and trace elements.[41]

Route of Administration

Nutritional support using the GI tract is the preferred approach whenever possible. Enteral administration of nutrients provides several advantages. First, interposition of the GI mucosa between the nutrient supply and the circulation allows absorptive function to provide a homeostatic control. Likewise, the flow of nutrients from the gut to the liver via the portal circulation before they reach the systemic circulation also allows for homeostatic control. The risk of bacteremia associated with parenteral infusions is avoided with enteral nutrition. Finally, the intestinal mucosa is dependent upon intraluminal absorption for much of its energy supply. Hence, provision of at least a small amount of enteral feeding may prevent energy deprivation of a major organ system and may simplify later introduction of full enteral feedings.[42,43]

Normal oral feeding is the most basic method for patients who are willing and able to eat or drink. Tube feedings may be used in patients whose GI motility, structure, and function are normal but whose oral feeding is prevented by an altered state of consciousness, incoordination of sucking and swallowing, or other conditions which prevent adequate oral ingestion. Tube feedings may be administered in intermittent boluses or by continuous infusion.

Bolus tube feedings more closely mimic the normal state. They periodically distend the stomach which aids in gastric secretion and emptying. In this method, the volume of formula required to provide sufficient calories for a 24-hour period is given by gravity through the tube in equal aliquots every two, three, or four hours. The frequency will depend upon gastric capacity and the ability of the patient to maintain a normal serum glucose between feedings. Intolerance to bolus tube feedings may be manifested as diarrhea, gastroesophageal reflux with emesis, or poor motility, which manifests as large volumes of feeding remaining in the stomach when the next feeding is due.

Continuous tube feedings may be attempted when bolus feedings have failed. In this method, the total daily feeding volume is given at a constant rate by infusion pump. This approach may be better tolerated by children with diarrhea.[44] Continuous tube feedings may be infused into the stomach or the duodenum. Feedings introduced directly into the duodenum should be nearly isosmolar with serum since hyperosmolar duodenal feedings may precipitate an osmotic diarrhea.

Patients with intrinsic GI disease such as those mentioned in Table 99.8 or with malabsorption may require total or supplemental parenteral nutrition. Concurrent administration of low-volume, hypocaloric enteral feedings may provide important nutrients to the gut mucosa even when the parenteral route supplies all of the necessary systemic nutrients.[42,43] Total parenteral nutrition is administered into a high-flow, central vein to dilute the hyperosmolar solution. Administration into a peripheral vein usually is limited to those receiving parenteral nutrition for short periods of time or those receiving low concentrations to supplement enteral intake.

Monitoring

When using any therapeutic intervention, including nutritional support, it is important to monitor the beneficial and adverse effects of therapy. The therapeutic benefit of a nutritional regimen is evaluated by repeating the nutritional assessment at regular intervals, generally weekly. The goal of therapy will depend upon the pre-existing nutritional status. If the patient previously was well nourished, the goal is to maintain that status until a normal diet can be resumed. In one who was previously malnourished, an effort should be made to promote ''catch-up'' growth in weight and anthropometric parameters and to normalize the biochemical nutritional measures.

To monitor for adverse effects of enteral and parenteral nutrition, the clinician must evaluate the patient for signs and symptoms of fluid overload, diarrhea, and metabolic imbalances. An excessive rate of weight gain, edema, or polyuria (>3 mL/kg/hour) may indicate a need to reduce the rate of administration. Each day, the patient should be weighed and the fluid intake, urine output, and stool output assessed. The latter also is used to detect diarrhea, a major adverse effect of enteral feeding.

To detect hyperglycemia, bedside blood and urine glucose determinations should be performed several times daily. Persistent hyperglycemia and glycosuria may require a reduced infusion rate.

Several laboratory tests also should be monitored routinely in those receiving parenteral nutrition because the nature of the solutions results in several adverse effects not commonly seen in enteral support. These include rickets, hepatotoxicity, azotemia, and acid-base disturbances. A scheme for laboratory monitoring of parenteral nutrition is provided in Table 99.9. The measurement of serum triglycerides shown in this table is necessary only in patients receiving parenteral fat emulsions.

Clinical Presentation: Nutritional Assessment

19. T.C., a 4-month-old, lethargic male, is seen in his pediatrician's office for routine well-baby care. At examination he

Table 99.9	Routine Laboratory Monitoring of Pediatric and Neonatal Parenteral Nutrition[a]
Test	Frequency
Electrolytes, glucose, BUN, SrCr	Daily until stable, then 2–3 times a week
Calcium	1–2 times a week
Phosphorous	1–2 times a week
Magnesium	1–2 times a week
Triglycerides	QOD until stable on maximum fat dose, then weekly
PA, RBP	Weekly
Total protein, albumin	Weekly if PA, RBP not available
Alkaline phosphatase	Weekly
Bilirubin	Weekly
Hgb, WBC count	Weekly
AST, ALT	Monthly

[a] ALT = Alanine aminotransferase; AST = Aspartate aminotransferase; BUN = Blood urea nitrogen; Hgb = Hemoglobin; PA = Prealbumin; RBP = Retinol binding protein; SrCr = Serum creatinine; WBC = White blood cell.

has a moderately distended abdomen and dry mucous membranes. There are no other remarkable abnormalities. His weight is 5 kg (5th percentile for age). At a previous well-baby visit when he was 2 months old, T.C. weighed 5.6 kg (75th percentile for age) and he was an alert, vigorous infant. His mother reports that for the last 4 weeks he has had 5–8 large, liquid stools per day. His diet has not been changed, and it consists of 5–6 ounces of a commercial, cow milk formula Q 4 hr around the clock. He is to be hospitalized for evaluation of his diarrhea and failure to thrive and for fluid and nutritional management.

A nutritional assessment has been performed, with these results: weight 5 kg (5th percentile); height 58 cm (<5th percentile); albumin 2.4 gm/dL (Normal: 4–5.3); prealbumin 10 mg/dL (Normal: 20–50); retinol binding protein 15.4 mg/dL (normal: 30–44). What does this show about the nature of T.C.'s malnutrition? [SI units: albumin 24 gm/L (Normal: 40–53)]

Though T.C.'s weight is at the 5th percentile for age, one already has learned that it declined during the period from two months to four months of age. Thus, while the 5th percentile weight otherwise would be acceptable, a decrease in weight at this age clearly is abnormal. His height, which is below the 5th percentile, marks this as malnutrition of long-standing duration. The low serum protein levels (albumin, prealbumin, and retinol binding protein) indicate this is a deficiency of both protein and calories.

Nutrient Requirements

20. It is decided to nourish T.C. parenterally while his diagnostic work-up proceeds. Determine his nutrient requirements.

The parenteral requirements for T.C. are shown in Table 99.10 with examples of how specific products can be used in compounding a final preparation. This regimen is designed for peripheral venous administration, while the course of his diarrheal disease is observed to determine whether long-term, central venous access will be required. The goal of therapy at this point is to prevent further deterioration of T.C.'s nutritional status until he is able to accept enteral nutrition.

In this regimen, fat, fluid, and caloric intakes differ from the daily need due to limitations imposed by the peripheral route of administration. High osmolality limits the concentration of glucose and, consequently, the calories which may be provided.

Partial compensation for this loss of calories is achieved by providing fluid and fat in excess of minimum needs. The additional fluid will allow administration of more glucose calories. The fat requirement shown in Table 99.1 represents the dose which will prevent essential fatty acid deficiency (4% to 5% of the caloric intake as linoleic acid);[45] this can be achieved with 1 gm/kg/day and will be exceeded in T.C. to provide additional calories. Table 99.10 outlines T.C.'s parenteral nutrition requirements.

Diarrheal disease may increase the loss of electrolytes, particularly sodium, potassium, bicarbonate, and the trace minerals, zinc and copper.[46] If T.C.'s diarrhea continues while he is being nourished parenterally, his losses of these substances should be quantitated and his intake adjusted to include his continuing losses plus his maintenance needs, as outlined in Questions 8 and 9.

Total Parenteral Nutrition (TPN)

21. Describe how a regimen of TPN should be instituted in T.C. What aspects of his disease may alter specific nutrient needs?

When initiating a parenteral nutrition regimen, the protein, glucose, fat, fluid and electrolyte, mineral, and vitamin components of the regimen are managed as separate entities. The fluids, electrolytes, minerals, and vitamins are initiated at full daily mainte-

Table 99.10		Parenteral Nutrition Regimen for T.C.
Nutrient	Daily Need	Provided As
Protein	12.5 gm	227 mL of 5.5% crystalline amino acids[a]
Sodium	15 mEq	6 mL of 2.5 mEq/mL NaCl
Potassium	15 mEq	1.7 mL of 4.4 mEq/mL K$^+$ phosphates plus 5 mL of 2 mEq/mL K$^+$ acetate
Chloride	15 mEq	Provided as NaCl above
Magnesium	2.5 mEq	0.6 mL of 50% MgSO$_4$
Calcium	5 mEq	10 mL of 10% Ca gluconate
Phosphorous	5 mmol	Provided as K$^+$ phosphates above
Zinc	500 µg	0.5 mL of 1 mg/mL ZnCl$_2$
Copper	100 µg	0.25 mL of 400 µg/mL CuCl$_2$
Manganese	50 µg	0.5 mL of 100 µg/mL MnCl$_2$
Chromium	1 µg	0.25 mL of 4 µg/mL CrCl$_2$
Selenium	15 µg	0.4 mL of 40 µg/mL selenious acid
Vitamins	Max requirement of all vitamins[b]	5 mL MVI Pediatric
Fat[c]	15 gm	72 mL of 20% soybean oil emulsion (3 mL/hr)
Fluid[c]	500 mL	72 mL of fat emulsion plus 528 mL 10% glucose amino acid solution
Calories[c]	500	144 calories from fat emulsion plus 179 calories from glucose

[a] Pediatric amino acid formula may be substituted.
[b] See Table 99.1.
[c] See text.

nance doses after correction of any pre-existing abnormalities. Protein, glucose, and fat are started at lower doses and increased daily until the desired daily dose is reached.

Protein will be started in T.C. at 1 gm/kg/day, and increased daily by 0.5 gm/kg/day until the desired dose of 2.5 gm/kg/day is reached.[47,48] Blood urea nitrogen should be monitored daily while the amino acid dose is being increased, and increases should be halted if abnormally high values are seen. Dose increases may resume when the BUN returns to normal. Likewise, fat will be started at 1 gm/kg/day and increased daily by 0.5 gm/kg/day until the maximum dose of 3 gm/kg/day[49] is reached. The serum triglycerides should be monitored every other day while the fat dose is being increased, and if abnormally high values are seen, further increases should be delayed until they return to normal. The daily fat dose will be infused at a constant rate over the full 24 hours since this method may be better tolerated.[50]

Parenteral glucose administration is initiated at 5 to 8 mg/kg/minute (7.2 to 11.5 gm/kg/day). This closely approximates normal endogenous glucose production[51] and should be tolerated. At normal maintenance fluid rates such as those planned for T.C., 10% glucose represents a generally well-tolerated starting solution for patients of virtually any age or size, except the extremely premature infant. In T.C.'s case, glucose will start and stay at 10% due to the limitations of the peripheral line. This will provide 7.3 mg/kg/minute. If a central line later becomes necessary, glucose can be advanced by 5% concentration each day until the caloric requirement is met. This advancement should be monitored using bedside blood glucose measurements and urine glucose checks. If blood glucose exceeds 150 mg/dL or urine glucose exceeds "trace," the total parenteral nutrition infusion rate should be decreased by at least 25% and a second solution should be added to provide adequate hydration and electrolyte intakes. Further decreases in TPN rate

may be needed after subsequent blood or urine monitoring to avoid serum hyperosmolality or osmotic diuresis resulting from the glycosuria.

22. Can the glucose-amino acid solution and the IV fat emulsion be infused through the same IV line?

Not only can they be infused through the same IV line, but doing so may prolong the patency of the IV site and reduce the likelihood of local complications, such as phlebitis, which occur when infusing the glucose-amino acid solution alone.[52,53] This protective effect is postulated to be due to a dilution of the osmolality of the glucose-amino acids by the fat emulsions which are isosmolar.[52] It also may be the result of a complex biophysical interaction between the fat product and the vascular endothelium or an effect of the fatty acids on prostaglandin and leukotriene mediators of inflammation.[53]

Role of Enteral Nutrition in Chronic Diarrhea

23. After receiving peripheral parenteral nutrition for 4 days, T.C.'s stool output has decreased dramatically. Is this characteristic of infants with chronic diarrhea? Should enteral intake be initiated?

A prompt decrease in stool output when enteral intake is stopped is typical of infants with chronic diarrhea. Nonetheless, evaluation of bowel function and adaption has shown that enteral nutrition is superior to parenteral nutrition with regard to histologic recovery, improvement of D-xylose absorption,[54] protein absorption, and disaccharidase activity.[55-58] In fact, some evidence suggests that no improvement in histology or absorptive function occurs until enteral nutrients are given.[55,56] Thus, for T.C., every effort should be made to provide some nutrition enterally, whether this route is used exclusively[55] or in combination with his supplemental parenteral nutrition.[57]

Choice of Formula

24. What type of enteral formula should be chosen for T.C.?

The enteral regimen should be initiated with an elemental formula. Carbohydrate absorption depends upon digestion of di- and polysaccharides to monosaccharides before assimilation takes place. This digestion, in turn, is dependent upon disaccharidase activity in the intestinal lumen. Infants with chronic diarrhea, regardless of the cause, have been shown to have small bowel mucosal damage and decreased disaccharidase activities.[56,57] While substitution of free glucose may overcome the problem of carbohydrate digestion and absorption, the administration of adequate amounts is limited by the osmotic effect of this small molecule.[59] Administration of other inadequately absorbed disaccharides or polysaccharides also can be associated with osmotic diarrhea. Incompletely absorbed carbohydrate is available to colonic bacteria for fermentation, the end products of which may produce diarrhea through colonic irritation.

The relative activity of the disaccharidases may be used to advantage in choosing a carbohydrate source. Maltase, which hydrolyzes glucose polymers, is present with twice the activity of sucrase and up to eight times the activity of lactase. Small chain glucose polymers which are hydrolyzed to glucose but do not present a large osmotic load, therefore, are the preferred enteral carbohydrate source for patients such as T.C.

Unlike carbohydrate, protein rarely causes diarrhea,[59] but the mucosal damage present in patients with chronic diarrhea, such as T.C., reduces the absorptive surface area so that protein malabsorption may occur. This can be minimized through the administration of a formula containing protein in the form of di- and tripeptides, which are absorbed more efficiently than free amino acids.[60]

Dilution of the formula to half-strength has been suggested to diminish the high osmolality of elemental formula.[55] Concentration is increased in a step-wise fashion to full strength if there is no carbohydrate malabsorption and if stool output is not excessive (defined by Orenstein as ≥40% of enteral intake).[55] Tolerance may be improved by continuous infusion of the enteral product.[44] If enteral refeeding results in a return of the diarrhea, fluid and electrolytes must be replaced with an equal volume of an intravenous solution of similar electrolyte composition to the stool loss.[55]

Monitoring

25. How can T.C.'s tolerance to the formula and his recovery of intestinal function be assessed?

Digestive and absorptive capacity can be evaluated roughly using stool pH, reducing substances, and fat content. Carbohydrate malabsorption can be manifested as reducing substances present in stool, and the bacterial fermentation products of malabsorbed carbohydrates may result in a decreased stool pH. Greater than 5% of ingested fat in a stool collection is indicative of fat malabsorption. D-xylose absorption may be of initial prognostic value in predicting which patients will require prolonged courses of treatment.[54] All of these tests may be followed serially during treatment to help guide the refeeding process.

Reinstitution of Standard Formula

26. Once the diarrhea has resolved and the elemental diet is well tolerated, how should standard infant formula be reinstituted in T.C.?

Standard formula feedings are restarted somewhat arbitrarily in patients such as T.C., although D-xylose absorption may be a useful guide.[54,55] The diarrhea should have resolved completely, and full maintenance fluid and caloric intake should be established on the enteral elemental formula. Regardless of the time chosen, a gradual step-wise conversion is suggested, substituting a small volume of standard formula for an equal volume of elemental formula and increasing the substitution daily until the elemental formula is eliminated completely from the regimen.

If a specific nutrient intolerance has been identified, a standard formula which does not contain that nutrient must be selected. For example, a patient with cow's milk protein intolerance may require a soy protein formula.

Special Considerations and Complications

27. J.H., a 28-day-old male infant, was born at 27 weeks of gestation. His birthweight was 970 gm, and he now weighs 900 gm. He has been mechanically ventilated since birth. His initial nutritional regimen was IV glucose and crystalline amino acids. Since the 14th day of life, he has received a commercial infant formula by orogastric tube in gradually increasing quantity. Now, on the 28th day of life, he has developed a distended abdomen and his stools contain bright red blood. An abdominal x-ray shows pneumatosis intestinalis (gas within the intestinal wall). All enteral feedings are stopped (NPO). What do these findings represent? What are the implications for J.H.'s nutritional management?

Abdominal distension, bloody stools, and pneumatosis intestinalis are characteristic of necrotizing enterocolitis.[22] The causes of this disorder are unclear, but it occurs more often in premature than term infants, may occur in clusters of cases, rarely is seen before enteral feeding is instituted, and may be associated with rapid increases in enteral intake.[61] However, it is clear that J.H. will remain NPO for a period of 10 to 21 days. Thus, he will require parenteral nutrition. The planned duration of the regimen will make central venous access a necessity.

Parenteral Nutrition

Goals of Long-Term Support

28. The following day, intestinal perforation requires the resection of ⅓ of J.H.'s jejunum, the entire ileum, the ileocecal valve, and the ascending colon to the hepatic flexure, with creation of a jejunostomy. During the operation, a central venous catheter is placed. What is the goal for parenteral nutrition in J.H.? Write a nutrition prescription designed to attain this goal and describe how the parenteral regimen will be started and advanced to reach this final prescription.

J.H. will be NPO for a prolonged period of time. The goals of his parenteral nutrition, therefore, must be to maintain his body composition, promote healing of his diseased gut and surgical wounds, and promote normal growth. Figures 99.2 and 99.3 present an example of a parenteral nutrition worksheet completed for J.H. This worksheet represents his nutrient intake after all components of the regimen are advanced to their final level of intake. It provides 113 kcal/kg/day. Figure 99.2 provides the information necessary to calculate J.H.'s parenteral nutrition orders.

The regimen will be initiated with 1 gm/kg/day of amino acids and advanced by 0.5 gm/kg/day each day until the desired dose is achieved. Glucose will be initiated at 10% and increased by 2.5% to 5% daily until the desired caloric intake is achieved. The electrolytes and minerals may be started immediately at the desired final daily doses.

Fat Emulsions: Complications

29. Fat has not been included in J.H.'s nutrient regimen as ordered in Figure 99.2. Does J.H. need parenteral fat emulsion? How should it be dosed and administered in J.H.? What special concerns must be considered in making these decisions?

Although J.H. can be provided with an adequate caloric intake using only glucose and crystalline amino acids, he will require fat as well to prevent essential fatty acid deficiency. Low birthweight infants have little stored fat and develop this deficiency rapidly.[62] Thus, J.H. should receive 4% to 5% of his total caloric requirement for linoleic acid.[45] Since linoleic acid represents 54% of the fatty acid in soybean oil and 77% of that in safflower oil,[63] this will require that 7% to 10% of his total caloric intake be from fat emulsions. This can be given daily, or the weekly fat requirement may be divided into two or three doses and given at intervals throughout the week. The latter approach may be more cost effective, since it promotes more complete use of the fat emulsion volumes commercially available.

Necrotizing enterocolitis, intestinal perforation, and surgery predispose J.H. to sepsis, which may alter the approach to the initiation of fat emulsion. Rapid IV infusion or *in vitro* incubation of leukocytes with fat emulsion results in impaired leukocyte chemotaxis and phagocytosis.[64] This may decrease his ability to clear a bacteremia should it occur. White cell function is normal when usual doses of IV fat are infused over a prolonged period of time.[65-67] However, the reticuloendothelial system may be impaired.[68] Hence, J.H. should receive his IV fat at the lowest dose necessary to prevent essential fatty acid deficiency. The fat emulsion should be infused daily over the full 24 hours to allow the slowest possible administration rate. This also should minimize the hyperlipidemia in preterm infants which results from inefficient fat clearance.[69]

Platelet dysfunction also presents a risk in a postoperative patient and has been cited as a complication of IV fat emulsions. However, supporting data are lacking and recent experience suggests that in doses used clinically, neither platelet function nor platelet numbers are affected adversely.[66,70]

In deciding how to administer fat to a preterm infant such as J.H., the possibility that unconjugated bilirubin (indirect) may be displaced from albumin binding sites by free fatty acids also should be considered.[71] The infusion rates outlined above, 1 gm/kg over 24 hours, are associated with minimal risk for decreased bilirubin binding,[72] though rapid infusion of this same dose has produced displacement. Given the low value for indirect bilirubin found on routine monitoring (see Question 37) and the planned fat infusion rate, this poses no threat to J.H. Finally, the clinician should be aware that inclusion of heparin in the infusate may cause an increased free fatty acid concentration through release of endogenous lipoprotein lipase.[73]

Glucose Intolerance

30. Parenteral nutrition is initiated in J.H. using 10% glucose and 1 gm/kg/day of amino acids as indicated above. On the 2nd day, he receives 15% glucose and 1.5 gm/kg/day of amino acids. On the 3rd day, glucose is increased to 20% and amino acids to 2 gm/kg. After this solution has infused for 8 hours, his urine tests at 1% for glucose (Normal: no glucose) and a blood glucose is reported as 210 mg/dL (Normal: <120). Explain this new finding and the problems it may cause. How should hyperglycemia be managed? [SI unit: 11.7 mmol/L (Normal: <6.66)]

At the prescribed fluid rate, 20% glucose represents 18.5 mg/kg/minute of glucose infusion. The hyperglycemia and glycosuria probably have occurred because the increases in the infusion rate have exceeded J.H.'s ability to adapt. However, infection must be ruled out as an explanation for his glucose intolerance.[74] Hyperglycemia and glycosuria may result in serum hyperosmolarity, osmotic diuresis, and dehydration.

Regardless of the cause, the hyperglycemia should be treated by reducing the glucose administration rate. We know that 15% glucose was tolerated. This represented a glucose infusion of 13.9 mg/kg/minute. The first step in managing the hyperglycemia would be to decrease J.H.'s total parenteral nutrition rate and add a second fluid with a lower glucose content so that the combination of the two fluids approximates this glucose dose. For example, the TPN could be decreased to 3 mL/hour to provide 11.1 mg/kg/minute of glucose, with 5% glucose added to provide another 1.9 mg/kg/minute. The sodium and potassium content of the supplemental fluid should be identical to the TPN to avoid electrolyte imbalance. After this new fluid combination is initiated, the blood and urine glucose should again be monitored at frequent intervals. Further adjustments in the rates should be made if the intolerance continues.

Parenteral Nutrition Orders for J.H.

Goal: kcal/day __90__ kcal   Protein/day __2.25__ gm   Fat/day __2.7__ gm   Volume/day = __90__

See Figure 99.3 for worksheet on calculating TPN.

Age __28 days__   Wt __0.9__ kg   Central Line ×   Peripheral Line

Dextrose Additives: __25__ %   Amino Acid __2.3__ %   Rate __3.4__ mL/hr[a]   for __24__ hr

Daily Requirements/kg		Amount/kg/day
Na	2–4 mEq	4
K	2–5 mEq	2
Ca[b]	0.5–1 mEq	1
Mg	0.2–1 mEq	0.3
Cl (leave blank if min or max acetate)	3–5 mEq	3
Phos	0.3–1 mM	1
Acetate[c] (min, max, balance)		balance
MVI-Pediatric	0.5 cc	0.5
Trace Elements-Pedi	0.2 cc	0.2
Heparin[c] (optional)		1 units/cc

Dextrose 12.5% or 3.5% amino acid is the maximum concentration for peripheral administration.

[a] If the amino acid concentration is <1%, then only one of the minerals (Ca, Phos, Mg) may be added to the TPN. Check Table 99.8 for the maximum allowable Ca and Phos concentration for the amino acid concentration.

[b] Anion in excess of specified Cl and Phos will be supplied as acetate. Acetate may be maximized for acidosis or minimized for alkalosis.

[c] Heparin may be added if the rate of the TPN through a central line is <10 mL/hr or <2 mL/hr through a peripheral line. Anticoagulant doses of heparin are 15–20 units/kg/hr.

[d] It is recommended that the rate not exceed 1.3 mL/kg/hr for infants and children or 0.8 mL/kg/hr for neonates. The patient should be monitored over the first 15 minutes of therapy when initiating fat therapy.

Fat Emulsion 20%[d] (2 kcal/mL):   Infuse at __0.5__ mL/hr   for __20__ hr

Information Printed on the Back of Form (See Figure 99.3)
1) Maximum achievable dextrose-amino acid concentrations (including kcal of dextrose/cc).
2) Maximum concentrations of Ca and Phos soluble in amino acid solutions.
3) Composition of Pediatric Multivitamin Injection and Pediatric Trace Element Solution.
4) Worksheet to calculate TPN.

Fig 99.2 Parenteral Nutrition Orders for J.H.

Table A. Maximum Achievable Dextrose Amino Acid Concentrations

kcal/cc (as Dex.)	% Dextrose (D %)	Max AA % (AA %)
0.34	10	7.5
0.43	12.5	7.25
0.51	15	7
0.60	17.5	6.5
0.68	20	6
0.85	25	5
1.02	30	4.5
1.19	35	3.5
1.36	40	3
1.53	45	2
1.70	50	1.5
1.87	55	0.5
2.04	60	0

Table B. Maximum Allowable Calcium and Phosphate Concentration in Amino Acid Solutions

Ca (mEq/L)	AA 1%–1.9% P (mM/L)	AA 2%–2.9% P (mM/L)	AA 3%–3.9% P (mM/L)	AA >4% P (mM/L)
2	35	40	40	40
5	12	40	40	40
8	7	15	20	30
10	5	10	15	20
12	3	7	10	15
15	3	6	8	9
18	0	5	5	7
20	0	4	5	6
22	0	0	0	5
25	0	0	0	4
28	0	0	0	0

If the AA concentration is <1%, only one of the following minerals (Ca, Phos, Mg) can be added to the TPN solution. If the amount of Ca or Phos to be added to any solution is between two numbers listed on this table, choose the corresponding amount of the next lower level.

To convert Ca and Phos to Amount/L:

$$\text{Amount/L} = \frac{(\text{Amount/kg/day}) \times \text{Weight (kg)}}{\text{Volume (L)/day}}$$

Table C. Composition of MVI-Pediatric (Per 0.5 cc)

A	230	units
D	40	units
C	8	mg
Thiamine B1	0.12	mg
Pyridoxine B6	0.1	mg
Riboflavin	0.14	mg
Niacin	1.7	mg
Pantothenic Acid	0.5	mg
E	0.7	units
Folic Acid	14	µg
B12	0.1	µg
Vitamin K	20	µg
Biotin	2	µg

Table D. Composition of Trace Element Solution-Pediatric Formula

Zinc	100	µg
Manganese	6	µg
Copper	20	µg
Chromium	0.2	µg

Minimal Biochemical Monitoring

See Table 99.5

Calories/Gram of Nutrition

Dextrose = 3.4 kcal/gm
Fat = 9 kcal/gm
Protein = 4 kcal/gm

Table E. Worksheet to Calculate PN in Stable Patients without Organ Failure

1. Calculate the goals of TPN.

   (See Table 99.1)

   Goal: kcal/day __90__ kcal   Protein/day __2.25__ gm   Maintenance Fluid __90__ mL

   __90__ mL Mt. Fluid – (__0__ mL IV + __0__ mL PO Fluid) = __90__ Nutritional Fluid

2. Lipids make up 20%–50% of the total calories and it is recommended fat not exceed 4 gm/kg/day or 60% of the total calories. Lipids are usually started at 0.5–1 gm/kg/day and infused over 20–24 hr.

   The lipids are increased by 0.5–1 gm/kg/day until the goal is reached.

   Fat Emulsion 20% = 2.0 kcal/cc. Fat = 9 kcal/gm

   __2__ gm/kg/day × 1 cc/0.2 gm Fat × __0.9__ kg = __9__ mL/day of 20% Fat

   Goal: Fat = __3__ gm/kg/day × 1 cc/0.2 gm Fat × __0.9__ kg = __13.5__ mL/day of 20% Fat

3. Nutritional Fluid __90__ mL – __9__ mL Fat = __81__ mL TPN

   __81__ mL TPN × 1 day/24 hr = __3.4__ cc/hr

4. Dextrose is started at the maximum tolerated concentration. (Usually 10%–15% dextrose)

   The dextrose concentration is then increased by 2.5%–5% daily until the caloric goal is reached. Dextrose makes up 50%–80% of the total daily calories.

   __90__ kcal/day × (0.8) = __72__ kcal Dextrose

   [__72__ kcal Dex. × 1 gm/3.4 kcal × 100%]/ __81__ mL TPN = __25__ % Dextrose Goal

5. Protein is usually started at 1 gm/kg/day and advanced as tolerated. Protein 4 kcal/gm

   __2.5__ gm/kg/day × __0.9__ kg = __2.25__ gm/day

   [__2.25__ gm/day × 100%]/ __99__ mL TNP = __2.3__ % Amino Acid

Fig 99.3 Parenteral Nutrition Orders for J.H. (*Continued*)

When the TPN prescription is written for the subsequent days, the glucose increments should be smaller. Frequent blood and urine glucose monitoring must be continued. Severe glucose intolerance in patients who require parenteral nutrition can be managed with insulin to normalize serum glucose. Although insulin is compatible with parenteral nutrient solutions, it does adsorb to glass, polyvinyl chloride, and filters, resulting in decreased delivery of insulin.[75]

The addition of albumin presumably decreases the binding of insulin to solution containers.[76] Frequently, pediatric patients have changing insulin requirements that prevent the addition of insulin (with albumin) to parenteral nutrient solutions. A separate continuous infusion of regular insulin (initial dose: 0.1 units/kg/hour) titrated to control serum glucose concentrations offers a practical solution to minimize waste of the parenteral nutrient solution.[77]

*Effects of Bronchopulmonary
Dysplasia (BPD) and Mechanical Ventilation*

31. J.H. remains dependent upon a mechanical ventilator due to immaturity of his lungs. He requires 75% oxygen to achieve an adequate arterial pO$_2$. How may J.H.'s respiratory disease influence his nutritional regimen?

At greater than 28 days of age, ventilator dependence defines J.H. as having bronchopulmonary dysplasia, a chronic lung disease of infancy. This disease is characterized by an increased resting energy expenditure, increased work of breathing, and growth failure.[78,79] This increased energy need is associated with biochemical evidence of protein calorie malnutrition.[79] Hence, J.H. may have a higher caloric requirement than expected.

J.H.'s dependence upon mechanical ventilation and high concentrations of supplemental oxygen also may alter the approach to his caloric supply. Very high carbohydrate loads have been associated with an increase in carbon dioxide production.[80,81] This, in turn, may make it difficult to wean J.H. from the mechanical ventilator. In infants, fat emulsion has been reported to impair oxygenation and to decrease arterial pO$_2$.[82] This occurred in infants under one week of age who received a fat infusion of 1 gm/kg over four hours. At slower infusion rates and with gradually increasing fat doses more closely resembling those used in clinical practice, no increase in the alveolar-arterial oxygen gradient was found.[83] Changes in pulmonary hemodynamics with increases in pulmonary vascular resistance also have been reported in infants over a wider range of fat infusion rates, including rates at the higher end of the spectrum used clinically.[84]

In summary, J.H.'s respiratory problems require that his blood gas values be considered when his carbohydrate load, fat dose, and infusion rate are established. A rise in pCO$_2$ should prompt a reevaluation of his glucose intake; and a fall in pO$_2$ should lead to reconsideration of his fat dose and fat infusion rate along with other potential causes for the deterioration. Within these confines, his caloric intake should be optimized and his growth monitored.

Pediatric Amino Acid Formulations (PAAFs)

32. Why would a specialized pediatric amino acid solution be preferable to a standard adult formulation for J.H.?

Two specifically designed amino acid solutions, TrophAmine and Aminosyn PF, are available for nutritional support of infants and children. They differ from conventional amino acid formulations in several ways. First, they contain a higher content of branch chain amino acids (leucine, isoleucine, and valine); and a lower content of glycine, methionine, and phenylalanine (see Table 99.11). In addition, pediatric amino acid formulations have a higher percentage of essential amino acids with a wider distribution of the nonessential amino acids. Finally, PAAFs are unique in that they contain taurine, tyrosine (as N-acetyl-L-tyrosine), and cysteine (added as L-cysteine HCl). TrophAmine (Kendall McGaw) is available as a 6% solution and has a pH of 5.5. Aminosyn-PF (Abbott Laboratories) is available as a 7% and 10% solution and has a pH of 5.8. The pH of these formulations decreases to 5.0 when 40 mg of cysteine per gram of protein is added.

Adult amino acid solutions lack cysteine and taurine and only contain minimal amounts of tyrosine because these are not considered to be essential for adults. However, cysteine, tyrosine, and taurine are essential amino acids for the neonate because neonates are not able to synthesize these important amino acids themselves due to immature liver function.[85] Hepatic cystathionase activity is decreased in neonates and they are unable to convert methionine to cysteine in substantial amounts.[86] Taurine is synthesized from cysteine and is markedly deficient in neonates receiving adult amino acid formulations. Taurine appears to have a role in retinal development, protection and stabilization of cell membranes, neurotransmission, regulation of cell volume, and bile acid conjugation. Taurine also may be important in decreasing or preventing cholestasis associated with long-term parenteral nutrition.

Pediatric amino acid formulations were developed in response to concern about the existence of abnormal plasma amino acid patterns in infants receiving adult amino acid formulations. PAAFs were designed with the specific goal of providing parenteral nutrition to produce plasma amino acid patterns closely matching those of two-hour postprandial, breast-fed infants. It has been proposed that the presence of normal plasma amino acid patterns will promote normal protein synthesis in growing infants.

Heard et al. and Helms et al. studied the clinical, nutritional, and biochemical effects of TrophAmine in term and preterm infants.[87-89] They were able to demonstrate that the use of the PAAF results in normal amino acid patterns. The authors felt that the patients receiving TrophAmine had greater weight gain and a statistically significant better nitrogen utilization than similar groups using the adult formulations. However, in one of the studies, some of the extremely low birthweight infants experienced a metabolic acidosis, suspected to be a result of the addition of cysteine HCl.[88] To avoid this problem, the authors suggested limiting the parenteral cysteine intake in these patients. A recent prospective, randomized multicenter study of 44 preterm infants compared TrophAmine to Aminosyn-PF.[90] Over a seven-day period, amino acid intake was approximately 2.6 gm/kg/day for both groups and nonprotein caloric intake approximately 90 kcal/kg/day. In both groups, weight gain averaged 15 gm/kg/day. Nitrogen retention averaged 67% and 69% with TrophAmine and Aminosyn-PF, respectively.

Unfortunately, there have been no long-term prospective trials comparing the parenteral nutrition-associated cholestasis occurring with conventional amino acid solutions to that seen in patients receiving PAAFs. In one study, the incidence of cholestasis in low birthweight infants receiving TrophAmine was reduced to 23% relative to historical controls of 30% to 50%.[91] In another study comparing these products, no difference in the incidence of cholestasis was found in infants less than one year old. These infants had an overall cholestasis incidence of 27%.[92]

To date, PAAFs have been effective in producing a positive weight gain, positive nitrogen balance, and normalizing amino acid patterns in a small population of preterm neonates. They also may increase the solubility of calcium and phosphate in solution, although the degree of increase may be relatively small.[93] Further study is needed to determine if the use of PAAFs results in improved clinical outcome and whether the potential benefits outweigh the additional cost ($\approx$10 times the cost of adult formulations). Larger long-term trials are needed to determine if normalized amino acid plasma levels result in less cholestasis, higher nitrogen retention, sustained weight gain, and improved patient outcome. Despite the lack of data showing dramatic differences, use of PAAFs in infants requiring parenteral nutrition currently is the standard of care. Many clinicians believe it is important to provide infants with an amino acid solution that offers the theoretical advantage of providing a more complete mix of amino acids. Since J.H. probably will remain on parenteral nutrition support for a prolonged period and no increase in morbidity has been documented with the use of PAAFs, it is justifiable to use a pediatric amino acid solution.

Protein Intolerance

33. On the 4th day of TPN, J.H. receives 2.5 gm/kg of amino acids, but his glucose remains at 15% due to his glucose intol-

Table 99.11	Pediatric Amino Acid Solutions	
	TrophAmine 6%	Aminosyn-PF 7%
Essential Amino Acids (EEA) (mg/1 gm total amino acids)		
Isoleucine	81.7	76.3
Leucine	140.0	118.7
Lysine	81.7	67.9
Methionine	33.3	17.9
Phenylalanine	48.3	42.9
Threonine	41.7	51.4
Tryptophan	20.0	17.9
Valine	78.3	64.6
Cysteine HCl[a]	3.3	0
Histidine	48.3	31.4
Tyrosine	23.3	6.3
Taurine	2.5	7.1
Nonessential Amino Acids (mg/1 gm total amino acids)		
Alanine	53.3	70.0
Arginine	121.7	123.0
Proline	68.3	81.4
Serine	38.3	49.6
Glycine	36.7	38.6
L-aspartic acid	31.7	52.9
L-glutamic acid	50.0	82.3
Sodium (mEq/L)	5.0	3.4
Acetate (mEq/L)	56.0	32.5
Chloride (mEq/L)	<3.0	0
% essential amino acid	60.1	50.2
% branched chain amino acid (gm amino acid/1 gm nitrogen)	30.0	26.0

[a] 40 gm of cysteine syringe available.

erance. He is alert and active. Routine laboratory monitoring reveals: BUN 12 mg/dL (Normal: <20), ammonia 240 µg/dL (Normal: <100), AST 14 U/L (Normal: <40), ALT 5 U/L (Normal: <28). Can hyperammonemia be explained by the parenteral nutrition regimen? How should it be managed? [SI units: BUN 4.3 mmol/L (Normal: <7.14); ammonia 140.1 µmol/L (Normal: <58); AST 14 U/L (Normal: <40); ALT 5 U/L (Normal: <28)]

Ammonia is a product of amino acid catabolism, and preterm infants become hyperammonemic when receiving infusions of crystalline amino acids.[94,95] The cause of this finding is unclear, but it has been observed with the infusion of adequate doses of arginine (which can facilitate ammonia metabolism) and in the absence of demonstrable liver disease. It has been suggested that an excessive intake of glycine may produce the hyperammonemia; thus, J.H.'s elevated blood ammonia concentration quite likely is related to his parenteral nutrients. Other possible causes of hyperammonemia include severe hepatic disease and inborn defects in the urea cycle enzymes. Neither is likely, since other laboratory abnormalities would be present in hepatic disease and urea cycle disorders generally present with vomiting and neurologic signs, such as seizures and coma.[96] In addition, a urea cycle defect would have been detected when protein was first introduced.

Since J.H. is asymptomatic and described as alert and active, treatment of his hyperammonemia can be limited to increasing his caloric intake as tolerated to promote more efficient protein utilization.[95] His blood ammonia level should be followed to assure that the hyperammonemia resolves. Should the blood ammonia remain elevated, reduction or discontinuation of the amino acids is indicated.

Septicemia

34. Because J.H. was diagnosed with necrotizing enterocolitis, he received 14 days of antibiotic therapy. On his 6th day off of antibiotics, he begins having 15–20 episodes of bradycardia per day. His physical examination is remarkable for cold extremities and slow capillary refill, but his chest x-rays show no acute change. Laboratory evaluation at this time includes electrolytes, blood glucose, complete blood count, and blood cultures, which were reported as follows: Na 139 mEq/L (Normal: 135–145), K 4.7 mEq/L (Normal: 3.5–5.0), Cl 112 mEq/L (Normal: 102–109), and HCO_3^- 17 mEq/L (Normal: 22–29); glucose 164 mg/dL (Normal: 70–105), platelet count 36,000/mm^3 (Normal: 150,000–450,000), WBC count 24,300 (Normal: 5500–18,000). WBC differential includes 52% segmented neutrophils (Normal: 20–50) and 27% immature neutrophils (Normal: 3–5). The blood cultures are placed in the laboratory to incubate; no results will be available for at least 24 hours. What is the likely cause of these findings? How might J.H.'s nutrition regimen affect the diagnostic evaluation and treatment selected? [SI units: Na 139 mmol/L (Normal: 135–145); K 4.7 mmol/L (Normal: 3.5–5.0); Cl 112 mmol/L (Normal: 102–109); HCO_3^- 17 mmol/L (Normal: 22–29); glucose 9.1 mmol/L (Normal: 3.9–5.8); platelet count 36 × 10^9/L (Normal: 150–450); WBC 24.3 × 10^6 cells/L (Normal: 5.5–18.0)]

The constellation of findings J.H. has developed, including metabolic acidosis, hyperglycemia, thrombocytopenia, leukocytosis, bradycardia, and poor perfusion, is nonspecific but could represent septicemia. His parenteral nutrition must be considered in the empiric determination of potential infecting organisms and the evaluation of culture results.

The presence of a central venous catheter predisposes J.H. to infection with coagulase-negative staphylococci normally found on the skin and gram negative species.[97] Cultures growing this organism must not be presumed to be the result of touch contamination of the culture medium in a symptomatic patient. The typical antimicrobial sensitivities of this organism dictate that vancomycin be among the empiric antibiotics chosen.[98]

The central venous catheter also may predispose J.H. to fungal infection.[99,100] Candidal infection may occur, and when fat emulsions are used, as in J.H., systemic infection with *Malassezia furfur* must be considered. The latter is a skin fungus which requires an exogenous source of fatty acids.[101,102] The empiric use of antifungal drugs is not indicated in these patients; however, the clinician should screen specifically for fungal infection by culture. *Malassezia furfur* requires specialized culture technique in that a fatty acid source must be added to the culture.[101]

Rickets

35. On the chest x-ray taken to evaluate the septic episode described above, the radiologist notes that J.H. has 2 rib fractures and that the bones appear undermineralized. The most recent laboratory values show a serum calcium (Ca) of 9.3 mg/dL (Normal: 8.5–10.5), a serum phosphorus of 3.6 mg/dL (Normal: 4.0–8.5), and an alkaline phosphatase of 674 U/L (Normal: <350). What diagnosis is suggested by these findings? How and why has J.H.'s nutrition regimen placed him at risk for this disease? [SI units: Ca 2.3 mmol/L (Normal: 2.1–2.6); phosphorus 1.16 mmol/L (Normal: 1.3–2.7); phosphatase 674 U/L (Normal: <350)]

Low serum phosphorus with high alkaline phosphatase, undermineralized bones, and fractures resulting from routine handling are consistent with a diagnosis of rickets. This is a common problem in low birthweight infants such as J.H.,[103] especially when they must be nourished parenterally. Parenteral nutrient solutions provide calcium and phosphorus in much smaller supply than the infant would accumulate *in utero*[104] due to the insolubility of their reaction product. It has been suggested that aluminum, which is found as a contaminant in some parenteral salt products (particularly calcium salts) and some infant formulas, also may play a role in this impaired bone mineraliziation.[105]

Many factors influence calcium and phosphorus solubility, including temperature, pH, amino acid complexation, and the salt form of calcium used.[106] Decreased pH, colder temperature, higher amino acid concentrations, and the use of relatively undissociated calcium salts such as calcium gluconate or gluceptate all allow higher calcium concentrations to be used. Addition of cysteine HCl to the amino acid solution may improve the solubility of calcium and phosphorus as well.[107] Charts indicating the solubility of calcium and phosphorus are available for all the available amino acid formulations and should be used to determine the maximum calcium content which can be added to the solution,[108,109] keeping in mind that small changes in the conditions noted above, such as running a length of tubing through a heated Isolette, can result in precipitation.

36. Calcium and Phosphorus Supplementation. How should the supply of these nutrients be altered to address J.H.'s rickets?

It is important to maintain the serum phosphorus concentrations since severe hypophosphatemia during parenteral nutrition has been associated with serious neurologic sequelae including lethargy, areflexia, tremor, and hypotonia.[110] Administration of 1.3 mmol/kg/day of phosphorus can avoid this problem.[110] In addition, adequate phosphorus supplementation minimizes calcium excretion in both adults and children.[111,112] J.H. is receiving this amount of phosphorus, and his serum phosphorus, while low, is not dangerously so. Given this, his calcium intake should be maximized (within the limits of solubility) in his parenteral nutrient solution.[113] It is preferable to maximize both minerals in one solution rather than supply two alternating solutions, one free of calcium and the other free of phosphorus.[114]

Although oral treatment of rickets would require supplemental vitamin D to enhance absorption of calcium and phosphorus, when the minerals are supplied parenterally, vitamin D doses similar to those in Table 99.1 are adequate to maintain normal vitamin D, calcium, and phosphorus homeostasis.[115] Serum phosphorus concentrations should be followed several times weekly and phosphorus intake adjusted to avoid symptomatic hypophosphatemia. Serum calcium is not useful as an indicator of disease activity since it will remain normal at the expense of bone mineralization. This is demonstrated by J.H.'s laboratory values at the time of his diagnosis (see Question 35).

Liver Disease in TPN

37. On the 56th day of life, J.H. is noted to be mildly jaundiced by physical examination. A review of the laboratory tests reveals the following:

Test	Age (days)				
	22	29	36	43	50
AST (U/L) (Normal: <40)	14	17	15	20	25
ALT (U/L) (Normal: <28)	6	7	10	10	11
Alkaline phosphatase (IU/L) (Normal: <350)	103	158	345	506	695
Bilirubin					
Indirect (Normal: <1 mg/dL)	0.9	0.9	0.8	0.8	0.9
Direct (Normal: <0.2)	0.1	0.1	0.8	1.6	2.1

Could this be related to his parenteral nutrition?

Hepatic damage has been reported in up to one-third of infants receiving parenteral nutrition,[116] with a higher prevalence (up to 50%) in very low birthweight infants such as J.H.[117] The laboratory abnormalities reported in J.H. are typical of such damage. The earliest abnormal finding in parenteral nutrition-induced liver disease in infants is an elevated direct or conjugated bilirubin, which occurs as early as two weeks after beginning the parenteral regi-

men.[118] Increases in the hepatic enzymes AST and ALT lag two weeks or more behind the rise in bilirubin.[118] Alkaline phosphatase also may rise, but it is a nonspecific indicator of liver disease for several reasons: it has been reported to rise during periods of growth,[118] it is derived primarily from bone in infants and children,[118] and it may be an indicator of rickets. Although the laboratory results observed in J.H. are consistent with the pattern associated with liver disease induced by parenteral nutrition, viral hepatitis must be ruled out.

38. Risk Factors. What clinical factors placed J.H. at high risk for developing cholestatic liver disease secondary to parenteral nutrition?

In addition to his prematurity, which has been mentioned already, J.H. has several other risk factors. As the duration of parenteral nutrition increases, so does the prevalence of hepatic disease in premature infants; 25% of infants nourished in this manner for ≥30 days show evidence of cholestasis.[117] Surgical patients have a greater likelihood of developing hyperbilirubinemia than medical patients, especially those requiring gastrointestinal surgery,[119,120] and a larger number of surgical procedures is associated with a higher risk of jaundice.[121] Prolonged enteral fasting may be the basis for all of these risk factors.[121] Stimulation of bile flow and gall bladder contraction may depend upon gut hormones which in turn depend upon enteral feeding for their release.[122] Absence of these secretogogues thus may promote cholestasis, which is the initial pathologic change in this disorder.[123–125] Finally, J.H.'s infection may increase the risk of cholestasis.[126]

In addition to the hepatic damage, gallstones have been reported in infants and children on parenteral nutrition.[127,128] The ileal resection performed during the acute phase of his necrotizing enterocolitis may put J.H. at increased risk for this hepatobiliary complication as well.[127]

One additional risk factor not present in J.H. is the administration of large amounts of protein. In one study, a high protein regimen (3.6 mg/kg/day) was associated with an earlier onset and greater degree of cholestasis than a low protein regimen (2.3 gm/kg/day).[129]

39. Do any of J.H.'s nutrients need to be modified in the presence of cholestasis?

Because they are eliminated in the bile and may accumulate in liver disease, the trace elements copper and manganese need to be removed from J.H.'s parenteral nutrition mixture.[130] Copper in particular may not only accumulate in this setting but may be hepatotoxic as well.

40. Prognosis. Project the course of J.H.'s liver disease if parenteral nutrition is discontinued and enteral feedings are instituted within 2 weeks. What may occur if enteral feedings cannot be instituted?

If parenteral nutrition can be stopped soon after the onset of cholestasis, the prospects for J.H. to recover normal hepatic function are good. Jaundice usually resolves within two weeks after parenteral nutrition is discontinued, and the biochemical abnormalities normalize soon thereafter, although this may lag behind for several months.[131] The pathological changes observed on biopsy resolve even more slowly. Biopsy evidence of cholestasis has been observed for up to 40 weeks after resolution of clinical and serologic evidence of hepatic disease.[131,132]

If enteral feedings cannot be instituted successfully in lieu of parenteral nutrition, the prognosis for J.H.'s liver function is not as good. Evaluation of biopsy or autopsy specimens obtained from infants at varying intervals after beginning parenteral nutrition revealed a progression of disease with increasing duration, from cholestasis to proliferation of the bile ductules to fibrosis.[124] Although the number of subjects was small, infants receiving parenteral nutrition for ≥90 days had biopsy evidence of some irreversible liver damage; one of these patients had cirrhosis.[124] In addition, hepatocellular carcinoma has been seen in the setting of long-term parenteral nutrition.[133] Thus, it clearly is advantageous to convert J.H.'s nutrition to the enteral route as soon as he tolerates such a change.

41. Tolerance of Conversion to Enteral Feeding. On day 60 of life, J.H.'s intestinal remnants are reanastomosed. Given the desirability of feeding J.H. enterally as soon as possible, what aspects of his disease and surgery will influence his ability to tolerate such a regimen?

J.H.'s surgery involved the resection of one-third of his jejunum, the entire ileum, and the ascending colon to the hepatic flexure. The absence of his ileum and ileocecal valve will have the most impact on his refeeding.

The terminal ileum is the site of absorption for vitamin B_{12}[134] and bile salts.[135] Depletion of the bile salt pool may impair fat absorption when enteral feeding is resumed, and passage of bile salts into the colon may precipitate diarrhea.[136] Absence of the ileocecal valve permits the overgrowth of colonic bacteria in the small intestine and may result in a malabsorption state by a variety of mechanisms.[136]

Even infants with necrotizing enterocolitis, but without perforation, may form strictures in areas of diseased intestine upon resolution of the acute illness.[22] Thus, feeding difficulties, surgery to correct strictures, and consequent periodic enteral starvation may become necessary for J.H. again in the future.

Not all infants with necrotizing enterocolitis will develop long-term nutritional difficulties. Indeed, in the absence of major intestinal resection, nutritional status and GI function are normal by one year of age.[137]

42. Enteral Refeeding. Plan a regimen for refeeding J.H. enterally.

The reinitiation of enteral feedings in a patient such as J.H. who has undergone resection of a large part of his small intestine can be viewed as an attempt to provide four separate nutrient components: protein, fat, carbohydrate, and micronutrients. Each is subject to its own regulatory mechanisms and may lead independently to the success or failure of the entire regimen. An important problem underlying the absorption of all nutrients is the decrease in surface area available for absorption which resulted from J.H.'s resection. Absorptive adaptation of the surgically shortened intestine is more efficient in the presence of enteral nutrient administration, even if it is carried out only in small amounts as a supplement of parenteral nutrition.[59] Thus, some enteral intake should be initiated as early as possible, however small the quantity.

A knowledge of the physiology of the small intestine underlies determination of the enteral prescription. It is important that the healthy sections of J.H.'s intestine have been reconnected since this procedure provides a larger total absorptive surface area.

Protein is unlikely to create diarrhea[59] but may be malabsorbed if the absorptive surface area is diminished. The malabsorption can be minimized by the administration of a formula containing protein in the form of short chain peptides which are absorbed more efficiently and are less osmotically active than free amino acids.[60]

Carbohydrate absorption has already been discussed (see Question 24). The same principles apply to the patient with a surgical short gut.

Ileal resection places J.H. at risk for excessive loss of bile acids and attendant fat malabsorption.[135] Administration of part or all of his fat intake as medium chain triglycerides may bypass the problem of fat absorption since these do not require bile for micelle formation, do not need to be re-esterified in the intestinal cell, and can be absorbed directly into the portal circulation bound to albumin.[138,139] Essential fatty acid deficiency will not be prevented by use of medium chain triglycerides, however, and a source of long chain fatty acids should be used in a quantity similar to that provided parenterally to satisfy this need (4% to 5% of total caloric intake as linoleic acid). In summary, an enteral feeding formula which is most likely to be tolerated by J.H. will contain small chain peptides, medium chain triglycerides, and short chain glucose polymers as nutrient sources.

Several aspects of J.H.'s micronutrient requirements deserve mention. Fat malabsorption is accompanied by malabsorption of fat-soluble vitamins as well,[59] so fat-soluble vitamins should be supplemented. This may be done by the oral route using a multivitamin product which supplies 100% of the recommended daily allowance in addition to whatever is absorbed from the formula. Vitamin B_{12} absorption requires an intact ileum. J.H. thus will require parenteral vitamin B_{12}, as a 100 µg intramuscular injection once monthly.

In addition to choosing a formula, it will be necessary to specify how it is to be given. In an infant who is able to coordinate the sucking and swallowing actions, oral feedings may be attempted; the infant who is incapable of such coordination will need to be fed through an orogastric or nasogastric tube. The tube feedings may be delivered by either continuous infusion or intermittent bolus administration. If patients on bolus feedings either orally or by tube develop diarrhea, substantial stool fluid and nutrient loss can occur. This can be minimized by changing the infant to a continuous feeding regimen.[44] Monitoring for carbohydrate and fat malabsorption can be achieved by measuring stool pH and reducing substances and quantitative fat excretion as outlined in Question 25.

References

1 **Santosham M et al.** Oral rehydration therapy of infantile diarrhea: a controlled study of well-nourished children hospitalized in the United States and Panama. N Engl J Med. 1983;306: 1070.

2 **Santosham M et al.** Oral rehydration therapy for acute diarrhea in ambulatory children in the United States: a double-blind comparison of four different solutions. Pediatrics. 1985;76: 159.

3 **Pizzaro D et al.** Oral rehydration in hypernatremic and hyponatremic diarrheal dehydration. Am J Dis Child. 1983;137:730.

4 **Meeuwisse GW.** High sugar worse than high sodium in oral rehydration solutions. Acta Paediatr Scand. 1983; 72:161.

5 **Guzman C et al.** Hypernatremic diarrheal dehydration treated with oral glucose—electrolyte solution containing 90 or 75 mEq/L of sodium. J Pediatr Gastroenterol Nutr. 1988;7:694.

6 **American Academy of Pediatrics, Committee on Nutrition.** On the feeding of supplemental foods to infants. Pediatrics. 1980;65:1178.

7 **Bucuvalas JC et al.** The neonatal gastrointestinal tract. In: Fanaroff AA et al., eds. Neonatal-Perinatal Medicine:

Disease of the Fetus and Infant. Washington: CB Mosby Co.; 1987:894.

8 **Greer FR et al.** Vitamin K_1 (phylloquinone) and vitamin K_2 (menaquinone) status in newborns during the first week of life. Pediatrics. 1988;81: 137.

9 **Chaou WT et al.** Intracranial hemorrhage and vitamin K deficiency in early infancy. J Pediatr. 1984;105:880.

10 **Garza C et al.** Special properties of human milk. Clin Perinatol. 1987;14: 11.

11 **Anderson GH.** Human milk feeding. Pediatr Clin North Am. 1985;32:335.

12 **Barness LA.** Infant feeding: formula,

solids. Pediatr Clin North Am. 1985; 32:355.

13 **Oski FA.** Iron deficiency—facts and fallacies. Pediatr Clin North Am. 1985; 32:493.

14 **American Academy of Pediatrics, Committee on Nutrition.** Fluoride supplementation. Pediatrics. 1986;77:758.

15 **Kramer MS.** Infant feeding, infection and public health. Pediatrics. 1988;81: 164.

16 **Brostrom K.** Human milk and infant formulas: nutritional and immunological considerations. In: Suskind RM, ed. Textbook of Pediatric Nutrition. New York: Raven Press; 1981:41.

17 Fomon SJ et al. Cow milk feeding in infancy: gastrointestinal blood loss and iron nutritional status. J Pediatr. 1981; 98:540.

18 Crump IM. Selected inborn errors of metabolism. In: Kelts DG, Jones EG, eds. Manual of Pediatric Nutrition. Boston: Little, Brown and Co.; 1984: 211.

19 Collins JE et al. The dietary management of inborn errors of metabolism. Hum Nutr Appl Nutr. 1985;39:255.

20 Heird WC et al. Intravenous alimentation in pediatric patients. J Pediatr. 1972;80:351.

21 Topper WH. Enteral feeding methods for compromised neonates and infants. In: Lebenthal E, ed. Textbook of Gastroenterology and Nutrition in Infancy. New York: Raven Press; 1981:645.

22 Kleigman RJ, Fanaroff A. Necrotizing enterocolitis. N Engl J Med. 1984; 310:1093.

23 Schuster SR. Omphalocele and gastroschisis. In: Welch KJ et al., eds. Pediatric Surgery. 4th ed. Chicago: Yearbook Medical Publishers; 1986:740.

24 Leleiko NS et al. Nutritional assessment of pediatric patients admitted to an acute-care pediatric service utilizing anthropometric measurements. J Parenter Enter Nutr. 1986;10:166.

25 Georgieff MK et al. Effect of neonatal caloric deprivation on head growth and 1-year developmental status in preterm infants. J Pediatr. 1985;107:581.

26 Galler JR et al. Long-term effects of early kwashiorkor compared with marasmus. II. Intellectual performance. J Pediatr Gastroenterol Nutr. 1987;6: 847.

27 Galler JR et al. Long-term effects of early kwashiorkor compared with marasmus. III. Fine motor skills. J Pediatr Gastroenterol Nutr. 1987;6:855.

28 Cooper A, Heird WC. Nutritional assessment of the pediatric patient including the low-birth-weight infant. Am J Clin Nutr. 1982;35:1132.

29 Lerner A et al. Computed axial tomography scanning of the thigh: an alternative method of nutritional assessment in pediatrics. Pediatrics. 1986;77: 732.

30 Trowbridge FL. Staehling N. Sensitivity and specificity of arm circumference indicators in identifying malnourished children. Am J Clin Nutr. 1980; 33:687.

31 Yoder MC et al. Comparison of serum fibronectin, prealbumin and albumin concentrations during nutritional repletion in protein calorie malnourished infants. J Pediatr Gastroenterol Nutr. 1987;6:84.

32 Thomas MR et al. Evaluation of transthyretin as a monitor of protein-energy intake in preterm and sick neonatal infants. J Parenter Enteral Nutr. 1988;12: 162.

33 Georgieff MK et al. Serum transthyretin levels and protein intake as predictors of weight gain velocity in premature infants. J Pediatr Gastroenterol Nutr. 1987;6:775.

34 Moskowitz SR et al. Prealbumin as a biochemical marker of nutritional adequacy in premature infants. J Pediatr. 1983;102:749.

35 Vanlandingham S et al. Prealbumin: a parameter of visceral protein levels during albumin infusion. J Parenter Enteral Nutr. 1982;6:230.

36 Ramsden DB et al. The interrelationship of thyroid hormones, vitamin A and the binding proteins following acute stress. Clin Endocrinol. 1978;8: 109.

37 Sandstedt S et al. Influence of total parenteral nutrition on plasma fibronectin in malnourished subjects with or without inflammatory response. J Parenter Enter Nutr. 1984;8:493.

38 Greene HL et al. Persistently low blood retinol levels during and after parenteral feeding of very low-birth-weight infants: examination of losses into intravenous administration sets and a method of prevention by addition to a lipid emulsion. Pediatrics. 1987; 79:84.

39 Greene HL et al. Evaluation of a pediatric multiple vitamin preparation for total parenteral nutrition. II. Blood levels of vitamins A, D, and E. Pediatrics. 1987;77:539.

40 Moore MC et al. Evaluation of a pediatric multiple vitamin preparation for total parenteral nutrition in infants and children. I. Blood levels of water soluble vitamins. Pediatrics. 1987;77:530.

41 Hambridge M. Trace element deficiencies in childhood. In: Suskind RM, ed. Textbook of Pediatric Nutrition. New York: Raven Press; 1981:163.

42 Dunn L et al. Beneficial effects of early hypocaloric enteral feeding on neonatal gastrointestinal function: preliminary report of a randomized trial. J Pediatr. 1988;112:622.

43 Slagle TA, Gross SJ. Effect of early low-volume enteral substrate on subsequent feeding tolerance in very low-birth-weight infants. J Pediatr. 1988; 113:526.

44 Parker P et al. A controlled comparison of continuous versus intermittent feeding in the treatment of infants with intestinal disease. J Pediatr. 1981;99: 360.

45 Hansen AE et al. Role of linoleic acid infant nutrition: clinical and chemical study of 438 infants feed on milk mixtures varying in kind and amount of fat. Pediatrics. 1963;31:171.

46 Castillo-Duran C et al. Trace mineral balance during acute diarrhea in infants. J Pediatr. 1988;113:452.

47 Zlotkin SH et al. Intravenous nitrogen and energy intakes required to duplicate in utero nitrogen accretion in prematurely born human infants. J Pediatr. 1981;99:115.

48 Zlotkin SH. Intravenous nitrogen intake requirements in full-term newborns undergoing surgery. Pediatrics. 1984;73:493.

49 Barness LA et al. Use of intravenous fat emulsions in pediatric patients. Pediatrics. 1981;68:738.

50 Kao LC et al. Triglycerides, free fatty acids, free fatty acids/albumin molar ratio and cholesterol levels in serum of neonates receiving long-term lipid infusions: controlled trial of continuous and intermittent regimens. J Pediatr. 1984;104:429.

51 Pildres RS, Lilien LD. Carbohydrate metabolism in the fetus and neonate. In: Fanaroff AA, Martin RJ, eds. Behrman's Neonatal-Perinatal Medicine. St. Louis: CV Mosby Co.; 1983;845.

52 Phelps SJ et al. Effect of the continuous administration of fat emulsion on the infiltration of intravenous lines in infants receiving peripheral nutrition solutions. J Parenter Enter Nutr. 1989;13:628.

53 Pineault M et al. Beneficial effect of coinfusing a lipid emulsion on venous patency. J Parenter Enteral Nutr. 1989; 13:637.

54 Hill R et al. An evaluation of D-xylose absorption measurements in children suspected of having small intestinal disease. J Pediatr. 1981;99:245.

55 Orenstein SR. Enteral versus parenteral therapy for intractable diarrhea of infancy: a prospective, randomized trial. J Pediatr. 1986;109:277.

56 Rossi TM et al. Extent and duration of small intestinal mucosal injury in tractable diarrhea of infancy. Pediatrics. 1980;66:730.

57 Green HL et al. Protracted diarrhea and malnutrition in infancy: changes in intestinal morphology and disaccharidase activities during treatment with total intravenous nutrition or oral elemental diets. J Pediatr. 1975;87:695.

58 Al-Jurf AS et al. Effect of nutritional method on adaptation of the intestinal remnant after massive bowel resection. J Pediatr Gastroenterol Nutr. 1985;4: 245.

59 Klish WJ, Putman TC. The short gut. Am J Dis Child. 1981;135:1056.

60 Adibi SA et al. Evidence for two different modes of tripeptide disappearance in human intestine. J Clin Invest. 1975;56:1355.

61 Zabielski PB et al. Necrotizing enterocolitis: feeding in endemic and epidemic periods. J Parenter Enteral Nutr. 1989;13:520.

62 Friedman Z et al. Rapid onset of essential fatty acid deficiency in the newborn. Pediatrics. 1976;58:640.

63 Pelham LD. Rational use of intravenous fat emulsions. Am J Hosp Pharm. 1981;18:198.

64 Fisher GW et al. Diminished bacterial defenses with Intralipid. Lancet. 1980; 2:819.

65 Usmani SS et al. Effect of a lipid emulsion (Intralipid) on polymorphonuclear leukocyte function in the neonate. J Pediatr. 1988;113:172.

66 Herson VC et al. Effect of intravenous fat infusion on neonatal neutrophil and platelet function. J Parenter Enteral Nutr. 1989;13:620.

67 Strunk RC et al. Normal macrophage function in infants receiving Intralipid by low-dose intermittent administration. J Pediatr. 1985;106:640.

68 Seidner DL et al. Effects of long-chain triglyceride emulsions on reticuloendothelial system function in humans. J Parenter Enteral Nutr. 1989;13:614.

69 Burckart GJ et al. Triglyceride and fatty acid clearance in neonates following safflower oil emulsion infusion. J Parenter Enteral Nutr. 1983;7:251.

70 Spear ML et al. Effect of fat infusions on platelet concentration in premature infants. J Parenter Enteral Nutr. 1990; 14:165.

71 Andrew G et al. Lipid metabolism in the neonate: II. The effect of Intralipid in bilirubin binding in vitro and in vivo. J Pediatr. 1976;88:279.

72 Spear ML et al. The effect of 15-hour fat infusions in varying dosage on bilirubin binding to albumin. J Parenter Enteral Nutr. 1985;9:144.

73 Spear ML et al. Effect of heparin dose and infusion rate on lipid clearance and bilirubin binding in premature infants receiving intravenous fat emulsions. J Pediatr. 1988;112:94.

74 Beisel WR. Metabolic response of the host to infections. In: Feigin RD, Cherry JD, eds. Textbook of Pediatric Infectious Disease. Philadelphia: WB Saunders Co.; 1981:1.

75 Weber SS et al. Availability of insulin from parenteral nutrient solutions. Am J Hosp Pharm. 1977;34:353–57.

76 Niemiec PW, Vanderveen TW. Compatibility considerations in parenteral nutrient solutions. Am J Hosp Pharm. 1984;41:893–911.

77 Sajbel TA et al. Use of separate insulin infusions with total parenteral nutrition. J Parenter Enteral Nutr. 1987;11: 97–9.

78 Yeh TF et al. Metabolic rate and energy balance in infants with bronchopulmonary dysplasia. J Pediatr. 1989; 114:448.

79 Kurzner SI et al. Growth failure in infants with bronchopulmonary dysplasia: nutrition and elevated resting metabolic expenditure. Pediatrics. 1988; 81:379.

80 Covelli HD et al. Respiratory failure precipitated by high carbohydrate loads. Ann Intern Med. 1981;95:579.

81 Askanazi J et al. Nutrition for the patient with respiratory failure: glucose versus fat. Anesthesiology. 1981;54: 373.

82 Pereira GR et al. Decreased oxygenation and hyperlipemia during intravenous fat emulsions in premature infants. Pediatrics. 1980;66:26.

83 Brans YW et al. Fat emulsion tolerance in very-low-birth-weight neonates: effect on diffusion of oxygen in the lungs and on blood pH. Pediatrics. 1986;78:79.

84 Lloyd TR, Boucek MM. Effect in Intralipid on the neonatal pulmonary bed: an echographic study. J Pediatr. 1986; 108:130.

85 Gaull GE. Taurine in the nutrition of the human infant. Acta Paediatr Scand. 1982;38(Suppl.):38–40.

86 Geggel HS et al. Nutritional requirement for taurine in patients receiving long-term parenteral nutrition. N Engl J Med. 1985;312:142–46.

87 Heird WC et al. Amino acid mixture designed to maintain normal plasma amino acid patterns in infants and children requiring parenteral nutrition. Pediatrics. 1987;80:401–08.

88 Heird WC et al. Pediatric parenteral amino acid mixture in low birth weight infants. Pediatrics. 1988;81:41–50.

89 Helms RA et al. Comparison of a pediatric versus standard amino acid formulation in preterm neonates requiring parenteral nutrition. J Pediatr. 1987; 110:466–70.

90 Adamkin D, McClead R. Comparison of two neonatal intravenous amino acid formulations in preterm infants: a multicenter study. J Perinatol. 1991;11:375.

91 Mauer E. Incidence of cholestasis in low birth weight neonates on Trophamine. J Parenter Enteral Nutr. 1991; 15(Suppl.):25S.

92 **Gura K, Forchielli M.** Incidence of cholestasis in infants receiving parenteral nutrition: comparison of Aminosyn-PF and TrophAmine. J Parenter Enteral Nutr. 1992;16(Suppl.):28S.

93 **Lenz GT, Mikrut BA.** Calcium and phosphate solubility in neonatal parenteral nutrient solutions containing Aminosyn-PF or TrophAmine. Am J Hosp Pharm. 1988;45:2367–371.

94 **Shohat M et al.** Plasma ammonia levels in preterm infants receiving parenteral nutrition with crystalline L-amino acids. J Parenter Enteral Nutr. 1984;8:178.

95 **Thomas DW et al.** Hyperammonemia in neonates receiving intravenous nutrition. J Parenter Enteral Nutr. 1982;6:503.

96 **Rezvani I, Auerbach VH.** Defects in metabolism of amino acids. In: Behrman RE et al., eds. Nelson Textbook of Pediatrics. Philadelphia: WB Saunders Co.; 1987:926.

97 **Baumgart S et al.** Sepsis with coagulase-negative staphylococci in critically-ill newborns. Am J Dis Child. 1983;137:461.

98 **Lowy FD, Hammer SM.** Staphylococcus epidermidis infection. Ann Intern Med. 1983;99:834.

99 **Johnson DE.** Systemic candidiasis in very low-birth-weight infants (1500 grams). Pediatrics. 1984;73:138.

100 **Baley JE et al.** Disseminated fungal infections in very low-birth-weight infants: clinical manifestations and epidemiology. Pediatrics. 1984;73:144.

101 **Powell DA et al.** Broviac catheter-related Malassezia furfur sepsis in five infants receiving intravenous fat emulsions. J Pediatr. 1984;105:987.

102 **Long JG, Keyserling HL.** Catheter-related infection in infants due to an unusual lipophylic yeast—Malassezia furfur. Pediatrics. 1985;76:896.

103 **Kulkarni PB et al.** Rickets in very low-birth-weight infants. J Pediatr. 1980;96:249.

104 **Ziegler EE et al.** Body composition of the reference fetus. Growth. 1976;40:329.

105 **Koo WWK et al.** Response of preterm infants to aluminum in parenteral nutrition. J Parenter Enteral Nutr. 1989;13:516.

106 **Niemiec PW, Vanderveen TW.** Compatibility considerations in parenteral nutrient solutions. Am J Hosp Pharm. 1984;41:893.

107 **Schmidt GL et al.** Cost containment using cysteine HCl acidification to increase calcium/phosphate solubility in hyperalimentation solutions. J Parenter Enteral Nutr. 1986;10:203.

108 **Fitzgerald KA, MacKay MW.** Calcium and phosphorus solubility in neonatal parenteral nutrient solutions containing TrophAmine. Am J Hosp Pharm. 1986;43:88.

109 **Eggert LD et al.** Calcium and phosphorus compatibility in parenteral nutrition solutions for neonates. Am J Hosp Pharm. 1982;39:49.

110 **Vileisis RA.** Effect of phosphorus intake in total parenteral nutrition infusates in premature neonates. J Pediatr. 1987;110:586.

111 **Wood RJ et al.** Reduction of total parenteral nutrition-induced urinary calcium loss by increasing phosphorus in the total parenteral nutrition prescription. J Parenter Enteral Nutr. 1986;10:188.

112 **Chessex P et al.** Calcuria in parenterally-fed preterm infants: role of phosphorus intake. J Pediatr. 1985;107:794.

113 **Koo WWK et al.** Parenteral nutrition for infants: effect of high versus low calcium and phosphorus content. J Pediatr Gastroenterol Nutr. 1987;6:96.

114 **Hoehn GJ et al.** Alternate day infusion of calcium and phosphate in very low-birth-weight infants: wasting of the infused mineral. J Pediatr Gastroenterol Nutr. 1987;6:752.

115 **Koo WWK et al.** Vitamin D requirements in infants receiving parenteral nutrition. J Parenter Enteral Nutr. 1987;11:172.

116 **Postuma R, Trevenen CL.** Liver disease in infants receiving total parenteral nutrition. Pediatrics. 1979;63:110.

117 **Pereira GR et al.** Hyperalimentation-induced cholestasis: increased incidence and severity in premature infants. Am J Dis Child. 1981;135:842.

118 **Vileisis RA et al.** Laboratory monitoring of parenteral nutrition-associated hepatic dysfunction in infants. J Parenter Enteral Nutr. 1981;5:67.

119 **Kattwinkel J et al.** The effects of age on alkaline phosphatase and other serologic liver function tests in normal subjects and patients with cystic fibrosis. J Pediatr. 1973;82:234.

120 **Bell RL et al.** Total parenteral nutrition-related cholestasis in infants. J Parenter Enteral Nutr. 1986;10:356.

121 **Drongowski RA et al.** An analysis of factors contributing to the development of total parenteral nutrition-induced cholestasis. J Parenter Enteral Nutr. 1989;13:586.

122 **Lucas A et al.** Metabolic and endocrine consequences of depriving preterm infants of enteral nutrition. Acta Paediatr Scand. 1983;72:245.

123 **Enzenauer RW et al.** Total parenteral nutrition cholestasis: a cause of mechanical biliary obstruction. Pediatrics. 1985;76:905.

124 **Cohen C, Olsen MM.** Pediatric total parenteral nutrition: liver histopathology. Arch Pathol Lab Med. 1981;105:152.

125 **Benjamin DR.** Hepatobiliary dysfunction in infants and children associated with long-term total parenteral nutrition: a clinicopathologic study. Am J Clin Pathol. 1981;76:276.

126 **Kubota A et al.** Hyperbilirubinemia in neonates associated with total parenteral nutrition. J Parenter Enteral Nutr. 1988;12:602.

127 **Roslyn JJ et al.** Increased risk of gallstones in children receiving total parenteral nutrition. Pediatrics. 1983;71:784.

128 **Suita S et al.** Cholelithiasis in infants: association with parenteral nutrition. J Parenter Enteral Nutr. 1984;8:568.

129 **Vileisis RA et al.** Prospective controlled study of parenteral nutrition-associated cholestatic jaundice: effect of protein intake. J Pediatr. 1980;96:893.

130 **Hambidge KM et al.** Plasma manganese concentrations in infants and children receiving parenteral nutrition. J Parenter Enteral Nutr. 1989;13:168.

131 **Dahms BB, Halpin TC.** Serial liver biopsies in parenteral nutrition-associated cholestasis of early infancy. Gastroenterology. 1981;81:136.

132 **Suita S et al.** Follow-up studies of children treated with long-term intravenous nutrition (IVN) during the neonatal period. J Pediatr Surg. 1982;17:37.

133 **Vileisis RA et al.** Liver malignancy after parenteral nutrition. J Pediatr. 1982;100:88.

134 **Scwarz KB.** Vitamins. In: Walk WA, Watkins JB, eds. Nutrition in Pediatrics—Basic Science and Clinical Application. Boston: Little, Brown and Co.; 1985:47.

135 **Tyor MP et al.** Metabolism and transport of bile salts in the intestine. Am J Med. 1971;51:614.

136 **Klish WJ.** Putnam TC. The short gut. Am J Dis Child. 1981;135:1056.

137 **Abbasi S et al.** Long-term assessment of growth, nutritional status and gastrointestinal function in survivors of necrotizing enterocolitis. J Pediatr. 1984;104:550.

138 **Record KE et al.** Long-chain versus medium-chain length triglycerides: a review of metabolism and clinical use. Nutr Clin Pract. 1986;1:129.

139 **Sucher KP.** Medium-chain triglycerides: a review of their enteral use in clinical nutrition. Nutr Clin Pract. 1986;1:146.

140 **Shires GT et al.** Fluid, electrolyte, and nutritional management of the surgical patient. In: Principles of Surgery. 4th ed. New York: McGraw-Hill; 1984:45.

Cystic Fibrosis

James W Jones

History 100-1	Acute Pulmonary Exacerbation 100-6
Genetic Basis/Epidemiology 100-1	Cleanout 100-6
Pathophysiology 100-1	Antibiotic therapy 100-7
Clinical Manifestations (See Table 100.1) 100-2	Intravenous (IV) antipseudomonal selection 100-7
Sweat Glands 100-2	Pharmacokinetic differences in CF patients
Sinus Involvement 100-2	(See Table 100.4) 100-7
Pancreatic Involvement 100-2	Monitoring therapy 100-8
Intestinal Involvement 100-2	Adverse effects 100-8
Hepatic Involvement 100-3	Mucoidal pseudomonas 100-9
Genitourinary Involvement 100-3	Prednisone Use in CF (See Question 24) 100-10
Pulmonary Involvement 100-3	Dornase Alpha (DNase) (See Question 25) 100-10
Neonatal Screening 100-3	Dosing and monitoring (See Question 26) 100-11
Diagnosis 100-3	Investigational Therapies (See Question 28) 100-11
Diagnostic Criteria 100-3	Chloride channel modifiers 100-11
Laboratory Testing 100-4	Anti-inflammatory agents 100-11
Pulmonary testing 100-4	Gene therapy 100-11
Gastrointestinal (GI) testing 100-4	**Atypical Infections** 100-9
Therapy 100-4	Allergic Bronchopulmonary Aspergillosis (ABPA) 100-9
Prophylactic Antibiotics 100-4	Clinical presentation and diagnosis 100-9
Chest Physiotherapy/Postural Drainage 100-5	Treatment 100-9
Pancreatic Enzymes (See Table 100.2) 100-5	Outpatient therapy 100-9
Dosing 100-5	Antibiotics aerosolized 100-9
Monitoring 100-5	Oral antipseudomonal antibiotics 100-10
Fat-Soluble Vitamin Supplementation	
(See Table 100.3) 100-6	

History

The genetic defect that causes the majority of cystic fibrosis (CF) cases is believed to have originated approximately four to five thousand years ago in Northern Europe. The first common description of the condition may have come from German folklore, which advised that infants whose foreheads taste of salt upon kissing will soon die. However, it was not until 1938 that CF was first described as a discrete clinical entity.[1] The term cystic fibrosis was used at that time to describe the characteristic appearance of the pancreas at postmortem. Initially it was thought to be predominantly a gastrointestinal (GI) disorder since patients died in infancy from meconium ileus, malnutrition, and inanition. Now CF is recognized as a multisystem disease. While CF is still the most common fatal inherited disease in Caucasians, survival since its first description has improved dramatically. (See Figure 100.1.)

Genetic Basis/Epidemiology

Cystic fibrosis is inherited as an autosomal recessive trait. In the U.S., approximately 1 in 20 Caucasians is a carrier of the defective allele with the incidence of CF in this group being about 1 in 2000 to 2500 live births.[2] In 1985, the defect was found to be localized to chromosome 7 and in 1989 the actual gene was identified.[3-9] The product of this gene is a 1480 amino acid protein called the cystic fibrosis transmembrane regulator (CFTR), which functions as a chloride channel throughout the body. While there are other channels that transport chloride, CFTR is thought to be the predominant route of transfer. CFTR is found in a variety of tissues providing different functions depending upon the site. For example, in the sweat glands, it reabsorbs chloride, while in the lung it excretes chloride. A dysfunctional or absent CFTR, therefore, has different pathologic consequences for different organs as discussed in greater detail later in this chapter.

There have been over 300 mutations described in this gene. The most common mutation is the deletion of a single amino acid, phenylalanine (abbreviated F), from the 508th position of the CFTR protein (delta F508). This deletion affects 70% of patients.[9,11] It is suspected that differences in disease severity and clinical course may be explained in part by the different mutations. However, an association between mutation type and the presence of pulmonary disease, which is responsible for most of the mortality, remains unclear.[12]

Pathophysiology

The consequence of these genetic defects is the production of an abnormal, dysfunctional CFTR protein and disruption of the normal transmembrane flow of chloride ions through the chloride channel. The result is abnormal movement of chloride, other ions (mostly sodium) and water across affected cellular membranes. In the exocrine glands, liver, lungs, and other organ systems, the defect in chloride transport leads to the production of altered secretions which either directly or indirectly cause the clinical manifestations. Two hallmarks of CF are chronic suppurative endobronchial (pulmonary) disease and pancreatic insufficiency. Of these, lung involvement leads to most of the morbidity and mortality in CF. The lungs in patients with CF are structurally normal at birth, but in greater than 90% of patients, chronic infection leads to lung tissue destruction. The clinical course between patients is variable. Factors that determine the speed of progression

Fig 100.1   Median Survival in Patients with Cystic Fibrosis   Source: CFF Data Registry, courtesy of Stacy FitzSimmons, Ph.D.

from mild pulmonary involvement to severe disease are unknown. Pancreatic insufficiency and the associated maldigestion and malabsorption are the other major causes of morbidity in these patients. Before the advent of exogenous pancreatic enzyme therapy, malabsorption was the major cause of mortality. Even with digestive enzyme supplementation many patients have difficulty gaining or maintaining weight. Many patients complain of a lack of appetite, which is probably secondary to concurrent pulmonary infection and associated malaise, or gastrointestinal complications such as gastroesophageal reflux or constipation. Another explanation for the lack of weight gain may be that these patients have a high basal metabolic rate, secondary to a variety of causes, inflammatory mediators (e.g., tumor necrosis factor or interleukin 1), elevated body temperature secondary to infection or an increased work of breathing with more advanced disease.[13] An abrupt loss of weight may signal the onset of diabetes mellitus.

Clinical Manifestations

Sweat Glands

The initial fluid secreted by the sweat glands in CF patients is normal. The defect is in the reabsorption of electrolytes by the sweat glands. CFTR is found in the apical membrane of the resorptive area of the gland. The dysfunctional ion channel leads to the inability to resorb chloride ions (the reabsorption of sodium also is deranged) and thus, a high level of salt in the sweat. This explains the "infant who tastes of salt" in German folklore and is the basis for sweat chloride testing, the primary diagnostic test for CF.

Sinus Involvement

Nasal polyps, these outgrowths of normal sinus epidermis, occur in up to 20% of older patients and may become large enough to block nasal passages. The pathogenesis of these polyps is unknown, but the obstruction of nasal passages may lead to infection. On x-ray, greater than 90% of adult aged CF patients have pansinusitis which may contribute to pulmonary exacerbations.[14]

Pancreatic Involvement

Both the exocrine and, ultimately, the endocrine function of the pancreas are affected in CF. The defect in chloride secretion leads to desiccation of pancreatic secretions, accumulation of secretory material within the pancreatic ducts, and ductal obstruction. The exocrine defect inhibits secretion of digestive enzymes and bicarbonate into the duodenum. Without these enzymes, there is poor digestion of fats and to a lesser extent, malabsorption of proteins

and carbohydrates. As a result, 85% of patients experience steatorrhea (fatty stools), decreased absorption of the fat soluble vitamins (ADEK), malnutrition, and failure to thrive. With blockage of the pancreatic ducts, the enzymes which normally flow down into the intestine to participate in digestion are trapped in the pancreas by ductal obstruction. Over time these enzymes (lipase, protease, amylase) accumulate and eventually begin to digest the pancreatic tissue. This leads to loss of functional tissue and the pancreas eventually becomes scarred and fibrotic. At postmortem this fibrotic appearance is characteristic which lead to the original term for the disease, fibrocystic disease of the pancreas. This was later shortened to cystic fibrosis. Early in life, elevations of serum amylase and lipase are seen secondary to pancreatic autodigestion. Ultimately this progressive destruction affects pancreatic endocrine function leading to glucose intolerance and finally diabetes mellitus in up to 15% of patients. A small number of patients also will experience either asymptomatic or painful chronic pancreatitis from this destructive process.

Intestinal Involvement

Meconium ileus occurs in approximately 10% to 15% of newborns with CF and is manifested by failure to pass meconium (the first stool) within the first 48 hours of life, abdominal distension, and bilious vomiting. Other less frequent complications during the neonatal period are intestinal volvulus, perforation, and jejunal and ileal atresias. Outside of the neonatal period, distal intestinal ob-

Table 100.1	Clinical Manifestations of Cystic Fibrosis[117]		
	Approximate Incidence (%)		
Manifestation	Infants	Children	Adults
Pancreatic			
Insufficiency	80–85	85	90
Pancreatitis	—	1–2	2–4
Abnormal glucose tolerance	—	5/yr[a]	30
Diabetes mellitus	—	2–4	8–15
Hepatobiliary			
Biliary cirrhosis	—	10–20	>20
Cholelithiasis	—	5	5–10
Biliary obstruction	—	1–2	5
Intestinal			
Meconium ileus	10–15	—	—
Meconium ileus equivalent	—	1–5	10–20
Rectal prolapse	—	10–15	1–2
Intussusception	—	1–5	1–2
Gastroesophageal reflux	—	1–5	>10
Appendiceal abscess	—	0–1	1–2
Respiratory			
Upper			
Nasal polyps	<1	4–10	15–20
Pansinusitis	—	—	90–100
Lower			
Bronchiectasis	—	30–50	>90
Pneumothorax	—	1–2	10–15
Hemoptysis[b]	—	5–15	50–60
Genitourinary			
Delayed puberty	—	—	85
Infertility			
Males	—	—	98
Females	—	—	70–80

a ↑ in glucose intolerance of ≈5% per year.
b Percentage includes both major and minor hemoptysis.

struction syndrome, (DIOS, also called meconium ileus equivalent) may occur at any age and results from the complete or partial obstruction of the intestine, usually in the cecum or terminal ileum. This obstruction is observed in 10% to 20% of patients and results from the inspissation of intestinal secretions and incompletely digested intestinal contents. A right lower quadrant mass, abdominal distention, failure to pass stools, and vomiting may accompany DIOS. Other intestinal complications seen are rectal prolapse, gastroesophageal reflux, intussusception, and appendiceal abscesses.

Hepatic Involvement

With abnormal chloride secretion, there is a reduction in the volume and flow of bile leading to stasis and obstruction of the biliary tree. With chronic obstruction there is inflammation which gives rise to the characteristic lesion of focal biliary cirrhosis.[15] Usually there is no clinically apparent disease observed with focal cirrhosis, but in approximately 2% of patients there is progression to multilobular cirrhosis. With this progressive cirrhosis there is associated portal hypertension, hypersplenism, esophageal varices, ascites, and, in a small number of patients, complete hepatic failure requiring transplantation. Approximately 45% of patients have abnormal gall bladder function and size (absent or small gall bladder) with 5% to 10% of patients developing gallstones.

Genitourinary Involvement

Approximately 98% of males with CF are infertile secondary to in utero obstruction of the vas deferens or related structures. Hormonal secretion and secondary sexual characteristics are normal. In the small number of CF patients in whom infertility is the only manifestation of disease, it may go undiagnosed until fertility testing is done. In females, the incidence of infertility is less, around 70% to 80%, and is thought to be related to the production of a thick and tenacious cervical mucus. Hundreds of pregnancies have been carried successfully to term, but not without risk, especially for the patient with moderate to severe pulmonary disease.[16]

Pulmonary Involvement

In the airway epithelium, there is failure of chloride secretion as well as enhanced sodium and water reabsorption. This results in a thick viscous mucus, airway plugging, bacterial adherence, and chronic bacterial colonization. Bacterial endobronchial infection incites an inflammatory response mediated predominately by neutrophils. Neutrophil protease and oxygen free radicals are released, as well as chemoattractants that perpetuate the immune response. Continued recruitment of neutrophils to the lungs and subsequent death of these cells, leads to an accumulation of host DNA which adds significantly to the viscosity of the sputum. With persistence of the immune response, the lungs' defenses (α_1-antitrypsin and secretory leukocyte protease inhibitor) are overwhelmed. Chronic bronchitis and the associated inflammation lead to progressive destruction of lung tissue, which over time results in fibrosis and bronchiectasis. Extensive loss of viable lung tissue and changes in lung architecture can cause hypoxemia, pulmonary hypertension, and cor pulmonale (hypertrophy of the right ventricle secondary to the pulmonary hypertension). Subsequently cardiorespiratory failure ensues, the cause of early death in 95% of CF patients. The exact sequence of events that translates the genetic defect at the cellular level to pulmonary infection is unknown, but all patients with CF eventually develop endobronchial colonization and infection. The clinical course of the infection is highly variable and despite intensive courses of antibiotics, the bacteria seldom are eradicated. The respiratory pathogens most commonly observed are Staphylococcus aureus, Haemophilus influenzae, and Pseudo-

monas aeruginosa. Of these, S. aureus (Staph) frequently is responsible for the first bronchopulmonary infection of CF and was historically the most commonly isolated organism. With the discovery and use of efficient antiStaph drugs, Pseudomonas aeruginosa has become the most common pathogen isolated in chronically colonized patients. Once established, P. aeruginosa seldom is eradicated. Because of this, P. aeruginosa becomes responsible for a repetitive cycle of infection, inflammation, and lung damage that ultimately leads to a high incidence of morbidity and mortality in CF. Burkholderia cepacia (formerly Pseudomonas cepacia) is another opportunistic pathogen which is cultured from patients with increasing frequency. Infection with this organism is problematic due to its high level of resistance to virtually all antibiotics. B. cepacia infections range from asymptomatic colonization to fulminant infection, bacteremia, and death. Viruses and fungi are also potential pathogens. Viruses may predispose patients to subsequent bacterial infection, and may be responsible for some of the acute pulmonary exacerbations. The fungus Aspergillus fumigatus has been associated with allergic bronchopulmonary aspergillosis (ABPA) in 5% to 25% of CF patients. ABPA is an immunologic reaction to Aspergillus that can lead to progressive pulmonary fibrosis if undiagnosed and untreated.

Neonatal Screening

In utero, obstruction of the pancreatic ducts leads to elevated fetal blood levels of immunoreactive trypsin (IRT). An IRT screening assay can detect this elevation of serum IRT, and has a sensitivity of 99% for the detection of CF in newborns.[17] There is no consensus that early treatment of CF in infants alters disease progression; therefore, routine large scale screening is not currently recommended.[18]

Diagnosis
Diagnostic Criteria

More than 70% of CF patients are diagnosed in their first year of life.[19] The gold standard for the diagnosis of CF is the pilocarpine iontophoresis test (sweat chloride test).[20] Because of the underlying chloride channel defect, elevated sweat chloride levels (>60 mEq/L) are seen in 98% of CF patients. This test may be unreliable in infants less than two months of age due to lack of sufficient sample volume obtainable. For the diagnosis of CF, both the abnormal sweat chloride and one or more of the associated clinical criteria are necessary. These criteria include: a) chronic obstructive airways disease (COAD), b) intestinal malabsorption, c) family history of CF, d) meconium ileus at birth, e) male infertility due to azoospermia, and f) presence of Staphylococcus aureus or mucoid Pseudomonas aeruginosa in the respiratory tract. The classic triad for the diagnosis of CF includes; a positive sweat test, malabsorption, and chronic pulmonary disease. With the discovery of the CF gene, DNA typing is now available for the delta F508 deletion, but this will detect only a few of the 30% nondelta F508 mutations. This would result in detection of the carrier state or a false negative result in these patients.

1. L.T., a 9-month-old male who has had sporadic well baby follow-up, is brought to the pediatric primary care clinic. His mother states: "he can't seem to eat enough food, he's always crying until I feed him." She says that he has 8–10 stools/day, but she thought this was because he ate so much. On further questioning, she says that the stools are large in amount, greasy, and foul smelling. He has never been hospitalized, but has had a lot of ear infections and 3 chest colds so far this winter that have been treated through the emergency room (ER) with antibiotics. When plotted on a standard growth

curve, L.T. is found to be in the fifth percentile for both weight and height. The pregnancy and delivery were uncomplicated and L.T.'s medical history is unremarkable except as noted above. Physical examination shows a poorly nourished, small for age infant in no apparent distress. Family history is unremarkable, but mom was adopted. Review of systems reveals diffuse crackles in the lower lung fields; all other systems are within normal limits. After taking this history, a sweat chloride test is ordered. The result is 110 mEq/L (Normal: <60 mEq/L). His chest x-ray is read as mild peribronchial thickening of both upper lobes. What subjective and objective data for L.T. is suggestive of the diagnosis of CF?

L.T. fulfills the classic triad for the diagnosis of CF: elevated sweat chloride, chronic recurrent pulmonary infections, and apparent pancreatic insufficiency. While not showing symptoms of pulmonary infection at the present time, he has had an abnormal number of chest colds and there are chest x-ray signs indicative of chronic inflammation. The earliest chest x-ray changes seen are peribronchial thickening in the upper zones. As the lung disease progresses, hyperinflation, as evidenced by increased antero-posterior diameter of the chest (barrel chest) and flattening of the diaphragm, is seen. Areas of collapse, consolidation, and eventually abscess formation and bronchiectasis are evident, indicating severe tissue destruction. L.T.'s pancreatic insufficiency is suggested by his multiple daily fatty stools and failure to thrive in spite of a voracious appetite. While there are no known first degree relatives with CF, mom's medical history is unknown. With a positive sweat test, evidence of malabsorption, and pulmonary involvement, as shown by recurrent infections and chest x-ray changes, L.T. fits the diagnosis of CF.

Laboratory Testing

2. What further testing can be done to confirm the diagnosis of CF in L.T.?

It is recommended that the sweat test be performed twice, on two different days for reliability and to rule out other conditions that can cause an elevated sweat chloride level such as hypothyroidism, adrenal insufficiency, anorexia nervosa, and severe malnutrition.

Pulmonary Testing

3. What testing and follow-up should be completed to define pulmonary involvement?

Baseline pulmonary function tests, chest x-ray, oxygen saturation, and respiratory cultures are a part of the normal workup. Spirometry should be done every six months and complete pulmonary function tests once a year. Arterial blood gases or pulse oximetry need to be completed on patients whose forced expiratory volume in one second (FEV_1) is less than 40% predicted. Unfortunately, children like L.T., who are less than five years of age are unable to adequately perform pulmonary function testing. Pulmonary function tests require voluntary cooperation, the ability to follow instructions and good respiratory muscle control. Children less than five years of age are largely unable to complete "adult" pulmonary function tests. Special techniques for performing pulmonary function tests in this age group are still being perfected and age related normals are currently being established. Discussion of pulmonary function testing in this age group is beyond the scope of this chapter but it is important to note that lack of accurate pulmonary function tests in these children make it difficult to assess the severity of their disease or to establish objective treatment endpoints. Chest x-rays should be obtained annually and on pulmonary-related hospital admissions or before any surgery. Respiratory tract cultures and sensitivities should be completed annually and before initiation of antibiotic therapy. As with pulmonary function

testing, obtaining an adequate sputum sample from infants like L.T. for testing is difficult since they cannot cooperate. One method for obtaining a sample in this age group is an oropharyngeal swab following a cough. However, the sample obtained actually may contain only normal upper airway flora rather than the true lower airway colonization; therefore one should interpret persistent normal flora results with caution.[21]

Gastrointestinal (GI) Testing

4. What testing and follow-up should be completed in L.T. to define GI and nutritional involvement?

Serum lipase and amylase should be measured. Quantification of fecal fat content may assist in titration of pancreatic enzyme doses. However, collection of the stool and obtaining an accurate diet history in patients like L.T. is difficult. In fact, in most centers these procedures are limited to patients whose enzyme dose requirements are excessive. Liver function tests, albumin, serum electrolytes, and vitamin A and E levels should be determined. L.T.'s height and weight should be plotted on standard growth charts at each visit. Nutritional assessments should be completed annually, especially if L.T. shows evidence of weight loss or poor weight gain. Other measures could include: 1) assessment of compliance to pancreatic enzyme and vitamin intake after these agents are prescribed; 2) measurement of albumin and/or prealbumin when indicated, to rule out frank protein-calorie malnutrition; 3) abdominal examination with particular attention to liver and spleen size and consistency; 4) evaluation of metabolic and liver status; and 5) a complete blood cell count.[22]

Therapy

5. Gram's stain of L.T.'s sputum reveals normal respiratory flora. The throat culture is pending. Significant laboratory findings include: serum vitamin E 2.5 mg/L (Normal: 3–15.8); vitamin A 26 μg/dL (Normal: 30–90); lipase 47 U/L (Normal: 0.1–208); amylase <30 U/L (Normal: 0–110); albumin 2.7 gm/dL (Normal: 3.4–5.1); all other labs are within normal limits. L.T. is admitted to the hospital for optimization of nutrition and family education to emphasize that CF is a lifelong chronic disease. What general treatment principles should be considered for L.T. at this time?

Since there is no specific cure for CF, the treatment is directed at preventing the progression of pulmonary disease, the primary cause of CF related morbidity and mortality. Since pancreatic insufficiency and malabsorption are seen in most patients, maintaining adequate nutrition is also a priority. As L.T. does not have evidence of a pulmonary infection at this time, no antibiotics are to be started, but chest physiotherapy is indicated to mobilize respiratory secretions. For correction of his nutritional status and pancreatic insufficiency, a high energy diet [120% to 150% of the recommended daily allowance (RDA)][23] should be started along with pancreatic enzyme replacement and vitamin supplementation.

Prophylactic Antibiotics

6. Is there a role for prophylactic antibiotics to prevent pseudomonal colonization in L.T.?

As discussed earlier, S. aureus is frequently responsible for the initial bacterial colonization/infection in CF and subsequent to the S. aureus is P. aeruginosa colonization. The mechanism(s) whereby S. aureus allows for subsequent P. aeruginosa colonization is not clear, but probably relate to epithelial damage.[24] While it has been suggested that preventing S. aureus colonization may prevent or delay P. aeruginosa colonization, there is a lack of proof and no consensus on the benefit of using prophylactic anti-Staph antibiotics. Frequent antibiotic administration has been shown in some studies to delay colonization or improve survival, while in others this practice promotes microbial resistance.[25–28] Since there is a lack of clear clinical efficacy, the use of prophylactic anti-Staph drugs is controversial. A multicenter trial of chemoprophylaxis with cephalexin is near completion and will hopefully shed more light on the value of prophylactic therapy.[29]

Chest Physiotherapy/Postural Drainage

7. What is chest physiotherapy (percussion and postural drainage) and what is its place in L.T.'s therapy?

Because of dehydration of the pulmonary secretions related to the CFTR defect, and the presence of large amounts of DNA, which is very viscous, the sputum in CF patients is difficult to mobilize. To facilitate removal of secretions, chest physiotherapy uses percussion on the chest wall with the cupped hand or a vibrator to shake loose secretions while the patient is in a head-lower-than-chest position. While the short term benefits have been established for many years,[30] it is only recently that the long-term benefits of percussion and postural drainage have been demonstrated.[31]

Pancreatic Enzymes

8. What is the source for pancreatic enzymes and what are the goals of therapy for L.T.?

The first available pancreatic enzymes were crude extracts from freeze dried porcine pancreas. It was necessary to use very large doses of these preparations because of degradation of the enzymes by gastric acidity. Pancreatic enzymes (particularly lipase) are very susceptible to acid degradation; by combining these agents with H_2-receptor antagonists or antacids, their efficacy is increased, but still suboptimal.[34] In the 1970s enteric-coated pancreatic enzymes were introduced. The enzymes were protected from gastric acidity and delivered to the site of activity in the duodenum relatively intact. Initially these were in tablet form, but tablets were too large to adequately disperse with food in the duodenum. Enteric-coated pancreatic microspheres (or Microtablets) are now the standard first-line therapy because of acid resistance and dispersion at the site of activity. The clinical efficacy and superiority of the microspheres over the original products has been shown in a number of studies.[35,36] The commercial pancreatic enzymes contain lipase, amylase, and protease. The ratios and amounts of these three digestive enzymes vary between the available products. Lipase content is considered the most important and thus the products names (e.g., Creon 10 = 10,000 units lipase) and conversion between them is based upon the lipase content. Protease digests proteins (it also may break down lipase) and amylase breaks down starches. The optimal amounts and ratios of protease and amylase to the lipase are unknown. Other considerations when choosing an enzyme preparation are: 1) microsphere size (optimal size is between 1 to 2 mm), 2) dissolution pH (optimal pH of dissolution of the enteric coating 5.5 to 6), and 3) cost. There has been no study to prove a definite clinical advantage of one enteric-coated microsphere product over another.

The goals of pancreatic enzyme supplementation are to: 1) improve weight gain, 2) minimize steatorrhea (it is seldom completely eliminated), and 3) eliminate abdominal cramping and bloating. Available products are listed in Table 100.2.

Dosing

9. How should L.T.'s pancreatic enzyme therapy be initiated?

There is wide patient variability in response to enzyme therapy; therefore, the final dosing must be individualized. Initial dosing is 2000 to 4000 units lipase per meal for infants less than one year

Table 100.2	Pancreatic Enzymes[a]		
Microencapsulated Microspheres			
Product[b]	Lipase	Protease	Amylase
Cotazym-S	5000	20,000	20,000
Creon 10	10,000	37,500	33,200
Creon 20	20,000	75,000	66,400
Pancrease	4000	25,000	20,000
Pancrease MT 4	4000	12,000	12,000
Pancrease MT 10	10,000	30,000	30,000
Pancrease MT 16	16,000	48,000	48,000
Pancrease MT 20	20,000	44,000	56,000
Ultrase MT 6	6000	19,500	19,500
Ultrase MT 12	12,000	39,000	39,000
Ultrase MT 18	18,000	58,500	58,500
Ultrase MT 20	20,000	65,000	65,000
Zymase	12,000	24,000	24,000

[a] Adapted from Drug Facts and Comparisons, Inc.; 1993.
[b] Dosing and comparison of products based on Lipase content.

of age and 4000 to 12,000 units lipase for children more than one year of age up through adults. Most patients' symptoms are controlled with 1500 to 2000 units lipase/kg/meal.[37] The full dose is taken with meals and half the prescribed dose is taken with snacks. L.T. is begun on one capsule of a product that contains 4000 units of lipase in enteric coated microtablets with meals and one-half capsule with snacks. For small children, the capsules may be opened and the microspheres poured onto a soft food, but the microspheres should not be chewed or put onto hot food or liquid as this will destroy the coating. In infants, if given with formula, enzymes should be administered with a small amount of formula separately before giving the rest of the bottle, to ensure that the child gets the full dose. One report published related high-strength pancreatic enzymes to colonic strictures.[38] The symptoms of strictures are the same as for DIOS and can only be differentiated by ultrasound or radiography. The causality has not been firmly established but use of products with greater than 20,000 units of lipase content/capsule and greater than 6500 units lipase/kg/meal of any product are not recommended at this time (6500 units/kg was the smallest dose associated with stricture formation). Because of these cases, all pancreatic enzymes with a lipase content of greater than 20,000 units per capsule have been removed from the market. More research is needed to establish the true causality of these strictures.

Monitoring

10. L.T. is stabilized over the next few days on 1 pancrease capsule with meals and has reduced stool frequency to 3/day with prompt weight gain. Parental teaching is completed and L.T. is discharged from the hospital after 4 days of inpatient therapy. He is scheduled for follow up in the clinic in 2 weeks. How should L.T.'s pancreatic enzyme therapy be monitored and adjusted?

The dose needs to be individualized. The above dosing provides starting recommendations. Dosing is adjusted based upon the presence of steatorrhea, abdominal cramping, the number of large frequent stools, and the degree of fullness reported by the patient or his parents. The doses are empirically increased to control these symptoms and to promote weight gain and growth. Once appropriate enzyme therapy is begun, a decrease in steatorrhea should be almost immediate. Weight gain should be seen in two to three days. In infants, a severe diaper rash may be caused by too large a dose of enzymes. This leads to active enzymes in the stool which, with prolonged contact, can irritate and breakdown the skin. If patients require more than 2000 units/kg/meal without control of symptoms or weight gain, fecal fat measurements should be assessed before any future adjustments. While not of proven efficacy with microsphere products, patients requiring high doses of enzymes may be given a trial of an H_2-receptor antagonist, omeprazole, or misoprostol as an adjunct to protect the enzymes from degradation.[39,40] Excessive enzyme therapy can be associated with constipation which also can be the result of a lack of sufficient enzyme therapy (producing DIOS). Differentiation as to the cause of constipation usually can be made by a careful dietary and compliance history.

Fat-Soluble Vitamin Supplementation

11. In addition to enzyme replacement, what fat soluble vitamin supplementation is appropriate for L.T.?

With the malabsorption of fats, deficiencies in the fat-soluble vitamins would be expected and have been observed in patients with CF. As seen in L.T.'s laboratory evaluation, deficiencies in vitamins A and E are relatively common in malabsorbing patients. His vitamin K and D levels were not measured since vitamin K deficiency usually occurs only in patients with cholestatic liver disease or as a complication of prolonged antibiotic therapy. While rare without liver disease or prolonged antibiotic therapy, if vitamin K deficiency is suspected, because of the difficulty of the assay, rather than measuring the vitamin directly the prothrombin time (PT) is measured. The PT is an indirect measure of vitamin K by assessing the activity of vitamin K dependent coagulation factors. Vitamin D deficiency has been reported, but is rarely clinically significant.[32] L.T. had no risk factors for vitamin K or D deficiency so they are not measured. The long-term effects of inadequate fat-soluble vitamin intake are unknown. Because of the theoretical benefits, low cost, and low risk, supplementation is routinely prescribed. Based upon the recommendations in Table 100.3, L.T. is begun on 1 cc once daily of a multivitamin liquid that contains vitamins A, D, E, and K in the amounts of 1500/400/40 units and 0.1 mg, respectively. Follow-up levels for vitamins A and E are recommended yearly, whereas measurement of D and K levels is not routinely recommended.[33]

Table 100.3	Guidelines for Fat Soluble Vitamins in Cystic Fibrosis[33]	
Vitamin	**Age**	**Dose**
A and D	<2 yr	A: 1500 international units D: 400 international units
	2–8 yr	A: 5000 international units D: 400 international units
E	0–6 months	25 international units
	6–12 months	50 international units
	1–4 yr	100 international units
	4–10 yr	100–200 international units
	>10 yr	200–400 international units
K[a]	0–12 months	2.5 mg/wk
		2.5 mg twice a week
	>1 yr	5 mg twice a week
Multi	Adolescent/adult	1–2 multivitamins QD

[a] Vitamin K is supplemented in: cholestatic liver disease, prolonged antibiotics dosing in active hemoptysis is higher.

Acute Pulmonary Exacerbation

12. B.W., a 19-year-old female, was diagnosed with CF at 3 years of age following a history of chronic pneumonias. She now presents to the pulmonary clinic with increasing cough and sputum production. B.W. seldom required hospitalization before age 12, but has since required hospitalization about twice a year. Over the past 2 weeks she has had an increase in cough and sputum, the sputum has changed from white to greenish in color. She relates a 4 pound weight loss over this period. She is noted to be a slightly thin adult female who is having labored breathing. Pulmonary function tests reveal an FEV_1 of 65% of predicted normal and a forced vital capacity (FVC) 60% of normal (her usual baselines are FEV_1 85% and FVC 80%). Two strains of _P. aeruginosa_ grew out of her clinic sputum sample from 4 months ago (see below for sensitivities). Other pertinent laboratory findings are: white blood cell (WBC) count 17,000/mm³ (Normal: 4.5–11) with bands 4% (Normal: 0–11), segs 35% (Normal: 36–66), lymphs 50% (Normal: 24–44), eosinophils 11% (Normal: 1–4); blood urea nitrogen (BUN) 7 mg/dL (Normal: 5–18); and creatinine 0.5 mg/dL (Normal: 0.6–1.3); all other bloodwork and electrolytes are within normal limits. Heart rate and blood pressure are normal. Temperature 99.2 °F orally (Normal: 98.6). Respiratory rate is 25 breaths/min (Normal: 12–16) with an oxygen saturation of 95% (Normal: 97–100) There are a number of new pulmonary infiltrates on chest x-ray. Her current medications include: 1 multiple vitamin QD, 2 microencapsulated pancreatic enzyme capsules (16,000 units lipase/capsule) with meals and 1 or 2 additional tablets with snacks as needed. How does B.W.'s clinical picture compare to the usual presentation of pulmonary infection in CF patients? [SI units: WBC count 17 × 10⁹/L (Normal: 4.5–11) with 0.04 bands (Normal: 0–0.11), 0.35 segs (Normal: 0.36–0.66), 0.5 lymphs (Normal: 0.24–0.44), and 0.11 eosinophils (Normal: 0.01–0.04); BUN 2.5 mmol/L urea (Normal: 1.79–6.43); creatinine 44.2 μmol/L (Normal: 53.04–114.92)]

The progression of pulmonary disease in CF is slow and inexorable. Superimposed on this chronic pulmonary disease are episodes of acute clinical deterioration. B.W. has had multiple infections in the past and now appears to have an acute exacerbation. The causative factors of these acute pulmonary exacerbations are unknown, but viruses, increased bacterial burden, irritants, and allergens have all been implicated.[41–43] The onset of an exacerbation usually is marked by an increase in symptoms that may include an increase in sputum production (usually purulent), increased cough, dyspnea, weight loss, and a decline in pulmonary function tests (15% to 20% decline over baseline is significant). All of these are present in B.W. An increase in WBC count and fever or appearance of a new infiltrate on chest x-ray may or may not be present. The traditional therapy for an acute exacerbation is nutritional repletion, antibiotics, and chest physiotherapy.

B.W. is diagnosed with an exacerbation on the basis of her 23% decrease in FEV_1, a 25% decrease in FVC, dyspnea, increased sputum production with color change, weight loss and chest radiographic changes. B.W. is admitted to the hospital for a "cleanout," consisting of aggressive chest physiotherapy, aggressive nutritional repletion and antipseudomonal antibiotics.

Cleanout

13. As stated in B.W.'s history, _P. aeruginosa_ was found in B.W.'s sputum 4 months ago. It is likely that she is still colonized with the same organisms since they rarely are eradicated in patients with CF despite the use of antipseudomonal antibiotics. Is there any value in giving antibiotics at this time?

In those patients with established _Pseudomonas_ infection, there is a hypothesis that tissue injury is related to bacterial load. With an increase in bacterial burden there is a commensurate increase over time in the immune response. Attempts to reduce the bacterial burden (i.e., by antibiotic administration) may be beneficial in slowing the production of lung disease.[44] A few studies have shown decreases in inflammatory markers after antibiotic administration, lending more credence to this hypothesis.[45,46] The current standard of care is to treat exacerbations with antibiotics.[47]

Antibiotic Therapy

14. Intravenous (IV) Antipseudomonal Selection. What are some considerations when choosing an antibiotic for B.W.?

There is little guidance in the literature to direct the choice of antibiotics because of a lack of demonstrated clinical superiority of one regimen over another. To begin, it is appropriate to exclude antibiotics to which the patient's organisms are resistant and to avoid those drugs that have previously caused an allergic response in the patient. The best initial choice is usually the most narrow spectrum antibiotic possible, while reserving broader spectrum drugs for the future since these patients receive lifelong intermittent antibiotic therapy and commonly develop multiresistant strains of *Pseudomonas* and other organisms. Ideally antibiotic therapy should be based upon the susceptibility of the isolated pathogen, but empiric therapy for the presumptive organism(s) being treated is common. If empiric therapy is initiated, there is a limited spectrum of infecting organisms to consider: *S. aureus*, *H. influenzae* and *P. aeruginosa* are found in an age-related sequence.[48] The use of monotherapy (e.g., ceftazidime against *P. aeruginosa*) has been shown to be clinically beneficial, but is thought to lead to increased bacterial resistance, so combination therapy is recommended.[49,50] Two drug combination therapies can include an aminoglycoside (amikacin, gentamicin, netilmicin, tobramycin) in addition to either a carboxypenicillin (carbenicillin, ticarcillin), a urideopenicillin (azlocillin, mezlocillin, piperacillin), a third-generation cephalosporin (ceftazidime), a monobactam (aztreonam), or a carbapenem (imipenem/cilastatin). Intravenous quinolones (e.g., ciprofloxacin) occasionally are used, but are generally less effective than the other agents. Quinolones are more typically used orally on an outpatient basis since most of the other effective agents are unavailable orally. Their use is discussed more completely in Question 23.

The choice of the antibiotic combination is made on susceptibility data or if known, previous patient response to a particular regimen since *in vitro* susceptibilities do not always correlate to clinical response.[51] In many cases the selection of antibiotics is based upon considerations of their relative advantages and disadvantages as they relate to a specific agent. Of the aminoglycosides, tobramycin has the most *in vitro* activity against clinical isolates of *P. aeruginosa* in CF patients, and should be used initially as empiric therapy until susceptibilities are known.[52] Ticarcillin has good anti-*P. aeruginosa* activity and the addition of clavulanate (Timentin) expands its *S. aureus* and *H. influenzae* coverage, a possible advantage relative to adding a separate third agent for coverage of these organisms. Ceftazidime is a good choice for home antibiotic therapy with every eight hour dosing compared to the every four to six hour dosing of the penicillins. Piperacillin has been associated with a high incidence of allergic reactions in CF patients,[53] where aztreonam has good *in vitro* activity and has been reported to be safe in treating patients who have a history of allergic reactions to beta-lactams.[54] As imipenem is a very broad spectrum agent and its use has been associated with the development of resistance, it is not recommended as first-line therapy.[55] An older drug, colistin (colistimethate sodium) may be used when there is resistance to aminoglycosides and beta-lactams, but it may cause nephrotoxicity and neurotoxicity when used intravenously.[56] While at present there is no consensus on the optimal length of therapy, the usual course should last 14 to 21 days, guided by assessment of the clinical response which should include an im-

provement in pulmonary function tests (if measurable), a decrease in sputum production, a decrease in dyspnea, normalization of white blood cell count (if initially elevated), an improvement in appetite and weight gain, and an overall improvement in sense of well being.

15. Antimicrobial sensitivities for B.W.'s cultured organisms are reported as follows: *P. aeruginosa* Strain 1 is resistant to all antibiotics tested except tobramycin and ceftazidime. Strain 2 was a mucoidal *P. aeruginosa* and is resistant only to gentamicin and mezlocillin. What antibiotic(s) are appropriate for B.W. based upon her microbial sensitivities?

The only antibiotics with activity against both strains of *P. aeruginosa* are tobramycin and ceftazidime. Rather than choosing only one agent, combination therapy is used to prevent the emergence of resistance.

16. Pharmacokinetic Differences in CF Patients. Based upon the above sensitivities and with a weight of 46 kg, B.W. is started on ceftazidime 150 mg/kg/day (1.5 gm: max of 6 gm/day) IV Q 6 hr and tobramycin 2.5 mg/kg (115 mg) Q 6 hr. Compared to treatment of other adult infectious diseases, these are large doses. Why are these doses appropriate for a CF patient?

The pharmacokinetics of many antibiotics are significantly different in CF compared to healthy nonCF individuals.[54–60] (See Table 100.4.) *Absorption*: CF patients manifest gastric hyperacidity and a decreased bicarbonate secretion along with pancreatic insufficiency and a prolonged small intestinal transit time. These changes will affect the solubility, rate, and extent of absorption of some drugs (e.g., ciprofloxacin). *Distribution*: The apparent volume of distribution (Vd) for some drugs (e.g., aminoglycosides, beta-lactams) is increased in CF patients, which may necessitate using higher doses to achieve therapeutic serum concentrations. *Elimination*: Individuals with CF manifest a higher clearance (Cl) of many drugs. This increased clearance is not limited to one particular route of elimination and can affect drugs eliminated by the kidneys without significant metabolism (e.g., aminoglycosides), those eliminated mostly by metabolism (e.g., theophylline), and those with a combination of renal and metabolic elimination (e.g., cloxacillin). Increased glomerular filtration rate, increased tubular secretion, and decreased tubular reabsorption all have been proposed as the mechanism for the increased renal Cl, but the actual mechanism is unknown. Metabolism of drugs takes place in a number of organs in the body, but the majority occurs in the liver. The increases in nonrenal Cl (i.e., hepatic biotransformation) of drugs can be explained in part by: 1) an increase in hepatic blood flow, which has been observed in CF patients, and which would increase metabolism of restrictively cleared drugs (those drugs whose clearance is dependent upon liver blood flow); and 2) the induction of various hepatic enzymes (e.g., cytochrome P450).[58] The result of these differences is that antibiotics need to be given more frequently and in larger doses.

The aminoglycosides, such as tobramycin chosen for B.W., have been shown to have an increased Cl, not completely explained by change in renal elimination alone. The changes of the Vd of aminoglycosides in studies have been variable. CF patients are leaner, so when calculated by weight, the Vd will appear large while if calculated by body surface area, the difference is less apparent. The aminoglycosides need to be administered more frequently due to enhanced elimination in CF. Improved efficacy has been shown with every six hour dosing when compared to every eight hours,[59] but administration more frequently than every six hours may be associated with toxicity.[60] Single daily dosing also has been shown to be effective in a pilot study,[61] suggesting that in addition to pharmacokinetic variables, the postantibiotic effect also apparently plays a role.[62] Increased clearance of beta-lactams, such as the ceftazidime used in B.W., also has been shown in CF. Some prac-

Table 100.4   Recommended Beginning Dosages of Antibiotics for the Treatment of Acute Exacerbations in Cystic Fibrosis[118]

Antibiotic	Dosage mg/kg/dose	Frequency	Daily Dose (mg/kg/day)	Therapeutic Serum Concentration (µg/cc)[a] Peak[b]	Trough
Aminoglycosides					
Amikacin	10	Q 6–8 hr	30	25–30	2–5
Gentamicin	2.5	Q 6–8 hr	7.5–10	8–12	<2
Netilmicin	2.5	Q 6–8 hr	7.5–10	8–12	<2
Tobramycin	2.5	Q 6–8 hr	7.5–10	8–12	<2
Cephalosporins					
Cefoperazone	25–50	Q 6–8 hr	75–200		
Ceftazidime	50	Q 6–8 hr	150–200		
Penicillins					
Carbenicillin	150–200	Q 4–6 hr	600–1200		
Methicillin	50	Q 4–6 hr	200–300		
Nafcillin	50	Q 4–6 hr	200–300		
Piperacillin	75–100	Q 4–6 hr	200–300		
Piperacillin/tazobactam	75–100	Q 4–6 hr	200–300		
Ticarcillin	75–100	Q 4–6 hr	200–300		
Ticarcillin/clavulanate	75–100	Q 4–6 hr	200–300		
Miscellaneous					
Aztreonam	30	Q 6–8 hr	90–120		
Ciprofloxacin	10	Q 8–12 hr	20–30		
Imipenem/cilastatin	10–15	Q 6 hr	40–60		

[a] Dependent upon the sensitivities of the organism.
[b] Extrapolated peak and trough by the Sawchuk-Zaske method.

titioners use probenecid when giving penicillins to decrease this renal clearance. In addition, the Vd of beta-lactams may be increased in CF.

B.W.'s renal function is in the normal range as assessed by admission BUN and creatinine, so initial dosage adjustment for renal function is not necessary. Because of rapid clearance of beta-lactams and aminoglycosides an every six hour interval is chosen. Based upon dosing guidelines (see Table 100.4) ceftazidime 1.5 gm IV every six hours and tobramycin 115 mg IV every six hours are begun.

17. Monitoring Therapy. What are the goals of antibiotic therapy for B.W. and how should she be monitored?

The typical endpoints of therapy in a normal patient with a pulmonary infection are eradication of the causative organism from the sputum and clearing of the chest x-ray. Neither of these conditions are achievable in CF lung disease. An improvement in pulmonary function tests is the most objective and clinically applicable measure.[66] An increase of 10% to 20% is considered a clinically significant response. Other parameters of success are increased appetite and weight gain, decreased cough and sputum production, a decrease in peripheral WBC count, and an overall improvement in subjective findings. When using aminoglycosides, it is important to monitor serum levels because of a narrow therapeutic window and wide pharmacokinetic variation between patients. Tobramycin and gentamicin peaks should be 8 to 10 µg/mL, but some practitioners aim for 10 to 12 µg/mL in nonresponding patients or in those with multiply resistant *Pseudomonas*. Troughs for tobramycin and gentamicin should be less than 2 µg/mL. For toxicity, a daily urine output should be monitored and BUN and creatinine should be obtained at baseline and weekly intervals. Every five to seven day trough serum aminoglycoside levels should be monitored. Amikacin peaks should be in the range of 25 to 30 µg/mL and trough concentrations in the range 2 to 5 µg/mL.

18. Adverse Effects. What adverse effects may be encountered with B.W.'s antibiotic therapy and how should she be monitored?

The ototoxic and nephrotoxic potentials of the aminoglycosides are well known.[67] Ototoxicity can be manifest in two ways: 1) loss of equilibrium and balance due to damage to the vestibular system or 2) hearing loss secondary to damage of cochlear hair cells. These toxicities are usually irreversible. There currently is no way to predict patients at risk of vestibular toxicity and there are no guidelines for audiometric testing in this population. It would be reasonable to perform audiometric testing in those patients who have elevated trough serum aminoglycoside levels, who have been on long-term antibiotic therapy (>21 days), and who are on other potentially ototoxic medications (e.g., furosemide). Yearly screening will identify those patients with hearing loss, but the lack of other effective good antipseudomonal antibiotics narrows the available options. A special population in whom to identify hearing loss is preschool and school age children. This would be important to prevent difficulties in language skills and schoolwork.

Unlike ototoxicity, the nephrotoxicity associated with aminoglycosides is usually reversible. Conditions predisposing patients to a greater risk of nephrotoxicity are: 1) long duration of therapy (>14 days), 2) prior aminoglycoside treatment or concurrent treatment with other nephrotoxic drugs (e.g., amphotericin B), 3) prior renal or hepatic insufficiency, 4) critically ill patients, 5) volume depletion or dehydration, and 6) more frequent administration (e.g., more frequently than Q 6 hr).[68] Since aminoglycosides are eliminated almost entirely by glomerular filtration, any decrease in the glomerular filtration rate (GFR) will result in a decrease in the clearance of the aminoglycoside as evidenced by an elevated or increasing trough serum concentration. Measuring trough levels is the most sensitive indicator of the patients renal function, and trough levels should be obtained at least once every five to seven days. Those patients with the above risk factors should be monitored more frequently. Also a baseline BUN and creatinine should be obtained (creatinine is the more sensitive indicator of renal function) and monitored weekly along with daily urine outputs. Some authors also recommend a weekly urinalysis looking for proteinuria and casts which would be indicative of tubular injury.[69]

The adverse effects most often seen with ceftazidime are an increase in liver function tests (e.g., aspartate aminotransferase and alanine aminotransferase), diarrhea (must rule out *Clostridia difficile*), hypersensitivity reactions, and fungal overgrowth (candidiasis). To monitor for the above side effects, urine output should be monitored daily in B.W. Serum electrolytes should be obtained several times a week along with physical examination for fungal overgrowth and allergic reactions. Weekly tobramycin trough level and serum creatinine concentration measurements are recommended.

Mucoidal Pseudomonas

19. What is a mucoidal *P. aeruginosa* and how does it impact on the progress of the disease and treatment?

The mucoid or slime layer protects *P. aeruginosa* from phagocytosis, decreases antibiotic penetration, and increases its virulence. Nonmucoid strains generally initiate the pseudomonal colonization in CF lungs. Transition to the mucoid strain is thought to be a result of selection pressure by the CF lung environment and antibiotic administration. There is a poor correlation between *in vitro* antibiotic susceptibilities and clinical outcomes of the mucoid variant, so these tests need to be interpreted along with clinical response. This switch to a mucoid variant also correlates to the production of a pronounced antibody response which is not associated with enhanced bacterial killing but rather with a poorer prognosis.[57]

Atypical Infections

Allergic Bronchopulmonary Aspergillosis (ABPA)

Clinical Presentation and Diagnosis

20. After 5 days of inpatient IV therapy B.W. has shown no improvement. A sputum culture taken at admission shows the same 2 strains of *P. aeruginosa* and sensitivities as previously reported results. The only new finding is rare *Aspergillus fumigatus* in the sputum. What additional testing should be completed in B.W. at this time?

The first step in the nonresponding patient is to ensure the appropriate antibiotics are being administered based upon current microbial sensitivities, the administration of correct doses given, and appropriate timing of serum level measurements. There are four problems in this simplified view, however: 1) occasionally *P. aeruginosa*, which grows rapidly, may obscure the growth of more fastidious organisms, such as *H. influenzae*; 2) often there are multiple strains of *P. aeruginosa* present with differing sensitivities; 3) many times the *P. aeruginosa* is multiply resistant; and 4) the *in vitro* sensitivities relate to concentrations achievable in the serum, but the site of this infection is the airway lumen. There are no good guidelines to fully address all of these problem areas. At this author's CF center, there is usually a good history of the patient's previous response to a given combination of antibiotics, and occasionally antibiotic synergy studies are utilized. If there is still no improvement in the patient after three to five days on appropriate antibiotics, an attempt is made to identify atypical infecting organisms. These would include *Mycobacteria* species, viral pathogens (e.g., influenza), *Burkholderia cepacia* (special culture techniques are necessary), *Mycoplasma*, *Legionella*, and fungal species.[70-72] In the case of B.W., *Aspergillus* is present in the sputum. Serum IgE concentrations are seen to increase in allergic *Aspergillus* is, so a measurement of serum IgE is indicated. In ad-

dition acid fast staining, cultures for mycobacteria and viruses as well as *Mycoplasma* and *Legionella* titers should be done.

21. Acid fast stain is negative, and all cultures are pending. *Mycoplasma* and *Legionella* titers are negative. Serum IgE is 3790 IU/mL (Normal: 0-257), and tobramycin levels are a peak of 9 µg/mL and a trough of 1.1 µg/mL. What are these results indicative of in B.W.? [SI units: IgE 9096 µg/L (Normal: 0-616.8); tobramycin peak 18.9 µmol/L; tobramycin trough 2.31 µmol/L]

B.W.'s tobramycin dosing is appropriate based upon the levels obtained. While a number of cultures are pending, the finding of an elevated IgE level is worrisome. This along with B.W.'s eosinophilia leads to a presumptive diagnosis of allergic bronchopulmonary aspergillosis. ABPA is seen almost exclusively in patients with asthma or CF. It is estimated to occur in approximately 5% to 25% of CF patients.[73,74] ABPA is characterized by a local inflammatory reaction to intraluminal antigens from *Aspergillus fumigatus*. However, colonization of the sputum with *Aspergillus* alone does not necessarily mean the patient will develop ABPA. Damage to the bronchial wall and surrounding tissues is thought to occur due to eosinophilic infiltration, but the precise mechanism remains unknown. Laboratory findings for the diagnosis of ABPA include chest x-ray infiltrates and proximal bronchiectasis, but these findings usually are present only in the later stages. Before chest x-ray changes there is an elevation of total serum IgE (>1000 µg/L) along with the expression of an immediate cutaneous reactivity on skin antigen testing, and precipitating antibodies to *Aspergillus*.[75] B.W. manifests new infiltrates on chest x-ray, peripheral eosinophilia, and a markedly elevated serum IgE. At this time a skin test is placed and B.W. reacts to an *Aspergillus* antigen and on immunoglobulin testing she is found to have an IgE specific for *Aspergillus*. B.W. is diagnosed with ABPA.

Treatment

22. How should ABPA be treated in B.W.?

The goal of therapy is to prevent the progression of pulmonary injury and preserve lung function. Oral prednisone, starting with 0.5 to 2 mg/kg as a single daily dose and tapered over a period of months is the drug of choice for treatment.[76] B.W. should be started on a dose of 40 mg. Serum IgE, chest x-rays for resolution of infiltrates, and pulmonary function tests should be followed. Of these, total serum IgE is the most reliable test for monitoring the response to ABPA therapy.[77] A greater than twofold increase in IgE during therapy or after a period of remission, in the absence of other symptoms, would indicate flare-up of the disease.[78] After initiating treatment it may take several months for the IgE to begin to decrease. Serum glucose should be monitored because of the high incidence of glucose intolerance in CF patients taking prednisone. The use of antifungals does not significantly alter the course of the disease and is not currently recommended.[79,80] The reader is referred to other resources for a more in-depth review of therapy.[73,81,82]

Outpatient Therapy

23. B.W. is now attending college and her ABPA has been in remission for 2 years. She calls into the clinic with complaints consistent with a pulmonary exacerbation, but she is in the middle of finals and refuses to consider hospitalization or IV antibiotics. What alternative therapy(s) is available to treat B.W.?

Two alternatives include aerosolized and oral antibiotics. Whether these are used alone or in combination is dependent upon the age of the patient (see Oral Antipseudomonal Antibiotics), severity of flareup, and the patient's wishes.

Antibiotic Aerosolization. The site of the infection in CF is the airway lumen, not the lung parenchyma. The goal is to achieve adequate levels of antibiotics in the sputum without causing toxicity. By aerosol delivery, high concentrations of the antibiotic can be delivered directly to the site of infection.

A variety of antibiotics have been aerosolized, including aminoglycosides, beta-lactams, amphotericin, and colistin. Most of the studies of aerosolized antibiotics have suffered from small sample sizes, as well as lack of placebo controls, and have yielded conflicting results.[83] Despite these limitations, these trials have shown decreased rates of hospitalization,[84] improvement in pulmonary function, and a decreased rate of decline or stabilization of pulmonary function;[85,86] however, in some patients the development of microbial resistance has been noted.[86] Aerosolized antibiotics have been used in combination with IV antibiotics in acute exacerbations. While an increased eradication of *P. aeruginosa* from the sputum has been shown using combined routes of therapy, the response was temporary and there appears to be no clinical advantage of adding aerosolized antibiotics to IV antibiotics.[90] In two studies, aerosolized tobramycin (80 mg BID or TID) either combined with IV carbenicillin or as sole therapy was considered as effective as IV therapy in acute exacerbations.[88,89] A study of aerosolized antibiotics evaluated the safety and efficacy of 600 mg of aerosolized tobramycin three times daily.[90] This study was a multicenter, double-blind trial using a crossover design in 71 stable CF patients. For administration, 600 mg of preservative-free tobramycin was dissolved in 30 mL of half-strength (0.45%) physiologic saline and delivered by an ultrasonic nebulizer. The results of the study showed that the FEV_1 and FVC were significantly increased, sputum density of *P. aeruginosa* was decreased, and there were no indications of toxicity or development of resistance. While the results are positive, because of a daily drug cost of approximately $110 (AWP), how this ''high dose'' aminoglycoside therapy fits into the routine management of patients has yet to be defined. At many centers, aerosolized therapy is reserved for those patients at serious risk for toxicity from intravenous aminoglycosides or those who lack IV access. While definitive well-controlled studies are lacking, there is a body of anecdotal experience and a few small studies showing improvements with aerosolized antibiotics. With the potential clinical benefit high and the risks low, B.W. is begun on aerosolized tobramycin 80 mg three times daily for one week.

Oral Antipseudomonal Antibiotics. Oral therapy can be considered either as an alternative to aerosolized antibiotics or as an adjunct therapy. Presently the quinolone family of antibiotics are the only option for oral coverage of *P. aeruginosa*. Ciprofloxacin is the most widely studied quinolone in CF, but ofloxacin also has been show to be efficacious.[91] Ciprofloxacin has good penetration into bronchi and activity against most strains of *P. aeruginosa*, but there are two concerns with the use of the quinolones. Emergence of resistance of *S. aureus* and *P. aeruginosa* has been observed and there is a potential for toxicity to cartilage in children. Initially, an irreversible cartilage toxicity was reported in the weight bearing joints of animals.[92,93] Fortunately, a growing body of evidence suggests that the quinolones probably are safe to use in children. A study of 634 children failed to demonstrate any arthropathy in the patients, although reversible arthralgias were noted.[94] Ciprofloxacin therapy has been studied for as long as three months without evidence of toxicity.[95] While this issue is not fully resolved, the quinolones are still recommended for use with caution in the pediatric population. In addition, because B.W. is of child bearing age, quinolones are relatively contraindicated because of possible effects on cartilage development in the fetus. If a quinolone is used, B.W. should be counseled to use appropriate birth control techniques.

In regard to the development of resistance, the minimum inhibitory concentrations (MICs) to Cipro have been seen to increase during therapy.[96,97] Treatment should be limited to two to four weeks because of concerns over the development of resistance.[98] Because of these potential problems Cipro is not recommended as first-line therapy in pediatric patients. The current role for oral quinolone therapy is for short-term therapy where IV access is not available or desirable and when the organism has been shown to be sensitive by culture and sensitivity testing. Because of the sensitivities of B.W.'s organisms and her situation, ciprofloxacin 750 mg orally twice daily for one week is begun. At the end of a week of the combined aerosol and oral therapies, she will be re-evaluated for hospital admission if she worsens or continuation of therapy if she shows some improvement.

Therapy

Prednisone Use in CF

24. J.J., an 18-year-old male with CF, returns to the clinic for a routine 6 month visit. He was diagnosed with CF following presentation with meconium ileus at birth. He now has mild pulmonary disease (FEV_1 85% of predicted normal and FVC 90% predicted) and mild chest x-ray changes. He is chronically colonized with a resistant *P. aeruginosa* and has a chronic productive cough, which currently is at baseline. Since the lung damage in CF is from inflammation secondary to the bacterial infection, does prednisone play a role in the treatment of CF patients such as J.J. without ABPA?

The progressive pulmonary damage seen in CF is thought to be related to an immune related inflammatory response.[99] Studies have suggested an association between the severity of pulmonary disease and markers of chronic inflammation.[100,101] Thus, therapy to reduce the magnitude of this inflammatory response should reduce the progression of pulmonary damage. A small initial study of prednisone in CF showed a beneficial response to therapy with no side effects.[102] A larger multicenter study to assess the long term effects of the use of every other day prednisone in CF was terminated secondary to corticosteroid side effects.[103] The study population contained three groups: 2 mg/kg every other day, 1 mg/kg every other day, and placebo. The 2 mg/kg arm had an increased frequency of glucose abnormalities, growth retardation, and cataracts leading to termination of this arm of the study. The 1 mg/kg group did not demonstrate any significant slowing of pulmonary disease. Based upon these findings, there is no role for routine, long-term oral corticosteroid therapy because of the adverse effects associated with systemic corticosteroids. Aerosolized corticosteroids may play a role in the future, but to date the only well-controlled study completed showed no benefit.[104]

Dornase Alpha (DNase)

25. J.J. wants to try DNase (Pulmozyme). What is DNase and what is the method of action?

The principle source of DNA in sputum of CF patients is from the nuclei of degenerating polymorphonuclear neutrophils which accumulate in the lung due to the chronic bacterial infection. This DNA has been shown to contribute significantly to the viscosity of CF sputum. DNase I is an endogenously produced enzyme in humans that is responsible for the breakdown of extracellular DNA. DNase is a recombinant human DNase I (rh DNase) that, when administered by aerosol to the lungs, degrades this intrapulmonary free DNA. By digesting the DNA, CF sputum has been shown *in vitro* to become less viscous.[105] Based upon these actions, dornase alpha should enable the patient to improve airway clearance, reduce obstruction, and reduce the severity of respiratory infections.

Safety and efficacy of dornase alpha has been demonstrated in a number of early trials,[106–108] but efficacy has only been evaluated in stable patients, older than five years of age, with FVCs ≥40% of predicted. The largest study, a Phase III trial contained a total of 968 patients and had three arms (2.5 mg BID, 2.5 mg QD, and placebo).[109] The study was blinded for 24 weeks and open labeled for 24 weeks. DNase reduced the relative risk of developing a respiratory tract infection by 27% and 29% for the 2.5 once daily and the 2.5 twice daily doses, respectively. FEV_1 was increased by 5.8% for once daily and 5.6% for twice daily; similar changes were seen with FVC. Patients on twice daily treatment spent 1.2 fewer hospital days and 2.4 fewer days on parenteral antibiotics when compared to placebo, while once daily treatment resulted in 1.4 fewer hospital days and 2.7 fewer days of parenteral antibiotic therapy. At the current time DNase has been studied only for safety in a small number of patients with FVC less than 40% and in acute exacerbations. These studies confirm its safety. There may be some patients in these groups who will benefit from this therapy. Before initiating dornase alpha therapy, the patient should have some indication of pulmonary inflammation and, if possible, a history of good compliance. The prophylactic use in patients without any evidence of pulmonary disease is not recommended.

Dosing/Monitoring

26. Is DNase indicated for J.J.? How should it be dosed in him and how should he be monitored?

Since J.J. is colonized with *P. aeruginosa*, has a productive cough, and meets the age and FVC indications for use stated above, he is a candidate for treatment. He should be started on the usual recommended starting dose of 2.5 mg aerosolized once daily. He should be instructed that no other drugs may be mixed with DNase, and only the approved nebulizers may be used. Since DNase is an enzyme, the effect of mixing it with other drugs, which may denature it, is unknown. Until further data are available, no drugs should be mixed with it. Only approved nebulizers can be recommended because of the variability of delivery of aerosolized medications from different nebulizers. Baseline pulmonary function tests should be obtained and J.J. should be followed-up at clinic in six weeks for re-evaluation. Evidence of improvement should include: diminished dyspnea and cough, an increase in sputum production, an increased appetite, improved subjective measures (e.g., perception of energy, ability to sleep), and an improvement in pulmonary function tests.

There are subgroups of patients who might benefit from twice daily dosing, but there is no way to prospectively identify them at present. Therefore, patients without obvious response at 2.5 mg once daily may warrant a trial of 2.5 mg twice daily. There are no guidelines for increasing the dose to greater than 2.5 mg twice daily, and it should be noted that clinical trial experience with doses greater than 20 mg/day is lacking. With the current cost of 2.5 mg once daily doses being approximately $10,000 per year, very high doses may be hard to justify. Adverse effects of DNase are mostly related to voice alteration (e.g., hoarseness) and pharyngitis, both of which appear to be dose related. While this product is a recombinant human protein, there is still the potential for severe allergic reactions and anaphylaxis; however, no cases have been reported in the 1500 patients studied so far. A small study reported an increase in serum IgG antibodies in approximately 5% of patients who received intermittent high dose (10 mg BID) therapy, but there was no production of serum IgE or allergic symptoms in these patients. How the addition of DNase will influence patient outcomes when combined with other therapies has yet to be defined.

Investigational Therapies

27. What other approaches may be tried to modify the course of B.W.'s or J.J.'s disease?

Chloride Channel Modifiers. Amiloride, a sodium channel blocker, has been given by nebulization on an investigational basis to inhibit the reabsorption of sodium (and water) into the lung epithelium in an attempt to prevent dehydration of pulmonary secretions. In two small studies, the ability to hydrate the lungs secretions was assessed and showed increased mucociliary and cough clearance and decreased sputum viscosity.[110,111] There was a mild decrease in pulmonary decline and this therapy is currently being evaluated in a large multicenter study. Other chloride channel modifiers are adenosine triphosphate (ATP) and uridine triphosphate (UTP) which both stimulate chloride secretion by increasing intracellular calcium. UTP and ATP, when combined with amiloride, enhance the hydration of pulmonary secretions.[112] Duramycin and isobutylmethylxanthine are two other compounds in early clinical trials that also act as chloride secretagogues.

Anti-Inflammatory Agents. Alpha$_1$-antitrypsin, an inhibitor of neutrophil elastase, and ibuprofen are both under current study with regard to the impact on the inflammatory component of lung disease.[113,114]

Immune Therapy. Early clinical trials have failed to demonstrate improvement in patients given *P. aeruginosa* vaccines,[115] but others are under investigation. Early trials with intravenous gammaglobulin (IVIG) in CF have yielded encouraging results and it is currently undergoing further study.[116]

Gene Therapy. With the discovery of the CF gene, there is the hope of someday being able to correct the defect at the genetic level. There are currently early phase I trials involving gene therapy ongoing which give the hope for an ultimate cure for CF. While none of these therapies are currently available for B.W. or J.J., they offer hope to both caregivers and patients that more definitive therapies will soon be available.

References

1 **Andersen DH.** Cystic fibrosis of the pancreas and its relation to celiac disease, a clinical and pathological study. Am J Dis Child. 1938;56:344.

2 **Wood RE et al.** Cystic fibrosis. Am Rev Resp Dis. 1976;113:841.

3 **Knowlton RB et al.** A polymorphic DNA marker linked to cystic fibrosis is located on chromosome 7. Nature. 1985;318:380.

4 **White R et al.** A closely linked genetic marker for cystic fibrosis. Nature. 1985;318:382.

5 **Wainwright BJ et al.** Localization of the cystic fibrosis locus to human chromosome 7 cen-q22. Nature. 1985; 318:384.

6 **Tsui LC et al.** Cystic fibrosis locus defined by a genetically linked polymorphic DNA marker. Science. 1985;230:1054.

7 **Rommens JM et al.** Identification of the cystic fibrosis gene: chromosome walking and jumping. Science. 1989; 245:1059.

8 **Riordan JR et al.** Identification of the cystic fibrosis gene: cloning and characterization of the complementary DNA. Science. 1989;245:1066.

9 **Kerem B et al.** Identification of the cystic fibrosis gene: genetic analysis. Science. 1989;245:1073.

10 **Collins FS.** The CF gene: perceptions, puzzles and promises. Pediatr Pulmonol. 1992;(Suppl. 8):63.

11 **Worldwide survey of the delta F508 mutation: report from the cystic fibrosis genetic analysis consortium.** Am J Hum Genet. 1990;47:354.

12 **The Cystic Fibrosis Genotype-Phenotype Consortium.** Correlation between genotype and phenotype in patients with cystic fibrosis. N Engl J Med. 1993;329:1308.

13 **Neijens HJ et al.** Influence of respiratory exacerbations on lung function variables and nutritional status in CF patients. Acta Pediatr Scand. 1984; (Suppl. 317):38.

14 **Umetsu DT et al.** Sinus disease in patients with severe cystic fibrosis: relation to pulmonary exacerbation. Lancet. 1990;335:1077.

15 **Kopelman H.** Gastrointestinal and nutritional aspects. Thorax. 1991;46:261.

16 **Geddes DM.** Cystic fibrosis and pregnancy. J Royal Soc Med. 1992;85 (Suppl. 19):36.

17 **Hammond KB et al.** Efficacy of statewide neonatal screening for cystic fibrosis by assay of trypsinogen concentrations. N Engl J Med. 1991;325(11):769.

18 **Committee on Genetics.** Newborn screening fact sheets. American Academy of Pediatrics. 1989;449.

19 **Cystic Fibrosis Foundation.** Patient Registry 1992 Annual Data Report. Bethesda, MD: 1993 Oct.

20 **Gibson LF, Cooke RE.** A test for concentration of electrolytes in sweat in cystic fibrosis of the pancreas utilizing pilocarpine iontophoresis. Pediatrics. 1959;23:545.

21 **Ramsey BW et al.** Predictive value of oropharyngeal cultures for identifying lower airway bacteria in cystic fibrosis patients. Am Rev Resp Dis. 1991;114:331.

22 **The Cystic Fibrosis Foundation Center Committee and Guidelines Subcommittee.** Cystic fibrosis foundation guidelines for patient services, evaluation and monitoring in cystic fibrosis centers. Am J Dis Child. 1990;144:1311.

23 **National Research Council, Recommended Dietary Allowances.** National Academy Press, Washington, DC: 1989.

24 **Abman SH et al.** Early Pseudomonas aeruginosa (PA) colonization in young infants with cystic fibrosis (CF) identified by newborn screening. Pediatr Res. 1987;21:491.

25 **Loening-Baucke VA et al.** A placebo controlled trial of cephalexin therapy in the ambulatory management of patients with cystic fibrosis. J Pediatr. 1979;95:630.

26 **Mearns MB et al.** Bacterial flora of the respiratory tract in patients with cystic fibrosis. Arch Dis Child. 1972;47:902.

27 **Pedersen S et al.** Management of Pseudomonas aeruginosa lung infection in Danish cystic fibrosis patients. Acta Pediatr Scand. 1987;76:955.

28 **Valerius N et al.** Prevention of chronic Pseudomonas aeruginosa colonization in cystic fibrosis by early treatment. Lancet. 1991;338:725.

29 **Stutman HR et al.** Cephalexin prophylaxis in newly diagnosed infants with cystic fibrosis. Pediatr Pulmonol. 1992;(Suppl. 12):147.

30 **Lorin MI, Denning CR.** Evaluation of postural drainage by measurement of sputum volume and consistency. Am J Phys Med Rehabil. 1971;50:215.

31 **Reisman JJ et al.** Role of conventional physiotherapy in cystic fibrosis. J Pediatr. 1988;113:632.

32 **Congden PJ et al.** Vitamin status in treated patients with cystic fibrosis. Arch Dis Child. 1981;81:708.

33 **Ramsey BW et al.** Nutritional assessment and management in cystic fibrosis: a consensus report. Am J Clin Nutr. 1992;55:108.

34 **George DE, Mangos JA.** Nutritional management and pancreatic enzyme therapy in cystic fibrosis patients: state of the art in 1987 and projections into the future. J Pediatr Gastroenterol Nutr. 1988;7(Suppl. 1):S49.

35 **Mischler EH et al.** Comparison of effectiveness of pancreatic enzyme preparations in cystic fibrosis. Am J Dis Child. 1982;136:1060.

36 **Bouquet J et al.** Malabsorption in cystic fibrosis: mechanisms and treatment. J Pediatr Gastroenterol Nutr. 1988;7 (Suppl. 1):30.

37 **Beker LT et al.** Comparison of weight based dosages of enteric coated microtablet enzyme preparations in patients with cystic fibrosis. J Pediatr Gastroenterol Nutr. 1994;19:191.

38 **Smyth RL et al.** Strictures of ascending colon in cystic fibrosis and high-strength pancreatic enzymes. Lancet. 1994;343:85.

39 **Heijerman HG et al.** Ranitidine compared with dimethylprostaglandin E2 analogue enprostil as adjunct to pancreatic enzyme replacement in adult cystic fibrosis. Scand J Gastroenterol. 1990;178(Suppl.):26.

40 **Heijerman HG et al.** Omeprazole enhances the efficacy of pancreatin (Pancrease) in cystic fibrosis. Ann Intern Med. 1991;114:200.

41 **Hoiby N.** Microbiology of lung infections in cystic fibrosis patients. Acta Pediatr Scand. 1982;301(Suppl.):33.

42 **Hordvik NL et al.** Effects of acute viral respiratory infections in patients with cystic fibrosis. Pediatr Pulmonol. 1989;7:217.

43 **Wood RE, Leigh MW.** What is a pulmonary exacerbation in cystic fibrosis? J Pediatr. 1987;841.

44 **Warren RE et al.** Reduction of sputum Pseudomonas aeruginosa density by antibiotics improves lung function in cystic fibrosis more than do bronchodilators and chest physiotherapy alone. Am Rev Resp Dis. 1990;141:914.

45 **Meyer KC et al.** Human neutrophil elastase and elastase/alpha1-antiprotease complex in cystic fibrosis: comparison with interstitial lung disease and evaluation of the effect of intravenously administered antibiotic therapy. Am Rev Resp Dis. 1991;144(3):580.

46 **Elborn JS et al.** In vitro tumour necrosis factor—alpha secretion by monocytes from patients with cystic fibrosis. Am Rev Resp Dis. 1991;6:207.

47 **Kerrebijn K et al.** Pulmonary infection and antibiotic treatment in cystic fibrosis. Chest. 1988;92(Suppl.):S97.

48 **Gilligan PH.** Microbiology of airway disease in patients with cystic fibrosis. Clin Microbiol Rev. 1991;4:35.

49 **Watkins J et al.** Does monotherapy of pulmonary infections in cystic fibrosis lead to early development of resistant strains of Pseudomonas aeruginosa? Scand J Gastroenterol. 1988;23(Suppl. 143):81.

50 **Bosso JA et al.** Changing susceptibility of Pseudomonas aeruginosa isolates from cystic fibrosis patients with the clinical use of newer antibiotics. Antimicrob Agents Chemother. 1989;33:526.

51 **Smith A.** Antibiotic resistance is not relevant in infections in cystic fibrosis. Pediatr Pulmonol. 1990;5(Suppl. 5):93.

52 **Kuhn RJ, Nahata MC.** Therapeutic management of cystic fibrosis. Clin Pharm. 1985;4:555.

53 **Steas RJ et al.** Adverse reactions to piperacillin in cystic fibrosis. Lancet. 1984;i:857.

54 **Jensen T et al.** Aztreonam for cystic fibrosis patients who are hypersensitive to other beta-lactams. Lancet. 1987;i:1319.

55 **Pedersen SS et al.** Combined imipenem/cilastatin and tobramycin therapy of multiresistant Pseudomonas aeruginosa in cystic fibrosis. J Antimicrob Chemother. 1987;19:101.

56 **Bosso JA et al.** Toxicity of colistin in cystic fibrosis patients. DICP. 1991;25:1168.

57 **Pressler T et al.** IgG subclass antibody responses to alginate from Pseudomonas aeruginosa in patients with cystic fibrosis and chronic P. aeruginosa infection. Pediatr Pulmonol. 1992;14:44.

58 **Kearns GL.** Hepatic drug metabolism in cystic fibrosis: recent developments and future directions. DICP. 1993;27:74.

59 **Winnie GB et al.** Comparison of 6 and 8 hourly tobramycin dosing intervals in treatment of pulmonary exacerbations in cystic fibrosis patients. Ped Infect Dis J. 1991;10:381.

60 **Hendeles L et al.** Individualizing gentamicin dosage in patients with cystic fibrosis: limitations to the pharmacokinetic approach. J Pediatr. 1987;110:303.

61 **Powell SH et al.** Once daily vs. continuous aminoglycoside dosing: efficacy and toxicity in animal and clinical studies of gentamicin, netilmicin and tobramycin. J Infect Dis. 1983;147:918.

62 **Morris G, Brown MRW.** Novel modes of action of aminoglycoside antibiotics against Pseudomonas aeruginosa. Lancet. 1988;i:1359.

63 **Spino M.** Pharmacokinetics of drugs in cystic fibrosis. Clin Rev Aller. 1991;9:169.

64 **Leitman PS.** Pharmacokinetics of antimicrobial drugs in cystic fibrosis: beta-lactam antibiotics. Chest. 1988;94 (Suppl.):115S.

65 **Horrevorts AM et al.** Pharmacokinetics of antimicrobial drugs in cystic fibrosis: aminoglycoside antibiotics. Chest. 1988;94(Suppl.):120S.

66 **Redding GJ et al.** Serial changes in pulmonary functions in children hospitalized with cystic fibrosis. Am Rev Respir Dis. 1982;126:31.

67 **Pedersen SS et al.** Cumulative and acute toxicity of repeated high-dose tobramycin treatment in cystic fibrosis. Antimicrob Agents Chemother. 1987;31:594.

68 **Appel GB.** Aminoglycoside nephrotoxicity. Am J Med. 1990;88(Suppl. 3C):16S.

69 **Lindsay CA et al.** Optimization of antibiotic therapy in cystic fibrosis patients. Clin Pharmacokinet. 1993;24:496.

70 **Smith MJ et al.** Mycobacterial isolations in young adults with cystic fibrosis. Thorax. 1984;39:369.

71 **Nikolaizik WH et al.** Aspergillus allergy and allergic bronchopulmonary aspergillosis in cystic fibrosis. Pediatr Allergy Immunol. 1991;2:83.

72 **Gladman G et al.** Controlled study of pseudomonas cepacia and pseudomonas maltophilia in cystic fibrosis. Arch Dis Child. 1992;67:192.

73 **Simmonds EJ et al.** Cystic fibrosis and allergic bronchopulmonary aspergillosis. Arch Dis Child. 1990;65:507.

74 **Hiller EJ.** Pathogenesis and management of aspergillosis in cystic fibrosis. Arch Dis Child. 1990;65:397.

75 **Rosenberg MAT et al.** Clinical and immunologic criteria for the diagnosis of allergic bronchopulmonary aspergillosis. Ann Intern Med. 1977;86:404.

76 **Greenberger PA, Patterson R.** Diagnosis and management of allergic bronchopulmonary aspergillosis. Ann Allergy. 1986;56:444.

77 **Patterson R et al.** Allergic bronchopulmonary aspergillosis: natural history and classification of early disease by serologic and roentgenographic studies. Arch Intern Med. 1986;146:916.

78 **Patterson R et al.** Allergic bronchopulmonary aspergillosis: staging as an aid to management. Ann Intern Med. 1982;96:296.

79 **Greenberger PA.** Allergic bronchopulmonary aspergillosis and funguses. Clin Chest Med. 1988;9:599.

80 **Ricketti AJ et al.** Allergic bronchopulmonary aspergillosis. Chest. 1984;86:773.

81 **Wang JLF et al.** Management of allergic bronchopulmonary aspergillosis. Am Rev Resp Dis. 1979;20:87.

82 **Vaughan LM.** Therapy review: allergic bronchopulmonary aspergillosis. Clin Pharm. 1993;12:24.

83 **Abramowsky CR, Swinehart GL.** Inhaled antibiotics in cystic fibrosis: is there a therapeutic effect? J Pediatr. 1986;108:861.

84 **Wall MA et al.** Inhaled antibiotics in cystic fibrosis. Lancet. 1983;1:1325.

85 **Carswell F et al.** A controlled trial of nebulized aminoglycoside and oral flucloxacillin verses placebo in the outpatient management of children with cystic fibrosis. Br J Dis Chest. 1987;81:356.

86 **MacLusky IB et al.** Long-term effects of inhaled tobramycin in patients with cystic fibrosis colonized with Pseudomonas aeruginosa. Pediatr Pulmonol. 1989;7:42.

87 **Stephens D et al.** Efficacy of inhaled tobramycin in the treatment of pulmonary exacerbations in children with cystic fibrosis. Pediatr Infect Dis. 1983;2:209.

88 **Cooper DM et al.** Comparison of intravenous and inhalation antibiotic therapy in acute pulmonary deterioration in cystic fibrosis. Am Rev Respir Dis. 1985;131:242.

89 **Semsarian C.** Efficacy of inhaled tobramycin in cystic fibrosis. J Paediatr Child Health. 1990;26:110.

90 **Ramsey BW et al.** Efficacy of aerosolized tobramycin in patients with cystic fibrosis. N Engl J Med. 1993;328:1740.

91 **Jensen T et al.** The efficacy and safety of ciprofloxacin and ofloxacin in chronic Pseudomonas aeruginosa infection in cystic fibrosis. J Antimicrob Chemother. 1987;205:585.

92 **Christ W et al.** Specific toxicologic aspects of the quinolones. Rev Infect Dis. 1988;10(Suppl. 1):141.

93 **Schluter G.** Ciprofloxacin: toxicologic evaluation of additional safety data. Am J Med. 1989;87(Suppl. 5A):37.

94 **Chysky V et al.** Safety of ciprofloxacin

in children: worldwide clinical experience based on compassionate use. Emphasis on joint evaluation. Infection. 1991;19:289.

95 **Schaad UB et al.** Clinical, radiologic and magnetic resonance monitoring for skeletal toxicity in pediatric patients with cystic fibrosis receiving a three month course of ciprofloxacin. Ped Infect Dis J. 1991;10:723.

96 **Bosso JA.** Use of ciprofloxacin in cystic fibrosis patients. Am J Med. 1989; 587(Suppl. 5A):123.

97 **Sorgel F et al.** High dose treatment with antibiotics in cystic fibrosis: a reappraisal with special reference to the pharmacokinetics of beta-lactams and new fluoroquinolones in adult CF patients. Infection. 1987;15:385.

98 **LeBel M.** Fluoroquinolones in the treatment of cystic fibrosis: a critical appraisal. Eur J Clin Microbiol Infect Dis. 1990;10:316.

99 **Doring G et al.** Immunologic aspects of cystic fibrosis. Chest. 1988;94 (Suppl.):109S.

100 **Wheeler WB et al.** Progression of cystic fibrosis lung disease as a function of serum immunoglobulin G levels: a 5-year longitudinal study. J Pediatr. 1984;104:695.

101 **Disis ML et al.** Circulating immune complexes in cystic fibrosis and their correlation to clinical parameters. Pediatr Res. 1986;20:385.

102 **Aurbach HS et al.** Alternate-day prednisone reduces morbidity and improves pulmonary function in cystic fibrosis. Lancet. 1985;2:686.

103 **Rosenstein BJ, Eigen H.** Risks of alternate day prednisone in patients with cystic fibrosis. Pediatrics. 1991;87:245.

104 **Schiotz PO et al.** Chronic Pseudomonas aeruginosa lung infection in cystic fibrosis. Acta Pediatr Scand. 1983;72:283.

105 **Shak S et al.** Recombinant human DNase I reduces the viscosity of cystic fibrosis sputum. Proc Natl Acad Sci. 1990;87:9188.

106 **Aitken ML et al.** Effect of inhaled recombinant human DNase on pulmonary function in normal and cystic fibrosis patients. JAMA. 1992;267:812.

107 **Hubbard RC et al.** A preliminary study of aerosolized recombinant human deoxyribose I in the sputum of cystic fibrosis. N Engl J Med. 1992; 326:812.

108 **Ramsey BW et al.** Efficacy and safety of short-term administration of aerosolized recombinant human deoxyribonuclease in patients with cystic fibrosis. Am Rev Respir Dis. 1993;148:145.

109 **Ramsey BW et al.** A summary of the results of the phase III multicenter clinical trial: aerosol administration of recombinant human DNase reduces the risk of respiratory tract infections and improves pulmonary function in patients with cystic fibrosis. Pediatr Pulmonol. 1993;(Suppl. 9):152. Abstract.

110 **Knowles MR et al.** A pilot study of aerosolized amiloride for the treatment of lung disease in cystic fibrosis. N Engl J Med. 1990;322:1189.

111 **App EM et al.** Acute and long-term amiloride inhalation in cystic fibrosis lung disease. Am Rev Respir Dis. 1990;141:605.

112 **Boucher RC et al.** Chloride secretory response of cystic fibrosis airway epithelia: presentation of calcium but not protein kinase C and A-dependent mechanism. J Clin Invest. 1989;84:1424.

113 **Konstan MW et al.** Ibuprofen in children with cystic fibrosis: pharmacokinetics and adverse effects. J Pediatr. 1991;118:956.

114 **McElvaney NG et al.** Aerosol alpha$_1$-antitrypsin treatment for cystic fibrosis. Lancet. 1991;337:392.

115 **Wood RE et al.** Intranasal administration of a Pseudomonas lipopolysaccharide vaccine in cystic fibrosis patients. Pediatr Infect Dis. 1983;2:367.

116 **Winnie GB et al.** Intravenous immune globulin treatment of pulmonary exacerbations in cystic fibrosis. Pediatr Pharmacol Therapeu. 1989;2:309.

117 **MacLusky I.** Spectrum of clinical manifestations of cystic fibrosis. Ped Annals. 1993;22:544.

118 **Kelly HW.** Recommended beginning dosages of antibiotics for the treatment of acute exacerbations in CF. Drug Intell Clin Pharm. 1984;18:722.

Geriatric Drug Use and Rehabilitation

Martin J Jinks
Robin H Fuerst

Geriatric Drug Use 101-1
  Overview 101-1
    Demographic considerations (See Table 101.1) 101-1
    Rate and cost of drug use in older adults
    (See Table 101.2) 101-2
    Age-related physiologic, pharmacokinetic, and
    pharmacodynamic changes (See Table 101.3) 101-2
      Absorption 101-2
      Distribution 101-3
      Altered protein binding 101-3
      Metabolism 101-3
      Reduction in hepatic reserve 101-3
      Excretion (See Tables 101.4 and 101.5) 101-4
      Pharmacodynamic changes (See Table 101.6) 101-4
        Homeostasis and postural hypotension 101-4
        Receptor sensitivity (See Table 101.7) 101-4
  Drug Use Problems in Older Adults 101-5
    Polytherapy 101-5
    Omnibus Budget Reconciliation Act (OBRA)
    (See Table 101.8) 101-6
    Specific examples 101-6
      Digoxin 101-6
      Antihypertensives 101-6
      Antiarthritics 101-6
      Psychotherapeutic agents 101-7
    Causes of polydrug therapy 101-7
  The Ambulatory Older Patient 101-7
    Medication management of the ambulatory
    older patient 101-7

Difficulties in obtaining a complete
  drug history 101-8
    Nonprescription drug use 101-8
    Conversion of legend drugs to
    nonprescription status 101-8
    Social drug use 101-8
    Hoarding, borrowing, and home remedies 101-8
  Compliance problems and medication errors
  (See Table 101.10) 101-8
    Types of noncompliance 101-8
    Barriers to compliance 101-9
    Compliance enhancement strategies
    (See Table 101.9) 101-9
    High-risk older adults (See Table 101.10) 101-10
  Adverse drug reactions and drug interactions 101-10
    Adverse drug reactions in older patients 101-10
    Strategies for healthy prescribing in older
    patients (See Table 101.11) 101-11
Geriatric Rehabilitation 101-11
  Role of Rehabilitative Medicine in Geriatrics 101-11
    Rehabilitation goals 101-11
    Functional assessment 101-11
    Team approach 101-11
    Assessment of drug therapy (See Table 101.12) . 101-11
  Effects of Drugs on Functional Ability 101-12
    Metoclopramide 101-12
    Ranitidine, cimetidine, and famotidine 101-13
    Digoxin 101-13
    Drug effects on other assessments
    (See Table 101.13) 101-13

Geriatric Drug Use

Demographic Considerations

The U.S. is a rapidly maturing society, a trend creating an unmistakable demographic imperative regarding the practitioner's knowledge of drug therapy in the older patient. Based upon 1990 census data, the American Association of Retired Persons and the U.S. Department of Health and Human Services (USDHHS) Administration on Aging have produced a profile of older Americans in the U.S. (see Table 101.1).[1]

In terms of impact on the health care system, the oldest-old category, (i.e., those >85 years of age) is the most important age group. The number of elderly in this group has increased faster than any other age category, over 200% during the last 25 years and more than double the rate of the next fastest-growing category. By 2050, at least one-half of Americans will survive to their 85th birthday and will comprise 15 million (5%) of the total U.S. population.[2–4] The oldest-old group incurs intractable problems of ill health, dependency, and loss, and demands the highest level of health services. They have the highest hospitalization rate, more than 50% higher than the general population.[5] Their use of physician services and hospital days is 30% and 380% greater, respectively. By the year 2000, the proportion of hospital days accounted for by the older patients will increase to 58%, up from the present 38%.[5,6] Five percent of the ≥65 population and 23% of the ≥85 population reside in long-term care facilities (LTCF). Ironically, LTCFs are staffed by only 10% of the total registered nurses (who primarily hold administrative positions), despite the existence of 1.5 million LTCF beds compared to 1 million acute care hospital beds.[5] With increasing numbers of the oldest-old, the LTCF patient population is projected to triple by 2030.[5,7]

Of older adults who live at home, about 10% in the 65- to 74-year-old age group and about 35% in the over 85-year-old age group require the help of a caregiver.[8] Children and other relatives of aging persons provide about 80% of all care, and these "informal caregivers" provide three times as much direct care for the aged as do all nursing homes, hospitals, and other institutions combined.[9] When serving a geriatric client who relies on a caregiver, it is important to include the caregiver in the counseling and monitoring activities when feasible.

In the future, health care reform is likely to result in an increase in managed health care or replacement with a single-payer system and an anticipated reduction in high-cost inpatient care. As the delivery of health care evolves, more emphasis will be placed on lower-cost alternative care, such as home health care, assisted living, and hospice care. In this climate, the challenges and opportunities for experts in geriatric pharmacotherapy will increase dramatically.[10]

Table 101.1	Profile of Older Americans[1]

Current Status of the Older Population
- The older population, persons ≥65 years of age, numbered 31.2 million in 1990, representing 12.6% of the U.S. population, or about 1 in 8 Americans. The number of older Americans has ↑ by 5.7 million or 22% since 1980, compared to an ↑ of 8% for the <65 population
- Since 1900, the percentage of Americans aged ≥65 tripled (4.1% in 1900 to 12.6% in 1990), and the number has ↑ 10-fold (from 3.1 million to 31.2 million in 1990)
- The older population is getting older. In 1990 the 65–74 age group (18.1 million) was 8 times larger than in 1900, but the 75–84 age group (10.1 million) was 13 times larger and the ≥85 age group (3.1 million) was 24 times larger
- In 1989 persons reaching age 65 had an average life expectancy of an additional 17.2 years (18.8 years for females and 15.2 years for males)
- About 2.2 million persons celebrated their 65th birthday in 1990 (6000/day). In the same year, ≈1.6 million persons aged ≥65 died, resulting in a net ↑ of 645,000 (1770/day)

Future Growth of the Older Population
- Although the rate of growth will slow during the 1990s due to the relatively small number of births during the Great Depression of the 1930s, the most rapid ↑ is expected between the years 2010 and 2030 when the "baby boom" generation reaches age 65
- By 2030, there will be about 66 million older persons, 2.5 times their number in 1980. If current fertility and immigration levels remain stable, the only age groups to grow significantly will be those >55 years of age
- By the year 2000, persons aged ≥65 are expected to represent 13% of the population; this will ↑ to 21.8% by 2030

Rate and Cost of Drug Use in Older Adults

Older adults have a higher rate of drug use compared to the general population. Those over 60 years of age comprise 17% of the population but consume nearly 40% of all prescription drugs, and the over 65 population (12%) consumes 32% of all prescription drugs.[11,12] Overall, older adults receive an average of 17 to 20 drugs annually.[13] Older nursing home patients receive an average of six to eight drugs daily, one-third receive 9 to 14 drugs daily, and 60% receive ≥four drugs daily compared to 35% of home-dwelling older persons.[13–17]

Prescription drug costs are a significant out-of-pocket expense for older adults. Prescription drug prices increased 88% from 1981 to 1988, during which time the Consumer Price Index increased only 28%, and over 15% of older patients who use prescription drugs report they are unable to pay for them.[18] Out-of-pocket expenses for the older patients for all health services dramatically increased from 12.3% of income in 1977 to 18.2% in 1988.[19] The high cost of medications has been associated with noncompliance in older patients.[20] Drug costs are the one discretionary part of health care costs over which older adults can exert control, and when forced into the untenable situation of choosing between expensive medications and other essentials, such as food or rent, the older patient often must choose the latter. Until prescription medication is covered by health care reform, discretionary noncompliance will continue to be a significant problem in geriatric pharmacotherapy.

A profile of drug use in the older population, presented at the Ninth National Conference on Prescription Medication Information and Education held in Washington, DC, May 1993, is provided in Table 101.2.[21]

Age-Related Physiologic, Pharmacokinetic, and Pharmacodynamic Changes

An important determinant of drug use problems in the aged is an increased physiological vulnerability to medication and im-paired ability to recover from drug-induced insults. Homeostatic mechanisms in the cardiovascular and nervous systems are less efficient; drug metabolism and excretion slow; body tissue composition and drug volume of distribution change; and drug receptor sensitivity may be altered. Age-related changes are progressive, occurring gradually over a lifetime, rather than abruptly at any given age (e.g., 65 years of age). The physiological processes of aging frequently result in an increased susceptibility to many diseases. However, older patients remain a heterogeneous group, with chronological age not always reflective of "functional age." Distinct separation of these interrelated factors is difficult, because all may contribute to variability in drug response. In particular, pharmacodynamic changes in the aging population is a research topic fraught with many methodological and logistical constraints, as is evidenced by the scarcity of information on aging and pharmacological effects (see Table 101.3).

Absorption. Changes in the gastrointestinal (GI) tract during aging may influence drug absorption. Gastric pH increases, intestinal blood flow diminishes, and some impairment of both active and passive transport mechanisms occurs.[22] However, the significance of these changes is not clear. Assessment of age-related changes in absorption necessitates careful attention to methodology. For example, samples must be collected for four to six half-lives in older subjects to obtain a complete area under the time-concentration curve (AUC). Also, intravenous (IV) and oral (PO) data must be compared in the same subject in order to validate the assumption that clearance is constant.

$$AUC = \frac{(S)(F)(Dose)}{Cl}$$

Eq 101.1

where (S)(F) is the fraction of dose administered that will reach systemic circulation, and Cl is clearance.

The following generalizations can be concluded: the completeness of absorption is similar in older patients and young adults; the rate of absorption is reduced or unaltered in older patients; and drugs that undergo first-pass metabolism are absorbed more completely in the older patient.

1. I.W., a 75-year-old female, 5'4", 120 pounds, serum creatinine (SrCr) 1.9 mg/dL, has an acute exacerbation of congestive heart failure (CHF). She is given furosemide 40 mg PO with minimal urine output or resolution of her symptoms. What might be an explanation for I.W.'s lack of response to furosemide? How might the desired response to furosemide be accomplished?

The extent of furosemide (Lasix) absorption is not changed in older patients, but the rate of absorption is slowed. This results in a diminished effect because active secretion into the urine or the rate of entry into the urine must reach the steep portion of the

Table 101.2	Facts About Drug Use in the Older Population[21]

≈90% of Americans (35.5 million) >60 years of age are taking ≥1 prescription drugs

The average older outpatient uses 2–4 different prescription drugs at the same time

Among people aged 65–84 who live in the community, 61% receive ≥3 different drugs in a year, 37% receive ≥5, and 19% receive ≥7

Each year, >9 million adverse drug reactions occur in older Americans

Unwanted side effects of drugs are 7 times more common in older patients than in younger adults

Nearly ¼ of all nursing home admissions result from the inability of older adults to take their medications properly

Table 101.3	Factors Which May Influence Functional Age
Poor versus good or adequate nutrition	
Smoking versus quit smoking versus never a smoker	
Acute or chronic diseases versus good health	
Acute or chronic drug therapy versus no drug use	
"Couch potato" versus lifelong habit of exercise	
Institutionalized versus living independently at home	

sigmoid dose/response curve for effect.[23] I.W. should be given a 40 mg dose of furosemide intravenously to bypass the problem of decreased rate of absorption and presentation to the renal tubules. High sodium intake or concurrent use of nonsteroidal anti-inflammatory drugs (NSAID) also can decrease the effectiveness of furosemide. Further increases in dosing of furosemide may be necessary, with consideration of a continuous infusion in patients with severe chronic renal insufficiency.[24]

Distribution. A number of changes may occur with aging which can affect the distribution of drugs in the body. Cardiac output decreases about 1% per year from ages 19 to 86.[25] In many older patients, this decline in cardiac output is accompanied by an increase in peripheral vascular resistance and a proportional decrease in hepatic and renal blood flow. However, noninstitutionalized older adults who are free of coronary artery disease or other debilitating health problems exhibit little age-related decline in cardiac output.[26] Body composition is altered during normal aging. Total body water and lean body mass both decline with age, and total fat content increases between ages 18 and 35 years from 18% to 36% in males and from 33% to 48% in females.[27,28] Thus, the volume of distribution (Vd) of drugs that are distributed primarily in body water or lean body mass (e.g., lithium or digoxin) is decreased in older adults; unadjusted dosing can result in higher blood levels. Conversely, the Vd of highly lipid-soluble drugs, such as long-acting benzodiazepines (e.g., diazepam), may be increased, thereby delaying maximal effects or resulting in accumulation with continued use.[29] Factors which may affect binding with special applicability in older patients include protein concentration, disease states, coadministration of other drugs, and nutritional status. Serum albumin concentrations also fall progressively for each decade beyond 40 years of age, reaching a mean of 3.58 gm/dL (normal: 4 gm/dL) in those older than 80 years of age.[30] Decreases in albumin are important because albumin is a major site of drug binding. Increases in α_1-acid glycoprotein in older patients affect the binding of weak bases such as lidocaine and propranolol. Data are lacking concerning age-related changes in tissue protein binding of drugs. However, the Vd of digoxin does decrease in subjects with impaired renal function, as does the myocardial:serum concentration ratio.[31] Finally, an important factor in determining the significance of changes in protein binding status is whether a drug is restrictively or nonrestrictively cleared (also see reference 32).

2. Altered Protein Binding. O.T., a 90-year-old female, 5′8″, 132 pounds, is brought to the emergency room (ER) for evaluation of a "shaking spell." In the ER, another "spell" is observed, starting with shaking of the left arm and proceeding into a generalized tonic-clonic seizure. Phenytoin (Dilantin) 1000 mg is given IV over 30 minutes. O.T. is admitted to the neurology unit for further evaluation, where phenytoin 300 mg Q HS is prescribed. What is your assessment of O.T.'s phenytoin therapy given her age? What laboratory tests should be monitored and when should these tests be ordered?

O.T. received an average phenytoin loading dose of 17 mg/kg (normal: 15 to 20 mg/kg) and is receiving the average daily dose.

A sodium serum concentration should be obtained to rule out hyponatremia-induced seizures, and an albumin serum concentration should be evaluated because of phenytoin's high level (90%) of protein binding. A phenytoin serum concentration should be measured before discharge from the hospital to document that the desired therapeutic serum concentration has been achieved. The serum phenytoin concentration also should be monitored if an adverse drug reaction or seizure occurs. A follow-up steady-state phenytoin serum concentration also should be obtained in 10 to 14 days.

3. The serum albumin concentration was determined to be 2.2 gm/dL (Normal: 3.2–5.2) and O.T. exhibits drowsiness and a wide-based, unsteady gait upon ambulation. Her phenytoin serum concentration is 15 mg/L (Normal: 10–20). What is the likely cause of her symptoms? [SI units: albumin 22 gm/L (Normal: 32–52); phenytoin 59.5 μmol/L (Normal: 40–80)]

O.T. could have a phenytoin free-fraction percentage of up to 18%, compared to the normal value of 10% because of her low albumin serum concentration.[32] This would produce a free-phenytoin concentration of 2.7 μg/mL (normal: 1 to 2 μg/mL) and explain O.T.'s symptoms. In O.T.'s case, free phenytoin concentration monitoring would be appropriate, if available, and her dose adjusted accordingly.

Metabolism. O.T.'s phenytoin metabolism also might possibly be affected. Factors shown to influence hepatic drug metabolism include disease states, concurrent drug use, nutritional status, environmental compounds, genetic differences, gender, liver mass, and blood flow. Hepatic microsomal enzyme activity is reduced with increasing age in animals, but the clinical significance of this is controversial in humans. Large interindividual variation in liver metabolism exists for any given drug and in most cases may be more important than the changes associated with aging.[22,33–36] Also, liver mass declines and hepatic blood flow decreases 45% between ages 25 and 65.[37] Unfortunately, clinical tools for assessment of hepatic metabolism are not readily available. Age-related changes in the liver metabolism of phenylbutazone, warfarin, and long-acting benzodiazepines have been reported in humans.[38–41] Compounds undergoing phase I metabolism (reduction, oxidation, hydroxylation, demethylation) have a decreased or unchanged clearance, while compounds metabolized by phase II (conjugation, acetylation, sulfonation, glucuronidation) processes have no change in clearance upon aging. Drugs with high hepatic-extraction ratios, such as the nitrates, barbiturates, lidocaine, and propranolol, may have reduced hepatic metabolism in older adults.[42]

4. Reduction in Hepatic Reserve. D.A., an independently living 65-year-old male, 70″ tall and weighing 260 pounds, has a chief complaint of severe shortness of breath [SOB (respirations 26 breaths/min)], palpitations [heart rate (HR) 120 beats/min], and nausea. He has a history of chronic obstructive airway disease (COAD) and CHF. D.A.'s current medications are theophylline-SR (Theo-Dur) 450 mg Q 8 hr, captopril (Capoten) 12.5 mg Q 8 hr, and furosemide (Lasix) 20 mg Q AM. At his last visit to his physician 2 months ago, his theophylline serum concentration was 15 μg/mL, and after a long history of heavy smoking, D.A. finally took his physician's advice and abruptly quit smoking. The diagnosis is acute CHF on the basis of the chest x-ray, 2+ pitting edema, and "junky" sounding lungs. Based upon the information given, what potential problem should be added to the differential diagnosis list to be ruled out?

Theophylline toxicity is a possibility for two reasons: 1) hepatic deinduction from the recent smoking cessation, and 2) the known reduction of theophylline hepatic metabolism secondary to acute CHF.[32] The theophylline dose should be withheld until the serum theophylline concentration is within the desired therapeutic range. To prevent future theophylline toxicity, the options of treating the

COAD with a beta agonist and/or ipratropium by inhalation should be considered (see Chapter 19: Asthma).

Although the potential for theophylline toxicity can be explained reasonably in D.A., the sudden appearance of clinical deterioration or an adverse effect often arises unexpectedly in many elderly patients. Patients often do well while medically stable only to abruptly experience a ''cascade of disasters'' when hospitalized or when they begin taking additional medications. As presented in the answer to Question 3, the process of aging can be associated with declining liver mass, decreased hepatic blood flow, altered nutritional status, and a host of other physiological changes. These alterations result in a loss of ''hepatic reserve'' and the patient is susceptible to increased risk of adverse effects because of competition for the same metabolic enzymes when drugs are added to the existing regimen.

The concept of a lost ''hepatic reserve'' in the elderly also applies in a similar fashion to other organ systems. Therefore, D.A.'s response to renally excreted drugs (e.g., captopril, furosemide) also should be considered during this episode of acute congestive failure.

Excretion. Age-related changes in renal function probably are the single most important physiological factor resulting in adverse drug reactions. In addition, arteriosclerotic changes and a declining cardiac output decrease renal perfusion by 40% to 50% between ages 25 and 65; this is accompanied by a corresponding decrease in glomerular filtration and urea clearance.[43] Urine concentrating ability declines with aging as does renal sodium conservation.[44,45] Tubular excretory capacity and creatinine clearance (Cl_{Cr}) also may be reduced in aging.[46,47] The kidney loses functioning cells during aging, and histological studies reveal a decline in the absolute number of nephrons.[48] All these measures of the function of the kidney decline uniformly, leading to the concept of the ''intact nephron.'' Significant variability can occur in the rate of decline in the renal function in a minority of elderly patients,[49] presumably in those older patients with ''younger'' functional age (see Table 101.3).

Prolongation of plasma half-lives of a number of renally excreted drugs has been shown consistently in healthy older adults. The highest-risk drugs are those that depend entirely upon the kidney for elimination. Examples of these are listed in Table 101.4.[50,51]

Table 101.4	Drugs Highly Dependent Upon Renal Function for Elimination[a]	
Acetazolamide	Colistimethate	Nitrosourea
Acyclovir	Diflunisal	Norfloxacin
Allopurinol	Digoxin	Penicillamine
Amantadine	Enalapril	Pentamidine
Amiloride	Ethambutol	Phenazopyridine
Aminoglycosides	Fluconazole	Plicamycin
Amphotericin B	Flucytosine	Probenecid
Atenolol	Furosemide	Procainamide
Aztreonam	Gallamine	Pyridostigmine
Bleomycin	Gold sodium thiomalate	Ranitidine
Bretylium	Imipenem	Spironolactone
Captopril	Lisinopril	Sulfamethoxazole
Cephalosporins (most)	Lithium	Sulfinpyrazone
Chlorpropamide	Methenamine	Thiazides
Cimetidine	Methotrexate	Ticarcillin
Ciprofloxacin	Metoclopramide	Trimethoprim
Cisplatin	Nadolol	Vancomycin
Clonidine	Netilmicin	

[a] This list is not comprehensive; see references 50 and 51 for additional details.

Age-related changes in renal function are measurable through creatinine clearance, an estimate of glomerular filtration rate. The most frequently used method for estimating creatinine clearance is the Cockcroft-Gault equation.[52] Controversy surrounds the use of actual versus lean body weight (LBW), actual versus rounding the serum creatinine to 1.0 mg/dL, or whether some other method may be less biased and more accurate in older patients.[53,54] The use of LBW may reflect serum creatinine production more accurately because creatinine is produced in muscle mass, which is decreased in older patients. Different subpopulations of older patients (i.e., ambulatory and healthy versus hospitalized, malnourished and/or critically ill) may require different methods of adjustment for renal function estimates.

Table 101.5 provides a composite picture of the age-related physiological changes, disease states, and pharmacological factors that affect pharmacokinetic processes in older adults.

Pharmacodynamic Changes. Homeostasis and Postural Hypotension. D.A. is susceptible not only to decreased clearance (i.e., hepatic metabolism, renal elimination) but also to pharmacodynamic changes. Pharmacodynamic changes are defined loosely in this chapter as changes in concentration/response relationships or receptor sensitivity. Drug side effects, which are mild or nonexistent in younger patients, may be significant in older adults due to inefficient homeostatic adjustments. For example, orthostatic hypotension seen with advanced age results from an impaired baroreceptor function and a failure of cerebral blood flow autoregulation. Orthostatic hypotension occurs in 20% of ambulatory older patients over 65 years of age and in 30% among those over 75,[55] and it often is aggravated by drugs with sympatholytic activity [e.g., guanethidine, reserpine, phenothiazines, and tricyclic antidepressants (TCA)], volume-depleting drugs (e.g., diuretics), and vasodilating agents (e.g., nitrates and alcohol).[56] In one study of 100 geriatric psychiatric outpatients, almost 40% complained of dizziness and falling which was attributed to psychiatric medication.[57] Patients with impaired cardiac output and patients taking concurrent diuretic therapy (e.g., D.A.) are especially vulnerable. Also, aging impairs balance and posture maintenance, and drug effects on posture control may contribute to drug-induced falls in older adults.[58] Table 101.6 reviews the therapeutic agents commonly associated with adverse drug reactions that may affect the mobility of older patients.

Receptor Sensitivity. An exaggerated response to some drugs may reflect an intrinsic, age-related change in receptor sensitivity. Evidence of receptor alterations exist for nitrazepam, heparin (in females), and warfarin.[59,60] The aging central nervous system (CNS) is particularly vulnerable to qualitative as well as quantitative alterations in drug response. The aging brain, like the aging kidney, loses a significant number of active cells during later life, and some brain atrophy is a common, although not necessarily pathological, finding in older adults. Normal aging also involves a reduction in cerebral blood flow and oxygen consumption, and an increased cerebrovascular resistance.[61] Older persons often have cerebral blood flow rates that are as much as 20% less than those of younger persons.[25] In addition, inhibitory and excitatory pathways in the CNS are delicately balanced to modulate cognitive functions and behavior. With aging, there is a selective decline in some pathways and the preservation of others. For example, cholinergic neurons in the neocortex and hippocampal areas of the brain normally decrease with age. Pathological cholinergic deficits are associated with memory loss, confusion, and other cognitive impairments.[62] Drugs with anticholinergic properties are particularly notorious for inducing mental fuzziness and confusion in

Table 101.5		Changes Affecting Pharmacokinetic Parameters[a]	
Parameter	Physiological Changes	Disease States	Pharmacological Factors
Absorption (bioavailability, first-pass metabolism)	↑ gastric pH ↓ absorptive surface ↓ splanchnic blood flow ↓ GI motility ↓ gastric emptying rate	Achlorhydria, diarrhea, gastrectomy, malabsorptive syndromes, pancreatitis	Drug interactions, antacids, anticholinergics, cholestyramine, food
Distribution	↓ cardiac output ↓ TBW ↓ lean body mass ↓ serum albumin ↑ α_1-acid glycoprotein ↑ body fat ↓ altered relative tissue perfusion	CHF; dehydration; edema, ascites; hepatic failure; malnutrition; renal failure	Drug interactions, protein binding displacement
Metabolism	↓ hepatic mass ↓ enzyme activity ↓ hepatic blood flow	CHF, fever, hepatic failure, malignancy, malnutrition, thyroid disease, viral infection, or immunization	Dietary makeup, drug interactions, insecticides, alcohol, smoking, induction of metabolism, inhibition of metabolism
Excretion	↓ renal blood flow ↓ GFR ↓ tubular secretion ↓ renal mass	Hypovolemia, renal insufficiency	Drug interactions

[a] CHF = Congestive heart failure; GFR = Glomerular filtration rate; GI = Gastrointestinal; TBW = Total body water.

older patients. Several examples of therapeutic classes with anticholinergic properties are listed in Table 101.7.

Both central and peripheral responsiveness of adrenergic receptors decline with aging.[63] Monoamine-oxidase activity increases with normal aging and this is reflected by a decline in norepinephrine and dopamine levels in aging brains.[64] The decline in CNS dopamine synthesis is associated with increased sensitivity to dopamine blocking agents (e.g., neuroleptics or metoclopramide). On the other hand, β-receptor sensitivity to both beta agonists and antagonists decreases, even if the number of β-receptors does not decrease in older patients. Since these neurological and biochemical reserves are reduced as a normal consequence of aging, it is not surprising that iatrogenic behavioral disorders are relatively common in older adults, and that drugs are one of the most common causes of sudden, unexplained mental impairment in the older adult. For example, in one study, 11% of 300 patients more than 65 years of age experienced cognitive impairment as a result of an adverse drug reaction, and the risk increased ninefold when patients were taking ≥four prescription drugs.[65] In conclusion, D.A. is susceptible to significant variations in response to his medications and needs to be monitored carefully because of both pharmacokinetic and pharmacodynamic alterations attributable to aging. His theophylline therapy in particular should be evaluated.

Drug Use Problems in Older Adults

Polytherapy

Polypharmacy (i.e., polydrug therapy) is common in older adults, and according to the Centers for Disease Control, multiple drug use perhaps is the single most important causative factor for drug use problems in the older population.[66] Although more than 85% of older ambulatory patients and almost 95% of older institutionalized patients receive medications, as much as 25% of prescribed medication may be ineffective or unnecessary.[7] The combining of several medications also can increase the risk of adverse drug reactions.

5. As a new health care provider to a 60-bed skilled-nursing facility, many multiple drug use problems become obvious during initial chart reviews. A typical case is B.J., an 80-year-old male who has resided there for the past 10 months. A synopsis of B.J.'s medical record is as follows: 1) cardiomegaly and a long history of heart disease; 2) hypertension; 3) depression; 4) constipation; 5) rheumatoid arthritis (RA); 6) organic brain syndrome that is long-standing, mild, and increasing in severity; and 7) dizziness.

Laboratory information includes: sodium (Na), potassium (K), chloride (Cl), carbon dioxide (CO_2), glucose, and blood urea nitrogen (BUN) all are within normal limits. Admission weight is 70 kg, blood pressure (BP) 105/60 mm Hg, and pulse is 80 beats/min. Subsequent measurements of vital signs are not recorded systematically into his medical record but occasional recordings in the nurses' notes indicate little change from admission values. No blood work or urinalysis has been done. There are no known allergies.

Current medications include: digoxin (Lanoxin) 0.125 mg/day; methyldopa 250 mg/hydrochlorothiazide 15 mg (Aldoril-15) TID; tolmetin (Tolectin) 200 mg TID; aspirin 10 gr

Table 101.6	Adverse Drug Reactions That May Affect Mobility of the Older Patient
Medication Class	Adverse Drug Reaction
TCAs[a]	Postural hypotension, tremor, cardiac arrhythmias, sedation
Benzodiazepines and sedative hypnotics	Sedation, weakness, ↓ coordination, confusion
Narcotic analgesics	Sedation, ↓ coordination, confusion
Antipsychotics	Postural hypotension, sedation, extrapyramidal effects
Antihypertensives	Postural hypotension
β-adrenergic blockers	↓ ability to respond to workload

[a] TCA = Tricyclic antidepressant.

Table 101.7	Categories of Anticholinergic Drugs Which Can Induce Confusion in Older Patients
Therapeutic Class	**Examples (Brand Name)**
Antispasmodic	Belladonna (Generic)
	Dicyclomine (Bentyl)
	Propantheline (Probanthine)
Antiparkinson	Benztropine (Cogentin)
	Trihexyphenidyl (Artane)
Antihistamine	Diphenhydramine (Benadryl)
	Chlorpheniramine (Chlortrimeton)
Antidepressant	Amitriptyline (Elavil)
	Imipramine (Tofranil)
Antiarrhythmic	Quinidine
	Disopyramide (Norpace)
Neuroleptic	Thioridazine (Mellaril)
	Chlorpromazine (Thorazine)
Hypnotic	Hydroxyzine (Vistaril)
OTC agents[a]	Antidiarrheals
	Doxylamine
	Cold remedies

[a] OTC = Over-the-counter.

TID; thioridazine (Mellaril) 25 mg TID; haloperidol (Haldol) 0.5 mg BID; benztropine (Cogentin) 1 mg BID; amitriptyline (Elavil) 25 mg HS; docusate (Colace) 100 mg BID; milk of magnesia (MOM) 30 cc/day; flurazepam (Dalmane) 15 mg HS; ibuprofen (Nuprin) 200 mg two tablets Q 4 to 6 hr PRN pain; and 2 gm sodium diet.

B.J. is ambulatory and receives his meals in the facility cafeteria. Although he is in no acute distress, the nurses' notes indicate that B.J. often is confused and complains of arthritic pain and intermittent dizziness when ambulating. What should be the expectations of this skilled nursing facility in medication monitoring, and what basic interventions should have been undertaken in the evaluation of B.J.'s drug therapy?

Omnibus Budget Reconciliation Act (OBRA)

Under the Omnibus Budget Reconciliation Act, the obligations of the "supervising pharmacist" in a long-term care facility are summarized in Table 101.8. The fulfillment of these responsibilities must include monthly reviews of each patient's drug regimen to determine the following:

- Is each drug clearly indicated?
- If indicated, are dosing and administration appropriate?
- Are the laboratory results and vital signs appropriate and available to adequately evaluate therapy?
- Are there existing or potential problems with drug side effects, interactions, or adverse reactions?
- What specific recommendations can be made to optimize this patient's drug therapy?
- Are there any unnecessary drugs?

The OBRA regulations further require that the pharmacist serves as a member of the pharmaceutical and infection control committees and participates in drug use evaluations. Medication errors and adverse drug reactions must be reported to the patient's physician and documented by the pharmacist or nurse. Very specific guidelines are provided for the monitoring and justification of the use of neuroleptic agents, as well as establishing therapeutic goals for other chronic drug therapy in older patients.

Specific Examples

Several examples of undesirable polytherapy and OBRA deficiencies can be illustrated in the review of B.J.'s medication profile.

Digoxin. B.J. apparently has been treated with digoxin for years for a "history" of heart disease. Treatment of patients with New York Heart Association (NYHA) Class II and III congestive heart failure with digoxin, with or without concomitant administration of a vasodilator, decreases symptoms and reduces the morbidity associated with CHF, particularly in patients with more advanced symptoms and ventricular dysfunction.[68] However, cardiomegaly (i.e., NYHA Class I, or "mild CHF") itself is not a sufficient indication for digoxin therapy if the patient is asymptomatic and in normal sinus rhythm.[69] In aged patients meeting the criteria for NYHA Class I heart failure, discontinuation of the digoxin often can be attempted safely. An appropriate strategy would be to physically examine the patient and obtain an electrocardiogram to seek out evidence of rhythm disturbances or congestive failure. If B.J. is asymptomatic, an attempt should be made to discontinue his digoxin cautiously over several weeks.

Antihypertensives. Under OBRA, monitoring for goals of antihypertensive therapy is required (e.g., blood pressures measured and documented in the patient's record by signature and date on a regular basis). With poorly documented vital signs, B.J.'s hypertension possibly is overtreated as evidenced by the low admission blood pressure and the presence of intermittent dizziness that could be a symptom of orthostatic hypotension. The use of the methyldopa/hydrochlorothiazide combination is questionable. Since methyldopa can aggravate B.J.'s depression and confusion, a logical goal is to discontinue it if possible. Although B.J. is not receiving full therapeutic doses of the methyldopa/hydrochlorothiazide combination, the potential hazard of hypokalemia should be considered, especially because of his concurrent digoxin therapy. If his blood pressure remains low, discontinue the methyldopa/hydrochlorothiazide (Aldoril-15) combination and observe. If hypertension recurs, reinstitute therapy with hydrochlorothiazide 12.5 mg, measure potassium concentrations periodically, and give potassium supplements if necessary. Alternatively, a calcium channel blocking agent or angiotensin-converting enzyme (ACE) inhibitor can be prescribed (also see Chapter 10: Essential Hypertension and Chapter 15: Congestive Heart Failure).

Antiarthritics. B.J.'s rheumatoid arthritis is a proper indication for either aspirin or tolmetin (Tolectin), but concurrent use is not reasonable because both act by the same mechanism (i.e., inhibition of cyclooxygenase to decrease prostaglandin synthesis). Furthermore, aspirin can decrease tolmetin blood levels.[70] The doses of both tolmetin and aspirin also are subtherapeutic and this may explain B.J.'s unsatisfactory anti-inflammatory response as well as his adjunctive use of nonprescription ibuprofen (Nuprin). Ibuprofen also is a cyclooxygenase inhibitor and is unnecessary if effective doses of aspirin or tolmetin are prescribed. The ibuprofen and

Table 101.8	Basic Requirements of OBRA 1990 Legislation[a,67]
Prospective DUR[a]	
Retrospective DUR	
Provide education and intervention programs	
Patient counseling and provision of information to patients/caregivers	
Documentation of DUR and educational activities	

[a] DUR = Drug utilization review; OBRA = Omnibus Budget Reconciliation Act.

either aspirin or tolmetin should be discontinued and monotherapy with the remaining drug should be prescribed in full anti-inflammatory doses.

Psychotherapeutic Agents. B.J.'s history of "organic brain disease" was described as long-standing and mild in the admission workup, but subsequent nursing notes suggest that the symptoms of confusion and disorientation worsened noticeably soon after admission. Rapid deterioration of mental acuity is atypical of chronic dementing disease (see Chapter 102: Geriatric Dementias) and raises the suspicion that a reversible factor could have precipitated B.J.'s mental decline. Psychotropic drugs, especially drugs with sedating and anticholinergic properties, are notorious for inducing mental fuzziness and confusion in older adults,[71,72] and overprescribing of psychotropic drugs in institutionalized older patients is well documented.[73] The cognitive impairment of chronic degenerative dementia can be exaggerated greatly by the flurazepam, thioridazine, haloperidol, benztropine, and amitriptyline presently being administered to B.J. Careful scrutiny of drug regimens in geriatric nursing home patients frequently enhances the rational use of psychotherapeutic drugs.[74]

Neuroleptics are some of the most commonly prescribed drugs in nursing home patients; however, the use of these drugs should be reserved for geriatric patients with psychotic behavioral disturbances, or impulsivity and agitation associated with functional or organic disorders, such as chronic degenerative dementia. Often, neuroleptics are prescribed unnecessarily for anxiety, insomnia, confusion, "senility," and nonconformity to the institutional lifestyle. However, OBRA regulations should reduce the potential for overuse of neuroleptics because these regulations mandate that these drugs be used for a specified condition, in the lowest dose possible, for the shortest time necessary, and that attempts at tapering the dose and all clinical assessments for ongoing need be documented carefully. In one neuroleptic use study, 57% of the institutionalized subjects studied received at least one neuroleptic, 12% did not have an appropriate indication, and 35% were without appropriate diagnoses and target symptoms.[75] When a neuroleptic agent is indicated, the use of two or more, as seen in B.J., is irrational. B.J.'s benztropine therapy also is not indicated unless extrapyramidal symptoms are documented clearly. Extrapyramidal symptoms are not likely to occur as long as the strongly anticholinergic amitriptyline continues to be administered for B.J. or if his haloperidol is discontinued.

Amitriptyline (Elavil) probably is not indicated for B.J. Even if indicated, amitriptyline is a poor choice in an elderly patient due to its significant anticholinergic and sedating side effects. B.J. is taking several sedating drugs (e.g., methyldopa, flurazepam, thioridazine) and these may induce a pseudodepression which will resolve with a reduction in the number of sedating drugs. Excessive digoxin also has been associated with a pseudodepressive syndrome.[76] Even if B.J. suffers from true depression, the use of low bedtime doses of antidepressant is irrational if his response is not monitored carefully and no attempt is made to titrate the dose to a reasonable therapeutic range. Most prescribers using antidepressants in this manner probably recognize they are achieving little antidepressant effect but do not have the time or interest to individualize the dose. The sleep-inducing effect of the sedating tricyclics often is used as a rationalization for this improper prescribing pattern.

Flurazepam (Dalmane), a long-acting benzodiazepine, may increase the risk of falls and bone fractures in the older population. Uninterrupted, nightly use of long-acting benzodiazepines increase the relative risk of hip fractures by 50% compared to shorter-acting benzodiazepines.[77] The need for chronically scheduled bedtime benzodiazepines should be evaluated thoroughly because older patients naturally sleep for a shorter period of time and their sleep is shallower and subject to frequent awakenings (see Chapter 74: Sleep Disorders).

In view of the atypical deterioration of B.J.'s cognitive function, the doses of all his psychotropic medications should be decreased gradually and the drugs discontinued eventually. A baseline assessment of cognitive function and psychiatric status should be undertaken by a geriatrician, psychiatrist, or clinical psychologist to establish the presence or absence of psychotic behavioral disturbances or depression. Each disorder then should be managed with a single drug in full therapeutic doses.

Causes of Polydrug Therapy

6. B.J.'s regimen was evaluated and revised over several weeks. The medication list was reduced to hydrochlorothiazide, a potassium supplement, tolmetin, docusate, and temazepam PRN. On these drugs, B.J. was much less confused and his dizziness disappeared. The elimination of drugs was thought to be responsible for improvement of his disabling symptoms. Why is polydrug therapy so prevalent in institutionalized geriatric patients?

Polydrug therapy thrives under conditions where multiple chronic diseases exist in unappealing patients with communication problems. These factors lead to imperfect diagnoses and unclear drug indications. For this reason, monitoring drug therapy in these patients is especially vexing. Busy health care providers all too frequently assign a low priority to nursing home patients in terms of individual attention, and much of the prescribing of medications and follow-up is done by telephone. Duplicative prescribing within the same drug class often results, or unrecognized drug side effects are treated with more drugs. With little actual patient contact, prescribers may continue drugs in stabilized patients long after the original problem has resolved to avoid the inconvenience of meticulous dose adjustments and follow-up monitoring. The practice of geriatrics often can be benefited by taking aged patients off of their unnecessary medications.

Underlying the difficult task of caring for institutionalized geriatric patients is the problem of gerontophobia. A common attitude among health professionals is that the older patient is less deserving than the young patient since the older patient is closer to death and has no distant future. Because of gerontophobia, health professionals often feel little needs to be done for the institutionalized old and that benign neglect is acceptable. One survey of physicians disclosed that 40% believe the nursing home is where old people go to die, and only 21% feel that they are actually in charge of their nursing home patients.[78] Gerontophobia includes indifference to the finer details of medication management.

As the proportion of the demented and the oldest-old grows in our population, difficult economic and ethical issues will confront society increasingly. The concern has been expressed that because approximately 40% of Medicare dollars go toward caring for older persons in their last year of life, it may be "difficult to maintain advocacy for these unappealing people."[79] It is important for health professionals to steadfastly maintain their advocacy role on behalf of the oldest-old.

The Ambulatory Older Patient

Medication Management of the Ambulatory Older Patient

In addition to the issues in B.J.'s case, several additional considerations must be incorporated into the medication assessment and pharmacotherapy of the ambulatory geriatric population. The common practice of self-medication adds to regimen complexity and its consequences. A complete drug history is difficult to obtain, and the ambulatory patient often is vulnerable due to physical, social, and economic factors. The resulting compliance problems and medication errors increase the older patient's risk of adverse drug reactions, drug interactions, and drug-induced illnesses.

Further compounding the difficulties of medication management in the ambulatory older patient is the problem of inappropriate prescribing. About 25% of older adults living in the community have been prescribed potentially inappropriate medications and subjected to increased risk for adverse drug effects such as cognitive impairment and sedation.[80] Improvements in medication management, therefore, are needed not only in nursing homes but also in the community.

Difficulties in Obtaining a Complete Drug History

7. K.S., an 81-year-old female, lives at home alone on a modest retirement income. She suffers from 4 chronic medical problems for which she sees different specialists and takes several prescription medications. She maintains an active social life hosting and visiting her elderly friends regularly and attending the seniors' congregate meal site program 3 times a week. She admits a high interest in matters pertaining to her health, and she frequently self-medicates with nonprescription medications and other home remedies she hears about through her network of senior friends. What difficulties might be encountered by health care providers who need to obtain a complete drug history in patients like K.S?

K.S.'s living situation is not atypical of today's geriatric population. Ninety-five percent of the older population are ambulatory, community-dwelling individuals. A significant problem in combating polydrug therapy in the independently living older adult is the difficulty in obtaining a complete drug history. Besides prescription drugs, K.S. may consume a significant number of nonprescription medications, social drugs, borrowed and hoarded drugs, and home remedies. Comprehensive consultation and medication management in the older patient is very problematical without a thorough knowledge of all self-medication.

Nonprescription Drug Use. Use of nonprescription drugs by the older population is common. Two-thirds of older ambulatory patients regularly self-medicate with nonprescription products, particularly with oral analgesics, such as aspirin, ibuprofen (Advil), acetaminophen (Tylenol), and naproxen sodium (Aleve). Although individuals more than 65 years of age only constitute 12% of the population, they consume 50% of the nonprescription drugs purchased. About 80% of the elderly use nonprescription drugs without consulting a physician.[81] Unfortunately, older adults as well as other consumers have the attitude that nonprescription ingredients are safe ''undrugs,'' not deserving of the same respect afforded prescription medications. In the older adult, this attitude can contribute to polydrug therapy and to an increased risk of adverse drug reactions. Prescribers often overlook or ignore nonprescription drug use by their older patients when prescribing medications, resulting in potentially negative consequences. In one study of geriatric admissions to the hospital due to drug-induced problems, one in five involved a nonprescription drug.[82]

Conversion of Legend Drugs to Nonprescription Status. The trend to increase the availability of prescription drugs by changing their status to nonprescription drugs has important implications for the older population. Many prescription drugs which are candidates for conversion to nonlegend over-the-counter status are indicated for chronic conditions. Four out of five older adults have at least one chronic health condition, and 40% have ≥two chronic conditions.[83] In the next several years, the Food and Drug Administration in the U.S. expects at least 48 petitions to change prescription drugs to nonprescription status, and by 1996, nonprescription drug sales are expected to increase by 66% due to the availability of previously prescription-only products.[84] The high rate of nonprescription drug use by the older adult and the increased availability of more potent agents will add to the problem of polydrug therapy and increase the challenge of optimizing medication management in older patients. For example, naproxen sodium (Aleve) has been converted to nonprescription status and NSAIDs, such as naproxen, are commonly associated with drug-related hospital admissions in older patients.[85]

Social Drug Use. The extent of K.S.'s use of social drugs also must be considered. Many social drugs have potent active ingredients which can contribute to drug-use problems. Alcohol, caffeinated beverages, and nicotine are the most commonly available ingredients in social drugs. Of the 100 most commonly prescribed drug products, about one-half have an ingredient that can interact with alcohol, either through additive CNS depression or GI irritation, and 18% of older patients admit to combining medications and alcohol regularly.[7] Excessive alcohol use can lead to premature cognitive impairment, gastric lesions, loss of appetite, falls, and social withdrawal. The stimulant effects of caffeine and nicotine are well known and produce additive effects with many prescription drugs. An accurate picture of social drug use is an important component of a complete drug history in the older patient.

Hoarding, Borrowing, and Home Remedies. Finally, older patients like K.S. are notorious for other forms of self-medication, including hoarding, borrowing, and using home remedies. Hoarding of old prescription drugs is common in older patients. Anyone who has participated in home health visitations to assess medication problems is well aware of the large inventories of hoarded prescriptions that are available (e.g., in medicine cabinets, shoeboxes, bedside drawers). In addition, older patients borrow medications from friends and relatives who exhibit similar symptoms, and the use of home remedies is common in the older patient, including such products as herbal drugs, dimethyl sulfoxide, special diets, and nutritional supplements.[16] In one survey, one-third of Americans had used at least one unconventional therapy during the past year (including nondrug therapies) with a national out-of-pocket expense of over $10 billion.[86] About 25% of older patients may be taking drugs not currently prescribed.[87]

Compliance Problems and Medication Errors

8. In addition to frequent self-medication, K.S.'s prescription regimen involves the use of several medications administered at different intervals throughout the day. How does regimen complexity predispose K.S. to compliance problems and medication errors?

Hippocrates once said that ''patients often lie when they state they have taken certain medications.''[88] However, confusion from polydrug therapy and regimen complexity are more characteristic of the older patient. Self-reporting of medication use becomes unreliable when the older patient receives ≥two prescription medications, suffers from ≥four active medical problems, or is depressed.[89] K.S. meets two of these criteria.

Noncompliance and medication errors are disturbingly common. Over one-half of the 1.6 billion prescriptions written annually in the U.S. are taken incorrectly, and 30% to 50% of prescribed medications fail to produce their intended results.[90] The economic consequences of medication noncompliance is in excess of $100 billion annually.[91]

Types of Noncompliance. Noncompliance exists in many forms, including: 1) failure to fill the original prescription; 2) failure to refill the prescription; and 3) failure to take the dose as prescribed.[90] Noncompliance in older patients is associated most often with incorrect dosing; however, in one survey 21% of respondents failed to have a new prescription filled.[92] One of the largest groups of older noncompliers are the ''partial'' compliers who set their own dosing schedule. These patients have been described as ''intelligent noncompliers'' because their noncompliance is intentional and based upon convenience, drug side effects, or drug expense.[93] Refill and compliance problems most often are associated with chronic drug therapy, and the average compliance rate for patients on chronic medication is about 50%.[87] This is a significant finding since older patients are more likely to be exposed to chronic rather than short-term patterns of drug administration, as in K.S.

Barriers to compliance have been identified as regimen complexity, miscommunication, and unresolved patient concerns.[90] Reduction of regimen complexity includes the use of specialized dosing formulations (e.g., transdermal systems) the selection of long-acting or fixed-combination products when therapeutically sound, and the use of user-friendly packaging (e.g., unit-of-use packaging, calendar blister packs). Compliance strategies employing transdermal systems, long-acting formulations, or blister packaging improve patient compliance.[94-97] Because compliance is such a significant problem and accounts for the loss of billions of dollars in retail prescription sales annually, it is predicted that novel delivery systems designed to reduce medication regimen complexity and to improve compliance will account for 40% of all pharmaceutical formulations marketed in the future.[90,94]

The other barriers to compliance, miscommunication and unresolved patient concerns, result from information gaps in the patient education process and the inability of the patient to express and resolve personal concerns. No single approach has been shown to be consistently effective in assuring compliance in the older adult, and practitioners must use a variety of patient educational tools and reminder devices tailored to the individual patient's abilities and needs.[98] Table 101.9 is a synthesis of the many patient education strategies, professional support programs, and compliance technologies available. (See reference 90 for a review of individual strategies.)

Physical disabilities also affect compliance to medication regimens and medication errors in older patients. Twenty-five to forty percent of persons over age 65 have impaired hearing, and in persons over age 90, more than 90% have a hearing handicap.[99,100] Hearing impairment is correlated with cognitive dysfunction in older patients and presumably with susceptibility to medication errors.[101] Vision impairment is the most common sensory deficit in the older population, with 90% requiring corrective lenses and 20% over age 80 unable to read a newspaper even with corrective lenses.[102] Glare intolerance and loss of color discrimination also are common.[103,104] Chronic diseases (e.g., arthritis, Parkinsonism) also can impair normal functioning. Thus, physical impairments can contribute substantially to medication errors in a variety of ways. Hearing impairment may interfere with the patient counseling process. Vision deficits may obviate the use of written information leaflets and make medication container labels difficult to read. Prescription labels with small type, low-density printing from computer-generated labels, and glossy surfaces all have been associated with decreased label readability.[102] Lack of color discrimination may lead to administration errors. And lastly, many older patients discontinue medications because of difficulty with child-resistant containers, or they may remove medications from the child-resistant container and store them under suboptimal conditions.

Table 101.9	Patient Compliance Enhancement Strategies[a,b]
Strategy	**Description**
Patient Education Tools	
APhA National Pharmacy Week	Patient information on the importance of talking with the pharmacist
NARD Consumer Information Corner Kits	News releases, flyers, brochures for patients
Pharma-Check Med Card System	Wallet-sized medication cards providing information about individual medications
Ask the Pharmacist 24-Hour Hotline	For-profit telephone hotline in which pharmacists provide medication information to patients and caregivers
Health Information Network	Brief telephone messages on medication and health topics derived from the *USP-DI*
NARD Diabetes Care Program	Medication and health information available to all people with diabetes
NARD Patient Information Leaflets (PIL)	Medication information leaflets abstracted from the *USP-DI*
Pharmacist-Patient Consultation Program (PPCP)	Educational materials developed by the Indian Health Service, University of Arizona, and Pfizer to train pharmacists in efficient medication counseling skills
Physician-Patient Communication Program (PPC)	Educational materials developed by Miles Laboratories to improve physician communication skills
Parke-Davis Elder-Care Program	Educational materials to enhance patient-pharmacist communication
NARD Regimen	Monthly newsletter for LTCF caregivers
National Eldercare Campaign	Administration on Aging program to improve patient and caregiver access to health and medication information
Reminder Devices	
Electronic counter caps	Container cap microcircuitry which alerts patient to single drug dosing time
Electronic pillboxes	Container microcircuitry which alerts patient to multiple drug dosage times and keeps a record of doses taken
Medisets	Weekly multiple drug dose pill organizers
Seiko RC-1000	Special programmable wrist watch alerting patient to dosing times, refills, or doctor appointments
Prescription label scratch offs	Dots that patients can scratch off the container after each dose is taken
Medi-Data Program	Credit card-sized portable medication profile on computer chip which requires card reader technology at each provider site
Smart Card (PDH, Inc., Sonex)	Credit card-sized comprehensive portable patient medical record on computer chip which requires card reader technology at each provider site
Postcard reminders	Sent automatically before refill is due; accompanied with telephone reminder "tickler" follow-up
Med-Minder Compliance Module	Computerized automatic telephone reminder system which connects to existing pharmacy computer

Continued

Table 101.9	Patient Compliance Enhancement Strategies^{a,b} (Continued)
Strategy	**Description**
Computer-generated printed patient education materials	Patient and professional printouts, on-screen information, specialized programs for illiterate, sight-impaired, or nonEnglish-speaking patients
Medication Event Monitoring System (MEMS)	Compliance monitor based upon container microcircuitry

^a Adapted from reference 90.
^b APhA = American Pharmacy Association; LTCF = Long-term care facility; NARD = National Association of Retail Druggists; USP-DI = United States Pharmacopoeia-Dispensing Information.

High-Risk Older Adults. Two types of ambulatory older patients are at especially high risk for drug-induced problems secondary to noncompliance and medication errors. The first high-risk group is characterized by K.S., who is representative of the over 9 million older adults living at home alone. The isolated community-dwelling older patient typically is female, ≥75 years of age, has multiple disorders, and takes multiple medications.[105] Lacking close support and a daily routine, she may not be fully cognizant of the time of the day or the day of the week. Without time awareness, adherence to complex regimens can decrease. Isolated older persons also may suffer from personal losses, such as loss of career, spouse, and ability to drive a car, and many turn to alcohol and other drug misuse. The misuse of alcohol or CNS depressants (mainly benzodiazepines) by this group may be as high as 10% and 5%, respectively.[106] The second high-risk group is comprised of older patients recently discharged from the hospital. The postdischarge period can be a time of confusion for the older patient, who often must cope with new drugs or replacement drugs added to his already complex prehospitalization regimen. Older patients frequently are readmitted to the hospital within a short time after discharge, and noncompliance with medications is a major responsible factor.[107,108]

A summary of the various factors contributing to noncompliance in the older patient is presented in Table 101.10.[109]

Adverse Drug Reactions and Drug Interactions

The adverse drug reaction rate in the aged is higher than that of young adults.[110–113] The overall adverse drug reaction rate per 100,000 population is 8.5, compared to 16.0 in persons ≥65 years of age, nearly double the average rate.[65] Adverse drug reactions in community-based older patients may be as high as 29% to 30%.[114] According to the Inspector General of the USDHHS, persons over 60 years of age (≈17% of the U.S. population) account for nearly 30% of drug-related hospitalizations and more than half the deaths from adverse drug reactions. The report further stated that 243,000 older adults were hospitalized in 1985 due to adverse drug reactions, and that an estimated 32,000 hip fractures, 163,000 cases of drug-induced cognitive impairment, and 61,000 cases of neuroleptic-induced parkinsonism occur annually.[115] Adverse drug reactions are a major cause of hospitalization of older adults and account for as many as 20% to 30% of hospital admissions.[116–118]

In older patients, adverse drug reactions can be difficult to detect because elderly patients often exhibit an atypical response and present with nonspecific symptoms, such as lethargy, confusion, lightheadedness, or falls, rather than the usual drug effects. Despite this, most adverse drug reactions are predictable extensions of a drug's pharmacological effect and are preventable. Nevertheless, adverse drug reactions are a significant problem,

with some experts placing the health care costs for adverse drug reactions at $3.4 billion annually.[13]

Ambulatory geriatric populations also experience a high rate of potential drug interactions in the moderate to severe categories, with the incidence ranging from 21% to 38%. The most common drug interactions involve digoxin, beta blockers, estrogens, oral hypoglycemics, diuretics, verapamil, and NSAIDs.[119–121]

Finally, age *per se* is not an independent risk factor for adverse drug reactions, but rather, increased risk is derived from age-related factors (e.g., physiological changes), polydrug therapy, and regimen complexity leading to medication errors and inappropriate prescribing.[122,123]

9. **Adverse Drug Reactions in Older Patients.** S.E., an 85-year-old female, 5'2" and 102 pounds, with a SrCr of 1.6 mg/dL, is admitted for chest pain, shortness of breath, and to rule out myocardial infarction. Her physician is concerned about over sedation with narcotics and prescribes ketorolac (Toradol) 30 mg Q 6 hr IV. She has a history of severe congestive heart failure and angina. She presently is being treated with captopril 12.5 mg Q 8 hr PO; furosemide 40 mg Q AM PO; aspirin 81 mg QD PO; and nitroglycerin SR 6 mg BID PO.

The captopril dose has been increased to 12.5 mg Q 6 hr and the furosemide to 40 mg BID. Her BP is 110/66 mm Hg and urine output has been 20 to 30 mL/hr for 4 hours since ketorolac was administered. What risk factors are present in S.E. for drug-induced renal problems? [SI units: SrCr 141.4 μmol/L]

S.E. has a number of risk factors for the development of drug-induced acute renal failure (ARF). ACE inhibitors may diminish efferent arteriole glomerular capillary filtration pressure and precipitate acute renal failure in predisposed patients. A low serum sodium concentration, high-dose diuretics, diabetes, severe CHF (i.e., NYHA class IV), use of a long-acting ACE inhibitor, and concurrent NSAID use are risk factors for drug-induced acute renal failure (see Chapter 29: Acute Renal Failure). Patients with these risk factors should be monitored closely when an ACE inhibitor is initiated and when the dose of an ACE inhibitor is increased. Renal prostaglandins (PGE_2, PGI_2) increase or help maintain renal blood flow when renal function is compromised by intrinsic renal disease, congestive heart failure, liver disease with ascites, or hypertension; therefore, the use of a prostaglandin inhibitor such as ketorolac places S.E. at an increased risk for acute renal failure. Furthermore, the ketorolac dose is excessive for S.E. based upon the recommended maximum dose of 15 mg every six hours for elderly patients.

Table 101.10	Factors Influencing the Ability to Comply with a Medication Regimen^a
≥3 chronic conditions	
>5 prescription medications	
≥12 medication dosages per day	
Medication regimen changed ≥4 times during the past 12 months	
≥3 prescribers involved	
Significant cognitive or physical impairments (e.g., memory, hearing, vision, color discrimination, child-resistant containers)	
Living alone in the community	
Recently discharged from the hospital	
Reliance on a caregiver	
Low literacy	
Medication cost	
Demonstrated poor compliance history	

^a Adapted from reference 108.

10. Strategies for Healthy Prescribing in Older Patients. What are some guidelines for medication prescribing that are useful for elderly patients?

Guidelines for healthy prescribing in the older patient are listed in Table 101.11.[124–126]

Geriatric Rehabilitation

Role of Rehabilitative Medicine in Geriatrics

Rehabilitative and geriatric medicine share a number of common objectives.[127] Both disciplines are concerned with preserving function in patients with multiple impairments and preventing secondary complications. Each uses a multidisciplinary team approach to accomplish holistic goals of maintaining overall health and functioning. The geriatric population forms a major part of rehabilitative medicine. Persons aged ≥65 have more than twice as much disability, have four times the activity limitation, and have about twice as many hospital stays that last about 50% longer than persons under 65.[128] The challenge to geriatric rehabilitation is to prevent or minimize functional impairments resulting from the various chronic and multiple illnesses to which older patients are prone.

Rehabilitation Goals

The goal of all rehabilitation programs is the development of a person to the fullest physical, psychological, social, vocational, avocational, and educational potential consistent with his physiological, anatomical, and environmental limitations. Realistic goals based upon functional activities that are important to the independence and well-being of the individual should be established mutually by the patient and the interdisciplinary rehabilitation team. In older patients, this often involves working to obtain optimal function despite residual disability, even if the impairment is caused by a pathological process that cannot be reversed with medical treatment.

Functional Assessment

The first step in a rehabilitation program is a meticulous clinical evaluation of the person as a whole, including medical and functional status.[129] A functional status evaluation should include an assessment of the personal care activities or activities of daily living appropriate to the age, gender, and environment of each person. Activities of daily living include dressing, eating, bathing, grooming, use of the toilet, and mobility within the home. Other important activities which determine functional independence are termed instrumental activities of daily living. These include food preparation, laundry, housekeeping, shopping, the ability to use the telephone, use of transportation, medication use, financial management, and child care when appropriate. Participation in leisure and recreational activities also can be viewed as instrumental activities of daily living important for the psychosocial and physical well-being of a person. Any deviation from the normal or characteristic ability of a person to perform tasks of living is called a disability or dysfunction. Impairments are defined as aberrations in organs or body systems which can lead to dysfunction. If the inability to perform tasks results in social disadvantage, the condition is viewed as a handicap.[130]

Team Approach

To accomplish such a comprehensive evaluation, an interdisciplinary "geriatric assessment" team is essential. A geriatric assessment team has a common goal, combines the skill of each discipline, and also must be able to work synergistically to contribute to the group effort on behalf of the patient. The team usually is lead by a physiatrist (i.e., a physician trained and certified in rehabilitation medicine). Other disciplines represented on the team

Table 101.11	Strategies for Healthy Prescribing in the Older Patient[124–126]

Assure a proper indication is established; do not just treat symptoms

Put the problem in context. Is it affecting the patient's quality of life or causing functional decline?

Know the patient. What is his overall health status? Is there known hepatic or renal impairment?

What drugs, including nonprescription drugs, social drugs, and other self-medication, is he taking? Who else is prescribing?

Consider nondrug alternatives to therapy (e.g., physical exercise, physical therapy, counseling, and relaxation techniques)

If drug treatment is necessary, know the drug well, including its mechanism of action, route of metabolism and excretion, and side effect profile in the elderly

Dose carefully. The well-known adage "start low and go slow" is appropriate. Adjust the dose according to the patient's response

Simplify the regimen as much as possible by minimizing dose frequency, using monotherapy or at least a minimum number of drugs possible, avoiding "PRN" orders, and reviewing the need for all prescribed medication periodically with the intent to eliminate unnecessary drugs

Try to anticipate and minimize adverse drug reactions by considering side-effect profiles in selecting a specific drug group

As a general rule, if an older patient receives a new drug and develops new symptoms (e.g., confusion, instability, or falls), seriously consider that the symptoms may be drug-induced

Determine whether the patient needs help using the medication. Pharmacists, nurses, and caregivers all can serve as resources for older patients who are living alone or are functionally or cognitively impaired. Written instruction, information leaflets, calendars, special containers, special packaging, and a variety of other reminder devices can enhance the appropriate use of medication

Educate the patient (and caregiver/family when needed) about intended therapeutic effects, possible adverse drug reactions, and signs of toxicity

Be sure to schedule regular follow-ups, constantly re-evaluate the older patient's medication regimen, and document the outcomes of your interventions based upon predetermined therapeutic goals

are pharmacy, physical therapy, occupational therapy, speech therapy, recreational therapy, behavioral medicine, and nursing. Weekly team staff meetings assess each patient's needs, establish goals, monitor progress, report problems, and sign off goals that have been attained. Interdisciplinary geriatric assessment teams, including a pharmacist member as the pharmacotherapy specialist, significantly reduce length of stay, readmissions, drug costs, and patient mortality.[126,131,132]

Assessment of Drug Therapy

As discussed earlier in this chapter, a complete medication history is essential, since polydrug therapy commonly is encountered in people with chronic disease, especially in older patients. Adverse reactions to medications can affect the functional assessment of the geriatric patient by further impeding cognition, psychological state, vascular reflexes, balance, bowel and bladder control, muscle tone and coordination that already are impaired by the present illness or injury. The pharmacist should alert the team to iatrogenic drug-induced problems, aid in compliance and medication education issues, discontinue medications no longer necessary in the recovery versus acute phase of the illness, screen for drug interactions, and recommend appropriate changes in therapy based upon altered pharmacokinetic and receptor sensitivity in older patients. A standardized comprehensive assessment of the ability of older persons to take medications does not exist, but several conditions or skills have been identified as possible indicators and are listed in Table 101.12.[133,134]

Table 101.12	Indicators of the Inability to Self-Medicate[133,134]

Cognitive impairments

>5 prescription medications

Inability to read prescription and auxiliary labels

Difficulty opening nonchildproof containers

Problems removing small tablets from containers

Inability to discriminate between medication colors and shapes

Effects of Drugs on Functional Ability

Many medications are capable of inducing functional impairments, especially in older adults.[135] Drugs depleting dopamine may produce extrapyramidal side effects and interfere with physical and occupational therapy goals. Postural hypotension increases the risk of falling and may be induced by neuroleptics, tricyclic antidepressants, or excessive doses of antihypertensives. Medications affecting the vestibular system, such as the aminoglycosides, loop diuretics, and high serum concentrations of aspirin may cause eighth cranial nerve damage, such as problems with balance or tinnitus. Long-term use of corticosteroids may bring about proximal muscle wasting and slow recovery of strength, despite aggressive therapies.

Drug-induced limitations in mental capacity also diminish the ability of an older person to respond maximally to therapy.[136,137] Oversedation with CNS medications decreases the capability to learn, ambulate, eat, or use the toilet. Reversible cognitive impairment or dementia has been reported with the use of benzodiazepines, antihypertensives, neuroleptics, H_2 blockers, and analgesics. Several benzodiazepines that bind tightly to the benzodiazepine-receptor complex have been associated with anterograde amnesia. Confusion, nightmares, delirium, or hallucinations may be the first manifestations of digoxin toxicity in the older patients. Medications increasing the prominence of dopamine or decreasing the influence of acetylcholine in the brain may be responsible for causing psychosis, hallucinations, or delirium.

Some antihypertensive drugs (e.g., reserpine, beta blockers, methyldopa) may cause depression. Metoclopramide (Reglan) is a frequently overlooked potential contributor to depression. Depression is an important adverse reaction in the rehabilitation area since it may mimic dementia on neuropsychological testing.

11. L.A., a 5'1", 95 pound, 75-year-old female, experienced an embolic stroke 5 days before transfer to the rehabilitation unit. Her past medical history is significant for atrial fibrillation. She was noncompliant with her digoxin 0.25 mg/day the week before admission because it made her "feel bad." Medications on transfer are: digoxin 0.25 mg/day, warfarin 5 mg/day, ranitidine 150 mg BID, metoclopramide 10 mg QID, acetaminophen 325 to 650 mg PRN pain, and MOM PRN constipation.

Laboratory results are: Na⁺ 135 mEq/L, K⁺ 4.0 mEq/L, SrCr 1.5 mg/dL, and BUN 23 mg/dL. Patient vital signs are: BP 110/60 mm Hg, HR 50 beats/min, T 98.4 °F. During the initial team staffing to discuss L.A., the physical therapist mentions that she walks with a stooped posture, shuffling gait, and has poor balance. Her nurse raises the problem of poor appetite. The speech therapist reports L.A. has difficulty in swallowing, noting the problem is out of proportion for the location of her stroke. A flat affect, crying episodes, fatigue, and drowsiness are reported in activities of daily living assessment by the occupational therapist. The psychologist notes confusion and potential dementia on neuropsychological testing. Can any of these problems be adverse reactions to L.A.'s drug therapy?
[SI units: Na 135 mmol/L; K 4.0 mmol/L; SrCr 132.6 μmol/L; BUN 8.2 mmol/L]

Metoclopramide. L.A. has a calculated creatinine clearance of less than 25 mL/minute, and several of the medications which she takes are partially or entirely excreted renally. Metoclopramide (Reglan) is metabolized only minimally and primarily is excreted renally. This agent has dopamine-blocking activity and can produce the pseudoparkinson symptoms noted by the physical therapist. Dopamine blockers also can disrupt the normal swallowing mechanisms. Metoclopramide also has produced mental depres-

Table 101.13		Drug Effects on Other Assessments[a,b]
Assessments	**Drug Effects**	**Drug Examples**
Functional	Movement disorders (extrapyramidal, tardive dyskinesia)	Neuroleptics, metoclopramide, amoxapine, methyldopa
	Balance (neuritis, neuropathies, tinnitis, dizziness; hypotension)	Metronidazole, phenytoin, aspirin, aminoglycosides, furosemide, ethacrynic acid; beta blockers, calcium channel blockers, neuroleptics, antidepressants, diuretics, vasodilators, benzodiazepines, levodopa, metoclopramide
Physical	Supporting structures (arthralgias, myopathies, osteoporosis, osteomalacia)	Corticosteroids, lithium, phenytoin, heparin
	Incontinence (urinary retention; secondary oversedation)	Anticholinergic agents, TCAs, neuroleptics, antihistamines, smooth muscle relaxants, nifedipine, phenylpropanolamine, prazosin; benzodiazepines, sedatives, hypnotics
	Sexual dysfunction	Hypotensive agents, CNS depressants
Social	Malnutrition	Drugs affecting appetite
	Poor dental health	Anticholinergic agents, glucose-containing oral liquid/chewable dosage forms
Psychological	Cognitive impairment (metabolic alterations; memory loss, dementia)	Beta blockers, corticosteroids, diuretics, sulfonylureas, methyldopa, propranolol, hydrochlorothiazide, reserpine, neuroleptics, opiates, cimetidine, amantadine, benzodiazepines, anticonvulsants
	Behavioral toxicity (insomnia, nightmares, sedation, agitation, delirium, psychosis, hallucinations)	Anticholinergics, cimetidine, ranitidine, famotidine, digoxin, bromocriptine, amantadine, baclofen, levodopa, opiates, sympathomimetics, corticosteroids
	Depression	Reserpine, methyldopa, beta blockers, metoclopramide, corticosteroids, CNS depressants

[a] Adapted from reference 135.
[b] CNS = Central nervous system; TCA = Tricyclic antidepressant.

sion in some patients that may or may not recur when the drug is reinstituted at lower doses. L.A. upon questioning revealed she used antacids at home on an as-needed basis to treat her reflux due to a small hiatal hernia. Metoclopramide should be discontinued and antacids should be reinstituted. Her difficulty in swallowing, decreased appetite, parkinsonian symptoms, and possibly her depression should improve within days of the discontinuation of her metoclopramide. If metoclopramide is needed, the dose should be decreased by 50% based upon L.A.'s creatinine clearance of less than 40 mL/minute.[138]

Ranitidine, Cimetidine, and Famotidine. Ranitidine (Zantac) is metabolized and excreted renally. A more reasonable dose in L.A. is 150 mg/day based upon her renal function. Ranitidine, as well as cimetidine and famotidine, has been reported to cause reversible confusion and agitation in older patients with decreased renal function.[139–141]

Digoxin (Lanoxin) also is an agent that is cleared hepatically and renally. The percent of digoxin eliminated renally per day would be only about 18% in L.A. compared with the normal of 35% (see Chapter 15: Congestive Heart Failure). Her heart rate of 50 beats/minute is a clinical sign that iatrogenically-induced bradycardia is a concern. Her maintenance dose of digoxin could be recalculated based upon her renal function (see Chapter 2: Clinical Pharmacokinetics and Chapter 32: Dosing of Drugs in Renal Failure).[142] A serum concentration of digoxin also should be obtained and the next dose of digoxin withheld until the laboratory test results are known. The gastrointestinal side effect of anorexia resulting in L.A.'s poor eating habits and her central nervous system effects of confusion, fatigue, and malaise are compatible with excessive digoxin effects.

Drug Effects on Other Assessments. Functional assessment of the geriatric patient is difficult enough without the confounding variable of multiple drug therapy. The influence of medication should never be overlooked as a potential source of functional deficits. Table 101.13 lists several examples of drugs which can interfere with the functional, physical, social, and psychological assessment of the older patient.

References

1   **Fowles DG.** A profile of older Americans: 1991. Washington, DC: 1991; USDHHSAoA/AARP Publication No. PF3049(1291)D996.

2   **Campbell WH.** Issues and priorities for research in geriatric pharmaceutical care. Drug Intell Clin Pharm. 1981;15:111.

3   **US Bureau of the Census.** Decennial census of population 1900–1983 and projection of the population of the U.S. 1982–2050. Washington, DC: US Bureau of the Census, 1982; publication no. 922. (Current population reports, Series P-25).

4   **Siegal JS, Taeber CM.** Demographic perspectives of the long-lived society. Daedalus. 1986;115:72.

5   **Simonson W.** Medications and the older patients: a guide for promoting proper use. Rockville, MD: Aspen Systems Corp.; 1984:8.

6   **Davis K.** Get ready for the era of geriatric care. Geriatrics. 1983;38:34.

7   **Lamy PP.** Prescribing for the older patients. 1st ed. Littleton, MA: PSG Publishing Co., Inc.; 1980:109.

8   **Schneider EL, Guralnik JM.** The aging of America: impact on health care costs. JAMA. 1990;263:2335.

9   **Perlman R.** Introduction to part I. In: Perlman R, ed. Family Home Care: Critical Issues for Services and Policies. New York: The Haworth Press; 1983.

10   **Shaughnessy PW, Kramer AM.** The increased needs of patients in nursing homes and patients receiving home health care. N Engl J Med. 1990;322:21.

11   **Lamy PP.** Geriatric drug therapy. Am Fam Physician. 1986;34:118.

12   **Baum C et al.** Prescription drug use in 1984 and changes over time. Med Care. 1988;26:105.

13   **Lamy PP.** Patterns of prescribing and drug use. In: Butler RN, Bearn AG, eds. The Aging Process: Therapeutic Implications. New York: Raven Press; 1985:53.

14   **Helling DK et al.** Medication use characteristics in the older patients: the Iowa 65+ Rural Health Study. J Am Geriatr Soc. 1987;35:4.

15   **May FE et al.** Prescribed and nonprescribed drug use in an ambulatory older patients population. South Med J. 1982;75:522.

16   **Hale WE et al.** Drug use in an ambulatory older patients population: a five year update. Drug Intell Clin Pharm. 1987;21:530.

17   **Benson JW.** Drug utilization patterns in geriatric drugs in the US—1986. J Geriatr Drug Ther. 1987;1:1.

18   **Anon.** US Senate Special Committee on Aging—Prescription drug prices: are we getting our money's worth? NARD Newsletter. 1989;3:1.

19   **Anon.** Health costs for older patients dramatically increase (study by the US House Select Committee on Aging). Pharmacy Today. 1990;29:2.

20   **Stewart RB, Caranasos GJ.** Medication compliance in the older patients. Med Clin North Am. 1989;73:1551.

21   **Facts about drug use in the older patients.** Am Pharm. 1993;NS33:6.

22   **Swift CG.** Clinical pharmacology in the older patients. Scott Med J. 1979; 24:221.

23   **Brater DC.** Resistance to loop diuretics. Drugs. 1985;30:427.

24   **Rudy DW et al.** Loop diuretics for chronic renal insufficiency. Ann Intern Med. 1991;115:360.

25   **Bender AD.** The effect of increasing age on the distribution of peripheral blood flow in man. J Am Geriatr Soc. 1965;13:192.

26   **Riesenberg DE.** Studies reshape some views of the aging heart. JAMA. 1986; 255:871.

27   **Shock NW et al.** Age differences in the water content of the body as related to basal oxygen consumption in males. J Gerontol. 1963;18:1.

28   **Novak IP.** Aging, total body potassium, fat-free mass, and cell mass in males and females between ages 18 and 35 years. J Gerontol. 1972;27:438.

29   **Greenblatt DJ et al.** Toxicity of high-dose flurazepam in the elderly. Clin Pharmacol Ther. 1977;21:355.

30   **Greenblatt DJ.** Reduced serum albumin concentration in the older patients: a report from the Boston Collaborative Drug Surveillance Program. J Am Geriatr Soc. 1979;27:20.

31   **Jusko WJ, Weintraub M.** Myocardial distribution of digoxin and renal function. Clin Pharmacol Ther. 1974;16:449.

32   **Mayersohn MB.** Special pharmacokinetic considerations in the elderly. In: Evans WE et al., eds. Applied Pharmacokinetics: Principles of Therapeutic Drug Monitoring. 3rd ed. Vancouver: Applied Therapeutics; 1992.

33   **Farah F et al.** Hepatic drug acetylation and oxidation: effects of aging in man. Br Med J. 1977;2:255.

34   **O'Malley K et al.** Effect of age and sex on human drug metabolism. Br Med J. 1971;3:607.

35   **Thompson EN et al.** Effect of age on liver function with particular reference to bromsulphalein excretion. Gut. 1965;6:266.

36   **Triggs EJ et al.** Pharmacokinetics in the older patients. Eur J Clin Pharmacol. 1975;8:55.

37   **Geokas MC et al.** The aging gastrointestinal tract. Am J Surg. 1969;117:881.

38   **Crooks J et al.** Pharmacokinetics in the older patients. Clin Pharmacokinet. 1976;1:280.

39   **Hewick DS et al.** The effect of age on sensitivity to warfarin sodium. Br J Pharmacol. 1975;2:189P.

40   **Shader RI et al.** Absorption and disposition of chlordiazepoxide in young and older patients male volunteers. J Clin Pharmacol. 1977;17:709.

41   **Klotz U et al.** Effects of age and liver disease on disposition and elimination of diazepam in adult man. J Clin Invest. 1975;55:347.

42   **Nies AS et al.** Altered hepatic blood flow and drug disposition. Clin Pharmacokinet. 1976;1:125.

43   **Rowe JW et al.** The effect of age on creatinine clearance in man: a cross sectional and longitudinal study. J Gerontol. 1976;31:155.

44   **Rowe JW et al.** The influence of age on renal response to water deprivation in man. Nephron. 1976;17:270.

45   **Epstein M et al.** Age as a determinant of renal sodium conservation. J Lab Clin Med. 1976;87:411.

46   **Baylis EM et al.** Effects of renal function on plasma digoxin levels in older patients ambulant patients in domiciliary practice. Br Med J. 1972;1:338.

47   **Leikola E et al.** On oral penicillin levels in young and geriatric patients. J Gerontol. 1957;12:48.

48   **de Wardener HE.** Renal function in relation to age. In: The Kidney. 4th ed. New York: Churchill Livingstone; 1973:100.

49   **Lindeman RD et al.** Longitudinal studies on the rate of decline in renal function with age. J Am Geriatr Soc. 1985;33:278.

50   **Bennett WM et al.** Drug prescribing in renal failure: Dosing guidelines for adults. American College of Physicians; 1991.

51   **Swan SK, Bennett WM.** Drug dosing guidelines in patients with renal failure. West J Med. 1992;156:633.

52   **Cockcroft DW, Gault MH.** Prediction of creatinine clearance from serum creatinine. Nephron. 1976;16:31.

53   **O'Connell MB et al.** Predictive performance of equations to estimate creatinine clearance in hospitalized elderly patients. Ann Pharmacother. 1992; 26:627.

54   **Smythe M et al.** Estimating creatinine clearance in elderly patients with low serum creatinine concentrations. Am J Hosp Pharm. 1994;51:198.

55   **Lipsitz LA.** Orthostatic hypotension in the older patients. N Engl J Med. 1989; 321:952.

56   **Davis TA et al.** Orthostatic hypotension: therapeutic alternatives for geriatric patients. DICP, Ann Pharmacother. 1989;23:750.

57   **Blumenthal MD et al.** Dizziness and

falling in elderly outpatients. Am J Psychiatry. 1980;137:203.

58 **Overstall PW et al.** Falls in the older patients related to postural imbalance. Br Med J. 1977;1:261.

59 **Anon.** Drugs in the older patients. Med Lett Drugs Ther. 1979;21:43.

60 **Castleden CM et al.** Increased sensitivity to nitrazepam in old age. Br Med J. 1977;1:10.

61 **Smith BH et al.** Aging and the nervous system. Geriatrics. 1975;30:109.

62 **Roth M.** Senile dementia and its borderlans. Proc Annu Meet Am Psychopathol Assoc. 1980;69:205.

63 **Heinsimer JA et al.** The impact of aging on adrenergic receptor function: clinical and biochemical aspects. J Am Geriatr Soc. 1985;33:184.

64 **Samorajski T.** Age-related changes in brain biogenic amines. In: Schneider EL, ed. Aging. Vol. I. Clinical, Morphologic and Neurochemical Aspects in the Aging Central Nervous System. New York: Raven Press; 1975:199.

65 **Larson EB et al.** Adverse drug reactions associated with global cognitive impairment in older patients persons. Ann Intern Med. 1987;107:169.

66 **Anon.** Surgeon General's workshop on health promotion and aging: summary recommendations of the medication working group. JAMA. 1989;262:1755.

67 **Canaday BR.** OBRA '90: A Practical Guide to Effecting Pharmaceutical Care. Washington, DC: American Pharmaceutical Association; 1994.

68 **Kelly A, Smith TW.** Digoxin in heart failure: implications of recent trials. J Am Coll Cardiol. 1993;22(Suppl. A): 107A.

69 **Chung EK.** Maintenance digitalization in asymptomatic older patients heart disease patients. JAMA. 1980;244:2561.

70 **Cressman WA et al.** Pharmacokinetics of tolmetin, a new antiinflammatory agent. Clin Pharmacol Ther. 1974;15: 203.

71 **Bartus RT et al.** The cholinergic hypothesis of geriatric memory dysfunction. Science. 1982;217:408.

72 **Rovner BW et al.** Self-care capacity and anticholinergic drug levels in nursing home patients. Am J Psychiatr. 1988;145:107.

73 **Beers M et al.** Psychoactive medication use in intermediate-care facility residents. JAMA. 1988;260:3016.

74 **Williams BR et al.** Improving medication use in the nursing home. In: Rubenstein LZ, Wieland D, eds. Improving Care in the Nursing Home: Comprehensive Reviews of Clinical Research. Newbury Park: Sage Publications; 1993:33.

75 **Cantu TG et al.** Prescription of neuroleptics for geriatric nursing home patients. Hosp Community Psychiatry. 1989;40:654.

76 **Wamboldt FS et al.** Digitalis intoxication misdiagnosed as depression by primary care physicians. Am J Psychiatry. 1986;143:219.

77 **Ray WA et al.** Benzodiazepines of long and short elimination half-life and the risk of hip fracture. JAMA. 1989; 262:3303.

78 **Miller DB et al.** Physicians' attitudes toward the ill, aged and nursing homes. J Am Geriatr Soc. 1976;24:498.

79 **Simmons K.** Caring for the older patients: challenge for now and the 21st-century medicine. JAMA. 1986;255: 3057.

80 **Wilcox SM et al.** Inappropriate drug-prescribing for the community-dwelling elderly. JAMA. 1994;272:292.

81 **Lamy PP.** Nonprescription drugs and the elderly. Am Fam Physician. 1989; 39:175.

82 **Hurwitz N.** Predisposing factors in adverse reactions to drugs. Br Med J. 1969;1:536.

83 **Evashwick CJ.** Aging and health: the role of self-medication. Nonprescription Drug Manufacturers Association. Washington, DC: 1991; publication no. VMW491-15M.

84 **FDA gets number on OTC workload.** NDMA Executive Newsletter. 1991; 25:2.

85 **Einarson TR.** Drug-related hospital admission. Ann Pharmacother. 1993; 27:832.

86 **Eisenberg DM et al.** Unconventional medicine in the United States—prevalence, cost, and patterns of use. N Engl J Med. 1993;328:246.

87 **Green LW et al.** Programs to reduce drug errors in the elderly: direct and indirect evidence from patient education. In: Improving Medication Compliance. Reston: National Pharmaceutical Council; 1985.

88 **Schering Report XIV: Improving patient compliance.** Kenilworth, NJ: Schering Laboratories; 1992.

89 **Jackson JE et al.** Reliability of drug histories in a specialized geriatric outpatient clinic. J Gen Intern Med. 1989; 4:39.

90 **Whitney HAK Jr et al.** Medication compliance: a healthcare problem. Ann Pharmacother. 1993;27(Suppl.):S1.

91 **Anon.** Emerging issues in pharmaceutical cost containment. Reston: National Pharmaceutical Council; 1992; 2:1.

92 **Anon.** Applied Research Techniques Survey. Washington, DC: American Association of Retired Persons; 1984.

93 **Weintraub M.** Compliance in the elderly. Clin Geriatr Med. 1990;6:445.

94 **Burris JF et al.** Therapeutic adherence in the elderly: transdermal clonidine compared to oral verapamil for hypertension. Am J Med. 1991;91(Suppl. 1A):22S.

95 **Dwyer MS et al.** Improving medication compliance through the use of modern dosage forms. J Pharm Technol. 1986;2:166.

96 **Morgan TO et al.** Compliance and the elderly's hypertensive. Drugs. 1986; 31(Suppl.):174.

97 **Hakitt RL.** Patient compliance: tapping into a billion-dollar drug market. Pharm Exec. 1989;46–52.

98 **Tett SE et al.** Impact of pharmacist interventions on medication management by the elderly: a review of the literature. Ann Pharmacother. 1993;27:80.

99 **Lichtenstein MJ et al.** Validation of screening tools for identifying hearing-impaired older patients in primary care. JAMA. 1988;259:2875.

100 **Bess FH et al.** Hearing impairment as a determinant of function in the older patients. J Am Geriatr Soc. 1989;37: 123.

101 **Uhlmann RF et al.** Relationship of hearing impairment to dementia and cognitive dysfunction in older adults. JAMA. 1989;261:1916.

102 **Jinks MJ et al.** Prescription label and container preferences in a geriatric population. J Geriatr Drug Ther. 1991; 5:55.

103 **Jinks MJ, Baker DE.** Addressing audiences of older adults. J Geriatr Drug Ther. 1989;1:89.

104 **Luscombe DK et al.** A survey of prescription label preferences among community pharmacy patrons. J Clin Pharm Ther. 1992;17:241.

105 **Lamy PP.** The elderly, communications and compliance. Pharm Times. 1992;58:33.

106 **Jinks MJ, Raschko RR.** A profile of alcohol and prescription drug abuse in a high-risk community-based elderly population. DICP, Ann Pharmacother. 1990;24:971.

107 **Hood JC, Murphy JE.** Patient noncompliance can lead to hospital readmissions. Hospitals. 1978;52:79.

108 **Bero LA et al.** Characterization of geriatric drug-related hospital readmissions. Medical Care. 1991;29:989.

109 **Mallet L.** Counseling in special populations: the elderly patient. Am Pharm. 1992;NS32:71.

110 **Tanner LA et al.** Spontaneous adverse reaction reporting in the older patients for 1986. J Geriatr Drug Ther. 1989;3: 31.

111 **Harper CM et al.** Drug-induced illness in the older patients. Postgrad Med. 1989;86:245.

112 **Lamy PP.** Hazards of drug use in the older patients. Postgrad Med. 1984;76: 50.

113 **Berlinger WG et al.** Adverse drug reactions in the older patients. Geriatrics. 1984;39:45.

114 **Darnell JC et al.** Medication use by ambulatory older patients—an in-home survey. J Am Geriatr Soc. 1986; 34:1.

115 **Kusserow R.** Drug misuse among the older patients. Report of the Inspector General of the U.S. Department of HHS: January 1989.

116 **Col N et al.** The role of medication noncompliance and adverse drug reaction in hospitalization of the elderly. Arch Intern Med. 1990;150:841.

117 **Colt HG, Shapiro AP.** Drug-induced illness as a cause for admission to a community hospital. J Am Geriatr Soc. 1989;37:323.

118 **Grymonpre RE et al.** Drug-associated hospital admissions in older medical patients. J Am Geriatr Soc. 1988;36: 1092.

119 **Geurian KL et al.** Potential drug-drug interactions in an ambulatory geriatric population. J Geriatr Drug Ther. 1992; 7:67.

120 **Costa AJ.** Potential drug interactions in an ambulatory geriatric population. Fam Pract. 1991;8:234.

121 **Schneider JK et al.** Adverse drug reactions in an elderly outpatient population. Am J Hosp Pharm. 1992;49:90.

122 **Carbonin P et al.** Is age an independent risk factor of adverse drug reactions in hospitalized medical patients? J Am Geriatr Soc. 1991;39:1093.

123 **Gurwitz JH, Avorn J.** The ambiguous relation between aging and adverse drug reactions. Ann Intern Med. 1991; 114:957.

124 **O'Brien JG, Kursch JE.** Health prescribing for the elderly. Postgrad Med. 1987;82:147.

125 **Montamat SC et al.** Management of drug therapy in the elderly. N Engl J Med. 1989;321:303.

126 **Karki SD et al.** Impact of a team approach on reducing polypharmacy. Consult Pharm. 1991;6:133.

127 **Wedgwood J.** The place of rehabilitation in geriatric medicine: an overview. Int Rehabil Med. 1985;7:107.

128 **Brotman HB.** Every ninth American: an analysis for the chairman of the select committee on aging, House of Representatives. Washington, D.C.: US Government Printing Office, 1982; Comm pub no. 1-97-332.

129 **DeLisa JA et al.** Rehabilitation medicine: past, present and future. In: DeLisa JA, ed. Rehabilitation Medicine: Principles and Practice. Philadelphia: Lippincott; 1988:3.

130 **World Health Organization.** International classification of impairments, disabilities, and handicaps: a manual of classification relating to the consequences of disease. Geneva: World Health Organization; 1980.

131 **Thomas DR et al.** Inpatient community-based geriatric assessment reduces subsequent mortality. J Am Geriatr Soc. 1993;41:101.

132 **Bjornson DC, Hiner WO Jr.** Evaluation of the effects of clinical pharmacists on inpatient health care outcomes. Presented at ASHP Midyear Clinical Meeting. Orlando, FL: 1992 Dec.

133 **Murray MD et al.** Factors contributing to medication noncompliance in older patients public housing tenants. Drug Intell Clin Pharm. 1986;20:146.

134 **Meyer ME et al.** Assessment of geriatric patients' functional ability to take medication. Drug Intell Clin Pharm. 1989;23:171.

135 **Owens NJ et al.** The relationship between comprehensive functional assessment and optimal pharmacotherapy in the older patient. DICP, Ann Pharmacother. 1989;23:847.

136 **Larson EB et al.** Adverse reactions associated with global cognitive impairment in older patients persons. Ann Intern Med. 1987;107:169.

137 **Gordon M et al.** Drugs and the aging brain. Geriatrics. 1988;5:69.

138 **Adams CD.** Metoclopramide and depression. Ann Intern Med. 1985;103: 960.

139 **Hughes JD et al.** Mental confusion associated with ranitidine. Med J Aust. 1983;2:12.

140 **Aldler LE et al.** Cimetidine toxicity manifested as paranoia and hallucinations. Am J Psychiatry. 1980;137: 1112.

141 **Henann NE et al.** Famotidine associated mental confusion in older patients. Drug Intell Clin Pharm. 1988;22:976.

142 **Reuning RH et al.** Digoxin. In: Evans WE et al., eds. Applied Pharmacokinetics: Principles of Therapeutic Drug Monitoring. 3rd ed. Vancouver: Applied Therapeutics; 1992.

Geriatric Dementias

Bradley R Williams

Prevalence 102-1
Clinical Diagnosis 102-1
Alzheimer's Disease 102-2
Etiology 102-2
Neuropathology 102-3
Clinical Presentation and Diagnosis 102-4
Prognosis 102-4
Treatment 102-5
Ergoloid mesylates 102-5
Tacrine 102-5
Investigational agents 102-6
Cholinergic agents 102-6
Nootropics 102-6
Monoamine oxidase inhibitors (MAOIs) 102-7
Vascular agents 102-7
Other agents 102-7
Vascular Dementias 102-7
Etiology 102-7
Neuropathology 102-7

Clinical Presentation 102-8
Diagnosis 102-8
Treatment 102-9
Smoking cessation 102-9
Antihypertensive therapy 102-9
Antiplatelet therapy 102-9
Hemorrheologic therapy 102-10
Behavioral Disturbances in Dementia 102-10
Anxiety 102-10
Psychosis 102-10
Aggressive Behaviors 102-11
Depression 102-11
Symptoms 102-11
Treatment 102-11
Social Support 102-12
Pseudodementia 102-12
Clinical Presentation and Diagnosis 102-12
Depression 102-12
Medications 102-12
Treatment 102-12

With the continuing increase in the elderly population, the prevalence of cognitive disorders will continue to rise. The majority of individuals with dementias suffer from primary degenerative dementia, or Alzheimer's disease. Although many people believe that dementia and Alzheimer's disease are synonymous, in fact, there are several other forms of dementia. Alzheimer's disease is the most common cause of dementia, accounting for about one-half of all diagnosed cases.[1] Vascular dementias, including multi-infarct dementia and Binswanger's disease are the second most common dementias, with Picks's disease, Parkinson's disease dementia, pseudodementia, and other forms occurring less frequently.[1]

Prevalence

The exact prevalence of dementia is difficult to determine for a number of reasons, including a lack of universally accepted diagnostic criteria, demographic variables, and the lack of well-designed epidemiologic studies.[2-5] Estimates have ranged from a prevalence of 2.5% in Great Britain to 24.6% in the former Soviet Union.[3] Studies in the U.S. have estimated the prevalence of dementias from 3.5% to 16.1% for the population aged 65 and older.[6,7] The worldwide prevalence of Alzheimer's disease appears to be about 1% of the elderly population, with an exponential age-related increase.[5,8] The prevalence in the U.S. may be over 10% of those aged 65 and above, increasing sharply with age, from 3% among those 65 to 74 years, to as much as 47.2% of those over 85 years of age.[9,10] The incidence of dementia for people age 30 and above in the U.S. has been estimated at 187 new cases/100,000 population per year, with 123/100,000 diagnosed as Alzheimer's disease.[11]

The cost of dementia is staggering. The average annual cost of treating a dementia patient is estimated to be over $22,000 in a nursing home and over $12,000 at home.[12,13] This translates into over $31 billion for the nation and possibly as high as $80 billion.[14,15] By the year 2040, the cost in 1985 dollars is expected to be as high as $149 billion.[16]

Clinical Diagnosis

Dementia is a syndrome, the most prominent feature of which is impaired short-term and long-term memory. According to DSM-IV diagnostic criteria, however, multiple cognitive deficits occur in a true dementia (see Table 102.1).[17] One important factor must be present before a disorder can be classified as a dementia: multiple cognitive deficits must be present, and these must be sufficiently severe to interfere with normal social functioning.

Table 102.1	Diagnostic Criteria for Dementia of the Alzheimer's Type[a,b]

1) The presence of multiple cognitive deficits manifested by both:
   - Impaired memory ($\downarrow$ ability to learn new information or to retrieve information previously learned), and

   - At least 1 of the following:
     Aphasia (language difficulties)
     Apraxia (diminished ability to perform motor activities in the presence of intact motor function)
     Agnosia (inability to recognize or name objects despite intact sensory function)
     Disruption of executive function (diminished ability to plan, organize)

2) The deficits above significantly interfere with normal work or social activities and represent a decline from previous ability to function

3) The deficits above cannot be attributed to any of the following:
   - CNS conditions that cause progressive cognitive or memory impairment (e.g., cerebrovascular disease)

   - Systemic conditions known to cause dementia (e.g., hypothyroidism, neurosyphilis, HIV infection)

   - Substance-induced conditions (e.g., drug toxicity)

4) The deficits do not occur exclusively during the course of a delirium

5) The disturbance is not better accounted for by another Axis I disorder (schizophrenia, major depressive disorder)

[a] Adapted from reference 17.
[b] CNS = Central nervous system; HIV = Human immunodeficiency virus.

The hallmark of dementia is impaired short- and long-term memory, which is frequently the primary complaint of patients or the first symptom noted by the family.[17] Memory loss frequently accompanies several diseases or disorders in elderly individuals; therefore, a complete history and physical examination is essential in excluding systemic illness as a cause of the dementia.[18] (See Table 102.2.) Laboratory and other tests to assist in differentiating dementia from other disorders are listed in Table 102.3. In patients with primary degenerative dementia, or Alzheimer's disease, test results will generally be normal; evidence of cerebrovascular disease will be present in those with vascular dementias.

Brain imaging, such as a computed tomography (CT) scan or magnetic resonance imaging (MRI), can be useful in establishing the presence of a dementia, but neither is diagnostic.[18] Computed tomography is useful when a space-occupying lesion, such as a tumor, is suspected as a possible cause. Magnetic resonance imaging is capable of identifying small infarcts such as those found in some vascular dementias, and atrophy of subcortical structures such as the brainstem.[18]

The initial test in mental status screening is generally the Folstein Mini-Mental Status Exam.[19] This test rapidly assesses orientation, registration, attention and calculation, recall, and language. Patients with dementia exhibit deficits in multiple areas. Those who score below the normal range on the Mini-Mental Status Exam or who exhibit symptoms characteristic of dementia (see Table 102.1) receive further testing. The Blessed Dementia Scale evaluates daily functional capacity (e.g., shopping, performing household tasks), activities of daily living (e.g., eating, dressing, toileting) and personality. The Blessed Information-Memory-Concentration Test evaluates orientation, memory, and concentration.[20] Both of these instruments are subject to error, reporting both false-positives and false-negatives.[18] Therefore, additional psychometric testing frequently is ordered to further establish the presence and type of dementia.

Dementias may be classified as cortical or subcortical, according to the areas of the brain preferentially affected by the disorder. Alzheimer's disease, a typical cortical dementia, disrupts the cerebral cortex. Patients with cortical dementias display impaired language rather than speech, a learning deficit (amnesia), reduced higher cortical functions (e.g., inability to perform calculations, poor judgment), and an unconcerned or disinhibited affect. Subcortical dementias such as multi-infarct dementia primarily affect the basal ganglia, thalamus, and brainstem. Deficits include ab-

Table 102.2	Disorders Causing Dementia Symptoms
CNS Disorders[a]	Systemic Illness
Adjustment disorder (e.g., inability to adjust to retirement)	Cardiovascular disease
	arrhythmia
Amnestic syndrome (e.g., isolated memory impairment)	heart failure
	vascular occlusion
Delirium	Deficiency states
Depression	vitamin B$_{12}$
Drugs and toxins	folate
antihypertensive agents	Infections
anxiolytics/sedatives	Metabolic disorders
CNS depressants	adrenal
H$_2$-blocking agents	glucose
hypoglycemics	renal failure
Intracranial causes	thyroid
brain abscess	
normal pressure hydrocephalus	
stroke	
subdural hematoma	
tumor	

^{a} CNS = Central nervous system.

Table 102.3	Dementia Screening Tests
Test	Rationale for Testing
CBC with sedimentation rate	Anemic anoxia; infection; neoplasms
Metabolic screen	
Serum electrolytes	Hypernatremia, hyponatremia; renal function
BUN, creatinine	Renal function
Bilirubin	Hepatic dysfunction (e.g., portal systemic encephalopathy, hepatocerebral degeneration)
Thyroid function	Hypothyroidism, apathetic hyperthyroidism
Iron, B$_{12}$, folate	Deficiency states (B$_{12}$, folate neuropathies), anemias
Stool occult blood	Blood loss, anemia
Syphilis serology	Neurosyphilis
UA	Infection, proteinuria
Chest roentgenogram	Neoplasms; infection; airway disease (anoxia)
ECG	Cardiac disease (stagnant anoxia)
Brain scan	Cerebral tumors; cerebrovascular disease
Mental status testing	General cognitive screen
Depression testing	Depression; pseudodementia

^{a} BUN = Blood urea nitrogen; CBC = Complete blood cell count; ECG = Electrocardiogram; UA = Urinalysis.

normal motor function, disrupted speech patterns rather than language difficulties, forgetfulness (impaired recall), slowed cognitive function, and an apathetic or depressed affect.[1]

Alzheimer's Disease

Etiology

Although a number of etiologies have been advanced for Alzheimer's disease [dementia of the Alzheimer type (DAT)], a definitive cause has yet to be determined. Aluminum toxicity, immunological abnormalities, hereditary predisposition, viral infection, and cellular dysfunction are among the more commonly proposed causes.[1] While elevated aluminum concentration has been noted in dementia of the Alzheimer type patients, this finding has not been consistent.[21-23] For example, patients with aluminum toxicity, as seen in dialysis dementia, do not exhibit dementia of the Alzheimer type-type lesions.[24] Increased concentrations of cerebral aluminum may be a secondary process resulting from underlying pathology.[15] Young (15 to 19 years) or old ($\geq$40 years) maternal age[25-28] and head trauma also seem to be associated with a propensity for Alzheimer's disease.

Genetics play a significant role in the development of dementia of the Alzheimer type. The high familial occurrence of Alzheimer's dementia is consistent with an autosomal dominant trait.[29,30] The risk to first-degree relatives of patients with Alzheimer's is 24% to 48%, and may be as high as 64% for offspring.[31-34] Familial dementia of the Alzheimer type is associated with an early onset, faster progression, family history of psychiatric problems, and more prominent language difficulties.[29,31,35,36] In families with a history of Down's syndrome or other defects on chromosome 21, the prevalence of dementia of the Alzheimer type is increased significantly. Alzheimer's disease affects virtually all Down's syndrome patients who survive into old age.[35,37,38] Differences in risk based upon age-at-onset and discordance for the disease among monozygotic twins, however, indicate some heterogeneity in the genetic etiology.[34,35,39] Clinically, patients with familial dementia of the Alzheimer type are indistinguishable from those with non-familial, or sporadic, forms of the disease, suggesting a combination of genetic and environmental causes.[26,36]

Abnormalities in serum protein and alterations in immune function are frequently found among patients with Alzheimer's disease. Amyloid precursor protein (APP), a normal protein found throughout the body (e.g., platelets and peripheral lymphocytes),[40] maps on chromosome 21 and is produced in excess in patients with Down's syndrome.[37] Due to overproduction or transcription errors, an abnormal subunit (i.e., beta-amyloid), is produced.[37,41] This finding is consistent in families with a high incidence of dementia of the Alzheimer type, especially those with early onset (before age 65) forms.[35,37,41]

Amyloid protein can be found commonly in the neuritic plaques which occur in dementia of the Alzheimer type; and cerebral amyloid angiopathy occurs in 50% to 90% of patients with progressive dementia and neurofibrillary degeneration.[42,43] Amyloid protein also is noted in blood vessel walls of patients with Alzheimer's disease.[40] Beta-amyloid protein deposits occur early in the course of Alzheimer's dementia and much current research focuses on its role in the etiology of the disease.[40] The beta-amyloid associated with dementia of the Alzheimer type is distinct from the amyloid proteins found in other amyloid disorders such as primary amyloidosis or multiple myeloma.[15]

Neuropathology

Brain atrophy is the most obvious finding among dementia of the Alzheimer type patients, with brain weight frequently less than 1 kg.[1] However, the presence of atrophy is not diagnostic for Alzheimer's or other dementias because some degree of atrophy accompanies normal aging.[44] Dementia of the Alzheimer type-induced atrophic changes are found primarily in the temporal, parietal, and frontal areas of the brain: the occipital region, primary motor cortex, and somatosensory areas generally are unaffected.[1] (See Figure 102.1.)

The cerebral cortex displays four major histologic findings in dementia of the Alzheimer type: neurofibrillary tangles, neuritic plaques, amyloid angiopathy, and granulovacuolar degeneration

Fig 102.1 Alzheimer's Disease: MRI Scan Ventricles are enlarged, there is generalized atrophy, with greater atrophy present near the temporal areas.

Figure 102.2 Numerous plaques (large, round bodies) and tangles (tear-shaped bodies) are found throughout the cortex in DAT.

(see Figure 102.2). *Neurofibrillary tangles* (NFTs) are found primarily in the pyramidal regions of the neocortex, hippocampus, and amygdala, but also are noted in areas of the brainstem and locus ceruleus.[1,45] Tangles are a prominent feature of dementia of the Alzheimer type, but can be found in several other brain disorders (e.g., Down's syndrome, postencephalitic Parkinson's disease) and even in normally aging brains, although they are generally less numerous and histologically different.[1,46] Conversely, dementia of the Alzheimer type also may occur in the absence of neurofibrillary tangles.[46]

Tangles are composed of paired helical filaments, combinations of fibrils with a characteristic width and contour, containing a tau protein with an abnormal pattern of phosphate deposition.[1,47,48] Although the nerve structures (axons, dendrites, and nerve terminals) found within neurofibrillary tangles contain amyloid deposits, abnormal axons may occur independently of amyloid deposition; thus, the presence of amyloid protein is not required for the development of tangles.[50] The presence of neurofibrillary tangles in the neocortical areas is associated with the presence of dementia of the Alzheimer type and their number in the nucleus basalis is correlated with the severity and duration of the disease.[51,52]

Neuritic plaques are spherical bodies of tissue composed of granular deposits and remnants of neuronal processes.[1] Plaques may develop from preamyloid deposits with subsequent deposition of amyloid protein and accumulation of oligosaccharide, aggregation of amyloid subunits, and beta-pleating of the protein.[53,54] Neuritic plaques exhibit a three-tiered structure: a central amyloid core, a middle region of swollen axons and dendrites, and an outer zone containing degenerating neuritic processes.[1] The plaques are concentrated in the cerebral cortex and hippocampus, but also are found in the corpus striatum, amygdala, and hypothalamus.[1,55] Rare plaques also have been found in nondemented elderly patients.[51]

Plaques contain an amyloid precursor protein that can be cleaved by a defective metabolic process to form beta-amyloid.[49,56,57] Although beta-amyloid is found in normal as well as dementia of the Alzheimer type subjects, neurofibrillary tangles occurring in the plaques of nondemented subjects do not contain the abnormal tau protein seen in demented individuals.[51] The deposition of amyloid in neuritic plaques correlates with the severity of dementia of the Alzheimer type, and the density of cortical plaques is associated with decreased choline acetyltransferase and the severity of cognitive impairment.[49,58] Beta-amyloid has been identified in plaques associated with Down's syndrome, and in both familial and sporadic forms of dementia of the Alzheimer type.[49,59] The process of development from the time of amyloid deposition to plaque formation may take as long as 30 years.[49,60]

In addition to neuritic plaques, amyloid precursor protein and beta-amyloid produce an *amyloid angiopathy* outside brain tissue. The amyloid precursor protein has been located in the adenohypophysis, adrenal gland, cardiac muscle, and peripheral nervous system.[56] Amyloid deposits, identical to those found in neuritic plaques, have been found in cerebral blood vessels as well as in the vasculature of skin, subcutaneous tissue, and intestine.[1,49,61]

A *granulovacuolar degeneration* is the other major histologic finding in dementia of the Alzheimer type. It consists of clusters of intracytoplasmic vacuoles that contain tiny granules. The vacuoles appear to be specifically located in the pyramidal neurons of the hippocampus. Granulovacuolar degeneration also can occur, albeit rarely, in individuals without dementia.[1]

The loss of cortical neurons that originate in the nucleus basalis and project into the cerebral cortex is the most significant histopathologic consequence of dementia of the Alzheimer type.[1,58,62,63] Cell loss, granulovacuolar degeneration, and neurons with neurofibrillary tangles are concentrated in this area.[1] Accompanying these changes are decreased concentrations of several neurotransmitters and enzymes. Choline acetyltransferase levels are reduced 60% to 90% in the cortical and hippocampal regions.[58] Acetylcholine and acetylcholinesterase also are decreased, while muscarinic receptors in the cortex and hippocampus remain at normal levels or are moderately decreased.[1,58,64] Nicotinic receptor proteins also may be reduced in dementia of the Alzheimer type patients when compared to age-matched controls.[65] Decreased choline acetyltransferase activity has been correlated with plaque density and disease severity;[58] and cortical synapse loss, especially in the midfrontal region, is associated with disease severity.[66]

Although cholinergic activity is the most significantly affected by dementia of the Alzheimer type, other neurochemical systems also are altered. Norepinephrine, serotonin, and gamma-aminobutyric acid levels may be normal or moderately decreased.[1,58,67] Somatostatin and corticotropin releasing factor also are reduced in dementia of the Alzheimer type patients.[58,68]

Clinical Presentation and Diagnosis

1. C.L., a 63-year-old female, complains of increasing memory problems over the past 2 years. She states that she began writing reminder notes to herself, but often forgot to look at the notes. Eventually, she began to lose items around her house, forgot appointments, and failed to pay some important bills. C.L. admits to becoming increasingly depressed over her memory problems, but denies appetite or sleep changes, or suicidal ideation. She also denies hallucinations, delusional thoughts, or symptoms of anxiety. C.L.'s medical history is significant for noninsulin dependent diabetes mellitus which is diet controlled, and bilateral open-angle glaucoma, treated with dipivefrin 0.1%, 1 drop BID. Her family history is negative for stroke and positive for diabetes mellitus and hypertension. She reports that two or three of her maternal relatives had "memory problems" and that one aunt was diagnosed with Alzheimer's disease 5 years ago.

Physical examination reveals a moderately obese woman, well dressed and groomed. Her blood pressure (BP) is 140/86 mm Hg supine and 132/82 mm Hg standing, with pulse rates of 74 beats/min and 78 beats/min, respectively. She is awake, cooperative, and oriented to place and person. The Folstein Mini-Mental score was 24/30, with errors in orientation, attention and calculation (inability to spell "world" backwards), recall and language (difficulty with word finding). Her score on the Blessed Dementia Scale was 25/33, with deficits in personality, memory and concentration and in habits. Neurologi-

cal examination revealed no deficits. The rest of the physical examination was within normal limits.

Laboratory tests performed include renal and liver chemistries, thyroid function tests, glycosylated hemoglobin, vitamin B_{12} and folate levels, syphilis and human immunodeficiency virus (HIV) tests, complete blood count (CBC) with sedimentation rate, and urinalysis. All results were normal with the exception of a fasting glucose level of 150 mg/dL and a glycosylated hemoglobin of 8.4%. Chest x-ray and electrocardiogram (ECG) were normal. Depression testing revealed a sad, mildly anxious individual who was not depressed. What is the most probable diagnosis for C.L.? [SI units: Fasting glucose 8.3 mmol/L; glycosylated hemoglobin 0.084%]

C.L. is in the early stages of Alzheimer's disease. Her score of 24/30 on the Folstein Mini-Mental state indicates mild cognitive impairment as evidenced by errors in orientation, calculation, recall, and language. Personality and habit changes and deficits in memory and concentration are revealed in C.L.'s score on the Blessed Dementia Scale. Secondary medical causes of cognitive impairment can be eliminated by C.L.'s generally normal physical examination and laboratory test results. C.L.'s fasting glucose and glycosylated hemoglobin levels are mildly elevated but cannot account for her significant cognitive decline. MRI or CT scanning may be useful in many cases to help eliminate brain pathology such as stroke, but the lack of any abnormal neurological findings renders imaging in C.L. unnecessary.

Secondary psychiatric causes for C.L.'s decline also can be discounted. Although she is sad and anxious, her absence of alterations in appetite or sleep patterns, absence of suicidal thoughts, and the results of psychological testing indicate C.L. is not depressed. She is fully conscious, alert, and oriented to place and person. She exhibits no psychotic behavior and no evidence of delirium.

C.L.'s slowly progressive decline, its impact on her social and occupational function (forgetting appointments, failing to pay bills), normal physical examination and laboratory findings, and family history meet the DSM-IV criteria for Alzheimer's disease (see Table 102.1); because she is younger than 65 years, she also may be classified as early onset type.[17] Her history and course-to-date satisfy the criteria for dementia of the Alzheimer type and do not indicate a likely alternative explanation for her condition. Thus, C.L. can be classified as probable dementia of the Alzheimer type according to the criteria established by the National Institute of Neurological and Communicative Disorders-Alzheimer's Disease and Related Disorders Association (NINCDS-ADRDA) Task Force (see Table 102.4).[69]

Prognosis

2. What is the likely prognosis for C.L.?

Alzheimer's disease follows a predictable course which may progress over a period of ten or more years.[70] Two common rating scales for dementia are the Global Deterioration Scale and the Clinical Dementia Rating Scale. According to the Global Deterioration Scale (see Table 102.5), C.L.'s impaired social functioning, anxiety, and objective cognitive decline and her continued ability to concentrate and perform some complex skills combined with her preserved affect and social interaction, are consistent with the features of stage three dementia of the Alzheimer type. This stage of Alzheimer's generally is associated with a period of mild cognitive decline.[71] The more general Clinical Dementia Rating Scale also places C.L. in the category of mild dementia.[72] Although she has been clinically diagnosed with dementia of the Alzheimer type, a definite diagnosis requires pathological confirmation at autopsy.[69] Clinical diagnoses of dementia of the Alzheimer type are accurate about 60% to 78% of the time.[73,74]

Table 102.4	NINCDS-ADRDA Criteria for Dementia of the Alzheimer Type[a,69]

Definite DAT

Clinical criteria for probable DAT

Histopathologic evidence for DAT (autopsy or biopsy confirmed)

Probable DAT

Dementia established by clinical examination and documented by mental status testing (e.g., history and physical examination, Folstein Mini-Mental)

Confirmation of dementia by neuropsychological tests (e.g., Blessed Dementia Screen and other tests)

Deficits in at least 2 areas of cognitive function (e.g., language and memory)

Progressive deterioration of memory and other cognitive function

Undisturbed consciousness

Onset between the ages of 40 and 90

Absence of systemic or other brain disease capable of producing dementia

Possible DAT

Atypical onset, presentation, or progression of dementia with an unknown etiology

Presence of a systemic or other brain disease capable of producing dementia, but not thought to be the cause of the dementia

Gradually progressive decline in one intellectual function in the absence of another identifiable cause

Unlikely DAT

Sudden onset

Focal neurological findings (e.g., ↑ DTRs, hemiparesis)

[a] DAT = Dementia of the Alzheimer type; DTRs = Deep tendon reflexes; NINCDS-ADRDA = National Institute of Neurological and Communicative Disorders-Alzheimer's Disease and Related Disorders Association.

Because of technological advances, it is possible to diagnose dementia earlier and to keep patients alive into the final stages of the disease. The early diagnosis of dementia of the Alzheimer type in C.L. will allow her condition to be followed closely and she can be moved into a sheltered environment (e.g., a relative's home, residential care facility, or nursing home) before suffering an injury caused by her poor judgment (e.g., failing to dress properly for the weather, falling). In the later stages, interventions ranging from tube feedings to life support can prolong life. Thus, the prognosis for length of survival for patients such as C.L. is dependent more on the stage at which dementia of the Alzheimer type is diagnosed rather than on the rate of progression of disease symptoms.[75] Death is frequently associated with the development of infections such as pneumonia, urinary tract infections, or decubitus ulcers.

Treatment

3. What is an appropriate initial treatment strategy for C.L.?

Maintaining independence as long as possible is an important goal in treating a patient with dementia. Remaining in familiar surroundings allows patients to function without the added burden of having to attempt to adapt to a strange environment. C.L. appears to be functioning reasonably well at home, although her forgetfulness is causing some problems for her. She is still eating well (her laboratory testing indicated no deficiencies in total protein or albumin, vitamin B$_{12}$, or folic acid) and performing normal daily activities such as dressing, grooming, bathing, and toileting. Some regular supervision from family members, neighbors, or household help will ensure that C.L. remains safe in her own home.

C.L.'s diabetes mellitus and general medical condition also should be monitored closely. Because both hyperglycemia and hypoglycemia can impair cognitive processes, either of these com-plications can exacerbate her memory problems. Concurrent diseases and many medications can reduce function and increase cognitive impairment in demented patients, so any new findings in C.L. must be carefully evaluated to distinguish new problems from a worsening of her dementia.

C.L.'s family needs to be educated about what to expect as her dementia progresses. They should be referred to the Alzheimer's Disease and Related Disorders Association (360 N. Michigan Avenue, Chicago, IL 60601). The association has local affiliates in most major cities which frequently sponsor support groups and will inform families of other resources available in the community.

4. What pharmacotherapeutic options are available for C.L.? Which is most appropriate for C.L. and why?

To date there are no drugs available which can halt or reverse the progression of dementia of the Alzheimer type. However, two agents, ergoloid mesylates (Hydergine) and tacrine (Cognex), have been approved by the Food and Drug Administration (FDA) for the treatment of memory deficits. Before initiating pharmacological treatment it is important to evaluate the potential risks and benefits in C.L. Because of her declining cognitive capacity, she will be at higher risk for noncompliance to therapy and may be unable to recognize or report possible adverse effects. Family supervision may be required for purposes of monitoring therapy.

Ergoloid Mesylates

Ergoloid mesylates are considered metabolic enhancers because of their effects on various neuronal processes and neurotransmitters.[76] The FDA-approved dosage is 1 mg three times daily, but doses up to 12 mg/day have been used.[77] Although a number of clinical trials have shown statistically significant improvement in mood, cognitive function, and physical symptoms, improvement in psychometric testing and overall functional capacity generally have been unimpressive.[77–79] A liquid-filled capsule, which has marginally improved bioavailability, has no clinical advantages over the oral or sublingual preparations.[80,81]

Tacrine

Because acetylcholine is significantly reduced in dementia of the Alzheimer type, several efforts have aimed at increasing its cerebral concentrations. This can be done by supplying choline as a substrate for synthesis, providing an agonist, or preventing its

Table 102.5	Stages of Dementia of the Alzheimer Type[a]	
Stage of Cognitive Decline	**Features**	
No cognitive decline	Normal cognitive state	
Very mild cognitive decline	Forgetfulness, subjective complaints only; no objective decline	
Mild cognitive decline	Objective decline through psychiatric testing; work and social impairment; mild anxiety and denial	
Moderate cognitive decline	Concentration, complex skills decline; flat affect and withdrawal	
Moderately-severe cognitive decline	Early dementia; difficulty in interactions; unable to recall or recognize people or places	
Severe cognitive decline	Requires assistance with bathing, toileting; behavioral symptoms present (agitation, delusions, aggressive behavior)	
Very severe cognitive decline	Loss of psychomotor skills and verbal abilities; incontinence; total dependence	

[a] Adapted from reference 71.

degradation with a cholinesterase inhibitor.[82] Tacrine, an acetylcholinesterase inhibitor, has been approved for the symptomatic treatment of mild to moderate dementia of the Alzheimer type. Tacrine, also known as THA (tetrahydroaminoacridine), began to receive attention as a potential treatment for dementia of the Alzheimer type following a report of its success in reversing symptoms in 17 patients.[83,84] Although the scientific validity of this report was questioned, it stimulated a great deal of research interest.[85] Early studies in patients with probable dementia of the Alzheimer type investigated the combination of tacrine plus lecithin, theorizing that supplying lecithin, a choline precursor, would increase acetylcholine synthesis in the central nervous system (CNS) and tacrine would inhibit acetylcholine metabolism.[86,87] Statistically significant improvement was noted in several subjects using lecithin in doses of up to 10.8 gm/day and tacrine doses up to 100 mg/day; however, clinically significant changes in subjects were not noted.[86,87] In a 12-week trial using up to 80 mg/day of tacrine, 51% of patients completing the trial improved when rated by both caregivers and physicians.[88] A 30-week trial in patients with mild to moderate dementia of the Alzheimer type, using doses up to 160 mg/day also demonstrated small, but significant, improvement in approximately one-third of subjects.[89]

It is unlikely that dramatic or long-lasting improvement will be seen in C.L.'s cognitive abilities with either ergoloid mesylates or tacrine. She has no contraindication to either medication so the choice of drug should be based upon which agent is more likely to produce a positive response. Ergoloid mesylates possess some α-adrenergic blocking activity and enhance brain metabolism in part through improved cerebral blood flow. Neither α-adrenergic function nor cerebral blood flow are compromised in Alzheimer's disease. In contrast, tacrine produces its effects by increasing central cholinergic activity which is directly and significantly reduced in dementia of the Alzheimer type. Therefore, tacrine would be the more appropriate agent to use in C.L. The primary concerns before initiating therapy are whether the patient will be able to tolerate the drug's adverse effects and be able to adhere to the strict requirements for clinical monitoring.

5. How should treatment with tacrine be instituted for C.L. and how should therapy be monitored?

Due to frequent and potentially serious adverse reactions, strict dosing guidelines have been developed for tacrine by the manufacturer and the FDA. Treatment should begin at a dose of 10 mg four times daily between meals and at bedtime. If after six weeks C.L. is not experiencing any adverse effects the dose should be increased to 20 mg four times daily. The dosage may be increased by 40 mg/day at six-week intervals until the patient experiences adverse effects or the maximum daily dosage of 160 mg is reached.[90] If C.L. exhibits side effects other than elevated hepatic enzymes at doses less than 40 mg four times daily, the tacrine dose should be reduced to the maximum amount tolerated and therapy continued.

Tacrine possesses significant cholinergic activity and causes typical cholinergic adverse effects. Nausea, vomiting, or diarrhea occur in over 5% of patients. Abdominal pain, dyspepsia, and rash also occur frequently.[88] The most important adverse effect, however, is hepatotoxicity which can be detected by elevations in alanine aminotransferase (ALT) serum levels. Serum concentrations of ALT increase above the normal range in almost 50% of patients treated with tacrine but return to the normal range after a brief period.[91] The ALT serum concentrations increase to more than three times the upper limit of normal in about 25% of patients being treated with tacrine. The risk of hepatotoxicity is greatest during the first 12 weeks of tacrine treatment.[91] The serum concentrations of ALT should be monitored weekly during the first 18 weeks of treatment; subsequently, the ALT serum concentrations can be

monitored every three months. ALT serum concentrations also should be monitored weekly for six weeks following any increase in the dose of tacrine.[90] When serum concentrations of ALT are increased, patients should be managed as outlined in Table 102.6. Patients experiencing jaundice and patients with a total bilirubin serum concentration in excess of 3.0 mg/dL should discontinue tacrine permanently.[90]

Investigational Agents

6. After 12 weeks of treatment with only mild nausea and elevation of ALT serum concentration to 100 IU/L, C.L. and her family decide to stop tacrine treatment because they observed no significant change in C.L.'s cognitive or functional abilities and the weekly blood tests have become burdensome. In addition, C.L. is beginning to exhibit some restlessness and agitated behavior, particularly in the afternoon and evening. What other drug therapy strategies are being investigated for dementia of the Alzheimer type, and which would be appropriate for C.L.? [SI unit: ALT 100 U/L]

Several other agents, including cholinergic agonists, monoamine oxidase inhibitors (MAOIs), and vascular agents are being studied. These protocols are aimed at treatments to modify the disease process rather than to treat associated behavioral problems such as C.L.'s restlessness and agitated behavior. The Alzheimer's Association and many of its local chapters can provide information regarding the studies and their eligibility requirements.

Cholinergic Agents. Efforts to influence cholinergic transmission are among the most well-studied areas for pharmacologic intervention. *Velnacrine maleate*, a hydroxy metabolite of tacrine, improves regional blood flow and modestly improves memory and attention in patients with Alzheimer's.[92-94] As with tacrine, however, hepatic effects of velnacrine maleate are a prominent feature.[93] Physostigmine, another cholinesterase inhibitor, also has been investigated in the treatment of dementia of the Alzheimer type, but results have been inconsistent.[95-97] Intracranial infusions of bethanechol, a cholinergic agonist, exhibited promising results in a pilot study, but a larger trial failed to replicate the findings.[98,99]

Nootropics. A group of gamma-aminobutyric acid (GABA) derivatives has been shown to stimulate brain metabolism and improve cognitive function.[100] The prototype, *piracetam*, has improved some memory function and information transmission in normal adults.[100] Early studies with *oxiracetam* noted improvement in memory and word fluency, attention, concentration, orientation, and improved scores on the Blessed Dementia Scale and other dementia tests;[101-103] however, poor results in other studies have led to the withdrawal of oxiracetam from clinical trials.[100]

Table 102.6	ALT Elevations with Tacrine[a,b]
Elevation	Action
≤3 × Upper limit of normal	Continue with normal dose of titration schedule
>3 to ≤5 × Upper limit of normal	Reduce dose by 40 mg/day. Resume dose titration schedule when ALT returns to normal level
>5 × Upper limit of normal	Stop treatment and monitor ALT levels. After levels have returned to normal, patient may begin treatment again at initial dose of 10 mg QID. Extreme caution should be used in restarting therapy in patients who experience ALT levels >10 × Upper limit of normal

a ALT = Alanine aminotransferase.
b Adapted from reference 90.

Monoamine Oxidase Inhibitors (MAOIs). Findings of decreased central norepinephrine and increased monoamine oxidase Type B (MAO-B) among dementia of the Alzheimer type patients has led to the investigation of the MAO-B inhibitor, *selegiline* (Eldepryl), as a potential treatment.[45,104] Improvement in memory, attention, and social interaction, as well as reductions in anxiety, depression, and tension, have been demonstrated in clinical trials, although a 15-month trial reported minimal improvement in only one neuropsychological measurement.[104–107] Mild improvement on dementia screening tests has been shown in a pilot study using selegiline in combination with tacrine or physostigmine.[108]

Vascular Agents. Both calcium channel blockers and angiotensin-converting enzyme (ACE) inhibitors have been investigated in dementia of the Alzheimer type patients. Calcium-activated enzymes play a role in several memory pathways and regional blood flow may be reduced in dementia.[100,109] One study noted improvement in the Mini-Mental Status Exam and Global Deterioration Scale when comparing nimodipine 30 mg three times daily to placebo.[110] Angiotensin II causes impaired memory function and exists at increased levels in dementia patients.[111] Studies with both captopril and the investigational ACE inhibitor ceranapril have improved memory and various cognitive tests following administration in both demented and nondemented patients.[100,111]

Other Agents. Several hormone and peptide agents have been studied for potential use in dementia of the Alzheimer type. Acetyl-*l*-carnitine is a naturally occurring substance synthesized in mitochondria.[100] Two long-term studies suggest that this agent, which possesses some cholinergic activity, improves several cognitive features of dementia of the Alzheimer type and has the potential to slow the course of the disorder.[112,113] Treatment with somatostatin, a neuropeptide deficient in dementia of the Alzheimer type, has shown disappointing results;[114] a naturally occurring phospholipid, phosphatidylserine, has produced mildly promising results.[115,116] In a retrospective study of aging and dementia, women treated with estrogen postmenopausally were less likely to develop dementia than untreated women.[117]

Two factors must be considered when referring C.L. for investigational treatments. The first is the appropriateness of individual therapies for her and the second is the likelihood that she will be able to comply with a research protocol. C.L. was able to tolerate the cholinergic adverse effects of tacrine and thus would probably not experience difficulty with other cholinergic drugs. Selegiline is currently available commercially as a treatment for Parkinson's disease (see Chapter 51: Parkinson's Disease). Nimodipine (Nimotop) and captopril (Capoten) also are readily available and possibly could be tried in C.L. Because C.L. is currently normotensive, the risk of orthostatic hypotension from selegiline and hypotension caused by the antihypertensive agents make these less desirable if used outside of a research protocol. Inasmuch as C.L. withdrew from tacrine treatment because of an unwillingness to adhere to the required blood tests, it is questionable whether she will be able to comply to a research protocol. Nevertheless, she should be referred to a local investigator to be evaluated for inclusion in a clinical trial. It is not likely that C.L.'s behavioral symptoms would be controlled successfully with any of the investigational drugs and must be addressed separately. (See Behavioral Disturbances in Dementia.)

Vascular Dementias
Etiology

Vascular dementia is a broad classification of cognitive disorders caused by vascular disease. The most common cause of vascular dementia is occlusion of cerebral blood vessels by thrombus or embolus, leading to ischemic brain injury.[1,118] The term multi-infarct dementia (MID) refers specifically to the cognitive decline that follows multiple small or large cerebrovascular occlusions.[119] A number of diseases, including atherosclerosis, arteriosclerosis, and vasculitis lead to the production of emboli and thrombi that have the potential to occlude brain vessels. Hemorrhagic phenomena and disorders such as hypertension or cardiac disease can produce episodes of cerebral ischemia or hypoxia, and are responsible for some cases of vascular dementia.[18,118] A partial list of etiologies is listed in Table 102.7. Specific risk factors for vascular dementias include diabetes mellitus, hypertension, heart disease, hyperlipidemia, cigarette smoking, and alcohol use.[120–122]

Neuropathology

Vascular dementias typically are subcortical. Most patients with multi-infarct dementia have blockage of multiple blood vessels and infarction of the cerebral tissue supplied by those vessels. When the distribution of a large artery or medium-sized arteriole is blocked, focal neurological deficits (see Chapter 53: Cerebrovascular Disorders) can be the result. Depending upon the area affected, there may be significant cognitive impairment. More frequently, however, a patient may have suffered transient ischemic attacks (TIAs) or multiple microinfarcts which have remained unrecognized.[123,124] Patients with subcortical vascular dementias frequently exhibit small, deep ischemic infarcts in arterioles of the basal ganglia, thalamus, and internal capsule.[1,125] A history of atherosclerosis, diabetes mellitus, or hypertension frequently is present without a history of stroke.[123,126,127] MRI scans can be very useful in diagnosing vascular dementias because areas of cerebral infarction are easier to visualize than with CT scanning (see Figure 102.3).

Lesions in white matter may occur in as many as 85% of patients with vascular dementia.[128] Deep white matter lesions known as leukoaraiosis frequently include demyelination and may represent early changes in dementia.[127,129,130] Although patients with dementia of the Alzheimer type also may exhibit leukoaraiosis, it is much more prevalent in those with multi-infarct type dementias.[131] Blood flow in patients with leukoaraiosis is reduced in all brain regions except parietal white matter, especially in the putamen and thalamus.[132] Patients with long-standing uncontrolled hypertension frequently develop multiple leukoaraiosis lesions leading to ischemic periventricular encephalopathy.[127] The lesions are too

Table 102.7	Vascular Dementia Etiologies[a]
Thrombotic Causes	**Embolic Causes[b]**
Atherosclerosis	Atherosclerotic stenosis
Arteriosclerosis	Artherosclerotic ulcerative plaques
Diabetes mellitus	Cardiac disease
Hematologic disorders	atrial fibrillation
hyperlipidemia	cardiac surgery
leukemia	cardiomyopathy
sickle cell disease	mitral valve prolapse
Inflammatory vascular disorders	MI with mural thrombus
giant cell arteritis	prosthetic valves
polyarteritis nodosa	rheumatic heart disease
rheumatoid arthritis with arteritis	rheumatic valve disease
scleroderma	Metastatic deposits
systemic lupus erythematosus	Parasites and ova
	Septic emboli

[a] Adapted from reference 1.
[b] MI = Myocardial infarction

small to be visualized grossly, but are evident on MRI scans.[118] Known as Binswager's disease, this disorder is characterized by focal neurological deficits, emotional lability, gait disturbances, and urinary incontinence.[127,133]

Vascular dementias typically have an earlier onset than dementia of the Alzheimer type.[70] Unlike Alzheimer's disease, males are affected more frequently than females, and survival is shorter for vascular dementia patients.[70,134]

Clinical Presentation

7. D.V., a 73-year-old male, is accompanied by his daughter for evaluation of "fuzzy thinking." Although his chief complaint is impaired memory, he denies significant impact on his daily routine. D.V. states his memory problem began 2 years ago following a dizzy spell and subsequent fall; however, his daughter states that the impairment began ≈1 year before that episode. The memory loss has been slowly progressive. D.V. states that he feels useless because of his memory problems and his "boring" daily routine. Although D.V. is generally independent, he relies on his daughter for assistance with most financial matters. He has voluntarily quit driving because of a lack of confidence in his abilities. D.V.'s daughter reports that according to her mother, D.V. is sometimes disoriented at night when he awakens to urinate. There is no history of urinary incontinence. D.V. has a questionable history of TIAs, but no focal neurological deficits. He has a long history of mild hypertension treated with a diuretic. He drinks alcohol occasionally and smokes about half a pack of cigarettes per day. His past medical history is unremarkable except for the possible TIAs, hypertension, and a mildly enlarged prostate. His family history is positive for diabetes and heart disease.

On physical examination, D.V. is found to be a mildly obese man who is well dressed and groomed, alert, and oriented to person. His BP is 160/92 mm Hg sitting and 168/95 mm Hg standing. Cardiac examination is normal. Neurological findings include somewhat diminished extraocular movements laterally, slightly asymmetric reflexes, with right greater than left. Muscle tone is normal in the lower extremities. He has a mild shuffling gait. Vibratory sensation is diminished, but within normal limits for his age. His score on the Folstein Mini-Mental Status Exam was 22/30, including errors in orientation and recall. His score on the Blessed Dementia Scale was 16/33,

Table 102.8	DSM-IV Criteria for Vascular Dementia[a,b]

1) The presence of multiple cognitive deficits manifested by both:

- Impaired memory (↓ ability to learn new information or to retrieve information previously learned)

- At least one of the following:
  Aphasia (language difficulties)
  Apraxia (diminished ability to perform motor activities in the presence of intact motor function)
  Agnosia (inability to recognize or name objects despite intact sensory function)
  Disruption of executive function (diminished ability to plan, organize)

2) The deficits above significantly interfere with normal work or social activities and represent a decline from previous ability to function

3) Focal neurological deficits (e.g., hyperactive DTRs, gait disturbances, weak extremities) or laboratory evidence indicating cerebrovascular disease (e.g., multiple infarctions of the cortex or white matter) judged to be etiologically linked to the disorder

4) The deficits do not occur exclusively during the course of a delirium

[a] Adapted from reference 17.
[b] DSM-IV = Diagnostic and Statistical Manual of Mental Disorders, 4th ed; DTRs = Deep tendon reflexes.

with errors in memory and orientation. Psychological evaluation found him mildly depressed.

A full laboratory analysis was generally within normal limits. D.V.'s serum potassium (3.8 mEq/dL) and sodium (138 mEq/dL) were in the low normal range and his blood urea nitrogen (BUN) (18 mg/dL) was in the upper normal range. Serum total cholesterol was 246 mg/dL and fasting triglycerides were 230 mg/dL. A chest x-ray revealed a mildly enlarged heart; ECG was normal. An MRI scan indicated generalized atrophy with enlarged ventricles, periventricular white matter ischemic changes, bilateral basal ganglion lacunar infarcts, and small cortical infarcts in the right parietal lobe. What subjective and objective evidence exists for a diagnosis of dementia in D.V.? [SI units: BUN 6.4 mmol/L of urea; total cholesterol 6.36 mmol/L; triglycerides 2.60 mmol/L]

D.V.'s major complaint is "fuzzy thinking" and impaired memory which he attributes to his dizzy spell and fall. His family, however, began to notice problems a full year before that episode, with progression over time. Although D.V. denies his impairment significantly affects his daily routine, he has voluntarily stopped driving and relies on his daughter for assistance with financial matters. His memory difficulties appear to have affected his mood and made him feel useless. D.V. is disoriented at night when he awakens to urinate. These factors satisfy the DSM-IV criteria for interference with normal activities.[17]

Multiple deficits are present on both the Folstein Mini-Mental Status Exam (orientation, recall) and on the Blessed Dementia Scale (memory, orientation), indicating impaired short-term and long-term memory. D.V.'s inability to drive reflects poor judgment behind the wheel of a car; a disturbance of higher cortical function is indicated by his need for assistance with financial matters. There is no evidence of a delirium being present. Evidence of an organic cause is provided by the MRI scan.

Diagnosis

8. What type of dementia does D.V. have?

There is sufficient evidence to indicate that D.V. suffers from a vascular dementia. Although DSM-IV provides diagnostic criteria for vascular dementia (see Table 102.8), it is not clear that D.V. satisfies the requirements.[17] With the exception of the dizzy spell and fall, his deterioration has been more of a downhill slide rather than stepwise. Although his cognitive deficits are "patchy" (e.g.,

Figure 102.3   A large stroke is visible to the right of the ventricles. There is evidence of atrophy in the right temporal area.

he appears to have no language difficulty), they are not particularly prominent. D.V. displays some neurological signs and symptoms including diminished extraocular movements, asymmetric reflexes, and a mild shuffling gait, but they are subtle and might be easily missed by an untrained observer as being related to a dementia. Reliance solely upon the clear presence of diagnostic criteria frequently may lead to a missed diagnosis.[135] The Hachinski Ischemic Scale (see Table 102.9) is used to help differentiate between dementia of the Alzheimer type and multi-infarct dementia.[136] Scores of ≤4 indicate a primary degenerative dementia, whereas scores of ≥7 signify multi-infarct dementia (or vascular dementia). According to this scale, D.V.'s score (7) would be classified as a vascular dementia.

D.V.'s history and clinical presentation do not suggest a dementia caused by a single large or several small strokes. Large strokes produce significant motor damage, typically on one side of the body (the side contralateral to the stroke). Multiple smaller strokes cause prominent motor deficits in discrete areas controlled by the affected areas. Neither of these patterns describes D.V.'s condition. However, he clearly is exhibiting signs of dementia and has significant cerebrovascular disease. He possesses several risk factors for a vascular dementia, including hypertension, smoking, and hyperlipidemia. His MRI indicates a lacunar state, multiple small infarcts in the deep penetrating arterioles at the base of the brain, particularly in the basal ganglia, internal capsule, thalamus, and pons (see Chapter 53: Cerebrovascular Disorders). These MRI findings are consistent with D.V.'s long-standing hypertension and neurological presentation. The absence of significant gait disturbance and urinary incontinence argues against Binswanger's disease. Because diagnostic criteria for vascular dementias are vague, arriving at a specific diagnosis is difficult. Diagnostic criteria (see Table 102.10) have been proposed for ischemic vascular dementia which would provide a structure for the most common type of these disorders.[118] According to this diagnostic scheme, D.V. suffers from probable ischemic vascular dementia.

Treatment

9. What treatment should be started for D.V.?

Smoking Cessation

Several treatment options are available which modify risk factors for vascular dementias. D.V. should be counseled to stop

Table 102.10	Proposed Diagnostic Criteria for Ischemic Vascular Dementia[a,b]

Definite IVD (Requires Histopathologic Examination of the Brain)
Clinical evidence of dementia

Pathologic confirmation of multiple infarcts, some extracerebellar

Probable IVD
Dementia

Evidence of at least 2 ischemic strokes by history, neurologic signs, or neuroimaging, or a single stroke with clearly documented temporal relationship to the dementia onset

Supporting evidence of multiple infarcts in regions affecting cognition, history of TIAs or vascular risk factors, elevated Hachinski score

Possible IVD
Dementia, plus one or more of the following:

- History or evidence of a single stroke (but not multiple strokes) without clearly documented temporal relationship to dementia onset
- Binswanger's disease (without multiple strokes), including all of the following:
  Early onset urinary incontinence unexplained by urologic disease, or gait disturbance not explained by peripheral cause,
  Vascular risk factors, and
  Extensive white matter change on neuroimaging

[a] Adapted from reference 118.
[b] IVD = Ischemic vascular dementia; TIAs = Transient ischemic attacks.

smoking because cigarette smoking reduces cerebral blood flow and increases the risk for stroke.[137] Among smokers with multi-infarct dementia, cessation of cigarette use improves cognitive performance.[138]

Antihypertensive Therapy

Hypertension and hyperlipidemia, both present in D.V., are additional risk factors for stroke and multi-infarct dementia. Control of systolic hypertension reduces the risk of stroke by 36% in elderly patients;[139] and maintenance of systolic blood pressure between 135 and 150 mm Hg is associated with improved cognition among multi-infarct dementia patients. Blood pressures greater than 150 mm Hg indicate inadequate control; systolic pressures below 135 mm Hg may provide inadequate cerebral perfusion.[138] As in nondemented individuals, nonpharmacologic treatment (e.g., diet, weight loss, exercise) is an essential component.[140] The antihypertensive agent must be chosen carefully in this population to maximize compliance and minimize adverse reactions. Both thiazide diuretics and β-adrenergic blockers may increase lipid levels, a potential complication in D.V. β-adrenergic blockers and sympatholytic agents may cause depression or impair cognitive activity. Calcium channel blockers or ACE inhibitors may be the preferred choices for control of hypertension in vascular dementia patients because they are well tolerated by elderly patients and may be of benefit in vascular dementia states.[100,141,142] The use of a vasodilating calcium channel blocker such as extended-release nifedipine (Procardia XL) 30 mg/day, is a reasonable first choice, as is benazepril (Lotensin) 10 mg/day. Both offer the additional advantage of single daily dosing over some other agents within their respective classes. This feature is important for compliance in patients with declining memory.

Antiplatelet Therapy

Prophylaxis against future cerebrovascular events is indicated in multi-infarct dementia, but few studies are available which have looked specifically at individuals with dementia. Cerebral perfusion and cognitive performance were improved in multi-infarct dementia patients receiving aspirin 325 mg/day for one year when

Table 102.9	Hachinski Ischemic Scale[a,b]	
Feature		**Score**
Abrupt onset		2
Stepwise deterioration		1
Fluctuating course		2
Nocturnal confusion		1
Relative preservation of personality		1
Depression		1
Somatic complaints		1
Emotional incontinence		1
History of hypertension		1
History of strokes		2
Evidence of associated atherosclerosis		1
Focal neurological symptoms		2
Focal neurological signs		2

[a] Adapted from reference 136.
[b] The Hachinski Ischemic Scale is used to help differentiate between dementia of the Alzheimer type and multi-infarct dementia.

compared to a control population.[143] Although aspirin doses as low as 30 mg/day reduce the incidence of transient ischemic attacks and are associated with fewer adverse effects than larger doses,[144] vascular dementia patients should receive aspirin 325 mg/day as prophylactic therapy based upon clinical trials.

Other agents which affect the coagulation process include dipyridamole (Persantin), ticlopidine (Ticlid), and warfarin (Coumadin). Dipyridamole has been used in patients with stroke and other thrombotic disorders, but has not been investigated for use in multi-infarct dementia.[140] Likewise, no data are available regarding the use of ticlopidine in this population, although the drug reduces subsequent stroke in patients with transient ischemic attacks (especially women).[145] The potential for significant leukopenia with ticlopidine cautions against its routine use until clear benefit is established. Warfarin is appropriate for patients with a vascular dementia secondary to multiple strokes or emboli associated with atrial fibrillation. Patients such as D.V. without these etiologies should be treated with aspirin rather than anticoagulants.[140] Aspirin 325 mg/day should be instituted in D.V.

Hemorrheologic Therapy

The use of hemorrheologic agents has been investigated in multi-infarct dementia patients. In two double-blind, placebo-controlled trials with pentoxifylline, global assessment ratings improved in patients with multi-infarct dementia.[146,147] Only subjects meeting the DSM-III-R criteria for multi-infarct dementia were included in the trials which may have excluded those without classic multi-infarct dementia.[17] Treatment gains were modest and patients with larger strokes seemed to benefit the most.[146] Some patients with mild dementia seemed to improve slightly with propentofylline, a pentoxifylline congener.[148] At present, treatment with hemorrheologic agents is investigational only and is not appropriate for D.V.

Behavioral Disturbances in Dementia

Several types of behavioral disturbances may develop during the course of a dementia, particularly during the later stages.[71] The disturbances can be classified into two broad categories of psychological behavior and nonpsychological behavior. *Psychologic behavior* includes anxiety, depression, withdrawal, psychotic behaviors, and aggression: these respond reasonably well to both nonpharmacologic and pharmacologic intervention. *Nonpsychologic behaviors* such as wandering, inappropriate motor activity, shouting, and incontinence respond better to environmental modification than to drug therapy.[149] The first step in evaluation of altered behavior in patients with dementia is to ensure that the problem is not due to an unrecognized medical problem or to an adverse effect of a medication (see Chapter 101: Geriatric Rehabilitation and Drug Use).

Anxiety

10. T.G., an otherwise healthy 62-year-old male, has recently been diagnosed with Alzheimer's disease. Recently he has refused to go on his daily walks around the neighborhood because he is afraid he will get lost. He also expresses worry about the burden he will place on his family as his condition worsens. His concerns keep him awake at night such that he is quite tired during the day. How should T.G.'s anxiety be managed?

Anxiety is a common problem in early stages of dementia. Patients are aware of their progressive cognitive decline and have sufficient insight to understand the consequences. Anxiety and apprehension are common reactions. T.G. exhibits a generalized anxiety disorder superimposed on his dementia which is interfering with his functional capacity more than his cognitive decline. Anxiolytic pharmacological therapy, therefore, would be appropriate.

Benzodiazepines are the most commonly used anxiolytics and are appropriate for T.G. Because of age-associated accumulation of long-acting benzodiazepines, the risk of acute toxicity is high. Long-acting benzodiazepines also are associated with an increased risk of falls and hip fractures.[150,151] Short half-life agents such as alprazolam (Xanax), lorazepam (Ativan), or oxazepam (Serax) are preferable and will help with his insomnia as well as his anxiety. Alprazolam 0.25 mg twice daily is appropriate for T.G. The dose may be increased by 0.25 mg/day at weekly intervals, up to a maximum daily dose of 1 mg if his symptoms do not respond. After two or three months the dose of alprazolam should be decreased gradually to determine if treatment is still necessary and to avoid seizures precipitated by sudden withdrawal.[149] All benzodiazepines carry the risk of causing confusion, impaired cognition, and paradoxical excitation which may be misinterpreted as a worsening of dementia symptoms.[152] Therefore, T.G.'s family should report any decrease in his functional capacity or increase in cognitive impairments, or any agitated behavior before increasing the alprazolam dose.

An alternative treatment is buspirone, which does not cause the cognitive impairments associated with the benzodiazepines. Dosage begins at 5 mg three times daily, and may be increased up to 15 mg three times daily. Buspirone however, will not concurrently manage T.G.'s insomnia because of its lack of sedative effect.[152] Additionally, the use of buspirone in individuals with dementia is not well studied.[153]

Psychosis

11. T.G. continues to decline and currently requires help with bathing and dressing. During a visit to his physician he states that his wife and children are stealing from him. He states that he cannot locate his coin collection which he placed in a "safe" location when his memory began to decline, and during the night he rummages through the house looking for it. He believes his family has been plotting to steal all of his assets and then turn him out onto the street. T.G.'s son reports that T.G. has been verbally abusive and has threatened several members of the family recently. How should T.G.'s psychotic behaviors be managed?

Delusions and hallucinations are common among demented individuals. Paranoid ideation occurs in approximately one-third of patients and delusions have been reported in almost one-half of dementia of the Alzheimer type patients.[154,155] Delusions typically involve suspicion of theft by family members, possibly secondary to the inability to remember where valuable items were placed and incorrectly concluding that they were stolen.[155] Another common delusion is the misidentification of people or objects. *Capgras syndrome*, the belief that a person has been "replaced" by an identical-looking imposter, or the belief that photographs or television pictures are real individuals, may occur in almost one-half of demented individuals.[155–157]

Psychotic symptoms respond best to neuroleptic agents although they are not highly effective, and no single antipsychotic is more effective than any other.[158,159] Delusions, hallucinations, aggression, and uncooperativeness symptoms respond best, but overall improvement occurs in only about 18% of patients.[157,159]

The choice of a neuroleptic agent should depend upon the symptoms displayed by the patient as well as the potential for adverse effects. Low potency neuroleptics (e.g., chlorpromazine, thioridazine) produce more sedation, which is useful in a patient exhibiting aggressive behavior. However, these agents are more likely to produce orthostatic hypotension or cardiac conduction defects and have significant anticholinergic properties. High potency neuroleptics (e.g., haloperidol) are more likely to cause pseudoparkinsonism, akathisia, and tardive dyskinesia.[160] Most clinicians prefer high potency neuroleptics because of less anticholinergic activity, a concern in dementia of the Alzheimer type patients.[160] At low doses, however, the anticholinergic effects of low potency neuroleptics are peripheral rather than central and should not interfere with cognitive function. Antipsychotic use places older adults at greater risk for falls, due in part to the α-adrenergic blocking effects of low potency agents and the extrapyramidal effects of the high potency drugs.[150]

Although psychotic symptoms in patients with dementia only minimally improve with neuroleptic agents, T.G. has no major contraindications (e.g., cardiovascular disease) to the use of a low potency agent. Therefore, thioridazine 25 mg at bedtime will facilitate T.G.'s ability to sleep at night as well as treat his paranoid delusions. If his symptoms do not respond within a few days the dosage of thioridazine may be increased in increments of 25 mg/day at intervals of five to seven days up to a maximum dose of 50 mg twice daily. While "as needed" doses may be appropriate for patients with occasional behavioral disturbances, they are not useful in patients with sustained psychotic symptoms due to the prolonged absorption phase for the neuroleptics.[149] The need for a rapid onset of therapeutic benefits in this kind of a situation usually requires a much larger neuroleptic dose which places the patient at increased risk for adverse effects once the total dose has reached the systemic circulation.

Because T.G. has no underlying cardiac disorders a baseline electrocardiogram is not necessary before initiating treatment. T.G. should be monitored by the family members for anticholinergic adverse effects such as dry mouth and constipation. T.G. is at relatively high risk for benign prostatic hyperplasia, so he also must be monitored for signs of urine retention (see Chapter 103: Geriatric Urological Disorders). Although pseudoparkinsonism is less probable with thioridazine than with the high potency neuroleptics, the appearance of muscle rigidity or akathisia should be reported to the physician.[160,161]

After two months the dose of thioridazine for T.G. should be reduced gradually (e.g., 25 mg/day every week) and his behavior assessed.[157] The chronic use of neuroleptics often impairs functional capacity in patients with dementia because of adverse effects. Withdrawal of neuroleptics after this short course of therapy actually may improve T.G.'s affect without an increase in behavior problems.[162]

Aggressive Behaviors

12. After 3 months, T.G.'s delusions have subsided, but he continues to be verbally abusive and frequently displays angry, emotional outbursts, especially when he requires help with bathing or toileting. At other times he is withdrawn and apathetic. He also has been found wandering in the neighborhood on 3 occasions. These behaviors persist despite 6-week trials each of thioridazine to a dose of 50 mg BID and of haloperidol to a dose of 5 mg/day. What alternative treatments can be attempted?

Although psychotic symptoms respond to neuroleptic agents, many other behaviors do not. More than 80% of patients with dementia exhibit at least one disruptive behavior such as angry outbursts, screaming, and abusive language, and more than 50% display multiple aggressive behaviors.[154,163,164] About 21% display assaultive or violent behavior.[154] Such behaviors typically are directed at caregivers, precipitated by receipt of assistance with activities of daily living such as bathing and toileting, and increase in frequency with dementia severity.[154,163,165] Several of these behaviors may be merely defensive responses to perceived threats in cognitively impaired individuals.[165] Behavioral disturbances must be addressed because they can have a negative effect on the patient's ability to perform activities of daily living.[166]

Some behaviors exhibited by T.G. are not likely to respond to medications. Wandering is typically unaltered by the use of medications unless the patient is oversedated. Nonpharmacological treatments such as periods of physical exercise and rest, or environmental modification are much more effective.[1,167] T.G.'s reactions to assistance with bathing and toileting may be caused by confusion and fear. Breaking the tasks down to step-by-step procedures, accomplished individually, frequently helps to modify aggressive behaviors.[167]

Verbal abuse and aggressiveness place both the patient and caregiver at risk for injury. Carbamazepine (Tegretol) 200 to 1000 mg/day is effective in reducing rage and aggressive behaviors in dementia patients resistant to treatment with neuroleptics.[168,169] It is not necessary to achieve the carbamazepine serum concentrations that usually are needed for anticonvulsant effect. Treatment with carbamazepine should begin at a dose of 100 mg twice daily and be increased at weekly intervals until the patient responds or until adverse effects require discontinuation. Significant adverse effects include dizziness, drowsiness, ataxia, and agranulocytosis. Patients should be monitored for CNS effects (e.g., increased confusion, daytime drowsiness) and require baseline and periodic complete blood counts with differentials. Carbamazepine also induces hepatic microsomal enzymes, causing more rapid metabolism of several drugs (see Chapter 3: Drug Interactions).

Lithium also has been employed in the treatment of aggressive behaviors, but results of the few trials have been generally disappointing.[153,170]

Depression

13. How should T.G.'s social withdrawal and apathetic features be treated?

Depression frequently accompanies dementia and may significantly impair a patient's functional capacity, cognitive abilities, and communication.[171,172] T.G. is withdrawn and apathetic, symptoms which are suggestive of depression. Screaming also is thought to be a symptom of depression in individuals with dementia, perhaps reflecting feelings of loneliness, boredom, or the need for attention.[163,173] Because a definite diagnosis of depression relies heavily on patient interview and response to questions, a formal diagnosis in patients with dementia is difficult if not impossible. Therefore, one must rely on observation of the patient to make a clinical evaluation.

Trazodone (Desyrel) reduces disruptive and aggressive behaviors in cognitively impaired patients and, thus, is a reasonable choice for treatment of depression in T.G.[174,175] This drug is sedating and may help with sleep disorders and is free of anticholinergic effects. It does, however, possess α-adrenergic blocking activity and may cause orthostasis. Doses of trazodone in T.G. should be initiated at 50 mg at bedtime and be increased to 100 mg at bedtime after several days. If necessary, doses for T.G. can be increased by 50 mg/day every five to seven days. Subsequent dose increases should divide the total daily dose into two or three doses up to a maximum daily dose of 600 mg.[176] The trazodone should provide T.G. restful sleep at night, increase his sociability, and decrease his abusive behaviors.

Tricyclic antidepressants also are appropriate agents. Desipramine (Norpramin) and doxepin (Sinequan) in low doses (25 to 75 mg/day) improve mood, activities of daily living, and vegetative symptoms in depressed patients with dementia.[177] The tricyclic antidepressants possess much more anticholinergic activity than trazodone and pose a greater risk for cardiac arrhythmias. Tertiary amines such as amitriptyline may interfere with cognitive function, possess very high anticholinergic and α-adrenergic activity,[171,176] and should be avoided in elderly patients. Therefore, a trial of trazodone is warranted for T.G.

Social Support

14. T.G.'s family indicates that caring for him at home has become a tremendous burden and they are considering placing him in an institution. What social support services are available to families facing this decision?

Institutionalization is a typical outcome for patients in the late stages of dementia. The total care required to manage a dementia patient usually becomes unmanageable for most families as the disease progresses. Caregiver stress often is exacerbated by declining memory in the patient, inability to communicate with the patient, physical decline of a loved one, incontinence, caregiver's loss of freedom, and depression in the caregiver.[178] Caregivers frequently experience anger, helplessness, guilt and worry, and suffer from physical stressors such as fatigue and illness.[167]

Outside assistance is essential to assist families in caring for a patient with dementia. Families should be referred to the Alzheimer's Disease and Related Disorders Association (360 N. Michigan Avenue, Chicago, IL 60601) as soon as a diagnosis of dementia is received. The association has local affiliates in most major cities. The book **The 36-Hour Day** is a valuable resource for families.[167] It describes the symptoms, behaviors, and problems that can be encountered when caring for a patient with dementia.

Support groups, individual and family counseling, and other sources of support are useful and may help families cope for a longer period of time.[179] However, the key intervention to reduce caregiver stress is respite care which allows a family time away from the responsibilities of taking care of a frail individual.[180] Respite care brings a person into the home or allows the patient to go to a day care or similar environment on a regular schedule. Such programs may delay the need to institutionalize a patient.

Pseudodementia

Clinical Presentation and Diagnosis

15. G.Y., an 86-year-old female, lives alone in a low-income housing unit. Over the course of the past 6 weeks she has become disoriented and confused. A neighbor brought her to the hospital after finding her wandering through the neighborhood in her nightclothes. She eats only 1 meal a day, a frozen pot pie, because she generally forgets to eat her other meals. Sev- eral bills remain unpaid. She has difficulty sleeping and expresses little desire to live because "all my friends are gone." Her score on the Folstein Mini-Mental Status Exam is 18/30 with multiple deficits. Most errors are attributable to answers of "I don't know" or "I can't." She currently takes propranolol 40 mg TID for high blood pressure, cimetidine 400 mg BID for gastroesophageal reflux disease, and temazepam 15 mg HS PRN insomnia. What subjective and objective data support a diagnosis of pseudodementia in G.Y.?

Depression

G.Y. clearly exhibits cognitive impairment as evidenced from her symptoms of confusion and disorientation, forgetting to eat, wandering, and score on the Folstein Mini-Mental Status Exam. However, the rapid course of her decline, lack of effort on mental status testing, and medications suggest that her impairment might be secondary to causes other than a true dementing illness.[181]

Depression is the most common cause of pseudodementia, accounting for at least 50% of cases.[1] Depressive symptoms in G.Y. include self-neglect, insomnia, loss of her desire to live, and lack of effort on mental status testing. When given a mental status screening test, depressed patients tend to give "I don't know" answers which reflect dysphoria or an inability to cooperate, whereas demented patients typically provide incorrect answers.[1,181]

Medications

Medications frequently are responsible for cognitive impairment in older adults, accounting for dementia symptoms in approximately 12% of patients with cognitive impairment. Psychotropic medications, analgesics, antihypertensives, corticosteroids, and cimetidine often are implicated.[18,182]

Treatment

16. What is the proper treatment for G.Y.'s pseudodementia?

Initial therapy should consist of the discontinuation of her medications, all of which may be contributing to her cognitive decline. Because all of the medications are relatively short acting, her mental status should improve markedly within 48 hours. At that time, her hypertension and gastroesophageal reflux disease can be reevaluated and more appropriate therapy instituted, if warranted.

G.Y. should be evaluated for depression, and psychotherapy should be initiated if she is in fact depressed. She also should be referred to a social services agency or senior center to provide her with assistance and to offer her opportunities for social interaction.

References

1 **Cummings J, Benson DF.** Dementia: A Clinical Approach. 2nd ed. Boston, MA: Butterworth-Heinemann; 1992:45.

2 **Cummings J et al.** Reversible dementia. Illustrative cases, definition, and review. JAMA. 1980;243:2434.

3 **Ineichen B.** Measuring the rising tide. How many dementia cases will there be by 2001? Br J Psychiatry. 1987;150: 193.

4 **Larson EB.** Alzheimer's disease in the community. JAMA. 1989;262:2591. Editorial.

5 **Henderson AS.** The epidemiology of Alzheimer's disease. Br Med Bull. 1986;42:3.

6 **Kokmen E et al.** Prevalence of medically diagnosed dementia in a defined United States population: Rochester, Minnesota, January 1, 1975. Neurology. 1989;39:773.

7 **Weissman MM et al.** Psychiatric disorders (DSM-III) and cognitive impairment among the elderly in a US urban community. Acta Psychiatr Scand. 1985;77:366.

8 **Rocca WA et al.** Frequency and distribution of Alzheimer's disease in Europe: a collaborative study of 1980–1990 prevalence findings. Ann Neurol. 1991;30:381.

9 **Evans DA et al.** Prevalence of Alzheimer's disease in a community of older persons: higher than previously reported. JAMA. 1989;262:2551.

10 **Wernicke TF, Reischies FM.** Prevalence of dementia in old age: clinical diagnoses in subjects aged 95 years and older. Neurology. 1994;44:250.

11 **Schoenberg BS et al.** Alzheimer's disease and other dementing illnesses in a defined United States population: incidence rates and clinical features. Ann Neurol. 1987;22:724.

12 **Hu T et al.** Evaluation of the costs of caring for the senile demented elderly: a pilot study. Gerontologist. 1986;26: 158.

13 **Coughlin TA, Liu K.** Health care costs of older persons with cognitive impairments. Gerontologist. 1989;29:173.

14 **Hay JW, Ernst RL.** The economic costs of Alzheimer's disease. Am J Public Health. 1987;77:1169.

15 **Selkoe DJ.** Alzheimer's disease: insights into an emerging epidemic. J Geriatr Psychiatry. 1992;25:211.

16 **Schneider EL, Guralnik JM.** The aging of America: impact on health care costs. JAMA. 1990;263:2335.

17 **American Psychiatric Association.** Diagnostic and Statistical Manual of Mental Disorders. 4th ed. Washington, DC: American Psychiatric Assoc.; 1994.

18 **Consensus Conference.** Differential diagnosis of dementing diseases. JAMA. 1987;258:3411.

19 **Folstein MF et al.** "Mini-mental state": a practical method for grading the mental state of patients for the clinician. J Psychiatr Res. 1975;12:189.

20 **Blessed G et al.** The association between quantitative measures of dementia and of senile change in the cerebral grey matter of elderly subjects. Br J

Psychiatry. 1968;114:797.

21 **Shore D et al.** Serum aluminum in primary degenerative dementia. Biol Psychiatry. 1980;15:971.

22 **Markesbery WR et al.** Instrumental neutron activation analysis of brain aluminum in Alzheimer disease and aging. Ann Neurol. 1981;10:511.

23 **Good PF et al.** Selective accumulation of aluminum and iron in the neurofibrillary tangles of Alzheimer's disease: a laser microprobe (LAMMA) study. Ann Neurol. 1992;31:286.

24 **Glenner GG.** The pathobiology of Alzheimer's disease. Ann Rev Med. 1989;40:45.

25 **Chandra V et al.** Head trauma with loss of consciousness as a risk factor for Alzheimer's disease. Neurology. 1989;39:1576.

26 **Edwards JK et al.** Are there clinical and epidemiological differences between familial and non-familial Alzheimer's disease? J Am Geriatr Soc. 1991;39:477.

27 **Mortimer JA et al.** Head trauma as a risk factor for Alzheimer's disease: a collaborative re-analysis of case-control studies. Int J Epidemiol. 1991;20:S28.

28 **Rocca WA et al.** Maternal age and Alzheimer's disease: a collaborative re-analysis of case-control studies. Int J Epidemiol. 1991;20:S21.

29 **Chui HC et al.** Clinical subtypes of dementia of the Alzheimer type. Neurology. 1985;35:1544.

30 **Frommelt P et al.** Familial Alzheimer disease: a large, multigeneration German kindred. Alzheimer Dis Assoc Disord. 1991;5:36.

31 **Huff FJ et al.** Risk of dementia in relatives of patients with Alzheimer's disease. Neurology. 1988;38:786.

32 **Farrer LA et al.** Assessment of genetic risk for Alzheimer's disease among first-degree relatives. Ann Neurol. 1989;25:485.

33 **Hoffman A et al.** History of dementia and Parkinson's disease in 1st-degree relatives of patients with Alzheimer's disease. Neurology. 1989;39:1589.

34 **Farrer LA et al.** Transmission and age-at-onset patterns in familial Alzheimer's disease: evidence for heterogeneity. Neurology. 1990;40:395.

35 **Van Duijn CM et al.** Familial aggregation of Alzheimer's disease and related disorders: a collaborative re-analysis of case-control studies. Int J Epidemiol. 1991;20:S13.

36 **Luchins DJ et al.** Are there clinical differences between familial and non-familial Alzheimer's disease? Am J Psychiatry. 1992;149:1023.

37 **St. George-Hyslop PH et al.** The genetic defect causing familial Alzheimer's disease maps on chromosome 21. Science. 1987;235:885.

38 **Lai F, Williams RS.** A prospective study of Alzheimer disease in Down syndrome. Arch Neurol. 1989;46:849.

39 **Creasey H et al.** Monozygotic twins discordant for Alzheimer's disease. Neurology. 1989;39:1474.

40 **Joachim CL, Selkoe DJ.** The seminal role of β-amyloid in the pathogenesis of Alzheimer's disease. Alzheimer Dis Assoc Disord. 1992;6:7.

41 **Murrell J et al.** A mutation in the amyloid precursor protein associated with hereditary Alzheimer's disease. Science. 1991;254:97.

42 **Glenner GG.** Current knowledge of amyloid deposits as applied to senile plaques and congophilic angiopathy. In: Katzman R, et al., eds. Alzheimer's Disease, Senile Dementia and Related Disorders. New York, NY: Raven Press; 1978:493.

43 **Chui HC.** The significance of clinically defined subgroups of Alzheimer's disease. J Neural Transm. 1987;24 (Suppl.):57.

44 **Poirier J, Finch CE.** Neurochemistry of the aging human brain. In: Hazzard WR et al., eds. Principles of Geriatric Medicine and Gerontology. New York: McGraw-Hill; 1990:905.

45 **Bondareff W et al.** Loss of neurons of origin of the adrenergic projection to cerebral cortex (nucleus locus ceruleus) in senile dementia. Neurology. 1982;32:164.

46 **Khachaturian ZS.** Diagnosis of Alzheimer's disease. Arch Neurol. 1985; 42:1097.

47 **Grundke-Iqbal I et al.** Abnormal phosphorylation of the microtubule-associated protein tau in Alzheimer cytoskeletal pathology. Proc Natl Acad Sci U S A. 1986;83:4913.

48 **Lee VMY et al.** A68: a major subunit of paired helical filaments and derivatized forms of normal tau. Nature. 1991;251:675.

49 **Beyreuther K et al.** Mechanisms of amyloid deposition in Alzheimer's disease. Ann N Y Acad Sci. 1991;640:129.

50 **Tabaton M et al.** The widespread alteration of neurites in Alzheimer's disease may be unrelated to amyloid deposition. Ann Neurol. 1989;26:771.

51 **McKee AC et al.** Neuritic pathology and dementia in Alzheimer's disease. Ann Neurol. 1991;30:156.

52 **Samuel WA et al.** Severity of dementia in Alzheimer disease and neurofibrillary tangles in multiple brain regions. Alzheimer Dis Assoc Disord. 1991;5:1.

53 **Bugiani O et al.** Preamyloid deposits, amyloid deposits, and senile plaques in Alzheimer's disease, Down syndrome, and aging. Ann N Y Acad Sci. 1991; 640:122.

54 **Mann DM.** Neuropathology of Alzheimer's disease: towards an understanding of the pathogenesis. Biochem Soc Trans. 1989;17:73.

55 **Lassman H et al.** Synaptic pathology of Alzheimer's disease. Ann N Y Acad Sci. 1993;695:59.

56 **Arai H et al.** Expression patterns of β-amyloid precursor protein (β-APP) in neural and nonneural human tissues from Alzheimer's disease and control subjects. Ann Neurol. 1991;30:686.

57 **Haass C et al.** Normal cellular processing of the β-amyloid precursor protein results in the secretion of the amyloid β peptide and related molecules. Ann N Y Acad Sci. 1993;695:109.

58 **Coyle JT et al.** Alzheimer's disease: a disorder of cortical cholinergic innervation. Science. 1983;219:1184.

59 **Rumble BR et al.** Amyloid A4 protein and its precursor in Down's syndrome and Alzheimer's disease. N Engl J Med. 1989;320:1446.

60 **Davies LB et al.** A4 amyloid protein deposition and the diagnosis of Alzheimer's disease: prevalence in aged brains determined by immunocytochemistry compared with conventional neuropathologic techniques. Neurology. 1988;38:1688.

61 **Joachim CL et al.** Amyloid β-protein deposition in tissues other than brain in Alzheimer's disease. Nature. 1989; 341:226.

62 **Whitehouse PJ et al.** Alzheimer's disease and senile dementia: loss of neurons in the basal forebrain. Science. 1982;215:1237.

63 **Whitehouse PJ et al.** Alzheimer disease: evidence for selective loss of cholinergic neurons in the nucleus basalis. Ann Neurol. 1981;10:122.

64 **Weinberger DR et al.** The distribution of cerebral muscarinic acetylcholine receptors in vivo in patients with dementia. Arch Neurol. 1991;48:169.

65 **Schröder H et al.** Cellular distribution and expression of cortical acetylcholine receptors in aging and Alzheimer's disease. Ann N Y Acad Sci. 1991;640: 189.

66 **Terry RD et al.** Physical basis of cognitive alterations in Alzheimer's disease: synapse loss is the major correlate of cognitive impairment. Ann Neurol. 1991;30:572.

67 **Francis PT et al.** Neurochemical studies of early-onset Alzheimer's disease: possible influence on treatment. N Engl J Med. 1985;313:7.

68 **Nemeroff CB et al.** Recent advances in the neurochemical pathology of Alzheimer's disease. Ann N Y Acad Sci. 1991;640:193.

69 **McKhann G et al.** Clinical diagnosis of Alzheimer's disease: report of the NINCDS-ADRDA Work Group, Department of Health and Human Services Task Force on Alzheimer's Disease. Neurology. 1984;34:939.

70 **Barclay LL et al.** Survival in Alzheimer's disease and vascular dementias. Neurology. 1985;35:834.

71 **Riesberg B et al.** The global deterioration scale for assessment of primary degenerative dementia. Am J Psychiatry. 1982;139:1136.

72 **Hughes CP et al.** A new clinical scale for the staging of dementia. Br J Psychiatry. 1982;140:566.

73 **Risse SC et al.** Neuropathological findings in patients with clinical diagnoses of probable Alzheimer's disease. Am J Psychiatry. 1990;147:168.

74 **Mendez MF et al.** Clinically diagnosed Alzheimer's disease: neuropathologic findings in 650 cases. Alzheimer Dis Assoc Disord. 1992;6:35.

75 **Drachman DA et al.** The prognosis in Alzheimer's disease: ''how far'' rather than ''how fast'' best predicts the course. Arch Neurol. 1990;47:851.

76 **Krassner MB.** Mechanism of action of Hydergine (ergoloid mesylates) in relation to organic brain disorders. Adv Ther. 1984;1:172.

77 **Hollister LE, Yesavage J.** Ergoloid mesylates for senile dementias: unanswered questions. Ann Intern Med. 1984;100:894.

78 **Hughes JR et al.** An ergot alkaloid preparation (Hydergine) in the treatment of dementia: critical review of the clinical literature. J Am Geriatr Soc. 1976;24:490.

79 **van Loveren-Huyben CMS et al.** Double-blind clinical and psychologic study of ergoloid mesylates (Hydergine) in subjects with senile dementia. J Am Geriatr Soc. 1984;32:584.

80 **Schran HF.** Bioavailability of ergoloid mesylates liquid capsule. Clin Ther. 1985;8:71.

81 **Thompson TL et al.** Lack of efficacy of Hydergine in patients with Alzheimer's disease. N Engl J Med. 1990; 323:445.

82 **Summers WK et al.** Use of THA in treatment of Alzheimer-like dementia: pilot study in twelve patients. Biol Psychiatry. 1981;16:145.

83 **Summers WK et al.** THA—a review of the literature and use in treatment of five overdose patients. Clin Toxicol. 1980;16:269.

84 **Summers WK et al.** Oral tetrahydroaminoacridine in long-term treatment of senile dementia, Alzheimer type. N Engl J Med. 1986;315:1241.

85 **Division of Neuropharmacological Drug Products, Food and Drug Administration.** Tacrine as a treatment for Alzheimer's dementia: an interim report from the FDA. N Engl J Med. 1991;324:349.

86 **Gauthier S et al.** Tetrahydroaminoacridine-lecithin combination treatment in patients with intermediate-stage Alzheimer's disease. N Engl J Med. 1990; 322:1272.

87 **Eagger SA et al.** Tacrine in Alzheimer's disease. Lancet. 1991;337:989.

88 **Farlow M et al.** A controlled trial of tacrine in Alzheimer's disease. JAMA. 1992;268:2523.

89 **Knapp MJ et al.** A 30-week randomized controlled trial of high-dose tacrine in patients with Alzheimer's disease. JAMA. 1994;271:985.

90 **Parke-Davis.** Cognex package insert. Morris Plains, NJ: 1993 Nov.

91 **Watkins PB et al.** Hepatotoxic effects of tacrine administration in patients with Alzheimer's disease. JAMA. 1994;271:992.

92 **Shutske GM et al.** (±)-9-amino-1,2,3,4-tetrahydroacridin-1-ol. A potential Alzheimer's disease therapeutic of low toxicity. J Med Chem. 1988;31: 1278. Letter.

93 **Murphy MF et al.** Evaluation of HP 029 (velnacrine maleate) in Alzheimer's disease. Ann N Y Acad Sci. 1991;640:253.

94 **Ebmeier KP et al.** Effects of a single dose of the acetylcholinesterase inhibitor velnacrine on recognition memory and regional cerebral blood flow in Alzheimer's disease. Psychopharmacology (Berl). 1992;108:103.

95 **Jenike ME et al.** Oral physostigmine for patients with presenile and senile dementia of the Alzheimer's type: a double-blind placebo-controlled trial. J Clin Psychiatry. 1990;51:3.

96 **Harrell LE et al.** The effect of long-term physostigmine administration in Alzheimer's disease. Neurology. 1990; 40:1350.

97 **Sano M et al.** Safety and efficacy of oral physostigmine in the treatment of Alzheimer disease. Clin Neuropharmacol. 1993;16:61.

98 **Harbaugh RE et al.** Preliminary report: intracranial cholinergic drug infusion in patients with Alzheimer's dis-

ease. Neurosurgery. 1984;15:514.

99 Penn RD et al. Intraventricular bethanechol infusion for Alzheimer's disease: results of double-blind and escalating-dose trials. Neurology. 1988;38:219.

100 Miller SW et al. Therapeutic frontiers in Alzheimer's disease. Pharmacotherapy. 1992;12:217.

101 Dysken MW et al. Oxiracetam in the treatment of multi-infarct dementia and primary degenerative dementia. J Neuropsychiatry Clin Neurosci. 1989;1:249.

102 Maina G et al. Oxiracetam in the treatment of primary degenerative and multi-infarct dementia: a double-blind, placebo-controlled study. Neuropsychobiology. 1989;21:141.

103 Parnetti L et al. Neuropsychological results of long-term therapy with oxiracetam in patients with dementia of Alzheimer type and multi-infarct dementia in comparison with a control group. Neuropsychobiology. 1989;22:97.

104 Tariot PN et al. L-deprenyl in Alzheimer's disease. Arch Gen Psychiatry. 1987;44:427.

105 Piccinin GL et al. Neuropsychological effects of l-deprenyl in Alzheimer's type dementia. Clin Neuropharmacol. 1990;13:147.

106 Lees AJ. Selegiline hydrochloride and cognition. Acta Neurol Scand. 1991; 84(Suppl. 136):91.

107 Burke WJ et al. L-deprenyl in the treatment of mild dementia of the Alzheimer type: results of a 15-month trial. J Am Geriatr Soc. 1993;41:1219.

108 Schneider LS et al. A double-blind crossover pilot study of l-deprenyl (selegiline) combined with cholinesterase inhibitor in Alzheimer's disease. Am J Psychiatry. 1993;150:321.

109 Cooper JK. Drug treatment of Alzheimer's disease. Arch Intern Med. 1991; 151:245.

110 Tollefson GD. Short-term effects of the calcium channel blocker nimodipine in the management of primary degenerative dementia. Biol Psychiatry. 1990;27:1133.

111 Sudilovsky A et al. A pilot clinical trial of the angiotensin-converting enzyme inhibitor ceranapril in Alzheimer disease. Alzheimer Dis Assoc Disord. 1993;7:105.

112 Carta A, Calvani M. Acetyl-l-carnitine: a drug able to slow the progress of Alzheimer's disease? Ann N Y Acad Sci. 1991;640:228.

113 Spagnoli A et al. Long-term acetyl-l-carnitine treatment in Alzheimer's disease. Neurology. 1991;41:1726.

114 Mouradian MM et al. Somatostatin replacement therapy for Alzheimer dementia. Ann Neurol. 1991;30:610.

115 Amaducci L et al. Phosphatidylserine in the treatment of Alzheimer's disease: results of a multicenter study. Psychopharmacol Bull. 1988;24:130.

116 Amaducci L et al. Use of phosphatidylserine in Alzheimer's disease. Ann N Y Acad Sci. 1991;640:245.

117 Henderson VW et al. Estrogen replacement and Alzheimer's disease. Soc for Neuroscience Abstracts. 1993; 19:1046.

118 Chui HC et al. Criteria for the diagnosis of ischemic vascular dementia proposed by the State of California Alzheimer's Disease Diagnostic and Treatment Centers. Neurology. 1992; 42:473.

119 Hachinski VC et al. Multi-infarct dementia: a cause of mental deterioration in the elderly. Lancet. 1974;2:207.

120 Tresch DD et al. Prevalence and significance of cardiovascular disease and hypertension in elderly patients with dementia. J Am Geriatr Soc. 1985;33: 530.

121 Meyer JS et al. Aetiological considerations and risk factors for multi-infarct dementia. J Neurol Neurosurg Psychiatry. 1988;51:1489.

122 Zimetbaum P et al. Lipids, vascular disease, and dementia with advancing age. Arch Intern Med. 1991;151:240.

123 Pullicino P et al. Small deep infarcts diagnosed on computed tomography. Neurology. 1980;30:1090.

124 Goto K et al. Diffuse white-matter disease in the geriatric population. Radiology. 1981;141:687.

125 Ishii N et al. Why do frontal lobe symptoms predominate in vascular dementia with lacunes? Neurology. 1986; 36:340.

126 Donnan GA et al. A prospective study of lacunar infarction using computerized tomography. Neurology. 1982;32:49.

127 Romàn GC. Senile dementia of the Binswanger type: a form of vascular dementia in the elderly. JAMA. 1987; 258:1782.

128 Wallin A, Blennow K. Pathogenetic basis of vascular dementia. Alzheimer Dis Assoc Disord. 1991;5:91-102.

129 Hachinski VC et al. Leuko-araiosis. Arch Neurol. 1987;44:21.

130 Munoz DG. The pathological basis of multi-infarct dementia. Alzheimer Dis Assoc Disord. 1991;5:77.

131 Inzitari D et al. Vascular risk factors and leuko-araiosis. Arch Neurol. 1987; 44:42.

132 Kawamura J et al. Leukoaraiosis correlates with cerebral hypoperfusion in vascular dementia. Stroke. 1991;22: 609.

133 Babikian V, Ropper AH. Binswanger's disease: a review. Stroke. 1987;18:2.

134 Rocca WA et al. Prevalence of clinically diagnosed Alzheimer's disease and other dementing disorders: a door-to-door survey in Appignano, Macerata Province, Italy. Neurology. 1990;40: 626.

135 Nussbaum M et al. DSM-III criteria for primary degenerative dementia and multi-infarct dementia. Alzheimer Dis Assoc Disord. 1992;6:111.

136 Hachinski VC et al. Cerebral blood flow in dementia. Arch Neurol. 1975; 32:632.

137 Rogers RL et al. Cigarette smoking decreases cerebral blood flow suggesting increased risk for stroke. JAMA. 1983;250:2796.

138 Meyer JS et al. Improved cognition after control of risk factors for multi-infarct dementia. JAMA. 1986;256:2203.

139 SHEP Cooperative Research Group. Prevention of stroke by antihypertensive drug treatment in older persons with isolated systolic hypertension. JAMA. 1991;265:3255.

140 Duthie EH, Glatt SL. Understanding and treating multi-infarct dementia. Clin Geriatr Med. 1988;4:749.

141 Harris RJ et al. The effects of a calcium antagonist, nimodipine, upon physiological responses of the cerebral vasculature and its possible influence upon focal cerebral ischaemia. Stroke. 1982;13:759.

142 Parnetti et al. Mental deterioration in old age: results of two multicenter, clinical trials with nimodipine. Clin Ther. 1993;15:394.

143 Meyer JS et al. Randomized clinical trial of daily aspirin therapy in multi-infarct dementia: a pilot study. J Am Geriatr Soc. 1989;37:549.

144 Dutch TIA Trial Study Group. A comparison of two doses of aspirin (30 mg vs. 283 mg a day) in patients after a transient ischemic attack or minor ischemic stroke. N Engl J Med. 1991; 325:1261.

145 Grotta JC et al. Prevention of stroke with ticlopidine: who benefits most? Neurology. 1992;42:111.

146 Black RS et al. Pentoxifylline in cerebrovascular disease. J Am Geriatr Soc. 1992;40:237.

147 Blume J et al. Treatment of chronic cerebrovascular disease in elderly patients with pentoxifylline. J Med. 1992; 23:417.

148 Saletu B et al. Propentofylline in adult-onset cognitive disorders: double-blind, placebo-controlled, clinical, psychometric and brain mapping studies. Neuropsychobiology. 1991;24:173.

149 Maletta GJ. Management of behavior in elderly patients with dementias. Clin Geriatr Med. 1988;4:719.

150 Ray WA et al. Psychotropic drug use and the risk of hip fractures. N Engl J Med. 1987;316:363.

151 Granek E et al. Medications and diagnoses in relation to falls in a long-term care facility. J Am Geriatr Soc. 1987;35:503.

152 Fankhauser M. Anxiolytic drugs and sedative-hypnotic agents. In: Bressler R, Katz MD, eds. Geriatric Pharmacology. New York: McGraw-Hill; 1993: 165.

153 Schneider LS, Sobin PB. Non-neuroleptic treatment of behavioral symptoms and agitation in Alzheimer's disease and other dementia. Psychopharmacol Bull. 1992;28:71.

154 Swearer JM et al. Troublesome and disruptive behaviors in dementia. J Am Geriatr Soc. 1988;36:784.

155 Binetti G et al. Delusions in Alzheimer's disease and multi-infarct dementia. Acta Neurol Scand. 1993;88:5.

156 Neitch SM, Zarraga A. A misidentification delusion in two Alzheimer's patients. J Am Geriatr Soc. 1991;39: 513.

157 Rapp MS et al. Behavioural disturbances in the demented elderly: phenomenology, pharmacotherapy and behaviour management. Can J Psychiatry. 1992;37:651.

158 Cowley LM, Glen RS. Double-blind study of thioridazine and haloperidol in geriatric patients with a psychosis associated with organic brain syndrome. J Clin Psychiatry. 1979;40:411.

159 Schneider LS et al. A meta-analysis of controlled trials of neuroleptic treatment in dementia. J Am Geriatr Soc. 1990;38:553.

160 Gelenberg AJ, Katz MD. Antipsychotic agents. In: Bressler R, Katz MD, eds. Geriatric Pharmacology. New York: McGraw-Hill; 1993:375.

161 Jenike MA. Tardive dyskinesia: special risk in the elderly. J Am Geriatr Soc. 1983;31:71.

162 Thapa PB et al. Effects of antipsychotic withdrawal in elderly nursing home residents. J Am Geriatr Soc. 1994;42:280.

163 Cohen-Mansfield J et al. Screaming in nursing home residents. J Am Geriatr Soc. 1990;38:785.

164 Cariaga J et al. A controlled study of disruptive vocalizations among geriatric residents in nursing homes. J Am Geriatr Soc. 1991;39:501.

165 Bridges-Parlet S et al. A descriptive study of physically aggressive behavior in dementia by direct observation. J Am Geriatr Soc. 1994;42:192.

166 Freels S et al. Functional status and clinical findings with Alzheimer's disease. J Gerontol. 1992;47:M177.

167 Mace NL, Rabins PV. The 36-Hour Day. Baltimore, MD: Johns Hopkins University Press; 1981:64.

168 Essa M. Carbamazepine in dementia. J Clin Psychopharmacol. 1986;6:234.

169 Gleason RP, Schneider LS. Carbamazepine treatment of agitation in Alzheimer's outpatients refractory to neuroleptics. J Clin Psychiatry. 1990;51: 115.

170 Williams KW, Goldstein G. Cognitive and affective responses to lithium in patients with organic brain syndrome. Am J Psychiatry. 1979;136:800.

171 Salzman C. Treatment of agitation, anxiety, and depression in dementia. Psychopharmacol Bull. 1988;24:39.

172 Fitz AG, Teri L. Depression, cognition, and functional ability in patients with Alzheimer's disease. J Am Geriatr Soc. 1994;42:186.

173 Carlyle W et al. ECT: an effective treatment in the screaming demented patient. J Am Geriatr Soc. 1991;39: 637. Letter.

174 Simpson DM, Foster D. Improvement in organically disturbed behavior with trazodone treatment. J Clin Psychiatry. 1986;47:191.

175 Pinner E, Rich C. Effects of trazodone on aggressive behavior in seven patients with organic mental disorders. Am J Psychiatry. 1988;145:1295.

176 Bressler R. Depression. In: Bressler R, Katz MD, eds. Geriatric Pharmacology. New York: McGraw-Hill; 1993: 329.

177 Reifler BV et al. Dementia of the Alzheimer's type and depression. J Am Geriatr Soc. 1986;34:855.

178 Williamson GM, Schulz R. Coping with specific stressors in Alzheimer's disease caregiving. Gerontologist. 1993; 33:747.

179 Mittelman MS et al. An intervention that delays institutionalization of Alzheimer's disease patients: treatment of spouse-caregivers. Gerontologist. 1993; 33:730.

180 Knight BG et al. A meta-analytic review of interventions for caregiver distress: recommendations for future research. Gerontologist. 1993;33:240.

181 Cole JO et al. Tricyclic use in the cognitively impaired elderly. J Clin Psychiatry. 1983;44:14.

182 Larson EB et al. Adverse drug reactions associated with cognitive impairment in elderly persons. Ann Intern Med. 1987;107:169.

Geriatric Urological Disorders

John F Thompson

Sexual Dysfunction 103-1
  Male Sexual Dysfunction 103-2
  Impotence 103-3
    Pathogenesis (See Table 103.1) 103-3
      Neurogenic disorders 103-3
      Hormonal disorders 103-3
      Vascular disorders 103-3
    Signs and symptoms 103-3
    Urological workup 103-4
    Relationship of medical history and impotence 103-4
      Hypertension 103-6
      Cigarette smoking 103-6
      Diabetes mellitus 103-6
    Gonadal function in impotence 103-6
      Gonadotropins 103-6
      Testicular size and aging 103-6
      Testosterone 103-6
      Endocrine disorders 103-7
    Medications that cause impotence
    (See Table 103.2) 103-7
    Pharmacotherapy 103-7
      Testosterone 103-7
      Bromocriptine and pergolide 103-8
      Yohimbine 103-8
      Pentoxifylline 103-8
      Trazodone 103-8
      Isoxsuprine and aldose-reductase inhibitors 103-8
      Intracavernous injections (ICI)
      (See Table 103.3) 103-8
        Papaverine-phentolamine combination 103-8
          Candidates for ICI therapy 103-9
          Dosing 103-9
          Extemporaneous compounding 103-9
          Patient instructions 103-10
          Adverse effects (See Table 103.4) 103-10
      Prostaglandin E_1 and atropine 103-10
Benign Prostatic Hyperplasia (BPH) 103-11
  Pathophysiology of Symptoms
  (See Tables 103.5 and 103.6) 103-11
  Clinical Findings 103-12
    Urinalysis (UA) 103-13
    Digital rectal examination (DRE) 103-13
  Radiologic and Imaging Studies 103-13
  Urodynamic Evaluation and Cystoscopy 103-13

Nonpharmacologic Treatment (See Table 103.7) 103-14
  Transurethral resection of the prostate (TURP) ..103-14
    Adverse effects 103-14
  Transurethral incision of the prostate (TUIP) 103-15
  Transurethral dilation of the prostate (TUDP)
  (See Table 103.7) 103-15
Drug Therapy (See Table 103.8) 103-15
  Alpha blockers 103-15
    Phenoxybenzamine 103-15
    Terazosin 103-16
    Alfuzosin 103-16
  Androgen suppression 103-16
  Finasteride 103-17
  Antiandrogens: flutamide 103-17
  Gonadotropin-releasing hormone (GnRH):
  Leuprolide 103-17
Effect of Androgen Suppression on Prostate
  Specific Antigen (PSA) 103-17
Urinary Incontinence (See Table 103.9) 103-18
  Neurophysiological Considerations
  (See Figure 103.5) 103-18
  Age-Related Changes (See Table 103.10) 103-18
  Classification 103-18
    Acute incontinence 103-18
    Persistent urinary incontinence (PUI) 103-18
      Urge incontinence 103-18
      Stress incontinence 103-19
      Overflow incontinence 103-19
      Functional incontinence 103-19
  Clinical Presentation and Evaluation 103-19
  Drug Therapy (See Table 103.11) 103-20
    Modifying bladder contractility 103-20
      Propantheline bromide 103-20
      Oxybutynin chloride 103-20
      Dicyclomine hydrochloride 103-20
      Flavoxate hydrochloride 103-21
      Terbutaline 103-21
      Imipramine hydrochloride 103-21
    Increasing bladder outlet resistance 103-21
      Imipramine hydrochloride 103-21
      Ephedrine 103-21
      Phenylpropanolamine 103-21
      Estrogens 103-22

Sexual Dysfunction

Advancing age is accompanied by a decrease in sexual function. Intercourse decreases from an average of once a week at the age of 65 to once every ten weeks at the age of 80.[1] The frequency of sexual intercourse among the elderly actually has increased over the past 40 years, but the frequency still is substantially less than in younger individuals.[1-4] Although individual variations in frequency are large, most studies show that sexual activity among the elderly depends upon the life pattern and past experiences of good or poor sexual function in each patient. Elderly patients may experience physiological changes and encounter additional interference with sexual activity because of disability, disease, and medications. Furthermore, the elderly have a decline in sexual interest with aging.[5]

Poor health often is cited by elderly women as a reason for not participating in sexual activity, and among men, impotence is the leading cause of a decline in activity.[1,6] The major factors correlated with reduced sexual activity include an older spouse, poor mental or physical health, marital difficulties, previous negative sexual experiences, and negative attitudes toward sexuality in the aged.[7] During the postmenopausal years, women undergo substantial physiologic change. The major physiological event of natural menopause is a decrease in estrogen production. There is little doubt that a decline in estrogen production is associated with many of the physiologic changes causing elderly women to report a low interest in sexual activity. The medical literature is replete with research and data on elderly male sexual dysfunction and little, if any, data on female sexual dysfunction.

Male Sexual Dysfunction

Men do not undergo an abrupt menopause, but do experience a decrease in testosterone, by as early as age 50.[8] The clinical impact of the decrease in testosterone that occurs with advancing age has been poorly investigated. However, with a decline in testosterone, libido and frequency of erections decline.[9]

Sexual function is considered to be an interaction between motivation, drive, desires, thoughts, fantasies, pleasures, experiences (referred to as the *libido*), penile vasocongestion, erection, orgasmic contractions, and ejaculations (referred to as potency).[10,11] Testosterone plays an important role in male libido and sexual behavior, and may play some role in penile erection. Elderly men show a strong correlation between advancing age and diminishing bioavailable serum testosterone levels.[12,13] Testosterone progressively declines after the seventh decade partly because of testicular and hypothalamic-pituitary dysfunction.[14]

Male sexual dysfunction, denoting the inability to achieve a satisfactory sexual relationship, may involve inadequacy of erection or problems with emission, ejaculation, or orgasm. Erectile impotence is the inability to achieve and maintain a firm erection. Premature ejaculation refers to uncontrolled ejaculation before or shortly after entering the vagina. Retarded ejaculation usually is synonymous with delayed ejaculation. Retrograde ejaculation denotes backflow of semen into the bladder during ejaculation due to an incompetent bladder neck mechanism.

The neurological structures in the brain most closely associated with sexual function and arousal are the limbic system and the hypothalamus. The psychogenic sexual arousal mechanism involving sensory organs (e.g., vision, auditory, olfactory, tactile) and imaginative stimuli participate in sexual function through the hypothalamus and limbic systems. Subsequent nerve transmission down the spinal cord to the autonomic nervous system and sacral and thoracolumbar centers mediates the penile erection. Furthermore, the reflexogenic mechanism of penile erection (stimulation of the genital area) also involves nerve transmission by the pudendal nerve to the sacral erection center. Neurotransmission in the peripheral nervous system is mediated by adrenergic and cholinergic stimulation and may be diminished in advanced age.[17] Neurochemical mediators also are involved with sexual function. For example, dopamine is associated with sexual arousal (stimulation), while serotonin has an inhibitory effect.[15,16] In the elderly, reduced onset of sexual arousal may be attributed to global cerebrovascular disease and diminished sensory input to the central nervous system (CNS). Peripheral mechanisms of sexual arousal also may be affected by aging.

Erectile impotence often is regarded as a benign disorder, but does have a profound impact on the quality of life. In the U.S. in 1985, impotence accounted for 400,000 outpatient visits to physicians and 30,000 hospitalizations, resulting in total direct costs of $146 million.[18] According to data from the Massachusetts Male Aging Study (MMAS), the combined prevalence of minimal, moderate, and complete impotence among all elderly men is 52%.[18] According to the Baltimore Longitudinal Study of Aging, impotence was a problem in 8% of all healthy men by age 55, and the prevalence of impotence increased to 25%, 55%, and 75% for men 65, 75, and 80 years of age, respectively.[37]

Erectile failure previously had been considered almost exclusively psychogenic; however, about 80% of all cases of impotence now are thought to be related to organic disease and subject to numerous influences.[10,19-21] In one study,[13] neurological and vascular disorders were the primary causes of impotence among elderly men, and psychogenic factors were the cause in less than 10%. The single most common etiology for erectile failure in the elderly is severe atherosclerosis (e.g., vascular disease and diabetes mellitus).[13] Cardiovascular disease, hypertension, diabetes mellitus, elevated low-density lipoprotein cholesterol, and cigarette smoking are associated with a greater probability of complete impotence in men.[18] Therefore, prevention of cardiovascular disorders by interventions such as low-fat and low-cholesterol diets and abstinence from tobacco should minimize the development of geriatric sexual impotence.

Different physiological mechanisms are involved in erection, emission, ejaculation, and orgasm. Except for nocturnal emissions, ejaculation requires stimulation of the external genitalia. Ejaculation occurs in three phases. The first phase is termed emission. Efferent signals traveling in the hypogastric nerve activate secretions and transport sperm from the distal epididymis, vas deferens, seminal vesicles, and prostate to the prostatic urethra (see Figure 103.1). The second phase is the coordinated closing of the internal urethral sphincter and relaxation of the external sphincter to direct the semen into the bulbous urethra. The coordinated closing of the internal sphincter and relaxation of the external sphincter is mediated by α- and β-adrenergic stimulation. The third phase, external ejaculation, involves the somatomotor efferent segment of the pudendal nerve to contract the bulbocavernosus muscle, which forces the semen through a pressurized conduit, the much-narrowed urethral lumen compressed by the engorged corpora cavernosa and corpus spongiosum (see Figure 103.2), to produce 2 to 5 mL of ejaculate.[20] In the elderly male, ejaculation is less vigorous and the total ejaculate is likely to be reduced.[23]

The hemodynamics of penile erection involve the pudendal artery (the major blood supply to the penis), of which the terminal portion divides into three branches: 1) the bulbourethral artery, 2) the dorsal artery, and 3) the cavernous artery. The cavernous artery supplies the corpora cavernosa; the dorsal artery, the glans

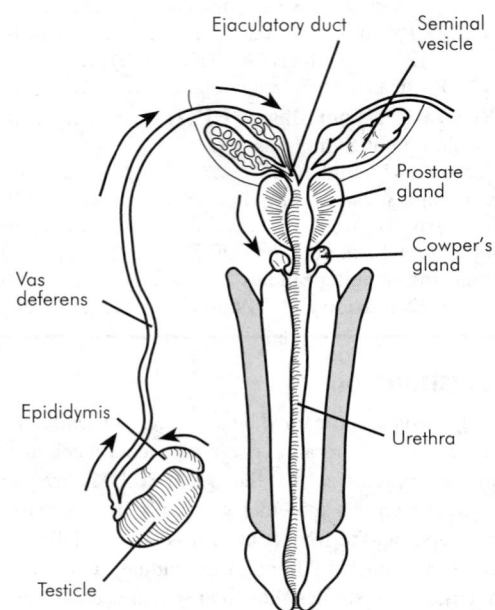

Fig 103.1   A Diagram Showing the Sources and Direction of Seminal Flow   Reprinted with permission from *Physical Assessment: A Guide for Evaluating Drug Therapy*. Vancouver; Applied Therapeutics: 1994.

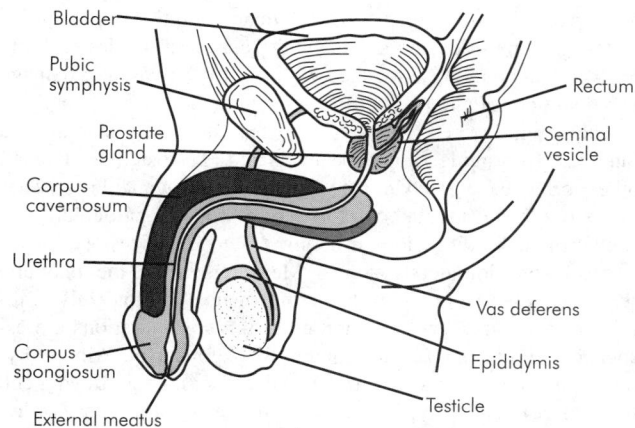

Fig 103.2 A Diagram Showing the Relations of the Bladder, Prostate, Seminal Vesicles, Penis, Urethra, and Scrotal Contents Reprinted with permission from Physical Assessment: A Guide for Evaluating Drug Therapy. Vancouver; Applied Therapeutics:1994.

penis; and the bulbourethral artery, the corpus spongiosum. The corpora cavernosa and the corpus spongiosum are the erectile muscle tissue and appear to be under β-adrenergic control.[10,20] Thoracolumbar or sacral erection-center stimulation shunts the blood to these structures and an erection ensues. The sympathetic nervous system also is involved in the constriction of veins in the erectile tissue that diminishes venous outflow. The resultant high intracavernous pressure converts a soft flaccid organ to a blood-distended erect penis. Distension of the erectile tissue further results in compression of the venules, reducing the venous capacity to minimum, which allows full erection of the penis. These actions will maintain erection in the corpora cavernosa without diverting too much cardiac output for penile erection.[22]

The process of orgasm is the least understood sexual process. Most likely the process involves cerebral interpretation of, and response to, sexual stimulation. Simultaneous with emission and ejaculation are involuntary rhythmic contractions of the anal sphincter, hyperventilation, tachycardia, and elevation of blood pressure.

Impotence

Pathogenesis

Erection involves the neurologic, psychologic, hormonal, arterial, and venous systems. In a study of 1500 elderly men over a period of ten years, organic impotence was diagnosed in more than 1050 subjects.[24] As a result of research in vascular physiology, neurophysiology, and neuropharmacology of the penis, most urologists today believe that up to 80% of elderly impotence cases are organic in origin and that the remainder are due to psychologic factors[25] (see Table 103.1). In the majority of elderly male sexual dysfunction studies, vascular damage is the leading cause of impotence.

Neurogenic Disorders. Erectile dysfunction can be caused by damage to the brain, spinal cord, cavernous and pudendal nerves, terminal nerve endings, and the receptors. Neurogenic impotence can be due to diabetes, spinal cord injury, cauda equina lesions, polyneuropathy, myelopathy, multiple sclerosis, dorsal nerve dysfunction from alcohol abuse or parkinsonism, and radical pelvic surgery.[25] Impotence was the presenting symptom in 12% of males with unrecognized diabetes mellitus.[26] Similarly, impotence can be the presenting symptom of temporal lobe epilepsy.[27]

Approximately 95% of patients with upper motor neuron lesions resulting from spinal injury are capable of erection through the reflexogenic mechanism,[28] while only 25% of patients with complete lower motor neuron lesions can have erections through the psychogenic mechanism.[28] With incomplete lesions, up to 90% of patients in both groups retain erectile ability. Patients who have a cerebrovascular accident, dementia, epilepsy, Parkinson's disease, or a brain tumor most likely will experience erectile failure through loss of sexual interest or overinhibition of the spinal erection centers.[25]

Hormonal Disorders. The incidence of impotence with a hormonal cause has been estimated to be 5% to 35%, depending upon which medical specialty is reporting the finding.[32] The most common hormonal disorder associated with impotence in the elderly is diabetes mellitus. About 75% of elderly male diabetics will experience impotence due to a combination of vascular, neurological, and psychological factors.[31] Insulin dosage, duration, and glycemic control are unrelated to sexual dysfunction.

Other hormonal disorders such as hypothyroidism, hyperthyroidism, Addison's disease, and Cushing's syndrome are associated with impotence. Patients with hypogonadism due to pituitary or hypothalamic tumors, antiandrogen therapy, or orchiectomy experience impotence. However, these patients can have a normal erection from visual stimulation, indicating that the erectile mechanism is intact.[29]

Vascular Disorders. Atherosclerosis is the leading vascular disease associated with male impotence. The age of onset of coronary artery disease parallels the onset of impotence, indicating a generalized atherosclerotic etiology for the impotence.[30] However, the degree of arteriolar narrowing and clinical presentation will differ from patient to patient. Some patients can have severe coronary artery disease but still retain the capability of a full erection. As long as the arterial flow into the penis exceeds the venous outflow, the patient can be potent. Narrowing of the arterial lumen lowers pressure in the cavernous arteries and poor arterial flow can only partially fill the sinusoidal system. Overall, the partial filling of the sinusoidal system causes inadequate expansion of the sinusoidal wall, resulting in partial compression of the venules. The net effect is a partial erection, difficulty in maintaining an erection, or the most common complaint, early detumescence. Intrapenile arterial disease resulting from diabetes mellitus, atherosclerosis, or aging does not respond to present surgical techniques.

Signs and Symptoms

1. **F.M., a 66-year-old male, was referred to a urologist because he was experiencing a loss of interest in sexual activity. He describes the inability to maintain a firm erection for the past 6 months in >75% of sexual attempts with his sexual part-**

Table 103.1	Causes of Impotence[a]	
Vascular	**Iatrogenic**
Atherosclerosis	Pelvic radiation
Penile Raynaud's phenomenon	Lumbar sympathectomy
	Prostatectomy
Neurologic	Renal transplantation
Cerebrovascular accident	Spinal cord resection
Spinal cord damage	
Autonomic neuropathy	**Psychogenic**
Peripheral neuropathy	Performance anxiety
	Depression
Endocrine	Widower's Syndrome
Diabetes mellitus	
Hypogonadism	
Prolactinomas	
Hyperthyroidism	
Hypothyroidism	

[a] Adapted with permission from reference 53.

ner. Physical examination was unremarkable except for an en-larged prostate gland and evidence of pubic and axillary hair loss. Vital signs were: blood pressure (BP) 160/95 mm Hg, pulse 88 beats/min, respirations 14 breaths/min, and temperature 98.7 °F. Current medications include ramipril 5 mg/day and glyburide 5 mg/day. The medical history is positive for ciga-rette smoking, hypertension, and diabetes mellitus. Significant laboratory results include: random blood sugar 200 mg/dL (Normal: 70–110), serum creatinine (SrCr) 1.5 mg/dL (Nor-mal: 0.6–1.2), blood urea nitrogen (BUN) 22 mg/dL (Normal: 8–18), total serum testosterone level 200 ng/dL, free testoster-one level 30 pg/mL (Normal: 52–280), luteinizing hormone (LH) 4 MU/mL (Normal: 1–8), follicle-stimulating hormone (FSH) level 40 mIU/mL (Normal: 4–25), and serum prolactin level 28 ng/mL (Normal: <20). What signs and symptoms does F.M. have that would suggest the need for a complete medical workup for impotence? [SI units: glucose 11.1 mmol/L (Normal: 3.9–6.1); SrCr 132.6 μmol/L (Normal: 50–110); BUN 7.9 mmol/L urea (Normal: 3.0–6.5); LH 4 IU/L (Normal: 1–8); FSH 40 IU/L (Normal: 4–25); serum prolactin 28 μg/L (Nor-mal: <20)]

F.M. presents with the complaint of loss of interest in sexual activity and the inability to maintain a full erection during 75% of sexual encounters with his partner. Upon physical examination F.M. has a noticeable loss of pubic and axillary body hair. With long-standing androgen deficiency there may be loss of hair in the androgen-dependent areas of the body, fine wrinkling of the skin around the mouth and eyes, noticeable loss of muscle mass and strength, altered body-fat distribution, and osteoporosis. In con-trast, overt hypogonadism will result in a change in the pattern of pubic hair from the male diamond shape to the female inverted triangle appearance. At this point it would appear that F.M.'s loss of pubic and axillary hair is the result of androgen deficiency, with the etiology yet to be determined. The laboratory results for go-nadal function coincide with what is expected in an elderly male with impotence (see Question 4).

Urological Work-Up

2. What clinical evaluations and laboratory tests should be included in the medical work-up of F.M. to determine the cause of his impotence?

A detailed medical and sexual history and thorough physical examination are essential in the evaluation of sexual dysfunction. General medical history and physical examination should consider drug-induced impotence (see Table 103.2); cigarette smoking (ci-gar and pipe tobacco have not been associated with sexual dys-function); prior surgery [e.g., transurethral resection of prostate (TURP), aortoiliac bypass, prostatectomy]; prior physical trauma (e.g., herniated disc, testicular trauma); voiding dysfunction; visual field defects (visual field changes may be one of the first presenting symptoms of diabetes mellitus, the most common endocrine ab-normality associated with male sexual dysfunction, and visual field changes may be associated with pituitary tumor pressure on the optic nerve); femoral artery bruits; testicular atrophy, Peyronie's plaques (a fibrous palpable plaque along the shaft of the penis, causing penile curvature and poor erection distal to the plaque, thought to be caused by atherosclerosis or severe vasculitis); pedal pulses; and neurological examination. Hormonal and metabolic screening should be included with the history and physical ex-amination.

F.M.'s endocrine status should include assessment of a glucose tolerance test (GTT), thyroid function tests, and a serum lipid profile. An abnormal GTT may be indicative of diabetes melli-tus. Neuropathy (as well as atherosclerosis) are common findings among male patients with diabetes mellitus, and both are potential causes of impotence. Patients experiencing hypothyroidism may have a decreased libido, and hypothyroidism is associated with

hyperprolactinemia, which can result in an inhibition in the release of testosterone. Elevated serum lipids (e.g., total cholesterol and triglycerides) may be associated with significant vascular damage that could contribute to erectile dysfunction.

The serum concentrations of free testosterone, prolactin, and luteinizing hormone should be evaluated. Testosterone, like all other hormones secreted into the plasma, is only available to tissues in the free form (i.e., unbound to serum proteins, particularly the sex hormone-binding globulin). Only 1% to 2% of testosterone is free and physiologically active. Measurement of the unbound serum testosterone provides the best estimate of biologically avail-able testosterone. Low testosterone serum concentrations are as-sociated with primary and secondary hypogonadism. Primary hy-pogonadism is associated with testicular disease (e.g., Leydig cell tumors). Secondary hypogonadism is the result of pituitary or hy-pothalamic disease.

The serum prolactin concentration should be determined be-cause a high serum concentration of prolactin inhibits release of testosterone from the testes. Therefore, a low serum testosterone concentration may be caused by hyperprolactinemia. Hyperprolac-tinemia may be due to prolactin adenomas, diabetes mellitus, or drug therapy (e.g., neuroleptics, metoclopramide).

Luteinizing hormone stimulates testicular steroidogenesis and secretion of testosterone. LH increases the conversion of choles-terol to pregnenolone, a precursor of testosterone. Follicle-stimu-lating hormone (FSH) is required for spermatogenesis in early pu-berty, but is not a required gonadotropin for the maintenance of spermatogenesis in adult men. Normal testicular function depends upon stimulation by the gonadotropin, luteinizing hormone which is secreted by the anterior pituitary gland. A low normal serum concentration of LH is associated with secondary hypogonadism.

In patients with symptoms of prostatic disease, expressed pro-static secretions (EPS) should be examined because prostate in-flammation has been associated with ejaculatory dysfunction. During prostatic inflammation, the EPS contains leukocytes and macrophages, and microscopic examination of the EPS can deter-mine the degree of prostate inflammation. The presence of more than 20 white blood cells (WBC) per high-powered field (HPF) in the EPS is abnormal, and indicative of prostatitis. Only about 5% of prostatitis cases can be attributed to a bacterial infection: the remaining 95% are due to unknown etiologies.

Ideally, assessment of erectile dysfunction should include uro-logical, endocrinological, psychiatric, and neurological evaluations as close together as possible.

The chief complaint of impotence must be identified carefully and described. Erectile impotence requires medical intervention if it occurs over a six-month period and in more than 50% of at-tempts.[20] A detailed history should determine whether impotence varies with partners, sexual settings, position, and masturbation and if morning and nocturnal erections also are impaired.

Clinicians should ask the patient to estimate the degree of penile rigidity, especially with regard to the ability for vaginal penetra-tion, and also should ask about nocturnal penile tumescence to differentiate psychogenic from organic causes of impotence. The examiner should ascertain the presence of associated problems (e.g., atherosclerosis, diabetes mellitus) and attempt to correlate these problems to identified concerns with libido, orgasm, and ejac-ulation. Ideally, the sexual partner should be present during history taking. A pattern of progressive impotence often indicates organic cause. A pattern of intermittent episodes of impotence with an abrupt onset suggests a psychogenic cause.

Relationship of Medical History and Impotence

3. What is the relationship between hypertension, cigarette smoking, diabetes mellitus, and F.M.'s impotence?

Table 103.2	Common Drug-Induced Alterations in Sexual Response[a]
Drug Categories	**Clinical Considerations**

Antihypertensives
Diuretics

Thiazides	Temporal association with sexual dysfunction. Reported incidence varies between 0%–32%;[68,69,75-77] however, impotence generally not considered common. Mechanism believed to be a "steal syndrome" whereby blood is routed from erectile tissues to skeletal muscle[71]
Spironolactone	Associated with ↓ libido, impotence, and gynecomastia. Mechanism may be hormone related. Incidence is dose related and reported to be 5%–67%[70,71,88] and much more commonly encountered than with the thiazides. May be due to antiandrogen effects of drug

Sympatholytics

Methyldopa	Central action mediated causing vasodilation resulting in erectile dysfunction. Reported incidence: 10%.[71,72] Also ↓ libido
Clonidine	Induces erectile dysfunction. Mechanism similar to methyldopa and other central α_2-agonists. Incidence reported to be 4%–70% and dose related.[78-80] Also ↓ libido
Guanabenz, guanfacine	Incidence and mechanism believed to be similar to other central α_2-agonists

Nonselective Beta Blockers

Propranolol	Associated with erectile dysfunction and ↓ libido. Mechanism believed to be due to ↓ vascular resistance and central effects. Erectile dysfunction reported to begin at doses of 120 mg/day. Incidence may be as high as 100% at higher doses[68,72,81]

Selective Beta Blockers

Atenolol, metoprolol, pindolol, timolol (drops)	Incidence of erectile dysfunction is significantly less than nonselective beta blockers[82]

Alpha Blockers

Prazosin, terazosin	Associated with erectile dysfunction and priapism.[72,83] Reported incidence: 0.6%–4%.[86] Mechanism is local α_1-blockade resulting in vasodilation
Phenoxybenzamine	Associated with priapism, retrograde ejaculation, and inhibited emissions during erection. Effects are dose related[84,85]

Direct Vasodilators

Hydralazine	Associated with erectile dysfunction. Mechanism is vascular smooth muscle relaxation. Incidence not reported[84]

Calcium Channel Blockers

Nifedipine	Associated with erectile dysfunction. Mechanism believed to be vasodilation and possibly muscle relaxation. Reported incidence: <2%[53]
Diltiazem, verapamil	Similar to nifedipine. Reported incidence: <1%

Antiarrhythmics
Class IA

Disopyramide	Associated with erectile dysfunction in patients treated for ventricular arrhythmias. Incidence not reported. Mechanism believed to be due to strong anticholinergic effect[71,84]

Antidepressants

Tricyclic antidepressants, monoamine oxidase inhibitors	Associated with impairment of sexual performance in both male and female: ↓ libido, anorgasmia, retrograde ejaculation, erectile dysfunction. Mechanism believed to be due to anticholinergic and serotonergic effects. Incidence not reported; several case studies in the literature[17]
Trazodone	Associated with priapism in men and ↑ libido in women. Mechanism similar to TCAs. Incidence not reported but believed to be dose related.[17] (*Note:* The literature reports that overall there is less sexual dysfunction with desipramine than with other antidepressants)

Antipsychotics

Phenothiazines	Frequently associated with sexual dysfunction. Commonly, ↓ libido is reported. Mechanism is due to hyperprolactinemia secondary to central dopamine antagonism. Thioridazine is the most often reported offender. Erectile and ejaculatory pain are very common with this drug class; the α-antagonism and anticholinergic effects are responsible. Priapism is common with this drug group, owing to the peripheral α-blockade property. Incidence for all sexual dysfunction with this drug class: ≈50% of users[17]

Anxiolytics

Short-acting barbiturates	Biphasic effect. At low doses, libido ↑, similar to ethanol, and at higher doses, CNS depression causes ↓ libido and performance[17]
Benzodiazepines	Biphasic effect. At low doses, libido ↑, while at higher doses, CNS depression causes performance failure. Some reports of anorgasmia (men and women) and ejaculatory failure[17]

Substances of Abuse

Cocaine	Biphasic effect. At low doses, there is enhanced sexual desire (similar to amphetamines) and possibly performance. At higher doses, there may be arousal dysfunction, ejaculatory dysfunction, anorgasmia. Freebasing has been associated with spontaneous orgasm. Continued use ("on a run") causes significant loss of sexual interest and performance ability. Chronic use associated with hyperprolactinemia resulting in ↓ libido[17]
Ethanol	At low doses actually may enhance libido. Sexual dysfunction is dose related and due to CNS depressant effects[71,72,83]
Hallucinogens	Biphasic effect for majority of drugs in this category. At low doses, libido is enhanced; at higher doses, libido is severely ↓. No reports on chronic use[17]
Marijuana	Biphasic effect similar to ethanol. With chronic use there is a ↓ in libido. Mechanism may be due to ↓ testosterone. Incidence not reported[17]

Continued

Table 103.2	Common Drug-Induced Alterations in Sexual Response[a] (Continued)
Drug Categories	Clinical Considerations
Opioids	Associated with sexual dysfunction: erection lubrication, orgasm, and ejaculation. Chronic use associated with ↓ libido. Mechanism may be due to α-antagonism, alterations in testosterone, and the intoxicating effects. Incidence not reported[72,73,83,90]
Miscellaneous	
Amyl nitrate	Associated with intense and prolonged orgasms in both male and female. Impotence has been reported in some cases due to vasodilation[17]
Cimetidine, ranitidine	Associated with ↓ libido and erectile dysfunction. Mechanism due to antiandrogen qualities and drug-induced elevation of prolactin. May be dose-related[72,89]
Metoclopramide	Associated with ↓ libido and erectile dysfunction. Mechanism is through CNS dopamine antagonism, resulting in hyperprolactinemia. Incidence not reported[72]

[a] CNS = Central nervous system; TCA = Tricyclic antidepressant.

Hypertension. Among elderly men, impotence most often is due to neurovascular diseases.[13] The high degree of arteriosclerosis among elderly American men is the leading cause of erectile impotence.[13,35,36] In the MMAS, heart disease with hypertension and low serum high-density lipoprotein correlated with impotence.[10] The hemodynamics of erection can be impaired in patients with myocardial infarction, coronary bypass surgery, cerebrovascular accidents, and peripheral vascular disease.[38-41] In several studies of impotent men, the number of abnormal penile vascular findings significantly increased when the history included hypertension and cigarette smoking.[42-44] In one report, 8% to 10% of all untreated hypertensive elderly males were impotent at the time of diagnosis of hypertension.[45] Control of blood pressure among hypertensive male patients does not necessarily improve erectile function, and antihypertensive medications can have a significant effect on impotence and sexual performances (see Table 103.2).[60-62]

Cigarette Smoking. The prevalence of cigarette smoking among men with erectile dysfunction is higher than in the general population.[43,56,57] When the relationship between cigarette smoking and erectile physiology was studied in 314 men with erectile dysfunction,[58] smoking was noted to further compromise penile physiology in men experiencing difficulty maintaining erections long enough for satisfactory intercourse. Several investigators report lower penile blood pressure indices, penile arterial insufficiency, and abnormal blood perfusion associated with cigarette smoking.[43,59] Clearly, cigarette smoking is counterproductive in men with existing erectile dysfunction.

Diabetes mellitus clearly has been associated with impotence. In the MMAS, male patients with diabetes mellitus were three times more likely to have impotence than patients without diabetes.[10] Other investigators using exclusively diabetic populations have found impotence as high as 75% among subjects.[46,47] The onset of impotence in the diabetic patient occurs at an earlier age when compared to the general population. In a few cases, impotence may be the presenting symptom of diabetes mellitus, and in most cases impotence will follow within ten years of the diagnosis, regardless of insulin-dependence status.[48,49] Researchers disagree as to the exact contribution of diabetes mellitus to impotence, but the majority of literature supports an atherosclerotic etiology.[50,51] Other causes also would include autonomic neuropathy and possible gonadal dysfunction.[48]

Gonadal Function in Impotence
4. What is the significance of the gonadal function results for F.M.?
Gonadotropins. Abnormalities of primary or secondary hypogonadism must be ruled out, particularly in those patients with a decreased libido with or without impotence. The results of F.M.'s gonadal function tests are relatively normal for an aged male. Tes-

testosterone serum levels decline with aging as a result of hypothalamic-pituitary changes or Leydig cell dysfunction. The understanding of changes that take place in the hypothalamic-pituitary level with advancing age is in a state of flux. For some time, most investigators focused on the increased serum concentration of male gonadotropins (LH, FSH), believing that all elderly males had some degree of primary hypogonadism.[52] In more recent studies, not only is testosterone serum concentration low in elderly males, but luteinizing hormone actually is less than the median in younger patients.[53] These findings show that LH levels do not increase in response to the decrease in testosterone serum concentrations in the aged male. This would indicate a defect in the hypothalamic-pituitary axis, leading to secondary hypogonadism.[54] Secondary hypogonadism results when there is a dysregulation of pituitary LH release, resulting in low serum testosterone levels.[25]

Testicular Size and Aging. Testicular size decreases with age; however, the testicular degeneration is sporadic, thereby allowing most elderly men to maintain a normal or slightly decreased sperm output.[52] Overall, spermatogenesis decreases and is accompanied by an increase in serum concentration of FSH. FSH elevation correlates well with a decline in Sertoli cell numbers. Sertoli cells secrete inhibin, which normally would decrease FSH.[55]

Testosterone. As a result of primary or secondary hypogonadism in the elderly male, there is a decline in available testosterone. Approximately 60% to 75% of circulating serum testosterone is bound to a beta-globulin known as sex hormone-binding globulin or as testosterone-binding globulin. About 20% to 40% of testosterone is bound to serum albumin, and 1% to 2% is unbound, or free. The unbound portion of testosterone is the only active portion of the total serum testosterone concentration. Testosterone serum concentrations are 20% higher in the morning than the evening, and this should be taken into consideration when evaluating laboratory results. In virtually all cases of male impotence, the serum concentration of testosterone should be measured in the morning.

The production of testosterone is regulated by feedback with the hypothalamus and pituitary. The hypothalamus produces gonadotropin-releasing hormone (GnRH) in response to low testosterone levels. GnRH induces the pituitary to secrete LH and FSH, which, in turn, stimulate the Leydig cells of the testes to secrete testosterone. Less than 10% of impotence cases studied are due strictly to hypogonadism.[13,34] The role of testosterone in male impotence is complex. After testosterone production decreases, libido eventually declines and precedes the decrease in frequency of erections.[9] Men given antiandrogens maintain their erectile capacity but have a decreased libido.[65] High doses of androgens to hypogonadal males clearly increase both the frequency of erections and libido.[66] It would seem reasonable to postulate that at physiological levels, testosterone modulates the cognitive processes associated with sexual arousal more than it contributes to erectile capability.

Endocrine Disorders. A number of endocrine disorders can result in impotence. Patients with prolactinomas commonly have impotence, but prolactinomas account for less than 1% of impotence cases.[63] Prolactin inhibits the release of testosterone, resulting in secondary hypogonadism. Hyperprolactinemia may be more prevalent in diabetic patients.[64] However, in the elderly, hyperprolactinemia often is secondary to the use of medications. F.M.'s serum prolactin level is elevated most likely due to his diabetes mellitus.

In summary, aged males have a decrease in testosterone due to defects at the testicular and hypothalamic-pituitary level. Secondary hypogonadism in elderly males is quite common, and the point at which this becomes pathologic has not yet been established. Correspondingly, the use of hormonal therapy to treat physiological secondary hypogonadism is extremely controversial. Therefore, the gonadal function tests for F.M. are normal for his age and do not provide an explanation for his impotence.

Medications That Cause Impotence

5. What medications are known to contribute to male impotence and is it likely that a medication is causing F.M.'s impotence?

There are several general statements that can be made regarding sexual function and medications. Drugs which affect libido generally have a central mode of action. For example, medication that blocks central dopamine transmission can decrease libido, and opiates have an antiandrogen effect.[73] Drugs that alter hemodynamics may interfere with erection. Excessive sympathetic tone is thought to cause the ''steal syndrome,'' which increases blood flow to muscles, drawing blood away from the erectile tissue.[71] Drugs that block the peripheral sympathetic system may cause retrograde ejaculation, or no ejaculation at all. There are well over 200 drugs that have been associated with altering sexual function[74] (see Table 103.2).

Few studies, if any, exist in the literature solely devoted to drug-induced impotence or sexual dysfunction.[61,62] However, a few studies and review articles list medications as one of many potential etiologies for male impotence.[10,15,25,37] Most studies documenting drug-induced impotence have been subjective and based upon case reports, uncontrolled studies, and clinical impressions. Nevertheless, 16 of the most common 200 drugs prescribed in the U.S. have been reported to cause impotence.[67]

In a study (MMAS) from the New England Research Institute at Boston University Medical Center, complete impotence was most significant for smokers being treated with cardiac drugs.[10] In this study, impotence was statistically correlated with antihypertensive, vasodilator, cardiac, and hypoglycemic drugs. The probability of moderate as well as complete impotence was particularly high for vasodilator drugs.[10] While the MMAS perhaps is one of the most well-designed studies to date, the medications reported are not considered to be the universe of all medications associated with impotence. Diagnosis of drug-induced sexual dysfunction should be restricted to a reproducible dose-related effect that disappears upon discontinuation of the drug.[72] A much larger survey of a controlled study in a clinical population would be required to establish any suspect medication as causative, rather than temporal.

F.M.'s sexual dysfunction (e.g., loss of interest in sexual activity and impotence) is not due to his current drug regimen, ramipril and glyburide. Even though the MMAS[10] reported a correlation between the use of antihypertensives and hypoglycemic drugs with impotence, clinicians must look at the individual drugs themselves and the conditions for which they are prescribed. Sexual dysfunction has not been reported for ramipril, or any of the other angiotensin-converting enzyme (ACE) inhibitors, as well as for glyburide. While ramipril is an antihypertensive, its pharmacological effects do not contribute to a decline in libido, or cause erectile dysfunction: an advantage that ACE inhibitors have over other antihypertensive medications. Similarly, the pharmacological action of glyburide does not contribute to F.M.'s decreased libido or impotence. In the majority of sexual dysfunction cases, it is less likely that the medication is the direct cause of the problem, but rather it is the medical condition for which the drugs were prescribed. The ability of a drug to induce sexual dysfunction simply is an extension of its pharmacologic actions. As a general rule, drugs that manipulate the sympathetic and/or the parasympathetic system, both centrally and peripherally, are associated with sexual dysfunction.

F.M. is a hypertensive diabetic patient who smokes cigarettes. These three factors (hypertension, diabetes, cigarettes) are more likely to be the etiology of F.M.'s sexual dysfunction. Again, in the MMAS[10] study, cigarette smoking combined with hypertension was determined to be the most significant cause of male impotence. Diabetes mellitus is the most common hormonal disorder associated with impotence in the elderly population.[31] The continued loss of interest in sexual activity experienced by F.M. most likely is the result of having experienced impotence during past and present sexual events.

F.M.'s subjective and objective findings are not unique, but rather quite common among elderly men. F.M.'s sexual dysfunction is due to atherosclerosis and possible neuropathy secondary to diabetes mellitus. Without a doubt, F.M.'s impotence is contributed to by his cigarette smoking. One immediate recommendation would be to stop the cigarette smoking, as erectile dysfunction is somewhat improved if the patient refrains from smoking during sexual performance.[17] There would be no need at this time to alter F.M.'s drug regimen.

Pharmacotherapy

Any therapy directed at male sexual dysfunction must include the elimination of drugs causing adverse sexual effects. Rational drug therapy involving geriatric sexual function is directed primarily toward treatment of male erectile dysfunction and impotence. Available pharmacotherapy for male sexual dysfunction includes hormonal therapy, bromocriptine, yohimbine, and intracavernosal injection of papaverine and phentolamine.

6. Testosterone. Should F.M. be treated with testosterone?

Primary hypogonadism with severely deficient serum levels of bioavailable testosterone is the only appropriate indication for the use of androgen hormone therapy.[91] The goal of androgen replacement therapy is to restore potency and libido by maintaining normal serum levels of testosterone.[92] Treatment of eugonadal or mildly hypogonadal elderly men is of no benefit and actually may enhance the growth of undiagnosed adenocarcinoma of the prostate, itself a cause of impotence.[19] F.M. would not be a candidate for testosterone therapy.

7. Which type of patient would benefit from testosterone therapy?

Testosterone replacement in patients with primary hypogonadism generally restores libido and potency. In some patients with secondary hypogonadism caused by disorders of the hypothalamus or pituitary, gonadotropin-releasing hormone analogues can be administered to differentiate between hypothalamic and pituitary abnormalities and to correct testosterone deficiency.[92] Libido and potency then are restored.

8. Why is the parenteral administration of testosterone preferred over oral administration?

Due to poor drug bioavailability, oral testosterone replacement therapy is less effective than parenteral testosterone in achieving normal serum testosterone levels. Oral administration also is associated with a higher incidence of hepatotoxicity and adverse serum lipid effects.[19,93] A long-acting testosterone intramuscular formulation such as the enanthate or the cypionate ester is the regimen of choice for the treatment of primary hypogonadism. A dose of 50 to 400 mg should be administered intramuscularly every two to four weeks. Side effects of testosterone therapy include early gynecomastia, increases in hematocrit (sometimes to the point of polycythemia), and fluid retention which may worsen hypertension or congestive heart failure (CHF).

9. Bromocriptine and Pergolide. Since F.M.'s prolactin serum concentration is 28 ng/mL, should bromocriptine or pergolide be prescribed to decrease his hyperprolactinemia and treat his impotence? [SI units: prolactin 28 µg/L]

Hyperprolactinemia may be treated with the ergot alkaloid, bromocriptine (Parlodel), or other dopamine agonists such as pergolide mesylate (Permax). Normalization of the serum prolactin level is mandatory if restoration of potency is to be achieved. However, even with normalization of prolactin levels, about 50% of elderly male patients are unable to achieve erectile function and desire.[92,93] Bromocriptine therapy may be initiated with twice-daily 1.25 mg doses taken with meals to minimize GI upset. Thereafter, doses may be increased on a weekly basis, at a rate of no more than 2.5 mg/day. As bromocriptine is associated with dizziness, drowsiness, hypotension, and cerebrovascular accidents, the patient should be forewarned.[19,92]

Pergolide mesylate, while not approved by the Food and Drug Administration (FDA) for sexual dysfunction, is quite useful for impotence associated with hyperprolactinemia associated with hypogonadism. Pergolide is many times more potent than bromocriptine. The initial dose is 0.05 mg/day for two days, then on the third day, the dose may be increased by 0.1 to 0.15 mg, and every third day thereafter for 12 days. From the 12th day on, the dose may be increased by 0.25 mg every third day until therapeutic effectiveness is noted. The average dose for pergolide is 1.0 mg three times a day. Maintenance doses of pergolide are administered three times a day to decrease the common side effect of nausea. As with bromocriptine, pergolide does cause hypotension and the patient should be forewarned.

F.M. is not a candidate for treatment with either bromocriptine or pergolide. F.M. does not have secondary hypogonadism, and his erectile dysfunction probably is secondary to atherosclerosis associated with his hypertension, diabetes, and cigarette smoking. Normalization of the prolactin serum level in F.M. would not correct his problem. Furthermore, the elevation of F.M.'s serum prolactin concentration is not significant enough to warrant drug therapy. With only a 50% (or less) response rate to bromocriptine or pergolide (in elderly males), the risk of adverse reactions (e.g., dyskinesia, dizziness, hallucinations, dystonia, confusion, cerebrovascular accidents) does not outweigh the benefit of this drug therapy.

10. What nonhormonal drug therapy is available for F.M.?

Yohimbine is an indole alkaloid derived from the bark of the West African yohimbine tree and has been classified as an aphrodisiac in many pharmacopoeias. Yohimbine hydrochloride is an α_2-adrenergic antagonist which decreases the outward blood flow from the penile corporal tissue. The effectiveness of yohimbine requires adequate penile blood supply. It has been used in treating impotence among diabetics with some degree of success.[97] A trial of yohimbine in psychogenic impotence noted a 47% response rate compared to 28% ($p = 0.42$) among placebo users.[98] This finding was affirmed in a subsequent study.[99] The response rate of psychogenic impotent men is marginal, at best. However, owing to its safety, availability, ease of administration, and the modest effect, it still is used in those patients who do not accept more invasive methods [e.g., intracavernous injections (ICI), penile implant]. Based upon the literature, those patients who have psychogenic and/or neurogenic impotence appear to have some response to yohimbine therapy.[97-99] As F.M. is experiencing vasculogenic, neurogenic, and psychogenic impotence, his response to yohimbine may be none to slight at best due to his atherosclerosis and resultant low penile blood supply. Again, the risk of side effects in comparison to the slight benefit that F.M. may experience would suggest that other therapies be considered. In some patients, yohimbine has been associated with nausea, tachycardia, a slight elevation in blood pressure, anxiety, and panic attacks.[93] The drug regimen used in clinical trials is 6 mg orally three times a day, and beneficial effects usually become apparent within two to three weeks.[15,97,98] In some of the trials, the point was made that perhaps the dose of 18 mg/day is too low; however, dose-response trials would be necessary before higher doses could be recommended.

Pentoxifylline (Trental) is a nonhormonal drug that holds some promise for the treatment of impotence. This drug decreases blood viscosity and increases red blood cell flexibility, which is believed to improve potency in penile artery disease.[100]

Trazodone. The antidepressant trazodone (Desyrel) has vasoactive potential. When injected directly into the corpora cavernosa, trazodone can initiate an erection;[100] however, a parenteral formulation of trazodone is not available in the U.S. When administered orally for depression, trazodone has been associated with priapism (i.e., persistent and painful erection of the penis).[101] Trazodone has been used with some success in treating impotence in patients due to primary and secondary psychological factors.[102]

Isoxsuprine and Aldose-Reductase Inhibitors. Other drugs that have been studied in the treatment of impotence are isoxsuprine and aldose reductase inhibitors. Isoxsuprine (Vasodilan) is a β-adrenergic stimulator that has been a moderately effective vasodilator in the treatment of impotence in some patients who are heavy cigarette smokers.[103] In patients with diabetic neuropathy, the administration of an aldose reductase inhibitor with inositol supplementation improved the impotence.[104] Reported results with these three drug therapies appear preliminary and at this time no recommendation for use can be made.

Intracavernous Injections (ICI). In 1982 inadvertent injection of papaverine into the penis was found to produce an erection.[105] This landmark observation ushered in a new methodology for the diagnosis and therapy of impotence. By 1986 papaverine injection into the penis had gained worldwide popularity for the treatment of impotence.[106] In 1983 the alpha blocker phenoxybenzamine also was noted to be effective.[107] Shortly thereafter, the combination of papaverine with another vasodilator, phentolamine, reportedly enhanced and prolonged the duration of erection.[108] These vasoactive drugs, when injected into the cavernosa, cause prolonged penile arterial vasodilation and venous compression, thus allowing the patient to achieve and maintain an erection. Erectile dysfunction responds favorably to the self-injection of vasoactive drugs into the penis.[106,109,110] Originally, the intracavernous regimen of papaverine with phentolamine was prescribed as a short-term measure while patients were awaiting the results of counseling or penile implant. Currently, self-injection of vasoactive drugs has become an accepted modality as a nonsurgical method of treating impotence (see Table 103.3).

Papaverine-Phentolamine Combination. Papaverine, a phosphodiesterase inhibitor, increases the serum concentration of cyclic adenosine monophosphate, resulting in penile arteriolar and corporal sinusoidal smooth muscle relaxation. In laboratory studies, papaverine blocks voltage-operated calcium channels, inhibits the release/storage of intracellular calcium, increases calcium efflux,

Table 103.3	Agents Used to Treat Vasculogenic Male Impotence	
Drugs	Route[a]	Mechanism
Papaverine	ICI	Phosphodiesterase inhibitor; penile arteriolar vasodilator
Phentolamine	ICI	α-adrenergic blockade; direct vasodilator
Prostaglandin E₁	ICI	α-blockade; vasodilator
Atropine	ICI	Antimuscarinic; smooth muscle relaxant

[a] ICI = Intracavernous injection.

and inhibits calcium-activated chloride and potassium currents in vascular smooth muscle.[120–122] Papaverine also may relax an elastic venous valve mechanism that is kept open by an α-adrenergically mediated smooth muscle contraction.[111–113]

Phentolamine exerts its relaxant effects by α-adrenergic receptor blockade of both α_1- and α_2-adrenoceptors. In addition, phentolamine also may have direct, nonspecific relaxant effect on vessels.[123] The combined use of papaverine with phentolamine exerts a greater effect than would be experienced with either drug alone.[114]

11. *Candidates for ICI Therapy.* **What objective data must be obtained to ensure that F.M. can receive ICIs safely?**

Patients who are candidates for the intracavernous injections of vasoactive drugs must have a complete medical work-up to include assessment of the penile arterial system. Doppler sonography of the penis will identify penile architecture, define the thickness of any plaques, measure the diameter of cavernous arteries (before and after vasodilation), as well as allow visualization of the penile arteries. This noninvasive assessment of the individual penile arteries is much more accurate than the penile brachial pressure index. The penile brachial pressure index (PBI) is the ratio of the penile systolic blood pressure (measured by continuous-wave Doppler analysis) to the brachial artery systolic pressure. This method of assessment measures all the penile arteries rather than signals from a single penile artery. PBI ratios that are normal (i.e., >0.6) do not always indicate normal penile blood flow, as the PBI is obtained while the penis is flaccid. F.M. should have sonography combined with Doppler analysis to assess his penile arteries.

In some urological practices, the functional evaluation of penile arteries is obtained by the intracavernous injection of vasoactive drugs at the office. If the patient develops a fully rigid erection within 12 minutes of injection of papaverine hydrochloride 30 to 60 mg or prostaglandin E₁ 10 to 20 µg and maintains a rigid erection for 30 minutes, adequate arterial flow and an intact venous mechanism can be assumed.[20] The patient then is a candidate for at-home intracavernous injection of vasoactive drugs.

12. The Doppler-sonography analysis of F.M.'s penile arteries showed severe atherosclerosis, indicating a vasculogenic etiology for his impotence. Is F.M. still a candidate for ICI therapy?

Patients with psychogenic and/or neurogenic impotence who respond to test doses of intracavernous injections of a vasoactive drug are the optimal candidates for continuing with ICI therapy.[100] Patients with vasculogenic impotence are less responsive to the intracavernous injections of vasoactive drugs and corporeal veno-occlusive dysfunction is the primary potential obstacle to this treatment.[118,119]

An abnormal veno-occlusive mechanism can result in penile venous incompetence, causing rapid detumescence or partial erection (referred to as venogenic impotence). The veno-occlusive mechanism of the corpora cavernosa can be assessed through an elaborate and quite painful invasive process, using angiocatheters and

iodinated contrast media. In a study to determine the effectiveness and safety of intracavernous therapy in vasculogenic impotent men, 40% of the participants had arterio-venogenic impotence, and 32% have venogenic impotence (i.e., they had a dysfunctional veno-occlusive mechanism), with only 28% of participants having pure arteriogenic impotence.[124] However, only 4% of the participants failed to achieve a sustained rigid erection, massive veno-occlusive mechanism dysfunction being cited as the reason. At a mean follow-up of 20 months, the remaining 96% of patients (including those with some degree of veno-occlusive mechanism dysfunction) still were using the intracavernous therapy. Given these findings, F.M. has a good chance of responding to intracavernous therapy, even if he is determined to have some veno-occlusive mechanism dysfunction. Absolute contraindications to ICI therapy are anticoagulant therapy, Peyronie's disease, and idiopathic priapism.

13. *Dosing.* **What is the protocol for starting a patient on an ICI therapy program for home use?**

The initial dose of the papaverine-phentolamine combination should take into consideration the underlying etiology for the impotence, the findings of the Doppler sonography, and the patient's response to a test dose of the ICI. Generally, patients with neurogenic impotence are started on the lowest doses (usually 0.5 mL) while patients with severely compromised penile arterial blood flow would receive larger doses (e.g., 1.0 mL). Keep in mind that there may be excessive sympathetic stimulation in an anxious patient while at the physician's office, and more drug may be required to overcome the vasoconstriction.[132] This would imply that at-home use may require a lower dose. The standard mixture for the most common vasoactive ICI solution is 30 mg/mL of papaverine and 1 mg/mL of phentolamine, for a total volume of 10 mL. The initial test dose administered in the physician's office generally is 0.5 mL (but may be as low as 0.25 mL) of the 30:1 mixture, using a tuberculin syringe with a 26-gauge needle. The patient is observed for not only therapeutic effects, but also for adverse effects such as bradycardia, hypertension, dizziness, or flushing. If any of these adverse effects are observed, atropine should be injected intracavernously.[126] In the event that the patient's erection becomes prolonged, usually rigid for more than 30 to 60 minutes, the subsequent dose of the papaverine-phentolamine should be reduced. Prolonged erection, which may progress to a pulsatile priapism, is the most significant complication of intracavernous injections of vasoactive drugs. Treatment should be instituted immediately with epinephrine 1 µg/mL 10 to 20 mL injected intracorporeally as an irrigant, and then aspirated.[100] Prolonged erections can lead to intracorporeal hypoxia, resulting in corporeal fibrosis.[126] In some cases the physician may choose single drug ICI with papaverine 25 to 60 mg, or prostaglandin E₁ 10 or 20 µg/dose.

14. *Extemporaneous Compounding.* **What procedures should be taken when extemporaneously compounding a papaverine-phentolamine injectable solution, and what expiration date is acceptable?**

The method of extemporaneous compounding of the papaverine-phentolamine mixture was developed in the early 1980s without consideration of pharmaceutical product stability. Today, the compounding of the papaverine-phentolamine solution has not changed much from those early days. The final product usually consists of a 10 mL vial of papaverine and phentolamine in a ratio of 30:1 mg/mL. Papaverine hydrochloride is available in a 30 mg/mL 10 mL multidose vial that also contains 0.5% chlorbutanol as a preservative. Phentolamine mesylate (Regitine) is available in vials containing 5 mg of active drug and 25 mg of mannitol, in a sterile lyophilized form. Extemporaneous compounding of this product requires sterile procedure technique. One vial of papaverine and two vials of phentolamine are needed to make the final product. Using a small gauge needle and 3 mL syringe, remove 2 mL (i.e., 60 mg) from the papaverine vial and use 1 mL to reconstitute the first vial of phentolamine. With the remaining 1 mL of papaverine solution in the syringe, reconstitute the second vial of phentolamine. Using the empty syringe, remove the solution from both phentolamine vials and instill this volume into the 10 mL papaverine multidose vial. Each milliliter of the final concentration in the papaverine vial should contain 30 mg of papaverine hydrochloride with 1 mg of phentolamine mesylate (plus 0.5% chlorbutanol and 5 mg of mannitol).

Currently, the FDA has not approved either papaverine or phentolamine alone or in combination as a treatment modality for erectile dysfunction. The addition of papaverine hydrochloride with phentolamine mesylate into a multidose vial for at-home patient use is not mentioned in the respective manufacturer's package inserts.[115,116] In a product stability study, the combination of papaverine and phentolamine was stable for at least 40 days when stored at room temperature.[117] In this study, the concentration of papaverine hydrochloride was 25 mg/mL and phentolamine mesylate was 0.83 mg/mL. It would seem that the already common practice of using a 30-day expiration date on the extemporaneously prepared papaverine-phentolamine multidose preparations is justified.

15. *Patient Instructions.* **What instructions should be provided to the patient for ICI therapy?**

Once the dose of ICI vasoactive drug is determined for the patient at the physician's office, the patient then is taught self-injection using a 26-gauge needle, 1 cc syringe.

Patients should be instructed to inject into the right side of the penis (lateral aspect), approximately 4 cm from the glans, after the area has been cleaned with an alcohol swab. The tip of the needle should be placed into the center of the right corpus cavernosum with a quick jab. The injection is administered within a one- to two-minute period. If pain is felt in the glans penis, the rate of injection should be slowed (next time) to perhaps three or four minutes. Upon withdrawal of the needle, the puncture site is compressed and the penis should be massaged gently by squeezing intermittently for about three minutes to distribute the drug throughout the shaft. A tourniquet at the base of the penis is not necessary. Sterile technique should be stressed when discussing this procedure with patients.

Patients are limited on the number of injections per month to prevent long-term complications, particularly when papaverine is used. In most cases the patient is prescribed a one-month supply of a 10 mL vial of 30:1 papaverine hydrochloride to phentolamine mesylate. The 10 mL volume will allow patients to have intercourse 10 to 20 times per month when doses of 0.5 mL to 1 mL are used.

16. *Adverse Effects.* **F.M. has been using papaverine-phentolamine 30:1 mixture at a dose of 1.0 mL per sexual episode over the past 6 months. He has injected himself 32 times. For the past month he has noticed a lateral deviation of his penis when rigid, and that he is able to feel a hard spot (induration) below the surface of the skin on the shaft. What are the adverse effects of repeated use of papaverine-phentolamine ICIs?**

Penile induration is a complication of intracavernous injections, particularly when papaverine hydrochloride is used. The appearance of induration is significantly correlated to the number of injections administered.[135] Men with penile induration injected the papaverine-phentolamine mixture two and one-half times more often than those who did not suffer this side effect. Similarly, men who administered higher doses also were more likely to develop penile induration ($p < 0.01$). Hence, a 10 mL solution of the papaverine-phentolamine combination should be dispensed on a

monthly basis to manage not only the frequency of use but the dose used. The patient should be educated about the complications and side effects of penile injection with vasoactive drugs (see Table 103.4).

During long-term treatment, corporeal fibrosis, which may result in Peyronie's disease, is the limiting factor with any combination of papaverine because the relative acidity of the drug (pH 3 to 4) is associated with sclerosis.[128–131] The frequency of intracavernous papaverine injections should be limited. At least 94% of patients using intracavernous self-injection will experience at least one complication, with 70% of users reporting at least two to three complications.[133] Pain at the site of injection is related more to the injection of the drugs than to the insertion of the needle.[134] The pain is described as a burning sensation in the glans penis occurring 30 seconds after the injection begins, and lasting for one to two minutes after the injection is stopped. The most devastating complication, priapism, will be experienced by about 4% of patients and require treatment. Of interest, none of the patients who experienced priapism were vasculogenic impotent. Self-administration side effects such as pain, bruising, and swelling usually do not occur when physicians inject the vasoactive drugs into the penis.[135]

Systemic effects of the papaverine-phentolamine initially were believed to be insignificant. However, the use of this mixture has been associated with abnormal liver function tests (LFTs) in 40% of recipients, mostly involving mild to moderate elevations of serum alkaline phosphatase and serum lactic dehydrogenase.[135] Hepatotoxicity, which may be an immune mechanism, has been associated with papaverine injection, infrequently. A patient may be well advised to discontinue the use of this medication if the LFTs are indicative of hepatocellular injury.

The adverse effects from the use of papaverine-phentolamine generally do not prevent continued use of this therapy. However, patients are instructed, after being treated for an episode of priapism, to not use the injection for at least one month.[133] Most patients who have experienced one or more adverse effects (e.g., bruising, pain, fibrosis, and priapism) from the papaverine-phentolamine injections generally still will resist penile implantation for as long as possible and continue with the injection therapy.[133]

Several studies have reported various degrees of satisfaction among users of intracavernous self-injection.[109,110,133] Eventually, the majority of users will discontinue the use of ICI vasoactive drugs, and will consider a penile implant. Complications as a result of intracavernous injection of vasoactive drugs do not prevent successful prosthetic implantation.[133]

17. *Prostaglandin E₁ and Atropine.* **What options are available for patients who no longer respond to the papaverine-phentolamine ICIs?**

Those patients who are more likely to not respond to the papaverine-phentolamine mixture have vasculogenic impotence. These patients generally require larger doses of papaverine-phentolamine and, thus, are more likely to develop penile induration. However, 96% of patients with vasculogenic impotence responded to a four-drug vasoactive mixture of papaverine hydrochloride 12.1

Table 103.4	Side Effects of Papaverine-Phentolamine ICI for Vasculogenic Impotence[a]
Prolonged erection	Penile induration
Priapism	Pain at injection site
Painless penile nodules	Bruising/bleeding at injection site
Peyronie's disease	Abnormal LFTs

[a] ICI = Intracavernous injection; LFTs = Liver function tests.

mg/mL, prostaglandin E$_1$ 10.1 μg/mL, phentolamine mesylate 1.01 mg/mL, and atropine sulfate 0.15 mg/mL. The solution was obtained by mixing 250 mg papaverine hydrochloride (14.4 mL), 200 μg of prostaglandin E$_1$ (0.4 mL), 20 mg of phentolamine mesylate (2 mL), and 3 mg of atropine sulfate (3 mL), for a total of 19.8 mL.[124] Doses administered were from 0.1 to 1.0 mL via a 27-gauge self-injection device.

Prostaglandin E$_1$ has alpha-blocking properties mediated through a membrane receptor. It relaxes the cavernous and arteriolar smooth muscle while restricting venous outflow.[100] Prostaglandin E$_1$ is an acceptable alternative to papaverine and patients experience few side effects.[136,137] Prostaglandin is metabolized in the local tissue and is unlikely to cause any systemic effects.[138] Penile induration has not yet been reported with use of prostaglandin E$_1$. Atropine, in low doses, will block the muscarinic receptors, thereby reducing cholinergic excitation of the nonadrenergic, noncholinergic neuroeffector systems that control neurogenic corporeal smooth muscle relaxation.[125] Multidrug intracavernous injections probably represent the future of erectile dysfunction management.

Benign Prostatic Hyperplasia (BPH)

Benign prostatic hyperplasia, a common cause of urinary dysfunctional symptoms in elderly men, results from proliferation of the stromal and epithelial cells of the prostate gland.[139,140] The term ''benign prostatic hypertrophy'' often is used inappropriately because the prostate gland pathology results from hyperplasia rather than hypertrophy. Benign prostatic hyperplasia rarely is detected in males less than 40 years of age. After age 40 the prevalence of BPH is age dependent.[141] Approximately 75% of men who live to the age of 70 will develop clinical symptoms of BPH that are sufficiently severe to necessitate medical attention and about 90% of octogenarians will have evidence of BPH. Essentially, all men will develop BPH if they live long enough. The microscopic incidence of BPH is fairly constant in several countries, both in Western and developing countries.[143] This suggests that the initiation of BPH may not be environmentally or genetically influenced. Although BPH and prostatic cancer often coexist, there is no compelling evidence that BPH predisposes patients to the development of prostate cancer.[142] However, the appearance of atypical prostatic hyperplasia correlates with the presence of latent prostatic carcinoma.[144]

The etiology of benign prostatic hyperplasia is unclear; however, most hypotheses are based upon hormonal and aging processes. Intact, normally functioning testes are essential for BPH to develop,[145] and castration before puberty prevents the development of BPH. The prostate is dependent upon androgens both for embryologic development and maintenance of size and function in the mature male.[241] Testosterone, the major circulating androgen, is metabolized to dihydrotestosterone (DHT) by 5-α-reductase, an enzyme contained in the prostatic epithelial cells (also found in high quantities in the liver, sebaceous glands, hair follicles, and skin of the external genitalia). For testosterone to be active in the prostate, it must be converted to dihydrotestosterone; therefore, DHT is the obligate androgen responsible for normal and hyperplastic prostate growth. Within the prostate, DHT initiates RNA synthesis, protein synthesis, and cell replication.

As males increase in age, testosterone serum concentrations will decrease and the peripheral conversion of testosterone to estrogen will increase. The role of estrogens may be to initiate stromal hyperplasia, which in turn induces epithelial hyperplasia. Stromal hyperplasia in the prostate periurethral glands is recognized as one of the earliest findings in human microscopic benign prostatic hyperplasia.[143] The exact role of testosterone may be only to initiate

fibroadenomatous hyperplasia, eventually resulting in glandular enlargement. Since the effects of testosterone within the prostate gland are dependent upon its metabolism to dihydrotestosterone by 5-α-reductase, the finding of males with a congenital absence of 5-α-reductase has increased the understanding of the actions of this enzyme. Male patients with 5-α-reductase deficiency are known commonly as pseudohermaphrodites (i.e., they possess a blind vaginal pouch, testes, vas deferens, epididymis, prostate gland, but no penis). These patients have normal to elevated testosterone serum levels, with an absence of DHT. Prostatic development or enlargement, acne, normal facial and body hair, and recession of the hairline do not occur in males affected with 5-α-reductase deficiency.

Pathophysiology of Symptoms

18. G.M., a 72-year-old male, presents to the emergency room with severe lower abdominal discomfort of 4 days duration. He gives a history of increasing difficulty initiating urination, a significant decrease in the force of his urinary stream, occasional midstream stoppage, and postvoiding dribbling. Physical examination is unremarkable except for the abdominal and rectal examination. Abdominal examination reveals distention, tenderness, and increased dullness in the hypogastrium with a large mass, believed to be the bladder. Upon rectal examination the prostate is severely enlarged, firm, and rubbery without nodules or undue hardness. G.M. gives a history of a nocturia approximately 4 to 5 times a night and a daytime urinary frequency of 8 to 10 times a day. G.M. indicates that when he is able to urinate he does not feel relieved. Laboratory findings are as follows: BUN 45 mg/dL, SrCr 3.2 mg/dL, serum prostatic acid phosphatase 3 IU/L (Normal: 2.5–11), and the serum prostate specific antigen (PSA) <4 ng/mL. A urethral catheter was inserted, and 900 mL of urine was obtained. G.M. subsequently was scheduled for a urological work-up. What is the pathophysiological basis for G.M.'s symptoms? [SI units: BUN 16.1 mmol/L urea; SrCr 282.9 μmol/L; serum prostatic acid phosphatase 3 units/L (Normal: 2.5–11)]

Symptoms of benign prostatic hyperplasia can be both obstructive and irritative and descriptions of the symptoms need a frame of reference for standardization. A questionnaire to quantify the severity of BPH[146] consisting of nine questions has been developed. Five questions are designed to assess obstructive symptoms and four to assess irritative symptoms. While there may be some limitations to the use of this questionnaire (see Table 103.5), it is one of the most common measures used to quantify symptoms in benign prostatic hyperplasia studies[143] and it correlates well with the pathophysiology of BPH. The format of the Boyarsky index is designed to assist the clinician in educating the patient about the obstructive and irritative symptoms of BPH.

The Boyarsky index was the first of three patient questionnaires developed for the quantitative assessment of benign prostatic hyperplasia and the effectiveness of individual treatment.[241] As such, this questionnaire has been used in numerous clinical trials to measure the outcome of interventions. The Boyarsky index is not useful in comparing different treatment therapies among BPH patients, as it has not been sufficiently validated for this purpose, but rather it is useful in evaluating an individual's response to therapy.

More recently, the Multidisciplinary Measurements Committee of the American Urologic Association (AUA) published its Urinary Symptom Index for Prostatism[242] (see Table 103.6). The AUA recognized the importance of a validated symptom index for assessing the baseline severity of prostatism, disease progression, and the effectiveness of different therapies. The AUA symptom index has been validated through internal consistency reliability, constructive reliability, test retest reliability, and criterion reliability. The AUA symptom index allows comparison between different

Table 103.5	BPH Symptom Scoring System (Boyarsky Index)[a,b]

Nocturia
0	Absence of symptoms
1	1 time/night
2	2–3 times/night
3	≥4 times/night

Daytime Frequency
0	Urinates 1–4 times/day
1	Urinates 5–7 times/day
2	Urinates 8–12 times/day
3	Urinates ≥13 times/day

Hesitance (Lasts ≥1 min)
0	Occasional (≤20% of the time)
1	Moderate (20%–50% of the time)
2	Frequent (≥50% of the time)
3	Always present

Intermittency (Lasts ≥1 min)
0	Occasional (≤20% of the time)
1	Moderate (20%–50% of the time)
2	Frequent (≥50% of the time)
3	Always present

Terminal Dribbling (At end of voiding)
0	Occasional (≤20% of the time)
1	Moderate (20%–50% of the time)
2	Frequent (≥50% of the time)
3	Always present (May wet clothes)

Urgency
0	Absence
1	Occasionally difficult to postpone urination
2	Frequently difficult to postpone urination
3	Always difficult to postpone urination

Impairment of Size and Force of Urinary Stream
0	Absence
1	Impaired trajectory
2	Most of time size and force are restricted
3	Urinates with great effort and stream is interrupted

Dysuria
0	Absence
1	Occasional burning sensation during urination
2	Frequent (>50% of the time) burning sensation
3	Frequent and painful burning sensation during urination

Sensation of Incomplete Voiding
0	Absence
1	Occasional sensation
2	Frequent (>50% of the time) sensation
3	Constant and urgent sensation, no relief on voiding

[a] Symptom scoring provides the clinician with a tool to measure the relative need for, and efficacy of, different interventions. No specific score is associated with the need for a specific intervention. A low symptom score in the absence of significant urine retention generally indicates that medical management can be attempted before considering surgical intervention.[146]
[b] BPH = Benign prostatic hyperplasia.

therapies. The preferred patient questionnaire today in benign prostatic hyperplasia intervention research is the AUA symptom index.[241] The AUA index, however, may not be BPH specific.[244] When 101 males and 96 females between the ages of 55 and 79 used the AUA index, urinary symptoms and severity of urinary symptoms were similar in both groups. Therefore, symptoms associated with prostatism can be associated with aging and with BPH.

G.M. presents with obstructive symptoms consistent with benign prostatic hyperplasia as follows: 1) a history of difficulty in initiating urination (hesitancy); 2) a decrease in urinary force; 3) occasional midstream stoppage; 4) postvoiding dribbling; and 5) feeling of incomplete bladder emptying. The common obstructive symptom of decreased force and size or urine stream is due to urethral compression from prostate gland hyperplasia. Hesitancy, another obstructive symptom, is the result of the bladder detrusor muscle taking a longer time to generate the initial increased pressure to overcome urethral resistance. Urinary stream intermittency is due to the inability of the bladder detrusor muscle to sustain the increased pressure until the end of voiding. Terminal dribbling and incomplete emptying occur for the same reason but also may be due to obstructive prostatic tissue at the bladder neck, causing a "ball valve" effect.

G.M. also has a history of classic irritative symptoms that are consistent with benign prostatic hyperplasia as follows: 1) nocturia approximately four to five times a night; and 2) daytime urinary frequency of eight to ten times a day. Incomplete emptying of the bladder results in shorter intervals between voiding, hence the complaint of frequency. Also, a large prostate gland provokes the bladder to trigger a voiding response more frequently. This response is more pronounced if the prostate is growing intravesically and compromising the bladder volume. Bladder detrusor muscle becomes hypertrophied as a result of the greater bladder residual urine volume, which can result in increased detrusor muscle excitability. Clinically this excitability may result in bladder instability. The symptoms of urinary frequency are more pronounced at night because cortical inhibitions are lessened and bladder sphincter tone is more relaxed during sleep. Obstructive symptoms are associated more with an enlarged prostate, and the predominance of irritative symptoms could suggest voiding dysfunctions in addition to those of benign prostatic hyperplasia.

Urinary incontinence is not a common symptom with benign prostatic hyperplasia. With advanced BPH, a large residual volume of urine in the bladder weakens the bladder sphincter and allows the escape of small amounts of urine, corresponding to bladder filling. As the residual bladder volume increases, the ureters will dilate, resulting in stasis of urine in the ureters. The end result may be ascending hydronephrosis with transmission of high pressure to nephrons resulting in renal damage (see Figure 103.3). As a result, abdominal discomfort and flank pain may occur during voiding. Ascending urinary tract infections are common in this scenario.

Acute urinary retention in benign prostatic hyperplasia may occur as a result of increasing size of the prostate gland. However, independent of gland size, drugs may precipitate acute urinary retention. Drugs such as alcohol, anticholinergics, α-adrenergic agents, and neuroleptics all have been associated with acute urinary retention in men with BPH. Commonly, in advanced benign prostatic hyperplasia, the ignoring of the first desire to void may result in acute urinary retention. G.M.'s acute bladder distention is not due to any of these medications as he is not taking drugs commonly associated with urinary retention.

Clinical Findings

19. What objective findings in G.M. are associated with BPH?

G.M. presents with classic symptoms of benign prostatic hyperplasia. The increasingly severe symptoms culminated in an episode of acute urinary retention as evidenced by inability to void and lower abdominal discomfort. Objective symptoms associated with G.M.'s benign prostatic hyperplasia are: 1) abdominal tenderness with increased dullness in the hypogastrium; 2) the finding of an enlarged bladder; 3) an enlarged, firm, and rubbery prostate gland; and 4) a return of 900 cc of urine via urinary catheter. The normal serum acid phosphatase, normal prostate specific antigen, and digital rectal examination of the prostate suggest that G.M.

Table 103.6	American Urological Association Urinary Symptom Index for Prostatism[a]						
		Score					
Symptom		Not at all	<1 in 5 times	<½ the time	≈½ the time	>½ the time	Almost always
1) Over the past month or so, how often have you had a sensation of not emptying your bladder completely after you finished urinating?		0	1	2	3	4	5
2) Over the past month or so, how often have you had to urinate again <2 hr after you finished urinating?		0	1	2	3	4	5
3) Over the past month or so, how often have you found you stopped and started several times when you urinated?		0	1	2	3	4	5
4) Over the past month or so, how often have you found it difficult to postpone urination?		0	1	2	3	4	5
5) Over the past month or so, how often have you had a weak urinary stream?		0	1	2	3	4	5
6) Over the past month or so, how often have you had to push or strain to begin urination?		0	1	2	3	4	5
7) Over the past month or so, how many times did you most typically get up to urinate from the time you went to bed at night until the time you got up in the morning?		0 times	1 time	2 times	3 times	4 times	5 times

Interpretation of AUA Symptom Index		AUA Symptom Score = Sum of questions 1–7 = _____
Mild prostatism	≤7	
Moderate prostatism	8–18	
Severe prostatism	>18	
Highest possible score	35	

[a] Reprinted with permission from reference 247.

does not have prostatic carcinoma at this time. The elevated BUN and serum creatinine may suggest that G.M. has hydronephrosis as a result of his BPH.

Urinalysis (UA)

As BPH patients also may have a urinary tract infection, a urinalysis with microscopic examination is essential. It is mandatory that G.M. give a urine specimen for urinalysis before the digital rectal examination (DRE) of the prostate gland. Examination of the prostate will cause prostatic secretions to be expelled into the urethra which may contaminate the urine specimen, making it difficult to determine the source of an infection. The presence of white blood cells and bacteria in the urine necessitates a work-up for infection. Similarly, hematuria requires a work-up for urinary tract pathology other than BPH. As BPH also may cause hydronephrosis, renal function and serum electrolytes should be evaluated.

Digital Rectal Examination (DRE)

Digital rectal examination of the prostate remains a fundamental part of the evaluation of a man with prostatism. The prostate examination should determine the size, shape, consistency, and nodularity of this gland. Prostatic hyperplasia results in a large palpable prostate with a smooth mucosal surface rectally. The discernability of the right and left prostate lobes is lost in benign prostatic hyperplasia. The digital rectal examination of a patient with BPH commonly finds asymmetry of the prostate with one side being larger than the other. Prostatic enlargement can be both in an anteroposterior and in a superioinferior direction. As a result, on digital rectal examination, the upper extent of prostate hyperplasia is not palpable. Occasionally, the degree of enlargement felt by digital rectal examination may be misleading, since a substantial portion of enlargement may be intravesical. The consistency of the gland may be soft or firm depending upon the predominance of glandular or fibromuscular elements.[147] The presence of firm to hard nodules, irregularities, induration, or a stony hard prostate suggest possible prostate cancer.

Radiologic and Imaging Studies

20. Why should G.M. have his urinary tract evaluated with radiologic and imaging studies?

Visualization of the kidneys, ureters, and bladder (KUB) with intravenous pyelography (IVP) in some institutions still remains a common investigation in benign prostatic hyperplasia. Currently, the routine use of IVP is being questioned because this procedure does not visualize the bladder outlet during voiding and, therefore, cannot detect obstruction directly. G.M. is suspected of having hydronephrosis as his BUN and serum creatinine are elevated, and the routine use of IVP for KUB visualization in this type of patient may be a risk that is greater than the potential benefit.[148–150] As G.M. has been scheduled for a transurethral resection of the prostate, it is important to determine the extent of urinary flow obstruction and the urinary flow rate. An accurate determination of the urinary peak flow rate and voided volume correlated with G.M.'s history will assist in determining the degree of G.M.'s urinary obstruction. Furthermore, when hydronephrosis is a concern, ultrasound is the preferred diagnostic maneuver, because it spares the patient exposure to radiation and the possible adverse reactions to the contrast agent.[151] Presently, the consensus is that IVP is warranted only if hematuria is present.[147]

Computerized tomographic (CT) scanning is of little benefit in benign prostatic hyperplasia evaluation. The effectiveness of magnetic resonance imaging (MRI) in BPH assessment is questionable. Presently, MRI has no place in the management of patients with symptomatic BPH.

Urodynamic Evaluation and Cystoscopy

21. Why should G.M. have urodynamic evaluation and cystoscopy for his BPH?

Urodynamic evaluation involves assessing the urinary flow rate, bladder volume, detrusor pressure, and visualization of voiding. Peak *urinary flow rate* to assess prostatism is a useful method of evaluation because it is noninvasive and requires only simple and inexpensive equipment.

Fig 103.3 Flow of Urine (Color) Is Interrupted by Compression from a Prostate That Has Enlarged from Normal Size In this diagram, the ureters and bladder are dilated by backed-up urine.

The urinary flow rate is dependent upon bladder volume,[152] and a nomogram which corrects for age has been developed.[153,154] Flow rate represents the contributions of bladder contraction and outlet opening during voiding. A low flow rate may reflect diminished bladder contractility (e.g., due to aging, disease, medications) or outlet obstruction. Thus, a low flow rate is not specific and cannot differentiate bladder outlet obstruction from an underactive detrusor muscle, nor does it discriminate well between those who will and those who will not benefit from transurethral resection of the prostate (TURP).[152–155] The use of urinary flow rates as predictors of TURP outcomes is controversial. Kadow et al. found no significant difference in symptomatic outcomes from TURP when comparing preTURP urinary flow rates.[156] In addition, although flow rates tend to improve following TURP, there is wide individual variation, and an increased postoperative peak flow does not always correlate with symptom relief.[157]

Voiding cystourethrography involves retrograde filling of the bladder with a contrast agent followed by visualization of the bladder and urethra during the resting, voiding, and postvoiding phases. While this procedure has the same problems as the IVP, it does have the advantage of providing a dynamic evaluation of the urethral outlet during micturition.[147] Voiding cystourethrography often is performed by technicians and read by radiologists who might not be well trained in lower urinary tract physiology and who, therefore, do not provide sensitive analyses.

In spite of its utility, pressure/flow analysis is not widely used in the evaluation of prostatism because the patient must be able to forestall voiding during bladder filling, and then void on command.

As a result, interpretable data are obtained in only 60% to 86% of cases analyzed in optimal laboratory settings.[159]

Cystoscopy is used in prostatism to rule out intravesical pathology such as tumors or stones that also cause voiding symptoms and to evaluate bladder trabeculation, prostatic length and size, the presence of an enlarged median lobe, and the degree of obstruction. Like an IVP, cystoscopy is required if hematuria is present and also should be considered whenever there is pelvic pain with voiding.

In making treatment decisions, the roles of intravenous urography, the visual appearance of the prostate via cystoscopy, urodynamic studies, urine flow measurements, and the degree of obstructive and irritative voiding symptoms, collectively, remain controversial and do not provide data sufficient to dictate the best treatment for the patient.[161,162] These tests, therefore, are not necessary for G.M.

Nonpharmacologic Treatment

Transurethral Resection of the Prostate (TURP)

22. What nonpharmacological treatment is best for G.M.? When should prostate surgery be undertaken in general?

G.M.'s subjective and objective findings, particularly the acute urinary retention and hydronephrosis, collectively indicate the need for a transurethral resection of the prostate gland. G.M. has been advised by his urologist that a TURP is the treatment of choice given the severity of his presentation (e.g., large prostate gland with acute urinary retention) and that the procedure will relieve his symptoms, allow him to lead a relatively normal life, and avoid sequelae of prolonged obstruction.

Transurethral resection of the prostate provides significant relief of benign prostatic hyperplasia symptoms in 86%, 83%, 75%, and 75% of patients at three months, one year, three years, and seven years, respectively.[162] For patients with severe BPH, 93% of patients report reduced symptoms one year following a TURP.[161] The TURP is considered the "gold standard" for the treatment of benign prostatic hyperplasia and is used in 90% of patients with symptoms of prostatism with residual urine and/or acute urinary retention.[143] As a result, surgical alternatives are always compared to the outcome studies of TURP.

The need for a transurethral resection of the prostate in G.M.'s situation is fairly clear; however, in the majority of cases, the need for a TURP is less clear. The symptoms of benign prostatic hyperplasia do not inevitably progress and men often are willing to live with their symptoms. Clinicians, therefore, need to be able to talk to patients and help them answer the question of whether the discomfort, risk, and problems during the postsurgical recovery period are outweighed by the high probability that surgery will relieve symptoms. After conditions that clearly require surgery have been ruled out, the severity of a patient's symptoms and the degree to which they interfere with living a normal life are the dominant factors in any decision to proceed with prostate surgery. Since surgery for prostate enlargement most often is performed to improve the patient's quality of life, it is critical for clinicians to counsel the patient and assist him in making the decision.

23. Adverse Effects. What are the adverse effects that G.M. may experience, after the TURP?

The adverse effects that G.M. may experience can be divided into those that are immediate in onset and those that are late in onset. The immediate adverse effects may depend more upon the size of G.M.'s prostate gland and the necessary time to complete the transurethral resection of his prostate as well as the surgical technique. One of the most devastating and potentially life-threatening adverse effects of the procedure is the postsurgical TURP syndrome.[143] Irrigating fluid (e.g., dextrose 5%) is forced through the urethra during the TURP procedure, and there is a certain

Table 103.7	Surgical Options for BPH[a]
Transurethral resection of the prostate (TURP)	
Transurethral incision of the prostate (TUIP)	
Transurethral (balloon) dilation of the prostate (TUDP)	
Visual laser ablation of the prostate (VLAP)[b]	

[a] BPH = Benign prostatic hyperplasia.
[b] Experimental.

amount of absorption via the venous sinuses that are created by the procedure. As most TURP procedures last 45 minutes (or less), approximately 1 to 2 L of fluid can be absorbed. If the procedure time is prolonged, the patient may become hypervolemic and hyponatremic, resulting in cerebral edema and seizures. Preventive measures require frequent monitoring of the patient's serum sodium concentration during the procedure, with correction of hyponatremia using 3% hypertonic saline and mannitol diuresis. The incidence of the postsurgical TURP syndrome is 2%. Other immediate complications of TURP include failure to void, hemorrhage, and urinary tract infections.

Late complications of the TURP are impotence, urinary incontinence, and bladder neck contractures. Impotence is the most devastating long-term adverse effect of the TURP procedure.[143] Impotence has been reported to afflict as many as 30% with some procedures; however, the incidence generally is lower. The etiologic mechanism may be arterial damage during the TURP procedure leading to arterial insufficiency. Similarly, electrocautery during the TURP may cause thermal damage to the arterial supply and the nerves of the corpora cavernosa resulting in fibrosis, or venous leakage. In most cases, the patient has other pathology associated with risk factors for impotence (e.g., atherosclerosis, peripheral vascular disease, hypertension).

Retrograde ejaculation (i.e., the ejaculation of semen into the urinary bladder) is a common outcome of the TURP, particularly after a "complete" TURP secondary to damage within the urethra at the location of the prostate gland. Retrograde ejaculation is not harmful; however, it is a strange sensation and patients will need to gradually become accustomed to the feeling.

24. Is the TURP the only procedure available for G.M.?

Transurethral Incision of the Prostate (TUIP)

A reasonable alternative to the TURP is the transurethral incision of the prostate. TUIP is a reasonable procedure for men with small prostates that nevertheless cause bladder outlet obstruction. The TUIP uses shallow incisions in the prostatic urethra area to relieve bladder outflow obstruction and preserve antegrade ejaculation[143] (retrograde ejaculation is a complication of TURP). The TUIP is advantageous in high-risk patients such as the elderly[163] because it can be performed under local anesthesia. The TUIP procedure does not provide a tissue specimen for pathology review, and the potential for missing an occult carcinoma is of real concern. In contrast, prostate tissue can be retrieved from a transurethral resection of the prostate and sent for pathology studies. Men, however, should not undergo a TURP purely to find out whether microscopic cancer is present because a TURP does not reduce the risk of developing prostate cancer which often develops in the outer shell of prostate tissue left behind at surgery. In terms of patient satisfaction, 88% of the TUIP group and 66% of the TURP group report good improvement in symptoms. Mean peak urinary flow improved by 67% in the TUIP group.[164] TUIP patients may undergo a TURP at a later time if the TUIP outcome is unacceptable.

Transurethral Dilation of the Prostate (TUDP)

Transurethral dilation of the prostate by balloon catheter may be another alternative for high-risk patients who are not candidates

for TURP (see Table 103.7). After satisfactory anesthesia has been achieved, the balloon catheter is positioned in the prostatic urethra. Balloon inflation, if not done properly, can damage the external sphincter and subsequent incontinence can occur. The balloon is inflated for 15 minutes to cause dilation of the tissue. Postoperatively, the patient is left with an indwelling urinary catheter, usually overnight. Balloon dilation is appropriate for patients with smaller prostates who wish to avoid potential side effects (i.e., retrograde ejaculation that is associated with TURP). The success rate of TUDP in comparison to TURP is uncertain.[165] Hospital stays are shorter and blood loss is less during TUDP surgery compared to a TURP.

The most recent innovation for an alternative to the TURP (which still is experimental) is the laser ablation of the prostate gland (VLAP) via the urethra. The VLAP has been shown to result in spontaneous urination in all patients treated, produce no operative complications, and result in a safe partial prostatectomy.[243] Patients who respond successfully to the VLAP generally have small prostate glands (i.e., ≤40 gm). As a minimally invasive method to remove an obstructing prostate, laser treatment warrants further study.

G.M. was determined to have a large prostate gland (i.e., most likely <80 gm and >40 gm), and is not a candidate for any of the alternative procedures (i.e., TUIP, TUDP, or VLAP). Currently, patients with prostate glands greater than 80 gm are not candidates for TURP, but rather open surgical removal of the prostate adenoma. TURP for large glands necessitates more than 45 minutes of procedure time, which exposes the patient to a much higher risk for the postsurgical TURP syndrome.

Drug Therapy

Alpha Blockers

25. What drug therapy should be prescribed to treat G.M.'s prostatic hyperplasia?

G.M. most likely will be scheduled for a TURP, as he presents with acute urinary retention, hydronephrosis, due to a moderately enlarged prostate gland (e.g., >40 gm and <80 gm). However, he should be started and maintained on terazosin to reduce the tension of the bladder neck, the prostate adenoma, and the prostatic capsule. Similarly, he should receive finasteride to induce atrophy of the prostate gland to halt progression of the disease (see Table 103.8). G.M. should be started on terazosin 1 mg orally at bedtime, and finasteride 5 mg orally daily. Adjusting the terazosin dose will depend upon G.M.'s response.

Phenoxybenzamine. The prostatic capsule and benign prostatic hyperplasia adenoma have plentiful α-adrenergic receptors, and blocking these receptors can reduce the smooth muscle tone of the

Table 103.8	Medical Treatment Options for BPH[a]	
Category	Drug	Mechanism
Antiandrogen	Flutamide	Inhibits binding of androgen to receptors
GnRH analogue	Leuprolide	Desensitization of LHRH receptor, preventing release of GnRH
5-α-reductase inhibitor	Finasteride	Competitive inhibition; prevents testosterone conversion to DHT
α-blockade	Prazosin, terazosin, alfuzosin	α₁-blockade; reduces tone of bladder neck and urethra

[a] BPH = Benign prostatic hyperplasia; DHT = Dihydrotestosterone; GnRH = Gonadotropin-releasing hormone; LHRH = Luteinizing hormone-releasing hormone.

prostatic urethra and, thereby, reduce the functional component of urethral constriction and obstruction. Phenoxybenzamine (Dibenzyline), a nonselective alpha blocker, has been 80% effective in increasing urinary flow rates, but its use is hampered by a 30% incidence of side effects (fatigue, dizziness, hypotension) which are exacerbated by its long half-life.[166,167] The dose of phenoxybenzamine is 5 to 20 mg/day orally. Prazosin (Minipress) 2 to 4 mg/day is more α_1-selective and is less likely to cause side effects compared to phenoxybenzamine. The clinical efficacy of prazosin in improving urinary flow rates also may be somewhat less impressive.[166-168] Terazosin (Hytrin) a long-acting α_1 blocker 1 to 5 mg/day has significantly improved obstructive symptoms and urinary flow rates.[170,241] However, orthostatic hypotension may occur. The dose of terazosin may need to be increased to 5 to 10 mg/day in some men to obtain desired results.

Terazosin maintained the level of improvement in BPH symptom scores over a 30-month period. Only 10% of the patients experienced treatment failure.[244] In this long-term study, the systolic blood pressure in normotensive and hypertensive patients was decreased by 4 mm Hg and 18 mm Hg, respectively. Apparently, terazosin typically only lowered the blood pressure significantly in the hypertensive patients.

Terazosin commonly is prescribed with finasteride to control the progression and symptoms of BPH despite the lack of adequate clinical studies.[196] The mechanisms of action for both of these drugs are different and the combined use of both produces a synergistic effect. When combined with finasteride, a smaller terazosin maintenance dose can be used, resulting in fewer dose-related side effects (e.g., orthostatic hypotension and dizziness).

Alfuzosin. Overall, alpha blockers reduce symptoms of benign prostatic hyperplasia in 50% to 70% of moderately symptomatic men and provide an acceptable first-line therapy for the man without an absolute indication for surgery (e.g., urinary retention, infection, or hydronephrosis).[166,167] A new quinazoline derivative, alfuzosin, acts as a selective and competitive α_1-adrenoreceptor inhibitor which mediates contraction of the prostatic capsule, bladder base, and proximal urethral smooth muscle, thereby reducing the tone of these structures. Alfuzosin is comparable to prazosin, but perhaps with fewer vasodilatory-related side effects. A potential advantage of alfuzosin is a greater affinity for α_1-adrenoreceptors of the genitourinary tract than for the vascular system.[169]

Androgen Suppression

In recent years, considerable information has accrued concerning the endocrine basis for control of benign prostatic hyperplasia (see Figure 103.4), the effect of age on hormone dynamics in men, and the hormonal changes in the hypertrophic human prostate. Maintenance of morphology and functional activity of the adult human prostate is controlled by, and dependent upon, androgens. Prostatic regression after androgen deprivation is not a passive process but, rather, requires the synthesis of macromolecules.[171] As a result of androgen deprivation,[172] the loss of stromal and epithelial prostate cells is disproportionate, with four times greater loss of epithelial cells. Testosterone serves as the prohormone for the two types of active metabolites: dihydrotestosterone (DHT) and 17-beta-estradiol. Testosterone is metabolized to DHT by the enzyme 5-α-reductase. Thus, conversion of testosterone to DHT precludes its conversion to estrogen by the enzyme, aromatase, and the relative activity of these two enzymes is of paramount importance in prostate homeostasis.[173]

Although the mean plasma testosterone level in men falls after the age of 60, the level of testosterone in subjects with BPH and age-matched controls is not different.[174] Moreover, the onset of BPH starts some 10 to 20 years before the decrease in plasma

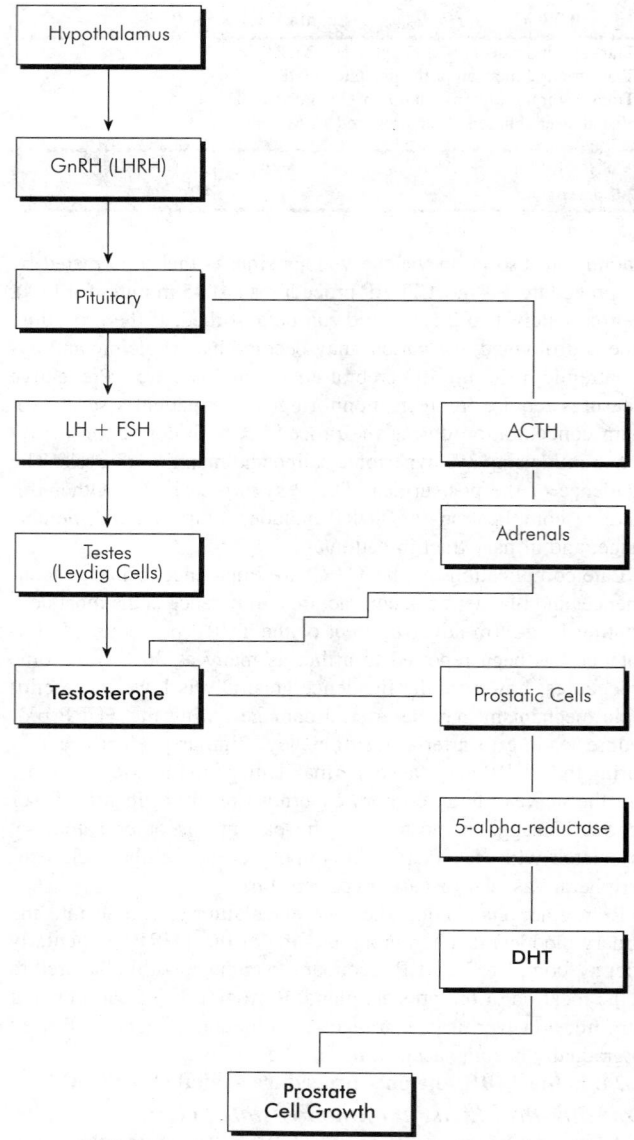

Fig 103.4   Pituitary-Gonadal Axis: Endocrine Basis for Control of Benign Prostatic Hyperplasia (BPH)   The pituitary-gonadal axis plays an important role in prostatic growth. Neurons in the preoptic area of the hypothalamus secrete gonadotropin-releasing hormone (GnRH), also known as luteinizing hormone-releasing hormone (LHRH). LHRH is a small peptide that interacts with surface receptor sites on the plasma membrane of the pituitary cells. LHRH stimulates the pituitary to release both luteinizing hormone (LH) and follicle-stimulating hormone (FSH). LH secretion causes the Leydig cells of the testicle to produce testosterone. Testosterone appears to inhibit LHRH at the hypothalamic level and luteinizing hormone at the pituitary level. The adrenals only contribute about 1% of circulating testosterone. Testosterone diffuses into the prostatic cells where it is converted to dihydrotestosterone (DHT) by 5-α-reductase. DHT binds to steroid receptor complexes in the nucleus of the prostate, which causes cell growth.[141]

testosterone levels. However, the serum concentration of dihydrotestosterone is increased in men with benign prostatic hyperplasia.[171,176,177] The mechanism responsible for accumulation of DHT has not been established. However, there is a significant increase in 5-α-reductase activity, which is known to produce DHT.[178,179]

One other major hormonal change associated with aging is the increased formation of estrogen from circulating androgens, both in the testes and the peripheral adipose tissue. Androgen conversion to estrogen via aromatase begins in males at about the third decade of life and increases with the aging process.[183] Although the amount of estrogen increases with aging in men, the plasma estrogen concentration in men with benign prostatic hyperplasia is not different to age-matched controls without BPH.[176] Estrogen receptors appear to be abundant in stroma[184,185] cells which may play a role in BPH. Estrogen stimulation of stromal tissue growth may explain why prostatic growth continues with age in spite of the decline in testosterone secretion by the testes. The effect of estrogen is augmented further by DHT in initiating the benign prostatic hyperplasia process.[186] The mechanism of estrogen in BPH is not fully understood. The number of prostate androgen receptors can be increased by estrogens and can be reversed by the administration of antiestrogens.[174] The increase in androgen receptors induced by estrogens may allow for continued androgen-mediated growth in spite of the declining amount of testosterone produced with old age.

Finasteride

The enzyme 5-α-reductase, which is present in high concentration in prostate tissue (see Figure 103.4), is responsible for converting testosterone to 5-α-dihydrotestosterone. DHT is the principal androgen responsible for stimulation of prostatic growth. Competitive inhibition of 5-α-reductase reduces DHT concentrations in the prostate and increases the serum and prostate concentrations of testosterone. When the 5-α-reductase inhibitor finasteride (Proscar) was administered in 1 and 5 mg doses to men with benign prostatic hyperplasia for a total of 12 months, symptom score and urinary flow improved significantly. Adverse effects in the finasteride groups occurred in less than 5% and side effects such as decreased libido and ejaculatory dysfunction were dose related.[190] The effectiveness of daily finasteride 5 mg in 298 men over a period of 24 months[191] noted slight improvement over the results reported at end of the 12-month period. The median DHT levels had declined by 74.5% compared to 69.3% at 12 months, and prostate volume declined by 25.2% as compared to 21.2% at 12 months. Patient symptom scores indicated slightly more improvement at 24 months, compared to 12 months. Obstructive symptom scores were responsible for the majority of improved symptoms reported. The prevalence of sexual adverse experiences at 24 months was similar to that at 12 months. Inhibition of dihydrotestosterone by 5-α-reductase inhibitors does not affect testosterone-mediated functions on muscle mass, libido, or spermatogenesis. Finasteride has an acceptable safety profile, halts disease progression, and improves the quality of life in patients with moderate BPH disease (i.e., enlarged prostate with symptoms of urinary obstruction, but not acute urinary retention). Although finasteride can reduce the size of an enlarged prostate gland in most patients, the majority of patients treated with the drug for one year do not have a clinically significant increase in urinary flow. Furthermore, at least six months of treatment may be necessary to determine whether a patient will respond to finasteride. For those who do respond, the drug must be continued indefinitely because DHT serum concentrations return to pretreatment levels within 14 days of discontinuing finasteride and prostate size returns to pretreatment levels within four months.[245,246] The cost to the pharmacist for a one-month supply of finasteride 5 mg tablets based upon 1995 Red Book price is $56.55.

Antiandrogens: Flutamide

The safety and effectiveness of flutamide were evaluated in a double-blind, placebo-controlled study of 31 males with symptomatic benign prostatic hyperplasia.[187] Flutamide (Eulexin) is an orally administered nonsteroidal antiandrogen that inhibits the binding of androgen to its receptor. The patients received a daily dose of 375 mg of active flutamide for 12 weeks. The efficacy of flutamide was evaluated based upon changes in symptoms, prostate size, residual urine, and uroflowmetry. A quantitative symptom index was not used. A significant difference in the treatment and placebo groups was not observed for any of the symptoms of prostatism (force of stream, frequency, nocturia). Based upon digital rectal examination, patients receiving flutamide were believed to have a significant reduction of prostate size. In 7 of the 15 patients treated with the flutamide, nipple tenderness and a decrease in libido developed. This study suggests that 375 mg/day of flutamide results in significant side effects; however, the dose may have been insufficient to achieve maximum reduction in prostate volume. Other studies using flutamide have not demonstrated a significant difference between active drug and the use of placebo.[188] In this same study, which used flutamide 250 mg three times daily, 53% of the patients experienced breast tenderness and 11% diarrhea. Flutamide also is associated with a 50% reduction in the serum concentration of prostate specific antigen.[195,196] Overall, flutamide results in toxicity and limited effectiveness. However, in those cases where the patient is not a candidate for surgery, and cannot tolerate finasteride with or without terazosin, flutamide may be justified.

Gonadotropin-Releasing Hormone (GnRH): Leuprolide

Analogs of gonadotropin-releasing hormone can cause regression of benign prostatic hyperplasia. Leuprolide acetate (Lupron) is a synthetic nonapeptide analog of natural occurring GnRH. It desensitizes luteinizing hormone releasing hormone receptors (when given continuously and in therapeutic doses), thereby preventing the release of gonadotropin. Chronic leuprolide acetate therapy will suppress testicular testosterone production, causing a "chemical-like" castration. As leuprolide acetate reversibly binds to GnRH receptors, testosterone production will resume upon discontinuance. In a double-blind, placebo-controlled study, patients received leuprolide 3.75 mg intramuscularly monthly for treatment of BPH for 24 weeks.[189] There were no statistical or clinically significant differences between the percent change in total, obstructive, or irritative symptoms at 24 weeks for the placebo and leuprolide groups. Detrusor muscle pressure at maximum urine flow at 24 weeks was improved, and prostate volume was reduced. However, of those patients receiving leuprolide acetate, 92% developed hot flashes, and of the sexually active patients, 95% experienced a loss of potency.

Leuprolide should be restricted to those patients who have prostate cancer. The high cost, questionable effectiveness, and castration-like adverse effects make leuprolide undesirable for treatment of benign prostatic hyperplasia.

Effect of Androgen Suppression on Prostate Specific Antigen (PSA)

26. What effect does androgen suppression have on PSA?

The FDA has approved Hybritech's prostate specific antigen test for the screening of prostate cancer. The possibility that antiandrogen treatment of benign prostatic hyperplasia could adversely affect the interpretation of the PSA screening test for prostate cancer is of concern. For example, androgen suppression with leuprolide acetate reduces prostate volume primarily by the involution of the epithelial elements of the prostate.[192] Since PSA is primarily produced by the epithelial cells of the prostate, these drugs can alter serum and prostate concentrations of PSA.[193] Finasteride 5 mg/day also can reduce the serum PSA level by 50%.[194] The serum PSA level reduction, however, is predictable and serum PSA levels can be recalculated during hormonal treatment for BPH. Nevertheless, patients receiving finasteride should have a digital rectal examination of their prostate periodically, have a PSA level measured, and have any suspicious findings investigated immediately.[191] Androgen suppression therapy should not be contraindicated in BPH solely on the basis of its effect on serum PSA levels.[195]

Urinary Incontinence

Urinary incontinence, both acute and chronic, is a common disorder among elderly individuals, affecting approximately 50% of the institutionalized elderly, and 20% of the community-dwelling elderly.[197,198] Neurologic impairment, immobility, and female gender are independent risk factors for incontinence, but neither advanced age nor chronic bacteriuria seem to be. The consequences of incontinence include not only economic costs, but also medical (e.g., cystitis, urosepsis, pressure sores, perineal rashes, and falls) and psychosocial (e.g., embarrassment, isolation, depression, and predisposition to institutionalization). Despite these considerations, incontinence often is neglected. Only a minority of patients whose lives are seriously disrupted seek medical attention; when they do, their incontinence often is attributed to aging and not evaluated further.[197,200] Incontinence is not an inevitable consequence of aging. It is a pathological condition that when rationally approached usually can be ameliorated or cured, often without invasive tests or surgery and almost invariably without an indwelling catheter[201,202] (see Table 103.9).

Neurophysiological Considerations

The bladder is considered to be a balloon with a narrow outlet, wrapped with a muscular layer, the detrusor muscle. The detrusor and the bladder outlet functions are coordinated neurologically to allow storage and expulsion of urine.[203] The detrusor muscle is innervated by the parasympathetic nervous system, and the bladder neck is innervated by the sympathetic nervous system (α-adrenergic) (see Figure 103.5). The proximal smooth-muscle (internal) sphincter in the bladder neck also is innervated through the sympathetic nervous system (α-adrenergic). The distal striated muscle (external) sphincter of the urethra is supplied by the somatic nervous system.

Urine storage is the result of detrusor muscle relaxation and closure of both the internal and external sphincters. Detrusor relaxation is accomplished by central nervous system inhibition of the parasympathetic tone; sphincter closure is mediated by a reflex increase in α-adrenergic and somatic activity. Voiding occurs when detrusor contraction is coordinated with sphincter relaxation. Detrusor contraction is mediated by the parasympathetic nervous system, and relaxation requires inhibition of somatic and sympathetic nerve impulses to the outlet. The bladder capacity is approximately 300 mL in the elderly and approximately 400 mL in young adults. The relationship between the detrusor and the outlet is coordinated by a micturition center, located in the CNS, perhaps the pons.[204] The cortex and diencephalon also permit inhibition of what would otherwise be a reflex contraction of the detrusor muscle in response to bladder distention.

Table 103.9	Causes of Incontinence[211]
Resnick's Mnemonic: DIAPPERS	
D	Delirium and dementia
I	Infections
A	Atrophic vaginitis, atrophic urethritis, atonic bladder
P	Psychological causes, depression
P	Pharmacological agents
E	Endocrine (diabetes, hypercalcemia, hypothyroidism)
R	Restricted mobility
S	Stool impaction

Age-Related Changes

Aging affects the lower urinary tract in several ways (see Table 103.10). Structural and functional changes have been observed. Bladder capacity, the ability to postpone voiding, urethral and bladder compliance, maximal urethral closure pressure, and urinary flow rate all are reduced with normal aging.[204,205] For women, these changes are correlated with the decline of estrogen production. Estrogen has trophic effects on the epithelium and tissues lining and surrounding the urethra, bladder outlet, and vagina. Atrophy of these tissues can result in friability, inflammation, susceptibility to infection, diminished periurethral blood flow, and prolapse of pelvic structures. All of these effects can precipitate symptoms of urinary incontinence. For men, the age-related changes in the prostate gland are responsible for many of the changes in urination. The most common age-related change, in both females and males, is involuntary bladder contractions (detrusor motor instability). These involuntary bladder contractions occur in up to 20% of asymptomatic, neurologically normal, continent elderly patients.[206–209]

In many elderly, nocturia is a common complaint and may stem from age-related increases in nocturnal urine production.[210] Each of these changes predisposes to incontinence, but none alone precipitates it. This predisposition to incontinence, coupled with the increased likelihood that an older person will be subjected to additional pathologic, physiologic, or pharmacologic insults, underlies the higher incidence of incontinence in the elderly. The onset or exacerbation of incontinence in an older person is likely to be due to a precipitating factor outside the lower urinary tract.[211]

Correspondingly, the reversal of the precipitating factor may be sufficient to restore continence without correction of the underlying urologic abnormality.

Classification

Urinary incontinence can be classified several different ways. The two most basic types of urinary incontinence are: 1) acute (or transient) and reversible; or 2) chronic and persistent. Persistent urinary incontinence (PUI), which refers to incontinence that is not acute and occurs over a long period of time, can be classified further into four subgroups: a) urge, b) stress, c) overflow, and d) functional.

Acute Incontinence

Urinary incontinence that is of relatively recent onset or associated with an acute medical problem should prompt a review for reversible factors. Factors that are associated with acute or abrupt onset urinary incontinence are: 1) cystitis, atrophic vaginitis, or urethritis; 2) congestive heart failure; 3) polyuria from diabetes; 4) delirium and acute confusional states; 5) immobility; and 6) medication side effects. Medications associated with acute onset urinary incontinence are: 1) diuretics; 2) α-adrenergic agonists (e.g., pseudoephedrine); 3) α-adrenergic antagonists (e.g., terazosin); 4) anticholinergics; and 5) neuroleptics. The management of acute forms of urinary incontinence depends upon the identification and elimination of the reversible factor.

For women with urethritis and atrophic vaginitis, with irritative voiding symptoms, estrogen replacement can be very helpful. An intravaginal estrogen cream administered nightly for seven days and followed by at least once a week application thereafter or oral conjugated estrogen 0.625 mg/day can be prescribed.[212] For women with an intact uterus, the conjugated estrogen should be given in a cyclic manner with a progestational agent.

Persistent Urinary Incontinence (PUI)

Urge incontinence is the most common form of incontinence affecting the elderly, and occurs when involuntary voiding is pre-

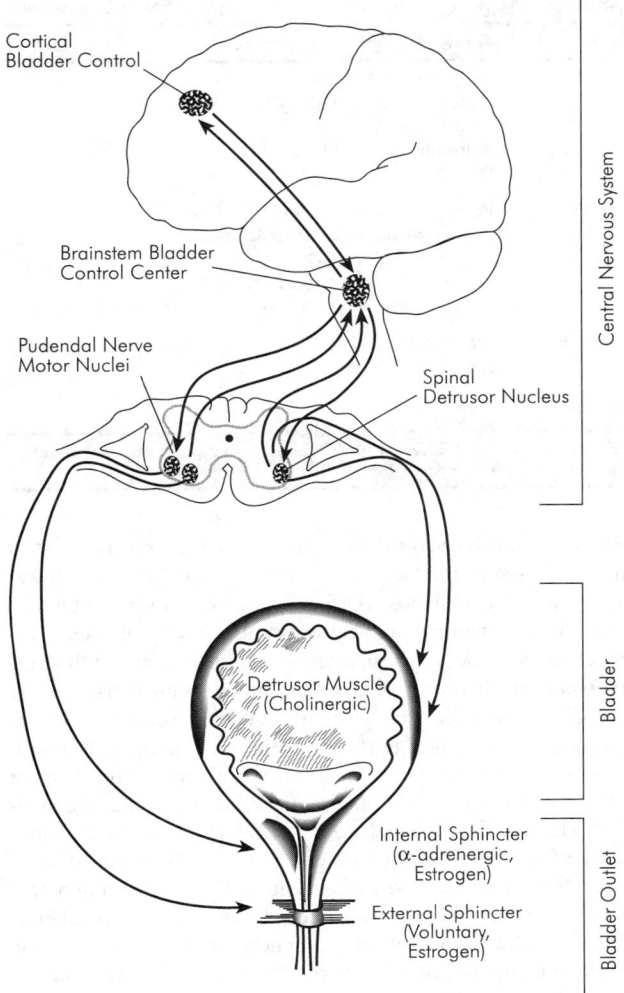

Cortical Bladder Control

Brainstem Bladder Control Center

Pudendal Nerve Motor Nuclei

Spinal Detrusor Nucleus

Central Nervous System

Detrusor Muscle (Cholinergic)

Bladder

Internal Sphincter (α-adrenergic, Estrogen)

External Sphincter (Voluntary, Estrogen)

Bladder Outlet

Fig 103.5 Neurologic Bladder Control   Three major components are involved in urine storage and release. 1) *Central nervous system:* Inhibition from the frontal lobe (cortical) micturition center permits bladder relaxation and filling, and sphincter closure to prevent leakage of urine. When cortical inhibition ceases (i.e., the patient wants to urinate), the brainstem (pontine) micturition center sends impulses down the spinal cord to the detrusor muscle, resulting in muscle contraction. 2) *Bladder:* Increase in bladder volume stimulates proprioception receptors in the bladder wall and sensory impulses are transmitted through the sacral nerves (S_2–S_4 roots) to trigger bladder contraction. This stimulus for bladder contraction is under inhibitory control by the CNS frontal lobe as described above. Cholinergic stimulation results in bladder contraction. 3) *Bladder outlet:* The two major factors in maintaining urethral pressure are the internal and external sphincters. *Internal sphincter:* α-adrenergic stimulation causes muscle contraction, preventing flow of urine. *External sphincter:* It consists of striated muscle under voluntary control. Contraction prevents flow of urine. Estrogen deficiency in women can result in decreased competence of the internal and external sphincters. Adapted from reference 248.

ceded by a warning of a few seconds to a few minutes. Urge persistent urinary incontinence is characterized by precipitous urine leakage, most often after the urge to void is perceived. Urge PUI can be caused by a variety of genitourinary and neurologic disorders. It most often, but not always, is associated with detrusor motor instability (involuntary contraction of the bladder) or detrusor hyperreflexia (detrusor motor instability caused by a neurologic disorder). The most common causes are local genitourinary conditions such as cystitis, urethritis, tumors, stones, bladder diverticuli, and outflow obstruction. Neurological disorders such as stroke, dementia, parkinsonism, and spinal cord injury can be associated with urge PUI.[213]

Stress incontinence, the involuntary leakage that occurs only during stress, is common in elderly women but uncommon in men

(unless the sphincter has been damaged during a transurethral resection of the prostate or prostatectomy). Stress incontinence occurs when an abrupt increase in intra-abdominal pressure (e.g., coughing, sneezing, laughing, lifting) overcomes urethral resistance. Typical stress PUI is characterized by daytime loss of small to moderate amounts of urine, infrequent nocturnal incontinence, and a low postvoiding residual volume in the absence of a large cystocele. The common cause of stress PUI is urethral hypermobility due to weakness and laxity of pelvic floor musculature, but other conditions, such as sphincter incompetence, urethral instability, or stress-induced detrusor instability, occasionally are responsible.[204] Estrogen deficiency in women, obesity, or transurethral resection of the prostate in men also can predispose individuals to stress incontinence.

Overflow incontinence occurs when the weight of urine in a distended bladder overcomes outlet resistance. Leakage of small amounts of urine are common throughout the day and night. The patient may complain of hesitancy, diminished and interrupted flow, a need to strain to void, and a sense of incomplete emptying. The bladder usually is palpable, and the residual urine volume is large. If the cause is neurologically mediated, control of the perianal sphincter may be impaired.[214]

Overflow incontinence results from an anatomic outlet obstruction or an acontractile bladder.[213] Common causes are benign prostatic hyperplasia, urethral stricture, bladder-sphincter dyssynergia, diabetic neuropathy, fecal impaction, and anticholinergic medication use.

Functional incontinence occurs when a continent individual is unable or unwilling to reach the toilet to urinate. Common causes are musculoskeletal disorders, muscle weakness, impaired mental status, use of physical restraints, psychological impairment, environmental barriers, and medications (e.g., sedatives, neuroleptics).

Clinical Presentation and Evaluation

27. H.K., a 83-year-old female resident of a nursing facility, developed urinary incontinence 3 years before admission to the nursing facility. She has been managed with adult diapers and bladder training. What objective and subjective data are needed to determine the pathophysiology (and hence the classification) of H.K.'s urinary incontinence?

The rationale for the clinical evaluation of H.K. is to classify the imbalance between bladder pressure and bladder sphincter resistance and, as a result, institute appropriate medical or surgical management of her urinary incontinence.

Documentation of H.K.'s urinary incontinence is accomplished most easily by having her or one of her nurses keep an incontinence record. Observations made every two hours should be recorded as to whether the patient is wet or dry, and be accompanied by comments regarding associated symptoms or circumstances. This record should be maintained over a three- to four-day period, which will then facilitate assessment of the voiding pattern. Establishment of the voiding pattern can assist bladder training programs, and help in detecting iatrogenic causes (e.g., diuretic in-

Table 103.10	Age-Related Changes in Urological Function
↓ bladder capacity	
↑ residual urine	
↑ uninhibited bladder contractions	
↑ nocturnal sodium and fluid excretion	
↓ urethral resistance in women	
↑ urethral resistance in men	
Weakness of pelvic floor muscles in women	

gestion, use of restraints). Successful bladder training depends upon estimating when the bladder is full.

Physical examination of H.K. is paramount in determining the etiology and classification of her urinary incontinence. A complete neurological examination is mandatory. Clinical findings may identify specific pathophysiologic abnormalities. H.K. should have a thorough pelvic examination to determine the contribution of atrophic vaginitis, uterine prolapse, and bladder anatomy. Funneling of the bladder neck suggests stress incontinence, and palpation of the bladder suggests overflow incontinence. The presence of physical restraints or musculoskeletal disability would suggest functional incontinence.

H.K should have bladder catheterization immediately following urination to determine residual urine volume. Volumes greater than 50 mL are abnormal and may indicate obstruction or an adynamic detrusor muscle. Although urodynamic studies are widely recommended and utilized, there is little evidence that these studies may assist in gathering clinically useful data for an institutionalized geriatric patient. H.K. should have a urinalysis, evaluation of blood chemistries, renal function, and a glucose tolerance test. An abnormal urinalysis may suggest pathology (e.g., infection) that can be managed medically. Urinary tract infection is common in the incontinent patient.

A number of treatment options exists for each type of urinary incontinence (see Table 103.11). Proper evaluation should guide the clinician in choosing the optimal course of drug therapy. Drug therapy should be based upon sound principles of neurophysiology, urology, and pharmacology. Basically, drug therapy is directed at decreasing bladder contractility (detrusor instability), and increasing outlet obstruction (bladder neck and proximal urethra).

28. The incontinence record maintained by the nursing staff indicates that H.K has urinary urges quite frequently, resulting in urine leakage. Throughout the day and night, H.K. will urinate 4 to 5 times. Physical examination reveals atrophic vaginitis, no funneling of the bladder neck, and no bladder distention. H.K. does have a history of stroke. The urinalysis is normal, as are the blood chemistries. Postvoiding bladder catheterization produced a residual urine volume of 30 mL. What is the pathophysiology and classification of H.K.'s incontinence?

H.K. is a stroke patient. Most neuropathic disease processes can change bladder function. A common disorder in the elderly associated with bladder dysfunction, and hence incontinence, is a cerebrovascular accident. Neurological injury above the level of the micturition center in the spinal cord, in most cases, will result in bladder spasticity. Sacral reflexes are intact, but loss of inhibition from higher CNS centers results in spastic bladder and inappropriate sphincter behavior. The degree of spasticity will vary between the bladder and sphincter, as well as from patient to patient with the same CNS lesions. H.K. is suffering from a detrusor muscle that is spastic due to an unchecked sacral reflex. H.K.'s bladder dysfunction is classified as urge urinary incontinence of the persistent type.

Drug Therapy

Modifying Bladder Contractility

29. What drug therapy should be prescribed for H.K.?

H.K. is suffering from detrusor instability and requires anticholinergic drug therapy. Detrusor muscle stabilization through pharmacological intervention and behavioral modification is the treatment of choice for urge PUI. The major neurohormonal stimulus for physiologic bladder muscle contraction is acetylcholine-induced stimulation of postganglionic parasympathetic cholinergic receptor sites on bladder smooth muscle.[215] Atropine and atropine-like substances will depress true involuntary bladder contractions of any etiology.[216]

Table 103.11	Drug Therapy of Persistent Urinary Incontinence
Type	**Treatment with Initial Doses**
Urge	Oxybutynin 2.5 mg QD–TID
	Flavoxate 100 mg TID–QID
	Imipramine 25 mg QD–TID
	Propantheline 15–30 mg TID
	Dicyclomine 10–20 mg TID
Stress	Phenylpropanolamine 50–75 mg QD–BID
	Pseudoephedrine 15–30 mg BID–TID
	Imipramine 25 mg QD
	Conjugated estrogens 0.625 mg QD[a]
	Vaginal estrogen cream 0.5–1.0 gm 2 times/week
Overflow	Prazosin 0.5–1.0 mg QD (usually at HS)
	Bethanechol 10 mg TID
Function	None

[a] If patient has uterus, consider cyclic therapy with a progestational agent to reduce risk for cervical cancer.

Propantheline bromide (Pro-Banthine) is the oral agent most commonly used to produce an anticholinergic effect in the lower urinary tract. The adult dose is 15 to 30 mg every four to six hours. Higher doses sometimes are necessary and are well tolerated. Propantheline bromide is a quaternary ammonium anticholinergic compound which does not cross the blood brain barrier.[217] As such, CNS side effects are insignificant. Oral administration of propantheline in the fasting state is preferred to improve bioavailability. The anticholinergic effects of propantheline on the detrusor muscle when compared to other anticholinergic agents are similar.[218] These anticholinergic agents differ primarily in their frequency of dosing and their side effect profile. However, there is no oral drug available whose direct anticholinergic binding potential approximates that of atropine better than that of propantheline bromide.[219] Other drugs with anticholinergic benefits are flavoxate, oxybutynin, and dicyclomine. Some drugs not only have anticholinergic properties, but also have the ability to relax smooth muscle sufficient to have earned the name of ''antispasmodic.'' The activity of these drugs is directly on smooth muscle at a site that is metabolically distal to the cholinergic receptor mechanism. Agents in this category are oxybutynin, flavoxate, and dicyclomine. Additionally, all three of these drugs possess local anesthetic properties. Clinically, their effectiveness in treating urge incontinence is due to their antispasmodic (muscle relaxant) property, rather than their anticholinergic effects.[217]

Oxybutynin chloride (Ditropan) has been described as a strong independent smooth muscle relaxant with local anesthetic activity as well as minor anticholinergic effects.[217,218] This agent has been used successfully to depress uninhibited detrusor contractions in patients with and without neurogenic bladder dysfunction. Oxybutynin improves total bladder capacity, neuropathic voiding dysfunction, and bladder filling pressure.[220,221] The dose of oxybutynin chloride suggested for the elderly is 2.5 mg up to three times a day. In some cases, the dose may need to be increased to 5 mg three times a day. As oxybutynin is a tertiary-amine anticholinergic compound, the potential for CNS toxicity increases as the dose is increased. In comparison to oral propantheline bromide 15 mg three times a day, full dose oral oxybutynin (5 mg TID) in one study produced a good response more frequently.[222]

Dicyclomine Hydrochloride. Another smooth muscle relaxant with anticholinergic properties is dicyclomine hydrochloride (Bentyl). Dicyclomine is a tertiary-amine and has dose-related CNS effects.[217] An oral dose of 20 mg three times a day will increase bladder capacity in patients with detrusor hyperreflexia. The dose for elderly patients is listed as 10 to 20 mg three times a day but the dose may need to be increased to 30 mg three times a day.[218,223] As the dose increases, the anticholinergic side effects become prominent.

Flavoxate hydrochloride (Urispas) is another smooth muscle relaxant with anticholinergic effects and local analgesic properties. Several studies, however, have reported conflicting results as to the efficacy of flavoxate. The recommended adult dose is 100 to 200 mg three to four times a day.

All agents in this group should be prescribed for a two-week trial period. If no improvement has been observed with one drug, trial with another may be appropriate. Based upon the literature and clinical experience, oxybutynin in fact may be the drug of choice for urge incontinence.

Terbutaline (Brethine) 5 mg orally three times a day reportedly benefits select patients with urge PUI and does not have significant effects on the bladders of normal humans without voiding difficulties.[230] The human bladder muscle has β-adrenergic receptors which when stimulated will increase the capacity of the bladder. However, few adequate studies are available on the effects of β-adrenergic stimulation in patients with detrusor hyperactivity. While any of the aforementioned anticholinergic drugs would be useful for H.K., oxybutynin is considered the drug of choice for the elderly. Oxybutynin has fewer anticholinergic effects and more prominent detrusor relaxation than any of the other drugs. This drug can be dosed, in some cases once a day, and in most cases, twice a day. All of the other drugs require at least three doses a day. The systemic anticholinergic side effects from oxybutynin, flavoxate, and dicyclomine are relatively mild when compared to propantheline. A beginning dose of oxybutynin for H.K. would be 2.5 mg/day and the dose can be increased by increments of 2.5 mg/day, not to exceed 5 mg three times a day.

Monitoring H.K. necessitates evaluating her urinary frequency through patient (and where possible nurse or caregiver) interviews. Specifically, a reduction in the urinary urgency sensation is the desired outcome. Too much anticholinergic therapy may result in urinary hesitancy and possibly urinary retention. If the patient has to concentrate on the act of micturition, perhaps the anticholinergic drug dose should be reduced. CNS and systemic side effects for the anticholinergic drug therapy should be assessed as often as possible. As with all urge incontinent patients, urinary tract infection is quite common. If symptoms of dysuria appear, or if urinary urgency reappears, a urinalysis should be obtained.

Increasing Bladder Outlet Resistance

30. M.K., a 68-year-old female, has been diagnosed with urinary stress incontinence. What drug therapy would be appropriate for this classification of PUI?

Imipramine hydrochloride (Tofranil) is useful for increasing bladder capacity and increasing bladder outlet resistance.[224] The pharmacological mechanism of tricyclic antidepressants (TCAs) in treating persistent urinary incontinence has been studied extensively.[225] The results and conclusions of the data reported demonstrate that, at best, the mechanism of action on the lower urinary tract is speculative. All of the TCAs have some degree of anticholinergic effects, both central and peripheral, but not at all sites. These drugs block the active transport system in the presynaptic nerve ending and prevent the uptake of norepinephrine and serotonin; they have varying degrees of CNS sedation. The TCAs all have some degree of histamine receptor antagonism, both H_1 and H_2; and they desensitize some α_2-adrenoceptors.[225,226] Imipramine has significant systemic anticholinergic effects but it has weak anticholinergic effects at the detrusor muscle.[227] However, imipramine has a significant inhibitory effect on the detrusor muscle, which is

neither anticholinergic nor adrenergic. Imipramine may have its detrusor inhibitory effect as a result of peripheral blockade of norepinephrine reuptake. The ability of imipramine to increase bladder outlet resistance is believed to be due to enhanced α-adrenergic effects in the smooth muscle of the bladder base and proximal urethra, where alpha receptors outnumber beta receptors. Imipramine 75 mg/day produced continence in 68% of women with stress PUI within four weeks.[237]

The initial dose for imipramine is 25 mg orally at bedtime. The dose can be increased every third day by 25 mg until the patient is continent, side effects occur, or a dose of 150 mg/day is reached.[224] Most patients will become continent within seven to ten days, and some patients may become continent in as little as three to five days. The usual adult dose for voiding dysfunction is 25 mg four times a day and for geriatric patients, the dose is 25 mg twice a day. The imipramine serum half-life is prolonged in the elderly.[228] Weakness, fatigue, and postural hypotension are significant problems with imipramine. There has been a threefold increase in hip fractures reported among elderly patients taking imipramine.[229]

Alpha-adrenergic receptor stimulation at the detrusor muscle and proximal urethra will increase the maximum urethral pressure (MUP) and the maximum urethral closure pressure (MUCP).[231] Several oral α-adrenergic agonist agents are available. All of them should be used with caution in the elderly due to side effects which include anxiety, insomnia, blood pressure elevation, headache, tremor, weakness, palpitations, cardiac arrhythmias, and respiratory difficulties.[232]

Ephedrine, a noncatecholamine sympathomimetic, in doses of 25 to 50 mg four times a day, directly stimulates both α- and β-adrenergic receptors.[232] Some tachyphylaxis develops to the peripheral actions of ephedrine, most likely as a result of depletion of norepinephrine stores. The benefit of ephedrine most often is achieved in patients with minimal to moderate wetting. Patients with severe stress persistent urinary incontinence derive little benefit from ephedrine. Cases that do not respond to drug therapy may require surgical intervention.

Phenylpropanolamine (Propadrine) 50 mg three times a day significantly improved stress PUI after four weeks of therapy.[233] Phenylpropanolamine is similar to ephedrine in its peripheral effects, but causes less CNS stimulation (i.e., anxiety, insomnia).[232] Phenylpropanolamine doses of 75 to 100 mg orally also increase the MUP and the MUCP in women with stress PUI. Not all patients with stress PUI responds to phenylpropanolamine or any combination thereof. Currently, the most frequently prescribed pharmaceutical agent for stress PUI for both females and males is Ornade Spansules. Ornade contains 75 mg of phenylpropanolamine hydrochloride and 12 mg of chlorpheniramine maleate in a sustained-release capsule. The dose is one capsule twice a day.[234] The original research data on the use of Ornade in treating stress incontinence were based upon the old formulation of phenylpropanolamine 50 mg, chlorpheniramine 8 mg, and isopropamide 2 mg; the dose was one capsule twice a day. Isopropamide is an anticholinergic agent and most likely was responsible for some of the benefits afforded by Ornade Spansules. Perhaps the current formula which has 50% more phenylpropanolamine and chlorpheniramine (anticholinergic effects) more than makes up for the elimination of the isopropamide 2 mg. In those patients with urge PUI, flavoxate was reported to be more effective than Ornade.[235]

A wide range of cardiovascular and CNS side effects have been attributed to phenylpropanolamine, both alone and in combination with other drugs. There are 17 reports, 21 separate studies, and nearly 50 controlled clinical trials on the efficacy and safety of phenylpropanolamine.[236] The effect of phenylpropanolamine on blood pressure is dose related, but at doses of 75 mg in a sustained-release formulation, the effect on blood pressure is considered to be clinically negligible, but nonetheless statistically reliable. Overall, the side effects reported with phenylpropanolamine are low when used at approved doses.

Estrogens affect many aspects of uterine smooth muscle, including excitability, receptor density, and transmitter metabolism, especially adrenergic nerves.[238] The detrusor and urethra are embryologically related to the uterus, and significant work has been done on estrogenic hormone effects on the lower urinary tract. Alpha-adrenergic stimulation of the urethra is estrogen dependent.[218] Several studies have demonstrated the relationship of estrogen to α-adrenergic receptor density in the lower urinary tract.[239] Estrogen therapy, in the form of vaginal suppositories (1 mg/day), is capable of facilitating urinary storage in some postmenopausal female patients by increasing urethral outlet resistance, and has an additive effect with α-adrenergic therapy (phenylpropanolamine 50 mg BID).[240]

The use of estrogen in the treatment of stress PUI requires further study. The use of long-term estrogen treatment must be considered carefully in light of the controversy over whether estrogen therapy predisposes to the development of endometrial carcinoma. If estrogen is combined with α-adrenergic agonist therapy, the lowest effective maintenance dose should be prescribed.

References

1   Kinsey A et al., eds. Sexual Behavior in the Human Male. Philadelphia, PA: WB Saunders; 1984.

2   Pfieffer E et al. Sexual behavior in aged men and women. Arch Gen Psychiatry. 1986;19:735.

3   Bretschneider JG, McCoy NL. Sexual interest and behavior in healthy 80 to 102 year olds. Arch Sex Behav. 1988;17:109.

4   Diokno AC et al. Correlates of sexual dysfunction in the elderly. J Urol. 1988;139:496A.

5   Tordarello O, Boscia FM. Sexuality in aging: a study of a group of 300 elderly men and women. J Endocrinol Invest. 1985;8(Suppl. 2):123.

6   Starr BD, Weiner MD. The Starr-Weiner Report on Sex and Sexuality in the Mature Years. New York, NY: Stein and Day; 1981.

7   Persson G. Sexuality in a 70-year-old urban population. J Psychosom Res. 1980;24:137.

8   Kaiser FE et al. Impotence and aging: clinical and hormonal factors. J Am Geriatr Soc. 1988;36:511.

9   Skakkeback N et al. Androgen replacement with oral testosterone in hypogonadal men: a double-blind controlled study. Clin Endocrinol (Oxf). 1981;14:49.

10 Feldman HA et al. Impotence and its medical and psychosocial correlates: results of the Massachusetts Male Aging Study. J Urol. 1994;151:54.

11 Melman. Evaluation of the first 70 patients in the center for male sexual dysfunction of Beth Israel Medical Center. J Urol. 1984;131:53.

12 Shrom SH et al. Clinical profile of experience with 130 consecutive cases of impotent men. Urology. 1980;13:511.

13 Mulligan T, Katz G. Why aged men become impotent. Arch Intern Med. 1989;149:1365.

14 Hsueh WA. Sexual dysfunction with aging and systemic hypertension. Am J Cardiol. 1988;61(Suppl.):18H.

15 Deamer RL, Thompson JF. The role of medications in geriatric sexual function. Clin Geriatr Med. 1991;7:95.

16 Mooradian AD et al. Endocrinology in aging. Dis Mon. 1988;34:398.

17 McWaine DE, Procci WR. Drug-induced sexual dysfunction. Med Toxicol. 1988;3:289.

18 Wein AJ, Van Arsdalen KN. Drug-induced male sexual dysfunction. Urol Clin North Am. 1988;15:23.

19 Krane RJ et al. Impotence. N Engl J Med. 1989;321:1648.

20 Lue TF. Male sexual dysfunction. In: Tanagho EA, McAinich JW, eds. Smith's General Urology. Norwalk: Appleton & Lange; 1992:696.

21 Deslypere JP, Vermeulen A. Leydig cell function in normal men: effect of age, life-style, residence, diet, and activity. J Clin Endocrinol Metab. 1984; 59:955.

22 Lue TF, Tanagho EA. Physiology of erection and pharmacological management of impotence. J Urol. 1987;137: 829.

23 Tesitouras PD. Effects of age on testicular function. Endocrinol Metab Clin North Am. 1987;16:1045.

24 Padam-Nathan H et al. Evaluation of the impotent patient. Semin Urol. 1986; 4:225–32.

25 Whitehead ED et al. Diagnostic evaluation of impotence. Postgrad Med. 1990;88:123.

26 Deutsch S et al. Previously unrecognized diabetes mellitus in sexually impotent men. JAMA. 1980;244:2430.

27 Spark RF et al. Hypogonadism, hyperprolactinaemia, and temporal lobe epilepsy in hyposexual men. Lancet. 1981;1:413.

28 Gerstenberg TC, Bradly WE. Nerve conduction velocity measurement of dorsal nerve of the penis in normal and impotent men. J Urol. 1985;21:90.

29 Bancroft J, Wu FCW. Changes in erectile responsiveness during androgen therapy. Arch Sex Behav. 1983;12: 59.

30 Michal V et al. Arterial lesions in impotence: phalloarteriography. Int Angiol. 1984;3:247.

31 Rubin A, Babbott D. Impotence and diabetes mellitus. JAMA. 1958;168:498.

32 Spark RF et al. Impotence is not always psychogenic: newer insights into hypothalamic-pituitary-gonadal dysfunction. JAMA. 1980;243:750.

33 Matsumoto AM. The testis and male sexual function. In: Wyngaarden JB et al., eds. Cecil's Textbook of Medicine. Philadelphia: WB Saunders; 1992: 1333.

34 Kaiser FE et al. Impotence and aging: clinical and hormonal factors. J Am Geriatr Soc. 1988;36:511.

35 Spina M et al. Age-related changes in the composition of and mechanical properties of the tunica media of the upper thoracic human aorta. Arteriosclerosis. 1983;3:64.

36 Smulyan H et al. Effect of age on arterial distensibility in asymptomatic humans. Arteriosclerosis. 1983;3:199.

37 Morley JE. Impotence. Am J Med. 1986;80:897.

38 Wabrek AJ, Burchell RC. Male sexual dysfunction associated with coronary heart disease. Arch Sex Behav. 1980;9:69.

39 Gundle MJ et al. Psychological outcome after aortocoronary artery surgery. Am J Psych. 1980;137:1591.

40 Agarwal A, Jain DC. Male sexual dysfunction after stroke. J Assoc Physicians India. 1989;37:505.

41 Ruzbarsky V, Michal V. Morphologic changes in the arterial bed of the penis with aging. Relationship to the pathogenesis of impotence. Invest Urol. 1977;15:194.

42 Morley JE et al. Relationship of penile brachial pressure index to myocardial infarction and cerebrovascular accidents in older men. Am J Med. 1988; 84:445.

43 Virag R et al. Is impotence an arterial disorder? Lancet. 1985;1:181.

44 Shabsigh R et al. Cigarette smoking and other vascular risk factors in vasculogenic impotence. Urology. 1991; 38:227.

45 Oaks WW, Moyer JH. Sex and hypertension. Med Aspects Hum Sex. 1972; 6:128.

46 Zemel P. Sexual dysfunction in the diabetic patient with hypertension. Am J Cardiol. 1988;61:27H.

47 Rubin A, Babbott D. Impotence and diabetes mellitus. JAMA. 1958;168: 498.

48 Whitehead ED, Klyde BJ. Diabetes-related impotence in the elderly. Clin Geriatr Med. 1990;6:771.

49 McCulloch DK et al. The prevalence of diabetic impotence. Diabetologia. 1980;18:279.

50 Kannel W et al. The role of diabetes in congestive heart failure: the Framingham study. Am J Cardiol. 1974; 34:29.

51 Lehman TP, Jacobs JA. Etiology of diabetic impotence. Urology. 1983; 129:291.

52 Morley JE, Kaiser FE. Testicular function in the aging male. In: Armbrecht HJ, ed. Endocrine Function and Aging. New York: Springer-Verlag; 1989:456.

53 Morely JE et al. Sexual function with advancing age. Med Clin North Am. 1989;73:1483.

54 Snyder PJ et al. Serum LH and FSH response to synthetic gonadotropins in normal men. J Clin Endocrinol Metab. 1975;41:938.

55 Tenover JS et al. Decreased serum inhibin levels in normal elderly men: evidence for a decline in Sertoli cell function with aging. J Clin Endocrinol Metab. 1988;67:455.

56 Wabrek AJ et al. Noninvasive penile arterial evaluation in 120 males with erectile dysfunction. Urology. 1983; 22:230.

57 Condra M et al. Prevalence and significance of tobacco smoking in impotence. Urology. 1986;27:495.

58 Hirshkowitz M et al. Nocturnal penile tumescence in cigarette smokers with erectile dysfunction. Urology. 1992; 34:101.

59 DePalma RG et al. A screening sequence for vasculogenic impotence. J Vasc Surg. 1987;5:228.

60 Bulpitt CJ et al. Changes in symptoms of hypertensive patients after referral to hospital clinic. Br Heart J. 1976;38: 121.

61 Report of Medical Research Council Working Party on Mild to Moderate Hypertension: Adverse reaction to bendroflumethiazide and propranolol for the treatment of mild hypertension. Lancet. 1981;2:539.

62 Veterans Administrative Cooperative Study Group on antihypertensive agents: Comparison of prazosin with hydralazine in patients receiving hydrochlorothiazide: A randomized double blind clinical trial. Circulation. 1981;64:722.

63 Morley JE. Impotence. Am J Med. 1986;80:897.

64 Mooradian AD et al. Hyperprolactinemia in male diabetics. Postgrad Med J. 1985;61:11.

65 Bancroft J. Endocrinology of sexual function. Clin Endocrinol Metab. 1980; 4:253.

66 Davidson JM et al. Hormonal changes and sexual function in aging men. J Clin Endocrinol Metab. 1983;57:71.

67 Morley JE. Impotence in older men. Hosp Pract. 1988;23:139.

68 MRC Working party on Mild to Moderate Hypertension: Adverse reactions to bendroflumethiazide and propranolol for the treatment of hypertension. Lancet. 1981;2:539.

69 Bulbitt DJ, Fletcher AE. Drug treatment and quality of life in the elderly. Clin Geriatr Med. 1990;6:309.

70 **Mallett EC, Badlani GH.** Sexuality in the elderly. Semin Urol. 1987;5:141.

71 **McWaine DE, Procci WR.** Drug-induced sexual dysfunction. Med Toxicol. 1988;3:289.

72 **Wein AJ, Van Arsdalen KN.** Drug-induced male dysfunction. Urol Clin North Am. 1988;15:23.

73 **Mirin SM, et al.** Opiate use and sexual function. Am J Psychiatry. 1980;137:909.

74 **Bissada NK, Finkbbeiner AE.** Urologic manifestations of drug therapy. Urol Clin North Am. 1988;15:725.

75 **Bauer GE et al.** Side-effects of antihypertensive treatment: a placebo-controlled study. Clin Sci Mol Med. 1978;55:341s.

76 **Bulpitt CJ, Dollery CT.** Side-effects of hypotensive agents evaluated by self-administered questionnaire. Am J Cardiol. 1973;3:485.

77 **Hogan MJ et al.** Antihypertensive therapy and male sexual dysfunction. Psychosomatics. 1981;21:234.

78 **Ebringer A et al.** The use of clonidine in the treatment of hypertension. 1970;1:524.

79 **Laver MC.** Sexual behavior patterns in male hypertensives. Aust N Z J Med. 1974;4:29.

80 **Onesti G et al.** Clonidine: a new antihypertensive agent. Am J Cardiol. 1971;28:74.

81 **Burnett WG, Chanine RA.** Sexual dysfunction as a complication of propranolol therapy in men. Cardiovasc Med. 1979;4:811.

82 **Buffum J.** Pharmacosexology: the effects of drugs on sexual function: a review. J Psychoactive Drugs. 1982;14:5.

83 **Troutman WG.** Drug-induced sexual dysfunction. In: Knoben JE, Anderson PO, eds. Handbook of Clinical Drug Data. 6th ed. Hamilton, IL: Drug Intelligence Publications; 1988:112.

84 **Van Arsdalen KN, Wein AJ.** Drug induced sexual dysfunction in older men. Geriatrics. 1984;39:63.

85 **Caine M et al.** Phenoxybenzamine for benign prostatic obstruction. Urology. 1981;17:542.

86 **Amery A et al.** Double-blind crossover study with a new vasodilator—prazosin—in the treatment of mild hypertension. Excerpta Medica International Congress Series. 1974;331:100.

87 **Hayes AH.** Clinical pharmacology of current and experimental drugs. In: Moser, ed. Hypertension—a practical approach. Boston: Little Brown and Co.; 1975.

88 **Zarren HS, Black PM.** Unilateral gynecomastia and impotence during low dose spironolactone administration in men. Milit Med. 1975;140:417.

89 **Beeley L.** Drug-induced sexual dysfunction and infertility. Adverse Drug React Acute Poisoning Rev. 1984;3:23.

90 **Buffum JC.** Pharmacosexology update: heroin and sexual function. J Psychoactive Drugs. 1983;15:317.

91 **Morley JE.** Impotence. Am J Med. 1986;80:897.

92 **Whitehead ED et al.** Treatment alternatives for impotence. Postgrad Med. 1990;88:139.

93 **Morley JE, Kaiser FE.** Sexual function with advancing age. Med Clin North Am. 1989;73:1483.

94 **Chiodoni P et al.** Size reduction of macroprolactinomas by bromocriptine or lisuride. J Clin Endocrinol Metab. 1981;53:737.

95 **Molitch ME et al.** Bromocriptine as primary therapy for prolactin secreting macroadenomas; results of a prospective multicenter study. J Clin Endocrinol Metab. 1985;60:698.

96 **Serri O et al.** Recurrence of hyperprolactinemia after selective transsphenoidal adenoidectomy in women with prolactinoma. N Engl J Med. 1983;309:280.

97 **Morales A et al.** Is yohimbine effective in the treatment of organic impotence? Results of a controlled trial. J Urol. 1987;137:1168.

98 **Morales A et al.** Oral and transcutaneous pharmacological agents in the treatment of impotence. Urol Clin North Am. 1988;15:87.

99 **Reid K et al.** Double blind trial of yohimbine in treatment of psychogenic impotence. Lancet. 1987;2:421.

100 **Lue T et al.** Physiology of erection and pharmacological management of impotence. J Urol. 1987;137:829.

101 **Carson CC, Mino RD.** Priapism associated with trazodone therapy. J Urol. 1988;139:369.

102 **Nelson RP.** Nonoperative management of impotence. J Urol. 1988;139:2.

103 **Elist J et al.** Evaluating medical treatment of impotence. Urology. 1984;27:74.

104 **Sacerdote A et al.** Recovery from diabetic impotence during improved diabetic control and inositol supplementation unassociated with improvement in bulbocavernous reflex latency. Diabetes. 1985;34:204A.

105 **Virag R.** Intracavernous injection of papaverine for erectile failure. Lancet. 1982;2:328.

106 **Sidi AA et al.** Intracavernous drug-induced erections in the management of male erectile dysfunction: experience with 100 patients. J Urol. 1986;135:704.

107 **Brindley GS.** Cavernosal alpha-blockade: a new technique for investigating and treating erectile impotence. Br J Psychiatry. 1983;143:332.

108 **Zorgniotti AW, Lefleur RS.** Auto-injection of the corpus cavernosum with a vasoactive drug combination for vasculogenic impotence. J Urol. 1985;133:39.

109 **Nelson RP.** Injections of papaverine and Regitine into the corpora cavernosa for erectile dysfunction: clinical results in 60 patients. South Med J. 1989;82:26.

110 **Watters GR et al.** Experience in the management of erectile dysfunction using the intracavernosal self-injection of vasoactive drugs. J Urol. 1988;140:1417.

111 **Brindley GS.** Neurophysiology of erection. In: Proceedings of the First World Meeting on Impotence. Paris, France: 1984:39.

112 **Brindley GS.** New treatment for priapism. Lancet. 1984;2:220.

113 **Juenemann KP et al.** Hemodynamics of papaverine and phentolamine induced penile erection. J Urol. 1986;136:158.

114 **Keogh E et al.** Treatment of impotence by intrapenile injections: a comparison of papaverine versus papaverine and phentolamine: a double-blind crossover study. J Urol. 1989;142:726.

115 **Eli Lilly and Company.** Papaverine Hydrochloride USP Injection, package insert. Indianapolis, IN: 1994 April.

116 **Ciba Pharmaceuticals.** Phentolamine Mesylate USP package insert. Woodbridge, NJ: 1994 April.

117 **Benson G, Seifert W.** Is phentolamine stable in solution with papaverine? J Urol. 1988;140:970.

118 **Lue T et al.** Functional evaluation of penile veins by cavernossography in papaverine induced erections. J Urol. 1986;135:479.

119 **Wespes E, Schulman C.** Systemic complications of intracavernous papaverine injections in patients with venous leakage. Urology. 1988;31:114.

120 **Brading AF et al.** The effects of papaverine on the electrical and mechanical activity of the guinea pig ureter. J Physiol. 1983;334:79.

121 **Huddart H et al.** Inhibition by papaverine of calcium movements and tension in the smooth muscle of rats vas deferens and urinary bladder. J Physiol. 1984;349:183.

122 **Wang Q, Large WA.** Modulation of noradrenaline-induced membrane currents by papaverine in rabbit vascular smooth muscle cells. J Physiol. 1991;439:501.

123 **Juenemann KP et al.** Further evidence of venous outflow restriction during erection. Br J Urol. 1986;58:320.

124 **Montorsi F et al.** Effectiveness and safety of multidrug intra-cavernous therapy for vasculogenic impotence. Urology. 1993;42:554.

125 **Hall S et al.** Use of atropine sulfate in pharmacologic erections: initial experience with one year follow up in the United States. J Urol. 1992;147:265A.

126 **Nelson RP.** Injections of Papaverine and Regitine into the corpora cavernosa for erectile dysfunction: clinical results in 60 patients. South Med J. 1989;82:26.

127 **Abber JC et al.** Diagnostic tests for impotence: comparison of papaverine injection with the penile brachial index and nocturnal tumescence monitoring. J Urol. 1986;135:923.

128 **Larsen EH et al.** Fibrosis of corpus cavernosum after intra-cavernous injection of phentolamine/papaverine. J Urol. 1987;137:292.

129 **Malloy TR, Malkowicz.** Pharmacologic treatment of impotence. Urol Clin North Am. 1987;14:297.

130 **Abozeid M et al.** Chronic papaverine treatment: the effect of repeated injections on the simian erectile and penile tissue. J Urol. 1987;138:1263.

131 **Fuchs M, Brawer M.** Papaverine-induced Fibrosis of the Corpus Cavernosum. J Urol. 1989;141:125.

132 **Katlowitz N et al.** Effect of multidose intracorporeal injection and audiovisual sexual stimulation in vasculogenic impotence. Urology. 1993;42:695.

133 **Girdley FM et al.** Intracavernous self-injection for impotence: a long-term therapeutic option? Experience in 78 patients. J Urol. 1988;140:972.

134 **Keogh EJ et al.** Treatment of impotence by intrapenile injections. A comparison of papaverine versus papaverine and phentolamine: a double-blind,

of papaverine versus papaverine and phentolamine: a double-blind crossover study. J Urol. 1989;142:726.

crossover trial. J Urol. 1989;142:726.

135 **Levine SB et al.** Side-effects of self-administration of intracavernous papaverine and phentolamine for the treatment of impotence. J Urol. 1989;141:54.

136 **Ishii N et al.** Therapeutic trial with prostaglandin E1 for organic impotence. Abstract presented at Second World Meeting on Impotence. Prague, Czechoslovakia: 1986.

137 **Sarsody M et al.** A prospective double-blind trial of intra-corporeal papaverine versus prostaglandin E1 in the treatment of impotence. J Urol. 1989;141:551.

138 **Hedlund H, Andersson K.** Contraction and relaxation induced by some prostanoids in isolated human penile erectile tissue and cavernous artery. J Urol. 1985;134:1245.

139 **Walsh PC.** Benign prostatic hyperplasia. In: Walch PC et al., eds. Campbell's Urology. 5th ed. Philadelphia: WB Saunders; 1986:1248.

140 **Standberg JD.** Comparative pathology of benign prostatic hypertrophy. In: Lepor H, Lawson RK, eds. Prostatic Diseases. Philadelphia: WB Saunders; 1993:212.

141 **Berry SJ et al.** The development of human benign prostatic hyperplasia with age. J Urol. 1984;132:474.

142 **Greenwald P et al.** Cancer of the prostate among men with benign prostatic hyperplasia. J Natl Cancer Inst. 1970:53;335.

143 **Narayan P.** Neoplasms of the prostate. In: Tanago EA and McAninch JW, eds. Smith's General Urology. Norwalk: Appleton & Lange; 1992:378.

144 **Takahashi S et al.** Latent prostatic carcinomas found at autopsy in men over 90 years old. Jap J Clin Oncol. 1992;22(2):117.

145 **Issacs JT, Coffey DS.** Etiology and disease process of benign prostatic hyperplasia. Prostate Suppl. 1989;2:34.

146 **Boyarsky S et al.** A new look at bladder neck obstruction by the Food and Drug Administration regulators: guidelines for the investigation of benign prostatic hypertrophy. Trans Am Assoc Genitourin Surg. 1977;68:29.

147 **DuBeau CE, Resnick NM.** Controversies in the diagnosis and management of benign prostatic hypertrophy. Adv Intern Med. 1991;37:55.

148 **Talner LB.** Specific causes of obstruction. In: Pollack HM, ed. Clinical Urology. 2nd ed. Philadelphia: WB Saunders; 1990:1629.

149 **Mushlin AI, Thornbury JR.** Intravenous pyelography. The case against its routine. Ann Intern Med. 1989;111:58.

150 **Wasserman NF et al.** Assessment of prostatism: role of intravenous urography. Radiology. 1987;165:831.

151 **Webb JAW.** Ultrasonography in the diagnosis of renal obstruction. Sensitive but not very specific. Br J Med. 1990;301:944.

152 **Siroky MB et al.** The flow rate nomogram: I. Development. J Urol. 1979;122:665.

153 **Haylen BT et al.** Maximum and average urine flow rates in normal male and female populations. Br J Urol. 1989;64:30.

154 **Marshall VR et al.** The use of urinary flow rates obtained from voided vol-

umes less than 150 mL in the assessment of voiding ability. Br J Urol. 1983;55:28.

155 **Lepor H, Rigaud C.** The efficacy of transurethral resection of the prostate in men with moderate symptoms of prostatism. J Urol. 1990;143:533.

156 **Kadow C et al.** Prostatectomy or conservative management in the treatment of benign prostatic hypertrophy. Br J Urol. 1988;61:432.

157 **Bruskewitz RC et al.** 3 year follow-up of urinary symptoms after transurethral resection of the prostate. J Urol. 1989; 142:1251.

158 **Coolsaet BLRA et al.** Prostatism: rationalization of urodynamic testing. World J Urol. 1984;2:216.

159 **Chancellor MB et al.** Bladder outlet obstruction and impaired detrusor contractility: a blinded comparison of the video-urodynamic diagnosis versus the diagnosis based on a detrusor contractility parameter, a urethral resistant parameter, and a sustained/fade index. Neurourol Urodyn. 1990;9:209.

160 **Isaacs JT.** Importance of the natural history of benign prostatic hyperplasia in the evaluation of pharmacologic intervention. Prostate. 1990;3(Suppl.):1.

161 **Fowler FJ et al.** Symptom status and quality of life following prostatectomy. JAMA. 1988;259:3018.

162 **Bruskewitz RC, Christensen MM.** Critical evaluation of transurethral resection and incision of the prostate. The Prostate. 1990;3:27.

163 **Loughlin KR et al.** Transurethral incisions and resection of the prostate under local anesthesia. Br J Urol. 1987; 60:105.

164 **Orandi A.** Transurethral incision of the prostate compared with transurethral resection of the prostate in 132 matching cases. J Urol. 1987;138:810.

165 **Keane PF et al.** Balloon dilation of the prostate: technique and early results. Br J Urol. 1990;65:354.

166 **Lepor H.** The role of alpha-adrenergic blockers in the treatment of benign prostatic hypertrophy. Prostate Suppl. 1990;3:75.

167 **Caine M.** The present role of alpha-adrenergic blockers in the treatment of benign prostatic hypertrophy. J Urol. 1986;136:1.

168 **Lepor H.** Nonoperative management of benign prostatic hypertrophy. J Urol. 1989;141:1283.

169 **Wilde MI et al.** Alfuzosin. A review of its pharmacodynamic and pharmacokinetic properties, and therapeutic potential in benign prostatic hyperplasia. Drugs. 1993;45:410.

170 **Dunzendorfer U.** Clinical experience: symptomatic management of BPH with terazosin. Urology. 1988;32(Suppl.): 27.

171 **Isaacs JT et al.** Changes in the metabolism of dihydrotestosterone in the hyperplastic human prostate. J Clin Endocrinol. 1983;56:139.

172 **DeKlerk DP, Coffey DS.** Quantitative determination of prostatic epithelial and stromal hyperplasia by a new technique: biomorphometrics. Invest Urol. 1978;16:240.

173 **Matzkin H, Braf Z.** Endocrine treatment of benign prostatic hypertrophy: Current concepts. Urology. 1991;37:1.

174 **Wilson JP.** The pathogenesis of benign

prostatic hyperplasia. Am J Med. 1980; 68:745.

175 **Ghanadian R.** Hormonal control and rationale for endocrine therapy of prostatic tumors. In: Ghanadian R, ed. The Endocrinology of Prostatic Tumors. Boston: The Hague, MTP Press; 1983: 59.

176 **Bartsh W et al.** Hormone blood levels and their interrelationships in normal men and men with benign prostatic hypertrophy. Acta Endocrinol (Copenh). 1979;90:727.

177 **Ghanadian et al.** Serum dihydrotestosterone in patients with benign prostatic hypertrophy. Br J Urol. 1977;49: 541.

178 **Siiteri PK, Wilson JD.** Dihydrotesterone in prostatic hypertrophy, the formation and content of DHT in the hypertrophic prostate of man. J Clin Invest. 1970;49:1737.

179 **Bruchovsky N, Lieskovsky G.** Increased ration of 5-alpha reductase: 3-alpha (Beta)-hydroxysteroid dehydrogenase activities in the hyperplastic human prostate. J Endocrinol. 1979;80: 289.

180 **Kreig M et al.** Stroma of human benign prostatic hyperplasia. Preferred tissue for androgen metabolism and estrogen binding. Acta Endocrinol (Copenh). 1981;96:422.

181 **Orlowski J and Clark AF.** Androgen metabolism and actions in rat ventral prostate epithelial and stromal cell cultures. Biochem Cell Biol. 1985;64:583.

182 **Bartsch G et al.** Correlative morphological and biochemical investigation on the stromal tissue of the human prostate. J Steroid Biochem. 1983;19: 147.

183 **Habenicht UF et al.** Development of a model for the induction of estrogen-related prostatic hyperplasia. Prostate. 1986;6:181.

184 **Geller J, Albert JD.** BPH and prostate cancer: results of hormonal manipulation. In: Bruchovsky N et al., eds. Regulation of Androgen Action. Berlin: Conrgessdruck R. Bruckner; 1985;51.

185 **Charisiri N, Pierrepoint CG.** Examination of the distribution of estrogen receptor between the stromal and epithelial compartments of the prostate. Prostate. 1980;1:357.

186 **DeKlerk DP et al.** Comparison of spontaneous and experimentally induced canine prostatic hypertrophy. J. Clin Endocrinol Metab. 1979;64:842.

187 **Caine M et al.** The treatment of benign prostatic hypertrophy with flutamide (SCH 13521): a placebo-controlled study. J Urol. 1975;114:564.

188 **Stone NN.** Flutamide in treatment of benign prostatic hypertrophy. Urology. 1989;34(Suppl.):64.

189 **Eri LM, Tveter KJ.** A prospective placebo controlled study of the luteinizing hormone releasing hormone agonist leuprolide as a treatment for patients with benign prostatic hyperplasia. J Urol. 1993;150:359.

190 **Gormley GJ et al.** The effect of finasteride in men with benign prostatic hyperplasia. The finasteride study group. N Engl J Med. 1992;327:1185.

191 **Stoner E et al.** Maintenance of clinical efficacy with finasteride therapy for 24 months in patients with benign pro-

static hyperplasia. Arch Intern Med. 1994;83:154.

192 **Keane PF et al.** Response of the benign hypertrophied prostate to treatment with an LHRH analogue. Br J Urol. 1988;62:163.

193 **Oesterling JE.** Prostate specific antigen: a critical assessment of the most useful tumor marker for adenocarcinoma of the prostate. J Urol. 1991;145: 907.

194 **Guess HA et al.** The effect of finasteride on prostate specific antigen in men with benign prostatic hyperplasia. Prostate. 1993;22:31.

195 **Lepor H.** Medical therapy for benign prostatic hyperplasia. Urology. 1993; 42:483.

196 **Lepor H, Machi G.** The relative efficacy of terazosin versus terazosin and flutamide for the treatment of symptomatic BPH. Prostate. 1992;20:89.

197 **Ouslander JG et al.** Urinary incontinence in elderly nursing home patients. JAMA. 1982;248:1194.

198 **Mohide EA.** The prevalence and scope of urinary incontinence. Clin Geriatr Med. 1986;2:639.

199 **Yarnell JWG et al.** The prevalence and severity of urinary incontinence in women. J Epidemiol Community Health. 1981;35:71.

200 **Thomas TM et al.** Prevalence of urinary incontinence. Br J Med. 1980; 281:1243.

201 **Marron et al.** The nonuse of urethral catheterization in the management of urinary incontinence in the teaching nursing home. J Am Geriatr Soc. 1983; 31:278.

202 **Colling J et al.** The effects of patterned urge-response toileting (PURT) on urinary incontinence among nursing home residents. J Am Geriatr Soc. 1992;40: 135.

203 **Gosling JA, Chilton CP.** The anatomy of the bladder, urethra, and pelvic floor. In: Mundy AR et al., eds. Urodynamics: Principles, Practice, and Application. New York: Churchill Livingstone; 1984:3.

204 **Resnick NM, Yalla SV.** Management of urinary incontinence in the elderly. N Engl J Med. 1985;313:800.

205 **Rud T.** Urethral pressure profile in continent women from childhood to old age. Acta Obstet Gynecol Scand. 1980;59:331.

206 **Jones KW, Schoenberg HW.** Comparison of the incidence of bladder hyperreflexia in patients with benign prostatic hypertrophy and age-matched female controls. J Urol. 1985;133:425.

207 **Ouslander JG et al.** Genitourinary dysfunction in a geriatric outpatient population. J Am Geriatr Soc. 1986;34: 507.

208 **Castleden CM et al.** Clinical and urodynamic studies in 100 elderly incontinent patients. Br J Med. 1981;282: 1103.

209 **Overstall PW et al.** Experience with an incontinence clinic. J Am Geriatr Soc. 1980;28:535.

210 **Ouslander JG, Bruskewitz R.** Disorders of micturition in the aging patient. Adv Intern Med. 1989;34:165.

211 **Resnick NM.** Voiding dysfunction in the elderly. In: Yalla SV et al., eds. Principles and practice of urodynamics

and neuro-urology. New York: MacMillan; 1986:180.

212 **Mandel FP et al.** Biological effects of various doses of vaginally administered conjugated equine estrogens in postmenopausal women. J Clin Endocrinol Metab. 1983;57:133.

213 **Ouslander JG.** Causes, assessment, and treatment of incontinence in the elderly. Urology. 1990;36(Suppl.):25.

214 **Blaivas JG et al.** The bulbocavernous reflex in urology: a prospective study of 299 patients. J Urol. 1981;126:197.

215 **Jensen D Jr.** Pharmacological studies of the uninhibited neurogenic bladder. Acta Neurol Scand. 1981;64:175.

216 **Blaivas J et al.** Cystometric response to propantheline in detrusor hyperreflexia: therapeutic implications. J Urol. 1980;124:259.

217 **Brown JH.** Atropine, scopolamine and related antimuscarinic drugs. In: Gilman AG et al., eds. Goodman and Gilman's The Pharmacological Basis of Therapeutics. New York: Pergamon Press; 1990:150.

218 **Wein AJ.** Pharmacological treatment of incontinence. J Am Geriatr Soc. 1990;38:317.

219 **Levin RM et al.** The muscarinic cholinergic binding kinetics of the human urinary bladder. Neurourol Urodyn. 1982;1:122.

220 **Moisey CU et al.** The urodynamic and subjective results of the treatment of detrusor instability with oxybutynin chloride. Br J Urol. 1980;52:472.

221 **Hehir M, Fitzpatrick JM.** Oxybutynin and the prevention of urinary incontinence in spina bifida. Eur Urol. 1985;11:254.

222 **Gajewski JB, Awad JA.** Oxybutynin versus propantheline in patients with multiple sclerosis and detrusor hyperreflexia. Urology. 1986;135:966.

223 **Marion Merrel Dow.** Bentyl package insert. Kansas City, MO: 1994 April.

224 **Castleden CM et al.** Imipramine—a possible alternative to current therapy for urinary incontinence in the elderly. J Urol. 1981;125:218.

225 **Hollister LE.** Current antidepressants. Ann Rev Pharmacol Toxicol. 1986;26: 23.

226 **Baldessarini RJ.** Drugs and the treatment of psychiatric disorders. Gilman AG et al., eds. Goodman and Gilman's The Pharmacological Basis of Therapeutics. New York: Pergamon Press; 1990:383.

227 **Levin RM et al.** Analysis of the anticholinergic and musculotropic effects of desmethylimipramine on the rabbit urinary bladder. Urol Res. 1983;11: 259.

228 **Abernethy DR et al.** Imipramine and desipramine disposition in the elderly. J Pharmacol Exp Ther. 1985;232:183.

229 **Ray WA et al.** Psychotropic drug use and the risk of hip fracture. N Engl J Med. 1987;316:363.

230 **Norlen L et al.** Beta-adrenoceptor stimulation of the human urinary bladder in vivo. Acta Pharmacol Toxicol (Copenh). 1981;43:5.

231 **Wein AJ, Barrett DM.** Voiding function and dysfunction: a logical and practical approach. Chicago, Illinois: Year Book Medical Publishers; 1988: 195.

232 **Hoffman BB, Lefkowitz RJ.** Catecho-

lamines and Sympathomimetic Drugs. Gilman AG et al., eds. Goodman and Gilman's The Pharmacological Basis of Therapeutics. New York: Pergamon Press; 1990:187.

233 **Awad S et al.** Alpha-adrenergic agents in urinary disorders of the proximal urethra: 1. Stress incontinence. Br J Urol. 1978;50:332.

234 **SmithKline Beechman.** Ornade Spansule package insert. Philadelphia, PA: 1994.

235 **Younglove RH et al.** Medical management of unstable bladder. J Reprod Med. 1980;24:215.

236 **Lasagna L.** Phenylpropanolamine—A review. New York: John Wiley & Sons; 1988:191.

237 **Gilja I et al.** Conservative treatment of female stress incontinence with imipramine. J Urol. 1984;132:909.

238 **Gibson A.** The influence of endocrine hormones on the autonomic nervous system. J Auton Pharmacol. 1981;1:331.

239 **Batra SC, Iosif CS.** Female urethra: a target for estrogen action. J Urol. 1983; 129:418.

240 **Beisland HO et al.** Urethral sphincter insufficiency in postmenopausal females: treatment with phenylpropanolamine and estriol separately and in combination. Urol Int. 1984;39:211.

241 **Lepor H.** Medical therapy for benign prostatic hyperplasia. Urology. 1993; 42;5:483.

242 **Barry MJ et al.** The American Urological Association symptom index for benign prostatic hyperplasia. J Urol. 1992;148:1549.

243 **Marks LS.** Serial endoscopy following visual laser ablation prostatectomy. Urology. 1993;42:66.

244 **Lepro H, Machi G.** Comparison of AUA Symptom Index in unselected males and females between fifty-five and seventy nine years of age. Urology. 1993;42:36.

245 **Anon.** Finasteride for benign prostatic hypertrophy. Med Lett Drugs Ther. 1992;34:83.

246 **MK-906C Finasteride Study Group.** One year experience in the treatment of benign prostatic hyperplasia with finasteride. J Androl. 1991;12:372.

247 **Longe RL, Calvert JC.** Physical Assessment: A Guide for Evaluating Drug Therapy. Vancouver, WA: Applied Therapeutics, Inc.; 1994.

248 **Ferri FF, Fretwell MD.** Practical Guide to the Care of the Geriatric Patient. St. Louis, MO: Mosby Year Book; 1992.

Clinical Toxicology

William A Watson

Definitions 104-2
Epidemiological Data (See Table 104.1) 104-2
  American Association of Poison Control
    Centers (AAPCC) and Drug Abuse Warning
    Network (DAWN) 104-2
  Age-specific 104-2
Information Resources 104-2
  Computerized databases 104-2
  Printed publications 104-2
  Poison control centers 104-2
  Established guidelines 104-3
Establishing Policies and Procedures 104-3
General Management 104-3
  Supportive Care and ''ABCs'' 104-3
    Gathering history of exposure 104-3
    Evaluating clinical presentation and toxidromes ...104-4
    Interpretation of laboratory data 104-4
      Qualitative drug screens 104-4
      Quantitative drug tests 104-4
      Pharmacokinetic considerations 104-4
    Decontamination 104-4
      Gastric decontamination 104-4
        Ipecac-induced emesis 104-5
        Activated charcoal 104-5
    Antidotes and specific treatments 104-5
    Enhancing systemic clearance 104-5
    Monitoring outcome 104-5
Assessments of Salicylate Ingestion 104-5
  Gathering History 104-5
  Evaluating Clinical Presentation 104-6
  Triage of Call 104-6
  Acute and Chronic Salicylism 104-6
    Signs and symptoms (See Table 104.2) 104-6
    Assessment of toxicity (See Figure 104.1) 104-8
    Laboratory evaluation 104-8
    Management 104-8
      Gastric decontamination and fluid therapy 104-8
      Sodium bicarbonate 104-8
      Seizures 104-8
      Coagulopathy 104-9
      Forced alkaline diuresis 104-9
Assessments of Iron Ingestion 104-9
  Gathering History and Communications 104-9
  Triage of Call 104-9
  Substance Identification 104-9
  Evaluating Severity of Toxicity 104-10
  Abdominal X-Rays 104-10
  Gastrointestinal Decontamination 104-10
    Emesis with ipecac 104-10
      Ipecac dosing 104-11
    Gastric lavage 104-11
    Monitoring effectiveness of treatment 104-11

Serum Iron Concentrations 104-12
Total Iron Binding Capacity (TIBC) 104-12
Blood Glucose and White Blood Cell (WBC) Count ..104-12
Deferoxamine Testing 104-12
Asymptomatic Period and Stages of Toxicity 104-12
  Stage I 104-13
  Stage II 104-13
  Stage III 104-13
  Stage IV 104-13
Deferoxamine 104-13
  Chelating 104-13
  Dose 104-13
  Monitoring and discontinuation 104-13
Assessments of Central Nervous System (CNS)
Depressant versus Antidepressant Ingestion 104-13
  Validation of Ingestion 104-13
  Interventions by Protocol 104-14
    Glucose and thiamine 104-14
    Naloxone 104-14
  Initial Treatment 104-14
  Antidotes: Flumazenil 104-14
  Organ-System Evaluations 104-15
    Central nervous system (CNS) function 104-15
    Cardiovascular function 104-15
    Pulmonary function 104-15
    Temperature 104-15
    Gastrointestinal function 104-16
    Skin and extremities 104-16
  Laboratory Tests 104-16
  Qualitative Screening 104-16
    Sensitivity, specificity, and practicality 104-17
  Quantitative Testing 104-17
  Assessment 104-17
  Antidepressant Toxicities 104-17
  Gastric Decontamination 104-18
    Activated charcoal 104-18
    Monitoring efficacy 104-18
  Sodium Bicarbonate and Hyperventilation 104-18
    Monitoring efficacy 104-18
  Seizures 104-19
  Interpretation of Urine Screens 104-19
  Duration of Hospitalization 104-19
Assessments of Acetaminophen Ingestion 104-19
  Complication of Pregnancy 104-19
  Mechanism of Hepatotoxicity 104-19
  Gastric Decontamination 104-19
  Estimating Potential Toxicity 104-20
  Matthew-Rumack Nomogram (See Figure 104.2) 104-20
  Acetylcysteine Administration 104-20
  Monitoring Efficacy of Acetylcysteine 104-20
Assessments of Health Food Ingestions 104-20

This chapter provides an overview of the management of poisoning and drug overdose, and presents several examples of approaches to problem-solving drug overdoses and poisonings. The detailed management of specific drug overdoses will not be presented and the reader needs to refer to other references or to an accredited poison control center if such information is needed.

Definitions

Clinical toxicology focuses on the effects of substances in patients caused by accidental poisonings or intentional overdoses of medications, drugs of abuse, household products, or various other chemicals. Environment exposures primarily involve the ingestion of plants and animal envenomations. Drug and chemical toxicities also can be secondary to intentional assaults, homicides, and weapons of war. *Intoxication* in this chapter is defined as toxicity associated with any chemical substance. *Poisoning* is defined as a clinical toxicity secondary to accidental exposure, and *overdose* as an intentional exposure with the intent of causing self-injury or death.[2,3]

Epidemiological Data

American Association of Poison Control Centers (AAPCC) and Drug Abuse Warning Network (DAWN). Toxicity secondary to drug and chemical exposure is common and has been described as a national epidemic.[2] The incidence of drug or chemical exposure, the agents involved, and the severity of the outcome varies with the reporting source (see Table 104.1). The incidence of toxic "exposures" in the U.S. in 1991 was approximately 1.8 million according to the regional poison control center members of the American Association of Poison Control Centers (AAPCC).[5] This "incidence" of about nine cases per thousand population during the 1991 calendar year is based upon the number of contacts (including telephone contacts) with poison control center members as noted by the AAPCC's Toxic Exposures Surveillance System (TESS).[5] In the majority of the cases, little or no toxicity was associated with the exposure; about 25% received treatment at a health care facility; 3% had moderate or severe symptoms; and 764 deaths were reported. The number of drug abuse, accidental poisonings, and intentional overdose cases treated in all U.S. emergency rooms in 1991 was about 400,000 according to the Drug Abuse Warning Network (DAWN).[6,7]

These disparate statistics from two national sources underscore the difficulty in determining the true incidence of poisoning and overdoses.[8,9] Nevertheless, epidemiological data are useful in identifying trends and in instigating public health interventions. For example, the rapid increase in cocaine use and toxicity during the 1980s stimulated research that studied mechanisms of cocaine toxicity, diagnosis and treatment of cocaine toxicity, prevention of cocaine abuse, and detoxification of the chronic cocaine abuser.[10,11] In another historical example of a public health intervention, epidemiological data on the intravenous abuse of pentaz-

ocine tablets prompted the manufacturer to add naloxone to pentazocine to decrease the potential for intravenous abuse.[12] The toxicity associated with specific occupations (e.g., tobacco picking) also has been identified based upon epidemiological data.[13]

Age-Specific. Grouping patients into age-defined categories can be useful in assessing the likelihood of severe adverse effects from exposure to a toxic substance. For example, the majority of accidental ingestions by patients between one and six years of age are the result of children becoming developmentally more mobile and able to explore their surroundings. Frequently, these explorations involve the insertion of objects or substances into their mouths and result in potential poisonings. These exposures usually involve the ingestion of a relatively small amount of a single substance without an intent to induce injury; therefore, severe toxicity is relatively uncommon despite the small body size of the child. Children less than one year of age have less ability to independently ingest substances and child abuse should be considered if the history of exposure is not consistent with the developmental age of the child. In children more than six years of age, the reason for the exposure becomes less clear. Although suicide attempts and ethanol abuse are unlikely, these potentialities should not be ignored entirely in older aged children. In adolescents and adults, potentially toxic exposures most commonly are attempts to cause death or to intentionally abuse toxic substances. These intentional overdoses frequently involve mixed exposures to illicit drugs, prescribed medications or ethanol, and produce more severe toxicity and death than accidental poisonings. In geriatric patients, overdoses tend to have a greater potential for severe adverse effects compared to overdoses in other age groups because of the greater likelihood of underlying cardiovascular or pulmonary disease.

Information Resources

Computerized Databases. An enormous number of different substances can be involved in a poisoning or overdose, and reliable data about the contents of products, toxicities of substances, and treatment approaches need to be readily accessible. *Poisindex*, a computerized CD-ROM database that is updated quarterly, is a primary resource for poison control centers. *Poisindex* lists more than 750,000 products and a large number of management protocols. A sister computerized-database is the Toxicologic, Occupational Medicine and Environmental Series (*Tomes*) which provides information on industrial chemicals.[14] Yearly subscriptions to *Poisindex* and *Tomes* are relatively expensive (several thousand dollars per year) and not generally available except in poison control centers and some medical centers.[15]

Printed Publications. Textbooks and manuals also provide useful clinical information about toxicity of substances, assessments of toxicities, and treatment approaches. *Medical Toxicology: Diagnosis and Treatment of Human Poisonings*,[143] *Clinical Management of Poisoning and Drug Overdose*,[144] *Goldfrank's Toxicologic Emergencies*,[145] and the pocket-sized *Poisoning and Drug Overdose*[146] are valuable, inexpensive alternatives to computerized database programs. Books, however, are less useful than computerized databases because of limits as to the amount of information that can be condensed into a publication and the inability of providing frequent updated information. Detailed information for specific toxicologic substances such as venomous snakebites,[147] ocular toxicity,[148] and plant toxicity[149] also are available.

Poison Control Centers. Poison control centers accredited by the AAPCC provide the most accurate, specific information for both the general public and health care providers. In an evaluation of the ability of poison control centers to accurately assess and rec-

Table 104.1	Substances Most Commonly Reported in Toxic Exposures[5–7]	
Cases	**Deaths**
Poison Centers	
1,837,939 Total	*764 Total*
1) Cleaning substances	1) Analgesics
2) Analgesics	2) Antidepressants
3) Cosmetics	3) Sedatives/hypnotics
4) Plants	4) Stimulants/street drugs
5) Cough/cold preparations	5) Cardiovascular agents
Emergency Departments	**Medical Examiner**
133,217 Total	*6601 Total*
1) Alcohol with other drugs	1) Cocaine
2) Cocaine	2) Alcohol with other drugs
3) Heroin/morphine	3) Heroin/morphine
4) Acetaminophen	4) Codeine
5) Analgesics	5) Diazepam

ommend appropriate treatment, nonaccredited poison control center personnel provided incorrect treatment recommendations nine times more frequently than accredited poison control centers.[16] Although pharmacies, drug information centers, and nonaccredited regional poison control centers frequently provide appropriate poison information in a timely manner, an accredited regional poison control center should be utilized whenever possible.[17–19] Pharmacists, nurses, and nonphysician clinical toxicologists can become certified as poison information specialists by the AAPCC or board certified as toxicologists by the American Board of Applied Toxicology; physicians can be certified by a medical board examination in clinical toxicology.

A poison control center's most important function is to provide event-specific toxicity information to individuals and health care providers. The poison information specialist must be able to accurately assess the toxicity and communicate usually by telephone without the benefit of observation of the patient. This assessment and communication should be conducted quickly, accurately, and professionally in a reassuring manner. Subsequent to the telephone consultation, the poison control center should initiate follow-up calls to determine the outcome, the effectiveness of the recommended treatment, and the need for additional evaluation or treatment.[19] The poison control center also should be able to coordinate treatment which may include facilitation of transportation to a health care facility that has appropriately trained personnel, equipment (e.g., hemoperfusion, hyperbaric oxygen), and an analytical toxicology laboratory.[20] Poison control centers also have the responsibility of promoting public awareness of the need for poison prevention and the responsibility to generate epidemiological data on toxicological exposures based upon documentation of their own experience with exposures, treatments, and clinical outcomes.[19]

Established Guidelines. The American College of Emergency Physicians has published guidelines for the initial approach to patients who present with acute toxic ingestions, or dermal or inhalation exposure.[1,4] The initial evaluation and diagnosis, stabilization, and management of the patient are included, however, specific antidotes are not included. There are also a number of position papers which currently are being prepared by the American Academy of Clinical Toxicology, and reviewed by other clinical toxicology and poison control groups. These position papers are intended to provide a critical review and consensus of the scientific and clinical data available for specific treatments, and recommendations for the role of various treatments. The initial position papers will address the methods available for gastrointestinal (GI) decontamination and enhanced drug elimination and should be released in 1995 or 1996.

Establishing Policies and Procedures

Requests for toxicological information in an acute situation often provoke considerable stress and anxiety which can be lessened by established policies and procedures. Although most institutional health care facilities are well acquainted with policies and procedures, physician offices, clinics, and community pharmacies are not as likely to have updated policies and procedures to assist staff who are faced with requests for assistance in assessing an accidental ingestion or overdose. These policies and procedures should be specific for each practice setting and should include consideration of the following: 1) steps for effective communications with the caller; 2) lists of patient-specific information needed for rapid triage assessments of toxicity; 3) sources for information on toxicities and management of ingested substances; and 4) processes to be initiated when more expert personnel or facilities are needed.[19,23]

Effective communications are extremely important in assessing potential poisonings. In most situations, the individual seeking guidance on the management of a potentially toxic exposure is the parent of a small child who may have ingested a substance. The caller will be anxious about the potential toxicity for the child and possibly have some feelings of guilt if the exposure could have been prevented. The health care provider should immediately reassure the parent that telephoning for assistance was very appropriate and that the best assistance possible will be provided in managing this situation. These reassurances usually calm the caller and allow for more effective communications. In the initial moments of the telephone conversation, the health care provider should attempt to determine the likelihood of effective communication with the caller. Foreign language barriers or other communication barriers sometimes can be alleviated by asking whether another responsible adult is in the household.

The health care provider should always first determine whether the patient who was exposed to the potentially toxic substance is conscious, breathing, and has a pulse. He or she must then coach the telephone caller as to actions to be undertaken to address the above deficits. If the health care provider cannot provide poison information because of a lack of knowledge or resources, the person requesting assistance should be put into contact with the closest accredited poison control center. Therefore, all policies and procedures should list the location and telephone number of the nearest accredited poison control center.

General Management
Supportive Care and "ABCs"

Management of poisoned or overdosed patients almost always centers around symptomatic and supportive care while the patient eliminates the substance. Specific antidotes exist for only a small percentage of the thousands of potential drugs and chemicals that could be ingested. The first aspect of patient management should always be basic support of airway, breathing, and circulation (the "ABCs"). A patent airway and adequate rate and depth of respiration must be assured and may necessitate endotracheal intubation and mechanical ventilation in patients with marked central nervous system (CNS) depression. Cardiac output, blood pressure, urine output, and peripheral perfusion must be maintained. The assessment and treatment of the potentially poisoned patient can be separated into seven primary functions: 1) gathering history of exposure; 2) evaluating clinical presentation (i.e., toxidromes); 3) evaluating clinical laboratory patient data; 4) removing toxic source (e.g., gastric decontamination); 5) considering antidotes and specific treatment; 6) enhancing systemic clearance; and 7) monitoring outcome.[2,3,21]

Gathering History of Exposure

Comprehensive historical information about the accidental ingestion or toxic exposure should be gathered from as many different sources as possible (e.g., patient, family, friends, prehospital health care providers). This information should be compared for consistency and evaluated relative to clinical findings and laboratory results. Although some claim that the patient's history is most likely to be inaccurate and should not be considered,[2,22] this opinion is not supported by scientific data, and historical information from the patient should be used until contradicted by objective clinical findings (see Question 27).

When obtaining the history of exposure, open-ended questions should be used to determine why the individual believes or knows that an accidental ingestion or overdose occurred. Specific information should be sought concerning: the state of consciousness of the patient, present symptoms, probable intoxicant(s), maximum amount of substance ingested, dosage form(s), and when the exposure occurred. Medications, allergies, and prior medical problems also should be ascertained (e.g., a history of renal failure may indicate the need for hemodialysis or hemoperfusion to compensate for decreased renal drug clearance).[19,23]

Evaluating Clinical Presentation and Toxidromes

A thorough physical examination should be performed to characterize the signs and symptoms of overdose. Physical examinations should be conducted serially to determine the evolution or resolution of the patient's intoxication. An evaluation of the presenting signs and symptoms can provide clues on the drug class causing the toxicity, confirm the historical data surrounding the toxic exposure, and suggest initial treatment.[2,24,25] The patient, however, may be asymptomatic upon presentation even though a potentially severe exposure has occurred if the drug or toxic substance was ingested a short time before the physical examination, or if absorption of the substance has been delayed.[26] Association of symptoms with a particular class of toxic substances also can be difficult when more than one substance has been ingested.

Different *toxidromes* (i.e., a constellation of signs and symptoms consistent with a syndrome) can be associated with some specific classes of drugs.[2,24] The most common probably are those associated with anticholinergic activity, increased sympathetic activity, central nervous system stimulation, or CNS depression. The anticholinergic effects of drugs can increase heart rate, decrease gastrointestinal motility, dilate pupils, and alter sensorium. Sympathomimetic drugs can increase CNS activity, sympathetic tone, heart rate, and blood pressure (BP). Opioids, sedatives, hypnotics, and antidepressants can depress the CNS, but the specific class of CNS depressant cannot be easily identified by a specific constellation of symptoms. Classic findings may not be present for all drugs within a therapeutic class. For example, opioids generally induce miosis, but meperidine can produce mydriasis instead. Clinicians should not focus on the presence or absence of a specific clinical finding's association with a toxidrome, but rather should focus on all subjective and objective data gleaned from the patient history, physical examination, and laboratory findings.

Interpretation of Laboratory Data

Qualitative Drug Screens. A qualitative urine drug screen can be useful in identifying the presence of drugs and metabolites in selected patients. A urine drug screen is not indicated in all cases of drug overdose, but it may be useful in a patient with coma of unknown etiology, when the presented history is inconsistent with clinical findings, or when more than one drug might have been ingested.[27–30] Gastric fluid and blood also can be screened for the presence of unknown substances, however, these evaluations are less likely to result in the identification of an ingested substance compared to urine screens. Urine generally contains a higher concentration of a drug and its metabolites compared to other body fluids and, as a result, is more likely to achieve the threshold concentration needed for detection.

A qualitative drug screen must be interpreted cautiously. A "positive" test cannot differentiate between an overdose and a therapeutic dose: it merely indicates the presence of the drug or its metabolites. A "negative" toxicological screening test does not necessarily rule out a drug overdose because the drug may have been present in an undetectable concentration at the time the sample was obtained or the laboratory method of analysis may not have been capable of detecting the substance in the sample. The sensitivity, specificity, and practicality of the test should be considered. When a specific ingested substance is suspected, the cli-

nician should communicate with the analytical toxicologist to ascertain whether the commonly utilized testing methodology is capable of identifying the suspected drug. Although urine toxicological screening tests can be useful in identifying the presence of a drug, these screening tests should not be used to quantify whether the drug is present in sufficient quantities to produce toxicity (see Question 33).

Quantitative Drug Tests. Measuring the amount of drug in serum or plasma is useful in the following situations: 1) if there is a known correlation between the concentration of the substance and toxic effects; 2) the turn-around time for results is rapid; and 3) treatment can be guided by the serum concentration of the drug. For example, drug serum concentrations are commonly used to estimate the potential toxicity of acetaminophen, salicylates, theophylline, iron, and ethanol (see Question 34).[2,29,31]

Pharmacokinetic Considerations. The absorption, distribution, metabolism, and elimination of drugs and compounds in the overdosed patient can be quite different than the pharmacokinetic parameters of a drug taken in usual therapeutic doses.[31,32] The pharmacodynamic and pharmacokinetic behavior of drugs can be substantially altered by large drug overdoses especially with drugs that are associated with dose-dependent pharmacokinetics. The rate of drug absorption generally is slowed by large overdoses and the time to reach peak serum drug concentrations can be prolonged. The volume of distribution of a drug can be increased with overdoses. Usual metabolic pathways can become saturated and secondary clearance pathways can become important. For example, large overdoses of acetaminophen can saturate glutathione mechanisms of detoxification and result in the production of greater quantities of a hepatotoxic metabolite.

These altered pharmacokinetic parameters of an overdosed drug suggest that measurements of serial plasma concentrations are necessary to better define the absorption, distribution, and clearance phases of the ingested substance. The usual (nonpatient-specific) pharmacokinetic parameters should not be used to predict whether absorption is complete or to predict the expected duration of intoxication from an intentionally overdosed drug.[31,32]

Decontamination

After the airway and the cardiopulmonary system have been supported, efforts should be directed to remove the toxic substance from the patient (i.e., decontamination). Decontamination is based upon the premise that both the dose and the duration of exposure to a toxin are important in determining the extent of toxicity, and prevention of continued exposure would potentially decrease the toxicity. This concept is clearly important with ocular, dermal, and respiratory exposures, especially when local tissue damage is the primary problem. Respiratory decontamination involves removing the patient from the toxic environment and providing fresh air or oxygen to the patient. Decontamination of skin and eyes involves the use of large volumes of fluid to physically remove the toxic substance from the surface. Decontamination should not be based upon neutralization of the substance because the chemical reaction of neutralization can produce heat which could further damage the exposed tissue.[33]

Gastric Decontamination. Since most intoxications result from oral ingestion of a substance, measures to decrease gastrointestinal absorption are commonly utilized in an attempt to limit the degree of patient exposure to the toxin. The intent of gastrointestinal decontamination is to prevent the continued absorption of substances remaining in the GI tract.[2,3,34–36] In this sense, gastrointestinal decontamination can be considered prophylactic therapy because it prevents the occurrence of toxicity which would result if all of the toxic substance remaining in the GI tract were to be absorbed.

Some method of gastrointestinal decontamination should be considered as treatment in all poisoned or overdosed patients if the ingestion is potentially large enough to produce clinically significant toxicity, or if the potential severity of the ingestion is unknown. Gastrointestinal decontamination can be accomplished by the following methods: 1) evacuation of gastric contents by emesis or lavage; 2) administration of activated charcoal as an adsorbent to bind the toxic substance in the GI tract; 3) whole bowel irrigation; or 4) combinations of the above. When the potential for toxicity from an ingestion is great, aggressive methods of GI decontamination should be selected. A history of spontaneous emesis before treatment should not negate the need to institute gastrointestinal decontamination and should be considered even when patients have abused drugs intravenously or by inhalation because of the possibility of concurrent oral routes of administration.

The best method of gastrointestinal decontamination is unclear because sound comparative data for different methods of gastrointestinal decontamination are unavailable. Clinical research in healthy subjects, by necessity, must use nontoxic doses of drugs. The alterations in GI absorption that can occur with large overdoses cannot be detected in studies utilizing nontoxic doses and these studies may not adequately account for the variances in absorption from different methods of gastrointestinal decontamination. Low-dose studies generally rely upon pharmacokinetic endpoints such as peak plasma concentrations, area under the plasma concentration-time curve, or quantity of drug recovered from the urine.[37,38] Clinical studies of gastrointestinal decontamination methods in patients who have ingested toxic doses of a substance frequently focus on clinical outcomes or on the directional change in serum drug concentrations (i.e., effective decontamination should result in no further increase in serum concentrations).[39,40] These latter studies, however, cannot standardize the trials as to the dose ingested or to the time of ingestion before initiation of gastric decontamination.[38]

Ipecac-induced emesis (see Questions 14 and 15) and gastric lavage (see Questions 16, 17, and 38) primarily remove substances from the stomach, and possibly from the proximal small bowel; however, these methods do not affect materials more distal in the small intestine. Whole bowel irrigation with a polyethylene glycol balanced electrolyte solution (e.g., CoLyte, GoLytely) can remove substances along the entire GI tract; however, this method of gastrointestinal decontamination takes much longer to complete than ipecac syrup or gastric lavage. Whole bowel irrigation is probably most effective (and may only be effective) with substances that disintegrate and dissolve very slowly (e.g., sustained-release dosage forms).[41] In extreme situations, surgical procedures can remove known fatal amounts of toxic substances from the GI tract after other gastrointestinal decontamination methods have failed.[36]

Activated Charcoal. Currently, the adsorption of substances to activated charcoal (see Questions 38 and 39) seems to be the preferred method of gastrointestinal decontamination.[36,42-43] The adsorption of substances to charcoal prevents absorption of the substance and the charcoal-drug complex can be recovered in stool. A cathartic such as sorbitol usually is administered concurrently with the activated charcoal to quickly remove the charcoal-drug complex from the intestinal tract and to prevent the possible disassociation of the toxic drug from the charcoal if this complex remains for a long period of time in the intestinal tract.[44] Cathartics alone are not effective for gastrointestinal decontamination.[36]

The effectiveness of gastrointestinal decontamination varies with the location of the toxic substance (i.e., stomach, proximal intestine, distal intestine) and with the amount of the substance that still might be present in the GI tract. The efficacy of gastrointestinal decontamination, therefore, needs to be monitored to provide some guidance to the clinician as to whether absorption and progression of the intoxication have been halted. Symptoms, serial plasma drug concentrations, visual inspection of vomitus or gastric lavage fluid, and the presence of activated charcoal in the stool can possibly serve as indicators of the effectiveness of gastrointestinal decontamination.[36,45]

Antidotes and Specific Treatments

An antidote is a substance which antagonizes the toxicity of another substance in a specific manner. These antidotes can be useful if they do not produce other effects that could pose even greater hazards for the patient. Antidotes can displace a drug from receptor sites (e.g., naloxone for opioids, flumazenil for benzodiazepines); inhibit the formation of toxic metabolites (e.g., acetylcysteine for acetaminophen, ethanol for methanol); and antibodies which bind a drug and prevent drug binding to the receptor (e.g., antidigoxin FAB fragment). Antidotes can be useful as selective diagnostic aids and as therapeutic agents (see Question 30).

Some specific treatments are highly effective for the management of individual drug overdoses, but do not meet the definition of an antidote. For example, sodium bicarbonate is useful in the treatment of the cardiotoxicity from tricyclic antidepressant overdoses (see Questions 40 and 41), and benzodiazepines are useful in the treatment of the CNS toxicity associated with cocaine overdoses. Replacement therapy with glucose also is a specific treatment for insulin or oral hypoglycemic overdoses.[2,10,21]

Enhancing Systemic Clearance

The systemic clearance of substances can be enhanced by increasing or decreasing urinary pH to prevent tubular reabsorption, increasing urine flow rates, hemodialysis, hemoperfusion, or gastrointestinal dialysis.[47] Generally, these interventions do not increase the total systemic clearance sufficient to clinically shorten the course of a drug overdose. Nevertheless, hemodialysis or hemoperfusion are successful for the treatment of some specific intoxications and should be considered for patients with renal dysfunction and diminished drug excretion.[3,21,46,48,76]

Monitoring Outcome

Selecting the appropriate parameters and length of time to monitor an intoxication requires knowledge of the types of toxicity which are of greatest concern and the time course of the intoxication. Most patients with potential moderate or severe toxicity are monitored in an intensive care unit (ICU) with careful assessment of cardiac, pulmonary, and central nervous system function.[49] Symptoms, laboratory parameters, observation, and findings such as electrocardiogram (ECG) abnormalities, changes in vital signs, and altered mental status should be monitored (see Question 44).

Assessments of Salicylate Ingestion

Gathering History

1. M.O., the mother of a 4-year-old child, inquires how to use ipecac syrup to cause vomiting. In response to further questioning she states that her daughter, D.O., has ingested some aspirin tablets. What additional information should be obtained from, or given to, M.O. at this point in time?

Requests for information about poisonings may focus on a single issue (e.g., dose of ipecac syrup); however, these requests for information should be evaluated more completely to determine whether a toxic substance has been ingested. The first information to be gleaned from a caller should focus on the function of the patient's airway, breathing, circulation, and mental status (especially with telephone calls when the patient is not available for observation). After this initial assessment of the patient's status, provide guidance to the caller for interventions that need to be undertaken immediately (e.g., calling 9-1-1 for Emergency Medical Services, or clearing an airway). The telephone number of the caller should be obtained in the event that the telephone call is disconnected, initial recommendations need to be modified, or subsequent follow-up is needed.

The initial dialogue with the caller should quickly establish the trust and cooperation that is needed for a successful outcome. The health care provider should ask for patient-specific information with questions and statements that are nonthreatening and nonjudgmental. For example, the caller could be asked to provide information about the ingestion with an explanation that better assistance could be provided as a result, rather than asking the caller whether she is sure that ipecac is necessary.

Evaluating Clinical Presentation

2. Upon further questioning, M.O. states that her daughter, D.O., is crying and complaining of a stomachache. D.O. otherwise appears to be acting as she normally would. M.O. apparently found her daughter sitting on the bathroom floor with an aspirin bottle in her hand and some partially chewed tablets on the floor next to her. D.O. was described as having the same look on her face that she does when she eats things that she does not like. The mother was gone no more than 5 minutes and had asked her 5- and 6-year-old sons to watch their sister. What additional information is needed to correctly assess the potential for toxicity in D.O.?

The information needed for a correct assessment of the potential for an accidental ingestion should focus on the presence of symptoms, identification of the substance ingested, and identification of all children who might have been involved in the accidental ingestion. This information should be gained by beginning with open-ended questions to determine what the caller is sure of versus what the caller may have assumed. Once this information is obtained, the answers usually will point out the more specific information that is needed to accurately assess the exposure.

The symptoms of D.O. do not appear to be life-threatening. Her complaints of a stomachache and her crying are not unusual behaviors for a child who is frightened. These behaviors probably are responses of the child to the actions and anxieties exhibited by her mother when the ingestion was discovered. After it has been established that the child is not likely to need immediate lifesaving treatment, the caller generally will become calmer and be more willing and able to answer additional questions.

Since M.O. already has provided information on the presence of symptoms, additional information is needed on the substance involved in the accidental ingestion, the route of ingestion, the maximum potential dose, and the time of ingestion. Further information needed would include: the brand of aspirin (to ensure that the product is not an aspirin-combination formulation), the dosage form, the number of dosage units in a full container, and the number of remaining dosage units. The actual number of remaining dosage units should be counted rather than estimated because most containers are not filled to the top when first purchased. Furthermore, the parent should be careful to look for uneaten tablets hidden under beds, under rugs, or in locations out of visual sight (e.g., wastepaper baskets). The dosage forms in the container should all be the same in appearance and the contents should be what is stated on the label, because individuals may put more than one type of drug in the same container.

If the ingested substance is a liquid, it can be more difficult to determine the amount ingested because the liquid is frequently spilled on, or around, the child. The caller may have witnessed the child actually drinking the liquid and be able to provide an estimate of how many swallows were ingested. In the average two-year-old child, each swallow of liquid will contain about 1.5 to 5 mL.[50]

When more than one child is present during an ingestion, the caller should be questioned as to whether an additional child also could have participated in the ingestion. Most poison information specialists have experienced ingestions that involved multiple children who equally shared in the missing dosage units of drug, fed all drug to one child (usually the youngest), or had the oldest or most aggressive child ingest all of the dosage units. When it is unclear how many missing dosage units of a substance may have been ingested among a group of children, each child should be evaluated and managed as if he or she may have ingested the total missing quantity.

Triage of Call

3. The caller, M.O., has now evaluated the exact number of tablets likely to have been ingested and has concluded that a total of 5 tablets containing 325 mg/tablet of aspirin are missing from the bottle. Since M.O. recalls having taken aspirin at one time from this bottle, it is likely that her daughter took no more than 3 tablets. Should M.O. now simply give the ipecac syrup so she need not worry about any possibility of toxicity?

The maximum dose of aspirin ingested by this child is likely to be much less than the minimum dose required to produce significant symptoms based upon the assumption that this 4-year-old girl is of average weight for her age. A dose of 150 mg/kg of aspirin is the lowest dose at which treatment or assessment at a health care facility is usually necessary.[51] The provision of this information to the mother will be reassuring and likely to foster her continued cooperation with further questioning.

Information concerning the child's weight, health status, and other medications is important. The weight can be used to determine the precise maximum mg/kg dose of aspirin that was ingested. Other medications and health conditions that could increase the toxicity produced by the ingestion also should be considered. If this child is healthy and takes no medications and is not allergic to aspirin, the mother does not have to administer ipecac syrup because the child has not taken a toxic dose of aspirin and the child need not undergo the unpleasantness of emesis. The mother should be instructed to continue to observe her daughter for any changes which would not be considered normal in the child, such as changes in mental status, nausea, vomiting, or diarrhea. With this history of ingestion, adverse effects would not be expected except possibly some mild nausea or emesis.

Follow-up of telephone consultations on toxic ingestions is important in identifying children who unexpectedly develop symptoms which might need to be treated. A follow-up telephone call to this mother would be professionally appropriate and be an opportunity to provide poison prevention information (e.g., the telephone number of the nearest accredited regional poison control center).[19,23]

Acute and Chronic Salicylism

Signs and Symptoms

4. V.K. is a 65-year-old, 55 kg female with a history of chronic headaches for which she has taken 10 to 12 aspirin/day for several months. On the evening of admission she became lethargic, disoriented, and combative. Additional history revealed that she had ingested up to 100 aspirin tablets on the morning of admission in a suicide attempt. Vital signs were BP 140/90 mm Hg, pulse 110 beats/min, respirations 36/min, and temperature 102.5 °F. V.K.'s laboratory data obtained on admission were as follows: serum sodium (Na) 148 mEq/L (Nor-

mal: 135–153), potassium (K) 3.0 mEq/L (Normal: 3.5–5.5), chloride (Cl) 105 mEq/L (Normal: 95–105), bicarbonate 12 mEq/L (Normal: 24–31), glucose 60 mg/dL (Normal: 70–110), blood urea nitrogen (BUN) 35 mg/dL (Normal: 5–25), and creatinine 2.1 mg/dL (Normal: 0.5–1.4). Arterial blood gases (ABGs) on room air were pH 7.25, pCO_2 20 mm Hg, and pO_2 95 mm Hg. A serum salicylate concentration measured ≈12 hours after the acute ingestion was 120 mg/dL. Describe the pathophysiology and clinical features of acute and chronic salicylism. [SI units: Na 148 mmol/L (Normal: 135–153); K 3 mmol/L (Normal: 3.5–5.5); Cl 105 mmol/L (Normal: 95–105); bicarbonate 12 mmol/L (Normal: 24–31); glucose 3.33 mmol/L (Normal: 3.89–6.11); BUN 12.50 mmol/L urea (Normal: 1.79–8.93); creatinine 185.64 μmol/L (Normal: 44.2–123.76); pCO_2 2.67 kPa; pO_2 12.66 kPa; salicylate 8.69 mmol/L]

For many years, aspirin was the most common cause of accidental poisoning and poisoning deaths among children. However, safety closure packaging and reduction of the total aspirin content in children's aspirin to approximately 3 gm has steadily reduced the frequency of aspirin poisoning and deaths.[151] While acute aspirin poisoning remains a problem, the largest percentage of life-threatening intoxications now results from "therapeutic overdose."[152]

Aspirin is readily available in almost all households. The use of methyl salicylate (oil of wintergreen) in topical liniments or as peppermint flavoring in homemade candy results in its occasional ingestion.

The symptoms and severity of salicylate intoxication depend upon the dose consumed, patient age, and whether the ingestion was acute or chronic. Children less than five years old seem especially susceptible to the toxic effects of salicylate and easily develop the severe acid-base and neurologic disturbances characteristic of advanced intoxication. Acute ingestion of 150 to 300 mg/kg of aspirin is likely to produce mild to moderate intoxication; more than 300 mg/kg leads to severe poisoning; over 500 mg/kg is potentially lethal (see Table 104.2).[153] V.K., who ingested approximately 600 mg/kg, has taken a potentially lethal dose. Chronic salicylate intoxication usually is associated with ingestion of more than 100 mg/kg/day for more than two to three days.[153] V.K. has been taking 70 mg/kg/day for her headaches.

Toxic doses of salicylate directly stimulate the medullary respiratory center and influence several key metabolic pathways. Direct stimulation of the respiratory drive results in an increased rate and depth of ventilation, producing a primary respiratory alkalosis. This causes increased renal excretion of bicarbonate resulting in mild diminution of buffering capacity. The patient usually presents clinically with a partially-compensated respiratory alkalosis. Occasionally, alkalosis may be of such a degree that the reduced fraction of ionized calcium can produce tetany.[154]

Table 104.2	Signs and Symptoms of Acute Salicylate Intoxication[153]	
Dose Ingested (mg/kg)	**Severity**	**Anticipated Symptoms**
<150	Asymptomatic	None
150–300	Mild to moderate	*Mild*: mild to moderate hyperpnea, occasional lethargy *Moderate*: severe hyperpnea, lethargy, agitation
300–500	Severe	Severe hyperpnea, coma, occasional convulsions
>500	Potentially lethal	Coma, convulsions, cardiovascular collapse

Gastrointestinal irritation caused by salicylate may produce nausea and vomiting; hyperventilation and increased GI fluid losses combine to produce mild dehydration. Hypokalemia may result from increased GI and renal losses and systemic alkalosis. Tinnitus is common when the salicylate concentration exceeds 25 to 30 mg/dL. While the marked metabolic and neurologic abnormalities are most commonly observed in young children with advanced salicylate intoxication, adolescents or adults acutely poisoned with a sufficiently large dose may develop the identical spectrum of problems, as demonstrated by V.K.

Acute salicylism in the young child often takes a more severe course than that typically seen in adults. Following acute ingestion, children quickly pass through the phase of pure respiratory alkalosis. Renal bicarbonate loss secondary to respiratory alkalosis reduces the buffering capacity more profoundly in a child and facilitates the development of metabolic acidosis.[155]

Salicylates also have toxic effects on several biochemical pathways which contribute to metabolic acidosis and other symptoms.[154] Oxidative phosphorylation is uncoupled resulting in an impaired ability to generate high-energy phosphates, increased oxygen utilization and carbon dioxide production, increased heat production and hyperpyrexia, and increased tissue glycolysis and a peripheral demand for glucose. Salicylates may inhibit key dehydrogenase enzymes within the Krebs cycle, resulting in increased levels of pyruvate and lactate. The increased demand for peripheral glucose causes increased glycogenolysis, gluconeogenesis, lipolysis, and free fatty acid metabolism. The latter results in enhanced formation of ketoacids (as in diabetic ketoacidosis).[153–155]

The patient may become severely volume depleted through several mechanisms. Hyperthermia and hyperventilation produce increased insensible water loss, vomiting may promote GI fluid losses, and the solute load caused by altered glucose metabolism results in an osmotic diuresis. Large amounts of sodium and potassium also may be lost through these mechanisms. However, depending upon the patient's acid-base balance and net fluid and electrolyte intake and output, serum sodium and potassium concentrations may be normal, elevated, or decreased. Hypernatremia and hypokalemia are most common.[153,154]

Blood glucose concentration is usually normal or slightly elevated, although hypoglycemia may accompany chronic salicylism or occur late in acute intoxication.[153] Central nervous system glucose levels may be markedly reduced in the presence of normal blood glucose concentrations.[156] This occurs because increased CNS glucose utilization to generate high-energy phosphate exceeds the rate at which glucose can be supplied. Clinical deterioration of the patient may be related to reduced CNS glucose concentrations.

Other manifestations of severe acute salicylism include a variety of neurologic signs and symptoms: disorientation, irritability, hallucinations, lethargy, stupor, coma, and seizures. Seizure activity may be due to direct salicylate effect, low brain glucose levels, hyponatremia, cerebral edema, or reduced amounts of ionized calcium accompanying alkalosis. Hyperthermia may be marked and has led to the inappropriate administration of aspirin as an antipyretic in cases where the etiology was not immediately recognized. A coagulopathy can occur because of impaired platelet function, salicylate-induced hypoprothrombinemia, reduced factor VII production, and increased capillary fragility.[154] Pulmonary edema and acute renal failure also are seen,[155] but the former occurs more commonly following chronic intoxication.[157]

In both adults and children, the principle manifestations of chronic salicylism are a partially compensated metabolic acidosis, increased anion gap, ketosis, dehydration, electrolyte loss, and encephalopathy.[153,154] Unless the history of salicylate intake is specifically sought, the problem may not be immediately apparent; this may be especially true in the elderly in whom the findings are likely to be attributed to other causes (e.g., encephalitis, meningitis, diabetic ketoacidosis, myocardial infarction).[158,159] Delay in diagnosis has been associated with increased mortality.[159] Plasma salicylate concentrations are often not as high in chronically-intoxicated patients and do not correlate with the degree of poisoning.[160]

Death in patients with salicylism, whether acute or chronic, is due to CNS dysfunction, severe dehydration and electrolyte loss, or pulmonary edema.[154] The severity of CNS manifestations is related to the cerebral spinal fluid salicylate concentration. This may increase in the presence of systemic acidosis because a greater fraction of the weak acid is un-ionized and can cross the blood-brain barrier.[161] Thus, metabolic acidosis can be especially dangerous in a salicylate-intoxicated patient.

Assessment of Toxicity

5. Explain V.K.'s signs, symptoms, and laboratory values.

V.K. demonstrates many of the findings typical of severe acute salicylism. Hyperventilation has resulted from the direct respiratory stimulant effects of salicylate and as compensation for her metabolic acidosis (pCO$_2$ 20 mm Hg, pH 7.25, serum bicarbonate 12 mEq/L, respiratory rate 36/minute). Hypokalemia (3.0 mEq/L) in the presence of metabolic acidosis represents severe potassium depletion due to increased renal and possibly GI losses. Hyperpyrexia caused by salicylate's effects on intermediary glucose metabolism and oxidative phosphorylation is present in V.K., although an infectious etiology also must be considered. Lastly, her neurologic symptoms of lethargy, disorientation, and combativeness are commonly seen in severe salicylate intoxication.

Laboratory Evaluation

6. What parameters should be measured to assess a patient with salicylate intoxication?

V.K.'s work-up illustrates a thorough initial patient evaluation. Laboratory evaluation should include ABGs and pH, serum electrolytes, and blood glucose. Physical examination should include an evaluation of cardiopulmonary and neurologic function and a measurement of urine output. Prothrombin and partial thromboplastin times may be useful in severe acute or chronic intoxication to assess the presence of salicylate-induced coagulopathy.

An appropriately-timed measurement of serum salicylate concentration, when interpreted using the nomogram in Figure 104.1,[162] is helpful in acute poisoning to identify the degree of intoxication, assess patient prognosis, and guide therapy. The nomogram cannot be used for patients with chronic intoxication. V.K.'s level was measured approximately 12 hours following ingestion; thus, it should accurately reflect her degree of intoxication. Serum concentrations obtained earlier than six hours after ingestion may be difficult to interpret and may result in an underestimation of the eventual degree of intoxication because gastrointestinal absorption of the ingested dose most likely will be incomplete. The salicylate concentration can continue to rise over approximately 24 hours if a large amount has been taken or enteric-coated tablets have been ingested.[163] Also, methyl salicylate appears to be more slowly absorbed than aspirin even though it is available in liquid form. Therefore, it may be useful to repeat a serum salicylate measurement in four to six hours to verify that the original concentration represented a peak level. V.K.'s salicylate concentration is clearly in the range associated with severe or potentially fatal intoxication following an acute overdose. Although her chronic salicylate therapy may be contributing to the serum salic-

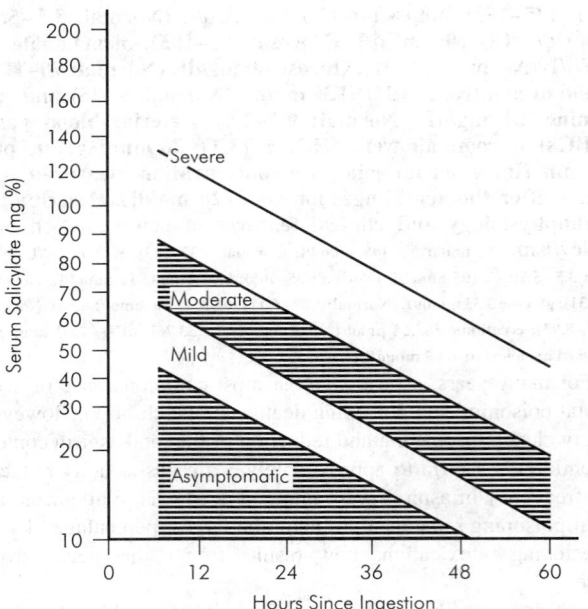

Fig 104.1   Done Nomogram for Interpretation of Severity of Acute Salicylate Poisoning   Reprinted with permission from Pediatrics, 1960;26:800.

ylate concentration, the presence of metabolic acidosis and encephalopathy are consistent with severe intoxication.

Management

7. Outline a management plan for V.K.

Management of acute or chronic salicylate intoxication depends upon the character and magnitude of acid-base and electrolyte disturbances which exist.

Gastric Decontamination and Fluid Therapy. V.K.'s initial management should include emptying the stomach by gastric lavage and/or administration of activated charcoal and a saline cathartic. Since V.K. is lethargic, emesis should be avoided. In V.K., hypokalemia, acidosis, and hypoglycemia must be corrected. This generally is accomplished through the administration of hypotonic saline solutions (¼ to ½ normal saline) combined with dextrose (5%) and potassium supplementation (20 to 40 mEq/L). This solution is administered at a rate of 4 to 8 mL/kg/hour, or at a rate which repletes the patient's deficits and keeps pace with continued losses. In hypotensive patients, initial therapy with normal saline at a rate of 10 to 15 mL/kg/hour is indicated. However, care should be taken to avoid overzealous fluid therapy which may predispose the patient to cerebral or pulmonary edema.[153] Because V.K. is hypoglycemic (60 mg/dL), administration of 25 gm dextrose IV is indicated.

Sodium Bicarbonate. It is also important to correct V.K.'s acidosis because acidosis may promote high cerebrospinal fluid (CSF) salicylate concentrations. This can be accomplished by adding 1 to 2 mEq/kg of sodium bicarbonate to each liter of IV fluids; occasionally, much larger doses will be necessary.[164] Care must be taken not to administer solutions which are excessively hypertonic, and the patient's serum sodium concentration should be monitored closely. Tromethamine should be avoided because it may elevate both intra- and extracellular pH. It could thereby trap ionized salicylate intracellularly and increase the brain salicylate concentration.[154]

Seizures. Other problems which may be encountered, but which are not yet apparent in V.K., are seizures and coagulopathy. Seizure activity in a patient with salicylate toxicity carries a very poor prognosis and usually indicates the presence of marked poisoning.[155] Occasionally, tetany or seizure-like activity can occur with marked alkalosis and will respond to calcium administration. If seizures are prolonged, they may be controlled initially with IV diazepam and subsequently with more long-acting anticonvulsants. Hypoglycemia or hyponatremia must be ruled out as a cause of seizures. The presence of seizures is an indication for hemodialysis (see below).[164]

Coagulopathy generally responds to the administration of phytonadione.[155] Vitamin K should be given if prothrombin time is prolonged, especially if evidence of gastrointestinal bleeding or other hemorrhage is found. The temperature may be elevated to such a degree that active cooling with cooling blankets and tepid water sponging is warranted.

8. Forced Alkaline Diuresis. What measures may be undertaken to enhance salicylate elimination? Which of these may be indicated in V.K.?

Because salicylate is a weak acid with a pKa of about 3, its renal elimination can be substantially increased in an alkaline urine. Thus, it has been previously recommended that salicylate intoxication be treated with forced alkaline diuresis.[155] While this measure shortens the apparent half-life of salicylate, it does not favorably influence the morbidity or mortality of patients with salicylism.[114,115] If bicarbonate is used, the risk of inducing pulmonary edema can be diminished and urinary salicylate excretion increased using alkaline diuresis without forced fluids.[116] One also should be aware that bicarbonate administration in the mildly poisoned patient with a primary respiratory alkalosis may further elevate extracellular pH causing marked degrees of alkalemia.[117,118]

It has been questioned whether it is possible to adequately alkalinize the urine (pH >7) in severely-intoxicated pediatric patients because of the marked acid load excreted.[117,153,155] Because systemic acidosis will increase intracellular penetration of salicylate and enhance its toxic effects, sodium bicarbonate is definitely indicated in these individuals to correct the arterial pH even if the goal of producing an alkaline urine is unachievable.[117,164] Vigorous sodium bicarbonate administration in an attempt to alkalinize the urine of severely intoxicated patients may result in sodium and fluid overload. However, because adequate urinary alkalinization may be possible in the severely-intoxicated adult, like V.K., it may be considered in this patient type.

Peritoneal dialysis, hemodialysis, or charcoal hemoperfusion should be considered in patients with severe salicylate intoxication and seizure activity, plasma salicylate concentrations in the potentially fatal range, or renal failure.[164] Peritoneal dialysis is much less effective than hemodialysis or hemoperfusion,[155] and hemodialysis is preferred to charcoal hemoperfusion because it also can be used to correct fluid and electrolyte imbalances.

Assessments of Iron Ingestion
Gathering History and Communications

9. The grandmother of F.E., a 20-month-old male, calls the poison control center because her grandson is vomiting and appears to have been playing with some red tablets. The boy was left alone in his room for about an hour to take a nap. Why might the consultation with this grandmother be expected to be more difficult than the consultation in Question 1?

Telephone calls to a poison control center from individuals other than the parent usually are more difficult to manage. The caller may not be able to provide all the patient-specific information needed to accurately assess the drug ingestion and supplemental information often is needed from a parent. Furthermore, nonparent callers tend to be more upset over an accidental ingestion because

they perceive that they have failed in their responsibility to protect the child. Establishing a positive rapport and effective communications is, therefore, even more important in these cases of accidental ingestions. In addition to the information generally gathered, the legal relationship of the caller to the substance-exposed child needs to be established if admission to a hospital is necessary. A grandparent, baby-sitter, or older sibling may have more difficulty than a parent in taking decisive action because they cannot take complete legal and financial responsibility for the child. Clinicians need to reassure these individuals that assistance will be provided in explaining the decision to the parent and to the medical care facility.

Triage of Call

10. Despite additional questioning, the grandmother cannot identify the tablets and cannot find any labeling or empty medicine containers that could help in identification of the tablets that presumably have been ingested. Her grandson, F.E., is still vomiting, and some of the vomitus is red. There are 3 children living at home with 2 adults who take medications for various chronic illnesses. According to the grandmother, F.E. is healthy and no one else in the household currently has the "flu" or other GI illness. The child's mother is now at her obstetrician for a postnatal visit after giving birth 3 weeks ago. What recommendations could be provided to this grandmother at this time?

With this history, the clinician should consider whether the information presented by F.E.'s grandmother is consistent with "classical" drug exposures and whether this incident is likely to be associated with a significant adverse outcome. Most 1.5 to 2-year-old children experience limited toxicity with accidental drug ingestions because only a relatively small amount of substance usually is ingested. Nevertheless, some substances (e.g., methanol, ethanol, ethylene glycol, nicotine and tobacco, clonidine, diphenoxylate-atropine, caustic substances, oral hypoglycemics, calcium channel blockers, tricyclic antidepressants, iron) can produce significant toxicity when only small amounts are ingested. As little as one dosage unit of camphor, chloroquine, tricyclic antidepressants, phenothiazines, quinine, methyl salicylate, or theophylline can be fatal in a 10-kg child. These compounds represented 42% of all childhood fatalities secondary to acute drug ingestions between 1983 and 1989 according to TESS data of the American Association of Poison Control Centers.[52]

Iron is currently the drug most commonly associated with childhood acute poisoning fatalities based upon TESS data.[52,53] Although the history of the presumed drug ingestion in F.E. is vague, the description of a red tablet, vomiting red material, and the recent pregnancy of his mother suggests possible ingestion of prenatal iron tablets. This exposure would be categorized as an unknown toxicity, with a realistic potential for severe toxicity if iron tablets were ingested. F.E. should be referred immediately to an emergency room (ER) for evaluation. The grandmother should be instructed to call 9-1-1 for emergency medical services transportation, rather than relying on other means of transportation because of the potential for significant toxicity in this case. The grandmother also should be instructed to give the red tablets to the paramedics to accompany the child to the emergency room for identification. Other medications which are in the house also should be taken to the emergency room and the mother should be contacted at the obstetrician's office.

Substance Identification

11. F.E.'s mother has been contacted and has confirmed that the only red tablets in the house are her prenatal iron supple-

ments. She is in close proximity to the hospital and will await the arrival of her son at the ER. Meanwhile, the poison control center telephoned the ER to prepare them for F.E.'s arrival. F.E. arrived 20 minutes later at the ER along with one red tablet and an empty prescription container that was found by his older brother. F.E. is still vomiting, and is awake and alert with a heart rate of 125 beats/min, respirations of 28 breaths/min, a temperature of 99.1 °F, and pulse oximetry of 99%. How can the maximum potential severity of this ingestion be estimated at this time?

These vital signs in an adult are abnormal and would impact considerably the initial management of the patient; however, the vital signs of F.E., when corrected for age, are normal. The vital signs and pulse oximetry of 99% indicate that F.E.'s airway, breathing, and circulation (ABCs) are normal, therefore, attention should focus on identifying the ingested substance and the maximum potential severity of the ingestion. Although this case was referred to the ER as an unknown intoxication with the potential for being a severe iron intoxication, the ingestion has not been verified. Therefore, assessment of F.E. and of the history of the exposure need to continue rather than assuming that the exposure is likely to be severe.

All solid dosage prescription drugs are required by the U.S. Food and Drug Administration to have identification markings on the dosage form. Reference books (e.g., *Facts and Comparisons*), computerized databases (e.g., *Identidex*), and the proprietary manufacturers can assist in the identification of solid dosage forms. The markings on the red tablet brought to the emergency room with F.E., the empty medication container, and the assistance of the mother should be sufficient to identify the tablet. Since most childhood ingestions usually involve only one substance, the identification of this one tablet can help establish the potential for toxicity in F.E.. After identification of the tablet, the maximum number of tablets ingested should be estimated. The label on the empty medication vial should provide information on the identity and number of tablets dispensed. If the medication container is unlabeled, the date the prescription was obtained, the number of estimated doses taken, and the number currently remaining in the medication vial usually can permit a rough approximation of the maximum number of tablets that were ingested.

F.E.'s vital signs and symptoms should be monitored at frequent intervals to evaluate whether his clinical status is consistent with expectations based upon the suspected ingestion. Nausea, vomiting, diarrhea, and abdominal pain are commonly encountered early in the course of iron intoxication. The caustic effects of iron may explain the presence of blood in the vomitus or stool. Central nervous system effects (e.g., lethargy, seizures) or cardiovascular symptoms (e.g., hypotension, tachycardia) are suggestive of more severe iron toxicity.[54] The absence of symptoms should not be interpreted as an indication that a poisoning has not occurred, especially if the patient is being evaluated a short period of time after the presumed ingestion.

Evaluating Severity of Toxicity

12. F.E. weights 21.5 pounds, appears to be in no apparent distress, and has stopped vomiting. About 30 mL of dark red vomitus was recovered, but no tablets are seen in the vomitus. Testing of the vomitus demonstrates that no blood is present. A maximum of 6 tablets were ingested based upon calculations described above. What degree of toxicity should be expected in F.E. because of his ingestion of 6 iron tablets?

The potential severity of ingestion can be estimated for commonly ingested drugs such as salicylates, iron, and tricyclic antidepressants[55] because of well established dose-toxicity relationships. When these relationships have not been established, animal

LD 50 (lethal dose in 50%) data can be considered. The LD 50 however, cannot predict severe morbidity and the 50% mortality associated with a dose might not be applicable to humans when extrapolated from animals. In this case, the dose-toxicity relationship for iron is known. Acute iron ingestions less than 20 mg/kg usually are nontoxic; 20 to 60 mg/kg doses result in mild to moderate toxicity, and greater than 60 mg/kg doses are severe and potentially fatal ingestions.[54,56,57]

The label on the prescription medication container, and independent verification of the tablet by F.E.'s mother and FDA-mandated imprinting on the tablet, indicate that each tablet that was ingested by F.E. contained 300 mg of ferrous sulfate in an enteric-coated formulation. The dose-toxicity relationship of iron is based upon the amount of elemental iron ingested rather than on the salt form.[56] Different iron salts contain different percentages of elemental iron; therefore, knowledge of the specific iron salt is important in calculating the ingested dose. Ferrous sulfate contains 20% elemental iron, ferrous gluconate 12%, and ferrous fumarate contains 33%. Since F.E. is presumed to have ingested a maximum of six ferrous sulfate 300 mg enteric-coated tablets, he would be exposed to about 360 mg of elemental iron (300 mg × 20% × 6 tablets = 360 mg). F.E., who weighs 21.5 pounds (about 10 kg) is likely to experience mild to moderate toxicity from his ingestion of 360 mg of elemental iron. Although F.E. is not demonstrating evidence of iron toxicity other than vomiting at this time, he did ingest 36 mg/kg of iron in an enteric-coated formulation.

Abdominal X-Rays

13. Since F.E. is expected to experience mild to moderate toxicity from his ingestion of iron, would an abdominal x-ray be useful to verify how many iron tablets actually were ingested?

Radiodense substances (e.g., iron and other heavy metals) in the GI tract can be visualized by an abdominal x-ray (also see Question 32). The ability of an x-ray to demonstrate the presence of a radiodense substance, however, is dependent upon the dosage form, concentration, and the molecular weight of the substance. The intact dosage form can be detected if the tablet has not already disintegrated or dissolved.[58,59]

An abdominal radiograph to verify the number of ingested iron tablets probably would not be of value in evaluating the probable toxicity in F.E. False negative results can occur even when whole tablets have not already started to disintegrate. Although visualization of iron tablets on x-ray can be useful in estimating the amount of unabsorbed iron, nonvisualization on x-ray may be the result either of tablets that already have disintegrated or that the iron already has been absorbed.[60] In this case, an x-ray procedure for F.E. would delay gastrointestinal decontamination unnecessarily. An abdominal x-ray after the completion of gastrointestinal decontamination could be helpful because it could demonstrate a need for further decontamination.

Gastrointestinal Decontamination

Emesis with Ipecac

14. Why would ipecac-induced emesis be the best choice for GI decontamination in F.E.?

The selection of a method for gastrointestinal decontamination (emesis, lavage, charcoal) should consider the availability of medication and equipment; substance ingested; drug dosage form; potential time course of toxicity commonly associated with the suspected drug; time elapsed between ingestion and the initiation of treatment; symptoms; and physical examination findings. Decontamination with activated charcoal would not be preferred over emesis because F.E. presumably has ingested iron tablets which do not adsorb to activated charcoal:[36,44] and gastric lavage would not be expected to be effective (see Question 13). The time from ingestion for F.E. is relatively short (i.e., probably <1 hour) and it is likely that the drug is still in the stomach. Therefore, induction of emesis would be the most reasonable choice for gastric decontamination at this point in time for F.E.

Induction of emesis should not be attempted by physical stimulation of the gag reflex by placing a finger towards the back of the patient's throat. Physical stimulation of emesis is seldom effective and generally does not generate sufficient propulsive force to bring up solid oral dosage forms of medications from the GI tract. Dishwashing detergent (e.g., Ivory) might be somewhat effective,[62] however, most dishwashing detergents contain toxic acids and automatic dishwashing detergent products are too caustic. Mustard powder, baking soda, egg whites, and other home remedies are not effective and also should not be attempted.

Syrup of ipecac is highly effective in inducing emesis and may be purchased without a prescription for use in the home. Induction of emesis with ipecac syrup is most frequently undertaken as a method of gastrointestinal decontamination in childhood poisoning either at home under the guidance of poison control center personnel or at the emergency room of a hospital.[34,36] Central nervous system depression, ingestion of caustic chemicals, ingestion of petroleum distillates, seizure activity, and other contraindications to emesis (see Table 104.3) are not factors in this case.

15. Ipecac Dosing. **How much ipecac syrup should be administered to F.E.?**

The administration of a 15 mL dose of ipecac syrup to children between one and ten years of age and 30 mL to older children and adults will induce emesis in 80% to 90%.[61] The 15 mL dose of ipecac for F.E. should be administered along with about two ounces of a clear liquid such as water. The administration of this fluid volume is useful in estimating the emptying of stomach contents. For example, the recovery of 15 mL of vomitus after the administration of two ounces of water would suggest that either

Table 104.3	Contraindications to Emesis

CNS Depression
Patients who are lethargic or unresponsive, lack a gag reflex, or are otherwise unable to adequately protect their airway are at risk of pulmonary aspiration

Caustic Ingestions
Esophageal and oropharyngeal mucous membranes can be further damaged when re-exposed to caustic solids or liquids upon emesis. Emesis also can cause gastric or esophageal perforation of the weakened visceral wall. Pulmonary aspiration of the caustic substance is a risk as well

Seizure Activity
The postictal patient is at risk of aspirating gastric contents should another seizure develop

Petroleum Distillates
Systemic toxicity from low viscosity agents (e.g., mineral seal oil) is low, but the risk of aspiration is high when vomiting is induced. Emesis also is not indicated when compounds of very high viscosity (e.g., motor oil, mineral oil) have been ingested because these agents also have low systemic toxicity.[119] In contrast, emesis may be induced when the following are ingested: halogenated hydrocarbons (e.g., carbon tetrachloride); large volumes (>1 mL/kg) of compounds with potent CNS activity (e.g., gasoline, paint thinner); or petroleum distillates serving as a base for a toxic chemical or pesticide.[119] For these agents, emesis carries a lower risk of aspiration than gastric lavage[120]

Foreign Body Ingestion
Can cause further damage to esophageal tissue or mucous membranes

the gastric emptying is incomplete or that gastric contents have already emptied into the small intestine. Although the volume of water does not impact the onset or efficacy of emesis in removing the ingested drug,[63] adults traditionally have been given about a cup of clear liquid to accompany their dose of ipecac in the hope that gastric distension might enhance the effectiveness of emesis.

Patients usually begin to vomit about 20 minutes after the administration of syrup of ipecac and will vomit about three or four times. If the patient has not vomited within 30 to 45 minutes after the ipecac dose, a second dose should be administered. Almost all patients will vomit after a second dose. The ingestion of antiemetics and drugs with antiemetic properties (e.g., phenothiazines) does not appear to inhibit the emetic effects of ipecac.[36,61]

Gastric Lavage

16. Why is gastric lavage less desirable than emesis for F.E.?

Gastric lavage would not be expected to be as effective as ipecac-induced emesis in F.E. because the removal of particles from the stomach is limited by the internal diameter of the gastric lavage tube. The commonly used adult gastric lavage tube (36 French size) has an internal diameter too small to allow recovery of large tablet or capsule fragments, and an even smaller diameter lavage tube is used for children. This smaller diameter tube can be easily occluded by foodstuffs and the recovery of tablet fragments would be even further limited.[36]

17. When is gastric lavage indicated and how should this process be implemented?

Gastric lavage generally is an alternative to ipecac-induced emesis in patients who, because of a decreased level of consciousness, may not be able to protect their airway from aspiration when vomiting. These patients generally require endotracheal intubation with a cuffed endotracheal tube before insertion of the lavage tube because passage of the lavage tube can stimulate emesis and place the patient at risk of aspiration.[36] After the gastric tube is in place, the gastric contents are initially aspirated and fluid is instilled (about 250 to 300 mL of fluid in adults and a correspondingly smaller amount in children) into the stomach and the fluid aspirated. This process is repeated several times until the gastric aspirate is clear. A total of several liters of fluid usually need to be instilled and aspirated. When gastric lavage is utilized for iron ingestions, solutions of sodium bicarbonate, phosphate, or deferoxamine (Desferal) have been used in an attempt to convert the iron to an insoluble form which would be less likely to be absorbed. Although this concept is appealing because of the theoretical chemical basis for this practice, gastric lavage with these solutions has not been effective clinically and probably is associated with some systemic toxicity. Therefore, lavage with these "enhanced" solutions is not recommended.[56]

The specific fluid used for lavage is unimportant in most situations and tap water is suitable for most adult patients. If more than 5 to 6 L are needed, dilutional hyponatremia can be encountered and should be avoided by alternating the instillation of the liter of tap water with one of normal saline. Following gastric lavage, activated charcoal and a cathartic should be placed down the orogastric tube and left in the stomach when dealing with substances that can be adsorbed by charcoal.

Monitoring Effectiveness of Treatment

18. How should the effectiveness of GI decontamination with ipecac for F.E. be assessed in the ER?

The simplest method of assessing gastrointestinal decontamination is to visually inspect the vomitus. Whole tablets of iron can sometimes be seen in the vomitus if the ipecac has been administered soon after an ingestion. Tablet fragments generally appear as soft, crumbly white particles that are easily distinguishable from partially digested food. It is not clear, however, whether vomited tablet fragments represent active drug or the inactive filler ingredients in the tablet dosage form.[45] Gastrointestinal decontamination can be variably effective based upon when the process can be initiated relative to the time of ingestion, dose, and other variables; therefore, the effectiveness of gastrointestinal decontamination ranges from 0% to 70%.[36]

In F.E.'s case, increasing serum iron concentrations, deteriorating clinical status, or evidence of radiodense tablets in the GI tract on abdominal x-ray would warrant more aggressive treatment.

Serum Iron Concentrations

19. F.E. was given 15 mL of ipecac syrup and 60 mL of water. No tablets were recovered in the 200 mL of vomitus and a subsequent abdominal x-ray did not demonstrate areas of radiodensity. F.E. has no evidence of GI, CNS, or cardiovascular symptoms that can occur with toxic iron ingestions. A serum iron concentration, obtained about 3 hours after the ingestion was 290 μg/dL (Normal: 60–160). What conclusions, as to severity or likely clinical outcome, can be derived from this serum concentration? [SI unit: 52.94 μmol/L (Normal: 10.75–28.66)]

The higher than normal serum concentration of iron confirms the suspicion that F.E. has ingested iron tablets in spite of both his lack of symptoms and the absence of tablet evidence in the vomitus or abdominal x-ray. The serum iron concentration also can provide an indication as to whether immediate more aggressive therapy is needed at this time. This one serum iron concentration, however, represents just one point in time and does not provide information as to whether the serum concentration will increase or decrease over the ensuing hours. Furthermore, in cases of poisonings and overdoses, absorption generally is slower and less predictable.[39,64–66] This decrease in absorption rate may be secondary to decreased tablet disintegration or dissolution when large number of tablets are ingested. The time course of absorption is probably the most difficult pharmacokinetic parameter to evaluate with toxic ingestions. This prolongation of absorption time is even further complicated when sustained-release or enteric-coated dosage forms have been ingested because symptoms from an overdose may not become apparent until such time as was intended by the release characteristics of the drug formulation.[64,66–68] For example, serum phenytoin concentrations can continue to rise for 48 to 72 hours after an overdose with extended-release phenytoin despite continued gastrointestinal decontamination.[65,69,70]

F.E.'s serum iron concentration of 290 μg/dL does not appear to be life-threatening at this point in time. Serum iron concentrations greater than 300 to 350 μg/dL usually are associated with toxicity and serum concentrations greater than 500 mg/dL usually are predictive of significant toxicity.[54,56,57] These serum concentration relationships are intended to reflect the peak serum iron concentration before distribution. Recommendations for when blood samples should be drawn for peak serum iron concentrations are inconsistent and, therefore, range from two to six hours after ingestion.[71] Since F.E.'s serum iron concentration was measured approximately three hours after ingestion, another serum iron measurement two to four hours after the first sample would be appropriate because F.E. ingested an enteric-coated iron formulation.

Total Iron Binding Capacity (TIBC)

20. Why would a laboratory assessment of the total iron-binding capacity be useful in evaluating the potential for iron toxicity in F.E.?

The total iron binding capacity traditionally has been utilized to improve interpretation of serum iron concentrations (see Chapter 88: Anemias). A TIBC less than the serum iron concentration could suggest that excess free iron from an iron ingestion would not be bound and be available to induce greater toxicity. In F.E. with a serum iron concentration of 290 μg/dL, a TIBC might be helpful in determining whether chelation therapy with deferoxamine (Desferal) should be initiated. Unfortunately, the specificity and sensitivity of laboratory measurements of TIBC are not good and TIBC determinations have not been of value in predicting the potential for iron toxicity.[72] As a result, a TIBC test for F.E. should not be ordered. Clinical signs and symptoms along with serum iron concentrations should be the determining factors for estimating the severity of iron intoxication.

Blood Glucose and White Blood Cell (WBC) Count

21. A second serum iron concentration has been ordered for 2 hours later (i.e., 5 hours postingestion); a TIBC was not ordered. What other laboratory tests could be helpful in assessing the potential toxicity of iron ingestion in F.E.?

Blood glucose concentrations and white blood cell counts usually are increased when serum iron concentrations are greater than 300 μg/dL. A white blood cell count greater than 15,000/mm³ and a blood glucose concentration greater than 150 mg/dL within six hours of an ingestion generally suggest a greater likelihood of severe iron intoxication.[60] Although these tests are not as specific as an increased iron serum concentration, they provide supplemental confirmation of iron intoxication, especially while awaiting the results of the serum iron concentration if delayed from the clinical laboratory. Since serum iron concentrations are much more specific, F.E. would benefit more from a repeat serum iron concentration.

Deferoxamine Testing

22. What is the role of a provocative deferoxamine test to determine the need for chelation therapy of iron toxicity?

A test dose of deferoxamine 50 mg/kg (up to 1 gm) has been suggested as a method of assessing the potential for iron toxicity when serum iron measurements are not readily available.[57] Deferoxamine is a chelating agent which will bind iron, resulting in the formation of ferrioxamine. Ferrioxamine is eliminated in the urine and will impart a "vin rose" color (i.e., orange-reddish brown) to the urine. Urine pH and urine concentration of ferrioxamine will affect this urine color change.

Asymptomatic Period and Stages of Toxicity

23. F.E. still has no evidence of CNS, cardiovascular, or GI symptoms (other than vomiting before initiation of ipecac) that would be expected from a toxic iron ingestion. His serum iron concentration that was obtained 3 hours after the presumed ingestion was 290 μg/dL and the results from his second serum iron concentration are not yet available. About 2 hours have elapsed since an intramuscular (IM) test dose of deferoxamine was administered to F.E. and his urine has not yet changed color. About 6 hours have elapsed since the time of his iron ingestion. Does this clinical presentation indicate that F.E. will be able to avoid severe toxicity from his iron ingestion? [SI unit: 51.94 μmol/L]

The time between the ingestion of an overdose of drugs and the development of severe toxicity often is delayed. It is unclear in some cases why there is an asymptomatic period, but it may be secondary to delayed absorption of the ingested drug, the time required for the drug to distribute to the sites of action, or the time needed for the formation of a metabolite which produces the severe toxicity. If the ingestion is not large enough to produce clinically severe toxicity, clinical symptoms also would not be expected to occur. As a result, it important not to interpret an early asymptomatic period as being indicative that severe toxicity will be avoided. F.E.'s absence of significant symptoms at this point in time should not be interpreted as if severe toxic symptoms will not occur. For some common exposures, distinct stages of toxicity can be recognized.

Stage I. The clinical manifestations of iron intoxication can be divided into four stages.[54,56,57] Stage I symptoms usually occur within six hours of ingestion. During this time, gastrointestinal effects of nausea, vomiting, diarrhea, and abdominal pain are most commonly encountered. These GI symptoms probably are secondary to the erosive effects of iron on the GI mucosa. The caustic effects of free iron also may result in bleeding, and blood in vomitus and stool. In more severe intoxications, CNS and cardiovascular toxicity may be present during Stage I.

Stage II of iron toxicity is described as a period of decreasing symptoms with apparent improvement in the clinical condition. This stage may last for up to 12 to 24 hours after the ingestion and can be misinterpreted as an indication that toxicity is resolving. The clinical course of iron intoxication, therefore, may not be an accurate reflection of the severity of the toxicity. Although this stage can be the genuine beginning of complete recovery, Stage II may progress to the more ominous Stage III. It is unknown why this stage of apparent improvement occurs with iron toxicity.

Stage III is the time period of the most severe toxicity and generally is encountered 12 to 48 hours after ingestion of iron. Central nervous system toxicity (e.g., lethargy, coma, seizures), cardiovascular toxicity (e.g., hypotension, pulmonary edema), metabolic acidosis, hypoglycemia, hepatic necrosis, renal damage, and coagulopathy can become manifested during this time.

Stage IV is apparent four to six weeks after acute iron ingestion and consists of late-appearing GI tract sequelae that are secondary to the initial local toxicity. In this stage, tissue damage can result in gastric scarring and strictures at the pylorus, with permanent abnormalities of function.

Deferoxamine

Chelating

24. The clinical laboratory has reported that the second serum iron concentration that was obtained 5 hours after ingestion from F.E. has increased from 290 µg/dL to 400 µg/dL. He still manifests no clinical symptoms. Should deferoxamine be administered? [SI units: 51.94 and 71.64 µmol/L, respectively]

Deferoxamine (Desferal) chelates iron by binding ferric ions in plasma to form the iron complex, ferrioxamine. Deferoxamine appears to have a greater affinity for iron than other chelating agents and probably also has additional mechanisms which decrease iron toxicity at the cellular level.[57,73] This may be important in explaining why deferoxamine is effective even though a relatively small amount of iron is bound ($\approx$85 mg of iron to 1 gm of deferoxamine). The iron-deferoxamine complex primarily is excreted renally as ferrioxamine.

Deferoxamine should be initiated when serum iron concentrations are greater than 400 µg/dL, when more than 180 to 300 mg of iron has been ingested, or when severe symptoms of iron toxicity (e.g., coma, shock, seizures) are present. Although F.E. is not experiencing severe symptoms, he presumably ingested up to 360 mg of elemental iron (see Question 12) and his serum iron concentration is perhaps still increasing based upon an increase of 110 µg/dL over the past two hours (i.e., increased from 290 µg/dL 3 hours postingestion to 400 µg/dL 5 hours postingestion). F.E., therefore, should be treated with deferoxamine.

Deferoxamine Dose

25. What dose of deferoxamine should be prescribed for F.E. and how should it be administered?

The usual intramuscular or intravenous (IV) dose of deferoxamine for the treatment of acute iron intoxication in adults is 1 gm followed by 500 mg at four-hour intervals for two doses. Depending upon the patient's clinical response, subsequent doses of 500 mg can be administered every 4 to 12 hours, but no more than 6 gm of deferoxamine should be given to adults or children in a 24-hour period. Children can be given an initial dose of 20 mg/kg IM or by slow IV infusion, followed by 10 mg/kg every 4 to 12 hours as needed.[150] Although deferoxamine can by given IM or IV, the manufacturer's product information warns in large capital letters that the IV route should be used only for patients in a state of cardiovascular collapse and then only by slow infusion not exceeding 15 mg/kg/hour. Following rapid IV injection, flushing, generalized erythema, urticaria, hypotension, shock, and seizures can occur and are thought to be manifestations of a histamine-liberating property of the drug. Deferoxamine, however, may be more effective when administered intravenously;[56,73] and a slow IV infusion, theoretically, should be similar to the gradual absorption of a drug from an IM injection. The intravenous route of administration is preferred clinically because the dose administered can be controlled more precisely. Adverse effects to deferoxamine are most likely related to rapid intravenous administration.[56] Deferoxamine should be administered to F.E. by slow IV infusion at a low dose (about 4 mg/kg/hour) and his clinical status should be monitored closely.

Monitoring and Discontinuation

26. F.E. is admitted to the pediatric ICU 1 hour after the initiation of a deferoxamine infusion at 4 mg/kg/hr. How should deferoxamine therapy be monitored, and when should it be discontinued?

The rate of deferoxamine infusion should be increased if symptoms of severe iron toxicity develop; and the dose should be decreased gradually if adverse effects develop. The infusion of deferoxamine should be continued until the serum iron concentration is within the normal range, and symptoms of iron toxicity are no longer present. The duration of deferoxamine infusion generally is about 6 to 12 hours; longer periods may be needed depending upon the dose of iron ingested. Chelation therapy that continues much longer than necessary should be avoided because it can result in the ironic need for supplemental iron therapy upon discharge from the hospital.

Deferoxamine can interfere with some laboratory methodologies that measure the serum iron concentration and cause falsely low serum iron concentrations.[56] When the deferoxamine is initiated, the clinical laboratory should be contacted to clarify whether deferoxamine would interfere with their serum iron tests. Disappearance of the "vin rose" color of urine also has been suggested as a method of determining adequacy of deferoxamine therapy.

Assessments of Central Nervous System (CNS) Depressant versus Antidepressant Ingestion
Validation of Ingestion

27. T.C., a 30-year-old very lethargic female, was found by her 12-year old daughter lying on the couch with a suicide note beside her. When the paramedics arrived in response to a call from her daughter, she stated that she took 25 of her pills. Her heart rate was 125 beats/min, BP was 110/70 mm Hg, and respirations were 12 shallow breaths/min. T.C. had vomitus in her mouth. The paramedics immediately started an IV with lactated Ringer's solution at 100 mL/hr after completing their

assessment of her airway, breathing, and circulation. Why does this drug overdose information from this suicidal patient need to be validated?

Assessing the accuracy of historical information in adult drug exposures is difficult and many health care professionals question the validity of verbal information, especially from patients who have stated suicidal intent.[2,22] The inaccurate history is sometimes due to an altered mental status that may prevent accurate recollection of what occurred, a conscious effort by the patient to deceive, or the patient impulsively may have ingested a large number of unidentified tablets. The supposition that the drug overdose history from a patient is unreliable primarily has been based upon studies that demonstrate poor correlation between stated drug ingestions with results of urine drug testing.[22,74,75] Urine drug testing, however, generally detects all recent drug and substance use, rather than just the overdosed drug. Although the history of a drug overdose from a patient may be inaccurate, this information should be used until contradicted by objective clinical findings. Information obtained from the patient should be validated with information from other sources. Assessment of a drug overdose and the potential severity in suicidal patients should consider all the drugs that may have been available to the patient, presenting symptoms, laboratory tests, and the history obtained from family members, police, paramedics, and other individuals who know the patient.

Interventions by Protocol

28. What pharmacological interventions should be authorized for the paramedics to administer to T.C. in addition to the lactated Ringer's solution?

Glucose and Thiamine

In addition to managing the ABCs of airway, breathing, circulation, and oxygenation, emergency medical service personnel often have standing protocols to treat patients with nontraumatic loss of consciousness of unknown cause with glucose, thiamine, and naloxone. T.C. should be given 50 mL of 50% dextrose in water to treat possible hypoglycemia if a blood glucose cannot be measured immediately by the paramedics. The risks of hyperglycemia from this dose of glucose are negligible relative to the significant benefits if the patient is hypoglycemic. If the dextrose bolus is to be administered, thiamine should be given because glucose can precipitate the Wernicke-Korsakoff complex in thiamine-deficient patients (see Chapters 25: Alcoholic Cirrhosis and 82: Alcohol Abuse). Wernicke's encephalopathy is a reversible neurological disturbance consisting of generalized confusion, ataxia, and ophthalmoplegia. Korsakoff's psychosis is believed to be irreversible and associated with a more prolonged deficiency of thiamine. Whether the thiamine must be administered before glucose administration, or whether it is still effective if given within a short period of time after glucose administration is unclear. In any case, thiamine should be given if glucose is to be administered.[77] The patient also should be evaluated for evidence of head trauma from a fall during this period of lethargy, and for blood loss and hypoxia.[2]

Naloxone

The pure opiate antagonists, naloxone (Narcan) and nalmefene are indicated for the treatment of respiratory depression induced by natural and synthetic opiates (e.g., codeine, morphine, meperidine).[80,170] Many emergency medical services protocols authorize paramedics to routinely administer naloxone to all patients with decreased mental status, however, naloxone is not necessary unless the use of opiates is suspected.[78] Although naloxone reportedly has reversed alcohol-induced coma and acute respiratory depression in intoxicated patients who have no evidence of opiate use, it seldom is effective in these patients.[79,80] The response to naloxone

in these patients might be secondary to either the presence of endogenous or exogenous opiates which have not been detected by the urine toxicology screens (e.g., oxycodone, fentanyl), or to the usual fluctuations in mental status that commonly are encountered with many drug overdoses.

Drug-induced CNS depression usually waxes and wanes, and reports of naloxone success in patients who have not used opiates could have been the result of responses to needle sticks, movement, or other stimuli rather than to naloxone. Although some patients might respond to naloxone, lack of consistent effectiveness, lack of clinical variables which could be useful in predicting when a patient should respond to naloxone, and lack of well-controlled clinical studies minimize the clinical usefulness of naloxone for nonopioid intoxications.[80] Furthermore, violent and aggressive patient behavior can be precipitated from sudden increased consciousness induced by naloxone which can complicate emergency care in an emergency transport vehicle and put caregivers and patients at risk for trauma.[79] Therefore, the empiric use of naloxone routinely for all patients lacking evidence of opiate use before the arrival of a patient at the emergency room of a medical facility is not appropriate. Since T.C. has no evidence of opiate use and is not comatose, naloxone should not be administered to T.C. in the emergency transport vehicle.

Initial Treatment

29. The paramedics arrive at the ER with T.C. 30 minutes after they were called by her daughter. T.C.'s heart rate in the ER is 115 to 130 beats/min, BP is 100/65 mm Hg, and respirations have decreased from 12 shallow breaths/min spontaneously to 7 breaths/min with assisted ventilation via a bag-valve mask. T.C.'s mental status has decreased and her current Glasgow coma score is 7. The paramedics were unable to find any prescriptions or other medications in the house. Her daughter thought that her mother was taking medications for her depression, but she could not be more specific. The police will notify T.C.'s husband and try to obtain additional information about the possible identity of the ingested substance. What initial treatment should be provided T.C. in the ER?

T.C. should be intubated and mechanically ventilated with 100% oxygen because of her shallow, slow respirations and the likelihood that vomitus has been aspirated into her lungs. The blood pressure taken by the paramedics was 110/70 mm Hg and now is 100/65 mm Hg in the ER. Since T.C.'s usual blood pressure is unknown at this time, the contribution of her hypotension to her mental status cannot be established. In this setting, the 100 mL/hour infusion of lactated Ringer's that was initiated by the paramedics should be increased to provide a 500 to 750 mL bolus to determine whether increasing T.C.'s intravascular fluid volume will increase her blood pressure and improve her mental status.

Antidotes: Flumazenil

30. T.C.'s husband reports that T.C. currently is under the care of a psychiatrist because of depression and 2 previous suicide attempts. He does not know the identity of her medications and attempts are underway to contact T.C.'s psychiatrist. What antidotes can be administered in the ER for diagnostic purposes and should flumazenil (Romazicon) be administered to T.C. because of her decreasing mental status?

Antidotes such as naloxone, flumazenil, deferoxamine, and antidigoxin FAB fragments can be administered in a hospitalized setting in the hope that a clinical response to these agents would be diagnostic. However, the costs, time required for administration, and increased risks from these antidotes precludes their use for diagnostic purposes without some plausible suspicion for a specific drug ingestion. Although naloxone and flumazenil can reverse

CNS depression caused by opiates and benzodiazepines respectively, their use is not appropriate without historical, clinical, or toxicological laboratory findings suggestive that these drugs may be the cause of T.C.'s intoxication.

Flumazenil, a specific benzodiazepine antagonist, has high affinity for benzodiazepine receptors. It can displace benzodiazepines from the receptor and does not have any intrinsic pharmacological effects.[81] The administration of flumazenil rapidly reverses benzodiazepine-induced central nervous system depression and is effective in most cases when more than one CNS depressant has been ingested.[81,82] Seizures after flumazenil administration can occur when a patient has ingested a benzodiazepine along with other drugs (e.g., antidepressants) which have the potential to induce seizures.[83] Patients, who intentionally overdose, frequently ingest more than one drug and antidepressant drugs commonly are involved. T.C.'s history of past suicide attempts and treatment by a psychiatrist increases the likelihood that antidepressants might have been ingested. Therefore, T.C. should not receive flumazenil or other antidotes for diagnostic purposes. An antidote may be appropriate as part of therapy after the diagnosis has been established.

Organ-System Evaluations

31. How can the initial physical assessment of T.C. by an organ-systems approach be helpful in identifying the ingested drugs?

The patient's airway, breathing, circulation, central nervous system, and cardiopulmonary function should be assessed with special attention to clinical manifestations that can be caused by toxicity from a specific class of drugs.[24] The epidemiology of drug toxicity in the local community and any historical patient-specific medical information should be considered in this evaluation. In T.C., with the information that is currently available, antidepressants, antipsychotics, lithium, or benzodiazepines could have been available to her for ingestion. These drugs should be strongly suspected of being ingested based upon T.C.'s history of a probable psychiatric disorder rather than on any presenting clinical findings. An organ-system evaluation of T.C. will help determine whether these (or other) drugs might have been ingested. Since adult drug ingestions usually involve more than one drug, clinical findings may be the result of more than one drug. Therefore, nonprescription medications such as aspirin, acetaminophen, decongestants, antihistamines, and vitamins which are commonly available in most households also should be considered in all drug intoxications.

Central Nervous System (CNS) Function

Changes in central nervous system function are probably the single most common finding associated with drug intoxication. CNS depression or stimulation, seizures, changes in sensorium, or any combination of these can be manifested in intoxicated patients. These CNS changes can be the sole direct result of an ingested drug or may be merely an additive effect to other underlying CNS processes. Many drug overdoses can produce different clinical manifestations at different times during the intoxication and different doses can produce different effects as well.

Drugs with anticholinergic properties can produce disorientation, confusion, delirium, and visual hallucinations early during the course of the intoxication: coma can become apparent as the toxicity develops. Generally, overdoses with anticholinergic drugs do not produce true hallucinations, but rather pseudohallucinations. When a patient with an intact sensorium presents with psychosis, paranoia, or visual hallucinations, CNS stimulants such as cocaine or amphetamines should be considered.[84] Drug intoxication-induced alterations in CNS function initially are difficult to distin-

guish from those caused by underlying psychiatric disorders, trauma, hypoxia, or metabolic disorders such as hepatic encephalopathy or hypoglycemia. With the passage of time, however, decreased CNS function secondary to drug toxicity is more likely to wax and wane in severity in contrast to the more constant CNS depression that occurs with significant trauma or metabolic disorders. Drug toxicity also rarely produces focal neurological findings with the exception of anisocoria (inequality of pupil diameter) which has been described with lysergic acid diethylamide (LSD).[84] Changes in pupil size, reflexes, and Glasgow coma score frequently will provide insights into the pharmacological class of drug involved in the intoxication.

CNS depression, seizures, disorientation, and other CNS changes that commonly are associated with drugs likely to be prescribed by psychiatrists should be evaluated carefully in T.C. For example, T.C.'s pupil size would be expected to be dilated if she had ingested a tricyclic antidepressant or a phenothiazine because of the anticholinergic effects of these drugs. Tricyclic antidepressant intoxications also can increase muscle tone and myoclonic spasms. These myoclonic spasms often are difficult to differentiate from seizure activity caused by tricyclic antidepressant overdoses, although these spasms often are asymmetrical and generally longer in duration.[55]

Cardiovascular Function

Assessments of heart rate, rhythm, conduction, and other parameters of cardiac function also can provide clues useful in identifying likely pharmacological classes of drugs that might have been ingested. For example, overdoses of sympathomimetic drugs usually increase heart rate, and overdoses of digitalis or beta blockers may slow heart rate. Changes in heart rate and conduction delays are encountered more commonly in drug overdoses than specific arrhythmias. Although drugs can increase or decrease heart rate directly, indirect cardiac effects (e.g., reflex tachycardia in response to hypotension) also need to be considered. Abnormal heart rates produced by drug overdoses usually are not treated unless hypotension or severe dysrhythmias are precipitated. The treatment of some drug intoxications might involve the management of central nervous system toxicities that coincidentally also might result in improvement in cardiac symptoms (e.g., cocaine).

Pulmonary Function

An evaluation of rate and depth of respiration and the effectiveness of gas exchange of an intoxicated patient also can provide clues for identifying drugs that might have been ingested. For example, a decrease in respiratory rate commonly is associated with ingestion of CNS depressants, and increased respiratory rate and depth generally is associated with CNS stimulant toxicity. An increase in respiratory rate also can be secondary to respiratory compensation for a drug-induced metabolic acidosis. Aspiration of gastric contents after emesis is a common event of drug ingestions, and pneumonitis and pneumonia are the most common pulmonary abnormalities associated with significant intoxications.[87,88] Noncardiogenic acute pulmonary edema commonly has been associated with drug overdoses of salicylates (especially with chronic intoxications), ethchlorvynol (Placidyl), tricyclic antidepressants, and the inhalation of drugs of abuse (e.g., cocaine).[88-91]

Temperature

Measuring body temperature is an important and sometimes overlooked aspect of the assessment of potential intoxications. Decreased mental status often is associated with a loss of thermoregulation which results in body temperature that falls toward the ambient temperature. Increased body temperature (hyperthermia) caused by overdoses of CNS stimulants (e.g., cocaine), salicylates, hallucinogens (e.g., phencyclidine), or anticholinergic drugs can have serious consequences.[10,24,84] The hyperthermia caused by drug overdoses commonly is encountered with conditions of high humidity and high ambient temperature, physical exertion, increased muscle tone, or seizures.

Gastrointestinal Function

The function of the gastrointestinal tract also should be assessed because identification of the presence of decreased motility suggests that drug absorption from the GI tract may be slowed. In this setting, GI decontamination may be beneficial following an oral ingestion even when a long period of time has elapsed since the ingestion. The ingestion of some drugs can irritate the GI tract and blood can be found in either emesis or stool. Nausea and vomiting are common events after the ingestion of potentially toxic amounts of many substances.

Skin and Extremities

Examination of the skin and extremities can provide evidence of intravenous or subcutaneous drug injections. Fluid-filled bullae at gravity-dependent sites which have been in contact with hard surfaces for a long time can sometimes be evident in comatose patients who have not moved. These bullae (''barbiturate burns'') at one time mistakenly were thought to be a direct pharmacological effect of barbiturates.[92] Muscle tone also needs to be assessed because increased tone or myoclonic spasms can be caused by some drug overdoses (e.g., tricyclic antidepressants) and can produce rhabdomyolysis or hyperthermia.

In summary, an organ-system assessment of T.C. can provide useful insights into the identity of drugs that might have been ingested, evaluate the viability of organ function that might have been adversely affected, and perhaps facilitate treatment (e.g., gastric decontamination).

Laboratory Tests

32. What laboratory tests should be ordered for T.C.?

The laboratory assessment of an intoxicated patient should be guided by the history of the events surrounding the ingestion, clinical presentation and past medical history of the patient. The status of oxygenation, acid-base balance, and blood glucose concentration must be determined, especially in patients with altered mental status such as T.C. Oxygenation can be assessed initially by pulse oximetry, and acid-base status by arterial blood gases and serum electrolyte concentrations. T.C. was administered oxygen and a bolus of intravenous fluid upon her arrival at the emergency room and a glucose load was administered by the paramedics before her arrival at the emergency room (see Questions 28 and 29). Presumably, oximetry, ABGs, serum electrolytes, and glucose concentrations already were evaluated, however, these tests should be ordered if not already available.

A past medical history of organ dysfunction or disorders (e.g., diabetes, hypertension) that can damage organs of elimination (e.g., kidney, liver) also would guide the need for laboratory tests. In this case, no past medical history was obtained from T.C. Therefore, a serum creatinine concentration and liver function tests [e.g., aspartate aminotransferase (AST), alanine aminotransferase (ALT)] also should be ordered for T.C. Other more specific tests reflective of her past medical history can be ordered subsequent to dialogue with her psychiatrist who already has been called. Until her medical records become available, a complete blood count (CBC), hemoglobin, SMA-chemistry panel, and other baseline laboratory tests (e.g., ECG) should be obtained as time and urgency permit. Measurement or calculation of an osmol or anion gap or of lactic acid serum concentration might be ordered if a substance

of high osmolality is suspected of being ingested (e.g., methanol, ethanol, propylene glycol); however, ingestion of these substances is not suspected in this case and these tests should not be ordered routinely.[93]

A baseline electrocardiogram should be obtained from any patient with suspected exposure to a cardiotoxic drug or with an alteration in cardiovascular or hemodynamic status. In these patients, continuous cardiac monitoring also is appropriate. Since T.C. is likely to have ingested a psychotropic agent, possibly a tricyclic antidepressant, a 12-lead ECG and continuous cardiac monitoring should be ordered because of the significant cardiotoxicity associated with overdoses of tricyclic antidepressants.

A chest x-ray would be useful when the potential exists for either direct pulmonary toxicity or aspiration in a patient with a toxic overdose of a substance. Since T.C. was noted by paramedics to have vomitus in her mouth, a chest x-ray would be helpful in this case to evaluate the possibility of aspiration. An abdominal x-ray would not be needed unless radiopaque substances are suspected to have been ingested. An endoscopy to evaluate possible caustic damage to the esophageal or gastric mucosa; an electroencephalogram to evaluate severe CNS toxicity; or a computerized tomography (CT) scan of the head to evaluate head trauma are not needed in this case at this point in time.

Qualitative Screening

33. Why should (or should not) urine, blood, and gastric fluid be screened in T.C. to assist in the identification of the ingested substance?

Toxicology laboratory testing can be used either to identify the substances involved in a toxic exposure, while excluding other substances, or to measure the concentration of substances in serum or other biological fluids.[28,94,95] The identification and quantification of compounds should be considered as two distinct types of toxicologic testing. Compared to other laboratory tests, *qualitative* screening is unique because it is intended to identify unknown substances which are not endogenous to the body. The test must be able to identify which substance, or class of substances, is involved in the toxic exposure. *Quantitative* testing is similar to therapeutic drug monitoring in that the presence of the substance usually is known, and the question being answered is how much is present.

Unknown substances can be identified by screening various biological fluids suspected of having high concentrations of a parent drug and its metabolites. As a result, urine is screened much more commonly than blood or gastric fluids. Urine testing generally utilizes a series of immunoassays which identify classes of compounds that have similar chemical structures and have common haptagenic sites on their molecular structure. *Immunoassays* have the advantage, compared to other analytic methods, of being able to detect very low concentrations of metabolites, and lend themselves well to automated methods of analysis. Another assay methodology to qualitatively detect the presence of drugs and toxins utilizes *thin layer chromatography* which identifies substances based upon their relative affinities for a polar solid stationary phase and a mobile liquid phase that is nonpolar. Depending upon these affinities, different compounds adsorb to the polar solid stationary phase differently and can be identified as the nonpolar solvent migrates up the stationary phase. When commercially available thin layer chromatography is combined with panels of immunoassays, over 100 classes of compounds and specific substances can be detected. A drug abuse screening panel that identifies metabolites of drugs of abuse (e.g., cocaine, marijuana, opiates, barbiturates), an alcohol screening panel, a heavy metals screening panel, and a comprehensive drug screening panel that identifies drugs commonly used for therapeutic purposes are commercially available.

Interpretation of the results of urine screening panels for drugs and other substances should include an understanding that the presence of a substance in urine is not necessarily related to concurrent toxicity. A positive result on a urine screening panel merely indicates that the patient has ingested or been exposed to the substance at some point in time before the collection of the urine sample. If a drug or its metabolites are eliminated slowly into the urine over a prolonged period of time, and if the testing methodology detects small concentrations of the substance, urine drug screening may identify the presence of a substance many days, weeks, or months after use or exposure to the substance.[96] The interpretation of both positive and negative results from a qualitative screening test should always include a consideration of assay methods and the limitations of these assay methods; an understanding of the elimination pharmacokinetic parameters of substances being assayed; and an appreciation of the clinical presentation of the patient.

Sensitivity, Specificity, and Practicality

An understanding of the sensitivity, specificity, and practicality of analytical tests is crucial to the interpretation of results from these tests. The *sensitivity* of a test reflects the minimum concentration required for detection of a substance. The *specificity* of a test reflects the ability of an assay method to identify an unknown compound and to distinguish it from other substances. When compounds with somewhat similar chemical structures cross-react with an assay, the assay is deemed to be of poor specificity. Cross-reactivity of compounds with an assay is acceptable in some instances. For example, the identity of a specific benzodiazepine is less important than knowing that a compound within the benzodiazepine pharmacological class is present. The *practicality* of an assay is determined by the cost, availability, and "turn-around time" for test results to be reported back to the clinician. Practicality is probably the most important determinant of whether toxicology testing is useful for assessment and management of drug intoxications.

The value of toxicology testing can be enhanced considerably when the analytical toxicologist and the clinician have discussed the potential drugs which are suspected to have been involved in the toxic exposure. This communication aids in the selection of the most appropriate qualitative tests that should be utilized for the individual patient.[94]

Qualitative toxicology screening is most useful when these tests can confirm the absence of suspected toxic substances. These tests also can be useful in those rare circumstances when they successfully identify the presence of toxic substances and alter the treatment plan of a patient.[97] As a result, the benefits of qualitative toxicology screening are controversial and toxicology screening should not be routinely ordered to assess all overdosed and poisoned patients. Toxicology screening is appropriate when the history of a suspected toxic exposure is unavailable, inaccurate, or inconsistent with clinical findings. A comprehensive qualitative urine drug screen should be ordered for T.C. because she is unable to provide information on the identity of the ingested toxic substance.

Quantitative Testing

34. Why should a quantitative toxicology laboratory test be ordered (or not ordered) for T.C. as well?

The qualitative screening of urine for drugs and other potentially toxic substances does not determine the amount of substance involve in an exposure; it only determines the presence of the substance or its metabolite. This limits the usefulness of qualitative

screening tests because knowledge of the concentration of a substance in serum or other biological fluids can assist in the determination of the severity of toxicity and of the need for aggressive interventions.[31] Quantitative tests that determine the amount of a substance, therefore, are much more useful. Quantitative tests are especially useful when assessing the potential toxicity of drugs with delayed clinical toxicity or when the toxicity primarily is caused by metabolites (e.g., acetaminophen, methanol). Furthermore, the concentration of a drug in serum is sometimes much more predictive of end-organ damage than clinically observed findings (e.g., ethanol effects on CNS).[98]

When blood samples are collected for the quantitation of potentially intoxicating substances, as much information as possible should be obtained about the time course of events to determine whether absorption and distribution of the substance has been completed, or whether these processes may still be occurring. Serial samples collected at three to six hour intervals may be needed to determine whether significant absorption is still occurring, and whether further gastrointestinal decontamination would be beneficial. In contrast to the interpretation of serum concentrations of chronically administered drugs, the serum concentration of a substance ingested in an overdose will not be at steady state. Furthermore, the pharmacokinetics of an ingested substance can be significantly affected by toxic concentrations of other drugs that could have been ingested concurrently. The pharmacokinetic behavior of drugs and other substances in the setting of clinical intoxications is sometimes referred to as "toxicokinetics."[31,32]

Quantitative toxicologic testing would not be of benefit to T.C. at this point in time because the identity of the ingested substance is unknown. Alcohol often is ingested concurrent with toxic drug overdoses and a quantitative measurement of the serum ethanol concentration would be useful in T.C. if the odor of an alcoholic beverage was noted on her breath or if there were other indications of alcohol use.

Assessment

35. T.C.'s clinical status has not changed over the last 10 minutes. A urine toxicology screen has been ordered along with an ABG. The 12-lead ECG noted a prolonged QRS interval of 0.14 sec (Normal: <0.1 sec). There is no odor of alcohol around T.C.'s mouth, face, or clothes, and a quantitative test for alcohol was not ordered. No antidotes have been administered. The physical examination of T.C. did not detect any evidence of trauma to her head. T.C.'s pupils were dilated and slowly responsive to light. Bowel sounds were hypoactive. What conclusions can be made at this time as to the likely substance ingested by T.C.?

Although the ingested substance still has not been specifically identified, the available data provide some clues as to the likely pharmacological class of drug that was ingested. The presence of CNS depression (T.C. is very lethargic); slowed ventricular conduction (prolonged QRS on ECG); tachycardia (heart rate 115 to 130 beats/minute); hypotension (BP 100/70 mm Hg); decreased gastrointestinal motility (hypoactive bowel sounds); and the history of a possible depressive illness (history from husband) are all consistent with a tricyclic antidepressant drug overdose. The antidepressant may have been ingested alone, or with other agents concomitantly.

Antidepressant Toxicities

36. How would the different toxicities of the various available antidepressants affect the treatment of T.C.?

As with most pharmacological classes of drugs, the major pharmacological effects and toxicities of the antidepressants are similar for all drugs within the same class. Small differences in toxicity among drugs within the same therapeutic class, however, can be magnified because of the large doses involved in toxic ingestions. Therefore, when a specific drug within a therapeutic class has not yet been identified, the overdose should be managed as if the ingested drug can produce the most severe toxicity of any drug in the class. In this light, T.C.'s presumed antidepressant drug overdose should be evaluated initially as if a tricyclic antidepressant such as imipramine (Tofranil), amitriptyline (Elavil), or doxepin (Sinequan) was ingested. These tricyclic antidepressants generally are associated with the most severe toxicities of all the available antidepressants.[99] New antidepressants such as trazodone (Desyrel), fluoxetine (Prozac), and sertraline (Zoloft) may not produce toxicity as severe as that of the tricyclic antidepressants; however, more experience and assessment of overdoses with these drugs are needed before conclusions about their overdose toxicities can become valid.[100,102] For example, maprotiline (Ludiomil) was initially thought not to result in cardiac toxicity, however, cardiotoxicity similar to that of the tricyclic antidepressants was subsequently encountered.[101]

Gastric Decontamination

37. In view of the fact that T.C. is now presumed to have ingested a tricyclic antidepressant, would GI decontamination be appropriate at this point in time?

Gastrointestinal decontamination should be initiated in all patients who have orally ingested overdoses whenever significant toxic symptoms are deemed to be likely. When the time from ingestion to the initiation of gastric decontamination is delayed, the effectiveness of decontamination is decreased because of the absorption that already has occurred. Nevertheless, absorption generally is slowed and more erratic after a toxic overdose. T.C. should undergo some form of gastrointestinal decontamination.

Activated Charcoal

38. What method of GI decontamination should be initiated for T.C.?

The best method for gastrointestinal decontamination for T.C. is a combination of gastric lavage followed by activated charcoal and sorbitol. T.C. will require endotracheal intubation with a cuffed endotracheal tube before the lavage tube is inserted because passage of the lavage tube can stimulate emesis and place her at risk of aspiration (see Question 17). Ipecac-induced emesis should not be initiated in suspected cases of tricyclic antidepressant overdoses because these patients can suddenly lose consciousness and be at risk for aspiration. T.C. already is very lethargic and would be vulnerable to aspiration during emesis. Furthermore, tricyclic antidepressant overdoses can induce seizures which are yet another contraindication to ipecac emesis (see Table 104.3). Although gastric lavage may not be as effective as emesis, it is not contraindicated in T.C. and greater than 300 mg of antidepressants have been recovered from overdosed patients by gastric lavage.[45]

A 50 gm dose of activated charcoal should be mixed into a slurry with water and sorbitol and given down the gastric tube after lavage has been completed. The adsorption of tricyclic antidepressants to charcoal prevents absorption and the charcoal-drug complex can be excreted in the stool. The sorbitol is administered to facilitate the removal of the charcoal-drug complex from the colon and to prevent the possible disassociation of the antidepressant from the charcoal. It is not clear whether a second dose of activated charcoal should always be administered at a later time, however, this is frequently undertaken.

Monitoring Efficacy

39. How should the effectiveness of GI decontamination be monitored in T.C.?

The tricyclic antidepressants frequently are absorbed very slowly when an overdose has been ingested.[55] As a result, gastrointestinal decontamination should be monitored to determine whether additional decontamination would be beneficial. Ideally, the clinical status of the patient would begin to improve after completion of decontamination because no further drug should be available for additional absorption. Therefore, the effectiveness of the activated charcoal and gastric lavage of T.C. should be monitored closely over the four to six hours after the completion of gastric decontamination. T.C. should have activated charcoal present in her stool within six hours of the charcoal administration.[104,105] Since activated charcoal can produce gastrointestinal obstruction, especially when administered to patients who have ingested drugs with anticholinergic activity,[103] sorbitol should be given to T.C. if no stool is apparent at this time.

Sodium Bicarbonate and Hyperventilation

40. T.C.'s psychiatrist has contacted the ER and provided the information that he prescribed the combination of amitriptyline with perphenazine (Triavil) for T.C.'s severe depression. How does this new information alter T.C.'s treatment plan?

This information from T.C.'s psychiatrist confirms the previous suspicion about the class of drugs most likely producing the toxicity in T.C. and specifically identifies the probable ingested drugs. T.C. should receive 50 mL of sodium bicarbonate at this time because of its ability to counteract the effects of amitriptyline on myocardial conduction. Since the suspicion of an antidepressant overdose was strong, the sodium bicarbonate could have been administered before receipt of this new information from her psychiatrist if her ECG demonstrated worsening myocardial conduction and her blood pressure continued to decline. The mechanism by which sodium bicarbonate decreases antidepressant-induced myocardial toxicity is not clear.[106–108] Hyperventilation of T.C. to a pH of about 7.5 also might decrease the cardiotoxicity of the antidepressants.[108]

The combination of a phenothiazine with an antidepressant has been associated with more severe cardiac toxicity than overdoses with antidepressants alone.[109] This increased toxicity has been attributed to the membrane-stabilizing effects of the phenothiazines. T.C. is, therefore, more likely to experience cardiotoxicity than previously expected because of her concurrent presumed ingestion of the phenothiazine, perphenazine. The treatment plan for T.C. has not been altered by this new information from her psychiatrist, but the information does reinforce the importance of continued monitoring and assessment of T.C.

Monitoring Efficacy

41. How should the sodium bicarbonate therapy in T.C. be monitored?

Drug therapy always needs to be monitored for both efficacy and toxicity. The efficacy of sodium bicarbonate can be evaluated by serial electrocardiograms to measure the QRS interval. A prolonged QRS interval generally will shorten to normal after the systemic pH has been increased to about 7.5. The toxicity of sodium bicarbonate administration can be evaluated by monitoring for systemic alkalosis and the production of carbon dioxide. The carbon dioxide is not a concern if pulmonary function is adequate to allow for excretion of this gas. Acid-base status should be monitored if more than 50 mL of sodium bicarbonate is administered, especially if the patient also is being ventilated mechanically. The combination of bicarbonate and mechanical ventilation is more likely to produce severe metabolic alkalosis.[110]

Seizures

42. T.C. suddenly experiences a generalized tonic-clonic seizure which lasts about 2 minutes and terminates spontaneously before treatment can be initiated. Should anticonvulsant therapy be initiated for T.C.?

Drug overdose-induced seizures are most commonly single seizures which frequently terminate before drug therapy can be administered.[111] If seizures do not stop within one to two minutes, a benzodiazepine should be administered parenterally. Chronic anticonvulsant therapy should not be administered to T.C. because there is no evidence that she will experience further seizures. Furthermore, the potential for drug-induced seizures will decrease as the clearance of the antidepressant continues.

Interpretation of Urine Screens

43. T.C.'s ECG normalized after the administration of 50 mL of sodium bicarbonate, her BP increased to 115/90 mm Hg, and no further seizures were experienced. The urine drug screen results came back positive for amitriptyline, nortriptyline, and phenothiazines. Does the presence of nortriptyline indicate that T.C. has ingested other drugs in addition to her combination of amitriptyline with perphenazine (Triavil)?

Nortriptyline is a metabolite of amitriptyline and for this reason was identified on the urine drug screen. Metabolites often are identified on comprehensive urine drug screens: the absence of nortriptyline on this drug screen should bring into question whether the assay was correctly interpreted by the clinical laboratory.

Duration of Hospitalization

44. How long should T.C. be monitored?

T.C. should be admitted into the intensive care unit from the emergency room and monitored until all evidence of CNS and cardiovascular toxicity has been reversed. As with all cases of tricyclic antidepressant overdoses, T.C. should be monitored until at least 12 hours have elapsed without any evidence of toxicity and that no further gastrointestinal absorption is likely based upon completion of gastrointestinal decontamination.[112,113] After the toxicity has completely resolved, T.C. should be evaluated by a psychiatrist to determine whether she should be admitted for inpatient treatment of her suicidal tendencies.

Assessments of Acetaminophen Ingestion
Complication of Pregnancy

45. L.P., a 23-year-old female who is about 32 weeks pregnant, presents to the ER 30 minutes after ingesting 50 acetaminophen 500 mg tablets. She is depressed and hoped to end her pregnancy by ingesting the acetaminophen. Her pregnancy was unplanned and she has not received any prenatal care. L.P. has thrown up twice since her ingestion of the acetaminophen. Her heart rate is 100 beats/min, BP 100/70 mm Hg, and temperature 97.5 °F. L.P. does not have any chronic diseases and the remainder of her medical history is unremarkable. How does L.P.'s pregnancy change the management of her acetaminophen ingestion?

Pregnancy should not change the initial approach to the assessment or treatment of potentially toxic ingestions. Assessment should initially focus on the mother. Overdoses during pregnancy often are associated with attempted abortions or with depression.[125]

The exposure of the fetus to the toxic ingestion will depend upon the ability of the ingested substance or its toxic metabolites to cross the placenta into the fetal circulation. The ability of the fetus to produce the toxic acetaminophen metabolite and the ability of the acetylcysteine antidote to cross the placenta also must be considered. Fetal and neonatal hepatotoxicity and death have occurred following maternal acetaminophen intoxications.[126-128] The fetal liver can begin to metabolize acetaminophen to its hepatotoxic metabolite sometime during the second trimester. The fetus also may be less able to detoxify the metabolite by conjugation with glutathione.[129]

The effects of the intoxication on maintaining the pregnancy and organogenesis also should be considered. The data on the impact of maternal poisonings on fetal outcome are sparse. In one series of 209 patients, a higher rate of stillbirths, lower birthweights, and increased likelihoods of CNS abnormalities were noted, but infant death rates, spontaneous abortions, or other congenital abnormalities were not noted.[130]

Mechanism of Hepatotoxicity

46. How do overdoses of acetaminophen cause hepatic necrosis?

Acetaminophen hepatotoxicity is secondary to the formation of a highly reactive toxic metabolite that is formed when cytochrome P450 metabolism of acetaminophen occurs to a greater extent than seen with therapeutic doses. Approximately 5% of a 335 mg dose of acetaminophen is metabolized via the P450 pathway, and detoxified by glutathione. Increased amounts of the metabolite depletes hepatic glutathione stores. When hepatic glutathione is depleted to about 30% of normal, the metabolite binds to hepatocytes, resulting in the characteristic centrilobular hepatic necrosis.[131]

Gastric Decontamination

47. What GI decontamination should be initiated for L.P.?

In the U.S., gastrointestinal decontamination of acetaminophen ingestions has been widely debated because acetylcysteine, the antidote used to prevent hepatotoxicity, is administered orally. In many other countries an intravenous dosage form of acetylcysteine obviates this debate. Ipecac-induced emesis could complicate oral acetylcysteine therapy by increasing the risk of emesis after acetylcysteine administration. (Nausea and vomiting are the most common adverse effects associated with acetylcysteine therapy.) Although gastric decontamination can be accomplished with activated charcoal, the activated charcoal has the potential to bind not only the unabsorbed acetaminophen, but also the absorption of the acetylcysteine which is administered as an "antidote." In clinical studies, acetylcysteine serum concentrations were decreased by activated charcoal, however, serum acetylcysteine concentrations do not adequately reflect the amount of acetylcysteine absorbed after an oral dose because acetylcysteine undergoes extensive first-pass metabolism.[132]

In the National Multicenter open study of oral acetylcysteine efficacy in the treatment of acetaminophen overdose, patients who had received activated charcoal were allowed to be entered into the study after gastric lavage had removed charcoal from the stomach. These patients did not appear to have experienced worse clinical outcomes.[133] Activated charcoal, therefore, is recommended in the management of all acetaminophen overdoses which present for treatment within four hours after ingestion; however, activated charcoal should not be administered at the same time as the administration of acetylcysteine.[134] Nevertheless, the clinical outcome in patients who received activated charcoal does not appear to be much different compared to patients who did not receive the activated charcoal.[135]

Activated charcoal 50 gm along with sorbitol should be administered to L.P. because her acetaminophen ingestion occurred only 30 minutes ago. If acetylcysteine therapy is needed later (e.g., 4 hours later; see Question 49), the activated charcoal already may have cleared from the stomach. Alternatively, the acetylcysteine can be given intravenously if patients are enrolled via telephone into investigational protocols (e.g., Rocky Mountain Poison Control Center). Acetylcysteine therapy is not influenced by the pregnancy.[128] According to preliminary data, acetylcysteine crosses the placenta and should protect the fetus from the development of hepatotoxicity.

Estimating Potential Toxicity

48. How should the potential toxicity of the acetaminophen ingestion be assessed?

While the acetaminophen dose correlates with toxicity somewhat with acute ingestions, serum acetaminophen concentrations are better predictors of the potential for hepatotoxicity.[136,137] The Matthew-Rumack nomogram (see Figure 104.2) is used in the U.S. to assess the potential for hepatotoxicity from acute overdoses of acetaminophen when the serum acetaminophen concentration is plotted on a graph against the time of ingestion.[133] This nomogram also is used to guide therapy. The nomogram, however, is only useful for acute ingestions, because it underestimates the potential for toxicity with chronic acetaminophen dosing.

In patients who are exposed to P450 enzyme induction which can increase the formation of the hepatotoxic acetaminophen metabolite, acetylcysteine therapy is initiated at lower acetaminophen serum concentrations based upon modified nomograms.[136,138,139] A hepatic P450 enzyme inhibitor (e.g., cimetidine) also can be added to the acetylcysteine therapy.[140]

49. A serum acetaminophen concentration is measured 4 hours after the ingestion for L.P. Why was this analysis of the serum acetaminophen concentration delayed for 4 hours when L.P. was in the ER within 30 minutes after her ingestion?

Absorption generally is completed within 1.5 to 2.5 hours after ingestion of solid or liquid dosage forms of acetaminophen.[141] The nomograms which are available to interpret serum acetaminophen concentrations and guide therapy are not applicable before four

hours postingestion because of the need to insure that acetaminophen absorption has been completed. The nomogram has not been shown to be useful with dosage forms except regular tablets and liquid (i.e., Extended Relief Tylenol). Since the dose ingested is not as accurate as serum concentrations in predicting hepatotoxicity, the acetaminophen dose should not be used to determine whether to initiate therapy with acetylcysteine. Most clinical laboratories can complete their assays and report acetaminophen serum concentration results within two hours of receipt of the four-hour postingestion blood sample. Acetylcysteine therapy is not more effective when administered sooner as long as it is initiated no later than eight hours after ingestion of the toxic dose. Therapy is not as effective when initiated after eight-hours postingestion; however, late administration of acetylcysteine still diminishes hepatotoxicity compared to historical controls who did not receive this antidote. Most acetaminophen ingestions do not require antidotal therapy and monitoring serum acetaminophen concentrations is much less costly if acetylcysteine therapy can be avoided.

Acetylcysteine Administration

50. The 4-hour acetaminophen concentration in L.P. was 245 mg/mL. How should acetylcysteine be administered to her; and what can be done if she vomits after acetylcysteine administration? [SI unit: 16,209 μmol/L]

The first dose of acetylcysteine is 140 mg/kg orally (about 7 to 10 gm for most adults). The acetylcysteine should be diluted to a concentration of ≥5% using whatever beverage is preferred by the patient. Carbonated beverages and fruit juices usually are used in an attempt to mask the odor of the acetylcysteine. With oral therapy, 17 additional 70 mg/kg doses of acetylcysteine are administered at four hour intervals following the initial dose for a total of 72 hours of therapy.

If L.P. vomits in the first hour after her acetylcysteine dose, the dose should be repeated. If she experiences protracted vomiting, the use of antiemetics, a duodenal feeding tube, and prokinetic agents can improve her gastrointestinal tolerance of acetylcysteine therapy.[121] Alternatively, she can be enrolled into an investigational protocol for intravenous acetylcysteine therapy (see Question 47).

Monitoring Efficacy of Acetylcysteine

51. How should the efficacy and toxicity of acetylcysteine therapy be monitored in L.P.?

With the exception of vomiting, acetylcysteine does not produce other toxicity when administered orally. The effectiveness of acetylcysteine intervention in L.P. should be monitored by daily assessment of her liver function tests and her prothrombin time. Prolonged prothrombin times are suggestive of poor prognosis.[142] Patients usually will experience an increase in the AST and ALT over the 24 to 72 hours after ingestion. As the hepatic damage continues, the liver enzymes may peak at several thousand units even with acetylcysteine therapy. In most patients, the AST and ALT will begin to decline after three days and return to baseline values. Patients who have a significant increase in serum bilirubin concentration and prothrombin time have a decreased likelihood of survival.[131]

Assessments of Health Food Ingestions

52. G.B., a 23-year-old exotic male dancer, is brought to the ER after being found having a generalized seizure in the restroom of a bar. Neurological examination is nonfocal, and he has no purposeful speech. His vital signs are as follows: BP 128/80 mm Hg, heart rate 85 beats/min, respirations 35 breaths/min, and temperature 100.2 °F. A blood ethanol con-

Fig 104.2 Matthew-Rumack Nomogram for Interpretation of Severity of Acetaminophen Poisoning Reprinted with permission from Pediatrics, 1975;871:55.

centration is only 120 mg/dL, and substances other than alcohol were not detected on qualitative urine drug screens for either substances of abuse or "comprehensive" drugs. His blood glucose is 110 mg/dL, and pulse oximetry is 98%. He does not respond to IV diagnostic doses of naloxone or flumazenil. The 2 coworkers who accompany him to the ER know that he has been healthy, has no history of seizure disorders, and is not currently on any medications. What are other types of drugs that could have been ingested by G.B.?

G.B. does not appear to have ingested an opioid or a benzodiazepine based upon his lack of response to naloxone and flumazenil, respectively. Since his urine drug screens for "comprehensive" drugs and for substances of abuse also are negative, unregulated chemicals and substances not generally considered as drugs of abuse should be considered. For example, anabolic steroids, vitamins, and health food supplements potentially used by weightlifters, body builders, individuals attempting to lose weight, and exotic dancers could have been ingested by G.B. In the past few years, poison control centers have been encountering toxic ingestions of these substances.

GHB (gamma hydroxybutyrate) has been sold in the U.S. as a health-food product since 1990. It is promoted as being able to enhance muscle mass, burn off fat, and stimulate growth hormone release. Adverse effects of GHB have been encountered especially when ingested with ethanol.[123] GHB had been evaluated as an anesthetic in Europe, however, the frequency of seizures and lack of analgesic effects resulted in loss of medical interest in this drug.[124]

Various substances, both legal and illicit, should be considered when evaluating G.B. Substances represented to the public as health-food products, natural remedies, or folk remedies can be toxic. Additional evaluation of the history, and expansion of questioning beyond prescription and nonprescription medications and common drugs of abuse must be considered for G.B. This is especially important since these substances will frequently not be identified in urine drug screening.

References

1 Herrington AM et al. Toxicology and management of acute drug ingestions in adults. Pharmacotherapy. 1995;15:182.

2 Kulig K. Current concepts—initial management of ingestions of toxic substances. N Engl J Med. 1992;326:1677.

3 Vale JA. Reviews in medicine—clinical toxicology. Postgrad Med J. 1993; 69:19.

4 American College of Emergency Physicians. Clinical policy for the initial approach to patients presenting with acute toxic ingestion or dermal or inhalation exposure. Ann Emerg Med. 1995;25:570.

5 Litovitz TL et al. 1991 annual report of the American Association of Poison Control Centers national data collection system. Am J Emerg Med. 1992; 10:452.

6 National Institute on Drug Abuse Statistical Series. Annual emergency room data 1991. Data from the drug abuse warning network (DAWN). Series I, Number 11-A. US Department of Health and Human Services.

7 National Institute on Drug Abuse Statistical Series. Annual medical examiner data 1991. Data from the drug abuse warning network (DAWN). Series I, Number 11-B. US Department of Health and Human Services.

8 Blanc PD et al. Surveillance of poisoning and drug overdose through hospital discharge coding, poison control center reporting, and the drug abuse warning network. Am J Emerg Med. 1993;11:14.

9 Soslow AR, Woolf AD. Reliability of data sources for poisoning deaths in Massachusetts. Am J Emerg Med. 1992;10:124.

10 Goldfrank LR, Hoffman RS. The cardiovascular effects of cocaine. Ann Emerg Med. 1991;20:165.

11 Watson WA. Longitudinal assessment of cocaine toxicity in emergency department patients. J Pharm Practice. 1993;6:74.

12 Baum C et al. The impact of the addition of naloxone on the use and abuse of pentazocine. Public Health Rep. 1987;102:426.

13 McKnight RH et al. Detection of green tobacco sickness by a regional poison center. Vet Hum Toxicol. 1994; 36:505.

14 Poisindex. Denver, CO: Micromedes.

15 Caravati EM, McElwee NE. Use of clinical toxicology resources by emergency physicians and its impact on poison control centers. Ann Emerg Med. 1991;20:147.

16 Thompson DF et al. Evaluation of regional and nonregional poison centers. N Engl J Med. 1983;308:191.

17 Litovitz T et al. Poison information providers: an assessment of proficiency. Am J Emerg Med. 1984;2:129.

18 Gellers RJ et al. American poison control centers: still not all the same? Ann Emerg Med. 1988;17:599.

19 Veltri JC. Regional poison control services. Hosp Forum. 1982;17:1469.

20 Anon. Facility assessment guidelines for regional toxicology treatment centers. Clin Toxicol. 1993;31:211.

21 Beckmann ML, Brass EP. Advances in managing drug overdoses. Hosp Forum. 1987;22:432.

22 Wright N. An assessment of the unreliability of the history given by self-poisoned patients. Clin Toxicol. 1980; 16:381.

23 Manoguerra AS. The poison information telephone call. In: Haddad LM, Winchester JF, eds. Clinical Management of Poisoning and Drug Overdose. 2nd ed. Philadelphia: WB Saunders; 1990:471.

24 Olson KR et al. Physical assessment and differential diagnosis of the poisoned patient. Med Toxicol. 1987;2:52.

25 Nice A et al. Toxidrome recognition to improve efficiency of emergency urine drug screens. Ann Emerg Med. 1988; 17:676.

26 Spyker DA, Minocha A. Toxicodynamic approach to management of the poisoned patient. J Emerg Med. 1988; 6:117.

27 Mahoney JD et al. Quantitative serum toxic screening in the management of suspected drug overdose. Am J Emerg Med. 1990;8:16.

28 Newton RW. The clinician's requirements from the laboratory in the treatment of the acutely poisoned patient. The Poisoned Patient: The Role of the Laboratory. Ciba Foundation Symposium 26 (new series). New York: Elsevier; 1974:5.

29 Watson WA. Identifying the acetaminophen overdose. Ann Emerg Med. 1989;18:1126. Editorial.

30 Hepler BR et al. Role of the toxicology laboratory in the treatment of acute poisoning. Med Toxicol. 1986;1:61.

31 Watson WA. Toxicokinetics and management of the poisoned patient. U.S. Pharm. 1990;15:H1.

32 Sue YJ, Shannon M. Pharmacokinetics of drugs in overdose. Clin Pharmacokinet. 1992;23:93.

33 Knopp R. Caustic ingestions. JACEP. 1979;8:329.

34 Easom JM, Lovejoy FH. Efficacy and safety of gastrointestinal decontamination in the treatment of oral poisonings. Pediatr Clin North Am. 1979;26: 827.

35 Cupit GC, Temple AR. Gastrointestinal decontamination in the management of the poisoned patient. Emerg Med Clin North Am. 1984;2:15.

36 Linden CH, Watson WA. Gastrointestinal decontamination. In: Harwood-Nuss A et al., eds. The Clinical Practice of Emergency Medicine. Philadelphia: JB Lippincott; 1991:438.

37 Dillon EC et al. Large surface area activated charcoal and the inhibition of aspirin absorption. Ann Emerg Med. 1989;18:547.

38 Krenzelok EP, Heller MB. Effectiveness of commercially available aqueous activated charcoal products. Ann Emerg Med. 1987;16:1340.

39 Comstock EG et al. Assessment of the efficacy of activated charcoal following gastric lavage in acute drug emergencies. J Toxicol Clin Toxicol. 1982; 19:149.

40 Kulig K et al. Management of acutely poisoned patients without gastric emptying. Ann Emerg Med. 1985;14:562.

41 Tenenbein M. Whole bowel irrigation as a gastrointestinal decontamination procedure after acute poisoning. Med Toxicol. 1988;3:77.

42 Park GD et al. Expanded role of charcoal therapy in the poisoned and overdose patient. Arch Intern Med. 1984; 144:48.

43 Palatnick W, Tenenbein M. Activated charcoal in the treatment of drug overdose. Drug Saf. 1992;7:3.

44 Neuvonen PJ, Olkkola KT. Oral activated charcoal in the treatment of intoxications—role of single and repeated doses. Med Toxicol. 1988;3:33.

45 Watson WA et al. Recovery of cyclic antidepressants with gastric lavage. J Emerg Med. 1989;7:373.

46 Todd JW. Do measures to enhance drug removal save life? Lancet. 1984; 1:331.

47 Garrettson LK, Geller RJ. Acid and alkaline diuresis: when are they of value in the treatment of poisoning. Drug Saf. 1990;5:220.

48 Lorch JA, Garella S. Hemoperfusion to treat intoxications. Ann Intern Med. 1979;91:301.

49 Kulling P, Persson H. Role of the intensive care unit in the management of the poisoned patient. Med Toxicol. 1986;1:375.

50 Watson WA et al. The volume of a swallow: correlation of deglutition with patient and container parameters. Am J Emerg Med. 1983;1:278.

51 Veltri JC, Thompson MIB. Salicylate intoxication. Clin Toxicol Consultant. 1980;2:111.

52 Koren G. Medications which can kill a toddler with one tablet or teaspoonful. Clin Toxicol. 1993;31:407.

53 Litovitz T, Manoguerra A. Comparison of pediatric poisoning hazards: an analysis of 3.8 million exposure incidents. A report from the American Association of Poison Control Centers. Pediatrics. 1992;89:999.

54 Schauben JL et al. Iron poisoning: report of three cases and a review of therapeutic intervention. J Emerg Med. 1990;8:309.

55 Callaham M. Tricyclic antidepressant overdose. JACEP. 1979;8:413.

56 Engle JP et al. Acute iron intoxication:

treatment controversies. Drug Intell Clin Pharm. 1987;21:153.

57 **Mann KV et al.** Management of acute iron overdose. Clin Pharm. 1989;8:428.

58 **Jaeger RW et al.** Radiopacity of drugs and plants in vivo— limited usefulness. Vet Hum Toxicol. 1981;23(Suppl. 1):2.

59 **Handy CA.** Radiopacity of oral non-liquid medications. Radiology. 1971;98:525.

60 **Lacouture PG et al.** Emergency assessment of severity of iron overdose by clinical and laboratory methods. J Pediatr. 1981;99:89.

61 **Manoguerra AS.** Rapid emesis from high-dose ipecac syrup in adults and children intoxicated with antiemetics or other drugs. Am J Hosp Pharm. 1978;35:1360.

62 **Geiseker DR, Troutman WG.** Emergency induction of emesis using liquid detergent products: a report of 15 cases. Clin Toxicol. 1981;18:277.

63 **Grbcich PA et al.** Effect of fluid volume on ipecac-induced emesis. J Pediatr. 1987;110:970.

64 **Buckley N et al.** Slow-release verapamil poisoning. Use of polyethylene glycol whole-bowel lavage and high-dose calcium. Med J Aust. 1993;158:202.

65 **Dolgin JG et al.** Pharmacokinetic modeling and simulation of the effect of multi-dose activated charcoal in phenytoin intoxication— report of two pediatric cases. DICP, Ann Pharmacother. 1991;25:463.

66 **Buckley NA et al.** Controlled release drugs in overdose— clinical consideration. Drug Saf. 1995;12:73.

67 **Shenfield GM.** Slow-release overdose. Med J Aust. 1993;158:150. Editorial.

68 **Minocha A, Spyker DA.** Acute overdose with sustained release drug formulations— perspectives in treatment. Med Toxicol. 1986;1:300.

69 **Jung D et al.** Effect of dose on phenytoin absorption. Clin Pharmacol Ther. 1980;28:479.

70 **Albertson TE et al.** A prolonged severe intoxication after ingestion of phenytoin and phenobarbital. West J Med. 1981;135:418.

71 **Ling LJ et al.** Absorption of iron after experimental overdose of chewable vitamins. Am J Emerg Med. 1991;9:24.

72 **Thompson DF.** Reassessment of measuring total iron binding capacity in acute iron overdose. Ann Pharmacother. 1994;28:63.

73 **Lovejoy FH.** Chelation therapy in iron poisoning. J Toxicol Clin Toxicol. 1982–83;19:871.

74 **Qirbi AA, Poznanski WJ.** Emergency toxicology in a general hospital. Can Med Assoc J. 1977;116:884.

75 **Ingelfinger JA et al.** Reliability of the toxic screen in drug overdose. Clin Pharmacol Ther. 1981;29:570.

76 **Pond SM et al.** Randomized study of the treatment of phenobarbital overdose with repeated doses of activated charcoal. JAMA. 1984;251:3104.

77 **Watson AJS et al.** Acute Wernicke's encephalopathy precipitated by glucose loading. Ir J Med Sci. 1981;150:301.

78 **Yealy DM et al.** The safety of prehospital naloxone administration by paramedics. Ann Emerg Med. 1990;19:902.

79 **Gaddis GM, Watson WA.** Naloxone-associated patient violence: an overlooked toxicity? Ann Pharmacother. 1992;26:196.

80 **Handal KA et al.** Naloxone. Ann Emerg Med. 1983;12:438.

81 **Klotz U, Kanto J.** Pharmacokinetics and clinical use of flumazenil (Ro 15-1788). Clin Pharmacokinet. 1988;14:1.

82 **Weinbroum A et al.** The use of flumazenil in the management of acute drug poisoning—a review. Intensive Care Med. 1991;17:S32.

83 **Spivey WH.** Flumazenil and seizures: analysis of 43 cases. Clin Ther. 1992;14:292.

84 **Leikin JB et al.** Clinical features and management of intoxication due to hallucinogenic drugs. Med Toxicol Adverse Drug Exp. 1989;4:324.

85 **Henry JA, Cassidy SL.** Hypothesis— membrane stabilizing activity: a major cause of fatal poisoning. Lancet. 1986;1:1414.

86 **Shannon M et al.** Hypotension in severe tricyclic antidepressant overdose. Am J Emerg Med. 1988;6:439.

87 **Jay SJ et al.** Respiratory complications of overdose with sedative drugs. Am Rev Respir Dis. 1975;112:591.

88 **Shannon M, Lovejoy FS.** Pulmonary consequences of severe tricyclic antidepressant ingestion. Clin Toxicol. 1987;25:443.

89 **Heffner JE, Sahn SA.** Salicylate-induced pulmonary edema. Ann Intern Med. 1981;95:405.

90 **Glauser FL et al.** Ethchlorvynol (Placidyl)-induced pulmonary edema. Ann Intern Med. 1976;84:46.

91 **Ettinger NA, Albin RJ.** A review of the respiratory effects of smoking cocaine. Am J Med. 1989;87:664.

92 **Parrish J, Arndt KA.** Skin lesions in barbiturate poisoning. Lancet. 1970;2:764.

93 **Linden CH.** General evaluation and management of the poisoned patient. In: Harwood-Nuss A et al., eds. The Clinical Practice of Emergency Medicine. Philadelphia: JB Lippincott; 1991:429.

94 **Garriott JC.** Interpretive toxicology. Clin Lab Med. 1983;3:367.

95 **Sohn D, Byers J.** Cost effective drug screening in the laboratory. Clin Toxicol. 1981;18:459.

96 **Ellis GM et al.** Excretion patterns of cannabinoid metabolites after last use in a group of chronic users. Clin Pharmacol Ther. 1985;38:572.

97 **Robinson MC et al.** Analysis of cost benefit of toxicology laboratory determinations. Vet Hum Toxicol. 1981;23(Suppl. 1):26.

98 **Starmer GA.** Effects of low to moderate doses of ethanol on human driving-related performance. In: Crow KE, Batt RD, eds. Human Metabolism of Alcohol. Vol. 1. Boca Raton: CRC Press; 1989:101.

99 **Cassidy S, Henry J.** Fatal toxicity of antidepressant drugs in overdose. Br Med J. 1987;295:1021.

100 **Crome P, Ali C.** Clinical features and management of self-poisoning with newer antidepressants. Med Toxicol. 1986;1:411.

101 **Bergman RN, Watson WA.** Cardiac toxicity associated with acute maprotiline poisoning. Am J Emerg Med. 1984;2:144.

102 **Borys DJ et al.** Acute fluoxetine overdose: a report of 234 cases. Am J Emerg Med. 1992;10:115.

103 **Watson WA et al.** Gastrointestinal obstruction associated with multiple-dose activated charcoal. J Emerg Med. 1986;4:401.

104 **Harchelroad F et al.** Gastrointestinal transit times of a charcoal/sorbitol slurry in overdose patients. Clin Toxicol. 1989;27:91.

105 **Krenzelok EP.** Gastrointestinal transit times of cathartics used with activated charcoal. Clin Pharm. 1985;4:446.

106 **Brown TCK et al.** The use of sodium bicarbonate in the treatment of tricyclic antidepressant-induced arrhythmias. Anaesth Intensive Care. 1973;1:203.

107 **Hoffman JR et al.** Effect of hypertonic sodium bicarbonate in the treatment of moderate-to-severe cyclic antidepressant overdose. Am J Emerg Med. 1993;111:336.

108 **Smilkstein MJ.** Reviewing cyclic antidepressant cardiotoxicity: wheat and chaff. J Emerg Med. 1990;8:645. Editorial.

109 **Wilens TE et al.** Adverse cardiac effects of combined neuroleptic ingestion and tricyclic antidepressant overdose. J Clin Psychopharmacol. 1990;10:51.

110 **Wrenn K et al.** Profound alkalemia during treatment of tricyclic antidepressant overdose. Am J Emerg Med. 1992;10:553.

111 **Olson KR et al.** Seizures associated with poisoning and drug overdose. Am J Emerg Med. 1993;11:565.

112 **Callaham M, Kassel D.** Epidemiology of fatal tricyclic antidepressant ingestion: implications of management. Ann Emerg Med. 1985;14:1.

113 **Tokarski GF, Young MJ.** Criteria for admitting patients with tricyclic antidepressant overdose. J Emerg Med. 1988;6:121.

114 **Whitten CF et al.** Managing salicylate poisoning in children. An evaluation of sodium bicarbonate therapy. Am J Dis Child. 1961;101:178.

115 **Berg KJ.** Acute acetylsalicylic acid poisoning; treatment with forced alkaline diuresis and diuretics. Eur J Clin Pharmacol. 1977;12:111.

116 **Prescott LF et al.** Diuresis or urinary alkalinization for salicylate poisoning. Br Med J (Clin Res). 1982;285:1383.

117 **Elenbaas RM.** Critical review of forced alkaline diuresis in acute salicylism. Crit Care Q. 1982;4:89.

118 **Fox GN.** Hypocalcemia complicating bicarbonate therapy for salicylate poisoning. West J Med. 1984;141:108.

119 **Wasserman GS.** Hydrocarbon poisoning. Crit Care Q. 1982;4:33.

120 **Ng R et al.** Emergency treatment of petroleum distillate ingestion. Can Med Assoc J. 1974;111:537.

121 **Reed MD, Marx CM.** Ondansetron for treating nausea and vomiting in the poisoned patient. Ann Pharmacother. 1994;28:331.

122 **Amitai Y et al.** Repetitive oral activated charcoal and control of emesis in severe theophylline toxicity. Ann Intern Med. 1986;105:386.

123 **Dyer JO.** Gamma- hydroxybutyrate: a health-food product producing coma
and seizure like activity. Am J Emerg Med. 1991;9:321.

124 **Snead OC.** Minireview: gamma hydroxybutyrate. Life Sci. 1977;20:1935.

125 **Lester D, Beck AT.** Attempted suicide and pregnancy. Am J Obstet Gynecol. 1988;158:1084.

126 **Haiback H et al.** Acetaminophen overdose with fetal demise. Am J Clin Pathol. 1984;82:240.

127 **Kurzel RB.** Can acetaminophen excess result in maternal and fetal toxicity? South Med J. 1990;83:953.

128 **Riggs BS et al.** Acute acetaminophen overdose during pregnancy. Obstet Gynecol. 1989;74:247.

129 **Rollins DE et al.** Acetaminophen: potentially toxic metabolite formed by human fetal and adult liver microsomes and isolated fetal liver cells. Science. 1979;205:1414.

130 **Czeizel A, Lendvay A.** Attempted suicide and pregnancy. Am J Obstet Gynecol. 1989;161:497. Letter.

131 **Lewis RK, Paloucek FP.** Assessment and treatment of acetaminophen overdose. Clin Pharm. 1991;10:765.

132 **Watson WA, McKinney PE.** Activated charcoal and acetylcysteine absorption: issues in interpreting pharmacokinetic data. Ann Pharmacother. 1991;25:1081.

133 **Smilkstein MJ et al.** Efficacy of oral n-acetylcysteine in the treatment of acetaminophen overdose— analysis of the national multicenter study (1976 to 1985). N Engl J Med. 1988;319:1557.

134 **Anon.** Acetaminophen Toxicologic Management. Poisindex. Micromedex. Vol. 77, exp 8/13/93.

135 **Spiller HA et al.** A prospective evaluation of the effect of the use of activated charcoal before oral N-acetylcysteine therapy in acetaminophen overdose. Vet Hum Toxicol. 1993;35:346. Abstract.

136 **Janes J, Routledge PA.** Recent developments in the management of paracetamol (acetaminophen) poisoning. Drug Saf. 1992;7:170.

137 **Flanagan RJ.** The role of acetylcysteine in clinical toxicology. Med Toxicol. 1987;2:93.

138 **Seeff LB et al.** Acetaminophen hepatotoxicity in alcoholics— a therapeutic misadventure. Ann Intern Med. 1986;104:399.

139 **Kumar S, Rex DK.** Failure of physicians to recognize acetaminophen hepatotoxicity in chronic alcoholics. Arch Intern Med. 1991;151:1189.

140 **McClements BM et al.** Management of paracetamol poisoning complicated by enzyme induction due to alcohol or drugs. Lancet. 1990;1:1526. Letter.

141 **Rose SR et al.** Simulated acetaminophen overdose: pharmacokinetics and effectiveness of activated charcoal. Ann Emerg Med. 1991;20:1064.

142 **Harrison PM et al.** Serial prothrombin time as prognostic indicator in paracetamol induced fulminant hepatic failure. Br Med J. 1990;301:964.

143 **Ellenhorn MJ, Barceloux DG.** Medical Toxicology: Diagnosis and Treatment of Human Poisonings. 1st ed. New York, NY; Elsevier Science Publishing Co.; 1988.

144 **Haddad LM, Winchester JF.** Clinical Management of Poisoning and Drug

Overdose. 2nd ed. Philadelphia: WB Saunders; 1990.

145 **Goldfrank LF et al.** Toxicologic Emergencies. 4th ed. Norwalk, CT; Appleton and Lange; 1990.

146 **Olson KR.** Poisoning and Drug Overdose. Norwalk, CT; Appleton and Lange; 1990.

147 **Russel FE.** Snake Venom Poisoning. Great Neck, NY; Scholium International; 1983.

148 **Grant WM.** Toxicology of the Eye. 3rd ed. Springfield, IL. Charles C Thomas; 1986.

149 **Spoerke DG, Smolinske SC.** Toxicity of Houseplants. Boca Raton, FL: CRC Press; 1990.

150 **McEvoy GK et al., eds.** American Hospital Formulary Service. American Society of Health Systems Pharmacists; 1994:1967.

151 **Clarke A, Walton WW.** Effect of safety packaging on aspirin ingestion by children. Pediatrics. 1979;63:687.

152 **Done AK.** Aspirin overdosage: incidence, diagnosis, and management. Pediatrics. 1978;62:890.

153 **Temple AR.** Acute and chronic effects of aspirin toxicity and their treatment. Arch Intern Med. 1981;141:364.

154 **Temple AR.** Pathophysiology of aspirin overdosage toxicity, with implications for management. Pediatrics. 1978; 62:873.

155 **Done AK, Temple AR.** Treatment of salicylate poisoning. Mod Treat. 1971; 8:528.

156 **Thurston JH et al.** Reduced brain glucose with normal plasma glucose in salicylate poisoning. J Clin Invest. 1970; 49:2139.

157 **Heffner JE, Sahn SA.** Salicylate-induced pulmonary edema. Clinical features and prognosis. Ann Intern Med. 1976;85:745.

158 **Paul BN.** Salicylate poisoning in the elderly: diagnostic pitfalls. J Am Geriatr Soc. 1972;20:387.

159 **Anderson RJ et al.** Unrecognized adult salicylate intoxication. Ann Intern Med. 1976;85:745.

160 **Gaudreault P et al.** The relative severity of acute versus chronic salicylate poisoning in children: a clinical comparison. Pediatrics. 1982;70:566.

161 **Hill JB.** Experimental salicylate poisoning: observations on the effects of altering blood pH on tissue and plasma salicylate concentrations. Pediatrics. 1971;47:658.

162 **Done AK.** Salicylate intoxication. Significance of measurements of salicylate in blood in cases of acute ingestion. Pediatrics. 1960;26:800.

163 **Kwong TC et al.** Self-poisoning with enteric-coated aspirin. Am J Clin Pathol. 1983;80:888.

164 **Klein-Schwartz W.** Salicylate poisoning. Ear Nose Throat J.

Nausea and Vomiting

Mary Anne Koda-Kimble
Lloyd Y Young

Definitions 105-1
Pathophysiology (See Figure 105.1) 105-1
Etiology (See Table 105.1) 105-2
Complications 105-3
Management 105-3
   Assessment 105-3
   Antiemetics (Also see Table 105.2) 105-3
   Specific management 105-5
      Gastroenteritis 105-5
      Mechanical obstruction 105-5
      Motion sickness 105-5
      Pregnancy 105-5
      Cancer chemotherapy 105-5
Chemotherapy-Associated Nausea
and Vomiting 105-5
   Treatment 105-5
      First-line antiemetics
      (See Tables 105.3 and 105.4) 105-5

Serotonin antagonists 105-6
Metoclopramide 105-7
Dexamethasone and methylprednisolone 105-7
Lorazepam 105-7
General management 105-7
Second-line antiemetics 105-7
   Prochlorperazine 105-7
   Haloperidol 105-8
   Dronabinol 105-8
Oral antiemetics 105-8
Outpatient therapy 105-8
   Parenteral antiemetics 105-8
   Patient education 105-8
   Brain metastases 105-8
Motion Sickness 105-8
Pediatric Cancer Chemotherapy 105-9

Nausea and vomiting are unpleasant consequences of a wide variety of both organic and psychogenic disorders which afflict most individuals from time to time. Although highly discomforting, nausea and vomiting usually are self-limiting events without serious sequelae. Severe and/or protracted nausea and vomiting, however, may result in serious medical complications such as dehydration, malnutrition, and metabolic disturbances. This is particularly true in infants and children. In such cases, treatment must be aimed at correction of the underlying disorder, symptomatic management of the nausea and vomiting, and correction of secondary complications.

Definitions

In most cases, vomiting is divided into three distinct stages. *Nausea* is a cerebral function and is manifested by a conscious perception of discomfort associated with an awareness of the urge to vomit.[1,2] A variety of stimuli may produce nausea, including labyrinthine stimulation, visceral pain, and unpleasant memories. During nausea there is a loss of gastric tone and peristalsis with contraction of the duodenum and reflux of the intestinal contents into the stomach.[2] Additional symptoms such as increased perspiration, salivation, tachycardia, anorexia, and headache often occur simultaneously. *Retching* is the rhythmic, labored, spasmodic respiratory movements involving the diaphragm, chest wall, and abdominal muscles which often precedes or alternates with episodes of vomiting.[2] *Vomiting* or emesis is the forceful expulsion of the gastrointestinal (GI) contents through the mouth. This act is considered to be a protective physiologic mechanism when it prevents the entry into the absorbing gut of ingested substances that are physically or chemically unsuitable. However, vomiting must be regarded as pathologic if it is not associated with this purpose.[3]

Pathophysiology

Although much of the pathophysiology involved in the vomiting process remains to be clearly elucidated, early investigators through the development of animal models recognized that it is a complicated act involving coordinated activities of the gastrointestinal tract and the respiratory and abdominal musculature.[4,5] This left little doubt that central mechanisms are important in the control of nausea and vomiting.

In 1949, Borison and Wang evoked projectile vomiting in a decerebrate cat by electrical stimulation of a cigar-shaped region in the reticular formation of the medulla oblongata.[6] This area is called the vomiting center (VC) or emetic center and is believed to be a final common pathway that mediates all vomiting. This center does not respond directly to chemical stimuli but is reflex-activated through the chemoreceptor trigger zone (CTZ) and other chemosensitive areas.[1] The CTZ is contained in the area postrema in the floor of the fourth ventricle where it is exposed to both blood and cerebrospinal fluid.[7] The chemoreceptor trigger zone incorporates various receptors (e.g., serotonin, dopamine, opiate) which appear to mediate the emetic effect of blood-borne drugs and toxins.[8-11] The CTZ is unable to cause vomiting without an intact vomiting center.

In addition to the chemoreceptor trigger zone, input from three other sources is known to stimulate the VC and cause emesis (see Figure 105.1). These sources are the vestibular apparatus, visceral afferent fibers in the pharynx and gastrointestinal tract, and supramedullary loci (higher brain stem and cortical structures).[12]

Disturbances in vestibular function are believed to stimulate the VC via direct central pathways. Motion sickness appears to be entirely a central nervous system (CNS) response to vestibular stimuli. Motion induces stress in the labyrinth which transmits impulses to the vestibular center located near the vomiting center. Norepinephrine and acetylcholine receptors are located within the vestibular center. The acetylcholine receptors are believed to mediate the impulses responsible for activating the VC while the norepinephrine receptors possibly produce a stabilizing influence when activated which resist motion sickness.[13]

Stimulation of the VC from outside the CNS is primarily from the pharynx and GI tract via afferent impulses carried primarily by

Stimuli	Agents Used for Treatment	Mechanism		Vomiting

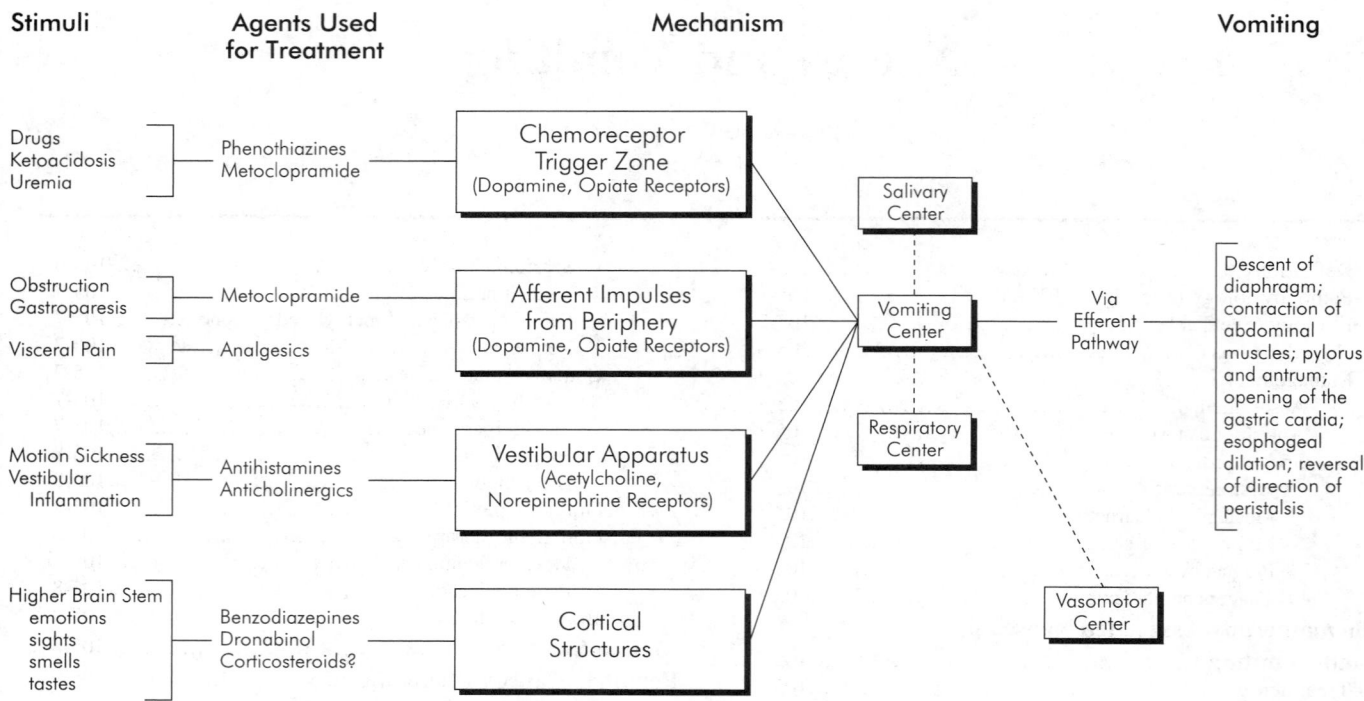

Fig 105.1 Causes, Treatments, and Mechanisms of Vomiting   Primary therapy should always include correction of the underlying disorder whenever possible.

the vagus and sympathetic nerves, without traversing the CTZ.[2] Chemical stimuli or physical factors such as irritation, distension, motility disorders, or obstruction may initiate this process. Visceral pain also may initiate vomiting through this mechanism.[5] Dopamine, serotonin (i.e., 5-HT$_3$), and opiate receptors also are found in gastrointestinal tissue and are believed to be mediators of the emetic effect.[1,2,11,14] Serotonin is believed to be a major mediator of chemotherapy-induced nausea and vomiting. One study demonstrated that following cisplatin administration, increased urinary excretion of 5-hydroxyin doleacetic acid (the major metabolite of serotonin) correlated with the onset of nausea and vomiting.[14] Serotonin is believed to be released from the gastrointestinal mucosal enterochromaffin cells as a result of cell damage following chemotherapy. The serotonin can then stimulate receptors on the visceral afferent fibers which in turn stimulate the CTZ. Elevated levels of serotonin also are seen in many vomiting patients (e.g., motion sickness, uremia, increased intracranial pressure), but it is unclear whether it is a mediator of the vomiting or a fluid conservation mechanism.[15–18]

Areas located in the higher brain stem or cortex seem able to initiate vomiting by sending impulses downstream to the VC.[12] Sights, smells, tastes, and unpleasant memories may stimulate these pathways.

Once the VC has been stimulated, efferent pathways are mainly somatic, involving the vagus and phrenic nerves.[19] A number of complex activities then occur which ultimately result in emesis. These include descent of the diaphragm with forceful contractions of the abdominal muscles, contraction of the pylorus and antrum, opening of the gastric cardia, relaxation of the proximal stomach, diminished esophageal-sphincter pressure, esophageal dilatation, and reversal of the direction of peristalsis in the small bowel and distal stomach.[1,5] The vomiting center is located in close proximity to the respiratory, vasomotor, vestibular, and salivary centers. Integrated activities between the VC and these centers are believed to mediate emesis as well as cause the symptoms which usually

accompany vomiting (e.g., nausea, salivation, dilatation of the pupils, perspiration, pallor, alterations in heart rate, blood pressure, and respiratory rate).[4]

Etiology

Given the number of pathways which are capable of stimulating the VC it is not surprising that a wide variety of disorders may be complicated by nausea and vomiting (see Table 105.1). As with most disorders, a thorough history usually provides clues to the primary pathological process and aids in the choice of a diagnostic approach.

The acute onset of vomiting in a previously healthy patient usually implicates an infectious or toxic (including drug) etiology. Viral gastroenteritis is the most common cause of acute onset nausea and vomiting in the U.S. Many drugs, such as cancer chemotherapeutic agents, opioids, and antibiotics may be responsible for the acute onset of nausea and vomiting through stimulation of the CTZ or local effects on the gastrointestinal tract. Metabolic disturbances (e.g., diabetic ketoacidosis, uremia), also may induce vomiting via stimulation of the CTZ.[5] Vestibular dysfunction (e.g., motion sickness) is believed to cause vomiting by a direct effect of the VC.[13] Visceral pain which frequently is associated with myocardial infarction, peritonitis, and renal biliary, or small bowel colic, also may cause vomiting mediated through afferent connections to the VC.[5]

Chronic nausea and vomiting (i.e., lasting more than 1 week) are most commonly a result of mechanical obstruction (e.g., peptic ulcer disease, gastric carcinoma) or motility disorders (e.g., gastroparesis, drug-induced gastric stasis, irritable bowel syndrome). The relationship of vomiting to meals may be helpful in distinguishing the etiology. The finding of vomiting of undigested food particles up to 12 hours after ingestion is classic for mechanical outlet obstruction. In contrast, patients suffering from gastroenteritis or psychogenic disorders usually vomit shortly after eating. The presence of bile in the vomitus is common during small bowel obstruction and after gastric surgery.[5]

Increased intracranial pressure also results in persistent vomiting. This vomiting may occur without nausea and retching. The mechanism of action is presumably related to pressure effects on the VC. A history of head trauma and/or an abnormal neurologic examination may aid in this diagnosis.[3]

Nausea is one of the most distressing side effects following anesthesia and often is followed by retching and vomiting. Studies suggest that in the absence of antiemetics, about 30% of patients experience these problems.[20] Postoperative nausea and vomiting probably are due to a variety of factors which stimulate both the CTZ and peripheral receptors in the gastrointestinal tract. Some characteristics of individual patients might influence the incidence of postoperative emesis (e.g., predisposition, sex, age, weight, concurrent illness). Factors directly associated with anesthesia may influence emesis (e.g., anesthetic agent, duration of exposure to the anesthetics, preoperative medications, anatomical site of surgery, amount of GI distension secondary to ventilation procedures, and type of anesthesia).

Persistent vomiting is also common during the first 14 to 16 weeks of pregnancy. Although the mechanism is unknown, various hormonal and psychogenic theories have been proposed. However, studies generally have failed to find any significant correlation between the onset of nausea and vomiting and blood levels of human chorionic gonadotropin, adrenocorticotropic hormone (ACTH), cortisol, 1-hydroxyprogesterone, luteinizing hormone (LH), follicle stimulating hormone (FSH), thyroid-stimulating hormone (TSH), growth hormone, and prolactin.[21-23]

The diagnosis of psychogenic vomiting should be considered only after other causes have been excluded. It may be a conscious and voluntary act, as it is in patients with bulimia who vomit in part to control their weight, or at a more subconscious level in otherwise healthy persons as a part of a strong emotional reaction. (See Chapter 80: Eating Disorders.) Psychogenic vomiting is more common in women than men.[5]

Complications

Serious medical complications secondary to severe and/or protracted nausea and vomiting include dehydration, malnutrition, and

Table 105.1	Causes of Nausea and Vomiting
Acute Onset of Symptoms	**Chronic Symptoms**
Gastroenteritis	*Motility Disorders*
Viral or bacterial	Gastroparesis
	Irritable bowel syndrome
Drugs	
Cancer chemotherapeutic agents	*Mechanical Obstruction*
Opioids	Peptic ulcer disease
Theophylline	Gastric ulcer
Digoxin	Gastric carcinoma
Antibiotics	Pancreatic carcinoma
Anticholinergics	Pancreatic pseudocyst
	Miscellaneous
Metabolic and Endocrine	Pregnancy
Disturbances	↑ intracranial pressure
Uremia	
Diabetic ketoacidosis	*Psychogenic*
Adrenal insufficiency	Bulimia
Hyperparathyroidism	Anorexia nervosa
	Rumination
Visceral Pain	
Myocardial infarction	
Renal, biliary, or small bowel colic	
Viral Hepatitis	
Vestibular Disorders	
Motion sickness	
Otitis interna	
Meniere's syndrome	
Migraine Headache	

metabolic disturbances. Anorexia and malnutrition may complicate the course of patients with cancer or obstruction, making them unable to tolerate aggressive therapy such as chemotherapy or surgery. Major metabolic disturbances resulting from vomiting include metabolic alkalosis, hyponatremia, hypochloremia, and hypokalemia. Dehydration and renal failure may further complicate the metabolic disturbances. Dehydration is the result of both gastric and renal losses as well as impaired oral intake. In severe cases, repletion of extracellular fluid volume and correction of electrolyte deficiencies may necessitate intravenous therapy.

Repeated vomiting or retching may be complicated by tears of the gastroesophageal junction (Mallory-Weiss syndrome) or in pathological bone fractures. Wound disruption may be precipitated if forceful vomiting follows soon after abdominal surgery.

Compliance with further treatment may become a significant factor in patients experiencing severe nausea and vomiting following cancer chemotherapy. In some instances, patients actually have declined potentially curative therapy.[24]

Aspiration pneumonias are most likely to occur during vomiting in patients with depressed levels of consciousness. Aspiration of gastric acid may produce a chemical pneumonitis which can be life-threatening.

Management

Assessment

Therapeutic efforts in the management of nausea and vomiting always should be directed at the underlying pathophysiological process. In situations where the nature of the underlying process is not readily apparent, a careful history and physical examination often may point to the correct diagnosis, avoiding the need for an in-depth evaluation of the GI tract. The history should include detailed characteristics of the symptoms including descriptions of the vomitus (e.g., presence of undigested food, blood, or bile), its volume, and the timing of vomiting in relationship to meals. The physical examination should include a neurologic assessment with attention to cranial nerves, vestibular and pupillary function, peripheral neuropathy, and extrapyramidal signs. Other tests that may be necessary in the diagnosis of unexplained vomiting include routine serum chemistries, drug screening, hormone levels, abdominal x-rays and computed tomography (CT) scans, upper gastrointestinal tract endoscopy, gastric emptying test, esophageal monography, and formal psychiatric assessment.[3]

Antiemetics

Palliation of the nausea and vomiting may be achieved with the use of antiemetic drugs. Unfortunately, many traditionally recommended antiemetic regimens are less than optimal in terms of both efficacy and incidence of side effects. Renewed interest in the management of nausea and vomiting and an increased level of understanding of the pathways of emetogenic stimuli have led to a proliferation of antiemetic drug trials and improvements in the overall management. This is especially true in the management of cancer chemotherapy-induced nausea and vomiting.

Antiemetics generally are classified either according to pharmacological class or by their proposed site of action (see Table 105.2). Phenothiazines and butyrophenones block dopamine receptors and are believed to act at the CTZ. Since these agents only partially block the CTZ, they are not completely effective. Halogenation of the R_1 side chain of the phenothiazines, thiethylperazine (Torecan) or prochlorperazine (Compazine), increases antiemetic activity and the frequency of extrapyramidal side effects, but decreases the incidence of sedation and hypotension.[2,27]

Antihistamines and anticholinergics are effective in managing vomiting associated with vestibular disturbances by blocking ace-

Table 105.2		Available Antiemetic Agents[a,25,26]	
Drug	Type of Emesis Used For	Available Dosage Forms	Recommended Dosage Regimen
Antihistamines			
Buclizine (Bucladin-S)	Motion sickness	Tab 50 mg	*Adults*: 50 mg PO 30 min before exposure and Q 4–6 hr
Cyclizine (Marezine)	Motion sickness	Tab 50 mg; Inj 50 mg/mL	*Adults*: 50 mg PO or IM 30 min before exposure and Q 4–6 hr (*max*: 200 mg/day)
			Children: 25 mg PO 30 min before exposure and Q 4–6 hr (*max*: 75 mg/day)
Dimenhydrinate (Dramamine, Dimetabs, Trav-Arex, Dimatē, Dramilin)	Motion sickness	Tab 50 mg; oral solution 15 mg/mL; Inj 50 mg/mL	*Adults*: 50–100 mg PO, IM or IV 30 min before exposure and Q 4 hr
			Children: 1.25 mg/kg PO or IM Q 4–6 hr (*max*: 300 mg/day)
Meclizine (Antivert Bonine)	Motion Sickness	Tab 12.5, 25, 50 mg	*Adults*: 25–50 mg PO 1 hr before exposure and Q 4–6 hr
Anticholinergics			
Scopolamine (Transderm-Scop)	Motion sickness, postoperative	Transdermal system 0.5 mg/72 hr; Inj 0.3, 0.4, 1 mg/mL	*Adults*: Apply 4 hr before exposure and Q 72 hr; preoperative 0.2–1 mg IM, IV, OR SQ
Butyrophenones			
Haloperidol (Haldol)	Chemotherapy, postoperative	Tab 0.5, 1, 2, 5, 10, 25 mg; oral solution 2 mg/mL; Inj 5 mg/mL	*Adults*: 1–2 mg PO or IM Q 8 hr
Droperidol (Inapsine)	Chemotherapy, postoperative	Inj 2.5 mg/mL	*Adults*: 0.5–1 mg IV Q 4 hr
Dopamine Antagonist			
Metoclopramide (Reglan)	Chemotherapy, gastric stasis	Tab 10 mg; oral solution 5 mg/mL; Inj 5 mg/mL	*Adults*: Chemotherapy: 1–2 mg/kg IV or PO 30–60 min before exposure and Q 2–3 hr (*max*: 12 mg/kg)
			Stasis: 10 mg PO, IM, or IV 30 min before meals and HS
Cannabinoid			
Dronabinol (Marinol)	Chemotherapy	Cap 2.5, 5, 10 mg	*Adults*: 5 mg/m² 1–3 hr before and Q 2–4 hr. May ↑ dose by 2.5 mg/m² to max of 15 mg/m²/dose
Nabilone (Cesamet)	Chemotherapy	Cap 1 mg	*Adults*: 1 or 2 mg PO Q 8 or 12 hr. Give 1st dose before chemotherapy
Phenothiazines			
Prochlorperazine (Compazine)	Chemotherapy, postoperative, general	Tab 5, 10, 25 mg; rectal suppository 2.5, 5, 25 mg; oral solution 5 mg/5 mL; Inj 5 mg/mL; extended release Cap 10, 15, 30 mg	*Adults*: 5–10 mg PO, IM or IV Q 6–8 hr
Promethazine (Phenergan, Anergan)	Postoperative, motion sickness	Tab 12.5, 25, 50 mg; oral solution 6.25, 25 mg/5 mL; Inj 25, 50 mg/mL; rectal suppository 12.55, 25, 50 mg	*Adults*: 25 mg PO or IM 30–60 min before exposure and Q 8–12 hr
			Children: 0.5 mg/kg PO 30–60 min before exposure and Q 8–12 hr
Thiethylperazine (Torecan)	Chemotherapy, postoperative, general	Tab 10 mg; rectal suppository 10 mg; Inj 5 mg/mL	*Adults*: 10 mg PO, IM, or PR Q 8 hr
Chlorpromazine (Thorazine)	Postoperative	Tab 10, 25, 50 mg; oral solution 10 mg/5 mL, 30, 100 mg/mL; Inj 25 mg/mL	*Adults*: 12.5–25 mg PO or IM Q 4–6 hr
			Children: 0.275–0.55 mg PO or IM Q 4–6 hr
Corticosteroids			
Dexamethasone (Decadron, Hexadrol, Dexone)	Chemotherapy	Tab 0.25, 0.5, 0.75, 1, 1.5, 2, 4, 6, mg; Inj 4 mg/mL	*Adults*: 10–20 mg PO or IV before chemotherapy
Serotonin Antagonists			
Granisetron (Kytril)	Chemotherapy	Inj 1 mg/mL	*Adults and Children >2 yr*: 10 µg/kg 30 min before chemotherapy
		Tab 1 mg	*Adults*: 1 mg Q 12 hr × 2 doses
Ondansetron (Zofran)	Chemotherapy	Inj 2 mg/mL	*Adults and Children >4 yr*: 0.15 mg/kg 30 min before chemotherapy and then 4 and 8 hr
			Adults: 32 mg before chemotherapy
		Tab 4, 8 mg	*Adults and Children >12*: 8 mg TID
			Children 4–14 yr: 4 mg TID
	Postoperative	Inj 2 mg/mL	*Adults*: 4 mg IV immediately before induction or postoperatively if symptoms occur
	Radiation	Tab 4, 8 mg	*Adults*: 8 mg TID
Miscellaneous			
Benzquinamide (Emete-Con)	Postoperative	Inj 25 mg/mL	*Adults*: 0.5–1 mg/kg IM Q 3–4 hr
Trimethobenzamide (Tigan)	General	Cap 100, 250 mg; Inj 100 mg/mL; rectal suppository 100, 200 mg	*Adults*: 250 mg PO Q 6–8 hr or 200 mg PR or IM Q 6–8 hr

[a] Cap = Capsule; HS = At bedtime; IM = Intramuscular; Inj = Injection; IV = Intravenous; PO = Oral; PR = Per rectum; Tab = Tablet.

tylcholine receptors in the vestibular center.[28] Metoclopramide (Reglan) is a dopamine antagonist which has both peripheral and central antiemetic actions. This agent accelerates gastric emptying, inhibits gastric relaxation, and appears to block the CTZ.[2] Ondansetron is a highly selective and potent antagonist of the 5-HT$_3$ receptors in the vagus or CTZ.[11]

Cannabinoids also have been used in the control of chemotherapy-induced vomiting. They are believed to inhibit emesis by blocking descending impulses from the cerebral cortex.[2]

The corticosteroids, dexamethasone and methylprednisolone, have demonstrated antiemetic activity in patients receiving cancer chemotherapy. Their mechanism of antiemetic effect is unknown; however, inhibition of prostaglandin synthesis or feedback inhibition may be involved.[29,30] The corticosteroids' ability to increase appetite and increase mood or sense of well-being also may contribute to their antiemetic effects.[31]

Specific Management

Gastroenteritis. The nausea and vomiting which accompany gastroenteritis are often refractory to drug therapy;[32] however, dietary manipulations may be helpful in alleviating some symptoms. In severe cases a trial of antiemetic agents may be warranted. Parental education is of major importance in the appropriate management of pediatric nausea and vomiting.[33] More than 700 children die annually in the U.S. from dehydration caused by acute gastroenteritis, and many more are hospitalized.[34] Parents should be made aware of the signs and symptoms of dehydration; no urination for 12 hours, dark circles under the eyes, weakness, a sticky mouth, thirst, and in infants, a sunken fontanel. Treatment of an infant or child with acute onset of vomiting consists of providing energy, water, and minerals in a clear liquid. Vomiting secondary to gastroenteritis usually subsides within 24 to 48 hours. Parents should be educated to seek medical attention if any of the following signs or symptoms occur along with vomiting: fever, severe headache, head injury, abdominal distension, abdominal pain, change in alertness or behavior, coughing or choking, toxic ingestion, or dehydration.

Mechanical Obstruction. Vomiting secondary to mechanical obstruction is relieved by management of the underlying process. Patients with active duodenal or gastric ulcer should initially be managed with intensive medical therapy including aggressive nasogastric suctioning, H$_2$-receptor antagonist or sucralfate therapy, rehydration, and total parenteral nutrition, if warranted. Patients who do not respond to an extended trial may require surgery, as do patients with obstruction secondary to tumor or chronic peptic ulcer disease.[5] Treatment of delayed gastric emptying without mechanical obstruction revolves around the use of "prokinetic" agents such as metoclopramide or bethanechol (Urecholine).

Motion Sickness. Antimotion sickness therapy may protect a high percentage of individuals from this unpleasant experience if the drug is given in sufficient dosages beginning one to two hours before an exposure and appropriately maintained throughout the duration of exposure.[28] Individuals differ in their susceptibility to motion sickness and their response to therapy; thus, therapy must be individualized. Antihistamines are generally the agents of choice for the mild to moderate stresses encountered in automobile, air, and moderate sea travel. Scopolamine, an anticholinergic agent, may be more efficacious in more stressful conditions (e.g., rough seas) or in individuals who are more prone to motion sickness.[28]

Pregnancy. The best treatment for nausea and vomiting associated with pregnancy is simple assurance. However, severe, protracted vomiting resulting in fluid and electrolyte disturbances (hy-

peremesis gravidarum) which affects approximately 2.5 of 1000 pregnancies may require intravenous fluid support.[5]

Cancer Chemotherapy. Nausea and vomiting are serious and occasionally limiting side effects of cancer chemotherapy. Standard antiemetics have proven to be of only marginal value and the use of more aggressive chemotherapeutic regimens has compounded the problem. Historically, chemotherapy-induced nausea and vomiting have been managed primarily with single agent therapy (i.e., phenothiazines and related compounds). Although such agents have demonstrated antiemetic activity superior to placebo, the outcome is frequently less than optimal, especially in patients receiving potent emetogenic chemotherapeutic agents such as cisplatin, doxorubicin, and dacarbazine.[27,35-37] It previously was proposed that most chemotherapeutic agents exert their emetogenic activity by stimulating the CTZ. However, the ineffectiveness of antiemetic agents that exert their effect on the CTZ has led to the theory that chemotherapy-induced emesis may be mediated through multiple sites. Consequently, combinations of antiemetic agents have evolved.[38] These regimens have included combinations of the following agents: metoclopramide, corticosteroids, phenothiazines, antihistamines, serotonin antagonists, and benzodiazepines. Antiemetic trials also have examined the dose-response relationship of several of these agents. In cisplatin-induced vomiting, metoclopramide has demonstrated a significant dose-response relationship. Attention also has been focused on the occurrence of nausea and vomiting in anticipation of therapy.[39,40]

Chemotherapy-Associated Nausea and Vomiting

Treatment

First-Line Antiemetics

1. A.H., a 63-year-old male who has smoked an average of 2 packs of cigarettes daily for the past 40 years, recently was found to have extensive small cell lung cancer. Initial staging procedures documented a 2 × 5 cm lesion in the periphery of the right middle lobe and metastatic involvement of the liver; however, bone marrow biopsy, bone scan, and CT scan of the brain were all negative. A.H. will receive combination chemotherapy with cisplatin (Platinol), doxorubicin (Adriamycin), cyclophosphamide (Cytoxan), and etoposide (VePesid) every 21 days. He is very anxious because he has heard that chemotherapy may cause severe nausea and vomiting. A.H. currently is hospitalized and about to begin chemotherapy. What would be an appropriate antiemetic regimen in view of A.H.'s anxiety and the chemotherapy regimen he will receive?

Several different emetic problems may be observed in patients such as A.H. who are receiving highly emetogenic cancer chemotherapy. The successful management of chemotherapy-associated nausea and vomiting is dependent, to a great extent, upon the recognition of and the individualized approach to each of these distinct problems. The most common emetic problem is that of *acute* chemotherapy-induced *nausea and vomiting* which usually occurs between one and two hours after chemotherapy administration. The potential of chemotherapeutic agents to cause nausea and vomiting differs greatly among agents (see Table 105.3), patients, and even treatment courses in the same patient. The dose and route of administration also can affect the incidence of nausea and vomiting. *Anticipatory emesis*, which is nausea and/or vomiting starting before the administration of chemotherapy, is a significant problem, especially in patients with previous inadequate antiemetic control or in patients receiving highly emetogenic regimens. The effect also may be observed in previously untreated patients as a result of adverse media exposure. The hospital or clinic environment or other treatment-related associations may trigger this re-

Table 105.3	Classification of Chemotherapeutic Agent Emetogenicity[a]	
Highly Emetogenic		
Cisplatin	≥ 70 mg/m^2	
Cytarabine	>1 gm/m^2	
Cyclophosphamide	≥ 1000 mg/m^2	
Dacarbazine	≥ 500 mg/m^2	
Carmustine	≥ 200 mg/m^2	
Streptozocin		
Mechlorethamine		
Dactinomycin		
Moderately High		
Carboplatin	200–400 mg/m^2	
Cisplatin	20–69 mg/m^2	
Dacarbazine	<500 mg/m^2	
Cyclophosphamide	600–999 mg/m^2	
Cytarabine	250 mg–1 gm/m^2	
Carmustine	<200 mg/m^2	
Doxorubicin	≥ 75 mg/m^2	
Methotrexate	≥ 250 mg/m^2	
Combination Therapy		
Cyclophosphamide	400–599 mg/m^2	
Doxorubicin	≥ 40 mg/m^2	
Moderately Emetogenic		
Methotrexate	100–250 mg/m^2	
Mitomycin C	≥ 8 mg/m^2	
Cyclophosphamide	<600 mg/m^2	
Doxorubicin	20–75 mg/m^2	
Combination Therapy		
Cyclophosphamide	100 mg/m^2 PO	
Methotrexate	40–60 mg/m^2 IV	
5-Fluorouracil	600–700 mg/m^2 IV	

[a] Adapted from reference 112.

sponse. Although most episodes of acute chemotherapy-induced emesis resolve or are controlled within 24 hours, some patients may experience persistent or delayed nausea and vomiting. In some cases, symptoms may persist for several days (in rare cases several weeks). The causes of this phenomenon are unclear; however, it is believed that metabolites of chemotherapeutic agents or associations similar to those observed with anticipatory emesis may be involved.[41] It is also important to consider that causes other than the chemotherapy may be responsible for the symptoms. A particularly protracted duration of vomiting following a course of chemotherapy should suggest the possibility of causes such as other medications which the patient may be receiving or the tumor itself.

The design of a comprehensive antiemetic regimen must consider each of these types of emetic problems. Although several antiemetic agents are superior to placebo in the control of chemotherapy-induced emesis (see Table 105.4), the results of single-agent antiemetic therapy in this setting have been far from optimal. As a result, combinations of antiemetic agents now are being used. This approach may be justified since most patients experience multiple emetic stimuli and receive multiple chemotherapeutic agents which may exert emetogenic activity through different mechanisms. In general, antiemetic combinations have been superior to single agents. Furthermore, anxiety now is recognized as a significant component in chemotherapy-associated nausea and vomiting, and an anti-anxiety agent may be added to the combination of antiemetic drugs. A.H.'s chemotherapy regimen contains three highly emetogenic agents (cisplatin, doxorubicin, and cyclophosphamide) and he also appears to be anxious regarding the prospect of receiving chemotherapy. Therefore, A.H. is at a very high risk of experiencing severe nausea and vomiting.

For maximum protection against these unpleasant side effects, A.H. should receive combination antiemetic therapy before the ad-

ministration of his chemotherapy. Antiemetic therapy generally is considered to be most effective when used prophylactically and least effective in controlling symptoms that have already become severe.

Metoclopramide (Reglan), ondansetron (Zofran), dexamethasone (Decadron), lorazepam (Ativan), prochlorperazine (Compazine), and thiethylperazine (Torecan) have been among the most widely used antiemetic agents in this setting. These agents and others have been evaluated in a variety of combinations. Ideally, agents included in combinations should exert different mechanisms of activity and not have overlapping toxicities.[38]

Serotonin Antagonists. Over the last few years, several serotonin antagonists have been studied extensively in the management of chemotherapy-associated emesis.[11,14,59–66,94–100] Ondansetron was the first of these agents available and is superior to placebo and metoclopramide (as a single agent) in controlling cisplatin-induced emesis.[14,59,94,95] Side effects following ondansetron have been mild to moderate and include headache, sedation, and transient elevations of liver function enzymes.[14,59–61] Like metoclopramide, ondansetron has been studied using both continuous infusion and intermittent schedules.[14,59–61,94–100] The manufacturer's original recommended dose was 0.15 mg/kg IV given 30 minutes before and then at four and eight hours after chemotherapy. More recently, a single 32 mg IV dose of ondansetron before chemotherapy has been added to official product information.[76] The dose response relationship of ondansetron is not well defined and lower doses of ondansetron have been reported to have equal efficacy to the 32 mg dose by some investigators,[77] but not others.[78] Ondansetron also is available in 4 and 8 mg tablets. Although one of the intravenous regimens of ondansetron recommends its administration before the administration of emetogenic chemotherapy, oral tablets may be used for two to three days following chemotherapy or in patients receiving external beam radiation therapy. The efficacy of the oral tablets in delayed chemotherapy-induced emesis has been challenged.[79] Although controlled clinical trials demonstrate benefits over placebo, ondansetron appears to be less effective than metoclopramide or dexamethasone.[103]

Granisetron is the newest serotonin antagonist available for the prevention of chemotherapy-induced emesis. The manufacturer's recommended dose of granisetron is 10 µg/kg administered intravenously 30 minutes before chemotherapy administration.[104] Alternatively, an oral dosing product has been marketed. Although unpublished at the time of writing, manufacturer's data demonstrate that 1 mg oral granisetron every 12 hours has efficacy equivalent to the intravenous product. Another unpublished study in-

Table 105.4	Agents with Demonstrated Antiemetic Activity Superior to Placebo in Chemotherapy-Associated Nausea and Vomiting	
Agent	Dose	Route
Metoclopramide[42,43]	1–2 mg/kg	IV
Ondansetron[a,14]	0.15 mg/kg	IV
Dronabinol[44–46]	7–10 mg/m^2	PO
	15 mg	PO
Granisetron[104]	10 µg/kg	IV
	1 mg BID	PO
	2 mg QD	PO
Dexamethasone[47,48]	10 mg	IV
Prochlorperazine[45,46,49]	10 mg	PO

[a] Single agent activity against cisplatin emesis.

dicates that 2 mg of oral granisetron before chemotherapy is equivalent to 1 mg every 12 hours on the day of chemotherapy. Unlike ondansetron, granisetron is not marketed or recommended for the treatment of delayed chemotherapy-induced emesis. Randomized controlled trials suggest that ondansetron and granisetron are equivalent in the prevention of chemotherapy-induced emesis.[105,106] However, therapeutic equivalence is hard to demonstrate due to the lack of large, well-controlled comparative trials which employ manufacturer's recommended dosage regimens. Ondansetron and granisetron are expensive products and impact significantly on institutional drug budgets. Therefore, formulary decisions often are based upon cost and usage patterns in the institution.

A number of studies have demonstrated the superiority of the combination of ondansetron or granisetron with dexamethasone in acute chemotherapy-induced emesis.[107] Complete response rates increase approximately 15% when dexamethasone is added to a serotonin antagonist. Currently, the combination of a serotonin antagonist with dexamethasone is considered the antiemetic regimen of choice in patients receiving moderate to highly emetogenic chemotherapy.

Metoclopramide. When given in high intravenous doses, metoclopramide generally has been shown to be superior, or at least equivalent, to most other antiemetic agents against cisplatin-induced emesis with the exception of serotonin antagonists.[42,43] (Cisplatin generally is considered to be the most emetogenic; therefore, most antiemetic regimens are evaluated based upon their activity against cisplatin-induced emesis.) The antiemetic activity of metoclopramide is dependent upon both the dose and the schedule of administration. The current dosage recommendation for intravenous metoclopramide is 1 to 2 mg/kg in a 15 minute infusion given every two hours for three to five doses.[41] The first dose should be given 30 minutes before chemotherapy. Metoclopramide also has been evaluated using continuous infusion schedules of a 2 to 3 mg/kg loading dose followed by an infusion of 0.5 mg/kg/hour for 8 to 12 hours. Results of controlled trials comparing infusion to intermittent dosing suggest the two methods of administration are equivalent in terms of efficacy and toxicity.[54-56] Extrapyramidal or acute dystonic reactions have been associated with metoclopramide, but may be prevented or reversed with diphenhydramine (Benadryl).[57] Diphenhydramine also may improve antiemetic control through its blockade of histamine receptors in the brain stem.[58]

Dexamethasone and Methylprednisolone. The corticosteroids, dexamethasone (Decadron) and methylprednisolone (Medrol), also have antiemetic activity.[29,47,48,50] Clinical trials have administered single doses (dexamethasone 4 to 20 mg) before chemotherapy or have continued doses every four to six hours for one to two days.[41] Toxicity with these short-course regimens has been mild (euphoria, insomnia, mild fluid retention). Therefore, dexamethasone is a good choice for inclusion in a combination regimen. In women with breast cancer receiving cyclophosphamide, methotrexate, and fluorouracil, dexamethasone 10 mg IV before chemotherapy was superior to placebo; 83% of patients who received dexamethasone did not experience GI side effects versus 57% of women who received placebo.[47] When dexamethasone and metoclopramide or a serotonin antagonist[106] are used in combination,[50] antiemetic control is improved and side effects are reduced.

Lorazepam. The benzodiazepine, lorazepam (Ativan), as a single agent has limited antiemetic effects; however, it is useful as an adjunct to other antiemetics.[52,67,68] The benzodiazepines, such as lorazepam, produce sedation and amnesia in addition to their anxiolytic activity which may make the unpleasant experience of receiving chemotherapy more tolerable for many patients. Dosages of lorazepam used in this setting are generally 1 to 2 mg intrave-

nously or orally given every four to six hours. In a double-blind, randomized trial, Kris et al. reported that the combination of metoclopramide, dexamethasone, and lorazepam was equivalent to the metoclopramide, dexamethasone, diphenhydramine regimen in controlling cisplatin-induced emesis. Interestingly, only 3% of patients receiving lorazepam experienced akathisia or acute dystonic reactions, as opposed to 21% of patients given diphenhydramine. Patients receiving lorazepam also reported less anxiety.[51] The use of both lorazepam and diphenhydramine may produce excessive sedation.

A reasonable initial antiemetic regimen for A.H. would include:

- Ondansetron 32 mg IV or granisetron 10 mg/kg IV, 30 minutes before administration of chemotherapy;
- Dexamethasone 20 mg IV before chemotherapy; plus or minus
- Lorazepam 1 mg IV before first dose of chemotherapy.

Alternatively, metoclopramide 2 mg/kg IV, 30 minutes before the administration of chemotherapeutic drugs with the dose repeated at two, four, and six hours after A.H. has received his chemotherapy treatment may be employed. Dexamethasone 20 mg IV should be administered before chemotherapy. Either diphenhydramine 50 mg IV before the first and third dose of metoclopramide or lorazepam, 1 mg IV before chemotherapy and every four hours thereafter as needed, may be added to the metoclopramide regimen to decrease the likelihood of the dystonic reaction.

General Management

2. What nonpharmacologic measures also may aid in the control of A.H.'s nausea and vomiting?

A.H. should not eat food and should restrict his intake to only liquids for several hours preceding chemotherapy. For several days following chemotherapy, he should eat small, light meals and maintain a bland diet, avoiding greasy, spicy, and sweet foods. If unable to tolerate solid foods, he should avoid them (ice chips and small sips of clear liquids may be tolerated) and advance his diet as he becomes more comfortable. A.H.'s hydrational status should be monitored closely until he is able to maintain an adequate oral intake. In general, he should avoid other unpleasant environmental stimuli such as stressful encounters and disturbing odors or sights. Restriction of activity to bed and chair rest (avoiding vestibular disturbances) also may be helpful in minimizing nausea and vomiting. Relaxation techniques, desensitization, and hypnosis also have been suggested in such situations.[69]

Second-Line Antiemetics

3. If the recommended antiemetic regimen is not sufficient to control A.H.'s nausea and vomiting, what are some possible alternative antiemetic agents?

Other antiemetic agents which are effective in chemotherapy-associated nausea and vomiting could be administered to A.H. if he fails to respond adequately to the prescribed regimen. For example, the phenothiazines such as prochlorperazine (Compazine) and thiethylperazine (Torecan), the butyrophenones such as haloperidol (Haldol) and droperidol (Inapsine), and the cannabinoid, dronabinol (Marinol), are useful alternatives. Although these agents have shown some activity, they generally are considered inferior to high-dose intravenous metoclopramide. Nevertheless, these agents may be useful as second-line therapy.

Prochlorperazine has been the most frequently used phenothiazine for nausea and vomiting and is available in a variety of dosage forms (oral, parenteral, and rectal).

Although clinical trials have shown prochlorperazine to be inferior to dronabinol and high-dose metoclopramide, preliminary trials have reported improved antiemetic activity with large doses (up to 40 mg) of intravenous prochlorperazine.[70,71]

Haloperidol. Intravenous haloperidol (3 mg IV Q 2 hr for 5 doses) and continuous infusion droperidol (1 to 1.5 mg/hour) also are effective against cisplatin-induced emesis.[72,73] Toxic effects (e.g., sedation, extrapyramidal effects) of these agents have been mild and similar to those that occur with the phenothiazines.

Dronabinol or alpha-9-tetrahydrocannabinol also has useful antiemetic activity. Clinical trials have reported dronabinol to be superior to placebo and equivalent or superior to oral prochlorperazine.[44,45] Doses of oral dronabinol are usually 5 to 10 mg/m² body surface area every three to four hours, with the first dose administered one to three hours before chemotherapy. The side effects of dronabinol, including sedation, a ''high,'' dizziness, ataxia, and orthostatic hypotension, have made it unacceptable in some older patients.[74] Dronabinol is recommended for use in patients who are refractory to standard antiemetics.

Oral Antiemetics

4. A.H. experienced moderate to severe nausea for the first 10 to 12 hours following chemotherapy and experienced actual retching and vomiting only twice during this period. Although he is unable to tolerate adequate amount of liquids 24 hours after chemotherapy, he still becomes nauseated at the sight of food. He is otherwise ready for discharge from the hospital. What therapeutic interventions might be useful in this situation?

Many patients experience prolonged nausea and/or vomiting following chemotherapy. Although parenteral antiemetics were needed to manage severe nausea and vomiting immediately following chemotherapy, oral antiemetics can be used in A.H. when symptoms are less intense. In A.H.'s case, the nausea seems to be stimulated by the sight and/or smell of food. The combination of metoclopramide 0.5 mg/kg orally four times a day plus dexamethasone 8 mg twice a day for two days, then 4 mg orally twice a day for two days can be used to control delayed emesis.[75] Oral lorazepam or oral or rectal prochlorperazine also may be effective in this situation. Serotonin antagonists have minimal activity in delayed emesis.

Outpatient Therapy

5. A.H. tolerated his first course of chemotherapy reasonably well and because he would prefer to be at home as much as possible, his oncologist would like to administer his second course of chemotherapy in the outpatient clinic. What antiemetic regimen would be acceptable for use in the outpatient clinic and what special instructions should A.H. and his family receive?

Parenteral Antiemetics. A.H. is receiving cisplatin in his chemotherapy regimen, therefore, he will require intense hydration both before and after his therapy. While A.H. is in the outpatient clinic, antiemetics can be administered parenterally. One regimen which was designed for outpatient management of cisplatin-induced nausea and vomiting consists of metoclopramide 3 mg/kg IV, dexamethasone 20 mg IV, and diphenhydramine 50 mg IV, all to be administered 30 minutes before therapy.[50] The metoclopramide is to be repeated 1.5 hours after the administration of chemotherapy drugs.

Following completion of his postchemotherapy hydration and second metoclopramide dose, A.H. may be discharged from the outpatient clinic when his condition is stable. Prescriptions for oral antiemetics such as metoclopramide 1 mg/kg orally every four hours and lorazepam 1 to 2 mg orally every four hours as needed were given to A.H.

Patient Education. A.H. and his wife should be instructed that he should follow the same dietary guidelines that he was given during his previous hospitalization and that he must maintain an adequate oral intake of liquids during this postchemotherapy period. If he is unable to maintain an oral intake to compensate for his emetic and urinary losses, or if he experiences symptoms of dehydration (e.g., postural hypotension, dry mucous membranes), A.H. should return to the outpatient clinic for evaluation.

Brain Metastases

6. Approximately 2 weeks after receiving his third course of chemotherapy, A.H.'s wife telephoned his oncologist to report that A.H. had been experiencing severe vomiting and slurred speech for about 3 hours. How should these symptoms in A.H. be managed?

Although nausea may persist for days following chemotherapy, it is unlikely that vomiting this severe would recur two weeks after chemotherapy. A patient with lung cancer who develops and CNS symptoms or signs of increased intracranial pressure should be evaluated immediately for evidence of brain metastases. (Lung cancer is the leading type of primary tumor associated with brain metastases.)

Upon arrival at the hospital, both A.H. and his wife denied that he had been taking any medications since his last course of chemotherapy except for occasional acetaminophen for his headaches. Computed tomography scan of A.H.'s head revealed three metastatic lesions which were believed to be causing increased intracranial pressure.

Corticosteroids and whole brain radiation are the principal treatment measures in most patients with brain metastases. For acute management of increased intracranial pressure, A.H. should receive dexamethasone 8 mg IV followed by 4 mg orally every six hours. Corticosteroids effectively reduce the edema associated with brain metastases and symptoms usually are relieved within several hours. Radiation therapy should be initiated as soon as possible and A.H. should receive 2000 to 3000 rad over two weeks. (Also see Chapter 90: Neoplastic Disorders and Their Treatment: General Principles.)

Motion Sickness

7. M.J. has experienced severe motion sickness whenever she has traveled by air or sea. In the past she has taken dimenhydrinate (Dramamine) or meclizine (Antivert) when symptoms have occurred; neither of these agents has afforded her much relief. M.J. has just won a Caribbean cruise for two (nontransferable) in a sweepstakes, but is considering forfeiting her prize unless her physician can offer her another alternative. What would be an effective treatment for M.J.?

Effective drugs in the management of motion sickness have strong CNS anticholinergic effects and act upon the receptors in the vomiting center and areas related to the vestibular system. Agents such as the phenothiazines exert their antiemetic activity primarily on the dopamine receptors of the chemoreceptor trigger zone and are ineffective against motion sickness. The possible exception is promethazine (Phenergan), a phenothiazine which is an effective antihistamine and reported to have strong central anticholinergic actions. The belladonna alkaloid, scopolamine, and antihistamines, such as dimenhydrinate, meclizine, and cyclizine (Marezine), exert central anticholinergic activity and generally are considered the most effective agents against motion sickness. While the antihistamines are useful in mild to moderate motion sickness, they are less effective in severe cases or in patients who are highly susceptible to motion sickness. Scopolamine is the most effective drug against motion sickness, however, toxicity following oral or parenteral administration has limited its usefulness by these routes.[28,80] Although the antiemetic effects of scopolamine may be maintained and the side effects diminished with smaller doses, the duration of action at these lower doses is relatively short.[28,81] Transdermal scopolamine (Transderm-Scop), however, alleviates these problems by allowing a constant delivery of drug to maintain a safe and effective blood level over a prolonged period of time. When applied to hairless, intact skin in the postauricular area, this transdermal patch delivers a priming dose of approximately 140 µg of scopolamine during the first few hours and 5 µg/hour for the remainder of the system's 72 hour lifetime.[80] In clinical trials, transdermal scopolamine has been superior to oral dimenhydrate or placebo in the control of motion-induced nausea and vomiting.[82,83] Side effects of the transdermal scopolamine system are minimal and generally limited to dry mouth, drowsiness, and blurred vision.

Because of M.J.'s history of susceptibility to motion sickness, her physician prescribed transdermal scopolamine with the instructions that she should apply the first patch two to three hours before her scheduled departure and replace it with a new patch every three days during her cruise. In addition, M.J. also should be advised to avoid alcohol and overindulgence of food for 24 hours before, and throughout, the duration of her trip. These factors are believed to predispose individuals to nausea and have an additive effect with the vestibular stimuli.[28]

Pediatric Cancer Chemotherapy

8. R.R., a 7-year-old male with stage III orbital rhabdomyosarcoma, will receive adjuvant chemotherapy with vincristine, dactinomycin, and cyclophosphamide subsequent to radiation therapy. What type of antiemetic therapy is recommended for pediatric patients?

Chemotherapy-associated nausea and vomiting pose significant management problems in pediatric oncology. Premature termination of chemotherapy secondary to severe nausea and vomiting has been reported in pediatric patient populations.[85] Although the selection of antiemetic regimens in children often is influenced by the result of adult trials, pediatric oncologists are at a disadvantage because few such trials have been completed in children and the validity of extrapolating the results from adult trials to children has not been tested. Pediatric chemotherapy-induced nausea and vomiting may differ significantly in the emetogenic potential of various antineoplastic agents, the chemotherapy regimens commonly utilized, the influence of behavioral factors, and the toxicities of various antiemetic agents.

The antiemetic efficacy and dose-related toxicities of the most commonly used antiemetic agents have not been objectively evaluated in children. A high incidence of extrapyramidal reactions (88%) to metoclopramide has been noted in children using recommended doses, however, when diphenhydramine was administered concomitantly, the incidence of these extrapyramidal reactions decreased.[86-88] Allen et al. reported a 14% incidence of neurological toxicity during the first 24 hours with an antiemetic regimen consisting of metoclopramide 2 mg/kg IV every two hours for four doses and diphenhydramine 0.5 mg/kg IV every four hours for two doses. Children who received two consecutive days of therapy experienced a higher frequency (43%) of extrapyramidal reactions.[87] Although the antiemetic effects of metoclopramide were not compared to other antiemetic therapy in this trial, the authors felt that the efficacy in children was very similar to that observed in adults. However, another randomized trial found chlorpromazine 0.5 mg/kg to be significantly more effective than metoclopramide. Extrapyramidal reactions were more common in the metoclopramide group; however, chlorpromazine produced more somnolence.[89]

Other phenothiazines also are widely prescribed antiemetics in children receiving chemotherapy although their efficacy is frequently less than optimal and the incidence of side effects is significant. Oral or rectal prochlorperazine (Compazine) 0.1 mg/kg, or chlorpromazine (Thorazine) 0.5 mg/kg, can be used beginning 30 to 60 minutes before chemotherapy and continuing every six hours until symptoms subside.[90]

In some cases, the prophylactic use of phenothiazine antiemetics has been associated with a higher incidence of postchemotherapy nausea and vomiting.[91] This paradoxical effect may represent an increased susceptibility to suggestion in children whose parents (or medical and nursing staff) encourage pretreatment antiemetics, repeatedly question the child as to the occurrence of symptoms, or place emesis basins nearby. Therefore, it may be advantageous to withhold antiemetics in some children (especially those who have not experienced symptoms with prior chemotherapy) until the onset of nausea.

Both granisetron and ondansetron are safe and well-tolerated antiemetics in pediatric patients receiving chemotherapy.[101-102] A number of well controlled studies have documented superior safety and efficacy of both of these agents compared to conventional antiemetics for acute chemotherapy induced emesis.[101,102,108-111]

Anticipatory nausea and vomiting is also a well recognized problem in children receiving chemotherapy.[92] In pediatric patients the susceptibility to these symptoms has been correlated to the emetic potential of the chemotherapy, and the degree of parental anxiety.[93] Behavioral intervention strategies using hypnosis or supportive counseling (distracting the child's attention during chemotherapy administration) have been beneficial in reducing postchemotherapy side effects and may be helpful in alleviating anticipatory components as well.[84]

Acknowledgment

We gratefully acknowledge Rebecca S. Finley and Celeste M. Lindley, whose work provided a foundation for this chapter.

References

1 **Borison HL, McCarthy LE.** Neuropharmacology of chemotherapy-induced emesis. Drugs. 1983;25(Suppl. 1):8.

2 **Seigel LJ, Longo DL.** The control of chemotherapy-induced emesis. Ann Intern Med. 1981;95:352.

3 **Malagelada JR, Camilleri M.** Unexplained vomiting: a diagnostic challenge. Ann Intern Med. 1984;101:211.

4 **Akwari OE.** The gastrointestinal tract in chemotherapy-induced emesis. A final common pathway. Drugs. 1983; 25(Suppl. 1):18.

5 **Hanson JS, McCallum RW.** The diagnosis and management of nausea and vomiting: a review. Am J Gastroenterol. 1985;80:210.

6 **Borison HL, Wang SC.** Functional localization of central coordinating mechanisms for emesis in cat. J Neurophysiol. 1949;12:305.

7 **Borison HL, Brizzee KR.** Morphology of emetic chemoreceptor trigger zone in cat medulla oblongata. Proc Soc Exp Biol Med. 1951;77:38.

8 **Costello DJ, Borison HL.** Naloxone antagonizes narcotic self-blockade of emesis in the cat. J Pharmacol Exp Ther. 1977;203:222.

9 **Kilpatrick GJ et al.** The distribution of specific binding of the 5-HT₃ receptor ligand ³H-GR65630 in rat brain using quantitative autoradiography. Neurosci Lett. 1988;94:156.

10 **Kilpatrick GJ et al.** The distribution of specific GR65630 binding to the brains of several species. Characterization of binding to rat area postrema and vagus nerve. Eur J Pharmacol. 1989;159:157.

11 **Tyers MB et al.** Pharmacological and antiemetic properties of ondansetron. Eur J Cancer Clin Oncol. 1989;25 (Suppl. 1):S15.

12 **Borison HL, Wang SC.** Physiology and pharmacology of vomiting. Pharmacol Rev. 1953;5:193.

13 **Wood CD, Graybiel A.** A theory of motion sickness based on pharmacological reactions. Clin Pharmacol Ther. 1970;11:621.

14 **Cubeddu L et al.** Efficacy of ondansetron (GR 38032F) and the role of serotonin in cisplatin-induced nausea and vomiting. N Engl J Med. 1990;322:810.

15 **Sorenson PS et al.** Cerebrospinal fluid vasopressin in benign intracranial hypertension. Neurology (NY). 1982;32:1255.

16 **Arieff AI.** Effects of water, electrolyte and acid base disorders on the central nervous system. In: Arieff AI, DeFronzo RA, eds. Fluid, Electrolyte and Acid-Base Disorders. New York: Churchill Livingstone; 1985:969–1040.

17 **Fox RA et al.** Vasopressin and motor sickness in cats. Aviat Space Environ Med. 1987;58:A143.

18 **Kohl RL et al.** Motion sickness susceptibility related to ACTH, ADH, and TSH. Physiologist. 1983;26:S117.

19 **Feldman M.** Nausea and vomiting. In: Sleisenger MH, Fordtran JS, eds. Gastrointestinal Disease. Pathophysiology, Diagnosis, Management. Philadelphia: WB Saunders; 1983:161.

20 **Palazzo MGA, Strunin L.** Anaesthesia and emesis. I: etiology. Can Anaesth Soc J. 1984;31:178.

21 **Kappila A.** The function of the anterior pituitary-adrenal cortex axis in hyperemesis gravidarum. Br J Obstet Gynaecol. 1976;83:11.

22 **Soules MR.** Nausea and vomiting of pregnancy: role of human chorionic gonadotropin and 17-hydroxyprogesterone. Obstet Gynecol. 1980;55:696.

23 **Ylikorkala O et al.** Follicle stimulating hormone, thyrotropin, human growth hormone and prolactin in hyperemesis gravidarum. Br J Obstet Gynaecol. 1976;83:528.

24 **Lazlo J.** Emesis as limiting toxicity in cancer chemotherapy. In: Lazlo J, ed. Antiemetics and Cancer Chemotherapy. Baltimore: Williams & Wilkins; 1982:1.

25 **American Hospital Formulary Service, Drug Information; 1990.**

26 **Olin BR et al, eds.** Facts and Comparisons; 1990.

27 **Wampler G.** The pharmacology and clinical effectiveness of phenothiazines and related drugs for managing chemotherapy-induced emesis. Drugs. 1983;25(Suppl. 1):35.

28 **Wood CD.** Antimotion sickness and antiemetic drugs. Drugs. 1979;17:471.

29 **Rich WM et al.** Methylprednisolone as an antiemetic during cancer chemotherapy—a pilot study. Gynecol Oncol. 1980;9:193.

30 **Curry SL et al.** The role of prostaglandins in the excessive nausea and vomiting after intravascular cisplatin therapy. Gynecol Oncol. 1981;12:89.

31 **Cersosimo RJ, Karp DD.** Adrenal corticosteroids as antiemetics during cancer chemotherapy. Pharmacotherapy. 1986;6:118.

32 **Barbezat GO.** The vomiting patient: a rational approach. Drugs. 1981;22:246.

33 **Book LS.** Vomiting and diarrhea. Pediatrics. 1984;74(Pt. 2):950.

34 **Snyder J.** From pedialyte to popsicles: a look at oral rehydration therapy used in the United States and Canada. Am J Clin Nutr. 1982;35:157.

35 **Lazlo J.** Nausea and vomiting as major complications of cancer chemotherapy. Drugs. 1983;25(Suppl. 1):1.

36 **Moertel CG et al.** A controlled clinical evaluation of antiemetic drugs. JAMA. 1963;186:116.

37 **Moertel CG, Reitemeier RJ.** Controlled clinical studies of orally-administered antiemetic drugs. Gastroenterology. 1969;57:262.

38 **Fortner CL et al.** Combination antiemetic therapy in the control of chemotherapy-induced emesis. Drug Intell Clin Pharm. 1985;19:21.

39 **Morrow GR.** Clinical characteristics associated with the development of anticipatory nausea and vomiting in cancer patients undergoing chemotherapy treatment. J Clin Oncol. 1984;2:1170.

40 **Stefanek ME et al.** Anticipatory nausea and vomiting: does it remain a significant clinical problem? Cancer. 1988;62:2654.

41 **Gralla RJ et al.** Antiemetic therapy: a review of recent studies and a report of a random assignment trial comparing metoclopramide with delta-9-tetrahydrocannabinol. Cancer Treat Rep. 1984;68:163.

42 **Gralla RJ et al.** Antiemetic efficacy of high-dose metoclopramide: randomized trials with placebo and prochlorperazine in patients with chemotherapy-induced nausea and vomiting. N Engl J Med. 1981;305:905.

43 **Homesley HD et al.** Double-blind placebo-controlled study of metoclopramide in cisplatin-induced emesis. N Engl J Med. 1982;307:250. Letter.

44 **Chang AE et al.** Delta-9-tetrahydrocannabinol as an antiemetic in patients receiving high-dose methotrexate: a prospective, randomized evaluation. Ann Intern Med. 1979;91:819.

45 **Orr LE et al.** Antiemetic effect of tetrahydrocannabinol. Arch Intern Med. 1980;140:1431.

46 **Frytak S et al.** Delta-9-tetrahydrocannabinol as an antiemetic in patients treated with cancer chemotherapy: a double comparison with prochlorperazine and a placebo. Ann Intern Med. 1979;91:825.

47 **Cassileth PA et al.** Antiemetic efficacy of dexamethasone therapy in patients receiving cancer chemotherapy. Arch Intern Med. 1983;143:1347.

48 **Cassileth PA et al.** Antiemetic efficacy of high-dose dexamethasone in induction therapy in acute nonlymphocytic leukemia. Ann Intern Med. 1984;100:701.

49 **Moertel CG.** A controlled clinical evaluation of antiemetic drugs. JAMA. 1963;186:116.

50 **Kris MG et al.** Improved control of cisplatin-induced emesis with high-dose metoclopramide and with combinations of metoclopramide, dexamethasone, and diphenhydramine. Cancer. 1985;55:527.

51 **Kris MG et al.** Antiemetic control and prevention of side effects of anticancer therapy with lorazepam or diphenhydramine when used in combination with metoclopramide plus dexamethasone. Cancer. 1987;60:2816.

52 **Kessler JR et al.** Five-drug antiemetic combination for prevention of chemotherapy-related nausea and vomiting. Proc Am Soc Clin Oncol. 1984;3:104. Abstract.

53 **Sridhar KS et al.** Combination antiemetic regimen (BIRD) including diphenhydramine (B:Benadryl), droperidol (I:Inapsine), Metoclopramide (R:Reglan), and dexamethasone (D:Decadron) in cisplatin (DDP)-based chemotherapy regimens. Proc Am Soc Clin Oncol. 1984;3:100. Abstract.

54 **Warrington PS et al.** Optimizing antiemesis in cancer chemotherapy. Efficacy of continuous versus intermittent infusion of high-dose metoclopramide in emesis induced by cisplatin. Br Med J (Clin Res). 1986;293:1334.

55 **Dana BW et al.** A randomized trial of high-dose bolus metoclopramide versus low-dose continuous infusion metoclopramide in the prevention of cisplatin-induced emesis. Am J Clin Oncol. 1987;10:253.

56 **Agostinucci WA et al.** Continuous IV infusion versus multiple bolus doses of metoclopramide for prevention of cisplatin-induced emesis. Clin Pharm. 1988;7:454.

57 **Kris MG et al.** Extrapyramidal reactions with high-dose metoclopramide. N Engl J Med. 1983;309:433.

58 **Peroutka SJ et al.** Antiemetics: neurotransmitter receptor binding predicts therapeutic actions. Lancet. 1982;1:658.

59 **Marty M et al.** Comparison of the 5-hydroxytryptamine3 (serotonin) antagonist ondansetron (GR 38032F) with high-dose metoclopramide in the control of cisplatin-induced emesis. N Engl J Med. 1990;322:816.

60 **Marty M et al.** GR38032F, a 5HT3 receptor antagonist, in the prophylaxis of acute cisplatin-induced nausea and vomiting. Cancer Chemother Pharmacol. 1989;23:389.

61 **Marty M.** Ondansetron in the prophylaxis of acute cisplatin-induced nausea and vomiting. Eur J Cancer Clin Oncol. 1989;24(Suppl. 1):S41.

62 **Hesketh PJ et al.** GR 38032F (GR-C507/75): a novel compound effective in the prevention of acute cisplatin-induced emesis. J Clin Oncol. 1989;7:700.

63 **Grunberg SM et al.** Dose ranging phase I study of the serotonin antagonist GR 38032F for prevention of cisplatin-induced nausea and vomiting. J Clin Oncol. 1989;7:1137.

64 **Kris MG et al.** Phase II trials of the serotonin antagonist GR38032F for the control of vomiting caused by cisplatin. J Natl Cancer Inst. 1989;81:42.

65 **Carmichael J et al.** The serotonin type 3 antagonist BRL 43694 and nausea and vomiting induced by cisplatin. Br Med J (Clin Res). 1988;297:110.

66 **Merrifield KR, Chaffee BJ.** Recent advances in the management of nausea and vomiting caused by antineoplastic agents. Clin Pharm. 1989;8:187.

67 **Kris MG et al.** Consecutive dose-finding trials adding lorazepam to the combination of metoclopramide plus dexamethasone: improved subjective effectiveness over the combination of diphenhydramine plus metoclopramide plus dexamethasone. Cancer Treat Rep. 1985;69:1257.

68 **Bishop JF et al.** Lorazepam: a randomized, double-blind, crossover study of a new antiemetic in patients receiving cytotoxic chemotherapy and prochlorperazine. J Clin Oncol. 1984;2:691.

69 **Billings AJ et al.** The management of common symptoms. In: Billings AJ, ed. Outpatient Management of Advance Cancer. New York: JB Lippincott; 1985:49.

70 **Carr BI et al.** Safety and efficacy of higher than conventional doses of prochlorperazine (Compazine) for chemotherapy-associated emesis. Proc Am Soc Clin Oncol. 1984;3:101.

71 **Carr BI et al.** High doses of prochlorperazine for cisplatin-induced emesis. Cancer. 1987;60:2165.

72 **Grunberg SM et al.** Comparison of the antiemetic effect of high-dose intravenous metoclopramide and high-dose intravenous haldol in a randomized double-blind crossover study. J Clin Oncol. 1984;2:782.

73 **Wilson J et al.** Continuous infusion droperidol: antiemetic therapy for cisplatin toxicity. Proc Am Soc Clin Oncol. 1981;22:421.

74 **Vincent BJ et al.** Review of cannabinoids and their antiemetic effectiveness. Drugs. 1983;25:52.

75 **Kris MG et al.** Controlling delayed vomiting: double-blind, randomized trial comparing placebo, dexamethasone alone, and metoclopramide plus dexamethasone in patients receiving cisplatin. J Clin Oncol. 1989;7:108.

76 **Brown GW et al.** The effectiveness of a single intravenous dose of ondansetron. Oncology. 1992;49:273–78.

77 **Seynaeve C et al.** Comparison of the anti-emetic efficacy of different doses of ondansetron, given as either a continuous infusion or a single intravenous dose, in acute cisplatin-induced emesis. A multicentre, double-blind, randomized, parallel group study. Br J Cancer. 1992;66:192–97.

78 **Beck TM et al.** Stratified, randomized double-blind comparison of intravenous ondansetron administered as a multiple-dose regimen versus two single-dose regimens in the prevention of cisplatin-induced nausea and vomiting. J Clin Oncol. 1992;10:1969–975.

79 **Kris MG et al.** Delayed emesis following anticancer chemotherapy. Support Care Cancer. 1994;2:297–300.

80 **Cronin CM et al.** Transdermal scopolamine in motion sickness. Pharmacotherapy. 1982;2:29.

81 **Brand JJ, Perry WLM.** Drugs used in motion sickness. Pharmacol Rev. 1966;18:895.

82 **McCauley ME et al.** Effect of transdermally-administered scopolamine in prevention of motion sickness. Aviat Space Environ Med. 1979;59:1108.

83 **Price NM et al.** Transdermal scopolamine in the prevention of motion sickness at sea. Clin Pharmacol Ther. 1981;29:414.

84 **Acute vomiting and diarrhea.** In: Walker-Smith JA et al., eds. Practical Pediatric Gastroenterology. Boston: Butterworths; 1984:57.

85 **Zeltzer L et al.** The effectiveness of behavioral intervention for reduction of nausea and vomiting in children and adolescents receiving chemotherapy. J Clin Oncol. 1984;6:683.

86 **Terrin BN et al.** Side effects of metoclopramide as an antiemetic in childhood cancer chemotherapy. J Pediatr. 1984;104:138.

87 **Allen JC et al.** Metoclopramide: dose-related toxicity and preliminary antiemetic studies in children receiving cancer chemotherapy. J Clin Oncol. 1985;3:1136.

88 **Howrie DL et al.** Metoclopramide as an antiemetic agent in pediatric oncology patients. Drug Intell Clin Pharm. 1986;20:122.

89 **Graham-Pole J et al.** Antiemetics in children receiving cancer chemotherapy: a double-blind prospective randomized study comparing metoclopramide with chlorpromazine. J Clin Oncol. 1986;4:1110.

90 **Karayalcin G.** Supportive care of the child with cancer. In: Lanzkowsky P, ed. Pediatric Oncology. New York: McGraw-Hill; 1983:436.

91 **Zeltzer L et al.** Paradoxical effects of prophylactic phenothiazine antiemetics in children receiving chemotherapy. J Clin Oncol. 1984;2:930.

92 **Frick SB et al.** Chemotherapy-associated nausea and vomiting in pediatric oncology patients. Cancer Nurs. 1988; 11:118.

93 **Dolgin MJ et al.** Anticipatory nausea and vomiting in pediatric cancer patients. Pediatrics. 1985;75:547.

94 **DeMulder DHM et al.** Ondansetron compared with high-dose metoclopramide in prophylaxis of acute and delayed cisplatin-induced nausea and vomiting. Ann Intern Med. 1990;113: 834.

95 **Bonneterre J et al.** A randomized double-blind comparison of ondansetron and metoclopramide in the prophylaxis of emesis induced by cyclophosphamide, fluorouracil, and doxorubicin or epirubicin chemotherapy. J Clin Oncol. 1990;8:1063.

96 **Cubeddu LX et al.** Antagonism of serotonin S3 receptors with ondansetron prevents nausea and emesis induced by cyclophosphamide-containing chemotherapy regimens. J Clin Oncol. 1990;21.

97 **Khojasteh A et al.** Ondansetron for the prevention of emesis induced by high-dose cisplatin. Cancer. 1990;66:1101.

98 **Smith DB et al.** A phase I/II study of the 5-HT3 antagonist GR38032F in the antiemetic prophylaxis of patients receiving high-dose cisplatin chemotherapy. Cancer Chemother Pharmacol. 1990;25:291.

99 **Viner CV et al.** Ondansetron—a new safe and effective antiemetic in patients receiving high-dose melphalan. Cancer Chemother Pharmacol. 1990;25:449.

100 **Einhorn LH et al.** Ondansetron: a new antiemetic for patients receiving cisplatin chemotherapy. J Clin Oncol. 1990; 8:731.

101 **Carden PA et al.** Prevention of cyclophosphamide/cytarabine-induced emesis with ondansetron in children with leukemia. J Clin Oncol. 1990;8:1531.

102 **Pinkerton CR et al.** 5-HT$_3$ antagonist ondansetron—an effective outpatient antiemetic in cancer treatment. Arch Dis Child. 1990;65:822.

103 **Jones AL et al.** Comparison of dexamethasone and ondansetron in the prophylaxis of emesis induced by moderately emetogenic chemotherapy. Lancet. 1991;338:483–87.

104 **Navari RM et al.** Efficacy and safety of granisetron, a selective 5-hydroxytryptamine-3 receptor antagonist, in the prevention of nausea and vomiting induced by high-dose cisplatin. J Clin Oncol. 1994;12:2204–210.

105 **Gebbia V et al.** Ondansetron versus granisetron in the prevention of chemotherapy-induced nausea and vomiting. Results of a prospective randomized trial. Cancer. 1994;74:1945–952.

106 **Ruff P et al.** Ondansetron compared with granisetron in the prophylaxis of cisplatin-induced acute emesis: a multicentre double-blind, randomized, parallel-group study. Oncology. 1994;51: 113–18.

107 **Anon.** Dexamethasone, granisetron, or both for the prevention of nausea and vomiting during chemotherapy for cancer. The Italian Group for Antiemetic Research. N Engl J Med. 1995;332: 1–5.

108 **Hahlen K et al.** A randomized comparison of intravenously administered granisetron versus chlorpromazine plus dexamethasone in the prevention of ifosfamide-induced emesis in children. J Pediatr. 1995;126:309–13.

109 **Palmer R.** Efficacy and safety of granisetron (Kytril) in two special patient populations: children and adults with impaired hepatic function. Semin Oncol. 1994;21(Suppl. 5):22–5.

110 **Miyajima Y et al.** Prevention of chemotherapy-induced emesis with granisetron in children with malignant diseases. Am J Pediatr Hematol Oncol. 1994;16:236–41.

111 **Jacobsen SJ et al.** The efficacy and safety of granisetron in pediatric cancer patients who had failed standard antiemetic therapy during anticancer chemotherapy. Am J Pediatr Hematol Oncol. 1994;16:231–35.

112 **Lindley CM et al.** Incidence and duration of chemotherapy-induced nausea and vomiting in the outpatient oncology population. J Clin Oncol. 1989; 8:1142–149.

Index

Abdominal trauma
infections 61.16
table of treatment regimens 61.17
Abscess
intra-abdominal 61.15–61.16
Absence seizures
See Seizures, absence
Absolute neutrophil count 67.2
Abstinence syndromes
See specific drugs of abuse
Abuse of drugs
See Drug abuse
Accidental deaths
alcohol 82.2
Accupril
See Quinapril
ACE inhibitors
See Angiotensin-converting
enzyme inhibitors; specific
agents
Acebutolol
Also see Beta blockers
adverse effects, teratogenicity 45.7
breast milk 45.23, 45.34
pharmacodynamic properties 10.19
pharmacokinetic properties 10.19,
10.20
use in hypertension 10.19
Acetaminophen
adverse effects
hemolysis 89.5
hepatotoxicity 7.7, 7.8, 26.5,
104.19
nephrotoxicity 7.8, 29.8
pulmonary 22.1
teratogenicity 45.7
breast milk 45.23
overdoses, treatment
104.19–104.20
pharmacokinetics
half-life, hepatitis 62.5
use in
analgesia 7.5–7.6
osteoarthritis 41.23
pediatric
analgesia 95.24
antipyresis 95.3
teething 95.2, 95.24
Acetazolamide
Also see Carbonic anhydrase
inhibitors
adverse effects 49.10–49.11
acidosis 28.14, 49.10
alkalinization, urine 40.13, 49.10
nephrotoxicity 29.8
ocular 49.11
renal tubular acidosis 27.5
breast milk 45.23
pharmacology 28.11
use in
glaucoma 49.10–49.11, 49.12
sleep apnea 20.11, 74.14
urine alkalinization 40.13
Acetic acid, topical 36.3
Acetohexamide 48.37–48.38
Also see Sulfonylureas
adverse effects, teratogenicity 45.7
Acetophenazine, teratogenicity 45.7
Acetylcysteine
adverse effects, anaphylactoid 6.16
use in acetaminophen overdoses
104.20

Acetylsalicylic acid
See Aspirin
Acid phosphatase 4.12
Acid-base disorders 27.1–27.13
Also see specific disorders
laboratory assessments 4.5–4.6
Acidosis, metabolic 27.4–27.7
Also see Diabetic ketoacidosis
associated with
cardiogenic shock 18.22
hyperchloremia 4.6
renal failure 30.4, 30.7
drug-induced 27.5
acetazolamide 28.14
carbonic anhydrase inhibitors
49.10
diuretics 28.13–28.14
salicylate 104.7
toxic shock syndrome 46.9
Acidosis, respiratory 27.9–27.10
Acne 37.1–37.7
clinical presentation 37.1, 37.4
drug-induced
anabolic steroids 87.4
corticosteroids 19.18
etiology 37.1
pathogenesis 37.1

contraceptives, oral 43.17
Acneiform drug eruptions 36.16
Acquired immunodeficiency
syndrome
See HIV infection; also see
Compromised host, infections in
ActHIB
See PRP-T
Action potential 16.1–16.2
Activated charcoal
See Charcoal, activated
Acute lymphocytic leukemia
See Leukemia, acute lymphocytic
Acute myelogenous leukemia
treatment allogenic bone marrow
transplant 94.4
Acute myocardial infarction
See Myocardial infarction
Acute stress disorder 73.27–73.28
Acyclovir
administration
oral 64.17–64.18, 68.20
parenteral 64.18, 64.21
topical 64.18
adverse effects
table of 70.5
nephrotoxicity 29.8, 54.14,
64.18, 68.21, 70.5, 70.7
neurotoxicity 54.14, 64.18
overview 70.3
phlebitis 54.14, 64.18
teratogenicity 45.7
breast milk 45.23
dosing 32.6, 70.2–70.3, 70.5
herpes
genital 64.18–64.19
simplex virus prophylaxis
94.18
renal failure 32.13
pharmacokinetics 70.2–70.3
clearance
dialysis 32.6, 32.14, 54.15
renal disease 54.18
renal failure 32.6, 32.13–32.14
concentrations, toxic 68.21

parameters 32.6
pharmacology
comparative 64.18
efficacy 64.18–64.21
use in
cytomegalovirus infection, prophylaxis 33.41, 67.17
herpes 64.18–64.19, 70.2–70.6
genital 64.18–64.21
neonatal 64.20–64.21
simplex 68.20–68.21
zoster 68.20–68.21
ocular 49.20
prophylaxis for
cytomegalovirus 94.18
herpes simplex 94.18
varicella zoster 70.6–70.7
Adapin
See Doxepin
Addiction
drug-induced
amphetamine 84.4
cocaine 84.14–84.16
hypnotics 83.10
in neonates 83.7, 96.26–96.28
opiates 83.3–83.9
Adenine arabinoside
See Vidarabine
Adenocard
See Adenosine
Adenosine
adverse effects
flushing 16.12
pulmonary 16.12
teratogenicity 45.7
dose supraventricular tachycardia
16.9, 16.12
interactions, drugs
dipyridamole 16.12
theophylline 16.12
use in paroxysmal supraventricular
tachycardia 16.12
ADH
See Antidiuretic hormone
Adrenal corticotrophic hormone
Also see Corticosteroids
use in
gout 40.5–40.6
ulcerative colitis 24.3
Adrenal function tests 42.8
Adrenal suppression 42.8
Adrenergic neuronal blocking drugs
Also see specigic agents
adverse effects 10.14, 10.28
comparison of
guanadrel 10.14, 10.28
guanethidine 10.14, 10.28
reserpine 10.14, 10.28
contraindications/precautions
10.14, 10.28
use in hypertension 10.14, 10.28
Adrenergics
See Beta-adrenergic agonists
Adverse drug reactions
Also see specific agents
anaphylaxis 6.1–6.4
drug allergies 6.1–6.21
Aerosols, topical
See specific agents
Affective disorders
See Depression, adulthood;
Affective disorders, bipolar
Affective disorders, bipolar

77.1–77.12
Also see Depression, adulthood
classification 77.1
clinical presentation 77.1–77.2
adolescents 78.5
children 78.5
complications of 77.2
diagnosis 77.1–77.3
drug-induced 77.3
target symptoms 77.1–77.2
treatment 77.4–77.9
children 78.5
Afterload 15.3
Age, altered drug response
See Geriatrics; Neonates;
Pediatrics
Aggression 79.1–79.5
anabolic steroids 87.4
clinical presentation 79.3
complication of geriatric dementia
102.11
diagnosis 79.3–79.4
drug-induced
amphetamines 84.3
clomipramine 78.7
in developmentally disabled
78.13–78.15
pathogenesis 79.2
treatment 79.3–79.5, 78.15
children 78.15–78.16
trazodone 102.11
Agranulcytosis
See Hematological disorders
AIDS
See HIV infection
AIDS-related complex 68.6
Airway disease
See Chronic obstructive airways
disease
Akathisia 75.16
use in pseudoparkinsonism 75.15
Albendazole
use in pinworms 71.9
Albumin
monitoring total parenteral nutrition 35.3
serum concentrations
assessment 4.11
cirrhosis 25.6
use in
cirrhosis 25.7
hepatorenal 25.14
hypovolemic shock 18.10–18.12,
18.15
Albuterol
Also see Beta-adrenergic agonists
adverse effects, teratogenicity 45.7
Alcohol
Also see Denatured alcohol;
Methanol
abuse 82.1–82.14
adverse effects
acidosis 27.7
amenorrhea 82.11
anemia 82.8–82.9
arrhythmias 82.11
atrial fibrillation 82.10–82.11
cardiovascular 82.11
cirrhosis 25.1–25.17
clotting 82.8, 82.9
delirium tremens 82.6
dyslipidemia 9.12, 9.20–9.21

Alcohol (continued)
  folate deficiency 63.16, 82.9,
    88.11
  gastrointestinal 23.3, 82.9–82.10
  gout 40.2
  hemosiderosis 82.9
  hepatotoxicity 25.1, 82.8, 82.9
  hypertension 10.11, 82.6, 82.11
  hyperuricemia 40.12, 82.4
  hypoglycemia 48.56, 82.3–82.4,
    82.5
  hypomagnesemia 28.26
  hypophosphatemia 28.24
  hypotension 82.5
  hypothermia 82.5, 82.11
  migraine headache 50.5
  musculoskeletal 82.11–82.12
  neurological 82.10–82.11
  osteoporosis 46.29
  pancreatitis 82.10
  platelet inhibition 82.9
  pulmonary 22.2, 82.4
  respiratory depression 82.4
  teratogenicity 45.5, 45.6, 45.12,
    81.8–81.9, 82.9
  testosterone deficiency
    82.11–82.12
  thrombocytopenia 89.7
  Wernicke-Korsakoff 82.10–82.11
  breast milk 45.25
  content and definitions 82.1
  effect on
    osteoporosis 46.29
    osmolality 28.2
  interactions, drugs
    benzodiazepines 82.6
    cimetidine 23.6, 23.8, 82.10
    disulfiram 82.7–82.8
    sulfonylureas 48.39, 48.43
  intoxication
    acute
      blood concentrations 82.4–82.5
      clinical presentation 82.4
      treatment 82.5
      withdrawal 82.5
    chronic
      diagnosis 82.7
      effect on organs 82.8–82.12
      etiology 82.6
      treatment 82.7–82.8
  pharmacokinetics
    absorption 82.2–82.3
    clearance 82.3–82.4
    concentrations
      definition of intoxication 82.1
      estimated by osmol gap 82.5
      estimated clinically 82.4
      plasma 82.4
    distribution 82.3
  use in
    angle closure glaucoma 49.12
    diabetes 48.8
  withdrawal, acute 82.5–82.6
Alcohol abuse 82.1–82.12
  assessment 81.4
  populations at risk 81.10–81.12
  screening 81.4–81.5
  societal impact 81.3
  treatment
    programs 81.6
    recovery support 81.6–81.8
Alcoholic cirrhosis 25.1–25.17
Alcoholism 82.1–82.12
  diagnosis
    DSM-IV 82.7
    ICD-10 82.7

  treatment
    drugs 82.7–82.8, 82.12
    programs 82.7
Aldactone
  See Spironolactone
Aldomet
  See Methyldopa
Aldose-reductase inhibitors 48.47
Aldosterone, cirrhosis 25.5
Alfentanil
  adverse effects, teratogenicity 45.7
  breast milk 45.23
Alfuzosin 103.16
ALG
  See Antilymphocyte globulin
Alkaline phosphatase
  overview 4.11
  ulcerative colitis 24.3
Alkalosis
  cirrhosis 25.5–25.6
  drug-induced
    antacids 23.8
    diuretics 15.13
Alkalosis
  metabolic, 27.8–27.9
    drug-induced, diuretics 28.13
  respiratory 27.9–27.11
Allergic reactions
  See Hypersensitivity reactions
Allergic rhinitis
  perennial 21.16–21.17
  seasonal 21.15–21.16
Allogenic bone marrow transplantation 94.1–94.5
Allopurinol
  Also see Probenecid
  adverse effects 40.10–40.11
    cataracts 40.10, 49.16
    drug fever 6.9
    gout 40.9
    hepatotoxicity 26.5, 40.10
    hypersensitivity 40.10
    nephrotoxicity 29.8, 40.10
    rash 40.10
    teratogenicity 45.7
    vasculitis 6.12, 40.10
  breast milk 45.23
  contraindications/precautions
    densitization 40.11
    renal insufficiency 40.10, 40.15
  dosing 32.6, 40.9
  interaction, drugs
    table of 40.10
    mercaptopurine 92.14
    vidarabine 70.5
    warfarin 12.20
  pharmacokinetics 40.9–40.10
    clearance
      dialysis 32.6
      renal failure 32.6
    parameters 32.6
  pharmacology
    indications 40.11
    initiation of therapy 40.9
    mechanism of action 40.9
    onset of effects 40.9
  use in
    hyperuricemia 40.9–40.11
    mucositis 91.7
    myocardial reperfusant 40.11
Alloxanthine 40.9–40.10
Alopecia 36.16
  drug-induced, chemotherapy
    agents 91.8–91.9

Alpha-adrenergic agonists, effect on
  lipids 9.12
Alpha$_1$-adrenergic inhibitors
  Also see specific agents
  adverse effects 10.14, 10.24–10.25
  use in
    diabetic hypertension 48.52
    hypertension 10.14, 10.24–10.25
    prostatic hyperplasia
      103.15–103.16
Alpha$_1$-antitrypsin
  pharmacology 20.2
Alpha$_2$-agonists
  Also see specific agents
  adverse effects 10.14, 10.25–10.26
  contraindications 10.25
  use in hypertension 10.14,
    10.25–10.26
Alpha-chymotrypsin
  adverse effects, ocular 49.3
Alpha fetoprotein 93.18
Alpha-interferon
  See Interferon
Alpha reductase inhibitors
  103.16–103.17
Alphaprodine, teratogenicity 45.7
Alprazolam
  adverse effects, teratogenicity 45.7
  breast milk 45.23
  interactions, drugs, nefazodone
    76.24
  pharmacokinetics 73.9, 73.12
  use in
    anxiety 73.7
    panic disorder 73.19–73.20
    premenstrual syndrome 46.16
ALT
  See Aminotransferase, alanine
Altace
  See Ramipril
Altretamine
  adverse effects 90.11
  pharmacokinetics 90.11
  pharmacology 90.11
Aluminum
  toxicity, renal failure, chronic 30.8,
    30.16
Aluminum acetate, topical 36.3
Aluminum antacids
  See Antacids, aluminum
Auminum hydroxide
  use in infectious diarrhea 60.2
Aluminum toxicity 31.7–31.8
  Also see Antacids; Aluminum
Alupent
  See Metaproterenol
Alzheimer's dementia
  behavioral disturbances
    102.10–102.12
  clinical presentation 102.3–102.4
  diagnosis 102.3–102.4
  pathogenesis 102.2–102.4
  treatment 102.5–102.7
    monoclonal antibodies 5.3
    nerve growth factor 5.3
Amantadine
  Also see Parkinson's disease
  adverse effects 51.4–51.5, 70.5,
    70.9
    table of 70.5
    anticholinergic 51.5
    central nervous system 51.4–51.5
    edema 51.5

    gastrointestinal 51.4–51.5
    livedo reticularis 51.5
    teratogenicity 45.7
  breast milk 45.23
  dosing
    Parkinson's disease 51.4
    renal insufficiency 51.4
  mechanism of action, Parkinson's
    disease 51.4
  pharmacokinetics 70.2–70.3
    clearance 51.4
  use in
    cocaine withdrawal 84.15
    herpes 70.2–70.5
    influenza 70.9–70.10
    Parkinson's disease 51.4–51.5
Ambien
  See Zolpidem
Amebiasis 71.4–71.8
  complications 71.7
  pathogenesis 71.4–71.7
  treatment 71.4–71.8
    also see specific agents
    table of 71.5–71.6
Amenorrhea
  drug-induced
    alcohol 82.11
    contraceptives 43.10, 43.12,
      43.13, 43.18, 43.19
    neuroleptics 75.20
Amidate
  See Etomidate
Amikacin
  Also see Aminoglycosides
  adverse effects
    nephrotoxicity 29.8
    teratogenicity 45.7
  breast milk 45.23
  dose 32.6
  pharmacokinetics
    clearance 32.6
      dialysis 32.6, 32.12–32.13
      renal failure 32.6, 32.11
    distribution 32.6
    half-life 32.6
    parameters 32.6
  use in
    cystic fibrosis 100.7–100.9
    pyelonephritis 63.8
Amikin
  See Amikacin
Amiloride 10.15–10.17
  Also see Diuretics; Diuretics,
    potassium-sparing
  adverse effects, teratogenicity 45.7
  use in
    cirrhosis 25.5
    congestive heart failure 15.15
    cystic fibrosis, nebulization
      100.11
Amino acids
  Also see Parenteral nutrition
  branched chain 25.11, 25.13, 34.6,
    35.13
  requirements 35.5–35.6
Aminoglutethimide 93.18
  adverse effects, teratogenicity 45.7
Aminoglycosides
  Also see specific agents
  table of 54.7
  administration
    aerosolized 58.13–58.14
    intermittent versus infusion 67.7
    intraperitoneal 61.5
    intrathecal 56.7, 56.16

Aminoglycosides (continued)
  intraventricular 56.7
  once a day 67.7–67.8
  adverse effects
    table of 54.13
    acute tubular necrosis 29.7, 29.15
    hypomagnesemia 28.26
    nephrotoxicity 29.7, 29.15
  dosing
    adjustments 54.12
    loading dose 54.18
    maintenance dose 54.18
    meningitis 56.9
    once a day dose 2.20, 54.17
    renal failure 32.5–32.10
  interactions, drugs
    cephalosporins 67.9
    cyclosporine 33.27
    penicillins 67.9
    penicillins, antipseudomonal 67.9
  pharmacokinetics
    clearance
      dialysis 31.10, 32.12–32.13,
        54.16
      hepatic 54.12
      peritoneal dialysis 32.17
      renal disease 54.12, 54.18
      renal failure 32.11
    concentrations
      bone 65.5
      bronchial secretions
        58.12–58.13
      serum
        peak 54.18
        trough 54.18
    CSF penetration characteristics
      56.7
    half-life 32.6–32.10
    once a day, high dose 2.20
    parameters 2.11, 32.5–32.10,
      32.12, 32.17
    peaks and troughs 2.17
    principles 2.11
  use in
    aspiration pneumonia 58.12
    cystic fibrosis 100.7–100.9
    empiric in immunocompromised
      67.6–67.13
    endocarditis
      culture negative 57.17
      enterococcal 57.11–57.15
      gram-negative 57.16
      prophylaxis 57.8–57.9,
        57.18–57.19
      S. aureus 57.9–57.11
      S. viridans 57.6–57.7
    meningitis 56.6, 56.9
    meningitis, neonatal 96.17–96.18
    necrotizing enterocolitis, neonate
      96.16
    neutropenia 67.4–67.12
    ophthalmic infections 49.17
    pelvic inflammatory disease 64.7
    peritonitis 31.10, 61.4, 61.5,
      61.6, 61.10
    pneumonia 58.7
    prosthetic valve 57.9–57.11
    pyelonephritis 63.8
  use with
    beta-lactams 67.4–67.7
    vancomycin 67.7
Aminophylline
  See Theophylline
Aminopterin, teratogenicity 45.6,
  45.7
Aminopyrine
  adverse effects, neutropenia 89.12

Aminosalicylic acid
  Also see Mesalamine
  breast milk 45.23
Aminotransferase, alanine
  aspirin effect 41.21
  cirrhosis 25.3
  overview 4.11
  ulcerative colitis 24.3
Aminotransferase, aspartate
  aspirin effects 41.21
  cirrhosis 25.3
  overview 4.11
Amiodarone
  adverse effects 16.6, 16.18–16.19
    gastrointestinal 16.18
    hepatic 16.18
    hepatotoxicity 26.5
    ophthalmic 49.12, 49.13
    pulmonary 16.18, 22.4,
      22.8–22.9
    teratogenicity 45.7
    thyroid disorders 16.19
  breast milk 45.23
  dose 16.18
  interactions, drugs
    digoxin 15.20
    mechanisms 3.2
    warfarin 12.20
  pharmacokinetics 16.6
    half-life 16.18
    parameters 16.6
  pharmacology
    effect on electrocardiograms 16.3
    effect on thyroid function tests
      47.5, 47.8, 47.27
  use in
    atrial fibrillation 16.10
    ventricular tachycardia 16.18
    Wolff-Parkinson-White syn-
      drome 16.13
Amitriptyline
  Also see Antidepressants, cyclic
  adverse effects, teratogenicity 45.7
  breast milk 45.23
  overdoses, treatment
    104.13–104.19
  use in
    anorexia 80.4
    bulimia 80.5
    depression, adulthood
      76.10–76.12
    diabetic neuropathy 48.47–48.48
    migraine headache 50.10,
      50.11–50.12
    pain 7.3, 7.16, 7.19–7.20
    tension headaches 50.16–50.17
Amlodipine 10.23, 13.14, 13.15,
  13.17
  adverse efects, teratogenicity 45.7
  use in congestive heart failure
    15.34
Ammonia, hepatic encephalopathy
  25.10
Ammonium chloride, use in phencyclidine toxicity 86.8
Amnesia, anterograde
  triazolam 74.6
Amobarbital, teratogenicity 45.7
Amoxapine
  Also see Antidepressants, cyclic;
    Depression, adulthood
  breast milk 45.23
  depression, adulthood 76.10–76.12
  depression, psychotic 76.22
Amoxicillin
  Also see Ampicillin

adverse effects
  nephrotoxicity 29.8
use in
  bronchitis 58.3
  chanchroid 64.15
  chlamydia 64.10
  endocarditis, prophylaxis
    57.18–57.19
  gonorrhea 64.4
  helicobacter 23.12
  Lyme 72.3–72.4
  otitis 97.8
  pediatric infections 97.4
  pneumonia, community acquired
    58.7
  sinusitis 97.10
  urinary tract infection 63.5
use with probenecid 64.4
Amoxicillin-clavulanate
  adverse effects, hepatotoxicity 26.6
  formulation storage/stability 97.10
  use in
    bronchitis 58.3
    otitis 97.8–97.9
    pediatric infections 97.4
    pneumonia, community acquired
      58.7
    sinusitis 97.10
    urinary tract infection 63.5
Amoxil
  See Amoxicillin
Amphetamine abuse
  clinical presentation 84.3–84.6
  complications 84.3
  table of street names 84.3
  treatment 84.3–84.5
Amphetamines
  abuse 84.1–84.5
  adverse effects
    cardiotoxicity 15.11
    nephrotoxicity 29.8
    psychoses 75.4–75.5
    teratogenicity 45.7, 81.9
  breast milk 45.22, 45.23, 84.6
  overdosage, treatment 84.5
  pharmacokinetics 84.4
  urine tests for 81.14
  use in
    attention deficit hyperactivity
      84.2
    narcolepsy 84.2
    narcotic-induced sedation 7.22
    weight reduction 84.2
Amphotericin B
  administration
    aerosolized 69.4
    bladder irrigation 69.13
    combined with intralipid 69.4,
      69.18
    drug fever 6.9
    intracisternal 69.17
    intrathecal 68.22, 69.17
    intravenous infusion 69.10–69.12
    oral 69.12
  adverse effects
    acute toxicities 68.21, 68.22
    acute tubular necrosis 29.16
    anemia 54.14
    drug fever 6.9
    electrolyte abnormalities 54.14
    hematological 54.14
    hypomagnesemia 28.26
    infusion related 68.22,
      69.10–69.12
    nephrotoxicity 29.8, 29.16,
      54.14, 69.11–69.12
    renal tubular acidosis 27.5

overview 69.11
teratogenicity 45.7
dosing 32.6, 32.16
  renal dysfunction 69.12
  renal failure 32.16
  usual 69.10–69.12
interactions, drugs
  cyclosporine 33.27
  mechanisms 3.2
pharmacokinetics 69.10–69.11
  absorption 32.6
  clearance 32.6
  dialysis 32.16
  half-life 32.6
  parameters 32.6
pharmacology 69.3–69.4
use in
  aspergillosis 69.18
  blastomycosis 69.15
  candidiasis 68.30, 69.10–69.13
  candiduria 69.13
  cryptococcal meningitis
    68.21–68.22
  cryptococcosis 69.19
  fungal endocarditis 57.16
  histoplasmosis 69.13
  renal failure 32.6, 32.16
  sporotrichosis 69.6
use with
  acetaminophen 68.22
  diphenhydramine 68.22
  flucytosine 68.21–68.22
Ampicillin
  adverse effects
    nephrotoxicity 29.8
    pseudomembranous colitis 60.10
  dosing, renal failure 32.6
  H. influenzae resistance 56.10
  interactions, drugs
    allopurinol 40.10
    contraceptives, oral 43.10–43.11
  pharmacokinetics
    clearance
      dialysis 32.6, 54.15
      renal disease 54.18
      renal failure 32.6
    parameters 32.6
    protein binding 32.6
  use in
    cholangitis (with aminoglyco-
      side) 61.2
    chronic bronchitis 58.3
    meningitis 56.10
    meningitis, neonate 96.17
    necrotizing enterocolitis, neonate
      96.16
    pediatric infections 97.4
    peritonitis 61.4, 61.6
    pneumonia, community acquired
      58.6, 58.7
    Salmonella gastroenteritis 60.2,
      60.14
    urinary tract infection 63.5,
      63.7–63.9
Ampicillin-sulbactam
  use in
    aspiration pneumonia 58.6
    lung abscess 58.6
Amrinone
  adverse effects 15.35, 18.20
  dose 15.35
  dosing 18.20
  pharmacokinetics 15.35
  pharmacology 15.35, 18.20–18.21
Amrinone (continued)
  use in
    congestive heart failure, severe

18.20–18.21
heart failure 15.35–15.36
Amyl nitrate, teratogenicity 45.7
Amyloidosis
dialysis 31.8
primary systemic 30.22–30.23
Anabolic steroids
Also see Androgens
abuse
adverse effects 87.3–87.5
table of 87.5
hepatotoxicity 26.6
banned drugs, table 87.2–87.3
clinical presentation 87.2–87.4
dosing 87.4
effect on tests
lipoprotein 87.4
substitute alternatives 87.5
urine tests for 87.5–87.6
use in osteoporosis 46.34
Anaerobic bacteria
peritonitis 61.13–61.14
Anafranil
See Clomipramine
Analgesia, patient controlled
use in pediatric analgesia 95.23
Analgesic nephropathy
clinical presentation 30.4
drug-induced
aspirin 30.4
NSAIDs 30.5
phenacetin 30.4
Analgesics
Also see specific agents; Pain
tables of
equianalgesic doses 7.6
mild analgesics 7.8
opioid analgesics 7.10
clinical uses 7.2–7.21
principles of use 7.4
use in
gout 40.8
myocardial infarction 14.6, 14.8,
14.19–14.20
Anaphylaxis 6.2–6.7
Anasarca 28.5
Ancef
See Cefazolin
Ancobon
See Flucytosine
Ancrod 53.11, 89.7
Androgens
Also see Anabolic steroids
adverse effects
hepatotoxicity 26.6
teratogenicity 45.6
effect on thyroid function tests
47.6
interactions, drugs
warfarin 12.20
use in anemia, renal failure 30.8
Anectine
See Succinylcholine
Anemia
Also see specific anemias;
Hematological disorders
aplastic 89.12–89.14
chloramphenicol 56.12
clinical presentation 89.13–89.14
drug-induced
table of 89.13
chloramphenicol 89.12–89.13
phenylbutazone 89.13
pathogenesis 89.12
treatment 89.14

B_{12} deficiency 88.8–88.11
also see Cyanocobalamin
clinical presentation 88.9–88.10
laboratory assessment 88.9
pathophysiology 88.8
treatment 88.10–88.11
chronic disease 88.13–88.15
renal failure 30.7
drug-induced
see Hematological disorders,
drug-induced; specific anemias
classification
morphologic 88.2
pathophysiologic 88.2
clinical presentation 88.2–88.4,
88.9, 88.12, 88.14
definition 88.1
diseases associated
hypothyroidism 47.8
toxic shock syndrome 46.9
ulcerative colitis 24.2
endocarditis 57.4
folate deficiency 88.11–88.12
also see Folic acid
cirrhosis 25.3
clinical presentation 88.11
drug-induced
alcohol 82.9
ethanol 63.16
phenytoin 63.16
trimethoprim-sulfamethoxazole
63.16
folate metabolism 88.11
laboratory assessment 88.11
pathogenesis
hypothyroidism 47.8
predisposing factors 88.11
alcohol 88.11
dialysis 30.8
nutritional 88.11
treatment 88.11–88.12
hemolytic
see Hemolytic anemia, G6PD;
Hemolytic anemia, immune;
Hemolytic disease, newborn;
Hemolytic uremic syndrome
hemosiderosis
alcohol induced 82.9
iron deficiency 88.3–88.7
also see Iron
clinical presentation 88.4–88.5
drug-induced, alcohol 82.9
etiology 88.5
laboratory diagnosis 88.4–88.5
pathogenesis, hypothyroidism
47.8
predisposing factors 88.4
preparations 88.5–88.6
treatment
oral 88.5–88.6
parenteral 88.7–88.8
laboratory assessment 88.2–88.4
megaloblastic
also see Anemia, folate deficiency; Anemia, B_{12} deficiency
B_{12} deficiency 88.8–88.11
folate deficiency 88.11–88.12
tapeworm induced 71.11
pathophysiology 88.1
pernicious 88.8–88.10
sickle cell 88.12–88.13
sideroblastic
alcohol-induced 82.9
Anesthesia
epidural 8.12, 8.20–8.22
local
pharmacokinetics, table of 8.13

pharmacology 8.11–8.13
uses 8.12
intravenous
adverse effects 8.6–8.7
characterictics, general 8.5–8.6
mechanisms of action 8.6
pharmacokinetics 8.6–8.7
table of 8.7
uses, table of 8.6
Angina
clinical presentation
chronic stable 13.4–13.5
microvascular ischemia (syndrome X) 13.20
Prinzmetal's variant 13.19–13.20
silent ischemia 13.20–13.21
unstable 13.21–13.22
definitions 13.1–13.2
diagnosis 13.5–13.6
drug-induced
alcohol 13.19
dopamine agonists 51.10
nifedipine 13.15
smoking 13.19
sumatriptan 50.9
thyroid hormone 47.14
vasopressin 25.9
pathophysiology 13.2–13.4
prognosis 13.6
treatment, drugs
also see specific drugs
antiplatelet therapy 13.18–13.19
beta blockers 13.11–13.13
calcium channel blockers
13.11–13.18
combination therapy 13.18
nitrates 13.6–13.11
treatment, nondrug
coronary angioplasty 13.22
coronary artery bypass 13.22
Angiograms
pulmonary 12.11
Angioplasty 13.22
Angiotensin 15.30
Angiotensin II antagonists
10.28–10.29
Angiotensin-converting enzyme
inhibitors
Also see specific agents
adverse effects
angioedema 6.16
cough 6.16
hemodynamic renal failure
29.17–29.18
hyperkalemia 10.14, 17.5
overview 10.22–10.23,
15.30–15.32, 17.5–17.6
pulmonary 22.2
teratogenicity 45.6, 45.33
contraindications/precautions
table of 10.14
hyperkalemia 10.14, 17.5
renal failure 10.14, 10.21
dosing
table of 10.22
heart failure 15.28, 15.30–15.32
hypertension 10.22–10.23
low dose 10.22
interactions, drugs
allopurinol 40.10
lithium 77.7
nonsteroidal anti-inflammatory
agents 3.4
potassium supplements 10.16
pharmacokinetic properties
10.21–10.23
pharmacology

comparison of agents
10.22–10.23
mechanisms of action 10.21,
15.30, 17.5
onset of action 17.5
preparations 15.31
benazepril 10.22
captopril 10.22–10.23
cilazapril 10.22
enalapril 10.22, 10.23
fosinopril 10.22
lisinopril 10.22, 10.23
quinapril 10.22
ramipril 10.22
use in
congestive heart failure 15.5,
15.12–15.13, 15.28–15.34
diabetic hypertension 48.52
diabetic nephropathy 48.53
glaucoma 49.11
hypertension 10.7, 10.12, 10.13,
10.14, 10.18, 10.21–10.23
hypertension, renal failure 30.12
hypertensive emergencies
17.5–17.6
myocardial infarction 14.4, 14.8,
14.15–14.16
pregnancy 44.18
vascular dementias 102.9
use with verapamil 49.11
Anion gap
calculation 4.6, 27.3
laboratory assessment 4.6, 27.3
Anistreplase
See APSAC
Anorexia nervosa
Also see Eating disorders; Bulimia
nervosa
clinical presentation 80.6, 84.6
comorbidity 80.6
complications 80.7
definitions 80.1
diagnosis 80.2, 80.6–80.7
treatment
drugs 80.3–80.4
goals 80.7
hospitalization 80.7
psychotherapy 80.4, 80.7
Ansacol
See Mesalamine
Ansaid
See Flurbiprofen
Antabuse
See Disulfiram
Antacids
Also see specific agents
adverse effects, table of 23.8
contraindications/precautions, renal
failure 23.8
dosing 23.8–23.9
interactions, drugs
table of 23.9
allopurinol 40.10
ciprofloxacin 23.9, 63.6
H_2 antagonists 23.9
iron 88.6–88.7
mechanisms 3.1, 3.2
quinolones 23.9
tetracyclines 23.9, 63.5
pharmacology
efficacy 23.8
mechanism of action 23.8
neutralizing capacity 23.9
Antacids (continued)
product selection
dosage form 23.9

neutralizing capacity 23.9
sodium content 23.9
use in
  aspiration pneumonia prophylax-
    is 8.5
  gastroesophageal reflux 23.17
  peptic ulcer 23.8–23.9
  stress ulcers 23.20
Antacids, aluminum
  Also see Antacids
  adverse effects
    table of 23.8
    constipation 23.8
    hypophosphatemia 23.8, 28.24
    osteoporosis 46.28–46.29
  preparations 30.13
  use in
    chronic renal failure 23.8
    hyperphosphatemia 23.8
    peptic ulcer 23.8–23.9
Antacids, calcium
  Also see Antacids
  adverse effects 23.8
  use in peptic ulcers 23.8
Antacids, magnesium 23.8–23.9
Antepar
  See Piperazine citrate
Anthracyclines
  See Doxorubicin
Anthralin, use in psoriasis 38.2
Antiarrhythmic agents
  Also see specific agents
  classification 16.4
  ECG effects 16.3
  pharmacology 16.3, 16.6
    table of 16.6
Antibiotic prophylaxis
  bowel decontamination 33.39
  bronchitis 58.3
  cystic fibrosis 100.4
  diarrhea, travelers' 60.2–60.6
  endocarditis 57.2–57.3,
    57.18–57.19
  immunocompromised hosts 33.39,
    67.13–67.14
  Shigella gastroenteritis 60.14
  surgical 55.1–55.5
  transplant 33.38
  transplant CMV infections 67.17
  use in bone marrow
    transplantation 94.5
Antibiotic-associated pseudomembranous colitis (AAPMC) 60.10–60.12
  clinical presentation and diagnosis
    60.10–60.11
  drug-induced, table 60.10
  pathophysiology 60.10
  treatment 60.11
Antibiotics
  Also see Antibiotic prophylaxis;
    specific agents and infections
  tables of
    accumulation in renal dysfunc-
      tion 54.18
    adverse effects 54.13–54.14
    aminoglycoside dosing 54.18
    available antibiotics 54.7
    biliary concentrations 61.3
    brain abscess therapy 56.19
    CNS infections, recommenda-
      tions 56.10
    CNS infections, regimens 56.9
    CNS penetration 56.7
    dosing guidelines 54.15–54.17
    drugs of choice 54.10–54.12
    intra-abdominal infection

penetrating wound, regimens
  61.17
peritonitis, regimens 61.12
pharmacokinetics in CAPD 61.6
susceptibilities 54.8–54.9
administration
  aerosolized 58.13–58.14
  endotracheally instilled 58.13
  into central nervous system 52.6,
    56.17–56.18
  intraperitoneal 61.5
  intravenous 56.18
  intraventricular 53.14, 56.18
  penetration into peritoneum
    61.16
aerosolized 100.10
costs of therapy 54.9, 54.12
dosing
  oral solution stabilities
    97.10–97.11
  pediatrics 97.4–97.7
  renal failure 32.5–32.10,
    32.12–32.16
factors for failure 54.18–54.19
pharmacokinetics
  penetration 56.6–56.7
    brain abscess fluid
      56.20–56.21
    bronchial secretions
      58.12–58.13
    cerebrospinal fluid 56.6–56.7
  renal elimination 32.6–32.10
postantibiotic effect 54.14
use in
  combination empirically
    67.4–67.13
  immunocompromised hosts
    67.1–67.18
  neutropenia 67.4–67.13
Anticholinergics
  Also see specific agents
  adverse effects 51.3–51.4
    blurred vision 51.4
    central nervous system 51.4
    glaucoma 49.3, 51.4
    ocular 49.13
    peripheral 51.4
    psychoses 49.18, 75.4–75.5
    teratogenicity
      see specific agents
    toxic megacolon 24.8
  interactions, drugs
    amantadine 51.5
    levodopa 51.9
  pharmacology
    comparative 51.3
    efficacy, Parkinson's disease
      51.3–51.4
    mechanism of action, Parkinson's
      disease 51.3
  use in
    akathisia 75.16
    asthma 19.7–19.9, 19.25
    chronic obstructive airways dis-
      ease 20.6–20.7
    dystonias 75.15–75.16
    emesis 105.3–105.5
    extrapyramidal syndromes
      75.13–75.19
    motion sickness 105.5,
      105.8–105.9
    Parkinson's disease 51.3–51.4
    pseudoparkinsonism 75.13–75.15
Anticholinesterases
  use in glaucoma 49.8–49.9
Anticoagulants
  Also see Anticoagulants, oral;

Heparin; Low molecular weight
  heparin; Thrombosis; Warfarin
use in
  myocardial infarction 14.4, 14.8,
    14.17–14.18
  thrombotic stroke 53.9–53.10
  transient ischemic attacks 53.10
Anticoagulants, oral
  interactions, drugs
    also see Warfarin, interactions,
      drugs
    allopurinol 40.10
    chloral hydrate 3.3
    cimetidine 23.6, 23.8
    contraceptives, oral 43.12
    disulfiram 82.7–82.8
    erythromycin 3.3
    mechanisms 3.2
    omeprazole 23.10
    phenylbutazone 3.1, 3.4
    rifampin 59.8
    sulfasalazine 24.7
    sulfonamides 24.7, 63.16
    thioamides 47.16
    thyroid hormone 3.4,
      47.15–47.16
    trimethoprim-sulfamethoxazole
      63.16
  use in
    atrial fibrillation 16.9
    thyroid disorders 47.15–47.16
Anticoagulation 12.1–12.22
  Also see Heparin; Thrombolytics;
    Thrombosis; Warfarin
  use in dialysis 31.4
Anticonvulsants
  See Antiepileptic drugs
Antidepressants
  Also see specific agents;
    Monoamine oxidase inhibitors;
    Affective disorders, bipolar;
    Depression, adulthood
  adverse effects, pulmonary 22.4,
    22.6
Antidepressants, cyclic
  adverse effects
    table of 76.11
    anxiogenesis, panic disorder
      73.21
    cardiovascular 76.9, 76.12–76.14
    hepatotoxicity 26.13
    hypotension 76.9, 76.12
    hypothyroidism 47.26–47.27
    interference skin testing 21.6
    mania 77.4, 78.5
      children 78.5
    ocular 49.13
    seizures 76.11, 76.14
    teratogenicity
      see specific agents
  breast milk 76.11
  dosing 76.10
  interactions, drugs
    table of 76.14
    guanethidine 3.3
    levodopa 51.8, 51.9
  overdose, treatment 104.13–104.19
  pharmacokinetics
    plasma concentrations
      therapeutic 76.12
  use in
    anorexia 80.4
    attention deficit hyperactivity
      78.3
    bulimia 80.4
    childhood

depression 78.4
  obsessive compulsive 78.6
  separation anxiety 78.6
cocaine addiction 84.16
depression, adulthood
  AIDS 76.15
  dementia 102.11
  elderly 76.15–76.16
  major 76.9–76.16
  psychotic 76.21
  refractory 76.22–76.23
diabetic neuropathy 48.47–48.48
generalized anxiety 73.7
insomnia 74.11–74.12
migraine headache 50.10,
  50.11–50.12
pain 7.3, 7.16, 7.19–7.20
panic disorders 73.19–73.21
posttraumatic stress 73.28
pregnancy 76.10
  see specific agents
premenstrual syndrome 46.16
sleep apnea 20.10–20.11
tension headaches 50.16
Tourette's 78.9
use with
  antipsychotics 76.21–76.23
  lithium 76.23
Antidiarrheals
  See Diarrhea
  use in
    cryptosporidiosis, AIDS 60.8
    E. coli, GI infections 60.10
    shigellosis 60.15
Antidiuretic hormone 15.4
  Also see Vasopressin; Syndrome of
    inappropriate antidiuretic hor-
    mone secretion
Antidotes 104.5, 104.14–104.15
  extravasation 91.12
Antiemetics
  Also see specific agents;
    Nausea/vomiting
  tables of 105.4, 105.6
  combination therapy 105.7, 105.8
  mechanism of action 105.3–105.5
  use in migraine headache 50.6
Antiepileptic drugs
  Also see Seizure disorders; specific
    agents
  adverse effects
    folic acid deficiency 88.11
    lupus 6.15
    teratogenicity 52.26
  education, patient 52.19
  effect on thyroid hormones 47.7
  efficacy, table of 52.4
  interactions, drugs
    contraceptives, oral 52.26
    lidocaine 16.9, 16.11, 16.17
  use in seizures
    absence 52.19–52.20
    complex partial 52.7–52.19
    febrile 52.22–52.23
    generalized tonic clonic
      52.19–52.22
  use, principles of
    discontinuation 52.6–52.7
    duration 52.6–52.7
    mono- versus polytherapy 52.6
    serum concentrations 52.4–52.6
Antihistamines
  adverse effects
    drug fever 6.9
    ocular 49.13
    teratogenicity
      see specific agents

breast milk
see specific agents
dosing, table of 21.9
pediatric doses 21.9
side effects 21.9
effects on
skin testing 21.6
pharmacokinetics 21.7–21.9
topical 36.14
use in
allergic conjunctivitis
49.16–49.17
allergies 6.5
anxiety 73.8
insomnia 74.5, 74.12
morning sickness 44.7
motion sickness 105.4, 105.5,
105.8–105.9
otitis 97.9
pregnancy 44.7
rhinitis 21.6–21.12
sinusitis 97.10
Antihypertensives
Also see specific agents
use in vascular dementias 102.9
Antilymphocyte globulin
administration 33.14
adverse effects 33.37
dose 33.14
pharmacology
duration of therapy 33.37
monitoring 33.37
use in
aplastic anemia 89.14
organ transplantation 33.14
Antimalarials
Also see specific agents
use in
juvenile rheumatoid arthritis
41.21
malaria 71.1–71.4
rheumatoid arthritis 41.3, 41.12
Antimicrobials
See Antibiotics; Antifungal agents;
Antivirals
Antimicrosomal antibodies 47.5
Antiminth
See Pyrantel pamoate
Antimycotics
Also see Azole antifungals;
specific agents
adverse effects, table of 54.14
approved drugs 69.3
mechanisms of action 69.3
pregnancy, use in 69.15
prophylaxis with 69.12
spectrum of activity 69.4
use in immunocompromised hosts
67.12–67.14
Antineoplastics
See specific agents; Chemotherapy
Antioxidants
use in
dyslipidemias 9.23
Parkinson's disease 51.13
Antiplatelet effects of drugs
table of 30.9
aspirin 53.6, 53.7, 53.8
dipyridamole 53.6, 53.7
ethanol 82.9
nicardipine 53.15
nimodipine 53.7, 53.13, 53.15
salicylates 7.7, 53.6, 53.7
sulfinpyrazone 53.6, 53.7
ticlopidine 53.6, 53.7, 53.8

Antiplatelet therapy
Also see Antiplatelet effects of
drugs; Thrombosis
aspirin 12.18
dipyridamole 12.18
use in
angina 13.18–13.19
hemolytic uremic syndrome
95.14–95.15
myocardial infarction
13.18–13.19
prosthetic valve 12.18
transient ischemic attacks
53.6–53.9
vascular dementia 102.10
Antipseudomonal penicillins
See Penicillins, antipseudomonal
Antipsychotics
See Neuroleptics
Antipyretics
Also see Acetaminophen; Aspirin
febrile seizures 52.3, 52.22–52.23
Antithymocyte globulin
administration 33.37
adverse effects 33.37
serum sickness 6.7
dosing 33.14
pharmacology 33.8, 33.37
use in
aplastic anemia 89.14
graft failure, bone marrow 94.11
graft versus host disease 94.13,
94.16
Antithyroglobulin 47.5
Antitussives 21.19
Antivirals
Also see specific agents
adverse effects, table of 54.14
Anxiety disorders 73.1–73.31
Also see Insomnia
children
classification 78.5
obsessive compulsive 78.6
separation anxiety 78.6
classification DSM-IV
acute stress disorder 73.27–73.28
generalized anxiety disorder
73.4–73.17
obsessive compulsive disorder
73.22–73.26
panic disorder 73.17–73.21
phobic disorder 73.21–73.22
posttraumatic stress disorder
73.27–73.28
diagnostic decision tree 73.3
in opioid withdrawal 83.9
treatment
table of, drug options 73.28
Anxiolytics
See Anxiety; specific agents
Aortic dissection 17.13
Aortic valve
anticoagulation 12.6
Apathy
clinical presentation 79.5–79.6
diagnosis 79.5
treatment 79.5–79.6
Apatite gout 40.4
Aplastic anemia
See Anemia, aplastic
Apnea
classification 20.10
treatment 20.10–20.11
Apnea, newborn
clinical presentation 96.21

pathogenesis 96.21–96.22
treatment 96.21–96.23
Appendectomy antibiotics
61.16–61.17
Apraclonidine 49.13
Apresoline
See Hydralazine
APSAC
contraindications/precautions, table
of 14.7
dosing in myocardial infarction
14.7, 14.9–14.10
selection 14.9
major thrombolytic trials 14.11
use in
elderly 14.13
myocardial infarction 14.7,
14.9–14.13
post cardiopulmonary resuscitation 14.12
reocclusion 14.12
Ara-A
See Vidarabine
Ara-C
See Cytarabine
Aralen
See Chloroquine
Arduan
See Pipecuronium
Arfonad
See Trimethaphan
Arrhythmias
Also see Cardiotoxicity;
Atrioventricular block; Atrial fibrillation; Supraventricular
arrhythmias; Ventricular arrhythmias; specific arrhythmias
bepridil 13.14, 13.18
classification 16.4
postinfarction 14.18
conduction blocks 16.13–16.14
drug-induced antiarrhythmics
16.6, 16.10, 16.15, 16.17
sotalol 16.17
verapamil 16.13
drug-induced
alcohol 82.11
amrinone 15.35, 18.20
beta agonists 19.10, 19.13, 20.7,
44.24–44.25
cocaine 84.12
dehydroemetine 71.8
diazepam (IV) 52.27–52.28
digoxin 15.16, 15.21–15.26
emetine 71.8
levodopa 51.5
milrinone 15.35
oxytocin 44.28
phenytoin (IV) 52.28–52.29
potassium 28.17–28.18
theophylline 19.13, 20.7
tricyclic antidepressants
76.13–76.14
pathophysiology 16.3–16.4, 16.5,
16.11
ventricular 16.14–16.19
Artane
See Trihexyphenidyl
Arterial blood gases 16.21, 27.3
in
asthma 19.1, 19.8, 19.15
respiratory failure 19.15
overview 19.1

Arteriosclerosis obliterans 11.2
Arteritis 42.3
Arthritis
Also see Osteoarthritis;
Rheumatoid arthritis; Septic
arthritis
Lyme 72.5
psoriatic 38.6
Ascites
Also see Cirrhosis; Hepatic disorders
clinical presentation 25.4
complication of cirrhosis
25.3–25.7
laboratory assessment 25.3
pathogenesis 25.4
treatment 25.4–25.7
Ascorbic acid
adverse effects
nephrotoxicity 29.8
use in dyslipidemia 9.23
Asendin
See Amoxapine
Asparaginase
See L-asparaginase
adverse effects 90.11
encephalopathy 91.15
hepatotoxicity 91.27
hypersensitivity 92.18
pancreatitis 92.17
pulmonary 22.2
teratogenicity 45.8
pharmacokinetics 90.11
pharmacology 90.11
use in acute lymphocytic leukemia
92.15
Aspartame
breast milk 45.23
teratogenicity 45.8
Aspergillosis 69.17–69.19
allergic bronchopulmonary 100.9
marijuana 86.5
Aspiration pneumonia
clinical presentation 58.8
common pathogens 58.9
pathogenesis 58.8
predisposing factors 58.8
alcohol 82.4, 82.6, 82.9–82.10
prophylaxis, perioperative 8.4–8.5
risk factors 8.4
treatment
antibiotics, table of 58.10
corticosteroids 58.9
Aspirin
Also see Salicylates
adverse effects
also see Toxic overdoses
angioedema 6.16
bleeding time 41.6
bronchospasm 6.16, 41.6
fetal effects 41.7
G6PD deficiency 71.4
gastrointestinal 7.8, 13.19, 23.3,
23.13, 41.6
hemolysis 89.5
hepatotoxicity 26.6, 41.21
hypersensitivity 41.6
Aspirin (continued)
adverse effects (continued)
hyperuricemia 40.12
nephrotoxicity 29.8
platelet function 7.7
pulmonary 22.2, 41.6
Reye's syndrome 41.21
teratogenicity 41.7, 45.8
tinnitus 41.5

transaminitis 41.21
breast milk 45.23
dosing
anti-inflammatory 41.5
juvenile rheumatoid arthritis 41.21
osteoarthritis 41.23
pain 7.8
patient education, transient ischemic attacks 53.8
stroke prevention 53.6, 53.7
tinnitus as endpoint 41.5
interactions, drugs
nonsteroidal anti-inflammatory drugs 41.7
probenecid 3.5
warfarin 12.18, 12.20
overdose, treatment 104.5–104.9
pharmacokinetics 41.5, 104.9
pharmacology 104.7–104.9
antiplatelet effects 13.18–13.19, 53.6
effect on thyroid function 47.6, 47.7
preparations/formulations 41.6
use in
angina 13.18–13.19
angioplasty, post 13.22
atrial fibrillation 12.18
dysmenorrhea 46.13
intermittent claudication 11.8
juvenile rheumatoid arthritis 41.21
Kawasaki's disease 97.18–97.19
microvascular angina 13.20
migraine headache prophylaxis 50.12
myocardial infarction 14.4, 14.8
osteoarthritis 41.23
pediatric
analgesia 95.24
teething 95.2, 95.24
pregnancy-induced hypertension 44.15–44.16
prosthetic valves 12.18
rheumatoid arthritis 41.5–41.9
silent myocardial ischemic 13.21
stroke
prophylaxis on atrial fibrillation 16.11
prevention 53.7
transient ischemic attacks 53.6–53.7
unstable angina 13.22
vascular dementias 102.9–102.10
use with
niacin 9.14–9.15, 9.19
AST
See Aminotransferase, aspartate
Astemizole
dosing 21.9
effects on
skin testing 21.6
interactions, drugs
itraconazole 69.7
ketoconazole 69.17
nefazodone 76.24
use in rhinitis 21.7–21.12
Asterixis 25.10
Asthma
classification
acute 19.6–19.18
chronic 19.19–19.25
drug-induced 19.28
exercise-induced 19.25–19.26
nocturnal 19.26–19.27
seasonal 19.20

clinical presentation 19.4–19.8
need for hospitalization 19.8
respiratory failure 19.15
definition 19.4
diagnosis 19.6
drug-induced
table of 22.2
aspirin 19.28, 41.6
beta-blockers 19.28
nonsteroidal anti-inflammatory drugs 19.28–19.29, 41.6
timolol 49.4
exercise-induced 21.5, 87.7
laboratory assessment
arterial blood gases 19.1, 19.8, 19.15
diffusion capacity 19.3
plethysmography 19.3
spirometry 19.2–19.3
V/Q mismatching 19.8
pathogenesis 19.5
pathophysiology 19.4
treatment
approach
goals 19.6, 19.19
patient education 19.27
stepwise 19.7
drugs
anticholinergics 19.13, 19.25
beta-adrenergics 19.7–19.15
corticosteroids 19.7, 19.14, 19.20–19.22
cromolyn 19.19–19.20
ipratropium 19.13
nedocromil 19.20
theophylline 19.15–19.25
Asystole 16.23
Atabrine
See Quinacrine
Atarax
See Hydroxyzine
Atenolol
Also see Beta blockers
adverse effects
nephrotoxicity 29.8
teratogenicity 44.17, 45.8
breast milk 45.23
dosing
in hypertension 10.19
in renal failure 32.6
pharmacodynamic properties 10.19–10.21
pharmacokinetics
absorption 32.6
clearance
half-life 32.6
dialysis 32.6
renal failure 32.6
parameters 32.6
properties, table of 10.20, 32.6
use in
alcohol withdrawal 82.6
hypertension 10.19–10.21
migraine headache 50.10
ATG
See Antithymocyte globulin
Atgam
See Antithymocyte globulin
Atherosclerosis
link to cholesterol 9.7–9.10
pathogenesis 9.7
Athlete drug abuse 87.1–87.9
Athlete's foot
See Tinea pedis
Ativan
See Lorazepam
Atovaquone
use in

pneumocystosis 68.16
toxoplasmosis 68.25
Atracurium 8.8–8.12
Atrial fibrillation 16.4–16.11
clinical presentation 16.5
induced by coronary artery bypass graft 16.11
in hyperthyroidism 47.16–47.17
treatment
adenosine 16.8
anticoagulation 12.4, 12.17–12.19, 16.11
beta-adrenergic blockers 16.7
calcium channel blockers 16.8
cardioversion 16.8
digitalis 16.7
quinidine 16.8, 16.10
Atrial natriuretic peptide 15.4
Atrioventricular block 16.13–16.14
Atromid-S
See Clofibrate
Atropine
adverse effects
ocular 49.13
teratogenicity 45.8
breast milk 45.23
use in
atrioventricular block 16.14
bronchopulmonary dysplasia 98.2
cardiac arrest 16.21
chronic obstructive airways disease 20.7
diarrhea, infectious 60.2, 60.3
impotence 103.10–103.11
Atrovent
See Ipratropium
Attention deficit hyperactivity 78.2–78.3, 84.2
Auranofin
Also see Gold
adverse effects 41.11
use in rheumatoid arthritis 41.10–41.11
Aurothioglucose 41.10
Also see Gold
Auspitz's sign 38.1, 38.4
Autism 78.10–78.11
Autoimmune disorders
Also see specific disorders
drug-induced, table of 6.15
Autologous bone marrow transplantation 94.5–94.7
Automaticity 16.2
Aventyl
See Nortriptyline
Axid
See Histamine₂-antagonists
Axsain
See Capsaicin
Azactam
See Aztreonam
Azatadine 21.9
Azathioprine
adverse effects
drug fever 6.9
hepatotoxicity 26.6, 33.38
leukopenia 33.38
myelosuppression 33.38
pancreatitis 33.38
teratogenicity 45.8
vasculitis 6.12
dosing 33.14

interactions, allopurinol 40.10
pharmacokinetics 33.5
pharmacology, mechanism of action 33.5
use in
Crohn's disease 24.11
graft versus host disease, chronic 94.17
hepatitis, autoimmune chronic active 62.14
lupus nephritis 30.21
organ transplantation 33.5, 33.14
rapidly progressive glomerulonephritis 29.5
rheumatoid arthritis 41.3
ulcerative colitis 24.7
Wegener's granulomatosis 30.26
Azithromycin
use in
bronchitis 58.3
chancroid 64.15
chlamydia 58.3, 64.9
Lyme 72.4
Mycobacterium avium infection 68.28–68.29
pertussis 97.17
sinusitis 97.11
Azlocillin
See Penicillins, antipseudomonal
Azole antifungals
Also see specific agents
adverse effects 69.16
interactions, drugs 69.16–69.17
pharmacokinetics 69.11
pharmacology 69.3–69.4
use in
blastomycosis 69.14
candiduria 69.13
onychomycosis 69.5
prophylaxis candidemia 69.12–69.13
Azotemia
Also see Renal failure, acute
drug-induced
diuretics 15.13
AZT
See Zidovudine
Aztreonam
adverse effects
nephrotoxicity 29.9
pharmacokinetics
clearance
dialysis 32.6, 54.15
renal disease 54.18
renal failure 32.6
concentration, bone 65.5
half-life 32.6
parameters 32.6
use in
cystic fibrosis 100.7–100.8
immunocompromised hosts 67.10, 67.15
pyelonephritis 63.8–63.9
travelers' diarrhea (oral) 60.4
urinary tract infection, hospital-acquired 63.7
Azulfidine
See Sulfasalazine
Bacitracin
adverse effects
nephrotoxicity 29.9
use in
corneal ulcers 49.17
pseudomembranous colitis 60.11
Baclofen
adverse effects, teratogenicity 45.8

breast milk 45.23
Bacteremia
  endocarditis 57.4
Bacteria
  antibiotic susceptibility, table of 54.8–54.9
  classification, table of 54.4
  pediatric pathogens 97.3
Bacterial vaginosis
  clinical presentation 64.15
  treatment 64.15–64.16
Bacteriuria
  Also see Urinary tract infection
  asymptomatic 63.9–63.10
Bactrim
  See Trimethoprim-sulfamethoxazole
Balloon tamponade 25.8
Band ligation 25.8, 25.10
Barbiturates
  abuse 83.10
  adverse effects
    ocular 49.15
    teratogenicity
      see specific agents
  interactions, drugs 3.2
    contraceptives, oral 43.11, 43.12
    corticosteroids 3.5
    quinidine 3.5, 3.6
    warfarin 12.20
  urine tests for 81.14
  use in
    benzodiazepine withdrawal 83.10
    neonatal opioid addiction 83.7
    prophylaxis, febrile seizures 52.23
    seizures 52.12, 52.29
Barium
  adverse effects, toxic megacolon 24.8
Bartter's syndrome 28.16
Basophils 4.16
BCG vaccine
  adverse effects, teratogenicity 45.8
  clinical use 59.14
  use in tuberculosis 59.14
BCNU
  See Carmustine
Beclomethasone
  adverse effects, teratogenicity 45.8
  nasal 21.14
Beconase
  See Beclomethasone
Bedrest
  congestive heart failure 15.5
  hepatitis 62.5
Belladonna alkaloids, teratogenicity 45.8
Bellergal
  See Ergotamine
Benazepril
  Also see Angiotensin-converting enzyme inhibitors
  adverse effects 10.22–10.23
    teratogenicity 45.8
  breast milk 45.23
  contraindications/precautions 10.14
  dose 10.22
  pharmacokinetic properties 10.21–10.23
  pharmacology, comparisons 10.22, 15.28
  use in
    hypertension 10.22

vascular dementia 102.9
Bendectin 44.7
Bendroflumethiazide
  Also see Diuretics
  adverse effects, teratogenicity 45.8
  breast milk 45.23
Benemid
  See Probenecid
Benign prostatic hyperplasia
  clinical findings 103.12–103.13
  diagnostic 103.13
  pathophysiology 103.11, 103.16
  symptoms 103.11–103.13
  treatment
    drugs 103.15–103.18
    TURP 103.14–103.15
Benzodiazepines
  Also see Anxiety; specific agents
  abuse 73.10–73.13
  administration
    intramuscular 73.10
  adverse effects
    addiction 83.10
    dependence 73.11, 74.9–74.10
    memory 73.11
    overdoses 73.16
    overview 73.10–73.13, 74.6–74.7
    paradoxical reactions 73.11
    psychomotor impairment 73.11
    respiratory depression 73.11
    teratogenicity 73.14–73.16
    withdrawal 73.10–73.13, 83.10
  available agents
    table of 73.7
    selection of 73.9
  dosing
    table of 74.8
    conversion to buspirone 73.17
    equivalent hypnotic dose 74.8
    interchanging benzodiazepines 73.14
  interactions, drugs
    table of 73.15
    alcohol 82.6, 82.7
    cigarettes 73.14, 85.3
    levodopa 51.9
  patient education 73.10, 73.13
  pharmacokinetics 74.8
    adults 73.9, 73.12
  pharmacology 74.9
    dependence 83.10
    fetal effects 81.9
    GABA-benzodiazepine receptor 73.6
    mechanism of action 73.6
    receptor subtypes to agents 73.6
  precautions
    elderly 74.12–74.13, 102.10
    sleep apnea 74.14
  use in
    aggression 78.15, 79.5
    alcohol withdrawal 82.6
    amphetamine intoxication 84.5
    anxiety 73.6, 73.9–73.16, 73.28
    chemotherapy-induced nausea 105.7
    cocaine intoxication 84.13, 84.15
    elderly 74.12–74.13
    insomnia 74.5–74.13
    jet lag 74.5
    mania 77.4
    nocturnal myoclonus 74.15
    opioid withdrawal 83.9
    panic disorders 73.20, 73.28
    schizophrenia, adjunctively 75.10

social phobias 73.22, 73.28
Benzoyl peroxide
  Also see Acne
  use in acne 37.2–37.5
Benzquinamide 105.4
Benzthiazide
  Also see Diuretics
  adverse effects, teratogenicity 45.8
  breast milk 45.23
Benztropine
  Also see Anticholinergics
  adverse effects, teratogenicity 45.8
  use in
    childhood dystonias 78.8
    extrapyramidal reactions 75.13–75.19
    Parkinson's disease 51.3, 51.4
Bepridil 13.14, 13.18
  adverse effects, teratogenicity 45.8
Beractant
  administration 96.9–96.10
  adverse effects 96.9–96.10
  dosing 96.9–96.10
  pharmacology 96.9–96.10
Berotec
  See Fenoterol
Beta-adrenergic agonists
  Also see specific agents
  administration
    inhalation 19.7, 19.9–19.13, 19.19, 20.7–20.8
    parenteral 19.15
    preferred routes 19.9
  adverse effects
    cardiovascular 19.10, 20.7, 44.24–44.25
    hyperglycemia 44.25, 48.54
    hypokalemia 19.11, 20.7, 28.16, 44.25
    hypoxia 19.11
    overuse 19.18
    pulmonary edema 44.25
    teratogenicity
      see specific agents
    tremors 19.11, 20.7, 44.25
  dosing in chronic obstructive airways disease 20.7–20.8, 20.11
  interactions, drugs
    theophylline 19.13
  pharmacology
    tolerance 19.14
  precautions
    theophylline 19.14
  preparations 19.11–19.13
  use in
    anaphylaxis 6.6–6.8
    asthma 19.7–19.15, 19.20
    bronchiolitis 97.14
    bronchopulmonary dysplasia 98.2–98.3
    combination with
      corticosteroids 19.14
      theophylline 19.14
    croup 97.14
    exercise-induced asthma 19.26
    hyperkalemia 28.19
    chronic obstructive airways disease 20.3, 20.7–20.9, 20.11
    preterm labor 44.23–44.25, 96.8
Beta-adrenergic blockers
  Also see Propranolol; specific agents
  adverse effects 10.19–10.21
    asthma 19.28
    bronchospasm 6.16
    central nervous system 13.13

dyslipidemia 9.12, 9.20
heart failure 15.10–15.11
hyperglycemia 48.51
hypoglycemia 48.51, 48.55, 48.58
  in diabetic patients 48.51
  lupus 6.15
  ophthalmic preparations 49.4, 49.7, 49.10
  psoriasis 38.5
  pulmonary 13.12, 22.2, 22.6
  respiratory acidosis 27.10
  teratogenicity 44.17, 47.24
    also see specific agents
  withdrawal syndrome 13.13
breast milk
  see specific agents
contraindications/precautions
  abrupt withdrawal 13.13
  CHF 14.14
  diabetes 14.14
  dyslipidemia 14.14
  intermittent claudication 11.6–11.7
  peripheral vascular disease 13.12
  pulmonary disorders 14.14
  Raynaud's phenomenon 11.9
  respiratory disease 13.12
  variant angina 13.20
dosing
  hypertension 10.19
  renal insufficiency 13.13
interactions, drugs
  alcohol 82.6
  cholestyramine/colestipol 9.14
  epinephrine 3.3
  monitoring parameters 13.12
  single versus multiple dosing 13.12
pharmacokinetics
  concentrations, breast 45.34
  in pregnancy 44.17
    fetal 44.17
  ophthalmic preparations 49.4–49.9
pharmacology
  table of 10.19
  comparative pharmacology 10.19–10.21, 13.12
  effect on breast feeding 45.34
  factors affecting response 13.12
    cardioselectivity 10.19
    intrinsic sympathomimetic activity 10.19, 13.12–13.13
    lipid solubility 10.19–10.20
    onset/duration 10.20
preparations 10.19
use in
  aggression 79.4–79.5
  alcohol withdrawal 82.6
  angina 13.8, 13.11–13.13
  anxiety 73.7–73.8
  atrial fibrillation 16.7, 16.11
  cocaine intoxication 84.11
  congestive heart failure 15.36–15.37
Beta-adrenergic blockers (continued)
use in (continued)
  diabetic, myocardial infarction 14.14
  disinhibition 79.4–79.5
  elderly 14.15
  esophageal varices 25.9–25.10
  glaucoma 49.4–49.9, 49.11
  hypertension 10.9–10.14, 10.18–10.21
  hyperthyroidism 47.19, 47.21
  microvascular angina 13.20

myocardial infarction 14.4, 14.8,
   14.14, 14.16
nonsustained ventricular tachycardia 16.16
Parkinson's tremor 51.13
portal hypertension 25.9–25.10
pregnancy 44.17
Prinzmetal's variant 13.20
supraventricular tachycardia
   16.12
surgery 13.13
unstable angina 13.22
ventricular tachycardia 16.17
use with calcium channel blockers
   13.15, 13.18
Beta agonists
   See Beta-adrenergic agonists
Beta blockers
   See Beta-adrenergic blockers
Beta human chorionic gonadotropin
   93.19
Beta-lactam antibiotics
   Also see specific antibiotics
   adverse effects, table of 54.13
Betamethasone
   Also see Corticosteroids
   adverse effects, teratogenicity 45.8
   use in respiratory distress,
      neonates 96.8
Betapace
   See Sotalol
Betaxolol 49.5, 49.7, 49.9
   adverse effects, teratogenicity 45.8
   pharmacodynamic properties
      10.19–10.21
   pharmacokinetic properties 10.20
   use in hypertension 10.18–10.21
Bethanechol
   breast milk 45.23
   use in
      gastroesophageal reflux 23.18
         pediatric 95.6
      urinary incontinence 103.20
Beuxalol
   See Beta-adrenergic blockers
Biaxin
   See Clarithromycin
Bicarbonate
   Also see Carbon dioxide, content
   acid-base balance 27.1–27.12
   concentration, serum 27.3
   laboratory interpretation 4.5
   serum concentration 4.5
   use in
      acid-base disorders 27.1–27.12
      hyperkalemia 28.19, 30.6
      cardiogenic shock 18.22
      cardiopulmonary arrest 16.21
      diabetic ketoacidosis
         48.35–48.36
Biguanides 48.36
   Also see Metformin
Bile acid resins
   Also see Colestipol and
      Cholestyramine
   administration 9.14, 9.17
   adverse effects 9.14, 9.17
   dose 9.14, 9.17
   efficacy 9.14
   interactions, drugs 9.14
   patient education 9.17
   pharmacology 9.14
   use in
      hypercholesterolemia 9.14,
         9.16–9.17

hypertriglyceridemia 9.22
mixed hyperlipidemia 9.22
Biliary atresia 33.29
Biliary pain
   treatment, analgesics 7.20
Biliary pseudolithiasis
   ceftriaxone 56.11–56.12
Biliary tract infections
   cholangitis and cholecystitis
      61.1–61.3
Bilirubin 4.12
Bioavailability
   in renal failure 32.1
   principles 2.3
Biotechnology 5.1–5.7
   gene therapy 5.5–5.7
   implications for clinical practice
      5.1–5.7
   monoclonal antibodies 5.1–5.5
   recombinant proteins 5.1
Biphosphonates
   use in
      prevention of osteoporosis 46.33
      hypercalcemia 28.22
Bipolar affective disorders
   See Affective disorders, bipolar
Bismuth subsalicylate
   adverse effects 60.5
      teratogenicity 45.8
   breast milk 45.23
   dosing
      prophylaxis, travelers' diarrhea
         60.3
      treatment, travelers' diarrhea 60.3
   use in travelers' diarrhea 60.3,
      60.4–60.5
Bismuth, colloidal
   use in
      helicobacter 23.5, 23.11
      peptic ulcer 23.11–23.13
Bisoprolol 10.19
   adverse effects, teratogenicity
      45.8
Bite wounds
   animal 66.8
   human 66.9
Bitolterol
   See Beta-adrenergic agonists
Bladder cancer
   chemotherapy
      adjuvant 93.14
      metastatic 93.14
      regimens 90.17
   clinical presentation 90.8, 93.14
   resection, endoscopic 93.14
   risk factors 93.14
Blastomycosis 69.13–69.15
Bleeding
   chemotherapy-associated 91.4–91.5
   disseminated intravascular clotting
      12.21
   heparin 12.9
   menstruation, warfarin 12.16
   pathogenesis
      uremia 30.8–30.9, 30.15
      warfarin 12.13
Bleeding time 12.6
   aspirin 41.6
Bleomycin 90.11
   adverse effects 90.11
      nephrotoxicity 29.9
      pulmonary toxicity 22.4, 22.7,
         91.22–91.24, 91.26
      teratogenicity 45.8

dosing
   alterations 90.11
   renal dysfunciton 91.20
   pharmacokinetics 90.11
   pharmacology 90.11
   use in pleural effusions 92.10
Blocadren
   See Timolol
Blood count 4.13
Blood disorders
   See Hematological disorders
Blood 18.13–18.14
   adverse effects 18.14
      coagulopathies 18.14
      hypocalcemia 18.14
Blood-brain barrier 56.2
Blood "doping" 87.6–87.7
Blood dyscrasias
   See Hematological disorders; spe-
      cific disorders
Blood gases
   See Arterial blood gases
Blood pressure
   See Hypertension
Blood transfusions
   use in bone marrow transplantation
      94.5
Blood typing 44.20–44.21
Blood urea nitrogen
   BUN/SrCr ratio 29.3
   cirrhosis 25.3
   overview 4.9
Bone marrow rescue 94.1
Bone marrow transplantation
   allogenic 94.1–94.5
   autologous 94.5–94.7
   bone marrow harvesting 94.3–94.4,
      94.6
   bone marrow rescue 94.1
   complications
      graft failure 94.11
      graft versus host disease
         acute 94.2, 94.11–94.15
         chronic 94.16–94.17
      infectious complications
         94.17–94.21
      regimen-related toxicities
         94.7–94.10
   immunosuppressive therapy
      94.2–94.3, 94.4, 94.6
   indications 93.3, 94.4–94.5
      acute myelogenous leukemia
         94.4–94.5
      nonHodgkin's lymphoma
         94.6–94.7
   preparative regimens 94.2–94.3, 94.4
   supportive care 94.5, 94.7
   use in
      aplastic anemia 89.14
      leukemia
         acute myelogenous 94.22
         acute nonlymphocytic 92.6
         chronic myelogenous 92.7
      metastatic breast cancer 93.6
Bone physiology
   antibiotic concentrations 65.5
   physiology 65.1–65.2
Boric acid
   use in candida vaginitis 46.7
Bowel decontamination
   transplant recipients 33.39
   use in bone marrow transplantation
      94.5

Brain abscess 56.18–56.21
   epidemiology 56.18
   infections 56.18–56.21
   predisposing factors 56.19
   treatment 56.20–56.21
Brain death 33.11
Breakthrough bleeding, drug-induced
   contraceptives, oral 43.12
Breast cancer
   chemotherapy
      adjuvant 93.3–93.5
      metastatic 93.5–93.6
      regimens 90.6
   drug-induced
      contraceptives, oral 43.13
      estrogens 46.32
      progestin 43.18
   metastatic sites 90.5
   prognostic factors, recurrence 93.4
   radiation, postsurgical 93.3
   risk factors 93.2
   screening 90.6, 93.2–93.3
   signs/symptoms 90.8
   staging 90.7
   surgery 93.3
Breast milk
   Also see Lactation
   content 99.5–99.6, 99.8
   contraindications, breast feeding
      45.22
   drugs excreted in
      table of 45.23–45.29
      lithium 77.8
      methadone 83.7
      timolol 49.4
   factors affecting 45.21
Brethine
   See Terbutaline
Bretylium
   adverse effects 16.6
   pharmacokinetics 16.6
   pharmacology
      effect on the ECG 16.3
   use in cardiac arrest 16.21
Bretylol
   See Bretylium
Brevicon
   See Contraceptives, oral
Brofaromine 73.19
Bromides, breast milk 45.23
Bromocriptine
   Also see Dopamine agonists;
      Parkinson's disease
   adverse effects
      dyskinesias 51.11
      gastrointestinal 44.30, 51.11
      general 51.11
      hypotension 44.30
      lactation suppression
         44.29–44.30
      neurological 44.30
      psychiatric 51.11
      pulmonary 22.4, 51.11
Bromocriptine (continued)
   breast milk 45.22, 45.23
   dosing, high/low doses
      51.10–51.11
   pharmacology
      effect on thyroid function tests
         47.6, 47.8
   use in
      apathy 79.6
      cocaine addiction 84.15, 84.17
      hepatic coma 25.14
      impotence 103.8

nocturnal myoclonus 74.15
Parkinson's disease 51.8,
    51.10–51.11
premenstrual syndrome 46.18
restless leg syndrome 74.15
short stature 95.16

Brompheniramine
    adverse effects, teratogenicity 45.8
    breast milk 45.23
    dosing 21.9
    use in rhinitis 21.7–21.12

Brompton's mixture 7.17

Bronchial infections
    classification
        acute bronchitis 58.2
        chronic bronchitis 58.2
    clinical presentation 58.2
    definition 58.2
    pathogens 58.2
    predisposing factors 58.2
    treatment 58.3

Bronchiolitis 70.10, 97.3,
    97.14–97.15
    obliterans 33.25

Bronchitis
    Also see Chronic obstructive air-
        ways disease
    antibiotic
        prophylaxis 58.3
        therapy 58.3
    clinical presentation 20.2
    diagnosis 20.2
    immunoprophylaxis 58.3

Bronchodilators
    Also see specific agents
    administration, metered-dose
        inhalers 19.27
    use in
        asthma 19.8–19.27
        bronchopulmonary dysplasia
            98.2–98.3
        chronic obstructive airways
            disease 20.6–20.9

Bronchopulmonary dysplasia
    definition 98.1
    nutritional needs, pediatric 99.16
    pathophysiology 98.1
    signs and symptoms 98.1
    therapy 98.1–98.4

Bronchospasm
    See specific pulmonary disorders

Bronkosol
    See Isoetharine

Brudzinski's sign 56.5

Buclizine
    adverse effects, teratogenicity 45.8
    use in motion sickness 105.4

Budd-Chiari 26.8

Budesonide, nasal 21.14

Bulimia nervosa
    Also see Eating disorders;
        Anorexia nervosa
    clinical presentation 80.8, 84.7
    comorbidity 80.10
    complications 80.9
    definitions 80.1
    diagnosis 80.2, 80.9–80.10
    prognosis 80.12
    treatment
        drugs 80.4–80.5, 80.10–80.12
        hospitalization 80.9
        psychotherapy 80.5, 80.10

Bumetanide
    Also see Diuretics, loop
    adverse effects, teratogenicity 45.8

use in
    congestive heart failure 15.15
    renal dysfunction 15.16

Bumex
    See Bumetamide

BUN
    See Blood urea nitrogen

Bupivicaine 8.20–8.21

Bupropion
    Also see Antidepressants
    adverse effects, teratogenicity 45.8
    breast milk 45.23
    use in
        adult attention deficit hyper-
            activity 78.3
        bulimia 80.5
        cocaine addiction 84.17
        depression, adulthood
            76.10–76.12

Burns 39.11–39.14

Buserelin
    endometriosis 46.21

Buspirone
    adverse effects 73.17
    pharmacology 73.7
        benzodiazepine comparison
            73.17
        benzodiazepine conversion 73.17
    use in
        aggression 73.17, 78.15–78.16,
            79.4–79.5
        anxiety 73.7, 73.17
        depression, adulthood 73.7,
            73.17
        premenstrual syndrome 46.16

Buspar
    See Buspirone

Busulfan
    adverse effects 90.11
        cataracts 49.14
        pulmonary toxicity 22.4, 91.24,
            91.26
        seizures 94.9
        teratogenicity 45.6, 45.8
    dosing in obese patients 94.8
    pharmacokinetics 90.11
    pharmacology 90.11
    use in
        leukemia
            acute myelogenous 94.22
            chronic myelogenous 92.7

Butalbital, teratogenicity 45.8

Butazolidin
    See Phenylbutazone

Butoconazole
    adverse effects, teratogenicity 45.8
    use in
        candidiasis, vaginal 69.5
        vaginitis 46.5–46.6

Butorphanol
    adverse effects
        cardiovascular 7.20
        psychosis 7.3, 7.14
        teratogenicity 45.8
        withdrawal reactions,
            precipitating 7.13, 7.14
    breast milk 45.23
    use in labor and delivery 7.13

Butyrophenones
    use in emesis 105.4

CABG
    See Coronary artery bypass graft

Cachectin
    See Tumor necrosis factor

Cachexia, cancer 93.11

Cafergot
    See Ergotamine

Caffeine
    abuse 85.8–85.13
    adverse effects 85.10
        anxiogenic 73.4
        hypertension 10.11
        increased intraocular pressure 49.3
        osteoporosis 46.29
        teratogenicity 45.9, 85.12
    breast milk 45.23, 85.12
    content in beverages 85.4
    dependence 85.11–85.12
    effect on athletes 85.13
    interactions, drugs
        table of 85.10
        ciprofloxacin 63.7
        lithium 77.6
    pharmacokinetics 85.9
    pharmacology 85.8–85.12
    use in
        apnea, newborn 96.23
        bronchopulmonary dysplasia
            98.2
        migraine headache 50.6, 50.8
        withdrawal 85.12

Calan
    See Verapamil

Calciferol
    adverse effects
        hypercalcemia 28.20–28.21
    use in
        cystic fibrosis 100.6
        hyperphosphatemia, renal failure
            30.14
        prevention of osteoporosis 41.20

Calcimar
    See Calcitonin

Calcipotriene 38.2

Calcitonin
    use in
        hypercalcemia 28.21–28.22
        osteoporosis 46.33–46.34

Calcitriol
    use in
        hyperphosphatemia 30.14
        hypocalcemia 30.14

Calcium
    Also see Hypercalcemia;
        Hypocalcemia
    content in foods 46.29–46.30
    dietary 28.20
    homeostasis 4.7–4.8, 28.19
    laboratory interpretation 4.7–4.8,
        28.19–28.20
    preparations 46.29
    use in
        cardiac arrest 16.23
        hypertension 10.11
        hyperkalemia 28.18–28.19, 30.6
        hypermagnesemia 28.27
        hyperphosphatemia 30.13
        neonatal seizures 96.25
        pregnancy 44.8
        prevention of osteoporosis 41.20,
            42.10, 46.29–46.30

Calcium channel blockers
    Also see specific agents
    table of 13.14
    adverse effects 10.24
        table of 13.16
        angina exacerbation 13.15
        bradycardia 13.16
        constipation 13.16
        edema 13.17, 13.18

fatigue 13.16
        headache 13.18
        heart block 13.16
        heart failure 15.11
        hyperglycemia 48.52
        hypotension 13.15
        ocular 49.15
    contraindications/precautions
        10.24, 13.16
    dosing
        table of 10.23
        hepatic insufficiency 13.17
        maintenance 13.15
        renal insufficiency 13.17
    interactions, drugs
        cimetidine 23.8
        differential effects on hepatic
            metabolism 3.4
        digoxin 13.16–13.17, 15.34
        lithium 77.7
    pharmacokinetics 13.17–13.18
    pharmacology
        comparative 10.23–10.24,
            13.13–13.15
        effect on
            nodal conduction 10.23–10.24
            vasodilation 10.23–10.24
        mechanism of action 10.23,
            13.14–13.15
    preparations
        amlodipine 10.23
        diltiazem 10.13, 10.23–10.24
        drugs 13.13–13.15
        felodipine 10.23
        isradipine 10.23
        nicardipine 10.23–10.24
        nifedipine 10.23–10.24
        sustained release 13.17–13.18
        verapamil 10.13, 10.23–10.24
    use in
        angina 13.13–13.18
        angioplasty, post 13.22
        atrial fibrillation 13.16, 16.8
        cluster headache 50.15
        congestive heart failure 15.34
        delayed cerebral ischemia 53.15
        diabetic hypertension 48.52
        diabetic nephropathy 30.20,
            48.53
        dysmenorrhea 46.14
        hypertensive emergencies 17.4,
            17.7
        ischemic stroke 53.12–53.13
        microvascular angina 13.20
        migraine headache 50.12–50.13
        myocardial infarction 14.5, 14.8,
            14.16
        paroxysmal supraventricular
            tachycardia 16.12
        preeclampsia 44.18, 44.20
        preterm labor 44.25–44.26
        Prinzmetal's angina 13.14, 13.20
        Raynaud's phenomenon 11.9
        unstable angina 13.14–13.15
        vascular dementias 102.9
    use with beta blockers 13.15, 13.18

Calcium hydroxyapatite,
    deposition 40.4

Calcium oxalate
    deposition 40.4
    stones 29.20

Calcium pyrophosphate,
    deposition 40.4

Calcium salts
    adverse effects
        nephrotoxicity 29.9

Calcium carbonate
   interactions, iron 88.7
Calorie calculations 35.6–35.8
Campylobacter
   helicobacter 23.11–23.13
   jejuni 60.9
Campylobacter enteritis 60.12
Cancer
   Also see specific cancers; specific
      drugs
   treatment
      gene therapy 5.6
      monoclonal antibodies 5.3–5.5
Candidiasis
   candida hypersensitivity 69.6
   diaper rash 95.3
   esophageal 68.30
   oral treatment 68.30
   peritonitis 61.14–61.15
   systemic
      clinical presentation 69.7
      diagnosis 69.7, 69.9
   urinary 69.13
   vaginal
      clinical presentation 1.11–1.12,
         46.2–46.4
      diagnosis 1.11–1.12, 46.3–46.4
      predisposing factors 46.4
      treatment 1.11–1.12
         systemic 46.5, 46.7, 69.6
         topical 1.11–1.12, 46.4–46.7,
            69.5–69.6
      risk factors 69.5
Candiduria 69.13
Cannabinoids 86.5–86.7
   Also see Dronabinol
   use as antiemetic 105.4, 105.5,
      105.7
CAPD
   See Peritoneal dialysis
Capoten
   See Captopril
Capreomycin
   adverse effects
      nephrotoxicity 29.9
   dosing 59.6
   pharmacokinetics
      concentration, plasma 59.6
Capsaicin 48.48
Captopril
   Also see Angiotensin-converting
      enzyme inhibitors
   adverse effects
      cough 15.31
      dermatological 15.31
      hematological 15.31
      hepatotoxicity 26.6
      hyperkalemia 10.22, 15.31, 17.5
      nephrotoxicity 15.32, 29.9
      overview 17.5–17.6
      rash 10.22, 15.31
      taste alterations 10.22
      teratogenicity 15.31, 45.9
   breast milk 45.23
   contraindications/precautions 15.31
      table of 10.14
      overview 17.6
   dosing 32.6
   interactions, drugs
      allopurinol 40.10
      digoxin 15.22
      potassium 10.22
      nonsteroidal anti-inflammatory
         drugs 3.4
   pharmacokinetics

clearance
   dialysis 32.6
   renal failure 32.6
   half-life 32.6
   parameters 32.6
pharmacology
   mechanism of action 10.23,
      15.30, 17.5, 17.6
   onset 17.5, 17.6
use in
   Alzheimer's 102.7
   congestive heart failure 15.5,
      15.12–15.13, 15.28–15.34
   diabetic nephropathy 30.19
   hypertension 10.13, 10.22–10.23
   hypertensive emergencies 17.5,
      17.6
   myocardial infarction 14.4, 14.8,
      14.15–14.16
   Raynaud's phenomenon 11.10
Carbachol 49.5, 49.8
Carbamazepine
   Also see Seizure disorders
   adverse effects 52.8–52.12
      drug fever 6.9
      hematological 52.8–52.9, 77.7
      hepatotoxicity 52.9
      nephrotoxicity 29.9
      neurotoxicity 77.7
      ocular 49.13
      pulmonary 22.6
      serum sickness 6.7
      syndrome of inappropriate secre-
         tion of antidiuretic hormone
         52.10
      teratogenicity 44.14, 45.6, 45.9,
         45.23
      vasculitis 6.12
   breast milk 45.23
   hematological routine monitoring
      52.8
   interactions, drugs
      cimetidine 23.8
      contraceptives 43.11
      corticosteroids 3.5
      erythromycin 3.9, 52.24
      felbamate 52.11
      lamotrigine 52.14
      lithium 77.7
      mechanism 3.2
      valproate 52.24
      warfarin 12.20
   pharmacokinetics
      autoinduction of metabolism
         52.9
      bioavailability 52.9–52.10
      bioequivalence, generics 52.9
      humidity effects 52.9
      parameters 52.9
      plasma concentrations 52.5–52.6,
         52.10
   pharmacology, effect on thyroid
      function tests 47.6–47.7
   use in
      aggression, dementia 102.11
      aggression/disinhibition
         79.4–79.5
      alcohol withdrawal 82.6
      bipolar disorders 77.9
      cocaine addiction 84.17
      diabetic neuropathy 48.48
      mood stabliziation 79.4
      posttraumatic stress 73.28
      pregnancy 44.14
      schizophrenia, adjunctively 75.11
      seizures 52.5, 52.8–52.12

Carbapenems
   See specific agents
Carbarsone, teratogenicity 45.9
Carbidopa
   Also see Levodopa
   combined with levodopa 51.5–51.7
Carbimazole
   adverse effects, teratogenicity 45.9
   breast milk 45.23
Carbinoxamine
   dosing
      adult and pediatric 21.9
   use in rhinitis 21.6–21.12
Carbon dioxide
   buffer system 27.1
   concentration, serum 27.3
   content 4.5
Carbonic anhydrase-inhibitors
   Also see specific agents
   adverse effects
      acidosis 49.10
      alkalinization, urine 40.13, 49.10
      ocular 49.15
   preparations 49.11
   use in glaucoma 49.10–49.11, 49.12
Carboplatin
   Also see Cisplatin
   adverse effects 90.11
   dosing
      alterations 90.11
      renal dysfunciton 91.20
   pharmacokinetics 90.11
   pharmacology 90.11
   use in ovarian cancer 93.13
Carboprost 44.28–44.29
Carcinoembryonic antigen, colon
   cancer 93.7–93.8
Carcinogens
   alcohol 82.10
   cigarettes 85.4
   coffee 85.11
   risks, table of 90.2
Carcinoma
   Also see specific cancers
   basal cell, sun exposure 39.4
   squamous cell, sun exposure 39.4
Cardiac arrhythmias
   See Arrhythmias
Cardiac Arrhythmia Suppression
   Trial 16.15–16.16
Cardiac dilation 15.3, 15.9
Cardiac hypertrophy 15.3, 15.9
Cardiac transplantation 33.9,
   33.17–33.23
Cardiogenic shock
   Also see Shock
   clinical presentation 18.16,
      18.22–18.23
   diagnosis 18.3–18.4, 18.22–18.23
   pathogenesis 18.3–18.5
   treatment 18.4, 18.16, 18.22–18.25
      bicarbonate 18.22
      fluids 18.16, 18.23
      inotropic agents 18.17–18.19,
         18.22–18.24
      intra-aortic balloon pump 18.24
      oxygen 18.22
      thrombolytics 18.22
      vasodilators 18.16, 18.22
      vasopressors 18.24
Cardiomyopathy
   alcohol-induced 82.11
Cardioplegic solutions 8.13–8.15,

33.12
Cardiopulmonary arrest 16.19–16.23
Cardiopulmonary resusitation
   16.19–16.23
Cardiotoxicity
   Also see Arrhythmias, drug-
      induced
   adverse effects, ocular 49.15
   drug-induced 85.2
      alcohol 82.11
      amiodarone 16.19
      amphetamine 15.11, 84.3
      amrinone 15.35, 18.20
      anabolic steroids 87.5
      antiarrhythmics 16.6, 16.10,
         16.16, 16.17
      antidepressants 16.17
         cyclic 76.9, 76.12–76.14
      antihistamine 16.17
      astemizole 21.12
      beta agonists 19.10, 19.13
      beta blockers, ophthalmic
         49.4–49.7, 49.10
      calcium channel blockers 13.14,
         13.15, 13.16
      cocaine 15.11, 84.10–84.12
      daunorubicin 15.11, 91.17–91.19
      diazepam (IV) 52.27–52.28
      digoxin 15.16
      dobutamine 18.18
      dopamine 18.17
      dopamine agonists 51.11
      doxorubicin 91.17–91.19
      erythropoietin 87.7
      idarubicin 91.7–91.19
      milrinone 15.35
      mitoxantrone 91.17–91.19
      nicotine 85.2, 85.4
      norepinephrine 18.24
      oxytocin 44.28
      phenylephrine, ophthalmic 49.18
      phenytoin (IV) 52.28–52.29
      potassium 28.17–28.18
      solvents, inhaled 83.12
      sotalol 16.17
      terfenadine 21.12, 69.16
      theophylline 19.13
      thyroid 47.14
      timolol 49.4
      vasopressin 25.9
      verapamil 16.13
Cardioversion
   anticoagulation 12.17
   in thyroid disorders 47.16–47.17
Cardizem
   See Diltiazem
Cardura
   See Doxazosin
Carmustine
   adverse effects 90.11
      encephalopathy 91.15
      hepatotoxicity 26.6, 91.27
      ocular 49.15
      pulmonary toxicity 22.4, 91.24,
         91.26
   dosing
      alterations 90.11
Carmustine (continued)
   in obese patients 94.8
   pharmacokinetics 90.11
   pharmacology 90.11
Carprofen 40.5
Carteolol
   adverse effects, teratogenicity 45.9
   pharmacodynamic properties 10.19
   pharmacokinetic properties 10.20

use in
glaucoma 49.5, 49.7
hypertension 10.18–10.21
Cartol
See Carteolol
Casanthranol
adverse effects, teratogenicity 45.9
breast milk 45.24
Cascara sagrada
adverse effects, teratogenicity 45.9
breast milk 45.23
Catapres
See Clonidine
Cataracts
drug-induced
allopurinol 49.16
busulfan 49.14
corticosteroids 49.15,
49.17–49.18
echothiophate 49.9
doxycycline 63.5
etiology 39.11
Cathartics
Also see Laxatives
Catheter-associated UTI 63.14–63.15
CAVH
See Continuous arteriovenous
hemofiltration
CBC
See Complete blood count
Cefaclor
Also see Cephalosporins
use in
otitis 97.8–97.9
pediatric infections 97.5
Cefadroxil
use in pediatric infections 97.4
Cefamandole
Also see Cephalosporins
interactions, drugs
warfarin 12.20
use in cardiac surgery 57.8
Cefazolin
Also see Cephalosporins
concentration, bone 65.5
dosing 32.6
clearance
dialysis 32.6
renal failure 32.6
half-life 32.6
parameters 32.6
pharmacokinetics
clearance
dialysis 54.15
renal disease 54.18
use in
endocarditis
prosthetic valve 57.8–57.10
S. aureus 57.10
S. viridans 57.6–57.7
meningitis 56.14
ophthalmic infections 49.17
osteomyelitis, acute 65.4
pneumonia 58.7, 58.10
pyelonephritis 63.8
surgical prophylaxis 55.2–55.5
transplant surgery 33.38
Cefepime
use in
cholangitis 61.3
febrile neutropenia 67.10
Cefixime
Also see Cephalosporins
dosing 32.6
clearance

dialysis 32.6
renal failure 32.6
half-life 32.6
use in
bronchitis 58.3
gonorrhea 64.3–64.8
otitis 97.8–97.9
pediatric infections 97.5
Cefmetazole
interactions, drugs
warfarin 12.20
Cefobid
See Cefoperazone
Cefonicid
Also see Cephalosporins
clearance
renal failure 54.18
protein binding 54.18
use in pyelonephritis 63.8
Cefoperazone
Also see Cephalosporins
dosing 32.6
clearance
dialysis 32.6
renal failure 32.6
half-life 32.6
parameters 32.6
interactions, drugs
warfarin 12.20
pharmacokinetics
renal disease 54.18
use in
cholangitis 61.3
immunocompromised hosts 67.9
pyelonephritis 63.8
Ceforanide
Also see Cephalosporins
clearance, renal disease 54.18
Cefotaxime
Also see Cephalosporins
dosing 32.6
pharmacokinetics
clearance
dialysis 32.6
renal failure 32.6
half-life 32.6
parameters 32.6
concentration, bone 65.5
protein binding 54.18
dialysis 54.15
use in
brain abscess 56.21
Lyme 72.3–72.4
meningitis 56.7–56.11,
56.14–56.16
neonates 96.17–96.18
osteomyelitis, acute 65.4
peritonitis 61.4, 61.10, 61.11
pyelonephritis 63.8–63.9
sepsis, neonates 96.17–96.18
transplant surgery 33.38
Cefotetan
Also see Cephalosporins
dosing 32.6
interactions, drugs
warfarin 12.20
pharmacokinetics
clearance
dialysis 32.6, 54.15
renal disease 54.18
renal failure 32.6
half-life 32.6
parameters 32.6
use in
pelvic inflammatory disease 64.6,
64.7
pyelonephritis 63.8

surgical prophylaxis 55.3, 55.5
Cefoxitin
Also see Cephalosporins
dosing 32.7
pharmacokinetics
clearance
dialysis 32.7, 54.15
renal disease 54.18
renal failure 32.7
half-life 32.7
parameters 32.7
concentration, bone 65.5
use in
pelvic inflammatory disease
64.6, 64.7
pyelonephritis 63.8
surgical prophylaxis 55.2, 55.3,
55.5
Cefpodoxime
Also see Cephalosporins
refrigeration 97.11
use in
otitis 97.9
pediatric infections 97.5
Cefprozil
Also see Cephalosporins
refrigeration oral solution 97.11
use in
otitis 97.9
pediatric infections 97.5
Ceftazidime
Also see Cephalosporins
dosing 32.5, 32.7
pharmacokinetics
clearance
dialysis 32.5, 32.7, 32.13, 54.15
renal disease 54.18
renal failure 32.5, 32.7
concentration, bone 65.5
parameters 32.7
pharmacology
combination 67.9–67.10
monotherapy 67.9–67.10
use in
cystic fibrosis 100.7–100.10
gram-negative meningitis 56.7,
56.10, 56.15
immunocompromised hosts
67.4–67.13
osteomyelitis, pseudomonal 65.4
peritonitis 31.10
pyelonephritis 63.8
UTI, hospital-acquired 63.7
Ceftizoxime
Also see Cephalosporins
dosing 32.7
pharmacokinetics
clearance
dialysis 32.7, 54.15
renal disease 54.18
renal failure 32.7
half-life 32.7
parameters 32.7
use in
aspiration pneumonia 58.12
meningitis 56.10, 56.16
pyelonephritis 63.8
Ceftriaxone
Also see Cephalosporins
adverse effects
biliary sludge 56.11–56.12
dosing 32.7
neonates 64.8
pharmacokinetics
clearance 32.7
dialysis 32.7
renal failure 32.7

half-life 32.7
parameters 32.7
use in
chancroid 64.15
chlamydia 64.10
gonorrhea 64.3–64.8
Lyme 72.3–72.4
meningitis 56.9–56.10
neonates 96.17–96.18
ophthalmia neonatorum 64.8
osteomyelitis, staph 65.4
otitis media 97.8
pelvic inflammatory disease 64.7
pregnancy 64.3
pyelonephritis 63.8
Salmonella enteritis 60.14
sepsis, neonates 96.17–96.18
septic arthritis 65.11
syphilis 64.4, 64.13
Cefuroxime
Also see Cephalosporins
dosing 32.7
pharmacokinetics
clearance
dialysis 32.7
renal failure 32.7
concentration, bone 65.5
half-life 32.7
parameters 32.7
refrigeration oral solution 97.11
use in
bronchitis 58.3
cardiac surgery 57.8
H. influenzae meningitis 56.10
Lyme 72.3–72.4
osteomyelitis, staph 65.4
otitis 97.8–97.9
pediatric infections 97.5
pyelonephritis 63.8
S. pneumoniae meningitis 56.14
surgical prophylaxis 55.4
Cefzil
See Cefprozil
Cellulitis
antibiotic spectrum of activity 66.3
definition 66.1
microbiology 66.2
pharmaceutical care 1.6, 1.7
treatment 66.2–66.5
empirical based on severity 66.2–66.5
IV drug abuser 66.5
penicillin allergic 66.4
topical 66.4
Central nervous system
infections 56.1–56.21
Also see Meningitis
brain abscess 56.18–56.21
meningitis 56.2–56.18
shunt infections 56.17–56.18
Central nervous system
penetration of drugs
Also see specific agents
antibiotics
table of 56.7
effect on meningitis 56.7–56.14,
56.19
Central nervous system penetration of
drugs (continued)
ethambutol 59.13
isoniazid 59.13
pyrazinamide 59.13
rifampin 59.13
CNS stimulant abuse 84.1–84.16
Centrax
See Prazepam

Cephalexin
Also see Cephalosporins
pharmacokinetics
clearance
dialysis 54.15
renal disease 54.18
concentration, bone 65.5
use in
pediatric infections 97.4
urinary tract infection 63.5
Cephalosporins
Also see specific agents; Beta-lactam antibiotics
table of generations 54.7
adverse effects
table of 54.13
coagulopathies 67.9
hemolysis 89.5
hypersensitivity 22.2
nephrotoxicity 29.9
neutropenia 89.10
pseudomembranous colitis 60.10
pulmonary 22.2
teratogenicity 45.9
breast milk 45.24
dosing 32.6–32.10
interactions, drugs
contraceptives, oral 43.11
mechanism 3.2
pharmacokinetics
clearance
dialysis 54.15
renal disease 54.18
concentration, bone 65.5
half-life 32.6–32.10
parameters 32.6–32.10
pharmacology
generations of products 63.8
use in
brain abscess 56.20, 56.21
chancroid 64.15
cholangitis 61.3
endocarditis
prosthetic valve 57.8–57.10
S. aureus 57.10
S. viridans 57.7
gonorrhea 64.3–64.8
immunocompromised hosts
67.4–67.13
meningitis
table of 56.9
neonatal 96.17–96.18
osteomyelitis 65.4–65.7
peritonitis 61.4, 61.5, 61.8,
61.10, 61.12, 61.13, 61.14,
61.15
pneumonia 58.7, 58.10
sepsis, neonatal 96.17–96.18
septic arthritis 65.10–65.11
syphilis 64.13
Cephalothin
Also see Cephalosporins
Cephapirin
Also see Cephalosporins
dosing 32.7
pharmacokinetics
clearance
renal failure 32.7
half-life 32.7
Cephradine
Also see Cephalosporins
pharmacokinetic parameters 32.7
use in
pediatric infections 97.4
urinary tract infection 63.5
Cephulac
See Lactulose

Ceranapril 102.7
Cerebral edema
etiology, dialysis disequilibrium
31.7
Cerebral hemorrhage
complications 53.14
treatment
delayed cerebral ischemia
53.14–53.15
hydrocephalus 53.14
rebleeding 53.14
seizures 53.14, 53.15
definition 53.1–53.2
drug-induced
amphetamine 84.4
cocaine 84.10
pathophysiology 53.2–53.3
Cerebral infarction
complications 53.13
definition 53.1
diagnosis 53.9
pathophysiology 53.2–53.3
treatment
anticoagulants 53.3, 53.9, 53.10
calcium channel blockers
53.12–53.13
corticosteroids 53.12
Cerebrospinal fluid 56.2
Cerebrovascular accident
See Thrombosis
Cerebrovascular disorders 53.1–53.15
Also see Cerebral hemorrhage;
Cerebral infarction; Transient
ischemic attacks
classifications
cerebral hemorrhage 53.1
cerebral infarction 53.1
cerebrovascular disease
53.1–53.15
reversible ischemic neurological
deficit 53.1
stroke 53.2
transient ischemic attacks
53.1–53.8
definition 53.1–53.2
epidemiology 53.2
pathophysiology 53.2–53.3
risk factors 53.2, 53.4
Cerebyx
See Phosphenytoin
Cervical cancer
drug-induced, contraceptives, oral
43.13
Cervical caps 43.4, 43.22
Cervical dysplasia 43.13
Cestodiasis 71.6, 71.9–71.11
Chancroid 64.15
Charcoal, activated
effect on elimination of drugs
theophylline 19.24
use in
acetaminophen overdoses
104.19–104.20
antidepressant overdoses 104.18
phencyclidine toxicity 86.8
Chemistries, blood 4.7–4.12
Chemo-embolization 93.9
Chemotherapy
Also see specific agents
adjuvant, breast cancer 93.3–93.5
administration guidelines 91.11
extravasation 91.11–91.12
adverse effects 91.1–91.33
allergic 91.13
cardiac 91.17–91.19

dermatological 91.8–91.12
drug fever 6.10
gastrointestinal 91.5–91.7
hematological 91.2–91.4
hepatic 91.23–91.24, 91.27
nausea/vomiting 105.5–105.9
neurological 91.14–91.17
pulmonary 91.22–91.25
renal 91.19–91.22
secondary malignancies 91.25
teratogenic 91.26–91.28
dosing in obese patients 94.8
use in
allogenic bone marrow transplantation 94.2–94.3, 94.4
autologous bone marrow transplantation 94.4, 94.6
Chemstrip bG
See Home blood glucose monitoring
Chemstrip uG
See Urine, glucose tests
Chenodiol, teratogenicity 45.9
Chickenpox 70.6–70.7, 95.25
Also see Varicella
China white 83.2
Chlamydia 64.8–64.10
clinical presentation
lymphogranuloma venereum
64.10
urethritis 64.9–64.10
treatment 64.9–64.10
doxycycline 63.9
ofloxacin 63.9
Chloral hydrate
Also see Benzodiazepines;
Insomnia
breast milk 45.24
dosing, neonates 96.30
interactions, drugs
warfarin 3.3, 12.20
use in
insomnia 74.11, 74.16
pediatrics 74.16
sedation 95.20–95.21
Chlorambucil
adverse effects 90.11
immune thrombocytopenia 92.8
pulmonary toxicity 22.5,
91.23–91.24
teratogenicity 45.9
pharmacokinetics 90.11
pharmacology 90.11
use in
chronic lymphocytic leukemia
92.8
rheumatoid arthritis 45.3
Chloramphenicol 56.6
adverse effects 97.20
anemia, aplastic 54.13, 56.12,
89.12–89.13
gray-baby syndrome 54.13
optic neuritis 49.14
teratogenicity 45.9
brain abscess 56.20–56.21
meningitis 56.6–56.7, 56.10
breast milk 45.24
interactions, drugs
contraceptives, oral 43.11, 43.12
mechanisms 3.2
sulfonylureas 48.39
warfarin 12.20
pharmacokinetics
half-life, hepatitis 62.5
use in
Rocky Mountain spotted fever
97.19–97.20

Salmonella gastroenteritis 60.13
Shigella gastroenteritis 60.2,
60.14
Chlordiazepoxide
Also see Benzodiazepines
administration, intramuscular
73.10
adverse effects
pulmonary 22.3
teratogenicity 45.9
pharmacokinetics 73.9, 73.12
half-life, hepatitis 62.5
use in
alcohol withdrawal, acute 82.6
generalized anxiety 73.7
Chlorhexidine, use in supportive care
94.5
Chloride, laboratory assessment 4.6
Chloroform, breast milk 45.24
Chloroquine
Also see Antimalarials;
Hydroxychloroquine
adverse effects 71.3–71.4
ocular 41.12, 49.14
psoriasis 38.5
teratogenicity 45.9, 71.3
breast milk 45.24
use in
juvenile rheumatoid arthritis
41.21
rheumatoid arthritis 41.12
malaria 71.3
pediatric patients 71.3
pregnancy 71.3
Chlorothiazide
Also see Diuretics
breast milk 45.24
teratogenicity 45.9
Chlorotrianisene
adverse effects, teratogenicity 45.9
breast milk 45.24
Chlorpheniramine
Also see Antihistamines
adverse effects
ocular 49.13
teratogenicity 45.9
dosing
adult and pediatric 21.9
use in rhinitis 21.7–21.12
Chlorpromazine
Also see Neuroleptics
adverse effects 75.7, 75.23
hemolysis 89.5
hepatotoxicity 26.7
lupus 6.15
neutropenia 89.10–89.11
ocular 49.12, 49.16
teratogenicity 45.9
breast milk 45.24
dose 75.8
effect of smoking 85.3
use in
lactation stimulation 44.29
migraine headache 50.8–50.9
nausea/vomiting 105.4
psychoses 75.7–75.8
Chlorpropamide
Also see Sulfonylureas
adverse effects
alcohol flush 48.43
antidiuretic effects (SIADH)
48.44
hepatotoxicity 26.6, 48.44
hemolysis 89.5
hypoglycemia 48.44–48.45
teratogenicity 45.9

breast milk 45.24
interactions, allopurinol 40.10
pharmacokinetics 48.37–48.38
use in elderly 48.46

Chlorprothixene, breast milk 45.24

Chlorthalidone
Also see Diuretics
adverse effects, teratogenicity 45.9
breast milk 45.24

Chlorzoxazone, teratogenicity 45.9

Cholangitis and cholecystitis
clinical presentation 61.2
diagnosis 61.2
microbiology, pathogens 61.2
treatment 61.2–61.3

Choledyl
See Theophylline

Cholelithiasis
drug-induced
contraceptives, oral 43.15
estrogens 46.32

Cholera vaccine, teratogenicity 45.9

Cholestasis
drug-induced
see Hepatic disorders, drug-
induced
laboratory interpretation 4.12
pathogenesis 26.2

Cholesterol
See Dyslipidemia
in thyroid disorders 47.6, 47.13
laboratory assessment 9.11–9.12
link to atherosclerosis 9.8–9.10

Cholestyramine
administration 9.14, 9.17
adverse effects 9.14, 9.17
bloating, constipation 9.14
malabsorption 9.14
teratogenicity 45.9
dosing for hypercholesterolemia
9.14–9.16, 9.17
interactions, drugs
digitoxin 15.22
digoxin 15.22
sulfasalazine 24.7
thyroxine 47.13
warfarin 12.20
interactions, drugs 3.1, 3.2, 9.14
pharmacology
effect on thyroid function 47.6
mechanism of action 9.14
use in
hypercholesterolemia 9.14, 9.15,
9.17, 9.19
pseudomembranous colitis 60.11,
60.12

Chorionic gonadotropin 44.2

Chromium
use in athletes 87.5

Chronic obstructive airways
disease 20.1–20.12
cautious use of narcotics in 7.21
clinical presentation 20.1
complications of
bacterial infection 20.6
cor pulmonale 20.2
polycythemia 20.2
definition 19.3, 20.1
pathogenesis 20.1–20.3
treatment
approaches
oxygen 20.8
principles 20.3
drugs
also see specific agents

anticholinergics 20.6–20.7
beta-adrenergic agonists 20.3,
20.7–20.9
bronchodilators 20.3–20.9
corticosteroids 20.3, 20.7–20.9
ipratropium 20.6–20.7
oxygen 20.8–20.9
progesterone 20.10
stimulants 20.9–20.10
theophylline 20.3, 20.7
vaccines 20.6

Chronic obstructive pulmonary disease
See Chronic obstructive airways
disease

Ciclopirox 69.3

Cigarettes
Also see Nicotine
adverse effects
teratogenicity 81.9, 85.3
cancers 90.1
cessation of 20.4–20.5, 85.6–85.8
effects on
bone mass 46.29
bronchitis, chronic 58.2
chronic obstructive airways disease 20.1–20.4
coronary heart disease 10.8
gastroesophageal reflux 23.17
intermittent claudication 11.2,
11.4
peptic ulcer 23.3
refractory ulcers 23.11
theophylline clearance
19.16–19.17
vascular dementias 102.9
interactions, drugs
table of 85.3
nicotine content 85.2–85.3

Cilazapril 10.22

Cimetidine
Also see Histamine₂-antagonists
adverse effects
confusion 23.4
drug fever 6.9
gynecomastia 23.4
impotence 23.4
nephrotoxicity 29.9
pulmonary 22.2
teratogenicity 45.9
vasculitis 6.12
breast milk 45.24
dosing 32.7
interactions, drugs
table of 23.8
alcohol 23.6, 23.8
antidepressants 23.8
benzodiazepines 23.8
beta blockers 23.8
calcium channel blockers 23.8
carbamazepine 23.8
ketoconazole 23.6, 23.8
lidocaine 16.17
mechanisms 3.2, 3.3
methadone 7.22–7.23
phenytoin 23.6, 23.8
procainamide 23.6, 23.8
propranolol 23.8
quinidine 23.8
sulfonylureas 48.39
theophylline 19.17, 19.24–19.25,
23.5, 23.8
warfarin 12.20, 23.6, 23.8
pharmacokinetics
clearance
dialysis 32.7
renal failure 32.7

half-life 32.7
parameters 32.7
pharmacology
comparisons histamine₂-antagonists 23.4
mechanism of action 23.4
use in
aspiration pneumonia prophylaxis 8.5
pediatric GERD 95.7

Cinchonism
quinine 11.11

Cinobac
See Cinoxacin

Ciprofloxacin
Also see Fluoroquinolones
adverse effects
anaphylactoid reaction 6.16
hepatotoxicity 26.8
nephrotoxicity 29.10
serum sickness 6.7
teratogenicity 45.9
vasculitis 6.12
breast milk 45.24
interactions, drugs
table of 63.7
antacids 23.9
cyclosporine 63.17
mechanism 3.2
theophylline 3.3, 19.17, 19.24
warfarin 12.20
pharmacokinetics
clearance
dialysis 32.7, 54.15
renal disease 54.18
renal failure 32.7
half-life 32.7
parameters 32.7
concentration, bone 65.5
use in
Campylobacter (Helicobacter)
60.12
chanchroid 64.15
cystic fibrosis 100.7–100.8,
100.10
gonorrhea 64.4, 64.8
Mycobacterium avium 68.29
Mycobacterium tuberculosis
68.26
pregnancy 64.15
Salmonella gastroenteritis 60.5,
60.13–60.14
Shigella gastroenteritis 60.5,
60.14–60.15
travelers' diarrhea 60.2, 60.3,
60.4–60.6
tuberculosis 59.10–59.11
urinary tract infection 63.5–63.8

Cirrhosis
Also see Hepatic disorders
classification 25.1
clinical presentation 25.1–25.3
complications
alkalosis 25.5
ascites 25.3–25.7
coma 25.10–25.14
diuretic resistance 28.15
encephalopathy 25.10–25.14
hepatorenal 25.14
hyponatremia 28.7
peritonitis 61.3–61.4
varices 25.7–25.10
definition 25.1
diagnosis 25.2
drug-induced, alcohol 82.8
laboratory assessment 25.3
pathogenesis 25.2

treatment 25.3–25.7

Cisapride
use in
aspiration pneumonia prophylaxis 8.5
diabetic gastroparesis 48.49
gastroesophageal reflux 23.18
pediatric GERD 95.7

Cisplatin
administration, hydration 93.22
adverse effects 90.11
hypomagnesemia 28.26
nephrotoxicity 29.10,
91.19–91.21
ototoxicity 91.16
breast milk 45.24
dosing
alterations 90.11
in obese patients 94.8
in renal dysfunction 91.20, 93.22
pharmacokinetics 90.11
pharmacology 90.11
use in
neuroblastoma 93.22
osteosarcoma 93.24
ovarian cancer 93.13
testicular cancer 93.19

Citalopram 73.19

Citirizine 21.6, 21.9

Cladribine
adverse effects 90.11
dosing/alterations 90.11
pharmacokinetics 90.11
pharmacology 90.11

Claforan
See Cefotaxime

Clarithromycin
interactions, drugs
terfenadine 21.12
use in
bronchitis 58.3
Lyme 72.4
Mycobacterium avium infection
68.28–68.29
pediatric infections 97.6, 97.11
pertussis 97.17
pneumonia, community acquired
58.7

Claritin
See Loratidine

Claudication, intermittent
clinical presentation 11.4
epidemiology 11.1
pathophysiology 11.2
risk factors 11.2
treatment
drugs 11.6–11.8
nondrug 11.4–11.5
surgery 11.8

Clavulanic acid, teratogenicity 45.9

Clearance
in renal failure 32.2
principles 2.5

Clemastine
adverse effects, teratogenicity 45.9
breast milk 45.24
dosing, adult and pediatric 21.9
use in rhinitis 21.6–21.12

Clenbuterol 87.5

Cleocin
See Clindamycin

Climacteric
See Menopause

Clindamycin
adverse effects

table of 54.13
pseudomembranous colitis 60.10
teratogenicity 45.9
breast milk 45.24
dosing
hepatic insufficiency 54.15
renal failure 32.7
necrotizing enterocolitis, perforated 96.16
pharmacokinetics
clearance
dialysis 54.15
renal disease 54.18
renal failure 32.7
concentration, bone 65.5
half-life 32.7
parameters 32.7
renal failure 32.7
preparations, vaginal 46.7
use in
acne 37.3, 37.5
aspiration pneumonia 58.10
cholangitis 61.2
endocarditis prophylaxis
57.18–57.19
nonspecific bacterial vaginitis
64.15
osteomyelitis, staph 65.4
pediatric infections 97.6
pelvic inflammatory disease
64.6, 64.7
peritonitis 61.10
pneumocystis prophylaxis 68.16,
68.17
toxoplasmosis suppression 68.25
vaginosis (vaginal cream) 46.7
Clinical pharmacokinetics
See Pharmacokinetics
Clinical toxicology 104.1–104.23
assessments of overdoses
104.3–104.5
acetaminophen 104.19–104.20
antidepressants, cyclic
104.13–104.19
aspirin 104.5–104.9
health food supplements
104.20
iron 104.9–104.13
theophylline 19.24–19.25
epidemiology 104.2
gastric decontamination
104.4–104.5, 104.10–104.11,
104.18, 104.19
general management 104.3–104.5
information resources 104.2
Clinitest
Also see Urine, glucose tests
Clinofloxacin 57.15
Clinoril
See Sulindac
Clistin
See Carbinoxamine
Clodronate 28.22
Clofazimine 68.28, 68.29
adverse effects, teratogenicity
45.10
breast milk 45.24
Clofibrate
adverse effects
nephrotoxicity 29.10
effect on thyroid function tests 47.6
interactions, drugs
sulfonylureas 48.39
warfarin 12.20
Clomiphene
adverse effects

ocular 49.15
teratogenicity 45.10
Clomipramine
adverse effects 73.26
aggression, children 78.7
paranoia, children 78.7
teratogenicity 45.10
breast milk 45.24
contraindications/precautions
MAOIs 73.26
interactions, drugs 73.26
patient education 73.26
use in
anorexia 80.4
children, obsessive compulsive
78.6–78.7
depression, adulthood
76.10–76.12
obsessive compulsive disorder
73.24
panic disorder 73.19
premenstrual syndrome 46.16
self-injurious behavior 78.15
self-restraint rituals 78.11
Clonazepam
Also see Benzodiazepines
absence seizures 52.4, 52.19
adverse effects, teratogenicity
45.10
breast milk 45.24
pharmacokinetics 73.9, 73.12
use in
anxiety 73.9
nocturnal myoclonus 74.15
Clonidine
Also see alpha$_2$-agonists
adverse effects 10.14, 10.18,
10.25–10.26
constipation 17.5
dizziness 17.5, 17.6
hyperglycemia 48.51–48.52
ocular 49.13
rebound withdrawal 10.25
sedation 17.5, 17.6
teratogenicity 45.10
breast milk 45.24
contraindications/precautions
10.25, 17.5, 17.6
dosing
oral 10.25
transdermal 10.25
interactions, drugs
cyclic antidepressants 3.3
pharmacology
mechanism of action 10.25, 17.5
onset/duration 17.5
preparations
oral 10.25
transdermal 10.25
use in
alcohol withdrawal 82.6
attention deficit hyperactivity
78.4
autism 78.11
cigarette cessation 10.25
diabetic neuropathy 48.48
glaucoma 49.11
hot flushes 46.26
hypertension 10.13, 10.14, 10.18,
10.24–10.27
hypertensive emergencies
17.5–17.6
migraine headache 50.12
nicotine withdrawal 85.7
opiate withdrawal 7.19, 83.9
premenstrual syndrome 46.16
short stature 95.16

Tourette's 78.9
Clorazepate
Also see Benzodiazepines
adjunct to antiepileptics 52.8
adverse effects, teratogenicity
45.10
breast milk 45.24
pharmacokinetics 73.9, 73.12
use in anxiety 73.7
Clot formation 12.2
Clotrimazole
adverse effects 46.6
teratogenicity 45.10
pharmacology 46.4–46.6
use in
candida vaginitis 46.5–46.6
candidiasis, oral 68.23
diaper rash 95.3
prophylaxis
candidemia 69.12–69.13
in immunocompromised hosts
67.14
trichomoniasis 64.16
Clotting factors 12.2
administration 12.10
cascade 12.2
Clotting tests 12.4–12.6
Cloxacillin
use in pediatric infections 97.4
Clozapine
Also see Neuroleptics
adverse effects
anticholinergic 75.7
cardiovascular 75.7
extrapyramidal 75.7
hematological 75.11–75.12
neutropenia 89.11–89.12
sedation 75.7
seizures 75.22
contraindications/precautions 75.11
pharmacological comparisons 75.2
use in
dyskinetic schizophrenics 75.11
refractory schizophrenia 75.11
Clozaril
See Clozapine
Cluster headache
See Headaches, cluster
CMV infections
See Cytomegalovirus
CMVIG, use in CMV infection 67.18
COAD
See Chronic obstructive airways
disease
Coal tar, use in psoriasis 38.2, 38.6
Cocaine
Also see Cocaine abuse
adverse effects
cardiovascular 15.11
mania 77.3
psychoses 75.4
teratogenicity 45.6, 45.10, 81.9
breast milk 45.22, 45.24
topical anesthesia 8.13
use in cluster headache 50.14
Cocaine abuse 84.7–84.16
administration 84.9
clinical presentation 84.10–84.16
in pregnancy 84.14
overdosage
acute 84.10–84.12
chronic 84.13–84.16
pharmacokinetics 84.9
pharmacology 84.9–84.10
street names, table of 84.8

support groups 84.17
treatment 84.11–84.17
monoclonal antibodies 5.4
Coccidioidomycosis 69.17
Codeine 7.5, 7.10
adverse effects, teratogenicity 45.10
breast milk 45.24
pharmacokinetics
clearance
dialysis 32.7, 32.18
renal failure 32.7, 32.18
half-life 32.7, 32.18
parameters 32.7
use in
cough suppression 21.19
pediatric analgesia 95.24
Coffee
See Caffeine
Cogentin
See Benztropine
Cognex
See Tacrine
Colace
See Docusate
Colchicine
Also see Gout; Hyperuricemia
administration
intravenous 40.7
oral 40.5, 40.7–40.8
with probenecid 40.11
adverse effects 40.7–40.8
teratogenicity 45.10
breast milk 45.24
dosing 40.5, 40.7–40.8
pharmacology 40.5, 40.7
toxicity/precautions 40.7–40.8
use in
amyloidosis 30.23
biliary cirrhosis 25.3
gout 40.5, 40.7–40.8
Mediterranean fever 40.7
Cold sores 70.5
Colds, common 21.18–21.19
Colestid
See Colestipol
Colestipol
administration 9.14, 9.17
adverse effects 9.14, 9.17
dose 9.14–9.16, 9.17
interactions, drugs 9.14
digitoxin 15.22
digoxin 15.22
warfarin 12.20
pharmacology
effect on thyroid function tests 47.6
mechanism of action 9.14
use in
hypercholesterolemia 9.14–9.15,
9.17, 9.19
secondary prevention of atherosclerosis 9.8–9.10
Colfosceril
administration 96.9–96.10
adverse effects 96.9–96.10
dosing 96.9–96.10
pharmacology 96.9–96.10
Colistimethate
breast milk 45.24
Colistin
adverse effects
nephrotoxicity 29.10
Colloids 18.10–18.12
use in hypovolemic shock 18.14
Colon cancer
chemo-embolization 93.9

chemotherapy
  adjuvant 93.8
  recurrent 93.8–93.9
  regimens 90.16
clinical presentation 90.8
metastatic sites 90.5, 93.9
screening 90.6, 93.8
staging 93.7
Colony stimulating factors 67.13
  Also see G-CSF; GM-CSF
  use in chemotherapy neutropenia 91.3–91.4
Communications
  consult note 1.16
Complete blood count 4.13
Complex-partial seizures
  See Seizures, complex-partial
Compliance enhancement 101.8–101.10
Compromised host, infections in 67.1–67.18
  Also see HIV infection
  clinical presentation 67.3–67.4
  diagnosis 67.3–67.4
  factors affecting response to therapy 67.5
  pathogenesis 67.2–67.4
  risk factors 67.2–67.4
  treatment
    double beta-lactam regimens 67.8–67.9
    duration 67.11
    empiric antibiotic therapy 67.4–67.12
    fungal prophylaxis therapy 67.12–67.15
    granulocyte-CSF 67.13
    synergistic combinations 67.6–67.9
    three drug therapy 67.7
    two drug therapy 67.6–67.7
Condoms 43.4, 43.22
Congestive heart failure 15.1–15.40
  altered, pharmacokinetics of drugs in
    lidocaine 16.17
    quinidine 16.10
  associated with hypothyroid 47.14
  classification
    diastolic dysfunction 15.2
    high output 15.2
    low output 15.2
    NYHA 15.10
    systolic dysfunction 15.2
  clinical presentation 15.8–15.10
    hemodynamic changes 18.19
  complications 15.2
    decreased diuretic absorption 28.15
    hyponatremia 28.7
    thrombosis 12.19
  drug-induced
    table of 15.11
    amantadine 51.5
    disopyramide 16.6
    hyperosmotic agents 49.12
    sodium-containing drugs, table of 15.10
    timolol ophthalmic 49.4
  etiology 15.2, 15.10
  pathogenesis 15.2–15.3
    hypertension 10.7
  pharmaceutical care 1.6–1.7
  treatment
    drugs
      also see specific agents

amrinone 15.35
angiotensin-converting enzyme inhibitors 15.5, 15.12–15.13, 15.28–15.34
beta-blockers 15.36–15.37
calcium channel blockers 15.34
digitalis 15.5–15.8, 15.11–15.13, 15.16–15.27
diuretics 15.5, 15.11–15.15
hydralazine plus nitroglycerin 15.5, 15.30
inotropic agents 15.6, 15.34–15.35
milrinone 15.35
nitrates 15.28–15.30
nitroprusside 18.20
prazosin 15.30
supportive care 15.5
vasodilators 15.5–15.6, 15.12, 15.27–15.30, 18.19–18.20, 18.21
  principles 15.4
  severe CHF
    amrinone 18.20–18.21
    digoxin 18.20
    diuretics 18.19–18.20
Conjugated estrogens
  See Estrogens
Conjunctivitis
  allergic 49.16–46.17
  bacterial 49.16
Connective tissue disorders 42.1–42.3
  Also see specific disorders
  juvenile rheumatoid arthritis 41.20–41.22
  osteoarthritis 41.22–41.23
  rheumatoid arthritis 41.1–41.20
Constipation
  drug-induced
    aluminum hydroxide 23.8
    amantadine 51.5
    anticholinergic agents 51.4
    antidepressants, cyclic 76.9
    bismuth subsalicylate 60.5
    sucralfate 23.9
    verapamil 13.16
    vincristine 91.5, 92.15
  opioid receptor relationship 83.1
  treatment
    also see Laxatives
    in myocardial infarction 14.6
    in pregnancy 44.9
Contact dermatitis 36.19
Contraception
  Also see Contraceptives, oral
  efficacy of methods 43.4–43.6
  menstrual cycle 43.2–43.4
    cervical caps 43.22
    condoms 43.22
    diaphragms 43.4, 43.20–43.22
    hormonal 43.2–43.19
    intrauterine devices 43.16, 43.19–43.20
    LHRH down regulators 43.23
    male oral contraceptives 43.22–43.23
    spermicides 43.22
    subdermal implants 43.19
Contraceptive sponge, toxic shock syndrome 46.10
Contraceptives, oral
  Also see Contraception; Estrogens; Progestins
  table of 43.5
  adverse effects

table of 43.8
amenorrhea 43.12, 43.15
breakthrough bleeding 43.12
breast cancer 43.13
cervical cancer 43.13
cervical dysplasia 43.13
chloasma 43.8
cholelithiasis 43.15
depression, adulthood 43.16
diabetes 43.13
dyslipidemia 9.12, 43.13–43.14
galactorrhea 43.15
headache 43.16, 50.5
hepatotoxicity 26.7, 43.13
hyperglycemia 43.13
hypertension 43.14
nausea and vomiting 43.17
nephrotoxicity 29.13
ocular 49.15
seizures 43.11
subarachnoid hemorrhage 43.14
teratogenicity 43.16, 45.16
thromboembolism 43.14
urinary tract infection 63.10
vaginal candidiasis 46.4
  benefits 43.16–43.17
    pelvic inflammatory disease 43.16
  breast milk 45.27
  contraindications/precautions
    table of 43.9
  education, patient
    combinations 43.8
    minipill 43.11
    missing pill 43.8
  interactions, drugs 43.10–43.12
    table of 43.12
    antiepileptic drugs 43.11, 52.26
    antimicrobials 43.11
    cigarettes 85.3
    metronidazole 64.16
    rifampin 59.8, 64.16
  pharmacology 43.4–43.5, 43.17
    comparative 43.7
    effect on thyroid function tests 47.6, 47.8
  preparations 43.5–43.6
    table of 43.5–43.6, 43.7
    biphasics 43.12–43.13
    minipill 43.9–43.11
    triphasics 43.12–43.13
  use in
    acne 37.4, 43.17
    contraception 43.2–43.19
    dysmenorrhea 46.12
    premenstrual syndrome 43.17, 46.16–46.17
  use of
    biphasics 43.12–43.13
    choice 43.6–43.8
    male contraceptives 43.22–43.23
    minipill 43.9–43.10
    morning after 43.17–43.18
    progestin implants 43.19
    progestin injections 43.18–43.19
    triphasics 43.12–43.13
Contractility 15.3
Contrast media
  adverse effects
    nephrotoxicity 29.10
    pulmonary 22.3
    teratogenicity
      see specific agents
Convulsions
  See Seizure disorders

Coombs' test 89.4–89.5
COPD
  See Chronic obstructive airways disease
Cordarone
  See Amiodarone
Corgard
  See Nadolol
Cornstarch
  diaper rash 95.3
Coronary angioplasty 13.22
Coronary artery bypass
  complications 16.11
  graft 13.22
    allopurinol reperfusion 40.11
Coronary artery disease
  risk factors
    table of 9.11
    cholesterol 9.8–9.10
    menopause 9.17–9.18
    triglycerides 9.20
Coronary heart disease
  Also see specific disorders
  association with
    cholesterol 10.8, 10.10
    cigarettes 10.8, 10.11
    gout 40.2
    hypertension 10.8
    obesity 10.8
    sodium 10.8
Corticosteroids
  administration
    aerosolized 19.22
    intra-articular 41.23
    intranasal 21.12–21.14, 21.18
    ophthalmic 49.17–49.19
    parenteral 24.3–24.4
    rectal 24.4
  adverse effects
    list of 19.18
    table of 42.10
    acne 37.4
    adrenal insufficiency 42.7–42.8
    cataracts 49.15, 49.18
    Cushing's disease 42.4
    cutaneous atrophy 24.4
    dermatological 42.10
    ecchymosis 42.10
    dyslipidemia 9.12
    fluid retention 33.34, 42.4
    gastrointestinal 33.35, 42.10
    glaucoma 49.15, 49.17–49.19
    growth retardation 24.4
    hepatotoxicity 26.8
    hyperglycemia 42.10, 48.54
    hypertension 10.16, 33.34, 42.4
    hypokalemia 15.23, 24.4
    immunosuppression 33.35, 67.3
    leukocytosis 42.8
    mania 77.3
    masks symptoms of
      infections 33.35, 54.4
      inflammation 24.4
Corticosteroids (continued)
  adverse effects (continued)
    mental 92.15
    mineralocorticoid 42.4
    neutrophilia 33.35
    osteoporosis 24.4, 33.35, 41.20, 42.9, 46.28–46.29
    psychosis 19.18, 33.30
    short-term 19.18
    teratogenicity 24.7, 45.13
      also see specific agents
    vaginal candidiasis 46.4
    weight gain 33.34

wound-healing impairment 24.4, 33.35
breast milk
    see specific agents
dosing 42.6–42.8
    alternate day 42.9
    divided daily dose 41.19–41.20
    during stress 42.8
    equivalent doses 42.5
    in asthma 19.7, 19.14, 19.20–19.22
    intra-articular 41.23
    once daily dose 41.19–41.20, 42.7
    pulse dose 41.20
    regimens, table of 42.6
    step-down bridge 41.15
    tapering dose 42.9
effect on allergen skin testing 21.6
interactions, drugs 3.5
    contraceptives, oral 43.12
    rifampin 59.8
intranasal 21.12–21.14
ophthalmic 49.17–49.18
    use in allergic conjunctivitis 49.16
pharmacokinetics 33.6, 42.5, 42.8
pharmacology
    effect on
        PPD skin test 59.13
        thyroid function tests 47.6
    mechanism of action
        anti-inflammatory 33.6, 42.6
        immune processes 33.6, 42.6
        mineralocorticoid potency 42.5
topical
    adverse effects 36.12–36. 13
    application principles 36.8–36.9
    occlusive dressings 36.12
    preparations 36.10–36.11
    use in psoriasis 38.1–38.2, 38.5–38.6
use in
    acne 37.4
    alcoholic hepatitis 82.9
    allergic aspergillosis 100.9
    amphotericin infusions 69.11
    anaphylaxis 6.8
    anemia, aplastic 89.14
    aspiration pneumonia 58.9
    asthma 19.7, 19.14, 19.20–19.22
        seasonal 19.20
    brain
        abscess 56.21
        metastases 105.8
    bronchiolitis 97.15
    bronchopulmonary dysplasia 98.2–98.3
    cerebral edema 105.8
    cerebral infarction 53.12
    cluster headache 50.14, 50.15
    COAD 20.3, 20.7–20.9
    combination with beta-agonists 19.14
    Crohn's disease 24.10–24.11
    croup 97.16
    cryptococcal meningitis 68.22
    cystic fibrosis 100.10
    giant cell arteritis 42.3
    Goodpasture's 30.24
    gout 40.5–40.6
    graft rejection 33.15–33.16
    graft versus host disease
        acute 94.14–94.16
        chronic 94.17
    Graves' ophthalmopathy 47.25
    hemorrhagic stroke 53.12
    hepatitis
        autoimmune chronic active 62.14

chronic 62.12
hepatorenal syndrome 25.14
hypercalcemia 28.23
interstitial nephritis 29.17
intracranial pressure elevations 56.4, 56.8
ITP 95.17–95.18
leukemia
    acute lymphocytic 92.13, 92.14
    chronic lymphocytic 92.8
    lupus nephritis 30.21
lymphoma, nonHodgkin's 92.9–92.10
meningitis 56.4, 56.8–56.10, 56.14
migraine headache 50.9
myxedema coma 47.14
nausea, chemotherapy-induced 105.4–105.7
nausea/vomiting 105.4–105.7
organ transplantation 33.6, 33.14
osteoarthritis 41.23
otitis 97.9
phenytoin hypersensitivity syndrome 52.25
pneumocystis 68.15, 68.17
rapidly progressive glomeru-lonephritis 29.5
respiratory distress syndrome 96.8
rheumatoid arthritis 41.3, 41.19–41.20
rhinitis, severe 21.14
serum sickness 6.6, 6.8
spinal cord
    decompression 93.18
    injury 53.12
systemic lupus erythematosus 42.6–42.7
temporal arteritis 42.3
thrombocytopenia 89.8
thyroid storm 47.26
toxic shock 46.10
tuberculosis meningitis 59.13
ulcerative colitis 24.3
Wegener's granulomatosis 30.25
Cosyntropin test 42.8
Cotrimoxazole
    See Trimethoprim-sulfamethoxazole
Cotton fever 83.4
Cough
    asthma-induced 19.6
    captopril 15.31
    COAD-induced 20.2
    drug-induced, angiotensin-converting enzyme inhibitors 22.2
Coumadin
    See Warfarin
Coumarin derivatives, teratogenicity 45.6
Cozaar
    See Losarten
"Crabs" 71.11
Crack
    See Cocaine
"Crack lung" 84.11
Creatine kinase
    effect of drugs, digoxin 15.21
    laboratory test 4.10, 14.2
Creatine phosphokinase
    See Creatine kinase
Creatinine
    clearance 4.9 29.2

serum 4.9
CREST syndrome 42.2
Crohn's disease
    clinical presentation 24.9
    treatment
        azathioprine 24.11
        corticosteroids 24.10–24.11
        cyclosporine 24.11
        immunosuppressive agents 24.11
        metronidazole 24.12
        sulfasalazine 24.10–24.11
        surgery 24.12
Cromoglycate, sodium
    use in allergic conjunctivitis 49.17
Cromolyn
    Also see Cromoglycate, sodium
    administration 19.20
        intranasal 21.16
    adverse effects 19.20
        pulmonary 22.6
    pharmacology
        comparative, theophylline 19.20
        mechanism of action 19.20
    use in
        asthma 19.19–19.20
            exercise-induced 19.25–19.26
            seasonal 19.20
        ulcerative colitis 24.8
Crotamiton, use in scabies 71.12
Croup 97.3, 97.15–97.17
Cryptococcal meningitis
    clinical presentation 68.21
    diagnosis 68.21–68.22
    treatment
        amphotericin B 68.21–68.22
        fluconazole 68.22
        flucytosine 68.21–68.22
        itraconazole 68.23
Cryptococcosis 69.19
Cryptosporidiosis
    clinical presentation 60.7, 68.30
    diagnosis 60.7
    pathophysiology 60.7
    treatment 60.7–60.8, 68.30
Crystalloids 18.10–18.13
Cuprimine
    See Penicillamine
Cyanide toxicity 17.9
Cyanocobalamin
    use in
        cirrhosis 25.3
        nitrous oxide abuse 83.16
        pernicious anemia 88.10–88.12
Cyclizine
    adverse effects, teratogenicity 45.10
    use in
        emesis, postoperative 8.17
        motion sickness 105.4
Cyclobenzaprine, teratogenicity 45.10
Cyclopenthiazide
    Also see Diuretics
    adverse effects, teratogenicity 45.10
    breast milk 45.24
Cyclophosphamide
    adverse effects 90.11
        cystitis, hemorrhagic 91.22, 94.9–94.10
        nephrotoxicity 29.10
        pulmonary toxicity 22.5, 91.23, 91.24, 91.26
        teratogenicity 45.6, 45.10
        breast milk 45.22, 45.24
    dosing

alterations 90.11
    hepatic dysfunction 91.28
    in obese patients 94.8
    renal dysfunction 91.20
interactions, allopurinol 40.10
pharmacokinetics 90.11
pharmacology 90.11
use in
    bone marrow priming for harvest 94.6
    Goodpasture's 30.24
    leukemia, acute myelogenous 94.22
    lupus nephritis 30.21–30.22
    neuroblastoma 93.22
    ovarian cancer 93.13
    rapidly progressive glomeru-lonephritis 29.5
    rhabdomyosarcoma 93.25
    rheumatoid arthritis 41.3
    Wegener's granulomatosis 30.25
Cycloserine 59.6
Cyclosporine
    administration 33.31
    adverse effects
        dyslipidemia 9.12, 33.23
        hepatotoxicity 26.8, 33.18
        hypertension 33.22
        hypertrichosis 33.18
        hyperuricemia 33.18, 40.14
        hypomagnesemia 28.26, 33.18
        nephrotoxicity 29.10, 30.22, 33.17, 40.14
        neurotoxicity 33.18
        pseudolymphoma 22.3
        pulmonary 22.3
    breast milk 45.22, 45.24
    dosing
        in renal failure 94.15
        organ transplantation 33.14
    interactions, drugs
        table of 33.27
        ciprofloxacin 63.17
        ketoconazole 33.26
        lovastatin 9.16
        plasticizers (IV bags) 33.31
        sulfonylureas 48.39
    pharmacokinetics 33.26, 33.31–33.32
        absorption 33.31
        bioavailability 33.26
        clearance 32.7
        concentrations
            assays 33.31–33.32
            blood 33.31–33.32
            serum 33.31–33.32
        distribution 32.7, 33.31–33.32
        monitoring 94.15
    pharmacology, mechanism of action 33.7
Cyclosporine (continued)
    use in
        bone marrow transplantation 94.2
        Crohn's disease 24.4
        graft versus host disease
            acute 94.14–94.16
            chronic 94.17
        lupus nephritis 30.22
        nephrotic syndrome 29.5
        organ transplantation 33.7, 33.14, 33.26–33.33
        type I diabetes 48.7, 48.33
        ulcerative colitis 24.8
Cyclothiazide
    Also see Diuretics
    breast milk 45.24
    teratogenicity 45.10

Cyclothymic disorder 77.1

Cyproheptadine
  adverse effects, teratogenicity
    45.10
  dosing 21.9
  use in
    anorexia 80.4
    migraine headache 50.12
    rhinitis 21.7–21.12

Cystic fibrosis 100.1–100.13
  altered drug distribution 100.7
  antibiotics, aerosolized 58.14
  clinical presentation 100.1–100.10
  complications of 100.1–100.3
    pneumonia 58.14
  diagnosis 100.3–100.4
  organ system involvement
    100.2–100.3
  pathophysiology 100.1–100.3
  patient assessments 100.2–100.5
  treatment 100.4–100.11

Cysticercosis 71.11

Cystine stones 29.20

Cystitis, hemorrhagic
  drug-induced
    cyclophosphamide 91.21–91.22
    ifosfamide 91.21–91.22
  prevention
    hydration 91.22
    Mesna 91.22
  treatment 91.22

Cytarabine
  adverse effects 90.11, 92.6
    diarrhea 91.5
    encephalopathy 91.15
    hepatotoxicity 91.27
    ocular 49.15
    pulmonary toxicity 91.24
    teratogenicity 45.10
  pharmacokinetics 90.11
  pharmacology 90.11
  use in leukemia, acute nonlympho-
    cytic 92.4–92.6

Cytokines 56.4, 56.8, 56.16

Cytomegalovirus infection 70.7–70.8
  clinical presentation 33.40, 70.7,
    94.20–94.21
  complication of HIV infection
    68.18–68.20
  transplant patients 67.16
  diagnosis 33.40, 70.7
  etiology 33.39
  gastrointestinal disease
    94.20–94.21
  interstitial pneumonitis 94.20
  pathogenesis 33.39
  predisposing factors 33.38–33.39
  prophylaxis for 67.17–67.18, 70.8,
    94.18
  transmission 67.17
  treatment 68.18–68.20, 70.7–70.8
    acyclovir 94.18
    foscarnet 33.40, 94.18,
      94.20–94.21
    ganciclovir 33.40, 94.18,
      94.20–94.21
    immune globulin 33.40, 94.18,
      94.20–94.21

Cytomel
  See Thyroid hormone;
    Triiodothyronine

Cytosine arabinoside
  See Cytarabine

Cytotoxic drugs, handling

90.21–90.22

Cytotoxic therapy
  See Chemotherapy

Cytoxan
  See Cyclophosphamide

Dacarbazine
  adverse effects 90.12
    hepatotoxicity 91.27
  dosing/alterations 90.12
  pharmacokinetics 90.12
  pharmacology 90.12

Dactinomycin
  adverse effects 90.12
    teratogenicity 45.10
  pharmacokinetics 90.12
  pharmacology 90.12
  use in
    rhabdomyosarcoma 93.25
    Wilm's tumor 93.23

Dalgan
  See Dezocin

Dalmane
  See Flurazepam

Danazol
  adverse effects 46.22–46.23
    teratogenicity 45.10
  pharmacology
    effect on thyroid function tests
      47.6
    mechanism of action 46.20
    onset/duration 46.22
  use in
    endometriosis 46.20–46.21,
      46.22–46.23
    premenstrual syndrome 46.18

Danocrine
  See Danazol

Danthron
  breast milk 45.24
  teratogenicity 45.10

Dantrolene
  adverse effects
    hepatotoxicity 26.8
    pulmonary 22.6
    teratogenicity 45.10

Dapsone
  use in *Pneumocystis carinii* pneu-
    monia 68.16–68.17
  use with trimethoprim 68.16–68.17

Darvon
  See Propoxyphene

Daunomycin
  See Daunorubicin

Daunorubicin
  adverse effects 90.12
    cardiotoxicity 91.17–91.19
    heart failure 15.11
    teratogenicity 45.10
  dosing
    alterations 90.12
    hepatic dysfunction 91.28
  pharmacokinetics 90.12
  pharmacology 90.12
  use in
    leukemia
      acute lymphocytic 92.15
      acute nonlymphocytic 92.4

Dawn phenomenon 48.24–48.25

DAWN reports 104.2

DDC
  See Dideoxycytidine

DDI
  See Dideoxyinosine

Dalteparin
  See Low molecular weight heparin

Decadron
  See Dexamethasone

Decongestants
  use in
    otitis 97.9
    rhinitis 21.10–21.11
    sinusitis 97.10

DEET 72.6

Deferoxamine
  adverse effects
    pseudoallergic 6.16
    teratogenicity 45.10
  use in
    iron toxicity 104.12–104.13
    neuroblastoma 93.22

Degenerative joint disease
  See Osteoarthritis

Dehydration
  Also see Fluids and electrolytes
  treatment, pediatric 95.5–95.6,
    99.3–99.5

Dehydroemetine
  adverse effects, cardiovascular 71.8
  use in amebiasis 71.7

Delirium tremens 82.6

Demecarium 49.8

Demeclocycline
  adverse effects, nephrotoxicity
    28.10
  use in SIADH 28.10

Dementias
  Alzheimer's 102.2–102.7
  behavioral problems
    102.10–102.12
  geriatric 102.1–102.14
    diagnostic studies 102.1–102.2
    disorders causing dementias,
      table of 102.2
  pseudodementias 102.12
  vascular 102.7
    also see Alzheimer's dementia;
      specific dementias
    behavioral disturbances
      102.10–102.12
    clinical presentation 102.8
    diagnostic criteria 102.8–102.9
      DSM-IV 102.8
      ischemic vascular dementia
        102.9
    risk factors 102.9
    treatment
      antiplatelet therapy 102.9
      blood pressure control 102.9
      hemorrheologics 102.10
      smoking cessation 102.9
      warfarin 102.10

Demerol
  See Meperidine

Demulen
  See Contraceptives, oral

Denatured alcohol 82.1

Densitization
  antithymocyte globulin 33.37

Dental procedures
  antibiotic regimens 57.19
  endocarditis 57.2–57.3

Deoxyspergualin 33.9

Depakene
  See Valproate

Depakoate
  See Valproate

Deprenyl
  See Selegiline

Depressant abuse 83.1–83.10

Depression, childhood
  clinical presentation 78.4
  concurrent with ADHD 78.3
  in developmentally disabled 78.13
  suicide, risk factors 78.4
  treatment 78.4–78.5, 78.16

Depressive disorders, major
  76.1–76.27
  Also see Affective disorders, bipo-
    lar
  classification 76.2
  clinical presentation 76.2–76.4,
    76.8–76.9
  depression, adulthood
    atypical 76.19
    psychotic 76.19
    refractory 76.22–76.23
  diagnosis 76.2–76.6, 76.8
  disease-induced 76.3
  drug-induced
    table of 76.4
    contraceptives, oral 43.16
    levodopa 51.8
  pathogenesis, stroke 53.13
  pathophysiology 76.3–76.6
  patient assessments 76.5
  target symptoms 76.8–76.9
  treatment 76.6–76.24
    drugs 76.9–76.24
    nondrug 76.6–76.7

Dermatological disorders
  Also see specific skin disorders
  acne 37.1–37.8
  burns 39.11–39.14
  contact dermatitis 36.19–36.21
  diaper rash 95.2–95.3
  drug eruptions 36.15–36.16
  dry skin 36.15
  eczema 36.9
  photosensitivity 39.1–39.11
  poison ivy 36.19–36.21
  poison oak 36.19–36.21
  pruritus 36.13
  psoriasis 38.1–38.7

Dermatological formulations
  36.2–36.5

Dermatological lesions 36.5–36.9

Dermatological reactions
  to drugs
  Also see specific skin disorders
  table of 36.18–36.19
  acne 37.1–37.7
  acyclovir 70.5
  allopurinol 40.10
  amiodarone 16.19
  aspirin 6.16
  auranofin 41.11

Dermatological reactions
  to drugs (continued)
  beta blockers 38.5
  beta-lactam antibiotics 54.13
  captopril 15.31
  carbamazepine 52.25
  chemotherapy agents 91.8–91.12
  chloroquine 38.5
  clofazamine 68.29
  corticosteroids 24.4, 42.10
  cytarabine 92.6
  gabapentin 52.11
  ganciclovir 70.5
  gold 41.10–41.11
  indomethacin 38.5
  insulin 48.27–48.28

lithium 38.5, 77.6
neuroleptics 75.21
nicotine patches 20.5
omeprazole 23.10
penicillamine 41.15
phenobarbital 52.25
phenytoin 52.25–52.26
sucralfate 23.9
sulfasalazine 24.6
sulfonamides 54.13, 63.5, 63.16, 68.29
sulfonylureas 48.43–48.44
tetracyclines 54.13, 63.5
thioamides 47.21
ticlopidine 53.7, 53.8
timolol 49.10
trimethoprim-sulfamethoxazole 68.15
vasculitis, table of 6.12–6.13
warfarin 6.13, 12.14
Dermatomyositis 42.3
Dermatotherapy 36.1–36.22
assessing patient 36.5
corticosteroids, topical 36.8–36.15
dermatitis, contact 36.19–36.21
drug delivery systems 36.2–36.5
drug eruptions 36.15–36.19
dry skin 36.15–36.16
DES
See Diethylstilbesterol
Desensitization
beta lactams 6.17–6.19
sulfamethoxazole 6.19
Designer drugs 83.3
Desipramine
Also see Antidepressants, cyclic
adverse effects, teratogenicity 45.10
breast milk 45.24
depression, adulthood 76.10–76.12
use in
attention deficit hyperactivity 78.3
bulimia 80.4, 80.11
cocaine addiction 84.16
Desmopressin
use in
enuresis 95.20
hemostasis, renal failure 30.9
Desyrel
See Trazodone
Detoxification
opioids 83.4–83.9
Developmentally disabled
aggression 78.13–78.15
depression, adulthood 78.13
schizophrenia 78.12
self-injurious behavior 78.14–78.15
Dexamethasone
adverse effects, teratogenicity 45.10
suppression test 76.6
use in nausea, chemotherapy-induced 105.7
Dexchlorpheniramine
dosing, adult and pediatric 21.9
use in rhinitis 21.6–21.12
Dexedrine
See Dextroamphetamine
Dextran 70
adverse effects
nephrotoxicity 29.11
pulmonary 22.3
use in ascites 25.6

Dextroamphetamine
use in
attention deficit hyperactivity 78.3
narcotic-induced sedation 7.22
Dextromethorphan 21.19
Dextronorgestrel
See Contraceptives, oral
Dezocine 7.9, 7.14
DHE
See Dihydroergotamine
Diabetes control and complications trial 48.6
Diabetes insipidus
Also see Syndrome of inappropriate antidiuretic hormone secretion
drug-induced, lithium 77.5, 77.6
Diabetes mellitus
Also see Diabetic ketoacidosis
classification 48.3–48.4
maturity onset diabetes of the young 48.4
type I, insulin-dependent 48.3
type II, noninsulin-dependent 48.3–48.4
clinical presentation
honeymoon period 48.31–48.32
in the elderly 48.45–48.46
in pharmacies 1.1–1.5, 1.8
in pregnancy 44.9–44.12
signs and symptoms 48.5
type I 48.13
type II 48.39
complications 48.6–48.54
dyslipidemia 48.53–48.54
effect of intensive insulin therapy 48.6
fetal morbidity and mortality 44.10
gastroparesis 48.49–48.50
hypertension 48.50–48.52
intermittent claudication 11.2
maternal morbidity and mortality 44.9–44.10
nephropathy 48.52
neuropathy 48.46–48.48
soft tissue infections 66.5–66.6
definition 48.2
diagnosis 48.5–48.6
drug-induced
also see Hyperglycemia, drug-induced
betamimetics 44.25
diazoxide 44.19
niacin 9.15, 9.17
factors affecting control 48.15
honeymoon period 48.3, 48.31–48.32
laboratory assessment
fructosamine 48.10
glucose
blood or plasma 48.8–48.9
urine 48.5, 48.8, 48.40
glycosylated hemoglobin 48.9–48.10
pathogenesis 48.3–48.5
carbohydrate metabolism 48.4–48.5
syndrome X 48.3
patient education
exercise 48.29
home blood glucose monitoring 48.18–48.19
insulin injection 48.17–48.18, 48.21
sick-day management 48.24
subjects, table of 48.9

prevention of 48.7
therapeutic goals
in elderly 48.46
intensive insulin therapy 48.14
overall 48.8
type I 48.13–48.14
type II 48.39
treatment
also see Insulin; Sulfonylureas
diet 48.7–48.8
during pregnancy 44.10–44.12
exercise 48.8, 48.29
immunosuppressants 48.7, 48.33
intensive insulin therapy 48.14–48.17
islet cell transplants 48.33
of fasting hyperglycemia 48.22–48.23
of dyslipidemia 48.53–48.54
of gastroparesis 48.49–48.50
of hypertension 48.50–48.52
of mid-morning hyperglycemia 48.23
of nephropathy 48.52
of peripheral neuropathy 48.46–48.48
pancreatic transplants 48.32–48.33
sick-day management 48.24
type I 48.13–48.35
type II 48.39–48.54
Diabetic gastroparesis 48.49–48.50
Diabetic ketoacidosis 48.33–48.35
clinical presentation 48.33–48.34
treatment
fluid and electrolytes 48.34
insulin 48.34–48.35
sodium bicarbonate 48.35–48.36
Diabetic nephropathy 30.18–30.20, 48.52
Diabetic neuropathy 48.46–48.48
Diabinese
See Chlorpropamide
Dialysate solutions 31.4
Dialysis
complications 31.7–31.8, 31.11–31.12
infection 61.5
drug removal 32.3
drugs
alcohol 82.5
antibiotics, table of 54.15–54.17
magnesium 28.27
potassium 28.19
salicylates 104.9
theophylline 19.24
types
hemodialysis 31.1–31.8, 31.12–31.13
hemofiltration 31.12, 32.4
hemoperfusion 32.4
high flux 32.4
peritoneal 31.8–31.12, 32.4
uric acid 40.13
use in
anemia, renal failure 30.8
hyperkalemia 30.6
Diaper dermatitis 95.2–95.3
Diaphragms 43.20–43.22
Diarrhea
Also see Antidiarrheals; Gastrointestinal infections; Pseudomembraneous colitis; Travelers' diarrhea; specific diseases
associated with
Crohn's disease 24.10

ulcerative colitis 24.1–24.3
complications
hypokalemia 28.7, 28.16
drug-induced
also see Gastrointestinal effects of drugs
table of 60.10
beta-lactam antibiotics 54.13
clindamycin 54.13
cytarabine 91.5
fluorouracil 91.5
lithium 77.5, 77.6
magnesium antacids 23.8
quinolones 54.14
sulfonamides 54.13
ticlopidine 53.8
pathogenesis
food poisoning 60.8
infectious 60.1–60.13
treatment
also see Antidiarrheals; specific conditions
anticholinergics 60.2
fluids and electrolytes 60.2
kaolin-pectin 60.2
opiates 60.2
pediatric 95.5–95.6, 99.4, 99.12
Diastix
See Urine, glucose tests
Diatrizoate, teratogenicity 45.10
Diazepam
Also see Benzodiazepines
administration
intramuscular infusion 52.28
intravenous infusion 52.27–52.28
adverse effects
cardiotoxicity 52.28
dependence/addiction 83.10
respiratory depression 52.28
teratogenicity 45.10
breast milk 45.24
interactions, drugs
alcohol 82.6
isoniazid 59.8
omeprazole 23.10
rifampin 59.8
intravenous compatibilities 52.27–52.28
pharmacokinetics 73.9, 73.12
half-life, hepatitis 62.5
use in
alcohol withdrawal, acute 82.6
anxiety 73.7
febrile seizures 52.23
LSD toxicity 86.4
pediatric sedation 95.21–95.22
seizures, neonatal 96.26
neonatal opiate withdrawal 96.28
status epilepticus 52.27–52.28
Diazoxide
administration 17.4, 17.12, 44.20
adverse effects
drug fever 6.9
hyperglycemia 17.12
hyperuricemia 17.11
neonatal hyperglycemia 44.19
ocular 49.13
teratogenicity 45.11
contraindications/precautions 17.4, 17.12
dosing in pregnancy 44.20
pharmacokinetics 17.12
pharmacology 17.12
effects on
fetus 44.19
uterine contractions 44.19
use in

hypertensive emergencies 17.4,
17.10–17.13
pregnancy, preeclampsia
44.19–44.20
DIC
See Disseminated intravascular
coagulation
Diclofenac
adverse effects, aplastic anemia
89.13
use in ophthalmics 49.18–49.19
Dicloxacillin
concentration, bone 65.5
use in pediatric infections 97.4
Dicumarol, breast milk 45.24
Dicyclomine
use in
GI hyperactivity 83.9
urinary incontinence
103.20–103.21
Didanosine
adverse effects
table of 54.14
gastrointestinal intolerance 68.14
use in HIV infection 68.7–68.8,
68.14
Dienestrol
adverse effects, teratogenicity
45.11
breast milk 45.24
Diet
Also see Sodium; Potassium
hypercholesterolemia 9.12–9.13
hypertriglyceridemia 9.21–9.22
interactions, drugs with foods
monoamine-oxidase inhibitors
76.20
warfarin 12.15
photosensitizing foods 39.6
pregnancy 44.6–44.8
use in
attention deficit hyperactivity
78.3
diabetes 48.7–48.8
diabetic nephropathy 30.20
dysmenorrhea 46.12
gout 40.1
heart failure 15.5, 15.10
hyperuricemia 40.1
osteodystrophy, renal 30.13
renal failure, chronic 30.3,
30.17–30.18
Diethylstilbesterol
Also see Estrogens
adverse effects, teratogenicity 45.6,
45.11
breast milk 45.24
use in
postcoital contraception
43.18–43.19
prostate cancer 93.17
Diffusion capacity 19.3
Diflucan
See Fluconazole
Diflunisal
adverse effects, teratogenicity
45.11
breast milk 45.24
Digibind 15.25–15.26
Digitalis
See Digoxin
Digitoxin
Also see Digoxin
factors affecting response
hepatic dysfunction 15.8

renal dysfunction 15.8
interactions, drugs
table of 15.22
cholestyramine/colestipol 9.14
quinidine 15.21
onset and duration 15.8
pharmacokinetics 15.7–15.8
plasma concentrations 15.8
Digoxin
Also see Digitoxin
administration
IM 15.21
IV 15.21
loading dose 15.17
maintenance dose 15.17
adverse effects
also see toxicity
arrhythmias 15.16
AV block 16.14
ocular 49.15
teratogenicity 45.11
ventricular arrhythmias 16.9
breast milk 45.25
contraindications/precautions
cardiogenic shock 15.34
myocardial infarction 15.34
dose, supraventricular arrhythmias
16.9, 16.12
dosing
in pediatrics 15.8, 15.26
in renal insufficiency 15.26, 32.7
intramuscular 15.21
intravenous 15.21
loading 15.16–15.17
maintenance 15.16–15.17
interactions, drugs
table of 15.22
antacids 23.9
calcium channel blockers 15.34
diltiazem 3.4
erythromycin 3.4
nifedipine 17.5
quinidine 3.5–3.7, 15.20, 16.10
sulfasalasine 24.7
verapamil 13.16–13.17, 15.34
pharmacokinetics
absorption 15.7, 15.19
clearance 15.7, 15.16–15.18,
32.7
excretion 15.7, 15.16–15.17,
32.7
metabolism 15.7, 15.20, 32.7
concentrations
assays 15.19
plasma 10.13, 15.18–15.19
distribution 15.7
parameters 15.7, 32.7
pharmacology 15.5
toxicity/poisoning
clinical presentation 15.21–15.23
monitoring 15.18
predisposing factors 15.23–15.24
treatment 15.24–15.25
use in
atrial fibrillation 16.7, 16.8, 16.9,
47.16
combination with vasodilators
15.32
congestive heart failure 15.5,
15.11–15.13, 15.16–15.27
postmyocardial infarction
15.34–15.35
severe congestive heart failure
18.20
thyroid disorders 47.16

Digoxin immune FAB 15.25–15.26
Dihydroergotamine
use in
cluster headache 50.14
intractable migraine headache
50.8
Diiodohydroxyquin
See Iodoquinol
Dilantin
See Phenytoin
Dilaudid
See Hydromorphone
Diloxanide furoate
adverse effects 71.8
use in amebiasis 71.7
Diltiazem
Also see Calcium channel blockers
adverse effects 10.24
table of 13.16
hepatotoxicity 26.8
nephrotoxicity 29.11
teratogenicity 45.11
breast milk 45.25
contraindications/precautions
10.24, 13.16
dose, supraventricular tachycardia
16.9
interactions, drugs
cyclosporine 33.27
digoxin 3.4 15.34
mechanism 3.2
pharmacology
comparisons 10.23–10.24, 13.14
monitoring 13.16
preparations
table of 13.15
sustained release 13.17–13.18
use in
angina 13.16
atrial fibrillation 16.8
heart failure 15.34
hypertension 10.13, 10.14,
10.23–10.24
hypertensive emergency 17.4,
17.7
hyperthyroidism 47.19, 47.21
migraine headache 50.12–50.13
myocardial infarction 14.5, 14.8,
14.16
paroxysmal ventricular tachycardia 16.12
Raynaud's phenomenon 11.9
Dimenhydrinate
Also see Antihistamines
adverse effects, teratogenicity
45.11
use in
morning sickness 44.8
motion sickness 105.4
Dimercaprol
use in gold toxicity 89.8
Dipentum
See Olsalazine
Diphenhydramine
Also see Antihistamines
adverse effects, teratogenicity
45.11
breast milk 45.25
dosing, adult and pediatric 21.9
use in
chemotherapy-induced nausea
105.7
childhood dystonias 78.8
extrapyramidal reactions
57.13–57.19
insomnia 73.8, 74.5

obsessive compulsive disorder
73.24
Parkinson's disease 51.3, 51.4
red man syndrome 56.18
rhinitis 21.6–21.12
use with amphotericin B 68.22
Diphenoxylate
adverse effects
teratogenicity 45.11
toxic megacolon 24.2
breast milk 45.25
use in travelers' diarrhea 60.3
Dipivefrin 49.5, 49.10
Dipravin
See Propofol
Dipyridamole
adverse effects
platelet inhibition 12.18
teratogenicity 45.11
breast milk 45.25
interactions, drugs
adenosine 16.12
use in
stroke prevention 53.7
transient ischemic attacks 53.7
Discoid lupus 42.2
Disinhibition 79.2–79.5
Disopyramide
adverse effects 16.6
anticholinergic 16.6
arrhythmia 16.6
congestive heart failure 16.6
heart failure 15.11
teratogenicity 45.11
breast milk 45.25
pharmacokinetics 16.6
clearance 16.6
parameters 16.6
pharmacology
effect on the ECG 16.3
Disseminated intravascular
coagulation
clinical presentation 12.21
etiology 12.22
table of 12.22
laboratory assessment 12.21
pathogenesis 12.22
pathophysiology 12.21–12.22
treatment 12.22
Disulfiram
interactions, drugs
alcohol 82.7–82.8
mechanism 3.2
metronidazole 60.11, 71.8
phenytoin 82.8
sulfonylureas 48.43
warfarin 12.20, 82.8
use in alcohol aversion 82.7–82.8
Diulo
See Metolazone
Diuretics
Also see Furosemide; Mannitol;
Diuretics, loop; Diuretics, potassium-sparing; Diuretics, thiazide;
specific agents
administration, continuous IV
18.19
adverse effects 10.15–10.17,
28.11–28.15
alkalosis 15.13, 27.8
aplastic anemia 89.13
azotemia 15.13
dyslipidemia 9.12, 9.21, 10.17,
48.50–48.51
hypercalcemia 10.17, 28.21
hyperglycemia 10.16–10.17,

15.13, 28.21, 48.50–48.51
hyperuricemia 10.16–10.17,
  15.14
hypochloremia 15.13
hypokalemia 10.15–10.16, 15.13,
  28.16
hypomagnesemia 10.17, 15.13,
  28.26
hyponatremia 10.17, 15.13
hypophosphatemia 28.24
nephrotoxicity 29.11
prerenal azotemia 25.6
pulmonary 22.3
SIADH 10.17
teratogenicity
  see specific agents
thrombocytopenia 89.7
breast milk
  see specific agents
contraindications/precautions 10.14
  hypercalcemia 10.17
dosing
  hypertension 10.13, 10.15
  renal insufficiency 10.15
interactions, drugs
  cholestyramine/colestipol 9.14
  lithium 77.7
  nonsteroidal anti-inflammatory
    drugs 3.3
pharmacology 15.6–15.7,
  28.10–28.11
  choice of 10.14–10.16
  combination diuretic therapy
    18.19
  comparative 10.14–10.15,
    30.10–30.12
  hemodynamic effects 18.19
  onset 10.15
  relative potencies 30.10–30.12
  sites of action 30.10–30.12
resistance to 28.14–28.15
use in
  ascites 25.4–25.6
  bronchopulmonary dysplasia
    98.2
  congestive heart failure 15.5,
    15.11–15.16
    severe 18.19
  edema, peripheral 25.5
  hypercalcemia 28.21
  hypertension 10.13–10.17
    pregnancy 44.8
  osteoporosis 41.20
  respiratory distress, neonates
    96.10
Diuretics, loop
  adverse effects
    hypokalemia 28.18
    volume depletion 28.11
  pharmacology 28.10
  use in
    hypercalcemia 28.13, 28.21
    hypermagnesemia 28.27
    SIADH 28.10
Diuretics, osmotic
  See Mannitol
Diuretics, potassium-sparing
  Also see specific agents
  contraindications/precautions 10.16
  pharmacology 28.10–28.11
  use in
    congestive heart failure 15.15
    cirrhosis 25.5
    hypertension 10.15–10.16
    hypokalemia 10.15–10.16, 15.15
Diuretics, thiazide
  Also see Diuretics

adverse effects, thrombocytopenia
  89.7
breast milk 45.29
interactions, drugs, mechanism 3.2
use in bone resorption 46.33
Dizziness
  See Hypotension
DNase
  See Dornase alpha
Dobutamine
  adverse effects 18.18
  cardiogenic shock 15.35
  dosing 18.18–18.19, 18.24
  pharmacology
    comparative 18.12, 18.18
    hemodynamic effects
      18.17–18.18
  use in
    cardiogenic shock 18.17–18.18
    septic shock 18.28
  use with dopamine 18.24
Docusate
  adverse effects
    teratogenicity 45.11
  breast milk 45.25
  use in constipation, MI 14.6
Dolophine
  See Methadone
Domperidone
  effect on thyroid function tests
    47.6, 47.8
Dopamine
  adverse effects 18.17
    teratogenicity 45.11
  dosing 18.17, 18.23, 18.24
  effect on TSH 47.5–47.6, 47.8
  pharmacology
    comparative 18.12, 18.18
    hemodynamic effects 18.17
  use in
    cardiogenic shock 15.35, 18.17,
      18.23–18.24
    hepatorenal 25.14
    septic shock 18.28
  use with dobutamine 18.24
Dopamine agonists
  Also see specific agents
  adverse effects 51.11
    dyskinesias 51.11
    gastrointestinal 51.11
    hypotension 51.11
    psychosis 51.11
    pulmonary 51.11
    vascular 51.11
  pharmacology
    comparative 51.11–51.12
    mechanism of action, Parkinson's
      disease 51.10
  use in
    apathy 79.6
    Parkinson's disease 51.10–51.12
Dopamine antagonists
  See Metoclopramide
Dopar
  See Levodopa
Dopram
  See Doxapram
Doral
  See Quazepam
Dornase alpha
  dosing 100.11
  pharmacology 100.10
  use in cystic fibrosis
    100.10–100.11

Dorzolamide 49.11
Dothiepin, breast milk 45.25
Doxacurium 8.8–8.12
Doxapram
  use in
    alcohol intoxication 82.4
    apnea, newborn 96.23
    COAD 20.10
    respiratory acidosis 27.11
Doxazosin 10.25
Doxepin
  Also see Depression, adulthood;
    Antidepressants, cyclic
  breast milk 45.25
  teratogenicity 45.11
  use in depression, adulthood
    76.10–76.12
Doxorubicin
  adverse effects 90.12
    cardiotoxicity 91.17–91.19
    ocular 49.15
    teratogenicity 45.11
  breast milk 45.22, 45.25
  dosing
    alterations 90.12
    hepatic dysfunction 91.28
  pharmacokinetics 90.12
  pharmacology 90.12
  use in
    breast cancer, metastatic 93.5
    leukemia, acute nonlymphocytic
      92.4
    neuroblastoma 93.22
    ovarian cancer 93.13
    prostate cancer, progressive
      93.18
    Wilm's tumor 93.23
Doxycycline
  adverse effects, teratogenicity
    63.5
  contraindications/precautions
    pediatrics 63.5, 63.10, 97.6
    pregnancy 63.10
  use in
    chlamydia 64.9–64.10
    gonorrhea 64.3
    Lyme 72.3–72.4
    lymphogranuloma venereum
      64.10
    malaria 71.3
    pelvic inflammatory disease
      64.6, 64.7
    pleural effusions 92.10
    pneumonia, community acquired
      58.7
    septic arthritis 65.11
    syphilis 64.13–64.14
    travelers' diarrhea, prophylaxis
      60.2, 60.5
    urinary tract infection 63.5
Doxylamine, teratogenicity 45.11
DPT cocktail
  pediatric sedation 95.21
Dronabinol
  antiemetic effect of cannabinoids
    105.5
  use in
    chemotherapy-induced nausea
      105.4, 105.8
    HIV-wasting 68.18
Droperidol
  adverse effects, teratogenicity
    45.11
  amphetamine intoxication 84.5
  antiemetic effect 105.3
  emesis, perioperative 8.17

use in postoperative emesis 105.4
Drug abuse
  Also see Alcohol abuse; Anabolic
    steroids, abuse; Caffeine abuse;
    CNS stimulant abuse;
    Depressants abuse; Drug abuse,
    athletes; Entactogen abuse;
    Inhalant abuse; Nicotine abuse;
    Psychoactive substance use
    disorders; see specific agents
  athletes 87.1–87.9
  athletic departments 87.7
  classification 81.2
  complications
    cellulitis 66.4
    endocarditis 57.9–57.11
    neonatal drug withdrawal
      96.26–96.28
    pulmonary 22.8
  confidentiality 81.14
  definitions 81.1–81.2
  diagnosis 81.2
  diagnostic specifiers 81.3
  drug testing 81.13–81.14
  drugs
    amphetamines 84.1–84.5
    anabolic steroids 87.2–87.5
    benzodiazepines 73.11–73.13
    caffeine 85.8–85.13
    cocaine 84.7–84.16
    designer drugs 83.3
    inhalants 83.11–83.17
    nicotine 85.1–85.7
    opioids 83.1–83.9
    phenylpropanolamine 84.6–84.7
    sedative-hypnotics 83.10–83.11
  drugs in workplace 81.12
  effect on neonates 81.8
  epidemiology 81.2–81.4
  health care professionals 81.11
  populations at risk 81.8–81.12
  treatment
    goals 81.5
    inpatient 81.6
    outpatient 81.6
    support 81.6–81.8
    twelve steps 81.7
Drug abuse, athletes 87.1–87.7
Drug addiction
  See Drug abuse; specific drugs
Drug administration, neonates
  96.30–96.31
Drug concentrations
  Also see individual drugs
  table of 4.19
Drug eruptions
  See Dermatological reactions to
    drugs
Drug fever
  See Fever
Drug interactions 3.1–3.9
  Also see specific drugs
  principles
    clinical outcomes 3.5–3.7
    decision support table 3.9
    literature evaluation 3.3–3.5
    mechanisms 3.1–3.2
    risk assessment 3.7–3.8
Drug screening 104.16–104.17
Dry skin 36.15–36.16
DTP vaccine 95.9
Duke's staging 93.7
Duragesic
  See Fentanyl

DynaCirc
  See Isradipine
Dyphylline 19.23
  Also see Theophylline
  adverse effects, teratogenicity
    45.11
  breast milk 45.25
Dysgeusia
  drug-induced
    captopril 10.22, 17.5
    chloroquine 71.7
Dyskinesias
  Also see Tardive dyskinesia
  drug-induced
    dopamine agonists 51.11
    levodopa 51.5
    neuroleptics 75.13–75.18
    rating system 75.18
    tardive 75.16–75.19
Dyslipidemia 9.1–9.23
  Also see Hypercholesterolemia;
    Hypertriglyceridemia
  associated with
    renal failure 30.3, 30.12
  classification 9.4
  complications of thyroid function
    47.6, 47.13
  diagnosis 9.5–9.6
  drug-induced
    table of 9.12
    contraceptives, oral 43.13–43.14
    corticosteroids 33.23, 33.35
    cyclosporine 33.25
    danazol 46.22
    disulfiram 82.8
    diuretics 10.17, 28.3
    isotretinoin 37.5–37.6
    ticlopidine 53.8
  effect of
    anabolic steroids 87.4
    cigarettes 85.4
    coffee 85.11
  effect on cardiovascular disease
    10.8
  laboratory assessment 9.2, 9.5–9.6,
    9.10–9.11, 9.19–9.20
  lipid metabolism 9.1–9.5
  pathogenesis 9.5–9.6
  treatment
    combination therapy 9.18–9.19,
      9.23
    cost effectiveness of 9.10
    efficacy 9.8–9.10
    estrogen replacement 9.18
    goals 9.13–9.14, 9.21
    hypercholesterolemia 9.10–9.19
    hypertriglyceridemia 9.19–9.23
    in diabetes 48.53–48.54
    mixed hyperlipidemia 9.19–9.23
    rationale 9.6–9.10
Dysmenorrhea
  clinical presentation 46.11
  pathogenesis 46.11
  treatment 46.11–46.12
    contraceptives, oral 43.17
    ibuprofen 7.23
Dyspareunia
  endometriosis 46.19
  vaginitis 46.3
Dysrhythmias
  See Arrhythmias; specific arrhyth-
    mias
Dyssomnias 74.1–74.13
Dysthymic disorder 76.3
Dystonias 75.13–75.18
  drug-induced

antipsychotics 78.8
  treatment in children 78.8
Dysuria
  See Urinary tract infections
Eating disorders 80.1–80.13
  classification
    anorexia nervosa 80.1–80.8
    bulimia nervosa 80.1–80.6,
      80.8–80.12
  definitions 80.1
  diagnosis 80.2
  pathogenesis 80.2
  pathophysiology 80.2–80.3
  treatment
    drugs 80.3–80.5, 80.7,
      80.10–80.11
    goals 80.7
    psychotherapy 80.6, 80.7
Echocardiography
  endocarditis 57.4
Echothiophate iodide 49.5, 49.8–49.9
Eclampsia 44.14–44.20
  hydralazine 17.7
Eczema 36.9, 36.17
Edecrin
  See Diuretics
Edema
  abdominal 25.5
  peripheral 25.5
Edrophonium, teratogenicity 45.11
Effexor
  See Venlafaxine
Eflornithine 68.16
Elderly
  See Geriatrics
Electrocardiogram 16.3
  in myocardial infarction 14.9
Electrocardiographic effects of drugs
  Also see Arrhythmias, drug-
    induced
  dehydroemetine 71.8
  emetine 71.8
Electrocardioversion
  atrial fibrillation 16.8–16.9
  hyperthyroid patient 47.17
Electroconvulsive therapy 76.6, 76.24
Electrolyte disorders 28.1–28.27
  Also see specific disorders
Electrolytes
  Also see specific electrolytes
  laboratory assessment 4.3–4.6
  nutrient requirements 35.10
Electrophysiology 16.1–16.3
Elimination rate constant 2.5
Elimite
  See Permethrin
Embolism
  See Thrombosis; Pulmonary
    embolus
Emesis
  Also see Nausea/vomiting
  contraindications 104.11
  treatment of overdoses 104.5,
    104.10
Emetine
  adverse effects, cardiovascular 71.8
  use in amebic dysentery 71.7
Eminase
  See Thrombolytic agents
EMLA 7.23, 95.24
Emphysema
  Also see Chronic obstructive air-

ways disease
  clinical presentation 20.1–20.2
  diagnosis 20.1–20.2
Enalapril
  Also see Angiotensin-converting
    enzyme inhibitors
  adverse effects
    hyperkalemia 10.22, 17.4
    nephrotoxicity 29.11
    teratogenicity 45.11, 45.33
  breast milk 45.25
  contraindications/precautions
    10.21, 17.4, 17.7
  dosing
    intravenous 17.4, 17.7
    oral 10.22
  pharmacokinetics
    elimination 10.22, 32.7
    properties 32.7
  pharmacology
    comparison of angiotensin-con-
      verting enzyme inhibitors
      10.21–10.23
    mechanism of action 10.21, 17.7
  use in
    heart failure 15.28, 15.30–15.32
    hypertension 10.22, 10.23
    hypertensive emergencies 17.4,
      17.7
    myocardial infarction 14.4, 14.16
Enalaprilat
  See Angiotensin-converting
    enzyme inhibitors; Enalapril
Encainide 16.10, 16.15
  breast milk 45.25
Encephalopathy
  hepatic 25.10–25.14
  uremic 30.16–30.17
End-stage renal disease 30.2
Endocarditis 57.1–57.23
  classification, causative organisms
    57.2
    culture negative endocarditis
      57.17
    enterococcal endocarditis
      57.11–57.15
    fungal endocarditis 57.15–57.16
    gram-negative bacillary endo-
      carditis 57.16–57.17
    S. aureus endocarditis
      57.9–57.11
    S. epidermidis endocarditis
      57.7–57.9
    S. viridans endocarditis
      57.3–57.6
  common pathogens 54.5
  diagnostic criteria
    criteria, table of 57.5
    definitions, table of 57.5
  epidemiology 57.2
  home therapy 57.19
  laboratory assessment 57.4
  microbiology, pathogens 57.2
  pathogenesis 57.1
    drug abuse 83.4
  predisposing factors 57.2
  principles, antibiotic use 57.4–57.7
  prophylaxis, antibiotics
    conditions/surgical, table of
      57.2–57.3
    postrheumatic fever 97.13
    rationale 57.18
    recommendations 57.18–57.19
    regimens, table of 57.19
  S. aureus endocarditis
    IV drug abuser 57.9
    antibiotic regimens 57.9–57.11

  S. epidermidis endocarditis
    antibiotic regimens 57.10
    prophylaxis, prosthetics
      57.7–57.10
  S. viridans endocarditis
    antibiotic regimens 57.6–57.7
    clinical presentation 57.3
  treatment
    culture negative endocarditis
      57.17
    enterccoccal endocarditis
      57.11–57.15
    fungal endocarditis 57.15–57.16
    gonorrheal 64.8
    gram-negative endocarditis
      57.16–57.17
    S. aureus endocarditis
      57.9–57.11
    S. epidermidis endocarditis
      57.8–57.9
    S. viridans endocarditis
      57.3–57.6
Endometrial cancer
  effect of contraceptives, oral 43.17
Endometrial carcinoma
  estrogen use 46.32
Endometriosis
  clinical presentation 46.19–46.20
  pathogenesis 46.18–46.19
  staging 46.19
  treatment 46.20–46.21
Endotracheal administration of drugs
  16.20
Engerix B
  See Hepatitis B vaccine
Enoxacin
  breast milk 45.25
  interactions, drugs
    theophylline 3.3
Enoxaparin 12.3–12.4
  use in thrombosis 89.9
Enoximone 15.35–15.36
Entactogen abuse 86.1–86.9
  Also see specific agents
  LSD 86.2–86.5
  marijuana 86.5–86.7
  MDA, MDEA, MDMA 86.2
  mescaline 86.1
  peyote 86.1
  phencyclidine 86.7–86.8
  psilocybin 86.2
Enteral nutrition 34.1–34.28
  Also see Fat emulsions;
    Malnutrition; Parenteral nutrition
Enteral nutrition (continued)
  administration 34.12–34.13, 34.26
  assessments, patients 34.1–34.3,
    34.18–34.26
  complications of
    table of 34.15
    gastrointestinal 34.15–34.16
    mechanical 34.15
    metabolic 34.15
  dosing regimens 34.12–34.13
  formula selection 34.3–34.9, 34.12
  medications by tube 34.17
  monitoring parameters 34.14,
    34.18–34.26
  nutritional needs 34.18–34.20,
    34.23
  use in
    adults 34.1–34.28
    pediatrics 99.1, 99.10–99.12
      hepatic failure 99.18–99.19

Enterobacter meningitis 56.16–56.17
Enterobiasis
    clinical presentation 71.9
    prevention 71.9
    treatment 71.9
Enterococcal endocarditis
    aminoglycoside resistant
        57.12–57.14
    antibiotic
        regimens 57.11–57.15
        synergy 57.11–57.15
Enterococcal peritonitis 61.13
Enterohemorrhagic *Escherichia coli*
    60.8–60.10
    clinical presentation 60.8–60.9
    diagnosis 60.9
    prevention 60.10
    transmission 60.9
    treatment 60.9–60.10
Enterovioform
    See Iodochlorhydroxyquin
Enuresis
    clinical presentation 95.19
    treatment
        desmopressin 95.20
        imipramine 95.20
        nondrug 95.19–95.20
        oxybutynin 95.20
Eosinophilia
    asthma 19.5
    Kawasaki's disease 97.18
    laboratory tests 4.15
    pulmonary 22.1, 22.7
Eosinophils 4.16
Ephedrine
    adverse effects, teratogenicity
        45.25
    breast milk 45.11
    use in urinary incontinence 103.21
Epidermal necrolysis 36.17
Epiglottitis 97.17
Epilepsy
    See Seizure disorders
Epinephrine
    Also see Epinephrine, ophthalmic
    administration
        endotracheal 16.20
        intravenous 16.20
    adverse effects
        pulmonary 22.3
        teratogenicity 45.11
    dose 16.20
    interactions, drugs
        beta blockers 3.3
    use in
        anaphylaxis 6.6–6.8
        cardiopulmonary arrest 16.20,
            16.21, 16.24
        croup, nebulized 97.16
        glaucoma 49.4–49.7, 49.9
Epinephrine, ophthalmic
    adverse effects 49.4, 49.10
    combined use with timolol 49.9
    mechanism of action 49.4, 49.9
    preparations 49.5, 49.10
    use in glaucoma 49.4–49.7, 49.9
Epinine 15.36
Epoetin
    See Erythropoietin
Epsilon aminocaproic acid, use in
    cerebral hemorrhage 53.14
Ergoloid mesylates
    use in Alzheimer's 102.5

Ergonovine
    use in
        diagnosis variant angina
            13.19–13.20
        migraine headache 50.7, 50.12
        postpartum hemorrhage 44.28
Ergostat
    See Ergotamine
Ergotamine
    administration 50.6
        caffeine concurrently 50.6
        routes of 50.6
    adverse effects
        gastrointestinal 50.6
        rebound headache 50.7
        teratogenicity 45.12
        vascular 50.7
    breast milk 45.22, 45.25
    contraindications/precautions 50.6
        ischemic disorders 50.6
        pregnancy 50.6
        Raynaud's phenomenon 11.9
    dosing
        determination 50.6
        dosage form selection 50.6
        schedule 50.6
    interactions, drugs
        erythromycin 50.6
        propranolol 50.7
        triacetyloleandomycin 50.6
    pharmacology 50.6
    preparations
        aerosolized 50.6
        oral 50.6
        rectal 50.6, 50.7
        sublingual 50.6, 50.7
    use in
        cluster headache 50.14, 50.15
        migraine headache 50.6–50.7,
            50.8
Ergotrate
    See Ergonovine
Erysipelas
    clinical presentation 66.7
    treatment 66.7
Erythema migrans 72.3
Erythema multiforme 36.17
    gabapentin 52.11
Erythema nodosum 36.17
Erythrocyte sedimentation rate 4.14
    acute osteomyelitis 65.3
    rheumatoid arthritis 41.4
    septic arthritis 65.9
    temporal arteritis 42.3
Erythromycin
    adverse effects
        table of 54.13
        hepatotoxicity 26.8
        nephrotoxicity 29.11
        teratogenicity 45.12
    breast milk 45.25
    formulations, oral 97.18
    interactions, drugs
        carbamazepine 3.7
        contraceptives, oral 43.11
        cyclosporine 33.26
        digoxin 3.4, 15.22
        lovastatin 9.16
        mechanism 3.2
        terfenadine 21.12
        theophylline 19.17, 19.24, 20.9
        warfarin 3.3, 12.20
    pharmacokinetics
        clearance
            dialyzability 32.7
            dialysis 54.15

renal disease 54.18
    parameters 32.7
    use in
        acne 37.3, 37.5
        Campylobacter diarrhea 60.2,
            60.12
        chancroid 64.15
        chlamydia 64.9–64.10
        chronic bronchitis 58.3
        diabetic gastroparesis 48.49
        endocarditis prophylaxis 57.19
        Legionaire's pneumonia 58.7
        Lyme 72.4
        lymphogranuloma venereum
            64.10
        ophthalmia neonatorum 64.8
        pediatric infections 97.5
        pertussis 97.17
        pneumonia, community acquired
            58.7
        pregnancy 44.14
        surgical prophylaxis 55.3
        syphilis 64.13
Erythromycin-sulfisoxazole
    use in
        otitis 97.8–97.9
        pediatric infections 97.6
Erythropoietin
    adverse effects 30.8
        teratogenicity 45.12
    use in
        anemia
            of AIDS 88.15
            of chronic disease 88.14–88.15
            renal failure 30.8
        athletes 87.6–87.7
        chemotherapy anemia 91.4
    use with zidovudine 68.12, 68.22
Eserine
    See Physostigmine
Esmolol
    breast milk 45.25
    dose
        atrial fibrillation 16.11
        supraventricular tachycardia 16.9
Esophageal cancer regimens 90.16
Esophageal varices
    Also see Cirrhosis; Hepatic disor-
        ders
    clinical presentation 25.2–25.6
    treatment 25.7–25.10
Esophagitis, reflux
    See Gastroesophageal reflux
Esophagoscopy 25.8
ESR
    See Erythrocyte sedimentation rate
Estazolam 74.8–74.9, 74.11
    Also see Benzodiazepines
    pharmacokinetics 73.9, 73.12
Estraderm
    See Estrogens
Estradiol
    Also see Estrogens;
        Contraceptives, oral
    breast milk 45.25
    teratogenicity 45.12
Estramustine
    adverse effects 90.12
    pharmacokinetics 90.12
    pharmacology 90.12
Estrogens
    Also see Contraceptives, oral
    administration
        oral 46.25–46.27
        transdermal 46.26–46.27

vaginal 46.27
    adverse effects 46.32
        headache 50.5
        hepatotoxicity 26.7
        teratogenicity 45.12
    breast milk 45.25
    combined with progestins
        46.32–46.33
    contraindications/precautions
        46.31–46.32
    effect on
        bone mass 46.31
        thyroid function 47.6, 47.8
    interactions, drugs
        warfarin 12.20
    use in
        contraception 43.2–43.19
        genitourinary atrophy 46.27
        hot flushes 46.25–46.26
        lactation suppression 44.30
        postcoital contraception
            43.17–43.18
        prevention of osteoporosis
            46.31–46.33
        urinary incontinence 103.20,
            103.22
Estrogens, replacement therapy
    adverse effects 9.18
        cancer 9.18
        dyslipidemia 9.18
        thrombosis 9.18
    contraindications 9.18
    use in dyslipidemia 9.17–9.18
Estrone
    breast milk 45.25
    teratogenicity 45.12
Ethacrynic acid
    Also see Diuretics, loop
    adverse effects, teratogenicity
        45.12
Ethambutol
    adverse effects 59.9
        nephrotoxicity 29.11
        optic neuritis 49.14
        teratogenicity 45.12, 59.12
    breast milk 45.25
    dosing
        in pediatrics 59.12
        in renal failure 32.7
        initial 59.3–59.4, 59.6
        maintenance 59.6
    pharmacokinetics
        clearance
            dialysis 32.7
Ethambutol (continued)
        renal failure 32.7
    concentrations
        central nervous system 59.13
        plasma 59.6
    dialysis 54.15
    use in
        drug-resistant tuberculosis 59.10
        meningitis tuberculosis 59.13
        Mycobacterium avium 68.27,
            68.28, 68.29
        Mycobacterium tuberculosis
            68.26
        short-course tuberculosis 59.6
        pregnancy 59.12
Ethanol
    Also see Alcohol
    interactions, drugs
        warfarin 12.20
Ethchlorvynol
    adverse effects, pulmonary 22.3

Ethinyl estradiol
Also see Estrogens;
Contraceptives, oral
adverse effects, teratogenicity 45.12
breast milk 45.25
Ethiodized oil, teratogenicity 45.12
Ethionamide
use in
Mycobacterium avium 68.28
tuberculosis 59.6
Ethisterone, teratogenicity 45.12
Ethmozine
See Moricizine
Ethosuximide
adverse effects
gastrointestinal 52.19–52.20
hematologic 52.19–52.20
sedation 52.19–52.20
teratogenicity 45.12
breast milk 45.25
interactions, contraceptives, oral
43.11, 43.12
use in seizures 52.4, 52.19–52.20
Ethotoin, teratogenicity 45.12
Ethyl biscoumacetate
Also see Anticoagulants
breast milk 45.25
Ethylene glycol
osmol gap 28.2, 82.5
Ethynodiol
Also see Contraceptives, oral;
Estrogens
adverse effects, teratogenicity
45.12
Etidronate
osteoporosis 46.34
use in hypercalcemia 28.22
Etomidate
adverse effects, myoclonus 8.7
use in anesthesia induction 8.7
Etoposide
adverse effects 90.12
hepatotoxicity 91.27
hypersensitivity 92.18
secondary leukemia 92.19
dosing
alterations 90.12
hepatic dysfunction 91.28
pharmacokinetics 90.12
pharmacology 90.12
use in
lung cancer 93.11–93.12
neuroblastoma 93.22
testicular cancer 93.19
Etretinate
adverse effects 38.3
teratogenicity 38.3, 45.6
pharmacology 38.3
use in psoriasis 38.2–38.3
Euro-Collins solution 33.12
Euthroid
See Thyroid hormone
Euthyroidism
Also see Hyperthyroidism;
Hypothyroidism; Thyroid
disorders
euthyroid sick syndrome 47.7
Evan's Blue, teratogenicity 45.12
Exelderm
See Sulconazole
Exercise
effect on
asthma 19.25
blood pressure 10.10

lipids 10.10
osteoporosis 46.29–46.30, 46.33
Exercise-induced asthma
See Asthma
Exfoliative dermatitis 36.17
Exophthalmometer 47.6
Exosurf
See Colfosceril
Expectorants 21.19
Extracellular fluid volume 28.1–28.2
Extrapyramidal reactions
Also see Neurotoxicity, drug-
induced
drug-induced
neuroleptics 75.13–75.18
rating scale 75.14
treatment 75.13–75.19
Extravasation
chemotherapy 91.12
norepinephrine 18.24
Eye disorders
Also see Glaucoma; Ocular
adverse effects of drugs; specific
agents; specific disorders
cataracts 39.11
chemical burns 49.12
conjunctivitis 49.16–49.17
corneal ulcers 49.17
drug-induced
also see Ocular adverse effects of
drugs
table of 49.13
glaucoma 49.3–49.11
herpetic keratitis 70.6
herpes simplex 49.18–49.19
ocular anatomy and physiology
49.1–49.2
ophthalmia neonatorum 64.8
ophthalmopathy, Graves' 47.25
stye 49.16
Famiciclovir
use in varicella zoster 68.21
Famotidine
Also see Histamine$_2$-antagonists
adverse effects, teratogenicity
45.12
breast milk 45.25
interactions, drugs
procainamide 3.3
use in aspiration pneumonia prophylaxis 8.5
Famvir
See Famiciclovir
Fanconi's syndrome, ifosfamide
93.26
Fansidar
Also see Pyrimethamine-sulfadoxine
Fasciitis, necrotizing 66.7
Fat emulsions 35.5, 35.9
adverse effects, pediatric
hyperbilirubinemia 99.13
infection 99.13
use in
low birth weight infants 99.13
pediatric pulmonary dysfunction
99.16
Febrile seizures 52.22–52.23
classification 52.22–52.23
prophylaxis 52.23
treatment 52.23
Feeding
enteral 34.1–34.28
parenteral 35.1–35.16

Felbamate
adverse effects
aplastic anemia 52.12
hepatotoxicity 52.12
insomnia 52.11
interactions, drugs 52.11–52.12
pharmacokinetics 52.6
use in seizures 52.4
Felbatol
See Felbamate
Feldene
See Piroxicam
Felodipine 10.23, 13.14, 13.15, 13.17
use in congestive heart failure
15.34
Felty's syndrome 41.4
Femstat
See Butoconazole
Fenfluramine
use in bulimia 80.5
Fenoprofen
Also see Nonsteroidal anti-inflammatory drugs
adverse effects
nephrotoxicity 29.11
teratogenicity 45.12
breast milk 45.25
interactions, drugs
aspirin 41.7
use in
gout 40.5
rheumatoid arthritis 41.8
Fenoterol
Also see Beta-adrenergic agonists
adverse effects, teratogenicity
45.12
Fentanyl
Also see Designer drugs; Opiate
abuse
adverse effects, teratogenicity
45.12
parenteral 7.10
patient controlled analgesia 7.10
transdermal 7.14–7.15
use in
anesthesia maintenance 8.7
epidural infusion 8.20–8.21
patient controlled analgesia 8.20
pediatric
analgesia 95.21–95.24
sedation 95.21–95.22
Ferritin 88.5
Ferrous fluconate 88.5–88.6
Ferrous fumarate 88.6
Ferrous gluconate
See Iron
Ferrous sulfate 88.5–88.6
Fertilization 44.3
Fetal alcohol syndrome 45.5, 81.9,
82.9
Also see Alcohol
Fetal anomalies, drug-induced
45.1–45.36
Fetal hydantoin syndrome 44.13,
45.30, 52.26–52.27
Fetal trimethadione syndrome 45.33
Fetal warfarin syndrome 45.30
Fetor hepaticus 25.10
Fever
clinical presentation, neutropenia
67.3
complications
see Febrile seizures

drug-induced 6.8–6.10
antilymphocyte globulin 33.37
characteristics, table of 6.8
drugs, table of 6.9–6.10
treatment
also see Acetaminophen; Aspirin
in pediatrics 95.3–95.4
Fibrocystic breast disease
effect of contraceptives, oral 43.17
Fibrosis, methylsergide-induced
50.11
Filgrastim 67.13
Also see GM-CSF
use in bone marrow transplantation
94.7
Finasteride
use in prostate hyperplasia 103.17
First-pass effect 2.3
Fish oils 9.17
Fixed drug eruptions 36.17
FK 506
See Tacrolimus
"Flag sign" 91.10
Flagyl
See Metronidazole
Flavoxate
use in urinary incontinence
103.20–103.21
Flaxedil
See Gallamine
Flecainide
adverse effects 16.6
arrhythmias 16.10, 16.15
sudden death 16.15
CAST trial 16.15
pharmacokinetics 16.6
pharmacology
effect on ECG 16.3
use in atrial fibrillation 16.10
Fleroxacin
use in travelers' diarrhea 60.4
Flosequinan 15.35–15.36
Floxuridine
adverse effects 90.12, 93.9
dosing/alterations 90.12
hepatic arterial infusion 93.9
pharmacokinetics 90.12
pharmacology 90.12
use in colon cancer 93.9
Fluconazole
adverse effects
table of 54.14
teratogenicity 45.12
breast milk 45.25
dosing, renal dysfunction 69.12
interactions, drugs
warfarin 12.20
pharmacokinetics
absorption 32.8
clearance 32.8
dialysis 32.8, 54.15
renal failure 32.8
parameters 32.8
pharmacology 69.3
use in
candida
esophagitis 68.30
oropharyngeal 67.14–67.15
candidiasis, vaginal 46.5,
69.5–69.6
candiduria 69.13
coccidioidomycosis 69.17
cryptococcal meningitis
68.22–68.23

cryptococcosis 69.19
endocarditis 57.16
peritonitis 31.10
prophylaxis, candidemia
69.12–69.13
Flucytosine
adverse effects 69.19
table of 54.14
teratogenicity 45.12
clearance
dialysis 54.16
renal disease 54.18
CSF penetration 69.17
use in
cryptococcal meningitis
68.21–68.23
cryptococcosis 69.19
dosing, renal dysfunction 69.19
fungal endocarditis 57.16
use with amphotericin B
68.21–68.23
Fludarabine
adverse effects 90.12
encephalopathy 91.15
pulmonary toxicity 91.24
pharmacokinetics 90.12
pharmacology 90.12
use in chronic lymphocytic
leukemia, refractory 92.8–92.9
Fluid retention
associated with renal failure,
chronic 30.5
drug-induced, corticosteroids
33.34, 42.4
Fluids and electrolytes
Also see specific electrolytes and
fluid disorders
assessment of
adult 28.2–28.10
pediatric 95.5–95.6
content of oral rehydration solutions 95.5
disorders of 28.1–28.27
effects of diuretics 28.11–28.15
principles
body water distribution
28.1–28.3
osmolality 28.2
requirements
pediatrics 99.2–99.3
use in
cardiogenic shock 18.16, 18.23
dehydration, pediatrics 99.3–99.5
diabetic ketoacidosis
48.34–48.35
diarrhea, pediatric patients
95.5–95.6
hypovolemic shock 18.10–18.15,
18.31
septic shock 18.26
Flumadine
See Rimantadine
Flumazenil
adverse effects 73.16
pharmacology 73.16
use in
benzodiazepine overdoses 73.16,
104.14–104.15
fluoxetine overdoses 104.18
hepatic encephalopathy 25.14
Flunisolide, nasal 21.14
Flunitrazepam, breast milk 45.25
Fluoride
requirements, pediatric 99.5
use in treatment of osteoporosis
46.34

Fluoroquinolones
Also see specific agents
table of 54.7
adverse effects
table of 54.14
hepatotoxicity 26.8
efficacy 63.5
antipseudomonal 63.5
interactions, drugs
antacids 63.5
cyclosporine 63.17
divalent cations 63.6
sucralfate 63.5
theophylline 3.3, 63.7
use in
febrile, neutropenic patients
67.10
gonorrhea 64.4, 64.6
pelvic inflammatory disease
64.6, 64.7
Salmonella gastroenteritis
60.13–60.14
Shigella gastroenteritis
60.14–60.15
travelers' diarrhea 60.2, 60.4,
60.5
tuberculosis 59.10–59.11
urinary tract infections
63.5–63.8, 63.17
Fluorouracil
adverse effects 90.12
diarrhea 91.5
encephalopathy 91.15
ocular 49.15
teratogenicity 45.12
dosing
alterations 90.12
hepatic dysfunction 91.28
pharmacokinetics 90.12
pharmacology 90.12
use in colon cancer 93.8–93.9
Fluoxetine
Also see Depression, adulthood;
Serotonin reuptake inhibitors
adverse effects
mania, children 78.5
self-injurious behavior 78.15
serum sickness 6.7
teratogenicity 45.12
breast milk 45.25
interactions, drugs
mechanism 3.2
use in
aggression/disinhibition
79.4–79.5
anorexia 80.4
bulimia 80.5, 80.11–80.12
children
anxiety disorders 78.16
obsessive compulsive disorder
78.7, 78.16
depression, adulthood
76.10–76.12
migraine headache 50.12
obsessive compulsive disorder
73.24, 73.28
pain 7.20
panic disorder 73.19
posttraumatic stress 73.28
premenstrual syndrome 46.16
tension headache 50.16
Fluoxymesterone
See Androgens
Flupenthixol, breast milk 45.25
Fluphenazine
Also see Neuroleptics
administration depot parenteral

75.9–75.10
adverse effects 75. 7
teratogenicity 45.12
dose 75.8
use in
diabetic neuropathy 48.48
psychoses 75.7–75.10
Flurazepam
Also see Benzodiazepines
adverse effects, teratogenicity
45.12
breast milk 45.25
pharmacokinetics 73.9, 73.12, 74.8
use in
elderly 74.13
insomnia 74.8
jet lag 74.5
sedation 73.7
Flurbiprofen
Also see Nonsteroidal anti-inflammatory drugs
use in gout 40.5
Flurocytosine
See Flucytosine
Flutamide
use in prostate
cancer 93.17
hyperplasia 103.17
Fluticasone, nasal 21.14
Fluvastatin 9.15, 9.16
Fluvoxamine
Also see Depression, adulthood;
Serotonin reuptake inhibitors
depression, adulthood 76.10–76.12
use in
alcoholism 82.7
children, obsessive compulsive
disorder 78.16
obsessive compulsive disorder
73.24, 73.28
panic disorder 73.19
Folate
Also see Folic acid
deficiency
also see Anemia, folate
deficiency
adults 82.9
Folic acid
Also see Anemia, folate deficiency
adverse effects, teratogenicity 45.12
deficiency
drug-induced, phenytoin 44.13,
44.14
fetus 44.13
interactions, drugs
sulfasalazine 24.7
metabolism 88.11
use in
anemia, folate deficient 88.11
cirrhosis 25.3
pregnancy 44.7–44.8, 44.14
Folinic acid
use with pyrimethamine-sulfadiazine 68.25
Food poisoning 60.8
Forced expiratory volume 19.2
in
asthma 19.2–19.3
COAD 20.1
Formoterol
See Beta-adrenergic agonists
Fortaz
See Ceftazidime
Foscarnet
adverse effects 33.41

table of 54.14, 70.5
nephrotoxicity 29.11, 68.19,
94.21
dosing 33.40
pharmacokinetics 70.2–70.3
pharmacology 33.40
use in cytomegalovirus
disease 33.40–33.41,
94.20–94.21
prophylaxis 67.17, 94.18–94.19
retinitis 68.18–68.20
Fosinopril
Also see Angiotensin-converting
enzyme inhibitors
adverse effects 10.22–10.23
teratogenicity 45.12
breast milk 45.25
contraindications/precautions 10.21
dose 10.22
pharmacokinetics 10.22
pharmacology, comparisons
10.22–10.23
use in hypertension 10.22
Fragmin
See Dalteparin
Freebase
See Cocaine
Fructose, alcohol toxicity 82.5
Fructosamine 48.10
Fungal endocarditis 57.15–57.16
Fungal infections 69.1–69.22
Also see specific infections;
specific antifungals
endocarditis 57.16
in the immunocompromised host
67.12–67.15
predisposing factors 67.12
superficial and cutaneous 69.4–69.7
systemic
aspergillosis 69.17–69.18
blastomycosis 69.13–69.15
candidiasis 69.7–69.12
coccidiodomycosis 69.17
cryptococcosis 69.19
histoplasmosis 69.15–69.17
treatment, systemic 67.13–67.15
Fungi
morphology, classification 69.2
infection sites 69.2
Fungoid
See Triacetin
Furamide
See Diloxanide furoate
Furazolidone
adverse effects
serum sickness 6.7
vasculitis 6.12
use in giardiasis 71.9
Furosemide
Also see Diuretics
administration
intravenous versus oral 15.15
single versus multiple doses 15.15
adverse effects
alkalosis 15.13
aplastic anemia 89.13
hyperglycemia 15.13
hyperuricemia 15.13
hypochloremia 15.13
hypokalemia 15.13
hypomagnesemia 15.13
nephrotoxicity 29.11
teratogenicity 45.12
vasculitis 6.12
breast milk 45.25

pharmacokinetics
  absorption 15.15
  bioavailability 15.15
pharmacology
  combined with other diuretics
    15.15–15.16
  effect on thyroid function 47.6
  hemodynamic effects 18.19
  monitoring efficacy 15.15
  onset/duration 15.15
  use in
    cirrhosis 25.5
    congestive heart failure
      15.6–15.7, 15.15–15.16
      severe 18.19
    hypertension 10.15
    hypertensive emergency 17.8
    renal insufficiency 15.16
    respiratory distress, neonates 96.7
Furoxone
  See Furazolidone
G6PD
  See Hemolytic anemia, G6PD
    deficiency
GABA benzodiazepine receptor 73.5,
  73.6
Gabapentin
  adverse effects 52.12
  pharmacokinetics 52.6
  use in seizures 52.4, 52.14
Group A beta-hemolytic streptococ-
  cus 97.11–97.13
Gadopentetate dimeglumine
  adverse effects, teratogenicity
    45.12
  breast milk 45.25
Galactorrhea
  Also see Lactation
  contraceptives, oral 43.15
  drug-induced
    neuroleptics 75.20
Gallamine 8.8–8.12
Gallium
  adverse effects 28.22
  use in hypercalcemia 28.22
Gallstones, contraceptives, oral 43.15
Gamimmune
  See Gamma globulin
Gamimmune-N
  See Immune globulin
Gamma amino butyric acid
  hepatic encephalopathy 25.11
Gamma benzene hexachloride
  See Lindane
Gamma globulin
  use in
    toxic shock 46.10
Gamma glutamyl transferase 4.12
Gamma hydroxybutyrate 87.5,
  104.21
  use in narcolepsy 74.15
Gammagard
  See Immune globulin IV (IVIG)
Ganciclovir
  administration
    intravenous 68.19
    intravitreal 68.20
    oral 68.20
  adverse effects 33.40–33.41
    table of 54.14, 70.5
    neutropenia 68.19, 94.21
    thrombocytopenia 94.21
  dialyzability 32.8
  dosing 32.8, 33.40

pharmacokinetics 70.2–70.3
  clearance 32.8
  parameters 32.8, 68.19
    dialysis 54.16
    renal disease 54.18
    renal failure 32.8
  use in cytomegalovirus
    33.40–33.41, 70.7–70.8
      prophylaxis 67.17, 94.18–94.19
      retinitis 68.18–68.20
Gangrene 66.7
Gantanol
  See Sulfamethoxazole
Garamycin
  See Gentamicin
Gardnerella vaginitis 46.2–46.3, 46.7
Gases
  See Arterial blood gases
Gastric cancer regimens 90.16
Gastric lavage
  drug overdoses 104.11
  use in alcohol toxicity 82.5
Gastric ulcer 23.5, 23.9, 23.13–23.14
  Also see Peptic ulcer disease
Gastroenteritis
  Also see Gastrointestinal infections
  common pathogens 54.5
Gastroesophageal reflux
  alcohol induced 82.10
  clinical presentation
    adults 23.16
    pediatrics 95.6
    pregnancy 44.9
  complications 23.16
  drug-induced, theophylline 20.11
  diagnosis, pediatrics 95.6
  pathogenesis
    adults 23.16
    pediatrics 95.6
  treatment
    adults 23.5, 23.7, 23.16–23.18
    pediatrics, table of 95.6–95.7
Gastrointestinal disorders
  Also see specific disorders
  bleeding 25.7
  esophageal varices 25.2–25.6
  gastric ulcer 23.13–23.14
  gastroesophageal reflux
    23.16–23.18
  infections 60.1
  peptic ulcer 23.1–23.14
  reflux, pediatric 95.6–95.7
  stress ulcer 23.18–23.20
Gastrointestinal effects of drugs
  Also see Nausea/vomiting; specific
    drugs
  acyclovir 64.19
  alcohol 23.3, 82.4, 82.9–82.10
  aluminum antacids 23.8
  amantadine 51.4, 70.5
  amiodarone 16.19
  antibiotics 60.10
  antineoplastics 60.10
  aspirin 7.8, 13.18, 41.6
  beta-lactam antibiotics 54.13
  bismuth subsalicylate 60.3–60.5
  bromocriptine 46.18, 51.11
  caffeine 23.3
  carbamazepine 52.10, 52.12
  carbonic anhydrase inhibitors
    49.10
  chemotherapy agents 91.5–91.8
  chloroquine 71.4
  cholestyramine 9.14, 9.17
  cigarettes 23.3

clindamycin 54.13
clofazamine 68.29
colchicine 40.8
corticosteroids 33.35, 42.10
digoxin 15.22
diiodohydroxyquine 71.8
diloxanide furoate 71.8
disulfiram 82.8
dopamine agonists 51.11
ergot 50.6
erythromycin 54.13
estrogens 46.32
ethosuximide 52.19–52.20
flucytosine 69.19
foscarnet 70.5
gemfibrozil 9.22
histamine$_2$-antagonists 23.4
HMG CoA reductase inhibitors
  9.16, 9.17
hydralazine 44.19
indomethacin 96.13
iron 88.7
ketoconazole 69.16
levodopa 51.5
lithium 77.5, 77.6
magnesium antacids 23.8
metformin 48.36
methysergide 50.11
metronidazole 71.8
morphine 7.22
niacin 9.15, 9.17, 9.19
nitrofurantoin 63.16–63.17
nonsteroidal anti-inflammatory
  drugs 7.8, 23.13, 40.5,
  41.8–41.9, 46.14
omeprazole 23.10
penicillamine 41.15
pergolide 51.11
phenylbutazone 40.5
plicamycin 28.22
primaquine 71.4
salicylates 41.6
sulfasalazine 24.6
sulfonamides 54.13
sulfonylureas 48.43
tetracyclines 54.13
theophylline 20.9
valproate 52.20, 52.21
Gastrointestinal hyperactivity
  opioid withdrawal 83.9
  treatment
    dicyclomine 83.9
    prochlorperazine 83.9
Gastrointestinal infections
  60.1–60.15
  Also see Food poisoning;
    Travelers' diarrhea; Viral gas-
    troenteritis; specific organisms
    table of 60.2
  normal flora 61.7
  pathogenesis 60.1
  predisposing factors 60.2
  treatment 60.1–60.2
    antibiotic-associated colitis
      60.10–60.12
    Campylobacter 60.12
    cryptosporidiosis 60.7–60.8
    enterohemorrhagic E. coli
      60.8–60.10
    food poisoning 60.8
    Helicobacter 60.13
    pseudomembranous colitis
      60.10–60.12
    Salmonella gastroenteritis
      60.13–60.14
    Shigella gastroenteritis
      60.14–60.15
    travelers' diarrhea 60.2–60.7

viral gastroenteritis 60.12–60.13
Gastroparesis, diabetic 48.49–48.50
G-CSF 67.13
  use in
    aplastic anemia 89.14
    HIV 68.12
    neutropenia 89.11
      chemotherapy 91.3–91.4
      ganciclovir 68.20
Gemfibrozil
  adverse effects 9.22
  interactions, lovastatin 9.16
  mechanism of action 9.22
  use in
    hypercholesterolemia 9.22
    hypertriglyceridemia 9.22
    mixed hyperlipidemia 9.22
Gender
  effect on benzodiazepines 73.12,
    73.14
Gene therapy 5.5–5.7
Generalized anxiety disorder
  clinical presentation 73.8
  diagnostic criteria 73.3, 73. 4
  etiology 73.5
  pathophysiology 73.5
  secondary causes of anxiety
    table of 73.4
    drug-induced 73.4
  treatment 73.6–73.17
Genital warts 64.21
Genitourinary atrophy 46.26–46.27
Gentamicin
  Also see Aminoglycosides
  administration
    aerosol 58.13–58.14
    intrathecal 56.16
  adverse effects
    nephrotoxicity 29.11,
      100.8–100.9
    ototoxicity 100.8
    pseudotumor cerebri 49.14
    teratogenicity 45.12
  breast milk 45.26
Gentamicin (continued)
  dosing
    neonates 96.7
    once a day 2.20
    renal failure 32.5, 32.8
  pharmacokinetics
    concentration, bone 65.5
  resistance 57.12
  use in
    cholangitis 61.2
    cystic fibrosis 100.7–100.9
    endocarditis
      culture negative 57.17
      enterococcal 57.12–57.15
      gram-negative 57.16
      prophylaxis 57.18–57.19
      prosthetic value 57.10
      S. aureus 57.9–57.11
      S. viridans 57.6–57.7
    meningitis 56.16
      neonate 96.17–96.18
    necrotizing enterocolitis 96.16
    osteomyelitis, neonatal 65.4
    peritonitis 61.10
    pyelonephritis 63.8
GERD
  See Gastroesophageal reflux
Geriatric urological disorders
  103.1–103.25
  benign prostate hyperplasia
    103.11–103.17

sexual dysfunction 103.1–103.10
urinary incontinence
103.18–103.22
Geriatrics
alcohol abuse 81.10–81.11
altered drug response
anticholinergics 51.4
benzodiazepines 73.12, 73.14,
74.13, 102.10
colchicine 40.8
digoxin 15.24
disopyramide 16.10
flurazepam 74.13
isoniazid 59.10
labetalol 17.11
narcotics 7.21–7.22
phenytoin 101.3
quinidine 16.10
sedative hypnotics 74.13
theophylline 19.17
thyroxine 47.2–47.3, 47.15
warfarin 12.13–12.14, 16.11
dosing
of antimicrobials 54.12
sulfonylureas 48.46
drug use considerations
adverse reactions 101.10
altered pharmacodynamics
101.2–101.4
altered pharmacokinetics
101.2–101.4
altered physiology 101.2–101.4
compliance 101.8–101.9
economic 101.1–101.2
functional abilities
101.12–101.13
medication errors 101.8
medication management
101.7–101.11
polytherapy 101.5
immunizations
influenza 58.3
medical problems and treatment
acute leukemia 92.6
benign prostate hyperplasia
103.11–103.17
schizophrenia 75.23
sexual dysfunction 103.1–103.10
urinary incontinence
103.18–103.22
pharmacokinetics
clearance 54.12
presentation in hypothyroidism
47.2–47.3, 47.15
rehabilitation 101.11–101.13
treatment of
Alzheimer's 102.2–102.7
anxiety 102.10
behavioral disturbances
102.10–102.12
dementias 102.1–102.11
depression, adulthood
76.15–76.16, 102.11
diabetes 48.46–48.47
insomnia 74.12–74.13
myocardial infarction 14.13,
14.15
pseudodementias 102.11–102.12
urinary incontinence 46.27
Gestational
See Pregnancy
Gestational diabetes 44.11–44.12
GGT
See Gamma glutamyl transferase
Giant cell arteritis 42.3
Giardiasis
clinical presentation and diagnosis

71.8
treatment 71.8–71.9
Ginghaosu 71.4
Gingival hyperplasia
drug-induced
cyclosporine 33.18
phenytoin 52.17
Glaucoma
Also see specific agents
clinical presentation 49.3
definitions 49.2
diagnosis 49.2–49.3
drug-induced 49.3
alphachymotrypsin 49.3
anticholinergics 49.3, 51.4
corticosteroids 49.17–49.18
trifluridine 70.5
treatment
also see Miotics; Mydriatics;
Ophthalmic drugs; specific
agents
angle closure 49.11–49.12
open angle 49.3–49.11
algorithm 49.6
anticholinesterases 49.8–49.9
apraclonidine 49.13
beta blockers 49.4
betaxolol 49.7, 49.9
carbachol 49.8
carbonic anhydrase inhibitors
49.10–49.11
carteolol 49.7
clonidine 49.13
dipivefrin 49.10
echothiophate 49.8
epinephrine 49.4–49.7,
49.9–49.10
guanethidine 49.11
isofluorophate 49.9
isoproterenol 49.11
levobunolol 49.4, 49.7
metipranolol 49.7
physostigmine 49.8
pilocarpine 49.4, 49.7–49.8,
49.11
prazosin 49.11
products table of 49.5
timolol 49.4–49.10, 49.11
Glipizide 48.36–48.38
Globulin, laboratory assessment 4.11
Glomerulonephritis
Also see Nephrotoxicity; Renal
failure
drug-induced 29.6
postinfectious 29.6
poststreptococcal 97.11
rapidly progressive 29.4–29.6
vasculitic 29.6
Glomerulopathies, chronic
amyloidosis, primary systemic
30.22–30.23
Goodpasture's 30.23–30.24
lupus nephritis 30.20–30.22
Wegener's granulomatosis
30.25–30.26
Glucagon 48.27
interactions, drugs
warfarin 12.20
use in hypotension 6.5, 6.8
Glucocorticoids
See Corticosteroids
Glucose
Also see Diabetes mellitus; Home
blood glucose monitoring;
Hyperglycemia; Hypoglycemia
alterations secondary to

dawn phenomenon 48.24–48.25
exercise 48.8
reactive hyperglycemia 48.22
Somogyi effect 48.22
blood versus plasma concentration
48.8–48.9
concentrations in diabetics
48.4–48.5
factors affecting 48.15, 48.20
fasting glucose concentrations
48.5, 48.8
laboratory assessment, effect of
levodopa 51.9–51.10
urine 48.5–48.6
see Urine, glucose tests
use in
hyperkalemia 30.6
hypoglycemia 48.26–48.27
Glucose-6-phosphate dehydrogenase
deficiency
See Hemolytic anemia, G6PD deficiency
Glucostix
See Home blood glucose
monitoring
Glucotrol
See Glipizide
Glue sniffing 83.12
Glyburide
Also see Sulfonylureas
adverse effects, teratogenicity
45.13
breast milk 45.26
hypoglycemia 48.44–48.45
pharmacokinetics 48.37–48.38
Glycerin 49.11
Glycocalyx 56.17–56.18
Glycogen storage disease 40.1
Glycosylated hemoglobin 48.9–48.10
GM-CSF 67.13
use as priming agent for bone marrow harvest 94.6
use in
aplastic anemia 89.14
HIV 68.12
neutropenia 89.11
chemotherapy 91.3–91.4
neutropenia 68.20
Goeckerman regimen 38.3, 38.6
Goiter 47.2–47.3, 47.28
Gold
Also see Auranofin
adverse effects 41.10–41.11
aplastic anemia 89.13
ocular 49.14
pulmonary 22.5
teratogenicity 45.13
thrombocytopenia 89.8
breast milk 45.26
dosing 41.10–41.11
preparations/formulations
41.10–41.11
use in
juvenile rheumatoid arthritis 41.22
rheumatoid arthritis 41.3,
41.10–41.11
Gold compounds
adverse effects
nephrotoxicity 29.11
Gonadotropin releasing hormone
adverse effects
osteoporosis 46.22
use in
endometriosis 46.21, 46.23
premenstrual syndrome 46.18

Gonadotropin, chorionic 44.3
Gonorrhea 64.2–64.8
clinical presentation
anorectal 64.5
arthritis 40.3, 65.10
disseminated 64.7–64.8
females 64.2
males 64.2
pelvic inflammatory disease
64.6–64.7
pharyngeal 64.5
diagnosis 64.3
prevention 64.6
ophthalmia neonatorum 96.21
treatment
anorectal 64.5–64.6
antibiotic-resistant neisseria
64.4–64.5
CDC recommendations
64.3–64.4
disseminated 64.7–64.8
endocarditis 64.8
gonococcal arthritis 64.7–64.8
in penicillin-allergic patients 64.4
meningitis 64.8
ophthalmic neonatorum 64.8
pharyngeal 64.5–64.6
prophylaxis of ophthalmia
neonatorum 64.8
septic arthritis 65.11
uncomplicated 64.3–64.4
Goodpasture's disease 30.23–30.24
Goserelin
endometriosis 46.21
use in prostate cancer 93.17
Gossypol 43.23
Gout
Also see Hyperuricemia; Uric acid
association with
coronary heart disease 40.2
lead toxicity 40.2
Gout (continued)
clinical presentation 40.2
definition 40.1
diagnosis 40.3
differential 40.4
drug-induced
allopurinol 40.9
ethanol 40.2
levodopa 51.9
niacin 9.15, 9.17
probenecid 40.11
laboratory assessment 40.3, 40.12
pathogenesis 40.1–40.3
treatment
drugs
colchicine 40.5, 40.7–40.8
corticosteroids 40.5–40.6
indomethacin 40.5–40.6
narcotics 40.8
nonsteroidal anti-inflammatory
drugs 40.5–40.6
phenylbutazone 40.5
goals 40.4
principles 40.4
Graft rejection 33.15–33.18,
33.20–33.21
Graft versus host disease
acute 94.12–94.15
chronic 94.16–94.17
stimulated by hematopoietic
growth factors 94.7
Gram-negative bacillary

meningitis 56.15–56.17
Gram-negative endocarditis 57.17
Gram's stain 54.6
    organisms, table of 54.4
Granisetron
    dosing as antiemetic 105.6–105.7
    use in
        chemotherapy-induced nausea
            and vomiting 105.6–105.7
        pediatric chemotherapy 105.9
Granulocyte-CSF
    Also see G-CSF
    use in immunocompromised hosts
        67.13
Granulocyte-macrophage CSF stimu-
    lating factor 67.13
    Also see GM-CSF
Granulocyte transfusions 67.12
Granulomatous enteritis 24.9–24.12
    Also see Crohn's disease
Graves' disease 47.2–47.3, 47.6,
    47.25
    Also see Hyperthyroidism
Gravida 44.4
Griseofulvin
    adverse effects, teratogenicity 45.13
    interactions, drugs
        contraceptives, oral 43.11, 43.12
        warfarin 12.20
    use in onychomycosis 69.5
Growth hormone 95.15–95.17
    use in HIV-wasting 68.18
Growth hormone releasing factor
    95.16
Guaiac, stool 93.7
Guaifenesin 21.19
Guanabenz 10.13, 10.14, 10.18,
    10.25, 10.26
    Also see Alpha₂-agonists
Guanadrel 10.14, 10.28
Guanethidine
    adverse effects, ocular 49.13
    interactions, drugs
        antidepressants 3.3
    use in
        glaucoma 49.11
        hypertension 10.14, 10.28
        Raynaud's phenomenon 11.9
        thyroid storm 47.26
Guanfacine 10.13, 10.14, 10.18,
    10.25, 10.26
    Also see Alpha₂-agonists
    adverse effects, teratogenicity
        45.13
    breast milk 45.26
Gynecologic disorders 46.1–46.34
    climacteric 46.23–46.27
    dysmenorrhea 46.10–46.14
    endometriosis 46.18–46.23
    HIV infection 68.32–68.35
    osteoporosis 46.27–46.34
    postcoital UTI 63.13
    premenstrual syndrome
        46.14–46.18
    toxic shock 46.7–46.10
    vaginitis 46.2–46.7
Gynecomastia, drug-induced
    alcohol, chronic 82.12
    anabolic steroids 87.3
    cimetidine 23.4
    digoxin 15.23
    ketoconazole 54.14
    omeprazole 23.10

Habitrol
    See Nicotine
Haemophilus influenzae
    meningitis 56.10–56.12
        prophylaxis
            rifampin 56.12
            vaccine 56.3, 56.12
        treatment
            ampicillin 56.10
            cefotaxime 56.10
            ceftriaxone 56.10
            cefuroxime 56.10
            chloramphenicol 56.7, 56.10
Haemophilus influenzae vaccine
    56.12–56.13, 95.10, 95.12
    adverse effects, serum sickness 6.7
    use in chronic bronchitis 58.3
Halazepam
    pharmacokinetics 73.9, 73.12
    use in anxiety 73.9
Halcion
    See Triazolam
Haldol
    See Haloperidol
Half-life 2.5
Hallucinogens
    See specific agents
    adverse effects, teratogenicity
        see specific agents
    breast milk
        see specific agents
Haloperidol
    Also see Neuroleptics
    adverse effects 75.7
        dystonias 75.15
        hepatotoxicity 26.8
        teratogenicity 45.13
        breast milk 45.26
    dosing
        decanoate 75.9–75.10
        traditional 75.6–75.8
    pharmacology
        comparison
            clozapine 75.2
            risperidone 75.2
        mechanism of action 75.2
        relative potency 75.7
    use in
        amphetamine intoxication 84.5
        autism 78.11
        childhood psychoses 78.8
        emesis 105.4, 105.8
        phencyclidine toxicity 86.8
        psychoses 75.2, 75.7–75.10
        Tourette's 78.9
Haloprogin 69.3
Halotestin
    See Fluoxymesterone
Halotex
    See Haloprogin
Halothane
    adverse effects, hepatotoxicity 26.9
Hamilton anxiety rating scale 73.8
Hamilton depressive scale 76.5
Hand foot syndrome 91.10
Hantavirus infections 70.11
Hashimoto's thyroiditis 47.2, 47.5
Havrix
    See Hepatitis A vaccine
Hay fever 21.15–21.16
HbOC immunization 56.12–56.13
Head injury
    treatment, analgesics 7.20

Headaches 50.1–50.17
    classification 50.1–50.3
    clinical presentation 50.2–50.17
    cluster
        clinical presentation 50.2,
            50.13–50.14
        pathophysiology 50.13
        prophylaxis
            corticosteroids 50.15
            drugs, table of 50.15
            ergotamine 50.15
            lithium 50.15
            methysergide 50.15
        treatment, acute
            dihydroergotamine 50.14
            drugs, table of 50.14
            ergotamine 50.14
            oxygen 50.14
            sumatriptan 50.14
    drug-induced 50.5
        calcium channel blockers 13.18
        chloroquine 71.4
        cluster 50.2, 50.13–50.15
        cocaine 50.5
        contraceptives, oral 43.16, 50.5
        estrogen 50.5
        hydralazine 44.19
        migraine headache 50.3, 50.13
        niacin 9.15, 9.17, 9.19
        nicardipine 17.4
        nifedipine 17.4
        nitrates 13.7, 13.9, 13.10
        nitroglycerin 50.5
        tension 50.2, 50.15–50.17
    migraine
        clinical presentation 50.2,
            50.3–50.4
        contraindications/precautions,
            contraceptives, oral 43.16
        diagnosis 50.5
        drug-induced
            ergot withdrawal 50.7
            estrogen 50.5
            oral contraceptives 50.5
        pathophysiology 50.3
        precipitating factors 50.5
        prophylaxis
            amitriptyline 50.11
            calcium channel blockers
                50.13–50.14
            drugs, table of 50.8, 50.12
            methysergide 50.11
            propranolol 50.10–50.11
            valproate 50.12
        treatment, acute
            analgesics 50.9
            chlorpromazine 50.9
            corticosteroids 50.9
            drugs, table of 50.9
            ergot 50.5–50.7, 50.8
            nonsteroidal anti-inflammatory
                drugs 50.7
            sumatriptan 50.7–50.8
    tension
        clinical presentation 50.2,
            50.15–50.16
        pathogenesis 50.16
        prophylaxis 50.16–50.17
        treatment, acute
            analgesics 50.16
            nonsteroidal anti-inflammatory
                drugs 50.16
        treatment, nonsteroidal anti-inflam-
            matory drugs 7.23
Health food, ingestions of
    toxicity 104.20–104.21
Heart failure
    See Congestive heart failure

Heart transplantation 33.9,
    33.17–33.23
Heat stroke
    See Hyperthermia
Heat treatment
    sporotrichosis 69.6
Helicobacter 60.13
    detection 23.12
    treatment 23.12–23.13
Hematemesis
    See Esophageal varices
Hematocrit 4.14
Hematological disorders
    Also see Anemia; Anemia, aplas-
        tic; Chemotherapy; G6PD defi-
        ciency; Hemolytic anemia;
        Neutropenia; Thrombocytopenia;
        specific disorders
    drug-induced 69.19, 89.1–89.14
        alcohol 82.9
        amphotericin 54.14, 67.13
        amrinone 15.35, 18.20
        antithymocyte globulin 33.37
        aspirin 41.6
        azathioprine 33.38
        beta-lactam antibiotics 54.13
        bepridil 13.18
        captopril 15.31
        carbamazepine 52.8, 52.12, 77.9
        cephalosporins 67.8–67.10
        chloramphenicol 54.13, 56.12,
            97.20
        clozapine 75.11–75.12
        colchicine 40.8
        corticosteroids 33.35, 42.8
        ethosuximide 52.19, 52.20
        felbamate 52.4
        flucytosine 54.14
        foscarnet 70.5
Hematological disorders
    (continued)
    drug-induced (continued)
        ganciclovir 33.40, 54.14, 68.19,
            68.20, 70.5, 94.21
        gold 41.11
        lithium 77.5
        methotrexate 41.13
        penicillamine 41.15
        pentamidine 68.16
        phenazopyridine 63.9
        phenylbutazone 40.5
        plicamycin 28.22
        pyrimethamine 68.24–68.25
        rifampin 59.8
        salicylates 41.6
        sulfasalazine 24.6
        sulfonamides 54.13, 63.15–63.16
        sulfonylureas 48.43
        thioamides 47.21–47.22
        ticlopidine 53.8, 102.10
        trimethoprim-sulfamethoxazole
            94.21–94.22
        valproate 52.24
        vidarabine 70.5
        zidovudine 54.14, 68.7, 68.8
Hematological effects of drugs
    Also see Hematological disorders,
        drug-induced
    chemotherapy agents 91.2–91.4
    G-CSF 91.3–91.4
    GM-CSF 91.3–91.4
Hematology, laboratory tests
    4.13–4.17, 88.3
Hematopoietic growth factors
    Also see specific agents
    use as priming agents for bone

marrow harvest 94.6
use in
  bone marrow transplantation
    94.6, 94.7
  graft failure, bone marrow 94.11
Hemodialysis 31.1–31.8, 31.12–31.13
  Also see Dialysis; specific drugs
  alcohol 82.5
  drugs, table of 32.6–32.10
  principles 31.1–31.8, 32.12
  use in
    hyperkalemia 28.19
    hypermagnesemia 28.27
Hemodilution, ischemic stroke 53.12
Hemodynamic monitoring
  18.7–18.10
Hemofiltration 31.12
  arteriovenous 31.13, 32.4
  ultrafiltration 31.13
  venovenous 31.13
Hemoglobin 4.14
Hemolytic anemia 89.2–89.6
  bilirubin concentrations 4.12
  complications
    hyperkalemia 28.18
  G6PD deficiency 89.2–89.4
    clinical presentation 89.3–89.4
    drug-induced
      table of 89.4
      antimalarials 71.4
      aspirin 71.4
      dapsone 68.16
      isoniazid 59.8
      methylene blue 71.4
      nalidixic acid 71.4
      nitrofurantoin 63.5, 71.4
      phenazopyridine 63.9
      primaquine 71.4
      quinidine 71.4
      quinine 71.4
      salicylates 71.4
      sulfasalazine 24.5
      sulfonamides 63.15, 71.4, 89.4
    pathogenesis 71.4, 89.2–89.3
    treatment 89.4
  immune 89.4–89.6
    classification 89.5
    clinical presentation 89.2, 89.5
    diagnosis 89.4–89.5
    drug-induced
      table of 89.5
      melthyldopa 89.6
      penicillin 89.5
      quinidine 89.5–89.6
    pathogenesis 89.2, 89.5–89.6
    treatment 89.6
Hemolytic disease, newborn
  44.20–44.21, 45.30
Hemolytic uremic syndrome 95.14
  clinical presentation 60.9
  enterohemorrhagic E. coli 60.9
Hemorrhage
  Also see Bleeding
  periventricular 96.24
  postpartum 44.28–44.29
Hemorrhoids, pregnancy 44.9
Hemosiderosis 82.9
  drug-induced
    alcohol 82.9
Heparin
  Also see Low molecular weight
    heparin; Thrombosis; Warfarin
  administration
    intravenous 12.7–12.8
    routes 12.3

subcutaneous 12.3, 12.10
  adverse effects
    bleeding 12.9
    hyperkalemia 12.10
    hypersensitivity reactions 12.10
    osteoporosis 12.10
    teratogenicity 45.6, 45.13,
      45.21–45.22
    thrombocytopenia 12.8,
      89.8–89.9
  breast milk 45.29
  dosing
    adjustments 12.8
    conversion to warfarin 12.12
    infusion 12.7–12.10
    loading dose 12.7, 12.12
    low dose 12.11
    monitoring 12.8–12.10
  interactions, drugs
    cigarettes 85.3
    protamine 12.10
    sulfonylureas 48.39
    warfarin 12.20
  overdose, treatment 12.10
  pharmacokinetics 12.3
  pharmacology 12.3
    duration therapy DVT 12.8
    mechanism of action 12.3
  use in
    amphotericin infusions 69.12
    cardiogenic thromboembolism
      12.17–12.19
    cardioversion 12.17
    deep venous thrombosis
      12.7–12.11
    DIC 12.22
    dialysis 31.4
    hemolytic uremic syndrome 95.15
    myocardial infarction 14.4, 14.8
    pregnancy 12.16
    pulmonary embolus 12.11–12.12
    "stroke" 53.10–53.11
    surgical prophylaxis 12.11
    thrombosis 12.3–12.19
    transient ischemic attacks
      53.10–53.11
    veno-occlusive disease of the
      liver 94.10
Hepatic coma 25.10–25.14
  clinical presentation 25.10–25.14
  drug-induced
    diuretics 25.6, 25.11
    opiates 7.21, 25.11
    sedatives 25.11
  pathogenesis 25.10–25.12
  predisposing factors 25.10–25.12
  treatment 25.12–25.14
    enteral nutrition 34.4, 34.6
    parenteral nutrition 35.13
Hepatic disorders
  Also see Hepatic coma
  altered drug disposition
    aminoglycosides 54.13
    benzodiazepines 73.12
    chloramphenicol 54.13
    clindamycin 59.7–59.8
    erythromycin 54.13
    nafcillin 54.13
    sulfamethoxazole 54.13
  altered drug pharmacokinetics
    table of 62.5
  autoimmune chronic active hepati-
    tis 62.14
  classification 26.1–26.3
    alcoholic cirrhosis 25.1–25.17
    cholestasis 26.2
    chronic active hepatitis 26.2
    cirrhosis 25.1–25.17, 26.2

drug-induced hepatotoxicity
  26.1–26.17
  encephalopathy 25.10–25.14
  fibrosis 26.2
  hepatic granulomas 26.3
  hepatitis, viral 62.1–62.16
  hepatocellular adenoma 26.3
  hepatorenal 25.14
  necroinflammatory 26.1
  phospholipidosis 26.2
drug-induced
  table of 26.5–26.13
  acetaminophen 7.7, 7.8, 104.19
  acyclovir 70.3, 70.5
  allopurinol 26.5, 40.10
  amiodarone 26.5
  amoxicillin clavulanate 26.6
  anabolic steroids 87.3, 87.5
  androgens 26.6
  antidepressants, tricyclic 26.12
  antineoplastic drugs, table of
    91.27
  aspirin 26.6, 41.21
  azathioprine 26.6
  beta-lactam antibiotics 54.13
  captopril 26.6
  carbamazepine 52.9
  carmustine 26.6
  chemotherapy 94.10
  chlorpromazine 26.7
  chlorpropamide 26.7
  contraceptives, oral 26.7, 43.13
  corticosteroids 26.8
  cyclosporine 26.8
  dantrolene 26.8
  diltiazem 26.8
  diuretics 15.14
  dopamine agonists 51.10–51.12
  erythromycin 26.8
  ethionamide 59.6
  felbamate 52.4
  flucytosine 54.14
  fluoroquinolones 26.8
  ganciclovir 54.14, 70.5
  haloperidol 26.8
  halothane 26.9
  HMG CoA reductase inhibitors
    9.16, 9.17
  isoniazid 26.9, 59.7–59.8
  ketoconazole 26.9, 54.14
  lovastatin 26.9
  mercaptopurine 26.9
  methimazole 26.9
  methotrexate 26.10, 41.13
  methoxyflurane 26.9
  methyldopa 26.10
  monoamine oxidase inhibitors
    26.10
  niacin 9.15, 9.17, 26.10
  nitrofurantoin 26.11
  nonsteroidal anti-inflammatory
    drugs 26.11
  oxacillin 26.11
  pediatric parenteral nutrition
    99.18
  penicillin 26.11
  pergolide 51.12
  phenindione 26.11
  phenylbutazone 26.12
  phenytoin 26.12
  plicamycin 26.10
  prochlorperazine 26.12
  propylthiouracil 26.12
  pyrazinamide 59.6
  quinidine 26.12
  retinol 26.13
  rifampin 26.12, 59.7–59.9
  sulfonamides 26.12, 54.13

sulfonylureas 48.44
  tetracyclines 26.13, 54.13
  thioamides 47.21
  total parenteral nutrition 35.13
  trifluoperazine 26.13
  trimethoprim-sulfamethoxazole
    26.12
  valproate 26.13, 52.20, 52.22
  vitamin A 26.13
  veno-occlusive disease
    94.10–94.11
Hepatic dysfunction, effect on drug
  dosing/pharmacokinetics
  calcium channel blockers 13.17
  narcotics 7.21
  sulfonylureas 48.45
Hepatitis A infection
  characteristics of virus 62.1
  clinical presentation 62.4
  diagnosis 62.2
  prophylaxis
    postexposure 62.9
    pre-exposure 62.6
  serologic markers 62.2–62.4
  transmission 62.2
  treatment 62.4–62.5
Hepatitis A vaccine 62.6
Hepatitis B immune globulin 62.9
Hepatitis B infection
  characteristics of virus 62.1
  clinical presentation 62.4
  complications
    chronic hepatitis 62.10–62.13
  diagnosis 62.2
  prophylaxis
    postexposure 62.8–62.10
    pre-exposure 62.5–62.8
Hepatitis B infection (continued)
  transmission 62.2
  treatment 62.5
Hepatitis B vaccine 62.6
  adverse effects, teratogenicity
    45.13
  dosing regimen 62.6–62.7
  efficacy 62.7
  immunizations, pediatric 62.8
  indications 62.8
  interchangeability HBV vaccines
    62.7
  pediatric immunization 95.7–95.9
Hepatitis C
  characteristics of virus 62.3
  clinical presentation 62.4
  diagnosis 62.3
  postexposure immune globulin
    62.10
  serologic markers 62.3–62.4
  transmission 62.3
  treatment 62.13
Hepatitis D
  characteristics of virus 62.3
  clinical presentation 62.4
  diagnosis 62.3
  serologic markers 62.3–62.4
  transmission 62.3
  treatment 62.13
Hepatitis E 62.3–62.4, 62.10
Hepatitis, chronic
  Also see specific viral hepatitis
  clinical presentation 62.11
  definitions 62.10
  diagnosis 62.11
  treatment approaches
    drugs 62.12
    goals 62.11

Hepatitis, viral 62.1–62.16
  Also see specific hepatitis viral
    infection
Hepatojugular reflex 15.10
Hepatomegaly
  in congestive heart failure 15.10
Hepatorenal syndrome 25.14
  Also see Hepatic disorders
Hepatotoxicity
  Also see Hepatic disorders
  drug-induced
    alcohol 82.8
    amphetamine abuse 84.3
    azathioprine 33.38
    cyclosporine 33.18
    diuretics 15.14
    flucytosine 69.19
    isotretinoin 37.5–37.6
    ketoconazole 69.16
    methotrexate 38.4–38.7
    neuroleptics 75.21
    phenazopyridine 63.9
    sulfasalazine 24.6
    tacrine 102.6
    tetracyclines 63.5
    valproate 77.9
Heroin
  Also see Opiate abuse
  abuse 83.3–83.9
  breast milk 45.22, 45.26
  effect on thyroid function tests
    47.6, 47.8
  pulmonary edema 22.3
Herpes, congenital 96.20–96.21
Herpes, genital 64.16–64.20
  clinical presentation 64.16
  complications 64.20
  diagnosis 64.17
  pathogenesis 64.16–64.17
  treatment 64.18
Herpes, neonatal 64.20
  clinical presentation 64.20–64.21
  treatment 64.20–64.21
Herpes simplex
  clinical presentation 64.16
    encephalitis 70.1–70.4
    in HIV 68.30
    in transplant patients 67.17
    keratitis 70.6
    neonatal 70.4–70.5, 96.20
    ocular herpes 49.18–49.19
  diagnosis 70.2–70.6
  prophylaxis 94.18
  treatment 70.2–70.6
    acyclovir 94.18
    keratitis 49.19–49.20
    neonatal 96.20
Herpes zoster
  clinical presentation, in HIV
    68.20–68.21
  transplant patients 67.17
  treatment 68.20–68.21
Hetastarch 18.15
Hexachlorophene, breast milk 45.26
HibTITER
  See HbOc
High blood pressure
  See Hypertension
Hirudin 89.9
Hismanal
  See Astemizole
Histamine$_2$-antagonists
  Also see specific agents
  administration 23.6–23.7

adverse effects 23.4
  infectious diarrhea 60.2, 60.3
dosing 23.6–23.7
  multiple daily 23.6–23.7
  night time 23.6–23.7
  renal insufficiency 23.4
  single daily 23.6–23.7
interactions, drug
  table of 23.8
  antacids 23.9
  overview 3.3
pharmacokinetics 23.4, 23.6–23.7
pharmacology
  comparison of H$_2$-antagonists
    23.4
  duration of therapy 23.7
  efficacy 23.7
  mechanism of action 23.4
use in
  allergic reactions 6.5, 6.8
  aspiration pneumonia prophylax-
    is 8.5
  combination with sucralfate
    23.10
  gastric ulcer 23.14
  gastroesophageal reflux disease
    23.7, 23.17
  peptic ulcer disease 23.4–23.8,
    23.11
  stress ulcers 23.19–23.20
  Zollinger-Ellison 23.7, 23.15
Histocompatibility 94.2
  antigens 33.3
Histrelin
  endometriosis 46.21
HIV infection
  complications
    cryptococcal meningitis
      68.21–68.24
    cytomegalovirus (CMV) retinitis
      68.18–68.20
    depression, adulthood 76.15
    enteric infections 68.29–68.31
    HIV-associated malignancies
      68.31–68.32
    HIV-wasting 68.18
    Mycobacterium avium complex
      (MAC) infection 68.27–68.29
    Mycobacterium tuberculosis
      68.25–68.27
    Pneumocystis carinii pneumonia
      (PCP) 68.14–68.18
    Toxoplasma encephalitis
      68.24–68.25
    tuberculosis 59.11
    varicella zoster virus 68.20–68.21
    vaginal candidiasis 46.14
  definitions 68.2, 68.4, 68.5
  diagnosis
    adults 68.4
    neonates 68.4–68.5
  epidemiology 68.5
  etiology, IV drug abuse 83.4
  pathophysiology 68.2–68.4
  pediatric HIV disease 68.34–68.38
  pharmacotherapy 68.6–68.18
  postexposure chemoprophylaxis
    68.32
  prognosis 68.5–68.6
  surrogate markers 68.6, 68.13
  therapeutic goals 68.6
  treatment 68.6–68.38
    gene therapy 5.6
  women and HIV disease
    68.32–68.34
Hivid
  See Zalcitabine

HLA complex 33.3
HMG CoA reductase inhibitors
  Also see Fluvastatin; Lovastatin;
    Pravastatin; Simvastatin
  adverse effects 9.16–9.17
  dose 9.15–9.16, 9.19
  efficacy 9.15–9.16
  pharmacology
    mechanism of action 9.16
  use in
    hypercholesterolemia 9.15–9.17,
      9.18–9.19
    hypertriglyceridemia 9.23
    mixed hyperlipidemia 9.22
Home blood glucose monitoring
  clinical use and interpretation
    48.18–48.21
    hospital bedside 48.31
    in elderly 48.46
    insulin dose adjustment 48.21
    sick-day management 48.24
    sliding scale 48.24, 48.30–48.31
  cost-saving measures 48.43
  indications 48.9, 48.18, 48.46
  patient education 48.20
  products, comparison of
    48.18–48.20
  sources of error 48.18–48.20
  testing frequency 48.20
Honeymoon period 48.31–48.32
Host versus graft disease 94.2–94.3
Hot flushes 46.24–46.26
Human chorionic gonadotropin 44.3
Human immunodeficiency virus
  infection
  See HIV infection
Human leukocyte antigen 33.3
Human placental lactogen 44.3–44.4
Humatin
  See Paromomycin
Humatrope
  See Somatotropin
Hyaline membrane disease 96.7
Hydergine
  See Ergoloid mesylates
Hydralazine
  Also see Vasodilators
  administration, parenteral 17.6,
    44.19
  adverse effects
    drug fever 6.9
    fetal effects 44.19
    headache 10.27, 44.19
    lupus 6.15
    nephrotoxicity 29.12
    systemic lupus erythematosus
      10.27, 42.3
    tachycardia 10.14, 44.19
    tachyphylaxis 10.26
    teratogenicity 45.13
    vasculitis 6.12
  breast milk 45.26
  contraindications/precautions
    10.14, 17.6
  dosing
    emergencies 17.4, 17.12–17.13
    preeclampsia 44.19
  use in
    congestive heart failure, com-
      bined with nitroglycerin 15.5,
      15.28–15.30
    hypertension 10.14, 10.24,
      10.26–10.27
    hypertensive emergencies 17.4,
      17.6, 17.12–17.13

    preeclampsia 44.19
    pregnancy 44.19
Hydrocephalus 53.14
Hydrochlorothiazide
  Also see Diuretics
  adverse effects
    hemolytic anemia 89.5
    teratogenicity 45.13
    vasculitis 6.12
  breast milk 45.26
  use in
    combination with furosemide
      15.16
    congestive heart failure 15.5,
      15.11–15.16
Hydrocodone
  Also see Morphine
  adverse effects, teratogenicity
    45.13
Hydrocortisone
  adverse effects, teratogenicity
    45.13
Hydrocortisone, topical
  See Corticosteroids, topical
Hydroflumethiazide
  Also see Diuretics
  adverse effects, teratogenicity
    45.13
  breast milk 45.26
Hydrogen peroxide, use in
  supportive care 94.5
Hydroiodic acid, teratogenicity 45.13
Hydromorphone 7.10–7.12
  Also see Morphine; Narcotics
  adverse effects, teratogenicity
    45.13
  use in
    epidural infusion 8.20–8.21
    patient controlled analgesia 8.20
Hydroxychloroquine
  Also see Chloroquine;
    Antimalarials
  adverse effects
    corneal toxicity 41.12
    retinal pigmentation 41.12
    teratogenicity 45.13
  breast milk 45.26
  dosing 41.12
  use in
    juvenile rheumatoid arthritis
      41.22
    rheumatoid arthritis 41.3, 41.12
Hydroxyprogesterone, teratogenicity
  45.13
Hydroxyurea
  breast milk 45.26
  use in chronic myelogenous
    leukemia 92.7
Hydroxyzine
  Also see Antihistamines
  analgesic potentiation 7.17–7.18
  use in anxiety 73.8
Hylorel
  See Guanadrel
Hyperalimentation
  See Parenteral nutrition
Hypercalcemia
  Also see Calcium
  clinical presentation 28.21
  digitalis toxicity 15.23
  drug-induced 28.21, 28.13
    diuretics 10.17
  etiology 28.20–28.21
  homeostasis 4.8

laboratory interpretation 4.8
pathogenesis 28.20–28.21
treatment 28.21–28.23
Hyperchloremia
laboratory assessment 4.6
metabolic acidosis 4.6, 27.4
Hypercholesterolemia 9.10–9.19
Also see Dyslipidemia
alcohol, effect on 9.12
complications 9.7–9.10
diagnosis 9.10–9.11
drug-induced 9.12
pathogenesis 9.5–9.6
treatment 9.12–9.19
also see specific drugs
combination therapy 9.18–9.19
diet 9.12–9.13
drugs 9.14–9.19, 9.22
gene therapy 5.6
goals 9.13–9.14
lifestyle changes 9.13
Hypergastrinemia 23.10
Hyperglycemia
drug-induced
table of 48.55
anabolic steroids 87.3, 87.5
beta-adrenergic blockers 48.51
beta-agonists 44.25, 48.54
calcium channel blockers 48.52
clonidine 48.51–48.52
contraceptives, oral 43.13, 48.55
corticosteroids 33.35, 42.10,
48.54
diazoxide 17.12, 44.19
diuretics 10.16–10.17, 15.13,
28.14, 48.50–48.51
levodopa 51.9
niacin 9.15, 9.17, 48.54
parenteral nutrition 35.9, 35.11
pentamidine 68.16
phenytoin 48.55
ritodrine 48.54
salbutamol 48.54
sympathomimetics 48.54
terbutaline 48.54
pathogenesis
renal failure, chronic 30.15
Hyperkalemia
Also see Potassium; Hypokalemia
associated with
acidosis 30.7
potassium-sparing diuretics 30.6
renal failure, chronic 30.7
clinical presentation 28.18, 30.6
complications of 28.18
drug-induced 28.18
angiotensin-converting enzyme
inhibitors 10.22
captopril 17.5
enalaprilat 17.5
heparin 12.10
indomethacin 40.5
potassium-sparing diuretics
15.15
ECG effects 30.6
laboratory assessment 4.3
pathogenesis 28.18
chronic renal failure 30.5–30.6
treatment 28.18–28.19, 30.6
Hyperlipidemia
See Dyslipidemia
Hypermagnesemia
associated with renal failure,
chronic 30.7, 30.16
clinical presentation 28.27, 44.19
drug-induced 28.27
magnesium sulfate 44.19

neonatal 44.19
etiology 28.27
treatment 28.27–28.28
Hypernatremia 4.3, 28.10
Hyperosmolar nonketotic coma
48.45–48.46
Hyperosmotics 49.11–49.12
Hyperparathyroidism
pathogenesis
renal failure, chronic 30.16
uremic encephalopathy 30.16
Hyperphosphatemia
associated with renal failure,
chronic 30.7
laboratory interpretation 4.8
treatment
aluminum antacids 30.13
calcium acetate 30.13
calcium antacids 30.13
Hyperpigmentation
drug-induced, chemotherapy
agents 91.8–91.10
Hypersensitivity reactions
Also see specific agents
candida 69.6
clinical presentation 6.1–6.21
dialysis membranes 31.7
drug-induced
antithymocyte globulin 33.37
asparaginase 92.18
aspirin 41.6
beta-lactam antibiotics 54.13
chemotherapy agents
91.13–91.14
etoposide 92.18
heparin 12.10
insulin 48.27–48.28
iron dextran 88.8
nonsteroidal anti-inflammatory
drugs 46.14
sulfonylureas 48.43–48.44
tetracyclines 54.13
trimethoprim-sulfamethoxazole
in HIV 68.15
overview 6.1–6.21
pathogenesis 6.2
pseudoallergic 6.13–6.14
Hypersensitivity vasculitis
See Vasculitis
Hypertension
Also see Hypertensive emergencies
classification 10.2–10.3
clinical presentation 10.5–10.8
complications
atherosclerosis 10.7, 10.21
cardiovascular 10.6–10.7
cerebrovascular accidents
10.6–10.7
eclampsia 44.14
fetal morbidity 44.16
heart failure 15.2
ocular 10.6–10.7
renal failure 10.6–10.7
retinopathy 10.7
stroke 10.6–10.7
definitions
accelerated hypertension 10.3
diastolic blood pressure 10.2
isolated systolic hypertension
10.3
malignant hypertension 10.3
office hypertension 10.3
secondary hypertension
10.3–10.4, 10.5
systolic blood pressure 10.2
diagnosis

blood pressure measurements
10.3, 10.4
secondary hypertension
10.3–10.4, 10.5, 10.6
drug-induced
table of 10.5
alcohol 82.6, 82.11
amphetamines 84.3
cocaine 84.12
contraceptives, oral 43.14
corticosteroids 10.5, 33.22, 42.4
cyclosporine 33.22, 33.34
estrogens 46.32
etiology 10.3–10.4
pathogenesis
in pregnancy 44.14–44.20
renal failure, chronic
30.10–30.12
pathophysiology 10.4–10.5
in diabetes 48.50
pharmaceutical care 1.5, 1.7
treatment
also see specific drugs
diabetic patients 48.50–48.52
drug selection 10.12, 10.13,
10.17–10.18
drugs
alpha₁-adrenergic antagonists
10.24, 10.28
alpha₂-agonists 10.12, 10.14,
10.18, 10.25–10.26
angiotensin II antagonists
10.28–10.29
angiotensin-converting enzyme
inhibitors 10.7, 10.12, 10.13,
10.14, 10.18, 10.21–10.23
beta blockers 10.9, 10.11,
10.12, 10.13, 10.14,
10.18–10.21
calcium channel blockers 10.7,
10.23–10.24, 10.26
diuretics 10.7, 10.9, 10.11,
10.12, 10.13–10.17, 10.18,
10.22, 10.24, 10.26, 10.27
peripheral neuronal blockers
10.28
vasodilators 10.12, 10.14,
10.24, 10.26, 10.27
goals 10.9–10.10
in dyslipidemia 9.21
individualized 10.10–10.14
in pregnancy 44.16–44.20
nondrug 10.10–10.11
principles 10.8–10.14,
10.17–10.18
stepped-care 10.12–10.13, 10.28
Hypertension, malignant
See Hypertensive emergencies
Hypertensive emergencies
17.1–17.16
Also see Hypertension
clinical presentation 17.1–17.2
complications 17.2
definitions 17.1–17.2
pathogenesis 17.1–17.2
treatment
drugs
table of 17.4
captopril 17.5–17.6
clonidine 17.5–17.6
diazoxide 17.4, 17.10–17.13
diltiazem 17.4, 17.7
enalaprilat 17.4, 17.7
hydralazine 17.4, 17.6,
17.12–17.13
labetalol 17.4–17.6,
17.10–17.11
nicardipine 17.4, 17.7

nifedipine 17.3–17.6
nitroglycerin 17.4, 17.11–17.12
nitroprusside 17.4, 17.8–17.11
prazosin 17.6
trimethaphan 17.4
verapamil 17.4
goals 17.3
principles 17.2–17.3
Hyperthermia
Also see Fever
drug-induced
amphetamines 84.3
cocaine 84.12
neuroleptics 75.21
Hyperthyroidism 47.15–47.26
Also see Thyroid disorders
altered drug disposition 47.16,
47.21
clinical presentation 47.2–47.3,
47.15–47.26
complications 47.15–47.26
diagnosis 47.2–47.6, 47.17
drug-induced 47.26–47.27
amiodarone 16.18
pathogenesis
classification of causes 47.16
Graves' disease 47.2
treatment 47.3, 47.15–47.26
table of 47.19
Hypertrichosis
drug-induced
cyclosporine 33.18, 33.27
minoxidil 10.27, 33.27
Hypertriglyceridemia
Also see Dyslipidemia
drug-induced
table of 9.12
estrogen 9.18
ethanol 9.21
laboratory assessment 9.19–9.20
parenteral nutrition 35.7
pathogenesis 9.20–9.23
insulin resistance 9.21
treatment
combination therapy 9.23
diet 9.21–9.22
fibric acid derivatives 9.22
Hyperuricemia
Also see Gout; Uric acid
associated with renal failure,
chronic 30.7
clinical significance 40.12
definition 40.12
drug-induced
table of 40.3
alcohol 82.4
cyclosporine 33.18, 40.14
diazoxide 17.11
diuretics 10.16–10.17 15.14,
28.13, 40.12
ethambutol 59.6
levodopa 51.9
liver tablets 40.1
niacin 9.15, 9.17
pyrazinamide 59.6
yeast tablets 40.1
laboratory assessment 4.8
pathogenesis, chronic renal failure
40.13
treatment
allopurinol 40.9–40.11
indications 40.6, 40.12
urinary alkalinization 40.13
Hyperventilation
use in antidepressant overdoses
104.18

Hypnotics
  Also see Benzodiazepines;
    Insomnia; specific agents
  selection for
    patient 74.11
    formulary 74.16–74.17
Hypoalbuminemia
  diuretic resistance 28.15
Hypocalcemia
  drug-induced, magnesium sulfate
    44.19
  laboratory interpretation 4.8, 28.19
  pathogenesis
    hyperphosphatemia 30.12
    renal failure, chronic 30.12
  treatment 30.14
    neonatal 96.25
Hypochloremia
  diuretic-induced 15.13
Hypoglycemia
  clinical presentation 48.25–48.27
  drug-induced
    table of 48.57
    alcohol 48.56, 82.3–82.5
    anabolic steroids 48.58
    beta-adrenergic blockers 48.51,
      48.55, 48.58
    disopyramide 48.58
    insulin 48.25–48.27, 48.55
    pentamidine 48.57, 68.16
    quinidine 48.57–48.58
    quinine 48.57–48.58
    ritodrine 48.55, 48.58
    salicylates 48.55, 48.56–48.57
    sulfonamides 48.58
    sulfonylureas 48.44–48.45, 48.55
  laboratory interpretation 4.8
  pathogenesis, hyperinsulinemia
    48.25–48.27, 48.55–48.56
  treatment
    glucagon 48.27
Hypogonadism
  alcohol-induced 82.12
Hypokalemia
  Also see Potassium
  clinical presentation 28.17
  complications of 28.12, 28.17
    cirrhosis 25.6
    digitalis toxicity 15.23
  drug-induced 28.11–28.12, 28.16
    amphotericin 69.11
    beta₂-agonists 19.11, 44.25
    bicarbonate 27.8
    corticosteroids 15.23, 24.4
    diuretics 10.15–10.16, 15.13
  laboratory interpretation 28.16
  pathogenesis 28.16
    also see drug-induced
    nasogastric suction 15.23
    renal tubular acidosis 27.6
    vomiting 15.23
  predisposing factors 28.18
  treatment 28.17
    dietary 10.16
    oral supplements 15.14
    oral tablets 10.16
    potassium-sparing diuretics
      10.16, 15.14
    salt substitutes 10.16
Hypomagnesemia
  clinical presentation 10.17,
    28.25–28.26
  complications 28.26
    digitalis toxicity 15.23
  drug-induced 28.26
    amphotericin 69.11
    cyclosporine 33.18

  diuretics 10.17, 15.13, 28.13
    overview 28.26
  etiology 28.26
  pathogenesis 28.25–28.26
  predisposing factors 10.18
  treatment 28.27
    neonatal 96.25
Hyponatremia
  Also see Sodium
  clinical presentation 28.4–28.9
  complications 28.8
  drug-induced 28.7–28.8
    also see syndrome of
      inappropriate antidiuretic
      hormone secretion
    carbamazepine 52.10
    diuretics 10.17, 15.13, 28.13
    neuroleptics 75.21
    vasopressin 25.9
  laboratory interpretation 4.3,
    28.4–28.9
  pathogenesis 28.4–28.9
  treatment 28.4–28.9
Hypophosphatemia
  Also see Phosphate; Phosphorus
  clinical presentation 28.24
  drug-induced 28.24
    parenteral nutrition 35.11
      pediatric 99.17–99.18
  etiology 28.23
  laboratory interpretation 4.8
  pathogenesis 28.24
  treatment 28.24–28.25
Hypotension
  complications of dialysis 31.7
  drug-induced
    alcohol 82.5, 82.11
    antidepressants 76.9, 76.12
    calcium channel blockers 13.15,
      13.16
    dopamine agonists 51.11
    levodopa 51.5
    monoamine oxidase inhibitors
      76.19
    nitrate 13.7–13.8
    pentamidine 68.16
    quinidine 16.6
Hypothermia
  drug-induced, alcohol 82.5, 82.11
Hypothyroidism 47.1–47.15
  Also see Thyroid disorders
  clinical presentation 47.2–47.15
  diagnosis 47.1–47.8
  drug-induced
    amiodarone 16.19, 47.5–47.6,
      47.8, 47.27
    antidepressants 47.26–47.27
    lithium 47.26–47.27, 77.6, 77.7
    radioactive iodides 47.24
    sulfonylureas 47.9
  pathogenesis 47.2–47.15
    renal failure, chronic 30.15
  prevalence 47.2
  treatment 47.8–47.15
    also see specific agents
Hypovolemia
  clinical presentation 25.7
  treatment 25.7
Hypovolemic shock
  Also see Shock
  clinical presentation 18.10, 18.14
  diagnosis 18.3, 18.10
  pathogenesis 18.3, 18.10, 18.14
  treatment 18.3, 18.10–18.15
    timing of fluid 18.31

Hytrin
  See Terazosin
Ibopamine 15.36
Ibuprofen
  Also see Nonsteroidal anti-inflam-
    matory drugs
  adverse effects
    drug fever 6.9
    nephrotoxicity 29.12
    ocular 49.13
    teratogenicity 45.13
  breast milk 45.26
  clearance 32.8
  dosing, renal dysfunction 32.19
  use in
    dysmenorrhea 46.13
    gout 40.5–40.6
    migraine headache 50.9
    tension headaches 50.16
    pediatric
      analgesia 95.24
      antipyresis 95.4
"Ice" 84.5
Idarubicin
  adverse effects 90.12
    cardiotoxicity 91.17–91.19
  pharmacokinetics 90.12
  pharmacology 90.12
Idiopathic thrombocytopenia purpura
  clinical presentation 95.17
  treatment 95.17–95.18
Idoxuridine
  adverse effects, teratogenicity 45.13
  use in ocular herpes simplex 49.19
Ifosfamide
  adverse effects 90.13
    Fanconi syndrome 93.26
    hemorrhagic cystitis 91.21–91.22
    nephrotoxicity 29.12,
      91.21–91.22
  dosing/alterations 90.13
  pharmacokinetics 90.13
  pharmacology 90.13
Iloprost 89.9
Imaging, endocarditis 57.4
Imazodan 15.35–15.36
Imipenem
  dosing 32.8
  pharmacokinetics
    clearance 32.8
      dialysis 54.16
      renal disease 54.18
    parameters 32.8
    renal failure 32.8
  use in
    brain abscess 56.21
    cystic fibrosis 100.7–100.8
    immunocompromised hosts
      67.10
    lung abscess 58.6
    meningitis 56.16
    pyelonephritis 63.8
Imipramine
  Also see Antidepressants, cyclic
  adverse effects, teratogenicity
    45.13
  breast milk 45.26
  overdoses, treatment
    104.13–104.19
  pharmacokinetics in children 78.5
  pulmonary infiltrates 22.6
  use in
    attention deficit hyperactivity
      78.3
    bulimia 80.5

  childhood depression 78.4–78.5
  depressive disorders 76.10–76.12
  enuresis 95.20
  narcolepsy 74.14–74.15
  pain 7.3, 7.16
  panic disorders 73.19
  posttraumatic stress 73.28
  urinary incontinence
    103.20–103.21
Immune globulin 100.11
  Also see Gamma globulin;
    RhoGAM
  adverse effects
    pseudoallergic 6.16
    serum sickness 6.7
  use in
    cytomegalovirus 33.40–33.41,
      67.17
      prophylaxis 94.19
    graft versus host disease, acute
      94.15
    HIV, pediatrics 68.37–68.38
    hypogammaglobinemia, CLL
      92.9
    immunogenic thrombocytopenic
      purpura 95.17–95.18
    Kawasaki's disease 97.19
    neonatal sepsis prevention 96.19
Immunizations
  Also see specific vaccines
  guidelines 95.7
  H. influenzae schedule 56.13
  in HIV children 68.35
  influenza 58.3
  schedule, table of 95.9
  use in immunocompromised hosts
    95.13–95.14
Immunocompetence, nutrition 35.3
Immunocompromised host infections
  67.1–67.21
  antibiotic regimens 67.6–67.10
  infectious disorders 67.1
    vaginal candidiasis 46.4
  neutropenic cancer patients 67.3
  prophylactic antibiotics 67.13
  risk factors, infection 67.1
  transplant patients 67.15–67.18
Immunodeficiency, infection
  during
    See Compromised host, infections in
Immunoglobulins
  use in
    cytomegalovirus prophylaxis
      67.17
    Kawasaki's disease 97.19
Immunology transplantation
  33.3–33.5
Immunoreactive trypsin 100.3
Immunostimulants
  Also see specific agents
Immunosuppressives
  Also see specific agents
  adverse effects
    economic costs 33.5
    infections 33.38–33.41
    vaginal candidiasis 46.4
  associated with renal failure,
    chronic 30.9
  use in
    allogenic bone marrow transplan-
      tation 94.2–94.3, 94.4,
      94.13–94.16
    autologous bone marrow trans-
      plantation 94.4, 94.6
    graft versus host disease
      94.13–94.17

organ transplants 33.5–33.38
rapidly progressive glomeru-
lonephritis 29.5
Imodium
See Loperamide
Impotence
Also see Sexual dysfunction
drug-induced
table of 103.5–103.6
gonadal function 103.6–103.7
pathogenesis 103.3
treatment 103.7–103.11
Imuran
See Azathioprine
Inappropriate ADH
See Syndrome of inappropriate
antidiuretic hormone secretion
Indapamide
adverse effects, teratogenicity
45.13
use in diabetes 48.50
Indigo carmine, teratogenicity 45.13
Indocin
See Indomethacin
Indomethacin
Also see Nonsteroidal anti-inflammatory drugs
adverse effects 40.5
anemia, aplastic 89.13
nephrotoxicity 7.8, 29.12
ocular 49.14
serum sickness 6.7
teratogenicity 45.13, 45.33
breast milk 45.26
interactions, drugs
antihypertensives 40.5
diuretics 40.5
triamterene 7.8
pharmacokinetics
clearance 32.8
mature adult parameters 32.8
use in
cluster headaches 50.15
dysmenorrhea 46.13–46.14
gout 40.5–40.6
hypercalcemia 28.23
patent ductus arteriosus
96.13–96.14
periventricular/intraventricular
hemorrhage 96.24
preterm labor 44.25
uremic pericarditis 30.10
Indoprofen 40.5
Infant formulas 99.6–99.7
table of 99.8–99.10
phenylketonuria formulas
99.6–99.7
therapeutic formulas 99.6–99.7
Infection, principles of
Also see specific infections
classification
sexually transmitted 64.1–64.20
tuberculosis 59.1–59.15
gastrointestinal infections
60.1–60.2
treatment considerations
immunocompromised hosts
67.1–67.6
alteration of therapy
67.11–67.12
antibiotic regimen selection
67.6–67.10
prophylaxis 67.13–67.14
transplant patients 67.15–67.18

Infectious diseases
central nervous system 56.1–56.23
endocarditis 57.1–57.23
fungal infections 69.1
gastrointestinal 60.1–60.16
hepatitis 62.1–62.16
human immunodeficiency virus
(HIV) 68.1–68.38
immunocompromised hosts 67.1
intra-abdominal infections
61.1–61.17
Lyme disease 72.1
osteomyelitis 65.1–65.8
osteomyelitis/septic arthritis 65.1
parasitic infections 71.1
pediatric 97.1–97.22
respiratory tract infections 58.1
septic arthritis 65.9–65.13
sexually transmitted 64.1
skin and soft tissue infections
66.1–66.10
surgical prophylaxis 55.1–55.6
tuberculosis 59.1
urinary tract infections 63.1–63.19
viral infections 70.1–70.13
Infectious diseases, principles
antibiogram tables 54.8–54.9
antimicrobial adverse effects
table of 54.13–54.14
antimicrobials of choice
table of 54.10–54.12
approach to infections
affirm diagnosis 54.4
assess antimicrobial costs 54.9
assess antimicrobial toxicities
54.9
determine administration route
54.12
determine dose 54.12–54.19
determine likely pathogens 54.5
determine pathogen susceptibility
54.6–54.7
determine site 54.5
establish presence of infection
54.1–54.2
establish severity 54.2–54.3
monitor efficacy 54.18–54.19
classification of micro-organisms
table of 54.4
microbiology tests
broth dilution 54.6
culture and sensitivity 54.7
Gram's stain 54.4, 54.6
MBC 54.7
MIC 54.7
SBT 54.7
pathogens to infections
table of 54.5
Infertility
cystic fibrosis 100.3
effect of chemotherapy agents
91.26–91.27
endometriosis 46.18
Inflammatory bowel disease
24.1–24.16
Also see Crohn's disease;
Ulcerative colitis
Influenza 70.8–70.10
flu-like, rifampin 59.8
treatment
gene therapy 5.7
Influenza vaccine
adverse effects, teratogenicity
45.13
use in
chronic bronchitis 58.3
chronic obstructive airways dis-

ease 20.6
Ingram's regimen 38.3, 38.6
INH
See Isoniazid
Inhalant abuse 83.11–83.17
clinical presentation 83.11–83.13
complications 83.14–83.15
treatment 83.12–83.15
Inhibace
See Cilazapril
Inocor
See Amrinone
Inotropes
table of 18.12
cardiogenic shock 18.17–18.19
myocardial infarction 18.17–18.19
septic shock 18.28
INR
See International normalized ratio
Insomnia 74.5–74.13
Also see Anxiety
drug-induced
amantadine 51.5
felbamate 52.12
in opioid withdrawal 83.9
treatment
see Benzodiazepines; Sedative-
hypnotics; specific agents
Insulin
Also see Diabetes mellitus;
Diabetic ketoacidosis
administration 48.17–48.18
injection devices 48.18, 48.32
insulin infusion pumps
48.14–48.15
intranasal 48.32
intravenous 48.14, 48.34–48.35
jet injectors 48.13, 48.32
subcutaneous 48.17–48.18
adsorption onto intravenous bottles
48.35
adverse effects
allergy and resistance
48.27–48.28
dermatologic 48.27–48.28
hypoglycemia 48.25–48.27,
48.55
hypokalemia 28.16, 28.19
teratogenicity 45.13
clearance, effect of renal failure
48.29–48.30
dosing
adjustment based on blood glucose tests 48.20–48.24
alterations with switch to less
antigenic forms 48.28
compensatory 48.22, 48.24
during illness 48.24
during pregnancy 44.11, 44.12
initial dose 48.16–48.17, 48.23,
48.42
low-dose infusion, ketoacidosis
48.34–48.35
perioperatively 48.30–48.31
rainbow/sliding scale 48.24,
48.30–48.31
renal failure 48.29–48.30
split dosing 48.14–48.17,
48.20–48.23
supplementary 48.22,
48.23–48.24
factors affecting response
also see Hyperglycemia and
Hypoglycemia, drug-induced
table of 48.13
absorption 48.10–48.11

cigarettes 85.3
exercise 48.8, 48.29
insulin antibodies 48.12, 48.13
renal function 48.29–48.30
human 48.12, 48.17
dose change with switch from
animal insulin 48.28
indications for 48.17
hyperinsulinemia 48.3–48.4
interactions, drug
contraceptives, oral 43.12–43.15
intensive therapy
goals 48.14
indications and precautions
48.14–48.17
mixtures, stability and clinical
effect 48.17, 48.21–48.22,
48.42–48.43
onset and duration of action
48.11–48.12
patient education
administration 48.18
measuring/mixing 48.17–48.18,
48.21
syringes 48.17
pharmacokinetics
table of 48.14
Insulin (continued)
pharmacokinetics (continued)
absorption 48.10–48.11
clearance 48.11, 48.29–48.30
duration of action 48.11–48.12
factors altering 48.11, 48.13,
48.29
pharmacology, comparative
48.10–48.13
antigenicity 48.12, 48.17, 48.24
biosynthetic versus semisynthetic
human 48.12, 48.27–48.28
NPH versus lente 48.17,
48.21–48.22
purity 48.11, 48.24
preparations 48.10
table of 48.11
Lys-Pro 48.12
resistance 48.3–48.4
stability/storage
effect of temperature 48.28
flocculation 48.28
in intravenous bottles 48.35
in syringes 48.43
of mixtures 48.17, 48.21–48.22,
48.42–48.43
syringes, re-use of 48.43
use in
diabetes
gestation 44.11–44.12
type I 48.10–48.32
type II 48.41–48.43
diabetic ketoacidosis
48.33–48.34
elderly 48.46
hyperkalemia 28.19, 30.6
ischemic cerebral infarction
53.10
prevention of diabetes, type I
48.7
use with sulfonylureas 48.42
Insulin resistance
dyslipidemia 9.21
syndrome X 9.21
Intal
See Cromolyn
Interactions, drugs 3.1–3.9
Also see individual drugs
Interferon
adverse effects, lupus 6.15

Interferon, alpha
α2a versus α2b 62.12
adverse effects 62.12
use in
chronic hepatitis B 62.12
chronic hepatitis C 62.13
chronic myelogenous leukemia 92.7
HIV infections 68.12
Kaposi's sarcoma 68.31
melanoma 93.15
Interleukin-1 56.4, 56.8, 56.16
Interleukin-2
adverse effects
ocular 49.16
pulmonary 22.3
use in
HIV infections 68.12
melanoma 93.15–93.16
septic shock 18.30
Intermittent claudication
See Claudication, intermittent
Intermittent positive-pressure breathing 19.9
International normalized ratio 12.5, 12.12–12.20
Interstitial fluid 28.2
Interstitial nephritis 29.16–29.17
drug-induced
table of 29.8–29.14, 29.16
ciprofloxacin 29.17
treatment 29.17
Interviewing 1.2–1.4
Intra-abdominal infections
See Peritonitis
common pathogens 54.5
gastrointestinal flora 61.7
treatment
table of regimens 61.12
types of
abdominal trauma infections 61.16
appendicitis 61.16
cholangitis 61.1–61.3
cholecystitis 61.1–61.3
peritonitis 61.3–61.14
Intracellular fluid volume 28.1–28.2
Intracerebral hemorrhage 53.3
Intracranial pressure 56.4, 56.5, 56.8
Intralipid
combined with amphotericin 69.4
Intraocular pressure 49.2
Intrauterine devices 43.4, 43.19–43.20, 43.22
Intravenous immune globulin
See Immune globulin
Intravenous therapy
chemotherapy administration 91.11–91.12
extravasation management 91.11–91.12
Iocetamic acid, teratogenicity 45.13
Iodamide, teratogenicity 45.13
Iodides
adverse effects
drug fever 6.9
teratogenicity
see specific agents
breast milk 45.26
pharmacology/pharmacodynamics
effect on thyroid function tests 47.6
mechanism of action 47.17
preparations 47.17

teratogenicity 71.23
use in
hyperthyroidism 47.17
preparation of thyroid surgery 47.17
Iodinated glycerol
teratogenicity 45.13
Iodine
See Iodides
Iodipamide, teratogenicity 45.13
Iodochlorhydroxyquin
subacute myelo-optic neuropathy 71.8
use in amebiasis 71.8
Iodoquinol
adverse effects 71.5, 71.7
use in amebiasis 71.5, 71.7
Iodoxamate, teratogenicity 45.14
Iopanoic acid
adverse effects, teratogenicity 45.14
breast milk 45.26
Iothalamate, teratogenicity 45.14
Ipecac
use in toxic overdoses 104.5, 104.10–104.11
Ipodate
adverse effects, teratogenicity 45.14
effect on thyroid function tests 47.6
use in hyperthyroidism 47.18
IPPB
See Intermittent positive-pressure breathing
Ipratropium
Also see Anticholinergics
use in
asthma 19.8–19.9, 19.12, 19.25
bronchopulmonary dysplasia 98.2
chronic obstructive airways disease 20.6–20.7
rhinitis, vasomotor 21.17
Iron
Also see Anemia, iron deficiency
absorption 88.3, 88.5
administration
oral 88.5
parenteral 88.7
adverse effects 88.6–88.7
content of salts 88.6
dietary requirements, in pregnancy 44.7
dosing in
adults 88.4–88.7
pediatrics 88.4
pregnancy 44.7
interactions, drugs
antacids 23.9, 88.7
levodopa 51.14
sulfasalazine 24.7
tetracycline 88.7
overdoses, treatment 104.9–104.13
patient education 88.6
use in
formula-fed infants 99.6
pregnancy 44.7
Iron binding capacity 88.5, 104.12
Iron dextran 88.7–88.8
adverse effects
drug fever 6.9
serum sickness 6.7
Irradiation therapy
breast cancer

decompression, spinal cord 93.6
postsurgical 93.3
craniospinal, ALL 92.15
dermatological effects 91.10
tumor sensitivities, table of 90.9
Ischemia attacks
See Transient ischemic attacks
Ischemic neurological deficit 53.1
Ischemic stroke 53.9–53.14
Ismelin
See Guanethidine
Isoetharine
See Beta-adrenergic agonists
Isometheptene 50.7, 50.9
Isoniazid
Also see Tuberculosis
adverse effects 59.7–59.9
drug fever 6.9
lupus 6.15
hemolytic anemia 89.5
hepatotoxicity 26.9
optic neuritis 49.14
teratogenicity 45.14, 59.11–59.12
allergy 59.8
breast milk 45.26
contraindications/precautions
alcoholics 59.7
elderly 59.9–59.10
dosing
in
acquired immunodeficiency syndrome 59.10–59.11
elderly 59.9
hepatic disorders 54.16
pediatrics 59.12
pregnancy 59.12
initial 59.3
maintenance 59.3–59.5
interactions, drug 3.2
antacids 23.9
diazepam 59.8
phenytoin 59.8
pharmacokinetics
clearance
dialysis 54.16
concentration
breast milk 59.12
central nervous system 59.13
serum 59.6
pharmacology 59.3–59.5
use in
Mycobacterium avium 68.28
Mycobacterium tuberculosis 59.3–59.14, 68.25–68.27
Isoproterenol
Also see Beta-agonists
use in
asthma 19.11–19.12
cardiac arrest 16.21
glaucoma 49.11
torsades de pointes 16.17
Isoptin
See Verapamil
Isosorbide dinitrate
Also see Nitrates; Nitroglycerin
use in
angina 13.9, 13.11
heart failure 15.29
Isosorbide mononitrate 13.11
Isotretinoin
Also see Acne
adverse effects 37.3, 37.6
table of 37.3
dyslipidemia 9.12, 37.5
hepatotoxicity 37.5

mucocutaneous drying 37.6
teratogenicity 37.6, 45.6, 45.14, 45.32
use in acne 37.3, 37.5–37.6
Isoxicam 40.5
Isoxsuprine
adverse effects, teratogenicity 45.14
use in impotence 103.8
Isradipine 10.23, 13.14, 13.15, 13.17
Also see Calcium channel blockers
use in congestive heart failure 15.34
Isuprel
See Isoproterenol
Itraconazole 67.15
dosing, renal dysfunction 69.12
use in
aspergillosis 69.18–69.19
blastomycosis 69.14
coccidioidomycosis 69.17
cryptococcal meningitis 68.23
histoplasmosis 69.16–69.17
Itraconazole (continued)
prophylaxis candidemia 69.12–69.13
sporotrichosis 69.6–69.7
IUD
See Intrauterine device
IVIG
See Immune globulin
Janeway lesions 57.4
Jarisch Herxheimer reaction 64.14
"Jet lag" 74.5
Jod-Basedow 47.27
Juvenile rheumatoid arthritis
Also see Rheumatoid arthritis
clinical presentation 41.20
definition 41.20
treatment 41.21–41.22
uveitis 41.22
Kanamycin
adverse effects
nephrotoxicity 59.6
neurotoxicity 59.6
ototoxicity 59.6
teratogenicity 45.14
breast milk 45.26
use in tuberculosis 59.6
Kantrex
See Kanamycin
Kaolin and pectin
adverse effects, teratogenicity 45.14
interactions, drugs 3.2
digoxin 15.22
use in infectious diarrhea 60.2
Kaopectate
See Kaolin and pectin
Kaposi's sarcoma 68.31
Kawasaki's disease 97.18–97.19
Kayexalate, 30.6
use in hyperkalemia 28.19
Keflex
See Cephalexin
Kefzol
See Cefazolin
Kerlone
See Betaxolol
Kernicterus, sulfonamide-induced

54.13
Kernig's sign 56.5
Ketamine
    use in
        analgesia, perioperative 8.6, 8.8
        anesthesia 8.6
Ketalar
    See Ketamine
Ketanserin
    use in Raynaud's phenomenon
        11.10
Ketoconazole
    absorption 67.15, 68.22
    adverse effects 46.6, 69.16
        table of 54.14
        hepatotoxicity 26.9, 54.14
        teratogenicity 45.14
    dosing 32.8
        renal dysfunction 69.12
    interactions, drugs 69.16–69.17
        table of 69.8
        astemizole 69.17
        cimetidine 23.6, 23.8
        cyclosporine 33.26
        mechanism 3.2
        rifampin 59.8, 68.29
        terfenadine 21.12, 69.17
        warfarin 12.20
    pharmacokinetics 32.8
    pharmacology 69.3
    use in
        blastomycosis 69.14
        candida esophagitis 68.30
        candida vaginitis 46.6
        candidiasis, oral 68.30
        candidiasis, vaginal 69.6
        cryptococcal meningitis 68.22
        histoplasmosis 69.16
        prophylaxis
            candidemia 69.12–69.13
            immunocompromised host
                67.15
        prostate cancer 93.18
Ketoprofen
    use in
        dysmenorrhea 46.14
        gout 40.5
Ketorolac
    administration
        intramuscular 7.7
        intravenous 7.18
    pharmacokinetics 7.7
    use in
        breakthrough epidural block 8.21
        pain 7.7
        pediatric analgesia 95.24
Kidney stones 29.19–29.20
Kidney transplantation 33.12–33.17
Köbner's phenomenon 38.1,
    38.4–38.5
Korsakoff's psychosis 82.11, 104.14
Kwashiorkor
    See Malnutrition
Kwell
    See Lindane
Labetalol
    Also see Beta blockers
    administration
        intravenous 44.19
        oral 10.25
    adverse effects 10.25
        fetal effects 44.18
        overview 17.12
        teratogenicity 45.14
    breast milk 45.26

contraindications/precautions
    10.25, 17.11
dosing
    in preeclampsia 44.17
    intravenous 17.4, 17.11
    oral 17.12
pharmacodynamics
    table of properties 10.20
    comparative 17.6
pharmacokinetic properties 10.20,
    10.25, 32.8
use in
    hypertension 10.20, 10.25
    hypertensive emergencies
        17.4–17.6, 17.10–17.11
    pregnancy 44.17–44.18
Labor and delivery
    analgesia in 7.13
    induction of 44.26–44.28
        amniotomy 44.28
        oxytocin 44.26–44.28
        prostaglandins 44.26
    preterm labor 44.21–44.26
        beta-agonists 44.23–44.25
        calcium channel blockers
            44.25–44.26
        magnesium sulfate 44.25
        prostaglandin synthetase
            inhibitors 44.25
        ritodrine 44.23–44.24
        terbutaline 44.24
Laboratory tests
    Also see specific chapters and tests
    tables of 4.4, 4.14, 4.18, 4.19
    acid phosphatase 4.12
    acid-base 27.3–27.5
    adrenal function 42.8
    alanine aminotransferase (ALT)
        4.11
    albumin 4.11, 35.3, 41.4
    alkaline phosphatase 4.11
    alpha fetoprotein 93.18
    aminotransferases 4.11
    anion gap 4.6, 27.3
    antinuclear antibodies 41.4
    arterial blood gases 16.21,
        19.2–19.3, 27.3
    aspartate aminotransferases 4.11
    basophils 4.16
    beta human chorionic
        gonadotropin 93.19
    bicarbonate 4.5
    bilirubin 4.12
    bleeding time 12.6
    blood urea nitrogen 4.9
    BUN/SrCr 29.3
    calcium 4.7–4.8, 28.19
    carbon dioxide content 4.5, 27.3
    carcinoembryonic antigen
        93.7–93.8
    CBC 4.13
    CD4+ cell count 68.2–68.4
    chemistries 4.7–4.12
    chloride 4.6
    clotting tests 4.17, 12.4–12.6
    coagulation 4.17
    creatine kinase 4.10, 14.2
    creatinine 4.9, 29.2
    creatinine clearance 29.2
    drug concentrations, table 4.19
    electrolytes 4.3–4.6
    eosinophils 4.16
    erythrocyte sedimentation rate
        4.15, 41.4
    ferritin 88.5
    fractional excretion, sodium 29.4
    fructosamine 48.10
    gamma glutamyl transferase 4.12

general principles 4.1–4.2
globulin 4.11
glucose 4.8, 48.5, 48.8–48.9
guaiac 93.7
hematocrit 4.14
hematology 88.3
hemoglobin 4.14
hepatitis serologic markers 62.2
HIV culture 68.4, 68.5
HIV p24 antigen 68.4, 68.5
immunoreactive trypsin 100.3
international normalized ratio 12.5,
    12.12–12.20
iron binding capacity 104.12
lactate dehydrogenase 4.10, 14.2
lymphocytes 4.16
magnesium 28.25
mean cell hemoglobin 4.15
mean cell hemoglobin concentra-
    tion 4.15
mean cell volume 4.15
monocytes 4.16
neutrophils 4.15
osmolal gap 4.6, 28.2
osmolality 4.6, 28.2
Papanicolaou test 93.12
partial thromboplastin time 12.5
phosphate 4.8, 28.23
potassium 4.3, 28.15
prostate specific antigen 93.18,
    103.17
prothrombin time 12.4
pulmonary function 19.1–19.3
renal function 2.7, 4.9
reticulocyte count 4.15, 88.5
rheumatoid factor 41.4
Schilling test (B_{12}) 88.9
Schlicter test 57.5
serum bactericidal titer 57.5
sodium 4.3, 28.6
spot test 71.4
streptococcal antigen 97.11
sweat chloride 100.3
Systeme International units
    4.2–4.5
technetium-99m-pyrophosphate
    14.2
thallium-201 14.2
thrombin time 12.6
thyroid function 47.3–47.8
TIBC 88.5
uric acid 4.8, 40.12
urinalysis 4.18–4.19
Lactate dehydrogenase 4.10, 14.2
Lactated Ringer's
    use in hypovolemic shock
        18.12–18.13
Lactation
    drug effects, table of 45.23–45.29
    hormonal control 44.29
    stimulation 44.29
    suppression 44.29–44.30
Lactic acidosis 27.7
    drug-induced
        biguanides 48.36
        metformin 48.36
Lactobacillus
    vaginal candidiasis 46.7
Lactulose
    use in
        hepatic coma 25.12
        upper gastrointestinal bleeding
            25.7
Laennec's cirrhosis 25.1
Lamictal
    See Lamotrigine

Lamisil
    See Terbinafine
Lamivudine
    use in HIV 68.9, 68.37
Lamotrigine
    adverse effects 52.14
    interactions, drugs
        carbamazepine 52.14
        valproate 52.11
    use in seizure disorders 52.4,
        52.11–52.14
Larium
    See Mefloquin
Larodopa
    See Levodopa
Laryngotracheobronchitis
    97.16–97.17
Lasix
    See Furosemide
Latex agglutination 56.6
Laxatives
    Also see specific agents
Laxatives (continued)
    breast milk
        see specific agents
    use in upper gastrointestinal bleed-
        ing 25.7
Lazeroids 53.12
LD
    See Lactate dehydrogenase
Lead
    gout 40.2
    renal tubular acidosis 27.5
Left ventricular diastolic dysfunction
    15.2, 15.36–15.37
Leg cramps
    associated with renal failure,
        chronic 30.17
    quinine 11.11–11.12
Legionaire's pneumonia
    treatment 58.7
Lennox-Gastaut 52.3
Lesch-Nyhan syndrome 40.5
Leucovorin rescue
    dosing, methotrexate concentra-
        tion-time 93.25
Leukemia, acute lymphoblastic
    clinical presentation 92.11
    etiology 92.10
    pathophysiology 92.11
    prognostic variables 92.11–92.13
        cytogenetic 92.13
        immunologic 92.12
    treatment
        CNS preventative 92.15
        duration 92.17
        high-risk ALL 92.17–92.19
        maintenance 92.16
        relapsed ALL 92.19
        remission induction 92.14–92.15
Leukemia, acute lymphocytic
    complications, hyperuricemia 40.2,
        40.13
Leukemia, acute myelogenous
    treatment, bone marrow transplan-
        tation 94.22
Leukemia, acute nonlymphocytic
    diagnosis 92.3
    drug-induced, chemotherapy
        agents 91.25–91.26
    signs and symptoms 92.3
    treatment 92.4–92.6

Leukemia, chronic lymphocytic
    prognosis 92.7
    signs and symptoms 92.6
    staging 92.7
    treatment 92.7
Leukemia, chronic myelogenous
    prognosis 92.7
    signs and symptoms 92.6
    staging 92.7
    treatment 92.7
Leukeran
    See Chlorambucil
Leukocytosis, corticosteroid-induced
    42.8
Leukopenia
    drug-induced
        carbamazepine 52.8
        ticlopidine 102.10
Leuprolide
    adverse effects, teratogenicity
        45.14
    use in
        endometriosis 46.21
        prostate hyperplasia 103.17
Levatol
    See Penbutolol
Levlen
    See Contraceptives, oral
Levobunolol 49.4–49.7
Levodopa
    Also see Parkinson's disease
    administration
        controlled-release product
            51.7–51.8
        drug holidays 51.8–51.9
        early/late initiation 51.5–51.6
    adverse effects
        arrhythmias 51.5
        dyskinesias 51.5–51.6
        gastrointestinal 51.5
        hemolysis 89.5
        hypotension 51.5
        mania 77.3
        "on/off" effect 51.6, 51.7
        psychiatric 51.5–51.8
    dosing, in Parkinson's disease
        51.5–51.7
    effect on thyroid function tests
        47.6, 47.8
    efficacy 51.5
        early/late initiation 51.5–51.6
        fluctuations 51.7
    interactions, drugs
        antidepressants 51.8
        benzodiazepines 51.9, 51.14
        imipramine 51.8
        iron 51.14
        metoclopramide 51.9, 51.14
        monoamine oxidase inhibitors
            51.8
        neuroleptics 51.9, 51.14
        pyridoxine 51.9, 51.14
    interference with laboratory tests
        51.9–51.10
        glucose 51.10
        ketones 51.10
        uric acid 51.10
    mechanism of action, Parkinson's
        disease 51.5
    use in
        combination with carbidopa
            51.5–51.8
        combination with dopamine ago-
            nists 51.8
        combination with monoamine
            oxidase-B inhibitors 51.8

hepatic coma 25.13
nocturnal myoclonus 74.15
Parkinson's disease 51.5–51.8
Levomethadyl 83.6–83.7
Levonorgestrel 43.19–43.20
Levophed
    See Norepinephrine
Levorphanol 7.10
Levothroid
    See Thyroid hormone; Thyroxine
Levothyroxine (T₄)
    Also see Thyroxine
    adverse effects, teratogenicity
        45.14
    breast milk 45.26
LHRH 43.22–43.23
LHRH analogs, use in prostate
cancer 93.17
Lice 71.11–71.12
    Also see Pediculosis
Licorice 15.11
Lidocaine
    adverse effects 16.6
        cardiovascular 16.17
        neurological 16.17
        overview 14.13
        pulmonary 22.3
    dose
        loading 2.8, 16.16
        maintenance 2.8, 16.17
    during discontinuation
        renal impairment 32.8
    factors affecting response
        congestive heart failure 16.17
    interactions, drugs
        antiepileptic drugs 16.17
        cimetidine 16.17
        phenytoin 16.17
        propranolol 16.17
    pharmacokinetics 16.6
        clearance 32.8
        half-life, hepatitis 62.5
        parameters 2.8, 32.8
        two-compartment model 2.8
    pharmacology
        effect on ECG 16.3
    plasma concentrations, MI 14.13
    use in
        cardiac arrest 16.20, 16.21
        digitalis toxicity 15.24
        myocardial infarction 14.6, 14.8
        ventricular arrhythmias 14.6,
            14.8
        ventricular tachycardia 16.16
        cluster headache 50.14
Lincomycin
    adverse effects, teratogenicity
        45.14
    breast milk 45.26
Lindane
    adverse effects 71.11–71.12
        teratogenicity 45.14
    breast milk 45.26
    use in
        lice 71.11–71.12
        scabies 71.12
Liothyronine (T₃)
    Also see Thyroid hormone
    adverse effects, teratogenicity
        45.14
    breast milk 45.26
Liotrix 47.10
    Also see Thyroid hormone
    adverse effects, teratogenicity
        45.14

breast milk 45.26
Lipid emulsions
    See Fat emulsions
Lipid peroxidation inhibition 53.12
Lipoproteins
    metabolism 9.1–9.5
    properties 9.4
Lisinopril
    Also see Angiotensin-converting
        enzyme inhibitors
    adverse effects, teratogenicity
        45.14
    breast milk 45.26
    interactions, drugs
        allopurinol 40.10
    use in
        heart failure 15.28, 15.30–15.32
        hypertension 10.22, 10.23
Listeria, in immunocompromised
patients 67.2
Lisuride
    Also see Dopamine agonists;
        Parkinson's disease
    adverse effects 51.12
    dosing 51.12
    use in Parkinson's disease 51.12
Lithium
    Also see Affective disorders, bipo-
        lar
    adverse effects 77.5–77.6
        table of 77.6
        hypermagnesemia 28.27
        hypothyroid 47.26–47.27
        leukocytosis 77.5
        nephropathy 30.5
        nephrotoxicity 28.7, 28.10, 29.12
        pediatric 78.5
        psoriasis 38.5
        renal tubular acidosis 27.5
        teratogenicity 45.6, 45.14, 77.8
    breast milk 45.22, 45.26
    contraindications/precautions
        pregnancy 77.8
    during discontinuation
        renal impairment 32.8
    interactions, drugs
        table of 77.7
        caffeine 85.10
        sulindac 3.4
    pharmacokinetics
        breast milk 77.8
        clearance 32.8
        parameters 32.8
        plasma, therapeutic 77.6
        renal failure 32.8
    pharmacology/pharmacodynamics
        factors affecting response
            see Interactions, drugs
    prelithium workup 77.4–77.5
    toxicity 77.7–77.8
    use in
        aggression 78.15, 79.5
        anorexia 80.4
        bipolar disorder 77.4–77.8
        bipolar, pediatric 78.5
        cluster headache 50.15
        depression, refractory 76.23
        hyperthyroidism 47.26–47.27
        schizophrenia, adjunctively 75.10
        self-injurious behavior 78.15
        syndrome of inappropriate antidi-
            uretic hormone secretion 28.10
    use with antipsychotics 77.4
Livedo reticularis, amantadine

induced 51.5
Liver disease
    See Hepatic disorders
Liver transplantation 33.28–33.38
Lodoxamide tromethamine 49.17
Loeffler's syndrome 22.1, 22.6
Loestrin
    See Contraceptives, oral
Lomefloxacin
    breast milk 45.26
Lomotil
    See Diphenoxylate
Lomustine
    adverse effects 90.13
        hepatotoxicity 91.27
    dosing/alterations 90.13
    pharmacokinetics 90.13
    pharmacology 90.13
Long-term care
    Omnibus Budget Reconciliation
        Act 101.6
Lo/Ovral
    See Contraceptives, oral
Loperamide
    adverse effects
        toxic megacolon 24.2
        teratogenicity 45.14
    use in
        cryptosporidiosis, AIDS 60.8
        shigellosis 60.15
        travelers' diarrhea 60.3–60.4
Lopid
    See Gemfibrizol
Lopressor
    See Metoprolol
Loprox
    See Ciclopirox
Lorabid
    See Loracarbef
Loracarbef
    use in
        otitis 97.8–97.9
        pediatric infections 97.5
        sinusitis 97.10–97.11
Loratadine
    dosing
        adult and pediatric 21.9
    use in rhinitis 21.7–21.12
Lorazepam
    Also see Benzodiazepines
    breast milk 45.26
    pharmacokinetics 73.9, 73.12
    use in
        acute alcohol withdrawal 82.6
        amphetamine intoxication 84.5
        anxiety 73.7
        mania 77.4
        nausea, chemotherapy-induced
            105.7
        pediatric sedation 95.21–95.22
        seizures, neonatal 96.26
        status epilepticus 52.27–52.28
Losarten 10.28–10.29
Lotensin
    See Benazepril
Lovastatin
    adverse effects 9.15–9.17, 9.19
        hepatotoxicity 26.9
        ocular 49.14
        teratogenicity 45.14
    breast milk 45.26
    dose 9.15, 9.16, 9.19
    interactions, drugs

cyclosporine 9.16, 33.27
erythromycin 9.16
gemfibrozil 9.16
niacin 9.16, 9.18–9.19
warfarin 9.16, 12.20
mechanism of action 9.16
use in hypercholesterolemia
9.15–9.17
Lovenox
See Enoxaparin
Low molecular weight heparin 12.3
adverse effects
thrombocytopenia 89.9
use in
ischemic cerebral stroke
53.10–53.11
thrombosis 89.9
Loxapine
Also see Neuroleptics
adverse effects 75.7
dose 75.8
use in psychosis 75.7–75.8
Loxitane
See Loxapine
LSD
See Lysergic acid diethylamide
adverse effects
psychoses 75.4
teratogenicity 45.14, 81.9
breast milk 45.26
L-thyroxine
See Thyroxine
Ludiomil
See Maprotiline
Lugol's solution 47.17
Lumbar puncture 56.5, 56.6, 56.16,
56.20
Lung abscess 58.6
Lung cancer
chemotherapy
combinations 93.11–93.12
regimens 90.17–90.18
risk factors 93.10
signs/symptoms 90.8, 93.9
staging 93.11
Lung scans 12.10–12.11
Lung transplantation 33.23–33.28
Lupron
See Leuprolide
Lupus erythematosus
See Systemic lupus erythematosus
Luteal phase dysphoric disorder
46.15
Luvox
See Fluvoxamine
Lyme disease 72.1–72.7
clinical presentation 72.2–72.4
diagnosis 72.2–72.4
etiology 72.1
prevention 72.6
treatment 72.3–72.5
Lymphocytes 4.16
Lymphoma, Hodgkin's disease,
chemotherapy regimens 90.18
Lymphoma, nonHodgkin's
adult 92.9–92.10
chemotherapy regimens 90.18
clinical presentation 90.8, 92.9
pediatric 92.20–92.22
treatment, bone marrow transplantation 94.6–94.7
Lymphoproliferative disorder, post-
transplant 33.27

Lynestrenol, teratogenicity 45.14
Lysergic acid diethylamide
abuse 86.2–86.5
teratogenicity 86.5
Macrolides
adverse effects
table of 54.13
Macrocytic anemias
See Anemia, folate deficiency
Maculopapular eruptions 36.17
Mafenide 39.14
Magnesium
Also see Antacids, magnesium;
Hypermagnesemia;
Hypomagnesemia
administration, intravenous 44.19
adverse effects
CNS depression 23.8
fetal effects 44.19
gastrointestinal 23.8
hypocalcemia 44.19
respiratory depression 44.19
dietary content 28.25
homeostasis 28.25
use in
hyperphosphatemia 30.13
hypertension 10.11
hypomagnesemia 28.27
myocardial infarction 14.14
neonatal seizures 96.25
preeclampsia 44.18–44.19
preterm labor 44.25, 96.8
torsades de pointes 16.19
Magnesium antacids
See Antacids, magnesium
Magnesium sulfate, breast milk 45.26
Magnesium trisilicate (talc) 22.7
Major depressive disorders
See Depressive disorders
Major histocompatibility complex
33.3
Malaria 71.1–71.4
pathogenesis 71.1–71.2
prophylaxis 71.3
treatment 71.2–71.4
also see specific drugs
Malathion, use in pediculosis 71.12
Malignant hyperthermia
Also see Hyperthermia, drug-
induced
Malnutrition
Also see Enteral nutrition; Fat
emulsions; Parenteral nutrition;
Vitamin, deficiency
clinical assessment 35.1–35.4,
99.7, 99.10
definition 35.3–35.4
nutritional requirements
table, pediatric 99.2
pathogenesis in children 99.2,
99.7, 99.10
predisposing factors, pediatrics
99.7, 99.10
Mammography, guidelines 90.6,
93.2–93.3
Mandelic acid, breast milk 45.26
Mandol
See Cefamandole
Manic depression
See Affective disorders, bipolar
Mania 77.1–77.9
drug-induced
monoamine oxidase inhibitors
76.20

Mannitol
pharmacology 28.11
use in angle closure glaucoma
49.11–49.12
Manoplax
See Flosequinan
MAO-B inhibitors
See Monoamine oxidase-B
inhibitors
Maprotiline
Also see antidepressants
breast milk 45.26
depression, adulthood 76.10–76.12
Marijuana
abuse 86.5–86.7
addiction 86.6
adverse effects
psychosis 75.4
teratogenicity 45.14, 81.9
breast milk 45.22, 45.26
teratogenicity 86.7
urine tests 81.9, 81.13, 86.7
Marasmus
See Malnutrition
Maxair
See Pirbuterol
Maxipime
See Cefepime
MCH 4.15
MCHC 4.15
MCV 4.15
MDA, MDEA, MDMA 86.2–86.3
Measles 97.17
Measles vaccine 95.10, 95.12
adverse effects, teratogenicity
45.14
Mebendazole
breast milk 45.26
use in
enterobiasis 71.9
pinworms 71.9
Mechlorethamine
adverse effects 90.13
teratogenicity 45.14
pharmacokinetics 90.13
pharmacology 90.13
Meclizine
adverse effects,
fetal 44.8
teratogenicity 45.14
use in
motion sickness 105.4
morning sickness 44.8
Meclofenamate
adverse effects, teratogenicity
45.14
use in gout 40.5
Mediterranean fever 40.7
Medium chain triglycerides 35.5
Medrol
See Methylprednisolone
Medroxyprogesterone
adverse effects
breakthrough bleeding 46.21
teratogenicity 45.14
breast milk 45.26
dose, menopause 9.18
use in
endometriosis 46.21
respiratory insufficiency 59.11
sleep apnea 20.10
use with estrogen replacement
46.32–46.33

Mefenamic acid
adverse effects
hematologic 46.17
hemolysis 89.5
nephrotoxicity 29.12
breast milk 45.26
pharmacology
comparative 46.12–46.13
mechanism of action 46.13
use in
dysmenorrhea 46.13
premenstrual syndrome 46.17
Mefloquine 71.3, 71.6
adverse effects
teratogenicity 45.14
vasculitis 6.12
breast milk 45.26
Mefoxin
See Cefoxitin
Megestrol acetate
use in
HIV-wasting 68.18
hot flushes 46.26
Melanoma
chemotherapy, metastatic
93.15–93.16
danger signs 90.8, 93.15
malignant, sun exposure 39.4
risk factors 93.16
Mellaril
See Thioridazine
Melphalan
adverse effects 90.13
pulmonary toxicity 22.5, 91.24
dosing/alterations 90.13
pharmacokinetics 90.13
pharmacology 90.13
use in amyloidosis 30.22
Menadiol, teratogenicity 45.14
Menadione, teratogenicity 45.15
Meningitis 56.2–56.18
Also see Central nervous system
infections
clinical presentation
bacterial 56.4–56.7, 56.12–56.13,
56.17
tubercular 59.12–59.13
complications
seizures 56.4, 56.5, 56.14, 56.16,
56.18, 56.20, 56.21
laboratory assessments 56.5–56.6
microbiology, pathogens
table of 56.3
pathogenesis and pathophysiology
56.3–56.4
common pathogens 54.5–54.6
predisposing factors 56.5, 56.13,
56.15, 56.19
prophylaxis 56.3, 56.12,
56.14–56.15
treatment
tables of
antibiotic CSF penetration 56.7
antibiotic regimens 56.9
empiric therapy 56.8
pathogens
gram-negative bacilli
56.15–56.16
H. influenzae 56.10–56.11
S. epidermidis 56.17–56.18
S. pneumoniae 56.12–56.14
principles 56.6–56.10
S. epidermis 56.20–56.21
Meningitis, neonatal 96.16–96.19
clinical presentation 96.17
microbiology

pathogens 96.17
treatment
  table of, dosage regimens 96.18
  antibiotic duration 96.19
  antibiotic selection 96.17
Meningococcal vaccine, teratogenicity 45.15
Meningoencephalitis 56.1
Menopause
  Also see Osteoporosis
  clinical presentation 46.24–46.25
  pathogenesis 46.24
  treatment 46.25–46.26
Menstrual cycle 43.2–43.4
  daily diary chart 46.17
  premenstrual syndrome 46.14–46.18
Menstruation, effect warfarin 12.16
Mental status exam 76.5–76.6
Meperidine
  Also see Morphine; Pain
  adverse effects 7.8–7.9
    addiction 83.3
    biliary spasms 7.20
    hepatic coma 25.12
    neonatal 7.13
    pseudoallergic 6.16
    seizures 7.9
    teratogenicity 45.15
    withdrawal symptoms 83.3
  breast milk 45.26
  contraindications/precautions, hepatic coma 25.10
  dosing
    guidelines 7.10
    renal failure 32.8, 32.17–32.18
  effect of renal failure 32.8, 32.17
  interactions, drug
    monoamine oxidase inhibitors 76.20
  pharmacokinetics 7.10–7.11
    absorption, intramuscular 7.13
    half-life 7.10, 32.8
    parameters 32.8
  pharmacology/pharmacodynamics 7.10
  use in
    amphotericin reactions 69.11
    epidural infusion 8.20–8.21
    morphine allergy 7.8–7.9
    myocardial infarction 14.6
    pain 7.9–7.15, 7.20–7.21
    patient-controlled analgesia 7.10–7.11, 8.20
    pediatric analgesic 95.21–95.24
    pediatric sedation 95.21–95.22
Mephenesin 22.6
Mephenytoin, teratogenicity 45.15
Mephobarbital, teratogenicity 45.15
Mepindolol
  adverse effects, teratogenicity 45.15
  breast milk 45.27
Meprobamate
  breast milk 45.27
Mepron
  See Atovaquone
Mercaptopurine
  adverse effects 90.13
    hepatotoxicity 26.9, 91.27
    pulmonary 22.5
    teratogenicity 45.15
  dosing/alterations 90.13
  interaction, drugs
    allopurinol 40.10, 92.14

pharmacokinetics 90.13
pharmacology 90.13
use in
  acute lymphocytic leukemia 92.17
  ulcerative colitis 24.8
Mesalamine
  administration 24.6
  adverse effects 24.6
    teratogenicity 45.15
  breast milk 45.27
  pharmacology 24.6
  preparations 24.7
  use in ulcerative colitis 24.6–24.7
Mesalazine
  See Mesalamine
Mescaline 86.1
Mesna 91.22
Mesoridazine
  adverse effects, teratogenicity 45.15
  breast milk 45.27
Mestranol
  adverse effects, teratogenicity 45.15
  breast milk 45.27
Metabolic acidosis
  Also see Acidosis, metabolic
  drug-induced
    toluene abuse 83.14
Metamucil
  See Psyllium
Metformin 48.36, 48.37, 48.58
  contraindications, lactic acidosis 48.58
  use with sulfonylureas 48.58
Metaproterenol
  See Beta-adrenergic agonists
Methadone
  adverse effects
    neonatal addiction 83.7
    neonatal withdrawal 45.15
    pulmonary 22.3
    teratogenicity 83.7
    therapeutic overdose 7.16, 7.19
  breast milk 45.27, 83.7
  dosing
    comparative 7.6, 7.10, 7.12
    elderly 7.17
    guidelines 7.6, 7.10
    maintenance 83.6
    neonates 83.7–83.8
    opioid detoxification 83.6
  effect on thyroid hormones 47.8
  interactions, drugs
    cimetidine 7.22–7.23
    phenytoin 7.22
  pharmacokinetics 7.16–7.17
  use in
    morphine allergy 7.8–7.9
    opioid addiction 83.5–83.7
    pain 7.5–7.23
  use with tricyclic antidepressants 7.16
Methanol
  Also see Alcohol
  intoxication 28.2
  metabolic acidosis 27.7
  osmol gap 28.2, 82.5
  poisoning 27.6–27.8
Methaqualone, urine tests for 81.13
Metharbital, breast milk 45.27
Methemoglobinemia, nitrate-induced

83.16
Methenamine, breast milk 45.27
Methicillin
  adverse effects
    nephrotoxicity 29.12
  staphylococci resistance 56.18
Methicillin-resistant staphylococci 57.9–57.10
Methimazole 47.3
  Also see Thioamides
  adverse effects, teratogenicity 45.15
  breast milk 45.27
Methocarbamol
  adverse effects, teratogenicity 45.15
  breast milk 45.27
Methohexital 8.6
Methotrexate
  administration, intrathecal 92.16
  adverse effects 41.13, 90.13
    encephalopathy 91.15
    hepatotoxicity 26.10, 38.4, 91.27
    myelosuppression 26.9, 38.4, 92.17
    nephrotoxicity 29.12
    neurotoxicity 92.16
    pulmonary toxicity 22.5, 38.4, 91.24–91.26
    renal tubular obstruction 91.21
    teratogenicity 38.4, 45.15
  breast milk 45.22, 45.27
  contraindications/precautions 38.4
  dosing alterations 90.13
    hepatic dysfunction 91.28
    renal dysfunction 91.20
  interactions, drugs
    list of 38.4
    mechanism 3.2
    nonsteroidal anti-inflammatory agents 3.5
    sulfonamides 94.22
  pharmacokinetics 32.8, 90.13
    serum concentration monitoring 92.19
    renal dysfunction 32.8
  pharmacology 90.13
  use in
    acute lymphoblastic leukemia 92.15–92.17
    Crohn's disease 24.8
    graft versus host disease 94.14
    osteosarcoma 93.24
    psoriasis 38.2–38.7
    rheumatoid arthritis 41.3, 41.13
    ulcerative colitis 24.8
Methoxyflurane
  adverse effects, hepatotoxicity 26.9
  use in cluster headache 50.14
Methsuximide, teratogenicity 45.15
Methyl mercury, teratogenicity 45.6, 45.15
Methylclothiazide
  Also see Diuretics
  adverse effects, teratogenicity 45.15
  breast milk 45.27
Methyldopa
  Also see Alpha$_2$-agonists
  adverse effects
    drug fever 6.9
    lupus 6.15
    hemolytic anemia 10.26, 89.5, 89.6
    hepatotoxicity 10.26, 26.10

teratogenicity 45.15
  breast milk 45.27
  dose in pregnancy 44.17
  interactions, drugs
    levodopa 51.9, 51.14
    sulfonylureas 48.39
  pharmacology, comparative 10.25, 10.26
  use in
    hypertension 10.13, 10.14, 10.18, 10.24–10.26
    pregnancy 44.17
Methylene blue
  adverse effects, teratogenicity 45.15
  use in methemoglobinemia 83.17
Methylphenidate
  adverse effects 78.2–78.3
  interactions, drugs
    morphine 7.22
    narcotic-induced sedation 7.22
  use in
    apathy 79.6
    attention deficit hyperactivity 78.2
Methylprednisolone
  See Corticosteroids
Methyprylon, breast milk 45.27
Methysergide
  adverse effects
    fibrosis 50.11
    gastrointestinal 50.11
    nephrotoxicity 29.12
    pulmonary toxicity 22.5, 50.11
    vascular 50.11
  contraindications/precautions 50.11
  use in
    cluster headache 50.15
    migraine headache 50.10, 50.11
Metipranolol 49.5–49.7
Metoclopramide
  adverse effects 48.50
    dystonias 48.50, 105.7
    extrapyramidal 48.50, 105.7
    teratogenicity 45.15
  antiemetic effect 105.7
  breast milk 45.27
  effect on thyroid function tests 47.6, 47.8
  interactions, drugs
    cyclosporine 33.27
    digoxin 15.22
    levodopa 51.9, 51.14
  use in
    aspiration pneumonia, prophylaxis 8.5
    chemotherapy-induced nausea 105.6–105.7
    diabetic gastroparesis 48.49
    emesis, perioperative 8.17
    gastroesophageal reflux 23.18
    pediatric 95.7
    lactation stimulation 44.29
    migraine headache 50.6, 50.8, 50.9
    morning sickness 44.8
Metolazone
  Also see Diuretics
  adverse effects, teratogenicity 45.15
  breast milk 45.27
  use in
    combination with furosemide 15.16
    congestive heart failure 15.6
    premenstrual syndrome 46.17

Metoprolol
Also see Beta blockers
adverse effects 10.19
teratogenicity 44.17, 45.15
breast milk 45.27
dose 16.6, 16.11
interactions, rifampin 59.8
pharmacodynamic properties 10.19
pharmacokinetic properties 10.20,
32.9
supraventricular tachycardia 16.9
use during pregnancy 44.17
use in
aggression 79.4–79.5
disinhibition 79.4–79.5
hypertension 10.19, 10.20
migraine headache 50.10
Metrizamide
adverse effects, teratogenicity
45.15
breast milk 45.27
Metronidazole 56.6, 56.9, 56.11
adverse effects 56.21, 60.11, 64.16,
71.8–71.9
disulfuram reaction 64.16
teratogenicity 24.7, 45.15, 64.16,
71.8
breast milk 45.22, 45.27
interactions, drugs
contraceptives, oral 43.12, 64.16
warfarin 12.20
pharmacokinetics
clearance
dialysis 54.16
renal disease 54.18
use in
acne 37.3
amebiasis 71.5, 71.7–71.8
bacterial vaginosis 46.7
brain abscess 56.20–56.21
Crohn's disease 24.12
giardiasis 71.8–71.9
helicobacter ulcers 23.12
nonspecific bacterial vaginitis
64.15–64.16
pediatric infections 97.6
pelvic inflammatory disease
64.6, 64.7
pseudomembranous colitis 60.10,
60.11
trichomoniasis 64.16
Mevacor
See Lovastatin
Mexican tar 83.2
Mexiletine
adverse effects 16.6
teratogenicity 45.15
breast milk 45.27
pharmacokinetics 16.6
pharmacology
effect on ECG 16.3
use in
diabetic neuropathy 48.48
ventricular tachycardia 16.18
Mezlocillin
Also see Penicillins,
antipseudomonal
pharmacokinetics
clearance
renal disease 54.18
parameters 32.9
use in cholangitis 61.3
Miconazole
adverse effects 46.6
dosing, vaginal 46.5
interactions, drugs
warfarin 12.20

pharmacology 46.5, 69.3
efficacy 46.5
onset/duration 46.5
preparations
vaginal creams 46.5
vaginal suppositories 46.5
vaginal tampon 46.5
use in
candidiasis, vaginal 46.4–46.6,
69.5
systemic fungal infections
67.14–67.15
Microalbuminuria 48.52–48.53
Micronase
See Glybunde
Micronor
See Contraceptives, oral
Micronutrients, in nutrition 35.5,
35.10
Microsporidiosis 68.30–68.31
Midazolam
adverse effects, teratogenicity
45.15
hypnotic dose 74.8
pharmacokinetics 73.9, 73.12
use in pediatric sedation
95.21–95.22
Midrin 50.7, 50.9
Mifepristone
Also see RU-486
adverse effects, teratogenicity
45.16
breast milk 45.27
Migraine
See Headaches, migraine
Milk alkali syndrome, antacid-
induced 23.8
Milrinone
adverse effects
arrhythmias 15.35
heart failure 15.36
pharmacology
compared to amrinone 15.35
mechanism of action 15.35
Mineral oil
adverse effects, teratogenicity
45.16
Mineral requirements
breast-fed infants 99.5
formula-fed infants 99.6
pediatric population 99.2
Minimal brain dysfunction
See Attention deficit hyperactivity
disorder
Minimum bactericidal concentration
54.7
Minimum inhibitory concentrations
54.7
Minipress
See Prazosin
Minocycline
adverse effects, pulmonary 22.6
Minoxidil
Also see Vasodilators
adverse effects
edema 10.27
hypertrichosis 10.27, 33.27
teratogenicity 45.16
breast milk 45.27
use in
hypertension 10.14, 10.27
hypertensive emergencies 17.6

Misoprostol
adverse effects, teratogenicity
45.16
contraindications/precautions 23.15
breast milk 45.27
use in
NSAID ulceration 23.15
peptic ulcers 23.15
Mite infection 71.12
Mitomycin
adverse effects
hepatotoxicity 91.27
nephrotoxicity 29.13
pulmonary toxicity 22.5, 91.25,
91.26
dosing in renal dysfunction 91.20
Mitotane
adverse effects 90.13
pharmacokinetics 90.13
pharmacology 90.13
Miotics
See specific agents
Mithramycin
See Plicamycin
Mitoxantrone
adverse effects 90.13
cardiotoxicity 91.17–91.19
pharmacokinetics 90.13
pharmacology 90.13
Mitral valve prolapse 12.6
Mitral valvular disease
anticoagulation 12.6
Mivacron
See Mivacurium
Mivacurium 8.8–8.12
Mixed hyperlipidemia 9.20–9.23
MMR vaccine 95.10, 95.12
Moclobemide 73.19
Modafinil 74.15
Modicon
See Contraceptives, oral
Molindone
Also see Neuroleptics
adverse effects 75.7
dose 75.8
use in psychoses 75.7–75.8
Monistat
See Miconazole
Monoamine-oxidase inhibitors
Also see specific agents
adverse effects 76.19–76.21
mania 77.3
contraindications/precautions
76.19–76.21
interactions
table of 76.21
clomipramine 73.26
foods and diet 76.20
meperidine 76.20
nefazodone 76.24
serotonin reuptake inhibitors
76.21
use in
attention deficit hyperactivity
78.3
depression, adulthood
76.19–76.23
panic disorders 73.19
posttraumatic stress disorder
73.28
Monoamine-oxidase B inhibitors
51.12
Also see Selegiline
use in Parkinson's disease 51.12

Monocid
Also see Cefonicid
Monoclonal antibodies 5.1–5.5
OKT3 33.33–33.34
Monoclonal antibodies to endotoxin
use in septic shock 18.29
Monoclonal antibodies to TNF
use in septic shock 18.29–18.30
Monocytes 4.16
Monopril
See Fosinopril
Monosialotetrahexosyl ganglioside,
ischemic stroke 53.13
Mood disorders
bipolar affective 77.1–77.12
classification 76.2
major depressive 76.1–76.27
Moricizine
adverse effects 16.6, 16.15
pharmacokinetics 16.6
pharmacology
effect on ECG 16.3
Morning sickness 44.7–44.8, 105.5
Morphine
Also see Opiate abuse; Narcotics
administration, feeding tube 7.16
adverse effects
addiction and withdrawal 7.12,
7.15, 7.19
allergy 7.8–7.9
hepatic coma 25.12
nausea 7.9
pseudoallergic 6.16
respiratory depression 7.12, 7.13,
7.21
reversal of, with naloxone 7.19
teratogenicity 45.16
breast milk 45.27
contraindications/precautions
chronic obstructive airways disease 7.21
head trauma 7.20
hepatic coma 25.12
tolerance 7.15
dosing 7.5–7.6, 7.10
comparative 7.5–7.6, 7.10
epidural 7.6, 7.12–7.13
oral 7.15
sustained release 7.15–7.16
parenteral infusion 7.17
patient controlled 7.9–7.11
rectal 7.16
renal failure 32.18
titration 7.15–7.16, 7.17
factors affecting response
age 7.21–7.22
dextroamphetamine 7.22
expectations 7.4–7.5
hydroxyzine 7.17–7.18
liver disease 7.21
methylphenidate 7.22
patient controlled 7.9–7.11
previous narcotic use 7.12, 7.13
renal function 32.18
interactions, drugs
dextroamphetamine 7.22
methylphenidate 7.22
narcotic antagonists 7.3
pentazocine 7.3
phenothiazines 7.17–7.18
pharmacokinetics 7.15–7.16
effect of renal failure 32.18
pharmacology/pharmacodynamics
comparative 7.2–7.22
cross tolerance 7.6
efficacy, monitoring 7.10–7.15,

7.18, 7.21
  onset/duration 7.5–7.6
  tolerance 7.15
preparations
  rectal suppository 7.16
  sustained-release 7.15–7.16
use in
  epidural infusion 8.20–8.21
  myocardial infarction 14.6, 14.8, 14.19–14.20
  patient controlled analgesia 8.20
  pediatric analgesia 95.21–95.24
  pediatric sedation 95.21–95.22
  ventilator assistance, neonatal 96.29
Motion sickness 105.5, 105.8
  Also see Nausea/vomiting
Motrin
  See Ibuprofen
Moxalactam
  Also see Cephalosporins
  adverse effects
    bleeding 67.9
    coagulopathies 67.9
MPTP
  parkinsonism 83.3
MRSA
  See Methicillin, staph resistance
MS Contin
  See Morphine
MSG
  See Monosodium glutamate
Mucocutaneous lymph node syndrome 97.18–97.19
Mucomyst
  See Acetylcysteine
Mucositis, chemotherapy-induced 91.5–91.8
Multiple myeloma, chemotherapy regimens 90.18
Mumps vaccine 95.10, 95.12
  adverse effects, teratogenicity 45.16
Murine monoclonal antibody
  See OKT3
Muromonab CD3
  See OKT3
Muscle disorders
  drug-induced
    alcohol 82.12
    colchicine 40.8
Mycobacterial infections, atypical
  Also see Tuberculosis
  clinical presentation in immunocompromised 67.3
  Mycobacterium avium infection
    clinical presentation in HIV 68.25–68.28
    treatment 68.26–68.29
    table of 68.29
Mycotic infections
  See Fungal infections
Mydriatics
  See specific agents
Myocardial infarction 14.1–14.19
  Also see Cardiogenic shock
  clinical presentation 14.2, 14.6–14.9
    anterior versus inferior 14.9
    cardiogenic shock 18.22–18.25
    Q wave versus non-Q wave 14.9
  complications 14.2–14.3
  diagnosis 14.2–14.6
  drug-induced

cocaine 84.10
  laboratory assessment 14.7–14.9
  pathophysiology 14.1–14.3
  right ventricular 14.18
  treatment 18.22–18.25
    approaches
      drugs 14.8–14.19
      goals 14.9
      lifestyle modifications 14.18
      long term 14.15–14.17
      overview 14.3–14.6
    drugs
      allopurinol ischemia reperfusion 40.11
      anticoagulation 12.6, 12.19
      aspirin 13.17–13.18
      bicarbonate 18.22
      inotropic agents 18.22
      oxygen 18.22
      thrombolytics 18.22
      vasodilators 18.22
    pain in 7.20
Myochrysine
  See Gold
Myoclonus, etomidate induced 8.7–89.8
Myopathy
  drug-induced
    colchicine 40.8
    ethanol 82.12
    gemfibrozil 9.22
    lovastatin 9.16–9.17, 9.19
    zidovudine 68.8
Mysoline
  See Primidone
Myxedema coma 47.13
Nabilone, use in emesis 105.4
N-acetylcysteine
  use in nitrate tolerance 13.9
Nadolol
  Also see Beta blockers
  adverse effects, teratogenicity 45.16
  breast milk 45.27
  pharmacodynamic properties 32.9
  use in
    aggression 79.4–79.5
    disinhibition 79.4–79.5
    glaucoma 49.11
    hypertension 10.19, 10.20
    migraine headache 50.10
    Parkinson's tremor 51.13
Nafarelin
  use in endometriosis 46.21
Nafcillin
  Also see Penicillins; Antistaphylococcal
  adverse effects
    nephrotoxicity 29.13
    neutropenia 89.10
  interactions, drugs
    warfarin 12.20
  pharmacokinetics
    clearance
      dialysis 54.16
      renal disease 54.18
    parameters 32.9
  use in
    cystic fibrosis 100.7–100.8
    endocarditis
      culture negative 57.17
      prosthetic valve 57.9
      S. aureus 57.9–57.11
    meningitis 56.21
    osteomyelitis, acute 65.3–65.4
    toxic shock 46.10

Naftine
  See Naftitine
Nalbuphine, teratogenicity 45.16
Nalfon
  See Fenoprofen
Nalidixic acid
  adverse effects
    G6PD deficiency anemia 89.4
    ocular 49.14
    breast milk 45.27
  interactions, drugs
    warfarin 12.20
  use in Shigella gastroenteritis 60.15
Nalmefene 104.4
Naloxone
  use in
    alcohol coma 104.14
    alcohol toxicity 82.4, 82.10, 82.11
    meperidine-induced seizures 7.9
    opioid overdoses 104.14
    overdoses 7.19, 83.4–83.5
    septic shock 18.30
Naltrexone
  use in
    alcoholism 82.12
    bulimia 80.5
    opiate addiction 83.8
    self-injurious behavior 78.15
Nandrolone decanoate
  See Androgens
NAPA 16.10
Naphazoline 21.10–21.11
Naprosyn
  See Naproxen
Naproxen
  Also see Nonsteroidal anti-inflammatory drugs
  adverse effects
    nephrotoxicity 29.13
    teratogenicity 45.16
    vasculitis 6.12
    breast milk 45.27
  use in
    dysmenorrhea 46.13
    gout 40.5
    migraine headache 50.12
    pediatric analgesia 95.24
Narcan
  See Naloxone
Narcolepsy 74.14–74.15, 84.2
Narcotics
  Also see Morphine; Opiate abuse; specific agents
  adverse effects
    addiction 7.15, 83.4
    allergy 7.8–7.9
    biliary spasm 7.20
    nausea/vomiting 7.22
    respiratory depression 7.12, 7.13, 7.19, 7.20, 7.21
    sedation 7.15–7.16, 7.19, 7.22
    seizure 7.9
    teratogenicity
      see specific agents
    tolerance/dependence 7.15
    toxic megacolon 24.8
  breast milk
    see specific agents
  contraindication/precautions
    head injury 7.20
    respiratory disorders 7.21
  dosing
    also see specific agents

tables of 7.6, 7.10
  initial 7.10, 7.15
  patient-controlled 7.10–7.12
pharmacokinetics, effect of liver disease 7.21
pharmacology/pharmacodynamics
  cardiovascular hemodynamics 7.20
  comparative 7.2–7.10
  factors affecting response 7.4–7.5
use in
  biliary colic 7.20–7.21
  labor and delivery 7.12–7.13
  migraine headache 50.9
  pain 7.2–7.23
use with
  central nervous system stimulants 7.22
  fluoxetine 7.20
  phenothiazines 7.17–7.18
  tricyclic antidepressants 7.16, 7.19–7.20
Nardil
  See Phenelzine
Nasal disorders
  drug-induced
    table of 21.20
    treatment 21.20–21.21
Nasal saline
  use in
    allergic rhinitis 21.7
    isotretinoin treated 37.8
Nasalcrome
  See Cromolyn
Nasalide
  See Flunisolide
Nausea
  pathogenesis
    renal failure, chronic 30.15
Nausea/vomiting 105.1–105.11
  Also see Antiemetics; Morning sickness; Motion sickness
  complications of 4.3, 105.3
  drug-induced
    also see Gastrointestinal effects of drugs
    antimicrobials, table of 54.13–54.14
    cancer chemotherapy 91.5
    ergot 50.6
    estrogens 43.17–43.18
    ethosuximide 52.19, 52.20
    methysergide 50.11
    narcotics 7.22
    nitrofurantoin 63.17
    valproate 52.20–52.21
  etiology
    migraine headache 50.6, 105.2
  pathophysiology 105.2
  treatment 105.4–105.9
    also see Antiemetics; specific agents
    diarrhea, infectious 60.1–60.12
    morning sickness 44.7–44.8
    perioperative 8.16–8.19
Navane
  See Thiethixene
Necroinflammatory liver disease 26.2
Necrotizing cellulitis 66.7
Necrotizing enterocolitis
  classification 96.15
  pathogenesis 96.14–96.15
  treatment 96.15–96.16

Necrotizing fasciitis 66.6–66.7
Necrotizing
    leukoencephalopathy 92.16
Nedcin
    See Aminoglycosides
Nedocromil 19.20
Nefazodone
    interactions, drugs 76.24
    use in depression 76.10–76.12,
        76.24
Neg-Gram
    See Nalidixic acid
Neomycin
    Also see Aminoglycosides
    adverse effects
        hypovitaminosis K 25.13
        nephrotoxicity 29.13
        teratogenicity 45.16
    interactions digoxin 15.22
    pharmacokinetics, absorption
        25.13
    use in
        hepatic coma 25.12–25.13
        surgical prophylaxis 55.3
Neonates
    Also see Pediatric patients;
        Pregnancy; Teratogenicity
    administration of drugs 96.30
        hypothyroidism 47.11–47.12
    dosing
        antimicrobials 54.12
        theophylline 19.16–19.17
    medical problems and treatment
        apnea 96.21–96.23
        drug abstinence syndrome
            83.7–83.8, 96.26–96.28
        gonorrhea ophthalmia 96.21
        hemolysis in newborn
            44.20–44.21
        hepatitis B 62.9, 96.21
        herpes 70.4, 96.20–96.21
        meningitis 96.18–96.19
        necrotizing enterocolitis
            96.14–96.16
        osteomyelitis, acute 65.4
        patent ductus arteriosus
            96.11–96.14
        periventricular/intraventricular
            hemorrhage 96.24
        phenylketonuria 99.6–99.7
        respiratory distress syndrome
            96.7–96.10
        rubella 96.21
        sedation during ventilation
            96.28–96.30
        seizure disorders 96.24–96.25
        sepsis 96.16–96.18
        syphilis 96.21
    monitoring parameters 96.2
    pharmacokinetics
        table of parameters 96.4
        absorption of drugs
            intramuscular 96.3
            oral 96.2
            percutaneous 96.3
            rectal 96.3
        distribution 96.4
        hepatic function 96.6
        pediatric patients 54.12
        protein binding 96.4
        renal function 96.6–96.7
        volume of distribution 96.4–96.5
    treatment of opioid addiction
        83.7–83.8
Neoplasms, general principles
    cancers, metastatic sites 90.5–90.6

detection/screening 90.6
etiology 90.1
handling cytotoxic drugs 90.21
paraneoplastic complications 90.9
prevention
    chemoprevention 90.2
    diet 90.4
    sun protection 90.4
signs/symptoms 90.8
staging 90.6
treatment
    biological therapy 90.20
    chemotherapy 90.9–90.21
    hormonal therapy 90.20
    irradiation 90.8
    surgical 90.8
tumor growth 90.5
Neoplastic disorders
    biologic therapy
        also see Cancer
        interferon alpha 90.20
        interleukin-2 90.20
        strategies 90.20
    chemotherapy
        administration
            intrathecal 92.1
            routes 90.20
            sites, localized 90.20
            systemic 90.19
        assessing response 90.19
        combination regimens
            90.15–90.18
            table of 90.16
        cytotoxic drugs
            clinical pharmacology, table of
                90.11
        cytotoxicity
            cell kill 90.4
            dose intensity 90.10
            drug resistance 90.15
            mechanisms of action 90.9
    hormonal therapy 90.19
    types
        hematological malignancies
            acute lymphoblastic leukemia
                92.10–92.19
            acute nonlymphocytic leukemia
                92.3–92.6
            chronic lymphocytic leukemia
                92.7–92.9
            chronic myelogenous leukemia
                92.6–92.7
            nonHodgkin's lymphoma
                adult 92.9–92.10
                pediatric 92.19–92.23
        solid tumors
            bladder cancer 93.13–93.14
            breast cancer 93.2–93.6
            colon cancer 93.7–93.9
            melanoma 93.14–93.16
            neuroblastoma 93.21–93.22
            osteosarcoma 93.24
            ovarian cancer 93.12–93.13
            prostate cancer 93.16–93.18
            rhabdomyosarcoma
                93.25–93.26
            small cell lung cancer
                93.9–93.12
            testicular cancer 93.18–93.19
            Wilm's tumor 93.22–93.23
Neostigmine 49.8
    adverse effects, teratogenicity
        45.16
    reversal neuromuscular blockade
        8.9

Nephrolithiasis 29.19–29.20
Nephron function 28.2
Nephrotic syndrome
    clinical presentation 28.5
    drug-induced, sulfasalazine 24.6
    treatment, loop diuretics 28.15
Nephrotoxicity, drug-induced
    acyclovir 32.1, 64.19, 68.21,
        70.3, 70.5, 70.7
    aminoglycosides 54.5, 100.8
    amphotericin B 32.16, 54.14,
        69.11–69.12
    analgesics 30.4
    angiotensin-converting enzyme-
        inhibitors 15.32
    beta-lactam antibiotics 54.13
    carbonic anhydrase inhibitors
        49.10
    cisplatin 91.19–91.21
    cocaine 84.12
    colchicine 40.8
    cyclophosphamide 94.9–94.10
    cyclosporine 30.22, 33.17, 40.14
    demeclocycline 28.10
    didanosine 68.8
    diuretics 15.13
    foscarnet 33.41, 68.19, 94.21
    ganciclovir 70.5
    gold 41.11
    ifosfamide 91.21
    indomethacin 40.5
    lithium 28.10, 30.5, 77.6
    methicillin 54.13
    methotrexate 91.20
    nonsteroidal anti-inflammatory
        drugs 7.8, 40.5
    penicillamine 41.15
    pentamidine 68.16
    phenazopyridine 63.9
    rifampin 59.9
    stavudine 54.14
    streptomycin 59.6
    tacrolimus 33.36
    tetracyclines 54.13
    vancomycin 54.13
Netilmicin
    See Aminoglycosides
    adverse effects
        nephrotoxicity 29.13
Neupogen 67.13
    Also see Colony stimulating
        factors
Neuroblastoma
    chemotherapy, table of 93.22
    clinical presentation 93.21
    staging 93.21
Neuroleptic malignant syndrome
    75.19
Neuroleptics
    Also see Phenothiazines; specific
        agents
    adverse effects
        akathisia 75.16
        amenorrhea 75.20
        anticholinergic 75.7
        cardiovascular 75.7
        cholestasis 75.21
        comparisons, table of 75.12
        dermatological 75.21
        drug fever 75.9
        dyskinesias 75.13–75.19
        dystonias 75.15
        galactorrhea 75.20
        hematological 75.19
        hyperthermia 75.21
        lupus 6.15

movement disorders 75.13–75.19
neuroleptic malignant syndrome
    75.19
ocular pigmentation 75.21
photosensitivity 75.21
sedative 75.17
seizures 75.22
sexual dysfunction 75.22
tardive dyskinesia 75.16–75.19
teratogenicity 75.22
    also see specific agents
weight gain 75.23
atypical neuroleptics 75.2
dosing
    depot injections 75.9–75.10
    dosing strategies 75.9
    duration of therapy 75.8
    evaluation of response
        75.10–75.12
    guidelines for maintenance 75.8
    rapid tranquilization 75.6
    traditonal 75.6
interactions, drugs
    levodopa 51.9, 51.14
    lithium 77.7
pharmacokinetics
Neuroleptics (continued)
    serum concentrations 75.13
    pharmacology
        comparisons of
            adverse effects 75.7–75.8
            dosages 75.8
            haloperidol/clozapine/risperi-
                done 75.2
            mechanisms of action 75.2
            neurochemistry 75.2
            potency 75.7–75.8
        dosing strategies 75.9
        duration of therapy 75.8
        goals of therapy 75.8
        onset 75.8
        response to therapy 75.10
        selection of drug 75.7
    use in
        aggression 78.15, 79.3
        bipolar disorders 77.4–77.5
        depression, adulthood
            76.21–76.22
        disinhibition 79.4
        elderly 75.23
        psychosis, dementia
            102.10–102.11
        schizophrenia 75.6–75.23
Neuromuscular blocking agents
    adverse effects, table of 8.10
    classification, table of 8.9
    contraindications/precautions 8.10
    monitoring degree 8.8
    perioperative use 8.8–8.10
    pharmacodynamics 8.9–8.10
        table of 8.11
    pharmacokinetics 8.9–8.11
        table of 8.11
    reversal 8.9
Neurontin
    See Gabapentin
Neuropathic pain 7.19–7.20
Neuropsychiatric disorders,
    secondary 79.1–79.7
    Also see Psychiatric disorders
Neuropsychiatric pharmacotherapy
    79.1–79.2
Neurotoxicity, drug-induced
    Also see CNS effects of drugs;
        Peripheral neuropathy;
        Psychosis, drug-induced

busulfan 94.9
central
  table of chemotherapy drugs
    91.16
  acyclovir 54.14, 64.19, 70.3
  alcohol 60.3–60.5
  amantadine 51.4–51.5, 70.5
  amiodarone 16.19
  amphetamine 84.3
  anabolic steroids 87.4
  anticholinergics 51.4
    ophthalmic 49.18
  antidepressants 76.11, 76.14
  antiepileptics 52.7, 52.12, 52.18
  asparaginase 91.15
  benzodiazepines 73.11
  beta-adrenergic blockers 13.13
  beta-lactam antibiotics 54.13
  bromocriptine 51.11
  calcium channel blockers 13.16
  carbamazepine 52.10
  carbonic anhydrase inhibitors
    49.10
  carmustine 91.15
  clozapine 75.22
  cocaine 84.12
  colchicine 40.8
  corticosteroids 33.30
  cycloserine 59.6
  cyclosporine 33.18
  cytarabine 91.14
  didanosine 68.8
  disulfiram 82.8
  ethosuximide 52.19–52.20
  fludarabine 91.15
  fluorouracil 91.15
  gamma hydroxy butyrate 87.5
  ganciclovir 70.5
  hydrocarbons 83.11
  indomethacin 40.5
  isoniazid 59.8
  levodopa 51.5–51.8
  lindane 71.11–71.12
  magnesium 28.27, 44.19
  meperidine 7.9
  methotrexate 91.15, 92.16
  metoclopramide 105.9
  neuroleptics 75.22, 77.7
  niacin 9.17, 9.19
  nitrous oxide 83.15
  nonsteroidal anti-inflammatory
    drugs 46.14
  opiates 7.9, 7.19
  penicillin 32.15
  phenobarbital 52.23
  phenytoin 52.17–52.18
  quinolones 54.14
  sedative-hypnotics 83.10
  streptomycin 59.6
  tacrolimus 33.36
  theophylline 19.24
  vidarabine 70.5
  zidovudine 68.8
peripheral
  carbamazepine 77.7
  cisplatin 91.17
  diazepam 52.28
  didanosine 68.7, 68.8
  isoniazid 59.6, 59.8
  lithium 77.7
  nifedipine 17.5
  nitrofurantoin 63.17
  phenytoin 52.28
  stavudine 68.7, 68.9
  vincristine 91.15–91.17, 92.15
  zalcitabine 68.7, 68.8, 68.9
Neutropenia
  absolute neutrophil count 67.2

clinical presentation 89.11, 89.12
drug-induced 89.9–89.12
  aminopyrine 89.12
  antilymphocyte globulin 33.37
  azathioprine 33.38
  carbamazepine 52.8, 52.12
  cephalosporins 89.10
  clozapine 75.11–75.12,
    89.11–89.12
  flucytosine 54.14
  ganciclovir 33.40, 68.19, 94.21
  penicillin 67.9, 89.10
  pentamidine 68.16
  phenothiazines 89.10–89.11
  sulfonamides 54.13
  ticlopidine 53.8
  zidovudine 54.14, 68.7, 68.8,
    68.14
pathogenesis 89.9–89.12
  risk factors for infection 67.2
treatment 89.11
  colony stimulating factors 67.13
  duration antibiotic 67.11
Neutrophils
  absolute neutrophil count 67.2
  laboratory assessment 4.15
  relation to mortality 67.4–67.5
Niacin
  adverse effects 9.15, 9.17
    hepatotoxicity 26.10
  dose 9.14, 9.16, 9.19
  efficacy 9.14–9.15
  interactions, lovastatin 9.16, 9.19
  patient education 9.19
  pharmacology
    mechanism of action 9.14–9.15
  use in
    hypercholesterolemia 9.14–9.15,
      9.18–9.19
    hypertriglyceridemia 9.22, 9.23
    mixed hyperlipidemia 9.22
    Raynaud's phenomenon 11.10
    secondary prevention of athero-
      sclerosis 9.8–9.10
Nicardipine 13.14, 13.15, 13.17
  Also see Calcium channel blockers
  adverse effects 10.24
    teratogenicity 45.16
  pharmacology, comparisons 10.24
  use in
    heart failure 15.34
    hypertension 10.23, 10.24
    hypertensive emergencies 17.4,
      17.7
    ischemic stroke 53.13
Niclocide 71.10
Niclosamide, use in cestodiasis 71.10
Nicoderm
  See Nicotine
Nicotinamide
  use in Type I diabetes 48.7
Nicotine
  Also see Cigarettes
  abuse 85.1–85.7
  adverse effects 85.2–85.6
    dermatological 20.5
  breast milk 45.22, 45.27, 85.4
  dependence 85.5
  effects on organ systems 85.2
  pharmacokinetics 85.1–85.2
    serum concentrations 20.4
  pharmacology 20.4, 85.2–85.6
  polacrilex 85.6–85.7
  preparations 85.6–85.7
    gums 20.4
    transdermal patches 20.5

use in cigarette cessation 20.4
  withdrawal 85.5–85.8
Nicotinic acid
  See Niacin
Nicotinyl alcohol, teratogenicity
  45.16
Nicotrol
  See Nicotine
Nifedipine
  Also see Calcium channel blockers
  administration 17.3
  adverse effects 10.24, 13.15–13.16
    table of 13.16, 17.5
    angina exacerbation 13.15
    ankle edema 17.5
    arrhythmias 17.5
    congestive heart failure 15.34
    drug fever 6.9
    edema 13.18
    headache 13.18
    hyperglycemia 48.52
    hypotension 13.15
    paresthesia 17.5
    teratogenicity 45.16
  breast milk 45.27
  contraindications/precautions
    table of 10.14, 13.16
    aortic stenosis 17.5
  dosing 10.23, 17.4–17.5
  interactions, drugs
    digoxin 17.5
  pharmacokinetic properties 17.3,
    32.9
  pharmacology
    comparisons 13.14
    mechanism of action 17.3
    onset/duration 17.4
  preparations
    table of 13.15
    sustained release 13.18
  use in
    heart failure 15.34
    hypertensive emergencies
      17.3–17.6
    migraine headache 50.12–50.13
    myocardial infarction 14.5, 14.8,
      14.16
    preterm labor 44.25
    Raynaud's phenomenon 11.9
Nimodipine
  Also see Calcium channel blockers
  administration, intracerebral 53.15
  mechanism of action 53.13
  use in
    Alzheimer's 102.7
    delayed cerebral ischemia 53.15
    ischemic stroke 53.13
    migraine headache 50.7, 50.13
    subarachnoid hemorrhage 53.15
Nipride
  See Nitroprusside
Nitrates
  See Nitroglycerin
  use in myocardial infarction 14.8,
    14.19
Nitrendipine
  See Calcium channel blockers
Nitrites
  abuse of inhalants 83.16
  adverse effects 83.16
Nitrofurantoin
  adverse effects
    drug fever 6.9
    G6PD deficiency anemia 89.4
    gastrointestinal 63.17–63.18
    hemolysis 63.5

hepatotoxicity 26.11
neurotoxicity 63.17
pulmonary toxicity 22.5–22.7,
  63.17
teratogenicity 45.16
breast milk 45.27, 63.5
pharmacokinetics 63.11, 63.17
  clearance, dialysis 54.16
use in
  postcoital UTI 63.13
  prophylaxis UTI 63.13
  recurrent UTI 63.10–63.11
Nitroglycerin
  administration
    intermittent 13.9
    intravenous 13.9, 13.21–13.22
    lingual 13.7–13.8
    ointment 13.10
    sublingual 13.7
    transdermal 13.9
  adverse effects
    headache 13.7, 13.9, 13.10; 50.5,
      50.8
    hypotension 13.7–13.8
    lingual 13.7–13.8
    methemoglobinemia 13.8
    ointment 13.10
Nitroglycerin (continued)
  sublingual 13.7
  teratogenicity 45.16
  dosing 13.7–13.11
    hypertension 17.12
  patient education 13.7, 13.9, 13.10
  pharmacokinetics 13.10
  pharmacology 17.12
    mechanism of action 13.6–13.7
    monitoring efficacy 13.8
    tolerance 13.8–13.9
  preparations
    table of 13.8
    lingual spray 13.7–13.8
    long-acting nitrates 13.8–13.9,
      15.29
    ointment 13.10, 15.29
    transdermal patches
      13.10–13.11, 15.29
    transmucosal 13.11, 15.29
  tolerance to 13.9
  use in
    angina 13.6–13.11
    congestive heart failure 15.28
    ergotamine-induced arterial con-
      striction 50.7
    esophageal varices 25.8
    hypertensive emergency 17.4,
      17.11–17.12
    microvascular angina 13.20
    myocardial infarction 14.8, 14.19
    Prinzmetal's angina 13.20
    unstable angina 13.20–13.21
  use in
    hydralazine 15.30
Nitroglycerin, ointment
  use in Raynaud's phenomenon
    11.10
Nitroprusside
  Also see Vasodilators
  administration 17.8–17.9, 17.4
  adverse effects 18.21
    cyanide toxicity 17.9
    hypothyroidism 47.9
    teratogenicity 45.16
    thiocynate toxicity 17.10
  dosing 17.4, 17.8–17.9
    congestive heart failure 18.21
  pharmacology 17.8–17.10
    comparative 18.20

hemodynamic effects 18.21
use in
congestive heart failure
15.27–15.28, 18.21
ergotamine-induced arterial constriction 50.7
hypertensive emergency 17.4,
17.8–17.11
Nitrosurea, dosing in renal dysfunction 91.20
Nitrous oxide abuse 83.15
NIX
See Permethrin
Nizatidine
Also see Histamine$_2$-antagonists
adverse effects, teratogenicity
45.16
breast milk 45.27
Nizoral
See Ketoconazole
Nocturnal leg cramps
clinical presentation 11.10
treatment
drug 11.11–11.12
nondrug 11.10
Nocturnal myoclonus 74.15
Nongonococcal urethritis 64.9–64.10
NonHodgkin's lymphoma
HIV association 68.31–68.32
Nonmenstrual toxic shock 46.8
Nonoxynol-9
adverse effects, teratogenicity
45.16
use in herpes genitalia 64.20
Nonsteroidal anti-inflammatory drugs
Also see specific agents
adverse effects 46.14
congestive heart failure 15.10
gastrointestinal 7.8, 23.13
hemodynamic renal failure
29.18–29.19
hepatotoxicity 26.11
masking gout 40.6
nephrotoxicity 7.8, 29.13, 32.19
platelet adhesiveness 7.7
pseudoallergic 6.17
pulmonary 22.2
teratogenicity
see specific agents
breast milk
see specific agents
contraindications/precautions 46.14
congestive heart failure 15.10
dosing
analgesic 7.5, 7.7
renal failure 32.19
interactions, drugs
antihypertensives 40.5
captopril 3.4
differential effects 3.4
lithium 3.4, 77.6
mechanism 3.4
methotrexate 3.5, 38.4
metoclopramide 50.7
sulfonylureas 48.39
thiazides 3.3
warfarin 3.4, 12.20
pharmacology/pharmacodynamics
comparative 7.2, 7.5, 7.7–7.8
mechanism of action 46.12
precautions, congestive heart
failure 15.10
preparations
ophthalmic 49.18, 49.19
use in

analgesia 7.2, 7.5, 7.7–7.8
bone pain 7.18
cystic fibrosis 100.11
diabetic neuropathy 48.47
dysmenorrhea 46.12–46.15
gout 40.5–40.6
hypercalcemia 28.23
juvenile rheumatoid arthritis
41.21
migraine headache 50.7
opioid withdrawal 83.9
osteoarthritis 41.23
pediatric analgesia 95.23
pericarditis 30.10
preterm labor 44.25
rheumatoid arthritis 41.2,
41.7–41.9
septic shock 18.30
tension headache 50.16
use with aspirin 41.7
Norcuron
See Vecuronium
Nordette
See Contraceptives, oral
Norepinephrine
administration, central IV 18.24
adverse effects 18.24
dosing
in cardiogenic shock 18.24
use in
anaphylaxis 6.5
cardiogenic shock 18.24
septic shock 18.27
Norethindrone
Also see Contraceptives, oral
adverse effects, teratogenicity
45.16
breast milk 45.27
Norethynodrel
Also see Contraceptives, oral
breast milk 45.27
adverse effects, teratogenicity
45.16
Norfloxacin
Also see Quinolones
breast milk 45.27
interactions, drugs
warfarin 12.20
use in
gonorrhea 64.4
Salmonella gastroenteritis 60.14
Shigella gastroenteritis 60.15
travelers' diarrhea 60.3–60.5
urinary tract infection, lower
63.5
Norgestrel
Also see Contraceptives, oral
breast milk 45.27
teratogenicity 45.16
Norinyl
See Contraceptives, oral
Norlestrin
See Contraceptives, oral
Normeperidine 7.9, 7.10, 7.12, 32.17
Normodyne
See Labetalol
Noroxin
See Norfloxacin
Norplant 43.19
See Levonorgestrel
Nortriptyline
Also see Antidepressants, cyclic
breast milk 45.27
teratogenicity 45.16
use in

childhood depression 78.4
depression, adulthood
76.10–76.12
Norvasc
See Amlodipine
Norwalk gastroenteritis 60.12
Nose
anatomy 21.1
congestion, drug-induced
21.19–21.21
physiology 21.1–21.2
rhinitis 21.1–21.21
Novobiocin, breast milk 45.27
NSAIDs
See Nonsteroidal
anti-inflammatory drugs
Nubain
See Nalbuphine
Numorphan
See Oxymorphone
Nuromax
See Atracurium
Nutrition
Also see Enteral nutrition; Fat
emulsions; Malnutrition;
Parenteral nutrition
assessment of 34.18–34.26,
35.2–35.8
drugs in breast milk 45.23–45.29
enteral 34.1–34.28
hepatic failure 35.13
parenteral 35.1–35.16
pediatric 99.1–99.21
renal failure 35.15
requirements
hepatic failure 34.6
renal failure 34.6
pregnancy 44.6–44.8
Nylidrin, teratogenicity 45.16
Nystatin
use in
candida vaginitis 46.5–46.6
candidiasis, oral 67.14, 68.30
diaper rash 95.3
prophylaxis
candidemia 69.12
immunocompromised host 67.14
Obesity
effect on dosing
benzodiazepine 73.12, 73.14
cardiovascular disease 10.10
chemotherapeutic agents 94.8
hypertension 10.8, 10.10
Obsessive compulsive disorders
clinical presentation 73.25
diagnostic criteria, DSM-IV
73.22–73.23
epidemiology 73.23
in children 78.6–78.7, 78.16
pathophysiology 73.23
treatment 73.24
Obstetrics
Also see Pregnancy
diabetes in pregnancy 44.9–44.12
epilepsy in pregnancy 44.12–44.14
hypertension in pregnancy
44.14–44.20
induction of labor 44.26–44.28
isoimmunization hemolysis
44.20–44.21
lactation 44.29
post-partum hemorrhage
44.28–44.29
pregnancy 44.1–44.30
prenatal care 44.5–44.6

preterm labor 44.21–44.26
Octoxynol, teratogenicity 45.16
Octreotide 23.16
use in
cryptosporidiosis 60.8
esophageal varices 25.8
Ocular adverse effects of drugs
Also see specific agents
adrenergic agents 49.3
allopurinol 40.12, 49.16
amantadine 49.14
amiodarone 16.19, 49.12, 49.13
anticholinergics 49.13, 51.4
anticholinesterases 49.8–49.9
antidepressants, cyclic 49.13, 76.9
atropine 49.13
barbiturates 49.15
betaxolol 49.7
busulfan 49.14
calcium channel blockers 49.15
carbamazepine 49.13, 52.8, 52.12
carbonic anhydrase inhibitors
49.11, 49.15
Ocular adverse effects of drugs
(continued)
carmustine 49.15
carteolol 49.7
chloramphenicol 49.14
chloroquine 41.12, 49.14
chlorpheniramine 49.13
chlorpromazine 49.12, 49.16
clomiphene 49.15
clonidine 49.13
contraceptives, oral 49.15
corticosteroids 49.15, 49.17–49.18
cytarabine 49.15, 92.6
diazoxide 49.13
digitalis 49.15
dipivefrin 49.10
doxorubicin 49.15
doxycycline 63.5
echothiophate 49.9
epinephrine 49.4–49.5, 49.10
estrogens 49.15
ethambutol 49.14, 59.9
fluorouracil 49.15
fluoxetine 49.13
gentamicin 49.14
gold 49.14
guanethidine 49.13
hydroxychloroquine 41.12
ibuprofen 49.13
idoxyuridine 49.19
indomethacin 49.14
interleukin-2 49.16
ipratropium 20.7
isoniazid 49.14
lovastatin 49.14
metipranolol 49.7
nalidixic acid 49.14
narcotics 49.13
neuroleptics 75.21
pentazocine 49.13
phenylbutazone 49.14
phenytoin 49.13, 52.15
physostigmine 49.8
pilocarpine 49.7–49.8
propofol 49.13
reserpine 49.14
ribavirin 70.5
sulfonamides 49.14
tamoxifen 49.15
tetracycline 49.14
theophylline 49.3
thiazides 49.12, 49.15
thioridazine 49.16
timolol 49.4, 49.10

trifluridine 49.20, 70.5
trimethadione 49.13
vidarabine 49.19
vincristine 49.15
Ocular disorders
 See Eye disorders
Ofloxacin
 Also see Quinolones
 adverse effects, vasculitis 6.12
 breast milk 45.27
 pharmacokinetics
  clearance, renal disease 54.18
 use in
  chlamydia 63.9, 64.10
  gonorrhea 64.4
  Legionaire's pneumonia 58.7
  pelvic inflammatory disease
   64.6, 64.7
  pneumonia, community acquired
   58.7
  travelers' diarrhea 60.2–60.4
  tuberculosis 59.10–59.11
  urinary tract infection 63.5
OKT3
 adverse effects
  table of 33.34
  hypersensitivity 33.33–33.34
  pulmonary 22.3
 biotechnology of 5.1–5.2
 dosing 33.34
 pharmacology 33.8
 use in
  graft versus host disease 94.16
  transplantation 33.14
Omeprazole
 adverse effects 23.10
  teratogenicity 45.16
 dosing 23.10
 interactions, drugs 23.10
 pharmacokinetics 23.10
 pharmacology
  hypergastrinemia 23.10
  mechanism of action 23.10
 use in
  aspiration pneumonia prophylaxis 8.5
  pediatric GERD 95.7
  peptic ulcer 23.7, 23.10–23.11
  reflux 23.7, 23.17
  refractory ulcers 23.10,
   23.12–23.13
  stress ulcers 23.20
  Zollinger-Ellison 23.7, 23.16
Oncology
 See Cancer
Ondansetron
 adverse effects 105.6
  anaphylactoid 6.17
  teratogenicity 45.16
 dosing as antiemetic 105.6, 105.7
 use in
  chemotherapy-induced nausea
   and vomiting 105.6–105.7
  emesis, perioperative 8.17
  pediatric chemotherapy 105.9
Onychomycosis 69.5
Ophthalmic disorders
 See Eye disorders
Ophthalmic drugs
 See specific drugs; Eye disorders;
  Contact lens care
Ophthalmopathy 47.25
Opioid abuse 83.1–83.9
 Also see Morphine; Narcotics;
  Pain
 addiction 83.3–83.10

medical complications 83.4
neonatal withdrawal 96.26–96.28
overdose 83.4
treatment 83.5–83.9
 clonidine 7.13
 withdrawal 7.12, 7.13, 7.15, 7.19,
  83.8–83.9
Opioid receptors 83.1
Opioids
 Also see Morphine; Narcotics;
  Opioid abuse
 adverse effects
  hepatic coma 25.12
  teratogenicity 81.9
 use in
  gout 40.8
  infectious diarrhea 60.2
 urine tests for 81.13
Opium
 adverse effects, teratogenicity
  45.16
 tincture of, use in neonatal narcotic
  addiction 83.8
Optipranolol
 See Metipranolol
Oragraffin
 See Ipodate
Oral contraceptives
 See Contraceptives, oral
Organ donation 33.10
Organ failure
 See Transplantation
Organ transplantation 33.1–33.44
Organidin
 See Iodinated glycerol
Orinase
 See Tolbutamide
ORLAAM 83.6
Ortho Novum
 See Contraceptives, oral
Orthoclone
 See OKT3
Orthostatic hypotension
 See Hypertension
Orudis
 See Ketoprofen
Osalazine
 use in
  Crohn's disease 24.11
  ulcerative colitis 24.6
Osmol gap
 calculated 82.5
 drug-induced
  alcohols 28.2, 82.5
  ethylene glycol 28.2
Osmolality
 Also see Osmol gap
 effect of
  alcohol 28.2, 82.5
  ethylene glycol 28.2
  methanol 28.2
 estimation of 28.2
 laboratory assessment 4.6
 regulation of 28.1–28.10
Osmoregulation disorders 28.6–28.10
Osteoarthritis
 Also see Rheumatoid arthritis; specific agents
 clinical presentation 41.22
 pathogenesis 41.22
 treatment 41.23

Osteodystrophy, renal 30.13
Osteomyelitis 65.1–65.8
 Also see septic arthritis
 characteristics, table of 65.2
 clinical presentation
  acute osteomyelitis 65.2
  chronic osteomyelitis 65.7
  prosthetic osteomyelitis 65.8
  secondary osteomyelitis 65.6
 common pathogens 54.5
 etiology 65.1–65.2
 risk factors 65.2
 treatment of
  also see specific agents
  acute osteomyelitis 65.3–65.5
  chronic osteomyelitis 65.7–65.8
  prosthetic osteomyelitis 65.8
  secondary osteomyelitis
   65.6–65.7
 treatment, principles
  bactericidal titers 65.4
  duration 65.4–65.5
  oral drugs 65.4–65.5, 65.8
Osteoporosis 46.27–46.34
 classification 46.28
 clinical presentation 46.28
 definition 46.27
 drug-induced 46.29
  corticosteroids 24.4, 33.35,
   41.20, 42.9
  GnRH agonists 46.23
  heparin 12.10
 pathogenesis 46.27
 predisposing factors 46.28–46.29
 prevention 46.29–46.33
 treatment 46.33–46.34
  calcium 41.20
Osteosarcoma
 chemotherapy 93.24
 clinical presentation 93.24
 prognostic factors 93.24
Otitis media
 clinical presentation 97.2
 pathogens 97.3
 treatment 97.4–97.9
Ototoxicity
 drug-induced
  aminoglycosides 54.13, 100.8
  cisplatin 91.17
  erythromycin 54.13
  kanamycin 59.6
  streptomycin 59.6
  tetracyclines 54.13
  vancomycin 54.13
Ovarian cancer
 chemotherapy
  intraperitoneal 93.13
  regimens 90.17
 effect of contraceptives, oral 43.17
 risk factors 93.12
 screening 93.12
 signs/symptoms 90.8, 93.12
Ovarian cysts
 effect of contraceptives, oral 43.17
Ovcon
 See Contraceptives, oral
Overdoses
 See Clinical toxicology
Ovrette
 See Contraceptives, oral
Oxacillin
 adverse effects, hepatotoxicity
  26.11
 use in
  endocarditis
   culture negative 57.17

prosthetic value 57.9–57.11
 S. aureus 57.9–57.11
osteomyelitis, acute 65.3–65.4
toxic shock 46.10
Oxaprenolol
 Also see Beta-adrenergic blockers
 adverse effects, teratogenicity
  45.16
 breast milk 45.28
Oxazepam
 Also see Benzodiazepines
 breast milk 45.27
 pharmacokinetics 73.9, 73.12
 use in anxiety 73.7
Oxcarbazine 52.13
Oxiconazole 69.3
Oxiracetam 102.6
Oxistat
 See Oxiconazole
Oxtriphylline 19.23
 Also see Theophylline
 adverse effects, teratogenicity
  45.16
Oxybutynin 95.20
 use in urinary incontinence 103.20
Oxycodone
 adverse effects, teratogenicity 45.16
 breast milk 45.28
Oxygen
 pulmonary 22.5
 use in
  acute myocardial infarction 18.22
  chronic obstructive airways
   disease 20.8–20.9
  cluster headache 50.14
  myocardial infarction 14.6
Oxygen saturation 19.2
Oxymetazoline 21.10–21.11
 adverse effects, teratogenicity
  45.16
Oxymorphone 7.10
 Also see Morphine;
  Phenylbutazone
 adverse effects, teratogenicity
  45.16
Oxyphenbutazone
 Also see Phenylbutazone
 adverse effects, teratogenicity 45.16
Oxypurinol 40.10
Oxytocin
 administration
  parenteral 44.27
 adverse effects 44.27–44.28
 contraindications 44.27
 pharmacology 44.26–44.27
 use in
  labor induction 44.26–44.27
  lactation stimulation 44.29
  postpartum hemorrhage 44.28
Ozone 39.2
PABA
 See Paraminobenzoic acid
Paclitaxel
 adverse effects 90.13
 dosing
  alterations 90.13
  hepatic dysfunction 91.28
 pharmacokinetics 90.13
 pharmacology 90.13
 use in
  breast cancer 93.5
  ovarian cancer 93.13
Pain 7.1–7.23
 Also see Analgesics

classification
  acute 7.3
  chronic 7.3–7.4
    malignant 7.4
    nonmalignant 7.4
  pathophysiology 7.2
treatment
  also see specific agents
  acute 7.6–7.14
  chronic
    malignant 7.14–7.18
    nonmalignant 7.18–7.19
  colic 7.20–7.21
  dysmenorrhea, primary 7.23
  geriatrics 7.21–7.22
  head injury 7.20
  headaches 7.23
  liver disease 7.21
  myocardial 7.20
  neonates and children 7.22
  neuropathic 7.19–7.20
  opiod abusers 83.4, 83.7
  patient controlled analgesia
    8.19–8.20
  postsurgical 8.19–8.21
  principles of 7.4–7.5
  respiratory disease 7.21
  types of
    postsurgical 8.19–8.21
  withdrawal, narcotic 7.12, 7.13,
    7.15, 7.19
Pain receptors 83.1
Palmar erythema 25.2
Pamidronate
  use in
    ESRD 28.22
    hypercalcemia 28.22
Pancreatic cancer regimens 90.17
Pancreatic enzymes
  preparations 100.5
  use in cystic fibrosis 100.5
Pancreatic insufficiency
  cystic fibrosis 100.2
  treatment 100.5
Pancreatic transplants 48.32–48.33
Pancreatitis
  drug-induced
    alcohol 82.10
    asparaginase 92.17
    azathioprine 33.38
    didanosine 68.7, 68.8
    sulfasalazine 24.6
    parenteral nutrition 35.14–35.15
Pancuronium 8.8–8.12
  use in ventilator assistance, neonatal 96.29
Panic disorders
  clinical presentation 73.19
  diagnostic criteria, DSM-IV
    73.17–73.18
  pathophysiology 73.18
  treatment 73.18–73.21
Papanicolaou test 93.12
Papaverine, use in impotence
  103.8–103.10
Para-aminosalicylic acid
  adverse effects
    drug fever 6.9
    pulmonary 22.6
Paracentesis 25.6
Paracetamol
  See Acetaminophen
Paralysis agitans
  See Parkinson's disease

Paramethadione, teratogenicity 45.6,
  45.16
Paranoia
  See Psychoses
Paraquat, pulmonary toxicity 22.6
Parasitic infections 71.1–71.12
  Also see specific infections
  amebiasis 71.4–71.8
  cestodiasis 71.9–71.11
  enterobiasis 71.9
  giardiasis 71.8–71.9
  malaria 71.1–71.4
  pediculosis 71.11–71.12
  scabies 71.12
Paregoric
  adverse effects
    camphor toxicity, neonates 96.28
    teratogenicity 45.16
  breast milk 45.28
  use in opiate withdrawal, newborns
    96.28
Parenteral nutrition 35.1–35.16
  Also see Enteral nutrition; Fat
    emulsions; Malnutrition
  administration 35.4–35.5
    enteral versus parenteral
      99.10–99.11
  adverse effects, pediatric
    hepatotoxicity 99.18
    hyperammonemia 99.17
    hyperglycemia 99.14–99.15
    hypophosphatemia
      99.17–99.18
    infection 99.17
    pulmonary effects 99.16
    rickets 99.17–99.18
  assessments of
    calories 35.8
    need 35.1–35.4
    nutrients 35.5–35.8
    proteins 35.8
    venous access 35.4–35.5
  compatibility problems
    35.11–35.12
  compatibility with
    calcium 99.18
    fat emulsions 99.13–99.14
  complications of
    alkalosis 35.11
    electrolyte disturbances 35.10
    fatty acid deficiency 35.9
    fluid imbalance 35.7
    hyperglycemia 35.9, 35.11
    hypertriglyceridemia 35.7
    hypokalemia 35.10
    hypophosphatemia 35.11
    infection 35.10
    metabolic 35.9
    phlebitis 35.7
    pulmonary 35.10
  dosing
    nutritional requirements, pediatric 99.2, 99.10–99.12
    rate of administration, pediatric
      99.10–99.12
  formulations
    design 35.7–35.10, 35.13–35.15
    pediatric amino acids 99.16
  goals of therapy
    adult 35.6
    pediatric 99.13
  medication incompatibilities 35.12
  monitoring, pediatric 99.11
  progression to enteral feedings
    35.15
  trace elements in 35.5, 35.10
  use in

adults 35.1–35.16
  diabetes 35.14
  fistula patients 35.12
  hepatic failure 35.13
  obesity 35.14
  pancreatitis 35.14–35.15
  pediatric patients 99.7–99.19
  renal failure 35.15
  short bowel 35.12
  use with vitamins 35.7
Parkinson's disease 51.1–51.14
  Also see specific agents
  clinical presentation 51.2
  definition 51.1
  drug-induced
    MPP 51.12, 83.3
    MPTP 51.1, 51.12, 83.3
    synthetic heroin 83.3
  pathogenesis 51.2, 51.12
  staging 51.2–51.3
  treatment
    adjunctive 51.13
    amantadine 51.4–51.5
    anticholinergics 51.3–51.4
    bromocriptine 51.10–51.11
    deprenyl 51.12
    dopamine agonists 51.10–51.12
    drug holidays 51.8–51.9
    levodopa 51.5–51.10,
      51.13–51.14
    lisuride 51.12
    monoamine oxidase B inhibitors
      51.12
    pergolide 51.11
    selegiline 51.3, 51.12
    surgery 51.13
    vitamin E 51.13
Parlodel
  See Bromocriptine
Paromomycin
  use in
    amebiasis 60.7, 71.5, 71.7
    cryptosporidiosis, AIDS 60.7
Paroxetine
  Also see Serotonin reuptake
    inhibitors; Depression, adulthood
  depression, adulthood 76.10–76.12
  use in aggression/disinhibition
    79.4–79.5
Paroxysmal supraventricular tachycardia
  See Supraventricular arrhythmias
Partial thromboplastin time 12.5
Parvolex
  See Acetylcysteine
Patent ductus arteriosus 96.11–96.14
  clinical presentation 96.12–96.13
  pathogenesis 96.12
  treatment 96.12–96.13
Pathogens
  table of 67.2
  colonization 67.3
Patient controlled analgesia 7.9–7.12,
  8.19–8.20
Patient education
  alcoholic cirrhosis 25.10
  amoxicillin-clavulanate 97.10
  antiepileptic drugs 52.19
  aspirin in
    arthritis 41.5
    transient ischemic atttacks 53.8
  benzodiazepines, anxiety 73.10,
    73.13
  childhood psychoses 78.8
  clomipramine, obsessive compulsive 73.26

corticosteroids, intranasal
  21.14–21.15
dry skin 36.16
gabapentin 52.14
glaucoma agents 49.7–49.8
hydrocortisone, topical 36.16
hypertension 10.6
insomnia 74.6
ipratropium 20.7
iron therapy 88.6
lithium therapy 77.6
metered-dose inhalers 19.27
nicotine gum 20.4
patient controlled analgesic pump
  8.19
penile injections 103.10
phenytoin 52.15
tanning booths 39.4–39.5
tretinoin use 39.5–39.6
vaginal candidiasis 46.6
warfarin 12.14
Patient profiles 1.1–1.6
Pavulon
  See Pancuronium
Paxil
  See Paroxetine
PCA
  See Patient controlled analgesia
PCB
  See Polychlorinated biphenyls
PCP
  See Phencyclidine
Peak expiratory flow 19.2, 20.8
Pedialyte 95.6
Pediatrics
  Also see Neonatal
  dosing
    of antimicrobials 54.12
  drug administration 95.25
  immunization
    adverse effects, table of 95.10
    hepatitis B 62.8
    recommended schedule, table of
      95.5
    varicella 70.6–70.7
  laboratory values, immunological
    97.2
  medical problems and treatment
    also see specific disorders
    absence seizures 52.19
    aggression 78.13–78.15, 78.16
    analgesia 95.6–95.7,
      95.22–95.24
    anxiety disorders 78.5–78.6
    asthma 19.1–19.31
    attention deficit hyperactivity
      78.2–78.3
    autism 78.10–78.11, 78.16
    biliary atresia 33.29
    bipolar affective 78.5
    bronchiolitis 70.10, 97.14–97.15
    bronchopulmonary dysplasia
      98.1–98.4
    chickenpox 70.6
    childhood absence epilepsy 52.3
    communicable diseases, table of
      95.8
    croup 97.15–97.17
    cystic fibrosis 100.1–100.13
    decongestants 21.11
    dehydration 95.5–95.6
    depression 78.4–78.5, 78.16
    developmentally disabled
      78.11–78.15
    diaper rash 95.2–95.3
    diarrhea 95.4–95.6, 99.4–99.5,

99.12
dystonias 78.8
enuresis 95.19–95.20
febrile seizures 52.22–52.23
fever 95.3
fluid replacement, oral 95.5
gastroenteritis 105.5
gastroesophageal reflux
    95.6–95.7
    insomnia 74.16
hemolytic uremic syndrome
    95.14–95.15
herpes, congenital 64.20–64.21
HIV infection 68.34–68.38
idiopathic thrombocytopenic pur-
    pura 95.17–95.18
infections 97.1–97.22
insomnia 74.16
Kawasaki's disease 97.18
lice 71.11
lymphoma, nonHodgkin's 92.20
malaria prophylaxis 71.3
measles 97.17
mental disorders in disabled
    78.11
mites 71.12
neuroblastoma 93.21–93.22
nausea/vomiting 105.5
    in chemotherapy 105.9
norwalk virus gastroenteritis
    60.12
ophthalmia neonatorum
    64.8–64.9
osteomyelitis, acute 65.4
osteosarcoma 93.24
otitis media 97.2–97.9
pain 7.22
pertussis 97.17
pharyngitis 97.11–97.12
photoprotection 39.11
pinworms 71.9
psychiatric disorders 78.1–78.18
rhabdomyosarcoma 93.25
rheumatic fever 97.13
rhinitis, antihistamines 21.9
Rocky Mountain spotted fever
    97.19–97.20
rotavirus gastroenteritis
    60.12–60.13
schizophrenia 78.7–78.8
sedation 95.20–95.22
self-injurious behavior
    78.13–78.15
short stature 95.15–95.16
sinusitis 97.9–97.10
tapeworm infection 71.9–71.11
teething 95.2
Tourette's 78.9
tuberculosis 59.12
urinary tract infection 63.5
varicella 70.6–70.7
vomiting 95.4
Wilm's tumor 93.22–93.23
nutrition 99.2–99.21
nutritional assessment
    99.7–99.11
nutritional requirements 99.2,
    99.10
    fluids and electrolytes
        99.2–99.5
    parenteral nutrition 99.2,
        99.13–99.19
sources
    breast milk 99.5–99.7
    infant formulas 99.6–99.9
    solid foods 99.6
    therapeutic formulas
        99.6–99.7, 99.12–99.19

special considerations
    bronchopulmonary dysplasia
        99.16
    diarrhea 99.4–99.5,
        99.12–99.13
    gastrointestinal anomalies 99.7
    hepatic disease 99.7,
        99.18–99.19
    metabolic disorders 99.6–99.7
    phenylketonuria 99.6
    prematurity 99.7
    protein intolerance 99.16
    renal failure 99.7
    respiratory distress 99.7
    rickets 99.18
    septicemia 99.17
pathogens 97.3
predisposition to metoclopramide
    toxicity 105.9
use of
    bronchodilators 19.12–19.13
    corticosteroids 19.22
    digoxin 15.26
    theophylline 19.16–19.17,
        19.22–19.23
Pediculosis 71.11–71.12
PedvaxHIB
    See PRP-OMP
PEEP
    See Positive end expiratory
        pressure
Peliosis hepatis 26.7
Pelvic inflammatory disease
    clinical presentation 64.6
    complications 64.6
    diagnosis 64.6
    etiology 64.6
    treatment
        Centers for Disease Control
            recommendations 64.6–64.7
        gonorrhea 64.6
        in pregnancy 64.7
        use of contraceptives, oral 43.16
Pemoline
    use in attention deficit hyper-
        activity 78.3
Penbutolol
    Also see Beta blockers
    adverse effects 10.19
        pharmacodynamic properties
            10.19
        pharmacokinetic properties 10.20
    use in hypertension 10.19
Penicillamine
    adverse effects 41.14–41.15
        lupus 6.15
        nephrotoxicity 29.13
        pulmonary 22.6
        teratogenicity 45.16
    dosing 41.14
    use in
        cirrhosis 25.3
        juvenile rheumatoid arthritis 41.22
        rheumatoid arthritis 41.3,
            41.14–41.15
Penicillin
    Also see Penicillins,
        antipseudomonal; specific agents
    adverse effects
        drug fever 6.9
        hepatotoxicity 26.11
        hemolytic anemia 89.5
        Jarisch-Herxheimer reaction
            64.14–64.15
        nephrotoxicity 29.13
        neurotoxicity 32.15

neutropenia 67.9, 89.10
pulmonary 22.2, 22.6
teratogenicity 45.17
vasculitis 6.12
breast milk 45.28
desensitization 6.17–6.19
dosing in
    meningitis 56.9, 56.13–56.14
    pediatrics 97.4
    renal failure 32.9
interactions, drug
    contraceptives, oral 43.12
pharmacokinetics
    clearance
        renal failure 32.9, 32.14
use in
    abscess, brain 56.20–56.21
    endocarditis, S. viridans
        57.6–57.7
    enterococcal endocarditis
        57.12–57.15
    gonorrhea 64.3, 64.4–64.5
    Lyme 72.3
    meningococcal meningitis 56.10
    peritonitis 61.5, 61.10, 61.13,
        61.14, 61.15
    pneumococcal meningitis 56.10,
        56.13–56.14
    pneumonia, community acquired
        58.7
    syphilis 64.13–64.15
    use with probenecid 64.13
Penicillins
    table of 54.7
    interactions, drugs
        mechanism 3.2
    pharmacokinetics
        clearance
            dialysis 54.16
            renal disease 54.18
Penicillins, antipseudomonal
    Also see Penicillin; specific agents
    dosing, renal failure 32.16
    gram-negative endocarditis 57.17
    incompatibility with aminoglyco-
        sides 67.8
    pharmacology
        comparative coagulopathies 67.9
        nephrotoxicity protection 67.7
    use in
        combination with aminoglyco-
            side 67.7–67.9
        neutropenia 67.4–67.12
        three drug combinations 67.7
Penicilloyl polylysine 6.4
Pentaerythritol, teratogenicity 45.17
Pentamidine
    administration
        aerosol 68.17
        parenteral 68.16
    adverse effects
        anaphylactoid 6.17
        hematologic 68.16
        hyperglycemia 48.57, 68.16
        hypocalcemia, with foscarnet
            68.19
        hypoglycemia 48.57, 68.16
        hypotension 68.16
        nephrotoxicity 29.13, 68.16
    dose
        in renal failure 68.16
    pharmacokinetics 32.7
    use in
        Pneumocystis carinii pneumonia
            68.16–68.17, 94.21–94.22
Pentasa
    See Mesalamine

Pentazocine
    adverse effects
        cardiovascular 7.20
        ocular 49.13
        psychotomimetic 7.3, 7.14, 7.17
        teratogenicity 45.17
        withdrawal reactions, precipita-
            tion of 7.13, 7.14
    dosing, comparative 7.6, 7.14
    opioid withdrawal 83.10
    pharmacology/pharmacodynamics,
        efficacy 7.3, 7.14
    use in
        cancer pain 7.17
        labor and delivery 7.13
Pentobarbital
    breast milk 45.28
    teratogenicity 45.17
    use in pediatric sedation
        95.21–95.22
Pentostatin
    adverse effects 90.13
    dosing/alterations 90.13
    pharmacokinetics 90.13
    pharmacology 90.13
Pentoxifylline
    adverse effects, serum sickness 6.7
    breast milk 45.28
    pharmacokinetics 11.7
    pharmacology 11.7
    use in
        diabetic neuropathy 48.48
        graft versus host disease 94.15
        impotence 103.8
        intermittent claudication 11.7
        multi-infarct dementia 102.10
        peripheral vascular disease 48.6
        septic shock 18.30
        veno-occlusive disease of the
            liver 94.11
Peptic ulcer disease 23.1–23.24
    Also see Gastric ulcers; Stress
        ulcers; Gastroesophageal reflux
    clinical presentation 23.3
    definition 23.1
    drug-induced
        alcohol 82.9–82.10
        auranofin 41.11
        cigarettes 23.3
        nonsteroidal anti-inflammatory
            drugs 23.13, 46.14
        salicylates 23.3
    pathogenesis
        epidemiology 23.2
        Helicobacter 23.11, 60.13
        renal failure, chronic 30.15
        risk factors 23.2
    pathophysiology 22.2
    prophylaxis
        H$_2$-antagonists 23.14
        misoprostil 23.14
        sucralfate 23.14
    treatment
        approaches
            goals 23.4
            options 23.4
            principles 23.3–23.4
        drugs
            also see specific agents
            antacids 23.8–23.9
            bismuth, colloidal 23.11–23.13
            H$_2$-antagonists 23.4–23.8
            misoprostil 23.14
            octreotide 23.16
            omeprazole 23.7, 23.10–23.11
            prostaglandins 23.11
            somatostatin 23.16

sucralfate 23.5, 23.9
nondrug
    diet 23.3
Pepto-Bismol
    See Bismuth subsalicylate
Percodan
    See Oxycodone
Pergolide
    Also see Dopamine agonists;
        Parkinson's disease
    adverse effects 51.11
    effectiveness comparisons 51.11
    use in
        impotence 103.8
        Parkinson's disease 51.11
Pericarditis, uremic 30.10
    renal failure, chronic 30.10
    treatment 30.10
Peridex
    See Chlorhexidine
Periodic limb movements 74.15
Perioperative care 8.1–8.24
    analgesics, postoperative 8.19–8.21
    anesthetics
        intravenous 8.5–8.8
        local/regional 8.11–8.13
    antiemetics 8.16–8.18
    cardioplegic solutions 8.13–8.15
    preoperative medications 8.2–8.5
        table of 8.3–8.4
Perphenazine
    adverse effects, teratogenicity 45.17
    use in emesis, postoperative 8.17
Peripheral blood stem cell rescue
    94.5–94.7
Peripheral neuropathy
    See Neurotoxicity; Dialysis
Peripheral vascular diseases
    bromocriptine-induced 51.11
    in diabetes 48.6
Peripheral vascular disorders
    11.1–11.13
    clinical presentation
        intermittent claudication 11.4
        nocturnal leg cramps 11.10
        Raynaud's phenomenon 11.9
    pathophysiology
        intermittent claudication 11.2
        nocturnal leg cramps 11.10
        Raynaud's phenomenon 11.8
    treatment
        intermittent claudication
            11.4–11.8
        nocturnal leg cramps
            11.10–11.12
        Raynaud's phenomenon
            11.9–11.10
Peritoneal dialysis 31.8–31.12
Peritonitis 31.7, 31.11–31.13
    classification
        primary peritonitis 61.3–61.5
        secondary peritonitis 61.7–61.16
    clinical presentation 61.4, 61.7
    microbiology, pathogens
        61.4–61.5, 61.7–61.16
    pathogenesis
        abdominal trauma 61.16
        appendicitis 61.16–61.17
        cirrhosis 61.3–61.4
        dialysis 61.5
    treatment 61.4–61.16
        table of single antibiotics 61.6
        table of combination regimens
            61.11, 61.12
        intra-abdominal abscess

61.15–61.16
Periventricular/intraventricular hem-
    orrhage
    clinical presentation 96.24
    pathogenesis 96.24
    treatment 96.24
Permanganate, potassium 36.3
Permethrin, use in scabies 71.12
Perphenazine
    See Neuroleptics
    teratogenicity 45.17
    use in emesis, postoperative 8.17
Persian Brown 83.2
Personality changes 79.1–79.2
Personality disorders 75.4
Pertussis 97.17
Pertussis vaccine 95.9–95.11
Petechial lesions, endocarditis 57.4
Pethidine
    See Meperidine
Petit mal seizures
    See Seizures, absence
Peyote 86.1
Pharmaceutical care 1.1–1.16
Pharmacokinetics
    Also see specific drugs
    antibiotics 54.12–54.19
    geriatrics 54.12, 101.2–101.5
    interactions, drugs 3.1–3.2
    neonates 96.2–96.7
    pediatrics 54.12
    principles 2.1–2.20
    renal failure 32.1–32.21
Pharyngitis 97.3, 97.11–97.12
Phenacetin
    adverse effects
        hemolysis 89.5
        nephrotoxicity 29.13
    breast milk 45.28
Phenazopyridine
    adverse effects 63.9
    use in symptomatic abacteriuria
        63.9
Phencyclidine
    abuse 84.8, 86.7–86.8
    adverse effects
        psychoses 75.4
        teratogenicity 45.17
    breast milk 45.22, 45.28
    overdose treatment 86.8
    urine tests for 81.13
Phenelzine
    Also see Depression, major
    adverse effects
        hepatotoxicity 26.11
        teratogenicity 45.17
    use in
        bulimia 80.5
        migraine headache prophylaxis
            50.12
        panic disorder 73.19
        posttraumatic stress 73.28
        social phobias 73.22
Phenindamine 21.9
Phenindione
    adverse effects, hepatotoxicity
        26.11
    breast milk 45.22, 45.28
Phenobarbital
    administration, IV 52.23, 52.29
    adverse effects
        hemorrhage in newborns 45.31
        hyperactivity 52.23

sedation 52.11, 52.20
        teratogenicity 45.17, 45.31
    breast milk 45.28
    dosing in neonates 83.11
    interactions, drugs
        contraceptives, oral 43.12
    pharmacokinetics
        adult parameters 32.9
    pharmacology/pharmacodynamics,
        effect on thyroid function 47.6,
        47.7
    use in
        benzodiazepine withdrawal 83.10
        neonatal
            drug withdrawal 96.28
            opioid addiction 83.8
        opioid withdrawal 83.9
        prophylaxis of febrile seizures
            52.23
        sedative withdrawal 83.10
        seizures 52.12, 52.23, 52.29
            neonatal 96.26
        status epilepticus 52.29
Phenolphthalein
    adverse effects, teratogenicity
        45.17
    breast milk 45.28
Phenothiazines
    Also see Neuroleptics; specific
        agents
    adverse effects
        neutropenia 89.10–89.11
        teratogenicity 44.8–44.9
        also see specific agents
    contraindications/precautions,
        hepatic coma 25.12
    pharmacology/pharmacodynamics,
        antiemetic effect 105.3
    use in
        lactation stimulation 44.29
        migraine headache 50.6
        morning sickness 44.9
        nausea/vomiting 105.3–105.9
        pain 7.17–7.18
        pediatric patients 105.9
Phenoxybenzamine
    teratogenicity 45.17
    use in
        male contraceptive 43.23
        prostate hyperplasia 103.16
Phensuximide, teratogenicity 45.17
Phentolamine
    teratogenicity 45.17
    use in impotence 103.8–103.10
Phenylbutazone
    adverse effects
        anemia, aplastic 89.13
        gastrointestinal 40.5
        hematological 40.5
        ocular 49.14
        pulmonary 22.4
        sodium retention 40.5
        teratogenicity 45.17
        uricosuria 40.5
        vasculitis 6.12
    breast milk 45.28
    interactions, drug
        sulfonylureas 48.39
        warfarin 3.1, 3.4, 12.20
    use in gout 40.5
Phenylephrine 21.10–21.11
    teratogenicity 45.17
    use in septic shock 18.28
Phenylketonuria 99.6–99.7
Phenylpropanolamine
    abuse 84.6

adverse effects 84.7
        teratogenicity 45.17
    contraindications/precautions 84.7
    dosing 21.8
    use in
        urinary incontinence
            103.20–103.21
        weight control 84.6–84.7
Phenytoin
    adverse effects
        table of 52.12
        aplastic anemia 89.13
        cardiac (IV) 52.28
        choreiform movements 52.18
        drug fever 6.9
        encephalopathy 52.17–52.18
        fetal hydantoin syndrome 44.13,
            45.30, 52.26–52.27
        fetal tumors 44.13
        folic acid deficiency 44.13
Phenytoin (continued)
        gingival hyperplasia 52.17
        hepatotoxicity 26.12
        hypersensitivity syndrome 52.25
        hypocalcemia 46.29
        hyperglycemia 48.55
        nephrotoxicity 29.14
        ocular 49.13, 52.15
        osteomalacia 52.12
        pulmonary 22.6
        serum sickness 6.7
        teratogenicity 45.6, 45.17,
            52.26–52.27
        thyroid function tests 47.6, 47.7
        vasculitis 6.12
    breast milk 45.28
    dosage forms 52.16
    dosing
        during withdrawal 52.6–52.7
        initial dose 52.14–52.15
        intramuscular 52.16–52.17
        intravenous 52.28
        loading 52.15, 52.28
        once a day 52.16
        oral suspension 52.16
        renal failure 32.9, 32.17
    education, patient 52.15, 52.16
    interactions, drugs
        allopurinol 40.10
        antacids 23.9
        cimetidine 23.6, 23.8
        contraceptives, oral 43.11, 43.12,
            52.26
        corticosteroids 3.5
        cyclosporine 33.27
        disulfiram 82.8
        felbamate 52.11
        isoniazid 59.8
        levodopa 51.9, 51.14
        lidocaine 16.17
        mechanisms 3.2
        methadone 7.22
        omeprazole 23.10
        quinidine 3.5, 3.6
        sulfonylureas 48.39
        theophylline 19.17, 19.25
        valproate 52.18
        warfarin 12.20
    intravenous compatibility 52.28
    pharmaceutical care 1.14–1.15
    pharmacokinetics
        adult parameters 32.9, 52.6
        bioequivalence dosage forms
            52.16
        concentrations 32.17
            effect of protein binding 52.6
            plasma 52.6, 52.16
            saliva 52.17

effect of
  renal failure 32.9, 32.17
  pregnancy 44.14
  geriatric patients 101.3
  protein binding 32.17
  parameters 52.6
use in
  alcohol withdrawal 82.6
  diabetic neuropathy 48.48
  digitalis toxicity 15.24
  meperidine-induced seizures 7.9
  migraine headache 50.12
  seizure disorders 52.4,
    52.14–52.19, 56.18, 56.21
    neonatal 96.26
  subarachnoid hemorrhage 53.15
  pregnancy 44.13–44.14
  syndrome of inappropriate anti-
    diuretic hormone secretion
    28.10
Phlebitis, drug-induced
  acyclovir 54.14, 64.19, 70.3, 70.5
  antilymphocyte globulin 33.37
  antithymocyte globulin 33.37
  beta-lactams 54.13
  colchicine 40.8
  ganciclovir 70.5
  parenteral nutrition 35.7
  vancomycin 54.14
Phobic disorders
  clinical presentation 73.22
  diagnostic criteria, DSM-IV 73.21
  epidemiology 73.21
  treatment 73.22
Phosphatase
  acid 4.12
  alkaline 4.11
Phosphates
  use in
    diabetic ketoacidosis 48.34
    hypercalcemia 28.23
Phosphenytoin 52.13
Phospholipidosis 26.2
Phosphorus
  Also see Hyperphosphatemia;
    Hypophosphatemia
  homeostasis 28.23
  laboratory assessment 4.8,
    28.23–28.25
  preparations 28.25
  use in
    hypercalcemia 28.23
    hypophosphatemia 28.24–28.25
Photoaging 39.5
Photoallergy 39.6–39.7
Photocarcinogenesis 39.3–39.4
Photochemotherapy, psoriasis 38.3,
  38.6
Photosensitivity 39.1–39.11
  drug eruptions 36.16
  drug-induced
    amiodarone 16.19
    chemotherapy agents
      91.10–91.11
    neuroleptics 75.21
    tetracyclines 54.13, 63.5
    tretinoin 37.5
Phototherapy
  depression, adulthood 76.6
  psoriasis 38.2–38.3
Phototoxicity 39.6
Physostigmine
  Also see Anticholinesterases
  adverse effects, teratogenicity
    45.17

use in
  Alzheimer's 102.6
  glaucoma 49.8
  pediculosis 71.11
PID
  See Pelvic inflammatory disease
Pilocarpine, ophthalmic
  adverse effects 49.7–49.8
  education, patient 49.7–49.8
  pharmacology 49.4
  preparations
    drops 49.4–49.8
    gel 49.8
    ocusert 49.8
  use in
    glaucoma 49.4–49.8, 49.11
    xerostomia 91.6
Pimozide 75.8, 78.9
Pindolol 10.19
  Also see Beta blockers
  adverse effects, pulmonary 22.6
  breast milk 45.28
  teratogenicity 45.17
  use in
    aggression 79.4–79.5
    disinhibition 79.4–79.5
Pinworms
  See Enterobiasis
Pipecuronium 8.8–8.12
Piperacillin
  Also see Penicillins,
    antipseudomonal
  dosing in renal failure 32.9, 32.15
  use in
    cholangitis 61.3
    cystic fibrosis 100.7
    peritonitis 61.10
    pyelonephritis 63.8
Piperacillin-tazobactam
  use in
    cystic fibrosis 100.7–100.8
    intra-abdominal infections 61.10
    lung abscess 58.6
Piracetam 102.6
Pirbuterol
  Also see Beta-adrenergic agonists
  use in obstructive airways disease
    20.11
Piroxicam
  Also see Nonsteroidal anti-inflam-
    matory drugs
  adverse effects
    nephrotoxicity 29.14
    teratogenicity 45.17
  breast milk 45.28
  use in gout 40.5
PLA
  See Analgesia, patient controlled
Placental development 44.2–44.3
Placental transfer, drugs 45.2–45.3
Plague vaccine, teratogenicity 45.17
Plaquenil
  See Hydroxychloroquine
Plasma concentration 2.2
Plasmapheresis
  use in
    Goodpasture's 30.24
    hemolytic uremia 95.15
    idiopathic thrombocytopenic pur-
      pura 95.17
    rapidly progressive glomeru-
      lonephritis 29.5

Plasmin 12.3, 12.21
Platelet activation 12.2
Platelet function
  See Antiplatelet effects of drugs
Plendil
  See Felodipine
Plethesmography 19.3
Pleural effusions, malignant 92.10
Plicamycin
  adverse effects 28.22
    hepatotoxicity 26.10, 91.27
  pharmacology 28.22
  use in hypercalcemia 28.22
PMS
  See Premenstrual syndrome
Pneumococcal meningitis
  56.12–56.15
Pneumococcal vaccine 56.14–56.15
  teratogenicity 45.17
  use in
    bronchitis 58.3
    chronic obstructive airways
      disease 20.6
    HIV 68.35
Pneumocystis carinii pneumonia
  clinical presentation 68.15–68.18
  diagnosis 68.15–68.16
  prophylaxis of 94.21–94.22
  treatment 68.15–68.18
    table of 68.16
Pneumonia
  Also see specific types
  classification
    aspiration 58.8–58.9
    community-acquired 58.6–58.7
    hospital-acquired 58.11–58.14
  clinical presentation 58.5
  complications 58.6
  microbiology 58.5
  pathogenesis 58.4–58.5
    cystic fibrosis 58.14
    stroke, neurologic 58.4
Pneumonia (continued)
  predisposing factors 58.4–58.5
  treatment 58.7–58.14
Pneumovax 23
  See Pneumococcal vaccine
Pnu-Immune
  See Pneumococcal vaccine
Podagra 40.3
Podophyllin, use in genital warts
  64.21
Poison ivy 36.19–36.21
Poison oak 36.19–36.21
Poisonings
  See specific agents; Clinical toxi-
    cology
Polio vaccine 95.10–95.12
  teratogenicity 45.17
Polychlorinated biphenyls,
  teratogenicity 45.6
Polyethylene glycol electrolyte solu-
  tion
  surgical prophylaxis 55.3
Polymethyl methacrylate 65.7
Polymyalgia rheumatica 42.3
Polymyositis 42.3
Polystyrene sulfonate, sodium
  See Kayexalate
Polythiazide
  breast milk 45.28
  teratogenicity 45.17

Ponstel
  See Mefenamic acid
Portal hypertension
  pathophysiology 25.2
  treatment 25.9
Postcoital contraception 43.18–43.19
  table of 43.18
Postpartum hemorrhage 44.28–44.29
Postsurgical emesis 8.16–8.18
Posttraumatic stress 73.27–73.28
Potassium
  Also see Hyperkalemia;
    Hypokalemia; specific agents
Potassium (continued)
  administration
    intravenous 28.17
    oral 28.12, 28.17–28.18
  concentration
    serum 4.3
    urine 25.4
  content
    foods 15.14
    salt substitutes 10.16
  dosing 10.16
  effect on blood pressure 10.5,
    10.11
  formulations 15.14
  homeostasis 28.15–28.16
  laboratory interpretation 4.3, 28.15
  preparations 10.16
  renal excretion 30.5
  use in
    cardioplegia 8.15
    diabetic ketoacidosis 48.34
    hypokalemia 10.15–10.16, 10.17,
      15.14–15.15
    hypertension 10.11, 10.15–10.16,
      10.17
Potassium iodide
  adverse effects, teratogenicity
    45.17
  hyperthyroidism 47.17
  use in sporotrichosis 69.6
Potassium-sparing diuretics
  See Diuretics, potassium-sparing;
    specific agents
PPD skin test 59.2–59.3
  booster phenomenon 59.13
  factors causing anergy 59.2
    acquired immunodeficiency
      syndrome 59.11
    steroids 59.11
  interpretation 59.3
Pravastatin 9.15–9.17
  effect on lipids 9.12
Prazepam
  Also see Benzodiazepines
  breast milk 45.28
  pharmacokinetics 73.9, 73.12
  use in anxiety 73.7
Praziquantel
  use in cestodiasis 71.10–71.11
Prazosin
  adverse effects 10.24–10.25
    syncope 15.30
    tachyphylaxis 15.30
    teratogenicity 45.17
  antihypertensive
    comparison to
      doxazosin 10.25
      terazosin 10.25
    mechanism of action
      10.24–10.25
  use in
    congestive heart failure 15.30

hypertension 10.14, 10.24–10.25
hypertensive emergencies 17.6
glaucoma 49.11
prostate hyperplasia 103.16
urinary incontinence 103.20
Preeclampsia
clinical presentation 44.14–44.16
definition 44.14–44.15
treatment 44.16–44.20
Prednisolone
Also see Corticosteroids
breast milk 45.28
teratogenicity 45.17
Prednisone
breast milk 45.28
adverse effects, teratogenicity
45.17
use in
acute lymphocytic leukemia 92.7
graft versus host disease
acute 94.11–94.16
chronic 94.17
Pregnancy
Also see Labor and delivery;
Lactation; Teratogenicity
clinical presentation 44.2–44.5
complications of
ABO isoimmunization
44.20–44.21
constipation 44.8
danger signs in 44.5
gestational diabetes 44.9–44.12
hemorrhoids 44.8
morning sickness 44.7–44.8
postpartum depression 76.10
preterm labor 44.21–44.26
reflux esophagitis 44.9
Rh isoimmunization 44.20–44.21
vaginal candidiasis 46.4
danger signs in 44.5
definitions 44.4
diagnosis 44.4–44.5
drug use in
HMG CoA reductase inhibitors
9.16
drugs in breast milk 45.23–45.29
ectopic 43.16
factors affecting fetal morbidity
and mortality
blood type incompatibility
44.20–44.21
diabetes 44.9–44.12
epilepsy 44.12–44.14
hypertension 44.14–44.20
factors affecting maternal morbidity and mortality
blood type incompatibility
44.20–44.21
diabetes 44.9–44.12
epilepsy 44.12–44.14
hypertension 44.14–44.20
gestational age 44.6
nutritional requirements 44.6–44.8
physiology of 44.2–44.5
postpartum hemorrhage
prenatal care 44.5–44.6
teratogenicity 45.1–45.36
treatment of
chlamydia 64.10
diabetes 44.9–44.12
epilepsy 44.12–44.14
fetal antigen incompatibility
44.20–44.21
fungal infections 69.15
gonorrhea 64.3
hemolytic disorder, fetal
44.20–44.21

herpes genitalia 64.20
hypertension 44.14–44.20
hyperthyroidism 47.18, 47.24
hypothyroidism 47.11
labor induction 44.26–44.28
lactation disturbance 44.29
malaria prophylaxis 71.3
morning sickness 44.7
nausea/vomiting 44.7, 105.5
postpartum hemorrhage
44.28–44.29
preeclampsia 44.14–44.20
preterm labor 44.21–44.26
syphilis 64.14
tuberculosis 59.11–59.12
urinary tract infection 63.5,
63.14
vaginal candidiasis 46.7
use of
acyclovir 64.20
aminoglycoside 64.7
angiotensin-converting enzyme
inhibitors 44.18
anticoagulants 12.16
antiemetics 44.8–44.9
antihistamines 44.8
aspirin 44.15–44.16
beta agonists 44.23–44.25
beta blockers 44.17, 44.19
bromocriptine 44.29–44.30
calcium 44.8
calcium channel blockers 44.18,
44.20, 44.25–44.26
carbamazepine 44.14
carboprost trometnamine
44.28–44.29
cefixime 64.3
ceftriaxone 64.3
chloroquine 71.3
ciprofloxacin 64.15
clindamycin 64.7
diazoxide 44.19–44.20
diuretics 44.18
ergot alkaloids 44.28
estrogen 44.30
folate 44.7–44.8
hydralazine 44.19
indomethacin 44.25
insulin 44.11, 44.12
iron 44.7
ketanserin 44.20
labetalol 44.19
laxatives 44.9
lithium 77.8
magnesium SO$_4$ 44.18–44.19,
44.25
methadone maintenance 83.7
methyldopa 44.17
metoclopramide 44.8, 44.29
oxytocin 44.26–44.28, 44.29
PGE$_2$ 44.26
phenothiazines 44.9, 44.29
phenytoin 44.13–44.14
primaquine 71.3
propylthiouracil 47.24
prostaglandin synthetase
inhibitors 44.25
pyridoxine 44.30
pyrimethamine-sulfadoxine 71.3
Rhogam 44.20–44.21
ritrodrine 44.23–44.24
spectinomycin 64.4
terbutaline 44.24
thyroxine 47.11
tocolytics 44.23–44.26
valproic acid 44.14
Preload 15.3
Premature ventricular

contractions 16.15–16.16
Premenstrual syndrome
clinical presentation 46.14–46.15
diagnosis, DSM-IV 46.15–46.16
pathogenesis 46.15
treatment 46.16–46.18
contraceptives, oral 43.17
Prenatal care 44.5–44.6
Preoperative medications
table of 8.3–8.4
administration
routes 8.2
timing 8.2
goals of 8.2
selection of 8.2
Prerenal azotemia, clinical
presentation 28.4–28.5
Prilosec
See Omeprazole
Primaquine
adverse effects
hemolysis 71.4
teratogenicity 45.17, 71.3
use in
malaria 71.3
pneumocystis 68.16, 68.17
Primaxin
See Imipenem
Primidone 52.8, 52.11, 52.12
Also see Antiepileptic drugs
adverse effects 52.8, 52.12
teratogenicity 45.17
breast milk 45.28
interactions, drugs 3.2
corticosteriods 3.5
use in seizures 52.12
Prinivil
See Lisinopril
Prinzmetal angina 13.19–13.20
Prioderm
See Malathion
Probenecid
Also see Gout; Hyperuricemia
adverse effects
hemolytic anemia 89.5
gout 40.11
contraindications/precautions
overexcretors 40.12
renal insufficiency 40.12
dosing 40.11
interactions, drugs
allopurinol 40.10
aspirin 3.5, 40.12
mechanism 3.2
methotrexate 38.4
pharmacokinetics
absorption 40.11
half-life 40.11
pharmacology
initiation of therapy 40.6, 40.11
mechanism of action 40.9
onset of effects 40.11
use in
hyperuricemia 40.9–40.12
urine masking agent 87.6
use with penicillin 64.13
Problem-oriented medical record
1.4–1.8
Probucol 9.23
Procainamide
adverse effects 16.6
drug fever 6.10
hemolysis 89.5
lupus 6.15
teratogenicity 45.17

vasculitis 6.12
breast milk 45.28
dosing
in renal failure 32.9, 32.19
maintenance 16.10
interactions, drugs
cimetidine 23.6, 23.8
famotidine 3.3
pharmacokinetics 16.6
concentrations
metabolites 32.19
metabolism 16.10, 32.9, 32.19
parameters 32.9, 32.19
Procainamide (continued)
pharmacology, effects on ECG
16.3
use in
atrial fibrillation 16.8, 16.10
cardiac arrest 16.21
digitalis toxicity 15.24
Wolff-Parkinson-White
syndrome 16.13
Procarbazine
adverse effects 90.14
pulmonary 22.6, 91.25
teratogenicity 45.18
dosing/alterations 90.14
pharmacokinetics 90.14
pharmacology 90.14
Procardia
See Nifedipine
Prochlorperazine
Also see Neuroleptics
adverse effects
hepatotoxicity 26.12
teratogenicity 45.18
use in
emesis, postoperative 8.17
morning sickness 44.9
nausea/vomiting 105.3, 105.4,
105.9
opioid withdrawal 83.9
Progestin
Also see Contraceptives, oral
adverse effects 46.16
amenorrhea 43.10, 43.18
hirsutism 43.17
irregular menses 43.17, 43.18
lipids 9.18
teratogenicity
see specific agents
weight gain 43.18
breast milk
see specific agents, table 45.23
use in
chronic obstructive airways
disease 20.10
contraception 43.4, 43.5,
43.18–43.19
endometriosis 46.21
hot flushes 46.25
menopause 9.17–9.18
premenstrual syndrome 46.16
respiratory insufficiency 27.11
sleep apnea 20.10
Progressive systemic sclerosis 42.2,
42.4
Prolastin
See Alpha-antitrypsin
Prolixin
See Fluphenazine
Proloid
See Thyroglobulin
Promazine
Also see Neuroleptics
teratogenicity 45.18

Promethazine
  Also see Neuroleptics
  adverse effects, teratogenicity
    45.18
  dosing 21.9
  pregnancy-induced hypertension
    44.14–44.20
  use in
    morning sickness 44.9
    nausea and vomiting 105.4
    rhinitis 21.6–21.12
Pronestyl
  See Procainamide
Propafenone
  adverse effects 16.6
  interactions, drugs
    digoxin 15.22
    quinidine 16.10
    warfarin 12.20
  pharmacokinetics 16.6
  pharmacology, effect on ECG 16.3
  use in atrial fibrillation 16.10
Propantheline, use in urinary incontinence 103.20
Propentofylline 102.10
Propofol
  breast milk 45.28
  teratogenicity 45.18
  use in
    anesthesia maintenance 8.7
    antiemetic effect 8.7
    eye surgery 8.7
    intensive care unit sedation 8.6
    preoperative sedation 8.6
Propoxyphene
  adverse effects
    pulmonary 22.4
    teratogenicity 45.18
  breast milk 45.28
  interactions, drugs
    mechanism 3.2
  pharmacokinetics, effect of renal
    failure 32.19
Propranolol
  Also see beta blockers
  adverse effects, teratogenicity
    45.18, 47.24
  breast milk 45.28
  dose, supraventricular arrhythmias
    16.9
  effect on thyroid function tests
    47.6
  interactions, drugs
    cigarettes 85.3
    cimetidine 23.8
    ergotamine 50.7
    lidocaine 16.17
    rifampin 59.8
  pharmacokinetics 10.20
  pharmacology/pharmacodynamics
    factors affecting response, thy-
      roid disorders 47.11
    properties 10.19–10.20
  use in
    adult ADHD 78.3
    aggression 79.4
    atrial fibrillation 16.11
    cocaine arrhythmias 84.5
    digitalis toxicity 15.24
    glaucoma 49.11
    hypertension 10.13, 10.19–10.20
    hyperthyroidism 47.19–47.20
    migraine headache 50.10–50.11
    schizophrenia, adjunctively 75.10
    self-injurious behavior 78.15
    thyroid storm 47.21

Propulsid
  See Cisapride
Propylthiouracil
  Also see Thioamides
  adverse effects
    drug fever 6.10
    hepatotoxicity 26.12
    teratogenicity 45.18
    vasculitis 6.12
  breast milk 45.28
  interactions, drugs
    warfarin 12.20
  use in
    hyperthyroidism 47.3,
      47.18–47.23
    pregnancy 47.3, 47.24
ProSom
  See Estazolam
Prostaglandin, use in glaucoma 49.11
Prostaglandin-E$_1$
  use in
    impotence 103.10–103.11
    veno-occlusive disease of the
      liver 94.11
Prostaglandin E$_2$
  use in
    endometriosis 46.11
    labor induction 44.26
Prostaglandins
  role in preeclampsia 44.15
  use in peptic ulcer disease 23.15
Prostaglandin inhibitors
  See specific agents
Prostate cancer
  chemotherapy, metastatic 93.18
  orchiectomy 93.17
  risk factors 93.16
  screening 90.6, 93.16
  signs/symptoms 90.8
  staging 93.16
  testosterone ablation 93.17
Prostate specific antigen 93.18,
  103.17
Prostatic hyperplasia 103.11–103.17
  complication, renal dysfunction
    29.21
Prostatitis 63.12–63.13
ProStep
  See Nicotine
Prosthetic valve endocarditis
  57.7–57.9
Protamine sulfate 12.10
Protein C 12.2, 12.4
Protein calorie calculation 35.6
Protein S 12.2, 12.4
Protein binding
  effect on antibiotics 54.18
  in renal failure 32.2
    table of drugs 32.1
  principles 2.2
Proteinuria
  diabetic nephropathy 30.19
  drug-induced
    gold 41.11
    penicillamine 41.15
  renal dysfunction 29.3
  renal hypertension 10.7, 10.21
  urinalysis 4.18
Protirelin
  See Thyrotropin releasing hormone
Prothrombin time
  laboratory test 12.4

Protirelin
  teratogenicity 45.18
Proton-pump inhibitors
  See Omeprazole
Protriptyline
  See Antidepressants, tricyclic
  use in
    depression, adulthood
      76.10–76.12
    sleep apnea 20.10–20.11
Protropin
  See Somatrem
Proventil
  See Albuterol
Provera
  See Medroxyprogesterone
Prozac
  See Fluoxetine
PRP-OMP immunization
  56.12–56.13
PRP-T immunization 56.12–56.13
Pruritus
  captopril 17.5
  dialysis 30.17
  uremic pruritus 30.17
Pseudoallergic reactions 6.13–6.14,
  6.16–6.17
Pseudodementia 102.12
Pseudoephedrine
  adverse effects, insomnia 74.6
  breast milk 45.28
  dosing 21.11
  use in decongestants 21.11
Pseudogout 40.4
Pseudohyponatremia 28.6
Pseudomembranous colitis
  60.10–60.12
  clinical presentation 60.10
  diagnosis 60.10
  drug-induced
    table of 60.10
    beta-lactam antibiotics 54.13
    clindamycin 54.13
  treatment 60.11–60.12
Pseudoparkinsonism 75.13–75.15
Psilocybin 86.2
Psoralens, psoriasis 38.3, 38.6
Psoriasis 38.1–38.7
  clinical presentation 38.1, 38.4,
    38.6
  drug-induced 38.5
  pathogenesis 38.1
  prognosis 38.1
  treatment
    drugs 38.1–38.6
    emotional 38.4–38.5
Psychiatric disorders
  anxiety disorders 73.1–73.28
  bipolar affective disorders
    77.1–77.12
  eating disorders 80.1–80.12
  in childhood, adolescents
    78.1–78.18
  major depressive disorders
    76.1–76.27
  schizophrenia 75.1–75.26
  secondary psychiatric disorders
    79.1–79.7
    apathy 79.5–79.6
    aggression 79.1–79.4
  sleep disorders 74.1–74.18
Psychoactive substance abuse
  See Drug abuse

Psychoactive substance use disorders
  81.1–81.16
  Also see specific disorders; Drug
    abuse
Psychogenic polydipsia 75.21
Psychoses
  Also see Affective disorders, bipo-
    lar; Depressive disorders, major;
    Neurotoxicity, drug-induced
  classification
    childhood schizophrenia
      78.7–78.9
Psychoses (continued)
    in developmentally disabled
      78.11
    Tourette's 78.9
  drug-induced
    amantadine 51.5
    amphetamine 84.3
    anabolic steroids 87.4
    anticholinergics 51.4
    barbiturate withdrawal 83.10
    bromocriptine 51.11
    butorphanol 7.3
    clomipramine 78.7
    cocaine 84.14
    corticosteroids 19.18, 33.30
    levodopa 51.8
    methylphenidate 78.3
    pentazocine 7.3, 7.14, 7.17
    triazolam 74.6
    zolpidem 74.7
Psychotherapy
  anorexia 80.4
  bipolar disorder 77.7
  bulimia 80.5
  depression, adulthood 76.6
Psyllium
  use in
    hypercholesterolemia 9.17
    ulcerative proctitis 24.2
  use with bile acid resins 9.17
PTU
  See Propylthiouracil
Pulmonary angiograms 12.11
Pulmonary disorders
  Also see specific disorders
  acidosis, respiratory 27.9–27.11
  alkalosis, respiratory 27.11–27.12
  drug-induced
    acetaminophen 22.1
    adenosine 16.12
    aerosolized drugs 22.2
    alcohol 22.2, 82.4
    amantadine 70.5
    aminosalicylic acid 22.6
    amiodarone 16.18, 22.4,
      22.8–22.9
    angiotensin-converting enzyme
      inhibitors 15.31 22.2
    antidepressants 22.4, 22.6
    asparaginase 22.2
    aspirin 6.17, 19.29, 22.2, 41.6
    beta-agonists 44.25
    beta blockers 6.16, 13.12, 19.28,
      22.2
    bleomycin 22.4, 22.7
    bromocriptine 22.4, 51.11
    busulfan 22.4
    carbamazepine 22.6
    carmustine 22.4
    cephalosporins 22.2
    chemotherapy drugs, table of
      91.24–91.25
    chlorambucil 22.5
    chlordiazepoxide 22.3

cimetidine 22.2
cocaine 84.11–84.12
contrast media 22.3
cromolyn 22.6
cyclophosphamide 22.5
cyclosporine 22.3
dantrolene 22.6
dextran 22.3
doxapram 82.4
epinephrine 22.3
ethychlorvynol 22.3
gold 22.5
heroin 22.3
hydrochlorothiazide 22.3
imipramine 22.6
interleukin-2 22.3
lidocaine 22.3
magnesium 44.19
magnesium trisilicate 22.7, 22.8
marijuana 86.6
melphalan 22.5
mephenesin 22.6
mercaptopurine 22.5
methadone 22.3
methotrexate 22.5, 38.4, 41.14
methysergide 22.5
minocycline 22.6
mitomycin 22.5
muromonab-CD3 22.3
narcotics 7.20
nitrites 83.12
nitrofurantoin 22.5–22.7, 63.17
nonsteroidal anti-inflammatory
drugs 19.29, 22.2, 46.14
oxygen 22.5
paraquat 22.6
penicillamine 22.6
penicillin 22.2, 22.6
phenylbutazone 22.4
phenytoin 22.6
pindolol 22.6
procarbazine 22.6
propoxyphene 22.4
ribavirin 70.5
ritodrine 22.4
salicylate 22.2, 22.4
sedatives 22.2
sulfasalazine 24.6
sulfites 22.2
sulfonamides 22.2, 22.7
tartrazine 22.2
terbutaline 22.4
tetracyclines 22.2
timolol 49.8
tocainide 22.6
vasopressin 25.9
types
apnea, neonates 96.21–96.23
asthma 19.1–19.29
chronic obstructive airways disease 20.1–20.12
obstructive diseases 19.3
pulmonary edema 22.3–22.4,
22.8
pulmonary embolism
12.11–12.17
pulmonary embolus 12.11–12.16
pulmonary eosinophilia 22.1,
22.6–22.7
pulmonary fibrosis 22.4–22.6,
22.7
drug-induced 22.7
respiratory distress syndrome
96.7–96.8
respiratory failure 19.15
restrictive diseases 19.3
sleep apnea 20.10

Pulmonary edema
drug-induced
betamimetics 44.25
opioids 83.5
volatile solvents 83.12
postlung transplant 33.24
Pulmonary embolus
clinical presentation 12.11
diagnosis 12.11
drug-induced, vasopressin 25.9
treatment
heparin 12.3–12.22
warfarin 12.3–12.21
Pulmonary eosinophilia 22.1, 22.6
Pulmonary fibrosis, cystic fibrosis
100.3
Pulmonary function tests 19.1–19.3
cystic fibrosis 100.4
Pulmonary surfactants 96.8–96.9
Pulmozyme
See Dornase alpha
Pulsus paradoxus 19.8
Purinethol
See Mercaptopurine
Purple toe syndrome 12.14
Purpura lesions 36.17
PUVA
See Phototherapy
PVCs
See Premature ventricular
contractions
Pyelonephritis
See Urinary tract infections
Pyrantel pamoate
dose 71.5, 71.9
use in pinworms 71.5, 71.9
Pyrazinamide
adverse effects 59.6
breast milk 45.28
dosing
initial 59.6
maintenance 59.6
pediatrics 59.6, 59.12
pharmacokinetics
concentrations
central nervous system 59.13
plasma 59.6
use in
Mycobacterium avium 68.28
Mycobacterium tuberculosis
68.26
tuberculosis 59.6, 59.10, 59.12
meningitis 59.13
pediatrics 59.12
Pyrethrin
teratogenicity 45.18
use in pediculosis 71.11
Pyridostigmine
breast milk 45.18
reversal neuromuscular blockade
8.9
teratogenicity 45.28
Pyridium
See Phenazopyridine
Pyridoxine
deficiency
renal failure, chronic 30.8
dosing 46.17
interactions, levodopa 51.9, 51.14
sideroblastic anemia 82.9
use in
lactation suppression 44.30
morning sickness 44.8
premenstrual syndrome 46.17

Pyrilamine
adverse effects, teratogenicity
45.18
dosing 21.9
use in rhinitis 21.6–21.12
Pyrimethamine
adverse effects
dermatologic 68.24
hematologic 68.24, 68.25
teratogenicity 45.18
breast milk 45.28
use in
pneumocystis 68.6
toxoplasmosis 68.24–68.25
Pyrimethamine-sulfadoxine
adverse effects
cutaneous reactions 71.3
teratogenicity 71.3
dosing 71.3, 71.6
use in
malaria
CRPF 71.2–71.4
prophylaxis 71.3
Pyrophosphate gout 40.4
Pyuria 63.6
Quazepam 74.8–74.9, 74.11
Also see Benzodiazepines
breast milk 45.28
pharmacokinetics 73.9
use as hypnotic 73.6, 73.7
Questran
See Cholestyramine
Quinacrine
adverse effects
anemia, aplastic 89.13
teratogenicity 45.18
use in giardiasis 71.9
Quinapril
Also see Angiotensin-converting
enzyme inhibitors
adverse effects, teratogenicity
45.18
breast milk 45.28
use in hypertension 10.22
Quinethazone
breast milk 45.28
teratogenicity 45.18
Quinidine
administration, oral 16.10
adverse effects 16.6
arrythmias 16.6, 16.9–16.10
cinchonism 16.6, 16.10
drug fever 6.10
gastrointestinal 16.6
hemolytic anemia 71.4,
89.5–89.6
hepatotoxicity 26.12
hypoglycemia 48.57–48.58
hypotension 16.6
lupus 6.15
syncope 16.6
teratogenicity 45.18
thrombocytopenia 16.10,
89.7–89.8
breast milk 45.28
dosing
maintenance 16.10
oral 16.10
interactions, drugs
antacids 23.9
barbiturates 3.5, 3.6
cimetidine 23.8
digoxin 3.5–3.7, 15.20, 16.10
mechanism 3.2
phenytoin 3.5, 3.6
propafenone 16.10

rifampin 59.8
pharmacokinetics 16.6
effect of heart failure 16.10
effect of old age 16.10
parameters 16.6
pharmacology, effect on electrocardiogram 16.3
use in
atrial fibrillation 16.8, 16.10
digitalis toxicity 15.24
malaria 71.2
Quinidine (continued)
premature atrial contractions
16.8
ventricular tachycardia 16.18
Quinine
adverse effects 11.11
hemolytic anemia 71.4, 89.5
hypoglycemia 48.57–48.58
thrombocytopenia 89.7–89.8
teratogenicity 45.18
breast milk 45.28
leg cramps 30.17
pharmacokinetics
half-life, hepatitis 62.5
use in
malaria
acute 71.2
CRPF 71.3
nocturnal leg cramps
11.11–11.12
Quinolones
See Fluoroquinolones
table of 54.7
adverse effects
table of 54.14
use in
gonorrhea 64.4, 64.6
pelvic inflammatory disease 64.7
Rabies vaccine
adverse effects
serum sickness 6.7
teratogenicity 45.18
Radio contrast media
adverse effects
acute tubular necrosis 29.6
anaphylactoid 6.17
Radioactive iodine 47.18, 47.24
uptake 47.5
Radiopharmaceuticals, breast milk
45.22, 45.28
Ramipril
Also see Angiotensin-converting
enzyme inhibitors
adverse effects, teratogenicity
45.18
breast milk 45.28
use in
hypertension 10.22
myocardial infarction 14.15
Ramoplanin 57.15
Ranitidine
Also see Histamine$_2$-antagonists
adverse effects
drug fever 6.10
teratogenicity 45.18
breast milk 45.28
use in
aspiration pneumonia
prophylaxis 8.5
pediatric GERD 95.7
Rapamycin 33.2, 33.9
Rash
See Dermatologic disorders;
Dermatologic reactions to drugs;

Hypersensitivity reactions
Raynaud's phenomenon
   bromocriptine-induced 51.11
   clinical presentation 11.9
   diagnosis 11.8
   pathophysiology 11.9
   treatment
      drug 11.9–11.10
      nondrug 11.9
RDS
   See Respiratory distress syndrome
Recombivax B
   See Hepatitis B vaccine
Re-entry arrhythmias 16.3, 16.12
Red cell indices 4.14
Red man syndrome 56.18
Reflux esophagitis
   See Gastroesophageal reflux
Reglan
   See Metoclopramide
Rehydration
   infectious diarrhea 60.1
   oral solutions 95.5–95.6
Reiter's syndrome 42.3
Renal failure, acute
   Also see Nephrotoxicity; Renal
      failure, chronic
   assessment of renal function
      29.2–29.4
   causes, table of 29.2
   clinical presentation 32.4–32.5
   dosing, drugs in 32.1–32.21
      amphotericin 69.12
      bleomycin 91.20
      carboplatin 91.20
      cisplatin 91.20
      cyclophosphamide 91.20
      methotrexate 91.20
      mitomycin 91.20
      nitrosurea 91.20
   drug-induced 29.8–29.14
      see Nephrotoxicity
   effect on drug dosing/pharmacoki-
      netics 54.12, 54.18
      also see specific drugs
      table of antibiotics 54.18
      table of drugs 32.6–32.10
      allopurinol 40.15
      amantadine 51.4–51.5
      benzodiazepines 73.12
      beta adrenergic blockers 13.13
      calcium channel blockers 13.17
      cyclosporine 94.15
      digoxin 15.26
      diuretics 15.16
      foscarnet 68.19
      insulin 48.29–48.30
      pentamidine 68.16
      probenecid 40.15
      procaineamide 16.10
      rifampin 59.6, 59.8
      sulfonylureas 48.45
   glomerulopathies 29.4–29.6
   hemodynamic renal failure 29.17
   hepatorenal 25.14
   laboratory assessment 2.7, 4.9
   pharmacodynamics 32.3
   postrenal 29.19–29.21
   predisposing factors, hypertension
      10.7
   treatment
      dialysis 31.1–31.13
      nutritional support 34.4, 34.6
      supportive 29.21
      tubulointerstitial diseases
         29.6–29.17

interstitial nephritis 29.16
tubular necrosis 29.6–29.16
Renal failure, chronic
   Also see Nephrotoxicity; Renal
      failure, acute
   clinical assessments 30.4–30.17
   clinical presentation 32.4
   complications of 30.2–30.7
      diuretic resistance 28.14
      hyperkalemia 28.18
      hyperphosphatemia 23.8
      hypertension 10.7
      hyponatremia 28.7
      hyperuricemia 40.13
      urinary tract infection 63.15
   definition 30.2
   dialysis 31.1–31.13
   dosing, drugs in 32.1–32.21
      amphotericin 69.12
      bleomycin 91.20
      carboplatin 91.20
      cisplatin 91.20
      cyclophosphamide 91.20
      methotrexate 91.20
      mitomycin 91.20
      nitrosurea 91.20
   effect on drug dosing/pharmacoki-
      netics 54.12, 54.18
      also see specific drugs
      table of antibiotics 54.18
      table of drugs 32.6–32.10
      allopurinol 40.15
      amantadine 51.4–51.5
      benzodiazepines 73.12
      beta adrenergic blockers 13.13
      calcium channel blockers 13.17
      cyclosporine 94.15
      digoxin 15.26
      diuretics 15.16
      foscarnet 68.19
      insulin 48.29–48.30
      pentamidine 68.16
      probenecid 40.15
      procaineamide 16.10
      rifampin 59.6, 59.8
      sulfonylureas 48.45
   end stage 31.1–31.13
   laboratory assessment 4.9
   nutritional requirements 34.4, 34.6,
      35.15
   pathogenesis 30.2–30.3
      diabetes 48.6–48.7
   pharmacodynamics 32.3
Renal function tests 2.7, 4.9
   neonates 95.6
Renal replacement therapy
   29.21–29.22
Renal transplantation 33.12–33.17
   Also see Transplantation
Renal tubular acidosis 27.5–27.6
   Also see Renal failure, acute
Renin-angiotensin system,
   congestive heart failure 15.4, 15.30
Reserpine
   adverse effects
      depression, adulthood 10.28
      gastrointestinal 10.18, 10.28
      nasal congestion 10.14, 10.28
      ocular 49.14
      pseudoallergic 6.17
      teratogenicity 45.18
   breast milk 45.28
   interactions, levodopa 51.9, 51.14
   use in
      hypertension 10.14, 10.18, 10.28
      Raynaud's phenomenon 11.9

Residual volume 19.2–19.3
Respiratory depression
   See Pulmonary disorders
Respiratory disorders
   See Pulmonary disorders
   asthma 19.1–19.31
   bronchopulmonary dysplasia
      98.1–98.4
   cystic fibrosis 100.1–100.10
   drug-induced pulmonary disorders
      22.1–22.11
   obstructive airways disease
      20.1–20.12
   pediatric infectious diseases
      97.1–97.19
   rhinitis, acute and chronic
      21.1–21.22
Respiratory distress syndrome
   96.7–96.10
   clinical presentation 96.7
   pathogenesis 96.7
   treatment 96.8–96.10
Respiratory failure 19.15
Respiratory infection, common
   pathogens 54.5
Respiratory stimulants 27.11
Respiratory syncytial virus
   70.10–70.11
Respiratory tract infections
   See Pulmonary disorders
   bronchial 58.2–58.3
   cold, common 21.18–21.19
   cystic fibrosis 100.3–100.4,
      100.6–100.10
   otitis media 58.1
   pneumonia 58.4–58.14
Restoril
   See Temazepam
Restrictive airway disease
   Also see specific airway diseases
   definition 19.3
Reticulocyte count, iron therapy 88.5
Reticulocytes 4.15
Retin-A
   See Tretinoin
Retinol
   adverse effects, hepatotoxicity
      26.13
   use in
      cystic fibrosis 100.6
      measles 97.17
Retinopathy
   diabetic 48.6
   hypertensive 10.7
Retroperitoneal fibrosis 50.11
Retrovir
   See Zidovudine
ReVia
   See Naltrexone
Reye's syndrome, aspirin induced
   41.21, 54.4
Rh isoimmunization 44.20–44.21
   management of fetus 44.21
   pathogenesis 44.20
   prophylaxis 44.20–44.21
Rhabdomyolysis
   cyclosporine 33.27
   drug-induced
      cocaine 84.12
      sedative-hypnotic withdrawal
         83.10
Rhabdomyosarcoma
   chemotherapy 93.25

clinical presentation 93.25
prognostic factors 93.25
Rheumatic disorders
   See specific disorders
Rheumatic fever 97.13
Rheumatoid arthritis
   Also see Juvenile rheumatoid
      arthritis
   definition 41.1–41.4
   diagnosis 41.1–41.4
Rheumatoid arthritis (continued)
   pathogenesis 41.1–41.4
   treatment
      combinations 41.15–41.16, 41.19
      drug 41.3–41.20
         monoclonal antibodies 5.5–5.6
      goals 41.2–41.3
      monitoring 41.4
      nondrug 41.4
Rheumatoid factor 41.4
Rhinitis 21.1–21.21
   assessment of patient 21.2–21.3
   classification 21.3
   clinical presentation
      allergic rhinitis 21.5
      eosinophilic nonallergic rhinitis
         21.18
      vasomotor rhinitis 21.16
      viral rhinitis 21.18
   diagnosis
      allergic rhinitis 21.2, 21.5, 21.15
      eosinophilic nonallergic rhinitis
         21.18
      vasomotor rhinitis 21.16
      viral rhinitis 21.18
   treatment
      allergic rhinitis 21.7– 21.16
         algorithm 21.8
      eosinophilic nonallergic rhinitis
         21.18
      vasomotor rhinitis 21.17
      viral rhinitis 21.18–21.19
Rhinitis medicamentosa 21.20–21.21
RhoGam 44.20–44.21
Rhythmol
   See Propafenone
Ribavirin
   administration 70.10–70.11, 97.15
   adverse effects 70.11
      table of 70.5
      environmental 70.11
      teratogenicity 70.11
   contraindications/precautions 70.11
   dose 70.10
   risks to health care workers 97.15
      teratogenicity 45.18
   use in
      chronic hepatitis C 62.13
      hantavirus 70.11
      respiratory syncytial virus
         70.10–70.11
      RSV bronchiolitis 97.15
Rickets 99.17–99.18
Ridaura
   See Auranofin
Rifabutin 68.28, 68.29
Rifampin
   Also see Tuberculosis
   adverse effects 59.6–59.9
      drug fever 6.10
      hemolysis 89.5
      hepatotoxicity 26.12, 59.8
      nephrotoxicity 29.14
      teratogenicity 45.18, 59.12
   breast milk 45.28

contraindications/precautions
  alcoholics 59.9
  elderly 59.9
dosing in
  elderly 59.10
  hepatic insufficiency 54.16, 59.8
  pediatrics 59.6, 59.12
  renal failure 59.6, 59.8
  initial 59.3–59.5
  maintenance 59.4–59.5
interactions, drugs
  contraceptives, oral 43.11, 43.12
  corticosteroids 3.5, 59.6
  cyclosporine 33.27
  diazepam 59.6
  ketoconazole 59.6, 68.29
  mechanism 3.2
  metoprolol 59.8
  sulfonylureas 48.39, 59.6
  theophylline 19.25
  warfarin 12.20, 59.6
pharmacokinetics
  clearance, dialysis 54.16
  concentration
    bone 65.5
    central nervous system 59.13
    serum 59.6
  half-life, hepatitis 62.5
pharmacology/pharmacodynamics
  59.3–59.7
  effect on thyroid function tests
    47.6, 47.7
use in
  atypical mycobacterial infections
    68.25–68.29
  H. influenzae meningitis,
    prophylaxis 56.12
  pediatric infections 97.7
  pseudomembranous colitis 60.10,
    60.12
  staphylococci endocarditis 57.10
  tuberculosis
    active 59.3–59.7
    drug-resistant 59.10
    meningitis 59.13
Rimactane
  See Rifampin
Rimantadine
  influenza prophylaxis 70.10
  pharmacokinetics 70.2–70.3
RIND
  See Ischemic neurological deficit
Risperidone 75.2, 75.7–75.8
Ritalin
  See Methylphenidate
Ritodrine
  administration
    intravenous 44.24
    oral 44.24
  adverse effects
    cardiovascular 44.24
    fetal 44.25
    hyperglycemia 44.25, 48.54
    hypoglycemia 48.55, 48.57
    pulmonary 22.4
    teratogenicity 45.19
    tremor 44.25
    vasculitis 6.13
  contraindications 44.23–44.24
  use in
    preeclampsia 44.23–44.24
    preterm labor 96.8
Robitussin
  See Guaifenesin
Rocephin
  See Ceftriaxone

Rocky Mountain spotted fever
  97.19–97.20
Rocuronium 8.8–8.12
Romazicon
  See Flumazenil
Rotavirus 95.4–95.5
  gastroenteritis, pediatric
    60.12–60.13
Roth spots, endocarditis 57.4
Rowasa
  See Mesalamine
Roxanol SR
  See Morphine
RU-486 43.23
Rubella vaccine 95.10, 95.12
  adverse effects, teratogenicity
    45.19
Sabril
  See Vigabatrin
Saccharin
  adverse effects, teratogenicity
    45.19
  breast milk 45.28
Salicylates
  Also see Aspirin
  adverse effects 41.6
    drug fever 6.10
    hepatotoxicity 26.6
    hypoglycemia 48.55,
      48.56–48.57
    pseudoallergic 6.16
    pulmonary 22.2
    Reye's syndrome 41.21
    teratogenicity 41.7
  effect on thyroid function tests
    47.6, 47.7
  interactions, drugs
    methotrexate 38.4
    probenecid 3.5, 40.12
    sulfonylureas 48.39
  overdose, treatment 104.5–104.9
  pharmacokinetics 41.5
  preparations/formulations 41.6
  use in acne 37.4
Salicylism 104.7
Saline
  See Sodium
  use in
    diabetic ketoacidosis 48.34
    hypovolemic shock 18.12–18.15,
      18.31
Salmeterol
  Also see Beta-adrenergic agonists
  use in obstructive airways disease
    20.11
Salmonella
  complications
    in HIV infection 68.30
    in pediatric HIV infection 68.35
Salmonella gastroenteritis
  60.13–60.14
Salt substitutes 28.12
Sandoglobulin
  See Immune globulin
Sansert
  See Methysergide
SAPHO 37.1
Saquinavir 68.10
Sargramostim
  Also see GM-CSF
  use in
    bone marrow transplants 94.7
    graft failure, bone marrow 94.11

Schilling test 88.9
Schizophrenia
  See Psychoses
  clinical features 75.3
  diagnostic criteria, DSM-IV 75.3
  differential diagnosis 75.4
  drug-induced 75.4–75.5
  pathophysiology 75.1–75.2
  prognosis 75.3–75.4
  target symptoms 75.5
  treatment 75.6–75.23
Schlicter test 57.5
Scleroderma 42.2
Sclerotherapy, esophageal varices
  25.8–25.9
Scopolamine
  adverse effects, teratogenicity
    45.19
  breast milk 45.28
  use in
    emesis, postoperative 8.17–8.18
    motion sickness 105.4, 105.5
    postoperative vomiting 105.4
SCUF 31.12
Secobarbital
  adverse effects, teratogenicity
    45.19
  breast milk 45.28
Sedation
  drug-induced
    antidepressants, cyclic 76.9
  pediatrics 95.20–95.22
  precautions, hepatic coma 25.12
  use in
    cirrhosis 25.12
    psychoses 75.7
Sectral
  See Acebutolol
Sedative-hypnotics
  Also see specific agents
  abuse 83.10
Sedatives
  adverse effects, pulmonary 22.2
  nonprescription 74.5
Sedimentation rate 4.15
Seizure disorders 52.1–52.29
  Also see Antiepileptic drugs; spe-
    cific seizure types
  absence
    clinical presentation 52.2, 52.19
    treatment 52.19
      ethosuximide 52.19
      trimethadione 52.19
      valproate 52.19, 52.20
  classification 52.2
    absence 52.2, 52.19
    childhood absence epilepsy 52.3
    complex partial 52.2, 52.7–52.19
    febrile seizures 52.22–52.23
    generalized tonic clonic 52.2,
      52.19–52.22
    juvenile myoclonic 52.3
    simple partial 52.2
  clinical presentation 52.2
  complex partial
    clinical presentation 52.2, 52.7
    treatment 52.7–52.19
      table of drugs 52.12
  diagnosis 52.3
  drug-induced
    also see Neurotoxicity
    amantadine 51.5
    antidepressants, cyclic 76.11,
      76.14, 104.19
    beta-lactam antibiotics 54.13

bromocriptine 44.30
bupropion 80.5
busulfan 94.9
carbamazepine 52.8–52.9, 52.10
clozapine 75.2
cocaine 84.9
ethosuximide 52.19–52.20
foscarnet 70.5
meperidine 7.9
Seizure disorders (continued)
  drug-induced (continued)
    neuroleptics 75.22
    phencyclidine 86.8
    quinolones 54.14
    salicylate overdoses 104.8
    sedative-hypnotic withdrawal
      83.10
    theophylline 19.25
  generalized tonic-clonic
    clinical presentation 52.2,
      52.19–52.20
    treatment
      table of drugs 52.12
      carbamazepine 52.20
      phenobarbital 52.20
      phenytoin 52.20
      primidone 52.12
      valproate 52.20–52.22
  neonatal 96.24–96.26
    treatment
      table of, drug regimens 96.26
      calcium 96.25
      glucose 96.24
      magnesium 96.25
  pathogenesis
    fevers 95.3
    stroke 53.13
  treatment
    absence 52.19
    complex partial 52.7–52.19
    febrile 52.22–52.23
    generalized tonic clonic
      52.19–52.22
    myoclonic 52.4
    principles 52.2–52.7
      duration of therapy 52.6–52.7
      mono- versus polytherapy 52.6
      use of serum drug concentra-
        tions 52.4–52.6
    status epilepticus 52.27–52.29
Seldane
  See Terfenadine
Selegiline
  dose 51.12
  efficacy in Parkinson's disease
    51.12
  mechanism of action 51.12
  use in
    Alzheimer's 102.7
    nocturnal myoclonus 74.15
    Parkinson's disease 51.12
Self-injurious behavior 78.14–78.15
Seminomas 93.19
Senna, breast milk 45.29
Separation anxiety, children 78.6
Sepsis
  neonatal 96.16–96.19
  pathophysiology 54.2–54.4
Septic arthritis 65.9–65.12
  clinical presentation
    gonococcal 40.3, 65.10
    nongonococcal 65.9–65.10
  treatment, principles
    antibiotic selection 65.9–65.11
    duration of therapy 65.10
    empirical 65.9–65.10

Septic shock
  Also see Cardiogenic shock;
    Hypovolemic shock
  clinical presentation 18.5–18.6,
    18.25
  goal of therapy 18.27
  hemodynamic profile 18.25
  pathogenesis 18.5–18.6
  treatment 18.6, 18.25–18.30
    also see specific agents
    antibiotics 18.25–18.26
    antiendotoxins 5.4–5.5
    fluids 18.26
    ibuprofen 18.30
    inotropes 18.27
    interleukin-2 18.30
    monoclonal antibodies 18.29
    naloxone 18.30
    pentoxifylline 18.30
    vasopressors 18.27–18.28
Septra
  See Trimethoprim-
    sulfamethoxazole
Serax
  See Oxazepam
Serotonin
  alcoholism 82.7
  association with eating disorders
    80.2
  depression, adulthood 76.4
Serotonin antagonists
  Also see Granisetron; Ondansetron
  use as antiemetics 105.6–105.7
Serotonin reuptake inhibitors
  Also see specific agents
  adverse effects 76.18
  interactions, drugs 76.18
    MAOIs 76.21
  pharmacokinetics 76.17
  use in
    aggression/disinhibition
      79.4–79.5
    anorexia 80.4
    bulimia 80.4
    depressive disorders 76.16–76.19
    panic disorders 73.19, 73.21
    pediatrics 78.16
Sertraline
  depression, adulthood 76.10–76.12
  toxicity 104.18
  use in
    obsessive compulsive disorder
      73.24–73.26, 73.28
    panic disorder 73.19
Serum bactericidal titer 57.5
Serum sickness
  clinical presentation 6.8
  drug-induced, table of 6.7
  treatment 6.6
Serzone
  See Nefazodone
Sexual dysfunction
  drug-induced
    table of 103.5–103.6
    alcohol, chronic 82.12
    antidepressants, cyclic 76.9
    antihypertensives 10.14, 10.19,
      10.28
    cimetidine 23.4
    ketoconazole 69.16
    monoamine oxidase inhibitors
      76.19–76.20
    neuroleptics 75.22
Sexually transmitted diseases
  64.2–64.21
  Also see HIV infection; specific

disorders
Sezolamide 49.11
SGOT
  See Aminotransferase, aspartate
SGPT
  See Aminotransferase, alanine
Shigella gastroenteritis 60.14–60.15
Shingles 70.7
Shock 85.2–85.7
  Also see Cardiogenic shock;
    Hemodynamic monitoring;
    Hypovolemic shock; Septic
    shock
  causes 18.2
  classification 18.2–18.6
    table of 18.2
    cardiogenic 18.3–18.5
    distributive 18.5
    hypovolemic 18.3
    septic 18.5
  clinical presentation 18.2, 18.25
  pathophysiology 18.2–18.3,
    18.28–18.30
  treatment 18.3–18.5, 18.25–18.30
Shohl's solution 27.6
Short stature 95.15–95.17
SI units 4.2–4.5
SIADH
  See Syndrome of inappropriate
    antidiuretic hormone secretion
Sickle cell anemia 88.12–88.13
Silver nitrate 36.3
  use in gonococcal ophthalmia 64.8
Silver sulfadiazine 39.14
Simethicone 23.8
  adverse effects, teratogenicity
    45.19
Simvastatin 9.15–9.17
Sinequan
  See Doxepin
Sinusitis
  clinical presentation 97.9–97.10
  cystic fibrosis 100.2
  diagnosis 97.9–97.10
  pathogens 97.3, 97.10
  treatment 97.10
    adjunctive 97.10
    antibiotic selection 97.10
Sjögren's syndrome 41.4
Skin
  Also see Dermatologic disorders;
    Dermatologic reactions to drugs
  structure and function 39.10
Skin disorders
  See Dermatologic reactions; spe-
    cific disorders
Skin infections, common pathogens
  54.5
Skin physiology 36.1
Skin tests
  Also see specific agents
  allergic rhinitis 21.5–21.6
  effect of
    antidepressants, cyclic 21.6
    antihistamines 21.6
    beta-agonists 21.6
    beta-adrenergic blockers 21.6
    corticosteroids 21.6
    phenothiazines 21.6
  immunocompetence 35.3
  penicillin allergy 6.3–6.4
  PPD 59.2–59.3

SLE
  See Systemic lupus erythematosus
Sleep apnea 20.10–20.11,
  74.13–74.14
Sleep disorders 74.1–74.18
  assessment 74.4
  classification 74.4
    dyssomnias 74.1–74.13
    narcolepsy 74.14–74.15
    nocturnal myoclonus 74.15
    pediatric insomnia 74.16
    periodic limb movements 74.15
    sleep apnea 74.13–74.14
  disease induced 74.8
  pathogenesis 74.2–74.4
  pathophysiology 74.2–74.4
  treatment 74.4–74.16
Smallpox vaccine, teratogenicity
  45.19
Smoking
  See Cigarettes
Sodium
  Also see Hypernatremia;
    Hyponatremia
  concentration, serum 4.3,
    28.4–28.10
  content in
    antacids 23.9
    diet 10.10
    drugs, table 15.10
  depletion 28.4, 28.6–28.10
  effect on
    cardiovascular disease 10.8
    hypertension 10.8
  excess 28.5
  fractional excretion of 29.4
  laboratory interpretation
    28.4–28.10
  restriction
    ascites 25.4
    congestive heart failure 15.5
    high blood pressure 10.10
  transport 28.1–28.3
  urine concentration 25.4
  use in
    hypercalcemia 28.21
    hyponatremia 28.7
Sodium bicarbonate
  See Bicarbonate
Sodium iodide, teratogenicity 45.19
Soft tissue infections
  diabetics 66.5–66.6
  necrotizing infections 66.6–66.7
Solganol
  See Gold
Solvents, abuse of 83.11–83.15
Somatostatin
  use in
    cluster headache 50.14
    esophageal varices 25.8
    Zollinger-Ellison 23.16
Somatrem 95.15
Somatropin 95.15
Somogyi effect 48.23
Sorbinil 48.47
Sotalol
  adverse effects 16.6
    teratogenicity 45.19
  breast milk 45.29
  pharmacokinetics 16.6, 16.17
  pharmacology, effect on ECG 16.3
  use in
    atrial fibrillation 16.10
    ventricular tachycardia 16.17

Spectinomycin
  adverse effects, teratogenicity
    45.19
  use in
    gonorrhea 64.3–64.4, 64.6, 64.8
    penicillin allergy 64.4, 64.6
"Speedballing" 83.9–83.10
Spermicides 43.22
Spider angiomas 25.2
Spinal cord decompression
  breast cancer, radiation 93.6
  prostate cancer, corticosteroids
    93.18
Spiramycin
  adverse effects, teratogenicity
    45.19
  breast milk 45.29
  use in
    cryptosporidiosis 68.30
      AIDS 60.7
Spirometry 19.2–19.3
Spironolactone
  Also see Diuretics, potassium-
    sparing
  adverse effects, gynecomastia 25.5
  breast milk 45.29
  contraindications/precautions 10.16
  use in
    acne 37.4
    ascites 25.5
    cirrhosis 25.5
    hypertension 10.15, 10.16
    premenstrual syndrome 46.17
    use with thiazides 10.16
Sporanox
  See Itraconazole
Sporotrichosis 69.6–69.7
Spot test 71.4
Sputum
  bronchial infection 58.2
  sample adequacy 58.2
SSKI 47.17
Stadol
  See Butorphanol
Staphylococcus epidermidis ventri-
  culitis/meningitis 56.17–56.18
  treatment 56.17–56.18
Starling curve 15.3
Status epilepticus 52.27–52.29
  definition 52.27
  treatment
    diazepam 52.27–52.28
    lorazepam 52.27–52.28
    phenobarbital 52.29
    phenytoin 52.28
Stavudine 68.7–68.9
  adverse effects, nephrotoxicity
    54.14
Steatosis 26.1
Stelazine
  See Trifluoperazine
Stevens-Johnson syndrome 36.17
Stimulants
  See specific agents; Cocaine;
    Amphetamines
Stoxil
  See Idoxuridine
Streptococcal antigen test 97.11
Streptogramin 57.15
Streptokinase
  adverse effects
    nephrotoxicity 29.14
    stroke 14.12–14.13

contraindications/precautions
  table of 14.7
dosing in myocardial infarction
  14.7, 14.9–14.10
pharmacology, comparative 14.3,
  14.7
selection of 14.9, 14.13
  major thrombolytic trials 14.11
use in
  myocardial infarction 14.3, 14.7,
    14.9–14.13
  reocclusion 14.12
Streptomycin
  adverse effects 59.6
    drug fever 6.10
    teratogenicity 45.19
  breast milk 45.29
  dosing
    in pediatrics 59.12
    in pregnancy 59.12
    initial 59.6
  pharmacokinetics
    concentration
      central nervous system 59.13
      plasma 59.6
    resistant organisms 57.12
  use in
    endocarditis 57.6–57.7,
      57.9–57.15
    tuberculosis 59.5, 59.13, 68.26
      meningitis 59.13
      pediatric 59.12
Streptozocin
  adverse effects 90.14
    hepatotoxicity 91.27
  dosing/alterations 90.14
  pharmacokinetics 90.14
  pharmacology 90.14
Stress disorder, acute 73.27–73.28
Stress ulcers
  clinical presentation 23.18
  pathogenesis 23.18
  risk factors 23.19
  treatment 23.19–23.20
Stroke
  Also see Cerebral Hemorrhage;
    Cerebral infection; Transient
    ischemic attacks
  cardioembolic, anticoagulation
    12.6
  definition 53.2
    ischemic stroke 53.9–53.14
  drug-induced
    cigarettes 85.5
    hypertension 10.7
    thrombolytics 14.12–14.13
Struvite stones 29.20
Stye 49.16
Subacute myelo-optic
  neuropathy 71.8
Subarachnoid hemorrhage
  clinical presentation 53.14
  complications of 53.14–53.15
  treatment 53.14–53.15
Sublimaze
  See Fentanyl
Substance abuse
  See Drug abuse; specific agents
Succinylcholine 8.8–8.12
Sucralfate
  administration 23.9
  adverse effects 23.9
    hypophosphatemia 28.24
    teratogenicity 45.19
  breast milk 45.29

dosing 23.9
interactions, drugs
  aluminum antacids 23.9
  fluoroquinolones 63.6
pharmacology, mechanism of
  action 23.9
use in
  combination with H$_2$-antagonists
    23.10
  gastric ulcer 23.9
  gastroesophageal reflux 23.18
  peptic ulcer disease 23.5, 23.7,
    23.9, 23.11, 23.14
  stress ulcer 23.20
  hyperphosphatemia 30.14
Sudafed
  See Pseudoephedrine
Sufenta
  See Sufentanil
Sufentanil
  use in epidural infusion 8.20–8.21
Suicide 78.4
  assessment 76.8
Sulconazole 69.3
Sulfadiazine
  adverse effects 68.24
    vasculitis 6.13
  use in toxoplasmosis 68.24–68.25
Sulfadoxine
  use in
    isosporiasis 68.30
    pneumocystosis 68.17
Sulfamethoxazole
  Also see Sulfonamides
  desensitization 6.19
  pharmacokinetics
    clearance
      dialysis 54.13
      renal failure 54.18
    parameters 32.9
Sulfasalazine
  Also see Sulfonamides
  adverse effects
    table of 24.6
    lupus 6.15
    teratogenicity 24.7, 45.19
  breast milk 24.7
  dosing 24.5
  interactions, drugs
    anticoagulants, oral 24.7
    cholestyramine 24.7
    digoxin 24.7
    ferrous sulfate 24.7
    folic acid 24.7
    sulfonylureas 24.7
  pharmacokinetics 24.5
  pharmacology
    efficacy versus steroids 24.4
    mechanism of action 24.4
  use in
    Crohn's disease 24.10–24.11
    rheumatoid arthritis 41.12
    ulcerative colitis 24.3–24.7
Sulfinpyrazone
  interactions, drugs
    mechanism 3.2
    warfarin 12.20
  use in
    angina 13.18
    transient ischemic attacks 53.6,
      53.7
Sulfisoxazole
  Also see Sulfonamides
  use in
    pregnancy 63.5
    urinary tract infection 63.5

Sulfites 22.2
Sulfonamides
  Also see specific agents
  adverse effects
    table of 54.13
    anemia, aplastic 89.13
    anemia, hemolytic 63.5,
      63.15–63.16, 71.4, 89.5
    crystalline nephropathy 68.24
    dermatological 63.16
    drug fever 6.10
    fever 68.15–68.16
    G6PD deficiency anemia 89.4
    hepatotoxicity 26.12
    kernicterus 54.13, 63.5
    nephrotoxicity 29.14
    ocular 49.14
    phototoxicity 63.5
    pulmonary 22.2, 22.7
    rash 54.13, 63.16, 68.15–68.16
    teratogenicity 45.19, 54.13, 63.5,
      63.14
    vasculitis 68.15–68.16
  breast milk 45.29
  contraindications/precautions,
    pregnancy 63.10
  interactions, drugs
    mechanism 3.2
    methotrexate 38.4
    sulfonylureas 48.39, 63.16
    warfarin 12.20, 63.16
  use in urinary tract infections
    63.4–63.6, 63.10–63.16
Sulfonylureas
  Also see Diabetes mellitus;
    specific agents
  adverse effects
    alcohol intolerance 48.43
    blood dyscrasias 89.13
    cardiovascular 48.44
    dermatological 48.43–48.44
    gastrointestinal 48.43
    hematological 48.43
    hepatotoxicity 26.7, 26.12, 48.44
    hypoglycemia 48.44–48.45, 48.55
    syndrome of inappropriate antidi-
      uretic hormone secretion 48.44
  teratogenicity
    see specific agents
  contraindications/precautions 48.41
    elderly 48.46
    hepatic dysfunction 48.45
    renal dysfunction 48.45
  cross-sensitivity with
    sulfonamides/sulfonylureas 48.44
  dosing 48.38, 48.41
    elderly 48.40–48.41
    hepatic dysfunction 48.45
    renal dysfunction 48.45
    switching to insulin 48.41–48.42
  drug of choice 48.41
  efficacy, secondary failure 48.41
  interactions, drugs 48.38–48.39
    table of 48.39
    mechanism 3.2
    rifampin 59.8
    sulfasalazine 24.7
    sulfonamides 24.7
  pharmacokinetics 48.37–48.38
  pharmacology
    comparative 48.36–48.38
    mechanism of action 48.36
  use
    in type II diabetes 48.40–48.42
    versus insulin in type II diabetes
      48.40
    with insulin 48.42
    with metformin 48.58

Sulfur, use in acne 37.4
Sulindac
  adverse effects
    drug fever 6.10
Sulindac (continued)
  adverse effects (continued)
    hepatotoxicity 26.13
    nephrotoxicity 7.8, 29.14, 41.9
    teratogenicity 45.19
  use in
    gout 40.5
    rheumatoid arthritis 41.9
Sulphasalazine
  See Sulfasalazine
Sumatriptan
  adverse effects 50.8
  dose 50.8, 50.9
  pharmacology 50.7
  use in
    cluster headache 50.14
    migraine headache 50.7–50.8
Sunburns 39.1–39.3
  Also see Sunscreens
  sunscreens 39.7–39.10
  treatment 39.11
Sunscreens
  chemical sunscreens 39.7–39.10
  effectiveness, substantivity 39.7
  physical sunscreens 39.10
  preparations 39.8, 39.10
  sun protection factor 39.7
Supportive care, immunosuppressed
  patients 94.5
Supraventricular arrhythmias
  16.4–16.13
  Also see Atrial fibrillation
  classification
    paroxysmal supraventricular
      tachycardia 16.12–16.13
    Wolff-Parkinson-White 16.13
Suprax
  See Cefixime
Suprofen
  See Nonsteroidal anti-
    inflammatory drugs
Suprol
  See Suprofen
Suramin 93.18
Surfactants, synthetic lung
  96.8–96.10
Surgical
  Also see Perioperative care
  adrenal support 42.8
  antibiotic prophylaxis 55.1–55.5
    table of regimens 55.3
    administration
      duration 55.4
      route 55.2–55.4
      timing 55.2
    adverse effects 55.5
    classification of wounds
      55.1–55.2
    decision for need 55.1
  bladder cancer
    cystectomy 93.14
    resection, endoscopic 93.14
  breast cancer 93.3
  cancers, general 90.8
  carotid endarterectomy 53.4
  colon cancer, cure rate 93.7
  Crohn's disease 24.12
  endometriosis 46.20
  hyperthyroidism 47.18, 47.22
  intermittent claudication 11.8
  orchiectomy

prostate cancer 93.17
testicular cancer 93.19
organ transplantation 33.9–33.10
also see Transplantation
osteomyelitis 65.7, 65.8
parathyroidectomy, renal failure
30.14
Parkinson's 51.13
pediatric GERD 95.7
portal hypertension 25.9
prostate hyperplasia
103.14–103.15
toxic megacolon 24.9
ulcerative colitis 24.9
Surmontil
See Trimipramine
Survanta
See Beractant
Swan Ganz catheter 18.7
Sweat chloride 100.3
Symmetrel
See Amantadine
Syndrome of inappropriate antidiuretic hormone secretion
clinical presentation 28.8
drug-induced 28.8
carbamazepine 52.10
chlorpropamide 48.44
diuretics 10.17
oxytocin 44.28
pathogenesis 28.8
treatment 28.8–28.10
Synovial fluid
See Septic arthritis
Synthroid
See Thyroid hormone; Thyroxine
Syphilis 64.10–64.15
clinical presentation 64.10–64.12
laboratory assessment 64.12–64.13
treatment 64.13–64.15
congenital 64.15
in penicillin allergy 64.13
in pregnancy 64.14
Systemic lupus erythematosus
classification 42.2
clinical presentation 42.5–42.6
drug-induced
table of characteristics 6.14
table of drugs 6.15
hydralazine 10.27, 42.2
isoniazid 59.8
sulfasalazine 24.6
thioamides 47.20
treatment
corticosteroids 42.5–42.7
complications, renal failure
30.20–30.22, 32.4
Systolic hypertension 10.3
TAC solution
use in pediatric topical anesthesia
95.24
Tacrine
adverse effects
hepatotoxicity 102.6
overview 102.6
use in Alzheimer's 102.5–102.6
Tacrolimus
adverse effects 33.36
dosing 33.36
pharmacokinetics 33.35–33.37
pharmacology 33.7
use in organ transplants 33.7,
33.14, 33.35–33.36
Tagamet
See Cimetidine

Talc
Also see Magnesium trisilicate
use in sclerosis 92.10
Talwin
See Pentazocine
Tamoxifen
adverse effects, ocular 49.15
effect on thyroid hormone 47.8
use in
breast cancer 93.4–93.7
melanoma 93.16
Tampon
miconazole impregnated 46.5
toxic shock 46.8, 46.10
Tanning 39.2–39.5
Also see Sunscreens
sunscreens 39.7–39.10
Tapeworms 71.6, 71.9–71.11
Tar
See Coal tar
Tardive dyskinesia 75.16–75.19
Tartrazine (FD&C yellow #5 dye)
22.2
Tavist
See Clemastine
Taxol
See Paclitaxel
TBG 47.2
Technetium-99m scan 14.2
Teething 95.2
Tegretol
See Carbamazepine
Teicoplanin 57.14
use in
pseudomembranous colitis 60.11
septic arthritis 65.10
Telepaque
See Ipodate
Temazepam
Also see Benzodiazepines
pharmacokinetics 73.9
use in
insomnia 74.8, 74.11
sedation 73.7
Temperature
See Fever
Tenex
See Guanfacine
Teniposide
adverse effects 90.14
dosing/alterations 90.14
pharmacokinetics 90.14
pharmacology 90.14
teratogenicity 45.19
Tenormin
See Atenolol
TENS
dysmenorrhea 46.12
Tension headaches
See Headaches, tension
Teratogenicity
Also see specific agents
table of drugs 45.7–45.20
table of proven human teratogens
45.6
alcohol 81.9
amphetamines 81.9
angiotensin-converting enzyme
inhibitors 44.18
anticoagulants 12.17
antiepileptic drugs 52.26–52.27
aspirin 41.7
benzodiazepines 73.14–73.16

beta-adrenergic agonists 44.25
beta-adrenergic blockers
44.17–44.18, 47.24
captopril 15.31
carbamazepine 44.14, 52.26–52.27
chemotherapy agents 91.26–91.27
cigarettes 81.9, 85.3–85.4
cocaine 81.9
contraceptives, oral 43.16
corticosteroids 24.7
dimenhydrinate 44.8
estrogens 43.18
heparin 12.17
hydralazine 44.19
iodides 47.24
lithium 77.8
LSD 81.9
marijuana 81.9
meclizine 44.8
methimazole 47.24
methyldopa 44.17
metoclopramide 44.8
metronidazole 24.7, 64.16, 71.8
nalidixic acid 63.14
neuroleptics 75.22
nitrofurantoin 63.14
norfloxacin 63.14
opiates 81.9
phenothiazines 44.8–44.9
phenytoin 44.13–44.14,
52.26–52.27
primaquine 71.3
propranolol 47.24
propylthiouracil 47.24
ribavirin 70.10
rifampin 59.12
sulfasalazine 24.7
sulfonamides 54.13, 63.5, 63.14
tetracycline 54.13, 63.14
thiomides 47.24
trimethoprim-sulfamethoxazole
63.14
valproic acid 44.14
warfarin 12.17
Terazol
See Terconazole
Terazosin
adverse effects 10.25
antihypertensive
comparison to prazosin 10.25
mechanism of action 10.25
use in
prostate hyperplasia 103.16
Terbinafine 69.3
Terbutaline
Also see Beta-adrenergic agonists
adverse effects
pulmonary 22.4
teratogenicity 45.19
vasculitis 6.13
breast milk 45.29
use in
asthma 19.13
preterm labor 44.24, 96.8
urinary incontinence 103.21
Terconazole
adverse effects, teratogenicity
45.19
use in candidiasis, vaginal
46.5–46.6, 69.5
Terfenadine
adverse effects
arrhythmias 16.17
cardiotoxicity 21.12
teratogenicity 45.19
dosing 21.9
interactions, drugs

adenosine 16.12
clarithromycin 21.12
erythromycin 21.12
Terfenadine (continued)
interactions, drugs (continued)
ketoconazole 21.12, 69.9
nefazodone 76.24
use in rhinitis 21.7–21.12
Terlipressin 25.8
Tes-Tape
See Urine, glucose tests
Testicular atrophy, anabolic steroid-
induced 87.3
Testicular cancer
chemotherapy
metastatic 93.19
regimens 90.17
clinical presentation 90.8, 93.19
orchiectomy 93.17
staging 93.19
Testosterone
use in impotence 103.7–103.8
Testosterone deficiency, ethanol-
induced 82.12
Tetanus 66.9–66.10
immunoglobulin 66.10
toxoid 66.9
vaccine 95.10, 95.11
Tetracyclines
adverse effects
table of 54.13
drug fever 6.10
hepatotoxicity 26.13, 54.13, 63.5
nephrotoxicity 29.14
ocular 49.14
photosensitivity 63.5
pulmonary 22.2
teratogenicity 45.6, 45.19, 54.13,
63.5, 63.14
vaginal candidiasis 46.4
bacterial, resistance to 64.3
breast milk 45.29
contraindications/precautions
children 63.5, 63.10
pregnancy 63.5, 63.10
pediatrics 97.6
interactions, drugs
antacids 23.9, 63.5
contraceptives, oral 43.11
dairy products 63.5
iron 63.5
use in
acne 37.3, 37.5
amebiasis 71.7
gonorrhea, uncomplicated 64.3,
64.4–64.5
Helicobacter ulceration 23.12
malaria 71.2
ophthalmia neonatorum 64.8
pelvic inflammatory disease 64.7
syphilis 64.13–64.14
urinary tract infections, acute
63.5
Tetrahydroaminoacridine
See Tacrine
Tetrahydrocannabinol
Also see Dronabinol
use in glaucoma 49.11
Tetrahydrozoline 21.10–21.11
Tetranitrate, teratogenicity 45.19
Thalidomide
adverse effects, teratogenicity 45.6
use in graft versus host disease,
chronic 94.17

Thallium-201 scan 14.2
THC
  See Dronabinol
Theophylline
  adverse effects
    cardiovascular 19.13
    esophageal reflux 20.11
    gastrointestinal 20.9
    seizures 19.25
    teratogenicity 45.19
  breast milk 45.29
  contraindications/precautions, beta-
    agonists 19.14
  dosing
    table of 19.17
    infants 19.22–19.23
    intravenous 19.15–19.18
    intravenous to oral 2.10, 19.18
    loading 2.8, 19.5–19.16
    maintenance 2.9, 19.16–19.18
    neonates 96.22–96.23
    pediatric 19.16–19.17, 19.23
    rectal 19.23
  interactions, drugs
    allopurinol 40.10
    beta-agonists 19.14
    cimetidine 19.17, 19.24–19.25,
      23.6, 23.8
    ciprofloxacin 3.3, 19.17, 19.24,
      63.7
    contraceptives, oral 43.12
    enoxacin 3.3
    erythromycin 19.17, 19.24, 20.9
    inducers 19.17, 19.25
    inhibitors 19.17, 19.24
    lithium 77.6
    smoking 19.16–19.17, 85.3
    vidarabine 70.5
  overdose, treatment 19.24
  pharmacokinetics 19.16–19.18
    bioequivalency 19.22–19.23
    clearance 19.16–19.17
    dialysis of 19.24
    geriatric patients 101.3–101.4
    half-life, hepatitis 62.5
    in elderly 19.17
    in pediatrics 19.16–19.17
    neonatal parameters 96.22
    sampling time 2.11, 19.17
    therapeutic drug monitoring
      19.15–19.18, 19.22–19.25
  pharmacology, mechanism of
    action 19.15
  preparations
    dyphylline 19.23
    oxtriphylline 19.23
    salts of 19.24
    sustained-release 19.22
  toxicity 19.24
  use in
    apnea, newborn 96.22–96.23
    bronchopulmonary dysplasia
      98.2–98.3
    asthma 19.15–19.25
    combination with beta-agonists
      19.14
    diuresis 28.11
    exercise-induced asthma 19.26
    respiratory failure 19.15
Thiamine
  adverse effects, anaphylactoid 6.17
  deficiency
    alcoholism 25.3
    Wernicke-Korsakoff 25.3
  use in
    bone resorption 46.33
    Korsakoff's prevention

      82.10–82.11
    Wernicke's encephalopathy
      104.14
hiazide diuretics
  See Diuretics, thiazide
Thiethylperazine 105.4
Thioamides
  administration 47.20
  adverse effects 47.19, 47.21–47.22
    hepatotoxicity 26.9
    teratogenicity 47.24
    see specific agents
  breast milk
    see specific agents
    table of 45.23
  contraindications/precautions 47.20
  dosing 47.20, 47.22–47.23
  pharmacokinetics, half-life 47.20
  pharmacology/pharmacodynamics
    47.3, 47.18–47.20
  use in
    cirrhosis 25.3
    hyperthyroidism 47.3,
      47.18–47.26
    pregnancy 47.24
Thiocyanate toxicity 17.10
Thioguanine
  adverse effects 90.14
    hepatotoxicity 91.27
    teratogenicity 45.19
  dosing/alterations 90.14
  pharmacokinetics 90.14
  pharmacology 90.14
Thiomalate, gold sodium 41.10
  Also see Gold
Thiopental, anesthesia induction 8.6,
  8.7
Thioridazine
  Also see Neuroleptics
  adverse effects 75.7, 75.23
    ocular 49.16
    teratogenicity 45.19
  dose 75.8
  use in psychoses 75.7–75.8
Thiosulfate, sodium
  use in
    combination with nitroprusside
      17.9
    cyanide toxicity 17.9–17.10
Thiotepa
  adverse effects 90.14
    teratogenicity 45.19
  dosing/alterations 90.14
  pharmacokinetics 90.14
  pharmacology 90.14
Thiothixene
  Also see Neuroleptics
  adverse effects 75.7
  dose 75.8
  use in psychoses 75.7
Thiouracil, breast milk 45.29
Thorazine
  See Chlorpromazine
Thrombin, pharmacology 12.3, 12.21
Thrombin time 12.6
Thrombocytopenia
  Also see Hematological disorders
  drug-induced 89.6–89.9
    alcohol 89.7
    amrinone 15.35, 18.20
    aspirin 41.6
    azathioprine 33.38
    beta-lactam antibiotics 54.13
    flucytosine 54.14
    ganciclovir 54.14, 94.21

    heparin 12.8–12.9, 89.8–89.9
      low molecular weight 89.9
    gold 41.11, 89.8
    phenylbutazone 40.5
    quinine 89.7–89.8
    rifampin 59.8
    thiazides 89.7
  pathogenesis 89.6–89.9
Thrombocytopenic purpura
  95.17–95.18
Thromboembolism
  See Thrombosis
Thrombolytics
  Also see Streptokinase; Tissue
    plasminogen activator;
    Antistreplase; Urokinase
  adverse effects, stroke 14.12–14.13
  contraindications/precautions
    table of 14.7
    thrombocytopenia 89.9
  dosing in myocardial infarction
    14.7, 14.9–14.10
  pharmacological comparisons 14.3,
    14.7
  selection of agent 14.9
  table of major studies 14.11
  use in
    acute ischemic stroke
      53.11–53.12
    elderly 14.12
    hemolytic uremic syndrome
      95.15
    myocardial infarction 14.3, 14.7,
      14.9–14.13
    postcardiopulmonary
      resuscitation 14.13
    reocclusion 14.12
Thrombophlebitis
  See Phlebitis
Thrombosis 12.1–12.22
  Also see Pulmonary embolus;
    Heparin; Warfarin;
    Thrombolytics
  clinical presentation
    cardiogenic thromboembolism
      12.17–12.21
    deep venous thrombosis 12.7
    disseminated intravascular coag-
      ulation 12.21
    pulmonary embolism 12.11
  clotting tests 12.4–12.6
  complications, dialysis 31.7
  diagnosis 12.7
  drug-induced
    contraceptives, oral 43.14
    estrogens 46.32
    vasopressin 25.9
  etiology 12.1–12.2
  pathogenesis
    clot formation 12.2
    platelet activation 12.2
    risk factors 12.7
  prophylaxis 12.11
  treatment
    general principles 12.1, 12.7
    heparin 12.7–12.12
    warfarin 12.4, 12.12, 12.17
Thymoxamine 11.9
Thyroglobulin 47.6
  teratogenicity 45.19
Thyroid disorders
  Also see Euthyroidism;
    Hyperthyroidism;
    Hypothyroidism; specific agents
  drug-induced 47.26–47.27
    iodoquinol 71.5

    lithium 77.6, 77.7
    hyperthyroid 47.15–47.26
Thyroid disorders (continued)
  hypothyroid 47.8–47.15
  nodular 47.28
Thyroid function tests 47.3–47.8
  effect of depression 76.4
  effect of drugs on 47.6
    table of 47.4
    androgens 87.4
Thyroid hormone 47.1–47.5
  Also see Thyroxine;
    Triiodothyronine
  adverse effects, teratogenicity
    45.19
  breast milk 45.29
  dessicated 47.9
  interactions, drugs
    warfarin 3.4, 12.20
  use in depression, refractory 76.24
Thyroid receptor antibodies 47.6
Thyroid stimulating hormone
  47.5–47.8
Thyroid stimulating immunoglobulins
  47.6, 47.8
Thyroid storm
  See Hyperthyroidism
Thyrolar
  See Liotrix
Thyrotoxicosis 47.17
Thyrotropin
  Also see Thyroid stimulating hor-
    mone
  adverse effects, teratogenicity
    45.19
Thyrotropin releasing hormone 47.5
  adverse effects, teratogenicity
    45.18
Thyroxine
  Also see Thyroid hormone;
    Triiodothyronine
  adverse effects
    cardiac 47.14
    teratogenicity 45.14
  bioequivalence 47.9
  breast milk 45.26
  dosing 47.10–47.15
  interactions, drugs
    cholestyramine 9.14
    warfarin 3.4
  pharmacology/pharmacodynamics
    47.2
  use in
    bipolar disorders 77.10
    depression, refractory 76.24
    hypothyroidism 47.2, 47.9–47.15
    pregnancy 47.11
TIA
  See Transient ischemic attacks
Tiagabine 52.13
Ticarcillin
  Also see Penicillins,
    antipseudomonal
  dose 63.8
  use in
    cystic fibrosis 100.7–100.8
    pyelonephritis 63.8
Ticarcillin-clavulanate 63.8
  use in
    cystic fibrosis 100.7–100.8
    lung abscess 58.6
Ticlopidine
  adverse effects
    diarrhea 53.8

hypercholesterolemia 53.8
neutropenia 53.8
rash 53.8
use in
intermittent claudication 11.8
stroke prevention 53.8
transient ischemic attacks 53.6–53.8, 102.10
Tidal volume 19.2
Total lung capacity 19.2
Time to sample 2.6–2.7
Timolol
Also see Beta-adrenergic blockers
adverse effects
ophthalmic 49.4, 49.10
systemic 49.4
tachyphylaxis 49.4
teratogenicity 45.19
breast milk 45.29
combined with epinephrine 49.9
interactions, drug 49.9
pharmacokinetic properties
breast milk 49.4
concentration 49.4, 49.8
pharmacology
comparative 10.19, 10.20, 49.4–49.7
mechanism of action 49.4, 49.9
use in
glaucoma 49.4–49.10
hypertension 10.19, 10.20
migraine 50.10
Timoptic
See Timolol
Timoptic XE 49.5, 49.7
Tinea pedis
clinical presentation 69.4
treatment 69.4
Tinea unguium 69.5
Tinea versicolor 69.2
Tinidazole 71.9
Tinnitus, aspirin-induced 41.5
Tioconazole
adverse effects 46.6
pharmacology
efficacy 46.6
onset/duration 46.6
use in candidal vaginitis 46.5–46.6
Tirilazad mesylate 53.12
Tissue plasminogen activator
adverse effects, stroke 14.12–14.13
contraindications/precautions, table of 14.7
dosing in myocardial infarction 14.7, 14.9–14.10
pharmacology, comparative 14.3, 14.7
selection 14.9, 14.13
major thrombolytic trials 14.11
use in
acute ischemic stroke 53.11–53.12
elderly 14.13
myocardial infarction 14.3, 14.7, 14.9–14.13
postcardiopulmonary resuscitation 14.12
reocclusion 14.12
veno-occlusive disease of the liver 94.11
TMP/SMX
See Trimethoprim-sulfamethoxazole
Tobacco
See Nicotine; Cigarettes

Tobramycin
Also see Aminoglycosides
adverse effects
nephrotoxicity 100.8–100.9
ototoxicity 100.8
teratogenicity 45.20
breast milk 45.29
dosing
once a day 2.20
during dialysis 31.10
pharmacokinetics
concentration, bone 65.5
use in cystic fibrosis 100.7–100.9
Tocainide
adverse effects 16.6
pulmonary 22.6
pharmacokinetics 16.6
pharmacology, effect on ECG 16.3
use in ventricular tachycardia 16.18
Tocolytics
Also see specific agents
beta-agonists 44.23–44.26
magnesium 44.18–44.19
ritodrine 44.23–44.24
terbutaline 44.24
Tocopherol
interactions, drugs
warfarin 12.20
use in
cystic fibrosis 100.6
hemolysis 89.4
hemolytic uremia 95.15
tardive dyskinesia 75.17
Tofranil
See Imipramine
Tolazamide 48.37–48.38
Also see Sulfonylureas
adverse effects, teratogenicity 45.20
Tolazoline, teratogenicity 45.20
Tolbutamide 48.37–48.38
Also see Sulfonylureas
adverse effects, teratogenicity 45.20
breast milk 45.29
interactions, drugs
omeprazole 23.10
Tolmetin
Also see Nonsteroidal anti-inflammatory drugs
adverse effects
drug fever 6.10
nephrotoxicity 29.14
teratogenicity 45.20
breast milk 45.29
use in gout 40.5
Tolrestat 48.47
Toluene
abuse 83.11–83.15
pharmacokinetics 83.14
toxicities 83.11–83.15
Topiramate 52.13
Toradol
See Ketorolac
TORCH titer 96.20
Tornalate
See Beta-adrenergic agonists
Torsades de pointes 16.17, 21.12
Torsemide
See Diuretics, loop
dosing 15.15
use in congestive heart failure 15.15
Tourette's syndrome 78.9–78.10

Toxic megacolon
clinical presentation 24.8
drug-induced
anticholinergic agents 24.8
antidiarrheals 24.2
barium enemas 24.8
cathartics 24.8
diphenoxylate 24.2
loperamide 24.2
opioids 24.8
predisposing factors 24.8
treatment 24.8
Toxic shock syndrome
CDC case definition 46.8
clinical presentation 70.8–70.10
diagnosis 70.8–70.9
pathogenesis 70.8
risk factors 46.10
treatment 70.9–70.10
Toxicology
See Clinical toxicology
Toxoplasmosis
clinical presentation 68.24
diagnosis 68.24
treatment 68.24–68.25
TPA
See Tissue plasminogen activator
TPN
See Parenteral nutrition
Trace minerals, use in parenteral nutrition 35.5, 35.10
Tracrium
See Atracurium
Tramadol 7.14
Trandate
See Labetalol
Transaminases
See Aminotransferases
Transient ischemic attacks
clinical presentation 53.3–53.4
definition 53.1
epidemiology 53.2
risk factors 53.2, 53.4
treatment
drugs
table of 53.7
anticoagulants 53.7, 53.8–53.9
antiplatelet agents 53.6–53.8
carotid endarterectomy 53.4
surgery 53.4, 53.6
ticlopidine 102.10
goals 53.4
Transplantation 33.1–33.49
Also see Bone marrow transplantation; Heart transplantation; Kidney transplantation; Liver transplantation; Lung transplantation
complications
infections 67.15–67.18
cytomegalovirus 67.16–67.18
prophylaxis of 67.17
transmission 67.17
herpes simplex virus 67.17
varicella zoster virus 67.17
histocompatibility 33.3
organs
heart 33.9, 33.18–33.23
liver 33.9, 33.28–33.38
lung 33.10, 33.23–33.28
pancreas 33.10
renal 33.9, 33.12–33.17
rejection reactions 33.15–33.18, 33.20–33.21
treatment, monoclonal antibodies 5.1–5.3

Tranxene
See Clorazepate
Tranylcypromine, teratogenicity 45.20
Trasicor
See Oxprenolol
Travelers' diarrhea 60.2–60.7
clinical presentation 60.6–60.7
pathogenesis 60.2–60.3
predisposing factors 60.2–60.3
prophylaxis 60.4–60.5
treatment 60.3–60.7
Trazodone
Also see Antidepressants, cyclic
adverse effects 76.16
breast milk 45.29
comparison to tricyclic antidepressants 76.16
use in
bulimia 80.5
depression 76.10–76.12, 76.16
dementia 102.11
insomnia 74.12
impotence 103.8
Tremors
drug-induced
beta-agonists 19.11
lithium 77.5
Trental
See Pentoxifylline
Treponema
See Syphilis
Tretinoin
Also see Acne
adverse effects
photosensitivity 37.5
teratogenicity 45.33
guidelines for use 37.3
use in
acne 37.2–37.5
aging 39.5–39.6
Trexan
See Naltrexone
Triacetin 69.3
Triamcinolone, nasal 21.14
Triamterene 10.15, 10.16
adverse effects
hyperkalemia 15.15
nephrotoxicity 29.14
interaction, drugs
indomethacin 7.8
use in
congestive heart failure 15.15
cirrhosis 25.5
Tri-Levlen
See Contraceptives, oral
Tri-Norinyl
See Contraceptives, oral
Triamterene 10.15, 10.16
Also see Diuretics; Diuretics, potassium-sparing
Triazolam 74.5–74.9
Also see Benzodiazepines
adverse effects 74.6
teratogenicity 45.20
breast milk 45.29
dose 74.8
interactions, drugs
nefazodone 76.24
pharmacokinetics 73.9, 74.6
use in
insomnia 74.5–74.11
sedation 73.7

Trichlormethiazide
  adverse effects, teratogenicity 45.20
  breast milk 45.29
Trichomoniasis
  clinical presentation 64.15
  treatment
    in pregnancy 64.16
    metronidazole 64.16
Tricyclic antidepressants
  See Antidepressants, cyclic
Trientine, teratogenicity 45.20
Trifluoperazine
  Also see Neuroleptics
  adverse effects
    hepatotoxicity 26.13
    teratogenicity 45.20
  adverse effects 75.7
  dose 75.8
  use in psychoses 75.8
Triflupromazine, teratogenicity 45.20
Trifluridine 70.4, 70.6
  use in ocular herpes simplex 49.19–49.20
Triglycerides
  Also see Dyslipidemias;
    Hypertriglyceridemia
  laboratory assessment of 9.20
  medium chain 35.5
Trihexyphenidyl
  Also see Anticholinergics
  use in
    extrapyramidal reactions 75.16
    Parkinson's disease 51.3–51.4
Triiodothyronine
  Also see Thyroid hormone;
    Thyroxine
  pharmacology/pharmacodynamics 47.1–47.10
  use in
    cardiac disease 47.15
    hypothyroid 47.9–47.15
    Raynaud's phenomenon 11.10
Trimeprazine
  Also see Neuroleptics
  adverse effects, teratogenicity 45.20
  breast milk 45.29
  dosing 21.9
  use in rhinitis 21.7–21.12
Trimethadione
  adverse effects
    fetal trimethadione syndrome 45.32–45.33
    teratogenicity 45.6, 45.20, 45.32–45.33
    ocular 49.13
Trimethaphan
  adverse effects 17.13
  dose 17.13
  use in
    aortic dissection 17.13
    hypertensive emergency 17.13
Trimethobenzamide 105.4
  adverse effects, teratogenicity 45.20
Trimethoprim
  adverse effects, teratogenicity 45.20, 63.16
  breast milk 45.29
  pharmacokinetics
    clearance
      hemodialysis 32.10, 54.16
      renal failure 32.10, 54.18
    parameters 32.10

  use in
    prostatitis 63.13
    travelers' diarrhea 60.3, 60.5
    urinary tract infection 63.5, 63.11
Trimethoprim-sulfamethoxazole
  adverse effects
    bacterial resistance 60.5
    dermatological 63.16
    folic acid deficiency 63.16
    hematological 63.5, 63.16
    hepatotoxicity 26.12
    hypersensitivity, human immun-odeficiency virus 68.15
    myelosuppression 94.20
    rash 94.22
    teratogenicity 63.5, 63.14
  interactions, drugs
    contraceptives, oral 43.11
    Depo-Provera 43.18–43.19
    methotrexate 94.22
    warfarin 12.20, 63.16
  pharmacology
    comparative, trimethoprim 63.5
  spectrum of antibacterial activity 63.6
  synergistic activity 63.5
  use in
    acne 37.3
    bronchitis 58.3
    chancroid 64.15
    gonorrhea 64.6
    immunocompromised hosts 67.14
    Isospora belli 68.30
    meningitis 56.9
    otitis 97.8
    pediatric infections 97.6
    Pneumocystis carinii 68.15–68.18, 94.17, 94.21–94.22
    pneumonia, community acquired 58.7
    prophylaxis, neutropenic patients 67.14
    pyelonephritis 63.9
    Salmonella gastroenteritis 60.13
    Shigella gastroenteritis 60.14
    travelers' diarrhea 60.3–60.4
    urinary tract infections
      hospital acquired 63.9
      prophylaxis 63.12
      recurrent 63.5, 63.12
Trimetrexate 68.16
  use in pneumocystosis 68.16
Trimipramine
  Also see Antidepressants, cyclic
  use in depression 76.10–76.12
Tripelennamine
  dosing 21.9
  use in rhinitis 21.6–21.12
Triphasil
  See Contraceptives, oral
Triprolidine
  breast milk 45.29
  dosing 21.9
  use in rhinitis 21.6–21.12
Trobicin
  See Spectinomycin
Tryptophan
  adverse effects, vasculitis 6.12
TSH
  See Thyroid stimulating hormone
Tube feeding
  See Enteral nutrition

Tuberculosis 59.1–59.15
  Also see Mycobacterial infections, atypical
  clinical presentation 59.2–59.3
    drug-resistant organisms 59.10–59.11
    extrapulmonary 59.12
    in acquired immunodeficiency syndrome 59.11
    in elderly 59.9–59.10
    in HIV 68.25–68.26
    meningitis 59.12–59.13
  diagnosis 59.2–59.3
  pathogenesis 59.1–59.2
    effect of steroids 59.11
  prophylaxis
    in HIV 59.11
    nonHIV 59.7
  transmission 59.1
  treatment 59.3–59.14
    also see specific drugs
Tubocurarine 8.8–8.12
Tubular necrosis, acute 29.6–29.16
  Also see Renal failure, acute
Tubulointerstitial disease
  Also see Renal failure, acute
Tularemia vaccine, teratogenicity 45.20
Tumor lysis syndrome 92.5
Tumor necrosis factor
  role in
    HIV-wasting 68.18
    septic shock 18.29–18.30
Tumors, solid 93.1–93.24
Turner's syndrome 95.17
Typhoid vaccine, teratogenicity 45.20
Tyropanoate, teratogenicity 45.20
Ulcerative colitis 24.1–24.9
  clinical presentation 24.1–24.3
  complications
    table of 24.2
    toxic megacolon 24.2, 24.8
  definition 24.1
  treatment
    corticosteroids 24.3
    cromolyn 24.8
    immunosuppressives 24.7–24.8
    mesalamine 24.6
    olsalazine 24.6
    sulfasalazine 24.3–24.7
    surgery 24.9
Ulcers
  See Peptic ulcer disease
Ultadol
  See Etodolac
Ultraviolet light, psoriasis 38.2–38.3
Ultraviolet radiation 39.1–39.3
Unipen
  See Nafcillin
Universal precautions, infection 62.6
Upper gastrointestinal disorders 23.1–23.24
Urapadil
  dosing 17.7
  pharmacology 17.7
  use in hypertensive emergency 17.7
Urea nitrogen
  See Blood urea nitrogen
Uremic encephalopathy 30.16
Uremic toxins 30.4
Uric acid
  Also see Gout; Hyperuricemia

disposition 40.1
laboratory interpretation 4.8
laboratory tests
  effect of levodopa 51.10
  serum 4.8, 40.12
  urine 40.8
Uricosurics
  See specific agents
Urinalysis 4.18
  anabolic steroids 87.5–87.6
  drugs screening 104.17
    anabolic steroids 87.5–87.6
    drugs of abuse, list of 81.13–81.14
    marijuana 81.9, 81.13
    masking results 81.14, 87.6
  erythropoietin limitations 87.7
  macroscopic 4.18, 63.3
  masking drug tests 81.14, 87.6
  microscopic 4.8, 63.3
    casts 29.4
    cells 29.4
    protein 4.18, 29.3
  specific gravity 4.18
  uric acid quantification 40.8
  urinary catheters 63.14–63.15
Urinary incontinence
  classification 103.18–103.19
  clinical presentation 103.19
  drug treatment 103.20–103.22
  neurophysiology 103.18–103.19
Urinary tract infections 63.1–63.17
  Also see Prostatitis
  clinical presentation 63.3
    asymptomatic bacteriuria 63.9
    pyelonephritis 63.7–63.9
    recurrent urinary tract infections 63.10–63.12
  common pathogens 54.5, 63.2
  definitions 63.1–63.2
  diagnosis 63.3–63.4
    interpretation of culture and sensitivity 63.6
    recurrent urinary tract infections 63.10–63.12
  epidemiology 63.2
  laboratory assessment 63.3–63.4
  pathogenesis
    community-acquired 63.2
    hospital-acquired 63.2, 63.7
  predisposing factors 63.10
  treatment of
    asymptomatic bacteriuria 63.9–63.10
    catheter associated 63.14–63.15
    hospital-acquired 63.7
    lower 63.4, 63.6–63.7
    postcoital 63.13
    pregnant women 63.13–63.14
    prostatitis 63.12–63.13
    pyelonephritis 63.7–63.9
    recurrent 63.10–63.12
    renal failure patients 63.15
    symptomatic abacteriuria 63.9
  treatment principles
    antibiotic selection 63.6
    chronic prophylaxis 63.2
    duration of therapy 63.4
    urine versus serum cidal levels 63.8
Urine
  Also see Urinalysis
  albumin tests 48.52–48.53
  alkalinization 40.13
    carbonic anhydrase inhibitors 49.10
  culture 63.3

discoloration
nitrofurantoin 63.5
phenazopyridine 63.9
rifampin 59.6, 59.8
drug screening, cannabinoids 86.7
electrolytes 25.4
glucose tests 48.5, 48.8, 48.40
levodopa 51.9
ketone tests, levodopa interference 51.10
Urokinase
contraindications/precautions, table of 14.7
dosing in myocardial infarction 14.7, 14.9–14.10
pharmacology, comparative 14.3, 14.7
use in
elderly 14.12
myocardial infarction 14.7, 14.9–14.13
post CPR 14.13
reocclusion 14.12
Ursodiol, teratogenicity 45.20
Urticaria 36.19
UW solution 33.12
V/Q mismatching 19.8
Vaccines
Also see Immunizations; specific infections
adverse effects 95.9
teratogenicity
see specific vaccines
contraindications/precautions 95.9
preparations
tables of 95.9, 95.10
BCG 59.13–59.14
chickenpox 95.25
hepatitis A 62.6
hepatitis B 62.6
influenza 58.3, 70.10
varicella 70.6–70.7
use in immunocompromised patients 95.13
Vaginal secretions 46.3–46.4
Vaginitis
Also see Urinary tract infections; Vaginosis
bacterial vaginosis 46.3, 46.4, 46.7
candidiasis, vaginal 46.2–46.7
treatment
bacterial vaginosis 64.15
trichomoniasis 64.16
trichomoniasis 64.15–64.16
Vagistat
See Tioconazole
Valproate
adverse effects
gastrointestinal 52.20, 52.21
hematological 52.24
hepatotoxicity 26.12, 52.20, 52.22, 77.9
teratogenicity 45.6, 45.20, 45.32, 52.26–52.27
vasculitis 6.13
weight gain 52.11, 52.20
breast milk 45.29
dosage forms 52.21
dosing
effect of enzyme inducers 52.24, 52.25, 52.26
monitoring serum 52.21–52.22
schedules 52.20, 52.21
interactions, drugs
carbamazepine 52.24
contraceptives, oral 43.11

felbamate 52.11
lamotrigine 52.11
mechanism 3.2
pharmacokinetics
bioavailability 52.21
concentrations 52.6, 52.21–52.22
parameters 52.6
pharmacology/pharmacodynamics, effect on thyroid hormones 47.7
use in
absence seizures 52.19, 52.20–52.21
aggression/disinhibition 79.5
bipolar disorders 77.9
cluster headaches 50.15
generalized tonic clonic seizures 52.20–52.22
migraine headache 50.10, 50.12
pregnancy 44.14
prophylaxis of febrile seizures 52.23
seizures, neonatal 96.26
Valve replacement, anticoagulation 12.6
Valvular disease, anticoagulation 12.6
Vancenase
See Beclomethasone
Vanceril
See Beclomethasone
Vancomycin
Also see Antibiotics
administration
intravenous 56.18, 57.8–57.9
intraventricular 56.18
surgical prophylaxis 57.9
adverse effects
table of 54.13
acute tubular necrosis 29.7
drug fever 6.10
hypotension 57.9
nephrotoxicity 29.7, 29.14, 56.14
red man syndrome 6.14, 6.17, 56.18, 57.8
red man syndrome 56.18, 57.8
breast milk 45.29
dose
intravenous 32.15, 56.18
intraventricular 56.18
renal failure 32.15–32.16
dosing 2.17–2.19, 54.17, 54.19
hemodialysis 54.17
pharmacokinetics 2.17–2.19
clearance
hemodialysis 32.10, 32.16
renal failure 32.10, 32.15–32.16, 54.19
concentrations
peak 32.15, 54.17
plasma 32.15
time to sample 32.16
trough 32.15, 54.17
half-life 32.15
pharmacology, three-drug combinations 67.7
resistant organisms 57.14–57.15
use in
central nervous system infections 56.9
endocarditis
enterococcal 57.12–57.15
prosthetic valve 57.8–57.10
S. aureus 57.9–57.11
S. viridans 57.6–57.7
meningitis, MRSA 56.10, 56.17–56.18
necrotizing enterocolitis, neonate 96.16

neutropenia 67.7
osteomyelitis 65.7
peritonitis 31.10–31.11
pseudomembranous colitis 60.11–60.12
septic arthritis 65.10
staphylococcus
methicillin-resistant staphylococcus 54.10, 57.9–57.11
surgical prophylaxis 55.3, 55.5
use in
aminoglycosides 57.13–57.14
diphenhydramine 56.18
rifampin 56.18, 57.10
Vantin
See Cefpodoxime
Varicella 70.6–70.7, 95.13, 95.25
vaccine 95.13, 95.25
Varicella zoster infections
clinical presentation, transplant patients 67.16
Varices, esophageal 25.2, 25.7–25.10
Vascor
See Bepridil
Vasculitis
complications of rheumatoid arthritis 41.4
drug-induced
table of 6.12–6.13
allopurinol 40.10
hypersensitivity 6.8
Vasodilators
Also see Amrinone; Angiotensin-converting enzyme inhibitors; Hydralazine; Minoxidil; Nitrates; Nitroprusside
adverse effects 10.12, 10.14, 10.24, 10.27
contraindications/precautions 10.14
intermittent claudication 11.6
use in
cardiogenic shock 18.16
congestive heart failure 15.5–15.6, 15.27–15.30, 15.32, 18.19–18.21
hypertension 10.12, 10.14, 10.24, 10.26
in combination with digoxin 15.32
Vasomotor rhinitis 21.16–21.17
Vasopressin
administration 25.8
adverse effects 25.9
use in varices 25.8–25.9
use with nitroglycerin 25.8
Vasopressors
Also see Dobutamine; Norepinephrine
table of 18.4
use in
cardiogenic shock 18.24
septic shock 18.27–18.28
Vasospasm, cerebral 53.14
Vasotec
See Enalapril
Vecuronium 8.8–8.12
Venlafaxine
Also see Serotonin reuptake inhibitors; Depression
pharmacology 76.10–76.12, 76.24
Venlafaxine (continued)
use in
depression, adulthood 76.10–76.12, 76.24
refractory depression 76.24

Veno-occlusive disease of the liver 94.10–94.11
Ventilator assistance, neonatal 96.26–96.29
Ventolin
See Albuterol
Ventricular arrhythmias 16.13–16.14
premature ventricular contractions 16.14
sustained ventricular tachycardia 16.16
torsade de pointes 16.17
ventricular fibrillation 16.19
ventricular tachycardia 16.16–16.19
Ventricular dysfunction, anticoagulation 12.6
Ventriculitis 53.14
Verapamil
Also see Calcium channel blockers
adverse effects 10.24, 10.27, 16.6
table of 13.16
atrioventricular block 16.13
bradycardia 13.16
congestive heart failure 15.10, 15.34
constipation 13.16
fatigue 13.16
teratogenicity 45.20
breast milk 45.29
dose
atrial fibrillation 16.11, 16.13
supraventricular tachycardia 16.9, 16.12
interactions, drugs
digoxin 13.16–13.17, 15.34
mechanism 3.2
pharmacology 13.14, 13.16
preparations
table of 13.15
sustained release 13.17
use in
angina 13.16
atrial fibrillation 16.8
bipolar disorders 77.10
cluster headache 50.15
glaucoma 49.11
heart failure 15.34
hypertension 10.13, 10.14, 10.23–10.24, 10.27, 10.28
hypertensive emergency 17.4, 17.7
hyperthyroid 47.19
migraine headache 50.10, 50.12–50.13
myocardial infarction 14.5, 14.8, 14.16
nocturnal leg cramps 11.12
premenstrual syndrome 46.17
Vermox
See Mebendazole
Versed
See Midazolam
Vesnarinone 15.35–15.36
Viaspan 33.12
Vidarabine
administration 70.5
adverse effects
list of 70.5
teratogenicity 45.20
dose 70.4
interactions, drugs
allopurinol 40.10, 70.5
theophylline 70.5
pharmacokinetics
absorption 70.5

clearance 70.5
parameters 70.2–70.3
use in
herpes 70.2–70.6
genital 64.18
congenital 64.21
ocular 49.19
Vigabatrin 52.13
Vinblastine
adverse effects 90.14
pulmonary toxicity 91.25, 91.26
teratogenicity 45.20
dosing
alterations 90.14
hepatic dysfunction 91.28
pharmacokinetics 90.14
pharmacology 90.14
Vincristine
adverse effects 90.14
autonomic neuropathy 91.17
constipation 91.5
ocular 49.15
peripheral nerve toxicity 91.15
teratogenicity 45.20
dosing, hepatic dysfunction 91.28
pharmacokinetics 90.14
pharmacology 90.14
use in
acute lymphoblastic leukemia
92.15
rhabdomyosarcoma 93.25
Wilm's tumor 92.34
Vinegar douche 64.16
Vinorelbine
adverse effects 90.14
pharmacokinetics 90.14
pharmacology 90.14
Vira-A
See Vidarabine
Viral gastroenteritis 60.12–60.13
Viral infections 70.1–70.13
Also see specific infections
cytomegalovirus 70.7–70.8
hantavirus 70.11
herpes simplex 70.1–70.6
influenza 70.8–70.10
respiratory syncytial virus
70.10–70.11
varicella zoster 70.6–70.7
Virazole
See Ribavirin
Virilization, anabolic steroids 87.3,
87.5
Viroptic
See Trifluridine
Visken
See Pindolol
Vistaril
See Hydroxyzine
Vital capacity 19.2–19.3
Vitamin
breast milk 45.29
induced vasculitis 6.13
requirements
adults 35.7
children 99.2, 99.5, 99.10
use in
cystic fibrosis 100.6
parenteral nutrition 35.10
Vitamin A
Also see Retinol
adverse effects, teratogenicity
45.20
use in dyslipidemia 9.23

Vitamin B$_{12}$
See Cyanocobalamin
Vitamin C
Also see Ascorbic acid
effect on glycosylated hemoglobin
48.10
Vitamin D
See Calciferol
Vitamin deficiency, cholestyramine-
induced 9.14
Vitamin E
Also see Tocopherol
effect on glycosylated hemoglobin
48.10
use in
dyslipidemia 9.23
Parkinson's 51.13
Vitamin K
pharmacology 12.4
use in
cirrhosis 25.7
cystic fibrosis 100.6
neonates 99.5
warfarin reversal 12.16, 12.20
Vivactil
See Protriptyline
Volatile inhalant abuse 83.11–83.17
Volume of distribution
See specific drugs
in renal failure 32.2
principles 2.3
Volume regulation disorders
28.4–28.6
Vomiting
Also see Nausea/vomiting
complications, hypokalemia 28.16
drug overdose 104.7
etiology, pediatric 95.4
pathogenesis
renal failure, chronic 30.15
treatment, pediatric 95.5–95.6
Warfarin
Also see Thrombosis; Heparin;
Pulmonary embolism
adverse effects
bleeding 12.13
fetal warfarin syndrome
45.21–45.22, 45.29–45.31
purple toe syndrome 12.14
skin necrosis 12.14
teratogenicity 12.16, 45.20,
45.21–45.22, 45.29–45.31
vasculitis 6.13
breast milk 45.29
dosing
adjustments 12.6–12.20
conversion from heparin 12.12
initiation 12.12
interactions, diet 12.15
interactions, drugs
table of 12.20
alcohol 12.15
allopurinol 40.10
amiodarone 12.20
antacids 23.9
aspirin 12.18–12.20
chloral hydrate 3.3
cholestyramine/colestipol 9.14
cimetidine 23.6, 23.8
disulfiram 82.8
erythromycin 3.3
lovastatin 9.16
nonsteroidal anti-inflammatory
agents 3.4, 12.20
omeprazole 23.10
phenylbutazone 3.1, 3.4

rifampin 59.8
sulfasalazine 24.7
sulfonamides 24.7, 63.16
sulfonylureas 48.39
thioamides 47.15–47.16
thyroid hormone 3.4,
47.15–47.16
trimethoprim-sulfamethoxazole
12.19–12.20, 63.16
overdose treatment 12.16
pharmacokinetics
absorption 12.5
clearance 12.5
distribution 12.5
parameters 12.5
thyroid disorders 47.15–47.166
pharmacology 12.4
duration of therapy 12.13
factors affecting response
elderly 12.13
intensity of therapy 12.13
use in
atrial fibrillation 12.4, 12.6,
12.17, 16.9
cardioembolic stroke 12.6
cardioversion 12.17
congestive heart failure 12.19
deep venous thrombosis
12.4–12.6
myocardial infarction 12.6,
12.19, 14.4, 14.8, 14.17–14.18
pregnancy 12.16
pulmonary embolism
12.12–12.16
thromboembolism 12.6
thrombotic stroke 53.9
transient ischemic attacks
53.8–53.9
valve replacement 12.6
valvular disease 12.6
vascular dementia strokes 102.10
ventricular dysfunction 12.6
Water reabsorption
body content 28.1–28.3
reabsorption 28.3
Wegener's granulomatosis
30.25–30.26
Weight gain, lithium-induced 77.6
Weight loss
amphetamines 84.2
phenylpropanolamine 84.6–84.7
Wellbutrin
See Bupropion
Wernicke's encephalopathy 104.14
Wernicke-Korsakoff 82.10–82.11
White blood cells 4.15
count 4.16
shift 42.8
Wilm's tumor
chemotherapy, dosing 93.23
clinical presentation 93.22–93.23
Withdrawal symptoms
See specific drugs of abuse
Wolff-Parkinson-White 16.13
Wound healing
effect of corticosteroids 34.35
Wound infections
trauma 66.8
bites 66.8–66.9
Wytensin
See Guanabenz
Xamaterol 15.33–15.36
Xerostomia, chemotherapy-induced

91.5–91.8
Xylometazoline 21.10–21.11
Yellow fever vaccine, teratogenicity
45.20
Yodoxin
See Diiodohydroxyquin
Yohimbine, use in impotence 103.8
Y-Protein
See Diiodohydroxyquin
Yutopar
See Ritodrine
Zalcitabine 68.7–68.9
adverse effects, table of 54.14
Zantac
See Rantidine
Zarontin
See Ethosuximide
Zaroxyln
See Metolazone
Zebeta
See Bisoprolol
Zemuron
See Rocuronium
Zentel
See Albendazole
Zidovudine
adverse effects 68.7
table of 54.13
teratogenicity 45.20
vasculitis 6.1
HIV resistance 68.14
pharmacokinetics 32.10, 68.7–68.8
pharmacology
efficacy 68.7–68.8
mechanism of action 68.7–68.8
use in
HIV 68.7–68.10, 68.13–68.14
pregnancy 68.34
renal failure 32.14
use with
alpha-interferon 68.12
erythropoietin 68.12
ganciclovir 68.12
interleukin-2 68.12
Zimelidine
use in
alcoholism 82.7
neonatal opioid addiction 83.8
opioid withdrawal 83.9
sedative withdrawal 83.10
Zinacef
See Cefuroxime
Zinc
hepatic failure 35.13
parental 35.1–35.16
renal failure 35.15
use in parenteral nutrition 35.5,
35.10
Zithromax
See Azithromycin
Zithromycin
use in pneumonia, community
acquired 58.7
Zollinger-Ellison
clinical presentation 23.15
diagnosis 23.15
pathogenesis 23.15
treatment
H$_2$-antagonists 23.7, 23.15
octreotide 23.16
omeprazole 23.7, 23.16
somatostatin 23.16

Zoloft
 See Sertraline
Zolpidem 74.6–74.9, 74.11
 use as hypnotic 73.6
Zoster
 See Varicella zoster
Zosyn
 See Piperacillin/tazobactam
Zovirax
 See Acyclovir
Zuclopenthixol, breast milk 45.29